# NET/SET

JRF & LECTURERSHIP

# Mathematical Sciences

Preeti Gupta (JRF)
Dr. Aditya Tomar
Dr. Naveen Sharma

**ARIHANT PUBLICATIONS (INDIA) LIMITED**



卐 **Administrative & Production Offices**

**Regd. Office**

'Ramchhaya' 4577/15, Agarwal Road, Darya Ganj, New Delhi -110002
Tele: 011- 47630600, 43518550

卐 **Head Office**

Kalindi, TP Nagar, Meerut (UP) - 250002
Tel: 0121-7156203, 7156204

卐 **Sales & Support Offices**

Agra, Ahmedabad, Bengaluru, Bareilly, Chennai, Delhi, Guwahati, Hyderabad, Jaipur, Jhansi, Kolkata, Lucknow, Nagpur & Pune.

卐 **PRICE** ₹995.00

PO No. :TXT-59-T062527-1 -25

Published by Arihant Publications (India) Ltd.

For further information about the books published by Arihant, log on to www.arihantbooks.com or e-mail at info@arihantbooks.com

Follow us on    

# Mathematical Sciences

# Preface

NET (National Eligibility Test) determines eligibility for lectureship and for award of Junior Research Fellowship (JRF) for Indian nationals in order to ensure minimum standards for the entrants in the teaching profession and research. The Council of Scientific and Industrial Research (CSIR) conducts the UGC-CSIR NET for other Science subjects, namely, Life Sciences, Physical Sciences, Chemical Sciences, Mathematical Sciences and Earth Sciences jointly with the UGC.

UGC-CSIR NET Tutor for Mathematical Sciences has been designed to help the students get away with their initial qualms & hiccups about the UGC-CSIR NET. In the course of preparation of this book we have followed the pattern & syllabus of the examination for the maximum benefit of the aspirants, difficulty level of the questions has also been kept in mind.

*Salient Features of The Book*

- Only book in the market which has complete & exhaustive theory exactly on the UGC-CSIR NET pattern & difficulty level.
- For complete understanding all units have been divided into individual chapters with sufficient number of Multiple Choice Questions.
- As per the nature & pattern of the questions Separate Exercises have been given for Part 'B' & Part 'C'.
- Only book in the market which has Previous Years' Papers

We are thankful to Arihant Publications (India) Limited for giving us this opportunity to make such a book which will help the students to get 100% success. We would like to thank Sorabh Chaudhary (Project Coordinator) for giving us their full support during this project. Any suggestion for the enhancement of the quality of this book is most welcome.

Pawan Sharma
Neha Sharma
Suraj Singh

# Contents

## UNIT I

## UNIT IV

## UNIT I

**Analysis** Elementary set theory, Finite, Countable and Uncountable sets, Real number system as a complete ordered field, Archimedean property, Supremum, Infimum. Sequences and series, Convergence, Limsup, Liminf. Bolzano Weierstrass theorem, Heine Borel theorem.

Continuity, Uniform continuity, Differentiability, Mean value theorem. Sequences and series of functions, Uniform convergence. Riemann sums and Riemann integral, Improper Integrals.

Monotonic functions, Types of discontinuity, Functions of bounded variation, Lebesgue measure, Lebesgue integral.

Functions of several variables, Directional derivative, Partial derivative, Derivative as a linear transformation, Inverse and implicit function theorems.

Metric spaces, Compactness, Connectedness. Normed linear spaces. Spaces of continuous functions as examples.

**Linear Algebra** Vector spaces, Subspaces, Linear dependence, Basis, Dimension, Algebra of linear transformations.

Algebra of matrices, Rank and determinant of matrices, Linear equations.

Eigen values and Eigen vectors, Cayley-Hamilton theorem.

Matrix representation of linear transformations. Change of basis, Canonical forms, Diagonal forms, Triangular forms, Jordan forms.

Inner product spaces, Orthonormal basis.

Quadratic forms, Reduction and classification of quadratic forms

## UNIT II

**Complex Analysis** Algebra of complex numbers, The complex plane, Polynomials, Power series, Transcendental functions such as exponential, Trigonometric and hyperbolic functions. Analytic functions, Cauchy Riemann equations.

Contour integral, Cauchy's theorem, Cauchy's integral formula, Liouville's theorem, Maximum modulus principle, Schwarz lemma, Open mapping theorem. Taylor series, Laurent series, Calculus of residues. Conformal mappings, Mobius transformations.

**Algebra** Permutations, Combinations, Pigeon hole principle, Inclusion exclusion principle, Derangements.

Fundamental theorem of arithmetic, Divisibility in Z, Congruences, Chinese remainder theorem, Euler's Ø- function, Primitive roots.

Groups, Subgroups, Normal subgroups, Quotient groups, Homomorphisms, Cyclic groups, Permutation groups, Cayley's theorem, Class equations, Sylow theorems.

Rings, Ideals, Prime and Maximal ideals, Quotient rings, Unique factorization domain, Principal ideal domain, Euclidean domain.

Polynomial rings and irreducibility criteria. Fields, Finite fields, Field extensions, Galois theory.

**Topology** Basis, Dense sets, Subspace and product topology, Separation axioms, Connectedness and compactness.

## UNIT III

**Ordinary Differential Equations (ODEs)** Existence and Uniqueness of solutions of initial value problems for first order ordinary differential equations, Singular solutions of first order ODEs, system of first order ODEs.

General theory of homogeneous and non-homogeneous linear ODEs, variation of parameters, Sturm-Liouville boundary value problem, Green's function.

**Partial Differential Equations (PDEs)** Lagrange and Charpit methods for solving first order PDEs, Cauchy problem for first order PDEs.

Classification of second order PDEs, General solution of higher order PDEs with constant coefficients, Method of separation of variables for Laplace, Heat and wave equations.

**Numerical Analysis** Numerical solutions of algebraic equations, Method of iteration and Newton Raphson method, Rate of convergence, Solution of systems of linear algebraic equations using Gauss elimination and Gauss Seidel methods, Finite differences, Lagrange, Hermite and spline interpolation, Numerical differentiation and integration, Numerical solutions of ODEs using Picard, Euler, Modified Euler and Runge Kutta methods.

**Calculus of Variations** Variation of a functional, Euler-Lagrange equation, Necessary and sufficient conditions for extrema.

Variational methods for boundary value problems in ordinary and partial differential equations.

**Linear Integral Equations** Linear integral equation of the first and second kind of Fredholm and Volterra type, Solutions with separable kernels. Characteristic numbers and eigen functions, Resolvent kernel.

**Classical Mechanics** Generalized coordinates, Lagrange's equations, Hamilton's canonical equations, Hamilton's principle and principle of least action, Two dimensional motion of rigid bodies, Euler's dynamical equations for the motion of a rigid body about an axis, Theory of small oscillations.

## UNIT IV

**Descriptive statistics, Exploratory data analysis** Sample space, Discrete probability, Independent events, Baye's theorem. Random variables and distribution functions (univariate and multivariate); Expectation and moments. Independent random variables, Marginal and conditional distributions. Characteristic functions. Probability inequalities (Tchebyshef, Markov, Jensen). Modes of convergence, Weak and strong laws of large numbers, Central limit theorems (iid case).

Markov chains with finite and countable state space, Classification of states, Limiting behaviour of n-step transition probabilities, Stationary distribution, Poisson and birth-and-death processes.

Standard discrete and continuous univariate distributions. Sampling distributions, Standard errors and asymptotic distributions, Distribution of order statistics and range.

Methods of estimation, Properties of estimators, Confidence intervals. Tests of hypothesis: most powerful and uniformly most powerful tests, Likelihood ratio tests. Analysis of discrete data and chi-square test of goodness of fit. Large sample tests.

Simple non-parametric tests for one and two sample problems, Rank correlation and test for independence. Elementary Bayesian inference.

Gauss Markov models, Estimability of parameters, Best linear unbiased estimators, Confidence intervals, Tests for linear hypothesis. Analysis of variance and covariance. Fixed, Random and mixed effects models.

Simple and multiple linear regression. Elementary regression diagnostics. Logistic regression.

Multivariate normal distribution, Wishart distribution and their properties. Distribution of quadratic forms. Inference for parameters, Partial and multiple correlation coefficients and related tests. Data reduction techniques: Principle component analysis, Discriminant analysis, Cluster analysis, Canonical correlation.

Simple random sampling, Stratified sampling and systematic sampling. Probability proportional to size sampling. Ratio and regression methods.

Completely randomized designs, Randomized block designs and Latin square designs. Connectedness and orthogonality of block designs, BIBD. $2k$ factorial experiments: Confounding and construction.

Hazard function and failure rates, Censoring and life testing, Series and parallel systems.

Linear programming problem, Simplex methods, Duality. Elementary queuing and inventory models.

Steady state solutions of Markovian queuing models: $M/M/1$, $M/M/1$ with limited waiting space, $M/M/C$, $M/M/C$ with limited waiting space, $M/G/1$.

**All students are expected to answer questions from Unit I. Students in mathematics are expected to answer additional question from Unit II and III. Students with in statistics are expected to answer additional question from Unit IV.**

# 1 Set Theory Real Number System

## Set

A set is a collection of well distinct objects. The objects of a set are called the members or elements of the set and their membership is defined by the certain conditions. The elements of the set can be anything pencil, apple, rubber, Sun etc.

Suppose, $S$ be the set *i.e.*, a collection of objects and $x$ is an object which belongs to $S$ *i.e.*, member of $S$, then we will write $x \in S$. We can also write $S = \{x : Q(x)\}$. It means $S$ is the set of objects for which the statement $Q(x)$ involving $x$ is true.

**Syllabus**

- Elementary Set Theorem
- Finite Countable and Uncountable Sets
- Real Number System as a Complete Ordered Field
- Archimedean Property
- Supremum, Infimum

> ***Note* (a)** Sets are generally denoted by capital letters $A, B, C, P, Q, X, Y$ etc.
> **(b)** Elements of the set are denoted by the small letters $a, b, c, p, q, x, y$ etc.
> **(c)** If $x$ is not the member of the set $S$, then it is written as $x \notin S$ and read as $x$ does not belong to $S$.

### Subsets

If every element of a set $A$ is also an element of a set $B$, then $A$ is called a subset of $B$ and it is denoted by $A \subseteq B$.

### Superset

If $A$ is a subset of $B$ means $A$ is contained in $B$, we can also say that $B$ contains $A$ or $B$ is superset of $A$, it can be written as $B \supset A$.

### Equality of Sets

If two sets $A$ and $B$ are equal, then symbollically it is written as $A = B$. If every element of $A$ belongs to $B$ and every element of $B$ belongs to $A$. *i.e.*, $A = B$ if and only if

$$x \in A \Leftrightarrow x \in B \quad \text{or} \quad A \subset B,\ B \subset A \Leftrightarrow A = B$$

### Proper Set

If every element of the set $A$ is an element of the set $B$ and $B$ contains atleast one element which does not belong to $A$, *i.e.*, if $A \subset B$ and $A \neq B$, then we can say that $A$ is proper subset of $B$ and it is denoted by $A \subset B$.

e.g., $\{2, 3, 6, 4\}$ is proper subset of $\{4, 3, 2, 6, 5, 8\}$

### Universal Set

We consider all the sets to be the subsets of a given fixed set known as universal set or universe of discourse. It is denoted by $U$ or $X$.

### Finite Set

If a set consist of finite number of elements, it is called a finite set.
e.g., $\{7, 9, 11\}$ is a finite set.

### Infinite Set

If a set consist of an infinite number of elements, it is called, infinite set.
e.g., Set of Natural numbers $N$, Set of Rational numbers $R$, etc.

### Power Set

Power set of the set is defined as the family consisting of all subsets of a set. It is denoted by $P$.
e.g., $\{A : A \subset B\}$ is power set of $B$. It can be written as

$$P = \{A : A \subset B\}$$

### Null Set

A set consisting of no points is called the empty set or null set. It is denoted by $\phi$ or $\{\}$.

### Indexed Set and Index Set

Let $S_t$ be a non-empty set for each $t$ in a set $\Delta$. The sets $A_1, A_2, A_3, \ldots, A_n$ are called indexed sets and the set $\Delta = \{1, 2, 3, \ldots, n\}$ is called index set. The suffix $t \in \Delta$ of $A_t$ is called an index and such a family of sets is denoted by

$$\{A_t : t \in \Delta\} \text{ or } \{A_t\},\ t \in \Delta.$$

### Singleton Set

A set consisting of a single element is called a singleton set.
e.g., $\{1\}, \{2\}, \{a\}$ etc., are singleton sets.

### Pairwise Disjoint Sets

A family $\{A_n\}$ of sets is said to be pairwise disjoint, if $A_t \cap A_s = \phi,\ \forall\ t, s \in \Delta$ s.t. $t \neq s$.

### Hereditary Property

A non-empty family $A = \{A_t\}$ of sets is said to have hereditary property, if

$$A_t \subset A_s,\ A_s \in A \Rightarrow A_t \in A$$

## Set Operations

### Union

Union of two sets $A$ and $B$ written as $A \cup B$. It means the set of points which belongs to one of the sets $A$ and $B$ i.e., which belongs to $A$ or to $B$ or to both.

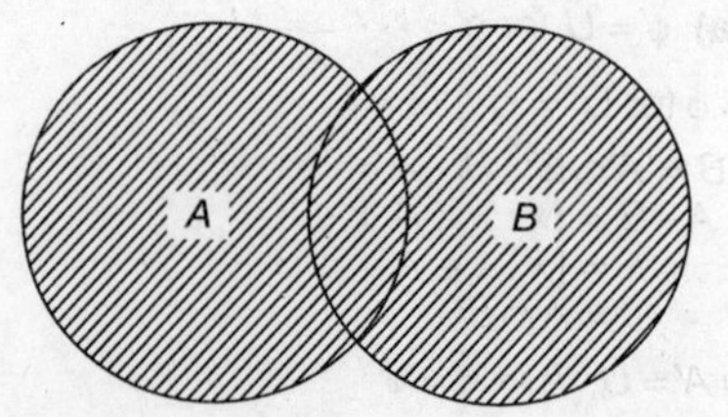


In the diagram shaded portion represents $A \cup B$.

$\therefore$ $A \cup B = \{x : x \in A \text{ or } x \in B \text{ or } x \in \text{ both } A \text{ and } B\}$

### Intersection

The intersection of two sets $A$ and $B$ written as $A \cap B$. It means the set of points which belongs to both $A$ and $B$.

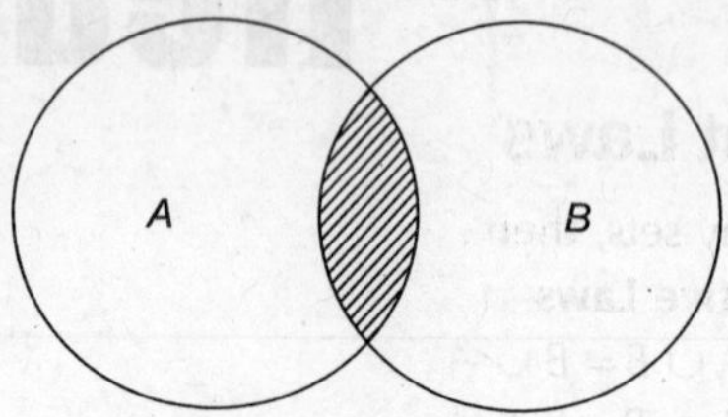


In the diagram shaded portion represents $A \cap B$.

$\therefore$ $A \cap B = \{x : x \in A \text{ and } x \in B\}$

If $A \cap B = \phi$, it means there is no common element in $A$ and $B$. In this case, the sets $A$ and $B$ are said to be disjoint.

> ***Note*** **(a)** Sometimes $A + B$ can be written in place of $A \cup B$.
> **(b)** Sometimes $A \cdot B$ can be written in place of $A \cap B$.
> **(c)** If $A = \{1, 2\}$, $B = \{3, 4, 5\}$, then $A \cup B = \{1, 2, 3, 4, 5\}$.
> **(d)** If $A = \{1, 2\}$, $B = \{2, 3, 4\}$, then $A \cap B = \{2\}$.
> **(e)** If $x \in A \Rightarrow x \in A \cup B$ and any $x \in B \Rightarrow x \in A \cup B$
> $\therefore A \subset A \cup B,\ B \subset A \cup B$
> **(f)** If $x \in A \cap B \Rightarrow x \in A$ and any $x \in A \cap B \Rightarrow x \in B$
> $\therefore A \cap B \subset A,\ A \cap B \subset B$

### Complement of a Set

The complement of a set $A$ is denoted by $A^C$ or $A'$ i.e., the set of all points in the universal set $U$ which do not belong to $A$. Symbollically, it can be written as

$$A^C = U - A = \{x : x \in U \text{ and } x \notin A\}$$

i.e., for any $x \in A' \Leftrightarrow x \notin A$

### Difference of Sets

The difference $A - B$ between two sets $A$ and $B$ is the set of points in $A$ which do not belong to $B$, i.e.,

$$A - B = A \cap B^C$$

### Symmetric Difference of Sets

The symmetric difference of two sets $A$ and $B$ is denoted by $A \Delta B$. It is defined as

$$A \Delta B = (A - B) \cup (B - A)$$

> ***Note*** **(a)** $\phi' = U$ for $\phi' = U - \phi = U$
> **(b)** $U' = \phi$ for $U' = U - U = \phi$
> **(c)** $A - B = A \cap B^C$, $B - A = B \cap A^C$
> For $A - B = \{x : x \in A, x \notin B\}$
> $= \{x : x \in A, x \in B'\}$
> $= A \cap B'$
> **(d)** $A \cup A' = U$, $A \cap A' = \phi$
> **(e)** $x \in A \cup B \Rightarrow x \in A$ or $x \in B$
> $x \notin A \cup B \Rightarrow x \notin A$ and $x \notin B$

e.g., If $A = \{2, 3, 4, 5\}$ and $B = \{4, 5, 6, 7\}$, then

$$A - B = \{2, 3\},\ B - A = \{6, 7\}$$
$$A \Delta B = (A - B) \cup (B - A) = \{2, 3\} \cup \{6, 7\}$$
$$= \{2, 3, 6, 7\}$$

## Important Laws

If $A, B, C$ be any sets, then

1. **Commutative Laws**
$$A \cup B = B \cup A$$
$$A \cap B = B \cap A$$
2. **Associative Laws**
$$(A \cup B) \cup C = A \cup (B \cup C)$$
$$(A \cap B) \cap C = A \cap (B \cap C)$$
3. **Distributive Laws**
$$A \cap (B \cup C) = (A \cap B) \cup (A \cap C)$$
$$A \cup (B \cap C) = (A \cup B) \cap (A \cup C)$$
4. **De-Morgan's Laws**
$$(A \cup B)' = A' \cap B'$$
$$(A \cap B)' = A' \cup B'$$
5. $$A - (B \cup C) = (A - B) \cap (A - C)$$
$$A - (B \cap C) = (A - B) \cup (A - C)$$

## Cartesian Product

Let $A$ and $B$ be two sets. Then,

$$A \times B = \{(x, y) : x \in A, y \in B\}$$

is known as cartesian product of $A$ and $B$.

In general

$$A \times B \neq B \times A$$

where

$$B \times A = \{(y, x) : y \in B, x \in A\}$$

### Properties of Cartesian Product

Let $A, B, C$ and $D$ are sets. Then,

**(i)** $(A \cup B) \times C = (A \times C) \cup (B \times C)$

**(ii)** $(A \cap B) \times C = (A \times C) \cap (B \times C)$

**(iii)** $(A - B) \times C = (A \times C) - (B \times C)$

**(iv)** $A \times B = \phi \Leftrightarrow A = \phi$ or $B = \phi$

**(v)** $A \times C \subseteq B \times C,\ C \neq \phi \Rightarrow A \subseteq B$

**(vi)** $(A \times B = B \times A) \Leftrightarrow (A = \phi$ or $B = \phi$ or $A = B)$

**(vii)** $(A \cap B) \times (C \cap D) = (A \times C) \cap (B \times D)$

**(viii)** $A \subseteq A \times A \Rightarrow A = \phi$

**(ix)** $A = A \times B \Rightarrow A = \phi$

**(x)** If $A$ contains $n$ elements and $B$ contains $m$ elements, then $A \times B$ contains $n \cdot m$ elements.

***Example 1.*** *If* $|A \cap B| = r$. *Then, find* $|(A \times B) \cap (B \times A)|$.

**Solution.** Let $A \cap B = D$. Then,

$$D \times D \subseteq A \times B \text{ and}$$
$$D \times D \subseteq B \times A$$
$$\Rightarrow \quad |D \times D| = r \times r = r^2$$
$$\Rightarrow \quad |(A \times B) \cap (B \times A)| = r^2$$

## Relation

A relation from set $A$ to set $B$ is a subset of $A \times B$. Similarly $A$ relation from set $B$ to set $A$ is a subset of $B \times A$.

e.g., Let $A = \{a, b\}$ and $B = \{1, 2\}$. Then, $A \times B = \{(a, 1), (a, 2), (b, 1), (b, 2)\}$ is a relation from $A$ to $B$. Thus, every subset of $A \times B$ is a relation from $A$ to $B$.

Similarly,

$B \times A = \{(1, a), (1, b), (2, a), (2, b)\}$ is a relation from $B$ to $A$. Thus, every subset of $B \times A$ is a relation from $B$ to $A$.

Since, $\phi$ is a subset of every set. Hence, $\phi$ is a relation from $A$ to $B$ (and $B$ to $A$) known as empty relation.

***Theorem*** **If a set $A$ has $n$ element and set $B$ has $m$ element, then total number of relations from set $A$ to set $B$ is $2^{n \cdot m} = 2^{|A| \times |B|}$.**

## Relation on a Set

A relation on a set $A$ is a subset of $A \times A$.

e.g., $\phi$ and $A \times A$ are relation on $A$.

e.g., $\Delta = \{(a, a) : a \in A\}$ is a relation on $A$ known as the diagonal relation on $A$.

e.g., Let $A = \{a, b, c\}$. Then,

$$R = \{(a, b), (b, a), (a, c)\}$$ is a relation on $A$.

e.g., Let $A$ be a set. Let $R = \{(X, Y) : X, Y \in P(A) \text{ and } X \subseteq Y\}$ is a relation on $P(A)$.

Now, let $R$ and $S$ be relations on $A$. Then, $R \cup S$, $R \cap S$ and $R - S$ are all subsets of $A \times A$ and hence they are also relations on $A$. The relation

$RoS = \{(a_1, a_2) \in A \times A : \exists\, a_3 \in X$ such that $(a_1, a_3) \in S$ and $(a_3, a_2) \in R\}$ is called the composition of $R$ and $S$.

### Properties of Relation

Let $R$, $S$ and $T$ be relations on $X$. Then,

**(i)** $(RoS)oT = Ro(SoT)$

**(ii)** $Ro\Delta = R = \Delta oR$

**(iii)** $Ro(S \cup T) = (RoS) \cup (RoT)$

**(iv)** $Ro(S \cap T) \subseteq (RoS) \cap (RoT)$

**(v)** $(R \cup S)oT = (RoT) \cup (SoT)$

**(vi)** $(R \cap S)oT \subseteq (RoT) \cap (SoT)$

## Inverse Relation

Let $R$ be a relation on $A$. Then, the relation

$$R^{-1} = \{(a_1, a_2) \in A \times A \mid (a_2, a_1) \in R\}$$

is called the inverse relation of $R$.

***Theorem*** Let $R$ and $S$ be relations on $A$. Then,

**(i)** $(R^{-1})^{-1} = R$

**(ii)** $(RoS)^{-1} = S^{-1}oR^{-1}$

## Types of Relations

Let $R$ be a relation on $A$. Then,

**(i)** $R$ is called reflexive, if $(a, a) \in R, \forall a \in A$ or equivalently $\Delta \subseteq R$.

**(ii)** $R$ is called symmetric, if $(a_1, a_2) \in R \Rightarrow (a_2, a_1) \in R$ or equivalently $R^{-1} = R$.

**(iii)** $R$ is called anti-symmetric, if $(a_1, a_2) \in R$ and $(a_2, a_1) \in R$ $\Rightarrow a_1 = a_2$ or equivalently $R \cap R^{-1} \subseteq \Delta$.

**(iv)** $R$ is called transitive, if $(a_1, a_2) \in R$ and $(a_2, a_3) \in R$ $\Rightarrow (a_1, a_3) \in R$ or equivalently $RoR \subseteq R$.

e.g., Let $A = \{a, b, c\}$ and

$$R = \{(a, a), (b, b), (c, c), (a, b), (b, c), (c, b)\}$$

Then, $R$ is reflexive but none of the rest of three.

e.g., Let $A = \{a, b, c\}$ and

$$R = \{(c, b), (a, c)\}$$

Then, $R$ is a anti-symmetric but none of the rest three.

e.g., Let $A = (a, b, c)$ and

$$R = \{(a, a), (b, b), (c, c), (a, b), (b, a), (b, c), (c, b)\}$$

Then, $R$ is reflexive , symmetric but neither anti-symmetric nor transitive.

## Equivalence Relation

A relation $R$ on a set $A$, which is reflexive, symmetric and transitive is called equivalence relation on $A$.

Let $R$ be an equivalence relation on $A$ and $a \in A$. The subset

$$R_a = \{b \in A : (a, b) \in R\}$$

is called the equivalence class of $A$ modulo $R$ determined by a.

***Theorem*** Let $R$ be an equivalence relation on $A$. Then,

**(i)** $R_a = R_b \Leftrightarrow (a, b) \in R$

**(ii)** $R_a \neq R_b \Leftrightarrow R_a \cap R_b = \phi$

## Partition of Set

Let $A$ be a set. A subset $P$ of the power set of $A$ is called partition of $A$, if

(i) union of member of $P$ is $A$

i.e., $\bigcup_{X \in P} = A$

(ii) $X, Y \in P, X \neq Y \Rightarrow X \cap Y = \phi$

## Function

Let $A$ and $B$ be two sets. A subset $f$ of $A \times B$ is called a function or a mapping (or a map) from $A$ to $B$, if

(i) $\forall a \in A, \exists b \in B$ such that $(a, b) \in f$

(ii) $(a, b_1) \in f$ and $(a, b_2) \in f$ $\Rightarrow b_1 = b_2$

$A$ is called the domain and $B$ is called the codomain of $f$. If $(a, b) \in f$, we write $b = f(a)$ and call it the image of the element a under the map $f$. Thus,

$$f = \{(a, f(a)) : a \in A\}$$

we also adopt the notations $f : A \rightarrow B$ to say that $f$ is a map from $A$ to $B$.

Let $f : A \rightarrow B$ and $g : B \rightarrow C$ be two maps.

Then, $gof : \{(a, c) : (a, b) \in f \text{ and } (b, c) \in g\}$

is a map from $A$ to $C$ called the composition of $f$ and $g$, given by

$$(gof)(a) = g(f(a)), \forall a \in A.$$

**Definition** The subset $\Delta$ of $A \times A$ is also a map from $A$ to $A$ called the identity map on $A$ and is denoted by $I_A$. Thus,

$$I_A(a) = a, \forall a \in A$$

and $\quad foI_A = f = I_Bof$

where $f : A \rightarrow B$ is a map.

**Definition** Let $X \subseteq A$. Then, $I_X = \{(x, x) : x \in X\}$ is a map from $X$ to $A$ called the inclusion map from $X$ to $A$.

**Definition** Let $A$ and $B$ be two sets and $b \in B$. Then, $A \times \{b\}$ is a map $f$ from $A$ to $B$ such that

$$f(a) = y, \forall a \in A$$

called constant map.

**Definition** Let $A$ and $B$ be two sets.

The map

$$p_1 : A \times B \rightarrow A$$

defined by

$$p_1(a, b) = a$$

is called the first projection and

$$p_2 : A \times B \rightarrow B$$

defined by

$$p_2(a, b) = b$$

is called the second projection map.

***Theorem*** Let $f : A \rightarrow B, g : B \rightarrow C$ and $h : C \rightarrow D$ be maps. Then,

$$(hog)of = ho(gof)$$

*i.e.,* The set of maps follows the associative law.

---

**Definition** Let $f : X \rightarrow Y$ be a map. Then,

$$f^{-1} = \{(b, a) : (a, b) \in f\} \subseteq B \times A$$

need not be a map from $B$ to $A$. But $f^{-1}$ will be a map iff

(i) $\forall\, b \in B, \exists\, a \in A$ such that $(a, b) \in f$

(ii) $(a_1, b) \in f$ and $(a_2, b) \in f$

$\Rightarrow \quad a_1 = a_2$

called inverse map of $f$.

**Definition** A map $f : A \to B$ is called injective or one-one, if

$$f(a_1) = f(a_2)$$

$$\Rightarrow \quad a_1 = a_2$$

or equivalently

$$a_1 \neq a_2$$

$$\Rightarrow \quad f(a_1) \neq f(a_2)$$

or equivalently

$$(a_1, b) \in f\ (a_2, b) \in f$$

$$\Rightarrow \quad a_1 = a_2$$

**Definition** A map $f : A \to B$ is called surjective map or onto map, if $\forall\, b \in B, \exists\, a \in A$ such that $(a, b) \in f$. Thus, $f$ is surjective, if $\forall\, b \in B, \exists\, a \in A$ such that $f(a) = b$.

**Definition** A map $f$ which is injective as well as surjective is called a bijective or one-one-onto map.

> **Note** The map $f^{-1}$ is a map iff $f$ is bijective.

***Example 2.*** *Show that a surjective map need be injective.*

**Solution.** Let $A = \{a, b, c\}$ and $B = \{x, y\}$

Define the map $f : A \to B$ by $f(a) = x = f(b)$, $f(c) = y$.

Then, $f$ is surjective but not injective for $f(a) = f(b)$ as $a \neq b$.

***Example 3.*** *Show that an injective map need not be surjective.*

**Solution.** Let $A = \{a, b\}$ and $B = \{x, y, z\}$

Define the map $f : A \to B$ by $f(a) = x$, $f(b) = y$. Then, $f$ is injective but not surjective for there is no element in $A$ whose image is $z$.

## Properties of Map

**(i)** Inverse of a bijective map is a bijective map.

**(ii)** Composition of any two injective maps is injective.

**(iii)** Composite of two surjective maps is surjective.

**(iv)** Composite of two bijective maps is bijective.

**(v)** Let $f : A \to B$ and $g : B \to C$ be maps. Then,

(a) If $gof$ is surjective, then $g$ is surjective.

(b) If $gof$ is injective, then $f$ is injective.

(c) If $gof$ is bijective, then $g$ is surjective and $f$ is injective.

**(vi)** A map $f : A \to B$ is injective iff $f$ can be left cancelled in the sense that

$$fog = foh \Rightarrow g = h$$

A map $f : A \to B$ is surjective iff $f$ can be right cancelled in the sense that

$$gof = hof$$

$$\Rightarrow \quad g = h$$

**(vii)** A map $f : A \to B$ is bijective iff it can be left as well as right cancelled.

**(viii)** Let $f : A \to B$ be a map. Then, $f$ is bijective iff $\exists$ a map $g : B \to A$ such that

$$gof = I_A \text{ and}$$

$$fog = I_B \text{ and then } g = f^{-1}$$

**(ix)** Let $f : A \to B$ and $g : B \to C$ be bijective maps. Then

$$(gof)^{-1} = f^{-1}og^{-1}$$

***Example 4.*** *Show that there is no surjective map from any set A to its power set P(A).*

**Solution.** Let $f : A \to P(A)$ be a map. Consider the set

$$X = \{a \in A : a \notin f(a)\}$$

Then, $X \in P(A)$. Suppose that $f(b) = X$ for some $b \in A$, if $b \notin X = f(b)$, then $b \in X$. If $b \in X = f(b)$, then $b \notin f(b) = X$. Hence, supposition that $f(b) = X$ for some $b \in A$ is false. This shows that $f$ cannot be surjective.

***Theorem*** Let $f$ be a map from $A$ to $B$ and $X \subseteq A$. Then, $X \subseteq f^{-1}(f(X))$. Also,

$$X = f^{-1}(f(X)), \forall\, X \subseteq A \text{ iff } f \text{ is injective.}$$

***Theorem*** Let $f : A \to B$ be a map and $Y \subseteq B$. Then, $f(f^{-1}(Y)) \subseteq Y$. Also,

$$Y = f(f^{-1}(Y)), \forall\, Y \in B \text{ iff } f \text{ is surjective.}$$

***Theorem*** Let $f : A \to B$ be a map. Let $X_1$ and $X_2$ be subsets of $A$. Then,

**(i)** $f(X_1 \cup X_2) = f(X_1) \cup f(X_2)$

**(ii)** $f(X_1 \cap X_2) \subseteq f(X_1) \cap f(X_2)$

***Theorem*** Let $f : A \to B$ be a map. Let $Y_1$ and $Y_2$ be subsets of $Y$. Then,

**(i)** $f^{-1}(B_1 \cap B_2) = f^{-1}(B_1) \cap f^{-1}(B_2)$

**(ii)** $f^{-1}(B_1 \cup B_2) = f^{-1}(B_1) \cup f^{-1}(B_2)$

**(iii)** $f^{-1}(B_1 - B_2) = f^{-1}(B_1) - f^{-1}(B_2)$

## Ordered Pair

Order pair is an element of the form $(a, b)$. The element $a$ is called first element and the element $b$ is called the second element of the ordered pair.

## Equality of Ordered Pairs

Let $(a, b)$ and $(c, d)$ be any two ordered pairs, then

$$(a, b) = (c, d) \Leftrightarrow a = c, b = d$$

## Cardinally Equivalent or Equivalent Sets

A set $A$ is said to be equivalent or cardinally equivalent to the set $B$ if there exist one-one map from $A$ to $B$. This relation is denoted by the symbol $\sim$. Therefore, $A \sim B \Leftrightarrow A$ and $B$ are equivalent.

e.g., The set of natural numbers $N = \{1, 2, \dots\}$ and set of all odd natural numbers $O = \{1, 3, 5, \dots\}$ are equivalent because $f$ is a map $f : N \to O$ by the formula $f(n) = (2n - 1), \forall\ n \in N$ which is one-one from $N$ onto $O$.

> ***Note*** **(a)** The relation ~ is an equivalent relation.
> **(b)** The relation $A \sim B$ in the family of sets is an equivalent relation.

## Cardinal Numbers (or Power or Potency)

The cardinal number of a equivalence sets is any representative of the class or we can say that every equivalence class defines a unique cardinal number.

If $S$ is any set consisting of $s$ elements, then the cardinal number is $s$.

The cardinal number of $\phi$ is defined as zero.

If $A \sim \{1, 2, 3, \dots, n\}$, then $n$ is called the cardinal number of $A$.

The cardinal number of the any set $A$ is denoted by card $A$ or $|A|$. Therefore, $|A|$ or card $A = n$.

> ***Note*** **(a)** If $A \sim B$, then by the definition of cardinal number $|A| = |B|$.
> **(b)** Cardinal number corresponding to a finite set is called a finite cardinal number.
> **(c)** Cardinal number corresponding to an infinite set is called transfinite cardinal number.
> **(d)** All transfinite cardinal numbers are greater than any finite cardinal numbers.

## Sum of Cardinal Numbers

Let $A$ and $B$ be any two sets with cardinality $n$ and $m$ s.t. their intersection is empty. Let

$$|A| = n,\ |B| = m \text{ and } A \cap B = \phi$$

Then, the sum of $n$ and $m$ is defined as $n + m = |A \cup B|$.

e.g.,

If $\quad A = \{a, b, c, d\},\ B = \{a, p, q, r, s, t\}$

Then, $\quad A \cup B = \{a, b, c, d\} \cup \{a, p, q, r, s, t\}$
$\quad = \{a, b, c, d, p, q, r, s, t\}$

$\therefore \quad |A \cup B| = 9$

and $\quad |A| = 4, |B| = 6, A \cap B \neq \phi$

$\therefore$ By the definition

$$|A \cup B| \neq |A| + |B|$$

> ***Note*** This example shows that $A \cap B$ is a necessary condition for the rule $|A \cup B| = |A| + |B|$.

## Product of Cardinal Numbers

Suppose $A$ and $B$ be any two sets s.t. $|A| = n$ and $|B| = m$, then the product of cardinal numbers $n$ and $m$ is defined as

$$n \times m = |A \times B|$$

e.g., Let $\quad A = \{a, b, c\},\ B = \{a, 2, 3, 4\}$

Then, $\quad |A| = 3$ and $|B| = 4$

$\therefore \quad |A \times B| = 3 \times 4 = 12$

Now, $|A \times B| = |\{(a, a), (a, 2), (a, 3), (a, 4), (b, a), (b, 2), (b, 3), (b, 4), (c, a), (c, 2), (c, 3), (c, 4)\}|$
$= 12$

$\therefore \quad |A \times B| = |A| \times |B| = n \times m$

## Denumerable (or Enumerable or Countably Infinite) Countable and Uncountable Sets

A set $A$ is called a denumerable set if $\exists$ a one-one mapping from the set $N$ of all natural numbers onto the set $A$ *i.e.*, if $A \sim N$.

A set $A$ is said to be countable set if either $A$ is denumerable or $A$ is finite *i.e.*, if either $A \sim N$ or $A$ is finite.

If the set $A$ is not countable, then it is said to be uncountable. *i.e.*, A set is called uncountable set, if $A$ is an infinite and $A$ is not cardinally equivalent to $N$.

> ***Note*** Uncountable sets are also called non-countable, non-denumerable, non-enumerable.

## Decimal Representation

The digits $0, 1, 2, \dots, 9$ are called the decimal digits. When the series

$$\frac{d_1}{10} + \frac{d_2}{10^2} + \frac{d_3}{10^3} + \frac{d_4}{10^4} + \dots + \frac{d_n}{10^n} + \dots$$

converges to $x$ with each $d_n$ as a decimal digit. Therefore, the decimal representation of $x$ is given by

$$x = 0 \cdot d_1 d_2 d_3 d_4 \dots$$

e.g., $\quad \frac{3}{10} + \frac{6}{10^2} + \frac{8}{10^3} + \dots$ represents $0.368\dots$

## Ternary Representation

The digits 0, 1, 2 are said to be ternary digits when the series

$$\frac{t_1}{3} + \frac{t_2}{3^2} + \frac{t_3}{3^3} + \frac{t_4}{3^4} + \dots + \frac{t_n}{3^n} + \dots$$

converges to $x$ with each $t_n$ as a ternary digit, then a ternary representation of $x$ is given by

$$x = 0 \cdot t_1 t_2 t_3 t_4 \dots$$

## Important Theorems on Countable and Uncountable Sets

1. Every subset of a finite set is finite.
2. Every superset of an infinite set is infinite.
3. If $A$ and $B$ are finite sets, then $A \cap B$ is also a finite set.
4. If $A$ and $B$ are finite sets, then $A \cup B$ is also a finite set.
5. Every subset of a countable set is countable.
6. Every infinite subset of a denumerable set is denumerable.
7. If $A$ and $B$ are countable sets, then $A \cap B$ is also a countable set.
8. Every superset of an uncountable set is uncountable.
9. Every infinite set has a denumerable subset.
10. Countably infinite sets are the smallest infinite sets.
11. The countable union of countable sets is countable.
12. Every infinite set is equivalent to one of its proper subsets.
13. The set of all rational numbers is countable.
14. The set of all rational numbers in $[0, 1]$ is countable.
15. The unit interval $[0, 1]$ is uncountable *i.e.*, the set of all real numbers in the closed interval $[0, 1]$ is not enumerable *i.e.*, the set of real numbers $x$ s.t. $0 \le x \le 1$ is not countable.
16. The set of real numbers is uncountable.
17. The set of irrational numbers is not countable.
18. Any open interval $]a, b[$ is equivalent to any other open interval $]c, d[$.
19. The set $N \times N$ is countable, where $N$ is the set of natural numbers.
20. The cartesian product of two countable sets is countable. *i.e.*, If $A$ and $B$ are countable sets, then $A \times B$ is countable.
21. (i) The intervals $]0, 1[$ and $[0, 1]$ are equivalent.
    (ii) The intervals $[0, 1]$ and $[0, 1[$ are equivalent.
    (iii) The intervals $[0, 1]$ and $]0, 1[$ are equivalent.
    (iv) Any open interval is equivalent to $[0, 1]$.
22. Any interval is equivalent to the set $R$ of real numbers. In particular, $R$ is equivalent to $[0, 1]$.

## Binary Representation

The digits 0 and 1 are said to be the binary digits when the series $\frac{b_1}{2} + \frac{b_2}{2^2} + \frac{b_3}{2^3} + \frac{b_4}{2^4} + \dots + \frac{b_n}{2^n} + \dots$ converges to $x$ with each $b_n$ as a binary digit, then the binary expression of $x$ is given by

$$x = 0 \cdot b_1 b_2 b_3 b_4 \dots$$

e.g., $$\frac{0}{2} + \frac{1}{2^2} + \frac{0}{2^3} + \frac{1}{2^4} + \dots = \frac{\frac{1}{4}}{1 - \frac{1}{4}} = \frac{1}{3}$$

Therefore, $$\frac{1}{3} = 0 \cdot 0101010101\dots$$

and similarly, $$\frac{1}{4} = 0 \cdot 010000\dots$$

> ***Note*** Suppose $A$ be a set of all sequences whose elements are the digits 0 and 1, then the set $A$ is countable.

## Cantor Set

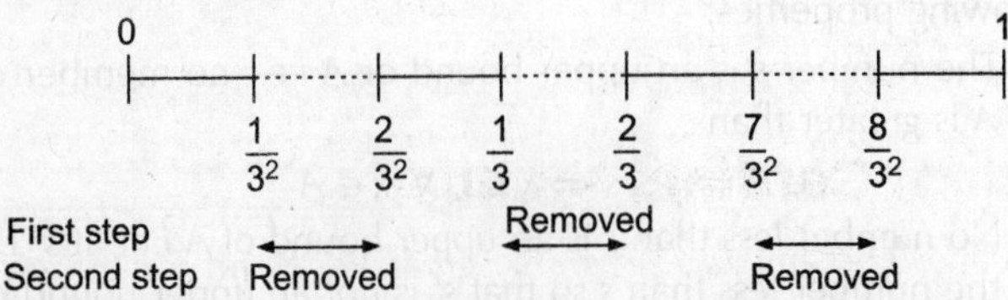


Consider the closed interval $[0, 1]$. Divide this closed interval into three equal parts and remove the middle one *i.e.* remove the open interval $\left(\frac{1}{3}, \frac{2}{3}\right)$. This is our first step of the construction of cantor set.

Now, again we divide the each of the remaining two intervals into three equal parts and remove the middle part means remove the open intervals $\left(\frac{1}{3^2}, \frac{2}{3^2}\right)$ and $\left(\frac{7}{9}, \frac{8}{9}\right)$. This is the second step of construction. On proceeding in this way infinitely many steps, at the $r$th step we have $2^{r-1}$ open intervals are removed each of the length $\frac{1}{3^r}$. The remaining set constitutes cantor set or cantor-ternary set.

Thus, the cantor set contains the points $0, 1, \frac{1}{3}, \frac{2}{3}, \frac{1}{9}, \frac{2}{9}, \frac{7}{9}$, etc. Therefore, cantor set is non-empty.

## Definition of Cantor Set

The cantor set is the set of all numbers in the interval [0, 1] which have a ternary expansion without the digit 1 *i.e.* ternary expansion involves only two digits 0 or 2.

Cantor set is the complement of an open set, therefore, cantor set is closed.

## Important Properties of Cantor Set

1. Cantor ternary set is measurable and its measure is zero.
2. Cantor set is equivalent to [0, 1].
3. Cantor set is uncountable.

# Real Number System as a Complete Ordered Field

The set $R$ of real numbers is an ordered field.

## Order Completeness of $R$

The set of upper bounds of a non-empty set of real numbers which is bounded above has a smallest number or we can also say that every non-empty set of real numbers which is bounded above admits of a least upper bound *i.e.*, supremum.

This property of the set $R$ of real numbers is referred to as its order-completeness. This property states that if $A$ be the set of real numbers which is bounded above there exists the smallest of the upper bounds of $A$. The fact of a number $s$ being the smallest of the upper bounds of $A$ can be described by the following properties:

1. The number $s$ is an upper bound of $A$ *i.e.*, no member of $A$ is greater than $s$.
$$x \in A \Rightarrow x \leq s \Leftrightarrow x \leq s, \forall x \in A$$
2. No number less than $s$ is an upper bound of $A$ *i.e.*, if $s'$ be the number less than $s$ so that $s'$ is not an upper bound of $A$, $\exists$ atleast one number $x \in A$ s.t. $x > s'$. Therefore, if $s' < s$, then there exist $x \in A$ s.t. $x > s'$.

Thus, we have completed the description of the set of real numbers as a complete ordered field.

> **Note** The ordered field of rational numbers is not order-complete.

## Irrational Number

A real number which is not rational is called irrational. e.g., $\sqrt{3}, \sqrt{10}$ etc.

> **Note** If we have a positive real number $m$ and a natural number $n$, then there exist one and only one positive real number $b$ s.t. $b^n = m$.

## Important Theorems on Real Numbers

***Theorem 1*** A non-empty subset of real numbers which is bounded below has the greatest lower bound (infimum) in $R$, the set of all real numbers.

***Theorem 2*** (Dedekind Property) Suppose $L$ and $U$ be two non-empty subsets of the ordered field $R$ s.t.

**(i)** $L \cup U = R$

**(ii)** each member of $L$ is less than each member of $U$ *i.e.*
$$x \in L \wedge y \in U \Rightarrow x < y$$

Then, either the subset $L$ has a greatest member or the subset $U$ has a smallest member.

### Subtraction and Division in $R$

1. $a - b = a + (-b)$
2. $a \div b = \frac{a}{b}$ or $a(b^{-1})$, $b \neq 0$

> **Note** The multiplicative inverse of $b \neq 0$ may be denoted as $b^{-1}$ or $\frac{1}{b}$.

## Archimedean Property of Real Numbers

***Theorem 1*** If $x$ and $y$ are two given real numbers with $x > 0$, then $\exists$ a natural number $n$ s.t. $nx > y$.

***Theorem 2*** For any real number $b$ $\exists$ a positive integer $n$ s.t. $n > b$.

***Theorem 3*** For any $\varepsilon > 0$ $\exists$ a positive integer $n$ s.t. $\frac{1}{n} < \varepsilon$

***Theorem 4*** For any real number $y$, $\exists$ two integers $p$ and $n$ s.t. $p < x < n$.

***Theorem 5*** For any real number $x$, $\exists$ a unique integer $n$ s.t. $n \leq x < n + 1$

***Theorem 6*** For any real number $x$, $\exists$ a unique integer $n$ s.t. $x - 1 < n < x$.

## Archimedean Ordered Field

Archimedean ordered field is an ordered field which has Archimedean property. For example, the field $R$ of the set of real numbers is an Archimedean ordered field.

# Important Theorems

## Denseness Property of Real Number System

***Theorem 1*** (The Density Theorem)
Between any two distinct numbers, there lies atleast one rational number and hence there lie infinitely many rational numbers.

***Theorem 2*** Between any two distinct real numbers, there lies atleast one irrational number also, and hence there lies infinitely many irrational numbers also.

***Theorem 3*** Between any two distinct rational numbers, there lies atleast one and hence infinite number of rational numbers.

---

## Supremum or least upper bound (lub)

If the set of all upper bounds of a set $S$ of real numbers has a smallest member $k$, then $k$ is said to be a least upper bound or supremum of $S$ and it is denoted by lub or Sup $S$.

## Infimum or greatest lower bound (glb)

If the set of all lower bounds of a set $S$ of real numbers has a greatest member $K$, then $K$ is said to be a infimum or greatest lower bound of $S$ and it is denoted by Inf $S$ or glb.

# Important Theorems on Supremum and Infimum

***Theorem 1*** lub or supremum of a non-empty set $S$ of real numbers, whenever it exists is unique.

***Theorem 2*** glb or infimum of a non-empty set $S$ of real numbers whenever it exists, is unique.

***Theorem 3*** The necessary and sufficient condition for a real number '$t$' to be the glb or infimum of a bounded below set $S$ is that '$t$' must satisfy the following conditions:

(i) $x \geq t, \forall\ x \in S$
(ii) For each positive real number $\varepsilon$, $\exists$ a real number $x \in S$ s.t. $x < 1 + \varepsilon$.

***Theorem 4*** The necessary and sufficient condition for a real number '$s$' to be the lub or supremum of a bounded above set $S$ is that '$s$' must satisfy the following conditions:

(i) $x \leq s, \forall\ x \in S$
(ii) For each positive real number $\varepsilon$, $\exists$ a real number $x \in S$ s.t. $x > s - \varepsilon$.

> ***Note*** The supremum or infimum if exist they are unique.

## Greatest Member of a Set Bounded above

A number $\eta$ is called the greatest member of the set $S$, if

(i) $\eta \in S \Rightarrow \eta$ is itself a member of $S$.
(ii) No member of $S$ is greater than $\eta$
$\Rightarrow$ $\eta$ is an upper bound of $S$, therefore

$$x \in S \Rightarrow x \leq \eta$$

Hence, the greatest member of a set is a member of the set bounded above and as well as an upper bound of the set.

## Smallest Number of a Set Bounded below

A number $\xi$ is called the smallest number of a set $S$, if

(i) $\xi \in S \Rightarrow \xi$ is itself a member of $S$.
(ii) No member of $S$ is smaller than $\xi$ *i.e.*, $\xi$ is a lower bound of $S$

$\therefore$ $$x \in S \Rightarrow x \geq \xi$$

Hence, the smallest member of a set is a member of the set bounded below and as well as lower bound of the set.

> ***Note*** **(a)** The smallest member of a set, if it exists, is the infimum or glb of the set.
> **(b)** The greatest member of a set, if it exists, is the supremum or lub of the set.

## Bounded Set

A set $S$ of real numbers is said to be bounded if it is bounded above as well as below. When the set $S$ is bounded, $\exists$ two real numbers $l$ and $m$ s.t.

$$l \leq x \leq m, \forall\ x \in S$$

> ***Note*** By saying that the set is bounded it means that $\exists$ an interval $I$ s.t. $S \subset I$.

e.g. (i) The sets $I$, $Q$ are neither bounded above nor bounded below.
(ii) The set $N$ of natural numbers is bounded below but not bounded above. The smallest number is 1.
Therefore, Inf $N = 1$.

# Limit Point of a Set

## Adherent Point

A point $p \in R$ is said to be an adherent point of a set $A \subset R$ if every neighbourhood of $p$ contains a point of $A$. The set of all adherent points of $A$ is called the adherence or closure of $A$ and it is denoted by Adh$(A)$. Adherent point is also called closure point.

## Limit Point

**(i)** A point $p \in R$ is said to be a limit point of the set $A \subset R$ if every neighbourhood of $p$ contains atleast one point of $A$ other than $p$. Or we can say that a point $p \in R$ is a limit point of $A \subset R$ if and only if for each neighbourhood $N$ of $p$, we have

$$(N \cap A) \sim \{p\} \neq \phi$$

**(ii)** A point $p \in R$ is called a limit point of a set $A \subset R$ if for each $\varepsilon > 0$, the open interval $]p - \varepsilon, p + \varepsilon[$ contains a point of $A$, other than $p$.

## Derived Set

The set of all limit points of a set $A \subset R$ is said to be derived set and it is denoted by $D(A)$ or $A'$. Therefore,

$$A' = D(A) = [p : p \text{ is a limit point of } A]$$

The derived set of $A'$ *i.e.*, $(A')'$ or $A''$.

## Isolated Point

A point $p \in R$ is called an isolated point of $A$, if it is not the limit point of $A$ *i.e.*, if there exist a neighbourhood of $p$ which contains no point of $A$ other than $p$.

> ***Note*** **(a)** A set $A$ is called the discrete set if all its points are isolated points.
>
> **(b)** Each point of a set $A$ is either an isolated point of $A$ or a limit point of $A$.

## Closed Set

**1.** A set $A$ is said to be closed set if it contains all its limit point.

**2.** A set $A$ is said to be closed if its complement is open.

e.g.,

(i) The null set $\phi$ is closed.

(ii) The set $Q$ is not a closed set.

(iii) Finite set is always closed.

## Closure of a Set

The smallest closed set containing $A$, is called the closure of $A$ and is denoted by $\overline{A}$.

## Dense Set

**1.** A set $A$ is said to be dense or everywhere dense in $R$, if $\overline{A} = R$.

**2.** A set $A$ is said to be nowhere dense in $R$ if interior of the closure of $A$ is empty *i.e.*, $(\overline{A})^{\circ} = \phi$.

# Important Theorems

***Theorem 1*** Interior of a set is an open set.

***Theorem 2*** A point $p \in R$ is a limit point of a set $A \subset R$ iff every neighbourhood of $p$ contains infinitely many points of $A$.

***Theorem 3*** If a non-empty subset $A$ of $R$ which is bounded above and has no maximum member, then its supremum is a limit point of the set $A$.

***Theorem 4*** The finite set has no limit point.

***Theorem 5*** If a non-empty subset $A$ of $R$, which is bounded below has no maximum member, then its infimum is a limit point of the set $A$.

***Theorem 6*** (Bolzano-Weierstrass Theorem) Every infinite bounded set of real numbers has a limit point.

***Theorem 7*** Every bounded infinite set has the smallest and the greatest limit point.

# Important Definitions

## Condensation Point

If every neighbourhood of a point contains an infinite number of points of $A$, then that point is called the condensation point of $A$. Thus, a finite set has no condensation point.

## Interior Point

The point $x \in A$ is called an interior point of $A$ if there exist a neighbourhood containing $x$ and contained in $A$. Evidently, $x$ must belong to $A$.

## Closed Set

If every limit point of a set is contained in the set itself, then such a set is called closed set. Thus, a closed set has the derived set as its subset, $D(A) \subseteq A$, $A$ is a closed set.

## Open Set

If every point of set $A$ is an interior point of $A$, then $A$ is always called an open set. Open interval is always an open set.

> ***Note*** **(a)** The cover $G$ is called an open cover, if every member of $G$ is an open set.
>
> **(b)** If $\exists\ G_1 \subset G$ s.t. $G_1$ is a cover of $A$, then $G_1$ is called a subcover of $G$. If every member of $G_1$ is open s.t. $G_1$ is finite set, then $G_1$ is called a finite open subcover of $G$.

## Important Theorems

1. The finite intersection of open subsets of $R$ is an open subset of $R$.
2. Suppose $A \subset R$, then
   (i) $A^\circ$ is an open subset of $R$.
   (ii) $A^\circ$ is the largest open set contained in $A$.
   (iii) $A^\circ$ is open if and only if $A^\circ = A$
   where $A^\circ$ represents the set of all interior point of $A$.
3. A subset $A$ of $R$ is closed if and only if its complement $A^c$ is open.
4. The arbitrary intersection of closed sets is a closed set.
5. The finite union of closed sets is a closed set.
6. (Heine-Borel Theorem) Suppose, $A \subset R$ and $G$ be the collection of subsets of $R$. Then, $G$ is called a cover of $A$ if $A \subset \bigcup_{G \in G} G$.

# SOLVED EXAMPLES

## Type I (*Only one correct option*)

***Example 1.*** *If $A = \{a, b, c\}$ and $R = \{(a, a), (a, b), (b, c), (b, b), (c, c), (c, a)\}$ is a binary relation on $A$, then which one of the following is correct?*

(a) $R$ is reflexive and symmetric, but not transitive
(b) $R$ is reflexive and transitive, but not symmetric
(c) $R$ is reflexive, but neither symmetric not transitive
(d) $R$ is reflexive, symmetric and transitive

**Solution.** (c) $\because (a, a), (b, b), (c, c) \in R$

$\therefore R$ is a reflexive relation

But $(a, b) \in R$ and $(b, a) \notin R$

$\therefore R$ is not a symmetric relation

Also, $(a, b), (b, c) \in R$

$\Rightarrow \quad (a, c) \notin R$

$\therefore R$ is not a transitive relation.

***Example 2.*** *If the cardinality of a set A is 4 and that of a set B is 3, then what is the cardinality of the set $A \Delta B$?*

(a) 1
(b) 5
(c) 7
(d) Cannot be determined as the sets $A$ and $B$ are not given.

**Solution.** (d) Since, the sets $A$ and $B$ are not known, thus cardinality of the set $A \Delta B$ cannot be determined.

***Example 3. Assertion (A)*** *If events, A, B, C and D are mutually exhaustive, then $(A \cup B \cup C)^c = D$*

***Reason (R)*** *$(A \cup B \cup C)^c = D$ implies if any element is excluded from the sets A, B and C, then it is included in D.*

(a) A and R are both correct, also R is the correct explanation of A.
(b) A and R are both correct, but R is not the correct explanation of A.
(c) A is correct but R is wrong.
(d) A is wrong but R is correct.

**Solution.** (a) Both (A) and (R) are true and (R) is the correct explanation of (A).

$\because \quad (A \cup B \cup C)^c = A^c \cap B^c \cap C^c = D$

***Example 4.*** *Elements of a population are classified according to the presence or absence of each of 3 attributes A, B and C. What is the number of smallest ultimate classes into which the population is divided?*

(a) 5 (b) 6
(c) 8 (d) 9

**Solution.** (d) Elements of a population are classified according to the presence or absence of each of 3 attributes $A$, $B$ and $C$. Then, the smallest number of smallest ultimate classes into which the population is divided, is 9.

***Example 5.*** *If A and B are subsets of a set X, then what is $\{A \cap (X - B)\} \cup B$ equal to?*

(a) $A \cup B$ (b) $A \cap B$
(c) $A$ (d) $B$

**Solution.** (a) $\because \ A \subseteq X$ and $B \subseteq X$

$$\therefore \quad \{(A \cap (X - B))\} \cup B \qquad (\because X - B = B')$$
$$= (A \cap B') \cup B = (A \cup B) \cap (B' \cup B) = (A \cup B) \cap X$$
$$= A \cup B$$

***Example 6.*** *The total number of subsets of a finite set A has 56 more elements, then the total number of subsets of another finite set B. What is the number of elements in the set A?*

(a) 5 (b) 6 (c) 7 (d) 8

**Solution.** (b) Let sets $A$ and $B$ have $m$ and $n$ elements, respectively.

$\therefore \quad 2^m - 2^n = 56$ (According to question)

$\Rightarrow \quad 2^n(2^{m-n} - 1) = 8 \times 7 = (2)^3 \times 7 = 2^3(2^3 - 1)$

On comparing

$\Rightarrow \quad n = 3$ and $m - n = 3$

$\Rightarrow \quad m = 6$ and $n = 3$

Number of subsets of $A = 2^3 + 56 = 64 = 2^6$

$\Rightarrow$ Number of elements in $A = 6$

***Example 7.*** *If* $f(x) = \begin{cases} 1, & \text{if } x \text{ is a rational number} \\ 0, & \text{if } x \text{ is an irrational number} \end{cases}$

*what is the value of* $(fof)(\sqrt{3})$?

(a) 0 (b) 1
(c) Both 0 and 1 (d) None of these

**Solution.** (b) $\because f(x) = \begin{cases} 1, & \text{if } x \text{ is a rational number} \\ 0, & \text{if } x \text{ is an irrational number} \end{cases}$

$(fof)\sqrt{3} = f\{f(\sqrt{3})\}$

$= f(0)$ ($\because \sqrt{3}$ is an irrational number)

$= 1$ ($\because 0$ is a rational number)

***Example 8.*** *Consider the following statement.*

*I. Parallelism of lines is an equivalence relation.*
*II. xRy, if x is a father of y, is an equivalence relation.*
*Which of the statements given above is/are correct?*

(a) I only (b) II only
(c) Both I and II (d) Neither I nor II

**Solution.** (a) I. Let $l, m, n$ are parallel lines and $R$ is a relation.

$\therefore \quad l \,||\, l$, then $R$ is reflexive.
and $l \,||\, m$ and $m \,||\, l$, the $R$ is symmetric.
Also, $l \,||\, m, m \,||\, n \Rightarrow l \,||\, n$,
then $R$ is transitive.
Hence, $R$ is an equivalence relation.

II. If $x$ is father of $y$ and $y$ is not father of $x$, then relation is not symmetric, thus relation is not equivalence.

***Example 9.*** *The function* $f: R \to R$ *defined by* $f(x) = (x^2 + 1)^{35}$ *for all* $x \in R$ *is*

(a) one-one but not onto
(b) onto but not one-one
(c) neither one-one nor onto
(d) both one-one and onto

**Solution.** (c) Since, $f(-1) = f(1) = 2^{35}$

*i.e.*, Two real number 1 and $-1$ have the same image. So, the function is not one-one and let

$$y = (x^2 + 1)^{35}$$

$$\Rightarrow \quad x = \sqrt{(y)^{1/35} - 1}$$

Thus, every real number has no pre-image. So, the function is not onto.

Hence, the function is neither one-one nor onto.

***Example 10.*** *If A and B are disjoint sets, then* $A \cap (A' \cup B)$ *is equal to which one of the following?*

(a) $\phi$ (b) $A$
(c) $A \cup B$ (d) $A - B'$

**Solution.** (a) $\because A \cap B = \phi$ (given)

$$A \cap (A' \cup B) = (A \cap A') \cup (A \cap B) = \phi \cup \phi = \phi$$

***Example 11.*** *Let* $U = \{1, 2, 3, \ldots, 20\}$. *Let A, B, C be the subsets of U. Let A be the set of all numbers, which are perfect squares, B be the set of all numbers which are multiples of 5 and C be the set of all numbers, which are divisible by 2 and 3.*

*Consider the following statements.*

*I. A, B, C are mutually exclusive.*
*II. A, B, C are mutually exhaustive.*
*III. The number of elements in the complement set of* $A \cup B$ *is 12.*

*Which of the statements given above the correct?*

(a) I and II (b) I and III
(c) II and III (d) I, II and III

**Solution.** (b) $U = \{1, 2, 3, \ldots, 20\}$

$A =$ Set of all natural numbers which are perfect square $= \{1, 4, 9, 16\}$

$B =$ Set of all natural numbers which are multiples of 5 $= \{5, 10, 15, 20\}$

$C =$ Set of all natural numbers which are divisible by 2 and 3 $= \{6, 12, 18\}$

$\because \quad A \cap B \cap C = \phi$

and $\quad A \cup B = \{1, 4, 9, 16, 5, 10, 15, 20\}$

$\Rightarrow \quad n(A \cup B) = 8$

$\Rightarrow \quad n(A \cup B)' = 20 - 8 = 12$

$\therefore A, B, C$ are mutually exclusive and the number of elements in the complement set of $A \cup B$ is 12.

***Example 12.*** *The function* $f(x) = e^x, x \in R$ *is*

(a) onto but not one-one
(b) one-one onto
(c) one-one but not onto
(d) neither one-one nor onto

**Solution.** (c) It is clear from the graph that $f(x) = e^x, \forall x \in R$ is one-one but not onto. Since, range $\neq$ codomain, so $f(x)$ is into.

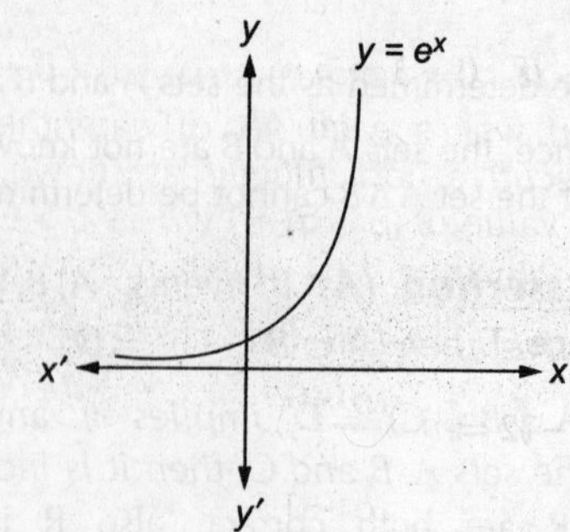

***Example 13.*** *If $A = P\{1, 2\}$ where P denotes the power set, then which one of the following is correct?*

(a) $\{1, 2\} \subset A$ (b) $1 \in A$ (c) $\phi \notin A$ (d) $\{1, 2\} \in A$

**Solution.** (d) $A = P\{1, 2\} = \{\phi, \{1\}, \{2\}, \{1, 2\}\}$

From above, it is clear that

$\{1, 2\} \in A$

***Example 14.*** *Let R and S be two equivalence relations on a set A. Then,*

(a) $R \cup S$ is an equivalence relation on A
(b) $R \cap S$ is an equivalence relation on A
(c) $R - S$ is an equivalence relation on A
(d) None of the above

**Solution.** (b) Given, R and S are relations on set A.

$\therefore$ $R \subseteq A \times A$ and $S \subseteq A \times A \Rightarrow R \cap C \subseteq A \times A$

$\Rightarrow$ $R \cap S$ is also a relation on A.

**Reflexivity** Let a be an arbitrary element of A. Then,

$a \in A \Rightarrow (a, a) \in R$ and $(a, a) \in S$, [$\because$ R and S are reflexive]

$\Rightarrow$ $(a, a) \in R \cap S$

Thus, $(a, a) \in R \cap S$ for all $a \in A$.

So, $R \cap S$ is a reflexive relation on A.

**Symmetry** Let $a, b \in A$ such that $(a, b) \in R \cap S$.

Then, $(a, b) \in R \cap S \Rightarrow (a, b) \in R$ and $(a, b) \in S$

$\Rightarrow$ $(b, a) \in R$ and $(b, a) \in S$ [$\because$ R and S are symmetric]

$\Rightarrow$ $(b, a) \in R \cap S$

Thus, $(a, b) \in R \cap S$

$\Rightarrow$ $(b, a) \in R \cap S$ for all $(a, b) \in R \cap S$.

So, $R \cap S$ is symmetric on A.

**Transitivity** Let $a, b, c \in A$ such that $(a, b) \in R \cap S$ and $(b, c) \in R \cap S$. Then, $(a, b) \in R \cap S$ and $(b, c) \in R \cap S$

$\Rightarrow$ $\{((a, b) \in R$ and $(a, b) \in S)\}$

and $\{((b, c) \in R$ and $(b, c) \in S)\}$

$\Rightarrow$ $\{(a, b) \in R, (b, c) \in R\}$ and $\{(a, b) \in S, (b, c) \in S\}$

$\Rightarrow$ $(a, c) \in R$ and $(a, c) \in S$

[$\because$ R and S are transitive. So
$(a, b) \in R$ and $(b, c) \in R \Rightarrow (a, c) \in R$
$(a, b) \in S$ and $(b, c) \in S \Rightarrow (a, c) \in S$]

$\Rightarrow$ $(a, c) \in R \cap S$

Thus, $(a, b) \in R \cap S$ and $(b, c) \in R \cap S \Rightarrow (a, c) \in R \cap S$.

So, $R \cap S$ is transitive on A.

Hence, R is an equivalence relation on A.

***Example 15.*** *If $(1 + 3 + 5 + \ldots + p) + (1 + 3 + 5 + \ldots + q) = (1 + 3 + 5 + \ldots + r)$ where each set of parentheses contains the sum of consecutive odd integers as shown, what is the smallest possible value of $(p + q + r)$ where $p > 6$?*

(a) 12 (b) 21 (c) 45 (d) 54

**Solution.** (b) Since, $T_n = a + (n-1)d$ ($\because$ nth term of an AP)

$$\therefore \quad p = 1 + (n-1)2 \Rightarrow n = \frac{p+1}{2},$$

$$q = 1 + (n-1)2 \Rightarrow n = \frac{q+1}{2}$$

and $r = 1 + (n-1)2 \Rightarrow n = \dfrac{r+1}{2}$

$\because$ Sum of n terms of an AP $= \dfrac{n}{2} = [2a + (n-1)d]$

$$\therefore \frac{\frac{p+1}{2}}{2}\left[2\times1 + \left(\frac{p+1}{2} - 1\right)2\right] + \frac{\left(\frac{q+1}{2}\right)}{2}\left[2\times1 + \left(\frac{q+1}{2} - 1\right)2\right]$$

$$= \frac{r+1}{4}\left[2\times1 + \left(\frac{r+1}{2} - 1\right)2\right]$$

$$\Rightarrow \quad \frac{p+1}{4}[2 + (p-1)] + \frac{q+1}{4}[2 + (q-1)] = \frac{r+1}{4}[2 + r - 1]$$

$$\Rightarrow \quad (p+1)^2 + (q+1)^2 = (r+1)^2$$

This the possible only when $p = 7, q = 5, r = 9$

[$\because p > 6$ (given)]

$$\therefore \quad p + q + r = 7 + 5 + 9 = 21$$

***Example 16.*** *Let $A = \{x \mid x \le 9, x \in N\}$. Let $B = \{a, b, c\}$ be the subset of A where $(a + b + c)$ is a multiple of 3. What is the largest possible number of subsets like B?*

(a) 12 (b) 21 (c) 27 (d) 30

**Solution.** (d) $A = \{x : x \le 9, x \in N\}$

$= \{1, 2, 3, 4, 5, 6, 7, 8, 9\}$

Total possible multiple of 3 are

3, 6, 9, 12, 15, 18, 21, 24, 27

But 3 and 27 are not possible.

$6 \to 1 + 2 + 3$

$9 \to 2 + 3 + 4, 5 + 3 + 1, 6 + 2 + 1$

$12 \to 9 + 2 + 1, 8 + 3 + 1, 7 + 1 + 4, 7 + 2 + 3, 6 + 4 + 2, 6 + 5 + 1, 5 + 4 + 3$

$15 \to 9 + 4 + 2, 9 + 5 + 1, 8 + 6 + 1, 8 + 5 + 2, 8 + 4 + 3, 7 + 6 + 2, 7 + 5 + 3, 6 + 5 + 4$

$18 \to 9 + 8 + 1, 9 + 7 + 2, 9 + 6 + 3, 9 + 5 + 4, 8 + 7 + 3, 8 + 6 + 4, 7 + 6 + 5$

$21 \to 9 + 8 + 4, 9 + 7 + 5, 8 + 7 + 6$

$24 \to 9 + 8 + 7$

Hence, total number of largest possible subsets are 30.

***Example 17.*** *A mapping $f : R \to R$ which is defined as $f(x) = \cos x$; $x \in R$ is*

(a) one-one only (b) onto only
(c) one-one onto (d) neither one-one nor onto

**Solution.** (d) Given, $f(x) = \cos x$

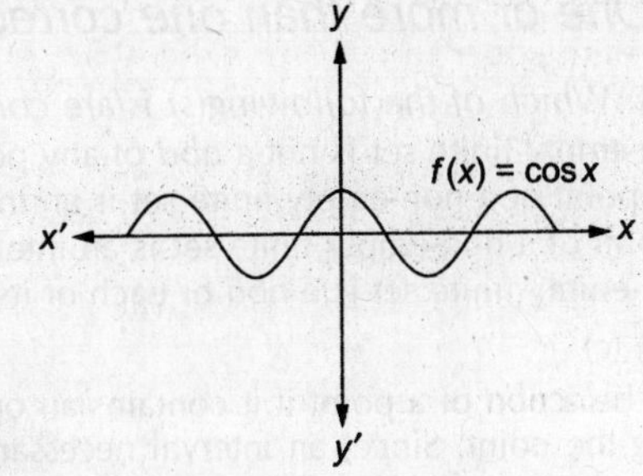

It is clear from the figure that $f(x)$ is neither one-one nor a onto function.

Since, whenever we drawn a line parallel to x-axis, then it intersects at infinite points to the curve. So, $f(x)$ is not one-one.

And, range of $f(x) = [-1, 1]$

Codomain of $f(x) = R$

Range of $f(x) \neq$ codomain of $f(x)$

$\therefore f(x)$ is not onto.

**Example 18.** *If $n(A) = 115, n(B) = 326, n(A - B) = 47$, then what is $n(A \cup B)$ equal to?*

(a) 373 (b) 165
(c) 370 (d) 394

**Solution.** (a) Now, $n(A-B) = n(A) - n(A \cap B)$

$\Rightarrow \quad 47 = 115 - n(A \cap B)$

$\Rightarrow \quad n(A \cap B) = 68$

$$n(A \cup B) = n(A) + n(B) - n(A \cap B) = 115 + 326 - 68 = 373$$

**Example 19.** *In a town of 10000 families it was found that 40% family buy newspaper A, 20% buy newspaper B and 10% families buy newspaper C, 5% families buy A and B, 3% buy B and C and 4% buy A and C. If 2% families buy all the three newspaper, then number of families which buy A only is*

(a) 3100 (b) 3300
(c) 2900 (d) 1400

**Solution.** (b) $n(A) = 40\%$ of $10000 = 4000$

$n(B) = 20\%$ of $10000 = 2000$

$n(C) = 10\%$ of $10000 = 1000$

$n(A \cap B) = 5\%$ of $10000 = 500$

$n(B \cap C) = 3\%$ of $10000 = 300$

$n(C \cap A) = 4\%$ of $10000 = 400$

$n(A \cap B \cap C) = 2\%$ of $10000 = 200$

We want to find $n(A \cap B^c \cap C^c) = n[A \cap (B \cup C)^c]$

$= n(A) - n[A \cap (B \cup C)] = n(A) - n[(A \cap B) \cup (A \cap C)]$

$= n(A) - [n(A \cap B) + n(A \cap C) - n(A \cap B \cap C)]$

$= 4000 - [500 + 400 - 200] = 4000 - 700 = 3300$

**Example 20.** *A survey shows that 63% of the Americans like cheese whereas 76% like apples. If x% of the Americans like both cheese and apples, then*

(a) $x = 39$ (b) $x = 63$
(c) $39 \le x \le 63$ (d) None of these

**Solution.** (c) Let $A$ denote the set of Americans who like cheese and let $B$ denote the set of Americans who like apples.

Let population of American be 100.

Then, $\quad n(A) = 63, n(B) = 76$

Now, $\quad n(A \cup B) = n(A) + n(B) - n(A \cap B)$

$\quad = 63 + 76 - n(A \cap B)$

$\therefore \quad n(A \cup B) + n(A \cap B) = 139$

$\Rightarrow \quad n(A \cap B) = 139 - n(A \cup B)$

But $\quad n(A \cup B) \le 100$

$\therefore \quad -n(A \cup B) \ge -100$

$\therefore \quad 139 - n(A \cup B) \ge 139 - 100 = 39$

$\therefore \quad n(A \cap B) \ge 39$ *i.e.*, $39 \le n(A \cap B)$ ...(i)

Again, $\quad A \cap B \subseteq A, A \cap B \subseteq B$

$\therefore \quad n(A \cap B) \le n(A) = 63$ and $n(A \cap B) \le n(B) = 76$

$\therefore \quad n(A \cap B) \le 63$ ...(ii)

Then, $\quad 39 \le n(A \cap B) \le 63 \Rightarrow 39 \le x \le 63$

**Example 21.** *The set of all limit point of the set*

$$S = \left\{\frac{1}{m} + \frac{1}{n} : m \in \mathbb{N}, n \in \mathbb{N}\right\} \text{ is}$$

(a) $\phi$ (b) $\{0\}$
(c) $\left\{\frac{1}{m} : m \in \mathbb{N}\right\}$ (d) None of these

**Solution.** (c) Let us fixed $m \in \mathbb{N}$. Then, for every $\delta > 0$. $\left(\frac{1}{m} - \delta, \frac{1}{m} + \delta\right)$ contains infinitely many elements of N.

Hence, the set of all limit point of $S$ is $\left\{\frac{1}{m} : m \in \mathbb{N}\right\}$.

**Example 22.** *The set of all limit points of the set*

$$S = \left\{\frac{1}{n} : n \in \mathbb{N}\right\} \text{ is}$$

(a) $\phi$ (b) $\{0\}$
(c) N (d) None of these

**Solution.** (b) For every $\delta > 0$, $(-\delta, \delta)$ contains infinite number of elements of set $S$. Hence, $\{0\}$ is the set of all limit point of the set $S$.

## Type II (*One or more than one correct option*)

**Example 23.** *Which of the following(s) is/are correct?*

(a) A non-empty finite set is not a *nbd* of any point
(b) Every point of a non-empty finite set is an interior point
(c) No point of a non-empty finite set is an interior point
(d) A non-empty finite set is a *nbd* of each of its points

**Solution.** (a), (c)

A set can be a *nbd* of a point if it contains an open interval containing the point. Since, an interval necessarily contains an infinite number of points. Therefore in order that a set be a *nbd* of a point it necessarily contain an infinity of points. Thus, a finite set cannot be a *nbd* of any points. Hence, no points of finite non-empty set is an interior point.

**Example 24.** *Which of the following(s) is/are correct?*

(a) The set of interior points of $N$ is empty
(b) The set of interior points of $I$ is empty
(c) The set of interior points of $Z$ is empty
(d) The set of interior points of $R$ is empty

**Solution.** (a), (b), (c)

Since, for the set $\mathbb{N}$, $I$ and $Z$ there is no open interval which is contained in $\mathbb{N}$ or $I$ or $Z$ as every open interval contains rational and irrational number but the set of interior points of $\mathbb{R}$ is $\mathbb{R}$.

***Example 25.*** *Which of the following(s) set is/are open?*

(a) $\mathbb{R}$ (b) $Q$ (c) $Z$ (d) $\phi$

**Solution.** (a), (d)

The set of real number $\mathbb{R}$ is an open set as every real number is an interior point of $\mathbb{R}$. Similarly the set $\phi$ is open as the set $\phi$ is a *nbd* of each of its points in the sense that there is no point in $\phi$ of which it is not *nbd*. But the set $\mathbb{Q}$ and $Z$ are not open as no points of $\mathbb{Q}$ or $Z$ is an interior points.

***Example 26.*** *Which of the following(s) is/are correct?*

(a) Every open interval is an open set

(b) Every open interval is a *nbd* of each of its points

(c) Every point of an open interval is an interior point

(d) The set $\left\{\frac{1}{n} : n \in \mathbb{N}\right\}$ is not open

**Solution.** (a), (b), (c), (d)

Let $(a, b)$ be an open interval and $x \in (a, b)$ which implies that $a < x < b$.

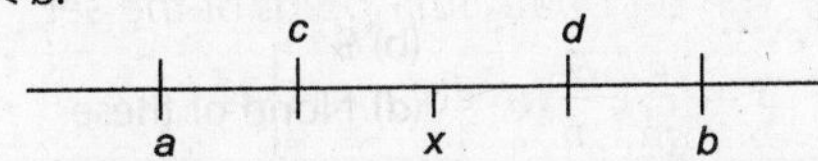


Let $c, d$ be two numbers such that $a < c < x$ and $n < d < b$

$\Rightarrow \quad a < c < x < d < b \Rightarrow x \in (c, d) \subset (a, b)$

Thus, the given interval $(a, b)$ contains an open interval containing the point $x$ and is therefore a *nbd* of $x$.

Hence, the open interval is a *nbd* of each of its points and is therefore an open set.

Hence, every point of an open interval is an interior point.

Now '$o$' is an interior point of the set $\left\{\frac{1}{n} : n \in \mathbb{N}\right\}$ which does not lie in this set.

Hence, the set $\left\{\frac{1}{n} : n \in \mathbb{N}\right\}$ is not open.

***Example 27.*** *Which of the following(s) is/are correct?*

(a) The intersection of any finite number of open sets is open

(b) The intersection of an arbitrary number of open sets is open

(c) The union of an arbitrary family of open sets is open

(d) Exactly one of the above is true

**Solution.** (a), (c)

Let $G_1$ and $G_2$ be two open sets. Then,

if $\quad G_1 \cap G_2 = \phi$, it is open

if $\quad G_1 \cap G_2 \neq \phi$, let $x \in G_1 \cap G_2$

$\Rightarrow \quad x \in G_1$ and $x \in G_2$

$\Rightarrow \quad G_1, G_2$ are *nbd* of $x$.

$\Rightarrow \quad G_1 \cap G_2$ is a *nbd* of $x$.

but since $x$ is any point of $G_1 \cap G_2$, therefore $G_1 \cap G_2$ is a *nbd* of each of its points. Hence, $G_1 \cap G_2$ is open.

Now, consider the open sets

$$G_n = \left(-\frac{1}{n}, \frac{1}{n}\right), n \in \mathbb{N}$$

$\Rightarrow \quad \bigcap_{n \in \mathbb{N}} G_n = \{0\}$, which is not an open set.

$\Rightarrow$ The intersection of arbitrary number of open set need not be open.

Next, let $G$ be the union of an arbitrary family $\mathbb{F} = \{G_\lambda : \lambda \in \Lambda\}$ of open sets, $\Lambda$ being an index set. To prove that $G$ is an open set, we shall show that for any point $x \in G$, it contains an open interval containing $x$.

Let $x \in G$

$\Rightarrow \quad \exists$ atleast one member, say

$G_{\lambda_1}$ of $\mathbb{F}$ such that

$x \in G_{\lambda_1}$

Since, $G_{\lambda_1}$ is an open set, $\exists$ an open interval $I_n$ such that

$$x \in I_n \subseteq G_{\lambda_1} \subseteq G$$

Thus, the set $G$ contains an open interval containing any point $x$ of $G$. Hence, $G$ is an open set.

***Example 28.*** *Which of the following(s) is/are correct?*

(a) The set $I$ has no limit point

(b) The set $\mathbb{N}$ has no limit point

(c) Every point of the set $Q$ is a limit point

(d) Every point of the set $\mathbb{R}$ is a limit point

**Solution.** (a), (b), (c), (d)

The set $I$ has no limit point, for a *nbd* $\left(m-\frac{1}{2}, m+\frac{1}{2}\right)$ of $m \in I$, contains no point of $I$ other than $m$. Thus the derived set of $I$ is the null set $\phi$.

The set $\mathbb{N}$ has no limit point, for a *nbd* $\left(m-\frac{1}{2}, m+\frac{1}{2}\right)$ of $m \in \mathbb{N}$, contains no points of $\mathbb{N}$ other than $m$. Thus, the derived set of $\mathbb{N}$ is null set $\phi$. Every point of the set $Q$ of rationals is a limit point, for between any two rationals there exist an infinity of rational.

Further every point of $\mathbb{R}$ is a limit point, for every *nbd* of any of its points contains an infinite member of $\mathbb{R}$.

***Example 29.*** *If $\bar{S}$ denotes the closure of the set $S$, then which of the following(s) is/are correct?*

(a) $\bar{I} = I$

(b) $\bar{Q} = \mathbb{R}$

(c) $\bar{R} = \mathbb{R}$

(d) If $S = \left\{\frac{1}{n} : n \in \mathbb{N}\right\}$, then $\bar{S} = \left\{\frac{1}{n} : n \in \mathbb{N}\right\} \cup \{0\}$

**Solution.** (a), (b), (c), (d)

Since, $I' = \phi$, $Q' = \mathbb{R}$, $\mathbb{R}' = \mathbb{R}$ and $S' = \{0\}$

Hence,

$$\bar{I} = I \cup I' = I \cup \phi = I$$

$$\bar{Q} = Q \cup Q' = Q \cup \mathbb{R} = \mathbb{R}$$

$$\bar{\mathbb{R}} = \mathbb{R} \cup \mathbb{R}' = \mathbb{R} \cup \mathbb{R} = \mathbb{R}$$

$$\bar{S} = S \cup S' = \left\{\frac{1}{n} : n \in \mathbb{N}\right\} \cup \{0\}$$

***Example 30.*** *Which of the following(s) is/are countable?*

(a) The set $\mathbb{R}$ of real number is uncountable
(b) The set of rational number in [0, 1] is countable
(c) The set of all rational numbers is countable
(d) None of the above

**Solution.** (a), (b), (c)

Let us suppose that the set of real number $\mathbb{R}$ is countable, then $\mathbb{R} = \{x_1, x_2, \dots, x_n, \dots\}$.

Enclose each member $x_n$ of $\mathbb{R}$ in an open interval

$$I_n = \left(x_n - \frac{1}{2^{n+1}}, x_n + \frac{1}{2^{n+1}}\right)$$

of length $\frac{1}{2^n}, n = 1, 2, 3, \dots$

where the sum of lengths of $I_n$'s is $\frac{1}{2} + \frac{1}{2^2} + \frac{1}{2^3} + \dots$

But $\quad x_n \in \mathbb{R}$ and $R = \bigcup_{n=1}^{\infty} \{x_n\} \subseteq \bigcup_{n=1}^{\infty} I_n$

$\Rightarrow$ The whole real line is contained in the union of intervals whose lengths add up to 1. Which is a contradiction. Hence, $\mathbb{R}$ is uncountable.

Arrange the set of rationals according to increasing denominators as $0, 1, \frac{1}{2}, \frac{1}{3}, \frac{2}{3}, \frac{1}{4}, \frac{3}{4}, \frac{1}{5}, \frac{2}{5}, \frac{3}{5}, \frac{4}{5}, \frac{1}{6}, \frac{5}{6}, \dots$

Then the one-one correspondence can be indicated as

$1 \leftrightarrow 0 \qquad 5 \leftrightarrow \frac{2}{3} \qquad 9 \leftrightarrow \frac{2}{5}$

$2 \leftrightarrow 1 \qquad 6 \leftrightarrow \frac{1}{4} \qquad 10 \leftrightarrow \frac{3}{5}$

$3 \leftrightarrow \frac{1}{2} \qquad 7 \leftrightarrow \frac{3}{4} \qquad 11 \leftrightarrow \frac{4}{5}$

$4 \leftrightarrow \frac{1}{3} \qquad 8 \leftrightarrow \frac{1}{5} \qquad \dots\dots\dots$

$\dots\dots\dots$

which shows that the set of rational numbers in [0, 1] is countable.

Now, the set of all rational numbers is the union $\bigcup_{i=1}^{\infty} A_i$, where $A_i$ is the set of rationals which can be written with denominator $i$. That is

$$A_i = \left\{\frac{0}{i}, \frac{-1}{i}, \frac{1}{i}, \frac{-2}{i}, \frac{2}{i}, \dots\right\}$$

Each $A_i$ is equivalent to the set of all positive integers and hence countable.

***Example 31.*** *Let $A = [1, 2, 3, 4]$ and $R$ be a relation in $A$ given by $R = \{(1, 1), (2, 2), (3, 3), (4, 4), (1, 2), (2, 1), (3, 1), (1, 3)\}$. Then, $R$ is*

(a) reflexive
(b) symmetric
(c) transitive
(d) an equivalence relation

**Solution.** (a), (b)

$(1, 1), (2, 2), (3, 3), (4, 4) \in R; \therefore R$ is reflexive.

$\because (1, 2), (3, 1) \in R$ and also $(2, 1), (1, 3) \in R$.

Hence, $R$ is symmetric. But clearly $R$ is not transitive.

***Example 32.*** *Let $X = \{1, 2, 3, 4, 5\}$ and $Y = \{1, 3, 5, 7, 9\}$. Which of the following(s) is/are relations from $X$ to $Y$?*

(a) $R_1 = \{(x, y) \mid y = 2 + x, x \in X, y \in Y\}$
(b) $R_2 = \{(1, 1), (2, 1), (3, 3), (4, 3), (5, 5)\}$
(c) $R_3 = \{(1, 1), (1, 3), (3, 5), (3, 7), (5, 7)\}$
(d) $R_4 = \{(1, 3), (2, 5), (2, 4), (7, 9)\}$

**Solution.** (a), (b), (c)

$R_4$ is not a relation from $X$ to $Y$, because $(7, 9) \in R_4$ but $(7, 9) \notin X \times Y$.

***Example 33.*** *In a class of 55 students, the number of students studying different subjects are 23 in Mathematics, 24 in Physics, 19 in Chemistry, 12 in Mathematics and Physics, 9 in Mathematics and Chemistry, 7 in Physics and Chemistry and 4 in all the three subjects. The number of students who have taken exactly one subject is*

(a) 6
(b) 9
(c) 7
(d) None of these

**Solution.** (a), (b), (c)

$$n(M) = 23, n(P) = 24, n(C) = 19$$
$$n(M \cap P) = 12, n(M \cap C) = 9, n(P \cap C) = 7$$
$$n(M \cap P \cap C) = 4$$

We have, to find

$$n(M \cap P' \cap C'), n(P \cap M' \cap C'), n(C \cap M' \cap P')$$

Now, $n(M \cap P' \cap C') = n[M \cap (P \cup C)']$
$= n(M) - n(M \cap (P \cup C))$
$= n(M) - n[(M \cap P) \cup (M \cap C)]$
$= n(M) - n(M \cap P) - n(M \cap C) + n(M \cap P \cap C)$
$= 23 - 12 - 9 + 4 = 27 - 21 = 6$

$n(P \cap M' \cap C') = n[P \cap (M \cup C)']$
$= n(P) - n[P \cap (M \cup C)] = n(P) - n[(P \cap M) \cup (P \cap C)]$
$= n(P) - n(P \cap M) - n(P \cap C) + n(P \cap M \cap C)$
$= 24 - 12 - 7 + 4 = 9$

$n(C \cap M' \cap P') = n(C) - n(C \cap P) - n(C \cap M) + n(C \cap P \cap M)$
$= 19 - 7 - 9 + 4 = 23 - 16 = 7$

# Exercise 1 (For Part 'B')

**Directions** (Q. Nos. 1-169) *All questions have only one correct option.*

**1.** If $A$ and $B$ are two sets satisfying $A - B = B - A$, then which one of the following is correct?
(a) $A = \phi$ (b) $A \cap B = \phi$
(c) $A = B$ (d) None of these

**2.** In a city 20% of the population travels by car, 50% travels by bus and 10% travels by both car and bus. Then, persons travelling by car or bus is
(a) 80% (b) 40%
(c) 60% (d) 70%

**3.** Sets $A$ and $B$ have $n$ elements in common. How many elements will $(A \times B)$ and $(B \times A)$ have in common?
(a) 0 (b) 1
(c) $n$ (d) $n^2$

**4.** A set $F$ is closed if
(a) it contains all of its points of closure
(b) it contains all of its accumulation point
(c) (a) is true, (b) is false
(d) Both (a) and (b) are true

**5.** If $(A - B) \cup (B - A) = A$ for subsets $A$ and $B$ of the universal set $U$, then which one of the following is correct?
(a) $B$ is a proper non-empty subset of $A$
(b) $A$ and $B$ are non-empty disjoint sets
(c) $B = \phi$
(d) None of the above

**6.** For real numbers $x$ and $y$, we write $xRy \Leftrightarrow x - y + \sqrt{2}$ is an irrational number. Then, the relation $R$ is
(a) reflexive (b) symmetric
(c) transitive (d) None of these

**7.** Let $A = \{x \in R \mid -9 \le x < 4\}$
$B = \{x \in R \mid -13 < x \le 5\}$ and
$C = \{x \in R \mid -7 \le x \le 8\}$
Then, which one of the following is correct?
(a) $-9 \in (A \cap B \cap C)$ (b) $-7 \in (A \cap B \cap C)$
(c) $4 \in (A \cap B \cap C)$ (d) $5 \in (A \cap B \cap C)$

**8.** "Every non-empty set $S$ of real numbers which is bounded above has supremum" is
(a) field axiom (b) ordered axiom
(c) completeness axiom (d) None of these

**9.** Which one of the following is correct?
(a) $A \cup P(A) = P(A)$ (b) $A \cap P(A) = A$
(c) $A - P(A) = A$ (d) $P(A) - \{A\} = P(A)$
Here, $P(A)$ denotes the power set of a set $A$.

**10.** The set of intelligent students in a class is
(a) a null set
(b) a singleton set
(c) a finite set
(d) not a well defined collection

**11.** The order of a set $A$ is 3 and that of a set $B$ is 2. What is the number of relations from $A$ to $B$?
(a) 4 (b) 6
(c) 32 (d) 64

**12.** If $X = \{4^n - 3n - 1 : n \in N\}$ and $Y = \{9(n-1) : n \in N\}$, then $X \cup Y$ is equal to
(a) $X$ (b) $Y$
(c) $N$ (d) None of these

**13.** If $N_a = \{ax \mid x \in N\}$, then what is $N_{12} \cap N_8$ equal to?
(a) $N_{12}$ (b) $N_{20}$
(c) $N_{24}$ (d) $N_{48}$

**14.** Which one of the following is the empty set?
(a) $\{x : x$ is a real number and $x^2 - 1 = 0\}$
(b) $\{x : x$ is a real number and $x^2 + 1 = 0\}$
(c) $\{x : x$ is a real number and $x^2 - 9 = 0\}$
(d) $\{x : x$ is a real number and $x^2 = x + 2\}$

**15.** In an examination out of 100 students, 75 passed in English, 60 passed in Mathematics and 45 passed in both English and Mathematics. What is the number of students passed in exactly one of the two subjects?
(a) 45 (b) 60
(c) 75 (d) 90

**16.** If the sets $A$ and $B$ are defined as
$A = \{(x, y) : y = \frac{1}{x}, 0 \ne x \in R\}$
$B = \{(x, y) : y = -x, x \in R\}$, then
(a) $A \cap B = A$ (b) $A \cap B = B$
(c) $A \cap B = \phi$ (d) None of these

**17.** Let $\mu$ = the set of all triangles, $P$ = the set of all isosceles triangles, $Q$ = the set of all equilateral triangles, $R$ = the set of all right angled triangles. What do the sets $P \cap Q$ and $R - P$ represents respectively?
(a) The set of isosceles triangles; the set of non-isosceles right angled triangles
(b) The set of isosceles triangles; the set of right angled triangles
(c) The set of equilateral triangles; the set of right angled triangles
(d) The set of isosceles triangles, the set of equilateral triangles

**18.** Let $A = \{x : x \in R, |x| < 1\}$; $B = \{x : x \in R, |x - 1| \ge 1\}$ and $A \cup B = R - D$, then the set $D$ is
(a) $\{x : 1 < x \le 2\}$ (b) $\{x : 1 \le x < 2\}$
(c) $\{x : 1 \le x \le 2\}$ (d) None of these

**19.** The function $f : A \to R$ where $A = \left\{x \in R, -\frac{\pi}{2} < x < \frac{\pi}{2}\right\}$ defined by $f(x) = \tan x$. Then which one of the following is correct?

(a) $f$ is injective (b) $f$ is not injective
(c) $f$ is bijective (d) $f$ is not bijective

**20.** Let $A = \{(x,y): y = e^x, x \in R\}$, $B = \{(x,y): y = e^{-x}, x \in R\}$. Then
(a) $A \cap B = \phi$ (b) $A \cap B \neq \phi$
(c) $A \cup B = R^2$ (d) None of these

**21.** If $A$, $B$ and $C$ are three sets and $U$ is the universal set such that $n(U) = 700$, $n(A) = 200$, $n(B) = 300$ and $n(A \cap B) = 100$, then what is the value of $(A' \cap B')$?
(a) 100 (b) 200
(c) 300 (d) 400

**22.** Let $A$ and $B$ be two sets such that $n(A) = 0.16$, $n(B) = 0.14$, $n(A \cup B) = 0.25$. Then, $n(A \cap B)$ is equal to
(a) 0.3 (b) 0.5
(c) 0.05 (d) None of these

**23.** $f: \{1, 2, 3\} \to \{4, 5\}$ is not a function, if it is defined by which one of the following?
(a) $\{(2, 4), (3, 5), (1, 5)\}$
(b) $\{(1, 4), (2, 5), (3, 4)\}$
(c) $\{(1, 4), (2, 5), (3, 4)\}$
(d) $\{(1, 4), (1, 5), (2, 4), (2, 5), (3, 4), (3, 5)\}$

**24.** 20 teachers of a school either teach Mathematics or Physics. 12 of them teach Mathematics while 4 teach both the subjects. Then, the number of teachers teaching Physics only is
(a) 12 (b) 8
(c) 16 (d) None of these

**25.** For non-empty subsets $A$, $B$ and $C$ of a set $X$ such that $A \cup B = B \cap C$, which one of the following is the strongest inference that can be derived?
(a) $A = B = C$ (b) $A \subseteq B = C$
(c) $A = B \subseteq C$ (d) $A \subseteq B \subseteq C$

**26.** In the set $A = \{1, 2, 3, 4, 5\}$, a relation $R$ is defined by $R = \{(x, y) \mid x, y \in A \text{ and } x < y\}$. Then, $R$ is
(a) reflexive (b) symmetric
(c) transitive (d) None of these

**27.** If $A$ and $B$ are two subsets of a set $X$, then what is $A \cap (A \cup B)'$ equal to?
(a) $A$ (b) $B$
(c) $\phi$ (d) $A'$

**28.** What is the inverse of the function $y = 5^{\log x}$?
(a) $x = 5^{1/\log y}$ (b) $x = y^{1/\log 5}$
(c) $x = 5^{\log y}$ (d) $x = y^{\log 5}$

**29.** In a battle 70% of the combatants lost one eye, 80% an ear, 75% an arm, 85% a leg, $x$% lost all the four limbs. Then, the minimum value of $x$ is
(a) 10 (b) 12
(c) 15 (d) None of these

**30.** In a class of 100 students, 55 students have passed in Mathematics and 67 students have passed in Physics. Then, the number of students who have passed in Physics only is
(a) 22 (b) 33
(c) 10 (d) 45

**31.** Let $R_1$ be a relation defined by $R_1 = \{(a, b) \mid a \geq b,\ a, b \in R\}$. Then, $R_1$ is
(a) an equivalence relation on $R$
(b) reflexive, transitive but not symmetric
(c) symmetric, transitive but not reflexive
(d) neither transitive not reflexive but symmetric

**32.** If $A$, $B$, $C$ are any three arbitrary events, then which one of the following expressions shows that both $A$ and $B$ occur but not $C$?
(a) $A \cap \bar{B} \cap \bar{C}$ (b) $A \cap B \cap \bar{C}$
(c) $\bar{A} \cap B \cap C$ (d) $A \cap B \cap C$

**33.** An integer $m$ is said to be related to another integer $n$, if $m$ is a multiple of $n$. Then, the relation is
(a) reflexive and symmetric
(b) reflexive and transitive
(c) symmetric and transitive
(d) equivalence relation

**34.** Every open set of real numbers is the union of
(a) countable collection of disjoint open intervals
(b) uncountable collection of disjoint open intervals
(c) countable collection of disjoint closed intervals
(d) uncountable collection of disjoint closed intervals

**35.** What is the number of proper subsets of a given finite set with $n$ elements?
(a) $2n - 1$ (b) $2n - 2$
(c) $2^n - 1$ (d) $2^n - 2$

**36.** Of the members of three athletic teams in a school 21 are in the cricket team, 26 are in the hockey team and 29 are in the football team. Among them, 14 play hockey and cricket, 15 play hockey and football, and 12 play football and cricket. 8 play all the three games. The total number of members in the three athletic teams is
(a) 43 (b) 76
(c) 49 (d) None of these

**37.** For a set $A$, consider the following statements
I. $A \cup P(A) = P(A)$
II. $\{A\} \cap P(A) = A$
III. $P(A) - \{A\} = P(A)$
where $P$ denotes power set.
Which of the statements given above is/are correct?
(a) I only (b) II only
(c) III only (d) I, II and III

**38.** Composite number $n$ is
(a) a prime number and $n > 1$
(b) non-prime number and $n < 1$
(c) non-prime number and $n > 1$
(d) a prime number and $n < 1$

**39.** In a class of 30 pupils, 12 take needle work, 16 take Physics and 18 take History. If all the 30 students take atleast one subject and no one takes all three, then the number of pupils taking 2 subjects is
(a) 16 (b) 6
(c) 8 (d) 20

**40.** The union of a finite or countable collection of countable sets is
(a) countable (b) uncountable
(c) infinite (d) None of these

**41.** The number of elements in the set $\{(a, b): 2a^2 + 3b^2 = 35,\ a, b \in Z\}$, where $Z$ is the set of all integer, is
(a) 2 (b) 4
(c) 8 (d) 12

**42.** If $x \in S$ a non-empty set of real numbers, then
(a) $\text{Inf}\, x = \text{Sup}\, x$ (b) $\text{Inf}\, x = -\text{Sup}(-x)$
(c) $\text{Inf}\, x = \text{Sup}(-x)$ (d) $\text{Inf}\ x = -\text{Sup}\ (x)$

**43.** If two sets $A$ and $B$ are having 99 elements in common, then the number of elements common to each of the sets $A \times B$ and $B \times A$ are
(a) $2^{99}$ (b) $99^2$
(c) 100 (d) 18

**44. Assertion (A)** $y = 2x + 3$ is a one-to-one real-valued function.
**Reason (R)** $x_1 \neq x_2 \Rightarrow y_1 \neq y_2$, $y_1 = 2x_1 + 3$, $y_2 = 2x_2 + 3$, for any two real $x_1$ and $x_2$
(a) A and R are both correct, also R is the correct explanation of A.
(b) A and R are both correct, but R is not the correct explanation of A.
(c) A is correct but R is wrong.
(d) A is wrong but R is correct.

**45.** An element a is an minimal element of set $S$, then
(a) $a \in S$
(b) $a \notin S$
(c) a is not lower bound of $S$
(d) a is not upper bound of $S$

**46.** If $n(A) = 3$, $n(B) = 6$ and $A \subseteq B$. Then, the number of elements in $A \cup B$ is equal to
(a) 3 (b) 9
(c) 6 (d) None of these

**47.** If $A$, $B$ and $C$ are three finite sets, then what is $[(A \cup B) \cap C]'$ equal to
(a) $A' \cup B' \cap C'$ (b) $A' \cap B' \cap C'$
(c) $A' \cap B' \cup C'$ (d) $A \cap B \cap C$

**48.** For every real number $x$, there is a positive integer $n$ such that
(a) $n > x$ (b) $n < x$
(c) $n = x$ (d) None of these

**49.** If $Q = \left\{x : x = \frac{1}{y}, \text{ where } y \in N\right\}$, then
(a) $0 \in Q$ (b) $1 \in Q$
(c) $2 \in Q$ (d) $\frac{2}{3} \in Q$

**50.** Consider the following statements
I. $\phi \in \{\phi\}$
II. $\{\phi\} \subseteq \phi$

Which of the statements given above is/are correct?
(a) I only (b) II only
(c) Both I and II (d) Neither I nor II

**51.** The set of real numbers in the closed interval {0, 1} is
(a) countable set (b) uncountable set
(c) finite set (d) None of these

**52.** A set contains $2n + 1$ elements. The number of subsets of this set containing more than $n$ elements is equal to
(a) $2^{n-1}$ (b) $2^n$
(c) $2^{n+1}$ (d) $2^{2n}$

**53.** What does the shaded region in the following diagram represent?

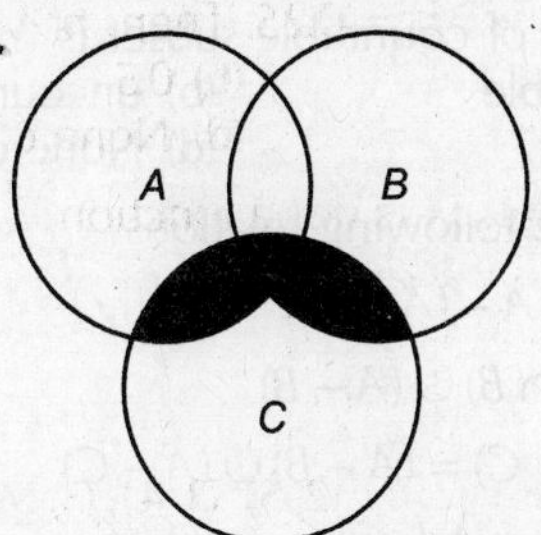


(a) $(A \cap B) \cap C$ (b) $(A \cup B) \cap C$
(c) $(A \cup B) - C$ (d) None of these

**54.** Every infinite set has a
(a) countable subset
(b) uncountable subset
(c) countable and uncountable both sets
(d) None of the above

**55.** Let $R$ be a relation on the set $N$ of natural numbers defined by $nRm \Leftrightarrow n$ is a factor of $m$(i.e., $n \mid m$). Then, $R$ is
(a) reflexive and symmetric
(b) transitive and symmetric
(c) equivalence
(d) reflexive, transitive but not symmetric

**56. Assertion (A)** Function $f: \{1, 2, 3\} \to \{a, b, c, d\}$ is defined by $f = \{(1, a), (2, b), (3, c)\}$ has no inverse.
**Reason (R)** Function '$f$' is not one-to-one.
(a) A and R are both correct, also R is the correct explanation of A.
(b) A and R are both correct; but R is not the correct explanation of A.
(c) A is correct but R is wrong.
(d) A is wrong but R is correct.

**57. Statement (A)** Set $S$ of real numbers is bounded above, if Sup $S$ is finite.
**Statement (B)** Set $S$ of real numbers is unbounded above, if Sub $S = \infty$
(a) A is true only (b) B is false only
(c) A and B both true (d) A and B both false

**58.** A class has 175 students. The following data shows the number of students obtaining one or more subjects Mathematics 100, Physics 70, Chemistry 40; Mathematics and Physics 30, Mathematics and Chemistry 28, Physics and Chemistry 23; Mathematics,

Physics and Chemistry 18. How many students have offered Mathematics alone
(a) 35 (b) 48
(c) 60 (d) 22

**59.** If $A = \{1, 2, 3, 4\}$ and
$R = \{(1, 1), (1, 3), (2, 2), (3, 1), (3, 4), (4, 3), (4, 4)\}$ is a relation on $A \times A$, then which one of the following is correct?
(a) $R$ is reflexive
(b) $R$ is symmetric and transitive
(c) $R$ is transitive, but not reflexive
(d) $R$ is neither reflexive nor transitive

**60.** Every subset of countable subset is
(a) countable (b) uncountable
(c) infinite (d) None of these

**61.** Consider the following relations
I. $A - B = A - (A \cap B)$
II. $A = (A \cap B) \cup (A - B)$
III. $A - (B \cup C) = (A - B) \cup (A - C)$
Which of these is/are correct?
(a) I and III (b) II only
(c) II and III (d) I and II

**62.** If $E$ is an non-empty set, then
(a) $\text{Inf}\, E < \text{Sup}\, E$ (b) $\text{Inf}\, E = \text{Sup}\, E$
(c) $\text{Inf}\, E > \text{Sup}\, E$ (d) None of these

**63.** The relation $R = \{(1, 1), (2, 2), (3, 3), (1, 2), (2, 3), (1, 3)\}$ on set $A = \{1, 2, 3\}$ is
(a) reflexive but not symmetric
(b) reflexive but not transitive
(c) symmetric and Transitive
(d) neither symmetric nor transitive

**64.** Let $R = \{(1, 3), (2, 2), (3, 2)\}$ and $S = \{(2, 1), (3, 2), (2, 3)\}$ be two relations of set $A = \{1, 2, 3\}$. Then, $RoS$ is equal to
(a) $\{(1, 3), (2, 2), (3, 2), (2, 1), (2, 3)\}$
(b) $\{(3, 2), (1, 3)\}$
(c) $\{(2, 3), (3, 2), (2, 2)\}$
(d) $\{(2, 3), (3, 2)\}$

**65.** If $A, B, C$ are three sets, then what is $A - (B - C)$ equal to
(a) $A - (B \cap C)$ (b) $(A - B) \cup C$
(c) $(A - B) \cup (A \cap C)$ (d) $(A - B) \cup (A - C)$

**66.** Every integer $n > 1$ is
(a) prime number
(b) prime number or product or prime numbers
(c) product of prime numbers
(d) sum of prime numbers

**67.** Let $S$ be the set of all real numbers. Then, the relation $R = \{(a, b) : 1 + ab > 0\}$ on $S$ is
(a) reflexive and symmetric but not transitive
(b) reflexive and transitive but not symmetric
(c) symmetric, transitive but not reflexive
(d) None of the above is true

**68.** If $A = \{x : f(x) = 0\}$ and $B = \{x : g(x) = 0\}$, then $A \cap B$ will be
(a) $\{f(x)\}^2 + \{g(x)\}^2 = 0$ (b) $\dfrac{f(x)}{g(x)}$
(c) $\dfrac{g(x)}{f(x)}$ (d) None of these

**69.** Let $R$ be the relation defined on the set of natural number $N$ as $aRb$; $a, b \in N$, if $a$ divides $b$. Then, which one of the following is correct?
(a) $R$ is reflexive only
(b) $R$ is symmetric only
(c) $R$ is transitive only
(d) $R$ is reflexive and transitive

**70.** If $A = \{(x, y) : x^2 + y^2 = 25\}$ and $B = \{(x, y) : x^2 + 9y^2 = 144\}$, then $A \cap B$ contains
(a) one point (b) three points
(c) two points (d) four points

**71.** If $A = \{4n + 2 \mid n$ is a natural number$\}$ and $B = \{3n \mid n$ is a natural number$\}$, then what is $(A \cap B)$ equal to?
(a) $\{12n^2 + 6n \mid n$ is a natural number$\}$
(b) $\{24n - 12 \mid n$ is a natural number$\}$
(c) $\{60n + 30 \mid n$ is a natural number$\}$
(d) $\{12n - 6 \mid n$ is a natural number$\}$

**72.** If $\mathbb{R}$ is a set of real numbers $x, y \in \mathbb{R}$, then
(a) $x > 0$ and $y > 0 \Rightarrow xy > 0$
(b) $x > 0$ and $y > 0 \Rightarrow xy < 0$
(c) $x > 0$ and $y > 0 \Rightarrow xy = 0$
(d) $x > 0$ and $y > 0 \Rightarrow xy = 1$

**73.** If $S$ is a set of real numbers, and $c_1$ and $c_2$ are two least upper bounds of $S$, then
(a) $c_1 = c_2$ (b) $c_1 > c_2$
(c) $c_1 < c_2$ (d) $c_1 \neq c_2$

**74.** If (1, 3), (2, 5) and (3, 3) are three elements of $A \times B$ and the total number of elements in $A \times B$ is 6, then the remaining elements of $A \times B$ are
(a) (1, 5); (2, 3); (3, 5) (b) (5, 1); (3, 2); (5, 3)
(c) (1, 5); (2, 3); (5, 3) (d) None of these

**75.** Solution set of $x \equiv 3 \pmod 7$, $p \in Z$, is given by
(a) $\{3\}$ (b) $\{7p - 3 : p \in Z\}$
(c) $\{7p + 3 : p \in Z\}$ (d) None of these

**76.** If $x, y, z \in \mathbb{R}$, the set of real numbers, then following relation does not hold
(a) $x > 0$ and $y > 0 \Rightarrow xy > 0$
(b) $x, y > 0 \Rightarrow x + y > 0$
(c) $x, y, z > 0 \Rightarrow x + y + z > 0$
(d) $x, y > 0 \Rightarrow x - y > 0$

**77.** A relation $R$ is defined over the set of non-negative integers as $xRy \Rightarrow x^2 + y^2 = 36$. What is $R$?
(a) $\{(0, 6)\}$
(b) $\{(0, 6), (\sqrt{11}, 5), (3, 3\sqrt{3})\}$
(c) $\{(6, 0), (0, 6)\}$
(d) $\{(\sqrt{11}, 5), (2, 4\sqrt{2}), (5, \sqrt{11}), (4\sqrt{2}, 2)\}$

**78.** If $\mathbb{R}^*$ is an extended real number system, then the $\text{Inf}\, \mathbb{R}^*$ is
(a) 0 (b) $+\infty$
(c) $-\infty$ (d) no infimum

**79.** Let a relation $R$ be defined by $R = \{(4, 5); (1, 4); (4, 6); (7, 6); (3, 7)\}$, then $R^{-1}oR$ is
(a) $\{(1, 1), (4, 4), (4, 7), (7, 4), (7, 7), (3, 3)\}$
(b) $\{(1, 1), (4, 4), (7, 7), (3, 3)\}$
(c) $\{(1, 5), (1, 6), (3, 6)\}$
(d) None of the above

**80. Assertion (A)** $\{x \in R \mid x^2 < 0\}$ is not a set. Here, $R$ is the set of real numbers.
**Reason (R)** For every real number $x$, $x^2 \geq 0$.
(a) A and R are both correct, also R is the correct explanation of A.
(b) A and R are both correct, but R is not the correct explanation of A.
(c) A is correct but R is wrong.
(d) A is wrong but R is correct.

**81.** If $A$ and $B$ are two non-empty set of $\mathbb{R}$. If $C = \{x + y : x \in A, y \in B\}$, then
(a) $\text{Inf } C = \text{Inf } A + \text{Inf } B$ (b) $\text{Inf } C \neq \text{Inf } A + \text{Inf } B$
(c) $\text{Inf } C < \text{Inf } A + \text{Inf } B$ (d) $\text{Inf } C > \text{Inf } A + \text{Inf } B$

**82.** If $X$ and $Y$ are any two non-empty sets, then what is $(X - Y)'$ equal to?
(a) $X' - Y'$ (b) $X' \cap Y$
(c) $X' \cup Y$ (d) $X - Y'$

**83.** The set of integer is
(a) ordered set
(b) non-ordered set
(c) set of irrational numbers
(d) does not satisfies principle of induction.

**84.** Let $R$ and $S$ be two non-void relations on a set $A$. Which of the following statements is false?
(a) $R$ and $S$ are transitive $\Rightarrow R \cup S$ is transitive
(b) $R$ and $S$ are transitive $\Rightarrow R \cap S$ is transitive
(c) $R$ and $S$ are symmetric $\Rightarrow R \cup S$ is symmetric
(d) $R$ and $S$ are reflexive $\Rightarrow R \cap S$ is reflexive

**85.** Composite number $n$ is
(a) a prime number and $n > 1$
(b) non-prime number and $n < 1$
(c) non-prime number and $n > 1$
(d) a prime number and $n < 1$

**86.** Consider the following statements
For non-empty sets $A$, $B$ and $C$
I. $A - (B - C) = (A - B) \cup C$
II. $A - (B \cup C) = (A - B) - C$
Which of the statements given above is/are correct?
(a) I only (b) II only
(c) Both I and II (d) Neither I nor II

**87.** The half interval $[0, 1)$ have
(a) maximal element only
(b) minimal element only
(c) maximal and minimal both element
(d) no maximal and no minimal element

**88.** Let $N$ be the set of integers. A relation $R$ on $N$ is defined as $R = \{(x, y) \mid xy > 0,\ x, y \in N\}$. Then, which one of the following is correct?
(a) $R$ is symmetric but not reflexive
(b) $R$ is reflexive but not symmetric
(c) $R$ is symmetric and reflexive but not transitive
(d) $R$ is an equivalence relation

**89.** The closed interval $S = [0, 1]$ is
(a) bounded above (b) unbounded below
(c) unbounded above (d) no maximal element

**90.** Which one of the following functions $f : R \to R$ is injective?
(a) $f(x) = |x|, \forall x \in R$ (b) $f(x) = x^2, \forall x \in R$
(c) $f(x) = 11, \forall x \in R$ (d) $f(x) = -x, \forall x \in R$

**91.** The relation $R$ defined on the set $A = \{1, 2, 3, 4, 5\}$ by $R = \{(x, y) : |x^2 - y^2| < 16\}$ is given by
(a) $\{(1, 1), (2, 1), (3, 1), (4, 1), (2, 3)\}$
(b) $\{(2, 2), (3, 2), (4, 2), (2, 4)\}$
(c) $\{(3, 3), (3, 4), (5, 4), (4, 3), (3, 1)\}$
(d) None of the above

**92.** Let $S = [0, 1)$, the least upper bound for $S$ is
(a) 0 (b) 1
(c) $\phi$ (d) 2

**93.** If $P(A)$ denotes the power set of $A$ and $A$ is the void set, then what is number of elements in $P\{P\{P\{P(A)\}\}\}$?
(a) 0 (b) 1
(c) 4 (d) 16

**94.** If $S$ is a set of real numbers which is bounded below, then Inf $S$ is
(a) a point of closure to $S$
(b) not a point of closure to $S$
(c) prime number
(d) None of the above

**95.** If $A$ is the set of even natural numbers less than 8 and $B$ is the set of prime numbers less than 7, then the number of relations from $A$ to $B$ is
(a) $2^9$ (b) $9^2$
(c) $3^2$ (d) $2^{9-1}$

**96.** If $S$ is non-empty set of real numbers and $S$ is unbounded below, then
(a) $\text{Inf } S = -\infty$ (b) $\text{Inf } S = +\infty$
(c) $\text{Sup } S = \infty$ (d) $\text{Sup } S = -\infty$

**97.** What does the shaded region in the Venn diagram given following represent?

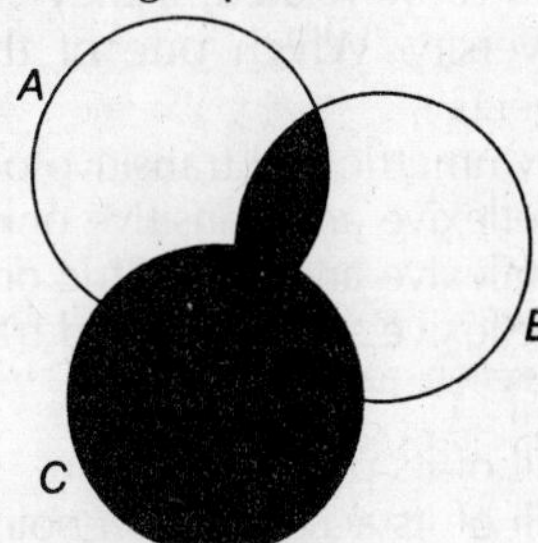


(a) $C \cap (A' \cap B')$
(b) $C \cup (C' \cap A \cap B)$
(c) $C \cup (C \cap A) \cup (C \cap B)$
(d) $C \cup (A \setminus B)$

**98.** If $\mathbb{R}$ is a set or real numbers $x, y \in R$, then
(a) $x+y \neq y+x$ (b) $x+y=y+x$
(c) $xy \neq xy$ (d) $x+y \geq y+x$

**99.** The function $f(x)=\dfrac{x}{x^2+1}$ from $R$ to $R$ is
(a) one-one as well as onto
(b) onto but not one-one
(c) Neither one-one nor onto
(d) one-one but not onto

**100.** An integer $n$ is a prime number, if
(a) $n>1$ and $n$ is divisible by itself only
(b) $n<1$ and $n$ is divisible by itself only
(c) $n=1$
(d) $n=1$ and $n/n$

**101.** Out of 32 persons, 30 invest in National savings Certificates and 17 invest in shares. What is the number of persons who invest in both?
(a) 13 (b) 15
(c) 17 (d) 19

**102.** Let $R$ be an equivalence relation on a finite set $A$ having $n$ elements. Then, the number of ordered pairs in $R$ is
(a) less than $n$
(b) greater than or equal to $n$
(c) less than or equal to $n$
(d) none of the above

**103.** The set of negative integers having the least upper bound is
(a) 1 (b) 0
(c) 2 (d) $-1$

**104.** Let $R=\{x \mid x \in N, x$ is a multiple of 3 and $x \leq 10\}$ and $S=\{x \mid x \in N, x$ is a multiple of 5 and $x \leq 100\}$
What is the number of elements in $(R \times S) \cap (S \times R)$
(a) 36 (b) 33
(c) 20 (d) 6

**105.** Every open set of real numbers is the union of
(a) countable collection of disjoint open intervals
(b) uncountable collection of disjoint open intervals
(c) countable collection of disjoint closed intervals
(d) uncountable collection of disjoint closed intervals

**106.** Let $X$ be the set of all graduates in India. Elements $x$ and $y$ in $X$ are said to be related, if they are graduates of the same university. Which one of the following statements is correct?
(a) Relation is symmetric and transitive only
(b) Relation is reflexive and transitive only
(c) Relation is reflexive and symmetric only
(d) Relation is reflexive symmetric and transitive

**107.** A set $F$ is closed, if
(a) it contains all of its points of closure
(b) it contains all of its accumulation point
(c) (a) is true, (b) is false
(d) Both (a) and (b) are true

**108.** In a college of 300 students, every student reads 5 newspaper and every newspaper is read by 60 students. The number of newspaper is
(a) atleast 30 (b) atmost 20
(c) exactly 25 (d) None of these

**109.** If $S$ is set of real numbers which is bounded above, then Sup $S$ is
(a) a point of closure to $S$
(b) not a point of closure to $S$
(c) prime number
(d) None of the above

**110.** If $X=\{(4^n-3n-1) \mid n \in N\}$ and $Y=\{9(n-1) \mid n \in N\}$, then what is $X \cup Y$ equal to
(a) $X$ (b) $Y$
(c) $N$ (d) a null set

**111.** The empty set $\phi$ is
(a) Both closed and open set
(b) open set only
(c) closed set only
(d) None of the above

**112.** Let $A=\{-1, 2, 5, 8\}$, $B=\{0, 1\ 3\ 6, 7\}$ and $R$ be the relation 'is one less than' from $A$ to $B$, then how many elements will $R$ contain?
(a) 2 (b) 3
(c) 5 (d) 9

**113.** The set $E$ which is a set of points of closure of $E$, then the false statement is
(a) $E \subset \bar{E}$ (b) $E \cap \bar{E}=E$
(c) $E \cap \bar{E}=\bar{E}$ (d) None of these

**114.** Consider the function $f: R \rightarrow \{0, 1\}$ such that
$$f(x)=\begin{cases} 1, \text{ if } x \text{ is rational} \\ 0, \text{ if } x \text{ is irrational} \end{cases}$$
Which one of the following is correct?
(a) The function is one-one into
(b) The function is many one into
(c) The function is one-one onto
(d) The function is many one onto

**115.** A finite set is
(a) open set (b) closed set
(c) uncountable set (d) None of these

**116.** Let $R$ be a relation over the set $N \times N$ and it is defined by $(a, b)R(c, d) \Rightarrow a+d=b+c$. Then, $R$ is
(a) reflexive only (b) symmetric only
(c) transitive only (d) an equivalence relation

**117.** The intersection of any collection of open sets is
(a) open set (b) closed set
(c) cannot defined (d) semi open

**118.** Let $N$ denote the set of natural numbers and $A=\{n^2 : n \in N\}$ and $B=\{n^{3/2} : n \in N\}$. Which one of the following is correct?
(a) $A \cup B=N$
(b) The complement of $(A \cup B)$ is an infinite set
(c) $A \cap B$ must be a finite set
(d) $A \cap B$ must be a proper subset of $\{m^6 : m \in N\}$

**119.** The set $E$ is nowhere dense, if
(a) closure of $E$ contains no non-empty open sets
(b) closure of $E$ contains non-empty open sets
(c) closure of $E$ contains empty open sets
(d) None of the above

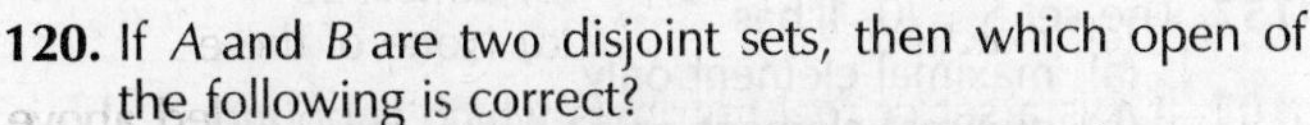



**120.** If $A$ and $B$ are two disjoint sets, then which open of the following is correct?
(a) $A - B = A - (A \cap B)$ (b) $B - A' = B \cap A$
(c) $A \cap B = (A - B) \cap B$ (d) All of these

**121.** If an element a is maximal element of set $S$, then
(a) $a \in S$
(b) $a \notin S$
(c) a is not upper bound of $S$
(d) a is lower bound of $S$

**122.** Let $M$ be the set of men and $R$ is a relation 'is son of' defined on $M$. Then, $R$ is
(a) an equivalence relation
(b) a symmetric relation only
(c) a transitive relation only
(d) None of the above

**123.** The closed interval (0, 1) have
(a) maximal element only
(b) minimal element only
(c) Both maximal and minimal elements
(d) None of the above

**124.** The relation $R = \{(1, 1), (2, 2), (3, 3), (1, 2), (2, 3), (1, 3)\}$ on a set $A = \{1, 2, 3\}$ is
(a) reflexive, transitive but not symmetric
(b) reflexive, symmetric but not transitive
(c) symmetric, transitive but not reflexive
(d) reflexive but neither symmetric nor transitive

**125.** The set of natural numbers has
(a) upper bound (b) lower bound
(c) maximal element (d) None of these

**126.** **Statement (A)** Between two real number, there is an integer.
**Statement (B)** Between two real number, there is a rational number.
(a) Both statements A and B are true
(b) Both statements A and B are false
(c) A is true but R is false
(d) None of the above

**127.** What is the range of $f(x) = \cos 2x - \sin 2x$?
(a) [2, 4] (b) [−1, 1]
(c) $[-\sqrt{2}, \sqrt{2}]$ (d) $(-\sqrt{2}, 2)$

**128.** Let $S = [0, 1)$ the maximal element of $S$ is
(a) 0 (b) 1
(c) $\phi$ (d) no maximal element

**129.** Consider the following with regard to a relation $R$ on a set of real numbers defined by $xRy$ if and only if $3x + 4y = 5$.
I. $_0R_1$
II. $_1R_{1/2}$
III. $_{2/3}R_{3/4}$
Which of the above are correct?
(a) I and II (b) I and II
(c) II and III (d) I, II and III

**130.** The set $\mathbb{R}^+ = (0, \infty)$ is
(a) bounded above (b) bounded below
(c) unbounded below (d) None of these

**131.** Let $f : \mathbb{R} \to \mathbb{R}$ be a function defined as $f(x) = x|x|$; for each $x \in \mathbb{R}$, $\mathbb{R}$ being the set of real numbers. Which one of the following is correct?
(a) $f$ is one-one but not onto
(b) $f$ is onto but not one-one
(c) $f$ is both one-one and onto
(d) $f$ is neither one-one nor onto

**132.** If $A$ is a non-empty open set, then
(a) its complement is open set
(b) its complement is closed set
(c) its complement is null set
(d) None of the above

**133.** If $x \in R$, then
(a) $\frac{x}{\infty} = \infty$ (b) $\frac{x}{\infty} = 0$
(c) $\frac{x}{\infty} = x$ (d) $\frac{x}{\infty} = -\infty$

**134.** The intersection of finite collection of open sets is
(a) open set (b) closed set
(c) empty set (d) unbounded set

**135.** The set of real numbers $\mathbb{R}$
(a) closed set (b) finite set
(c) bounded set (d) None of these

**136.** If $S, T \subset \mathbb{R}$ and $\forall\, s \in S, t \in T, s \le t$, if $S$ and $T$ have infimum, then
(a) $\operatorname{Inf} S \ge \operatorname{Inf} T$ (b) $\operatorname{Inf} S \le \operatorname{Inf} T$
(c) $\operatorname{Inf} S = \operatorname{Inf} T$ (d) None of these

**137.** If $x < 0$, then
(a) $x(-\infty) = -\infty$ (b) $x(-\infty) = \infty$
(c) $x(-\infty) = 0$ (d) $x(-\infty) = x$

**138.** The intersection of all sets of the form,
$$O_n = \left(-\frac{1}{n}, \frac{1}{n}\right), n = 1, 2, \ldots, \text{ is}$$
(a) open set (b) {0}
(c) not a open set (d) None of these

**139.** If $\mathbb{R}^*$ is an extended real number system, then the least upper bound of $\mathbb{R}^*$ is
(a) $+\infty$ (b) $-\infty$
(c) 0 (d) no least upper bound

**140.** If $A = \{1, 2, 5, 6\}$ and $B = \{1, 2, 3\}$, then what is $(A \times B) \cap (B \times A)$ equal to
(a) $\{(1, 1), (2, 1), (6, 1), (3, 2)\}$
(b) $\{(1, 1), (1, 2), (2, 1), (2, 2)\}$
(c) $\{(1, 1), (2, 2)\}$
(d) $\{(1, 1), (1, 2), (2, 5), (2, 6)\}$

**141.** The set of real numbers $\mathbb{R}$ is
(a) open set (b) finite set
(c) bounded set (d) None of these

**142.** The set of real numbers is
(a) unbounded (b) bounded from below
(c) bounded from above (d) bounded

**143.** The intersection of any collection of closed sets is
(a) closed set (b) open set
(c) null set (d) None of these

**144.** The set of real numbers $\mathbb{R}$ is
(a) countable (b) uncountable
(c) infinite (d) bounded

**145.** The intersection of finite collection of any closed set is
(a) closed set (b) open set
(c) null set (d) None of these

**146.** The set $\mathbb{R}^+ = (0, +\infty)$ is
(a) bounded above (b) unbounded above
(c) unbounded below (d) None of these

**147.** Let $N$ denote the set of all natural numbers and $R$ be the relation on $N \times N$ defined by $(a, b)R(c, d)$ if $ad(b+c) = bc(a+d)$, then $R$ is
(a) symmetric only (b) reflexive only
(c) transitive only (d) an equivalence relation

**148.** If $A$ is non-empty and bounded from below, then
(a) $\text{Inf } A = -\text{ Sup } |A|$ (b) $\text{Inf } A = -\text{ Sup } |-A|$
(c) $\text{Inf } A = \text{Sup } |A|$ (d) None of these

**149.** If $S, T \subset \mathbb{R}$ and $A = \{x + y : x \in S \text{ and } y \in T\}$, then
(a) $\text{Sup } A = \text{Sup } S + \text{Sup } T$
(b) $\text{Sup } A > \text{Sup } S + \text{Sup } T$
(c) $\text{Sup } A < \text{Sup } S + \text{Sup } T$
(d) $\text{Sup } A \neq \text{Sup } S + \text{Sup } T$

**150.** If $\mu$ is the universal set and $P$ is a subset of $\mu$, then what is $P \cap \{(P - \mu) \cup (\mu - P)\}$ equal to?
(a) $\phi$ (b) $P'$
(c) $\mu$ (d) $P$

**151.** The half closed interval $[a, \infty)$ is
(a) open set (b) closed set
(c) empty set (d) unbounded set

**152.** If $x \in \mathbb{R}$, then
(a) $x + (-\infty) = -\infty$ (b) $x + (-\infty) = +\infty$
(c) $x + (-\infty) = x$ (d) $x + (-\infty) = 0$

**153.** Let $F_n = \left[-\frac{1}{n}, \frac{1}{n}\right]$ be a given interval, then $\bigcap_{n=1}^{\infty} F_n$ is
(a) closed set (b) open set
(c) null set (d) None of these

**154.** In a certain town 25% families own a phone and 15% own a car, 65% families own neither a phone nor a car. 2000 families own both a car and a phone. Consider the following statements in this regard:
I. 10% families own both a car and a phone.
II. 35% families own either a car or a phone.
III. 40000 families live in the town.
Which of the above statements are correct?
(a) I and II (b) I and III
(c) II and III (d) I, II and III

**155.** "Every non-empty set $S$ of real number which is bounded below, has infimum" is stated in
(a) field axiom (b) ordered axiom
(c) completeness axiom (d) None of these

**156.** If $S$ is a non-empty set and $S$ has no upper bound, then
(a) $\text{Sup } S = \infty$ (b) $\text{Inf } S = \infty$
(c) $\text{Sup } S = -\infty$ (d) $\text{Inf } S = -\infty$

**157.** The set $S = [0, 1]$ has
(a) maximal element only
(b) minimal element only
(c) Both maximal and minimal element
(d) None of the above

**158.** If $A$, $B$ and $C$ are non-empty sets such that $A \cap C = \phi$, then what is $(A \times B) \cap (C \times B)$ equal to?
(a) $A \times C$ (b) $A \times B$
(c) $B \times C$ (d) $\phi$

**159.** For the set of negative real numbers
$$A = \{x \in R;\ x < 0\}$$
Then, Sup $A$ is equal to
(a) $-1$ (b) 1 (c) 0 (d) 2

**160.** Let $S = [0, 1]$, the maximal element of $S$ is
(a) 0 (b) 1 (c) $\phi$ (d) 2

**161.** Two finite sets have $m$ and $n$ elements. The total number of subsets of the first set is 56 more than the total number of subsets of the second set. The values of $m$ and $n$ are
(a) 7, 6 (b) 6, 3 (c) 5, 1 (d) 8, 7

**162.** The solution set of $8x \equiv 6 \pmod{14}$, $x \in Z$, are
(a) $[8] \cup [6]$ (b) $[8] \cup [14]$
(c) $[6] \cup [13]$ (d) $[8] \cup [6] \cup [13]$

**163.** Suppose $A_1, A_2, A_3, \ldots, A_{30}$ are thirty sets each having 5 elements and $B_1, B_2, \ldots, B_n$ are $n$ sets each with 3 elements. Let $\bigcup_{i=1}^{30} A_i = \bigcup_{j=1}^{n} B_j = S$ and each elements of $S$ belongs to exactly 10 of the $A_i$s and exactly 9 of the $B_j$s. Then, $n$ is equal to
(a) 15 (b) 3
(c) 45 (d) None of these

**164.** Singleton set $\{x_0\}$ is
(a) open (b) closed
(c) uncountable (d) None of these

**165.** If $x < y < 0$ and $0 < z < w$, then
(a) $xz < yw$ (b) $xz > yw$
(c) $xz < y$ (d) $xz < w$

**166.** The union of any collection of open sets is
(a) open set (b) closed set
(c) $\{0\}$ (d) $\phi$

**167.** The value of $(0, \infty)$ is
(a) $\infty$ (b) 0
(c) undefined (d) None of these

**168.** The complement of open set is
(a) closed set (b) open set
(c) countable (d) None of these

**169.** Out of 800 boys in a school, 224 played cricket, 240 played hockey and 336 played basketball. Of the total, 64 played both basketball and hockey; 80 played cricket and basketball and 40 played cricket and hockey; 24 played all the three games. The number of boys who did not play any game is
(a) 128 (b) 216
(c) 240 (d) 160

# Exercise 2 (For Part 'C')

**Directions (Q. Nos. 1-46)** *Questions may have one or more than one correct option.*

1. Let $a, b \in \mathbb{R}$ and $a \le b + \frac{1}{n}, \forall n \in N$, then
   (a) $a < b$ (b) $a > b$
   (c) $a \le b$ (d) $a \ge b$
2. Let $a, b \in \mathbb{R}$ and $a < c$ for each $c > b$. Then,
   (a) $a < b$ (b) $a = b$
   (c) $a > b$ (d) $a \ge b$
3. Which of the following(s) is/are correct?
   (a) Superset of a *nbd* of a point x is also a *nbd* of x
   (b) Finite intersection of *nbd* of x is also a *nbd* of x
   (c) Finite union of *nbds* of a point x is again a *nbd* of x
   (d) Arbitrary union of *nbds* of a point x is again a *nbd* of x
4. Which of the following(s) is/are correct?
   (a) The derived set of $\{x : 0 \le x < 1\}$ is $[0, 1]$
   (b) The derived set of $\{x : 0 < x < 1, x \in \mathbb{Q}\}$ is $[0, 1]$
   (c) The derived set of $\left\{1, -1, 1\frac{1}{2}, -1\frac{1}{2}, \ldots\right\}$ is $\{1, -1\}$
   (d) The derived set of $\left\{\frac{1}{m} + \frac{1}{n} : m \in \mathbb{N}, n \in \mathbb{N}\right\}$ is $\left\{\frac{1}{m} : m \in \mathbb{N}\right\}$
5. Which of the following statement(s) is/are true?
   (a) A non-empty finite set is not open
   (b) The set $\mathbb{N}$ is not open
   (c) The set $\mathbb{Z}$ is not open
   (d) the set $\mathbb{R}$ is not open
6. Which of the following(s) is/are correct?
   (a) The interior of a set S does not contains every open subset of S
   (b) The interior of a set S contains every open subset of S
   (c) The interior of a set S is the largest open subset of S
   (d) Interior of a set is the union of all open subset of S
7. Which of the following(s) is/are correct?
   (a) The intersection of any finite number of open sets is open
   (b) The intersection of an arbitrary family of open set is open
   (c) Both (a) and (b)
   (d) Exactly only one of (a) and (b)
8. Which of the following(s) is/are correct?
   (a) A finite set cannot have a limit point
   (b) An infinite set must posses a limit point
   (c) An infinite set cannot have a limit point
   (d) A finite set must posses a limit point
9. Which of the following(s) is/are correct?
   (a) A set may have no limit point
   (b) A set must have a limit point
   (c) A set may have unique limit point
   (d) A set may have finite number of limit points
10. Which of the following(s) is/are correct?
    (a) The set $[0, 1] \cup [2, 3]$ which is not an interval is closed
    (b) $[a, b]$ is a set which is closed but not open
    (c) The set of real numbers $\mathbb{R}$ is open as well as closed
    (d) The set $\left\{\frac{1}{n} : n \in \mathbb{N}\right\}$ is closed
11. Let S and T are subsets of real numbers. Then,
    (a) $S \subseteq T \Rightarrow S' \subseteq T'$
    (b) $(S \cap T)' \subseteq S' \cap T'$
    (c) $(S \cup T)' = S' \cup T'$
    (d) $(S \cap T)'$ and $S' \cap T'$ may or may not be equal
12. Which of the following(s) is/are correct?
    (a) The set $S = \left\{1, -1, \frac{1}{2}, -\frac{1}{2}, \frac{1}{3}, -\frac{1}{3}, \ldots\right\}$ is neither open nor closed
    (b) Boundedness is not necessary in order for an infinite set S to have a limit point
    (c) Both (a) and (b)
    (d) Exactly one of (a) or (b)
13. Which of the following(s) is/are correct?
    (a) The set $S = \left\{1, -1, 1\frac{1}{2}, -1\frac{1}{2}, 1\frac{1}{3}, -1\frac{1}{3}, \ldots\right\}$ is open but not closed
    (b) The set $S = \left\{1, -1, 1\frac{1}{2}, -1\frac{1}{2}, 1\frac{1}{3}, -1\frac{1}{3}, \ldots\right\}$ is closed but not open
    (c) Exactly one of (a) or (b)
    (d) All of the above
14. Which of the following(s) is/are correct?
    (a) The set $\mathbb{R}$ of real numbers is a perfect set
    (b) The set $\mathbb{R}$ of real numbers is dense is itself and closed
    (c) Both (a) and (b)
    (d) Exactly only one of (a) or (b)
15. Which of the following(s) is/are correct?
    (a) The set $\{x : a \le x \le b\}$ is a perfect set
    (b) The set $\mathbb{Q}$ of rationals is dense in itself but not closed
    (c) Exactly only one of (a) of (b)
    (d) None of the above
16. Which of the following(s) is/are correct?
    (a) The empty set is not perfect
    (b) The empty set is perfect
    (c) The empty set is closed
    (d) The empty set is open

**17.** Which of the following(s) is/are correct?
(a) The union of two closed sets is a closed set
(b) The union of a finite number of closed sets is closed
(c) The union of an arbitrary family of closed sets may not always be a closed set
(d) Exactly only one of the above

**18.** Which of the following(s) is/are correct?
(a) The derived set of a set is not closed
(b) The derived set of a set is closed
(c) Both (a) and (b)
(d) Either (a) or (b)

**19.** Which of the following(s) is/are correct?
(a) For every set $S$ the closure $\bar{S}$ is closed
(b) The derived set of derived set is closed
(c) Both (a) and (b)
(d) None of the above

**20.** Which of the following(s) is/are correct?
(a) The supremum of a bounded non-empty set $S(\subseteq R)$. When not a member of $S$ is a limit point of $S$
(b) The infimum of a bounded non-empty set $S(\subseteq R)$. When not a member of $S$ is a limit point of $S$
(c) Neither (a) nor (b)
(d) Both (a) and (b)

**21.** Which of the following(s) is/are correct?
(a) The supremum $M$ of a bounded set $S$ is a member of the closure $\bar{S}$ of $S$
(b) The infimum $M$ of a bounded set $S$ is always a member of the closure $\bar{S}$ of $S$
(c) Neither (a) nor (b)
(d) Exactly only one of (a) or (b)

**22.** Which of the following(s) is/are correct?
(a) Every bounded infinite set does not has smallest limit point
(b) Every bounded infinite set has smallest limit point
(c) Every bounded infinite set has greatest limit point
(d) None of the above

**23.** Which of the following(s) is/are correct?
(a) The set $\{1, 4, 9, 16, \ldots\}$ is countable
(b) The set of all integers is countable
(c) Both (a) and (b)
(d) Exactly only one of (a) and (b)

**24.** Which of the following(s) is/are correct?
(a) The set of all ordered pairs of integers is countable
(b) The set of all polynomial functions with integer coefficients is countable
(c) Both (a) and (b)
(d) Either (a) or (b)

**25.** Which of the following(s) is/are correct?
(a) The set of all real number is countable
(b) The set of all real number is uncountable
(c) Both (a) and (b)
(d) Either (a) or (b)

**26.** Which of the following(s) is/are correct?
(a) The set of real number in $\mathbb{R} \cap \mathbb{Q}$ is countable
(b) The set of real number in $\mathbb{R} \cap \mathbb{Q}^c$ is uncountable
(c) Both (a) and (b)
(d) Neither (a) nor (b)

**27.** Which of the following(s) is/are countable?
(a) A countable union of countable set
(b) The cartesian product of two countable set
(c) The set $\mathbb{R}$ of real number
(d) The set of all rational number

**28.** Let $L$ be the set of all straight lines in the Euclidean plane. Two lines $l_1$ and $l_2$ are said to be related by the relation $R$ iff $l_1$ is parallel to $l_2$. Then, the relation $R$ is
(a) reflexive (b) symmetric
(c) transitive (d) equivalence

**29.** Let $n$ be a fixed positive integer. Define a relation $R$ on the set $Z$ of integers by, $aRb \Leftrightarrow n|a-b|$. Then, $R$ is
(a) reflexive (b) symmetric
(c) transitive (d) equivalence

**30.** Let $A$ be the non-void set of the children in a family. The relation '$x$ is a brother of $y$' on $A$ is
(a) reflexive (b) symmetric
(c) transitive (d) None of these

**31.** Let $R$ and $S$ be two relation on a set $A$. Then,
(a) $R$ and $S$ are transitive, then $R \cup S$ is also transitive
(b) $R$ and $S$ are transitive, then $R \cap S$ is also transitive
(c) $R$ and $S$ are reflexive, then $R \cap S$ is also reflexive
(d) $R$ and $S$ are symmetric, then $R \cup S$ is also symmetric

**32.** If $P$, $Q$ and $R$ are subsets of a set $A$, then $R \times (P^c \cup Q^c)^c$ is equal to
(a) $(R \times P) \cap (R \times Q)$ (b) $(R \times Q) \cap (R \times P)$
(c) $(R \times P) \cup (R \times Q)$ (d) None of these

**33.** For the set of real numbers $\mathbb{R}$.
(a) $\text{Sup}\,\mathbb{R} = +\infty$ (b) $\text{Inf}\,\mathbb{R} = -\infty$
(c) $+\infty, -\infty \in \mathbb{R}$ (d) $+\infty, -\infty \notin \mathbb{R}$

**34.** Which of the following(s) is/are correct?
(a) The open interval is an open set
(b) The open interval is closed set
(c) The open interval is not an open set
(d) The open interval is null set

**35.** $S = (0, 1]$ is
(a) bounded above by 1 and maximal element is 1
(b) bounded below by 0 and no minimal element
(c) bounded above by 0 and minimal element is 0
(d) bounded below by 1 and no maximal element

**36.** Let $\bar{E}$ is the set of point of closure of $E$,
(a) $\bar{E}$ is closed (b) $\bar{E}$ is open
(c) $\bar{E}$ is null (d) $\bar{E}$ is closed interval

**37.** Which of the following(s) is/are correct?
(a) The open interval is an open set
(b) Open interval is an closed set
(c) Open interval is a null set
(d) Open interval is singleton set

**38.** Let $O_n = \left(-\frac{1}{n}, \frac{1}{n}\right)$, $n = 1, 2, \ldots$. Then
(a) $\left(\bigcap_{n=1}^{\infty} O_n\right)$ is not a open set

(b) $\left(\bigcap_{n=1}^{\infty} O_n\right)$ is closed set

(c) $\left(\bigcap_{n=1}^{\infty} O_n\right) = \{0\}$

(d) $\left(\bigcap_{n=1}^{\infty} O_n\right) = (0, 0)$

**39.** If $A$ is open set and $B$ is closed set, then

(a) $A - B$ is open set (b) $B - A$ is closed set

(c) $A - B$ is closed set (d) $B - A$ is open set

**40.** Which of the following(s) is/are correct?

(a) The closed interval is a closed set

(b) Closed interval is open set

(c) Closed interval is null set

(d) Closed interval contains its closure points

**41.** Let $O_n = \left(-\frac{1}{n}, \frac{1}{n}\right)$, $n = 1, 2, \ldots$. Then $\left(\bigcap_{n=1}^{\infty} O_n\right)$ is

(a) open set (b) closed set

(c) singleton set (d) null set

**42.** Which of the following(s) is/are correct?

(a) Null set is open set

(b) Null set is semi-open set

(c) Null set is closed interval

(d) Null set is open interval

**43.** Which of the following(s) is/are correct?

(a) The null set is open set

(b) $\mathbb{R}^c = \phi$

(c) $\mathbb{R}$ is closed set

(d) complement of closed set is closed

**44.** Which of the following(s) is/are correct?

(a) A set of integer is countable

(b) A set of integer is uncountable

(c) A set of rational number is countable

(d) A set of rational number is uncountable

**45.** $\mathbb{R}^+ = (0, +\infty)$ is

(a) unbounded above, has no upper bounds and no maximal element

(b) bounded below by 0 and no minimal element

(c) unbounded below by 0

(d) bounded above by 0

**46.** Which of the following(s) is/are correct?

(a) The closed interval is a closed set

(b) Closed interval is open set

(c) Closed interval contains all its closure points

(d) Closed interval does not contains all its closure points

# Answers

## Exercise 1

| **1.** (c) | **2.** (c) | **3.** (d) | **4.** (d) | **5.** (c) | **6.** (a) | **7.** (b) | **8.** (c) | **9.** (c) | **10.** (d) |
|---|---|---|---|---|---|---|---|---|---|
| **11.** (d) | **12.** (b) | **13.** (c) | **14.** (b) | **15.** (a) | **16.** (c) | **17.** (a) | **18.** (b) | **19.** (a) | **20.** (a) |
| **21.** (c) | **22.** (c) | **23.** (d) | **24.** (a) | **25.** (d) | **26.** (c) | **27.** (c) | **28.** (b) | **29.** (a) | **30.** (d) |
| **31.** (b) | **32.** (b) | **33.** (b) | **34.** (a) | **35.** (c) | **36.** (a) | **37.** (b) | **38.** (c) | **39.** (a) | **40.** (a) |
| **41.** (c) | **42.** (b) | **43.** (b) | **44.** (a) | **45.** (d) | **46.** (c) | **47.** (c) | **48.** (a) | **49.** (b) | **50.** (d) |
| **51.** (b) | **52.** (d) | **53.** (b) | **54.** (a) | **55.** (d) | **56.** (a) | **57.** (c) | **58.** (c) | **59.** (d) | **60.** (a) |
| **61.** (d) | **62.** (a) | **63.** (a) | **64.** (c) | **65.** (c) | **66.** (b) | **67.** (a) | **68.** (a) | **69.** (d) | **70.** (d) |
| **71.** (d) | **72.** (a) | **73.** (a) | **74.** (a) | **75.** (c) | **76.** (d) | **77.** (c) | **78.** (c) | **79.** (a) | **80.** (a) |
| **81.** (a) | **82.** (c) | **83.** (a) | **84.** (a) | **85.** (c) | **86.** (b) | **87.** (b) | **88.** (d) | **89.** (a) | **90.** (d) |
| **91.** (d) | **92.** (b) | **93.** (d) | **94.** (a) | **95.** (a) | **96.** (a) | **97.** (c) | **98.** (b) | **99.** (d) | **100.** (a) |
| **101.** (b) | **102.** (b) | **103.** (d) | **104.** (a) | **105.** (a) | **106.** (d) | **107.** (d) | **108.** (c) | **109.** (a) | **110.** (b) |
| **111.** (a) | **112.** (b) | **113.** (c) | **114.** (d) | **115.** (b) | **116.** (d) | **117.** (c) | **118.** (d) | **119.** (a) | **120.** (d) |
| **121.** (a) | **122.** (d) | **123.** (d) | **124.** (a) | **125.** (b) | **126.** (d) | **127.** (c) | **128.** (c) | **129.** (c) | **130.** (b) |
| **131.** (c) | **132.** (b) | **133.** (b) | **134.** (a) | **135.** (a) | **136.** (a) | **137.** (a) | **138.** (b) | **139.** (a) | **140.** (b) |
| **141.** (a) | **142.** (a) | **143.** (a) | **144.** (a) | **145.** (a) | **146.** (b) | **147.** (d) | **148.** (b) | **149.** (b) | **150.** (a) |
| **151.** (b) | **152.** (a) | **153.** (a) | **154.** (c) | **155.** (d) | **156.** (a) | **157.** (c) | **158.** (d) | **159.** (c) | **160.** (b) |
| **161.** (b) | **162.** (c) | **163.** (c) | **164.** (b) | **165.** (b) | **166.** (a) | **167.** (b) | **168.** (a) | **169.** (d) | |

## Exercise 2

| **1.** (a,c) | **2.** (a,b) | **3.** (a,b,c,d) | **4.** (a,b,c,d) | **5.** (a,b,c) | **6.** (b,d) | **7.** (a,d) | **8.** (a,c) | **9.** (a,c,d) | **10.** (a,b,c) |
|---|---|---|---|---|---|---|---|---|---|
| **11.** (a,b,c,d) | **12.** (a,b) | **13.** (b,c) | **14.** (a,b,c) | **15.** (a,b) | **16.** (a,b,c,d) | **17.** (a,b,c) | **18.** (b) | **19.** (a,b,c) | **20.** (a,b,d) |
| **21.** (a,b) | **22.** (b,c) | **23.** (a,b,c) | **24.** (a,b) | **25.** (b) | **26.** (a,b,c) | **27.** (a,b,d) | **28.** (a,b,c,d) | **29.** (a,b,c,d) | **30.** (b,c) |
| **31.** (b,c,d) | **32.** (a,b) | **33.** (a,b,c) | **34.** (a) | **35.** (a,b) | **36.** (a) | **37.** (a) | **38.** (a,b,c,d) | **39.** (a,b) | **40.** (a,d) |
| **41.** (b,d) | **42.** (a) | **43.** (a,b,c) | **44.** (a,c) | **45.** (a,b) | **46.** (a,c) | | | | |

# Hints & Solutions

## Exercise 1

**1.** $\because$ $A$ and $B$ are two sets satisfying $A-B=B-A$, which is possible only if $A=B$.

**2.** $n(C)=20$, $n(B)=50$, $n(C\cap B)=10$

Now, $n(C\cup B)=n(C)+n(B)-n(C\cap B)$

$=20+50-10=60$

Hence, required number of persons = 60%

**3.** The total number of elements common in $(A\times B)$ and $(B\times A)$ is $n^2$. (by property)

**5.** $A=(A-B)\cup(B-A)$ ...(i)

$=(A\cap B')\cup(B\cap A')$

$=\{(A\cap B')\cup B\}\cap\{(A\cap B')\cup A'\}$

$=\{(A\cup B)\cap(B'\cup B)\}\cap\{(A\cup A')\cap(B'\cup A')\}$

$=\{(A\cup B)\cap U\}\cap\{U\cap(B'\cup A')\}$

$=\{A\cup B\}\cap\{B'\cup A'\}$

$=(A\cup B)\cap(A\cap B)'$

$=\phi$

or $A=\phi$

Here, $B=\phi$ satisfy the given condition (i)

$\Rightarrow$ $(A-\phi)\cup(\phi-A)=A$

$\Rightarrow$ $A\cup\phi=A$

$\Rightarrow$ $A=A$

**6.** For any $x\in R$, we have $x-x+\sqrt{2}=\sqrt{2}$ an irrational number.

$\Rightarrow$ $xRx$ for all $x$. So, $R$ is reflexive.

$R$ is not symmetric, because ${}_{\sqrt{2}}R_1$ but ${}_1R_{\sqrt{2}}$, $R$ is not transitive also because ${}_{\sqrt{2}}R_1$ and ${}_1R_{2\sqrt{2}}$ but ${}_{\sqrt{2}}R_{2\sqrt{2}}$

**7.** $\because$ $A=\{x\in R\,|\,-9\le x<4\}=\{-9,-8,-7,\ldots,3,4\}$

$B=\{x\in R\,|\,-13<x\le 5\}=\{-13,-12,-11,\ldots,4,5\}$

and $C=\{x\in R\,|\,-7\le x\le 8\}=\{-7,-6,-5,\ldots,7,8\}$

$\therefore$ $A\cap B\cap C=\{x\in R\,|\,-7\le x<4\}=\{-7,-6,-5,\ldots,3,4\}$

Hence, $-7\in(A\cap B\cap C)$

**9.** $A-P(A)=A$

Which is correct as $A$ and $P(A)$ are disjoint sets.

**10.** Since, intelligency is not defined for students in a class *i.e.,* not a well defined collection.

**11.** $\because$ $n(A)=3$ and $n(B)=2$

$\therefore$ Number of relations from $A$ to $B=2^{[n(A)\times n(B)]}$

$=2^{(3\times 2)}=2^6$

$=64$

**12.** Since, $4^n-3n-1=(3+1)^n-3n-1$

$=3^n+{}^nC_1 3^{n-1}+{}^nC_2 3^{n-2}+\ldots+{}^nC_{n-1}3+{}^nC_n-3n-1$

$={}^nC_2 3^2+{}^nC_3\cdot 3^3+\ldots+{}^nC_n 3^n$, $({}^nC_0={}^nC_n,\ {}^nC_1={}^nC_{n-1}$ etc.)

$=9[{}^nC_2+{}^nC_3(3)+\ldots+{}^nC_n 3^{n-1}]$

$\therefore 4^n-3n-1$ is a multiple of 9 for $n\ge 2$

For $n=1$, $4^n-3n-1=4-3-1=0$

For $n=2$, $4^n-3n-1=16-6-1=9$

$\therefore 4^n-3n-1$ is a multiples of 9 for all $n\in N$

$\therefore X$ contains elements, which are multiples of 9 and clearly $Y$ contains all multiples of 9.

$\therefore X\subseteq Y$ *i.e.,* $X\cup Y=Y$

**13.** Given, $N_a=\{ax\,|\,x\in N\}$

$\therefore$ $N_{12}=\{12,24,36,48,\ldots\}$

and $N_8=\{8,16,24,\ldots\}$

$\therefore N_8\cap N_{12}=\{24,48,\ldots\}$

$=N_{24}$

**14.** Since, $x^2+1=0$, gives $x^2=-1\Rightarrow x=\pm i$

$\therefore x$ is not real but $x$ is real (given)

$\therefore$ No value of $x$ is possible.

**15.** $\because$ $n(E)=75$, $n(M)=60$ and $n(E\cap M)=45$

$\therefore$ $n(E\cup M)=n(E)+n(M)-n(E\cap M)$

$=75+60-45=90$

Required number of students $=90-45=45$

**16.** Since, $y=\frac{1}{x}$, $y=-x$ meet when $-x=\frac{1}{x}\Rightarrow x^2=-1$,

which does not give any real value of $x$.

Hence, $A\cap B=\phi$

**17.** $\mu$ = the set of all triangles

$P$ = the set of all isosceles triangles

$Q$ = the set of all equilateral triangles

$R$ = the set of all the right angled triangles

$\therefore P\cap Q$ represents the set of isosceles triangles and $R-P$ represents the set of non-isosceles right angled triangles.

**18.** $A=[x:x\in R,\,-1<x<1]$

$B=[x:x\in R:x-1\le -1 \text{ or } x-1\ge 1]$

$=[x:x\in R:x\le 0 \text{ or } x\ge 2]$

$\therefore A\cup B=R-D$, where $D=[x:x\in R,\,1\le x<2]$

**19.** $\because$ $f(x)=\tan x$

$\therefore f'(x)=\sec^2 x$

$f(x)$ is increasing in the interval $\left(-\frac{\pi}{2},\frac{\pi}{2}\right)$

Hence, $f(x)$ is injective in the interval $\left(-\frac{\pi}{2},\frac{\pi}{2}\right)$

And, codomain of $f(x)\ne$ range of $f(x)$

$\therefore$ It is not onto.

**20.** $\because y=e^x$, $y=e^{-x}$ will meet, when $e^x=e^{-x}$

$\Rightarrow$ $e^{2x}=1$,

$\therefore$ $x=0,\ y=1$

$\therefore$ $A$ and $B$ meet on $(0,1)$,

$\therefore$ $A\cap B=\phi$

**21.** Given that, $n(U) = 700$, $n(A) = 200$, $n(B) = 300$ and $n(A \cap B) = 100$

We know that,

$$n(A \cup B) = n(A) + n(B) - n(A \cap B)$$
$$= 200 + 300 - 100 = 400$$

Now, $n(A' \cap B') = n(U) - n(A \cup B)$
$$= 700 - 400 = 300$$

**22.** $n(A \cup B) = n(A) + n(B) - n(A \cap B)$
$$0.25 = 0.16 + 0.14 - n(A \cap B)$$
$$\Rightarrow n(A \cap B) = 0.30 - 0.25 = 0.05$$

**23.** If the relation is defined by option (d), then each 1, 2 and 3 has two images. So, it is not a function.

**24.** Let $n(P)$ = Number of teachers in Physics.

$n(M)$ = Number of teachers in Maths

$$n(P \cup M) = n(P) + n(M) - n(P \cap M)$$
$$20 = n(P) + 12 - 4 \Rightarrow n(P) = 12$$

**25.** $\because A \cup B = B \cap C$

From above strong inference is

$$A \subseteq B \subseteq C$$

e.g., $A = \{a\}$, $B = \{a, b\}$, $C = \{a, b, c\}$

$A \cup B = \{a, b\}$, $B \cap C = \{a, b\}$

**26.** Since, $x \not< x$, therefore $R$ is not reflexive. Also, $x < y$ does not imply that $y < x$. So, $R$ is not symmetric. Let $xRy$ and $yRz$. Then, $x < y$ and $y < z \Rightarrow x < z$ i.e., $xRz$. Hence, $R$ is transitive.

**27.** $A \cap (A \cup B)' = A \cap (A' \cap B')$ [De Morgan's law]

$= (A \cap A') \cap B'$ [Associative law]

$= \phi \cap B' = \phi$

**28.** Given that, $y = 5^{\log x}$

$\Rightarrow$ $\log y = \log x \cdot \log 5$

or $\log x = \dfrac{\log y}{\log 5} = \log(y)^{(1/\log 5)} \Rightarrow x = y^{1/\log 5}$

**30.** $n(M) = 55$, $n(P) = 67$, $n(M \cup P) = 100$

Now, $n(M \cup P) = n(M) + n(P) - n(M \cap P)$
$$100 = 55 + 67 - n(M \cap P)$$
$\therefore$ $n(M \cap P) = 122 - 100 = 22$

Now, $n(P \text{ only}) = n(P) - n(M \cap P) = 67 - 22 = 45$

**31.** For any $a \in R$, we have $a \geq a$. Therefore, the relation $R$ is reflexive but it is not symmetric as $(2, 1) \in R$ but $(1, 2) \notin R$. The relation $R$ is transitive also, because $(a, b) \in R$, $(b, c) \in R$ imply that $a \geq b$ and $b \geq c$ which is turn imply that $a \geq c$.

**33.** For any integer $n$, we have $n \mid n \Rightarrow nRn$

So, $nRn$ for all $n \in Z \Rightarrow R$ is reflexive

Now, $2 \mid 6$ but $6 \nmid 2$, $\Rightarrow (2, 6) \in R$ but $(6, 2) \notin R$

So, $R$ is not symmetric.

Let $(m, n) \in R$ and $(n, p) \in R$

Then, $\left.\begin{array}{l}(m, n) \in R \Rightarrow m \mid n \\ (n, p) \in R \Rightarrow n \mid p\end{array}\right] \Rightarrow m \mid p \Rightarrow (m, p) \in R$

So, $R$ is transitive.

Hence, $R$ is reflexive and transitive but it is not symmetric.

**36.** Let $B$, $H$, $F$ denote the sets of members who are on the basketball team, hockey team and football team, respectively.

Then, we are given $n(B) = 21$, $n(H) = 26$, $n(F) = 29$

$n(H \cap B) = 14$, $n(H \cap F) = 15$, $n(F \cap B) = 12$

and $n(B \cap H \cap F) = 8$

We have to find $n(B \cup H \cup F)$

To find this, we use the formula

$$n(B \cup H \cup F) = n(B) + n(H) + n(F) - n(B \cap H) - n(H \cap F) - n(F \cap B) + n(B \cap H \cap F)$$

Hence, $n(B \cup H \cup F) = (21 + 26 + 29) - (14 + 15 + 12) + 8 = 43$

Thus these are 43 members in all.

**37.** Let $A = \{1, 2\}$ and $\{A\} = \{(1, 2)\}$

$\Rightarrow$ $P(A) = \{\{1\}, \{2\}, \{1, 2\}, \phi\}$

Then, $A \cup P(A) \neq P(A)$

and $\{A\} \cap P(A) = \{\{1, 2\}\} \cap \{\{1\}, \{2\}, \{1, 2\}, \phi\}$
$$= \{1, 2\} = A$$

**39.** Given, $n(N) = 12$, $n(P) = 16$, $n(H) = 18$, $n(N \cup P \cup H) = 30$

From $n(N \cup P \cup H) = n(N) + n(P) + n(H) - n(N \cap P) - n(P \cap H) - n(N \cap H) + n(N \cap P \cap H)$

$\therefore$ $n(N \cap P) + n(P \cap H) + n(N \cap H) = 16$

Now, number of pupils taking two subjects
$$= n(N \cap P) + n(P \cap H) + n(N \cap H) - 3n(N \cap P \cap H)$$
$$= 16 - 0 = 16$$

**41.** Given set is $\{(a, b) : 2a^2 + 3b^2 - 35, a, b \in Z\}$

We can see that, $2(\pm 2)^2 + 3(\pm 3)^2 = 35$

and $2(\pm 4)^2 + 3(\pm 1)^2 = 35$

$\therefore (2, 3), (2, -3), (-2, -3), (-2, 3), (4, 1), (4, -1), (-4, -1), (-4, 1)$ are 8 elements of the set.

$\therefore$ $n = 8$

**43.** $n((A \times B) \cap (B \times A))$
$$= n((A \cap B) \times (B \cap A)) = n(A \cap B) \cdot n(B \cap A)$$
$$= n(A \cap B) \cdot n(A \cap B) = (99)(99) = 99^2$$

**44.** Given, $y = 2x + 3 = f(x)$

For one-to-one function, $f(x_1) \neq f(x_2)$

$\Rightarrow$ $2x_1 + 3 \neq 2x_2 + 3$

$\Rightarrow$ $2x_1 \neq 2x_2 \Rightarrow x_1 \neq x_2$

So, function is one-to-one.

**47.** We know that,

$[(A \cup B) \cap C]' = (A \cup B)' \cup C' = (A' \cap B') \cup C'$

$= A' \cap B' \cup C'$ (by De Morgan's law)

**49.** Since, $\dfrac{1}{y} \neq 0$, $\dfrac{1}{y} \neq 2$, $\dfrac{1}{y} \neq \dfrac{-2}{3}$ $[\because y \in N]$

$\therefore$ $\dfrac{1}{y}$ can be 1. $[\because y$ can be 1$]$

**52.** Let the original set contains $(2n + 1)$ elements, then subsets of this set containing more than $n$ elements, i.e., subsets containing $(n + 1)$ elements, $(n + 2)$ elements,...... $(2n + 1)$ elements.

$\therefore$ Required number of subsets
$$= {}^{2n+1}C_{n+1} + {}^{2n+1}C_{n+2} + \ldots + {}^{2n+1}C_{2n} + {}^{2n+1}C_{2n+1}$$

$$= {}^{2n+1}C_n + {}^{2n+1}C_{n-1} + \ldots + {}^{2n+1}C_1 + {}^{2n+1}C_0$$

$${}^{2n+1}C_0 + {}^{2n+1}C_1 + {}^{2n+1}C_2 + \ldots + {}^{2n+1}C_{n-1} + {}^{2n+1}C_n$$

$$= \frac{1}{2}[(1+1)^{2n+1}] = \frac{1}{2}[2^{2n+1}] = 2^{2n}$$

**55.** Since, $n \mid n$ for all $n \in N$, therefore $R$ is reflexive. Since, $2 \mid 6$ but $6 \nmid 2$, therefore $R$ is not symmetric.

Let $nRm$ and $mRp \Rightarrow n \mid m$ and $m \mid p \Rightarrow n \mid p \Rightarrow nRp$.

So, $R$ is transitive.

**56.**

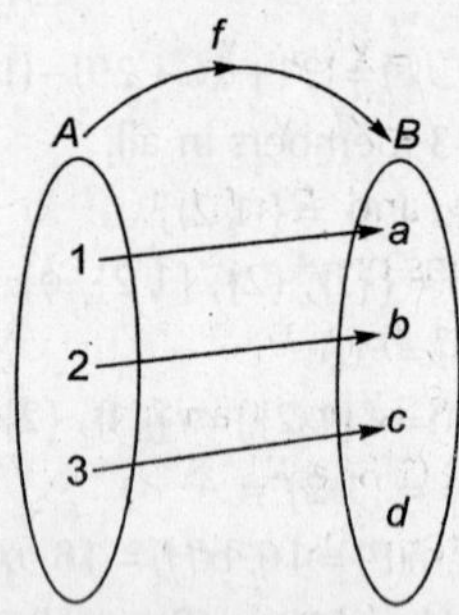


Since, the image of the each element of $A$ is belonging to only one element in $B$. But $d$ has no pre-image in $A$. Therefore, function is one-one but not onto.

So, its inverse does not exist.

**58.** $n(M \text{ alone}) = n(M) - n(M \cap C) - n(M \cap P) + n(M \cap P \cap C)$

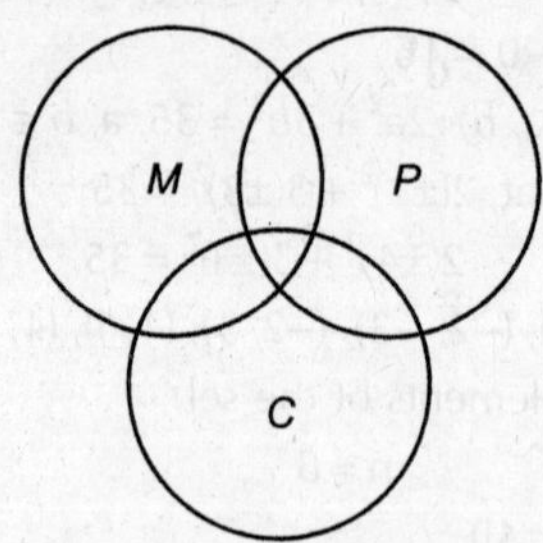


$$= 100 - 28 - 30 + 18 = 60$$

**59.** Since, $3 \in A$

But $(3, 3) \notin R$

So, it is not reflexive.

and $(3, 4) \in R$ and $(4, 3) \in R$

But $(3, 3) \notin R$

So, it is also not transitive.

Hence, $R$ is neither reflexive nor transitive.

**61.** $A - B = A - (A \cap B)$ is correct.

$A = (A \cap B) \cup (A - B)$ is correct.

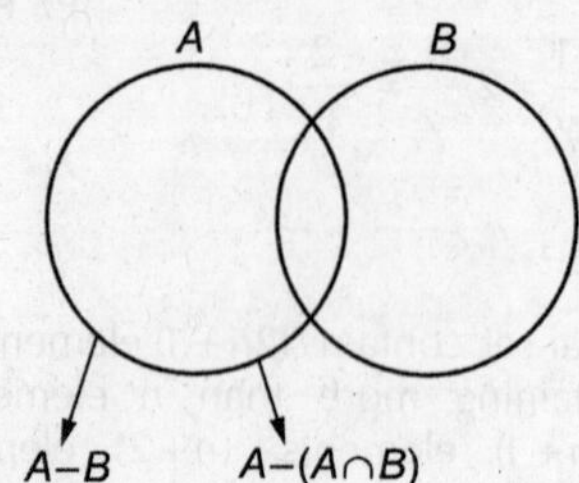


III is false.

$\therefore$ I and II are true.

**63.** (a) Since, $(1, 1); (2, 2); (3, 3) \in R$ therefore $R$ is reflexive.

$(1, 2) \in R$ but $(2, 1) \notin R$, therefore $R$ is not symmetric.

It can be easily seen that $R$ is transitive.

(c) Here, $R = \{(1, 3), (2, 2); (3, 2)\}$, $S = \{(2, 1); (3, 2); (2, 3)\}$

Then $RoS = \{(2, 3); (3, 2); (2, 2)\}$

**65.**

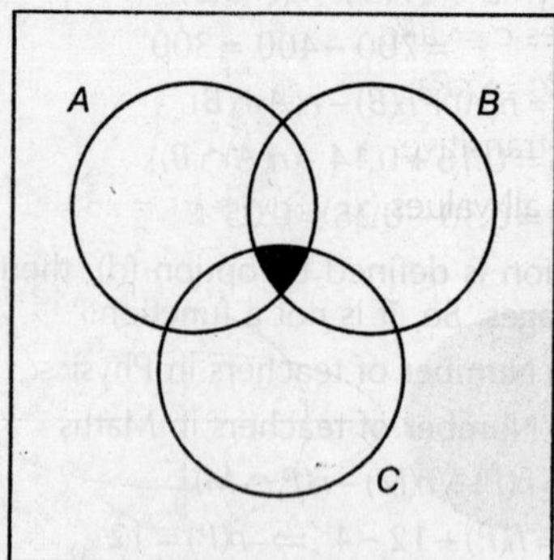


In the above Venn diagram, shaded area shows $A - (B - C)$

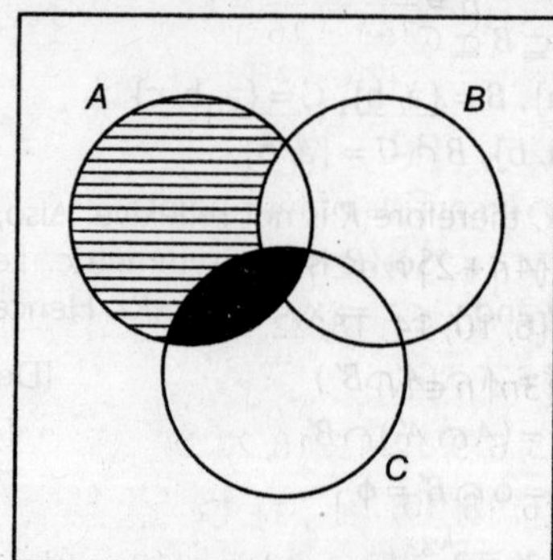


In the above Venn diagram, horizontal lines mean $(A - B)$ and vertical lines mean $(A \cap C)$.

Total shaded portion $= (A - B) \cup (A \cap C)$

$\therefore \quad (A - B) \cup (A \cap C) = A - (B - C)$

**67.** Since, $1 + a \cdot a = 1 + a^2 > 0, \forall a \in S$,

$\therefore$ $(a, a) \in R$

$\therefore$ $R$ is reflexive.

Also, $(a, b) \in R \Rightarrow 1 + ab > 0 \Rightarrow 1 + ba > 0 \Rightarrow (b, a) \in R$,

$\therefore$ $R$ is symmetric.

$\because$ $(a, b) \in R$ and $(b, c) \in R$ need not imply $(a, c) \in R$.

Hence, $R$ is not transitive.

**68.** $A \cap B = \{x : x \in A \text{ and } x \in B\}$

$= [x : f(x) = 0 \text{ and } g(x) = 0] = [f(x)]^2 + [g(x)]^2 = 0$

**69.** For reflexive

$aRa \Rightarrow a$ divides $a$

$\therefore$ $R$ is reflexive.

For symmetric

$aRb \Rightarrow a$ divides $b$

$bRa \Rightarrow b$ divides $a$

which may not be possible.

$\therefore R$ is not symmetric.

For transitive

$aRb \Rightarrow a$ divides $b \Rightarrow b = ka$

$bRc \Rightarrow b$ divides $c \Rightarrow c = lb$

Now, $c = lka$

$\Rightarrow a$ divides $c \Rightarrow aRc$

$\Rightarrow aRb, bRc \Rightarrow cRa$

Thus, $R$ is transitive.

**70.** $A =$ Set of all values $(x, y) : x^2 + y^2 = 25 = 5^2$

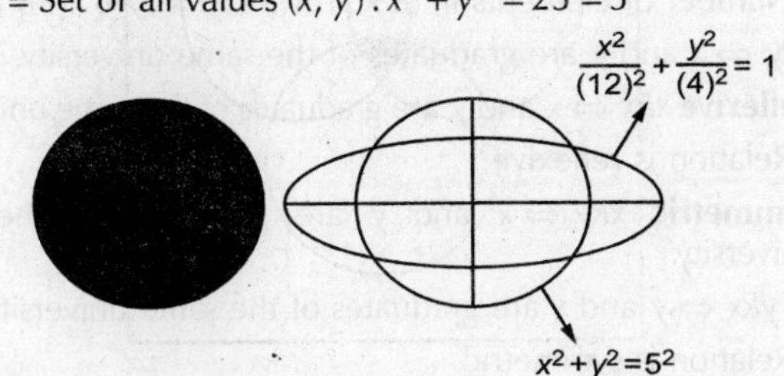


$$B = \frac{x^2}{144} + \frac{y^2}{16} = 1$$

i.e., $$\frac{x^2}{(12)^2} + \frac{y^2}{(4)^2} = 1$$

Clearly, $A \cap B$ consists of four points.

**71.** (d) $\because A = \{4n + 2 \mid n \in N\}$

$- \{6, 10, 14, 18, 22, 26, 30, \ldots\}$

and $B = \{3n \mid n \in N\}$

$= \{3, 6, 9, 12, 15, 18, 21, 24, \ldots\}$

$\therefore A \cap B = \{6, 18, 30, \ldots\}$

$= \{6 + (n-1)12 \mid n \in N\} = \{12n - 6 \mid n \in N\}$

(c) $x \equiv 3(\text{mod}\, 7) \Rightarrow x - 3 = 7p, (p \in z)$

$\Rightarrow x = 7p + 3, p \in z$ i.e., $\{7p + 3 : p \in z\}$

**74.** Since, $R$ is defined over the set of non-negative inegers, then $R = \{(6, 0), (0, 6)\}$ because the options (b) and (c) does not have integers in all pairs. Also in option (a) and (c), the most appropriate option is (c).

**75.** We first find $R^{-1}$, we have

$R^{-1} = \{(5, 4); (4, 1); (6, 4); (6, 7); (7, 3)\}$. We now obtain the elements of $R^{-1}oR$ we first pick the element of $R$ and then of $R^{-1}$. Since, $(4, 5) \in R$ and $(5, 4) \in R^{-1}$, we have

$(4, 4) \in R^{-1}oR$

Similarly, $(1, 4) \in R, (4, 1) \in R^{-1} \Rightarrow (1, 1) \in R^{-1}oR$

$(4, 6) \in R, (6, 4) \in R^{-1} \Rightarrow (4, 4) \in R^{-1}oR,$

$(4, 6) \in R, (6, 7) \in R^{-1} \Rightarrow (4, 7) \in R^{-1}oR$

$(7, 6) \in R, (6, 4) \in R^{-1} \Rightarrow (7, 4) \in R^{-1}oR,$

$(7, 6) \in R, (6, 7) \in R^{-1} \Rightarrow (7, 7) \in R^{-1}oR$

$(3, 7) \in R, (7, 3) \in R^{-1} \Rightarrow (3, 3) \in R^{-1}oR$

Hence, $R^{-1}oR = \{(1, 1); (4, 4); (4, 7); (7, 4); (7, 7); (3, 3)\}$

**80.** Both (A) and (R) are true and (R) is the correct explanation of (A).

$\because x^2$ is never negative but it can be positive or zero.

**82.** From the figure, it is clear that

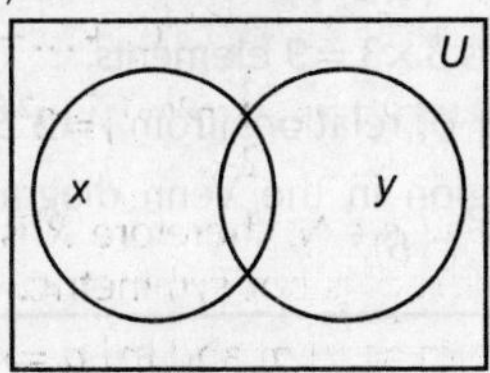


$(X - Y)' - X' \cup Y'$

**Alternate** $(X - Y)' = (X \cap Y')'$

$= X' \cup (Y')'$

$= X' \cup Y$

**84.** Let $A = \{1, 2, 3\}$ and $R = \{(1, 1), (1, 2)\}$, $S = \{(2, 2), (2, 3)\}$ be transitive relations on $A$.

Then, $R \cup S = \{(1, 1); (1, 2); (2, 2); (2, 3)\}$

Obviously, $R \cup S$ is not transitive. Since, $(1, 2) \in R \cup S$ and $(2, 3) \in R \cup S$ but $(1, 3) \notin R \cup S$.

**86.** In the given statements, statement (I) is correct.

(I) $A - (B - C) = A - (B \cap C') = A \cap (B \cap C')' = A \cap (B' \cup C)$

$(\because A - B = A \cap B')$

$(A - B) \cup C = (A \cap B') \cup C = C \cup (A \cap B')$

(II) $A - (B \cup C) = A \cap (B \cup C)' = A \cap (B' \cap C') = (A \cap B' \cap C')$

$(A - B) - C = (A \cap B') - C = (A \cap B') \cap C' = (A \cap B' \cap C')$

**88.** $\because R = \{(x, y) \mid xy > 0, x, y \in N\}$

**Reflexive**

$\because$ $x, y \in N$

$\therefore$ $x, x \in N \Rightarrow x^2 > 0$

$\therefore R$ is reflexive.

**Symmetric**

$\because$ $x, y \in N$

and $xy > 0 \Rightarrow yx > 0$

$\therefore R$ is also symmetric.

**Transitive**

$\because$ $x, y, z \in N$

$\Rightarrow$ $xy > 0, yz > 0 \Rightarrow xz > 0$

$\therefore R$ is also transitive

Thus, $R$ is an equivalence relation.

**90.** An injective function means one-one.

In option (d), $f(x) = -x$

For every values of $x$, we get a different value of $f$.

Hence, it is injective.

**91.** Here, $R = \{(x, y) : |x^2 - y^2| < 16\}$

and given $A = \{1, 2, 3, 4, 5\}$

$\therefore R = \{(1, 2)(1, 3)(1, 4); (2, 1)(2, 2)(2, 3)(2, 4); (3, 1)(3, 2)(3, 3)$

$(3, 4); (4, 1)(4, 2)(4, 3); (4, 4)(4, 5)(5, 4)(5, 5)\}$

**93.** The number of elements in power set of $A$ is 1.

$[\because P(A) = 2^0 = 1]$

$\therefore$ $P\{P(A)\} = 2^1 = 2$

$\Rightarrow$ $P\{P\{P(A)\}\} = 2^2 = 4$

$\Rightarrow$ $P\{P\{P\{P(A)\}\}\} = 2^4 = 16$

**95.** $A = \{2, 4, 6\}$, $B = \{2, 3, 5\}$

$\therefore$ $A \times B$ contains $3 \times 3 = 9$ elements.

Hence, number of relations from $A$ to $B = 2^9$.

**97.** The shaded region in the Venn diagram is represented by $C \cup (C \cap A) \cup (C \cap B)$.

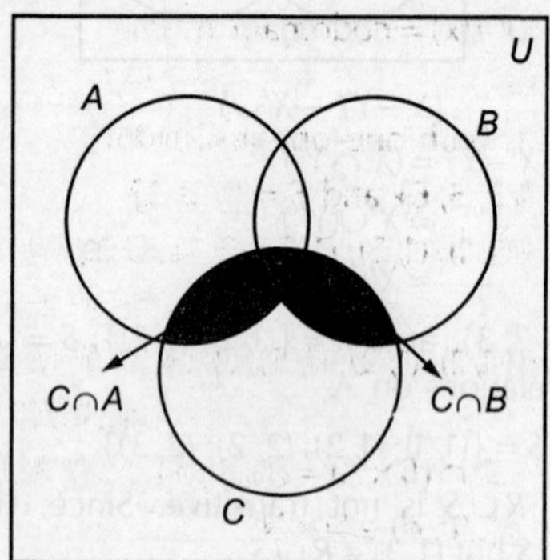


**99.** Given function, $f(x) = \frac{x}{x^2+1}$

For the function $f(x)$ is one-one

$$f(x_1) = f(x_2)$$

$\Rightarrow$ $\frac{x_1}{x_1^2+1} = \frac{x_2}{x_2^2+1}$

$\Rightarrow$ $x_1 x_2^2 + x_1 = x_1^2 x_2 + x_2$

$\Rightarrow$ $x_1 x_2 (x_1 - x_2) - (x_1 - x_2) = 0$

$\Rightarrow$ $(x_1 - x_2)(x_1 x_2 - 1) = 0$

$\Rightarrow$ $x_1 = x_2$ and $x_1 x_2 \neq 1$

So, the function is one-one.

Let $y = \frac{x}{x^2+1} \Rightarrow yx^2 + y = x$

$\Rightarrow$ $x^2 y - x + y = 0$

$\Rightarrow$ $x = \frac{1 \pm \sqrt{1-4y^2}}{2y}$; $1 - 4y^2 \geq 0$

$(1-2y)(1+2y) \geq 0$

$(2y-1)(2y+1) \leq 0$

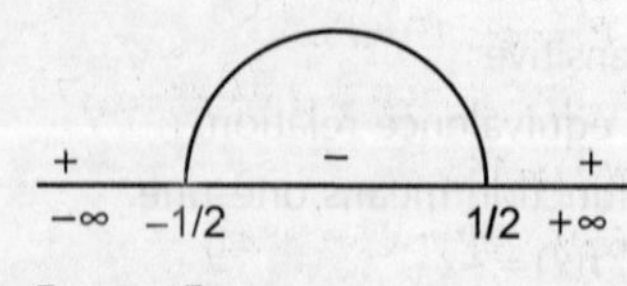


$y \in \left[-\frac{1}{2}, \frac{1}{2}\right] \sim \{0\}$

Here, the range of $f(x) = \left[-\frac{1}{2}, \frac{1}{2}\right] \sim \{0\}$ and codomain $= R$

$\Rightarrow$ Range $\neq$ Codomain

$\therefore$ $f(x)$ is not onto.

Hence, $f(x)$ is one-one but not onto.

**101.** $n(N \cup S) = 32$, $n(N) = 30$, $n(S) = 17$

$\because$ We know that,

$$n(N \cup S) = n(N) + n(S) - n(N \cap S)$$

$\Rightarrow$ $32 = 30 + 17 - n(N \cap S)$

$\Rightarrow$ $n(N \cap S) = 47 - 32 = 15$

Since, $R$ is an equivalence relation on set $A$, therefore $(a, a) \in R$ for all $a \in A$. Hence, $R$ has atleast $n$ ordered pairs.

**104.** $\because$ $R = \{3, 6, 9, 12, 15, \ldots, 99\}$

and $S = \{5, 10, 15, \ldots, 95\}$

Now, $(R \times S) \cap (S \times R)$

$= (R \cap S) \times (S \cap R)$

$= (15, 30, 45, 60, 75, 90) \times (15, 30, 45, 60, 75, 90)$

$\therefore$ Number of elements in $(R \times S) \cap (S \times R) = 6 \times 6 = 36$

**106.** $xRy \Leftrightarrow x$ and $y$ are graduates of the same university.

**Reflexive** $xRx \Leftrightarrow x$ and $y$ are graduates of the same university.

$\therefore$ Relation is reflexive.

**Symmetric** $xRy \Leftrightarrow x$ and $y$ are graduates of the same university.

$\Rightarrow yRx \Leftrightarrow y$ and $x$ are graduates of the same university.

$\therefore$ Relation is symmetric.

**Transitive** $xRy$, $yRz \Leftrightarrow xRz$

It means $x$ and $y$, $y$ and $z$ are graduates of the same university, then $x$ and $z$ are also graduates of the same university.

$\therefore$ Relation is transitive.

Hence, relation is reflexive, symmetric and transitive.

**108.** Let number of newspapers be $x$. If every students reads one newspaper, the number of students would be $x(60) = 60x$

Since, every students reads 5 newspapers

$\therefore$ Number of students $= \frac{x \times 60}{5} = 300$, $x = 25$

**110.** $X = \{(4^n - 3n - 1) \mid n \in N\}$

and $Y = \{9(n-1) \mid n \in N\}$

$\Rightarrow$ $X = \{0, 9, 54, \ldots\}$

and $Y = \{0, 9, 18, 27, 36, 54, \ldots\}$

$\therefore$ $X \cup Y = \{0, 9, 18, 27, 36, 54, \ldots\}$

$= Y$

**112.** Given, $A = \{-1, 2, 5, 8\}$ and $B = \{0, 1, 3, 6, 7\}$

$R = \{(-1, 0), (2, 3), (5, 6)\}$

($\because$ $R = A$ is one less than from $B$)

Hence, total number of elements in $R$ is 3.

**114.** Since, on taking a straight line parallel to $x$-axis, the group of given function intersect it at many points.

$\therefore f(x)$ is many one.

And as range of $f(x) =$ codomain

$\therefore f(x)$ is onto.

Hence, $f(x)$ is many one onto.

**116.** We have $(a, b)R(a, b)$ for all $(a, b) \in N \times N$

Since, $a + b = b + a$. Hence, $R$ is reflexive.

$R$ is symmetric for we have $(a, b)R(c, d) \Rightarrow a + d = b + c$

$\Rightarrow d + a = c + b \Rightarrow c + b = d + a \Rightarrow (c, d)R(e, f)$

Then, by definition of $R$, we have

$a + d = b + c$ and $c + f = d + e$

whence by addition, we get

$$a+d+c+f=b+c+d+e \text{ or } a+f=b+e$$

Hence, $(a, b)R(e, f)$

Thus, $(a, b)R(c, d)$ and $(c, d)R(e, f) \Rightarrow (a, b)R(e, f)$

**118.** $\because$ $A=\{n^2 : n \in N\}$ and $B=\{n^3 : n \in N\}$

$A=\{1, 4, 9, 16, 25, 49, 64, 81, \ldots\}$

$B=\{1, 8, 27, 64, 125, \ldots\}$

$A \cap B=\{1, 64, \ldots\}$

$\therefore$ $A \cap B$ must be a proper subset of $\{m^6 : m \in N\}$

**120.** $\because$ $A \cap B=\phi$ (given)

$\therefore$ $A-B=A-(A \cap B)$ $(\because A-B=A)$

Now, $B-A'=\phi$

and $B \cap A=\phi$

or $B-A'=B \cap A$

and $(A-B) \cap B=A \cap B$

So, option (d) is correct.

**122.** $M$ = set of men and $R$ is a relation 'is son of' defined on $M$.

Reflexive relation $aRa$.

Since, $a$ cannot be a son of $a$.

**Symmetric relation**

$aRb \Rightarrow bRa$

which is also not possible

**Transitive relation**

$aRb, bRc \Rightarrow cRa$

which is not possible.

**124.** $\because R=\{(1,1),(2,2),(3,3),(1,2),(2,3),(1,3)\}$

**Reflexive**

$\because$ 1R1, 2R2, 3R3

$\therefore R$ is a reflexive relation.

**Symmetric**

$\because$ 1R2 but 2R1

$\therefore$ $R$ is not a symmetric relation.

**Transitive**

$\because$ 1R2, 2R3 $\Rightarrow$ 1R3

$\therefore$ $R$ is a transitive relation.

**127.** $\because f(x)=\cos 2x-\sin 2x$

$[\because f(x)=a\cos x+b\sin x, -\sqrt{a^2+b^2} \le f(x) \le \sqrt{a^2+b^2}]$

$$-\sqrt{1+1} \le \cos 2x-\sin 2x \le \sqrt{1+1}$$

$$-\sqrt{2} \le \cos 2x-\sin 2x \le \sqrt{2}$$

So, Range of $f(x)$ is $[-\sqrt{2}, \sqrt{2}]$

**129.** Since, on the set of real numbers, $R$ is a relation defined by $xRy$ if and only if $3x+4y=5$ for which $1R\frac{1}{2}$ and $\frac{2}{3}R\frac{3}{4}$.

*i.e.*, $1R\frac{1}{2} \Rightarrow 3 \cdot 1+4 \cdot \frac{1}{2}=5$,

and $\frac{2}{3}R\frac{3}{4} \Rightarrow 3\times\frac{2}{3}+\frac{3}{4}\times 4=5$

Hence, both the statements II and III are correct.

**131.** $\because$ $f(x)=x|x|$

If $f(x_1)=f(x_2)$

$\Rightarrow$ $x_1|x_1|=x_2|x_2|$

$\Rightarrow$ $x_1=x_2$

$\therefore$ $f(x)$ is one-one.

Also, range of $f(x)$ = codomain of $f(x)$

$\therefore$ $f(x)$ is onto.

Hence, $f(x)$ is both one-one and onto.

**140.** $\because$ $A=\{1, 2, 5, 6\}$ and $B=\{1, 2, 3\}$

$\therefore$ $A \times B=\{(1,1),(1,2),(1,3),(2,1),(2,2),(2,3),(5,1),(5,2),(5,3),(6,1),(6,2),(6,3)\}$

and $B \times A=\{(1,1),(1,2),(1,5),(1,6),(2,1),(2,2),(2,5),(2,6),(3,1),(3,2),(3,5),(3,6)\}$

$\Rightarrow$ $(A \times B) \cap (B \times A)=\{(1,1),(1,2),(2,1),(2,2)\}$

**147.** For $(a, b), (c, d) \in N \times N$

$(a, b)R(c, d) \Rightarrow ad(b+c)=bc(a+d)$

**Reflexive** Since, $ab(b+a)=ba(a+b), \forall\, ab \in N$,

$\therefore$ $(a, b)R(a, b)$, $\therefore R$ is reflexive.

**Symmetric** For $(a, b), (c, d) \in N \times N$, let $(a, b)R(c, d)$

$\therefore$ $ad(b+c)=bc(a+d) \Rightarrow bc(a+d)=ad(b+c)$

$\Rightarrow$ $cb(d+a)=da(c+b) \Rightarrow (c, d)R(a, b)$

$\therefore$ $R$ is symmetric

**Transitive** For $(a, b), (c, d), (e, f) \in N \times N$,

Let $(a, b)R(c, d)$, $(c, d)R(e, f)$

$\therefore$ $ad(b+c)=bc(a+d)$, $cf(d+e)=de(c+f)$

$\Rightarrow$ $adb+adc=bca+bcd$ ...(i)

and $cfd+cfe=dec+def$ ...(ii)

Eq. (i) $\times ef$ + Eq. (ii) $\times ab$ gives,

$$adbef+adcef+cfdab+cfeab$$
$$=bcaef+bcdef+decab+defab$$

$\Rightarrow$ $adcf(b+e)=bcde(a+f) \Rightarrow af(b+e)=be(a+f)$

$\Rightarrow$ $(a, b)R(e, f)$

$\therefore$ $R$ is transitive.

Hence, $R$ is an equivalence relation.

**150.** $(P-\mu) \cup (\mu-P)=\phi \cup P'=P'$

Now, $P \cap \{(P-\mu) \cup (\mu-P)\}=P \cap P'=\phi$

**154.** $n(P)=25\%$, $n(C)=15\%$

$n(P^c \cap C^c)=65\%$, $n(P \cap C)=2000$

Since, $n(P^c \cap C^c)=65\%$

$\therefore$ $n(P \cup C)^c=65\%$ and $n(P \cup C)=35\%$

Now, $n(P \cup C)=n(P)+n(C)-n(P \cap C)$

$35=25+15-n(P \cap C)$

$\therefore$ $n(P \cap C)=40-35=5$. Thus, $n(P \cap C)=5\%$

But $n(P \cap C)=2000$

$\therefore$ Total number of families $=\frac{2000\times 100}{5}=40000$

Since, $n(P \cup C)=35\%$

and total number of families = 40000

and $n(P \cap C)=5\%$.

Hence, (II) and (III) are correct.

**158.** $\because$ *A, B, C* are non-empty sets such that $A \cap C = \phi$

$\therefore (A \times B) \cap (C \times B) = (A \cap C) \times B = \phi \times B = \phi$

**161.** Since, $2^m - 2^n = 56 = 8 \times 7 = 2^3 \times 7$

$\Rightarrow 2^n(2^{m-n} - 1) = 2^3 \times 7$

$\therefore n = 3$ and $2^{m-n} = 8 = 2^3$

$\Rightarrow m - n = 3 \Rightarrow m - 3 = 3 \Rightarrow m = 6;$

$\therefore \quad m = 6, n = 3$

**162.** $8x - 6 = 14P, (x \in Z)$

$\Rightarrow \quad x = \frac{1}{8}[14P + 6], (x \in Z)$

$\Rightarrow \quad x = \frac{1}{4}[7P + 3] \Rightarrow x = 6, 13, 20, 27, 34, 41, 48, \ldots$

$\therefore$ Solution set $= \{6, 20, 34, 48, \ldots\} \cup \{13, 27, 41, \ldots\}$

$= [6] \cup [13],$

where [6], [13] are equivalence classes of 6 and 13, respectively.

**163.** $O(S) = O\left(\bigcup_{i=1}^{30} A_i\right) = \frac{1}{10}(5 \times 30) = 15$

Since, element in the union *S* belongs to 10 of $A_i$'s

Also, $O(S) = O\left(\bigcup_{j=1}^{n} B_j\right) = \frac{3n}{9} = \frac{n}{3}, \therefore \frac{n}{3} = 15 \Rightarrow n = 45$

**169.** Here, $n(C) = 224, n(H) = 240, n(B) = 336$

$n(H \cap B) = 64, n(B \cap C) = 80$

$n(H \cap C) = 40, n(C \cap H \cap B) = 24$

$n(C^c \cap H^c \cap B^c) = n[(C \cup H \cup B)^c]$

$= n(\cup) - n(C \cup H \cup B)$

$= 800 - [n(C) + n(H) + n(B) - n(H \cap C)$

$- n(H \cap B) - n(C \cap B) + n(C \cap H \cap B)]$

$= 800 - [224 + 240 + 336 - 64 - 80 - 40 + 24]$

$= 800 - 640 = 160$

## Exercise 2

1. We have assume that $a \le b + \frac{1}{n}, \forall n \in \mathbb{N}$ and $a > b$.

   Then, $a - b > 0$ and by the Archimedean property we have

   $n_0(a - b) > 1$ for some $n_0 \in \mathbb{N}$

   Then, $\quad a > b + \frac{1}{n_0}$

   which is a contradiction to our assumption. Hence, $a \le b$.

2. Assume that *a* and *b* satisfy the hypothesis but not the conclusion. Then, $a > b$ and so there is a $c \in \mathbb{R}$ such that $a > c > b$. Now $c > b \Rightarrow a < c$ in contradiction to $a > c$.

3. Let $M \supseteq N$ and *N* be a *nbd* of a point *x*. Then there exists an open interval *I* such that $x \in I \subseteq N \subseteq M$

   $\Rightarrow$ *M* is *nbd* of *x*.

   Now, let *M* and *N* be *nbds* of *x*, then there exists open intervals enclosing the point *x* such that

   $x \in (x - \delta_1, x + \delta_1) \subseteq M$ and

   $x \in (x - \delta_2, x + \delta_2) \subseteq N$

   Let $\delta = \min(\delta_1, \delta_2)$. Then,

   $(x - \delta, x + \delta) \subseteq (x - \delta_1, x + \delta_2) \subseteq M$

   and $(x - \delta, x + \delta) \subseteq (x - \delta_1, x + \delta_2) \subseteq N$

   $\Rightarrow \quad (x - \delta, x + \delta) \subseteq M \cap N$

   $\Rightarrow M \cap N$ is a *nbd* of *x*.

   Clearly, arbitrary and finite union of *nbds* of *x* is again a *nbd* of *x*.

6. We know that the interior $S^0$ of a set *S* is an open subset of *S*. Let us now proceed to show that any open subset $G_1$ of *S* is contained in $S^0$.

   Let $x \in G_1$ since an open set is a *nbd* of each of its points, therefore $G_1$ is a *nbd* of *x* but *S* is superset of $G_1$. Hence, *S* is also a *nbd* of *x*. Hence, *x* is an interior point of *S*. Hence, $x \in S^0$.

7. Let $G_1$ and $G_2$ be two open set. Then,

   If $\quad G_1 \cap G_2 = \phi$, it is an open set.

   If $\quad G_1 \cap G_2 \ne \phi$,

   let $\quad x \in G_1 \cap G_2$

   $\Rightarrow \quad x \in G_1$ and $x \in G_2$

   $\Rightarrow \quad G_1$ and $G_2$ are *nbds* of *x*.

   $\Rightarrow G_1 \cap G_2$ is a *nbd* of *x* but, since *x* is any point of $G_1 \cap G_2$, therefore $G_1 \cap G_2$ is a *nbd* of each of its points.

   Hence, $G_1 \cap G_2$ is open.

   Now, consider the open sets

   $G_n = \left(-\frac{1}{n}, \frac{1}{n}\right), n \in N$

   $\Rightarrow \quad \bigcap_{n \in N} G_n = \{0\}$

   which is not open. Hence, arbitrary intersection of open set need not be open.

11. If $S' = \phi$, then $S' \subseteq T'$.

    If $S' \ne \phi$, let $x \in S'$ and *N* be a *nbd* of *x*. Then, *N* contains an infinite number of members of *S*. But $S \subseteq T$.

    Hence, *N* contains infinitely many members of *T*. Hence, *x* is a limit point of *T*.

    *i.e.*, $\quad x \in T'$. Hence, $S' \subseteq T'$.

    Now, $S \cap T \subseteq S$

    $\Rightarrow \quad (S \cap T)' \subseteq S'$

    and $\quad S \cap T \subseteq T$

    $\Rightarrow \quad (S \cap T)' \subseteq T'$

    $\therefore \quad (ST)' \subseteq S' \cap T'$

    Next, let $\quad x \notin S' \cap T'$

    $\Rightarrow \quad x \notin S'$ or $x \notin T'$

    $\Rightarrow$ *x* is not a limit point of *S* or *T*.

    Hence there exists *nbds* $N_1$, $N_2$ of *x* such that $N_1$ contains no point of *S* other than *x* and $N_2$ contains no points of *T* other than possible *x*.

    Now, since, $\quad N_1 \cap N_2 \subseteq N_1$

    and $\quad N_1 \cap N_2 \subseteq N_2$

Hence, there exists a *nbd* $N_1 \cap N_2$ of $x$ which contains no point other than $x$ of $S$ or of $T$ and thus of $S \cup T$.

$\Rightarrow x$ is not a limit point of $S \cup T$.

$\Rightarrow x \notin (S \cup T)'$

Thus, $(S \cup T)' \subseteq S' \cup T'$

Let $S = (1, 2)$ and $T = (2, 3)$

Then, $S \cap T = \phi$

$\Rightarrow (S \cap T)' = \phi' = \phi$

Also, $S' = [1, 2]$ and $T' = [2, 3]$

Hence, $S' \cap T' = \{2\}$

$\Rightarrow (S \cap T)' \neq S' \cap T'$

**12.** The members of $S$ heap or cluster near zero on bothe sides of it and every *nbd* of zero contains an infinite number of points of $S$. Hence, $0 \notin S$ is a limit point. Hence, $S$ is not closed. Also $S$ is not open, for it does not contain any *nbd* of any of its point.

Next, the set $S = \left\{\frac{1}{2}, 2, \frac{1}{3}, 3, \frac{1}{4}, 4, \frac{1}{5}, 5, \ldots\right\}$ is unbounded and infinite and has the limit point 0.

**13.** Since, 1 and $-1$ are the only limit points of the set and are in the set. Hence, the set $S$ is closed. Again all member of the set except 1 and $-1$, are not the interior points of the set. Thus, the set is not open.

**17.** Let $F_1$ and $F_2$ be two closed sets and

$$F = F_1 \cup F_2$$

Let $x$ be a limit point of $F$ let if possible $x \notin F$, thus $x \notin S$ and $x \notin I$. Also, as $F_1, F_2$ are closed sets, the point $x$ which does not belong to them, cannot be a limit point of either.

Hence, there exists *nbds* $N_1$ and $N_2$ of $x$ such that

$$N_1 \cap F_1 = \phi \text{ and } N_2 \cap F_2 = \phi \quad \ldots \text{(i)}$$

Let $N_1 \cap N_2 = N$, where $x \in N$

Then, from Eq. (i), we have

$$N \cap (F_1 \cup F_2) = \phi \Rightarrow N \cap F = \phi$$

Hence, there exists a *nbd* $N$ of $x$ which contains no point of $F$. Hence, $x$ is not a limit point of $F$ which is a contradiction. Hence, $F$ is closed.

**18.** Let $S'$ be denote the derived set of $S$. We have to show that the derived set $S''$ of $S'$ is contained in $S'$, if $S'' = \phi$, then $S'' = \phi \subseteq S'$ and $S'$, if is closed. If $S'' \neq \phi$, let $x \in S''$. Hence, every *nbd* $N$ of $x$ contains atleast one point $y \neq x$ of $S'$. Again, $y \in S'$. Hence, every *nbd* of $y$, $N$ being such a *nbd*, contains infinitely many points of $S$. Hence, $x$ is a limit point of $S$. Hence,

$$S'' \subseteq S'$$

$\Rightarrow S'$ is a closed set.

**19.** We have,

$$(\bar{S})' = (S \cup S')'$$
$$= S' \cup S''$$
$$= S'$$
$$\subset \bar{S}$$

Hence, $\bar{S}$ is closed.

Now, since

$$\bar{S}' = S'$$

Hence, derived set of derived set of $S$ is closed.

**20.** Let $M$ be the supremum of the bounded set $S (\subseteq \mathbb{R})$, which must exists by the order. Completeness property of $\mathbb{R}$. If $M \notin S$, then for any number $\varepsilon > 0$, however small, there exists atleast one member $x$ of $S$ such that

$$M - \varepsilon < x < M$$

Hence, every *nbd* of $M$ contains atleast one member $x$ of the set $S$ other than $M$. Hence, $M$ is a limit of $S$.

**21.** If $M \notin S$

$\Rightarrow M \in S'$

$\Rightarrow M \in S \cup S' = \bar{S}$

If $M \in S$

$\Rightarrow M \in S \cup S' = \bar{S}$

Hence, $M \in \bar{S}$

**28.** Here, $l_1 R l_2$

$l_1$ is parallel $l_2$ and also $l_2$ is parallel to $l_1$, so it is symmetric. Clearly, it is also reflexive and transitive. Hence, it is equivalence relation.

**32.** $R \times (P^c \cup Q^c) = R \times [(P^c)^c \cap (Q^c)^c]$

$$= R \times (P \cap Q)$$
$$= (R \times P) \cap (R \times Q) = (R \times Q) \cap (R \times P)$$

**34.** Let $(a, b)$ be an open interval.

If $x \in (a, b)$, then $a < x < b$

Choose $\delta = \min\{x - a, b - x\}$

Thus, $\forall x \in (a, b), \delta > 0$, whenever $|x - y| < \delta$, $y \in (a, b)$, *i.e.*, $(a, b)$ is open set.

**36.** $\bar{E}$ is closed, if it contains all its points of closure, *i.e.*, if $x$ is a point of closure of $\bar{E}$, then $x \in \bar{E}$.

Let $x$ be a point of closure of $\bar{E}$, then for every $\delta > 0$, there is $y \in \bar{E}$ such that $|x - y| < \delta/2$.

Since, $y \in \bar{E}$, for $\delta > 0$, there is $z \in E$ such that $|y - z| < \delta/2$.

Also, $|x - z| = |x - y + y - z| \leq |x - y| + |y - z| < \delta/2 + \delta/2$

$\Rightarrow |x - z| < \delta$

*i.e.*, for $\delta > 0$, $z \in E : |x - z| < \delta$, we have $x$ is a point of closure of $E$.

$\Rightarrow x \in \bar{E}$

**37.** Let $(a, b)$ be an open interval.

If $x \in (a, b)$, then $a < x < b$.

Choose $\delta = \min\{x - a, b - x\}$

Thus, $\forall x \in (a, b), \delta > 0$, whenever $|x - y| < \delta$, $y \in (a, b)$, *i.e.*, $(a, b)$ is open set.

**38.** Here, $O_1 = (-1, 1)$

$$O_2 = \left(-\frac{1}{2}, \frac{1}{2}\right)$$
$$O_3 = \left(-\frac{1}{3}, \frac{1}{3}\right)$$
$$O_\infty = \left(-\frac{1}{\infty}, \frac{1}{\infty}\right)$$
$$= (0, 0) = \{0\} \qquad \left(\because \frac{x}{-\infty} = 0, x \in \mathbb{R}\right)$$

$\therefore \bigcap_{n=1}^{\infty} O_n = \{0\}$, a closed set.

**39.** $A - B = \{x : x \in A \text{ and } x \notin B\}$
$= \{x : x \in A \text{ and } x \in B^c\}$
$= A \cap B^c$

Since, $B$ is closed set, its complement $B^c$ is open set.

$\therefore A - B$ is open set, because intersection of two open sets is open set.

$B - A = \{x : x \in B \text{ and } x \notin A\}$
$= \{x : x \in B \text{ and } x \in A^c\}$
$= B \cap A^c$

Since $A$ is closed, $A^c$ is open and intersection of two closed sets is closed, *i.e.*, $B - A$ is closed.

**40.** Let $x$ be a point of closure of $[a, b]$, then for every $\delta > 0$, there is $y \in [a, b]$, such that $|x - y| < \delta$.

A closed interval $[a, b]$ is closed set, if it contains all its points of closure, *i.e.*, $x \in [a, b]$.

On the contrary, let $x \notin [a, b]$.

Choose $\delta = \min\{b - y, y - a\}$, for every $y \in [a, b]$,

Such that $|x - y| < \delta$, $x \in [a, b]$,

which is the contradiction.

Thus, $x \in [a, b]$.

$\Rightarrow [a, b]$ contains all its closure points.

$\Rightarrow [a, b]$ is a closed set.

**41.** Here,

$$O_1 = (-1, 1)$$

$$O_2 = \left(-\frac{1}{2}, \frac{1}{2}\right)$$

$$O_3 = \left(-\frac{1}{3}, \frac{1}{3}\right)$$

$$O_\infty = \left(-\frac{1}{\infty}, \frac{1}{\infty}\right)$$

$$= (0, 0) = \{0\} \qquad \left(\because \frac{x}{-\infty} = 0, x \in \mathbb{R}\right)$$

$$\therefore \bigcap_{n=1}^{\infty} O_n = \{0\}, \text{ a closed set.}$$

**42.** Since, $\mathbb{R}$ is a closed set, it contains all its points of closure, and $\mathbb{R}^c = \phi$, a complement of closed set is open, therefore $\phi$ is a open set.

**43.** Since $R$ is a closed set, it contains all its points of closure, and $\mathbb{R}^c = \phi$, a complement of closed set is open, therefore $\phi$ is a open set.

**44.** $Q = \{x/n : x, n \text{ are integers}, n \neq 0\}$

Let $A_n = \{n : n \text{ is the denominator}\}$

$$\Rightarrow \bigcup_{n=1}^{\infty} A_n = Q$$

$\because A_n$ is the set of integer it is countable.

$\therefore \bigcup_{n=1}^{\infty} A_n$ is also countable and so $Q$ is countable.

# 2 Sequences and Series

**Syllabus**

- Sequences and Series
- Convergence
- lim sup
- lim inf
- Bolzano Weiertrase Theorem
- Heine Borel Theorem

## Sequences

A sequence of real numbers (or a real sequence) is defined as a function $S:N\to R$, where $N$ is the set of natural numbers and $R$ is the set of real numbers.

If $S:N\to R$ is a sequence, then for each $n\in N$, $S(n)$ is a real number. It is customary to write $S(n)$ as $S_n$. A sequence may be written as

$$< s_1, s_2, s_3, \ldots, s_n > \text{ or } < S_n > \text{ or } \{S_n\}$$

the real numbers $s_1, s_2, \ldots, s_n, \ldots$ are called the terms or elements of the sequence. $S_1$ is called the first term; $S_2$, the second term ...; $S_n$, the $n$th term of the sequence $< S_n >$. We can write all the terms of a sequence, if its $n$th term is known.

*e.g.* (i) $< \frac{1}{n} >$ is the sequence $< 1, \frac{1}{2}, \ldots, \frac{1}{n}, \ldots >$

(ii) $< -5n >$ is the sequence $< -5, -10, -15, \ldots, -5n, \ldots >$

(iii) $< \frac{(-1)^n}{n} >$ is the sequence $< -1, \frac{1}{2}, \frac{-1}{3}, \ldots >$

(iv) $< (-1)^n >$ is the sequence $< -1, 1, -1, 1, \ldots >$

> ***Note*** **(a)** A sequence may be formed by a recurrence relation.
> *e.g.* If $x_n = x_{n-1} + x_{n-2}$ for $n \ge 2$ and $x_0 = x_1 = 1$, then a sequence $< x_n >$ is generated and is known as the Fibonacci sequence.
> **(b)** The terms of a sequence may be all distincts (as in example (i), (ii), (iii)) or repeating (as in example (iv)).

### Range Set of a Sequence

The set of all distinct elements of a sequence is called the range set of the given sequence.

*e.g.* (i) The range set of the sequence $< \frac{1}{n} > = \left\{\frac{1}{n} : n \in N\right\}$.

(ii) The range set of the sequence $< (-1)^n > = \{-1, 1\}$ which is a finite set.

> ***Note*** **(a)** The range set of the sequences may be finite or infinite but the sequences has always an infinite number of elements.
> **(b)** The range of a sequence may or may not be a set at all for example, the sequence $< (-1)^n >$ is often called the range set of the sequence $< (-1)^n >$. Thus, we shall distinguish the range from the range set of a sequence.

### Constant Sequence

If the range of a sequence is a singleton set, it is called a constant sequence. In other words, a sequence $< S_n >$ defined by $S_n = a$ for all $n \in N$ is called a constant sequence.

*e.g.*, If $S_n = 5$, then $< S_n >$ is a constant sequence.

### Equality of Two Sequences

Two sequences $<S_n>$ and $<t_n>$ are said to be equal, if $S_n = t_n, \forall n \in N$.

## Algebra of Sequences

Let $<S_n>, <t_n>$ be two sequences, then the sequences having $n$th terms $\langle S_n + t_n \rangle, \langle S_n - t_n \rangle$ and $\langle S_n \cdot t_n \rangle$ are respectively called the sum, difference and product of the sequence $<S_n>$ and $<t_n>$. These sequences are denoted by $<S_n + t_n>, <S_n - t_n>, <S_n \cdot t_n>$ respectively.

If $t_n \neq 0, \forall n$, then the sequence where $n$th term is $<\frac{1}{t_n}>$ is known as the reciprocal of the sequence $<t_n>$ and is denoted by $<1/t_n>$. Also the sequence where $n$th term is $<\frac{S_n}{t_n}>$ is called the quotient of the sequence $<S_n>$ by the sequence $<t_n>$ and is denoted by $\frac{<S_n>}{<t_n>}$.

If $c \in R$, then the sequence have $n$th term $c\,S_n$ is called the scalar multiple of $<S_n>$ by c. This sequence is denoted by $<c\,S_n>$.

## Bounds of a Sequence

### Definitions

1. A sequence $<S_n>$ is said to be bounded above, if there exists a real number $k$ such that $S_n \leq k, \forall n \in N$. $k$ is called an upper bound of the sequence $<S_n>$.
2. A sequence $<S_n>$ is said to be bounded below, if there exists a real number $k$ such that $k \leq S_n, \forall n \in N$. $k$ is called the lower bound of the sequence $<S_n>$.
3. A sequence $<S_n>$ is said to be bounded, if it is both bounded above and bounded below.

   Equivalently, $<S_n>$ is bounded, if there exists two real numbers $k$ and $K$ such that $k \leq S_n \leq K, \forall n \in N$.
4. A sequence $<S_n>$ is said to be unbounded, if it is either unbounded below or unbounded above.
5. The least number $M$(say), if it exists of the set of upper bounds of $<S_n>$ is called the least upper bound (lub) or supremum (Sup) of the sequence $<S_n>$.
6. The greatest number $m$(say), if it exists, of the set of lower bounds of $<S_n>$ is called the greatest lower bounds (glb) or the infimum (Inf) of the sequence $<S_n>$.

> **Note** (a) It is not necessary that a sequence be bounded above or bounded below.
>
> (b) If the range of a sequence is a finite set, then the sequence is bounded because a finite set is always bounded.

e.g. (i) The sequence $<n^2> = <1, 4, 9, 16, \ldots>$ is bounded below by 1 but is not bounded above.

(ii) The sequence $<\frac{1}{n}> = <1, \frac{1}{2}, \frac{1}{3}, \ldots>$ is bounded as

$$0 < \frac{1}{n} \leq 1, \forall n \in N$$

(iii) The sequence $<(-1)^n> = <-1, 1, -1, 1, \ldots>$ is bounded, $-1$ being a lower bound and 1 an upper bound.

(iv) The sequence $<(-n)^2> = <-1, -4, -9, -16, \ldots>$ is bounded above by $-1$, but is not bounded below.

(v) The sequence $<(-1)^n n> = <-1, 2, -3, 4, -5, \ldots>$ is neither bounded above nor bounded below.

## Convergent Sequence

Suppose, $<S_n>$ be a sequence and $l$ be a real number. Let $]l - \varepsilon, l + \varepsilon[$ be a nbd of $l$, where $\varepsilon$ is positive and is as small as we please.

Suppose, $S_{10000}, S_{10001}, S_{10002}, \ldots$ belongs to $]l - \varepsilon, l + \varepsilon[$

$\Rightarrow \quad S_n \in ]l - \varepsilon, l + \varepsilon[, \forall n \geq 10000$

$\Rightarrow \quad l - \varepsilon < Sn < l + \varepsilon, \forall n \geq m, m = 10000$ ...(i)

> **Note** That with the exception of the elements $S_1, S_2, \ldots, S_{9999}$; the rest of the elements of the given sequence $<S_n>$ are scattered in $]l - \varepsilon, l + \varepsilon[$ and are extremely close to $l$ *i.e.,* Such elements are approaching to $l$ or converging to $l$. We express the property as
>
> The sequence $<S_n>$ converges to $l$. we may write Eq. (i)
>
> as $-\varepsilon < S_n - l < \varepsilon, \forall n \geq m$
>
> $\Rightarrow \quad |S_n - l| < \varepsilon, \forall n \geq m$
>
> with this motivation, we are now in a position to give the proper definition of a convergent sequence.

### Definition

A sequence $<S_n>$ is said to converge to a real number $l$ (or to have the real number $l$ as its limit) if for each $\varepsilon > 0$, there exists a positive integer $m$ (depending on $\varepsilon$), such that $|S_n - l| < \varepsilon, \forall n \geq m$.

In such a case, we write this fact as $\lim_{n \to \infty} S_n = l$ or $\lim S_n = l$ or simply as $S_n \to l$ we read $S_n \to l$ as $S_n$ tends (or approaches) to $l$, and the number $l$ is called the limit of the sequence $S_n$.

***Example 1.*** *Show that the sequence* $<\frac{1}{n}>$ *has the limit* 0.

**Solution.** Let $\varepsilon > 0$ be given. If $S_n = \frac{1}{n}$, then we have

$$|S_n - 0| = \left|\frac{1}{n} - 0\right| = \frac{1}{n} < \varepsilon, \text{ if } n > 1/\varepsilon$$

Let us choose a positive integer $m = \left[\frac{1}{\varepsilon}\right] + 1$

[Where [P] denotes the greatest integer not greater than P]. Then we have,

$$|S_n - 0| < \varepsilon, \quad \forall\ n \geq m$$

$\therefore\ < S_n > = < \frac{1}{n} >$ converges to 0 *i.e.* $< \frac{1}{n} >$ has the limit 0.

# Non-convergent Sequences

Non-convergence of a sequence may occur in two ways by oscillation and by divergence. A sequence may oscillate finitely or infinitely. Similarly, a sequence may diverge to $+\infty$ or to $-\infty$.

## Definitions

1. Let $< S_n >$ be the sequence of real numbers $< S_n >$ is said to diverge to plus infinity ($\infty$), if for any real number $M > 0$, however large, there exists a positive integer $m \in N$, such that $S_n > M, \forall\ n \geq m$. We write as $\lim_{n \to \infty} S_n = \infty$ or $\lim S_n = \infty$ or $S_n \to \infty$ as $n \to \infty$ or simply $S_n \to \infty$.
2. Let $< S_n >$ be the sequence of real number $< S_n >$ is said to diverge to minus infinity ($-\infty$), if for any real number $N > 0$, however small, there exists a positive integer $m \in N$, such that $S_n < N, \forall\ n \geq m$. We write as $\lim_{n \to \infty} S_n = -\infty$, or $\lim S_n = -\infty$ or $S_n \to -\infty$ as $n \to \infty$ or simply $S_n \to -\infty$.
3. A sequence $< S_n >$ which diverges either to plus infinity ($+\infty$) or minus infinity ($-\infty$) is said to be divergent sequence or a sequence $S_n$ diverges, then we say that $\lim S_n$ exists infinitely.
4. A sequence which diverges to neither to plus infinity ($+\infty$) nor to minus infinity ($-\infty$) is said to be non-divergent sequence.

***Example 2.*** *Prove that the sequence $< 2^n >$ diverges to plus infinity.*

**Solution.** Let $M > 0$ be a real number.

Now, if $2^n > M$, then $n \log 2 > \log M$ *i.e.*, $n > \frac{\log M}{\log 2}$.

Let us choose a positive integer $m = \left[\frac{\log M}{\log 2}\right] + 1$.

Then, $2^n > M, \forall\ n \geq m$. Hence, the sequence $< 2^n >$ diverges to infinity.

# Oscillatory Sequences

## Definitions

1. A sequence is said to oscillate finitely, if
   (i) It is bounded.
   (ii) It neither converges nor diverges.
2. A sequence is said to oscillate infinitely, if
   (i) It is not bounded.
   (ii) It neither converges nor diverges.

***Note*** **(a)** A bounded sequence either converges or oscillates finitely.
**(b)** An unbounded sequence either diverges to $+\infty$ to $-\infty$
or oscillates infinitely. *e.g.*
(i) The sequence $< (-1)^n >$ oscillates finitely.
(ii) The sequence $< (-1)^n \cdot n >$ oscillates infinitely.

***Example 3.*** *Let $< S_n >$ and $< t_n >$ be two sequences such that $< S_n + t_n >, < S_n \cdot t_n >$ converges. Show by an example that the sequence $< S_n >$ and $< t_n >$ may fail to converge.*

## Important Theorems on Convergent and Non-convergent Sequence

1. (Uniqueness theorem) A sequence can not converge to more than one limit.
   or Every convergent sequence has a unique limit.
2. If $< S_n >$ is a sequence of non-negative numbers such that $\lim S_n = l$, then $l \geq 0$.
3. Every convergent sequence is bounded but the converse is not.
4. Let $\lim S_n = l$ and $\lim t_n = l'$, then $\lim(S_n + t_n) = l + l'$.
   In other words, the limit of the sum of two convergent sequences is the sum of their limit.
5. Let $\lim S_n = l$ and $\lim t_n = l'$, then $\lim(S_n - t_n) = l - l'$.
6. Let $\lim S_n = l$ and $\lim t_n = l'$, then $\lim(S_n \cdot t_n) = l \cdot l'$.
   In other words, the limit of the product of two convergent sequences is the product of their limits.
7. If $\lim t_n = l', l' \neq 0$ and $t_n \neq 0, \forall\ n$, then $\lim(1/t_n) = 1/l'$.
8. If $\lim S_n = l$ and $\lim t_n = l', l' \neq 0, t_n \neq 0, \forall\ n$, then $\lim(S_n/t_n) = l/l'$.
9. Let $< S_n >$ and $< t_n >$ be two sequences such that $S_n \leq t_n, \forall\ n \in N$, then $\lim S_n \leq \lim t_n$.
10. Let $\lim S_n = l$ and $c \in R$, then $\lim(cS_n) = cl$.
11. Let $\lim S_n = 0$ and the sequence $< t_n >$ is bounded, then $\lim(S_n \cdot t_n) = 0$.
12. Let $\lim S_n = l$ and $l \neq 0$, then there exists a positive number $k$ and a positive integer $m$, such that $|S_n| > k, \forall\ n \geq m$.
13. Let the sequence $< S_n >$ diverges to infinity and the sequence $< t_n >$ is bounded, then $< S_n + t_n >$ diverges to infinity.
14. Let the sequence $< S_n >$ and $< t_n >$ both diverges to infinity, then the sequence $< S_n + t_n >$ and $< S_n \cdot t_n >$ diverges to infinity.
15. Let the sequence $< S_n >$ converges to $l$, then the sequence $|S_n|$ converges to $|l|$.

**Solution.** Let $< S_n > = < (-1)^n > = < -1, 1, -1, 1, ....>$

$< t_n > = < (-1)^{n+1} > = < 1, -1, 1, -1, 1, ....>$

Clearly, $< S_n >$ and $< t_n >$ both do not converge, but

$< S_n + t_n > = < 0, 0, 0, ....>$ converges to 0.

$< S_n \cdot t_n > = < -1, -1, -1, ....>$ converges to $-1$.

## General Theorem on Limits

***Theorem 1*** (Sandwitch Theorem) If $< S_n >, < u_n >$ and $< t_n >$ be three sequences such that

(i) $S_n \le u_n \le t_n, \forall n \in N$

(ii) $\lim_{n\to\infty} S_n = l = \lim_{n\to\infty} t_n$, then $\lim_{n\to\infty} u_n = l$.

***Theorem 2*** (Cauchy's First Theorem on Limits) If $\lim_{n\to\infty} S_n = l$, then $\lim_{n\to\infty} \frac{S_1 + S_2 + \ldots + S_n}{n} = l$.

***Theorem 3*** (Cauchy's Second Theorem on Limits) If $< S_n >$ is a sequence such that $S_n > 0, \forall n$ and $\lim S_n = l$, then $\lim (S_1, S_2, \ldots, S_n)^{1/n} = l$.

***Theorem 4*** Suppose $< S_n >$ is a sequence of positive real numbers such that $\lim_{n\to\infty} \frac{S_{n+1}}{S_n} = l, (l > 0)$.

Then, $\lim_{n\to\infty} (S_n)^{1/n} = l$.

***Theorem 5*** (Cesaro's Theorem) If $\lim S_n = l$ and $\lim t_n = l'$, then

$$\lim \left[ \frac{S_1 t_n + S_2 t_{n-1} + \ldots + S_n t_1}{n} \right] = l \cdot l'$$

---

***Example 4.*** *Show that* $\lim_{n\to\infty} \frac{1}{n}\left[1 + \frac{1}{2} + \frac{1}{3} + \ldots + \frac{1}{n}\right] = 0$.

**Solution.** Let $S_n = \frac{1}{n}$. Then, $\lim_{n\to\infty} S_n = \lim_{n\to\infty} \frac{1}{n} = 0$

Since, $\lim_{n\to\infty} S_n = 0$. So by Cauchy's first theorem on limits.

$$\lim_{n\to\infty} \frac{1}{n}(a_1 + a_2 + \ldots + a_n) = 0$$

Hence, $\lim_{n\to\infty} \frac{1}{n}\left[1 + \frac{1}{2} + \frac{1}{3} + \ldots + \frac{1}{n}\right] = 0$

***Example 5.*** *Show that* $\lim_{n\to\infty} \frac{1}{n}[1 + 2^{1/2} + 3^{1/3} + \ldots + n^{1/n}] = 1$.

**Solution.** Let $S_n = n^{1/n}$ Clearly, $S_n > 0, \forall n \in N$

$\Rightarrow \lim_{n\to\infty} S_n = \lim_{n\to\infty} n^{1/n} = 1$

By Cauchy's first theorem on limits, we have

$$\lim_{n\to\infty} \frac{S_1 + S_2 + \ldots + S_n}{n} = 1$$

Hence, $\lim_{n\to\infty} \frac{1}{n}[1 + 2^{1/2} + 3^{1/3} + \ldots + n^{1/n}] = 1$.

***Example 6.*** *Prove that*

$$\lim_{n\to\infty} \left[ \left(\frac{2}{1}\right)\left(\frac{3}{2}\right)^2\left(\frac{4}{3}\right)^3 \cdots \left(\frac{n+1}{n}\right)^n \right]^{1/n} = e.$$

**Solution.** Let $S_n = \left(\frac{n+1}{n}\right)^n = \left(1 + \frac{1}{n}\right)^n$

Then, $\lim S_n = e$. Clearly, $S_n > 0, \forall n$.

By Cauchy's second theorem on limits, we have

$$\lim_{n\to\infty} (s_1, s_2, s_3, \ldots, s_n)^{1/n} = e$$

Hence, $\lim_{n\to\infty} \left[ \left(\frac{2}{1}\right)\left(\frac{3}{2}\right)^2\left(\frac{4}{3}\right)^3 \cdots \left(\frac{n+1}{n}\right)^n \right]^{1/n} = e$

## Important Theorems on Limit

***Theorem 1*** Let $< S_n >$ be a sequence, such that $S_n \neq 0, \forall n$ and

$\lim_{n\to\infty} \frac{S_{n+1}}{S_n} = l$. If $|l| < 1$, then $\lim_{n\to\infty} S_n = 0$

***Theorem 2*** Let $< S_n >$ be a sequence such that $S_n \neq 0$, $\forall n \in N$ and $\lim_{n\to\infty} \frac{S_{n+1}}{S_n} = l$, if $l > 1$, then $\lim_{n\to\infty} S_n = \infty$.

---

***Example 7.*** *Show that, if x be any real number, then* $\lim_{n\to\infty} \frac{x^n}{n!} = 0$.

**Solution.** Let $S_n = \frac{x^n}{n!}$. Here, two case arises

***Case 1*** If $x = 0$, then $S_n = 0, \forall n \in N$ and so $\lim_{n\to\infty} S_n = 0$.

***Case 2*** If $x \neq 0$, then $S_n \neq 0, \forall n \in N$ we know that if $S_n \neq 0, \forall n \in N$ and $\lim_{n\to\infty} \frac{S_{n+1}}{S_n} = l$, where $|l| < 1$, then $\lim_{n\to\infty} S_n = 0$

Now, we have $\frac{S_{n+1}}{S_n} = \frac{x^{n+1}}{(n+1)!} \cdot \frac{n!}{x^n} = \frac{x^{n+1} \cdot n!}{(n+1) \cdot n! x^n} = \frac{x}{(n+1)}$

$\Rightarrow \lim_{n\to\infty} \frac{S_{n+1}}{S_n} = \lim_{n\to\infty} \frac{x}{(n+1)} = 0 < 1$ and $|0| = 0 < 1$.

Hence, $\lim_{n\to\infty} S_n = 0$ i.e., $\lim_{n\to\infty} \frac{x^n}{n!} = 0, \forall x \in R$

***Example 8.*** *Show that* $\lim_{n\to\infty} \frac{2^n}{n} = \infty$.

**Solution.** Let $S_n = \frac{2^n}{n}$. Clearly, $S_n \neq 0, \forall n \in N$.

We know that, if $S_n \neq 0, \forall n \in N$ and $\lim_{n\to\infty} \frac{S_{n+1}}{S_n} = l > 1$, then $\lim_{n\to\infty} S_n = \infty.$

Now, we have $\frac{S_{n+1}}{S_n} = \frac{2^{n+1}}{(n+1)} \cdot \frac{n}{2^n} = \frac{2\cdot n}{(n+1)} = \frac{2}{(1+1/n)}$

$\Rightarrow \quad \lim_{n\to\infty} \frac{S_{n+1}}{S_n} = \lim_{n\to\infty}\left[\frac{2}{\left(1+\frac{1}{n}\right)}\right] = 2 > 1$

Hence, $\lim_{n\to\infty} S_n = \infty$ *i.e.,* $\lim_{n\to\infty} \frac{2^n}{n} = \infty$

## Subsequences

Let $< S_n > = < S_1, S_2, S_3, S_4, \ldots >$ be a sequence in $R$. A subsequence of a sequence is a sequence whose terms are chosen from the original sequence in the same order as in the original sequence. Thus, $< S_2, S_5, S_7, S_{11}, S_{13}, S_{25}, S_{27}, \ldots >$ or $< S_6, S_9, S_{13}, S_{26}, S_{31}, \ldots >$ are subsequences of the sequence $< S_1, S_2, S_3, \ldots >$. But $< S_3, S_7, S_4, S_1, \ldots >$ or $< S_{10}, S_7, S_9, S_4, \ldots >$ are not the subsequences of the sequence $< S_1, S_2, S_3, \ldots >$ because in $< S_3, S_7, S_4, S_1, \ldots >$ the order of the terms is last and in $< S_{10}, S_7, S_9, S_1, \ldots >$ a particular term $S_9$ appears more than once which should not be. The formal definition may be given as

Let $< S_n >$ be any sequence. Let $< n_1, n_2, \ldots, nk, \ldots >$ be a sequence of positive integers. Such that, $i > j \Rightarrow n_i > n_j$. Then, the sequence $< S_{n1}, S_{n2}, S_{n3}, \ldots, S_{nk} >$, written as $< S_{nk} >$, is called a subsequence of $< S_n >$.

> **Note** The condition $i > j \Rightarrow n_i > n_j$ guarantees that the order of the terms of a subsequence is the same as that of the given sequence.
>
> *e.g.* (i) $< 1, 27, 125, \ldots, (2n-1)3, \ldots >$ is a subsequence of $< n^3 >$.
>
> (ii) $< 1, \frac{1}{3}, \frac{1}{5}, \frac{1}{7}, \ldots >$ is a subsequence of $< \frac{1}{2n-1} >$.

## Important Theorems on Subsequence

***Theorem 1*** If a sequence $< S_n >$ converges to $l$, then every subsequence of $< S_n >$ converges to $l$.

> **Note** The converge of the above theorem may not be true. *e.g.* The sequence $< 1 + (-1)^n > = < 0, 2, 0, 2, \ldots >$ does not converge but its subsequence $< 0, 0, 0, \ldots >$ converges to 0.

***Theorem 2*** All subsequence of a convergent sequence converge to the same limit.

> **Note** To show that a given sequence is not convergent it is enough to show that two of its subsequence converge to different limits. *e.g.* The sequence $< 2 + (-1)^n > = < 1, 3, 1, 3, \ldots >$ is not convergent. The two subsequences $< 1, 1, 1, 1, 1, \ldots >$ and $< 3, 3, 3, \ldots >$ of the given sequence converge respectively 1 and 3, which are different.

***Theorem 3*** If subsequences $< S_{2n-1} >$ and $< S_{2n} >$ of the sequence $< S_n >$ converge to the same limit $l$, then the sequence $< S_n >$ converges to $l$.

***Example 9.*** *Show that $< \frac{1}{n!} >$ is a subsequence of the sequence $< \frac{1}{n} >$.*

**Solution.** Let $S_n = \frac{1}{n}$ and $t_n = \frac{1}{n!}, \forall n \in N$

Then, we have $t_n = \frac{1}{n!} = Sa_n$, where $a_n = n!, \forall n \in N$.

Now, we have $\frac{a_{n+1}}{a_n} = \frac{(n+1)!}{n!} = (n+1) > 1, \forall n \in N.$

$\Rightarrow \quad a_{n+1} > a_n, \forall n \in N$

Thus, we have got a sequence $< a_n >$ of natural numbers, such that $a_n < a_{n+1}$ *i.e.,* $< a_n >$ is a monotonically increasing sequence of natural numbers. Hence, the sequence $< \frac{1}{n!} >$ is a subsequence of the sequence $< \frac{1}{n} >$.

***Example 10.*** *Show that the sequence $< S_n >$, we have $S_n = \frac{(-1)^{n-1}}{n}$, converges to 0.*

**Solution.** We have $S_n = \begin{vmatrix} \frac{1}{n} & n \text{ is odd} \\ \frac{-1}{n}, & n \text{ is even} \end{vmatrix}$

The sequence $< S_{2n-1} >$ and $< S_{2n} >$ are subsequences of $< S_n >$.

$$< S_{2n-1} > = < 1, \frac{1}{3}, \frac{1}{5}, \ldots >, < S_{2n} > = < \frac{-1}{2}, \frac{-1}{4}, \frac{-1}{6}, \ldots >$$

But $< 1, \frac{1}{3}, \frac{1}{5}, \ldots >$ and $< \frac{1}{2}, \frac{1}{3}, \frac{1}{5}, \ldots >$ are subsequences of the sequence $< \frac{1}{n} >$, which converges to zero.

$\therefore$ $< S_{2n-1} >$ and $< S_{2n} >$ both converge to the same limit 0. Hence, $< S_n >$ converges to 0.

## Limit Points of a Sequence

A real number $P$ is said to be a limit point of a sequence, if every neighbourhood of $P$ contains an infinite number of elements of the given sequence. In other words, a real number $P$ is a limit point of a sequence $< S_n >$, if for a given $\varepsilon > 0$.

$S_n \in ]P - \varepsilon, P + \varepsilon[$ for infinitely many values of $n$.

> **Note (a)** In the case of set of real numbers, limit point of a sequence may also be called accumulation, cluster or condensation points.
>
> **(b)** A real number $P$ is not a limit point of the sequence $< S_n >$, if there exists atleast one neighbourhood of $P$ which contains only finite number of elements of $< S_n >$.

(c) Limit point of a sequence need not be a member of the sequence.

(d) A limit point of a sequence may or may not be a limit point of the range of the sequence but the limit point of the range of a sequence is always a limit point of the sequence.

*e.g.* (i) The sequence $< \frac{1}{n} > = < 1, \frac{1}{2}, \frac{1}{3}, \frac{1}{4}, \ldots >$ has only 0 as its limit point.

(ii) The sequence $< n^2 > = < 1, 4, 9, 16, 25, \ldots >$ has no limit point.

(iii) The sequence $< (-1)^n > = < -1, 1, -1, 1, -1, \ldots >$ has only two limit points $-1$ and 1.

## Balzano Weierstrass Theorem

Every bounded real sequence has a limit point.

**Note** An unbounded sequence may or may not have limit point.
*e.g.* (i) $< n^2 > = < 1, 4, 9, 16, 25, \ldots >$ is an unbounded sequence having no limit point.
(ii) $< S_n > = < 1, 2, 1, 4, 1, 6, \ldots >$ is an unbounded sequence having 1 as its limit point.

## Limit Superior and Limit Inferior

Recall that "Every bounded sequence must have a limit point".

### Definitions

1. The greatest limit point of a bounded sequence $< S_n >$ is called the limit superior of $< S_n >$. It is written as $\lim_{n \to \infty} \text{Sup } S_n$, or $\overline{\lim_{n \to \infty}} S_n$.
2. The smallest limit point of a bounded sequence $< S_n >$ is called the limit inferior of $< S_n >$. It is written as $\lim_{n \to \infty} \text{Inf } S_n$, or $\underline{\lim_{n \to \infty}} S_n$.

**Note** $\lim_{n \to \infty} \text{Inf } S_n \le \lim_{n \to \infty} \text{Sup } S_n$.

*e.g.* (i) Let $< S_n > = < 2 + (-1)^n > = < 1, 3, 1, 3, 1, 3, \ldots >$. Its set of limit points $= \{1, 3\}$. The greatest and the smallest limit points are 3 and 1, respectively.

$\therefore \quad \lim_{n \to \infty} \text{Sup } S_n = 3, \quad \lim_{n \to \infty} \text{Inf } S_n = 1$

(ii) Let $< S_n > = < \frac{1}{n} > = < 1, \frac{1}{2}, \frac{1}{3}, \frac{1}{4}, \frac{1}{5}, \ldots >$

It has exactly one limit point 0.

$\therefore \quad \lim_{n \to \infty} \text{Sup } S_n = 0, \quad \lim_{n \to \infty} \text{Inf } S_n = 0$

(iii) Let $< S_n > = < 1, 2, 3, 1, 2, 3, 1, 2, 3, \ldots >$

Its set of limit points $= \{1, 2, 3\}$

$\therefore \quad \lim_{n \to \infty} \text{Sup } S_n = 3, \quad \lim_{n \to \infty} \text{Inf } S_n = 1.$

**Note** A sequence $< S_n >$ is said to have a limit $l$, if for a given $\varepsilon > 0$, there exists a positive integer $m$, such that $|S_n - l| < \varepsilon, \forall n \ge m$.

## Monotonic Sequences

### Definitions

1. A sequence $< S_n > = < S_1, S_2, S_3, \ldots >$ is said to be monotonically increasing, if
$$S_{n+1} \ge S_n, \forall n \in N$$
*i.e.*, $a_2 \ge a_1$, $a_3 \ge a_2$, $a_4 \ge a_3$ and so on.
2. A sequence $< S_n > = < S_1, S_2, S_3, \ldots >$ is said to be monotonically decreasing, if $S_{n+1} \le S_n$, $\forall n \in N$ *i.e.*, $a_2 \le a_1$, $a_3 \le a_2$, $a_4 \le a_3$ and so on.
3. A sequence $< S_n >$ is said to be monotonic, if it is either monotonically increasing or monotonically decreasing.
4. A sequence $< S_n >$ is said to be strictly monotonically increasing sequence, if $S_{n+1} > S_n, \forall n \in N$.
*i.e.*, $a_2 > a_1$, $a_3 > a_2$, $a_4 > a_3$ and so on.
5. A sequence $< S_n >$ is said to be strictly monotonically decreasing sequence, if $S_{n+1} < S_n, \forall n \in N$.
*i.e.*, $a_2 < a_1$, $a_3 < a_2$, $a_4 < a_3$ and so on.
6. A sequence $< S_n >$ is said to be strictly monotonic, if it is either strictly monotonically increasing or monotonically decreasing.

*e.g.* (i) The sequence $< 3^n > = < 3, 9, 27, \ldots >$ is monotonically increasing.

(ii) The sequence $< \frac{1}{n} > = < 1, \frac{1}{2}, \frac{1}{3}, \frac{1}{4}, \frac{1}{5}, \ldots >$ is monotonically decreasing.

(iii) The sequence $< (-1)^n > = < -1, 1, -1, 1, -1, \ldots >$ is neither monotonically increasing nor monotonically decreasing therefore $< (-1)^n >$ is not monotonic sequence.

## Important Theorems on Monotonic Sequence

***Theorem 1*** A monotonic increasing sequence which is bounded above is convergent and convergence to its least upper bound.

***Theorem 2*** A monotonic decreasing sequence which is bounded below is convergent and converges to its greatest lower bound.

**Note** Combining the theorems (1) and (2) we note that a monotonic sequence converges if and only if it is bounded.

***Theorem 3*** A monotonic increasing sequence which is not bounded above diverges to plus infinity $(+\infty)$.

***Theorem 4*** A monotonic decreasing sequence which is not bounded below diverges to minus infinity $(-\infty)$.

***Example 11.*** *Show that* $< S_n >$ *is convergent whose* $S_n = 2 - \frac{1}{2^{n-1}}$.

**Solution.** We have,

$$S_{n+1} - S_n = \left(2 - \frac{1}{2^n}\right) - \left(2 - \frac{1}{2^{n-1}}\right)$$

$$= \frac{1}{2^{n-1}} - \frac{1}{2^n} = \frac{1}{2^n} > 0, \forall n.$$

Hence, the sequence $< S_n >$ is monotonically increasing.

Also, $S_n = 2 - \frac{1}{2^{n-1}} < 2, \forall n$

$\therefore$ $< S_n >$ is bounded above.

Since, $< S_n >$ is a bounded above, monotonically increasing sequence, hence it converges.

We have $\lim_{n\to\infty} S_n = \lim_{n\to\infty}\left(2 - \frac{1}{2^{n-1}}\right) = 2$

***Example 12.*** *Show that the sequence* $< S_n >$, *where* $S_n = 1 + \frac{1}{1!} + \frac{1}{2!} + \ldots + \frac{1}{n!}$ *is convergent.*

**Solution.** We have,

$$S_{n+1} - S_n = \frac{1}{(n+1)!} > 0, \forall n$$

Hence, the sequence $< S_n >$ is monotonically increasing.

Now, we shall show that $< S_n >$ is bounded.

Now, we have

$$S_n = 1 + \frac{1}{1!} + \frac{1}{2!} + \ldots + \frac{1}{(n-1)!} + \frac{1}{n!}$$

$$\le 1 + \frac{1}{1} + \frac{1}{2} + \frac{1}{2^2} + \ldots + \frac{1}{2^{n-1}}$$

$$[\because n! > 2^{n-1}, \forall n \in N]$$

$$= 1 + 1 + \frac{1}{2} + \frac{1}{2^2} + \ldots + \frac{1}{2^{n-1}} = 1 + \frac{1 - \left(\frac{1}{2}\right)^n}{1 - \frac{1}{2}}$$

$$[\because 1 + \frac{1}{2} + \frac{1}{2^2} + \ldots + \frac{1}{2^{n-1}} \text{ is GP with common ratio } = \frac{1}{2}]$$

$$= 1 + 2\left[1 - \left(\frac{1}{2}\right)^n\right] = 3 - \frac{1}{2^{n-1}} < 3 \quad \left[\because \frac{1}{2^{n-1}} > 0\right]$$

Also, $S_1 = 2 < 3$

$\therefore$ $S_n < 3 \; \forall n \in N$

Therefore $< S_n >$ is bounded above.

Since, $< S_n >$ is bounded above and monotonically increasing therefore $< S_n >$ is convergent.

# Cauchy Sequence

The main aim of this section is to prove Cauchy's criterion for the convergence of a sequence of real numbers. This criterion helps to prove the convergence of a sequence without knowing its limit.

A sequence $< S_n >$ is said to be a Cauchy's sequence if for every $\varepsilon > 0$, there exists a positive integer $m$ such that $|S_n - S_m| < \varepsilon$, whenever $n \ge m$.

Note that for large value of $n$ and $m$, the terms of the sequence are close together.

## Important Theorems on Cauchy Sequence

***Theorem 1*** Every Cauchy sequence is bounded.

> ***Note*** Converge of the above theorem is not true. *e.g.* The sequence $< (-1)^n >$ is bounded, but not Cauchy sequence.

***Theorem 2*** (Cauchy's General Principle of Convergence) A sequence of real numbers converges if and only if it is a Cauchy sequence.

> ***Note*** The above theorem may be restated as a necessary and sufficient condition for the convergence of a sequence $< S_n >$ is that, for each $\varepsilon > 0$ there exists a positive integer $m$ such that
> $$|S_{n+p} - S_n| < \varepsilon, \forall n > m \text{ and } p \ge 1$$

***Example 13.*** *Show that the sequence* $< S_n >$ *defined by* $S_n = \frac{(-1)^n}{n}$ *converges.*

**Solution.** We shall show that the given sequence is a Cauchy sequence.

By Cauchy's general principle of convergence, let $\varepsilon > 0$ be given.

If $n \ge m$, then $\frac{1}{n} \le \frac{1}{m}$ and

$$|S_n - S_m| = \left|\frac{(-1)^n}{n} - \frac{(-1)^m}{m}\right| \le \left|\frac{(-1)^n}{n}\right| + \left|\frac{(-1)^m}{m}\right|$$

$$= \frac{1}{n} + \frac{1}{m} \le \frac{1}{m} + \frac{1}{m} = \frac{2}{m}$$

$$|S_n - S_m| < \varepsilon, \text{ if } \frac{2}{m} < \varepsilon \text{ i.e., } m > \frac{2}{\varepsilon}$$

Let us choose a positive integer $m = \left[\frac{2}{\varepsilon}\right] + 1$, such that

$$|S_n - S_m| < \varepsilon, \forall n \ge m$$

Hence, $< S_n >$ is a Cauchy sequence and so is convergent.

***Example 14.*** *Show that the sequence* $< S_n >$, *where*

$$S_n = 1 + \frac{1}{2} + \frac{1}{3} + \ldots + \frac{1}{n} \text{ is not convergent.}$$

**Solution.** Let if possible $< S_n >$ be convergent. By Cauchy's general principle of convergence, for $\varepsilon = 1/2$, there exists a positive integer $m$ such that $|S_n - S_m| < \frac{1}{2}, \forall n \ge m$.

If we take $n = 2m$, then $n > m$ and we have,

$$|S_n - S_m| = |S_{2m} - S_m| < 1/2 \quad \text{...(i)}$$

Now, we have

$$|S_{2m} - S_m| = \left|\left(1 + \frac{1}{2} + \frac{1}{3} + \dots + \frac{1}{m} + \frac{1}{(m+1)} + \dots + \frac{1}{2m}\right) - \left(1 + \frac{1}{2} + \frac{1}{3} + \dots + \frac{1}{m}\right)\right|$$

$$= \frac{1}{(m+1)} + \frac{1}{(m+2)} + \dots + \frac{1}{2m} > \frac{1}{2m} + \frac{1}{2m} + \dots + \frac{1}{2m}$$

$$= \frac{1}{2m} \cdot m = \frac{1}{2}$$

Thus, $|S_{2m} - S_m| > \frac{1}{2}$, which contradicts Eq. (i).

Hence, the given sequence $< S_n >$ is not convergent.

## Series of Non-negative Terms

A series is an expression of the form $u_1 + u_2 + u_3 + u_4 + \dots + u_n + \dots$ in which every term is followed by another according to some definite law. If in a series the number of terms are infinite. *i.e.*, unlimited then it is called an infinite series. If the series contains a finite number of terms, then it is called a finite series.

The series $u_1 + u_2 + u_3 + \dots + u_n + \dots$ is symbolically written as $\sum_{n=1}^{\infty} u_n$.

If $R_n = u_{n+1} + u_{n+2} + \dots$, then $R_n$ is called remainder after $n$ terms of the series.

If $S_n = u_1 + u_2 + u_3 + \dots + u_n$, where, $S_n$ denotes the sum of the first $n$ terms of the infinite series $\sum u_n$. Thus, we can express the series $\sum u_n$ as a sequence $< S_n >$ of the partial sums $\{S_n\}$. Thus, we can say that the behaviour of the series $\sum u_n$ is same as the behaviour of the sequence $S_1, S_2, S_3, \dots, S_n$.

**Note** **(a)** The infinite series $\sum u_n$ is said to be convergent if the sequence $< S_n >$ of its partially sum is convergent. $S$ is called the sum of the series $\sum u_n$, if $\lim S_n = S$ and this $S$ is called the sum of the series $\sum u_n^{\infty}$ and symbolically it can be written as $S = \sum u_n$.
If the sequence $< S_n >$ of partial sums of $\sum u_n$ is divergent, then the series $\sum u_n$ is said to be divergent.
If the sequence $< S_n >$ of the partial sums of $\sum u_n$ oscillates, then the series $\sum u_n$ is said to be oscillates.

**(b)** The convergence of the series remains same if each of its term is multiplied by a non-zero constant.

**(c)** The addition, omission and replacement of finite number of terms of a series $\sum u_n$ does not has any effect on its convergence.

## Definition

General series are those series whose terms are both positive and negative. A series of positive terms either converges or diverges and cannot oscillate. But the series with infinite number of positive and negative terms may either (i) converge (ii) diverge (iii) oscillate

A series is denoted by $\sum u_n$, whether it contains all positive, some positive, some negative terms and its partial sum $u_1 + u_2 + \dots + u_n$ is denoted by $S_n$ and its limiting sum by $S$ and after $n$ terms its remainder is denoted by $R_n$ *i.e.*, $R_n = S - S_n = u_{n+1} + u_{n+2} + \dots$

## Important Theorems on Series of Non-negative Terms

***Theorem 1*** The necessary condition for the convergence of an infinite series, If the series $\sum_{n=1}^{\infty} u_n$ converges, then $\lim_{n \to \infty} u_n = 0$ but the converse is not true.

***Theorem 2*** Cauchy's General Principal of convergence for series. The necessary and sufficient condition for the convergence of an infinite series $\sum u_n$ is that corresponding to an arbitrary chosen positive number $\varepsilon$, however small, there exists a positive integer $m$, such that $|u_{n+1} + u_{n+2} + \dots + u_{n+p}| < \varepsilon$ for every $n \geq m$ and every $p \geq 0$.

***Theorem 3*** The necessary and sufficient condition for the convergence of a positive term series $\sum_{n=1}^{\infty} u_n$ is that the sequence $< S_n >$ of the partial sums of the series defined by $S_n = u_1 + u_2 + \dots + u_n$ is bounded above.

***Theorem 4*** A series $\sum u_n$ of positive terms converges if and only if there exist a number $K$, such that $u_1 + u_2 + u_3 + \dots + u_n < K, \forall n \in N$.

**Note** **(a)** If we want to show that a series of positive term converges it is sufficient to show that the sequence of its partial sums is bounded.

**(b)** If we want to show that a series of positive term diverges for this show that the sequence of its partial sums is not bounded.

***Theorem 5*** A series of positive terms is divergent, if each term after a fixed stage is greater than some fixed positive number.

***Theorem 6*** A series of positive terms is divergent, if $\lim u_n > 0$.

***Example 15.*** *Prove that the series* $\sum \frac{1}{4^n}$ *converges to* $1/3$.

**Solution.** We have,

$$S_n = \frac{1}{4} + \frac{1}{4^2} + \frac{1}{4^3} + \dots + \frac{1}{4^n}$$

$$= \frac{1}{4}\frac{\left[1-\left(\frac{1}{4}\right)^n\right]}{1-1/4}$$

$$\Rightarrow \quad S_n = \frac{1}{3}\left[1-\frac{1}{4^n}\right]$$

$$\Rightarrow \quad \lim S_n = \lim \frac{1}{3}\left[1-\frac{1}{4^n}\right] = \frac{1}{3} \qquad \left[\because \lim \frac{1}{4^n} = 0\right]$$

$\therefore$ The sequence $< S_n >$ converges to 1/3 and therefore, $\sum u_n$ converges to 1/3.

## Comparison Test for the Convergence of Positive Term Series

1. **First Type** Let $\sum u_n$ and $\sum v_n$ be two series of positive terms such that $u_n < M v_n, \forall n$, where $M$ is a fixed positive number. If $\sum v_n$ converges, then $\sum u_n$ is also converges and if $\sum u_n$ diverges, then $\sum v_n$ also diverges.
2. **Second Type** Let $\sum u_n$ and $\sum v_n$ be two series of positive terms and let $m$ and $M$ be positive real numbers such that

$$m v_n < u_n < M v_n, \forall n$$

Then, the series $\sum u_n$ and $\sum v_n$ converge or diverge together.

3. **Third Type** If $\sum u_n$ and $\sum v_n$ be two series of positive terms and let $M$ be a positive number such that $u_n < M v_n, \forall n > p$, $p$ being a fixed positive integer. Then, $\sum u_n$ is divergent, then the series $\sum v_n$ is also divergent.
4. **Fourth Type** Suppose, $\sum u_n$ and $\sum v_n$ be the two series of positive terms such that $\lim\limits_{n\to\infty} \frac{u_n}{v_n} = l$, $l$ is finite and non-zero, then both the series diverge or converge together *i.e.*, the two series $\sum u_n$ and $\sum v_n$ are either both convergent or both divergent.
5. **Fifth Type** Let $\sum u_n$ and $\sum v_n$ be the two series of positive terms and let $m$ and $M$ be the positive real numbers such that $m v_n < u_n < M v_n, \forall n > p$, where $p$ is a fixed positive integer. Then, the series $\sum u_n$ and $\sum v_n$ converge or diverge together.
6. **Sixth Type** Suppose, $\sum u_n$ and $\sum v_n$ be the two series of positive terms such that $\frac{u_n}{u_{n+1}} > \frac{v_n}{v_{n+1}}, \forall n \geq p$

Then, $\sum v_n$ converges $\Rightarrow \sum u_n$ converges
and $\sum u_n$ diverges $\Rightarrow \sum v_n$ diverges.

> ***Note*** From the above test the third and fourth type of the comparison test are more useful.

## Important Results on Comparison Test

1. If each term of a series $\sum u_n$ of positive terms does not exceed the corresponding term of a convergent series $\sum v_n$ of positive terms, then $\sum u_n$ is convergent.
   If each term of $\sum u_n$ equals or exceeds the corresponding term of a divergent series of positive terms, then $\sum u_n$ is divergent.
2. If $\sum u_n$ and $\sum v_n$ are two convergent series, then $\sum(u_n + v_n)$ and $\sum(u_n - v_n)$ are also convergent.
3. If $\sum u_n$ converges and $\sum v_n$ diverges, then $\sum(u_n + v_n)$ diverges.
4. If $\sum u_n$ is a series of positive terms such that $\lim\limits_{n\to\infty} u_n \neq 0$, then $\sum u_n$ diverges.

## The Auxiliary Series $\sum 1/n^p$

The infinite series $\sum \frac{1}{n^p}$ *i.e.*, $\frac{1}{1^p} + \frac{1}{2^p} + \frac{1}{3^p} + \ldots + \frac{1}{n^p} + \ldots$ is convergent, if $p > 1$ and divergent, if $p \leq 1$.

> **Important Results**
>
> 1. $\lim\limits_{n\to\infty} n^{1/n} - 1$
> 2. $\lim\limits_{n\to\infty}\left(1+\frac{x}{n}\right)^n = e^x$
> 3. $\lim\limits_{n\to\infty}\left(1+\frac{x}{n}\right)^{n+p} = e^x$
> 4. $\lim\limits_{n\to\infty}\left(1+\frac{x}{n}\right)^p = 1$, where $p$ is finite number
> 5. $\lim\limits_{n\to\infty} \frac{\log n}{n} = 0$

## d'Alembert Ratio Test

Suppose, $\sum u_n$ be a positive term series such that

1. $\lim\limits_{n\to\infty} \frac{u_{n+1}}{u_n} = l$, then the series is
   (i) Convergent, if $l > 1$.
   (ii) Divergent, if $l < 1$.
   (iii) The test fails to decide the nature of the series, if $l = 1$.
2. If $\lim\limits_{n\to\infty} \frac{u_{n+1}}{u_n} = \infty$, then $\sum u_n$ is divergent.

> ***Note*** **(a)** d'Alembert test can also be stated as. If $\lim \frac{u_n}{u_{n+1}} > 1$, then the series $\sum u_n$ is convergent and if $\lim \frac{u_n}{u_{n+1}} < 1$, then the series $\sum u_n$ is divergent and if $\lim \frac{u_n}{u_{n+1}} = 1$, then the test fails.
>
> **(b)** $\sum u_n$ is convergent, if $\lim\limits_{n\to\infty} \frac{u_n}{u_{n+1}} = \infty$

***Example 16.*** *Test the convergence of the series whose nth term is* $\dfrac{\sqrt{n}}{n^2+1}$.

**Solution.** Here, $u_n = \dfrac{\sqrt{n}}{n^2+1}$

Let us take $v_n = \dfrac{\sqrt{n}}{n^2} = \dfrac{1}{n^{3/2}}$

$\therefore$ The auxiliary series is $\Sigma v_n = \Sigma \dfrac{1}{n^{3/2}}$

Now, $\lim \dfrac{u_n}{v_n} = \lim \left\{\dfrac{\sqrt{n}}{n^2+1} \cdot n^{3/2}\right\} = \lim \dfrac{n^2}{n^2+1}$

$= \lim \dfrac{1}{1+(1/n^2)} = 1$

But the series $\Sigma \dfrac{1}{n^{3/2}}$ is convergent as $p = \dfrac{3}{2} > 1$.

Hence, the series $\Sigma \dfrac{\sqrt{n}}{n^2+1}$ is convergent.

***Example 17.*** *Test the convergence of the following series* $\dfrac{1}{3} + \dfrac{1\cdot 2}{3\cdot 5} + \dfrac{1\cdot 2\cdot 3}{3\cdot 5\cdot 7} + \dfrac{1\cdot 2\cdot 3\cdot 4}{3\cdot 5\cdot 7\cdot 9} + \ldots$

**Solution.** Here, $u_n = \dfrac{1\cdot 2\cdot 3\cdot 4\ldots n}{3\cdot 5\cdot 7\cdot 9\ldots(2n+1)}$ $\left[\begin{array}{l}\because 3, 5, 7, \ldots \text{ are in AP} \\ \therefore n\text{th term is} \\ = 3+(n-1)\times 2 \\ = 2n+1\end{array}\right]$

$\Rightarrow \quad u_{n+1} = \dfrac{1\cdot 2\cdot 3\cdot 4\ldots(n+1)}{3\cdot 5\cdot 7\cdot 9\ldots(2n+1)(2n+3)}$

Now, $\lim\limits_{n\to\infty} \dfrac{u_n}{u_{n+1}} = \lim\limits_{n\to\infty} \dfrac{2n+3}{n+1} = \lim\limits_{n\to\infty} \dfrac{2+3/n}{1+1/n} = 2,$

which is greater than 1.

Therefore, by ratio test, the given series is convergent.

***Example 18.*** *For all positive values of x test, the convergence of the series*

$$1 + \frac{x^2}{2} + \frac{x^4}{4} + \frac{x^6}{6} + \ldots$$

**Solution.** On omitting the first term of series, the nature of the series remains the same.

Now, $u_n = \dfrac{x^{2n}}{2n}$ and $u_{n+1} = \dfrac{x^{2n+2}}{2n+2}$

$\Rightarrow \lim \dfrac{u_n}{u_{n+1}} = \lim\limits_{n\to\infty} \dfrac{1}{x^2} \times \dfrac{2n+2}{2n}$

$= \lim\limits_{n\to\infty} \dfrac{1}{x^2}\left(1+\dfrac{1}{n}\right) = \dfrac{1}{x^2}$

By Ratio test, the given series converges, if $\dfrac{1}{x^2} > 1$,

*i.e.* if $x^2 < 1$ *i.e.*, if $x < 1$ (as $x > 0$),

diverges if $\dfrac{1}{x^2} < 1$, *i.e.*, if $x^2 > 1$ *i.e.*, if $x > 1$ and the test fails if $1/x^2 = 1$ *i.e.*, if $x = 1$.

Now, when $x = 1$, $u_n = 1/2n$ we take $v_n = 1/n$

$\therefore \quad \lim\limits_{n\to\infty} \dfrac{u_n}{v_n} = \lim\limits_{n\to\infty} \dfrac{1}{2} = \dfrac{1}{2}$, which is finite and non-zero.

$\because \quad \Sigma v_n$ diverges, so by comparison test, the given series also diverges, if $x = 1$. Therefore, the given series converges, if $x < 1$ and diverges, if $x \geq 1$.

***Example 19.*** *Test the convergence of the following series* $\Sigma\left(\dfrac{x^n}{x+n}\right)$.

**Solution.** Here, $u_n = \dfrac{x^n}{x+n} \Rightarrow u_{n+1} = \dfrac{x^{n+1}}{x+n+1}$

$\dfrac{u_n}{u_{n+1}} = \dfrac{x^n}{x+n} \cdot \dfrac{x+n+1}{x^{n+1}} = \dfrac{1}{x} \cdot \dfrac{n[1+\{(1+x)/n\}]}{n[1+(x/n)]}$

$= \dfrac{1}{x} \cdot \dfrac{[1+\{(1+x)/n\}]}{[1+(x/n)]}$

$\therefore \quad \lim\limits_{n\to\infty} \dfrac{u_n}{u_{n+1}} = \dfrac{1}{x}$

$\therefore$ By d'Alembert ratio test, $\Sigma u_n$ is convergent, if $\dfrac{1}{x} > 1$ *i.e.*, if $x < 1$ and $\Sigma u_n$ is divergent if $1/x < 1$ *i.e.*, if $x > 1$

for $x = 1$, we have $u_n = \dfrac{1}{n+1} = \dfrac{1}{n} \cdot \dfrac{1}{[1+(1/n)]}$

Let us take $v_n = \dfrac{1}{n}$. Then, $\lim\limits_{n\to\infty} \dfrac{u_n}{v_n} = \lim\limits_{n\to\infty} \dfrac{1}{1+\dfrac{1}{n}} = 1$

which is finite and non-zero.

$\therefore$ By comparison test $\Sigma u_n$ and $\Sigma v_n$ are either both convergent or both divergent.

But for $v_n = \dfrac{1}{n} = \dfrac{1}{n^p}$, here $p = 1$

which is finite and non-zero.

$\because$ The auxiliary series $\Sigma v_n = \Sigma \dfrac{1}{n^{3/2}}$ is convergent $(p = 3/2 > 1)$, therefore by comparison test the given series $\Sigma u_n$ is also convergent.

***Example 20.*** *Test the convergence of the following series*

$$1 + \frac{1}{2^2} + \frac{2^2}{3^3} + \frac{3^3}{4^4} + \frac{4^4}{5^5} + \ldots$$

**Solution.** Omitting the first term. If the given series is denoted by $\Sigma u_n$, then

$$\Sigma u_n = \frac{1}{2^2} + \frac{2^2}{3^3} + \frac{3^3}{4^4} + \ldots$$

$\Rightarrow \quad \Sigma u_n = \Sigma \dfrac{n^n}{(n+1)^{n+1}} \Rightarrow u_n = \dfrac{n^n}{(n+1)^{n+1}}$

Now, take $v_n = \dfrac{n^n}{n^{n+1}} = \dfrac{1}{n}$

$\therefore \quad \lim \dfrac{u_n}{v_n} = \lim \left\{\dfrac{n^n}{(n+1)^{n+1}} \cdot n\right\}$

$= \lim \left\{\dfrac{1}{(1+1/n)^n \cdot (1+1/n)}\right\} = \dfrac{1}{e}$

which is finite and non-zero. $\left[\because \lim\left(1+\frac{1}{n}\right)^n = e\right]$

The auxiliary series $\Sigma v_n = \Sigma \frac{1}{n}$ is divergent as $p = 1$.
Therefore, by comparison test the given series is divergent.

## Cauchy's *n*th Root Test

Suppose, $\Sigma u_n$ be a series of positive terms such that $\lim u_n^{1/n} = l$.
(where $u_n^{1/n}$ stands for positive *n*th root of $u_n$), then

**(i)** $\Sigma u_n$ is convergent, if $l < 1$.
**(ii)** $\Sigma u_n$ is divergent, if $l > 1$.
**(iii)** The test fails to decide the nature of the series, if $l = 1$, then it may converge or diverge.

> ***Note*** Cauchy's root test is generally used when powers are involved.

***Example 21.*** *Test the convergence of the series*

$$\left(\frac{2^2}{1^2}-\frac{2}{1}\right)^{-1}+\left(\frac{3^3}{2^3}-\frac{3}{2}\right)^{-2}+\left(\frac{4^4}{3^4}-\frac{4}{3}\right)^{-3}+\ldots$$

**Solution.** For the given series the *n*th term, $u_n$ is

$$u_n = \left\{\left(\frac{n+1}{n}\right)^{n+1}-\left(\frac{n+1}{n}\right)\right\}^{-n}$$

$$\therefore \quad (u_n)^{1/n} = \left\{\left(\frac{n+1}{n}\right)^{n+1}-\left(\frac{n+1}{n}\right)\right\}^{-1}$$

$$= \left(\frac{n+1}{n}\right)^{-1}\left\{\left(\frac{n+1}{n}\right)^{n}-1\right\}^{-1}$$

$$\Rightarrow \quad \lim_{n\to\infty}(u_n)^{1/n} = \lim_{n\to\infty}\left(1+\frac{1}{n}\right)^{-1}\left\{\left(1+\frac{1}{n}\right)^{n}-1\right\}^{-1}$$

$$= 1+(e-1)^{-1} = \frac{1}{e-1} < 1 \quad [\because e = 2.71]$$

Therefore, by cauchy's root test, the given series is convergent.

***Example 22.*** *Test the convergence of the series* $\Sigma\left(1+\frac{1}{n}\right)^{-n^2}$.

**Solution.** We have,

$$u_n = \left(1+\frac{1}{n}\right)^{-n^2}$$

$$\Rightarrow \quad (u_n)^{1/n} = \left(1+\frac{1}{n}\right)^{-n}$$

$$\therefore \quad \lim(u_n)^{1/n} = \lim\left(1+\frac{1}{n}\right)^{-n}$$

$$\Rightarrow \quad \lim(u_n)^{1/n} = \lim\frac{1}{\left(1+\frac{1}{n}\right)^n}$$

$$\Rightarrow \quad \lim(u_n)^{1/n} = \frac{1}{e} < 1$$

Therefore, by Cauchy's root test, the given series is convergent.

## Cauchy's Condensation Test

If the function $f(n)$ is positive for all positive integral value of *n* and monotonically decreases as *n* increases, then the two infinite series $\Sigma f(n)$ and $\Sigma a^n f(a^n)$ converge or diverge together, '*a*' being a positive integer greater than unity.

> ***Note*** The auxiliary series $1+\frac{1}{2(\log 2)^p}+\frac{1}{3(\log 3)^p}+\ldots+\frac{1}{n(\log n)^p}+\ldots$ is convergent, if $p > 1$ and divergent, if $p \le 1$.

***Example 23.*** *Test the convergence of the series*

$$\frac{1}{(\log 2)^p}+\frac{1}{(\log 3)^p}+\ldots+\frac{1}{(\log n)^p}+\ldots$$

**Solution.** If $p \le 0$, the given series is obviously divergent. Now, consider the case when $p > 0$.

$$f(n) = \frac{1}{(\log n)^p} > 0, \ \forall\, n \ge 2$$

$f(n)$ decreases continuously as *n* increases.

$$\text{Now,} \quad a^n f(a^n) = \frac{a^n}{(\log a^n)^p} = \frac{a^n}{n^p(\log a)^p} \qquad (a > 1)$$

Now, consider the series $\Sigma\, a^n f(a^n)$

$$\Rightarrow \quad \Sigma\, a^n f(a^n) = \sum\frac{a^n}{n^p(\log a)^p} = \sum v_n \quad \text{(say)}$$

$$\therefore \quad v_n = \frac{a^n}{n^p(\log a)^p} \text{ and } v_{n+1} = \frac{a^{n+1}}{(n+1)^p(\log a)^p}$$

$$\text{Now,} \quad \frac{v_n}{v_{n+1}} = \frac{a^n}{n^p(\log a)^p}\cdot\frac{(n+1)^p(\log a)^p}{a^{n+1}} = \left(1+\frac{1}{n}\right)^p\cdot\frac{1}{a}$$

$$\Rightarrow \quad \lim\frac{v_n}{v_{n+1}} = \frac{1}{a} < 1 \text{ as } a > 1$$

$\therefore$ By d'Alembert Ratio test the series $\Sigma v_n = \Sigma\, a^n f(a^n)$ is divergent.

$\therefore$ By Cauchy's condensation test, the given series $\Sigma f(n)$ is also divergent.

***Example 24.*** *Test the convergence of the series*

$$\frac{(\log 2)^2}{2^2}+\frac{(\log 3)^2}{3^2}+\frac{(\log 4)^2}{4^2}+\ldots+\frac{(\log n)^2}{n^2}+\ldots$$

**Solution.** On adding a term $\frac{(\log 1)^2}{1^2}$ to the given series, the *n*th term *f*(*n*) is given by

$$f(n) = \frac{(\log n)^2}{n^2}$$

Now, $a^n f(a^n) = \frac{a^n(\log a^n)^2}{(a^n)^2} = \frac{(n\log a)^2}{a^n} = \frac{n^2(\log a)^2}{a^n}, \quad a > 1$

Now, suppose $\Sigma u_n = \Sigma a^n f(a^n) = \sum \frac{n^2(\log a)^2}{a^n}$

Then, $u_n = \frac{n^2(\log a)^2}{a^n}$ and $u_{n+1} = \frac{(n+1)^2(\log a)^2}{a^{n+1}}$

$$\therefore \quad \lim_{n\to\infty} \frac{u_n}{u_{n+1}} = \lim_{n\to\infty}\left\{a\cdot\left(\frac{n}{n+1}\right)^2\right\} = \lim_{n\to\infty} \frac{a}{[1+1/n]^2} = a > 1$$

Therefore, by d'Alembert Ratio test, $\Sigma u_n$, *i.e.*, $\Sigma a^n f(a^n)$ is convergent. Then, by cauchy's condensation test, the given series $\Sigma f(n)$ is convergent.

## Raabe's Test

Let $\Sigma u_n$ be the series of positive terms and

$$\lim\left[n\left(\frac{u_n}{u_{n+1}} - 1\right)\right] = l$$

Then,

**(i)** The series is convergent, if $l > 1$.
**(ii)** The series is divergent, if $l < 1$.
**(iii)** The test fails to decide the nature, if $l = 1$.

> ***Note*** Raabe's test is applied when d'Alembert's Ratio test fails.

***Example 25.*** *Test the convergence of the following series*

$$x^2 + \frac{2^2}{3\cdot4}x^4 + \frac{2^2\cdot4^2}{3\cdot4\cdot5\cdot6}x^6 + \frac{2^2\cdot4^2\cdot6^2}{3\cdot4\cdot5\cdot6\cdot7\cdot8}x^8 + \ldots$$

**Solution.** Omission of the first term of the series will not affect the nature of the series

$$u_n = \frac{2^2\cdot4^2\cdot6^2\ldots(2n)^2}{3\cdot4\cdot5\cdot6\cdot7\cdot8\ldots(2n+1)(2n+2)}x^{2n+2}$$

and $u_{n+1} = \frac{2^2\cdot4^2\cdot6^2\ldots(2n)^2(2n+2)^2}{3\cdot4\cdot5\cdot6\cdot7\cdot8\ldots(2n+1)(2n+2)(2n+3)(2n+4)}x^{2n+4}$

$$\Rightarrow \quad \frac{u_n}{u_{n+1}} = \frac{1}{x^2}\cdot\frac{(2n+3)(2n+4)}{(2n+2)^2} = \frac{1}{x^2}\cdot\frac{4n^2+14n+12}{4n^2+8n+4}$$

$$\therefore \quad \lim_{n\to\infty}\frac{u_n}{u_{n+1}} = \frac{1}{x^2}$$

By Ratio test, $\Sigma u_n$ is convergent if $\frac{1}{x^2} > 1 \Rightarrow x^2 < 1$ and $\Sigma u_n$ is divergent, if $\frac{1}{x^2} < 1 \Rightarrow x^2 > 1$.

For $\frac{1}{x^2} = 1 \Rightarrow x^2 = 1$, the Ratio test fails and we apply Raabe's test in this case.

When $x^2 = 1$,

we have $\frac{u_n}{u_{n+1}} = \frac{4n^2+14n+12}{4n^2+8n+4}$

$$\Rightarrow \quad n\left(\frac{u_n}{u_{n+1}} - 1\right) = n\left(\frac{4n^2+14n+12}{4n^2+8n+4} - 1\right) = \frac{6n^2+8n}{4n^2+8n+4}$$

$$\Rightarrow \lim_{n\to\infty} n\left(\frac{u_n}{u_{n+1}} - 1\right) = \lim_{n\to\infty}\frac{6n^2+8n}{4n^2+8n+4} = \frac{6}{4} = \frac{3}{2} > 1$$

Therefore, by Raabe's test $\Sigma u_n$ is convergent for $x^2 = 1$. Thus, the given series is convergent, if $x^2 \le 1$ and is divergent, if $x^2 > 1$.

## Logarithmic Test

Let $\Sigma u_n$ be the series of the positive term and

$$\lim_{n\to\infty}\left(n\log\frac{u_n}{u_{n+1}}\right) = l.$$

Then,

(i) The series is convergent, if $l > 1$.
(ii) The series is divergent, if $l < 1$.
(iii) The test fails to decide the nature, if $l = 1$.

> ***Note*** **(a)** This test is an alternative to Raabe's test and should be used, when the d'Alembert's ratio test fails.
>
> **(b)** It can also be used when *n* occurs as an exponent in $\frac{u_n}{u_{n+1}}$, so that it is not convenient to find $\frac{u_n}{u_{n+1}} - 1$.
>
> **(c)** On taking the logarithmic of $\frac{u_n}{u_{n+1}}$, the evaluation of limits becomes easier.

***Example 26.*** *Test the convergence of the series*

$$x + \frac{2^2x^2}{2!} + \frac{3^3x^3}{3!} + \frac{4^4x^4}{4!} + \frac{5^5x^5}{5!} + \ldots$$

**Solution.** We have, $u_n = \frac{n^n\cdot x^n}{n!}$ and $u_{n+1} = \frac{(n+1)^{n+1}\cdot x^{n+1}}{(n+1)!}$

$$\Rightarrow \quad \frac{u_n}{u_{n+1}} = \frac{1}{x}\cdot\frac{n^n}{n!}\cdot\frac{(n+1)!}{(n+1)^{n+1}} = \frac{1}{x}\cdot\frac{n^n\cdot(n+1)}{(n+1)^{n+1}}$$

$$= \frac{1}{x}\cdot\frac{n^n}{(n+1)^n} = \frac{1}{x}\cdot\frac{n^n}{n^n\{1+(1/n)\}^n}$$

$$\Rightarrow \quad \frac{u_n}{u_{n+1}} = \frac{1}{x}\cdot\frac{1}{[1+1/n]^n}$$

$$\Rightarrow \quad \lim\frac{u_n}{u_{n+1}} = \frac{1}{x}\lim\frac{1}{\left[1+\frac{1}{n}\right]^n} = \frac{1}{ex} \qquad \left[\because \lim_{n\to\infty}\left[1+\frac{1}{n}\right]^n = e\right]$$

Therefore, by Ratio test, $\Sigma u_n$ is convergent, if $\frac{1}{ex} > 1$

$\Rightarrow$ If $x < \frac{1}{e}$ and $\Sigma u_n$ is divergent if $\frac{1}{ex} < 1 \Rightarrow$ if $x > \frac{1}{e}$

For $\frac{1}{ex} = 1 \Rightarrow x = \frac{1}{e}$, the d'Alembert ratio test fails and now, we apply the logarithmic test in this case.

When $x = \frac{1}{e}$, we have $\frac{u_n}{u_{n+1}} = e \cdot \frac{1}{\left\{1 + \left(\frac{1}{n}\right)\right\}^n}$

$$\Rightarrow \quad n \log \frac{u_n}{u_{n+1}} = n[1 - n \log\{1 + (1/n)\}]$$

$$= n\left[1 - n\left(\frac{1}{n} - \frac{1}{2n^2} + \frac{1}{3n^3} - \dots\right)\right]$$

$$= n\left(\frac{1}{2n} - \frac{1}{3n^2} + \dots\right)$$

$$\Rightarrow \quad n \log \frac{u_n}{u_{n+1}} = \frac{1}{2} - \frac{1}{3n} + \dots \Rightarrow \lim_{n \to \infty} n \log \frac{u_n}{u_{n+1}} = \frac{1}{2} < 1$$

Therefore, by logarithmic test, $\Sigma u_n$ is divergent for $x = \frac{1}{e}$.

Thus, the given series is convergent if $x < \frac{1}{e}$ and is divergent if $x \geq \frac{1}{e}$.

# De Morgan's and Bertrand's Test

Suppose, $\Sigma u_n$ is the series of positive terms and

$$\lim\left[\left\{n\left(\frac{u_n}{u_{n+1}} - 1\right) - 1\right\} \log n\right] = l,$$

Then,

(i) The series is convergent, if $l > 1$.
(ii) The series is divergent, if $l < 1$.
(iii) The test fails to decide the nature, if $l = 1$.

**Note** This test is applied when d'Alembert ratio test and Raabe's test both are failed.

***Example 27.*** *Test the convergence of the following series*

$$\frac{1^2}{2^2} + \frac{1^2 \cdot 3^2}{2^2 \cdot 4^2} x + \frac{1^2 \cdot 3^2 \cdot 5^2}{2^2 \cdot 4^2 \cdot 6^2} x^2 + \dots$$

**Solution.** We have,

$$u_n = \frac{1^2 \cdot 3^2 \cdot 5^2 \dots (2n-1)^2}{2^2 \cdot 4^2 \cdot 6^2 \dots (2n)^2} x^{n-1}$$

and

$$u_{n+1} = \frac{1^2 \cdot 3^2 \cdot 5^2 \dots (2n-1)^2 \cdot (2n+1)^2}{2^2 \cdot 4^2 \cdot 6^2 \dots (2n)^2 \cdot (2n+2)^2} \cdot x^n$$

$$\Rightarrow \quad \frac{u_n}{u_{n+1}} = \frac{(2n+2)^2}{(2n+1)^2} \cdot \frac{1}{x} = \left\{\frac{2 + 2/n}{2 + 1/n}\right\}^2 \frac{1}{x}$$

$$\Rightarrow \quad \lim \frac{u_n}{u_{n+1}} = \lim\left[\left\{\frac{2 + 2/n}{2 + 1/n}\right\}^2 \cdot \frac{1}{x}\right] = \frac{2^2}{2^2} \cdot \frac{1}{x} = \frac{1}{x}$$

Therefore, by d'Alembert ratio test, the series $\Sigma u_n$ is convergent, if $\frac{1}{x} > 1 \Rightarrow x < 1$ and is divergent, if $\frac{1}{x} < 1 \Rightarrow x > 1$ and the test fails, if $\frac{1}{x} = 1 \Rightarrow x = 1$.

When $x = 1$,

$$\frac{u_n}{u_{n+1}} = \frac{(2n+2)^2}{(2n+1)^2}$$

$$\Rightarrow \quad n\left\{\frac{u_n}{u_{n+1}} - 1\right\} = n\left\{\frac{(2n+2)^2}{(2n+1)^2} - 1\right\} = \frac{n(4n+3)}{(2n+1)^2} = \frac{4 + 3/n}{(2 + 1/n)^2}$$

$$\Rightarrow \quad \lim n\left\{\frac{u_n}{u_{n+1}} - 1\right\} = \lim \frac{4 + 3/n}{(2 + 1/n)^2} = \frac{4}{2^2} = 1$$

Therefore, the Raabe's test is also fails, when $x = 1$, so on. We apply De Morgan's test

$$n\left\{\frac{u_n}{u_{n+1}} - 1\right\} - 1 = \frac{n(4n+3)}{(2n+1)^2} - 1 = \frac{-n-1}{(2n+1)^2}$$

$$\Rightarrow \quad \lim\left[\left\{n\left(\frac{u_n}{u_{n+1}} - 1\right) - 1\right\} \log n\right] = \lim\left[\left\{\frac{-n-1}{(2n+1)^2}\right\} \log n\right]$$

$$= \lim\left[\frac{-1 - 1/n}{(2 + 1/n)^2} \cdot \frac{\log n}{n}\right] = \frac{-1}{2^2} \cdot 0 \qquad \left(\because \lim \frac{\log n}{n} = 0\right)$$

$$= 0 < 1$$

Therefore, by De Morgan's test $\Sigma u_n$ is divergent, when $x = 1$.

$\Rightarrow$ The given series $\Sigma u_n$ is convergent, if $x < 1$ and divergent, if $x \geq 1$.

# Second Logarithmic Ratio Test (or An Alternative to Bertrand's Test)

Let $\Sigma u_n$ be the series of positive terms and

$$\lim_{n \to \infty}\left\{\left(n \log \frac{u_n}{u_{n+1}}\right) \log n\right\} = l$$

Then,

(i) The series is convergent, if $l > 1$.
(ii) The series is divergent, if $l < 1$.
(iii) The test fails to decide the nature of the series, if $l = 1$.

**Note** This test is used when the logarithmic test fails *i.e.*, when $\lim \frac{u_n}{u_{n+1}} = 1$ and $\lim n \log \frac{u_n}{u_{n+1}} = 1$.

***Example 28.*** *Test the convergence of the series*

$$1^p + \left(\frac{1}{2}\right)^p + \left(\frac{1 \cdot 3}{2 \cdot 4}\right)^p + \left(\frac{1 \cdot 3 \cdot 5}{2 \cdot 4 \cdot 6}\right)^p + \dots$$

**Solution.** On omitting the first term, we get

$$u_n = \left[\frac{1 \cdot 3 \cdot 5 \dots (2n-1)}{2 \cdot 4 \cdot 6 \dots (2n)}\right]^p \text{ and}$$

$$u_{n+1}=\left[\frac{1\cdot 3\cdot 5\ldots(2n-1)(2n+1)}{2\cdot 4\cdot 6\ldots(2n)(2n+2)}\right]^p$$

$$\Rightarrow \quad \frac{u_n}{u_{n+1}}=\left(\frac{2n+2}{2n+1}\right)^p=\left(\frac{1+1/n}{1+1/2n}\right)^p \qquad \ldots\text{(i)}$$

$$\Rightarrow \quad \lim_{n\to\infty}\frac{u_n}{u_{n+1}}=1$$

Therefore, the ratio test fails .
Now, we shall apply the logarithmic test.
From Eq. (i), we get

$$\log\frac{u_n}{u_{n+1}}=p\log\left[\frac{1+1/n}{1+1/2n}\right]$$

$$=p[\log(1+1/n)-\log(1+1/2n)]$$

$$=p\left\{\left(\frac{1}{n}-\frac{1}{2n^2}+\frac{1}{3n^3}-\ldots\right)-\left(\frac{1}{2n}-\frac{1}{2\cdot 2^2\cdot n^2}+\frac{1}{3\cdot 2^3\cdot n^3}+\ldots\right)\right\}$$

$$=p\left(\frac{1}{2n}-\frac{3}{8n^2}+\frac{7}{24n^3}-\ldots\right)$$

$$\Rightarrow \quad n\log\frac{u_n}{u_{n+1}}=p\left[\frac{1}{2}-\frac{3}{8n}+\frac{7}{24n^2}-\ldots\right] \qquad \ldots\text{(ii)}$$

$$\Rightarrow \quad \lim_{n\to\infty} n\cdot\log\frac{u_n}{u_{n+1}}=\frac{p}{2}$$

Therefore, $\Sigma u_n$ converges, if $\frac{p}{2}>1 \Rightarrow$ if $p>2$ and diverges, if $\frac{p}{2}<1 \Rightarrow p<2$ and the test fails when $p=2$.

For $p=2$, from Eq. (ii),

$$n\log\frac{u_n}{u_{n+1}}=2\left(\frac{1}{2}-\frac{3}{8n}+\frac{7}{24n^2}-\ldots\right)=1-\frac{3}{4n}+\frac{7}{12n^2}-\ldots$$

$$\Rightarrow \quad n\log\frac{u_n}{u_{n+1}}-1=-\frac{3}{4n}+\frac{7}{12n^2}\ldots$$

$$=\left(-\frac{3}{4}+\frac{7}{12n}-\ldots\right)\times\frac{1}{n}$$

$$\Rightarrow \quad \lim_{n\to\infty}\left(n\log\frac{u_n}{u_{n+1}}-1\right)\log n=\lim_{n\to\infty}\left(-\frac{3}{4}+\frac{7}{12n}-\ldots\right)\frac{\log n}{n}$$

$$=\frac{3}{4}\,0 \qquad \left[\because \lim_{n\to\infty}\frac{\log n}{n}=0\right]$$

$$=0<1$$

Therefore, by second logarithmic ratio test, the series $\Sigma u_n$ diverges for $p=2$.

Hence, the given series converges, if $p>1$ and is diverges if $p\le 2$.

## Gauss's Test

Suppose, $\Sigma u_n$ be the series of positive terms and let there exist two positive numbers $\rho$, $\delta$ and a bounded sequence $<a_n>$, such that

$$\frac{u_n}{u_{n+1}}=1+\frac{\rho}{n}+\frac{a_n}{n^{1+\delta}}$$

Then, the series $\Sigma u_n$ converges, if $\rho>1$ and diverges, if $\rho\le 1$.

> ***Note*** **(a)** If there exists $\delta>0$, such that $\lim_{n\to\infty}\left[n^\delta\left\{n\left(\frac{u_n}{u_{n+1}}-1\right)\right\}\right]$ exists finitely, then the series $\Sigma u_n$ is divergent.
>
> **(b)** Gauss's test can be applied after the failure of ratio test and when it is possible to expand $\frac{u_n}{u_{n+1}}$ in powers of $\frac{1}{n}$ by binomial theorem.
>
> $$(1+x)^n=1+nx+\frac{n(n-1)}{2!}x^2+\ldots$$
>
> **(c)** We apply ratio test, if the terms of the given series $\Sigma u_n$ involve $x$ and then try Gauss's test. But Gauss's test applied directly, if the terms of the series $\Sigma u_n$ free from $x$.

***Example 29.*** *Test the convergence of the series*

$$1+\left(\frac{1}{2}\right)^p+\left(\frac{1\cdot 3}{2\cdot 4}\right)^p+\left(\frac{1\cdot 3\cdot 5}{2\cdot 4\cdot 6}\right)^p+\ldots$$

**Solution.** On the omission of first term of the series, we get

$$u_n=\frac{1\cdot 3\cdot 5\ldots(2n-1)}{2\cdot 4\cdot 6\ \ldots\ 2n}$$

$$u_{n+1}=\left\{\frac{1\cdot 3\cdot 5\ \ldots\ (2n-1)(2n+1)}{2\cdot 4\cdot 6\ldots(2n)(2n+1)}\right\}^p$$

$$\Rightarrow \quad \frac{u_n}{u_{n+1}}=\frac{(2n+2)^p}{(2n+1)^p}=\frac{(1+1/n)^p}{(1+1/2n)^p} \qquad \ldots\text{(i)}$$

$$\Rightarrow \quad \lim_{n\to\infty}\frac{u_n}{u_{n+1}}=\lim_{n\to\infty}\frac{(1+1/n)^p}{(1+1/2n)^p}=1$$

$\therefore$ The d'Alembert ratio test fails.

Now, by Eq. (i)

$$\frac{u_n}{u_{n+1}}=\left(1+\frac{1}{n}\right)^p\left(1+\frac{1}{2n}\right)^{-p}$$

$$=\left\{1+\frac{p}{n}+\frac{p(p-1)}{2!}\frac{1}{n^2}+\ldots\right\}\times\left\{1-\frac{p}{2n}+\frac{p(p+1)}{2!}\cdot\frac{1}{4n^2}+\ldots\right\}$$

$$=1+\frac{p}{2n}+0\left(\frac{1}{n^2}\right)$$

Here, $\rho=$ coefficient of $\frac{1}{n}=\frac{p}{2}$. Therefore, by Gauss's test the given series converges, if $\frac{p}{2}>1 \Rightarrow p>2$ and diverges, if

$$\frac{p}{2}\le 1 \Rightarrow p\le 2.$$

Hence, the given series converges, if $p>2$ and diverges, if $p\le 2$.

## Cauchy's Integral Test

Before starting the test which is based on the comparison of a positive term series with an infinite integral we give some preliminaries.

**Improper Integrals** Integrals of the form $\int_a^\infty f(x)\,dx$, where $a \in R$ are called improper integrals.

Let $F(t) = \int_a^t f(x)\,dx$ for $a \le t < \infty$.

If $\lim_{t\to\infty} F(t)$ exists and is equal to $l \in R$, the improper integral $\int_a^t f(x)\,dx$ is said to converge to $l$, otherwise it is called divergent integral.

***Theorem*** Suppose, $u(x)$ be a non-negative monotonically decreasing integrable function on $[1, \infty[$. Then, the series $\sum_{n=1}^{\infty} u_n$ and the improper integral $\int_1^\infty u(x)\,dx$ converge or diverge together *i.e.*, the series $\sum u_n$ converges or diverges according as the integral $\int_1^n u(x)\,dx$ tends to finite limit or diverge to $\infty$ as $n \to \infty$.

> ***Note*** The series $\sum u_n$ and the integral $\int_a^\infty f(x)\,dx$ converge or diverge together for $a \ge 1$.

***Example 30.*** *Test the convergence of the series using Cauchy's integral test.*

$$\sum \frac{1}{n^2+1}.$$

**Solution.** Let $u(x) = \dfrac{1}{x^2+1}$, $\forall\ x \in [1, \infty[$, then $u(x) > 0$ and $u(x)$ is monotonically decreasing on $[1, \infty[$.

Now,
$$\int_1^n \frac{dx}{x^2+1} = [\tan^{-1} x]_1^n\ \tan^{-1} n - \frac{\pi}{4}$$

$$\Rightarrow \quad \lim_{n\to\infty} \int_1^n \frac{dx}{x^2+1} = \lim_{n\to\infty}\left[\tan^{-1} n - \frac{\pi}{4}\right]$$

$$= \frac{\pi}{2} - \frac{\pi}{4} = \frac{\pi}{4}$$

$$\therefore \quad \int_1^\infty u(x)\,dx \text{ converges to } \frac{\pi}{4}.$$

Therefore, by Cauchy's integral test, the series
$$\sum f(n) = \sum \frac{1}{n^2+1} \text{ converges.}$$

***Example 31.*** *Using integral test, show that the series* $\sum_{n=2}^{\infty} \dfrac{1}{n(\log n)^p}$ *is convergent, if $p > 1$ and divergent, if $0 < p < 1$.*

**Solution.** We have, $u_n = \dfrac{1}{n\,(\log n)^p} = u(n),\ \forall\ n \in N$

$$\therefore \quad u(x) = \frac{1}{x(\log x)^p}$$

For $n \ge 2$, $u(x)$ is a non-negative and monotonically decreasing function. Therefore, the Cauchy's integral test can be applied.

**Case I** Suppose, $p = 1$, then $u(x) = \dfrac{1}{x\log x}$

$$\therefore \quad \int_2^s u(x)\,dx = \int_2^s \frac{1}{x\log x}\,dx = [\log(\log x)]_2^s$$
$$= \log\log s - \log\log 2$$
$$\Rightarrow \quad \int_2^s u(x)\,dx = \lim_{s\to\infty} \int_2^s u(x)\,dx$$
$$= \lim_{s\to\infty}(\log\log s - \log\log 2) = \infty$$
$$\Rightarrow \quad \int_2^\infty u(x)\,dx \text{ diverges} \Rightarrow \sum_{n=2}^{\infty} u_n \text{ diverges,}$$

By using Cauchy's integral test.

**Case II** Suppose, $p > 1 \Rightarrow (p-1) > 0$

$$\therefore \quad \int_2^s u(x)\,dx = \int_2^s \frac{dx}{x(\log x)^p} = \left[\frac{(\log x)^{1-p}}{1-p}\right]_2^s$$
$$= \left[-\frac{(\log x)^{1-p}}{p-1}\right]_2^s$$
$$= \frac{1}{p-1}\left[\frac{1}{(\log 2)^{p-1}} - \frac{1}{(\log s)^{p-1}}\right]$$
$$\Rightarrow \quad \int_2^\infty u(x)\,dx = \lim_{s\to\infty} \int_0^s u(x)dx$$
$$= \lim_{s\to\infty} \frac{1}{p-1}\left[\frac{1}{(\log 2)^{p-1}} - \frac{1}{(\log s)^{p-1}}\right]$$
$$= \frac{1}{(p-1)(\log 2)^{p-1}} = \text{finite}$$
$$\Rightarrow \quad \int_2^\infty u(x)\,dx \text{ converges} \to \text{By Cauchy's integral test } \sum_2^\infty u_n \text{ converges.}$$

**Case III** Suppose, $0 < p < 1 \Rightarrow (1-p) > 0$. Then, we have

$$\int_2^s u(x)\,dx = \int_2^s \frac{dx}{x(\log x)^p} = \left[\frac{(\log x)^{1-p}}{1-p}\right]_2^s$$
$$= \frac{1}{1-p}[(\log s)^{1-p} - (\log 2)^{1-p}]$$
$$\Rightarrow \quad \int_2^\infty u(x)\,dx = \lim_{s\to\infty} \int_2^s u(x)dx$$
$$= \lim_{s\to\infty} \frac{1}{1-p}[(\log t)^{1-p} - (\log 2)^{1-p}] = \infty$$
$$\Rightarrow \quad \int_2^\infty u(x)\,dx \text{ diverges.}$$

$\therefore$ By Cauchy's integral test $\sum_2^\infty u_n$ diverges.

Hence, $\sum_{n=2}^{\infty} u_n$ converges, if $p > 1$ and diverges, if $0 < p \le 1$.

# Alternating Series

A series of the type $u_1 - u_2 + u_3 - u_4 + \ldots$, where $u_n > 0$, $\forall\ n \in N$, is called an alternating series and is denoted by $\sum(-1)^{n-1}u_n$.

Some example of alternating series are

$$1 - \frac{1}{\sqrt{2}} + \frac{1}{\sqrt{3}} - \frac{1}{\sqrt{4}} + \ldots\ldots,\ 2 - \frac{3}{2} + \frac{4}{3} - \frac{5}{4} + \ldots$$

## Leibnitz Test for Testing the Convergence of an Alternating Series

An infinite series in which the terms are alternately positive and negative is convergent if (i) each terms is numerically less than the preceding term and (ii) $\lim_{n\to\infty} u_n = 0$.

## Absolute Convergence and Conditional Convergence of Series

A series $\Sigma u_n$ is said to be an absolutely convergent series, if the series of absolute value of terms, *i.e.*, $\Sigma|u_n|$ is convergent. Note that, if $\Sigma u_n$ is a series of positive terms, then $\Sigma|u_n|$ is nothing but the same as $\Sigma u_n$.

Thus, the notion of absolute convergence is applicable to the series of positive and negative terms (like alternating series).

For instance, if given series is $1-\frac{1}{2^2}+\frac{1}{3^2}-\frac{1}{4^2}+\ldots\ldots$, then series $\Sigma|u_n| = \Sigma\frac{1}{n^2}$. This is convergent.

Hence, the series $1-\frac{1}{2^2}+\frac{1}{3^2}-\frac{1}{4^2}+\ldots$ is absolutely convergent.

Note that every absolutely convergent series is convergent, but the converse is not necessarily true,

*i.e.*, a convergent series may and may not be absolutely convergent. For example, the series

$$\Sigma u_n = 1-\frac{1}{2}+\frac{1}{3}-\frac{1}{4}+\ldots+(-1)^{n-1}\cdot\frac{1}{n}+\ldots$$

is convergent by Leibnitz's test but the absolute series is

$$\Sigma|u_n| = 1+\frac{1}{2}+\frac{1}{3}+\frac{1}{4}+\ldots$$

is a divergent series as it is of the form $\Sigma\frac{1}{n^p}$, $p = 1$.

## Conditionally Convergent or Semi-convergent Series

A series $\Sigma u_n$ is said to be semi-convergent or conditionally convergent, if $\Sigma u_n$ is convergent while $\Sigma|u_n|$ is divergent. Thus, above series $\Sigma(-1)^{n-1}\cdot\frac{1}{n}$ conditionally convergent.

***Example 32.*** *Test the convergency of the series*

$$\frac{1}{x}-\frac{1}{x+a}+\frac{1}{x+2a}-\frac{1}{x+3a}+\ldots$$

*and a being positive quantity.*

**Solution.** Here, we observe that

(i) the terms are alternately positive and negative.

(ii) the terms are continually decreasing and [Since, $x<(x+a)<(x+2a)<\ldots$]

(iii) $\lim_{n\to\infty} u_n = \lim_{n\to\infty}\frac{1}{x+(n-1)a} = \lim_{n\to\infty}\frac{1}{\infty} = 0$

Hence, all the three conditions of the alternating series test are satisfied. Therefore, the given series is convergent.

***Example 33.*** *Test the convergence of the series*

$$\sum_{n=1}^{\infty}\left[\frac{1}{n}+\frac{(-1)^{n+1}}{\sqrt{n}}\right].$$

**Solution.** We know that $\Sigma(u_n+v_n) = \Sigma u_n + \Sigma v_n$,

Therefore, given series

$$\sum_{n=1}^{\infty}\left[\frac{1}{n}+\frac{(-1)^{n+1}}{\sqrt{n}}\right] = \sum_{n=1}^{\infty}\frac{1}{n}+\sum_{n=1}^{\infty}\frac{(-1)^{n+1}}{\sqrt{n}}$$

Now, second series $\Sigma(-1)^{n+1}/\sqrt{n}$ is a convergent series, by Leibnitz's test and hence its sum is a finite quantity.

But first series $\Sigma\frac{1}{n}$ is a series of positive terms of the form $\Sigma\frac{1}{n^p}$, where $p = 1$. So by *p*-test, it is a divergent series and hence, it sum is $\infty$. So the sum of the given series is also $\infty$ and hence given series is divergent.

***Example 34.*** *Test for convergence of the series*

$$1-\frac{1}{1!}+\frac{1}{2!}-\frac{1}{3!}+\frac{1}{4!}-\ldots$$

**Solution.** Here, we observe that

(i) The terms of the series are alternately positive and negative,

(ii) Each terms is numerically less than its preceding terms, *i.e.*, $u_{n+1}<u_n$, $\forall\ n\in N$ and

(iii) $\lim_{n\to\infty} u_n = \lim_{n\to\infty}\frac{1}{n!} = 0$

Hence, the given series is convergent.

***Example 35.*** *Show that the series $\Sigma\sin n\theta/n^2$ is absolutely convergent.*

**Solution.** Here, $|u_n| = \left|\frac{\sin(n\theta)}{n^2}\right| \le \frac{1}{n^2}$ as $|\sin n\theta| \le 1$

$\Rightarrow$ $\Sigma|u_n| \le \Sigma\frac{1}{n^2}$, which is a finite quantity as series $\Sigma\frac{1}{n^2}$ is convergent.

$\Rightarrow$ $\Sigma|u_n|$ is also finite and hence convergent.

$\Rightarrow$ Given series is absolutely convergent.

***Example 36.*** *Test the convergent and the absolute convergence of the series*

$$1-\frac{1}{2\sqrt{2}}+\frac{1}{3\sqrt{3}}-\frac{1}{4\sqrt{4}}+\ldots$$

**Solution.** The given series is $\sum_{n=1}^{\infty}(-1)^{n-1}u_n$,

where $u_n = \frac{1}{n\sqrt{n}} > 0$, $\forall\ n$.

We have, $u_{n+1}<u_n$, $\forall\ n$ because

$$\frac{1}{(n+1)\sqrt{n+1}} < \frac{1}{n\sqrt{n}}$$

$\Rightarrow$ Each term of the given series numerically less than the preceding term.

Also, $\lim_{n\to\infty} u_n = \lim_{n\to\infty} \frac{1}{n\sqrt{n}} = 0$

$\Rightarrow$ By Leibnitz's test for alternating series, the given series is convergent.

Further, the series

$$\sum_{n=1}^{\infty} |(-1)^{n-1} u_n| = \sum \frac{1}{n\sqrt{n}} = \frac{1}{n^{3/2}} = \sum \frac{1}{n^{p'}}$$

where $p = (3/2) > 1$

$\therefore$ The series $\sum |(-1)^{n-1} u_n|$ is convergent and hence the given series is absolutely convergent also.

# SOLVED EXAMPLES

## Type I (*Only one correct option*)

***Example 1.*** *The sequence* $< 1 + (-1)^n >$ *has*

(a) exactly one constant subsequence
(b) exactly two constant subsequence
(c) exactly three constant subsequence
(d) exactly four constant subsequence

**Solution.** (b) We have

$< 1 + (-1)^n > = < 0, 2, 0, 2, 0, 2, \ldots >$

whose subsequence are

$< 0, 0, 0, 0, \ldots >$

and $< 2, 2, 2, 2, \ldots >$

which are constants.

Hence, $< 1 + (-1)^n >$ has exactly two constant subsequences.

***Example 2.*** *Which one of the following sequence is convergent?*

(a) $< 2^n >$ (b) $< \left(\frac{1}{3}\right)^n >$

(c) $< 3^n >$ (d) None of these

**Solution.** (b) Since, we know that the sequence $< r^n >$ is convergent if $r < 1$ and divergent if $r \geq 1$. Hence, only the sequence $< \left(\frac{1}{3}\right)^n >$ is convergent.

***Example 3.*** *The value of*

$$\lim_{n\to\infty} \frac{1}{n}\left[\left(\frac{1}{2}\right)^n + \left(\frac{1}{2}\right)\left(\frac{1}{2}\right)^{n-1} + \left(\frac{1}{3}\right)\left(\frac{1}{2}\right)^{n-2} + \ldots + \left(\frac{1}{n}\right)\left(\frac{1}{2}\right)\right]$$

*is*

(a) 0 (b) does not exist

(c) 1 (d) None of these

**Solution.** (a) Let $S_n = \left(\frac{1}{2}\right)^n$ and $t_n = \frac{1}{n}$

Then $\lim_{n\to\infty} S_n = \lim_{n\to\infty} \left(\frac{1}{2}\right)^n = 0$

and $\lim_{n\to\infty} t_n = \lim_{n\to\infty} \frac{1}{n} = 0$

Hence, by Cesaro's theorem

$$\lim_{n\to\infty} \frac{1}{n}\left[\left(\frac{1}{2}\right)^n + \left(\frac{1}{2}\right)\left(\frac{1}{2}\right)^{n-1} + \left(\frac{1}{3}\right)\left(\frac{1}{2}\right)^{n-2} + \ldots + \left(\frac{1}{n}\right)\left(\frac{1}{2}\right)\right] = 0$$

***Example 4.*** *The sequence*

$$S_n = \begin{cases} 2, & \textit{when } n \textit{ is even} \\ \textit{Lowest prime factor } (\neq 1) \textit{ of } n, & \textit{when } n \textit{ is odd} \end{cases}$$

*has limit point*

(a) 2 (b) 1, 2, 3, 4, 5, ....

(c) countable in number (d) uncountable in number

**Solution.** (c) Clearly 2, 3, 5, 7, 11, ... are limit point of the sequence $S_n$, which are countable in numbers.

***Example 5.*** *The limit of the sequence*

$$S_n = \frac{3 + 2\sqrt{n}}{\sqrt{n}}$$

*is*

(a) 0 (b) 1

(c) 2 (d) None of these

**Solution.** (c) Let $\varepsilon > 0$ be given number

$\therefore$ $\left|\frac{3 + 2\sqrt{n}}{\sqrt{n}} - 0\right| < \varepsilon$ if $\left|\frac{3}{\sqrt{n}}\right| < \varepsilon$ or if $n > \frac{9}{\varepsilon^2}$

Let $m$ be a positive integer greater than $\frac{9}{\varepsilon^2}$. Thus, to $\varepsilon > 0$, $\exists$ a positive integer $m$, such that $\left|\frac{3 + 2\sqrt{n}}{\sqrt{n}} - 2\right| < \varepsilon \;\forall\; n \geq m$.

$\therefore$ $\lim_{n\to\infty} \frac{3 + 2\sqrt{n}}{\sqrt{n}} = 2$

***Example 6.*** *The limit of the sequence*

$$S_n = \left\{\frac{(3n+1)(n-2)}{n(n+3)}\right\}$$

*is*

(a) 0 (b) 1 (c) 2 (d) 3

**Solution.** (d) We know that the sequence $\left\{\frac{1}{n}\right\}$ converges to zero.

Now,

$$\lim_{n\to\infty} S_n = \lim_{n\to\infty} \frac{(3n+1)(n-2)}{n(n+3)} = \lim_{n\to\infty} \frac{n^2\left(3+\frac{1}{n}\right)\left(1-\frac{2}{n}\right)}{n^2\left(1+\frac{3}{n}\right)}$$

$$= \lim_{n\to\infty} \frac{\left(3+\frac{1}{n}\right)\left(1-\frac{2}{n}\right)}{\left(1+\frac{3}{n}\right)} = \frac{3\cdot 1}{1} = 3$$

***Example 7.*** *Consider the statements*

(A) $\lim_{n\to\infty} \frac{(3n)!}{(n!)^3} = 27$

(B) $\lim_{n\to\infty} \frac{n^n}{(n+1)(n+2)(n+n)} = \frac{e}{4}$

*Then*

(a) (A) is true but (B) is false.
(b) (A) is false but (B) is true.
(c) (A) and (B) both are true.
(d) Neither (A) nor (B) is true.

**Solution.** (c) (A) We have

$$a_n = \frac{(3n)!}{(n!)^3}$$

$$\Rightarrow \quad a_{n+1} = \frac{(3(n+1))!}{((n+1)!)^3}$$

$$\therefore \quad \lim_{n\to\infty} \frac{a_{n+1}}{a_n} = \lim_{n\to\infty} \frac{(3n+3)!}{((n+1)!)^3} \cdot \frac{(n!)^3}{(3n)!}$$

$$= \lim_{n\to\infty} \frac{(3n+3)(3n+2)(3n+1)}{(n+1)^3} = 27$$

Hence, $\lim_{n\to\infty} a_n^{1/n} = \lim_{n\to\infty} \frac{a_{n+1}}{a_n} = 27$

(B) We have

$$b_n = \frac{n^n}{(n+1)(n+2)\ldots(n+n)}$$

$$\Rightarrow \quad b_{n+1} = \frac{(n+1)^{(n+1)}}{(n+2)(n+3)\ldots 2n(2n+1)(2n+2)}$$

$$\therefore \quad \lim_{n\to\infty} \frac{b_{n+1}}{b_n} = \lim_{n\to\infty} \frac{(n+1)^{(n+1)}(n+1)(n+2)\ldots(2n)}{(n+2)(n+3)\ldots(2n+1)(2n+2)n^n}$$

$$= \lim_{n\to\infty} \frac{\left(1+\frac{1}{n}\right)^n\left(1+\frac{1}{n}\right)^2}{\left(2+\frac{1}{n}\right)\left(2+\frac{2}{n}\right)} = \frac{e}{4}$$

$$\therefore \quad \lim_{n\to\infty} b_n^{1/n} = \lim_{n\to\infty} \frac{b_{n+1}}{b_n} = \frac{e}{4}$$

Hence, both the statements are true.

***Example 8.*** *Consider the statements*

(A) *The series* $\Sigma \sin\frac{1}{n}$ *is divergent.*

(B) *The series*

$$\frac{1}{3^2}\cdot\frac{2}{4^2} + \frac{3\cdot 4}{5^2\cdot 6^2} + \frac{5\cdot 6}{7^2\cdot 8^2} + \ldots \text{ is convergent.}$$

*Then*

(a) Both the statements (A) and (B) are true.
(b) (A) is true but (B) is false.
(c) (A) is false but (B) is true.
(d) Neither (A) nor (B) is true.

**Solution.** (a) Let $\quad u_n = \sin\frac{1}{n}$

Then its auxiliary series is

$$v_n = \frac{1}{n}$$

Now, $\quad \lim_{n\to\infty} \frac{u_n}{v_n} = \lim_{n\to\infty} \frac{\sin 1/n}{1/n} = 1 \neq 0$

Therefore, by comparison test, the two series behave alike. But the series

$$\Sigma \frac{1}{n}$$

is divergent.

Hence, the series

$$\Sigma \sin\left(\frac{1}{n}\right)$$

is divergent.

Next, let $\quad u_n = \frac{(2n-1)(2n)}{(2n+1)^2(2n+2)^2} \equiv \frac{1}{n^2}$

Then its auxiliary series is given by

$$v_n = \frac{1}{n^2}$$

$$\therefore \quad \lim_{n\to\infty} \frac{u_n}{v_n} = \lim_{n\to\infty} \frac{\left(2-\frac{1}{n}\right)(2)}{\left(2+\frac{1}{n}\right)^2\left(2+\frac{2}{n}\right)^2} = \frac{1}{4}$$

Hence, by comparison test both the two series behave alike, but the series $\Sigma\frac{1}{n^2}$ is convergent.

$\therefore \quad \Sigma u_n$ is convergent.

***Example 9.*** *Which of the following is convergent series?*

(a) $\sum_{n=1}^{\infty} \cos\left(\frac{1}{n}\right)$

(b) $\sqrt[7]{\frac{1}{1+1}} + \sqrt[7]{\frac{2}{2+1}} + \sqrt[7]{\frac{3}{3+1}} + \ldots + \sqrt[7]{\frac{n}{n+1}} + \ldots$

(c) $\sum_{n=1}^{\infty} \left(n\log\left(\frac{3n+2}{3n-2}\right)-1\right)$

(d) None of the above

**Solution.** (d); (a) Let $u_n = \cos\left(\frac{1}{n}\right)$

$$\Rightarrow \quad \lim_{n\to\infty} u_n = \lim_{n\to\infty} \cos\left(\frac{1}{n}\right) = \cos 0 = 1 \neq 0$$

$$\Rightarrow \quad \Sigma \cos\left(\frac{1}{n}\right) \text{ is divergent.}$$

(b) Let $\quad u_n = \sqrt[7]{\frac{n}{n+1}}$

$$\therefore \quad \lim_{n\to\infty} u_n = \lim_{n\to\infty} \sqrt[7]{\frac{n}{n+1}} = \lim_{n\to\infty} \sqrt[7]{\frac{n}{1+\frac{1}{n}}}$$

$$= \left(\frac{1}{1+0}\right)^{1/7} = 1 \neq 0$$

Hence, $\Sigma u_n$ is divergent.

(c) Let $\quad u_n = n \log\left(\frac{3n+2}{3n-2}\right) - 1$

$$\therefore \quad \lim_{n\to\infty} u_n = \lim_{n\to\infty} n \log\left(\frac{3n+2}{3n-2}\right) - 1$$

$$= \lim_{n\to\infty} n \log \frac{1+\frac{2}{3n}}{1-\frac{2}{3n}} - 1$$

$$= \lim_{n\to\infty} n \left\{\log\left(1+\frac{2}{3n}\right) - \log\left(1-\frac{2}{3n}\right)\right\} - 1$$

$$= \lim_{n\to\infty} n\left(2\left(\frac{2}{3n} + \frac{8}{3\cdot 27n^3} + \dots\right)\right) - 1$$

$$\left(\because \log(1+x) - \log(1-x) = 2\left(x + \frac{x^3}{3} + \frac{x^5}{5} + \dots\right)\right)$$

$$= \lim_{n\to\infty} \left(\frac{4}{3} + \frac{16}{81n^2} + \dots\right) - 1$$

$$= \left(\frac{4}{3} + 0 + 0 + \dots\right) - 1 = \frac{1}{3} \neq 0$$

$\therefore$ $\Sigma u_n$ is divergent.

## Type II (*One or more than one correct option*)

***Example 10.*** *Which of the following(s) is/are correct?*

(a) $\lim_{n\to\infty} \frac{x^n}{n!} = 0 \ \ \forall\ x \in \mathbb{R}$ (b) $\lim_{n\to\infty} \frac{x^n}{n!} = \infty \ \ \forall\ x \in \mathbb{R}$

(c) $\lim_{n\to\infty} \frac{x^n}{n} = 0 \ \ \forall\ x > 1$ (d) $\lim_{n\to\infty} \frac{x^n}{n} = \infty \ \ \forall\ x > 1$

**Solution.** (a), (d)

Let $x = 0$, then $\lim_{n\to\infty} \frac{x^n}{n!} = \lim_{n\to\infty} 0 = 0$

Let $x \neq 0$, then $\frac{x^n}{n!} \neq 0$

Let $\quad S_n = \frac{x^n}{n!} \Rightarrow S_{n+1} = \frac{x^{n+1}}{(n+1)!}$

$$\therefore \quad \lim_{n\to\infty} \frac{S_{n+1}}{S_n} = \lim_{n\to\infty} \frac{x^{n+1}}{(n+1)!} \cdot \frac{n!}{x^n}$$

$$= \lim_{n\to\infty} \frac{x}{n+1} = 0 < 1$$

$$\Rightarrow \quad \lim_{n\to\infty} S_n = \lim_{n\to\infty} \frac{x^n}{n!} = 0$$

Next, $\quad$ if $x = 0$, then

$$\lim_{n\to\infty} \frac{x^n}{n} = \lim_{n\to\infty} 0 = 0$$

and if $x \neq 0$, then $\frac{x^n}{n} \neq 0$

Let $\quad S_n = \frac{x^n}{n} \Rightarrow S_{n+1} = \frac{x^{n+1}}{n+1}$

$$\therefore \quad \lim_{n\to\infty} \frac{S_{n+1}}{S_n} = \lim_{n\to\infty} \frac{x^{n+1}}{n+1} \cdot \frac{n}{x^n} = \lim_{n\to\infty} \frac{nx}{n+1}$$

$$= \lim_{n\to\infty} \frac{x}{\left(1+\frac{1}{n}\right)} = x > 1 \text{ (given)}$$

$$\Rightarrow \quad \lim_{n\to\infty} S_n = \lim_{n\to\infty} \frac{x^n}{n} = \infty.$$

***Example 11.*** *Let $< S_n >$ and $< t_n >$ be two sequences such that*

$$\lim_{n\to\infty} \frac{S_{n+1}}{S_n} = \frac{1}{2}, \ S_n \neq 0 \ \forall\ n$$

*and* $$\lim_{n\to\infty} \frac{t_{n+1}}{t_n} = \frac{3}{2}, \ t_n \neq 0 \ \forall\ n$$

*Then*

(a) $\lim_{n\to\infty} S_n = 0$

(b) $\lim_{n\to\infty} S_n$ does not exists finitely

(c) $\lim_{n\to\infty} t_n = 0$

(d) $\lim_{n\to\infty} t_n$ does not exists finitely

**Solution.** (a), (d)

Since, we know that if $< S_n >$ be a sequence such that $S_n \neq 0 \ \forall\ n$ and

$$\lim_{n\to\infty} \frac{S_{n+1}}{S_n} = l$$

Then if $|l| < 1$, $\quad \lim_{n\to\infty} S_n = 0$

and if $\quad l > 1$, $\quad \lim_{n\to\infty} S_n = \infty$

Hence, $\quad \lim_{n\to\infty} S_n = 0$ as $l = \frac{1}{2} < 1$

and $\quad \lim_{n\to\infty} t_n = \infty$ as $l = \frac{3}{2} > 1$

***Example 12.*** *Which of the following(s) is/are correct?*

(a) $\lim_{n\to\infty} \frac{1}{n}\left[\frac{1}{2}+\frac{1}{2^2}+\frac{1}{2^3}+\ldots+\frac{1}{2^n}\right]=0$

(b) $\lim_{n\to\infty} \frac{1}{n}\left[\frac{1}{2}+\frac{1}{2^2}+\frac{1}{2^3}+\ldots+\frac{1}{2^n}\right]$ does not exists

(c) $\lim_{n\to\infty}\left[\left(\frac{1}{2}\right)\left(\frac{1}{2}\right)^2\left(\frac{1}{2}\right)^3\cdots\left(\frac{1}{2}\right)^n\right]^{1/n}=0$

(d) $\lim_{n\to\infty}\left[\left(\frac{1}{2}\right)\left(\frac{1}{2}\right)^2\left(\frac{1}{2}\right)^3\cdots\left(\frac{1}{2}\right)^n\right]^{1/n}$ does not exists

**Solution.** (a), (c)

Let $S_n=\left(\frac{1}{2}\right)^n$. Then $\lim_{n\to\infty} S_n=0$

Hence, by Cauchy first theorem on limits, we have

$$\lim_{n\to\infty} \frac{1}{n}\left[\frac{1}{2}+\frac{1}{2^2}+\frac{1}{2^3}+\ldots+\frac{1}{2^n}\right]=0$$

and by Cauchy second theorem on limits, we have

$$\lim_{n\to\infty}\left[\left(\frac{1}{2}\right)\left(\frac{1}{2}\right)^2\left(\frac{1}{3}\right)^3\cdots\left(\frac{1}{2}\right)^n\right]^{1/n}=0$$

***Example 13.*** *Which of the following sequence(s) is/are convergent?*

(a) $S_n=\left\{1+\frac{1}{n}\right\}$ (b) $S_n=\left\{\frac{(-1)^n}{n^2}\right\}$

(c) $S_n=\left\{\frac{(-1)^{n-1}}{n!}\right\}$ (d) $S_n=\left\{(-1)^n\left(1+\frac{1}{n}\right)\right\}$

**Solution.** (b), (c)

(a) Given that

$$S_n=1+\frac{1}{n}=\left\{2,1\frac{1}{2},1\frac{1}{3},1\frac{1}{4},1\frac{1}{5},\ldots\right\}$$

$\therefore$ $\overline{\lim} S_n=2$ and $\underline{\lim} S_n=1$

$\therefore$ $\overline{\lim} S_n \neq \underline{\lim}\, S_n$

Hence, $S_n=\left\{1+\frac{1}{n}\right\}$ is divergent.

(b) $\underline{\lim} S_n=\sup_n \inf\left\{\frac{(-1)^n}{n^2},\frac{(-1)^{n+1}}{(n+1)^2},\ldots\right\}$

$$=\sup_n\begin{cases}-\frac{1}{n^2} & \text{if } n \text{ is odd}\\ -\frac{1}{(n+1)^2} & \text{if } n \text{ is even}\end{cases}$$

$=0$

Similarly,

$\overline{\lim} S_n=0$

$\therefore$ $\underline{\lim} S_n=\overline{\lim} S_n=0$

$\therefore$ $S_n=\left\{\frac{(-1)^n}{n^2}\right\}$ is convergent.

(c) Given, $S_n=\left\{\frac{(-1)^{n-1}}{n!}\right\}$ has

$$\overline{\lim} S_n=0=\underline{\lim}\, S_n=0$$

Hence, $S_n$ is convergent.

(d) Given that

$$S_n=\left\{(-1)^n\left(1+\frac{1}{n}\right)\right\}$$

$$=-2,1\frac{1}{2},-1\frac{1}{3},1\frac{1}{4},-1\frac{1}{5},\ldots$$

$\therefore$ $\underline{\lim}\, S_n=-2,\ \overline{\lim} S_n=1$

Hence, $S_n$ is divergent.

***Example 14.*** *The limit point of the sequence*

$$\left\{m+\frac{1}{n}\right\}$$

*is*

(a) countable in number (b) uncountable in number

(c) 0 (d) 1, 2, 3, 4,5, ....

**Solution.** (a), (d)

Clearly, 1, 2, 3,4, 5,.... are only limit point of the sequence $S_n=\left\{m+\frac{1}{n}\right\}$ which are countable in number.

***Example 15.*** *The limit point of the sequence* $\left\{\frac{1}{m}+\frac{1}{n}\right\}$ *is/are*

(a) 0 (b) 1, 2, 3, 4, ...

(c) $1,\frac{1}{2},\frac{1}{3},\frac{1}{4},\frac{1}{5},\ldots$ (d) countable in numbers

**Solution.** (c), (d)

Clearly $1,\frac{1}{2},\frac{1}{3},\frac{1}{4},\frac{1}{5},\ldots$ are limit point of the sequence $S_n=\left\{\frac{1}{m}+\frac{1}{n}\right\}$ which are countable in numbers.

***Example 16.*** *The sequence*

$$S_n=\begin{cases}2 & \text{, when } n \text{ is even}\\ \text{Lowest prime factor } (\neq 1) \text{ of } n, & \text{when } n \text{ is odd}\end{cases}$$

*is*

(a) convergent
(b) divergent
(c) oscillates
(d) bounded on the left but not on the right

**Solution.** (b), (d)

Given sequence is

$$S_n=\begin{cases}2 & \text{, when } n \text{ is even}\\ \text{Lowest prime factor } (\neq 1) \text{ of } n, & \text{when } n \text{ is odd}\end{cases}$$

$=\{1, 2, 3, 2, 5, 2,7, 2, 3, 2, 11, 2, 13, \ldots\}$

Which is bounded on left but not on right and $\overline{\lim}\, S_n=+\infty$ and $\underline{\lim} S_n=2$. Hence, divergent.

**Example 17.** *Which of the following(s) is/are correct?*

(a) The sequence $\{S_n\}$, where $S_n = 1, \frac{1}{2}, \frac{1}{3}, \frac{1}{4}, \ldots$ is convergent

(b) The sequence $\{S_n\}$, where $S_n = 1, \frac{1}{2}, \frac{1}{3}, \frac{1}{4}, \ldots$ is divergent

(c) The sequence $\{S_n\}$, where $S_n = 1 + \frac{1}{2} + \frac{1}{3} + \frac{1}{4} + \ldots$ is convergent

(d) The sequence $\{S_n\}$, where $S_n = 1 + \frac{1}{2} + \frac{1}{3} + \frac{1}{4} + \ldots$ is divergent

**Solution.** (a), (d)

We have $\{S_n\}$, where

$$S_n = 1, \frac{1}{2}, \frac{1}{3}, \frac{1}{4}, \ldots$$

$$\therefore \quad \lim_{n\to\infty} S_n = 0 \quad \Rightarrow \quad S_n \text{ is convergent.}$$

Next, we have $\{S_n\}$, where

$$S_n = 1 + \frac{1}{2} + \frac{1}{3} + \frac{1}{4} + \ldots$$

Let if possible, the sequence $\{S_n\}$ is convergent. Let us take $\varepsilon = \frac{1}{2}$, and $n = m$ and $p = m$ in Cauchy's General principle of convergence, so that

$$|S_{2m} - S_m| < \frac{1}{2}$$

But
$$S_{2m} - S_m = \frac{1}{m+1} + \frac{1}{m+2} + \ldots + \frac{1}{2m}$$
$$> \frac{1}{2m} + \frac{1}{2m} + \ldots + \frac{1}{2m} = \frac{m}{2m} = \frac{1}{2}$$

i.e.,
$$|S_{2m} - S_m| > \frac{1}{2}$$

which contradicts the Cauchy's General principle of convergence. Hence, $\{S_n\}$ is divergent.

**Example 18.** *Which of the following(s) is/are correct?*

(a) The series $\frac{1}{(\log 2)^p} + \frac{1}{(\log 3)^p} + \ldots + \frac{1}{(\log n)^p} + \ldots$ converges for $p > 0$

(b) The series $\frac{1}{(\log 2)^p} + \frac{1}{(\log 3)^p} + \ldots + \frac{1}{(\log n)^p} + \ldots$ diverges for $p > 0$

(c) The series $1 + \frac{1}{2!} + \frac{1}{3!} + \frac{1}{4!} + \ldots$ is convergent

(d) The series $1 + \frac{1}{2!} + \frac{1}{3!} + \frac{1}{4!} + \ldots$ is divergent

**Solution.** (b), (c)

We have for $p > 0$

$$\lim_{n\to\infty} \frac{(\log n)^p}{n} = 0 \quad \Rightarrow \quad (\log n)^p < n \;\forall\; n > 1$$

$$\Rightarrow \quad \frac{1}{(\log n)^p} > \frac{1}{n} \;\forall\; n > 1$$

Let us compare the given series with the divergent series

$$\frac{1}{2} + \frac{1}{3} + \frac{1}{4} + \ldots$$

Since, each term of the given series is greater than the corresponding term of the divergent series, therefore, the given series diverges.

Next, we have

$$\frac{1}{2!} = \frac{1}{2}$$
$$\frac{1}{3!} < \frac{1}{2^2}$$
$$\frac{1}{4!} < \frac{1}{2^3}$$
$$\ldots\ldots\ldots$$
$$\ldots\ldots\ldots$$
$$\frac{1}{n!} < \frac{1}{2^{n-1}}$$

$$\therefore \quad 1 + \frac{1}{2!} + \frac{1}{3!} + \frac{1}{4!} + \ldots + \frac{1}{n!} + \ldots < 1 + \frac{1}{2} + \frac{1}{2^2} + \ldots$$

Thus, each term of the given series after the second is less than the corresponding term of the convergent geometric series,

$$1 + \frac{1}{2} + \frac{1}{2^2} + \frac{1}{2^3} + \ldots$$

Hence, the given series is convergent.

**Example 19.** *Which of the following(s) is/are correct?*

(a) For $p > 0$, the series $\frac{1}{1^p} - \frac{1}{2^p} + \frac{1}{3^p} - \frac{1}{4^p} + \ldots$ is convergent

(b) The series $1 - \frac{1}{2^3} + \frac{1}{3^3} - \frac{1}{4^3} + \ldots$ is absolutely convergent

(c) The series $1 - \frac{1}{2} + \frac{1}{3} - \frac{1}{4} + \ldots$ is conditionally convergent

(d) None of the above

**Solution.** (a), (b), (c)

For $p > 0$. Let

$$u_n = \frac{1}{n^p} \quad \Rightarrow \quad u_{n+1} \le u_n \;\forall\; n$$

and
$$\lim_{n\to\infty} u_n = \lim_{n\to\infty} \frac{1}{n^p} = 0$$

Hence, by Leibnitz test

The series

$$\frac{1}{1^p} - \frac{1}{2^p} + \frac{1}{3^p} - \frac{1}{4^p} + \ldots$$

is convergent.

Next, the series

$$1 + \frac{1}{2^3} + \frac{1}{3^3} + \frac{1}{4^3} + \ldots = \Sigma \frac{1}{n^3}$$

is convergent as $p = 3 > 1$.

Hence, the given series

$$1 - \frac{1}{2^3} + \frac{1}{3^3} - \frac{1}{4^3} + \ldots$$

is absolutely convergent.

Next, the series

$$1-\frac{1}{2}+\frac{1}{3}-\frac{1}{4}+\ldots.$$

is convergent by Leibnitz test, but the series

$$1+\frac{1}{2}+\frac{1}{3}+\frac{1}{4}+\ldots.$$

obtained on taking every term with a positive sign is divergent.

Thus, the given series is conditionally convergent.

***Example 20.*** *The series*

$$x+\frac{x^2}{2!}+\frac{x^3}{3!}+\ldots$$

*is*

(a) convergent $\forall$ x

(b) divergent $\forall$ x

(c) conditionally convergent $\forall$ x

(d) absolutely convergent $\forall$ x

**Solution.** (a), (d)

Let $$u_n=\frac{x^n}{n!}$$

Now, $$\lim_{n\to\infty}\frac{|u_n|}{|u_{n+1}|}=\lim_{n\to\infty}\frac{n+1}{n}$$

$$=\infty \quad \text{except at } x=0$$

Hence, by ratio test, the series converges absolutely for all $x$ except possibly at zero. But for $x=0$, the series evidently converges absolutely. Hence, the given series is absolutely convergent $\forall$ x. Hence, convergent $\forall$ x.

# Exercise 1 (For Part 'B')

**Directions** (Q. Nos. 1-219) *All questions have only one correct option.*

**1.** The sequence $\left\{\frac{n}{n+1}\right\}$ is
(a) increasing sequence (b) decreasing sequence
(c) unbounded (d) None of these

**2.** The sequence $\{(-1)^n\}_{n=1}^{\infty}$ is
(a) bounded and convergent
(b) convergent and unbounded
(c) bounded and divergent
(d) divergent and unbounded

**3.** The series $\sum_{n=1}^{\infty}\left[\frac{(-1)^n}{(2n-1)}\right]$ is
(a) convergent (b) divergent
(c) unbounded (d) None of these

**4.** The radius of convergent of the series
$$\frac{1+0.2}{1}+\frac{(x+0.2)^2}{2}+\ldots+\frac{(x+0.2)^n}{2}+\ldots$$
(a) 1 (b) $\infty$
(c) zero (d) None of these

**5.** The radius of convergent of the series
$$1-\frac{x}{1}+\frac{x^2}{2!}-\frac{x^3}{3!}$$ is
(a) $\infty$ (b) zero
(c) 1 (d) None of these

**6.** The sequence $\left\{\frac{1}{n}\right\}$ is
(a) unbounded and convergent
(b) bounded and convergent
(c) bounded and divergent
(d) unbounded and divergent

**7.** The sequence $\left\{a+\frac{(-1)^n b}{n}\right\}$
(a) bounded (b) unbounded
(c) divergent (d) None of these

**8.** The series $\sum_{n=1}^{\infty}\frac{1}{\left(1+\frac{1}{n}\right)^{n^2}}$ is
(a) convergent (b) divergent
(c) oscillatory (d) None of these

**9.** If $p$ and $q$ are positive real numbers, the series $\frac{2^p}{1^q}+\frac{3^p}{2^q}+\frac{4^p}{3^q}+\ldots$ is convergent for
(a) $p<q-1$ (b) $p<q+1$
(c) $p\geq q-1$ (d) $p\geq q+1$

**10.** If a sequence of real number has a cluster points, then
(a) it is convergent
(b) it is divergent
(c) limit exist
(d) existence of limit not definite

**11.** Following inequality is false
(a) $\underline{\lim}\, x_n+\underline{\lim}\, y_n\leq \underline{\lim}\, x_n+\overline{\lim}\, y_n$
(b) $\underline{\lim}\, x_n+\underline{\lim}\, y_n\leq \underline{\lim}\,(x_n+y_n)$
(c) $\underline{\lim}\, x_n+\overline{\lim}\, y_n\leq \overline{\lim}\, x_n+\overline{\lim}\, y_n$
(d) $\underline{\lim}\, x_n+\overline{\lim}\, y_n\geq \overline{\lim}\, x_n+\overline{\lim}\, y_n$

**12.** The domain of convergence for $x-\frac{x^2}{2}+\frac{x^3}{3}-\frac{x^4}{4}+\ldots$ is
(a) $(-1, 1)$ (b) $(-1, 1]$
(c) $(-1, 2)$ (d) $[-1, 1)$

**13.** Let $<a_n>\to a$. Let for every positive integer $k$, $A_k$ be the set of all positive integers $n$ such that $|a_n-a|<\frac{1}{k}$. Then
(a) $A_k$ is finite for all $k$
(b) $A_k$ is finite for some $k$
(c) every $A_k$ contains all but finitely many positive integers
(d) $A_k$ contains all positive integers

**14.** If sequences $\{a_n\}_{n=1}^{\infty}$ and $\{b_n\}_{n=1}^{\infty}$ are convergent, then
(a) $\{a_n+b_n\}_{n=1}^{\infty}$ is always convergent
(b) $\{a_n+b_n\}_{n=1}^{\infty}$ is always divergent
(c) $\{a_n+b_n\}_{n=1}^{\infty}$ is sometimes divergent
(d) None of the above

**15.** Let $<a_n>$ be a sequence of real numbers such that liminf $(a_n)=0$ and limsup $(a_n)=1$. Then
(a) all the terms should lie between 0 and 1
(b) there must be infinitely many terms between 0 and 1
(c) there are only finitely many terms between $-1$ and 2
(d) there are only finitely many terms outside of $[0, 1]$

**16.** If $\forall\, x_n, y_n\in\mathbb{R}$, $x_n\leq y_n$, then
(a) $\underline{\lim}\; x_n\geq\underline{\lim}\; y_n$ (b) $\underline{\lim}\; x_n\leq\underline{\lim}\; y_n$
(c) $\overline{\lim}\; x_n\leq\overline{\lim}\; y_n$ (d) $\overline{\lim}\, x_n\leq\underline{\lim}\; y_n$

**17.** The sequence diverges to $+\infty$ iff
(a) $\underline{\lim}\, x_n=\overline{\lim}\, x_n=+\infty$ (b) $\underline{\lim}\; x_n\leq+\infty$
(c) $\overline{\lim}\; x_n\leq+\infty$ (d) $\underline{\lim}\, x_n=\overline{\lim}\; x_n<+\infty$

**18.** If $(a_n)_{n=1}^{\infty}$ is a sequence of real numbers satisfying $a_{n+1}^2 = 2a_n - 1$, then

(a) $\lim_{n\to\infty} a_n = 2$ (b) $\lim_{n\to\infty} a_n = 1$

(c) $\lim_{n\to\infty} a_n$ does not exists (d) $(a_n)_{n=1}^{\infty}$ oscillates finitely

**19.** If $f : N \to R$ is a sequence, what is $f(x)$ for each $x \in n$?

(a) $f(x)$ is a real number

(b) $f(x)$ is a natural number

(c) $f(x)$ is a complex number

(d) None of the above

**20.** Following statement is true

(a) $\underline{\lim}\ x_n \le \overline{\lim}\ x_n$ (b) $\overline{\lim}\ x_n \le \underline{\lim}\ x_n$

(c) $\underline{\lim}\ x_n \ge \lim x_n$ (d) $\overline{\lim}\ x_n \le \lim x_n$

**21.** If $\lim x_n = l$ exists, then

(a) $\underline{\lim}\ x_n = \overline{\lim}\ x_n = l$ (b) $\underline{\lim}\ x_n \ne \overline{\lim}\ x_n = l$

(c) $l = \underline{\lim}\ x_n \ne \overline{\lim}\ x_n$ (d) $\underline{\lim}\ x_n \le \overline{\lim}\ x_n \le l$

**22.** Let $a_n = \begin{cases} \dfrac{1}{n^2}, & \text{if } n \text{ is even} \\ \dfrac{1}{n}, & \text{if } n \text{ is odd} \end{cases}$

Then $\sum_{n=1}^{\infty} a_n$ is

(a) convergent (b) divergent

(c) oscillatory (d) None of these

**23.** What is the set of all the distinct elements of a sequence called?

(a) The domain set of the given sequence

(b) Element set of the given sequence

(c) Upper bound of a sequence

(d) The range set of the given sequence

**24.** Let $\{a_n\}_{n=0}^{\infty}$ and $\{b_n\}_{n=0}^{\infty}$ be two sequence such that $\{a_n\}_{n=0}^{\infty}$ and $\{a_nb_n\}_{n=0}^{\infty}$ converges respectively to $A$ and $AB$, then $\{b_n\}_{n=0}^{\infty}$ converges iff

(a) $A \ne 0$ (b) $A = 0$

(c) $B = 0$ (d) None of these

**25.** Let $a_n = \begin{cases} 1 + \dfrac{1}{n}, & n \text{ is even} \\ -1 - \dfrac{1}{n}, & n \text{ is odd} \end{cases}$

Then

(a) $\limsup_{n\to\infty} a_n = \liminf_{n\to\infty} a_n = 1$

(b) $\limsup_{n\to\infty} a_n = \liminf_{n\to\infty} a_n = -1$

(c) $\limsup_{n\to\infty} a_n = 1$, $\liminf_{n\to\infty} a_n = -1$

(d) $\limsup_{n\to\infty} a_n = -1$, $\liminf_{n\to\infty} a_n = 1$

**26.** The sequence {1, 0, 1, 0, 1, 0,....} is

(a) increasing sequence (b) decreasing sequence

(c) monotonic sequence (d) None of these

**27.** If $u_n = \sqrt{n+1} - \sqrt{n}$ and $v_n = \sqrt{n^4 + 1} - n^2$, then

(a) $\sum_{n=1}^{\infty} u_n$ converges but $\sum_{n=1}^{\infty} v_n$ diverges

(b) $\sum_{n=1}^{\infty} u_n$ diverges but $\sum_{n=1}^{\infty} v_n$ converges

(c) $\sum_{n=1}^{\infty} u_n$ and $\sum_{n=1}^{\infty} v_n$ both converges

(d) $\sum_{n=1}^{\infty} u_n$ and $\sum_{n=1}^{\infty} v_n$ both diverges

**28. Statement (A)** Every convergent sequence is bounded.

**Statement (B)** Every bounded sequence is convergent.

(a) A is true, B is false (b) B is true, A is false

(c) A and B both true (d) A and B both false

**29.** Let $\{a_n\}$ be a sequence of real numbers. Then $\lim_{n\to\infty} a_n$ exists if and only if

(a) $\lim_{n\to\infty} a_{2n}$ and $\lim_{n\to\infty} a_{2n+1}$ exists

(b) $\lim_{n\to\infty} a_{2n}$ and $\lim_{n\to\infty} a_{2n+2}$ exists

(c) $\lim_{n\to\infty} a_{2n}$ and $\lim_{n\to\infty} a_{2n+1}$ and $\lim_{n\to\infty} a_{3n}$ exists

(d) None of the above

**30.** If $\{a_n\}_{n=1}^{\infty}$ converges to $a$, for all $n$, $a \ge 0$, then $\{\sqrt{a_n}\}_{n=0}^{\infty}$ is

(a) converges to $\sqrt{a}$ (b) diverges to $\sqrt{a}$

(c) converges to a (d) diverges to a

**31.** If $\Sigma a_n$ be the alternative series and $\Sigma q_n$, $\Sigma p_n$ are series of negative and positive terms respectively if $\Sigma a_n$ is conditionally convergent, then

(a) $\Sigma p_n$ is convergent but $\Sigma q_n$ not

(b) $\Sigma p_n$ is divergent but $\Sigma q_n$ not

(c) $\Sigma p_n$ and $\Sigma q_n$ both are convergent

(d) $\Sigma p_n$ and $\Sigma q_n$ both are divergent

**32.** If $\{a_n\}_{n=1}^{\infty}$ is decreasing and bounded, then $\{a_n\}_{n=1}^{\infty}$ is

(a) convergent sequence

(b) divergent sequence

(c) non-cauchy sequence

(d) None of the above

**33.** Let $a_n$ = least power of 2 that divides $n$. Then $< a_n >$ is

(a) divergent to infinity

(b) bounded

(c) having a subsequence converging to 3

(d) convergent

**34.** Let sequence $\{a_n\}_{n=1}^{\infty}$ and $\{b_n\}_{n=1}^{\infty}$ converges to $A$ and $B$ respectively, then $\{a_n/b_n\}_{n=1}^{\infty}$ converges to $A/B$, if

(a) $b_n \ne 0$ for all $n$ and $B = 0$

(b) $b_n \ne$ for some $n$

(c) $b_n \ne 0$ for all $n$ and $B \ne 0$

(d) None of the above

35. If $< a_n >$ is decreasing sequence of positive number $\Sigma a_n$ converge, then $\lim_{n\to\infty} na_n$ is

(a) $\infty$ (b) 0
(c) 1 (d) may not exist

36. A series $\sum_{n=1}^{\infty} a_n$ converges, then sequence $\{a_n\}_{n=1}^{\infty}$ is

(a) diverges
(b) converges to zero
(c) converges to any number
(d) None of the above

37. The sequence $\left\{\frac{(-1)^n}{n}\right\}$ is

(a) bounded (b) decreasing
(c) increasing (d) None of these

38. The series $\sum_{n=1}^{\infty} (-1)^n$ is

(a) divergent (b) convergent
(c) unbounded (d) None of these

39. The series $1\cdot x + 1\cdot 2x^2 + 1\cdot 2\cdot 3x^3 + ... + n!\cdot x^n + ...$ is

(a) divergent everywhere except $x = 0$
(b) convergent everywhere except $x = 0$
(c) divergent for $x = 0$
(d) None of the above

40. The series $1 + 3 + 5 + 7 + ....$ is

(a) divergent (b) convergent
(c) unbounded (d) None of these

41. The series $2 + 4 + 6 + 8 + ....$ is

(a) divergent (b) convergent
(c) unbounded (d) None of these

42. The series $\frac{1}{1\cdot 3} + \frac{1}{2\cdot 4} + \frac{1}{3\cdot 5} + ...$ is

(a) convergent (b) divergent
(c) decreasing (d) None of these

43. The series $\sum_{n=1}^{\infty} \frac{n^2}{3^n}$ is

(a) divergent (b) convergent
(c) unbounded (d) None of these

44. The sequence $\left\{\frac{(-1)^n}{n}\right\}$ converges to

(a) Zero (b) 1
(c) 2 (d) None of these

45. The series $\sum_{n=1}^{\infty} (-1)^n \frac{x^n}{n}$, for $|x| > 1$ is

(a) convergent
(b) divergent
(c) oscillatory
(d) None of the above

46. A sequence $\{a_n\}$ may be defined by a recursion formula

(a) $\langle 1, \sqrt{2}, \sqrt{2\sqrt{2}}, ... \rangle$ (b) $< f_1, f_2, f_3, ... >$
(c) $a_{n+1} = \sqrt{2a_n}, a_1 = 1$ (d) $f : N \to R$

47. For real number $\alpha$, if $\sum_{n=1}^{\infty} a_n$ and $\sum_{n=1}^{\infty} b_n$ converges to $A$ and $B$ respectively, then $\sum_{n=1}^{\infty} (a_n + \alpha b_n)$

(a) converges to $A + \alpha B$ (b) diverges
(c) converges to $\alpha A + B$ (d) None of these

48. If $a_n = \frac{1}{n \log n}$, then

(a) $\Sigma a_n$ is convergent
(b) $< a_n >$ is convergent
(c) $\Sigma a_n$ is divergent as $< a_n >$ does not converges to 0
(d) $\Sigma a_n$ is divergent

49. Let $\{a_n\}_{n=1}^{\infty}$ be a sequence converges to 0 and $\{b_n\}_{n=1}^{\infty}$ be a sequence that is bounded, then $\{a_n b_n\}_{n=1}^{\infty}$ is a sequence that

(a) converges to one (b) converges to zero
(c) is divergent sequence (d) None of these

50. If $\{b_n\}_{n=1}^{\infty}$ is an increasing bounded sequence, then for the sequence $\{b_n\}_{n=1}^{\infty}$ is following statement is false

(a) $\{b_n\}_{n=1}^{\infty}$ is a convergent sequence
(b) $\{b_n\}_{n=1}^{\infty}$ is a divergent sequence
(c) $\{b_n\}_{n=1}^{\infty}$ is a monotone sequence
(d) $\{b_n\}_{n=1}^{\infty}$ is a Cauchy sequence

51. If $a_n = \begin{cases} \frac{1}{n} & \text{when } n \text{ is perfect square} \\ \frac{1}{n^2} & \text{when } n \text{ is not perfect square} \end{cases}$

then $\Sigma a_n$ is

(a) convergent
(b) divergent
(c) divergent as $\lim_{n\to\infty} na_n \neq 0$
(d) $\lim_{n\to\infty} na_n \neq 0$

52. If a sequence is not a Cauchy sequence, then it is a

(a) divergent sequence (b) convergent sequence
(c) bounded sequence (d) None of these

53. For infinite series $\sum_{n=1}^{\infty} a_n$ and $\sum_{n=1}^{\infty} b_n$, $b_n \geq 0$ for $n$, and there is a real number $N$, such that for $n \geq N \Rightarrow |a_n| \leq b_n$. If $\sum_{n=1}^{\infty} b_n$ converges, then

(a) $\sum_{n=1}^{\infty} b_n$ is absolutely convergent

(b) $\sum_{n=1}^{\infty} a_n$ is absolutely convergent

(c) $\sum_{n=1}^{\infty} a_n$ is absolutely divergent

(d) $\sum_{n=1}^{\infty} b_n$ is absolutely divergent

**54.** Let $\Sigma a_n$ be series of real number and $\Sigma p_n$ and $\Sigma q_n$ be the series of positive and negative terms of $\Sigma a_n$ respectively, then select the correct statement

(a) $\Sigma q_n$ may be convergent if $\Sigma a_n$ is conditionally convergent

(b) $\Sigma p_n$ or $\Sigma q_n$ is divergent then $\Sigma a_n$ is divergent

(c) $\Sigma a_n$ is absolutely convergent if $\Sigma P_n$ and $\Sigma q_n$ are convergent. But converse may be true

(d) $\Sigma a_n$ is absolutely convergent then $\Sigma p_n$ and $\Sigma q_n$ are convergent

**55.** If $\{a_n\}_{n=0}^{\infty}$ converges to A, then

(a) $\{|a_n|\}_{n=0}^{\infty}$ converges to A

(b) $\{|a_n|\}_{n=0}^{\infty}$ converges to $|A|$

(c) $\{|a_n|\}_{n=0}^{\infty}$ is divergent sequence

(d) None of the above

**56.** Let $b_n = 2 - \dfrac{(-1)^n}{n}$ and $a_n = b_n - b_{n+1}$, then the series $\Sigma a_n$

(a) converges to 2 (b) diverges to $+\infty$

(c) converges to 1 (d) oscillates

**57.** Which amongst the following expressions is not true?

(a) $\lim_{n\to\infty} \dfrac{3n+2}{n+1} = 1$

(b) $\lim_{n\to\infty} \dfrac{1+3+5+\ldots+(2n-1)}{n^2} = 1$

(c) $\lim_{n\to\infty} \dfrac{3+2\sqrt{n}}{\sqrt{n}} = 2$

(d) $\lim_{n\to\infty} \sqrt[n]{n} = 1$

**58.** The sequence $\left[\dfrac{\cos(n\pi/2)}{n}\right]_{n=1}^{\infty}$ is

(a) convergent to 0 (b) divergent

(c) convergent to 1 (d) None of these

**59.** If a sequence $\{a_n\}_{n=1}^{\infty}$ converges to a real number A, then $\{a_n\}_{n=1}^{\infty}$ is

(a) unbounded sequence

(b) bounded sequence

(c) divergent sequence

(d) None of the above

**60.** Let $a = \min\{x^2 + 2x + 3, x \in R\}$ and $b = \lim_{\theta\to\infty} \dfrac{1-\cos\theta}{\theta^2}$, then the value of $\sum_{r=0}^{n} a^r \cdot b^{n-r}$ is

(a) $\dfrac{2^{n+1}-1}{3(2^n)}$ (b) $\dfrac{2^{n+1}+1}{3(2^n)}$

(c) $\dfrac{4^{n+1}-1}{3(2^n)}$ (d) None of these

**61.** Let sequence $\{a_n\}_{n=1}^{\infty}$ converges to A and sequence $\{b_n\}_{n=1}^{\infty}$ converges to B, with $a_n \le b_n$ for all n, then

(a) $A \Delta B$ (b) $A = B$

(c) $A \ge B$ (d) None of these

**62.** The series $1 + \dfrac{x}{1^2} + \dfrac{x^2}{2^2} + \dfrac{x^3}{3^2} + \ldots$

(a) diverges for $|x| > 1$ (b) converges for $|x| < 1$

(c) diverges for $|x| = 1$ (d) None of these

**63.** The series $1 + x + x^2 + \ldots + x^n + \ldots$

(a) converges for $|x| < 1$

(b) diverges for $|x| > 1$

(c) converges for $|x| = 1$

(d) None of the above

**64.** If $b_n = \begin{cases} \dfrac{1}{\sqrt{n}}, & \text{if } n \text{ is odd} \\ \dfrac{1}{n}, & \text{if } n \text{ is even} \end{cases}$

then

(a) both $< b_n >$ and $\Sigma b_n$ are convergent

(b) both $< b_n >$ and $\Sigma b_n$ are divergent

(c) $< b_n >$ is convergent but $\Sigma b_n$ is not

(d) $\Sigma b_n$ is convergent but $< b_n >$ is not

**65.** Which amongst the following statements is not true?

(a) A sequence cannot converge to more than one limit

(b) Every convergent sequence is bounded

(c) Every bounded sequence is convergent

(d) Limit of a sequence is unique

**66.** Every Cauchy sequence of real numbers, if

(a) convergent (b) divergent

(c) limit does not exist (d) None of these

**67.** The series $\sum_{n=1}^{\infty} \left(\dfrac{1}{n} - \sin\dfrac{1}{n}\right)^a$ converges, if

(a) $a > \dfrac{1}{3}$ (b) $a < \dfrac{1}{3}$

(c) $a < \dfrac{1}{2}$ (d) $a > \dfrac{1}{2}$

**68.** The domain of convergence for $1 + x + x^2 + \ldots$ is

(a) $(-1, +1)$ (b) $[-1, +1]$

(c) $(-2, 2)$ (d) None of these

**69.** Let $\Sigma a_n$ be a convergent series of positive terms and let $\Sigma b_n$ be a divergent series of positive terms. Then

(a) the sequence $< a_n >$ is convergent and $< b_n >$ is not convergent

(b) the sequence $< a_n >$ converges to 0

(c) the sequence $< b_n >$ does not converge to 0

(d) the sequence $< b_n >$ diverges to $\infty$

**70.** A : Cauchy sequence is convergent.

B : Cauchy sequence is bounded.

(a) A and B both true (b) A is false

(c) B is false (d) A and B both false

**71.** A : Sequence $< x_n >$ is convergent.
B : Sequence $< x_n >$ is bounded.
(a) $A \Rightarrow B$ (b) $B \Rightarrow A$
(c) $A \Leftrightarrow B$ (d) None of these

**72.** Which of the following series is absolutely convergent?
(a) $\Sigma \frac{(-1)^n}{n}$ (b) $\Sigma \frac{1}{\sqrt{n}}$
(c) $\Sigma \frac{1}{\log(n+1)}$ (d) $\Sigma \frac{(-1)^n}{n^{3/2}}$

**73.** What will be the value of $\lim_{n\to\infty} \frac{2n^2+3}{3n^2+5n}$ ?
(a) $\frac{2}{3}$ (b) $\frac{3}{2}$
(c) $\frac{3}{5}$ (d) $\frac{5}{8}$

**74.** Let $\Sigma a_n$ be a convergent series of positive terms and let $\Sigma b_n$ be a divergent series of positive terms. Then
(a) the sequence $< a_n >$ is convergent and $< b_n >$ is not convergent
(b) the sequence $< a_n >$ converges to 0
(c) the sequence $< b_n >$ does not converge to 0
(d) the sequence $< b_n >$ diverges to $\infty$

**75.** Which amongst the following expresses the Cauchy's first theorem on limits?
(a) If $a_n \geq 0 \,\forall\, n$ and $\lim_{n\to\infty} a_n = l$, then $l \geq 0$
(b) If $\lim_{n\to\infty} a_n = l$, then $\lim_{n\to\infty} \frac{a_1+a_2+\ldots+a_n}{n} = l$
(c) If $\lim \frac{a_1+a_2+\ldots+a_n}{n} = l$, then $\lim_{n\to\infty} a_n = l$
(d) If $< a_n >$ and $< b_n >$ be two sequences such that $a_n \leq b_n \,\forall\, n$, then $\lim a_n \leq \lim b_n$

**76.** The series $\left(\frac{2^2}{1^2}-\frac{2}{1}\right)^{-1}+\left(\frac{3^3}{2^3}-\frac{3}{2}\right)^{-2}+\left(\frac{4^4}{3^4}-\frac{4}{3}\right)^{-3}+\ldots$ is
(a) convergent (b) divergent
(c) oscillating finitely (d) oscillating infinitely

**77.** If $\lim_{n\to\infty} a_n = l$, where $a_n > 0 \,\forall\, n$, then $(a_1 a_2 a_3 \ldots a_n)^{\frac{1}{n}} = l$.
Above theorem is known as
(a) Cauchy's first theorem on limits
(b) Cauchy's second theorem on limits
(c) Maclaurin's theorem
(d) Leibnitz theorem

**78.** For which real number '$t$' does the infinite series $\Sigma \frac{\sqrt{n+1}-\sqrt{n}}{n^t}$ converge
(a) $t > \frac{1}{3}$ (b) $t > \frac{1}{2}$
(c) $t > 1$ (d) $t > \frac{3}{2}$

**79.** The series $\Sigma \frac{1}{4}\{1+(-1)^{n+1}(2n+1)\}$ is
(a) convergent (b) divergent
(c) oscillating infinitely (d) oscillating finitely

**80.** If $a_n \geq 0 \,\forall\, n$ and $\lim_{n\to\infty} a_n = l$, then which of the following relation is correct?
(a) $l \geq 0$ (b) $l \leq 0$
(c) $l = 1$ (d) $l = \infty$

**81.** $\lim_{n\to\infty}\left(\frac{1}{n+1}+\frac{1}{n+2}+\ldots+\frac{1}{2n}\right)$ is equal to
(a) 0 (b) 1
(c) 2 (d) $\log_e 2$

**82.** What is true for the sequence $< a_n >$ given by $a_n = \frac{n+1}{n}$ ?
(a) It oscillates (b) It diverges
(c) It converges to 1 (d) Converges to $\frac{3}{2}$

**83.** The $n$th term of the sequence $\left\{2, \frac{-3}{2}, \frac{4}{3}, \frac{-5}{4}, \ldots\right\}$ is
(a) $1+\frac{1}{n}$ (b) $(-1)^{n-1}\left(1-\frac{1}{n}\right)$
(c) $(-1)^{n-1}\left(1+\frac{1}{n}\right)$ (d) None of these

**84.** The series $1^3+2^3+3^3+\ldots$ is
(a) divergent (b) convergent
(c) bounded (d) None of these

**85. Assertion (A)** $\Sigma \frac{n}{n+1}$ is not convergent.
**Reason (R)** If the series $\Sigma \frac{n}{n+1}$ converges, then $\lim_{n\to\infty} \frac{n}{n+1} = 0$
(a) Both (A) and (R) are true and (R) is correct reason of (A).
(b) Both (A) and (R) are true but (R) is not correct reason of (A).
(c) (A) is true but (R) is false.
(d) (A) is false but (R) is true.

**86.** If $a_n > 0$ for all $n$, then $\lim_{n\to\infty} |a_n|^{1/n}$ is equal to
(a) $\lim_{n\to\infty}\left(\frac{a_n}{a_{n+1}}\right)$
(b) $\lim_{n\to\infty}\left(\frac{a_n}{a_{n+1}+1}\right)$
(c) $\lim_{n\to\infty}\left(\frac{a_n}{a_{n-1}+1}\right)$
(d) $\lim_{n\to\infty}\left(\frac{a_n}{a_{n-1}}\right)$ provided the later limit exist

**87.** A real number $P$ is a cluster point of a sequence $< a_n >$ if for any $\varepsilon > 0$,
(a) $a_n \in ]P-\varepsilon, P+\varepsilon[$ for infinitely many values of $n$
(b) $a_n \in [P-\varepsilon, P+\varepsilon]$ for infinitely many values of $n$
(c) $a_n \in ]P-\varepsilon, P+\varepsilon[$ for unique value of $n$
(d) $a_n \in [P-\varepsilon, P+\varepsilon]$ for unique value of $n$

**88.** If for a given series $\Sigma u_n$, $\dfrac{u_n}{u_{n+1}} = \alpha + \dfrac{\beta}{n} + 0\left(\dfrac{1}{n^p}\right)$, $p > 1$; $\alpha, \beta \in R$. Then
(a) $\Sigma u_n$ converges, if $\beta > 1 \forall \alpha$
(b) $\Sigma u_n$ diverges to $\infty$, if $\alpha > 1$ for any $\beta$
(c) $\Sigma u_n$ converges, if $\alpha \geq 1$ but $\beta > 1$
(d) $\Sigma u_n$ converges, if $\alpha > 1$ for any $\beta$

**89.** Let $\Sigma u_n$ be a series of positive terms such that $\lim\limits_{n\to\infty} \left\{ n\left(\dfrac{u_n}{u_{n+1}} - 1\right) \right\} = l$.

Then, (i) if $l > 1$, the series converges;
(ii) if $l < 1$, the series diverges;
(iii) if $l = 1$, the series may either converge or diverge, and therefore the test fails.

This theorem is known as
(a) d'Alembert's test (b) Cauchy test
(c) Raabe's test (d) Kummer's test

**90.** Let $A_1 \geq A_2 \geq ... \geq A_k \geq 0$, then $\lim\limits_{n\to\infty} [A_1^n + A_2^n + ... + A_k^n]^{\frac{1}{n}}$ is equal to
(a) 1 (b) 0
(c) $A_t$ (d) $A_k$

**91.** If $\dfrac{a_n}{a_{n+1}} > \dfrac{b_n}{b_{n+1}} (a_n > 0,\ b_n > 0)$, then
(a) $\Sigma\, a_n$ and $\Sigma\, b_n$ diverge or converge together
(b) $\Sigma\, a_n$ diverges $\Rightarrow \Sigma\, b_n$ converges
(c) $\Sigma\, b_n$ diverges $\Rightarrow \Sigma\, a_n$ diverges
(d) $\Sigma\, b_n$ converges $\Rightarrow \Sigma\, a_n$ converges

**92.** Bolzano-Weierstrass Theorem is
(a) every bounded sequence has a limit point
(b) the set of limit points of a bounded sequence is bounded
(c) an unbounded sequence may or may not have a limit point
(d) None of the above

**93.** If $\lim\limits_{n\to\infty} \dfrac{S_n}{n} = l \neq 0$, then $< S_n >$
(a) is not bounded
(b) may or may not be bounded
(c) convergent
(d) may or may not be convergent

**94.** There is given a sequence $< S_n >$ of partial sums of the series $\dfrac{1-2^n}{1-2} = 2^n - 1$, where
(a) $S_n = 1 - 2^n$ (b) $S_n = \left(\dfrac{1-2^n}{1-2}\right)^n$
(c) $S_n = 2^n - 1$ (d) None of these

**95.** The sequence $< S_n >$, where $S_n = 1 + \dfrac{1}{3} + \dfrac{1}{5} + ... + \dfrac{1}{2n-1}$ is
(a) convergent
(b) monotonically decreasing
(c) not cauchy
(d) None of the above

**96.** If for any $\varepsilon > 0$, there exists a positive integer $m$ such that $|a_n - a_m| < \varepsilon$ whenever $n \geq m$. The sequence $< a_n >$ is called
(a) monotonic sequence (b) convergent sequence
(c) cauchy sequence (d) divergent sequence

**97.** The limit superior and limit inferior of $< (-1)^n >$ is respectively given by
(a) $-1, -1$ (b) $1, -1$
(c) $0, -1$ (d) $1, -2$

**98.** A sequence $< a_n >$ converges to $l$ concludes
(a) some subsequence of $< a_n >$ converge to $l$
(b) every subsequence of $< a_n >$ converges to $l$
(c) no subsequence of $< a_n >$ converges to $l$
(d) None of the above

**99.** The limit superior and limit inferior of $\left\langle \dfrac{(-1)^n}{n^2} \right\rangle$ are respectively equal to
(a) $-1, -1$ (b) $1, 0$
(c) $0, 0$ (d) $1, 1$

**100.** A real number $l$ is a limit point of a sequence $< a_n >$ if and only if there exists
(a) $k$ such that $k \leq a_n \ \forall\ n \in N$
(b) $k$ such that $k \geq a_n \ \forall\ n \in N$
(c) a subsequence of $< a_n >$ converging to $l$
(d) None of the above

**101.** If $S_n = \dfrac{1}{n+1} + \dfrac{1}{n+2} + ... + \dfrac{1}{n+n}$, then $< S_n >$ is
(a) monotonic increasing sequence
(b) monotonic decreasing sequence
(c) divergent sequence
(d) None of the above

**102.** If $n^{\frac{1}{n}} \to 1$ as $n \to \infty$, then the series $\sum\limits_{n=1}^{\infty} \left(n^{\frac{1}{n}} - 1\right)^n$
(a) converges
(b) diverges
(c) neither converges nor diverges
(d) the test fails

**103.** Which one of the following is incorrect?
(a) every bounded sequence has a convergent subsequence

(b) every sequence has a monotonic subsequence
(c) every sequence has a limit point
(d) every sequence has a countable number of terms

**104.** Which of the following inequalities will be used in showing the series $\sum_{n=1}^{\infty} e^{-n^2}$ converges?

(a) $e^n < x$, if $n = 0$ (b) $e^n < x$, if $n > 0$
(c) $e^n > x$, if $n > 0$ (d) None of these

**105.** Let $< a_n >$ and $< b_n >$ be two sequences of real numbers such that $a_n = b_n - b_{n+1}$ for $n = 1, 2, 3, 4, \ldots$ if $\Sigma b_n$ is convergent, then which is always true?

(a) $\Sigma a_n$ may not be convergent
(b) $\Sigma a_n$ is convergent and $\Sigma a_n = b_1$
(c) $\Sigma a_n$ is convergent and $\Sigma a_n = 0$
(d) $\Sigma a_n$ is convergent and $\Sigma a_n = a_1 - b_1$

**106.**

| A (sequence) | B (converges to ) |
|---|---|
| (α) $\langle r^n \rangle$ if $\lvert r\rvert < 1$ | (1) $+\infty$ |
| (β) $\left\langle 1 + \frac{1}{n} \right\rangle$ | (2) c |
| (γ) $\langle c, c, c, \ldots \rangle$ | (3) 1 |
| (δ) $\langle r^n \rangle$ if $r > 1$ | (4) 0 |

**Codes**

| | α | β | γ | δ |
|---|---|---|---|---|
| (a) | 1 | 2 | 3 | 4 |
| (b) | 2 | 3 | 4 | 1 |
| (c) | 3 | 2 | 1 | 4 |
| (d) | 4 | 3 | 2 | 1 |

**107.** If the sequence $< a_n >$ be defined by $a_1 = 1$ and $a_{n+1} = \sqrt{6 + a_n}$ for $n > 1$, then $\lim_{n\to\infty} a_n$ is equal to

(a) 1 (b) 2
(c) 3 (d) 4

**108.** Which of the following series is alternating series?

(a) $1 + 2 + 1 + 2 + 1 + \ldots$
(b) $1 + \frac{2}{3} + \frac{3}{2} + \frac{4}{5} + \frac{5}{4} + \ldots$
(c) $1 - \frac{1}{2} + \frac{1}{3} - \frac{1}{4} + \ldots$
(d) $1 - \frac{2}{3} - \frac{3}{2} + \frac{4}{5} + \frac{5}{4} + \ldots$

**109.** If $< a_n >$ be a sequence such that $\lim_{x\to\infty} (a_{n+1} - a_n) = l$, then the sequence $< b_n >$ where $b_n = \frac{a_n}{n}$

(a) converges to 0
(b) may or may not be converge
(c) converges to $l$
(d) bounded but may not be converge

**110.** Let $\Sigma u_n$ be a series of positive terms and let $\lim_{n\to\infty} u_n^{1/n} = l$, then which among the following does not express the condition for the Cauchy's $n$th root test?

(a) If $l < 1$, $\Sigma u_n$ converges
(b) If $l > 1$, $\Sigma u_n$ diverges
(c) If $l = 1$, the test fails and the series may either converge or diverge
(d) If $l = 0$, the series neither converges nor diverges

**111.** The inf and sup of the set $\left\{\frac{3n+2}{2n+1} : n \in N\right\}$ are respectively

(a) $\frac{2}{3}, \frac{5}{3}$ (b) $\frac{3}{2}, \frac{5}{3}$
(c) $-\frac{3}{2}, \frac{5}{2}$ (d) $\frac{2}{3}, \frac{5}{2}$

**112.**

| A (sequence) | B (limit points) |
|---|---|
| (α) $< (-1)^n \left(1 + \frac{1}{n}\right) >$ | (1) 0 |
| (β) $\langle n^2 \rangle$ | (2) no |
| (γ) $\langle 1, 2, 1, 4, 1, 6, \ldots \rangle$ | (3) 1 |
| (δ) $< \frac{1}{n} >$ | (4) 1 and −1 |

**Codes**

| | α | β | γ | δ |
|---|---|---|---|---|
| (a) | 4 | 2 | 3 | 1 |
| (b) | 1 | 3 | 2 | 4 |
| (c) | 1 | 2 | 3 | 4 |
| (d) | 4 | 3 | 2 | 1 |

**113.** If $A_i = \frac{x - a_i}{\lvert x - a_i \rvert}$; $i = 1, 2, \ldots, n$ and $a_1 < a_2 < \ldots < a_n$, then $\lim_{x\to a_m} (A_1 A_2 \ldots A_n)$, $1 \le m \le n$

(a) is equal to $(-1)^m$ (b) is equal to $(-1)^{m+1}$
(c) is equal to $(-1)^{m-1}$ (d) does not exist

**114.** A conditionally converges series is a series which is

(a) absolutely convergent
(b) convergent but not absolutely convergent
(c) absolutely divergent
(d) None of the above

**115.** Select the incorrect

(a) $\lim\sup (a_n + b_n) \le \lim\sup a_n + \lim\sup b_n$; $< a_n >$ and $< b_n >$ are bounded
(b) $\lim\inf (a_n + b_n) \ge \lim\inf a_n + \lim\inf b_n$; $< a_n >$ and $< b_n >$ are bounded
(c) $\lim\sup (a_n)^{1/n} \ge \lim\sup \frac{a_{n+1}}{a_n}$, $a_n > 0$
(d) $\lim\inf (a_n)^{1/n} \ge \lim\inf \frac{a_{n+1}}{a_n}$, $a_n > 0$

**116.**

| A (sequence) | B (name) |
|---|---|
| (α) $< \frac{n}{n+1} >$ | (1) monotonically increasing |
| (β) $< 1, 2, 3, \ldots >$ | (2) monotonically decreasing |
| (γ) $< 1, -1, -2, \ldots >$ | (3) Cauchy |

**Codes**

| | α | β | γ |
|---|---|---|---|
| (a) | 1 | 2 | 3 |
| (b) | 2 | 3 | 1 |
| (c) | 1 and 3 | 1 | 2 |
| (d) | 3 | 2 | 1 |

**117.** If $f(x) = \begin{cases} \sin\left(\frac{1}{x}\right), & x \neq 0 \\ 0, & x = 0 \end{cases}$ $x \in [-1, 1]$

then select the incorrect

(a) There exists a sequence $< a_n >$ s.t. $< a_n > \to 0$ and $< f(a_n) > \to 0$

(b) There exists a sequence $< a_n >$ s.t. $< a_n > \to 0$ and $< f(a_n) > \to -1$

(c) There exists a sequence $< a_n >$ s.t. $< a_n > \to 0$ and $< f(a_n) > \to 1/2$

(d) None of the above

**118.** $\Sigma u_n$ is a series of positive terms. If $S_n = u_1 + u_2 + \ldots + u_n$, then

(a) $S_n - S_{n-1} = u_n$ (b) $S_n = S_{n-1}$

(c) $S_n - S_{n-1} = 0$ (d) $S_n + S_{n-1} = 0$

**119.** The set of limit points of a bounded sequence is

(a) unbounded

(b) bounded

(c) not necessarily bounded

(d) neither bounded nor unbounded

**120.** If $< a_n >$ is bounded and $b_n \to 0$, choose the appropriate conclusion from the following options

(a) $(a_n \pm b_n) \to 0$ (b) $\frac{a_n}{b_n} \to 0$

(c) $a_n b_n \to 0$ (d) $a_n \to b_n$

**121.** Which amongst the following statements is not true?

(a) If $\lim_{n \to \infty} a_n = l$, then $l$ is the only limit point of $< a_n >$

(b) If $l$ is the only limit point of $< a_n >$, then $\lim_{n \to \infty} a_n = l$

(c) Every bounded sequence has a limit point

(d) The set of limit points of a bounded sequence is bounded

**122.** What is true about the geometric series $1 + r + r^2 + \ldots (r > 0)$?

(a) It diverges if $0 < r < 1$ and converges if $r \geq 1$

(b) It converges if $0 < r < 1$ and diverges if $r \geq 1$

(c) It does not converge

(d) It does not diverge

**123. Assertion (A)** $\lim_{n \to \infty} \frac{(1+y)^n}{n!} = 0$ for all $y$.

**Reason (R)** If $< a_n >$ be a sequence such that $\lim_{n \to \infty} \frac{a_{n+1}}{a_n} = l$, where $|l| < 1$, then $\lim_{n \to \infty} a_n = 0$

(a) Both (A) and (R) are true and (R) is correct reason of (A).

(b) Both (A) and (R) are true and (R) is not correct reason of (A).

(c) (A) is true but (R) is false.

(d) (A) is false but (R) is true.

**124.** Which of the following series is divergent?

(a) $\Sigma \frac{1}{n} \sin \frac{1}{n}$ (b) $\Sigma \frac{1}{n^2} \sin \frac{1}{n}$

(c) $\Sigma \frac{1}{\sqrt{n} + \sqrt{n+1}}$ (d) $\Sigma \left( \frac{n}{n^2 + 3} \right)$

**125.** The series $1 + \frac{3}{1!} + \frac{5}{3!} + \frac{7}{4!} + \ldots$ is

(a) convergent (b) divergent

(c) oscillatory (d) None of these

**126.** The series $\frac{1}{3^p} + \frac{1}{5^p} + \frac{1}{7^p} + \frac{1}{9^p} + \ldots$ converges, if

(a) $p < 1$ (b) $p = 1$

(c) $p > 1$ (d) None of these

**127.** The series $\Sigma \frac{1}{n^p}$ is

(a) convergent (b) divergent

(c) oscillatory (d) None of these

**128.** The series $1 + r + r^2 + r^3 + \ldots$ is oscillatory, if

(a) $r < 1$ (b) $r > 1$ (c) $r = 1$ (d) $r = -1$

**129.** The series $\Sigma \frac{1}{n(\log x)^p}$ is divergent, if

(a) $p > 1$ (b) $p < 1$ (c) $p \leq 1$ (d) $p = 1$

**130.** Which of the following statement is true?

(a) For any positive number ε, there is a natural number $n$, such that $\frac{1}{n} < \varepsilon$.

(b) Between any two real number there is no irrational number.

(c) Convergent sequence is not bounded.

(d) None of the above is true.

**131.** The series $x + \frac{2^2 x^2}{2!} + \frac{3^3 x^3}{3!} + \frac{4^4 x^4}{4!} + \ldots$ is convergent, if

(a) $0 < x < 1/e$ (b) $x > 1/e$

(c) $2/e < x < 3/e$ (d) $3/e < x < 4/e$

**132.** The $\frac{3}{5} x^4 + \frac{8}{10} x^6 + \frac{15}{17} x^8 + \ldots + \frac{n^2 - 1}{n^2 + 1} x^{2n} + \ldots$ is

(a) convergent, if $x^2 \geq 1$ and divergent, if $x^2 < 1$

(b) convergent, if $x^2 \leq 1$ and divergent, if $x^2 > 1$

(c) convergent, if $x^2 < 1$ and divergent, if $x^2 \geq 1$

(d) convergent, if $x^2 > 1$ and divergent, if $x^2 \leq 1$

**133.** $\lim_{n\to\infty}\left[\frac{n}{n^2}+\frac{n}{(n^2+1^2)}+\frac{n}{(n^2+2^2)}+\ldots\right]$ is equal to

(a) $-\pi/4$ (b) 0
(c) $\pi/4$ (d) $\pi/3$

**134.** If $S_n$ denoted the sum of $n$ term of the series $1+\frac{1}{\sqrt{2}}+\frac{1}{\sqrt{3}}+\ldots+\frac{1}{\sqrt{n}}+\ldots$, then

(a) $S_n > n^2$ (b) $S_n > n$
(c) $S_n > \sqrt{n}$ (d) $S_n = \infty$

**135.** Let $\Sigma u_n$ be a series of positive terms. Given that $\Sigma u_n$ is convergent and also $\lim_{n\to\infty}\frac{u_n+1}{u_n}$ exists, then the said limit is

(a) necessarily equal to $-1$
(b) necessarily greater than $-1$
(c) may be equal to 1 or less than 1
(d) necessarily less than 1

**136.** The series $\frac{2}{1^2}+\frac{3}{2^2}+\frac{4}{3^2}+\frac{5}{4^2}+\ldots$ is

(a) conditional convergent (b) absolutely convergent
(c) divergent (d) None of these

**137.** The series $\Sigma\frac{4\cdot7\ldots(3n+1)}{1\cdot2\ldots n}x^n$ is convergent, if

(a) $|x|<1$ (b) $|x|<1/3$
(c) $|x|<\frac{1}{4}$ (d) $|x|<\frac{1}{2}$

**138.** The series $\Sigma\frac{n!2^n}{n^n}$ is

(a) convergent (b) divergent
(c) conditional convergent (d) None of these

**139.** If a sequence $<a_n^2>$ converges to $a^2$, then the sequence $<a_n>$ converges to

(a) a (b) $a^2$
(c) $\sqrt{a}$ (d) None of these

**140.** $\lim_{n\to\infty}\frac{1}{n}(1+2^{1/2}+3^{1/3}+\ldots+n^{1/n})$ is

(a) 1 (b) 2
(c) 0 (d) None of these

**141.** Let $\Sigma a_n$ be a convergent series of positive terms and let $\Sigma b_n$ be a divergent series of positive terms. Then,

(a) the sequence $<a_n>$ is convergent and $<b_n>$ is not convergent
(b) the sequence $<a_n>$ converges to 0
(c) the sequence $<b_n>$ does not converge to 0
(d) the sequence $<b_n>$ diverges to $\infty$

**142.** Which of the following is absolutely convergent?

(a) $\Sigma\frac{(-1)^n}{n}$ (b) $\Sigma\frac{1}{\sqrt{n}}$
(c) $\Sigma\frac{1}{\log(n+1)}$ (d) $\Sigma\frac{(-1)^n}{n^{3/2}}$

**143.** Consider the sequence $a_n = \sin n$

(a) the sequence is convergent as $n\to\infty$
(b) the sequence is divergent to $\infty$ as $n\to\infty$
(c) $\liminf_{n\to\infty}\sin(n)=0$
(d) $\lim_{n\to\infty}\sin(n)=-1$

**144.** The series $\sum_{n=1}^{\infty}\frac{2n+1}{(n^2+n)^2}$

(a) converges to 1
(b) converges to a number>1
(c) diverges to $\infty$
(d) has an oscillating sequences of partial sums

**145.** Let $a_n$ = least power of 2 that divides $n$. For instance, $a_1=0, a_2=1, a_3=0, a_4=2$. Then, the sequence $(a_n)$ is

(a) diverging to infinity
(b) bounded
(c) having a subsequence converging to 3
(d) convergent

**146.** Which of the following statement is/are correct?

(a) Every bounded sequence $a_n$ has atleast one limit point.
(b) Every bounded sequence has no limit point.
(c) The set of limit points of a bounded sequence $a_n$ is unbounded.
(d) None of the above

**147.** The series $x-\frac{x^2}{2}+\frac{x^3}{3}-\frac{x^4}{4}+\ldots$ is convergent for

(a) all real value of x (b) $|x|<1$ only
(c) $|x|\le 1$ (d) $-1<x\le 1$

**148.** For a positive term series $\Sigma a_n$, the ratio test states that

(a) the series convergent, if $\lim_{n\to\infty}\frac{a_{n+1}}{a_n}>1$
(b) the series converges, if $\lim_{n\to\infty}\frac{a_{n+1}}{a_n}<1$
(c) the series diverges, if $\lim_{n\to\infty}\frac{a_{n+1}}{a_n}=1$
(d) None of the above

**149.** Match list I with list II and select the correct answer

| | List I | | List II |
|---|---|---|---|
| A. | $\sum_1^{\infty}(-1)^{n-1}\frac{n^2}{n+1!}$ | 1. | Diverges |
| B. | $\sum_1^{\infty}\frac{n^n}{n!}$ | 2. | Converges |
| C. | $\sum_1^{\infty}\frac{(-1)^n\log n}{n^2}$ | 3. | Converges conditionally |
| D. | $\sum_1^{\infty}\frac{(-1)^n}{\log n}$ | 4. | Converges absolutely |

| | A | B | C | D |
|---|---|---|---|---|
| (a) | 2 | 4 | 1 | 3 |
| (b) | 4 | 3 | 2 | 1 |
| (c) | 4 | 1 | 2 | 3 |
| (d) | 3 | 1 | 4 | 2 |

**150.** The series $1+\frac{2}{6}+\frac{2\cdot 5}{6\cdot 12}+\frac{2\cdot 5\cdot 8}{6\cdot 12\cdot 18}+\ldots$ is

(a) divergent (b) convergent
(c) oscillates finitely (d) oscillates infinitely

**151.** The series whose $n$th term is $t_n=\sqrt{n^2+1}-n$

(a) converges to the sum 0
(b) converges to the sum 1/2
(c) converges to the sum 1
(d) diverges

**152.** Which one of the following tests does not give absolute convergence of a series?

(a) Root test (b) Comparision test
(c) Ratio test (d) Leibnitz test

**153.** If $u_n=\sqrt{n+1}-\sqrt{n}$, $v_n=\sqrt{n^4+1}-n^2$, then

(a) $\sum_{n=1}^{\infty} u_n$ converges but $\sum_{n=1}^{\infty} v_n$ diverges
(b) $\sum_{n=1}^{\infty} u_n$ diverges but $\sum_{n=1}^{\infty} u_n$ converges
(c) $\sum_{n=1}^{\infty} u_n$ and $\sum_{n=1}^{\infty} v_n$ both converges
(d) $\sum_{n=1}^{\infty} u_n$ and $\sum_{n=1}^{\infty} v_n$ both diverges

**154.** The series $\frac{x}{1\cdot 2}+\frac{x^2}{2\cdot 3}+\frac{x^3}{3\cdot 4}+\ldots$ is convergent, if

(a) $|x|\leq 1$ (b) $|x|\leq 2$
(c) $|x|>2$ (d) $|x|\geq 4$

**155.** If $\sum_{n=1}^{\infty} a_n$ converges, then $\lim_{n\to\infty}\frac{a_n-1}{n\sqrt{n}}$ is equal to

(a) 0 (b) 1
(c) $-1$ (d) $\frac{-1}{n\sqrt{n}}$

**156.** If $S_1=\sum_{n=1}^{\infty}\frac{(n!)^n}{(n^n)^2}$ and $S_2=\sum_{n=1}^{\infty}\frac{1}{(2n-1)(2n+1)}$, then which one of the following statement is correct?

(a) Both $S_1$ and $S_2$ are convergent
(b) $S_1$ is divergent and $S_2$ is convergent
(c) $S_1$ is convergent and $S_2$ is divergent
(d) Both $S_1$ and $S_2$ are divergent

**157.** If $<x_n>$ and $<y_n>$ are sequences of real numbers, which of the following is/are true?

(a) $\lim_n \text{Sup}(x_n+y_n)\leq \lim_n \text{Sup}\, x_n+\lim_n \text{Sup}\, y_n$
(b) $\lim_n \text{Sup}(x_n+y_n)\geq \lim_n \text{Sup}\, x_n+\lim_n \text{Sup}\, y_n$
(c) $\lim_n \text{Inf}(x_n+y_n)\leq \lim_n \text{Inf}\, x_n+\lim_n \text{Inf}\, y_n$
(d) None of the above

**158.** If $\frac{u_n}{u_{n+1}}>\frac{v_n}{v_{n+1}}$ $(u_n>0, v_n>0)$, then

(a) $\Sigma u_n$ and $\Sigma v_n$ diverge or converge together
(b) $\Sigma u_n$ diverges $\Rightarrow \Sigma v_n$ diverges
(c) $\Sigma v_n$ diverges $\Rightarrow \Sigma u_n$ diverges
(d) $\Sigma v_n$ converges $\Rightarrow \Sigma u_n$ converges

**159.** If $u_n>0$, $\forall n$, then $\lim_{n\to\infty}(u_n)^{1/n}$ is equal to

(a) $\lim_{n\to\infty}\left(\frac{u_n}{u_{n+1}}\right)$
(b) $\lim_{n\to\infty}\left(\frac{u_n}{u_{n+1}+1}\right)$
(c) $\lim_{n\to\infty}\left(\frac{u_n}{u_{n-1}+1}\right)$
(d) $\lim_{n\to\infty}\left(\frac{u_n}{u_{n-1}}\right)$ provided the later limit exists

**160.** The series $\left(\frac{2^2}{1^2}-\frac{2}{1}\right)^{-1}+\left(\frac{3^3}{2^3}-\frac{3}{2}\right)^{-2}+\left(\frac{4^4}{3^4}-\frac{4}{3}\right)^{-3}+\ldots$ is

(a) convergent (b) divergent
(c) oscillating finitely (d) oscillating infinitely

**161.** If $x_1=4$ and $x_{n+1}=\sqrt{7+x_n}$, then the sequence $\{x_n\}$ converges to the positive root of the equation

(a) $x^2-x+7=0$ (b) $x^2+x+7=0$
(c) $x^2-x-7=0$ (d) $x^2+x-7=0$

**162.** The sequence $\{x_n\}$, where $x_n=n^{1/n}$, converge to

(a) 0 (b) 1
(c) 1/2 (d) None of these

**163.** The sequence $\{x_n\}$, where $x_n=\left(1+\frac{1}{3n}\right)^{2n}$, converge to

(a) $e^{2/3}$ (b) $e^{3/2}$
(c) $e^{1/3}$ (d) None of these

**164.** The sequence $\{x_n\}$, where $x_n=\frac{2n+5}{3n+1}$ converge to

(a) 0 (b) 1
(c) 2/3 (d) None of these

**165.** The sequence $\{x_n\}$, where $x_n=\left(1+\frac{1}{n+1}\right)^n$ converge to

(a) e (b) 0
(c) 1 (d) None of these

**166.** If $x_1=4$ and $x_{n+1}=\sqrt{2+x_n}$, $\forall n\in N$, then the sequence $\{x_n\}$ converge to

(a) 1 (b) 2
(c) $\sqrt{2}$ (d) None of these

**167.** If $x_1=1$ and $x_{n+1}=\sqrt{3x_n}$, $\forall n\in N$, then the sequence $\{x_n\}$ converge to

(a) 1 (b) $\sqrt{3}$
(c) 3 (d) None of these

**168.** For which real number $m$ does the infinite series $\sum \frac{\sqrt{(n+1)}+\sqrt{n}}{n^m}$ converge

(a) $m>\frac{1}{3}$ (b) $m>\frac{1}{2}$

(c) $m>1$ (d) $m>\frac{3}{2}$

**169.** The series $\Sigma\left(1+\frac{1}{n}\right)^{-n^2}$ is

(a) convergent (b) divergent

(c) oscillatory (d) None of these

**170.** The series $\Sigma 3^{-n+(-1)^n/n}$ is

(a) convergent (b) divergent

(c) oscillatory (d) None of these

**171.** For what value of $x$ the infinite series $\sum \frac{\left(1+\frac{1}{n}\right)^{n^2}}{x^n}$ converge?

(a) $x<e$ (b) $x>e$ (c) $x=e$ (d) $x=1$

**172.** For what value of $x$ the infinite series $\sum \frac{n!\,x^n}{n^n}$ diverges?

(a) $x<e$ (b) $x>e$

(c) $x=\sqrt{e}$ (d) None of these

**173.** If $a_1, a_2, a_3, \ldots$ be a sequence of non-zero integers satisfying

I. $|a_n|<|a_{n+1}|, \forall n$

II. $a_n$ divides $a_{n+1}$, $\forall n$ and

III. every integer is a divisor of some $a_n$, then $\frac{1}{a_1}+\frac{1}{a_2}+\frac{1}{a_3}+\ldots$ is

(a) absolutely convergent and its sum is rational number

(b) absolutely convergent and its sum is an irrational number

(c) absolutely convergent and its sum is positive number

(d) None of the above

**174.** The series $\sum\left(\sin\frac{1}{n}+\frac{1}{n^2}\right)$ is

(a) convergent (b) divergent

(c) oscillatory (d) None of these

**175.** The series $\sum \frac{1}{\sqrt{n}+\sqrt{n+1}+\sqrt{n+2}+\sqrt{n+3}}$ is

(a) convergent (b) divergent

(c) oscillatory (d) None of these

**176.** The series $\sum \frac{1}{n^p+n^{-p}}$ converges, if

(a) $|p|>1$ (b) $p=1$

(c) $|p|<1$ (d) None of these

**177.** The series $\sum \frac{1}{n \log n (\log n)^p}$ converges, if

(a) $p>1$ (b) $p=1$

(c) $p\le 1$ (d) $p<1$

**178.** For what value of $x$ the infinite series $\sum [\sqrt[3]{n^3+1}-n]\,x^n$ converges, if

(a) $|x|>1$ (b) $|x|\le 1$

(c) $x=e$ (d) $x>e$

**179.** If $\{x_n\}$ is a sequence of real number, then match list I with list II and select the correct answer using codes given below the lists

**List I** (sequences)

(A) $x_1=4, x_{n+1}=\sqrt{12+x_n}$ (B) $x_n=\left(1+\frac{1}{3n}\right)^n$

(C) $x_n=\frac{3n+2}{5n+6}$ (D) $x_1=4,\ x_{n+1}=\sqrt{3x_n}$

**List II** (Limit of sequences)

(1) 3/5 (2) 3

(3) 4 (4) $e^{1/3}$

**Codes**

| | A | B | C | D |
|---|---|---|---|---|
| (a) | 3 | 4 | 1 | 2 |
| (b) | 2 | 4 | 3 | 1 |
| (c) | 3 | 1 | 2 | 4 |
| (d) | 4 | 3 | 1 | 2 |

**180.** Let $x_n=1+\frac{1}{2}+\ldots+\frac{1}{n}-\log n$, then

(a) $\{x_n\}$ is increasing sequence and $x_n\ge 0, \forall n\in N$

(b) $\{x_n\}$ is decreasing sequence and $x_n\le 0, \forall n\in N$

(c) $\{x_n\}$ is increasing sequence and $x_n\le 0, \forall n\in N$

(d) $\{x_n\}$ is decreasing sequence and $x_n\ge 0, \forall n\in N$

**181.** The sequence $\{x_n\}$, where

$$x_n=1+\frac{1}{2}+\frac{1}{2^2}+\ldots+\frac{1}{2^{n-1}},$$

(a) increasing but not bounded

(b) increasing and bounded

(c) decreasing but not bounded

(d) decreasing and bounded

**182.** The sequence $\{x_n\}$, where $x_n=\frac{1}{n+1}+\frac{1}{n+2}+\ldots+\frac{1}{2n}$ is

(a) increasing but not bounded

(b) increasing and bounded

(c) decreasing and bounded

(d) decreasing but not bounded

**183.** The sequence $\{x_n\}$, where

$$x_n=1+\frac{1}{1!}+\frac{1}{2!}+\frac{1}{3!}+\ldots+\frac{1}{n-1!}$$ is

(a) increasing and bounded

(b) decreasing and bounded

(c) increasing but not bounded

(d) decreasing but not bounded

**184.** The sequence $\{x_n\}$, where $x_n = \frac{1}{n} + \frac{1}{n+1} + \frac{1}{n+2} + \ldots + \frac{1}{2n-1}$ is

(a) increasing but not bounded
(b) decreasing and bounded
(c) increasing and bounded
(d) decreasing but not bounded

**185.** The sequence $\{x_n\}$, where $x_n = \left(1+\frac{1}{n}\right)^{2n}$ converge to

(a) e (b) $e^{1/2}$
(c) $e^2$ (d) None of these

**186.** The sequence $\{x_n\}$, where $x_n = \left(1+\frac{1}{2n}\right)^{n}$ converge to

(a) e (b) $e^{1/2}$
(c) $e^2$ (d) None of these

**187.** If $x_1 = 1$ and $x_{n+1} = \sqrt{20 + x_n}, \forall x \in N$, then the sequence $\{x_n\}$ converge to

(a) 3 (b) 4
(c) 5 (d) None of these

**188.** If $\{x_n\}$ and $\{y_n\}$ are two convergent sequence such that $x_n < y_n, \forall n \in N$, then

(a) $\lim_{n\to\infty} x_n < \lim_{n\to\infty} y_n$ (b) $\lim_{n\to\infty} x_n \le \lim_{n\to\infty} y_n$
(c) $\lim_{n\to\infty} x_n = \lim_{n\to\infty} y_n$ (d) None of these

**189.** If $\{x_n\}$ is a strictly increasing sequence which converge to 3, then for all $n \in N$,

(a) $x_n < 3$ (b) $x_n \le 3$
(c) $x_n > 3$ (d) $x_n \ge 3$

**190.** If $x_1 = a > 1$ and $x_{n+1} = \sqrt{b + x_n}$ for all $n \in N$, then sequence $\{x_n\}$ converges to the positive root of the equation

(a) $x^2 - x - b = 0$ (b) $x^2 + x + b = 0$
(c) $x^2 - x + b = 0$ (d) $x^2 + x - b = 0$

**191.** If a sequence $\{x_n\}$ converge to x and $x_n > 0$ for all $n \in N$, then

(a) $x > 0$ (b) $x \ge 0$
(c) $x \le 0$ (d) None of these

**192.** If $\{x_n\}$ is a sequence of real numbers, then match list I with list II and select the correct answer using codes given below the lists

**List I** (sequences)

(A) $x_n = \left(1+\frac{1}{n}\right)^{n-1}$ (B) $x_1 = 1, x_{n+1} = \sqrt{6 + x_n}$
(C) $x_n = n^{1/n}$ (D) $x_1 = 1, x_{n+1} = \sqrt{2x_n}$

**List II** (limit of sequences)

(1) 2 (2) 1
(3) 4 (4) 3

**Codes**

| | A | B | C | D |
|---|---|---|---|---|
| (a) | 3 | 1 | 2 | 4 |
| (b) | 3 | 4 | 2 | 1 |
| (c) | 2 | 4 | 1 | 3 |
| (d) | 4 | 2 | 3 | 1 |

**193.** If $\{x_n\}$ is a decreasing sequence which converges to 2, then for all $n \in N$,

(a) $x_n \ge 2$ (b) $x_n > 2$
(c) $x_n < 2$ (d) $x_n \le 2$

**194.** $\lim_{n\to\infty} (2^n + 3^n)^{1/n}$ is equal to

(a) 2 (b) 3
(c) 6 (d) None of these

**195.** $\lim_{n\to\infty}\left(\frac{2}{1}\cdot\frac{3}{2}\cdot\frac{4}{3}\cdots\frac{n+1}{n}\right)^{1/n}$ is equal to

(a) 0 (b) 1
(c) e (d) None of these

**196.** $\lim_{n\to\infty}\left(\frac{1}{n!}\right)^{1/n}$ is equal to

(a) 0 (b) 1
(c) e (d) None of these

**197.** If $\lim_{n\to\infty} a^n = 0$, then

(a) $|a| < 1$ (b) $|a| \le 1$
(c) $|a| > 1$ (d) $|a| \ge 1$

**198.** $\lim_{n\to\infty} \frac{1}{n}\left(1 + \frac{1}{2} + \frac{1}{3} + \ldots + \frac{1}{n}\right)$ is equal to

(a) 1 (b) 0
(c) e (d) None of these

**199.** If $x_n = \sum_{t=0}^{\infty} r^t$ with $|r| < 1$, then the sequence $\{x_n\}$ converges to

(a) 0 (b) 1
(c) $\frac{1}{1-r}$ (d) $\frac{1}{r-1}$

**200.** $\lim_{n\to\infty} \frac{1}{n}\left(\frac{2}{1} + \frac{3}{2} + \frac{4}{3} + \ldots + \frac{n+1}{n}\right)$ is equal to

(a) 0 (b) 1
(c) e (d) None of these

**201.** $\lim_{n\to\infty} \frac{e + e^{1/2} + e^{1/3} + \ldots + e^{1/n}}{n}$ is equal to

(a) 0 (b) 1
(c) e (d) None of these

**202.** $\lim_{n\to\infty} \frac{1}{n}[(m+1)(m+2)\ldots(m+n)]^{1/n}$, where $m$ is a fixed positive integer is equal to

(a) 1 (b) e
(c) 1/e (d) 4/e

**203.** $\lim_{n\to\infty} \frac{1}{n}(1+2^{1/2}+3^{1/3}+...+n^{1/n})$ is equal to

(a) 0 (b) 1
(c) e (d) None of these

**204.** For the sequence $\{x_n\}$, where $x_n = 1+\frac{1}{2}+\frac{1}{3}+...+\frac{1}{n}$, consider the following statements

(I) $\{x_n\}$ is a Cauchy sequence.
(II) $\{x_n\}$ is not convergent.
(III) $\{x_n\}$ is not bounded.

Select the correct answer using the codes given below

(a) (II) and (III) (b) (I) and (III)
(c) (I) and (II) (d) (I), (II) and (III)

**205.** Let $\{x_n\}$ be a sequence of positive terms, such that $\lim_{n\to\infty} \frac{x_{n+1}}{x_n}$ does not exist, then

(a) $\lim_{n\to\infty} x_n^{1/n}$ exists
(b) $\lim_{n\to\infty} x_n^{1/n}$ may exist
(c) $\lim_{n\to\infty} x_n^{1/n}$ does not exists
(d) $\lim_{n\to\infty} x_n^{1/n}$ exist infinitely

**206.** Consider the following statement

(a) every convergent sequence is a Cauchy sequence
(b) every Cauchy sequence of rational number is convergent
(c) every Cauchy sequence of real number is convergent
(d) every convergent sequence is bounded

**207.** For the sequence $\{x_n\}$, where $x_n = 1+\frac{1}{3}+\frac{1}{5}+...+\frac{1}{2n-1}$, consider the following statement

(I) $\{x_n\}$ is a Cauchy sequence
(II) $\{x_n\}$ is a convergent sequence
(III) $\{x_n\}$ is a bounded sequence

Select the correct answer using the codes given below

(a) (II) and (III) (b) (I) and (III)
(c) (I) and (II) (d) None of these

**208.** $\lim_{n\to\infty} \frac{x_1+x_2+...+x_n}{n} = \lim_{n\to\infty} x_n$ only of

(a) $\{x_n\}$ is a convergent sequence of positive terms
(b) $\{x_n\}$ is a convergent sequence of non-negative terms
(c) $\{x_n\}$ is a convergent sequence of negative terms
(d) $\{x_n\}$ is a convergent sequence

**209.** A sequence contains a convergent subsequence, if it is

(a) bounded above (b) bounded below
(c) bounded (d) monotone

**210.** $\lim_{n\to\infty} x_n = 0$, if

(a) $\left|\lim_{n\to\infty} \frac{x_n+1}{x_n}\right| < 1$
(b) $\lim_{n\to\infty} \frac{x_n+1}{x_n} < 1$
(c) $\left|\lim_{n\to\infty} \frac{x_n+1}{x_n}\right| < 1$ and $x_n > 0, \forall n \in N$
(d) $\lim_{n\to\infty} \frac{x_n+1}{x_n} < 1$ and $x_n > 0, \forall n \in N$

**211.** $\lim_{n\to\infty} x_n^{1/n} = \lim_{n\to\infty} \frac{x_{n+1}}{x_n}$, if

(a) $\lim_{n\to\infty} \frac{x_{n+1}}{x_n}$ exists finitely and $x_n > 0, \forall n \in N$
(b) $\lim_{n\to\infty} \frac{x_{n+1}}{x_n}$ exists finitely or infinitely and $x_n > 0, \forall n \in N$
(c) $\lim_{n\to\infty} \frac{x_{n+1}}{x_n}$ exists finitely and $x_n$ need not be positive
(d) $\lim_{n\to\infty} \frac{x_{n+1}}{x_n}$ exists finitely or infinitely and $x_n$ need not be positive

**212.** A Cauchy sequence is convergent, if it is a

(a) sequence of real numbers
(b) sequence of rational numbers
(c) sequence of irrational numbers
(d) bounded sequence of rational numbers

**213.** A convergent sequence is a Cauchy sequence, if it is a

(a) sequence of real numbers
(b) sequence of rational numbers
(c) sequence of irrational numbers
(d) None of the above

**214.** Consider the following statement

(I) Every cauchy sequence contains convergent subsequence
(II) If a subsequence of a cauchy sequence converges to a real numbers, $l$, then the original sequence also converge to $l$.
(III) Every monotone sequence contains a convergent subsequence.
(IV) Every bounded sequence contains a convergent subsequence

Select the correct answer using the codes given below

(a) (II), (III) and (IV)
(b) (I), (III) and (IV)
(c) (I), (II) and (IV)
(d) (I), (II) and (III)

**215.** The series $\sum_{n=1}^{\infty}(-1)^n n$ is

(a) bounded (b) convergent
(c) divergent (d) None of these

**216.** Which of the following series is divergent?

(a) $\Sigma \sin\frac{1}{n}$ (b) $\Sigma \sin\frac{1}{n^2}$

(c) $\frac{1}{\sqrt{n}}\tan\frac{1}{n}$ (d) None of these

**217.** If $\Sigma u_n$ is a positive term series such that $\lim_{n\to\infty} u_n \neq 0$, then $\Sigma u_n$

(a) converges (b) diverges

(c) oscillatory (d) None of these

**218.** If $p > 0$, then $\lim_{n\to\infty} p^{1/n}$ is

(a) 0 (b) 1 (c) 2 (d) e

**219.** For any sequence $< a_n >, < b_n >$ of real numbers, we always have

(a) $\lim_{n\to\infty} \text{Sup} < a_n + b_n > = \lim_{n\to\infty} \text{Sup}\, a_n + \lim_{n\to\infty} \text{Sup}\, b_n$

(b) $\lim_{n\to\infty} \text{Sup} < a_n + b_n > \leq \lim_{n\to\infty} \text{Sup}\, a_n + \lim_{n\to\infty} \text{Sup}\, b_n$

(c) $\lim_{n\to\infty} \text{Sup} < a_n + b_n > > \lim_{n\to\infty} \text{Sup}\, a_n + \lim_{n\to\infty} \text{Sup}\, b_n$

(d) There is no relation between $\lim_{n\to\infty} \text{Sup} < a_n + b_n >$, $\lim_{n\to\infty} \text{Sup}\, a_n$ and $\lim_{n\to\infty} \text{Sup}\, b_n$

# Exercise 2 (For Part 'C')

**Directions** (Q. Nos. 1-40) *Questions may have one or more than one correct option.*

**1.** Let the sequences $< S_n >$ and $< t_n >$ are not convergent. Then,

(a) the sequence $< S_n + t_n >$ may or may not be convergent

(b) the sequence $< S_n + t_n >$ is never convergent

(c) the sequence $< S_n \cdot t_n >$ may or may not be convergent

(d) the sequence $< S_n \cdot t_n >$ is never convergent

**2.** Let the sequences $< S_n >$ and $< t_n >$ are divergent. Then,

(a) the sequence $< S_n + t_n >$ may or may not be convergent

(b) the sequence $< S_n + t_n >$ is always divergent

(c) the sequence $< S_n \cdot t_n >$ may or may not be convergent

(d) the sequence $< S_n \cdot t_n >$ is always divergent

**3.** Which of the following(s) is/are correct?

(a) $\lim_{n\to\infty}\left(\frac{1}{1\cdot 2\cdot 3\ldots n}\right)^{1/n} = 0$

(b) $\lim_{n\to\infty}\left(\frac{1}{1\cdot 2\cdot 3\ldots n}\right)^{1/n}$ does not exists

(c) $\lim_{n\to\infty}\frac{1}{n}\left[2+\left(\frac{3}{2}\right)^2+\left(\frac{4}{3}\right)^3+\ldots+\left(\frac{n+1}{n}\right)^n\right] = e$

(d) $\lim_{n\to\infty}\frac{1}{n}\left[2+\left(\frac{3}{2}\right)^2+\left(\frac{4}{3}\right)^3+\ldots+\left(\frac{n+1}{n}\right)^n\right]$ does not exists

**4.** Which of the following sequence(s) is/are convergent?

(a) $\left\langle\left(\frac{1}{2}\right)^n\right\rangle$ (b) $\left\langle\left(\frac{1}{3}\right)^n\right\rangle$

(c) $\left\langle\left(\frac{1}{r}\right)^n\right\rangle, r < 1$ (d) All of these

**5.** Let $< S_n >$ and $< t_n >$ be two sequences such that $\lim_{n\to\infty}\frac{S_{n+1}}{S_n} = 0.750, S_n \neq 0, \forall\, n$ and $\lim_{n\to\infty}\frac{t_{n+1}}{t_n} = 1.750, t_n \neq 0, \forall\, n.$

Then,

(a) $\lim_{n\to\infty} S_n = 0$ (b) $\lim_{n\to\infty} S_n = \infty$

(c) $\lim_{n\to\infty} t_n = 0$ (d) $\lim_{n\to\infty} t_n = \infty$

**6.** Which of the following(s) is/are correct?

(a) $\lim_{n\to\infty}\frac{3^n}{n} = 0$ (b) $\lim_{n\to\infty}\frac{(0.05)^n}{n} = 0$

(c) $\lim_{n\to\infty}\frac{3^n}{n} = \infty$ (d) $\lim_{n\to\infty}\frac{(0.05)^n}{n} = \infty$

**7.** Which of the following(s) is/are correct?

(a) $\lim_{n\to\infty}\frac{2^n}{n!} = 0$

(b) $\lim_{n\to\infty}\frac{(0.30)^n}{n!} = 0$

(c) $\lim_{n\to\infty}\frac{2^n}{n!} = \infty$

(d) $\lim_{n\to\infty}\frac{(0.30)^n}{n!} = \infty$

**8.** The subsequence(s) of the sequence $< \sin\left(\frac{1}{n}\right) >$ is/are

(a) $< \sin\left(\frac{1}{n!}\right) >$ (b) $< \sin\left(\frac{1}{n^2}\right) >$

(c) $< \sin\left(\frac{1}{2n+1}\right) >$ (d) $< \sin\left(\frac{1}{2n}\right) >$

**9.** Which of the following(s) is/are correct?

(a) The sequence $< \frac{1}{n} >$ has exactly one limit point

(b) The sequence $< \frac{1}{n} >$ has infinitely limit point

(c) The sequence $< 1+(-1)^n >$ has exactly two limit point

(d) The sequence $< (-1)^n >$ has exactly only one limit point

**10.** Sequence $a_n = \sin\frac{n\pi}{2} + \frac{(-1)^n}{n}$, $n \in \mathbb{N}$ has

(a) $\underline{\lim}\, a_n = -1$ (b) $\overline{\lim}\, a_n = 1$

(c) $\underline{\lim}\, a_n = 1$ (d) $\overline{\lim}\, a_n = 2$

**11.** Given sequence $\left\{\frac{1}{2^n}\right\}$

(a) an increasing sequence

(b) a decreasing sequence

(c) the $n$th term is $\frac{1}{2^n}$

(d) the $(n+1)$th term is $\frac{1}{2^{n+1}}$

**12.** Which of the following(s) is/are correct?

(a) A sequence can have atmost one limit

(b) A sequence can have more than one limit

(c) A sequence can have distinct limit

(d) Every sequence is bounded

**13.** Which of the following(s) is/are correct?

(a) Every Cauchy sequence is bounded

(b) Every Cauchy sequence is unbounded

(c) Every Cauchy sequence is convergent

(d) Every Cauchy sequence is divergent

**14.** Given a sequence $\left\{\frac{n}{n+1}\right\}$

(a) a convergent sequence

(b) a divergent sequence

(c) an increasing sequence

(d) a bounded sequence

**15.** The series $\sum_{n=1}^{\infty} \frac{n!}{n^n}$ is

(a) convergent (b) divergent

(c) unbounded (d) None of these

**16.** Which of the following(s) is/are correct?

(a) Every Cauchy sequence is bounded

(b) Every Cauchy sequence is not bounded

(c) Every Cauchy sequence is unbounded

(d) Some Cauchy sequence are bounded

**17.** Given sequence $\left\{\frac{1}{n}\right\}$

(a) the $n$th term is $\frac{1}{n}$

(b) the sequence is bounded below

(c) the sequence is bounded above

(d) the sequence is a bounded sequence

**18.** Which of the following(s) is/are bounded sequence?

(a) $S_n = \{(-n)^n\}, \forall\, n$ (b) $S_n = \left\{\left(1+\frac{1}{n}\right)^n\right\}, \forall\, n$

(c) $S_n = \{1\}, \forall\, n$ (d) $S_n = \{1+(-1)^n\}, \forall\, n$

**19.** Which of the following statement(s) is/are correct?

(a) Every convergent sequence is bounded

(b) A sequence cannot converge to more than one limit

(c) Every convergent sequence is bounded and has a unique limit

(d) All of the above

**20.** Which of the following(s) is/are correct?

(a) A limit point of the range set of a sequence is also a limit point of the sequence

(b) A limit point of a sequence is also a limit point of the range set of the sequence

(c) Both (a) and (b) are correct

(d) Exactly only one of (a) and (b) is correct

**21.** Which of the following(s) is/are correct?

(a) The sequence $S_n = \{1+(-1)^n\}$ has limit point 0 and 2

(b) The sequence $S_n = \{1+(-1)^n\}$ has countable number of limit point

(c) The range set of sequence $S_n = \{1+(-1)^n\}$ has limit point 0 and 2

(d) The range set of sequence $S_n = \{1+(-1)^n\}$ has not limit point

**22.** If $\{a_n\}$ is a sequence, then

(a) $\underline{\lim}\,(-a_n) = \underline{\lim}\, a_n$ (b) $\underline{\lim}\,(-a_n) = -\overline{\lim}\, a_n$

(c) $\overline{\lim}\,(-a_n) = \overline{\lim}\, a_n$ (d) $\overline{\lim}\,(-a_n) = -\underline{\lim}\, a_n$

**23.** If $\{a_n\}$ is a sequence, where $a_n = \sin\frac{n\pi}{3}$, $\forall\, n \in \mathbb{N}$.

Then,

(a) $\underline{\lim}\, a_n = -\frac{\sqrt{3}}{2}$ (b) $\underline{\lim}\, a_n = \frac{\sqrt{3}}{2}$

(c) $\overline{\lim}\, a_n = \frac{\sqrt{3}}{2}$ (d) $\overline{\lim}\, a_n = \frac{3}{2}$

**24.** Which of the following(s) is/are correct?

(a) Every bounded sequence with unique limit point is convergent

(b) A bounded sequence $\{a_n\}$ converges to a real number $a$ iff

$$\underline{\lim}\, a_n = \overline{\lim}\, a_n$$

(c) Exactly only one of (a) and (b)

(d) Both (a) and (b)

**25.** If $\{a_n\}$ and $\{b_n\}$ are two sequences such that $\lim_{n\to\infty} a_n = a$ and $\lim_{n\to\infty} b_n = b$. Then,

(a) $\lim_{n\to\infty}(a_n \pm b_n) = \lim_{n\to\infty} a_n \pm \lim_{n\to\infty} b_n$

(b) $\lim_{n\to\infty}(a_n b_n) = (\lim_{n\to\infty} a_n)(\lim_{n\to\infty} b_n)$

(c) $\lim_{n\to\infty}\left(\frac{a_n}{b_n}\right) = \frac{(\lim_{n\to\infty} a_n)}{(\lim_{n\to\infty} b_n)}$, if $b \neq 0$, $b_n \neq 0$, $\forall\ n$

(d) None of the above

**26.** If $\{a_n\}$ and $\{b_n\}$ are bounded sequences, then

(a) $\underline{\lim}\, a_n + \underline{\lim}\, b_n \le \underline{\lim}\,(a_n + b_n)$

(b) $\underline{\lim}\,(a_n + b_n) \le \underline{\lim}\, a_n + \overline{\lim}\,(b_n)$

(c) $\underline{\lim}\, a_n + \overline{\lim}\, b_n \le \overline{\lim}\,(a_n + b_n)$

(d) $\overline{\lim}\,(a_n + b_n) \le \overline{\lim}\, a_n + \overline{\lim}\, b_n$

**27.** If $\{a_n\}$ and $\{b_n\}$ are bounded sequences, then

(a) $\underline{\lim}\, a_n - \overline{\lim}\, b_n \le \underline{\lim}\,(a_n - b_n)$

(b) $\underline{\lim}\,(a_n - b_n) \le \underline{\lim}\, a_n - \underline{\lim}\,(b_n)$
or $\le \overline{\lim}\, a_n - \overline{\lim}\, b_n$

(c) $\left.\begin{array}{l}\underline{\lim}\, a_n - \underline{\lim}\, b_n \\ \text{or } \overline{\lim}\, a_n - \overline{\lim}\, b_n\end{array}\right\} \le \overline{\lim}(a_n - b_n)$

(d) $\overline{\lim}\,(a_n - b_n) \le \overline{\lim}\, a_n + \underline{\lim}\, b_n$

**28.** If $\{a_n\}$ and $\{b_n\}$ are two bounded sequence of non-negative real numbers. Then,

(a) $(\underline{\lim}\, a_n)(\underline{\lim}\, b_n) \le \underline{\lim}\,(a_n b_n)$

(b) $\underline{\lim}\,(a_n b_n) \le (\underline{\lim}\, a_n)(\overline{\lim}\, b_n)$

(c) $(\underline{\lim}\, a_n)(\overline{\lim}\, b_n) \le \overline{\lim}\,(a_n b_n)$

(d) $\overline{\lim}\,(a_n b_n) \le (\overline{\lim}\, a_n)(\overline{\lim}\, b_n)$

**29.** If $\{a_n\}$ is a bounded sequence such that $a_n > 0$, $\forall\ n \in 1\mathbb{N}$, then

(a) $\underline{\lim}\left(\frac{1}{a_n}\right) = \frac{1}{\overline{\lim}\, a_n}$, if $\overline{\lim}\, a_n > 0$

(b) $\overline{\lim}\left(\frac{1}{a_n}\right) = \frac{1}{\underline{\lim}\, a_n}$, if $\underline{\lim}\, a_n > 0$

(c) $\underline{\lim}\left(\frac{1}{a_n}\right) = \frac{1}{\overline{\lim}\, a_n}$, if $\overline{\lim}\, a_n < 0$

(d) $\overline{\lim}\left(\frac{1}{a_n}\right) = \frac{1}{\underline{\lim}\, a_n}$, if $\underline{\lim}\, a_n < 0$

**30.** If $\{a_n\}$ and $\{b_n\}$ are bounded sequence, $a_n \ge 0$, $b_n > 0$, $\forall\ n \in \mathbb{N}$. Then,

(a) $\underline{\lim}\left(\frac{a_n}{b_n}\right) \ge \frac{\underline{\lim}\, a_n}{\overline{\lim}\, a_n}$, if $\overline{\lim}\, b_n > 0$

(b) $\underline{\lim}\left(\frac{a_n}{b_n}\right) \le \frac{\underline{\lim}\, a_n}{\overline{\lim}\, a_n}$, if $\overline{\lim}\, b_n > 0$

(c) $\overline{\lim}\left(\frac{a_n}{b_n}\right) \le \frac{\overline{\lim}\, a_n}{\underline{\lim}\, b_n}$, if $\underline{\lim}\, b_n > 0$

(d) $\overline{\lim}\left(\frac{a_n}{b_n}\right) \ge \frac{\overline{\lim}\, a_n}{\underline{\lim}\, b_n}$, if $\underline{\lim}\, b_n > 0$

**31.** Given that $\lim_{n\to\infty} a_n = a$ and $\lim_{n\to\infty} b_n = b$ and $\{S_n\}$ and $\{T_n\}$ are two sequences such that $S_n = \max(a_n, b_n)$ and $T_n = \min\{a_n, b_n\}$, then

(a) $\{S_n\}$ is convergent
(b) $\{T_n\}$ is convergent
(c) $\lim_{n\to\infty} S_n = \max(a, b)$
(d) $\lim_{n\to\infty} T_n = \min(a, b)$

**32.** The sequence $\{S_n\}$ defined by the recursion relation $S_{n+1} = \sqrt{3S_n}$, $S_1 = 1$

(a) converge to 3
(b) monotonic increasing sequence
(c) monotonic decreasing sequence
(d) bounded sequence

**33.** The sequence $\{a_n\}$ defined by

$$a_{n+1} = \frac{1}{2}\left(a_n + \frac{9}{a_n}\right),\ n \ge 1,\ a_1 > 0.\ \text{Then,}$$

(a) converges to 3
(b) monotonic increasing sequence, if $a_n \le 3, \forall\ n$
(c) monotonic decreasing sequence, if $a_n \ge 3, \forall\ n$
(d) bounded sequence

**34.** Which of the following(s) is/are correct?

(a) The infinite series $\Sigma \frac{1}{n^{1+\frac{1}{n}}}$ is convergent

(b) The infinite series $\Sigma\{n^3 + 1)^{1/3} - n\}$ is convergent

(c) (a) is convergent while (b) is divergent

(d) (a) is divergent while (b) is convergent

**35.** Which of the following(s) is/are correct?

(a) The infinite series $\Sigma\left(1 + \frac{1}{\sqrt{n}}\right)^{-n^{3/2}}$ is convergent

(b) The infinite series $\Sigma \frac{n^2 - 1}{n^2 + 1} x^n$, $x > 0$ is convergent, if $x < 1$

(c) The infinite series $\Sigma \frac{n^2 - 1}{n^2 + 1} x^n$, $x > 0$ is divergent, if $x \ge 1$

(d) None of the above

**36.** The series

$$\Sigma \frac{3 \cdot 6 \cdot 9 \ldots 3n}{7 \cdot 10 \cdot 13 \ldots (3n + 4)} x^n,\ x > 0$$

is

(a) converges, if $x > 1$
(b) diverges, if $x \le 1$
(c) converges, if $x \le 1$
(d) diverges, if $x > 1$

**37.** Which of the following(s) is/are correct?

(a) The series $\Sigma \frac{(n^3 + 1)^{1/3} - n}{\log n}$ is converges

(b) The series $1 - \frac{1}{3 \cdot 2^2} + \frac{1}{5 \cdot 3^2} - \frac{1}{7 \cdot 4^2} + \ldots$ is converges

(c) (a) is converges but (b) is diverges

(d) (a) is diverges but (b) is converges

**38.** According to Riemann's theorem by an appropriate rearrangement of terms, a conditionally convergent series $\Sigma u_n$ can be made

(a) to converge to any number
(b) to diverge to $+\infty$
(c) to diverge to $-\infty$
(d) to oscillate finitely

**39.** Which of the following(s) is/are correct?

(a) $\Sigma u_n$ is a convergent series $\Rightarrow \Sigma \dfrac{u_n}{1+u_n}$ is also convergent series
(b) $\Sigma u_n^2$ is convergent $\Rightarrow \Sigma \dfrac{u_n}{n}$ is convergent
(c) $\Sigma u_n$ is convergent $\Rightarrow \Sigma u_n^2$ is convergent
(d) None of the above

**40.** Which of the following series is convergent?

(a) $\dfrac{1}{2}+\dfrac{\sqrt{2}}{5}+\dfrac{\sqrt{3}}{10}+\ldots+\dfrac{\sqrt{n}}{n^2+1}+\ldots$ is convergent
(b) $\Sigma \dfrac{n(n+4)}{(n+2)(n+3)(n+5)}$ is convergent
(c) (a) is convergent but (b) is divergent
(d) (a) is divergent but (b) is convergent

# Answers

## Exercise 1

**1.** (a) **2.** (c) **3.** (a) **4.** (a) **5.** (a) **6.** (b) **7.** (a) **8.** (a) **9.** (a) **10.** (d)
**11.** (c) **12.** (b) **13.** (d) **14.** (a) **15.** (b) **16.** (b) **17.** (a) **18.** (b) **19.** (a) **20.** (a)
**21.** (a) **22.** (b) **23.** (d) **24.** (a) **25.** (c) **26.** (d) **27.** (b) **28.** (a) **29.** (c) **30.** (a)
**31.** (d) **32.** (a) **33.** (b) **34.** (c) **35.** (b) **36.** (b) **37.** (a) **38.** (a) **39.** (a) **40.** (a)
**41.** (a) **42.** (a) **43.** (b) **44.** (a) **45.** (b) **46.** (c) **47.** (c) **48.** (d) **49.** (b) **50.** (b)
**51.** (a) **52.** (a) **53.** (b) **54.** (d) **55.** (b) **56.** (c) **57.** (a) **58.** (a) **59.** (b) **60.** (c)
**61.** (a) **62.** (a) **63.** (a) **64.** (c) **65.** (c) **66.** (a) **67.** (a) **68.** (a) **69.** (b) **70.** (a)
**71.** (c) **72.** (d) **73.** (a) **74.** (b) **75.** (b) **76.** (a) **77.** (b) **78.** (b) **79.** (c) **80.** (a)
**81.** (d) **82.** (c) **83.** (c) **84.** (a) **85.** (a) **86.** (d) **87.** (a) **88.** (d) **89.** (a) **90.** (c)
**91.** (d) **92.** (a) **93.** (a) **94.** (c) **95.** (c) **96.** (c) **97.** (b) **98.** (b) **99.** (c) **100.** (c)
**101.** (a) **102.** (a) **103.** (c) **104.** (c) **105.** (b) **106.** (a) **107.** (c) **108.** (c) **109.** (c) **110.** (d)
**111.** (b) **112.** (c) **113.** (d) **114.** (b) **115.** (c) **116.** (c) **117.** (d) **118.** (a) **119.** (b) **120.** (d)
**121.** (a) **122.** (c) **123.** (a) **124.** (d) **125.** (a) **126.** (c) **127.** (d) **128.** (d) **129.** (c) **130.** (a)
**131.** (a) **132.** (b) **133.** (c) **134.** (c) **135.** (d) **136.** (a) **137.** (c) **138.** (a) **139.** (d) **140.** (a)
**141.** (d) **142.** (d) **143.** (d) **144.** (a) **145.** (a) **146.** (a) **147.** (d) **148.** (b) **149.** (c) **150.** (b)
**151.** (d) **152.** (b) **153.** (c) **154.** (a) **155.** (c) **156.** (b) **157.** (a) **158.** (c) **159.** (d) **160.** (a)
**161.** (c) **162.** (a) **163.** (a) **164.** (c) **165.** (a) **166.** (b) **167.** (c) **168.** (d) **169.** (a) **170.** (a)
**171.** (a) **172.** (a) **173.** (b) **174.** (b) **175.** (b) **176.** (a) **177.** (a) **178.** (b) **179.** (a) **180.** (a)
**181.** (b) **182.** (a) **183.** (b) **184.** (c) **185.** (a) **186.** (b) **187.** (d) **188.** (a) **189.** (c) **190.** (c)
**191.** (b) **192.** (b) **193.** (d) **194.** (b) **195.** (c) **196.** (c) **197.** (d) **198.** (a) **199.** (c) **200.** (b)
**201.** (b) **202.** (c) **203.** (a) **204.** (a) **205.** (c) **206.** (c) **207.** (c) **208.** (a) **209.** (c) **210.** (a)
**211.** (d) **212.** (a) **213.** (b) **214.** (b) **215.** (a) **216.** (b) **217.** (a) **218.** (b) **219.** (b)

## Exercise 2

**1.** (a,c) **2.** (b,d) **3.** (a,c) **4.** (a,b) **5.** (a,d) **6.** (b,c) **7.** (a,b) **8.** (a,b,c,d) **9.** (a,c) **10.** (a,b)
**11.** (b,c,d) **12.** (a) **13.** (a,c) **14.** (a,c,d) **15.** (a) **16.** (a) **17.** (a,b,c,d) **18.** (b,c,d) **19.** (a,b,c,d) **20.** (a,d)
**21.** (a,b,d) **22.** (b,d) **23.** (a,c) **24.** (a,b,d) **25.** (a,b,c) **26.** (a,b,c,d) **27.** (a,b,c,d) **28.** (a,b,c,d) **29.** (a,b) **30.** (a,c)
**31.** (a,b,c,d) **32.** (a,b,d) **33.** (a,b,c,d) **34.** (b,d) **35.** (a,b,c) **36.** (c,d) **37.** (a,b) **38.** (a,b,c,d) **39.** (a,b,c) **40.** (a,c)

# Hints with Solutions

## Exercise 1

**1.** We have $x_n = \frac{n}{n+1}$

$\Rightarrow \quad x_{n+1} = \frac{n+1}{n+1+1} = \frac{n+1}{n+2}$

$\therefore \quad x_{n+1} - x_n = \frac{n+1}{n+2} - \frac{n}{n+1}$

$= \frac{(n+1)^2 - n(n+2)}{(n+2)(n+1)}$

$= \frac{1}{(n+2)(n+1)}$

$\Rightarrow \quad x_{n+1} - x_n > 0$

$\Rightarrow \quad x_{n+1} > x_n$

$\Rightarrow \quad \left\{\frac{n}{n+1}\right\}$ is increasing sequence.

**2.** $x_n = (-1)^n, \forall\ n \in N$

$\forall\ n \in N, \quad -1 \le x_n$

and $\forall\ n \in N, \quad 1 \ge x_n$

$\Rightarrow \{(-1)^n\}$ is bounded

For even number, $\lim_{n\to\infty} (-1)^n = 1$

For odd number, $\lim_{n\to\infty} (-1)^n = -1$

Hence, series is divergent.

**3.** The *n*th term $a_n = \frac{(-1)^n}{2n-1}$

$\Rightarrow \quad \lim_{n\to\infty} a_n = \lim_{n\to\infty} \left|\frac{(-1)^n}{2n-1}\right| = 0$

$\Rightarrow \quad \{|a_n|\}$ is a convergent sequence.

$\Rightarrow \quad \Sigma |a_n|$ is convergent.

$\Rightarrow \quad \Sigma a_n$ is convergent and converges to zero.

**4.** Here, $x_0 = 0.2$ and $a_n = \frac{1}{n}$

$\therefore \quad \left|\frac{a_{n+1}}{a_n}\right| = \frac{1}{n+1} \cdot \frac{n}{1} = \frac{n}{n+1} = \frac{1}{1+\frac{1}{n}}$

$\Rightarrow \quad L = \lim_{n\to\infty} \frac{1}{1+\frac{1}{n}} = 1$

and the radius of convergence

$R = \frac{1}{L} = 1$

**5.** Here, $\quad a_n = \frac{(-1)^n}{n!}$

and $\left|\frac{a_{n+1}}{a_n}\right| = \frac{1}{(n+1)!} \times \frac{n!}{1} = \frac{1}{n}$

Hence, $\quad L = \lim_{n\to\infty} \left|\frac{a_{n+1}}{a_n}\right| = \lim_{n\to\infty} \frac{1}{n} = 0$

and the radius of convergence

$R = \frac{1}{L} = \frac{1}{0} = \infty$

**6.** We have $x_n = \frac{1}{n}, \ \forall\ n \in N$

$\forall\ n \in N, \quad 1 \ge x_n$

$\forall\ n \in N, \quad 0 \le 0$

$\Rightarrow \quad \left\{\frac{1}{n}\right\}$ is bounded.

Now, $x_n = \frac{1}{n} \Rightarrow x_{n+1} = \frac{1}{n+1}$

$\Rightarrow \quad x_{n+1} - x_n = \frac{1}{n+1} - \frac{1}{n} = \frac{n-n-1}{(n+1)n}$

$= \frac{-1}{(n+1)n}$

$\Rightarrow x_{n+1} - x_n \le 0$

$\Rightarrow x_{n+1} \le x_n, \ \forall\ n \in N$ decreasing sequence

$\therefore \quad \left\{\frac{1}{n}\right\}$ is bounded and monotone sequence.

Hence, $\quad \left\{\frac{1}{n}\right\}$ is convergent.

**7.** $\forall\ n \in N, \quad a \le x_n$

$\forall\ n \in N, a - b \ge x_n$

Hence, $\{x_n\}$ is bounded.

**8.** Here, $a_n = \frac{1}{\left(1+\frac{1}{n}\right)^{n^2}}$

By root test

$\lim_{n\to\infty} \sqrt[n]{a_n} = \lim_{n\to\infty} \frac{1}{\left(1+\frac{1}{n}\right)^n} = \frac{1}{e} < 1$

Hence, the series is convergent.

**37.** We have $x_n = \frac{(-1)^n}{n}$

$x_{n+1} = \frac{(-1)^{n+1}}{n+1}$

$x_{n+1} - x_n = \frac{(-1)^{n+1}}{n+1} - \frac{(-1)^n}{n}$

$= \frac{n(-1)^{n+1} - (n+1)(-1)^n}{(n+1)n}$

$$= \frac{(-1)^n(-n-n+1)}{(n+1)n}$$

$$= \frac{(-1)^n}{n(n+1)}, \begin{array}{l}\text{Increasing } n \text{ even}\\ \text{Decreasing } n \text{ odd}\end{array}$$

$\forall\ n \in N,\ \ -1 \le x_n \le 0$, bounded.

**38.** $S_n = \sum_{n=1}^{n} (-1)^n = 1$ or 0 as $n$ is odd or even

$\Rightarrow \{S_n\} = (1, 0, 1, 0, \ldots)$

It is divergent sequence.

$\Rightarrow \Sigma(-1)^n$ is divergent.

**39.** Here, $\quad a_n = n!$

and $\left|\frac{a_{n+1}}{a_n}\right| = \frac{(n+1)!}{n!} = n+1$

$\Rightarrow \qquad L = \lim_{n\to\infty}\left|\frac{a_{n+1}}{a_n}\right| = \infty$

The radius of convergence $R = 0$

Hence, the series converges only at $x = 0$.

**40.** The partial sum

$$S_n = \frac{1}{2}n[2(1) + (n-1)(1)]$$

$$= \frac{1}{2}n(n+1),\ \forall\ n \in N$$

$\therefore\ \forall\ n \in N,\ \ 1 \le S_n$ (bounded below)

and there is $n\theta\ M : M \ge S_n$

Hence, $\{S_n\}$ is unbounded sequence.

Also, $S_{n+1} - S_n = \frac{1}{2}(n+1)(n+2) - \frac{1}{2}n(n+1)$

$$= \frac{1}{2}(n+1)(n+2-n) = n+1$$

$\Rightarrow \quad S_{n+1} - S_n \ge 0$

$\Rightarrow \{S_n\}$ is increasing sequence.

$\because \quad \{S_n\}$ is increasing and unbounded.

Hence, $\{S_n\}$ is divergent.

$\Rightarrow 1+3+5+\ldots$ is divergent.

**41.** The $n$th term $a_n = 2n$

$$\lim_{n\to\infty} a_n = \lim_{n\to\infty}(2n) = \infty \ne 0$$

$\because\ \{a_n\}$ is does not converges to zero.

Hence, $\Sigma\, a_n$ is divergent.

**42.** The $n$th term $\quad a_n = \frac{1}{n(n+2)}$

$$= \frac{1}{2}\left[\frac{1}{n} - \frac{1}{n+2}\right]$$

$$S_n = \sum_{k=1}^{n} a_k = \frac{1}{2}\left[\frac{3}{2} - \frac{1}{n+1} - \frac{1}{n+2}\right]$$

$\forall\ n \in N, \qquad S_n \ge \frac{1}{6}$ and $S_n \le \frac{3}{4}$

$\therefore\ \{S_n\}$ is bounded and also $S_n$ is monotone sequence.

$\Rightarrow \{S_n\}$ is convergent.

Hence, the series is convergent.

**43.** We have $\frac{a_{n+1}}{a_n} = \frac{1}{3}\left(1+\frac{1}{n}\right)^2$

$\Rightarrow \qquad \frac{a_{n+1}}{a_n} = \frac{1}{3} < 1$

Hence, series is convergent.

**44.** We have $x_n = a_n b_n = (-1)^n \cdot \left(\frac{1}{n}\right),\ \forall\ n \in N$

$$a_n = (-1)^n$$

$\Rightarrow \qquad \forall\ n \in N\ -1 \le a_n$ and $1 \ge a_n$

$\Rightarrow \{a_n\}$ is a bounded sequence.

$$\lim_{n\to\infty} b_n = \lim_{n\to\infty}\frac{1}{n} = 0$$

$\Rightarrow \{b_n\}$ is converges to zero.

Since, $\{a_n\}$ is bounded sequence and $\{b_n\}$ converges to zero.

Hence, $\{a_n b_n\}$ converges to zero.

**45.** By ratio test

$$\left|\frac{a_{n+1}}{a_n}\right| = \left|(-1)^{n+1}\frac{x^{n+1}}{n+1} \times \frac{n}{(-1)^n x^n}\right|$$

$$= \left|\frac{x \cdot n}{n+1}\right| = x\left|\frac{1}{1+\frac{1}{n}}\right|$$

$$\lim_{n\to\infty}\left|\frac{1}{1+\frac{1}{n}}\right| = x > 1, \text{ when } |x| > 1$$

Hence, the series diverges for $|x| > 1$.

**83.** Here, $a_1 = 2 = 1 + \frac{1}{1}$

$$a_2 = -\frac{3}{2} = (-1)^{2-1}\left(1+\frac{1}{2}\right)$$

$$a_3 = \frac{4}{3} = (-1)^{3-1}\left(1+\frac{1}{3}\right)$$

$$a_4 = -\frac{5}{4} = (-1)^{4-1}\left(1+\frac{1}{4}\right)$$

...... ...... ......

...... ...... ......

$$a_n = (-1)^{n-1}\left(1+\frac{1}{n}\right)$$

**84.** The partial sum $S_n = \sum_{k=1}^{n}(n)^n$

$\{S_n\}$ is increasing sequence and unbounded from above.

$\therefore$ It is divergent sequence.

Hence, the series is divergent series.

**131.** If $\Sigma u_n$ be the given series, then we have

$$u_n = \frac{n^n x^n}{n!} \text{ and } u_{n+1} = \frac{(n+1)^{n+1}x^{n+1}}{n+1!}$$

$$\therefore \quad \frac{u_n}{u_{n+1}} = \frac{n^n x^n}{n!} \times \frac{n+1!}{(n+1)^{n+1}x^{n+1}} = \frac{n^n(n+1)}{(n+1)^{n+1}x}$$

$$=\left(\frac{n}{n+1}\right)^n\cdot\frac{1}{x}=\frac{1}{\left[1+\frac{1}{n}\right]^n}\cdot\frac{1}{x}$$

$$\therefore \quad \lim_{n\to\infty}\frac{u_n}{u_{n+1}}=\lim_{n\to\infty}\left[\frac{1}{[1+1/n]^n}\cdot\frac{1}{x}\right]=\frac{1}{ex}$$

$\therefore$ From ratio test, the given series $\Sigma u_n$ is convergent or divergent according as $\frac{1}{ex}>0$

or $<1$ *i.e.*, $\frac{1}{e}>$ or $<x$ *i.e.*,

Hence, for convergent $x<\frac{1}{e}$

**132.** Here, given series is

$$\frac{3}{5}x^4+\frac{8}{10}x^6+\frac{15}{17}x^8+\ldots+\frac{n^2-1}{n^2+1}x^{2n}+\ldots$$

$\therefore$ If $\Sigma u_n$ be the given series, then we have

$$u_n=\frac{n^2-1}{n^2+1}x^{2n} \text{ and } u_{n+1}=\frac{(n+1)^2-1}{(n+1)^2+1}x^{2(n+1)}$$

$$=\frac{n^2+2n}{n^2+2n+2}x^{2(n+1)}$$

$$\frac{u_n}{u_{n+1}}=\frac{(n^2-1)}{(n^2+1)}x^{2n}\times\frac{(n^2+2n+2)}{(n^2+2n)x^{2n+1}}$$

$$=\frac{\left[1-\frac{1}{n^2}\right]\left[1+\frac{2}{n}+\frac{2}{n^2}\right]}{\left[1+\frac{1}{n^2}\right]\left[1+\frac{2}{n}\right]x}$$

$$\therefore \quad \lim_{n\to\infty}\frac{u_n}{u_{n+1}}=\frac{1}{x}$$

Therefore, from ratio test, we conclude that the given series $\Sigma u_n$ is convergent or divergent according as $\frac{1}{x}>1$ or $<1$

*i.e.*, according as $x<1$ or $>1$ ...(i)

If $n=1$, this test fails and the given series reduces to $\Sigma u_n$, whose $n$th term $u_n=\frac{n+1}{n}$ and can be proved to be divergent.

Hence, we conclude that the given series is convergent. If $x^2\le 1$ and divergent, if $x^2>1$.

**133.** Here, it is given that

$$\lim_{n\to\infty}\left[\frac{n}{n^2}+\frac{n}{n^2+1^2}+\ldots+\frac{n}{n^2+(n-1)^2}\right]$$

$$=\lim_{n\to\infty}\sum\frac{n}{n^2+r^2}=\int_0^1\frac{1}{1+n^2}\,dn$$

$$=[\tan^{-1}n]_0^1$$

$$=[\tan^{-1}1-\tan^{-1}0]$$

$$=[\pi/4-0]$$

$$=\pi/4$$

**134.** If $S_n$ denoted the sum of $n$ terms of the series

$$1+\frac{1}{\sqrt{2}}+\frac{1}{\sqrt{3}}+\ldots+\frac{1}{\sqrt{n}}+\ldots,\text{ then } S_n \text{ will be } <\sqrt{n}.$$

**135.** Let $S_n=u_1+u_2+u_3+\ldots+u_{n-1}+u_n$

Then, $S_{n-1}=u_1+u_2+u_3+\ldots+u_{n-1}$

$\therefore \quad u_n=S_n-S_{n-1}$ ...(i)

Now, the given series $\Sigma u_n$ is convergent, if $\lim_{n\to\infty}S_n$ is finite and unique, therefore let $\lim_{n\to\infty}S_n=S$, a finite and unique quantity.

Then, from Eq. (i) we have

$$\therefore \lim_{n\to\infty}u_n=\lim_{n\to\infty}(S_n-S_{n-1})$$

$$=\lim_{n\to\infty}S_n-\lim_{n\to\infty}S_{n-1}$$

$$=S-S=0$$

It is necessarily less than 1.

**136.** Let the given series be denoted by $\Sigma u_n$, then

$$\Sigma|u_n|=\frac{2}{1^2}+\frac{3}{2^2}+\frac{4}{3^2}+\frac{5}{4^2}+\ldots$$

$$=\Sigma\frac{n+1}{n^2}=\Sigma v_n \text{ (say)}$$

Compare this series $\Sigma v_n$ with the auxiliary series,

$$\Sigma w_n=\Sigma 1/n$$

$$\text{Then,}\quad \lim_{n\to\infty}\frac{v_n}{w_n}=\lim_{n\to\infty}\left[\frac{n+1}{n^2}\times\frac{n}{1}\right]=\lim_{n\to\infty}\left(1+\frac{1}{n}\right)=1$$

Which is finite quantity.

Hence, $\Sigma u_n$ and $\Sigma w_n$ are either both convergent or both divergent. But $\Sigma w_n=\Sigma\frac{1}{n}$ is divergent as the series $\Sigma\frac{1}{n^p}$ is divergent, if $p=1$.

Hence, the series $\Sigma v_n$ is divergent.

Also, in the series $\Sigma u_n$, we find that its term are alternately positive and negative, its terms are continuously decreasing and

$$\lim_{n\to\infty}u_n=\lim_{n\to\infty}\left(\frac{n+1}{n^2}\right)$$

$$=\lim_{n\to\infty}\left(\frac{1}{n}+\frac{1}{n^2}\right)=0$$

Thus, all condition of Leibnitz's test are satisfied and as such $\Sigma u_n$ is convergent. Hence, the given series $\Sigma u_n$ is conditionally convergent.

**137.**
$$u_n=\frac{4\cdot 7\ldots(3n+1)}{1\cdot 2\ldots n}x^n$$

$$\Rightarrow \quad u_{n+1}=\frac{4\cdot 7\ldots(3n+1)+1}{1\cdot 2\ldots n+1}x^{n+1}$$

$$\text{Now,}\quad \frac{u_n}{u_{n+1}}=\frac{4\cdot 7\ldots(3n+1)}{1\cdot 2\ldots n}x^n\times\frac{1\cdot 2\ldots(n+1)}{4\cdot 7\ldots(3n+4)}\times\frac{1}{x^{n+1}}$$

$$=\frac{n+1}{3n+4}\cdot\frac{1}{x}$$

$$\text{Hence,}\quad \lim_{n\to\infty}\frac{u_n}{u_{n+1}}=\frac{1}{4x}$$

By d'Alembert's ratio test, the series $\Sigma u_n$ is convergent.

$$|4x|<1 \text{ or } |x|<\frac{1}{4}$$

**138.** Let $u_n = \frac{n!2^n}{n^n}$

$\Rightarrow \quad u_{n+1} = \frac{(n+1)!2^{n+1}}{(n+1)^{n+1}}$

$\Rightarrow \quad \frac{u_n}{u_{n+1}} = \frac{n!2^n}{n^n} \times \frac{(n+1)^{n+1}}{(n+1)!2^{n+1}}$

$= \frac{n+1}{n^n} \cdot \frac{1}{2} = \frac{1}{2}\left(1+\frac{1}{n}\right)^n$

$\lim_{n\to\infty} \frac{u_n}{u_{n+1}} = \frac{1}{2} \lim_{n\to\infty} \left(1+\frac{1}{n}\right)^n = \frac{1}{2} e > 1$

Hence, by d'Alembert's ratio test, it is convergent.

**147.** The series $x - \frac{x^2}{2} + \frac{x^3}{3} - \frac{x^4}{4} + \ldots$ is convergent. If $-1 < x \le 1$.

**148.** For ratio test

$\Sigma a_n$ is convergent if

$\lim_{n\to\infty} \frac{a_n}{a_{n+1}} > 1 \Rightarrow \lim_{n\to\infty} \frac{a_{n+1}}{a_n} < 1$

**149.** (A) $u_n = \sum_1^{\infty} (-1)^{n-1} \frac{n^2}{n+1}$ is a convergent series and $|u_n| = \frac{n^2}{n+1!}$ is also convergent series.

$\therefore u_n$ is also convergent series.

(B) $u_n = \frac{n^n}{n!}$ and $u_{n+1} = \frac{(n+1)^{n+1}}{n+1!}$

$\Rightarrow \quad \frac{u_n}{u_{n+1}} = \frac{n^n}{n!} \times \frac{n+1!}{(n+1)^{n+1}}$

$= \frac{n^n(n+1)}{(n+1)^n} = \frac{1}{\left(1+\frac{1}{n}\right)^n}$

Hence, by d'Alembert test

$\lim_{n\to\infty} \frac{u_n}{u_{n+1}} = \lim_{n\to\infty} \frac{1}{\left(1+\frac{1}{n}\right)^n} = \frac{1}{e} < 1$

$\Rightarrow u_n$ is divergent series.

(C) $u_n = \frac{(-1)^n \log n}{n^2}$

Also, $u_{n+1} < u_n$

By Cauchy condensation test, $\Sigma u_n$ is convergent series.

(D) $u_n = \sum_1^{\infty} \frac{(-1)^n}{\log n}$

By Leibnitz's test, the series is convergent.

Also, $|\Sigma u_n| = \Sigma \frac{1}{\log x}$ is divergent series.

So, the given series is converges conditionally.

**150.** Here, given series is

$$1 + \frac{2}{6} + \frac{2\cdot 5}{6\cdot 12} + \frac{2\cdot 5\cdot 8}{6\cdot 12\cdot 18} + \ldots$$

$\Rightarrow \quad u_n = \frac{2\cdot 5\cdot 8 \ldots (3n-1)}{6\cdot 12\cdot 18 \ldots 6n}$

and $\quad u_{n+1} = \frac{2\cdot 5\cdot 8 \ldots (3n-1)(3n+2)}{6\cdot 12\cdot 18 \ldots 6n\cdot 6(n+1)}$

$\Rightarrow \quad \frac{u_n}{u_{n+1}} = \frac{(3n-1)}{6n} \times \frac{6n\cdot 6(n+1)}{(3n-1)(3n+2)} = \frac{6(n+1)}{(3n+2)}$

Hence, by comparison test

$\lim_{n\to\infty} \frac{u_n}{u_{n+1}} = \lim_{n\to\infty} \frac{6(n+1)}{3n+2} = \lim_{n\to\infty} \frac{6n\left(1+\frac{1}{n}\right)}{3n\left(1+\frac{2}{3}n\right)} = 2 > 1$

Hence, $\Sigma u_n$ is convergent series.

**151.** Here, it is given that

$t_n = \sqrt{n^2+1} - n$

$= \frac{\sqrt{n^2+1}-n}{\sqrt{n^2+1}+n} \times \sqrt{n^2+1}+n$

$= \frac{(\sqrt{n^2+1})^2 - n^2}{\sqrt{n^2+1}+n} = \frac{n^2+1-n^2}{\sqrt{n^2+1}+n} = \frac{1}{\sqrt{n^2+1}+n}$

Now, taking auxiliary series $\Sigma v_n = \frac{1}{n}$

$\Rightarrow \quad \lim_{n\to\infty} \frac{u_n}{v_n} = \lim_{n\to\infty} \frac{1}{\sqrt{n^2+1}+n} \cdot n = \frac{1}{2}$

Which is finite and non-zero. Since, $v_n$ is divergent. Hence, $t_n$ is also divergent.

**152.** The comparison test does not give absolute convergence of a series.

**153.** Here, it is given that

$u_n = \sqrt{n+1} - \sqrt{n}$

and $\quad v_n = \sqrt{n^4+1} - n^2$

$u_n = \sqrt{n+1} - \sqrt{n}$

$= \frac{\sqrt{n+1}-\sqrt{n}}{\sqrt{n+1}+\sqrt{n}} \times \sqrt{n+1}+\sqrt{n}$

$= \frac{(\sqrt{n+1})^2 - (\sqrt{n})^2}{\sqrt{n+1}+\sqrt{n}} = \frac{n+1-n}{\sqrt{n+1}+\sqrt{n}} = \frac{1}{\sqrt{n+1}+\sqrt{n}}$

Now, taking auxiliary series $v_n = \frac{1}{\sqrt{n}}$.

$\Rightarrow \quad \lim_{n\to\infty} \frac{u_n}{v_n} = \frac{\frac{1}{\sqrt{n+1}+\sqrt{n}}}{1/\sqrt{n}} = \frac{\sqrt{n}}{\sqrt{n+1}+\sqrt{n}} = 1,$

finite and non-zero.

$\therefore \Sigma v_n = \frac{1}{n^{1/2}}$ is a $p$ series as $p = \frac{1}{2}$

Hence, $\Sigma v_n$ is divergent and $\Sigma u_n$ is also divergent and

$v_n = \sqrt{n^4+1} - n^2$

$= \frac{\sqrt{n^4+1}-n^2}{\sqrt{n^4+1}+n^2} \times \sqrt{n^4+1}+n^2$

$= \frac{1}{\sqrt{n^4+1}+n^2}$

Now, taking auxiliary series $\Sigma v_n = \frac{1}{n^2}$

$$\because \lim_{n\to\infty}\frac{u_n}{v_n} = \lim_{n\to\infty}\frac{n^2}{\sqrt{n^4+1+n^2}} = 1,$$

finite and non-zero

$\because \Sigma v_n = \frac{1}{n^2}$ is a $p$-series at $p = 2$

$\Sigma v_n$ is convergent and

Hence, $\Sigma u_n$ is also convergent.

**154.** Here, given series is

$$\frac{x}{1\cdot 2}+\frac{x^2}{2\cdot 3}+\frac{x^3}{3\cdot 4}+\ldots \text{ is convergent}$$

$$\Rightarrow \quad u_n = \frac{x^n}{n(n+1)}$$

Then, $$u_{n+1} = \frac{x^{n+1}}{(n+1)(n+2)}$$

$$\Rightarrow \quad \frac{u_n}{u_{n+1}} = \frac{x^n}{n(n+1)}\times\frac{(n+1)(n+2)}{x^{n+1}}$$

$$= \frac{n+2}{nx^{n+1-n}} = \frac{n+2}{nx}$$

$$\Rightarrow \quad \lim_{n\to\infty}\frac{u_n}{u_{n+1}} = \lim_{n\to\infty}\frac{n+2}{2}\cdot\frac{1}{x} = \frac{1}{x}$$

$\therefore$ The given series will be convergent, if $\left|\frac{1}{x}\right| > 1$ i.e., $|n| < 1$

$\therefore$ If $n = 1$, then

By comparison test

$$u_n = \frac{1}{n(n+1)} \text{ and take } v_n = \frac{1}{n^2}$$

$$\therefore \quad \frac{u_n}{v_n} = 1 \qquad \text{(finite and non-zero)}$$

$\therefore$ [ $v_n = \frac{1}{n^2}$ is $p$-series, where $p = 2 > 1$]

Hence, $v_n$ is convergent series, so $u_n$ is also convergent.

$\therefore$ The given series is convergent, if $|x| \le 1$.

**155.** Since, $\sum_{n=1}^{\infty} a_n$ convergent, then $\lim_{n\to\infty} a_n = 0$

$$\Rightarrow \quad \lim_{n\to\infty} a_{n-1} = -1$$

$$\therefore \quad \lim_{n\to\infty}\frac{a_n - 1}{n^{1/n}} = \frac{0-1}{1} = -1$$

**156.** Here, $S_1 = \sum_{n=1}^{\infty}\frac{(n!)^n}{(n^n)^2}$ and $S_2 = \sum_{n=1}^{\infty}\frac{1}{(2n-1)(2n+1)}$

So, we can see that from $S_1$ and $S_2$ that $S_1$ is divergent and $S_2$ is convergent.

**159.** The $n$th term of the given series is

$$u_n = \left[\left(\frac{n+1}{n}\right)^{n+1} - \left(\frac{n+1}{n}\right)\right]^{-n}$$

Now, $$u_n^{1/n} = \left[\left(\frac{n+1}{n}\right)^{n+1} - \left(\frac{n+1}{n}\right)\right]^{-1}$$

$$= \left(\frac{n+1}{n}\right)^{-1}\left[\left(\frac{n+1}{n}\right)^{n} - 1\right]^{-1}$$

$$= \left(1+\frac{1}{n}\right)^{-1}\left[\left(1+\frac{1}{n}\right)^{n} - 1\right]^{-1}$$

Hence, $\lim_{n\to\infty} u_n^{1/n} = 1(e-1)^{-1} = \frac{1}{e-1} < 1\,(e = 2.718)$

Hence, by Cauchy's root test, the given series converges.

**168.** The $n$th term of the given series is

$$u_n = \frac{\sqrt{(n+1)}+\sqrt{n}}{n^m}$$

and $$v_n = \frac{1}{n^{m-\frac{1}{2}}}$$

$$\Rightarrow \lim_{n\to\infty}\frac{u_n}{v_n} = \lim_{n\to\infty}\frac{\sqrt{(n+1)}+\sqrt{n}}{n^m}\cdot\frac{n^{m-\frac{1}{2}}}{1}$$

$$= \lim_{n\to\infty}\left[\sqrt{\left(1+\frac{1}{n}\right)}+1\right]$$

$$= 2$$

Which is finite and non-zero.

If $m - \frac{1}{2} > 1$ i.e., $m > \frac{3}{2}$ then the series $\Sigma v_n$ and $\Sigma u_n$ are convergent.

**169.** The $n$th term of the given series is

$$u_n = \left(1+\frac{1}{n}\right)^{-n^2} \Rightarrow u_n^{1/n} = \left(1+\frac{1}{n}\right)^{-n}$$

$$\lim_{n\to\infty} u_n^{1/n} = e^{-1} < 1,$$

Hence, $\Sigma u_n$ is convergent.

**170.** Here, $$u_n = 3^{-n+\frac{(-1)^n}{n}}$$

$$u_n^{1/n} = 3^{-1+\frac{(-1)^n}{n^2}}$$

$$\lim u_n^{1/n} = \frac{1}{3} < 1$$

Hence, by Cauchy's root test, the series convergent.

**171.** Here, $$u_n = \frac{\left(1+\frac{1}{n}\right)^{n^2}}{x^n}$$

$$\Rightarrow \quad u_n^{1/n} = \frac{1}{x}\left(1+\frac{1}{n}\right)^n$$

$$\lim_{n\to\infty} u_n^{1/n} = \frac{e}{x}$$

If $\frac{e}{x} > 1$ i.e., $x < e$, then the given series converges.

**172.** Here, $u_n = \frac{n!x^n}{n^n}$

and $u_{n+1} = \frac{n+1!x^{n+1}}{(n+1)^{n+1}}$

$$\Rightarrow \frac{u_n}{u_{n+1}} = \frac{n!x^n}{n^n} \cdot \frac{(n+1)^{n+1}}{n+1!x^{n+1}} = \frac{\left(1+\frac{1}{n}\right)^n}{x}$$

$$\lim \frac{u_n}{u_{n+1}} = \lim \left[\frac{\left(1+\frac{1}{n}\right)^n}{x}\right] = \frac{e}{x}$$

If $\frac{e}{x} > 1$ *i.e.*, $x < e$, then the given series diverges.

**173.** Here, $2|a_n| < |a_{n+1}|$, $\forall n$ and so $2^k|a_n| < |a_{n+k}|$ gives that $\lim\left(\frac{a_n}{a_{n+1}}\right) \le \frac{1}{2}$, So that $\Sigma\frac{1}{|a_n|}$ is convergent.

Thus, $\Sigma\frac{1}{a_n}$ is absolutely convergent.

Let the sum $\Sigma\frac{1}{a_n} = A$, be rational, then for some $a_n$, $a_n A$ is integral, and so

$a_n A - a_n\left(\frac{1}{a_1}+\frac{1}{a_2}+\ldots+\frac{1}{a_n}\right)$ is integral.

*i.e.*, $a_n\left(\frac{1}{a_{n+1}}+\frac{1}{a_{n+2}}+\frac{1}{a_{n+3}}+\ldots+\right)$ is integral.

But $\left|a_n\left(\frac{1}{a_{n+1}}+\frac{1}{a_{n+2}}+\frac{1}{a_{n+3}}+\ldots\right)\right|$ positive integer

$$< \left|\frac{a_n}{a_{n+1}}\right| + \left|\frac{a_n}{a_{n+2}}\right| + \left|\frac{a_n}{a_{n+3}}\right| + \ldots$$

$< \frac{1}{2}+\frac{1}{2^2}+\frac{1}{2^3}+\ldots(=1)$ is a contradiction chair, and so, $A$ is an irrational number.

**174.** Here, $u_n = \sin\frac{1}{n}+\frac{1}{n^2}$

Let $v_n = \frac{1}{n}$

$\lim\limits_{n\to\infty}\frac{u_n}{v_n} = \lim\limits_{n\to\infty}\left[n\left(\sin\frac{1}{n}+\frac{1}{n^2}\right)\right] = 1$, which is finite and non-zero.

Since, $\Sigma\frac{1}{n}$ is divergent, therefore $\sum\left(\sin\frac{1}{n}+\frac{1}{n^2}\right)$ is divergent.

**175.** Here, $u_n = \frac{1}{\sqrt{n}+\sqrt{n+1}+\sqrt{n+2}+\sqrt{n+3}}$

Let $v_n = \frac{1}{\sqrt{n}}$

$$\therefore \lim_{n\to\infty}\frac{u_n}{v_n} = \lim_{n\to\infty}\left[\frac{1}{1+\sqrt{\left(1+\frac{1}{n}\right)}+\sqrt{\left(1+\frac{2}{n}\right)}+\sqrt{\left(1+\frac{3}{n}\right)}}\right] = \frac{1}{4},$$

which is finite and none-zero.

Since, $\Sigma v_n$ is divergent, therefore $\Sigma u_n$ is also divergent.

**176.** Hence,

$$\frac{1}{n^p+n^{-p}} < \frac{1}{n^{|p|}}$$

If $|p| > 1$, then $\Sigma\frac{1}{n^{|p|}}$ is convergent, therefore $\Sigma\frac{1}{n^p+n^{-p}}$ is also convergent.

**178.** Here,

$$\left|\left[3\sqrt{(n^3+1)}-n\right]x^n\right| \le \sqrt[3]{(x^3+1)}-n[|x| \le 1 \text{ (say)}]$$

$$= \frac{1}{(n^3+1)^{2/3}+(n^3+1)^{1/3}n+n^2} < \frac{1}{3n^2}$$

Since, $\Sigma\frac{1}{3n^2}$ is convergent, therefore $\Sigma[3\sqrt{n^3+1}-n]$ is also convergent.

## Exercise 2

**2.** We have,

$$\lim_{n\to\infty} S_n = \infty \text{ and } \lim_{n\to\infty} t_n = \infty$$

Hence,

$$\lim_{n\to\infty}(S_n+t_n) = \lim_{n\to\infty} S_n + \lim_{n\to\infty} t_n = \infty$$

and $\lim\limits_{n\to\infty}(S_n \cdot t_n) = \lim\limits_{n\to\infty} S_n \cdot \lim\limits_{n\to\infty} t_n = \infty$

Hence, the sequences $< S_n + t_n >$ and $< S_n \cdot t_n >$ always divergent.

**3.** Let $S_n = \frac{1}{n} \Rightarrow \lim\limits_{n\to\infty} S_n = \lim\limits_{n\to\infty}\frac{1}{n} = 0$

Hence, by Cauchy's second theorem on limits, we have

$$\lim_{n\to\infty}\left(1\cdot\frac{1}{2}\cdot\frac{1}{3}\cdot\frac{1}{4}\cdots\frac{1}{n}\right)^{1/n} = 0$$

$$= \lim_{n\to\infty}\left(\frac{1}{1\cdot2\cdot3\cdot4\ldots n}\right)^{1/n} = 0$$

Next, let

$$S_n = \left(\frac{n+1}{n}\right)^n = \left(1+\frac{1}{n}\right)^n$$

$$\Rightarrow \lim S_n = \lim_{n\to\infty}\left(1+\frac{1}{n}\right)^n = e$$

Hence, by Cauchy's first theorem on limits, we have

$$\lim_{n\to\infty}\frac{1}{n}\left[2+\left(\frac{3}{2}\right)^2+\left(\frac{4}{3}\right)^3+\ldots+\left(\frac{n+1}{n}\right)^n\right] = 0$$

**5.** We have,

$$\lim_{n\to\infty}\frac{S_{n+1}}{S_n} = 0.750, \quad S_n \ne 0, \forall\ n$$

but $0.750 < 1$

Hence, $\lim\limits_{n\to\infty} S_n = 0$

and $\lim_{n\to\infty}\frac{t_{n+1}}{t_n}=1.750,\quad t_n\neq 0, \forall\ n$

But $1.750>1$

Hence, $\lim_{n\to\infty} t_n=\infty$

**6.** Let $S_n=\frac{3^n}{n}\Rightarrow S_{n+1}=\frac{3^{n+1}}{n+1}$

$$\Rightarrow \lim_{n\to\infty}\frac{S_{n+1}}{S_n}=\lim_{n\to\infty}\frac{3^{n+1}}{n+1}\cdot\frac{n}{3^n}=\lim_{n\to\infty}\frac{3n}{n+1}$$

$$=\lim_{n\to\infty}\frac{3}{1+\frac{1}{n}}=3>1$$

$$\Rightarrow \lim_{n\to\infty}\frac{3^n}{n}=\infty$$

Next, let $t_n=\frac{(0.05)^n}{n}$

$$\Rightarrow t_{n+1}=\frac{(0.05)^{n+1}}{n+1}$$

$$\Rightarrow \lim_{n\to\infty}\frac{t_{n+1}}{t_n}=\lim_{n\to\infty}\frac{(0.05)^{n+1}}{n+1}\cdot\frac{n}{(0.05)^n}$$

$$=\lim_{n\to\infty}\frac{(0.05)}{1+\frac{1}{n}}=0.05<1$$

$$\Rightarrow \lim_{n\to\infty} t_n=\lim_{n\to\infty}\frac{(0.05)^n}{n}=0$$

**7.** Since, $\lim_{n\to\infty}\frac{x^n}{n!}=0, \forall\ x\in\mathbb{R}$

$$\Rightarrow \lim_{n\to\infty}\frac{2^n}{n!}=0=\lim_{n\to\infty}\frac{(0.30)^n}{n!}$$

**9.** The sequence $<\frac{1}{n}>$ has only one limit point '0'. The sequence $<1+(-1)^n>$ has two limit points '0' and '2'. The sequence $<(-1)^n>$ has two limit points '1' and '–1'.

**11.** $x_n=\frac{1}{2^n}, \forall\ n\in N$

$$x_{n+1}=\frac{1}{2^{n+1}}, \forall\ n\in N$$

$$\Rightarrow x_{n+1}-x_n=\frac{1}{2^{n+1}}-\frac{1}{2^n}$$

$$=\frac{1-2}{2^{n+1}}=\frac{-1}{2^{n+1}}\ \forall\ n\in N$$

$$\Rightarrow x_{n+1}-x_n<0$$

$$\Rightarrow x_{n+1}<x_n$$

Hence, $\left\{\frac{1}{2^n}\right\}$ is a decreasing sequence.

**12.** Let $l_1$ and $l_2$ are the distinct limit of the sequence $<x_n>$.

$\lim x_n=l_1\Rightarrow \varepsilon>0,\ \exists\ N_1:\ \forall\ n\geq N_1, |x_n-l_1|<\varepsilon$

$\lim x_n=l_2\Rightarrow \varepsilon>0,\ \exists\ N_2:\ \forall\ n\geq N_2, |x_n-l_2|<\varepsilon$

Choose $N=\min\{N_1, N_2\}$, we have

for $\varepsilon>0$ and $\forall\ n\geq N$, $|x_n-l_1|<\varepsilon$ and $|x_n-l_2|<\varepsilon$

$\because |l_1-l_2|=|l_1-x_n+x_n-l_2|\leq|x_n-l_n|+|x_n-l_2|<\varepsilon+\varepsilon$

$\Rightarrow |l_1-l_2|<2\varepsilon$

$\Rightarrow l_1=l_2$, which contradicts the statement that $l_1$ and $l_2$ are distinct. Thus, the sequence $<x_n>$ have atmost one limit.

**13.** Let sequence $<x_n>$ is a Cauchy's sequence,

for $\varepsilon>0,\ \exists\ N: n\geq N,\ m\geq N$

$\Rightarrow \quad |x_n-x_m|<\varepsilon$

$\because \quad |x_n-x_m|\leq|x_n|-|x_m|$

$\Rightarrow \quad |x_n|-|x_m|<\varepsilon$

$\Rightarrow \quad |x_n|<|x_m|+\varepsilon$ ...(i)

Choose $M=\min(|x_m|)+\varepsilon$

$\therefore$ By Eq. (i), we have

$\varepsilon>0,\ \exists\ N: n\geq N, |x_n|<M$

The sequence $<x_n>$ is bounded.

**14.** Here, $x_n=\frac{n}{n+1}$

and $x_{n+1}=\frac{n+1}{n+1+1}=\frac{n+1}{n+2}$

$$\Rightarrow x_{n+1}-x_n=\frac{n+1}{n+2}-\frac{n}{n+1}$$

$$=\frac{(n+1)^2-(n+2)n}{(n+2)(n+1)}$$

$$=\frac{1}{(n+2)(n+1)}$$

$\Rightarrow \quad x_{n+1}-x_n\geq 0$

$\Rightarrow \quad x_{n+1}\geq x_n,\ \forall\ n\in N$, increasing sequence

$\forall\ n\in N, \frac{1}{2}\leq x_n$

$\forall\ n\in N, 1\geq x_n$

$\therefore \left\{\frac{n}{n+1}\right\}$ is bounded.

Since, $x_n$ is increasing sequence and bounded too it is convergent.

**15.** $$\frac{a_{n+1}}{a_n}=\frac{(n+1)!}{(n+1)^{n+1}}=\frac{n^n}{n!}=\frac{n^n}{(1+n)^n}=\frac{1}{\left(1+\frac{1}{n}\right)^n}$$

$$\Rightarrow \lim\left|\frac{a_{n+1}}{a_n}\right|=1+\left\{\lim_{n\to\infty}\left(1+\frac{1}{n}\right)^n\right\}=\frac{1}{e}<1$$

Hence, the series is convergent.

**16.** Let sequence $<x_n>$ is a Cauchy sequence,

for $\varepsilon>0,\ \exists\ N: n\geq N,\ m\geq N$

$\Rightarrow \quad |x_n-x_m|<\varepsilon$

$\because \quad |x_n-x_m|\leq|x_n|-|x_m|$

$\Rightarrow \quad |x_n|-|x_m|<\varepsilon$

$\Rightarrow \quad |x_n|<|x_m|+\varepsilon$ ...(i)

Choose $M=\min(|x_m|)+\varepsilon$

$\therefore$ By Eq. (i), we have

$\varepsilon>0,\ \exists\ N: n\geq N, |x_n|<M$

The sequence $<x_n>$ is bounded.

**17.** If $x_n = \frac{1}{n}$,

then $\{x_n\} = \left\{\frac{1}{n}\right\}$

$x_n \geq 0$ for, $\forall\ n \in N$ (Bounded below)

$x_n \leq 1$ for, $\forall\ n \in N$ (Bounded above)

$\Rightarrow$ $0 \leq x_n \leq 1$, $\forall\ n \in N$ (Bounded below and above)

Hence, $\left\{\frac{1}{n}\right\}$ is bounded.

**18.** We have,

$$S_n = \{(-n)^n\}$$
$$= \{-1, 2, -3, 4, -5, 6, \ldots\}$$

which is neither bounded below nor bounded above. Hence, $S_n$ is not bounded.

Next,

$$S_n = \left\{\left(1 + \frac{1}{n}\right)^n\right\} = 2, 1\frac{1}{2}, 1\frac{1}{3}, 1\frac{1}{4}, \ldots$$

which is bounded below by 1 and bounded above by 2. Hence, $S_n$ is bounded sequence.

Next,

$$S_n = \{1\}, \forall\ n$$

which is bounded below by 1 and bounded above by 1 also. Hence, $S_n$ is bounded sequence.

Next,

$$S_n = \{1 + (-1)^n\} = \{0, 2, 0, 2, 0, 2, \ldots\}$$

which is bounded below by 0 and bounded above by 2. Hence, $S_n$ is bounded sequence.

**21.** Clearly the sequence

$$S_n = \{1 + (-1)^n\}$$

has two limit points 0 and 2 which are countable in number.

Now, the range of the sequence $S_n = \{1 + (-1)^n\}$ is $\{0, 2\}$ which has no limit point.

**22.** Let us consider the sequence $b_n = -a_n$, $\forall\ n \in \mathbb{N}$. Then, we have

$$\underline{B_n} = \text{Inf}\ \{b_n, b_{n+1}, \ldots\}$$
$$= -\text{Sup}\ \{a_n, a_{n+1}, \ldots\} = -\overline{A_n}$$

Hence,

$$\underline{\lim}\ (-a_n) = \underline{\lim}\ b_n$$
$$= \text{Sup}\{B_1, B_2, \ldots\}$$
$$= \text{Sup}\ \{-\overline{A_1}, -\overline{A_2}, \ldots\}$$
$$= -\text{Inf}\ \{\overline{A_1}, \overline{A_2}, \ldots\}$$
$$= -\text{Inf}\ \overline{A_n} = -\overline{\lim}\ a_n$$

$\Rightarrow$ $\underline{\lim}\ (-a_n) = -\overline{\lim}\ a_n$

Similarly,

$$\overline{\lim}(-a_n) = -\underline{\lim}\ (a_n)$$

**23.** We have,

$$a_n = \sin\frac{n\pi}{3},\ \forall\ n \in \mathbb{N}$$
$$= \left\{\frac{\sqrt{3}}{2}, \frac{\sqrt{3}}{2}, 0, -\frac{\sqrt{3}}{2}, -\frac{\sqrt{3}}{2}, 0, \frac{\sqrt{3}}{2}, \frac{\sqrt{3}}{2}, \ldots\right\}$$

$\Rightarrow$ $\underline{A_n} = -\frac{\sqrt{3}}{2}$ and $\overline{A_n} = \frac{\sqrt{3}}{2}$, $\forall\ n \in \mathbb{N}$

Hence, $\underline{\lim}\ a_n = -\frac{\sqrt{3}}{2}$ and $\overline{\lim}\ a_n = \frac{\sqrt{3}}{2}$

**31.** We have,

$$\lim_{n\to\infty} S_n = \lim_{n\to\infty} \max(a_n, b_n)$$
$$= \lim_{n\to\infty} \left\{\frac{1}{2}(a_n + b_n) + \frac{1}{2}|a_n - b_n|\right\}$$
$$= \frac{1}{2}\left(\lim_{n\to\infty} a_n + \lim_{n\to\infty} b_n\right) + \frac{1}{2}\left|\lim_{n\to\infty} a_n - \lim_{n\to\infty} b_n\right|$$
$$= \frac{1}{2}(a + b) + \frac{1}{2}|a - b| = \max(a, b)$$

Hence, $\{S_n\}$ is convergent.

Similarly,

$$\lim_{n\to\infty} T_n = \lim_{n\to\infty} \min(a_n, b_n)$$
$$= \lim_{n\to\infty} \left\{\frac{1}{2}(a_n + b_n) - \frac{1}{2}|a_n - b_n|\right\}$$
$$= \frac{1}{2}\left(\lim_{n\to\infty} a_n + \lim_{n\to\infty} b_n\right) - \frac{1}{2}\left|\lim_{n\to\infty} a_n - \lim_{n\to\infty} b_n\right|$$
$$= \frac{1}{2}(a + b) - \frac{1}{2}|a - b|$$
$$= \min(a, b)$$

Hence, $\{T_n\}$ is convergent.

**32.** We have,

$$\{S_n\} = 1, \sqrt{3}, \sqrt{3\sqrt{3}}, \sqrt{3\sqrt{3\sqrt{3}}}, \ldots$$

Hence,

$$S_2 > S_1$$
$$S_3 > S_2$$

and

$$S_{m+1} > S_m \Rightarrow \sqrt{3S_{m+1}} > \sqrt{3S_m}$$
$$\Rightarrow S_{m+2} > S_{m+1}$$

Hence, by induction, the sequence $\{S_n\}$ is monotonic increasing sequence.

Next,

$$S_1 < 3$$
$$S_2 < 3$$
$$S_3 < 3$$

and $S_m < 3 \Rightarrow \sqrt{3S_m} < \sqrt{3 \cdot 3}$

$\Rightarrow S_{m+1} < 3$

Hence, again by induction

$$0 < S_n < 3, \forall\ n$$

Hence, $\{S_n\}$ is bounded sequence.

Hence, $\{S_n\}$ is bounded monotonic increasing sequence and hence convergent.

Now,

let $\lim_{n\to\infty} S_n = l$

$\Rightarrow$ $\lim_{n\to\infty} S_{n+1} = l$

But we have,

$$S_{n+1} = \sqrt{3S_n}$$

Taking limit on both sides,
we get,

$$\lim_{n\to\infty} S_{n+1} = \lim \sqrt{3S_n} \Rightarrow l = \sqrt{3l}$$

$$\Rightarrow \quad l(l-3) = 0 \Rightarrow l = 0 \text{ or } l = 3$$

But $l \neq 0$, since $S_n \geq 1, \forall\, n \Rightarrow \lim_{n\to\infty} S_n = 3$

**33.** We have,

$$a_2 - a_1 = \frac{1}{2}\left(a_1 + \frac{9}{a_1}\right) - a_1$$

$$= \frac{9 - a_1^2}{2a_1}$$

$$\geq 0, \text{ if } a_1 \leq 3$$

$$\Rightarrow \quad a_2 \geq a_1, \text{ if } a_1 \leq 3$$

Now, $a_{n+1} - a_n = \frac{1}{2}\left(a_n + \frac{9}{a_n}\right) - a_n = \frac{9 - a_n^2}{2a_n} \geq 0$, if $a_n \leq 3$

Hence, the sequence $\{a_n\}$ is monotonically increasing, if $a_n \leq 3, \forall\, n$ and decreasing, if $a_n \geq 3, \forall\, n$.

Thus, the sequence $\{a_n\}$ is bounded and monotonic and hence convergent.

Let $\lim_{n\to\infty} a_n = l$

Then, $\lim_{n\to\infty} a_{n+1} = \lim_{n\to\infty} \frac{1}{2}\left(a_n + \frac{9}{a_n}\right) = \frac{1}{2}\left(l + \frac{9}{l}\right)$

$$\Rightarrow \quad l = \frac{1}{2}\left(l + \frac{9}{l}\right) \Rightarrow l^2 = 9 \Rightarrow l^2 = \pm 3$$

But $l \neq -3$ as $a_n > 0, \forall\, n$.

Hence, $l = 3$. Hence, $\{a_n\}$ converges to 3.

**34.** Let $u_n = \frac{1}{n^{1+\frac{1}{n}}}$ and $v_n = \frac{1}{n}$

$$\therefore \lim_{n\to\infty} \frac{u_n}{v_n} = \lim_{n\to\infty} \frac{1}{n^{\frac{1}{n}}} = 1 \neq 0$$

Hence, the two series $\Sigma u_n$ and $\Sigma v_n$ be have alike.

But the series $\Sigma v_n = \Sigma \frac{1}{n}$ is divergent. Hence, the series $\Sigma \frac{1}{n^{1+\frac{1}{n}}}$ is divergent.

Next, let $u_n = (n^3+1)^{1/3} - n$

$$= n\left\{\left(1 + \frac{1}{n^3}\right)^{1/3} - 1\right\}$$

$$= n\left\{\frac{1}{3n^3} + \ldots\right\} = \frac{1}{3n^2} + \ldots \cong \frac{1}{n^2}$$

and $v_n = \frac{1}{n^2}$

$$\therefore \quad \lim_{n\to\infty} \frac{u_n}{v_n} = \frac{1}{3}$$

Hence, the two series converges and diverges together. But the series $\Sigma v_n = \Sigma \frac{1}{n^2}$ is convergent.

Hence, the given series is also convergent.

**35.** Let $u_n = \frac{1}{\left(1 + \frac{1}{\sqrt{n}}\right)^{n^{3/2}}}$

Then, $\lim_{n\to\infty} (u_n)^{1/n} = \lim_{n\to\infty} \frac{1}{\left(1 + \frac{1}{\sqrt{n}}\right)^{\sqrt{n}}} = \frac{1}{e} < 1$

Hence, the given series is convergent.

Next, let $u_n = \frac{n^2-1}{n^2+1} \cdot x^n$

$$\Rightarrow \quad \lim_{n\to\infty} \frac{u_{n+1}}{u_n} = \lim_{n\to\infty} \frac{n^2+1}{n^2-1} \cdot \frac{(n+1)^2 - 1}{(n+1)^2+1} \cdot \frac{x^{n+1}}{x^n} = x$$

Hence by d'Alembert's ratio test the series converges, if $x < 1$ and diverges, if $n > 1$. The test fails to give any information when $x = 1$. When $x = 1$, we get

$$u_n = \frac{n^2-1}{n^2+1} \text{ and } \lim_{n\to\infty} u_n = 1 \neq 0$$

Hence, the series is divergent.

Hence, the given series is convergent, if $x < 1$ and divergent, if $x \geq 1$.

**36.** We have, $\frac{u_n}{u_{n+1}}$

$$= \frac{3\cdot 6\cdot 9 \ldots 3n}{7\cdot 10\cdot 13 \ldots (3n+4)} \cdot x^n \cdot \frac{7\cdot 10\cdot 13 \ldots (3n+4)(3n+7)}{3\cdot 6\cdot 9 \ldots 3n(3n+3)} \cdot \frac{1}{x^{n+1}}$$

$$= \frac{3n+7}{3n+3} \cdot \frac{1}{x}$$

$$\therefore \lim_{n\to\infty} \frac{u_{n+1}}{u_n} = x$$

Hence, by ratio test, the series converges, if $x < 1$ and diverges, if $x > 1$. The test fails, if $x = 1$.

But when $x = 1$

$$\frac{u_n}{u_{n+1}} = \frac{3n+7}{3n+3}$$

$$\Rightarrow \lim_{n\to\infty} n\left(\frac{u_n}{u_{n+1}} - 1\right) = \lim_{n\to\infty} \frac{4n}{3n+3} = \frac{4}{3} > 1$$

Hence, by Raabe's test. The series converges.

Hence, the given series converges, if $x \leq 1$ and diverges, if $x > 1$.

**37.** Let $u_n = (n^3+1)^{1/3} - n$ and $b_n = \frac{1}{\log n}$

Hence, the given series can be written as $\Sigma\, b_n u_n$.

Since, $\Sigma u_n$ converges and $\{b_n\}$ is a positive monotonic decreasing sequence. Therefore, by Abel's test, the given series converges.

Next, let

$$\Sigma u_n = \frac{1}{1^2} - \frac{1}{2^2} + \frac{1}{3^2} - \frac{1}{4^2} + \ldots$$

and $b_n = \frac{1}{2n-1}$

Then the given series can be written as $\Sigma\, b_n u_n$. Since, $\Sigma u_n$ converges and $b_n$ is positive and monotonic decreasing, therefore by Abel's test, the given series converges.

# 3 Limit, Continuity Differentiability Mean Value Theorem

**Syllabus**

- Continuity
- Uniform Continuity
- Differentiability
- Mean Value Theorem

## Limit of a Function

A function $f$ is said to tend to limit $l$ as $x$ tends to $a$ written as $\lim_{x\to a} f(x) = l$, if for arbitrary $\varepsilon > 0$ (however small), there exists some $\delta > 0$ (depending upon $\varepsilon$) such that

$$|f(x) - l| < \epsilon, \text{ whenever } 0 < |x - a| < \delta.$$

> **Note** $\lim_{x\to a} f(x)$ should not be understood as substituting $x = a$ in $f(x)$. In fact, $f(x)$ may not be defined at $x = a$. We are not to check the difference of $f(x)$ and $l$ at $x = a$, because $0 < |x - a|$.

### Important Definitions

Let $f(x)$ and $g(x)$ be two real-valued functions with a common domain $D$, i.e., $f, g: D \to R$. We define

**Sum** $(f + g)(x) = f(x) + g(x), \forall x \in D$

**Difference** $(f - g)(x) = f(x) - g(x), \forall x \in D$

**Product** $(fg)(x) = f(x) \cdot g(x), \forall x \in D$

**Quotient** $\left(\frac{f}{g}\right)(x) = \frac{f(x)}{g(x)}, \forall x \in D, g(x) \neq 0, \forall x \in D.$

## Important Theorems on Limit of a Function

***Theorem 1*** $\lim_{x\to a} f(x)$, if it exists, then it is unique.

***Theorem 2*** If $\lim_{x\to a} f(x) = l$ and $\lim_{x\to a} g(x) = m$, then $\lim_{x\to a} [f(x) \pm g(x)] = l \pm m$.

***Theorem 3*** $\lim_{x\to a} [f(x) \cdot g(x)] = lm = \lim_{x\to a} f(x) \cdot \lim_{x\to a} g(x)$.

***Theorem 4*** If $\lim_{x\to a} f(x) = l \neq 0$, then there exists a $\delta > 0$ such that $|f(x)| > \frac{1}{2}|l|$, when $0 < |x - a| < \delta$.

***Theorem 5*** $\lim_{x\to a}\left[\frac{f(x)}{g(x)}\right] = \frac{l}{m}$, provided $m \neq 0$.

***Theorem 6*** If $\lim_{x\to a} f(x) = l$, then $\lim_{x\to a} |f(x)| = |l|$.

## Functional Value of a Function at a Point and Limiting Value of a Function

Suppose, $y = f(x)$ is a function of $x$. Then, the value of $f(x)$ obtained by putting $x = a$ in this, is called functional value of $f(x)$ at $x = a$ or value of the function at $x = a$ and denoted by symbol $f(a)$.

e.g., If $f(x) = 3x + 1$, then

$f(3) = 3 \cdot 3 + 1 = 10$ [functional value of $f(x)$ at $x = 3$]

## Limiting Value of a Function

Consider a function $y = f(x) = 3x + 1$. We have already learnt $f(3)$, the value of $f(x)$ at exactly $x = 3$.

Now, consider its values at a point very close to $x = 3$

| Table I | | Table II | |
|---|---|---|---|
| $x$ | $f(x)$ | $x$ | $f(x)$ |
| 3.1 | $3 \times 3.1 + 1 = 10.3$ | 2.9 | $3 \times 2.9 + 1 = 9.7$ |
| 3.01 | $3 \times 3.01 + 1 = 10.03$ | 2.99 | $3 \times 2.99 + 1 = 9.97$ |
| 3.001 | $3 \times 3.001 + 1 = 10.003$ | 2.999 | $3 \times 2.999 + 1 = 9.997$ |
| $x \to 3$ (from right) | $f(x) \to 10$ | $x \to 3$ (from left) | $f(x) \to 10$ |

From first table we observe that as $x$ approaches to 3 (means $x$ becomes closer and more closer to $x = 3$) from the right side of point $x = 3$, the functional value continuously approaches to 10 (meaning becomes more and more close to 10). We say that when $x$ becomes very close to 3 on the right side, $f(x)$ almost becomes 10. This is called "Right hand limit" of $f(x)$ at $x = 3$ is 10 and written as $\lim_{x\to 3^+} f(x) = 10$.

Similarly, the second table shows that as $x$ approaches to $x = 3$ from the left hand side of point $x = 3$, even then $f(x)$ approaches to 10, this is called "left hand limit" of $f(x)$ at $x = 3$ is 10 and written as $\lim_{x\to 3^-} f(x) = 10$.

In general, the limit of a function at $x = a$ is nothing but the value of a function at a point very-very close to $a$.

**Definition** If the value of a function $f(x)$ approaches to a number '$l$' when $x$ approaches to $a (x \to a)$ from the right, then '$l$' is called the right hand limit of $f(x)$ at $x = a$, denoted by $Rf(a)$ or $f(a + 0)$. To determine this we make $h \to 0$ in the value of $f(x)$ at $x = a + h$. Thus,

$$Rf(a) = f(a + 0) = \lim_{x\to a^+} f(x) = \lim_{h\to 0} f(a + h).$$

Similarly, if the value of a function $f(x)$ approaches to number '$m$' as $x \to a$ from the left, then '$m$' is called the left hand limit of $f(x)$ at $x = a$, denoted by $f(a - 0)$ or $Lf(a)$. To determine this we make $h \to 0$ in the value of $f(x)$ at $x = a - h$. Thus,

$$Lf(a) = f(a - 0) = \lim_{x\to a^-} f(x) = \lim_{h\to 0} f(a - h)$$

If left hand limit of a function at $x = a$ is equal to its right hand limit at $x = a$, then we say that limit of $f(x)$ at $x = a$ exists and common value is called the limiting value of $f(x)$ at $x = a$, written as $\lim_{x\to a} f(x) = l$.

### Important Limits

**1.** $\lim_{\theta\to 0} \frac{\sin\theta}{\theta} = 1$; $\lim_{\theta\to 0} \frac{\theta}{\sin\theta} = 1$

$\lim_{\theta\to 0} \frac{\tan\theta}{\theta} = 1$; $\lim_{\theta\to 0} \cos\theta = 1$

**2.** $\lim_{x\to a} \frac{x^n - a^n}{x - a} = na^{n-1}$

**3.** $\lim_{x\to 0} (1 + x)^{1/x} = e$

**4.** $\lim_{x\to\infty} \left(1 + \frac{1}{x}\right)^x = e$

**5.** $\lim_{x\to\infty} \left(1 + \frac{a}{x}\right)^x = e^a$

**6.** $\lim_{x\to b} \frac{a^x - 1}{x} = \log_e a$

**7.** $\lim_{x\to 0} \frac{e^{ax} - 1}{x} = a$

### Important Expansions

**1.** $e^x = 1 + \frac{x}{1!} + \frac{x^2}{2!} + \frac{x^3}{3!} + \ldots$

**2.** $e^{-x} = 1 - \frac{x}{1!} + \frac{x^2}{2!} - \frac{x^3}{3!} + \ldots$

**3.** $\log_e (1 + x) = x - \frac{x^2}{2} + \frac{x^3}{3} - \frac{x^4}{4} + \ldots$

provided $|x| < 1$ or $x = 1$

**4.** $\log_e (1 - x) = -x - \frac{x^2}{2} - \frac{x^3}{3} - \frac{x^4}{4} \ldots$

provided $|x| < 1$ or $x = -1$

**5.** $(1 + x)^n = 1 + \frac{n}{1!} \cdot x + \frac{n(n-1)}{2!} \cdot x^2 + \frac{n(n-1)(n-2)}{3!} \cdot x^3 + \ldots$

provided $|x| < 1$

**6.** $\sin x = x - \frac{x^3}{3!} + \frac{x^5}{5!} - \ldots$

**7.** $\cos x = 1 - \frac{x^2}{2!} + \frac{x^4}{4!} - \ldots$

**8.** $\tan x = x + \frac{x^3}{3} + \frac{2}{15} x^5 + \ldots$

***Example 1.*** *Prove that the limit of the function f defined by*

$$f(x)=\begin{cases}\dfrac{|x|}{x}, & \text{if } x\neq 0\\ 0, & \text{otherwise}\end{cases}$$ *does not exist*

**Solution.** We have,

$$RHL = f(0+0)$$

$$= \lim_{h\to 0} f(0+h) = \lim_{h\to 0} f(h) = \lim_{h\to 0}\frac{|h|}{h} = \lim_{h\to 0}\frac{h}{h} = 1$$

$$LHL = f(0-0) = \lim_{h\to 0} f(0-h) = \lim_{h\to 0} f(-h) = \lim_{h\to 0}\frac{|-h|}{(-h)}$$

$$= \lim_{h\to 0}\frac{h}{(-h)} = -1$$

Since, LHL is not equal to RHL, the $\lim_{x\to 0}\frac{|x|}{x}$ does not exist.

Similarly, we can prove that $\lim_{x\to 0}\frac{x}{|x|}$ also does not exist.

***Example 2.*** *Let* $f(x)=\begin{cases}\dfrac{\sin[x]}{[x]}, & [x]\neq 0\\ 0, & [x]=0\end{cases}$

*where, [x] denotes the greatest integer less than or equal to x, then find* $\lim_{x\to 0} f(x)$.

**Solution.** We have,

$$RHL = f(0+0) = \lim_{h\to 0} f(0+h) = \lim_{h\to 0} f(h) = \lim_{h\to 0} 0 = 0 \quad [\because [h]=0]$$

$$LHL = f(0-0) = \lim_{h\to 0} f(0-h) = \lim_{h\to 0} f(-h) = \lim_{h\to 0}\frac{\sin[-h]}{[-h]}$$

$$= \lim_{h\to 0}\frac{\sin(-1)}{(-1)} = \lim_{h\to 0}\sin 1 = \sin 1 \neq 0 \quad [\because [-h]=-1\neq 0]$$

Since, LHL ≠ RHL, therefore $\lim_{x\to 0} f(x)$ does not exist.

***Example 3.*** *Let* $f(x)=\begin{cases}x, & \text{if } x \text{ is rational}\\ -x, & \text{if } x \text{ is irrational}\end{cases}$

*Show that* $\lim_{x\to a} f(x)$ *exists only when* $a=0$.

**Solution. *Case* I.** If $a$ is non-zero rational number. In this case,

$$f(a-0) = \lim_{h\to 0} f(a-h)$$

$$= \lim_{h\to 0}(a-h) \text{ or } \lim_{h\to 0}[-(a-h)]$$

[According as $(a-h)$ is rational or irrational]

$= a$ or $-a$ *i.e.*, is not unique.

$\therefore f(a-0)$ does not exist.

$\Rightarrow \lim_{x\to a} f(x)$ does not exist.

***Case* II.** If $a=0$. In this case $f(a-0)=\lim_{h\to 0} f(a-h)$

$$\Rightarrow \quad f(a-0) = \lim_{h\to 0} f(-h)$$

$$= \lim_{h\to 0}(-h) \text{ or } h=0$$

[According as $-h$ is rational or irrational]

Again, $f(0+0) = \lim_{h\to 0} f(0+h) = \lim_{h\to 0} f(h)$

$$= \lim_{h\to 0} h \text{ or } \lim_{h\to 0}(-h) = 0$$

[According as $h$ is rational or irrational]

Since, $f(0+0)=f(0-0)=0$; $\lim_{x\to 0} f(x)$ exists and is equal to zero.

***Case* III.** If $a$ is an irrational number. In this case

$$f(a-0) = \lim_{h\to 0} f(a-h)$$

$$= \lim_{h\to 0}(a-h) \text{ or } \lim_{h\to 0}[-(a-h)]$$

[According to $(a-h)$ is rational or irrational]

$= a$ or $-a$ *i.e.* is not unique.

$\therefore f(a-0)$ does not exist.

$\Rightarrow \lim_{x\to a} f(x)$ does not exist.

Thus, we see that $\lim_{x\to a} f(x)$ exists only when $a=0$.

# Continuity of a Function

Consider a function $f:[a, b]\to R$. Let $a<c<b$. A function $f(x)$ is said to be continuous at $x=c$, if $\lim_{x\to c} f(x) = f(c)$.

In other words, a function $f(x)$ is said to be continuous at a point $c$, if for any $\epsilon>0$, there exists some $\delta>0$ such that $|f(x)-f(c)|<\epsilon$, when $|x-c|<\delta$.

Equivalently, a function $f(x)$ is said to be continuous at a point $c$, if $f(c+0)=f(c-0)=f(c)$.

> ***Note*** **(a)** The graph of a continuous function is continuous at $x=c$.
>
> **(b)** A function $f(x)$ is continuous in an interval $[a, b]$, if it is continuous at every point of the interval $[a, b]$.
>
> **(c)** A function $f(x)$ is discontinuous at a point $x=c$, if $f(x)$ is not continuous at $x=c$.
>
> **(d)** A function $f(x)$ is said to be continuous at the left end point $a$, if
>
> $$\lim_{x\to a^+} f(x) = f(a+0) = f(a)$$
>
> **(e)** A function $f(x)$ is said to be continuous at the right end point $b$, if
>
> $$\lim_{x\to b^-} f(x) = f(b-0) = f(b)$$

# Discontinuity

If a function is not continuous at a point, then it is said to be discontinuous at that point and the point is called a point of discontinuity of this function.

> **Note** The discontinuity of a function $f(x)$ at $x = c$ is obtained in either of the following cases:
> (i) $\lim_{x\to c} f(x)$ exists but $\lim_{x\to c} f(x) \neq f(c)$.
> (ii) $\lim_{x\to c} f(x)$ does not exist.
> (iii) $f$ is not defined at $x = c$.

## Kinds of Discontinuity

### 1. Removable Discontinuity

If either $f(a)$ is not defined or $f(a) \neq \lim_{x\to a} f(x)$, then $f(x)$ is said to have removable discontinuity at $x = a$, because the discontinuity at $x = a$ can be removed by redefining $f(a)$ such that $\lim_{x\to a} f(x) = f(a)$.

### 2. Discontinuity of First Kind

If $\lim_{x\to a^-} f(x)$ and $\lim_{x\to a^+} f(x)$ both exists finitely but not equal, then $f(x)$ is said to have discontinuity of the first kind at $x = a$.

### 3. Discontinuity of Second Kind

If either $\lim_{x\to a^-} f(x)$ or $\lim_{x\to a^+} f(x)$ or both do not exist, then $f(x)$ is said to have discontinuity of second kind at $x = a$.

> **Note** Possible point of discontinuity, if $f(x)$ is defined differently to the left of $a$ and to the right of $a$, then $a$ is possible point of discontinuity.

## Important Results on Continuity

Let $f(x)$ and $g(x)$ be two continuous functions at $x = a$, then

1. $f(x)+g(x)$ is continuous at $x = a$.
2. $f(x)-g(x)$ is continuous at $x = a$.
3. $f(x)\cdot g(x)$ is continuous at $x = a$.
4. $f(x)/g(x)$ is continuous at $x = a$, provided $g(a) \neq 0$.
5. $c\cdot f(x)$ is continuous at $x = a$, where c is any real number.
6. If $f(x)+g(x)$ is continuous at $x = a$, then we can't conclude that $f(x)$ and $g(x)$ are continuous at $x = a$. Similarly, conclusion holds for $f(x)-g(x)$, $f(x)\cdot g(x)$ and $f(x)/g(x)$.
7. If $f(x)$ and $g(x)$ are continuous, then $f(x)+g(x)$, $f(x)-g(x)$, $f(x)\cdot g(x)$ are continuous on $D_f \cap D_g$, $f(x)/g(x)$ is continuous on $D_f \cap D_g$ except at those points, where $g(x) = 0$.
8. (i) Every constant function is continuous.
   (ii) Every polynomial function is continuous.
   (iii) Every rational function is continuous in its domain.
   (iv) Trigonometric, inverse trigonometric, exponential and logarithmic functions are continuous in their respective domains.
   (v) If $f(x)$ is continuous function and $f(x) \neq 0$, then $\frac{1}{f(x)}$ is also a continuous function.
   (vi) If $f(x)$ is continuous, then $|f(x)|$ is also continuous.
   (vii) The graph of a continuous function is a continuous curve without any breaks in it.

**Theorem** Let $f$ and $g$ be real-valued functions. If $f$ is continuous at $x = a$ and $g$ is continuous at $f(a)$, then the composite function $gof$ is also continuous at $x = a$.

**Example 4.** *Show that the function defined by*

$$f(x) = \begin{cases} (1+2x)^{1/x}, & \text{for } x \neq 0 \\ e^2, & \text{for } x = 0 \end{cases}$$

*is continuous at $x = 0$.*

**Solution.** We have, $f(0) = e^2$

Now, $f(0+0) = \lim_{h\to 0} f(0+h) = \lim_{h\to 0} f(h)$

$$= \lim_{h\to 0}(1+2h)^{1/h} = e^2 \qquad \left[\because \lim_{x\to 0}(1+ax)^{1/x} = e^a\right]$$

and $f(0-0) = \lim_{h\to 0} f(0-h) = \lim_{h\to 0} f(-h)$

$$= \lim_{h\to 0}[1-2h]^{-1/h} = \lim_{h\to 0}[1+2(-h)]^{1/(-h)}$$

$$= \lim_{p\to 0}[1+2p]^{1/p}, \qquad \text{(where } p = -h\text{)}$$

$$= e^2$$

Since, $f(0-0) = f(0) = f(0+0)$, the function $f(x)$ is continuous at $x = 0$.

**Example 5.** *If*
$$f(x) = \begin{cases} -2\sin x, & -\pi \le x \le -\pi/2 \\ a\sin x + b, & -\pi/2 < x < \pi/2 \\ \cos x, & \pi/2 \le x \le \pi \end{cases}$$
*is continuous on $[-\pi, \pi]$, find the values of a and b.*

**Solution.** At $x = -\pi/2$

$$f\left(-\frac{\pi}{2}-0\right) = \lim_{h\to 0} f\left(-\frac{\pi}{2}-h\right) = \lim_{h\to 0} -2\sin\left(-\frac{\pi}{2}-h\right)$$

$$= \lim_{h\to 0} 2\sin\left(\frac{\pi}{2}+h\right) = 2\sin\left(\frac{\pi}{2}\right) = 2$$

and $$f\left(-\frac{\pi}{2}+0\right) = \lim_{h\to 0} f\left(-\frac{\pi}{2}+h\right)$$

$$= \lim_{h\to 0}\left[a\sin\left(-\frac{\pi}{2}+h\right)+b\right] = -a+b$$

But $f(x)$ is given continuous at $x = -\pi/2$.

So, we must have

$$-a+b = 2 \qquad \text{...(i)}$$

Further at $x = \pi/2$,

$$f\left(\frac{\pi}{2}-0\right) = \lim_{h\to 0} f\left(\frac{\pi}{2}-h\right) = \lim_{h\to 0}\left[a\sin\left(\frac{\pi}{2}-h\right)+b\right]$$

$$= a\sin\pi/2 + b = a+b$$

and $$f\left(\frac{\pi}{2}+0\right) = \lim_{h\to 0} f\left(\frac{\pi}{2}+h\right) = \lim_{h\to 0}\cos\left(\frac{\pi}{2}+h\right)$$

$$= \cos\pi/2 = 0$$

For continuity at $x = \pi/2$, we must have

$$a+b = 0 \qquad \text{...(ii)}$$

Solving Eqs. (i) and (ii), we get

$$b = 1, a = -1$$

## Uniform Continuity

A function $f$ defined on an interval $I$ is said to be uniformly continuous in the interval $I$, if for each $\varepsilon > 0$, $\exists$ some $\delta > 0$ such that

$$|f(x_2) - f(x_1)| < \varepsilon, \text{ when } |x_2 - x_1| < \delta, \ \forall\ x_1, x_2 \in I.$$

***Note*** **(a)** In case of continuity of a function at a point $C$, the choice of $\delta > 0$ depends up on $\varepsilon > 0$ and the point $C$. But in case of uniform continuity of a function in an interval, the choice of $\delta > 0$ depends only on $\varepsilon > 0$ and not on a pair of points of the given interval.

**(b)** A function $f$ is not uniformly continuous in an interval $I$, if $\exists$ some $\varepsilon > 0$, such that for any $\delta > 0\ \exists$ a pair of points $x, y \in I$ for which $|f(x) - f(y)| \geq \varepsilon$, when $|x-y| < \delta$.

**(c)** Continuity of a function is defined at a point, whereas the uniform continuity of a function is defined in an interval. When we say that the function $f$ is continuous in an interval, then its meaning $f$ is continuous at all points of the interval.

## Important Theorems on Uniform Continuity

***Theorem 1*** Every uniformly continuous function on an interval is continuous on that interval but the converse is not true.

***Theorem 2*** If a function $f$ is continuous on a closed and bounded interval $[a, b]$, then it is uniformly continuous on $[a, b]$.

***Theorem 3*** If $f$ is uniformly continuous on a bounded interval $I$, then $f$ is bounded on $I$.

***Theorem 4*** If $f$ is uniformly continuous in an interval $I$ and $< x_n >$ is a cauchy sequence of elements in $I$, then $< f(x_n) >$ is a cauchy sequence.

***Theorem 5*** The product of two uniformly continuous functions may not be uniformly continuous.

***Theorem 6*** If $f$ and $g$ are uniformly continuous on an interval $I$, then $f - g$ is uniformly continuous on $I$.

***Theorem 7*** If $f$ is uniformly continuous on an interval $I_1$ and $k \in R$, then $kf$ is uniformly continuous on $I$.

***Example 6.*** *Prove that $f(x) = x^2$ is not uniformly continuous on $[0, \infty[$.*

**Solution.** Suppose, $\varepsilon = 1/2$ and $\delta$ be any positive number, then we can choose a positive integer $n$ s.t.

$$n > \frac{1}{4\delta^2} \Rightarrow \frac{1}{4n} < \delta^2 \qquad \text{...(i)}$$

Let $x_1 = \sqrt{n}$ and $x_2 = \sqrt{n+1} \in [0, \infty[$,

then $|f(x_2) - f(x_1)| = |x_2^2 - x_1^2| = |(n+1) - n| = 1 > \varepsilon$,

and $$|x_2 - x_1| = |\sqrt{n+1} - \sqrt{n}|$$

$$= \left|\frac{(\sqrt{n+1}-\sqrt{n})(\sqrt{n+1}+\sqrt{n})}{\sqrt{n+1}+\sqrt{n}}\right|$$

$$= \frac{n+1-n}{\sqrt{n+1}+\sqrt{n}} = \frac{1}{\sqrt{n+1}+\sqrt{n}} < \frac{1}{2\sqrt{n}} < \delta$$

[Using Eq. (i) $\because \sqrt{n+1}+\sqrt{n} > \sqrt{n}+\sqrt{n} = 2\sqrt{n}$]

$\Rightarrow \quad |f(x_2) - f(x_1)| > \varepsilon$, when $|x_2 - x_1| < \delta$

Therefore, $f$ is not uniformly continuous on $[0, \infty[$.

***Example 7.*** *Is the function $f(x) = \dfrac{x}{x+1}$ uniformly continuous for $x \in [0, 2]$? Justify you answer.*

**Solution.** Let $x, y$ be two arbitrary points in $[0, 2]$. Then, $x \geq 0$, $y \geq 0$.

$\Rightarrow \quad x+1 \geq 1$ and $y+1 \geq 1 \Rightarrow (x+1)(y+1) \geq 1$

$$\therefore \quad |f(x) - f(y)| = \left|\frac{x}{x+1} - \frac{y}{y+1}\right|$$

$$= \frac{|x-y|}{(x+1)(y+1)} \leq |x-y|$$

[using Eq. (i)]

Let $\varepsilon > 0$ be given, let us take $\delta = \varepsilon$, we observe that

$$|f(x) - f(y)| < \varepsilon,$$

whenever $|x-y| < \delta, \forall\ x, y \in [0, 2]$

Therefore, $f$ is uniformly continuous on $[0, 2]$.

***Example 8.*** *Show that $f(x) = 1/x^2$ is uniformly continuous on $[a, \infty[$, $a > 0$.*

**Solution.** For $x, y \geq a > 0$; we observe that

$$|f(x) - f(y)| = \left|\frac{1}{x^2} - \frac{1}{y^2}\right| = \left|\frac{1}{x} - \frac{1}{y}\right|\left|\frac{1}{x} + \frac{1}{y}\right|$$

$$\Rightarrow |f(x) - f(y)| = \left|\frac{y-x}{yx}\right|\left(\frac{1}{x} + \frac{1}{y}\right) \leq \frac{2}{a} \cdot \frac{|x-y|}{|xy|} \quad [\because x, y \geq a > 0]$$

$$\leq \frac{2}{a^3}|x-y|$$

$$\left[\because x \geq a,\ y \geq a \Rightarrow xy \geq a^2 \Rightarrow \frac{1}{xy} \leq \frac{1}{a^2}\right]$$

Let $\varepsilon > 0$ be given. Let $\delta = \varepsilon a^3/2$

Then, $|f(x) - f(y)| < \varepsilon$, when $|x-y| < \delta$, $\forall x, y \geq a$.

Therefore, $f$ is uniformly continuous on $[a, \infty[$.

***Example 9.*** *Prove that $\sin x$ is uniformly continuous on $[0, \infty[$.*

**Solution.** Let $\varepsilon > 0$ be given and $x, y$ be any two points in $[0, \infty[$.

Let $f(x) = \sin x$. Then,

$$|f(x) - f(y)| = |\sin x - \sin y| = \left|2 \sin\frac{x-y}{2} \cos\frac{x+y}{2}\right|$$

$$= 2\left|\sin\frac{(x-y)}{2}\right|\left|\cos\frac{(x+y)}{2}\right|$$

$$\leq 2\left|\frac{x-y}{2}\right| \cdot 1 \quad \left[\because |\sin\theta| \leq |\theta|,\ |\cos\theta| \leq |\theta|, \forall\theta\right]$$

$\because |f(x) - f(y)| \leq |x-y|$

$\Rightarrow |f(x) - f(y)| < \varepsilon$, when $|x-y| < \delta, (\delta = \varepsilon), \forall x, y \in [0, \infty[$.

Therefore, $f(x) = \sin x$ is uniformly continuous on $[0, \infty[$.

***Theorem 8*** **If $f$ is a continuous function at $x = a$. Then, $|f|$ is also continuous at $x = a$, but the converse is not true in general.**

***Theorem 9*** **A function defined on an external $I$, is continuous at a point $c \in I$ if and only if for every sequence $< sn >$ converging to $c$, we have**

$$\lim_{n \to \infty} f(x_n) = f(c)$$

***Theorem 10*** **If a function is continuous on a closed interval $[a, b]$, then it is bounded on that interval and attains its bounds.**

## Differentiability of a Function

The value of the $\lim\limits_{h \to 0} \dfrac{f(a+h) - f(a)}{h}$ or $\lim\limits_{x \to a^+} \dfrac{f(x) - f(a)}{x - a}$, if exists, is called right hand or progressive derivative of $f(x)$ at $x = a$ and denoted by $Rf'(a)$.

Similarly, the value of the $\lim\limits_{h \to 0} \dfrac{f(a-h) - f(a)}{-h}$ or $\lim\limits_{x \to a^-} \dfrac{f(x) - f(a)}{x - a}$ if exists is called left hand or progressive derivative of $f(x)$ at $x = a$ and is denoted by $Lf'(a)$.

A function $f(x)$ is said to be differentiable at $x = a$ if $Rf'(a) = Lf'(a)$.

## Necessary Condition for the Existence of the Finite Derivative

Continuity is a necessary but not a sufficient condition for the existence of a finite derivative. But the converse is not necessarily true.

## Important Theorems on Differentiability

***Theorem 1*** If functions $f$ and $g$ are derivable at a point $x$, then so are $(f \pm g)$, $fg$, $f/g$, $g(x) \neq 0$ and

**(i)** $(f \pm g)'(x) = f'(x) \pm g'(x)$

**(ii)** $(fg)'(x) = f'(x)g(x) + f(x)g'(x)$

**(iii)** $\left(\dfrac{f}{g}\right)'(x) = \dfrac{f'(x)g(x) - f(x)g'(x)}{[g(x)]^2}$,

provided $g(x) \neq 0$ in (iii).

***Theorem 2*** If $f$ and $g$ are derivable at $g(x)$ and $x$ respectively, then $(fog)$ is derivable at $x$ and $(fog)'(x) = f'(y)g(x)$, where $y = g(x)$.

***Theorem 3*** If $f$ is derivable at $x$ and is one-one on some *nbd* of $x$, then the inverse functions of $f$ is derivable at $f(x)$ and $(f^{-1})'(f(x)) = 1/f'(x)$; provided $f'(x) \neq 0$.

***Example 10.*** *Show that the function defined by*

*$f(x) = |x| - 1, \forall x \in R$ is not differentiable at $x = 0$.*

**Solution.** From the definition of mod function, we have

$$f(x) = \begin{cases} x - 1, & \text{if } x \geq 0 \\ -x - 1, & x < 0 \end{cases}$$

Now, $$Rf'(0) = \lim_{h \to 0} \frac{f(0+h) - f(0)}{h} = \lim_{h \to 0} \frac{f(h) - f(0)}{h}$$

$$= \lim_{h \to 0} \frac{(h-1) - (-1)}{h} = \lim_{h \to 0} \frac{h}{h} = \lim_{h \to 0} 1 = 1$$

and $$Lf'(0) = \lim_{h \to 0} \frac{f(0-h) - f(0)}{h} = \lim_{h \to 0} \frac{f(-h) - f(0)}{(-h)}$$

$$= \lim_{h \to 0} \frac{[-(h) - 1] - (-1)}{(-h)} = \lim_{h \to 0} \frac{h}{(-h)} = \lim_{h \to 0} (-1) = -1$$

Since, $Rf'(0) \neq Lf'(0)$

$\therefore f(x)$ is not differentiable at $x = 0$.

***Example 11.*** *Find the value of a and b, so that $f(x)$ may be differentiable at $x = 1$, where*

$$f(x) = \begin{cases} x^2 + 3x + a, & \text{if } x \leq 1 \\ bx + 2, & \text{if } x > 1 \end{cases}$$

**Solution.** Since, the function $f(x)$ is differentiable, so it will be continuous also.

Now, $f(1+0) = \lim_{h\to 0} f(1+h) = \lim_{h\to 0} b(1+h) + 2 = b + 2$

and $f(1-0) = \lim_{h\to 0} f(1-h) = \lim_{h\to 0} [(1-h)^2 + 3(1-h) + a]$

$= 1 + 3 + a = a + 4$

For continuity, we must have

$$a + 4 = b + 2 \text{ or } a - b = -2 \qquad \ldots\text{(i)}$$

Now, $Rf'(1) = \lim_{h\to 0} \dfrac{f(1+h) - f(1)}{h}$

$= \lim_{h\to 0} \dfrac{b(1+h) + 2 - (4+a)}{h}$

$= \lim_{h\to 0} \dfrac{(b-2-a) + bh}{h}$

For this limit to exist, we must have $b - 2 - a = 0$ [which is same as Eq. (i)] and $Rf'(1) = b$

Also, $Lf'(1) = \lim_{h\to 0} \dfrac{f(1-h) - f(1)}{-h}$

$= \lim_{h\to 0} \dfrac{[(1-h)^2 + 3(1-h) + a] - [4+a]}{-h}$

$= \lim_{h\to 0} \dfrac{[1 - 2h + h^2 + 3 - 3h + a - 4 - a]}{-h}$

$= \lim_{h\to 0} \dfrac{h(-5+h)}{-h} = 5$

For the function $f(x)$ to be differentiable, we must have

$$Rf'(1) = Lf'(1) \Rightarrow b = 5$$

Putting this in Eq. (i), $a = b - 2 = 5 - 2 = 3 \Rightarrow a = 3$

***Theorem 4*** (Darboux Theorem) If $f$ is derivable on $[a,b]$ and $f'(a) \neq f'(b)$, then for each $k$ lying between $f'(a)$ and $f'(b)$, there exists a point $c \in [a,b]$ such that $f'(c) = k$.

***Theorem 5*** If $f$ is derivable on $[a,b]$ and $f'(a)f'(b) < 0$ then there exists a point $c \in (a,b)$ such that $f'(c) = 0$.

***Theorem 6*** If $f$ is derivable on an interval $I$, then the range of $f'$ on $I$, *i.e.*, $f'(I)$ is either an interval or singleton.

***Theorem 7*** If $f'(x) \neq 0, \forall x \in (a,b)$, then $f'(x)$ retains the same sign, positive or negative in $(a,b)$.

***Theorem 8*** If $f$ is derivable on $[a,b]$, $f(a) = f(b) = 0$ and $f'(a)f'(b) > 0$, then $\exists\ c \in (a,b)$, such that $f(c) = 0$.

# Rolle's Theorem

If a function $f(x)$ defined on $[a, b]$ is such that

**(i)** $f(x)$ is continuous in the closed interval $[a, b]$.

**(ii)** $f'(x)$ exists, *i.e.*, $f(x)$ is differentiable for every point in the open interval $]a, b[$ and

**(iii)** $f(a) = f'(b)$, then there exists atleast one point or say one value of $x$, say $c$ where $a < c < b$ such that $f'(c) = 0$.

> ***Note*** Converse of Rolle's theorem is not true, *i.e.*, the conditions of Rolle's theorem are sufficient only but not necessary. For example, the function $f(x) = \dfrac{1}{x} + \dfrac{1}{2-x}$ is continuous on $[0, 2]$ and differentiable on $]0, 2[$ and $f(0) = f(2) =$ undefined, although $f'(1) = 0$.

## Geometric Interpretation of Rolle's Theorem

Rolle's theorem has a nice geometric implication. If a function is continuous on a closed and bounded interval, *i.e.*, its graph has no break and is derivable *i.e.*, has no sharp bend, then there exists atleast one point on the graph, the tangent at which is parallel to the x-axis.

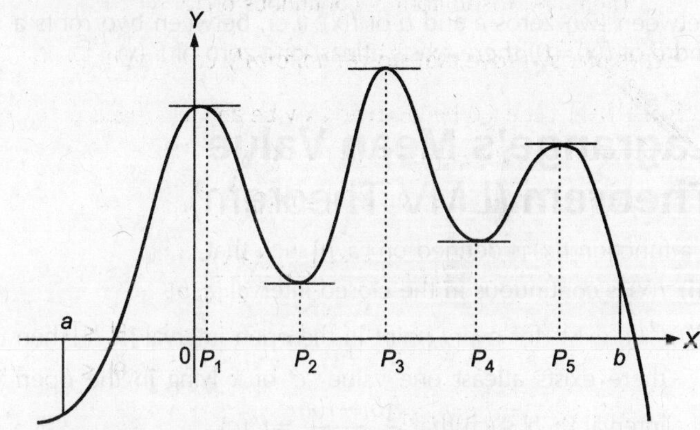


In the graph, there are five such points $P_1, P_2, P_3, P_4, P_5$, where the tangents drawn are parallel to the x-axis.

***Example 12.*** *Show that between any two distinct roots of* $e^x \cos x = 1$, *there exists atleast one root of* $e^x \sin x - 1 = 0$.

**Solution.** Let $\alpha$ and $\beta$ be any two distinct roots of $e^x \cos x = 1$.

$$\therefore \quad e^\alpha \cos\alpha = 1 \text{ and } e^\beta \cos\beta = 1 \qquad \ldots\text{(i)}$$

Define a function $f$ as follows

$$f(x) = e^{-x} - \cos x, \quad \forall\ x \in [\alpha, \beta] \qquad \ldots\text{(ii)}$$

Obviously, $f$ is continuous in $[\alpha, \beta]$ as $e^{-x}$ and $\cos x$ both are continuous.

Indeed, $f'(x) = -e^{-x} + \sin x, \forall x \in ]\alpha, \beta[$

$\Rightarrow f(x)$ is derivable also in $]\alpha, \beta[$.

From Eq. (ii), $f(\alpha) = e^{-\alpha} - \cos\alpha = \dfrac{1 - e^\alpha \cos\alpha}{e^\alpha} = 0$, [from Eq. (i)]

Similarly, $f(\beta) = 0$ and hence $f(\alpha) = f(\beta)$

Thus, $f$ satisfies all the conditions of Rolle's theorem in $[\alpha, \beta]$ and so there exists some $\gamma \in ]\alpha, \beta[$ such that $f'(\gamma) = 0$

$\Rightarrow \sin\gamma - e^{-\gamma} = 0 \Rightarrow \sin\gamma = e^{-\gamma} = 1/e^\gamma$

$\Rightarrow e^\gamma \sin\gamma - 1 = 0$, where $\alpha < \gamma < \beta$

Hence, $\gamma$ is a root of $e^x \sin x - 1 = 0, \alpha < \gamma < \beta$.

$\Rightarrow$ We get atleast one root of $e^x \sin x - 1 = 0$.

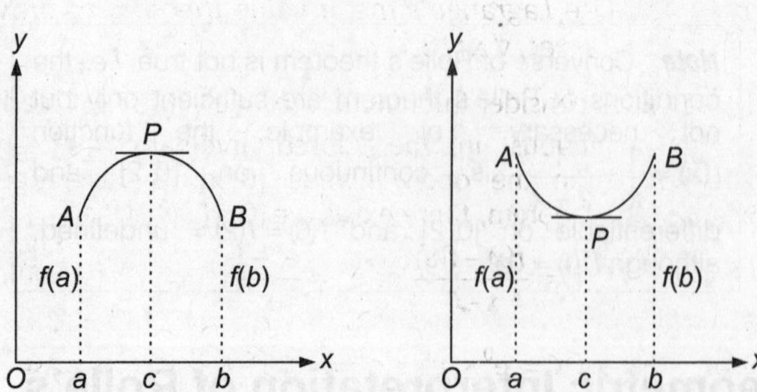


In the above graphs there is one point $P$, where the tangents drawn are parallel to the $x$-axis.

## Algebraic Interpretation of Rolle's Theorem

Between two zeros $a$ and $b$ of $f(x)$, (*i.e.*, between two roots $a$ and $b$ of $f(x)=0$) there exists atleast one zero of $f'(x)$.

## Lagrange's Mean Value Theorem (LMV Theorem)

If a function $f(x)$ is defined on $[a, b]$ such that

**(i)** $f(x)$ is continuous in the closed interval $[a, b]$.

**(ii)** $f'(x)$ exists for every point in the open interval $]a, b[$, then there exists atleast one value '$c$' of $x$ lying in the open interval $]a, b[$ such that $\dfrac{f(b)-f(a)}{b-a}=f'(c)$.

## Another Form of Lagrange's Mean Value Theorem

The result $f(b)-f(a)=(b-a)f'(c)$ is also known as the formulae for finite increments, if we put $b=a+h$, we get

$$f(a+h)-f(a)=hf'(a+\theta h)$$

or $$f(a+h)=f(a)+hf'(a+\theta h),\text{ where } 0<\theta<1$$

and $f$ is continuous on $[a, a+h]$ and differentiable on $]a, a+h[$.

> **Note** Lagrange's mean value theorem is also called as "First mean value theorem of differential calculus".

## Geometrical Interpretation of the Mean Value Theorem

If the curve $y=f(x)$ is continuous from $x=a$ to $x=b$ and has a definite tangent at each point on the curve between $x=a$ and $x=b$, then geometrically, Lagrange's mean value theorem means that there is atleast one point between $x=a$ and $x=b$ on the curve where the tangent to the curve is parallel to the chord joining the points $[a, f(a)]$ and $[b, f(b)]$.

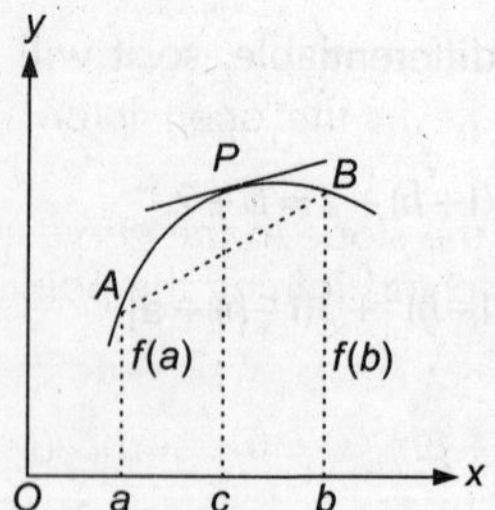


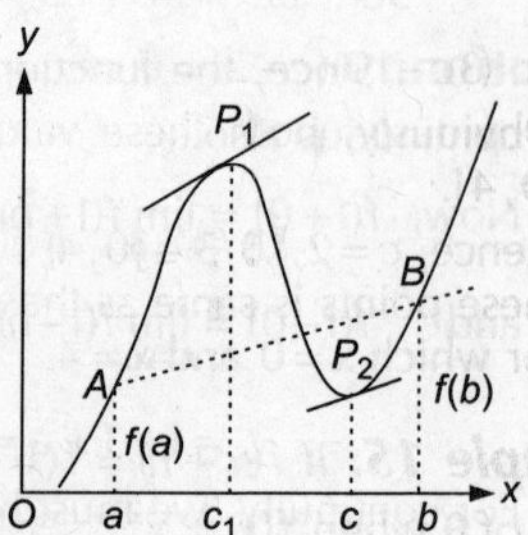


## Important Deductions from Lagrange's Mean Value Theorem

1. If a function $f$ is (i) continuous on $[a, b]$ and (ii) derivable on $(a, b)$, then
$f'(x)=0, \forall x\in[a, b] \Rightarrow f$ is constant on $[a, b]$.
2. If two functions $f$ and $g$ are (i) continuous on $[a, b]$ and (ii) derivable on $(a, b)$, then $f'(x)=g'(x), \forall x\in[a, b] \Rightarrow f-g$ is constant on $[a, b]$.
3. If a function $f$ is (i) continuous on $[a, b]$ and (ii) derivable on $(a, b)$, then $f'(x)>0, \forall x\in[a, b] \Rightarrow f$ is strictly increasing on $[a, b]$.
4. If a function $f$ is (i) continuous on $[a, b]$ and (ii) derivable on $(a, b)$, then $f'(x)<0, \forall x\in[a, b]$
$\Rightarrow f$ is strictly decreasing on $[a, b]$.

***Example 13.*** *Test if Lagrange's mean value theorem holds for the function $f(x)=|x|$ in the interval $[-1, 1]$.*

**Solution.** Clearly, the function $f(x)=|x|$ is continuous on the closed interval $[-1, 1]$ but not differentiable at $x=0$ which is a point of the open interval $]-1, 1[$. Thus, $f(x)$ is not differentiable in $]-1, 1[$. Hence, Lagrange's mean value theorem does not hold for the function $f(x)=|x|$ in the interval $[-1, 1]$.

***Example 14.*** *If $f(x)=(x-1)(x-3)(x-5)$, $a=0, b=4$. Find the value of $c$ such that $f'(c)$ has the same value as the slope of the chord joining the points for which $x=0$ and $x=4$.*

**Solution.** We know that a polynomial function is continuous as well as differentiable for all $x$. Since,

$$f(x)=(x-1)(x-3)(x-5)=x^3-9x^2+23x-15$$

is a polynomial in $x$, therefore it is continuous in $[0, 4]$ and differentiable in $]0, 4[$.

Since, $f(x)$ satisfies all the conditions of Lagrange's mean value theorem, therefore there must exist some $c\in]0, 4[$ such that $\dfrac{f(4)-f(0)}{4-0}=f'(c)$

$$\Rightarrow \frac{(-3)-(-15)}{4-0}=f'(c) \Rightarrow \frac{12}{4}=f'(c) \Rightarrow 3=f'(c) \quad \text{...(i)}$$

Since, $f(x)=x^3-9x^2+23x-15$,

therefore, $f'(x)=3x^2-18x+23$

$$\Rightarrow \quad f'(c)=3c^2-18c+23=3$$

or $$3c^2-18c+20=0 \quad \text{...(ii)}$$

or $3c^2-6c-10c+20=0$ or $3c(c-2)-10(c-2)=0$

or $(3c-10)(c-2)=0$ or $c=2, 10/3$

Obviously, both these values of c lie in the open interval $]0,4[$.

Hence, $c=2, 10/3 \in ]0,4[$ such that the slope to the curve at these points is same as the slope of chord joining the points for which $x=0$ and $x=4$.

***Example 15.*** *If $f(x+h)=f(x)+hf'(x+\theta h)$, $0<\theta<1$, find the value of $\theta$ when $f(x)=x^2$.*

**Solution.** $f(x)=x^2, f'(x)=2x, f(x+h)=(x+h)^2$

$\Rightarrow \quad (x+h)^2 = x^2+h\cdot 2\cdot(x+\theta h)$

$\Rightarrow \quad 2xh+h^2 = 2h(x+\theta h)$

$\Rightarrow \quad h^2 = 2h^2\theta \Rightarrow 1=2\theta \Rightarrow \theta = 1/2$

***Example 16.*** *Given $f(x)=\sin^2 x, x\in]0,\pi[$, on what subintervals of $[0,\pi]$ is f increasing or decreasing?*

**Solution.** $f(x)=\sin^2 x \Rightarrow f'(x)=2\sin x\cos x=\sin 2x$

$\Rightarrow$ $f(x)$ is an increasing function, if $f'(x)>0$.

$\Rightarrow \sin 2x>0 \Rightarrow 0<2x<\pi \Rightarrow 0<x<\pi/2$

Thus, $f(x)$ is increasing in the subinterval $]0,\pi/2[$. Now, $f(x)$ is increasing function, if $f'(x)<0$.

or if $\sin 2x<0$ or $\pi<2x<2\pi$ or $\pi/2<x<\pi$.

Hence, $f(x)$ is decreasing in the subinterval $]\pi/2,\pi[$.

***Example 17.*** *Show that the function f defined as $f(x)=x^3-6x^2+12x-4, \forall x\in R$, is increasing in every interval.*

**Solution.** Given, $f(x)=x^3-6x^2+12x-4$

$\therefore \quad f'(x)=3x^2-12x+12$

$= 3(x^2-4x+4)=3(x-2)^2, \forall x\in R$

$\Rightarrow f'(x)>0$ when $x\neq 2$ and $f'(2)=0$ consider any interval $[c,2], c\in R$. Clearly, $f$ is continuous in $[c,2]$ and $f'(x)>0$ for all $x$ in $]c,2[$. Therefore, $f$ is strictly increasing in $[c,2[$. Similarly, $f$ is strictly increasing in $[2,d], d\in R$.

***Example 18.*** *Use the function $f(x)=x^{1/x}, x>0$ to determine the bigger of the two numbers $e^\pi$ and $\pi^e$.*

**Solution.** Let $f(x)=x^{1/x} \Rightarrow \log f(x)=\frac{1}{x}\log x$

Differentiating *wrt* $x$, we get

$$\frac{1}{f(x)}\cdot f'(x)=\frac{1}{x}\cdot\frac{1}{x}+\frac{(-1)}{x^2}\cdot\log_e x$$

or $\quad f'(x)=\frac{x^{1/x}}{x^2}[1-\log_e x]$

for $x>e, f'(x)<0$ $\quad [\because \log e^x>1$ for $x>e]$

$\therefore f(x)$ is a decreasing function of $x$ for $x>e$.

Hence, as $\pi>e \Rightarrow f(\pi)<f(e)\Rightarrow \pi^{1/\pi}<e^{1/e}$

$\Rightarrow (\pi^{1/\pi})^{e\pi}<(e^{1/e})^{e\pi} \Rightarrow \pi^e<e^\pi$

$\Rightarrow e^\pi$ is bigger than $\pi^e$.

***Example 19.*** *Use Lagrange's mean value theorem to prove that $1+x<e^x<1+xe^x, \forall x>0$.*

**Solution.** Let us consider the function $f(x)=e^x$ in $]0,x[$. Clearly, $f(x)$ is continuous in the closed interval $[0,x]$ and differentiable in the open interval $]0,x[$. By Lagrange's means value theorem, there exists $c\in]0,x[$ such that

$$f'(c)=\frac{f(x)-f(0)}{x-0} \text{ or } e^c=\frac{e^x-1}{x}$$

Now, $0<c<x \Rightarrow e^0<e^c<e^x \Rightarrow e^0<\frac{e^x-1}{x}<e^x, \forall x>0$

$\Rightarrow x<e^x-1<xe^x$ or $1+x<e^x<1+xe^x$

Hence, $1+x<e^x<1+xe^x, \forall x>0$

***Example 20.*** *Prove that $\tan x>x$, whenever $0<x<\frac{\pi}{2}$.*

**Solution.** Let c be any real number such that $0<c<\pi/2$.

Let $\quad f(x)=\tan x-x, \forall x\in[0,c]$

Clearly, $f(x)$ is continuous as well as differentiable on $[0,c]$.

Now, $f'(x)=\sec^2 x-1=\tan^2 x>0$ for $0<x<c$

Thus, $f(x)$ is strictly increasing in $[0,c]$.

$\Rightarrow \quad f(x)>f(0)$, for $c>0$

But $f(0)=0$. Therefore, $f(c)>0 \Rightarrow \tan c-c>0$, since c is any real number such that $0<c<\pi/2$, therefore $\tan x>x$ whenever $0<x<\pi/2$.

***Example 21.*** *Let $f(x)$ be defined for all $x\in R$ and let $|f(x)-f(y)|\le(x-y)^2, \forall x,y\in R$. Show that $f(x)$ is a constant function.*

**Solution.** We have, $|f(x)-f(y)|\le(x-y)^2, \forall x,y\in R$ ...(i)

$[\because |x|^2=x^2, \forall x\in R]$

Let x be any real number and let y be chosen arbitrarily close to x but not equal to x. Then, Eq. (i) gives

$$\left|\frac{f(x)-f(y)}{x-y}\right|\le|x-y|$$

Taking limit when $y\to x$, we get

$$\lim_{y\to x}\left|\frac{f(x)-f(y)}{x-y}\right|\le\lim_{y\to x}|x-y|$$

$\Rightarrow \quad f'(x)\le 0 \quad [\because \lim_{y\to x}\frac{f(x)-f(y)}{x-y}=f'(x)]$

But $\quad |f'(x)|\ge 0$,

therefore $\quad |f'(x)|=0 \Rightarrow f'(x)=0$

$\Rightarrow f(x)$ is constant.

## Cauchy's Mean Value Theorem

If two functions $f(x)$ and $g(x)$ are defined on $[a, b]$ such that

**(i)** $f(x)$ and $g(x)$ both are continuous on $[a, b]$.

**(ii)** $f(x)$ and $g(x)$ both are differentiable on $]a, b[$.

**(iii)** $g'(x)$ does not vanish on $]a, b[$ *i.e.*, $g'(x)\neq 0$ for every point of the open interval $]a, b[$, then there exists atleast one value '$c$' of $x$ in the open interval $]a, b[$ *i.e.*, $c \in ]a, b[$ such that

$$\frac{f(b)-f(a)}{g(b)-g(a)} = \frac{f'(c)}{g'(c)}, \quad a < c < b.$$

***Note*** **(a)** If we take $g(x) = x, \forall x \in [a, b]$ in cauchy's mean value theorem. We obtain $\frac{f(b)-f(a)}{b-a} = f'(c)$ [$\because g'(c) = 1$] which is the result of Lagrange's mean value theorem.

**(b)** The theorem can be stated alternatively as follows:

If $f(x)$ and $g(x)$ are two real functions such that

(i) $f(x)$ and $g(x)$ are both continuous on $[a, a+h]$, $h > 0$.

(ii) $f(x)$ and $g(x)$ are both differentiable in $]a, a+h[$.

(iii) $g'(x)$ does not vanish on $]a, a+h[$.

Then, there exists a number $\theta \in ]0, 1[$ such that

$$\frac{f(a+h)-f(a)}{g(a+h)-g(a)} = \frac{f'(a+\theta h)}{g'(a+\theta h)}$$

**(c)** A theorem close to Cauchy's theorem can be deduced using Lagrange's theorem to $f(x)$ and $g(x)$ separately where one gets $c_1$ and $c_2$ so that

$$\frac{f(a+h)-f(a)}{g(a+h)-g(a)} = \frac{f'(c_1)}{g'(c_2)},$$

where $c_1 \neq c_2$ in general and $a < c_1, c_2 < a+h$.

***Example 22.*** *Use Cauchy's mean value theorem to show that* $\frac{\sin\alpha - \sin\beta}{\cos\beta - \cos\alpha} = \cot\theta$ *for some such that* $0 < \alpha < \theta < \beta < \pi/2$.

**Solution.** Let $f(x) = \sin x$ and $g(x) = \cos x$ and interval is $[\alpha, \beta]$.

We know that functions $\sin x$ and $\cos x$ both are continuous and differentiable in the interval $[\alpha, \beta]$. Therefore, by LMV theorem we shall get $\theta$ such that

$$\alpha < \theta < \beta \text{ and } \frac{f'(\theta)}{g'(\theta)} = \frac{f(\beta)-f(\alpha)}{g(\beta)-g(\alpha)}$$

$$\Rightarrow \quad \frac{\cos\theta}{-\sin\theta} = \frac{\sin\beta - \sin\alpha}{\cos\beta - \cos\alpha}$$

$$\Rightarrow \quad \frac{\sin\alpha - \sin\beta}{\cos\beta - \cos\alpha} = \cot\beta$$

***Example 23.*** *Show that c of cauchy's mean value theorem for the interval (a, b) is the geometric mean of a, b if* $\phi(x) = \sqrt{x}$ *and* $f(x) = 1/\sqrt{x}$; *and is the harmonic mean of a, b if* $\phi(x) = 1/x^2$ *and* $f(x) = 1/x$.

**Solution.** (i) Since, $f(x) = 1/\sqrt{x}$, $\phi(x) = \sqrt{x}$

We have, $$\frac{\phi(b)-\phi(a)}{f(b)-f(a)} = \frac{\sqrt{b}-\sqrt{a}}{(1/\sqrt{b})-(1/\sqrt{a})} = -\sqrt{ab}$$

and $$\frac{\phi'(x)}{f'(x)} = \frac{\frac{d}{dx}(\sqrt{x})}{\frac{d}{dx}(1/\sqrt{x})} = \frac{\frac{1}{2}x^{-1/2}}{\frac{-1}{2}x^{-3/2}}$$

$$\Rightarrow \quad \frac{\phi'(c)}{f'(c)} = \frac{-c^{-1/2}}{c^{-3/2}} = -c$$

According to Cauchy's mean value theorem, we get

$$\frac{\phi'(c)}{f'(c)} = \frac{\phi(b)-\phi(a)}{f(b)-f(a)}$$

$$\Rightarrow \quad -c = -\sqrt{ab} \Rightarrow c = \sqrt{ab}$$

$\Rightarrow$ $c$ is the geometric mean of $a$, $b$.

(ii) Here, $$\frac{\phi(b)-\phi(a)}{f(b)-f(a)} = \frac{(1/b^2)-(1/a^2)}{(1/b)-(1/a)} = \frac{a+b}{ab}$$

and $$\frac{\phi'(x)}{f'(x)} = \frac{-2x^{-3}}{-x^{-2}} \Rightarrow \frac{\phi'(c)}{f'(c)} = \frac{-2c^{-3}}{-c^{-2}} = \frac{2}{c}.$$

According to Cauchy's mean value theorem, we get

$$\frac{2}{c} = \frac{a+b}{ab} \Rightarrow c = \frac{2ab}{a+b} = \text{HM of } a, b$$

## Taylor's Theorem or Taylor's Series (Infinite Form)

Let $f(x)$ be a function of $x$ which possesses continuous derivatives of all orders in the interval $[a, a+h]$. Assuming that $f(a+h)$ can be expanded as an infinite power series in $h$, we have

$$f(a+h) = f(a) + hf'(a) + \frac{h^2}{2!}f''(a) + \ldots + \frac{h^n}{n!}f^n(a) + \ldots \quad \ldots\text{(i)}$$

***Note*** **(a)** Putting $h = x - a$ in Eq. (i), we get the following expansion of $f(x)$ in powers of $(x-a)$ which is given below

$$f(x) = f(a) + (x-a)f'(a) + \frac{(x-a)^2}{2!}f''(a) + \frac{(x-a)^3}{3!}f'''(a) + \ldots + \frac{(x-a)^n}{n!}f^n(a) + \ldots$$

**(b)** If we expand $f(x+h)$ by Taylor's theorem as a power series in $h$, then the result is as follows

$$f(x+h) = f(x) + hf'(x) + \frac{h^2}{2!}f''(x) + \ldots + \frac{h^n}{n!}f^n(x) + \ldots$$

**(c)** Putting $a = 0$ and $h = x$ in Eq. (i), we get

$$f(x) = f(0) + xf'(0) + \frac{x^2}{2!}f''(0) + \ldots + \frac{x^n}{n!}f^n(0) + \ldots$$

which is nothing but the Maclaurin's series.

## Taylor's Theorem with Lagrange's Remainder

If a function $f$ defined on $[a, a+h]$ is such that

**(i)** All the derivatives of orders upto $(n-1)$th order are continuous in $[a, a+h]$.

**(ii)** The $(n-1)$th derivative $f^{n-1}$ is derivable in $]a, a+h[$, then there exists some $\theta$, $0 < \theta < 1$, such that

$$f(a+h) = f(a) + hf'(a) + \frac{h^2}{2!}f''(a) + \ldots + \frac{h^{n-1}}{(n-1)!}f^{n-1}(a) + R_n$$

where, $R_n = \frac{h^n}{n!}f^n(a+\theta h)$. (Lagrange's Remainder)

## Taylor's Theorem With Cauchy's Form of Remainder

If a function $f$ defined on $[a, a+h]$ is such that

**(i)** All the derivatives upto $(n-1)$th order are continuous in $[a, a+h]$.

**(ii)** The $(n-1)$th derivative $f^{n-1}$ is derivable in $]a, a+h[$, then there exists some $\theta$, $0<\theta<1$, such that

$$f(a+h) = f(a) + hf'(a) + \frac{h^2}{2!}f''(a) + \ldots + \frac{h^{n-1}}{(n-1)!}f^{n-1}(a) + R_n$$

where, $R_n = h^n \dfrac{(1-\theta)^{n-1}}{(n-1)!} f^n(a+\theta h)$

(Cauchy's form of Remainder)

## Maclaurin's Theorem

On taking $a=0$ in Taylor theorem, we get Maclaurin's theorem, which may be stated as follows

$$f(x) = f(0) + xf'(0) + \frac{x^2}{2!}f''(0) + \ldots + \frac{x^{n-1}}{(n-1)!}f^{n-1}(0) + \frac{x^n}{n!}f^n(\theta x) \quad \text{(Lagrange's Remainder)}$$

$$f(x) = f(0) + xf'(0) + \frac{x^2}{2!}f''(0) + \ldots + \frac{x^{n-1}}{(n-1)!}f^{n-1}(0) + \frac{x^n(1-\theta)^{n-1}}{(n-1)!}f^n(\theta x) \quad \text{(Cauchy's Remainder)}$$

### Maclaurin's Infinite Series

Let $S_n = f(0) + xf'(0) + \dfrac{x^2}{2!}f''(0) + \ldots + \dfrac{x^{n-1}}{(n-1)!}f^{n-1}(0)$

$$R_n = \frac{x^n}{n!}f^n(\theta x) \text{ or } R_n = \frac{x^{n-1}}{(n-1)!}(1-\theta)^{n-1}f^n(\theta x)$$

$\therefore \quad f(x) = S_n + R_n$

Now, $R_n \to 0$ as $n \to \infty$ if and only if

$$f(x) = \lim_{n\to\infty} S_n$$

Thus, we have the following

If a function $f$ defined on $[0, h]$ is such that

**(i)** $f^n$ exists for each $n$, *i.e.*, $f$ has derivatives of all orders.

**(ii)** $R_n \to 0$ as $n \to \infty$, then

$$f(x) = f(0) + xf'(0) + \frac{x^2}{2!}f''(0) + \frac{x^3}{3!}f'''(0) + \ldots + \frac{x^n}{n!}f^n(0) + \ldots$$

This is called Maclaurin's infinite series expansion of $f(x)$.

***Example 24.*** *Expand* $\sin x$ *in the powers of* $\left(x - \dfrac{\pi}{2}\right)$ *by Taylor's series.*

**Solution.** Let $f(x) = \sin x$ and $a = \dfrac{\pi}{2}$ ...(i)

Now, $f(x) = \sin x \Rightarrow f(a) = f(\pi/2) = 1$

$f'(x) = \cos x \Rightarrow f'(a) = f'(\pi/2) = 0$

$f''(x) = -\sin x \Rightarrow f''(a) = f''(\pi/2) = -1$

$f'''(x) = -\cos x \Rightarrow f'''(a) = f'''(\pi/2) = 0$

$f^{iv}(x) = \sin x \Rightarrow f^{iv}(a) = f^{iv}(\pi/2) = 1$ and so on.

Hence, applying Taylor's theorem, we have

$$f(x) = f(\pi/2) + (x-\pi/2)f'(\pi/2) + \frac{[x-(\pi/2)]^2}{2!}f''(\pi/2) + \ldots \quad \text{...(ii)}$$

Substituting the values of $f(\pi/2)$, $f'(\pi/2)$, $f''(\pi/2)$, $f'''(\pi/2)$, $f^{iv}(\pi/2)$ and so on in Eq. (ii), we obtain

$$\sin x = 1 + \left(x - \frac{\pi}{2}\right)\cdot 0 + \frac{1}{2!}\left(x-\frac{\pi}{2}\right)^2(-1) + \frac{1}{3!}\left(x - \frac{\pi}{2}\right)^3 \cdot 0 + \ldots$$

$$= 1 - \left(\frac{1}{2!}\right)(x-\pi/2)^2 + \left(\frac{1}{4!}\right)(x-\pi/2)^4 - \ldots$$

***Example 25.*** *Prove that*

$$f\left(\frac{x^2}{1+x}\right) = f(x) - \frac{x}{1+x}f'(x) + \frac{x^2}{(1+x)^2}\cdot\frac{1}{2!}f''(x) - \ldots$$

**Solution.** We have, $f\left(\dfrac{x^2}{1+x}\right) = f\left(x - \dfrac{x}{1+x}\right) = f(x+h)$

where, $h = \dfrac{-x}{1+x}$

Expanding $f(x+h)$ by Taylor's series, we get

$$f(x+h) = f(x) + h\cdot f'(0) + \frac{h^2}{2!}f''(0) + \ldots$$

Putting the value of $h$ in both sides, we get

$$f\left(x + \frac{-x}{1+x}\right) = f(x) - \frac{x}{1+x}f'(x) + \frac{1}{2!}\cdot\frac{x^2}{(1+x)^2}f''(x) - \ldots$$

$$\Rightarrow \quad f\left(\frac{x^2}{1+x}\right) = f(x) - \frac{x}{1+x}f'(x) + \frac{1}{2!}\frac{x^2}{(1+x)^2}f''(x) - \ldots$$

## Maxima and Minima of Functions of Two Independent Variables

Let $f(x, y)$ be any function of two independent variables $x$ and $y$ supposed to be continuous for all values of these variables in the neighbourhood of their values $a$ and $b$, respectively. Then, $f(a, b)$ is said to be a maximum or minimum value of $f(x, y)$ according as $f(a+h, b+k)$ is less or greater than $f(a, b)$ for all sufficiently small independent values of $h$ and $k$, positive or negative provided both of them are not equal to zero.

## Necessary Conditions

The necessary conditions that $f(x, y)$ should be maximum or minimum at $x = a$, $y = b$ is that

$$\left.\frac{\partial f}{\partial x}\right|_{\substack{x=a\\y=b}} = 0 \quad \text{and} \quad \left.\frac{\partial f}{\partial y}\right|_{\substack{x=a\\y=b}} = 0$$

## Sufficient Condition

Let $r = \left(\frac{\partial^2 f}{\partial x^2}\right)_{\substack{x=a\\y=b}}$; $s = \left(\frac{\partial^2 f}{\partial x \partial y}\right)_{\substack{x=a\\y=b}}$; $t = \left(\frac{\partial^2 f}{\partial y^2}\right)_{\substack{x=a\\y=b}}$

***Case* I** $f(x, y)$ will have a maximum or a minimum value at $x = a, y = b$, if $rt > s^2$. Further, $f(x, y)$ is maximum or minimum according as $r$ is negative or positive.

***Case* II** If $f(x, y)$ will have neither maximum or minimum at $x = a, y = b$, if $rt < s^2$, *i.e.*, $x = a, y = b$ is a saddle point.

***Case* III** If $rt = s^2$, this case is doubtful case and further advanced investigation is needed to determine whether $f(x, y)$ is a maximum or minimum at $x = a, y = b$ or not. This case is very rarely used.

# Relative or Local Maxima and Minima (of Function of a Single Independent Variable)

**Definition** A function $f(x)$ is said to be a local or relative maximum at $x = a$, if $\exists$ a positive number $\delta$ such that $f(a + \delta) < f(a)$ for all values of $\delta$ other than zero in the interval $(-\delta, \delta)$.

A function $f(x)$ is said to be a local or relative minimum at $x = a$, if $\exists$ a positive number $\delta$ such that $f(a + \delta) > f(a)$ for all values of $\delta$ other than zero in the interval $(-\delta, \delta)$.

Maximum and minimum values of a function are together also called extreme values or turing values and the points at which they are attained are called points of maxima and minima. The points at which a function has extreme value are called turing points.

## Important Properties of Relative Maxima and Minima

**(i)** Atleast one maximum or one minimum must lie between two equal values of a function.

**(ii)** Maximum and minimum values must occur alternatively.

**(iii)** There may be several maximum or minimum values of same function.

**(iv)** A function $y = f(x)$ is maximum at $x = a$, if $\frac{dy}{dx}$ changes sign from positive to negative as $x$ passes through $a$.

**(v)** A function $y = f(x)$ is minimum at $x = a$, if $\frac{dy}{dx}$ changes sign from negative and positive as $x$ passes through $a$.

**(vi)** If the sign of $\frac{dy}{dx}$ does not change while $x$ passes through $a$, then $y$ is neither maximum nor minimum at $x = a$.

## Conditions for Maximum or Minimum Values

The necessary condition that $f(x)$ should have a maximum or a minimum at $x = a$ is that $f'(a) = 0$.

## Definition of Stationary Values

A function $f(x)$ is said to be stationary at $x = a$, if $f'(a) = 0$. Thus, for a function $f(x)$ to be a maximum or minimum at $x = a$, it must be stationary at $x = a$.

## Sufficient Conditions of Maximum or Minimum Values

There is a maximum of $f(x)$ at $x = a$, if $f'(a) = 0$ and $f''(a)$ is negative.

Similarly, there is a minimum of $f(x)$ at $x = a$, if $f'(a) = 0$ and $f''(a)$ is positive.

## Working Rule for Maxima and Minima of *f*(*x*)

**(i)** Find $f'(x)$ and equate it to zero.

**(ii)** Solve the resulting equation of $x$. Let its roots be $a_1, a_2, \ldots, a_n$. Then, $f(x)$ is stationary at $x = a_1, a_2, \ldots$ Thus, $x = a_1, a_2, \ldots$ are the only points at which $f(x)$ can be maximum or minimum.

**(iii)** Find $f''(x)$ and substitute it by terms $x = a_1, a_2, \ldots$ wherever $f''(x)$ is negative we have a maximum and whenever $f''(x)$ is positive we have a minimum.

**(iv)** If $f''(a_1) = 0$, find $f'''(x)$ put $x = a_1$ in it. If $f'''(a_1) \neq 0$, there is neither a maximum nor a minimum at $x = a_1$. If $f'''(a_1) = 0$. Find $f^{iv}(x)$ and put $x = a_1$ in it. If $f^{iv}(a_1)$ is negative, we have maximum at $x = a_1$, if it is positive there is a minimum at $x = a_1$. If $f^{v}(a_1)$ is zero, we must find $f^{v}(x)$ and so on. Repeat the above process for each root of the equation $f'(x) - 0$.

***Example 26.*** *A function is given as* $f(x, y) = 4x^2 + 6y^2 - 8x - 4y + 8$. *Find the optimal value of* $f(x, y)$.

**Solution.** $f(x, y) = 4x^2 + 6y^2 - 8x - 4y + 8$

$$\frac{\partial f}{\partial x} = 8x - 8, \frac{\partial f}{\partial y} = 12y - 4$$

Putting $\frac{\partial f}{\partial x} = 0$ and $\frac{\partial f}{\partial y} = 0$

$$\Rightarrow \quad 8x - 8 = 0 \Rightarrow x = 1$$

$$\Rightarrow \quad 12y - 4 = 0 \Rightarrow y = \frac{1}{3}$$

Therefore, $\left(1, \frac{1}{3}\right)$ is the only stationary point.

$$r = \left[\frac{\partial^2 f}{\partial x^2}\right]_{x=1} = 8,$$

$$s = \left[\frac{\partial^2 f}{\partial x \partial y}\right]_{\substack{x=1\\y=1/3}} = 0,$$

$$t = \left[\frac{\partial^2 f}{\partial y^2}\right]_{y=1/3} = 12$$

$$rt = 8 \times 12 = 96, s^2 = 0$$

Since, $rt > s^2$, we have either a maxima or minima at $\left(1, \frac{1}{3}\right)$.

Also, since $r = 8 > 0$, the point $\left(1, \frac{1}{3}\right)$ is a point of minima.

The minimum value is

$$f\left(1, \frac{1}{3}\right) = 4(1)^2 + 6 \times \left(\frac{1}{3}\right)^2 - 8(1) - 4\left(\frac{1}{3}\right) + 8 = \frac{10}{3}$$

So, the optimal value of $f(x, y)$ is minimum and equal to $\frac{10}{3}$.

***Example 27.*** *Find the distance between the origin and the point nearest to its surface $z^2 = 1 + xy$?*

**Solution.** (b) Let the point be $(x, y, z)$ on surface $z^2 = 1 + xy$

Distance from origin $= l$

$$= \sqrt{(x-0)^2 + (y-0)^2 + (z-0)^2}$$

$$= \sqrt{x^2 + y^2 + z^2}$$

$$= \sqrt{x^2 + y^2 + 1 + xy} \qquad (\because z^2 = 1 + xy)$$

The distance is shortest when $l$ is minimum we need to find minima of $x^2 + y^2 + 1 + xy$.

Let $\quad u = x^2 + y^2 + 1 + xy$

$$\frac{\partial u}{\partial x} = 2x + y, \frac{\partial u}{\partial y} = 2y + x$$

But $\quad \frac{\partial u}{\partial x} = 0 = 2x + y,$

$$\frac{\partial u}{\partial y} = 2y + x = 0$$

$\Rightarrow \quad x = -2y$

$\Rightarrow \quad 2(-2y) + y = 0$

$\Rightarrow \quad y = 0, x = 0$

is the only solution and so, $(0, 0)$ is the only stationary point.

Now, $\quad r = \frac{\partial^2 u}{\partial x^2} = 2, s = \frac{\partial^2 u}{\partial x \partial y} = 1,$

$$t = \frac{\partial^2 u}{\partial y^2} = 2$$

$$rt = 2 \times 2 = 4 > 0, s = 1 > 0$$

$\Rightarrow \quad rt > s^2$

We have Case I, *i.e.*, either a maximum or minimum exists at $(0, 0)$.

Now, since $r = 2 > 0$, so it is a minima at $(0, 0)$.

Now, at $x = 0, y = 0, z = \sqrt{1 + xy} = \sqrt{1 + 0} = 1$

So, the point nearest to the origin on surface $z^2 = 1 + xy$ is $(0, 0, 1)$. Hence, the distance $l = \sqrt{0^2 + 0^2 + 1^2} = 1$

## Working Rule for Finding (Absolute) Maximum and Minimum in Range $[a, b]$

If a function $f$ is differentiable in $[a, b]$ except at finitely many points, then to find (absolute) maximum and minimum values adopt the following procedure

**(i)** Evaluate $f(x)$ at the points, where $f'(x) = 0$.

**(ii)** Evaluate $f(x)$ at the points, where derivative fails to exist.

**(iii)** Find $f(a)$ and $f(b)$.

Then, the maximum of these values is the absolute maximum of the given function $f$ and the minimum of these values is the absolute minimum of the given function $f$.

# SOLVED EXAMPLES

## Type I (*Only one correct option*)

***Example 1.*** *Let $f$ be continuous on $[0, 1]$ and let $f(x)$ be in $[0, 1], \forall x \in [0, 1]$. Then,*

(a) $f(x) = x$ for some $x \in [0, 1]$

(b) $f(x) = x^2, \forall x \in [0, 1]$

(c) $f(x) = x - 1, \forall x \in [0, 1]$

(d) None of the above

**Solution.** (a) If $f(0) = 0$ or $f(1) = 1$, then we have done. Let us consider the case when $f(0) \neq 0$ and $f(1) \neq 1$.

Consider

$$g(x) = f(x) - x$$

Now, since $f$ is continuous on $[0, 1]$. Therefore, $g$ is also continuous on $[0, 1]$.

Also, $g(0) = f(0) > 0$. Since, $f(0) \in [0, 1]$ and $f(0) \neq 0$. Again, $g(1) = f(1) - 1 < 0$. Since, $f(1) \in [0, 1], f(1) \neq 1$.

Since, $g(0)$ and $g(1)$ are opposite signs, therefore by the intermediate value theorem $g(x) = 0$ for some $x \in [0, 1]$.

Hence,

$$f(x) - x = 0 \text{ for some } x \in [0, 1]$$

$\Rightarrow \quad f(x) = x$ for some $x \in [0, 1]$

***Example 2.*** *The number of continuous functions on $R$ which satisfy $(f(x))^2 = x^2, \forall x \in R$, is*

(a) 1 (b) 2

(c) 3 (d) 4

**Solution.** (d) Since, $(f(x))^2 = x^2, \forall x \in R$, therefore $f(0) = 0$ ...(i)

Let us now consider the form of $f$ on the interval $I = (0, \infty)$. Since, $f$ is continuous on $I$ and $f(x) \neq 0$ (because $(f(x))^2 \neq 0$) for any $x \in I$, therefore either

$$f(x) = x, \forall x \in I \quad \text{...(ii)}$$

or

$$f(x) = -x, \forall x \in I \quad \text{...(iii)}$$

Next, let us consider the form of $f$ on the interval $J = (-\infty, 0)$. Since, $f$ is continuous on $J$ and $f(x) \neq 0$ (because $(f(x))^2 \neq 0$) for any $x \in J$, therefore either

$$f(x) = x, \forall x \in J \quad \text{...(iv)}$$

or

$$f(x) = -x, \forall x \in J \quad \text{...(v)}$$

Combining Eqs. (i), (ii), (iii), (iv) and (v), we have the following four possibilities

(i) $f(x) = x, \forall x \in R$

(ii) $f(x) = -x, \forall x \in R$

(iii) $f(x) = x$, when $x \geq 0$, $f(x) = -x$, when $x < 0$

(iv) $f(x) = -x$, when $x \geq 0$, $f(x) = x$, when $x < 0$

Since, the functions described in (i) to (iv) above are all continuous and hence we find that there are four continuous functions on $R$, satisfying $(f(x))^2 = x^2, \forall x \in R$, *viz.*, $f(x) = x$, $f(x) = -x$, $f(x) = |x|$ and $f(x) = -|x|$.

***Example 3.*** *Let f be the function defined on R as follows*

$$f(x) = \begin{cases} 1-2x, & \text{when } x<0 \\ 0, & \text{when } x=0 \\ 1+3x, & \text{when } x>0 \end{cases}$$

*Then,*

(a) *f* is continuous at 0

(b) *f* is discontinuous at 0

(c) *f* is nowhere continuous

(d) *f* is everywhere discontinuous

**Solution.** (a) ***Case I*** Let $x < 0$. Given, $\varepsilon > 0$,

$$|f(x)-1| = |-2x| = -2x$$

$$< \varepsilon \text{ iff } x > -\frac{\varepsilon}{2}$$

Now, taking $\delta = \frac{\varepsilon}{2}$, we find that $|f(x)-1| < \varepsilon$, whenever $-\delta < x < 0$.

$$\Rightarrow \lim_{x \to 0^-} f(x) = 1$$

***Case II*** Let $x > 0$. Given, $\varepsilon > 0$,

$$|f(x)-1| = |3x| = 3x$$

$$< \varepsilon \text{ iff } x < \frac{\varepsilon}{3}$$

Now, taking $\delta = \frac{\varepsilon}{3}$, we find that $|f(x)-1| < \varepsilon$, whenever $0 < x < \delta$.

$$\Rightarrow \lim_{x \to 0^+} f(x) = 1$$

Hence, $f$ is continuous at 0 and hence continuous everywhere.

***Example 4.*** *Let f be defined on R by setting*

$$f(x) = \begin{cases} x\dfrac{e^{1/x} - e^{-1/x}}{e^{1/x} + e^{-1/x}}, & \text{if } x \neq 0 \\ 0, & \text{if } x = 0 \end{cases}$$

*Then,*

(a) *f* is derivable at 0

(b) *f* is not derivable at 0

(c) $Lf'(0) = -1$

(d) $Rf'(0) = +1$

**Solution.** (b) We have,

$$Rf'(0) = \lim_{\substack{h\to 0\\ h>0}} \frac{f(0+h) - f(0)}{h}$$

$$= \lim_{\substack{h\to 0\\ h>0}} \frac{h \cdot \dfrac{e^{1/h} - e^{-1/h}}{e^{1/h} + e^{-1/h}} - 0}{h}$$

$$= \lim_{\substack{h\to 0\\ h>0}} \frac{e^{1/h} - e^{-1/h}}{e^{1/h} + e^{-1/h}}$$

$$= \lim_{\substack{h\to 0\\ h>0}} \frac{1 - e^{-2/h}}{1 + e^{-2/h}}$$

$$= 1, \text{ as } e^{-1/h} \to 0 \text{ as } h \to 0$$

and

$$Lf'(0) = \lim_{\substack{h\to 0\\ h>0}} \frac{f(0-h) - f(0)}{-h}$$

$$= \lim_{\substack{h\to 0\\ h>0}} \frac{(-h) \cdot \dfrac{e^{-1/h} - e^{1/h}}{e^{-1/h} + e^{1/h}} - 0}{(-h)}$$

$$= \lim_{\substack{h\to 0\\ h>0}} \frac{e^{-1/h} - e^{1/h}}{e^{-1/h} + e^{1/h}}$$

$$= \lim_{\substack{h\to 0\\ h>0}} \frac{e^{-2/h} - 1}{e^{-2/h} + 1}$$

$$= -1, \text{ as } e^{-2/h} \to 0 \text{ as } h \to 0$$

Hence, $f$ is not derivable at 0 as $Rf'(0) \neq Lf'(0)$.

***Example 5.*** *The value of 'C' of Lagrange's mean value theorem, if*

$$f(x) = x(x-1)(x-2);\ a = 0,\ b = \frac{1}{2} \text{ is}$$

(a) $\frac{1}{4}$

(b) $\frac{1}{3}$

(c) $\frac{6-\sqrt{21}}{6}$

(d) $\frac{6+\sqrt{21}}{6}$

**Solution.** (c) Since, $f(x) = x(x-1)(x-2)$ is a polynomial. Hence, $f(x)$ is continuous on $\left[0, \frac{1}{2}\right]$ and differentiable on $\left(0, \frac{1}{2}\right)$.

Now,

$$f(0) = 0,\ f\left(\frac{1}{2}\right) = \frac{1}{2}\left(\frac{1}{2}-1\right)\left(\frac{1}{2}-2\right) = \frac{3}{8}$$

Also, $\quad f'(x) = 3x^2 - 6x + 2$

Putting $a=0, b=\frac{1}{2}$ in

$$f(b)-f(a)=(b-a)f'(C)$$

we have,

$$\frac{3}{8}=\frac{1}{2}(3C^2-6C+2)$$

$$\Rightarrow 12C^2-24C+5=0$$

$$\Rightarrow \quad C=\frac{6\pm\sqrt{21}}{6}$$

Since, $\frac{6+\sqrt{21}}{6}\notin\left(0,\frac{1}{2}\right)$, therefore this value of C has to be discarded. Hence, the required value of C is $\frac{6-\sqrt{21}}{6}$.

***Example 6.*** *Which of the following is correct?*

(a) $\frac{2}{\pi}>\frac{\sin x}{x}<1, 0<x<\frac{\pi}{2}$ (b) $\frac{2}{\pi}>\frac{\sin x}{x}>1, 0<x<\frac{\pi}{2}$

(c) $\frac{2}{\pi}<\frac{\sin x}{x}<1, 0<x<\frac{\pi}{2}$ (d) $\frac{2}{\pi}<\frac{\sin x}{x}>1, 0<x<\frac{\pi}{2}$

**Solution.** (c) Let $f$ be defined as follows

$$f(x)=\begin{cases}\frac{\sin x}{x}, & x\neq 0\\ 1 & x=0\end{cases}$$

Now, since $\lim_{x\to 0}f(x)=\lim_{x\to 0}\frac{\sin x}{x}=1=f(0)$. Therefore, $f$ is continuous at $x=0$. Also, $f$ is continuous in $\left]0,\frac{\pi}{2}\right]$.

Therefore, $f$ is continuous in $\left[0,\frac{\pi}{2}\right]$

$$\text{when } x\neq 0, f'(x)=\frac{(x\cos x-\sin x)}{x^2}$$

$$=\frac{(x-\tan x)\cos x}{x^2}$$

If $0<x<\frac{\pi}{2}$, then $\tan x>x$ and $\cos x>0$. Therefore, $f'(x)<0$, whenever $0<x<\frac{\pi}{2}$. Consequently, $f$ is strictly decreasing in $\left[0,\frac{\pi}{2}\right]$. So, that whenever $0<x<\frac{\pi}{2}$, we have

$$f(0)>f(x)>f\left(\frac{\pi}{2}\right)$$

$$\Rightarrow \quad 1>\frac{\sin x}{x}>\frac{2}{\pi}$$

***Example 7.*** *Applying Lagrange's mean value theorem to the function defined by*

$$f(x)=\log(1+x), \forall\, x\geq 0$$

*Then,*

(a) $0<[\log(1+x)]^{-1}-x^{-1}>1$, whenever $x>0$

(b) $0<[\log(1+x)]^{-1}-x^{-1}<1$, whenever $x>0$

(c) $0<[\log(1+x)]^{-1}-x^{-1}>1$, whenever $x<0$

(d) $0<[\log(1+x)]^{-1}-x^{-1}<1$, whenever $x<0$

**Solution.** (b) Let $x$ be any positive real number. Then, the function $f$, given by

$$f(x)=\log(1+x), \forall\, x\geq 0$$

is continuous on $[0, x]$ and derivable on $(0, x)$.

Therefore, by Lagrange's mean value theorem, there exists a number $\theta$ between 0 and 1 such that

$$f(x)-f(0)=xf'(\theta x)$$

$$\Rightarrow \quad \log(1+x)=\frac{x}{1+\theta x} \quad \text{...(i)}$$

Since, $0<\theta<1$ and $x>0$, hence

$$\frac{x}{1+x}<\frac{x}{1+\theta x}<x \quad \text{...(ii)}$$

From Eqs. (i) and (ii), we get

$$\frac{x}{1+x}<\log(1+x)<x$$

$$\Rightarrow \quad \frac{1+x}{x}>[\log(1+x)]^{-1}>x^{-1}$$

$$\Rightarrow \quad 0<[\log(1+x)]^{-1}-x^{-1}<1$$

***Example 8.*** *A function f is continuous in the interval [0, 1] and assumes only rational values in the entire interval. If $f(x)=\frac{1}{2}$ when $x=\frac{1}{2}$. Then,*

(a) $f(x)=1$, everywhere (b) $f(x)=\frac{1}{2}$, everywhere

(c) $f(x)=\frac{1}{2}$, nowhere (d) None of these

**Solution.** (b) Suppose, if possible, that there exists a point $c\in[0,1]$ such that $f(c)\neq\frac{1}{2}$. It is obvious that $c\neq\frac{1}{2}$. By the law of trichotomy, either $c<\frac{1}{2}$ or $\frac{1}{2}<c$. Without loss of generality, let us assume that $c<\frac{1}{2}$. The function $f$ is continuous in $[c,\frac{1}{2}]$ and hence by intermediate value theorem it must take every value lying between $f(c)$ and $f\left(\frac{1}{2}\right)$. But this is not possible, because $f(c)$ and $f\left(\frac{1}{2}\right)$ are two distinct rational numbers between which there lie infinitely many irrational numbers, and $f(x)$ does not take any irrational values. Which shows that there does not exists any $c\in[0,1]$ such that $f(c)\neq\frac{1}{2}$. Hence, $f(x)=\frac{1}{2}$ everywhere.

***Example 9.*** *Solve* $\lim_{x\to\infty}\frac{x-\sin x}{x+\cos x}$.

(a) $-1$ (b) 1 (c) $\pi$ (d) $\sin x$

**Solution.** (b) We have $\lim_{x\to\infty}\frac{x-\sin x}{x+\cos x}=\lim_{x\to\infty}\frac{1-\sin x/x}{1+\cos x/x}$

$$=\frac{\lim_{x\to\infty}\left(1-\frac{\sin x}{x}\right)}{\lim_{x\to\infty}\left(1+\frac{\cos x}{x}\right)}=\frac{1-\lim_{x\to\infty}\frac{\sin x}{x}}{1+\lim_{x\to\infty}\frac{\cos x}{x}}=\frac{1-0}{1+0}=1$$

***Example 10.*** *The value of* $\lim_{x\to 0} \frac{\sinh x - \sin x}{x \sin^2 x}$ *is*

(a) $\frac{1}{2}$ (b) $\frac{1}{4}$ (c) $\frac{1}{3}$ (d) $\frac{1}{6}$

**Solution.** (c) We know that

$$\frac{\sinh x - \sin x}{x \sin^2 x} = \frac{\sinh x - \sin x}{x^3} \cdot \left(\frac{x}{\sin x}\right)^2$$

Hence, $\lim_{x\to 0} \frac{\sinh x - \sin x}{x \sin^2 x} = \lim_{x\to 0} \frac{\sinh x - \sin x}{x^3} \lim_{x\to 0} \left(\frac{x}{\sin x}\right)^2$

$$= \lim_{x\to 0} \frac{\sinh x - \sin x}{x^3} \quad \left(\frac{0}{0} \text{ form}\right)$$

$$= \lim_{x\to 0} \frac{\cosh x - \cos x}{3x^2} \quad \left(\frac{0}{0} \text{ form}\right)$$

$$= \lim_{x\to 0} \frac{\cosh x - \cos x}{3x^2} \quad \left(\frac{0}{0} \text{ form}\right)$$

$$= \lim_{x\to 0} \frac{\sinh x + \sin x}{6x} \quad \left(\frac{0}{0} \text{ form}\right)$$

$$= \lim_{x\to 0} \frac{\cosh x + \cos x}{6} = \frac{1}{3}$$

***Example 11.*** *At t = 0, the function* $f(t) = \frac{\sin t}{t}$ *has*

(a) a minimum (b) a discontinuity

(c) a point of inflection (d) a maximum

**Solution.** (d) Given, $f(t) = \frac{\sin t}{t}$

At $t = 0$, first we will check continuity of the function.

Now, LHL $= f(0-h) = \lim_{h\to 0} \frac{\sin(0-h)}{(0-h)}$

$$= \lim_{h\to 0} \frac{-\sin h}{-h} \quad [\because \sin(-\theta) = -\sin\theta]$$

$$= 1 \quad \left[\because \lim_{\theta\to 0} \frac{\sin\theta}{\theta} = 1\right]$$

and RHL $= f(0+h) = \lim_{h\to 0} \frac{\sin(0+h)}{(0+h)}$

$$= \lim_{h\to 0} \frac{\sin h}{h} = 1$$

and $f(0) = 1$

Since, LHL = RHL = $f(0)$

So, the function is continuous at $t = 0$.

Now, we check the function is maximum or minimum.

$$f'(t) = \frac{1}{t}\cos t - \frac{1}{t^2}\sin t$$

and $$f''(t) = -\frac{1}{t}\sin t - \frac{1}{t^2}\cos t - \frac{1}{t^2}\cos t + \frac{2\sin t}{t^3}$$

$$= -\frac{\sin t}{t} - \frac{2\cos t}{t^2} + \frac{2\sin t}{t^3}$$

For maximum or minimum value of $f(x)$

$$f'(x) = 0$$

$$\frac{\cos t}{t} - \frac{\sin t}{t^2} = 0 \Rightarrow \frac{\tan t}{t} = 1$$

Now, $\lim_{t\to 0} f''(t) = -\lim_{t\to 0}\left(\frac{\sin t}{t}\right) + \lim_{t\to 0} \frac{(2\sin t - 2t\cos t)}{t^3}$ $\left[\because \left(\frac{0}{0}\right) \text{form}\right]$

$$= -1 + \lim_{t\to 0} \frac{(2\cos t - 2\cos t + 2t\sin t)}{3t^2}$$

[$\because$ Using L'Hospital's rule]

$$= -1 + \lim_{t\to 0} \frac{2t\sin t}{3t}$$

$$= -1 + \frac{2}{3}\lim_{t\to 0}\left(\frac{\sin t}{t}\right)$$

$$= -1 + \frac{2}{3} \times 1 = -\frac{1}{3} < 0 \quad \text{(Maximum)}$$

So, function $f(t)$ is maximum at $t = 0$.

***Example 12.*** *Find the absolute maximum and minimum value of* $f(x) = 2x^3 - 9x^2 + 12x - 5$ *in [0, 3]. Also, find points of maxima and minima.*

(a) Max value = 4 at max point 3
Min value = −5 at min point 0

(b) Max value = 4 at max point 2
Min value = −5 at min point −1

(c) Max value = 4 at max point 3
Min value = −5 at min point 0

(d) Max value = 5 at max point 0
Min value = 0 at min point −2

**Solution.** (a) Given, $f(x) = 2x^3 - 9x^2 + 12x - 5$

Differentiating the polynomial *wrt x*, we get

$$f'(x) = 6x^2 - 18x + 12 = 0$$

$$\Rightarrow \quad 6(x^2 - 3x + 2) = 0$$

$$\Rightarrow \quad x^2 - 2x - x + 2 = 0$$

$$\Rightarrow \quad (x-2)(x-1) = 0 \Rightarrow x = 1, 2$$

1 and 2 both are in between (0, 3), therefore 1 and 2 both are stationary points or turing points.

$$f(1) = 2(1)^3 - 9(1)^2 + 12(1) - 5$$

$$= 2 - 9 + 12 - 5 = 14 - 14 = 0$$

$$f(2) = 2(2)^3 - 9(2)^2 + 12(2) - 5$$

$$= 16 - 36 + 24 - 5 = 40 - 41 = -1$$

$$f(0) = -5$$

$$f(3) = 2(3)^3 - 9(3)^2 + 12(3) - 5$$

$$= 54 - 81 + 36 - 5 = 90 - 86 = 4$$

Therefore, the absolute maximum value = 4 the absolute minimum value = −5

The point of maxima is 3 and the point of minima is 0.

***Example 13.*** *It is given that at x = 1, the function* $x^4 - 62x^2 + ax + 9$ *attains its maximum value in the interval [0, 2]. Find the value of a.*

(a) 12 (b) 120 (c) 100 (d) 20

**Solution.** (b) Let $f(x) = x^4 - 62x^2 + ax + 9$

Differentiating given polynomial *wrt* $x$, we get

$$f'(x) = 4x^3 - 124x + a = 0$$

$$f'(1) = 4 - 124 + a = 0$$

$$\Rightarrow \quad a = 120$$

(Given that at $x = 1$, the polynomial has maximum value)

***Example 14.*** *What should be the value of $\lambda$ such that the function defined below is continuous at $x = \frac{\pi}{2}$?*

$$f(x) = \begin{cases} \dfrac{\lambda \cos x}{\pi/2 - x}, & \text{if } x \neq \pi/2 \\ 1, & \text{if } x = \pi/2 \end{cases}$$

(a) 1 (b) −1

(c) 2 (d) −2

**Solution.** (a) If $f(x)$ is continuous at $x = \frac{\pi}{2}$, then

$$\lim_{x \to \pi/2} \frac{\lambda \cos x}{\frac{\pi}{2} - x} = \frac{0}{0} \text{ and } f\left(\frac{\pi}{2}\right) = 1$$

Since, the limit is in indeterminate form. Then, applying L'Hospital rule,

$$\lim_{x \to \pi/2} \frac{-\lambda \sin x}{-1} = \lambda \cdot 1 = \lambda$$

and $\quad f\left(\frac{\pi}{2}\right) = 1 \Rightarrow \lambda = 1$

***Example 15.*** *The distance between the origin and the point nearest to it on the surface $z^2 = 1 + xy$ is*

(a) 1 (b) $\frac{\sqrt{3}}{2}$

(c) $\sqrt{3}$ (d) 2

**Solution.** (a) The given equation of surface is

$$z^2 = 1 + xy \quad \text{...(i)}$$

Let, $P(x, y, z)$ be the nearest point on the surface Eq. (i), then the distance of $P$ from origin is

$$L = \sqrt{(x-0)^2 + (y-0)^2 + (z-0)^2}$$

$$L^2 = x^2 + y^2 + z^2$$

$$z^2 = L^2 - x^2 - y^2 \quad \text{...(ii)}$$

From Eqs. (i) and (ii), we get

$$L^2 - x^2 - y^2 = 1 + xy$$

$$L^2 = x^2 + y^2 + xy + 1 \quad \text{...(iii)}$$

Let $\quad f(x, y) = L^2 = x^2 + y^2 + xy + 1 \quad \text{...(iv)}$

The value of $f(x, y)$ will be maximum or minimum, if $L^2$ is maximum or minimum.

Now, differentiating partially *wrt* $x$ and $y$ of Eq. (iv) respectively, we get

$$\frac{\partial f}{\partial x} = 2x + y \text{ and } \frac{\partial f}{\partial y} = 2y + x$$

For maximum and minimum value of $f(x, y)$,

$$\frac{\partial f}{\partial x} = 0 \text{ and } \frac{\partial f}{\partial y} = 0$$

$\Rightarrow \quad 2x + y = 0$ and $2y + x = 0$

$\Rightarrow \quad (x, y) = (0, 0)$

Only one stationary point.

Also, $\quad r = \frac{\partial^2 f}{\partial x^2} = 2, s = \frac{\partial^2 f}{\partial x \partial y} = 1$

$$t = \frac{\partial^2 f}{\partial y^2} = 2$$

Now, $rt - s^2 = 4 - 1 \Rightarrow 3 > 0$ and $r$ is positive.

So, $\quad f(x, y) = L^2$ is minimum at $(0, 0)$

Now, minimum value of $L^2$ at $(0, 0)$

$$L^2 = x^2 + y^2 + xy + 1$$

$$L^2 = 0 + 0 + 0 + 1$$

$$L = +1 \text{ or } f(x, y) = 1$$

and the nearest point is

$$z^2 = 1 + xy \Rightarrow 1 + 0$$

$$z = \pm 1$$

$\Rightarrow \quad (x, y, z) = (0, 0, 1)$ or $(0, 0, -1)$

Hence, the required distance is $= \sqrt{0^2 + 0^2 + 1^2} = 1$

## Type II *(One or more than one correct option)*

***Example 16.*** *Which of the following(s) is/are correct?*

(a) The identity function is continuous

(b) The constant function is continuous

(c) The function $f(x) = x^2, \forall x \in R$ is continuous

(d) None of the above

**Solution.** (a), (b), (c)

(a) Let $f$ be the identity function defined on $R$ by

$$f(x) = x, \forall x \in R$$

If $x$ be any point of $R$ and $< x_n >$ be a sequence in $R$ converging to $x$, then $f(x_n) = x_n, \forall n$. Therefore,

$$\lim_{n \to \infty} f(x_n) = \lim_{n \to \infty} x_n = x = f(x)$$

Since, $\lim_{n \to \infty} x_n = x \Rightarrow \lim_{n \to \infty} f(x_n) = f(x)$

Therefore, $f$ is continuous at $\forall x \in R$.

(b) Let $f$ be constant function defined on $R$ by

$$f(x) = c, \forall x \in R$$

If $x$ be any point of $R$ and $< x_n >$ be a sequence in $R$ converging to $x$, then $f(x_n) = c, \forall n$ and $< f(x_n) >$ is a constant sequence converging to $c$, which is the same as $f(x)$.

Since, $x_n \to x \Rightarrow f(x_n) \to f(x)$, Therefore, $f$ is continuous, $\forall x \in R$.

(c) If $x$ be any point of $R$ and $< x_n >$ be a sequence converging to $x$, then

$$\lim_{n\to\infty} f(x_n) = \lim_{n\to\infty} x_n^2 = \left(\lim_{n\to\infty} x_n\right)\left(\lim_{n\to\infty} x_n\right) = x^2 = f(x)$$

Since, $\lim_{n\to\infty} x_n = x \Rightarrow \lim_{n\to\infty} f(x_n) = f(x)$.

Hence, $f$ is continuous, $\forall\, x \in R$.

**Example 17.** *Let f be the function defined on $[0, \infty)$ by*

$$f(x) = [x]$$
$$= \text{The greatest integer not exceeding } x,\ \forall\, x \ge 0$$

*Then,*

(a) $f$ is continuous at $x = 1, 2, 3, \ldots$

(b) $f$ is discontinuous at $x = 1, 2, 3, \ldots$

(c) $f$ is continuous at countably many points

(d) $f$ is discontinuous at countably many points

**Solution.** (b), (d)

We have,

$$f(x) = [x],\ \forall\, x \ge 0$$

$$\Rightarrow\quad f(x) = \begin{cases} 0, 0 \le x < 1 \\ 1, 1 \le x < 2 \\ 2, 2 \le x < 3 \\ 3, 3 \le x < 4 \\ \vdots \\ k, k \le x < k+1 \end{cases}$$

To show that $f$ is discontinuous at $x = k, k = 1, 2, 3, \ldots$, we have only to consider the sequence $< x_n >$ defined by $x_n = k - \frac{1}{n}, \forall\, n$.

Hence, $\lim_{n\to\infty} x_n = k$ but

$$\lim_{n\to\infty} f(x_n) = k - 1 \ne f(k)$$

Hence, $f$ is not continuous at $x = k, k = 1, 2, 3, \ldots$ which are countably many points.

**Example 18.** *Let f be the function defined on R by*

$$f(x) = \begin{cases} \dfrac{e^{1/x}}{1+e^{1/x}}, & x \ne 0 \\ 0, & x = 0 \end{cases}$$

*Then,*

(a) $f$ is continuous at $x = 0$

(b) $f$ is discontinuous at $x = 0$

(c) $f$ has discontinuity of first kind from left at $x = 0$

(d) $f$ has discontinuity of first kind from right at $x = 0$

**Solution.** (b), (d)

We have,

$$f(0+0) = \lim_{\substack{h\to 0\\ h>0}} \frac{e^{1/h}}{1+e^{1/h}}$$
$$= \lim_{\substack{h\to 0\\ h>0}} \frac{1}{e^{-1/h}+1} = 1$$

and $$f(0-0) = \lim_{\substack{h\to 0\\ h>0}} \frac{e^{-1/h}}{1+e^{-1/h}} = 0$$

Since, $f(0-0) = f(0) \ne f(0+0)$

Hence, $f$ is continuous from left at $x = 0$ and has a discontinuity of the first kind from right at $x = 0$.

Hence, $f$ is discontinuous at $x = 0$.

**Example 19.** *Let f be the function defined on R by*

$$f(x) = |x-1| + |x+1|,\ \forall\, x \in R$$

*Then,*

(a) $f$ is derivable at $x = 1$

(b) $f$ is not derivable at $x = 1$

(c) $f$ is derivable at $x = -1$

(d) $f$ is not derivable at $x = -1$

**Solution.** (b), (d)

We have,

$$|x-1| = \begin{cases} x-1 & , x-1 \ge 0 \\ -(x-1), & x-1 < 0 \end{cases}$$

and $$|x+1| = \begin{cases} x+1 & , x+1 \ge 0 \\ -(x+1), & x+1 < 0 \end{cases}$$

Therefore, we may rewrite the given function as follows

If $x + 1 < 0$, then

$$f(x) = |x-1| + |x+1|$$
$$= -(x-1) + [-(x+1)]$$
$$= -2x$$

If $x + 1 \ge 0$, then

$$f(x) = -(x-1) + (x+1)$$
$$= 2$$

If $x - 1 \ge 0$, then

$$f(x) = (x-1) + (x+1)$$
$$= 2x$$

Hence,

$$f(x) = \begin{cases} -2x, & x < -1 \\ 2 & , -1 \le x < 1 \\ 2x\ , & x \ge 1 \end{cases}$$

The graph of $f$ is given below.

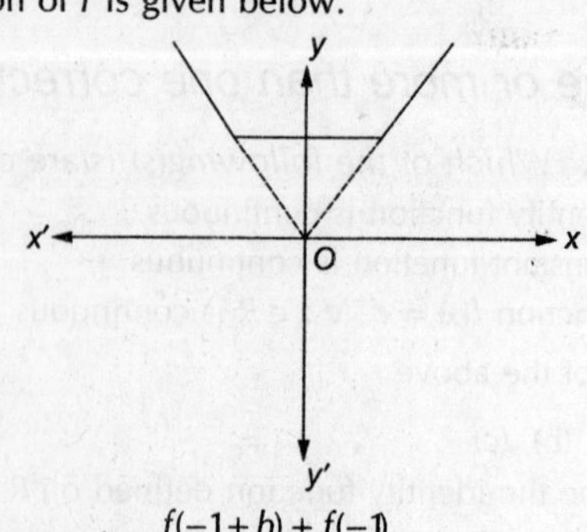


Now $$Rf'(-1) = \lim_{\substack{h\to 0\\ h>0}} \frac{f(-1+h) + f(-1)}{h}$$
$$= \lim_{\substack{h\to 0\\ h>0}} \frac{2-2}{h} = 0$$

$$Lf'(-1) = \lim_{\substack{h\to 0\\ h>0}} \frac{f(-1-h)-f(-1)}{-h}$$

$$= \lim_{\substack{h\to 0\\ h>0}} \frac{-2(-1-h)-(2)}{-h}$$

$$= -2$$

Since, $Rf'(-1) \neq Lf'(-1)$. Hence, $f$ is not derivable at $x = -1$.

Again,

$$Rf'(1) = \lim_{\substack{h\to 0\\ h>0}} \frac{f(1+h)+f(1)}{h}$$

$$= \lim_{\substack{h\to 0\\ h>0}} \frac{2(1+h)-2}{h}$$

$$= 2$$

and

$$Lf'(1) = \lim_{\substack{h\to 0\\ h>0}} \frac{f(1-h)-f(1)}{-h} = \lim_{\substack{h\to 0\\ h>0}} \frac{2-2}{-h} = 0$$

Since, $Rf'(1) \neq Lf'(1)$. Hence, $f$ is not derivable at $x = 1$.

***Example 20.*** *Let $f$ be the function defined on $R$ by*

$$f(x) = \begin{cases} x^2 \sin\frac{1}{x}, & x \neq 0 \\ 0 & , x = 0 \end{cases}$$

*Then,*

(a) $f$ is derivable $\forall, x \in R$

(b) $f$ is not derivable $\forall, x \in R$

(c) $f'$ is continuous at $x = 0$

(d) $f'$ is not continuous at $x = 0$

**Solution.** (a), (d)

Since, the function $x \to \frac{1}{x}$ and $x \to \sin x$ are both derivable. Whenever $x \neq 0$, hence the function $x \to \sin\frac{1}{x}$ is derivable when $x \neq 0$. Therefore, the product function $x \to x^2 \sin\frac{1}{x}$ is derivable when $x \neq 0$.

Also, for $x \neq 0$, by the rule for the product of two functions and the chain rule we find that

$$f'(x) = 2x\sin\frac{1}{x} + x^2\left(\cos\frac{1}{x}\right)\left(-\frac{1}{x^2}\right)$$

$$= 2x\sin\frac{1}{x} - \cos\frac{1}{x}$$

Now, at $x = 0$

$$Rf'(0) = \lim_{\substack{h\to 0\\ h>0}} \frac{f(0+h)+f(0)}{h}$$

$$= \lim_{\substack{h\to 0\\ h>0}} \frac{h^2\sin\frac{1}{h}}{h}$$

$$= \lim_{\substack{h\to 0\\ h>0}} h\sin\frac{1}{h}$$

$$= 0$$

and

$$Lf'(0) = \lim_{\substack{h\to 0\\ h>0}} \frac{f(0-h)-f(0)}{-h}$$

$$= \lim_{\substack{h\to 0\\ h>0}} \frac{(-h)^2\sin\frac{1}{-h}}{-h}$$

$$= \lim_{\substack{h\to 0\\ h>0}} \left(h\sin\frac{1}{h}\right)$$

$$= 0$$

Since, $Rf'(0) = Lf'(0) = 0$, hence $f$ is derivable at $x = 0$, and $f'(0) = 0$ observe that while $\lim_{x\to 0} x\sin\frac{1}{x}$ exists and equal to zero, $\lim_{x\to 0}\cos\frac{1}{x}$ does not exists. Hence, $\lim_{x\to 0} f'(x)$ does not exists. Hence, $f'$ is not continuous at $x = 0$.

# Exercise 1 (For Part 'B')

**Directions** (Q. Nos. 1-342) *All questions have only one correct option.*

**1.** $\lim_{x\to\infty} x\sin\frac{1}{x}$ equals to

(a) 1 (b) 0
(c) −1 (d) $-\infty$

**2.** If $f(x) = \begin{cases} x^n \cos\frac{1}{x}, & x \neq 0 \\ 0, & x = 0 \end{cases}$ is differentiable at $x = 0$, then

(a) $n < 1$ (b) $n > 1$
(c) $n = 1$ (d) $n$ may be positive or zero

**3.** A continuous function $f$ from a bounded closed interval $[a, b]$ to $R$

(a) is always unbounded
(b) may be bounded or unbounded
(c) is always bounded and attains its bounds
(d) is always bounded but may or may not attain its bounds

**4.** The function $f(x) = \frac{2[x]}{3x - [x]}$ is

(a) continuous at $x = -\frac{1}{2}$ and $x = 1$
(b) continuous at $x = -\frac{1}{2}$ and discontinuous $x = 1$
(c) discontinuous at $x = -\frac{1}{2}$ and continuous $x = 1$
(d) discontinuous at $x = -\frac{1}{2}$ and $x = 1$

**5.** Let $f$ be a real-valued function defined as follows
$f(x) = x$, when $-1 \leq x \leq 1$
$f(x + 2) = f(x)$, for all $x \in R$. Then, the function $f(x)$ is

(a) continuous all even integers
(b) continuous all odd integers
(c) continuous all integers
(d) None of the above

**6.** The function $f(x) = x|x|$ is

(a) not monotonic
(b) strictly decreasing function
(c) differentiable, $\forall x \in R$
(d) differentiable, $\forall x \in R$ except at $x = 0$

**7.** The values of $a$ and $b$ for which the function

$$f(x) = \begin{cases} 2x + 1, & \text{if } x \leq 1 \\ ax^2 + b, & \text{if } 1 < x < 3 \\ 5x + 2a, & \text{if } x \geq 3 \end{cases}$$

is continuous everywhere.

(a) $a = 2, b = 1$ (b) $a = 1, b = 2$
(c) $a = 3, b = 2$ (d) $a = 2, b = 3$

**8.** The function
$f(x) = |x| + |x + 1| + |x + 2| + |x - 1| + |x - 2|$ is

(a) continuous, $\forall x \in R$
(b) differentiable, $\forall x \in R$
(c) only differentiable at $x = 0, -1, -2, 1, 2$
(d) None of the above

**9.** The function $f(x) = \begin{cases} x, & \text{when } x \text{ is rational} \\ 1 - x, & \text{when } x \text{ is irrational} \end{cases}$ is

(a) continuous only at $x = \frac{1}{2}$
(b) continuous, $\forall x \in R$
(c) differentiable, $\forall x \in R$
(d) None of the above

**10.** The function $f(x) = \lim_{n\to\infty} \left(\frac{x^{2n} - 1}{x^{2n} + 1}\right)$ is

(a) continuous, $\forall x \in R$
(b) continuous, $\forall x \in R - \{-1, 1\}$
(c) continuous, $\forall x \in Z$
(d) None of the above

**11.** The function $f(x) = \lim_{n\to\infty} \left[\frac{x^{2n}}{1 + x^{2n}}\right]$ is continuous

(a) $\forall, x \in R$ (b) $\forall, x \in R - \{-1, 1\}$
(c) $\forall, x \in Z$ (d) None of these

**12.** If $f(x) = \begin{cases} \frac{\sin[x]}{[x]}, & [x] \neq 0 \\ 0, & [x] = 0 \end{cases}$

where $[x]$ denotes the greatest integer less than or equal to $x$, then $\lim_{x\to 0} f(x)$ is

(a) 1 (b) 0
(c) −1 (d) None of these

**13.** If $f(x)$ and $g(x)$ are continuous functions everywhere and $f(x) = \lim_{n\to\infty} \frac{f(x) + x^{2n} g(x)}{1 + x^{2n}}$.

Then, $f(x)$ is continuous everywhere except at which of the following points

(a) 2 (b) −2
(c) $\pm 1$ (d) $\infty$

**14.** The function $f(x) = \begin{cases} \sin\frac{1}{x}, & x \neq 0 \\ 1, & x = 0 \end{cases}$ has

(a) removable discontinuity at $x = 0$
(b) non-removal discontinuity at $x = 0$
(c) mined discontinuity at $x = 0$
(d) continuity at $x = 0$

**15.** Let $f : R \to R$ be a monotonically decreasing function (defined everywhere on the real line) and let $f$ be discontinuous at certain point $x = a$. What is the nature of discontinuity?
(a) Removable discontinuity
(b) Either removable or discontinuity of the second kind
(c) Discontinuity of first kind
(d) Either discontinuity of first kind or the second kind

**16.** If $f(x) = \begin{cases} x & , 0 < x < 1 \\ 3 - x, & 1 \le x \le 2 \end{cases}$, then
I. $\lim_{x \to 1^-} f(x) = 1$
II. $\lim_{x \to 1^+} f(x) = 2$
III. $\lim_{x \to 1} f(x) = 2$

Which of these statement(s) is/are correct?
(a) I and III are correct
(b) I, II and III are correct
(c) I and II are correct
(d) II alone is correct

**17.** Consider the function $f(x) = |x|^3$, where $x$ is real. Then, the function $f(x)$ at $x = 0$ is
(a) continuous but not differentiable
(b) once differentiable but not twice
(c) twice differentiable but not thrice
(d) thrice differentiable

**18.** Let $f : R \to R$ defined by
$$f(x) = \begin{cases} x, \text{if } x \in Q \\ \sin x, \text{if } x \in R - Q \end{cases}, \text{ then}$$
(a) $f$ is differentiable exactly at one point
(b) $f$ is differentiable exactly at two points
(c) $f$ is nowhere differentiable because nowhere continuous
(d) $f$ is continuous only at one point

**19.** If $f(x) = \begin{cases} a + \sin^{-1}(x + b), x \ge 1 \\ x \qquad , x < 1 \end{cases}$ is differentiable at $x = 1$, then
(a) $a = 1, b = 1$ (b) $a = -1, b = -1$
(c) $a = 1, b = -1$ (d) None of these

**20.** If $f(x) = (x^2 - 1)|x^2 - 3x + 2| + \cos(|x|)$, then set of point of non-differentiability is
(a) $\{1, 0, 2\}$ (b) $\{1, 2\}$
(c) $\{2\}$ (d) $\{0, 2\}$

**21.** If $f(x) = \begin{cases} x^2, \text{if } x \in Q \\ 0 \ , \text{otherwise} \end{cases}$, then
(a) $f$ is continuous but not differentiable at $x = 0$
(b) $f$ is differentiable at $x = 0$
(c) $f$ is continuous but not differentiable at $x = 1$
(d) $f$ is differentiable at $x = 1$

**22.** Consider the function $f(x) = \frac{|\sin x|}{\sin x}$, then which one of the following is correct?
(a) $f(x)$ is everywhere differentiable except $x = 0$.
(b) $\left\{x : f(x) > \frac{1}{2}\right\}$ is empty set.
(c) Set of point for which $f(x) \ge -1$ is countable.
(d) None of the above

**23.** Consider the function $f(x) = x + x^2$, which one of the following is correct?
(a) $f(x)$ is monotonic in its domain and $f^{-1}$ also monotonic.
(b) $f(x)$ is continuous in $R$ and monotonic only in $R^+$.
(c) $f(x)$ is everywhere differentiable and invertible in $\left]-\frac{1}{2}, \infty\right[$ with range $R$.
(d) $f(x)$ is invertible in $\left[-\frac{1}{2}, \infty\right[$ and $f^{-1} = (-1 + \sqrt{1 + 4y})/2$.

**24.** Consider $f(x) = \begin{cases} 0, & \text{if } x \text{ is rational} \\ \sin|x|, & \text{if } x \text{ irrational} \end{cases}$

the set of point of continuity is
(a) countable (b) bounded
(c) $\phi$ (d) None of these

**25.** Let $f(x) = ax + b$ be monotonic function in $R$ and satisfies condition $f(x) = f^{-1}(x)$, then the value of $a$ and $b$ are
(a) $a = 2, b = -1$ (b) $a = -1, b \in R$
(c) $a = 1, b \in R$ (d) $a = 1, b = -1$

**26.** The function $f$ defined by $f(x) = \begin{cases} \frac{x^2}{a} - a, \text{ if } 0 < x < a \\ a - \frac{a^3}{x^2}, \text{ if } x \ge a \end{cases}$
(a) is not continuous on $]0, \infty[$
(b) is not differentiable on $]0, \infty[$
(c) is differentiable on $]0, \infty[$
(d) is differentiable on $]0, \infty[$ except at $x = a$

**27.** Consider the following statements
I. A differentiable function is continuous.
II. A continuous function is differentiable.
III. A continuous function on a closed interval $[a, b]$ of finite length is uniformly continuous on $[a, b]$.

Which of these statements are correct?
(a) I, II and III (b) II and III
(c) I and III (d) I and II

**28.** The function $f(x) = |x + 2|$ is not differentiable at a point
(a) $x = 2$ (b) $x = -2$
(c) $x = -1$ (d) $x = 1$

**29.** Consider the following conditions
I. $f(x)$ is well defined at $x = a$.
II. $\lim_{x \to a} f(x)$ must exist.

III. $f(x)$ is continuous.
IV. $f(x) \neq 0$ at $x = a$.

Which of these conditions are necessary for a function $f(x)$ to be derivable at a point $x = a$ of its domain?
(a) I and II (b) III and IV
(c) I, II and III (d) I, II and IV

**30.** The function $f(x) = |x|$ at $x = 0$ is
(a) continuous and differentiable
(b) continuous but not differentiable
(c) not continuous but differentiable
(d) neither continuous nor differentiable

**31.** A function $f$ defined such that for all real $x, y$
(i) $(x + y) = f(x) \cdot f(y)$, (ii) $f(x) = 1 + x\, g(x)$
where $\lim_{x \to 0} g(x) = 1$. What is $\frac{d f(x)}{dx}$ equal to?
(a) $g(x)$ (b) $f(x)$
(c) $g'(x)$ (d) $g(x) + xg'(x)$

**32.** We define a function $f: R \to R$ as follows $f(x) = 2x^2 + 3x + 4$ if $x \in ]-\infty, 1[$ and $f(x) = kx + 9 - k$ if $x \in [1, \infty[$. If this function is differentiable on the whole real line, then the value of $k$ must be
(a) 4 (b) 5
(c) 6 (d) 7

**33.** Consider the following functions
I. $y = x\sin(1/x)$, if $x \neq 0$ and $y = 0$ if $x = 0$
II. $y = x^2 \sin(1/x)$; if $x \neq 0$ and $y = 0$ if $x = 0$
III. $y = x^2 \cos(1/x)$, if $x \neq 0$ and $y = 0$ if $x = 0$
IV. $y = x\cos(1/x)$, if $x \neq 0$ and $y = 0$ if $x = 0$
The functions differentiable at $x = 0$ are
(a) I and II (b) II and III
(c) III and II (d) IV and I

**34.** The number of points at which the function $f(x) = \text{Max}\{a - x, a + x, b\}, -\infty < x < \infty, 0 < a < b$ cannot be differentiable
(a) 2 (b) 3
(c) 1 (d) 0

**35.** Which one is uniformly continuous in $[0, \infty[$?
(a) $x^2$ (b) $\sin x$
(c) $\sin x^2$ (d) None of these

**36.** Let $f(x) = \lim_{n \to \infty} \left[\frac{\log(2 + x) - x^{2n} \sin x}{1 + x^{2n}}\right], 0 \leq x \leq \frac{\pi}{2}$ $x \in R$, then the nature of $f(x)$ at $x = 1$, is
(a) differentiable
(b) continuous but not differentiable
(c) discontinuous
(d) None of the above

**37.** If $f(x) = \begin{cases} e^{-\frac{1}{x^2}}, & x \neq 0, \\ 0, & x = 0 \end{cases}$ then
(a) is not differentiable at $x = 0$
(b) $f^n(0) = 0, \forall n$
(c) $f^n(0)$ does not exist for some $n$
(d) $f^n(0) \neq 0, \forall n$

**38.** If $f$ is a differentiable function on the real line such that $f(0) = 5$ and $f(x) < 5, \forall x \neq 0$, then
(a) $f'(0) = 5$ (b) $f'(0) = -5$
(c) $f'(0) = 0$ (d) $f'(0) = 25$

**39.** Let $f(x + y) = f(x)f(y)$ for all $x$ and $y$ and $f(5) = -2$ and $f'(0) = 3$. What is the value of $f'(5)$?
(a) 3 (b) 1
(c) $-6$ (d) 6

**40.** Under which of the following conditions does the function $f(x) = [(x^2)^m \sin(x^{-2})^m]$, $x \neq 0$ and $x > 0$ and $f(0) = 0$ have a derivative at $x = 0$?
(a) $m \geq -1/2$ (b) $m > 0$
(c) $m > 1/2$ (d) $m \geq 1/2$

**41.** If $f(x) = \begin{cases} \frac{|x|}{2} + 1, & \text{if } x < 1 \\ \frac{x}{2} + 1, & \text{if } 1 \leq x \leq 2 \\ \frac{-|x|}{2} + 1, & \text{if } 2 < x \end{cases}$

Then, the function is
(a) discontinuous at $x = 1, 2$
(b) continuous at $x = 0, 2$
(c) continuous as well as differentiable at $x = 0$
(d) neither continuous nor differentiable at $x = 2$

**42.** Let $f(x)$ be continuous and differentiable over $(a - h, a + h), a \in R$.

Let $F(x) = \begin{cases} \frac{f'(x)}{f(x) - f(a)} - \frac{1}{x - a}; & \text{if } x \neq a \\ \alpha & ; \text{if } x = a \end{cases}$

when $F(x)$ is continuous at $x = a$
(a) $\alpha = 1$ (b) $\alpha = \frac{f'(a)}{f(a)}$
(c) $\alpha = 0$ (d) $\alpha = \frac{f''(a)}{2f'(a)}$

**43.** Let $f(x) = x - [x]$, $x > 0$, where $[x]$ denotes the integral part of $x$
I. $f(x)$ is continuous for all integral values of $x$.
II. $f(x)$ is not differentiable for positive integral values of $x$.
III. $\lim_{x \to 2} f(x)$ does not exist.
Which of the above statements are correct?
(a) I and II only
(b) II and III only
(c) I and III only
(d) I, II and III

**44.** Let $f(x) = x^n |x|$ for real $x$. Then, $f(x)$ is differentiable at origin, if $x$ is equal to which one of the following?
(a) 1 (b) 0
(c) any real number (d) any positive integer

**45.** If the function defined by $f(x) = 2x^2 + 3x - m\log x$ is a monotonically decreasing function on the open interval (0, 1), then the least possible value of the parameter $m$ is

(a) 7 (b) $\frac{15}{2}$

(c) $\frac{31}{4}$ (d) 8

**46.** If the function $f$ and $g$ be defined and continuous on $[l, m]$ and be differentiable on $]l, m[$, then which one of the following is not correct?

(a) When $f(l) = f(m)$, there is $p \in ]l, m[$ such $f'(p) = 0$

(b) There is $p \in ]l, m[$ such that $f(m) - f(l) = f'(p)(m - l)$

(c) There is $p \in ]l, m[$ such that $f(m) - f(l) = f'(p)[g(m) - g(l)]$

(d) There is $p \in ]l, m[$ such that $\frac{f(m) - f(l)}{g(m) - g(l)} = \frac{f'(p)}{g'(p)}$, where $g(m) \neq g(l)$ and $f'(p), g'(p)$ are not simultaneously zero.

**47.** The value of 'c' in Rolle's theorem, where $-\pi/2 < c < \pi/2$ and $f(x) = \cos x$ is equal to

(a) $\pi/4$ (b) $\pi/3$

(c) $\pi$ (d) 0

**48.** The expansion of $\tan x$ in powers of $x$ by Maclaurin's theorem is valid in the interval

(a) $(-\infty, \infty)$ (b) $(-3\pi/2, 3\pi/2)$

(c) $(-\pi, \pi)$ (d) $(-\pi/2, \pi/2)$

**49.** If we expand $\sin x$ by Taylor's series about $\frac{\pi}{2}$, then $a_2, a_7, a_4, a_3$ are

(a) $-\frac{1}{2}, 0, \frac{1}{24}, 0$ (b) $-\frac{1}{2}, 0, -\frac{1}{24}, 0$

(c) $\frac{1}{2}, 0, \frac{1}{24}, 0$ (d) $0, -\frac{1}{7!}, 0, \frac{1}{6}$

**50.** Consider the function

$$f(x) = \begin{cases} x - \sin x, & \text{if } x \text{ is rational} \\ 0, & \text{if } x \text{ is irrational} \end{cases}$$

(a) $f(x)$ is everywhere discontinuous

(b) $f(x)$ is continuous at one point

(c) $f(x)$ is continuous more than one point but at countable points

(d) None of the above

**51.** Let $f(x) = x^3 + 3x^2 - 10x$, so that $f(1) = -6$ and $f(2) = 0$. By the mean value theorem, there exists a number $y$ in the open interval (0, 1) such that $f'(1 + y) = 6$. The value of $y$ turns out to be

(a) greater than 3/4 (b) between 1/2 and 3/4

(c) between 1/4 and 1/2 (d) less than 1/4

**52.** If $f(x) = x^5 - 20x^3 + 240x$, then $f(x)$ is

(a) monotonically decreasing everywhere

(b) monotonically decreasing on $(0, \infty)$

(c) monotonically increasing everywhere

(d) monotonically increasing only in $(-\infty, 0)$

**53.** If $f(x) = \begin{cases} -x^{1/3}, & -1 \le x \le 0 \\ x^{1/3}, & 0 < x \le 1 \end{cases}$, then

(a) Rolle's theorem does not apply to $f$ in $[-1, 1]$

(b) Rolle's theorem applies to $f$ in $[-1, 1]$

(c) $f$ is not continuous at $x = 0$

(d) $f'(0) = 0$

**54.** The function $f(x) = -2x^3 - 9x^2 - 12x + 1$ is an increasing function in the interval

(a) $-2 < x < -1$ (b) $-2 < x < 1$

(c) $-1 < x < 2$ (d) $1 < x < 2$

**55.** If a quadratic function defined on $[a, b]$ by $f(x) = \alpha x^2 + \beta x + \gamma$, $\alpha \neq 0$. Then, the real number 'c' guaranteed by Lagrange's mean value theorem is equal to

(a) $\frac{a + b}{2}$ (b) $\sqrt{ab}$

(c) $\frac{2ab}{a + b}$ (d) $\frac{a}{b} + \frac{b}{a}$

**56.** Using Rolle's theorem, the equation $a_0x^n + a_1x^{n-1} + \ldots + a_n = 0$ has atleast one root between 0 and 1, if

(a) $\frac{a_0}{n} + \frac{a_1}{n-1} + \ldots + a_{n-1} = 0$

(b) $\frac{a_0}{n-1} + \frac{a_1}{n-2} + \ldots + a_{n-2} = 0$

(c) $na_0 + (n-1)a_1 + \ldots + a_{n-1} = 0$

(d) $\frac{a_0}{n+1} + \frac{a_1}{n} + \ldots + a_n = 0$

**57.** If $4a + 2b + c = 0$, the equation $3ax^2 + 2bx + c = 0$ has the one real root between which of the following

(a) 0 and 1 (b) 1 and 2

(c) 0 and 2 (d) None of these

**58.** $f(x) = x^6 - x - 1$, $x \in [1, 2]$, consider the following statements

I. $f$ is increasing on [1, 2].

II. $f$ has root in [1, 2].

III. $f$ is decreasing in [1, 2].

IV. $f$ has no root in [1, 2].

Which of the above is/are correct?

(a) I and II (b) I and IV

(c) II and III (d) III and IV

**59.** If the tangent to the curve $f(x) = x^2$ at any point $(c, f(c))$ is parallel to the line joining $(a, f(a))$ and $(b, f(b))$ on the curve, then which one of the following is true?

(a) $a, c, b$ in AP

(b) $a, c, b$ in GP

(c) $a, c, b$ in HP

(d) $a, c, b$ do not follow definite sequence

**60.** What is abscissa of the point at which the tangent to the curve $y = e^x$ is parallel to the chord joining the extrimities of the curve in the interval [0, 1]?

(a) 1/2 (b) $\ln(1/e)$

(c) $\ln(e - 1)$ (d) $1/e$

**61.** Consider the function (i) $\sqrt{x}$ (ii) $\sin^2 x$ (iii) $e^x$ (iv) $\sin x^2$ on $[0, \infty)$, then which one of the following is correct?
(a) $\sqrt{x}$ and $\sin^2 x$ are uniformly continuous on $[0, \infty)$ only.
(b) $\sqrt{x}, \sin^2 x, e^x$ are uniformly continuous on $[0, \infty)$ only.
(c) All are uniformly continuous on $[0, \infty)$ only.
(d) $\sqrt{x}, e^x, \sin x^2$ are only uniformly continuous on $[0, \infty)$.

**62.** If $\alpha$ is a repeated root of the polynomial equation $f(x) = 0$, then
(a) $f(\alpha) = 0$ but $f'(\alpha) \neq 0$ (b) $f(\alpha) \neq 0$ but $f'(\alpha) = 0$
(c) $f'(\alpha) \neq 0$ and $f''(\alpha) = 0$ (d) $f(\alpha) = 0$ and $f'(\alpha) = 0$

**63.** $f : [0, 1] \to R$ is a function which of the following is possible?
(a) $f$ is unbounded and continuous
(b) $f$ is differentiable but not continuous
(c) $f$ is continuous and bounded
(d) $f$ is differentiable but not bounded

**64.** The value of '$c$' of Rolle's theorem for the function $f(x) = \sin x$ in $[0, \pi]$ is given by
(a) $\pi/3$ (b) $\pi/6$
(c) $\pi/2$ (d) None of these

**65.** The function for which Rolle's theorem is true?
(a) $f(x) = \log x$ in the interval $[1/2, 2]$.
(b) $f(x) = |x + 1|$ in the interval $[-2, 2]$.
(c) $f(x) = |x|$ in the interval $[-1, 1]$.
(d) None of the above

**66.** The value of '$c$' of Lagrange's mean value theorem for $f(x) = x(x - 1)$ in $[1, 2]$ is given by
(a) 5/4 (b) 3/2
(c) 7/4 (d) 11/6

**67.** Lagrange's form of remainder after $n$ terms in Taylor's development of the function $e^x$ in a finite form in the interval $[a, a + h]$ is
(a) $\frac{h^n}{n!} e^{a+\theta h}$ (b) $\frac{h^n}{n!} e^{\theta h}$
(c) $\frac{h^n(1-\theta)e^{a+\theta h}}{n!}$ (d) $\frac{h^n(1+\theta)^n}{n!} e^{a+\theta h}$

**68.** In Taylor's development of $f(a + h)$ in ascending integral form of $h$ with cauchy's form of remainder after $n$ terms, we have

$$f(a+h) = f(a) + hf'(a) + \frac{h^2}{2!} f''(a) + \ldots + \frac{h^{n-1}}{(n-1)!} f^{(n-1)}(a) + R_n, \text{ where}$$

(a) $R_n = \frac{h^n}{(n-1)!}(1-\theta)^{n-1} f^n(a + \theta h),\ 0 < \theta < 1$
(b) $R_n = \frac{h^n}{(n-1)!}(1-\theta)^{n-1} f^{n-1}(a + \theta h),\ 0 < \theta < 1$
(c) $R_n = \frac{h^n}{n!}(1-\theta)^{n-1} f^n(a + \theta h),\ 0 < \theta < 1$
(d) $R_n = \frac{h^n}{(n-1)!}(1-\theta)^n f^n(a + \theta h),\ 0 < \theta < 1$

**69.** If $f(x + y) = f(x) \cdot f(y)$ for all $x$ and $y$. Suppose, that $f(3) = 3$ and $f'(0) = 11$. Then, $f'(3)$ is equal to
(a) 22 (b) 33
(c) 28 (d) None of these

**70.** Select (a), (b), (c) and (d) which is correct?
(a) Divergent sequence is not bounded.
(b) A function which is not continuous at a point may be differentiable at that point.
(c) Least upper bound of a bounded set is an element of the set.
(d) Bounded sequence is always convergent.

**71.** If $f'(a)$ exists, then $\lim_{h \to 0} \frac{f(a+h) - f(a-h)}{h}$ is equal to
(a) $\frac{f'(a)}{2}$ (b) $f'(a)$
(c) $2f'(a)$ (d) None of these

**72.** If $f$ and $g$ are continuous on $[a, b]$ and have equal finite derivatives in $[a, b]$, then $f - g$ is
(a) constant (b) $f/g$
(c) $g$ (d) $\infty$

**73.** Function $f(x) = |x|$ is defined on $[-2, 2]$. The points at which $f$ is differentiable are
(a) $-1, 0$ (b) $-1, 0, 1$
(c) $-1, 0, 1, 2$ (d) None of these

**74.** If $f(x)$ be real-valued function and differentiable on $R$ and $f(x + y) = \frac{f(x) + f(y)}{1 - f(x)f(y)}$, then $f(x)$ is equals to
(a) $\tan^{-1}[x f'(0)]$ (b) $\tan[x f(0)]$
(c) $\cot[x f(0)]$ (d) $\cot^{-1}[x f'(0)]$

**75.** If $f(x)$ be defined on $[a, b]$ such that for $\alpha > 0$ $|f(x) - f(y)| \leq |x - y|^{1+\alpha}$, $\forall\ x, y \in [a, b]$, then $f(x)$ is
(a) constant on $[a, b]$
(b) continuous but not differentiable on $[a, b]$
(c) continuous but not uniformly continuous on $[a, b]$
(d) None of the above

**76.** If $f(x)$ is differentiable on $(a, b)$ and $f(a) = 0$, and there exists a real number $k$ such that $|f'(x)| \leq k|f(x)|$ on $[a, b]$, then $f(x)$ is
(a) non-zero, $\forall\ x \in [a, b]$
(b) zero, $\forall\ x \in [a, b]$
(c) discontinuous at $x = \frac{a+b}{2}$
(d) continuous but not differentiable, $\forall\ x \in [a, b]$

**77.** Let $f(x) = \begin{cases} x, & \text{when } 0 \leq x < 1/2 \\ 1, & \text{when } x = 1/2 \\ 1 - x, & \text{when } 1/2 < x < 1 \end{cases}$,

then $f$ is
(a) continuous at $x = 1/2$
(b) not defined at $x = 1/2$
(c) discontinuous at $x = 1/2$
(d) continuous for all $x$, $0 \leq x < 1$

**78.** Let $f : R \to R$ be a monotonically decreasing function (defined everywhere on the real line) and let $f$ be discontinuous at certain point $x = a$. What is the nature of discontinuity?
(a) Removable discontinuity.
(b) Either removable or discontinuity of the second kind.
(c) Discontinuity of first kind.
(d) Either discontinuity of first kind or of second kind.

**79.** If $f(x) = x^2$ for all $x \in R$, $f$ is
(a) not continuous on $R$
(b) uniformly continuous on $R$
(c) not uniformly continuous on $R$
(d) None of the above

**80.** The points at which $f(x) = [x]$ is discontinuous are (Here, $[x]$ is the greatest integer less then or equal to x)
(a) set of all rational numbers
(b) set of all irrational numbers
(c) set of all integers
(d) set of all prime numbers

**81.** For $m \in N$ such that $n \geq m$, the function $f(x) = \dfrac{x^{2n+2} - \sin x - 1}{x^{2n} + 1}$, $\forall\, x \in [1, 2]$ with $f(1) \cdot f(2) < 0$ has
(a) no zero in [1, 2]
(b) exactly zeros in [1, 2]
(c) exactly two zeros in [1, 2]
(d) countable zeros in [1, 2]

**82.** Which of the following is correct?
(a) $\dfrac{x}{1+x^2} > \tan^{-1} x > x, \forall\, x > 0$
(b) $\dfrac{x}{1+x^2} < \tan^{-1} x < x, \forall\, x > 0$
(c) $\dfrac{x}{1+x^2} < x < \tan^{-1} x, \forall\, x > 0$
(d) None of the above

**83.** If $f(x + y) = f(x) + f(y), \forall\, x, y \in R$ and $f(x)$ is differentiable at one point of $R$, then $f(x)$ is
(a) differentiable, $\forall\, R$
(b) differentiable, $\forall\, Q$
(c) differentiable, $\forall\, R ^\wedge Q$
(d) None of the above

**84.** The function $f(x) = \sin 1/x$ at $x = 0$ has a
(a) discontinuity of first kind
(b) discontinuity of second kind
(c) mixed continuity
(d) removable discontinuity

**85.** For function $f(x) = \sin 1/x$, $x \neq 0$ at the origin
(a) left limit is $-1$
(b) right limit is $+1$
(c) limit is zero
(d) None of these

**86.** If $f(x) = x^2$ for all $x \in R$, $f$ is
(a) not continuous on $R$
(b) uniformly continuous on $R$
(c) not uniformly continuous on $R$
(d) None of the above

**87.** Function $f(x) = \dfrac{|x|}{x}$, $x \neq 0$ may be continuous at origin, if
(a) $f(0) = 0$
(b) $f(0) = -1$
(c) $f(0) = \infty$
(d) Cannot be continuous for any value of $f(0)$

**88.** If $f(x)$, $g(x)$ are differentiable on $(a, b)$ and are continuous on $[a, b]$ and $f(a) = g(b) = 0$, then $\exists$ a point $c \in (a, b)$ such that
(a) $f(c) + f'(c)g'(c) = 0$
(b) $f'(c) + f(c)g'(c) = 0$
(c) $f'(c)g(c) + f(c) = 0$
(d) $f(c)f'(c) + g(c) = 0$

**89.** If $f(x)$ is differentiable on interval $I$ and $\exists\ \alpha > 0$, such that $|f'(x)| \leq \alpha$ on $I$, then $f(x)$ is
(a) continuous but not uniformly continuous on $I$
(b) uniformly continuous but not continuous on $I$
(c) uniformly continuous but not differentiable on $I$
(d) continuous, uniformly continuous and differentiable on $I$

**90.** If $f(x)$ and $g(x)$ are two functions such as $f'(x) = g'(x)$ on an interval $I$, then there difference functions is
(a) zero function on $I$
(b) constant function on $I$
(c) polynomial of degree one on $I$
(d) None of the above

**91.** If $f(x)$ and $g(x)$ are real functions defined on $[0, \pi/2]$ and $-\dfrac{\pi}{2} < f(x) \pm g(x) < \dfrac{\pi}{2}$, then which of following is correct?
(a) $\cos(f(x)) = \sin(g(x)), \forall\, x \in [0, \pi/2]$
(b) $\cos(f(x)) > \sin(g(x)), \forall\, x \in [0, \pi/2]$
(c) $\cos(f(x)) < \sin(g(x)), \forall\, x \subset [0, \pi/2]$
(d) None of the above

**92.** If $1 > x > y > 0$ or $x > y > 1$, then which of the following is correct?
(a) $x^{y^x}/y^{x^y} > x/y > x^y/y^x$
(b) $x^{y^x}/y^{x^y} < x/y < x^y/y^x$
(c) $\dfrac{x}{y} < x^y/y^x < x^{y^x}/y^{x^y}$
(d) $\dfrac{x}{y} > x^y/y^x > x^{y^x}/y^{x^y}$

**93.** If $f''(x) \geq 0$ on an interval $I$. Then, which of the following is correct?
(a) $f\left(\dfrac{x_1 + x_2 + \ldots + x_n}{n}\right) \geq \dfrac{f(x_1) + f(x_2) + \ldots + f(x_n)}{n}$, $\forall\, x_1, x_2, \ldots, x_n \in I$
(b) $f\left(\dfrac{x_1 + x_2 + \ldots + x_n}{n}\right) \leq \dfrac{f(x_1) + f(x_2) + \ldots + f(x_n)}{n}$, $\forall\, x_1, x_2, \ldots, x_n \in I$
(c) $f\left(\dfrac{x_1 + x_2 + \ldots + x_n}{n}\right) = \dfrac{1}{n}[f(x_1) + f(x_2) + \ldots + f(x_n)]$
(d) None of the above

**94.** If $f(x)$ is twice differentiable and $|f(x)| < \alpha$, $|f''(x)| < \beta$, in the range $x > a$, then which of the following is correct?
(a) $|f'(x)| > 2\sqrt{(\alpha\beta)}, \forall\, x > a$

(b) $|f'(x)| \leq 2\sqrt{(\alpha\beta)}, \forall x > a$
(c) $|f'(x)| < 2\sqrt{(\alpha\beta)}, \forall x > a$
(d) $|f'(x)| = 2\sqrt{(\alpha\beta)}, \forall x > a$

**95.** If $f(x)$ is twice differentiable real function on $]0, \infty[$ and $\alpha$, $\beta$ and $\gamma$ are the supremum of $|f|, |f'|, |f''|$, respectively on $]0, \infty[$
(a) $\beta^2 = \alpha\gamma$ (b) $\beta^2 < \alpha\gamma$
(c) $\beta^2 \leq \alpha\gamma$ (d) $\beta^2 > \alpha\gamma$

**96.** If $f(x) = \begin{cases} \sin^2 x \sin\left(\dfrac{1}{\sin x}\right), & \text{if } 0 < x < \pi \\ 0, & \text{if } x = 0 \end{cases}$. Then, $f(x)$ is
(a) continuous but not differentiable, $\forall x \in [0, \pi[$
(b) differentiable, $\forall x \in ]0, \pi[$
(c) not differentiable, $\forall x \in [0, \pi[$
(d) None of the above

**97.** A function $f : R \to R$ satisfies the equation
$f(x+y) = f(x) \cdot f(y), \forall x, y \in R$ and $f(x) \neq 0, \forall x \in R$.
If $f(x)$ is differentiable at 0 and $f'(0) = 2$. Then, $f'(x)$ is equals to
(a) $2f(x), \forall x \in R$
(b) $4f(x), \forall x \in R$
(c) $0, \forall x \in R - \{0\}$
(d) None of the above

**98.** If $f(x+y) = f(x) \cdot f(y)$ on $R$ and $f(x)$ is continuous at $x = 0$, then $f(x)$ is
(a) differentiable at $x = 0$
(b) not differentiable at $x = 0$
(c) differentiable, $\forall x \in Q$
(d) None of the above

**99.** If $f(x+y) = f(x) + f(y), \forall x, y \in R$ and $f$ is continuous at one point of $R$, then $f(x)$ is/are
(a) not continuous, $\forall x \in R$
(b) uniformly continuous, $\forall x \in R$
(c) differentiable, $\forall x \in R$
(d) None of the above

**100.** $\lim_{x \to 0^+} x^n e^{-\frac{1}{x^m}} = l, \forall n \in R$ and $m > 0$. Then, the value of $l$ is
(a) 0 (b) 1
(c) $-1$ (d) None of these

**101.** Which of the following statement is correct?
(a) $|\sin x - \sin y| = |x - y|$ (b) $|\sin x - \sin y| < |x - y|$
(c) $|\sin x - \sin y| \leq |x - y|$ (d) $|\sin x - \sin y| > |x - y|$

**102.** If $f(x)$ is real-valued function defined on $]0, \infty[$ such that $f(0) = 0$ and $f''(x) > 0, \forall x$, then the function $h(x) = \dfrac{f(x)}{x}$ is
(a) increasing in $]0, \infty[$
(b) decreasing in $[0, 1]$
(c) increasing in $]0, 1[$ and decreasing in $[1, \infty[$
(d) decreasing in $]0, 1]$ and increasing in $[1, \infty[$

**103.** Let $f : (0, \infty) \to R$ be a twice differentiable function and $|f(x)| \leq 1, |f''(x)| \leq 2, \forall x$, then
(a) $|f'(x)| \leq 2\sqrt{2}, \forall x$ (b) $|f'(x)| < \sqrt{2}, \forall x$
(c) $|f'(x)| < 2, \forall x$ (d) None of these

**104.** Let $f$ be a continuous real-valued function on $[0, 1]$ such that $f(0) = -1$ and $f(1) = 1/2$, then there always exists a $t \in [0, 1]$ such that
(a) $f(t) = -2$ (b) $f(t) = 1$
(c) $f(t) = 3/2$ (d) $f(t) = -1/2$

**105.** The function $f(x) = \dfrac{1}{x}$, $x \geq 1$ is
(a) uniformly continuous
(b) not continuous at $x = 1$
(c) not uniformly continuous
(d) not differentiable

**106.** The function $f(x) = \begin{cases} x\sin\dfrac{1}{x}, & x \neq 0 \\ 0, & x = 0 \end{cases}$ is
(a) continuous at $x = 0$ but not differentiable at $x = 0$
(b) differentiable at $x = 0$
(c) discontinuous at $x = 0$
(d) twice differentiable at $x = 0$

**107.** The function $f(x) = 1 - |1 - x|$ on $R$ is
(a) not continuous
(b) continuous but not differentiable
(c) differentiable but not continuous
(d) differentiable at only one point

**108.** Which one of the following functions has exactly two points of discontinuity?
(a) $f(x) = \begin{cases} 1, & \text{if } x > 0 \\ 0, & \text{if } x \leq 0 \end{cases}$
(b) $f(x) = \begin{cases} 1, & \text{if } 0 \leq x \leq 1 \\ 0, & \text{otherwise} \end{cases}$
(c) $f(x) = \begin{cases} x, & \text{if } 0 \leq x \leq 1 \\ 0, & \text{otherwise} \end{cases}$
(d) $f(x) = \begin{cases} 1, & \text{if } x \text{ is rational} \\ 0, & \text{if } x \text{ is irrational} \end{cases}$

**109.** The graph of the function $f$ is given below.

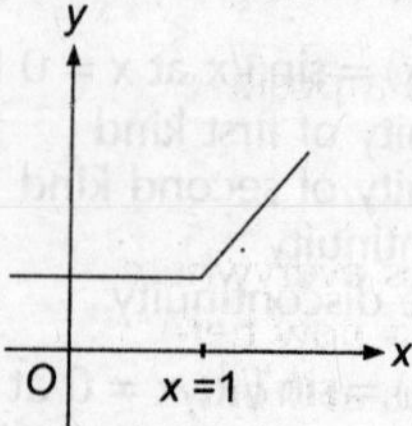


The derivative of $f$
(a) exists everywhere except at $x = 1$
(b) does not exists anywhere
(c) exists only at $x = 1$
(d) exists everywhere and is continuous

**110.** Let $f:[0, 1] \to (0, \infty)$ be a continuous function. Suppose, $f(0) = 1$ and $f(1) = 7$. Then,
(a) $f$ is uniformly continuous and is not onto
(b) $f$ is increasing and $f([0, 1]) = [1, 7]$
(c) $f$ is not uniformly continuous
(d) $f$ is not bounded

**111.** Let $f:[a, b] \to [c, d]$ be a monotonic and bijective function, then
(a) $f$ is continuous, but $f^{-1}$ need not be
(b) $f$ and $f^{-1}$ are both continuous
(c) If $(b-a) > (d-c)$, then $f$ is decreasing function
(d) $f$ is not uniformly continuous

**112.** Let $f: R \to R$ be defined by

$$f(x) = \begin{cases} x^2 \sin\frac{1}{x^2}, & x \neq 0 \\ 0, & x = 0 \end{cases}, \text{ then}$$

(a) $f$ is differentiable everywhere with continuous derivative
(b) $f$ is differentiable everywhere other than the point zero
(c) $f$ is now here differentiable
(d) $f$ is differentiable but its derivative is not continuous

**113.** Let $f: R \to R$ be defined by $f(x) = [x^2]$, where $[x]$ is greatest integer function. The points of discontinuity of $f$ are
(a) only the integral points
(b) all rational numbers
(c) $\{\pm\sqrt{n} : n \text{ is positive integer}\}$
(d) all real numbers

**114.** The function $f(x) = |x| + 3$ is
(a) continuous as well as differentiable on $R$
(b) continuous on $R$ but not differentiable anywhere on $R$
(c) not continuous on $R$
(d) continuous on $R$ and differentiable at all points on $R$ except $x = 0$

**115.** Let $f: R \to R$ be defined by

$$f(x) = \begin{cases} 0, & \text{if } x \text{ is not a positive integer} \\ \frac{1}{n}, & \text{if } x \text{ is a positive} \end{cases}$$

Then, $f$ is
(a) continuous everywhere
(b) continuous now here
(c) continuous at 0 only
(d) continuous everywhere except at positive integers

**116.** A monotonic function
(a) is always continuous
(b) is continuous only, if it intermediate value property
(c) can be nowhere continuous
(d) can be discontinuous at infinitely many points

**117.** Let $f(x) = |\sin \pi x|, \forall x \in R$. Then,
(a) $f$ is continuous nowhere
(b) $f$ is continuous everywhere and differentiable nowhere
(c) $f$ is continuous everywhere and differentiable everywhere except at integral values of $x$
(d) $f$ is differentiable everywhere

**118.** The function $f(x) = 1/x$, $x > 0$ is
(a) continuous but not uniformly continuous
(b) discontinuous everywhere
(c) neither continuous not uniformly continuous
(d) uniformly continuous but not continuous

**119.** If $f$ is a differentiable function on the real line such as $f(0) = 50$ and $f(x) < 50$ for $x \neq 0$, then
(a) $f'(0) = 50$ (b) $f'(0) = -50$
(c) $f'(0) = 0$ (d) None of these

**120.** $f:[0, 1] \to R$ is a function, which of the following is possible?
(a) $f$ is differentiable but not continuous.
(b) $f$ is unbounded and continuous.
(c) $f$ is differentiable but its derivative is not continuous.
(d) $f$ is uniformly continuous but not continuous.

**121.** Suppose, $f: R \to R$ and $g: R \to R$ are uniformly continuous functions with $g(x) > 0, \forall x$. Then, which of the following is true?
(a) $f \cdot g$ is uniformly continuous, $\forall f$ and $g$.
(b) $f + g$ is uniformly continuous, $\forall f$ and $g$.
(c) $f/g$ is uniformly continuous, $\forall f$ and $g$.
(d) $f \cdot g$ is never continuous.

**122.** The limit of $\frac{x^3 - 1}{x - 1}$ as $x \to 1$ is
(a) $\infty$ (b) 0
(c) 1 (d) 3

**123.** An example of a function on the real line $R$ i.e., continuous but not uniformly continuous is
(a) constant function (b) identity function
(c) $\sin x$ (d) $x^2$

**124.** Let $f:[a, b] \to R$ be a continuous function and let $f(a) < f(b)$. Then, by intermediate value theorem
(a) $f([a, b]) = [f(a), f(b)]$ (b) $f([a, b]) \supseteq [f(a), f(b)]$
(c) $f([a, b]) \subseteq [f(a), f(b)]$ (d) $f([a, b]) \neq [f(a), f(b)]$

**125.** Let $f: R \to R$ be differentiable. Which of these will follow from mean value theorem?
(a) $\forall\, a, b \in R$, if $a < c < b$, then $\frac{f(b) - f(a)}{b \quad a} = f'(c)$
(b) for same $a, b$ in $R$ and for all $c \in ]a, b[$, $\frac{f(b) - f(a)}{b - a} = f'(c)$
(c) $\forall\, a, b \in R$ there is some $c$ in $(a, b)$ such that $\frac{f(b) - f(a)}{b - a} = f'(c)$
(d) $\forall\, a, b \in R$, there is a unique element $c$ in $(a, b)$ such that $\frac{f(b) - f(a)}{b - a} = f'(c)$

**126.** The function $f(x) = \begin{cases} x\sin\frac{1}{x}, & x \neq 0 \\ 0, & x = 0 \end{cases}$ is

(a) differentiable at 0 but not continuous
(b) has 2nd derivative at the origin
(c) continuous at the origin but not differentiable
(d) neither continuous nor differentiable at the origin

**127.** Suppose, $f$ is a real-valued function on the interval $[-1, 1]$ such that $|f|$ is continuous. Which of the following is true?

(a) $f$ is continuous
(b) $f$ is not continuous
(c) $f$ need not be continuous
(d) $f$ is bounded

**128.** Which of the following functions is not uniformly continuous in $[2, \infty[$?

(a) $e^x$ (b) $\frac{1}{x}$
(c) $\frac{1}{x^2}$ (d) $\sin x$

**129.** Which of the following statements is true?

(a) All continuous functions from $R \to R$ are uniformly continuous.
(b) All continuous functions from $R \to [0, 1]$ are uniformly continuous.
(c) All continuous functions from $[0, 1] \to R$ are uniformly continuous.
(d) All continuous functions from $[0, \infty[$ to $R$ are uniformly continuous.

**130.** Let $f: R \to R$ be a function and $A = \{x : x \in R \text{ and } x > 0\}$, $B = \{x : x \in R \text{ and } x \leq 0\}$, then

(a) if $f$ is continuous on $R$, then $f$ is continuous on $A$ and $f$ is continuous on $B$ but converse is false
(b) if $f$ is continuous on $A$ and $f$ is continuous on $B$, then $f$ is continuous on $R$ but converse is not true
(c) if $f$ is continuous on $R$, then $f$ is continuous on $A$ and $f$ is continuous on $B$
(d) no relatives between continuity of $f$ on $R$ and continuity of $f$ on $A$ and $B$

**131.** The value of $\lim_{x \to \infty}[\sqrt{x^2+1} - x]$ is

(a) $\infty$ (b) 1
(c) 0 (d) does not exists

**132.** Let $f(x)$ be defined as
$f(x)$ = distance of $x$ from its nearest integer, then

(a) $f$ is continuous everywhere but differentiable now here
(b) $f$ is neither continuous nor differentiable
(c) $f$ is continuous everywhere but not differentiable at $\{n/2 : n \in I\}$
(d) $f$ is continuous and differentiable everywhere

**133.** If $f$ is differentiable on $[a, b]$ and $f(a) = f(b) = 0$, then

(a) $f\left(\frac{a+b}{2}\right) = 0$
(b) $f'(t) = 0$ for some $t \in (a, b)$
(c) $f(x) = 0, \forall x \in [a, b]$
(d) $f(x) = 0$ for some $x \in (a, b)$

**134.** Let $f: R \to R$ be defined as
$f(x) = \begin{cases} x, & \text{if } x \text{ is rational number} \\ -x, & \text{if } x \text{ is irrational number} \end{cases}$, then

(a) $f$ is continuous nowhere
(b) $f$ is continuous exactly at one point
(c) $f$ is continuous everywhere
(d) $f$ is continuous only at irrational points

**135.** Let $f: R \to R$ be differentiable everywhere. Then,

(a) if $f$ is strictly increasing, then $f'(x) = 0, \forall x$ but converse is false
(b) $f'(x) > 0, \forall x$, then $f(x)$ is strictly increasing
(c) $f'(x) > 0, \forall x$, then $f$ is strictly increasing, but converse is also true
(d) there is no relation between positivity of $f'(x)$ and monotonicity of $f$.

**136.** Let a function $f(x)$ is defined as
$f(x) = \begin{cases} 2, & x = 2 \\ 1, & x \neq 2 \end{cases}$, then

(a) $\lim_{x \to \infty} f(x) = -\infty$ and $\lim_{x \to \infty} f(x) = \infty$
(b) $f(x)$ is continuous
(c) $\lim_{x \to \infty} f(x)$ does not exists
(d) $f(x)$ is discontinuous

**137.** Let $p_n(x)$ be a Taylor's polynomial of degree $n \geq 0$ for the function $e^x$ about $x = 0$. Then, the error in this approximation is

(a) $\frac{x^n}{n!}e^t$ for some $0 < t < x$
(b) $\frac{x^n}{(n+1)!}e^t$ for some $0 < t < x$
(c) $\frac{x^{n+1}}{n!}e^t$ for some $0 < t < x$
(d) $\frac{x^{n+1}}{(n+1)!}e^t$ for some $0 < t < x$

**138.** Let $f: R \to R$ be given by $f(x) = [x]$, the greatest integer less than or equal to $x$. Then,

(a) the points at which $f$ is not continuous is countable
(b) the points at which $f$ is not continuous is $R$
(c) $f$ is strictly increasing
(d) $f$ is strictly decreasing

**139.** Let $f: [0, 1] \to [0, 1]$ be a strictly increasing onto function. Then,

(a) $f$ is continuous but $f^{-1}$ is not
(b) $f$ and $f^{-1}$ are both continuous
(c) $f^{-1}$ is continuous but $f$ is not
(d) $f$ and $f^{-1}$ both not continuous

**140.** The set of points where $f(x) = |\sin x|$ is not differentiable is

(a) empty (b) $\{0\}$
(c) $\{k\pi : k \in Z\}$ (d) $\{k\pi/2 : k \in Z\}$

**141.** Let $I = \{1\} \cup \{2\} \subseteq R$. For $x \in R$, let $\phi(x) = \text{dis}(x, I) = \text{Inf}\{|x-y| : y \in I\}$. Then,
(a) $\phi$ is discontinuous somewhere on $R$
(b) $\phi$ is continuous on $R$ but not differentiable only at $x = 1$
(c) $\phi$ is continuous on $R$ but not differentiable only at $x = 1$ and 2
(d) $\phi$ is continuous on $R$ but not differentiable only at $x = 1, \frac{3}{2}$ and 2

**142.** Consider the function $f(x) = |\cos x| + |\sin(2-x)|$
At which of the following points is $f$ not differentiable?
(a) $\{(2n+2)\frac{\pi}{2} : n \in Z\}$ (b) $\{n\pi : n \in Z\}$
(c) $\{n\pi + 2 : n \in Z\}$ (d) $\{\frac{n\pi}{2} : n \in Z\}$

**143.** Which of the following is correct?
(a) $(n+1)\log\left(1+\frac{1}{n+1}\right) \to 1$ as $n \to \infty$
(b) $(n+1)\log\left(1+\frac{1}{n}\right) \to 1$ as $n \to \infty$
(c) $n^2 \log\left(1+\frac{1}{n}\right) \to 1$ as $n \to \infty$
(d) $n\log\left(1+\frac{1}{n^2}\right) \to 1$ as $n \to \infty$

**144.** Let $F = \{f : R \to R : |f(x) - f(y)| \le k|(x-y)|^{\alpha}\}$ for all $x, y \in R$ and for some $\alpha > 0$ and some $k > 0$. Which of the following is/are true?
(a) Every $f \in F$ is not continuous.
(b) Every $f \in F$ is not uniformly continuous.
(c) Every differentiable function $f$ is in $F$.
(d) Every $f \in F$ is differentiable.

**145.** Which of the following statement is true?
(a) $\lim_{x\to\infty} \frac{\log x}{x^{1/2}} = 0$ and $\lim_{x\to\infty} \frac{\log x}{x} = \infty$
(b) $\lim_{x\to\infty} \frac{\log x}{x^{1/2}} = \infty$ and $\lim_{x\to\infty} \frac{\log x}{x} = 0$
(c) $\lim_{x\to\infty} \frac{\log x}{x^{1/2}} = 0$ and $\lim_{x\to\infty} \frac{\log x}{x} = 0$
(d) $\lim_{x\to\infty} \frac{\log x}{x^{1/2}} = 0$ but $\lim_{x\to\infty} \frac{\log x}{x}$ does not exists

**146.** Which of the following real-valued function $f$ defined on $R$ have the property that $f$ is continuous and $fof = f$?
(a) $f(x) = \begin{cases} |x|, \text{ if } x \in [-1, 1] \\ x^2, \text{ if } x \notin [-1, 1] \end{cases}$ (b) $f(x) = \begin{cases} x, \text{ if } x \in [0, 1] \\ -x, \text{ if } x \ge 1 \\ 0, \text{ if } x < 0 \end{cases}$
(c) $f(x) = \begin{cases} x, \text{ if } x \in [-1, 1] \\ 1, \text{ if } x \ge 1 \\ -1, \text{ if } x < -1 \end{cases}$ (d) $f(x) = \begin{cases} 1, \text{ if } x \in [-23, 27] \\ 22 + x, \text{ if } x \le -23 \\ -26 + x, \text{ if } x \ge 27 \end{cases}$

**147.** Define $f : R \to R$ by $f(x) = \begin{cases} x^2, \text{ if } x < 0 \\ 2x + x^2, \text{ if } x \ge 0 \end{cases}$
Then, which of the following statements are correct?
(a) $f''(x) = 2, \forall x \in R$.
(b) $f''(0)$ does not exists.
(c) $f'(x)$ exists for each $x \neq 0$.
(d) $f'(0)$ does not exists.

**148.** $\lim_{x\to 0} \left[\frac{(1+x)^{1/2} - e + \frac{1}{2}ex}{x^2}\right]$ is
(a) $\frac{24}{11}e$ (b) $\frac{11}{24}e$
(c) $\frac{1}{11}e$ (d) $\frac{1}{24}e$

**149.** $\lim_{x\to 0} \frac{(1+x)^{1/x} - e}{x}$ is
(a) $e$ (b) $-e$
(c) $-2e$ (d) $-\frac{e}{2}$

**150.** $f(x) = x|x|$, then choose the correct statement
(a) $f(x)$ is strictly decreasing function
(b) $f(x)$ is not monotonic
(c) $f(x)$ is differentiable, $\forall x \in R$ except $x = 0$
(d) $f(x)$ is differentiable, $\forall x \in R$

**151.** The continuous function $f : R \to R$ defined by $f(x) = (x^2 + 1)^{2011}$ is
(a) onto but not one-one
(b) one-one but not onto
(c) Both one-one and onto
(d) Neither one-one nor onto

**152.** If $f(x) = \lim_{n\to\infty} \frac{1}{1 + n\sin^2 \pi x}$, then $f(x)$ is
(a) discontinuous, $\forall x \in R$
(b) discontinuous, $\forall x \in Q$
(c) discontinuous, $\forall x \in R - Q$
(d) discontinuous, $\forall x \in Z$

**153.** $\lim_{x\to a} \frac{1}{(x-a)^2}$, $a > 0$ is
(a) $\infty$ (b) $-\infty$
(c) exists finitely (d) does not exists

**154.** $f(x) = (x + |x|)|x|, \forall x \in R$, then which of the following is incorrect?
(a) $f$ is continuous
(b) $f'$ is continuous
(c) $f$ is not differentiable for some $x$
(d) $f'$ is differentiable

**155.** If $f(x) = \begin{cases} x, \; x \text{ is rational} \\ 1 - x, \; x \text{ is irrational} \end{cases}$
then which of the following is incorrect?
(a) $fof(x)$ is monotonic.
(b) $f(x) + f(1-x)$ is constant.

(c) $f(x)$ assumes every value between 0 and 1.
(d) None of the above

**156.** Let $f:[0,1]\to[0,1]$ be a continuous function, then
(a) $f$ has atleast one fixed point
(b) $f$ has atleast nine fixed points
(c) $f$ has atleast ten fixed points
(d) $f$ need not to have any fixed point

**157.** If $f(x)=\lim_{n\to\infty}\left[\lim_{t\to 0}\frac{\sin^2(n!\pi x)}{\sin^2(n!\pi x)+t^2}\right]$. Then,
(a) $f(x)$ is nowhere continuous
(b) $f(x)$ is continuous everywhere
(c) $f(x)$ has only 2 point of continuity
(d) $f(x)$ has only 2 point of discontinuity

**158.** What is the value of $\lim_{x\to 0}\frac{e^x-x-1}{x^2}$?
(a) 0 (b) $\frac{1}{2}$
(c) 2 (d) e

**159.** Which of the following function is continuous at origin?
(a) $f(x)=\begin{cases}\cos\left(\frac{1}{x}\right), & x\neq 0\\ 0, & x=0\end{cases}$
(b) $f(x)=\begin{cases}x+\sin\frac{1}{x}, & x\neq 0\\ 1, & x=0\end{cases}$
(c) $f(x)=\begin{cases}\sin x\sin\frac{1}{x}, & x\neq 0\\ 0, & x=0\end{cases}$
(d) $f(x)=\begin{cases}x\sin\frac{1}{x}, & x\neq 0\\ 1, & x=0\end{cases}$

**160.** If $f(x)$ and $g(x)$ are differentiable function for $0\le x\le 1$ such that $f(1)-f(0)=k[g(1)-g(0)]$, $k\neq 0$, then there exists c satisfying $0<c<1$. Then, $\frac{f'(c)}{g'(c)}$ is equal to
(a) $2k$ (b) $k$
(c) $-k$ (d) $\frac{1}{k}$

**161.** If $f(x)=\begin{cases}x^{\frac{1}{k}-1}\cos\frac{1}{x}, & \text{if } x\neq 0\\ 0, & \text{if } x=0\end{cases}$

then under what condition is $f(x)$ differentiable at $x=0$?
(a) $k>\frac{1}{2}$ (b) $k\ge\frac{1}{2}$
(c) $k\le\frac{1}{2}$ (d) $k<\frac{1}{2}$

**162.** Given that the function
$$f(x)=\lim_{n\to\infty}n(x^{1/n}-1),\ x>0$$
if f satisfies $f(1/x)=kf(x)$, then what is/are the value/s of k?
(a) 1 (b) −1
(c) 0 (d) ±1

**163.** Under which one of the following conditions does the function $f(x)=[(x^2)^m\sin(x^{-2})^n]$, $x\neq 0$, $n>0$ and $f(0)=0$, have a derivative at $x=0$?
(a) $m\ge-\frac{1}{2}$ (b) $m>0$
(c) $m>\frac{1}{2}$ (d) $m\ge\frac{1}{2}$

**164.** Which of the following is/are correct for the function?
$$f(x)=\begin{cases}x^2\sin\frac{1}{x}, & x\neq 0\\ 0, & x=0\end{cases},\ x\in[-1,1]$$
(a) Continuous (b) Uniformly continuous
(c) Bounded (d) Absolutely continuous

**165.** $\lim_{x\to 0}\frac{(1+x)^{1/2}-e+\frac{1}{2}ex}{x^2}$ is
(a) $\frac{24}{11}e$ (b) $\frac{11}{24}e$
(c) $\frac{1}{11}e$ (d) $\frac{1}{24}e$

**166.** $f(x)=(x+|x|)|x|,\forall x\in R$, then which of the following is incorrect?
(a) $f$ is continuous
(b) $f$ is not differentiable for some $x$
(c) $f'$ is continuous
(d) $f'$ is differentiable

**167.** Let $f:[0,10]\to[0,10]$ be a continuous function, then
(a) $f$ need not to have any fixed point
(b) $f$ has atleast 10 fixed points
(c) $f$ has atleast 9 fixed points
(d) $f$ has atleast one fixed point

**168.** Let $f$ be an infinitely differentiable function from $R$ to $R$. Suppose that for some positive integer $n$,
$$f(0)=f(1)=f'(0)=f''(0)\ldots f^n(0)=0,$$
then
(a) all the subsequent derivative has atleast one zero in the interval (0, 1)
(b) $f^{n+1}(x)\neq 0$ for any x in (0, 1)
(c) $f^{n+1}(x)=0$ for some x in (0, 1)
(d) $f^{n+1}(x)$ is constant in [0, 1]

**169.** If $f$ is monotonic increasing on $(a,b)$, then for each $c\in(a,b)$ which of the following is incorrect?
(a) $\lim_{x\to c^-}f(x)=\sup_{x\in(a,c)}f(x)<f(c)$
(b) $\lim_{x\to c^+}f(x)=\inf_{x\in(c,b)}f(x)>f(c)$
(c) $\sup_{x\in(a,c)}f(x)=\inf_{x\in(c,b)}f(x)$
(d) $\lim_{x\to c^-}f(x)$ and $\lim_{x\to c^+}f(x)$ both exists but may not be equal

**170.** Let $f:[0,10] \to [0,10]$ be a continuous mapping, then
(a) $f$ need not to have any fixed point
(b) $f$ has atleast 10 fixed points
(c) $f$ has atleast 9 fixed points
(d) $f$ has atleast one fixed point

**171.** Let $y$ be a continuously differentiable function which satisfies the differential equation
$y'' + y' - y = 0, \forall x \in [0, a]$, where $a$ is a positive real number, if $y(0) = y(a) = 0$, then on $[0, a]$
(a) $y$ is strictly increasing
(b) $y$ is strictly decreasing
(c) $y$ is monotonic
(d) $y$ has finite/countably infinite number is zero

**172.** If $f(x) = [x] + x\sin 1/x$. Then, in $[-2\pi, 2\pi]$
(a) $f(x)$ is discontinuous but limit exist at every point
(b) $f(x)$ is continuous
(c) $f(x)$ is monotonic
(d) limit does not exist at some points of the interval $[-2\pi, 2\pi]$

**173.** Let $f(x) = \begin{cases} e^{-1/x^2} \sin 1/x, & x \neq 0 \\ 0, & x = 0 \end{cases}$

then
(a) $\lim_{x\to 0} f(x)$ does not exist
(b) $\lim_{x\to 0} f(x)$ exist but $f(x)$ is discontinuous there
(c) $f(x)$ is continuous at $x = 0$ but not differentiable
(d) $f(x)$ is differentiable

**174.** If $f(x)$ is differentiable function, $\forall x \in R$ s.t. $f(1) = 5$ and $f(x) < 5, \forall x \neq 1$. Then,
(a) $f(x)$ is monotonically increasing
(b) $f(x)$ is monotonically decreasing
(c) $f(x)$ is bounded
(d) $f(x)$ is not monotonic

**175.** $\lim_{n\to\infty} \sin(\pi\sqrt{n^2 + 1})$ is
(a) 1 (b) −1
(c) 0 (d) doesn't exist

**176.** The function $f$ defined as

$$f(x) = \begin{cases} x^p \cos\left(\frac{1}{x}\right), & x \neq 0 \\ 0, & x = 0 \end{cases}$$

many have a differential coefficient at $x = 0$
(a) for all $p$
(b) for $p > 1$
(c) for $p < 1$
(d) for $p < 0$

**177.** Let $f:[0,1] \to R$ be a discontinuous monotonic function. Then, the range set of $f$ is
(a) a bounded set that is not an interval
(b) a bounded interval
(c) an unbounded connected set
(d) a set that is neither bounded nor connected

**178.** The local minimum and maximum of the function $f:[-2,2] \to R$ defined by $f(x) = e^x(1 + x^2)$ are respectively,
(a) 0, −1 (b) −1, 2
(c) −1, −2 (d) −2, 2

**179.** Assume $f'$ exists and is monotonic on an open interval $(a, b)$, then on $(a, b)$
(a) $f$ is bounded
(b) $f(x)$ can have only first kind discontinuity
(c) $f(x)$ is continuous
(d) $f(x)$ is continuous only when length of interval is finite

**180.** If $f$ is defined by

$$f(x) = |x| + |x^2 - 1|, \forall x \in R, \text{ then}$$

(a) $f$ is discontinuous on $R$
(b) $f$ has local minima at $x = \pm 1/2$
(c) $f$ has local maxima at $x = \pm 1/2$
(d) $f$ has no local extrema

**181.** Let $f: D \to R$; $D \subseteq R$ is a function for which the set $\left\{\frac{f(x) - f(y)}{x - y}; \forall x, y \in D \text{ and } x \neq y\right\}$ is bounded, then
(a) $f$ is continuous but not uniformly on $D$
(b) $f$ is differentiable over $D$
(c) $f$ is uniformly continuous
(d) $f$ is constant

**182.** Let $f: R \to R$ be a discontinuous function and $D = \{x_0 \in R : f(x) \text{ has discontinuity of 1st kind at } x_0\}$, then
(a) $D$ is finite
(b) $R$-$D$ is finite
(c) $R$-$D$ is countable
(d) $D$ does not contain interval

**183.** $f(x) = x(x-1)(x-2)$ and $g(x) = x(x-2)(x-3)$ in $[0, 1/2]$, then the value of $c$ defined in the Cauchy's mean value theorem is
(a) $\frac{(5 + \sqrt{13})}{6}$ (b) $\frac{(5 - \sqrt{13})}{6}$
(c) $\frac{1}{4}$ (d) None of these

**184.** Let $f$ and $g$ be two non-negative continuous function on $[0, 1]$ and satisfying the condition

$$\sup_{0\le x\le 1} f(x) = \sup_{0\le x\le 1} g(x)$$

(a) either $f(0) = g(0)$ or $f(1) = g(1)$
(b) $f(x) \neq g(x), \forall x \in [0, 1]$
(c) $f(x) = g(x)$ for some $x$ in $[0, 1]$
(d) $f(x) = g(x), \forall x \in [0, 1]$

**185.** If $f(x) = e^{-x}$ and $g(x) = e^x$, then in the Cauchy's mean value theorem the value of $c$ is
(a) geometric mean of $a$ and $b$
(b) $\frac{a + b}{ab}$
(c) $\frac{a + b}{2}$
(d) $\frac{ab}{a + b}$

**186.** Let $f : R \to R$ be a continuous function. If $f(Q) \subseteq N$, then
(a) $f(R) = N$
(b) $f(R) \subseteq N$ but $f$ need not be constant
(c) $f$ is unbounded
(d) $f$ is a constant function

**187.** If $\phi(x)$ and $\psi(x)$ are continuous functions defined on $R$ and $\phi(1) \neq \psi(1)$ and $\phi(-1) \neq \psi(-1)$, then the function
$$f(x) = \lim_{n\to\infty} \frac{x^n \phi(x) + \psi(x)}{x^n + 1}$$
(a) is continuous on $R$
(b) is discontinuous at exactly two points
(c) has only one point of discontinuity
(d) is nowhere continuous

**188.** $\lim_{x\to 0} \frac{(1+x)^{1/x} - e}{x}$ is
(a) e (b) $-$ e
(c) $-2$e (d) $-$e/2

**189.** Select the correct statement
(a) If $f$ and $g$ are uniformly continuous on $I$, then their product is uniformly continuous
(b) If $f$ and $g$ are uniformly continuous on $I$, then $f/g$ is uniformly continuous provided $g(x) \neq 0, \forall\ x \in I$
(c) If $f$ is differentiable in $(a, b)$ and $f'(x)$ is bounded on $(a, b)$, then $f(x)$ is uniformly continuous
(d) None of the above

**190.** The function $f(x) = \frac{|x|}{1+|x|}$ is
(a) increasing in $(0, \infty)$ and decreasing in $(-\infty, 0)$
(b) decreasing in $(0, \infty)$ and increasing in $(-\infty, 0)$
(c) increasing in $R$
(d) decreasing in $R$

**191.** Which of following inequality is true for $x > 0$?
(a) $\log(1+x) < \frac{x}{1+x} < x$ (b) $\frac{x}{1+x} < x < \log(1+x)$
(c) $x < \log(1+x) < \frac{x}{1+x}$ (d) $\frac{x}{1+x} < \log(1+x) < x$

**192.** $\lim_{x\to 2} \frac{1}{(x-2)^2}$ is
(a) $+\infty$ (b) $-\infty$
(c) exists finitely (d) does not exist

**193.** If $x + |y| = 2y$, which of the following statements is/are true about $y$ as a function of $x$?
I. it is defined for all real $x$
II. it is continuous at $x = 0$
III. it is differentiable for all $x$
IV. $\frac{dy}{dx} = \frac{1}{3}$ for $x < 0$
(a) Only I (b) Only I and II
(c) Only I, II and IV (d) All are true

**194.** The equation $x^6 - x - 1 = 0$ has
(a) no positive real roots
(b) exactly one positive real root
(c) exactly two positive real roots
(d) all positive real roots

**195.** If $f(x) = \lim_{n\to\infty} \frac{1}{1 + n\sin^2 \pi x}$, then $f(x)$ is
(a) discontinuous at all rational
(b) discontinuous at all integers
(c) discontinuous at all irrationals
(d) discontinuous at all reals

**196.** If $f$ is twice difference and $|f| < \alpha$, $|f''| < \beta$ in the range $x > a$, then which may be an upper bound by $|f'|$?
(a) $\sqrt{\alpha\beta}$ (b) $2\sqrt{\alpha\beta}$
(c) $\frac{1}{2}\sqrt{\alpha\beta}$ (d) $4\sqrt{\alpha\beta}$

**197.** If $f$ is non-negative and has a finite third derivative in the open interval $(0, 1)$, then $f'''(c) = 0$ for some $c \in (a, b)$, if
(a) $f(x) = 0$ for atleast two values of $x$ in $(0, 1)$
(b) $f(x) = 0$ for atleast one values of $x$ in $(0, 1)$
(c) $f'(x) = 0$ for atleast two values of $x$ in $(0, 1)$
(d) None of the above

**198.** Let $f'(\sin x) < 0$ and $f''(\sin x) > 0$, $\forall\, x \in (0, \pi/2)$, then $g(x) = f(\sin x) + f(\cos x)$ is decreasing in Note $g'(\pi/4) = 0$ and $g''(x) > 0$
(a) $\left(\frac{\pi}{4}, \frac{\pi}{2}\right)$ (b) $\left(0, \frac{\pi}{4}\right)$
(c) $\left(0, \frac{\pi}{2}\right)$ (d) $\left(\frac{\pi}{6}, \frac{\pi}{2}\right)$

**199.** Let $f$ be a continuous real-valued function on $[0, 1]$ such that $f(0) = -1$ and $f(1) = 1/2$, then there always exists a $t \in (0, 1)$ such that
(a) $f'(t) = -2$ (b) $f'(t) = 1$
(c) $f'(t) = 3/2$ (d) $f'(t) = -1/2$

**200.** Let $f : [0, \infty) \to [0, \infty)$ and $g : [0, \infty) \to [0, \infty)$ be non-increasing and non-decreasing functions, respectively.
Define $h(x) = gof(x)$
If $f$ and $g$ are differentiable for all points in their respectively, domains and $h(0) = 0$, then $h(x)$
(a) an strictly increasing function
(b) strictly decreasing function
(c) may not be monotonic
(d) identically zero

**201.** If $f(x) = \lim_{n\to\infty} \left[\lim_{t\to 0} \frac{\sin^2(n!\pi x)}{\sin^2(n!\pi x) + t^2}\right]$
Then,
(a) $f(x)$ is nowhere continuous
(b) $f(x)$ has only 2 point of discontinuity
(c) $f(x)$ has only 2 point of continuity
(d) $f(x)$ is continuous everywhere

**202.** $f(x) = x|x|$, then choose the correct statement
(a) $f(x)$ is strictly decreasing function
(b) $f(x)$ is not monotonic
(c) $f(x)$ is differentiable, $\forall x \in R$ except at $x = 0$
(d) $f(x)$ is differentiable, $\forall x \in R$

**203.** The value of $\theta$ in the first mean value theorem $f(x+h) = f(x) + hf'(x+\theta h)$ for the function $f(x) = ax^2 + bx + c$ is
(a) $\frac{1}{3}$ (b) $\frac{1}{2}$
(c) $\frac{3}{4}$ (d) $\sqrt{b^2 - 4ac}$

**204.** If $x = \pi^3$ and $y = 3^\pi$, then
(a) $x < y$ (b) $y < x$
(c) can't be related (d) None of these

**205.** If $f$ has a finite second order derivative in $[a, b]$ and the line segment joining the points $A(a, f(a))$ and $B(b, f(b))$ intersects the graph of $f$ in a third point $P$ different from $A$ and $B$, then
(a) $f'(x)$ is monotonic in $[a, b]$ but not strictly
(b) $f'(x)$ is strictly increasing
(c) $f''(x)$ has no root in $(a, b)$
(d) $f''(x)$ has atleast one root in $(a, b)$

**206.** $f(x) = \left\{\sin\frac{1}{x} : x \in (0, 1) \cup \{2\}\right\}$, then
(a) $f(x)$ is continuous
(b) $f(x)$ has only one point of discontinuity
(c) $f(x)$ has two points of discontinuity
(d) $f(x)$ has three points of discontinuity

**207.** Let $F(x)$ is twice differentiable function defined in $[0, 1]$ and satisfies the equation $F''(x) = e^x F(x)$, then
(a) $F$ has positive local maxima in $(0, 1)$ but not negative local minima in $(0, 1)$
(b) $F$ has negative local minima in $(0, 1)$ but not positive local maxima
(c) $F$ has positive local maxima as well as negative local minima in the interval $(0, 1)$
(d) $F$ has neither positive local maxima nor negative local minima in $(0, 1)$

**208.** In the Q. 207, if $F(0) = F(1) = 0$, then
(a) $F$ is strictly increasing in $[0, 1]$
(b) $F$ is strictly decreasing in $[0, 1]$
(c) $F$ is identically zero in $[0, 1]$
(d) $F$ is not monotonic

**209.** Which of the following is not correct?
(a) The set of points of ordinary (first kind) discontinuities of a function is countable
(b) The set of points of discontinuity of the function defined by
$f(x) = \lim_{n\to\infty} \lim_{m\to\infty} [\cos^{2n}(m!\pi x)]$ is uncountable
(c) There cannot be a function defined on $R$, which is continuous on $R$ but nowhere differentiable
(d) None of the above

**210.** In which interval the polynomial $2x^3 - 15x^2 + 36x + 1$ is decreasing
(a) $(-\infty, 2)$ (b) $(3, \infty)$
(c) $(2, 3)$ (d) None of these

**211.** If $f(x) = \begin{cases} x, & x \text{ is rational} \\ 1 - x, & x \text{ is irrational} \end{cases}$
then which of the following is incorrect?
(a) $fof(x)$ is monotonic
(b) $f(x) + f(1-x)$ is constant
(c) $f(x)$ assumes every value between 0 and 1
(d) None of the above

**212.** If $f(x)$ is real-valued function defined on $[0, \infty]$ such that $f(0) = 0$ and $f''(x) > 0$ for all $x$, then the function $h(x) = \frac{f(x)}{x}$ is
(a) increasing in $[0, \infty]$
(b) decreasing in $[0, 1]$
(c) increasing in $[0, 1]$ and decreasing in $[1, \infty]$
(d) decreasing in $[0, 1]$ and increasing in $[1, \infty]$

**213.** Let $X = (0, 1) \cup (2, 3)$ be an open set in $R$. Let $f$ be a continuous function on $X$ such that the derivative $f'(x) = 0$ for all $x$. Then, the range of $f$ has
(a) uncountable number of points
(b) countably infinite number of points
(c) atmost 2 points
(d) atmost 1 point

**214.** If $f(x) - f(a) = p(x) - q(x)$ and $v(f; a, x) = p(x) + q(x)$ where $v(f; a, x)$ is variation function and $f$ is function of bounded variation, then
(a) $p(x)$ is non-decreasing and $q(x)$ is non-increasing on $[a, b]$
(b) $p(x)$ is non-increasing and $q(x)$ is non-decreasing on $[a, b]$
(c) $p(x)$ and $q(x)$ both are non-decreasing on $[a, b]$
(d) $p(x)$ and $q(x)$ both are non-increasing on $[a, b]$

**215.** $D^- f(x)$ is equal to
(a) $\overline{\lim_{h\to0^+}} \frac{f(x+h) - f(x)}{h}$ (b) $\overline{\lim_{h\to0^+}} \frac{f(x) - f(x-h)}{h}$
(c) $\lim_{h\to0^+} \frac{f(x+h) - f(x)}{h}$ (d) $\lim_{h\to0^+} \frac{f(x+h) - f(x-h)}{h}$

**216.** Select the correct statement about
$$f(x) = \begin{cases} x\sin\left(\frac{1}{x}\right), & x \neq 0 \\ 0, & x = 0 \end{cases}$$
(a) $f(x) \in R[a, b]$ but not continuous
(b) $f(x)$ is of bounded variation but $f(x) \notin R[a, b]$
(c) $f(x)$ is not of bounded variation but $f(x) \in R[a, b]$
(d) $f(x) \in R[a, b]$ as $f(x)$ is of bounded variation

**217.** $D^+ f(x)$ is equal to
(a) $\overline{\lim_{h\to0^+}} \frac{f(x+h) - f(x)}{h}$ (b) $\overline{\lim_{h\to0^+}} \frac{f(x) - f(x-h)}{h}$
(c) $\lim_{h\to0^+} \frac{f(x+h) - f(x)}{h}$ (d) $\lim_{h\to0^+} \frac{f(x+h) - f(x-h)}{h}$

**218.** $D_+f(x)$ is equal to

(a) $\lim\limits_{h\to 0^+}\dfrac{f(x+h)-f(x)}{h}$ (b) $\lim\limits_{h\to 0^+}\dfrac{f(x)-f(x-h)}{-h}$

(c) $\lim\limits_{h\to 0^+}\dfrac{f(x+h)-f(x)}{h}$ (d) None of these

**219.** The continuous function $f: R\to R$ defined by $f(x)=(x^2+1)^{2008}$ is

(a) onto but not one-one
(b) one-one but not onto
(c) both one-one and onto
(d) neither one-one nor onto

**220.** Every subspace of a separable metric space is

(a) separable (b) non-separable
(c) incomplete (d) None of these

**221.** Let $Q$ be the set of rational numbers. Then,

(a) there is no one-one function from [0, 1] to $Q$
(b) there is no onto function from [0, 1] to $Q$
(c) there is no one-one function from $Q$ to [0, 1]
(d) there is bijection between $Q$ and [0, 1]

**222.** If a function $f$ is increasing function, then

(a) $-f$ is increasing function
(b) $-f$ is decreasing function
(c) $-f$ is constant function
(d) None of the above

**223.** If $f$ is absolutely continuous on $[a, b]$ and $f'(x)=0$ almost everywhere

(a) then $f$ is constant
(b) then $f$ is increasing function
(c) then $f$ is decreasing function
(d) None of the above

**224.** If $f$ is increasing function $n$ closed interval, then for $c\in(a, b)$

(a) $f(c^+)$ and $f(c^-)$ exists
(b) $f(c^+)$ and $f(c^-)$ does not exist
(c) $(c^+)\le f(c^-)$
(d) None of the above

**225.** If $f$ is integrable on $[a, b]$, then the function $F(x)=\int_a^x f'(t)\,dt$

(a) A continuous function of bounded variation on $[a, b]$
(b) A discontinuous function of bounded variation on $[a, b]$
(c) A discrete function of bounded variation on $[a, b]$
(d) None of the above

**226.** If $f$ is decreasing function on closed interval, then for $c\in(a, b)$

(a) $f(c^+)$ and $f(c^-)$ does not exist
(b) $f(c^+)$ and $f(c^-)$ both exist
(c) $f(c^+)\le f(c)$
(d) None of the above

**227.** A function $f$ is an indefinite integral

(a) then $f$ is absolutely continuous
(b) then $f$ is increasing function
(c) then $f$ is decreasing function
(d) None of the above

**228.** If $f$ is increasing function on closed interval $[a, b]$, then for $a<c<b$, we have

(a) $f(c^+)\le f(c)\le f(c^+)$ (b) $f(c^+)\le f(c)$
(c) $f(c^-)\ge f(c)$ (d) None of these

**229. Statement (A)** $f$ is continuous.

**Statement (B)** $f$ is differentiable.

(a) If A is true, then B is true
(b) If A is false, then B is false
(c) If B is true, then A is true
(d) If B is true, then A is false

**230.** If $f$ is increasing function on closed interval $[a, b]$, then at end points

(a) $f(a)\le f(a^+)$ and $f(b)\le f(b^+)$
(b) $f(a^+)\ge f(a^+)$ and $f(b)\ge f(b^+)$
(c) $f(a^+)\le f(a)$ and $f(b^+)\le f(b)$
(d) $f(a^+)\ge f(a)$ and $f(b^+)\le f(b)$

**231.** $f: E\to Q$ and $g: E\to R$ and both are continuous at $x_0$, then

(a) $f/g$ is continuous at $x_0$
(b) $f/g$ is discontinuous at $x_0$
(c) $f/g$ is continuous at $x_0$, if $g(x_0)\neq 0$
(d) None of the above

**232.** If $f$ is one-to-one and continuous on $[a, b]$, then

(a) $f$ is strictly monotonic (b) $f$ is monotonic
(c) $f$ is constant (d) None of these

**233.** The function $f(x)$ is continuous on closed interval $[a, b]$, then

(a) $f$ is bounded on $[a, b]$ (b) $f$ is unbounded on $[a, b]$
(c) $f$ is constant on $[a, b]$ (d) None of these

**234.** If $f$ is strictly increasing on $E\subset\mathbb{R}$, then

(a) $f^{-1}$ exist and it is strictly decreasing on $E$
(b) $f^{-1}$ exist and it is strictly increasing on $E$
(c) $f^{-1}$ does not exist
(d) None is true

**235.** A function $f(x)=\dfrac{x^2-1}{x-1}$ is

(a) discontinuous at $x=1$ (b) discontinuous at $x=2$
(c) continuous at $x=1$ (d) continuous at $x=2$

**236.** If $f$ is one-to-one and continuous on $[a, b]$, then

(a) $f$ is strictly increasing on $[a, b]$
(b) $f$ is strictly decreasing on $[a, b]$
(c) $f$ is strictly increasing on $[a]$
(d) None of the above

**237.** A function $f(x)=|x|$ is

(a) continuous and differentiable at $x=0$
(b) continuous but not differentiable at $x=0$
(c) discontinuous and differentiable at $x=0$
(d) None of the above

**238.** If $f'$ is exist and is monotonic on $(a, b)$, then

(a) $f'$ is continuous on $[a, b]$
(b) $f'$ is discontinuous on $[a, b]$
(c) $f'$ is constant
(d) None of the above

**239.** The function $f(x)$ is continuous on closed interval $[a, b]$ and $m = \min f(x)$ and $M = \max f(x)$. If for any $A$, $m \le A \le M$, there is $x_0 \in [a, b]$ for which
(a) $f(x_0) = A$ (b) $f(x_0) = 0$
(c) $f(x_0) \neq A$ (d) None of these

**240.** If $f$ is continuous on $[a, b]$ and $f'$ exist at each $x \in (a, b)$, if $f' > 0$ in $(a, b)$, then
(a) $f$ is strictly increasing (b) $f$ is strictly decreasing
(c) $f$ is constant (d) None of these

**241.** A function $f(x) = |x|$ is
(a) discontinuous
(b) discontinuous at $x = 0$
(c) continuous everywhere
(d) None of the above

**242.** If $f$ is continuous on $[a, b]$ and $f'$ exist at each $x \in (a, b)$, then if $f' = 0$
(a) $f$ is increasing (b) $f$ is decreasing
(c) $f$ is constant (d) None of these

**243.** Let $f : E \to R$ and $x_0 \in E$ and $x_0$ an accumulation point of $E$. If every sequence $\{x_n\}_{n=1}^{\infty}$ converges to $x_0$ with $x_n \in E$ for all $n$, $\{f(x_n)\}_{n=1}^{\infty}$ converges to $f(x_0)$, then
(a) $f$ is continuous at $x_0$
(b) $f$ is discontinuous at $x_0$
(c) $f$ is differentiable at $x_0$
(d) None of the above

**244.** If $f$ is strictly increasing on $E \subset \mathbb{R}$, then
(a) $f^{-1}$ exist
(b) $f^{-1}$ does not exist
(c) $f^{-1}$ is strictly decreasing on $f(E)$
(d) None of the above

**245.** $f : D \to R$, following statement is false
(a) If $f$ is differentiable, then it is continuous too
(b) If $f$ is continuous, then it is differentiable too
(c) Polynomial function is differentiable and continuous both
(d) Every differentiable function is continuous

**246.** If $f$ is differentiable on $[a, b]$ and $f'(x) \neq 0$ for all $x \in (a, b)$. Then, for all $x \in [a, b]$, $f(x)$ is
(a) either increasing or decreasing function
(b) neither increasing nor decreasing
(c) a constant function
(d) None of the above

**247.** Let $f$ be the function defined on $R$ by setting $f(x) = x - [x]$, for all $x \in R$. Here, $f$ will be continuous at the points
(a) 0 (b) $\pm 1$
(c) $\pm 2$ (d) None of these

**248.** Let $f$ and $g$ be defined on an interval $I$. If $f$ and $g$ are continuous at $P \in I$, then
(a) $f + g$ is discontinuous at $P$
(b) $f + g$ is continuous at $P$
(c) $f + g$ may be continuous at $P$
(d) None of the above

**249.** Let $f$ be the function defined on $R$ by setting $f(x) = x - [x] - \frac{1}{2}$, when $x$ is not an integer, $f(x) = 0$, when $x$ is an integer.
At what point will be function be continuous?
(a) At all points of $Z$ (b) At all points of $R \sim Z$
(c) At all points of $R$ (d) whenever $x \in Z$

**250.** Let $f : [a, b] \to R$ is continuous on $[a, b]$ and $f$ is differentiable on $(a, b)$. If $f(a) = f(b) = 0$ there exist $c$ such that $f'(c) = 0$, then
(a) $c \in [a, b]$ (b) $c \in (a, b)$
(c) $c \in [a, b)$ (d) $c \in (a, b]$

**251.** Let $f$ be defined on $R$ by setting $f(x) = \dfrac{x}{1 + e^{\frac{1}{n}}}$, when $x \neq 0$, $f(0) = 0$, the function $f$ is continuous at
(a) $n = 0$ (b) $n = 1$
(c) $n = 2$ (d) $n = 3$

**252.** Suppose $f : [a, b] \to R$ and $f$ have relative maximum at $x_0 \in (a, b)$. If $f$ is differentiable at $x_0$, then
(a) $f'(x_0) \neq 0$ (b) $f'(x_0) = 0$
(c) $f'(x_0) =$ constant (d) None of these

**253.** Let $f : D \to R$. A point $x_0 \in D$ is a relative minimum of $f$, iff there is a neighbourhood $Q$ of $x_0$ such that $x \in Q \cap D$, then
(a) $f(x) \le f(x_0)$ (b) $f(x) \ge f(x_0)$
(c) $f(x) \not\le f(x_0)$ (d) $f(x) \not\ge f(x_0)$

**254.** Let $f$ and $g$ be defined on an interval $I$. If $f$ and $g$ are continuous at $P \in I$, then
(a) $fg$ may be continuous at $P$
(b) $fg$ is discontinuous at $P$
(c) $fg$ is continuous at $P$
(d) None of the above

**255.** A rational function (the quotient of two polynomial functions) is
(a) differentiable everywhere
(b) not differentiable anywhere
(c) differentiable at each point, where denominator is non-zero
(d) None of the above

**256.** Suppose $f$ and $g$ are differentiable function on $(a, b)$ and $f'(x) = g'(x)$, for all $x \in (a, b)$. There exist real number $k$
(a) $f(x) = \dfrac{g(x)}{k}$ (b) $f(x) = kg(x)$
(c) $f(x) = g(x) + k$ (d) None of these

**257.** The following discontinuity is not removal discontinuity
(a) discontinuity of first kind
(b) discontinuity of second kind
(c) jump discontinuity
(d) None of the above

**258.** Given a function $f(x) = |x|$ for all $x \in R$. The function $f$ is
(a) differentiable at zero
(b) continuous at zero
(c) (a) is true (b) is false
(d) Both (a) and (b) are true

**259.** Let $f : D \to R$. A point $x_0 \in D$ is relative maximum of $f(x)$ if there is a neighbourhood $Q$ of $x_0$ such that
(a) $f(x) \le f(x_0)$ for $x \in D \cap Q$
(b) $f(x) \ge f(x_0)$ for $x \in D \cap Q$
(c) $f(x) > f(x_0)$ for $x \in D \cap Q$
(d) None of the above

**260.** If $f$ is continuous, which of the following conclusions is true for $|f|$?
(a) $|f|$ is discontinuous
(b) $|f|$ is continuous
(c) $|f|$ may be continuous
(d) $|f|$ has removable discontinuity

**261.** Let $f : D \to R$ be differentiable at $x_0$
(a) $f$ is continuous at $x_0$
(b) $f$ is discontinuous at $x_0$
(c) $f$ is constant at $x_0$
(d) None of the above

**262.** If $f$ is continuous on $I(= [a, b])$, then there exists a real number $u$ such that
(a) $f(x) = u$ for all $x \in I$
(b) $f(x) \ge u$ for all $x \in I$
(c) $f(x) \le u$ for all $x \in I$
(d) $f(x) = \frac{a^2 + b^2}{u^2}$ for all $x \in I$

**263.** Suppose $f : [a, b] \to R$ is continuous on $[a, b]$ and $f$ is differentiable on $(a, b)$. If $f(a) = f(b) = 0$, there is $c \in (a, b) : f'(c) = 0$
(a) Rolle's theorem
(b) Mean value theorem
(c) Intermediate value theorem
(d) None of the above

**264.** Let $f$ be continuous on $[a, b]$ and let $x_0$ be such that $a < x_0 < b$. Then, $f(x_0) < 0$ implies that
(a) there exist a $\delta_0 > 0$ such that $f(x) < 0$ for all $x$ in $]x_0 - \delta_0, x_0 + \delta_0[$
(b) there exists a $\delta_0 > 0$ such that $f(x) < 0$ for all $x$ in $[a, a + \delta_0[$
(c) there exists a $\delta_0 > 0$ such that $f(x) < 0$ for all $x$ in $]b - \delta_0, b[$
(d) None of the above

**265.** If $f, g : D \to R$ are differentiable at $x_0$, then $(f / g)$ is differentiable at $x_0$, if
(a) $g(x_0) \ne 0$ (b) $g(x_0) = 0$
(c) $g(x_0) = \infty$ (d) None of these

**266.** If a function $f$, continuous on $x_0$, is such that given $\varepsilon > 0$ we can find $\delta > 0$ and $f$ is uniformly continuous, then $\delta$ depends
(a) only on $x_0$ (b) on $x_0$ and $\varepsilon$
(c) only on $\varepsilon$ (d) None of these

**267.** Suppose $f : [a, b] \to R$ and is differentiable on $(a, b)$. Then, if $f'(x) = 0$ for all $x \in (a, b)$, we have
(a) $f$ is constant (b) $f$ is increasing
(c) $f$ is decreasing (d) None of these

**268.** If $f$ is decreasing function on $E \subset \mathbb{R}$, then for $x, y \in E$, we have
(a) $x < y \Rightarrow f(x) \le f(y)$ (b) $x < y \Rightarrow f(x) \ge f(y)$
(c) $x < y \Rightarrow f(x) < f(y)$ (d) None of these

**269.** The derivative of a differentiable odd function is
(a) odd function (b) even function
(c) constant function (d) None of these

**270.** Let $f$ be a continuous function on $[-1, 1]$ such that $(f(x))^2 + x^2 = 1$, for all $x \in [-1, 1]$. What will be $f(x)$ for all $x \in [-1, 1]$?
(a) $f(x) = \sqrt{1 - x^2}$
(b) $f(x) = -\sqrt{1 - x^2}$
(c) $f(x) =$ either $\sqrt{1 - x^2}$ or $-\sqrt{1 - x^2}$
(d) $f(x) = 1 - x^2$

**271.** If $f'(x) \ge 0$ for all $x \in (a, b)$, then
(a) $f$ is increasing function
(b) $f$ is decreasing function
(c) $f$ is a constant function
(d) None of the above

**272.** A uniformly continuous function $f$ is defined as $f(x) = x^3, 0 < x < 1$. Choose the correct expression of $\delta$ that will work corresponding to a given $\varepsilon$ from the codes given below.
(a) $\delta = \frac{\varepsilon}{2}$ (b) $\delta = \frac{\varepsilon}{27}$
(c) $\delta = \frac{\varepsilon}{3}$ (d) $\delta = \varepsilon^3$

**273.** The derivative of a periodic function with period $T$ is
(a) constant function
(b) periodic function with period $T$
(c) non-periodic function
(d) None of the above

**274.** Let $n$ be a fixed positive integer and let $f$ be the function defined on $R$ by $f(x) = x^n$, for all $n \in R$, then
(a) $f'(x)$ exists for all $x \in R$
(b) $f'(x)$ does not exists
(c) $f'(x)$ exists but not for all $x \in R$
(d) $f'(x)$ exists for all $x \notin R$

**275.** $f'(c) < 0 \Rightarrow \exists$ some $\delta > 0$ such that
I. $f(x) < f(c), \forall x \in ]c, c + \delta[$
II. $f(x) < f(c), \forall x \in [c, c + \delta]$
III. $f(x) > f(c), \forall x \in [c - \delta, c]$
IV. $f(x) > f(c), \forall x \in ]c - \delta, c[$

**Codes**
(a) I and II (b) II and III
(c) I and IV (d) III and IV

**276.** The derivative of a differentiable even function is
(a) odd function (b) even function
(c) constant function (d) None of these

**277.** $f'(c) > 0 \Rightarrow \exists$ some $\delta > 0$ such that
I. $f(x) > f(c), \forall x \in ]c, c + \delta[$
II. $f(x) > f(c), \forall x \in [c, c + \delta]$
III. $f(x) < f(c), \forall x \in [c - \delta, c]$
IV. $f(x) < f(c), \forall x \in ]c - \delta, c[$

**Codes**

(a) I and II (b) II and III
(c) I and IV (d) III and IV

**278.** A function $F(x) = f(x)g(x)$ have derivatives at $x_0$, if
(a) $f(x)$ has derivative at $x_0$, but $g(x)$ has not
(b) $g(x)$ has derivative at $x_0$, but $f(x)$ has not
(c) $f(x)$ and $g(x)$, both have derivatives at $x_0$
(d) None of the above

**279.** Which of the following conclusions is/are true for the function defined as

$f(x) = |x-1| + |x+1|, \forall x \in R$?

I. x is derivable at the points $x = -1$ and $x = 1$
II. x is not derivable at the points $x = -1$ and $x = 1$
III. x is derivable at every other point except $-1$ and $1$
IV. x is not derivable at any other point except $-1$ and $1$

Choose the correct answer from the codes given below.

**Codes**

(a) I and II (b) II and III
(c) III and IV (d) I and IV

**280.** The function $f(x)$ is continuous on closed interval $[a, b]$ and $f(a) \cdot f(b) < 0$, if at some point $c, f(c) = 0$, then
(a) $c \notin (a, b)$ (b) $c \in (a, b)$
(c) $c \in [a, b]$ (d) None of these

**281.** If $f$ derivable in $[a, b]$ and $f'(a)f'(b)$, then for each $k$ lying between $f'(a)$ and $f'(b)$, $\exists$ some point $c \in ]a, b[$ such that
(a) $f'(c) = k$ (b) $f'(c) > k$
(c) $f'(c) < k$ (d) None of these

**282.** A function $f$ defined by

$$f(x) = \begin{cases} x^m \sin\frac{1}{x}, & \text{if } x \neq 0 \\ 0, & \text{if } x = 0 \end{cases}$$

is given. What is the value of $m$ when $f$ is continuous at $x = 0$?
(a) $m \geq 3$ (b) $m \leq 2$
(c) $0 \leq m < 2$ (d) $0 \leq m < 1$

**283.** Rolle's theorem does not hold if
I. $f'$ does not exist even at one point of $]a, b[$
II. $f$ is continuous in $]a, b[$ only
III. $f(a) \neq f(b)$
IV. $f(a) = f(b)$

**Codes**

(a) I and II (b) I, II and III
(c) I, II, III and IV (d) I and IV

**284.** If $f$ and $g$ are absolutely continuous functions, then $f/g$ is
(a) $g$ is bounded away from zero
(b) $f$ is bounded away from zero
(c) Both (a) and (b) are true
(d) Both (a) and (b) are false

**285.** Lagrange's mean value theorem says that there exists a point $x = c$ on the curve $y = f(x)$ lying between $A$ and $B$ at which the tangent to the curve is
(a) parallel to x-axis
(b) perpendicular to x-axis
(c) parallel to the chord $AB$
(d) perpendicular to the chord $AB$

**286.** Every absolutely continuous function is
(a) continuous
(b) constant
(c) absolutely discontinuous
(d) None of the above

**287.** If $f, F$ are absolutely continuous, then
(a) $f$ has derivative almost everywhere
(b) $F$ is an indefinite integral
(c) $f$ has no derivative
(d) None of the above

**288.** If $f$ is absolutely continuous on $[a, b]$ and $f'(x) = 0$, then
(a) $f$ is constant almost everywhere
(b) $f$ is non-constant
(c) $f$ is not continuous
(d) None of the above

**289.** If $f$ satisfies the conditions of Lagrange's mean value theorem and, if $f'(x) > 0, \forall x \in ]a, b[$, then what is true for the given function?
(a) $f$ is constant on $[a, b]$ (b) $f$ is increasing in $[a, b]$
(c) $f$ is decreasing in $[a, b]$ (d) None of these

**290.** If $f$ and $g$ are absolutely continuous functions, then following is false.
(a) $f + g$ is absolutely continuous
(b) $f g$ is absolutely continuous
(c) $f - g$ is absolutely continuous
(d) $f / g$ is absolutely continuous

**291.** Which amongst the following is correct by mean value theorem?
(a) $1 + x > e^x > 1 + xe^x, \forall x > 0$
(b) $1 + x = e^x = 1 + xe^x, \forall x > 0$
(c) $1 + x < e^x < 1 + xe^x, \forall x > 0$
(d) None of the above

**292.** Examine the validity of the hypothesis and the conclusions of Rolle's theorem for the function

$f(x) = 1 - (x-1)^{2/3}$ on $[0, 2]$

And choose the correct results from the codes given below

**Results**

I. It satisfies the hypothesis of Rolle's theorem.
II. It does not satisfy all the conditions of Rolle's theorem.
III. Rolle's theorem is not valid for the given function.
IV. Rolle's theorem is valid for the given function.

**Codes**

(a) I and II (b) II and III
(c) III and IV (d) I and IV

**293.** Let $f$ be defined for all real $x$ such that $|f(x) - f(y)| < (x-y)^2$ for all real $x$ and $y$, then
(a) $f$ is constant (b) $f$ is increasing
(c) $f$ is decreasing (d) None of these

**294.** A function $f$ is strictly decreasing on $E \subset \mathbb{R}$, if $x, y \in E$.

(a) $x<y \Rightarrow f(x)<f(y)$ (b) $x<y \Rightarrow f(y)<f(x)$
(c) $x<y \Rightarrow f(y) \le f(x)$ (d) $x<y \Rightarrow f(y) \ge f(x)$

**295.** The function $f(x) = x\sin\left(\frac{1}{x}\right)$, if $x = 0$ and $f(0) = 1$ has discontinuity at

(a) 0 (b) 1
(c) 2 (d) None of these

**296.** A

(Functions)

(α) $f(n) = \begin{cases} \frac{n^2+9}{n-3}, & n \ne 3 \\ 6, & n = 3 \end{cases}$

(β) $f(n) = \begin{cases} n\sin\frac{1}{n}, & n \ne 0 \\ 0, & n = 0 \end{cases}$

(γ) $f(n) = \begin{cases} \frac{|n-a|}{n-a}, & n \ne a \\ 1, & n = a \end{cases}$

(δ) $f(n) = \begin{cases} \frac{ne^{\frac{1}{n}}}{1+e^{\frac{1}{n}}}, & n \ne 0 \\ 0, & n = 0 \end{cases}$

B

(Continuity)

(1) continuous at $n = 3$ (2) continuous at $n = 0$
(3) continuous at $n = 0$ (4) discontinuous at $n = 0$

**Codes**

| | α | β | γ | δ |
|---|---|---|---|---|
| (a) | 1 | 2 | 3 | 4 |
| (b) | 2 | 1 | 4 | 3 |
| (c) | 1 | 2 | 4 | 3 |
| (d) | 4 | 3 | 2 | 1 |

**297.** If $f(0) = 0$ and $f''(x)$ exists on $[0, \infty[$, then $f'(x) - \frac{f(x)}{x}$ is equal to

(a) $\frac{1}{2}xf'(\xi),\ 0<\xi<x$ (b) $f''(\xi),\ 0<\xi<x$
(c) $x^2f''(\xi),\ 0<\xi<x$ (d) $x^3f''(\xi),\ 0<\xi<x$

**298.** If $f$ is an increasing function, then

(a) $-f$ is decreasing function
(b) $-f$ is increasing function
(c) $-f$ is constant
(d) None of the above

**299.** A

(Functions)

(a) $\lim_{n\to c^-} f(x) \ne \lim_{n\to c^+} f(x)$ (b) $\lim_{n\to c^-} f(x)$ does not exist
(c) $\lim_{n\to c} f(x) \ne f(c)$ (d) $\lim_{n\to c^-} f(x) \ne f(c)$

B

(Types of Discontinuity)

(1) Removable discontinuity
(2) Discontinuity of first kind from left
(3) Discontinuity of second kind from left
(4) Discontinuity of first kind

**Codes**

| | α | β | γ | δ |
|---|---|---|---|---|
| (a) | 1 | 2 | 3 | 4 |
| (b) | 4 | 3 | 1 | 2 |
| (c) | 4 | 3 | 2 | 1 |
| (d) | 1 | 2 | 4 | 3 |

**300.** A function is a monotonic function, if

(a) $f$ is only a decreasing function
(b) $f$ is only an increasing function
(c) $f$ is either increasing or decreasing function
(d) None of the above

**301.** The function $f(x) = \begin{cases} e^{1/x}, & x \ne 0 \\ 0, & x = 0 \end{cases}$ has

(a) removable discontinuity at $x = 0$
(b) irremovable discontinuity at $x = 0$
(c) continuity at $x = 0$
(d) None of the above

**302.** For $f(x) = 4 + 2x - x^2$, the error term is

(a) $f(2)$ (b) $(x-2)^2$
(c) $-(x-2)^2$ (d) 4

**303.** Singular monotonic function on $[a, b]$ have

(a) $f(x) = 0,\ \forall x \in [a, b]$ (b) $f'(x) = 0,\ \forall x \in [a, b]$
(c) $f'(x) \ne 0,\ \forall x \in [a, b]$ (d) None of these

**304.** If we take $h(x) = 1$ in the general mean value theorem, we obtain

(a) Lagrange's mean value theorem
(b) Cauchy's mean value theorem
(c) Rolle's theorem
(d) None of the above

**305.** The function $f(x) = \frac{1}{x-a}\sin\frac{1}{x-a}$ has

(a) discontinuity at first kind at $x = 0$
(b) discontinuity of second kind at $x = 0$
(c) continuity at $x = 0$
(d) None or the above

**306.** If $f$ is an increasing function on closed interval $[a, b]$, then $c \in [a, b]$, we have

(a) $f(c^-) \ge f(c) \ge f(c^+)$ (b) $f(c^-) \le f(c) \le f(c^+)$
(c) $f(c^-) = f(c) = f(c^+)$ (d) None of these

**307.** If $f$ is an increasing function on $[a, b]$, then

(a) $f(a) \le f(a^+)$ and $f(b) \le f(b^+)$
(b) $f(a) \le f(a^+)$ and $f(b^-) \le f(b)$
(c) $f(a) \le f(a^-)$ and $f(b^+) \le f(b)$
(d) None of the above

**308.** A function $f$ is monotonic function, if

(a) $f$ is increasing or decreasing function
(b) $f$ is constant function
(c) $f$ is zero function
(d) None of the above

**309.** Choose the correct statement
(a) $f(x) = f(a) - Df(a)(x - a)$
(b) $f(x) \cong f(a) + Df(a)(x - a)$
(c) $f(x) \cong f(a) - Df(x)(a - x)$
(d) None of the above

**310.** The function $f(x) = \begin{cases} x\sin(1/x), & x \neq 0 \\ 1 & x = 0 \end{cases}$ has
(a) removal discontinuity at $x = 0$
(b) non-removal discontinuity at $x = 0$
(c) mixed discontinuity at $x = 0$
(d) continuity at $x = 0$

**311.** A saltus at point of discontinuity is equal to
(a) positive number (b) negative number
(c) zero (d) None of these

**312.** Let $f$ and $g$ be two functions defined on $[a, b]$ such that
I. $f$ and $g$ are continuous in $[a, b]$
II. $f$ and $g$ are derivable in $]a, b[$
III. $g'(x) \neq 0$ for each $x \in ]a, b[$.
Then, there exists atleast one point $c \in ]a, b[$ such that $\dfrac{f(b) - f(a)}{g(b) - g(a)} = \dfrac{f'(c)}{g'(c)}$. This theorem is known as
(a) Rolle's theorem
(b) Cauchy's mean value theorem
(c) Lagrange's mean value theorem
(d) None of the above

**313.** If $f$ is increasing function on $E \subset \mathbb{R}$, then for $x, y \in E$, we have
(a) $x < y \Rightarrow f(x) \leq f(y)$ (b) $x < y \Rightarrow f(x) \geq f(y)$
(c) $x < y \Rightarrow f(x) > f(y)$ (d) None of these

**314.** Error term is represented by
(a) $\in(x, a) = f(x) - f(a) - f'(a)(x - a)$
(b) $\in(x, a) = f(x) - f(a)$
(c) $\in(x, a) = f(a) - f(x) - f'(a)(a - x)$
(d) $\in(x, a) = f(a) + f(x) - f'(a)(a - x)$

**315.** The function $f(x) = \begin{cases} \sin 1/x, & x \neq 0 \\ 1, & x = 0 \end{cases}$ has
(a) removal discontinuity at $x = 0$
(b) non-removal discontinuity at $x = 0$
(c) mixed discontinuity at $x = 0$
(d) continuity at $x = 0$

**316.** Choose Maclaurin's series expansion of $\cos x$ from the following alternatives.
(a) $1 + x + \dfrac{x^2}{2!} + \dfrac{x^3}{3!} + \ldots, \forall\ x \in R$
(b) $x - \dfrac{x^3}{3!} + \dfrac{x^5}{5!} \ldots, \forall\ x \in R$
(c) $1 - \dfrac{x^2}{2!} + \dfrac{x^4}{4!} \ldots, \forall\ x \in R$
(d) $x - \dfrac{x^2}{2} + \dfrac{x^3}{3} + \ldots, \forall\ x \in R$

**317.** Assume Rolle's theorem for the function $f(x) = \cos x$ in $\left[\dfrac{-\pi}{2}, \dfrac{\pi}{2}\right]$. If there exists a real number $c \in \left]\dfrac{-\pi}{2}, \dfrac{\pi}{2}\right[$, what is the value of $c$?
(a) $\dfrac{\pi}{4}$ (b) $\dfrac{3\pi}{4}$
(c) $\pi$ (d) 0

**318.** The function $f(x) = \begin{cases} \cos x, & x \geq 0 \\ -\cos x, & x < 0 \end{cases}$ has
(a) continuity at $x = 0$
(b) removal discontinuity at $x = 0$
(c) irremovable discontinuity at $x = 0$
(d) None of the above

**319.** A function $f(x)$ has the continuity at $x = a$, if
(a) $f(a^+) = f(a^-) = f(a)$ (b) $f(a^+) = f(a^-) \neq f(a)$
(c) $f(a^+) \neq f(a^-)$ (d) $f(a^+) \neq f(a)$

**320.** If a function $f$ defined in $[a, b]$ is such that
I. $f$ is derivable in $[a, b]$
II. $f'(a)$ and $f'(b)$ are of opposite signs, then there exists some points $c \in ]a, b[$ such that
(a) $a < f'(c) > b$ (b) $a = f'(c) = b$
(c) $a \geq f'(c) \geq b$ (d) $f'(c) = 0$

**321.** A saltus at point of continuity is equal to
(a) positive number (b) negative number
(c) zero (d) None of these

**322.** If a continuous curve is drawn in $[a, b]$ such that the coordinates at $a$ and $b$ are equal, then there exists atleast one point $c$ lying between $a$ and $b$ such that the tangent at $c$ is
(a) parallel to the x-axis
(b) perpendicular to the x-axis
(c) passing through origin and neither parallel nor perpendicular to x-axis
(d) None of the above

**323.** The function $f(x) = \begin{cases} \dfrac{\sin x}{x}, & x \neq 0 \\ 0, & x = 0 \end{cases}$ has
(a) discontinuity of first kind at $x = 0$
(b) discontinuity of second kind at $x = 0$
(c) continuity at $x = 0$
(d) None of the above

**324.** A real-valued function $f(x)$ has discontinuity of first kind at $x = a$, if
(a) $f(a^+)$ and $f(a^-)$ does not exist
(b) $f(a^+) = f(a^-)$
(c) $f(a^+) \neq f(a^-)$
(d) $f(a^+) = f(a^-) \neq f(a)$

**325.** If $f''$ be continuous on $[a, b]$ and derivable on $]a, b[$, then for some real number $d$ between $a$ and $b$ the expression
$$f(b) - f(a) - \frac{1}{2}(b - a)\{f'(a) + f'(b)\}$$
is equivalent to

(a) $\frac{(b-a)^2}{6} f'''(d)$
(b) $\frac{b^2-a^2}{2} f'''(d)$
(c) $\frac{(b-a)^3}{6} f'''(d)$
(d) $\frac{-(b-a)^3}{12} f'''(d)$

**326.** A function $f$ is increasing function on $E \subset \mathbb{R}$, if $x, y \in E$.
(a) $x < y \Rightarrow f(x) \le f(y)$ (b) $x < y \Rightarrow f(y) \le f(x)$
(c) $x < y \Rightarrow f(x) = f(y)$ (d) None of these

**327.** If $f$ satisfies the conditions of Lagrange's mean value theorem and if $f'(x) = 0, \forall\ x \in ]a, b[$, then which of the following statements is correct?
(a) $f$ is constant on $[a, b]$
(b) $f$ is strictly increasing in $[a, b]$
(c) $f$ is strictly decreasing in $[a, b]$
(d) None of the above

**328.** If the function $f(x) = \sqrt{x^2 - 4}$ in $[2,4]$ satisfies the Lagrange's mean value theorem, then there exists some $c \in ]2, 4[$. What is the value of $c$?
(a) 12 (b) 6
(c) $\sqrt{2}$ (d) $\sqrt{6}$

**329.** If $a_0, a_1, \ldots, a_n$ are real numbers such that $\frac{a_0}{n+1} + \frac{a_1}{n} + \ldots + \frac{a_{n-1}}{2} + a_n = 0$, then there exists atleast one real number $x$ between 0 and 1 such that
(a) $a_0x^n - a_1x^{n-1} + \ldots + a_n = 0$
(b) $-a_0x^n + a_1x^{n-1} + \ldots + a_n = 0$
(c) $a_0x^n + a_1x^{n-1} + \ldots + a_n = 0$
(d) $+\frac{a_0x^n}{n} + \frac{a_1x^{n-1}}{n-1} + \ldots + a_n = 0$

**330.** If we take $g(x) = x$ and $h(x) = 1$ in general mean value theorem, we obtain
(a) Lagrange's mean value theorem
(b) Cauchy's mean value theorem
(c) Rolle's theorem
(d) None of the above

**331.** A function $f(x)$ have no jump discontinuity at $x = a$, if
(a) $f(a^+) = f(a^-) = f(a)$ (b) $f(a^+) \ne f(a^-)$
(c) $f(a^+) \ne f(a)$ (d) $f(a^+) = f(a^-) \ne f(a)$

**332.** A real-valued function $f$ has discontinuity of second kind at $x = a$, if
(a) neither $f(a^+)$ nor $f(a^-)$ exist
(b) $f(a^+)$ exist only
(c) $f(a^-)$ exist only
(d) $f(a^+)$ and $f(a^-)$ both exist

**333.** If $f$ is uniformly continuous mapping of metric space $X$ into metric space $Y$, then
(a) $\langle x_n \rangle$ is Cauchy sequence in $X \Rightarrow \langle f(x_n) \rangle$ is Cauchy sequence in $Y$
(b) $\langle x_n \rangle$ is a sequence in $X \Rightarrow \langle f(x_n) \rangle$ is Cauchy sequence in $Y$
(c) $\langle x_n \rangle$ is Cauchy sequence in $X \ne \langle f(x_n) \rangle$ is Cauchy sequence in $Y$
(d) None of the above

**334. Assertion (A)** Rolle's theorem does not hold.
If $f$ is continuous in $]a, b[$ only.
**Reason (R)** $f'(x) \ne a, \forall\ x \in ]a, b]$.
(a) Both A and R are correct and R is correct reason of A
(b) Both A and R are correct and R is not correct reason of A
(c) A is true but R is false
(d) A is false but R is true

**335. Assertion (A)** If $f$ is continuous on $[a, b]$, then there exists a real number $u$ such that $f(x) \le u, \forall\ x \in [a, b]$
**Reason (R)** If $f$ is continuous in $[a, b]$, then it attains its bounds in $[a, b]$.
(a) Both A and R are correct and R is correct reason of A
(b) Both A and R are correct and R is not correct reason of A
(c) A is true but R is false
(d) A is false but R is true

**336.** The derivative of the function $f(x) = x^{2m-1}$ is
(a) even function (b) odd function
(c) constant function (d) None of these

**337.** The derivative of the function $f(x) = x^{2m}$ is
(a) even function (b) odd function
(c) constant function (d) None of these

**338.** The function $f(x) = \begin{cases} \cos x, & x \ge 0 \\ -\cos x, & x < 0 \end{cases}$ has
(a) continuity at $x = 0$
(b) removable discontinuity at $x = 0$
(c) irremovable discontinuity at $x = 0$
(d) None of the above

**339.** A function $f(x)$ has left hand jump discontinuity at $x = a$, if $f(a^+)$ and $f(a^-)$ exist and
(a) $f(a^+) - f(a^-) = 0$ (b) $f(a^+) + f(a^-) \ne 0$
(c) $f(a^+) - f(a) = 0$ (d) $f(a) - f(a^-) = 0$

**340.** The derivative of the function $f(x) = \sin nx$ is
(a) odd function
(b) constant function
(c) even function
(d) None of the above

**341.** The function $y = |\log x|$ is
(a) discontinuous at $x = 1$
(b) differentiable at $x = 1$
(c) not differentiable at $x = 1$
(d) None of the above

**342.** The function $\sin x^n$ is
(a) differentiable
(b) non-differentiable
(c) discontinuous
(d) None of the above

# Exercise 2 (For Part 'C')

**Directions** (Q. Nos. 1-35) *Questions may have one or more than one correct option.*

**1.** Given function $f(x)=|x|$, then

(a) differentiable at $x=0$
(b) not differentiable at $x=0$
(c) $f'(0^+)=f'(0^-)$
(d) $f'(0^+)\neq f'(0^-)$

**2.** If $L$ is a lattice of continuous real-valued functions on a compact space $X$, and suppose that the function $h$ defined by

$$h(x)=\operatorname*{Inf}_{f\in L} f(x)$$

is continuous, then

(a) Given $\varepsilon>0$, there is a $g\in L$ such that $0\leq g(x)-h(x)<\varepsilon$ for all $x\in X$
(b) Given $\varepsilon>0$, there is no such $g\in L: 0\leq g(x)-h(x)<\varepsilon$ for all $x\in X$
(c) $f(x)$ and $h$ are continuous
(d) $f(x)$ and $h$ are not continuous

**3.** Given the function

$$f(x)=\begin{cases} x\tan^{-1}\left(\frac{1}{x}\right) & x\neq 0 \\ 0 & , x=0\end{cases}, \text{ then}$$

(a) differentiable at $x=0$
(b) not differentiable at $x=0$
(c) $f'(0^+)=\frac{\pi}{2}$
(d) $f'(0^-)=\frac{\pi}{2}$

**4.** Given the function

$$f(x)=\begin{cases} x^2\sin\left(\frac{1}{x}\right), & \text{if } x\neq 0 \\ 0 & , \text{if } x=0\end{cases}$$

(a) differentiable at $x=0$
(b) $f'(0^-)=0$
(c) $f'(0^+)=0$
(d) $f'(0^-)\neq f'(0^+)$

**5.** Given the function

$$f(x)=\begin{cases}\frac{1}{x} & \text{at } x\neq 0 \\ a & \text{at } x=0\end{cases}, \text{ then}$$

(a) $f(x)$ is continuous
(b) $f(x)$ has discontinuity of first kind
(c) $f(x)$ has discontinuity of second kind
(d) $f(0)=f(0^+)=f(0^-)$

**6.** Given the function $f(x)=x^n$, then

(a) differentiable at $x=0$
(b) not differentiable at $x=0$
(c) $f'(0^+)\neq f'(0^-)$
(d) $f'(0^+)=f'(0^-)$

**7.** In Lagrange's mean value theorem, the differential function exists

(a) in an open interval $]a,b[$
(b) in a closed interval $[a,b]$
(c) in a semi-open interval
(d) None of the above

**8.** If $f$ is continuous on $[a,b]$ and $f'(x)\geq 0$ in $]a,b[$, then

(a) $f$ is increasing in $[a,b]$
(b) $f$ is increasing in $]a,b[$
(c) $f$ is decreasing in $[a,b]$
(d) $f$ is decreasing in $]a,b[$

**9.** If $f(x)=x^2$ and $g(x)=x^3$ in the interval $[1,2]$, then by Cauchy's mean value theorem, the value of $c$ is given by

(a) $\frac{14}{4}$
(b) $\frac{14}{9}$
(c) $\frac{3}{7}$
(d) $\frac{2}{3}$

**10.** Find a point on the equation $y=x^3$, where the tangent is parallel to the chord joining $(1,1)$ and $(3,27)$. The value of $c$ is given by

(a) 3
(b) 13
(c) 23
(d) 31

**11.** Does the mean value theorem apply to $f(x)=x^{1/3}$, $-1\leq x\leq 1$?

(a) Yes
(b) No
(c) Can't say anything
(d) None of the above

**12.** The value of $c$ in $f(x)=px^2+qx+r$, $p\neq 0$ in $[1,b]$ by Lagrange's mean value theorem is

(a) 5
(b) 15
(c) 25
(d) None of these

**13.** Given the function

$$f(x)=\begin{cases}2^{1/x}, & x\neq 0 \\ 0 & , x=0\end{cases}, \text{ then}$$

(a) $f(0^+)=\infty$
(b) $f(0^-)=0$
(c) $f(0)=0$
(d) it has mixed discontinuity of second kind

**14.** Given the function $f(x)=x-[x]$, then

(a) $f$ has discontinuity of first kind for integer value of $x$
(b) $f$ has discontinuity of second kind for integer value of $x$
(c) $f$ is continuous for integer value of $x$
(d) $f$ has irremovable discontinuity for integer value of $x$

**15.** Given the function $f(x) = \begin{cases} \dfrac{x}{|x|}, & x \neq 0 \\ a, & x = 0 \end{cases}$, then
(a) $f(x)$ is continuous
(b) $f(x)$ is discontinuous
(c) $f(x)$ has jump at $x = 0$
(d) The measure of discontinuity is 2

**16.** Given the function $f(x) = \begin{cases} 1, & x \neq 0 \\ 0, & x = 0 \end{cases}$, then
(a) $f$ has removal discontinuity of first kind
(b) $f$ has removal discontinuity of second kind
(c) $f(x)$ has a jump at $x = 0$
(d) $f(x)$ is continuous

**17.** Let $X$ be an indiscrete topological space containing more than one element. Then,
(a) every non-empty set is dense
(b) the interior of a proper subset of $X$ is $\phi$
(c) no non-empty set in $X$ is nowhere dense
(d) every non-empty set in $X$ is nowhere dense

**18.** Let $X = \{a, b, c\}$ be an indiscrete topological space. Then,
(a) $cl\{a\} = X$
(b) $cl\{b\} = X$
(c) $cl(\{a\} \cap \{b\}) = \phi$
(d) $cl(\{a\} \cap \{b\}) \neq cl\{a\} \cap cl\{b\}$

**19.** Let $X = \{a, b, c\}$ be an indiscrete topological space. Then,
(a) $\text{Inf}\{a\} = \phi$
(b) $\text{Inf}\{b, c\} = \phi$
(c) $\text{Inf}(\{a\} \cup \{b, c\}) = X$
(d) $(\text{Inf}\{a\}) \cup (\text{Inf}\{b, c\}) \neq \text{Inf}(\{a\} \cup \{b, c\})$

**20.** Let $X$ be a discrete topological space and $A$ is subset of $X$, then
(a) $cl\,A = A$
(b) $cl\,A \neq A$
(c) every proper subset of $X$ is dense
(d) no proper subset of $X$ is dense

**21.** The values of $a$ and $b$ in order that

$$\lim_{x \to 0} \frac{x(1 - a\cos x) + b\sin x}{x^3} = \frac{1}{3}$$

are
(a) $a = \frac{1}{2}$ (b) $b = \frac{1}{2}$
(c) $a = -\frac{1}{2}$ (d) $b = -\frac{1}{2}$

**22.** The function $f(x, y) = 2x^2 + 2xy - y^3$ has
(a) only one stationary point at $(0, 0)$
(b) two stationary points at $(0, 0)$ and $\left(\frac{1}{6}, -\frac{1}{3}\right)$
(c) two stationary points at $(0, 0)$ and $(1, -1)$
(d) no stationary point

**23.** Given a function $f(x, y) = 4x^2 + 6y^2 - 8x - 4y + 8$. The optimal value of $(x, y)$ is
(a) a minimum equal to $10/3$
(b) a maximum equal to $10/3$
(c) a minimum equal to $8/3$
(d) a maximum equal to $8/3$

**24.** The function $f(x, y) = x^2 + y^2 - xy - x - y + 5$ has the
(a) maximum at $(1, 1)$
(b) saddle point at $(1, 1)$
(c) minimum at $(1, 1)$
(d) None of the above at $(1, 1)$

**25.** Let $f$ be a real-valued function defined by
$f(x) = [x]$
= greatest integer less than or equal to x.
Then,
(a) $f$ is monotonic function
(b) Domain of $f = \mathbb{R}$
(c) Domain of continuity of $f = \mathbb{R} - \mathbb{Z}$
(d) None of the above

**26.** Let $f$ be a real-valued function defined by

$$f(x) = \{x\} = x - [x]$$

where $[x]$ is greatest integer less than or equal to $x$, then
(a) $f$ is monotonic function
(b) domain of $f$ is $\mathbb{R}$
(c) domain of Continuity of $f$ is $\mathbb{R} - \mathbb{Z}$
(d) None of the above

**27.** Let $f$ be a real-valued function defined by

$$f(x) = \text{Sig}(x) = \begin{cases} \dfrac{|x|}{x}, & x \neq 0 \\ 0, & x = 0 \end{cases}$$

Then,
(a) domain of $f$ is $\mathbb{R}$
(b) domain of continuity of $f$ is $\mathbb{R} - \{0\}$
(c) $\lim_{x \to 0} f(x)$ exists
(d) $\lim_{x \to 0} f(x)$ does not exists

**28.** Let $f : \mathbb{R} \to \mathbb{R}$ defined by

$$f(x) = \begin{cases} 1, & x \in Q \\ -1, & x \in Q^c \end{cases}$$

Then,
(a) domain of $f$ is $\mathbb{R}$
(b) domain of continuity of $f$ is null set
(c) $\lim_{x \to a} f(x)$ does not exists for all $a \in \mathbb{R}$
(d) $\lim_{x \to a} f(x)$ exists for some $a \in \mathbb{R}$

**29.** Which of the following(s) is/are correct?
(a) $f(x) = \sin x^2$ is not uniformly continuous in $[0, \infty)$
(b) $f(x) = \sin x$ is uniformly continuous in $[0, \infty)$
(c) $f(x) = x^2$ is uniformly continuous in $[-1, 1]$
(d) None of the above

**30.** Which of the following(s) is/are correct?

(a) $\frac{\tan x}{x} > \frac{x}{\sin x}, \forall\ 0 < x < \frac{\pi}{2}$

(b) $\cos x < \left(\frac{\sin x}{x}\right)^2, \forall\ 0 < x < \frac{\pi}{2}$

(c) $\frac{x^2}{2(1+x)} < x - \log(1+x) < \frac{x^2}{2}, x > 0$

(d) None of the above

**31.** For the function

$$f(x) = (x-3)^5 (x+1)^4$$

(a) $x = -1$ is a point of maximum value

(b) $x = 3$ is neither a maximum nor a minimum

(c) $x = \frac{7}{9}$ is a point of minimum value

(d) None of the above

**32.** Let $g$ be a real-valued function defined by

$$g(x) = \text{Sig}\,(f(x)) = \begin{cases} \frac{|f(x)|}{f(x)}, & f(x) \neq 0 \\ 0\ , & f(x) = 0 \end{cases}$$

where $f$ is also a real-valued function, then

(a) domain of $g$ is same as domain of $f$

(b) domain of $g$ is different from domain of $f$ at some point

(c) domain of continuity of $g$ = domain of continuity of $f - \{x \in D_f \,|\, f(x) = 0\}$

(d) None of the above

**33.** For the real-valued function given by

$$f(x) = \sin(\sin x) = \begin{cases} -1, & \sin x < 0 \\ 1, & \sin x > 0 \\ 0, & \sin x = 0 \end{cases}$$

Then,

(a) domain of $f = \mathbb{R}$.

(b) domain of continuity of $f = \mathbb{R} - \{n\pi : n \in \mathbb{Z}\}$

(c) domain of continuity of $f = \mathbb{R} - \{(2n+1)\pi : n \in \mathbb{Z}\}$

(d) None of the above

**34.** Let $f$ be a real-valued function given by

$$f(x) = \begin{cases} p \sin \frac{1}{q}, & x = \frac{p}{q} \text{ in } [0, 1] \\ x\ , & \text{else} \end{cases}$$

Then,

(a) domain of $f$ is $\mathbb{R}$

(b) domain of $f$ is $[0, 1]$

(c) domain of continuity of $f$ is $[0, 1] \cap Q^c \cup \{0\}$

(d) domain of continuity of $f$ is $Q^c \cup \{0\}$

**35.** Let $f : \mathbb{R} \to \mathbb{R}$ be given by

$$f(x) = \begin{cases} \sqrt{\frac{1+p^2}{1+q^2}}, & x = \frac{p}{q} \neq 0 \\ x\ , & \text{else} \end{cases}$$

Then,

(a) $f$ is continuous on $(0, \infty) \cap Q^c \cup \{0, 1\}$

(b) $f$ is discontinuous on $\mathbb{R}$ – Domain of continuity of $f$

(c) If $a \in (-\infty, 0)$, then $\lim_{x \to a} f(x)$ does not exists

(d) If $a \in [0, \infty)$, then $\lim_{x \to a} f(x) = a$

# Answers

## Exercise 1

| | | | | | | | | | |
|---|---|---|---|---|---|---|---|---|---|
| **1.** (b) | **2.** (b) | **3.** (c) | **4.** (c) | **5.** (a) | **6.** (c) | **7.** (a) | **8.** (a) | **9.** (a) | **10.** (b) |
| **11.** (b) | **12.** (d) | **13.** (c) | **14.** (b) | **15.** (c) | **16.** (c) | **17.** (c) | **18.** (c) | **19.** (c) | **20.** (c) |
| **21.** (b) | **22.** (d) | **23.** (d) | **24.** (a) | **25.** (b) | **26.** (c) | **27.** (c) | **28.** (b) | **29.** (c) | **30.** (b) |
| **31.** (b) | **32.** (d) | **33.** (b) | **34.** (a) | **35.** (b) | **36.** (c) | **37.** (b) | **38.** (b) | **39.** (c) | **40.** (c) |
| **41.** (d) | **42.** (d) | **43.** (b) | **44.** (d) | **45.** (a) | **46.** (c) | **47.** (d) | **48.** (d) | **49.** (a) | **50.** (b) |
| **51.** (b) | **52.** (c) | **53.** (a) | **54.** (a) | **55.** (a) | **56.** (d) | **57.** (c) | **58.** (a) | **59.** (a) | **60.** (a) |
| **61.** (b) | **62.** (d) | **63.** (c) | **64.** (c) | **65.** (d) | **66.** (b) | **67.** (a) | **68.** (a) | **69.** (b) | **70.** (c) |
| **71.** (c) | **72.** (a) | **73.** (d) | **74.** (b) | **75.** (a) | **76.** (b) | **77.** (c) | **78.** (c) | **79.** (c) | **80.** (c) |
| **81.** (a) | **82.** (b) | **83.** (a) | **84.** (b) | **85.** (d) | **86.** (c) | **87.** (d) | **88.** (b) | **89.** (d) | **90.** (b) |
| **91.** (b) | **92.** (a) | **93.** (b) | **94.** (c) | **95.** (c) | **96.** (b) | **97.** (a) | **98.** (a) | **99.** (b) | **100.** (a) |
| **101.** (c) | **102.** (a) | **103.** (a) | **104.** (d) | **105.** (a) | **106.** (a) | **107.** (b) | **108.** (b) | **109.** (a) | **110.** (b) |
| **111.** (b) | **112.** (d) | **113.** (c) | **114.** (d) | **115.** (d) | **116.** (b) | **117.** (c) | **118.** (a) | **119.** (b) | **120.** (c) |
| **121.** (a) | **122.** (d) | **123.** (d) | **124.** (a) | **125.** (c) | **126.** (c) | **127.** (c) | **128.** (a) | **129.** (b) | **130.** (c) |
| **131.** (c) | **132.** (d) | **133.** (b) | **134.** (b) | **135.** (b) | **136.** (d) | **137.** (a) | **138.** (a) | **139.** (b) | **140.** (c) |
| **141.** (d) | **142.** (c) | **143.** (b) | **144.** (d) | **145.** (c) | **146.** (c) | **147.** (c) | **148.** (b) | **149.** (d) | **150.** (d) |
| **151.** (d) | **152.** (d) | **153.** (d) | **154.** (d) | **155.** (b) | **156.** (a) | **157.** (a) | **158.** (b) | **159.** (c) | **160.** (b) |

| | | | | | | | | | |
|---|---|---|---|---|---|---|---|---|---|
| **161.** (d) | **162.** (b) | **163.** (c) | **164.** (b) | **165.** (b) | **166.** (d) | **167.** (d) | **168.** (c) | **169.** (c) | **170.** (a) |
| **171.** (c) | **172.** (d) | **173.** (c) | **174.** (d) | **175.** (c) | **176.** (b) | **177.** (a) | **178.** (d) | **179.** (c) | **180.** (c) |
| **181.** (c) | **182.** (d) | **183.** (b) | **184.** (c) | **185.** (c) | **186.** (d) | **187.** (b) | **188.** (d) | **189.** (c) | **190.** (a) |
| **191.** (d) | **192.** (a) | **193.** (c) | **194.** (b) | **195.** (b) | **196.** (b) | **197.** (a) | **198.** (b) | **199.** (c) | **200.** (b) |
| **201.** (a) | **202.** (d) | **203.** (b) | **204.** (a) | **205.** (d) | **206.** (a) | **207.** (d) | **208.** (c) | **209.** (c) | **210.** (c) |
| **211.** (d) | **212.** (a) | **213.** (c) | **214.** (c) | **215.** (b) | **216.** (c) | **217.** (a) | **218.** (c) | **219.** (d) | **220.** (a) |
| **221.** (a) | **222.** (a) | **223.** (a) | **224.** (a) | **225.** (a) | **226.** (b) | **227.** (a) | **228.** (a) | **229.** (c) | **230.** (a) |
| **231.** (c) | **232.** (a) | **233.** (a) | **234.** (b) | **235.** (a) | **236.** (c) | **237.** (b) | **238.** (a) | **239.** (a) | **240.** (a) |
| **241.** (c) | **242.** (c) | **243.** (b) | **244.** (a) | **245.** (b) | **246.** (a) | **247.** (a) | **248.** (c) | **249.** (d) | **250.** (b) |
| **251.** (b) | **252.** (b) | **253.** (b) | **254.** (b) | **255.** (c) | **256.** (c) | **257.** (d) | **258.** (c) | **259.** (a) | **260.** (c) |
| **261.** (a) | **262.** (a) | **263.** (a) | **264.** (c) | **265.** (a) | **266.** (c) | **267.** (a) | **268.** (b) | **269.** (b) | **270.** (c) |
| **271.** (a) | **272.** (c) | **273.** (b) | **274.** (a) | **275.** (d) | **276.** (a) | **277.** (c) | **278.** (c) | **279.** (c) | **280.** (b) |
| **281.** (b) | **282.** (b) | **283.** (a) | **284.** (a) | **285.** (d) | **286.** (a) | **287.** (a) | **288.** (a) | **289.** (c) | **290.** (d) |
| **291.** (b) | **292.** (c) | **293.** (c) | **294.** (b) | **295.** (a) | **296.** (b) | **297.** (c) | **298.** (a) | **299.** (a) | **300.** (c) |
| **301.** (a) | **302.** (c) | **303.** (b) | **304.** (b) | **305.** (b) | **306.** (b) | **307.** (b) | **308.** (a) | **309.** (b) | **310.** (a) |
| **311.** (a) | **312.** (a) | **313.** (a) | **314.** (a) | **315.** (b) | **316.** (b) | **317.** (a) | **318.** (c) | **319.** (a) | **320.** (a) |
| **321.** (c) | **322.** (b) | **323.** (b) | **324.** (b) | **325.** (c) | **326.** (a) | **327.** (a) | **328.** (a) | **329.** (a) | **330.** (b) |
| **331.** (a) | **332.** (a) | **333.** (a) | **334.** (a) | **335.** (a) | **336.** (a) | **337.** (b) | **338.** (c) | **339.** (d) | **340.** (c) |
| **341.** (c) | **342.** (a) | | | | | | | | |

## Exercise 2

| | | | | | | | | | |
|---|---|---|---|---|---|---|---|---|---|
| **1.** (b,d) | **2.** (a,c) | **3.** (b,c) | **4.** (a,b,c) | **5.** (c) | **6.** (a,c,d) | **7.** (a) | **8.** (a) | **9.** (b) | **10.** (b) |
| **11.** (b) | **12.** (a) | **13.** (a,b,c,d) | **14.** (a,d) | **15.** (b,c,d) | **16.** (a,c) | **17.** (a,b,c) | **18.** (a,b,c,d) | **19.** (a,b,c,d) | **20.** (a,d) |
| **21.** (a,d) | **22.** (a) | **23.** (a) | **24.** (c) | **25.** (a,b,c) | **26.** (b,c) | **27.** (a,b,d) | **28.** (a,b,c) | **29.** (a,b,c) | **30.** (a,b,c) |
| **31.** (a,b,c) | **32.** (a,c) | **33.** (a,b) | **34.** (a,c) | **35.** (a,b,c,d) | | | | | |

# Hints & Solutions

## Exercise 1

**2.** Here, $f(x) = x^n \cos\frac{1}{x},\ x \neq 0,\ f(x) = 0,\ x = 0$

Hence, $f'(0) = \lim_{h\to 0} \frac{f(0+h) - f(0)}{h}$

$$= \lim_{h\to 0} \frac{h^n \cos\frac{1}{h} - 0}{h}$$

$$= \lim_{h\to 0} h^{n-1} \cos\frac{1}{h}$$

limit exist only, if $n - 1 > 0 \Rightarrow n > 1$.

**6.** Given that $f(x) = x|x|$

$$= \begin{cases} x^2, & x \geq 0 \\ -x^2, & x \leq 0 \end{cases}$$

Obviously, the rule of the function is changing at $x = 0$. So, we shall test the differentiable of $f(x)$ only at the point $x = 0$. Obviously, being polynomial, at all other points the function is differentiable.

$$Rf'(0) = \lim_{h\to 0} \frac{f(0+h) - f(0)}{h}$$

$$= \lim_{h\to 0} \frac{h^2 - 0}{h} = 0$$

and $Lf'(0) = \lim_{h\to 0} \frac{f(0-h) - f(0)}{-h}$

$$= \frac{-h^2 - 0}{-h} = 0$$

Since, $Rf'(0) = Lf'(0)$, therefore $f(x)$ is differentiable at $x = 0$. Hence, $f(x)$ is differentiable, $\forall\, x \in R$.

**7.** Given that $f(x) = \begin{cases} 2x + 1, & \text{if } x \leq 1 \\ ax^2 + b, & \text{if } 1 < x < 3 \\ 5x + 2a, & \text{if } x \geq 3 \end{cases}$

Clearly, the rule of the function is changing at $x = 1$ and 3. Now, we have

$$f(1+0) = f(1-0)$$

$\Rightarrow \quad \lim_{h\to 0} f(1+h) = \lim_{h\to 0}(1-h)$

$\Rightarrow \quad \lim_{h\to 0}[a(1+h)^2+b] = \lim_{h\to 0}[2(1-h)+1]$

$\Rightarrow \quad a+b=3 \quad \text{...(i)}$

and $\quad f(3+0) = f(3-0)$

$\Rightarrow \quad \lim_{h\to 0} f(3+h) = \lim_{h\to 0} f(3-h)$

$\Rightarrow \quad \lim_{h\to 0}[5(3+h)+2a] = \lim_{h\to 0}[a(3-h)^2+b]$

$\Rightarrow \quad 15+2a = 9a+b$

$\Rightarrow \quad 7a+b=15 \quad \text{...(ii)}$

Solving Eqs. (i) and (ii), we get

$$a=2, b=1$$

**9.** Given that

$$f(x) = \begin{cases} x, & \text{when } x \text{ is rational} \\ 1-x, & \text{when } x \text{ is irrational} \end{cases}$$

Here, three cases arises

***Case I.*** When $x = \frac{1}{2}$

We have

$$f\left(\frac{1}{2}+0\right) = \lim_{h\to 0} f\left(\frac{1}{2}+h\right)$$

$$\lim_{h\to 0}\left(\frac{1}{2}-h\right) \text{ or } \lim_{h\to 0}\left[1-\left(\frac{1}{2}-h\right)\right]$$

$$= \frac{1}{2} \text{ or } \frac{1}{2} = \frac{1}{2}$$

and $f\left(\frac{1}{2}-0\right) = \lim_{h\to 0} f\left(\frac{1}{2}-h\right)$

$$= \lim_{h\to 0} f\left(\frac{1}{2}-h\right) \text{ or } \lim_{h\to 0}\left[1-\left(\frac{1}{2}-h\right)\right]$$

$$= \frac{1}{2} \text{ or } \frac{1}{2} = \frac{1}{2}$$

But $\quad f\left(\frac{1}{2}\right) = \frac{1}{2}$

Since, $f\left(\frac{1}{2}+0\right) = f(0) = f\left(\frac{1}{2}-0\right)$, therefore $f(x)$ is continuous at $x = \frac{1}{2}$.

***Case II.*** When $x = a$ is rational number and $x \neq \frac{1}{2}$.

We have, $f(a+0) = \lim_{h\to 0} f(a+h)$

$$= \lim_{h\to 0}[a+h] \text{ or } \lim_{h\to 0}[1-(a+h)]$$

$$= a \text{ or } 1-a$$

Since, limit is not unique, therefore $f(x)$ is not continuous at $x = a$.

***Case III.*** When $x = a$ is irrational number

We have, $f(a+0) = \lim_{h\to 0} f(a+h)$

$$= \lim_{h\to 0}[a+h] \text{ or } \lim_{h\to 0}[1-(a+h)]$$

$$= a \text{ or } 1-a$$

Since, limit is not unique, therefore $f(x)$ is not continuous at $x = a$.

Hence, $f(x)$ is continuous only at $x = 1/2$.

**10.** Let $x = 2n$, where $n$ is any integer. So that $x = \pm 2, \pm 4, \pm 4, \ldots$ *i.e.,* any even integers. We have,

$$f(2n+0) = \lim_{n\to 0} f(2n+n) = \lim_{n\to 0} f(h) \quad [\because f(2+x) = f(x)]$$

$$= \lim_{n\to 0}(n) = 0$$

and $\quad f(2n-0) = \lim_{n\to 0} f(2n-n) = \lim_{n\to 0} f(-n)$

$$= \lim_{n\to 0}(-n) = 0$$

and $\quad f(2n+0) = f(0) = 0$

Since, $f(2n+0) = f(0) = f(2n-0)$, therefore $f(x)$ is continuous at $x = 2n$, *i.e.,* even integers.

Again, let $x = 2n+1$, where $n$ is any integer, so that $x = \pm 1, \pm 3, \pm 5, \ldots$ *i.e.,* any odd integer. We have,

$$f(2n+1+0) = \lim_{n\to 0} f(2n+1+n) = \lim_{n\to 0} f(1+n) \quad [\because f(x+2) = f(x)]$$

$$= \lim_{n\to 0} f[2+(-1+n)]$$

$$= \lim_{n\to 0} f(-1+n)$$

$$= \lim_{n\to 0}(-1+n) = -1$$

and $f(2n+1-0) = \lim_{n\to 0} f(2n+1-n) = \lim_{n\to 0} f(1-n)$

$$= \lim_{n\to 0}(1-n) = 1$$

Since, $f(2n+1-0) \neq f(2n+1+0)$, therefore $f(x)$ is not continuous at $x = 2n+1$.

*i.e.,* odd integers.

Hence, $f(x)$ is continuous only even integers.

**12.** Given that

$$f(x) = \begin{cases} \dfrac{\sin[x]}{[x]}, & [x] \neq 0 \\ 0, & [x] = 0 \end{cases}$$

Now, we have

$$f(0+0) = \lim_{h\to 0} f(0+h)$$

$$= \lim_{h\to 0} f(h)$$

$$= \lim_{h\to 0}\left[\frac{\sin[h]}{[h]}\right]$$

$$= \lim_{h\to 0}(0) = 0 \quad [\because [h] = 0]$$

and $\quad f(0-0) = \lim_{h\to 0} f(0-h) = \lim_{h\to 0} f(-h) = \lim_{h\to 0} \frac{\sin[-h]}{[-h]}$

$$= \lim_{h\to 0} \frac{\sin(-1)}{(-1)} = \lim_{h\to 0} \sin 1 = \sin 1 \neq 0$$

Since, $f(0-0) \neq f(0+0)$; therefore, $\lim_{x\to 0} f(x)$ does not exists.

**16.** Given that $f(x) = \begin{cases} x, & 0 < x < 1 \\ 3-x, & 1 \le x \le 2 \end{cases}$

Clearly, the value of functions is changing at $x = 1$, therefore we check limit at $x = 1$.

$$\lim_{x\to 1^-} f(x) = \lim_{h\to 0} f(1-h) = \lim_{h\to 0}(1-h) = 1$$

and $$\lim_{x\to 1^+} f(x) = \lim_{h\to 0} f(1+h) = \lim_{h\to 0}[3-(1+h)] = 2$$

**17.** Given that $f(x) = |x|^3 = \begin{cases} x^3, & x \geq 0 \\ -x^3, & x \leq 0 \end{cases}$

It is clear that the function is twice differentiable at $x = 0$ and the other points the function is a polynomial. Therefore, it is obviously differentiable.

**20.** Given that $f(x) = (x^2-1)|x^2-3x+2| + \cos(|x|)$

$$= (x^2-1)|(x-1)(x-2)| + \cos|x|$$

$$= (x^2-1)|x-1||x-2| + \cos x \quad [\because \cos|x| = \cos x]$$

$$= \begin{cases} (x^2-1)(1-x)(2-x)+\cos x, & x \leq 1 \\ (x^2-1)(x-1)(2-x)+\cos x, & 1 \leq x \leq 2 \\ (x^2-1)(x-1)(x-2)+\cos x, & x \geq 2 \end{cases}$$

$$= \begin{cases} (x-1)^2(x+1)(x-2)+\cos x, & x \leq 1 \\ -(x-1)^2(x+1)(x-2)+\cos x, & 1 \leq x \leq 2 \\ (x-1)^2(x+1)(x-2)+\cos x, & x \geq 2 \end{cases}$$

Clearly, the rule of the function is changing at $x = 1$ and 2. So, we shall test the differentiability of $f(x)$ only at the points $x = 1$ and 2.

Clearly, $Rf'(1) = Lf'(1)$ and $Rf'(2) \neq Lf'(2)$

Hence, $f(x)$ is not differentiable at $x = 2$.

**21.** Given that $f(x) = \begin{cases} x^2, & \text{if } x \in Q \\ 0, & \text{otherwise} \end{cases}$

$$Rf'(0) = \lim_{h\to 0} \frac{f(0+h)-f(0)}{h} = \lim_{h\to 0} \frac{f(h)}{h}$$

$$= \lim_{h\to 0}\left(\frac{h^2}{h}\right) \text{ or } \lim_{h\to 0}\left(\frac{0}{h}\right)$$

$$= 0 \text{ or } 0$$

$$= 0$$

Similarly, $Lf'(0) = 0$

Hence, $f(x)$ is differentiable at $x = 0$.

**22.** Given that

$$f(x) = \frac{|\sin x|}{\sin x}$$

$$= \begin{cases} \vdots & \vdots \\ \frac{\sin x}{\sin x}, & 0 < x < \pi \\ -\frac{\sin x}{\sin x}, & \pi < x < 2\pi \\ \frac{\sin x}{\sin x}, & 2\pi < x < 3\pi \\ -\frac{\sin x}{\sin x}, & 3\pi < x < 4\pi \\ \vdots & \vdots \end{cases}$$

$$= \begin{cases} \vdots & \vdots \\ 1, & 0 < x < \pi \\ -1, & \pi < x < 2\pi \\ 1, & 2\pi < x < 3\pi \\ -1, & 3\pi < x < 4\pi \\ \vdots & \vdots \end{cases}$$

It is clear that $f(x)$ is not continuous at the points $x = n\pi, n \in Z$, therefore it is not differentiable at that points.

Also, there are infinite many point for which $f(x) > \frac{1}{2}$, and $f(x) \geq -1$, also these points are not countable.

**23.** Given that, $f(x) = x + x^2$

$$\Rightarrow \quad f(x) = (x + 1/2)^2 - \frac{1}{4}$$

$$\Rightarrow \quad f(x) + \frac{1}{4} = (x + 1/2)^2,$$

which is the equation of the parabola.

The graph of the function is

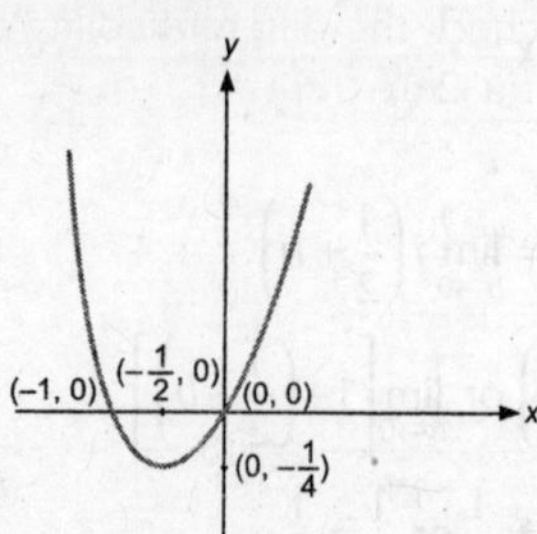


It is clear from the graph the given function $f(x)$ is invertible in $[-\frac{1}{2}, \infty[$ and $f^{-1} = \left[\frac{-1+\sqrt{1+4y}}{2}\right]$.

**24.** $f(x) = \begin{cases} 0, & \text{if } x \text{ is rational} \\ \sin|x|, & \text{if } x \text{ is irrational} \end{cases}$

The points of continuity are $0, \pm\pi, \pm 2\pi, \pm 3\pi, \ldots$ These points are countable.

**25.** Since, $f(x)$ is monotonic in $R$ such that

$$f(x) = f^{-1}(x) \qquad \ldots\text{(i)}$$

Since, $$f(x) = ax + b \qquad \ldots\text{(ii)}$$

$$\Rightarrow \quad y = ax + b \Rightarrow x = \frac{y-b}{a}$$

$$\Rightarrow \quad f^{-1}(y) = \frac{y-b}{a}$$

$$\Rightarrow \quad f^{-1}(x) = \frac{x-b}{a} \qquad \ldots\text{(iii)}$$

From Eqs. (ii) and (iii) in Eq. (i), we get

$$ax + b = \frac{x-b}{a} \Rightarrow a^2x + ab = x - b$$

Comparing on both sides, we get

$$a^2 = 1 \text{ and } ab = -b$$

$$\Rightarrow \quad a = \pm 1 \text{ and } ab = -b$$

If $a = -1$, then $ab = -b$ is possible.

Hence, $a = -1, b \in R$

**26.** Here, it is given that

$$f(x)=\begin{cases}\dfrac{x^2}{a}-a, & (0<x<a)\\[2mm] a-\dfrac{a^3}{x^2}, & (x\ge a)\end{cases}$$

Continuity at $x=a$, $f(a)=0$

Hence, LHL $=\lim_{x\to a^-} f(x)=\lim_{h\to 0} f(a-h)=\lim_{h\to 0}\dfrac{(a-h)^2}{a}-a$

$$=\lim_{h\to 0}\frac{(a-h)^2-a^2}{a}=\frac{a^2-a^2}{a}=0$$

and RHL $=\lim_{x\to a^+} f(x)=\lim_{h\to 0} a-\dfrac{a^3}{(a+h)^2}$

$$=\lim_{h\to 0}\frac{a(a+h)^2-a^3}{(a+h)^2}=\frac{a^3-a^3}{a^2}=0$$

Hence, LHL $=f(a)=$ RHL

Hence, $f(x)$ is continuous.

Hence, $f(x)$ is continuous on $]0,\infty[$.

Now, we can check the differentiability at $x=a$

$$Lf'(a)=\lim_{h\to 0}\frac{f(a-h)-f(a)}{-h}$$

$$=\lim_{h\to 0}\frac{\dfrac{(a-h)^2}{a}-a-0}{-h}$$

$$=\lim_{h\to 0}\frac{(a-h)^2-a^2}{-ah}=\lim_{h\to 0}\frac{a^2+h^2-2ah-a^2}{-ah}$$

$$=\lim_{h\to 0}\frac{h(h-2a)}{-ah}=\frac{-2a}{-a}=2$$

and $Rf'(a)=\lim_{h\to 0}\dfrac{f(a+h)-f(a)}{h}$

$$=\lim_{h\to 0}\frac{a-\dfrac{a^3}{(a+h)^2}-0}{h}$$

$$=\lim_{h\to 0}\frac{a(a+h)^2-a^3}{h(a+h)^2}$$

$$=\lim_{h\to 0}\frac{a^3+ah^2+2a^2h-a^3}{h(a+h)^2}$$

$$=\lim_{h\to 0}\frac{ah(h+2a)}{h(a+h)^2}=\lim_{h\to 0}\frac{ah+2a^2}{(a+h)^2}=\frac{2a^2}{a^2}=2$$

Hence, $Lf'(a)=Rf'(a)$

Hence, $f(x)$ is differentiable at $x=a$.

Therefore, $f(x)$ is differentiable at $(0,\infty)$.

**27.** In given these statements

A continuous function is differentiable and a continuous function on a closed interval $[a, b]$ of finite length is uniformly continuous on $[a, b]$ is true but a differentiable function is continuous, is a false statement.

Since, differentiable function need not be continuous e.g., $f(x)=|x|$.

**28.** Given that,

$$f(x)=|x+2|=\begin{cases}-(x+2), & x\le -2\\ x+2, & x\ge -2\end{cases}$$

Clearly, the rule of the function is changing at $x=0$. So, we shall test the differentiability of $f(x)$ only at the point $x=-2$. Obviously, being polynomial, at all other points the function is differentiable.

At $x=-2$.

$$Rf'(-2)=\lim_{h\to 0}\frac{f(-2+h)-f(-2)}{h}$$

$$=\lim_{h\to 0}\frac{(-2+h+2)-0}{h}=1$$

$$Lf'(-2)=\lim_{h\to 0}\frac{f(-2-h)-f(-2)}{h}=\lim_{h\to 0}\left[\frac{[-(-2+h+2)]-0}{h}\right]=-1$$

Since, $Lf'(-2)\ne Rf'(-2)$, therefore $f(x)$ is not differentiable at $x=-2$.

**29.** The necessary condition for a function $f(x)$ to be derivable at a point $x=a$ of its domain.

I. $f(x)$ is well defined at $x=a$

II. $\lim_{x\to a} f(x)$ must exist

III. $f(x)$ is continuous

**31.** Here, it is given that

(i) $f(x+y)=f(x)\cdot f(y)$ and

(ii) $f(x)=1+x\,g(x)$, where $\lim_{x\to 0} g(x)=1$

Now, writing for $y$ in the given condition. We have,

$$f(x+h)=f(x)\cdot f(h)$$

Then, $f(x+h)-f(x)=f(x)f(h)-f(x)$

or $\dfrac{f(x+h)-f(x)}{h}=\dfrac{f(x)[f(h)-1]}{h}$

$$=\frac{f(x)h\cdot g(h)}{h}=f(x)\cdot g(h)$$

Hence, $\lim_{h\to 0}\dfrac{f(x+h)-f(x)}{h}=\lim_{h\to 0} f(x)\cdot g(h)=f(x)\cdot 1$

Since, by hypothesis $\lim_{h\to 0} g(h)=1$

It follows that $f'(x)=f(x)$

Since, $f(x)$ exists, $f'(x)$ also exists

and $f'(x)=f(x)\Rightarrow \dfrac{d}{dx}f(x)=f(x)$

**34.** Given that

$$f(x)=\text{Max}\{a-x,\ a+x,\ b\},\ 0<a<b$$

The graph of the function is

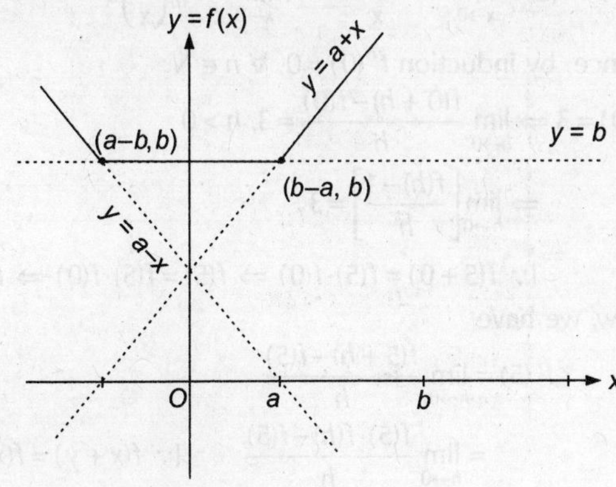

From the graph it is clear that the graph of the function $f(x)$ has two sharp edges, therefore $f(x)$ is not differentiable at that points. Hence, the number of points at which the function is not differentiable is 2.

**38.** Given that

$$f(x)=\lim_{n\to\infty}\left[\frac{\log(2+x)-x^{2n}\sin x}{1+x^{2n}}\right],\ 0\le x\le\frac{\pi}{2}$$

$$=\begin{cases}\log(2+x), & \text{if } 0\le x<1\\ \dfrac{\log 3-\sin 1}{2}, & \text{if } x=1\\ -\sin x, & \text{if } 1<x\le\dfrac{\pi}{2}\end{cases}\quad\left[\because \lim_{n\to\infty}x^{2n}=\begin{cases}0, & 0\le x<1\\ 1, & x=1\\ \infty, & 1<x\le\dfrac{\pi}{2}\end{cases}\right]$$

Now, $f(1)=\dfrac{1}{2}(\log 3-\sin 1)$

$$f(1-0)=\lim_{n\to 0}f(1-n)$$
$$=\lim_{n\to 0}\log(2+(1-n))$$
$$=\log 3$$

and $f(1+0)=\lim_{n\to 0}f(1+n)$

$\lim_{n\to 0}[-\sin(1+n)]=-\sin 1$

Since, $f(1-0)\ne f(1+0)$, therefore the limit does not exist at $x=1$. Hence, $f(x)$ is not continuous at $x=1$.

**37.** If $x\ne 0$, $f^n(x)=e^{-\frac{1}{x^2}}p_{3n}(1/x)$, where $p_{3n}(1/x)$ is a polynomial of degree $3n$ in $(1/x)$. We have,

$$f'(0)=\lim_{x\to 0}\frac{f(x)-f(0)}{x}=\lim_{x\to 0}\frac{e^{-1/x^2}}{x}=0$$

for, $e^{1/x^2}>\left(\dfrac{1}{x^2}\right)^m\Big/m!$

$\Rightarrow\quad m!\cdot|x^{2m-n}|>|x^{-n}e^{-1/x^2}|$

Let $2m>n$, then $\lim_{x\to 0}|x^{-n}e^{-1/x^2}|=0$

*e.g.*, $\lim_{x\to 0}x^{-n}e^{-1/x^2}=0,\ \forall n\in N$

If we assume $f^n(0)=0$, we get

$$f^{n+1}(0)=\lim_{x\to 0}\frac{f^n(x)-f^n(0)}{x}=\lim_{x\to 0}\frac{1}{x}P_{3n}\left(\frac{1}{x}\right)e^{-1/x^2}=0$$

Hence, by induction $f^n(0)=0,\ \forall\ n\in N$

**39.** $f'(0)=3\Rightarrow\lim_{h\to 0}\dfrac{f(0+h)-f(0)}{h}=3,\ h>0$

$$\Rightarrow\lim_{h\to 0}\left[\frac{f(h)-1}{h}\right]=3\qquad\text{...(i)}$$

$[\because f(5+0)=f(5)\cdot f(0)\Rightarrow f(5)=f(5)\cdot f(0)\Rightarrow f(0)=1]$

Now, we have

$$f'(5)=\lim_{h\to 0}\frac{f(5+h)-f(5)}{h}$$
$$=\lim_{h\to 0}\frac{f(5)\cdot f(h)-f(5)}{h}\qquad[\because f(x+y)=f(x)\cdot f(y)]$$
$$=f(5)\lim_{h\to 0}\left(\frac{f(h)-1}{h}\right)$$
$$=f(5)\cdot 3\qquad\text{[by Eq. (i)]}$$
$$=(-2)\times 3=-6$$

Hence, $f'(5)=-6$

**41.** Given that $f(x)=\begin{cases}\dfrac{|x|}{2}+1, & \text{if } x<1\\ \dfrac{x}{2}+1, & \text{if } 1\le x\le 2\\ \dfrac{-|x|}{2}+1, & \text{if } 2<x\end{cases}$

$$=\begin{cases}\dfrac{-x}{2}+1, & x\le 0\\ \dfrac{x}{2}+1, & 0\le x<1\\ \dfrac{x}{2}+1, & 1\le x\le 2\\ -\dfrac{x}{2}+1, & x>2\end{cases}$$

$$=\begin{cases}-\dfrac{x}{2}+1, & x\le 0\\ \dfrac{x}{2}+1, & 0\le x\le 2\\ -\dfrac{x}{2}+1, & x>2\end{cases}$$

Clearly, the rule of the function is changing at $x=0, 2$. So, we shall test the continuity and differentiability at $x=0, 2$. Obviously being polynomial, at all other points, the function is continuous as well as differentiable.

Continuity at $x=0$

$$f(0+0)=\lim_{h\to 0}f(0+h)=\lim_{h\to 0}f(h)=\lim_{h\to 0}\left(\frac{h}{2}+1\right)=1$$

$$f(0-0)=\lim_{h\to 0}f(0-h)=\lim_{h\to 0}f(-h)=\lim_{h\to 0}\left(\frac{h}{2}+1\right)=1$$

and $f(0)=1$

Since, $f(0+0)=f(0)=f(0-0)$, therefore $f(x)$ is continuous at $x=0$.

Differentiability at $x=0$

$$Rf'(0)=\lim_{h\to 0}\frac{f(0+h)-f(0)}{h}=\lim_{h\to 0}\left[\frac{f(h)-f(0)}{h}\right]$$

$$=\lim_{h\to 0}\frac{\left(\frac{h}{2}+1\right)-1}{h}=\lim_{h\to 0}\left(\frac{1}{2}\right)=\frac{1}{2}$$

$$Lf'(0)=\lim_{h\to 0}\frac{f(0-h)-f(0)}{(-h)}=\lim_{h\to 0}\left[\frac{f(-h)-f(0)}{(-h)}\right]$$

$$=\lim_{h\to 0}\left[\frac{\left(\frac{h}{2}+1\right)-1}{h}\right]=\lim_{h\to 0}\left(-\frac{1}{2}\right)=-\frac{1}{2}$$

Since, $Rf'(0)\ne Lf'(0)$, therefore $f(x)$ is not differentiable at $x=0$.

Continuity at $x = 2$.

$$f(2+0) = \lim_{h\to 0} f(2+h) = \lim_{h\to 0}\left[\frac{-(2+h)}{2}+1\right] = \lim_{h\to 0}(-1) = -1$$

$$f(2-0) = \lim_{h\to 0} f(2-h) = \lim_{h\to 0}\left[\frac{(2-h)}{2}+1\right] = \lim_{h\to 0}\left[2-\frac{h}{2}\right] = 2$$

Since, $f(2-0) \neq f(2+0)$, therefore $f(x)$ is not continuous at $x = 2$.

We know that, $f(x)$ is not continuous at $x = a$, then it is not differentiable at $x = a$.

Hence, $f(x)$ is neither continuous nor differentiable at $x = a$.

**42.** Since, $f(x)$ is continuous at $x = a$, therefore we have

$\lim_{x\to a} f(x) = f(a)$

$$\Rightarrow \quad \lim_{x\to a}\left[\frac{f'(x)}{f(x)-f(a)} - \frac{1}{(x-a)}\right] = \alpha$$

$$\Rightarrow \quad \lim_{x\to a}\left[\frac{f'(x)\cdot(x-a)-f(x)+f(a)}{[f(x)-f(a)](x-a)}\right] = \alpha$$

$$\Rightarrow \quad \lim_{x\to a}\left[\frac{f''(x)(x-a)+f'(x)-f'(x)}{[f(x)-f(a)]+f'(x)(x-a)}\right] = \alpha$$

$$\Rightarrow \quad \lim_{x\to a}\left[\frac{f''(x)}{\frac{f(x)-f(a)}{(x-a)}+f'(x)}\right] = \alpha$$

$$\Rightarrow \quad \frac{f''(a)}{\lim_{x\to a}\left(\frac{f(x)-f(a)}{x-a}\right)+f'(a)} = \alpha$$

$$\Rightarrow \quad \frac{f''(a)}{f'(a)+f'(a)} = \alpha$$

$$\Rightarrow \quad \frac{f''(a)}{2f'(a)} = \alpha$$

**44.** Given that $f(x) = x^n\,|x| = \begin{cases} x^{n+1}, & x \geq 0 \\ -x^{n+1}, & x \leq 0 \end{cases}$

Since, $f(x)$ is differentiable at $x = 0$, therefore, we have

$$Rf'(0) = \lim_{h\to 0}\frac{f(0+h)-f(0)}{h}$$

$$= \lim_{h\to 0}\frac{h^{n+1}-0}{h}$$

$$= \lim_{h\to 0}(h^n)$$

$= 0$, if $n$ is any positive integer

**47.** Clearly, $f(x) = \cos x$ is continuous as well as differentiable in interval $\left[-\frac{\pi}{2}, \frac{\pi}{2}\right]$ and $f\left(-\frac{\pi}{2}\right) = f\left(\frac{\pi}{2}\right) = 0$. Then, by Rolle's theorem, we have

$$f'(c) = 0 \Rightarrow \sin c = 0 \Rightarrow c = 0$$

**49.** Given function $f(x) = \sin x$

$$f(x) = f[\pi/2 + (x-\pi/2)]$$

$$= f(\pi/2) + \frac{(x-\pi/2)}{1!}f'(\pi/2) + \frac{(x-\pi/2)^2}{2!}f''(\pi/2)$$

$$+ \frac{(x-\pi/2)^3}{3!}f'''(\pi/2) + \frac{(x-\pi/2)^4}{4!}f^{iv}(\pi/2)$$

$$+ \frac{(x-\pi/2)^5}{5!}f^{v}(\pi/2) + \frac{(x-\pi/2)^6}{6!}f^{vi}(\pi/2)$$

$$+ \frac{(x-\pi/2)^7}{7!}f^{vii}(\pi/2) + \ldots \quad \ldots(i)$$

$f(x) = \sin x \quad f(\pi/2) = 1 \quad f^{iv}(x) = \sin x \quad f^{iv}(\pi/2) = 1$

$f'(x) = \cos x \quad f'(\pi/2) = 0 \quad f^{v}(x) = \cos x \quad f^{v}(\pi/2) = 0$

$f''(x) = -\sin x \quad f''(\pi/2) = -1 \quad f^{vi}(x) = -\sin x \quad f^{vi}(\pi/2) = -1$

$f'''(x) = -\cos x \quad f'''(\pi/2) = 0 \quad f^{vii}(x) = -\cos x \quad f^{vii}(\pi/2) = 0$

The values of $a_2, a_7, a_4, a_3$ in Eq. (i) are

$$\frac{f''(\pi/2)}{2!}, \frac{f^{vii}(\pi/2)}{7!}, \frac{f^{iv}(\pi/2)}{4!}, \frac{f'''(\pi/2)}{3!}$$

*i.e.,* $\quad -\frac{1}{2}, 0, \frac{1}{24}, 0$

**52.** Given that, $\quad f(x) = x^5 - 20x^3 + 140x$

$\Rightarrow \quad f'(x) = 5x^4 - 60x^2 + 140$

$\quad = 5[(x^2-6)^2 + 12]$

$\Rightarrow \quad f'(x) > 0, \forall x \in R$

Hence, $f(x)$ is increasing, $\forall x \in R$.

**53.** Given that,

$$f(x) = \begin{cases} -x^{1/3}, & -1 \leq x \leq 0 \\ x^{1/3}, & 0 < x \leq 1 \end{cases}$$

Clearly, the given function is not differentiable at $x = 0$. Therefore, Rolle's theorem does not apply to $f$ in $[-1, 1]$.

**54.** Given that,

$$f(x) = -2x^3 - 9x^2 - 12x + 1$$

(sign scheme: $-$ before $-2$, $+$ between $-2$ and $-1$, $-$ after $-1$)

$\Rightarrow \quad f'(x) = -6x^2 - 18x - 12$

$\quad = -6[x^2 + 3x + 2]$

$\quad = -6(x+1)(x+2)$

$\Rightarrow \quad f'(x) > 0, \forall x \in (-2, -1)$

Hence, $f(x)$ is increasing in the interval $(-2, -1)$.

**56.** Consider the function $f$ defined by

$$f(x) = a_0\frac{x^{n+1}}{(n+1)} + a_1\frac{x^n}{n} + \ldots + a_{n-1}\frac{x^2}{2} + a_n x$$

Since, $f(x)$ is a polynomial, it is continuous and differentiable $\forall x$. Consequently $f(x)$ is continuous in the closed interval $[0, 1]$ and differentiable in the open interval $]0, 1[$. Also, $f(0) = 0$ and

$$f(1) = \frac{a_0}{n+1} + \frac{a_1}{n} + \ldots + \frac{a_{n-1}}{2} + a_n = 0 \text{ (say)}$$

*i.e.,* $\quad f(0) = f(1)$

Thus, all the three conditions of Rolle's theorem are satisfied. Hence, there is atleast one value of $x$ in the open interval $]0, 1[$, where $f'(x) = 0$

*i.e.,* $\cos x^n + a_1x^{n-1} + \ldots + a_{n-1}x + a_n = 0$.

**58.** Given that $f(x) = x^6 - x - 1$

$\Rightarrow \quad f'(x) = 6x^5 - 1$

$\Rightarrow \quad f'(x) > 0, \forall x \in [1, 2]$

Hence, $f(x)$ is increasing in the interval $[1, 2]$.

Clearly, $f(x)$ is continuous in the interval $[1, 2]$ such that $f(1)f(2) < 0$, therefore $f(x)$ has atleast one root between $[1, 2]$.

**61.** We know that $\sin x^2$ and $e^x$ are not uniformly continuous in the interval $[0, \infty[$.

**62.** Since, $\alpha$ is the repeated root of the polynomial equation. $f(x)=0$, then $f(\alpha)=0$ and $f'(\alpha)=0$.

Clearly, $f(x)=\sin x$ is continuous in the interval $[0, \pi]$ and differentiable in the open interval $]0, \pi[$

Also, $f(0)=f(\pi)=0$. Then, by Rolle's theorem

$$f'(c)=0 \Rightarrow \cos c=0 \Rightarrow c=\frac{\pi}{2}$$

**66.** Clearly, $f(x)=x^2-x$ is continuous in the interval $[1, 2]$ and differentiable in the open interval $]1, 2[$. Therefore,

$$\frac{f(2)-f(1)}{2-1}=f'(c) \Rightarrow \frac{2-0}{1}=2c-1$$

$$\Rightarrow \quad 2=2c-1$$

$$\Rightarrow \quad c=\frac{3}{2}$$

**69.** Given that,

$$f'(0)=11$$

$$\Rightarrow \quad \lim_{h\to 0}\frac{f(0+h)-f(0)}{h}=11$$

$$\Rightarrow \quad \lim_{h\to 0}\frac{f(h)-f(0)}{h}=11$$

$$\Rightarrow \quad \lim_{h\to 0}\left[\frac{f(h)-1}{h}\right]=11 \quad \text{...(i)}$$

$$[\because f(3+0)=f(3)\cdot f(0) \Rightarrow f(3)=f(3)\cdot(0) \Rightarrow f(0)=1]$$

Now, we have

$$f'(3)=\lim_{h\to 0}\frac{f(3+h)-f(3)}{h}$$

$$=\lim_{h\to 0}\frac{f(3)\cdot f(h)-f(3)}{h}$$

$$=f(3)\cdot \lim_{h\to 0}\left[\frac{f(h)-1}{h}\right]$$

$$=3\times 11=33 \quad \text{[by Eq. (i)]}$$

**71.** Since, $f'(a)$ exists. Then, we have

$$Lf'(a)=f'(a) \text{ and } Rf'(a)=f'(a)$$

$$\Rightarrow \quad \lim_{h\to 0}\frac{f(a-h)-f(a)}{-h}=f'(a)$$

and $$\lim_{h\to 0}\frac{f(a+h)-f(a)}{h}=f'(a)$$

Adding these two, we get

$$\lim_{h\to 0}\frac{f(a+h)-f(a-h)}{h}=2f'(a)$$

**74.** Given that

$$f(x+y)=\frac{f(x)+f(y)}{1-f(x)\cdot f(y)} \quad \text{...(i)}$$

Here, $x=0, y=0$ gives $f(0)=0$ and $y=-x$ gives

$$f(-x)=-f(x)$$

and $$\frac{f(y-x)}{y-x}=\frac{f(y)-f(x)}{1-f(y)\cdot f(-x)}\cdot\frac{1}{y-x}$$

$$=\frac{f(y)-f(x)}{y-x}\cdot\frac{1}{1+f(y)\cdot f(x)}, \text{ as } y\to x$$

$$\Rightarrow \quad f'(0)=f'(x)\cdot\frac{1}{1+[f(x)]^2}$$

$$\Rightarrow \quad \frac{df}{1+f^2}=f'(0)dx$$

On integrating, we obtain

$$\tan^{-1}f(x)=xf'(0)+C \quad \text{...(i)}$$

When $x=0$, then $f(x)=0$

$$0=0+C \Rightarrow C=0$$

From Eq. (ii), we obtain

$$\Rightarrow \quad \tan^{-1}f(x)=xf'(0)$$

$$f(x)=\tan(xf'(0))$$

**75.** For $\varepsilon>0$, when $|x-y|<\varepsilon^{1/\delta}$

We have, $\quad |f(x)-f(y)|\le|x-y|^{1+\delta}$

$$\Rightarrow \quad \frac{|f(x)-f(y)|}{|x-y|}\le|x-y|^{\delta}$$

$$\Rightarrow \quad \frac{|f(x)-f(y)|}{|x-y|}<(\varepsilon^{1/\delta})^{\delta}$$

$$\Rightarrow \quad \left|\frac{f(x)-f(y)}{x-y}\right|<\varepsilon$$

$$\Rightarrow \quad \left|\frac{f(x)-f(y)}{x-y}-0\right|<\varepsilon$$

$$\Rightarrow \quad f'(x)=0, \forall x\in[a, b]$$

Hence, $f(x)$ is constant on $[a, b]$.

**76.** Choose $x_1>a$ such that $k(x_1-a)<1$. Let $\alpha=\text{Sup}|f(t)|$ on $a<t<x_1$, then by Lagrange's mean value theorem

$$\frac{f(x)-f(a)}{x-a}=f'(t), \text{ where } a<t<x\le x_1$$

$$\Rightarrow \quad f(x)-f(a)=(x-a)f'(t)$$

$$\Rightarrow \quad f(x)=(x-a)f'(t) \quad [\because f(a)=0]$$

$$\Rightarrow \quad |f(x)|\le k(x-a)|f(t)|\le k(x-a)\alpha$$

$$\Rightarrow \quad \alpha\le k(x-a)\alpha<\alpha$$

$$\Rightarrow \quad \alpha=0$$

$$\Rightarrow \quad f(x)=0, \forall a\le x\le x_1$$

Proceeding with $a=x_1$, we get $x_2>x_1$, so as $f(x)=0$, $\forall x_1\le x\le x_2$ and so on. Thus, we get $x_1, x_2, \ldots, x_n=b$, so that $f(x)=0, \forall x\in[a, b]$.

**77.** $$f(x)=\begin{cases} x, \text{ when } 0\le x<\frac{1}{2} \\ 1, \text{ when } x=\frac{1}{2} \\ 1-x, \text{ when } \frac{1}{2}<x<1 \end{cases}$$

At $x=\frac{1}{2}$

$$f\left(\frac{1}{2}\right)=1$$

$$f\left(\frac{1}{2}+0\right)=\lim_{h\to 0}f\left(\frac{1}{2}+h\right)=\lim_{h\to 0}\left[1-\left(\frac{1}{2}+h\right)\right]$$

$$=\lim_{h\to 0}\left[\frac{1}{2}-h\right]=\frac{1}{2}$$

and $f\left(\frac{1}{2}-0\right)=\lim_{h\to0} f\left(\frac{1}{2}-h\right)=\lim_{h\to0}\left(\frac{1}{2}-h\right)=\frac{1}{2}$

Since, $f\left(\frac{1}{2}-0\right)=f\left(\frac{1}{2}+0\right)\neq f\left(\frac{1}{2}\right)$,

Therefore, $f(x)$ is not continuous $x=\frac{1}{2}$.

**88.** Let us consider a function $F(x)$ such as

$$F(x)=f(x)e^{g(x)}$$

Clearly, $F(x)$ satisfies the conditions of Rolle's theorem on $[a, b]$. So, that there exists a point $c\in\,]a, b[$ such that

$$F'(c)=0$$

$\Rightarrow$ $f'(c)e^{g(c)}+f(c)g'(c)e^{g(c)}=0$

$\Rightarrow$ $[f'(c)+f(c)g'(c)]e^{g(c)}=0$

Since, $e^{g(c)}\neq0$, therefore

$$f'(c)+f(c)g'(c)=0$$

**89.** For $x, y\in I$, by Lagrange's mean value theorem

$$\frac{f(x)-f(y)}{x-y}=f'(c),\text{ where } x<c<y$$

$\Rightarrow$ $f(x)-f(y)=(x-y)f'(c)$

$\Rightarrow$ $|f(x)-f(y)|=|x-y||f'(c)|$

For a given $\varepsilon>0\ \exists,\ \delta=\frac{\varepsilon}{\alpha}>0$ such that

$$|f(x)-f(y)|<\varepsilon,\ \forall\,|x-y|<\delta,\ x, y\in I$$

Hence, $f(x)$ is uniformly continuous on $I$

We know that every uniformly continuous function is also continuous.

**91.** Here, $\forall\, x\in\left[0,\frac{\pi}{2}\right]$

$\cos(f(x))-\sin(g(x))=\sin\left(\frac{\pi}{2}-f(x)\right)-\sin(g(x))$

$$=2\sin\frac{1}{2}\left(\frac{\pi}{2}-f(x)-g(x)\right)\cos\frac{1}{2}\left(\frac{\pi}{2}-f(x)+g(x)\right) \quad ...(i)$$

Since, $-\frac{\pi}{2}<f(x)\pm g(x)<\frac{\pi}{2}$

$\Rightarrow$ $\frac{\pi}{2}>-[f(x)\pm g(x)]>-\frac{\pi}{2}$

$\Rightarrow$ $\pi>\frac{\pi}{2}-[f(x)\pm g(x)]>0$

$\Rightarrow$ $0<\frac{1}{2}\left[\frac{\pi}{2}-(f(x)\pm g(x))\right]<\frac{\pi}{2}$ ...(ii)

Using Eq. (ii) in Eq. (i), then we obtain

$$\cos(f(x))-\sin(g(x))>0$$

$\Rightarrow$ $\cos(f(x))>\sin(g(x)),\ \forall\, x\in\left[0,\frac{\pi}{2}\right]$

**94.** Let $x>a$ and $n$ a positive number; then

$$f(x+h)=f(x)+hf'(x)+\frac{h^2}{2!}f''(x+\theta h)$$

$\Rightarrow$ $hf'(x)=f(x+h)-f(x)-\frac{h^2}{2!}f''(x+\theta h)$

$\Rightarrow$ $|hf'(x)|=\left|f(x+h)-f(x)-\frac{h^2}{2!}f''(x+\theta h)\right|$

$$\leq|f(x+h)|+|-f(x)|+\frac{h^2}{2!}|-f''(x+\theta h)|$$

$$\leq\alpha+\alpha+\frac{h^2}{2}\beta$$

$\Rightarrow$ $|f'(x)|<\frac{2\alpha}{h}+\frac{\beta h}{2}=\phi(h)$ (say)

Now, $|f'(x)|$ is independent of $n$ and also less than $\phi(h)$ for all values of $h$. Hence, $|f'(x)|$ must be less than the least value of $\phi(h)$, For maxima or minima of $\phi(h)$, we have

$$0=\phi'(h)=-\frac{2A}{h^2}+\frac{B}{2}$$

or $h=\pm2\sqrt{\frac{A}{B}}$

and $\phi''(h)=\frac{4A}{h^3}>0$ when $h=2\sqrt{\frac{A}{B}}$

Hence, the least value of $\phi(h)$

$$=2A\frac{1}{2}\sqrt{\frac{B}{A}}+\frac{B}{2}\cdot2\sqrt{\frac{A}{B}}$$

$$=2\sqrt{AB}$$

Thus, $|f'(x)|<2\sqrt{AB}$

**97.** We have,

$$f'(x)=\lim_{h\to0}\frac{f(x+h)-f(x)}{h}$$

$\Rightarrow$ $f'(x)=\lim_{h\to0}\frac{f(x)\cdot f(h)-f(x)}{h}$

$\Rightarrow$ $f'(x)=f(x)\lim_{h\to0}\frac{f(h)-1}{h}$ ...(i)

Again, $f'(0)=f(0)\lim_{h\to0}\frac{f(h)-1}{h}$

$\Rightarrow$ $2=f(0)\lim_{h\to0}\frac{f(h)-1}{h}$ ...(ii)

Now, $f(0+0)=f(0)\cdot f(0)\Rightarrow f(0)=[f(0)]^2$

$$\Rightarrow f(0)[f(0)-1]=0$$

$$\Rightarrow f(0)=1\ [\because\ f(x)\neq0,\ \forall\, x\in R]$$

From Eq. (ii), we get

Gives, $2=\lim_{h\to0}\frac{f(h)-1}{h}$

$$2=\frac{f'(x)}{f(x)}\quad\text{[by Eq. (i)]}$$

$$f'(x)=2f(x),\ \forall\, x\in R$$

**102.** Given that, $h(x)=\frac{f(x)}{x}, x>0$

$\Rightarrow$ $h'(x)=\frac{xf'(x)-f(x)}{x^2}$

Let $g(x)=xf'(x)-f(x)$

$\Rightarrow$ $g'(x)=xf''(x)+f'(x)-f'(x)$

$\Rightarrow$ $g'(x)=xf''(x)$

Since, $f''(x)>0$ and $x>0$, therefore $g'(x)>0,\ \forall\, x>0$

$\Rightarrow$ $g(x)$ is strictly increasing function in $]0,\infty[$.

Since, $h'(x)=\frac{g(x)}{x^2}\Rightarrow h'(x)>0,\ \forall\, x>0$

$\Rightarrow$ $h(x)$ is increasing in $]0,\infty[$.

**103.** By Taylor's theorem, we have

$$f(x+h)=f(x)+hf'(x)+\frac{h^2}{2}f''(x+\theta h);$$

$$x+\theta h\in[x,x+h] \text{ and } 0<\theta<1$$

$$\Rightarrow \quad f'(x)=\frac{\left[f(x+h)-f(x)-\frac{h^2}{2}f''(x+\theta h)\right]}{h}$$

$$\Rightarrow \quad f'(x)=\frac{[f(x+h)-f(x)]}{h}-\frac{h}{2}f''(x+\theta h)$$

$$\Rightarrow \quad |f'(x)|=\left|\frac{1}{h}[f(x+h)-f(x)]-\frac{h}{2}f''(x+\theta h)\right|$$

$$\le\frac{1}{h}[|f(x+h)|+|f(x)|]+\frac{h}{2}|f''(x+\theta h)|$$

$$\le\frac{1}{h}[1+1]+\frac{h}{2}\cdot 2$$

Hence, $|f'(x)|<\frac{2}{h}+h$

Since, $f'(x)$ is independent of $h$ and the inequality is true for all $h>0$, therefore the inequality is also true for least value of $\left(\frac{2}{h}+h\right)$.

Let $\quad u=\frac{2}{h}+h$

$$\Rightarrow \quad \frac{du}{dh}=\frac{-2}{h^2}+1$$

and $\quad \frac{d^2u}{dh^2}=\frac{4}{h^3}$

Putting $\quad \frac{du}{dh}=0 \Rightarrow \frac{-2}{h^2}+1=0$

$$\Rightarrow \quad h=\pm\sqrt{2}$$

But $\left(\frac{d^2u}{dh^2}\right)_{h=\sqrt{2}}$ is positive, therefore $u$ is minimum at $h=\frac{1}{\sqrt{2}}$

Hence, the minimum value of $u=\frac{2}{\sqrt{2}}+\sqrt{2}=2\sqrt{2}$

Hence, $\quad |f'(x)|\le 2\sqrt{2}$

**104.** We know that, a function $f(x)$ is continuous on $[a, b]$ and $f(a)\ne f(b)$, then $f$ takes on $[a, b]$ atleast once every value between $f(a)$ and $f(b)$.

**109.** Clearly, the graph of the function has sharp edge at $x=1$. Therefore, $f(x)$ is not differentiable at $x=1$.

**113.** Given that

$$f(x)=[x^2]$$

$$=\begin{cases}2, & -\sqrt{3}<x<-\sqrt{2}\\ 1, & -\sqrt{2}<x\le -1\\ 0, & -1<x\le 0\\ 0, & 0\le x<1\\ 1, & 1\le x<\sqrt{2}\\ 2, & \sqrt{2}\le x<\sqrt{3}\\ 3, & \sqrt{3}\le x<\sqrt{4}\end{cases}$$

Clearly, $f(x)$ is not continuous at $x=\pm\sqrt{n}, n\in I^+$.

**117.** The graph of the function $f(x)=|\sin \pi x|$ is

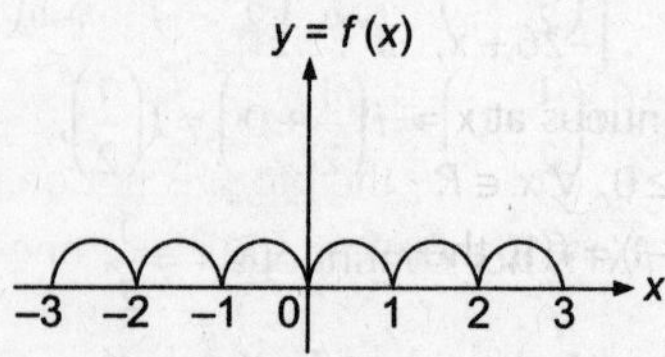


Clearly, the graph have sharp edges at the points $0, \pm1, \pm2, \pm3, \ldots$ therefore function is continuous everywhere but not differentiable everywhere except at integral values of $x$.

**121.** The product of two uniformly continuous functions may not be uniformly continuous.

We know that $f(x)=x+1$ and $g(x)=x-1$ are uniformly continuous on $R$ but $f(x)\cdot g(x)=x^2-1$ is not uniformly continuous on $R$.

**138.** The graph of the greatest integer function is

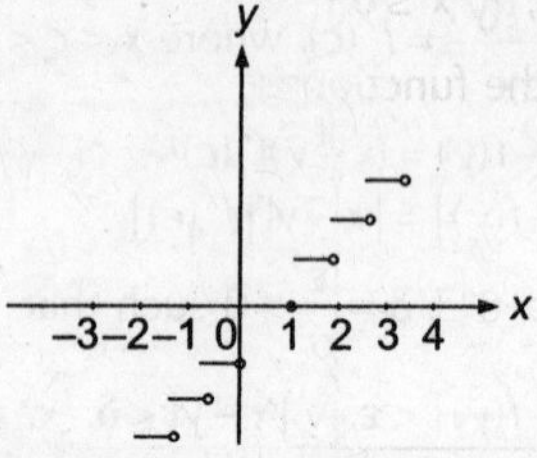


Clearly, the function $y=f(x)=[x]$ is discontinuous at the points $0, \pm1, \pm2, \pm3, \ldots$

The points of discontinuity are countable.

**141.** Given that, $\quad \phi=\text{dis}(x, I)$

$$=\text{Inf}\{|x-y|: y\in I\}, \text{ where } I=\{1\}\cup\{2\}$$

$$=\text{Inf}\{|x-1|, |x-2|\}$$

The graph of the $\phi(x)$ is given by.

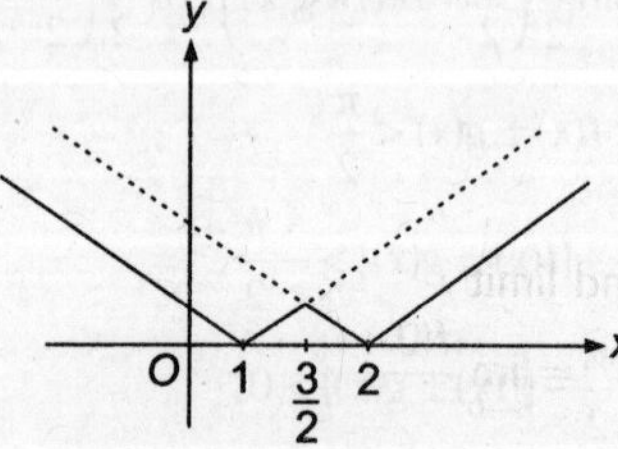


Clearly, the graph of the function have sharp edges at $x=1, \frac{3}{2}$ and 2. Therefore, $f(x)$ is not differentiable at $x=1, \frac{3}{2}$ and 2.

Hence, $\phi(x)$ is continuous on $R$ but not differentiable at $x=1, \frac{3}{2}$ and 2.

**143.** Use the following expansion, we obtain required results.

$$\log(1+x)=x-\frac{x^2}{2}+\frac{x^3}{3}-\ldots$$

**146.** Clearly, $f(x)=\begin{cases}|x|, \text{ if } x\in[-11, 1]\\ x^2, \text{ if } x\notin[-1, 1)\end{cases}$

is not satisfy the property $fof=f$ and the function

$$f(x)=\begin{cases}1, & \text{if } x\in[-23, 27]\\ 22+x, & \text{if } x\le -23\\ -26+x, & \text{if } x\ge 27\end{cases}$$

is not continuous at $x=-23$.

**151.** Since, $f(x)\ge 0$, $\forall\, x\in R$, therefore is not onto and

$f(-1)=f(1)$, therefore $f(x)$ is not one-one.

**152.** Given that,

$$f(x)=\lim_{n\to\infty}\frac{1}{1+n\sin^2\pi x}$$

$$\Rightarrow \quad f(x)=\begin{cases}1, & x\in Z\\ 0, & x\notin Z\end{cases} \quad [\because \sin n\pi=0, \forall\, n\in Z]$$

Clearly, $f(x)$ is discontinuous for, $\forall\, x\in Z$.

**154.** $f(x)=(x+|x|)|x|$

$$=\begin{cases}(x+x)x, & x\ge 0\\ (x-x)(-x), & x\le 0\end{cases}$$

$$=\begin{cases}2x^2, & x\ge 0\\ 0, & x\le 0\end{cases}$$

The graph of the function is

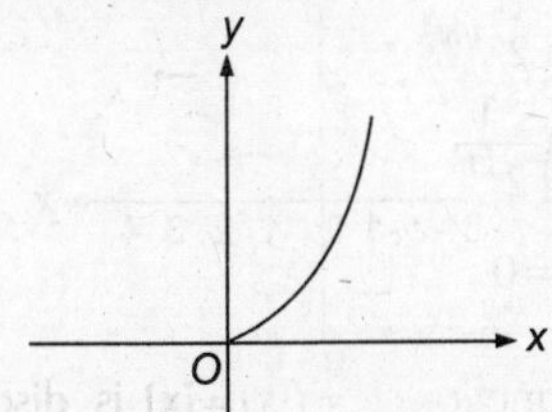


Clearly, $f(x)$ is continuous as well as differentiable in $R$ and $f'$ is continuous but not differentiable.

**156.** We know that, if continuous function $f(x):[0, 1]\to[0, 1]$, then there exists a point $c\in[0, 1]$, such that $f(c)=c$

**157.** Given that,

$$f(x)=\lim_{n\to\infty}\left\{\lim_{t\to\infty}\frac{\sin^2 n!\pi x}{\sin^2 n!\pi x+t^2}\right\},$$

then $f(x)=\begin{cases}0, & \text{if } x\in Q\\ 1, & \text{if } x\in R-Q\end{cases}$

Clearly, $f(x)$ is nowhere continuous.

**336.** Here, $f(x)=x^{2m-1}$ is odd function

and $f'(x)=(2m-1)x^{2(m-1)}$ is even function.

**337.** Here, $f(x)=x^{2m}$ is an even function

$f'(x)=2mx^{2m-1}$ is an odd function.

**338.** $f(0^+)=\lim_{x\to 0^+}f(x)=\lim_{h\to 0}\cos(0+h)=1$

$f(0^-)=\lim_{x\to 0^-}f(x)=\lim_{h\to 0}-\cos(0-h)=-1$

$f(0^+)\ne f(0^-)$

Irremovable discontinuity.

**340.** Here, $f(x)=\sin nx$ is an odd function.

$f'(x)=\cos nx$, which is an even function.

**341.** At $x=1$

$\Delta y=|\log(1+\Delta x)|-|\log 1|$

$=|\log(1+\Delta x)|$

*i.e.,* $\Delta y=|\log(1+\Delta x)|$

$$=\begin{cases}\log(1+\Delta x), & x\ge 0\\ -\log(1+\Delta x), & x<0\end{cases}$$

$$\Rightarrow \quad \frac{\Delta y}{\Delta x}=\begin{cases}\dfrac{\log(1+\Delta x)}{\Delta x} & \text{at } \Delta x>0\\ -\dfrac{\log(1+\Delta x)}{\Delta x} & \text{at } \Delta x<0\end{cases}$$

$$\Rightarrow \lim_{\Delta x\to^+ 0}\frac{\Delta y}{\Delta x}=+1 \text{ and } \lim_{\Delta x\to^- 0}\frac{\Delta y}{\Delta x}=-1$$

Hence, the function $y=|\log x|$ is not differentiable at $x=1$.

**342.** $\sin x$ is differentiable and $x^n$ is also differentiable.

Hence, $\sin x^n$ is also differentiable.

# Exercise 2

**1.** The right hand limit

$$f'(0^+)=\lim_{h\to 0}\frac{f(0+h)-f(0)}{h}$$

$$=\lim_{h\to 0}\frac{|h|-0}{h}$$

$$=\lim_{h\to 0}\frac{h}{h}=1, h>0$$

The left hand limit

$$f'(0^-)=\lim_{h\to 0}\frac{f(0-h)-f(0)}{-h}$$

$$=\lim_{h\to 0}\frac{|h|-0}{-h}$$

$$=\lim_{h\to 0}\frac{h}{-h}=-1, h>0$$

$\Rightarrow \quad f'(0^+)\ne f'(0^-)$

Hence, the function $f(x)$ is not differentiable at $x=0$.

**2.** For each $x\in X$ there is a function $f_x$ in $L$ such that $f_x(x)<h(x)+\varepsilon/3$.

Since, $f_x$ and $h$ are continuous there is an open set $O_x$ containing $x$ such that

$$|f_x(y)-f_x(x)|<\frac{\varepsilon}{3} \text{ and } |h(y)-h(x)|<\frac{\varepsilon}{3}$$

for all $y\in O_x$.

Hence, $f_x(y)-h(y)<\varepsilon$ for all $y$ in $O_x$. Now, since the sets $O_x$ cover $X$, and by compactness there are a finite number of them, say $\{O_{x_1}, \ldots, O_{x_n}\}$, which cover $X$. Let $g=f_{x_1}\wedge f_{x_2}\wedge\ldots\wedge f_{x_n}$. Then, $g\in L$ and given $y\in X$, we may choose $i$, so that $y\in O_{x_i}$, whence

$$g(y)-h(y)\le f_{x_i}(y)-h(y)<\varepsilon$$

**3.** $$f'(0^+)=\lim_{\Delta x\to 0^+}\frac{f(0+\Delta x)-f(0)}{\Delta x}$$

$$=\lim_{\Delta x\to 0^+}\frac{(0+\Delta x)\tan^{-1}[1/(0+\Delta x)]-0}{\Delta x}$$

$$= \lim_{\Delta x \to 0^+} \tan^{-1}\left(\frac{1}{0+\Delta x}\right)$$

$$= \tan^{-1}(\infty) = \frac{\pi}{2}$$

$$f'(0^-) = \lim_{\Delta x \to 0^-} \frac{f(0-\Delta x) - f(0)}{-\Delta x}$$

$$= \lim_{\Delta x \to 0^-} \frac{(0-\Delta x)\tan^{-1}[1/(0-\Delta x)] - 0}{-\Delta x}$$

$$= \lim_{\Delta x \to 0^-} \tan^{-1}\left(\frac{1}{-\Delta x}\right)$$

$$= -\tan^{-1}(\infty) = -\frac{\pi}{2}$$

Since, $f'(0^+) \neq f'(0^-)$

$\Rightarrow$ The function $f(x)$ is not differentiable at $x = 0$.

**4.** $$f'(0^+) = \lim_{\Delta x \to 0^+} \frac{f(0+\Delta x) - f(0)}{\Delta x}$$

$$= \lim_{\Delta x \to 0^+} \frac{(0+\Delta x)^2 \sin[1/(0+\Delta x)] - 0}{\Delta x}$$

$$= \lim_{\Delta x \to 0^+} \left\{\frac{(\Delta x)^2}{\Delta x} \sin\left(\frac{1}{\Delta x}\right)\right\}$$

$$= \lim_{\Delta x \to 0^+} (\Delta x) \sin\left(\frac{1}{\Delta x}\right)$$

$= 0 \times$ (a finite quantity between $-1$ and $+1$)

$= 0$

$$f'(0^-) = \lim_{\Delta x \to 0^-} \frac{f(0-\Delta x) - f(0)}{\Delta x}$$

$$= \lim_{\Delta x \to 0^-} \frac{(-\Delta x)^2 \sin(1/\Delta x)}{\Delta x}$$

$$= \lim_{\Delta x \to 0^-} \Delta x \sin\left(\frac{1}{\Delta x}\right)$$

$= 0 \times$ (a finite quantity between $-1$ and $+1$)

$= 0$

Since, $f'(0^+) = f'(0^-)$

Hence, $f(x)$ is differentiable at $x = 0$.

**5.** Here,

$$f(0) = 0$$

and $f(0^+)$ and $f(0^-)$ does not exist.

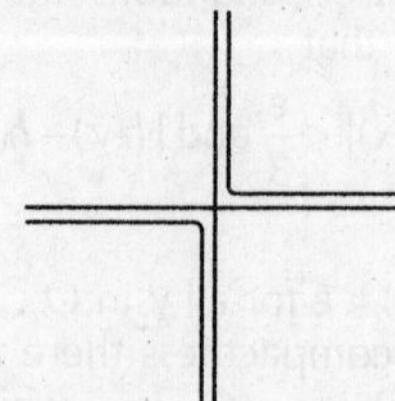

(a) $f(x)$ has discontinuity of second kind at $x = 0$.

(b) $f(x)$ has irremovable discontinuity at $x = 0$.

**6.** $$f'(0^+) = \lim_{\Delta x \to 0^+} \frac{f(0+\Delta x) - f(0)}{\Delta x}$$

$$= \lim_{\Delta x \to 0^+} \frac{(0+\Delta x)^n - 0}{\Delta x}$$

$$= \lim_{\Delta x \to 0^+} \frac{(\Delta x)^2}{\Delta x} = \lim_{\Delta x \to 0^+} (\Delta x)^{n-1}$$

$$= 0$$

$$f'(0^-) = \lim_{\Delta x \to 0^-} \frac{f(0-\Delta x) - f(0)}{\Delta x}$$

$$= \lim_{\Delta x \to 0^-} \frac{(0-\Delta x)^n - 0}{\Delta x}$$

$$= \lim_{\Delta x \to 0^-} \frac{(-\Delta x)^n}{\Delta x} = \lim_{\Delta x \to 0^-} \frac{(-1)^n (\Delta x)^n}{\Delta x}$$

$$= \lim_{\Delta x \to 0^-} (-1)^n (\Delta x)^{n-1}$$

$$= 0$$

Since, $f'(0^+) = f'(0^-)$

$\Rightarrow$ $f(x) = x^n$ is differentiable at $x = 0$.

**13.** $$f(0^+) = \lim_{x \to 0^+} 2^{1/x} = \lim_{h \to 0} 2^{1/0+h}$$

$$= \lim_{h \to 0} 2^{1/h} = \infty$$

$$f(0^-) = \lim_{x \to 0^-} 2^{1/x} = \lim_{h \to 0} 2^{1/0-h}$$

$$= \lim_{h \to 0} 2^{-1/h}$$

$$= \lim_{h \to 0} \frac{1}{2^{1/h}}$$

$$= \frac{1}{\infty} = 0$$

and $f(0) = 0$

Here, $f(0^+)$ does not exist, so $f$ has a mixed discontinuity of second kind and it is irremovable discontinuity.

**14.** For the integer $n$. We have,

$$f(x) = x - (n-1),\ n-1 < x < n$$
$$= 0, \qquad x = n$$
$$= x - n,\ n < x < n+1$$

$$f(n) = 0$$

$$f(n^+) = \lim_{x \to n^+} f(x) = \lim_{h \to 0} f(n+h)$$

$$= \lim_{h \to 0} [(n+h) - n] = 0$$

$$f(n^-) = \lim_{x \to n^-} f(x) = \lim_{h \to 0} f(n-h)$$

$$= \lim_{h \to 0} [(n-h) - (n-1)] = 1$$

Since, $f(n^+) \neq f(n^-)$

$f$ has discontinuity of first kind and it is irremovable discontinuity.

**15.** Here,

(i) $f(x) = 0$ at $x = 0$

(ii) $f(0^+) = 1$

(iii) $f(0^-) = -1$

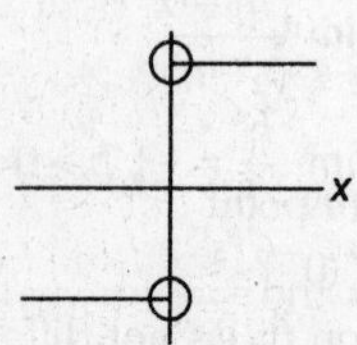

(a) $f(x)$ has jump at $x=0$

Since, $f(0^+)-f(0^-)=1-(-1)=2\neq 0$

(b) $f(x)$ has discontinuity of first kind.

(c) Measure of discontinuity is 2.

**16.** Here,

$$f(x)=0 \text{ at } x=0$$

and $f(0^+)=1$

$f(0^-)=1$

(a) $f(x)$ has jump at $x=0$

Since, $f(0^+)-f(0^-)=1-(-1)=2\neq 0$

(b) $\because f(0^+)=f(0^-)\neq f(0)$

Hence, $f$ has removal discontinuity of first kind.

**21.** $\dfrac{x(1-a\cos x)+b\sin x}{x^3}$ is of the form $\dfrac{0}{0}$ as $x\to 0$, whatever values $a$ and $b$ may have. Hence, by L'Hospital's rule.

$$\lim_{x\to 0}\frac{x(1-a\cos x)+b\sin x}{x^3}=\lim_{x\to 0}\frac{1-a\cos x+ax\sin x+b\cos x}{3x^2} \quad \text{...(i)}$$

Since, the denominator of the expression on the right has the value 0, when $x=0$. Therefore, in order that the limit of the expression on the right be finite as $x\to 0$, it is necessary that the numerator of the expression on the right has the value 0 when $x=0$. Hence,

$$1-a+b=0 \quad \text{...(ii)}$$

From Eq. (ii), the expression on the right hand side of Eq. (i) is $\dfrac{0}{0}$ as $x\to 0$ and consequently its limit as $x\to 0$.

We have,

$$\lim_{x\to 0}\frac{1-a\cos x+ax\sin x+b\cos x}{3x^2}$$

$$=\lim_{x\to 0}\frac{2a\sin x+ax\cos x-b\sin x}{6x} \quad \left(\frac{0}{0}\text{ form}\right)$$

$$=\lim_{x\to 0}\frac{3a\cos x-ax\sin x-b\cos x}{6}$$

$$=\frac{3a-b}{6}$$

Hence,

$$\frac{3a-b}{6}=\frac{1}{3}$$

$$\Rightarrow \quad 3a-b=2 \quad \text{...(iii)}$$

Hence, from Eqs. (ii) and (iii), we have

$$a=\frac{1}{2},\ b=-\frac{1}{2}$$

**22.** The given function,

$$f(x,y)=2x^2+2xy-y^3$$

Partially, differentiating *wrt* $x$ and $y$

$$\frac{\partial f}{\partial x}=4x+2y$$

and $$\frac{\partial f}{\partial y}=2x-3y^2$$

Now, for stationary point of the $f(x,y)$

$$\frac{\partial f}{\partial x}=0 \text{ and } \frac{\partial f}{\partial y}=0$$

Hence, $4x+2y=0 \Rightarrow 2x+y=0$ ...(i)

and $2x-3y^2=0$ ...(ii)

From Eqs. (i) and (ii), we get

$$-y-3y^2=0 \Rightarrow y=0 \text{ and } x=0$$

So, the only one stationary point is (0, 0) or origin.

**23.** $f(x,y)=4x^2+6y^2-8x-4y+8$ ...(i)

We know that, $r=\dfrac{\partial^2 f}{\partial x^2},\ s=\dfrac{\partial^2 f}{\partial x\partial y},\ t=\dfrac{\partial^2 f}{\partial y^2}$

From Eq. (i), differentiate partially *wrt* $x$ and $y$, we get

$$\frac{\partial f}{\partial x}=8x-8;\ \frac{\partial f}{\partial y}=12y-4$$

For maximum and minimum values of $f(x,y)$

$$\frac{\partial f}{\partial y}=0 \text{ and } \frac{\partial f}{\partial y}=0$$

$$8(x-1)=0 \text{ and } 4(3y-1)=0$$

$$\Rightarrow \quad x=1 \Rightarrow y=\frac{1}{3}$$

So, here only one stationary point is (1, 1/3).

Now, $r=\dfrac{\partial^2 f}{\partial x^2}=8,\ r=\dfrac{\partial^2 f}{\partial x\partial y}=0,\ t=\dfrac{\partial^2 f}{\partial y^2}=12$

$$rt-s^2=(8)(12)-0$$

$$\Rightarrow \quad 96>0 \text{ (minima)}$$

So, at stationary point (1, 1/3), the value of $(rt-s^2)$ positive and $r$ is also positive. Therefore, the function $f(x,y)$ is minimum value at (1, 1/3).

Now, the minimum value of $f(x,y)$ at (1, 1/3) is

$$f(1,1/3)=4(1)^2+6(1/3)^2-8(1)-4(1/3)+8$$
$$=4+2/3-8-4/3+8=4-2/3=10/3$$

**24.** $f(x,y)=x^2+y^2-xy-x-y+5$

$$\frac{\partial f}{\partial x}=2x-y-1=0$$

$$\frac{\partial f}{\partial y}=2y-x-1=0$$

Now, we have point (1, 1)

$$r=\frac{\partial^2 f}{\partial x^2}=2$$

$$s=\frac{\partial^2 f}{\partial y\partial x}=-1$$

$$t=\frac{\partial^2 f}{\partial y^2}=2$$

Here, $r>0, t>0$

Also, $rt-s^2>0$

$\Rightarrow f$ has minimum at (1, 1).

**29.** (a) Let $\varepsilon=\dfrac{1}{2}$ and $\delta$ be any positive number such that

for $$n>\frac{\pi}{\delta^2}.$$

$$\left|\sqrt{\frac{n\pi}{2}}-\sqrt{\frac{(n+1)\pi}{2}}\right|<\delta$$

Hence, by taking $x_1 = \sqrt{\frac{n\pi}{2}}$ and $x_2 = \sqrt{\frac{(n+1)\pi}{2}}$ as any two points of the interval $[0, \infty)$, we have

$$|f(x_1) - f(x_2)| = \left|\sin\frac{n\pi}{2} - \sin\frac{(n+1)\pi}{2}\right| = 1 > \varepsilon$$

whenever $|x_1 - x_2| < \delta$.

Hence, $f(x) = \sin x^2$ is not uniformly continuous on $[0, \infty)$.

(b) Let $\varepsilon > 0$ be given. Let $x, y \in [0, \infty)$. Then,

$$|\sin x - \sin y| = \left|2\sin\left(\frac{x-y}{2}\right)\cos\left(\frac{x+y}{2}\right)\right|$$

$$\leq 2\left|\frac{x-y}{2}\right| = |x-y|$$

$$< \varepsilon, \text{ whenever } |x-y| < \varepsilon$$

Hence, taking $\delta = \varepsilon$, we have

$$|\sin x - \sin y| < \varepsilon, \text{ whenever } |x-y| < \delta.$$

Hence, $\sin x$ is uniformly continuous on $[0, \infty)$.

(c) Let $\varepsilon > 0$ be given. Let $x_1, x_2$ be any two points of $[-1, 1]$, then

$$|f(x_1) - f(x_2)| = |x_1^2 - x_2^2|$$

$$= |x_1 - x_2||x_1 + x_2|$$

$$< \varepsilon, \text{ whenever } |x_1 - x_2| < \frac{\varepsilon}{2} = \delta$$

where $\delta$ is independent of $x_1$ and $x_2$.

Hence, for given $\varepsilon > 0$, $\exists$ a $\delta = \frac{\varepsilon}{2}$ such that for any choice of $x_1, x_2$ in $[-1, 1]$, we have

$$|f(x_1) - f(x_2)| < \varepsilon, \text{ when } |x_1 - x_2| < \frac{\varepsilon}{2} = \delta$$

$\Rightarrow$ $f$ is uniformly continuous in $[-1, 1]$.

**31.** Let

$$f(x) = (x-3)^5(x+1)^4$$

$$\Rightarrow \quad f'(x) = (x-3)^4(x+1)^3(9x-7)$$

$\therefore$ The function is derivable for all $x \in R$ and the derivative $f'$ vanishes for $x = -1, 3, \frac{7}{9}$, which may now be tested for extreme values.

(a) $x = -1$, $f'$ is positive for a value of $x$ slightly less then $-1$ and negative for slightly greater than $-1$.

Hence, $f'$ changes sign from positive to negative as $x$ passes through $-1$.

Hence, $x = -1$ is a point of maximum value.

(b) $x = 3$, $f'$ remains positive as $x$ passes through 3. Hence, $x = 3$ is neither a maximum nor a minimum.

(c) $x = \frac{7}{9}$, $f'$ changes sign from negative to positive as $x$ passes through $\frac{7}{9}$. Hence, $x = \frac{7}{9}$ is a point of minimum value.

# The Riemann Integral and Improper Integral

**Syllabus**

- Riemann Sums and Riemann Integral
- Improper Integrals

## Partitions

Suppose, $I = [a, b]$ is a closed and bounded interval. Then, by a partition (dissection or net) of $I$, means a finite set of real numbers $P = \{x_0, x_1, x_2, \ldots, x_{n-1}, x_n\}$ having the property that $a = x_0 < x_1 < x_2 < \ldots < x_{n-1} < x_n = b$. The closed sub-intervals

$$I_1 = [x_0, x_1], I_2 = [x_1, x_2], I_3 = [x_2, x_3], \ldots, I_{n-1} = [x_{n-2}, x_{n-1}], I_n = [x_{n-1}, x_n]$$

determined by $P$ constitute the segments of partition.

The length of the segment $[x_{r-1}, x_r]$ is denoted by $\Delta x_r$ and is given by $\Delta x_r = x_r - x_{r-1}$, $r = 1, 2, 3, \ldots, n$.

**Norm or Mesh** The greatest of the lengths of the segments of a partition $P$ is called norm or mesh of $P$. It is denoted by $\| P \|$ and can be written as

$$\| P \| = \max\ (\Delta x_r : r = 1, 2, \ldots, n)$$

Sometimes $\| P \|$ can also be denoted by $\mu(P)$.

**Refinement** A partition $P^*$ is called a refinement of other partition $P$ or we can say that $P^*$ is finer than $P$ if and only if $P^* \supset P$ *i.e.*, if every point of $P$ is used in the construction of $P^*$.

If we have two partitions $P_1$ and $P_2$, then $P^*$ is their common refinement if $P^* = P_1 \cup P_2$.

## Riemann Sums

Suppose, $f$ is a bounded function defined on a close interval $[a, b]$ and suppose $P = \{x_0, x_1, x_2, \ldots, x_n\}$ be any partition of $[a, b]$.

Suppose, $m_r = \text{Inf}\ \{f(x) : x_{r-1} \le x \le x_r\}$ and
$M_r = \text{Sup}\ \{f(x) : x_{r-1} \le x \le x_r\}$, $r = 1, 2, 3, \ldots, n$

Form the sums,

$$L(P, f) = \sum_{r=1}^{n} m_r \cdot \Delta x_r \text{ and } U(P, f) = \sum_{r=1}^{n} M_r \cdot \Delta x_r$$

$L(P, f)$ is called the lower Riemann sum of $f$ on $[a, b]$ with respect to the partition $P$ and $U[P, f]$ is called the upper Riemann sum. Lower Riemann sum is also called lower Darboux sums and upper Riemann sum is called upper Darboux sums.

> ***Note*** **(a)** $L(P, f)$ and $U(P, f)$ are also called lower and upper R-sums respectively.
> **(b)** $L(P, f) \le U(P, f)$
> **(c)** $L(P, -f) = -U(P, f)$
> **(d)** $U(P, -f) = -L(P, f)$
> **(e)** Family of all the partitions of interval $[a, b]$ is denoted by $P[a, b]$.

## Important Theorems on Riemann Sums

***Theorem 1*** Suppose, $f$ be a bounded function defined on $[a, b]$ and let $m$ and $M$ be the infimum and supremum of $f(x)$ in $[a, b]$. Then, for any partition $P$ of $[a, b]$ we have

$$m(b-a) \le L(P, f) \le U(P, f) \le M(b-a)$$

***Theorem 2*** For all partitions $P$ of $[a, b]$; $L(P, f) \le U(P, f)$

***Theorem 3*** Suppose, $f$ be a bounded function defined on $[a, b]$ and $P$ be the partition of $[a, b]$. If the refinement of $P$ is $P^*$, then

$$L(P^*, f) \ge L(P, f) \text{ and } U(P^*, f) \le U(P, f)$$

***Theorem 4*** Suppose, $P_1$ and $P_2$ be the two partitions of $[a, b]$, then

$$U(P_1, f) \ge L(P_2, f)$$

*i.e.*, every upper sum for $f$ is greater than or equal to every lower sum for $f$.

***Theorem 5*** Suppose, $f$ and $g$ be the two bounded functions defined on $[a, b]$ and suppose $P$ is any partition of $[a, b]$. Then,

$$L(P, f+g) \ge L(P, f) + L(P, g)$$

and $$U(P, f+g) \le U(P, f) + U(P, g)$$

## Lower and Upper R-Integrals

Suppose, $f$ be a bounded function defined on the interval $[a, b]$. The set of all numbers $L(P, f)$ is bounded above by $M(b-a)$ and so that it possesses a supremum of $L(P, f)$. The supremum of $L(P, f)$ is called the lower R-integral of $f$ or lower Riemann integral on $[a, b]$. It is denoted by

$$\underline{\int_a^b} f(x)\,dx \quad \text{or} \quad \underline{\int_a^b} f$$

The set of numbers $U(P, f)$ is bounded below by $m(b-a)$ so it possesses an infimum of $U(P, f)$. The infimum of $U(P, f)$ is called the upper Riemann integral or upper R-integral of $f$ on $[a, b]$ and denoted by

$$\overline{\int_a^b} f(x)\,dx \quad \text{or} \quad \overline{\int_a^b} f$$

> ***Note*** **(a)** $\underline{\int_a^b} f(x)dx = \text{Sup}\,\{L(P, f) : P \text{ is partition of } [a, b]\}$
>
> $\overline{\int_a^b} f(x)\,dx = \text{Inf}\,\{U(P, f) : P \text{ is partition of } [a, b]\}$
>
> **(b)** $\because L(P, -f) = -U(P, f)$ and $U(P, -f) = -L(P, f)$ from this we have
>
> $$\underline{\int_a^b} (-f) = -\overline{\int_a^b} f \quad \text{and} \quad \overline{\int_a^b} (-f) = -\underline{\int_a^b} f$$
>
> **(c)** $\underline{\int_a^b} f \le \overline{\int_a^b} f$ *i.e.*, the lower R-integral cannot exceed the upper R-integral.

## Darboux Theorem

Suppose, $f$ be a bounded function defined on the interval $[a, b]$. Then, for every $\varepsilon > 0, \exists\, \delta > 0$

s.t. $$U(P, f) < \overline{\int_a^b} f + \varepsilon \text{ and } L(P, f) > \underline{\int_a^b} f - \varepsilon,$$

$\forall$ partitions $P$ with $\|P\| \le \delta$.

> ***Note*** $\lim_{\|P\|\to 0} L(P, f) = \underline{\int_a^b} f$ and $\lim_{\|P\|\to 0} U(P, f) = \overline{\int_a^b} f$

## Riemann Integral or R-integrability

Suppose, $f$ be a bounded function defined on the bounded interval $[a, b]$, then $f$ is Riemann integrable on $[a, b]$ if and only if

$$\underline{\int_a^b} f = \overline{\int_a^b} f$$

their common value is called R-integral of $f$ on $[a, b]$ and it is denoted by $\int_a^b f$ *i.e.*,

$$\underline{\int_a^b} f = \int_a^b f = \overline{\int_a^b} f$$

The class of all bounded functions $f$ which are R-integrable on $[a, b]$ is denoted by $R[a, b]$, where $a$ and $b$ are called lower and upper limit of integration respectively.

> ***Note*** **(a)** $\int_a^b f$ exist it implies that the function is bounded and integrable over the interval $[a, b]$.
>
> **(b)** Every bounded function is not always integrable *i.e.*, there may exists a bounded function for which
>
> $$\underline{\int_a^b} f \ne \overline{\int_a^b} f$$

***Theorem*** Suppose, $f$ be a bounded function defined on a bounded interval $[a, b]$ and suppose $f$ is R-integrable on the interval $[a, b]$. Then, for every $\varepsilon > 0, \exists\, \delta > 0$ s.t. for every partition.

$P = \{a = x_0, x_1, x_2, \ldots, x_n = b\}$ with $\|P\| < \delta$ and for every choice of $\eta_r \in [x_{r-1}, x_r]$

$$\left| \sum_{r=1}^{n} f(\eta_r)(x_r - x_{r-1}) - \int_a^b f(x)\,dx \right| < \varepsilon$$

> ***Note*** From the above theorem, we can also define Riemann integral as
>
> A function $f$ is integrable if and only if
>
> $$\lim_{\|P\|\to 0} \sum_{r=1}^{n} f(\eta_r)\Delta x_r$$
>
> exists and is independent of the choice of the interval $\Delta x_r$ and of the point $\eta_r \in [x_{r-1}, x_r]$, where $P = \{a = x_0, x_1, x_2, \ldots, x_n = b\}$ be any partition of $[a, b]$. If the limit exists, then it is called the integral of $f$ over $[a, b]$.

## Oscillatory Sum

We know that

$$U(P, f) = \sum_{r=1}^{n} M_r \cdot \Delta x_r$$

and $$L(P, f) = \sum_{r=1}^{n} m_r \cdot \Delta x_r$$

Suppose, $W_r = M_r - m_r \Rightarrow W_r$ is the oscillation of $f$ on $[x_{r-1}, x_r]$.

Therefore, $$U(P, f) - L(P, f) = \sum_{r=1}^{n} (M_r - m_r)\Delta x_r = \sum_{r=1}^{n} W_r \cdot \Delta x_r$$

Then, $\sum_{r=1}^{n} W_r \cdot \Delta x_r$ is called the oscillatory sum for the function $f$ corresponding to the partition $P$. Oscillatory sum is denoted by $W(P, f)$.

## Riemann's Necessary and Sufficient Conditions for R-Integrability

Suppose, $f$ be a bounded function defined on the bounded interval $[a, b]$. Then, $f \in R[a, b]$ iff for every $\varepsilon > 0$, $\exists$ a partition $P$ of $[a, b]$ s.t. $U(P, f) - L(P, f) < \varepsilon \Rightarrow$ the oscillatory sum $W(P, f) < \varepsilon$.

> ***Note*** Alternate form of necessary and sufficient condition for R-integrability is a bounded function $f$ is said to be integrable over $[a, b]$ is that $\lim_{\|P\| \to 0} W(P, f) = 0$.

***Example 1.*** *Show that if f is defined on [a, b] by*

$$f(x) = K, \ \forall \ x \in [a, b]$$

*where, K is a constant, then* $f \in R[a, b]$ *and* $\int_a^b K = K(b-a)$.

**Solution.** Suppose, $P = \{a = x_0, x_1, \ldots, x_n = b\}$ be any partition of $[a, b]$, Then,

$$\int_a^{\bar{b}} f = \text{Inf}\,[K\Delta x_1 + K\Delta x_2 + \ldots + K\Delta x_n]$$
$$= \text{Inf}\,K[\Delta x_1 + \Delta x_2 + \ldots + \Delta x_n]$$
$$= \text{Inf}\,K(b-a) = K(b-a)$$

and $$\int_{\underline{a}}^{b} f = \text{Sup}\,[K\Delta x_1 + K\Delta x_2 + \ldots + K\Delta x_n]$$
$$= \text{Sup}\,K[\Delta x_1 + \Delta x_2 + \ldots + \Delta x_n]$$
$$= \text{Sup}\,K(b-a) = K(b-a)$$

Therefore, $K \in R[a, b]$ and $\int_a^b K = K(b-a)$.

***Example 2.*** *Let* $f(x) = x$ *on [0, 1].*

*Calculate* $\int_{\underline{0}}^{1} x\,dx$ *and* $\int_0^{\bar{1}} x\,dx$ *by dissecting [0, 1] into n equal parts and hence, show that* $f \in R[0, 1]$.

**Solution.** Let $P = \left\{0, \frac{1}{n}, \frac{2}{n}, \ldots, \frac{r-1}{n}, \ldots, \frac{n}{n} = 1\right\}$.

Here, $$m_r = \frac{r-1}{n},$$

$$M_r = \frac{r}{n} \text{ and } \Delta x_r = \frac{1}{n} \qquad (r = 1, 2, \ldots, n)$$

Now, $$L(P, f) = \left[0 \cdot \frac{1}{n} + \frac{1}{n}\cdot\frac{1}{n} + \frac{2}{n}\cdot\frac{1}{n} + \ldots + \frac{n-1}{n}\cdot\frac{1}{n}\right]$$
$$= \frac{1}{n^2}[1 + 2 + 3 + \ldots + (n-1)]$$
$$= \frac{(n-1)}{2n^2}\cdot n = \frac{n-1}{2n}$$

and $$U(P, f) = \left[\frac{1}{n}\cdot\frac{1}{n} + \frac{2}{n}\cdot\frac{1}{n} + \ldots + \frac{n}{n}\cdot\frac{1}{n}\right]$$
$$= \frac{1}{n^2}(1 + 2 + 3 + \ldots + n) = \frac{n(n+1)}{2n^2} = \frac{n+1}{2n}$$

As we know that

$$\lim_{\|P\| \to 0} U(P, f) = \int_a^{\bar{b}} f \text{ and } \lim_{\|P\| \to 0} L(P, f) = \int_{\underline{a}}^{b} f$$

From this, we get

$$\int_{\underline{0}}^{1} x\,dx = \lim_{\|P\| \to 0} L(P, f) = \lim_{n \to \infty} \frac{n-1}{2n} = \frac{1}{2}$$

and

$$\int_0^{\bar{1}} x\,dx = \lim_{\|P\| \to 0} U(P, f) = \lim_{n \to \infty} \frac{n+1}{2n} = \frac{1}{2}$$

$$\because \int_{\underline{0}}^{1} f = \int_0^{\bar{1}} f.$$

Hence, $f \in R[0, 1]$ and $\int_0^1 x\,dx = \frac{1}{2}$

***Example 3.*** *Let f be the function defined on [0, 1] by*

$$f(x) = \begin{cases} 0, & \text{when } x \text{ is irrational} \\ 1, & \text{when } x \text{ is rational} \end{cases}$$

*Calculate* $\int_{\underline{0}}^{1} f$ *and* $\int_0^{\bar{1}} f$ *and hence, show that* $f \notin R[0, 1]$.

**Solution.** Since $f$ is bounded for $0 \le f(x) \le 1$, $\forall \ x \in [0, 1]$. If $P$ is any partition, then for any sub-interval $[x_{r-1}, x_r]$ of $P$, we have $m_r = 0$ and $M_r = 1$, $r = 1, 2, \ldots, n$ [because, rational as well as irrational points are everywhere dense].

Also, $$L(P, f) = [0 \cdot \Delta x_1 + 0 \cdot \Delta x_2 + \ldots + 0 \cdot \Delta x_n] = 0$$

and $$U(P, f) = [1 \cdot \Delta x_1 + 1 \cdot \Delta x_2 + \ldots + 1 \cdot \Delta x_n]$$
$$= [\Delta x_1 + \Delta x_2 + \ldots + \Delta x_n] = 1$$

Therefore,

$$\int_{\underline{0}}^{1} f = \lim_{n \to \infty} L(P, f) = 0$$

and $$\int_0^{\bar{1}} f = \lim_{n \to \infty} U(P, f) = 1$$

$$\because \int_{\underline{0}}^{1} f \ne \int_0^{\bar{1}} f \Rightarrow f \notin R[0, 1]$$

***Example 4.*** *Find the upper and lower R-integrals for the function f defined on [0, 1] as follows.*

$$f(x) = \begin{cases} \sqrt{1-x^2} & , \text{ when } x \text{ is rational} \\ 1-x & , \text{ when } x \text{ is irrational} \end{cases}$$

**Solution.** We have,

$$(1-x^2)-(1-x)^2 = 2x-2x^2 = 2x(1-x) > 0, \forall\ x \in ]0, 1[$$

$$\Rightarrow \quad \sqrt{1-x^2} > 1-x, \forall\ x \in ]0, 1[$$

Hence,

$$\underline{\int_0^1} f = \int_0^1 (1-x)\,dx = \left[x - \frac{x^2}{2}\right]_0^1$$

$$= 1 - \frac{1}{2} = \frac{1}{2}$$

and

$$\overline{\int_0^1} f = \int_0^1 \sqrt{(1-x^2)}\,dx$$

$$= \left[\frac{1}{2}x\cdot\sqrt{1-x^2} + \frac{1}{2}\sin^{-1}x\right]_0^1$$

$$= \frac{1}{2}\cdot\frac{\pi}{2} = \frac{\pi}{4}$$

Therefore, $\underline{\int_0^1} f \neq \overline{\int_0^1} f$

It follows that $f \notin R\ [0, 1]$.

## Important Theorems on R-Integrals

***Theorem 1*** If $f$ is continuous on $[a, b]$, then $f \in R\ [a,b]$.

***Theorem 2*** If $f$ is monotonic on $[a, b]$, then $f \in R[a, b]$.

***Theorem 3*** If the set of points of discontinuities of a bounded function $f$ defined on the interval $[a, b]$ is finite, then $f \in R\ [a, b]$.

***Theorem 4*** If a function $f$ defined on $[a, b]$ is R-integrable, then $f$ is continuous almost everywhere on $[a, b]$ *i.e.*, the set of the points of discontinuity of $f$ is of measure zero.

***Theorem 5*** If the set of points of discontinuity of a bounded function $f$ defined on $[a, b]$ has only a finite number of limit points, then $f \in R\ [a, b]$.

***Theorem 6*** Suppose, $f$ be a bounded function defined on $[a, b]$ and let $f$ is continuous everywhere on $[a, b]$ *i.e.*, suppose the set of discontinuity points of $f$ on $[a, b]$ is of measure zero, then $f \in R[a,b]$.

***Theorem 7*** The necessary and sufficient condition that a bounded function $f$ defined on $[a, b]$ is R-integrable is that $f$ is continuous almost everywhere on $[a, b]$ *i.e.*, the set of discontinuity points of $f$ is of measure zero.

***Example 5.*** *Let f be a function defined by*

$$f(x) = \begin{cases} 1+x, & 0 \le x \le 1/2,\ 1/2 < x \le 1 \\ 0, & x = 1/2 \end{cases}$$

*Then,* $f \in R[0, 1]$ *and* $\int_0^1 f = \frac{3}{2}$,

*but there is no point c in [0, 1] s.t.* $\int_0^1 f = f(c)$

**Solution.** $\because f$ is bounded and has only one point of discontinuity 1/2. Therefore, $f \in R[0, 1]$.

Now, consider the partition $P = \left\{0, \frac{1}{n}, \frac{2}{n}, \ldots, \frac{n}{n} = 1\right\}$,

which is obtained by dissecting [0, 1] into $n$ equal parts

take $\eta_r = \frac{r}{n}$. Also, $\Delta x_r = \frac{1}{n}$ for $r = 1, 2, \ldots, n$

$$\therefore \quad \int_0^1 f = \lim_{n\to\infty} \sum_{r=1}^{n} \frac{1}{n}\left(1+\frac{r}{n}\right)$$

$$= \lim_{n\to\infty}\left[\frac{1}{n}\left\{\left(1+\frac{1}{n}\right)+\ldots+\left(1+\frac{1}{n}\right)\right\}\right]$$

$$= \lim_{n\to\infty} \frac{1}{n}\left\{n + \frac{1}{n}\frac{n(n+1)}{2}\right\}$$

$$= \lim_{n\to\infty} \frac{3n+1}{2n} = \frac{3}{2}$$

But there is no point of [0, 1] at which $f$ takes this value. The only likely candidate for the point $c$ is the point $\frac{1}{2}$, but $f\left(\frac{1}{2}\right) = 0$.

## Algebra for Integrals

If $b < a$, then we can define $\int_a^b f$ to be $-\int_b^a f$ provided that $f \in R[a, b]$.

Also, $\quad \int_a^a f = 0$

## Important Theorems on Algebra for Integrals

1. Suppose, $f \in R[a, b]$ and let $m$ and $M$ be bounds of $f$ on $[a, b]$. Then,
$$m(b-a) \le \int_a^b f(x)\,dx \le M(b-a), \text{ if } b \ge a, \text{ if } b \le a, \text{ then } m(b-a) \ge \int_a^b f(x)\,dx \ge M(b-a).$$
2. (First Mean Value Theorem of Integral Calculus) Suppose, $f \in R[a, b]$. Then, $\exists$ a number $\mu$ lying between the bounds $m$ and $M$ of $f$, such that
$$\int_a^b f(x)\,dx = \mu\,(b-a)$$
3. Let $f$ be continuous on $[a, b]$, then $\exists$ a point $c \in [a, b]$ s.t.
$$\int_a^b f = (b-a)\ f(c)$$
4. Let $f \in R\ [a, b]$ and let $N$ be a number, such that $|\ f(x)| \le N\ |\ b-a|$
5. Let $f,\ g \in R\ [a, b]$. Then,
$$f \ge g \Rightarrow \begin{cases} \int_a^b f(x)\,dx \ge \int_a^b g(x)\,dx, \text{ if } b \ge a \\ \int_a^b f(x)\,dx \le \int_a^b g(x)\,dx, \text{ if } b \le a \end{cases}$$
6. Suppose, $f \in R[a, b]$ and let $a < c < b$, then $f \in R[a, c]$, $f \in R[c, b]$ and $\int_a^b f = \int_a^c f + \int_c^b f$
7. Suppose, $f \in R[a, b]$ and $[c, d] \subset [a, b]$, then $f \in R[c, d]$
8. If $f \in R[a, b]$ and $l \in R$, then if $f \in R[a, b]$ and $\int_a^b lf = l \int_a^b f$.
9. If $f \in R[a, b]$, then $-f \in R[a, b]$ and $\int_a^b (-f) = -\int_a^b f$.
10. If $f \in R\ [a, b]$ and $g \in R\ [a, b]$, then $f + g \in R[a, b]$, $f - g \in R\ [a, b]$.
Also, $\int_a^b (f+g) = \int_a^b f + \int_a^b g$ and $\int_a^b f - g = \int_a^b f - \int_a^b g$.
11. If $f, g \in R[a, b]$, then $l_1 f + l_2 g \in R[a, b]$
Moreover $\int_a^b (l_1 f_1 + l_2 f_2) = l_1 \int_a^b f_1 + l_2 \int_a^b f_2$.
12. If $f \in R[a, b]$ and $g \in R[a, b]$ and if $f(x) \le g(x)$, $\forall\ x \in [a, b]$, then $\int_a^b f \le \int_a^b g$.
13. If $f \in R[a, b]$, then $|f| \in R[a, b]$ and $|\int_a^b f| \le \int_a^b |f|$
14. If $f \in R[a, b]$ and $g \in R[a, b]$, then $fg \in R[a, b]$.
15. Let $f \in R[a, b]$ and $g \in R[a, b]$
$$|g(x)| \ge l,\ l > 0,\ \forall x \text{ in } [a, b], \text{ then } \frac{f}{g} \in R\ [a, b].$$

## Primitive or Anti-derivative

A differentiable function $\phi$ defined on $[a, b]$ s.t. its derivative $\phi'$ equals to a given function $f$ on $[a, b]$ is called a primitive or anti-derivative of $f$ on $[a, b]$.

> ***Note*** **(a)** The primitive of a function is not unique. If $\phi$ is primitive of $f$, then $\phi + c$ is also primitive of $f$, where $c$ is an arbitrary constant.
> **(b)** If $b < a$, then we define
> $$\int_a^b f = -\int_a^b f$$

## Important Theorems on Primitive

***Theorem 1*** Let $f \in R[a, b]$. Then, the function $F$ defined on $[a, b]$ by $F(x) = \int_a^x f(t)\,dt$ is continuous on $[a, b]$.

***Theorem 2*** Suppose, $f$ be continuous on $[a, b]$ and suppose, $F(x) = \int_a^x f(t)\,dt,\ \forall\ x \in [a, b]$.

Then, $F'(x) = f(x),\ \forall\ x \in [a, b]$.

***Theorem 3*** Suppose, $f \in R[a, b]$ and let $f$ be continuous at $x_0 \in [a, b]$. If $F(x) = \int_a^x f(t)\,dt,\ a \le x \le b$, then

$$F'(x_0) = f(x_0)$$

***Theorem 4*** (Fundamental Theorem) Suppose, $f \in R[a, b]$ and suppose $\phi$ be a differentiable function on $[a, b]$ s.t. $\phi'(x) = f(x),\ \forall\ x \in [a, b]$. Then,

$$\int_a^b f(x)\,dx = \phi(b) - \phi(a)$$

***Theorem 5*** Suppose, $f$ be continuous function on $[a, b]$ and suppose $\phi$ be a differentiable function on $[a, b]$ s.t.

$$\phi'(x) = f(x), \forall\ x \in [a, b]$$

Then, $$\int_a^b f(t)dt = \phi(b) - \phi(a)$$

***Example 6.*** *Evaluate* $\int_1^2 x^3 dx$.

**Solution.** Let $f(x) = x^3, 1 \le x \le 2$. Then, $f$ is continuous on $[a, b]$.

If $\phi(x) = \frac{x^4}{4}[1 \le x \le 2]$, then $\phi'(x) = x^3 = f(x),\ (1 \le x \le 2)$

Therefore, by Fundamental theorem

$$\int_1^2 x^3 dx = \phi(2) - \phi(1) = \frac{2^4}{4} - \frac{1}{4} = \frac{15}{4}.$$

## Mean Value Theorems

***Theorem 1*** (First Mean Value Theorem) Suppose, $f \in R[a, b]$, then $\exists$ a number $\mu$ lying between $m$ and $M$ of $f$ s.t.

$$\int_a^b f(x)\,dx = \mu(b - a)$$

Moreover, if $f$ is continuous, then

$$\int_a^b f(x)\,dx = (b - a) f(c),\ a \le c \le b$$

***Theorem 2*** (Second Mean Value Theorem) Let $f \in R[a, b]$ and $g \in R[a, b]$ and $g(x) \ge 0$ or $\le 0,\ \forall\ x \in [a, b]$, then $\exists$ a number $\mu$ with $m \le \mu \le M$ s.t.

$$\int_a^b f(x) g(x)\,dx = \mu \int_a^b g(x)\,dx$$

where $m$ and $M$ are the bounds of $f$ on $[a, b]$.

***Theorem 3*** If in addition to the continuous of the above theorem $f$ is continuous as well, then $\exists\ \eta \in [a, b]$ s.t.

$$\int_a^b f(x) g(x)\,dx = f(\eta) \int_a^b g(x)\,dx$$

***Theorem 4*** (Bonnet's Mean Value Theorem) Suppose, $g \in R[a, b]$ and suppose $f$ be monotonic and non-negative on $[a, b]$, then for some $\xi$ or $\eta \in [a, b]$

$$\int_a^b f(x)\,g(x)\,dx = f(a) \int_a^\xi g(x)\,dx$$

or $$\int_a^b f(x) g(x)\,dx = f(b) \int_\eta^b g(x)\,dx$$

According as $f$ is monotonically non-increasing or non-decreasing on $[a, b]$.

***Theorem 5*** [Weierstrass's (Second) Mean Value Theorem]

Suppose, $g \in R[a, b]$ and suppose $f$ be bounded and monotonic on $[a, b]$, then

$$\int_a^b fg = f(a) \int_a^\xi g + f(b) \int_\xi^b g$$

***Theorem 6*** Suppose, $g$ be a real-valued function on the closed bounded interval $[a, b]$ s.t. $g'$ is continuous on $[a, b]$. Let $\alpha = g(a)$ and $\beta = g(b)$

If $f$ is continuous function on $[a, b]$, then

$$\int_\alpha^\beta f = \int_a^b (fog) \cdot g'$$

*i.e.* $$\int_\alpha^\beta f(x)\,dx = \int_a^b f[g(u)] g'(u)\,du$$

***Theorem 7*** Let $f$ and $g$ be continuous on $[a, b]$ and have, bounded and continuous derivatives on $[a, b]$. Then,

$$\int_a^b f(x) g'(x)\,dx = f(b) g(b) - f(a) g(a) - \int_a^b g(x) f'(x)\,dx$$

***Theorem 8*** If $f \in R[a, b]$, then

**(i)** $\lim_{n \to \infty} \sum_1^n h f(a + rh) = \int_a^b f$, where $b - a = nh$

**(ii)** $\lim_{n \to \infty} \sum_1^n f(ah^r) = (ah^r - ah^{r-1}) = \int_a^b f$,

where $h^n = \frac{b}{a} \in R_+$.

***Example 7.*** *A function f is defined on* $[0, 1]$ *by* $f(x) = \frac{1}{2^n}$ *for* $\frac{1}{2^{n+1}} < x \le \frac{1}{2^n}$, $n = 0, 1, 2, \ldots$ *and* $f(0) = 0$. *Show that* $f \in R[0, 1]$ *and calculate the value of* $\int_a^x f(t)\,dt$ *where x lies between* $\frac{1}{2^m}$ *and* $\frac{1}{2^{m-1}}$.

**Solution.** Clearly, $f$ is discontinuous at $x = \frac{1}{2^n}$

$$f\left(\frac{1}{2^n} + 0\right) = \frac{1}{2^{n-1}} \text{ and } f\left(\frac{1}{2^n} - 0\right) = \frac{1}{2^n}$$

There are points of discontinuity which are $1, \frac{1}{2}, \frac{1}{2^2}, \frac{1}{2^3}, \ldots$

$\therefore$ Points of discontinuity of $f$ have only one limiting point at $x = 0$, it follows that $f \in R[0, 1]$.

Now, $$\int_0^x f(t)\,dt = \int_{1/2^m}^x f + \int_{1/2^{m+1}}^{1/2^m} f + \int_{1/2^{m+2}}^{1/2^{m+1}} f + \ldots$$

$$= \int_{1/2^m}^x \frac{1}{2^{m-1}} + \int_{1/2^{m+1}}^{1/2^m} \frac{1}{2^m} + \int_{1/2^{m+2}}^{1/2^{m+1}} \frac{1}{2^{m+1}} + \ldots$$

$$= \frac{1}{2^{m-1}}\left[x - \frac{1}{2^m}\right] + \frac{1}{2^m}\left(\frac{1}{2^m} - \frac{1}{2^{m+1}}\right)$$

$$+ \frac{1}{2^{m+1}}\left(\frac{1}{2^{m+1}} - \frac{1}{2^{m+2}}\right) + \dots$$

$$= \frac{1}{2^{m-1}}\left(x - \frac{1}{2^m}\right) + \frac{1}{2^{2m+1}} + \frac{1}{2^{2m+3}} + \frac{1}{2^{2m+5}} + \dots$$

$$= \frac{x}{2^{m-1}} - \frac{1}{2^{2m-1}} + \frac{\frac{1}{2^{2m+1}}}{1 - \frac{1}{4}}$$

$$= \frac{x}{2^{m-1}} - \frac{1}{2^{2m-1}} + \frac{1}{3 \cdot 2^{2m-1}} = \frac{x}{2^{m-1}} - \frac{1}{3 \cdot 2^{2m+2}}$$

***Example 8.*** *A function f is defined on [0, 1] by* $f(x) = \frac{1}{n}$ *for* $\frac{1}{n} \ge x > \frac{1}{(n+1)}$, $n = 1, 2, 3, \dots$. *Prove that* $f \in R[0, 1]$ *and evaluate* $\int_0^1 f(x)\, dx$.

**Solution.** Clearly, $f$ is discontinuous at the points

$$1, \frac{1}{2}, \frac{1}{3}, \frac{1}{4}, \dots \qquad \dots \text{(i)}$$

$\because$ The set Eq. (i) has only one limit point at $x = 0$,

$\therefore$ $f \in R[0, 1]$

Now,

$$\int_0^1 f(x)\, dx = \lim_{n\to\infty} \sum_{r=1}^{n} \int_{1/(r+1)}^{1/r} \frac{1}{r}\, dr = \lim_{n\to\infty} \sum_{r=1}^{n} \frac{1}{r}\left(\frac{1}{r} - \frac{1}{r+1}\right)$$

$$= \lim_{n\to\infty}\left[\left(1 - \frac{1}{2}\right) + \frac{1}{2}\left(\frac{1}{2} - \frac{1}{3}\right) + \dots + \frac{1}{n}\left(\frac{1}{n} - \frac{1}{n+1}\right)\right]$$

$$= \lim_{n\to\infty}\left[\left(1 + \frac{1}{2^2} + \dots + \frac{1}{n^2}\right) - \left(\frac{1}{2} + \frac{1}{2} - \frac{1}{3} + \frac{1}{3} - \frac{1}{4} + \dots + \dots \frac{1}{n} - \frac{1}{n+1}\right)\right]$$

$$= \lim_{n\to\infty}\left[\left(1 + \frac{1}{2^2} + \dots + \frac{1}{n^2}\right) - \left(1 - \frac{1}{n+1}\right)\right]$$

$$= \frac{\pi^2}{6} - 1$$

[$\because$ The series $1 + \frac{1}{2^2} + \frac{1}{3^2} + \dots$ is known to converge to $\frac{\pi^2}{6}$]

## Improper Integrals

If the function $f$ becomes unbounded on $[a, b]$ or if the limits of integration become infinite, then the integral $\int_a^b f(x)\,dx$ is called an improper integral. If either one or both the limits of integration become infinite and the integrand bounded, then $\int_a^b f(x)\,dx$ is called an improper integral of first kind. If $f$ becomes unbounded on $[a, b]$ and the limits of integration are finite, then $\int_a^b f(x)\, dx$ is an improper integral of second kind.

## Integral with Infinite Limits

If the function $f$ is bounded and integrable for $x \ge a$, then

$$\int_a^\infty f(x)\,dx = \lim_{t\to\infty} \int_a^t f(x)\,dx,$$

or

$$\int_a^\infty f(x)\, dx = \lim_{\varepsilon\to 0} \int_a^{1/\varepsilon} f(x)\, dx$$

The above integral $\int_a^\infty f(x)\,dx$ is said to converge, if the above limit exists. Otherwise, it is called a divergent integral.

The integral $\int_a^\infty f(x)\,dx$ is said to converge to the value $l$, if for any given $\varepsilon > 0$, $\exists\, m > 0$ s.t. $\left| \int_a^r f(x)\,dx - l \right| < \varepsilon$, for every $r \ge m$.

***Theorem*** The necessary and sufficient condition for the convergence of the integral $\int_a^\infty f(x)\,dx$ is that for a given $\varepsilon$, however small, a number $m$ can be found s.t.

$$\left|\int_{x_1}^{x_2} f(x)\,dx\right| < \varepsilon, \forall\, x_1 \text{ and } x_2 \text{ for which } x_2 > x_1 > m.$$

## Test for Convergence of $\int_a^\infty f(x)\,dx$

### 1. Comparison Test

Suppose, $f(x)$ and $\phi(x)$ are two functions which are bounded and integrable in the interval $[a, \infty[$. Let $f(x)$ be positive and $|\phi(x)| \le f(x)$, when $x \ge a$. Then, if $\int_a^\infty f(x)\,dx$ is convergent it follows that $\int_a^\infty \phi(x)$ is also convergent and that $\int_a^\infty \phi(x)\,dx \le \int_a^\infty f(x)\,dx$ and if $|\phi(x)| \ge f(x)$ for all values of $x$ greater than some number $x_0 > a$ and $\int_a^\infty f(x)\,dx$ is divergent, then $\int_a^\infty \phi(x)\,dx$ is also divergent.

### Test of Convergence for the Integral $\int_a^\infty \frac{dx}{x^n}$, $a > 0$

$$\int_a^\infty \frac{dx}{x^n} = \lim_{\varepsilon\to 0} \int_0^{1/\varepsilon} \frac{dx}{x^n} = \begin{cases} \frac{a^{1-n}}{n-1}, & n > 1 \\ \infty, & n < 1 \end{cases}$$

when $n = 1$, we have

$$\int_a^\infty \frac{dx}{x^n} = \lim_{\varepsilon\to 0} \int_a^{1/\varepsilon} \frac{dx}{x}$$

$$= \lim_{\varepsilon\to 0}\left[\log \frac{1}{\varepsilon} - \log a\right] = \infty$$

Therefore, when $n > 1$, the integral converges and when $n \le 1$, then the integral is not convergent.

***Example 9.*** *Test the convergence of* $\int_0^\infty \frac{\sin x}{1+x^2}dx$

**Solution.** We have, $f(x) = \frac{\sin x}{1+x^2}$,

Suppose, $\phi(x) = \frac{1}{1+x^2}$

$$\left|\frac{\sin x}{1+x^2}\right| \le \frac{1}{1+x^2} \qquad [\because |\sin x| \le 1]$$

and $\int_0^\infty \frac{1}{1+x^2} = \lim_{\varepsilon\to 0}\int_0^{1/\varepsilon} \frac{dx}{1+x^2} = \lim_{\varepsilon\to 0}[\tan^{-1} x]_0^{1/\varepsilon} = \frac{\pi}{2}$

$\therefore$ $\int_0^\infty \frac{dx}{1+x^2}$ is convergent.

$\therefore$ By comparison test, we have

$\int_0^\infty \frac{\sin x}{1+x^2}dx$ is also convergent.

## 2. μ-Test

Suppose, $f$ be a bounded and integrable function in the interval $[a, \infty[$, where $a>0$

If there is a number $\mu > 1$, s.t. $\lim_{x\to\infty} x^\mu f(x)$ exists, then $\int_a^\infty f(x)dx$ converges absolutely.

If $\mu \le 1$ s.t. $\lim_{x\to\infty} x^\mu f(x)$ exists and is not zero, then the integral $\int_a^\infty f(x)dx$ is divergent and the same is hold, if $\lim_{x\to\infty} x^\mu f(x)$ is $+\infty$ or $-\infty$.

## 3. Abel's Test

If $\int_a^\infty f(x)dx$ converges and $\phi(x)$ is bounded and monotonic for $x>a$, then $\int_a^\infty f(x)\phi(x)dx$ is convergent.

## 4. Dirichlet's Test

If $f(x)$ be bounded and monotonic in $[a, \infty[$ and if $\lim_{x\to\infty} f(x)=0$, then integral $\int_a^\infty f(x)\cdot\phi(x)dx$ converges provided

$|\int_a^x \phi(x)dx|$ is bounded as $x$ takes all finite values.

***Example 10.*** *Examine the convergence of* $\int_0^\infty \frac{dx}{x^{1/3}(1+x^{1/2})}$.

**Solution.** We have, $\int_0^\infty \frac{dx}{x^{1/3}(1+x^{1/2})}$, here $f(x) = \frac{1}{x^{1/3}(1+x^{1/2})}$

Take $\mu = \frac{5}{6}$; then

$$\lim_{x\to\infty} x^\mu f(x) = \lim_{x\to\infty} x^{5/6}\frac{1}{x^{1/3}(1+x^{1/2})}$$

$$= \lim_{x\to\infty}\frac{x^{5/6}}{x^{1/3}\cdot x^{1/2}\{1+(1/x^{1/2})\}} = \lim_{x\to\infty}\frac{1}{1+(1/x^{1/2})}$$

$\because$ $\mu<1$ and the limit is non-zero, therefore from μ-test, the given integral is divergent.

***Example 11.*** *Test the convergence of* $\int_a^\infty (1-e^{-x})\frac{\cos x}{x^2}dx$.

**Solution.** We have, $\int_a^\infty (1-e^{-x})\frac{\cos x}{x^2}$, for this we apply Abel's test

Take $\phi(x) = 1-e^{-x}$

$\because$ $\frac{\cos x}{x^2} \le \frac{1}{x^2}$ and $\frac{1}{x^2}$ is convergent, therefore by comparison test, $\int_0^\infty \frac{\cos x}{x^2}$ is also convergent. Also, $(1-e^{-x})$ is monotonic increasing and bounded function for $x>a$. Therefore, by Abel's test $\int_a^\infty (1-e^{-x})\frac{\cos x}{x^2}$ is convergent.

***Example 12.*** *Show that the integral* $\int_0^\infty e^{-ax}\frac{\sin x}{x}dx$, $a\ge 0$ *is convergent.*

**Solution.** We have,

$$\int_0^\infty e^{-ax}\frac{\sin x}{x}dx = \int_0^\alpha e^{-ax}\frac{\sin x}{x}dx + \int_\alpha^\infty e^{-ax}\frac{\sin x}{x}dx,\ \alpha>0$$

$\because$ $\lim_{x\to 0} e^{-ax}\frac{\sin x}{x} = 1$ and $\int_0^\alpha e^{-\alpha x}\frac{\sin x}{x}dx$ is a proper integral.

Therefore, we only consider

$$\int_\alpha^\infty e^{-ax}\frac{\sin x}{x}dx$$

Suppose, $f(x) = \frac{e^{-ax}}{x}$ and $\phi(x) = \sin x$. Clearly, $f(x)$ is bounded and monotonic decreasing function of $x$, when $x$ takes all finite values greater than zero.

Also, $\lim_{x\to\infty} f(x) = \lim_{x\to\infty}\frac{e^{-ax}}{x} = 0$

and $|\int_a^x \phi(x)dx| = |\int_a^x \sin x dx|$ is bounded for all finite values of $x$. Therefore, By Dirichlet's test, the integral $\int_a^\infty f(x)\phi(x)dx$ is convergent, *i.e.*,

$\int_a^\infty e^{-ax}\frac{\sin x}{x}dx$ is convergent.

Hence, $\int_0^\infty e^{-ax}\frac{\sin x}{x}dx$ is convergent.

# Absolute Convergence

If $f$ is bounded and integrable on $[a, x]$, $\forall\, x\ge a$ and if $\int_a^\infty |f(x)|\,dx$ exists, then $\int_a^\infty f(x)\,dx$ also exists. Or we can say that the integral $\int_a^\infty f(x)dx$ will converges, if it converges absolutely.

> ***Note*** Absolute convergence gives a sufficient but not a necessary condition for the convergence of an infinite integral.

***Example 13.*** *Test the integral* $\int_0^\infty f(x)\,dx$ *for absolute convergence, where f(x) is defined as*

$$f(x) = \begin{cases} 1 & , \quad 0 \le x \le 1 \\ 0 & , \quad n-1 < x \le n - \dfrac{1}{n} \\ (-1)^{n+1} & , \quad n - \dfrac{1}{n} < x \le n \end{cases}$$

*when n = 2, 3, 4,...*

**Solution.** We have,

$$\int_a^\infty f(x)\,dx = \int_0^1 f(x)\,dx + \int_1^{1\frac{1}{2}} f(x)\,dx + \int_{1\frac{1}{2}}^2 f(x)\,dx + \ldots$$

$$= \int_0^1 dx + \int_1^{1\frac{1}{2}} 0\,dx - \int_{1\frac{1}{2}}^2 dx + \ldots$$

$$= 1 - \frac{1}{2} + \frac{1}{3} - \frac{1}{4} + \ldots$$

We know that the series on the right hand side is convergent. Its value being log 2.

Therefore, the given integral is convergent. *i.e.,*

$$\int_0^\infty |f(x)|\,dx = \int_0^1 |f(x)|\,dx + \int_1^{1\frac{1}{2}} |f(x)|\,dx + \int_{1\frac{1}{2}}^2 f(x)\,dx + \ldots$$

$$= 1 + \frac{1}{2} + \frac{1}{3} + \ldots$$

The series is divergent.

$\therefore \int_0^\infty |f(x)|\,dx$ is divergent. It follows that given integral converges but not absolutely.

> ***Note*** $\int_a^\infty f(x)dx$ is said to be converges conditionally, if $\int_a^\infty f(x)\,dx$ converges but not absolutely.

# Tests for the Convergence of the Improper Integral $\int_a^b f(x)dx$

## 1. Comparison Test

Let $f(x)$ be positive and $|\phi(x)| \le f(x)$ in the interval $[a+\varepsilon, b]$. Then, $\int_a^b \phi(x)\,dx$ is convergent provided $\int_a^b f(x)\,dx$ is convergent. If $|\phi(x)| \ge f(x)$, $\forall$ x in $[a+\varepsilon, b]$, then $\int_a^b \phi(x)\,dx$ is divergent provided $\int_a^b f(x)\,dx$ is divergent.

## 2. Test the Convergence of $\int_a^b \dfrac{dx}{(x-a)^n}$

We have, $\displaystyle\int_a^b \frac{dx}{(x-a)^n} = \lim_{\varepsilon\to 0}\int_{a+\varepsilon}^b \frac{dx}{(x-a)^n}$

$$= \lim_{\varepsilon\to 0} \frac{1}{1-n}[(b-a)^{1-n} - \varepsilon^{1-n}]$$

$$= \begin{cases} \dfrac{1}{1-n}(b-a)^{1-n}, & \text{if } n<1 \\ \infty & , \text{if } n>1 \end{cases}$$

When $n = 1$, we have

$$\int_a^b \frac{dx}{(x-a)} = \lim_{\varepsilon\to 0}\int_{a+\varepsilon}^b \frac{dx}{(x-a)}$$

$$= \lim_{\varepsilon\to 0} [\log(b-a) - \log\varepsilon] = \infty$$

Therefore, the integral is convergent, if $n < 1$ and divergent, if $n \ge 1$.

## 3. The μ-Test

Suppose, $f(x)$ be unbounded at a and integrable in the arbitrary interval $[a+\varepsilon, b]$, where $0 < \varepsilon < b - a$. If there is a number μ between zero and 1 s.t. $\lim_{x\to a+0} (x-a)^\mu f(x)$ exists, then $\int_a^b f(x)\,dx$ converges absolutely. If there is a number $\mu \ge 1$ s.t. $\lim_{x\to a+0} (x-a)^\mu f(x)$ exists and is not zero, then $\int_a^b f(x)\,dx$ diverges and the same is true, if $\lim_{x\to a+0} (x-a)^\mu f(x) = \pm\infty$.

> ***Note*** If $f(x)$ is unbounded at $x = b$, then we find $\lim_{x\to b-0} (b-x)^\mu f(x)$, and the other conditions remaining the same.

## 4. Abel's Test

If $\int_a^b f(x)\,dx$ converges and $\phi(x)$ bounded monotonic on $[a, b]$. Then, $\int_a^b f(x)\cdot\phi(x)\,dx$ converges.

## 5. Dirichlet's Test

If $\int_{a+\varepsilon}^b f(x)\,dx$ be bounded and $\phi(x)$ be bounded and monotonic on $[a, b]$, converging to zero as x tends to a, then $\int_a^b f(x)\cdot\phi(x)\,dx$ is convergent.

***Example 14.*** *Prove that the integral* $\int_0^1 \dfrac{\sec x}{x}dx$ *is divergent.*

**Solution.** We have, $\int_0^1 \dfrac{\sec x}{x}dx$

$\because$ $|\sec x| \ge 1$, $\forall$ x and therefore, we have $\left|\dfrac{\sec x}{x}\right| \ge \dfrac{1}{x}$ and the integral $\int_0^1 \dfrac{1}{x}dx$ is divergent. Therefore, the integral $\int_0^1 \dfrac{\sec x}{x}dx$ is also divergent.

***Example 15.*** *Test the convergence of* $\int_0^1 \frac{dx}{\sqrt{x(1-x)}}$.

**Solution.** The integrand $f(x) = \frac{1}{\sqrt{x(1-x)}}$ is unbounded at $x=0$ and $x=1$.

Now, $\int_0^1 \frac{dx}{\sqrt{x(1-x)}} = \int_0^a \frac{dx}{\sqrt{x(1-x)}} + \int_a^1 \frac{dx}{\sqrt{x(1-x)}}$

Now, we apply $\mu$-test

Let $f(x) = \frac{1}{\sqrt{x(1-x)}}$, then $\int_0^a \frac{dx}{\sqrt{x(1-x)}}$ converges.

$\because \lim_{x\to 0} x^{1/2} f(x) = \lim_{x\to 0} \frac{1}{\sqrt{1-x}} = 1$

and $\int_a^1 \frac{dx}{\sqrt{x(1-x)}}$ also convergent.

because $\lim_{x\to 1-0} [(1-x)^{1/2} f(x)] = \lim_{x\to 1-0} \frac{1}{x^{1/2}} = \lim_{h\to 0} \frac{1}{(1-h)^{1/2}} = 1$

$\therefore$ The given integral converges.

***Example 16.*** *Test the convergence of the integral*

$$\int_0^{\pi/2} \log \sin x\, dx.$$

**Solution.** We have, $\int_0^{\pi/2} \log \sin x\, dx$, the only point of infinite discontinuity is $x=0$.

Now, $\lim_{x\to 0} x^{\mu} \log \sin x$, where $\mu > 0$

$$= \lim_{x\to 0} \frac{\log \sin x}{x^{-\mu}} \qquad \left[\text{form } \frac{\infty}{\infty}\right]$$

$$= \lim_{x\to 0} \frac{\cot x}{-\mu x^{-\mu-1}} \qquad \text{[by D'L'Hospital rule]}$$

$$= \lim_{x\to 0} \frac{-1}{\mu} \frac{x^{\mu+1}}{\tan x} \qquad \left[\text{form } \frac{0}{0}\right]$$

$$= \lim_{x\to 0} \frac{-1}{\mu} \frac{(\mu+1)\, x^{\mu}}{\sec^2 x} = 0, \text{ if } \mu > 0$$

Choose $0 < \mu < 1$, it follows from $\mu$-test that the given integral is convergent.

***Example 17.*** *Show that the integral* $\int_0^{\infty} e^{-a^2x^2} \cos bx\, dx$ *is absolutely convergent.*

**Solution.** We have,

$$\int_0^{\infty} |e^{-a^2x^2} \cos bx|\, dx \le \int_0^{\infty} |e^{-a^2x^2}|\, dx$$
$$= \int_0^{\infty} e^{-a^2x^2} dx$$
$$= \int_0^{\alpha} e^{-a^2x^2} dx + \int_{\alpha}^{\infty} e^{-a^2x^2} dx$$

But the integral $\int_0^{\alpha} e^{-a^2x^2} dx$ is a proper integral and $\int_{\alpha}^{\infty} e^{-a^2x^2} dx$ is convergent by $\mu$-test, we have

$$\lim_{x\to\infty} x^{\mu} e^{-a^2x^2} = \lim_{x\to\infty} \frac{x^{\mu}}{1 + a^2x^2 + \frac{a^4x^4}{2!} + \ldots} = 0, \ \forall\, \mu$$

Choose $\mu > 1$, we observe that $\int_{\alpha}^{\infty} e^{-a^2x^2} dx$ is convergent. Therefore, $\int_0^{\infty} |e^{-a^2x^2} \cos bx|\, dx$ is also convergent, by Comparison test. Hence, the given integral $\int_0^{\infty} e^{-a^2x^2} \cos bx\, dx$ is absolutely convergent.

***Example 18.*** *Prove that the integral* $\int_0^{\infty} \frac{\sin x}{x} dx$ *converges but not absolutely.*

**Solution.** We have,

$$\int_0^{\infty} \frac{\sin x}{x} dx = \int_0^{\alpha} \frac{\sin x}{x} dx + \int_{\alpha}^{\infty} \frac{\sin x}{x} dx, \ \alpha > 0$$

$$\because \quad \lim_{x\to 0} \frac{\sin x}{x} = 1,$$

$\therefore \int_0^{\alpha} \frac{\sin x}{x} dx$ is proper integral. So, we only consider $\int_{\alpha}^{\infty} \frac{\sin x}{x} dx.$

Suppose, $\quad f(x) = \frac{1}{x}$ and $\phi(x) = \sin x$.

Clearly, $f(x)$ is bounded and monotonic decreasing function and $\lim_{x\to\infty} f(x) = \lim_{x\to\infty} \frac{1}{x} = 0.$

Also, $\quad \left|\int_{\alpha}^{\infty} \phi(x)\, dx\right| = \left|\int_{\alpha}^{x} \sin x\, dx\right|$

is bounded for all finite values of $x$. Therefore, by Dirichlet's test, the integral $\int_{\alpha}^{\infty} f(x)\cdot\phi(x)\, dx \Rightarrow \int_{\alpha}^{\infty} \frac{\sin x}{x} dx$ is convergent.

Hence, $\int_0^{\infty} \frac{\sin x}{x} dx$ is convergent.

## Operations with Improper Integrals

The integral $\int_a^{\infty} f(x, \alpha)\, dx$ is said to be converge uniformly, in the interval $\alpha_0 \le \alpha \le \alpha_1$, if given $\varepsilon > 0$, $\exists$ a number $m$, independent of $\alpha$, s.t.

$\left|\int_p^{\infty} f(x, \alpha)\, dx\right| < \varepsilon$, for every value of $\alpha$ in the interval $[\alpha_0, \alpha_1]$, where $p \ge m$.

## Integration under the Integral Sign

If $f(x, \alpha)$ is continuous in $x$ and $\alpha$ for $\alpha_0 \le \alpha < \alpha_1$ and for all values of $x \ge \alpha_1$, then

$F(\alpha) = \int_{\alpha}^{\infty} f(x, \alpha)\, dx$ can be integrated under the integral sign with respect to $\alpha$ in any interval $[\beta_1, \beta_2]$ contained in $[\alpha_0, \alpha_1]$ to give

$$\int_{\beta_1}^{\beta_2} F(\alpha)\, dx = \int_{\alpha}^{\infty} \int_{\beta_1}^{\beta_2} f(x, \alpha)\, dx\, d\alpha$$

provided $\int_a^{\infty} f(x, \alpha)\, dx$ converges uniformly on $[\alpha_0, \alpha_1]$.

# SOLVED EXAMPLES

## Type I (*Only one correct option*)

***Example 1.*** *The integral* $\int_{-1}^{1}|x|\,dx$ *is*

(a) $-1$ (b) 1

(c) 0 (d) None of these

**Solution.** (b) The given function is bounded and continuous on $[-1,1]$ and given by

$$f(x)=\begin{cases} x, x\geq 0 \\ -x, x\leq 0\end{cases}$$

Let $P=\{-1=x_0,x_1,\ldots,x_n=0=y_0,y_1,\ldots,y_n=1\}$

be a partition of $[-1,1]$ which divide $[-1,1]$ into $2n$ equal sub-intervals each of length $\frac{1}{n}$, so that $\mu(P)=\frac{1}{n}\to 0$ as $n\to\infty$.

$$x_i=-1+\frac{i}{n}, i=1,2,\ldots,n$$

$$y_i=\frac{i}{n}, i=1,2,\ldots,n$$

$$\Delta x_i=\frac{1}{n}=\Delta y_i$$

Also, $\Sigma\Delta x_i=\frac{1}{n}=\Sigma\Delta y_i$

Now, let $t_i\in\Delta x_i$ and $t_i'\in\Delta y_i$ and $t_i=n_i, t_i'=y_i$ where $i=1,2,\ldots,n$

Then,

$$S(P,f)=\sum_{i=1}^{n}f(t_i)\Delta x_i+\sum_{i=1}^{n}f(t_i')\Delta y_i$$

$$=\sum_{i=1}^{n}(-x_i)\Delta x_i+\sum_{i=1}^{n}y_i\Delta y_i$$

$$=\sum_{i=1}^{n}\left(1-\frac{i}{n}\right)\Delta x_i+\sum_{i=1}^{n}\frac{i}{n}\Delta y_i$$

$$=\sum_{i=1}^{n}\Delta x_i-\frac{1}{n^2}\sum_{i=1}^{n}i+\frac{1}{n^2}\sum_{i=1}^{n}i$$

$$\Rightarrow \lim_{\mu(P)\to 0}S(P,f)=1$$

$$\Rightarrow \int_{-1}^{1}|x|\,dx=\lim_{\mu(P)\to 0}S(P,t)=1$$

***Example 2.*** *If* $f(x)/\phi(x)\to l$ *where* $x\to a$ *and* $l$ *is neither 0 nor infinite and given two integrals*

(A) $\int_a^b f(x)\,dx$ *and* (B) $\int_a^b \phi(x)\,dx$

(a) (A) converge but (B) does not

(b) (B) converge but (A) does not

(c) Either both converges or both do not converges

(d) None of them converges

**Solution.** (c) Since, $f(x)/\phi(x)$ is positive, $\forall\, x$ limit $f(x)/\phi(x)=l$ cannot be negative.

Let $\delta$ be a positive number less than $l$ so that there exists a number $c$, $(a<c<b)$, such that

$$l-\delta<\frac{f(x)}{\phi(x)}<l+\delta$$

when $a<x\leq c$

i.e. $\forall\, x\in(a,c]$

we have $\forall\, x\in(a,c]$

(i) $(l-\delta)\phi(x)<f(x)$

and $f(x)<(l+\delta)\phi(x)$ ...(i)

Now, $\int_a^b f(x)\,dx$ converges

$\Rightarrow \int_a^c f(x)\,dx$ converges;

$\Rightarrow (l-\delta)\int_a^c f(x)\,dx$ converges;

$\Rightarrow \int_a^c \phi(x)\,dx$ converges;

$\Rightarrow \int_a^b \phi(x)\,dx$ converges.

It may similarly be shown that

$\int_a^b \phi(x)\,dx$ does not converge $\Rightarrow \int_a^b f(x)\,dx$ does not converge.

Also, from Eq. (ii), we get

$\int_a^b \phi(x)\,dx$ converges $\Rightarrow \int_a^b f(x)\,dx$ converges,

$\int_a^b f(x)\,dx$ does not converge $\Rightarrow \int_a^b \phi(x)\,dx$ does not converge.

***Example 3.*** *Let the function f is defined as follows*

$$f(x)=\begin{cases}\dfrac{1}{2^n}, & \dfrac{1}{2^{n+1}}<x\leq\dfrac{1}{2^n}, n=0,1,2,\ldots \\ 0, & else\end{cases}$$

*Then,* $\int_0^1 f(x)\,dx$ *is*

(a) 1 (b) 0

(c) $\frac{2}{3}$ (d) $\frac{3}{2}$

**Solution.** (c) We have,

$$\int_0^1 f(x)\,dx=\lim_{n\to\infty}\int_{1/2^n}^{1}f(x)\,dx$$

$$=\lim_{n\to\infty}\left\{\int_{1/2}^{1}f(x)\,dx+\int_{1/2^2}^{1/2}f(x)\,dx+\int_{1/2^3}^{1/2^2}f(x)\,dx+\ldots+\int_{1/2^n}^{1/2^{n-1}}f(x)\,dx\right\}$$

$$= \lim_{n\to\infty}\left\{\int_{1/2}^{1} dx + \frac{1}{2}\int_{1/2^2}^{1/2} dx + \frac{1}{2^2}\int_{1/2^3}^{1/2^2} dx + \ldots + \frac{1}{2^{n-1}}\int_{1/2^n}^{1/2^{n-1}} dx\right\}$$

$$= \lim_{n\to\infty}\left\{\frac{1}{2} + \frac{1}{2}\left(\frac{1}{2} - \frac{1}{2^2}\right) + \frac{1}{2^3}\left(\frac{1}{2^2} - \frac{1}{2^3}\right) + \ldots + \frac{1}{2^{n-1}}\left(\frac{1}{2^{n-1}} - \frac{1}{2^n}\right)\right\}$$

$$= \lim_{n\to\infty}\left[\frac{1}{2}\left\{1 + \frac{1}{2^2} + \left(\frac{1}{2^2}\right)^2 + \left(\frac{1}{2^2}\right)^3 + \ldots + \left(\frac{1}{2^2}\right)^{n-1}\right\}\right]$$

$$= \lim_{n\to\infty}\left[\frac{1}{2}\,\frac{1-\left(\frac{1}{4}\right)^n}{1-\frac{1}{4}}\right] = \lim_{n\to\infty}\left[\frac{2}{3}\left(1-\frac{1}{4^n}\right)\right] = \frac{2}{3}$$

***Example 4.*** *Which one of the following is true?*

(a) A constant function is Riemann integrable
(b) Constant function is not Riemann integrable
(c) A constant function may or may not be Riemann integrable
(d) None of the above

**Solution.** (a) Let a function $f$ be defined on $[a, b]$, by

$$f(x) = c, \forall x \in [a, b]$$

where $c$ is a constant.

Let $P$ be a partition of $[a, b]$ given by

$$P = \{a = x_0, x_1, x_2, \ldots, x_r, \ldots, x_n = b\}$$

Let its sub-intervals be given by

$$I_r = [x_{r-1}, x_r] \text{ for } r = 1, 2, \ldots, n$$

If $\delta_r$ be the length of this interval $I_r$, then

$$\delta_r = x_r - x_{r-1}$$

Also, if $M_r$ and $m_r$ be the lub and glb of the function $f$ in $I_r$ respectively, then

$$M_r = c, m_r = c, \text{ as } f(x) = c, \forall x \in (a, b)$$

Hence, $U(P, f) = \sum_{r=1}^{n} M_r \delta_r$

$$= \sum_{r=1}^{n} c(x_r - x_{r-1}) = c\sum_{r=1}^{n}(x_r - x_{r-1})$$

$$= c[(x_1 - x_0) + (x_2 - x_1) + \ldots + (x_n - x_{n-1})]$$

$$= c(x_n - x_0) = c(b - a)$$

$$= \text{constant}$$

and $L(P, f) = \sum_{r=1}^{n} m_r \delta_r$

$$= \sum_{r=1}^{n} c(x_r - x_{r-1}) = c(b-a), \text{ as above}$$

$$= \text{constant}$$

Hence, $\overline{\int_a^b} f(x)\, dx = \text{glb}\{U(P, f)\}$

$$= \text{glb}\{c(b-a)\}$$

$$= c(b-a) \qquad \ldots\text{(i)}$$

and $\underline{\int_a^b} f(x)\, dx = \text{lub}\{L(P - f)\}$

$$= \text{lub}\{c(b-a)\}$$

$$= c(b-a) \qquad \ldots\text{(ii)}$$

Hence, From Eqs. (i) and (ii), we get

$$\overline{\int_a^b} f(x)\, dx = \underline{\int_a^b} f(x)\, dx$$

$$= c(b-a)$$

and so we conclude that $f \in R[a, b]$ and $\int_a^b f(x)\, dx = c(b-a)$

*i.e.*, the function $f$ is Riemann integrable.

***Example 5.*** *The integral* $\int_0^3 [x]dx$ *(where* $[x]$ *is greatest integer function) is*

(a) 0 (b) 1
(c) 2 (d) 3

**Solution.** (d) Since, the function $f(x) = [x]$ is bounded and has only three points of discontinuity at $x = 1, 2, 3$.

Let $\varepsilon > 0$ be given number and

$$P = \{0 = x_0, x_1, \ldots, x_i, y_0, y_1, \ldots, y_m, z_0, z_1, \ldots, z_n = 3\}$$

be a partition of $[0, 3]$ where $y_0 = 1, z_0 = 2$.

Hence,

$$U(P, f) = \Sigma 0 \cdot \Delta x_i + 1\cdot(y_0 - x_i) + \Sigma 1 \cdot \Delta y_i + 2(z_0 - y_m) + \Sigma 2\cdot \Delta z_i + 3(z_n - z_{n-1})$$

$$= 1 + 2 + \{(y_0 - x_i) + (z_0 - y_m) + (z_n - z_{n-1})\}$$

Now, select $P$ such that

$$(y_0 - x_i) + (z_0 - y_m) + (z_n - z_{n-1}) < \varepsilon$$

$$\Rightarrow \qquad U(P, f) < 3 + \varepsilon$$

Similarly,

$$L(P, f) = \Sigma 0 \cdot \Delta x_i + \Sigma 1 \cdot \Delta y_i + (z_0 - y_m) + \Sigma 2 \cdot \Delta z_i = 3$$

Hence,

$$U(P, f) - L(P, f) < \varepsilon$$

Hence, $f(x) = [x]$ is integrable in $[0, 3]$ and

$$\overline{\int_0^3} [x]dx = \underline{\int_0^3} [x]dx = 3$$

***Example 6.*** *The value of integral* $\int_0^\infty e^{-x^2} \cos\alpha x\, dx$ *is*

(a) $\frac{1}{2}\sqrt{\pi}e^{-\frac{1}{4}\alpha^2}$ (b) $\frac{1}{2}\sqrt{\pi}$
(c) $\sqrt{\pi/6}$ (d) $\frac{1}{2}\alpha^2$

**Solution.** (a) Since,

$$|xe^{-x^2} \sin\alpha x| \le xe^{-x^2}$$

We see that the differentiation under the integral sign is justified.

Hence, $f'(\alpha) = -\int_0^\infty xe^{-x^2} \sin\alpha x dx$

On Integrating by parts, we have

$$f'(\alpha) = \left|\frac{1}{2}e^{-x^2} \sin\alpha x\right|_0^\infty - \frac{\alpha}{2}\int_0^\infty e^{-x^2} \cos\alpha x dx$$

$$= -\frac{\alpha}{2} f(\alpha)$$

Hence, $\log f(\alpha) = -\frac{1}{4}\alpha^2 + C_1$

$\Rightarrow \quad f(\alpha) = Ce^{\frac{1}{4}\alpha^2}$

Now, $\quad f(0) = \int_0^{\infty} e^{-x^2} dx = \frac{\sqrt{\pi}}{2}$

Hence $\quad C = f(0) = \frac{\sqrt{\pi}}{2}$

So that $\quad f(\alpha) = \frac{1}{2}\sqrt{\pi} e^{-\frac{1}{4}\alpha^2}$

**Example 7.** *Given*

$$\int_0^1 x^{m-1}(1-x)^{n-1} dx$$

(a) integral exist when $m > 0, n < 0$
(b) integral exist when $m < 0, n < 0$
(c) integral exist when $m, n > 0$
(d) integral exist when $m, n = 0$

**Solution.** (c) The integral is proper, if $m \geq 1$ and $n \geq 1$.

The number, 0 is a point of infinite discontinuity, if $m < 1$ and the number 1, is a point of infinite discontinuity, if $n < 1$.

Let $\quad m < 1$

and $\quad n < 1$

We take any number, say $\frac{1}{2}$, between 0 and 1 and examine the convergence of the two improper integrals

$$\int_0^{1/2} x^{m-1}(1-x)^{n-1} dx \text{ and } \int_{1/2}^1 x^{m-1}(1-x)^{n-1} dx$$

at 0 and 1, respectively.

**Convergence at 0** We have,

$$f(x) = x^{m-1}(1-x)^{n-1} = \frac{(1-x)^{n-1}}{x^{1-m}}$$

and let $\quad \phi(x) = \frac{1}{x^{1-m}}$

Hence $\quad \frac{f(x)}{\phi(x)} \to 1 \text{ as } x \to 0$

as $\quad \int_0^{1/2} \phi(x)\, dx = \int_0^{1/2} \frac{1}{x^{1-m}} dx$

is convergent at 0, if and only if,

$$1 - m < 1$$

$$\Leftrightarrow \quad 0 < m$$

$$\Rightarrow \quad \int_0^{1/2} x^{m-1}(1-x)^{n-1} dx$$

is convergent at 0, if and only if, $m > 0$.

**Convergence at 1** We have,

$$f'(x) = x^{m-1}(1-x)^{n-1} = \frac{x^{m-1}}{(1-x)^{1-n}}$$

and let $\phi(x) = \frac{1}{(1-x)^{1-n}}$

Hence $\quad \frac{f(x)}{\phi(x)} \to 1 \text{ as } x \to 1$

as $\quad \int_{1/2}^1 \phi(x)\, dx = \int_{1/2}^1 \frac{1}{(1-x)^{1-n}} dx$

is convergent, if and only if

$$1 - n < 1 \Leftrightarrow 0 < n$$

$$\Rightarrow \quad \int_{1/2}^1 x^{m-1}(1-x)^{n-1} dx$$

converges if and only if

$$n > 0$$

Thus, $\int_0^1 x^{m-1}(1-x)^{n-1} dx$ exists for positive values of $m, n$ only.

## Type II (*One or more than one correct option*)

***Example 8.*** *If $f(x)$ be defined on $(0, 2)$ as follows*

$$f(x) = x + x^2, \text{ when } x \text{ is rational}$$
$$= x^2 + x^3, \text{ when } x \text{ is irrational}$$

(a) the value of upper Riemann integrals in $(0, 2)$ is 8/3
(b) the value of upper Riemann integrals in $(0, 2)$ is 83/12
(c) the value of lower Riemann integral in $(0, 2)$ is 5/3
(d) the value of lower Riemann integral in $(0, 2)$ is 53/12

**Solution.** (b), (d)

As, $(x + x^2) - (x^2 + x^3) = x - x^3$

$$= x(1 - x^2)$$

So, $(x + x^2) - (x^2 + x^3) \begin{cases} > 0, \text{ if } 0 < x < 1 \\ < 0, \text{ if } 1 < x < 2 \end{cases}$

If $M_r$ and $m_r$ be the upper and lower bounds of the given function $f(x)$ in $I_r$ respectively where $I_r$ has its usual meaning, then for all values of $r$, we have

$$M_r = \begin{cases} x + x^2, \text{ if } 0 < x < 1 \\ x^2 + x^3, \text{ if } 1 < x < 2 \end{cases}$$

and $\quad m_r = \begin{cases} x^2 + x^3, \text{ if } 0 < x < 1 \\ x + x^2, \text{ if } 1 < x < 2 \end{cases}$

Hence, the upper Riemann integral is

$$= \int_0^1 (x + x^2)\, dx + \int_1^2 (x^2 + x^3)\, dx$$

$$= \left(\frac{x^2}{2} + \frac{x^3}{3}\right)_0^1 + \left(\frac{x^3}{3} + \frac{x^4}{4}\right)_1^2$$

$$= \left(\frac{1}{2} + \frac{1}{3}\right) + \left[\left\{\left(\frac{8}{3}\right) + \left(\frac{16}{4}\right)\right\} - \left(\frac{1}{3} + \frac{1}{4}\right)\right]$$

$$= \left(\frac{83}{12}\right)$$

and the lower Riemann integral is

$$= \int_0^1 (x^2 + x^3)\, dx + \int_1^2 (x + x^2)\, dx$$

$$= \left(\frac{x^3}{3} + \frac{x^4}{4}\right)_0^1 + \left(\frac{x^2}{2} + \frac{x^3}{3}\right)_1^2$$

$$=\left(\frac{1}{3}+\frac{1}{4}\right)+\left[\left\{\left(\frac{4}{2}\right)+\left(\frac{8}{3}\right)\right\}-\left(\frac{1}{2}+\frac{1}{3}\right)\right]$$

$$=\left(\frac{53}{12}\right)$$

***Example* 9.** *Given,*

(A) $f_1(x)=\frac{1}{2^n}, x\in\left(\frac{1}{2^{n+1}},\frac{1}{2^n}\right], n=0,1,2,\ldots$

$=0, \quad x=0$

(B) $f_2(x)=\frac{1}{n}, x\in\left(\frac{1}{n+1},\frac{1}{n}\right], n=0,1,\ldots$

$=0,\ x=0$

*Then*

(a) $f_1(x)$ is Riemann integrable on interval $[0,1]$

(b) $f_1(x)$ is not Riemann integrable on interval $[0,1]$

(c) $f_1(x)$ is bounded and monotonically increasing in $[0,1]$

(d) $f_2(x)$ is discontinuous at $1,\frac{1}{2},\frac{1}{3},\ldots$

**Solution.** (a), (c), (d)

(a) Here, $f_1(0)=0$ and $f_1(1)=1$

and lower and upper bounds for $f_1(x)$ in $[0,1]$ are 0 and 1, respectively.

Hence, the function is bounded and monotonically increasing in $[0,1]$, so $f_1(x)$ is Riemann integrable on $[0,1]$.

(b) We have, $f_2\left(\frac{1}{n}\right)=\frac{1}{n}$

and $f_2\left(\frac{1}{n}-0\right)=\frac{1}{n}$

and $f_2\left(\frac{1}{n}+0\right)=\frac{1}{n+1}$

$\Rightarrow f_2(x)$ is discontinuous at each point $1,\frac{1}{2},\frac{1}{3},\frac{1}{4},\ldots$

Also, $f_2(0)=0, f_2(0+0)=0$, so function $f_2(x)$ is continuous on the right of $x=0$.

Hence, $\left(1,\frac{1}{2},\frac{1}{3},\ldots\right)$ are the point of discontinuity of $f_2(x)$ and $f_2(x)$ has one limit point, so $f_2(x)$ is Riemann integrable.

***Example* 10.** *If f(x) be defined on [0, 1] as follows*

$$f(x)=\begin{cases}1, \text{ when } x \text{ is rational}\\ -1, \text{ when } x \text{ is irrational}\end{cases}$$

*Then,*

(a) $f$ is Riemann integrable over $[0,1]$

(b) $f$ is not Riemann integrable over $[0,1]$

(c) $\int_0^{\bar{1}} f(x)\,dx=1$

(d) $\int_0^{1} f(x)=-1$

**Solution.** (a), (c), (d)

Let $P$ be a partition of $[0,1]$ given by

$$P=\{0=x_0,x_1,x_2,\ldots,x_r,\ldots,x_n=1\}$$

Let its sub-intervals be given by

$$I_r=[x_{r-1},x_r] \text{ for } r=1,2,\ldots,n$$

If $\delta_r$ be the length of this interval $I_r$, then

$$\delta_r=x_r-x_{r-1}$$

Let $M_r$ and $m_r$ be respectively the lub and glb of the function $f$ in $I_r$, respectively.

Then, $f(x)$ will have the values 1 as well as $-1$ in every interval $I_r$, however small it may be, so we have

$$M_r=1 \text{ and } m_r=1 \text{ as } M_r\ge m_r$$

Now we have,

$$U(P,f)=\sum_{r=1}^{n}M_r\delta_r=\sum_{r=1}^{n}1(x_r-x_{r-1})$$

$$=(x_1-x_0)+(x_2-x_1)+\ldots+(x_n-x_{n-1})$$

$$=x_n-x_0=1-0=1$$

and $$L(P,f)=\sum_{r=1}^{n}m_r\delta_r$$

$$=\sum_{r=1}^{n}(-1)(x_r-x_{r-1})$$

$$=\sum_{r=1}^{n}(x_{r-1}-x_r)$$

$$=(x_0-x_1)+(x_1-x_2)+\ldots+(x_{n-1}-x_n)$$

$$=x_0-x_n=0-1=-1$$

Hence, $\int_0^{\bar{1}} f(x)\,dx=\text{glb}\{U(P,f)\}=1$ ...(i)

and $\int_{\underline{0}}^{1} f(x)\,dx=\text{lub}\{L(P,f)\}=-1$ ...(ii)

Hence, from Eqs. (i) and (ii), we find that

$$\int_0^{\bar{1}} f(x)\,dx\ne\int_{\underline{0}}^{1} f(x)\,dx$$

$\Rightarrow f$ is not Riemann integrable over $[0,1]$.

***Example* 11.** *If f is a function defined on [0, 1] by*

$$f(x)=\begin{cases}1, \text{ if } x\ne\frac{1}{2}\\ 0, \text{ if } x=\frac{1}{2}\end{cases}$$

*Then*

(a) the function $f$ is Riemann integrable over $[0,1]$

(b) the function $f$ is not Riemann integrable over $[0,1]$

(c) $f(x)$ is bounded in $[0,1]$

(d) $f(d)$ is not bounded in $[0,1]$

**Solution.** (a), (c)

Since, $0\le f(x)\le 1$

For every $x\in[0,1]$

Therefore, the function $f(x)$ is bounded in $[0,1]$

Let $P$ be a partition of $[0,1]$ given by

$$P=\{0=x_0,x_1,\ldots,x_n=1\} \text{ such that the point}$$

$$\frac{1}{2}\in(x_{s-1},x_s)$$

Also, $M_r=m_r=1,\ r=1,2,\ldots,n$

and $\quad r \neq s$

$$M_s = 1, m_s = 0$$

Hence, $U(P, f) - L(P, f)$

$$= \sum_{\substack{r=1 \\ r \neq s}}^{n} (M_r - m_r)(x_r - x_{r-1}) + (M_s - m_s)(x_s - x_{s-1})$$

$$= \sum_{\substack{r=1 \\ r \neq s}}^{n} (1-1)(x_r - x_{r-1}) + (1-0)(x_s - x_{s-1})$$

$$= (x_s - x_{s-1}) \quad \text{...(i)}$$

Let a positive number ε be given, then a partition $P$ of $[0, 1]$ can be so chosen that $x_{s-1} < \frac{1}{2} < x_s$ and $x_s - x_{s-1} < \varepsilon$.

Hence, from Eq. (i), we have $U(P, f) - L(P, f) < \varepsilon$, which implies that $f$ is Riemann integrable over $[0, 1]$.

***Example 12.*** *If $f$ is bounded and integrable in $[a, b]$ and $M, m$ are the bounds of $f$ in $[a, b]$.*

(a) $m(b-a) \leq \int_a^b f(x)\,dx \leq M(b-a)$, if $b \geq a$

(b) $m(b-a) \geq \int_a^b f(x)\,dx \geq M(b-a)$, if $b \leq a$

(c) $m(b-a) \geq M(b-a)$, if $b \geq a$

(d) $m(b-a) \leq M(b-a)$, if $b \leq a$

**Solution.** (a), (b)

(i) For $a = b$, the result is trivial.

(ii) If $b > a$, then for any partition $P$, we have

$$m(b-a) \leq L(f, P) \leq \int_a^b f(x)dx$$

$$\leq U(f, P) \leq M(b-a)$$

$$\Rightarrow \quad m(b-a) \leq \int_a^b f(x)\,dx \leq M(b-a)$$

If $b < a$ i.e., $\quad a > b$,

then as proved above,

$$m(a-b) \leq \int_b^a f(x)\,dx \leq M(a-b)$$

$$\Rightarrow \quad -m(a-b) \geq -\int_b^a f(x)dx \geq -M(a-b)$$

$$\Rightarrow \quad m(b-a) \geq \int_a^b f(x)\,dx \geq M(b-a)$$

***Example 13.*** *Given $\int_a^\infty \frac{x\,dx}{1 + x^4 \sin^2 x}$, then*

(a) it is convergent (b) it is divergent

(c) it does not converges (d) it does not diverges

**Solution.** (b), (c)

We have,

$$\int_a^{n\pi} \frac{x\,dx}{1 + x^4 \sin^2 x} = \sum_{r=1}^{n} \int_{(r-1)\pi}^{r\pi} \frac{x\,dx}{1 + x^4 \sin^2 x}$$

Now, $\forall\, x \in [(r-1)\pi, r\pi]$, we have

$$\frac{(r-1)\pi}{1 + (r\pi)^4 \sin^2 x} \leq \frac{x}{1 + x^4 \sin^2 x}$$

Hence, $$\int_{(r-1)\pi}^{r\pi} \frac{(r-1)\pi}{1 + (r\pi)^4 \sin^2 x}\,dx \leq \int_{(r-1)\pi}^{r\pi} \frac{x}{1 + x^4 \sin^2 x}\,dx$$

Now, $$\int_{(r-1)\pi}^{r\pi} \frac{(r-1)\pi}{1 + (r\pi)^4 \sin^2 x}\,dx$$

$$= (r-1)\pi \int_0^{\pi} \frac{dy}{1 + (r\pi)^4 \sin^2 y}$$

$$= 2(r-1)\pi \int_0^{\pi/2} \frac{dy}{1 + (r\pi)^4 \sin^2 y}$$

$$= 2(r-1)\pi \frac{\pi}{2} \frac{1}{\sqrt{1 + (r\pi)^4}}$$

$$= \frac{(r-1)\pi^2}{\sqrt{1 + (r\pi)^4}}$$

The infinite series $\sum \frac{(r-1)\pi^2}{\sqrt{1 + (r\pi)^4}}$ diverges, as we may see on comparison with the series $\sum \left(\frac{1}{r}\right)$.

Hence, the given integral does not converge.

***Example 14.*** *Given $\int_0^1 \frac{\sin(1/x)}{\sqrt{x}}\,dx$, then*

(a) integral is convergent

(b) integral is divergent

(c) integral is absolutely convergent

(d) integral is not absolutely convergent

**Solution.** (a), (c)

Let $f(x) = \frac{\sin(1/x)}{\sqrt{x}}$. Now, there is no neighbourhood of the point, 0, in which $f(x)$ constantly keeps the same sign.

Now, $\forall\, x \in (0, 1]$, we have

$$\left|\frac{\sin \frac{1}{x}}{\sqrt{x}}\right| = \frac{\left|\sin \frac{1}{x}\right|}{\sqrt{x}} \leq \frac{1}{\sqrt{x}}$$

Also, $\int_0^1 \frac{1}{\sqrt{x}}\,dx$ is convergent. It follows that

$\int_0^1 \left|\frac{\sin \frac{1}{x}}{\sqrt{x}}\right| dx$ is convergent $\Rightarrow$ $\int_0^1 \frac{\sin \frac{1}{x}}{\sqrt{x}}\,dx$ is absolutely convergent.

***Example 15.*** *Given integrals*

(A) $\int_1^\infty \frac{dx}{x^2}$ (B) $\int_{-1}^1 \frac{dx}{x^{2/3}}$

*Then,*

(a) (A) exist and converges to 1

(b) (A) does not exist

(c) (B) exist in general sense

(d) (A) and (B) both exist

**Solution.** (a), (c), (d)

(a) We have, $\int_1^\infty \frac{dx}{x^2}$

Since, $\quad \frac{d}{dx}\left(-\frac{1}{x}\right) = \frac{1}{x^2}$

We have, $\int_1^{\infty} \frac{dx}{x^2} = \lim_{b\to\infty} \int_1^b \frac{dx}{x^2}$

$$= \lim_{b\to\infty} \left[-\frac{1}{x}\right]_1^b$$

$$= \lim_{b\to\infty} \left(1-\frac{1}{b}\right) = 1$$

Hence, the integral exist and converges to 1.

(b) We have, $\int_{-1}^{1} \frac{dx}{x^{2/3}}$

Here the given function becomes unbounded at $x=0$.

$$\int_{-1}^{1} \frac{dx}{x^{2/3}} = \lim_{\varepsilon\to 0} \int_{-1}^{-\varepsilon} \frac{dx}{x^{2/3}} + \lim_{\delta\to a} \int_{\delta}^{1} \frac{dx}{x^{2/3}}$$

$$= \lim_{\varepsilon\to 0} [3x^{1/3}]_{-1}^{-\varepsilon} + \lim_{\delta\to 0} [3x^{1/3}]_{\delta}^{1}$$

$$= \lim_{\varepsilon\to 0} [-3\varepsilon^{1/3} + 3] + \lim_{\delta\to 0} [3 - 3\delta^{1/3}]$$

$$= 3+3 = 6$$

Hence, the given integral exists in the general sense.

***Example 16.*** *Given integral* $\int_0^{\infty} \frac{\sin x}{x} dx$, *then*

(a) integral converges
(b) integral is not converges
(c) integral converges but not absolutely
(d) integral also converges absolutely

**Solution.** (a), (c)

We have,

$$\int_0^{\infty} \frac{\sin x}{x} dx = \int_0^{a} \frac{\sin x}{x} dx + \int_0^{\infty} \frac{\sin x}{x} dx,\ a>0$$

Now, $\lim_{x\to 0^+} \frac{\sin x}{x} = 1$

Hence, the integral $\int_0^{a} \frac{\sin x}{x} dx$ is proper and hence convergent.

Also, in $\int_a^{\infty} \frac{\sin x}{x} dx$, $\frac{1}{x}$ is bounded and monotonic in the interval $(a, \infty)$ and $\lim_{x\to\infty} (1/x) = 0$.

Now, $\left|\int_a^{\infty} \sin x\, dx\right| = \lim_{x\to\infty} \left|\int_a^{x} \sin x\, dx\right|$

$$= \lim_{x\to\infty} |\cos a - \cos x| \le 2$$

Hence, $\int_a^{\infty} \sin x\, dx$ is bounded; hence $\int_0^{\infty} \frac{\sin x}{x} dx$ is convergent.

***Example 17.*** *Given the integral* $\int_0^{\infty} \frac{|\sin x|}{x} dx$, *then*

(a) it is convergent
(b) it is not convergent
(c) it is divergent
(d) it is convergent but absolutely

**Solution.** (a), (d)

To prove $\int_0^{\infty} \frac{|\sin x|}{x} dx$ is divergent, it is only necessary to consider.

$$\lim_{n\to\infty} \int_0^{n\pi} \frac{|\sin x|}{x} dx$$

$$\int_0^{n\pi} \frac{|\sin x|}{x} dx = \int_0^{\pi} \frac{|\sin x|}{x} dx + \int_0^{2\pi} \frac{|\sin x|}{x} dx + \ldots + \int_{(n-1)\pi}^{n\pi} \frac{|\sin x|}{x} dx$$

$$= \sum_{r=1}^{n} \int_{(r-1)p}^{r\pi} \frac{|\sin x|}{x} dx \quad \ldots(i)$$

In $\int_{(r-1)\pi}^{r\pi} \frac{|\sin x|}{x} dx$

Put $x = (r-1)\pi + y$

and $dx = dy$

Hence, $\int_{(r-1)\pi}^{r\pi} \frac{|\sin x|}{x} dx = \int_0^{\pi} \frac{\sin y}{(r-1)\pi + y} dy \quad \ldots(ii)$

Now, in the interval $(0, \pi)$, $\frac{1}{r\pi + (y-\pi)} > \frac{1}{r\pi}$, for all values of $y$.

Therefore, from the first mean value theorem, we have

$$\int_0^{\pi} \frac{\sin y\, dy}{r\pi + (y-\pi)} > \frac{1}{r\pi} \int_0^{\pi} \sin y\, dy = \frac{2}{r\pi}$$

$$\Rightarrow \int_{(r-1)n}^{\pi} \frac{|\sin x|}{x} dx > \frac{2}{r\pi} \quad \text{[from Eq. (ii)]}$$

Hence, from Eq. (i), we have

$$\int_0^{n\pi} \frac{|\sin x|}{x} dx = \frac{2}{\pi} \sum_1^n \frac{1}{r}$$

But the series, $\sum_1^n \frac{1}{r} = 1 + \frac{1}{2} + \frac{1}{3} + \ldots$ is divergent when $n\to\infty$.

Therefore, $\lim_{x\to\infty} \int_0^{n\pi} \frac{|\sin x|}{x} dx$ is divergent.

Hence, from above it is evident that $\int_0^{\infty} \frac{|\sin x|}{x} dx$ is also divergent. Thus, the given integral converges but not absolutely.

***Example 18.*** *Given integral*

$$\int_0^{\frac{1}{2}\pi} x^m \operatorname{cosec}^n x\, dx \quad \ldots(i)$$

*Then,*

(a) it exist when $n > (m+1)$
(b) it exist when $n < (m+1)$
(c) it exist when $n = m+1$
(d) it does not exist

**Solution.** (b) Let $f(x) = x^m \operatorname{cosec}^n x$

$$= \frac{x^m}{(\sin x)^n}$$

$$= \left(\frac{x}{\sin x}\right)^n \cdot x^{m-n}$$

$$= \left(\frac{x}{\sin x}\right)^n \frac{1}{x^{n-m}}$$

Here,

$$\lim_{x\to 0} f(x) = \begin{cases} 0, \text{ if } m-n>0 \\ 1, \text{ if } m-n=0 \\ \infty, \text{ if } m-n<0 \end{cases}$$

Thus, $\int_0^{\pi/2} f(x)dx$ is a proper integral, if $(m-n) \geq 0$ and improper, if $(m-n) < 0$, 0 being the only point of infinite discontinuity of the integrand in this case.

Let $(m-n) < 0$

$\Leftrightarrow$ $(n-m) > 0$

Let $\varphi(x) = \dfrac{1}{x^{n-m}}$

Then, $\dfrac{f(x)}{\varphi(x)} \to 1$ as $x \to 0$

Also, $\int_0^{\frac{1}{2}\pi} \varphi(x)\, dx = \int_0^{\frac{1}{2}\pi} \dfrac{1}{x^{n-m}} dx$

Converges if and only if,

$$(n-m) < 1$$

$$\Leftrightarrow \quad n < (m+1)$$

Therefore, the integral $\int_0^{\pi/2} f(x)\, dx$ converges if and only if $n < (m+1)$, which also includes the case $n \leq m$ when the integral is proper.

***Example 19.*** *Which of the following(s) is/are correct?*

(a) $\int_0^{\infty} e^{-x}dx$ is convergent

(b) $\int_{-\infty}^{0} e^{-x}dx$ is convergent

(c) $\int_0^{\infty} e^{-x^2} dx$ is convergent

(d) $\int_0^{\infty} e^{-x^2} dx$ is divergent

**Solution.** (a), (b), (c)

(a) We have,

$$\int_0^{\infty} e^{-x}dx = \lim_{x\to\infty} \int_0^{x} e^{-x}dx = \lim_{x\to\infty} (1-e^{x}) = 1$$

Hence, the given integral is convergent.

(b) We have,

$$\int_{-\infty}^{0} e^{x}dx = \lim_{x\to-\infty} \int_x^{0} e^{x}dx = \lim_{x\to-\infty} (1-e^{x}) = 1$$

Hence, convergent.

(c) We have, $\int_0^{\infty} e^{-x^2} dx$

Here, we have

$$\lim_{x\to\infty} x^2 \cdot e^{-x^2} = \lim_{x\to\infty} \frac{x^2}{e^{x^2}}$$

$$= \lim_{x\to\infty} \frac{x^2}{1+x^2+(x^2)^2/2!+\ldots} = 0$$

Hence, the given integral converges.

# Exercise 1 (For Part 'B')

**Direction** (Q. Nos. 1-43) *All questions have only one correct option.*

**1.** If $f$ is a non-negative continuous function on $[a, b]$ and $\int_a^b f(x)\,dx = 0, \forall x \in [a, b]$.

Then,

(a) $f(x) = c, \forall x \in [a, b]$ (b) $f(x) = x, \forall x \in [a, b]$
(c) $f(x) = 0, \forall x \in [a, b]$ (d) $f(x) = 1, \forall x \in [a, b]$

**2.** If a function $f$ is continuous on $[0, 1]$, then $\lim_{n\to\infty} \int_0^1 \frac{nf(x)}{1+n^2x^2}\,dx$ is

(a) $\frac{\pi}{2}$ (b) $\frac{\pi}{2} f(0)$
(c) $\pi f(0)$ (d) $\frac{2}{\pi} f(0)$

**3.** Let $c$ is a fixed point in $[0, 1]$. A function $f : [0, 1] \to R$ is defined by
$f(x) = \begin{cases} c, & \text{if } 0 \le x \le c \\ 2c, & \text{if } c < x \le 1 \end{cases}$. It is given that the Riemann integral $\int_0^1 f(x)\,dx$ is $\frac{7}{16}$. Then, the value of $c$ is

(a) $\frac{1}{2}$ (b) $\frac{1}{3}$
(c) $\frac{1}{4}$ (d) $\frac{1}{5}$

**4.** The integral $\int_0^2 \frac{dx}{(2x - x^2)}$ is

(a) divergent (b) convergent
(c) 0 (d) 1

**5.** The integral $\int_2^\infty \frac{2x^2}{x^4 - 1}\,dx$ is

(a) convergent and equal to $\frac{\pi}{2}$

(b) convergent and equal to $\frac{\pi}{2} - \tan^{-1} 2$

(c) convergent and equal to $\frac{\pi}{2} - \tan^{-1} 2 + \frac{1}{2}\log 3$

(d) divergent

**6.** If $f_1$ and $f_2$ are Riemann integral functions, then $\int_a^b f_1 dx + \int_a^b f_2 dx$ is equal to

(a) $\int_b^a (f_1 + f_2)dx$ (b) zero
(c) $\int_a^b (f + f_2)dx$ (d) None of these

**7.** $\lim_{n\to\infty} \left[(n+1)\int_0^1 x^n \ln(1+x)dx\right]$ is equal to

(a) 0 (b) $\ln 2$
(c) $\ln 3$ (d) $\infty$

**8.** $f : [0, 1] \to R$, such that $f(x) = \begin{cases} 0, & x \text{ is rational} \\ 1, & x \text{ is irrational} \end{cases}$

Then,

(a) the upper and lower integral of $f$ does not exist
(b) $f$ is Riemann integrable
(c) $f$ is not Riemann integrable
(d) None of the above

**9.** Let $f : [0, 1] \to R$ and $g : [0, 1] \to R$ be two functions defined by

$f(x) = \begin{cases} 1/n, & \text{if } x = 1/n, n \in N \\ 0, & \text{otherwise} \end{cases}$ and

$g(x) = \begin{cases} n, & \text{if } x = 1/n, n \in N \\ 0, & \text{otherwise} \end{cases}$

Then,

(a) both $f$ and $g$ are Riemann integrable
(b) $f$ is Riemann integrable but $g$ is not
(c) $g$ is Riemann integrable but $f$ is not
(d) Neither $f$ nor $g$ is Riemann integrable

**10.** Consider the following improper integrals
$I_1 = \int_1^\infty \frac{dx}{(1+x^2)^{1/2}}$ and $I_2 = \int_1^\infty \frac{dx}{(1+x^2)^{3/2}}$. Then,

(a) $I_1$ converges but not $I_2$
(b) $I_2$ converges but not $I_1$
(c) both $I_1$ and $I_2$ converge
(d) Neither $I_1$ nor $I_2$ converges

**11.** The integral $\int_0^\infty \sin x\,dx$ is

(a) exists (b) exists and equal zero
(c) exists and equal 1 (d) does not exists

**12.** The integral $\int_{-\infty}^\infty \frac{dx}{(x^2+1)^2}$ is

(a) exist and equal to zero (b) exists and equal to $\frac{\pi}{2}$
(c) exists and equal to $\frac{2}{\pi}$ (d) does not exists

**13.** If $f$ is real-valued bounded function on $[a, b]$ and $m$ and $M$ are greatest lower bound and least upper bound respectively, then

(a) $m(b-a) = M(b-a)$ (b) $m(b-a) \ge M(b-a)$
(c) $m(b-a) \le M(b-a)$ (d) None of these

**14.** A real-valued bounded function $f(x)$ is Riemann integral on $[a, b]$. Then,

(a) $\int_{\underline{a}}^b f(x)\,dx$ and $\int_a^{\bar{b}} f(x)\,dx$ exist

(b) $\int_{\underline{a}}^b f(x)\,dx = \int_a^b f(x)\,dx$

(c) 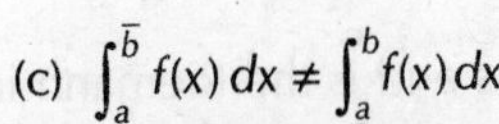 $\int_a^{\bar{b}} f(x)\,dx \neq \int_{\underline{a}}^{b} f(x)\,dx$

(d) None of the above

**15.** If $f$ is a Riemann integrable function on $[a, b]$ and $c$ is any real number, then which of the following holds?

(a) $c\int_a^b f(x)\,dx = \int_a^b c\,f(x)\,dx$

(b) $c\int_a^b f(x)\,dx \neq \int_a^b c\,f(x)\,dx$

(c) $c\int_a^b f(x)\,dx \geq \int_a^b c\,f(x)\,dx$

(d) None of the above

**16.** If $\int_a^b f(x)\,dx$ and $\int_a^b f\,dx$ are lower and upper Riemann integrable on $[a, b]$. Then,

(a) $\int_a^b f\,dx \geq \int_a^{\bar{b}} f(x)\,dx$ (b) $\int_a^b f dx = \int_a^{\bar{b}} f\,dx$

(c) $\int_a^b f\,dx \leq \int_a^b f\,dx$ (d) None of these

**17.** If $f_1$ and $f_2$ are two real-valued bounded functions defined on $[a, b]$. Then for every partition $P$ on $[a, b]$

(a) $U(P, f_1 + f_2) = U(P, f_1) + U(P, f_2)$

(b) $U(P, f_1 + f_2) \leq U(P, f_1) + U(P, f_2)$

(c) $U(P, f_1 + f_2) \geq U(P, f_1) + U(P, f_2)$

(d) None of the above

**18.** Let lower Riemann integral be $f(x)$ on $[a, b]$ and $L(P, f)$ is the lower Riemann sum over all partitions on $[a, b]$, then

(a) $\int_{\underline{a}}^{b} f(x)\,dx = \text{lub}\{L(P, f)\}$

(b) $\int_{\underline{a}}^{b} f(x)\,dx = \text{glb}\{L(P, f)\}$

(c) $\int_{\underline{a}}^{b} f(x)\,dx = \{L(P, f)\}$

(d) None of the above

**19.** $f : [a, b] \to R$, $P$ and $Q$ are partitions of $[a, b]$ such that $P \subset Q$, then

(a) $L(P, f) \leq L(Q, f)$

(b) $L(P, f) \geq L(Q, f)$

(c) (a) is true and (b) is false

(d) (b) is true and (a) is false

**20.** A function $f$ is Riemann integrable on $[a, b]$ iff

(a) Only $\int_a^{\bar{b}} f\,dx$ exist (b) Only $\int_{\underline{a}}^{b} f\,dx$ exist

(c) $\int_a^{\bar{b}} f\,dx \neq \int_{\underline{a}}^{b} f\,dx$ (d) $\int_a^{\bar{b}} f\,dx = \int_{\underline{a}}^{b} f\,dx$

**21.** If $f : [0, 1] \to R$, such that $f(x) = \begin{cases} 0, & x \text{ is rational} \\ 1, & x \text{ is irrational} \end{cases}$

Then,

(a) the upper and lower integral of $f$ do not exist

(b) $f$ is Riemann integrable

(c) $f$ is not Riemann integrable

(d) None of the above

**22.** If $f : [a, b] \to R$ is continuous and monotonic function, then

(a) $f$ is Riemann integrable on $[a, b]$

(b) $f$ is not Riemann integrable on $[a, b]$

(c) $f$ is Riemann integrable on $R$

(d) None of the above

**23.** If $f_1$ and $f_2$ are Riemann integral functions, then $\int_a^b f_1 dx + \int_a^b f_2\,dx$ is equal to

(a) $\int_b^a (f_1 + f_2)\,dx$ (b) $\int_a^b (f_1 + f_2)\,dx$

(c) Both (a) and (b) (d) Neither (a) nor (b)

**24.** $f : [a, b] \to R$, $f$ is Riemann integrable, then

(a) $\left|\int_a^b f(x)dx\right| \leq \int_a^b |f(x)|\,dx$

(b) $\int_a^b |f(x)|\,dx \leq \left|\int_a^b f(x)\,dx\right|$

(c) $\int_a^b |f(x)|\,dx = \int_a^b f(x)\,dx|$

(d) None of the above

**25.** If $f_1$ is Riemann integrable, then $\int_a^b f_1 dx + \int_b^c f_1 dx$ is

(a) $\int_a^c f_1\,dx + C$ (b) $\int_a^b f_1\,dx + C$

(c) $\int_a^c f_1\,dx$ (d) None of these

**26.** Let $f$ be a bounded function defined on the bounded interval $[a, b]$. Then, $f$ is Riemann integrable on $[a, b]$ iff

(a) $\int_{\underline{a}}^{b} f \leq \int_a^{\bar{b}} f$ (b) $\int_{\underline{a}}^{b} f \geq \int_a^{\bar{b}} f$

(c) $\int_{\underline{a}}^{b} f = \int_a^{\bar{b}} f$ (d) $\int_a^{\bar{b}} f + \int_{\underline{a}}^{b} f = 0$

**27.** Let $f$ be a bounded function defined on $[a, b]$ and let $P$ be a partition of $[a, b]$. If $P^*$ is a refinement of $P$, then

(a) $L(P^*, f) \leq L(P, f)$ (b) $U(P^*, f) \leq U(P, f)$

(c) $U(P^*, f) \geq U(P, f)$ (d) $L(P^*, f) = U(P, f)$

**28.** If $f$ is Riemann integrable on $[a, b]$, then

(a) $\left|\int_a^b f(x)\,dx\right| = \int_a^b |f(x)|\,dx$

(b) $\left|\int_a^b f(x)\,dx\right| \geq \int_a^b |f(x)|\,dx$

(c) $\left|\int_a^b f(x)\,dx\right| = -\int_a^b |f(x)|\,dx$

(d) $\left|\int_a^b f(x)\,dx\right| \leq \int_a^b |f(x)|\,dx$

**29.** Let $f$ and $g$ be bounded functions defined on $[a, b]$ and let $P$ be any partition of $[a, b]$. Then,

(a) $U(P, f + g) \leq U(P, f) + U(P, g)$

(b) $U(P, f + g) \geq U(P, f) + U(P, g)$

(c) $U(P, f + g) = U(P, f) + U(P, g)$

(d) $L(P, f + g) \leq L(P, f) + L(P, g)$

**30.** The integral $\int_0^\infty x^{n-1}e^{-x}\,dx$ is divergent, when

(a) $n > 0$ (b) $n > 1$

(c) $n \leq 0$ (d) $n = 1/2$

**31.** The integral $\int_a^\infty \frac{dx}{x^n}$, where $a > 0$ is convergent, when

(a) $n = 1$ (b) $n < 1$

(c) $n \leq 1$ (d) $n > 1$

**32.** The integral $\int_0^1 x^{m-1}(1-x)^{n-1}dx$ is convergent, when
(a) $m>0$ (b) $n>0$
(c) $m>0,\ n>0$ (d) $m=0,\ n>1$

**33.** The integral $\int_a^b \frac{dx}{(x-a)^n}$ is convergent, when
(a) $n<1$ (b) $n>1$
(c) $n=1$ (d) $n\geq 1$

**34.** Let $f:[0,2]\to R$ be defined by
$$f(x)=\begin{cases}0, & \text{if } x \text{ is rational}\\ \frac{1}{2}, & \text{if } x \text{ is irrational}\end{cases}$$
Let $A$ and $B$ be the upper Riemann integral and the lower Riemann integral respectively of $f$ on $[0, 2]$. Then,
(a) $A=B=0$ (b) $A=1$ and $B=0$
(c) $A=\frac{1}{2}$ and $B=0$ (d) $A=B=\frac{1}{2}$

**35.** There are four statements
(A) Every continuous function is integrable.
(B) Every continuous function is differentiable.
(C) Every Riemann integrable function is continuous.
(D) Every differentiable function is continuous.
Then,
(a) Both (A) and (B) are correct
(b) Both (A) and (D) are correct
(c) Both (A) and (C) are correct
(d) Both (B) and (D) are correct

**36.** Consider the improper integrals
$I_1=\int_1^{\infty}\frac{dx}{x\sqrt{x^2+1}}$ and $I_2=\int_0^{\infty}e^{-x^2}dx$. Then,
(a) $I_1$ is convergent but $I_2$ is divergent
(b) $I_1$ is divergent but $I_2$ is convergent
(c) both $I_1$ and $I_2$ are convergent
(d) Neither $I_1$ nor $I_2$ are convergent

**37.** The value of integral $\int_1^4 [\log x]dx$ where [ ] denotes greatest integer
(a) log 4 (b) 1/2
(c) 4 − e (d) 4 + e

**38.** The limit $\lim_{n\to\infty}\sum_{k=1}^{n}\frac{k}{n^2}$ exists and is the Riemann integral of the function
(a) $f(x)=x^2,\ 0\leq x\leq 1$
(b) $f(x)=k$ for all $x, 0\leq x\leq 1$
(c) $f(x)=3x,\ 0\leq x\leq \frac{1}{3}$
(d) $f(x)=x,\ 0\leq x\leq 1$

**39.** If $f$ is Riemann integrable with respect to $\alpha$ on $[a, b]$, then
(a) $f$ is increasing and $\alpha$ is bounded function
(b) $f$ is bounded and $\alpha$ is increasing function
(c) $f$ and $\alpha$ are both bounded
(d) $f$ and $\alpha$ are both increasing

**40.** $f:[a,b]\to R$ is continuous, then $f$ is Riemann integrable on $[a, b]$
(a) the statement is true (b) the statement is false
(c) neither true nor false (d) partially true

**41.** Choose the correct statement for Riemann integral
(a) $\iint f(x,y)\,dA=\lim_{\max\Delta A_k\to 0}\sum_{k=1}^{n}f(x_k^*)\Delta x_k$
(b) $\iint f(x,y)\,dA=\lim_{\max\Delta A_k\to 0}\sum_{k=1}^{n}f(x_k^*,y_k^*)\Delta A_k$
(c) $\iint f(x,y)\,dA=\lim_{\max\Delta x_k\to 0}\sum_{k=1}^{n}f(x_k^*)\Delta x_k$
(d) None of the above

**42.** If $\underline{\int_a^b} fdx$ and $\overline{\int_a^b} fdx$ are lower and upper Riemann integrable on $[a, b]$. Then,
(a) $\underline{\int_a^b} fdx\geq\overline{\int_a^b} fdx$ (b) $\underline{\int_a^b} fdx=\overline{\int_a^b} fdx$
(c) $\underline{\int_a^b} fdx\leq\overline{\int_a^b} fdx$ (d) None of these

**43.** Consider the statements
I. It $f_1$ and $f_2$ are both integrable on $[a, b]$, then $f_1f_2$ is also integrable on $[a, b]$.
II. If $f$ is integrable on $[a, b]$, then $f^2$ is also integrable on $[a, b]$.
(a) Both (I) and (II) are true
(b) (I) is true but (II) is false
(c) (I) is false but (II) is true
(d) Neither (I) nor (II) is true

# Exercise 2 (For Part 'C')

**Direction** (Q. Nos. 1-34) *Questions may have one or more than one correct option.*

**1.** Let $f(x)=\begin{cases}0, & x \text{ irrational}\\ 1, & x \text{ rational}\end{cases}$, then
(a) $R\overline{\int_a^b} f(x)dx=b-a$ (b) $R\underline{\int_a^b} f(x)dx=0$
(c) $R\overline{\int_a^b} f(x)dx=0$ (d) $R\underline{\int_a^b} f(x)dx=b-a$

**2.** Which of the following(s) is/are correct?
(a) If $f$ is monotonic in $[a, b]$, then it is integrable in $[a, b]$
(b) If $f$ is monotonic in $[a, b]$, then $f$ is not integrable in $[a, b]$
(c) If $f$ is monotonic in $[a, b]$, then it is bounded
(d) If $f$ is monotonic in $[a, b]$, then it is not bounded

**3.** Which of the following(s) is/are correct?
(a) Every monotonic increasing function $f$ is Riemann integrable
(b) Every monotonic increasing function $f$ is not Riemann integrable
(c) If function is increasing in an interval, it is increasing in each of its sub-interval
(d) If function is increasing in an interval, it is not increasing in each of its sub-interval

**4.** If the function $f$ is defined in the interval (0, 1) as

$$f(x) = \begin{cases} \sqrt{(1-x^2)}, \text{ when } x \text{ is irrational} \\ (1-x), \text{ when } x \text{ is rational} \end{cases}$$

(a) $f(x)$ is not Riemann integrable in (0, 1)
(b) the lower Riemann integral of $f$ is $\frac{1}{2}$
(c) the function $f$ is Riemann integral of $f$ is $\frac{\pi}{4}$
(d) the function $f$ is not Riemann integrable

**5.** Given, $\int_0^1 x^{m-1}(1-x)^{n-1}dx$, then
(a) for $m, n > 1$, the integral is bounded
(b) for $m > 1, n < 1$, the points $x = 0, x = 1$ are the points of infinite discontinuities
(c) For $m, n > 1$, the integral is convergent
(d) $m, n > 0$ the integral is convergent

**6.** The function $f(x) = x^2$ is
(a) integrable on [0, 1]
(b) integrable on [0, 2]
(c) integrable on [0, 5]
(d) integrable on [0, 10]

**7.** If $f$ and $g$ are bounded and integrable on $[a, b]$, such that $f \geq g$, then
(a) $\int_a^b fdx \geq \int_a^b gdx$ when $b \geq a$
(b) $\int_a^b fdx \leq \int_a^b gdx$ when $b \leq a$
(c) Exactly one of above
(d) Neither (a) nor (b)

**8.** The oscillation of a bounded function $f$ on an interval $[a, b]$ is
(a) supremum of $\{|f(x_1) - f(x_2)| : x_1, x_2 \in [a, b]\}$
(b) infimum of $\{|f(x_1) - f(x_2)| : x_1, x_2 \in [a, b]\}$
(c) Both (a) and (b)
(d) Neither (a) nor (b)

**9.** Consider the statements
I. If $f_1$ and $f_2$ are two bounded and integrable functions on $[a, b]$, then $f_1 f_2$ is also integrable on $[a, b]$.
II. If $f_1$ and $f_2$ are two bounded and integrable functions on $[a, b]$ and there exists a number $\lambda > 0$ such that $|f_2(x)| \geq \lambda, \forall x \in [a, b]$, then $f_1/f_2$ is bounded and integrable on $[a, b]$.
(a) (I) is true but (II) is false
(b) (I) is false but (II) is true
(c) Both (I), (II) are false
(d) Neither (I) nor (II) is true

**10.** Which of the following(s) is/are correct?
(a) $f(x) = 3x + 1$ is Riemann integrable on [1, 2]
(b) $\int_1^2 f(x)dx = \frac{11}{2}$
(c) $\int_1^2 f(x)dx = \frac{2}{11}$
(d) None of the above

**11.** Consider the following statements
I. If $f_1 \in \mathbb{R}[a, b]$ and $f_2 \in \mathbb{R}[a, b]$ and $c_1, c_2$ are arbitrary constants, then $c_1 t_1 + c_2 t_2 \in \mathbb{R}[a, b]$.
II. If a function $f$ is bounded and integrable on each of the intervals $[a, c]$, $[c, b]$, $[a, b]$ where $c$ is a point of $[a, b]$, then $\int_a^b fdx = \int_a^c fdx + \int_c^b fdx$
(a) (I) is true but (II) is false
(b) (I) is false but (II) is true
(c) Both (I) and (II) are true
(d) Neither (I) nor (II) is true

**12.** Which of the following(s) is/are correct?
(a) If a function $f$ is monotonic on $[a, b]$, then it is integrable on $[a, b]$
(b) If a function $f$ is continuous, then to every $\varepsilon > 0$, there exists $\delta > 0$ such that

$$\left| \sum_{i=1}^{n} f(t_i)\Delta x_i - \int_a^b fdx \right| < \varepsilon$$

for every partition $P$ of $[a, b]$ with $\mu(P) < \delta$ and for every choice of points $t_i$ in $[x_{i-1}, x_i]$
(c) Exactly one of (a) and (b)
(d) None of the above

**13.** Consider the statements
I. A bounded function $f$, having a finite number of points of discontinuity on $[a, b]$ is integrable on $[a, b]$.
II. A bounded function $f$ is integrable on $[a, b]$, if the set of its points of discontinuity has only a finite number of limit points.
(a) (I) is true but (II) is false
(b) (I) is false but (II) is true
(c) Both (I) and (II) are true
(d) Neither (I) nor (II) is true

**14.** Consider the function

$$f(x) = \begin{cases} 0, \text{ when } x \text{ is irrational or zero} \\ \frac{1}{q}, \text{ when } x \text{ is any non-zero rational number } \frac{p}{q}, \\ \text{with least positive integers } p \text{ and } q. \end{cases}$$

Then,
(a) $f$ is $\mathbb{R}[0, 1]$
(b) $\int_0^1 f(x)dx = 0$
(c) $\int_0^1 f(x)dx = \frac{p}{q}, q \neq 0, p, q \in \mathbb{Z}$
(d) None of the above

**15.** Consider the function $f$ defined on $[-1, 1]$ as follows

$$f(x) = \begin{cases} k, & x \neq 0 \\ 0, & x = 0 \end{cases}$$

Then,

(a) $f$ is not Riemann integrable
(b) $f$ is Riemann integrable
(c) $\int_0^1 f(x)dx = 0$
(d) $\int_0^1 f(x)dx = 2k$

**16.** Consider the function $f$ defined as follows

$$f(x) = \begin{cases} \frac{1}{2^n}, & \frac{1}{2^{n+1}} < x \le \frac{1}{2^n}, n = 0, 1, 2, \ldots \\ 0, & \text{else} \end{cases}$$

Then,

(a) $f$ has infinite number of points of discontinuity
(b) $f$ has finite number of points of discontinuity
(c) the set of points of discontinuity of $f$ has only one limit point
(d) every member of set of points of discontinuity of $f$ is a limit point

**17.** Consider the function $f$ on [0, 1] defined as follows

$$f(x) = \begin{cases} 2x\sin(1/x) - \cos(1/x), & x \ne 0 \\ 0, & x = 0 \end{cases}$$

Then,

(a) $f$ is continuous at $x = 0$
(b) $f$ is discontinuous at $x = 0$
(c) $f$ has primitive $F$, where $F(x) = \begin{cases} x^2 \sin(1/x), & x \ne 0 \\ 0, & x = 0 \end{cases}$
(d) $f$ has primitive $F$, where $F(x) = \begin{cases} x^2 \cos(1/x), & x \ne 0 \\ 0, & x = 0 \end{cases}$

**18.** Which of the following(s) is/are improper integrals?

(a) $\int_{-\infty}^{\infty} \frac{dx}{1+x^2}$ (b) $\int_0^1 \frac{dx}{x(1-x)}$
(c) $\int_1^{\infty} \frac{dx}{x^2}$ (d) $\int_0^1 \frac{\sin x}{x} dx$

**19.** The improper integral $\int_0^1 \frac{dx}{x(1-x)}$ has

(a) point of infinite discontinuity at 0
(b) point of infinite discontinuity at 1
(c) point of infinite discontinuity at 0, 1
(d) point of infinite discontinuity at $\infty$

**20.** Which of the following improper integral is/are convergent?

(a) $\int_{-2}^{2} \frac{dx}{(1-x)x^2}$ (b) $\int_0^{\pi} \frac{dx}{\sin x}$
(c) Both (a) and (b) (d) Neither (a) nor (b)

**21.** Which of the following(s) improper integral is/are convergent?

(a) $\int_0^1 \frac{dx}{\sqrt{1-x^2}}$ (b) $\int_1^2 \frac{xdx}{\sqrt{x-1}}$
(c) Exactly one of above (d) Neither (a) nor (b)

**22.** Consider the improper integrals

I. $\int_{-1}^{1} \frac{dx}{(2-x)\sqrt{1-x^2}}$ II. $\int_{-1}^{1} \frac{x-1}{x^{5/3}} dx$

(a) (I) is convergent but (II) is divergent
(b) (I) is divergent but (II) is convergent
(c) Both (I) and (II) are convergent
(d) Neither (I) nor (II) is convergent

**23.** Consider the improper integrals

I. $\int_0^1 \frac{dx}{\sqrt{1-x}}$ II. $\int_0^1 \frac{dx}{x^2}$

Then,

(a) (I) is convergent but (II) is divergent
(b) (I) is divergent but (b) is convergent
(c) Both (I) and (II) are convergent
(d) Neither (I) nor (II) is convergent

**24.** Consider the improper integrals

I. $\int_1^2 \frac{\sqrt{x}}{\log x} dx$ II. $\int_0^1 \frac{\log x}{\sqrt{x}} dx$

Then,

(a) (I) is convergent but (II) is divergent
(b) (I) is divergent but (II) is convergent
(c) Both (I) and (II) are convergent
(d) Neither (I) nor (II) is convergent

**25.** Consider the improper integral $I = \int_0^{\pi/2} \log \sin x dx$.

Then,

(a) $I$ is convergent (b) $I$ is divergent
(c) $I = \frac{\pi}{2} \log 2$ (d) $I = -\frac{\pi}{2} \log 2$

**26.** Which of the following(s) improper integral is/are convergent?

(a) $\int_2^3 \frac{x^2+1}{x^2-4} dx$ (b) $\int_0^1 \frac{\sin x}{x^{3/2}} dx$
(c) Both (a) and (b) (d) Neither (a) nor (b)

**27.** Which of the following(s) improper integral is/are divergent?

(a) $\int_0^{\pi} \frac{\sqrt{x}}{\sin x} dx$
(b) $\int_0^1 \frac{x^n \log x}{(1+x)^2} dx, n > -1$
(c) Both (a) and (b)
(d) Exactly only one of (a) and (b)

**28.** Which of the following(s) improper integral is/are convergent?

(a) $\int_0^{\infty} x^3 e^{-x^2} dx$
(b) $\int_{-\infty}^{\infty} \frac{dx}{1+x^2}$
(c) Exactly one of (a) and (b)
(d) Exactly only one of (a) and (b)

**29.** Which of the following(s) improper integral is/are convergent?

(a) $\int_{\sqrt{2}}^{\infty} \frac{dx}{x\sqrt{x^2-1}}$ (b) $\int_0^{\infty} x \sin x dx$
(c) Both (a) and (b) (d) Either (a) or (b)

**30.** Which of the following(s) improper integral is/are convergent?

(a) $\int_0^\infty \frac{x^2\,dx}{\sqrt{1+x^5}}$

(b) $\int_1^\infty \frac{\log x}{x^2}\,dx$

(c) Both (a) and (b)

(d) Exactly only one of (a) and (b)

**31.** Which of the following(s) improper integral is/are convergent?

(a) $\int_0^\infty \frac{x\tan^{-1}x}{(1+x^4)^{1/3}}\,dx$ (b) $\int_{e^2}^\infty \frac{dx}{x\log x}$

(c) Both (a) and (b) (d) Neither (a) nor (b)

**32.** Let $f$ and $\phi$ be two functions such that, $\forall\, x \in\, ]a, b[$, $f(x) \geq 0$, $\phi(x) \geq 0$

Also, let $f(x) \leq \phi(x)$, then

(a) $\int_a^b \phi(x)dx$ converges $\Rightarrow \int_a^b f(x)dx$ converges

(b) $\int_a^b f(x)dx$ does not converges $\Rightarrow \int_a^b \phi(x)dx$ does not converge

(c) $\int_a^b \phi(x)dx$ converges $\Rightarrow \int_a^b f(x)dx$ diverges

(d) $\int_a^b f(x)dx$ diverges $\Rightarrow \int_a^b \phi(x)dx$ converges

**33.** Which of the following(s) is/are correct?

(a) Every continuous function is Riemann integrable

(b) Every continuous function is not Riemann integrable

(c) If function is continuous in an interval it is bounded and uniformly continuous on that interval

(d) If function is continuous in an interval it is not neither bounded nor uniformly continuous on that interval

**34.** Given,

$$\int_0^\infty e^{-x}x^{n-1}dx, \text{ then}$$

(a) the integral is divergent when $n \leq 0$

(b) the integral is convergent when $0 < n < 1$

(c) the integral is convergent when $n \geq 1$

(d) the integral is divergent when $n \geq 1$

# Answers

## Exercise 1

| | | | | | | | | | |
|---|---|---|---|---|---|---|---|---|---|
| **1.** (c) | **2.** (b) | **3.** (c) | **4.** (a) | **5.** (c) | **6.** (c) | **7.** (a) | **8.** (b) | **9.** (h) | **10.** (b) |
| **11.** (d) | **12.** (b) | **13.** (c) | **14.** (b) | **15.** (a) | **16.** (c) | **17.** (b) | **18.** (a) | **19.** (a) | **20.** (d) |
| **21.** (b) | **22.** (a) | **23.** (c) | **24.** (b) | **25.** (c) | **26.** (c) | **27.** (b) | **28.** (d) | **29.** (a) | **30.** (c) |
| **31.** (d) | **32.** (c) | **33.** (a) | **34.** (b) | **35.** (b) | **36.** (c) | **37.** (c) | **38.** (d) | **39.** (b) | **40.** (a) |
| **41.** (b) | **42.** (c) | **43.** (a) | | | | | | | |

## Exercise 2

| | | | | | | | | | |
|---|---|---|---|---|---|---|---|---|---|
| **1.** (a,b) | **2.** (a,c) | **3.** (a,c) | **4.** (a,b,c,d) | **5.** (a,b,c,d) | **6.** (a,b,c,d) | **7.** (a,b) | **8.** (a) | **9.** (c) | **10.** (a,b) |
| **11.** (c) | **12.** (a,b) | **13.** (c) | **14.** (a,b) | **15.** (b,d) | **16.** (a,c) | **17.** (b,c) | **18.** (a,b,c) | **19.** (a,b,c) | **20.** (d) |
| **21.** (a,b) | **22.** (a) | **23.** (a) | **24.** (b) | **25.** (a,d) | **26.** (b) | **27.** (b,d) | **28.** (a,b) | **29.** (a) | **30.** (b,d) |
| **31.** (d) | **32.** (a,b) | **33.** (a,c) | **34.** (a,b,c) | | | | | | |

# Hints & Solutions

## Exercise 1

**1.** Suppose that for some $c \in (a, b)$, $f(c) > 0$. Then, for given $\varepsilon = \frac{f(c)}{2} > 0$, continuity of $f$ at $c$ implies that there exists a $\delta > 0$ such that

$$f(x) > \frac{f(c)}{2}, \forall\, x \in (c-\delta, c+\delta)$$

Hence, $\int_a^b f(x)dx = \int_a^{c-\delta} f(x)dx + \int_{c-\delta}^{c+\delta} f(x)dx + \int_{c+\delta}^b f(x)dx$

$$\geq \int_{c-\delta}^{c+\delta} f(x)dx \qquad \text{[as } f(x) \text{ is non-negative } \forall\, x]$$

$$> \frac{f(c)}{2}\int_{c-\delta}^{c+\delta} dx = \delta f(c) > 0$$

which contradict the fact that $\int_a^b f(x)dx = 0$

Similarly, $f(a) \not> 0$, $f(b) \not> 0$. Hence, $f(x) = 0$, $\forall\, x \in [a, b]$.

**2.** We have,

$$\int_0^1 \frac{nf(x)}{1+n^2x^2}dx = \int_0^{\frac{1}{\sqrt{n}}} \frac{nf(x)}{1+n^2x^2}dx + \int_{\frac{1}{\sqrt{n}}}^1 \frac{nf(x)}{1+n^2x^2}dx$$

Hence, by mean value theorem, $\exists\, t,\ 0 \leq t \leq \frac{1}{\sqrt{n}}$,

$$\int_0^{\frac{1}{\sqrt{n}}} \frac{nf(x)}{1+n^2x^2}dx = f(t)\int_0^{\frac{1}{\sqrt{n}}} \frac{n}{1+n^2x^2}dx$$

$$= f(t)\tan^{-1}\sqrt{n}$$

Hence, $$\lim_{n\to\infty}\int_0^{\frac{1}{\sqrt{n}}} \frac{nf(x)}{1+n^2x^2}dx = \frac{\pi}{2}f(0)$$

Now, since $f$ is continuous on [0, 1].

Hence, $f$ is bounded and therefore, there exists a constant $k$ such that

$$|f(x)| \leq k,\ \forall\, x \in [0, 1]$$

Hence, $$\left|\int_{\frac{1}{\sqrt{n}}}^1 \frac{nf(x)}{1+n^2x^2}dx\right| \leq k\left|\int_{\frac{1}{\sqrt{n}}}^1 \frac{n}{1+n^2x^2}dx\right|$$

$$= k\,|\tan^{-1} n - \tan^{-1}\sqrt{n}\,|$$

Hence, $$\lim_{n\to\infty}\left|\int_{\frac{1}{\sqrt{n}}}^1 \frac{nf(x)}{1+n^2x^2}dx\right| = 0.$$

$$\Rightarrow \quad \lim_{n\to\infty}\int_{\frac{1}{\sqrt{n}}}^1 \frac{nf(x)}{1+n^2x^2}dx = 0$$

Therefore,

$$\lim_{n\to\infty}\int_0^1 \frac{nf(x)}{1+n^2x^2}dx = \frac{\pi}{2}f(0) + 0$$

$$= \frac{\pi}{2}f(0)$$

**4.** Since, 0 and 2 are only the points of infinite discontinuity in [0, 2]. Hence,

$$\int_0^2 \frac{dx}{2x-x^2} = \lim_{\varepsilon\to 0^+}\int_\varepsilon^1 \frac{dx}{x(2-x)} + \lim_{\gamma\to 0^+}\int_1^{2-\gamma} \frac{dx}{x(2-x)}$$

$$= \frac{1}{2}\lim_{\varepsilon\to 0^+}\left[\log\frac{x}{2-x}\right]_\varepsilon^1 + \frac{1}{2}\lim_{\gamma\to 0^+}\left[\log\frac{x}{2-x}\right]_1^{2-\gamma}$$

$$= -\frac{1}{2}\lim_{\varepsilon\to 0^+}\log\frac{\lambda}{2-\lambda} + \frac{1}{2}\lim_{\gamma\to 0^+}\log\frac{2-\mu}{\mu} = \infty$$

Hence, the given integral is divergent.

**5.** We have,

$$\int_2^\infty \frac{2x^2}{x^4-1}dx = \lim_{\varepsilon\to\infty}\int_2^\varepsilon \frac{2x^2}{x^4-1}dx$$

$$= \lim_{\varepsilon\to\infty}\left[\tan^{-1}\varepsilon - \tan^{-1}2 + \frac{1}{2}\log\frac{\varepsilon-1}{\varepsilon+1} + \frac{1}{2}\log 3\right]$$

$$= \frac{\pi}{2} - \tan^{-1}2 + \frac{1}{2}\log 3$$

Since, the limit exists. Hence, given integral is convergent and equal to

$$\frac{\pi}{2} - \tan^{-1}2 + \frac{1}{2}\log 3$$

**11.** We have,

$$\int_0^\infty \sin x dx = \lim_{\varepsilon\to\infty}\int_0^\varepsilon \sin x dx$$

$$= \lim_{\varepsilon\to\infty}(1-\cos\varepsilon)$$

Hence, the improper integral does not exists, since $\cos\varepsilon$ has no limit when $\varepsilon \to \infty$.

**12.** We have,

$$\int_{-\infty}^\infty \frac{dx}{(1+x^2)^2} = \int_{-\infty}^0 \frac{dx}{(1+x^2)^2} + \int_0^\infty \frac{dx}{(1+x^2)^2}$$

$$= 2\int_0^\infty \frac{dx}{(1+x^2)^2}$$

$$= \lim_{\varepsilon\to\infty} 2\int_0^\varepsilon \frac{dx}{(1+x^2)^2}$$

$$= \lim_{\varepsilon\to\infty} 2\left[\tan^{-1}\varepsilon + \frac{\varepsilon}{1+\varepsilon^2}\right] = \frac{\pi}{2}$$

Hence, exists and equal to $\frac{\pi}{2}$.

**36.** $I_1$ Let $f(x) = \frac{1}{x\sqrt{x^2+1}}$

and $g(x) = \frac{1}{x^2}$

Hence, $$\lim_{x\to\infty}\frac{f(x)}{g(x)} = \lim_{x\to\infty}\frac{x^2}{x\sqrt{x^2+1}} = 1 \neq 0$$

but the integral $\int_1^\infty \frac{dx}{x^2}$ is convergent. Hence, $I_1 = \int_1^\infty \frac{dx}{x\sqrt{x^2+1}}$ is convergent.

$I_2$ Since, 0 is not a point of infinite discontinuity and so we have to examine convergence at $\infty$ only.

we know that

$$e^{x^2} > x^2,\ \forall\, x \in \mathbb{R}$$

$$\Rightarrow \quad e^{-x^2} < \frac{1}{x^2},\ \forall\, x \in \mathbb{R}$$

but $\int_1^\infty \frac{1}{x^2}dx$ is convergent. Hence, $\int_1^\infty e^{-x^2}dx$ is convergent.

Hence, $\int_0^\infty e^{-x^2}dx$ is convergent.

**43.** Given that $f$ is bounded on $[a, b]$. Hence, $|f|$ is also bounded on $[a, b]$. Hence, there exists $M > 0$ such that $|f(x)| \leq M$, $\forall\, x \in [a, b]$.

Again, since $f$ is integrable, therefore $|f|$ is also integrable on $[a, b]$ and for given $\varepsilon > 0$, there exists a partition $P$ of $[a, b]$ such that

$$U(P, |f|) - L(P, |f|) < \frac{\varepsilon}{2M}$$

Since, $|f^2(x)| = |f(x)|^2 \le M^2$

$\Rightarrow$ $f^2$ is bounded

Let $M_i, m_i$ be the bounds of $|f|$ and $M_i', m_i'$ be bounds of $f^2$ in $\Delta x_i$. Then,

$$M_i' = M_i^2, m_i' = m_i^2$$

Also,

$$U(P, f^2) - L(P, f^2) = \sum_{i=1}^{n} (M_i' - m_i')\Delta x_i$$

$$= \sum_{i=1}^{n} (M_i^2 - m_i^2)\Delta x_i$$

$$= \sum_{i=1}^{n} (M_i - m_i)(M_i + m_i)\Delta x_i$$

$$\le 2M\left[\sum_{i=1}^{n} (M_i - m_i)\Delta x_i\right]$$

$$= 2M\{U(P,|f|) - L(P,|f|)\}$$

$$< 2M \cdot \frac{\varepsilon}{2M}$$

$$= \varepsilon$$

$\Rightarrow$ $f^2$ is Riemann integrable.

$\Rightarrow$ $f_1^2, f_2^2$ and $(f_1 + f_2)^2$ are also Riemann integrable on [a, b].

Also,

$$f_1 f_2 = \frac{1}{2}\{(f_1 + f_2)^2 - f_1^2 - f_2^2\}$$

$\Rightarrow$ $f_1 f_2$ is also Riemann integrable.

## Exercise 2

**1.** Let $a = x_1 < x_2 < \ldots < x_n = b$ be a sub-division of [a, b]. Then, we have

$$R\bar{\int_a^b} f(x)dx = \text{Inf}\sum_{i=1}^{n} (x_i - x_{i-1})M_i$$

where $$M_i = \sup_{x_i < x < x_{i-1}} f(x) = 1$$

$$= \text{Inf}\sum_{i=1}^{n} (x_i - x_{i-1})$$

$$= (x_n - x_i)$$

$$= b - a$$

Also, $$R\underline{\int_a^b} f(x)dx = \text{Sup}\sum_{i=1}^{n} (x_i - x_{i-1})m_i$$

where $$m_i = \inf_{x_i < x < x_{i-1}} f(x) = 0$$

$$= \sum_{i=1}^{n} (x_i - x_{i-1}) \cdot 0 = 0$$

**2.** Since, $f$ is monotonic in [a, b] it is bounded and $f(a)$, $f(b)$ are its two bounds.

Let $\varepsilon$ be a positive number.

Suppose that $f$ is monotonically increasing.

Divide [a, b] so that the length of each sub-interval is

$$< \varepsilon/[f(b) - f(a) + 1]$$

Let $P = D\{a = x_0, x_1, x_2, \ldots, x_{r-1}, x_r, \ldots, x_n = b\}$ be any partition.

Let $\delta_r = x_r - x_{r-1}$

Here, $M_r = f(x_r)$

$m_r = f(x_{r-1})$

Thus, we have

$$\omega(D) = \Sigma(M_r - m_r)\delta_r$$

$$= \Sigma[f(x_r) - f(x_{r-1})\delta_r]$$

$$< \frac{\varepsilon}{f(b) - f(a) + 1} \cdot \Sigma[f(x_r) - f(x_{r-1})]$$

$$= \frac{\varepsilon}{f(b) - f(a) + 1} \cdot [f(b) - f(a)] < \varepsilon$$

Hence, $f$ is integrable in [a, b].

**3.** Let us assume function $f$ is increasing function on [a, b].

Now for a given positive number $\varepsilon$; there exists a partition $P = \{a = x_0, x_1, x_2, \ldots, x_n = b\}$ of [a, b] such that

$$(x_r - x_{r-1}) < \frac{\varepsilon}{[f(b) - f(a) + 1]} \text{ for } r = 1, 2, \ldots, n$$

Since, the function $f$ being increasing on [a, b], it is bounded and increasing on each sub-interval $[x_{r-1}, x_r]$.

Let the bounds of the function $f$ on the sub-interval $[x_{r-1}, x_r]$, be $M_r$ and $m_r$, then

$$M_r = f(x_r)$$

and $$m_r = f(x_{r-1})$$

Hence, for this partition $P$, we have

$\Rightarrow$ $$U(P, f) - L(P, f)$$

$$= \sum_{r=1}^{n} (M_r - m_r)(x_r - x_{r-1})$$

$$< \frac{\varepsilon}{[f(b) - f(a) + 1]} \sum_{r=1}^{n} [f(x_r) - f(x_{r-1})]$$

$\Rightarrow$ $$U(P, f) - L(P, f) < \frac{\varepsilon}{[f(b) - f(a) + 1]}[f(x_n) - f(x_0)]$$

$\Rightarrow$ $$U(P, f) - L(P, f) < \frac{\varepsilon}{[f(b) - f(a) + 1]}[f(b) - f(a)],$$

$(\because x_0 = a, x_n = b)$

$\Rightarrow$ $U(P, f) - L(P, f) < \varepsilon$

*i.e.,* the function $f$ is Riemann integrable on [a, b].

**4.** As,

$$\{\sqrt{(1 - x^2)}\}^2 (1 - x)^2 = 1 - x^2 - 1 + 2x - x^2$$

$$= 2x - 2x^2$$

$$= 2x(1 - x) > 0$$

For all values of $x$ in the open interval (0, 1).

So, $$\{\sqrt{(1 - x^2)}\}^2 > (1 - x)^2$$

$\Rightarrow$ $$\sqrt{(1 - x^2)} > (1 - x) \text{ for } 0 < x < 1 \quad \ldots\text{(i)}$$

Now, if $P = \{0 = x_0, x_1, x_2, \ldots, x_n = 1\}$ is any partition of (0, 1), then for any sub-interval.

$I_r = (x_{r-1}, x_r)$ however small it may be, the values of $f(x)$ range between $(1-x)$ and $\sqrt{(1-x)^2}$.

Therefore, for all $r$, we have

$$\left.\begin{aligned} M_r &= \text{upper bound of } f(x) \text{ in } I_r = \sqrt{(1-x^2)} \\ m_r &= \text{lower bound of } f(x) \text{ in } I_r = (1-x) \end{aligned}\right\} \quad \ldots\text{(ii)}$$

Hence, the lower Riemann integral

$$= \int_0^1 f(x)dx$$

$$= \lim_{\|P\| \to 0} L(P, f)$$

$$= \lim_{\|P\| \to 0} \sum_{r=1}^{n} m_r \delta_r$$

$$= \int_0^1 (1-x)dx \quad \text{[from Eq. (ii)]}$$

$$= \left[x - \frac{1}{2}x^2\right]_0^1 = 1 - \frac{1}{2} = \frac{1}{2} \quad \ldots\text{(iii)}$$

and the upper Riemann integral

$$= \int_0^1 f(x)dx$$

$$= \lim_{\|P\| \to 0} U(P, f)$$

$$= \lim_{\|P\| \to 0} \sum_{r=1}^{n} M_r \delta_r$$

$$= \int_0^1 \sqrt{(1-x^2)}dx \quad \text{[from Eq. (ii)]}$$

$$= \left[\frac{1}{2}x\sqrt{(1-x^2)} + \frac{1}{2}\sin^{-1} x\right]_0^1$$

$$= \frac{1}{2}(\sin^{-1} 1)$$

$$= \left(\frac{1}{2}\right)\left(\frac{\pi}{2}\right) = \frac{\pi}{4} \quad \ldots\text{(iv)}$$

From Eqs. (iii) and (iv), we find that the lower and upper Riemann integrals are not equal, hence the function $f$ is not Riemann integrable in (0, 1).

**5.** ***Case* I** When $m > 1, n > 1$, the integrand is bounded and therefore, the integral is convergent when $m > 1$ and $n > 1$.

***Case* II** When $m > 1, n < 1$, the points $x = 0$ and $x = 1$ are the points of infinite discontinuities.

At $x = 0$, we have,

$$\lim_{x \to 0^+} [x^{1-m} \cdot f(x)] = 1$$

where $$f(x) = x^{m-1}(1-x)^{n-1}$$

Hence, the limit is finite and non-zero and therefore, the integral will be convergent by $\mu$-test.

If $$\mu = 1 - m < 1$$

or $$m > 0$$

At $x = 1$ we have

$$\lim_{x \to 1^-} [(1-x)^{1-n} \cdot f(x)] = 1$$

which is finite and $\neq 0$.

**6.** Let us consider the interval $[0, k]$ where $k = 1, 2, 5, 10$. Let $P$ be the partition of interval $[0, k]$ obtained by dividing the interval into $n$ equal parts.

Thus,

$$P = \left\{0, \frac{k}{n}, \frac{2k}{n}, \ldots, \frac{nk}{n}\right\}$$

where

$$\left[(i-1)\cdot\frac{k}{n}\right]^2 \text{ and } \left[\frac{ik}{n}\right]^2$$

are the lower and upper bounds of the function in $\Delta x_i$ (as $f(x) = x^2$ is increasing in $[0, k]$, $k > 0$) and the length of each such interval is $\frac{k}{n}$.

Hence, $$U(P, x^2) = \sum_{i=1}^{n} M_i \Delta x_i$$

$$= \sum_{i=1}^{n} \left[\frac{ik}{n}\right]^2 \Delta x_i$$

$$= \sum_{i=1}^{n} \left[\frac{ik}{n}\right]^2 \cdot \frac{k}{n}$$

$$= \frac{k^3}{n^3} \sum_{i=1}^{n} i^2$$

$$= \frac{k^3}{n^3} \cdot \frac{n}{6}(n+1)(2n+1)$$

$$= \frac{k^3}{6}\left(1 + \frac{1}{n}\right)\left(2 + \frac{1}{n}\right)$$

Hence, $$\int_0^{\bar{k}} f(x)dx = \int_0^{\bar{k}} x^2 dx$$

$$= \operatorname*{Inf}_{\text{over } P} U(P, x^2)$$

$$= \lim_{\|\mu(P)\| \to 0} U(P, x^2)$$

$$= \lim_{n \to \infty} \mu(P, x^2)$$

$$= \lim_{n \to \infty} \frac{k^3}{6}\left(1 + \frac{1}{n}\right)\left(2 + \frac{1}{n}\right) = \frac{k^3}{3}$$

Now, $$L(P, x^2) = \sum_{i=1}^{n} m_i \Delta x_i$$

$$= \sum_{i=1}^{n} \left[(i-1)\frac{k}{n}\right]^2 \frac{k}{n}$$

$$= \frac{k^3}{n^3} \sum_{i=1}^{n} (i-1)^2$$

$$= \frac{k^3}{n^3} \cdot \frac{(n-1)}{6} \cdot n \cdot (2n-1)$$

$$= \frac{k^3}{3}\left(1 - \frac{1}{n}\right)\left(2 - \frac{1}{n}\right)$$

Hence, $$\int_{\underline{0}}^{k} f(x)dx = \int_{\underline{0}}^{k} x^2 dx$$

$$= \operatorname*{Sup}_{\text{over } P} L(P, x^2)$$

$$= \lim_{\|\mu(P)\| \to 0} L(P, x^2)$$

$$= \lim_{n\to\infty} L(P, x^2) = \frac{k^3}{3}$$

Hence, $\int_0^{\bar{k}} f(x)dx = \int_{\underline{0}}^{k} f(x)dx$

$\Rightarrow f(x) = x^2$ is Riemann integrable in $[0, k]$, $\forall\, k > 0$.

**7.** Since, $\quad f \geq g$

$\Rightarrow \quad f - g \geq 0, \forall\, x \in [a, b]$

Hence,

$$\int_a^b (f - g)dx \geq 0, \text{ if } b \geq a$$

$$\Rightarrow \quad \int_a^b fdx \geq \int_a^b gdx, \text{ if } b \geq a$$

Also,

$$\int_a^b (f - g)dx \leq 0, \text{ if } b \leq a$$

$$\Rightarrow \quad \int_a^b fdx \leq \int_a^b gdx, \text{ if } b \leq a$$

**8.** Suppose $m$ and $M$ are the bounds of $f$ on $[a, b]$. Then,

$$m \leq f(x_1), f(x_2) \leq M, \forall\, x_1, x_2 \in [a, b]$$

$$\Rightarrow \quad |f(x_1) - f(x_2)| \leq M - m, \forall\, x_1, x_2 \in [a, b] \quad \text{...(i)}$$

$\Rightarrow M - m$ is an upper bound of the set

$$\{|f(x_1) - f(x_2)| : x_1, x_2 \in [a, b]\}$$

Let $\varepsilon > 0$ be a given number.

Since, $M$ is supremum of $f$.

Hence, there exists $x' \subset [a, b]$ such that

$$f(x') = M - \frac{1}{2}\varepsilon \quad \text{...(ii)}$$

Similarly, there exists $x'' \in [a, b]$ such that

$$f(x'') < m + \frac{1}{2}\varepsilon \quad \text{...(iii)}$$

From Eqs. (ii) and (iii), we have

$x', x'' \in [a, b]$ such that

$f(x') - f(x'') > M - m - \varepsilon$

$$\Rightarrow \quad |f(x') - f(x'')| > M - m - \varepsilon \quad \text{...(iv)}$$

Thus, from Eqs. (i) and (iv) $M - m$ is an upper bound and no number less than $M - m$ can be an upper bound of the set

$\{|f(x_1) - f(x_2)| : x_1, x_2 \in [a, b]\}$

$$\Rightarrow \quad M - m = \text{Sup}\{|f(x_1) - f(x_2)| : x_1, x_2 \in [a, b]\}$$

**10.** Let us consider the partition

$P = \{1 = x_0, x_1, x_2, \ldots, x_n = 2\}$ of interval $[1, 2]$, which divides the interval $[1, 2]$ into $n$ equal sub-interval, each of length $\frac{2-1}{n} = \frac{1}{n}$, so that

$$\mu(P) = \frac{1}{n} \to 0 \text{ as } n \to \infty$$

$$x_i = 1 + \frac{i}{n}, i = 1, 2, \ldots, n$$

$$\Delta x_i = \frac{1}{n}, i = 1, 2, \ldots, n$$

and $\quad \sum_{i=1}^{n} \Delta x_i = n \cdot \frac{1}{n} = 2 - 1 = 1$

Let $\quad t_i = x_i;\ i = 1, 2, \ldots, n$

Then, $\quad S(P, f) = S(P, 3x + 1)$

$$= \sum_{i=1}^{n} f(t_i)\Delta x_i = \sum_{i=1}^{n} f(x_i)\Delta x_i$$

$$= \sum_{i=1}^{n} (3x_i + 1)\Delta x_i$$

$$= 4\sum_{i=1}^{n} \Delta x_i + \frac{3}{n^2}\sum_{i=1}^{n} i$$

$$= 4 + \frac{3}{n^2}\frac{n(n+1)}{2} = \frac{11}{2} + \frac{3}{2n}$$

Hence, $\quad \lim_{\mu(P)\to 0} S(P, 3x + 1) = \frac{11}{2}$

Since, the limit exists and hence $f$ is Riemann integrable and

$$\int_1^2 fdx = \lim_{\mu(P)\to 0} S(P, 3x + 1) = \frac{11}{2}$$

**14.** Given function $f$ is bounded with bounds 0 and 1. Let $\varepsilon > 0$ be a given number. Then, there exists a largest integer $q \in N$ such that $\frac{1}{q} > \frac{1}{2}\varepsilon \Rightarrow q < \frac{2}{\varepsilon}$.

Hence, there are only finite number of points $\frac{p}{q}$ for which $\frac{1}{q} > \frac{1}{2}\varepsilon$, which are exceptional points.

Therefore at those rational points which are exceptional points, $f$ has a value $\frac{1}{q} > \frac{1}{2}\varepsilon$, while at the other rational points, the value of $f$ is $\frac{1}{q} < \frac{1}{2}\varepsilon$ and the value of $f$ at irrational points.

But every interval contains rational as well as irrational points. Hence, the oscillation of $f$ in any interval which includes no exceptional points is less than $\frac{\varepsilon}{2}$ and that in an interval. Which includes the exceptional points it is at the most equal to 1.

Let $P$ be a partition of $[0, 1]$ so as to enclose the exceptional points which are finite in numbers in sub-intervals, the sum of whose length is less than $\frac{\varepsilon}{2}$. Hence, the contribution to $\{U(P, f) - L(P, f)\}$ made by these is less than $\frac{\varepsilon}{2}$. But the contribution to

$$[U(P, f) - L(P, f)]$$

by remaining portion of $[0, 1]$ is evidently less than $\frac{\varepsilon}{2}$.

Hence, $\quad U(P, f) - L(P, f) < \varepsilon$

$\Rightarrow \quad f$ is Riemann integrable and

$$\int_0^1 f(x)dx = 0$$

**17.** Clearly, $f$ is discontinuous at $x = 0$

Now, consider the function

$$F(x) = \begin{cases} x^2 \sin(1/x), & x \neq 0 \\ 0 & , x = 0 \end{cases}$$

$$\Rightarrow \quad F'(x) = \begin{cases} 2x\sin(1/x) - \cos(1/x), & x \neq 0 \\ 0 & , x = 0 \end{cases}$$

$$= f(x)$$

Hence, $f$ has primitive

$$F(x) = \begin{cases} x^2 \sin(1/x), & x \neq 0 \\ 0 & , x = 0 \end{cases}$$

**23.** (I) Since, 1 is the only point of infinite discontinuity in [0, 1]. Hence,

$$\int_0^1 \frac{dx}{\sqrt{1-x}} = \lim_{\varepsilon \to 0^+} \int_0^{1-\varepsilon} \frac{dx}{\sqrt{1-x}}, \ 0 < \varepsilon < 1$$

$$= \lim_{\varepsilon \to 0^+} [-2\sqrt{1-x}]_0^{1-\varepsilon}$$

$$= -\lim_{\varepsilon \to 0^+} [2(\sqrt{\varepsilon} - 1)] = 2$$

Hence, the improper integral exists and is equal to 2.

(II) Since, 0 is the only point of infinite discontinuity in [0, 1]. Hence,

$$\int_0^1 \frac{dx}{x^2} = \lim_{\varepsilon \to 0^+} \int_{0+\varepsilon}^1 \frac{dx}{x^2}, \quad 0 < \varepsilon < 1$$

$$= \lim_{\varepsilon \to 0^+} \left(\frac{1}{\varepsilon} - 1\right) = \infty$$

Hence, the improper integral is divergent.

**24.** (I) Since, 1 is the only point of infinite discontinuity. Let

$$f(x) = \frac{\sqrt{x}}{\log x} \text{ and } g(x) = \frac{1}{x-1}$$

$$\Rightarrow \quad \lim_{x \to 1^+} \frac{f(x)}{g(x)} = \lim_{x \to 1^+} \frac{(x-1)\sqrt{x}}{\log x}$$

$$= \lim_{x \to 1^+} \frac{\frac{3}{2}x^{1/2} - \frac{1}{2}x^{-1/2}}{1/x} = 1 \neq 0$$

But the integral

$$\int_1^2 \frac{dx}{x-1} \text{ is divergent.}$$

Hence,

$$\int_1^2 \frac{\sqrt{x}}{\log x} \text{ is divergent.}$$

(II) Since, $\frac{\log x}{\sqrt{x}}$ is less than zero in [0, 1]. Hence, we take

$$f(x) = -\frac{\log x}{\sqrt{x}} = \frac{\log(1/x)}{\sqrt{x}}$$

Here, 0 is the only point of infinite discontinuity.

Let $\quad g(x) = \dfrac{1}{x^{3/4}}$

$$\Rightarrow \quad \lim_{x \to 0^+} \frac{f(x)}{g(x)} = \lim_{x \to 0^+} \frac{\frac{\log(1/x)}{\sqrt{x}}}{1/x^{3/4}}$$

$$= \lim_{x \to 0^+} x^{1/4} \log(1/x) = 0$$

but the integral $\int_0^1 \frac{dx}{x^{3/4}}$ convergent at 0. Hence, $\int_0^1 \frac{\log x}{\sqrt{x}} dx$ is convergent.

**25.** Since, $f$ is less than or equal to zero in [0, 2]. Hence, we consider the function $(-f)$ for testing convergence of the interval.

Let

$$f(x) = -\log \sin x$$

Since, 0 is the only point of infinite discontinuity of $f$.

Let $\quad g(x) = \dfrac{1}{x^m}, \ m < 1$

$$\Rightarrow \quad \lim_{x \to 0^+} \frac{f(x)}{g(x)} = \lim_{x \to 0^+} -x^m \log \sin x$$

$$= 0$$

but $\int_0^{\pi/2} \frac{dx}{x^m}$ is convergent, if $m < 1$.

Hence, $\int_0^{\pi/2} -\log \sin x dx$ is convergent.

$\Rightarrow \int_0^{\pi/2} \log \sin x dx$ is convergent.

Let $\quad I = \int_0^{\pi/2} \log \sin x dx$

Since, $\quad \log \sin 2x = \log 2 + \log \sin x + \log \cos x$

Hence, $\int_0^{\pi/2} \log \sin 2x dx = \int_0^{\pi/2} (\log 2) dx + \int_0^{\pi/2} \log \sin x dx + \int_0^{\pi/2} \log \cos x dx$

$$= \frac{\pi}{2} \log 2 + I + \int_0^{\pi/2} \log \cos x dx$$

Putting $t = 2x$ in first and $x = \frac{\pi}{2} - y$ in the last integral, we have

$$I = \frac{\pi}{2} \log 2 + I + I \ \Rightarrow \ I = -\frac{\pi}{2} \log 2$$

**28.** We have,

$$\int_0^\infty x^3 e^{-x^2} dx = \lim_{\varepsilon \to \infty} \int_0^\varepsilon x^3 e^{-x^2} dx$$

$$= \lim_{\varepsilon \to \infty} \left[\frac{1}{2} - \frac{1}{2}(\varepsilon^2 + 1)e^{-\varepsilon^2}\right] = \frac{1}{2}$$

Hence, convergent.

Next, we have

$$\int_{-\infty}^\infty \frac{dx}{1+x^2} = \lim_{\substack{\varepsilon \to \infty \\ \gamma \to -\infty}} \int_\gamma^\varepsilon \frac{dx}{1+x^2}$$

$$= \lim_{\substack{\varepsilon \to \infty \\ \gamma \to -\infty}} [\tan^{-1} x]_\gamma^\varepsilon$$

$$= \lim_{\substack{\varepsilon \to \infty \\ \gamma \to -\infty}} \tan^{-1} \varepsilon - \tan^{-1} \gamma$$

$$= \frac{\pi}{2} - \left(-\frac{\pi}{2}\right) = \pi$$

Hence, convergent.

**30.** (I) We have,

$$f(x) = \frac{x^2}{\sqrt{1+x^5}} \simeq x^{-1/2}$$

and let $\quad g(x) = \dfrac{1}{\sqrt{x}}$

Then, $\lim_{x\to\infty}\frac{f(x)}{g(x)}=\lim_{x\to\infty}\frac{x^{5/2}}{\sqrt{1+x^5}}$

$=\lim_{x\to\infty}\frac{1}{\sqrt{1+x^5}}=1$

but the integral $\int_0^\infty \frac{dx}{\sqrt{x}}$ is divergent.

Hence, $\int_0^\infty \frac{x^2dx}{\sqrt{1+x^5}}$ is divergent.

(II) We have,

$$f(x)=\frac{\log x}{x^2}$$

Let $\quad g(x)=\frac{1}{x^{3/2}}$

Then,

$$\lim_{x\to\infty}\frac{f(x)}{g(x)}=\lim_{x\to\infty}x^{3/2}\frac{\log x}{x^2}=\lim_{x\to\infty}\frac{\log x}{x^{1/2}}=0$$

but the integral $\int_1^\infty \frac{dx}{x^{3/2}}$ is convergent.

Hence, $\int_1^\infty \frac{\log x}{x^2}$ is convergent.

**32.** It is assumed that $f$ and $\phi$ are both bounded and integrable in $[a+\varepsilon, b]$, $0<\varepsilon\le(b-a)$, and a, is the only point of infinite discontinuity $[a, b]$. We have, $\forall\ \varepsilon\in\,]0, b-a[$.

$$\int_{a+\varepsilon}^b f(x)dx\le\int_{a+\varepsilon}^b \phi(x)dx \qquad \text{...(i)}$$

Let $\int_a^b\phi(x)dx$ converge so that there exists a number $k$ such that, $\forall\ \varepsilon\in\,]0, b-a]$.

$$\int_{a+\varepsilon}^b \phi(x)dx<k \qquad \text{...(ii)}$$

From Eqs. (i) and (ii), we have $\forall\ \varepsilon\in\,]0, b-a]$,

$$\int_{a+\varepsilon}^b f(x)dx<k$$

$\Rightarrow \int_a^b f(x)dx$ converges at a.

For the second part, we see that, if $\int_a^b f(x)dx$ does not converge at a, then $\int_{a+\varepsilon}^b f(x)dx$ is not bounded above and consequently, from Eq. (i) $\int_{a+\varepsilon}^b \phi(x)dx$ is also not bounded above so that $\int_a^b\phi(x)dx$ does not converge.

**33.** Let $f$ be a continuous function on $[a, b]$, then evidently $f$ is bounded and uniformly continuous on $[a, b]$.

Hence, for a given positive number $\varepsilon$, there exists a partition $P=\{a=x_0, x_1, x_2, \ldots, x_n=b\}$ of $[a, b]$ such that the oscillation $(M_r-m_r)$ of the function $f$ in the sub-interval $(x_{r-1}, x_r)$ is less than

$$\frac{\varepsilon}{b-a},\ r=1, 2, \ldots, n$$

Now, $U(P, f)-L(P, f)=\sum_{r=1}^n M_r(x_r-x_{r-1})-\sum_{r=1}^n m_r(x_r-x_{r-1})$

$$=\sum_{r=1}^n(M_r-m_r)(x_r-x_{r-1})$$

$$<\sum_{r=1}^n\frac{\varepsilon}{b-a}(x_r-x_{r-1})\qquad\left(\because M_r-m_r=\frac{\varepsilon}{b-a}\right)$$

$$\Rightarrow U(P, f)-L(P, f)<\frac{\varepsilon}{b-a}[(x_1-x_0)+(x_2-x_1)+\ldots+(x_n-x_{n-1})]$$

$$\Rightarrow U(P, f)-L(P, f)<\frac{\varepsilon}{b-a}(x_n-x_0)$$

$$\Rightarrow U(P, f)-L(P, f)<\frac{\varepsilon}{b-a}(b-a)\qquad(\because x_0=a, x_n=b)$$

$$\Rightarrow U(P, f)-L(P, f)<\varepsilon$$

Hence, the function $f$ is Riemann integrable on $[a, b]$.

**34.** ***Case I*** $n>1$

$$\int_0^\infty e^{-x}x^{n-1}dx=\int_0^a e^{-x}x^{n-1}dx+\int_a^\infty e^{-x}x^{n-1}dx,\ a\ge0 \qquad \text{...(i)}$$

The integrand $e^{-x}x^{n-1}$ is bounded in $(0, a)$ when $n\ge1$, therefore, the first integral on the right is proper and hence we need consider the convergence of $\int_a^\infty e^{-x}x^{n-1}dx$ only.

Now,

$$\lim_{x\to\infty}\frac{x^\mu\cdot x^{n-1}}{e^x}=\lim_{x\to\infty}\frac{x^{\mu+n-1}}{1+x+x^2/2!+\ldots}$$

$=0$, for all values of $\mu>1$ and all values of $n$.

Hence, $\int_a^\infty e^{-x}x^{n-1}dx$ is convergent.

Also, $\quad \lim_{n\to\infty}\frac{x^{\mu+n-1}}{1+x+\frac{x^2}{2!+\ldots}}=0$

If $\quad \mu\le1$

But the integral cannot be divergent as the limit is zero, which violates the condition of divergence.

Therefore, $\int_0^\infty e^{-x}x^{n-1}dx$ is convergent, when $n\ge1$.

***Case II*** $0<n<1$

In this case the point $x=0$ is a point of infinite discontinuity; hence in this case we have to consider both the integrals on the right of Eq. (i)

Now, $\quad \lim_{x\to0}x^\mu x^{n-1}e^{-x}=1$

If $\quad \mu+n-1=0$

or if $\quad \mu=1-n$

Hence, $\quad 0<\mu<1$

Thus, $\int_0^a e^{-x}\cdot x^{n-1}dx$ is convergent. Also, $\int_0^\infty e^{-x}x^{n-1}dx$ is convergent from Case I.

Hence, the integral is convergent when $0<n<1$

***Case III*** $n\le0$. In this case

$$\lim_{x\to0}x^\mu\cdot x^{n-1}e^{-x}=1$$

If $\quad \mu+n-1=0$

*i.e.*, if $\quad \mu=1-n\ge1$

Hence, the first integral on the right of Eq. (i) is divergent. Consequently the given integral

$$\int_0^\infty e^{-x}\cdot x^{n-1}dx \text{ is divergent, when } n\le0.$$

# 5 Uniform Convergence of Sequences & Series of Functions

Syllabus

- Sequences and Series of Function
- Uniform Convergence

## Sequence in a Set

A sequence in a set $X$ is a mapping of the set $N$ of positive integers into $X$. The image $S_{(n)}$ of $n \in N$ is denoted by $S_n$ where $S_n$ is called the $n$th term of the sequence. The sequence is written as $\{S_1, S_2, S_3, \ldots, S_n, \ldots\}$ and it is denoted by $\{S_n\}$.

## Convergence of Sequences in a Metric Space

A sequence $\{S_n\}$ in a metric space $(X, d)$ is said to converge to a point $x_0 \in X$ iff for every $\varepsilon > 0$, $\exists$ a positive integer $m(\varepsilon)$ s.t. $n \geq m(\varepsilon) \Rightarrow d(x_0, S_n) < \varepsilon$ or equivalently for each open sphere $S(x_0, \varepsilon)$ with centre $x_0$ and arbitrary radius $\varepsilon$, $\exists$ a positive integer $m(\varepsilon)$ s.t. $n \geq m(\varepsilon) \Rightarrow S_n \in S(x_0, \varepsilon)$ symbolically it can be expressed as

$$S_n \to x_0 \text{ or } \lim S_n = x_0.$$

## Cauchy's Sequences in a Metric Space

Suppose $(X, d)$ be a metric space and $S = \{S_n\}$ be a sequence in $X$. Then, $S$ is said to be Cauchy sequence in $X$ iff for every $\varepsilon > 0$, $\exists$ a positive integer $m(\varepsilon)$ s.t.

$$p \geq m(\varepsilon),\ n \geq m(\varepsilon) \Rightarrow d(S_p, S_n) < \varepsilon$$

Clearly, we observe that every convergent sequence in a metric space is a Cauchy sequence but in general the converge is not true.

## Uniformly Bounded Sequence

A sequence $\{f_n\}$ of real-valued functions defined on a metric space $X$ is said to be uniformly bounded on $X$, if $|f_n(x)| < M$ for every $x \in X$ and for every positive integer $n$.

e.g.,

(i) The sequence $\{f_n\}$, where $f_n(x) = \dfrac{1}{nx}$ is bounded but not uniformly bounded.

(ii) $\because |\cos nx| \leq 1$, $\forall\ x \in R$ and $n \in N$, therefore the sequence defined by $\{\cos nx\}$ is uniformly bounded on $R$.

## Point-wise Convergence

For each $a \in S$, there corresponds a real number sequence $\{f_n(a)\}$ with values

$$f_1(a),\ f_2(a),\ f_3(a),\ \ldots,\ f_n(a), \ldots$$

Suppose that this sequence is convergent. Actually, we assume that each of the sequences arising for different members of $S$ is convergent. Therefore, we define in a natural way a real-valued function say $f$, with domain $S$ s.t. its value $f(a)$ for $a \in S$ is $\lim\{f_n(a)\}$.

The function $f$ defined is referred to as the point-wise limit of the sequence $\{f_n\}$ of functions. Thus, we say that in this case the sequence is point-wise convergent.

If a function $f$ is the point-wise limit of the point-wise convergent sequence $\{f_n\}$ of functions defined in $S$, at $a \in S$. Then, to each $\varepsilon > 0$, there corresponds an integer $m$ s.t.,

$$|f_n(a) - f(a)| < \varepsilon, \forall\ n \geq m.$$

# Uniform Convergence

A sequence $\{f_n\}$ of real-valued functions with domain $S$ is uniformly convergent, if there exist a real-valued function $\phi$ with domain $S$ and for each $\varepsilon > 0$, there corresponds an integer $p$ s.t., $\forall\ x \in S$ and $n \geq p$. $|f_n(x) - \phi(x)| < \varepsilon$.

In this case, we can say that the function $f$ is the uniform limit of the sequence $\{f_n\}$.

Thus, it can be observe that

Uniform convergence $\Rightarrow$ Point-wise convergence and

Uniform limit = Point-wise limit

We denote the uniform limit of $\{f_n\}$ by $f$ instead of $\phi$.

> **Note** Every point-wise convergent sequence need not be uniformly convergent.

e.g., Suppose, $f_n(x) = \dfrac{nx}{1+n^2x^2},\ x \in R$

$$\lim_{n\to\infty} f_n(x) = \lim_{n\to\infty} \frac{nx}{1+n^2x^2} = \lim_{n\to\infty} \frac{x}{nx^2 + 1/n} = 0, \quad \forall\ x \in R.$$

which shows that the sequence $\{f_n\}$ is point-wise convergent with point-wise limit $f$ s.t. $f(x) = 0,\ \forall\ x \in R$.

Now, we show that the convergence is not true in any interval $[a, b]$ with 0 as an interior point.

Let $\{f_n\}$ is uniformly convergent in $[a, b]$ therefore, the point-wise limit $f$ is also the uniform limit.

Suppose, $\varepsilon > 0$ be given, then $\exists\ p$ s.t., $\forall\ x \in [a, b]$ and $\forall\ n \geq p$.

$$\left|\frac{nx}{1+n^2x^2} - 0\right| < \varepsilon$$

Choose $\varepsilon = \dfrac{1}{4}$. Now, $\exists$ an integer $m$ s.t. $m \geq p$ and $\dfrac{1}{m} \in [a, b]$.

Choose $n = m$ and $x = \dfrac{1}{2}$, we have

$$\frac{nx}{1+n^2x^2} = \frac{1}{2} \not< \frac{1}{4}$$

which is a contradiction and therefore, the sequence is not uniformly convergent in any interval $[a, b]$ with 0 as an interior point even though it is point-wise convergent.

## Point of Non-uniform Convergence

A point is said to be non-uniform convergence of sequence, if it is such that the sequence does not converge uniformly in any neighbourhood of it however small.

> **Note** The series $\sum_{n=1}^{\infty} u_n(x)$ is said to converge uniformly on $X$, if the sequence $\{f_n(x)\}$, where $f_n(x) = u_1(x) + u_2(x) + u_3(x) + \ldots + u_n(x)$ converges uniformly on $X$.

## Cauchy's General Principal of Uniform Convergence

Suppose $\{f_n\}$ be a sequence of real-valued functions defined on a metric space $X$. Then, $\{f_n\}$ converges uniformly on $X$ iff for every $\varepsilon > 0$, $\exists$ a positive integer $m$ s.t. $n \geq m$, $p \geq m$, $x \in X$ s.t. $|f_n(x) - f_p(x)| < \varepsilon$

**Example 1.** *Show that the sequence $\{f_n\}$, where $f_n(x) = x^n$ is uniformly convergent in $[0, k]$ where $k$ is a number less than 1 and only point-wise convergent in $[0, 1]$.*

**Solution.** The given sequence is point-wise convergent in $[0, 1]$ and the point-wise limit $f$ is given by

$$f(x) = \begin{cases} 0, & 0 \leq x < 1 \\ 1, & x = 1 \end{cases}$$

Suppose, $\varepsilon > 0$ be given. Let $\varepsilon > 1$ we have, when $x \neq 1$

$$|f_n(x) - f(x)| = x^n < \varepsilon$$

$$\Rightarrow \quad (1/x)^n > (1/\varepsilon) \Rightarrow n\log(1/x) > \log(1/\varepsilon),\ x \neq 0$$

$$\Rightarrow \quad n > \log(1/\varepsilon) \div \log(1/x)$$

Again, if $x = 0$, $|f_n(x) - f(x)| = 0 < \varepsilon$, when $n > 1$.

Suppose, $m(\varepsilon, x)$ denote the integer next greater than 1 and $\log(1/\varepsilon) \div \log(1/x)$.

Also, $m(\varepsilon, x)$ increases and $\to \infty$ as $x \to 1$.

Therefore, there does not exist an $m$ s.t., $\forall\ n \geq m$ and $\forall\ x \in [0, 1]$. Therefore, the convergence is not uniform in $[0, 1]$.

Again now, we suppose that $k$ is a number s.t. $0 \leq k < 1$. We observe that in $[0, k]$, the greatest value of $\log(1/\varepsilon) \div \log(1/x)$ is $\log(1/\varepsilon) \div \log(1/k)$.

Suppose, any integer greater than this value is denoted by $m$. Then, we observe that, $\forall\ n \geq m$ and $\forall\ x \in [0, k]$, $|f_n(x) - f(x)| < \varepsilon$.

Therefore, the convergence is uniform in $[0, k]$.

**Example 2.** *Prove that the sequence $\{f_n\}$ of functions, where $f_n(x) = \dfrac{n}{(x+n)}$ is uniformly convergent in $[0, k]$, whatever $k$ may be but not uniformly convergent in $[0, \infty)$.*

**Solution.** The sequence $\{f_n\}$ is point-wise convergent, $\forall\ x \geq 0$ and the point-wise limit $f$ is given by $f(x) = 1,\ \forall\ x \geq 0$.

Suppose $\varepsilon > 0$ is given, then we have

$$|f_n(x) - f(x)| = \frac{x}{x+n} < \varepsilon, \text{ if } n > x\left(\frac{1}{\varepsilon} - 1\right).$$

Suppose $m(\varepsilon, x)$ denote the integer just greater than $x\left(\frac{1}{\varepsilon}-1\right)$.

Definitely $m(\varepsilon, x)$ increases as $x$ increases and $\to \infty$ as $x \to \infty$ so that it is not possible to choose any number $m$ s.t., $\forall\ n \geq m$ and $\forall\ x \geq 0\ |f_n(x) - f(x)| < \varepsilon$.

So that the convergence is not uniform in $[0, \infty)$.

Now, consider the interval $[0, k]$.

Suppose $m$ is an integer greater than $k(1/\varepsilon - 1)$, then we observe that, $\forall\ n \geq m$ and $\forall\ x \in [0, k]$

$$|f_n(x) - f(x)| < \varepsilon.$$

Hence, the convergence is uniform in $[0, k]$.

# Test for Uniform Convergence

## $M_n$-Test

Let $\{f_n\}$ be a sequence of functions defined on a metric space $X$.

Suppose $\lim_{n\to\infty} f_n(x) = f(x),\ \forall\ x \in X$.

Set $M_n = \text{Sup}\{|f_n(x) - f(x)| : x \in X\}$.

Then, $\{f_n\}$ converges uniformly to $f$ iff $M_n \to 0$ as $n \to \infty$.

***Example 3.*** *Show that the sequence* $\{f_n\}$, *where* $f_n(x) = \dfrac{x}{1+nx^2}$ *converges uniformly on only closed intervals I.*

**Solution.** Point-wise limit $= f(x) = \lim_{n\to\infty} f_n(x) = 0,\ \forall\ x \in I$

$$\therefore \quad |f_n(x) - f(x)| = \left|\frac{x}{1+nx^2} - 0\right| = \left|\frac{x}{1+nx^2}\right| = |t| \text{ (say)} \quad \text{...(i)}$$

where,
$$t = \frac{x}{1+nx^2} \quad \text{...(ii)}$$

$$\Rightarrow \quad \frac{dt}{dx} = \frac{(1+nx^2)\cdot 1 - x\cdot 2nx}{(1+nx^2)^2} = \frac{1-nx^2}{(1+nx^2)^2} \quad \text{...(iii)}$$

For max and min values of $t$, we have

$$\frac{dt}{dx} = 0$$

$$\Rightarrow \quad 1 - nx^2 = 0 \quad \Rightarrow \quad x = \frac{1}{\sqrt{n}} \in I$$

Using Eq. (iii), we get

$$\frac{d^2t}{dx^2} = \frac{(1+nx^2)^2\cdot(-2nx) - (1-nx^2)\cdot 2(1+nx^2)\cdot 2nx}{(1+nx^2)^4}$$

$$\Rightarrow \quad \frac{d^2t}{dx^2} = \frac{-2nx(1+nx^2) - 4nx(1-nx^2)}{(1+nx^2)^3}$$

Put $x = \dfrac{1}{\sqrt{n}}$,

$$\Rightarrow \quad \frac{d^2t}{dx^2} = -\left(\frac{\sqrt{n}}{2}\right) < 0$$

$\therefore$ $t$ is maximum, when $x = \dfrac{1}{\sqrt{n}}$ and using Eq. (ii), the maximum value of $t = \dfrac{1}{2\sqrt{n}}$.

$$\therefore \ M_n = \text{Sup}\{|f_n(x) - f(x)| : x \in I\} = \text{Sup}\{|t| : x \in I\} = \frac{1}{2\sqrt{n}}$$

$\because$ $M_n \to 0$ as $n \to \infty$, $\{f_n\}$ is uniformly convergent on any closed interval $I$.

***Example 4.*** *Prove that the sequence* $\{f_n\}$ *where* $f_n(x) = nx(1-x)^n$ *is not uniformly converges on* $[0, 1]$.

**Solution.** When $x = 0$, $f_n(x) = 0,\ \forall\ n \in N$ and

when $x = 1$, $f_n(x) = 0,\ \forall\ n \in N$

$\therefore$ $f(x) = \lim_{n\to\infty} f_n(x) = 0$, when $x = 0$ and $x = 1$.

Now, for $0 < x < 1$, we have

$$f(x) = \lim_{n\to\infty} f_n(x) = \lim_{n\to\infty} nx(1-x)^n = \lim_{n\to\infty} \frac{nx}{(1-x)^{-n}} \quad \left(\frac{\infty}{\infty}\text{ form}\right)$$

$$= \lim_{n\to\infty} \frac{x}{-(1-x)^{-n}\log(1-x)} = \lim_{n\to\infty} \frac{-x(1-x)^n}{\log(1-x)}$$

[by using D'L Hospital rule]

$$= 0 \text{ as } 0 < x < 1$$

$$\therefore \quad (1-x)^n \to 0 \text{ as } n \to \infty$$

Hence, we have $f(x) = 0,\ \forall\ x \in [0, 1]$.

Therefore,

$$|f_n(x) - f(x)| = |nx(1-x)^n - 0| = nx(1-x)^n = t \text{ (say)} \quad \text{...(i)}$$

where
$$t = nx(1-x)^n \quad \text{...(ii)}$$

$$\therefore \quad \frac{dt}{dx} = n(1-x)^n - n^2x(1-x)^n$$

$$= n(1-x)^{n-1}\{1-(n+1)x\} \quad \text{...(iii)}$$

Now, for max and min value of $t$, we have

$$\frac{dt}{dx} = 0$$

$$\Rightarrow \quad x = \frac{1}{(n+1)}$$

Using Eq. (iii), we get

$$\frac{d^2t}{dx^2} = -n(n-1)(1-x)^{n-2}\{1-(n+1)x\} - n(n+1)(1-x)^{n-1}$$

Now, when $x = \dfrac{1}{n+1}$, $\dfrac{d^2t}{dx^2} = -n(n+1)\cdot\left(\dfrac{n}{n+1}\right)^{n-1} < 0$ ...(iv)

$\Rightarrow$ $t$ is maximum, when $x = \dfrac{1}{(n+1)}$

Now, using Eq. (ii), the maximum value of

$$t = \frac{n}{n+1}\left(1 - \frac{1}{n+1}\right) = \left(1 - \frac{1}{n+1}\right)^{n+1}$$

$$\therefore \ M_n = \text{Sup}\{|f_n(x) - f(x)| : x \in [0, 1]\}$$

$$= \text{Sup}\{|t| : x \in [0, 1]\} = \left[1 - \frac{1}{n+1}\right]^{n+1} \quad \text{[using Eq. (iv)]}$$

$$\therefore \ M_n \to \frac{1}{e} \text{ as } n \to \infty.$$

$\because$ $M_n$ does not tend to zero as $n \to \infty$, the sequence $\{f_n\}$ is not uniformly convergent on $[0, 1]$. Here, zero is the point of non-uniform convergence, since as $n \to \infty$, $x \to 0$.

## Uniform Convergence and Continuity

Let $\{f_n\}$ be a sequence of real-valued functions on a metric space $(X, d)$ which converges uniformly to the function $f$ on $X$. If each $f_n (n = 1, 2, 3, 4, ...)$ is continuous on $X$, then $f$ is also continuous on $X$.

***Example 5.*** *Prove that the sequence $\{f_n\}$, where $f_n(x) = \tan^{-1} nx$ is not uniformly convergent.*

**Solution.** The limit function $f$ is given by

$$f(x) = \lim_{n\to\infty} f_n(x)$$

$$= \lim_{n\to\infty} \tan^{-1} nx = \frac{\pi}{2}, \quad 0 < x \le 1$$

when $x = 0$, the sequence $\{f_n\}$ converges to zero.

Therefore, $f(x) = \begin{cases} \frac{\pi}{2}, & 0 < x \le 1 \\ 0, & x = 0 \end{cases}$

As we seen that $f$ is discontinuous at $x = 0$ and so $f$ is discontinuous on $[0, 1]$ and also $f_n(x) = \tan^{-1} nx$, $0 \le x \le 1$ is continuous on $[0, 1]$, $\forall\ n \in N$. Hence, $\{f_n\}$ is a sequence of continuous function and its limit function $f$ is discontinuous on $[0, 1]$.

Therefore, $\{f_n\}$ is not uniformly convergent on $[0, 1]$.

## Uniform Convergence and Differentiability

Suppose, the sequence $< f_n >$ is a uniformly convergent sequence with uniform limit $f$ on $[a, b]$ and suppose $f_n$ be differentiable on $[a, b]$, $\forall\ n \in \mathbb{N}$. Then, $f$ may not be differentiable; but if the sequence $< f_n'(x) >$ converges uniformly $g(x)$ (say). Then,

$$g(x) = f'(x)$$

*i.e.*, $f(x)$ is differentiable.

## Uniform Convergence and Integration

***Theorem 1*** Suppose, the sequence $< f_n >$ is a uniformly convergent sequence with uniform limit $f$ on $[a, b]$ and suppose $f_n$ be integrable on $[a, b]$, $\forall\ n \in N$. Then, the limit $f$ is itself integrable and

$$\int_a^b f(x)dx = \lim_{n\to\infty} \int_a^b f_n(x)dx$$

***Theorem 2*** The sequence $< \int_a^t f_n(x)dx >$ of functions is uniformly convergent with limit $\int_a^t f(x)dx$, $t \in [a, b]$.

> ***Note*** **(a)** The converse of the theorem 2 is not true means a sequence may converge to an integrable limit without being uniformly convergent.
>
> **(b)** If $\{f_n\}$ is a sequence of integrable function converges to $f$ on $[a, b]$ and if $\int_a^b f(x)dx \ne \lim_{n\to\infty} \int_a^b f_n(x)dx$, then $\{f_n\}$ cannot converge uniformly to $f$.

***Example 6.*** *If $< g_n >$ and $< f_n >$ are two sequences of functions defined for $0 \le x \le 1$ by*

$$g_n(x) = \frac{nx}{1 + n^3x^2} \text{ and } f_n(x) = \frac{\{\log(1 + n^3x^2)\}}{2n^2}.$$

*Prove that $< g_n >$ converges uniformly to zero on $[0, 1]$ and hence obtain the uniform convergence of $< f_n >$.*

**Solution.** When $x \ne 0$,

$$\lim_{n\to\infty} g_n(x) = \lim_{n\to\infty} \frac{nx}{1+n^3x^2}$$

$$= \lim_{n\to\infty} \frac{x/n^2}{(1/n)^3 + x^2} = 0$$

When $x = 0$, $\quad g_n(0) = 0, \ \forall\ n \in N.$

$\therefore \quad \lim_{n\to\infty} g_n(0) = 0, \ \forall\ n \in N$

$\therefore \quad g(x) = \lim_{n\to\infty} g_n(x) = 0, \ \forall\ x \in [0, 1].$

Thus, $$|g_n(x) - g(x)| = \left|\frac{nx}{1+n^3x^2} - 0\right| = \frac{nx}{1+n^3x^2} = t \text{ (say)} \quad ...(i)$$

$$\Rightarrow \quad \frac{dt}{dx} = \frac{n(1+n^3x^2) - nx\cdot 2n^3x}{(1+n^3x^2)^2} = \frac{n(1-n^3x^2)}{(1+n^3x^2)^2} \quad ...(ii)$$

For max and min of $t$, $\frac{dt}{dx} = 0 \Rightarrow 1 - n^3x^2 = 0$

$$\Rightarrow x = \frac{1}{n^{3/2}}$$

Using Eq. (ii), we get

$$\frac{d^2t}{dx^2} = \frac{nx - 2n^3x(1+n^3x^2) - (1-n^3x^2)\cdot 2(1+n^3x^2)\cdot 2n^3x}{(1+n^3x^2)^4}$$

$$\Rightarrow \quad \frac{d^2t}{dx^2} = \frac{-2n^4x\cdot(3 - n^3x^2)}{(1+n^3x^2)^3}$$

$\because \quad$ At $x = \frac{1}{n^{3/2}}$, $\frac{d^2t}{dx^2} = -n^{5/2} < 0$

$\Rightarrow$ $t$ is maximum, when $x = \frac{1}{n^{3/2}}$ and therefore, the maximum value of $t = \frac{n \times (1/n^{3/2})}{1+1} = \frac{1}{2n^{1/2}}$

Therefore, $\quad M_n = \text{Sup}\{|g_n(x) - g(x)| : x \in [0, 1]\} = \frac{1}{n^{3/2}}$

$\because \ M_n \to 0$ as $n \to \infty$, therefore, $\{g_n\}$ uniformly converges to $g(x) = 0, \forall\ x \in [0, 1]$

Now, we show that $\{f_n\}$ is converges uniformly, we have

$$f_n(x) = \frac{\{\log(1+n^3x^2)\}}{2n^2} \quad ...(iii)$$

Using Eq. (iii), we get

$$f_n'(x) = \frac{1}{2n^2} \cdot \frac{2n^3x}{1+n^3x^2} = \frac{nx}{1+n^3x^2} = g_n(x) \quad \text{...(iv)}$$

$\because$ The sequence $\{g_n\}$ uniformly converges to $g(x)$, where $g(x) = 0$ on $[0, 1]$.

$\because$ Each $g_n(x)$ is continuous on $[0, 1]$ and therefore, integrable on $[0, 1]$

Hence, $\left\{\int_0^1 g_n(x)dx\right\}$ i.e., $\left\{\int_0^1 f_n'(x)dx\right\} \Rightarrow \{f_n(x)\}$

is converges uniformly and the uniform limit is zero.

***Example* 7.** *Prove that the sequence $\{f_n\}$, where $f_n(x) = nxe^{-nx^2}$ is not uniformly convergent on [0, 1].*

**Solution.** We have,

$$f(x) = \lim_{n\to\infty} f_n(x) = \lim_{n\to\infty} \frac{nx}{e^{nx^2}} = \lim_{n\to\infty} \frac{nx}{1+\frac{nx^2}{1!}+\frac{n^2x^4}{2!}}$$

$$= 0, \ \forall \ x \in [0, 1]$$

Therefore, $$\int_0^1 f(x)dx = \int_0^1 0 \cdot dx = 0 \quad \text{...(i)}$$

$$\int_0^1 f_n(x)dx = \int_0^1 nxe^{-nx^2}dx$$

Put $t = nx^2 \Rightarrow dt = 2nxdx$

$\therefore$ $$\int_0^1 f_n(x)\,dx = \frac{1}{2}\int_0^n e^{-t}dt = \frac{(1-e^n)}{2}$$

$\therefore$ $$\lim_{n\to\infty} \int_0^1 f_n(x)\,dx = \lim_{n\to\infty} \frac{1}{2}(1-e^{-n}) = \frac{1}{2} \quad \text{...(ii)}$$

Using Eqs. (i) and (ii), we get

$$\lim_{n\to\infty} \int_0^1 f_n(x)\,dx = \frac{1}{2} \neq 0$$

$$= \int_0^1 f(x)\,dx = \int_0^1 \lim_{n\to\infty} f_n(x)$$

The integral of the point-wise limit is not equal to the limit of the sequence of the integrals.

Hence, the sequence $\{f_n\}$ is not uniformly convergent is [0, 1].

# Infinite Series of Functions

Let us consider the series whose terms are functions defined in some set $S$. Suppose $f_1 + f_2 + f_3 + \ldots + f_n + f_{n+1} + \ldots$ be such a series.

Then, we can write $S_n(x) = f_1 + f_2 + f_3 + \ldots + f_n$

$\therefore$ $< S_n(x) >$ is a sequence of partial sum of functions.

> ***Note*** **(a)** The series is point-wise convergent, if the sequence $< S_n(x) >$ is point-wise convergent.
>
> **(b)** The series is said to be uniformly convergent, if the sequence $< S_n(x) >$ is uniformly convergent.
>
> **(c)** The point-wise limit or the uniform limit of $< S_n(x) >$ is said to be the point-wise sum or the uniform sum of the series and it is denoted by $S(x)$.

# Test for Uniform Convergence of a Series

## 1. Cauchy's General Principal of Convergence

The necessary and sufficient condition for the uniform convergence in $[a, b]$ of a series $\Sigma f_n$ is that to every positive number $\varepsilon$, there corresponds a positive integer $m$ s.t., $\forall \ n \geq m$ and $\forall \ x \in [a, b]$,

$$| f_{n+1}(x) + f_{n+2}(x) + \ldots + f_{n+p}(x) | < \varepsilon.$$

## 2. Weierstrass's $M$-Test for Uniform Convergence

A series $\Sigma f_n$ will converge uniformly in the interval $[a, b]$, if $\exists$ a convergent series $\Sigma M_n$ of positive numbers s.t., $\forall \ x \in [a, b]$,

$$| f_n(x) | \leq M_n.$$

***Example* 8.** *Prove that the series $\sum_{n=1}^{\infty} \frac{x}{n(1+nx^2)}$ converges.*

**Solution.** We have,

$$f_n(x) = \frac{x}{n(1+nx^2)} \quad \text{...(i)}$$

$\Rightarrow$ $$\frac{df_n}{dx} = \frac{1}{n} \frac{(1+nx^2)\cdot 1 - x \cdot 2nx}{(1+nx^2)^2} = \frac{1-nx^2}{n(1+nx^2)^2} \quad \text{...(ii)}$$

Now, for maximum or minimum values

$$\frac{df_n(x)}{dx} = 0$$

$\Rightarrow$ $$1 - nx^2 = 0 \Rightarrow x = \frac{1}{\sqrt{n}}$$

Using, Eq. (ii), we get

$$\frac{d^2f_n}{dx^2} = \frac{\frac{1}{n}(1+nx^2)^2 \cdot (-2nx) - (1-nx^2) \cdot 2(1+nx^2) \cdot 2nx}{(1+nx^2)^4}$$

$\Rightarrow$ $$\frac{d^2f_n}{dx^2} = \frac{-2x\{(1+nx^2) + 2(1-nx^2)\}}{(1+nx^2)^3}$$

When $$x = \frac{1}{\sqrt{n}}, \ \frac{d^2f_n}{dx^2} = \frac{-1}{2\sqrt{n}} < 0$$

$\therefore$ $f_n(x)$ is maximum at $x = \frac{1}{\sqrt{n}}$ and the maximum value of $f_n(x)$ is obtained from Eq. (i) is $\frac{\frac{1}{\sqrt{n}}}{n(1+1)} = \frac{1}{2n^{3/2}}$.

Therefore, $| f_n(x) | \leq \frac{1}{2n^{3/2}} < \frac{1}{n^{3/2}} = M_n$ (say)

$\because$ $\sum_{n=1}^{\infty} M_n = \sum_{n=1}^{\infty} \frac{1}{n^{3/2}}$ is convergent. Therefore, by Weierstrass's $M$-test, the given series converges uniformly for all real values of $x$.

***Example 9.*** *Prove that the following series are converges uniformly for real values of x.*

(i) $\sum_{n=1}^{\infty}\frac{\sin(x^2+nx^2)}{n(n+1)}$ (ii) $\sum_{n=1}^{\infty}\frac{\sin nx}{n^p},\ p>1$

**Solution.** (i) We have $f_n(x)=\frac{\sin(x^2+nx^2)}{n(n+1)}$

$$\Rightarrow \quad |f_n(x)|=\left|\frac{\sin(x^2+nx^2)}{n(n+1)}\right|=\frac{|\sin(x^2+nx^2)|}{n^2(1+1/n)}$$

$$\le\frac{1}{n^2}=M_n,\ \forall\ x\in R$$

$\because \quad \sum_{n=1}^{\infty}M_n=\sum_{n=1}^{\infty}\frac{1}{n^2}$ is convergent. Therefore, by Weierstrass's *M*-test, the given series converges uniformly for all real values of *x*.

(ii) We have, $f_n(x)=\frac{\sin(nx)}{n^p}$

$$\Rightarrow \quad |f_n(x)|=\left|\frac{\sin nx}{n^p}\right|\le\frac{1}{n^p}=M_n\ \text{(say)},\qquad \forall\ x\in R$$

$\because \quad \sum_{n=1}^{\infty}M_n=\sum_{n=1}^{\infty}\frac{1}{n^p}$ is convergent for $p>1$. Therefore, by weierstrass's *M*-test, the given series is uniformly convergent for all real values of *x*.

## 3. Abel's Test for Uniform Convergence

If $v_n(x)$ is a positive, monotonic decreasing function of *n* for each fixed value of *x* in the interval $[a,b]$ and $v_n(x)$ is bounded for all values of *n* and *x* concerned and if the series $\Sigma u_n(x)$ is uniformly convergent on $[a,b]$, then so also is the series $\Sigma v_n(x)u_n(x)$.

***Example 10.*** *Prove that the series* $\Sigma\frac{(-1)^n}{n}|x|^n$ *is uniformly convergent in* $|x|\le 1$.

**Solution.** Since, $|x|^n$ is positive monotonic decreasing and bounded for $|x|\le 1$ and the series $\Sigma\frac{(-1)^n}{n}$ is uniformly convergent, therefore the given series is convergent in $|x|\le 1$.

## 4. Dirichlet's Test for Uniform Convergence

If $v_n(x)$ is a monotonic function of *n* for each fixed value of *x* in $[a,b]$ and $v_n(x)$ tends uniformly to zero for $a\le x\le b$ and if $\Sigma u_n(x)$ either uniformly converges or oscillates finitely in $[a,b]$, then the series $\Sigma v_n(x)u_n(x)$ is uniformly convergent on $[a,b]$.

***Example 11.*** *Prove that the series* $\Sigma\{\log(n+1)\}^{-x}\cos nx$ *is uniformly convergent in* $[a,b]$, *where* $0<a\le x\le b<2\pi$.

**Solution.** When $x\in[a,b]$, $\{\log(n+1)\}^{-x}$ is a positive monotonic decreasing function of *n*. Also since,

$$\{\log(n+1)\}^{-x}\le\{\log(n+1)\}^{-a},$$

The function $\{\log(n+1)\}^{-x}$ tends uniformly to zero as $n\to\infty$.

Now, $$\left|\sum_{r=1}^{n}\cos rx\right|\le\frac{1}{\sin\left(\frac{x}{2}\right)}\le\max\left\{\frac{1}{\sin\left(\frac{a}{2}\right)},\frac{1}{\sin\left(\frac{b}{2}\right)}\right\}$$

both of which are independent of *x* and *n*.

Hence, by Dirichlet's test the series

$$\Sigma\{\log(n+1)\}^{-x}\cos nx$$

is uniformly convergent in $[a,b]$.

***Example 12.*** *Show that the series* $\Sigma(-1)^n\frac{x^2+n}{n^2}$

*Converges uniformly in every bounded interval, but does not converge absolutely for any value of x.*

**Solution.** Let the bounded interval be $[x_1,x_2]$, so that there exists a number *M* such that for all $x\in[x_1,x_2]$, $|x|<M$.

Let us take

$$\Sigma u_n=\Sigma(-1)^n$$

Which oscillates finitely and

$$b_n=\frac{x^2+n}{n^2}<\frac{M^2+n}{n^2}$$

Clearly $b_n$ is positive, monotonic decreasing function of *n* for each *x* in $[x_1,x_2]$ and tends to zero uniformly for $x_1\le x\le x_2$. Thus, by Dirichlet's test, the series

$$\Sigma(-1)^n\frac{x^2+n}{n^2}$$

Converges uniformly on $[x_1,x_2]$.

But

$$\Sigma\left|(-1)^n\frac{x^2+n}{n^2}\right|=\Sigma\frac{x^2+n}{n^2}$$

$$\sim\Sigma\frac{1}{n}$$

Which is a divergent series. Thus, the given series is not absolutely convergent for any value of *x*.

# Solved Examples

## Type I (*Only one correct option*)

***Example 1.*** *Let $\{f_n(x)\}, \forall x \in \mathbb{Z}$ be a sequence of real-valued function. Then, the number of point-wise sequence is*

(a) $\phi$ (b) finite
(c) countably infinite (d) uncountably infinite

**Solution.** (c) Since, for each different value of $x$, we get different point-wise sequence. Hence, the number of point-wise sequence $\{f_n(x)\}, \forall x \in \mathbb{Z}$ is countably infinite.

***Example 2.*** *The sequence of real-valued function*

$$f_n(x) = x^n, x \in [0, 1] \cup \{2\}$$

*is*

(a) point-wise convergent
(b) uniformly convergent
(c) does not uniformly convergent
(d) point-wise limit is $f(x) = \begin{cases} 0, x=0 \\ 1, x \neq 0 \end{cases}$

**Solution.** (c) Let $\alpha \in [0, 1] \cup \{2\}$, then

***Case I*** If $\alpha = 0$, then

$$f(x) = \lim_{n\to\infty} f_n(\alpha) = \lim_{n\to\infty} f_n(0) = \lim_{n\to\infty} 0 = 0$$

***Case II*** If $\alpha = 1$, then

$$f(x) = \lim_{n\to\infty} f_n(\alpha) = \lim_{n\to\infty} f_n(1) = \lim_{n\to\infty} 1 = 1$$

***Case III*** If $0 < \alpha < 1$, then

$$f(\alpha) = \lim_{n\to\infty} f_n(\alpha) = \lim_{n\to\infty} \alpha^n = 0 \quad (\because 0 < \infty < 1)$$

***Case IV*** If $\alpha = 2$. Then,

$$f(x) = \lim_{n\to\infty} f_n(\alpha) = \lim_{n\to\infty} f_n(2) = \lim_{n\to\infty} 2^n = \text{does not exist}$$

Hence, $f_n(x)$ is not point-wise convergent.
$\Rightarrow$ $f_n(x)$ is not uniformly convergent.

***Example 3.*** *The point-wise limit of sequence of real-valued function*

$$f_n(x) = \sin x + \frac{x}{n}, \forall x \in \mathbb{R}$$

*is*

(a) $f(x) = 0, \forall x \in \mathbb{R}$ (b) $f(x) = \begin{cases} 0, & x=0 \\ 1, & \text{else} \end{cases}$
(c) $f(x) = \sin x, \forall x \in \mathbb{R}$ (d) does not exists

**Solution.** (c) Let $\alpha \in \mathbb{R}$, then

$$a_n(\alpha) = f_n(\alpha) = \sin\alpha + \frac{\alpha}{n}$$

$$\therefore \quad f(\alpha) = \lim_{n\to\infty} a_n(\alpha) = \lim_{n\to\infty} \sin\alpha + \frac{\alpha}{n} = \sin\alpha$$

$\therefore$ The point-wise limit $f(x) = \sin x, \forall x \in R$

***Example 4.*** *$f_{n,m}(x) = \cos^{2n}(m!)\pi x$, $x \in [0, 1]$ be a sequence of real-valued function. Then,*

(a) $f_{n,m}(x)$ is point-wise convergent
(b) $f_{n,m}(x)$ is uniformly convergent
(c) $f_{n,m}(x)$ does not converge point-wise
(d) None of the above

**Solution.** (a) Let $\alpha = \frac{p}{q} \in [0, 1]$, where $q \neq 0$.

Then,

$$a_n(\alpha) = f_{n,m}(\alpha) = \cos^{2n}(m!)\pi\alpha$$

$$\therefore \quad f(\alpha) = \lim_{n\to\infty} a_n(\alpha) = \lim_{n\to\infty} \cos^{2n}(m!)\frac{p}{q}\pi = 1$$

and if $\alpha$ is an irrational number. Then,

$$f(\alpha) = \lim_{n\to\infty} a_n(\alpha) = 0$$

Hence,

$$f(x) = \begin{cases} 1, & x \in \mathbb{Q} \\ 0, & x \in \mathbb{Q}^c \end{cases}$$

which is nowhere continuous function. Hence, $f_{n,m}(x)$ is not uniformly convergent but it is point-wise convergent.

***Example 5.*** *The uniform limit of the sequence of real-valued function*

$$f_n(x) = x - \frac{x^n}{n}, \forall x \in [0, 1]$$

*is*

(a) $f(x) = 0, \forall x$ (b) $f(x) \begin{cases} 0, & x=0 \\ 1, & \text{else} \end{cases}$
(c) $f(x) = \begin{cases} 0, & x=0 \\ 1, & x=1 \\ x, & 0<x<1 \end{cases}$ (d) $f(x) = x, \forall x$

**Solution.** (c) Let $\alpha \in [0, 1]$. Then,

***Case I*** If $\alpha = 0$, then

$$f(\alpha) = \lim_{n\to\infty} f_n(\alpha) = \lim_{n\to\infty} 0 = 0$$

**Case II** If $\alpha = 1$, then

$$f(\alpha) = \lim_{n\to\infty} f_n(\alpha)$$
$$= \lim_{n\to\infty}\left(1-\frac{1}{n}\right) = 1$$

**Case III** If $0 < \alpha < 1$, then

$$f(\alpha) = \lim_{n\to\infty} f_n(\alpha)$$
$$= \lim_{n\to\infty} \alpha - \frac{\alpha^n}{n}$$
$$= \alpha - \lim_{n\to\infty} \frac{\alpha^n}{n}$$
$$= \alpha - \lim_{n\to\infty} \alpha^n \cdot \lim_{n\to\infty}\left(\frac{1}{n}\right)$$
$$= \alpha - 0 = \alpha$$

Hence, point-wise limit is

$$f(x) = \begin{cases} 0, & x = 0 \\ 1, & x = 1 \\ x, & 0 < x < 1 \end{cases}$$

which is defined $\forall\ x \neq 0, 1$ but depends on $x$. Hence, $f_n(x)$ is point-wise converge to $f(x)$ but not uniformly.

## Type II (*One or more than one correct option*)

***Example 6.*** $f_n(x) = \dfrac{2+nx^2}{2+nx}$, $x \in [0, 1]$

*be a sequence of real-valued function, then*

(a) Point-wise limit of $f_n(x)$ is $f(x) = 0$

(b) Point-wise limit of $f_n(x)$ is

$$f(x) = \begin{cases} 1, & x = 1, 0 \\ x, & 0 < x < 1 \end{cases}$$

(c) $f_n(x)$ is point-wise convergent

(d) $f_n(x)$ is not uniformly convergent

**Solution.** (b), (c), (d)

Let $\alpha \in [0, 1]$. Then,

**Case I** If $\alpha = 0$, then

$$f(\alpha) = \lim_{n\to\infty} f_n(\alpha) = \lim_{n\to\infty} 1 = 1$$

**Case II** If $\alpha = 1$, then

$$f(\alpha) = \lim_{n\to\infty} f_n(\alpha) = \lim_{n\to\infty} \frac{2+n}{2+n}$$
$$= 1$$

**Case III** If $0 < \alpha < 1$, then

$$f(\alpha) = \lim_{n\to\infty} f_n(\alpha) = \lim_{n\to\infty} \frac{2+n\alpha^2}{2+n\alpha}$$
$$= \lim_{n\to\infty}\left(\frac{\frac{2}{n}+\alpha^2}{\frac{2}{n}+\alpha}\right)$$
$$= \alpha$$

$\therefore$ Point-wise limit is

$$f(x) = \begin{cases} 1, & x = 0, 1 \\ x, & 0 < x < 1 \end{cases}$$

Next, if $\alpha = 0$ or $1$, then

$|f_n(x) - f(x)| = |1 - 1| = 0 < \varepsilon,\ \forall\ n$

Hence, take $\alpha \neq 0, 1$, then

$$|f_n(x) - f(x)| = \left|\frac{2+nx^2}{2+nx} - x\right|$$
$$= \left|\frac{2-2x}{2+nx}\right| < \varepsilon$$

If $\qquad n > \dfrac{2(1-x-\varepsilon)}{x\varepsilon}$

***Example 7.*** *Let* $f_n(x) = \dfrac{x^{2n}}{n^2+x^{2n}}$, $x \in [-1, 1]$

*be a sequence of real-valued function, then*

(a) Point-wise limit of $f_n(x)$ is $f(x) = 0$

(b) Uniform limit of $f_n(x)$ is $f(x) = 0$

(c) $f_n(x)$ does not converge point-wise

(d) $f_n(x)$ converge point-wise and point-wise limit is

$$f(x) = \begin{cases} 1, & x = 1, -1 \\ 0, & -1 < x < 1 \end{cases}$$

**Solution.** (a), (b)

Let $\alpha \in [-1, 1]$, then

**Case I** If $\alpha = 1, -1$, then

$$f(\alpha) = \lim_{n\to\infty} a_n(\alpha) = \lim_{n\to\infty} \frac{1}{n^2+1} = 0$$

**Case II** If $-1 < \alpha < 1$, then

$$f(\alpha) = \lim_{n\to\infty} a_n(\alpha) = \lim_{n\to\infty} \frac{\alpha^{2n}}{n^2+\alpha^{2n}} = 0$$

Hence, $f(x) = 0$ is the point-wise limit of the sequence.

Now,

$$M_n = \sup_{x\in[-1,1]}\left|\frac{x^{2n}}{n^2+x^{2n}}\right| = \frac{1}{n^2+1}$$

$$\therefore \quad \lim_{n\to\infty} M_n = \lim_{n\to\infty} \frac{1}{n^2+1} = 0$$

$\therefore \quad f_n(x)$ is uniformly converge to $f(x) = 0$.

***Example 8.*** *Let* $f_n(x) = \dfrac{x^n}{x(x+1)}$, $x \in [-1, 1]$

*be a sequence of real-valued function. Then,*

(a) number of point-wise sequence is countable

(b) number of point-wise sequence is uncountable

(c) $f_n(x)$ uniformly converge to $f(x) = 0$

(d) $f_n(x)$ does not uniformly convergent

**Solution.** (b), (c)

Let $\alpha \in [-1, 1]$. Then,

$$f(\alpha) = \lim_{n\to\infty} f_n(\alpha) = \lim_{n\to\infty} \frac{\alpha^n}{n(n+1)} = 0$$

Now,

$$M_n = \sup_{x\in[-1,1]}\left|\frac{x^n}{n(n+1)}\right|$$

$$= \frac{1}{n(n+1)}$$

$$\therefore \quad \lim_{n\to\infty} M_n = \lim_{n\to\infty}\frac{1}{n(n+1)} = 0$$

Hence, $f_n(x)$ is uniformly convergent to $f(x) = 0$.

***Example 9.*** *Let* $f_n(x) = \dfrac{x}{1+n^2x^2},\ x\in[0,1]$

*be a sequence of real-valued function. Then,*

(a) $f_n(x)$ is uniformly convergent

(b) $f_n'(x)$ is uniformly convergent

(c) uniform limit of $f_n'(x)$ is $f(x) = 0$

(d) uniform limit of $f_n(x)$ is $f(x) = 0,\ \forall\ x$

**Solution.** (a), (d)

We have

$$f_n(x) = \frac{x}{1+n^2x^2},\ x\in[0,1]$$

Let $\alpha\in[0,1]$. Then,

$$f(\alpha) = \lim_{n\to\infty} f_n(\alpha)$$

$$= \lim_{n\to\infty}\frac{\alpha}{1+n^2\alpha^2}$$

$$= 0$$

$\therefore$ Point-wise limit of $f_n(x)$ is $f(x) = 0,\ \forall\ x\in[0,1]$.

Now, $M_n = \sup_{x\in[0,1]} |f_n(x) - f(x)|$

$$= \sup_{x\in[0,1]}\left|\frac{x}{1+n^2x^2}\right|$$

Let $y = \dfrac{x}{1+n^2x^2} \Rightarrow \dfrac{dy}{dx} = \dfrac{(1+n^2x^2)\cdot 1 - x\cdot(2n^2x)}{(1+n^2x^2)^2} = \dfrac{1-n^2x^2}{(1+n^2x^2)^2}$

Now, $\dfrac{dy}{dx} = 0 \Rightarrow 1-n^2x^2 = 0 \Rightarrow x = \pm\dfrac{1}{n}$

Next $\dfrac{d^2y}{dx^2} = \dfrac{(1+n^2x^2)^2\cdot(-2n^2x) - (1-n^2x^2)\cdot 2(1+n^2x^2)(2n^2x)}{(1+n^2x^2)^4}$

$$= \frac{2n^2x(n^2x^2-3)}{(1+n^2x^2)^4}$$

At $x = \dfrac{1}{n}$, $\dfrac{d^2y}{dx^2} = -\dfrac{n}{4} < 0$

$\therefore$ *y* is maximum at $x = \dfrac{1}{n}$

and at $x = -\dfrac{1}{n}$, $\dfrac{d^2y}{dx^2} = \dfrac{n}{4} > 0$

$\therefore$ *y* is minimum at $x = -\dfrac{1}{n}$

$$\therefore M_n = \frac{1/n}{1+n^2\cdot\frac{1}{n^2}} = \frac{1}{2n}$$

$$\therefore \lim_{n\to\infty} M_n = \lim_{n\to\infty}\frac{1}{2n} = 0$$

Hence, $f_n(x)$ is uniformly convergent to $f(x) = 0$.

Now,

$$f'_n(x) = \frac{(1+n^2x^2)\cdot 1 - x(2n^2x)}{(1+n^2x^2)^2}$$

$$= \frac{1-n^2x^2}{(1+n^2x^2)^2}$$

Let $\alpha\in[0,1]$. Then,

***Case* I** If $\alpha = 0$, then

$$f(\alpha) = \lim_{n\to\infty} a_n(\alpha)$$

$$= \lim_{n\to\infty} 1 = 1$$

***Case* II** If $\alpha = 1$, then

$$f(\alpha) = \lim_{n\to\infty} a_n(\alpha)$$

$$= \lim_{n\to\infty} a_n(1)$$

$$= \lim_{n\to\infty}\frac{1-n^2}{(1+n^2)^2}$$

= does not exist

Hence, $f'_n(x)$ is not convergent.

$\Rightarrow f_n'(x)$ is not uniformly convergent.

***Example 10.*** *Let*

$$f_n(x) = nxe^{-nx^2},\ x\in[0,1]$$

*be a sequence of real-valued function. Then,*

(a) $f_n(x)$ is not uniformly convergent

(b) $f_n'(x)$ is not uniformly convergent

(c) $\int_0^x f_n(x)\,dx$ is not uniformly convergent

(d) $\int_0^x f_n(x)\,dx$ is point-wise convergent

**Solution.** (a), (b), (c)

We have

$$f_n(x) = nxe^{-nx^2},\ x\in[0,1]$$

Let $\alpha\in[0,1]$. Then,

$$f(\alpha) = \lim_{n\to\infty} a_n(\alpha)$$

$$= \lim_{n\to\infty} n\alpha e^{-n\alpha^2}$$

= does not exists

$\Rightarrow f_n(x)$ is not convergent.

$\Rightarrow f_n(x)$ is not uniformly convergent.

Now, $f_n'(x) = ne^{-nx^2} - 2n^2xe^{-nx^2},\ x\in[0,1]$

Let $\alpha\in[0,1]$, then

$$f'(\alpha) = \lim_{n\to\infty} a_n'(\alpha)$$

$$= \lim_{n\to\infty} ne^{-n\alpha^2} - 2n^2\alpha e^{-n\alpha^2}$$

= does not exists

$\Rightarrow f_n'(x)$ is not uniformly convergent.

Now, $\int_0^x f_n(x)\,dx = \int_0^x nxe^{-nx^2}\,dx$

put $-nx^2 = t \Rightarrow -2nx\,dx = dt$

$$\Rightarrow \quad nx\,dx = \frac{dt}{-2n}$$

$$= \int_0^{-nx^2} e^t \frac{dt}{(-2n)} = -2n \int_0^{-nx^2} e^t dt$$

$$= -2n\,[e^t]_0^{-nx^2} = -2ne^{-nx^2} + 2n$$

$$= 2n(1 - e^{-nx^2})$$

Let $\alpha \in [0, 1]$. Then,

$$\int_0^x f(\alpha)\,d\alpha = \lim_{n\to\infty} \int_0^x a_n(\alpha)\,d\alpha$$

$$= \lim_{n\to\infty} 2n\,(1 - e^{-n\alpha^2})$$

= does not exists

$\therefore \int_0^x f_n(x)\,dx$ does not converges uniformly.

***Example 11.*** *Let*

$$u_n(x) = \frac{nx}{1+n^2x^2} - \frac{(n-1)\,x}{1+(n-1)^2x^2}$$

*be a series of real-valued function. Then,*

(a) $\Sigma\, u_n(x) = \dfrac{nx}{1+n^2x^2}$

(b) $\Sigma\, u_n(x) = \dfrac{(n-1)\,x}{1+(n-1)^2x^2}$

(c) $\Sigma\, u_n(x)$ is uniformly convergent

(d) $\Sigma\, u_n(x)$ is not uniformly convergent

**Solution.** (a), (d)

We have

$$S_n(x) = u_1(x) + u_2(x) + \ldots + u_n(x)$$

$$= \frac{x}{1+x^2} + \frac{2x}{1+2^2x^2} - \frac{x}{1+x^2} + \frac{3x}{1+3^2x^2} - \frac{2x}{1+2^2x^2} + \ldots + \frac{(n-1)\,x}{1+(n-1)^2x^2} - \frac{(n-2)\,x}{1+(n-2)^2x^2} + \frac{nx}{1+n^2x^2} - \frac{(n-1)\,x}{1+(n-1)^2x^2}$$

$$\therefore \quad \Sigma\, u_n(x) = \frac{nx}{1+n^2x^2}$$

Now,

$$\lim_{n\to\infty} S_n(x) = \lim_{n\to\infty} \frac{nx}{1+n^2x^2} = 0$$

Now, $\dfrac{nx}{1+n^2x^2}$ attains the maximum value $\dfrac{1}{2}$ at $x = \dfrac{1}{n}$, $\dfrac{1}{n} \to 0$ as $n \to \infty$.

Let us take an interval $[a, b]$ containing 0. Thus,

$$M_n = \sup_{x\in[a,b]} \left| f_n(x) - f(x) \right|$$

$$= \sup_{x\in[a,b]} \left| \frac{nx}{1+n^2x^2} \right|$$

$$= \frac{1}{2}$$

Which does not tend to zero as $n \to \infty$.

Hence, $\Sigma u_n(x)$ is not uniformly convergent.

# Exercise 1 (For Part 'B')

**Direction** (Q. Nos. 1-16) *All questions have only one correct option.*

**1.** Let $f_n(x)$ be a sequence of real-valued function and converges uniformly to $f(x)$. Then, which one of the following is correct?
(a) If each $f_n(x)$ is continuous $\Rightarrow f$ is continuous
(b) If each $f_n(x)$ is continuous $\Rightarrow f$ may not be continuous
(c) If each $f_n(x)$ is differentiable $\Rightarrow f$ is differentiable
(d) None of the above

**2.** Let $f_n(x), \forall\, x \in \mathbb{Q}$ be a sequence of real-valued function. Then,
(a) the number of point sequence is zero
(b) the number of point sequence is finite
(c) the number of point sequence is countably infinite
(d) None of the above

**3.** Let $f_n(x) = x\pi^n$, $x \in [0, 1]$ be a sequence of real-valued function. Then,
(a) $f_n(x)$ is point-wise convergent
(b) $f_n(x)$ does not converge point-wise
(c) $f_n(x)$ is uniformly convergent
(d) None of the above

**4.** Let $f_n(x)$ be a sequence of real-valued function converges uniformly to $f(x)$. Then,
(a) if each $f_n(x)$ is continuous $\Rightarrow f$ may not be continuous
(b) if each $f_n(x)$ is differentiable $\Rightarrow f$ is differentiable
(c) if $f(x)$ is not continuous $\Rightarrow f_n(x)$ is not uniformly convergent
(d) None of the above

**5.** Let $f_n(x) = nxe^{-nx^2}$, $x \in [0, 1]$, then which one of the following is not a point sequence?
(a) $a_n = 0$ (b) $a_n = ne^{-n}$
(c) $a_n = 2ne^{-4n}$ (d) $a_n = 2ne^{-2n}$

**6.** Let $f_n(x) = \tan^{-1} nx$, $n \in [0, 1]$, whose point-wise limit is

$$f(x) = \begin{cases} 0, & x = 0 \\ \dfrac{\pi}{2}, & x \in (0, 1] \end{cases}$$

Then,
(a) $f(x)$ is continuous (b) $f(x)$ is not differentiable
(c) $f(x)$ is differentiable (d) None of these

**7.** The series $\Sigma \dfrac{\log n}{n^x}$ is
(a) converges uniformly for all $x \in [0, \infty)$
(b) converges uniformly for all $x \in [1, \infty)$
(c) converges uniformly for all $x \in (1, \infty)$
(d) None of the above

**8.** The series $\Sigma \dfrac{\sin nx}{n}$
(a) converges uniformly on $[5, 2\pi - 5]$
(b) converges uniformly on $[10, 2\pi - 10]$
(c) converges uniformly on $\left[\dfrac{\pi}{2}, \dfrac{3\pi}{2}\right]$
(d) does not converges uniformly

**9.** The series $\Sigma \dfrac{\cos nx}{n}$
(a) converges uniformly on $[10, 2\pi - 10]$
(b) converges uniformly on $[4, 2\pi - 4]$
(c) converges uniformly on $\left[\dfrac{\pi}{4}, \dfrac{7\pi}{4}\right]$
(d) None of the above

**10.** The sequence

$$f_n(x) = \left(\frac{\sin x}{x}\right)^{1/n}, \; x \in [0, \pi]$$

(a) converges point-wise
(b) does not Converges point-wise
(c) converges uniformly
(d) None of the above

**11.** The sequence

$$f_n(x) = \begin{cases} n(1 - nx), & 0 < x < \dfrac{1}{n} \\ 0, & \text{else} \end{cases}$$

(a) converges point-wise to $f(x) = 0$
(b) converges uniformly to $f(x) = 0$
(c) $\lim\limits_{n \to \infty} \int_0^1 f_n(x)\,dx = \int_0^1 f(x)\,dx$
(d) None of the above

**12.** The sequence

$$f_n(x) = \begin{cases} n^2 x, & 0 \le x \le \dfrac{1}{n} \\ -n^2 x + 2n, & \dfrac{1}{n} \le x \le \dfrac{2}{n} \\ 0, & \dfrac{2}{n} \le x \le 1 \end{cases}$$

(a) converges uniformly
(b) the point-wise limit is $f(x) = x$
(c) $\lim\limits_{n \to \infty} \int_0^1 f_n(x)\,dx = \int_0^1 f(x)\,dx$
(d) $\lim\limits_{n \to \infty} \int_0^1 f_n(x)\,dx \neq \int_0^1 f(x)\,dx$

**13.** Let $f_n(x) = x^n$, $\forall\, x \in [0, 1]$ and for all positive integers $n$. Then,
(a) $< f_n >$ does not converge at any point
(b) $< f_n >$ converges at some points, but does not converge at some other points
(c) $< f_n >$ converges uniformly
(d) $< f_n >$ converges at every point, but does not converge uniformly

**14.** Let $< f_n >$ be a sequence of functions converging to $f$, then
(a) if the convergence is uniform and if $f$ is continuous, then each $f_n$ is continuous
(b) if each $f_n$ is continuous and if $f$ is continuous, then the convergence is uniform
(c) if the convergence is uniform and if each $f_n$ is continuous, then $f$ is continuous
(d) if the convergence is not uniform, $f$ is not continuous

**15.** If $f_n(x) = < x^n >, \forall x \in [0, 1]$, then the sequence $< f_n(x) >$
(a) converges to the zero function on [0, 1]
(b) converges uniformly
(c) does not converge point-wise
(d) converges point-wise to a discontinuous function

**16.** Let $f_n : [0, 1] \to R$ be defined by

$$f_n(x) = \begin{cases} 1 - n^2x^2, & 0 \le |x| \le \frac{1}{n} \\ 0, & \frac{1}{n} \le |x| \le 1 \end{cases} \text{ for } n = 1, 2, 3, \ldots$$

Then, the sequence of functions $< f_n >$
(a) converges point-wise but not uniformly
(b) converges uniformly
(c) converges point-wise and the limit function is continuous
(d) does not converge point-wise

# Exercise 2 (For Part 'C')

**Direction** (Q. Nos. 1-16) *Questions may have one or more than one correct option.*

**1.** Let $f_n(x) = \frac{1}{x + n}$, $x \in [0, b]$, $b > 0$ be a sequence of real-valued function. Then,
(a) point-wise limit of $f_n(x)$ is $f(x) = 0$
(b) uniform limit of $f_n(x)$ is $f(x) = 0$
(c) $f_n(x)$ is not uniformly convergent
(d) $f_n(x)$ is uniformly convergent and $f(x) = x, \forall x$

**2.** Which of the following(s) is/are correct?
(a) The interval of uniform convergence is always to be a closed interval.
(b) The interval of uniform convergence can be of any type.
(c) The interval of point-wise convergence is always to be a closed interval.
(d) The interval of point-wise convergence can be of any type.

**3.** Let $f_n(x) = n^2 e^{\cos x}$, $x \in [0, 2\pi]$ be a sequence of real-valued function. Then, which of the following(s) is/are point-wise sequence?
(a) $a_n = n$ (b) $a_n = n^2 e$
(c) $a_n = \frac{n^2}{e}$ (d) $a_n = \ln \frac{n}{e}$

**4.** The sequence of real-valued function

$$f_n(x) = \frac{nx}{1 + n^3x^2}, \; x \in [0, 1]$$

is
(a) point-wise convergent
(b) uniformly convergent
(c) has uncountable number of point sequence
(d) does not uniformly convergent

**5.** The series $\Sigma f_n$, where $n$th partial sum

$$S_n(x) = nxe^{-nx^2}, \; x \in [0, k], \; k > 0$$

is
(a) point-wise convergent
(b) does not point-wise convergent
(c) uniformly convergent
(d) does not uniformly convergent

**6.** The sequence

$$f_n(x) = \begin{cases} n^2x, & 0 \le x < \frac{1}{n} \\ -n^2x + 2x, & \frac{1}{n} \le x < \frac{2}{n} \\ 0, & \frac{2}{n} \le n \le 1 \end{cases}$$

be a sequence of real-valued function on [0, 1]. Then,
(a) uniform limit of $f_n(x)$ is $f(x) = 0$
(b) point-wise limit of $f_n(x)$ is $f(x) = 0$
(c) $f_n(x)$ does not uniformly convergent
(d) $f_n(x)$ does not point-wise convergent

**7.** The series

$$\frac{2x}{1+x^2} + \frac{4x^3}{1+x^4} + \frac{8x^7}{1+x^8} + \ldots. -\frac{1}{2} \le x \le \frac{1}{2}$$

is
(a) does not converge uniformly on $-\frac{1}{2} \le x \le \frac{1}{2}$
(b) converge uniformly on $-\frac{1}{2} \le x \le \frac{1}{2}$
(c) converge uniformly on $0 \le x \le \frac{1}{2}$
(d) converge uniformly on $-\frac{1}{2} \le x \le 0$

**8.** The series

$$\Sigma \frac{\sin(x^2 + n^2 x)}{n(n+1)}$$

is

(a) convergent uniformly only for finite real number.
(b) convergent uniformly only for countable real number
(c) convergent uniformly only for rational number
(d) convergent uniformly for all real number

**9.** Let $f_n(x) = e^{-nx}$ be a sequence of real-valued function. Then,

(a) $f_n(x)$ is point-wise convergent in $[0, k]$, $k > 0$
(b) $f_n(x)$ is uniformly convergent in $[0, k]$, $k > 0$
(c) $f_n(x)$ is uniformly convergent in $[a, b], a > 0, b > 0$.
(d) $f_n(x)$ is not uniformly convergent in $[a, b]$, $a > 0$, $b > 0$

**10.** The series

$$\Sigma \frac{x}{n^p + x^2 n^q}$$

is uniformly convergent over any finite interval $[a, b]$ for

(a) $p > 1, q \geq 0$
(b) $p > 1, q \leq 0$
(c) $0 < p \leq 1, p + q > 2$
(d) None of the above

**11.** The series

$$\Sigma \frac{\cos n\theta}{n^p}$$

is

(a) uniformly convergent for all real $\theta$ and $p > 1$
(b) absolutely convergent for all real $\theta$ and $p < 1$
(c) uniformly convergent for all real $\theta$ and $p < 1$
(d) absolutely convergent for all real $\theta$ and $p > 1$

**12.** The series

$$\Sigma (-1)^n \cdot \frac{1}{n}$$

is

(a) uniformly convergent
(b) does not uniformly convergent
(c) the sum of partial sum $S_n(x)$ is uniformly bounded
(d) None of the above

**13.** The series

$$\Sigma \frac{(-1)^n x^{2n}}{n^p (1 + x^{2n})}$$

is

(a) converges uniformly, $\forall\ x \in \mathbb{R}, p > 1$
(b) converges uniformly, $\forall\ x \in \mathbb{R}, p < 1$
(c) converges absolutely, $\forall\ x \in \mathbb{R}, p > 1$
(d) converges absolutely, $\forall\ x \in \mathbb{R}, p < 1$

**14.** The series

$$\Sigma (-1)^n \cos \frac{1}{n}$$

is

(a) uniformly convergent
(b) does not converge uniformly
(c) $\lim_{n \to \infty} \cos \frac{1}{n}$ does not exists
(d) $\lim_{n \to \infty} \cos \frac{1}{n}$ exists

**15.** The series

$$\Sigma\, n^{-x}$$

is

(a) uniformly convergent in $[1 + \delta, \infty)$, $\delta \geq 0$
(b) uniformly convergent in $[1 + \delta, \infty)$, $\delta > 0$
(c) uniformly convergent in $[\delta, \infty)$, $\delta \geq 0$
(d) uniformly convergent in $[\delta, \infty)$, $\delta > 0$

**16.** Let $f_n(x)$ be a sequence of real-valued function converges uniformly to $f(x)$. Then, which of the following(s) is/are true?

(a) If each $f_n(x)$, $\forall\ n \in \mathbb{N}$ is continuous $\Rightarrow f$ is continuous.
(b) $\lim_{n \to \infty} \lim_{x \to a} f_n(x) = \lim_{x \to a} \lim_{x \to \infty} f_n(x)$ provided the limit exists.
(c) If each $f_n(x)$ is differentiable, $\forall\ n \in \mathbb{N} \Rightarrow f$ may not be differentiable.
(d) None of the above

# Answers

## Exercise 1

| | | | | | | | | | |
|---|---|---|---|---|---|---|---|---|---|
| **1.** (a) | **2.** (c) | **3.** (b) | **4.** (c) | **5.** (d) | **6.** (b) | **7.** (c) | **8.** (c) | **9.** (c) | **10.** (a) |
| **11.** (a) | **12.** (d) | **13.** (d) | **14.** (c) | **15.** (d) | **16.** (a) | | | | |

## Exercise 2

| | | | | | | | | | |
|---|---|---|---|---|---|---|---|---|---|
| **1.** (a,b) | **2.** (a,d) | **3.** (b,c) | **4.** (a,b,c) | **5.** (a,d) | **6.** (b,c) | **7.** (b,c,d) | **8.** (d) | **9.** (a,c) | **10.** (a,c) |
| **11.** (a,d) | **12.** (a,c) | **13.** (a,c) | **14.** (b,c) | **15.** (b) | **16.** (a,b,c) | | | | |

# Hints & Solutions

## Exercise 1

**2.** As for different value of x, we get different point sequence. Since, $\mathbb{Q}$ is countably infinite. Hence, the number of point sequence of given sequence of real-valued function is countable infinite.

**3.** We have,

$$f(x) = \lim_{n\to\infty} f_n(x)$$
$$= \lim_{n\to\infty} x\pi^n$$
$$= x \lim_{n\to\infty} \pi^n$$
$$= \text{does not exists}$$

Hence, the given sequence of real-valued function does not converge point-wise.

**5.** For $x = 0$, we have

$$a_n = 0$$

For $x = 1$, we have

$$a_n = ne^{-n}$$

For $x = 2$, we have

$$a_n = 2ne^{-4n}$$

but there does not exists any $x \in [0, 1]$, such that

$$a_n = 2ne^{-2n}$$

**6.** We have,

$$f(x) = \begin{cases} 0, & x = 0 \\ \dfrac{\pi}{2}, & x \in (0, 1] \end{cases}$$

Clearly $f(x)$ is discontinuous at 0.

$\Rightarrow$ $f(x)$ is not differentiable at 0.

**8.** Since, $\Sigma \dfrac{\sin nx}{n}$ converges uniformly in $[\alpha, 2\pi - \alpha]$ where $\alpha$ is any fixed positive number less than $\pi$. Hence, by taking $\alpha = \dfrac{\pi}{2}$, the given series converges uniformly on $\left[\dfrac{\pi}{2}, \dfrac{3\pi}{2}\right]$.

**9.** Since, $\Sigma \dfrac{\cos nx}{n}$ converges uniformly on $[\alpha, 2\pi - \alpha]$, where $\alpha$ is any fixed positive number less than $\pi$. Hence, by taking $\alpha = \dfrac{\pi}{4}$, the given series converges uniformly $\left[\dfrac{\pi}{4}, \dfrac{7\pi}{4}\right]$.

**12.** The sequence converges point-wise to $f(x) = 0$, $\forall\ x \in [0, 1]$, each function $f_n$ and $f$ are continuous on $[0, 1]$.

Also,

$$\int_0^1 f_n(x)\,dx = \int_0^{1/n} -n^2x\,dx + \int_{1/n}^{2/n} (-n^2x + 2n)\,dx + \int_{2/n}^1 0\,dx$$
$$= 1$$

but $\displaystyle\int_0^1 f(x)\,dx = 0$

$\Rightarrow$ $\displaystyle\lim_{n\to\infty} \int_0^1 f_n(x)\,dx \neq \int_0^1 f(x)\,dx$

**13.** We have, $f_n(x) = x^n$, $\forall\ x \in [0, 1]$

$\Rightarrow$ $f(x) = \begin{cases} 0, & 0 \le x < 1 \\ 1, & x = 1 \end{cases}$

$\therefore$ $M_n = \sup_{x\in[0,1]} \{|f_n(x) - f(x)|\}$

$$= \sup_{x\in[0,1]} \{|x^n|\} = 1$$

$\therefore$ $\lim_{n\to\infty} M_n = 1$

$\Rightarrow$ $f_n(x)$ is not uniformly convergent but convergent at every point.

**15.** We have,

$$f(x) = \lim_{n\to\infty} x^n$$
$$= \begin{cases} 0, & 0 \le x < 1 \\ 1, & x = 1 \end{cases}$$

$\Rightarrow$ $f(x)$ is discontinuous at $x = 1$.

## Exercise 2

**1.** Let $\alpha \in [0, b]$, $b > 0$, then

$$f(\alpha) = \lim_{n\to\infty} f_n(\alpha)$$
$$= \lim_{n\to\infty} \frac{1}{\alpha + n} = 0$$

$\therefore$ $f(x) = 0$, $\forall\ x$ is point-wise limit of $f_n(x)$.

Now,

$$M_n = \sup_{x\in[0,b]} |f_n(x) - f(x)|$$
$$= \sup_{x\in[0,b]} \left|\frac{1}{x+n}\right|$$

Let $y = \dfrac{1}{x+n} \Rightarrow \dfrac{dy}{dx} = \dfrac{(x+n)\cdot 0 - 1\cdot 1}{(x+n)^2}$

$$= -\frac{1}{(x+n)^2}$$

$\Rightarrow$ $y$ is decreasing. Hence,

$$M_n = \frac{1}{n}$$

$\therefore$ $$\lim_{n\to\infty} M_n = \lim_{n\to\infty} \frac{1}{n} = 0$$

$\therefore$ $f_n(x)$ is uniformly convergent and uniform limit is $f(x) = 0$.

**3.** For $x = 0$, we get

$$a_n = n^2 e^{\cos 0} = n^2 e$$

For $x = \pi$, we get

$$a_n = n^2 e^{\cos \pi} = n^2 e^{-1} = \frac{n^2}{e}$$

Hence, $a_n = n^2 e$ and $a_n = \dfrac{n^2}{e}$ are point-wise sequence.

**5.** The point-wise sum

$$S(x) = \lim_{n\to\infty} S_n(x)$$
$$= 0, \forall\ x \geq 0$$

Thus, the series converges point-wise to 0 in $[0, k]$.

If possible let the series converges uniformly on $[0, k]$. Thus, for any given $\varepsilon > 0$, $\exists\, \mathbb{N}$ such that, $\forall\ x \geq 0$

$$|S_n(x) - S(x)| = nxe^{-nx^2}$$
$$< \varepsilon,\ \forall\ n \geq \mathbb{N}$$

Let $N_0$ be an integer greater than $N$ and $\varepsilon^2 e^2$. Then, for $x = \dfrac{1}{\sqrt{N_0}}$ and $n = N_0$, we get

$$\frac{\sqrt{N_0}}{e} < \varepsilon$$

$\Rightarrow$ $$N_0 < e^2 \varepsilon^2$$

Which is a contradiction. Therefore, the series is not uniformly convergent in $[0, k]$.

**6.** Clearly,

$$f(x) = \lim_{n\to\infty} f_n(x)$$
$$= 0, \forall\ n \in [0, 1]$$

Now,

$$M_n = \sup_{x\in[0,1]} |f_n(x) - f(x)|$$

$$= \sup_{x\in[0,1]} \left\{ \sup_{x\in\left[0,\frac{1}{n}\right)} |f_n(x) - f(x)|,\ \sup_{x\in\left[\frac{1}{n},\frac{2}{n}\right)} |f_n(x) - f(x)|,\ \sup_{x\in\left[\frac{2}{n},1\right]} |f_n(x) - f(x)|, \right\}$$

$$= \sup_{x\in[0,1]} \left\{ \sup_{x\in\left[0,\frac{1}{n}\right)} |n^2 x|,\ \sup_{x\in\left[\frac{1}{n},\frac{2}{n}\right)} |-n^2 x + 2n|, 0 \right\}$$

$$= \sup_{x\in[0,1]} \{n, n, 0\} = n$$

$\therefore$ $\lim_{n\to\infty} M_n = \lim_{n\to\infty} n =$ does not exists.

Hence, $f_n(x)$ is not uniformly convergent but point-wise convergent.

**7.** We have,

$$S_n(x) = \frac{2^n\, x^{2n-1}}{1 + x^{2n}}$$

$\Rightarrow$ $$|f_n(x)| \leq 2^n (\alpha)^{2n-1}$$

where $$|x| \leq \alpha \leq \frac{1}{2}$$

but the series $\Sigma\, 2^n (\alpha)^{2n-1}$ converges and hence by $M$-test the given series converges uniformly on $\left[-\frac{1}{2}, \frac{1}{2}\right]$, and hence converges uniformly on $\left[0, -\frac{1}{2}\right]$ and $\left[-\frac{1}{2}, 0\right]$.

**8.** We have,

$$|f_n(x)| = \left| \frac{\sin(x^2 + n^2 x)}{n(n+1)} \right|$$
$$\leq \frac{|\sin(x^2 + n^2 x)|}{n(n+1)}$$
$$= \frac{1}{n(n+1)} = M_n,\ \forall\ x \in \mathbb{R}$$

but the series $\Sigma \dfrac{1}{n(n+1)}$ is convergent.

Hence, the series $\Sigma \dfrac{\sin(x^2 + n^2 x)}{n(n+1)}$ is uniformly convergent, $\forall\ x \in \mathbb{R}$.

**10.** When $p > 1$, $q \geq 0$, we have

$$|f_n(x)| = \left| \frac{x}{n^p + x^2 n^q} \right| \leq \frac{\alpha}{n^p}$$

where $\alpha \geq \max\{|a|, |b|\}$

but the series $\Sigma \left(\dfrac{\alpha}{n^p}\right)$ is convergent for $p > 1$. Therefore, by $M$-test, the given series converges uniformly over the interval $[a, b]$.

Now, when

$$0 < p \leq 1,\ p + q > 2$$

We have,

$|f_n(x)|$ attains the maximum value $\dfrac{1}{2n^{\left(\frac{p+q}{2}\right)}}$ at the point, where $x^2 n^q = n^p$. Hence,

$|f_n(x)| \leq \dfrac{1}{2n^{\left(\frac{p+q}{2}\right)}}$ which is a convergent series for $p + q > 2$.

Hence, given series converges uniformly over any finite interval $[a, b]$.

**11.** We have,

$$|f_n(\theta)| = \left|\frac{\cos\theta}{n^p}\right| \le \frac{1}{n^p}, \forall \theta$$

but the series $\Sigma \frac{1}{n^p}$ is convergent for $p > 1$. Hence, the given series converges uniformly and absolutely for all real θ and $p > 1$.

**12.** We have,

$$v_n(x) = \frac{1}{n} \text{ and } u_n(x) = (-1)^n$$

Hence, $$\lim_{n\to\infty} v_n(x) = \lim_{n\to\infty} \frac{1}{n} = 0$$

and $v_n(x)$ is monotonic decreasing sequence.

Now, sum of partial sum of $\Sigma u_n(x)$ is

$$S_n(x) = \begin{cases} -1, & n \text{ is odd} \\ 0, & n \text{ is even} \end{cases}$$

Therefore, $$|S_n(x)| \le 1$$

Hence, $S_n(x)$ is uniformly bounded. Therefore, the given series $\Sigma (-1)^n \cdot \frac{1}{n}$ converges uniformly.

**13.** We have,

$$|f_n(x)| = \left|\frac{(-1)^n x^{2n}}{n^p(1+x^{2n})}\right|$$

$$\le \frac{1}{n^p}, \forall\ x \in \mathbb{R}$$

but the series $\Sigma \frac{1}{n^p}$ is convergent for $p > 1$.

Hence, the given series converges uniformly and absolutely $\forall\ x \in \mathbb{R}$ and $p > 1$.

**14.** We have

$$u_n = (-1)^n$$

and $$v_n = \cos\frac{1}{n}$$

$$\therefore \quad \lim_{n\to\infty} v_n = \lim_{n\to\infty} \cos\frac{1}{n}$$

$$= \text{does not exists}$$

Hence, by Leibnitz test the given series is not uniformly convergent.

# Functions of Several Variables

**Syllabus**

- Functions of Several Variables
- Directional Derivative
- Partial Derivative
- Derivative as a Linear Transformation

## Functions of Two Variables

Let $R$ denotes the set of real numbers and $R^2 = R \times R = \{(x, y) : x \in R, y \in R\}$

Suppose, $S \subseteq R^2$

If $f : S \to R$, then $f$ is called a real-valued function of two real variables.

The set $S$ is called the domain of this function and range of this function is a subset of $R$.

> ***Note*** $z = f(x, y)$ is a real-valued function of two independent real variables $x$ and $y$, if for each pair of values of $x$ and $y$ of a set $\{(x, y)\}$ over which the point $(x, y)$ ranges, there exists a unique real value of $z$.
>
> *e.g.*, $z = x\cos y + y\sin x$.
>
> $z = 2x^2 + 2y^2 - 3xy$ are real-valued functions of independent variables $x$ and $y$.

## Neighbourhood (*nbd* or *nhd*) of a Point

### Rectangular Neighbourhood of a Point

Let $(a, b)$ be any point of $R^2$.

The set $N(a, b) = \{(x, y) : x \in R, y \in R, a - h < x < a + h, b - k < y < b + k\}$ is called a rectangular neighbourhood of the point $(a, b)$, where $h$ and $k$ are arbitrarily small positive real numbers.

A neighbourhood of a point $(a, b)$ is denoted by $N(a, b)$.

### Deleted *nbd* of a Point

If we delete the point $(a, b)$ from the neighbourhood $N(a, b)$ of the point $(a, b)$, then the remaining set is called the deleted *nbd* of $(a, b)$.

### Circular *nbd* of a Point

The set $N(a, b) = \{(x, y) : x \in R, y \in R$ and $\sqrt{(x - a)^2 + (y - b)^2} < \delta\}$ is called a circular neighbourhood of a point $(a, b)$, where $\delta$ is an arbitrarily small positive real number.

> ***Note*** Every circular *nbd* of a point contains a rectangular neighbourhood and *vice-versa*.

## Simultaneous and Iterated Limits (or Repeated Limit)

We can define several kinds of limit for a function $f(x, y)$ of two variables $x$ and $y$.

Suppose, $(a, b)$ is limit point of a set of values in two dimensional space, then we have the following limits

**(i)** $\lim_{(x,y)\to(a,b)} f(x, y)$ it can also be written as $\lim_{\substack{x\to a\\ y\to b}} f(x, y)$ this is called simultaneous limit.

**(ii)** $\lim_{x\to a}\lim_{y\to b} f(x,y)$; $\lim_{y\to b}\lim_{x\to a} f(x, y)$ this is called iterated limits or repeated limits. These two limits may or may not be equal.

> ***Note*** **(a)** The simultaneous limit of $f(x, y)$ exists and is equal to $A$ as $(x, y)\to(a, b)$, if for every $\varepsilon > 0$, there exists a $\delta > 0$, such that
> $$|f(x, y) - A| < \varepsilon$$
> for all values of $x$ and $y$ in the *nbd* of $(a, b)$ defined by $|x - a| < \delta, |y - b| < \delta$.
>
> **(b)** If the repeated limits are not equal, the simultaneous limit cannot exist.

***Example 1.*** *Prove that the simultaneous limit* $\lim_{(x,y)\to(0,0)} y\sin\frac{1}{x}$ *exists and is equal to* 0 *but the single limit* $\lim_{x\to 0} y_1\sin\frac{1}{x}\ (y_1 \neq 0)$ *does not exist.*

**Solution.** First we show that the simultaneous limit $\lim_{(x,y)\to(0,0)} y\sin\frac{1}{x}$ exists.

Let $\varepsilon > 0$ be given. Let us take $\delta = \varepsilon$, we observe that for all $x, y$ satisfying the inequalities $0 < |x| < \delta$, $0 < |y| < \delta$, we have

$$|y\sin\frac{1}{x} - 0| = |y\sin\frac{1}{x}| = |y|\,|\sin\frac{1}{x}| \le |y| \quad [\because |\sin\frac{1}{x}| \le 1]$$
$$< \delta = \varepsilon$$

$$\therefore \quad \lim_{(x,y)\to(0,0)} y\sin\frac{1}{x} = 0$$

$\Rightarrow$ Simultaneous limit exists.

But for any constant value of $y = y_1 \neq 0$, we get $\lim_{x\to 0} y_1\sin\frac{1}{x} = y_1\lim_{x\to 0}\sin\frac{1}{x}$, which does not exist.

***Example 2.*** *Prove that the simultaneous limit*

$$\lim_{(x,y)\to(0,0)} \frac{xy^3}{x^2+y^6} \text{ does not exist.}$$

**Solution.** Let us suppose $(x, y)$ approaches $(0, 0)$ along the line $y = x$, which is a line through the origin. Put $y = x$ and allows $x\to 0$, we get

$$\lim_{x\to 0}\frac{x^4}{x^2+x^6} = \lim_{x\to 0}\frac{x^2}{1+x^4} = 0$$

Again, let $(x, y)$ approach $(0, 0)$ along the curve $y^3 = x$, put $y^3 = x$ and allows $x\to 0$, we get

$$\lim_{x\to 0}\frac{x\cdot x}{x^2+x^2} = \frac{1}{2}$$

Since, along two paths we get different limiting values. Therefore, the simultaneous limit does not exist.

***Theorem*** Suppose the simultaneous limit $\lim_{(x,y)\to(a,b)} f(x, y)$ exists and be equal to $A$ and let the $\lim_{x\to a} f(x, y)$ exist for each constant value of $y$ in the *nbd* of $b$ and likewise. Suppose the $\lim_{y\to b} f(x, y)$ exist for each constant value of $x$ in the *nbd* of $a$.

Then, $\lim_{x\to a}\lim_{y\to b} f(x, y) = \lim_{y\to b}\lim_{x\to a} f(x, y) = A.$

***Example 3.*** *Prove that* $\lim_{(x,y)\to(0,0)} xy\cdot\frac{x^2-y^2}{x^2+y^2} = 0.$

**Solution.** Let $\varepsilon > 0$ be given, $\forall\ (x, y) \neq (0, 0)$, we have

$$\left|xy\frac{(x^2-y^2)}{x^2+y^2} - 0\right| = \left|\frac{xy\,(x^2-y^2)}{x^2+y^2}\right| = |x^2-y^2|\cdot\frac{|xy|}{x^2+y^2} \quad \text{...(i)}$$

Now, for all $x$ and $y$, we have $(|x| - |y|)^2 \ge 0$

$\Rightarrow\ |x^2| + |y^2| - 2\,|x|\cdot|y| \ge 0$

$$\Rightarrow \quad x^2 + y^2 \ge 2\,|xy|$$

$$\Rightarrow \quad \frac{|xy|}{x^2+y^2} \le \frac{1}{2},\ \text{if } (x, y) \neq (0, 0) \quad \text{...(ii)}$$

Using Eqs. (i) and (ii) for all $(x, y) \neq (0, 0)$, we have

$$\left|xy\frac{(x^2-y^2)}{x^2+y^2} - 0\right| \le \frac{1}{2}|x^2-y^2| \le \frac{1}{2}|x^2+y^2|$$
$$= \frac{1}{2}(x^2+y^2) < \varepsilon, \text{ if } x^2 < \varepsilon \text{ and } y^2 < \varepsilon$$

$\Rightarrow$ If $|x| < \sqrt{\varepsilon}$ and $|y| < \sqrt{\varepsilon}$

If we take $\delta = \sqrt{\varepsilon}$, then we see that for any $\varepsilon > 0$, $\exists\ \delta > 0$ s.t.

$$\left|\frac{xy(x^2-y^2)}{x^2+y^2} - 0\right| < \varepsilon, \text{ whenever } |x| < \delta, |y| < \delta$$

$$\therefore \quad \lim_{(x,y)\to(0,0)} xy\cdot\frac{x^2-y^2}{x^2+y^2} = 0$$

***Example 4.*** *Prove that the simultaneous limit exists at the origin but the repeated limit does not, where*

$$f(x, y) = \begin{cases} x\sin\frac{1}{y} + y\sin\frac{1}{x} & , xy \neq 0 \\ 0 & , xy = 0 \end{cases}$$

**Solution.** $\lim_{y\to 0} f(x, y)$, $\lim_{x\to 0} f(x, y)$ do not exist and therefore, both the repeated limits $\lim_{x\to 0}\lim_{y\to 0} f(x, y)$ and $\lim_{y\to 0}\lim_{x\to 0} f(x, y)$ do not exist.

However, the simultaneous limit $\lim_{(x, y)\to(0, 0)} f(x, y)$ exists and equal to zero as shown below

Now, let us take any given

$\varepsilon > 0, \forall (x, y) \neq (0, 0)$ s.t. $xy = 0$, we have

$$|f(x, y) - 0| = |0 - 0| = 0 < \varepsilon$$

Now, $\forall (x, y) \neq (0, 0)$ s.t. $xy \neq 0$, we get

$$|f(x, y) - 0| = |f(x, y)| = \left|x \sin\frac{1}{y} + y \sin\frac{1}{x}\right|$$

$$\leq \left|x \sin\frac{1}{y}\right| + \left|y \sin\frac{1}{x}\right| \quad [\because |a+b| \leq |a| + |b|]$$

$$= |x| \left|\sin\frac{1}{y}\right| + |y| \left|\sin\frac{1}{x}\right| \quad [\because |ab| = |a|\,|b|]$$

$$\leq |x| + |y| \quad \left[\because \left|\sin\frac{1}{y}\right| \leq 1 \text{ and } \left|\sin\frac{1}{x}\right| \leq 1\right]$$

$$\leq 2\sqrt{x^2 + y^2} \quad [\because |x| \leq \sqrt{x^2 + y^2} \text{ and } |y| \leq \sqrt{x^2 + y^2}]$$

$$< \varepsilon, \text{ if } x^2 < \frac{\varepsilon^2}{8} \text{ and } y^2 < \frac{\varepsilon^2}{8}.$$

*i.e.* $\quad |x| < \dfrac{\varepsilon}{2\sqrt{2}}$ and $|y| < \dfrac{\varepsilon}{2\sqrt{2}}$

If we take $\delta = \dfrac{\varepsilon}{2\sqrt{2}}$, then we observe that for any given $\varepsilon > 0, \exists\, \delta > 0$ s.t. $|f(x, y) - 0| < \varepsilon$, whenever $|x| < \delta$ and $|y| < \delta$

Therefore, $\lim_{(x, y)\to(0, 0)} f(x, y) = 0$

## Continuity of Functions of Two Variables

The function $f(x, y)$ is said to be continuous at $(a, b)$, if for every $\varepsilon > 0, \exists\, \delta > 0$ s.t.

$|f(x, y) - f(a, b)| < \varepsilon, \forall\, |x - a| < \delta, |y - b| < \delta$

or we can say that, $f(x, y)$ is said to be continuous at $(a, b)$, if the simultaneous limit $\lim_{(x, y)\to(a, b)} f(x, y)$ exists and is equal to its functional value $f(a, b)$ at $(a, b)$.

$f$ is said to be continuous on the domain $D$, if $f$ is continuous at each point of $D$. $f$ is not continuous at $(a, b) \in D \subseteq R^2$, then $f$ is called discontinuous on $(a, b)$.

***Example 5.*** *Prove that the function $f : R^2 \to R$ defined by $f(x, y) = \dfrac{(y^2 - x^2)yx}{x^2 + y^2}$ for $f(x, y) \neq (0, 0)$ and $f(0, 0) = 0$ is continuous at the point $(0, 0)$.*

**Solution.** Firstly, we show that $\lim_{(x, y)\to(0, 0)} f(x, y) = 0$

Let us take the given $\varepsilon > 0, \forall (x, y) \neq (0, 0)$, we have

$$|f(x, y) - 0| = \left|\frac{(y^2 - x^2)yx}{x^2 + y^2}\right| = |y^2 - x^2| \cdot \frac{|xy|}{x^2 + y^2} \quad \text{...(i)}$$

Now, for all $x$ and $y$, we have $(|x| - |y|)^2 \geq 0$

$$\Rightarrow \quad |x|^2 + |y|^2 - 2|x|\cdot|y| \geq 0 \Rightarrow x^2 + y^2 \geq 2|xy|$$

$$\Rightarrow \quad \frac{|xy|}{x^2 + y^2} \leq \frac{1}{2}, \text{ if } (x, y) \neq (0, 0) \quad \text{...(ii)}$$

Using Eqs. (i) and (ii) for all $(x, y) \neq (0, 0)$, we have

$$|f(x, y) - 0| \leq \frac{1}{2}|y^2 - x^2| \leq \frac{1}{2}|y^2 + x^2| = \frac{1}{2}(x^2 + y^2)$$

$$< \varepsilon, \text{ if } x^2 < \varepsilon, y^2 < \varepsilon$$

*i.e.*, $\quad |x| < \sqrt{\varepsilon}, |y| < \sqrt{\varepsilon}$

If we take $\delta = \sqrt{\varepsilon}$, then we observe that for any given $\varepsilon > 0, \exists\, \delta > 0$ s.t.

$$|f(x, y) - 0| < \varepsilon, \text{ whenever } |x| < \delta \text{ and } |y| < \delta$$

$\therefore \quad \lim_{(x, y)\to(0, 0)} f(x, y) = 0$

But it is given that $f(0, 0) = 0$

$\Rightarrow \quad \lim_{(x, y)\to(0, 0)} f(x, y) = f(0, 0)$

$\therefore \quad f(x, y)$ is continuous at the origin.

***Example 6.*** *Test the continuity at (1, 2) of the function*

$$f(x, y) = \begin{cases} x^2 + 4y, & (x, y) \neq (1, 2) \\ 0, & (x, y) = (1, 2) \end{cases}$$

**Solution.** We have,

$$\lim_{(x, y)\to(1, 2)} f(x, y) = \lim_{(x, y)\to(1, 2)} x^2 + 4y = 1^2 + 4 \times 2 = 9,$$

$\Rightarrow$ Limit exists and is equal to 9.

$$\left[\because f(1, 2) = 0 \text{ and } \lim_{(x, y)\to(1, 2)} f(x, y) = 9\right]$$

Clearly, $\quad \lim_{(x, y)\to(1, 2)} f(x, y) \neq f(1, 2)$

Therefore, the functions is not continuous at (1, 2).

***Example 7.*** *Prove that the function*

$$f(x, y) = \begin{cases} \dfrac{xy}{\sqrt{x^2 + y^2}}, & (x, y) \neq (0, 0) \\ 0, & (x, y) = (0, 0) \end{cases}$$

*is continuous at the origin in x-y together.*

**Solution.** Firstly, we prove that $\lim_{(x, y)\to(0, 0)} f(x, y) = 0$

Let $\varepsilon > 0$ be given, for all $(x, y) \neq (0, 0)$, we have

$$|f(x, y) - 0| = \left|\frac{xy}{\sqrt{x^2 + y^2}} - 0\right| = \left|\frac{xy}{\sqrt{x^2 + y^2}}\right|$$

Put $x = r\cos\theta$, $y = r\sin\theta$

$$\Rightarrow \quad |f(x, y) - 0| = \left|\frac{r\cos\theta \cdot r\sin\theta}{r}\right|$$

$$= r\,|\cos\theta|\,|\sin\theta|$$

$$\leq r \quad [\because |\cos\theta| \leq 1, |\sin\theta| \leq 1]$$

$$= \sqrt{x^2 + y^2} < \varepsilon, \text{ if } x^2 < \frac{\varepsilon^2}{2}, y^2 < \frac{\varepsilon^2}{2}$$

*i.e.* $\quad |x| < \dfrac{\varepsilon}{\sqrt{2}}, \; |y| < \dfrac{\varepsilon}{\sqrt{2}}$

If we take $\delta = \dfrac{\varepsilon}{\sqrt{2}}$, then we observe that for any given $\varepsilon > 0, \exists\, \delta > 0$ s.t.

$|f(x, y) - 0| < \varepsilon$, whenever $|x| < \delta$ and $|y| < \delta$.

$$\therefore \quad \lim_{(x, y) \to (0, 0)} f(x, y) = 0$$

But it is given that $\quad f(0, 0) = 0$

$$\therefore \quad \lim_{(x, y) \to (0, 0)} f(x, y) = f(0, 0)$$

Therefore, $f(x, y)$ is continuous at $(0, 0)$ in $x$-$y$ together.

# Directional Derivative

Let $f$ is defined on $S \subseteq \mathbb{R}^2$ and $c \in S$. Let $u = (u_1, u_2) \in \mathbb{R}^2$, then the directional derivative of $f$ at $c$ in the direction of $u$ is defined as $\lim_{h \to 0} \frac{f(c + hu) - f(c)}{h}$ provided this limit exists denoted by $f'(c, u)$.

***Example 8.*** *Let*

$$f(x, y) = \begin{cases} \dfrac{xy^2}{x^2 + y^4}, & (x, y) \neq (0, 0) \\ 0 & , (x, y) = 0 \end{cases}$$

*find the directional derivative along* $u = (\sqrt{2}, \sqrt{2})$ *at* $(0, 0)$.

**Solution.** We have,

$$f'(c, u) = \lim_{h \to 0} \frac{f(c + hu) - f(c)}{h}$$

$$= \lim_{h \to 0} \frac{f[(0, 0) + h(\sqrt{2}, \sqrt{2})] - f(0, 0)}{h}$$

$$= \lim_{h \to 0} \frac{f(h\sqrt{2}, h\sqrt{2})}{h}$$

$$= \lim_{h \to 0} \frac{\frac{h\sqrt{2} \cdot 2h^2}{2h^2 + 4h^4}}{h}$$

$$= \lim_{h \to 0} \frac{2\sqrt{2}}{2(1 + 2h^2)}$$

$$= \frac{2\sqrt{2}}{2}$$

$$= \sqrt{2}$$

# Partial Derivatives

Suppose, $z = f(x, y)$ be a function of two independent variables $x$ and $y$. Then, the partial derivative of $z$ with respect to $x$ is the ordinary derivative of $z$ with respect to $x$, when $y$ is treated as a constant and it is denoted by

$$f_x \text{ or } \frac{\partial z}{\partial x} \text{ or } \frac{\partial y}{\partial x}$$

Therefore, if $\lim_{h \to 0} \frac{f(a + h, b) - f(a, b)}{h}$ exists, then this limit is called the partial derivative of $f(x, y)$ with respect to $x$ at the point $(a, b)$ and it is denoted by

$$\left(\frac{\partial f}{\partial x}\right)_{(a, b)} \text{ or } \left(\frac{\partial z}{\partial x}\right)_{(a, b)} \text{ or } f_x(a, b).$$

Similarly, if $\lim_{k \to 0} \frac{f(a, b + k) - f(a, b)}{k}$ exists, then this limit is called the partial derivative of $f(x, y)$ with respect to $y$ at $(a, b)$ and it is denoted by

$$\left(\frac{\partial f}{\partial y}\right)_{(a, b)} \text{ or } f_y(a, b) \text{ or } \left(\frac{\partial z}{\partial y}\right)_{(a, b)}$$

***Note*** **(a)** When we consider the functions of two variables, the existence of partial derivatives at a point need not imply continuity at that point.

**(b)** By the definition of partial derivatives, we have

$$f_x(a, b) = \lim_{h \to 0} \frac{f(a + h, b) - f(a, b)}{h}$$

$$= \lim_{x \to a} \frac{f(x, b) - f(a, b)}{x - a}$$

and

$$f_y(a, b) = \lim_{k \to 0} \frac{f(a, b + k) - f(a, b)}{k}$$

$$= \lim_{y \to b} \frac{f(a, y) - f(a, b)}{y - b}$$

***Example 9.*** *If* $f(x, y) = \begin{cases} \dfrac{x^3 + y^3}{x - y}, & x \neq 0 \\ 0 \ , & x = y \end{cases}$

*then, show that f is discontinuous at the origin but the partial derivative exist at the origin.*

**Solution.** Suppose, $(x, y) \to (0, 0)$ through the curve $y = x - mx^3$, we get

$$\lim_{(x, y) \to (0, 0)} f(x, y) = \lim_{(x, y) \to (0, 0)} f(x, x - mx^3)$$

$$= \lim_{x \to 0} \frac{x^3 + (x - mx^3)^3}{x - (x - mx^3)}$$

$$= \lim_{x \to 0} \frac{x^3\{1 + (1 - mx^2)^3\}}{mx^3}$$

$$= \lim_{x \to 0} \frac{1}{m}\{2 - m^3x^6 - 3mx^2 + 3m^2x^4\}$$

$$= \lim_{x \to 0} \left\{\frac{2}{m} - m^2x^6 - 3x^2 + 3mx^4\right\} = \frac{2}{m}$$

Which depends on $m$, therefore the simultaneous limit does not exist. Hence, the function $f(x, y)$ is not continuous in $x - y$ at the origin.

Now, we have

$$f_x(0, 0) = \lim_{h \to 0} \frac{f(0 + h, 0) - f(0, 0)}{h}$$

$$= \lim_{h \to 0} \frac{\frac{h^3}{h} - 0}{h} = \lim_{h \to 0} h = 0$$

and

$$f_y(0, 0) = \lim_{k \to 0} \frac{f(0, 0 + k) - f(0, 0)}{k}$$

$$= \lim_{k \to 0} \frac{\frac{k^3}{-k} - 0}{k} = \lim_{k \to 0} (-k) = 0$$

Clearly, partial derivatives exist at the origin.

***Example 10.*** *Using definition calculate $f_x(0, 0)$ and $f_y(0, 0)$, if $f : R^2 \to R$ be a function defined by $f(x, y) = \frac{xy^2}{x^2 + y^4}$ for $(x, y) \neq (0, 0)$ and $f(0, 0) = 0$.*

**Solution.** We know that by the definition of partial derivatives.

$$f_x(0, 0) = \lim_{h\to 0} \frac{f(0+h, 0) - f(0, 0)}{h}$$

$$= \lim_{h\to 0} \frac{f(h, 0) - f(0, 0)}{h}$$

$$= \lim_{h\to 0} \frac{0-0}{h} = \lim_{h\to 0} 0 = 0$$

$$\left[\because f(h, 0) = \frac{h\cdot 0^2}{h^2 + 0^4} = 0 \text{ and } f(0, 0) = 0\right]$$

and $$f_y(0, 0) = \lim_{k\to 0} \frac{f(0, 0+k) - f(0, 0)}{k}$$

$$\Rightarrow \quad f_y(0, 0) = \lim_{k\to 0} \frac{f(0, k) - f(0, 0)}{k}$$

$$\Rightarrow \quad f_y(0, 0) = \lim_{k\to 0} \frac{0-0}{k} = \lim_{k\to 0} 0 = 0$$

$$\left[\because f(0, k) = \frac{0\cdot k^2}{0^2 + k^4} = 0 \text{ and } f(0, 0) = 0\right]$$

## Matrix of a Derivative

Let $f : \mathbb{R}^n \to \mathbb{R}^m$ be given by

$$f(x_1, x_2, \ldots, x_n) = (f_1, f_2, f_3, \ldots, f_m),$$

where

$$f_i : \mathbb{R}^n \to \mathbb{R}, \forall\, i = 1, 2, \ldots, m.$$

Then, the matrix of derivative $\partial f$ is defined as

$$\partial f = \begin{bmatrix} \partial_1 f_1 & \partial_2 f_1 & \ldots & \partial_n f_1 \\ \partial_1 f_2 & \partial_2 f_2 & \ldots & \partial_n f_2 \\ \ldots & \ldots & \ldots & \ldots \\ \partial_1 f_m & \partial_2 f_m & \ldots & \partial_n f_m \end{bmatrix}_{m\times m}$$

where $\partial_i f_j = \frac{\partial f_j}{\partial x_i} \forall\, i, j$

***Example 11.*** *Find the matrix of derivative of $f : \mathbb{R}^2 \to \mathbb{R}^2$ given by $f(x, y) = (x + y, xy)$ under what condition it will be singular?*

**Solution.** We have,

$$\partial_1 f_1 = \frac{\partial}{\partial x}(x+y) = 1$$

$$\partial_1 f_2 = \frac{\partial}{\partial x}(xy) = y$$

$$\partial_2 f_1 = \frac{\partial}{\partial y}(x+y) = 1$$

$$\partial_2 f_2 = \frac{\partial}{\partial y}(xy) = x$$

$\therefore$ The matrix of derivative of $f$ is

$$\partial f = \begin{bmatrix} 1 & 1 \\ y & x \end{bmatrix}$$

which is singular, if $x = y$.

## Differentiability

Let us consider a function $z = f(x, y)$ of two independent variables $x$ and $y$.

Let $f(x, y)$ possesses a determinate value at a point $(a, b)$ and at any point $(a + h, b + k)$ in the neighbourhood of $(a, b)$. The function $f(x, y)$ is said to be totally differentiable or simply differentiable at $(a, b)$, if there exist two numbers $A$ and $B$ independent of $h$, $k$ such that

$$f(a+h, b+k) - f(a, b) = Ah + Bk + \sqrt{(h^2 + k^2)}\, \phi(h, k)$$

where, $\lim_{(h, k)\to(0,0)} \phi(h, k) = 0$. Then

The part $Ah + Bk$ is called the derivative of $f(x, y)$ at $(a, b)$.

The distance between the fixed point $(a, b)$ and the variable point $(a + h, b + k)$ is $\sqrt{h^2 + k^2}$, which can be regarded as a simultaneous increment of the two variables.

> ***Note*** **(a)** If $f(x, y)$ is a function which is differentiable at the point $(a, b)$, then it is continuous in $x$-$y$ together at $(a, b)$.
>
> **(b)** The continuity in the two variables is a necessary condition for differentiability. But it is not sufficient condition.
>
> **(c)** Let us consider a function $z = f(x, y)$ which is differentiable at $(a, b)$, then the partial derivatives $f_x(a, b)$ and $f_y(a, b)$ both exist and are finite. But the converse is need not be true means, if $f$ is continuous and possesses partial derivatives at a point, then $f$ need not be differentiable.

***Example 12.*** *Prove that the function defined by*

$$f(x, y) = \begin{cases} \frac{xy}{\sqrt{x^2 + y^2}}, & (x, y) \neq (0, 0) \\ 0, & (x, y) = (0, 0) \end{cases}$$

*is continuous in x-y at the origin but is not differentiable in x-y at the origin.*

**Solution.** We have already shown that the function is continuous in $x$-$y$ at the origin. Now, we show that $f(x, y)$ is not differentiable at the origin.

We have,

$$f(0+h, 0+k) = \frac{hk}{\sqrt{h^2+k^2}}$$

$$\therefore\ f(0+h, 0+k) - f(0, 0) = 0\cdot h + 0\cdot k + \sqrt{h^2+k^2}\cdot \frac{hk}{(h^2+k^2)}$$

So that, $A = 0, B = 0$ and $\phi(h, k) = \frac{hk}{h^2+k^2}$

Therefore, $A$ and $B$ are independent of $h$ and $k$.

Now, $$\lim_{(h, k)\to(0, 0)} \phi(h, k) = \lim_{(h, k)\to(0, 0)} \frac{hk}{h^2+k^2}$$

Let us take $k = mh$, we have

$$\lim_{(h, k)\to(0, 0)} \frac{hk}{h^2+k^2} = \lim_{h\to 0} \frac{mh^2}{h^2+m^2h^2} = \lim_{h\to 0} \frac{mh^2}{h^2(1+m^2)}$$

$$= \lim_{h\to 0} \frac{m}{1+m^2} = \frac{m}{1+m^2}$$

which depends upon $m$.

If $m=0$, then $\lim_{(h,\ k)\to(0,\ 0)} \frac{m}{1+m^2} = \frac{0}{1+0} = 0$

If $m=1$, then $\lim_{(h,\ k)\to(0,\ 0)} \frac{m}{1+m^2} = \frac{1}{1+1} = \frac{1}{2}$

$\because$ Along two paths the limiting value is different, hence the simultaneous limit does not exist.

Therefore, $f$ is not differentiable at the origin.

***Example 13.*** *Suppose*

$$f(x, y) = \begin{cases} \frac{xy}{\sqrt{x^2+y^2}}, & (x, y) \neq (0, 0) \\ 0, & (x, y) = (0, 0) \end{cases}$$

*then, prove that f has partial derivatives at (0, 0) but is not differentiable at the origin.*

**Solution.** We know that,

$$f_x(0, 0) = \lim_{h\to0} \frac{f(0+h, 0)-f(0, 0)}{h}$$

$$= \lim_{h\to0} \frac{f(h, 0)-f(0, 0)}{h}$$

$$= \lim_{h\to0} \frac{0-0}{h} = \lim_{h\to0} 0 = 0$$

and

$$f_y(0, 0) = \lim_{k\to0} \frac{f(0, 0+k)-f(0, 0)}{k}$$

$$= \lim_{k\to0} \frac{f(0, k)-f(0, 0)}{k}$$

$$= \lim_{k\to0} \frac{0-0}{k} = 0$$

Therefore, $f$ has partial derivatives at (0, 0) see the above example.

***Example 14.*** *Prove that*

$$f(x, y) = \begin{cases} xy\left(\frac{x^2-y^2}{x^2+y^2}\right), & (x, y) \neq (0, 0) \\ 0, & (x, y) = (0, 0) \end{cases}$$

*is differentiable at the origin.*

**Solution.** $f(0+h, 0+k) = f(h, k) = hk\left(\frac{h^2-k^2}{h^2+k^2}\right)$

$$\Rightarrow f(0+h, 0+k) - f(0, 0)$$

$$= 0\cdot h + 0\cdot k + \sqrt{h^2+k^2}\cdot\frac{hk(h^2-k^2)}{(h^2+k^2)^{3/2}}$$

So that, $A=0$, $B=0$ and $\phi(h, k) = \frac{hk(h^2-k^2)}{(h^2+k^2)^{3/2}}$

Therefore, $A$ and $B$ are independent of $h$ and $k$.

Now, we show that $\phi(h, k) \to 0$ as $(h, k) \to (0, 0)$

Suppose, $\varepsilon > 0$ be given

For all $(h, k) \neq (0,0)$, we have

$$|\phi(h, k) - 0| = \left|\frac{hk}{\sqrt{h^2+k^2}}\cdot\frac{h^2-k^2}{h^2+k^2}\right|$$

$$= \left|\frac{hk}{\sqrt{h^2+k^2}}\right|\cdot\frac{|h^2-k^2|}{h^2+k^2}$$

$$\leq \left|\frac{hk}{\sqrt{h^2+k^2}}\right| \qquad [\because |h^2-k^2| \leq h^2+k^2]$$

$$= \frac{|hk|}{h^2+k^2}\cdot\sqrt{h^2+k^2} \qquad \text{...(i)}$$

Now, for all $h$ and $k$, we have $(|h| - |k|)^2 \geq 0$

$$\Rightarrow |h|^2+|k|^2-2|h||k| \geq 0 \Rightarrow h^2+k^2 \geq 2|hk|$$

$$\Rightarrow \frac{|hk|}{h^2+k^2} \leq \frac{1}{2}, \text{ if } (h, k) \neq (0, 0) \qquad \text{...(ii)}$$

Using Eqs. (i) and (ii) for all $(h, k) \neq (0, 0)$, we get

$$|\phi(h, k) - 0| \leq \frac{1}{2}\sqrt{h^2+k^2}$$

$$< \sqrt{h^2+k^2} < \varepsilon, \text{ if } h^2 < \frac{\varepsilon^2}{2} \text{ and } k^2 < \frac{\varepsilon^2}{2}$$

*i.e.* $|h| < \frac{\varepsilon}{\sqrt{2}}, |k| < \frac{\varepsilon}{\sqrt{2}}$

If we take $\delta = \frac{\varepsilon}{\sqrt{2}}$, then we observe that for any given $\varepsilon > 0$, there exists $\delta > 0$ s.t.

$$|\phi(h, k) - 0| < \varepsilon, \text{ whenever } |h| < \delta \text{ and } |k| < \delta$$

$$\Rightarrow \lim_{(h,\ k)\to(0,\ 0)} \phi(h, k) = 0$$

Hence, $f$ is differentiable at (0, 0) and the derivative of $f$ at $(0, 0) = Ah + Bk = 0$.

# Important Theorems

***Theorem 1*** **Mean Value Theorem** If $f: X \to R$, $X \subseteq R^2$ and $(a, b) \in X$, such that

**(i)** $f_y(a, b)$ exists

**(ii)** $f_x$ exists throughout a *nbd* of $(a, b)$,

then for every point $(a+h, b+k) \in N(a, b)$

$$f(a+h, b+k) - f(a, b) = hf_x(a+\theta h, b+k) + k[f_y(a, b) + \phi(k)]$$

where $0 < \theta < 1$ and $\lim_{k\to0} \phi(k) = 0$

***Theorem 2*** **Sufficient Condition for Continuity** If $f: X \to R$, $X \subseteq R^2$, $(a, b) \in X$ is such that

**(i)** $f_x$ exists and bounded on $N(a, b)$ and

**(ii)** $f_y(a, b)$ exists,

then $f$ is continuous at $(a, b)$.

***Theorem 3*** **Sufficient Condition for Differentiability** If $f: X \to R$, $X \subseteq R^2$, $(a, b) \in X$ is such that

**(i)** $f_x$ is continuous at $(a, b)$

**(ii)** $f_y(a, b)$ exists,

then $f$ is differentiable at $(a, b)$.

***Example 15.*** *Suppose f be a function defined by*

$$f(x, y) = x^2 \sin\frac{1}{x} + y^2 \sin\frac{1}{y}; \quad (x, y) \neq (0, 0)$$

$$f(x, 0) = x^2 \sin\frac{1}{x}; \quad x \neq 0$$

$$f(0, y) = y^2 \sin\frac{1}{y}; \quad y \neq 0$$

*and* $f(0, 0) = 0$

**Solution.** For $x \neq 0$, $f_x(x, y) = 2x \sin\frac{1}{x} + x^2 \cos\frac{1}{x} \cdot \left(-\frac{1}{x^2}\right)$

$$= 2x \sin\frac{1}{x} - \cos\frac{1}{x}$$

and $\quad f_y(x, y) = 2y \sin\frac{1}{y} - \cos\frac{1}{y}$ for $y \neq 0$

$$f_x(0, y) = 0, \; f_y(x, 0) = 0$$

Therefore, $\quad f_x(x, y) = \begin{cases} 2x \sin\frac{1}{x} - \cos\frac{1}{x}; & x \neq 0 \\ 0 \quad ; & x = 0 \end{cases}$

$\therefore \quad \lim_{(x, y) \to (0, 0)} f_x(x, y) = \lim_{x \to 0} 2x \sin\frac{1}{x} - \lim_{x \to 0} \cos\frac{1}{x}$

which does not exist because $\lim_{x \to 0} \cos\frac{1}{x}$ does not exist.

Therefore, $f_x(x, y)$ is not continuous at (0, 0).

Similarly, we may show that $f_y(x, y)$ is not continuous at (0, 0).

Now, $f(0 + h, 0 + k) - f(0, 0) = h^2 \sin\frac{1}{h} + k^2 \sin\frac{1}{k}$

$$= 0 \cdot h + 0 \cdot k + \sqrt{h^2 + k^2}\left\{\frac{h^2}{\sqrt{h^2 + k^2}} \cdot \sin\frac{1}{h} + \frac{k^2}{\sqrt{h^2 + k^2}} \cdot \sin\frac{1}{k}\right\}$$

So that, $A = 0$, $B = 0$

$\therefore \quad$ A and B are independent of h, k.

And $\quad \phi(h, k) = \frac{h^2}{\sqrt{h^2 + k^2}} \sin\frac{1}{h} + \frac{k^2}{\sqrt{h^2 + k^2}} \sin\frac{1}{k}$

$$(\because \lim_{h \to 0} h \sin\frac{1}{h} = 0 \text{ and } \lim_{k \to 0} k \sin\frac{1}{k} = 0)$$

and $\frac{h}{\sqrt{h^2 + k^2}}, \frac{k}{\sqrt{h^2 + k^2}}$ are bounded.

$\therefore \quad \lim \phi(h, k) = 0$ as $(h, k) \to (0, 0)$

Hence, $f$ is differentiable at (0, 0).

## Partial Derivatives of Higher Order

The derivatives functions $f_x$, $f_y$ are in general functions of $x$ and $y$ and hence can be further differentiated partially with respect to $x$ or $y$ which lcd higher order partial derivatives.

$$\frac{\partial}{\partial x}\left(\frac{\partial f}{\partial x}\right) = \frac{\partial^2 f}{\partial x^2} = f_{xx}$$

$$\frac{\partial}{\partial y}\left(\frac{\partial f}{\partial y}\right) = \frac{\partial^2 f}{\partial y^2} = f_{yy}$$

$$\frac{\partial}{\partial x}\left(\frac{\partial f}{\partial y}\right) = \frac{\partial^2 f}{\partial x \partial y} = f_{xy}$$

$$\frac{\partial}{\partial y}\left(\frac{\partial f}{\partial x}\right) = \frac{\partial^2 f}{\partial y \partial x} = f_{yx}$$

These are second order partial derivatives of $f$.

Further, the second order partial derivatives at a particular point $(a, b)$ are denoted by

$$\left(\frac{\partial^2 f}{\partial x^2}\right)_{(a,b)} \text{ or } f_x(a, b) \text{ or } \frac{\partial^2 f}{\partial x^2}(a, b)$$

and $\left(\frac{\partial^2 f}{\partial x \partial y}\right)_{(a,b)}$ or $f_{xy}(a, b)$ or $\frac{\partial^2 f}{\partial x \partial y}(a, b)$ etc.

Thus,

$$f_{xx}(a, b) = \lim_{h \to 0} \frac{f_x(a + h, b) - f_x(a, b)}{h}$$

$$f_{xy}(a, b) = \lim_{h \to 0} \frac{f_y(a + h, b) - f_y(a, b)}{h}$$

$$f_{yx}(a, b) = \lim_{k \to 0} \frac{f_x(a, b + k) - f_x(a, b)}{k}$$

$$f_{yy}(a, b) = \lim_{k \to 0} \frac{f_y(a, b + k) - f_y(a, b)}{k}$$

Provided the limits exists.

Now, we have

$$f_{xx}(a, b) = \lim_{h \to 0} \frac{f_x(a + h, b) - f_x(a, b)}{h}$$

$$= \lim_{h \to 0} \frac{1}{h}\left[\lim_{h \to 0} \frac{f(a + 2h, b) - f(a + h, b)}{h} - \lim_{h \to 0} \frac{f(a + h, b) - f(a, b)}{h}\right]$$

$$\Rightarrow \quad f_{xx}(a, b) = \lim_{h \to 0} \frac{f(a + 2h, b) - 2f(a + h, b) + f(a, b)}{h^2}$$

Similarly,

$$f_{yy}(a, b) = \lim_{k \to 0} \frac{f(a, b + 2k) - 2f(a, b + k) + f(a, b)}{k^2},$$

$$f_{yx}(a, b) = \lim_{h \to 0} \left[\lim_{k \to 0} \frac{f(a + h, b + k) - f(a + h, b) - f(a, b + k) + f(a, b)}{hk}\right]$$

and

$$f_{xy}(a, b) = \lim_{k \to 0} \left[\lim_{h \to 0} \frac{f(a + h, b + k) - f(a + h, b) - f(a, b + k) + f(a, b)}{hk}\right]$$

***Example 16.*** *Let* $f(x, y) = x \sin\frac{1}{x} + y \sin\frac{1}{y}, \; (x, y) \neq (0, 0);$

$$f(0, y) = y \sin\frac{1}{y}, \; y \neq 0 \text{ and } f(x, 0) = x \sin\frac{1}{x}, x \neq 0.$$

**Solution.** $f_x(0, 0) = \lim_{h\to 0} \frac{f(0+h, 0) - f(0, 0)}{h}$

$$= \lim_{h\to 0} \frac{h \sin \frac{1}{h} - 0}{h} = \lim_{h\to 0} \sin \frac{1}{h}$$

which does not exist. Therefore, $f_x(0, 0)$ does not exist.

$$f_{yx}(0, 0) = \lim_{k\to 0}\left[\lim_{h\to 0}\left\{\frac{f(h,k) - f(h,0) - f(0,k) + f(0,0)}{hk}\right\}\right]$$

$$= \lim_{k\to 0}\lim_{h\to 0} \frac{h \sin 1/h + k \sin 1/k - h \sin 1/h - k \sin 1/k + 0}{hk}$$

$$= \lim_{k\to 0}\lim_{h\to 0} \frac{0}{hk} = 0$$

Therefore, the limit used for the second derivative $f_{yx}$ does exist. But inspite of this fact $f_{yx}(0, 0)$ can not said to exist because $f_x(0, 0)$ does not exist.

## Interchange of the Order of Differentiation

Suppose, $z = f(x, y)$ be a function of two independent variables $x$ and $y$, then $\frac{\partial^2 z}{\partial x \partial y}$ and $\frac{\partial^2 z}{\partial y \partial x}$ always do not have the same value but under the certain conditions $\frac{\partial^2 z}{\partial x \partial y} = \frac{\partial^2 z}{\partial y \partial x}$ holds.

***Example 17.*** *If* $f(x, y) = \begin{cases} \frac{xy(x^2 - y^2)}{x^2 + y^2}; & (x, y) \neq (0, 0) \\ 0\,; & (x, y) = (0, 0) \end{cases}$, *then show that* $f_{xy}(0, 0) \neq f_{yx}(0, 0)$.

**Solution.** We have,

$$f_{xy}(0, 0) = \lim_{h\to 0} \frac{f_y(0+h, 0) - f_y(0, 0)}{h}$$

where $f_y(0+h, 0) = f_y(h, 0) = \lim_{k\to 0} \frac{f(h, 0+k) - f(h, 0)}{k}$

$$= \lim_{k\to 0} \frac{\frac{hk(h^2 - k^2)}{h^2 + k^2} - 0}{k}$$

$$= \lim_{k\to 0} \frac{h(h^2 - k^2)}{h^2 + k^2} = h$$

and $f_y(0, 0) = \lim_{k\to 0} \frac{f(0, 0+k) - f(0, 0)}{k}$

$$= \lim_{k\to 0} \frac{0}{k} = \lim_{k\to 0} 0 = 0$$

Therefore,

$$f_{xy}(0, 0) = \lim_{h\to 0} \frac{h - 0}{h} = \lim_{h\to 0} 1 = 1$$

Again, $f_{yx}(0, 0) = \lim_{k\to 0} \frac{f_x(0, 0+k) - f_x(0, 0)}{k}$

where $f_x(0, 0+k) = f_x(0, k) = \lim_{h\to 0} \frac{f(0+h, k) - f(0, k)}{h}$

$$= \lim_{h\to 0} \frac{\frac{hk(h^2 - k^2)}{h^2 + k^2} - 0}{h}$$

$$= \lim_{h\to 0} \frac{k(h^2 - k^2)}{h^2 + k^2} = -k$$

and $f_x(0, 0) = \lim_{h\to 0} \frac{f(h, 0) - f(0, 0)}{h} = \lim_{h\to 0} 0 = 0$

Therefore, $f_{yx}(0, 0) = \lim_{k\to 0} \frac{-k - 0}{k} = \lim_{k\to 0} (-1) = -1$

Hence, $f_{xy}(0, 0) \neq f_{yx}(0, 0)$

## Sufficient Conditions for the Equality of $f_{xy}$ and $f_{yx}$

(i) **Schwarz's Theorem** If $f: X \to R$, $X \subseteq R^2$ and $(a, b) \in X$ is such that

(a) $f_x$ exists in $N(a, b)$.

(b) $f_{xy}$ is continuous at $(a, b)$,

then $f_{yx}(a, b)$ exists and is equal to $f_{xy}(a, b)$.

(ii) **Young's Theorem** If $f: X \to R$, $X \subseteq R^2$ and $(a, b) \in X$ is s.t. $f_x, f_y$ are differentiable at $(a, b)$, then $f_{xy}(a, b) = f_{yx}(a, b)$.

***Example 18.*** *Let*

$$f(x, y) = \begin{cases} \frac{1}{4}(x^2 + y^2)\log(x^2 + y^2); & \text{for } (x, y) \neq (0, 0) \\ 0; & \text{for } (x, y) = (0, 0) \end{cases}$$

*Show that* $f_{xy} = f_{yx}$ *at all points* $(x, y)$. *Also, prove that neither of the derivatives is continuous in x-y at the origin.*

**Solution.** For $(x, y) \neq (0, 0)$

$$f_x = \frac{1}{2} x \{1 + \log(x^2 + y^2)\}$$

$$f_y = \frac{1}{2} y \{1 + \log(x^2 + y^2)\}$$

Therefore, $f_{xy} = f_{yx} = \frac{xy}{x^2 + y^2}$

For $x = 0$, $y = 0$ by using the definition of partial derivatives, we can easily shown that

$$f_x = f_y = f_{xy} = f_{yx} = 0$$

Therefore, $f_{xy} = f_{yx}$ at all points of $(x, y)$ but $f_{xy} = f_{yx}$ is not continuous at $(0, 0)$.

Also, we find that the simultaneous limit $\lim_{(x, y)\to(0, 0)} \frac{xy}{x^2 + y^2}$ does not exist which is shown below.

Suppose, $(x, y) \to (0, 0)$ along the line $y = mx$, then

$$\lim_{(x, y)\to(0, 0)} \frac{xy}{x^2 + y^2} = \lim_{x\to 0} \frac{x \cdot mx}{x^2 + m^2 x^2} = \frac{m}{1 + m^2}$$

which depends on $m$ and give different values for different values of $m$. It implies that $f_{xy} = f_{yx}$ is not continuous at the origin.

## Composite Functions

If $x = \phi(t)$ and $y = \psi(t)$ are differentiable functions of $t$ for a given $t$ and $z = f(x, y)$ is a differentiable function of $(x, y)$ for the corresponding $(x, y)$, then $z = f(\phi(t), \psi(t))$ is differentiable function of $t$ and $\frac{dz}{dt} = \frac{\partial z}{\partial x}\cdot\frac{dx}{dt} + \frac{\partial z}{\partial y}\cdot\frac{dy}{dt}$.

## Taylor's Theorem for Functions of Two Variables

If $f(x, y)$ and all its partial derivatives upto the $n$th order are finite and continuous for all points $(x, y)$ where $a \le x \le a+h,\ b \le y \le b+k$.

Then, $f(a+h, b+k) = f(a, b) + \left(h\frac{\partial}{\partial x} + k\frac{\partial}{\partial y}\right)f$

$$+\frac{1}{2!}\left(h\frac{\partial}{\partial x} + k\frac{\partial}{\partial y}\right)^2 f + \frac{1}{3!}\left(h\frac{\partial}{\partial x} + k\frac{\partial}{\partial y}\right)^3 f + \ldots$$

## Extreme Values

**Definition** A point $(a_1, a_2, \ldots, a_n)$ is said to be an extreme point and $f(a_1, a_2, \ldots, a_n)$ an extreme value of a function $f : \mathbb{R}^n \to \mathbb{R}$, if for every point $(x_1, x_2, \ldots, x_n)$, other than $(a_1, a_2, \ldots, a_n)$ of some neighbourhood of $(a_1, a_2, \ldots, a_n)$. The difference $f(x_1, x_2, \ldots, x_n) - f(a_1, a_2, \ldots, a_n)$ keeps the same sign. The extreme value is minimum or maximum according as the sign is positive or negative.

## Necessary Condition for Extreme Value

The necessary conditions for $f(a_1, a_2, \ldots, a_n)$ to be an extreme value of the function $f$ are that all the partial derivatives $f_{x_1}, f_{x_2}, \ldots, f_{x_n}$ in case they exists, vanish at $(a_1, a_2, \ldots, a_n)$ and the point $(a_1, a_2, \ldots, a_n)$ is called a stationary point. Thus, the stationary points are determined by solving the following $n$ equations simultaneously.

$$\begin{aligned} f_{x_1}(x_1, x_2, \ldots, x_n) &= 0 \\ f_{x_2}(x_1, x_2, \ldots, x_n) &= 0 \\ \ldots \quad \ldots & \quad \ldots \\ \ldots \quad \ldots & \quad \ldots \\ f_{x_n}(x_1, x_2, \ldots, x_n) &= 0 \end{aligned}$$

For a function $f$ of $n$ independent variables $x_1, x_2, \ldots, x_n$, the condition can be given in a more compact form.

Hence, if $(a_1, a_2, \ldots, a_n)$ is a stationary point, then $df(a_1, a_2, \ldots, a_n) = 0$

$$\Rightarrow \quad f_{x_1}(a_1, a_2, \ldots, a_n)dx_1 + f_{x_2}(a_1, a_2, \ldots, a_n)dx_2 + \ldots + f_{x_n}(a_1, a_2, \ldots, a_n)dx_n = 0$$

$\Rightarrow$ The coefficient of the differential $dx_1, dx_2, \ldots, dx_n$ of independent variables are separately equal to zero.

Further investigations are necessary to decide whether a stationary point is an extreme point or not or whether it is a maxima or a minima. We now state rules.

## Rules for Three Independent Variables

For a function of three independent variables, $f(x, y, z)$ sufficient conditions for $(a, b, c)$ to be an extreme point are that

**(i)** $df(a, b, c) = f_x dx + f_y dy + f_z dz = 0$

$\Rightarrow \quad f_x = f_y = f_z = 0$ and

**(ii)** $d^2 f(a, b, c) = f_{xx}(dx)^2 + f_{yy}(dy)^2 + f_{zz}(dz)^2 + 2f_{xy}dxdy + 2f_{yz}dydz + 2f_{zx}dzdx$

keep the same sign for arbitrary values of $dx, dy, dz$; the extreme point $(a, b, c)$ being a maxima or a minima according as the sign of $d^2 f$ is negative or positive.

The point at which $d^2 f$ does not keep the same sign will be neither a maxima nor a minima and requires further investigation, if $d^2 f$ keeps the same sign but vanishes at some points of a *nbd* of $(a, b, c)$.

The conditions for $d^2 f$ keeps the same sign may be stated in terms of matrices as follows

**(i)** $d^2 f$ will always be positive if and only if

$$f_{xx} > 0, \begin{vmatrix} f_{xx} & f_{xy} \\ f_{yx} & f_{yy} \end{vmatrix} > 0 \text{ and } \begin{vmatrix} f_{xx} & f_{xy} & f_{xz} \\ f_{yx} & f_{yy} & f_{yz} \\ f_{zx} & f_{zy} & f_{zz} \end{vmatrix} > 0$$

**(ii)** $d^2 f$ will always be negative if and only if

$$f_{xx} < 0, \begin{vmatrix} f_{xx} & f_{xy} \\ f_{yx} & f_{yy} \end{vmatrix} > 0 \text{ and } \begin{vmatrix} f_{xx} & f_{xy} & f_{xz} \\ f_{yx} & f_{yy} & f_{yz} \\ f_{zx} & f_{zy} & f_{zz} \end{vmatrix} < 0$$

## Rules for Two Independent Variables

For function of two independent variables $f(x, y)$ sufficient conditions for $(a, b)$ to be an extreme point are that

**(i)** $df(a, b) = f_x dx + f_y dy = 0$

$\Rightarrow \quad f_x = f_y = 0$ and

**(ii)** $d^2 f(a, b) = f_{xx}(dx)^2 + f_{yy}(dy)^2 + 2f_{xy}dxdy$

keep the same sign for arbitrary values of $dx, dy, dz$; the extreme point being a maxima or minima according as the sign of $d^2 f$ is negative or positive. The point at which $d^2 f$ does not keep the same sign will be neither maxima nor minima and requires.

Further investigation, if $d^2 f$ keeps the same sign but vanishes at some points of a *nbd* of $(a, b)$.

The conditions for $d^2 f$ keeps the same sign may be stated in terms of matrices as follows

**(i)** $d^2 f$ will be always negative if and only if

$$f_{xx} > 0 \text{ and } \begin{vmatrix} f_{xx} & f_{xy} \\ f_{yx} & f_{yy} \end{vmatrix} > 0 \text{ and}$$

**(ii)** $d^2 f$ will be always positive if and only if

$$f_{xx} < 0 \text{ and } \begin{vmatrix} f_{xx} & f_{xy} \\ f_{yx} & f_{yy} \end{vmatrix} > 0$$

> ***Note*** The points at which neither maxima nor minima are called saddle points.

*Example 19.* *Prove that*

$$f(x, y) = y^2 + x^2y + x^4$$

*has a minimum at (0, 0).*

**Solution.** We have,

$$f_x = 2xy + 4x^3$$
$$f_{xx} = 2y + 12x^2$$
$$f_{xy} = 2x$$
$$\Rightarrow \quad (f_{xx})_{(0,0)} = 0 \text{ and } (f_{xy})_{(0,0)} = 0$$

and

$$f_y = 2y + x^2$$
$$f_{yx} = 2x$$
$$f_{yy} = 2$$
$$\Rightarrow \quad (f_{yx})_{(0,0)} = 0 \text{ and } (f_{yy})_{(0,0)} = 2$$

Thus, at $(0, 0)$ $f_{xx}f_{yy} - (f_{xy})^2 = 0$

So that it is a doubtful case and requires further investigation. But we can write

$$f(x, y) = (y + \frac{1}{2}x^2)^2 + \frac{3}{4}x^4$$

and $f(x, y) - f(0, 0) = (y + \frac{1}{2}x^2)^2 + \frac{3}{4}x^4$

which is greater than zero for all values of $(x, y)$. Hence, $f$ has a minimum value at the origin.

## Important Definitions

**(i)** Let $X$ be a subset of $R^n$. Then, $X$ is said to be a vector space, if $x \in X$, $y \in X \Rightarrow x + y \in X$ and $cx \in X$ for all scalars $c$.

**(ii)** If $x_1, x_2, \ldots, x_m \in R^n$ and $c_1, c_2, \ldots, c_m$ are scalars, then the vector $c_1x_1 + c_2x_2 + \ldots + c_mx_m$ is called a linear combination of $x_1, x_2, \ldots, x_m$.

**(iii)** If $S \subset R^n$ and if $A$ is the set of linear combinations of elements of $S$, then we say that $S$ spans $A$ or that $A$ is the span of $S$.

**(iv)** We say that the set of vectors $\{x_1, x_2, \ldots, x_n\}$ is independent, if $c_1x_1 + c_2x_2 + \ldots + c_nx_n = 0$

$$\Rightarrow \quad c_1 = c_2 = \ldots = c_n = 0.$$

**(v)** A vector space $X$ is said to have dimension $K$, if $X$ contains an independent set of $K$ vectors but no independent set of $K + 1$ vectors, then we write $\dim X = K$.

The set consisting of 0 alone is a vector space. Its dimension is 0.

**(vi)** A subset $B$ of a vector space $X$ is said to be a basis of $X$, if $B$ is independent and spans $X$.

*Example 20.* *The set* $B = \{e_1, e_2, \ldots, e_n\}$ *consisting of* $n$ *vectors in* $R^n$, *where*

$$e_1 = (1, 0, \ldots, 0), \; e_2 = (0, 1, \ldots, 0), \ldots, e_n = (0, 0, \ldots, 1)$$

*is a basis of the vector space* $R^n$.

**Solution.** If $c_1, c_2, \ldots, c_n$ are any scalars, then

$$c_1e_1 + c_2e_2 + \ldots + c_ne_n = 0$$
$$\Rightarrow \quad c_1(1, 0, \ldots, 0) + \ldots + c_n(0, \ldots, 1) = (0, 0, \ldots, 0)$$
$$\Rightarrow \quad (c_1, 0, \ldots, 0) + \ldots + (0, \ldots, c_n) = (0, 0, \ldots, 0)$$
$$\Rightarrow \quad (c_1, c_2, \ldots, c_n) = (0, 0, \ldots, 0)$$
$$\Rightarrow \quad c_1 = 0, c_2 = 0, \ldots, c_n = 0$$

$\Rightarrow$ $B$ is linearly independent.

Moreover, if $X = (x_1, \ldots, x_n)$ is any vector in $R^n$, then we may write

$$X = x_1(1, 0, \ldots, 0) + x_2(0, 1, \ldots, 0) + \ldots + x_n(0, \ldots, 1)$$
$$= x_1e_1 + x_2e_2 + \ldots + x_ne_n$$

This shows that $B$ spans $X$. Hence, $B$ is a basis for $R^n$ called the standard basis.

## Important Theorems

***Theorem 1*** Every span is a vector space.

***Theorem 2*** Any set containing the zero vector is dependent or equivalently, no independent set contains the zero vector.

***Theorem 3*** If $B = \{x_1, x_2, \ldots, x_m\}$ is a basis of a vector space $X$, then every $x \in X$ can be expressed uniquely in the form

$$x = \sum_{i=1}^{m} c_ix_i$$

It follows from the fact that $B$ spans $X$ and that $B$ is independent. The numbers $c_1, c_2, \ldots, c_m$ are called coordinates of $x$ with respect to the basis $B$.

***Theorem 4*** If a vector space $X$ is spanned by a set of $K$ vectors, then $\dim X \leq K$.

***Theorem 5*** Let $X$ be a vector space with $\dim X = n$. Then,

**(i)** A set $A$ of $n$ vectors in $X$ spans $X$ iff $A$ is independent.

**(ii)** $X$ has a basis and every basis consists of $n$ vectors.

**(iii)** If $1 \leq K \leq n$ and $(y_1, y_2, \ldots, y_K)$ is an independent set of vectors in $X$, then $X$ has a basis containing $\{y_1, y_2, \ldots, y_k\}$.

---

## Linear Transformation

Let $X$ and $Y$ be two vector spaces. A mapping $T : X \rightarrow Y$ is said to be a linear transformation, if $T(x_1 + x_2) = Tx_1 + Tx_2$, $T(cx) = cTx$, $\forall \; x_1, x_2, x \in X$ and all scalars $c$. Linear transformation of $X$ into $X$ will be called linear operator on $X$.

We see that $T0 = 0$ for any linear transformation $T$.

Therefore, we can say that a linear operator $T$ on $X$ is invertible, if $T$ is one-one and onto . If $T$ is invertible, then we can define an operator $T^{-1}$ on $X$ by taking $T^{-1}(Tx) = x$, $\forall \; x \in X$, then we also have $T(T^{-1}x) = x$, $\forall \; x \in X$ and that $T^{-1}$ is linear.

***Theorem*** A linear operator $T$ on a finite dimensional vector space $X$ is one-one iff the range of $T$ is all of $X$, *i.e.*, if and only if $T$ is onto.

# SOLVED EXAMPLES

## Type I (*Only one correct option*)

***Example 1.*** *If*

$$f(x, y) = \begin{cases} 3x + 4y, (x, y) \neq (1, 2) \\ 6, \quad else \end{cases}.$$

*Then,*

$$\lim_{(x, y) \to (e, \frac{1}{e})} f(x, y) \text{ is}$$

(a) $e(3e^2 + 4)$ (b) $e^{-1}(3e^2 + 4)$

(c) $e(3 + 4e^2)$ (d) $e^{-1}(3 + 4e^2)$

**Solution.** (b) We have,

$$\lim_{(x, y) \to (e, \frac{1}{e})} f(x, y) = 3 \cdot e + 4 \cdot \frac{1}{e}$$

$$= e^{-1}(3e^2 + 4)$$

***Example 2.*** *If*

$$f(x, y) = \begin{cases} x + y, x \text{ or } y = 0 \\ 0 \text{ , else} \end{cases}$$

*Then, the directional derivative at* $c = (0, 0)$ *along the direction* $u = (a, b)$, $a \neq 0 \neq b$ *is*

(a) 0 (b) 1

(c) 2 (d) $ab$

**Solution.** (a) $f(c, u) = \lim_{h \to 0} \frac{f((0, 0) + h(a, b)) - f(0, 0)}{h}$

$$= \lim_{h \to 0} \frac{f(ha, hb)}{h}$$

$$= \lim_{h \to 0} 0$$

$$= 0$$

***Example 3.*** *If*

$$f(x, y) = \begin{cases} xy \sin \frac{1}{x}, x \neq 0 \\ 0 \quad , x = 0 \end{cases}$$

*Then,*

(a) $f_x(0, 0) = 0 = f_y(0, 0)$

(b) $f_x(0, 0) = 1 = f_y(0, 0)$

(c) $f_x(0, 0)$ and $f_y(0, 0)$ does not exists

(d) None of the above

**Solution.** (a) We have $f_x(0, 0) = \lim_{h \to 0} \frac{f(0 + h, 0) - f(0, 0)}{h}$

$$= \lim_{h \to 0} \frac{f(h, 0)}{h}$$

$$= \lim_{h \to 0} 0 = 0$$

and $f_y(0, 0) = \lim_{k \to 0} \frac{f(0, 0 + k) - f(0, 0)}{k}$

$$= \lim_{k \to 0} \frac{f(0, k)}{k}$$

$$= \lim_{k \to 0} 0 = 0$$

$\therefore$ $f_x(0, 0) = f_y(0, 0) = 0$

***Example 4.*** *For what value of k, the function*

$$f(x, y) = \begin{cases} \frac{\sin^{-1}(xy - 2)}{\tan^{-1}(3xy - 6)}, (x, y) \neq (1, 2) \\ k, \quad (x, y) = (1, 2) \end{cases}$$

*is continuous?*

(a) $\frac{1}{2}$ (b) $\frac{1}{3}$

(c) $\frac{1}{4}$ (d) $\frac{3}{4}$

**Solution.** (b) $\lim_{(x, y) \to (1, 2)} f(x, y) = \lim_{(x, y) \to (1, 2)} \frac{\sin^{-1}(xy - 2)}{\tan^{-1}(3xy - 6)}$

Putting $xy - 2 = t$,

$$= \lim_{t \to 0} \frac{\sin^{-1} t}{\tan^{-1} 3t} = \lim_{t \to 0} \frac{1/\sqrt{1 - t^2}}{3/(1 + 3t^2)}$$

$$= \frac{1}{3}$$

$\therefore$ $k = \frac{1}{3}$

***Example 5.*** *If*

$$f(x, y) = x^3 y + e^{xy^2}$$

*Then, which one of the following is correct?*

(a) $f_{xy} > f_{yx}$ (b) $f_{xy} < f_{yx}$

(c) $f_{xy} = f_{yx}$ (d) $f_{xy} \geq f_{yx}$

**Solution.** (c) *We have,*

$$f_y = x^3 + 2xye^{xy^2}$$

$\therefore$ $f_{xy} = 3x^2 + 2ye^{xy^2} + 2xy^3 e^{xy^2}$

Again,

$$f_x = 3x^2 y + y^2 e^{xy^2}$$

$\therefore$ $f_{yx} = 3x^2 + 2ye^{xy^2} + 2xy^3 e^{xy^2}$

$\Rightarrow$ $f_{xy} = f_{yx}$

## Type II (*One or more than one correct option*)

***Example 6.*** *Let* $f(x, y) = \sqrt{|xy|}$. *Then,*

(a) $f(x, y)$ is continuous at origin
(b) $f(x, y)$ is discontinuous at origin
(c) $f_x$ exists at origin and equal to zero
(d) $f_y$ exists at origin and equal to zero

**Solution.** (a), (c), (d)

Let us take given $\varepsilon > 0$ and $(x, y) \neq 0$

Consider

$$|f(x,y) - 0| = |\sqrt{xy}|$$

Let $x = r\cos\theta, y = r\sin\theta$

$$\therefore \quad |f(x,y) - 0| = |\sqrt{r\cos\theta r\sin\theta}|$$
$$= |r||\sqrt{\cos\theta}||\sqrt{\sin\theta}|$$
$$\leq |r|$$
$$= x^2 + y^2$$
$$< \varepsilon$$

If $x^2 < \frac{\varepsilon}{2}$ and $y^2 < \frac{\varepsilon}{2}$

or If $x < \sqrt{\frac{\varepsilon}{2}} = \delta$ and $y = \sqrt{\frac{\varepsilon}{2}} = \delta$

$\therefore$ For given $\varepsilon > 0$, there exists $\delta > 0$, such that

$$|f(x,y) - 0| < \varepsilon$$

whenever $0 < |x| < \delta, 0 < |y| < \delta$

$$\therefore \quad \lim_{(x,y)\to(0,0)} f(x,y) = 0$$
$$= f(0,0)$$

$\therefore$ $f(x, y)$ is continuous at $(0, 0)$.

Now,

$$f_x(0,0) = \lim_{h\to 0}\frac{f(0+h,0) - f(0,0)}{h}$$
$$= \lim_{h\to 0}\frac{f(h,0)}{h}$$
$$= \lim_{h\to 0} 0$$
$$= 0$$

$\therefore$ $f_x$ exists at origin and equal to zero.

and

$$f_y(0,0) = \lim_{k\to 0}\frac{f(0,0+k) - f(0,0)}{k}$$
$$= \lim_{k\to 0}\frac{f(0,k)}{k}$$
$$= \lim_{k\to 0} 0$$
$$= 0$$

$\therefore$ $f_y$ exists at origin and equal to zero.

***Example 7.*** Let

$$f(x,y) = \begin{cases} \dfrac{xy}{x^2+y^2}, & x^2+y^2 \neq 0 \\ 0, & x = y = 0 \end{cases}$$

Then,

(a) $f(x, y)$ is continuous at origin
(b) $f(x, y)$ is discontinuous at origin
(c) $f(x, y)$ has removable discontinuity at origin
(d) $f(x, y)$ is not differentiable at origin

**Solution.** (b), (d)

Let us approaches along the line $y = mx$, we get

$$\lim_{x\to 0} f(x, mx) = \lim_{x\to 0}\frac{x\cdot mx}{x^2 + m^2x^2}$$
$$= \lim_{x\to 0}\frac{m}{1+m^2}$$

which depends on $m$. Hence, $\lim_{(x,y)\to(0,0)} f(x, y)$ does not exists and hence $f(x, y)$ is discontinuous at origin.

Now,

$$f(0+h, 0+k) - f(0,0)$$
$$= 0\cdot h + 0\cdot k + \sqrt{h^2+k^2}\cdot\frac{hk}{(h^2+k^2)^{3/2}}$$

So that $A = 0, B = 0$ which does not depends on $h$ and $k$ and

$$\phi(h,k) = \frac{hk}{(\sqrt{h^2+k^2})^3}$$

Now approaching along the line $h = mk$, we have

$$\lim_{k\to 0}\phi(h,k) = \lim_{k\to 0}\frac{mk\cdot k}{(m^2k^2+k^2)^{3/2}}$$
$$= \lim_{k\to 0}\frac{m}{k(m^2+1)^{3/2}}$$

which does not exists.

$\therefore$ $f(x, y)$ is not differentiable at origin.

***Example 8.*** Let

$$f(x,y) = \begin{cases} \dfrac{xy}{\sqrt{x^2+y^2}}, & x^2+y^2 \neq 0 \\ 0, & x = y = 0 \end{cases}$$

(a) $f(x, y)$ is continuous at origin
(b) $f(x, y)$ is not differentiable at origin
(c) $f_x(0, 0) = f(0, 0)$
(d) $f_y(0, 0) = f(0, 0)$

**Solution.** (a), (b), (c), (d)

Let us take given $\varepsilon > 0$ and $x^2 + y^2 \neq 0$.

Consider $|f(x,y) - 0| = \left|\dfrac{xy}{\sqrt{x^2+y^2}}\right| = \dfrac{|x||y|}{\sqrt{x^2+y^2}}$

$\because \quad |x| \le \sqrt{x^2+y^2} \Rightarrow \dfrac{|x|}{\sqrt{x^2+y^2}} \le 1$

$\therefore \quad |f(x,y)-0| \le |y|$

$= 0 \cdot |x| + 1 \cdot |y|$

$\therefore \quad \delta = \dfrac{\varepsilon}{0+1} = \varepsilon$

$\therefore$ For given $\varepsilon > 0$, we get $\delta > 0$, such that

$|f(x,y)-0| < \varepsilon$, whenever $0 < |x| < \delta, 0 < |y| < \delta$

$\therefore \quad \lim_{(x,y)\to(0,0)} f(x,y) = 0 = f(0,0)$

$\Rightarrow$ $f(x,y)$ is continuous at $(0,0)$

Now,

$$f(0+h, 0+k) - f(0,0) = f(h,k) - f(0,0)$$

$$= 0\cdot h + 0\cdot k + \sqrt{h^2+k^2}\cdot \frac{h\cdot k}{h^2+k^2}$$

So that $A = 0, B = 0$ which does not depends on $h$ and $k$ and

$$\phi(h,k) = \frac{hk}{h^2+k^2}$$

Now, approaching along $h = mk$, we get

$$\lim_{k\to 0} \phi(mk,k) = \lim_{k\to 0} \frac{mk^2}{k^2(1+m^2)}$$

$$= \lim_{k\to 0} \frac{m}{1+m^2}$$

which depends on $m$. Hence, $\lim_{(h,k)\to(0,0)} \phi(h,k)$ does not exists.

Hence, $f(x,y)$ is not differentiable at origin.

***Example 9.*** *If*

$$f(x,y) = \begin{cases} \dfrac{xy^2}{x^2+y^4}, & x^2+y^4 \ne 0 \\ 0, & else \end{cases}$$

*Then, the directional derivative at $c = (0,0)$ in the direction $u = (a_1, a_2)$ is/are*

(a) $f(c,u) = \dfrac{a_2^2}{a_1}, a_1 \ne 0$

(b) $f(c,u) = 0, a_1 = 0$

(c) $f(c,u) = \dfrac{1}{\sqrt{3}}, a_1 = a_2 = \dfrac{1}{\sqrt{3}}$

(d) None of these

**Solution.** (a), (b), (c)

We have,

$$f(c,u) = \lim_{h\to 0} \frac{f(c+hu)-f(c)}{h}$$

$$= \lim_{h\to 0} \frac{f(a_1h, a_2h)}{h}$$

$$= \lim_{h\to 0} \frac{h^3 a_1 a_2^2}{h(h^2a_1^2 + h^4a_2^4)}$$

$$= \begin{cases} \dfrac{a_2^2}{a_1}, & a_1 \ne 0 \\ 0, & a_1 = 0 \end{cases}$$

$\therefore \quad f(c,u) = \dfrac{1}{\sqrt{3}}$, if $a_1 = a_2 = \dfrac{1}{\sqrt{3}}$

# Exercise 1 (For Part 'B')

**Direction** (Q. Nos. 1-19) *All questions have only one correct option.*

**1.** Let

$$f(x, y) = \begin{cases} \dfrac{xy}{x^2 + y^2}; & (x, y) \neq (0, 0) \\ 0 & ; (x, y) = (0, 0) \end{cases}$$

Then,

(a) $f$ is continuous at (0, 0) and the partial derivatives $f_x, f_y$ exists at every point of $R^2$

(b) $f$ is discontinuous at (0, 0) and $f_x, f_y$ does not exists at every point of $R^2$

(c) $f$ is discontinuous at (0, 0) and $f_x, f_y$ exists at only at (0,0)

(d) None of the above

**2.** Let $f = R^2 \to R$ be defined by

$$f(x, y) = \begin{cases} x^2 + y^2, & \text{if } x \text{ and } y \text{ are rational} \\ 0 \quad , & \text{otherwise} \end{cases}.$$

Then,

(a) $f$ is not continuous at (0, 0)

(b) $f$ is continuous at (0, 0) as well as differentiable at (0, 0)

(c) $f$ is differentiable only at (0, 0)

(d) $f$ is differentiable everywhere

**3.** Let $f: R^2 \to R$ be defined by

$$f(x, y) = \begin{cases} \dfrac{x^2 y}{x^4 + y^2}; & (x, y) \neq (0, 0) \\ 0 & ; (x, y) = (0, 0) \end{cases}$$

Then, the directional derivative of $f$ at (0, 0) in the direction of the vector $\left(\dfrac{1}{\sqrt{2}}, \dfrac{1}{\sqrt{2}}\right)$ is

(a) $\dfrac{1}{\sqrt{2}}$ (b) $\dfrac{1}{2}$

(c) $\dfrac{1}{2\sqrt{2}}$ (d) $\dfrac{1}{4\sqrt{2}}$

**4.** For $(x, y) \in R^2$, let

$$f(x, y) = \begin{cases} \dfrac{2xy}{x^2 + y^2}; & \text{if } (x, y) \neq (0, 0) \\ 0 & ; \text{if } (x, y) = (0, 0) \end{cases}.$$

Then,

(a) $f_x$ and $f_y$ exists at (0, 0) and $f$ is continuous at (0, 0)

(b) $f_x$ and $f_y$ exists at (0, 0) and $f$ is discontinuous at (0, 0)

(c) $f_x$ and $f_y$ does not exist at (0, 0) and $f$ is continuous at (0, 0)

(d) $f_x$ and $f_y$ exists at (0, 0) and $f$ is discontinuous at (0, 0)

**5.** Let

$$f(x, y) = \begin{cases} \dfrac{xy}{(x^2 + y^2)^{5/2}}[1 - \cos(x^2 + y^2)]; & (x, y) \neq (0,0) \\ k & ; (x, y) = (0, 0) \end{cases}$$

Then, the value of $k$ for which $f(x, y)$ is continuous at (0, 0) is

(a) 0 (b) 1/2

(c) 1 (d) 3/2

**6.** Let $f: R^2 \to R$ be such that $\dfrac{\partial f}{\partial x}$ and $\dfrac{\partial f}{\partial y}$ exist at all points. Then,

(a) the total derivative of $f$ exists at all points of $R^2$

(b) $f$ is continuous on $R^2$

(c) the function $f(x, y)$ as a function of $x$ for every fixed $y$ and $f(x, y)$ as a function of $y$ for every fixed $x$ are continuous

(d) all directional derivative of $f$ exist at all points of $R^2$

**7.** Let

$$f(x, y) = \frac{xy}{\sqrt{x^2 + y^2}}, \ (x, y) \neq (0, 0).$$

Then,

(a) $f(x, y)$ is discontinuous at (0, 0)

(b) $f(x, y)$ is continuous at (0, 0)

(c) $f_x(0, 0) = 1$

(d) $f_y(0, 0) = 1$

**8.** Let

$$f(x, y) = \begin{cases} \dfrac{xy^2}{x^2 + y^4}; & (x, y) \neq (0, 0) \\ 0 & ; (x, y) = (0, 0) \end{cases}.$$

Then,

(a) $f(x, y)$ is not defined at the origin

(b) $f_x(0, 0) = 1$

(c) $f_x(0, 0) = 0$

(d) $f_y(0, 0)$ does not exists

**9.** Let if possible, $\alpha = \lim\limits_{(x,y) \to (0,0)} \dfrac{\sin(x^2 + y^2)}{x^2 + y^2}$,

$\beta = \lim\limits_{(x,y) \to (0,0)} \dfrac{x^2 - y^2}{x^2 + y^2}$. Then,

(a) $\alpha$ exists but $\beta$ does not exists

(b) $\alpha$ does not exists but $\beta$ exists

(c) $\alpha, \beta$ do not exists

(d) Both $\alpha, \beta$ exist

**10.** Let $f: R^2 \to R$ be a function defined by

$$f(x, y) = \begin{cases} \dfrac{xy^2}{x^2 + y^4}; & (x, y) \neq (0,0) \\ 0 & ; (x, y) = (0,0) \end{cases}$$

Then, the value of $f_x(0,0)$ and $f_y(0,0)$ is

(a) 0, 1
(b) 1, 0
(c) 0, 0
(d) None of the above

**11.** Let

$f: R^2 \to R$ be defined by

$$f(x, y) = \begin{cases} \dfrac{xy}{\sqrt{x^2 + y^2}}; & (x, y) \neq (0, 0) \\ 0 & ; (x, y) = (0, 0) \end{cases}$$

Then,

(a) $f$ is not continuous at (0, 0)
(b) $f$ is continuous at (0, 0) but not differentiable at (0, 0)
(c) $f$ is differentiable only at (0, 0)
(d) $f$ is differentiable everywhere

**12.** If $f(x, y)$ is differentiable at $(a, b)$, then the partial derivatives $f_x$ and $f_y$ at $(a, b)$

(a) $f_x$ exists but $f_y$ does not exists
(b) $f_x$ does not exists but $f_y$ exists
(c) $f_x$ and $f_y$ both are exists
(d) $f_x$ and $f_y$ both are not exists

**13.** Let

$$f(x, y) = \begin{cases} \dfrac{xy(x^2 - y^2)}{x^2 + y^2}; & (x, y) \neq (0, 0) \\ 0 & ; (x, y) = (0, 0) \end{cases}.$$

Then,

(a) $f_{xy}(0,0) = f_{yx}(0,0) = 0$
(b) $f_{xy}(0,0) \neq f_{yx}(0,0)$
(c) $f_{xy}(0,0) = f_{yx}(0,0)$
(d) None of the above

**14.** Let

$$f(x, y) = \begin{cases} \dfrac{x^2 y^2}{x^2 + y^2}; & (x, y) \neq (0, 0) \\ 0 & ; (x, y) = (0, 0) \end{cases}$$

Then,

(a) $f_{xy}(0,0) = f_{yx}(0,0) = 0$ (b) $f_{xy}(0,0) \neq f_{yx}(0,0)$
(c) $f_{xy}(0,0) = f_{yx}(0,0) = 1$ (d) None of these

**15.** If $f_{xy}$ and $f_{yx}$ are both continuous at $(a, b)$. Then,

(a) $f_{xy}(a, b) \neq f_{yx}(a, b)$ (b) $f_{xy}(a, b) = f_{yx}(a, b)$
(c) $f_{xy}(a, b) = 0, f_{yx}(a, b) = 1$ (d) None of these

**16.** Which of the following statement(s) is/are correct?

(a) If the function $f(x, y)$ is continuous at the point $(a, b)$, it must also be differentiable at $(a, b)$
(b) If a function $f(x, y)$ is differentiable at $(a, b)$, it must be continuous at $(a, b)$
(c) If a function $f(x, y)$ possesses both the partial derivatives $f_x(a, b)$ and $f_y(a, b)$ it must be differentiable at $(a, b)$
(d) If $f_{xy}$ and $f_{yx}$ are both continuous at $(a, b)$, then $f_{xy}(a, b) \neq f_{yx}(a, b)$

**17.** Which of the following statement(s) is/are correct?

(a) If $f: X \to R$, $X \subseteq R^2$ and $(a, b) \in X$ is such that $f_x$, $f_y$ are differentiable at $(a, b)$, then $f_x(a, b) = f_y(a, b)$
(b) If a function $f(x, y)$ is differentiable at $(a, b)$, then the partial derivatives $f_x(a, b)$ and $f_y(a, b)$ both exists at $(a, b)$
(c) If a function $f(x, y)$ is discontinuous at $(a, b)$, then both the partial derivatives $f_x(a, b)$ and $f_y(a, b)$ do not exists
(d) If $f_{xy}$ and $f_{yx}$ are both continuous at $(a, b)$, then $f_{xy}(a, b) \neq f_{yx}(a, b)$

**18.** Let

$$f(x, y) = \sqrt{|xy|},$$

then the value of $f_x(0, 0)$ and $f_y(0, 0)$ is

(a) 0, 0 (b) 0, 1
(c) 1, 0 (d) 1, 1

**19.** For the function $f(x, y) = 2x^4 - 3x^2 y + y^2$ has

(a) maximum at (0, 0)
(b) minimum at (0, 0)
(c) neither maxima nor minima at (0, 0)
(d) doubtful case at (0, 0) always

# Exercise 2 (For Part 'C')

**Direction** (Q. Nos. 1-31) *Questions may have one or more than one correct option.*

**1.** If

$$f(x, y) = \begin{cases} \dfrac{x^2 - xy}{x + y}; & (x, y) \neq (0, 0) \\ 0 & ; (x, y) = (0, 0) \end{cases}$$

Then,

(a) $f_x(0, 0) = 1$ (b) $f_y(0, 0) = 0$
(c) $f_x(0, 0) = 0$ (d) $f_y(0, 0) = 1$

**2.** If

$$f(x, y) = \begin{cases} \frac{2xy}{x^2 + y^2}; (x, y) \neq (0, 0) \\ 0 \quad ; (x, y) = (0, 0) \end{cases}$$

Then,

(a) $f_x$ exist at origin
(b) $f_x$ does not exist at origin
(c) $f_y$ exist at origin
(d) $f_y$ does not exist at origin

**3.** If

$$f(x, y) = 2x^2 - xy + 2y^2.$$

Then, at (1, 2)

(a) $\frac{\partial f}{\partial x} = 2$ (b) $\frac{\partial f}{\partial y} = 7$
(c) $\frac{\partial f}{\partial x} = \frac{\partial f}{\partial y}$ (d) $\frac{\partial f}{\partial x} \neq \frac{\partial f}{\partial y}$

**4.** Given the function

$$f(x, y) = x^2 - 2xy + y^2 + x^3 - y^3 + x^5$$

Then,

(a) has maximum value at origin
(b) has minimum value at origin
(c) has neither maximum nor minimum value at origin
(d) has maximum value but no minimum value at origin

**5.** Given the function

$f(x, y) = x^3 + y^3 - 63(x + y) + 12xy$

(a) the function has four stationary points
(b) the function is maximum at (–7, – 7)
(c) the function is minimum at (3, 3)
(d) the function has neither minimum nor a maximum at (5, – 1)

**6.** Let

$$f(x, y) = \begin{cases} \frac{xy}{x^2 + y^2}; (x, y) \neq (0, 0) \\ 0 \quad ; (x, y) = (0, 0) \end{cases}$$

Then,

(a) $f(x, y)$ is continuous at origin
(b) $f(x, y)$ is discontinuous at origin
(c) both the partial derivative exists at origin
(d) both the partial derivative does not exists

**7.** Let

$$f(x, y) = \begin{cases} xy\frac{(x^2 - y^2)}{(x^2 + y^2)}; x^2 + y^2 \neq 0 \\ 0 \quad ; x = y = 0 \end{cases}$$

Then,

(a) $f_x(x, 0) = 0$ (b) $f_y(x, 0) = x$
(c) $f_x(0, y) = -y$ (d) $f_y(0, y) = 0$

**8.** Let

$$f(x, y) = \begin{cases} x^3 + y^3; x \neq y \\ 0 \quad ; x = y \end{cases}$$

Then,

(a) $f(x, y)$ is continuous at origin
(b) $f(x, y)$ is discontinuous at origin
(c) $f_x$ exists at every point including origin
(d) $f_y$ exists at every point including origin

**9.** Let

$$f(x, y) = \begin{cases} \frac{x^2 y}{x^3 + y^3}; x^3 + y^3 \neq 0 \\ 0 \;; x = y = 0 \end{cases}$$

Then,

(a) $f(x, y)$ is continuous at (0, 0)
(b) $f(x, y)$ is discontinuous at (0, 0)
(c) $f(0, y)$ is continuous at origin
(d) $f(x, 0)$ is continuous at origin

**10.** Let

$$f(x, y) = \begin{cases} \frac{xy^3}{x^2 + y^6}; x \neq 0, y \neq 0 \\ 0 \quad ; x = y = 0 \end{cases}$$

Then,

(a) $f(x, y)$ is continuous at origin
(b) $f(x, y)$ is discontinuous at origin
(c) $f(0, y)$ is continuous at origin
(d) $f(x, 0)$ is continuous at origin

**11.** Let

$$f(x, y) = \begin{cases} x^2 + 2y; \; (x, y) \neq (1, 2) \\ 0 \;; \; (x, y) = (1, 2) \end{cases}$$

Then,

(a) $f(x, y)$ is continuous at (1, 2)
(b) $f(x, y)$ is discontinuous at (1, 2)
(c) $f(x, y)$ has removable discontinuity at (1, 2)
(d) $\lim_{(x,y)\to(1,2)} f(x, y)$ does not exists

**12.** Let

$$f(x, y) = \begin{cases} \frac{xy}{\sqrt{x^2 + y^2}}; (x, y) \neq (0, 0) \\ 0 \quad ; (x, y) = (0, 0) \end{cases}$$

Then,

(a) $f(x, y)$ is continuous at (0, 0)
(b) $f(x, y)$ is discontinuous at (0, 0)
(c) only one function of single variable is continuous at origin
(d) both the function of single variable are continuous at origin

**13.** Let

$$f(x, y) = \begin{cases} y + x\sin\left(\frac{1}{y}\right); & y \neq 0 \\ 0 & ; y = 0 \end{cases}$$

Then,

(a) $\lim_{x\to 0}\lim_{y\to 0} f(x, y)$ does not exists

(b) $\lim_{y\to 0}\lim_{x\to 0} f(x, y)$ exists

(c) $\lim_{(x,y)\to(0,0)} f(x, y)$ does not exists

(d) $\lim_{(x,y)\to(0,0)} f(x, y)$ exists

**14.** Let

$$f(x, y) = \begin{cases} \frac{2xy}{x^2 + y}; & (x, y) \neq (0, 0) \\ 0 & ; (x, y) = (0, 0) \end{cases}$$

Then,

(a) $\lim_{x\to 0} f(x, 0) = f(0, 0)$

(b) $\lim_{y\to 0} f(0, y) = f(0, 0)$

(c) $\lim_{(x,y)\to(0,0)} f(x, y) = f(0, 0)$

(d) $\lim_{(x,y)\to(0,0)} f(x, y) \neq f(0, 0)$

**15.** Let

$$f(x, y) = \begin{cases} y\sin(1/x) + \frac{xy}{x^2 + y^2}; & x \neq 0 \\ 0 & ; x = 0 \end{cases}$$

Then,

(a) one repeated limit exists but other does not exists
(b) double limit exists
(c) double limit does not exists
(d) any two of the above are correct

**16.** Let

$$f(x, y) = \begin{cases} 1; & xy \neq 0 \\ 0; & xy = 0 \end{cases}$$

Then,

(a) $\lim_{x\to 0}\lim_{y\to 0} f(x, y) = 1$

(b) $\lim_{y\to 0}\lim_{x\to 0} f(x, y) = 1$

(c) $\lim_{(x,y)\to(0,0)} f(x, y)$ does not exists

(d) $\lim_{(x,y)\to(0,0)} f(x, y) = 1$

**17.** Let

$$f(x, y) = \frac{y - x}{y + x}\cdot\frac{1 + x}{1 + y}.$$

Then,

(a) $\lim_{x\to 0}\lim_{y\to 0} f(x, y) = 1$

(b) $\lim_{y\to 0}\lim_{x\to 0} f(x, y) = 1$

(c) $\lim_{(x,y)\to(0,0)} f(x, y)$ does not exists

(d) $\lim_{(x,y)\to(0,0)} f(x, y)$ exists

**18.** Let

$$f(x, y) = \begin{cases} x\sin\left(\frac{1}{y}\right) + y\sin\left(\frac{1}{x}\right); & xy \neq 0 \\ 0 & ; xy = 0 \end{cases}$$

Then,

(a) $\lim_{x\to 0}\lim_{y\to 0} f(x, y)$ does not exists

(b) $\lim_{y\to 0}\lim_{x\to 0} f(x, y)$ does not exists

(c) $\lim_{(x,y)\to(0,0)} f(x, y)$ exists and equal to 0

(d) $\lim_{x\to 0} f(x, y)$ and $\lim_{y\to 0} f(x, y)$ both does not exists

**19.** Let

$$f(x, y) = \begin{cases} \frac{x^2 y}{x^4 + y^2}, & \text{if } x^4 + y^2 \neq 0 \\ 0, & \text{if } x^4 + y^2 = 0 \end{cases}$$

Then,

(a) $\lim_{(x,y)\to(0,0)} f(x, y)$ does not exists

(b) $\lim_{(x,y)\to(0,0)} f(x, y)$ exists

(c) the function posses no limit at the origin, but a straight line approach gives the limit zero

(d) None of the above

**20.** Which of the following(s) is/are true?

(a) $\lim_{(x,y)\to(0,0)} xy\frac{x^2 - y^2}{x^2 + y^2} = 0$

(b) $\lim_{(x,y)\to(0,0)} \frac{2xy^2}{x^2 + y^4}$ does not exists

(c) $\lim_{(x,y)\to(0,0)} \frac{\sqrt{x^2y^2 + 1} - 1}{x^2 + y^2} = 0$

(d) $\lim_{(x,y)\to(0,0)} \left(\frac{1}{xy}\right)\sin(x^2 y + xy^2) = 0$

**21.** Consider

$$f(x, y) = \begin{cases} x\sin 1/x + y\sin 1/x, & xy \neq 0 \\ x\sin 1/x, & y = 0, x \neq 0 \\ y\sin 1/y, & x = 0, y \neq 0 \\ 0, & x = y = 0 \end{cases}$$

Then,

(a) $f(x, y)$ is continuous at origin
(b) $f(x, y)$ is discontinuous at origin
(c) $f(x, y)$ is differentiable at origin
(d) both partial derivative exists at origin

**22.** Let

$$f(x, y) = \begin{cases} |x| + |y|, (x, y) \neq (0, 0) \\ 0 \quad , (x, y) = (0, 0) \end{cases}$$

Then,
(a) $f(x, y)$ is continuous at origin
(b) $f(x, y)$ is discontinuous at origin
(c) $f(x, y)$ is differentiable at origin
(d) $f(x, y)$ is not differentiable at origin

**23.** If

$$f(x, y) = \begin{cases} xy \tan(y/x), (x, y) \neq (0, 0) \\ 0 \quad , (x, y) = (0, 0) \end{cases}$$

Then, at (0, 0)
(a) $xf_x + yf_y = 2f$ (b) $xf_x - yf_y = 2f$
(c) $yf_x + xf_y = 2f$ (d) $yf_x - xf_y = 2f$

**24.** If

$$f(x, y) = x^y,$$

then
(a) $f_x(a, 0) = 1$, where a is constant
(b) $f_y(e, 0) = 1$
(c) $f_{xy}(1, 0) = 1$
(d) $f_{yx}(1, 1) = 1$

**25.** If

$$f(x, y) = \begin{cases} \dfrac{1}{x^2 + y^2}, (x, y) \neq (0, 0) \\ 0 \quad , (x, y) = (0, 0) \end{cases}$$

Then,
(a) $f$ is differentiable at (0, 0)
(b) $f$ is not differentiable at (0, 0)
(c) $f$ is continuous at (0, 0)
(d) $f$ is discontinuous at (0, 0)

**26.** For what value of $k$, the function

$$f(x, y) = \begin{cases} 3xy, (x, y) \neq (2, 3) \\ k, (x, y) = (2, 3) \end{cases}$$

is discontinuous?
(a) 6 (b) 9
(c) 16 (d) 18

**27.** If

$$f(x, y) = \frac{xy}{\sqrt{x^2 + y^2}} \text{ when } (x, y) \neq (0, 0),\ f(0, 0) = 0$$

at (0, 0), then
(a) $f$ is continuous
(b) $f$ process partial derivatives
(c) $f$ is not continuous
(d) $f$ is not differentiable

**28.** If

$$f(x, y) = \begin{cases} \dfrac{x^3 + y^3}{x - y} & ; x \neq y \\ 0 & ; x = y \end{cases}.$$

Then,
(a) $f$ is discontinuous at the origin
(b) $f_x(0, 0)$ exist
(c) $f_y(0, 0)$ exist
(d) $f$ is continuous at the origin

**29.** If $f(x, y) = xy(x^2 - y^2)/(x^2 + y^2)$,
when $(x, y) \neq (0, 0)$ and $f(0, 0) = 0$
(a) $f_{xy}(0, 0) = 1$ (b) $f_{yx}(0, 0) = -1$
(c) $f_{xy}(0, 0) = f_{yx}(0, 0)$ (d) $f_{xy}(0, 0) \neq f_{yx}(0, 0)$

**30.** Let us consider the pair of ordered pair of sequences $(a_n, b_n)$ and $(c_n, d_n)$ such that $\lim_{n\to\infty}(a_n, b_n) = (a, b)$ and $\lim_{n\to\infty}(c_n, d_n) = (a, b)$, then

$$\lim_{(x,y)\to(a,b)} f(x, y) \text{ does not exists, if}$$

(a) $\lim_{n\to\infty} f(a_n, b_n) = \lim_{n\to\infty} f(c_n, d_n)$
(b) $\lim_{n\to\infty} f(a_n, b_n) \neq \lim_{n\to\infty} f(c_n, d_n)$
(c) $\lim_{n\to\infty} f(a_n, b_n) > \lim_{n\to\infty} f(c_n, d_n)$
(d) $\lim_{n\to\infty} f(a_n, b_n) < \lim_{n\to\infty} f(c_n, d_n)$

**31.** For the function $f(x, y) = x^3 + y^3 - 3x - 12y + 20$ has
(a) minima at (1, 2)
(b) maxima at (–1, – 2)
(c) neither maxima nor minima at (1, – 2) and (–1, 2)
(d) the saddle points are (–1, 2) and (1, – 2)

# Answers

## Exercise 1

**1.** (c) **2.** (b) **3.** (a) **4.** (d) **5.** (a) **6.** (c) **7.** (b) **8.** (c) **9.** (a) **10.** (c)
**11.** (b) **12.** (c) **13.** (b) **14.** (a) **15.** (b) **16.** (b) **17.** (c) **18.** (a) **19.** (c)

## Exercise 2

| | | | | | | | | | |
|---|---|---|---|---|---|---|---|---|---|
| **1.** (a,b) | **2.** (a,c) | **3.** (a,b,d) | **4.** (c) | **5.** (a,b,c,d) | **6.** (b,c) | **7.** (a,b,c,d) | **8.** (a,c,d) | **9.** (b,c,d) | **10.** (b,c,d) |
| **11.** (b,c) | **12.** (a,d) | **13.** (a,b,d) | **14.** (a,b,d) | **15.** (a,c,d) | **16.** (a,b,c) | **17.** (b,c) | **18.** (a,b,c,d) | **19.** (a,c) | **20.** (a,b,c,d) |
| **21.** (a,d) | **22.** (a,d) | **23.** (a,b,c,d) | **24.** (a,b,c,d) | **25.** (b,d) | **26.** (a,b,c) | **27.** (a,b,d) | **28.** (a,b,c) | **29.** (a,b,d) | **30.** (b) |
| **31.** (a,b,c,d) | | | | | | | | | |

# Hints & Solutions

## Exercise 1

**1.** Let us suppose $(x, y)$ approaches $(0, 0)$ along the line $y = mx$. Which is a line through the origin. Put $y = mx$ and allows $x \to 0$, we get

$$\lim_{x\to 0} \frac{x \cdot mx}{x^2 + m^2x^2} = \lim_{x\to 0} \frac{m}{1+m^2}$$

which depends on $m$, therefore the limit of $f(x, y)$ at $(0, 0)$ does not exists. Hence, $f(x, y)$ is discontinuous at origin.

Now, $$f_x(0, 0) = \lim_{h\to 0} \frac{f(0+h, 0) - f(0, 0)}{h}$$

$$= \lim_{h\to 0} \frac{f(h, 0)}{h}$$

$$= \lim_{h\to 0} 0 = 0$$

$\therefore$ $f_x$ exists at origin.

And $$f_y(0, 0) = \lim_{k\to 0} \frac{f(0, 0+k) - f(0, 0)}{k}$$

$$= \lim_{k\to 0} \frac{f(0, k)}{k}$$

$$= \lim_{k\to 0} 0 = 0$$

$\therefore$ $f_y$ exists at origin.

**2.** We have,

$$\lim_{(x,y)\to(0,0)} f(x, y) = \lim_{(x,y)\to(0,0)} x^2 + y^2 = 0$$

But $f(0, 0) = 0$

Hence, $\lim_{(x,y)\to(0,0)} f(x, y) = f(0, 0)$

$\Rightarrow f(x, y)$ is continuous at $(0, 0)$

Now,

$$f(0+h, 0+k) - f(0, 0) = 0 \cdot h + 0 \cdot k + \sqrt{h^2 + k^2} \cdot \sqrt{h^2 + k^2}$$

where $A = 0$, $B = 0$ which does not depends on $h$ and $k$ and

$$\phi(h, k) = \sqrt{h^2 + k^2}$$

and $$\lim_{(h,k)\to(0,0)} \phi(h, k) = \lim_{(h,k)\to(0,0)} \sqrt{h^2 + k^2}$$

$$= 0$$

Hence, $f(x, y)$ is continuous as well as differentiable at $(0, 0)$.

**3.** Given that $u = \left(\frac{1}{\sqrt{2}}, \frac{1}{\sqrt{2}}\right)$ and $a = (0, 0)$

we have directional derivative at $a$ in the direction $u$ as

$$f'(a, u) = \lim_{h\to 0} \frac{f(a+hu) - f(a)}{h}$$

$$= \lim_{h\to 0} \frac{f\left(0 + \frac{h}{\sqrt{2}}, 0 + \frac{h}{\sqrt{2}}\right) - f(0, 0)}{h}$$

$$= \lim_{h\to 0} \frac{f\left(\frac{h}{\sqrt{2}}, \frac{h}{\sqrt{2}}\right)}{h}$$

$$= \lim_{h\to 0} \frac{\left(\dfrac{\frac{h^3}{2\sqrt{2}}}{\frac{h^4}{4} + \frac{h^2}{2}}\right)}{h}$$

$$= \lim_{h\to 0} \frac{2h^3}{\sqrt{2}\, h(h^4 + 2h^2)}$$

$$= \lim_{h\to 0} \frac{2}{\sqrt{2}(h^2 + 2)}$$

$$= \frac{2}{2\sqrt{2}} = \frac{1}{\sqrt{2}}$$

**4.** Let us approaches $(0, 0)$ along the line $y = mx$ which passes through origin. Put $y = mx$, we get

$$\lim_{x\to 0} f(x, y) = \lim_{x\to 0} \frac{2 \cdot x \cdot mx}{x^2 + m^2x^2}$$

$$= \lim_{x\to 0} \frac{2m}{1+m^2}$$

which depends on $m$. Hence, $\lim_{(x,y)\to(0,0)} f(x, y)$ does not exists, therefore $f(x, y)$ is discontinuous at $(0, 0)$.

Now,

$$f_x(0, 0) = \lim_{h\to 0} \frac{f(0+h, 0) - f(0, 0)}{h}$$

$$= \lim_{h\to 0} \frac{f(h, 0)}{h} = \lim_{h\to 0} 0 = 0$$

and

$$f_y(0, 0) = \lim_{k\to 0} \frac{f(0, 0+k) - f(0, 0)}{k}$$

$$= \lim_{k\to 0} \frac{f(0, k)}{k} = \lim_{k\to 0} 0 = 0$$

Hence, $f(x, y)$ is discontinuous at $(0, 0)$. But both the partial derivative $f_x$ and $f_y$ exists at origin.

**7.** Let us take given $\varepsilon > 0$ and $(x, y) \neq (0, 0)$.

Consider

$$|f(x, y) - 0| = \left|\frac{xy}{\sqrt{x^2+y^2}}\right|$$

$$= \frac{|xy|}{\sqrt{x^2+y^2}}$$

$$= \frac{|x|\cdot|y|}{\sqrt{x^2+y^2}}$$

Now, since $y^2 \leq x^2 + y^2$

$\Rightarrow$ $|y| \leq \sqrt{x^2+y^2}$

$\Rightarrow$ $\dfrac{|y|}{\sqrt{x^2+y^2}} \leq 1$

$\therefore$ $|f(x, y) - 0| \leq |x|$

$$= 1\cdot|x - 0| + 0\cdot|y - 0|$$

$\therefore$ $\delta = \dfrac{\varepsilon}{1+0} = \varepsilon$

$\therefore$ For every given $\varepsilon > 0$, $\exists\ \delta = \varepsilon > 0$ such that $|f(x, y) - 0| < \varepsilon$ whenever $0 < |x| < \delta$ and $0 < |y| < \delta$.

$\Rightarrow f(x, y)$ is continuous at $(0, 0)$.

**8.** Here,

$$f_x(0, 0) = \lim_{h\to 0} \frac{f(0+h, 0) - f(0, 0)}{h}$$

$$= \lim_{h\to 0} \frac{f(h, 0)}{h}$$

$$= \lim_{h\to 0} 0$$

$$= 0$$

**9.** $\alpha = \lim\limits_{(x,y)\to(0,0)} \dfrac{\sin(x^2+y^2)}{x^2+y^2}$

Put $x^2 + y^2 = t$, $\therefore (x, y) \to (0, 0) \Rightarrow t \to 0$

$$= \lim_{t\to 0} \frac{\sin t}{t}$$

$$= 1$$

$\therefore$ $\alpha$ exists.

Now,

$$\beta = \lim_{(x,y)\to(0,0)} \frac{x^2-y^2}{x^2+y^2}$$

Let us approaches along $y = mx$, which is passing through $(0, 0)$. Hence,

$$\beta = \lim_{x\to 0} \frac{x^2 - m^2\cdot x^2}{x^2 + m^2\cdot x^2}$$

$$= \lim_{x\to 0} \frac{1-m^2}{1+m^2}$$

which depends on $m$. Hence, $\beta$ does not exists.

**10.** We have,

$$f_x(0, 0) = \lim_{h\to 0} \frac{f(0+h, 0) - f(0, 0)}{h}$$

$$= \lim_{h\to 0} \frac{f(h, 0)}{h} = \lim_{h\to 0} 0 = 0$$

and

$$f_y(0, 0) = \lim_{k\to 0} \frac{f(0, 0+k) - f(0, 0)}{k}$$

$$= \lim_{k\to 0} \frac{f(0, k)}{k}$$

$$= \lim_{k\to 0} 0 = 0$$

**11.** Let us take given $\varepsilon > 0$ and $(x, y) \neq (0, 0)$.

Consider

$$|f(x, y) - 0| = \left|\frac{xy}{\sqrt{x^2+y^2}}\right|$$

$$= \frac{|x|\cdot|y|}{\sqrt{x^2+y^2}}$$

Since, $y^2 \leq x^2 + y^2$

$\Rightarrow$ $|y| \leq \sqrt{x^2+y^2}$

$\therefore$ $|f(x, y) - 0| \leq |x|$

$$= 1\cdot|x| + 0\cdot|y|$$

$\therefore$ $\delta = \dfrac{\varepsilon}{1+0} = \varepsilon$

$\therefore$ For given $\varepsilon > 0$, we get $\delta = \varepsilon > 0$ such that $|f(x, y) - 0| < \varepsilon$, whenever $0 < |x| < \delta$ and $0 < |y| < \delta$.

$\therefore f(x, y)$ is continuous at $(0, 0)$.

Now,

$$f(0+h, 0+k) - f(0, 0) = 0\cdot h + 0\cdot k + \sqrt{h^2+k^2}\cdot\frac{h\cdot k}{(h^2+k^2)}$$

So that $A = 0$, $B = 0$, which does not depends on $h$ and $k$ and

$$\phi(h, k) = \frac{hk}{h^2+k^2}$$

Let us take $h = mk$, we get

$$\lim_{k\to 0} \frac{m\cdot k^2}{(m^2+1)k^2} = \lim_{k\to 0} \frac{m}{1+m^2}$$

which depends on $m$. Hence, $\lim\limits_{(h,k)\to(0,0)} \phi(h, k)$ does not exists.

Hence, $f$ is not differentiable at $(0, 0)$.

**13.** Here,

$$f_{xy}(0, 0) = \lim_{k\to 0}\left[\lim_{h\to 0} \frac{f(0+h, 0+k) - f(0+h, 0) - f(0, 0+k) + f(0, 0)}{hk}\right]$$

$$= \lim_{k\to 0}\left[\lim_{h\to 0} \frac{\dfrac{hk(h^2-k^2)}{h^2+k^2} - 0 - 0 + 0}{hk}\right]$$

$$= \lim_{k\to 0}\left[\lim_{h\to 0} \frac{h^2-k^2}{h^2+k^2}\right]$$

$$= \lim_{k\to 0} -1 = -1$$

and

$$f_{yx}(0,0)=\lim_{h\to 0}\left[\lim_{k\to 0}\frac{f(0+h,0+k)-f(0,0+k)-f(0+h,0)+f(0,0)}{hk}\right]$$

$$=\lim_{h\to 0}\left[\lim_{k\to 0}\frac{\frac{hk(h^2-k^2)}{h^2+k^2}}{hk}\right]$$

$$=\lim_{h\to 0}\left[\lim_{k\to 0}\frac{h^2-k^2}{h^2+k^2}\right]$$

$$=\lim_{h\to 0}1=1$$

$\therefore f_{xy}(0,0)\neq f_{yx}(0,0)$

**14.** Here,

$$f_{xy}(0,0)=\lim_{k\to 0}\left[\lim_{h\to 0}\frac{f(0+h,0+k)-f(0+h,0)-f(0,0+k)+f(0,0)}{hk}\right]$$

$$=\lim_{k\to 0}\left[\lim_{h\to 0}\frac{f(h,k)-0-0+0}{hk}\right]$$

$$=\lim_{k\to 0}\left[\lim_{h\to 0}\frac{\frac{h^2k^2}{h^2+k^2}}{hk}\right]$$

$$=\lim_{k\to 0}\left[\lim_{h\to 0}\frac{hk}{h^2+k^2}\right]=\lim_{k\to 0}0=0$$

and

$$f_{yx}(0,0)=\lim_{h\to 0}\left[\lim_{k\to 0}\frac{f(0+h,0+k)-f(0,0+k)-f(0+h,0)+f(0,0)}{hk}\right]$$

$$=\lim_{h\to 0}\left[\lim_{k\to 0}\frac{f(h,k)-0-0+0}{hk}\right]$$

$$=\lim_{h\to 0}\left[\lim_{k\to 0}\frac{\frac{h^2k^2}{h^2+k^2}}{hk}\right]$$

$$=\lim_{h\to 0}\left[\lim_{k\to 0}\frac{hk}{h^2+k^2}\right]$$

$$=\lim_{h\to 0}0=0$$

$\therefore f_{xy}(0,0)=f_{yx}(0,0)=0$

**19.** We have,

$$f_x(x,y)=8x^3-6xy$$
$$f_y(x,y)=-3x^2+2y$$
$$\therefore\quad f_x(0,0)=0=f_y(0,0)$$

Also,

$$f_{xx}(x,y)=24x^2-6y=0 \text{ at } (0,0)$$
$$f_{xy}(x,y)=-6x=0 \text{ at } (0,0)$$
$$f_{yy}(x,y)=2 \text{ at } (0,0)$$

Thus, at (0, 0)

$$f_{xx}(0,0)\cdot f_{yy}(0,0)-(f_{xy}(0,0))^2=0$$

So, it is a doubtful case and so requires further investigation. Again,

$$f(x,y)=(x^2-y)(2x^2-y),\ f(0,0)=0$$
$$\Rightarrow\quad f(x,y)-f(0,0)=(x^2-y)(2x^2-y)$$
$$>0 \text{ for } y<0 \text{ or } x^2>y>0$$
$$<0 \text{ for } y>x^2>\frac{y}{2}>0$$

So that $f(x,y)-f(0,0)$ does not keep the same sign near the origin. Therefore, $f$ has neither a maximum nor a minimum value at the origin.

# Exercise 2

**1.** We have,

$$f_x(0,0)=\lim_{h\to 0}\frac{f(0+h,0)-f(0,0)}{h}$$

$$=\lim_{h\to 0}\frac{\frac{h^2-h\cdot 0}{h+0}-0}{h}$$

$$=\lim_{h\to 0}1=1$$

$$f_y(0,0)=\lim_{k\to 0}\frac{f(0,0+k)-f(0,0)}{k}$$

$$=\lim_{k\to 0}\frac{0-0}{k}$$

$$=\lim_{k\to 0}0=0$$

**2.** We have, $f_x(0,0)=\lim\limits_{h\to 0}\dfrac{f(0+h,0)-f(0,0)}{h}$

$$=\lim_{h\to 0}\frac{0-0}{h}=\lim_{h\to 0}0=0, \text{ exists}$$

and $f_y(0,0)=\lim\limits_{k\to 0}\dfrac{f(0,0+k)-f(0,0)}{k}=\lim\limits_{k\to 0}\dfrac{0}{k}$

$$=\lim_{k\to 0}0=0, \text{ exists}$$

**3.** Since, $\left(\dfrac{\partial f}{\partial x}\right)_{(1,2)}=\lim\limits_{h\to 0}\dfrac{f(1+h,2)-f(1,2)}{h}$

$$=\lim_{h\to 0}\frac{\{2(1+h)^2-(1+h)^2+2\cdot 2^2\}-\{2\cdot 1^2-1\cdot 2+2\cdot 2^2\}}{h}$$

$$=\lim_{h\to 0}\frac{2h^2+2h}{h}=\lim_{h\to 0}(2h+2)=2$$

$$\left(\frac{\partial f}{\partial y}\right)_{(1,2)} = \lim_{k\to 0}\frac{f(1, 2+k)-f(1, 2)}{k}$$

$$= \lim_{k\to 0}\frac{\{2-(2+k)+2(2+k)^2\}-\{2-2+8\}}{k}$$

$$= \lim_{k\to 0}\frac{2k^2+7k}{k}$$

$$= \lim_{k\to 0}(2k+7)=7$$

**Alternative method**

We have,

$$f(x, y)=2x^2-xy+2y^2$$

$$\Rightarrow \quad \frac{\partial f}{\partial x}=4x-y \quad \text{and} \quad \frac{\partial f}{\partial y}=-x+4y$$

Hence,

$$\left(\frac{\partial f}{\partial x}\right)_{(1,2)} =4\cdot 1-2=2$$

and

$$\left(\frac{\partial f}{\partial y}\right)_{(1,2)} =-1+4\cdot 2=7$$

**4.** It may be easily seen that at (0, 0)

$$f_x=0$$
$$f_y=0$$
$$f_{xx}=2$$
$$f_{xy}=-2$$
$$f_{yy}=0$$

so that $f_{xx}f_{yy}-(f_{xy})^2=0$

Thus, we need to further examine the question.

Now, we have

$$f(0, 0)=0$$

Since, $\quad f(x, y)=(x-y)^2+(x-y)(x^2+xy+y^2)+x^5$

we see that for points along the line $y-x=0$, we have

$$f(x, y)=x^5$$

and accordingly in every neighbourhood of (0, 0) there are points where for $f(x, y)$ is positive and there are points where for $f(x, y)$ is negative.

Hence, $f(0, 0)$ is neither a maximum nor a minimum value.

**5.** We have,

$$f_x(x, y)=3x^2-63+12y$$
$$f_y(x, y)=3y^2-63+12x$$
$$f_{xx}(x, y)=f_{xy}(x, y)=12$$
$$f_{yy}(x, y)=6y$$

The equations

$$f_x(x, y)=3x^2-63+12y=0$$
$$f_y(x, y)=3y^2-63+12x=0$$

$$\Leftrightarrow \begin{cases} f_x(x, y)=3x^2-63+12y=0 \\ f_x(x, y)-f_y(x, y)=3(x^2-y^2)+12(y-x)=0 \end{cases}$$

$$\Leftrightarrow \begin{cases} x^2-21+4y=0 \\ (y-x)(4-y-x)=0 \end{cases}$$

$$\Leftrightarrow \begin{cases} x^2-21+4x=0 \\ y-x=0 \end{cases} \text{and} \begin{cases} x^2-21+4y=0 \\ 4-y-x=0 \end{cases}$$

These give

$$(-7, -7), (3, 3), (5, -1), (-1, 5)$$

as 4 pairs of solutions. Thus, the function has four stationary points.

At (−7, −7),

$$f_{xx}=42<0$$

and $\quad f_{xy}f_{yy}-(f_{xy})^2=1620>0$

so that the function is maximum at (−7, −7).

At (3, 3),

$$f_{xx}=18>0$$

and $\quad f_{xx}f_{yy}-(f_{xy})^2=180>0$

so that the function is minimum at (3, 3).

At each of the other points (5, − 1) and (−1, 5),

$$f_{xx}f_{yy}-(f_{xy})^2=-324<0$$

So that the function is neither a maximum nor a minimum.

**6.** Putting $y=mx$, we have

$$\lim_{x\to 0} f(x, y)=\frac{m}{1+m^2}$$

So that the limit depends on the value of $m$ *i.e.*, on the path of approaches and is different for the different paths followed and therefore does not exists. Hence, the function $f(x, y)$ is not continuous at $(0, 0)$.

Now, $\quad f_x(0, 0)=\lim_{h\to 0}\frac{f(0+h, 0)-f(0, 0)}{h}$

$$=\lim_{h\to 0}\frac{f(h, 0)}{h}$$

$$=\lim_{h\to 0} 0=0$$

and $\quad f_y(0, 0)=\lim_{k\to 0}\frac{f(0, 0+k)-f(0, 0)}{k}$

$$=\lim_{k\to 0}\frac{f(0, 0+k)}{k}$$

$$=\lim_{k\to 0} 0=0$$

Hence, both partial derivative exists at origin.

**9.** Let approaches along the line $y=mx$, which is passes through origin. Put $y=mx$, we get

$$\lim_{x\to 0} f(x, mx)=\lim_{x\to 0}\frac{x^2\cdot mx}{x^3+m^3x^3}=\lim_{x\to 0}\frac{m}{1+m^2}$$

which depends on $m$. Hence, $\lim_{(x, y)\to (0, 0)} f(x, y)$ does not exists.

Hence, $f(x, y)$ is discontinuous at origin.

Now, $\quad \lim_{y\to 0} f(0, y)=\lim_{y\to 0} 0=0$

and $\quad \lim_{x\to 0} f(x, 0)=\lim_{x\to 0} 0=0$

$\therefore$ $f(0, y)$ and $f(x, 0)$ are continuous at origin.

**11.** We have

$$\lim_{(x,y)\to(1,2)} f(x,y) = \lim_{(x,y)\to(1,2)} x^2+2y$$

$$= 1^2 + 2\cdot 2 = 5$$

But $f(1, 2) = 0$

$$\therefore \quad \lim_{(x,y)\to(1,2)} f(x,y) \neq f(1,2)$$

Hence, $f(x, y)$ is discontinuous at (1, 2).
Now, if we define

$$f(x,y) = \begin{cases} x^2+2y & (x,y)\neq(1,2) \\ 5 & (x,y)=(1,2) \end{cases}$$

$\Rightarrow$ $f(x, y)$ is continuous.
Hence, $f(x, y)$ has removable discontinuity at (1, 2).

**14.** We have,

$$\lim_{x\to 0} f(x,0) = \lim_{x\to 0} 0 = 0$$

$$= f(0,0)$$

and $$\lim_{y\to 0} f(0,y) = \lim_{y\to 0} 0 = 0$$

$$= f(0,0)$$

Again, we approaches along line $y = mx$, we have

$$\lim_{x\to 0} f(x,mx) = \lim_{x\to 0} \frac{2\cdot x\cdot mx}{x^2+mx}$$

$$= \lim_{x\to 0} \frac{2m\cdot x^2}{x^2\left(1+\frac{m}{x}\right)}$$

$$= \lim_{x\to 0} \frac{2m}{1+\frac{m}{x}}$$

which does not exists. Hence, $f(x, y)$ is discontinuous at origin.

$$\therefore \quad \lim_{(x,y)\to(0,0)} f(x,y) \neq f(0,0)$$

**16.** We have

$$\lim_{y\to 0} f(x,y) = \begin{cases} 1 \text{ if } x\neq 0 \\ 0 \text{ if } x = 0 \end{cases}$$

$$\therefore \quad \lim_{x\to 0}\lim_{y\to 0} f(x,y) = 1$$

Similarly

$$\lim_{y\to 0}\lim_{x\to 0} f(x,y) = 1$$

Again, since there are points arbitrary near (0, 0) at which $f$ is equal to 0 and points arbitrary near (0, 0) at which $f$ is equal to 1. Therefore, there is an $\varepsilon > 0$, such that

$$|f(x,y) - f(0,0)| = |f(x,y)| \not< \varepsilon$$

for all points in any *nbd* of (0, 0).
Hence, $\lim_{(x,y)\to(0,0)} f(x,y)$ does not exists.

**20.** (a) Putting $x = r\cos\theta, y = r\sin\theta$

$$\therefore \quad |f(x,y)-0| = \left|xy\frac{x^2-y^2}{x^2+y^2}\right|$$

$$= |r^2\sin\theta\cos\theta\cos 2\theta|$$

$$= \left|\frac{r^2}{4}\sin 4\theta\right|$$

$$\leq \frac{r^2}{4}$$

$$= \frac{x^2+y^2}{4} < \varepsilon$$

If $\frac{x^2}{4} < \frac{\varepsilon}{2}$ and $\frac{y^2}{4} < \frac{\varepsilon}{2}$

or if $|x| < \sqrt{2\varepsilon} = \delta, |y| = \sqrt{2\varepsilon} = \delta$

$\therefore$ For given $\varepsilon > 0, \exists\, \delta > 0$, such that

$$\left|xy\frac{x^2-y^2}{x^2+y^2} - 0\right| < \varepsilon \text{ whenever } |x| < \delta, |y| < \delta$$

$$\Rightarrow \quad \lim_{(x,y)\to(0,0)} xy\frac{x^2-y^2}{x^2+y^2} = 0$$

(b) If we put $x = my^2$ and let $y \to 0$, we get

$$\lim_{y\to 0} \frac{2my^4}{(1+m^2)y^4} = \frac{2m}{1+m^2}$$

which is different for different value of $m$.

Hence, $\lim_{(x,y)\to(0,0)} \frac{2xy^2}{x^2+y^4}$ does not exists.

(c) Since, x, y are small

$$\therefore \quad \frac{\sqrt{x^2y^2+1}-1}{x^2+y^2} = \frac{(1+x^2y^2)^{1/2}-1}{x^2+y^2}$$

$$\simeq \frac{\frac{1}{2}x^2y^2}{x^2+y^2}$$

by changing in polar coordinates, we get

$$\lim_{(x,y)\to(0,0)} \frac{\frac{1}{2}x^2y^2}{x^2+y^2} = 0$$

(d) $$\lim_{(x,y)\to(0,0)} \left(\frac{1}{xy}\right)\sin(x^2y+xy^2) = 0$$

**23.** We have

$$f_x(0,0) = \lim_{h\to 0} \frac{f(0+h,0)-f(0,0)}{h}$$

$$= \lim_{h\to 0} \frac{f(h,0)}{h}$$

$$= \lim_{h\to 0} 0$$

$$= 0$$

and $$f_y(0,0) = \lim_{k\to 0} \frac{f(0,0+k)-f(0,0)}{k}$$

$$= \lim_{k\to 0} \frac{f(0,k)}{k}$$

$$= \lim_{k\to 0} 0$$

$$= 0$$

$\therefore$ $xf_x + yf_y = 2f$

$xf_x - yf_y = 2f$

$yf_x + xf_y = 2f$

$yf_x - xf_y = 2f$

**24.** Given that

$f(x, y) = x^y$

$\therefore$ $f_x(x, y) = yx^{y-1}$

$\therefore$ $f_x(a, 1) = 1$

and $f_y(x, y) = x^y \log_e x$

$\therefore$ $f_y(e, 0) = 1$

and $f_{xy}(x, y) = yx^{y-1}(\log_e x) + x^y \cdot \dfrac{1}{x}$

$\therefore$ $f_{xy}(1, 0) = 1$

and $f_{yx}(x, y) = x^{y-1} + yx^{y-1} \cdot \log_e x$

$\therefore$ $f_{yx}(1, 1) = 1$

**25.** Let us approaches along the line $y = mx$, we get

$$\lim_{x\to 0} f(x, mx) = \lim_{x\to 0} \frac{1}{x^2 + m^2x^2}$$

$$= \lim_{x\to 0} \frac{1}{x^2(1+m^2)}$$

which does not exists. Hence, $f(x, y)$ discontinuous at origin and hence $f(x, y)$ is not differentiable at origin.

**26.** We have $(x, y) \neq (2, 3)$

$$\therefore \lim_{(x,y)\to(2,3)} f(x, y) = \lim_{(x,y)\to(2,3)} 3xy$$

$$= 3 \times 2 \times 3 = 18$$

**27.** We have

$$\left| \frac{xy}{\sqrt{x^2+y^2}} - 0 \right| = \frac{|xy|}{\sqrt{x^2+y^2}}$$

Also,

$$x^2 + y^2 - |xy| = \left(|x| - \frac{1}{2}|y|\right)^2 + \frac{1}{2}|y^2| \geq 0$$

$$\Rightarrow x^2 + y^2 - |xy| \geq 0$$

$$\Rightarrow \frac{|xy|}{\sqrt{x^2+y^2}} \leq \sqrt{x^2+y^2}$$

for all $(x, y) \neq (0, 0)$

Thus, $\left| \dfrac{xy}{\sqrt{x^2+y^2}} - 0 \right| < \varepsilon$, if $\sqrt{x^2+y^2} < \varepsilon$

and accordingly $f$ is continuous at $(0, 0)$.

Also, it is easy to see that $f_x(0, 0) = 0 = f_y(0, 0)$ so that if $f$ were differentiable at $(0, 0)$, we should have, by definition,

$$\frac{hk}{\sqrt{h^2+k^2}} = 0 \cdot h + 0 \cdot k + \sqrt{h^2+k^2}\,\phi(h, k) \quad \text{...(i)}$$

where $\phi(h, k) \to 0$ as $(h, k) \to (0, 0)$.

We have $\phi(h, k) = \dfrac{hk}{h^2+k^2}$

where $\displaystyle\lim_{(h,k)\to(0,0)} \phi(h, k) = 0$

Thus, we arrive at a contradiction in as much as $\displaystyle\lim_{(h,k)\to(0,0)} \frac{hk}{h^2+k^2}$ does not exist.

**28.** $\displaystyle\lim_{\substack{(x,y)\to(0,0)\\ y=x-mx^3}} f(x, y) = \lim_{x\to 0} f(x, x - mx^3)$

$$= \lim_{x\to 0} \frac{x^3 + (x - mx^3)^3}{x - (x - mx^3)}$$

$$= \lim_{x\to 0} \frac{x^3\{1 + (1 - mx^2)^3\}}{mx^3}$$

$$= \lim_{x\to 0} \frac{1}{m}\{2 - m^3x^6 - 3mx^2 + 3m^2x^4\}$$

$$= \lim_{x\to 0} \left\{\frac{2}{m} - m^2x^6 - 3x^2 + 3mx^4\right\}$$

$$= \frac{2}{m}$$

$\therefore$ The limit depends on the value of $m$ and hence is not unique.

$\therefore$ $\displaystyle\lim_{(x,y)\to(0,0)} f(x, y)$ does not exist and so $f$ is not continuous at the origin.

But $\displaystyle f_x(0, 0) = \lim_{h\to 0} \frac{f(0+h, 0) - f(0, 0)}{h}$

$$= \lim_{h\to 0} \frac{\frac{h^3}{h} - 0}{h} = \lim_{h\to 0} h = 0$$

and $\displaystyle f_y(0, 0) = \lim_{k\to 0} \frac{f(0, 0+k) - f(0, 0)}{k}$

$$= \lim_{k\to 0} \frac{\frac{k^3}{-k} - 0}{k}$$

$$= \lim_{k\to 0}(-k) = 0 \text{ exist}$$

**29.** (i) $\displaystyle f_{xy}(0, 0) = \lim_{h\to 0} \frac{f_y(0+h, 0) - f_y(0, 0)}{h}$

But $\displaystyle f_y(0, 0) = \lim_{k\to 0} \frac{f(0, 0+k) - f(0, 0)}{k}$

$$= \lim_{k\to 0} \frac{0}{k} = 0$$

and $\displaystyle f_y(h, 0) = \lim_{k\to 0} \frac{f(h, 0+k) - f(h, 0)}{k}$

$$= \lim_{k\to 0} \frac{hk(h^2 - k^2)}{k(h^2 + k^2)} = h$$

$\therefore$ $\displaystyle f_{xy}(0, 0) = \lim_{h\to 0} \frac{h - 0}{h} = 1$

(ii) $\displaystyle f_{yx}(0, 0) = \lim_{k\to 0} \frac{f_x(0, 0+k) - f_x(0, 0)}{k}$

But $\displaystyle f_x(0, 0) = \lim_{h\to 0} \frac{f(0+h, 0) - f(0, 0)}{h}$

$$= 0$$

and $f_x(0, k) = \lim_{h\to 0} \dfrac{f(0+h, k) - f(0, k)}{h}$

$= \lim_{h\to 0} \dfrac{hk(h^2 - k^2)}{h(h^2 + k^2)}$

$= -k$

$\therefore \quad f_{yx}(0, 0) = \lim_{k\to 0} \dfrac{-k-0}{k}$

$= -1$

**31.** We have

$f_x(x, y) = 3x^2 - 3 = 0$, when $x = \pm 1$

$f_y(x, y) = 3y^2 - 12 = 0$, when $y = \pm 2$

Thus, the function has four stationary points given by

$(1, 2), (-1, -2), (1, -2), (-1, 2)$

Now, $f_{xx}(x, y) = 6x$

$f_{xy}(x, y) = 0$

$f_{yy}(x, y) = 6y$

At (1, 2),

$f_{xy} = 6 > 0$ and $f_{xx}f_{yy} - (f_{xy})^2 = 72 > 0$

Thus, (1, 2) is a point of minima.

At (−1, −2)

$f_{xx} = -6 < 0$ and $f_{xx}f_{yy} - (f_{xy})^2 = 72 > 0$

Thus, (1, 2) is a point of minima.

At (−1, −2),

$f_{xx} = -6 < 0$ and $f_{xx}f_{yy} - (f_{xy})^2 = 72 > 0$

Thus, (−1, −2) is a point of maxima.

At (−1, 2),

$f_{xx} = -6 < 0$ and $f_{xx}f_{yy} - (f_{xy})^2 = -72 < 0$

Thus, the function has neither maxima nor minima at (−1, 2).

At (1, −2)

$f_{xx} = 6 > 0$ and $f_{xx}f_{yy} - (f_{xy})^2 = -72 < 0$

Thus, the function has neither maxima nor minima at (1, −2).

Therefore, (−1, 2) and (1, −2) are saddle points.

# 7 Functions of Bounded Variation, Lebesgue Measure and Metric Space

## Function of Bounded Variation

**Syllabus**

- Functions of Bounded Variation
- Lebesgue Measure
- Lebesgue Integral
- Metric Space
- Connectedness
- Compactness
- Normed Linear Space

Suppose a real-valued function is defined on a closed interval [a, b]. The interval [a, b] is divided by means of points.

$$a = x_0 < x_1 < x_2 < x_3 < \ldots < x_n = b$$

Define $V = \sum_{k=0}^{n-1} |f(x_{k+1} - f(x_k)|$

The least upper bound of the set of all possible sums $V$ is called the total variation of $f$ and is denoted by $\overset{b}{\underset{a}{V}}(f)$.

i.e., $\overset{b}{\underset{a}{V}}(f) = \text{Sup } V$. If $\overset{b}{\underset{a}{V}}$ = finite, then $f$ is called a function of finite variation or function of bounded variation. This can also be say that $f$ has finite variation in [a, b].

## Important Theorems on Function of Bounded Variation

***Theorem 1*** If $f$ is function of bounded variation on $[a, b]$, then it is bounded on $[a, b]$.

***Theorem 2*** If the derivative $f'(x)$ exists and is bounded in closed interval $[a, b]$, then the function $f$ is function of bounded variation.

***Theorem 3*** If $c \in [a, b]$, then $f$ is function of bounded variation on $[a, c]$ and $[c, b]$, if $f$ is function of bounded variation on $[a, b]$.

Also, $$V(f, [a, b]) = V(f, [a, c]) + V(f, [c, b])$$

## Absolutely Continuous Functions

A real-valued function $f$ defined on $[a, b]$ is said to be absolutely continuous on $[a, b]$, if for any arbitrary $\varepsilon > 0$ however small $\exists\ a,\ \delta > 0$ such that

$$\sum_{r=1}^{n} |f(b_r) - f(a_r)| < \varepsilon, \text{ whenever } \sum_{r=1}^{n} [(b_r) - (a_r)] < \delta,$$

where $a_1 < b_1 \le a_2 < b_2 \le \ldots \le a_n < b_n$ that is $a_i$'s and $b_i$'s are forming finite collection $\{(a_i, b_i) : i = 1, 2, 3, \ldots, n\}$ of pairwise disjoint (non-overlapping) intervals.

Definitely every absolutely continuous function is continuous.

## Lipschitz Condition

A function $f$ is said to satisfy Lipschitz condition, if $\exists$ positive constant $M$ s.t.

$$|f(x) - f(y)| \le M\,|x - y|$$

## Variation Function

Let $f$ be a function of bounded variation on $[a, b]$ and $x \in [a, b]$. The total variation of $f$ on $[a, x]$ is denoted by $V(f, [a, x])$, which is obviously a function of $x$.

Now, $v(x) = V_f(x) = V(f, [a, x])$

Then, $V_f(x)$ is defined as variation function or total variation function of $f$.

> ***Note*** $v(x)$ is monotonic non-decreasing function on $[a, b]$.

## Important Theorems on Variation Function

1. The variation function $v(x)$ of a function of bounded variation is continuous if and only if $f$ is continuous function.
2. A monotonic function is a function of bounded variation or we can say that, every increasing function on $[a, b]$ is of bounded variation.
3. A function $f$ is of bounded variation iff it is expressible as a difference of two monotonic functions both non-increasing or both non-decreasing.
4. If $f$ and $g$ are functions of bounded variation on $[a, b]$, then their sum $f + g$, product $fg$ and difference $f - g$ are functions of bounded variation on $[a, b]$.
5. If a function $f$ is of bounded variation of $[a, b]$ and if $\exists\ k > 0$ s.t. $|f(x)| \ge k,\ \forall\ x \in [a, b]$, then $1/f$ is also of bounded variation.
6. A function of bounded variation is expressible as a difference of two monotonic increasing functions.
7. Every absolute continuous function $f$ defined on $[a, b]$ is bounded variation.
8. If a function $f$ is of bounded variation of $[a, b]$ and if $\exists,\ k > 0$ s.t. $|f(x)| \ge k,\ \forall\ x \in [a, b]$, then $1/f$ is also of bounded variation.
9. A function $f$ of bounded variation is expressible as a difference of two monotonic increasing functions.

## Lebesgue Outer Measure of a Set

The outer lebesgue measure of a set $A \subseteq R$ is defined by

$$m*(A) = \begin{cases} 0, & \text{if } A = \phi \\ \text{Inf } \{y : y = \Sigma |I_i|\}, & \end{cases}$$

(where, $\{I_i\}$ is a countable family of disjoint open intervals s.t. $\cup I_i \supseteq A$, when $A \ne \phi$ and is denoted by $m*(A)$.

> ***Note*** **(a)** Outer lebesgue measure is also known as lebesgue exterior measure and is also denoted by $m_c(A)$ or $\overline{m}(A)$.
>
> **(b)** $m^*(A)$ is non-negative *i.e.* $m^*(A) \ge 0$.
>
> **(c)** For every set $A$, $m^*(A)$ is unique.
>
> **(d)** If $A = \{a\}$, then $m^*(A) = 0$
>
> **(e)** If $A \subseteq [a, b]$, then $m^*(A) \le (b - a)$
>
> **(f)** If $G$ is an open set of real number, then $m^*(G) = |G|$.
>
> **(g)** If $I$ is an interval of the real line, then $m^*(I) =$ length of $I$.
>
> **(h)** If $A \subseteq B \Rightarrow m^*(A) \subseteq m^*(B)$

## Important Theorems on Outer Measure

***Theorem 1*** If $\{A_1, A_2, A_3, \ldots\}$ is a countable family of subsets on $R$, then $m^d(\bigcup_n A_n) \le \sum_{n=1}^{\infty} m^d(A_n)$

[This property is known as countably subadditive]

***Theorem 2*** If $A$ is countable set, then $m^d(A) = 0$.

***Theorem 3*** If $A$ and $B$ are any two disjoint subsets of $R$, then

$$m^d(A \cup B) = m^d(A) + m^d(B)$$

***Theorem 4*** The outer measure of an interval is its length.

> ***Note*** **(a)** A set without measure different from zero is uncountable.
>
> **(b)** A set with outer measure zero may or may not be countable.

## Lebesgue Inner Measure of a Set

A inner measure of a set $A$, denoted by $m_*(A)$ and is defined as

$$m_*(A) = b - a - m^*(A^c)$$

where, $A^c$ is the complement of $A$ relative to $[a, b]$ s.t. $A \subset [a, b]$.

> **Note** **(a)** Lebesgue inner measure is also known as lebesgue interior measure and is also denoted by $m_c(A)$ or $\underline{m}(A)$.
> **(b)** $m_*(A)$ is non-negative *i.e.*, $m_*(A) \geq 0$.
> **(c)** For every set $A$, $m_*(A)$ is unique.
> **(d)** If $H$ is closed set, then $m_*(H) = |H|$.
> **(e)** $m_*(\phi) = 0$

***Theorem*** For any set $A \subset R$, $m^*(A) \geq m_*(A)$.

## Lebesgue Measurable Sets

The set $A$ is said to be lebesgue measurable, if $m^*(A) = m_*(A)$ and the common value is called its measure and is denoted by $m(A)$. Thus, if $A$ is lebesgue measurable, then

$$m^*(A) = m_*(A) = m(A)$$

> ***Note*** The set $A$ is said to be lebesgue measurable, if for each set $E$, we have
> $$m^*(E) = m^*(E \cap A) + m^*(E \cap A^c)$$

### Important Theorems on Lebesgue Measurable Set

1. A linear set $A$ of outer measure zero is lebesgue measurable.
2. Any subset of $A$ whose outer measure is zero, is also measurable.
   For $B \subseteq A \Rightarrow m^*(B) \leq m^*(A) \Rightarrow m^*(B) \leq 0$. Also, $m^*(B) \geq 0 \Rightarrow m^*(B) = 0$, therefore $B$ is measurable.
3. Every countable set is $\alpha$-measurable and its measure is zero.
4. Let $A$ and $B$ be two sets s.t. $A \subseteq B$, then
   (i) $m^*(A) \leq m^*(B)$ (ii) $m_*(A) \leq m_*(B)$
5. Every bounded open set and every bounded closed set is measurable.
6. Any set $A$ is measurable if and only if an open set $G$ containing $A$ and a closed set $H$ contained in $A$ can be so determined, that $|G| - |H| < \varepsilon$, where $\varepsilon$ is an arbitrary positive real number.
7. Union of two measurable sets is also measurable.
8. The union of a finite number of measurable sets is also measurable.
9. If a measurable set $G_1$ contains another measurable set $G_2$, then the set $G_1 - G_2$ is measurable and its measure is $m(G_1) - m(G_2)$.
10. (First Fundamental Theorem) If $E_1, E_2, E_3, \ldots$ are pairwise disjoint measurable sets and $E = E_1 \cup E_2 \cup \ldots$, then $E$ is measurable and $m(E) = \sum_{k=1}^{\infty} m(E_k)$.
11. If $E_1, E_2, E_3, \ldots$ are any measurable sets of real numbers, then $\bigcup_{n=1}^{\infty} E_n$ is measurable and $m\left(\bigcup_{n=1}^{\infty} E_n\right) \leq \sum_{n=1}^{\infty} m(E_n)$.
12. (Second Fundamental Theorem) If $E_1, E_2, \ldots$ are measurable sets, then the set $\bigcap_{k=1}^{\infty} E_k$ is measurable.
13. Suppose, that $< E_n >$ is a monotonic increasing or non-decreasing sequence of measurable sets, let $E = \bigcup_{k=1}^{\infty} E_k$, then $m(E) = \lim_{n \to \infty} m(E_n)$.
14. If $E_1, E_2, \ldots$ is a monotonic decreasing or non-increasing sequence of measurable sets and $E = \bigcap_{k=1}^{\infty} E_k$, then $m(E) = \lim_{n \to \infty} m(E_n)$.
15. Cantor ternary set is measurable and its measure is zero.
16. A set $A$ is lebesgue measurable if and only if its complement $A^C$ is measurable.
17. If set $A$ is lebesgue measurable and $m^*(A \Delta B) = 0$, then $B$ is also measurable.

## Partition

By a measurable partition of $[a, b]$, we mean any finite collection $[S_r, r = 1, 2, 3, \ldots, n]$ of measurable subsets of $[a, b]$ s.t.

$$\bigcup_{r=1}^{n} S_r = [a, b]$$

and s.t. $m(S_i \cap S_j) = 0, \ \forall \ i, j = 1, 2, 3, \ldots, n, \ (i \neq j)$. The partition of an interval is denoted by $P$.

**Note** **(a)** The sets $S_1, S_2, \ldots, S_n$ are called components of the partition $P$. i.e., $P = \{S_1, S_2, S_3, \ldots, S_n\}$.
**(b)** A measurable partition $P$ of an interval $[a, b]$ is nothing but a finite collection of subsets of $[a, b]$ whose union is the whole $[a, b]$ and whose pairwise intersection have the measure zero.

### Refinement of a Partition

Let $P$ be a measurable partition of the closed interval $[a, b]$ and $P^*$ be another measurable partition of $[a, b]$ s.t. every component of $P$; then $P^*$ is called a refinement of $P$.

### Supremum and Infimum of a Function on a Set

Let $E$ be a subset of $[a, b]$ and $f$ be a bounded function on $[a, b]$. Then, we define

$$M[f; E] = \sup\{f(x) : x \in E\}$$
$$m[f; E] = \inf\{f(x) : x \in E\}$$

## Lower and Upper Lebesgue Sums

Let $P = \{S_1, S_2, \ldots, S_n\}$ be a measurable partition of the closed interval $[a, b]$ and $f$ be a bounded function defined on $[a, b]$, then we define

$$U[f; P] = \text{Upper Lebesgue Sum} = \sum_{r=1}^{n} M[f; S_r] \cdot m(S_r)$$

and

$$L[f; P] = \text{Lower Lebesgue Sum} = \sum_{r=1}^{n} M[f; S_r] \cdot m(S_r)$$

where, $m(S_r)$ is the lebesgue measure of $S_r$.

**Note** $L[f; P] \le U[f; P]$

## Upper and Lower Lebesgue Integrals

Let $f$ be a bounded function defined on $[a, b]$. The supremum of $L[f : Q]$ is called the lower lebesgue integral on $[a, b]$ and is denoted by $L\underline{\int_a^b} f(x)\,dx$.

Supremum is taken overall measurable partitions $Q$ of $[a, b]$. The infimum of $U[f; P]$ is called the upper lebesgue integral and is denoted by $L\overline{\int_a^b} f(x)\,dx$.

Therefore, $L\underline{\int_a^b} f(x)dx = \sup\{L[f; Q] : Q$ is a measurable partition of $[a, b]\}$

and $L\overline{\int_a^b} f(x)\,dx = \inf\{U[f; P]: P$ is a measurable partition of $[a, b]\}$.

**Note** **(a)** $L(-f; Q) = -U[f; Q]$ and $U[-f, P] = -L[f, P]$

**(b)** $L\underline{\int_a^b}(-f) = -\left(L\overline{\int_a^b} f\right)$ and $L\overline{\int_a^b}(-f) = -L\underline{\int_a^b} f$

**(c)** $L\underline{\int_a^b} f \ge [f; Q], \forall Q$

**(d)** $L\overline{\int_a^b} f \le U[f; P], \forall P$

**(e)** For every $\varepsilon > 0$, however small, there always exists atleast one partition $P'$ s.t.

$$L\overline{\int_a^b} f + \varepsilon > U[f; P']$$

**(f)** For every $\varepsilon > 0$, however small, there always exists atleast one partition $Q'$ s.t.

$$L\underline{\int_a^b} f - \varepsilon > U[f; Q'].$$

## Lebesgue Integral

Let $f$ be a bounded function defined on the interval $[a, b]$; we say that $f$ is lebesgue integral on $[a, b]$ iff

$$L\underline{\int_a^b} f = L\overline{\int_a^b} f$$

and their common value is called the L-integral of $f$ on $[a, b]$ and is denoted by $\int_a^b f$.

## Important Theorems on Lebesgue Integral

***Theorem 1*** Let $f$ be a bounded function defined on $[a, b]$. Then, every upper sum is greater than or equal to every lower sum for $f$.

***Theorem 2*** If $f$ is a bounded function defined on $[a, b]$ and $f$ is R-integrable on $[a, b]$, then $f$ is also L-integrable on $[a, b]$ and $L\int_a^b f = R\int_a^b f$.

***Theorem 3*** (First Mean Value Theorem) Let $f$ be a bounded measurable real-valued function s.t. $a \le f(x) \le b$ on a measurable set $E[p, q] \subset R$.
Then,

$$a \cdot m(E) \le \int_E f(x)\,dx \le b \cdot m(E)$$

***Theorem 4*** Let $f$ be a bounded function defined on $[a, b]$. Then, the function $f$ is L-integrable if and only if for each $\varepsilon > 0$, however small, $\exists$ a measurable partition $P$ of $[a, b]$ s.t.

$$U[f; P] - L[f; P] < \varepsilon$$

## Metric Space

Suppose $X$ be a non-empty set. We have,

$$X \times X = \{(x, y) : x \in X, y \in X\}$$

A real-valued function $d$ defined on $X \times X$ *i.e.,* $d : X \times X \to R$ is called a metric on $X$, if it satisfies the following axioms

(i) $M_1 : d(x, y) \geq 0, \ \forall \ x, y \in X$
(ii) $M_2 : d(x, y) = 0 \Leftrightarrow x = y$
(iii) $M_3 : d(x, y) = d(y, x), \ \forall \ x, y \in X$ (symmetry)
(iv) $M_4 : d(x, z) \leq d(x, y) + d(y, z), \ \forall \ x, y, z \in X$ (triangle inequality)

The pair $(X, d)$ is called a metric space and $d(x, y)$ is called the distance between the points $x$ and $y$.

***Example 1.*** *Show that the Euclidean plane $R^2$ is a metric space wrt the metric $d^*$ defined by*

$$d^*(x, y) = \max\{|x_1 - y_1|, |x_2 - y_2|\}$$

*where,* $x = (x_1, x_2) \in R^2$ *and* $y = (y_1, y_2) \in R^2$.

**Solution.** We have,

$$d^*(x, y) = \max\{|x_1 - y_1|, |x_2 - y_2|\} \quad \text{...(i)}$$

Clearly, $d^*(x, y) \geq 0, \ \forall \ x, y \in R^2$

Now, $d^*(x, y) = 0 \Leftrightarrow \max\{|x_1 - y_1|, |x_2 - y_2|\} = 0$

$\Leftrightarrow x_1 = y_1$ and $x_2 = y_2$

$\Leftrightarrow (x_1, x_2)$ and $(y_1, y_2)$

$\Leftrightarrow x = y$

$$d^*(x, y) = \max\{|x_1 - y_1|, |x_2 - y_2|\}$$
$$= \max\{|y_1 - x_1|, |y_2 - x_2|\}$$
$$= d^*(y, x)$$

Now, we shall prove triangle inequality $M_4$.

Let $x = (x_1, x_2)$, $y = (y_1, y_2)$, $z = (z_1, z_2)$ be the three points of $R^2$.

We have,

$$|x_1 - z_1| = |(x_1 - y_1) + (y_1 - z_1)|$$
$$\leq |x_1 - y_1| + |y_1 - z_1|$$
$$\leq \max\{|x_1 - y_1|, |x_2 - y_2|\} + \max\{|y_1 - z_1|, |y_2 - z_2|\} \quad \text{...(ii)}$$

$\therefore$ $|x_1 - z_1| \leq d^*(x, y) + d^*(y, z)$ [using Eq. (i)]

Again, $|x_2 - z_2| = |(x_2 - y_2) + (y_2 - z_2)|$

$$\leq |x_2 - y_2| + |y_2 - z_2|$$
$$\leq \max\{|x_1 - y_1|, |x_2 - y_2|\} + \max\{|y_1 - z_1|, |y_2 - z_2|\}$$

$\therefore$ $|x_2 - z_2| \leq d^*(x, y) + d^*(y, z)$ ...(iii)

Using Eqs. (ii) and (iii), we get

$$\max\{|x_1 - z_1|, |x_2 - z_2|\} \leq d^*(x, y) + d^*(y, z)$$

$\Rightarrow$ $d^*(x, z) \leq d^*(x, y) + d^*(y, z)$

Hence, $(R^2, d^*)$ is a metric space.

## Open Ball or Open Sphere

Let $(X, d)$ be a metric space and $a \in X$. If $r > 0$, then the set $\{x \in X : d(a, x) < r\}$ is called open ball or open sphere of radius $r$ centred at a.

It is denoted by $B(a, r)$ or $S_r(a)$. Therefore,

$$B(a, r) = \{x \in X : d(a, x) < r\}$$

## Closed Ball or Closed Sphere

Let $(X, d)$ be a metric space and $a \in X$. If $r > 0$, then the set $\{x \in X : d(a, x) \leq r\}$ is closed a $d$-closed ball or closed ball or closed sphere of radius $r$ centred at a. It is denoted by

$$B^*(a, r) \text{ or } S_r[a] \text{ or } B^*(a, r : a).$$

Therefore,

$$B^*(a, r) = \{x \in X : d(a, x) \leq r\}$$

Clearly, $B(a, r) \subset B^*(a, r)$, for each $a \in X$ and for every $r > 0$.

***Example 2.*** *Explain geometrically the open ball with centre* (0, 0) *and radius* 2 *in* $(R^2, d)$.

**Solution.** An open ball with centre (0, 0) and radius 1 in $(R^2, d)$, where, $d\{(x_1, x_2), (y_1, y_2)\} = |x_1 - y_1| + |x_2 - y_2|$ is given by $B[(0, 0), 1] = \{(x_1, x_2) \in R^2 : |x_1| + |x_2| < 1\}$

Geometrically, this open ball can be described as

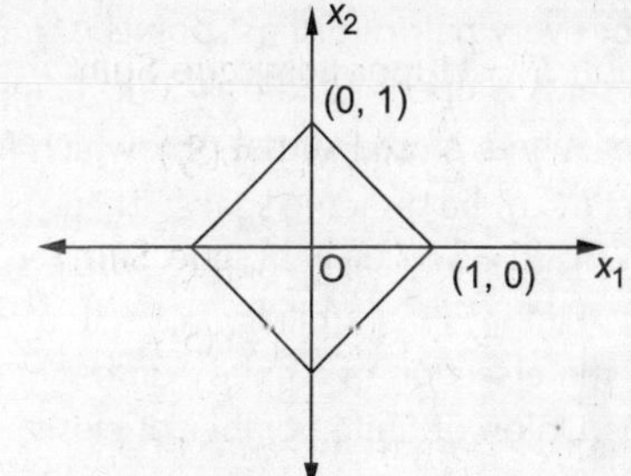


# Neighbourhoods, Limit Points Open and Closed Sets, Neighbourhood of a Point

Let $(X, d)$ be a metric space and $S \subset X$. The set $S$ is called a neighbourhood of a point $a \in X$, if $\exists$ some $\varepsilon > 0$ s.t. $B(a, \varepsilon) \subset S$. In abbrivated form neighbourhood is written as *nhd* or *nbd*. *e.g.,* $]a, b[$ is a neighbourhood of all its points except a.

## Limit Point

A point $a$ is said to be a limit point of the set $A$, if every neighbourhood of a contains a point of $A$ other than a. The set of all limit points of $A$ is called the derived set of $A$ and shall be denoted by $D(A)$.

*e.g.,* The set $\left\{1, \frac{1}{2}, \frac{1}{3}, \ldots\right\}$ has exactly one limit point 0, thus $S' = \{0\}$.

## Open Set

Let $(X, d)$ be a metric space and $S \subset X$. Then, $S$ is called an open set or $d$-open set, if it is a *nhd* of all its points. We can also say that, $S$ is an open set if for each $x \in S$, there exists some $\varepsilon > 0$ s.t. $B(x, \varepsilon) \in S$. It is noted that, if a set $S \subset X$ will not be an open set, if it is not a *nbd* of even one point of it.

e.g., Any metric space $X$ is open, since for each $x \in X$ and any $\varepsilon > 0$, $B(x, \varepsilon) \subset X$.

## Closed Sets

Let $(X, d)$ be a metric space. A set $S \subset X$ is called a closed set if and only if its complement $X \sim S$ is open.

Thus, $S$ is closed $\Leftrightarrow X \sim S$ is open.

e.g., Any metric space $X$ is closed.

$\because \quad X \sim X = \phi$, which is open.

## Important Theorems on Neighbourhood of a Point, Limit Points, Open and Closed Sets

1. Let $(X, d)$ be a metric space and $M \subset X$. If $M$ is a *nbd* of a point $p \in X$ and $N \supset M$, then N is also a *nhd* of p.
2. In a metric space $(X, d)$ the intersection of two neighbourhoods of a point $p \in X$ is a neighbourhood of $p$.
3. The intersection of a finite number of neighbourhoods of a point $p \in X$ is a *nbd* of p, however, the intersection of an arbitrary family of neighbourhoods of a point $p \in X$ may not be a *nhd* of p.

   e.g., $S = \left\{ \left] -\frac{1}{n}, \frac{1}{n} \right[ : n \in N \right\}$ is a family of infinite number of *nbds* of zero.

   But $\bigcap_{n=1}^{\infty} \left] -\frac{1}{n}, \frac{1}{n} \right[ = \{0\}$, which is not a neighbourhood of 0.
4. In a metric space every neighbourhood is an open set.
5. A subset of a metric space $(X, d)$ is open if and only, if it is a union of open balls.
6. For every pair of distinct points $p, q$ in a metric space $(X, d)$, $\exists$ disjoint open sets $U, V$ s.t. $p \in U$, $q \in V$.
7. A set $A$ is open if and only if its complement is closed.
8. Let $A$ be a closed subset of $R$ which is bounded above. If $u$ be the lub of $A$, then $u \in A$.
9. Let $(X, d)$ be a metric space. Then,
   (i) The empty set $\phi$ and the whole space $X$ are open as well as closed.
   (ii) Union of an arbitrary collection of open sets is open.
   (iii) Intersection of a finite number of open sets is open.
   (iv) Union of finite number of closed sets is closed.
   (v) Intersection of an arbitrary collection of closed sets is closed.
10. A subset of a metric space $(X, d)$ is closed iff it contains all its limit points.
11. Let $(X, d)$ be a metric space and $S \subset X$. A point $p \in X$ is a limit point of $S$ iff every neighbourhood of $p$ contains infinitely many points of $S$.
12. Finite sets in a metric space have no limit points.
13. In a metric space $(X, d)$, every finite set is closed.
14. In a metric space every singleton set $\{p\}$ is closed.

***Example 3.*** *Prove that in a metric space, every finite set is closed.*

**Solution.** Let $S = \{x_1, x_2, x_3, \ldots, x_n\}$ be any finite set in a metric space $(X, d)$, then

$$S = \{x_1\} \cup \{x_2\} \cup \ldots \cup \{x_n\} \quad \ldots\text{(i)}$$

Since, every singleton in a metric space is $X$, is closed. Therefore, $\{x_1\} \cup \{x_2\} \cup \{x_3\} \cup \ldots \cup \{x_n\}$ is closed. Hence, $S$ is closed.

# Connectedness

## Subspace of X

Let $(X, d)$ be a metric space and let $A$ be a subset of $X$. Let $d^*$ denote restriction of $d$ to $A \times A$,

i.e. $\quad d^*(x, y) = d(x, y)$

where $x, y$ are points of $A$. Then, $d^*$ is a metric for $A$ called the reduced matrix and the set $A$ with metric $d^*$ is called subspace of $X$.

## Separated Sets

Two non-empty subsets $P$ and $Q$ of a metric space $(X, d)$ are said to be separated if and only if $P \cap \overline{Q} = \phi$ and $\overline{P} \cap Q = \phi$.

> **Note** If $P$ and $Q$ are two separated sets, $S \subset P, T \subset Q$, then $S$ and $T$ are also separated sets because $S \cap \overline{T} \subset P \cap \overline{Q} = \phi$ and $\overline{S} \cap T \subset \overline{P} \cap Q = \phi$.
> *e.g.,* $P = ]0, 2[$ and $Q = ]2, 3[$ are separated subsets of $R$, because $\overline{P} = [0, 2]$ and $\overline{Q} = [2, 3]$, $P \cap \overline{Q} = \phi$ and $\overline{P} \cap Q = \phi$.

## Disconnected Metric Space

A metric space $(X, d)$ is called disconnected, if $X$ can be expressed as union of two separated sets s.t.

$X = P \cup Q$, where $P \cap \overline{Q} = \phi$ and $\overline{P} \cap Q = \phi$. Thus, we say that the pair $(P, Q)$ is a separation or disconnection of $X$.

*e.g.,* The metric space $Q$ of all rationals with usual metric is disconnected.

## Connected Metric Space

A metric space $(X, d)$ is called connected, if it is not disconnected means $X$ cannot be expressed, as the union of two separated sets.

*e.g.,* The bounded intervals $]a, b[$, $]a, b]$ and $[a, b]$ are connected.

## Connected Set

A subset $S$ of a metric space $(X, d)$ is said to be disconnected if and only if the subspace $(S, ds)$ is disconnected, where $ds(x, y) = d(x, y), \ \forall \ x, y \in S$.

> **Note** Every singleton set is a connected set.

## Important Theorems on Connectedness

***Theorem 1*** $R$ is connected.

***Theorem 2*** A subset $A$ of $R$ is connected iff it is an interval.

***Theorem 3*** Let $(X, d)$ be a metric space. The following conditions are equivalent

**(i)** $(X, d)$ is disconnected.

**(ii)** is expressed as the union of two disjoint, non-empty open sets.

**(iii)** $X$ is expressed as the union of two disjoint non-empty closed sets.

**(iv)** There exists a non-empty, proper subset of $X$, which is both open and closed.

***Theorem 4*** A metric space $(X, d)$ is connected if and only if $X$ and $\phi$ are the only subsets of $X$, which are both open and closed.

***Theorem 5*** A metric space $(X, d)$ is connected if and only if $X$ is not the union of two non-empty, disjoint, closed sets.

***Theorem 6*** A metric space $(X, d)$ is connected if and only if $X$ is not the union of two non-empty, disjoint, open sets.

***Theorem 7*** A subset $S$ of a metric space $(X, d)$ is disconnected if and only if $S$ is expressible as the union of two non-empty separated subsets of $X$.

***Example 4.*** *Prove that the metric space $Q$ with the usual metric is disconnected.*

**Solution.** Since, $Q = A \cup B$, where

$$A = \{x \in Q : x < \sqrt{2}\} \text{ and } B = \{x \in Q : x > \sqrt{2}\}$$

which are non-empty, disjoint open sets.

Therefore, $Q$ is disconnected.

# Compactness

## Open Cover

A family of open sets $\{G_\lambda : \lambda \in \Delta\}$ of a metric space $(X, d)$ is called an open cover of $X$, if $X = \bigcup_{\lambda \in \Delta} G_\lambda$, where $\Delta$ is an index set.

*e.g.,* $\{ ]-n, n[ \ : n \in Z^+\}$ is an open cover of $R$

$$R = ]-1, 1[ \cup ]-2, 2[ \cup ]-3, 3[ \cup \ldots$$

## Compact Metric Space

A subset $A$ of a metric space $X$ is said to be compact, if every open cover of $A$ has a finite subcover *i.e.,* if for every collection $\{G_\lambda : \lambda \in \Delta\}$ of open sets for which $A \subset U\{G_\lambda : \lambda \in \Delta\}$, $\exists$ finitely many sets $G_{\lambda_1}, G_{\lambda_2}, G_{\lambda_3}, \ldots, G_{\lambda_n}$ among the $G_\lambda$'s s.t.

$$A \subset G_{\lambda_1} \cup G_{\lambda_2} \cup \ldots \cup G_{\lambda_n}$$

In particular, the metric space $X$ is said to be compact, if for every collection $\{G_\lambda : \lambda \in \Delta\}$ of open sets for which $X = U \ \{G_\lambda : \lambda \in \Delta\}$, $\exists$ finitely many sets $G_{\lambda_1}, G_{\lambda_2}, \ldots, G_{\lambda_n}$ among the $G_\lambda$'s s.t.

$$X = G_{\lambda_1} \cup G_{\lambda_2} \cup \ldots \cup G_{\lambda_n}.$$

> **Note** **(a)** Every closed interval is compact.
> **(b)** The metric space $(X, d)$, where $X$ is any non-empty finite set is compact.

***Example 5.*** *Prove that the real line is not compact.*

**Solution.** We have,

$F = \{]-n, n[ \ : n \in Z^+\}$ is an open cover of $R$.

Suppose,

$S = \{]-n_1, n_1[, ]-n_2, n_2[, \ldots, ]-n_k, n_k[\}$ be any finite subfamily of $S$.

Let $m = \max\{n_1, n_2, n_3, \ldots, n_k\}$. Then,

$$]-n_i, n_i[ \subseteq ]-m, m[ \text{ for } i = 1, 2, 3, \ldots, k$$

$$\Rightarrow \bigcup_{i=1}^{k} ]-n_i, n_i[ \subseteq ]-m, m[$$

Therefore, $S$ is not a finite subcover of $R$ and so open cover $F$ has no finite subcover. Therefore, $R$ is not compact.

## Important Theorems on Compactness

***Theorem 1*** Suppose $Y$ be a subspace of a metric space $X$ and suppose $A \subset Y$. Then, $A$ is compact relative to $X$ iff $A$ is compact relative to $Y$.

***Theorem 2*** Closed subsets of compact sets are compact.

***Theorem 3*** Every compact subset of a metric space is closed.

***Theorem 4*** If $F$ is closed and $Y$ is compact, then $F \cap Y$ is compact.

## Finite Intersection Property

A collection $C$ of sets is said to have the finite intersection property or said to be finitely common, if the intersection of members of each finite subcollection of $C$ is non-empty.

## Bolzano Weierstrass Property

A metric space $X$ is said to have Bolzano Weierstrass property, if every infinite set $A$ has a limit point.

## Important Theorems on Finite Intersection Property and Bolzano Weierstrass Theorem

***Theorem 1*** Every collection of compact subsets of a metric space with the finite intersection property has a non-empty intersection.

***Theorem 2*** If $< A_n >$ is a sequence of non-empty compact sets s.t. $A_n \supset A_{n+1} (n = 1, 2, \ldots)$, then $\cap\{A_n : n \in N\} \neq \phi$.

***Theorem 3*** If $A$ is an infinite subset of a compact set $Y$, then $A$ has a limit point in $Y$ *i.e.*, compact sets have Bolzano Weierstrass Property.

***Theorem 4*** Every bounded infinite subset $A$ of $R^n$ has a limit point in $R^n$.

***Theorem 5*** Let $A$ be subset of $R^n$. Then, the following statements are equivalent

**(i)** $A$ is closed and bounded.

**(ii)** $A$ is compact.

**(iii)** Every infinite subset of $A$ has a limit point in $A$.

## Normed Linear Spaces

Let $N$ be a complex or real linear space and let $|| \ ||$ be a function from $N$ into $R$ s.t. for all $x, y \in N$ and all $\alpha \in C$ (or $R$), we have

(i) $||x|| \geq 0$

(ii) $||x|| = 0 \Leftrightarrow x = 0$

(iii) $||x + y|| \leq ||x|| + ||y||$

(iv) $||\alpha x|| = |\alpha| \ ||x||$

Then, the function $|| \ ||$ is called a norm on $N$ and the pair $(N, || \ ||)$ is called a complex or real normed linear space. The real number $||x||$ is called the norm of the vector $x$. Property $[n\ 3]$ is called subadditivity and property $[n\ 4]$ is called absolute homogeneity.

If the condition $[n\ 2]$ is left, then $|| \ ||$ is called a semi-norm or Pseudo norm on $N$, then $N$ is called a semi-normed linear space.

***Theorem 1*** Suppose, $N$ be a normed linear space and let $d$ be a function from $N \times N$ into $R$ defined by $d(x, y) = ||x - y||$. Then, $d$ is a metric on $N$.

***Theorem 2*** If $x, y, z \in N$ and $\lambda$ is any scalar, then

$$d(x + z, y + z) = ||(x + z) - (y + z)|| = ||x - y|| = d(x, y)$$

and

$$d(\lambda x, \lambda y) = ||\lambda x - \lambda y|| = ||\lambda(x - y)|| = |\lambda| \ ||x - y|| = |\lambda| \ d(x, y)$$

## Convergence in Normed Linear Space

Suppose, $(N, || \ ||)$ be a normed linear space. Then,

**(i)** A sequence $< x_n >$ in $N$ is said to converge to an element $x_0 \in N$ if, given $\varepsilon > 0$, $\exists$ a positive integer $m_0$ s.t. $n \geq m_0 \Rightarrow ||x_n - x_0|| < \varepsilon$. If $x_n$ converges to $x_0$, we can write $\lim_{n \to \infty} x_n = x_0$ or $x_n \to x_0$ as $n \to \infty$ it follows that $x_n \to x_0$ if and only if $||x_n - x_0|| \to 0$.

**(ii)** A sequence $< x_n >$ in $N$ is called a Cauchy sequence, if gives $\varepsilon > 0$, $\exists$ a positive integer $m_0$ s.t. $m, n \geq m_0 \Rightarrow ||x_n - x_m|| < \varepsilon$, $\forall\ n, m \geq m_0$.

**(iii)** A normed linear space $N$ is called complete if and only if every Cauchy sequence in $N$ is convergent *i.e.*, if and only if for each Cauchy sequence $< x_n >$ in $N$, there exists an element $x_0$ in $N$ s.t. $x_n \to x_0$.

***Theorem*** In a normed linear space, every convergent sequence is a Cauchy sequence.

## Continuity and Joint Continuity

If $N$ and $M$ are normed linear spaces, a mapping $f : N \to M$ is continuous at $x_0 \in N$ if and only if to each $\varepsilon > 0$, $\exists$ a $\delta > 0$ s.t.

$$||x - x_n|| < \delta \Rightarrow ||f(x) - f(x_0)|| < \varepsilon$$

Also, we say that $f$ is continuous on $N$ if and only if it is continuous at each point of $N$.

> **Note** If $N$ and $M$ are normed linear spaces, a mapping $f : N \to M$ is continuous at $x_0 \in N$ iff for every sequence $< x_n >$ in $N$ converging to $x_0$, the sequence $< f(x_n) >$ in $M$ converges to $f(x_0) \in M$ *i.e.*, if and only if $x_n \to x_0 \Rightarrow f(x_n) \to f(x_0)$.

***Example 6.*** *Suppose N be a normed linear space and let x, y ∈ N. Then,* $|\,||x|| - ||y||\,| \le ||x - y||$.

**Solution.** We have,

$$||x|| - ||(x-y) + y|| \le ||x-y|| + ||y||$$

*i.e.,* $\quad ||x|| - ||y|| \le ||x-y|| \quad$ ...(i)

Similarly, $\quad ||y|| - ||x|| \le ||y-x|| \quad$ ...(ii)

But $\quad ||y-x|| = ||(-1)(x-y)|| = |-1|\,||x-y||$

$$= ||x-y|| \quad \text{...(iii)}$$

Using Eqs. (ii) and (iii), we get

$$||y|| - ||x|| \le ||x-y|| \quad \text{...(iv)}$$

Using Eqs. (i) and (iv), we get

$$|\,||x|| - ||y||\,| \le ||x-y||$$

***Example 7.*** *Suppose N be a normed linear space with the norm || ||. Then, the mapping* $f : N \to R;\ f(x) = ||x||$ *is continuous, i.e., the norm || || on N is a continuous function.*

**Solution.** Let $x \in N$ and Suppose $< x_n >$ be a sequence in $N$ s.t.

$$x_n \to x \text{ as } n \to \infty \quad \text{...(i)}$$

$$|f(x_n) - f(x)| = |\,||x_n|| - ||x||\,| < ||x_n - x|| \to 0$$

as $n \to \infty$ [using Eq. (i)]

Therefore, $f(x_n) \to f(x)$ as $n \to \infty$.

Hence, $f$ is continuous.

# SOLVED EXAMPLES

## Type I (*Only one correct option*)

***Example 1.*** *If f is a continuous mapping of a compact metric space X into a metric space Y, then*

(a) $f$ is uniformally continuous
(b) $f$ is not continuous
(c) $f$ has a jump at $x = 0$
(d) $f$ is a step function

**Solution.** (a) Given, $\varepsilon > 0$ and $x \in X$, there is a $\delta_x > 0$ such that $\rho(x, y) < \delta_x \Rightarrow \sigma(f(x), f(y)) < \varepsilon/2$. Let $O_x$ be the spheroid $\{y : \rho(x, y) < \frac{1}{2}\delta_x\}$.

Then, $\{O_x : x \in X\}$ is an open covering of $X$ and so has a finite subcovering $\{O_{x_1}, \ldots, O_{x_n}\}$. Let $\delta = \frac{1}{2}\min\{\delta_{x_1}, \ldots, \delta_{x_n}\}$. Then, $\delta > 0$. Given, two points $y$ and $z$ in $X$ such that $\rho(y, z) < \delta$, the point $y$ must belong to some $O_{x_i}$ and hence $\rho(y, x_i) < \frac{1}{2}$, $\delta x_i$. Consequently, $\rho(z, x_i) \le \rho(z, y) + \rho(y, x_i) < \frac{1}{2}$, $\delta x_i + \delta \le \delta x_i$.

Thus, we have $\sigma(f(y), f(x_i)) < \varepsilon/2$ and $\sigma(f(z), f(x_i)) < \varepsilon/2$. This implies that $\sigma(f(z), f(y)) < \varepsilon$, hence $f$ is uniformly continuous on $X$.

***Example 2.*** *Which one of the following is true?*

(a) Every open cover of a set admits of a countable subcover.
(b) Every open cover of a set does not admits of a countable subcover.
(c) Both (a) and (b)
(d) Neither (a) nor (b)

**Solution.** (a) Let $\zeta$ be any open cover of a set $A$, so that every points of $A$ belongs to some member of $\zeta$.

Let $\beta$ denote the countable family of rational sphere and $a \in A$.

Now, there exists a member, say $F$ of $\zeta$ containing $a$ and a sphere $S(a, r)$ such that

$$a \in S(a, r) \subset F$$

Hence, there exists a rational sphere $S(p, \rho)$ such that

$$a \in S(p, \rho) \subset S(a, r) \subset F$$

Therefore, we associate with the set $A$ a subset of the countable set $\beta$ consisting of rational spheres and with this latter subset of $\beta$ a subset of $\zeta$. A subset of a countable set being countable, we arrive at a countable subset of $\zeta$ converging $A$.

***Example 3.*** *Given the collection G of open intervals of the form* $\left(-\frac{1}{n}, \frac{1}{n}\right)$, *then*

(a) it is a covering of $(-1, 2)$
(b) it is not a covering of $(-1, 2)$
(c) Both (a) and (b)
(d) Neither (a) nor (b)

**Solution.** (b) We have

$$O_1 = (-1, 1), O_2 = \left(-\frac{1}{2}, \frac{1}{2}\right), \ldots,$$

$$O_n = \left(-\frac{1}{n}, \frac{1}{n}\right), \ldots, O_\infty = (0, 0)$$

and $\bigcup_{k=1}^{n} O_n = (-1, 1)$

and $(-1, 2) \not\subset (-1, 1)$

Hence, $G$ does not provides covering to $(-1, 2)$.

***Example 4.*** *If $\phi = \sum_{i=1}^{n} a_i \chi_{E_i}$ for mutually disjoint sets $E_i$, which are measurable sets of finite measure, then*

(a) $\int \phi(x)\, dx = \sum_{i=1}^{n} a_i mE_i$ (b) $\int \phi(x)\, dx = \sum_{i=1}^{n} a_i$

(c) $\int \phi(x)\, dx = 0$ (d) $\int \phi(x)\, dx = 1$

**Solution.** (a) The set $A_a = \{x : \phi(x) = a\}$

$$= \bigcup_{a_i = a} E_i$$

Hence, $$mA_a = m\left(\bigcup_{a_i=a} E_i\right) = \sum_{a_i=a} mE_i$$

and $$amA_a = \sum_{a_i=a} a_i mE_i$$

$$\Rightarrow \int \phi(x)dx = \Sigma\, a_i mE_i$$

***Example 5.*** *If $\phi$ is a convex function on $(-\infty, \infty)$ and $f$ an integrable function on $[0, 1]$, then*

(a) $\int \phi(f(t))dt \geq \phi[\int f(t)dt]$ (b) $\int \phi(f(t))dt = \phi[\int f(t)dt]$

(c) $\int \phi(f(t))dt \leq \phi[\int f(t)dt]$ (d) $\int \phi(f(t))dt < \phi[\int f(t)dt]$

**Solution.** (a) Let $\alpha = \int f(t)dt$ and $y = m(x - \alpha) + \phi(\alpha)$ be the equation of supporting line at $\alpha$. Then,

$$\phi(f(t)) \geq m(f(t) - \alpha) + \phi(\alpha)$$

On integrating, we get

$$\int \phi(f(t))dt \geq m(\int f(t)\, dt - \int f(t)dt) + \phi(\alpha) = \phi[\int f(t)dt]$$

***Example 6.*** *Let $X$ be a complete metric space. Then, no non-empty open subset of $X$ is of first category, i.e., the union of a countable collection of nowhere dense subsets, then*

(a) A Baire category theorem

(b) Bolzano Weierstrass theorem

(c) Intermediate value theorem

(d) Cauchy's theorem

**Solution.** (a) Let $E_n$ be a countable collection of nowhere dense subsets and $U$ a non-empty open set. Then, $O_n = \sim E_n$ is a dense open subset of $X$ and by the theorem of Baire there is a point $x \in U$ which is in $\cap O_n$. But this means that $x \notin \cup E_n$ and so $\cup$ is not contained in $\cup E_n$.

***Example 7.*** *Suppose $f$ is integrable on $[a, b]$ and $\int_a^x f(t)dt = 0$ for all $x \in [a, b]$, then $f(t) = 0$ almost everywhere in $[a, b]$, if*

(a) $f(t) = 0$ almost everywhere in $[a, b]$

(b) $f(t) > 0$ almost everywhere in $[a, b]$

(c) $f(t) < 0$ almost everywhere in $[a, b]$

(d) $f(t) \neq 0$ almost everywhere in $[a, b]$

**Solution.** (a) Let $f(t) > 0$, almost everywhere in $[a, b]$.

Since, the interval $[a, b]$ is a measurable.

$\therefore$ For $\varepsilon > 0$ there exist closed set $F \subset [a, b]$ with $m([a, b] \sim F) < \varepsilon$.

Let $0 = (a, b) \sim F$. Then, either

$$\int_a^b f \neq 0 \text{ or } \int_a^b f = 0$$

If $\int_a^b f = 0$, then $\int_a^b f = \int_0 f + \int_F f = 0$

$$\Rightarrow \int_0 f = -\int_F f \neq 0.$$

Since, 0 is the disjoint union of countable collection $\{(a_n, b_n)\}$ of open intervals, so,

$$\int_0 f = \Sigma \int_{a_n}^{b_n} f \text{ and for some } n,$$

$$\int_{a_n}^{b_n} f \neq 0 \text{ and either } \int_a^{a_n} f \neq 0 \text{ or } \int_a^{b_n} f \neq 0$$

Since, $f > 0$, then for some $\int_a^x f(x) \neq 0$

Hence, $f(t) = 0$, when $\int_a^x f(t)dt = 0$

***Example 8.*** *If $\langle E_i \rangle$ is a sequence of disjoint Lebesgue measurable sets and $A$ is any set, then*

(a) $m^*\left(A \cap \left[\bigcup_{i=1}^{\infty} E_i\right]\right) \geq \sum_{i=1}^{\infty} m^*(A \cap E_i)$

(b) $m^*\left(A \cap \left[\bigcup_{i=1}^{\infty} E_i\right]\right) \leq \sum_{i=1}^{\infty} m^*(A \cap E_i)$

(c) Both (a) and (b)

(d) Neither (a) nor (b)

**Solution.** (a) If $\langle E_i \rangle$ is a finite sequence of disjoint Lebesgue measurable sets, then for any set $A$,

$$m^*\left(A \cap \left[\bigcup_{i=1}^{n} E_i\right]\right) \geq \sum_{i=1}^{n} m^*(A \cap E_i)$$

Since, $$\bigcup_{i=1}^{n} E_i \subset \bigcup_{i=1}^{\infty} E_i,$$

$$\Rightarrow A \cap \left(\bigcup_{i=1}^{n} E_i\right) \subset A \cap \left(\bigcup_{i=1}^{\infty} E_i\right)$$

$$\Rightarrow m^*\left(A \cap \left[\bigcup_{i=1}^{n} E_i\right]\right) = \sum_{i=1}^{n} m^*(A \cap E_i) \leq m^*\left[A \cap \left(\bigcup_{i=1}^{\infty} E_i\right)\right]$$

Since, right hand side of inequality is independent of $n$, we have

$$\sum_{i=1}^{\infty} m^*(A \cap E_i) \leq m^*\left(A \cap \left[\bigcup_{i=1}^{\infty} E_i\right]\right).$$

***Example 9.*** *If $E_1$ and $E_2$ are Lebesgue measurable sets,*

(a) $E_1 \cup E_2$ are also Lebesgue measurable sets

(b) $E_1 \cup E_2$ is not Lebesgue measurable set

(c) Both (a) and (b) are true

(d) Neither (a) nor (b) is true

**Solution.** (a) Let $E_1 \cup E_2$ are Lebesgue measurable. Then, for any set $A$ it is sufficient to prove that

$$m^*A \geq m^*(A \cap (E_1 \cup E_2)) + m^*(A \cap (E_1 \cup E_2)^c) \quad \text{...(i)}$$

Since, $E_2$ is Lebesgue measurable,

$$m^*(A \cap E_1^c) = m^*(A \cap E_1^c \cap E_2) + m^*(A \cap E_1^c \cap E_2^c)$$

$$\Rightarrow \quad m^*(A \cap (E_1 \cup E_2)^c) = m^*(A \cap E_1^c) - m^*(A \cap E_1^c \cap E_2) \quad \text{...(ii)}$$

Also, $$A \cap (E_1 \cup E_2) = (A \cap E_1) \cup (A \cap E_2) = (A \cap E_1) \cup (A \cap E_2 \cap E_1^c)$$

This gives

$$m^*(A \cap (E_1 \cup E_2)) \leq m^*(A \cap E_1) + m^*(A \cap E_2 \cap E_1^c) \quad \text{...(iii)}$$

By adding Eqs. (ii) and (iii), we have

$$m^*(A \cap (E_1 \cup E_2)^c) + m^*(A \cap (E_1 \cup E_2))$$
$$\leq m^*(A \cap E_1) + m^*(A \cap E_1^c) + m^*(A \cap E_2 \cap E_1^c) - m^*(A \cap E_2 \cap E_1^c)$$
$$\leq m^*(A \cap E_1) + m^*(A \cap E_1^c) = m^*A$$

By the measurability of $E_1$ and we have finally

$$m^*(A) \geq m^*(A \cap (E_1 \cup E_2)^c + m^*(A \cap (E_1 \cup E_2))$$

This proves $E_1 \cup E_2$ is measurable.

## Type II (*One or more than one correct option*)

***Example 10.*** *If $\langle f_n \rangle$ is an equicontinuous sequence of mappings from a metric space X to a complete metric space Y. If the sequences $\langle f_n(x) \rangle$ converge for each point x of a dense subset D of X, then*

(a) $\langle f_n \rangle$ converges at each point of $X$
(b) the limit function is continuous
(c) $\langle f_n \rangle$ does not converges to each point of $X$
(d) the limit function is not continuous

**Solution.** (a), (b)

Given $x$ in $X$ and $\varepsilon > 0$, we can find an open set $O$ containing $x$ such that $\sigma[f_n(x), f_n(y)] < \varepsilon/3$ for all $y \in O$. Since, $D$ is dense, there must be a point $y \in D \cap O$ and since $\langle f_n(y) \rangle$ converges, so it must be a Cauchy sequence, so for $N > 0$, we have $m, n \geq N$

$$\sigma[f_n(y), f_m(y)] < \varepsilon/3$$

Hence, for all $m, n \geq N$

$$\sigma[f_n(x), f_m(x)] \leq \sigma[f_n(x), f_n(y)] + \sigma[f_n(y), f_m(y)] + \sigma[f_m(x), f_m(y)] < \varepsilon$$

Thus, $\langle f_n(x) \rangle$ is a Cauchy sequence and converges by the completeness of $Y$.

Let $f(x) = \lim f_n(x)$. To prove $f$ is continuous at $x$, let $\varepsilon > 0$ be given. By equicontinuity there is an open set $O$ containing $x$ such that $\sigma[f_n(x), f_n(y)] < \varepsilon$ for all $n$ and all $y$ in $O$. Hence, for all $y$ in $O$, we have

$$\sigma[f(x), f(y)] = \lim \sigma[f_n(x), f_n(y)] \leq \varepsilon$$

and $f$ is continuous at $x$.

***Example 11.*** *Given a metric space X also there is a countable family $\{O_i\}$ of open sets such that for any open set $O \subset X$,*

$$O = \bigcup_{O_i \subset O} O_i, \text{ then}$$

(a) metric space $X$ is separable
(b) metric space $X$ is not separable
(c) if metric space $X$ has a countable subset which is every where dense, then it is separable
(d) if metric space $X$ is separable, if every Cauchy sequence in metric space converges

**Solution.** (a), (c)

Given the countable collection $\{O_i\}$. Let $x_i$ be a point of $O_i$ and let $D$ be the set of all these points $x_i$. We shall now see that $D$ is dense. Let $x$ be any point of $X$ and $S$ any spheroid centred at $x$. Then, we must show that $S$ contains a point of $D$. But since $S$ is an open set and so we must have some $O_i$ so $x \in O_i \subset S$. Hence, $x_i \in S$ and we see that $x \in \overline{D}$.

***Example 12.*** *Which of the following(s) is/are true?*

(a) The compact subset of a metric space is closed.
(b) The compact subset of a metric space is open.
(c) The compact subset of a metric space is bounded.
(d) The compact subset of a metric space is unbounded.

**Solution.** (a), (c)

Suppose that $K$ is a compact subset of a metric space $X$, and let $y$ be a point of closure of $K$. Then, $f(x) = p(x, y)$ is a continuous function on $K$ whose infimum is 0.

Since, $f$ assumes its minimum on $K$, there is a $z \in K$ such that $f(z) = \min f(x) = 0$. Hence, $p(z, y) = 0$ and so $y = z \in K$. Thus, $K$ is closed.

To see that $K$ is bounded, we have $\rho(x_0, x)$ a continuous function of $x$ on $K$ and so bounded by some number $M$. Then, $K \subset B_{x_0, M}$.

***Example 13.*** *If f is a continuous real-valued function on a (sequentially) compact space, then*

(a) $f$ is bounded (b) $f$ assumes its maximum
(c) $f$ is unbounded (d) $f$ assumes its minimum

**Solution.** (a), (b)

Let $M = \text{Sup } \{f(x) : x \in X\}$. Then, (even if $M = \infty$) there is a sequence $\langle x_n \rangle$ of points of $X$ such that $M = \lim f(x_n)$. Since, $X$ is sequentially compact, there is a subsequence $\langle x_{nk} \rangle$ that converges to a point $z \in X$. Then, $f(z) = \lim f(x_{nk}) = M$. Thus, $M$ is a real number and $f(z) = M$.

Hence, $M$ is the maximum of $f$ and is assumed at $z$.

***Example 14.*** *Which of the following(s) is/are correct?*

(a) Open ball is open set in $\mathbb{R}^n$
(b) Open ball is closed set in $\mathbb{R}^n$
(c) Open ball is half closed set in $\mathbb{R}^n$
(d) Open ball is an open interval in $\mathbb{R}^n$

**Solution.** (a), (d)

Let $\bar{a} \in \mathbb{R}^n, r > 0$, then the open ball with centre $\bar{a}$ is $B(\bar{a}, r)$.

and $$B(\bar{a}, r) = \{x \mid \|\bar{x} - \bar{a}\| < r\}$$

$\bar{x}$ is an interior of $B(\bar{a}, r)$, if $\bar{x} \in B(\bar{a}, r)$ and there is an open ball $O(\bar{x}, \delta) \subset B(\bar{a}, r)$.

Let $\bar{x} \in B(\bar{a}, r)$

$\Rightarrow$ $||\bar{x}-\bar{a}||<r$

choose $\delta = r - ||x-y||$

We have, $O(\bar{x}, \delta) = \{y| \ ||\bar{x}-\bar{y}||<\delta\}$

$\forall \bar{y} \in O(\bar{x}, \delta)$

$\Rightarrow$ $||\bar{x}-\bar{y}||<r-||\bar{x}-\bar{a}||$

$\Rightarrow ||\bar{x}-\bar{y}||+||\bar{x}-\bar{a}||<r$

$\Rightarrow$ $||\bar{a}-\bar{y}||<r$

$\Rightarrow$ $y \in B(\bar{a}, r)$

Hence, $O(\bar{x}, \delta) \subset B(\bar{a}, r)$

This proves open ball are open intervals.

***Example 15.*** *(α) If $A \subset \mathbb{R}^n$ and F is an open covering of A. (β) there is a countable subcollection of F which also covers A, then*

(a) $\alpha \Rightarrow \beta$

(b) $\alpha \not\Rightarrow \beta$

(c) If $\alpha \Rightarrow \beta$, then it states Lendel θf covering theorem

(d) If $\alpha \not\Rightarrow \beta$, then it states Lendel θf covering theorem

**Solution.** (a), (c)

Let $G = \{A_1, A_2, \ldots\}$ is a countable collection of open balls having rational number and centres at points with rational coordinate in $\mathbb{R}^n$.

Suppose, $\bar{x} \in A$, then since F is an open covering A, there exist an open set $S \in F$ such that $\bar{x} \in S$.

Also, since $\bar{x} \in S$, there exist atleast one open ball $A_k$ in G, such that

$$\bar{x} \in A_k \subset S$$

Hence, $\forall \bar{x} \in A$

We have some $A_k$ in G and $A_k \subset S$, an open set in F

i.e., $A \subset \cup A_k$

A countable sub-collection of open balls in G, which are contained in F.

***Example 16.*** *Which of the following(s) is /are correct?*

(a) $S \subset \mathbb{R}^n$ is closed, if it contains all its accumulation points

(b) $S \subset \mathbb{R}^n$ is closed, if it does not contains all its accumulation points

(c) $S \subset \mathbb{R}^n$ is contains all its accumulation points so it is closed

(d) $S \subset \mathbb{R}^n$ is closed iff it contains all its accumulation points

**Solution.** (a), (c), (d)

If $\bar{S}$ and $S'$ are closure and derived set of set S, then

$$\bar{S} = S \cup S'$$

S is closed iff $S = \bar{S}$

$\Rightarrow$ $S = S \cup S' \Rightarrow S' \subset S$

$S'$ is a set which contains all its accumulation points and so S contains all its accumulation points.

If S contains all its accumulation points and $S'$ is also a set which contains all the accumulation points of S.

Hence, $S' \subset S$

and since $\bar{S} = S \cup S' \Rightarrow \bar{S} = S \Rightarrow S$ is closed.

***Example 17.*** *If K is a compact metric space and $\langle f_n \rangle$ an equicontinuous sequence of functions to a metric space Y that converges at each point of K to a function f, then*

(a) $< f_n >$ converges to f on K

(b) $< f_n >$ does not converges to f on K

(c) $< f_n >$ converges to f uniformally on K

(d) $< f_n >$ does not converges to f uniformally on K

**Solution.** (a), (c)

Choose $\varepsilon > 0$.

By equicontinuity each $x \in K$ is contained in an open set $O_x$ such that $\sigma[f_n(x), f_n(y)] < \varepsilon/3$ for all $y \in O_x$ and all n. Form this it also follows that $\sigma[f(x), f(y)] \le \varepsilon/3$ for all y in $O_x$

By the compactness of K there is a finite collection $\{O_{x_1}, \ldots, O_{x_n}\}$ of these sets which covers K.

Choose N so large that for all $n \ge N$ we have $\sigma[f_n(x_i), f(x_i)] < \varepsilon/3$ for each $x_i$ corresponding to this finite collection. Then, for any $y \in K$ there is an $i \le k$ such that $y \in O_{x_i}$. Hence

$$\sigma[f_n(y), f(y)] \le \sigma[f_n(y), f_n(x_i)] + \sigma[f_n(x_i), f(x_i)] + \sigma[f(y), f(x_i)] < \varepsilon$$

for $n \ge N$. Thus, $< f_n >$ converges to f uniformly on K.

***Example 18.*** *Let m be a countable additive measure defined on all sets in σ-algebra M. Then,*

(a) $A, B \in M$ such that $A \subset B$, then $mA \le mB$

(b) if $A \in M$ such that $mA < \infty$, then $m\phi = 0$

(c) $A, B \in M$ such that $A \subset B$, then $mA \ge mB$

(d) if $A \in M$ such that $mA < \infty$, then $m\phi = \infty$

**Solution.** (a), (b)

(a) We have, $A \subset B$ so A and $B - A$ are mutually disjoint and belongs to M. By the definition of countable additive measure,

$$m(A \cup (B-A)) = mA + m(B-A)$$

$$\Rightarrow \quad mB = mA + m(B-A) \Rightarrow mB \ge mA$$

(b) Since, $A \cap \phi = \phi$, A and $\phi$ are mutually disjoint sets. By definition of countable additive measure.

$$m(A \cup \phi) = mA + m\phi \Rightarrow mA = mA + m\phi$$

Since, $mA < \infty$, we have $m\phi = 0$.

***Example 19.*** *If f is an extended real-valued function whose domain is measurable. The following are equivalent, for each real number, α.*

(a) set $\{x : f(x) > \alpha\}$ is measurable

(b) set $\{x : f(x) \ge \alpha\}$ is measurable

(c) set $\{x : f(x) < \alpha\}$ is measurable

(d) set $\{x : f(x) \le \alpha\}$ is measurable

**Solution.** (a), (b), (c), (d)

Let the domain of f is D.

(a) $\Rightarrow$ (d), $\{x : f(x) \le \alpha\} = D \sim \{x : f(x) > \alpha\}$

The difference of two measurable sets is a measurable set.

(d) $\Rightarrow$ (a), $\{x : f(x) > \alpha\} = D \sim \{x : f(x) \le \alpha\}$

The difference of two measurable sets.

Hence, (a) $\Leftrightarrow$ (d)

(a) $\Rightarrow$ (b), $\{x : f(x) \geq \alpha\} = \bigcap_{i=1}^{\infty} \{x : f(x) > \alpha - \frac{1}{n}\}$

The intersection of a sequence of measurable sets is measurable set.

(b) $\Rightarrow$ (a), $\{x : f(x) > \alpha\} = \bigcup_{i=1}^{\infty} \{x : f(x) \geq \alpha + \frac{1}{n}\}$

The union of a sequence of measurable sets is measurable.

Hence, (a) $\Leftrightarrow$ (b)

(c) $\Rightarrow$ (b), $\{x : f(x) \geq \alpha\} = D \sim \{x : f(x) < \alpha\}$

The difference of two measurable sets is measurable.

(b) $\Rightarrow$ (c), $\{x : f(x) < \alpha\} = D \sim \{x : f(x) \geq \alpha\}$

The difference of two measurable sets is measurable.

Hence, (c) $\Leftrightarrow$ (b)

So that we have (a) $\Leftrightarrow$ (b) $\Leftrightarrow$ (c) $\Leftrightarrow$ (d).

***Example 20.*** *Given two non-empty sets A and B, if* $m^*A = 0$, *then*

(a) $m^*(A \cup B) = m^*B$ (b) $m^*(A \cup B) \neq m^*B$

(c) $m^*(A \cup B) = m^*A$ (d) $m^*(A \cup B) \leq m^*(B)$

**Solution.** (a), (d)

We have,

$$m^*(A \cup B) \leq m^*A + m^*B$$
$$\leq m^*B \quad \text{...(i)}$$

Since, $B \subset A \cup B$

$\Rightarrow$ $m^*B \leq m^*(A \cup B)$ ...(ii)

By Eqs. (i) and (ii), we have

$$m^*(A \cup B) = m^*B$$

***Example 21.*** *If* $\phi$ *and* $\psi$ *are simple functions which vanish outside a set of finite measure, then*

(a) $\int (a\phi + b\psi) = a\int \phi + b\int \psi$

(b) $\int (a\phi + b\psi) \neq a\int \phi + b\int \psi$

(c) $\phi$ and $\psi$ can be represented by canonical representation

(d) $\phi$ and $\psi$ cannot be represented by canonical representation

**Solution.** (a), (c)

Since, $\phi$ and $\psi$ are simple functions, it can be represented by canonical representation.

$$\phi = \Sigma a_i \chi_{A_i}, A_i = \{x : \phi(x) = a_i\}$$

where $A_i \cap A_j = \phi$, $a_i = a_j$ for $i \neq j$

and $\psi = \Sigma b_i \chi_{B_i}$ $B_i = \{x : \psi(x) = b_i\}$

where $B_i \cap B_j = \phi$, $b_i \neq b_j$, for $i \neq j$

Let $E_k = A_i \cap B_j$, then they form a disjoint collection of measurable sets and can be represented as,

$$\phi = \Sigma a_k \chi_{E_k} \text{ and } \psi = \Sigma b_k \chi_{E_k}$$

and so $a\phi + b\psi = \Sigma (aa_k + bb_k) \chi_{E_k}$

$\Rightarrow$ $\int (a\phi + b\psi) = a\Sigma a_k \chi_{E_k} + b\Sigma b_k \chi_{E_k} = a\int \phi + b\int \psi$

***Example 22.*** *If f and g are two measurable real-valued functions defined on same domain, then*

(a) $f + g$ is measurable

(b) $f + g$ is not measurable

(c) $fg$ is measurable

(d) $fg$ is not measurable

**Solution.** (a), (c)

If $f(x) + g(x) < \alpha$, then $f(x) < \alpha - g(x)$ and by axiom of Archimedes there is a rational number $r$ such that

$$f(x) < r < \alpha - g(x)$$

Hence,

$$\{x : f(x) + g(x) < \alpha\} = \cup(\{x : f(x) < r\} \cap \{x : g(x) < \alpha - r\})$$

Since, the rationals are countable this is measurable and so $f + g$ is measurable.

The function $f^2$ is measurable, since

$$\{x : f^2(x) > \alpha\} = \{x : f(x) > \sqrt{\alpha}\} \cup \{x : f(x) < -\sqrt{\alpha}\}$$

for $\alpha \geq 0$ and $\{x : f^2(x) > \alpha\} = D$

If $\alpha < 0$, where $D$ is the domain of $f$. Thus,

$$fg = \frac{1}{2}\{(f + g)^2 - f^2 - g^2\} \text{ is measurable.}$$

***Example 23.*** *Let A and B be any two subsets of a metric space* $(X, d)$, *then*

(a) $A \subseteq B \Rightarrow \inf A \subseteq \inf B$

(b) $\inf (A \cap B) = (\inf A) \cap (\inf B)$

(c) $\inf (A \cup B) \supseteq \inf A \cup \inf B$

(d) None of the above

**Solution.** (a), (b), (c)

(a) Let $x \in \inf A$, then $\exists$, $r > 0$ such that

$S_r(x) \subseteq A$

$\Rightarrow$ $S_r(x) \subseteq B$ $(\because A \subseteq B)$

$\Rightarrow$ $x \in \inf B$

$\Rightarrow$ $\inf A \subseteq \inf B$

(b) We know that

$\inf A \subseteq A$ and $\inf B \subseteq B$

$\therefore$ $\inf A \cap \inf B$, being the intersection of two open sets is open. Hence,

$\inf A \cap \inf B \subseteq \inf (A \cap B)$

Also, $A \cap B \subseteq A \Rightarrow \inf (A \cap B) \subseteq \inf A$

and $\inf(A \cap B) \subseteq \inf B$

$\therefore$ $\inf(A \cap B) \subseteq \inf A \cap \inf B$

(c) Since, $A \subseteq A \cup B \Rightarrow \inf A \subseteq \inf(A \cup B)$

and $B \subseteq A \cup B \Rightarrow \inf B \subseteq \inf (A \cup B)$

$\therefore$ $\inf A \cup \inf B \subseteq \inf (A \cup B)$

***Example 24.*** *Which of the following(s) is/are connected subset of the Euclidean space $R^2$?*

(a) $D = \{(x, y) : x \neq 0 \text{ and } -1 \leq y \leq 1\}$
(b) $E = \{(x, y) : x = 0 \text{ and } -1 \leq y \leq 1\} \cup D$
(c) Both (a) and (b)
(d) Neither (a) nor (b)

**Solution.** Let $A = \{(x, y) : x > 0 \text{ and } y = \sin\frac{1}{x}\}$

and $B = \{(x, y) : x < 0\} \text{ and } y = \sin\frac{1}{x}\}$

Then, $D = A \cup B$ and $A \cap B = \phi$

Now since,

$$A = D \cap \{(x, y) : x > 0\}$$

and $B = D \cap \{(x, y) : x < 0\}$

and the sets $\{(x, y) : x > 0\}$ and $\{(x, y) : x < 0\}$ are pairwise disjoint open subset of $R^2$. Hence, $A$ and $B$ are open in $D$ and

$$A \neq \phi, B \neq \phi$$

Hence, $\{A, B\}$ is disconnection of $D$.

$\Rightarrow$ $D$ is disconnected subset of $R^2$.

Next, let $F = \{(0, y) : -1 \leq y \leq 1\}$

Then, $E = A \cup B \cup F$

Now, from graph of $y = \sin\frac{1}{x}$

$$\overline{A} = A \cup F \text{ and } \overline{B} = B \cup F$$

Hence, $E = \overline{A} \cup B$

Also, $\overline{A} \cap \overline{B} = F \neq \phi$

Now, define a function $f : (0, \infty) \to R^2$ given by

$$f(x) = (x, \sin 1/x)$$

which is continuous and the set $A$, being the continuous image of the connected set $(0, \infty)$ is connected. Hence, $\overline{A}$ is connected. Similarly the function $g : (-\infty, 0) \to R^2$ given by

$$g(x) = (x, \sin 1/x)$$

is continuous and $B$ is connected. Therefore, $E$ is a connected subset of $R^2$.

***Example 25.*** *Consider the functions*

$$f(x) = \begin{cases} \frac{1}{x^{2/3}}, & 0 < x \leq 1 \\ 0, & x = 0 \end{cases}$$

*and* $$g(x) = \begin{cases} \frac{1}{x}, 0 < x \leq 1 \\ 9, x = 0 \end{cases}$$

*Then,*

(a) $f$ is Lebesgue integrable on $[0, 1]$
(b) $f$ is not Lebesgue integrable on $[0, 1]$
(c) $g$ is Lebesgue integrable on $[0, 1]$
(d) $g$ is not Lebesgue integrable on $[0, 1]$

**Solution.** (a), (d)

(a) Since, $\frac{1}{x^{2/3}} \to \infty$ as $x \to 0$. Hence, $f$ is unbounded in $[0, 1]$. Now, define

$$F(x, n) = \begin{cases} \frac{1}{x^{2/3}}, \frac{1}{n^{3/2}} \leq x \leq 1 \\ n \quad, 0 < x < \frac{1}{n^{3/2}} \\ 0 \quad, x = 0 \end{cases}$$

Now, $$\int_0^1 F(x, n)dx = \int_0^{\frac{1}{n^{3/2}}} F(x, n)dx + \int_{\frac{1}{n^{3/2}}}^1 F(x, n)dx$$

$$= \int_0^{\frac{1}{n^{3/2}}} ndx + \int_{\frac{1}{n^{3/2}}}^1 \frac{1}{x^{2/3}}dx$$

$$= \frac{1}{\sqrt{n}} + 3\left[1 - \left(\frac{1}{n^{3/2}}\right)^{\frac{1}{3}}\right]$$

$$= 3 - \frac{2}{\sqrt{n}}, \forall n$$

Hence, by definition of the Lebesgue integral of unbounded functions, we have

$$\int_0^1 f(x)dx = \lim_{x \to \infty} \int_0^1 F(x, n)dx$$

$$= \lim_{n \to \infty}\left(3 - \frac{2}{\sqrt{n}}\right) = 3$$

Hence, $f$ is Lebesgue integrable in $[0, 1]$.

Next, define

$$G(x, n) = \begin{cases} \frac{1}{x}, \frac{1}{n} \leq x \leq 1 \\ n, 0 < x < \frac{1}{n} \\ \min(9, n), x = 0 \end{cases}$$

$$\therefore \quad \int_0^1 G(x, n)dx = \int_0^{\frac{1}{n}} ndx + \int_{\frac{1}{n}}^1 \frac{1}{x}dx$$

$$= 1 + \log n, \forall n$$

$$\therefore \quad \int_0^1 g(x)dx = \lim_{n \to \infty} \int_0^1 G(x, n)dx$$

$$= \lim_{n \to \infty}(1 + \log n)$$

$$= \infty$$

Hence, $g$ is not Lebesgue integrable.

# Exercise 1 (For Part 'B')

**Direction** (Q. Nos. 1-158) *All questions have only one correct option.*

**1.** Which one of the following is true?
(a) There exists a rational sphere containing a point contained in any spherical neighbourhood of the points.
(b) There does not exists a rational sphere containing a point contained in spherical neighbourhood of the points.
(c) Both (a) and (b)
(d) Neither (a) nor (b)

**2.** Which one of the following is correct?
(a) The intersection of an arbitrary collection of closed sets is closed.
(b) The intersection of arbitrary collection of closed sets is open.
(c) The intersection of arbitrary collection of closed sets is not closed.
(d) The intersection of arbitrary collection of closed sets is empty.

**3.** Which one of the following is correct?
(a) The union of any collection of open sets is an open set.
(b) The union of any collection of open sets is an closed set.
(c) The union of any collection of open sets is not an open set.
(d) The union of any collection of open set is an empty set.

**4.** If $\bar{x}$ and $\bar{y}$ belongs to $\mathbb{R}^n$, then
(a) $||\bar{x}+y|| \le ||x|| + ||\bar{y}||$ (b) $||\bar{x}+\bar{y}|| = ||\bar{x}|| + ||y||$
(c) $||\bar{x}+\bar{y}|| < ||\bar{x}|| + ||y||$ (d) $||\bar{x}+\bar{y}|| > ||\bar{x}|| + ||y||$

**5.** If $A$ is an open set and $B$ is a closed set in $\mathbb{R}^n$, then
(a) $B-A$ is closed set (b) $B-A$ is open set
(c) $B-A$ is null set (d) $B-A$ is semi-open set

**6.** Which one of the following is true?
(a) A function continuous on a compact domain is uniformly continuous.
(b) A function continuous on a compact domain is not uniformly continuous.
(c) Both (a) and (b)
(d) Neither (a) nor (b)

**7.** The collection $\mathcal{C}$ of open intervals of the form $\left(\frac{1}{n}, \frac{2}{n}\right)$, $n = 2, 3, \ldots$ is an open covering of the open interval $(0, 1)$, then
(a) finite subcollection covers (0, 1)
(b) finite subcollection does not covers (0, 1)
(c) Both (a) and (b)
(d) Neither (a) nor (b)

**8.** Which one of the following is true?
(a) A sequentially compact metric space is totally bounded.
(b) A sequentially compact metric space is totally unbounded.
(c) Both (a) and (b)
(d) Neither (a) nor (b)

**9.** Which one of the following is true?
(a) The continuous image of a compact set is compact.
(b) The continuous image of a compact set is not compact.
(c) Both (a) and (b)
(d) Neither (a) nor (b)

**10.** Given $\varepsilon > 0$, there is a polynomial $P$ in one variable, such that for all $x \in [-1, 1]$, then
(a) $|P(s)|-|s|| < \varepsilon$ (b) $|P(x)|-|s|| > 0$
(c) $|P(x)|-|s|| = 0$ (d) $|P(x)|-|s|| \ge \varepsilon$

**11.** Let $X$ be a complete metric space and $\{O_k\}$ a countable collection of dense open subsets of $X$, then
(a) $\cap O_n$ is dense (b) $\cup O_n$ is dense
(c) $\cap O_n$ is not dense (d) $\cap O_n$ is not dense

**12.** Which one of the following is true?
(a) The collection $M$ of Lebesgue measurable sets is a $\sigma$-algebra.
(b) The collection $M$ of Lebesgue measurable sets is not a $\sigma$-algebra.
(c) Both (a) and (b)
(d) Neither (a) nor (b)

**13.** If $E$ is a measurable set of finite measure, $\langle f_n \rangle$, a sequence of measurable functions defined on $E$.
If $f$ is a real-valued function such that for each $x \in E$, $f_n(x) \to f(x)$, then
(a) Given $\varepsilon > 0$ and $\delta > 0$, there is a measurable set $A \subset E$ with $mA < \delta$
(b) Given $\varepsilon > 0$ and $\delta > 0$, there does not exist a measurable set $A \subset E$ with $mA < \delta$
(c) Both (a) and (b)
(d) Neither (a) nor (b)

**14.** If $\langle E_i \rangle$ is a sequence of Lebesgue measurable sets, then
(a) Lebesgue measure $m(\cup E_i) \le \Sigma mE_i$
(b) $m(\cup E_i) = \Sigma mE_i$
(c) $m(\cup E_i) > \Sigma mE_i$
(d) $m(\cup E_i) = 0$

**15.** Let $S = \{(x, y) \in R^2 : x^2 - y = 0.3\}$. Then,
(a) $S$ is connected but not compact
(b) $S$ is not connected and not compact
(c) $S$ is not connected but compact
(d) $S$ is connected and compact

**16.** Which one of the following is true?
(a) Intersection of two Lebesgue measurable sets is a Lebesgue measurable set.
(b) The intersection of two Lebesgue measurable set is not Lebesgue measurable.
(c) Both (a) and (b)
(d) Neither (a) nor (b)

**17.** Which one of the following is true?
(a) $(-\infty, b)$ is Lebesgue measurable set.
(b) $(-\infty, b)$ is not Lebesgue measurable set.
(c) Both (a) and (b)
(d) Neither (a) nor (b)

**18.** Which one of the following is true?
(a) Interval $(a, \infty)$ is Lebesgue measurable.
(b) Interval $(a, \infty)$ is not Lebesgue measurable.
(c) $m^*(a, \infty) = 0$
(d) $m^*(a, \infty) \neq \infty$

**19.** If $E_1$ and $E_2$ are Lebesgue measurable, then
(a) $m(E_1 \cup E_2) + m(E_1 \cap E_2) = mE_1 + mE_2$
(b) $m(E_1 \cup E_2) + m(E_1 \cap E_2) \neq mE_1 + mE_2$
(c) Both (a) and (b)
(d) Neither (a) nor (b)

**20.** Which one of the following is true?
(a) Family $M$ of Lebesgue measurable sets is an algebra of sets.
(b) Family $M$ of Lebesgue measurable sets is not an algebra of sets.
(c) Both (a) and (b)
(d) Neither (a) nor (b)

**21.** If $A$ is any set, and $E_1, E_2, \ldots, E_n$ is a finite sequence of disjoint Lebesgue measurable sets, then
(a) $m^*\left(A \cap \left[\bigcup_{i=1}^{n} E_i\right]\right) \geq \sum_{i=1}^{n} m^*(A \cap E_i)$
(b) $m^*\left(A \cap \left[\bigcup_{i=1}^{n} E_i\right]\right) = 0$
(c) $m^*\left(A \cap \left[\bigcup_{i=1}^{n} E_i\right]\right) = \infty$
(d) $m^*\left(A \cap \left[\bigcup_{i=1}^{n} E_i\right]\right) \leq \sum_{i=1}^{n} m^*(A \cap E_i)$

**22.** If $\langle E_i \rangle$ is a sequence of disjoint measurable sets and $A$ any set, then
(a) $m^*\left(A \cap \bigcup_{i=1}^{\infty} E_i\right) = \sum_{i=1}^{\infty} m^*(A \cap E_i)$
(b) $m^*\left(A \cap \bigcup_{i=1}^{\infty} E_i\right) = 0$
(c) $m^*\left(A \cap \bigcup_{i=1}^{\infty} E_i\right) = \infty$
(d) $m^*\left(A \cap \bigcup_{i=1}^{\infty} E_i\right) \geq \sum_{i=1}^{\infty} m^*(A \cap E_i)$

**23.** If Lebesgue outer measure of a set $E$, $m^* E = 0$, then
(a) $E$ is measurable (b) $E$ is not measurable
(c) Both (a) and (b) (d) Neither (a) nor (b)

**24.** Which one of the following is true?
(a) Lebesgue outer measure $m^*$ is translation invariant.
(b) Lebesgue outer measure $m^*$ is not translation invariant.
(c) Both (a) and (b)
(d) Neither (a) nor (b)

**25.** For a set A of rational numbers between 0 and 1. If $\{I_n\}$ is a finite collection of open intervals that covers $A$, then
(a) $\Sigma l(I_n) \geq 1$ (b) $\Sigma l(I_n) \leq 1$
(c) $\Sigma l(I_n) = \infty$ (d) $\Sigma l(I_n) = 0$

**26.** If $A$ is countable, then
(a) $m^* A = 0$ (b) $m^* A = \infty$
(c) $m^* A \neq 0$ (d) $m^* A = 1$

**27.** If $\{A_n\}$ is a countable collection of sets of real number, then
(a) $m^*(\cup A_n) \leq \Sigma m^* A_n$ (b) $m^*(\cup A_n) = \infty$
(c) $m^*(\cup A_n) \geq \Sigma m^* A_n$ (d) $m^*(\cup A_n) = 0$

**28.** Let $\langle F_n \rangle$ is a sequence of measurable functions (on the some domain), then
(a) $\overline{\lim} f_n$ is measurable (b) $\overline{\lim} f_n$ is not measurable
(c) Both (a) and (b) (d) Neither (a) nor (b)

**29.** Prove that if $f$ is measurable function and $f = g$ almost everywhere,
(a) $g$ is measurable
(b) $g$ is not measurable
(c) Both (a) and (b) are true
(d) Neither (a) nor (b) is true

**30.** If $f$ is bounded variation on $[a, b]$ and $c \in (a, b)$, then
(a) $V_f(a, b) \leq V_f(a, c) + V_f(c, b)$
(b) $V_f(a, b) \geq V_f(a, c) + V_f(c, b)$
(c) $V_f(a, b) = V_f(a, c) + V_f(c, b)$
(d) None of the above

**31.** $f$ is of bounded variation on $[a, b]$ iff
(a) $f$ is the difference of two monotone real-valued functions on $[a, b]$
(b) $f$ is the product of two monotone real-valued functions on $[a, b]$
(c) $f$ is the quotient of two monotone real-valued functions on $[a, b]$
(d) None of the above

**32.** If $f$ is of bounded variation on $[a, b]$ and $c \in (a, b)$, then
(a) $f$ is of bounded variation on $[a, c]$ and on $[c, b]$
(b) $f$ is not of bounded variation on $[a, c]$ and on $[c, b]$
(c) $f$ is constant on $[a, c]$ and $[c, b]$
(d) None of the above

**33.** If $f$ is of bounded variation on $[a, b]$, then total variation of $f$ on $[a, b]$ is
(a) finite number (b) infinite
(c) zero (d) None of these

**34.** If $f : [a, b] \to \mathbb{R}$ is monotonic, then
(a) $f$ is of bounded variation
(b) $f$ is unbounded
(c) the set of discontinuities of $f$ are uncountable
(d) None of the above

**35.** If $f$ is continuous on $[a, b]$. Then, $f$ is of bounded variation on $[a, b]$ iff
(a) $f$ is the difference of two monotonic continuous function on $[a, b]$
(b) $f$ is the product of two monotonic continuous function on $[a, b]$
(c) $f$ is the quotient of two monotonic continuous functions on $[a, b]$
(d) None of the above

**36.** If $f$ is of bounded variation, then $f / g$ is of bounded variation, if
(a) $f$ is of bounded above from zero
(b) $f$ is of bounded below from zero
(c) $f$ is not bounded from zero
(d) None of the above

**37.** If $f$ and $g$ are of bounded variation, then following is flase.
(a) $f + g$ is of bounded variation
(b) $f - g$ is of bounded variation
(c) $fg$ is of bounded variation
(d) $f/g$ is of bounded variation

**38.** If $f$ is constant function on $[a, b]$, then total variation of $f$ on $[a, b]$ is
(a) $V_f(a, b) = 0$ (b) $V_f(a, b) \geq 0$
(c) $V_f(a, b) \leq 0$ (d) None of these

**39.** The total variation of $f$ on $[a, b], V_f(a, b) = 0$ then
(a) $a = b$
(b) $f$ is constant on $[a, b]$
(c) $f$ is monotonic on $[a, b]$
(d) None of the above

**40.** If $f$ is an absolutely continuous function on $[a, b]$, then
(a) $f$ is of bounded variation
(b) $f$ is not of bounded variation
(c) $f$ is not continuous
(d) None of the above

**41.** The total variation on $[a, b]$ is
(a) non-negative finite number
(b) non-positive finite number
(c) extended real number
(d) None of the above

**42.** The total variation on $[a, b]$ is
(a) $V_f(a, b) < 0$ (b) $V_f(a, b) \geq 0$
(c) $V_f(a, b) = 0$ (d) None of these

**43.** If $f$ is absolutely continuous on $[a, b]$, then
(a) it is of bounded variation on $[a, b]$
(b) it is not of bounded variation on $[a, b]$
(c) Both (a) and (b)
(d) Neither (a) nor (b)

**44.** A function $f$ is of bounded variation on $[a, b]$ iff
(a) $f$ is a difference of two monotone real-valued function on $[a, b]$
(b) $f$ is a product of two monotone real-valued function on $[a, b]$
(c) $f$ is a ratio of two monotone real-valued function on $[a, b]$
(d) None of the above

**45.** A function of bounded variation is
(a) necessarily bounded
(b) necessarily unbounded
(c) may be bounded or bounded
(d) None of the above

**46.** The total variation of the function $\sin x$ on the interval $[0, 2\pi]$
(a) 1 (b) 2
(c) $2\pi$ (d) 4

**47.** If $f(x) = \sin x$. Then, the total variation of $f(x)$ on $[0, 2]$ is
(a) $\infty$ (b) 1
(c) 2 (d) 3

**48.** If $f(x) = \begin{cases} x, & x \in [0,1) \\ 1 + x, & x \in [1, 2] \end{cases}$. Then,
(a) $f(x) \notin R[a, b]$ but $f(x)$ is of bounded variation
(b) $f(x)$ is not of bounded variation as it is discontinuous at $x = 1$
(c) $f(x)$ is of bounded variation
(d) $f(x)$ is not of bounded variation as it is not monotonic

**49.** If $\alpha > 0$ and $\beta > 0$, the function
$f(x) = \begin{cases} x^{\alpha} \sin \dfrac{1}{x^{\beta}}, & \text{when } x \neq 0 \\ 0, & \text{when } x = 0 \end{cases}$, then $f(x)$ is of bounded variation in $[0, 1]$, if
(a) $\alpha > \beta$ (b) $\alpha < \beta$
(c) $1 + \alpha < \beta$ (d) None of these

**50.** A continuous function
(a) is always a function of bounded variation
(b) is never a function of bounded variation
(c) may or may not be a function of bounded variation
(d) None of the above

**51.** Let $F(x)$ is defined on $[a, b]$ s.t. $F(x) = x + \frac{1}{20} f(x)$ where $f(x)$ is differentiable on $[a, b]$ and $|f'(x)| < 10$, then from following statements select the correct statement /statements:
I. $F(x)$ is of bounded variation
II. $F(x)$ is one-one
III. $F(x)$ is decreasing
(a) Only I
(b) Only II and III
(c) Only I and II
(d) All are correct

**52.** If $f$ be of bounded variation function with variation function $g(x)$ such that $\lim_{x\to t} g(x)$ exists for all $t \in [a, b]$, then

(a) $g(x)$ is discontinuous on a non-empty finite subset of $[a, b]$
(b) $g(x)$ is continuous but not uniformly
(c) $g(x)$ is uniformly continuous
(d) None of the above

**53.** Select the incorrect statement.

(a) If $f$ is of bounded variation on $[a, b]$ to $[c, d]$ and one-one, then $f^{-1}$ is of bounded variation on $[c, d]$, provided $f^{-1}$ exist
(b) If $f$ is defined from $[a, b]$ onto itself and satisfies LMVT conditions, then $f$ is of bounded variation
(c) If $f(x) = \int_a^x g(t)\,dt, \forall x \in (a, b]$, then $f$ is of bounded variation if $g(t)$ is Riemann integrable
(d) If $g(x) \in R[a, b]$, then $g(x)$ is of bounded variation on $[a, b]$

**54.** If $g \in R[a, b]$ and $f(x) = \int_a^x b(t)dt, \forall x \in (a, b]$, then select the correct statement

(a) $f(x)$ is differentiable
(b) variation function of $f$ is given by $\int_a^x g(t)\,dt$
(c) the variation function of $f$ is given by $\int_a^x |g(t)|\,dt$
(d) $f$ may not be of bounded variation

**55.** For a subset $A$ of a metric space, which of the following implies the other three?

(a) $A$ is closed
(b) $A$ is bounded
(c) Closure of $B$ is compact for every $B \subseteq A$
(d) $A$ is compact

**56.** Set $S$ and $T$ are subsets of $R$. Then, select the incorrect statement.

(a) $(\text{int } S) \cap (\text{int } T) = \text{int}(S \cap T)$
(b) $(\text{int } S) \cup (\text{int } T) \subseteq \text{int}(S \cup T)$
(c) $\bar{S}$ is closed in $R$
(d) $\bar{T}$ is the largest closed set containing $T$

**57.** Which is not correct about the cantor ternary set?

(a) It is closed (b) It is uncountable
(c) It is dense (d) It is perfect set

**58.** Which statement is correct?

(a) Any two norm metrics on a finite-dimensionals are equivalent.
(b) Any finite dimensional *lss* of a *nls* $X$ provides *ba's* to any $x \in X$.
(c) If $X$ is complete and $A \in bL(X, Y)$ is bounded below, then *ran* $A$ is closed.
(d) All of the above

**59.** Which of the following sets is not countable?

(a) The set of range of all the sequences in a countable set of real sequences.
(b) The domain of a one-one function onto a countable set.
(c) The range of an onto function with countable domain.
(d) None of the above

**60.** A real number set $E$ is compact, if

(a) $E$ is bounded and open
(b) $E$ is unbounded and closed
(c) $E$ is bounded and closed
(d) $E$ is unbounded and open

**61.** If $F = \{A_1, A_2, ....\}$ is a countable collection of sets let $G = \{B_1, B_2, ....\}$ where $B_1 = A_1$ and for $n > 1$; $B_n = A_n \to \bigcup_{k=1}^{n-1} A_k$. Then, from the following statements which is/are true?

I. $G$ is a collection of disjoint sets
II. $\bigcup_{k=1}^{\infty} A_k = \bigcup_{k=1}^{\infty} B_k$
III. $\bigcup_{k=1}^{\infty} B_k$ is countable

Codes
(a) Only (I) (b) (I) and (III)
(c) (II) and (III) (d) All three

**62.** The collection $\mathbb{C}$ of sets is an open cover of set $A$ if

(a) every $B \in \mathbb{C}$ is open (b) every $B \in \mathbb{C}$ is closed
(c) some $B \in \mathbb{C}$ is open (d) None of these

**63.** Let $F$ be an open covering of $A$, then

(a) there exist countable sub-collection of $F$ which covers $A$
(b) there exist uncountable collection of $F$ which covers $A$
(c) Both (a) and (b) are true
(d) Both (a) and (b) are false

**64.** Scale invariance of metric space is

(a) $d(\alpha, y) = |\alpha|(x, y)$ (b) $d(\alpha x, \alpha y) = |\alpha|\, d(x, y)$
(c) $d(\alpha y, \beta x) = |\beta|\, d(x, y)$ (d) All of these

**65.** A set $E \subset R$ is compact, then

(a) it is closed and bounded
(b) it is open and bounded
(c) it is open and unbounded
(d) it is closed and unbounded

**66.** For Lebesgue measure, which property is not correct

(a) $\mu(I) = l(I)$
(b) $0 \le (A) \le \mu(B) \le \infty$
(c) $\mu(A + x_0) = \mu(A) + \mu(x_0)$
(d) $\mu(A \cup B) = \mu(A) + \mu(B)$

**67.** Mesh size of the part is

(a) $\Delta x_k$ (b) $\Delta x_k = 1$
(c) $\Delta x_k + 1$ (d) $\dfrac{\Delta x_k}{k}$

**68.** A set $E \subset R$ is called Lebesgue measurable, if for every subset $A$ of $R$, then

(a) $\mu^*(A) = \mu^*(A \cap E) + \mu^*(A \cap E)$
(b) $\mu^*(A) = \mu^*(A \cup E) + \mu^*(A \cap E)$
(c) $\mu^*(A) = \mu(A \cap E)$
(d) None of the above

**69.** A metric space $X$ satisfies Bolzano Weierstrass property, then
(a) every infinite sequence $\langle x_n \rangle$ in $X$ has no cluster point
(b) every infinite sequence $\langle x_n \rangle$ in $X$ has atleast one cluster point
(c) $X$ is not sequentially compact
(d) $X$ is not compact

**70.** Let $\langle x_n \rangle$ be a sequence from metric space $(X, \rho)$
A : $x$ is a limit of $x_n$, then $x$ is a cluster point.
B : $x$ is a cluster point of $x_n$, then $x$ is a limit of $x_n$.
(a) Only A is true (b) Only B is true
(c) Both A and B are true (d) Both A and B are false

**71.** If every sequence $\langle x_n \rangle$ in metric space $X$ is convergent, then every Cauchy sequence is $\langle x_n \rangle$ also
(a) convergent (b) divergent
(c) constant (d) None of these

**72.** The completeness axiom states
(a) every non-empty set $S$ of real numbers which is bounded above has supremum
(b) every non-empty set $S$ of real numbers which is bounded above has infimum
(c) every non-empty set $S$ of real numbers which is bounded have no supremum
(d) every non-empty set $S$ of real numbers which is bounded have no infimum

**73.** A metric space $X$ is compact
(a) it is sequentially compact
(b) it is not sequentially compact
(c) it does not satisfies Bolzano Weierstrass property
(d) None of the above

**74.** A sequentially compact metric space is
(a) totally bounded (b) unbounded
(c) non-compact (d) None of these

**75.** A collection $F$ of sets have finite intersection property, if
(a) any finite sub-collection of $F$ has empty intersection
(b) any finite sub-collection of $F$ has non-empty intersection
(c) any finite sub-collection of $F$ has empty set
(d) None of the above

**76.** The union of any finite collection of non-empty closed sets is
(a) open set (b) closed set
(c) null set (d) None of these

**77.** If $A$ is an open subset of complete metric space $X$, then
(a) $A$ is complete
(b) $A$ is incomplete
(c) complement of $A$ is closed
(d) None of the above

**78.** A metric space $(X, \rho)$ is complete, if
(a) every sequence in $X$ is convergent
(b) every sequence in $X$ is divergent
(c) every Cauchy sequence in $X$ is convergent
(d) every Cauchy sequence in $X$ is divergent

**79.** A metric space $X$ is sequentially compact, if
(a) every sequence $\langle x_n \rangle$ from $X$ have convergent subsequence
(b) every sequence $\langle x_n \rangle$ from $X$ have divergent subsequence
(c) Both (a) and (b) are false
(d) Both (a) and (b) are true

**80.** If $A$ is closed subset of complete metric space, then
(a) $A$ is complete metric space
(b) $A$ is incomplete metric space
(c) undefined
(d) None of the above

**81.** A set is of second category (non-merger), if
(a) it is of first category (b) it is not of first category
(c) it is empty (d) None of these

**82.** If there is a countable family $\{O_i\}$ of open sets in metric space $(X, \rho)$ such that $O \subset X$, $O = \bigcap_{O_i \subset O} O_i$, then
(a) $X$ is separable (b) $X$ is non-separable
(c) $X$ is closed (d) None of these

**83.** A continuous image of compact set is
(a) compact (b) non-compact
(c) unbounded (d) None of these

**84.** If $f$ is continuous real-valued function on compact space, then
(a) $f$ is unbounded (b) $f$ is bounded
(c) $f$ is constant (d) None of these

**85.** If $F$ is a closed and bounded set of real numbers, then each open covering of $F$ have
(a) finite sub-covering of $F$
(b) infinite sub-covering of $F$
(c) no finite sub-covering
(d) no infinite sub-covering

**86.** If $X$ is a complete metric space, $E$ is non-empty open subset of $X$, then
(a) $E$ is of first category
(b) $E$ is of second category
(c) $E$ is null set
(d) None of the above

**87.** A set $E$ is of first category, if
(a) $E$ is the union of countable collection of nowhere dense sets
(b) $E$ is the union of collection of nowhere dense sets
(c) $E$ is not the union of countable collection of nowhere dense sets
(d) None of the above

**88.** If $F = \{F_1, ..., F_n\}$ is a countable collection of sets, then *FQETP* finite intersection property of

(a) $\bigcap_{i=1}^{n} F_i = \phi$ (b) $\bigcap_{i=1}^{n} F_i \neq \phi$

(c) $\bigcup_{i=1}^{n} F_i = \phi$ (d) None of these

**89.** The empty set of a metric space $(X, \rho)$ is

(a) open set and closed set both
(b) neither open nor closed
(c) does not exist
(d) None of the above

**90.** A set $O$ of a metric space $(X, \rho)$ is open, if $x \in O, \exists \delta > 0$, such that

(a) all $y$ with $\rho(x, y) < \delta$ belongs to $O$
(b) all $y$ with $\rho(x, y) < \delta$ belongs to $X$
(c) all $y$ with $\rho(x, y) = \delta$ belongs to $X$
(d) None of the above

**91.** If $(X, \rho)$ is a metric space, then diameter of non-empty set $E \subset X$ is equal to

(a) $\sup\{\rho(x, y) : x, y \in E\}$ (b) $\inf\{\rho(x, y) : x, y \in E\}$
(c) $\{\rho(x, y) : x, y \in E\}$ (d) None of these

**92.** The collection e of sets covers a set $S$, if

(a) $F \subset \cup\{A : A \in \mathbb{G}\}$ (b) $F \supset \cup\{A : A \in \mathbb{G}\}$
(c) $F \subset \cap\{A : A \in \mathbb{G}\}$ (d) None of these

**93.** The function $\rho : X \to \mathbb{R}$ is called pseudo metric, if

(a) $\rho(x, y) = 0$ iff $x = y$
(b) $\rho(x, y) = 0$ for some $x \neq y$
(c) $\rho(x, y) \neq 0$ for $x = y$
(d) None of the above

**94.** The metric space $(X, \rho)$ is

(a) Both open and closed sets
(b) Neither open nor closed
(c) null set
(d) None of the above

**95.** A metric space $X$ is compact, if

(a) it is complete
(b) it is incomplete
(c) It is unbounded
(d) None of the above

**96.** If $\rho$ is an extended metric on set $x$, then for some $x, y \in X$

(a) $\rho(x, y) < \infty$ (b) $\rho(x, y) = +\infty$
(c) $\rho(x, y) > \infty$ (d) None of these

**97.** If $F$ is an open covering of a closed and bounded set $A$, then

(a) there exist a infinite sub-collection of $F$ which covers $A$
(b) there exist a uncountable sub-collection of $F$ which covers $A$
(c) there exist a finite sub-collection of $F$ which cover $A$
(d) None of the above

**98.** The union of two non-empty closed sets of metric space is

(a) open set (b) closed set
(c) null set (d) None of these

**99.** A function $f$ of metric space $\langle X, \rho_1 \rangle$ onto $\langle Y, \rho_2 \rangle$ is homomorphism, if

(a) $f(X) = Y$ (b) $f(X) \subset Y$
(c) $f(X) \neq Y$ (d) None of these

**100.** A set $F$ of metric space $(X, \rho)$ is closed

(a) if it contains all its point of closure
(b) if its complement is open
(c) (a) is true, (b) is false
(d) Both (a) and (b) are true

**101.** The complement of non-empty open set of metric space is

(a) open set (b) closed set
(c) null set (d) None of these

**102.** The closure of any non-empty set $E$ of a metric space is

(a) closed set (b) open set
(c) null set (d) None of these

**103.** Let $F$ be an open covering of $A$, then

(a) there exist countable sub-collection of $F$ which covers $A$
(b) there exist uncountable collection of $F$ which covers $A$
(c) Both (a) and (b) are true
(d) Both (a) and (b) are false

**104.** The collection $\mathbb{G}$ of sets is an open cover of set $A$ if

(a) every $B \in \mathbb{G}$ is open (b) every $B \in \mathbb{G}$ is closed
(c) some $B \in \mathbb{G}$ is open (d) None of the above

**105.** If $\mathbb{G}$ is a collection of open sets of real numbers, then there is a countable sub-collection $\{O_i\}$ of $\mathbb{G}$ such that

(a) $\bigcup_{O \in \mathbb{G}} O \subset \bigcup_{i=1}^{\infty} O_i$ (b) $\bigcup_{O \in \mathbb{G}} O \supset \bigcup_{i=1}^{\infty} O_i$

(c) $\bigcup_{O \in \mathbb{G}} O = \bigcup_{i=1}^{\infty} O_i$ (d) None of these

**106.** The union of any collection of open sets of metric space is

(a) open set (b) closed set
(c) null set (d) None of these

**107.** If $X$ and $Y$ are metric spaces and for every open-set of $YO \subset Y, f^{-1}(O) \subset X$ is open, then

(a) $f$ is continuous function
(b) $f$ is constant function
(c) $f$ is increasing function
(d) $f$ is decreasing function

**108.** If $(X, \rho)$ is metric space, then for all $x, y \in X$

(a) $\rho(x, y) \leq 0$
(b) $\rho(x, y) = 0$ for some $x \neq y$
(c) $\rho(x, y) = 0$ if $x = y$
(d) None of the above

**109.** If $X$ is a non-empty set, $\rho: X \to \mathbb{R}, (X, \rho)$ is pseudometric, then $\forall x, y \in X$

(a) $x = y \Rightarrow \rho(x, y) = 0$
(b) $x \neq y \Rightarrow \rho(x, y) = 0$
(c) $\rho(x, y) = 0$ for some $x \neq y$
(d) None of the above

**110.** If $\langle X, \rho \rangle$ is metric space, then for all $x, y, z \in X$

(a) $\rho(x, y) \leq \rho(x, z) + \rho(z, y)$ (b) $\rho(x, y) \geq \rho(x, z) + \rho(z, y)$
(c) $\rho(x, y) \leq 0$ (d) None of these

**111.** If $(X, \rho)$ is metric space, then for all $x, y \in X$

(a) $\rho(x, y) = 0$, then $x = y$
(b) $\rho(x, y) = 0$, then some $x \neq y$
(c) $\rho(x, y) < 0$ for some $x \neq y$
(d) $\rho(x, y) < 0$ for some $x = y$

**112.** Let $f_n(x) = \begin{cases} 1/x, n < x < n+1 \\ 0, \quad \text{otherwise} \end{cases}$

If $f(x) = \lim_{n \to \infty} f_n(x)$, then $\int_{(0,\infty)} f(x)dx = \lim_{n \to \infty} \int_{(0,\infty)} f_n(x)dx$ follows by

(a) bounded convergence theorem
(b) monotone convergence theorem
(c) dominated convergence theorem
(d) None of the above

**113.** Given set $S \subseteq R$ with the property that for every $x \subset S$ the intersection of $S$ with any interval containing $x$ is countable, then $S$ is

(a) uncountable and not of measure zero
(b) uncountable but of measure zero
(c) countable
(d) None of the above

**114.** Any countable set of points on the real axis has

(a) no measure (b) measure one
(c) measure zero (d) None of these

**115.** Let $f:(\Omega, F) \to [0, +\infty]$ be a non-negative and measurable map, then

(a) $\int f d\mu = 0$ (b) $\int f d\mu = I^{\mu}(f)$
(c) $\int f d\mu = g \int dr$ (d) $\int f d\mu = 1$

**116.** If $f$ is a measurable function and $f = g$ almost everywhere, then $g$ is

(a) measurable
(b) not measurable
(c) neither measurable nor not measurable
(d) None is true

**117.** If $f$ is integrable on $[a, b]$ and $\int_a^x f(t)dt = 0$ for all $x \in |a, b|$, then

(a) $f(t) = 0$ almost everywhere in $[a, b]$
(b) $f(t) = 0$ nowhere in $[a, b]$
(c) $f(t)$ is not equal to zero almost everywhere in $[a, b]$
(d) None of the above

**118.** $\int (-f) d\mu$ is equal to

(a) 0 (b) 1
(c) $-\int f d\mu$ (d) $-\int f(-d\mu)$

**119.** I. If $f$ is bounded and measurable on $[a, b]$ and $F(x) = \int_a^x f'(t)dt + F(a)$, then $F'(x) = f(x)$ for almost all $x \in [a, b]$.

II. If $f$ is an integrable function on $[a, b]$ and suppose that $F(x) = F(a) + \int_a^x f(t)dt$. Then, $F'(x) = f(x)$ for almost all $x \in [a, b]$.

(a) Only I is true (b) Only II is true
(c) Both I and II are true (d) Both I and II are false

**120.** A sequence $< f_n >$ of measurable functions is ..., if given $\varepsilon > 0$, there is an $N$ such that for all $m, n \geq N$, we have $m\{x: | f_n(x) - f_m(x) | \geq \varepsilon\} < \varepsilon$

(a) Cauchy sequence in measure
(b) Lebesgue sequence
(c) Differentiable sequence
(d) None of the above

**121.** Which of the following statement is true?

I. If $E$ is a set of finite outer measure and $J$ a collection of intervals that cover $E$ in the sense of Vitali. Then, given $\varepsilon > 0$, there is a finite disjoint collection $\{I_1, ..., I_N\}$ of intervals in $J$ such that $m^* \left[ E \sim \bigcup_{n=1}^{N} I_n \right] < \varepsilon$

II. If $f$ is continuous on $[a, b]$ and one of its derivatives (say $D^+$) is everywhere non-negative on $(a, b)$, then $f$ is non-decreasing on $[a, b]$; *i.e.*, $f(x) \leq f(y)$ for $x \leq y$.

III. If $f$ is an increasing real-valued function on the interval $[a, b]$. Then, $f$ is differentiable almost everywhere. The derivative $f'$ is measurable, and $\int_a^b f'(x)dx \leq f(b) - f(a)$

(a) Statement I is true only
(b) Statement II is true only
(c) Statement III is true only
(d) Statements I, II and III are all true

**122.** Which of the following statements are false?

I. If $< f_n >$ is a sequence of measurable functions that converges in measure to $f$. Then, there is a subsequence $< f_{nk} >$ that converges to $f$ almost everywhere.

II. If $< f_n >$ is a sequence of measurable functions defined on a measurable set $E$ of finite measure. Then, $< f_n >$ converges of $f$ in measure iff every subsequence of $< f_n >$ has in turn a subsequence that converges almost everywhere to $f$.

(a) Only I is false
(b) Only II is false
(c) Both I and II are false
(d) None of the statement is false

**123.** If $< g_n >$ is a sequence of integrable functions which converges almost everywhere to an integrable function $g$. If $< f_n >$ is a sequence of measurable functions such that $|f_n| \leq g_n$ and $< f_n >$ converges to $f$ almost everywhere. If $\int g = \lim \int g_n$, then

(a) $\int f = \lim \int f_n$ (b) $\int f > \lim \int f_n$
(c) $\int f < \lim \int f_n$ (d) None of these

**124.** If $f$ and $g$ are integrable over $E$. Then,

I. the function $cf$ is integrable over $E$ and $\int_E cf = c\int_E f$,

II. the function $f+g$ is integrable over $E$ and $\int_E (f+g) = \int_E f + \int_E g$.

(a) Only I is true
(b) Only II is true
(c) Both I and II are true
(d) None is true

**125.** If $g$ is integrable over $E$ and $< f_n >$ is a sequence of measurable functions such that $|f_n| \leq g$ on $E$ and for almost all $x \in E$ we have $f(x) = \lim f_n(x)$. Then, $\int_E f \leq \lim \int_E f_n$

(a) Lebesgue convergence theorem
(b) Lebesgue divergence theorem
(c) Cauchy convergence theorem
(d) None of the above

**126.** If $f$ is a measurable function, then $f$ is integrable over $E$

(a) if $f^+$ and $f^-$ are both integrable over $E$,
(b) if $\int_E f(x)\,dx = \int_E f^+(x)dx + \int_E f^-(x)dx$
(c) Both (a) and (b)
(d) None of the above

**127.** If $f$ and $g$ are integrable over $E$. Then

I. if $f \leq g$ almost everywhere, then $\int_E f \leq \int_E g$

II. if $A$ and $B$ are disjoint measurable sets contained in $E$, then $\int_{A\cup B} f = \int_A f + \int_B f$

(a) Only I is true (b) Only II is true
(c) Both I and II are true (d) None is true

**128.** A sequence $< f_n >$ of measurable functions is said to ... to $f$ in measure, if given $\varepsilon > 0$, there is an $N$ such that for all $n \geq N$, we have $m\{x: |f(x) - f_n(x)| \geq \varepsilon\} < \varepsilon$.

(a) converge (b) diverge
(c) oscillate (d) None of these

**129.** If $f^+(x) = \max\{f(x), 0\}$ and $f^-(x) = \max\{-f(x), 0\}$, then

(a) $|f| = f^+ + f^-$ (b) $|f| = f^+ - f^-$
(c) $|f| = f^+$ (d) $|f| = f^-$

**130.** The positive part of function $f$ is defined as

(a) $f^+(x) = \max\{f(x), 0\}$
(b) $f^-(x) = \max\{-f(x), 0\}$
(c) $f = f^+ - f^-$
(d) $f = f^+ + f^-$

**131.** Let $f$ and $g$ be two non-negative measurable functions. If $f$ is integrable over $E$ and $g(x) < f(x)$ on $E$, then $g$ is also integrable on $E$

(a) integrable (b) not integrable
(c) Both (a) and (b) (d) Neither (a) nor (b)

**132.** If $< u_n >$ is a sequence of non-negative measurable functions and $f = \sum_{n=1}^{\infty} u_n$. Then,

(a) $\int f = \int u_n$ (b) $\int f = \sum_{n=1}^{\infty} \int u_n$
(c) $\int f < \sum_{n=1}^{\infty} \int u_n$ (d) $f > \sum_{n=1}^{\infty} \int u_n$

**133.** Given following statements

I. If $< E_i >$ is a sequence of Lebesgue measurable set and if the sets $E_i$'s are pairwise disjoint, then for Lebesgue measure $m(\cup E_i) = \Sigma m E_i$

II. Let $< E_n >$ be an infinite decreasing sequence of Legesgue measurable sets, *i.e.*, $E_{n+1} \subset E_n$ for each $n$. Let Lebesgue measure $mE_i$ is finite. Then, $m\left(\bigcup_{n=1}^{\infty} E_i\right) = \lim_{n\to\infty} mE_n$.

(a) Only I is true (b) Only II is true
(c) Both I and II are true (d) Neither I nor II is true

**134.** If $f$ is a non-negative function and $< E_i >$ a disjoint sequence of measurable sets. Let $E = \cup E_i$. Then,

(a) $\int_E f = \cup \int_{E_i} f$ (b) $\int_E f > \Sigma \int_{E_i} f$
(c) $\int_E f < \Sigma \int_{E_i} f$ (d) $\int_E f = \Sigma \int_{E_i} f$

**135.** Following is the Littlewood's Three Principles;

I. Every (measurable) set is nearly a finite union of intervals.

II. Every (measurable) set is nearly continuous.

III. Every convergent sequence of (measurable) functions is nearly uniformly convergent.

(a) Only I (b) Only II
(c) Only III (d) All the three I, II, III

**136.** If $f$ is a non-negative function which is integrable over a set $E$. Then, given $\varepsilon > 0$ there is $\delta > 0$ such that for every set $A \subset E$ with $mA < \delta$ one have

(a) $\int_A f = \varepsilon$ (b) $\int_A f > \varepsilon$
(c) $\int_A f < \varepsilon$ (d) None of these

**137.** Given following statements

I. The length of an interval I is the difference of end points of the interval.

II. The Lebesgue outer measure of an interval is its length.

(a) Only I is true (b) Only II is true
(c) Both I and II are true (d) Neither I nor II is true

**138.** If $f^+(x) = \max\{f(x), 0\}$ and $f^-(x) = \max\{-f(x), 0\}$, then

(a) $f = f^+ - f^-$ (b) $f = f^{+-}$
(c) $f = -f^-$ (d) $f = f^+ + f^-$

**139.** If $f$ is a measurable functions, then
(a) $\int_E cf < c\int_E f, c>0$ (b) $\int_E cf > c\int_E f, c>0$
(c) $\int_E cf = c\int_E f, c>0$ (d) None of these

**140.** A non-negative measurable function $f$ is integrable over the measurable set $E$, if
(a) $\int_E f = \infty$ (b) $\int_E f > \infty$
(c) $\int_E f < \infty$ (d) None of these

**141.** If $<f_n>$ is a sequence of Lebesgue measurable functions (with the same domain of definition). Then
(a) the functions sup $\{f_1, ...., f_n\}$ and inf $\{f_1, ... f_n\}$ are Lebesgue measurable
(b) the functions $\sup_n f_n$ and $\inf_n f_n$ are Lebesgue measurable
(c) the functions $\overline{\lim}\ f_n$ and $\underline{\lim} f_n$ are Lebesgue measurable
(d) All (a), (b), (c) are true

**142.** The negative part of function $f$ is defined as
(a) $f^+(x) = \max\{f(x), 0\}$ (b) $f^-(x) = \max\{-f(x), 0\}$
(c) $f = f^+ - f^-$ (d) $|f| = f^+ + f^-$

**143.** If $f$ and $g$ are measurable functions and $f \le g$ almost everywhere, then
(a) $\int_E f = \int_E g$ (b) $\int_E f > \int_E g$
(c) $\int_E f \le \int_E g$ (d) None of these

**144.** Egorff's theorem state
(a) If $E$ is a measurable set of finite measure and $<f_n>$ a sequence of measurable functions defined on $E$. If $f$ is real-valued function such that for each $x \in E$, we have $f_n(x) \to f(x)$. Then, given $\varepsilon > 0$ and $\delta > 0$, there is a measurable set $A \subset E$ with $mA < \delta$ and an integer $N$ such that for all $x \notin A$ and all $n \ge N$. $|f_n(x) - f(x)| < \varepsilon$.
(b) If $<f_n>$ is a sequence of measurable functions that converge to a real-valued function $f$ almost everywhere on a measurable set $E$ of finite measure, then given $\eta > 0$, there is a subset $A \subset E$ with $mA < \eta$ such that $f_n$ converges to $f$ uniformly on $E \sim A$.
(c) If $f_n$ is a measurable real-valued function on an interval $[a, b]$. Then, given $\delta > 0$, there is a continuous function $\phi$ on $[a, b]$ such that $m\{x : f(x) \ne \phi(x)\} < \delta$
(d) None of the above

**145.** A real-valued function $\phi$ is ... function, if it is Lebesgue measurable and assume only a finite number of values.
(a) simple (b) complex
(c) discrete (d) None of these

**146.** If $f$ and $g$ are measurable functions, then
(a) $\int_E f + g > \int_E f + \int_E g$ (b) $\int_E f + g < \int_E f + \int_E g$
(c) $\int_E f + g = \int_E f + \int_E g$ (d) None of these

**147.** If $c$ is a constant and $f$ and $g$ are two Lebesgue measurable real-valued functions defined on the same domain. Then,
(a) the functions $f + c$ and $cf$, also Lebesgue measurable
(b) the functions $f + g$ and $g - f$ are also Lebesgue measurable
(c) the function $fg$ is also Lebesgue measurable
(d) All (a), (b), (c) are true

**148.** Let $f$ and $g$ be two non-negative measurable functions. If $f$ is integrable over $E$ and $g(x) < f(x)$ on $E$, then
(a) $\int_E (f-g) < \int_E f - \int_E g$ (b) $\int_E (f-g) = \int_E f - \int_E g$
(c) $\int_E (f-g) > \int_E f - \int_E g$ (d) None of these

**149.** Given following statements
I. The collection $M$ of Lebesgue measurable sets is a σ-algebra.
II. Every set with Lebesgue outer measure zero is Lebesgue measurable.
III. The interval $(a, \infty)$ is Lebesgue measurable.
(a) Only I is true (b) Only II is true
(c) Only III is true (d) All I, II and III are true

**150. Statement I.** Let $\phi = \sum_{i=1} a_i \chi_{E_i}$, with $E_i \cap E_j = \phi$ for $i \ne j$. Suppose, each set $E_i$ is a measurable set of finite measure. Then, $\int \phi = \sum_{i=1}^{n} a_i mE_i$.

**Statement II.** If $\phi$ and $\psi$ is simple function which vanish outside a set of finite measure, then $\int (a\phi + b\psi) = a\int \phi + b\int \psi$ and if $\phi \ge \psi$ almost everywhere, then $\int \phi \ge \int \psi$.

**Statement III.** If $f$ is defined and bounded on a measurable set $E$ with $mE$ and $\inf_{f \le \psi} \int_E \psi(x)dx = \sup_{f > \phi} \int_E \psi(x)dx$ for all simple functions $\phi$ and $\psi$. Then, $f$ is measurable function.
(a) Only I is true (b) Only II is true
(c) Only III is true (d) All I, II, III are true

**151.** Given following statements
I. The set [0, 1] is not countable.
II. If $E_1$ and $E_2$ are Lebesgue measurable, so $E_1 \cup E_2$
III. The family $M$ of Lebesgue measurable sets is an algebra of sets.
(a) Only I is true (b) Only II is true
(c) Only III is true (d) All I, II and III are true

**152.** Fatou's lemma states If $<f_n>$ is a sequence of non-negative measurable functions and $f_n(x) \to f(x)$, almost everywhere on a set $E$, then
(a) $\int_E f \le \underline{\lim} \int_E f_n$ (b) $\int_E f \le \int_E f_n$
(c) $\int_E f \ge \underline{\lim} \int_E f_n$ (d) None of these

**153.** A real-valued function of set $E$, defined as
$$\chi_E = \begin{cases} 1, x \in E \\ 0, x \notin E \end{cases} \text{ is}$$
(a) Characteristic function (b) Simple function
(c) Both (a) and (b) (d) Neither (a) nor (b)

**154.** Lusin's theorem states
(a) If $E$ is a measurable set of finite measure and $< f_n >$ a sequence of measurable functions defined on $E$. If $f$ is real-valued function such that for each $x \in E$, we have $f_n(x) \to f(x)$. Then, given $\varepsilon > 0$ and $\delta > 0$, there is a measurable set $A \subset E$ with $mA < \delta$ and an integer $N$ such that for all $x \notin A$ and all $n \geq N$, $|f_n(x) - f(x)| < \varepsilon$.
(b) If $< f_n >$ is a sequence of measurable functions that converge to a real-valued function $f$ almost everywhere on a measurable set $E$ of finite measure, then given $\eta > 0$, there is a subset $A \subset E$ with $mA < \eta$ such that $f_n$ converges to $f$ uniformly on $E \sim A$.
(c) If $f_n$ is a measurable real-valued function on an interval $[a, b]$. Then, given $\delta > 0$, there is a continuous function $\phi$ on $[a, b]$ such that $m\{x : f(x) \neq \phi(x)\} < \delta$
(d) None of the above

**155.** Given following statements
I. Every Borel set is Lebesgue measurable.
II. Each open set and closed set is Lebesgue measurable.
III. If $< E_i >$ is a sequence of Lebesgue measurable set. Then, for Lebesgue measure $m(\cup E_i) \leq \Sigma m E_i$.

(a) Only I is true (b) Only II is true
(c) Only III is true (d) All I, II and III are true

**156.** If $f$ is a non-negative measurable function defined on a measurable set $E$, then Integral of non-negative measurable function $f$ is defined as
(a) $\int_E f = \sup_{h \leq f} \int_E h$, where $h$ is a unbounded measurable function such that $m\{x : h(x) \neq 0\} > \infty$
(b) $\int_E f = \inf_{h \leq f} \int_E h$, where $h$ is a bounded measurable function such that $m\{x : h(x) \neq 0\} > \infty$
(c) $\int_E f = \sup_{h \leq f} \int_E h$, where $h$ is a bounded measurable function such that $m\{x : h(x) \neq 0\} < \infty$
(d) $\int_E f = \sup_{h \leq f} \int_E h$, where $h$ is a unbounded measurable function such that $m\{x : h(x) \neq 0\} = \infty$

**157.** Monotone convergence theorem states: If $< f_n >$ is an increasing sequence of non-negative measurable functions and let $f = \lim f_n$ almost everywhere, then
(a) $\int f = \int f_n$ (b) $\int f = \lim \int f_n$
(c) $\int f < \int f_n$ (d) None of these

**158.** Let $C$ be the standard Cantor's middle thirds set. Then,
(a) $C$ is not measurable
(b) $C$ is countable and of measure zero
(c) $C$ is uncountable and of measure zero
(d) $C$ is uncountable and of positive measure

# Exercise 2 (For Part 'C')

**Direction** (Q. Nos. 1-51) *Questions may have one or more than one correct option.*

**1.** If $f$ is integrable on closed interval $[a, b]$, then the function $F$ defined by $F(x) = \int_a^x f(t)\,dt$ is
(a) continuous function of bounded variation on $[a, b]$
(b) discontinuous function of bounded variation on $[a, b]$
(c) function of bounded variation
(d) continuous function

**2.** If $f$ is of bounded variation on $[a, b]$, then
(a) total variation is the sum of positive and negative variations of $f$ over $[a, b]$
(b) total variation is equal to positive variations of $f$ over $[a, b]$
(c) total variation is equal to negative variations of $f$ over $[a, b]$
(d) total variation is not equal to the sum of positive and negative variations of $f$ over $[a, b]$

**3.** A function $f$ is of bounded variation on $[a, b]$
(a) if it is the difference of two monotone real-valued function on $[a, b]$
(b) if it is not the difference of two monotone real-valued function on $[a, b]$
(c) Both (a) and (b) are true
(d) Neither (a) nor (b) is true

**4.** If function $f$ is the difference of two monotone real-valued functions on $[a, b]$, then
(a) $f$ is of bounded variation
(b) $f$ is not bounded variation
(c) Both (a) and (b) are true
(d) Neither (a) nor (b) is true

**5.** The collection $\mathbb{C}$ of open intervals of the form $\left(\frac{1}{n}, \frac{2}{n}\right)$, $n = 2, 3, \ldots$ is an open covering of the open interval $(0, 1)$, then

(a) finite sub-collection covers (0, 1)
(b) finite sub-collection does not cover (0, 1)
(c) the union of intervals is (0, 1)
(d) the union of intervals is (0, 0)

**6.** Let $A$ and $B$ be two sets of positive real numbers bounded above, Let $a = \text{Sup } A$ and $b = \text{Sup} B$ and $C = \{xy : x \in A\}$ and $y \in B\}$, then
(a) $x > 0, y > 0 \Rightarrow xy \le ab$
(b) $ab$ is an upper bound for $c$
(c) $ab = \text{Sup } c$
(d) $ab$ is an lower bound for $c$

**7.** Let $f$ be bounded and integrable in $[-\pi, \pi]$ and monotonic in $[-\alpha, 0[$ and $]0, \alpha]$, (not necessarily in the same sense), where $\alpha$, is some positive number less than $\pi$. Then,
(a) $\frac{1}{2}a_0 + \sum_{n=1}^{\infty} a_n = \frac{f(+0) + f(-0)}{2}$
(b) $\frac{1}{2}a_0 + \sum_{n=1}^{\infty} a_n \ne \frac{f(+0) + f(-0)}{2}$
(c) $\frac{1}{2}a_0 + \sum_{n=1}^{\infty} a_n = \frac{1}{2\pi}\int_{-\pi}^{+\pi} f(x)\,dx + \frac{1}{\pi}\int_{-\pi}^{+\pi} f(x) \sum_{n=1}^{m} \cos n\pi dx$
(d) $\frac{1}{2}a_0 + \sum_{n=1}^{\infty} a_n = \frac{1}{\pi}[f(-0) + f(+0)] \int_0^{\infty} \frac{\sin x}{x}\,dx$ as $m \to \infty$

**8.** If $A$ and $B$ are respectively open and closed set in $\mathbb{R}^n$, then
(a) $A - B$ is open (b) $B - A$ is closed
(c) $A - B$ is closed (d) $B - A$ is open

**9.** If $x$ is an accumulation point of $S \subset \mathbb{R}^n$, then
(a) every open ball $B(x)$ contains infinitely many points
(b) every open ball $B(x)$ contains finitely many points
(c) every open ball $B(x)$ does not contain many of its points
(d) every open ball $B(x)$ contains $x$

**10.** Which of the follwoing(s) is/are true?
(a) $S \subset \mathbb{R}^n$ is closed, if it contains all its adherent points
(b) $S \subset \mathbb{R}^n$ is closed, if it does not contain all its adherent points
(c) $S \subset \mathbb{R}^n$ is closed, if some adherent points does not belong to $S$
(d) $S \subset \mathbb{R}^n$ is closed, if $\mathbb{R}^n - S$ is open

**11.** Which of the following(s) is/are true?
(a) If a set $S \subset \mathbb{R}^n$ contains all its adherent points, then $S$ is closed set.
(b) If a set $S \subset \mathbb{R}^n$ contains all its adherent points, then $S$ is not a closed set.
(c) If $\mathbb{R}^n - S$ is open, then $S \subset \mathbb{R}^n$ is closed.
(d) If $\mathbb{R}^n - S$ is open, then $S \subset \mathbb{R}^n$ is open.

**12.** Given collection $\mathbb{C}$ of oven intervals of the form $\left(-\frac{1}{n}, \frac{1}{n}\right)$, then
(a) $\mathbb{C}$ is a covering of $(-1, 2)$
(b) $\mathbb{C}$ is not a covering of $(-1, 2)$
(c) union of intervals is $(-1, 1)$
(d) union of intervals is $(1, -1)$

**13.** If $S \subset \mathbb{R}^n$, then
(a) $S$ is compact $\Rightarrow$ $S$ is closed and bounded
(b) $S$ is closed and bounded $\Rightarrow$ $S$ is compact
(c) $S$ is closed and bounded $\Leftrightarrow$ $S$ is compact
(d) $S$ is closed and bounded, then there is an open covering of $S$ such that a finite subcollection of open covering also covers $S$.

**14.** If $\{Q_1, Q_2, \ldots\}$ is a countable collection of non-empty sets in $\mathbb{R}^n$. Such that
I. $Q_{k+1} \subset Q_k$
II. each set $Q_k$ is closed and bounded
(a) $\bigcap_{k=1}^{\infty} Q_k$ is open (b) $\bigcap_{k=1}^{\infty} Q_k$ is closed
(c) $\bigcap_{k=1}^{\infty}$ is empty (d) $\bigcap_{k=1}^{\infty}$ is non-empty

**15.** Let $X$ is metric space
(a) if $X$ is sequentially compact, then $X$ is compact
(b) if $X$ is sequentially compact, then $X$ is not compact
(c) if $X$ is compact, $X$ is totally bounded
(d) if $X$ is compact, $X$ is totally unbounded

**16.** If $X$ is a compact space and $L$ a lattice of continuous real-valued functions on $X$ with the following properties
I. $L$ separates points; that is, if $x \ne y$, there is an $f \in L$ with $f(x) \ne f(y)$.
II. If $f \in L$, and $c$ is any real number, then $cf$ and $c + f$ also belong to $L$.

Then, given any continuous real-valued function $h$ on $X$ and any $\in > 0$.
(a) There is a function $g \in L$ such that for all $x \in X$ $0 \le g(x) - h(x) < \varepsilon$
(b) If $L$ is non-empty, then constant functions belong to $L$
(c) If $L$ is non-empty, then constant functions does not belong to $L$
(d) There is a function $g \in L$ such that for all $x \in X$ $0 \ge g(x) - h(x) > \varepsilon$

**17.** Which of the following(s) is/are true?
(a) A metric space $X$ has the Bolzano-Weierstrass property, if $X$ is sequentially compact.
(b) A metric space $X$ is sequentially compact, if $X$ has Bolzano-Weierstrass property.
(c) A metric space $X$ has the Bolzano-Weierstrass property iff $X$ is sequentially compact.
(d) A metric space $X$ is sequentially compact, if $X$ does not satisfies Bolzano-Weierstrass property.

**18.** Which of the following(s) is/are true?
(a) Closed subset of a compact space is compact.
(b) If $X$ is compact, $F$ is closed subset of $X$ and $U$ an open coverig for $F$. Then, $U \cup \{\tilde{F}\}$ is an open covering for $X$.
(c) A closed subset of compact at space is not compact.
(d) If $X$ is compact, $F$ is closed subset of $X$ and $U$ an open covering for $F$, then $U$ has a finite subcovering.

**19.** Let $X$ be a compact space and $A$ an algebra of continuous real-valued functions on $X$ that separates the points of $X$ and contains the constant functions. Then, given any continuous real-valued function $f$ on $X$ and any $\varepsilon > 0$
(a) If a function $g$ in $A$ such that for all $x$ in $X$ we have $|g(x) - f(x)| < \varepsilon$
(b) $A$ is a dense subset of $C(X)$
(c) $C(X)$ is the space of continuous real functions on $X$
(d) $\bar{A}$, the closure of $A$ is a lattice and equal to $C(X)$

**20.** If $F$ is a family of real-valued continuous functions on a complete metric space $X$, and suppose that for each $x \in X$ there is a number $M_x$ such that $|f(x)| \le M_x$ for all $f \in F$.
(a) There is a non-empty open set $O \subset X$ and a constant $M$ such that $|f(x)| \le M$ for all $f \in F$ and all $x \in O$.
(b) There is an empty set $\phi \subset X$ and a constant $M$ such that $|f(x)' \le M|$ for all $f \in F$ and all $x \in \phi$.
(c) Since, $X$ is complete metric space there is a set $E_m$ which is nowhere dense.
(d) Since, $X$ is complete metric space there is a set $E_m$ which is not nowhere dense.

**21.** If $E$ is a subset of a topological space $X$ and $f: E \to Y$ a continuous map into a complete metric space $(Y, \sigma)$
(a) then $f$ may be extended to a continuous function $f^*: E^* \to Y$ defined on a set $E^*$ that is a $G_\delta$ containing $E$
(b) then $f$ may not be extended to a continuous function $f^*: E^* \to Y$ defined on a set $E^*$
(c) $f^*(x) = f(x)$ for $x \in E$ and $f^*$ is continuous
(d) $f^*(x) \ne f(x)$ for $x \in E$ and $f^*$ is continuous

**22.** If $(X, \rho)$ be a complete metric space and $E \subset XaG_\delta$, then
(a) there is a metric $\sigma$ for $E$, equivalent on $E$ to $\rho$
(b) $(E, \sigma)$ is a complete metric space
(c) $(E, \sigma)$ is not a complete metric space
(d) there is no metric $\sigma$ of $E$ which is equivalent on $E$ to $\rho$.

**23.** If $\langle f_n \rangle$ is a sequence of mappings of a countable set $D$ into a metric space $Y$ such that for each $x \in D$ the closure of the set $\{f_n(x): 0 \le n < \infty\}$ is compact, then
(a) there is a subsequence $\langle f_m \rangle$ that converges for each $x$ in $D$
(b) there is no subsequence $\langle f_m \rangle$ that diverges for each $x \in D$
(c) for each $x \in D$, there is subsequence $\langle f_m \rangle$ that converges
(d) for each $x \in D$, there is subsequence $\langle f_m \rangle$ that diverges

**24.** If metric space $X$ is separable, then there is a countable family $\{O_i\}$ of open sets such that for any open set $O \subset X$, then
(a) $O = \bigcup_{O_i \subset O} O_i$
(b) $O \subset \bigcup_{O_i \subset O} O_i$
(c) $O \supset \bigcup_{O_i \subset O} O_i$
(d) $O \in \bigcup_{O_i \subset O} O_i$

**25.** Which of the following(s) is/are correct?
(a) Every integer $n > 1$ is either prime or product of primes.
(b) If $n$ is not prime there is $1 < d < n$ such that $d / n$
(c) $n = 4, 6, 8, 9, 10$ .... are prime numbers
(d) $n = 2, 3, 5$ .... are product of prime numbers

**26.** If $S \subset \mathbb{R}^n$ and if every infinite subset of $S$ has an accumulation point in $S$, then
(a) $S$ is bounded
(b) $S$ is not bounded
(c) $S$ contains all its accumulation points
(d) $S$ does not contains all its accumulation points

**27.** If $S$ is a subset of $\mathbb{R}^n$, if $S$ is closed and bounded, then
(a) every infinite subset of $S$ has an accumulation point in $S$
(b) every infinite subset of $S$ has no accumulation point in $S$
(c) if $S$ is bounded, then its subset is bounded
(d) if $S$ is bounded, then its subset is not bounded

**28.** If the functions $f$ and $\phi$ are bounded and integrable in $[a, b]$, then
(a) $\left[\int_a^b f(x)\phi(x)dx\right]^2 \le \int_a^b [f(x)]^2\, dx \int_a^b [\phi(x)]^2\, dx$
(b) the sign of equality hold in (a), if $f, \phi$ are constant
(c) the sign of equality hold in (a), if $f, \phi$ are constant
(d) the inequality in (a) does not holds

**29.** If $f$ is bounded and measurable on closed interval $[a, b]$, then
(a) $F(x) = \int_a^x f(t)dt + F(a)$
(b) $F'(x)$ exist for almost all $x \in [a, b]$
(c) $F'(x) = f(x)$ almost everywhere in $[a, b]$
(d) $F'(x) - f(x) = 0$ almost everywhere in $[a, b]$

**30.** Let $\langle f_n \rangle$ be a sequence of measurable functions (with the same domain), then
(a) $\text{Inf}\{f_1, f_1, \ldots, f_n\}$ is measurable
(b) $\text{Inf}\{f_1, f_1, \ldots, f_n\}$ is not measurable
(c) $\text{Inf}_n f_n$ is measurable
(d) $\text{Inf}_n f_n$ is not measurable

**31.** If $\langle f_n \rangle$ is a sequence of measurable functions (with the same domain), then
(a) $\text{Sup}\{f_1, f_2, \ldots, f_n\}$ is measurable
(b) $\text{Sup}\{f_1, f_2, \ldots, f_n\}$ is not measurable
(c) $\text{Sup}_n f_n$ is measurable
(d) $\text{Sup}_n f_n$ is not measurable

**32.** If $c$ is a constant and $f$ is measurable real-valued function, then
(a) $f + c$ is measurable
(b) $f + c$ is non-measurable
(c) $cf$ is measurable
(d) $cf$ is not measurable

**33.** Which of the following(s) is/are true?
(a) Closed set is Lebesgue mesurable
(b) Closed set is not Lebesgue mesurable
(c) Open set is Lebesgue measurable
(d) Open set is not Lebesgue measurable

**34.** Which of the following(s) is/are true?
(a) Closed set is Lebesgue measurable
(b) Closed set is not Lebesgue measurable
(c) Open set is Lebesgue measurable
(d) Open set is not Lebesgue measurable

**35.** If $E$ is a Lebesgue measurable set, then
(a) each translate $E + y$ is also measurable
(b) each translate $E + y$ are not measurable
(c) $E + y$ is measurable, if for some set $A$ $m^* A = m^*(A \cap (E+y)) + m^*(A \cap (E+y)^c)$
(d) $E + y$ is measurable, if for some set $A$ $m^* A = 0$

**36.** Which of the following(s) is/are true?
(a) The set of rational numbers is Lebesgue measurable.
(b) The set of rational numbers have Lebesgue outer measure equal to zero.
(c) The set of rational numbers is not Lebesgue measurable.
(d) The set of rational numbers have Lebesgue out measure equal to one.

**37.** Which of the following(s) is/are true?
(a) The set [0, 1] is not countable
(b) The set [0, 1] is countable
(c) $m^*[0, 1] = 1$
(d) $m^*[0, 1] = 0$

**38.** Which of the following(s) is/are correct?
(a) Cantor set is a perfect set
(b) Cantor set is nowhere dense set
(c) Measure of cantor set is zero
(d) None of the above

**39.** Which of the following(s) is/are true?
(a) The Euclidean space $\mathbb{R}^n$ is separable.
(b) The metric space $l_\infty$ of all bounded sequences with submetric is not separable.
(c) Every dense subset is uncountable in $l_\infty$.
(d) None of the above

**40.** Let $(Q, d)$ be a metric space, where $Q$ is the set of rational number and metric $d$ is defined by
$$d(x, y) = |x - y|, \forall x, y \in Q$$
Then,
(a) the sequence $\left\{\frac{1}{3^n}\right\}$ is a cauchy sequence
(b) the sequence $\left\{\frac{1}{3^n}\right\}$ converges to a point of $Q$
(c) the sequence $\left\{\left(1+\frac{1}{n}\right)^n\right\}$ is a cauchy sequence
(d) the sequence $\left\{\left(1+\frac{1}{n}\right)^n\right\}$ does not converge to a point in $Q$

**41.** Which of the following(s) is/are corret?
(a) The discrete space $(X, d)$ is a complete metric space.
(b) The space $(R, d)$ is a complete metric space, where $d$ is usual metric.
(c) The space $R^n$ of all $n$-tuples with metric $d$, defined by $d(x, y) = \left(\sum_{i=1}^{n} (x_i - y_i)^2\right)^{1/2}$ is a complete metric space.
(d) None of the above

**42.** Which of the following(s) is/are true?
(a) $Q$ is of first category in $R$ wrt usual metric.
(b) If $X$ is of second category and if $X = A \cup B$, then either $A$ or $B$ must be of second category.
(c) Every countable sub-space of $R$ is of first category in $R$.
(d) None of the above

**43.** Which of the following(s) is/are continuous map from $R$ to $R$, where $(R, d)$ is usual metric?
(a) $f(x) = x^2$
(b) $f(x) = \sin x$
(c) Both (a) and (b)
(d) Neither (a) nor (b)

**44.** Which of the following(s) is/are true?
(a) Any closed interval with usual metric is not compact.
(b) Any closed interval with usual metirc is compact.
(c) The discrete space $(X, d)$, where $X$ is finite set, is compact.
(d) The usual metric space $(R, d)$ is not compact.

**45.** Let $X = \{x : 0 < d(0, x) \leq 1$, and $x \in \mathbb{R}^2\}$ where $0 = (0, 0)$ and $d$ is the usual metric on $X$. Then,
(a) $X$ is closed
(b) $X$ is bounded
(c) $X$ is compact
(d) $X$ is not compact

**46.** Which of the following(s) is/are true?
(a) The interval $[a, \infty)$ is measurable.
(b) Every interval is measurable.
(c) Every open set in $\mathbb{R}$ is measurable
(d) Every closed set in $\mathbb{R}$ is measurable

**47.** Which of the following(s) is/are correct?
(a) Singleton set is measurable.
(b) Measure of singleton set is zero.
(c) Countable set is measurable
(d) Measure of countable set is zero.

**48.** Which of the following(s) is/are correct?
(a) If $f$ is measurable, then $|f|$ is measurable.
(b) If $f$ is a measurable function on $[a, b]$ and if $\mathbb{R} \in \mathbb{R}$, then $f + k$ and $kf$ are measurable.
(c) Constant functions are measurable.
(d) None of the above

**49.** If $\{f_n\}$ is a sequence of measurable functions on $[a, b]$ such that the sequence $\{f_n(x)\}$ is bounded for every $x \in [a, b]$. Then, the functions
(a) $G(x) = \text{lub}\{f_1(x), f_2(x), f_3(x), \ldots\}$ is measurable
(b) $g(x) = \text{glb}\{f_1(x), f_2(x), f_3(x), \ldots\}$ is measurable
(c) $G(x) = \text{lub}\{f_1(x), f_2(x), f_3(x), \ldots\}$ is not measurable
(d) $g(x) = \text{glb}\{f_1(x), f_2(x), f_3(x), \ldots\}$ is not measurable

**50.** If $\{f_n\}$ is a sequence of measurable functions on $[a, b]$ such that the sequence $\{f_n(n)\}$ is bounded for every $n \in [a, b]$, then the functions
(a) $H(n) = \lim\limits_{n\to\infty} \text{Sup}\, f_n(n)$ is measurable
(b) $H(n) = \lim\limits_{n\to\infty} \text{Sup}\, f_n(n)$ is not measurable
(c) $h(n) = \lim\limits_{n\to\infty} \text{Inf}\, f_n(n)$ is measurable
(d) $h(n) = \lim\limits_{n\to\infty} \text{Inf}\, f_n(n)$ is not measurable

**51.** Which of the following(s) is/are true?
(a) $S \subset \mathbb{R}^n$ is closed $\Rightarrow S = \bar{S}$
(b) $S = \bar{S} \Rightarrow S \subset \mathbb{R}^n$ is closed
(c) $S \subset \mathbb{R}^n$ is closed $\Leftrightarrow S = \bar{S}$
(d) $S = \bar{S} \Leftrightarrow S \subset \mathbb{R}^n$ is open

# Answers

## Exercise 1

| | | | | | | | | | |
|---|---|---|---|---|---|---|---|---|---|
| **1.** (a) | **2.** (a) | **3.** (a) | **4.** (a) | **5.** (a) | **6.** (a) | **7.** (b) | **8.** (a) | **9.** (a) | **10.** (a) |
| **11.** (a) | **12.** (a) | **13.** (a) | **14.** (a) | **15.** (a) | **16.** (a) | **17.** (a) | **18.** (a) | **19.** (a) | **20.** (a) |
| **21.** (a) | **22.** (a) | **23.** (a) | **24.** (a) | **25.** (a) | **26.** (a) | **27.** (a) | **28.** (a) | **29.** (a) | **30.** (c) |
| **31.** (a) | **32.** (a) | **33.** (a) | **34.** (a) | **35.** (a) | **36.** (b) | **37.** (d) | **38.** (a) | **39.** (b) | **40.** (a) |
| **41.** (a) | **42.** (b) | **43.** (a) | **44.** (a) | **45.** (a) | **46.** (d) | **47.** (d) | **48.** (c) | **49.** (a) | **50.** (c) |
| **51.** (c) | **52.** (c) | **53.** (d) | **54.** (c) | **55.** (d) | **56.** (d) | **57.** (c) | **58.** (d) | **59.** (d) | **60.** (c) |
| **61.** (d) | **62.** (a) | **63.** (a) | **64.** (b) | **65.** (a) | **66.** (c) | **67.** (a) | **68.** (a) | **69.** (b) | **70.** (a) |
| **71.** (a) | **72.** (a) | **73.** (a) | **74.** (a) | **75.** (a) | **76.** (b) | **77.** (c) | **78.** (c) | **79.** (a) | **80.** (a) |
| **81.** (b) | **82.** (a) | **83.** (a) | **84.** (b) | **85.** (a) | **86.** (a) | **87.** (a) | **88.** (a) | **89.** (a) | **90.** (a) |
| **91.** (a) | **92.** (a) | **93.** (b) | **94.** (a) | **95.** (a) | **96.** (b) | **97.** (c) | **98.** (b) | **99.** (a) | **100.** (a) |
| **101.** (b) | **102.** (a) | **103.** (a) | **104.** (a) | **105.** (c) | **106.** (a) | **107.** (a) | **108.** (c) | **109.** (c) | **110.** (a) |
| **111.** (a) | **112.** (c) | **113.** (c) | **114.** (c) | **115.** (b) | **116.** (a) | **117.** (a) | **118.** (c) | **119.** (c) | **120.** (a) |
| **121.** (d) | **122.** (c) | **123.** (a) | **124.** (c) | **125.** (a) | **126.** (c) | **127.** (c) | **128.** (a) | **129.** (a) | **130.** (a) |
| **131.** (a) | **132.** (b) | **133.** (c) | **134.** (d) | **135.** (d) | **136.** (c) | **137.** (c) | **138.** (a) | **139.** (c) | **140.** (c) |
| **141.** (d) | **142.** (b) | **143.** (c) | **144.** (b) | **145.** (a) | **146.** (c) | **147.** (d) | **148.** (b) | **149.** (d) | **150.** (d) |
| **151.** (d) | **152.** (a) | **153.** (a) | **154.** (c) | **155.** (d) | **156.** (c) | **157.** (b) | **158.** (c) | | |

## Exercise 2

| | | | | | | | | | |
|---|---|---|---|---|---|---|---|---|---|
| **1.** (a,c,d) | **2.** (a) | **3.** (a) | **4.** (a) | **5.** (b,c) | **6.** (a,b,c) | **7.** (a,c,d) | **8.** (a,b) | **9.** (a,d) | **10.** (a,d) |
| **11.** (a,c) | **12.** (b,c) | **13.** (a,b,c,d) | **14.** (b,d) | **15.** (a,c) | **16.** (a,b) | **17.** (a,b,c) | **18.** (a,b,c,d) | **19.** (a,b,c,d) | **20.** (a,d) |
| **21.** (a,c) | **22.** (a,b) | **23.** (a,c) | **24.** (a,b,c) | **25.** (a,b) | **26.** (a,c) | **27.** (a,c) | **28.** (a,b) | **29.** (a,b,c,d) | **30.** (a,c) |
| **31.** (a,c) | **32.** (a,c) | **33.** (a,c) | **34.** (a,c) | **35.** (a,c) | **36.** (a,b) | **37.** (a,c) | **38.** (a,b,c) | **39.** (a,b,c) | **40.** (a,b,c,d) |
| **41.** (a,b,c) | **42.** (a,b,c) | **43.** (a,b,c) | **44.** (b,c,d) | **45.** (a,b,d) | **46.** (a,b,c) | **47.** (a,b,c,d) | **48.** (a,b,c) | **49.** (a,b) | **50.** (a,c) |
| **51.** (a,b,c) | | | | | | | | | |

# Hints & Solutions

## Exercise 1

**1.** Let $a$ be any given point and let $S(a, r)$ be any spherical neighbourhood of the point.

We have to show that there exists a rational sphere containing a and contained in $S(a, r)$.

Let $\quad a = (a_1, \ldots, a_n)$

and let $p_1, \ldots, p_n$ be rational numbers such that

$$a_i - \frac{1}{2n}r < p_i < a_i + \frac{1}{2n}r, \ 1 \le i \le n$$

We write $\quad P = (p_1, \ldots, p_n)$

We have,

$$\|a-p\|^2 < \frac{nr^2}{4n^2}$$

$$= \frac{r^2}{4n_1} \le \frac{r^2}{4}$$

$$\Rightarrow \quad \|a-p\| < \frac{1}{2}r$$

Let $\rho$ be a rational number such that

$$\|a-p\| < \rho < \frac{1}{2}r$$

Now, consider the rational sphere $S(p, \rho)$,

We have $\|a-p\| \le \rho$

$\Rightarrow \quad a \in S(p, \rho)$

Let $x$ be any point of $S(p, \rho)$. We have,

$$\|x-a\| \le \|x-p\| + \|p-a\|$$

$$< \rho + \|p-a\| < \frac{1}{2}r + \frac{1}{2}r = \|x-a\| < r$$

$\Rightarrow \quad x \in S(a, r)$

Thus, $S(p, \rho) \subset S(a, r)$.

**2.** Let $\{S_\alpha\}$ be an arbitrary collection of closed sets in $\mathbb{R}^n$ and let $S = \cup S_\alpha$.

We have $\mathbb{R}^n - \cap S_\alpha = \cup(\mathbb{R}^n - S_\alpha)$ and $\mathbb{R}^n - S_\alpha$ is an open set and union of open sets is an open set.

Hence, $\mathbb{R}^n - \cap S_\alpha$ is an open set.

$\Rightarrow \cap S_\alpha$ is closed set.

**3.** Let $F$ be an open collection of open sets and let $S = \underset{A \in F}{\cup} A$.

Suppose $x \in S$

$\Rightarrow$ x must belong to atleast one of the sets in $F$ say $A$.

Since, $A$ is open and $\bar{x} \in A$, there exist an open ball $B(\bar{x}) \subseteq A$.

But, since $A \subseteq S \Rightarrow B(\bar{x}) \subset S$ and hence $\bar{x}$ is an interior point of $S$.

Since, $\forall\, x \in S$ is an interior point.

Hence, $S$ is open.

**4.** We have,

$$\|\bar{x}+\bar{y}\|^2 = \sum_{k=1}^{n}(x_k + y_k)^2$$

$$= \sum_{k=1}^{n}(x_k^2 + y_k^2 + 2x_k y_k)$$

$$= \|x\|^2 + \|y\|^2 + 2\bar{x}\cdot\bar{y}$$

$$\le \|x\|^2 + \|y\|^2 + 2\|x\|\|y\|$$

$$= (\|x\| + \|y\|)^2$$

**5.** We have,

$$B - A = \{x \mid x \in B \text{ and } x \notin A\}$$

$$= \{x \mid x \in B \text{ and } x \in \mathbb{R}^n - A\}$$

$$= B \cap (\mathbb{R}^n - A)$$

$(\mathbb{R}^n - A)$ is closed set since $A$ is an open set.

Since, $B$ and $(\mathbb{R}^n - A)$ are closed sets and intersection of closed sets is closed set, thus $B - A$ is closed set.

**6.** Let the domain $D$ of a continuous function $f$ be compact and let $E$ be the range of $f$.

Then for given $\varepsilon > 0$ and

$$x \in D$$

There exists $\delta(x) > 0$ such that

$$\|x-t\| < \delta(x)$$

$$\Rightarrow \quad |f(x) - f(t)| < \frac{1}{2}\varepsilon$$

Now, the spheres

$$S\left(x, \frac{1}{2}\delta(x)\right) x \in D$$

constitute an open cover of the compact set $D$. Thus, there exists a finite sub-cover. Let this finite sub-cover consist of the spheres

$$S\left(x_1, \frac{1}{2}\delta(x_1)\right), \ldots, S\left(x_p, \frac{1}{2}\delta(x_p)\right)$$

We write $\delta = \frac{1}{2}\min[\delta(x_1), \ldots, \delta(x_p)]$

Now, suppose that $x$, $y$ are two points of $D$ such that

$$\|x-y\| < \delta$$

Suppose that $x \in S\left[x_i, \frac{1}{2}\delta(x_i)\right]$

We have,

$$\|y-x_i\| \le \|y-x\| + \|x-x_i\| < \delta + \frac{1}{2}\delta(x) < \delta(x_i)$$

Thus, the point x and y belong to the same sphere *viz.*

$$S[x_i, \delta(x_i)]$$

$$|f(x)-f(y)| \le |f(x)-f(x_i)| + |f(x_i)-f(y)|$$

$$< \frac{1}{2}\varepsilon + \frac{1}{2}\varepsilon = \varepsilon$$

Thus, we have shown that given $\varepsilon > 0$, there exist $\delta > 0$ such that

$$\|x-y\| < \delta \Rightarrow |f(x)-f(y)| < \varepsilon$$

**7.** Here,

$$O_2 = \left(\frac{1}{2}, 1\right), O_3 = \left(\frac{1}{3}, \frac{2}{3}\right), \ldots,$$

$$O_\infty = \left(\frac{1}{\infty}, \frac{2}{\infty}\right) = (0, 0)$$

and $\cup\{O_n : O_n \in \mathcal{C}, n = 2, 3, \ldots\}$

$$= \left(\frac{1}{2}, 1\right) \cup \left(\frac{1}{3}, \frac{2}{3}\right) \cup \ldots \cup (0, 0)$$

$$= (0, 1)$$

and $(0, 1) = \cup\{O_n : n = 2, \ldots\}$

For $k \neq \infty$

$$\bigcup_{n=2}^{k}\{O_n : O_n \in \mathcal{C}, n = 2, 3, \ldots\}$$

$$= \left(\frac{1}{2}, 1\right) \cup \left(\frac{1}{3}, \frac{2}{3}\right), \ldots, \left(\frac{1}{k}, \frac{2}{k}\right) = \left(\frac{1}{k}, 1\right)$$

and $(0, 1) \not\subset \left(\frac{1}{k}, 1\right)$

Hence, finite sub-collection does not cover (0, 1).

**8.** On the contrary suppose that $X$ is not totally bounded. Then, for some $\varepsilon > 0$ we cannot cover $X$ by a finite number of balls of radius $\varepsilon$.

Hence, we can pick $x_1, x_2, \ldots, x_n$ in turn so that $\rho(x_n, x_k) \geq \varepsilon$ for $n > k$. Then, the sequence $< x_n >$ can have no convergent subsequence, since any two different terms in it are at distance $\varepsilon$ or more. Thus, $X$ is not sequentially compact. Thus, a sequentially compact metric space is totally bounded.

**9.** Let $f$ be a continuous function mapping the compact set $K$ onto a space $Y$. If $U$ is an open covering for $Y$, then the collection of sets $f^{-1}[O]$ for all $O \in U$ is an open covering of $K$. By the compactness of $K$, there are a finite number $O_1, \ldots, O_n$ of sets of $U$ such that the sets $f^{-1}[O_i]$ cover $K$. Since, $f$ is onto, the sets $O_1, \ldots, O_n$ cover $Y$. Thus, the continuous image of a compact set is compact.

**10.** Let $\bigcap_{n=0}^{\infty} c_n r^n$ be the binomial series for $(1-t)^{1/2}$. This series converges uniformly for $i$ in the interval [0, 1]. Hence, given $\varepsilon > 0$, we can choose $N$ so that for all $t \in [0, 1]$ we have

$$|(1-t)^{1/2} - Q_N(t)| < \varepsilon,$$

where $Q_N = \sum_{n=0}^{N} c_n t^n$. Let $P(s) = Q_N(1 - s^2)$. Then, $P$ is a polynomial in $s$, and $||s| - P(s)| < \varepsilon$ for $s \in [-1, 1]$.

**11.** Given, an open set $U$, let $x_1$ be a point of $O_1 \cap U$ and $S_1$ a ball (of radius $r_1$) centred at $x_1$ and contained in $O_1 \cap U$. Since, $O_2$ is dense, there must be a point $x_2$ in $O_2 \cap S_1$. Since, $O_2$ is open, there is a small ball $S_2$ centred at $x_2$ and contained in $O_2$, and we may take the radius $r_2$ of $S_2$ to be smaller than $\frac{1}{2} r_1$ and smaller than $r_1 - \rho(x_1, x_2)$. Then, $\bar{S}_2 \subset S_1$.

Proceeding inductively, we obtain a sequence $< S_n >$ of balls such that $\bar{S}_n \subset \bar{S}_{n-1}$ and $S_n \subset O_n$ and whose radii $< r_n >$ tend to zero. Let $< x_n >$ be the sequence of centres of these balls. Then, for $n, m \geq N$ we have $x_n \in S_N$ and $x_m \in S_N$. Therefore, $\rho(x_n, x_m) \leq 2r_N$ and $< x_n >$ is a Cauchy sequence, since $r_n \to 0$. By the completeness of $X$ there is a point $x$ such that $x_n \to x$. Since, $x_n \in S_{N+1}$ for $n > N$, we have $x \in \bar{S}_{N+1} \subset S_N \subset O_N$. Consequently, $x \in \cap O_n$ and $x \in U$. Since, $U$ was an arbitrary open $\cap O_n$ is dense in $X$.

**12.** The collection $M$ of Lebesgue measurable sets is a $\sigma$-algebra it satisfies

(a) If $E_1$ and $E_2$ are Lebesgue measurable set, then $E_1 \cup E_2$ is Lebesgue measurable.

(b) The measurable set $E$ and its complement $E^c$ is also measurable set. Now, we have only to prove that if $E$ is the union of countable collection of measurable set, then $E$ is measurable set.

Let $< E_i >$ be a sequence of mutually disjoint measurable sets and let

$F_n = \bigcup_{i=1}^{N} E_i$. Then, for any set $A$,

$$m^*(A \cap F_n) = m^*\left(A \cap \left[\bigcup_{i=1}^{n} F_i\right]\right)$$

$$= \sum_{i=1}^{n} m^*(A \cap E_i)$$

Let $\quad E = \bigcup_{i=1}^{\infty} E_i$, then $F_n \subset E$ and $E^c \subset F_n^c$.

Since, $F_n = \bigcup_{i=1}^{n} E_i$ it is a measurable set

Hence, $m^*(A) = m^*(A \cap F_n) + m^*(A \cap F_n^c)$

$\geq m^*(A \cap F_n) + m^*(A \cap E^c) \qquad (\because F_n^c \subset E^c)$

$\Rightarrow m^*(A) = m^*(A \cap F_n) + m^*(A \cap F^c)$

$$= \sum_{i=1}^{n} m^*(A \cap E_i) + m^*(A \cap E^c)$$

Since, left hand side is independent of $n$, we have

$$m^* A = \sum_{i=1}^{\infty} m^*(A \cap E_i) + m^*(A \cap E^c)$$

$$= m^*\left(A \cap \left[\bigcup_{i=1}^{\infty} E_i\right]\right) + m^*(A \cap E^c)$$

$$\geq m^*(A \cap E) + m^*(A \cap E^c)$$

**13.** Since, $f$ is a real-valued function such that for each $x \in E$, $f_n(x) \to f(x)$, let

$$G_n = \{x \in E : |f_n(x) - f(x)| \geq \varepsilon\}$$

Also, let

$$A = E_N = \bigcup_{n=N}^{\infty} G_n$$

$$= \{x \in E : |f_n(x) - f(x)| \geq \varepsilon \text{ for some } n \geq N\}$$

So, we have $E_{N+1} \subset E_n$ and $< E_N >$ forms a decreasing sequence of measurable sets.

For some $N$, $\exists\, E_n : x \notin E_N$ but $x \in E \qquad [\because f_n(x) \to f(x)]$

Hence, $\cap E_N = \phi$ and we have

$$m(\cap E_N) = \lim_{n \to \infty} mE_n = 0.$$

Hence, given $\delta > 0$, $\exists\, N$ so that $mE_N < \delta$, i.e.,

$m\{x \in E : |f_n(x) - f(x)| \geq \varepsilon \text{ for some } n \geq N\} < \delta$

$\Rightarrow \qquad mA < \delta$

**14.** Since, $<E_i>$ is sequence of set, we have Lebesgue outer measure $m^*(\cup E_n) \le \Sigma m^* E_n$, also since these sets are Lebesgue measurable, the Lebesgue outer measure is Lebesgue measure, *i.e.*,

$$m(\cup E_i) \le \Sigma\, mE_i$$

**16.** Let $A$ and $B$ be Lebesgue measurable sets. Then, $A^c$, $B^c$ and $A^c \cup B^c$ is also Lebesgue measurable set.

Since, $A^c \cup B^c = (A \cap B)^c$, a Lebesgue measurable set.

$\Rightarrow$ $A \cap B$ is a Lebesgue measurable set.

**17.** The interval $(b, \infty)$ is Lebesgue measurable set and its complements $(-\infty, b]$ too

Since, $(-\infty, b) = \bigcup_{i=1}^{\infty} (-\infty, b - \frac{1}{n}]$ it is measurable too.

$\because$ The countable union of Lebesgue measurable set is Lebesgue measurable and $\left(-\infty, b - \frac{1}{n}\right]$ is Lebesgue measurable, since $\left(b - \frac{1}{n}, \infty\right)$ is Lebesgue measurable.

**18.** Let $A$ be any set. Then, $(a, \infty)$ is Lebesgue measurable, if

$$m^* A \ge m^*(A \cap (a, \infty)) + m^*(A \cap (-\infty, a])$$

If $m^* A = \infty$ it is proved.

If $m^* A < \infty$, then given $\varepsilon > 0$, there is a countable collection $\{I_n\}$ of open intervals, which covers $A$ and for which

$$\Sigma\, l(I_n) \le m^* A + \varepsilon,\ \varepsilon > 0$$

Let $I_n' = I_n \cap (a, \infty)$ and $I_n'' = I_n \cap (-\infty, a]$

Then $I_n'$ and $I_n''$ are either empty or intervals and

$l(I_n) = l(I_n') + l(I_n'') = m^*(I_n) + m^*(I_n'')$

$\because [A \cap (a, \infty)] \subset \cup I_n'$

$\Rightarrow m^*[A \cap (a, \infty)] \le m^*(I_n') \le m^* I_n$

Also $\because [A \cap (-\infty, a)] \subset \cup I_n''$

$\Rightarrow m^*[A \cap (-\infty, a)] \le m^*(\cup I_n'') \le \Sigma m^* I_n''$

Thus,

$m^*[A \cap (a, \infty)] + m^*[A \cap (-\infty, a)]$

$\le \Sigma m^* I_n' + \Sigma m^* I_n'' \le \Sigma l(I_n) \le m^* A + \varepsilon$

$\because \varepsilon > 0$, we have

$m^* A \ge m^*[A \cap (a, \infty)] + m^*[A \cap (-\infty, a]]$

Hence, $(a, \infty)$ is measurable.

**19.** $E_1$ is Lebesgue measurable.

$$\begin{aligned} m(E_1 \cup E_2) &= m((E_1 \cup E_2) \cap E_1) + m((E_1 \cup E_2) \cap E_1^c) \\ &= m((E_1 \cap E_1) \cup (E_2 \cap E_1)) + m((E_1 \cap E_1^c) \cup (E_2 \cap E_1^c)) \\ &= m(E_1 \cup (E_2 \cap E_1)) + m(E_2 \cap E_1^c) \quad \text{...(i)} \end{aligned}$$

$E_2$ is Lebesgue measurable.

$$\begin{aligned} m(E_1 \cap E_2) &= m(E_1 \cap E_2 \cap E_2) + m(E_1 \cap E_2 \cap E_2^c) \\ &= m(E_1 \cap E_2) + m(\phi) \\ &= m(E_1 \cap E_2) \quad \text{...(ii)} \end{aligned}$$

Adding Eqs. (i) and (ii), we have

$$\begin{aligned} m(E_1 \cup E_2) + m(E_1 \cap E_2) &= m(E_1 \cup (E_2 \cap E_1)) + m(E_2 \cap E_1) + m(E_2 \cap E_1^c) \quad \text{...(iii)} \\ &= m(E_1 \cup (E_2 \cap E_1)) + mE_2 \end{aligned}$$

Also, since $E_2$ is Lebesgue measurable,

$$\begin{aligned} m(E_1 \cup (E_2 \cap E_1)) &= m((E_1 \cup (E_2 \cap E_1)) \cap E_2) + m((E_1 \cup (E_2 \cap E_1)) \cap E_2^c) \\ &= m((E_1 \cap E_2) \cup (E_2 \cap E_1 \cap E_2)) \\ &\quad + m(E_1 \cap E_2^c) \cup (E_2 \cap E_1 \cap E_2^c) \\ &= m((E_1 \cap E_2) \cup (E_1 \cap E_2)) + m((E_1 \cap E_2^c) \cup \phi) \\ &= m(E_1 \cap E_2) + m(E_1 \cap E_2^c) \\ &= m(E_1) \quad \text{...(iv)} \end{aligned}$$

Substituting this in Eq. (iii), we have

$$m(E_1 \cup E_2) + m(E_1 \cap E_2) = mE_1 + mE_2$$

**20.** Let $M$ is the family of measurable sets,

(a) If $E_1, E_2 \in M$, then $E_1 \cup E_2$ is a measurable set, so $E_1 \cup E_2 \in M$.

(b) Since, set $E_1$ and it complement $E^c$ are both measurable sets

$\therefore \forall E \in M, E^c \in M.$

This proves the family $M$ of Lebesgue measurable sets is an algebra of sets.

**21.** By induction $n = 1$, $m^*(A \cap E_1) = m^*(A \cap E_1)$ is true.

For $n = 2$, since $E_1$ and $E_2$ are disjoints

$A \cap (E_1 \cup E_2) \cap E_2 = A \cap E_2$

$A \cap (E_1 \cup E_2) \cap E_2^c = A \cap E_1$

Adding we have

$$\begin{aligned} m^*(A \cap (E_1 \cup E_2) \cap E_2) + m^*(A \cap (E_1 \cup E_2) \cap E_2^c) \\ = m^*(A \cap E_1) + m^*(A \cap E_2) \end{aligned}$$

or $m^*(A \cap (E_1 \cup E_2)) = m^*(A \cap E_1) + m^*(A \cap E_2)$

Assume it is true for $(n-1)$ sets $E_i$. Since, $E_i'$ s are disjoint.

$$A \cap \left[\bigcup_{i=1}^{n} E_i\right] \cap E_n = A \cap E_n$$

and $$A \cap \left[\bigcup_{i=1}^{n} E_i\right] \cap E_n^c = A \cap \left[\bigcup_{i=1}^{n-1} E_i\right]$$

Adding, we have

$$\begin{aligned} m^*\left(A \cap \left[\bigcup_{i=1}^{n} E_i\right]\right) &= m^*(A \cap E_n) + m^*\left(A \cap \left[\bigcup_{i=1}^{n-1} E_i\right]\right) \\ &= m^*(A \cap E_n) + \sum_{i=1}^{n-1} m^*(A \cap E_i) \\ &= \sum_{i=1}^{n} m^*(A \cap E_i) \end{aligned}$$

**22.** If $\langle E_i \rangle$ is a sequence of finite of number of disjoint measurable sets, then for any set $A$, suppose that this is true for $n-1$ disjoint sets $E_i$, then

$$A \cap \left[\bigcup_{i=1}^{n} E_i\right] \cap E_n = A \cap E_n$$

and $$\begin{aligned} A \cap \left[\bigcup_{i=1}^{n} E_i\right] \cap E_n^c &= A \cap \left[\bigcup_{i=1}^{n-1} E_i \cup E_n\right] \cap E_n^c \\ &= A \cap \left[\left(\left(\bigcup_{i=1}^{n-1} E_i\right) \cap E_n^c\right) \cup (E_n \cap E_n^c)\right] \\ &= A \cap \left[\bigcup_{i=1}^{n-1} E_i\right] \end{aligned}$$

(Since, $E_n \cap E_n^c = \phi$ and $\overset{n-1}{\underset{i=1}{\cup}} E_i$ and $E_n$ are disjoint, so $\overset{n-1}{\underset{i=1}{\cup}} E_i \cap E_n = \overset{n-1}{\underset{i=1}{\cup}} E_i$)

And by the definition of measurability of $E_n$,

$$m^*\left[A \cap \left(\overset{n}{\underset{i=1}{\cup}} E_i\right)\right]$$

$$= m^*(A \cap E_n) + m^*\left[A \cap \left(\overset{n-1}{\underset{i=1}{\cup}} E_i\right)\right]$$

$$= m^*(A \cap E_n) + \sum_{i=1}^{n-1} m^*[A \cap E_i]$$

$$= \sum_{i=1}^{n} m^*(A \cap E_i)$$

Also, since $A \cap \left[\overset{n}{\underset{i=1}{\cup}} E_i\right] \subset A \cap \left[\overset{\infty}{\underset{i=1}{\cup}} E_i\right]$

$$\Rightarrow \quad m^*\left[A \cap \left(\overset{n}{\underset{i=1}{\cup}} E_i\right)\right] \le m^*\left[A \cap \left[\overset{\infty}{\underset{i=1}{\cup}} E_i\right]\right]$$

$$\therefore \quad m^*\left[A \cap \left(\overset{\infty}{\underset{i=1}{\cup}} E_i\right)\right] \ge \sum_{i=1}^{n} m^*(A \cap E_i)$$

Since, the left hand side is independent of $n$.

$$m^*\left[A \cap \left(\overset{\infty}{\underset{i=1}{\cup}} E_i\right)\right] \ge \sum_{i=1}^{\infty} m^*(A \cap E_i)$$

Also, since $\Sigma m^*(A \cap E_i) \le m^*(A \cap (\cup E_i))$

We have $m^*(A \cap (\cup E_i)) = \Sigma m^*(A \cap E_i)$

**23.** Let $A$ be any set. Then, $A \cap E \subset E$ and we have $m^*(A \cap E) \le m^* E = 0$. Also, $A \supset A \cap E^c$

$\Rightarrow m^* A \ge m^*(A \cap E^c) = m^*(A \cap E^c) + m^*(A \cap E)$

$\therefore$ $E$ is measurable.

**24.** Let $E$ be a set on which $m^*$ is defined and $E + y = \{x + y : x \in E\}$ is a given set.

$m^*(E + y) = m^* E + m^* y = m^* E$

Since, $m^* y = 0$

This shows $m^*$ is translation invariant.

**25.** Let $\{I_n\}$ is a finite collection of open intervals that covers [0, 1], then it will also cover $A$, since $A \subset [0, 1]$.

$\therefore \quad A \subset [0, 1] \subset \cup I_n$

$\Rightarrow \quad m^* A \le m^*[0, 1] \le m^*(\cup I_n)$

$\Rightarrow \quad 0 \le 1 \le \Sigma\, l(I_n)$

(Since, $A$ is a set of rational numbers it is countable. So $m^* A = 0$)

**26.** Let $A = \{a_1, a_2, \dots\}$ is a countable set.

$\{a_1\}, \{a_2\}, \dots$ is a collection of countable subsets of $A$.

$\therefore m^*(\cup a_n) \le m^* a_n = 0$ (Lebesgue outer measure of single element set is equal to zero)

$\Rightarrow m^* A = 0$

**27.** If one the set $A_n$ is such that

$m^*(A_n = \infty$, the result holds. If $m^* A_n < \infty$, given $\varepsilon > 0$, there is a countable collection $\{I_n, i\}$ of open intervals such that

$$A_n \subset = \underset{i}{\cup} I_{n,i} \text{ and } \underset{i}{\Sigma}\, l(I_n, i) < m^* A_n + \frac{\varepsilon}{2^n}$$

Since, $\quad A_n \subset \underset{i}{\cup} I_{n,i} \Rightarrow \underset{n}{\cup} A_n \subset \underset{n}{\cup}\left(\underset{i}{\cup} I_{n,i}\right)$

$\therefore \left(\underset{i}{\cup} I_{n,i}\right)$ is a union of countable collection $\{I_{nj}\}$ it is countable and so $\underset{n}{\cup}\left(\underset{i}{\cup} I_{n,i}\right)$ is countable too.

Since it covers $(\cup A_n)$,

$$m^*(\cup A_n) \le \underset{n}{\Sigma}\underset{i}{\Sigma}\, l(I_{n,i}) < \underset{n}{\Sigma}\left(m^* A_n + \frac{\varepsilon}{2^n}\right)$$

$$= \underset{n}{\Sigma}\, m^* A_n + \varepsilon$$

$$\Rightarrow \quad m^*(\cup A_n) \le \Sigma m^* A_n$$

**28.** Let $h(x) = \underset{n}{\lim} f_n(x) = \operatorname{Inf} \underset{k \ge n}{\sup} f_n$. Since, $g_k = \underset{k \ge n}{\operatorname{Sup}} f_n(x)$ is a measurable function and in then inf $g_k$ is a measurable function too and so $\overline{\lim} f_n(x) = \operatorname{Inf} g_k = \operatorname{Inf} \underset{k \ge n}{\operatorname{Sup}}$ is also measurable.

**29.** Let $E = \{x : f(x) \ne g(x)\}$ the functions $f = g$ almost everywhere, we have $mE = 0$, and so

$$\{x : g(x) > \alpha\} = [\{x : f(x) > \alpha\} \cup \{x \in E : g(x) > \alpha\}] \sim \{x \in E : g(x) \le \alpha\}$$

Here, $\{x : f(x) > \alpha\}$ is a measurable set, since $f$ is a measurable function.

The sets $\{x : f(x) > \alpha\}$ and $\{x \in E : g(x) \le \alpha\}$ are subsets of $E$ and $mE = 0$ so they are measurable.

Thus, $\{x : g(x) > \alpha\}$ is measurable for each $\alpha$ and so $g$ is measurable.

# Exercise 2

**1.** The function $f$ is integrable on closed interval $[a, b]$. Then, for given $\varepsilon > 0$, there is $\delta > 0$ such that for every closed interval $[a, x] \subset [a, b]$ with $m[a, x] < \delta$, we have $\int_a^x f(x)\, dx < \varepsilon$.

This shows $f$ is continuous function.

To prove $f$ is of bounded variation, let $a = x_0 < x_1 < \dots < x_n = b$ be any sub-division of $[a, b]$.

Then, $\quad \displaystyle\sum_{i=1}^{n} |F(x_i) - F(x_{i-1})| = \sum_{i=1}^{n} \left|\int_{x_{i-1}}^{x_i} f(t)\, dt\right|$

$$\le \sum_{i=1}^{n} \int_{x_{i-1}}^{x_i} |f(t)|\, dt$$

$$= \int_a^b |f(t)|\, dt$$

$$\Rightarrow \quad T_a^b(F) \le \int_a^b |f(t)| < \infty$$

Hence, $\quad F = \int_0^x f(t)\, dt$

is of bounded variation.

So, $F(x) = \int_a^x f(t)\,dt$ is a continuous function of bounded variation whenever $f$ is integrable on closed interval $[a, b]$.

**2.** For any sub-division of $[a, b]$,

$$p - n = f(b) - f(a)$$

and taking suprema over all possible sub-divisions, we have

$$P = N + f(b) - f(a) \quad \text{...(i)}$$

Also, $\quad t = p + n = p + p - \{f(b) - f(a)\}$

taking suprema, we have

$$T = 2P - \{f(b) - f(a)\}$$
$$= P + N \quad \text{[by Eq. (i)]}$$

**3.** Let $f$ be bounded variation on $[a, b]$ and let $g(x) = P_a^x$, positive variation of $f$ over $[a, x] \subset [a, b]$ and $h(x) = Na^x$, negative variation of $f$ over $[a, x) \subset [a, b]$. Then, $g$ and $h$ are monotone increasing functions which are real-valued, since

$$0 \le P_a^x \le T_a^x \le T_a^b < \infty$$

and $\quad 0 \le N_a^x \le T_a^x \le T_a^b < \infty$

Hence, $\quad P - N = f(b) - f(a)$

$\Rightarrow \quad g(x) - h(x) = f(x) - f(a)$

$\Rightarrow \quad f(x) = g(x) - h(x) + f(a)$

Since, $h - f(a)$ is a monotone function.

Hence, $\quad f(x) = g(x) - (h(x) - f(a))$

is difference monotone function.

**4.** Since, $f = g - h$ on $[a, b]$ where $g$ and $h$ are increasing functions, then for any sub-division, we have

$$\Sigma |f(x_i) - f(x_{i-1})| \le \Sigma[g(x_i) - g(x_{i-1})] + \Sigma[h(x_i) - h(x_{i-1})]$$
$$= g(b) - g(a) + h(b) - h(a)$$

$\Rightarrow \quad T_a^b(f) \le g(b) + h(b) - g(a) - h(a),$

which shows $f$ is of bounded variation on $[a, b]$.

**5.** Here,

$$O_2 = \left(\frac{1}{2}, 1\right),\ O_3 = \left(\frac{1}{3}, \frac{2}{3}\right) \ldots$$

$$O_\infty = \left(\frac{1}{\infty}, \frac{2}{\infty}\right) = (0, 0)$$

and $\quad \cup\{O_n : O_n \in \mathcal{C}, n = 2, 3, \ldots\}$

$$= \left(\frac{1}{2}, 1\right) \cup \left(\frac{1}{3}, \frac{2}{3}\right) \cup \ldots \cup (0, 0)$$

$$= (0, 1)$$

and $\quad (0, 1) = \cup\{O_n : n = 2, 3, \ldots\}$

For $k \ne \infty$

$$\bigcup_{n=2}^{k} \{O_n : O_n \in \mathcal{C}, n = 2, 3, \ldots\}$$

$$= \left(\frac{1}{2}, 1\right) \cup \left(\frac{1}{3}, \frac{2}{3}\right) \ldots \left(\frac{1}{k}, \frac{2}{k}\right)$$

$$= \left(\frac{1}{k}, 1\right)$$

and $\quad (0, 1) \not\subset \left(\frac{1}{k} - 1\right)$

Hence, finite sub-collection does not covers $(0, 1)$.

**6.** Let $\quad x \in A \quad \Rightarrow \quad 0 < x \le a$

$\quad y \in B \quad \Rightarrow \quad 0 < y \le b$

Since, $\quad x > 0$ and $y > 0 \quad \Rightarrow \quad xy \le ab$

$\Rightarrow$ $ab$ is an upper bound for $C$.

$\Rightarrow$ $C$ is bounded above.

$\Rightarrow$ By completeness axiom, $C$ has a Sup $C = c$ (say)

$$c \text{ is a Sup } C \Rightarrow \quad c \le ab \quad \text{...(i)}$$

Now, we have to prove $c \ge ab$.

Let $x \in A$ and $y \in B$

$\Rightarrow \quad xy \le ab$

Choose $\varepsilon > 0$ : $\quad xy > ab - \varepsilon$

Then, we have $\quad c = \text{Sup } C \ge xy > ab - \varepsilon$

$\Rightarrow \quad c > ab - \varepsilon$

$\Rightarrow \quad x + \varepsilon > ab$

$\Rightarrow \quad c > ab \quad \text{...(ii)}$

By Eqs. (i) and (ii), we get

$$c = ab = \text{Sup } C$$

**7.** We have,

$$\frac{1}{2}a_0 + \sum_{n=1}^{m} a_n$$

$$= \frac{1}{2\pi}\int_{-\pi}^{\pi} f(x)\,dx + \frac{1}{\pi}\int_{-\pi}^{\pi} f(x) \sum_{n=1}^{m} \cos n\pi\,dx$$

$$= \frac{1}{2\pi}\int_{-\pi}^{+\pi} f(x)\left[1 + 2\sum_{n=1}^{m} \cos nx\right] dx$$

$$= \frac{1}{2\pi}\int_{-\pi}^{\pi} f(x) \frac{\sin\left(m + \frac{1}{2}\right)x}{\sin\frac{1}{2}x}\,dx$$

$$= \frac{1}{2\pi}\int_{0}^{\pi} f(-x) \frac{\sin\left(m + \frac{1}{2}\right)x}{\sin\frac{1}{2}x}\,dx$$

$$+ \frac{1}{2\pi}\int_{0}^{\pi} f(x) \frac{\sin\left(m + \frac{1}{2}\right)x}{\sin\frac{1}{2}x}\,dx$$

$$= \frac{1}{2\pi} \cdot 2\int_0^{\frac{1}{2}\pi} f(-2x) \frac{\sin(2m+1)x}{\sin x}\,dx$$

$$+ \frac{1}{2\pi} \cdot 2\int_0^{\frac{1}{2}\pi} f(2x) \frac{\sin(2m+1)x}{\sin x}\,dx$$

$$= \frac{1}{\pi}[f(-0) + f(+0)]\int_0^\infty \frac{\sin x}{x}\,dx \text{ as } m \to \infty,$$

Taking $f(x) = 1, \forall\ x$, we see that

$$\frac{1}{2}a_0 = \frac{1}{2\pi}\int_{-\pi}^{+\pi} 1\,dx = 1$$

and $\quad a_n = \frac{1}{\pi}\int_{-\pi}^{+\pi} \cos nx\,dx = 0$

so that we obtain

$$1 = \frac{1+1}{\pi}\int_0^\infty \frac{\sin x}{x}\,dx$$

$$\Rightarrow \quad \int_0^\infty \frac{\sin x}{x}\,dx = \frac{\pi}{2}$$

**8.** We have,

$$A-B=\{\bar{x} \mid \bar{x}\in A \text{ and } \bar{x}\notin B\}$$
$$=\{\bar{x} \mid \bar{x}\in A \text{ and } \bar{x}\in \mathbb{R}^n - B\}$$
$$=A\cap(\mathbb{R}^n - B)$$

$\mathbb{R}^n - B$ is open since $B$ is closed and intersection of open set $A$ and $(\mathbb{R}^n - B)$ is open.

Hence, $A-B$ is open.

**9.** On the contrary assume $B(x)$ exist such that it contains finite number of points of $S$ distinct from $x$, say $a_1, a_2, \ldots, a_n$.

If $\quad r=\min\{\|x-a_i\|\}$

Then, an open ball $B\left(x, \frac{r}{2}\right)$ about $x$ contain no point of $S$ distinct from $x$. So, $x$ is not an accumulation point of $S$, which is a contradiction.

**10.** Suppose, $S\subset\mathbb{R}^n$ is closed and $x$ is an adherent point of $S$. On the contrary let assume $x\notin S$.

If $\quad x\notin S$

$\Rightarrow \quad x\in\mathbb{R}^n - S$

and $\quad \mathbb{R}^n - S$ is open

$\Rightarrow \quad \exists$ an open ball $B(x)\subset\mathbb{R}^n - S$

$\Rightarrow \quad B(x)$ contains no points of $S$.

which is contradiction, since $x$ is an adherent point of $S$ and open ball on $x$ may contain atleast one point of $S$.

Hence, $\forall$ adherent point of $S$, $x\in S$, if $S$ is closed.

**11.** Let $S$ contains all its adherent points.

and suppose $\quad \bar{x}\in\mathbb{R}^n - S$

$\Rightarrow \quad \bar{x}\notin S$

and $\bar{x}$ will not adhere to $S$.

Hence, there is some open ball

$$B(\bar{x}) : B(\bar{x})\cap S=\phi$$

$\Rightarrow \quad B(\bar{x})\subset\mathbb{R}^n - S$

$\Rightarrow \quad \mathbb{R}^n - S$ is open

$\Rightarrow \quad S$ is closed.

**12.**
$$O_1=(-1,1),\ O_2=\left(-\frac{1}{2},\frac{1}{2}\right),\ldots$$
$$O_n=\left(-\frac{1}{n},\frac{1}{n}\right),\ldots,O_\infty=(0,0)$$

and $\quad \bigcup_{k=1}^{n} O_n=(-1,1)$

and $\quad (-1,2)\not\subset(-1,1)$

Thus, $\mathcal{C}$ does not provides covering to $(-1,2)$.

**13.** Suppose, $\mathcal{C}$ is closed and bounded by of Heine Borel theorem there is an open covering $F$ of $S$ such that a finite subcollection of $F$ also covers $S$, so $S$ is compact by definition of compactness.

Suppose, $S$ is compact to prove $S$ is bounded, choose $\bar{x}\in S$, then $\{B(\bar{x},k), k=1,2,\ldots,\}$ a collection of open covering of $S$. Since, $S$ is compact, a finite sub-collection also cover $S$ and hence $S$ is bounded.

To prove $S$ is closed. Suppose, $S$ is not closed, there is an accumulation point $y$ of $S$ such that $y\notin S$.

If $\quad x\in S$

and let $\quad r_x=\dfrac{\|x-y\|}{2}$

Then, the collection $\{B(x,r_x) : x\in S\}$ is an open covering of $S$. Since, $S$ is compact there is a finite sub-collection which cover $S$,

i.e., $\quad S\subseteq\bigcup_{k=1}^{p} B(x_k, r_k),$

Choose $\quad r=\min\{r_1, r_2, \ldots, r_p\}$

Then, for open ball $B(y,r)$

If $\quad x\in B(y,r)$

$\Rightarrow \quad \|x-y\|<r\le r_k$ (for some $r_k$).

Also, we have

$$\|y-x_k\|\le\|y-x\|+\|x-x_k\|$$
$$\Rightarrow \quad \|x-x_k\|\ge\|y-x_k\|-\|x-y\|$$
$$=2r_k-\|x-y\|$$

**14.** Let $S=\bigcap_{k=1}^{\infty} Q_k$ is closed, since intersection of arbitrary collection of closed sets is closed.

To prove $\bigcap_{k=1}^{\infty}$ is non-empty.

Assume each $Q_k$ contains infinitely many points and $A=\{\bar{x}_1,\bar{x}_2,\ldots\}$ is a collection of distinct $\bar{x}_i$ where $\bar{x}_k\in Q_k$.

Since, $A$ is an infinite set contained in $Q_1$, a bounded set, it has an accumulation point, say $\bar{x}$.

Since, $\bar{x}$ is an accumulation point of $A$, then every open ball $B(\bar{x})$ contains infinitely many points of $A$.

Since, number of points of $A$ belongs $Q_k$, the open ball $B(\bar{x})$ contains infinitely many points of $Q_k$. Therefore, $\bar{x}$ is an accumulation point of $Q_k$.

Since, $Q_k$ is closed it contains accumulation point $\bar{x}$.

So, $\bar{x}$ is contained in $\bigcap_{i=1}^{\infty} Q_k$, since it is contained in each $Q_k$.

Thus, $\bigcap_{i=1}^{\infty} Q_k$ is non-empty.

**15.** If $X$ is sequentially compact and $U$ is an open covering of $X$. Since, $X$ is compact, $X$ is totally bounded, we can find a finite number of balls $B_{x_i,\delta}\ldots, B_{x_n,\delta}$ of radius $\delta$ which cover $X$. Since, each ball $B_{x_k,\delta}$ is contained in a set $O_k\in U$ the collection $\{O_1,\ldots,O_n\}$ is a finite sub-collection of $U$ which covers $X$.

**16.** Since, $L$ is non-empty, it follows from (b) that the constant functions belong to $L$. Given $g\in C(x)$, let $L'=\{f : f\in L$ and $f\ge g\}$. For each $p\in X$ have $g(p)=\text{Inf } f(p)$, $f\in L'$. Choose a positive real number $\eta$. Since, $g$ is continuous, the set

$$F=\{x : g(x)\ge g(p)+\eta\}$$

is closed. Since, $X$ is compact, $g$ is bounded on $X$, say by $M$ have a function $f\in L$ such that $f\ge g(p)+\eta$, $f(p)=g(p)+\eta$ and $f(x)>M$ on $F$. Since, $g<g(b)+\eta$ on $\widetilde{F}$ we have $g<f$ on $X$. Thus, $f\in L'$ and $f(p)\le g(p)+\eta$. Since, $\eta$ was an arbitrary positive number, we have $g(p)=\text{Inf } f(p)$, $f\in L$.

**17.** Since, every limit of a subsequence of $<x_n>$, sequential compactness implies the Bolzano-Weierstrass property. Conversely, if $<x_n>$ has $x$ for a cluster point, then for each $k$ we can find an $n_k>n_{k-1}$ such that the ball of radius $1/k$ about $x$ contains $x_{nk}$. Then, $x_{nk}\to x$. Thus, a metric space with the Bolzano Weierstrass property is sequentially compact.

**18.** Let $X$ be compact, $F$ a closed subset of $X$ and $U$ an open covering for $F$. Then, $U, \cup\{\widetilde{F}\}$ is an open covering for $X$ and so must have a finite subcovering $\{\widetilde{F}, O_1, ..., O_N\}$. Then, the sets $O_1, O_2, ..., O_n$ cover $F$, and so $U$ has a finite sub-covering.

**19.** Let $\bar{A}$ denote the closure of $A$ considered as a subset of $C(X)$. Thus, $\bar{A}$ consists of those function on $X$ that are uniform limits of sequences of functions from $A$. Since, $\bar{A}$ is itself an algebra of continuous real-valued functions on $X$.The theorem is equivalent to the statement that $\bar{A} = C(X)$. Thus, we can show that $\bar{A}$ is a lattice. Let $f \in \bar{A}$ and $||f|| \le 1$.Then given $\varepsilon > 0$, $|||f| - P(f)|| < \varepsilon$, where $P$ is the polynomial in one variable for all $|f| \le 1$. Since, $\bar{A}$ is an algebra containing the constants, $P(f) \in \bar{A}$ ,and since $\bar{A}$ is a closed subset of $C(X)$, we have $|f| \in A$. If now $f$ is any function in $A$, then $f/||f||$ has norm 1, and so $|f|/||f||$ and hence also $|f|$ belong to $\bar{A}$. Thus, $\bar{A}$ contains the absolute value of each function which is in $A$. But

$$f \vee g = \frac{1}{2}(f+g) + \frac{1}{2}|f-g| \quad \text{and} \quad f \wedge g = \frac{1}{2}(f+g) - \frac{1}{2}|f-g|$$

Thus, $\bar{A}$ is a lattice and must be equal to $C(X)$.

**20.** For each integer $m$, let $E_{m,f} = \{x : |f(x)| \le m\}$ and set $E_m = \bigcap_F E_{mf}$. Since, each $f$ is continuous, $E_{m,f}$ is closed and consequently $E_m$ is closed. For each $x \in X$, there is an $m$ such that $|f(x)| \le m$ for all $f \in F$; *i.e.*, there is an $m$ such that $x \in E_m$. Hence,

$$X = \bigcup_{m=1}^{\infty} E_m$$

Since, also $X$ is a complete metric space, there is a set $E_m$ which is not nowhere dense. Since, this $E_m$ is a closed set, it must contain some ball $O$. But, for every $x \in O$ we have $|f(x)| \le m$ for all $f \in F$.

**21.** Let $O_n = \{x \in X : \exists$ a neighbourhood $U$ of $x$ such that $U \cap E \ne \phi$ and the diameter of $f[U \cap E]$ is less than $1/n\}$.Then $O_n$ is open and $E \subset O_n$. Let $E^* = \cap O_n$. Then, $E^*$ is a $G_\delta$ and $E \subset E^*$.

Let $x \in E^*$. Then, for each $n$ there is a neighbourhood $U$ of $x$ with $U \cap E \ne \phi$ and diam $f[E \cap U]$ less than $1/n$. Choose $x_n \in U$. Then, the sequence $\langle x_k \rangle$ has the property that $\sigma(f(x_k), f(x_j)) \le 1/n$ for $k, 1 \ge n$.

Hence, $\langle f(x_k) \rangle$ is a Cauchy sequence and so converges to a point $y \in Y$.

Define $f^*(x)$ to be $y$. Then, the value of $f^*(x)$ is readily seen to be independent of the choice of the sequence $(x_k)$.Thus, $f^*(x) = f(x)$ for $x \in E$ , and $f^*$ is continuous.

**22.** Let $E = \bigcap_{n=1}^{\infty} O_n$ with $O_n$ open. Let $\sigma_n$ be a metric for $O_n$ which is bounded by 1, equivalent on $O_n$ to $\rho$, and for which $(O_n, \rho_n)$ is complete set

$$\sigma = \Sigma 2^{-n} \sigma_n.$$

Then, $\sigma$ is a metric on $E$ which is equivalent to $\rho$.

Let $\langle x_k \rangle$ be a Cauchy sequence in $\sigma$. Then, since $2^n \sigma \ge \sigma_n$. $\langle x_k \rangle$ must be a Cauchy sequence for $\sigma_n$. Hence, $\langle x_k \rangle$ converges in $(O_n . \sigma_n)$ to a point $y_n \in O'n$. Since, $\sigma_n$ and $\rho$ are equivalent on $O_n, x_k \to y_n$ in $(X, p)$. Since, limits of sequences in metric spaces are unique, we have $y_n = y_m$ for all $m, n$. Let this common value be $y$. Then $x_n \to y$ in $X$. Since, $y = y_n \in O_n, y \in E = \cap O_n$. The equivalence of $\rho$ and $\sigma$ implies that $\langle x_k \rangle$ converges to $y$ in $(E, \sigma)$ and so $(E, \sigma)$ is complete.

**23.** Let $D = \{x_k\}$. By the sequential compactness of the closure of $\{f_n(x_1) : 0 \le n < \infty\}$ we can pick a subsequence $< f_{1n} >$ of $< f_n >$ such that $< f_{1n}(x_1) >$ converges. Choose a subsequence $< f_{2n} >$ of $< f_{1n} >$ such that $< f_{2n}(x_2) >$ converges. Continuing this, we obtain a subsequence $< f_{jn} >$ convergent of $x_j$. Consider the 'diagonal' sequence $< f_{nn} >$. Thus, we have $< f_{nn} >_{n=j}^{\infty}$ a subsequence of $< f_{in} >$ and so $< f_{nn}(x_j) >$ converges.

**24.** Given $X$ is separable, let $D$ be a countable dense set. And we have a balls at $x$ with radius $\delta$,

$$S_{x,\delta} = \{y : p(x, y) < \delta\}.$$

Let $\{O_i\}$ consist of those balls $S_{x,\delta}$ for which $x \in D$ and $\delta$ is rational. Then $_i\{O_i\}$ is a countable collection of open sets. If $O$ is any open set and $y \in O$, then we have to show that for some $O_i$ we have $y \in O_i \subset O$. Since, $O$ is open, there is a ball $S_{y,\delta}$ such that $S_{y,\delta} \subset O$. By taking $\delta$ even smaller, we may assume $\delta$ is rational. Since, $y$ is a point of closure of $D$, there is a point $x \in D$ such that $p(x, y) < \delta/2$. Hence,

$$S_{x,\delta/2} \subset S_{y,\delta} \subset O.$$

But $S_{x,\delta/2}$ is one of the $\{O_i\}$.

$\Rightarrow \quad \cup O_i \subset O.$

**25.** By induction on $n$

for $n = 2$, 2 is a prime number

for $n = 3$, 3 is a prime number

for $n = 4$ 4 is the product of 2.

Assume this holds every integer $k, 1 < k < n$.

In $n$ is not a prime, there is $1 < d < n : d/n$

$\Rightarrow n = cd$ for some $1 < c < n$, each $c$ and $d$ are prime or product of prime, thus $n$ is a product of prime.

**26.** Let on the contrary $S$ is unbounded, then for every $m > 0$ there exist a point $\bar{x}_m \in S$ such that $||\bar{x}_m|| \ge m$.

The collection $F = \{x_1, x_2, ...\}$ is an infinite subset of $S$. And $F$ has an accumulation point $y \in S$. But for $m > 1 + ||y||$, we have $||x_m - y|| \ge ||x_m|| - ||y|| \ge m - ||y|| > 1$ contradicting the fact that $y$ is an accumulation point of $F$. This proves $S$ is bounded.

*i.e.*, $||x - x_k|| \ge 2r_k - ||x - y|| > r_k$

Hence, $x \notin B(x_k, r_k)$

*i.e.*, if $x \in B(y, r)$,

then $x \notin B(x_k, r_k)$

and so $x \notin \cup B(x_k, r_k)$

and we have also $x \notin S$

Hence, $B(y, r) \cap S = \phi$ an empty set.

Contradicting the fact that $y$ is an accumulation point of $S$. This is a contradiction so $S$ is closed.

**27.** Suppose, $S$ is bounded. If $T$ is an infinite subset of $S$, then $T$ is bounded (since $S$ is bounded set) and hence by Bolzano-Weierstrass theorem there is atleast one point $x \in \mathbb{R}^n$ which is also an accumulation point of $T$ and $x$ is also accumulation point of $S$.

Since, $S$ is closed, therefore, $x \in S$. which proves the given statement.

**28.** We have,

$$\left[\int_a^b f(x)\,\phi(x)\,dx\right]^2 = \lim \sum (x_r - x_{r-1}) f(\xi_r)\phi(\xi_r)]^2$$

$$\int_a^b [f(x)]^2 dx = \lim \sum [\sqrt{x_r - x_{r-1}}\, f(\xi_r)]^2$$

$$\int_a^b [\phi(x)]^2 dx = \lim [\sum \sqrt{x_r - x_{r-1}}\phi(\xi_r)]^2$$

Now, putting

$$a_r = \sqrt{x_r - x_{r-1}}\, f(\xi_r), \quad b_r = \sqrt{x_r - x_{r-1}}\,\phi(\xi_r)$$

in the Cauchy's inequality

$$(\sum a_r b_r)^2 \le \sum a_r^2 \sum b_r^2$$

We get the required result.

The sign of equality holds only when

$$\frac{a_1}{b_1} = \frac{a_2}{b_2} = \ldots$$

$$\Leftrightarrow \frac{f(\xi_1)}{\phi(\xi_1)} = \frac{f(\xi_2)}{\phi(\xi_2)} = \ldots$$

$\Leftrightarrow$ $f, \phi$ are both constant functions.

**29.** Since, $\int_a^x f(t)\,dt$ is of bounded variation, then so $F(x) = \int_a^x f(t)\,dt + F(a)$ and so $F'(x)$ exist for almost all $x$ in $[a, b]$.

Since, $f$ is bounded, there is some $M \ge 0$ such that $|f| \le M$, set

$$f_n(x) = \frac{F(x+h) - F(x)}{h} \text{ with } h = \frac{1}{n}$$

We have,

$$f_n(x) = \frac{1}{h}\int_x^{x+h} f(t)\,dt$$

and so $|f_n| \le M$

Since, $f_n(x) \to F'(x)$ almost everywhere, we have

$$\int_a^c F'(x)\,dx = \lim \int_a^c f_n(x)\,dx$$

$$= \lim_{h\to 0} \int_a^c (F(x+h) - F(x))\,dx$$

$$= \lim \left[\frac{1}{h}\int_c^{c+h} F(x)\,dt - \frac{1}{h}\int_a^{a+h} F(x)\,dx\right]$$

$$= F(c) - F(a) = \int_a^c f(x)\,dx$$

Since, $F$ is continuous. Hence,

$\int_a^c \{F'(x) - f(x)\}\,dx = 0$ for all $c \in [a, b]$

Then, $F'(x) - f(x) = 0$ almost everywhere in $[a, b]$

$\Rightarrow F'(x) = f(x)$ almost everywhere in $[a, b]$.

**30.** Let $g(x) = \text{Inf}\,\{f_1(x), f_2(x), \ldots, f_n(x)\}$, then

$$\{x : g(x) < \alpha\} = \bigcup_{i=1}^{n} \{x : f_i(x) < \alpha\}$$

Since, $f_i(x)$ are measurable, the union of measurable functions is also measurable. So, $g$ is measurable.

Let $\qquad h(x) = \inf_n f_n(x)$,

then $\qquad \{x : h(x) < \alpha\} = \bigcup_{i=1}^{\infty} \{x : F_i(x) < \alpha\}$

Since, $f_i(x)$ are measurable, the union of measurable functions is also measurable. So, $h$ is measurable.

**31.** Let $h(x) = \text{Sup}\,\{f_1(x), f_2(x), \ldots, f_n(x)\}$,

then $\{x : h(x) > \alpha\} = \bigcup_{i=1}^{\infty} \{x : f_i(x) > \alpha\}$

Since, $f_i(x)$ are measurable the union of measurable functions is also measurable. So, $h$ is measurable.

Let $\qquad g(x) = \text{Sup}_n\, f_n(x)$

then $\qquad \{x : g(x) > \alpha\} = \bigcup_{i=1}^{\infty} \{x : f_i(x) > \alpha\}$

Since, $f_i(x)$ are measurable, the union of measurable functions is also measurable. So, $g$ is measurable.

**32.** Since, $f$ is a measurable real-valued function, then for real number $\alpha$ the $\{x : f(x) < \infty\}$ is measurable.

$$\{x : f(x) + c < \alpha\} = \{x : f(x) < \alpha - c\}$$

So, $f + c$ is measurable.

$$\{x : c\,f(x) < \alpha\} = \left\{x : f(x) < \frac{\alpha}{c}\right\}$$

So, $cf$ is measurable.

**33.** Let $(a, b)$ be an open set.

Then, $(a, b) = (-\infty, b) \cup (a, \infty)$

$\because$ $(-\infty, b)$ and $(a, \infty)$ are Lebesgue measurable sets.

$\therefore$ $(a, b)$ which is a intersection of two Lebesgue measurable sets is also Lebesgue measurable.

**34.** $[a, b] = (-\infty, b] \cap [a, \infty)$ and since $(-\infty, b]$ and $[a, \infty)$ is Lebesgue measurable $[a, b]$ is Lebesgue measurable.

**35.** Let $E + y$ is Lebesgue measurable, then for some set $A$

$$m^*A = m^*(A \cap (E+y)) + m^*(A \cap (E+y)^c) \qquad \ldots(i)$$

Since, $E$ is measurable, we have

$$m^*(A \cap (E+y))$$
$$= m^*(A \cap (E+y) \cap E) + m^*(A \cap (E+y) \cap E^c)$$
$$m^*(A \cap (E+y)^c)$$
$$= m^*(A \cap (E+y)^c \cap E) + m^*(A \cap (E+y)^c \cap E^c)$$

Adding these, we have

$$m^*(A \cap (E+y)) + m^*(A \cap (E+y)^c)$$
$$= m^*(A \cap E \cap (E+y)E) + m^*(A \cap E \cap (E+y)^c)$$
$$+ m^*(A \cap E^c \cap (E+y)) + m^*(A \cap E^c \cap (E+y))$$
$$= m^*(A \cap E) + m^*(A \cap E^c) = m^*A$$

This proves $(E + y)$ is Lebesgue measurable.

**36.** Since the set of rational number is countable, it is Lebesgue measurable and its Lebesgue outer measure is equal to zero.

**37.** $\qquad m^*[0, 1] = 1 \ne 0$

Since, $\quad m^*[0, 1] \ne 0$, it is not countable.

**51.** We know, if $\bar{S}$ is a closure of $S$, then $S \subset \bar{S}$.

$\bar{S}$ is a closure of $S$, it contains all its adherents points, and set $S$ is closed, if it contains all its adherent points.

*i.e.*, $\qquad \bar{S} \subset S$

So, we have $\quad \bar{S} = S$ iff $S$ is closed.

Hence, by $\mu$-test, the given integral is convergent at $x = 1$, if

$$1 - n < 1 \quad i.e., \quad n > 0$$

Therefore, the given integral is convergent for all positive values of $m$ and $n$.

*i.e.*, when $\qquad m > 0$

$\qquad\qquad\qquad n > 0$

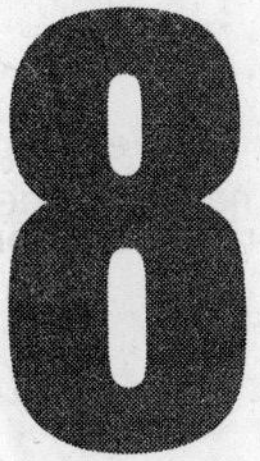

# Matrices and Vector Space

## Matrix

A system of $mn$ numbers (real or complex) arranged in rectangular array in $m$ horizontal lines (called rows) and $n$ vertical lines (called columns) is called an $m \times n$ matrix and to be read as $m$ by $n$ matrix.

An $m \times n$ matrix is usually written as

$$\begin{bmatrix} a_{11} & a_{12} & \dots & a_{1n} \\ a_{21} & a_{22} & \dots & a_{2n} \\ \vdots & \vdots & \dots & \vdots \\ am_1 & am_2 & \dots & amn \end{bmatrix}$$

The symbol $a_{ij}$ represents any entry $a_{ij}$ lies in the $i$th row (from left) and $j$th column (from top).

**Note** **(a)** A matrix may be represented by the symbols $[a_{ij}], ([a_{ij}]), ||a_{ij}||$ or by a single capital letter $A$; say

$$A = [a_{ij}]_{m \times n} \quad \text{or} \quad (a_{ij})_{m \times n} \quad \text{or} \quad ||a_{ij}||_{m \times n}$$

**(b)** A matrix has no numerical value. It is only a convenient way of storing information.

**(c)** Each of the $mn$ numbers constituting an $m \times n$ matrix is known as an element of the matrix.

**Syllabus**

- Algebra of Matrices
- Rank and Determinant of Matrices
- Linear Equations
- Eigen Values and Eigen Vectors
- Cayley-Hamilton Theorem
- Vector Spaces
- Subspaces
- Linear Dependences
- Basis
- Dimensions

## Various Kinds of Matrices

### 1. Row Matrix

If a matrix has only one row and any number of columns is called row matrix or row vector.

*e.g.*, $[4 \quad 5 \quad 6]$ is a row matrix of order $1 \times 3$.

### 2. Column Matrix

If a matrix has only one column and any number of rows is called column matrix.

*e.g.*, $\begin{bmatrix} 1 \\ 2 \\ 4 \\ 9 \end{bmatrix}$ is a column matrix of order $4 \times 1$.

### 3. Square Matrix

A matrix is said to be a square matrix, if it has number of rows equal to number of columns.

e.g., $\begin{bmatrix} 1 & 2 & 3 \\ 4 & 5 & 6 \\ 9 & 10 & 12 \end{bmatrix}$ is a square matrix of order 3.

### 4. Diagonal Matrix

A square matrix is called diagonal matrix, if all its non-diagonal elements are zero.

e.g., $\begin{bmatrix} 4 & 0 & 0 \\ 0 & 6 & 0 \\ 0 & 0 & 1 \end{bmatrix}$ is a diagonal matrix.

### 5. Scalar Matrix

A diagonal matrix is called scalar matrix, if all the non-diagonal elements are equal to zero and all the diagonal elements are equal to a scalar say $k$.

e.g., $\begin{bmatrix} 5 & 0 & 0 \\ 0 & 5 & 0 \\ 0 & 0 & 5 \end{bmatrix}$ is a scalar matrix.

### 6. Unit or Identity Matrix

A square matrix is said to be unit or identity matrix, if all the diagonal elements are equal to unity and non-diagonal elements are zero.

e.g., $\begin{bmatrix} 1 & 0 & 0 \\ 0 & 1 & 0 \\ 0 & 0 & 1 \end{bmatrix}$, $\begin{bmatrix} 1 & 0 \\ 0 & 1 \end{bmatrix}$ etc., are unit matrices.

### 7. Null Matrix or Zero Matrix

A matrix is said to be null matrix or zero matrix, if all the elements are zero.

e.g., $\begin{bmatrix} 0 & 0 \\ 0 & 0 \end{bmatrix}$, $\begin{bmatrix} 0 & 0 & 0 \\ 0 & 0 & 0 \end{bmatrix}$ are null matrices.

### 8. Horizontal Matrix

A matrix is said to be horizontal matrix, if the number of columns are more than the number of rows.

e.g., $\begin{bmatrix} 1 & 2 & 7 & 4 & 6 \\ 9 & 3 & 2 & 10 & 5 \\ 7 & 9 & 3 & 8 & 4 \end{bmatrix}$ is a horizontal matrix.

### 9. Vertical Matrix

A matrix is said to be vertical matrix, if the number of rows are more than number of columns.

e.g., $\begin{bmatrix} 1 & 3 \\ 7 & 10 \\ 8 & 5 \end{bmatrix}$ is a vertical matrix.

### 10. Sub-matrix

A matrix which is obtained from a given matrix by deleting any number of rows or columns is called a sub-matrix of the given matrix.

e.g., $\begin{bmatrix} 2 & 5 & 7 \\ 8 & 1 & 3 \end{bmatrix}$ is a sub-matrix of $\begin{bmatrix} 2 & 5 & 7 \\ 8 & 1 & 3 \\ 5 & 7 & 9 \end{bmatrix}$.

### 11. Upper Triangular Matrix

A square matrix is said to be upper triangular matrix if all elements below the leading diagonal are zero.

e.g., $\begin{bmatrix} 4 & 5 & 2 & 7 \\ 0 & 3 & 7 & 0 \\ 0 & 0 & 1 & 3 \\ 0 & 0 & 0 & 5 \end{bmatrix}$ → Leading diagonal

is an upper triangular matrix.

### 12. Lower Triangular Matrix

A square matrix is said to be lower triangular matrix if all elements above the leading diagonal are zero.

e.g., $\begin{bmatrix} 3 & 0 & 0 & 0 \\ 7 & 5 & 0 & 0 \\ 5 & 2 & 2 & 0 \\ 8 & 7 & 3 & 1 \end{bmatrix}$ → Leading diagonal

is a lower triangular matrix.

### 13. Transpose Matrix

If we interchange the rows and the corresponding columns in a given matrix $A$, the new matrix obtained is called transpose of the matrix $A$ and denoted by $A^T$ or $A'$.

e.g., Transpose of $A = \begin{bmatrix} 3 & 4 & 5 \\ 2 & 1 & 6 \\ 7 & 8 & 0 \end{bmatrix}$ is

$$\Rightarrow \quad A^T = \begin{bmatrix} 3 & 2 & 7 \\ 4 & 1 & 8 \\ 5 & 6 & 0 \end{bmatrix}$$

### 14. Symmetric Matrix

A square matrix $A$ is said to be symmetric matrix, if $A' = A$ i.e., if for all the values of $i$ and $j$, $a_{ij} = a_{ji}$.

e.g., $\begin{bmatrix} a & h & g \\ h & b & f \\ g & f & e \end{bmatrix}$ is a symmetric matrix.

### 15. Skew-symmetric Matrix

A square matrix $A$ is said to be skew-symmetric matrix, if $A' = -A$ i.e., if for all the values of $i$ and $j$

$$a_{ij} = -a_{ji}$$

e.g., $\begin{bmatrix} 0 & -h & -g \\ h & 0 & -f \\ g & f & 0 \end{bmatrix}$ is a skew-symmetric matrix.

## 16. Orthogonal Matrix

A square matrix $A$ is said to be an orthogonal matrix, if $AA' = I = A'A$, where $I$ is a unit matrix.

## 17. Conjugate Matrix

If we replace each element of given matrix $A$ by its complex conjugate, then the new matrix obtained is called conjugate matrix of $A$ and is denoted by $\overline{A}$.

e.g., Let $A = \begin{bmatrix} 2+i & 3-4i & 5 \\ 8+3i & -2i & 4-5i \end{bmatrix}$,

then the conjugate matrix of $A$ is

$$\overline{A} = \begin{bmatrix} 2-i & 3+4i & 5 \\ 8-3i & 2i & 4+5i \end{bmatrix}$$

## 18. Tranjugate Matrix

The transpose of a conjugate matrix is called tranjugate matrix and is denoted by $A^\theta$ i.e.,

$$A^\theta = (\overline{A})'$$

e.g., Let $A = \begin{bmatrix} 4+5i & 3-4i & 2 \\ 5+6i & 0 & 7+3i \\ 5-4i & 6+9i & 7+8i \end{bmatrix}$,

then $\overline{A} = \begin{bmatrix} 4-5i & 3+4i & 2 \\ 5-6i & 0 & 7-3i \\ 5+4i & 6-9i & 7-8i \end{bmatrix}$

Hence, $A^\theta = (\overline{A})' = \begin{bmatrix} 4-5i & 5-6i & 5+4i \\ 3+4i & 0 & 6-9i \\ 2 & 7-3i & 7-8i \end{bmatrix}$

## 19. Hermitian Matrix

A square matrix $A$ is called Hermitian matrix, if $A = (\overline{A})'$. i.e., if every $i$-$j$th element of $A$ is equal to complex conjugate $j$-$i$th element of $A \Rightarrow a_{ij} = \overline{a}_{ji}$

> **Note** Every diagonal element of Hermitian matrix is real.

e.g., $\begin{bmatrix} a & c-id \\ c+id & b \end{bmatrix}$, $\begin{bmatrix} 1 & 1-i & 2 \\ 1+i & 3 & i \\ 2 & -i & 0 \end{bmatrix}$ are Hermitian matrix.

## 20. Skew-Hermitian Matrix

A square matrix $A$ is called Skew-Hermitian matrix, if $A = -(\overline{A})'$ i.e., if every $i$-$j$th element of $A$ is equal to negative of complex conjugate of $j$-$i$th elements of $A \Rightarrow a_{ij} = -\overline{a}_{ji}$.

> **Note** Diagonal elements of a Skew-Hermitian matrix are either purely imaginary or zero.

e.g., $\begin{bmatrix} 0 & 5+4i \\ 5-4i & 0 \end{bmatrix}$ and $\begin{bmatrix} -i & 3+2i & -2-i \\ -3+2i & 0 & 3-4i \\ 2-i & -3-4i & 2i \end{bmatrix}$ are Skew-Hermitian matrix.

## 21. Unitary Matrix

A square matrix $A$ is said to be unitary matrix, if $AA^\theta = I = A^\theta A$.

## 22. Periodic Matrix

A matrix is called periodic matrix, if

$$A^{n+1} = A$$

Where, $n$ is a positive integer if $n$ is the least positive integer, for which $A^{n+1} = A$, then $n$ is called the period of $A$.

## 23. Idempotent Matrix

A matrix is said to be idempotent matrix, if $A^2 = A$.

## 24. Nilpotent Matrix

A square matrix is called nilpotent matrix, if $A^n = 0$, where $n$ is a positive integer, if $n$ is least positive integer for which $A^n = 0$, then $n$ is called index of the nilpotent matrix.

## 25. Involuntary Matrix

A matrix $A$ is said to be involuntary matrix, if $A^2 = I$. Unit matrix is always an involuntary matrix, since $I^2 = I$.

## 26. Singular and Non-singular Matrix

The matrix $A$ is said to be singular matrix, if $|A| = 0$ and the matrix $A$ is said to be non-singular matrix, if $|A| \neq 0$.

# Algebra of Matrix

## Addition of Matrix

If two matrices $A$ and $B$ are of the same order, then addition of matrices $A + B$ is defined as the matrix which is obtained by the addition of the corresponding elements of $A$ and $B$.

More clearly, we can say that

$$A = \begin{bmatrix} a_{11} & a_{12} & a_{13} \\ a_{21} & a_{22} & a_{23} \\ a_{31} & a_{32} & a_{33} \end{bmatrix} \text{ and } B = \begin{bmatrix} b_{11} & b_{12} & b_{13} \\ b_{21} & b_{22} & b_{23} \\ b_{31} & b_{32} & b_{33} \end{bmatrix}$$

$$\Rightarrow A + B = \begin{bmatrix} a_{11}+b_{11} & a_{12}+b_{12} & a_{13}+b_{13} \\ a_{21}+b_{21} & a_{22}+b_{22} & a_{23}+b_{23} \\ a_{31}+b_{31} & a_{32}+b_{32} & a_{33}+b_{33} \end{bmatrix}$$

### Properties of Matrix Addition

Let $A = [a_{ij}]$, $B = [b_{ij}]$ and $C = [c_{ij}]$ be the matrices of the same order say $m \times n$. Then

**(i)** $A + B = B + A$ [Commutative law]

**(ii)** $A + (B + C) = (A + B) + C$ [Associative law]

(iii) $k(A+B)=kA+kB$, where $k$ is scalar [Distributive law]
(iv) $A+0=A=0+A$ [Additive identity]
(v) $A+B=0=B+A$, here 0 is a zero matrix [Additive inverse]
(vi) (a) $A+B=A+C \Rightarrow B=C$ [Left cancellation law]
(b) $B+A=C+A \Rightarrow B=C$ [Right cancellation law]
(vii) The equation $A+X=0$ has a unique solution $X=-A$, where $X$ has order $m \times n$.

## Subtraction of Matrices

If $A$ and $B$ be two matrices of the same order, then their difference $A-B$ is defined as the matrix, each element of which is the difference of the corresponding elements of $A$ and $B$ i.e.,

$$A-B=[a_{ij}-b_{ij}], \text{ where } A=[a_{ij}] \text{ and } B=[b_{ij}]$$

More clearly, we can say that, if

$$A=\begin{bmatrix} a_{11} & a_{12} & a_{13} \\ a_{21} & a_{22} & a_{23} \\ a_{31} & a_{32} & a_{33} \end{bmatrix} \text{ and } B=\begin{bmatrix} b_{11} & b_{12} & b_{13} \\ b_{21} & b_{22} & b_{23} \\ b_{31} & b_{32} & b_{33} \end{bmatrix}$$

$$\Rightarrow \quad A-B=\begin{bmatrix} a_{11}-b_{11} & a_{12}-b_{12} & a_{13}-b_{13} \\ a_{21}-b_{21} & a_{22}-b_{22} & a_{23}-b_{23} \\ a_{31}-b_{31} & a_{32}-b_{32} & a_{33}-b_{33} \end{bmatrix}$$

## Scalar Multiplication of a Matrix

Let $A$ be any matrix and $k$ be any scalar, then the matrix obtained by multiplying every element of the matrix $A$ by $k$ is called scalar multiplication of $A$ by $k$ and denoted by $kA$.

e.g., $k=3$ and $A=\begin{bmatrix} 1 & 2 & 5 \\ 3 & -3 & 1 \end{bmatrix}$, then $3A=\begin{bmatrix} 3 & 6 & 15 \\ 9 & -9 & 3 \end{bmatrix}$

## Equality of Matrices

Two matrices $A$ and $B$ are said to be equal, if

(i) They are of same order and
(ii) All the corresponding elements are equal i.e., $a_{ij}=b_{ij}$

e.g., Let $A=\begin{bmatrix} 1 & 2 \\ 4 & 5 \end{bmatrix}$ and $B=\begin{bmatrix} 1 & 2 \\ 4 & 5 \end{bmatrix}$, then $A=B$.

## Matrix Multiplication

If $A$ and $B$ be two matrices such that the number of columns in $A$ is equal to the number of rows in $B$ i.e., if $A=[a_{ij}]$ be an $m \times n$ matrix and $B=[b_{ij}]$ be an $n \times P$ matrix, then the product $AB$ of these matrices is $m \times p$ matrix $C=[c_{ij}]$, where

$$c_{ij}=a_{i1}b_{1j}+a_{i2}b_{2j}+\ldots+a_{in}b_{nj}$$

The rule for multiplication of two comformable matrices is called row-by-column method.

> **Note** If the number of columns in $A$ is same as the number of rows in $B$, then the product $AB$ is defined, and such matrices are said to be comformable for multiplication otherwise non-comformable for multiplication.

e.g., $A=\begin{bmatrix} a_{11} & a_{12} & a_{13} \\ a_{21} & a_{22} & a_{23} \end{bmatrix}$, $B=\begin{bmatrix} b_{11} & b_{12} \\ b_{21} & b_{22} \\ b_{31} & b_{32} \end{bmatrix}$

$$AB=\begin{bmatrix} a_{11}b_{11}+a_{12}b_{21}+a_{13}b_{31} & a_{11}b_{12}+a_{12}b_{22}+a_{13}b_{32} \\ a_{21}b_{11}+a_{22}b_{21}+a_{23}b_{31} & a_{21}b_{12}+a_{22}b_{22}+a_{23}b_{32} \end{bmatrix}_{2\times 2}$$

### Properties of Matrix Multiplication

(i) **Matrix multiplication is associative** If $A$, $B$ and $C$ are three $m \times n$, $n \times p$, $p \times q$ matrices respectively, then

$$(AB)C=A(BC)$$

(ii) Multiplication of matrices is distributive with respect to addition of matrices.

$$A(B+C)=AB+AC$$

(iii) **Multiplication of matrices is not necessarily commutative** For some matrices $AB$ may be equal to $BA$ but for some matrices $AB \neq BA$ in general.

## Positive Integral Power of Matrices

If $A$ is a square matrix and $p$ is a positive integer, then $A^p$ is defined by the recurrence relation $A^p=A \cdot A^{p-1}$.

If $m$ and $n$ are any arbitrary positive integers.

We have,

$A^m \cdot A^n=(AA\ldots A, m \text{ times}).(AA\ldots A, n \text{ times})$

[Since, the product of any number of matrices is associative]

$=A^{m+n}$

Again, $(A^m)^n=A^m \cdot A^m \ldots A^m$, $n$ times

$=(AA\ldots A, m \text{ times})(AA\ldots A, m \text{ times})\ldots n$ times

$=AAA\ldots A$, $mn$ times

$=(A^n)^m$

***Example 1.*** *If* $A=\begin{bmatrix} 2 & 3 \\ -1 & 2 \\ 4 & 3 \end{bmatrix}$ *and* $B=\begin{bmatrix} 1 & -2 & 4 \\ 2 & 3 & 1 \end{bmatrix}$, *find AB.*

**Solution.** Since, the number of columns of matrix $A$ is equal to the number of rows of matrix $B$, hence the product $AB$ is possible and

$$AB=\begin{bmatrix} 2\times1+3\times2 & 2\times(-2)+3\times3 & 2\times4+3\times1 \\ -1\times1+2\times2 & -1\times(-2)+2\times3 & -1\times4+2\times1 \\ 4\times1+3\times2 & 4\times(-2)+3\times3 & 4\times4+3\times1 \end{bmatrix}$$

$$=\begin{bmatrix} 8 & 5 & 11 \\ 3 & 8 & -2 \\ 10 & 1 & 19 \end{bmatrix}$$

# Determinants, Adjoint and Inverse of Matrix

## Determinant

Every square matrix can be associated to an expression or a number which is known as determinant. The determinant of a square matrix $A=[a_{ij}]$ of order $n$ is denoted by $|A|$ and is given by

$$|A|=\begin{vmatrix} a_{11} & a_{12} & \cdots & a_{1n} \\ a_{21} & a_{22} & \cdots & a_{2n} \\ \vdots & \vdots & \vdots & \vdots \\ a_{n1} & a_{n2} & \cdots & a_{nn} \end{vmatrix}$$

> ***Note*** A matrix which is not square matrix does not possess determinant.

## Determinant of a Square Matrix of Order 2

Let $A=\begin{bmatrix} a_{11} & a_{12} \\ a_{21} & a_{22} \end{bmatrix}$ be a square matrix of order 2, then $|A|$ is given by

$$|A|=\begin{vmatrix} a_{11} & a_{12} \\ a_{21} & a_{22} \end{vmatrix}=a_{11}a_{22}-a_{21}a_{12}$$

The number $a_{11}a_{22}-a_{21}a_{12}$ is called the value of the determinant. The number $a_{11}, a_{12}, a_{21}, a_{22}$ is called the elements of the determinant. In a determinant of order 2 there are two rows and two columns.

## Determinant of Square Matrix of Order 3

Let $A=\begin{bmatrix} a_{11} & a_{12} & a_{13} \\ a_{21} & a_{22} & a_{23} \\ a_{31} & a_{32} & a_{33} \end{bmatrix}$ be a square matrix of order 3, then $|A|$ is given by

$$|A|=\begin{vmatrix} a_{11} & a_{12} & a_{13} \\ a_{21} & a_{22} & a_{23} \\ a_{31} & a_{32} & a_{33} \end{vmatrix}$$

$$=(-1)^{1+1}a_{11}\begin{vmatrix} a_{22} & a_{23} \\ a_{32} & a_{33} \end{vmatrix}+(-1)^{1+2}a_{12}\begin{vmatrix} a_{21} & a_{23} \\ a_{31} & a_{33} \end{vmatrix}+(-1)^{1+3}a_{13}\begin{vmatrix} a_{21} & a_{22} \\ a_{31} & a_{32} \end{vmatrix}$$

$$=a_{11}\begin{vmatrix} a_{22} & a_{23} \\ a_{32} & a_{33} \end{vmatrix}-a_{12}\begin{vmatrix} a_{21} & a_{23} \\ a_{31} & a_{33} \end{vmatrix}+a_{13}\begin{vmatrix} a_{21} & a_{22} \\ a_{31} & a_{32} \end{vmatrix}$$

This is called the expansion of the determinant along its first row. We can find the value of the determinant by expanding along any of its row or any of its column.
If we expand $|A|$ along the third row, then

$$|A|=(-1)^{3+1}\begin{vmatrix} a_{12} & a_{13} \\ a_{22} & a_{23} \end{vmatrix}+(-1)^{3+2}\begin{vmatrix} a_{11} & a_{13} \\ a_{21} & a_{23} \end{vmatrix}+(-1)^{3+3}\begin{vmatrix} a_{11} & a_{21} \\ a_{21} & a_{22} \end{vmatrix}$$

Similarly, if we expand $|A|$ along the second column, we get

$$|A|=(-1)^{1+2}a_{12}\begin{vmatrix} a_{21} & a_{23} \\ a_{31} & a_{33} \end{vmatrix}+(-1)^{2+2}a_{22}\begin{vmatrix} a_{11} & a_{13} \\ a_{31} & a_{33} \end{vmatrix}+(-1)^{3+2}\begin{vmatrix} a_{11} & a_{12} \\ a_{21} & a_{22} \end{vmatrix}$$

To fix positive or negative sign before the element $a_{ij}$ occurring in the $i$th row and the $j$th column, we should multiply it by $(-1)^{i+j}$.

> ***Note*** **(a)** The determinant of a square matrix is also denoted by $\Delta$.
> **(b)** Expand a determinant along that row or column which has maximum number of zero.

***Example 2.*** *Evaluate the following determinant*

$$\begin{vmatrix} 1 & 2 & 4 \\ 4 & 5 & 6 \\ 7 & 8 & 9 \end{vmatrix}$$

**Solution.** We have,

$$\begin{vmatrix} 1 & 2 & 4 \\ 4 & 5 & 6 \\ 7 & 8 & 9 \end{vmatrix}=(-1)^{1+1}\cdot 1\begin{vmatrix} 5 & 6 \\ 8 & 9 \end{vmatrix}+(-1)^{1+2}\cdot 2\begin{vmatrix} 4 & 6 \\ 7 & 9 \end{vmatrix}+(-1)^{1+3}\cdot 4\begin{vmatrix} 4 & 5 \\ 7 & 8 \end{vmatrix}$$

$$=(45-48)-2(36-42)+4(32-35)$$

$$=-3+12-12=-3$$

## Properties of Determinants

**(i)** The value of a determinant does not change when rows and columns are interchanged.

**(ii)** If any row (or column) of a matrix $A$ is completely zero, then $|A|=0$
Also, if any two rows (or columns) of a matrix $A$ are identical, then $|A|=0$

**(iii)** If any two rows or two columns of a determinant are interchanged, the value of determinant is multiplied by (–1).

**(iv)** If all elements of the one row (or one column) of a determinant are multiplied by same number $k$ the value of determinant is $k$ times the value of given determinant.

**(v)** If $A$ be $n$-rowed square matrix and $k$ be any scalar, then $|kA|=k^n|A|$

**(vi)** In a determinant the sum of the products of the elements of any row (or column) with the cofactors of corresponding elements of any row or (column) is equal to the determinant value.

**(vii)** In determinant the sum of the products of the elements of any row (or column) with the cofactors of corresponding elements of other row or column is zero.

**(viii)** If to the elements of a row (or column) of a determinant are added $m$ times the corresponding elements of another row (or column) the value of determinant thus obtained is equal to the value or original determinant.

**(ix)** $|AB|=|A|\times|B|$ and based on this we can say the following

$$|A^n|=(|A|)^n$$

# Minors and Co-factors

## Minors

If we delete the $i$th row and the $j$th column passing through the element $a_{ij}$ of the matrix $A$ of order $n$, then the determinant of the square sub-matrix of order $(n-1)$ obtained is called the minor of the element $a_{ij}$ and is denoted by $M_{ij}$.

*e.g.*, Let us consider a matrix $A$.

$$A = \begin{bmatrix} a_{11} & a_{12} & a_{13} \\ a_{21} & a_{22} & a_{23} \\ a_{31} & a_{32} & a_{33} \end{bmatrix}$$

The minor of element $a_{21} = \begin{vmatrix} a_{12} & a_{13} \\ a_{32} & a_{33} \end{vmatrix} = M_{21}$

The minor of element $a_{32} = \begin{vmatrix} a_{11} & a_{13} \\ a_{21} & a_{23} \end{vmatrix} = M_{32}$

The minor of element $a_{11} = \begin{vmatrix} a_{22} & a_{23} \\ a_{32} & a_{33} \end{vmatrix} = M_{11}$

and so on.

## Co-factor of an Element of a Matrix

If the minor $M_{ij}$ multiplied by $(-1)^{i+j}$, then it is called the co-factor of the element $a_{ij}$. It is denoted by $A_{ij}$ or $C_{ij}$.

*e.g.*, The co-factor of the element

$$a_{21} = A_{21} = (-1)^{2+1} M_{21} = -\begin{vmatrix} a_{12} & a_{13} \\ a_{32} & a_{33} \end{vmatrix}$$

The co-factor of the element

$$a_{13} = A_{13} = (-1)^{1+3} M_{13} = \begin{vmatrix} a_{21} & a_{22} \\ a_{31} & a_{32} \end{vmatrix}$$

The co-factor of the element

$$a_{32} = A_{32} = (-1)^{3+2} M_{32} = -\begin{vmatrix} a_{11} & a_{13} \\ a_{21} & a_{23} \end{vmatrix}$$

and so on.

***Example 3.*** *If* $A = \begin{bmatrix} 2 & 3 \\ 4 & 5 \end{bmatrix}$, *then find the minors.*

**Solution.** We have, $A = \begin{bmatrix} 2 & 3 \\ 4 & 5 \end{bmatrix}$

The minors of $a_{11} = M_{11} = 5$

The minors of $a_{12} = M_{12} = 4$

The minors of $a_{21} = M_{21} = 3$

The minors of $a_{22} = M_{22} = 2$

***Example 4.*** *Find the co-factors of the matrix,*

$$A = \begin{bmatrix} 3 & -6 \\ 8 & 2 \end{bmatrix}$$

**Solution.** We have, $A = \begin{bmatrix} 3 & -6 \\ 8 & 2 \end{bmatrix}$

The co-factor of $a_{11} = A_{11} = (-1)^{1+1} \cdot 2 = 2$

The co-factor of $a_{12} = A_{12} = (-1)^{1+2} \cdot 8 = -8$

The co-factor of $a_{21} = A_{21} = (-1)^{2+1} \cdot (-6) = 6$

The co-factor of $a_{22} = A_{22} = (-1)^{2+2} \cdot 3 = 3$

# Adjoint of a Square Matrix

Let $A = [a_{ij}]$ be any $n \times n$ matrix, then adjoint of $A$ is defined as the transpose of the matrix $[A_{ij}]_{n\times n}$, where $A_{ij}$ denotes the co-factor of the element $a_{ij}$ in the determinant $|A|$. The adjoint of the matrix $A$ is denoted by the symbol adj $(A)$.

Let $A = \begin{bmatrix} a_{11} & a_{12} & a_{13} \\ a_{21} & a_{22} & a_{23} \\ a_{31} & a_{32} & a_{33} \end{bmatrix}$ be a $3 \times 3$ matrix, then

$$\text{co-factor matrix or Cof } (A) = \begin{bmatrix} A_{11} & A_{12} & A_{13} \\ A_{21} & A_{22} & A_{23} \\ A_{31} & A_{32} & A_{33} \end{bmatrix}$$

$$\therefore \quad \text{adj}(A) = [\text{Cof}(A)]' = \begin{bmatrix} A_{11} & A_{21} & A_{31} \\ A_{12} & A_{22} & A_{32} \\ A_{13} & A_{23} & A_{33} \end{bmatrix}$$

> ***Note*** The product of a matrix $A$ and its adjoint is equal to unit matrix multiplied by the determinant $A$ *i.e.*, $(\text{adj } A)A = A(\text{adj } A) = |A|I$

# Inverse of a Matrix

A square matrix $A$ of order $n$ is said to be invertible, if $\exists$ a square matrix $B$ of order $n$, such that

$$AB = BA = I$$

$B$ is called the inverse of $A$, we have $B = A^{-1}$. The inverse of $A$ is given by

$$A^{-1} = \frac{\text{adj}(A)}{|A|}, \text{ provided } |A| \neq 0$$

*i.e.*, the necessary and sufficient condition for a square matrix $A$ to possess the inverse is that $|A| \neq 0$.

## Properties of Inverse Matrix

**(i)** Inverse of a square matrix $A$ exists iff $A$ is non-singular *i.e.*, $|A| \neq 0$.

**(ii)** Inverse of a square matrix if it exists is unique.

**(iii)** $A$ and $B$ are inverse of each other iff $AB = BA = I$, where $A$ and $B$ are non-singular square matrices of same order.

**(iv)** $AA^{-1} = A^{-1}A = I$, where $A$ is non-singular square matrix.

**(v)** If $A$ and $B$ are square matrices of same order, then $AB$ is invertible iff both $A$ and $B$ are non-singular and

$$(AB)^{-1} = B^{-1}A^{-1}$$

In general,

$$(ABCD\ldots XYZ)^{-1} = Z^{-1}Y^{-1}X^{-1}\ldots D^{-1}C^{-1}B^{-1}A^{-1}$$

where $A, B, C, D, \ldots, X, Y, Z$ are invertible square matrices of same order.

**(vi)** $(A^{-1})^{-1} = A$, where $A$ is non-singular square matrices.

**(vii)** $(A')^{-1} = (A^{-1})'$, where $A$ is non-singular square matrix.

**(viii)** Only for a $2 \times 2$ matrix

$$A = \begin{bmatrix} a & b \\ c & d \end{bmatrix}, A^{-1} = \frac{1}{ad - bc}\begin{bmatrix} d & -b \\ -c & a \end{bmatrix}$$

$$= \frac{1}{|A|}\begin{bmatrix} d & -b \\ -c & a \end{bmatrix}$$

**Example 5.** *If* $A = \begin{bmatrix} 3 & -3 & 4 \\ 2 & -3 & 4 \\ 0 & -1 & 1 \end{bmatrix}$. *Find* $A^{-1}$.

**Solution.** We have, $A = \begin{bmatrix} 3 & -3 & 4 \\ 2 & -3 & 4 \\ 0 & -1 & 1 \end{bmatrix}$

$$\Rightarrow \quad |A| = \begin{vmatrix} 3 & -3 & 4 \\ 2 & -3 & 4 \\ 0 & -1 & 1 \end{vmatrix}$$

$$= 3(-3 + 4) + 3(2 - 0) + 4(-2 - 0)$$

$$= 3 + 6 - 8 = 1$$

The co-factors of elements of various rows of $|A|$ are

$$\begin{bmatrix} (-3+4) & (-2-0) & (-2-0) \\ (3-4) & (3-0) & (3-0) \\ (-12+12) & (-12+8) & (-9+6) \end{bmatrix}$$

Therefore, the matrix formed by the co-factors of $|A|$ is

$$\text{Cof}(A) = \begin{bmatrix} 1 & -2 & -2 \\ -1 & 3 & 3 \\ 0 & -4 & -3 \end{bmatrix}$$

Now, $\quad \text{adj}(A) = [\text{Cof}(A)]' = \begin{bmatrix} 1 & -1 & 0 \\ -2 & 3 & -4 \\ -2 & 3 & -3 \end{bmatrix}$

$$\therefore \quad A^{-1} = \frac{1}{|A|}\text{adj}(A) = \frac{1}{1}\begin{bmatrix} 1 & -1 & 0 \\ -2 & 3 & -4 \\ -2 & 3 & -3 \end{bmatrix}$$

$$= \begin{bmatrix} 1 & -1 & 0 \\ -2 & 3 & -4 \\ -2 & 3 & -3 \end{bmatrix}$$

# To Find Inverse of Matrix by Elementary Transformation

## Elementary Transformation

Any of the three operations applied on the rows or columns of a matrix is known as elementary row or column transformation.

**(i)** Interchange of any two rows or columns. This transformation is indicated by $R_i \leftrightarrow R_j$, if the $i$th row and the $j$th row are interchanged, and $C_i \leftrightarrow C_j$, if the $i$th column and the $j$th column are interchanged.

**(ii)** Multiplying every element of any row or column of a matrix by a non-zero number. This transformation is indicated by $R_i \to kR_i$, if the elements of $i$th row multiplied by $k (k \neq 0)$, and $C_i \to kC_i$, if the elements of $i$th column multiplied by $k$, $(k \neq 0)$.

**(iii)** Adding to the elements of a row or column to the corresponding elements of any other row or column multiplied by any scalar $k$. This transformation is indicated by $R_i \to R_i + kR_j$ and $C_i \to C_i + kC_j$.

## Elementary Matrix

A matrix obtained from an identity matrix by applying a single elementary transformation is called an elementary matrix.

e.g., $\begin{bmatrix} 1 & 0 & 0 \\ 0 & 1 & 0 \\ 0 & 0 & 1 \end{bmatrix}$ is an identity matrix.

Using $R_1 \to R_1 + 3R_2$, we get

$\begin{bmatrix} 1 & 3 & 0 \\ 0 & 1 & 0 \\ 0 & 0 & 1 \end{bmatrix}$ this matrix is called the elementary matrix.

## Working Rule to Find Inverse of a Matrix by Elementary Row Transformation (Gauss-Jordan Method)

**(i)** Write the given matrix as

$$A = I_n A \quad \ldots(i)$$

where, $I_n$ is the identity matrix of order $n$, which is equal to the order of the matrix $A$.

**(ii)** Perform elementary row transformation on $A$ of left hand side of Eq. (i) to reduce it into the identity matrix.

**(iii)** Apply the same elementary row transformation on the $I$ of the right hand side, so that $I$ is reduced to $B$.

**(iv)** The transformation reduce the Eq. (i) *i.e.*,

$$A = I_n A \text{ into } I_n = BA,$$

where $B$ denote the inverse of $A$.

***Example 6.*** *Find the inverse of the matrix A by using the elementary transformations, where*

$$A = \begin{bmatrix} 1 & 2 & -2 \\ -1 & 3 & 0 \\ 0 & 2 & 1 \end{bmatrix}$$

**Solution.** The given matrix can be written as

$$A = IA$$

$$\Rightarrow \quad \begin{bmatrix} 1 & 2 & -2 \\ -1 & 3 & 0 \\ 0 & 2 & 1 \end{bmatrix} = \begin{bmatrix} 1 & 0 & 0 \\ 0 & 1 & 0 \\ 0 & 0 & 1 \end{bmatrix} A, \; R_2 \to R_2 + R_1$$

$$\Rightarrow \quad \begin{bmatrix} 1 & 2 & -2 \\ 0 & 5 & -2 \\ 0 & -2 & 1 \end{bmatrix} = \begin{bmatrix} 1 & 0 & 0 \\ 0 & 1 & 0 \\ 0 & 0 & 1 \end{bmatrix} A, \; \begin{matrix} R_1 \to R_1 - R_3, \\ R_2 \to R_2 - 2R_3 \end{matrix}$$

$$\Rightarrow \begin{bmatrix} 1 & 0 & -1 \\ 0 & 1 & 0 \\ 0 & -2 & 1 \end{bmatrix} = \begin{bmatrix} 1 & 0 & 1 \\ 1 & 1 & 2 \\ 0 & 0 & 1 \end{bmatrix} A, R_3 \to R_3 + 2R_2$$

$$\Rightarrow \begin{bmatrix} 1 & 0 & -1 \\ 0 & 1 & 0 \\ 0 & 0 & 1 \end{bmatrix} = \begin{bmatrix} 1 & 0 & 1 \\ 1 & 1 & 2 \\ 2 & 2 & 5 \end{bmatrix} A, R_1 \to R_1 + R_3$$

$$\Rightarrow \begin{bmatrix} 1 & 0 & 0 \\ 0 & 1 & 0 \\ 0 & 0 & 1 \end{bmatrix} = \begin{bmatrix} 3 & 2 & 6 \\ 1 & 1 & 2 \\ 2 & 2 & 5 \end{bmatrix} A,$$

Hence, $A^{-1} = \begin{bmatrix} 3 & 2 & 6 \\ 1 & 1 & 2 \\ 2 & 2 & 5 \end{bmatrix}$

# Properties of Various Kind of Matrices

## Properties of Symmetric Matrix

**(i)** In a symmetric matrix the $(i\text{-}j)$th element above the principal diagonal and $(j\text{-}i)$th element below the principal diagonal are same.

**(ii)** Square null matrix, diagonal matrix, scalar matrix and identity matrix are symmetric matrices.

**(iii)** Every symmetric matrix is necessarily be square matrix.

**(iv)** Transpose of symmetric matrix need not be symmetric matrix. For, $(A')' = A \neq A'$.

**(v)** Symmetric matrix may be singular or non-singular according as its determinant is zero or non-zero, respectively.

**(vi)** If $A$ is symmetric matrix, then $kA$ is also symmetric matrix for any scalar $k$.

**(vii)** If $A$ and $B$ are symmetric matrices of same order. Then, $\lambda_1 A \pm \lambda_2 B$ are also be symmetric matrices for scalars $\lambda_1$ and $\lambda_2$.

**(viii)** If $A$ and $B$ are both symmetric matrices of same order. Then, $AB$ is symmetric matrix iff $AB = BA$.

**(ix)** If $A$ be any square matrix. Then, $AA'$ and $A'A$ both will be symmetric matrix.

**(x)** If $A$ and $B$ are symmetric matrices of same order. Then, $AB + BA$ must be symmetric matrix.

For,
$$\begin{aligned}(AB + BA)' &= (AB)' + (BA)' \\ &= B'A' + A'B' \\ &= BA + AB \\ &= AB + BA\end{aligned}$$

**(xi)** If $A$ is symmetric matrix, then all positive integral powers of $A$ are symmetric matrices. For,
$$(A^n)' = A^n$$

**(xii)** If $A$ is any square matrix, then $A + A'$ is always symmetric matrix. For,
$$\begin{aligned}(A + A')' &= A' + (A')' \\ &= A' + A = A + A'\end{aligned}$$

## Properties of Skew-symmetric Matrix

**(i)** In a skew-symmetric matrix the $(i\text{-}j)$th elements below the principal diagonal are negatively equal to the $(j\text{-}i)$th elements above the principal diagonal.

**(ii)** All the principal diagonal elements of a skew-symmetric matrix are zero, *i.e.*, $a_{ij} = 0$. For let $A = [a_{ij}]_{n \times n}$ be a skew-symmetric matrix. Then,
$$a_{ij} = -a_{ji}$$
Putting $j = i$, we get
$$a_{ii} = -a_{ii}$$
$$\Rightarrow \quad 2a_{ii} = 0$$
$$\Rightarrow \quad a_{ii} = 0$$

**(iii)** Square null matrix is a skew-symmetric matrix but none of diagonal matrix, scalar matrix and identity matrix are skew-symmetric matrix.

**(iv)** Every skew-symmetric matrix is necessarily be square matrix.

**(v)** If $A$ is a skew-symmetric matrix, then $kA$ is also skew-symmetric matrix for any scalar $k$.

**(vi)** If $A$ and $B$ are skew-symmetric matrices of same order, then $\lambda_1 A \pm \lambda_2 B$ are also skew-symmetric matrix for any scalar $\lambda_1$ and $\lambda_2$. For,
$$\begin{aligned}(\lambda_1 A + \lambda_2 B)' &= \lambda_1 A' + \lambda_2 B' \\ &= -\lambda_1 A - \lambda_2 B = -(\lambda_1 A + \lambda_2 B)\end{aligned}$$

**(vii)** If $A$ and $B$ are both skew-symmetric matrices of same order, then $AB$ is skew-symmetric iff $AB + BA = 0$. For,
$$\begin{aligned}(AB)' &= B'A' \\ &= (-B)(-A) \\ &= BA = -AB\end{aligned}$$

**(viii)** If $A$ and $B$ are symmetric matrices of same order, then $AB - BA$ must be skew-symmetric matrix. For,
$$\begin{aligned}(AB - BA)' &= (AB)' - (BA)' \\ &= B'A' - A'B' \\ &= BA - AB \\ &= -(AB - BA)\end{aligned}$$

**(ix)** If $A$ is any skew-symmetric matrix, then all positive odd integral powers of $A$ are skew-symmetric matrix. For,
$$(A^n)' = (A')^n = (-A)^n = -A^n \qquad (\because n \text{ is odd})$$

**(x)** If $A$ is any square matrix, then $A - A'$ is always skew-symmetric. For, $(A - A')' = A' - (A')'$
$$= A' - A = -(A - A')$$

**(xi)** Any square matrix $A$ is uniquely expressed as the sum of a symmetric matrix and a skew-symmetric matrix. The symmetric part is $\frac{1}{2}(A + A')$ and skew-symmetric part is $\frac{1}{2}(A - A')$. Thus
$$A = \underbrace{\frac{1}{2}(A + A')}_{\text{Symmetric matrix}} + \underbrace{\frac{1}{2}(A - A')}_{\text{Skew-symmetric matrix}}$$

e.g., Let $A=\begin{bmatrix}1&2&3\\4&5&6\\7&8&9\end{bmatrix}$, then $A'=\begin{bmatrix}1&4&7\\2&5&8\\3&6&9\end{bmatrix}$

$\therefore$ Symmetric part $=\frac{1}{2}(A+A')$

$$=\frac{1}{2}\left\{\begin{bmatrix}1&2&3\\4&5&6\\7&8&9\end{bmatrix}+\begin{bmatrix}1&4&7\\2&5&8\\3&6&9\end{bmatrix}\right\}$$

$$=\frac{1}{2}\begin{bmatrix}2&6&10\\6&10&14\\10&14&18\end{bmatrix}=\begin{bmatrix}1&3&5\\3&5&7\\5&7&9\end{bmatrix}$$

and skew-symmetric part

$$=\frac{1}{2}(A-A')$$

$$=\frac{1}{2}\left\{\begin{bmatrix}1&2&3\\4&5&6\\7&8&9\end{bmatrix}-\begin{bmatrix}1&4&7\\2&5&8\\3&6&9\end{bmatrix}\right\}$$

$$=\frac{1}{2}\begin{bmatrix}0&-2&-4\\2&0&-2\\4&2&0\end{bmatrix}=\begin{bmatrix}0&-1&-2\\1&0&-1\\2&1&0\end{bmatrix}$$

Therefore,

$$A=\begin{bmatrix}1&2&3\\4&5&6\\7&8&9\end{bmatrix}=\underbrace{\begin{bmatrix}1&3&5\\3&5&7\\5&7&9\end{bmatrix}}_{\text{Symmetric matrix}}+\underbrace{\begin{bmatrix}0&-1&-2\\1&0&-1\\2&1&0\end{bmatrix}}_{\text{Skew-symmetric matrix}}$$

## Properties of an Orthogonal Matrix

**(i)** If $A$ is orthogonal matrix, then $A$ is non-singular and $A^{-1}=A'$.

For, $A'A=I\Rightarrow A(A'A)=AI=A$

$\Rightarrow (AA')A=A\Rightarrow AA'=I\Rightarrow A$ is non-singular and $A^{-1}=A'$.

**(ii)** If $A$ is an orthogonal matrix, then $|A|=\pm 1$. For,

$A'A=I\Rightarrow |A'A|=1\Rightarrow |A'||A|=1\Rightarrow |A|^2=1$

$\Rightarrow \quad |A|=\pm 1$

**(iii)** Transpose of an orthogonal matrix is orthogonal. *i.e.*, If $A$ is orthogonal matrix, then $A'$ is also orthogonal matrix. For,

$AA'=A'A=I\Rightarrow (AA')'=(A'A)'=I$

$\Rightarrow \quad AA'=A'A=I.$

**(iv)** Product of two orthogonal matrices is orthogonal matrix. *i.e.*, if $A$ and $B$ are orthogonal matrices, then $AB$ and $BA$ are orthogonal matrices. For,

$$(AB)(AB)'=(AB)(B'A')=A(BB')A'$$
$$=AIA'=AA'=I$$

Similarly,

$$(BA)(BA)'=(BA)(A'B')$$
$$=B(AA')B'$$
$$=BIB'$$
$$=BB'=I$$

**(v)** Inverse of an orthogonal matrix is orthogonal. *i.e.*, if $A$ is orthogonal matrix, then $A^{-1}$ is also orthogonal. For,

$$AA'=A'A=I$$
$$\Rightarrow \quad (AA')^{-1}=(A'A)^{-1}=I$$
$$\Rightarrow (A')^{-1}A^{-1}=A^{-1}(A')^{-1}=I$$
$$\Rightarrow (A^{-1})'A^{-1}=A^{-1}(A^{-1})'=I$$

## Properties of Conjugate of a Matrix

Let $\bar{A}$ and $\bar{B}$ be the conjugate matrix of matrices $A$ and $B$, respectively. Then,

**(i)** $\bar{\bar{A}}=A$

**(ii)** $\overline{(A+B)}=\bar{A}+\bar{B}$

**(iii)** $\overline{(kA)}=\bar{k}\,\bar{A}$, $k$ being any scalar number.

**(iv)** $\overline{AB}=\bar{A}\,\bar{B}$, $A$ and $B$ are conformable to multiplication.

**(v)** $\overline{(A^n)}=(\bar{A})^n$

**(vi)** $\bar{A}=A$ iff $A$ is purely real matrix.

**(vii)** $\bar{A}=-A$ iff $A$ is purely imaginary matrix.

## Properties of Transpose Conjugate of Matrix

Let $A^\theta$ and $B^\theta$ are transpose conjugate of matrices $A$ and $B$, respectively. Then,

**(i)** $(A^\theta)^\theta=A$

**(ii)** $(A+B)^\theta=A^\theta+B^\theta$

**(iii)** $(kA)^\theta=\bar{k}A^\theta$

**(iv)** $(AB)^\theta=B^\theta A^\theta$, $A$ and $B$ are conformable for multiplication.

**(v)** $(A^n)^\theta=(A^\theta)^n$

## Properties of Unitary Matrix

**(i)** If $A$ is an unitary matrix, then $A'$ is also unitary matrix. For,

$$AA^\theta=A^\theta A=I$$
$$\Rightarrow \quad (AA^\theta)'=(A^\theta A)'=I$$
$$\Rightarrow \quad (A^\theta)'A'=A'(A^\theta)'=I$$
$$\Rightarrow \quad (A')^\theta A'=A'(A')^\theta=I$$

**(ii)** If $A$ and $B$ are two unitary matrices of same order, then $AB$ and $BA$ are also unitary matrices of same order. For,

$$(AB)(AB)^\theta=AB(B^\theta A^\theta)$$
$$=A(BB^\theta)A^\theta=AIA^\theta$$
$$=AA^\theta=I$$

Similarly,

$$\begin{aligned}(BA)(BA)^\theta &= (BA)(A^\theta B^\theta)\\ &= B(AA^\theta)B^\theta\\ &= BIB^\theta\\ &= BB^\theta = I\end{aligned}$$

**(iii)** If $A$ is unitary matrix, then $A^{-1}$ is also unitary matrix. For,

$$AA^\theta = A^\theta A = I$$

$$\Rightarrow \quad (AA^\theta)^{-1} = (A^\theta A)^{-1} = I$$

$$\Rightarrow \quad (A^\theta)^{-1}A^{-1} = A^{-1}(A^\theta)^{-1} = I$$

$$\Rightarrow \quad (A^{-1})^\theta A^{-1} = A^{-1}(A^{-1})^\theta = I$$

## Properties of Hermitian Matrix

**(i)** A square matrix $A = [a_{ij}]_{n\times n}$ is Hermitian iff $\bar{a}_{ij} = a_{ji}$.

**(ii)** In a Hermitian matrix, the elements on the principal diagonal all are real numbers *i.e.*, $\bar{a}_{ii} = a_{ii}$. For,

$$\bar{a}_{ij} = a_{ji}$$

Putting $j = i$, we get

$$\bar{a}_{ii} = a_{ii}$$

**(iii)** If $A$ is Hermitian matrix, then $kA$ is also Hermitian matrix, $k$ is any real number. For,

$$(kA)^\theta = \bar{k}A^\theta = kA.$$

**(iv)** If $A$ and $B$ are Hermitian matrices of same order, then $\lambda_1 A \pm \lambda_2 B$ are also Hermitian matrices for any real scalar $\lambda_1$ and $\lambda_2$.

**(v)** If $A$ and $B$ are Hermitian matrices of same order, then $AB$ is also Hermitian iff $AB = BA$. For,

$$(AB)^\theta = B^\theta A^\theta = BA = AB.$$

**(vi)** If $A$ be any square matrix, then $AA^\theta$ and $A^\theta A$ are also Hermitian matrices. For,

$$(AA^\theta)^\theta = (A^\theta)^\theta A^\theta = AA^\theta$$

Similarly,

$$(A^\theta A)^\theta = A^\theta (A^\theta)^\theta = A^\theta A.$$

**(vii)** If $A$ and $B$ are Hermitian matrices of same order, then $AB + BA$ is also Hermitian matrix. For,

$$\begin{aligned}(AB + BA)^\theta &= (AB)^\theta + (BA)^\theta = B^\theta A^\theta + A^\theta B^\theta\\ &= BA + AB = AB + BA.\end{aligned}$$

**(viii)** If $A$ is a Hermitian matrix, then $\bar{A}$ is also Hermitian matrix.

**(ix)** If $A$ is any square matrix, then all positive integral power of $A$ are Hermitian matrix.

**(x)** If $A$ is any square matrix, then $A + A^\theta$ is a Hermitian matrix.

**(xi)** Any square matrix can be expressed as $A + iB$, where, $A$ and $B$ are Hermitian matrices.

## Properties of Skew-Hermitian Matrix

**(i)** A square matrix $A = [a_{ij}]_{n\times n}$ is Skew-Hermitian iff $\bar{a}_{ij} = -a_{ji}$

**(ii)** In a Skew-Hermitian matrix, the element on the principal diagonal must be purely imaginary numbers are zero. For,

$$\bar{a}_{ij} = -a_{ji}$$

Putting $j = i$, we get

$$\bar{a}_{ii} = -a_{ii}$$

$$\Rightarrow \quad \bar{a}_{ii} + a_{ii} = 0$$

$\Rightarrow$ Real part of $a_{ii} = 0$.

**(iii)** If $A$ is Skew-Hermitian matrix, then $(kA)$ is also Skew-Hermitian matrix for any real scalar $k$. For,

$$(kA)^\theta = \bar{k}A^\theta = -kA.$$

**(iv)** If $A$ and $B$ are Skew-Hermitian matrices of same order, then $\lambda_1 A \pm \lambda_2 B$ are also Skew-Hermitian matrices of same order for any real numbers $\lambda_1$ and $\lambda_2$.

**(v)** If $A$ and $B$ are Hermitian matrices of same order, then $AB - BA$ is Skew-Hermitian. For,

$$\begin{aligned}(AB - BA)^\theta &= (AB)^\theta - (BA)^\theta = B^\theta A^\theta - A^\theta B^\theta\\ &= BA - AB = -(AB - BA).\end{aligned}$$

**(vi)** If $A$ is any square matrix, then $A - A^\theta$ is Skew-Hermitian. For,

$$\begin{aligned}(A - A^\theta)^\theta &= A^\theta - (A^\theta)^\theta\\ &= A^\theta - A = -(A - A^\theta).\end{aligned}$$

**(vii)** If $A$ is a Skew-Hermitian matrix, then $\bar{A}$ is also Skew-Hermitian matrix.

**(viii)** If $A$ is Hermitian matrix, then $iA$ is Skew-Hermitian matrix. For,

$$(iA)^\theta = \bar{i}A^\theta = -iA.$$

**(ix)** If $A$ is Skew-Hermitian matrix, then $iA$ is Hermitian matrix. For,

$$(iA)^\theta = \bar{i}A^\theta = (-i)(-A) = iA$$

**(ix)** Every square matrix can be uniquely represented as the sum of a Hermitian matrix and a Skew-Hermitian matrix. *i.e.*,

$$A = \underbrace{\frac{1}{2}(A + A^\theta)}_{\text{Hermitian matrix}} + \underbrace{\frac{1}{2}(A - A^\theta)}_{\text{Skew-Hermitian matrix}}$$

## Properties of Idempotent Matrix

**(i)** An idempotent matrix is necessarily be square matrix.

**(ii)** If $A$ and $B$ are idempotent matrices of same order, then $AB$ is idempotent iff $AB = BA$. For,

$$\begin{aligned}(AB)^2 &= (AB)(AB) = A(BA)B\\ &= A(AB)B = A^2B^2 = AB\end{aligned}$$

**(iii)** If $A$ and $B$ are idempotent matrices of same order, then $A + B$ is idempotent iff $AB = BA = O$. For,

$$\begin{aligned}(A + B)^2 &= A^2 + AB + BA + B^2\\ &= A^2 + B^2 = A + B\end{aligned}$$

**(iv)** If $A$ is an idempotent matrix and $A + B = I$, then $B$ is idempotent and $AB = BA = O$. For,

$$\begin{aligned}B = I - A \Rightarrow B^2 &= (I - A)^2\\ &= I - A - A + A^2 = I - A\end{aligned}$$

$\Rightarrow \quad B^2 = I - A \Rightarrow B^2 = B$

and $\quad AB = A(I - A) = A - A^2 = A - A = 0$

Similarly, $\quad BA = (I - A)A = A - A^2 = A - A = 0$

**(v)** Diag (1, 1, 1, ..., 1) is an idempotent matrix. For,

$$[\text{Diag }(1,1,1,\ldots,1)]^2 = \text{Diag }(1,1,1,\ldots,1)$$

**(vi)** If $\lambda_1, \lambda_2, \lambda_3$ are direction cosines, then the matrix

$$\begin{bmatrix} \lambda_1^2 & \lambda_1\lambda_2 & \lambda_1\lambda_3 \\ \lambda_1\lambda_2 & \lambda_2^2 & \lambda_2\lambda_3 \\ \lambda_1\lambda_3 & \lambda_2\lambda_3 & \lambda_3^2 \end{bmatrix}$$

is an idempotent matrix.

**(vii)** If $AB = A$ and $BA = B$, then $A$ and $B$ are idempotent matrices. For,

$AB = A \Leftrightarrow BAB = BA \Leftrightarrow BAB = B \Leftrightarrow AB = I \Leftrightarrow A^{-1} = B$

Thus,

$AB = A \Leftrightarrow AA^{-1} = A \Leftrightarrow A = I \Leftrightarrow A^2 = I \Leftrightarrow A^2 = A$

Similarly,

$BA = B \Leftrightarrow B = I \Leftrightarrow B^2 = I \Leftrightarrow B^2 = B$

## Properties of Involuntory Matrix

**(i)** Identity matrix is always involutory matrix.

**(ii)** $A$ is involutory matrix iff

$$(A - I)(A + I) = 0$$

For, $\quad A^2 = I \Leftrightarrow A^2 - I = 0$

$\Leftrightarrow \quad (A - I)(A + I) = 0$

***Example 7.*** *Show that* $\begin{bmatrix} 4 & 3 & 3 \\ -1 & 0 & -1 \\ -4 & -4 & -3 \end{bmatrix}$ *is involutory matrix*

**Solution.** From $A^2 = A \times A$,

$$= \begin{bmatrix} 4 & 3 & 3 \\ -1 & 0 & -1 \\ -4 & -4 & -3 \end{bmatrix}\begin{bmatrix} 4 & 3 & 3 \\ -1 & 0 & -1 \\ -4 & -4 & -3 \end{bmatrix}$$

$$= \begin{bmatrix} 16-3-12 & 12+0-12 & 12-3-9 \\ -4+0+4 & -3+0+4 & -3+0+3 \\ -16+4+12 & -12+0+12 & -12+4+9 \end{bmatrix}$$

$$= \begin{bmatrix} 1 & 0 & 0 \\ 0 & 1 & 0 \\ 0 & 0 & 1 \end{bmatrix} = I$$

Hence, $A$ is involutory matrix.

# Rank of Matrix

A number $r$ is said to be the rank of a matrix $A$, if it possesses the following two properties

**(i)** The determinant of atleast one minor of order $r$ is non-zero

**(ii)** The determinant of every minor of $A$ of order higher than $r$ is zero.

Rank of a matrix $A$ is denoted by $\rho(A)$.

## Properties of Rank

**(i)** The rank of every non-singular matrix of order $n$ is $n$.

**(ii)** The rank of a square matrix $A$ of order $n$ can be less than $n$ if and only if $A$ is singular *i.e.*, $|A| = 0$

**(iii)** The rank $r$ of an $m \times n$ matrix can atmost be equal to the smaller of the numbers $m$ and $n$, but it may be less.

**(iv)** The rank of zero matrix is taken as zero.

**(v)** If $I$ is a unit matrix of order $n$, then its rank is equal to $n$.

**(vi)** Elementary transformation do not alter the rank of a matrix.

**(vii)** If $A$ is a square matrix of order $m$, then $m$-rank $A$ is called the nullity of the matrix $A$ and is denoted by $N(A)$.

**(viii)** Rank of a matrix is same as the number of linearly independent row vectors in the matrix as well as the number of linearly independent column vectors in the matrix.

**(ix)** The rank of a matrix $A$ does not change by pre-multiplication or post-multiplication with any non-singular matrix.

**(x)** If $A$ and $B$ are matrices of same order, then

$$\rho(A + B) \le \rho(A) + \rho(B)$$

**(xi)** If $A$ and $B$ are matrices of same order, then

$$\rho(AB) \le \min\{\rho(A), \rho(B)\}$$

where, $A$ and $B$ are conformable for multiplication.

Thus, $\quad \rho(AB) \le \rho(A)$

and $\quad \rho(AB) \le \rho(B)$

**(xii)** If $A'$ is a transpose of matrix $A$, then

$$\rho(A') = \rho(A) \text{ and } \rho(AA') = \rho(A)$$

**(xiii)** If $A^\theta$ is the conjugate transpose of $A$, then

$$\rho(A^\theta) = \rho(A) \text{ and } \rho(AA^\theta) = \rho(A)$$

**(xiv)** If $A$ is a matrix of order $m \times n$, then

$$\rho(A) \le \min\{m, n\}$$

Thus, $\quad \rho(A) \le m$ and $\rho(A) \le n$

**(xv)** The rank of a skew-symmetric matrix cannot be one.

**(xvi)** If $A$ and $B$ are two $n$-rowed square matrices, then

$$\rho(AB) \ge \rho(A) + \rho(B) - n$$

***Example 8.*** *Find the rank of the matrix*

$$\begin{bmatrix} 1 & 2 & 3 \\ 2 & 3 & 4 \\ 3 & 5 & 7 \end{bmatrix}.$$

**Solution.** Highest order minor = 3rd order minor

$$= \begin{vmatrix} 1 & 2 & 3 \\ 2 & 3 & 4 \\ 3 & 5 & 7 \end{vmatrix}$$

$$= 1\begin{vmatrix} 3 & 4 \\ 5 & 7 \end{vmatrix} - 2\begin{vmatrix} 2 & 4 \\ 3 & 7 \end{vmatrix} + 3\begin{vmatrix} 2 & 3 \\ 3 & 5 \end{vmatrix}$$

$$= 1(21-20) - 2(14-12) + 3(10-9)$$
$$= 1 - 2\times 2 + 3\times 1 = 1 - 4 + 3 = 0$$

Its 3rd order minor is zero. So, we calculate the second order minors.

One second order minor is

$$\begin{vmatrix} 1 & 2 \\ 2 & 3 \end{vmatrix} = 3 - 4 = -1 \neq 0$$

$\therefore$ Rank of the given matrix is 2.

# Normal Form of a Matrix

## (Canonical Form of a Matrix)

By performing a series of elementary (row or column) transformations any non-zero matrix $A$ can be reduced to one of the following four forms, called the normal forms of $A$.

**(i)** $I_r$ **(ii)** $[I_r \ 0]$ **(iii)** $\begin{bmatrix} I_r \\ 0 \end{bmatrix}$ **(iv)** $\begin{bmatrix} I_r & 0 \\ 0 & 0 \end{bmatrix}$

The number $r$, so obtained is called the rank of the matrix $A$ i.e., $\rho(A) = r$.

### Procedure to Obtain Normal Form

**(i)** Interchange rows or column to obtain a non-zero element in first row and first column of the given matrix.

**(ii)** If this non-zero element is not 1, then make it 1.

**(iii)** Obtain zeros in the remainder of Ist row and Ist column.

**(iv)** Repeat the above three steps starting with element in IInd row and IInd column.

**(v)** Continue the procedure down the main diagonal either until the end of the diagonal is reached or all the elements which are zero.

***Example 9.*** *Find the rank of matrix by normal form, where*

$$A = \begin{bmatrix} -2 & -1 & -3 & -1 \\ 1 & 2 & 3 & -1 \\ 1 & 0 & 1 & 1 \\ 0 & 1 & 1 & -1 \end{bmatrix}$$

**Solution.** We have,

$$A = \begin{bmatrix} -2 & -1 & -3 & -1 \\ 1 & 2 & 3 & -1 \\ 1 & 0 & 1 & 1 \\ 0 & 1 & 1 & -1 \end{bmatrix} \quad R_1 \leftrightarrow R_2$$

$$A = \begin{bmatrix} 1 & 2 & 3 & -1 \\ -2 & -1 & -3 & -1 \\ 1 & 0 & 1 & 1 \\ 0 & 1 & 1 & -1 \end{bmatrix}$$

$$R_2 \to R_2 + 2R_1,\ R_3 \to R_3 - R_1$$

$$A = \begin{bmatrix} 1 & 2 & 3 & -1 \\ 0 & 3 & 3 & -3 \\ 0 & -2 & -2 & 2 \\ 0 & 1 & 1 & -1 \end{bmatrix}$$

$$C_2 \to C_2 - 2C_1,\ C_3 \to C_3 - 3C_1,\ C_4 \to C_4 + C_1$$

$$\Rightarrow \quad A = \begin{bmatrix} 1 & 0 & 0 & 0 \\ 0 & 3 & 3 & -3 \\ 0 & -2 & -2 & 2 \\ 0 & 1 & 1 & -1 \end{bmatrix} \quad R_4 \leftrightarrow R_2$$

$$\Rightarrow \quad A = \begin{bmatrix} 1 & 0 & 0 & 0 \\ 0 & 1 & 1 & -1 \\ 0 & -2 & -2 & 2 \\ 0 & 3 & 3 & -3 \end{bmatrix}$$

$$R_3 \to R_3 + 2R_2,\ R_4 \to R_4 - 3R_2$$

$$= \begin{bmatrix} 1 & 0 & 0 & 0 \\ 0 & 1 & 1 & -1 \\ 0 & 0 & 0 & 0 \\ 0 & 0 & 0 & 0 \end{bmatrix} \quad C_3 \to C_3 - C_2,\ C_4 \to C_4 + C_2$$

$$= \left[\begin{array}{cc|cc} 1 & 0 & 0 & 0 \\ 0 & 1 & 0 & 0 \\ \hline 0 & 0 & 0 & 0 \\ 0 & 0 & 0 & 0 \end{array}\right]$$

$\therefore$ Rank of $A = 2$

# Echelon Form or Triangular Form

A matrix is said to be in Echelon form, if

**(i)** All the non-zero rows, if any precede the zero rows.

**(ii)** The number of zeros preceding the Ist non-zero element in a row is less than that the number of such zeros in the next row.

**(iii)** The first non-zero element in every row is unity, *i.e.*, the elements of main diagonal must be unit if possible.

**(iv)** The number of zeros precede the first non-zero element in rows.

**(v)** The number of non-zero rows is then rank of given matrix.

# Rank of Matrix by Triangular Form

## (Echelon Form)

Rank = Number of non-zero row in upper triangular matrix.

> ***Note*** Non-zero row is that row which does not contain all the elements as zero.

***Example 10.*** *Find the rank of the matrix.*

$$\begin{bmatrix} 1 & 2 & 3 & 2 \\ 2 & 3 & 5 & 1 \\ 1 & 3 & 4 & 5 \end{bmatrix}$$

**Solution.** Let $A = \begin{bmatrix} 1 & 2 & 3 & 2 \\ 2 & 3 & 5 & 1 \\ 1 & 3 & 4 & 5 \end{bmatrix}$

$$\sim \begin{bmatrix} 1 & 2 & 3 & 2 \\ 0 & -1 & -1 & -3 \\ 0 & 1 & 1 & 3 \end{bmatrix} \begin{matrix} R_2 \to R_2 - 2R_1 \\ R_3 \to R_3 - R_1 \end{matrix}$$

$$\sim \begin{bmatrix} 1 & 2 & 3 & 2 \\ 0 & -1 & -1 & -3 \\ 0 & 0 & 0 & 0 \end{bmatrix} R_3 \to R_3 + R_2$$

$\therefore$ Rank = Number of non-zero rows = 2

> ***Note*** The rank of the product matrix $AB$ of two matrices $A$ and $B$ is less than the rank of the either of the matrices $A$ and $B$.

## System of Linear Equation

Suppose, we have the system of $m$ linear equations with $n$ variables $x_1, x_2, \ldots, x_n$.

$$\begin{aligned} a_{11}x_1 + a_{12}x_2 + \ldots + a_{1n}x_n &= b_1 \\ a_{12}x_1 + a_{12}x_2 + \ldots + a_{2n}x_n &= b_2 \\ \vdots \quad\quad \vdots \quad\quad\quad\quad \vdots \quad\; & \quad \vdots \\ a_{m1}x_1 + a_{m2}x_2 + \ldots + a_{mn}x_n &= b_n \end{aligned}$$

These equations can be written in matrix form as

$$\begin{bmatrix} a_{11} & a_{12} & \cdots & a_{1n} \\ a_{21} & a_{22} & \cdots & a_{2n} \\ \vdots & \vdots & \vdots & \vdots \\ a_{m1} & a_{m2} & \cdots & a_{mn} \end{bmatrix} \begin{bmatrix} x_1 \\ x_2 \\ \vdots \\ x_n \end{bmatrix} = \begin{bmatrix} b_1 \\ b_2 \\ \vdots \\ b_n \end{bmatrix} \Rightarrow AX = B,$$

where $A = \begin{bmatrix} a_{11} & a_{12} & \cdots & a_{1n} \\ a_{21} & a_{22} & \cdots & a_{2n} \\ \vdots & \vdots & \vdots & \vdots \\ a_{m1} & a_{m2} & \cdots & a_{mn} \end{bmatrix}$, $X = \begin{bmatrix} x_1 \\ x_2 \\ \vdots \\ x_n \end{bmatrix}$ and $B = \begin{bmatrix} b_1 \\ b_2 \\ \vdots \\ b_n \end{bmatrix}$

## Homogeneous and Non-homogeneous Linear Equations

A system of equation of the form $AX = B$, $B \neq 0$ is called a system of non-homogeneous linear equation.

If $B = 0$, the matrix equation $AX = B$ reduced to $AX = 0$, such a system of equation is called a system of homogeneous linear equations. A system of equations having one or more solution is called a consistent system of equations.

A system of equations having no solution is called an inconsistent system of equations.

## Criterion of Consistency

Let $AX = B$ be a system of $m$ linear equations in $n$ variables.

**(a)** If $|A| \neq 0$, then the system is consistent and has unique solution is given by

$$X = A^{-1}B$$

**(b)** If $|A| = 0$ and $\text{adj}(A) \cdot B = 0$, then system is consistent and has infinite number of solutions.

**(c)** If $|A| = 0$ and $(\text{adj}(A)) \cdot B \neq 0$, then system is inconsistent and has no solution.

## Working Rule to Find Solution of Linear Equations (Matrix Method)

**(i)** Write the given system of equations in matrix form $AX = B$.

**(ii)** Find $|A|$.

**(iii)** If $|A| \neq 0$, then compute $A^{-1}$ by using $A^{-1} = \frac{1}{|A|}(\text{adj}(A))$ and use the relation $X = A^{-1}B$ to find $X$.

**(iv)** If $|A| = 0$, then find $(\text{adj}(A)) \cdot B$.

**(v)** If $(\text{adj}(A)) \cdot B = 0$, then system has infinitely many solutions and if $(\text{adj}(A)) \cdot B \neq 0$, then the system has no solution.

**(vi)** If the system has infinitely many solutions, then choose a real number $k$ for one of the variable, this will reduce the number of variables by one. Now, take any two equations and solve by using matrix method.

## Solution of a System of Linear Equations by Reducing in Echelon Form

Suppose, we have a system of equations

$$\begin{aligned} a_{11}x_1 + a_{12}x_2 + \ldots + a_{1n}x_n &= b_1 \\ a_{21}x_1 + a_{22}x_2 + \ldots + a_{2n}x_n &= b_2 \\ \vdots \quad\quad \vdots \quad\quad\quad\quad \vdots \quad\; & \quad \vdots \\ a_{m1}x_1 + a_{m2}x_2 + \ldots + a_{mn}x_n &= b_n \end{aligned}$$

$$\Rightarrow \begin{bmatrix} a_{11} & a_{12} & \cdots & a_{1n} \\ a_{21} & a_{22} & \cdots & a_{2n} \\ \vdots & \vdots & \vdots & \vdots \\ a_{m1} & a_{m2} & \cdots & a_{mn} \end{bmatrix} \begin{bmatrix} x_1 \\ x_2 \\ \vdots \\ x_n \end{bmatrix} = \begin{bmatrix} b_1 \\ b_2 \\ \vdots \\ b_n \end{bmatrix} \Rightarrow AX = B,$$

where $A = \begin{bmatrix} a_{11} & a_{12} & \cdots & a_{1n} \\ a_{21} & a_{22} & \cdots & a_{2n} \\ \vdots & \vdots & \vdots & \vdots \\ a_{m1} & a_{m2} & \cdots & a_{mn} \end{bmatrix}$

is called the coefficient matrix.

$X = \begin{bmatrix} x_1 \\ x_2 \\ \vdots \\ x_n \end{bmatrix}$ is called the column matrix of the unknowns.

$$B = \begin{bmatrix} b_1 \\ b_2 \\ \vdots \\ b_n \end{bmatrix}$$ is called the column matrix of the constant.

and $$C = [A : B] = \begin{bmatrix} a_{11} & a_{12} & \cdots & a_{1n} & \vdots & b_1 \\ a_{21} & a_{22} & \cdots & a_{2n} & \vdots & b_2 \\ \vdots & & & \vdots & & \vdots \\ a_{m1} & a_{m2} & \cdots & a_{mn} & \vdots & b_n \end{bmatrix}$$

is called augmented matrix.

The rank of augmented matrix $C$ cannot be less than the rank of matrix $A$, because every sub-matrix of $A$ is also a sub-matrix of $B$.

## Criteria for a System of Non-homogeneous Linear Equation $AX = B$

**(i)** If Rank $C \neq$ Rank of $A$, then the system is inconsistent has no solutions.

**(ii)** If Rank of $C$ = Rank of $A$ = number of unknowns, then the system has unique solution.

**(iii)** If Rank of $C$ = Rank of $A <$ number of unknowns, then the system has infinite number of solutions.

## For a System of Homogeneous Linear Equation $AX = 0$

A system of homogeneous equations can either the trivial solution or an infinite number of solutions.

**(i)** If rank $A = n$, number of unknowns, then the system has only the trivial solution or unique solution (each unknown equal to zero).

**(ii)** If rank $A < n$, number of unknowns, then the system has an infinite number of non-trivial solution.

***Example 11.*** *Solve the following linear system of equations*

$$x + y + z = -3$$
$$3x + y - 2z = -2$$
$$2x + 4y + 7z = 7$$

**Solution.** The given equation can be written as

$$AX = B$$

i.e., $$\begin{bmatrix} 1 & 1 & 1 \\ 3 & 1 & -2 \\ 2 & 4 & 7 \end{bmatrix} \begin{bmatrix} x \\ y \\ z \end{bmatrix} = \begin{bmatrix} -3 \\ -2 \\ 7 \end{bmatrix}$$

The augmented matrix is $C = [A : B]$

$$C = \begin{bmatrix} 1 & 1 & 1 & : & -3 \\ 3 & 1 & -2 & : & -2 \\ 2 & 4 & 7 & : & 7 \end{bmatrix} \begin{matrix} R_2 \to R_2 - 3R_1 \\ R_3 \to R_3 - 2R_1 \end{matrix}$$

$$\sim \begin{bmatrix} 1 & 1 & 1 & : & -3 \\ 0 & -2 & -5 & : & 7 \\ 0 & 2 & 5 & : & 13 \end{bmatrix} R_3 \to R_3 + R_2$$

$$\sim \begin{bmatrix} 1 & 1 & 1 & : & -3 \\ 0 & -2 & -5 & : & 7 \\ 0 & 0 & 0 & : & 20 \end{bmatrix}$$

$\Rightarrow$ Rank $C = 3$, Rank $A = 2$, we observe that $\rho(C) \neq \rho(A)$

$\therefore$ The given system is inconsistent and has no solution.

***Example 12.*** *Investigate the values of $\lambda$ and $\mu$, so that the equations*

$$2x + 3y + 5z = 9$$
$$7x + 3y - 2z = 8$$
$$2x + 3y + \lambda z = \mu \text{ have}$$

*(i) No solution*
*(ii) A unique solution*
*(iii) An infinite number of solutions*

**Solution.** Here, we have

$$2x + 3y + 5z = 9$$
$$7x + 3y - 2z = 8$$
$$2x + 3y + \lambda z = \mu$$

The above equations in the matrix form can be written as

$$\begin{bmatrix} 2 & 3 & 5 \\ 7 & 3 & -2 \\ 2 & 3 & \lambda \end{bmatrix} \begin{bmatrix} x \\ y \\ z \end{bmatrix} = \begin{bmatrix} 9 \\ 8 \\ \mu \end{bmatrix}$$

$$AX = B$$

$$\therefore \quad C = (A : B) = \begin{bmatrix} 2 & 3 & 5 & : & 9 \\ 7 & 3 & -2 & : & 8 \\ 2 & 3 & \lambda & : & \mu \end{bmatrix}$$

$$= \begin{bmatrix} 2 & 3 & 5 & : & 9 \\ 0 & -15/2 & -39/2 & : & -47/2 \\ 0 & 0 & \lambda - 5 & : & \mu - 9 \end{bmatrix} \begin{matrix} R_2 \to R_2 - \frac{7}{2}R_1 \\ R_3 \to R_3 - R_1 \end{matrix}$$

(i) **No solution**

Rank $(A) \neq$ Rank $(C)$

$\lambda - 5 = 0$ or $\lambda = 5$ and $\mu - 9 \neq 0 \Rightarrow \mu \neq 9$

(ii) **Unique Solution**

Rank $A$ = Rank $C$ < Number of unknowns

$\lambda - 5 \neq 0 \Rightarrow \lambda \neq 5$ and $\mu$ may have any value.

(iii) **An Infinite Number of Solution**

Rank $A$ = Rank $C = 2$

$\therefore$ $\lambda - 5 = 0$ and $\mu - 9 = 0$

$\Rightarrow$ $\lambda = 5$ and $\mu = 9$

## Cramer's Rule

Let us consider the equations

$$a_1x + b_1y + c_1z = d_1$$
$$a_2x + b_2y + c_2z = d_2$$
$$a_3x + b_3y + c_3z = d_3,$$

then $$D = \begin{vmatrix} a_1 & b_1 & c_1 \\ a_2 & b_2 & c_2 \\ a_3 & b_3 & c_3 \end{vmatrix}, \quad D_1 = \begin{vmatrix} d_1 & b_1 & c_1 \\ d_2 & b_2 & c_2 \\ d_3 & b_3 & c_3 \end{vmatrix}$$

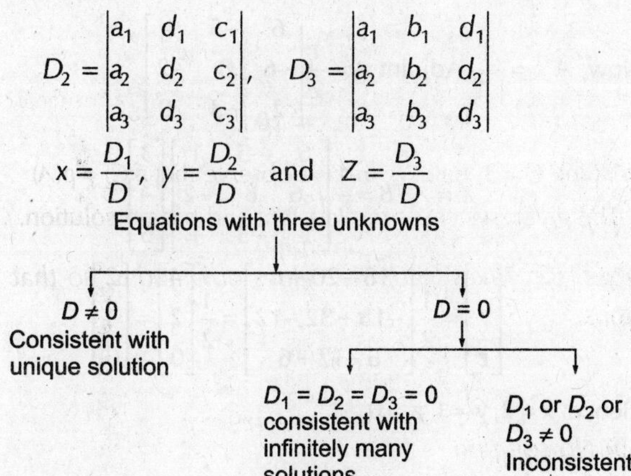


## Vectors

An $n$-tuple is a set of $n$ similiar things. If the place of every members of a set is fixed, then it is called an ordered set. Any ordered $n$-tuple of numbers is called a $n$-vector. Thus, the coordinates of a point in space is called 3-vector $(x, y, z)$.

The members of a set are called the components of a vector. So, $x, y, z$ in a 3-vector are called components.

$x_1, x_2, \ldots, x_n$ are the components of a $n$-vector

$$X = (x_1, x_2, \ldots, x_n)$$

Each column of a matrix is a vector and each row of a matrix is also a vector.

## Linear Independence and Dependence of Vectors

Vectors (matrices) $X_1, X_2, X_3, \ldots, X_n$ are said to be dependent, if

**(i)** All the vectors (row or column matrices) are of same order.

**(ii)** $n$ scalars $\lambda_1, \lambda_2, \lambda_3, \ldots, \lambda_n$ not all zero exist such that $\lambda_1 X_1 + \lambda_2 X_2 + \lambda_3 X_3 + \ldots + \lambda_n X_n = 0$ otherwise, they are linearly independent.

> ***Note*** If in a set of vectors any vector of the set is the linear combination of the remaining vectors, then the vectors are called dependent vectors.

***Example 13.*** *Examine for linear dependence* [1, 0, 2, 1], [3, 1, 2, 1], [4, 6, 2, – 4], [–6, 0, – 3, – 4] *and find the relation between them, if possible.*

**Solution.** Consider the matrix equation

$$\lambda_1 x_1 + \lambda_2 x_2 + \lambda_3 x_3 + \lambda_4 x_4 = 0 \qquad \ldots(i)$$

$$\lambda_1(1,0,2,1) + \lambda_2(3,1,2,1) + \lambda_3(4,6,2,-4) + \lambda_4(-6,0,-3,-4) = 0$$

$$\begin{aligned} \lambda_1 + 3\lambda_2 + 4\lambda_3 - 6\lambda_4 &= 0 \\ 0\lambda_1 + \lambda_2 + 6\lambda_3 + 0\lambda_4 &= 0 \\ 2\lambda_1 + 2\lambda_2 + 2\lambda_3 - 3\lambda_4 &= 0 \\ \lambda_1 + \lambda_2 - 4\lambda_3 - 4\lambda_4 &= 0 \end{aligned}$$

$$\begin{bmatrix} 1 & 3 & 4 & -6 \\ 0 & 1 & 6 & 0 \\ 2 & 2 & 2 & -3 \\ 1 & 1 & -4 & -4 \end{bmatrix} \begin{bmatrix} \lambda_1 \\ \lambda_2 \\ \lambda_3 \\ \lambda_4 \end{bmatrix} = \begin{bmatrix} 0 \\ 0 \\ 0 \\ 0 \end{bmatrix} \quad \begin{matrix} R_3 \to R_3 - 2R_1 \\ R_4 \to R_4 - R_1 \end{matrix}$$

$$\begin{bmatrix} 1 & 3 & 4 & -6 \\ 0 & 1 & 6 & 0 \\ 0 & -4 & -6 & 9 \\ 0 & -2 & -8 & 2 \end{bmatrix} \begin{bmatrix} \lambda_1 \\ \lambda_2 \\ \lambda_3 \\ \lambda_4 \end{bmatrix} = \begin{bmatrix} 0 \\ 0 \\ 0 \\ 0 \end{bmatrix} \quad \begin{matrix} R_3 \to R_3 + 4R_2 \\ R_4 \to R_4 + 2R_2 \end{matrix}$$

$$\begin{bmatrix} 1 & 3 & 4 & -6 \\ 0 & 1 & 6 & 0 \\ 0 & 0 & 18 & 9 \\ 0 & 0 & 4 & 2 \end{bmatrix} \begin{bmatrix} \lambda_1 \\ \lambda_2 \\ \lambda_3 \\ \lambda_4 \end{bmatrix} = \begin{bmatrix} 0 \\ 0 \\ 0 \\ 0 \end{bmatrix} \quad R_4 \to R_4 - \frac{2}{9}R_3$$

$$\begin{bmatrix} 1 & 3 & 4 & -6 \\ 0 & 1 & 6 & 0 \\ 0 & 0 & 18 & 9 \\ 0 & 0 & 0 & 0 \end{bmatrix} \begin{bmatrix} \lambda_1 \\ \lambda_2 \\ \lambda_3 \\ \lambda_4 \end{bmatrix} = \begin{bmatrix} 0 \\ 0 \\ 0 \\ 0 \end{bmatrix}$$

$$\begin{aligned} \lambda_1 + 3\lambda_2 + 4\lambda_3 - 6\lambda_4 &= 0 \\ \lambda_2 + 6\lambda_3 &= 0 \\ 18\lambda_3 + 9\lambda_4 &= 0 \end{aligned}$$

Let $\lambda_4 = t$, $\quad 18\lambda_3 + 9t = 0 \Rightarrow \lambda_3 = t/2$

$$\lambda_2 - 3t = 0 \Rightarrow \lambda_2 = 3t$$

$$\lambda_1 + 9t - 2t - 6t = 0 \Rightarrow \lambda_1 = -t$$

Put the values of $\lambda_1, \lambda_2, \lambda_3$ and $\lambda_4$ in Eq. (i), we get

$$-tX_1 + 3tX_2 - \frac{t}{2}X_3 + tX_4 = 0$$

$$\Rightarrow \quad 2X_1 - 6X_2 + X_3 - 2X_4 = 0$$

## Linearly Dependence and Independence of Vectors by Rank Method

**(i)** If the rank of the matrix of the given vectors is less than the number of vectors, then the vectors are linearly dependent.

**(ii)** If the rank of the matrix of the given vectors is equal to the number of vectors, then the vectors are linearly independent.

***Example 14.*** *By using matrix prove that the set of vectors*

$$X = [1, 2, -3, 4], Y = [3, -1, 2, 1], Z = [1, -5, 8, -7]$$

*is linearly dependent.*

**Solution.** We have,

$X = [1, 2, -3, 4], Y = [3, -1, 2, 1], Z = [1, -5, 8, -7]$

By using above vectors, let us form a matrix.

$$\begin{bmatrix} 1 & 2 & -3 & 4 \\ 3 & -1 & 2 & 1 \\ 1 & -5 & 8 & -7 \end{bmatrix} \quad \begin{matrix} R_2 \to R_2 - 3R_1 \\ R_3 \to R_3 - R_1 \end{matrix}$$

$$\sim\begin{bmatrix}1 & 2 & -3 & 4\\0 & -7 & 11 & -11\\0 & -7 & 11 & -11\end{bmatrix} R_3 \to R_3 - R_2$$

$$\sim\begin{bmatrix}1 & 2 & -3 & 4\\0 & -7 & 11 & -11\\0 & 0 & 0 & 0\end{bmatrix}$$

Hence, the rank of matrix $= 2 <$ Number of vectors

$\therefore$ Vectors are linearly dependent.

## Another Method (Adjoint Method) to Solve Linear Equations

Let the equations be

$$a_1x + a_2y + a_3z = d_1$$
$$b_1x + b_2y + b_3z = d_2$$
$$c_1x + c_2y + c_3z = d_3$$

Write the above equations in the matrix form,

$$\begin{bmatrix}a_1 & a_2 & a_3\\b_1 & b_2 & b_3\\c_1 & c_2 & c_3\end{bmatrix}\begin{bmatrix}x\\y\\z\end{bmatrix} = \begin{bmatrix}d_1\\d_2\\d_3\end{bmatrix}$$

$$\Rightarrow \qquad AX = B \qquad \text{...(i)}$$

where, $A = \begin{bmatrix}a_1 & a_2 & a_3\\b_1 & b_2 & b_3\\c_1 & c_2 & c_3\end{bmatrix}$, $X = \begin{bmatrix}x\\y\\z\end{bmatrix}$ and $B = \begin{bmatrix}d_1\\d_2\\d_3\end{bmatrix}$

Multiplying Eq. (i) by $A^{-1}$

$$A^{-1}(AX) = A^{-1}B \Rightarrow IX = A^{-1}B \Rightarrow X = A^{-1}B$$

***Example 15.*** *Solve the following simultaneous equations by using matrices*

$$x + y + z = 3, \quad x + 2y + 3z = 4, \quad x + 4y + 9z = 6$$

**Solution.** We have,

$$x + y + z = 3, \quad x + 2y + 3z = 4, \quad x + 4y + 9z = 6$$

The above equations in the matrix form can be written as

$$\begin{bmatrix}1 & 1 & 1\\1 & 2 & 3\\1 & 4 & 9\end{bmatrix}\begin{bmatrix}x\\y\\z\end{bmatrix} = \begin{bmatrix}3\\4\\6\end{bmatrix} \Rightarrow AX = B$$

where, $A = \begin{bmatrix}1 & 1 & 1\\1 & 2 & 3\\1 & 4 & 9\end{bmatrix}$, $X = \begin{bmatrix}x\\y\\z\end{bmatrix}$ and $B = \begin{bmatrix}3\\4\\6\end{bmatrix}$

$$\text{Now, } |A| = \begin{vmatrix}1 & 1 & 1\\1 & 2 & 3\\1 & 4 & 9\end{vmatrix} \begin{aligned}&= 1\times 6 + 1\times(-6) + 1\times 2\\&= 6 - 6 + 2 = 2\end{aligned}$$

$$\text{Matrix of co-factors} = \begin{bmatrix}6 & -6 & 2\\-5 & 8 & -3\\1 & -2 & 1\end{bmatrix},$$

$$\text{Adjoint } A = \frac{1}{2}\begin{bmatrix}6 & -5 & 1\\-6 & 8 & -2\\2 & -3 & 1\end{bmatrix}$$

$$\text{Now, } A^{-1} = \frac{1}{|A|}\text{ Adjoint } A = \frac{1}{2}\begin{bmatrix}6 & -5 & 1\\-6 & 8 & -2\\2 & -3 & 1\end{bmatrix}$$

$$X = A^{-1}B = \frac{1}{2}\begin{bmatrix}6 & -5 & 1\\-6 & 8 & -2\\2 & -3 & 1\end{bmatrix}\begin{bmatrix}3\\4\\6\end{bmatrix}$$

$$\Rightarrow \begin{bmatrix}x\\y\\z\end{bmatrix} = \frac{1}{2}\begin{bmatrix}18 - 20 + 6\\-18 + 32 - 12\\6 - 12 + 6\end{bmatrix} = \frac{1}{2}\begin{bmatrix}4\\2\\0\end{bmatrix} = \begin{bmatrix}2\\1\\0\end{bmatrix}$$

Hence, $x = 2, y = 1, z = 0$

## Eigen Values

Let us consider the system of equations in matrix form, we have

$$\begin{bmatrix}a_{11} & a_{12} & a_{13} & \cdots & a_{1n}\\a_{21} & a_{22} & a_{23} & \cdots & a_{2n}\\a_{31} & a_{32} & a_{33} & \cdots & a_{3n}\\a_{41} & a_{42} & a_{43} & \cdots & a_{4n}\\\vdots & \vdots & \vdots & & \vdots\\a_{n1} & a_{n2} & a_{n3} & \cdots & a_{nn}\end{bmatrix}\begin{bmatrix}x_1\\x_2\\x_3\\\vdots\\x_n\end{bmatrix} = \begin{bmatrix}y_1\\y_2\\y_3\\\vdots\\y_n\end{bmatrix}$$

$$\Rightarrow \qquad AX = Y \qquad \text{...(i)}$$

where $A$ is matrix, $X$ and $Y$ are column vectors. Here, we transformed column vector $X$ into the column vector $Y$ by means of the square matrix $A$. Suppose, $X$ be such vector which transforms into $\lambda X$ by means of the transformation (i). Let the linear transformation $Y = AX$ transforms $X$ into $\lambda X$, a scalar multiple of itself.

Now, we have

$$AX = Y = \lambda X$$

$$\Rightarrow \quad AX = \lambda X \Rightarrow AX - \lambda IX = 0$$

$$\Rightarrow \quad (A - \lambda I)X = 0 \qquad \text{...(ii)}$$

The scalar $\lambda$ is known as eigen value of the matrix $A$ and the corresponding non-zero vector $X$ is known as eigen vector.

## Characteristic Polynomial

The determinant $|A - \lambda I|$ when expanded will give a polynomial in $\lambda$ which is called characteristic polynomial of matrix $A$.

## Characteristic Equation

The equation $|A - \lambda I| = 0$ is called the characteristic equation of the matrix $A$.

e.g.,

$$\text{Let} \qquad A = \begin{bmatrix}1 & 2 & 2\\2 & 1 & -2\\2 & -2 & 1\end{bmatrix}$$

$$\text{then} \qquad |A - \lambda I| = \begin{vmatrix}1-\lambda & 2 & 2\\2 & 1-\lambda & -2\\2 & -2 & 1\end{vmatrix} = \lambda^3 - 3\lambda^2 - 9\lambda + 27$$

This is called characteristic polynomial.

Put $|A - \lambda I| = 0$

$\Rightarrow \lambda^3 - 3\lambda^2 - 9\lambda + 27 = 0$, this is called characteristic equation.

## Characteristic Roots or Latent Roots or Eigen Values

The roots of the characteristic equation $|A - \lambda I| = 0$ are called eigen values of the matrix $A$.

*e.g.*, The characteristic equation is

$$\lambda^3 - 3\lambda^2 - 9\lambda + 27 = 0$$

$$\Rightarrow \quad (\lambda - 3)^2(\lambda + 3) = 0$$

$$\Rightarrow \quad \lambda = 3, 3, -3$$

$\therefore$ The eigen values of the matrix $A$ are 3, 3, −3.

### Properties of Eigen Values

**(i)** The sum of the eigen values of a matrix is equal to the trace of the matrix. [The sum of elements on the principal diagonal of matrix is called trace of matrix].

**(ii)** Any square matrix $A$ and its transpose matrix $A'$ have the same eigen values.

**(iii)** The product of the eigen values of a matrix $A$ is equal to the determinant of $A$.

**(iv)** If $\lambda_1, \lambda_2, \lambda_3, \ldots, \lambda_n$ are the eigen values of $A$, then the eigen values of

(a) $A^m$ are $\lambda_1^m, \lambda_2^m, \lambda_3^m, \ldots, \lambda_n^m$

(b) $KA$ are $K\lambda_1, K\lambda_2, K\lambda_3, \ldots, K\lambda_n$

(c) $A^{-1}$ are $\dfrac{1}{\lambda_1}, \dfrac{1}{\lambda_2}, \dfrac{1}{\lambda_3}, \ldots, \dfrac{1}{\lambda_n}$

> ***Note*** **(a)** If $A$ and $P$ be square matrices of the same type and if $P$ be invertible, then the matrices $A$ and $P^{-1}AP$ have the same eigen values.
>
> **(b)** If $A$ and $B$ be the square matrices of order $n$ and if $A$ be invertible, then the matrices $A^{-1}B$ and $BA^{-1}$ have the same eigen values.
>
> **(c)** If $A$ and $B$ be the two square invertible matrices, then $AB$ and $BA$ have same eigen values.
>
> **(d)** Zero is the eigen value of a matrix, iff the matrix is singular.
>
> Eigen values of a triangular matrix are just the diagonal elements of the matrix.
>
> **(e)** If $\lambda$ is an eigen value of an orthogonal matrix, then $\frac{1}{\lambda}$ is also eigen value.
>
> [Two vectors $X$ and $Y$ are said to be orthogonal, if $X_1^T X_2 = X_2^T X_1 = 0$]
>
> **(f)** The eigen values of a Hermitian matrix are all real.
>
> **(g)** The eigen values of real symmetric matrix are all real, in this case real symmetric matrix will be Hermitian.
>
> **(h)** Eigen values of a Skew-Hermitian matrix is either zero or a pure imaginary number.
>
> **(i)** Eigen values of an idempotent matrix are either zero or unity.

### Spectrum of Eigen Values of Various Matrices

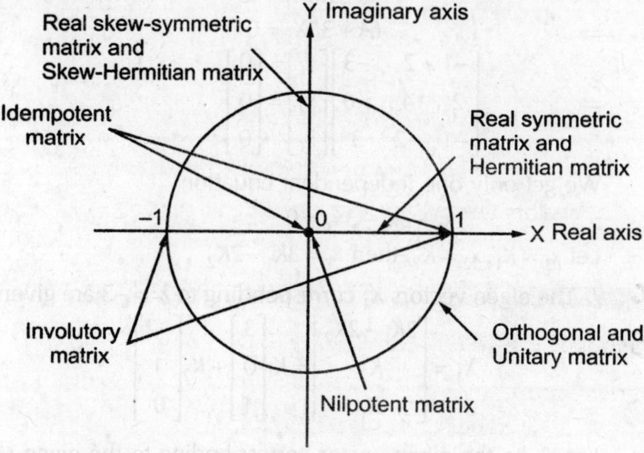


## Eigen Vectors or Latent Vectors or Characteristic Vectors

If $\lambda$ is a eigen value of an $n \times n$ matrix $A$, then a non-zero vector $X$ s.t. $AX = \lambda X$ is called a characteristic vector or eigen vector of the matrix $A$ corresponding to the eigen value $\lambda$.

### Properties of Eigen Vectors

**(i)** The eigen vector $X$ of a matrix $A$ is not unique.

**(ii)** If two or more eigen values are equal it may or may not be possible to get linearly independent eigen vectors corresponding to the equal roots.

**(iii)** If $\lambda_1, \lambda_2, \lambda_3, \ldots, \lambda_n$ be distinct eigen values of an $n \times n$ matrix, then corresponding eigen vectors $X_1, X_2, \ldots, X_n$ form a linearly independent set.

**(iv)** Eigen vectors of a symmetric matrix corresponding to different eigen values are orthogonal.

**(v)** Two eigen vectors $X_1$ and $X_2$ are called orthogonal vectors, if $X_1' X_2 = 0$.

***Example 16.*** *Find the eigen values and eigen vectors of the matrix* $A = \begin{bmatrix} -2 & 2 & -3 \\ 2 & 1 & -6 \\ -1 & -2 & 0 \end{bmatrix}$

**Solution.** The characteristic equation of the given matrix is

$$|A - \lambda I| = 0$$

$$\Rightarrow \quad \begin{vmatrix} -2-\lambda & 2 & -3 \\ 2 & 1-\lambda & -6 \\ -1 & -2 & 0-\lambda \end{vmatrix} = 0$$

$$(-2-\lambda)[-\lambda(1-\lambda) - 12] - 2[-2\lambda - 6] - 3[-4 + 1(1-\lambda)] = 0$$

$$\Rightarrow \quad \lambda^3 + \lambda^2 - 21\lambda - 45 = 0$$

$$\Rightarrow \quad (\lambda + 3)(\lambda^2 - 2\lambda - 15) = 0$$

$$\Rightarrow \quad (\lambda + 3)(\lambda + 3)(\lambda - 5) = 0 \Rightarrow \lambda = -3, -3, 5$$

$\therefore$ The eigen values of the matrix $A$ are −3, −3, 5.

Let $X_1$ be the eigen vectors corresponding to the eigen value $\lambda = -3$ is given by

$$(A-\lambda I)X_1 = 0$$

$$\Rightarrow \quad (A+3I)X_1 = 0$$

$$\Rightarrow \begin{bmatrix} -1 & 2 & -3 \\ 2 & 4 & -6 \\ -1 & -2 & 3 \end{bmatrix}\begin{bmatrix} x_1 \\ x_2 \\ x_3 \end{bmatrix} = \begin{bmatrix} 0 \\ 0 \\ 0 \end{bmatrix}$$

We get only one independent equation

$$x_1 + 2x_2 - 3x_3 = 0$$

Let $x_3 = K_1, x_2 = K_2$, then $x_1 = 3K_1 - 2K_2$

$\therefore$ The eigen vectors $X_1$ corresponding to $\lambda = -3$ are given by

$$X_1 = \begin{bmatrix} 3K_1 - 2K_2 \\ K_2 \\ K_1 \end{bmatrix} = K_1\begin{bmatrix} 3 \\ 0 \\ 1 \end{bmatrix} + K_2\begin{bmatrix} -2 \\ 1 \\ 0 \end{bmatrix}$$

Let $X_2$ be the eigen vector corresponding to the eigen value $\lambda = 5$, then

$$(A-\lambda I)X_2 = 0 \quad \Rightarrow \quad (A-5I)X_2 = 0$$

$$\Rightarrow \begin{bmatrix} -2-5 & 2 & -3 \\ 2 & 1-5 & -6 \\ -1 & -2 & -5 \end{bmatrix}\begin{bmatrix} x_1 \\ x_2 \\ x_3 \end{bmatrix} = \begin{bmatrix} 0 \\ 0 \\ 0 \end{bmatrix}$$

$$\begin{bmatrix} -7 & 2 & -3 \\ 2 & -4 & -6 \\ -1 & -2 & -5 \end{bmatrix}\begin{bmatrix} x_1 \\ x_2 \\ x_3 \end{bmatrix} = \begin{bmatrix} 0 \\ 0 \\ 0 \end{bmatrix}$$

$$\Rightarrow \quad -7x_1 + 2x_2 - 3x_3 = 0$$

$$x_1 - 2x_2 - 3x_3 = 0$$

$$-x_1 - 2x_2 - 5x_3 = 0$$

Now, from first two equations

$$\frac{x_1}{10-6} = \frac{x_2}{3+5} = \frac{x_3}{-2-2}$$

$$\Rightarrow \quad \frac{x_1}{4} = \frac{x_2}{8} = \frac{x_3}{-4}$$

$$\Rightarrow \quad \frac{x_1}{1} = \frac{x_2}{2} = \frac{x_3}{-2} = k_3 \text{ (say)}$$

$$\therefore \quad x_1 = k_3, \quad x_2 = 2k_3, \quad x_3 = -k_3$$

$\therefore$ The eigen vectors $X_2$ corresponding to $\lambda = 5$ are given by

$$X_2 = \begin{bmatrix} k_3 \\ 2k_3 \\ -k_3 \end{bmatrix} \Rightarrow X_2 = k_3\begin{bmatrix} 1 \\ 2 \\ -1 \end{bmatrix}$$

***Example 17.*** *Find the eigen values and eigen vectors of the matrix.*

$$A = \begin{bmatrix} 3 & 1 & 4 \\ 0 & 2 & 6 \\ 0 & 0 & 5 \end{bmatrix}$$

**Solution.** We have,

$$|A-\lambda I| = \begin{vmatrix} 3-\lambda & 1 & 4 \\ 0 & 2-\lambda & 6 \\ 0 & 0 & 5-\lambda \end{vmatrix} = (3-\lambda)(2-\lambda)(5-\lambda)$$

The characteristic equation $|A-\lambda I| = 0$

$$\Rightarrow \quad (3-\lambda)(2-\lambda)(5-\lambda) = 0 \Rightarrow \lambda = 2, 3, 5$$

$\therefore$ The eigen values of the matrix $A$ are 2, 3, 5.

Let $X_1$ be the eigen vector corresponding to the eigen value $\lambda = 2$ s.t.

$$(A-\lambda I)X_1 = 0$$

$$\Rightarrow \begin{bmatrix} 3-\lambda & 1 & 4 \\ 0 & 2-\lambda & 6 \\ 0 & 0 & 5-\lambda \end{bmatrix}\begin{bmatrix} x_1 \\ x_2 \\ x_3 \end{bmatrix} = \begin{bmatrix} 0 \\ 0 \\ 0 \end{bmatrix}$$

$$\Rightarrow \begin{bmatrix} 1 & 1 & 4 \\ 0 & 0 & 6 \\ 0 & 0 & 3 \end{bmatrix}\begin{bmatrix} x_1 \\ x_2 \\ x_3 \end{bmatrix} = \begin{bmatrix} 0 \\ 0 \\ 0 \end{bmatrix}$$

$$\Rightarrow \quad x_1 + x_2 + 4x_3 = 0$$

and

$$0x_1 + 0x_2 + 6x_3 = 0$$

$$0x_1 + 0x_2 + 3x_3 = 0$$

From first two equations, we have

$$\frac{x_1}{6-0} = \frac{x_2}{0-6} = \frac{x_3}{0-0} = k$$

$$\Rightarrow \quad \frac{x_1}{1} = \frac{x_2}{-1} = \frac{x_3}{0} = k$$

$$\Rightarrow \quad x_1 = k, \ x_2 = -k, \ x_3 = 0$$

Therefore,

$$X_1 = \begin{bmatrix} k \\ -k \\ 0 \end{bmatrix} \Rightarrow X_1 = k\begin{bmatrix} 1 \\ -1 \\ 0 \end{bmatrix}$$

Let $X_2$ be the eigen vector corresponding to the eigen value $\lambda = 3$, then

$$(A-\lambda I)X_2 = 0$$

$$\Rightarrow \begin{bmatrix} 3-3 & 1 & 4 \\ 0 & 2-3 & 6 \\ 0 & 0 & 5-3 \end{bmatrix}\begin{bmatrix} x_1 \\ x_2 \\ x_3 \end{bmatrix} = \begin{bmatrix} 0 \\ 0 \\ 0 \end{bmatrix}$$

$$\Rightarrow \begin{bmatrix} 0 & 1 & 4 \\ 0 & -1 & 6 \\ 0 & 0 & 2 \end{bmatrix}\begin{bmatrix} x_1 \\ x_2 \\ x_3 \end{bmatrix} = \begin{bmatrix} 0 \\ 0 \\ 0 \end{bmatrix}$$

$$\Rightarrow \quad 0x_1 + x_2 + 4x_3 = 0$$

$$0x_1 - x_2 + 6x_3 = 0$$

$$0x_1 + 0x_2 + 2x_3 = 0$$

From first two equations, we have

$$\frac{x_1}{6+4} = \frac{x_2}{0-0} = \frac{x_3}{0-0}$$

$$\Rightarrow \quad \frac{x_1}{10} = \frac{x_2}{0} = \frac{x_3}{0} = k \text{ (say)}$$

$$\Rightarrow \quad x_1 = 10k, \ x_2 = 0, \ x_3 = 0$$

$$\Rightarrow \quad X_2 = \begin{bmatrix} 10k \\ 0 \\ 0 \end{bmatrix} \Rightarrow X_2 = k\begin{bmatrix} 10 \\ 0 \\ 0 \end{bmatrix}$$

When $\lambda = 5$,

Let $X_3$ be the eigen vector corresponding to the eigen value $\lambda = 5$, then

$$(A-\lambda I)X_3 = 0$$

$$\Rightarrow \begin{bmatrix} 3-5 & 1 & 4 \\ 0 & 2-5 & 6 \\ 0 & 0 & 5-5 \end{bmatrix}\begin{bmatrix} x_1 \\ x_2 \\ x_3 \end{bmatrix} = \begin{bmatrix} 0 \\ 0 \\ 0 \end{bmatrix}$$

$$\Rightarrow \begin{bmatrix} -2 & 1 & 4 \\ 0 & -3 & 6 \\ 0 & 0 & 0 \end{bmatrix}\begin{bmatrix} x_1 \\ x_2 \\ x_3 \end{bmatrix} = \begin{bmatrix} 0 \\ 0 \\ 0 \end{bmatrix}$$

$$\Rightarrow \quad -2x_1 + x_2 + 4x_3 = 0$$
$$-3x_2 + 6x_3 = 0$$

On solving these equations by cross multiplication, we have

$$\frac{x_1}{6+12} = \frac{x_2}{0+12} = \frac{x_3}{6-0}$$

$$\Rightarrow \quad \frac{x_1}{18} = \frac{x_2}{12} = \frac{x_3}{6} \Rightarrow \frac{x_1}{3} = \frac{x_2}{2} = \frac{x_3}{1} = k \text{ (say)}$$

$$\Rightarrow \quad x_1 = 3k, \quad x_2 = 2k, \; x_3 = k$$

$$\therefore \quad X_3 = \begin{bmatrix} 3k \\ 2k \\ k \end{bmatrix} \Rightarrow X_3 = k\begin{bmatrix} 3 \\ 2 \\ 1 \end{bmatrix}$$

**Example 18.** *Find all the eigen values and eigen vectors of the matrix* $\begin{bmatrix} 2 & -1 & 1 \\ -1 & 2 & -1 \\ 1 & -1 & 2 \end{bmatrix}$.

**Solution.** The characteristic equation $|A - \lambda I| = 0$ is

$$\begin{vmatrix} 2-\lambda & -1 & 1 \\ -1 & 2-\lambda & -1 \\ 1 & -1 & 2-\lambda \end{vmatrix} = 0$$

$$\Rightarrow \quad (2-\lambda)[(2-\lambda)^2 - 1] + 1[-2+\lambda+1] + 1[1-2+\lambda] = 0$$

$$\Rightarrow \quad (2-\lambda)[4 - 4\lambda + \lambda^2 - 1] + (\lambda - 1) + \lambda - 1 = 0$$

$$\Rightarrow \quad 8 - 8\lambda + 2\lambda^2 - 2 - 4\lambda + 4\lambda^2 - \lambda^3 + \lambda + 2\lambda - 2 = 0$$

$$\Rightarrow \quad -\lambda^3 + 6\lambda^2 - 9\lambda + 4 = 0$$

$$\Rightarrow \quad \lambda^3 - 6\lambda^2 + 9\lambda - 4 = 0 \qquad \text{...(i)}$$

$$\Rightarrow \quad (\lambda - 1)(\lambda^2 - 5\lambda + 4) = 0$$

$$\Rightarrow \quad (\lambda - 1)(\lambda - 1)(\lambda - 4) = 0$$

$$\Rightarrow \quad \lambda = 1, 1, 4$$

$\therefore$ Eigen values are $\lambda = 1, 1, 4$

Let $X_1$ be eigen vector corresponding to the eigen value $\lambda = 1$

$$\therefore \quad [A - \lambda I]X_1 = 0$$

$$\Rightarrow \begin{bmatrix} 2-4 & -1 & 1 \\ -1 & 2-4 & -1 \\ 1 & -1 & 2-4 \end{bmatrix}\begin{bmatrix} x_1 \\ x_2 \\ x_3 \end{bmatrix} = \begin{bmatrix} 0 \\ 0 \\ 0 \end{bmatrix}$$

$$\Rightarrow \begin{bmatrix} -2 & -1 & 1 \\ -1 & -2 & -1 \\ 1 & -1 & -2 \end{bmatrix}\begin{bmatrix} x_1 \\ x_2 \\ x_3 \end{bmatrix} = \begin{bmatrix} 0 \\ 0 \\ 0 \end{bmatrix}$$

$$-2x_1 - x_2 + x_3 = 0 \qquad \text{...(i)}$$
$$-x_1 - 2x_2 - x_3 = 0 \qquad \text{...(ii)}$$
$$+x_1 - x_2 - 2x_3 = 0 \qquad \text{...(iii)}$$

From Eqs. (i) and (iii) equations

$$-2x_1 - x_2 + x_3 = 0$$
$$x_1 - x_2 - 2x_3 = 0, \text{ we have}$$

$$\frac{x_1}{2+1} = \frac{x_2}{1-4} = \frac{x_3}{2+1}$$

$$\Rightarrow \quad \frac{x_1}{3} = \frac{x_2}{-3} = \frac{x_3}{3}$$

$$\Rightarrow \quad \frac{x_1}{1} = \frac{x_2}{-1} = \frac{x_3}{1} = k \text{(say)}$$

$$\Rightarrow \quad x_1 = k, \; x_2 = -k, \; x_3 = k$$

$$\therefore \quad X_1 = \begin{bmatrix} k \\ -k \\ k \end{bmatrix} \Rightarrow X_1 = k\begin{bmatrix} 1 \\ -1 \\ 1 \end{bmatrix}$$

or $X_1 = \begin{bmatrix} 1 \\ -1 \\ 1 \end{bmatrix}$ [put $k = 1$]

When $\lambda = 1$, let $X_2$ be the eigen vector corresponding to the eigen value $\lambda = 1$ s.t. $(A - \lambda I)X_2 = 0$

$$\begin{bmatrix} 2-1 & -1 & 1 \\ -1 & 2-1 & -1 \\ 1 & -1 & 2-1 \end{bmatrix}\begin{bmatrix} x_1 \\ x_2 \\ x_3 \end{bmatrix} = \begin{bmatrix} 0 \\ 0 \\ 0 \end{bmatrix}$$

$$\Rightarrow \begin{bmatrix} 1 & -1 & 1 \\ -1 & 1 & -1 \\ 1 & -1 & 1 \end{bmatrix}\begin{bmatrix} x_1 \\ x_2 \\ x_3 \end{bmatrix} = \begin{bmatrix} 0 \\ 0 \\ 0 \end{bmatrix}$$

$$R_2 \to R_2 + R_1$$
$$R_3 \to R_3 - R_1$$

$$\Rightarrow \begin{bmatrix} 1 & -1 & 1 \\ 0 & 0 & 0 \\ 0 & 0 & 0 \end{bmatrix}\begin{bmatrix} x_1 \\ x_2 \\ x_3 \end{bmatrix} = \begin{bmatrix} 0 \\ 0 \\ 0 \end{bmatrix}$$

$$\Rightarrow \quad x_1 - x_2 + x_3 = 0$$

Let $x_1 = k_1$ and $x_2 = k_2$

$$\Rightarrow \quad k_1 - k_2 + x_3 = 0 \Rightarrow x_3 = k_2 - k_1$$

$$\therefore \quad X_2 = \begin{bmatrix} k_1 \\ k_2 \\ k_2 - k_1 \end{bmatrix}$$

$$\Rightarrow \quad X_2 = \begin{bmatrix} 1 \\ 1 \\ 0 \end{bmatrix} \qquad [\text{Take } k_1 = 1, k_2 = 1]$$

Let $X_3 = \begin{bmatrix} l \\ m \\ n \end{bmatrix}$

As, $X_3$ is orthogonal to $X_1$, since the given matrix is symmetric.

$$\therefore \quad [1 \;\; -1 \;\; 1]\begin{bmatrix} l \\ m \\ n \end{bmatrix} = 0 \text{ or } l - m + n = 0 \qquad \text{...(ii)}$$

As, $X_3$ is orthogonal to $X_2$, since the given matrix is symmetric.

$$[1\ 1\ 0]\begin{bmatrix} l \\ m \\ n \end{bmatrix} = 0 \quad \text{or} \quad l + m + 0 \cdot n = 0 \qquad \text{...(iii)}$$

On solving Eqs. (ii) and (iii), we get

$$\frac{l}{0-1} = \frac{m}{1-0} = \frac{n}{1+1} \Rightarrow \frac{l}{-1} = \frac{m}{1} = \frac{n}{2}$$

$$\therefore \quad X_3 = \begin{bmatrix} -1 \\ 1 \\ 2 \end{bmatrix}$$

## Algebraic Multiplicity and Geometric Multiplicity

Let $A = [a_{ij}]_{n \times n}$ be a square matrix of order $n$ whose characteristic equation is

$$\text{charc}(x) = 0$$

If $x = \lambda$ is a root of $\text{ch}'(x) = 0$ s.t.,

$$\text{ch}(\lambda) = \text{ch}'(\lambda) = \ldots = \text{ch}^{r-1}(\lambda) = 0$$

but $\quad \text{ch}^r(\lambda) \neq 0$

Then, $r$ is called algebraic multiplicity of $\lambda$.

In other words, the multiplicity of an eigen value is called algebraic multiplicity of that eigen value *i.e.*, if

$$\text{ch}(x) = (x - \lambda)^r \phi(x)$$

Then, $r$ is algebraic multiplicity of eigen value $\lambda$.

Now, construct the matrices $B_r = A - \lambda_r I$ (distinct), where $\lambda_1, \lambda_2, \ldots, \lambda_k$ are eigen values of matrix $A$. Thus, we get system of homogeneous equations.

$$B_r X = 0; \quad r = 1 \text{ to } k.$$

Now, $\quad W_r = \text{solution set of } B_r X = 0$

$$= \{X : B_r X = 0\}$$

$W_r$ is called eigen space corresponding to eigen value $\lambda_r$. Moreover, $W_r$ is null space of $B_r$. Thus,

$$\dim B_r = \text{Nullity of } B_r$$
$$= n - \text{Rank } B_r = m_r$$

This $m_r$ is called the geometric multiplicity of $\lambda_r$, which is equal to the number of linearly independent eigen vector of matrix $A$.

Thus, geometric multiplicity of $\lambda_r$

$$= \text{Number of linearly independent eigen vector of } A$$
$$= n - \rho(B_r) = n - \rho(A - \lambda_r I) = m_r$$

Clearly, algebraic multiplicity (AM) of $\lambda_r$ is greater than or equal to the geometric multiplicity of $\lambda_r$.

***Example 19.*** *Find the AM and GM of eigen values for the matrix*

$$A = \begin{bmatrix} 1 & 2010 & 2011 \\ 0 & -1 & 2010 \\ 0 & 0 & 1 \end{bmatrix}$$

**Solution.** $\because \text{ch}(x) = (x-1)^2(x+1)$

$\therefore$ The eigen values of the given matrix are 1, 1 and $-1$.

$\therefore$ AM of $\lambda = 1$ is 2

and AM of $\lambda = -1$ is 1.

Now, constructing

$$B_1 = A - I = \begin{bmatrix} 0 & 2012 & 2011 \\ 0 & -2 & 2010 \\ 0 & 0 & 0 \end{bmatrix}$$

$$B_{-1} = A + I = \begin{bmatrix} 2 & 2012 & 2011 \\ 0 & 0 & 2010 \\ 0 & 0 & 2 \end{bmatrix}$$

$$\therefore \quad \rho(B_1) = 2$$
$$\rho(B_{-1}) = 3$$

$\therefore$ GM of $\lambda = 1$ is $3 - 2 = 1$

and GM of $\lambda = -1$ is $3 - 3 = 0$

Thus, the number of eigen vector corresponding to $\lambda = 1$ is 1 while corresponding to $\lambda = -1$ is zero.

## Cayley-Hamilton Theorem

Every square matrix satisfies its characteristic equation *i.e.*, if for a square matrix $A$ of order $n$,

$$|A - \lambda I| = (-1)^n[\lambda^n + a_1\lambda^{n-1} + a_2\lambda^{n-2} + \ldots + a_n],$$

then the matrix equation

$$x^n + a_1 x^{n-1} + a_2 x^{n-2} + a_3 x^{n-3} + \ldots + a_n I = 0$$

is satisfied by $X = A$ *i.e.*,

$$A^n + a_1 A^{n-1} + a_2 A^{n-2} + \ldots + a_n I = 0$$

***Example 20.*** *Find the characteristic equation of the matrix*

$$A = \begin{bmatrix} 4 & 3 & 1 \\ 2 & 1 & -2 \\ 1 & 2 & 1 \end{bmatrix}. \text{ Hence, find } A^{-1}.$$

**Solution.** The characteristic equation of the matrix $A$ is

$$|A - \lambda I| = 0 \Rightarrow \begin{vmatrix} 4-\lambda & 3 & 1 \\ 2 & 1-\lambda & -2 \\ 1 & 2 & 1-\lambda \end{vmatrix} = 0$$

$$\Rightarrow (4-\lambda)[1 + \lambda^2 - 2\lambda + 4] - 3[2 - 2\lambda + 2] + 1(4 - 1 + \lambda) = 0$$
$$\Rightarrow (4-\lambda)(\lambda^2 - 2\lambda + 5) - 3[-2\lambda + 4] + (3 + \lambda) = 0$$
$$\Rightarrow 4\lambda^2 - 8\lambda + 20 - \lambda^3 + 2\lambda^2 - 5\lambda + 6\lambda - 12 + 3 + \lambda = 0$$
$$\Rightarrow -\lambda^3 + 6\lambda^2 - 6\lambda + 11 = 0$$
$$\Rightarrow \lambda^3 - 6\lambda^2 + 6\lambda - 11 = 0$$

which is the characteristic equation. Now, by Cayley-Hamilton theorem, we have

$$A^3 - 6A^2 + 6A - 11I = 0$$

Multiplying both sides by $A^{-1}$, we get

$$A^2 - 6A + 6I - 11A^{-1} = 0$$

$$\Rightarrow \quad 11A^{-1} = A^2 - 6A + 6I$$

$$\Rightarrow \quad 11A^{-1} = \begin{bmatrix} 4 & 3 & 1 \\ 2 & 1 & -2 \\ 1 & 2 & 1 \end{bmatrix}\begin{bmatrix} 4 & 3 & 1 \\ 2 & 1 & -2 \\ 1 & 2 & 1 \end{bmatrix} - 6\begin{bmatrix} 4 & 3 & 1 \\ 2 & 1 & -2 \\ 1 & 2 & 1 \end{bmatrix} + 6\begin{bmatrix} 1 & 0 & 0 \\ 0 & 1 & 0 \\ 0 & 0 & 1 \end{bmatrix}$$

$$= \begin{bmatrix} 23 & 17 & -1 \\ 8 & 3 & -2 \\ 9 & 7 & -2 \end{bmatrix} + \begin{bmatrix} -24 & -18 & -6 \\ -12 & -6 & 12 \\ -6 & -12 & -6 \end{bmatrix} + \begin{bmatrix} 6 & 0 & 0 \\ 0 & 6 & 0 \\ 0 & 0 & 6 \end{bmatrix}$$

$$= \begin{bmatrix} 5 & -1 & -7 \\ -4 & 3 & 10 \\ 3 & -5 & -2 \end{bmatrix}$$

$$\therefore \quad A^{-1} = \frac{1}{11}\begin{bmatrix} 5 & -1 & -7 \\ -4 & 3 & 10 \\ 3 & -5 & -2 \end{bmatrix}$$

***Example 21.*** *Find the characteristic equations of the matrix*

$$A = \begin{bmatrix} 2 & 1 & 1 \\ 0 & 1 & 0 \\ 1 & 1 & 2 \end{bmatrix}$$

*Verify Cayley-Hamilton theorem and hence evaluate the matrix equation.*

$$A^8 - 5A^7 + 7A^6 - 3A^5 + A^4 - 5A^3 + 8A^2 - 2A + I$$

**Solution.** The characteristic equation of the matrix $A$ is

$$|A - \lambda I| = 0$$

$$\Rightarrow \quad \begin{vmatrix} 2-\lambda & 1 & 1 \\ 0 & 1-\lambda & 0 \\ 1 & 1 & 2-\lambda \end{vmatrix} = 0$$

$$\Rightarrow \quad (2-\lambda)[(1-\lambda)(2-\lambda)] - 1(0) + 1(0 - 1 + \lambda) = 0$$

$$\Rightarrow \quad \lambda^3 - 5\lambda^2 + 7\lambda - 3 = 0$$

Which is the characteristic equation.

Now, by the Cayley-Hamilton theorem, we get

$$A^3 - 5A^2 + 7A - 3I = 0$$

$$\text{Now, } A^2 = A \cdot A = \begin{bmatrix} 2 & 1 & 1 \\ 0 & 1 & 0 \\ 1 & 1 & 2 \end{bmatrix}\begin{bmatrix} 2 & 1 & 1 \\ 0 & 1 & 0 \\ 1 & 1 & 2 \end{bmatrix} = \begin{bmatrix} 5 & 4 & 4 \\ 0 & 1 & 0 \\ 4 & 4 & 5 \end{bmatrix}$$

$$\text{and} \quad A^3 = A^2 \cdot A = \begin{bmatrix} 5 & 4 & 4 \\ 0 & 1 & 0 \\ 4 & 4 & 5 \end{bmatrix} \cdot \begin{bmatrix} 2 & 1 & 1 \\ 0 & 1 & 0 \\ 1 & 1 & 2 \end{bmatrix} = \begin{bmatrix} 14 & 13 & 13 \\ 0 & 1 & 0 \\ 13 & 13 & 14 \end{bmatrix}$$

$$\therefore A^3 - 5A^2 + 7A - 3I = \begin{bmatrix} 14 & 13 & 13 \\ 0 & 1 & 0 \\ 13 & 13 & 14 \end{bmatrix} - 5\begin{bmatrix} 5 & 4 & 4 \\ 0 & 1 & 0 \\ 4 & 4 & 5 \end{bmatrix} + 7\begin{bmatrix} 2 & 1 & 1 \\ 0 & 1 & 0 \\ 1 & 1 & 2 \end{bmatrix} - 3\begin{bmatrix} 1 & 0 & 0 \\ 0 & 1 & 0 \\ 0 & 0 & 1 \end{bmatrix}$$

$$= \begin{bmatrix} 14-25+14-3 & 13-20+7+0 & 13-20+7+0 \\ 0+0+0+0 & 1-5+7-3 & 0-0+0-0 \\ 13-20+7+0 & 13-20+7 & 14-25+14-3 \end{bmatrix}.$$

$$= \begin{bmatrix} 0 & 0 & 0 \\ 0 & 0 & 0 \\ 0 & 0 & 0 \end{bmatrix} = 0 \quad \text{...(i)}$$

$\therefore$ Cayley-Hamilton theorem is verified.

Now, we have

$$A^8 - 5A^7 + 7A^6 - 3A^5 + A^4 - 5A^3 + 8A^2 - 2A + I$$
$$= A^5(A^3 - 5A^2 + 7A - 3I) + A(A^3 - 5A^2 + 7A - 3I) + A^2 + A + I$$
$$= A^5 \times 0 + A \times 0 + A^2 + A + I = A^2 + A + I$$
$$= \begin{bmatrix} 5 & 4 & 4 \\ 0 & 1 & 0 \\ 4 & 4 & 5 \end{bmatrix} + \begin{bmatrix} 2 & 1 & 1 \\ 0 & 1 & 0 \\ 1 & 1 & 2 \end{bmatrix} + \begin{bmatrix} 1 & 0 & 0 \\ 0 & 1 & 0 \\ 0 & 0 & 1 \end{bmatrix} = \begin{bmatrix} 8 & 5 & 5 \\ 0 & 3 & 0 \\ 5 & 5 & 8 \end{bmatrix}$$

## Minimal Polynomial

The smallest degree monic polynomial $m_A(x)$ is called the minimal polynomial for the matrix $A$, if

$$m_A(A) = 0$$

## Properties of Minimal Polynomial

**(i)** For every matrix minimal polynomial is unique.

**(ii)** For any matrix $A$, minimal polynomial divides the characteristic polynomial of $A$ *i.e.*,

$$\deg m_A(x) \leq \deg \text{ch}(x)$$

**(iii)** The deg $m_A(x) - 1$ iff $A$ is scalar matrix.

Thus, if $A$ is not scalar. Then, deg $m_A(x) \geq 2$

**(iv)** If $x - \lambda$ divides $m_A(x)$ or $m_A(\lambda) = 0$, then $\lambda$ is an eigen value of $A$ *i.e.*, every root of $m_A(x)$ is an eigen value of $A$ which does not give algebraic multiplicity of eigen value.

**(v)** The order of $\lambda$ as zero of $m_A(x)$ may not be algebraic multiplicity of eigen value.

**(vi)** If $A = [a_{ij}]_{n \times n}$ is a square matrix of order $n$, then ch$(x)$ divides $[m_A(x)]^n$ *i.e.*, every irreducible factor of ch$(x)$ is also a factor of $m_A(x)$.

Hence, all the eigen values of $A$ without algebraic multiplicitv can be root of $m_A(x) = 0$.

Hence, if

$$\text{ch}(x) = \pi(x - \lambda_i)^{ni}, \ \Sigma n_i = n$$

Then, $m_A(x) = \pi(x - \lambda_i)^{mi}, \ \Sigma m_i \leq n$

***Example 22.*** *Find the minimal polynomial for the matrix*

$$A = \begin{bmatrix} 1 & 1 & 1 & \dots & 1 \\ 1 & 1 & 1 & \dots & 1 \\ \dots & \dots & \dots & \dots & \\ \dots & \dots & \dots & \dots & \\ \dots & \dots & \dots & \dots & \\ 1 & 1 & 1 & \dots & 1 \end{bmatrix}_{10 \times 10}$$

**Solution.** We have,

$$A^2 = \begin{bmatrix} 10 & 10 & \dots & 10 \\ 10 & 10 & \dots & 10 \\ \dots & \dots & \dots & \dots \\ \dots & \dots & \dots & \dots \\ \dots & \dots & \dots & \dots \\ 10 & 10 & \dots & 10 \end{bmatrix}_{10\times10} = 10\,A$$

$$\Rightarrow \quad A^2 - 10A = 0$$

$$\Rightarrow \quad m_A(x) = x^2 - 10x = 0$$

## Similarity Transformation

Let $A$ and $B$ be two square matrices of order $n$. Then, $B$ is said to be similar to $A$, if there exists a non-singular matrix $P$ such that

$$B = P^{-1}AP \qquad \dots(i)$$

Eq. (i) is called a similar transformation.

## Diagonalisation of a Matrix

Diagonalisation of a matrix $A$ is the process of reducing the matrix $A$ into a diagonal form '$D$. If matrix $A$ is related to $D$ by a similarity transformation such that $D = P^{-1}AP$, then the matrix $A$ is reduced to the diagonal matrix $D$ through modal matrix $P$.

> ***Note*** **(a)** The matrix $D$ is called spectral matrix of $A$.
>
> **(b)** If a square matrix $A$ of order $n$ has $n$ linearly independent eigen vectors, then a matrix $P$ can be found such that $P^{-1}AP$ is a diagonal matrix.
>
> **(c)** The square matrix $P$, which diagonalises $A$, is found by grouping the eigen vectors of $A$, into square matrix and the resulting diagonal matrix has the eigen values of $A$ as its diagonal elements.
>
> **(d)** The reduction of $A$ to a diagonal matrix is, obviously a particular case of similarity transformation.
>
> **(e)** The matrix $P$ which diagonalises $A$ is called the modal matrix of $A$ and the resulting diagonal matrix $D$ is known as the spectra matrix of $A$.

***Example 23.*** Let $A = \begin{bmatrix} -2 & 2 & -3 \\ 2 & 1 & -6 \\ -1 & -2 & 0 \end{bmatrix}$

*Find a similarity transformation that diagonalises the matrix A.*

**Solution.** Let $A = \begin{bmatrix} -2 & 2 & -3 \\ 2 & 1 & -6 \\ -1 & -2 & 0 \end{bmatrix}$

The characteristic equation is $|A - \lambda I| = 0$

$$\Rightarrow \begin{vmatrix} -(2+\lambda) & 2 & -3 \\ 2 & 1-\lambda & -6 \\ -1 & -2 & -\lambda \end{vmatrix} = 0$$

$$\Rightarrow -(2+\lambda)[(1-\lambda)(-\lambda)-12] - 2[-2\lambda-6] - 3[-4+(1-\lambda)] = 0$$

$$\Rightarrow -(2+\lambda)[-\lambda+\lambda^2-12] + 4\lambda + 12 + 12 - 3 + 3\lambda = 0$$

$$\Rightarrow 2\lambda - 2\lambda^2 + 24 + \lambda^2 - \lambda^3 + 12\lambda + 4\lambda + 12 + 12 - 3 + 3\lambda = 0$$

$$\Rightarrow -\lambda^3 - \lambda^2 + 21\lambda + 45 = 0$$

$$\Rightarrow \lambda^3 + \lambda^2 - 21\lambda - 45 = 0$$

$$\Rightarrow (\lambda-5)(\lambda^2+6\lambda+9) = 0$$

$$\Rightarrow (\lambda-5)(\lambda+3)^2 = 0 \Rightarrow \lambda = 5, -3, -3$$

$\therefore$ The eigen values are 5, −3, −3.

Now, Let $X_1$ be the eigen vector corresponding to the eigen value $\lambda = 5$ is given by $(A - \lambda I)X = 0$

$$\begin{bmatrix} -7 & 2 & -3 \\ 2 & -4 & -6 \\ -1 & -2 & -5 \end{bmatrix}\begin{bmatrix} x \\ y \\ z \end{bmatrix} = \begin{bmatrix} 0 \\ 0 \\ 0 \end{bmatrix}$$

$$-7x + 2y - 3z = 0$$

$$2x - 4y - 6z = 0$$

$$\Rightarrow \frac{x}{-12-12} = \frac{y}{-6-42} = \frac{z}{28-4}$$

$$\Rightarrow \frac{x}{-24} = \frac{y}{-48} = \frac{z}{24}$$

$$\Rightarrow \frac{x}{-1} = \frac{y}{-2} = \frac{z}{1}$$

$$\therefore \quad X_1 = \begin{bmatrix} -1 \\ -2 \\ 1 \end{bmatrix}$$

For $\lambda = -3$

$$\begin{bmatrix} 1 & 2 & -3 \\ 2 & 4 & -6 \\ -1 & -2 & 3 \end{bmatrix}\begin{bmatrix} x \\ y \\ z \end{bmatrix} = \begin{bmatrix} 0 \\ 0 \\ 0 \end{bmatrix} \quad \begin{matrix} R_2 \to R_2 - 2R_1 \\ R_3 \to R_3 + R_1 \end{matrix}$$

$$\sim \begin{bmatrix} 1 & 2 & -3 \\ 0 & 0 & 0 \\ 0 & 0 & 0 \end{bmatrix}\begin{bmatrix} x \\ y \\ z \end{bmatrix} = \begin{bmatrix} 0 \\ 0 \\ 0 \end{bmatrix}$$

$$\Rightarrow \quad x + 2y - 3z = 0$$

Let $z = 0, y = -1, x - 2 + 0 = 0 \Rightarrow x = 2$

$$\therefore \quad X_2 = \begin{bmatrix} 2 \\ -1 \\ 0 \end{bmatrix}$$

Let $z = 1, y = 0, x = 0 - 3 = 0 \Rightarrow x = 3$

$$\therefore \quad X_3 = \begin{bmatrix} 3 \\ 0 \\ 1 \end{bmatrix}$$

$\therefore$ The required transformation matrix is

$$P = \begin{bmatrix} -1 & 2 & 3 \\ -2 & -1 & 0 \\ 1 & 0 & 1 \end{bmatrix} \text{ and } P^{-1} = \frac{1}{8}\begin{bmatrix} -1 & -2 & 3 \\ 2 & -4 & -6 \\ 1 & 2 & 5 \end{bmatrix}$$

$$\therefore \quad P^{-1}AP = \frac{1}{8}\begin{bmatrix} -1 & -2 & 3 \\ 2 & -4 & -6 \\ 1 & 2 & 5 \end{bmatrix}\begin{bmatrix} -2 & 2 & -3 \\ 2 & 1 & -6 \\ -1 & -2 & 6 \end{bmatrix}\begin{bmatrix} -1 & 2 & 3 \\ -2 & -1 & 0 \\ 1 & 0 & 1 \end{bmatrix}$$

$$= \frac{1}{8}\begin{bmatrix} -5 & -10 & 15 \\ -6 & 12 & 18 \\ -3 & -6 & -15 \end{bmatrix}\begin{bmatrix} -1 & 2 & 3 \\ -2 & -1 & 0 \\ 1 & 0 & 1 \end{bmatrix}$$

$$= \frac{1}{8}\begin{bmatrix} 40 & 0 & 0 \\ 0 & -24 & 0 \\ 0 & 0 & -24 \end{bmatrix} = \begin{bmatrix} 5 & 0 & 0 \\ 0 & -3 & 0 \\ 0 & 0 & -3 \end{bmatrix}$$

## Powers of a Matrix

### (By Diagonalisation)

We can obtain powers of a matrix by using diagonalisation.

We have, $\quad D = P^{-1}AP$

Where, $A$ is the square matrix and $P$ is a non-singular matrix.

$$D^2 = (P^{-1}AP)(P^{-1}AP) = P^{-1}A(PP^{-1})AP$$
$$= P^{-1}A^2P$$

Similarly, $\quad D^3 = P^{-1}A^3P$

$\therefore$ In general $\quad D^n = P^{-1}A^nP \quad$ ...(i)

On pre-multiplying Eq. (i) by $P$ and on post multiplying the Eq. (i) by $P^{-1}$, we get

$$PD^nP^{-1} = P(P^{-1}A^nP)P^{-1}$$
$$= (PP^{-1})A^n(PP^{-1}) = A^n$$

***Example 24.*** *Find a matrix P which transform the matrix* $A = \begin{bmatrix} 1 & 0 & -1 \\ 1 & 2 & 1 \\ 2 & 2 & 3 \end{bmatrix}$ *to diagonal form. Hence, find* $A^4$.

**Solution.** We have,

$$|A - \lambda I| = 0 \Rightarrow \begin{vmatrix} 1-\lambda & 0 & -1 \\ 1 & 2-\lambda & 1 \\ 2 & 2 & 3-\lambda \end{vmatrix} = 0$$

$$\Rightarrow \quad \lambda^3 - 6\lambda^2 + 11\lambda - 6 = 0$$
$$\Rightarrow \quad (\lambda-1)(\lambda-2)(\lambda-3) = 0$$
$$\Rightarrow \quad \lambda = 1, 2, 3$$

Let $X_1$ be eigen vector corresponding to the eigen value $\lambda = 1$, we have $(A - \lambda I)X_1 = 0$

$$\therefore \quad \begin{bmatrix} 1-1 & 0 & -1 \\ 1 & 2-1 & 1 \\ 2 & 2 & 3-1 \end{bmatrix}\begin{bmatrix} x_1 \\ x_2 \\ x_3 \end{bmatrix} = \begin{bmatrix} 0 \\ 0 \\ 0 \end{bmatrix}$$

$$\Rightarrow \quad \begin{bmatrix} 0 & 0 & -1 \\ 1 & 1 & 1 \\ 2 & 2 & 2 \end{bmatrix}\begin{bmatrix} x_1 \\ x_2 \\ x_3 \end{bmatrix} = \begin{bmatrix} 0 \\ 0 \\ 0 \end{bmatrix}$$

$$\Rightarrow \quad 0x_1 + 0x_2 - x_3 = 0 \quad \text{...(i)}$$
$$x_1 + x_2 + x_3 = 0 \quad \text{...(ii)}$$
and
$$2x_1 + 2x_2 + 2x_3 = 0 \quad \text{...(iii)}$$

From Eqs. (i) and (ii), we get

$$\frac{x_1}{0+1} = \frac{x_2}{-1+0} = \frac{x_3}{0}$$

$$\Rightarrow \quad x_1 = 1, \; x_2 = -1 \text{ and } x_3 = 0$$

$$\therefore \quad X_1 = \begin{bmatrix} 1 \\ -1 \\ 0 \end{bmatrix}$$

For $\lambda = 2$, Let $X_2$ be the eigen vector corresponding to the eigen value $\lambda = 2$, we have $(A - \lambda I)X_2 = 0$

$$\therefore \quad \begin{bmatrix} 1-2 & 0 & -1 \\ 1 & 2-2 & 1 \\ 2 & 2 & 3-2 \end{bmatrix}\begin{bmatrix} x_1 \\ x_2 \\ x_3 \end{bmatrix} = \begin{bmatrix} 0 \\ 0 \\ 0 \end{bmatrix}$$

$$\Rightarrow \quad \begin{bmatrix} -1 & 0 & -1 \\ 1 & 0 & 1 \\ 2 & 2 & 1 \end{bmatrix}\begin{bmatrix} x_1 \\ x_2 \\ x_3 \end{bmatrix} = \begin{bmatrix} 0 \\ 0 \\ 0 \end{bmatrix}$$

$$\Rightarrow \quad \begin{bmatrix} 0 & 0 & 0 \\ 1 & 0 & 1 \\ 2 & 2 & 1 \end{bmatrix}\begin{bmatrix} x_1 \\ x_2 \\ x_3 \end{bmatrix} = \begin{bmatrix} 0 \\ 0 \\ 0 \end{bmatrix} \quad R_1 \to R_1 + R_2$$

$$\Rightarrow \quad 0x_1 + 0x_2 + 0x_3 = 0 \quad \text{...(iv)}$$
$$x_1 + 0x_2 + x_3 = 0 \quad \text{...(v)}$$
and
$$2x_1 + 2x_2 + x_3 = 0 \quad \text{...(vi)}$$

From Eqs. (v) and (vi), we have

$$-2x_1 + 0x_2 - x_3 = 0$$
and
$$x_1 - x_2 + x_3 = 0$$

On solving these we get

$$\frac{x_1}{0-1} = \frac{x_2}{-1+2} = \frac{x_3}{2-0}$$

$$\Rightarrow \quad x_1 = -1, \; x_2 = 1, \; x_3 = 2$$

$$\therefore \quad X_2 = \begin{bmatrix} -1 \\ 1 \\ 2 \end{bmatrix}$$

$$\therefore \text{ Modal matrix, } P = \begin{bmatrix} 1 & -2 & -1 \\ -1 & 1 & 1 \\ 0 & 2 & 2 \end{bmatrix}$$

and
$$P^{-1} = \frac{-1}{2}\begin{bmatrix} 0 & 2 & -1 \\ 2 & 2 & 0 \\ -2 & -2 & -1 \end{bmatrix}$$

$$\Rightarrow \quad P^{-1}AP = -\frac{1}{2}\begin{bmatrix} 0 & 2 & -1 \\ 2 & 2 & 0 \\ -2 & -2 & -1 \end{bmatrix}\begin{bmatrix} 1 & 0 & -1 \\ 1 & 2 & 1 \\ 2 & 2 & 3 \end{bmatrix}\begin{bmatrix} 1 & -2 & -1 \\ -1 & 1 & 1 \\ 0 & 2 & 2 \end{bmatrix}$$

$$= \begin{bmatrix} 1 & 0 & 0 \\ 0 & 2 & 0 \\ 0 & 0 & 3 \end{bmatrix} = D$$

Now, we have

$$A^4 = PD^4P^{-1} = \begin{bmatrix} 1 & -2 & -1 \\ -1 & 1 & 1 \\ 0 & 2 & 2 \end{bmatrix}\begin{bmatrix} 1 & 0 & 0 \\ 0 & 16 & 0 \\ 0 & 0 & 81 \end{bmatrix}\begin{bmatrix} 0 & -1 & 1/2 \\ -1 & -1 & 0 \\ 1 & 1 & 1/2 \end{bmatrix}$$

$$= \begin{bmatrix} -49 & -50 & -40 \\ 65 & 66 & 40 \\ 130 & 130 & 81 \end{bmatrix}$$

## Vector Space

A non-empty set $V$ is called a real vector space (or a real linear space or a linear vector space) if the following properties are satisfied

**(i)** There is defined an internal composition in $V$ called the addition of vectors and denoted by '+'. Also, for this composition $V$ is an abelian group.

**(ii)** There is an external composition in $V$ over the field $F$ [or $(F, +, \cdot)$] called scalar multiplication and denoted multiplicatively *i.e.*, $a\alpha \in V, \forall a \in F$ and $\forall \alpha \in V$. We can say that $V$ is closed with respect to scalar multiplication.

**(iii)** The two compositions *i.e.*, addition of vectors and scalar multiplication satisfy the following postulates

(a) $a(\alpha + \beta) = a\alpha + a\beta, \forall a \in F$ and $\forall \alpha, \beta \in V$

(b) $(a + b)\alpha = a\alpha + b\alpha, \forall \alpha \in V$ and $a, b \in F$

(c) $(ab)\alpha = a(b\alpha), \forall \alpha \in V$ and $a, b \in F$

(d) $1\alpha = \alpha, \forall \alpha \in V$ and 1 is the unity element of the field $F$.

> ***Note*** **(a)** The real or complex numbers used for scalar multiplication in the definition.
>
> **(b)** If $F$ is any field, then $F$ itself is a vector space over the field $F$ of a vector space are called scalars. Throughout we shall deal with only real vector spaces and complex vector spaces.

***Example 25.*** *A field $K$ can be regarded as a vector space over any subfield $F$ of $K$.*

**Solution.** We have, $K$ is the set of vectors. Addition of vectors is the addition composition in the field $K$. Since, $K$ is a field, therefore $(K, +)$ is an abelian group. The elements of the subfield $F$ constitute the set of scalars. The composition of scalar multiplication is the multiplication composition in the field $K$. $K$ is a field, therefore $a\alpha \in K, \forall \alpha \in K$ and $\forall a \in F$ because both a and $\alpha$ are elements of $K$. If 1 is the unity element of $K$, then 1 is also the unity element of the subfield $F$. We have the following observations

(i) $a(\alpha + \beta) = a\alpha + a\beta, \forall \alpha, \beta \in K$ and $\forall a \in F$.
This result comes from the left distributive law in $K$.

(ii) $(a + b)\alpha = a\alpha + b\alpha, \forall \alpha \in K$ and $a, b \in F$. This result comes from the right distributive law in $K$.

(iii) $(ab)\alpha = a(b\alpha), \forall \alpha \in K$ and $a, b \in F$. This result comes from the associativity of multiplication in $K$.

(iv) $1\alpha = \alpha, \forall \alpha \in K$ and 1 is the unity element of the sub-field $F$. Since, 1 is also the unity element of the field $K$, therefore $1\alpha = \alpha, \forall \alpha \in K$. Therefore, $K(F)$ is a vector space.

***Example 26.*** *Let $V$ be the set of all pairs $(x, y)$ of real numbers and let $F$ be the field of real numbers. Define $(x, y) + (x_1, y_1) = (x + x_1, 0)$, $c(x, y) = c(x, 0)$. Is $V$, with these operations, a vector space over the field of real numbers?*

**Solution.** Suppose, the ordered pair $(x_1, y_1)$ is to be the identity element for the operation of addition of vectors. Then, we must have

$$(x, y) + (x_1, y_1) = (x, y), \forall x, y \in R$$

$$\Rightarrow \quad (x + x_1, 0) = (x, y), \forall x, y \in R$$

But if $y \neq 0$, then we cannot have $(x + x_1, 0) = (x, y)$. Thus, there exists no element $(x_1, y_1)$ of $V$ such that $(x, y) + (x_1, y_1) = (x, y), \forall (x, y) \in V$.

$\therefore$ The identity element does not exist and hence $V$ is not a vector space over the field $R$.

***Example 27.*** *Let $V$ be the set of all pairs $(x, y)$ of real numbers and let $F$ be the field of real numbers. Define*

$$(x, y) + (x_1, y_1) = (3y + 3y_1, -x - x_1)$$

$$c(x, y) = (3cy, -cx)$$

*Verify that $V$, with these operations, is not a vector space over the field of real numbers.*

***Solution.*** Let $\alpha = (1, 2)$, $\beta = (2, 3)$ and $\gamma = (1, 3)$,

then $(\alpha + \beta) + \gamma = \{(1, 2) + (2, 3)\} + (1, 3)$
$= (15, -3) + (1, 3) = (0, -16)$

and $\alpha + (\beta + \gamma) = (1, 2) + \{(2, 3) + (1, 3)\}$
$= (1, 2) + (18, -3) = (-3, -19)$

Therefore, we conclude that in general $(\alpha + \beta) + \gamma \neq \alpha + (\beta + \gamma)$. Hence, $V$ is not a vector space over the field of real numbers.

## Important Theorems on Vector Space

***Theorem 1*** Let $V(F)$ be a vector space and 0 be the zero vector of $V$, then

**(i)** $a0 = 0, \forall a \in F$

**(ii)** $0\alpha = 0, \forall \alpha \in V$

**(iii)** $a(-\alpha) = -(a\alpha), \forall a \in F, \forall \alpha \in V$

**(iv)** $(-a)\alpha = -(a\alpha), \forall a \in F, \forall \alpha \in V$

**(v)** $a(\alpha - \beta) = a\alpha - a\beta, \forall a \in F$ and $\alpha, \beta \in V$

**(vi)** $a\alpha = 0 \Rightarrow a = 0$ or $\alpha = 0$

***Theorem 2*** Let $V(F)$ be a vector space, then

**(i)** If $a, b \in F$ and $\alpha$ is a non-zero element of $V$, we have $a\alpha = b\alpha \Rightarrow a = b$.

**(ii)** If $\alpha, \beta \in V$ and is a non-zero element of $F$, we have $a\alpha = a\beta \Rightarrow \alpha = \beta$.

## Vector Subspaces

Let $V$ be a vector space over the field $F$ and $W \subseteq V$. Then, $W$ is called a subspace of $V$ if $W$ itself is a vector space over $F$ with respect to the operations of vector addition and scalar multiplication in $V$.

## Important Theorems on Vector Subspaces

***Theorem 1*** The necessary and sufficient condition for a non-empty subset $W$ of a vector space $V(F)$ to be a subspace of $V$ is that $W$ is closed under vector addition and scalar multiplication in $V$.

***Theorem 2*** (Two Step Test) The necessary and sufficient conditions for a non-empty subset $W$ of a vector space $V(F)$ to be a subspace of $V$ are

**(i)** $\alpha \in W, \beta \in W \Rightarrow \alpha - \beta \in W$

**(ii)** $a \in F, \alpha \in W \Rightarrow a\alpha \in W$

***Theorem 3*** (Single Step Test) The necessary and sufficient conditions for a non-empty subset $W$ of a vector space $V(F)$ to be a subspace of $V$ is

$$a, b \in F \text{ and } \alpha, \beta \in W \Rightarrow a\alpha + b\beta \in W.$$

***Theorem 4*** A non-empty subset $W$ of a vector space $V(F)$ is a subspace of $V$ iff for each pair of vectors $\alpha, \beta$ in $W$ and each scalar $a$ in $F$ the vector $a\alpha + \beta$ is again in $W$.

***Example 28.*** *The set $W$ of ordered triads $(a_1, a_2, 0)$, where $a_1, a_2 \in F$ is a subspace of $V_3(F)$.*

**Solution.** $W$ is non-empty, since $0 = (0, 0, 0) \in W$. Let $\alpha = (a_1, a_2, 0)$ and $\beta = (b_1, b_2, 0)$ be any two elements of $W$. Then, $a_1, a_2, b_1, b_2 \in F$. If $a, b$ be any two elements of $F$, we have

$$\begin{aligned} a\alpha + b\beta &= a(a_1, a_2, 0) + b(b_1, b_2, 0) \\ &= (aa_1, aa_2, 0) + (bb_1, bb_2, 0) \\ &= (aa_1 + bb_1, aa_2 + bb_2, 0) \in W \end{aligned}$$

$\because$ $aa_1 + bb_1, aa_2 + bb_2 \in F$ and the last coordinate of this triad is zero.

Hence, $W$ is a subspace of $V_3(F)$.

***Example 29.*** *Let $R$ be the field of real numbers. Which of the following are subspaces of $V_3(R)$?*

(i) $\{(x, 2y, 3z) : x, y, z \in R\}$

(ii) $\{(x, y, z) : x, y, z$ *are rational numbers*$\}$

**Solution.** (i) Suppose, $W = \{(x, 2y, 3z) : x, y, z \in R\}$. Let $x_1, y_1, z_1, x_2, y_2, z_2$ are real numbers. If $a$ and $b$ are any two real numbers, then

$$\begin{aligned} a\alpha + b\beta &= a(x_1, 2y_1, 3z_1) + b(x_2, 2y_2, 3z_2) \\ &= (ax_1 + bx_2, 2ay_1 + 2by_2, 3az_1 + 3bz_2) \\ &= (ax_1 + bx_2, 2[ay_1 + by_2], 3[az_1 + bz_2]) \in W \end{aligned}$$

Since, $ax_1 + bx_2, ay_1 + by_2, az_1 + bz_2$ are real numbers.

Therefore, $a, b \in R$ and $\alpha, \beta \in W \Rightarrow a\alpha + b\beta \in W$

$\therefore$ $W$ is a subspace of $V_3(R)$.

(ii) Suppose, $W = \{(x, y, z) : x, y, z$ are rational numbers$\}$

Now, $\alpha = (3, 4, 5)$ is an element of $W$.

Also, $a = \sqrt{7}$ is an element of $R$. But

$a\alpha = \sqrt{7}(3, 4, 5) = (3\sqrt{7}, 4\sqrt{7}, 5\sqrt{7}) \notin W$

$\because$ $3\sqrt{7}, 4\sqrt{7}, 5\sqrt{7}$ are not rational numbers.

$\therefore$ $W$ is not closed under scalar multiplication.

Hence, $W$ is not a subspace of $V_3(R)$.

***Example 30.*** *If a vector space $V$ is the set of all real-valued continuous functions over the field of real numbers $R$, then show that the set $W$ of solutions of differential equation.*

$$2\frac{d^2y}{dx^2} - 9\frac{dy}{dx} + 2y = 0 \text{ is a subspace of } V.$$

**Solution.** We have, $W = \left\{y : 2\frac{d^2y}{dx^2} - 9\frac{dy}{dx} + 2y = 0\right\}$, where $y = f(x)$

Definitely $y = 0$ satisfies the given differential equation and as such it belongs to $W$ and thus $W \neq \phi$.

Now, Let $y_1, y_2 \in W$, then

$$2\frac{d^2y_1}{dx^2} - 9\frac{dy_1}{dx} + 2y_1 = 0 \quad \text{...(i)}$$

and

$$2\frac{d^2y_2}{dx^2} - 9\frac{dy_2}{dx} + 2y_2 = 0 \quad \text{...(ii)}$$

Let $a, b \in R$. If $W$ is to be a subspace, then we should show that $ay_1 + by_2$ also belongs to $W$ *i.e.*, it is a solution of the given differential equation.

We have, $2\frac{d^2}{dx^2}(ay_1 + by_2) - 9\frac{d}{dx}(ay_1 + by_2) + 2(ay_1 + by_2)$

$$\begin{aligned} &= 2a\frac{d^2y_1}{dx^2} - 2b\frac{d^2y_2}{dx^2} - 9a\frac{dy_1}{dx} - 9b\frac{dy_2}{dx} + 2ay_1 + 2by_2 \\ &= a\left[2\frac{d^2y_1}{dx^2} - 9\frac{dy_1}{dx} + 2y_1\right] + b\left[2\frac{d^2y_2}{dx^2} - 9\frac{dy_2}{dx} + 2y_2\right] \\ &= a \cdot 0 + b \cdot 0 \quad \text{[By using Eqs. (i) and (ii)]} \\ &= 0 \end{aligned}$$

Therefore, $ay_1 + by_2$ is a solution of the given differential equation and so it belongs to $W$.

Thus, $W$ is a subspace of $V$.

***Theorem 5*** The intersection of any two subspaces $W_1$ and $W_2$ of a vector space $V(F)$ is also a subspace of $V(F)$.

***Theorem 6*** The union of two subspaces is a subspace iff one is contained in other.

***Theorem 7*** Arbitrary intersection of subspaces *i.e.*, the intersection of any family of subspaces of a vector space is a subspace.

> ***Note*** The union of two subspaces of $V(F)$ may not be a subspace of $V(F)$. For example, if $R$ be the field of real numbers, then
>
> $W_1 = \{(0, 0, z) : z \in R\}$ and $W_2 = \{(0, y, 0) : y \in R\}$
>
> are two subspaces of $V_3(R)$.
>
> We have, $(0, 0, 3) \in W_1$ and $(0, 5, 0) \in W_2$
>
> But $(0, 0, 3) + (0, 5, 0) = (0, 5, 3) \notin W_1 \cup W_2$, since neither $(0, 5, 3) \in W_1$ nor $(0, 5, 3) \in W_2$. Thus, $W_1 \cup W_2$ is not closed under vector addition. Hence, $W_1 \cup W_2$ is not a subspace of $V_3(R)$.

## Linear Combination of Vectors and Linear Span of a Set

### Linear Combination

Let $V(F)$ be a vector space. If $\alpha_1, \alpha_2, \ldots, \alpha_n \in V$, then any vector

$$\alpha = a_1\alpha_1 + a_2\alpha_2 + \ldots + a_n\alpha_n, \text{ where, } a_1, a_2, a_3, \ldots, a_n \in F$$

is called linear combination of the vectors $\alpha_1, \alpha_2, \alpha_3, \ldots, \alpha_n$.

## Linear Span

Let $V(F)$ be a vector space and $S$ be any non-empty subset of $V$. Then, the linear span of $S$ is the set of all linear combinations of finite sets of elements of $S$ and is denoted by $L(S)$. Thus, we have

$$L(S) = \{a_1\alpha_1 + a_2\alpha_2 + \dots + a_n\alpha_n : \alpha_1, \alpha_2, \alpha_3, \dots, \alpha_n \text{ is any arbitrary finite subset of } S \text{ and } a_1, a_2, a_3, \dots, a_n \text{ is any arbitrary finite subset of } F\}.$$

***Theorem*** The linear span $L(S)$ of any subset $S$ of a vector space $V(F)$ is a subspace of $V$ generated by $S$ *i.e.*, $L(S) = \{S\}$.

> ***Note*** **(a)** In any case we are to prove that $L(S) = V$, then we should prove that $V \subseteq L(S)$ because $L(S) \subseteq V$. Since, $L(S)$ is a subspace of $V$. In order to prove that $V \subseteq L(S)$. We should prove that each element of $V$ can be expressed as a linear combination of a finite number of elements of $S$. Then, each element of $V$ will also be an element of $L(S)$ and we shall have $V \subseteq L(S)$. Finally, $V \subseteq L(S)$ and $L(S) \subseteq V \Rightarrow L(S) = V$
>
> **(b)** Suppose, $S$ is a non-empty subset of a vector space $V(F)$. Then, a vector $\alpha \in V$ will be in the subspace of $V$ generated by $S$ if it can be expressed as a linear combination over $F$ of a finite number of vectors belonging to $S$.
>
> *e.g.*, The subset $S = \{(1, 0, 0), (0, 1, 0)\}$ of $V_3(F)$ generates or spans the entire vector space $V_3(F)$ *i.e.*, $L(S) = V$
>
> If $(a, b, c)$ be any element of $V$, then
>
> $$(a, b, c) = a(1, 0, 0) + b(0, 1, 0) + c(0, 0, 1)$$
>
> Therefore, $(a, b, c) \in L(S)$. Hence, $V \subseteq L(S)$.
>
> Also, $L(S) \subseteq V$. Therefore, $L(S) = V$.

# Linear Sum of Two Subspaces

Let $W_1$ and $W_2$ be two subspaces of the vector space $V(F)$. Then, the linear sum of the subspaces $W_1$ and $W_2$, denoted by $W_1 + W_2$, is the set of all sums $\alpha_1 + \alpha_2$ such that $\alpha_1 \in W_1$, $\alpha_2 \in W_2$. Therefore,

$$W_1 + W_2 = \{\alpha_1 + \alpha_2 : \alpha_1 \in W_1, \alpha_2 \in W_2\}$$

For any subspace $W$ of a vector space $V$, we have $W + W = W$.

## Important Theorems on Linear Sum

***Theorem 1*** If $W_1$ and $W_2$ are subspaces of the vector space $V(F)$, then

**(i)** $W_1 + W_2$ is a subspace of $V(F)$

**(ii)** $W_1 + W_2 = \{W_1 \cup W_2\}$

*i.e.*, $L(W_1 \cup W_2) = W_1 + W_2$

***Theorem 2*** If $S$ and $T$ are subsets of $V(F)$, then

**(i)** $S \subseteq T \Rightarrow L(S) \subseteq L(T)$

**(ii)** $L(S \cup T) = L(S) + L(T)$

**(iii)** $S$ is a subspace of $V \Leftrightarrow L(S) = S$

**(iv)** $L(L(S)) = L(S)$

***Theorem 3*** Let $V$ be the vector space of all functions from $R$ into $R$; let $V_e$ be the subset of even functions, $f(-x) = f(x)$, let $V_o$ be the subset of odd functions $f(-x) = -f(x)$, then

**(i)** $V_e$ and $V_o$ are subspaces of $V$.

**(ii)** $V_e + V_o = V$

**(iii)** $V_e \cap V_o = \{0\}$

---

***Example 31.*** *For what value of m, the vector $(m, 3, 1)$ is a linear combination of the vectors $(3, 2, 1)$ and $(2, 1, 0)$?*

**Solution.** Let $\alpha_1 = (3, 2, 1)$ and $\alpha_2 = (2, 1, 0)$

Let $(m, 3, 1) = a \cdot \alpha_1 + b \cdot \alpha_2$ where $a, b \in R$

Then, $(m, 3, 1) = a(3, 2, 1) + b(2, 1, 0)$

$= (3a, 2a, a) + (2b, b, 0)$

$= (3a + 2b, 2a + b, a)$

$\therefore \quad 3a + 2b = m,\ 2a + b = 3,\ a = 1$

$\Rightarrow \quad a = 1, b = 1, m = 5$

Therefore, the required value of $m$ is 5.

# Linear Dependence and Independence

## Linear Dependence

Let $V(F)$ be a vector space. A finite set $(\alpha_1, \alpha_2, \alpha_3, \dots, \alpha_n)$ of vectors of $V$ is said to be linearly dependent, if there exist scalars $a_1, a_2, a_3, \dots, a_n \in F$ not all of them 0 (some of them may be zero). Such that

$$a_1\alpha_1 + a_2\alpha_2 + a_3\alpha_3 + \dots + a_n\alpha_n = 0$$

## Linear Independence

Let $V(F)$ be a vector space. A finite set $(\alpha_1, \alpha_2, \alpha_3, \dots, \alpha_n)$ of vectors of $V$ is said to be linearly independent if every relation of the form

$$a_1\alpha_1 + a_2\alpha_2 + a_3\alpha_3 + \dots + a_n\alpha_n = 0,\ a_i \in F,\ 1 \le i \le n$$

$\Rightarrow \quad a_i = 0$ for each $1 \le i \le n$

Any infinite set of vectors of $V$ is said to be linearly independent if its every finite subset is linearly independent, otherwise it is linearly dependent.

> ***Note*** The empty set $\phi$ is defined as a linearly independent set.

## Important Theorems on Linear Dependence and Independence

***Theorem 1*** If two vectors are linearly dependent one of them is a scalar multiple of the other.

***Theorem 2*** A system consisting of a single non-zero vector is always linearly independent.

***Theorem 3*** Every superset of a linearly dependent set of vectors is linearly dependent.

***Theorem 4*** If the set $S = \{\alpha_1, \alpha_2, \alpha_3, \ldots, \alpha_n\}$ of vectors of $V(F)$ is linearly independent, then none of the vectors $\alpha_1, \alpha_2, \ldots, \alpha_n$ can be zero vector.

***Example 32.*** *In the vector space $V_n(F)$, the system of n vectors $e_1 = (1, 0, 0, \ldots, 0)$, $e_2 = (0, 1, 0, \ldots, 0, 0)$, $e_n = (0, 0, \ldots, 0, 1)$ is linearly independent where 1 denotes the unity of the field F.*

**Solution.** If $a_1, a_2, a_3, a_4, \ldots, a_n$ be any scalars, then

$$a_1e_1 + a_2e_2 + \ldots + a_ne_n = 0$$
$$\Rightarrow a_1(1,0,0,\ldots,0) + a_2(0,1,0,\ldots,0) + \ldots + a_n(0,0,\ldots,0,1) = 0$$
$$\Rightarrow (a_1, a_2, a_3, \ldots, a_n) = (0,0,0,\ldots,0)$$
$$\Rightarrow a_1 = 0,\ a_2 = 0, \ldots, a_n = 0$$

Therefore, the given set of $n$ vectors is linearly independent.

In particular, $\{(1,0,0), (0,1,0), (0,0,1)\}$ is a linearly independent subset of $V_3(F)$.

***Example 33.*** *Prove that the system of three vectors (1, 3, 2), (1, – 7, – 8), (2, 1, – 1) of $V_3(R)$ is linearly dependent.*

**Solution.** Let a, b, c be scalars *i.e.*, real numbers such that

$$a(1,3,2) + b(1,-7,-8) + c(2,1,-1) = (0,0,0)$$
$$\Rightarrow (a+b+2c, 3a-7b+c, 2a-8b-c) = (0,0,0)$$

$\therefore$ $a + b + 2c = 0$ ...(i)

$3a - 7b + c = 0$ ...(ii)

and $2a - 8b - c = 0$ ...(iii)

The coefficient matrix A of the system of Eqs. (i), (ii) and (iii) is

$$A = \begin{bmatrix} 1 & 1 & 2 \\ 3 & -7 & 1 \\ 2 & -8 & -1 \end{bmatrix}$$

We have, $\det(A) = \begin{vmatrix} 1 & 1 & 2 \\ 3 & -7 & 1 \\ 2 & -8 & -1 \end{vmatrix} \begin{matrix} C_2 \to C_2 - C_1 \\ C_3 \to C_3 - 2C_1 \end{matrix}$

$$= \begin{vmatrix} 1 & 0 & 0 \\ 3 & -10 & -5 \\ 2 & -10 & -5 \end{vmatrix} = 50 - 50 = 0$$

$\therefore$ Rank $A < 3 \Rightarrow$ rank $A <$ number of unknowns $a, b, c$ in the Eqs. (i), (ii) and (iii)

Therefore, the Eqs. (i), (ii) and (iii) must possess a non-zero solution. Therefore, the given vectors are linearly dependent.

***Example 34.*** *If α, β and γ are linearly independent vectors of V(F) where F is any subfield of the field of complex numbers, then so also are α + β, β + γ, γ + α.*

**Solution.** Let a, b, c be scalars such that

$$a(\alpha+\beta) + b(\beta+\gamma) + c(\gamma+\alpha) = 0$$

$\Rightarrow (a+c)\alpha + (a+b)\beta + (b+c)\gamma = 0$ ...(i)

But α, β and γ are linearly independent. Therefore, from Eq. (i), we have

$$a + 0\cdot b + c = 0,\ a + b + 0\cdot c = 0,\ 0\cdot a + b + c = 0$$

The coefficient matrix A of these equations is

$$A = \begin{bmatrix} 1 & 0 & 1 \\ 1 & 1 & 0 \\ 0 & 1 & 1 \end{bmatrix}$$

We have rank $A = 3$ *i.e.*, the number of unknowns $a, b, c$. Therefore, $a = 0, b = 0, c = 0$ is the only solution of the given equations.

Hence, $\alpha+\beta, \beta+\gamma, \gamma+\alpha$ are also linearly independent.

***Theorem 5*** Let V(F) be a vector space. If $\alpha_1, \alpha_2, \ldots, \alpha_n$ are non-zero vectors $\in V$, then either they are linearly independent or some $\alpha_k, 2 \le k \le n$, is a linear combination of the preceding ones $\alpha_1, \alpha_2, \alpha_3, \ldots, \alpha_{k-1}$.

***Theorem 6*** If in a vector space V(F); a vector β is a linear combination of the set of vectors $\alpha_1, \alpha_2, \ldots, \alpha_n$, then the set of vectors $\beta, \alpha_1, \alpha_2, \alpha_3, \ldots, \alpha_n$ is linearly dependent.

***Theorem 7*** The set of non-zero vectors $\alpha_1, \alpha_2, \alpha_3, \ldots, \alpha_n$ of V(F) is linearly dependent if some $\alpha_k, 2 \le k \le n$, is a linear combination of the preceding ones $\alpha_1, \alpha_2, \alpha_3, \ldots, \alpha_{k-1}$.

***Theorem 8*** The set of non-zero vectors $\alpha_1, \alpha_2, \ldots, \alpha_n$ of V(F) is linearly dependent if and only if one of these vectors is a linear combination of the remaining $(n - 1)$ vectors.

***Theorem 9*** Let S be a linearly independent subset of a vector space V. Suppose, β is a vector in V which is not in the subspace spanned by S. Then, the set obtained by adjoining β to S is linearly independent.

## Basis of a Vector Space

A subset S of a vector space V(F) is said to be a basis of V(F), if

**(i)** S consists of linearly independent vectors.

**(ii)** S generates V(F) *i.e.*, $L(S) = V$, each vector in V is a linear combination of a finite number of elements of S.

***Example 35.*** *A system S consisting of n vectors $e_1 = (1,0,0,0,\ldots,0)$, $e_2 = (0,1,0,0,\ldots,0), \ldots,$ $e_n = (0,0,0,\ldots,0,1)$ is a basis of $V_n(F)$.*

**Solution.** First of all we shall show that S is a linearly independent set of vectors.

If $a_1, a_2, \ldots, a_n$ be any scalars, then

$$a_1e_1 + a_2e_2 + a_3e_3 + \ldots + a_ne_n = 0$$
$$\Rightarrow a_1(1,0,0,\ldots,0) + a_2(0,1,0,\ldots,0) + \ldots + a_n(0,0,\ldots,0,1) = 0$$
$$\Rightarrow (a_1, a_2, \ldots, a_n) = (0,0,\ldots,0) \Rightarrow a_1 = 0, a_2 = 0, \ldots, a_n = 0$$

$\therefore$ The given set fo $n$ vectors is linearly independent.

Now, we shall show that $L(S) = V_n(F)$. We have always, $L(S) \subseteq V_n(F)$. So we shall prove that $V_n(F) \subseteq L(S)$ *i.e.*, each vector in $V_n(F)$ is a linear combination of elements of $S$.

Let $\alpha = (a_1, a_2, \dots, a_n)$ be any vector in $V_n(F)$, then we can write

$$(a_1, a_2, a_3, \dots, a_n) = a_1(1, 0, \dots, 0) + a_2(0, 1, \dots, 0) + \dots + a_n(0, 0, \dots, 0, 1)$$

$$\Rightarrow \quad \alpha = a_1e_1 + a_2e_2 + \dots + a_ne_n$$

Therefore, $S$ is a basis of $V_n(F)$. We can call this particular basis the standard basis of $V_n(F)$.

## Finite Dimensional Vector Space

The vector space $V(F)$ is said to be finite dimensional or finitely generated, if there exists a finite subset $S$ of $V$ such that $V = L(S)$.

***Note*** **(a)** The vector space $V_n(F)$ of $n$-tuples is a finite dimensional vector space.

**(b)** The dimension of the zero space {0} is defined to be zero. It is generated by $\phi$.

### Existence of Basis of a Finite Dimensional Vector Space

There exists a basis for each finite dimensional vector space.

### Invarient Theorem For Vector Spaces

If $V(F)$ is a finite dimensional vector space, then any two basis of $V$ have the same number of elements.

### Dimension of a Finitely Generated Vector Space

The number of elements in any basis of a finite dimensional vector space $V(F)$ is called the dimension of the vector space $V(F)$ and will be denoted by $\dim V$.

### Important Theorems on Dimension

1. **Existence Theorem** Every linearly independent subset of a finitely generated vector space $V(F)$ is either a basis of $V$ or can be extended to form a basis of $V$.

   OR

   Every linearly independent subset of a finitely generated vector space $V(F)$ forms a part of a basis of $V$.
2. Let $V$ be a vector space which is spanned by a finite set of vectors $\beta_1, \beta_2, \dots, \beta_m$. Then, any linearly independent set of vectors in $V$ is finite and contains no more than $m$ vectors.
3. Each set of $(n+1)$ or more vectors of a finite dimensional vector space $V(F)$ of dimension $n$ is linearly dependent.
4. If a set $S$ of $n$ vectors of a finite dimensional vector space $V(F)$ of dimension $n$ generates $V(F)$, then $S$ is a basis of $V$.
5. If $V(F)$ is a finite dimensional vector space of dimension $n$, then any set of $n$ linearly independent vectors in $V$ forms a basis of $V$.
6. (Dimension of a subspace) Each subspace $W$ of a finite dimensional vector space $V(F)$ of dimension $n$ is a finite dimensional space with dim $m \le n$.
7. Let $S = \{\alpha_1, \alpha_2, \dots, \alpha_n\}$ be a basis of a finite dimensional vector space $V(F)$ of dimension $n$. Then, every element $\alpha$ of $V$ can be uniquely expressed as $\alpha = a_1\alpha_1 + a_2\alpha_2 + \dots + a_n\alpha_n$ where $a_1 a_2, \dots, a_n \in F$.
8. If $W$ is a subspace of a finite dimensional vector space $V$, every linearly independent subset of $W$ is finite and is part of a finite basis for $W$.
9. If $W_1$ and $W_2$ are two subspaces of a finite dimensional vector space $V(F)$, then
$$\dim(W_1 + W_2) = \dim W_1 + \dim W_2 - \dim(W_1 \cap W_2).$$

***Example* 36.** *Prove that, if* $S = \{\alpha, \beta, \gamma\}$ *is a basis of* $C^3(C)$, *then the set* $S' = \{\alpha+\beta, \beta+\gamma, \gamma+\alpha\}$ *is also a basis of* $C^3(C)$.

**Solution.** The vector space $C^3(C)$ is of dimension 3. Any subset of $C^3$ having three linearly independent vectors will form a basis of $C^3$. We have shown in one of the previous examples that if $S$ is a linearly independent subset of $C^3$, then $S'$ is also a linearly independent subset of $C^3$. Therefore, $S'$ is also a basis of $C^3$.

***Example* 37.** *Prove that the vectors* (1, 2, 1), (2, 1, 0), (1, −1, 2) *form a basis of* $R^3$.

**Solution.** We know that the set {(1, 0, 0), (0, 1, 0), (0, 0, 1)} forms a basis for $R^3$. Therefore, $\dim R^3 = 3$. If we prove that the set $S = \{(1, 2, 1), (2, 1, 0), (1, -1, 2)\}$ is linearly independent, then this set will also form a basis for $R^3$.

Now, we have

$$a_1(1, 2, 1) + a_2(2, 1, 0) + a_3(1, -1, 2) = (0, 0, 0)$$

$$\Rightarrow \quad (a_1 + 2a_2 + a_3, 2a_1 + a_2 - a_3, a_1 + 2a_3) = (0, 0, 0)$$

$\therefore$
$$a_1 + 2a_2 + a_3 = 0 \quad \text{...(i)}$$
$$2a_1 + a_2 - a_3 = 0 \quad \text{...(ii)}$$
$$a_1 + 2a_3 = 0 \quad \text{...(iii)}$$

Solving these equations,

Multiply 2 by Eq. (ii), then subtracting Eq. (ii) from Eq. (i), we have

$$-3a_1 + 3a_3 = 0 \Rightarrow -a_1 + a_3 = 0 \quad \text{...(iv)}$$

On adding Eqs. (iii) and (iv), we get

$$3a_3 = 0 \Rightarrow a_3 = 0$$

Put $a_3 = 0$ in Eq. (iii), we get

$a_1 = 0$, put $a_3 = 0$ and $a_1 = 0$ in Eq. (i), we get $a_2 = 0$

Therefore, on solving Eqs. (i), (ii) and (iii) we get

$a_1 = 0,\ a_2 = 0, a_3 = 0$. Therefore, $S$ is linearly independent. Hence, it forms a basis for $R^3$.

## Homomorphism of Vector Spaces or Linear Transformation

Let $U(F)$ and $V(F)$ be two vector spaces. Then, a mapping $f: U \to V$ is called a homomorphism or a linear transformation of $U$ into $V$, if

**(i)** $f(\alpha + \beta) = f(\alpha) + f(\beta),\ \forall\ \alpha, \beta \in U$

**(ii)** $f(a\alpha) = af(\alpha),\ \forall\ a \in F, \forall\ \alpha \in U$

The conditions (i) and (ii) can be combined into a single condition.

$$f(a\alpha + b\beta) = af(\alpha) + bf(\beta),\ \forall\ a, b \in F \text{ and } \alpha, \beta \in U$$

If $f$ is a homomorphism of $U$ onto $V$, then $V$ is called a homomorphic image of $U$.

> **Note** If $f$ is a homomorphism of $U(F)$ into $V(F)$, then
> (i) $f(0) = 0'$ where 0 and $0'$ are the zero vectors of $U$ and $V$ respectively.
> (ii) $f(-\alpha) = -f(\alpha),\ \forall\ \alpha \in U$.

## Isomorphism of Vector Spaces

Let $U(F)$ and $V(F)$ be two vector spaces. Then, a mapping $f: U \to V$ is called an isomorphism of $U$ onto $V$, if

**(i)** $f$ is one-one

**(ii)** $f$ is onto

**(iii)** $F(a\alpha + b\beta) = af(\alpha) + bf(\beta),\ \forall\ a, b \in F$ and $\alpha, \beta \in V$

Also, then the two vector spaces $U$ and $V$ are said to be isomorphic and symbolically we write $U(F) \underline{f} V(F)$. The vector space $V(F)$ is also called the isomorphic image of the vector space $U(F)$.

If $f$ is a homomorphism of $U(F)$ into $V(F)$, then $f$ will become an isomorphism of $U$ into $V$ if $f$ is one-one. Also, in addition if $f$ is onto $V$, then $f$ will become an isomorphism of $U$ onto $V$.

## Important Theorems on Homomorphism

***Theorem 1*** Two finite dimensional vector spaces over the same field are isomorphic iff they are of same dimension.

***Theorem 2*** Every $n$-dimensional vector space $V(F)$ is isomorphic to $V_n(F)$.

***Example 38.*** *Let $V(R)$ be the vector space of all complex numbers $a + ib$ over the field of reals $R$ and let $T$ be a mapping from $V(R)$ to $V_2(R)$ defined as $T(a + ib) = (a, b)$, then prove that $T$ is an isomorphism.*

**Solution.** ***T* is one-one**

Suppose, $\alpha = a + ib, \beta = c + id$ be any two members of $V(R)$. Then, $a, b, c, d \in R$.

We have, $T(\alpha) = T(\beta) \Rightarrow (a, b) = (c, d) \quad [\because\ T(\alpha) = (a, b)]$

$$\Rightarrow a = c, b = d \Rightarrow \alpha = \beta$$

$\therefore$ $T$ is one-one.

***T* is onto**

Let $(a, b)$ be an arbitrary member of $V_2(R)$, then $\exists$ a vector $a + ib \in V(R)$ such that $T(a + ib) = (a, b)$. Therefore, $T$ is onto.

***T* is a Linear Transformation**

Let $\alpha = a + ib, \beta = c + id$ be any two members of $V(R)$ and $m_1, m_2$ be any two elements of the field $R$. Then, we have

$$m_1\alpha + m_2\beta = m_1(a + ib) + m_2(c + id) = (m_1a + m_2c) + i(m_1b + m_2d)$$

Now, we have

$$T(m_1\alpha + m_2\beta) = (m_1a + m_2c, m_1b + m_2d) \quad \text{[by the definition of } T]$$
$$= (m_1a, m_1b) + (m_2c, m_2d)$$
$$= m_1T(a + ib) + m_2T(c + id) \quad \text{[by the definition of } T]$$
$$= m_1T(\alpha) + m_2T(\beta)$$

Therefore, $T$ is a linear Transformation

Hence, $T$ is an isomorphism.

***Example 39.*** *Prove that the mapping $f: V_3(F) \to V_2(F)$ defined by $f(a_1, a_2, a_3) = (a_1, a_2)$ is a homomorphism of $V_3(F)$ onto $V_2(F)$.*

**Solution.** Suppose, $\alpha = (a_1, a_2, a_3)$ and $\beta = (b_1, b_2, b_3)$ be any two elements $V_3(F)$. Also, let $a, b$ be any two elements of $F$.

Now, we have

$$f(a\alpha + b\beta) = f[a(a_1, a_2, a_3) + b(b_1, b_2, b_3)]$$
$$= f[(aa_1 + bb_1, aa_2 + bb_2, aa_3 + bb_3)]$$
$$= (aa_1 + bb_1, aa_2 + bb_2)$$
$$= a(a_1, a_2) + b(b_1, b_2) = af(a_1, a_2, a_3) + bf(b_1, b_2, b_3)$$
$$= af(\alpha) + bf(\beta)$$

$\therefore$ $f$ is a linear transformation.

Now, we shall show that $f$ is onto $V_2(F)$.

Suppose, $(a_1, a_2)$ be any element of $V_2(F)$. Then, since $(a_1, a_2, 0) \in V_3(F)$ and therefore $f(a_1, a_2, 0) = (a_1, a_2)$

$\Rightarrow$ $f$ is onto $V_2(F)$.

Hence, $f$ is a homomorphism of $V_3(F)$ onto $V_2(F)$.

## Quotient Space

Suppose, $W$ be any subspace of a vector space $V(F)$ and let $\alpha$ be any element of $V$. Then, the set $W + \alpha = \{l + \alpha : l \in W\}$ is called a right coset of $W$ in $V$ generated by $\alpha$.
Similarly, $\alpha + W = \{\alpha + l : l \in W\}$ is called a left coset of $W$ in $V$ generated by $\alpha$.
Definitely, $W + \alpha$ and $\alpha + W$ are both subsets of $V$. As addition in $V$ is commutative, therefore we have $W + \alpha = \alpha + W$.
Thus, we can call $W + \alpha$ as simply a coset of $W$ in $V$ generated by $\alpha$.

> **Note** (a) We have, $0 \in V$ and $W + 0 = W$
> $\therefore$ $W$ itself is a coset of $W$ in $V$.
>
> (b) $\alpha \in W \Rightarrow W + \alpha = W$
>
> (c) If $W + \alpha$ and $W + \beta$ are two cosets of $W$ in $V$, then $W + \alpha = W + \beta \Leftrightarrow \alpha - \beta \in W$.

## Important Theorems on Quotient Space

***Theorem 1*** *If $W$ is any subspace of a vector space $V(F)$, then the set $V/W$ of all cosets $W + \alpha$, where $\alpha$ be any arbitrary element of $V$, is a vector space over $F$ for the addition and scalar multiplication composition defined as*

**(i)** $(W + \alpha) + (W + \beta) = W + (\alpha + \beta), \forall \alpha, \beta \in V$

**(ii)** $a(W + \alpha) = W + a\alpha, \forall \alpha \in V$ and $a \in F$

***Theorem 2*** If $W$ be a subspace of a finite dimensional vector space $V(F)$, then $\dim V/W = \dim V - \dim W$.

## Direct Sum of Spaces

Let $V(F)$ be a vector space and suppose $W_1, W_2, W_3, \ldots, W_m$ be subspaces of $V$. Then, $V$ is said to be the direct sum of $W_1, W_2, W_3, \ldots, W_m$, if every element $\alpha \in V$ can be written in one and only one way as $\alpha = \alpha_1 + \alpha_2 + \alpha_3 + \ldots + \alpha_m$, where $\alpha_1 \in W_1, \alpha_2 \in W_2, \alpha_3 \in W_3, \ldots, \alpha_m \in W_m$

> **Note** If a vector space $V(F)$ is the direct sum of its two subspaces $W_1$ and $W_2$, then we must have not only $V = W_1 + W_2$ but also each vector of $V$ can be uniquely expressed as the sum of an element of $W_1$ and an element of $W_2$. Direct sum, symbolically represented by $V = W_1 \oplus W_2$.

e.g., Suppose, $W_1 = \{(a, b, 0) : a, b \in R\}$ and
$W_2 = \{(0, 0, c) : c \in R\}$ be two subspaces of $R^3$.
Any vector $(a, b, c) \in R^3$ can be uniquely expressed as the sum of a vector in $W_1$ and a vector in
$W_2 : (a, b, c) = (a, b, 0) + (0, 0, c)$

$\therefore$ $R^3$ is the direct sum of $W_1$ and $W_2$.

Also, we see that the only element common to both $W_1$ and $W_2$ is the zero vector $(0, 0, 0)$.

### Disjoint Subspaces

Two subspaces $W_1$ and $W_2$ of vector space $V(F)$ are called disjoint if their intersection is the zero subspace means, if $W_1 \cap W_2 = \{0\}$.

***Theorem*** The necessary and sufficient conditions for a vector space $V(F)$ to be a direct sum of its two subspaces $W_1$ and $W_2$ are that

**(i)** $V = W_1 + W_2$

**(ii)** $W_1 \cap W_2 = \{0\}$

$\Rightarrow$ $W_1$ and $W_2$ are disjoint.

### Dimension of a Direct Sum

If a finite dimensional vector space $V(F)$ is a direct sum of two subspaces $W_1$ and $W_2$, then $\dim V = \dim W_1 + \dim W_2$

***Theorem*** Suppose, $V$ be a finite dimensional vector space and suppose $W_1, W_2$ be subspaces of $V$ such that $V = W_1 + W_2$ and $\dim V = \dim W_1 + \dim W_2$, then we have $V = W_1 \oplus W_2$.

### Complementary Subspaces

Let $V(F)$ be a vector space and $W_1, W_2$ be two subspaces of $V$. Then, the subspace $W_2$ is said to the complement of $W_1$ in $V$, if $V$ is the direct sum of $W_1$ and $W_2$.

## Important Theorems on Direct Sum

***Theorem 1*** Corresponding to each subspace $W_1$ of a finite dimensional vector space $V(F)$, there exists a subspace $W_2$ such that $V$ is the direct sum of $W_1$ and $W_2$.

***Theorem 2*** If $W_1$ and $W_2$ are complementary subspaces of a vector space $V$, then the mapping $f$ which assigns to each vector $\beta$ in $W_2$ the coset $W_1 + \beta$ is an isomorphism between $W_2$ and $V/W_1$.

***Theorem 3*** If $W$ is an $m$-dimensional subspace of an $n$-dimensional vector space $V$, then the dimension of the quotient space $V/W$ is $n$-$m$.

### Independence of Subspaces

Suppose, $W_1, W_2, \ldots, W_m$ are subspaces of the vector space $V$. Then, we can say that $W_1, W_2, W_3, \ldots, W_m$ are independent, if $\alpha_1 + \alpha_2 + \ldots + \alpha_m = 0, \alpha_i \in W_i \Rightarrow$ Each $\alpha_i = 0$.

***Theorem 1*** Let $V(F)$ be a vector space. Let $W_1, W_2, W_3, \ldots, W_m$ be subspaces of $V$ and let $W_1 + W_2 + W_3 + \ldots + W_m$ are independent, then we have

**(i)** $W_1, W_2, W_3, \ldots, W_m$ are independent.

**(ii)** Each vector $\alpha$ in $W$ can be uniquely expressed in the form $\alpha = \alpha_1 + \alpha_2 + \alpha_3 + \ldots + \alpha_m$ with $\alpha_i$ in $W_i; i = 1, 2, \ldots, m$.

**(iii)** For each $j$, $2 \le j \le m$ the subspace $W_j$ is disjoint from the sum $(W_1 + W_2 + \ldots + W_{j-1})$.

> **Note** If any (and hence all) of the three conditions of the above theorem holds for $W_1, W_2, \ldots, W_k$, then we shall say that $W$ is the direct sum of $W_1, W_2, \ldots, W_m$ and we can write $W = W_1 \oplus W_2 \oplus \ldots \oplus W_m$.

***Theorem 2*** Suppose, $V(F)$ be a vector space. Suppose, $W_1, W_2, \ldots, W_n$ be subspaces of $V$. Let $V = W_1 + W_2 + \ldots + W_n$ and that $W_i \cap (W_1 + W_2 + \ldots + W_{i-1} + W_{i+1} + \ldots + W_n) = \{0\}$ for every $i = 1, 2, 3, \ldots, n$. Then, $V$ is the direct sum of $W_1, W_2, \ldots, W_n$.

***Theorem 3*** Let $V(F)$ be a finite dimensional vector space and let $W_1, W_2, \ldots, W_m$ be subspaces of $V$. Then, the following two statements are equivalent.

**(i)** $V$ is the direct sum of $W_1, W_2, \ldots, W_m$.

**(ii)** If $B_i$ is a basis of $W_i, i = 1, 2, \ldots, m$ then the union $B = \bigcup_{i=1}^{m} B_i$ is also a basis for $V$.

> **Note** If a finite dimensional vector space $V(F)$ is the direct sum of its subspaces $W_1, W_2, \ldots, W_m$, then
> $$\dim V = \dim W_1 + \dim W_2 + \ldots + \dim W_m$$

***Example 40.*** *If $W_1 = \{(x, 0, z) : x, z \in R\}$, $W_2 = \{(0, y, z) : y, z \in R\}$ be two subspaces of $R^3$, then prove that $R^3 = W_1 + W_2$ but $R^3 \ne W_1 \oplus W_2$.*

**Solution.** We show that any $(x, y, z) \in R^3$ may be written as a sum of a vector of $W_1$ and a vector of $W_2$

We have, $(x, y, z) = \left(x, 0, \frac{z}{2}\right) + \left(0, y, \frac{z}{2}\right)$

where, $\left(x, 0, \frac{z}{2}\right) \in W_1$ and $\left(0, y, \frac{z}{2}\right) \in W_2$

Therefore, $R^3 = W_1 + W_2$

Now, we have $(x, y, z) = \left(x, 0, \frac{z}{4}\right) + \left(0, y, \frac{3}{4}z\right)$

where $\left(x, 0, \frac{z}{4}\right) \in W_1$ and $\left(0, y, \frac{3}{4}z\right) \in W_2$

Which follows that representation of $(x, y, z)$ as a sum of a vector of $W_1$ and a vector of $W_2$ is not unique.

Therefore, $R^3 \ne W_1 \oplus W_3$.

# Coordinates

Let $V(F)$ be a finite dimensional vector space. Let $B = \{\alpha_1, \alpha_2, \alpha_3, \ldots, \alpha_n\}$ be an ordered basis for $V$. By an ordered basis we mean that the vectors of $B$ have been enumerate in some well defined way. This implies that the vectors occupying the first, second, third,..., $n$th places in the set $B$ are fixed.

Let $\alpha \in V$. Then, $\exists$ a unique $n$-tuple $(x_1, x_2, \ldots, x_n)$ of scalars such that

$$\alpha = x_1\alpha_1 + x_2\alpha_2 + \ldots + x_n\alpha_n = \sum_{i=1}^{n} x_i\alpha_i$$

The $n$-tuple $(x_1, x_2, \ldots, x_n)$ is called the $n$-tuple of coordinates of $\alpha$ relative to the ordered basis $B$. The scalar $x_i$ is called the $i$th coordinate of $\alpha$ relative to the ordered basis $B$. The $n \times 1$

$$\text{matrix } X = \begin{bmatrix} x_1 \\ x_2 \\ x_3 \\ \vdots \\ x_n \end{bmatrix}$$

is called the coordinated matrix of $\alpha$ relative to the ordered basis $B$.

The coordinate matrix of the vector $\alpha$ relative to the ordered basis is denoted by $[\alpha]_B$.

> **Note** If $V(F)$ is a vector space of dimension $n$, then coordinate vector of $0 \in V$ relative to any basis of $V$ is always the zero $n$-tuple $(0, 0, 0, \ldots, 0)$.

***Example 41.*** *Find the coordinates of the vector $(2, 1, -6)$ of $R^3$ relative to the basis*

$$\alpha_1 = (1, 1, 2), \alpha_2 = (3, -1, 0), \alpha_3 = (2, 0, -1)$$

**Solution.** For this, we shall express the vector $(2, 1, -6)$ as the linear combination of the vectors $\alpha_1, \alpha_2, \alpha_3$. Suppose, $l, m, n$ be scalars in $R$ such that

$\Rightarrow \quad (2, 1, -6) = l\alpha_1 + m\alpha_2 + n\alpha_3$

$\Rightarrow \quad (2, 1, -6) = l(1, 1, 2) + m(3, -1, 0) + n(2, 0, -1)$

$\Rightarrow \quad (2, 1, -6) = (l + 3m + 2n, l - m, 2l - n)$

$\Rightarrow \quad l + 3m + 2n = 2, \quad$ ...(i)

$l - m = 1 \quad$ ...(ii)

and $\quad 2l - n = -6 \quad$ ...(iii)

On solving Eqs. (i), (ii) and (iii), we get

$l = -7/8, \ m = -15/8, \ n = 17/4$

Therefore, the required coordinates of the vector $(2, 1, -6)$ relative to the ordered basis $\{\alpha_1, \alpha_2, \alpha_3\}$ are $(l, m, n)$ means $(-7/8, -15/8, 17/4)$.

# SOLVED EXAMPLES

## Type I (*Only one correct option*)

***Example 1.*** *For which value of x will the matrix given below become singular?*

$$\begin{bmatrix} 8 & x & 0 \\ 4 & 0 & 2 \\ 12 & 6 & 0 \end{bmatrix}$$

(a) 4 (b) 6
(c) 8 (d) 12

**Solution.** (a) Since, a matrix is said to be singular, if $|A| = 0$

$$\Rightarrow \quad \begin{vmatrix} 8 & x & 0 \\ 4 & 0 & 2 \\ 12 & 6 & 0 \end{vmatrix} = 0$$

$$\Rightarrow \quad 8(0-12) - x(0-24) + 0(24-0) = 0$$

$$\Rightarrow \quad x = 4$$

***Example 2.*** *Real matrices* $[A]_{3\times1}, [B]_{3\times3}, [C]_{3\times5}, [D]_{5\times3}, [E]_{5\times5}$ *and* $[F]_{5\times1}$ *are given.*
*Matrices [B] and [E] are symmetric.*
*Following statements are made with respect to these matrices*

(i) *Matrix product* $[F]^T[C]^T[B][C][F]$ *is a scalar.*

(ii) *Matrix product* $[D]^T[F][D]$ *is always symmetric.*

*With reference to above statements, which of the following applies?*

(a) Statement (i) is true but (ii) is false.
(b) Statement (i) is false but (ii) is true.
(c) Both the statements are true.
(d) Both the statements are false.

**Solution.** (d) Both the statements are false. (i) is false because the product of two or more matrices is always a matrix and statement $[D]^T[F][D]$ does not exist because it is not compitable for matrix product. Hence, the statement (ii) is also false.

***Example 3.*** *If* $A = \begin{bmatrix} -5 & -8 & 0 \\ 3 & 5 & 0 \\ 1 & 2 & -1 \end{bmatrix}$, *then* $A^2$ *is*

(a) idempotent (b) nilpotent
(c) involutory (d) periodic

**Solution.** (c) $\because \; A^2 = \begin{bmatrix} -5 & -8 & 0 \\ 3 & 5 & 0 \\ 1 & 2 & -1 \end{bmatrix}\begin{bmatrix} -5 & -8 & 0 \\ 3 & 5 & 0 \\ 1 & 2 & -1 \end{bmatrix}$

$$= \begin{bmatrix} 1 & 0 & 0 \\ 0 & 1 & 0 \\ 0 & 0 & 1 \end{bmatrix} = I$$

Hence, $A^2$ is involutory.

***Example 4.*** *Let* $f(x) = x^2 - 5x + 6$, *and* $A = \begin{bmatrix} 2 & 0 & 1 \\ 2 & 1 & 3 \\ 1 & -1 & 0 \end{bmatrix}$, *then* $f(A)$ *is equal to*

(a) $\begin{bmatrix} 1 & -1 & -3 \\ -1 & -1 & -10 \\ -5 & 4 & 4 \end{bmatrix}$ (b) $\begin{bmatrix} 1 & -1 & -5 \\ -1 & -1 & 4 \\ -3 & -10 & 4 \end{bmatrix}$

(c) $\begin{bmatrix} 1 & -1 & 4 \\ -1 & 4 & -10 \\ 4 & -3 & -5 \end{bmatrix}$ (d) None of these

**Solution.** (a) $\because \; f(A) = A^2 - 5A + 6I$

$$= \begin{bmatrix} 2 & 0 & 1 \\ 2 & 1 & 3 \\ 1 & -1 & 0 \end{bmatrix}\begin{bmatrix} 2 & 0 & 1 \\ 2 & 1 & 3 \\ 1 & -1 & 0 \end{bmatrix} - 5\begin{bmatrix} 2 & 0 & 1 \\ 2 & 1 & 3 \\ 1 & -1 & 0 \end{bmatrix} + 6\begin{bmatrix} 1 & 0 & 0 \\ 0 & 1 & 0 \\ 0 & 0 & 1 \end{bmatrix}$$

$$= \begin{bmatrix} 1 & -1 & -3 \\ -1 & -1 & -10 \\ -5 & 4 & 4 \end{bmatrix}$$

***Example 5.*** $X = [X_1 \; X_2 \; \dots \; X_n]'$ *is an n-tuple non-zero vector. The* $n \times n$ *matrix* $V = XX'$

(a) has rank zero (b) has rank 1
(c) is orthogonal (d) has rank $n$

**Solution.** (b) $\because \; X = [X_1 \; X_2 \; \dots \; X_n]'$

$$V = XX' = \begin{bmatrix} X_1 \\ X_2 \\ \vdots \\ X_n \end{bmatrix}[X_1 \; X_2 \; \dots \; X_n]$$

$$= \begin{bmatrix} X_1^2 & X_1X_2 & X_1X_3 & \dots & X_1X_n \\ X_2X_1 & X_2^2 & X_2X_3 & \dots & X_2X_n \\ X_3X_1 & X_3X_2 & X_3^2 & \dots & X_3X_n \\ \vdots & \vdots & \vdots & & \vdots \\ X_nX_1 & X_nX_2 & X_nX_3 & \dots & X_n^2 \end{bmatrix}$$

Now, if we perform following elementary operations on above $(\because X_1, X_2, \dots, X_n \neq 0)$

$$R_2 \to \frac{R_2}{X_2} - \frac{R_1}{X_1}$$

$$R_3 \to \frac{R_3}{X_3} - \frac{R_1}{X_1}$$

$$\dots\dots\dots\dots\dots$$

$$R_n \to \frac{R_n}{X_n} - \frac{R_1}{X_1}$$

We get $\begin{bmatrix} x_1^2 & x_1x_2 & x_1x_3 & \dots & x_1x_n \\ 0 & 0 & 0 & \dots & 0 \\ 0 & 0 & 0 & \dots & 0 \\ \dots & \dots & \dots & \dots & \dots \\ 0 & 0 & 0 & \dots & 0 \end{bmatrix}$

$\because \quad x_1^2 \neq 0$

Hence, rank of matrix $= 1$

***Example 6.*** *Consider a non-homogeneous system of linear equations representing mathematically an over determined system. Such a system will be*

(a) consistent having a unique solution
(b) consistent having many solutions
(c) inconsistent having no solution
(d) All of the above

**Solution.** (d)

In an over determined system having more equations than variables all three possibilities can exist

(a) Consistent and unique, if $r = n$
(b) Consistent and infinite, if Rank of $\tilde{A}$ = Rank of $A \neq$ number of unknowns
(c) inconsistent and no solution, if Rank of $[A : B] \neq$ Rank of $[A]$.

***Example 7.*** *Consider the system of equations $A_{(n\times n)}X_{(n\times t)} = \lambda(n \times l)$ where, $\lambda$ is a scalar. Let, $(\lambda_i, x_i)$ be an eigen pair of an eigen value and its corresponding eigen vector for real matrix A. Let I be a $(n \times n)$ unit matrix. Which one of the following statements is not correct?*

(a) For a homogeneous $n \times n$ system of linear equations, $(A - \lambda I)x = 0$ having a non-trivial solution, the rank of $(A - \lambda I)$ is less than $n$.
(b) For matrix $A^m$, $m$ being a positive integer, $(\lambda_i^m, x_i^m)$ will be the eigen pair for all $i$.
(c) If $A^T = A^{-1}$, then $|\lambda_i| = 1$ for all $i$
(d) If $A^T = A$, then $\lambda_i$ is real for all $i$.

**Solution.** (b) For matrix $A^m$, $m$ being a positive integer $(\lambda_i^m X_i^m)$ will be the eigen pair for all $i$.

Although $\lambda_i^m$ will be the corresponding eigen values of $A^m$, $X_i^m$ will not be corresponding eigen vectors.

***Example 8.*** *Eigen values of a matrix $S = \begin{bmatrix} 3 & 2 \\ 2 & 3 \end{bmatrix}$ are 5 and 1.*

*What is the eigen values of the matrix $S^2 = SS$?*

(a) 1 and 25 (b) 6 and 4
(c) 5 and 1 (d) 2 and 10

**Solution.** (a) $\because$ If $\lambda_1, \lambda_2, \dots, \lambda_n$ are the eigen values of $A$, then the eigen values of $A^m$ are $\lambda_1^m, \lambda_2^m, \dots, \lambda_n^m$.

$\because$ S has eigen values 1 and 5, so $S^2$ has eigen values $1^2$ and $5^2$.

$\Rightarrow \quad$ 1 and 25

***Example 9.*** *If A is non-scalar, non-identity idempotent matrix of order $n \geq 2$. Then, minimal polynomial $m_A(x)$ is*

(a) $x(x-1)$ (b) $x(x+1)$
(c) $x(1-x)$ (d) $x^2(1+x)$

**Solution.** (a) We have,

$$A^2 = A$$
$$\Rightarrow \quad A^2 - A = 0$$
$$\Rightarrow \quad m_A(x) = x^2 - x = x(x-1)$$

***Example 10.*** *If A is non-scalar, non-identity involutory matrix, then minimal polynomial $m_A(x)$ is*

(a) $x(x-1)$ (b) $(x-1)(x+1)$
(c) $x(1-x)$ (d) $x+1$

**Solution.** (b) We have,

$$A^2 = I$$
$$\Rightarrow \quad A^2 - I = 0$$
$$\Rightarrow \quad m_A(x) = x^2 - 1 = (x-1)(x+1)$$

***Example 11.*** *All the four entries of the $2 \times 2$ matrix $P = \begin{bmatrix} p_{11} & p_{12} \\ p_{21} & p_{22} \end{bmatrix}$ are non-zero, and one of its eigen values is zero. Which one of the following statements is true?*

(a) $p_{11}p_{22} - p_{12}p_{21} = 1$ (b) $p_{11}p_{22} - p_{12}p_{21} = -1$
(c) $p_{11}p_{22} - p_{12}p_{21} = 0$ (d) $p_{11}p_{22} + p_{12}p_{21} = 0$

**Solution.** (c) $\because$ All entries of given matrix are non-zero, then $|P| = 0$.

or $$\begin{vmatrix} p_{11} & p_{12} \\ p_{21} & p_{22} \end{vmatrix} = 0$$

$$\Rightarrow \quad p_{11}p_{22} - p_{12}p_{21} = 0$$

***Example 12.*** *In the matrix equation $PX = q$, which of the following is a necessary condition for the existence of atleast one solution for the unknown vector.*

(a) Augmented matrix $[pq]$ must have the same rank as matrix $p$.
(b) Vector $q$ must have only non-zero elements.
(c) Matrix $p$ must be singular.
(d) Matrix $p$ must be square.

**Solution.** (a) $\because$ Rank $[pq]$ = Rank $[p]$ is necessary for existence of atleast one solution.

***Example 13.*** *The square matrix A is defined as*

$$A = \begin{bmatrix} 1 & 2 & -2 \\ 1 & 2 & 1 \\ -1 & -1 & 0 \end{bmatrix}$$, *the diagonal matrix D of A is*

(a) $\begin{bmatrix} 1 & 0 & 0 \\ 0 & 2 & 0 \\ 0 & 0 & 3 \end{bmatrix}$ (b) $\begin{bmatrix} 0 & 0 & 0 \\ 0 & -1 & 0 \\ 0 & 0 & 2 \end{bmatrix}$

(c) $\begin{bmatrix} 1 & 0 & 0 \\ 0 & -1 & 0 \\ 0 & 0 & 3 \end{bmatrix}$ (d) $\begin{bmatrix} 3 & 0 & 0 \\ 0 & 1 & 0 \\ 0 & 0 & 8 \end{bmatrix}$

**Solution.** (c) The characteristic roots are $|A-\lambda I|=0$

$$\Rightarrow \begin{vmatrix} 1-\lambda & 2 & -2 \\ 1 & 2-\lambda & 1 \\ -1 & -1 & -\lambda \end{vmatrix} = 0$$

$$\Rightarrow (1-\lambda)\begin{vmatrix} 2-\lambda & 1 \\ -1 & -\lambda \end{vmatrix} - 2\begin{vmatrix} 1 & 1 \\ -1 & -\lambda \end{vmatrix} - 2\begin{vmatrix} 1 & 2-\lambda \\ -1 & -1 \end{vmatrix} = 0$$

$$\Rightarrow (1-\lambda)\{(2-\lambda)X-\lambda+1\}-2\{-\lambda+1\}-2\{-1+2-\lambda\}=0$$

$$\Rightarrow (1-\lambda)[-2\lambda+\lambda^2+1]-2(1-\lambda)-2(1-\lambda)=0$$

$$\Rightarrow (1-\lambda)[\lambda^2-2\lambda+1-4]=0$$

$$\Rightarrow \lambda = 1, -1, 3$$

Now, eigen vectors

At $\lambda = 1 \Rightarrow [A-I]X_1 = 0$

$$\begin{bmatrix} 0 & 2 & -2 \\ 1 & 1 & 1 \\ -1 & -1 & -1 \end{bmatrix}\begin{bmatrix} x_1 \\ x_2 \\ x_3 \end{bmatrix} = \begin{bmatrix} 0 \\ 0 \\ 0 \end{bmatrix}$$

$$\Rightarrow x_2 - x_3 = 0 \Rightarrow x_2 = x_3$$

$$\Rightarrow x_1 + x_2 + x_3 = 0 \Rightarrow x_1 = -2x_3$$

$$\Rightarrow X_1 = \begin{bmatrix} -2 \\ 1 \\ 1 \end{bmatrix}$$

At $\lambda = -1 \Rightarrow [A+I]X_2 = 0$

$$\Rightarrow \begin{bmatrix} 2 & 2 & -2 \\ 1 & 3 & 1 \\ -1 & -1 & 1 \end{bmatrix}\begin{bmatrix} x_1 \\ x_2 \\ x_3 \end{bmatrix} = \begin{bmatrix} 0 \\ 0 \\ 0 \end{bmatrix}$$

$$\Rightarrow \left.\begin{aligned} x_1 + x_2 - x_3 &= 0 \\ x_1 + 3x_2 + x_3 &= 0 \end{aligned}\right\}$$

$$\Rightarrow 2x_1 + 4x_2 = 0$$

$$\Rightarrow 2x_2 = -x_1 \Rightarrow x_3 = x_2$$

$$\Rightarrow X_2 = \begin{bmatrix} -2 \\ 1 \\ 1 \end{bmatrix}$$

At $\lambda = 3 \Rightarrow [A-3I]X_3 = 0$

$$\Rightarrow \begin{bmatrix} -2 & 2 & -2 \\ 1 & -1 & 1 \\ -1 & -1 & -3 \end{bmatrix}\begin{bmatrix} x_1 \\ x_2 \\ x_3 \end{bmatrix} = \begin{bmatrix} 0 \\ 0 \\ 0 \end{bmatrix}$$

$$\Rightarrow \left.\begin{aligned} x_1 - x_2 + x_3 &= 0 \\ -x_1 - x_2 - 3x_3 &= 0 \end{aligned}\right\}$$

$$\Rightarrow -2x_2 - 2x_3 = 0$$

$$\Rightarrow x_3 = -x_2$$

$$\Rightarrow x_1 = 2x_2$$

$$\Rightarrow X_3 = \begin{bmatrix} -2 \\ -1 \\ 1 \end{bmatrix}$$

So, model matrix

$$P = [X_1 \quad X_2 \quad X_3] = \begin{bmatrix} -2 & -2 & -2 \\ 1 & 1 & -1 \\ 1 & 1 & 1 \end{bmatrix}$$

So, diagonal matrix of

$$A = D = \begin{bmatrix} \lambda_1 & 0 & 0 \\ 0 & \lambda_2 & 0 \\ 0 & 0 & \lambda_3 \end{bmatrix} = \begin{bmatrix} 1 & 0 & 0 \\ 0 & -1 & 0 \\ 0 & 0 & 3 \end{bmatrix}$$

***Example 14.*** *The rank of the following $(n+1)\times(n+1)$ matrix where a is real number*

$$\begin{bmatrix} 1 & a & a^2 & \dots & a^n \\ 1 & a & a^2 & \dots & a^n \\ \vdots & \vdots & \vdots & & \vdots \\ 1 & a & a^2 & \dots & a^n \end{bmatrix} \textit{ is}$$

(a) 1 (b) 2

(c) $n$ (d) Depends on 'a'

**Solution.** (a) Given matrix is

$$A = \begin{bmatrix} 1 & a & a^2 & \dots & a^n \\ 1 & a & a^2 & \dots & a^n \\ \dots & \dots & \dots & \dots & \dots \\ \dots & \dots & \dots & \dots & \dots \\ \dots & \dots & \dots & \dots & \dots \\ \dots & \dots & \dots & \dots & \dots \\ 1 & a & a^2 & \dots & a^n \end{bmatrix}_{(n+1)\times(n+1)}$$

Applying the following row operation, we get

$$R_2 \to R_2 - R_1$$
$$R_3 \to R_3 - R_1$$
$$R_4 \to R_4 - R_1$$
$$\dots\dots\dots\dots$$
$$\dots\dots\dots\dots$$
$$R_n \to R_n - R_1$$
$$R_{n+1} \to R_{n+1} - R_1$$

$$\sim \begin{bmatrix} 1 & a & a^2 & \dots & a^n \\ 0 & 0 & 0 & \dots & 0 \\ 0 & 0 & 0 & \dots & 0 \\ \dots & \dots & \dots & \dots & \dots \\ \dots & \dots & \dots & \dots & \dots \\ \dots & \dots & \dots & \dots & \dots \\ 0 & 0 & 0 & \dots & 0 \end{bmatrix}_{(n+1)\times(n+1)}$$

which is in echelon form and the number of non-zero rows is 1. Hence, $\rho(A) = 1$.

***Example 15.*** *Multiplication of matrices E and F is G. Matrices E and G are as follows*

$$E = \begin{bmatrix} \cos\theta & -\sin\theta & 0 \\ \sin\theta & \cos\theta & 0 \\ 0 & 0 & 1 \end{bmatrix}, G = \begin{bmatrix} 1 & 0 & 0 \\ 0 & 1 & 0 \\ 0 & 0 & 1 \end{bmatrix}$$

*Then, the value of matrix F is*

(a) $\begin{bmatrix} \cos\theta & -\sin\theta & 0 \\ \sin\theta & \cos\theta & 0 \\ 0 & 0 & 1 \end{bmatrix}$ (b) $\begin{bmatrix} \cos\theta & \cos\theta & 0 \\ -\cos\theta & \sin\theta & 0 \\ 0 & 0 & 1 \end{bmatrix}$

(c) $\begin{bmatrix} \cos\theta & \sin\theta & 0 \\ -\sin\theta & \cos\theta & 0 \\ 0 & 0 & 1 \end{bmatrix}$ (d) $\begin{bmatrix} \sin\theta & -\cos\theta & 0 \\ \cos\theta & \sin\theta & 0 \\ 0 & 0 & 1 \end{bmatrix}$

**Solution.** (c) $\because$ Given that $E \times F = G$

$$\Rightarrow \begin{bmatrix} \cos\theta & -\sin\theta & 0 \\ \sin\theta & \cos\theta & 0 \\ 0 & 0 & 1 \end{bmatrix} \times F = \begin{bmatrix} 1 & 0 & 0 \\ 0 & 1 & 0 \\ 0 & 0 & 1 \end{bmatrix}$$

$$\Rightarrow \quad F = \begin{bmatrix} \cos\theta & -\sin\theta & 0 \\ \sin\theta & \cos\theta & 0 \\ 0 & 0 & 1 \end{bmatrix}^{-1}$$

[Because the product of any matrix and unit matrix is the matrix itself.]

So, $$|E| = \cos\theta \begin{vmatrix} \cos\theta & 0 \\ 0 & 1 \end{vmatrix} - (-\sin\theta) \begin{vmatrix} \sin\theta & 0 \\ 0 & 1 \end{vmatrix} + 0 \begin{vmatrix} \sin\theta & \cos\theta \\ 0 & 0 \end{vmatrix}$$

$$= \cos^2\theta + \sin^2\theta = 1$$

Matrix of cofactors of $E = C = \begin{bmatrix} \cos\theta & -\sin\theta & 0 \\ \sin\theta & \cos\theta & 0 \\ 0 & 0 & 1 \end{bmatrix}$

So, adjoint of $E = C' = \begin{bmatrix} \cos\theta & \sin\theta & 0 \\ -\sin\theta & \cos\theta & 0 \\ 0 & 0 & 1 \end{bmatrix}$

Hence, $$F = \frac{\text{adj}(E)}{|E|} = \begin{bmatrix} \cos\theta & \sin\theta & 0 \\ -\sin\theta & \cos\theta & 0 \\ 0 & 0 & 1 \end{bmatrix}$$

***Example 16.*** *The linear operation $L(x)$ is defined by the cross product $L(x) = bX_x$, where $b = [0\ 1\ 0]^T$ and $x = [x_1\ \ x_2\ \ x_3]^T$ are three dimensional vectors. The $3 \times 3$ matrix $M$ of this operation satisfies $L(x) = M \begin{bmatrix} x_1 \\ x_2 \\ x_3 \end{bmatrix}$*

*Then, the eigen values of $M$ are*

(a) $0, +1, -1$ (b) $1, -1, 1$

(c) $i, -i, 1$ (d) $i, -i, 0$

**Solution.** (d) $\because$ The cross product of $b = [0\ \ 1\ \ 0]^T$ and $x = [x_1\ \ x_2\ \ x_3]^T$ is

$$b \times X = \begin{vmatrix} \mathbf{i} & \mathbf{j} & \mathbf{k} \\ 0 & 1 & 0 \\ x_1 & x_2 & x_3 \end{vmatrix} = x_3\mathbf{i} + 0\,\mathbf{j} - x_1\mathbf{k}$$

$$= [x_3\ \ 0\ \ -x_1]$$

Now, we have $L(x) = b \times X = M \begin{bmatrix} x_1 \\ x_2 \\ x_3 \end{bmatrix}$

where $M$ is a $3 \times 3$ matrix

Let $$M = \begin{bmatrix} c_{11} & c_{12} & c_{13} \\ c_{21} & c_{22} & c_{23} \\ c_{31} & c_{32} & c_{33} \end{bmatrix}$$

Now, $$M \begin{bmatrix} x_1 \\ x_2 \\ x_3 \end{bmatrix} = b \times X$$

$$\Rightarrow \begin{bmatrix} c_{11} & c_{12} & c_{13} \\ c_{21} & c_{22} & c_{23} \\ c_{31} & c_{32} & c_{33} \end{bmatrix} \begin{bmatrix} x_1 \\ x_2 \\ x_3 \end{bmatrix} = \begin{bmatrix} x_3 \\ 0 \\ -x_1 \end{bmatrix}$$

By matching LHS and RHS, we get

$$\begin{bmatrix} 0 & 0 & 1 \\ 0 & 0 & 0 \\ -1 & 0 & 0 \end{bmatrix} \begin{bmatrix} x_1 \\ x_2 \\ x_3 \end{bmatrix} = \begin{bmatrix} x_3 \\ 0 \\ -x_1 \end{bmatrix}$$

So, $$M = \begin{bmatrix} 0 & 0 & 1 \\ 0 & 0 & 0 \\ -1 & 0 & 0 \end{bmatrix}$$

Now, we have to find the eigen values of $M$ as

$$|M - \lambda I| = 0$$

$$\begin{vmatrix} -\lambda & 0 & 1 \\ 0 & -\lambda & 0 \\ -1 & 0 & -\lambda \end{vmatrix} = 0$$

$$\Rightarrow \quad -\lambda(\lambda^2 - 0) + 1(0 - \lambda) = 0$$

$$\Rightarrow \quad \lambda^3 + \lambda = 0$$

$$\Rightarrow \quad \lambda = 0 \text{ and } \lambda^2 = -1$$

$$\Rightarrow \quad \lambda^2 = \pm i$$

Hence, $\lambda - 0, \pm i$

So, the eigen values are $0, i, -i$.

***Example 17.*** *Let $V$ be a 3 dimensional vector space with $A$ and $B$ its subspaces of dimensions 2 and 1, respectively. If $A \cap B = \{0\}$, then*

(a) $V = A - B$ (b) $V = A + B$

(c) $V = A \cdot B$ (d) None of these

**Solution.** (b) Since, $A \cap B = \{0\}$

$$\Rightarrow \quad \dim(A \cap B) = 0$$

Now, $$\dim(A + B) = \dim A + \dim B - \dim(A \cap B)$$

$$= 2 + 1 - 0 = 3$$

$$\therefore \quad \dim(A + B) = \dim V$$

$$\Rightarrow \quad V = A + B$$

***Example 18.*** $\dim V$, *where*

$$V = \{a_1, a_2, \ldots, a_{100} : a_1 + a_2 = 0,\ a_3 + a_4 = 0\}$$

*is*

(a) 97 (b) 98

(c) 99 (d) 100

**Solution.** (b) Since,

total number of variables – dependent variable = 4 – 2 = 2

Hence, $\dim V = 100 - 2 = 98$

## Type II (*One or more than one correct option*)

***Example 19.*** *Which of the following(s) is/are correct?*

(a) The transpose of a symmetric matrix need not be symmetric matrix.

(b) If $A$ and $B$ are symmetric matrix of same order, then $AB+BA$ must be symmetric matrix.

(c) If $A$ is symmetric matrix, then all positive integral powers of $A$ are symmetric matrices.

(d) If $A$ is any square matrix, then $A+A'$ is always symmetric matrix.

**Solution.** (a), (b), (c), (d)

(a) Since, $(A')' = A \neq A'$. Hence, transpose of a symmetric matrix need not be symmetric matrix.

(b) Since, $(AB+BA)' = (AB)' + (BA)'$

$$= B'A' + A'B'$$
$$= BA + AB$$
$$= AB + BA$$

Hence, $AB+BA$ must be symmetric matrix.

(c) Since, $(A^n)' = A^n$.

Hence, all the integral powers of a symmetric matrix $A$ are symmetric.

(d) Since, $(A+A')' = A' + (A')'$

$$= A' + A$$
$$= A + A'$$

Hence, $A+A'$ is always symmetric matrix.

***Example 20.*** *Which of the following(s) is/are correct?*

(a) If $A$ is orthogonal matrix, then $A$ is non-singular and $A^{-1} = A'$

(b) If $A$ is orthogonal matrix, then $|A| = \pm 1$

(c) Transpose of an orthogonal matrix is orthogonal

(d) None of the above

**Solution.** (a), (b), (c)

(a) We have,

$$A'A = I$$
$$\Rightarrow \quad A(A'A) = AI = A$$
$$\Rightarrow \quad (AA')A = A$$
$$\Rightarrow \quad AA' = I$$

$\Rightarrow$ $A$ is non-singular and $A^{-1} = A$.

(b) We have,

$$A'A = I$$
$$\Rightarrow \quad |A'A| = 1$$
$$\Rightarrow \quad |A'||A| = 1$$
$$\Rightarrow \quad |A|^2 = 1$$
$$\Rightarrow \quad |A| = \pm 1$$

(c) We have,

$$AA' = A'A = I$$
$$\Rightarrow \quad (AA')' = (A'A)' = I$$
$$\Rightarrow \quad AA' = A'A = I$$

***Example 21.*** *Which of the following(s) is/are correct?*

(a) If $A$ is unitary matrix, then $A'$ is also unitary matrix.

(b) Inverse of unitary matrix is unitary matrix.

(c) $A = \frac{1}{\sqrt{3}}\begin{bmatrix} 1 & 1+i \\ 1-i & -1 \end{bmatrix}$ is unitary matrix.

(d) None of the above

**Solution.** (a), (b), (c)

(a) We have,

$$AA^{\Theta} = A^{\Theta}A = I$$
$$\Rightarrow \quad (AA^{\Theta})' = (A^{\Theta}A)' = I$$
$$\Rightarrow \quad (A^{\Theta})'A' = A'(A^{\Theta})' = I$$
$$\Rightarrow \quad (A')^{\Theta}A' = A'(A')^{\Theta} = I$$

Hence, transpose of unitary matrix is matrix.

(b) We have,

$$AA^{\Theta} = A^{\Theta}A = I$$
$$\Rightarrow \quad (AA^{\Theta})^{-1} = (A^{\Theta}A)^{-1} = I$$
$$\Rightarrow \quad (A^{\Theta})^{-1}A^{-1} = A^{-1}(A^{\Theta})^{-1} = I$$
$$\Rightarrow \quad (A^{-1})^{\Theta}A^{-1} = A^{-1}(A^{-1})^{\Theta} = I$$

Hence, inverse of unitary matrix is unitary matrix.

(c) Given that

$$A = \frac{1}{\sqrt{3}}\begin{bmatrix} 1 & 1+i \\ 1-i & -1 \end{bmatrix}$$
$$\Rightarrow \quad A^{\Theta} = \frac{1}{\sqrt{3}}\begin{bmatrix} 1 & 1+i \\ 1-i & -1 \end{bmatrix}$$
$$\Rightarrow \quad AA^{\Theta} = \frac{1}{\sqrt{3}}\begin{bmatrix} 1 & 1+i \\ 1-i & -1 \end{bmatrix} \times \frac{1}{\sqrt{3}}\begin{bmatrix} 1 & 1+i \\ 1-i & -1 \end{bmatrix}$$
$$= \frac{1}{3}\begin{bmatrix} 3 & 0 \\ 0 & 3 \end{bmatrix} = \begin{bmatrix} 1 & 0 \\ 0 & 1 \end{bmatrix}$$

$\Rightarrow$ $A$ is unitary matrix.

***Example 22.*** *Which of the following(s) is/are correct?*

(a) In a Skew-Hermitian matrix, the element on the principle diagonal must be purely imaginary.

(b) If $A$ is Hermitian matrix, then $iA$ is Skew-Hermitian matrix.

(c) If $A$ is any square matrix, then $A - A^{\Theta}$ is Skew-Hermitian matrix.

(d) All of the above

**Solution.** (d)

(a) We have,

$$\bar{a}_{ij} = -a_{ji}$$

On putting $j = i$, we get

$$\bar{a}_{ii} = -a_{ii}$$

$\Rightarrow$ $\bar{a}_{ii} + a_{ii} = 0$

$\Rightarrow$ Real part of $a_{ii} = 0$

$\Rightarrow$ $a_{ii}$ is purely imaginary.

Hence, the element on the principal diagonal of a Skew-Hermitian matrix are purely imaginary.

(b) Since,

$$(iA)^{\Theta} = \bar{i}A^{\Theta} = -iA$$

Hence, $iA$ is Skew-Hermitian matrix.

(c) Since,

$$(A - A^{\Theta})^{\Theta} = A^{\Theta} - (A^{\Theta})^{\Theta}$$
$$= A^{\Theta} - A$$
$$= -(A - A^{\Theta})$$

Hence, $A - A^{\Theta}$ is Skew-Hermitian matrix.

***Example 23.*** *Which of the following(s) is/are correct?*

(a) The eigen values of a real symmetric matrix are all real.
(b) The modulus of each eigen value of a unitary matrix is unity.
(c) The eigen value of a Skew-Hermitian matrix is either zero or a pure imaginary number.
(d) None of the above

**Solution.** (a), (b), (c)

(a) Let $A$ be a unitary matrix, then

$$A^{\Theta}A = A\cdot A^{\Theta} = I$$

Now, since $\lambda$ is an eigen value of $A$.

$\Rightarrow \quad AX = \lambda X$

$\Rightarrow \quad (AX)^{\Theta} = (\lambda X)^{\Theta}$

$\Rightarrow \quad X^{\Theta}A^{\Theta} = \bar{\lambda}X^{\Theta}$

$\Rightarrow \quad X^{\Theta}A^{\Theta}AX = \bar{\lambda}X^{\Theta}\lambda X$

$\Rightarrow \quad X^{\Theta}A^{\Theta}AX = \bar{\lambda}\lambda X^{\Theta}X$

$\Rightarrow \quad X^{\Theta}IX = \bar{\lambda}\lambda X^{\Theta}X \quad (\because A^{\Theta}A = I)$

$\Rightarrow \quad (1 - \lambda\bar{\lambda})X^{\Theta}X = 0$

But $\because \quad X \neq 0 \Rightarrow X^{\Theta} \neq 0$

$\therefore \quad 1 - \lambda\bar{\lambda} = 0$

$\Rightarrow \quad \lambda\bar{\lambda} = 1$

$\Rightarrow \quad |\lambda|^2 = 1$

(b) We have,

$$A' = A$$

$\Rightarrow \quad (\bar{A'}) = A$

$\Rightarrow \quad A^{\Theta} = A$

$\Rightarrow$ $A$ is Hermitian matrix.

$\Rightarrow$ All eigen values are real.

(c) Let $A$ be a Skew-Hermitian matrix, then $iA$ is Hermitian matrix.

Now, if $\lambda$ is an eigen value of $A$

$\Rightarrow \quad AX = \lambda X$

$\Rightarrow \quad (iA)X = (i\lambda)X$

$\Rightarrow$ $i\lambda$ is an eigen value of $(iA)$.

$\Rightarrow$ $i\lambda$ should be real, which is possible only when $\lambda$ is either zero or a pure imaginary number.

***Example 24.*** *Consider the matrix*

$$A = \begin{bmatrix} 1 & 2010 & 2011 \\ 0 & -1 & 2010 \\ 0 & 0 & -1 \end{bmatrix}$$

*Then,*

(a) the eigen values of $A$ are $\pm 1$
(b) sum of AM = 3
(c) sum of GM = 1
(d) None of the above

**Solution.** (a), (b), (c)

Since, $ch_A(x) = (x-1)^2(x+1)$

$\therefore$ The eigen values of the given matrix are $\pm 1$.

$\therefore$ AM of $\lambda = 1$ is 2.

AM of $\lambda = -1$ is 1

$\therefore$ Sum of AM $= 2 + 1 = 3$

Now,

$$B_1 = A - I = \begin{bmatrix} 0 & 2010 & 2011 \\ 0 & -2 & 2010 \\ 0 & 0 & 0 \end{bmatrix}$$

and

$$B_{-1} = A + I = \begin{bmatrix} 2 & 2010 & 2011 \\ 0 & 0 & 2010 \\ 0 & 0 & 2 \end{bmatrix}$$

Hence,

$$\rho(B_1) = 2$$
$$\rho(B_{-1}) = 3$$

$\therefore$ GM of $\lambda = 1$ is $3 - 2 = 1$

GM of $\lambda = -1$ is $3 - 3 = 0$

Hence, sum of GM $= 1 + 0 = 1$

***Example 25.*** *Let $V$ be a vector space over $F$. The zero vector is denoted by $\mathbf{0}$ to distinguish it from $0 \in F$. Then,*

(a) $\alpha\mathbf{0} = \mathbf{0}$, $\alpha \in F$
(b) $0x = \mathbf{0}$, $x \in V$
(c) $(-\alpha)(x) = -(\alpha x) = \alpha(-x), \alpha \in F, x \in V$
(d) $\alpha x = \mathbf{0} \Rightarrow \alpha = 0$ or $x = \mathbf{0}$

**Solution.** (a), (b), (c), (d)

(a) We have,

$$\alpha\mathbf{0} = \alpha(\mathbf{0} + \mathbf{0})$$
$$= \alpha\mathbf{0} + \alpha\mathbf{0}$$

$\Rightarrow \quad \alpha\mathbf{0} + \mathbf{0} = \alpha\mathbf{0} + \alpha\mathbf{0}$

$\Rightarrow \quad \mathbf{0} = \alpha\mathbf{0}$ (by left cancellation law)

(b) Similarly, $0x = \mathbf{0}$, $x \in V$

(c) We have,

$$(-\alpha)x + \alpha x = ((-\alpha) + \alpha)x$$
$$= 0x$$
$$= \mathbf{0}$$

$\Rightarrow$ Additive inverse of $\alpha x$ is $(-\alpha)x$

$\Rightarrow \quad -(\alpha x) = (-\alpha)x$

Similarly, $-(\alpha x) = \alpha(-x)$

(d) Let $\alpha x = 0$ and $\alpha \neq 0$, then $\alpha^{-1}$ exists.

$\Rightarrow \quad \alpha^{-1}(\alpha x) = \alpha^{-1}\mathbf{0} = \mathbf{0}$

$\Rightarrow \quad (\alpha^{-1}\alpha)x = \mathbf{0}$

$\Rightarrow \quad 1\cdot x = \mathbf{0} \Rightarrow x = 0$

Now, let $x \neq 0$, then we have to prove

$$\alpha x = \mathbf{0} \Rightarrow \alpha = 0$$

Let if possible $\alpha \neq 0$, then $\alpha^{-1}$ exists.

$\Rightarrow \quad \alpha x = \mathbf{0}$

$\Rightarrow \quad (\alpha^{-1})(\alpha x) = \alpha^{-1}\mathbf{0}$

$\Rightarrow \quad (\alpha^{-1}\alpha)\, x = \mathbf{0}$

$\Rightarrow \quad 1 \cdot x = \mathbf{0} \Rightarrow x = \mathbf{0}$

which is a contradiction as $x \neq 0$.

Hence, $\quad \alpha = 0$

***Example 26.*** *Which of the following(s) is/are subspace of F[x]?*

(a) $W_1 = \{f(x) \in F(x) : f(x+1) = f(x)\}$
(b) $W_2 = \{f(x) \in F(x) : 2f(0) = f(1)\}$
(c) Both (a) and (b)
(d) Neither (a) nor (b)

**Solution.** (c)

Let $f(x), g(x) \in W$, then

$$f(x+1) = f(x),\ g(x+1) = g(x) \qquad \text{...(i)}$$

Let $\alpha, \beta \in F$ and $\alpha f(x) + \beta g(x) = h(x)$

$$\Rightarrow \quad h(x+1) = \alpha f(x+1) + \beta g(x+1)$$
$$= \alpha f(x) + \beta g(x) \qquad \text{[by Eq. (i)]}$$
$$= h(x)$$
$$\Rightarrow \quad h(x) = \alpha f(x) + \beta g(x) \in W_1$$

Hence, $W_1$ is a subspace of $F[x]$.

Next, let $f(x), g(x) \in W_2$, then

$$2f(0) = f(1) \text{ and } 2g(0) = g(1) \qquad \text{...(ii)}$$

Let $\alpha, \beta \in F$ and $\alpha f(x) + \beta g(x) = h(x)$

Then, $\quad 2h(0) = 2\alpha f(0) + 2\beta g(0)$
$$= \alpha f(1) + \beta g(1) \qquad \text{[by Eq. (ii)]}$$
$$= h(1)$$
$$\Rightarrow \quad h(x) = \alpha f(x) + \beta g(x) \in W_2$$

$\Rightarrow$ $W_2$ is a subspace of $F[x]$.

Hence, both (a) and (b) are subspace of $F[x]$.

***Example 27.*** *Which of the following(s) is/are linearly independent set of vectors in $R^3$?*

(a) $\{(1,0,0),(1,1,0),(1,1,1)\}$
(b) $\{(1,1,1),(-1,0,1),(0,-2,1)\}$
(c) $\{(1,0,0),(0,1,0),(1,1,1),(-1,1,-1)\}$
(d) All of the above

**Solution.** (a), (b)

(a) Let $a, b, c \in R$ such that
$$a(1,0,0) + b(1,1,0) + c(1,1,1) = (0,0,0)$$
$$\Rightarrow \quad a+b+c=0,\ b+c=0,\ c=0$$
$$\Rightarrow \quad a=0,\ b=0,\ c=0$$
Hence, $\{(1,0,0),(1,1,0),(1,1,1)\}$ is linearly independent set of vectors.

(b) Let $a, b, c \in R$ such that
$$a(1,1,1) + b(-1,0,1) + c(0,-2,1) = (0,0,0)$$
$$\Rightarrow \quad a-b=0,\ a-2c=0,\ a+b+c=0$$
$$\Rightarrow \quad a=b, \quad c=\frac{1}{2}b, \quad b+b+\frac{1}{2}b=0$$
$$\Rightarrow \quad b=0, \quad a=0, \quad c=0.$$
Hence, $\{(1,1,1),(-1,0,1),(0,-2,1)\}$ is linearly independent set of vectors.

(c) Let $a, b, c, d \in R$ such that
$$a(1,0,0) + b(0,1,0) + c(1,1,1) + d(-1,1,-1) = (0,0,0)$$
$$\Rightarrow \quad a+c-d=0,\ b+c+d=0,\ c-d=0$$
$$\Rightarrow \quad c=b, \quad b=-2d, \quad a=0$$
taking $d=1$, we get
$$a=0, \quad b=-2, \quad c=1, \quad d=1$$
Hence, $\{(1,0,0),(0,1,0),(1,1,1),(-1,1,-1)\}$ is linearly dependent set of vectors.

***Example 28.*** *Let V is a vector space of dimensional 100. A and B are two subspaces of V of dimensions 60 and 63, respectively. Then,*

(a) maximum dimension of $A \cap B$ is 23
(b) maximum dimension of $A \cap B$ is 60
(c) minimum dimension of $A \cap B$ is 23
(d) minimum dimension of $A \cap B$ is 60

**Solution.** (a), (b), (c)

Since $\quad \dim(A \cap B) \leq \dim A$

and $\quad \dim(A \cap B) \leq \dim B$

$\Rightarrow \quad \dim(A \cap B) \leq 60$

and $\quad \dim(A \cap B) \leq 63$

Hence, $\quad \dim(A \cap B) \leq 60$.

Hence, dim of $A \cap B = 60$.

Again, we know that
$$\dim(A+B) = \dim A + \dim B - \dim(A \cap B)$$
$$\Rightarrow \quad \dim(A \cap B) = \dim A + \dim B - \dim(A+B)$$
$$= 60 + 63 - \dim(A+B)$$
$$\Rightarrow \text{minimum } \dim(A \cap B) = 60 + 63 - 100 = 23$$
[$\because$ maximum dim of $A+B = 100$ (dimv)]

# Exercise 1 (For Part 'B')

**Directions** (Q. Nos. 1-318) *All questions have only one correct option.*

**1.** Consider the real vector space $V = \mathbb{R}^3$ and following of its subsets

I. $S = \{(x, y, z) \in V : x = y = 0\}$
II. $T = \{(x, y, z) \in V : x = 0\}$
III. $W = \{(x, y, z) \in V : z \neq 0\}$

Which one of the following statement is correct?
(a) $S, T$ and $W$ are subspaces
(b) Only $S$ and $W$ are subspaces
(c) Only $T$ and $W$ are subspaces
(d) Only $S$ and $T$ are subspaces

**2.** Let $V$ be a vector space over the field $F$ of dimension $n$. Consider the following statements

I. Every subset of $V$ containing $n$ elements is a basis of $V$.
II. No linearly independent subset of $V$ contains more than $n$ elements.

Which of the above statement is/are correct?
(a) I only (b) II only
(c) Both I and II (d) Neither I nor II

**3.** If $A$ and $B$ are two odd order skew-symmetric matrices such that $AB = BA$, then what is the matrix $AB$?
(a) An orthogonal matrix
(b) A skew-symmetric matrix
(c) A symmetric matrix
(d) An identity matrix

**4.** Consider the vector space $V$ over the field of real numbers spanned by the set
$S = \{(0, 1, 0, 0), (1, 1, 0, 0), (1, 0, 1, 0), (0, 0, 1, 0), (1, 1, 1, 0)$ $(1, 0, 0, 0)\}$
What is the dimension of $V$?
(a) 1 (b) 2
(c) 3 (d) 4

**5.** Let $X = (3, 2, -1), Y = (2, 4, 1), Z = (4, 0, -3)$ and $W = (10, 4, -5)$ be vector in $\mathbb{R}^3$, a real vector space. Which one of the following is correct?
(a) $2X + Z = W, Y + Z = W$
(b) $2X - Y = Z, Y + 2Z = W$
(c) $X + Z = W, 2X + Y = Z$
(d) $Y + 2Z = W, X - Y = Z$

**6.** If $V$ is the real vector space of all mapping from $\mathbb{R}$ to $\mathbb{R}$, $V_1 = \{f \in V / f(-x) = f(x)\}$ and $V_2 = \{f \in V / f(-x) = -f(x)\}$, then which one of the following is correct?
(a) Neither $V_1$ nor $V_2$ is a subspace of $V$.
(b) $V_1$ is a subspace of $V$, but $V_2$ is not a subspace of $V$.
(c) $V_1$ is not a subspace of $V$, but $V_2$ is a subspace of $V$.
(d) Both $V_1$ and $V_2$ are subspace of $V$.

**7.** Let $f[x]$ be the ring of polynomials in one variable $x$ over a field $f$ with the relation $x^n = 0$, for a fixed $n \in N$.
What is the dimension of $f[x]$ over $f$?
(a) 1 (b) $n - 1$
(c) $n$ (d) infinite

**8.** Which one of the following is correct? The set $S = \{a + ib, c + id\}$ is a basis for the vector space $c$ over $R$ iff
(a) $ad - bc = 0$ (b) $ad + bc = 0$
(c) $ad + bc \neq 0$ (d) $ad - bc \neq 0$

**9.** If $A$ and $B$ are symmetric matrices of the same order, then which one of the following is not correct?
(a) $A + B$ is a symmetric matrix.
(b) $AB - BA$ is a symmetric matrix.
(c) $AB + BA$ is a symmetric matrix.
(d) $A + A^T$ and $B + B^T$ are symmetric matrices.

**10.** If $A = \begin{bmatrix} 3 & -2 \\ 4 & -2 \end{bmatrix}$ satisfies the matrix equation $A^2 - kA + 2I = 0$, then what is the value of $k$?
(a) 0 (b) 1
(c) 2 (d) 3

**11.** Under which one of the following condition does the system of equations

$$\begin{bmatrix} 1 & 2 & 4 \\ 2 & 1 & 2 \\ 1 & 2 & a-4 \end{bmatrix} \begin{bmatrix} x \\ y \\ z \end{bmatrix} = \begin{bmatrix} 6 \\ 4 \\ a \end{bmatrix}$$

have a unique solution?
(a) For all $a \in R$ (b) $a = 8$
(c) For all $a \in Z$ (d) $a \neq 8$

**12.** Consider the equation $2x + 2y = 1$ and $2x - y = 1$ over $Z_3$. What is the solution of $(x, y)$?
(a) $(1, 1)$ but not $(2, 0)$ (b) $(2, 0)$ but not $(1, 1)$
(c) Both $(1, 1)$ and $(2, 0)$ (d) $(1/2, 0)$

**13.** Let $S = \{(1, i, o), (2i, 1, 1), (0, 1 + i, 1 - i)\}$ be a subset of the complex vector space $c^3$ and $T = \{(1, 1, 1), (1, 1, 0), (1, 0, 0)\}$ be a subset of the real vector space $\mathbb{R}^3$. Which one of the following statements is correct?
(a) $S$ and $T$ are both basis.
(b) $S$ is a basis but $T$ is not a basis.
(c) $S$ is not a basis but $T$ is a basis.
(d) Neither $S$ nor $T$ is a basis.

**14.** Consider the real vector space $\mathbb{R}^3$. The subspace $\{(x, y, z) \in \mathbb{R}^3 : y = x\}$ of $\mathbb{R}^3$ is generated by which one of the following?

(a) $\{(1,1,0),(0,0,1)\}$ (b) $\{(1,1,0), (1,0,0)\}$
(c) $\{(1,0,0), (0,1,0)\}$ (d) $\{(1,0,1),(0,0,1)\}$

**15.** What is the dimension of the vector space over the field *IR*?

(a) 1 (b) Infinite
(c) 2 (d) 4

**16.** Let $V$ be a vector space over a field and $\alpha \in F$ and $u \in V$. Which of the following statement is not correct?

(a) $\alpha u = \theta \Rightarrow$ either $\alpha = 0$ or $u = \theta$
(b) $|-1u| = |-1|u$ for all $u \in v$
(c) $\alpha\theta = \theta$
(d) $0u = \theta$

**17.** Which one of the following polynomials lies in the linear span of $S = \{1, 1 + x + x^2\}$?

(a) $5x^2 + 5x + 1$
(b) $100x^2 + 10x + 10$
(c) $\pi(x^2 + 1)$
(d) $7x^2 + \pi x + 3$

**18.** What is the dimension of the vector space formed by the solution of the system of the following equations?

$$x_1 + x_2 + x_3 = 0$$
$$x_1 + 2x_2 = 0$$
$$x_2 - x_3 = 0$$

(a) 1 (b) 2
(c) 3 (d) 0

**19.** Given the vector

$\alpha = (1,2,3)$, $\beta = (3,1,0)$, $\gamma = (2,1,3)$ and $\delta = (-1,3,6)$

Consider the following statements

I. $\gamma$ is a linear combination of $\alpha$ and $\beta$.
II. $\delta$ is a linear combination of $\alpha$ and $\beta$.

Which of the following statement given above is/are correct?

(a) I only (b) II only
(c) Both I and II (d) Neither I nor II

**20.** Let $A$ and $B$ be any two $n \times n$ matrices and $\text{tr}(A) = \sum_{i=1}^{n} a_{ij}$ and $\text{tr}(B) = \sum_{i=1}^{n} b_{ii}$.

Consider the following statement

I. $\text{tr}(AB) = \text{tr}(BA)$
II. $\text{tr}(A + B) = \text{tr}(A) + \text{tr}(B)$

Which of the following statement given above is/are correct?

(a) I only (b) II only
(c) Both I and II (d) Neither I nor II

**21.** Let $A = \begin{pmatrix} 2 & 0 \\ 3 & 5 \end{pmatrix}$ be expressed as $P + Q$, where $P$ is symmetric matrix and $Q$ is skew-symmetric matrix. Which one of the following is correct?

(a) $Q = \begin{pmatrix} 1/2 & -3/2 \\ 3/2 & 0 \end{pmatrix}$ (b) $Q = \begin{pmatrix} 0 & 3/2 \\ 3/2 & 0 \end{pmatrix}$

(c) $Q = \frac{1}{2}\begin{pmatrix} 0 & -3 \\ 3 & 0 \end{pmatrix}$ (d) $Q = \frac{1}{2}\begin{pmatrix} 2 & 3 \\ 0 & 5 \end{pmatrix}$

**22.** What is the determinant of the following matrix?

$$\begin{vmatrix} 1 & 0 & 0 & \dots & \dots & 0 \\ 1 & 1/2 & 0 & \dots & \dots & 0 \\ 1 & 1/2 & 1/3 & \dots & \dots & 0 \\ 1 & 1/2 & 1/3 & 1/4 & \dots & 0 \\ \dots & \dots & \dots & \dots & \dots & \dots \\ 1 & 1/2 & 1/3 & 1/4 & \dots & 1/n \end{vmatrix}$$

(a) $n^2 + n + 1$ (b) $\frac{1}{n^2} + \frac{1}{n} + 1$

(c) $\frac{1}{n!}$ (d) $\frac{n(n+1)}{2}$

**23.** If the system of equations

$x - 2y - 3z = 1$, $(P + 2)z = 3$, $(2P + 1)y + z = 2$ is inconsistent, then what is the value of $P$?

(a) $-2$ (b) $-1/2$
(c) 0 (d) 2

**24.** Let $R$ be the set of all real number and $\mathbb{R}^2 = \{(x_1, x_2) : x_1 \in \mathbb{R}, x_2 \in \mathbb{R}\}$. Then, which one of the following is a subspace of $\mathbb{R}^2$ over $\mathbb{R}$?

(a) $\{(x_1, x_2) : x_1 > 0, x_2 > 0\}$
(b) $\{(x_1, x_2) : x_1 \in \mathbb{R}, x_2 > 0\}$
(c) $\{(x_1, x_2\} : x_1 < 0, x_2 < 0\}$
(d) $\{(x_1, 0) : x_1 \in \mathbb{R}\}$

**25.** If $W_1 = \{(0, x_2, x_3, x_4, x_5) : x_2, x_3, x_4, x_5 \in \mathbb{R}\}$ and $W_2 = \{(x_1, 0, x_3, x_4, x_5) : x_1, x_3, x_4, x_5 \in \mathbb{R}\}$ be subspace of $R^5$, then $\dim(W_1 \cap W_2)$ is equal to

(a) 5 (b) 4
(c) 3 (d) 2

**26.** If $A$ be a non-zero square matrix of orders $n$, then

(a) the matrix $A + A'$ is anti-symmetric, but the matrix $A - A'$ is symmetric.
(b) the matrix $A + A'$ is symmetric, but the matrix $A - A'$ is anti-symmetric.
(c) Both $A + A'$ and $A - A'$ are symmetric.
(d) Both $A + A'$ and $A - A'$ are anti-symmetric.

**27.** If $x, y, z$ are in AP with common difference $d$ and the rank of the matrix $\begin{bmatrix} 4 & 5 & x \\ 5 & 6 & y \\ 6 & k & z \end{bmatrix}$ is 2, then the value of $d$ and $k$ are

(a) $d = x/2$; $k$ is an arbitrary number
(b) $d$ an arbitrary number; $k = 7$
(c) $d = k$; $k = 5$
(d) $d = x/2$; $k = 6$

**28.** Square matrix $A$ of order $n$ over $\mathbb{R}$ has rank $n$. Which one of the following statement is not correct?

(a) $A^T$ has rank $n$
(b) $A$ has $n$ linearly independent columns
(c) $A$ is non-singular
(d) $A$ is singular

**29.** If C is a non-singular matrix and $B = C\begin{bmatrix} 0 & x & y \\ 0 & 0 & z \\ 0 & 0 & 0 \end{bmatrix}C^{-1}$, then

(a) $B^2 = 1$ (b) $B^2 = 0$
(c) $B^3 = 1$ (d) $B^3 = 0$

**30.** Suppose, $X = \left\{\begin{bmatrix} a \\ b \\ c \\ d \end{bmatrix} : b - c = 4\right\}$; $Y = \left\{\begin{bmatrix} a \\ b \\ c \\ d \end{bmatrix} : a = b + c\right\}$

and $Z = \left\{\begin{bmatrix} a \\ b \\ c \\ d \end{bmatrix} : b = 0,\ c = d\right\}$

Which of these subset of the vector space $\mathbb{R}^4$ is/are subspace(S)?

(a) X only (b) Y and Z
(c) X, Y and Z (d) X and Z

**31.** Suppose, $P$ is an $n \times n$ matrix such that the $k$th diagonal element of $PP^T$ is zero.
Consider the following statement

I. The $k$th row of $P$ is zero.
II. The $k$th row of $PP^T$ is zero.
III. The $k$th column of $P$ is zero.
IV. The $k$th column of $PP^T$ is zero.

Select the correct answer using the codes given below
(a) I and III (b) I, II and IV
(c) II, III and IV (d) I, II and III

**32.** If $X = \begin{bmatrix} 0 & 1 & 0 & 0 \\ 0 & 0 & 1 & 0 \\ 0 & 0 & 0 & 1 \\ 0 & 0 & 0 & 0 \end{bmatrix}$, then the rank of $X^TX$, where $X^T$ denotes the transpose of $X$, is

(a) 0 (b) 2
(c) 3 (d) 4

**33.** Let $W_1, W_2, W_3$ be subspace of a vector space $V$ such that $W_3 \subset W_1$. Then, which one of the following is correct?

(a) $W_1 \cap (W_2 + W_3) = W_2 + W_1 \cap W_3$
(b) $W_1 \cap (W_2 + W_3) = W_3 + W_1 \cap W_2$
(c) $W_1 \cup (W_2 + W_3) = W_2 + W_1 \cup W_3$
(d) None of the above

**34.** Let $\xi_1$, $\xi_2$ and $\xi_3$ be vector space $V$ over the field $F$. If $r$ and $S$ are arbitrary element of $F$ and the set $(\xi_1, \xi_2, r\xi_1 + S\xi_2 + \xi_3)$ is linearly dependent, then $(\xi_1, \xi_2, \xi_3)$ is

(a) linearly dependent set
(b) a null set
(c) linearly independent set
(d) None of the above

**35.** The dimension of the subspace of $\mathbb{R}^3$ spanned by $(-3, 0, 1)$, $(1, 2, 1)$ and $(3, 0, -1)$

(a) 0 (b) 1
(c) 2 (d) 3

**36.** If $V$ is a vector space over an infinite field $F$ such that $\dim V = 2$, then the number of distinct subspace $V$ has is

(a) 2 (b) 3
(c) 4 (d) infinite

**37.** The set $S_1 = \left\{\alpha = \begin{bmatrix} 1 & -2 & 4 \\ 3 & 0 & -1 \end{bmatrix}, \beta = \begin{bmatrix} 2 & -4 & 8 \\ 6 & 0 & -2 \end{bmatrix}\right\}$ and $S_2 = (f = u^3 + 3u + 4,\ g = u^3 + 4u + 3)$ are

(a) both linearly dependent
(b) both linearly independent
(c) $S_1$ is linearly dependent but $S_2$ is not
(d) $S_2$ is linearly dependent but $S_1$ is not

**38.** Let $M_{2\times 2}(R)$ be the vector space of $2 \times 2$ matrices over $R$ and $W_1 = \left\{\begin{bmatrix} x & x \\ 0 & x \end{bmatrix} : x, y \in R\right\}$ and

$W_2 = \left\{\begin{bmatrix} x & y \\ z & 0 \end{bmatrix} : x, y, z \in R\right\}$,

then $\dim(W_1 \cap W_2)$ is equal to

(a) 0 (b) 1
(c) 2 (d) 3

**39.** Consider the following assertions

I. Rank $(ST)$ = Rank $S$ = Rank $T$
II. Rank $(ST)$ = Rank $S$, if $T$ is non-singular
III. Rank $(ST)$ = Rank $T$, if $T$ is non-singular

where $S, T : V \to V$ are linear transformations of a finite dimensional vector space $V$. Which of these is/are correct?

(a) only I (b) only II
(c) I and II (d) II and III

**40.** If $S = \{(1, 1, 0), (2, 1, 3)\} \subseteq \mathbb{R}^3$, then which one of the following vectors of $R^3$ is not in the span $[S]$?

(a) (0, 0, 0) (b) (3, 2, 3)
(c) (1, 2, 3) (d) (4/3, 1, 1)

**41.** The system of equation $kx + y + z = 1$, $x + ky + z = k$ and $x + y + kz = k^3$ does not have a solution, if $k$ is equal to

(a) 0 (b) 1
(c) −1 (d) −2

**42.** The system of equations

$$4x_1 + x_2 - 3x_3 - x_4 = 0$$
$$2x_1 + 3x_2 + x_3 - 5x_4 = 0$$
$$x_1 - 2x_2 - 2x_3 + 3x_4 = 0 \text{ has}$$

(a) no solution
(b) only one solution (0, 0, 0, 0)
(c) infinite number of solutions
(d) only two solution (0, 0, 0, 0) and (3/5, 1, 4/5, 1)

**43.** If $W_1 = \{(0, a_2, a_3)\}$ and $W_2 = \{b_1, 0, b_3\}$ are two subspace of $F^3$, where $F^n$ is a vector space of dimension $n$. Then, the subspace $W_1 \cap W_2$ is isomorphic to the vector space.

(a) $F^1$ (b) $F^2$
(c) $F^3$ (d) $2F^4$

**44.** If the set of all triples $(x_1, x_2, x_3)$ of real number $R$ form a vector space $V_3$, then a subspace denoted by a vertical plane $y = x$ can be obtained by a linear combination of the sets.

(a) (1, 1, 0) and (0, 0, 1)
(b) (1, 1, 0) and (1, 0, 0)
(c) (1, 0, 0) and (0, 1, 0)
(d) (1, 0, 1) and (0, 0, 1)

**45.** In $\mathbb{R}^3$, consider the following three statement about the subset

$E = \{(1, 0, 0), (0, 1, 0), (0, 0, 1), (1, 1, 1), (1, 1, 0)\}$

I. $E$ is linearly dependent set.
II. Any three vector of $E$ are linearly independent.
III. Any four vectors of $E$ are linearly dependent.

Which of the above statement are correct?

(a) I, II and III (b) I and II
(c) I and III (d) II and III

**46.** The system of equations

$$x - y + 3z = 4$$
$$x + z = 2$$
$$x + y - z = 0 \text{ has}$$

(a) a unique solution
(b) finitely many solutions
(c) infinitely many solutions
(d) no solution

**47.** Which of the following sets of vectors in $\mathbb{R}^3$ are linearly independent?

I. [(1, 0, 0), (0, 1, 0), (1, 1, 0)]
II. [(1, 0, 0), (0, 1, 0), (0, 0, 1)]
III. [(0, 1, 0), (1, 0, 1), (1, 1, 0)]
IV. [(0, 0, 1), (0, 1, 0), (0, 1, 1)]

Select the correct answer using the codes given below

(a) I and II (b) II and III
(c) III and IV (d) I and IV

**48.** Which one of the following statement is correct?

(a) There is no vector space of dimension 1.
(b) Any three vectors of a vector space of dimension 3 are linearly independent.
(c) There is one and only one basis of a vector space of finite dimension.
(d) If a non-zero vector space $V$ is generated by a finite set $S$, then $V$ can be generated by a linearly independent subset of $S$.

**49.** Consider the equation $AX = B$, where $A = \begin{bmatrix} -1 & 2 \\ 2 & -1 \end{bmatrix}$ and $B = \begin{bmatrix} 3 \\ 1 \end{bmatrix}$, then

(a) the equation has no solution
(b) $\begin{bmatrix} 0 \\ 0 \end{bmatrix}$ is a solution of the equation
(c) there exists a non-zero unique solution
(d) the equation has infinitely many solutions

**50.** Consider the following statement

**Assertion (A)** If $M$ is an $n \times n$ matrix with rank $(n-1)$, then $M$ can be made non-singular by changing one element.

**Reason (R)** An $n \times n$ matrix with rank $n-1$, has a non-vanishing minor of order $n-1$ of these statement.

(a) Both A and R are true and R is the correct explained of A.
(b) Both A and R are true, but R is not a correct explained of A.
(c) A is true but R is false.
(d) A is false but R is true.

**51.** The system of equation

$$2x + y = 5$$
$$x - 3y = -1$$

$3x + 4y = k$ is consistent, when $k$ is

(a) 1 (b) 2
(c) 5 (d) 10

**52.** The value of $\alpha$ for which the system of equation

$$x + y + z = 0$$
$$y + 2z = 0$$

$\alpha x + z = 0$ has more than one solution is

(a) $-1$ (b) 0
(c) $1/2$ (d) 1

**53.** The system of the equations

$$x + 2y + z = 9$$
$$2x + y + 3z = 7$$

can be expressed as

(a) $\begin{bmatrix} 1 & 2 & 1 \\ 2 & 1 & 3 \end{bmatrix} \begin{bmatrix} 9 \\ 7 \end{bmatrix} = \begin{bmatrix} x \\ y \\ z \end{bmatrix}$ (b) $\begin{bmatrix} 1 & 2 & 1 \\ 2 & 1 & 3 \end{bmatrix} \begin{bmatrix} 9 \\ 7 \end{bmatrix} = \begin{bmatrix} x \\ y \\ z \end{bmatrix}$

(c) $\begin{bmatrix} 1 & 2 & 1 \\ 2 & 1 & 3 \end{bmatrix} \begin{bmatrix} x \\ y \\ z \end{bmatrix} = \begin{bmatrix} 9 \\ 7 \end{bmatrix}$ (d) None of these

**54.** Let $A$ be an $n \times n$ matrix from the set of numbers and $A^3 - 3A^2 + 4A - 6I = 0$, where $I$ is $n \times n$ unit matrix. If $A^{-1}$ exist, then

(a) $A^{-1} = A - I$ (b) $A^{-1} = A + 6I$
(c) $A^{-1} = 3A - 6I$ (d) $A^{-1} = \frac{1}{6}(A^2 - 3A + 4I)$

**55.** If $3x+2y+z=0$
$x+4y+z=0$
$2x+y+4z=0$
be a system of equation, then
(a) it is inconsistent
(b) it has only the trivial solution $x=0, y=0, z=0$
(c) it can be reduced to a single equation and so a solution does not exist
(d) the determinant of the matrix of coefficient is zero

**56.** Let $M$ be a $m\times n(m<n)$ matrix with rank $m$. Then,
(a) for every $b$ in $\mathbb{R}^m$, $M_x=b$ has unique solution
(b) for every $b$ in $\mathbb{R}^m$, $M_x=b$ has a solution but it is not unique
(c) there exists $b\in\mathbb{R}^m$ for which $M_x=b$ has no solution
(d) None of the above

**57.** Let $M=\begin{bmatrix}1 & 1 & 0\\ -1 & 1 & 2\\ 2 & 2 & 0\\ -1 & 0 & 1\end{bmatrix}$. Then, the rank of $M$ is equal to
(a) 3 (b) 4
(c) 2 (d) 1

**58.** All the eigen value of the matrix $\begin{bmatrix}1 & 2 & 0\\ 2 & 1 & 0\\ 0 & 0 & -1\end{bmatrix}$ lie in the disc
(a) $|\lambda+1|\le 1$ (b) $|\lambda-1|\le 1$
(c) $|\lambda+1|\le 0$ (d) $|\lambda-1|\le 2$

**59.** Let $A$ be a $m\times n$ matrix with row rank $=r=$ column rank. The dimension of the space of solutions of the system of linear equation $AX=0$ is
(a) $r$ (b) $n-r$
(c) $m-r$ (d) $\min(m,n)-r$

**60.** A matrix $M$ has eigen value 1 and 4 with corresponding eigen vectors $(1,-1)^T$ and $(2,1)^T$, respectively. Then, $M$ is
(a) $\begin{pmatrix}-4 & -8\\ 5 & 9\end{pmatrix}$ (b) $\begin{pmatrix}9 & -8\\ 5 & -4\end{pmatrix}$
(c) $\begin{pmatrix}2 & 2\\ 1 & 3\end{pmatrix}$ (d) $\begin{pmatrix}3 & 2\\ 1 & 2\end{pmatrix}$

**61.** Let $A$ and $B$ be $n\times n$ matrices with the same minimal polynomial. Then,
(a) $A$ is similar to $B$
(b) $A$ is diagonalizable, if $B$ is diagonalizable
(c) $A$-$B$ is singular
(d) $A$ and $B$ commute

**62.** Let $A\in C^{m\times n}$ and $A'$, $A^*$ denote, respectively the transpose and conjugate transpose of $A$. Then,
(a) rank $(AA^*A)=$ rank $(A)$
(b) rank $(A)=$ rank $(A^2)$
(c) rank $(A)=$ rank $(A'A)$
(d) rank $(A^2)-$ rank $(A)=$ rank $(A^3)-$ rank $(A^2)$

**63.** Let $A$ be an $n\times n$ matrix which is both Hermitian and unitary. Then,
(a) $A^2=I$
(b) $A$ is real
(c) the eigen value of $A$ are $0, 1, -1$
(d) the characteristic and minimal polynomials of $A$ are the same

**64.** Let $P$ be a matrix of order $m\times n$ and $Q$ be a matrix of order $n\times P$, $n\ne P$. If rank $(P)=n$ and rank $(Q)=P$, then rank $(PQ)$ is
(a) $n$ (b) $P$
(c) $nP$ (d) $n+P$

**65.** The following statement is correct.
(a) The matrix $A$ and its transpose $A^T$ have the same characteristic polynomials.
(b) Similar matrices have not the same characteristic polynomials.
(c) The trace of two similar matrices are not same.
(d) The determinant of two similar matrices are not same.

**66.** If $A=\begin{bmatrix}1 & -1\\ 2 & -1\end{bmatrix}$, then the model matrix $P$ is
(a) $\begin{bmatrix}-1 & 1\\ 1+i & 1+i\end{bmatrix}$ (b) $\begin{bmatrix}1 & 1\\ 1-i & 1+i\end{bmatrix}$
(c) $\begin{bmatrix}1 & -1\\ 1+i & 1-i\end{bmatrix}$ (d) $\begin{bmatrix}-1 & -1\\ 1-i & 1+i\end{bmatrix}$

**67.** If $A=\begin{bmatrix}1 & -3 & 3\\ 3 & -5 & 3\\ 6 & -6 & 4\end{bmatrix}$, then $P^{-1}AP$ is
(a) $\begin{bmatrix}-2 & 0 & 0\\ 0 & -2 & 0\\ 0 & 0 & 4\end{bmatrix}$ (b) $\begin{bmatrix}-4 & 0 & 0\\ 0 & -4 & 0\\ 0 & 0 & 2\end{bmatrix}$
(c) $\begin{bmatrix}-4 & 0 & 0\\ 0 & 2 & 0\\ 0 & 0 & 2\end{bmatrix}$ (d) $\begin{bmatrix}2 & 0 & 6\\ 0 & -2 & 0\\ 0 & 0 & 4\end{bmatrix}$

**68.** The determinant of the matrix
$$\begin{bmatrix}1 & 0 & 0 & 0 & 0 & 2\\ 0 & 1 & 0 & 2 & 2 & 0\\ 0 & 0 & 1 & 2 & 0 & 0\\ 0 & 0 & 2 & 1 & 0 & 0\\ 0 & 2 & 0 & 0 & 1 & 0\\ 2 & 0 & 0 & 0 & 0 & 1\end{bmatrix}$$ is
(a) 0 (b) $-9$ (c) $-27$ (d) 1

**69.** Let $A$ be a $3\times 3$ matrix with real entries such that $\det(A)=6$ and the trace of $A$ is 0. If $\det(A+I)=0$, where $I$ denotes the $3\times 3$ identity matrix, then the eigen values of $A$ are
(a) $-1, 2, 3$ (b) $-1, 2, -3$
(c) $1, 2, -3$ (d) $-1, -2, 3$

**70.** Let $n$ be a positive integer and let $H_n$ be the space of all $n \times n$ matrices $A = (a_{ij})$ with entries in $\mathbb{R}$ satisfying $a_{ij} = a_{rs}$ whenever $i + j = r + s$ $(i, j, r, s = 1, 2, \ldots, n)$. Then, the dimension of $H_n$, as a vector space over $R$ is

(a) $n^2$ (b) $n^2 - n + 1$
(c) $2n + 1$ (d) $2n - 1$

**71.** Let $\omega$ be a complex number such that $\omega^3 = 1$, but $\omega \neq 1$. If $A = \begin{bmatrix} 1 & \omega & \omega^2 \\ \omega & \omega^2 & 1 \\ \omega^2 & \omega & 1 \end{bmatrix}$, then which of the following statement are true?

(a) $A$ is invertible
(b) rank $(A) = 2$
(c) 0 is an eigen value of $A$
(d) There exists linearly independent vectors $v, \omega \in C^3$ such that $Av = A\omega = 0$

**72.** Let $A$ be a $4 \times 4$ matrix with real entries such that $-1, 1, 2, -2$ are its eigen values. If $B = A^4 - 5A^2 + 5I$, where $I$ denotes the $4 \times 4$ identity matrix, then which of the following statements are correct?

(a) $\det(A + B) = 0$ (b) $\det(B) = 1$
(c) trace of $A - B$ is 0 (d) trace of $A + B$ is 4

**73.** Consider a matrix $A = [a_{ij}]_{n \times n}$ with integer entries such that $a_{ij} = 0$ for $i > j$ and $a_{ii} = 1$ for $i = 1, \ldots, n$. Which of the following properties must be true?

(a) $A^{-1}$ exists and it has integer entries.
(b) $A^{-1}$ exists and it has some entries that not integers.
(c) $A^{-1}$ is a polynomial function of $A$ with rational coefficients.
(d) $A^{-1}$ is not a power of $A$ unless $A$ is the identity matrix.

**74.** The number of vectors of maximum set of linearly independent eigen vectors of $A = \begin{bmatrix} 4 & 1 & -1 \\ 2 & 5 & -2 \\ 1 & 1 & 2 \end{bmatrix}$ is

(a) 1 (b) 2
(c) 3 (d) None of these

**75.** Which one of the following is correct?

(a) $R$ is a vector space over $N$.
(b) $R$ is a vector space over $C$.
(c) $R$ is a vector space over $Z$.
(d) None of the above

**76.** Let $V$ be the vector space of $m \times n$ matrices over a field $k$, then the dimension of $V$ is

(a) $n$ (b) $m$
(c) $mn$ (d) $m - n$

**77.** The dimension of $C(R)$ is

(a) 1 (b) 2
(c) 3 (d) 4

**78.** Let $V$ be the vector space of ordered pairs of complex numbers over the real field $\mathbb{R}$. Then, the dimension of $V$ is

(a) 1 (b) 2 (c) 3 (d) 4

**79.** The dimension of $R(Q)$ is

(a) 1 (b) finite
(c) infinite (d) None of these

**80.** Let $A$ be an $m \times n$ matrix where $m < n$. Consider the system of linear equation $A\underline{X} = \underline{b}$, where $b$ is an $n \times 1$ column vector and $b \neq 0$. Which of the following is always true?

(a) The system of equations has no solution.
(b) The system of equations has a solution if and only if it has infinitely many solutions.
(c) The system of equations has a unique solution.
(d) The system of equations has atleast one solution.

**81.** The set of all solutions to the system of equations $(1 - i)x_1 - ix_2 = 0$, $2x_1 + (1 - i)x_2 = 0$ is given by

(a) $(x_1, x_2) = (0, 0)$
(b) $(x_1, x_2) = (1, 1)$
(c) $(x_1, x_2) = C\left(1, \cos\frac{5\pi}{4} + i\sin\frac{5\pi}{4}\right)$, where $C$ is any complex number
(d) $(x_1, x_2) = C\left(\cos\frac{3\pi}{4}, i\sin\frac{3\pi}{4}\right)$, where $C$ is any complex number

**82.** The characteristic polynomial of the $3 \times 3$ real matrix $A = \begin{bmatrix} 0 & 0 & -c \\ 1 & 0 & -b \\ 0 & 1 & -a \end{bmatrix}$ is

(a) $\lambda^3 + a\lambda^2 + b\lambda + c$ (b) $(\lambda - a)(\lambda - b)(\lambda - c)$
(c) $(\lambda - 1)(\lambda - abc)^2$ (d) $(\lambda - 1)^2(\lambda - abc)$

**83.** Let $A$ be $n \times n$ matrix over $R$. Consider the following statements

I. Rank $A = n$
II. Det $(A) \neq 0$

Then,

(a) I $\Rightarrow$ II but II does not imply I
(b) II $\Rightarrow$ I but I does not imply II
(c) I $\Leftrightarrow$ II
(d) There is no relation between the statements

**84.** Let $S$ be the relation space of a set of $m$ homogeneous linear equations with real coefficients in $n$ unknowns. If $A$ is the matrix of this system of equations, then

(a) dimension $S = n -$ rank $A$
(b) dimension $S$ is always $n$
(c) dimension $S$ is infinite
(d) dimension $S = n +$ rank $A$

**85.** If the characteristic roots of $\begin{bmatrix} 3 & 7 \\ 2 & 5 \end{bmatrix}$ are $\lambda_1$ and $\lambda_2$, the characteristic roots of $\begin{bmatrix} 5 & -7 \\ -2 & 3 \end{bmatrix}$ are

(a) $\lambda_1 + \lambda_2, \lambda_1 - \lambda_2$ (b) $\frac{1}{\lambda_1}$ and $\frac{1}{\lambda_2}$
(c) $2\lambda_1$ and $2\lambda_2$ (d) $\lambda_1 + \lambda_2$ and $|\lambda_1 - \lambda_2|$

**86.** If $A$ and $B$ are two $n \times n$ matrices over $\mathbb{R}$ and $\alpha \in \mathbb{R}$, then

(a) $\det(\alpha A + B) = \alpha \det(A) + \det(B)$
(b) $\det(\alpha A - B) = \alpha \det(A) + \det(B)$
(c) $\det(\alpha A \cdot B) = \alpha \det(A) + \det(B)$
(d) $\det(\alpha A \cdot B) = \alpha^n \det(A) + \det(B)$

**87.** Let $V$ be the vector space of real polynomials of degree not exceeding 2. Let $f(x) = x - 1$, $g(x) = x + 1$, $h(x) = x^2 - 1$, $f(x) = x^2 + 1$. Then, the set $\{f, g, h, j\}$ is

(a) linearly independent
(b) linearly dependent $fg = h$
(c) linearly dependent because $f + g - h = 0$
(d) linearly dependent because $f - g - h + j = 0$

**88.** If $A = \begin{bmatrix} 2 & 1 \\ 3 & -1 \end{bmatrix}$ and $I = \begin{bmatrix} 1 & 0 \\ 0 & 1 \end{bmatrix}$. Which of the following is the zero matrix?

(a) $A^2 - A - 5I$
(b) $A^2 + A - 5I$
(c) $A^2 + A - I$
(d) $A^2 - 3A + 5I$

**89.** Let $W_1$ and $W_2$ be finite dimensional subspaces of a vector space $V$. If $\dim W_1 = 2$, $\dim W_2 = 2$, $\dim(W_1 + W_2) = 3$, then $\dim(W_1 \cap W_2)$ is

(a) 1 (b) 2
(c) 3 (d) 4

**90.** In the vector space $\mathbb{R}^3$, the coordinate vector of $(3, 5, -2)$ relative to the ordered basis $\{(1, 0, 0), (0, 1, 0), (0, 0, 1)\}$ is

(a) $(5, 3, -2)$ (b) $(3, 5, -2)$
(c) $(-2, 5, 3)$ (d) $(-2, 3, 5)$

**91.** Let $T$ be an arbitrary linear transformation from $\mathbb{R}^n$ to $\mathbb{R}^n$, which is not one-one, then

(a) rank $T > 0$ (b) rank $T = n$
(c) rank $T < n$ (d) rank $T = n - 1$

**92.** Let the characteristic equation of a matrix $M$ be $\lambda^2 - \lambda - 1 = 0$, then

(a) $M^{-1}$ does not exist
(b) $M^{-1}$ exists but cannot be determined from the data
(c) $M^{-1} = M - 1$
(d) $M^{-1} = M + 1$

**93.** The zero vector in the vector space $R^4$ is

(a) $(0, 0)$ (b) $(0, 0, 0)$
(c) $(0, 0, 0, 0)$ (d) None of these

**94.** Let $V$ be the vector space of all $2 \times 2$ matrices over the field $F$. The dimension of $V$ is

(a) 2 (b) 3
(c) 4 (d) None of these

**95.** The dimension of the vector space spanned by $(1, -2, 3, -1)$ and $(1, 1, -2, 3)$ is

(a) 1 (b) 2
(c) 4 (d) None of these

**96.** Consider the matrix $M = \begin{bmatrix} a^2 & ab & ac \\ ab & b^2 & bc \\ ac & bc & c^2 \end{bmatrix}$, where $a$, $b$ and $c$ are non-zero real numbers. Then, the matrix has

(a) three non-zero real eigen values
(b) complex eigen values
(c) two non-zero eigen values
(d) only one non-zero eigen value

**97.** If $W$ be a subspace of a finite dimensional vector space $V(F)$, then $\dim V/W$ is equal to

(a) $\dim V - \dim W$ (b) $\dim V + \dim W$
(c) $\dfrac{\dim V}{\dim W}$ (d) None of these

**98.** The vector space $V_3(\mathbb{R})$ is of dimension

(a) 1 (b) 3
(c) 2 (d) None of these

**99.** Let $M = \begin{bmatrix} 1 & 1+i & 2i & 9 \\ 1-i & 3 & 4 & 7-i \\ -2i & 4 & 5 & i \\ 9 & 7+i & -i & 7 \end{bmatrix}$, then

(a) $M$ has purely imaginary eigen values
(b) $M$ has only real eigen values
(c) $M$ is not diagonalizable
(d) $M$ has eigen values which are neither real nor purely imaginary

**100.** The dimension of the vector space $C(R)$ is

(a) 1 (b) 2
(c) 4 (d) None of these

**101.** The dimension of the vector space $C^{-2}(R)$ is

(a) 2 (b) 4
(c) 1 (d) None of these

**102.** If $(m, 3, 1)$ is a linear combination of vectors $(3, 2, 1)$ and $(2, 1, 0)$ in $\mathbb{R}^3$, then the value of $m$ is

(a) 1 (b) 3
(c) 5 (d) None of these

**103.** The set $V = \{(x, y) \in \mathbb{R}^2 : xy \geq 0\}$ is

(a) a vector subspace of $\mathbb{R}^2$
(b) not a vector subspace of $\mathbb{R}^2$, since every element does not have an inverse in $V$
(c) not a vector subspace of $\mathbb{R}^2$, since it is not closed under scalar multiplication
(d) not a vector subspace of $\mathbb{R}^2$, since it is not closed under vector addition

**104.** If $M$ is a $7 \times 5$ matrix of rank 3 and $N$ is a $5 \times 7$ matrix of rank 5, then rank $(MN)$ is

(a) 5 (b) 3
(c) 2 (d) 1

**105.** The dimension of the vector space spanned by $(1, -2, 3, -1)$ and $(1, 1, -2, 3)$ is

(a) 1 (b) 2
(c) 4 (d) None of these

**106.** The number of elements in the vector space of polynomials of degree atmost $n$ in which the coefficients are the elements of the field $I(P)$ over the field $I(P)$, $P$ being a prime number is

(a) $p^{n+1}$ (b) $p^n$

(c) $p^{n-1}$ (d) None of these

**107.** Let $S$ and $T$ be two subspaces of $R^{24}$ such that $\dim(S) = 19$ and $\dim(T) = 17$, then the

(a) smallest possible value of $\dim(S \cap T)$ is 2

(b) largest possible value of $\dim(S \cap T)$ is 18

(c) smallest possible value of $\dim(S + T)$ is 19

(d) largest possible value of $\dim(S + T)$ is 22

**108.** The set of all $x \in \mathbb{R}$ for which the vectors $(1, x, 0)$, $(0, x^2, 1)$ and $(0, 1, x)$ are linearly independent in $\mathbb{R}^3$ is

(a) $\{x \in R : x = 0\}$ (b) $\{x \in R : x \neq 0\}$

(c) $\{x \in R : x \neq 1\}$ (d) $\{x \in R : x \neq -1\}$

**109.** Consider the system of linear equations

$x + y + z = 3$, $x - y - z = 4$, $x - 5y + kz = 6$

Then, the value of $k$ for which this system has an infinite number of solutions is

(a) $k = -5$ (b) $k = 0$

(c) $k = 1$ (d) $k = 3$

**110.** For which value of $\lambda$ will the matrix given below become singular?

$$\begin{bmatrix} 8 & \lambda & 0 \\ 4 & 0 & 2 \\ 12 & 6 & 0 \end{bmatrix}$$

(a) 4 (b) 6

(c) 8 (d) 12

**111.** Given matrix $[A] = \begin{bmatrix} 4 & 2 & 1 & 3 \\ 6 & 3 & 4 & 7 \\ 2 & 1 & 0 & 1 \end{bmatrix}$, the rank of the matrix is

(a) 4 (b) 3

(c) 2 (d) 1

**112.** Let $V_n(Z_p)$ be a vector space over the field $Z_p$. Then, the total number of distinct basis are

(a) $\dfrac{(p^n - 1)(p^n - p)\ldots(p^n - p^{n-1})}{n!}$

(b) $\dfrac{(p^n - 1)(p^n - p)\ldots(p^n - p^{n-1})}{p!}$

(c) $\dfrac{(p^n - 1)(p^n - p)\ldots.(p^n - p^{n-1})}{(n! - p!)^2}$

(d) None of the above

**113.** Let $V_n(Z_p)$ be a vector space over the field $Z_p$. Then, the total number of subspace of dimension $r$ are

(a) $\dfrac{(p^n - 1)(p^n - p)\ldots..(p^n - p^{n-1})}{(p^r - 1)(p^r - p)\ldots..(p^r - p^{r-1})}$

(b) $\dfrac{(p^n - 1)(p^n - p)\ldots..(p^n - p^{n-1})}{r!}$

(c) $\dfrac{(p^n - 1)(p^n - p)\ldots..(p^n - p^{n-1})}{p!}$

(d) $\dfrac{(p^n - 1)(p^n - p)\ldots..(p^n - p^{n-1})}{(p^n - 1)(p^n - p)\ldots..(p^n - p^{r-1})}$

**114.** The total number of basis of the vector space $V_3(Z_3)$ are

(a) 11232 (b) 11223

(c) 1024 (d) None of these

**115.** The total number of subspace of the vector space $V_2(Z_5)$ is/are

(a) 1 (b) 2

(c) 3 (d) 4

**116.** It is given that $X_1, X_2, \ldots, X_N$ are $N$ non-zero, orthogonal vectors. The dimension of the vector space spanned by the $2N$ vectors $X_1, X_2, \ldots, X_N$, $-X_1, -X_2, \ldots, -X_N$ is

(a) $2N$

(b) $N + 1$

(c) $N$

(d) dependent on the choice of $X_1, X_2, \ldots, X_N$

**117.** If the rank of a $(5 \times 6)$ matrix $A$ is 4, then which one of the following statements is correct?

(a) $A$ will have four linearly independent rows and four linearly independent columns

(b) $A$ will have four linearly independent rows and five linearly independent columns

(c) $AA^T$ will be invertible

(d) $A^TA$ will be invertible

**118.** Consider the set of vectors (columns) defined by $X = \{x \in R^3 : x_1 + x_2 + x_3 = 0$, where $x^T = [x_1, x_2, x_3]^T\}$. Which of the following is true?

(a) $\{[1, -1, 0]^T, [1, 0, -1]^T\}$ is a basis for the subspace $X$.

(b) $\{[1, -1, 0]^T, [1, 0, -1]^T\}$ is a linearly independent set, but it does not span $X$ and therefore is not a basis of $X$.

(c) $X$ is not a subspace for $R^3$.

(d) None of the above

**119.** Let $M_{n \times n}(R)$ be the set of all $n \times n$ matrices. Then, the subset $S =$ diagonal $(d_1, d_2, \ldots, d_n)$ where $d_i \in R$ of $M_{n \times n}(R)$ where Trace (Diagonal) = 0 where $A \in S$.

(a) The set $S$ does not forms a subspace of $V = M_{n \times n}$.

(b) The set $S$ is not closed *wrt* multiplication.

(c) Set $S$ form a subspace of dimension $(n - 1)$.

(d) Set $S$ form a subspace of dimension $(n^2 - 1)$.

**120.** Find the value of $k$ for which the following simultaneous equations

$$x + y + z = 3; x + 2y + 3z = 4; x + 4y + kz = 6$$

will not have a unique solution.

(a) 0 (b) 5

(c) 6 (d) 7

**121.** In the matrix equation $AX = B$, which of the following is a necessary condition for the existence of atleast one solution for the unknown vector $X$?

(a) Augmented matrix $[A : B]$ must have the same rank as matrix $P$.
(b) Vector $B$ must have only non-zero elements.
(c) Matrix $A$ must be singular.
(d) Matrix $A$ must be square.

**122.** Solution for the system defined by the set of equations $4y + 3z = 8$; $2x - z = 2$ and $3x + 2y = 5$ is

(a) $x = 0; y = 1; z = 4/3$
(b) $x = 0; y = 1/2; z = 2$
(c) $x = 1; y = 1/2; z = 2$
(d) not exist

**123.** Consider the system of simultaneous equations

$$x + 2y + z = 6;\ 2x + y + 2z = b;\ x + y + z = 5$$

This system has

(a) unique solution
(b) infinite number of solutions
(c) no solution
(d) exactly two solutions

**124.** The collection of all polynomial of degree $\le 5$, consider the derivative $DP = P'$. Then, which one of the following is correct?

(a) 0 must be eigen value for matrix $D$.
(b) 1 must be eigen value for matrix $D$.
(c) 5 must be eigen value for matrix $D$.
(d) None of the above

**125.** $A_{2\times2}$ matrix which satisfy $A^2 - A = 0$, then

(a) $A$ is either $\begin{bmatrix}1 & 0\\ 0 & 1\end{bmatrix}$ or $\begin{bmatrix}-1 & 0\\ 0 & -1\end{bmatrix}$
(b) $\exists$ infinite such matrix
(c) $\exists$ no such matrix
(d) must be diagonal

**126.** A is any $n \times n$ matrix with entries equal to 1, then

(a) multiplicity of 0 is $n - 1$
(b) multiplicity of 0 is 1
(c) multiplicity of 0 is $n$
(d) multiplicity of 0 is 0

**127.** $S = \{(x_1, x_2, \ldots, x_{100}) \in \mathbb{R}.$ s.t. $x_1 = x_2 = \ldots = x_{50},$ $x_{51} + x_{52} + \ldots + x_{100} = 0\}$.

Then, dim $S$ is

(a) 49 (b) 50
(c) 47 (d) 51

**128.** $A$ is any matrix which satisfy $A^3 - A^2 + A - I = 0$ and $A_{3\times3}$, then $A^4$ is

(a) $A = 0$ (b) $A = I$
(c) $\exists$ no such matrix (d) $A^3 + A^2 - A + I$

**129.** Consider the system $x + y + z = 0; x - y - z = 0$, then the system of equation have

(a) no solution
(b) infinite number of solution
(c) unique solution
(d) None of the above

**130.** Consider $S = \{a_0 + a_1x + a_2x^2 + a_3x^3 : a_i \in \mathbb{R}, i = 0, 1, 2, 3\}$ with usual addition and multiplication

(a) $S$ does not form a vector space
(b) for vector space with dim 4
(c) $S$ does not form vector space because does not have identity
(d) form a vector space with dim 3

**131.** For the set of equations

$$x_1 + 2x_2 + x_3 + 4x_4 = 2$$
$$3x_1 + 6x_2 + 3x_3 + 12x_4 = 6$$

The following statement is true

(a) only the trivial solution $x_1 = x_2 = x_3 = x_4 = 0$ exists
(b) there are no solution
(c) a unique non-trivial solution exists
(d) multiple non-trivial solutions exists

**132.** The eigen values of the matrix $\begin{bmatrix}4 & -2\\ -2 & 1\end{bmatrix}$ are

(a) 1, 4 (b) −1, 2
(c) 0, 5 (d) Cannot be determined

**133.** Which one of the following is an eigen vector of the matrix $\begin{bmatrix}5 & 0 & 0 & 0\\ 0 & 5 & 5 & 0\\ 0 & 0 & 2 & 1\\ 0 & 0 & 3 & 1\end{bmatrix}$

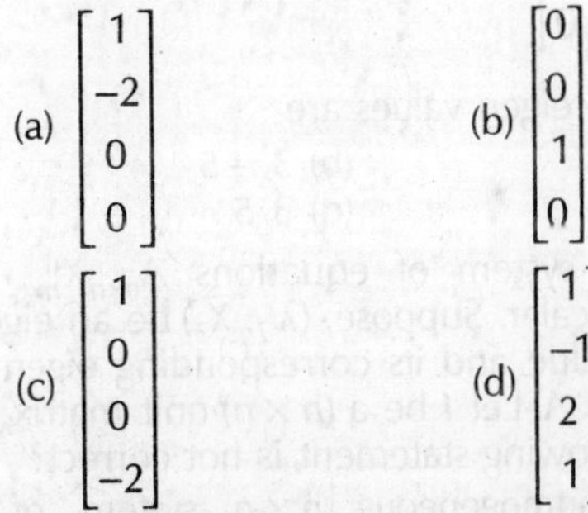

(a) $\begin{bmatrix}1\\ -2\\ 0\\ 0\end{bmatrix}$ (b) $\begin{bmatrix}0\\ 0\\ 1\\ 0\end{bmatrix}$

(c) $\begin{bmatrix}1\\ 0\\ 0\\ -2\end{bmatrix}$ (d) $\begin{bmatrix}1\\ -1\\ 2\\ 1\end{bmatrix}$

**134.** The linear operation $L(X)$ is defined by the cross product $L(X) = bX_X$, where $b = [0 \ \ 1 \ \ 0]^T$ and $X = [x_1 \ \ x_2 \ \ x_3]^T$ are three dimensional vectors. The $3 \times 3$ matrix $A$ of this operation satisfies. $L(X) = A\begin{bmatrix}x_1\\ x_2\\ x_3\end{bmatrix}$.

Then, the eigen values of $A$ are

(a) $0, 1, -1$ (b) $1, -1, 1$
(c) $i, -i, 1$ (d) $i, -i, 0$

**135.** Let $A$ be a $4 \times 3$ matrix whose columns form a linearly independent set which conclusion is justified *i.e.*, which are true?

(a) The set of rows in $A$ is linearly dependent.
(b) The equation $Ax = b$ is consistent for every $b$ in $\mathbb{R}^4$.
(c) The equation $Ax = 0$ has a non-trivial solution.
(d) There is a matrix $B$ s.t. $AB = I_4$.

**136.** The eigen vectors of the matrix $\begin{bmatrix} 1 & 2 \\ 0 & 2 \end{bmatrix}$ are written in the form $\begin{bmatrix} 1 \\ a \end{bmatrix}$ and $\begin{bmatrix} 1 \\ b \end{bmatrix}$. What is $a+b$?

(a) 0 (b) 1/2
(c) 1 (d) 2

**137.** The number of different $n \times n$ symmetric matrices with each element being either 0 or 1 where $n = 5$

(a) 5! (b) $5^5$
(c) $2^{15}$ (d) $5^{15}$

**138.** An eigen vector of $A = \begin{bmatrix} 1 & 1 & 0 \\ 0 & 2 & 2 \\ 0 & 0 & 3 \end{bmatrix}$ is

(a) $[-1 \;\; 1 \;\; 1]^T$ (b) $[1 \;\; 2 \;\; 1]^T$
(c) $[1 \;\; -1 \;\; 2]^T$ (d) $[2 \;\; 1 \;\; -1]^T$

**139.** How many of the following have an eigen value 1?

$$\begin{bmatrix} 1 & 0 \\ 0 & 0 \end{bmatrix}\begin{bmatrix} 0 & 1 \\ 0 & 0 \end{bmatrix} \text{ and } \begin{bmatrix} -1 & 0 \\ 1 & -1 \end{bmatrix}$$

(a) one (b) two
(c) three (d) four

**140.** For the matrix

$$A = \begin{bmatrix} 2 & -2 & 3 \\ -2 & -1 & 6 \\ 1 & 2 & 0 \end{bmatrix} \text{ one of the eigen values is 3.}$$

The other two eigen values are

(a) 2, – 5 (b) 3, – 5
(c) 2, 5 (d) 3, 5

**141.** Consider the system of equations $A_{n \times n} X_{n \times t} = \lambda_{n \times 1}$ where $\lambda$ is a scalar. Suppose, $(\lambda_i, X_i)$ be an eigen pair of an eigen value and its corresponding eigen vector for real matrix $A$. Let $I$ be a $(n \times n)$ unit matrix, which one of the following statement is not correct?

(a) For a homogeneous $n \times n$ system of linear equations $(A - \lambda I)X = 0$ having a non-trivial solution, the rank of $(A - \lambda I)$ is less than $n$.
(b) For a matrix $A^m$, $m$ being a positive integer $(\lambda_i^m, x_i^m)$ will be the eigen pair for all $i$.
(c) If $A^T = A^{-1}$, then $|\lambda_i| = 1, \forall i$
(d) If $A^T = A$, then $\lambda_i$ is real, $\forall i$

**142.** Consider the following matrix $A = \begin{bmatrix} 2 & 3 \\ x & y \end{bmatrix}$.

If the eigen values of $A$ are 4 and 8, then

(a) $x = 4, y = 10$ (b) $x = 5, y = 8$
(c) $x = -3, y = 9$ (d) $x = -4, y = 10$

**143.** The eigen values of the matrix $\begin{bmatrix} -1 & 3 & 5 \\ -3 & -1 & 6 \\ 0 & 0 & 3 \end{bmatrix}$ are

(a) $3, 3 + 5i, 6 - i$ (b) $-6 + 5i, 3 + i, 3 - i$
(c) $3 + i, 3 - i, 5 + i$ (d) $3, -1 + 3i, -1 - 3i$

**144.** The eigen values of a skew-symmetric matrix are

(a) always zero
(b) always pure imaginary
(c) either zero or pure imaginary
(d) always real

**145.** The characteristic equation of a $(3 \times 3)$ matrix $A$ is defined as $a(\lambda) = |\lambda I - A| = \lambda^3 + \lambda^2 + 2\lambda + 1 = 0$. If $I$ denotes identity matrix, then the inverse of matrix $A$ will be

(a) $A^2 + A + 2I$ (b) $A^2 + A + I$
(c) $-(A^2 + A + I)$ (d) $-(A^2 + A + 2I)$

**146.** If $A = \begin{bmatrix} -3 & 2 \\ -1 & 0 \end{bmatrix}$, then calculate $A^9$.

(a) $511A + 510I$ (b) $309A + 104I$
(c) $154A + 155I$ (d) $\exp(9A)$

**147.** If $A = \begin{bmatrix} -3 & 2 \\ -1 & 0 \end{bmatrix}$, then $A$ satisfies the relation

(a) $A + 3I + 2A^{-1} = O$ (b) $A^2 + 2A + 2I = O$
(c) $(A + I)(A + 2I) = O$ (d) $\exp(A) = 0$

**148.** If $V$ and $W$ are subspaces of $\mathbb{R}^n$, then

(a) $V \cup W$ is necessarily a subspace of $\mathbb{R}^n$
(b) $V \cup W$ is never a subspace of $\mathbb{R}^n$
(c) $V \cup W$ is a subspace of $\mathbb{R}^n$ if and only if one of $V, W$ is contained in the other
(d) $V \cup W$ is a subspace of $\mathbb{R}^n$ if and only if one of $V, W$ in $\{0\}$

**149.** Let $V_1, V_2, V_3$ be three non-zero vectors in $\mathbb{R}^n$ are linearly dependent, then

(a) $V_3$ must be a linear combination of $V_1$ and $V_2$
(b) $V_2$ must be a linear combination of $V_1$ and $V_3$
(c) $V_1$ must be a linear combination of $V_2$ and $V_3$
(d) None of the above

**150.** Let $S, T$ be subsets of a vector space $V$ and $S \subseteq T$. Consider the following statements.

I. If $T$ is linearly independent, then $S_0$ is $S$.
II. If $T$ generates $V$, then $S$ also must generate $V$.
III. If $S$ is linearly independent, then $T$ must be linearly independent.
IV. If $S$ generates $V$, then $S_0$ does $T$.

Then,

(a) I and III are true, but I and IV are false
(b) I and IV are true, but II and III are false
(c) I and III are true, but II and IV are false
(d) II and IV are true, but I and III are false

**151.** Let $V$ and $W$ be subspaces of $\mathbb{R}^n$. Then,

(a) $\dim(V + W)$ must be $\dim V + \dim W$
(b) $\dim(V + W) > \dim V + \dim W$
(c) $\dim(V + W) < \min(\dim V > \dim W)$
(d) $\dim(V + W) \geq \max\{\dim V, \dim W\}$

**152.** Let $V$ be vector spaces of $n \times n$ matrices over $\mathbb{R}$, and $W$ be the subspace. Then, $T$ is a linear transformation if and only if of matrices with entries in each row adding upto zero. Then, the dimension of $W$ is

(a) $n$ (b) $\frac{n(n-1)}{2}$

(c) $n-1$ (d) $n(n-1)$

**153.** If $A$ is a $3\times3$ matrix over $\mathbb{R}$ and $\alpha, \beta, \alpha\neq\beta$ are the only characteristic roots (eigen values) of $A$ in $\mathbb{R}$, then the characteristic polynomial of $A$ is

(a) $(x-\alpha)(x-\beta)$

(b) $(x-\alpha)^3+(x-\beta)^3$

(c) $(x-\alpha)(x-\beta)(x-\gamma)$ for some $\gamma\neq\alpha,\beta$

(d) $(x-\alpha)^2(x-\beta)$ or $(x-\alpha)(x-\beta)^2$

**154.** Let $A, B, C$ be $m\times n$ matrices. Then, rank $\begin{bmatrix} A & B \\ 0 & C\end{bmatrix}$ is

(a) equal to [rank $k(A)$ + rank $(B)$ + rank $(C)$]

(b) equal to [rank $(A)$ + rank $(B)$ − rank $(C)$]

(c) equal to [rank $(A)$ + rank $(C)$ − rank $(B)$]

(d) atleast rank $A$ + rank $C$

**155.** Let $A$ be an $m\times n$ matrix, $\bar{b}\in\mathbb{R}^m$, then the system of equations $A\bar{x}=\bar{b}$ has a solution if and only if

(a) $\bar{b}\in$ column space of $A$

(b) $\bar{b}\in$ row space of $A$

(c) $\bar{b}=0$

(d) rank $[A,\bar{b}]>$ rank $A$

**156.** Let $S=\{(0,1,\alpha),(\alpha,1,0),(1,\alpha,1)\}$. Then, $S$ is a basis for $\mathbb{R}^3$ if and only if

(a) $\alpha\neq0$ (b) $\alpha\neq1$

(c) $\alpha\neq0$ and $\alpha^2\neq2$ (d) $-1\leq\alpha\leq1$

**157.** Let $A$ be a $3\times3$ matrix and consider the system of equation

$Ax=\begin{bmatrix}1\\0\\-1\end{bmatrix}$. Then,

(a) if the system is consistent, then it has a unique solution.

(b) if A is singular, then the system has infinitely many solution

(c) if the system is consistent, then the $|A|\neq0$

(d) if the system has a unique solution, then $A$ is non-singular

**158.** The characteristic polynomial of $3\times3$ matrix $A$ is $|\lambda I-A|=\lambda^3+3\lambda^2+4\lambda+3$

Let $x=$ trace $(A)$ and $y=|A|$, the determinant of $A$. Then,

(a) $\frac{x}{y}=\frac{3}{4}$ (b) $\frac{x}{y}=\frac{4}{3}$

(c) $x=y=-3$ (d) $x=3$ and $y=-3$

**159.** Let $S=\{(-1,0,1),(2,1,4)\}$. The value of $k$ for which the vector $(3k+2,3,10)$ belongs to the linear span of $S$ is

(a) −2 (b) 2

(c) 8 (d) 3

**160.** Let $S=\{x_1x_2\ldots x_m\}$ and $T=\{y_1y_2\ldots y_n\}$ be subsets of the vector space $V$. Then,

(a) if $S$ and $T$ are both linearly independent, then $m=n$

(b) if $S$ is a basis for $V$ and if $T$ spans $V$. Then, $m\geq n$

(c) if $S$ is a basis for $V$ and if $T$ in linearly independent, then $m\leq n$

(d) if $S$ is linearly independent and if $T$ spans $V$, then $m\leq n$

**161.** Let $A$ and $B$ be $n\times n$ matrices. Then, the incorrect statement among the following is

(a) trace $(AB)$ = trace $(BA)$

(b) $|AB|=|BA|$

(c) rank $(AB)$ = rank $(BA)$

(d) if $AB=0$, then rank $(A)$ + rank $(B)<2n$

**162.** Let $A$ be a real $4\times4$ matrix with characteristic polynomial $P(T)=(T^2+1)^2$. Which of the following is true?

(a) $A$ is diagonalizable over complex number but not over real numbers.

(b) $A$ is nilpotent.

(c) $A$ is invertible.

(d) there is no such matrix $A$.

**163.** The characteristic vector of the matrix $\begin{bmatrix}2&3\\1&4\end{bmatrix}$ corresponding to characteristic root 1 is

(a) $(-1,1)$ (b) $(3,1)$

(c) $(-3,1)$ (d) $(1,-3)$

**164.** Which one of the following is not a basis of $R^3$?

(a) $\{(3,0,0),(0,-1,0),(0,0,\frac{1}{2})$

(b) $(0,0,-3),(1,2,3),(1,2,1)$

(c) $(1,2,-1),(1,1,1),(1,3,5)$

(d) $(1,1,0),(1,2,3)(0,0,1)$

**165.** A system of linear equations $x+2y-z=11$, $3x+y-2z=10$, $x-3y=5$ has

(a) no solution

(b) exactly one solution

(c) exactly 3 solutions

(d) infinitely many solution

**166.** The constant term of the characteristic polynomial of the matrix $\begin{bmatrix}1&2&6&5\\2&4&12&10\\-1&3&2&-5\\3&-2&1&-4\end{bmatrix}$ is

(a) 0 (b) 1

(c) trace $A$ (d) 2

**167.** $W$ is a 3-dimensional subspace of a finite dimensional vector space $V$. If the quotient space $V/W$ has dimension 8, the dimension of $V$ is

(a) 3 (b) 8

(c) 11 (d) 5

**168.** Which of the following sets of function is linearly dependent in the vector space $C[0, 1]$ of real continuous functions over $[0, 1]$?

(a) $\{1, x, x^2 + 1\}$ (b) $\{\sqrt{2}, x^2, x^3, 3x^2 + \sqrt{2}\}$
(c) $\{x + 1, x^2 + 1\}$ (d) $\{x^2 + 1, x^2 + 5\}$

**169.** The minimal polynomial of the $3 \times 3$ real matrix $\begin{bmatrix} a & 0 & 0 \\ 0 & a & 0 \\ 0 & 0 & b \end{bmatrix}$ is

(a) $(x - a)(x - b)$ (b) $(x - a)^2(x - b)$
(c) $(x - a)^2(x - b)^2$ (d) $(x - a)(x - b)^2$

**170.** If $\dim \frac{V}{W} = 8$ and $\dim W = 3$. Then, $\dim V$ is

(a) 11 (b) 5
(c) 10 (d) 1

**171.** Consider the two statements

I. Rank $(A)$ + Rank $(B)$ = max {Rank $(A)$, Rank $(B)$}
II. Rank $(A)$ + Rank $(B) \leq$ min {Rank $(A)$, Rank $(B)$}

Then,

(a) I is true but II is false (b) II is true but I is false
(c) Both are true (d) Both are false

**172.** Let $A = \begin{bmatrix} 0 & 1 & 1 \\ 1 & 0 & 1 \\ 1 & 1 & 0 \end{bmatrix}$, then the eigen values of $A$ are

(a) 2, 1 and 0 (b) 2, $(1 + i)$ and $(1 - i)$
(c) 2, $-1$ and $-1$ (d) 1, $-1$ and 0

**173.** Let $\{e_1, e_2, e_3\}$ be a basis of a vector space $V$ over $R$. Consider the following sets

$A = \{e_2, e_1 + e_2, e_1 + e_2 + e_3\}$

$B = \{e_1, e_1 - e_2, e_1 - e_2 + e_3\}$

$C = \{2e_1, 3e_2 + e_3, 6e_1 + 3e_2 + e_3\}$, then

(a) $A$ and $B$ are basis of $V$ (b) $A$ and $C$ are basis of $V$
(c) $B$ and $C$ are basis of $V$ (d) only $B$ is a basis of $V$

**174.** Let $A$ be an $n \times m$ matrix and $b = (b_1, b_2, \ldots, b_n)^t$ be a fined vector. Consider a system of $n$ linear equations $Ax = b$, where $x = (x_1, x_2, \ldots, x_n)^t$. Consider the following statements.

I. If rank $A = n$, the system has a unique solution.
II. If rank $A < n$, the system has infinitely many solutions.
III. If $b = 0$, the system has atleast one solution.

Which of the following is correct?

(a) I and II are true (b) I and III are true
(c) Only I is true (d) Only II is true

**175.** Let $A = \begin{bmatrix} \cos\theta & -\sin\theta \\ \sin\theta & \cos\theta \end{bmatrix}$ be such that $A$ has real eigen values, then

(a) $\theta = n\pi$ for some integer $n$
(b) $\theta = 2n\pi + \frac{\pi}{2}$ for some integer $n$
(c) there is no restriction on $\theta$
(d) $\theta = 2n\pi + \frac{\pi}{4}$ for some integer $n$

**176.** Let $A = [a_{ij}]$ be an $n \times n$ matrix with real entries such that the sum of all the entries in each row is zero. Consider the following statements.

I. $A$ is non-singular.
II. $A$ is singular.
III. 0 is an eigen value of $A$.

Which of the following is correct?

(a) Only I is true (b) I and III are true
(c) II and III are true (d) Only III is true

**177.** Let $A = [a_{ij}]$ be an $n \times n$ matrix such that $a_{ij} = 3, \forall\, i$ and $j$. Then, the nullity of $A$ is

(a) $n - 1$ (b) $n - 3$
(c) $n$ (d) 0

**178.** Let $A$ be a non-zero matrix of order 8 with $A^2 = 0$. Then, one of the possible value for rank of $A$ is

(a) 5 (b) 6
(c) 4 (d) 8

**179.** Let $V$ be the vector space of all $5 \times 5$ real skew-symmetric matrices. Then, the dimension of $V$ is

(a) 20 (b) 15
(c) 10 (d) 5

**180.** A homogeneous system of 5 linear equation in 6-variables admits

(a) no solution in $\mathbb{R}^6$
(b) a unique solution in $\mathbb{R}^6$
(c) infinitely many solutions in $\mathbb{R}^6$
(d) finite, but more than 2 solutions in $\mathbb{R}^6$

**181.** Let $V = \{(x_1, x_2, \ldots, x_{100}) \in R^{100} : x_1 = 2x_2 = 3x_3$ and $x_{51} - x_{52} - \ldots - x_{100} = 0\}$. Then, $\dim V$ is

(a) 98 (b) 49
(c) 99 (d) 97

**182.** A square matrix $A$ is said to be idempotent, if $A^2 = A$. An idempotent matrix is non-singular if and only if

(a) all eigen values are real
(b) all eigen values are non-negative
(c) all eigen values are either 1 or 0
(d) all eigen values are 1

**183.** The system of simultaneous linear equations

$$x + y + z = 0$$
$$x - y - z = 0 \text{ has}$$

(a) no solution in $\mathbb{R}^3$
(b) a unique solution in $\mathbb{R}^3$
(c) infinitely many solution in $\mathbb{R}^3$
(d) more than 2 but finitely many solutions in $\mathbb{R}^3$

**184.** Let $P(3) = \{a_0 + a_1x + a_2x^2 + a_3x^3 : a_i \in R, i = 0, 1, 2, 3\}$. Under the standard operation of addition (+) and scalar multiplication $(\cdot)$, $P(3)$ is

(a) not a vector space
(b) a vector space of infinite dimension
(c) a vector space of dimension 3
(d) a vector space of dimension 4

**185.** Let $V = \{(x_1, x_2, ..., x_{100}) \in R^{100} : x_1 = ... = x_{50}$ and $x_{51} + x_{52} + ... + x_{100} = 0\}$. Then, dim$V$ is
(a) 98 (b) 51
(c) 49 (d) 50

**186.** If $A$ is a symmetric matrix $\lambda_1, \lambda_2, ..., \lambda_n$ be the eigen values of $A$ and $a_{11}, a_{22}, a_{33}, ..., a_{nn}$ is the diagonal entries of $A$. Then, which of the following is correct?
(a) $\Sigma a_{ii} < \Sigma \lambda_i$ (b) $\Sigma a_{ii} = \Sigma \lambda_i$
(c) $\Sigma a_{ii} > \Sigma \lambda_i$ (d) $\Sigma a_{ii} \le \Sigma \lambda_i$

**187.** Let $S = \{A : A = [a_{ij}]_{5\times 5}, a_{ij} = 0$ or $1, \forall i, j, \Sigma a_{ij} = 1, \forall i$ and $\sum_j a_{ij} = \forall j\}$. Then, the number of elements in $S$ is
(a) $5^2$ (b) $5^5$
(c) 5! (d) 55

**188.** Let $D$ be a non-zero $n \times n$ real matrix with $n \ge 2$. Which of the following implications is valid?
(a) Det $(D) = 0 \Rightarrow$ rank $(D) = 0$
(b) Det $(D) = 1 \Rightarrow$ rank $(D) \ne 1$
(c) Rank $(D) = 1 \Rightarrow$ det $(D) \ne 0$
(d) Rank $(D) = n \Rightarrow$ det $(D) \ne 1$

**189.** The dimension of the vector space of all symmetric matrices of order $n \times n (n \ge 2)$ with real entries and trace equal to zero is
(a) $\left(\frac{n^2 - n}{2}\right) - 1$ (b) $\left(\frac{n^2 + n}{2}\right) - 1$
(c) $\left(\frac{n^2 - 2n}{2}\right) - 1$ (d) $\left(\frac{n^2 + 2n}{2}\right) - 1$

**190.** Let $A$ be an $n \times n$ complex matrices whose characteristic polynomial is given by $f(t) = t^n + C_{n-1}t^{n-1} + ... + C_1 t + C_0$. Then,
(a) det $(A) = C_{n-1}$ (b) det $(A) = C_0$
(c) det $(A) = (-1)^n C_{n-1}$ (d) det $(A) = (-1)^n C_0$

**191.** Consider the subspace $W = \{[a_{ij}] : a_{ij} = 0$ if $i$ is even$\}$ of all $10 \times 10$. Then, dimension of $W$ is
(a) 25 (b) 50
(c) 75 (d) 100

**192.** Minimal polynomial $m(x)$ of $A_{n\times n}$, each of whose element is 1, is
(a) $x - 1$ (b) $x^2 + x$
(c) $x^2 + nx$ (d) $x^2 - nx$

**193.** The minimum polynomial $m(\lambda)$ of

$$M = \begin{bmatrix} 2 & 8 & 0 & 0 & 0 & 0 & 0 \\ 0 & 2 & 0 & 0 & 0 & 0 & 0 \\ 0 & 0 & 2 & 4 & 0 & 0 & 0 \\ 0 & 0 & 0 & 5 & 0 & 0 & 0 \\ 0 & 0 & 0 & 0 & 0 & 3 & 0 \\ 0 & 0 & 0 & 0 & 0 & 0 & 0 \\ 0 & 0 & 0 & 0 & 0 & 0 & 5 \end{bmatrix} \text{ is}$$

(a) $\lambda^2(\lambda - 2)^2(\lambda - 5)$ (b) $\lambda(\lambda - 2)^2(\lambda - 5)$
(c) $\lambda(\lambda - 2)(\lambda - 5)$ (d) $\lambda^2(\lambda - 2)(\lambda - 5)$

**194.** Let $A$ be an improper orthogonal matrix, then adj $A$ is equal to
(a) $A$ (b) $A^T$ (c) $-A$ (d) $-A^T$

**195.** If the characteristic polynomial of $A_{3\times 3}$ is given by $\Delta(\lambda) = \lambda^3 - \lambda^2 + 2\lambda + 28$. Then, trace of $A$ and determinant of $A$ are, respectively
(a) 1 and 28 (b) −1 and 28
(c) 1 and −28 (d) −1 and −28

**196.** If $\begin{bmatrix} 1 \\ -1 \end{bmatrix}$ is an eigen vector $\begin{bmatrix} 1 & -n \\ -3 & 2n \end{bmatrix}$, then $n$ is
(a) 1 (b) −2
(c) 3 (d) 4

**197.** If $x_1 = \begin{bmatrix} 1 \\ i \end{bmatrix}, x_2 = \begin{bmatrix} i \\ 1 \end{bmatrix}$ are given vectors and $A = \begin{bmatrix} \cos\theta & \sin\theta \\ -\sin\theta & \cos\theta \end{bmatrix}$ and if $P = [x_1, x_2]$, then $P^{-1}AP$
(a) $\begin{bmatrix} e^{i\theta} & 0 \\ 0 & e^{-i\theta} \end{bmatrix}$ (b) $\begin{bmatrix} e^{-i\theta} & 0 \\ 0 & e^{i\theta} \end{bmatrix}$
(c) $\begin{bmatrix} 1 & 0 \\ 0 & 1 \end{bmatrix}$ (d) $\begin{bmatrix} -1 & 0 \\ 0 & -1 \end{bmatrix}$

**198.** Let $A = \begin{bmatrix} 2 & 3 & 4 \\ 0 & 5 & 6 \\ 0 & 0 & 7 \end{bmatrix}$. Then,
(a) $A$ is diagonalizable but not $A^2$
(b) $A^2$ is diagonalizable but not $A$
(c) Both $A$ and $A^2$ are diagonalizable
(d) Neither $A$ nor $A^2$ is diagonalizable

**199.** For the matrix $A = \begin{bmatrix} 5 & -1 \\ 1 & 3 \end{bmatrix}$ which of the following is not correct?
(a) $A$ is non-singular
(b) $A$ is not diagonalizable
(c) (1, 1) is an eigen vector
(d) It has an eigen space of dimension 2

**200.** Let $A$ be a $2 \times 2$ real matrix of rank 1. If $A$ is not diagonalizable, then
(a) $A$ is nilpotent
(b) $A$ is not nilpotent
(c) the minimal polynomial of $A$ is linear
(d) $A$ has a non-zero eigen value

**201.** Let $A$ be an $n \times n$ matrix and has $r$ distinct eigen values $(r < n)$, then the degree of its minimal polynomial is
(a) atleast $n$ (b) atleast $r$
(c) atleast $n - r$ (d) atmost $r$

**202.** Consider the matrix $A = \begin{bmatrix} 0 & 1 & 2 & 0 \\ 1 & 0 & 1 & 0 \\ 2 & 1 & 0 & 2 \\ 0 & 0 & 2 & 0 \end{bmatrix}$. Then,
(a) $A$ has no real eigen value
(b) all real eigen values of $A$ are positive
(c) all real eigen values of $A$ are negative
(d) $A$ has both positive and negative real eigen values

**203.** If $A$ and $B$ are two matrices such that $AB$ and $BA$ both exist, then which is not correct?
(a) Eigen values of $AB$ and $BA$ are same
(b) $|AB| = |BA|$
(c) Either $|AB| = |BA|$ or atleast one eigen value of $AB$ or $BA$ is zero
(d) None of the above

**204.** If $A$ is a $3 \times 3$ real matrix that satisfies $A^3 = A$, then
(a) $A$ is diagonalizable
(b) $A$ can't be diagonalized
(c) $A$ is invertible
(d) the characteristic polynomial of $A$ is different from its minimal polynomial

**205.** Consider the set of all functions $f$ defined on [0, 1] such that

I. $f(x) = 0$ at a finite number of points in [0, 1]
II. $f$ has a local maxima at $x = \frac{1}{2}$
III. $f$ has a local extrema at $x = \frac{1}{2}$

Then, the correct code is
(a) only (I) is vector space over $R$
(b) only (II) is a vector space over $R$
(c) only (III) is a vector space over $R$
(d) None of the above

**206.** Let the characteristics equation of a matrix $M$ be $\lambda^2 - \lambda - 1 = 0$, then
(a) $M^{-1}$ does not exist
(b) $M^{-1}$ exists but cannot be determined from the data
(c) $M^{-1} = M + 1$
(d) $M^{-1} = M - 1$

**207.** The convex hull $H$ of three vectors $u, v$ and $w$ in $V$ is
(a) circle passing through $u, v, w$
(b) triangle with $u, v, w$ as the mid-points of the sides
(c) triangular lamina with $u, v$ and $w$ as vertices
(d) None of the above

**208.** Let $A$ be a matrix with complex entries. If $A$ is Hermitian as well as unitary and $\alpha$ is an eigen value of $A$, then
(a) $\alpha$ can be any real number
(b) $\alpha = 1$ or $-1$
(c) $\alpha$ can be any complex number of absolute value 1
(d) None of the above

**209.** Which of the following sets are subspaces of $P$ (the vector space of all polynomials)
(a) $\{p \in P : \text{degree of } p = 4\}$
(b) $\{p \in P : \text{degree of } p \geq 3\}$
(c) $\{p \in P : \text{degree of } p \leq 4 \text{ and } p'(0) = 1\}$
(d) None of the above

**210.** Let $u_1 = (2, 5, 2), u_2 = (4, 2, 3)$ and $u_3 = (1, 1, 4)$ in $\mathbb{R}^3$. Then, the vectors $u_1, u_2$ and $u_3$ taken in order form
(a) right handed coordinate system
(b) left handed coordinate system
(c) orthogonal coordinate system
(d) all coplanar hence does not form coordinate system at all

**211.** A matrix $M$ has eigen values 1 and 4 with corresponding eigen vectors $[1, -1]^T$ and $[2, 1]^T$, respectively. Then, $M$ is
(a) $\begin{bmatrix} -4 & -8 \\ 5 & 9 \end{bmatrix}$ (b) $\begin{bmatrix} 9 & -8 \\ 5 & -4 \end{bmatrix}$
(c) $\begin{bmatrix} 2 & 2 \\ 1 & 3 \end{bmatrix}$ (d) $\begin{bmatrix} 3 & 2 \\ 1 & 2 \end{bmatrix}$

**212.** Which of the following sets are subspaces of the space $C(a, b)$ of all real-valued continuous functions defined on the open interval $(a, b)$
(a) $\{f \in C(a, b) : f(x_0) = 0,\ x_0 \in (a, b)\}$
(b) $\{f \in C(a, b) : f'(x) \neq 0, \text{ for all } x \in (a, b)\}$
(c) $\left\{f \in C(a, b) : f\left(\frac{a+b}{2}\right) = 1\right\}$
(d) None of the above

**213.** Let $A$ be an $n \times n$ matrix which is both Hermitian and unitary. Then,
(a) $A^2 = I$
(b) $A$ is real
(c) the eigen values of $A$ are 0, 1 and $-1$
(d) the characteristic and minimal polynomials of $A$ are same

**214.** Which of the following sets are subspaces of the space $C(a, b)$ of all real-valued continuous functions defined on the open interval $(a, b)$
(a) $\{f \in C(a, b) : f(x) = x^2 f(x)\}$
(b) $\{f \in C(a, b) : 2f'''(x) + 3xf^2(x) - f'(x) + x^2 f(x) = 0\}$
(c) $\{f \in C(a, b) : \int_a^b f(x)\,dx = 0\}$
(d) All of the above

**215.** Let $P$ and $Q$ be square matrices such that $PQ = I$, the identity matrix. Then, zero is an eigen value of
(a) $P$ but not $Q$ (b) $Q$ but not $P$
(c) Both $P$ and $Q$ (d) Neither $P$ nor $Q$

**216.** Consider $2 \times 2$ matrix $A = \begin{bmatrix} a & b \\ c & d \end{bmatrix}$. If $a + d = 1 = ad - bc$, then $A^3$ equals
(a) 0 (b) $-I$
(c) $3I$ (d) None of these

**217.** Which of the following sets is not a subspace of $C(a, b)$
(a) $\{f \in C(a, b) : \lim_{x \to \frac{a+b}{2}} f(x) = 0\}$
(b) $\{f \in C(a, b) : \lim_{x \to \frac{a+b}{2}} f(x) = 1\}$
(c) $\{f \in C(-\infty, \infty) : f(x) = f(-x)\}$
(d) All of the above

**218.** The eigen values of a $3\times3$ real matrix $A$ are 1, 2 and −3. Then,

(a) $A^{-1}=-\frac{1}{6}A^2$ (b) $A^{-1}=\frac{1}{6}(7I-A^2)$

(c) $A^{-1}=-\frac{1}{6}(7I-A^2)$ (d) $A^{-1}=\frac{1}{6}(-7I-A^2)$

**219.** Let $V$ be the vector space of all $2\times2$ matrices over $\mathbb{R}$. Then, the set $W$, consisting of all matrices $A$ for which $A^2=A$,

(a) is a subspace of $V$

(b) is not a subspace of $V$ as it is not closed with respect to vector addition

(c) is not a subspace of $V$ as it is not closed *wrt* scalar multiplication

(d) Both (b) and (c)

**220.** The minimal polynomial of

$$\begin{pmatrix}1&0&0&0\\1&1&0&0\\0&0&2&0\\0&0&0&2\end{pmatrix}\text{ is}$$

(a) $(x-1)^2(x-2)$ (b) $(x-1)(x-2)^2$

(c) $(x-1)(x-2)$ (d) $(x-1)^2(x-2)^2$

**221.** Let $V$ be the vector space of all $n\times n$ matrices over $R$. Then, the set $W$, consisting of all matrices which commute with a given matrix $M$ *i.e.*, $W=\{M\in V: AM=MA\}$

(a) is a subspace of $V$

(b) is not a subspace of $V$ as it is not closed *wrt* vector addition

(c) is not a subspace of $V$ as it is not closed *wrt* scalar multiplication

(d) None of the above

**222.** Let $A$ be a $3\times3$ real matrix such that $A^2=-I_3$, where $I_3$ is the $3\times3$ identity matrix. Then, a matrix $A$ is

(a) diagonalizable (b) orthogonal

(c) does not exist (d) symmetric

**223.** The set $V=\{(x,y)\in\mathbb{R}^2: xy\geq0\}$ is

(a) a vector subspace of $\mathbb{R}^2$

(b) not a vector subspace of $\mathbb{R}^2$, since every element does not have an inverse in $V$

(c) not a vector subspace of $\mathbb{R}^2$, since it is not closed under scalar multiplication

(d) not a vector subspace of $\mathbb{R}^2$, since it is not closed under vector addition

**224.** Let $A=\begin{pmatrix}0&a\\0&0\end{pmatrix}$ where $0\neq\alpha\in\mathbb{R}$. If $B$ is another $2\times2$ real matrix which commutes with $A$, then the eigen values of $B$ are always

(a) equal (b) distinct

(c) equal to 0 (d) equal to 1

**225.** The number of distinct bases of a two dimensional vector spaces over $Z_3$ is

(a) 24 (b) 27 (c) 9 (d) 48

**226.** Let $A$ be $3\times3$ matrix whose characteristic roots are 3, 2, − 1.
If $B=A^2-A$, then $|B|$ is

(a) 24 (b) −2

(c) 12 (d) −12

**227.** If $A$ is a real $n\times n$ matrix satisfying $A^3=A$, then trace of $A$ is always

(a) $n$

(b) 0

(c) $-n$

(d) an integer in the set $\{-n,-(n-1),\ldots,-1,0,1,\ldots,n\}$

**228.** If $A=\begin{bmatrix}a&-b\\b&a\end{bmatrix}\in K^{2\times2}, b\neq0$, then $A$ has eigen values if $K$ is

(a) $R$ (b) $C$

(c) $Q$ (d) All of these

**229.** Which is not correct, if $T_r(A)$ = Trace of $A$, then

(a) $T_r(A+B)=T_r(A)+T_r(B)$

(b) $T_r(AB)=T_r(BA)$

(c) $T_r(A)=T_r(CAC^{-1})$, $C$ is non-singular

(d) For any $A$, $\exists$ $B$ (both are square of same order) s.t. $(AB-BA)=I_n$

**230.** If $M$ is a $3\times3$ real matrix that satisfies $M^3=M$, then

I. $M$ is invertible

II. Eigen values of $M$ are distinct

III. $M$ is singular

Select the correct code

(a) I and II (b) II and III

(c) only I (d) only III

**231.** Which of the following is not a vector subspace of the vector space of polynomials with real coefficient

(a) $W$ consists of all polynomials divisible by $x$

(b) $W=\{p(x)\in V: p(3)=0\}$

(c) $W=\{p(x)\in V: p(a)=p(1-a), a\in R\}$

(d) $W$ consists of all polynomials with integral coefficient

**232.** Let

$v_1=(1,2,0,3,0)$,

$v_2=(1,2,-1,-1,0)$,

$v_3=(0,0,1,4,0)$

$v_4=(2,4,1,10,1)$ and

$v_5=(0,0,0,0,1)$. The dimension of the linear span of $\{v_1,v_2,v_3,v_4,v_5\}$ is

(a) 2 (b) 3

(c) 4 (d) 5

**233.** The set $\{e^{2x},e^{3x}\}$, $x\in\mathbb{R}$, is

(a) LI over $\mathbb{R}$

(b) LD over $\mathbb{R}$

(c) LI over any interval $(a,b)$, only when $0\notin(a,b)$

(d) None of the above

**234.** If $B$ is a non-singular matrix and $A$ is a square matrix. Then, $\det(B^{-1}AB)$ is equal to

(a) $\det(BAB)$ (b) $\det(A)$
(c) $\det(B^{-1})$ (d) $\det(A^{-1})$

**235.** Consider the set of all functions $f$ defined on [0, 1] such that

I. $f(1/2) = 0$
II. $f(3/4) = 1$
III. $f(x) = xf(x)$
IV. $f(0) = f(1)$

Then, the correct code is

(a) only I is vector spaces
(b) only I and IV are vector spaces
(c) only I, III and IV are vector spaces
(d) all are vector spaces

**236.** Let $V$ be the subspace of $\mathbb{R}^3$ spanned by $u = (1, 1, 1)$ and $v = (1, 1, -1)$

The orthonormal basis of $V$ obtained by the Gram-Schmidt process on the ordered basis $\{u, v\}$ of $V$ is

(a) $\{(1/\sqrt{3}, 1/\sqrt{3}, 1/\sqrt{3}), (2/3, 2/3, -4/3)\}$
(b) $\{(1, 1, 0), (1, 0, 1)\}$
(c) $\{(1/\sqrt{3}, 1/\sqrt{3}, 1/\sqrt{3}), (1/\sqrt{6}, 1/\sqrt{6}, -2/\sqrt{6})\}$
(d) $\{(1/\sqrt{3}, 1/\sqrt{3}, 1/\sqrt{3}), (2/\sqrt{6}, -1/\sqrt{6}, -1/\sqrt{6})\}$

**237.** Choose the correct statement

(a) Every subset of a LI set is LI
(b) Every superset of a LI set is LI
(c) Every subset of a LD set is LD
(d) Every subset of a LD set is LI

**238.** Let $M$ be a square matrix of the order 2, such that rank of $M$ is 1. Then, $M$ is

(a) diagonalizable and non-singular
(b) diagonalizable and nilpotent
(c) Neither diagonalizable nor nilpotent
(d) Either diagonalizable or nilpotent but not both

**239.** Let $Q[\sqrt{3}] = \{a + b\sqrt{3} : a, b \in Q\}$, then which of the following is correct?

(a) $Q[\sqrt{3}]$ is infinite dimensional vector space over $R$
(b) $Q[\sqrt{3}]$ is two-dimensional vector space over $R$
(c) $Q[\sqrt{3}]$ is two-dimensional vector space over $Q$
(d) $R$ is finite dimensional vector space over $Q[\sqrt{3}]$

**240.** The dimension of the vector space of all real numbers $\mathbb{R}$ over the field of rational numbers is

(a) 1 (b) 2
(c) 3 (d) None of these

**241.** Every skew-symmetric matrix of odd order is

(a) singular (b) non-singular
(c) invertible (d) Skew-Hermitian

**242.** Consider the $2 \times 2$ matrix $T = \begin{pmatrix} 0 & 1 \\ 0 & 0 \end{pmatrix}$ which of the following is not true?

(a) $T$ is in Jordan canonical form
(b) $T$ has zero image
(c) All eigen values of $T$ are zero
(d) $T$ is nilpotent

**243.** Let $U$ and $W$ be the following subspaces of $\mathbb{R}^4$

$U = \{(a, b, c, d) : b + c + d = 0\}$
$W = \{(a, b, c, d) : a + b = 0,\ c = 2d\}$

Then, dim of $U, W$ and $U \cap W$ are, respectively

(a) 2, 3, 1 (b) 3, 2, 1
(c) 2, 2, 2 (d) 1, 2, 3

**244.** Let $A$ is nilpotent of index 2 with rank $(A) = 2$. Then, Jordan canonical nilpotent matrix $M$, which is similar to $A$, contains

(a) 3 diagonal blocks each of order 2
(b) 3 diagonal blocks; 2 of order 2 and 1 of order 1
(c) 3 diagonal blocks; 1 of order 2 and 2 of order 1
(d) all of the above are possible

**245.** The vectors $u = [3 + \sqrt{2}, 1 + \sqrt{2}]^T$ and $v = [7, 1 + 2\sqrt{2}]^T$ in $R^2$ are

(a) LI over $R$ (b) LI over $C$
(c) LI over $Q$ (d) All of these

**246.** Let $u, v, w$ are LI' vectors. Then, consider the statements

I. $u + v - 2w, u - v - w$ and $u + w$ are LI
II. $u + v - 3w, u + 3v - w$ and $v + w$ are LD

Choose the correct code

(a) I is true but II is false
(b) I is false but II is true
(c) both I and II are true
(d) both I and II are false

**247.** If a square matrix of order 10 has exactly 4 distinct eigen values, then the degree of its minimal polynomial is

(a) atleast 4 (b) atmost 4
(c) atleast 6 (d) atmost 6

**248.** Let $M$ be a skew-symmetric, orthogonal real matrix. Then, only possible eigen values are

(a) $-1, 1$ (b) $-i, i$
(c) 0 (d) $1, i$

**249.** The set of all $x \in \mathbb{R}$ for which the vectors $(1, x, 0), (0, x^2, 1)$ and $(0, 1, x)$ are linearly independent in $R^3$ is

(a) $\{x \in \mathbb{R} : x = 0\}$ (b) $\{x \in \mathbb{R} : x \neq 0\}$
(c) $\{x \in \mathbb{R} : x \neq 1\}$ (d) $\{x \in \mathbb{R} : x \neq -1\}$

**250.** If $S = \{(1, 1, 0), (2, 1, 3)\} \subset \mathbb{R}^3$, then which one of the following vectors of $R^3$ is not in the span $< S >$?

(a) $(0, 0, 0)$ (b) $(3, 2, 3)$
(c) $(1, 2, 3)$ (d) $(4/3, 1, 1)$

**251.** Let $V$ be the space of $2 \times 2$ matrices over $R$ and let $W$ be the subspace generated by

$\begin{bmatrix} 1 & -5 \\ -4 & 2 \end{bmatrix}, \begin{bmatrix} 1 & 1 \\ -1 & 5 \end{bmatrix}, \begin{bmatrix} 2 & -4 \\ -5 & 7 \end{bmatrix}$ and $\begin{bmatrix} 1 & -7 \\ -5 & 1 \end{bmatrix}$. Then, dimension of $W$ is

(a) 2 (b) 3
(c) 4 (d) 5

**252.** The characteristic polynomial of a $3\times 3$ matrix $A$ is $|\lambda I - A| = \lambda^3 + 3\lambda^2 + 4\lambda + 3$. Let $x =$ trace $(A)$ and $y = |A|$, the determinant of $A$. Then,

(a) $\frac{x}{y} = \frac{3}{4}$ (b) $\frac{x}{y} = \frac{4}{3}$

(c) $x = 3$ and $y = -3$ (d) $x = y = -3$

**253.** Which of the following sets of vectors is a basis for $\mathbb{R}^3$

I. $\{(1,2,3),(3,5,7),(5,8,11)\}$

II. $\{(1,0,1),(0,1,0),(-1,0,1)\}$

III. $\{(1,2,3),(2,3,4),(2,4,6)\}$

(a) only I and II (b) only II

(c) only I and III (d) only I

**254.** For a $3\times 3$ real matrix let $C(A)$ denote the set of the real characteristic roots of $A$. Suppose, $C(B) = C(B^{-1})$ for a non-singular matrix $B$ with no repeated eigen values. Then,

(a) either 1 or $-1$ must be an eigen value of $B$.

(b) $I = B^2$

(c) 1 and $-1$ are the only possible real eigen values of $B$

(d) $-1$ must be an eigen values of $B$

**255.** Let $S = \{(1,2,3),(1,0,-1)\}$. The value of $k$ for which the vector $(2,1,k)$ belongs to the linear span of $S$ is

(a) 1 (b) $-1$

(c) 2 (d) 0

**256.** Let $f$ and $g$ be two elements of the vector space of all continuous functions defined on $[a,b]$ over real field $\mathbb{R}$. Consider the following statements

I. $f$ and $g$ are LI on $[a,b]$ implies that they are LI on each subinterval of $[a,b]$

II. $f$ and $g$ are LD on $[a,b]$ implies that they are LD on each subinterval of $[a,b]$

III. $f$ and $g$ are LI on any subinterval of $[a,b]$ implies that they are LI on $[a,b]$

IV. $f$ and $g$ are LD on any subinterval of $[a,b]$ implies that they are LD on $[a,b]$

Then,

(a) only I and II are true

(b) only II and III are true

(c) only III and IV are true

(d) only I and IV are true

**257.** Let $V$ be the vector space of polynomials of degree $\le 3$; $W_1 \subset V$ be the subspace of polynomials of degree $\le 2$; $W_2 \subset V$ is the subspace of polynomials vanishing at 0. Then, which of the following is not true?

(a) Span of $W_1$ and $W_2$ is $V$

(b) $W_1$ is isomorphic to $W_2$

(c) Dim $(W_1 \cap W_2) = 2$

(d) Dim $W_1 <$ dim $W_2$

**258.** Let $A$ be an $m\times n$ matrix, $\bar{b} \in \mathbb{R}^m$. Then, the system of equations $A\bar{X} = \bar{b}$ has a solution if and only if

(a) $\bar{b} \in$ column space of $A$

(b) $\bar{b} \in$ row space of $A$

(c) $\bar{b} = 0$

(d) rank $[A\bar{b}] >$ rank $A$

**259.** In $\mathbb{R}^3$, consider the following three statements about the subsets $E = \{(1,0,0),(0,1,0),(0,0,1),(1,1,1),(1,1,0)\}$

I. $E$ is a linearly dependent set

II. Any three vectors of $E$ are linearly independent

III. Any four vectors of $E$ are linearly dependent

Which of the above statements are correct?

(a) I, II and III (b) I and II

(c) I and III (d) II and III

**260.** Let $M_1 = \begin{bmatrix} 3 & 0 & 0 \\ 1 & 3 & 0 \\ 0 & 0 & 3 \end{bmatrix}$,

$M_2 = \begin{bmatrix} -3 & 0 \\ 1 & -3 \end{bmatrix}$

$M_3 = \begin{bmatrix} 0 & 0 \\ 1 & 0 \end{bmatrix}$

Then, the minimal polynomial of the matrix $\begin{bmatrix} M_1 & 0 & 0 \\ 0 & M_2 & 0 \\ 0 & 0 & M_3 \end{bmatrix}$ is

(a) $x^2(x-3)^3(x+3)^2$ (b) $x^2(x^2-9)$

(c) $x^2(x^2-9)^2$ (d) $x(x-3)^4(x+3)^2$

**261.** If $\alpha$ is a characteristic root of a non-singular matrix, then characteristic root of adj $(A)$ is

(a) $\alpha|A|$ (b) $\alpha$

(c) $\frac{|A|}{\alpha}$ (d) $\frac{|\text{adj }(A)|}{\alpha}$

**262.** Let $A = \begin{bmatrix} a_1 & a_2 & a_3 \\ b_1 & b_2 & b_3 \\ c_1 & c_2 & c_3 \end{bmatrix}$ be an idempotent matrix with rank 2. Then, the rank of $B = \begin{bmatrix} a_1-1 & a_2 & a_3 \\ b_1 & b_2-1 & b_3 \\ c_1 & c_2 & c_3-1 \end{bmatrix}$ is

(a) 2 (b) 1

(c) 3 (d) $\le 2$

**263.** Let $A$ be the matrix of the quadratic form $(a_1x_1 + a_2x_2 + \ldots + a_nx_n)^2$. Then, the sum of all the entries of $A$ is

(a) $a_1^2 + a_2^2 + \ldots + a_n^2$

(b) $(a_1 + a_2 + \ldots + a_n)^2$

(c) $a_1 + a_2 + \ldots + a_n$

(d) $a_1^2 + a_2^2 + \ldots + a_n^2 + \frac{1}{2}\sum_{i\ne j} a_i a_j$

**264.** Let the two matrices $A$ and $B$ represent a linear operator from $V_4$ to $V_4$ with basis $(v_1, v_2, v_3, v_4)$ and $\{v_1, 2v_2, 3v_3, 4v_4\}$, respectively. Then, if trace of $A$ is $k$, then the trace of $B$ is

(a) $k$ (b) $k+10$

(c) $k+6$ (d) $k+24$

**265.** Let $V$ be the space of $n \times n$ matrices over $\mathbb{R}$ and let $W$ be the subspace of matrices with entries in each row adding up to zero. Then, the dimension of $W$ is

(a) $n$ (b) $\frac{n(n-1)}{2}$

(c) $n-1$ (d) $n(n-1)$

**266.** Let $A$ be the matrix of quadratic form $(x_1 - x_2 + 2x_3)^2$. Then, trace of $A$ is

(a) 2 (b) 4

(c) 6 (d) 0

**267.** Let $S$ be the set of all $n \times n$ matrices over $\mathbb{R}$ with zero trace. Then,

(a) $S$ is not a vector space

(b) $S$ is a vector space of dimension $n-1$

(c) $S$, together with the identity matrix, form a vector space

(d) $S$ is vector space and it has a basis consisting of $n^2 - 1$ matrices

**268.** For $0 < \theta < \pi$, the matrix $\begin{bmatrix} \cos\theta & -\sin\theta \\ \sin\theta & \cos\theta \end{bmatrix}$

(a) has no real eigen value

(b) is orthogonal

(c) is symmetric

(d) is skew-symmetric

**269.** If $A$ and $B$ are square matrices of different order, $C_x(A)$ and $C_x(B)$ are characteristic polynomials of $A$ and $B$, respectively and it is given that $C_x(B)$ is minimal polynomial of $A$ as well, then

(a) $A$ is invertible implies $B$ is invertible but $B$ may be invertible even, if $A$ is not so

(b) $B$ is invertible implies $A$ is invertible but $A$ may be invertible even, if $B$ is not so

(c) A and $B$ are invertible together or fail together to be so

(d) No such relation is necessary

**270.** Suppose, $\{x_1, -x_2, x_3\}$ is a basis for $\mathbb{R}^3$. Let $T = \{x_1 + x_3, x_1 - x_2, 2x_2 - x_3 + x_1\}$. Then,

(a) Both $S$ and $T$ are basis for $\mathbb{R}^3$

(b) $S$ is not a basis for $\mathbb{R}^3$ btu $T$ is a basis for $\mathbb{R}^3$

(c) $T$ is not a basis for $\mathbb{R}^3$ but $S$ is a basis for $\mathbb{R}^3$

(d) Neither $S$ nor $T$ is a basis for $\mathbb{R}^3$

**271.** The eigen values of a $3 \times 3$ real matrix $P$ are $1, -2, 3$. Then,

(a) $P^{-1} = \frac{1}{6}(5I + 2P - P^2)$ (b) $P^{-1} = \frac{1}{6}(5I - 2P + P^2)$

(c) $P^{-1} = \frac{1}{6}(5I - 2P - P^2)$ (d) $P^{-1} = \frac{1}{6}(5I + 2P + P^2)$

**272.** Consider the system of equations $Ax = 0$ where $A$ is a $2 \times 3$ matrix. Then, it must be true that

(a) there is a solution $x \neq 0$

(b) there are atleast two linearly independent solutions

(c) any solution $x$ satisfies $x_1 + x_2 + x_3 = 0$

(d) any two solutions are linearly dependent

**273.** Let $A, B$ be two $n \times n$ matrices. Then, incorrect statement is

(a) trace $(AB) =$ trace $(BA)$

(b) $\rho(AB) = \rho(BA)$

(c) $|AB| = |BA|$

(d) if $AB = 0$, then $r(A) + r(B) < 2n$

**274.** If $(A + B)^{-1}$ exists, then

(a) $A^{-1}$ and $B^{-1}$ both exist

(b) $A^{-1}$ and $B^{-1}$ do not exist

(c) atleast one of $A^{-1}$ and $B^{-1}$ exists

(d) nothing can be said

**275.** Let $A$ be a $3 \times 3$ matrix and consider the system of equations $Ax = \begin{bmatrix} 1 \\ 0 \\ -1 \end{bmatrix}$. Then,

(a) if the system is consistent then it has a unique solution

(b) if $A$ is singular, then the system has infinitely many solutions

(c) if the system is consistent, then the $|A| \neq 0$

(d) if the system has a unique solution, then $A$ is non-singular

**276.** Let $S = \{(0, 1, \alpha), (\alpha, 1, 0), (1, \alpha, 1)\}$. Then, $S$ is a basis for $\mathbb{R}^3$ if and only if

(a) $\alpha \neq 0$ (b) $\alpha \neq 1$

(c) $\alpha \neq 0$ and $\alpha^2 \neq 2$ (d) $-1 \leq \alpha \leq 1$

**277.** Let $U$ be a $3 \times 3$ complex Hermitian matrix which is unitary. Then, the distinct eigen values of $U$ are

(a) $\pm i$ (b) $1 \pm i$

(c) $\pm 1$ (d) $1/2(1 \pm i)$

**278.** All the eigen values of the matrix $\begin{bmatrix} 1 & 2 & 0 \\ 2 & 1 & 0 \\ 0 & 0 & -1 \end{bmatrix}$ lie in the disc

(a) $|\lambda + 1| \leq 1$ (b) $|\lambda - 1| \leq 1$

(c) $|\lambda + 1| \leq 0$ (d) $|\lambda - 1| \leq 2$

**279.** $A$, $B$, $(A + B)$ are non-singular matrices. Then, $[B(A + B)^{-1} A]^{-1}$ is equal to

(a) $A + B$ (b) $A^{-1} + B^{-1}$

(c) $A^{-1} + B^{-1} + I$ (d) $AB$

**280.** $A$ basis for the eigen space of the matrix $\begin{bmatrix} 1 & 0 \\ 0 & 1 \end{bmatrix}$ consist of

(a) $\begin{bmatrix} 1 \\ 1 \end{bmatrix}$ (b) $\begin{bmatrix} 0 \\ 0 \end{bmatrix}$ and $\begin{bmatrix} 1 \\ 1 \end{bmatrix}$

(c) $\begin{bmatrix} 0 \\ 1 \end{bmatrix}$ (d) $\begin{bmatrix} 0 \\ 1 \end{bmatrix}$ and $\begin{bmatrix} 1 \\ 0 \end{bmatrix}$

**281.** Which of the following sets of vectors in $\mathbb{R}^3$ are linearly independent

I. $[(1, 0, 0), (0, 1, 0), (1, 1, 0)]$

II. $[(1,0,0),(0,1,0),(0,0,1)]$
III. $[(0,1,0),(1,0,1),(1,1,0)]$
IV. $[(0,0,1),(0,1,0),(0,1,1)]$

Select the correct answer
(a) I and II (b) II and III
(c) III and IV (d) I and IV

**282.** A matrix $M$ has eigen values 1 and 4 with corresponding eigen vectors $(1,-1)^r$ and $(2,1)^T$, respectively. Then, $M$ is
(a) $\begin{pmatrix}-4 & -8\\ 5 & 9\end{pmatrix}$ (b) $\begin{pmatrix}9 & -8\\ 5 & -4\end{pmatrix}$
(c) $\begin{pmatrix}2 & 2\\ 1 & 3\end{pmatrix}$ (d) $\begin{pmatrix}3 & 2\\ 1 & 2\end{pmatrix}$

**283.** Let $M$ be a $m\times n$ $(m<n)$ matrix with rank $m$. Then,
(a) for every $b$ in $\mathbb{R}^m$, $Mx=b$ has unique solution
(b) for every $b$ in $\mathbb{R}^m$, $Mx=b$ has a solution but it is not unique
(c) there exists $b\in\mathbb{R}^m$ for which $Mx=b$ has no solution
(d) None of the above

**284.** In context of a matrix, which one of the following is not an elementary row operation?
(a) Interchanging of two rows
(b) To multiply any row by a scalar
(c) $R_i=R_j+kR_s$, where $R_i=i$th row, $k$ any scalar
(d) None of the above

**285.** If $A$ and $B$ are square matrices of same order, then
(a) $AB$ is invertible iff $BA$ is invertible
(b) $AB$ and $BA$ have same eigen vectors
(c) $A$ and $B$ have same eigen vector, if $AB=BA$
(d) $AB$ and $BA$ have same eigen values iff $AB=BA$

**286.** If $A$ and $B$ are two matrices of the same order such that $AB=BA$, then
(a) $A$ is diagonal and $B$ is any matrix
(b) $A$ and $B$ are both diagonal
(c) $A$ is scalar and $B$ is diagonal matrix
(d) None of the above

**287.** Consider the matrix

$$M=\begin{pmatrix}0 & 1 & 2 & 0\\ 1 & 0 & 1 & 0\\ 2 & 1 & 0 & 2\\ 0 & 0 & 2 & 0\end{pmatrix}$$

(a) $M$ has no real eigen values
(b) All real eigen values of $M$ are positive
(c) All real eigen values of $M$ are negative
(d) $M$ has both positive and negative real eigen values

**288.** If $\lambda_1,\lambda_2,\ldots,\lambda_n$ are eigen values of matrix $A$, then trace of $A$ is
(a) $\lambda_1\lambda_2\ldots\lambda_n$ (b) $\lambda_1+\lambda_2+\ldots+\lambda_n$
(c) $\dfrac{1}{\lambda_1\lambda_2\ldots\lambda_n}$ (d) $\lambda_1^2+\lambda_2^2+\ldots+\lambda_n^2$

**289.** Let $W$ be the space spanned by $f=\sin x$ and $g=\cos x$. Then, for any real value of $\theta$, $f_1=\sin(x+\theta)$ and $g_1=\cos(x+\theta)$.
(a) are vectors in $W$
(b) are linearly independent
(c) do not form a basis for $W$
(d) form a basis for $W$

**290.** Let $A$ be a $3\times 3$ matrix with eigen values $1,-1,0$. Then, the determinant of $I+A^{100}$ is
(a) 6 (b) 4
(c) 9 (d) 100

**291.** Let $A\in\mathbb{R}^{n\times n}$ be such that the sum of enteries of each row is equal to 0 and the rank of $A$ is non-zero. Then,
(a) $A$ is diagonalizable (b) $A$ is idempotent
(c) $A$ is singular (d) $A$ is involuntary

**292.** The roots of the equation

$$\begin{vmatrix}a+x & h & g\\ h & b+x & f\\ g & f & c+x\end{vmatrix}=0;$$

where $a,b,c,f,g,h$ are real, are
(a) all real
(b) only one real
(c) cannot be determined
(d) of same sign

**293.** Let $M$ be the real $5\times 5$ matrix having all of its entries equal to 1. Then,
(a) $M$ is not diagonalizable
(b) $M$ is idempotent
(c) $M$ is nilpotent
(d) the minimal polynomial and the characteristic polynomial of $M$ are not equal

**294.** Let $A$ be an $m\times n$ matrix with rank $r$. Then, dimension of the solution space of the system $Ax=0$ is
(a) $r$ (b) $n-r$
(c) $m-r$ (d) $\min(m,n)-r$

**295.** If $A$ and $B$ are Hermitian, then select the incorrect one
(a) $AB+BA$ is Hermitian
(b) $AB-BA$ is Skew-Hermitian
(c) $B^\theta B$ is Hermitian
(d) $A+A^\theta$ is Skew-Hermitian

**296.** Let $A$ be a $2\times 2$ orthogonal matrix of trace and determinant 1. Then, the angle between $Au$ and $u$ $(u=[1,0]^t)$ is
(a) 15° (b) 30°
(c) 45° (d) 60°

**297.** If $F(x)$, $G(x)$ and $H(x)$ are three polynomials of degree 2, then

$$f(x)=\begin{vmatrix}F(x) & G(x) & H(x)\\ F'(x) & G'(x) & H'(x)\\ F''(x) & G''(x) & H''(x)\end{vmatrix}$$

is a polynomial of degree

(a) 1 (b) 2
(c) 0 (d) $f(x)$ is zero polynomial

**298.** Let $A$ be a non-zero upper triangular matrix all of whose eigen values are 0. Then, $I + A$ is

(a) invertible (b) singular
(c) idempotent (d) nilpotent

**299.** Consider the matrix

$$M = \begin{pmatrix} 1 & 0 & -1 \\ 0 & 1 & 0 \\ 1 & 1 & -1 \end{pmatrix} \text{ and}$$

let $S_M$ be the set of $3 \times 3$ matrices $N$, such that $MN = 0$. Then, the dimension of the real vector space $S_M$ is equal to

(a) 0 (b) 1
(c) 2 (d) 3

**300.** If $M$ is a $7 \times 5$ matrix of rank 3 and $N$ is a $5 \times 7$ matrix of rank 5, then rank $(MN)$ is

(a) 5 (b) 3
(c) 2 (d) 1

**301.** The columns of an orthogonal matrix forms

(a) an orthogonal set of vectors
(b) an orthonormal set of vectors
(c) a linearly independent set
(d) All of the above

**302.** Consider the matrix

$$M = \begin{pmatrix} a^2 & ab & ac \\ ab & b^2 & bc \\ ac & bc & c^2 \end{pmatrix}$$

where $a, b$ and $c$ are non-zero real number. Then, the matrix has

(a) three non-zero real eigen values
(b) complex eigen values
(c) two non-zero eigen value
(d) only one non-zero eigen value

**303.** The dimension of the vector space of all $3 \times 3$ real symmetric matrices is

(a) 3 (b) 9 (c) 6 (d) 4

**304.** If $A = \begin{bmatrix} 2 & 6 \\ 3 & 9 \end{bmatrix}$, $B = \begin{bmatrix} 3 & x \\ y & 2 \end{bmatrix}$, then in order that $AB = 0$. The values of $x$ and $y$ will be, respectively

(a) $-6$ and $-1$ (b) 6 and 1
(c) $-6$ and $-3$ (d) $-5$ and 4

**305.** The rank of the $4 \times 4$ skew-symmetric matrix

$$\begin{bmatrix} 0 & 1 & 0 & 1 \\ -1 & 0 & 1 & 0 \\ 0 & -1 & 0 & 1 \\ -1 & 0 & -1 & 0 \end{bmatrix} \text{ is}$$

(a) 1 (b) 2 (c) 3 (d) 4

**306.** Let $S$ and $T$ be two subspaces of $\mathbb{R}^{24}$ such that $\dim(S) = 19$ and $\dim(T) = 17$. Then, the

(a) smallest possible value of dim $(S \cap T)$ is 2
(b) largest possible value of dim $(S \cap T)$ is 18
(c) smallest possible value of dim $(S + T)$ is 19
(d) largest possible value of dim $(S + T)$ is 22

**307.** Let $A$ be a matrix of order $m \times n$ and $B$ be a matrix of order $n \times p$, $n > p$. If rank $(A) = n$ and rank $(B) = p$, then the rank $(AB)$ is

(a) $n$ (b) $p$
(c) $np$ (d) $n + p$

**308.** The dimension of the subspace $\{(x_1, x_2, x_3, x_4, x_5) : 3x_1 - x_2 + x_3 = 0\}$ of $\mathbb{R}^5$ is

(a) 1 (b) 2
(c) 3 (d) 4

**309.** Let $(A, B)$ be a pair of $n \times n$ matrices such that $AB - BA = I_n$ where $I_n$ is the $n \times n$ identity matrix.

(a) Then, $A$ and $B$ are simultaneously diagonalizable
(b) Such a pair $(A, B)$ does not exist
(c) Rank $A$ = rank $B$
(d) det $(AB) = 1$

**310.** Consider the non-homogeneous system of linear equations $Ax = b$, where $A$ is $m \times n$, $X \in \mathbb{R}^n$, $b \in \mathbb{R}^m$, then

I. the corresponding homogeneous system $Ax = 0$ has unique solution $\Rightarrow Ax = b$ has infinitely many solutions for each vector $b$ in $R^m$.

II. the corresponding homogeneous system $Ax = 0$ has a non-zero solution $\Rightarrow$ there is a vector $b$ in $R^m$ for which $Ax = b$ has no solution

Choose the correct code

(a) I and II are true (b) I is true but II is false
(c) I is false but II is true (d) both I and II are false

**311.** The system of equations

$$x + y + z = 0$$
$$3x + 6y + z = 0$$
$$\alpha x + 2y + z = 0$$

has infinitely many solutions, then $\alpha$ is equal to

(a) 7 (b) $\frac{7}{5}$
(c) $\frac{5}{7}$ (d) 4

**312.** Let $M = \begin{pmatrix} 1 & 1+i & 2i & 9 \\ 1-i & 3 & 4 & 7-i \\ -2i & 4 & 5 & i \\ 9 & 7+i & -i & 7 \end{pmatrix}$

Then,

(a) $M$ has purely imaginary eigen values
(b) $M$ is no diagonalizable
(c) $M$ has eigen values which are neither real nor purely imaginary
(d) $M$ has only real eigen values

**313.** Let $\{v_1, v_2, v_3, v_4\}$ be a basis of $\mathbb{R}^4$ and $v = a_1v_1 + a_2v_2 + a_3v_3 + a_4v_4$, where $a_i \in R, i = 1, 2, 3, 4$.

Then, $\{v_1 - v, v_2 - v, v_3 - v, v_4 - v\}$ is a basis of $\mathbb{R}^4$ if and only if

(a) $a_1 = a_2 = a_3 = a_4$ (b) $a_1a_2a_3a_4 = -1$
(c) $a_1 + a_2 + a_3 + a_4 \neq 1$ (d) $a_1 + a_2 + a_3 + a_4 \neq 0$

**314.** Let $V$ be the vector space of all real polynomials. Consider the subspace $W$ spanned by

$t^2 + t + 2, t^2 + 2t + 5, 5t^2 + 3t + 4$ and $2t^2 + 2t + 4$

Then, the dimension of $W$ is

(a) 4 (b) 3
(c) 2 (d) 1

**315.** The eigen values of a skew-symmetric matrix are

(a) negative
(b) real
(c) purely imaginary or zero
(d) None of the above

**316.** Consider the system of linear equation

$x + y + z = 3, x - y - z = 4, x - 5y + kz = 6$

Then, the value of $k$ for which this system has an infinite number of solutions is

(a) $k = -5$ (b) $k = 0$
(c) $k = 1$ (d) $k = 3$

**317.** If $A$ be an $n \times n$ matrix of rank $n - 2$; $n > 2$, then the rank of adj $A$ is

(a) $n$ (b) $n - 1$
(c) 2 (d) 0

**318.** Let $A$ be an $m \times n (m < n)$ matrix with rank $m$. Then,

(a) for every $b$ in $R^m$, $Ax = b$ has unique solution
(b) for every $b$ in $R^m$, $Ax = b$ has a solution but it is not unique
(c) there exists $b \in R^m$ for which $Ax = b$ has no solution
(d) None of the above

# Exercise 2 (For Part 'C')

**Directions** (Q. Nos. 1-86) *Questions may have one or more than one correct option.*

**1.** Given, $A = \begin{bmatrix} 5 & -6 & -6 \\ -1 & 4 & 2 \\ 3 & -6 & -4 \end{bmatrix}$,

(a) the characteristic polynomial is det $(xI - A)$
(b) the characteristic polynomial is det $(A)$
(c) the characteristic polynomial is $(x - 2)^2 (x - 1)$
(d) the characteristic polynomial is $(x - 2)(x + 1)x$

**2.** Which of the following sets of vectors $x = (x_1, x_2, x_3)$ in $\mathbb{R}^3$ are subspaces of $\mathbb{R}^3$?

(a) All $x$ such that $x_1$ is an integer
(b) All $x$ such that $x_1 + 2x_2 = 0$
(c) All $x$ such that $x_1$ is not an integer
(d) All $x$ such that $x_1 + 2x_2 \neq 0$

**3.** Given, $A = \begin{bmatrix} 5 & -6 & -6 \\ -1 & 4 & 2 \\ 3 & -6 & -4 \end{bmatrix}$,

(a) characteristic polynomial of $A$ is $(x - 2)^2 (x - 1)$
(b) characteristic polynomial of $A$ is det $(xI - A)$
(c) characteristic polynomial of $A$ is $(x^2 - 3)$
(d) characteristic polynomial of $A$ is det $(xA)$

**4.** Given, $D = \begin{vmatrix} a_{11} & a_{12} & a_{13} \\ a_{21} & a_{22} & a_{23} \\ a_{31} & a_{32} & a_{33} \end{vmatrix}$

The minors are

(a) $\begin{vmatrix} a_{22} & a_{23} \\ a_{32} & a_{33} \end{vmatrix}$ (b) $\begin{vmatrix} a_{12} & a_{13} \\ a_{32} & a_{33} \end{vmatrix}$

(c) $\begin{vmatrix} a_{12} & a_{13} \\ a_{22} & a_{23} \end{vmatrix}$ (d) $\begin{vmatrix} a_{11} & a_{12} \\ a_{13} & a_{22} \end{vmatrix}$

**5.** Given, $A = \begin{bmatrix} 8 & -6 & 2 \\ -6 & 7 & -4 \\ 2 & -4 & 3 \end{bmatrix}$

(a) the characteristic equation is $|A - \lambda I| = 0$
(b) the characteristic equation is $|A + I| = 0$
(c) the characteristic roots are 0, 3, 15
(d) No characteristic roots exist

**6.** Given, $A = \begin{bmatrix} a & h & g \\ 0 & b & f \\ 0 & 0 & c \end{bmatrix}$

(a) the characteristic equation is $|A - \lambda I| = 0$
(b) the latent roots are $a, b, c$
(c) the latent roots are $h, g, f$
(d) the characteristic equation is $(a - \lambda)(b - \lambda)(c - \lambda) = 0$

**7.** The value of the determinant

$\begin{vmatrix} a & h & g \\ h & b & f \\ g & f & c \end{vmatrix}$

(a) $abc + 2fgh - af^2 - bg^2 - ch^2$

(b) $ab + a + c + d$
(c) $abc + ab - bc - cg$
(d) $a + b + c$

**8.** Given, $A = \begin{bmatrix} 1 & 2 & 3 \\ 1 & 4 & 2 \\ 2 & 6 & 5 \end{bmatrix}$ is

(a) $|A| = 0$ (b) $|A| \neq 0$
(c) rank $(A) = 2$ (d) rank $(A) = 3$

**9.** The value of the determinant $\begin{vmatrix} 67 & 19 & 21 \\ 39 & 13 & 14 \\ 81 & 24 & 26 \end{vmatrix}$ is

(a) −43 (b) 48 (c) 62 (d) 39

**10.** Given, $A = \begin{vmatrix} 1 & a & b & 0 \\ 0 & c & d & 1 \\ 1 & a & b & 0 \\ 0 & c & d & 1 \end{vmatrix}$

(a) $|A| = 0$ (b) two rows are identical
(c) rank $(A) = 2$ (d) rank $(A) = 3$

**11.** Given, $A = \begin{bmatrix} 2 & 1 & -1 \\ 0 & 3 & -2 \\ 2 & 4 & -3 \end{bmatrix}$ is

(a) $|A| = 0$ (b) $|A| \neq 0$
(c) rank $(A) = 2$ (d) rank $(A) = 5$

**12.** Given, $A = \begin{bmatrix} 1+i & 2-3i & 2 \\ 3-4i & 4+5i & 1 \\ 5 & 3 & 3-i \end{bmatrix}$

(a) $\begin{bmatrix} 1-i & 2+3i & 2 \\ 3+4i & 4+5i & 2 \\ 1 & 0 & 1 \end{bmatrix}$ is conjugate of $A$

(b) $\begin{bmatrix} 1-i & 2+3i & 2 \\ 3+4i & 4-5i & 1 \\ 5 & 3 & 3+i \end{bmatrix}$ is conjugate of $A$

(c) $\begin{bmatrix} 1-i & 3+4i & 5 \\ 2+3i & 4-5i & 3 \\ 2 & 3 & 3+i \end{bmatrix}$ is transpose of $A$

(d) $\begin{bmatrix} 1+i & 3-4i & 5 \\ 2-3i & 4+5i & 3 \\ 2 & 1 & 3-i \end{bmatrix}$ is transpose of $A$

**13.** Let $A = \begin{bmatrix} \cos\theta & \sin\theta \\ -\sin\theta & \cos\theta \end{bmatrix}$

(a) $AA^T = \begin{bmatrix} 1 & 0 \\ 0 & 1 \end{bmatrix}$
(b) $AA^T = 1$
(c) $A$ is orthogonal matrix
(d) $A$ is not a orthogonal matrix

**14.** Let $A = \begin{bmatrix} 3 & 1+2i \\ 1-2i & 2 \end{bmatrix}$, then

(a) $\bar{A} = \begin{bmatrix} 3 & 1-2i \\ 1+2i & 2 \end{bmatrix}$ (b) $A^* = \begin{bmatrix} 2 & 1+2i \\ 1-2i & 2 \end{bmatrix}$
(c) $A^* = A$ (d) $A$ is hermitian matrix

**15.** Which of the following(s) is/are not vector space?
(a) $V = \{< a_n > : a_n \in \mathbb{R}\}$ over $\mathbb{R}$
(b) $V = \{f : f:[0,1] \to \mathbb{R}$ and $f(x) = 0$ at finitely many points in $[0,1]\}$
(c) $V = \{f : f:[0,1] \to \mathbb{R}$ and $f$ has a local extrema at $x = 1/2\}$
(d) None of the above

**16.** Let $V$ be a vector space of all functions from $R$ into $R$. Let $V_e$ be the subset of even functions, $f(-x) = f(x)$ and $V_o$ be the subset of odd functions $f(-x) = -f(x)$.
(a) $V_e$ is subspaces of $V$
(b) $V_o$ is subspaces of $V$
(c) $V_e$ is not a subspaces of $V$
(d) $V_o$ is not a subspaces of $V$

**17.** Let $\bar{a}_1 = (1,0,0,0), \bar{a}_2 = (0,1,0,0), \bar{a}_3 = (0,0,1,0)$ and $\bar{a}_4 = (0,0,0,1)$
(a) linearly independent
(b) linearly dependent
(c) $\Sigma c_i a_i = 0$ for all $c_i = 0,\ i = 1,2,3,4$
(d) $\Sigma c_i a_i \neq 0$ for some $c_i \neq 0,\ i = 1,2,3,4$

**18.** Given $V_1$ and $V_2$ are subspace of $R^4$,
$$V_1 = \{(a,b,c,d) : b - 2c + d = 0\}$$
$$V_2 = \{(a,b,c,d) : a = d, b = 2c\}$$
(a) $V_1$ has dimension three
(b) $V_1$ has dimension two
(c) $\{(0,-1,0,1),(0,2,1,0),(1,0,0,0)\}$ is a basis of $V_1$
(d) $\{(0,2,1,0),(1,0,0,1)\}$ is a basis of $V_2$

**19.** Given vectors $(1,1,0,0), (0,1,-1,0)$ and $(0,0,0,3)$ in $F^{(4)}$
(a) vectors are linearly dependent
(b) vectors are linearly independent
(c) the sum of vectors is $(0,0,0,0)$
(d) the sum of vectors is $(1,2,-1,3)$

**20.** Let $\bar{a}_1 = (3,0,2,2),\ \bar{a}_2 = (-6,42,24,54)$ and $\bar{a}_3 = (21,-21,0,-15)$
(a) $\Sigma c_i a_i = 0$ for some $c_i \neq 0,\ i = 1,2,3$
(b) $\Sigma c_i a_i = 0$ for some $c_i = 0, i = 1,2,3$
(c) linearly independent
(d) linearly dependent

**21.** Given $\bar{a}_1 = (3,1,-4), \bar{a}_2 = (2,2,-3)$ and $\bar{a}_3 = (0,-4,1)$
(a) $\bar{a}_1, \bar{a}_2$ and $\bar{a}_3$ are linearly dependent
(b) $\bar{a}_1, \bar{a}_2$ and $\bar{a}_3$ are linearly independent
(c) for some $c_1 = 2, c_2 = -3, c_3 = -1, \Sigma c_1\bar{a}_1 = \bar{0}$
(d) for some $c_1 = c_2 = c_3 \neq 0,\ \Sigma c_1\bar{a}_1 = \bar{0}$

**22.** Given $\bar{a} = (3,1,-5),\ \bar{b} = (2,2,-3)$
(a) $\bar{a}$ and $\bar{b}$ are linearly independent vectors
(b) $\bar{a}$ and $\bar{b}$ are linearly dependent vectors
(c) $c_1\bar{a} + c_2\bar{b} = 0$ only when $c_1 = c_2 = 0$
(d) $c_1\bar{a} + c_2\bar{b} = 0$ for some $c_1 \neq 0$ or $c_2 \neq 0$

**23.** Which of the following(s) is/are true?
(a) The determinant of an orthogonal matrix has the value 1
(b) The determinant of an orthogonal matrix has the value –1
(c) The determinant of an orthogonal matrix has the value ±1
(d) The determinant of an orthogonal matrix has the value 0

**24.** If $V_1$ and $V_2$ are subspace of $R^4$ given by
$V_1 = \{(a, b, c, d) : b - 2c + d = 0\}$
$V_2 = \{(a, b, c, d) : a = d, b = 2c\}$, then
(a) the dimension of $V_1$ is 1
(b) the dimension of $V_2$ is 2
(c) the dimension of $V_1$ is 3
(d) the dimension of $V_2$ is 3

**25.** Given set of unit vector $\{(1,0,0),(0,1,0),(0,0,1)\}$
(a) This set consist independent vectors
(b) This set consist of dependent vectors
(c) This set span space $V_3$
(d) This set is a basis of $V_3$

**26.** Which of the following(s) is/are vector space?
(a) $V = \{(a_1, a_2, \ldots, a_n) : a_i \in \mathbb{R}\}$ over $\mathbb{R}$
(b) $V = \{f : f : [0,1] \to \mathbb{R}$ and $f(1/2) = 0\}$ over $\mathbb{R}$
(c) $V = \{f : f : [0,1] \to \mathbb{R}$ and $f(0) = f(1)\}$ over $\mathbb{R}$
(d) $V = \{f : f : [0,1] \to \mathbb{R}$ and $f(2/3) = 1\}$ over $\mathbb{R}$

**27.** Which of the following(s) is/are vector space?
(a) $V = \{p(x) = a_0 + a_1x + \ldots + a_nx^n : a_i \in \mathbb{R}\}$ over $\mathbb{R}$
(b) $V = \{f : f : [0,1] \to \mathbb{R}$ and $f$ has a local maxima at $x = 1/2\}$ over $\mathbb{R}$.
(c) $V = \{[a_{ij}]_{m\times n} : a_{ij} \in \mathbb{R}\}$ over $F = (\mathbb{R}, +, ;)$
(d) $V = \{f : f$ is real-valued function$\}$ over $\mathbb{R}$

**28.** Given the vector space $C(R)$ of the complex number over real numbers
(a) set $\{1, i\}$ form a basis for $C$
(b) 1 and $i$ are linearly independent
(c) 1 and $i$ are linearly dependent
(d) $\{1, i\}$ span $C(R)$

**29.** If $\bar{x}$ is an eigen vector of a matrix $A$ corresponding to an eigen value $\lambda$, then
(a) for some $k \neq 0$, $k\bar{x}$ is also an eigen vector
(b) for some $k \neq 0$, $k\bar{x}$ is not an eigen vector
(c) Both (a) and (b) are true
(d) Neither (a) nor (b) is true

**30.** Given $\{\alpha + i\beta, a + ib\}$, $\alpha, \beta, a, b \in R$
(a) $a\beta = b\alpha$, then this set form a basis for vector space $C$ over $R$
(b) $\dfrac{a}{\beta} = \dfrac{b}{\alpha}$, then this set form a basis for vector space $C$ over $R$
(c) Both (a) and (b) are true
(d) Neither (a) nor (b) is true

**31.** If $V$ is a vector space of $n \times n$ matrix over field of real numbers and $V_1$ and $V_2$ are the subspaces of symmetric and anti-symmetric matrices, respectively.
(a) $V = V_1 \oplus V_2$
(b) $V_1 \cap V_2 = \{0\}$
(c) $V = V_1 + V_2$
(d) $V = \frac{1}{2}(V_1 + V_2)$

**32.** Let $V$ is a finite dimensional vector space, with direct sum of its subspaces, $U$ and $W$
(a) $\dim(U + W) = \dim U + \dim V$
(b) $U$ and $W$ are independent
(c) $U \cap W = \{0\}$
(d) $\dim(U \cap W) = 0$

**33.** Given a subspace of $R^3$
$V = \{a_0 + a_1x + a_2x^2 + a_3x_i^2,\ x \in R\}$.
(a) $S = \{1, x, x^2, x^3\}$ is a basis
(b) $V$ has dimension 2
(c) $V$ has dimension 3
(d) $V$ has dimension 4

**34.** If the set $\{\alpha_1, \ldots, \alpha_n\}$ is linearly independent set and if $a_1, \ldots, a_n, b_1, \ldots, b_n \in F$. Such that $\Sigma a_i\alpha_i = \Sigma b_i\alpha_i$
(a) when $a_i = b_i$, $i = 1, 2, \ldots$
(b) when $a_i \neq b_i$, $i = 1, 2, \ldots$
(c) when $a_i = \frac{1}{2}b_i$, $i = 1, 2, \ldots$
(d) when $a_i - b_i = 0$, $i = 1, 2, \ldots$

**35.** Which of the following(s) is/are not vector space?
(a) $V = \{(a, b) : a, b \in \mathbb{R}$ and $ab \geq 0\}$ over $\mathbb{R}$
(b) $V = \{(a, b) : a, b \in \mathbb{R}$ and $ab \leq 0\}$ over $\mathbb{R}$
(c) $V = \{(a, b) : a, b \in \mathbb{R}$ and $a + b \geq 0\}$ over $\mathbb{R}$
(d) $V = \{(a, b) : a, b \in \mathbb{R}$ and $a + b \leq 0\}$ over $\mathbb{R}$

**36.** Which of the following(s) is/are not vector space?
(a) $V = \left\{\begin{bmatrix} a & b \\ c & d \end{bmatrix} : a, b, c, d \in \mathbb{R}\right\}$ over the field
$F = \left\{\begin{bmatrix} a & a \\ a & a \end{bmatrix} : a \in \mathbb{R}\right\}$
(b) $V = \mathbb{Z}_{10}$ over the field $F = \{0, 2, 4, 6, 8, +_{10}, \times_{10}\}$
(c) Any field over its subfield
(d) None of the above

**37.** If $F[x]$ is the vector space of all polynomials in one indeterminate $x$ over the field $F$, the
(a) infinite set $\{1, x, x^2, \ldots, x^n, \ldots\}$ is a basis of vector space $F[x]$
(b) infinite set $\{1, x, \ldots, x^n, \ldots\}$ is not a basis of vector space $F[x]$
(c) $\{1, x, \ldots, x^n, \ldots\}$ spans $F[x]$
(d) $\{1, x, \ldots, x^n, \ldots\}$ does not spans $F[x]$

**38.** If $F[x]$ is the vector space of all polynomials in one indeterminate $x$ over the field $F$, the infinite set $1, x, x^2, \ldots$ is
(a) linearly independent
(b) linearly dependent
(c) Both (a) and (b)
(d) Neither (a) nor (b)

**39.** Let $T$ be any linear operator on finite dimensional vector space $V$. $c_1, ..., c_k$ be distinct characteristic values of $T$, $W_i$ be the space of characteristic vector associated with the characteristic value $c_i$

(a) $W_1, ..., W_k$ are linearly independent
(b) if $T$ is diagonalizable, then $V = W_1 \oplus W_2 \oplus ... \oplus W_k$.
(c) $V = W_1 + W_2 + ... + W_k$
(d) $\dim V = \dim W_1 + ... + \dim W_k$

**40.** Given the linear span $[S]$ of any subset $S$ of a linear space $L(F)$

(a) $[S]$ is a subspace of $L$
(b) $[S]$ is not a subspace of $L$
(c) $[S]$ is subspace of $L$ generated by $S$
(d) $S$ is not a subspace of $L$ generated by $S$

**41.** Let $V = \mathbb{R}^n$ be a vector space over $\mathbb{R}$. Then, which of the following(s) is/are subspace of $V$?

(a) $W = \{(a_1, a_2, ..., a_n) : \Sigma a_n = i\}$
(b) $W = \{(a_1, a_2, ..., a_n) : \Sigma\, ia_i = 0\}$
(c) $W = \{(a_1, a_2, ..., a_n) : a_i \geq 0\}$
(d) $W = \{(a_1, a_2, ..., a_n) : a_i \text{ is eventually zero}\}$

**42.** Let $V = \mathbb{R}^n$ be a vector space over $\mathbb{R}$. Then, which of the following is/are not subspace of $V$?

(a) $W = \{(a_1, a_2, ..., a_n) : a_i = 0, \ i \text{ is even}\}$
(b) $W = \{(a_1, a_2, ..., a_n) : \Sigma a_i^2 \leq 1\}$
(c) $W = \{(a_1, a_2, ..., a_n) : \Sigma a_i^2 = 0\}$
(d) $W = \{(a_1, a_2, ..., a_n) : \frac{a_1}{a_2} = \lambda, \ \lambda \text{ is real number}\}$

**43.** Let $V$ be a finite dimensional vector space, $W_1, ..., W_k$ be subspaces of $V$ such that

$V = W_1 + .. + W_k$ and $\dim V = \dim W_1 + ... + \dim W_k$

(a) $V = W_1 \oplus ... \oplus W_k$
(b) $W_1, ..., W_k$ are linearly independent
(c) $W_1, ..., W_k$ are linearly dependent
(d) $V \neq W_1 \oplus ... \oplus W_k$

**44.** If $M_1$ and $M_2$ are subspaces of the linear space L(F), then

(a) $M_1 + M_2$ is a subspace of $L$
(b) $M_1 + M_2$ is not a subspace of $L$
(c) $x, y \in M_1 + M_2 \Rightarrow x + y \in M_1 + M_2$
(d) $x, y \in M_1 + M_2 \Rightarrow x + y \notin M_1 + M_2$

**45.** If a finite dimensional vector space $V(F)$ be the direct sum of its subspace $U$ and $W$, *i.e.*, $V = U \oplus W$,

(a) $\dim(U \oplus W) = \dim U + \dim W$
(b) $U \cap W = \{0\}$
(c) $\dim V = \dim U + \dim W$
(d) $\dim U \cap W = 0$

**46.** Given the set of vectors $v_1 = (1, 2, 3); v_2 = (1, 0, 1)$ and $v_3 = (0, 1, 0)$

(a) the set of vectors are linearly independent
(b) The set of vectors are linearly dependent
(c) $(1, 2, 3) + (1, 0, 1) + (0, 1, 0) = 0$
(d) $(1, 2, 3) + (1, 0, 1) + (0, 1, 0) \neq 0$

**47.** If $V$ be the vector space of all functions from $\mathbb{R}$ to $\mathbb{R}$ and $W = \{f : f(4) = 3 + f(2)\}$,

(a) $W$ is a subspace of $V$
(b) $W$ is not a subspace of $V$
(c) $W$ is not closed under scalar multiplication
(d) $W$ is closed under scalar multiplication

**48.** Let $V = \{p(x) : p(x) = a_0 + a_1x + a_2x^2 + ... + a_nx^n : a_r \in \mathbb{R}\}$ be a vector space over $\mathbb{R}$. Then, which of the following(s) is/are subspace of $V$?

(a) $W = \{p(x) : \Sigma a_r = 0$ where $a_r$ is the coefficient of $n^r\}$
(b) $W = \{p(x) : p(0) = p(1)\}$
(c) $W = \{p(x) : a_r = 0 \text{ where } r \text{ is odd}\}$
(d) $W = \{p(x) : p(i) = 0, \forall\, i = 1, 2, ..., n\}$

**49.** Let $V = \{p(x) : p(x) = a_0 + a_1x + a_2x^2 + ... + a_nx^n : a_r \in \mathbb{R}\}$ be a vector space over $\mathbb{R}$. Then, which of the following(s) is/are not subspace of $V$?

(a) $W = \{p(x) : a_i \neq 0 \text{ when } i \text{ is odd}\}$
(b) $W = \{p(x) : \text{graph of } p(x) \text{ passes through the origin}\}$
(c) $W = \{p(x) : a_i \neq 0 \text{ when } i \text{ is even}\}$
(d) $W = \{p(x) :$ the graph of $y = p(x)$ intersects the x-axis atleast three given points say $x = \alpha$, $x = \beta$ and $x = \gamma\}$

**50.** If $V = \mathbb{R}^3 = \{(x, y, z) : x, y, z \in \mathbb{R}\}$ and $W = \{(x, y, z) : x - 2y \ \ 3z = 0\}$,

(a) $W$ is a subspace of $V$
(b) $W$ is not a subspace of $V$
(c) $\alpha, \beta \in W \Rightarrow \alpha + \beta \in W$
(d) $\alpha, \beta \in W \Rightarrow \alpha + \beta \notin W$

**51.** If $V$ be the vector space of all $n \times n$(*i.e.*, square) matrices over a field $F$ and $W$ consists of the symmetric matrices $A = [a_{ij}]_{n \times n}$ for which $A' = A$ (where $A'$ is the transposed matrix of $A$), then

(a) $W$ is a subspace of $V(F)$
(b) $W$ is not a subspace of $V(F)$
(c) $A, B \in W \Rightarrow A + B \in W$
(d) $A, B \in W \Rightarrow A + B \notin W$

**52.** Let the set $\{v_1, v_2, ..., v_n\}$ is linearly independent set and if $a_1, a_2, ..., a_n, b_1, b_2, ..., b_n \in F$, such that $\Sigma a_i v_j = \Sigma b_i v_i$,

(a) $a_i = b_i, \ i = 1, 2, ..., n$
(b) $a_i \neq b_i, \ i = 1, 2, ..., n$
(c) $a_i - b_i = 0, \ i = 1, 2, ..., n$
(d) $a_i - b_i \neq 0, \ i = 1, 2, ..., n$

**53.** Given $W = \{(x, 3x, 3x + 2) \cdot x \in \mathbb{R}\}$

(a) $W$ form a subspace of $\mathbb{R}^3(\mathbb{R})$
(b) $W$ does not form a subspace of $\mathbb{R}^3(\mathbb{R})$
(c) $\alpha, \beta \in W \Rightarrow \alpha + \beta \in W$
(d) $\alpha, \beta \in W \Rightarrow \alpha + \beta \notin W$

**54.** If $M_1$ and $M_2$ are subspaces of a linear space $L(F)$,

(a) $M_1 + M_2 = M_1 \cup M_2$
(b) $M_1 + M_2 \neq M_1 \cup M_2$
(c) $M_1 + M_2$ is also a subspace
(d) $M_1 + M_2$ is not a subspace

**55.** Given non-empty subset $W$ of a vector space $V(F)$ is a vector subspace of $V(F)$
(a) $\alpha, \beta \in W$ and $a, b \in F \Rightarrow a\alpha + b\beta \in W$
(b) $W$ is closed under addition
(c) $W$ is closed under scalar multiplication
(d) $\alpha, \beta \in W \Rightarrow \alpha + \beta \in W$

**56.** Let $L$ be a finite dimensional linear space and let $M_1, M_2$ be subspaces of $L$ such that $L = M_1 + M_2$ and $\dim L = \dim M_1 + \dim M_2$.
(a) $L = M_1 \oplus M_2$ (b) $L \neq M_1 \oplus M_2$
(c) $M_1 \cap M_2 = \{0\}$ (d) $M_1 \cap M_2 = \phi$

**57.** If $V$ be the vector space of all square $n \times n$ matrices over a field $F$ and $W = (A \in V : AM = MA)$, for a given matrix $M$,
(a) $W$ is a subspace of $V(F)$
(b) $W$ is not a subspace of $V(F)$
(c) $x, y \in F$ and $A, B \in W$, then $xA + yB \in W$
(d) $A, B \in W \Rightarrow A + B \in W$

**58.** Let $S = \{v_1, v_2, \ldots, v_n\}$ be a basis of a finite dimensional space $V(F)$ and $\dim V(F) = n$,
(a) every element $u \in V$ can be uniquely expressed as $u = a_1v_1 + a_2v_2 + \ldots + a_nv_n$, where $a_1, \ldots, a_n \in F$
(b) $S$ is a linearly independent set
(c) $S$ is not a linearly independent set
(d) $L(S) = V$

**59.** Which of the following(s) is/are true?
(a) The singleton set $\{v_1\}$ is linearly independent, if $v_1 \neq 0$
(b) If $v_1 \neq 0$, then the singleton set $\{v_1\}$ is linearly independent
(c) If $v_1 \neq 0$, then $\{v_1\}$ is linearly independent
(d) If $v_1 \neq 0$, then $\{v_1\}$ is not linearly independent

**60.** If $V$ be the vector space of all functions from $\mathbb{R}$ to $\mathbb{R}$ and $W = \{f : f(5) = 0\}$.
(a) $W$ is a subspace of $V$
(b) $W$ is not a subspace of $V$
(c) $W$ is closed under multiplication
(d) $W$ is not closed under multiplication

**61.** Which of the following statements is/are true?
(a) The intersection of any two subspaces of a vector space $V(F)$ is again a subspace of $V(F)$
(b) The intersection of any two subspaces of a vector space $V(F)$ is not a subspace of $V(F)$
(c) $V(F)$ is the subspace of intersection of any two subspace of $V(F)$
(d) If $V_1$ and $V_2$ are two subspaces of $V$, then $v_1 \in V_1$ and $v_2 \in V_2$, then $v_1 + v_2 \in V_1 \cap V_2$

**62.** Let $\mathbb{R}$ be the field of real numbers and $Q$ be the field of rational numbers and show that $W = \{(x, y, z) : x, y, z \in Q\}$
(a) $W$ is not a subspace of $V_3(\mathbb{R})$
(b) $W$ is not a subspace of $V_3(\mathbb{R})$
(c) $W$ is closed under multiplication
(d) $W$ is not closed under multiplication

**63.** Prove that, if $A$ is an $m \times n$ matrix over field $F$ and $B$, $C$ are $n \times p$ matrices over field $F$, then
(a) $A(dB + C) = d(AB) + AC$
For each scalar $d \in F$
(b) $A(dB + C) \neq d(AB) + AC$
For each scalar $d \in F$
(c) $A(dB + C) = d(AB)$
(d) $A(dB + C) - AC = d(AB)$

**64.** The set $M_{mn}$ of all $m \times n$ matrices (where $m$ and $n$ are fixed positive integers) over the set $\mathbb{R}$ of real numbers is an abelian group with respect to matrix addition.
(a) $M_{mn}$ is a vector space over $\mathbb{R}$ with respect to matrix addition and multiplication matrices by a scalar (real number)
(b) $M_{mn}$ is not a vector space over $R$ with respect to matrix addition and matrices multiplication by a scalar (real number)
(c) $A \in M_{mn}, a \in \mathbb{R} \Rightarrow aA \in M_{mn}$
(d) $a, b \in \mathbb{R}$ and $a \in M_{mn}$, then $(a + b)A = aA + bA$

**65.** Given the vectors (1, 1, 0), (3, 1, 3) and (5, 3, 3)
(a) the vectors are linearly independent
(b) the vectors are linearly dependent
(c) $(1, 1, 0) + (3, 1, 3) + (5, 3, 3) = 0$
(d) $(1, 1, 0) + (3, 1, 3) + (5, 3, 3) \neq 0$

**66.** Let $V = \mathbb{R}^3$, also $W = \{(x, y, 0) : x, y \in \mathbb{R}\}$
(a) $W$ is a subspace of $V$
(b) $W$ is not a subspace of $V$
(c) $\alpha, \beta \in W \Rightarrow \alpha + \beta \in W$
(d) $\alpha + 2\beta \in W \Rightarrow \alpha + 2\beta \in W$

**67.** If $V$ be the vector space of all functions from $\mathbb{R}$ to $\mathbb{R}$ and $W = \{f : 2f(3) = f(1)\}$
(a) $W$ is a subspace of $V$
(b) $W$ is not a subspace of $V$
(c) $\alpha + \beta \in W \Rightarrow \alpha + \beta \in W$
(d) $\alpha + \beta \in W \Rightarrow \alpha + 3\beta \in W$

**68.** If $E_1, \ldots, E_k$ are $k$ linear operators on $V$ which satisfy conditions
(i) Each $E_i$ is a projection ($E_i^2 = E_i$);
(ii) $E_iE_j = 0$, if $i \neq j$;
(iii) $I = E_1 + \ldots + E_k$;
(iv) The range of $E_i$ is $W_i$ and if $W_i$ be the range of $E_i$,
(a) $V = W_i \oplus \ldots \oplus W_k$
(b) $V$ is the direct sum of $W_i$
(c) $V$ is the sum of $W_i$
(d) $V$ is not the sum of $W_i$

**69.** Which of the following statements is/are true?
(a) The vectors (1, 0, 0), (1, 1, 0), (1, 1, 1) form a basis for $\mathbb{R}^3$
(b) The vectors (1, 0, 0), (1, 1, 0), (1, 1, 1) does not form a basis for $\mathbb{R}^3$
(c) If $\{e_1, e_2, e_3\}$ is a basis for $\mathbb{R}^3$, then $\{e_1 + e_2, e_1 + e_3, e_2 + e_3\}$ is also a basis for $\mathbb{R}^3$
(d) If $\{e_1, e_2, e_3\}$ is a basis for $\mathbb{R}^3$, then $(e_1 + e_2, e_1 + e_3, e_2 + e_3)$ is not a basis for $\mathbb{R}^3$

**70.** Given system of three vectors $v_1 = (1, 3, 2)$, $v_2 = (1, -7, -8)$, $v_3 = (2, 1, -1)$ of $V_3(\mathbb{R})$, where $\mathbb{R}$ is the field of real numbers.

(a) The set of vectors are linearly dependent
(b) The set of vectors are linearly independent
(c) $a_1v_1 + a_2v_2 + a_3v_3 = 0 \Rightarrow a_1 = a_2 = a_3 = 0$
(d) $a_1v_1 + a_2v_2 + a_3v_3 \neq 0 \Rightarrow a_1 = a_2 = a_3 = 0$

**71.** Which of the following statements is/are true?

(a) For each subspace $M$ of a finite dimensional linear space $L$ of dimension $n$ is a finite dimensional space.
(b) For each subspace $M$ of a finite dimensional space $L$ of dimension $n$ is $\dim M \leq n$.
(c) For each subspace $M$ of a finite dimensional space $L$, $L = M$, if $\dim L = \dim M$.
(d) For each subspace $M$ of a finite dimensional space $L$, $\dim L = \dim M$, if $L = M$.

**72.** If $V$ be the vector space of all functions from $\mathbb{R}$ to $\mathbb{R}$ and

$$W = \{f(x) : f(-x) = f(x),\ x \in V\}$$
$$f(-x) = f(x),\ \forall x \in V, \text{ then}$$

(a) $W$ is a subspace of $V(\mathbb{R})$
(b) $W$ is not a subspace of $V(\mathbb{R})$
(c) $\forall f_1 g \in W$ and $a, b \in \mathbb{R}$ $f_1 g \in W \Rightarrow af + bg \in W$
(d) $\forall f_1 g \in W$ and $a, b \in \mathbb{R}$ $f_1 g \in W \Rightarrow af + bg \notin W$

**73.** Each subspace $W$ of a finite dimensional vector space $V$, over a field $F$ of dimension $n$

(a) is a finite dimensional space
(b) is of infinite dimension
(c) $\dim W \leq n$
(d) $V = W$ iff $\dim V = \dim W$

**74.** Which of the following statements is/are true?

(a) Linear space $F^n$ is of dimension $n$
(b) The linear space $F^n$ is not of dimension $n$
(c) The linear space $F^n$ is of infinite dimension
(d) The linear space $F^n$ is not of infinite dimension

**75.** Let $V$ be the set of all ordered $n$-tupples $V = \{(a_1, a_2, \ldots, a_n) : a_1, a_2, \ldots, a_n \in F\}$ under the operation of addition and scalar multiplication in $V$ defined as

I. Let $a = (a_1, a_2, \ldots, a_n)$
$b = (b_1, b_2, \ldots, b_n)$
then $a, b \in V$
$a + b = (a_1 + b_1, a_2 + b_2, \ldots, a_n + b_n) \in V$
$(\because a_i + b_i \in V, 1 \leq i \leq n)$

II. Let $a = (a_1, a_2, \ldots, a_n) \in V$ and $\alpha \in F$,
then $\alpha a = (\alpha a_1, \alpha a_2, \ldots, \alpha a_n) \in V$
$(\because \alpha a_i \in V, \forall 1 \leq i \leq n)$

(a) $V$ is a vector space under the defined operation of addition and scalar multiplication
(b) $V$ is not a vector space under the defined operation of addition and scalar multiplication
(c) $V$ under the defined operation of addition is an abelian group
(d) $V$ under the defined operation of multiplication is not an abelian group

**76.** Let $W = \{(x - y, x + y, x + y + z) : x \in \mathbb{R}\}$

(a) $W$ is a subspace of $\mathbb{R}^3(\mathbb{R})$
(b) $W$ is not a subspace of $\mathbb{R}^3(\mathbb{R})$
(c) $\alpha, \beta \in W$ and $a, b \in \mathbb{R} \Rightarrow a\alpha + b\beta \in W$
(d) $\alpha, \beta \in W$ and $a, b \in \mathbb{R} \Rightarrow a\alpha + b\beta \notin W$

**77.** Let $L$ be the real linear space of all bounded continuous real-valued functions defined on the closed interval $[-1, 1]$. Which of the following sets in $L$ are subspaces of $L$?

(a) All $f$ such that $f(0) = 0$
(b) All $f$ such that $f(0) \neq 0$
(c) All $f$ such that $f(x) \geq 0$ for all $x \in [-1, 1]$
(d) All $f$ such that $f(x) \leq 0$ for all $x \in [-1, 1]$

**78.** Let $P$ be the real linear space of all polynomials with real coefficients defined on the closed unit interval $[0, 1]$.

(a) $P$ is an infinite dimensional linear space
(b) $P$ is not an infinite dimensional linear space
(c) The infinite set is a basis for $P$
(d) The infinite set is not a basis for $P$

**79.** If (i) $L = M_1 + M_2$ and (ii) $M_1 \cap M_2 = (0)$ *i.e.*, $M_1$ and $M_2$ are disjoint subspaces of $L$.

(a) A linear space $L$ is a direct sum of its two subspaces $M_1$ and $M_2$
(b) A linear space $L$ is not direct sum of its two subspaces $M_1$ and $M_2$
(c) $L = M_1 \oplus M_2$
(d) $L \neq M_1 \oplus M_2$

**80.** Let $L$ be the real linear space of all bounded continuous real-valued functions defined on the closed interval $[-1, 1]$. Which of the following set is $L$ are subspace of $L$?

(a) All $f$ such that $f(0) = 1$.
(b) All $f$ such that $f$ is differentiable.
(c) All $f$ such that $f$ is a polynomial of degree 3
(d) All $f$ such that $f(0) \neq 1$

**81.** Let $M_1$ and $M_2$ are two subspaces of a linear space $L(F)$. If $L = M_1 + M_2$ and $M_1 \cap M_2 = \{0\}$

(a) $L = M_1 \oplus M_2$
(b) $L \neq M_1 \oplus M_2$
(c) $L$ can be expressed as a sum of an element of $M_1$ and an element of $M_2$
(d) $L$ cannot be expressed as a sum of an element of $M_1$ and an element of $M_2$

**82.** Which of the following set of vectors $x = (x_1, x_2, x_3)$ in $\mathbb{R}^3$ is/are subspaces of $\mathbb{R}^3$?

(a) All $x$ such that $x_1 = 0$ or $x_2 = 0$
(b) All $x$ such that $x_1 + 2x_2 = 1$
(c) All $x$ such that $x_1 = x_2 \neq 0$
(d) All $x$ such that $x_1 + 2x_2 \neq 1$

**83.** For the three equations

$$-2x + y + z = a$$
$$x - 2y + z = b$$
$$x + y - 2z = c$$

(a) have no solution unless $a + b + c = 0$
(b) when $a + b + c = 0$, then solution exist
(c) have solution when $a + b + c \neq 0$
(d) when $a + b + c \neq 0$, then solution exist

**84.** Given the equation

$$x + y + z = 1$$
$$ax + by + cz = k$$
$$a^2x + b^2y + c^2z = k^2$$

(a) $x = \dfrac{(k-b)(c-k)}{(a-b)(c-a)}$ (b) $y = \dfrac{(a-k)(k-c)}{(a-b)(b-c)}$

(c) $z = \dfrac{(b-k)(k-a)}{(b-c)(c-a)}$ (d) $x = y = z$

**85.** The values of $\lambda$ for which the equations

$$(\lambda - 1)x + (3\lambda + 1)y + 2\lambda z = 0$$
$$(\lambda - 1)x + (4\lambda - 2)y + (\lambda + 3)z = 0$$
$$2x + (3\lambda + 1)y + 3(\lambda - 1)z = 0$$

are consistent

(a) 1, 1, 1 (b) 2, 2, 2
(c) 0, 3, 3 (d) 1, 2, 3

**86.** Given $\begin{bmatrix} 1 & -1 & 1 \\ 1 & 2 & -1 \\ 2 & 1 & 3 \end{bmatrix} \begin{bmatrix} x_1 \\ x_2 \\ x_3 \end{bmatrix} = \begin{bmatrix} 0 \\ 0 \\ 0 \end{bmatrix}$

(a) the given equation have only trivial solution
(b) the given equation have no trivial solution
(c) $x_1 = x_2 = x_3 = 0$
(d) $x_1 = x_2 = x_3 \neq 0$

# Answers

## Exercise 1

**1.** (d) **2.** (b) **3.** (c) **4.** (c) **5.** (b) **6.** (d) **7.** (c) **8.** (d) **9.** (b) **10.** (b)
**11.** (d) **12.** (d) **13.** (b) **14.** (a) **15.** (c) **16.** (b) **17.** (b) **18.** (c) **19.** (b) **20.** (c)
**21.** (c) **22.** (c) **23.** (b) **24.** (d) **25.** (d) **26.** (b) **27.** (b) **28.** (d) **29.** (d) **30.** (b)
**31.** (c) **32.** (c) **33.** (c) **34.** (a) **35.** (c) **36.** (b) **37.** (c) **38.** (b) **39.** (b) **40.** (c)
**41.** (d) **42.** (c) **43.** (a) **44.** (a) **45.** (a) **46.** (c) **47.** (b) **48.** (d) **49.** (c) **50.** (d)
**51.** (d) **52.** (a) **53.** (c) **54.** (b) **55.** (b) **56.** (b) **57.** (c) **58.** (d) **59.** (b) **60.** (d)
**61.** (b) **62.** (c) **63.** (a) **64.** (b) **65.** (a) **66.** (b) **67.** (a) **68.** (c) **69.** (d) **70.** (d)
**71.** (b) **72.** (c) **73.** (a) **74.** (c) **75.** (b) **76.** (c) **77.** (b) **78.** (d) **79.** (c) **80.** (b)
**81.** (a) **82.** (a) **83.** (c) **84.** (a) **85.** (b) **86.** (a) **87.** (d) **88.** (a) **89.** (a) **90.** (b)
**91.** (d) **92.** (c) **93.** (c) **94.** (c) **95.** (b) **96.** (a) **97.** (a) **98.** (b) **99.** (b) **100.** (b)
**101.** (b) **102.** (c) **103.** (d) **104.** (b) **105.** (a) **106.** (a) **107.** (c) **108.** (a) **109.** (a) **110.** (a)
**111.** (c) **112.** (a) **113.** (a) **114.** (a) **115.** (a) **116.** (c) **117.** (a) **118.** (a) **119.** (c) **120.** (d)
**121.** (a) **122.** (d) **123.** (c) **124.** (a) **125.** (d) **126.** (a) **127.** (b) **128.** (b) **129.** (b) **130.** (d)
**131.** (d) **132.** (c) **133.** (a) **134.** (d) **135.** (a) **136.** (b) **137.** (c) **138.** (b) **139.** (a) **140.** (b)
**141.** (b) **142.** (d) **143.** (d) **144.** (c) **145.** (d) **146.** (a) **147.** (a) **148.** (c) **149.** (d) **150.** (d)
**151.** (d) **152.** (d) **153.** (d) **154.** (d) **155.** (c) **156.** (c) **157.** (d) **158.** (c) **159.** (b) **160.** (d)
**161.** (d) **162.** (c) **163.** (c) **164.** (b) **165.** (a) **166.** (a) **167.** (c) **168.** (b) **169.** (a) **170.** (a)
**171.** (a) **172.** (c) **173.** (a) **174.** (b) **175.** (a) **176.** (c) **177.** (a) **178.** (c) **179.** (c) **180.** (c)
**181.** (d) **182.** (d) **183.** (c) **184.** (d) **185.** (d) **186.** (b) **187.** (c) **188.** (b) **189.** (b) **190.** (b)
**191.** (a) **192.** (d) **193.** (a) **194.** (d) **195.** (c) **196.** (b) **197.** (a) **198.** (c) **199.** (d) **200.** (a)
**201.** (b) **202.** (d) **203.** (c) **204.** (a) **205.** (d) **206.** (d) **207.** (c) **208.** (b) **209.** (d) **210.** (a)
**211.** (a) **212.** (a) **213.** (a) **214.** (d) **215.** (d) **216.** (b) **217.** (b) **218.** (b) **219.** (d) **220.** (c)
**221.** (a) **222.** (c) **223.** (b) **224.** (a) **225.** (a) **226.** (a) **227.** (d) **228.** (b) **229.** (d) **230.** (b)
**231.** (d) **232.** (b) **233.** (c) **234.** (b) **235.** (c) **236.** (c) **237.** (a) **238.** (d) **239.** (c) **240.** (d)
**241.** (a) **242.** (b) **243.** (b) **244.** (b) **245.** (c) **246.** (c) **247.** (a) **248.** (b) **249.** (a) **250.** (c)
**251.** (b) **252.** (d) **253.** (b) **254.** (a) **255.** (d) **256.** (b) **257.** (d) **258.** (a) **259.** (c) **260.** (a)
**261.** (c) **262.** (b) **263.** (b) **264.** (a) **265.** (d) **266.** (c) **267.** (d) **268.** (b) **269.** (c) **270.** (b)
**271.** (a) **272.** (a) **273.** (b) **274.** (d) **275.** (d) **276.** (c) **277.** (c) **278.** (d) **279.** (b) **280.** (d)
**281.** (b) **282.** (d) **283.** (d) **284.** (d) **285.** (c) **286.** (d) **287.** (d) **288.** (b) **289.** (b) **290.** (b)
**291.** (c) **292.** (a) **293.** (a) **294.** (b) **295.** (d) **296.** (c) **297.** (c) **298.** (a) **299.** (d) **300.** (b)

| | | | | | | | | | |
|---|---|---|---|---|---|---|---|---|---|
| **301.** (d) | **302.** (d) | **303.** (c) | **304.** (a) | **305.** (d) | **306.** (c) | **307.** (b) | **308.** (d) | **309.** (b) | **310.** (d) |
| **311.** (b) | **312.** (d) | **313.** (c) | **314.** (c) | **315.** (c) | **316.** (a) | **317.** (d) | **318.** (b) | | |

## Exercise 2

| | | | | | | | | | |
|---|---|---|---|---|---|---|---|---|---|
| **1.** (a,c) | **2.** (a,b) | **3.** (a,c) | **4.** (a,b,c) | **5.** (a,c) | **6.** (a,b,d) | **7.** (a) | **8.** (a,c) | **9.** (a) | **10.** (a,b,c) |
| **11.** (a,c) | **12.** (a,d) | **13.** (a,b,c) | **14.** (a,b,c,d) | **15.** (b,c) | **16.** (a,b) | **17.** (a,c) | **18.** (a,b,c) | **19.** (b,d) | **20.** (a,d) |
| **21.** (a,c) | **22.** (a,c) | **23.** (a,b,c) | **24.** (b,c) | **25.** (a,c,d) | **26.** (a,b,c) | **27.** (a,c,d) | **28.** (a,b,d) | **29.** (a) | **30.** (a) |
| **31.** (a,b,c) | **32.** (a,b,c,d) | **33.** (a,d) | **34.** (a,d) | **35.** (a,b,c,d) | **36.** (a,b) | **37.** (a,c) | **38.** (a) | **39.** (a,b,c) | **40.** (a,c) |
| **41.** (b,d) | **42.** (b,d) | **43.** (a,b) | **44.** (a,c) | **45.** (a,b,c,d) | **46.** (a,d) | **47.** (b,c) | **48.** (a,b,c,d) | **49.** (a,c) | **50.** (a,c) |
| **51.** (a,c) | **52.** (a,c) | **53.** (b,d) | **54.** (a,c) | **55.** (a,b,c,d) | **56.** (a,c) | **57.** (a,c,d) | **58.** (a,b,d) | **59.** (a,b,c) | **60.** (a,c) |
| **61.** (a,d) | **62.** (b,d) | **63.** (a,d) | **64.** (a,c,d) | **65.** (b,d) | **66.** (a,c,d) | **67.** (a,c,d) | **68.** (a,c) | **69.** (a,c) | **70.** (a,c) |
| **71.** (a,b) | **72.** (a,c) | **73.** (a,c,d) | **74.** (a,d) | **75.** (a,c) | **76.** (a,c) | **77.** (a,c) | **78.** (a,c) | **79.** (a,c) | **80.** (a,b,c) |
| **81.** (a,c) | **82.** (a,b) | **83.** (a,b) | **84.** (a,b,c) | **85.** (c) | **86.** (a,c) | | | | |

# Hints & Solutions

## Exercise 1

**1.** Here, it is given that vector space $V = R^3$ and its subset are

$$S = \{(x, y, z) \in V \ : \ x = y = 0\}$$
$$T = \{(x, y, z)\} \in V : x = 0\}$$
$$W_1 = \{(x, y, z) \in V : \ z \neq 0\}$$

Let $W_1 = (2, 1, -3)$, $W_2 = (1, 2, 3) \in W$

Hence, $W_1 + W_2 = (3, 3, 0) \notin W$

So, it is not a subspace of $R^3$ but $S$ and $T$ both are subspaces.

Since, $\alpha S_1 + \beta S_2 \in S$ and $\alpha T_1 + \beta T_2 \in T$

where $S_1$ and $S_2 \in S$ and $T_1, T_2 \in T$, $\alpha, \beta \in F$ (field)

**2.** (I) Every subset of $V$ containing $n$ elements is a basis of $V$ is not true.

Let $R^3$ be vector space of dimension 3. But $\{(2, 2, 4), (1, 1, 2), (1, 0, 1)\}$ is not a basis for $R^3$ because these are linearly dependent.

(II) But we know that, no linearly independent subset of $V$ contains more than $n$ elements. So, it is true because we have not any linearly dependent set which has $n$ elements.

**3.** If $A$ and $B$ are both order skew-symmetric matrices, then

$$A = -A^T \text{ and } B = -B^T \quad \ldots(i)$$

Also, given that $AB = BA$

$$= (-B^T)(-A^T) \quad \text{[from Eq. (i)]}$$
$$= B^T A^T$$
$$= (AB)^T$$

$\Rightarrow$ $AB = (AB)^T$ i.e., $AB$ is a symmetric matrix.

**4.** Here, it is given that vector space $V$ over the field of real numbers spanned by the set

$$S = \{(0, 1, 0, 0), (1, 1, 0, 0), (1, 0, 1, 0), (0, 0, 1, 0)$$
$$(1, 1, 1, 0), (1, 0, 0, 0)\}$$

$\Rightarrow$ $(1, 1, 1, 0) = (0, 1, 0, 0) + (1, 0, 0, 0) + (0, 0, 1, 0)$

So, it can be omitted.

$(1, 1, 0, 0) = 1(1, 0, 0, 0) + 1(0, 1, 0, 0) + 0\,(0, 0, 1, 0)$

It can also be omitted.

Similarly, $(1, 0, 1, 0)$ will be omitted.

Since, $\{(1, 0, 0, 0), (0, 1, 0, 0), (0, 0, 1, 0)\}$ are linearly independent and span whole set $V$.

It is a of given set

Hence, Dimension = 3

**5.** Let
$$X = (3, 2, -1)$$
$$Y = (2, 4, 1)$$
$$Z = (4, 0, -3)$$
$$W = (10, 4, -5)$$

(i) $2X + Z = 2(3, 2, -1) + (4, 0, -3)$
$$= (6, 4, -2) + (4, 0, -3)$$
$$= (10, 4, -5)$$
$$= W$$

and $Y + Z = (2, 4, 1) + (4, 0, -3)$
$$= (6, 4, -2) \neq W$$

Thus, first option is wrong.

(ii) $2X - Y = 2(3, 2, -1) - (2, 4, 1)$
$$= (6, 4, -2) - (2, 4, 1)$$
$$= (4, 0, -3) = Z$$

and $Y + 2Z = (2, 4, 1) + 2(4, 0, -3)$
$$= (2, 4, 1) + (8, 0, -6)$$
$$= (10, 4, -5) = W$$

Thus, $2X - Y = Z$ and $Y + 2Z = W$

$\Rightarrow$ Second option is right.

**6.** We have, $V$ is the real vector space of all mapping from $R$ to $R$ and $V_1 = \{f \in V \,/\, f(-x) = f(x)\}$

$$V_2 = \{f \in V \,/\, f(-x) = -f(x)\}$$

vector subspace. Let $V$ be a vector space over field $F$ and let $W \subseteq V$. Then, $W$ is called a subspace of $V$ iff $W$ itself is a vector space over $F$ with respect to operations of vector addition and scalar multiplication in $V$.

The necessary and sufficient condition for a non-empty subset $W$ of a vector space $V(F)$ to be subspace of $V$ is $a, b \in F$ and $\forall \alpha, \beta \in W \Rightarrow a\alpha + b\beta \in W$ ...(i)

To show $V_1$ and $V_2$ as subspace of $V$. Suppose, $f, g \in V_1$ and a is any scalar *i.e.,* $a \in R$. Then,

$$(af+g)(-x) = af(-x) + g(-x)$$
$$= af(x) + g(x)$$
$$= (af+g)(x)$$
$$\Rightarrow \quad af + g \in V_1$$

Thus, $a \in R$ and $f, g \in V_1 \Rightarrow af + g \in V_1$. Hence, $V_1$ is a subspace of $V$. Again suppose $f_0, g_0 \in V_2$ and a is any scalar, then

$$(af_0 + g_0)\ (-x) = af_0(-x) + g_0(-x)$$
$$= a[-f_0(x) - g_0(x)]$$
$$= -[a f_0(x) + g_0(x)]$$
$$= -[af_0 + g_0]x$$
$$\Rightarrow \quad af_0 + g_0 \in V_2$$

Hence, $V_2$ is subspace of $V$.

A ring $R$ is said to be field, if it has

(i) unity element

(ii) commutative

(iii) each non-zero element possesses multiplication inverse.

The dimension of $f[x]$ over $f$ is $n-1$.

**8.** A subset $S$ of a vector space $V(F)$ is said to be a basis of $V(F)$, if

(i) $S$ consists of linearly independent vectors.

(ii) $S$ generates $V(F)$ *i.e.,* $L(S) = V$ *i.e.,* each vector in $V$ is a linear combination of a finite number of element of $S$.

Now, set $S = \{a+ib,\ c+id\}$ is a basis for the vector space $V$ over $R$, then by (i) $S$ should be linearly independent *i.e.,* If $x(a+ib) + y(c+id) = 0$, then $x=0, y=0$

or $xa + yc + i(xb + yd) = (0, 0)$, then $x = 0, y = 0$

or
$$xa + yc = 0$$
$$xb + yd = 0$$

This system of equation have a unique solution *i.e.,* $x = 0, y = 0$ iff

$$\begin{vmatrix} a & c \\ b & d \end{vmatrix} \neq 0 \quad \Rightarrow \quad ad - bc \neq 0$$

(i) A matrix is said to be symmetric, if matrix is equal to its transpose

*i.e.,* $A = A^T$

Thus, $A$ is symmetric matrix iff

$$A^T = A$$

We have, $A$ and $B$ are symmetric matrices of same order.

Hence, $A^T = A$ and $B^T = B$

Now, $(A+B)^T = A^T + B^T = A + B$

Hence, $A + B$ is a symmetric matrix

$$(AB - BA)^T = (AB)^T - (BA)^T$$
$$= B^T A^T - A^T B^T$$
$$= BA - AB \qquad (\text{since } A^T = A, B^T = B)$$
$$= -(AB - BA)$$

Here, $(AB - BA)$ is anti-symmetric matrix and this is not a symmetric matrix.

**10.** By Cayley Hamilton Theorem "every square matrix satisfies its characteristic equation".

We have, $A = \begin{bmatrix} 3 & -2 \\ 4 & -2 \end{bmatrix}$

Here, $A - \lambda I = \begin{vmatrix} 3-\lambda & -2 \\ 4 & -2-\lambda \end{vmatrix} = 0$

$$\Rightarrow (3-\lambda)(-2-\lambda) - 4(-2) = 0$$
$$\Rightarrow \quad -(3-\lambda)(\lambda+2) + 8 = 0$$
$$\Rightarrow \quad \lambda^2 - \lambda - 6 + 8 = 0$$
$$\Rightarrow \quad \lambda^2 - \lambda + 2 = 0$$

Hence, by Cayley Hamilton theorem

$$A^2 - A + 2I = 0$$

Comparing $A^2 - kA + 2I = 0$

We get $k = 1$

**11.** The system of equation, $AX = B$ has a solution, if Rank of $A$ = Rank $[A:B]$.

This solution is unique, if rank of A is equal to number of $U_n$ known.

So, for unique solution $|A| \neq 0$.

Here, $|A| = \begin{vmatrix} 1 & 2 & 4 \\ 2 & 1 & 2 \\ 1 & 2 & a-4 \end{vmatrix} \neq 0 \Rightarrow R_3 \to R_3 - R_1$

$$= \begin{vmatrix} 1 & 2 & 4 \\ 2 & 1 & 2 \\ 0 & 0 & a-8 \end{vmatrix}$$

The rank of $A$ will be 3, if $a - 8 \neq 0 \quad \Rightarrow \quad a \neq 8$

**12.** We have, $2x + 2y = 1$

$2x - y = 1$ over $z_3$

$$\Rightarrow \quad y = 0, \ x = 1/2$$

Hence, solution is $\left(\frac{1}{2}, 0\right)$.

**13.** Here, it is given that

$S = \{(1, i, 0)\ (2i, 1, 1), (1, 1+i, 1-i)\}$ be a subset of the complex vector space $C^3$ and

$T = \{(1, 1, 1), (1, 1, 0), (1, 0, 0)\}$ be a subset of the real vector space $\mathbb{R}^3$.

Hence, any element of $C^3$ is

$$(a + ib,\ c + id, e + if)$$

We know that any three complex trial which is linearly independent can generate it and any real trial (linearly independent) will also generate.

Therefore, $S = \{(1, i, 0)(2i, 1, 1), (0, 1+i, 1-i)\}$ is linearly independent, so $S$ is basis. Hence, $S$ is a basis but $T$ is not a basis.

**14.** Here, it is given that $\mathbb{R}^3$ is a real vector space and subspace $\{(x, y, z) \in \mathbb{R}^3 : y = x\}$

Hence, generators are $\{(1, 1, 0), (0, 0, 1)\}$.

**15.** The dimension of the vector space $c$ over the field $IR$ will be equal to 2.

**16.** $|-1u|=|-1|u, \forall u \in V$ is false statement.

**17.** Here, given linear span

$$S=\{1, 1+x+x^2\}$$

Hence, polynomials lies on this span will be

$$100x^2+10x+10$$

**18.** Here, given equations are

$$x_1+x_2+x_3=0$$
$$x_1+2x_2=0$$
$$x_2-x_3=0$$

or $(x_1+x_2+x_3, x_1+2x_2, x_2-x_3)=(0,0,0)$

$\Rightarrow x_1(1,1,0)+x_2(1,2,1)+x_3(1,0,-1)=(0,0,0)$

$\Rightarrow$ So, here we can see that $x_1, x_2, x_3 \in R$

Hence, we will prove that $R^3=3$.

**19.** Here, it is given that

$\alpha=(1,2,3), \beta=(3,1,0), \gamma=(2,1,3)$ and $\delta=(-1,3,6)$

We have, $2\alpha-1\beta=2(1,2,3)-1(3,1,0)$

$=(-1,3,6)=\delta$

Hence, $\delta$ is a linear combination of $\alpha$ and $\beta$.

**20.** Here, $A$ and $B$ be any two $n\times n$ matrices

and $\quad \text{tr}(A)=\sum_{i=1}^{n} a_{ii}$ and $\text{tr}(B)=\sum_{i=1}^{n} b_{ii}$

Then, given statement (I)

$\text{tr}(AB)=\text{tr}(BA)$ is true,

because it show commutative law and statement (II)

$\text{tr}(A+B)=\text{tr}(A)+\text{tr}(B)$

is also true by distributive law. So, both (I) and (II) are true statements.

**21.** Here, it is given that, $A=\begin{pmatrix}2 & 0\\ 3 & 5\end{pmatrix}$ be expressed as $P+Q$

where

$P\rightarrow$ symmetric matrix and

$Q\rightarrow$ skew-symmetric matrix

(i) $A'=-A$

(ii) All the diagonal element of a skew-symmetric matrix are zero.

Hence, $\quad Q=\frac{1}{2}\begin{pmatrix}0 & -3\\ 3 & 0\end{pmatrix}$

**22.** Here, given matrix is

$$\begin{bmatrix}1 & 0 & 0 & \dots & \dots & 0\\ 1 & 1/2 & 0 & \dots & \dots & 0\\ 1 & 1/2 & 1/3 & \dots & \dots & 0\\ 1 & 1/2 & 1/3 & 1/4 & \dots & 0\\ \dots & \dots & \dots & \dots & \dots & \\ 1 & 1/2 & 1/3 & 1/4 & \dots & 1/n\end{bmatrix}$$

$$1\cdot\frac{1}{2}\cdot\frac{1}{3}\cdots\cdot\frac{1}{n}\begin{bmatrix}1 & 0 & 0 & \dots & 0\\ 1 & 1 & 0 & \dots & 0\\ 1 & 1 & 1 & \dots & 0\\ \dots & \dots & \dots & \dots & \dots\\ 1 & 1 & 1 & 1 & 1\end{bmatrix} \Rightarrow \frac{1}{n!}$$

**23.** Here, system of the equations are

$$x+2y-3z=1$$
$$(P+2)z=3$$
$$(2P+1)y+z=2$$

Hence, $\quad A=\begin{vmatrix}1 & 2 & -3\\ 0 & 0 & P+2\\ 0 & (2P+1) & 1\end{vmatrix}=0$

$$1(2P+1)(P+2)-2(0-0)+(-3)(0-0)=0$$
$$2P^2+P+4P+2=0$$
$$\Rightarrow \quad 2P^2+5P+2=0$$
$$\Rightarrow \quad 2P^2+4P+P+2=0$$
$$\Rightarrow \quad 2P(P+2)+1(P+2)=0$$
$$(P+2)(2P+1)=0$$

Hence, $\quad P=-2, -1/2$

But at $P=-2$, rank $A$ is same to other matrix form

Therefore, $P=-1/2$

**24.** Here, $R$ is the set of real numbers

and $\quad R^2=\{(x_1, x_2): x_1 \in R, x_2 \in R\}$

$a=\{(x_1, 0): x_1 \in R\}$

$b=\{(y_1, 0): y_1 \in R\}$

Hence, $\alpha a+\beta b=\{\alpha x_1, \beta_1 y_1, 0: x, y \in R\}$

**25.** Here, it is given that

$W_1=\{(0, x_2, x_3, x_4, x_5): x_2, x_3, x_4, x_5 \in R\}$

and $\quad W_2=\{(x_1, 0, x_3, x_4, x_5): x_1, x_3, x_4, x_5 \in R\}$

which is subspace of $R^5$

Hence, $W_1 \cap W_2$ will be equal to 2.

**26.** Here, if $A$ be a non-zero square matrix of order $n$, then the matrix $A+A'$ is symmetric, but $A-A'$ will be anti-symmetric.

**27.** It is given that $x, y, z$ are in AP with common difference $d$

$$x=x, y=x+d, z=x+2d$$

Let $\quad |A|=\begin{vmatrix}4 & 5 & x\\ 5 & 6 & y\\ 6 & k & z\end{vmatrix}=\begin{vmatrix}4 & 5 & x\\ 5 & 6 & x+d\\ 6 & k & x+2d\end{vmatrix}$

$$=\begin{vmatrix}4 & 5 & x\\ 1 & 1 & d\\ 1 & k-6 & d\end{vmatrix}$$

Applying $R_2-R_1=R_2$ and $R_3-R_2=R_3$

$$=\begin{vmatrix}4 & 5 & x\\ 1 & 1 & d\\ 0 & k-7 & 0\end{vmatrix} \quad R_3=R_3-R_2$$

$$|A|=0 \Rightarrow (k-7)(4d-x)=0$$

$\Rightarrow \quad d=\frac{x}{4}, k=7$

**28.** Since, if $A$ is a square matrix of rank $n$, then it cannot be a singular.

**29.** Here, $c$ is a non-singular matrix and

$$B = c\begin{bmatrix} 0 & x & y \\ 0 & 0 & z \\ 0 & 0 & 0 \end{bmatrix} c^{-1}, \quad \text{(given)}$$

Now, we can see that $B$ is similar to $\begin{bmatrix} 0 & x & y \\ 0 & 0 & z \\ 0 & 0 & 0 \end{bmatrix}$ and the eigen value of $\begin{bmatrix} 0 & x & y \\ 0 & 0 & z \\ 0 & 0 & 0 \end{bmatrix}$ are all zeros.

Hence, $B^k = 0$ for $k = 3$

$\Rightarrow \quad B^3 = 0$

**32.** Here, $X = \begin{bmatrix} 0 & 1 & 0 & 0 \\ 0 & 0 & 1 & 0 \\ 0 & 0 & 0 & 1 \\ 0 & 0 & 0 & 0 \end{bmatrix}$ (given)

and transpose of $X = X^T = \begin{bmatrix} 0 & 0 & 0 & 0 \\ 1 & 0 & 0 & 0 \\ 0 & 1 & 0 & 0 \\ 0 & 0 & 1 & 0 \end{bmatrix}$

Here, we can see that rank of matrix $X = 3$.

Hence, we will get the rank of $X^TX$.

Let $Y = X \cdot X^T$, the rank of $Y \leq$ rank of $X$

Also, $X^{-1}Y = X^T$ and so we have

Rank $X$ = Rank $X^T \leq$ Rank of $Y$

Hence, from Eqs. (i) and (ii), we get

Rank of $X$ = Rank of $Y$

Hence, rank of $X \cdot X^T = 3$

**33.** If $W_1, W_2, W_3$ be subspace of a vector space $V$ such that $W_3 \subset W_1$, then $W_1 \cup (W_2 + W_3) = W_2 + W_1 \cup W_3$ will be correct.

**34.** Here, $\xi_1, \xi_2, \xi_3$ be vectors of a vector space $V$ over the field $F$ and $r$ and $s$ are arbitrary elements.

Since $(\xi_1, \xi_2, r\xi_1 + s\xi_2 + \xi_3)$ is linearly dependent (given)

There exist scalar $\alpha, \beta, \gamma$ not all zero such that

$$\alpha\xi_1 + \beta\xi_2 + \gamma(r\xi_1 + s\xi_2 + \xi_3) = 0$$

$$\Rightarrow \quad (\alpha + \gamma r)\xi_1 + (\beta + \gamma s)\xi_2 + \gamma\xi_3 = 0$$

If $V \neq 0$, then it is clear that $\xi_1, \xi_2, \xi_3$ will be linearly dependent.

If $V = 0$, then one of the $\alpha$ or $\beta$ will be non-zero and in this case also $\xi_1, \xi_2$ and $\xi_3$ are linearly dependent.

**35.** Here, we can see that vectors $(-3, 0, 1)$ and $(3, 0, -1)$ are linearly dependent.

Hence, dim = 2.

**36.** Here, $V$ has a subspace of dimension 0, 1 and 2. Thus, there are three subspaces.

**37.** Here, the sets

$$S_1 = \left\{\alpha = \begin{bmatrix} 1 & -2 & 4 \\ 3 & 0 & -1 \end{bmatrix}, \beta = \begin{bmatrix} 2 & -4 & 8 \\ 6 & 0 & -2 \end{bmatrix}\right\}$$

or $S_1 = \left\{\alpha = \begin{bmatrix} 1 & -2 & 4 \\ 3 & 0 & -1 \end{bmatrix}, \beta = 2\begin{bmatrix} 1 & -2 & 4 \\ 3 & 0 & -1 \end{bmatrix}\right\}$

So, we can see that in set $S_1$, $\beta = 2\alpha$

Hence, $S_1$ is linearly dependent.

and set $\quad S_2 = \{f = u^3 + 3u + 4, g = u^3 + 4u + 3\}$

then, $\quad f = u^3 + 3u + 4$

and $\quad g = u^3 + 4u + 3$

Now, $af + bg = 0$

Hence, $a(u^3 + 3u + 4) + b(u^3 + 4u + 3) = 0$

or $\quad au^3 + 3au + 4a + bu^3 + 4bu + 3b = 0$

or $\quad (a + b)u^3 + (3a + 4b)u + (4a + 3b) = 0$

$\Rightarrow \quad a + b = 0 \quad$ ...(i)

$3a + 4b = 0 \quad$ ...(ii)

and $\quad 4a + 3b = 0 \quad$ ...(iii)

Hence, from Eq. (i), $\quad a = -b$

Putting this value Eq. (ii), we get

$$3(-b) + 4b = 0$$
$$-3b + 4b = 0$$
$$b = 0,$$

then $\quad a = 0$

and $\quad af + bg = 0 \Rightarrow a = 0$ and $b = 0$

Hence, $f$ and $g$ are linearly independent.

**38.** Here, $\quad W_1 = \left\{\begin{bmatrix} x & y \\ 0 & x \end{bmatrix} : x, y \in R\right\}$

and $\quad W_2 = \left\{\begin{bmatrix} x & y \\ z & 0 \end{bmatrix} : x, y, z \in R\right\}$

Then, $(W_1 \cap W_2) = \left\{\begin{bmatrix} x & y \\ 0 & 0 \end{bmatrix} : x, y \in R\right\}$

Hence, $\dim(w_1 \cap w_2) = 1$

**39.** Suppose, $T$ be a non-singular, then $T$ is invertible.

Now, $\quad \xi(S) = \xi(STT^{-1}) = \xi[(ST)T^{-1}] < \xi(ST)$

or $\quad (S) \leq \xi(ST)$

Hence, $\quad \xi(ST) = \xi(T)$

But $\quad \xi(ST) \leq \xi(S)$

Hence, $\quad \xi(ST) = \xi(T)$, if $T$ is non-singular.

Therefore, correct answer is rank $(ST)$ = Rank $S$, if $T$ is non-singular.

**40.** Here, we cannot consider (1, 2, 3) as linear combination of element of $S$.

If possible, let $(1, 2, 3) = a(1, 1, 0) + b(2, 1, 3) \quad$ ...(i)

or $\quad (1, 2, 3) = (a + 2b, a + b, 3b)$

$\Rightarrow \quad a + 2b = 1$

$$a + b = 2$$
$$3b = 3$$

These equations are inconsistent.

Hence, there exist no $a, b \in R$ for which Eq. (i) is true.

**41.** Here, the system of equations are

$$kx + y + z = 1 \quad \text{...(i)}$$
$$x + ky + z = k \quad \text{...(ii)}$$
$$x + y + kz = k^2 \quad \text{...(iii)}$$

We can write it in the form

$$AX = B$$

i.e.,
$$\begin{bmatrix} k & 1 & 1 \\ 1 & k & 1 \\ 1 & 1 & k \end{bmatrix}\begin{bmatrix} x \\ y \\ z \end{bmatrix} = \begin{bmatrix} 1 \\ k \\ k^2 \end{bmatrix}$$

where
$$A = \begin{bmatrix} k & 1 & 1 \\ 1 & k & 1 \\ 1 & 1 & k \end{bmatrix}$$

Hence, augmented matrix

$$[A : B] = \begin{bmatrix} k & 1 & 1 & \vdots & 1 \\ 1 & k & 1 & \vdots & k \\ 1 & 1 & k & \vdots & k^2 \end{bmatrix}$$

The system of equation have no solution, if rank of $A <$ rank $[A : B]$. Therefore,

This is possible, if $k = -2$.

**42.** Here, given system of equations are

$$4x_1 + x_2 - 3x_3 - x_4 = 0 \quad \text{...(i)}$$
$$2x_1 + 3x_2 + x_3 - 5x_4 = 0 \quad \text{...(ii)}$$
$$x_1 - 2x_2 - 2x_3 + 3x_4 = 0 \quad \text{...(iii)}$$

Hence, let $A$ be the coefficient matrix given by

$$A = \begin{vmatrix} 4 & 1 & -3 & -1 \\ 2 & 3 & 1 & -5 \\ 1 & -2 & -2 & 3 \end{vmatrix}$$

We consider the submatrix

$$B = \begin{vmatrix} 4 & 1 & 3 \\ 2 & 3 & 1 \\ 1 & -2 & -2 \end{vmatrix}$$

$$= 4(-6+2) + 1(1+4) - 3(-4-3)$$
$$= -16 + 5 + 21 \neq 0$$

Hence, rank of $A = 3 < 4$ (number of unknowns)

$\Rightarrow$ The system of equation has infinite number of solutions.

**43.** If $W_1 = \{0, a_2, a_3\}$ and $W_3 = \{b_1, 0, b_3\}$ are two subspace of $F^3$, where $F^n$ is a vector space of dimension $n$. Then, the subspace $W_1 \cap W_2$ is isomorphic to the vector space $F'$.

**44.** Here, it is given that set of all triples $(x_1, x_2, x_3)$ of real numbers $R$ from a vector space $V_3$.

And a subspace denoted by a vertical plane $y = x$.

Hence, $(x_1, x_2, x_3) = (x_1, x_2, x_3)$
$$= (x_1, x_1, 0) + (0, 0, x_3)$$
$$= x_1(1, 1, 0) + x_3(0, 0, 1)$$

$\Rightarrow$ The linear combination of the sets is (1, 1, 0) and (0, 0, 1).

**45.** Here, it is given that

$E = \{(1, 0, 0), (0, 1, 0), (0, 0, 1), (1, 1, 1), (1, 1, 0)\}$

Let a, b, c, d, e be the scalar, such that

$a(1, 0, 0) + b(0, 1, 0) + c(0, 0, 1) + d(1, 1, 1) + e(1, 1, 0) = (0, 0, 0)$

i.e., $(a + d + e, b + d + e, c + d) = (0, 0, 0)$

i.e.,
$$a + 0 \cdot b + 0 \cdot c + d + e = 0$$
$$0 \cdot a + b + 0 \cdot c + d + e = 0 \quad \text{...(i)}$$
$$0 \cdot a + 0 \cdot b + c + d + 0 \cdot e = 0$$

Hence, the coefficient matrix of Eq. (i), is

$$\begin{bmatrix} 1 & 0 & 0 & 1 & 1 \\ 0 & 1 & 0 & 1 & 1 \\ 0 & 0 & 1 & 1 & 0 \end{bmatrix} = 0$$

$\Rightarrow$ Rank of coefficient matrix < number of unknowns.

Hence, $E$ is linearly dependent.

Also, for any four vector $E$ is linearly dependent and any three vector of $E$ is linearly independent.

**46.** Here, given equation are

$$x - y + 3z = 4$$
$$x + z = 2$$
$$x + y - z = 0$$

write the system of equation in matrix form $AX = B$.

we get
$$\begin{bmatrix} 1 & -1 & 3 \\ 1 & 0 & 1 \\ 1 & 1 & -1 \end{bmatrix}\begin{bmatrix} x \\ y \\ z \end{bmatrix} = \begin{bmatrix} 4 \\ 2 \\ 0 \end{bmatrix}$$

Hence, coefficient matrix
$$A = \begin{bmatrix} 1 & -1 & 3 \\ 1 & 0 & 1 \\ 1 & 1 & -1 \end{bmatrix}$$

Augmented matrix $[A : B]$

$$= \begin{bmatrix} 1 & -1 & 3 & \vdots & 4 \\ 1 & 0 & 1 & \vdots & 2 \\ 1 & 1 & -1 & \vdots & 0 \end{bmatrix}$$

Rank of $A = 2$

$$= \begin{bmatrix} 1 & -1 & 3 & \vdots & 4 \\ 0 & 1 & -2 & \vdots & -2 \\ 0 & 1 & -2 & \vdots & -2 \end{bmatrix}$$

By $R_2 \to R_2 - R_1$
$R_3 \to R_3 - R_2$

$$= \begin{bmatrix} 1 & -1 & 3 & \vdots & 4 \\ 0 & 1 & -2 & \vdots & -2 \\ 0 & 0 & 0 & \vdots & 0 \end{bmatrix}$$

By $R_3 \to R_3 - R_2$

$\Rightarrow$ Rank $[A : B] = 2$

Rank of $A =$ Rank $[A : B] <$ number of unknowns.

Therefore, the given system of equation has infinite many solutions.

**47.** II. Let a, b, c be scalar, such that

$$a(1, 0, 0) + b(0, 1, 0) + c(0, 0, 1) = (0, 0, 0)$$
$$\Rightarrow \quad (a, 0, 0) + (0, b, 0) + (0, 0, c) = (0, 0, 0)$$
$$\Rightarrow \quad a = 0, b = 0, c = 0$$

Therefore, the given system of vector is linearly independent.

III. Let a, b, c be scalar such that

$$a(0, 1, 0) + b(1, 0, 1) + c(1, 1, 0) = (0, 0, 0)$$

$\Rightarrow \quad (0, a, 0)+(b, 0, b)+(c, c, 0)=(0, 0, 0)$

$\Rightarrow \quad b+c=0, a+c=0, b=0$

Hence, $\quad a=0, \; b=0, \; c=0$

Therefore, the given system of vectors is linearly independent.

**48.** If a non-zero vector space $V$ is generated by a finite set $S$, then $V$ can be generated by a linearly independent subset of $S$.

**49.** Here, it is given that the equation $AX = B$,

where $A=\begin{bmatrix}-1 & 2\\ 2 & -1\end{bmatrix}$ and $B=\begin{bmatrix}3\\1\end{bmatrix}$

Hence, $|A|=\begin{vmatrix}-1 & 2\\ 2 & -1\end{vmatrix}=1-4=-3$

Hence, rank of $A$ *i.e.*, $\rho(A)=2$

Now, augmented matrix

$$A:B=\begin{bmatrix}-1 & 2 & : & 3\\ 2 & -1 & : & 1\end{bmatrix}$$

Hence, $\rho(A)=\rho(A:B)=2=$ number of unknowns.

$\Rightarrow$ There exist a non-zero unique solution.

**50.** Here, in a given statement, Assertion (A).If $M$ is an $n\times n$ matrix with rank $n-1$, then $M$ can be made non-singular by changing one element is correct but given Reason (R) that an $n\times n$ matrix with rank $(n-1)$ has a non-vanishing minor of order $(n-1)$ is correct statement.

**51.** Here, given system of equation are

$$2x+y=5 \quad \text{...(i)}$$
$$x-3y=-1 \quad \text{...(ii)}$$
$$3x+4y=k \quad \text{...(iii)}$$

Since, it is given that these are consistent, so

$$\begin{vmatrix}2 & 1 & 5\\ 1 & -3 & -1\\ 3 & 4 & k\end{vmatrix}=0$$

$\Rightarrow \quad 2(-3k+4)+1(-3-k)+5(4+9)=0$

$\Rightarrow \quad -6k+8-3-k+20+45=0$

$-7k+70=0$

$k=\dfrac{70}{7}=10$

$k=10$

**52.** Here, given system of equation is $x+y+z=0$, $y+2z=0$ and $\alpha x+z=0$, since it has more than one solution, then determinant of coefficient matrix must be zero.

*i.e.*, $\begin{vmatrix}1 & 1 & 1\\ 0 & 1 & 2\\ \alpha & 0 & 1\end{vmatrix}=0$

$\Rightarrow \quad 1(1-0)-1(0-2\alpha)+1(0-\alpha)=0$

$\Rightarrow \quad 1+2\alpha-\alpha=0$

$\Rightarrow \quad 1+\alpha=0$

$\Rightarrow \quad \alpha=-1$

**53.** Here, given equations are

$x+2y+z=9$ and $2x+y+3z=7$

Hence, we can expressed it as

$$\begin{bmatrix}1 & 2 & 1\\ 2 & 1 & 3\end{bmatrix}\begin{bmatrix}x\\y\\z\end{bmatrix}=\begin{bmatrix}9\\7\end{bmatrix}$$

**54.** If $A$ is $n\times n$ matrix from the set of real numbers and $A^3-3A^2+4A-6I=0$, then $A^{-1}$ is equal to

$\dfrac{1}{6}(A^2-3A+4I)$

or $\quad A^{-1}=\dfrac{1}{6}(A^2-3A+4I)$

**55.** Here, given equations are

$$3x+2y+z=0 \quad \text{...(i)}$$
$$x+4y+z=0 \quad \text{...(ii)}$$
$$2x+y+4z=0 \quad \text{...(iii)}$$

$$\Rightarrow \frac{x}{\begin{vmatrix}0 & 2 & 1\\ 0 & 4 & 1\\ 0 & 1 & 4\end{vmatrix}}=\frac{y}{\begin{vmatrix}3 & 0 & 1\\ 1 & 0 & 1\\ 2 & 0 & 4\end{vmatrix}}=\frac{z}{\begin{vmatrix}3 & 2 & 0\\ 1 & 4 & 0\\ 2 & 1 & 0\end{vmatrix}}=\frac{1}{\begin{vmatrix}3 & 2 & 1\\ 1 & 4 & 1\\ 2 & 1 & 4\end{vmatrix}}$$

$$=\frac{x}{0}=\frac{y}{0}=\frac{z}{0}=\frac{1}{\begin{vmatrix}3 & 2 & 1\\ 1 & 4 & 1\\ 2 & 1 & 4\end{vmatrix}}$$

Hence, $\quad x=0, y=0, z=0$

$\Rightarrow$ It has only the trivial solution.

$x=0, y=0, z=0$

**110.** For singularity of matrix $=\begin{vmatrix}8 & \lambda & 0\\ 4 & 0 & 2\\ 12 & 6 & 0\end{vmatrix}=0$

$\Rightarrow 8(0-12)-\lambda(0-2\times 12)=0 \Rightarrow \lambda=4$

**111.** Consider $3\times 3$ minors, $\because$ maximum possible rank is 3.

$$\begin{vmatrix}4 & 2 & 1\\ 6 & 3 & 4\\ 2 & 1 & 0\end{vmatrix}=0, \begin{vmatrix}2 & 1 & 3\\ 3 & 4 & 7\\ 1 & 0 & 1\end{vmatrix}=0, \begin{vmatrix}4 & 1 & 3\\ 6 & 4 & 7\\ 2 & 0 & 1\end{vmatrix}=0$$

and $\begin{vmatrix}4 & 2 & 3\\ 6 & 3 & 7\\ 2 & 1 & 1\end{vmatrix}=0$

Since, all $3\times 3$ minors are zero. Now, we consider $2\times 2$ minors

$$\begin{vmatrix}4 & 2\\ 6 & 3\end{vmatrix}=0, \begin{vmatrix}2 & 1\\ 3 & 4\end{vmatrix}=8-3=5\neq 0$$

Hence, $\quad$ Rank $=2$

**116.** Since $(X_1, X_2, X_3, \ldots, X_N)$ are orthogonal, they span a vector space of dimension $N$.

And $(-X_1, -X_2, -X_3, \ldots, -X_N)$ are linearly dependent on $X_1, X_2, X_3, \ldots, X_N$, the set $(X_1, X_2, \ldots, X_N, -X_1, -X_2, \ldots, -X_N)$ will also span a vector space of dimension $N$ only.

**117.** If rank of $(5\times 6)$ matrix is 4, then surely it must have exactly 4 linearly independent rows as well as 4 linearly independent columns.

Hence, Rank = Row rank = Column rank

**118.** Two conditions must be satisfied to be basis for subspace $X$.

1. The vectors have to be linearly independent (LI).
2. They must span $X$.

Now, $\{[1, -1, 0]^T, [1, 0, -1]^T\}$ is LI set because one cannot be obtained from other by scalar multiplication. They are independent this can also be seen from the rank of $\begin{bmatrix} 1 & -1 & 0 \\ 1 & 0 & -1 \end{bmatrix}$ which is 2.

Next, we check, if the set spans $X$.

$$X = \{x \in R^3 : x_1 + x_2 + x_3 = 0\}$$

Now, the general infinite solution of $X = \begin{bmatrix} -k_1 - k_2 \\ k_1 \\ k_2 \end{bmatrix}$

Take $k_1, k_2$ as $\begin{bmatrix} k_1 \\ k_2 \end{bmatrix} = \begin{bmatrix} 0 \\ k \end{bmatrix}$ and $\begin{bmatrix} k_1 \\ k_2 \end{bmatrix} = \begin{bmatrix} k \\ 0 \end{bmatrix}$ we will get two independent solutions for $X$.

$X = \begin{bmatrix} -k \\ 0 \\ k \end{bmatrix}$ or $\begin{bmatrix} -k \\ k \\ 0 \end{bmatrix}$ both of these can be generated by the linear combination of $[1, -1, 0]^T$ and $[1, 0, -1]^T$, the set spans $X$.

Therefore, by the definition it is a basis for the subspace of $X$ as we have shown that the set is not only LI but also spans $X$.

**120.** The augmented matrix $[A : B]$ is

$$\begin{bmatrix} 1 & 1 & 1 & \vdots & 3 \\ 1 & 2 & 3 & \vdots & 4 \\ 1 & 4 & k & \vdots & 6 \end{bmatrix} \begin{matrix} R_2 \to R_2 - R_1 \\ R_3 \to R_3 - R_1 \end{matrix}$$

$$\sim \begin{bmatrix} 1 & 1 & 1 & \vdots & 3 \\ 0 & 1 & 2 & \vdots & 1 \\ 0 & 3 & k-1 & \vdots & 3 \end{bmatrix} R_3 \to R_3 - 3R_2 \sim \begin{bmatrix} 1 & 1 & 1 & \vdots & 3 \\ 0 & 1 & 2 & \vdots & 1 \\ 0 & 0 & k-7 & \vdots & 0 \end{bmatrix}$$

Now, rank of $A$ = rank $[A : B] = 3$, if $k \neq 7$, then solution is unique.

But rank $A$ = rank $[A : B] = 2$, if $k = 7$, then system has infinite solution and therefore unique solution is not possible.

**121.** Rank $[A : B]$ = Rank $[A]$ is necessary for existence of atleast one solution to $PX = q$.

**122.** The augmented matrix

$$[A : B] = \begin{bmatrix} 0 & 4 & 3 & \vdots & 8 \\ 2 & 0 & -1 & \vdots & 2 \\ 3 & 2 & 0 & \vdots & 5 \end{bmatrix} R_1 \leftrightarrow R_2$$

$$\sim \begin{bmatrix} 2 & 0 & -1 & \vdots & 2 \\ 0 & 4 & 3 & \vdots & 8 \\ 3 & 2 & 0 & \vdots & 5 \end{bmatrix} R_3 \to R_3 - \frac{3}{2} R_1$$

$$\sim \begin{bmatrix} 2 & 0 & -1 & \vdots & 2 \\ 0 & 4 & 3 & \vdots & 8 \\ 0 & 2 & 3/2 & \vdots & 2 \end{bmatrix} R_3 \to R_3 - \frac{2}{4} R_2$$

$$\sim \begin{bmatrix} 2 & 0 & -1 & \vdots & 8 \\ 0 & 4 & 3 & \vdots & 8 \\ 0 & 0 & 0 & \vdots & -2 \end{bmatrix}$$

for the last row, we observe that $0 = -2$ which is inconsistence. Also, $r(A) = 2$ and $r[A : B] = 3$ *i.e.*, $r(A) \neq r[A : B]$ which is inconsistent. Therefore, solution is not exist.

**132.** The characteristic equation is

$$|A - \lambda I| = 0$$

$$\begin{vmatrix} 4-\lambda & -2 \\ -2 & 1-\lambda \end{vmatrix} = 0 \Rightarrow (4-\lambda)(1-\lambda) - [(-2)\times(-2)] = 0$$

$$\Rightarrow \lambda^2 - 5\lambda = 0 \Rightarrow \lambda(\lambda - 5) = 0$$

$$\Rightarrow \lambda = 0, 5 \text{ are the eigen value}$$

**133.** The characteristic equation is $|A - \lambda I| = 0$

$$\Rightarrow \begin{vmatrix} 5-\lambda & 0 & 0 & 0 \\ 0 & 5-\lambda & 5 & 0 \\ 0 & 0 & 2-\lambda & 1 \\ 0 & 0 & 3 & 1-\lambda \end{vmatrix} = 0$$

$$\Rightarrow (5-\lambda)(5-\lambda)[(2-\lambda)(1-\lambda) - 3] = 0$$

$$\Rightarrow (5-\lambda)(5-\lambda)(\lambda^2 - 3\lambda - 1) = 0 \Rightarrow \lambda = 5, 5, \frac{3 \pm \sqrt{3}}{2}$$

Put $\lambda = 5$ in $[A - \lambda I]X = 0$

$$\Rightarrow \begin{bmatrix} 5-5 & 0 & 0 & 0 \\ 0 & 5-5 & 5 & 0 \\ 0 & 0 & 2-5 & 1 \\ 0 & 0 & 3 & 1-5 \end{bmatrix} \begin{bmatrix} x_1 \\ x_2 \\ x_3 \\ x_4 \end{bmatrix} = \begin{bmatrix} 0 \\ 0 \\ 0 \\ 0 \end{bmatrix}$$

$$\Rightarrow \begin{bmatrix} 0 & 0 & 0 & 0 \\ 0 & 0 & 5 & 0 \\ 0 & 0 & -3 & 1 \\ 0 & 0 & 3 & -4 \end{bmatrix} \begin{bmatrix} x_1 \\ x_2 \\ x_3 \\ x_4 \end{bmatrix} = \begin{bmatrix} 0 \\ 0 \\ 0 \\ 0 \end{bmatrix}$$

$$\Rightarrow \begin{aligned} 5x_3 &= 0 \\ -3x_3 + x_4 &= 0 \\ 3x_3 - 4x_4 &= 0 \end{aligned}$$

On solving above equations, we get $x_3 = 0$, $x_4 = 0$, $x_1$ and $x_2$ may be anything, suppose $x_1 = k_1$ and $x_2 = k_2$.

Hence, the eigen vector corresponding to the eigen value $\lambda = 5$ is

$$X = \begin{bmatrix} x_1 \\ x_2 \\ x_3 \\ x_4 \end{bmatrix} = \begin{bmatrix} k_1 \\ k_2 \\ 0 \\ 0 \end{bmatrix}$$

Let $k_1 = 1, k_2 = -2$

Hence, $X = \begin{bmatrix} 1 \\ -2 \\ 0 \\ 0 \end{bmatrix}$, so that (a) is correct.

**134.** Cross product of $b=[0\ \ 1\ \ 0]^T$ and $X=[x_1\ \ x_2\ \ x_3]^T$ is given by

$$b\times X=\begin{vmatrix}\mathbf{i} & \mathbf{j} & \mathbf{k}\\ 0 & 1 & 0\\ x_1 & x_2 & x_3\end{vmatrix}=x_3\mathbf{i}+0\,\mathbf{j}-x_1\mathbf{k}$$

$$=[x_3\ \ 0\ \ -x_1]$$

and $L(X)=b\times X=A\begin{bmatrix}x_1\\ x_2\\ x_3\end{bmatrix}$, where $A$ is $3\times 3$ matrix.

Suppose, $A=\begin{bmatrix}a_1 & a_2 & a_3\\ a_4 & a_5 & a_6\\ a_7 & a_8 & a_9\end{bmatrix}$

Now, $A\begin{bmatrix}x_1\\ x_2\\ x_3\end{bmatrix}=b\times X$

$$\Rightarrow \begin{bmatrix}a_1 & a_2 & a_3\\ a_4 & a_5 & a_6\\ a_7 & a_8 & a_9\end{bmatrix}\begin{bmatrix}x_1\\ x_2\\ x_3\end{bmatrix}=\begin{bmatrix}x_3\\ 0\\ -x_1\end{bmatrix}$$

By matching LHS and RHS, we get

$$\begin{bmatrix}0 & 0 & 1\\ 0 & 0 & 0\\ -1 & 0 & 0\end{bmatrix}\begin{bmatrix}x_1\\ x_2\\ x_3\end{bmatrix}=\begin{bmatrix}x_3\\ 0\\ -x_1\end{bmatrix}$$

Hence, $A=\begin{bmatrix}0 & 0 & 1\\ 0 & 0 & 0\\ -1 & 0 & 0\end{bmatrix}$

Now, eigen values of $A$ are given by

$$|A-\lambda I|=0 \Rightarrow \begin{vmatrix}-\lambda & 0 & 1\\ 0 & -\lambda & 0\\ -1 & 0 & -\lambda\end{vmatrix}=0$$

$$\Rightarrow -\lambda(\lambda^2-0)+1(0-\lambda)=0$$

$$\Rightarrow \lambda^3+\lambda=0$$

$$\Rightarrow \lambda(\lambda^2+1)=0$$

$$\Rightarrow \lambda=0,\pm i$$

**136.** $|A-\lambda I|=0$

$$\Rightarrow \begin{vmatrix}1-\lambda & 2\\ 0 & 2-\lambda\end{vmatrix}=0 \Rightarrow \lambda=1,2$$

Put $\lambda=1 \Rightarrow \begin{bmatrix}0 & 2\\ 0 & 1\end{bmatrix}\begin{bmatrix}1\\ a\end{bmatrix}=0 \Rightarrow a=0$

Put $\lambda=2 \Rightarrow \begin{bmatrix}-1 & 2\\ 0 & 0\end{bmatrix}\begin{bmatrix}1\\ b\end{bmatrix}=0$

$\Rightarrow -1+2b=0 \Rightarrow b=1/2 \ \therefore\ a+b=1/2$

**138.** Since, $A$ is triangular matrix, therefore the eigen values are diagonal elements $\lambda=1, 2, 3$.

Suppose, $X_1$ be the eigen vector corresponding to the eigen value $\lambda=1$.

Hence, $(A-\lambda I)X_1=0$

$$\Rightarrow \begin{bmatrix}1-\lambda & 1 & 0\\ 0 & 2-\lambda & 2\\ 0 & 0 & 3-\lambda\end{bmatrix}\begin{bmatrix}x_1\\ x_2\\ x_3\end{bmatrix}=\begin{bmatrix}0\\ 0\\ 0\end{bmatrix}$$

Put $\lambda=1$

$$\Rightarrow \begin{bmatrix}0 & 1 & 0\\ 0 & 1 & 2\\ 0 & 0 & 2\end{bmatrix}\begin{bmatrix}x_1\\ x_2\\ x_3\end{bmatrix}=\begin{bmatrix}0\\ 0\\ 0\end{bmatrix}$$

$\Rightarrow$ $x_2=0,\ x_2+2x_3=0,\ 2x_3=0$

Let $x_1=k,\ x_2=0,\ x_3=0$

Hence, $X_1=\begin{bmatrix}k\\ 0\\ 0\end{bmatrix}$

Suppose, $X_2$ be the eigen vector corresponding to the eigen value $\lambda=2$

$\Rightarrow$ $(A-\lambda I)X_2=0$

$$\Rightarrow \begin{bmatrix}-1 & 1 & 0\\ 0 & 0 & 2\\ 0 & 0 & 1\end{bmatrix}\begin{bmatrix}x_1\\ x_2\\ x_3\end{bmatrix}=\begin{bmatrix}0\\ 0\\ 0\end{bmatrix}$$

$$\Rightarrow -x_1+x_2=0$$

$$2x_3=0$$

$$x_3=0$$

Let $x_1=k$ $\therefore$ the solution is $x_1=k,\ x_2=k,\ x_3=0$

Hence, $X_2=\begin{bmatrix}k\\ k\\ 0\end{bmatrix}$

Let $k=1 \Rightarrow X_2=\begin{bmatrix}1\\ 1\\ 0\end{bmatrix}$

Further, suppose $X_3$ is eigen vector corresponding to the eigen value $\lambda=3$

Hence, $(A-\lambda I)X_3=0.$

$$\Rightarrow \begin{bmatrix}-2 & 1 & 0\\ 0 & -1 & 2\\ 0 & 0 & 0\end{bmatrix}\begin{bmatrix}x_1\\ x_2\\ x_3\end{bmatrix}=\begin{bmatrix}0\\ 0\\ 0\end{bmatrix}$$

$$\Rightarrow -2x_1+x_2=0$$

$$-x_2+2x_3=0$$

Let $x_1=k$

Hence, the solution is $x_1=k,\ x_2=2k$ and $x_3=x_2/2=k$

$$\Rightarrow X_3=\begin{bmatrix}k\\ 2k\\ k\end{bmatrix} \text{ put } k=1 \Rightarrow X_3=\begin{bmatrix}1\\ 2\\ 1\end{bmatrix}$$

$\Rightarrow$ The correct answer is (b).

**139.** The characteristic equation is $|A-\lambda I|=0$

when $A=\begin{bmatrix}1 & 0\\ 0 & 0\end{bmatrix}$; $|A-\lambda I|=\begin{vmatrix}1-\lambda & 0\\ 0 & 0-\lambda\end{vmatrix}=0 \Rightarrow \lambda=0,1$

when $A=\begin{bmatrix}0 & 1\\ 0 & 0\end{bmatrix}$; $|A-\lambda I|=\begin{vmatrix}0-\lambda & 1\\ 0 & 0-\lambda\end{vmatrix}=0 \Rightarrow \lambda=0,0$

when $A=\begin{bmatrix}1 & -1\\ 1 & 1\end{bmatrix}$; $|A-\lambda I|=\begin{vmatrix}1-\lambda & -1\\ 1 & 1-\lambda\end{vmatrix}=0$

$\Rightarrow \quad \lambda = 1-i, 1+i$

when $A=\begin{bmatrix}-1 & 0\\ 1 & -1\end{bmatrix}$; $|A-\lambda I|=\begin{vmatrix}-1-\lambda & 0\\ 1 & -1-\lambda\end{vmatrix}=0$

$\Rightarrow \quad \lambda = -1, -1$

$\Rightarrow$ Only matrix $\begin{bmatrix}1 & 0\\ 0 & 0\end{bmatrix}$ has eigen value $\lambda = 1$.

Hence, the correct answer is (a).

**140.** We know that

Trace $A = \Sigma \lambda_i$

$\lambda_1 + \lambda_2 + \lambda_3 = \text{Trace } A = 2 + (-1) + 0 = 1$

Now, $\quad \lambda_1 = 3$

Hence, $3 + \lambda_2 + \lambda_3 = 1 \Rightarrow \lambda_2 + \lambda_3 = -2$

$\Rightarrow$ Option (b) satisfies this conditions.

**141.** $\lambda_i^m$ will be the corresponding eigen values of $A^m$, $x_i^m$ will not be corresponding eigen vectors.

**142.** Since Trace $A$ = sum of eigen values

$\Rightarrow$ Sum of eigen values $= 2 + y$

and the product of eigen values $= |A| = 2y - 3x$

Hence $\quad 4 + 8 = 2 + y$ and $4 \times 8 = 2y - 3x$

$\Rightarrow \quad 2 + y = 12 \quad$ ...(i)

and $\quad 2y - 3x = 32 \quad$ ...(ii)

From Eqs. (i) and (ii), we get

$x = -4, y = 10$

**143.** Sum of eigen values = Trace of the matrix $A$

$= -1 + (-1) + 3 = 1$

Option (d) $3, -1+3i, -1-3i$ satisfies this condition.

**145.** The characteristic equation is

$$\lambda^3 + \lambda^2 + 2\lambda + 1 = 0$$

Now, by Cayley Hamilton theorem

$$A^3 + A^2 + 2A + I = 0 \Rightarrow I = -A^3 - A^2 - 2A$$

Multiplying by $A^{-1}$ on both sides, we get

$$A^{-1} = -A^2 - A - 2I = -(A^2 + A + 2I)$$

**146.** We have,

$$A = \begin{bmatrix}-3 & 2\\ -1 & 0\end{bmatrix}$$

The characteristic equation is $|A - \lambda I| = 0$

$\Rightarrow \quad \begin{vmatrix}-3-\lambda & 2\\ -1 & 0-\lambda\end{vmatrix}=0$

$\Rightarrow \quad (-3-\lambda)(-\lambda) + 2 = 0$

$\lambda^2 + 3\lambda + 2 = 0$

By Cayley Hamilton theorem,

$A^2 + 3A + 2I = 0$

$\Rightarrow \quad A^2 = -3A - 2I$

$A^4 = A^2 \times A^2 = (-3A - 2I)(-3A - 2I)$

$= 9A^2 + 12A + 4I$

$= 9(-3A - 2I) + 12A + 4I$

$= -15A - 14I$

$A^8 = A^4 \times A^4 = (-15A - 14I)(-15A - 14I)$

$= 225A^2 + 420A + 196I$

$= 225(-3A - 2I) + 420A + 196I$

$= -255A - 254I$

$A^9 = A \times A^8 = A(-255A - 254I)$

$= -255A^2 - 254A$

$= -255(-3A - 2I) - 254A$

$= 511A + 510I$

## Exercise 2

**1.** The characteristic polynomial $f(x) = \det(xI - A)$

Hence, $f(x) = \begin{vmatrix}x & 0 & 0\\ 0 & x & 0\\ 0 & 0 & x\end{vmatrix} - \begin{vmatrix}5 & -6 & -6\\ -1 & 4 & 2\\ 3 & -6 & -4\end{vmatrix}$

$= \begin{vmatrix}x-5 & 6 & 6\\ 1 & x-4 & -2\\ -3 & 6 & x+4\end{vmatrix}$

$= \begin{vmatrix}x-5 & 0 & 6\\ 1 & x-2 & -2\\ -3 & -1 & x+4\end{vmatrix}$

$= (x-2)\begin{vmatrix}x-5 & 0 & 6\\ 1 & 1 & -2\\ -3 & -1 & x+4\end{vmatrix}$

$= (x-2)\begin{vmatrix}x-5 & 0 & 6\\ 1 & 1 & -2\\ -2 & 0 & x+2\end{vmatrix}$

$= (x-2)\begin{vmatrix}x-5 & 6\\ -2 & x+2\end{vmatrix}$

$= (x-2)(x^2 - 3x + 2)$

$= (x-2)^2(x-1)$

**2.** (i) Let $M = \{x : x \in \mathbb{R}^3$ and $x_1$ is an integer$\}$

Let $\quad x = \{x_1, x_2, x_3\}$

$y = \{y_1, y_2, y_3\}$

be any two members of $M$.

Then, $x_1$ is an integer and $y_1$ is an integer.

If $\quad \alpha, \beta \in \mathbb{R}$

Then, $\alpha x + \beta y = (\alpha x_1 + \beta y_1, \alpha x_2 + \beta y_2, \alpha x_3 + \beta y_3)$

Now, $\alpha x_1 + \beta y_1$ is not necessarily an integer.

e.g., if we take

$$\alpha = \frac{7}{3}, \ \beta = \frac{5}{8}$$

$$x_1 = 4, \ y_1 = 5$$

Then, $\alpha x_1 + \beta y_1$ is not an integer.

Thus, $\alpha, \beta \in \mathbb{R}$
and $x, y \in M$
$\Rightarrow \alpha x + \beta y \notin M$
Hence, $M$ is not a subspace of $\mathbb{R}^3$.

(ii) Let $M = \{x : x \in \mathbb{R}^3 \text{ and } x_1 + 2x_2 = 0\}$
Let $x = \{x_1, x_2, x_3\}$
and $y = \{y_1, y_2, y_3\}$
be any two members of $M$.
Then, $x_1 + 2x_4 = 0$ and $y_1 + 2y_2 = 0$
If $\alpha, \beta \in \mathbb{R}$, then
$$\alpha x + \beta y = (\alpha x_1 + \beta y_1, \alpha x_2 + \beta y_2, \alpha x_3 + \beta y_3)$$
We have,
$$\alpha x_1 + \beta y_1 + 2(\alpha x_2 + \beta y_3) = \alpha(x_1 + 2x_2) + \beta(y_1 + 2y_2) = 0$$
Thus, according to the definition of $M$
$$\alpha x + \beta y \in M$$
In this way $\alpha, \beta \in \mathbb{R}$ and $x, y \in M$
$$\Rightarrow \alpha x + \beta y \in M$$
Hence, $M$ is a subspace of $\mathbb{R}^3$.

**3.** The characteristic polynomial $f(x) = \det(xI - A)$

$$\therefore \quad f(x) = \begin{bmatrix} x & 0 & 0 \\ 0 & x & 0 \\ 0 & 0 & x \end{bmatrix} - \begin{bmatrix} 5 & -6 & -6 \\ -1 & 4 & 2 \\ 3 & -6 & -4 \end{bmatrix}$$
$$= \begin{bmatrix} x-5 & 6 & 6 \\ 1 & x-4 & -2 \\ -3 & 6 & x+4 \end{bmatrix}$$
$$= \begin{bmatrix} x-5 & 0 & 6 \\ 1 & x-2 & -2 \\ -3 & -1 & x+4 \end{bmatrix}$$
$$= (x-2)\begin{bmatrix} x-5 & 0 & 6 \\ 1 & 1 & -2 \\ -3 & -1 & x+4 \end{bmatrix}$$
$$= (x-2)\begin{bmatrix} x-5 & 0 & 6 \\ 1 & 1 & -2 \\ -2 & 0 & x+2 \end{bmatrix}$$
$$= (x-2)\begin{bmatrix} x-5 & 6 \\ -2 & x+2 \end{bmatrix}$$
$$= (x-2)(x^2 - 3x + 2)$$
$$= (x-2)^2(x-1)$$

**4.**
$$\begin{vmatrix} a_{11} & a_{12} & a_{13} \\ a_{21} & a_{22} & a_{23} \\ a_{31} & a_{32} & a_{33} \end{vmatrix} = a_{11}\begin{vmatrix} a_{22} & a_{23} \\ a_{32} & a_{33} \end{vmatrix} - a_{21}\begin{vmatrix} a_{12} & a_{13} \\ a_{32} & a_{33} \end{vmatrix} + a_{31}\begin{vmatrix} a_{12} & a_{13} \\ a_{22} & a_{23} \end{vmatrix}$$

The minors are $M_{11} = \begin{vmatrix} a_{22} & a_{23} \\ a_{32} & a_{33} \end{vmatrix}$,
$$M_{21} = \begin{vmatrix} a_{12} & a_{13} \\ a_{32} & a_{33} \end{vmatrix} \text{ and } M_{31} = \begin{vmatrix} a_{12} & a_{13} \\ a_{22} & a_{23} \end{vmatrix}$$

and cofactors are $C_{11} = +M_{11}$
$$C_{21} = -M_{21}$$
$$C_{31} = M_{31}$$

**5.** The characteristic equation is
$$|A - \lambda I| = 0$$
$$\Rightarrow \begin{vmatrix} 8-\lambda & -6 & 2 \\ -6 & 7-\lambda & -4 \\ 2 & -4 & 3-\lambda \end{vmatrix} = 0$$
$$\Rightarrow (8-\lambda)\begin{vmatrix} 7-\lambda & -4 \\ -4 & 3-\lambda \end{vmatrix} + 6\begin{vmatrix} -6 & -4 \\ 2 & 3-\lambda \end{vmatrix} + 2\begin{vmatrix} -6 & 7-\lambda \\ 2 & -4 \end{vmatrix} = 0$$
$$\Rightarrow (8-\lambda)(\lambda^2 - 10\lambda + 5) + 6(-6(3-\lambda) + 8) + 2[24 - 2(7-\lambda)] = 0$$
$$\Rightarrow -\lambda^3 + 18\lambda^2 - 45\lambda = 0$$
$$\Rightarrow -\lambda(\lambda - 3)(\lambda - 15) = 0$$
$$\Rightarrow \lambda = 0, 3, 15$$
Hence, the characteristic roots are
$$\lambda_1 = 0, \lambda_2 = 3, \lambda_3 = 15$$

**6.** The characteristic equation is $|A - \lambda I| = 0$
$$\Rightarrow \begin{vmatrix} a-\lambda & h & g \\ 0 & b-\lambda & f \\ 0 & 0 & c-\lambda \end{vmatrix} = 0$$
$$\Rightarrow (a-\lambda)(b-\lambda)(c-\lambda) = 0$$
Substituting $\lambda = a, b, c$ gives the characteristic root.
$$\lambda_1 = a, \lambda_2 = b \text{ and } \lambda_3 = c$$

**7.**
$$\begin{vmatrix} a & h & g \\ h & b & f \\ g & f & c \end{vmatrix} = a\begin{vmatrix} b & f \\ f & c \end{vmatrix} - h\begin{vmatrix} h & f \\ g & c \end{vmatrix} + g\begin{vmatrix} h & b \\ g & f \end{vmatrix}$$
$$= a(bc - f^2) - h(hc - fg) + g(hf - gb)$$
$$= abc - af^2 - h^2c + hfg + ghf - g^2b$$
$$= abc + 2fgh - af^2 - bg^2 - ch^2$$

**8.** Here, $A = \begin{bmatrix} 1 & 2 & 3 \\ 1 & 4 & 2 \\ 2 & 6 & 5 \end{bmatrix}$

Performing operation $R_{31}(-1)$, we get $A \sim \begin{bmatrix} 1 & 2 & 3 \\ 1 & 4 & 2 \\ 1 & 4 & 2 \end{bmatrix}$

By operation $R_{32}(-1)$, we get $A \sim \begin{bmatrix} 1 & 2 & 3 \\ 1 & 4 & 2 \\ 0 & 0 & 0 \end{bmatrix}$

$$\Rightarrow |A| = 0$$
and $\begin{vmatrix} 1 & 2 \\ 1 & 4 \end{vmatrix} \neq 0$
$$\Rightarrow \text{Rank}(A) = 2$$

**9.** Determinant $= 67\begin{vmatrix} 13 & 14 \\ 24 & 26 \end{vmatrix} - 19\begin{vmatrix} 39 & 14 \\ 81 & 26 \end{vmatrix} + 21\begin{vmatrix} 39 & 13 \\ 81 & 24 \end{vmatrix}$
$$= 134 + 2280 - 2457$$
$$= -43$$

**10.** Here, $|A| = 0$

All minors of order 3 are zero, since two rows are identical.

The second minor $\begin{vmatrix} 1 & 0 \\ 0 & 1 \end{vmatrix} \neq 0$

Hence, $\text{Rank}(A) = 2$

**11.** Here, $|A| = 2(-9+8)+2(-2+3)$

$= 0$

But $\begin{vmatrix} 2 & 1 \\ 0 & 3 \end{vmatrix} \neq 0$

Hence, Rank $(A) = 2$

**13.** $AA^T = \begin{bmatrix} \cos\theta & \sin\theta \\ -\sin\theta & \cos\theta \end{bmatrix}\begin{bmatrix} \cos\theta & -\sin\theta \\ \sin\theta & \cos\theta \end{bmatrix}$

$= \begin{bmatrix} \cos^2\theta + \sin^2\theta & -\cos\theta\sin\theta + \sin\theta\cos\theta \\ -\sin\theta\cos\theta + \cos\theta\sin\theta & \sin^2\theta + \cos^2\theta \end{bmatrix}$

$= \begin{bmatrix} 1 & 0 \\ 0 & 1 \end{bmatrix}$

$= I$, Hence $A$ is orthogonal matrix.

**14.** $\overline{A}$ = conjugate of $A$

$= \begin{bmatrix} 3 & 1-2i \\ 1+2i & 2 \end{bmatrix}$

and $A^* = (\overline{A})^T$ = transpose of $\overline{A}$

$= \begin{bmatrix} 3 & 1+2i \\ 1-2i & 2 \end{bmatrix}$

Since, $A^* = A$

Hence, $A$ is hermitian matrix.

**16.** (I) $V_e$ is a subspace of $V$.

$f_1, f_2 \in V_e$ and $c$ any scalar

Now, $(cf_1 + f_2)(-x) = c_1f_1(-x) + f_2(-x)$

$= c_1f_1(x) + f_2(x)$

$= (c_1f_1 + f_2)(x)$

(II) $V_0$ is a subspace of $V$

$f_1, f_2 \in V_0$, $c$ any scalar

$(cf_1 + f_2)(-x) = c_1f_1(-x) + f_2(-x)$

$= c_1f_1(x) + f_2(x)$

$= (c_1f_1 + f_2)(x)$

**17.** Here, $0(1, 0, 0, 0) + 0(0, 1, 0, 0) + 0(0, 0, 1, 0)$

$+ 0(0, 0, 0, 1) = (0, 0, 0, 0, 0)$

Since, all $c_i$'s are zero, then only the linear combination is equal to zero.

Hence, linearly independent vector.

**18.** If $V_1$ taking $a$, $c$, $d$ as free variable and

$a = c = 0, d = 1; a = d = 0, c = 1; c = d = 0, a = 1$

We get the set $\{(0, -1, 0, 1), (0, 2, 1, 0), (1, 0, 0, 0)\}$ as the basis of $V_1$ and its dimensions therefore is three.

If $V_2$ have $a = d$, $b = 2c$, so $c$, $d$ are free variables and then taking $c = 0, d = 1$ and $c = 1, d = 0$, we get the set $\{(0, 2, 1, 0), (1, 0, 0, 1)\}$ as basis of $V_2$ and its dimension is two.

**19.** $a(1, 1, 0, 0) + b(0, 1, -1, 0) + c(0, 0, 0, 3) = (0, 0, 0, 0)$

$\Rightarrow (a+0+0, a+b+0, 0-b+0, 0+0+3c) = (0, 0, 0, 0)$

$\Rightarrow a = 0, a+b = 0, -b = 0, 3c = 0$

$\Rightarrow a = b = c = 0$

**20.** $\bar{a}_1$, $\bar{a}_2$ and $\bar{a}_3$ are linearly dependent *i.e.*, $\sum_{i=1}^{3} c_i\bar{a}_i = \bar{0}$ for some none zero $c_i$'s.

Here, $6(3, 0, 2, 2) - \frac{1}{2}(-6, 42, 24, 54) - (21, -21, 0, -15)$

$= (0, 0, 0, 0)$

Hence, they are linearly dependent.

**21.** $c_1\bar{a}_1 + c_2\bar{a}_2 + c_3\bar{a}_3 = c_1(3, 1, -4) + c_2(2, 2, -3) + c_3(0, -4, 1)$

$= (3c_1 + 2c_2, c_1 + 2c_2 - 4c_3, -4c_1 - 3c_2 + c_3)$

$= (0, 0, 0)$

$\Rightarrow 3c_1 + 2c_2 = 0$

$c_1 + 2c_2 - 4c_3 = 0$

$-4c_1 - 3c_2 + c_3 = 0$

$\Rightarrow c_1 = 2, c_2 = -3, c_3 = -1$

Since, $c_1$, $c_2$ and $c_3$ are not all zero

Hence, $\bar{a}_1$, $\bar{a}_2$ and $\bar{a}_3$ are linearly dependent.

**22.** $c_1\bar{a}_1 - c_2\bar{a}_2 = 0$

$\Rightarrow c_1(3, 1, -5) + c_2(2, 2, -3) = 0$

$\Rightarrow 3c_1 + 2c_2 = 0$

$c_1 + 2c_2 = 0$

$-5c_1 - 3c_2 = 0$

$\Rightarrow c_1 = 0, c_2 = 0$

Hence, $\bar{a}$ and $\bar{b}$ are independent vectors.

**23.** $1 = \det(I) = \det(AA^{-1})$

Since, $A$ is orthogonal.

$\Rightarrow A^T = A^{-1}$

$\Rightarrow 1 = \det(AA^T)$

$= \det(A)\det(A^T)$

$= (\det A)^2$

$\Rightarrow \det(A) = \pm 1$

**24.** If $V_1$ taking a, c, d as free variable and

$a = c = 0, d = 1; a = d = 0, c = 1; c = d = 0, a = 1$

We get the set $\{(0, -1, 0, 1), (0, 2, 1, 0), (1, 0, 0, 0)\}$ as the basis of $V_1$ and its dimensions therefore is three.

If $V_2$ have $a = d$, $b = 2c$, so $c$, $d$ are free variables and then taking $c = 0, d = 1$ and $c = 1, d = 0$, we get the set $\{(0, 2, 1, 0), (1, 0, 0, 1)\}$ as basis of $V_2$ and its dimension is two.

**25.** For scalar $c_1$, $c_2$, $c_3$

$c_1(1, 0, 0) + c_2(0, 1, 0) + c_3(0, 0, 1)$

$= (c_1, 0, 0) + (0, c_2, 0) + (0, 0, c_3)$

$= (c_1, c_2, c_3)$

$(c_1, c_2, c_3) = (0, 0, 0) \Leftrightarrow c_1 = c_2 = c_3$

$\Rightarrow \{(1, 0, 0), (0, 1, 0), (0, 0, 1)\}$ is linearly independent set.

Since, this set spans the space $V_3$.

Hence, this set is a basis of $V_3$.

**28.** Set $\{1, i\} \subset C$ forms a basis for $C$

Since, $a \cdot 1 + b \cdot i = 0 \Rightarrow a = 0,\ b = 0,\ a, b \in R$

Hence, 1, $i$ are linearly independent.

$\forall\ a + b_i \in C,\ a, b \in R \Rightarrow \{1, i\}$ span $C(R)$.

**29.** $\bar{x}$ is an eigen vector of matrix $\bar{A}$ corresponding to $\lambda$

$$\Leftrightarrow \quad \bar{A}\bar{x} = \lambda\bar{x}$$
$$\Rightarrow \quad k(A\bar{x}) = k\lambda\bar{x}$$
$$\Rightarrow \quad A(k\bar{x}) = \lambda(k\bar{x})$$

**30.** $(\alpha + i\beta)$ and $(a + ib)$ to the linearly independent.

$$\Rightarrow \quad \theta_1(a+ib) + \theta_2(\alpha + i\beta) = 0$$
$$\Rightarrow \quad \theta_1 a + \theta_2 \alpha = 0$$
$$\theta_1 b + \theta_2 \beta = 0$$
$$\Rightarrow \quad \theta_1(a\beta - b\alpha) = 0$$
$$\theta_2(a\beta - b\alpha) = 0$$
$$\Rightarrow \theta_1 = 0 = \theta_2 \Leftrightarrow a\beta - b\alpha = 0$$

Hence, If $a\beta = b\alpha$, then $\{\alpha + i\beta,\ a + ib\}$ is a basis.

**31.** Matrix $A$ is symmetric $\Rightarrow A = A^T$

Matrix $A$ is anti-symmetric.

$\Rightarrow A = -A^T$, where $A^T$ is the transpose of $A$.

$V_1$ and $V_2$ are two subspaces of $V \Rightarrow V_1 \cap V_2$ is also a subspace.

Let $A \in V_1 \cap V_2$

$\Rightarrow A \in V_1$ and $A \in V_2$

$$\Rightarrow \quad A = A^T \text{ and } A = -A^T$$
$$\Rightarrow \quad A = 0$$
$$\Rightarrow \quad V_1 \cap V_2 = \{0\} \qquad \text{...(i)}$$

$\Rightarrow V_1$ and $V_2$ are independent subspaces.

Also, $$A = \frac{1}{2}(A + A^T) + \frac{1}{2}(A - A^T) \qquad \text{...(ii)}$$

where $\frac{1}{2}(A + A^T)$ is symmetric and $\frac{1}{2}(A - A^T)$ is anti-symmetric.

Hence, Eq. (ii) $\Rightarrow$ $$V = V_1 + V_2 \qquad \text{...(iii)}$$

By Eqs. (iii) and (i), we get
$$V = V_1 \oplus V_2$$

**32.** If $U$ and $W$ are the subspaces of $V$

$\Rightarrow \dim(U + W) = \dim U + \dim W - \dim(U \cap W)$

Since, $U$ and $W$ are direct

$\Rightarrow U$ and $W$ are independent

$$\Rightarrow \quad U \cap W = \{0\}$$

$\Rightarrow \dim(U \cap W) = 0$

Hence, $\dim(U + W) = \dim U + \dim V$

**33.** $S = \{1, x, x^2, x^3\}$ is a basis and $V$ has, therefore, dimension four.

**34.**
$$\Sigma a_i \alpha_i = \Sigma b_i \alpha_i$$
$$\Rightarrow \Sigma a_i \alpha_i - \Sigma b_i \alpha_i = 0$$
$$\Rightarrow \quad \Sigma (a_i - b_i)\alpha_i = 0$$
$$\Rightarrow \quad (a_i - b_i) = 0,\ i = 1, \dots, n,$$
(as the given set is independent)
$$\Rightarrow \quad a_i = b_i,\ i = 1, 2, \dots, n$$

**37.** $f(x) = a_0 + a_1 x + a_2 x^2 + \dots + a_n x^n \in F[x]$ and $\{1, x, \dots, x^n, \dots\}$ are linearly independent set.

Since $\{1, x, \dots, x^n, \dots\}$ spans $F[x]$ *i.e.*, every polynomial in $F[x]$ can be expressed as linear combination of a elements of $\{1, x, \dots, x^n, \dots\}$

*i.e.*, $f(x) = a_0(1) + a_1(x) + a_2(x^2) + \dots + a_n(x^n) + \dots$

Hence, $\{1, x, x^2, \dots\}$ is a basis.

**38.** $f(x) = a_0 + a_1 x + a_2 x^2 + \dots + a_n x^n \in F[x]$

If $f(x)$ is a zero polynomial,

$\Rightarrow a_0 + a_1 x + a_2 x^2 + \dots + a_n x^n = 0$

$\Rightarrow a_0 = a_1 = \dots = a_n$, if $x \neq 0$

$\Rightarrow \{1, x, x^2, \dots, x^n\}$ are independent.

**39.** (I) Since, $W_i$ is the space of characteristic vectors associated with characteristic value $C_i$ and $C_i$ are distinct characteristic values of $T$, linear operation on $V$, we have

$$\dim W_1 + \dots + \dim W_k = \dim V$$

$\Rightarrow$ There exist $V = W_1 + W_2 + \dots + W_k$

$\Rightarrow W_1 \dots W_k$ are linear independent.

(II) $T$ is diagonalizable.

$\Rightarrow \dim V = \dim W_1 + \dots + \dim W_k$

$\Rightarrow W_1 \dots W_k$ are independent.

$\Rightarrow V = W_1 \oplus W_2 \oplus \dots \oplus W_k$.

**40.** Let $x$, $y$ be any two elements of $[S]$. Then,

$$x = \alpha_1 x_1 + \alpha_2 x_2 + \dots + \alpha_m x_m$$
and $$y = \beta_1 y_1 + \beta_2 y_2 + \dots + \beta_n y_n$$

where the $\alpha$'s and $\beta$'s are elements of $F$ and the $x$'s and $y$'s are elements of $S$. If $\alpha$, $\beta$ be any two elements of $F$, then

$$\alpha x + \beta y = \alpha(\alpha_1 x_1 + \alpha_2 x_2 + \dots + \alpha_m x_m) + \beta(\beta_1 y_1 + \beta_2 y_2 + \dots + \beta_n y_n)$$
$$= (\alpha\alpha_1)x_1 + (\alpha\alpha_2)x_2 + \dots + (\alpha\alpha_m)x_m$$
$$+ (\beta\beta_1)y_1 + \dots + (\beta\beta_n)y_n$$

Hence, $\alpha x + \beta y$ has been expressed as a linear combination of a finite set $x_1, x_2, \dots, x_m, y_1, y_2, \dots, y_n$ of the elements of $S$. Consequently $\alpha x + \beta y \in [S]$. Thus,

$$\alpha, \beta \in F \text{ and } x, y \in [S] \Rightarrow \alpha x + \beta y \in [S].$$

Therefore, $[S]$ is a subspace of $L$.

Also, each element of $S$ belongs to $[S]$ because, if $x_r \in S$, then $x_r = 1x_r$ and this implies that $x_r \in [S]$. Thus, $[S]$ is a subspace of $L$ and $S$ is contained in $[S]$.

Now, if $M$ is any subspace of $L$ containing $S$, then each element of $[S]$ must be in $M$ because $M$ is to be closed under vector addition and scalar multiplication. Therefore, $[S]$ will be contained in $M$. Hence, $[S]$ is the smallest subspace of $L$ containing $S$ and thus $[S]$ is the subspace of $L$ generated by $S$.

**43.** $V = W_1 + \dots + W_k$

$\Rightarrow \dim V \le \dim W_1 + \dots + \dim W_k$

This inequality converts into equality, if $W_1, \dots, W_k$ are linearly independent.

$\Rightarrow W = W_1 \oplus W_2 \oplus \dots \oplus W_k$ is the direct sum of $W_1 \dots W_k$.

**44.** Let $x, y$ be any two elements of $M_1 + M_2$. Then, $x = x_1 + x_2$, $y = y_1 + y_2$ where $x_1, y_1 \in M_1$ and $x_2, y_2 \in M_2$. If $\alpha, \beta \in F$, we have

$$\alpha x + \beta y = \alpha(x_1 + x_2) + \beta(y_1 + y_2)$$
$$= (\alpha x_1 + \beta y_1) + (\alpha x_2 + \beta y_2)$$

Since, $M_1$ is a subspace of $L$, therefore $\alpha, \beta \in F$ and $x_1, y_1 \in M_1$

$\Rightarrow \alpha x_1 + \beta y_1 \in M_1$. Similarly, $\alpha x_2 + \beta y_2 \in M_2$.

Consequently,

$$\alpha x + \beta y = (\alpha x_1 + \beta y_1) + (\alpha x_2 + \beta y_2) \in M_1 + M_2$$

Thus, $\alpha, \beta \in F$ and $x, y \in M_1 + M_2$

$\Rightarrow \alpha x + \beta y \in M_1 + M_2$

Hence, $M_1 + M_2$ is a subspace of $L$.

**45.** Given, $V = U \oplus W$

$\Rightarrow V = U + W$

and $U \cap W = \{0\}$

Hence, $\dim U + \dim W = \dim(U + W) + \dim(U \cap W)$

$= \dim(U + W) + 0$

$= \dim(U + W) = \dim V \quad (\because V = U + W)$

$\Rightarrow \dim V = \dim U + \dim W$

or $\dim(U \oplus W) = \dim U + \dim W$

**46.** Let $a_1(1, 2, 3) + a_2(1, 0, 1) + a_3(0, 1, 0) = 0$

$\Rightarrow (a_1 + a_2, 2a_1 + a_3, 3a_1 + a_2) = (0, 0, 0)$

Hence, we have

$$a_1 + a_2 = 0 \quad \text{...(i)}$$

$$2a_1 + a_3 = 0 \quad \text{...(ii)}$$

and $3a_1 + a_2 = 0$ ...(iii)

Solving the Eqs. (i), (ii) and (iii), we find that

$$a_1 = 0, a_2 = 0, a_3 = 0$$

*i.e.*, all the coefficients are zero.

Hence, the given set of vectors are linearly independent.

**47.** We have $f, g \in W$

$$f(4) = 3 + f(2)$$

and $g(4) = 3 + g(2)$ ...(i)

If $a, b \in \mathbb{R}$, then

$(af + bg)(4) = af(4) + bg(4)$

$= a[3 + f(2)] + b[3 + g(2)]$, [from Eq. (i)]

$= af(2) + bg(2) + 3a + 3b$

$= (af + bg)(2) + 3(a + b)$

$\neq 3 + (af + bg)(2)$

$\Rightarrow (af + bg)(4) \neq W$

Hence, $W$ is not a subspace of $V$.

**50.** Let $\alpha = (x_1, y_1, z_1)$

and $\beta = (x_2, y_2, z_2)$

be two arbitrary elements of W. Then, $x_1, y_1, z_1$ and $x_2, y_2, z_2$ must satisfy the given condition

$$x - 2y - 3z = 0$$

or $x = 2y + 3z$

$\Rightarrow x_1 = 2y_1 + 3z_1$

and $x_2 = 2y_2 + 3z_2$ ... (i)

Consequently, $\alpha = (2y_1 + 3z_1, y_1, z_1)$

and $\beta = (2y_2 + 3z_2, y_2, z_2)$

Now, if $a, b \in \mathbb{R}$, then

$a\alpha + b\beta = a(2y_1 + 3z_1, y_1, z_1) + b(2y_2 + 3z_2, y_2, z_2)$

$= (a \cdot 2y_1 + a \cdot 3z_1, ay_1, az_1) + (b \cdot 2y_2 + b \cdot 3z_2, by_2, bz_2)$

$= (2ay_1 + 3az_1, ay_1, az_1) + (2by_2 + 3bz_2, by_2, bz_2)$

$= (2ay_1 + 3az_1 + 2by_2 + 3bz_2, ay_1 + by_2, az_1 + bz_2)$

$= (a(2y_1 + 3z_1) + b(2y_2 + 3z_2), ay_1 + by_2, az_1 + bz_2)$,

(by associative law of addition in $\mathbb{R}$)

$= (ax_1 + bx_2, ay_1 + by_2, az_1 + bz_2)$, [from Eq. (i)]

$= (x', y', z')$

where $x' = ax_1 + bx_2$

$y' = ay_1 + by_2$

$z' = az_1 + b\dfrac{z'}{2}$

Further

$x' - 2y' - 3z'$

$= (ax_1 + bx_2) - 2(ay_1 + by_2) - 3(az_1 + bz_2)$

$= (ax_1 - 2ay_1 - 3az_1) + (bx_2 - 2by_2 - 3bz_2)$

$= a(x_1 - 2y_1 - 3z_1) + b(x_2 - 2y_2 - 3z_2)$

$= a(0) + b(0)$, [from Eq. (i)]

$= 0$

Hence, $a\alpha + b\beta \in W$

Hence, $W$ is a subspace of $V$.

**51.** Let $A = [a_{ij}]_{n \times n}$ and $B = [b_{ij}]_{n \times n}$ be any two elements of $W$. Then, $A$ and $B$ are symmetric matrices, and so

$$a_{ij} = a_{ji} \text{ and } b_{ij} = b_{ji} \quad \text{... (i)}$$

If $x, y \in F$, then

$xA + yB = x[a_{ij}]_{n \times n} + y[b_{ij}]_{n \times n}$

$= [xa_{ij} + yb_{ij}]_{n \times n}$

$= [xa_{ji} + yb_{ji}]_{n \times n}$ [from Eq. (i)]

*i.e.*, $xA + yB \in W$

*i.e.*, $A, B \in W$

and $x, y \in F$

$\Rightarrow xA + yB \in W$

Hence, $W$ is a subspace of $V(F)$.

**52.** We have $\Sigma a_i v_i = \Sigma b_i v_i$

$\Rightarrow (\Sigma a_i v_i) - (\Sigma b_i v_i) = 0$

$\Rightarrow \Sigma(a_i - b_i)v_i = 0$

$\Rightarrow a_i - b_i = 0, i = 1, 2, \ldots, n.$

(As the given set in linearly independent)

$\Rightarrow a_i = b_i, i = 1, 2, 3, \ldots, n.$

**53.** Let

$$\alpha = (x_1, 3x_1, 3x_1 + 2)$$

and $\beta = (x_2, 3x_2, 3x_2 + 2)$

be any two elements of $W$

If $a, b \in \mathbb{R}$, then

$a\alpha + b\beta$

$= a(x_1, 3x_1, 3x_1 + 2) + b(x_2, 3x_2, 3x_2 + 2)$

$= (ax_1, a \cdot 3x_1, a \cdot 3x_1 + a \cdot 2) + (b \cdot x_2, b \cdot 3x_2, b \cdot 3x_2 + b \cdot 2)$

$= (ax_1, 3ax_1, 3ax_1 + 2a) + (bx_2, 3bx_2, 3bx_2 + 2b)$

$= (ax_1 + bx_2, 3ax_1 + 3bx_2, 3ax_1 + 2a + 3bx_2 + 2b)$

$= (ax_1 + bx_2, 3[ax_1 + bx_2], 3[ax_1 + bx_2] + 2a + 2b)$

$= (x', 3x', 3x' + [2a + 2b])$

where $x' = ax_1 + bx_2 \in \mathbb{R}$

or $a\alpha + b\beta \notin W$

Since, $2a + 2b$ is not necessarily equal to 2

Hence, $\alpha, \beta \in W$ and $a, b \in \mathbb{R}$

does not imply that

$a\alpha + b\beta \in W$

Hence, $W$ is not a vector subspace of $\mathbb{R}^3(\mathbb{R})$.

**54.** Since, $0 \in M_2$, therefore, if $x_1 \in M_1$, $x_1 = x_1 + 0 \in M_1 + M_2$. Thus, $M_1 \subset M_1 + M_2$,

Similarly, $M_2 \subset M_1 + M_2$.

Hence, $M_1 \cup M_2 \subset M_1 + M_2$

Therefore, $M_1 + M_2$ is a subspace of $L$ containing $M_1 \cup M_2$.

Now, in order to prove that $M_1 + M_2 = [M_1 \cup M_2]$ we should prove that $M_1 + M_2 \subset [M_1 \cup M_2]$ and $[M_1 \cup M_2] \subset M_1 + M_2$

Let $x = x_1 + x_2$ be any element of $M_1 + M_2$.

Then, $x_1 \in M_1$ and $x_2 \in M_2$, therefore $x_1, x_2 \in M_1 \cup M_2$. We can write

$$x_1 + x_2 = 1x_1 + 1x_2$$

Thus, $x_1 + x_2$ is a linear combination of finite number of elements $x_1, x_2 \in M_1 \cup M_2$

Therefore, $x_1 + x_2 \in [M_1 \cup M_2]$

Hence, $M_1 + M_2 \subset [M_1 \cup M_2]$

Also, $[M_1 \cup M_2]$ is the smallest subspace containing $M_1 \cup M_2$ and $M_1 + M_2$ is a subspace containing $M_1 \cup M_2$. Therefore, $[M_1 \cup M_2]$ must be contained in $M_1 + M_2$.

Consequently, $[M_1 \cup M_2] \subset M_1 + M_2$

Hence, $M_1 + M_2 = [M_1 \cup M_2]$

**55.** (i) Let $W$ be a vector subspace.

Then, $\alpha \in W$ and $a \in F \Rightarrow a\alpha \in W, \beta \in W$ and

$$b \in F \rightarrow b\beta \in W$$

Thus, $a\alpha \in W$ and $b\beta \in W \Rightarrow a\alpha + b\beta \in W$

(ii) Let $\alpha, \beta \in W$ and $a, b \in F$

$\Rightarrow \quad a\alpha + b\beta \in W$ ...(i)

Substituting $a = 1$, $b = 1$ in Eq. (i), we get

$\alpha, \beta \in W \Rightarrow 1\alpha + 1\beta \in W$

$\Rightarrow \quad \alpha + \beta \in W$

Hence, $W$ is closed under addition.

Also, taking $b = 0$ in Eq. (i), we get

$\alpha, \beta \in W \Rightarrow a\alpha + 0\beta \in W$

$\Rightarrow \quad a\alpha \in W$

Hence, $a \in F, \alpha \in W \Rightarrow a\alpha \in W$

$\Rightarrow$ $W$ is closed under scalar multiplication.

Hence, $W$ is a subspace of $V(F)$.

**56.** Let

$\dim M_1 = l$ and $\dim M_2 = m$

Then, $\dim L = l + m$

Let $S_1 = \{x_1, x_2, \ldots, x_l\}$

be a basis of $M_1$ and

$S_2 = (y_1, y_2, \ldots, y_m)$

be a basis of $M_2$. We shall show that $S_1 \cup S_2$ is a basis of $L$.

Let $x \in L$ Since, $L = M_1 + M_2$. Therefore, we can write

$$x = y + z \text{ where } y \in M_1, z \in M_2$$

Now, $y \in M_1$ can be expressed as a linear combination of the elements of $S_1$ and $z \in M_2$ can be expressed as a linear combination of the elements of $S_2$. Therefore, $x \in L$ can be expressed as a linear combination of the elements of $S_1 \cup S_2$.

Hence, $L = [S_1 \cup S_2]$

Since, $\dim L = l + m$ and $[S_1 \cup S_2] = L$

Hence, the number of distinct elements in $S_1 \cup S_2$ cannot be less than $l + m$. Thus, $S_1 \cup S_2$ has $l + m$ distinct elements and therefore, $S_1 \cup S_2$ is a basis of $L$. Therefore, the set

$$\{x_1, x_2, \ldots, x_l, y_1, y_2, \ldots, y_m\}$$

is linearly independent.

Now, we shall show that

$$M_1 \cap M_2 = \{0\}$$

Let $x \in M_1 \cap M_2$. Then, $x \in M_1$, $x \in M_2$

Hence, $x = \alpha_1 x_1 + \alpha_2 x_2 + \ldots + \alpha_l x_l$

and $x = \beta_1 y_1 + \beta_2 y_2 + \ldots + \beta_m y_m$

for some $\alpha$'s and $\beta$'s $\in F$.

Hence, $\alpha_1 x_1 + \alpha_2 x_2 + \ldots + \alpha_l x_l = \beta_1 y_1 + \beta_2 y_2 + \ldots + \beta_m y_m$

$\Rightarrow \alpha_1 x_1 + \alpha_2 x_2 + \ldots + \alpha_l x_l - \beta_1 y_1 - \beta_2 y_2 - \ldots - \beta_m y_m = 0$

$\Rightarrow \alpha_1 = 0, \alpha_2 = 0, \ldots, \alpha_l = 0, \beta_1 = 0, \beta_2 = 0, \ldots, \beta_m = 0$

$\Rightarrow x = 0$

Hence, $M_1 \cap M_2 = \{0\}$

Now, $L = M_1 + M_2$

and $M_1 \cap M_2 = \{0\} \Rightarrow L = M_1 \oplus M_2$

**57.** Let $A = [a_{ij}]_{n \times n}$

and $B = [b_{ij}]_{n \times n}$

be two arbitrary elements of $W$, then

$AM = MA$

and $BM = MB$

...(i)

If $x, y \in F$, then

$$\begin{aligned}(xA + yB)M &= (xA)M + (yB)M \\ &= x(AM) + y(BM) \\ &= x(MA) + y(MB) \\ &= M(xA) + M(yB) \\ &= M(xA + yB)\end{aligned}$$

This shows that

$xA + yB \in W$

i.e., $A, B \in W$

and $x, y \in F$

$\Rightarrow \quad xA + yB \in W$

Hence, $W$ is a subspace of $V(F)$.

**58.** Given, $S = \{v_1, v_2, \ldots, v_n\}$ a basis of $V(F)$, therefore, we have

(i) $L(S) = V$

(ii) $S$ is a linearly independent set.

Since, $L(S) = V$

Hence, any vector $u$ of $V$ can be expressed as a linear combination of vector of $S$

i.e., $u = a_1 v_1 + a_2 v_2 + \ldots + a_n v_n$

where $a' S \in F$

Then, $a_1v_1 + a_2v_2 + \ldots + a_nv_n$
$$= b_1v_1 + b_2v_2 + \ldots + b_nv_n$$
$$\Rightarrow (a_1 - b_1)v_1 + (a_2 - b_2)v_2 + \ldots + (a_n - b_n)v_n = 0$$
$$\Rightarrow a_1 - b_1 = 0,\ a_2 - b_2 = 0, \ldots, a_n - b_n = 0$$
Because $S$ being a basis of $V(F)$ is a linearly independent set,
$$\Rightarrow a_1 = b_1,\ a_2 = b_2, \ldots, a_n = b_n$$
Hence, $u = a_1v_1 + a_2v_2 + \ldots + a_nv_n$
where $a_1, a_2, \ldots, a_n \in F$, is unique.

**59.** Let $\quad v_1 \neq 0$

Then, $\quad av_1 = 0 \ \Rightarrow\ a = 0$.

Hence, the set $\{v_1\}$ is linearly independent.

If $v_1 = 0$, then $\{v_1\}$ is evidently linearly dependent.

**60.** Let $f, g \in W$
$$f(5) = 0 \text{ and } g(5) = 0 \qquad \ldots(i)$$
If $a, b \in \mathbb{R}$, then
$$(af + bg)(5) = (af)(5) + (bg)(5)$$
$$= af(5) + bg(5)$$
$$= a\cdot 0 + b\cdot 0 \qquad \text{[from Eq. (i)]}$$
$$= 0$$
$$\Rightarrow af + bg \in W$$
*i.e.*, $f, g \in W$ and $a, b \in \mathbb{R} \Rightarrow af + bg \in W$

Hence, $W$ is a subspace of $V$.

**61.** Let $V_1, V_2$ be two subspaces of the vector space $V$ over a field $F$.

Let $v_1, v_2 \in V_1 \cap V_2,\ a, b \in F$

Then, $\quad v_1 \in V_1 \cap V_2 \Rightarrow v_1 \in V_1$ and $v_1 \in V_2$
$$v_2 \in V_1 \cap V_2 \Rightarrow v_2 \in V_1 \text{ and } v_2 \in V_2$$
$v_1, v_2 \in V_1 \Rightarrow av_1 + bv_2 \in V_1$ (Since, $V_1$ is a subspace)

and $v_1, v_2 \in V_2 \Rightarrow av_1 + bv_2 \in V_2$ (Since, $V_2$ is a subspace)

As, $av_1 + bv_2 \in V_1$ and $av_1 + bv_2 \in V_2$
$$\Rightarrow av_1 + bv_2 \in V_1 \cap V_2$$
Thus, $V_1 \cap V_2$ is subspace of a vector space $V$ over a field $F$.

**62.** Let $\quad \alpha = \left(\frac{1}{2}, \frac{3}{5}, 7\right)$

and $\quad a = \sqrt{3}$, a real number

Then, $\quad a\alpha = \sqrt{3}\left(\frac{1}{2}, \frac{3}{5}, 7\right)$
$$= \left(\frac{\sqrt{3}}{2}, \frac{3\sqrt{3}}{5}, 7\sqrt{3}\right) \notin W$$
Since, $\frac{\sqrt{3}}{2}, \frac{3\sqrt{3}}{5}, 7\sqrt{3}$ are not rational numbers.

Hence, $W$ is not closed under scalar multiplication, consequently it does not form a vector space of $V_3(\mathbb{R})$.

**63.**
$$[A(dB + C)]_{ij} = \sum_k A_{ik}(dB + C)_{kj}$$
$$= \sum_k (dA_{ik}B_{kj} + A_{ik}C_{kj})$$
$$= d\sum_k A_{ik}B_{kj} + \sum_k A_{ik}C_{kj}$$
$$= d(AB)_{ij} + (AC)_{ij}$$
$$= [d(AB) + AC]_{ij}$$

**64.** Since, it is an Abelian group, for vector space it have to satisfy the following

(I) Scalar multiplication

If $\quad A \in M_{mn}$ and $a \in \mathbb{R}$

Then, the matrix
$$aA \in M_{mn}$$
(II) Distributive laws

If $\quad a, b \in \mathbb{R}$

and $\quad A = [a_{ij}]_{m\times n}$
$$B = \{b_{ij}\}_{m\times n} \in M_{mn}, \text{ then}$$
$$(V_1): a(A + B) = a([a_{ij}]_{m\times n} + [b_{ij}]_{m\times n})$$
$$= a([a_{ij} + b_{ij}]_{m\times n})$$
$$= [aa_{ij} + ab_{ij}]_{m\times n}$$
$$= [aa_{ij}]_{m\times n} + [ab_{ij}]_{m\times n}$$
$$= a[a_{ij}]_{m\times n} + a[b_{ij}]_{m\times n}$$
$$= aA + aB$$
$$(V_2): (a + b)A = (a + b)[a_{ij}]_{m\times n}$$
$$= [aa_{ij} + ba_{ij}]_{m\times n}$$
$$= [aa_{ij}]_{m\times n} + [ba_{ij}]_{m\times n}$$
$$= a[a_{ij}]_{m\times n} + b[a_{ij}]_{m\times n}$$
$$= aA + bA$$
$(V_3)$ Associativity
$$a(bA) = a(b[a_{ij}]_{m\times n}) = a[ba_{ij}]_{m\times n}$$
$$= [ab\, a_{ij}]_{m\times n} = (ab)[a_{ij}]_{m\times n}$$
$$= (ab)A$$
$(V_4)$ Existence of identity
$$1A = 1[a_{ij}]_{m\times n} = [1a_{ij}]_{m\times n}$$
$$= [a_{ij}]_{m\times n} = A$$
where 1 is the unity of the field $\mathbb{R}$ of real numbers.

Hence, all the postulates of vector space are satisfied and therefore, the given set $M_{mn}$ is a vector space.

**65.** Let
$$a_1(1, 1, 0) + a_2(3, 1, 3) + a_3(5, 3, 3) = 0$$
$$\Rightarrow (a_1 + 3a_2 + 5a_3,\ a_1 + a_2 + 3a_3,\ 3a_2 + 3a_3) = (0, 0, 0)$$
Hence, we have, $a_1 + 3a_2 + 5a_3 = 0 \qquad \ldots(i)$
$$a_1 + a_2 + 3a_3 = 0 \qquad \ldots(ii)$$
and $\quad 3a_2 + 3a_3 = 0 \qquad \ldots(iii)$

Subtracting Eq. (ii) from Eq. (i), we get
$$2a_2 + 2a_3 = 0 \Rightarrow a_2 + a_3 = 0 \qquad \ldots(iv)$$
Subtracting Eq. (iv) from Eq. (ii), we get
$$a_1 + 2a_3 = 0 \qquad \ldots(v)$$
Hence, from Eqs. (iv) and (v), we get
$$a_1 = -2a_3,\ a_2 = -a_3$$
Hence, $a_1(1, 1, 0) + a_2(3, 1, 3) + a_3(5, 3, 3) = 0$

where $\quad a_1 = -2a_3,\ a_2 = -a_3$

and $a_3$ can take any value.

Hence, the given system of vectors in linearly dependent.

**66.** Let $\alpha = (x_1, y_1, 0)$ and $\beta = (x_2, y_2, 0)$ belongs to $W$

If $\quad a, b \in \mathbb{R}$, then
$$a\alpha + b\beta = a(x_1, y_1, 0) + b(x_2, y_2, 0)$$

$$= (ax_1, ay_1, 0) + (bx_2, by_2, 0)$$
$$= (ax_1 + bx_2, ay_1 + by_2, 0 + 0)$$
$$= (x', y', 0)$$

where $x' = ax_1 + bx_2$

$y' = ay_1 + by_2 \in \mathbb{R} \in W$

*i.e.*, $\alpha, \beta \in W$

and $a, b \in \mathbb{R}$

$\Rightarrow a\alpha + b\beta \in W$

Hence, $W$ is a subspace of $V$.

**67.** Let $f, g \in W$

Then, $2f(3) = f(1)$ and $2g(3) = g(1)$ ...(i)

If $a, b \in \mathbb{R}$, then

$$2(af + bg)(3) = 2af(3) + 2bg(3)$$
$$= a[2f(3)] + b[2g(3)]$$
$$= af(1) + bg(1), \quad \text{[from Eq. (i)]}$$
$$= (af + bg)(1)$$

$\Rightarrow af + bg \in W$

*i.e.*, $f, g \in W$ and $a, b \in \mathbb{R}$

$\Rightarrow af + bg \in W$

Hence, $W$ is a subspace of $V$.

**68.** Suppose, $E_1, \ldots, E_k$ are $k$ linear operators on $V$ which satisfy the first three conditions and let $W_i$ be the range of $E_i$. Then, certainly

$$V = W_1 + \ldots + W_k\alpha$$

For by condition (iii), we have

$$\alpha = E_1\alpha + \ldots + E_k\alpha$$

for each $\alpha$ in $V$, and $E_i\alpha$ is in $W_i$. This expression for $\alpha$ is unique, because, if

$$\alpha = \alpha_1 + \ldots + \alpha_k$$

with $\alpha_i$ in, if $W_i$, say $\alpha_i = E_i\beta_i$, then using (i) and (ii), we have

$$E_j\alpha = \sum_{i=1}^{k} E_j\alpha_i$$
$$= \sum_{i=1}^{k} E_jE_i\beta_i$$
$$= E_j^2\beta_j = E_j\beta_j$$
$$= \alpha_j$$

which shows that $V$ is the direct sum of the $W_i$.

**69.** Let

$$B = \{(1, 0, 0), (1, 1, 0), (1, 1, 1)\}$$

First we shall show that $B$ is linearly independent.

We have,

$$\alpha(1, 0, 0) + \beta(1, 1, 0) + \gamma(1, 1, 1) = (0, 0, 0)$$
$$\Rightarrow \quad (\alpha + \beta + \gamma, \beta + \gamma, \gamma) = (0, 0, 0)$$
$$\Rightarrow \quad \alpha + \beta + \gamma = 0$$
$$\beta + \gamma = 0, \gamma = 0$$
$$\Rightarrow \quad \gamma = 0$$
$$\beta = 0, \alpha = 0$$

$\Rightarrow$ The vectors (1, 0, 0), (1, 1, 0), (1, 1, 1) are linearly independent.

Now, we shall show that the set $B$ generates $\mathbb{R}^3$.

Let $x = (\alpha, \beta, \gamma)$ be any element of $\mathbb{R}^3$. Let

$(\alpha, \beta, \gamma) = \alpha_1(1, 0, 0) + \alpha_2(1, 1, 0) + \alpha_3(1, 1, 1)$.

Then $(\alpha, \beta, \gamma) = (\alpha_1 + \alpha_2 + \alpha_3, \alpha_2 + \alpha_3, \alpha_3)$

$$\Rightarrow \quad \alpha_1 + \alpha_2 + \alpha_3 = \alpha$$
$$\alpha_2 + \alpha_3 = \beta$$
$$\alpha_3 = \gamma$$

On solving these equations, we get

$$\alpha_3 = \gamma, \alpha_2 = \beta - \gamma, \alpha_1 = \alpha - \beta$$

Hence, $(\alpha, \beta, \gamma) = (\alpha - \beta)(1, 0, 0) + (\beta - \gamma)(1, 1, 0) + \gamma(1, 1, 1)$

Therefore, $B$ generates $\mathbb{R}^3$.

Hence, $B$ is a basis for $\mathbb{R}^3$.

Now, suppose that $B_1 = \{e_1, e_2, e_3\}$ is a basis for $\mathbb{R}^3$. Then, to show that $B_2 = \{e_1 + e_2, e_1 + e_3, e_2 + e_3\}$ is also a basis for $\mathbb{R}^3$. We shall show that $B_2$ is linearly independent. We have,

$$\alpha(e_1 + e_2) + \beta(e_1 + e_3) + \gamma(e_2 + e_3) = 0$$
$$\Rightarrow \quad (\alpha + \beta)e_1 + (\alpha + \gamma)e_3 + (\beta + \gamma)e_3 = 0$$
$$\Rightarrow \quad \alpha + \beta = 0, \alpha + \gamma = 0, \beta + \gamma = 0$$

[$\because e_1, e_2, e_3$ are linearly independent]

The only solution of these equations is

$$\alpha = 0, \beta = 0, \gamma = 0$$

Hence, the set $B_2$ is linearly independent. Now, $\dim \mathbb{R}^3 = 3$ and $B_2$ is a linearly independent set containing 3 vectors. Hence, $B_2$ must be a basis for $\mathbb{R}^3$.

**70.** Let $a_1(1, 3, 2) + a_2(1, -7, -8) + a_3(2, 1, -1) = 0$

$\Rightarrow (a_1 + a_2 + 2a_3, 3a_1 - 7a_2 + a_3, 2a_1 - 8a_2 - a_3) = (0, 0, 0)$

Hence, we have, $a_1 + a_2 + 2a_3 = 0$

$$3a_1 - 7a_2 + a_3 = 0$$
$$2a_1 - 8a_2 - a_3 = 0$$

Solving these, we get

$$a_2 = \frac{1}{3}a_1, a_3 = -\frac{2}{3}a_1$$

Hence, $a_1v_1 + a_2v_2 + a_3v_3 = 0$

where $a_2$ and $a_3$ are given by above results and $a_1$ can take any value in $\mathbb{R}$.

Hence, the given system of vectors in linearly dependent.

**71.** Let $L$ be a finite dimensional linear space of dim $n$. Let $M$ be a subspace of $L$. Any subset of $M$ containing $(n+1)$ or more vectors is also a subset of $L$ and any $(n+1)$ vectors in $L$ are linearly dependent. Therefore, any linearly independent set of vectors in $M$ can contain, at the most $n$ vectors. Let

$$S = \{x_1, x_2, \ldots, x_n\}$$

be a linearly independent subset of $M$ with a maximum number of elements. We claim that $S$ is a basis of $M$.

Now,

(i) $S$ is a linearly independent subset of $M$.

(ii) $[S] = M$. Let $x$ be any element of $M$.

Then, the $(m+1)$ vectors $x, x_1, x_2, \ldots, x_m$ belonging to $M$ are linearly dependent because we have supposed that the largest independent subset of $M$ contains $m$ vectors.

Now, $\{x_1, x_2, \ldots, x_m, x\}$ is a linearly dependent set. Therefore, there exists a vector belonging to it which can be expressed as a linear combination of the preceding vectors. Since, $x_1, x_2, \ldots, x_m$ are linearly independent, therefore, this vector cannot be any of these $m$ vectors. So it must be $x$ itself. Thus, $x$ can be expressed as a linear combination of $x_1, x_2, \ldots, x_m$. Hence, $S$ generates $M$.

i.e., $[S] = M$

Hence, $S$ is a basis of $M$.

$\Rightarrow$ $\dim M = m$ and $m \le n$.

Now, if $L = M$, then every basis of $L$ is also a basis of $M$.

Hence, $\dim L = \dim M = n$

Conversely, let $\dim M = \dim$

$L = n$

Then, to prove that $M = L$.

Let $S$ be a basis of $M$. Then, $[S] = M$ and $S$ contains $n$ vectors. Since, $S$ is also a subset of $L$ and $S$ contains $n$ linearly independent vectors, therefore $S$ will also be a basis of $L$.

Therefore, $[S] = L$

$\Rightarrow$ $M = L$

Thus, if $M$ is a proper subspace of a finite dimensional linear space $L$, then $M$ is finite dimensional and $\dim M < \dim L$.

**72.** Let $f(-x) = -f(x)$ and $g(-x) = -g(x)$ ...(i)

If $a, b \in \mathbb{R}$, then

$$(af + bg)(-x) = af(-x) + bg(-x)$$
$$= a[-f(x)] + b[-g(x)], \quad \text{[from Eq. (i)]}$$
$$= -[af(x) + bg(x)]$$
$$= -(af + bg)(x)$$

i.e., $af + bg \in W$

i.e., $f, g \in W$ and $a, b \in \mathbb{R}$

$\Rightarrow$ $af + bg \in W$

Hence, $W$ is a subspace of $V(\mathbb{R})$.

**73.** Let $V(F)$ be a finite dimensional vector space that $\dim V = n$. Let $W$ be a subspace of $V(F)$.

Each subset of $n+1$ or more vectors of $W$, being a subset of $V$ is linearly dependent. Thus, a linearly independent set of vectors in $W$ can contain at the most $n$ vectors.

Let $S = \{v_1, v_2, \ldots, v_m\}$ be a linearly independent subset of $W$ with a maximum number of elements. Then, $S$ is a basis set for $W$ as

(i) $S$ is a linearly independent subset of $W$,

(ii) $L(S) = W$, for if $v$ be any element of $W$, then the set $\{v_1, v_2, \ldots, v_m, v\}$ is linearly dependent as the set $\{v_1, v_2, \ldots, v_m\}$ is a maximal linearly independent set. So, it follows that $v$ is a linear combination of $v_1, v_2, \ldots, v_m$.

Hence, $L(S) = W$

Hence, $S$ is a basis set for $W$.

So that $\dim W = m$ and $m \le n$

Again, if $V = W$, then every basis of $V$ is also a basis of $W$

i.e., $\dim V = \dim W = n$

Conversely, if $\dim V = \dim W$, then if $S$ be a basis of $W$, we have $L(S) = W$ and $S$ contains $n$ vectors.

Since, $S$ is a subset of $V$ and there are $n$ linearly independent vectors in $S$, so $S$ is also a basis on $V$ i.e., $L(S) = V$

Hence, from $L(S) = W$

and $L(S) = V$

Hence, $W = V$

**74.** We shall show that the set

$$B = \{e_1, e_2, \ldots, e_n\}$$

where $e_1 = (1, 0, \ldots, 0)$, $e_2 = (0, 1, \ldots, 0), \ldots, e_n = (0, 0, \ldots, 0, 1)$ is a basis for $F^n$. First we shall show that the set $B$ is linearly independent. If $\alpha_1, \alpha_2, \ldots, \alpha_n$ be any scalars, then

$$\alpha_1 e_1 + \alpha_2 e_2 + \ldots + \alpha_n e_n = 0$$
$$\Rightarrow \alpha_1(1, 0, 0, \ldots, 0) + \alpha_2(0, 1, 0, \ldots, 0) + \ldots + \alpha_n(0, 0, \ldots, 0, 1) = 0$$
$$\Rightarrow (\alpha_1, \alpha_2, \ldots, \alpha_n) = (0, 0, \ldots, 0)$$
$$\Rightarrow \alpha_1 = 0$$
$$\alpha_2 = 0, \ldots, \alpha_n = 0$$

Therefore, the set $B$ is linearly independent. Now, we shall show that the set $B$ generates the linear space $F^n$. Let $x = (\alpha_1, \alpha_2, \ldots, \alpha_n)$ be any vector in $F^n$. We can write

$$(\alpha_1, \alpha_2, \ldots, \alpha_n) = \alpha_1(1, 0, \ldots, 0) + \alpha_2(0, 1, 0, \ldots, 0) + \ldots + \alpha_n(0, 0, \ldots, 0, 1)$$

i.e., $x = \alpha_1 e_1 + \alpha_2 e_2 + \ldots + \alpha_n e_n$

Therefore, the set $B$ generates $F^n$. Hence, $B$ is a basis of $F^n$.

**75.** Since,

$V = \{(a_1, a_2, \ldots, a_n); a_1, a_2, a_3, \ldots, a_n \in F\}$

$V_1$ $(V, +)$ is an Abelian group

$V$ is closed with respect to addition

i.e., $a + b = (a_1 + b_1, a_2 + b_2, \ldots, a_n + b_n) \in V$

Since, $a_r + b_r \in F$ for all $a_r, b_r \in F$

If $a, b, c \in V$

$a + (b + c) = (a + b) + c$

Since, addition is associative in $F$.

$0 = (0, 0, \ldots, 0) \in V$ is the identity element i.e., $\forall\, a \in V$

$$a + 0 = (a_1, a_2, \ldots, a_n) + (0, 0, \ldots, 0)$$
$$= (a_1 + 0, a_2 + 0, \ldots, a_n + 0)$$
$$= (a_1, a_2, \ldots, a_n) \quad \text{(by property of } 0 \in F)$$
$$= a$$

Similarly, $0 + a = a$

Thus, $a + 0 = 0 + a = a$

$a = (-a_1, -a_2, \ldots, -a_n)$ is the inverse of $a = (a_1, a_2, \ldots, a_n)$ because

$$a + (-a) = (a_1 - a_1, a_2 - a_2, \ldots, a_n - a_n)$$
$$= (0, 0, 0, \ldots, 0) = 0$$

Similarly,

$(-a) + a = 0$

$\therefore$ $a + (-a) = 0 = (-a) + a$

Let $a, b \in V$.

then $a + b = b + a$ (because commutative law holds in $F$)

$(V_2)$ Let $a = (a_1, a_2, \ldots, a_n) \in V$ and $b = (b_1, b_2, \ldots, b_n) \in V$ and $\alpha \in F$, then

$$\alpha(a + b) = \alpha(a_1 + b_1, a_2 + b_2, \ldots, a_n + b_n)$$
$$= [\alpha(a_1 + b_1), \alpha(a_2 + b_2), \ldots, \alpha(a_n + b_n)]$$
$$= (\alpha a_1 + \alpha b_1, \alpha a_2 + \alpha b_2, \ldots, \alpha a_n + \alpha b_n)$$
$$= (\alpha a_1 + \alpha a_2, \ldots, \alpha a_n) + (\alpha b_1, \alpha b_2, \ldots, \alpha b_n)$$
$$= \alpha(a_1, a_2, \ldots, a_n) + \alpha(b_1, b_2, \ldots, b_n)$$
$$= \alpha a + \alpha b$$

$(V_3)$ For $\alpha, \beta \in F$ and $a \in V$, we have

$$(\alpha+\beta)a = (\alpha+\beta)(a_1, a_2, \ldots, a_n)$$
$$= ((\alpha+\beta)a_1, (\alpha+\beta)a_2, \ldots, (\alpha+\beta)a_n)$$
$$= (\alpha a_1 + \beta a_1, \alpha a_2 + \beta a_2, \ldots, \alpha a_n + \beta a_n)$$

(by right distributive law in $F$)

$$= (\alpha a_1, \alpha a_2, \ldots, \alpha a_n) + (\beta a_1, \beta a_2, \ldots, \beta a_n)$$
$$(\alpha+\beta)a = \alpha a + \beta a$$

$(V_4)$ For $\alpha, \beta \in F$ and $a \in V$, we have

$$(\alpha\beta)a = ((\alpha\beta)a_1, (\alpha\beta)a_2, \ldots, (\alpha\beta)a_n)$$
$$= (\alpha(\beta a_1), \alpha(\beta a_2), \ldots, \alpha(\beta a_n))$$

(by associative law in $F$)

$$= \alpha[\beta(a_1, a_2, \ldots, a_n)]$$
$$\therefore \quad (\alpha\beta)a = \alpha(\beta a).$$

$(V_5)$ If 1 is the unity of $F$ and $a \in V$, then

$$1\cdot a = (1\cdot a_1, 1\cdot a_2, \ldots, 1\cdot a_n)$$
$$= (a_1, a_2, \ldots, a_n) = a \qquad (\because 1\cdot a_n = a_n)$$
$$\therefore \quad 1\cdot a = a\cdot 1 = a$$

Hence, $V$ is a vector space over $F$.

**76.** Let $\alpha = (x_1 - y_1, x_1 + y_1, x_1 + y_1 + z_1)$

and $\beta = (x_2 - y_2, x_2 + y_2, x_2 + y_2 + z_2)$

be any two elements of $W$.

If $a, b \in \mathbb{R}$, then

$$a\alpha + b\beta = a(x_1 - y_1, x_1 + y_1, x_1 + y_1 + z_1) + b(x_2 - y_2, x_2 + y_2, x_2 + y_2 + z_2)$$
$$= (ax_1 - ay_1, ax_1 + ay_1, ax_1 + ay_1 + az_1) + (bx_2 - by_2, bx_2 + by_2, bx_2 + by_2 + bz_2)$$
$$= ([ax_1 - ay_1 + bx_2 - by_2], [ax_1 + ay_1 + bx_2 + by_2], [ax_1 + ay_1 + az_1 + bx_2 + by_2 + bz_2])$$
$$= ([ax_1 + bx_2] - [ay_1 + by_2], [ax_1 + bx_2] + [ay_1 + by_2], [ax_1 + bx_2] + [ay_1 + by_2] + [az_1 + bz_2])$$
$$= (x' - y', x' + y', x' + y' + z')$$

where $x' = ax_1 + bx_2$, $y' = ay_1 + by_2$, $z' = az_1 + bz_2$

and $x', y', z' \in \mathbb{R} \in W$ i.e., $\alpha, \beta \in W$

and $a, b \in \mathbb{R} \Rightarrow a\alpha + b\beta \in W$

Hence, $W$ is a subspace of $\mathbb{R}^3(\mathbb{R})$.

**77.** (i) Let $M = \{f : f \in L \text{ and } f(0) = 0\}$

Let $f, g$ be any two members of $M$.

Then, $f(0) = 0$

$g(0) = 0$

Let $\alpha, \beta \in R$

Then, $(\alpha f + \beta g)(0) = \alpha f(0) + \beta g(0)$

$= \alpha(0) + \beta(0) = 0$

Therefore, $\alpha f \cdot \beta g \in M$

Hence, $M$ is a subspace of $L$.

(ii) Let $M = \{f : f \in L \text{ and } f(x) \geq 0 \text{ for all } x\}$

Let $f, g \in M$

Then, $f(x) \geq 0$

and $g(x) \geq 0$ for all $x$

Let $\alpha, \beta \in R$

Then, $(\alpha f + \beta g)(x) = \alpha f(x) + \beta g(x)$

Now, if $f(x) \geq 0$, $g(x) \geq 0$ and $\alpha, \beta$ are any real numbers, then it is not necessary that

$$\alpha f(x) + \beta g(x) \text{ is } \geq 0$$

Therefore, $\alpha f + \beta g$ is not necessarily member of $M$. Hence, $M$ is not a subspace of $L$.

**78.** We shall show that the infinite set $B = \{1, x, x^2, x^3, \ldots\}$ is a basis for $P$. First we shall show that $B$ is linearly independent.

Let $B' = \{x^{m_1}, x^{m_2}, \ldots, x^{m_n}\}$

be any finite subset of $B$ having $n$ vectors. Here, $m_1, m_2, \ldots, m_n$ are some non-negative integers. Let $\alpha_1, \alpha_2, \ldots, \alpha_n$ be scalars such that

$$\alpha_1 x^{m_1} + \alpha_2 x^{m_2} + \ldots + \alpha_n x^{m_n} = 0 \qquad \ldots(i)$$

(i.e., zero polynomial)

By the definition of equality of two polynomials, we have from Eq. (i) $\alpha_1 = 0, \alpha_2 = 0, \ldots, \alpha_n = 0$. Thus, every finite subset of $B$ is linearly independent and therefore, $B$ is linearly independent. Now, we shall show that $B$ generates $P$, i.e., each polynomial in $P$ can be expressed as a linear combination of finite number of elements of $B$.

Let $f(x) = \alpha_0 + \alpha_1 x + \alpha_2 x^2 + \ldots + \alpha_t x^t$

be a polynomial of degree $t$. Then,

$$f(x) = \alpha_0 + \alpha_1 x + \alpha_2 x^2 + \ldots + \alpha_t x^t$$

Hence, $B$ generates $P$. Therefore, $B$ is a basis for $P$ and $P$ is infinite dimensional.

**79.** Let $L$ be direct sum of its two subspaces $M_1$ and $M_2$. Then, each element of $L$ is expressible uniquely as sum of an element of $M_1$ and an element of $M_2$. Therefore, we have

$$L = M_1 + M_2$$

Let, if possible $0 \neq x \in M_1 \cap M_2$. Then, $x \in M_1$, $x \in M_2$. Also, $x \in L$ and we can write

$$x = 0 + x, \text{ where } 0 \in M_1, x \in M_2$$

and $x = x + 0$, where $x \in M_1$, $0 \in M_1$.

Thus, $x \in L$ can be expressed in atleast two different ways as sum of an element of $M_1$ and an element of $M_2$. This contradicts the fact that $L$ is the direct sum of $M_1$ and $M_2$. Hence, 0 is the only vector common to both $M_1$ and $M_2$ i.e., $M_1 \cap M_2 = \{0\}$.

**80.** (i) Let $f, g \in M$ in this case.

Then, $f(0) = 1$

$g(0) = 1$

Let $\alpha, \beta \in R$

Then, $(\alpha f + \beta g)(0) = \alpha f(0) + \beta g(0) = \alpha(1) + \beta(1)$

which is not necessarily equal to 1 for all $\alpha, \beta \in R$.

Hence, $\alpha f + \beta g$ is not necessarily a member of $M$ and therefore, $M$ is not a subspace of $L$.

(ii) If $f$ and $g$ are differentiable functions and $\alpha, \beta \in R$, then of $\alpha f + \beta g$ is also a differentiable function. Hence, in this case $M$ is a subspace of $L$.

(iii) If $f$ and $g$ are two polynomials of degree 3 and $\alpha, \beta \in R$, then $\alpha f + \beta g$ is not necessarily a polynomial of degree 3. Hence, in this case $M$ is not a subspace of $L$.

**81.** Let $L = M_1 + M_2$

and $M_1 \cap M_2 = \{0\}$

Then, to show that $L$ is the direct sum of $M_1$ and $M_2$. We have $L = M_1 + M_2 \Rightarrow$ that each element of $L$ can be expressed as sum of an element of $M_1$ and an element of $M_2$. Now, to show that this expression is unique.

Let, if possible,

$$x = x_1 + x_2, x \in L, x_1 \in M_1, x_2 \in M_2$$

and $\quad x = y_1 + y_2, y_1 \in M_1, y_2 \in M_2$

Then, to show that $x_1 = y_1$

and $\quad x_2 = y_2$

We have $x_1 + x_2 = y_1 + y_2$

$\Rightarrow \quad x_1 - y_1 = y_2 - x_2$

Since, $M_1$ is a subspace, therefore

$$x_1 \in M_1, y_1 \in M_1$$

$\Rightarrow \quad x_1 - y_1 \in M_1$

Similarly, $\quad y_2 - x_2 \in M_2$

Therefore, $x_1 - y_1 = x_2 \in M_1 \cap M_2$

But 0 is the only vector which belongs to

$$M_1 \cap M_2$$

Therefore, $x_1 - y_1 = 0$

$\Rightarrow \quad x_1 = y_1$

Also, $\quad y_2 - x_2 = 0$

$\Rightarrow \quad x_2 = y_2$

Thus, each vector $x \in L$ is uniquely expressible as sum of an element of $M_1$ and an element of $M_2$.

Hence, $L = M_1 \oplus M_2$

**82.** (i) Let

$$M = \{x : x \in \mathbb{R}^3 \text{ and } x_1 = 0 \text{ or } x_2 = 0\}$$

Let $\quad x = (x_1, x_2, x_3)$

$\quad y = (y_1, y_2, y_3)$

be any two members of $M$. Then, $x_1 = 0$ or $x_2 = 0$ and $y_1 = 0$ or $y_2 = 0$, if $\alpha, \beta \in \mathbb{R}$, then

$$\alpha x + \beta y = (\alpha x_1 + \beta y_1, \alpha x_2 + \beta y_2, \alpha x_3 + \beta y_3)$$

Now, it is not necessarily that, we must have

$$\alpha x_1 + \beta y_1 = 0$$

or $\quad \alpha x_2 + \beta y_2 = 0$

e.g., if $\quad \alpha = 7, \beta = 6, x_1 = 5, x_2 = 0, y_1 = 0, y_2 = 4$

Then, $\quad \alpha x_1 + \beta y_1 = 35$

or $\quad \alpha x_2 + \beta y_2 = 24$

**83.** Here $A = \begin{bmatrix} -2 & 1 & 1 \\ 1 & -2 & 1 \\ 1 & 1 & -2 \end{bmatrix}$

$$\tilde{A} = (A;\, b)$$

$$= \begin{bmatrix} -2 & 1 & 1 & : & a \\ 1 & -2 & 1 & : & b \\ 1 & 1 & -2 & : & c \end{bmatrix}$$

Since, $|A| = \begin{vmatrix} -2 & 1 & 1 \\ 1 & -2 & 1 \\ 1 & 1 & -2 \end{vmatrix} \sim \begin{vmatrix} 1 & 1 & -2 \\ 0 & -3 & 3 \\ 0 & 0 & 0 \end{vmatrix}$

Hence, $\quad$ Rank (A) $\neq 3$

$$\begin{vmatrix} -2 & 1 \\ 1 & -2 \end{vmatrix} \neq 0$$

$\Rightarrow \quad$ Rank (A) $= 2$

$$\tilde{A} = \begin{bmatrix} 1 & 1 & -2 & : & a \\ 0 & -3 & 3 & : & b \\ 0 & 0 & 0 & : & c \end{bmatrix}$$

$\Rightarrow \quad$ Rank $\tilde{A} = 3$

and when $a + b + c = 0$,

then rank $\quad \tilde{A} = 2$

$\because$ If rank $(A;\, b) =$ rank $(A)$,

then only it have solution

$\therefore \quad a + b + c = 0$

**84.** $\begin{bmatrix} 1 & 1 & 1 \\ a & b & c \\ a^2 & b^2 & c^2 \end{bmatrix} \begin{bmatrix} x \\ y \\ z \end{bmatrix} = \begin{bmatrix} 1 \\ k \\ k^2 \end{bmatrix}$ by Cramer's rule,

$$\frac{x}{\begin{bmatrix} 1 & 1 & 1 \\ k & b & c \\ k^2 & b^2 & c^2 \end{bmatrix}} = \frac{y}{\begin{bmatrix} 1 & 1 & 1 \\ a & k & c \\ a^2 & k^2 & c^2 \end{bmatrix}} = \frac{z}{\begin{bmatrix} 1 & 1 & 1 \\ a & b & c \\ a^2 & b^2 & c^2 \end{bmatrix}} = \frac{1}{\begin{bmatrix} 1 & 1 & 1 \\ a & b & c \\ a^2 & b^2 & c^2 \end{bmatrix}}$$

$$x = \frac{\begin{bmatrix} 1 & 1 & 1 \\ k & b & c \\ k^2 & b^2 & c^2 \end{bmatrix}}{\begin{bmatrix} 1 & 1 & 1 \\ a & b & c \\ a^2 & b^2 & c^2 \end{bmatrix}}$$

$$= \frac{(k-b)(c-k)(b-c)}{(a-b)(c-a)(b-c)} = \frac{(k-b)(c-k)}{(a-b)(c-a)}$$

Similarly, $\quad y = \dfrac{(a-k)(k-c)}{(a-b)(b-c)}, \quad z = \dfrac{(b-k)(k-a)}{(b-c)(c-a)}$

**85.** The given equation is consistent, if

Hence, $\quad \begin{vmatrix} \lambda-1 & 3\lambda+1 & 2\lambda \\ \lambda-1 & 4\lambda-2 & \lambda+3 \\ 2 & 3\lambda+1 & 3(\lambda-1) \end{vmatrix} = 0$

Operation $R_2 - R_1$ gives

$$\begin{vmatrix} \lambda-1 & 3\lambda+1 & 2\lambda \\ 0 & \lambda-3 & 3-\lambda \\ 2 & 3\lambda+1 & 3(\lambda-1) \end{vmatrix} = 0$$

Operation $C_3 - C_2$ gives

$$\begin{vmatrix} \lambda-1 & 3\lambda+1 & 5\lambda+1 \\ 0 & \lambda-3 & 0 \\ 2 & 3\lambda+1 & 6\lambda-2 \end{vmatrix} = 0$$

$\Rightarrow \quad (\lambda-3)\begin{vmatrix} \lambda-1 & 5\lambda+1 \\ 2 & 6\lambda-2 \end{vmatrix} = 0$

$\Rightarrow 2(\lambda-3)[(\lambda-1)(3\lambda-1) - (5\lambda+1)] = 0$

$\Rightarrow \quad 6\lambda(\lambda-3)^2 = 0 \quad \Rightarrow \quad \lambda = 0, 3, 3$

**86.** $|A| = \begin{vmatrix} 1 & -1 & 1 \\ 1 & 2 & -1 \\ 2 & 1 & 3 \end{vmatrix} \neq 0$

Hence, Rank $(A) = 3$ and hence the given equation have only trivial solutions.

# Linear Transformations

**Syllabus**

- Linear Transformation
- Matrix Representation of Linear Transformation
- Change of Basis
- Rank and Nullity
- Dual Space
- Annihilators
- Cayley-Hamilton Theorem

## Linear Transformation

Suppose, $U(F)$ and $V(F)$ are two vector spaces over the same field $F$. A linear transformation from $U$ into $V$ is a function $T$ from $U$ into $V$ such that

$$T(a\alpha + b\beta) = aT(\alpha) + bT(\beta), \forall \ \alpha, \beta \text{ in } U, a, b \text{ in } F. \qquad \text{...(i)}$$

The Eq. (i) is called the linearity property.

> ***Note*** **(a)** Eq. (i) is equivalent to the condition $T(a\alpha + \beta) = aT(\alpha) + T(\beta), \forall \alpha, \beta$ in $U$ and all scalars $a$ in $F$.
> **(b)** Linear transformation is also called vector space homomorphism.

## Linear Operator

Let $V(F)$ be a vector space. A linear operator on $V$ is a function $T$ from $V$ into $V$ such that

$$T(a\alpha + b\beta) = aT(\alpha) + bT(\beta), \forall \ \alpha, \beta \in V \text{ and } \forall \ a, b \in F$$

Therefore, $T$ is a linear operator on $V$ if $T$ is a linear transformation from $V$ into $V$ itself.

***Example 1.*** *Let $V(F)$ be the vector space of all $m \times n$ matrices over the field $F$. Let $P$ be a fixed $m \times m$ matrix over $F$ and let $Q$ be a fixed $n \times n$ matrix over $F$. The correspondence $T$ from $V$ into $V$ defined by $T(A) = PAQ, \forall \ A \in V$ is a linear operator on $V$.*

**Solution.** If $A$ is an $m \times n$ matrix over the field $F$, then $PAQ$ is also an $m \times n$ matrix over the field $F$. Therefore, $T$ is a function from $V$ into $V$. Now, let $A, B \in V$ and $a, b \in F$. Then,

$$\begin{aligned} T(aA + bB) &= P(aA + bB)Q \qquad \text{[by the definition of } T] \\ &= (aPA + bPB) = aPAQ + bPBQ \\ &= aT(A) + bT(B) \end{aligned}$$

$\therefore T$ is a linear transformation from $U$ into $V$.

Thus, $T$ is a linear operator on $V$.

## Important Transformations

### 1. Zero Transformation

Let $U(F)$ and $V(F)$ be two vector spaces. The function $T$ from $U$ into $V$ defined by

$$T(\alpha) = 0 \text{ (zero vector of } V), \forall \ \alpha \in U$$

is a linear transformation from $U$ into $V$.

Let $\alpha, \beta \in U$ and $a, b \in F$. Then, $a\alpha + b\beta \in U$

We have, $T(a\alpha + b\beta) = 0 = a0 + b0$ [by definition of $T$]
$= aT(\alpha) + bT(\beta)$

$\therefore$ $T$ is a linear transformation from $U$ into $V$.

It is called zero transformation and we shall denote it by $\hat{0}$.

## 2. Indentity Operator

Let $V(F)$ be a vector space. The function $I$ from $V$ into $V$ defined by $I(\alpha) = \alpha$, $\forall\ \alpha \in V$ is a linear transformation from $V$ into $V$. If $\alpha, \beta \in V$ and $a, b \in F$, then $a\alpha + b\beta \in V$ and we have

$$I(a\alpha + b\beta) = a\alpha + b\beta = aI(\alpha) + bI(\beta)$$

$\therefore$ $I$ is a linear transformation from $V$ into $V$. The transformation $I$ is called identity operator on $V$ and it is denoted by $I$.

## 3. Negative of a Linear Transformation

Let $U(F)$ and $V(F)$ be two vector spaces. Let $T$ be a linear transformation from $U$ into $V$. The corresponding $\sim T$ defined by $(-T)\alpha = -[T(\alpha)], \forall\ \alpha \in U$ is a linear transformation from $U$ into $V$.

$\because$ $T(\alpha) \in V \Rightarrow -T(\alpha) \in V$,

$\therefore -T$ is a function from $U$ into $V$.

Let $\alpha, \beta \in U$ and $a, b \in F$. Then, $a\alpha + b\beta \in U$ and we have

$$(-T)(a\alpha + b\beta) = -[T(a\alpha + b\beta)] \quad \text{[by the definition of } -T]$$
$$= -[aT(\alpha) + bT(\beta)]$$
$$[\because T \text{ is a linear transformation}]$$
$$= a[-T(\alpha)] + b[-T(\beta)]$$
$$= a[(-T)\alpha] + b[(-T)\beta]$$

$\therefore -T$ is a linear transformation from $U$ into $V$. The linear transformation $-T$ is called negative of linear transformation $T$.

***Theorem*** Let $T$ be a linear transformation from a vector space $U(F)$ into a vector space $V(F)$. Then, we have

**(i)** $T(0) = 0$, where 0 on the left hand side is zero vector of $U$ and 0 on the right hand side is zero vector of $V$.

**(ii)** $T(-\alpha) = -T(\alpha), \forall\ \alpha \in U$

**(iii)** $T(\alpha - \beta) = T(\alpha) - T(\beta), \forall\ \alpha, \beta \in U$

**(iv)** $T(a_1\alpha_1 + a_2\alpha_2 + \ldots + a_n\alpha_n) = a_1T(\alpha_1) + a_2T(\alpha_2) + \ldots + \ldots a_nT(\alpha_n)$

where, $\alpha_1, \alpha_2, \alpha_3, \ldots, \alpha_n \in U$ and $a_1, a_2, a_3, \ldots, a_n \in R$

## Range of a Linear Transformation

Let $U(F)$ and $V(F)$ be two vector spaces and let $T$ be a linear transformation from $U$ into $V$. Then, the range of $T$ written as $R(T)$ is the set of all vectors $\beta$ in $V$ such that $\beta = T(\alpha)$ for some $\alpha$ in $U$. Therefore, the range of $T$ is the image set of $U$ under $T$ *i.e.*,

$$\text{Range } T = \{T(\alpha) \in V : \alpha \in U\}$$

## Null Space of Linear Transformation

Let $U(F)$ and $V(F)$ be two vector spaces and let $T$ be a linear transformation from $U$ into $V$. Then, the null space of $T$ written as $N(T)$ is the set of all vectors $\alpha$ in $U$ such that $T(\alpha) = 0$ (zero vector of $V$). Therefore,

$$N(T) = \{\alpha \in U : T(\alpha) = 0 \in V\}$$

If we regard the linear transformation $T$ from $U$ into $V$ as a vector space homomorphism of $U$ into $V$. Then, the null space of $T$ is also called the kernel of $T$.

# Important Theorems on Range and Null Space

***Theorem 1*** If $U(F)$ and $V(F)$ be two vector spaces and $T$ is a linear transformation from $U$ into $V$, then the kernel of $T$ or the null space of $T$ is a subspace of $U$.

***Theorem 2*** If $U(F)$ and $V(F)$ are two vector spaces and $T$ is a linear transformation from $U$ into $V$, then the range of $T$ is a subspace of $V$.

***Theorem 3*** Let $T$ be a linear transformation from a vector space $U(F)$ into a vector space $V(F)$. If $U$ is finite dimensional, then the range of $T$ is a finite dimensional subspace of $V$.

---

## Rank and Nullity of a Linear Transformation

Let $T$ be a linear transformation from a vector space $U(F)$ into a vector space $V(F)$ with $U$ as finite dimensional. The rank of $T$ denoted by $\rho(T)$ is the dimension of the range of $T$ *i.e.*,

$$\rho(T) = \dim R(T)$$

The nullity of $T$ denoted by $V(T)$ is the dimension of the null space of $T$ *i.e.*,

$$V(T) = \dim N(T)$$

## Rank Nullity Theorem

Let $U$ and $V$ be vector spaces over the field $F$ and let $T$ be a linear transformation from $U$ into $V$. Suppose that $U$ is finite dimensional. Then, rank $(T)$ + nullity $(T) = \dim U$

***Example 2.*** *Prove that the mapping $T : V_2(R) \to V_3(R)$ defined as $T(a, b) = (a + b, a - b, b)$ is a linear transformation from $V_2(R)$ into $V_3(R)$. Find the range, rank, nullspace and nullity of $T$.*

**Solution.** Let $\alpha = (a_1, b_1), \beta = (a_2, b_2) \in V_2(R)$

Then, $T(\alpha) = T(a_1, b_1) = (a_1 + b_1, a_1 - b_1, b_1)$

and $T(\beta) = T(a_2, b_2) = (a_2 + b_2, a_2 - b_2, b_2)$

Let $a, b \in R$

Then, $a\alpha + b\beta \in V_2(R)$

and $T(a\alpha + b\beta) = T[a(a_1, b_1) + b(a_2, b_2)]$

$$= T(aa_1 + ba_2, ab_1 + bb_2)$$
$$= (aa_1 + ba_2 + ab_1 + bb_2, aa_1 + ba_2 - ab_1 - bb_2, ab_1 + bb_2]$$

$= (a[a_1 + b_1] + b[a_2 + b_2],\ a[a_1 - b_1] + b[a_2 - b_2], ab_1 + bb_2]$

$= a(a_1 + b_1, a_1 - b_1,\ b_1) + b(a_2 + b_2,\ a_2 - b_2,\ b_2)$

$= aT(\alpha) + bT(\beta)$

$\therefore T$ is a linear transformation from $V_2(R)$ into $V_3(R)$

Now, $\{(1, 0),\ (0, 1)\}$ is a basis for $V_2(R)$.

We have $T(1, 0) = (1+0, 1-0, 0) = (1, 1, 0)$

and $T(0, 1) = (0+1, 0-1, 1) = (1, -1, 1)$

The vectors $T(1, 0)$, $T(0, 1)$ span the range of $T$.

Therefore, the range of $T$ is the subspace of $V_3(R)$ spanned by the vectors (1, 1, 0), (1, −1, 1).

The vectors $(1, 1, 0), (1, -1, 1) \in V_3(R)$ are linearly independent because if $x, y \in R$, then we have

$$x(1, 1, 0) + y(1, -1, 1) = (0, 0, 0)$$

$$\Rightarrow \quad (x+y,\ x-y,\ y) = (0, 0, 0)$$

$$\Rightarrow \quad x+y=0,\ x-y=0,\ y=0 \Rightarrow x=0, y=0$$

$\therefore$ The vectors (1, 1, 0), (1, −1, 1) from a basis for the range of $T$. Therefore, the rank $T = \dim$ of range of $T = 2$

Nullity of $T = \dim$ of $V_2(R)$ − rank $T = 2 - 2 = 0$

$\Rightarrow$ Null space of $T$ must be zero subspace of $V_2(R)$ otherwise, $(a, b) \in$ null space of $T$

$$\Rightarrow \quad T(a, b) = (0, 0, 0) \Rightarrow (a+b,\ a-b,\ b) = (0, 0, 0)$$

$$\Rightarrow \quad a+b=0,\ a-b=0,\ b=0$$

$$\Rightarrow \quad a=0,\ b=0$$

$\therefore$ (0, 0) is the only element of $V_2(R)$ which belongs to the null space of $T$.

$\therefore$ Null space of $T$ is the zero subspace of $V_2(R)$.

***Example 3.*** *Consider the basis* $S = \{\alpha_1, \alpha_2, \alpha_3\}$ *of* $R^3$ *where* $\alpha_1 = (1, 1, 1),\ \alpha_2 = (1, 1, 0),\ \alpha_3 = (1, 0, 0)$

*Express* (2, − 3, 5) *in terms of the basis* $\alpha_1, \alpha_2, \alpha_3$

*Suppose* $T : R^3 \to R^2$ *be defined as*

$$T(\alpha_1) = (1, 0);\ T(\alpha_2) = (2, -1);\ T(\alpha_3) = (4, 3)$$

*Find* $T(2, -3, 5)$.

**Solution.** Let $(2, -3, 5) = a\alpha_1 + b\alpha_2 + c\alpha_3$

$$\Rightarrow \quad (2, -3, 5) = a(1, 1, 1) + b(1, 1, 0) + c(1, 0, 0)$$

$$\Rightarrow \quad a+b+c=2,\quad a+b=-3,\quad a=5$$

On solving the above equations, we get

$$a=5,\ b=-8,\ c=5$$

$$\therefore \quad (2, -3, 5) = 5\alpha_1 - 8\alpha_2 + 5\alpha_3$$

$$\Rightarrow \quad T(2, -3, 5) = T(5\alpha_1 - 8\alpha_2 + 5\alpha_3)$$

$$= 5T(\alpha_1) - 8T(\alpha_2) + 5T(\alpha_3)$$

[$\because$ $T$ is a linear transformation]

$$= 5(1, 0) - 8(2, -1) + 5(4, 3)$$

$$= (5, 0) - (16, -8) + (20, 15)$$

$$= (9, 23)$$

> ***Note*** Let $V$ be a vector space and $T$ is a linear transformation from $V$ into $V$. Then, the following two statements about $T$ are equivalent
>
> (i) The intersection of the range of $T$ and the null space of $T$ is the zero subspace of $V$ *i.e.*, $R(T) \cap N(T) = \{0\}$
>
> (ii) $T[T(\alpha)] = 0 \Rightarrow T(\alpha) = 0$.

# Linear Transformations as Vectors

Suppose, $L(U, V)$ or Hom$(U, V)$ be the set of all linear transformations from a vector space $U(F)$ into the vector space $V(F)$. If we wish to impose a vector space structure on the set $L(U, V)$ over the same field $F$, then for this purpose we have to define scalar multiplication and addition in $L[U, V]$ over $F$.

## Scalar Multiplication in $L(U, V)$ Over $F$ and Addition in $L(U, V)$ Over $F$

Let $U$ and $V$ be the two vector spaces over the field $F$. Let $C$ be any element of $F$, the function $(CT)$ defined by

$$(CT)(\alpha) = CT(\alpha), \forall\ \alpha \in U$$

is a linear transformation from $U$ into $V$.

Let $T_1$ and $T_2$ be linear transformations from $U$ into $V$. The function $T_1 + T_2$ defined by

$$(T_1 + T_2)(\alpha) = T_1(\alpha) + T_2(\alpha), \forall\ \ \alpha \in U$$

is a linear transformation from $U$ into $V$.

The set $L[U, V]$ of all linear transformations from $U$ into $V$, together with the addition and scalar multiplication defined above is a vector space over the field $F$.

### Dimension of $L(U, V)$

If $U(F)$ and $V(F)$ are finite dimensional, then the vector space of linear transformations from $U$ into $V$ is also finite dimensional.

# Important Theorems on $L(U,V)$

***Theorem 1*** Suppose $U$ be a finite dimensional vector space over the field $F$ and suppose

$$\beta = \{\alpha_1, \alpha_2, \alpha_3, \ldots, \alpha_n\}$$

be an ordered basis for $U$.

Suppose, $V$ be the vector space over the same field $F$ and let $\beta_1, \beta_2, \ldots, \beta_n$ be any vectors in $V$. Then, $\exists$ a unique linear transformation $T$ from $U$ into $V$ such that

$$T(\alpha_i) = \beta_i,\ i = 1, 2, \ldots, n$$

***Theorem 2*** Suppose, $U$ be an $n$-dimensional vector space over the field $F$, and let $V$ be an $m$-dimensional vector space over $F$. Then, the vector space $L[U, V]$ of all linear transformations from $U$ into $V$ is finite dimensional and is of dimension $mn$.

***Theorem 3*** The vector space $L[U, U]$ of all linear operators on an $n$-dimensional vector space $U$ is of dimension $n^2$.

***Theorem 4*** Let $U, V$ and $W$ be vector spaces over the field $F$. Let $T$ be a linear transformation from $U$ into $V$ and $S$ a linear transformation from $V$ into $W$. Then, the composite function $ST$ (called product of linear transformations) defined by

$$(ST)(\alpha) = S[T(\alpha)], \forall \alpha \in U$$

is a linear transformation from $U$ into $W$.

> ***Note*** **(a)** From theorem 1 we observe that if $T$ is a linear transformation from a finite dimensional vector space $U(F)$ into a vector space $V(F)$, then $T$ is completely defined under the images of the elements of a basis set of $U$. If $S$ and $T$ are two linear transformations from $U$ into $V$ s.t.
>
> $S(\alpha_i) = T(\alpha_i)$, $\forall \alpha_i \in$ to the basis of $U$, then
>
> $S(\alpha) = T(\alpha), \forall \alpha \in U$
>
> $\Rightarrow \quad S = T$
>
> Therefore, two linear transformations from $U$ into $V$ are equal if they agree on a basis of $U$.
>
> **(b)** If $T$ and $S$ are linear operators on a vector space $V(F)$, then both the products $ST$ as well as $TS$ exists and each is a linear operator on $V$. But in general $ST \neq TS$.

***Example 4.*** *Suppose $T_1$ and $T_2$ be the linear operators on $R^2$ s.t. $T_1(x_1, x_2) = (x_1, x_2)$ and $T_2(x_1, x_2) = (x_1, 0)$, then prove that $T_1T_2 \neq T_2T_1$*

**Solution.** $(T_1T_2)(x_1, x_2) = T_1[T_2(x_1, x_2)]$

$= T_1(x_1, 0)$ [By the definition of $T_2$]

$= (0, x_1)$ [By the definition of $T_1$] ...(i)

and $(T_2T_1)(x_1, x_2) = T_2[T_1(x_1, x_2)]$ [By definition of $T_2T_1$]

$= T_2(x_2, x_1)$ [By the definition of $T_1$]

$= (x_2, 0)$ [By the definition of $T_2$] ...(ii)

From Eqs. (i) and (ii), we have

$$T_1T_2 \neq T_2T_1$$

# Polynomials

Let $T$ be a linear transformation on a vector space $V(F)$. Then, $TT$ is also a linear transformation on $V$. We can write $T^1 = T$ and $T^2 = TT$. As we know that the product of linear transformations is an associative operation. Therefore, if $n$ is a positive integer, then we define

$$T^n = TTT \ldots \text{ upto } n \text{ times}$$

Definitely, $T^n$ is linear transformation on $V$.

We can also define $T^0 = I$ (which is identity transformation)

Suppose, $n$ and $l$ are non-negative integers, then

$$T^nT^l = T^{n+l} \text{ and } (T^n)^l = T^{nl}$$

The set $L(V, V)$ of all linear transformation on $V$ is a vector space over the field $F$.

Suppose $a_0, a_1, a_2, \ldots, a_n \in F$, then

$$p(T) = a_0I + a_1T + a_1T + a_2T^2 + a_3T^3 + \ldots + a_nT^n \in L(V, V)$$

$\Rightarrow p(T)$ is also a linear transformation on $V$ because it is a linear combination over $F$ of elements of $L(V, V)$. $p(T)$ is called a polynomial in linear transformation $T$.

# Invertible Linear Transformations

Suppose, $U$ and $V$ are the vector spaces over the field $F$. Suppose, $T$ is a linear transformation from $U$ into $V$ s.t. $T$ is one-one onto. Then, $T$ is called invertible.

Suppose, $T$ is a function from $U$ into $V$, then $T$ is said to be one-one if

$$\alpha_1, \alpha_2 \in U \text{ and } \alpha_1 \neq \alpha_2$$

$$\Rightarrow \quad T(\alpha_1) \neq T(\alpha_2)$$

or we can say that $T$ is one-one if

$$\alpha_1, \alpha_2 \in U \text{ and } T(\alpha_1) = T(\alpha_2) \Rightarrow \alpha_1 = \alpha_2$$

Again, $T$ is onto if

$$\beta \in V \Rightarrow \exists\, \alpha \in U \text{ s.t. } T(\alpha) = \beta$$

# Inverse of $T$

If $T$ is one-one and onto, then we define a function $T^{-1}$ (inverse of $T$) from $V$ into $U$ as follows

Let $\gamma$ be any vector in $V$. As $T$ is onto,

$\therefore \quad \gamma \in V \Rightarrow \exists\, \alpha \in U$ s.t. $T(\alpha) = \gamma$

$\because \quad T$ is one-one, so that $\alpha$ is a unique element of $U$.

$\therefore \quad \alpha, \beta \in U$ and $\alpha \neq \beta \Rightarrow \gamma = T(\alpha) \neq T(\beta)$

So that we define $T^{-1}(\gamma)$ to be $\alpha$.

$\Rightarrow \quad T^{-1} : V \to U$ s.t.

$$T^{-1}(\gamma) = \alpha \Leftrightarrow T(\alpha) = \gamma$$

$T^{-1}$ is one-one and onto.

## Important Results on Invertible Linear Transformation

1. Suppose, $U$ and $V$ are vector spaces over the field $F$ and suppose $T$ be the linear transformation from $U$ into $V$. If $T$ is one-one and onto, then $T^{-1}$ (inverse function) is a linear transformation from $V$ into $U$.
2. Suppose, $A$, $B$ and $C$ are linear transformations on a vector space $V(F)$ s.t. $AB = CA = I$, then $A$ is said to be invertible and $A^{-1} = B = C$
3. Suppose $T$ be an invertible linear transformation on a vector space $V(F)$. Then, $T^{-1}T = I = TT^{-1}$
4. (Uniqueness of Inverse) suppose, $A$ be an invertible linear transformation on a vector space $V(F)$, then $A$ have unique inverse.
5. The necessary and sufficient condition for a linear transformation $A$ on a vector space $V(F)$ to be invertible is that $\exists$ a linear transformation $B$ on $V$ such that $AB = I = BA$
6. Let $V(F)$ be a vector space and let $A$, $B$ be linear transformation on $V$, then
   (i) If $A$ and $B$ are invertible, then $AB$ is invertible and $(AB)^{-1} = B^{-1}A^{-1}$
   (ii) If $A$ is invertible and $a \neq 0 \in F$, then $aA$ is invertible and $(aA)^{-1} = \frac{1}{a}A^{-1}$
   (iii) If $A$ is a invertible, then $A^{-1}$ is invertible and $(A^{-1})^{-1} = A$

# Non-singular and Singular Transformations

Suppose, $T$ be a linear transformation from a vector space $U(F)$ into a vector space $V(F)$. Then, $T$ is said to be non-singular if the null space of $T$ *i.e.*, $\ker T$ consists of the zero vector alone means, if

$$\alpha \in U \text{ and } T(\alpha) = 0 \Rightarrow \alpha = 0$$

On the other hand, if $\exists$ a vector $0 \neq \alpha \in U$ s.t. $T(\alpha) = 0$, then $T$ is called to be singular.

## Important Theorems on Singular and Non-singular Transformation

***Theorem 1*** Suppose, $T$ is a linear transformation from $U$ into $V$. Then, $T$ is non-singular iff $T$ carries each linearly independent subset of $U$ onto a linearly independent subset of $V$.

***Theorem 2*** Let $T$ be a linear transformation from a vector space $U(F)$ into a vector space $V(F)$. Then, $T$ is non-singular iff $T$ is one-one.

***Theorem 3*** Let $U$ and $V$ be finite dimensional vector spaces over the field $F$ s.t. $\dim U = \dim V$

If $T$ is a linear transformation from $U$ into $V$, the following are equivalent

**(i)** $T$ is invertible.

**(ii)** $T$ is non-singular.

**(iii)** The range of $T$ is $V$.

**(iv)** If $\{\alpha_1, \alpha_2, \ldots, \alpha_n\}$ is any basis for $U$, then

$$\{T(\alpha_1), T(\alpha_2), \ldots, T(\alpha_n)\} \text{ is a basis for } V.$$

**(v)** There is some basis $(\alpha_1, \alpha_2, \ldots, \alpha_n)$ for $U$ s.t.

$$\{T(\alpha_1), T(\alpha_2), \ldots, T(\alpha_n)\} \text{ is a basis for } V.$$

***Theorem 4***

**(i)** A linear transformation $T$ on a finite dimensional vector space is invertible iff $T$ is onto.

**(ii)** A linear transformation $T$ on a finite dimensional vector space is invertible if and only if $T$ is non-singular.

> ***Note*** If $T$ is a linear transformation on a finite dimensional vector space $V$, then $T$ is one-one $\Rightarrow T$ must be onto. Also, $T$ is onto $\Rightarrow T$ is one-one. But it fails when $V$ is not finite dimensional. *e.g.*,
>
> Suppose, $V(F)$ be the vector space of all polynomials in $x$ with coefficients in $F$. Let $D$ be the differentiation operator on $V$. The range of $D$ is all of $V$ and so $D$ is onto but $D$ is not one-one since all constant polynomials are sent into 0 by $D$.
> Suppose, $T$ is the linear transformation on $V$ defined by
> $$T[f(x)] = xf(x), \forall f(x) \in V$$
> $\Rightarrow T$ is one-one.
> But, $T$ is not onto $V$. Suppose, if $f(x)$ is a non-zero constant polynomial in $V$, then $f(x)$ will not be the image of any element in $V$ under the function $T$.

***Example 5.*** *If $A$ is a linear transformation on a vector space $V$ s.t. $A^2 - A + I = \hat{0}$, then prove that $A$ is invertible.*

**Solution.** We have,

$$A^2 - A + I = \hat{0} \quad \Rightarrow \quad A^2 - A = -I \qquad \ldots(i)$$

Let $\alpha_1, \alpha_2 \in V$

$$\Rightarrow \quad A(\alpha_1) = A(\alpha_2) \Rightarrow A[A(\alpha_1)] = A[A(\alpha_2)]$$
$$\Rightarrow \quad A^2(\alpha_1) = A^2(\alpha_2)$$
$$\Rightarrow \quad A^2(\alpha_1) - A(\alpha_1) = A^2(\alpha_2) - A(\alpha_2)$$
$$\Rightarrow \quad (A^2 - A)(\alpha_1) = (A^2 - A)(\alpha_2)$$
$$\Rightarrow \quad (-I)\alpha_1 = (-I)\alpha_2 \qquad \text{[using Eq. (i)]}$$
$$\Rightarrow \quad -[I(\alpha_1)] = -[I(\alpha_2)]$$
$$\Rightarrow \quad -\alpha_1 = -\alpha_2 \quad \Rightarrow \alpha_1 = \alpha_2$$

$\Rightarrow$ $A$ is one-one. ...(ii)

Now, we shall prove that $A$ is onto.

Suppose, $\alpha \in V \Rightarrow \alpha - A(\alpha) \in V$

$\Rightarrow \quad A[\alpha - A(\alpha)] = A(\alpha) - A^2(\alpha)$

$= (A - A^2)(\alpha) = I(\alpha)$

$[\because A^2 - A = -I \Rightarrow A - A^2 = I]$

$= \alpha$

Thus, $\alpha \in V \Rightarrow \exists\, \alpha - A(\alpha) \in V$ s.t.

$A[\alpha - A(\alpha)] = \alpha \quad \Rightarrow A$ is onto. ...(iii)

From Eqs. (ii) and (iii), we conclude that $A$ is invertible.

**Example 6.** *If $T : U \to V$ be a linear transformation and $U$ is finite dimensional, then prove that $U$ and range of $T$ have the same dimension if and only if $T$ is non-singular. Determine all non-singular linear transformations.*

$$T : V_4(R) \to V_3(R)$$

**Solution.** Since, $\dim U = \text{rank}(T) + \text{nullity}(T)$

$= \dim$ of range of $T +$ dim of null space of $T$

$\Rightarrow \quad \dim U = \dim$ of range of $T$

If and only if dim of null space of $T$ is zero.

$\Rightarrow$ If and only if null space of $T$ consists of zero vector alone.

$\Rightarrow$ If and only if $T$ is non-singular.

Suppose, $T$ be a linear transformation from $V_4(R)$ into $V_3(R)$. Then, $T$ will be non-singular if and only if

dim of $V_4(R) =$ dim of range of $T$.

Now, dim $V_4(R) = 4$ and dim of range of $T \le 3$ because range of $T \subseteq V_3(R)$

$\therefore$ $\dim V_4(R)$ may not be equal to dim of range of $T$. Therefore, $T$ cannot be non-singular. So, there can be no non-singular linear transformation from $V_4(R)$ into $V_3(R)$.

**Example 7.** *Suppose $T_1$ be a linear transformation on a vector space $V(F)$. Show that the set of all linear transformations $S$ on $V$ for which $T_1S = \hat{0}$ is a subspace of the vector space of all linear transformations.*

**Solution.** Suppose, $L$ be the vector space of all linear transformations on the vector space $V$.

Suppose that $W = \{S : S$ is a linear transformation on $V$ and $T_1S = \hat{0}\}$. Now, we shall prove that $W$ is a subspace of $L$. Let $a, b \in F$ and $S_1, S_2 \in W$. Then, by using the definition of $W$, we have $T_1S_1 = \hat{0}$ and $T_1S_2 = \hat{0}$. Now, we shall prove that

$$T_1(aS_1 + bS_2) = \hat{0}$$

Let $\alpha \in V$. Then, we have

$[T_1(aS_1 + bS_2)](\alpha) = T_1[(aS_1 + bS_2)(\alpha)]$

[by using the definition of linear transformation]

$= T_1[(aS_1)(\alpha) + (bS_2)(\alpha)]$

$= T_1[a\,S_1(\alpha) + bS_2(\alpha)]$

$= aT_1[S_1(\alpha) + bT_1[S_2(\alpha)]$

$[\because T$ is a linear transformation$]$

$= a(T_1S_1)(\alpha) + b(T_1S_2)(\alpha)$

$= a\hat{0}(\alpha) + b\hat{0}(\alpha)$

$= a \cdot 0 + b \cdot 0 = 0 = \hat{0}(\alpha)$

$\therefore \quad [T_1(aS_1 + bS_2)](\alpha) = \hat{0}(\alpha), \forall\, \alpha \in W$

Therefore, $T_1(aS_1 + bS_2) = \hat{0}$.

Hence, by definition of $W$, $aS_1 + bS_2 \in W$.

Therefore, $a, b \in F$ and $S_1, S_2 \in W \Rightarrow aS_1 + bS_2 \in W$.

Hence, $W$ is a subspace of $L$.

## Matrix Representation of Linear Transformations

Let $U$ and $V$ be vector spaces of dimension $n$ and $m$ respectively. Let $B_1 = \{\alpha_1, \alpha_2, \ldots, \alpha_n\}$ and $B_2 = \{\beta_1, \beta_2, \ldots, \beta_n\}$ be ordered bases of $U$ and $V$ respectively. Let $T : U \to V$ be a linear transformation defined by

$$T(\alpha_j) = a_{1j}\beta_1 + a_{2j}\beta_2 + \ldots + a_{mj}\beta_m,\ j = 1, 2, \ldots, n$$

So that the coordinate vector of $T(\alpha_j)$ written as a column vector is $[a_{1j} \ \ a_{2j} \ \ a_{3j} \ldots a_{mj}]^T$

Write the column vector of $T(\alpha_1), T(\alpha_2), \ldots, T(\alpha_n)$ successively as column vectors in the form of a rectangular array as follows

$$\begin{bmatrix} a_{11} & a_{12} & a_{13} & \ldots & a_{1n} \\ a_{21} & a_{22} & a_{23} & \ldots & a_{2n} \\ \vdots & & & & \\ a_{m1} & a_{m2} & a_{m3} & \ldots & a_{mn} \end{bmatrix}$$

This rectangular array is called the matrix of $T$ relative to the ordered bases $B_1$ and $B_2$ and is denoted by $(T : B_1, B_2)$.

*e.g.*, Determine the matrix $(T : B_1, B_2)$ for the linear transformation $T : V_2 \to V_3$,

$T(x_1, x_2) = (x_1 + x_2, 2x_1 - x_2, 7x_2)$ and the bases

$$B_1 = \{(1, 0), (0, 1)\},$$
$$B_2 = \{(1, 0, 0), (0, 1, 0), (0, 0, 1)\}$$
$$T(1, 0) = (1, 2, 0) = 1(1, 0, 0) + 2(0, 1, 0) + 0(0, 0, 1)$$
$$T(0, 1) = (1, -1, 7) = 1(1, 0, 0) - 1(0, 1, 0) + 7(0, 0, 1)$$

$$\therefore \quad (T; B_1, B_2) = \begin{bmatrix} 1 & 1 \\ 2 & -1 \\ 0 & 7 \end{bmatrix}$$

*e.g.*, Let a linear transformation $T : V_2 \to V_2$ be defined by $T(x_1, x_2) = (x_1, -x_2)$. Let us calculate the matrix of $T$ relative to the bases $B_1 = \{(1, 0), (0, 1)\}$ and $B_2 = \{(1, 1), (1, -1)\}$.

$$T(1, 0) = (1, 0) = \frac{1}{2}(1, 1) + \frac{1}{2}(1, -1)$$

$$T(0, 1) = (0, -1) = -\frac{1}{2}(1, 1) + \frac{1}{2}(1, -1)$$

$$\therefore \quad [T; B_1, B_2] = \begin{bmatrix} \frac{1}{2} & -\frac{1}{2} \\ \frac{1}{2} & \frac{1}{2} \end{bmatrix}$$

## Important Theorems on Matrix Representation

***Theorem 1*** Let $U$ be an $n$-dimensional vector space over the field $F$ and let $V$ be an $m$-dimensional vector space over $F$. Let $B$ and $B'$ be ordered bases for $U$ and $V$, respectively. Then, corresponding to every matrix $[a_{ij}]_{m\times n}$ of $mn$ scalars belonging to $F$ these corresponds to a unique linear transformation $T$ from $U$ into $V$ such that

$$[T : B : B'] = [a_{ij}]_{m\times n}$$

***Theorem 2*** Let $T$ be a linear transformation from an $n$-dimensional vector space $U$ into an $m$-dimensional vector space $V$ and let $B$ and $B'$ be ordered bases for $U$ and $V$ respectively. If $A$ is the matrix of $T$ relative to $B$ and $B'$, then $\forall\ \alpha \in U$, we have

$$[T(\alpha)]_{B'} = A[\alpha]_B$$

where $[\alpha]_B$ is the coordinate matrix of $\alpha$ with respect to ordered basis $B$ and $[T(\alpha)]_{B'}$ is coordinate matrix of $T(\alpha) \in V$ with respect to $B'$.

***Theorem 3*** Let $V(F)$ be an $n$-dimensional vector space and $B$ be any ordered basis for $V$. If $I$ be the identity transformation and $\hat{0}$ be the zero transformation as $V$, then

**(i)** $[I : B] = I$ (unit matrix of order $n$) and

**(ii)** $[\hat{0} : B] =$ Null matrix of order $n$

***Theorem 4*** Let $T$ and $S$ be linear transformations from an $n$-dimensional vector space $U$ into an $m$-dimensional vector space $V$ and let $B$ and $B'$ be ordered bases for $U$ and $V$, respectively. Then,

**(i)** $[T + S :\ B';\ B'] = [T : B, B'] + [S : B; B']$

**(ii)** $[CT, B, B'] = C\ [T : B; B']$, where $C$ is any scalar.

***Theorem 5*** Let $V$ be an $n$-dimensional vector space over the field $F$. Let $T$ and $S$ be linear transformation of $V$. Further, let $B$ be an ordered basis for $V$. If $A$ is the matrix of $T$ relative to $B$ and $D$ is the matrix of $S$ relative to $B$, then the matrix of the composite transformation $ST$ relative to $B$ in the product matrix

$$C = DA \ \ i.e.,\ [ST]_B = [S]_B\,[T]_B$$

***Theorem 6*** Let $U$ be an $n$-dimensional vector space over the field $F$ and let $V$ be an $m$-dimensional vector space over $F$. For each pair of ordered basis $B$, $B'$ or relative to $B$, $B'$ is an isomorphic between the space $L(U, V)$ and the space of all $m \times n$ matrices over the field $F$.

***Theorem 7*** Let $T$ be an linear operator on an $n$-dimensional vector space $V$ and let $B$ be an ordered basis for $V$. Prove that $T$ is invertible iff $[T]_B$ is an invertable matrix. Also, if $T$ is invertible, then

$$[T^{-1}]_B = [T]_B^{-1}$$

*i.e.*, the matrix of $T^{-1}$ relative to $B$ is the inverse of the matrix of $T$ relative to $B$.

## Change of Basis (Transition) Matrix

Let $B = \{\alpha_1, \alpha_2, \ldots, \alpha_n\}$ and $B' = \{\beta_1, \beta_2, \ldots, \beta_n\}$ be two ordered bases for the $n$-dimensional vector space $V(F)$.

Suppose,

$$\begin{aligned} \beta_1 &= a_{11}\alpha_1 + a_{12}\alpha_2 + \ldots + a_{1n}\alpha_n \\ \beta_2 &= a_{21}\alpha_1 + a_{22}\alpha_2 + \ldots + a_{2n}\alpha_n \\ &\vdots \\ \beta_n &= a_{n1}\alpha_1 + a_{n2}\alpha_2 + \ldots + a_{nn}\alpha_n \end{aligned}$$

Then, the transpose $P$ of the above matrix of coefficients is called the change-of-basis matrix or the transition matrix from the old basis $\{\alpha_i\}$ to the new basis $\{\beta_i\}$.

***Theorem 1*** Let $V(F)$ be an $n$-dimensional vector space over the field $F$ and let $B$ and $B'$ be two ordered basis for $V$. Then, there is a unique necessarily invertible, $n \times n$ matrix $A$ when entries in $F$ such that

**(i)** $[\alpha]_B = A[\alpha]_{B'}$

**(ii)** $[\alpha]_{B'} = A^{-1}[\alpha]_B$ for every vector $\alpha$ in $V$.

***Theorem 2*** Let $B = \{\alpha_1, \alpha_2, \ldots, \alpha_n\}$ and $B' = \{\beta_1, \beta_2, \ldots, \beta_n\}$ be two ordered bases for an $n$-dimensional vector space $V(F)$. If $(x_1, x_2, \ldots, x_n)$ is an ordered set of $n$ scalars. Let $\alpha = \sum_{i=1}^{n} x_i\alpha_i$ and $\beta = \sum_{i=1}^{n} x_i\beta_i$.

Then, $T(\alpha) = \beta$, where $T$ is the linear operator on $V$ defined by

$$T(\alpha_i) = \beta_i,\ i = 1, 2, \ldots, n.$$

## Similarity of Matrices

Let $A$ and $B$ be square matrices of order $n$ over the field $F$. Then, $B$ is said to be similar to $A$ if there exists an $n \times n$ invertible square matrix $C$ with elements in $F$ such that

$$B = C^{-1}AC$$

> ***Note*** **(a)** The relation of similarity is an equivalence relation in the set of all $n \times n$ matrices over the field $F$.
> **(b)** Similar matrices have the same determinant.

## Similarity of Linear Transformations

Let $A$ and $B$ be two linear transformations on a vector space $V(F)$. Then, $B$ is said to be similar to $A$ if there exists an invertible linear transformation $C$ on $V$ such that

$$B = CAC^{-1}$$

> ***Note*** The relation of similarity is an equivalence relation in the set of all transformations on a vector space $V(F)$.

## Important Theorem on Similarity of Linear Transformation

***Theorem 1*** Let $T$ be a linear operator on an $n$-dimensional vector space $V(F)$ and let $B$ and $B'$ be two ordered bases for $V$. Then, the matrix of $T$ relative to $B'$ is similar to the matrix of $T$ relative to $B$.

***Theorem 2*** Let $V$ be an $n$-dimensional vector space over the field $F$ and $T_1$ and $T_2$ be two linear operator on $V$. If there exist two ordered bases $B$ and $B'$ for $V$ such that $[T_1]_B = [T_2]_{B'}$, then $T_2$ is similar to $T$.

# Determinant of a Linear Transformation on a Finite Dimensional Vector Space

Let $T$ be a linear operator on an $n$-dimensional vector space $V(F)$. Then, the determinant of $T$ is the determinant of the matrix of $T$ relative to any ordered basis for $V$.

### Scalar Transformation

Let $V(F)$ be a vector space. A linear transformation $T$ on $V$ is said to be a scalar transformation of $V$ if

$$T(\alpha) = c\alpha, \forall\ \alpha \in V$$

where $c$ is a fixed scalar in $F$.

### Trace of a Matrix

Let $A$ be a square matrix of order $n$ over a field $F$. The sum of the elements of $A$ lying along the principal diagonal is called the trace of $A$. It is denoted by trace $A$. If $A = [a_{ij}]_{n\times n}$, then

$$\text{tr } A = \sum_{i=1}^{n} a_{ii} = a_{11} + a_{22} + \ldots + a_{nn}$$

> ***Note*** **(a)** Let $A$ and $B$ be two square matrices of order $n$ over a field $F$ and $\lambda \in F$. Then,
> (i) $\text{tr}(\lambda A) = \lambda\, \text{tr}(A)$
> (ii) $\text{tr}(A+B) = \text{tr}(A) + \text{tr}(B)$
> (iii) $\text{tr}(AB) = \text{tr}(BA)$
> **(b)** Similar matrices have the same trace.

### Trace of a Linear Transformation

Let $T$ be a linear operator on an $n$-dimensional vector space $V(F)$. Then, the trace of $T$ is the trace of the matrix $T$ relative to any ordered basis for $V$.

***Example 8.*** *Suppose, $T$ be the linear operator on $R^3$ defined by $T(x_1, x_2, x_3) = (3x_1 + x_3 - 2x_1 + x_2, - x_1 + 2x_2 + 4x_3)$, then prove that $T$ is invertible.*

**Solution.** Suppose,

$$\beta = \{\rho_1 = (1,0,0), \rho_2 = (0,1,0), \rho_3 = (0,0,1)\}$$

is an ordered basis of $R^3$. Then,

$$[T]_\beta = \begin{bmatrix} 3 & 0 & 1 \\ -2 & 1 & 0 \\ -1 & 2 & 4 \end{bmatrix} = A$$

$$\det(A) = \begin{vmatrix} 3 & 0 & 1 \\ -2 & 1 & 0 \\ -1 & 2 & 4 \end{vmatrix}$$

$$= 3(4-0) - 0(-8+0) + 1(-4+1)$$
$$= 9 \neq 0$$

$\therefore$ $A$ is invertible.

Hence, $T$ is invertible.

***Example 9.*** *Suppose, $T$ is the linear operator on $R^2$ defined by $T(x_1, x_2) = (-x_2, x_1)$.*

*Let* $\beta = \{\rho_1 = (1, 0), \rho_2 = (0, 1)\}$

$\beta' = \{\alpha_1 = (1, 2), \alpha_2 = (1, -1)\}$

*be ordered basis for $R^2$. Find a matrix $P$ such that*

$$[T]_{\beta'} = P^{-1}[T]_\beta P$$

**Solution.** $T(\rho_1) = T(1, 0) = (0, 1) = 0\rho_1 + 1\rho_2$

$T(\rho_2) = T(0, 1) = (-1, 0) = -1\rho_1 + 0\rho_2$

$$\therefore \quad [T]_\beta = \begin{bmatrix} 0 & -1 \\ 1 & 0 \end{bmatrix}$$

Now, we define $S : R^2 \to R^2$

s.t. $S(\rho_i) = \alpha_i,\ i = 1, 2$

Now, $\alpha_1 = (1, 2) = 1\,\rho_1 + 2\,\rho_2$

$\alpha_2 = (1, -1) = 1\,\rho_1 + (-1)\,\rho_2$

$\Rightarrow$ $S(\alpha_1) = 1\alpha_1 + 2\alpha_2$ and $S(\alpha_2) = 1\alpha_1 + (-1)\alpha_2$

$$\Rightarrow \quad [S]_{\beta'} = \begin{bmatrix} 1 & 1 \\ 2 & -1 \end{bmatrix}$$

$$\Rightarrow \quad P = \begin{bmatrix} 1 & 1 \\ 2 & -1 \end{bmatrix} \text{ and } P^{-1} = \begin{bmatrix} \frac{1}{3} & \frac{1}{3} \\ \frac{2}{3} & -\frac{1}{3} \end{bmatrix}$$

$$\Rightarrow P^{-1}[T]_\beta P = \begin{bmatrix} \frac{1}{3} & \frac{1}{3} \\ \frac{2}{3} & -\frac{1}{3} \end{bmatrix} \begin{bmatrix} 0 & -1 \\ 1 & 0 \end{bmatrix} \begin{bmatrix} 1 & 1 \\ 2 & -1 \end{bmatrix}$$

$$= \begin{bmatrix} \frac{1}{3} & -\frac{1}{3} \\ -\frac{1}{3} & -\frac{2}{3} \end{bmatrix} \begin{bmatrix} 1 & 1 \\ 2 & -1 \end{bmatrix} = \begin{bmatrix} -\frac{1}{3} & \frac{2}{3} \\ -\frac{5}{3} & \frac{1}{3} \end{bmatrix}$$

$$= [T]_{\beta'}$$

# Characteristic Values and Characteristic Vectors

Suppose $V$ be a vector space over $F$. Let $T$ be a linear operator on $V$. If $\exists\ 0 \neq v \in V$ s.t. $T(v) = cv$ for some $c \in F$, then $v$ is called an eigen vector or characteristic vector of $T$ and $c$ is called an eigen value or characteristic value of $T$.

## Important Theorems on Characteristics Value & Vector

***Theorem 1*** If $\alpha$ is a characteristic vector of $T$ corresponding to the characteristic value $c$, then $k\alpha$ is also a characteristic vector of $T$ corresponding to the same characteristic value $c$ and here, $k$ is any non-zero scalar.

***Theorem 2*** If $\alpha$ is a characteristic vector of $T$, then $\alpha$ cannot correspond to more than one characteristic values of $T$.

***Theorem 3*** Suppose, $T$ be a linear operator on a finite dimensional vector space $V$ and let $c$ be a characteristic value of $T$. Then, the set $W_c = \{\alpha \in V : T\alpha = c\alpha\}$ is a subspace of $V$.

***Theorem 4*** Distinct characteristic vectors of $T$ corresponding to distinct characteristic values of $T$ are linearly independent.

***Theorem 5*** If $T$ is a linear operator on an $n$-dimensional vector space $V$, then $T$ cannot have more than $n$ distinct characteristic values.

***Theorem 6*** Suppose, $T$ be a linear operator on a finite-dimensional vector space $V$. Then, the following are equivalent

**(i)** $c$ is a characteristic value of $T$.

**(ii)** The operator $T - cI$ is singular (not invertible)

**(iii)** $\det(T - cI) = 0$

***Theorem 7*** Let $T$ be a linear operator on an $n$-dimensional vector space $V$ and $A$ be the matrix of $T$ relative to any ordered basis $B$. Then, a vector $\alpha$ in $V$ is an eigen vector of $T$ corresponding to its eigen value $c$ iff its coordinate vector $X$ relative to the basis $B$ is an eigen vector of $A$ corresponding to its eigen value $c$.

***Theorem 8*** Similar matrices $A$ and $B$ have the same characteristic polynomial and hence the same eigen values. If $X$ is an eigen vector of $B$ corresponding to the eigen value $c$, where $B = P^{-1}AP$, $P$ is non-singular matrix.

## Algebraic Multiplicity

Algebraic multiplicity of an eigen value is the number of times of repetition of an eigen value. It is denoted by $\text{mult}_a(\lambda)$.

## Geometric Multiplicity

Geometric multiplicity of an eigen value is the number of linearly independent eigen vector corresponding to $\lambda$. It is denoted by $\text{mult}_g(\lambda)$.

## Regular Eigen Value

If the algebraic multiplicity and geometric multiplicity of an eigen value are equal then the eigen value is called the regular eigen value.

***Example 10.*** *Let $T$ be a linear operator on $R^3$ which is represented in the standard basis by the matrix*

$$\begin{bmatrix} -2 & 2 & -3 \\ 2 & 1 & -6 \\ -1 & -2 & 0 \end{bmatrix}.$$

**Solution.** The eigen values of the matrix are $-3, -3, 5$

$\therefore$ $\text{mult}_a(-3) = 2$ and $\text{mult}_a(5) = 1$

The two linearly independent eigen vectors corresponding to $\lambda = -3$ are $\begin{bmatrix} 0 \\ 3 \\ 2 \end{bmatrix}$ and $\begin{bmatrix} 3 \\ 0 \\ 1 \end{bmatrix}$.

The eigen vector corresponding to the eigen value $\lambda = 5$ is $\begin{bmatrix} 1 \\ 2 \\ -1 \end{bmatrix}$.

$\therefore$ $\text{mult}_g(-3) = 2$ and $\text{mult}_g(5) = 1$.

## Linear Functionals

Let $V(F)$ be a vector space. A function $f$ from $V$ into $F$ is said to be a linear functional on $V$ if

$$f(a\alpha + b\beta) = a f(\alpha) + bf(\beta), \forall\ a,\ b \in F \text{ and } \alpha,\ \beta \in V$$

***Example 11.*** *Let $V_n(F)$ be the vector space of ordered $n$-tuples of the elements of the field $F$.*

**Solution.** Let $x_1, x_2, x_3, \ldots, x_n$ be $n$ elements of field $F$. If $\alpha = (a_1, a_2, a_3, \ldots, a_n) \in V_n(F)$

Let $F$ be a function from $V_n(F)$ into $F$ defined by $f(\alpha) = x_1a_1 + x_2a_2 + \ldots + x_na_n$. If $a, b \in F$, then we have,

Let $\beta = (b_1, b_2, \ldots, b_n) \in V_n(F)$

$$\begin{aligned} f(a\alpha + b\beta) &= f[a(a_1, a_2, \ldots, a_n) + b(b_1, b_2, \ldots, b_n)] \\ &= f(aa_1 + bb_1 + \ldots + aa_n + bb_n) \\ &= x_1(aa_1 + bb_1) + \ldots + x_n(aa_n + bb_n) \\ &= a(x_1a_1 + \ldots + x_na_n) + b(x_1b_1 + \ldots + x_nb_n) \\ &= af(a_1, a_2, \ldots, a_n) + bf(b_1, b_2, \ldots, b_n) \\ &= af(\alpha) + bf(\beta) \end{aligned}$$

$\therefore$ $f$ is a linear functional on $V_n(F)$.

## Particular Linear Functionals

### 1. Zero Functional

Let $V$ be a vector space over the field $F$. The function $f$ from $V$ into $F$ defined by

$$f(\alpha) = 0, \forall\ (\alpha \in V)$$

is a linear functional on $V$.

### 2. Negative of a Linear Functional

Let $V$ be a vector space over the field $F$. Let $f$ be a linear functional on $V$. The correspondence $-f$ defined by

$$(-f)(\alpha) = -[f(\alpha)], \forall \alpha \in V$$

is a linear functional on $V$.

***Theorem*** Suppose, $f$ be a linear functional on a vector space $V(F)$. Then,

**(i)** $f(0) = 0$, where 0 on the left hand side is zero vector of $V$, and 0 on the right hand side is zero element of $F$.

**(ii)** $f(-\alpha) = -f(\alpha), \forall \alpha \in V$

## Dual Space

Let $V$ be a vector space over the field $F$. Then, the set $V^*$ of all linear functionals on $V$ is also a vector space over the field $F$. The vector space $V^*$ is called the dual space of $V$.

## Important Theorems on Dual Space

***Theorem 1*** Let $V$ be an $n$-dimensional vector space over the field $F$ and let $B = \{\alpha_1, \alpha_2, \ldots, \alpha_n\}$ be an ordered basis for $V$. If $\{x_1, x_2, \ldots, x_n\}$ is any ordered set of $n$ scalars, then there exists a unique linear functional $f$ on $V$ such that $f(\alpha_i) = x_i$, $i = 1, 2, \ldots, n$.

***Theorem 2*** Suppose, $V$ be an $n$-dimensional vector space over the field $F$ and let $B = \{\alpha_1, \alpha_2, \ldots, \alpha_n\}$ be a basis for $V$. Then, there is a uniquely determined basis $B' = \{f_1, f_2, \ldots, f_n\}$ for $V^*$ such that $f_i(\alpha_j) = \delta_{ij}$. Consequently the dual space of an $n$-dimensional space is $n$-dimensional.

The basis $B'$ is called the dual basis of $B$.

***Theorem 3*** If $V$ is an $n$-dimensional vector space over the field $F$, then $V$ is isomorphic to its dual space $V^*$.

***Theorem 4*** Let $V$ be an $n$-dimensional vector space over the field $F$ and let $B = \{\alpha_1, \alpha_2, \ldots, \alpha_n\}$ be a basis for $V$. Let $B' = \{f_1, f_2, \ldots, f_n\}$ be the dual basis of $B$. Then, for each linear functional $f$ on $V$, we have $f = \sum_{i=1}^{n} f(\alpha_i) f_i$ and for each vector $\alpha$ in $V$, we have $\alpha = \sum_{i=1}^{n} f_i(\alpha)\alpha_i$.

***Theorem 5*** Suppose, $V$ be an $n$-dimensional vector space over the field $F$. If $\alpha$ is a non-zero vector in $V$, then $\exists$ a linear functional $f$ on $V$ such that $f(\alpha) \neq 0$.

***Theorem 6*** Let $V$ be an $n$-dimensional vector space over the field $F$. If $f(\alpha) = 0$ for all $f \in V^*$, then $\alpha = 0$.

***Theorem 7*** Let $V$ be an $n$-dimensional vector space over the field $F$. If $\alpha$, $\beta$ be any two different vectors in $V$, then $\exists$ a linear functional $f$ on $V$ s.t. $f(\alpha) \neq f(\beta)$

## Second Dual Space

We know that every vector space $V$ possesses a dual space $V^*$ consisting of all linear functionals on $V$. Now, $V^*$ is also a vector space. Therefore, it will also possesses a dual space $(V^*)^*$ consisting of all linear functionals on $V^*$. This dual space of $V^*$ is called the second dual space of $V$. It is denoted by $V^{**}$.

If $V$ is finite-dimensional, then

$$\dim V = \dim V^* = \dim V^{**}$$

## Important Theorems on Second Dual Space

***Theorem 1*** Suppose, $V$ be a finite dimensional vector space over the field $F$. If $\alpha$ is any vector in $V$, the function $L\alpha$ on $V^*$ defined by

$$L\alpha(f) = f(\alpha), \forall f \in V^*$$

is a linear functional on $V^*$ *i.e.*, $L\alpha \in V^{**}$

Also, the mapping $\alpha \longrightarrow L\alpha$ is an isomorphism of $V$ onto $V^{**}$.

***Theorem 2*** Let $V$ be a finite dimensional vector space over the field $F$. If $L$ is a linear functional on the dual space $V^*$ of $V$, then there is a unique vector $\alpha$ in $V$ such that

$$L(f) = f(\alpha), \forall f \in V^*$$

***Theorem 3*** Suppose, $V$ be a finite dimensional vector space over the field $F$. Each basis for $V^*$ is the dual of some basis for $V$.

***Theorem 4*** Suppose $V$ be a finite dimensional vector space over the field $F$. Let $B$ be a basis for $V$ and $B'$ be the dual basis of $B$. Then,

$$B'' = (B')' = B$$

---

***Example 12.*** *Find the dual basis of the basis set*
$B = \{(1, -1, 3), (0, 1, -1), (0, 3, -2)\}$ *for* $V_3(R)$.

**Solution.** Suppose, $\alpha_1 = (1, -1, 3)$, $\alpha_2 = (0, 1, -1)$, $\alpha_3 = (0, 3, -2)$

$\Rightarrow \quad B = \{\alpha_1, \alpha_2, \alpha_3\}$

If $B' = \{f_1, f_2, f_3\}$ is a dual basis of $B$, then we have

$$f_1(\alpha_1) = 1, \; f_1(\alpha_2) = 0, \; f_1(\alpha_3) = 0$$
$$f_2(\alpha_1) = 0, \; f_2(\alpha_2) = 1, \; f_2(\alpha_3) = 0$$
and
$$f_3(\alpha_1) = 0, \; f_3(\alpha_2) = 0, \; f_3(\alpha_3) = 1$$

Now, we find $f_1, f_2, f_3$.

Let $(a, b, c) \in V_3(R)$

Let $(a, b, c) = x(1, -1, 3) + y(0, 1, -1) + z(0, 3, -2)$ ...(i)

$= x\alpha_1 + y\alpha_2 + z\alpha_3$

$\therefore \quad f_1(a, b, c) = x$, $f_2(a, b, c) = y$ and $f_3(a, b, c) = z$

Now, we find the values of $x$, $y$, $z$ using Eq. (i), we have

$$x = a, \; -x + y + 3z = b, \; 3x - y - 2z = c$$

On solving the above equations, we get

$$x = a,\ y = 7a - 2b - 3c,\ z = b + c - 2a$$

$\therefore$ $f_1(a, b, c) = a,\ f_2(a, b, c) = 7a - 2b - 3c$

and $f_3(a, b, c) = -2a + b + c$

Hence, $B' = \{f_1, f_2, f_3\}$ is a dual basis of $B$.

## Annihilators

If $V$ is the vector space over the field $F$ and $S$ is the subset of $V$, then the annihilator of $S$ is the set $S^0$ of all linear functionals $f$ on $V$ s.t.

$$f(\alpha) = 0, \forall\ \alpha \in S$$

The annihilator of $S$ sometimes can also be denoted by $A(S)$.

$$\therefore S^0 = \{f \in V^* : f(\alpha) = 0, \forall\ \alpha \in S\}$$

We defined the annihilator of $S$ which is a subset of $V$. It should not be necessarily that $S$ be the subspace of $V$.

If $S$ is zero subspace of $V$, then $S^0 = V^*$

If $S = V$, then $S^0 = V^0$ = zero subspace of $V^*$.

If $S$ contains a non-zero vector and $V$ is finite dimensional, then $S^0 \neq V^*$. If $0 \neq \alpha \in S$, then there is a linear functional $f$ on $V$ such that $f(\alpha) \neq 0$, so that there is $f \in V^*$ s.t.

$$f \notin S^0.\ \text{Therefore,}\ S^0 \neq V^*.$$

## Annihilator of on Annihilator

Suppose, $V$ is a vector space over the field $F$. If $S$ be any subspace of $V$, then $S^0$ is a subspace of $V^*$. Now, by the definition of an annihilator, we have

$$(S^0)^0 = S^{00} = \{L \in V^{**} : L(f) = 0, \forall\ f \in S^0\}$$

Infinitely $S^{00}$ is a subspace of $V^n$. But if $V$ is finite dimensional, then we have identified $V^{**}$ with $V$ through the natural isomorphism $\alpha \leftrightarrow L\alpha$. Thus, we may regard $S^{00}$ as a subspace of $V$. Therefore,

$$S^{00} = \{\alpha \in V : f(\alpha) = 0, \forall\ f \in S^0\}$$

## Important Theorems on Annihilator

***Theorem 1*** If $S$ is any subset of vector space $V(F)$, then $S^0$ is a subspace of $V^*$.

***Theorem 2*** Suppose, $V$ be a finite dimensional vector space over the field $F$, and suppose $W$ be a subspace of $V$, then

$$\dim W + \dim W^0 = \dim V$$

***Theorem 3*** If $V$ is finite dimensional and $W$ is a subspace of $V$ then $W^*$ is isomorphic to $V^*/W^0$.

***Theorem 4*** Suppose $V$ be a finite dimensional vector space over the field $F$ and suppose $W$ be the subspace of $V$. Then, $W^{00} = W$.

*e.g.*, Suppose, $W_1$ and $W_2$ be the subspaces of a finite dimensional vector space $V$. Then, prove that

**(i)** $(W_1 + W_2)^0 = W_1^0 \cap W_2^0$

**(ii)** $(W_1 \cap W_2)^0 = W_1^0 + W_2^0$

**(i)** Let $f \in W_1^0 \cap W_2^0 \Rightarrow f \in W_1^0,\ f \in W_2^0$

Let $\alpha$ be any vector in $W_1 + W_2$. Then,

$$\alpha = \alpha_1 + \alpha_2 \ \text{ where } \alpha_1 \in W_1,\ \alpha_2 \in W_2$$

$$\Rightarrow \quad f(\alpha) = f(\alpha_1 + \alpha_2) = f(\alpha_1) + f(\alpha_2)$$

$$= 0 + 0\ [\because \alpha_1 \in V \text{ and } f \in W_1^0 \Rightarrow f(\alpha_1) = 0$$

$$= 0 \text{ and similarly } f(\alpha_2) = 0$$

Therefore, $f(\alpha) = 0, \forall\ \alpha \in W_1 + W_2$

$$\therefore \quad f \in (W_1 + W_2)^0$$

$$\Rightarrow \quad W_1^0 \cap W_2^0 \subseteq (W_1 + W_2)^0 \quad \text{...(i)}$$

Now, we prove that $(W_1 + W_2)^0 \subseteq W_1^0 \cap W_2^0$,

we have

$$W_1 \subseteq W_1 + W_2$$

$$\therefore \quad (W_1 + W_2)^0 \subseteq W_1^0 \quad \text{...(ii)}$$

Similarly, $W_2 \subseteq W_1 + W_2$

$$\therefore \quad (W_1 + W_2)^0 \subseteq W_2^0 \quad \text{...(iii)}$$

By using Eqs. (ii) and (iii), we get

$$(W_1 + W_2)^0 \subseteq W_1^0 \cap W_2^0 \quad \text{...(iv)}$$

By using Eqs. (i) and (iv), we have

$$(W_1 + W_2)^0 = W_1^0 \cap W_2^0$$

**(ii)** Now, we use the result (i) proved above for the vector space $V^*$ in place of vector space $V$.

Therefore, replacing $W_1$ by $W_1^0$ and $W_2$ by $W_2^0$ in Eq. (i),

we get

$$(W_1^0 + W_2^0)^0 = W_1^{00} \cap W_2^{00}$$

$$\Rightarrow \quad (W_1^0 + W_2^0)^0 = W_1 \cap W_2 \qquad (\because W_1^{00} = W_1 \text{ etc.})$$

$$\Rightarrow \quad (W_1^0 + W_2^0)^{00} = (W_1 \cap W_2)^0$$

$$\Rightarrow \quad W_1^0 + W_2^0 = (W_1 \cap W_2)^0$$

# Minimal Polynomial and Minimal Equation of a Linear Operator or of a Matrix

## Annihilating Polynomials

Let us consider a linear operator $T$ on a finite dimensional vector space over the field $F$ and $p(x)$ is a polynomial over $F$. If $F(T) = \hat{0}$, then we can say that polynomial $p(x)$ annihilates the linear operator $T$. Again, suppose $M$ is a square matrix of order $n$ over the field $F$ and $p(x)$ is a polynomial over $F$. If $p(M) = 0$, then we can say that the polynomial $p(x)$ annihilates the matrix $M$. We also know that every linear operator $T$ on an $n$-dimensional vector space $V(F)$ satisfies it characteristic equation. Also, the characteristic polynomial of $T$ is a non-zero polynomial means, a polynomial in which the coefficients of various terms are not all zero.

> ***Note*** If $M$ is the matrix of $T$ in some ordered basis, then the characteristic polynomial of $T$ is given by $|M-xI|$ in which the coefficient of $x^n$ is $(-1)^n$ which is not zero. We observe that atleast the characteristic polynomial of $T$ is a non-zero polynomial which annihilates $T$. Hence, the set of those non-zero polynomials which annihilates $T$ is not empty.

## Monic Polynomial

A polynomial in $x$ over a field $F$ is called a monic polynomial if the coefficient of the highest power of $x$ in it is unity .

For e.g., $x^4 - 2x^3 + 3x^2 + \frac{5}{6}x + 7$ is a monic polynomial of degree 3 over the field of rational numbers.

## Minimal Polynomial of a Linear Operator

Let $T$ is a linear operator on an $n$-dimensional vector space $V(F)$. The monic polynomial of lowest degree over the field $F$ that annihilates $T$ is called the minimal polynomial of $T$. Also, if $f(x)$ is the minimal polynomial of $T$, the equation $f(x)=0$ is called the minimal equation of the linear operator $T$.

In the same way we may define the minimal polynomial of a matrix. Let $A$ be the square matrix of order $n$ over the field $F$. The monic polynomial of lowest degree over the field $F$ that annihilates $A$ is called the minimal polynomial of $A$.

## Important Results on Minimal Polynomial of Linear Transformation

1. The minimal polynomial of a linear operator or a matrix is unique.
2. Suppose $T$ be a linear operator on an $n$-dimensional vector space $V$ [or suppose $M$ be an $n\times n$ matrix]. The characteristic and minimal polynomials for $T$ [ for $M$] have the same roots, except for multiplicities.
3. The minimal polynomial of a linear operator or a matrix is a divisor of every polynomial that annihilates the linear operator or matrix.
4. The minimal polynomial of a matrix is a divisor of the characteristic polynomial of that matrix.
5. Suppose, $T$ is a diagonalizable linear operator and suppose $c_1, c_2, \dots, c_m$ be the distinct characteristic values of $T$. Then, the minimal polynomial for $T$ is the polynomial.
$$p(x) = (x-c_1)\ (x-c_2), \dots, (x-c_m)$$
6. If the roots of the characteristic equation of a linear operator $T$ are all distinct, $c_1, c_2, c_3, \dots, c_t$, then the minimal polynomial for $T$ is the polynomial
$$p(x) = (x-c_1)\ (x-c_2), \dots, (x-c_t)$$

***Example 13.*** *Find the minimal polynomial for the real matrix.*

$$A = \begin{bmatrix} 7 & 4 & -1 \\ 4 & 7 & -1 \\ -4 & -4 & 4 \end{bmatrix}$$

**Solution.** We know that the characteristic polynomial of $T$ is given by $|A-xI|$

$$\therefore \quad |A-xI| = \begin{vmatrix} 7-x & 4 & -1 \\ 4 & 7-x & -1 \\ -4 & -4 & 4-x \end{vmatrix} \text{ by } R_3 \to R_3 + R_2$$

$$= \begin{vmatrix} 7-x & 4 & -1 \\ 4 & 7-x & -1 \\ 0 & 3-x & 3-x \end{vmatrix}$$

$$= (3-x)\begin{vmatrix} 7-x & 4 & -1 \\ 4 & 7-x & -1 \\ 0 & 1 & 1 \end{vmatrix} \text{ by } C_3 \to C_3 - C_2$$

$$= (3-x)\begin{vmatrix} 7-x & 4 & -5 \\ 4 & 7-x & x-8 \\ 0 & 1 & 0 \end{vmatrix}$$

Now, expanding along third row.

$$= (3-x)\,[0\,\{4(x-8)+5\} - 1\{(7-x)(x-8)+20\} + 0\,\{(7-x)^2-16\}]$$
$$= -(3-x)\,[(7-x)(x-8)+20]$$
$$= -(3-x)\,[7x-56-x^2+8x+20]$$
$$= -(3-x)\,[-x^2+15x-36]$$
$$= +(3-x)\,[x^2-15x+36]$$
$$= -(3-x)^2(x-12)$$

$\therefore$ Roots of the equation $|A-xI|=0$ are 3, 3, 12, these are characteristic roots of the matrix $A$.

Now, we find the minimal polynomial of $A$. As we know that characteristic root of $A$ is also a root of its minimal polynomial.

Therefore, if $m(x)$ is the minimal polynomial for $A$ then $(x-3)$ and $(x-12)$ are factors of $m(x)$. Now, we test whether the polynomial

$$p(x) = (x-3)(x-12) = x^2 - 15x + 36$$

annihilates $A$ or not

$$A^2 = \begin{bmatrix} 69 & 60 & -15 \\ 60 & 69 & -15 \\ -60 & -60 & 24 \end{bmatrix}$$

$$\therefore\ A^2-15A+36I=\begin{bmatrix}69 & 60 & -15\\ 60 & 69 & -15\\ -60 & -60 & 24\end{bmatrix}-15\begin{bmatrix}7 & 4 & -1\\ 4 & 7 & -1\\ -4 & -4 & 4\end{bmatrix}+\begin{bmatrix}36 & 0 & 0\\ 0 & 36 & 0\\ 0 & 0 & 36\end{bmatrix}$$

$$=\begin{bmatrix}105 & 60 & -15\\ 60 & 105 & -15\\ -60 & -60 & 60\end{bmatrix}-\begin{bmatrix}105 & 60 & -15\\ 60 & 105 & -15\\ -60 & -60 & 60\end{bmatrix}=0$$

Therefore, $p(x)$ annihilates $A$. Thus, $p(x)$ is the monic polynomial of lowest degree which annihilates $A$.

Therefore, $p(x)$ is the minimal polynomial for $A$.

***Example 14.*** *Prove that the similar matrices have the same minimal polynomial.*

**Solution.** Suppose, $M$ and $N$ are two similar matrices, then $\exists$ a non- singular matrix $P$ s.t.

$$N=P^{-1}MP$$

Now, we shall show that the matrices $M$ and $P^{-1}MP$ have the same monic polynomial. Firstly, we prove that a monic polynomial $f(x)$ annihilates $A$ iff it annihilates $P^{-1}MP$. Now, we have

$$(P^{-1}MP)^2=P^{-1}MP\,P^{-1}MP=P^{-1}M^2P$$

Similarly, we can prove that

$$(P^{-1}MP)^m=P^{-1}M^mP$$

where $m$ is any positive integer.

Suppose, $\quad f(x)=x^r+a_1x^{r-1}+\ldots+a_{r-1}x+a_r$

$\Rightarrow\quad f(M)=M^r+a_1M^{r-1}+\ldots+a_{r-1}M+a_rI$

and $\quad f(P^{-1}MP)=(P^{-1}MP)^r+\ldots+a_{r-1}(P^{-1}MP)+a_rI$

$$=P^{-1}M^rP+\ldots+a_{r-1}(P^{-1}MP)+a_rP^{-1}P$$

$$=P^{-1}(M^r+\ldots+a_{r-1}M+a_rI)\,P$$

$$=P^{-1}f(M)\,P$$

$\because$ $P$ is non-singular. So that

$$P^{-1}f(M)P=0\ \text{ iff }\ f(M)=0$$

$\Rightarrow$ $f(x)$ annihilates $M$ iff it annihilates $P^{-1}MP$.

$\therefore$ If $f(x)$ is the polynomial of lowest degree that annihilates $P^{-1}MP$, then it annihilates $M$ and conversely. Therefore, $M$ and $P^{-1}MP$ have the same minimal polynomial.

## Cayley-Hamilton Theorem

Let $T$ be a linear operator on $n$-dimensional vector space $V(F)$, then $T$ satisfies its characteristic equations.

## Diagonalizable Operators

Let $T$ be a linear operator on the finite dimensional vector space $V$. Then, $T$ is said to be diagonalizable if there is a basis $B$ for $V$ each vector of which is a characteristic vector of $T$.

## Matrix of a Diagonalizable Operator

Let $T$ be a diagonalizable operator on an $n$-dimensional vector space $V$. Let $B=\{\alpha_1,\alpha_2,\ldots,\alpha_n\}$ be an ordered bases for $V$ s.t. each $\alpha_j$ is a characteristic vector of $T$. Let $T\alpha_i=C_i\alpha_i$. Then,

$$T\alpha_1=C_1\alpha_1=C_1\alpha_1+0\,\alpha_2+\ldots+0\,\alpha_n$$
$$T\alpha_2=C_2\alpha_2=0\,\alpha_1+C_2\,\alpha_2+\ldots+0\,\alpha_n$$
$$\ldots\quad\ldots\quad\ldots\quad\ldots$$
$$\ldots\quad\ldots\quad\ldots\quad\ldots$$
$$T\alpha_n=C_n\alpha_n=0\,\alpha_1+0\,\alpha_2+\ldots+0\,\alpha_{n-1}+C_n\alpha_n$$

$\therefore$ The matrix of $T$ relative to $B$ is

$$[T]_B=\begin{bmatrix}C_1 & 0 & \ldots & 0\\ 0 & C_2 & \ldots & 0\\ \ldots & \ldots & \ldots & \ldots\\ 0 & 0 & \ldots & C_n\end{bmatrix}$$

This matrix is a diagonal matrix.

***Theorem*** **A linear operator $T$ on an $n$-dimensional vector space $V(F)$ is diagonalizable iff its matrix $A$ relative to any ordered basis $B$ of $V$ is diagonalizable.**

***Example 15.*** *Suppose, $T$ be a linear operator on a finite dimensional vector space $V$ and let $\lambda$ be a characteristic value of $T$. Show that the characteristic space of $\lambda$ i.e., $W_\lambda$ invariant under $T$.*

**Solution.** We know that $W_\lambda=\{\alpha\in V:\ T_\alpha=\lambda_\alpha\}$

Let $\alpha\in W_\lambda$.

Then, $\quad T_\alpha=\lambda_\alpha$

$\because$ $W_c$ is a subspace,

$\therefore$ $\quad\lambda\in F$ and $\alpha\in W_\lambda\Rightarrow\lambda_\alpha\in W_\lambda$

$\therefore$ $\quad\alpha\in W_\lambda\Rightarrow T_\alpha\in W_\lambda$

Hence, $W_\lambda$ is invariant under $T$.

***Example 16.*** *If $T$ be a linear operator on a finite dimensional vector space $V$ and $\lambda$ be a characteristic value of $T$, then prove that the characteristic space of $\lambda$ i.e., $W_\lambda$ is the null space of the operator $T-\lambda I$.*

**Solution.** Suppose, $\alpha\in W_\lambda\Rightarrow(T-\lambda I)\alpha=0$

$\Rightarrow\quad\alpha\in$ null space of $T-\lambda I$

Let $\alpha\in$ the null space $T-\lambda I$, then $(T-\lambda I)\alpha=0\Rightarrow T\alpha=\lambda\alpha$

$\Rightarrow\quad\alpha\in W_\lambda$

Hence, $W_\lambda=$ The nullspace of $T-\lambda I$.

# SOLVED EXAMPLES

## Type I (*Only one correct option*)

***Example 1.** Let $T : R^2 \to R^3$ be a linear transformation given by*

$$T(x_1, x_2) = (x_1 + x_2, x_1 - x_2, x_2)$$

*Then, Rank T is*

(a) 0 (b) 1 (c) 2 (d) 3

**Solution.** (c) Let $(x_1, x_2) \in \ker T$

$$\begin{aligned}
\Rightarrow \quad & T(x_1, x_2) = (0, 0, 0) \\
\Rightarrow \quad & (x_1 + x_2, x_1 - x_2, x_2) = (0, 0, 0) \\
\Rightarrow \quad & x_1 + x_2 = 0, x_1 - x_2 = 0, x_2 = 0 \\
\Rightarrow \quad & x_1 = x_2 = 0 \\
\therefore \quad & \ker T = \{(0, 0)\} \\
\therefore \quad & \text{Nullity } T = \dim(\ker T) = 0 \\
\therefore \quad & \text{Rank } T = \dim(R^2) - \text{Nullity } T \\
& = 2 - 0 = 2
\end{aligned}$$

***Example 2.** The linear transformation $T : R^3 \to R^4$ whose image is generated by $\{(1, 2, 0, -4), (2, 0, -1, -3)\}$ is*

(a) $T(x, y, z) = (x - 2y, x, -y, -4x - 3y)$
(b) $T(x, y, z) = (x - 2y, -x, y, -4x - 3y)$
(c) $T(x, y, z) = (x + 2y, -x, y, 4x + 3y)$
(d) $T(x, y, z) = (x + 2y, 2x, -y, -4x - 3y)$

**Solution.** (d) Since, $\{e_1 = (1, 0, 0), e_2 = (0, 1, 0), e_3 = (0, 0, 1)\}$ is a usual basis of $R_3$.

Define the map $T : \{e_1, e_2, e_3\} \to R^4$ as follows

$$T(1, 0, 0) = (1, 2, 0, -4)$$
$$T(0, 1, 0) = (2, 0, -1, -3)$$

and

$$T(0, 0, 1) = (0, 0, 0, 0)$$

Now, such linear transformation $T$ exists and is unique.

$$\begin{aligned}
T(x, y, z) &= T(x(1, 0, 0) + y(0, 1, 0) + z(0, 0, 1)) \\
&= xT(1, 0, 0) + yT(0, 1, 0) + zT(0, 0, 1) \\
&= x(1, 2, 0, 4) + y(2, 0, -1, -3) + z(0, 0, 0, 0) \\
&= (x + 2y, 2x, -y, -4x - 3y)
\end{aligned}$$

which is required linear transformation.

***Example 3.** If V and U be vector spaces of dimension 4 and 6, respectively. Then, $\dim \hom(V, U)$ is*

(a) 4 (b) 6 (c) 10 (d) 24

**Solution.** (d) We have

$$\dim(V, U) = \dim V \cdot \dim U = 4.6 = 24$$

***Example 4.** Let T and S be linear transformations on a finite dimensional vector space V, where S is non-singular. Then,*

(a) rank $(ST)$ = rank $(TS)$ = rank $T$
(b) rank $(ST) \neq$ rank $(TS)$ = rank $T$
(c) rank $(ST)$ = rank $(TS) \neq$ rank $T$
(d) rank $(ST) \neq$ rank $(TS) \neq$ rank $T$

**Solution.** (a) Since, $\text{Im}(ST) = (ST)(V) = S(T(V))$

$$\Rightarrow \quad \text{Rank } (ST) = \dim(S(T(V)))$$

Now, consider the linear map $S : T(V) \to V$, where $S$ is non-singular.

Then,

$$\begin{aligned}
& \text{Rank } S = \dim(T(V)) \\
\Rightarrow \quad & \dim S(T(V)) = \dim T(V) \\
\Rightarrow \quad & \text{Rank } (ST) = \dim T(V) \\
& = \text{Rank } T \quad \text{...(i)}
\end{aligned}$$

Again, $S : V \to V$ is non-singular

$\Rightarrow$ $S : V \to V$ is injective

$\Rightarrow$ $S : V \to V$ is surjective ($\because$ $V$ is finite dimensional)

Hence, $S(V) = V$

$$\begin{aligned}
\Rightarrow \quad & T(S(V)) = T(V) \\
\Rightarrow \quad & (TS)(V) = T(V) \\
\therefore \quad & \dim \text{Im}(TS) = \dim T(V) \\
\Rightarrow \quad & \text{Rank } (TS) = \text{Rank } T \quad \text{...(ii)}
\end{aligned}$$

Hence, from Eqs. (i) and (ii), we have

$$\text{Rank } (ST) = \text{Rank } (TS) = \text{Rank } T$$

***Example 5.** Let T be a linear transformation on V such that*

$$T^3 - T^2 - T + I = 0$$

*Then, $T^{-1}$ is*

(a) $I - T - T^2$ (b) $I + T - T^2$
(c) $I + T + T^2$ (d) None of these

**Solution.** (b) We have,

$$\begin{aligned}
& T^3 - T^2 - T + I = 0 \\
\Rightarrow \quad & I = T + T^2 - T^3 \\
& = T(I + T - T^2) \quad \text{...(i)}
\end{aligned}$$

Now,

$$(I + T - T^2)T = T + T^2 - T^3 = I \quad \text{...(ii)}$$

From Eqs. (i) and (ii), we have

$$T^{-1} = I + T - T^2$$

***Example 6.** Let $\phi$ be the linear functional on $R^2$ defined by $\phi(x, y) = x - 2y$. Then, the transpose of the linear transformation T on $R^2$ given by*

$$T(x, y) = (2x - 3y, 5x + 2y)$$

*is*

(a) $-8x - 7y$ (b) $8x - 7y$
(c) $8x + 7y$ (d) None of these

**Solution.** (a)

$$(T^t(\phi))(x,y) = \phi(T(x,y))$$
$$= \phi(2x-3y, 5x+2y)$$
$$= 2x-3y-2(5x+2y)$$
$$= -8x-7y$$

***Example 7.*** *Let T be a linear transformation on $R^3$ given by*

$$T(x,y,z) = (a_1x + a_2y + a_3z, b_1x + b_2y + b_3z, c_1x + c_2y + c_3z)$$

*Then, the matrix of T relative to the usual basis of $R^3$ is*

(a) $\begin{bmatrix} a_1 & a_2 & a_3 \\ b_1 & b_2 & b_3 \\ c_1 & c_2 & c_3 \end{bmatrix}$ (b) $\begin{bmatrix} a_1 & b_1 & c_1 \\ a_2 & b_2 & c_2 \\ a_3 & b_3 & c_3 \end{bmatrix}$

(c) $\begin{bmatrix} a_1 & b_1 & b_2 \\ c_1 & a_2 & b_3 \\ c_2 & c_3 & a_3 \end{bmatrix}$ (d) None of these

**Solution.** (a) We have,

$$T(1,0,0) = (a_1, b_1, c_1)$$
$$= a_1(1,0,0) + b_1(0,1,0) + c_1(0,0,1)$$
$$T(0,1,0) = (a_2, b_2, c_2)$$
$$= a_2(1,0,0) + b_2(0,1,0) + c_2(0,0,1)$$
$$T(0,0,1) = (a_3, b_3, c_3)$$
$$= a_3(1,0,0) + b_3(0,1,0) + c_3(0,0,1)$$

Hence, the required matrix is

$$\begin{bmatrix} a_1 & a_2 & a_3 \\ b_1 & b_2 & b_3 \\ c_1 & c_2 & c_3 \end{bmatrix}$$

***Example 8.*** *Let V be the vector space of polynomials in x over the field F of degree ≤ 3 and $\{1, x, x^2, x^3\}$ is a basis of V. Then, the matrix of differentiation transformation $D: V \to V$ relative to the basis $\{1, x, x^2, x^3\}$ is*

(a) $\begin{bmatrix} 1 & 0 & 0 & 0 \\ 0 & 1 & 0 & 0 \\ 0 & 0 & 1 & 0 \\ 0 & 0 & 0 & 1 \end{bmatrix}$ (b) $\begin{bmatrix} 0 & 0 & 0 & 1 \\ 0 & 0 & 1 & 0 \\ 0 & 1 & 0 & 0 \\ 1 & 0 & 0 & 0 \end{bmatrix}$

(c) $\begin{bmatrix} 0 & 1 & 0 & 0 \\ 0 & 0 & 2 & 0 \\ 0 & 0 & 0 & 3 \\ 0 & 0 & 0 & 0 \end{bmatrix}$ (d) None of these

**Solution.** (c) We have,

$$D(1) = 0 = 0\cdot 1 + 0\cdot x + 0\cdot x^2 + 0\cdot x^3$$
$$D(x) = 1 = 1\cdot 1 + 0\cdot x + 0\cdot x^2 + 0\cdot x^3$$
$$D(x^2) = 2x = 0\cdot 1 + 2\cdot x + 0\cdot x^2 + 0\cdot x^3$$
$$D(x^3) = 3x = 0\cdot 1 + 3\cdot x + 0\cdot x^2 + 0\cdot x^3$$

Hence, the required matrix is

$$\begin{bmatrix} 0 & 1 & 0 & 0 \\ 0 & 0 & 2 & 0 \\ 0 & 0 & 0 & 3 \\ 0 & 0 & 0 & 0 \end{bmatrix}$$

***Example 9.*** *The linear map whose matrix with respect to usual basis is*

$$\begin{bmatrix} 0 & 0 & 1 & 0 \\ 0 & 1 & 0 & 0 \\ 1 & 0 & 0 & 0 \\ 0 & 0 & 0 & 1 \end{bmatrix}$$

*is*

(a) $T(x,y,z,w) = (z,y,x,w)$

(b) $T(x,y,z,w) = (0,x,w,y)$

(c) $T(x,y,z,w) = (x-y,0,y,w)$

(d) None of the above

**Solution.** (a) Let $T: F^4 \to F^4$ be linear map. Then,

$$T(1,0,0,0) = (0,0,1,0)$$
$$T(0,1,0,0) = (0,1,0,0)$$
$$T(0,0,1,0) = (1,0,0,0)$$
$$T(0,0,0,1) = (0,0,0,1)$$

$\Rightarrow$ If $(x,y,z,w) \in F^4$, then

$$T(x,y,z,w) = xT(1,0,0,0) + yT(0,1,0,0) + zT(0,0,1,0) + wT(0,0,0,1)$$
$$= x(0,0,1,0) + y(0,1,0,0) + z(1,0,0,0) + w(0,0,0,1)$$

$\Rightarrow$ $T(x,y,z,w) = (z,y,x,w)$

Which is required linear transformation.

***Example 10.*** *Let V be a vector space of all polynomial of degree ≤ 3. Then, the transition matrix from $\{1, x, x^2, x^3\}$ to $\{x^3, x^2, x, 1\}$ is*

(a) $\begin{bmatrix} 0 & 0 & 0 & 1 \\ 0 & 0 & 1 & 0 \\ 0 & 1 & 0 & 0 \\ 1 & 0 & 0 & 0 \end{bmatrix}$ (b) $\begin{bmatrix} 0 & 0 & 1 & 0 \\ 0 & 0 & 0 & 1 \\ 1 & 0 & 0 & 0 \\ 0 & 1 & 0 & 0 \end{bmatrix}$

(c) $\begin{bmatrix} 1 & 1 & 0 & 0 \\ 0 & 1 & 1 & 0 \\ 0 & 0 & 1 & 1 \\ 1 & 0 & 0 & 1 \end{bmatrix}$ (d) None of these

**Solution.** (a) We have,

$$x^3 = 0\cdot 1 + 0\cdot x + 0\cdot x^2 + 1\cdot x^3$$
$$x^2 = 0\cdot 1 + 0\cdot x + 1\cdot x^2 + 0\cdot x^3$$
$$x = 0\cdot 1 + 1\cdot x + 0\cdot x^2 + 0\cdot x^3$$
$$1 = 1\cdot 1 + 0\cdot x + 0\cdot x^2 + 0\cdot x^3$$

Hence, the transition matrix from $\{1, x, x^2, x^3\}$ to $\{x^3, x^2, x, 1\}$ is

$$\begin{bmatrix} 0 & 0 & 0 & 1 \\ 0 & 0 & 1 & 0 \\ 0 & 1 & 0 & 0 \\ 1 & 0 & 0 & 0 \end{bmatrix}$$

***Example 11.*** *Let $V = \{f(x) \in R[x] \mid \deg f(x) \le 1\}$ where R is field of real numbers. Define*

*$e_1^*, e_2^* : V \to R$ by*

$$e_1^*[f(x)] = \int_0^1 f(x)dx \text{ and } e_2^*[f(x)] = \int_0^2 f(x)dx$$

*Then, the basis of V whose dual basis is $\{e_1^*, e_2^*\}$ is*

(a) $\{1+x, 1-x\}$ (b) $\left\{2-2x, -\frac{1}{2}+x\right\}$

(c) $\left\{2+2x, \frac{1}{2}-x\right\}$ (d) $\left\{\frac{1-x}{2}, \frac{1+x}{2}\right\}$

**Solution.** (b) Let $\{e_1, e_2\}$ be the required basis of V given by

$$e_1 = a_1 + b_1x, e_2 = a_2 + b_2x$$

Then, $1 = e_1^*(e_1) = \int_0^1 (a_1 + b_1x)dx = a_1 + \frac{1}{2}b_1$

$$0 = e_1^*(e_2) = \int_0^1 (a_2 + b_2x)dx = a_2 + \frac{1}{2}b_2$$

$$0 = e_2^*(e_1) = \int_0^2 (a_1 + b_1x)dx = 2a_1 + 2b_1$$

$$1 = e_2^*(e_2) = \int_0^2 (a_2 + b_2x)dx = 2a_2 + 2b_2$$

On solving, we get

$$a_1 + \frac{1}{2}b_1 = 0 \text{ and } a_2 + \frac{1}{2}b_2 = 0$$

$$2a_1 + 2b_1 = 0 \qquad 2a_2 + 2b_2 = 1$$

$\Rightarrow$ $a_1 = 2$ and $a_2 = -\frac{1}{2}$

$$b_1 = -2 \qquad b_2 = 1$$

Hence, $\left\{2-2x, -\frac{1}{2}+x\right\}$ is the required basis of V whose dual basis is $\{e_1^*, e_2^*\}$.

***Example 12.*** *The dual of the basis*

$\{e_1 = (1, -1, 3), e_2 = (0, 1, -1), e_3 = (0, 3, -2)\}$ *of $R^3$ is*

(a) $(x, 7x-2y-3z, 2x-y-z)$

(b) $(x, 7x-2y-3z, -2x+y-z)$

(c) $(x, 7x+2y+3z, -2x+y+z)$

(d) $(x, 7x+2y-3z, 2x-y-z)$

**Solution.** (b) Let $(e_1^*, e_2^*, e_3^*)$ be dual basis given by

$$e_1^*(x, y, z) = a_1x + a_2y + a_3z$$
$$e_2^*(x, y, z) = b_1x + b_2y + b_3z$$
$$e_3^*(x, y, z) = c_1x + c_2y + c_3z$$

where $a_i, b_i, c_i \in R$ are to be determined which will make $\{e_1^*, e_2^*, e_3^*\}$ a basis of $(R^3)^*$

Now,

$$1 = e_1^*(e_1) = e_1^*(1, -1, 3) = a_1 - a_2 + 3a_3$$
$$0 = e_1^*(e_2) = e_1^*(0, 1, -1) = a_2 - a_3$$
$$0 = e_1^*(e_3) = e_1^*(0, 3, -2) = 3a_2 - 2a_3$$

On solving, we get

$$a_1 = 1, a_2 = 0, a_3 = 0$$

$\therefore$ $e_1^*(x, y, z) = 1\cdot x + 0\cdot y + 0\cdot z = x$

Similarly,

$$e_2^*(x, y, z) = 7x - 2y - 3z$$

and

$$e_3^*(x, y, z) = -2x + y - z$$

Hence, the required dual basis is $(x, 7x-2y-3z, -2x+y-z)$

***Example 13.*** *The number of all non-singular linear transformation $T : R^4 \to R^3$ is*

(a) 0 (b) 1 (c) 3 (d) 4

**Solution.** (a) Since, T is non-singular.

Hence, Rank $T = \dim R^4$

or $\dim T(R^4) = 4$

But $T(R^4)$ is a subspace of $R^3$.

$\Rightarrow$ $\dim T(R^4) \le 3$

Hence, there exists no non-singular linear transformation $T : R^4 \to R^3$.

## Type II (*One or more than one correct option*)

***Example 14.*** *Let $T : F[x] \to F[x]$ be a map. Then, which of the following(s) is/are linear transformation?*

(a) $T(f(x)) = -f(x)$ (b) $T(f(x)) = f(-x)$

(c) $T(f(x)) = f(0)$ (d) $T(f(x)) = f(x) + f(-x)$

**Solution.** (a), (b), (c), (d)

Let $f(x), g(x) \in F[x]$ and $\alpha, \beta \in F$, then

(a) We have,

$$\begin{aligned} T(\alpha f(x) + \beta g(x)) &= -[\alpha f(x) + \beta g(x)] \\ &= -\alpha f(x) - \beta g(x) \\ &= \alpha(-f(x)) + \beta(-g(x)) \\ &= \alpha T(f(x)) + \beta T(g(x)) \end{aligned}$$

$[\because T(f(x)) = -f(x) \text{ and } T(g(x)) = -g(x)]$

Hence, T is linear transformation.

(b) We have,

$$\begin{aligned} T(\alpha f(x) + \beta g(x)) &= T((\alpha f + \beta g)(x)) \\ &= (\alpha f + \beta g)(-x) \\ &= \alpha f(-x) + \beta g(-x) \\ &= \alpha T(f(x)) + \beta(T(g(x))) \end{aligned}$$

$[\because T(f(x)) = f(-x); T(g(x)) = g(-x)]$

Hence, T is linear transformation.

(c) We have,

$$\begin{aligned} T(\alpha f(x) + \beta g(x)) &= T((\alpha f + \beta g)(x)) \\ &= (\alpha f + \beta g)(0) \\ &= \alpha f(0) + \beta g(0) \\ &= \alpha T(f(x)) + \beta T(g(x)) \end{aligned}$$

$[\because T(f(x)) = f(0), T(g(x)) = g(0)]$

Hence, T is linear transformation.

(d) We have,

$$T(\alpha f(x)+\beta g(x)) = T((\alpha f+\beta g)(x))$$
$$= (\alpha f+\beta g)(x)+(\alpha f+\beta g)(-x)$$
$$= \alpha[f(x)+f(-x)]+\beta[g(x)+g(-x)]$$
$$= \alpha T(f(x))+\beta T(g(x))$$
$$[\because T(f(x)) = f(x)+f(-x), T(g(x)) = g(x)+g(-x)]$$

Hence, $T$ is linear transformation.

***Example 15.*** *Let $T:\mathbb{R}^2\to\mathbb{R}^2$ be a map, then which of the following(s) is/are linear transformation?*

(a) $T(x_1, x_2) = (x_1^2, x_2)$ (b) $T(x_1, x_2) = (x_2, x_1)$

(c) $T(x_1, x_2) = (x_1 - x_2, 0)$ (d) None of these

**Solution.** (b), (c)

Let $(x_1, x_2), (y_1, y_2) \in \mathbb{R}^2$ and $\alpha, \beta \in \mathbb{R}$. Then,

(a) $T[\alpha(x_1, x_2)+\beta(y_1, y_2)] = T(\alpha x_1+\beta y_1, \alpha x_2+\beta y_2)$
$$= ((\alpha x_1+\beta y_1)^2, \alpha x_2+\beta y_2) \quad \text{...(i)}$$

Now,

$$\alpha T(x_1, x_2)+\beta T(y_1, y_2) = \alpha(x_1^2, x_2)+(y_1^2, y_2)$$
$$= (\alpha x_1^2+\beta y_1^2, \alpha x_2+\beta y_2) \quad \text{...(ii)}$$

From Eqs. (i) and (ii), we get

$$T[\alpha(x_1, x_2)+\beta(y_1, y_2)] \neq T[\alpha(x_1, x_2)+\beta(y_1, y_2)]$$

Hence, $T$ is not linear transformation.

(b) $T[\alpha(x_1, x_2)+\beta(y_1, y_2)] = T(\alpha x_1+\beta y_1, \alpha x_2+\beta y_2)$
$$= (\alpha x_2+\beta y_2, \alpha x_1+\beta y_1)$$
$$= \alpha(x_2, x_1)+\beta(y_2, y_1)$$
$$= \alpha T(x_1, x_2)+\beta T(y_1, y_2)$$
$$[\because T(x_1, x_2) = (x_2, x_1), T(y_1, y_2) = (y_2, y_1)]$$

Hence, $T$ is linear transformation.

(c) $T[\alpha(x_1, x_2)+\beta(y_1, y_2)] = T(\alpha x_1+\beta y_1, \alpha x_2+\beta y_2)$
$$= ((\alpha x_1+\beta y_1)-(\alpha x_2+\beta y_2), 0)$$
$$= (\alpha(x_1-x_2)+\beta(y_1-y_2), 0)$$
$$= \alpha T(x_1, x_2)+\beta T(y_1, y_2)$$
$$[\because T(x_1, x_2) = (x_1-x_2, 0), T(y_1, y_2) = (y_1-y_2), 0]$$

Hence, $T$ is linear transformation.

***Example 16.*** *Let $V$ be a finite dimensional vector space. Then,*

(a) for the identity linear map $I: V\to V$, Rank $I = \dim V$ and Nullity $I = 0$

(b) for the zero linear map $O: V\to W$, Rank $O = 0$, and Nullity $O = \dim V$

(c) Either (a) or (b) is true

(d) Neither (a) nor (b) is true

**Solution.** (a), (b)

(a) We have,

$$I: V\to V \text{ given by}$$
$$I(x) = x, \forall x\in V$$

where $V$ is finite dimensional vector space.

Then,

$$\ker T = \{x\in V: T(x) = 0\}$$
$$= \{x\in V: x = 0\} = \{0\}$$

Hence,

$$\text{Nullity } I = 0$$
$$\Rightarrow \quad \text{Rank } I = \dim V - \text{Nullity } I$$
$$= \dim V$$

(b) We have, $O: V\to V$ given by

$$O(x) = 0, \forall x\in V$$

where $V$ is finite dimensional vector space.

Then,

$$\ker O = \{x\in V: O(x) = 0\}$$
$$= V$$

$\therefore$ Nullity $O = \dim V$

$\Rightarrow$ Rank $O = \dim V - \text{Nullity } O$
$$= \dim V - \dim V$$
$$= 0-0$$
$$= 0$$

***Example 17.*** *Let $T: V\to W$ be a linear transformation, where $V$ is finite dimensional. Let $B$ be a subspace of $W$. Then,*

(a) $T^{-1}(B)$ is a subspace of $V$

(b) $T^{-1}(B)$ is not a subspace of $V$

(c) $\dim T^{-1}(B) \geq \dim(\ker T)$

(d) $\dim T^{-1}(B) \leq \dim(\ker T)$

**Solution.** (a), (c)

Since, $T(0) = 0$, so $T^{-1}(B) \neq \phi$

Let $x_1, x_2 \in T^{-1}(B)$

$\Rightarrow$ $T(x_1)\in B, T(x_2)\in B$

$\Rightarrow$ $\alpha_1 T(x_1)+\alpha_2 T(x_2)\in B$, where $\alpha_1, \alpha_2 \in F$

(Since, $B$ is a subspace of $W$)

$\Rightarrow$ $T(\alpha_1 x_1+\alpha_2 x_2)\in B$ ($\because T$ is linear)

$\Rightarrow$ $\alpha_1 x_1+\alpha_2 x_2 \in T^{-1}(B)$

Hence, $T^{-1}(B)$ is a subspace of $V$.

Now, $x\in\ker T \Rightarrow T(x) = 0\in B$

$\Rightarrow x\in T^{-1}(B)$

So, $\ker T \subseteq T^{-1}(B)$

Hence,

$$\dim T^{-1}(B) \geq \dim(\ker T)$$

***Example 18.*** *Let $V$ and $U$ be vector spaces of the same dimension $n$. Let $T: V\to U$ be a linear map. Then,*

(a) $T$ is injective iff $\ker T = \{0\}$

(b) $T$ is injective iff $T$ is surjective

(c) Either (a) or (b) is true

(d) Neither (a) nor (b) is true

**Solution.** (a), (b)

Let $\ker T = \{0\}$

Then, $T(x) = T(y), x, y\in V$

$\Rightarrow$ $T(x)-T(y) = 0$

$\Rightarrow$ $T(x-y) = 0$

$\Rightarrow$ $x-y \in \ker T = \{0\}$

$\Rightarrow$ $x-y = 0$

$\Rightarrow \quad x = y$

Hence, $\quad T(x) = T(y) \Rightarrow x = y$

$\Rightarrow T$ is injective

Now, let $T$ be injective;

and $\quad x \in \ker T$

$\Rightarrow \quad T(x) = 0 = T(0)$

$\Rightarrow \quad x = 0 \quad (\because T \text{ is injective})$

$\therefore \quad \ker T = \{0\}$

Next, let $T$ is injective, then

$\ker T = \{0\}$

$\Rightarrow$ Nullity $T = 0$. Hence, Rank $T = \dim V = \dim U$

$\Rightarrow \quad \dim T(V) = \dim U$

$\Rightarrow \quad T(V) = U$

$\Rightarrow T$ is surjective.

Now, let $T$ be surjective,

Then, $\quad T(V) = U$

$\therefore \quad \dim T(V) = \dim U = \dim V$

$\therefore \quad$ Rank $T = \dim V$

$\Rightarrow$ Nullity $T = 0$

$\Rightarrow \quad \ker T = \{0\}$

$\Rightarrow T$ is injective.

***Example 19.*** *Let $V$ and $U$ be vector spaces of dimensions $m$ and $n$ respectively and $T : V \to U$ be a linear map. Then,*

(a) $m > n \Rightarrow T$ is not injective

(b) $m < n \Rightarrow T$ is not surjective

(c) $m = n \Rightarrow T$ is injective iff $T$ is surjective

(d) None of the above

**Solution.** (a), (b), (c)

We have,

$T(V) \subseteq U$

$\Rightarrow \quad \dim T(V) \le \dim U$

$\Rightarrow \quad$ Rank $T \le n < m$

$\Rightarrow \quad$ Nullity $T > 0$

$\Rightarrow \quad \ker T \ne \{0\}$

$\Rightarrow T$ is not injective.

Also, we know that

Rank $T \le m < n$

$\Rightarrow \quad \dim T(V) < \dim U$

$\Rightarrow \quad T(V) \subseteq U$

$\Rightarrow T$ is not surjective.

Next, let $T$ be injective, then

$\ker T = \{0\}$

$\Rightarrow \quad$ Nullity $T = 0$

$\Rightarrow \quad$ Rank $T = \dim V$

$= \dim U$

$\Rightarrow \quad \dim T(V) = \dim U$

$\Rightarrow \quad T(V) = U$

$\Rightarrow T$ is surjective.

Now, let $T$ be surjective;

$\Rightarrow \quad T(V) = U$

$\Rightarrow \quad \dim T(V) = \dim U = \dim V$

$\Rightarrow \quad$ Rank $T = \dim V$

$\Rightarrow \quad$ Nullity $T = 0$

$\Rightarrow \quad \ker T = \{0\}$

$\Rightarrow T$ is injective.

***Example 20.*** *Let $T : \mathbb{R}^4 \to \mathbb{R}^3$ be the linear map defined by*

$$T(x_1, x_2, x_3, x_4) = (x_1 - x_2 + x_3 + x_4, x_1 + 2x_3 - x_4, x_1 + x_2 + 3x_3 - 3x_4)$$

*Then,*

(a) $\dim(T(V)) = 1$

(b) $\dim(T(V)) = 2$

(c) $\{(2, 1, -1, 0), (1, 2, 0, 1)\}$ is basis of $\ker T$

(d) $\dim(\ker T) = 2$

**Solution.** (b), (c), (d)

Since,

$\{(1, 0, 0, 0), (0, 1, 0, 0), (0, 0, 1, 0), (0, 0, 0, 1)\}$ is a basis of $\mathbb{R}^1\mathbb{R}^4$.

Now,

$$T(1, 0, 0, 0) = (1, 1, 1)$$
$$T(0, 1, 0, 0) = (-1, 0, 1)$$
$$T(0, 0, 1, 0) = (1, 2, 3)$$
$$T(0, 0, 0, 1) = (1, -1, -3)$$

$\Rightarrow \quad \{(1, 1, 1), (-1, 0, 1), (1, 2, 3), (1, -1, -3)\}$

generates $T(V)$ and a basis of $T(V)$ will be the maximal subset of linearly independent vectors of the above generating set of $T(V)$ and this will be the maximal set of linearly independent rows of the matrix $A$ whose rows are generating vectors of $T(V)$ that is, it will be the row rank of the matrix.

$$A = \begin{bmatrix} 1 & 1 & 1 \\ -1 & 0 & 1 \\ 1 & 2 & 3 \\ 1 & -1 & -3 \end{bmatrix}$$

$$\sim \begin{bmatrix} 1 & 1 & 1 \\ 0 & 1 & 2 \\ 0 & 1 & 2 \\ 0 & -2 & -4 \end{bmatrix}$$

$$\sim \begin{bmatrix} 1 & 1 & 1 \\ 0 & 1 & 2 \\ 0 & 0 & 0 \\ 0 & 0 & 0 \end{bmatrix}$$

$\Rightarrow \quad$ Rank $A = 2 = \dim(T(V))$

Next, let $(x_1, x_2, x_3, x_4) \in \ker T$

$\Rightarrow \quad T(x_1, x_2, x_3, x_4) = (x_1 - x_2 + x_3 + x_4, x_1 + 2x_3 - x_4, x_1 + x_2 + 3x_3 - 3x_4)$

$= (0, 0, 0)$

$\Rightarrow \quad x_1 - x_2 + x_3 + x_4 = 0$

$x_1 + 2x_3 - x_4 = 0$

$x_1 + x_2 + 3x_3 - 3x_4 = 0$

which is a set of linear equations having two linearly independent solutions $(2,1,-1,0)$ and $(1,2,0,1)$ which will be a basis of ker $T$ and hence

$$\dim(\ker T) = 2$$

***Example 21.*** *Let $V, U, Z$ be finite dimensional vector spaces over the same field $F$ and let $T: V \to U$ and $S: U \to Z$ be linear maps. Then,*

(a) rank $ST$ cannot exceed rank $S$ or rank $T$
(b) rank $ST$ must exceed rank $S$ or rank $T$
(c) nullity $(ST) \geq$ nullity $T$
(d) nullity $(ST) \leq$ nullity $T$

**Solution.** (a), (c)

Since, $ST: V \to Z$ is a linear map.

Now, $T(V) \subseteq U$

$\Rightarrow$ $S(T(V)) \subseteq S(U)$

$\Rightarrow$ $(ST)(V) \subseteq S(U)$

Now, $(ST)(V)$ and $S(U)$ are both subspaces of $Z$.

$\Rightarrow$ $(ST)(V)$ is a subspace of $S(U)$.

$\Rightarrow$ $\dim(ST)(V) \leq \dim S(U)$

$\Rightarrow$ Rank $(ST) \leq$ Rank $S$

Again, $T(V)$ is subspace of $U$.

Hence, the restriction of $S$ to $T(V)$ may be considered as a linear map $S: T(V) \to Z$. Hence, we have

$\dim S(T(V)) \leq \dim T(V)$

$\Rightarrow$ $\dim(ST)(V) \leq \dim T(V)$

$\Rightarrow$ Rank $(ST) \leq$ Rank $T$

Next, let $x \in \ker T$

$\Rightarrow$ $T(x) = 0$

$\Rightarrow$ $S(T(x)) = S(0) = 0$

$\Rightarrow$ $(ST)(x) = 0$

$\Rightarrow$ $x \in \ker(ST)$

$\Rightarrow$ $\ker T \subseteq \ker(ST)$

Now, both ker $T$ and ker$(ST)$ are subspaces of $V$. Hence, ker $T$ is a subspace of ker$(ST)$.

$\Rightarrow$ $\dim(\ker T) \leq \dim \ker(ST)$

$\Rightarrow$ Nullity $T \leq$ Nullity $(ST)$

***Example 22.*** *Let $T: V \to U$ be a linear transformation. Then,*

(a) $T$ is non-singular $\Rightarrow$ image of a linearly independent set is linearly independent
(b) image of a linearly independent set is linearly independent $\Rightarrow T$ is non-singular
(c) either (a) or (b) is true
(d) Neither (a) nor (b) is true

**Solution.** (a), (b)

Let $T: V \to U$ be non-singular linear transformation and let $\{v_1, v_2, \ldots, v_n\}$ be a linearly independent set of $V$. Then,

$a_1T(v_1) + a_2T(v_2) + \ldots + a_nT(v_n) = 0$

$\Rightarrow$ $T(a_1v_1 + a_2v_2 + \ldots + a_nv_n) = 0$ ($\because T$ is linear transformation)

$\Rightarrow$ $a_1v_1 + a_2v_2 + \ldots + a_nv_n = 0$ ($\because \ker T = 0$)

$\Rightarrow$ $a_i = 0, \forall i$ ($\because \{v_1, v_2, \ldots, v_n\}$ is linear independent)

$\Rightarrow$ $\{T(v_1), T(v_2), \ldots, T(v_n)\}$ is linearly independent set.

Conversely suppose that image of a linearly independent set is linearly independent. Thus,

$\{v\}$ where $v \neq 0$ is linearly independent.

$\Rightarrow$ $\{T(v)\}$ is also linearly independent.

$\Rightarrow$ $T(v) \neq 0$

$\Rightarrow$ $v \neq 0 \Rightarrow T(v) \neq 0$

or $T(v) = 0 \Rightarrow v = 0$

$\Rightarrow$ $T$ is non-singular.

***Example 23.*** *If $T_1, T_2$ are invertible linear transformations on a vector space $V$, then*

(a) $T_2T_1$ is invertible and $(T_2T_1)^{-1} = T_1^{-1}T_2^{-1}$
(b) $\alpha(\neq 0) \in F, \alpha T_1$ is invertible and $(\alpha T_1)^{-1} = \alpha^{-1}T^{-1}$
(c) Either (a) or (b) is true
(d) Neither (a) nor (b) is true

**Solution.** (a), (b)

Since, $T_1$ and $T_2$ are invertible linear transformations. Hence, $T_1^{-1}$ and $T_2^{-1}$ exists.

Now, $(T_2T_1)(T_1^{-1}T_2^{-1}) = T_2(T_1T_1^{-1})T_2^{-1}$

$= (T_2I)T_2^{-1}$

$= I$

Again, $(T_1^{-1}T_2^{-1})(T_2T_1) = T_1^{-1}(T_2^{-1}T_2)T_1$

$= T^{-1}(IT_1) = I$

Hence, $T_2T_1$ is invertible and

$(T_2T_1)^{-1} = T_1^{-1}T_2^{-1}$

Next, $(\alpha T_1)(\alpha^{-1}T_1^{-1}) = \alpha(T_1\alpha^{-1})T_1^{-1}$

$= \alpha(\alpha^{-1}T_1)T_1^{-1}$

$= (\alpha\alpha^{-1})T_1T_1^{-1}$

$= I$

$\therefore$ $\alpha T_1$ is invertible and

$(\alpha T_1)^{-1} = \alpha^{-1}T_1^{-1}$

***Example 24.*** *Let $T$ be a linear transformation on a vector space $V$ such that*

$$T^2 - T + I = 0$$

*Then,*

(a) $T$ is singular
(b) $T$ is non-singular
(c) $T$ is invertible
(d) $T$ is not invertible

**Solution.** (b), (c)

We have,

$T^2 - T + I = 0$

$\Rightarrow$ $I = T - T^2 = T(I - T)$ ...(i)

Again, $(I - T)T = IT - T^2 = T - T^2 = I$ ...(ii)

From Eqs. (i) and (ii), we get

$T(I - T) = (I - T)T = I$

Hence, $T$ is invertible and

$$T^{-1} = I - T$$

Hence, $T$ is non-singular.

***Example 25.*** *Let $\mathbb{C}^2$ be a vector space over $\mathbb{C}$ the field of complex numbers. Let $T : \mathbb{C}^2 \to \mathbb{C}^2$ be a linear transformation defined by*

$$T(z_1, z_2) = (\alpha z_1 + \beta z_2, \gamma z_1 + \delta z_2)$$

*where $\alpha, \beta, \gamma, \delta$ are fixed scalar, then $T$ is non-singular, if*

(a) $\alpha\delta - \beta\gamma = 0$  (b) $\alpha\delta - \beta\gamma \neq 0$

(c) $\beta\gamma - a\delta = 0$  (d) $\beta\gamma - \alpha\delta \neq 0$

**Solution.** (b), (d)

Since, $T$ is non-singular;

$\Rightarrow$ $\ker T = \{0\}$

Now, let $z_1, z_2 \in \ker T$

$\Rightarrow$ $T(z_1, z_2) = (0, 0)$

$\Rightarrow$ $(\alpha z_1 + \beta z_2, \gamma z_1 + \delta z_2) = (0, 0)$

$\Rightarrow$ $\alpha z_1 + \beta z_2 = 0$

$\gamma z_1 + \delta z_2 = 0$

These equations will have non-zero solution $(z_1, z_2)$, if

$$\begin{vmatrix} \alpha & \beta \\ \gamma & \delta \end{vmatrix} \neq 0$$

$\Rightarrow$ $\alpha\delta - \beta\gamma \neq 0$

$\Rightarrow$ $\beta\gamma - \alpha\delta \neq 0$

***Example 26.*** *Let $T$ be a linear transformation on $R^3$ given by*

$$T(x, y, z) = (2x, 4x - y, 2x + 3y - z)$$

*Then,*

(a) *$T$ is singular*

(b) *$T$ is non-singular*

(c) *$T$ is invertible*

(d) $T^{-1}(x, y, z) = \left(\frac{x}{2}, 2x - y, 7x - 3y - z\right)$

**Solution.** (b), (c), (d)

Let $(x, y, z) \in \ker T$

$\Rightarrow$ $T(x, y, z) = (0, 0, 0)$

$\Rightarrow$ $(2x, 4x - y, 2x + 3y - z) = (0, 0, 0)$

$\Rightarrow$ $2x = 0, 4x - y = 0, 2x + 3y - z = 0$

$\Rightarrow$ $x = 0, y = 0, z = 0$

Hence, $\ker T = \{(0, 0, 0)\}$

$\Rightarrow$ $T$ is one-one

$\Rightarrow$ $T$ is onto (as $\dim R^3 = 3$)

Hence, $T$ is non-singular.

$\Rightarrow$ $T$ is invertible.

Now, let $T(x, y, z) = (r, s, t)$

$\Rightarrow$ $(2x, 4x - y, 2x + 3y - z) = (r, s, t)$

$\Rightarrow$ $2x = r, 4x - y = s, 2x + 3y - z = t$

$\Rightarrow$ $x = \frac{r}{2}, y = 2r - s, z = 7r - 3s - t$

Hence,

$$T^{-1}(r, s, t) = \left(\frac{r}{2}, 2r - s, 7r - 3s - t\right)$$

$\therefore$

$$T^{-1}(x, y, z) = \left(\frac{x}{2}, 2x - y, 7x - 3y - z\right)$$

***Example 27.*** *Let $\{e_1 = (1, 0, 0), e_2 = (0, 1, 0), e_3 = (0, 0, 1)\}$ and $\{f_1 = (1, 1, 1), f_2 = (1, 1, 0), f_3 = (1, 0, 0)\}$ are basis of $R^3$. Then,*

(a) transition matrix $\mu$ from $\{e_i\}$ to $\{f_i\}$ is

$$\mu = \begin{bmatrix} 1 & 1 & 1 \\ 1 & 1 & 0 \\ 1 & 0 & 0 \end{bmatrix}$$

(b) transition matrix $\nu$ from $\{f_i\}$ to $\{e_i\}$ is

$$\nu = \begin{bmatrix} 0 & 0 & 1 \\ 0 & 1 & -1 \\ 1 & -1 & 0 \end{bmatrix}$$

(c) $\nu = \mu^{-1}$

(d) None of the above

**Solution.** (a), (b), (c)

We have,

$$f_1 = (1, 1, 1) = 1 \cdot e_1 + 1 \cdot e_2 + 1 \cdot e_3$$
$$f_2 = (1, 1, 0) = 1 \cdot e_1 + 1 \cdot e_2 + 0 \cdot e_3$$
$$f_3 = (1, 0, 0) = 1 \cdot e_1 + 0 \cdot e_2 + 0 \cdot e_3$$

Hence, the transition matrix $\mu$ from $\{e_i\}$ to $\{f_i\}$ is

$$\mu = \begin{bmatrix} 1 & 1 & 1 \\ 1 & 1 & 0 \\ 1 & 0 & 0 \end{bmatrix}$$

Next $e_1 = (1, 0, 0) = a_1(1, 1, 1) + b_1(1, 1, 0) + c_1(1, 0, 0)$

$= (a_1 + b_1 + c_1, a_1 + b_1, a_1)$

$\Rightarrow$ $a_1 + b_1 + c_1 = 1, a_1 + b_1 = 0, a_1 = 0$

$\Rightarrow$ $a_1 = 0, b_1 = 0, c_1 = 1$

Hence,

$$e_1 = 0 \cdot f_1 + 0 \cdot f_2 + 1 \cdot f_3$$

Similarly,

$$e_2 = 0 \cdot f_1 + 1 \cdot f_2 - f_3$$
$$e_3 = 1 \cdot f_1 - 1 \cdot f_2 + 0 \cdot f_3$$

Hence, the transition matrix $\nu$ from $\{f_i\}$ to $\{e_i\}$ is

$$\nu = \begin{bmatrix} 0 & 0 & 1 \\ 0 & 1 & -1 \\ 1 & -1 & 0 \end{bmatrix}$$

Now, $$(\mu)(\nu) = \begin{bmatrix} 1 & 1 & 1 \\ 1 & 1 & 0 \\ 1 & 0 & 0 \end{bmatrix}\begin{bmatrix} 0 & 0 & 1 \\ 0 & 1 & -1 \\ 1 & -1 & 0 \end{bmatrix}$$

$$= \begin{bmatrix} 1 & 0 & 0 \\ 0 & 1 & 0 \\ 0 & 0 & 1 \end{bmatrix} = I$$

$\Rightarrow$ $\nu = (\mu)^{-1}$

# Exercise 1 (For Part 'B')

**Directions** (Q. Nos. 1-183) *All questions have only one correct option.*

**1.** If $T: R^2 \to R^3$ is a linear transformation $T(1,0) = (2, 3, 1)$ and $T(1, 1) = (3, 0, 2)$, then which one of the following statement is correct?

(a) $T(x, y) = (x + y, 2x + y, 3x - 3y), \forall (x, y) \in R^2$
(b) $T(x, y) = (2x + y, 3x - 3y, x + y), \forall (x, y) \in R^2$
(c) $T(x, y) = (2x - y, 3x + 3y, x - y), \forall (x, y) \in R^2$
(d) $T(x, y) = (x - y, 2x - y, 3x + 3y), \forall (x, y) \in R^2$

**2.** Let $T: R^3 \to R^2$ be the linear transformation given by

$$T(x, y, z) = (x, y), \forall (x, y, z) \in R^3$$

with respect to standard basis of $R^3$ and the basic $\{(1,0), (1,1)\}$ of $R^2$. What is the matrix representation of $T$?

(a) $\begin{bmatrix} 1 & 0 \\ -1 & 1 \\ 0 & 0 \end{bmatrix}$ (b) $\begin{bmatrix} 0 & 1 & 1 \\ 0 & 0 & 1 \end{bmatrix}$

(c) $\begin{bmatrix} 1 & -1 & 0 \\ 0 & 1 & 0 \end{bmatrix}$ (d) $\begin{bmatrix} 0 & 0 \\ 1 & 0 \\ 1 & 1 \end{bmatrix}$

**3.** Let $T: R^3 \to R^3$ be defined by $T(x, y, z) = (x, y, 0)$ and $S: R^2 \to R^2$ be defined by $S(x, y) = (2x, 3y)$, be linear transformations on the real vector spaces $R^3$ and $R^2$, respectively. Then, which one of the following is correct?

(a) $T$ and $S$ are both singular.
(b) $T$ and $S$ are both non-singular.
(c) $T$ is singular and $S$ is non-singular.
(d) $S$ is singular and $T$ is non-singular.

**4.** Consider, the linear transformation $T: R^4 \to R^4$ given by

$T(x, y, z, u) = (x, y, 0, 0), \forall (x, y, z, u) \in R^4$

Then, which one of the following is correct?

(a) Rank of $T >$ Nullity of $T$
(b) Nullity of $T >$ Rank of $T$
(c) Rank of $T =$ Nullity of $T = 3$
(d) Rank of $T =$ Nullity of $T = 2$

**5.** Let $V$ be the vector space of all $2 \times 2$ matrix over the field $R$ of real numbers and $B = \begin{bmatrix} 1 & 2 \\ 0 & 3 \end{bmatrix}$. If $T: V \to V$ is a linear transformation defined by $T(A) = AB - BA$, then what is the dimensional of the kernel of $T$?

(a) 1 (b) 2
(c) 3 (d) 4

**6.** What is the rank of the linear transformation $T: R^3 \to R^3$ defined by $T(x, y, z) = (y, 0, z)$?

(a) 3 (b) 2
(c) 1 (d) 0

**7.** Consider the vector space $C$ over $R$ and let $T: C \to C$ be a linear transformation given by $T(Z) = \bar{Z}$. Then, which one of the following is correct?

(a) $T$ is one-one, but not onto.
(b) $T$ is onto, but not one-one.
(c) $T$ is one-one as well as onto.
(d) $T$ is neither one-one nor onto.

**8.** Let $T: R^3 \to R^3$ be a linear transformation given by $T(x, y, z) = (x, y, 0)$. Then, the null space is generated by which one of the following?

(a) (0, 0, 1) (b) (0, 1, 0)
(c) (1, 0, 0) (d) None of these

**9.** Let $T: R^3 \to R^3$ be a linear transformation given by $T(x, y, z) = \left(\frac{x}{2}, \frac{y}{2}, 0\right)$. What is the rank of $T$?

(a) 4 (b) 3
(c) 2 (d) 1

**10.** Consider the mapping

(I) $T: R^3 \to R^2$, $T(x, y, z) = (x + 1, y + z)$
(II) $T: R^3 \to R$, $T(x, y) = xy$
(III) $T: R^3 \to R^2$, $T(x, y, z) = (|x|, 0)$

Which of the above are linear transformation?

(a) (I), (II) and (III)
(b) (I) and (II), only
(c) (II) and (III) only
(d) None of these

**11.** Let $T: R^2 \to R^3$ be defined by

$$T(x, y) = (x + y, x - y)$$

Which one of the following is the matrix of $T$ for (0, 1) and (1, 0) as a basis for both domain and range of $T$?

(a) $\begin{pmatrix} 1 & 1 \\ 1 & -1 \end{pmatrix}$ (b) $\begin{pmatrix} -1 & 1 \\ 1 & 1 \end{pmatrix}$

(c) $\begin{pmatrix} 1 & -1 \\ 1 & 1 \end{pmatrix}$ (d) $\begin{pmatrix} 1 & 1 \\ -1 & 1 \end{pmatrix}$

**12.** Let $T: R^2 \to R^2$ be a map defined by

$$T(x, y) = (x + y, x - y)$$

Which of the following statement is correct?

(a) $T$ is linear and its kernel has infinite number of element of $R^2$.
(b) $T$ is not linear.
(c) The kernel of $T$ consist of only two element of $R^2$.
(d) Nullity of $T$ is zero.

**13.** Let $T: R^2 \to R^2$ be a linear transformation such that

$$T\left[\begin{pmatrix} 1 \\ 0 \end{pmatrix}\right] = \begin{pmatrix} 1 \\ 2 \end{pmatrix} \text{ and } T\left[\begin{pmatrix} 0 \\ 1 \end{pmatrix}\right] = \begin{pmatrix} 2 \\ 1 \end{pmatrix}$$

What is the value of $T\left[\begin{pmatrix}1\\1\end{pmatrix}\right]$?

(a) $\begin{pmatrix}1\\2\end{pmatrix}$ (b) $\begin{pmatrix}2\\1\end{pmatrix}$

(c) $\begin{pmatrix}3\\3\end{pmatrix}$ (d) $\begin{pmatrix}2\\2\end{pmatrix}$

**14.** Define $T$ on $\mathbb{R}^4$ into $\mathbb{R}^4$ by

$$T(x_1, x_2, x_3, x_4) = (x_1 + x_2 + x_3, x_2 + x_3 + x_4, x_3 + x_4 + x_2)$$

Then, rank of $T$ is equal to ($\mathbb{R}$ being the set of real number)

(a) 1 (b) 2
(c) 3 (d) 4

**15.** Let $T$ be linear transformation on $R^2$ into itself such that $T(1, 0) = (1, 2)$ and $T(1, 1) = (0, 2)$. Then, $T(a, b)$ is equal to

(a) $(a, 2b)$ (b) $(2a, b)$
(c) $(a - b, 2a)$ (d) $(a - b, 2b)$

**16.** If $T : V \to V$ is a linear transformation of vector space $V$ and the composite $ToT = 0$, then

(a) kernel of $T \subseteq$ image of $T$
(b) image of $T \subseteq$ kernel of $T$
(c) $T$ is 0 linear transformation
(d) $T$ is a non-singular linear transformation

**17.** Define $T$ on $R^2$ into itself by

$$T(x_1, x_2) = (x_1 + x_2, x_1 - x_2).$$

Then, matrix of $T^{-1}$ relative to the standard basis for $R^2$ is

(a) $\begin{bmatrix}1 & 1\\1 & -1\end{bmatrix}$ (b) $\begin{bmatrix}-1 & -1\\-1 & 1\end{bmatrix}$

(c) $\begin{bmatrix}1/2 & 1/2\\1/2 & -1/2\end{bmatrix}$ (d) $\begin{bmatrix}-1/2 & -1/2\\-1/2 & 1/2\end{bmatrix}$

**18.** Let $T$ be a linear transformation from a 3-dimensional vector space $V$ into a 2-dimensional vector space $W$. Then, $T$

(a) can be both injective and surjective
(b) can be neither injective nor surjective
(c) can be surjective but cannot be injective
(d) can be injective but cannot be surjective

**19.** Which of the following mapping $\mathbb{R}^2 \to \mathbb{R}^2$ is not a linear mapping?

(a) $(x_1, x_2) \to (x_2, x_1)$ (b) $(x_1, x_2) \to (x_1 + x_2, x_2)$
(c) $(x_1, x_2) \to (x_1 + 1, x_2)$ (d) $(x_1, x_2) \to (0, 0)$

**20.** $R$ is the set of real number. In $R^2$, let $f_1$ and $f_2$ be the two transformations defined by

$$f_1(x, y) = (0, y)$$
$$f_2(x, y) = (y, x)$$

Then, the product of the mapping $(f_2 o f_1)(x, y)$ gives the projection of the $x$-$y$ plane on the

(a) $y$-axis (b) $x$-axis
(c) line $y = x$ (d) line $y = -x$

**21.** Consider the following linear transformation from the vector space $\mathbb{R}^2$ into the vector space $\mathbb{R}^3$

$$T(x, y) = (-x - y, 3x + 8y, 9x - 11y)$$

Then, the rank and nullity of $T$ are respectively

(a) 2 and 0 (b) 1 and 0
(c) 1 and 1 (d) None of these

**22.** If the linear transformation $T : R^2 \to R^3$ is such that $T(1,0) = (2, 3, 1)$ and $T(1, 1) = (3, 0, 2)$, then

(a) $T(x, y) = (x + y, 2x + y, 3x - 3y)$
(b) $T(x, y) = (2x + y, 3x - 3y, x + y)$
(c) $T(x, y) = (2x - y, 3x + 3y, x - y)$
(d) $T(x, y) = (x - y, 2x - y, 3x + 3y)$

**23.** If $T : R^3 \to R^3$ is given by

$$T(x, y, z) = (x - y, y + 3z, x + 2y), \text{ then } T^{-1} \text{ is}$$

(a) $\frac{1}{3}\left(2x + z, -x + z, \frac{x}{3} + y - \frac{z}{3}\right)$

(b) $\frac{1}{3}\left(2x + y, -x + y, \frac{1}{3}x - \frac{1}{3}y + z\right)$

(c) $\frac{1}{3}\left(x + 2y, x - y, -\frac{1}{3}x + \frac{1}{3}y - z\right)$

(d) $\frac{1}{3}\left(x - 2y, x + y, \frac{x}{3} - \frac{y}{3} - z\right)$

**24.** Let $V$ be a vector space of $2 \times 2$ matrices over $R$. Let $T$ be the linear mapping $T : V \to V$, such that $T(A) = AB - BA$, $B = \begin{bmatrix}2 & 1\\0 & 3\end{bmatrix}$, then the nullity of $T$ is

(a) 1 (b) 2
(c) 3 (d) 4

**25.** Let $P_2[x]$ be the vector space of all polynomials over $R$ of degree less than or equal to 2. Let $D$ be the differential operator on $P_2[x]$. Then, matrix of $D$ relative to the basis $[x_2, 1, x]$ is equal to

(a) $\begin{bmatrix}0 & 0 & 0\\0 & 0 & 1\\2 & 0 & 0\end{bmatrix}$ (b) $\begin{bmatrix}0 & 0 & 0\\2 & 0 & 0\\0 & 0 & 1\end{bmatrix}$

(c) $\begin{bmatrix}0 & 0 & 2\\0 & 0 & 0\\0 & 1 & 0\end{bmatrix}$ (d) $\begin{bmatrix}0 & 0 & 0\\0 & 0 & 2\\0 & 1 & 0\end{bmatrix}$

**26.** If $T : V \to V$ is a linear operator, for $\dim V = n$ and $T$ has $n$ distinct eigen values, then

(a) $T$ must be invertible
(b) $T$ must be diagonalizable
(c) $T$ must be invertible as well as diagonalizable
(d) $T$ is not diagonalizable

**27.** Let $V$ and $W$ be vector spaces over $R$. $T : V \to W$ be a map. Then, $T$ is a linear transformation if and only if

(a) $T(x + y) = T(x) + T(y), \forall\ x, y \in V$
(b) $T(\alpha x) = \alpha T(x), \forall\ x \in V, \alpha \in R$
(c) $T(\alpha x + y) = \alpha T(x) + T(y), \forall\ x, y \in V, \alpha \in R$
(d) $T(x - y) = T(x) - T(y), \forall\ x, y \in V$

**28.** The transformation
$(x, y, z) \to (x+y, y+z) : R^3 \to R^2$ is
(a) linear and has zero kernel
(b) linear and has a proper subspace as kernel
(c) neither linear nor one-one
(d) neither linear nor onto

**29.** For a linear transformation $T : R^{10} \to R^6$, the kernal is having dimension 5. Then, the dimension of the range of $T$ is
(a) 5 (b) 6
(c) 4 (d) 2

**30.** Let $M_1 = \begin{bmatrix} 3 & 0 & 0 \\ 1 & 3 & 0 \\ 0 & 0 & 3 \end{bmatrix}$, $M_2 = \begin{bmatrix} -3 & 0 \\ 1 & -3 \end{bmatrix}$, $M_3 = \begin{bmatrix} 0 & 0 \\ 1 & 0 \end{bmatrix}$

Then, the minimal polynomial of the matrix
$\begin{bmatrix} M_1 & 0 & 0 \\ 0 & M_2 & 0 \\ 0 & 0 & M_3 \end{bmatrix}$ is
(a) $x^2(x-3)^3(x+3)^2$ (b) $x^2(x^2-9)$
(c) $x^2(x^2-9)^2$ (d) $x(x-1)^4(x+3)^2$

**31.** The unique linear transformation $T : R^2 \to R^2$ such that $T(1, 2) = (2, 3)$ and $T(0, 1) = (1, 4)$. Then, the rule for $T$ is
(a) $T(a, b) = (b, -5a+4b)$
(b) $T(a, b) = (-5a+4b, b)$
(c) $T(a, b) = (a, -5a+4b)$
(d) $T(a, b) = (-4a+5b, b)$

**32.** A linear transformation $T : R^2 \to R^2$ such that $T(3, 1) = (2, -4)$ and $T(1, 1) = (0, 2)$. Then, the $T(7, 8)$ is
(a) $(-1, 3)$ (b) $(3, -1)$
(c) $(2, -3)$ (d) $(-3, 2)$

**33.** Let $F$ be any field and let $T$ be a linear operator on $F^2$ defined by $T(a, b) = (a+b, a)$, then $T^{-1}(a, b)$ is equal to
(a) $(b, a-b)$ (b) $(a-b, b)$
(c) $(a, a+b)$ (d) None of these

**34.** If $S$ is any subset of a vector space $V(F)$, then $S$ is a subspace of
(a) $V$ (b) $V'$
(c) $V''$ (d) None of these

**35.** If $U(F)$ and $V(F)$ are two vector spaces and $T$ is a linear transformation from $U$ into $V$, then range of $T$ is a subspace of
(a) $U$ (b) $V$
(c) $U \cup V$ (d) None of these

**36.** The transition matrix $P$ from the standard ordered basis to the ordered basis $\{(1, 1), (-1, 0)\}$ is
(a) $\begin{bmatrix} 1 & 1 \\ -1 & 0 \end{bmatrix}$ (b) $\begin{bmatrix} 1 & -1 \\ 1 & 0 \end{bmatrix}$
(c) $\begin{bmatrix} 0 & 1 \\ 1 & 0 \end{bmatrix}$ (d) $\begin{bmatrix} 1 & 0 \\ 0 & 1 \end{bmatrix}$

**37.** If $T : V_2(R) \to V_3(R)$ defined as $T(a, b) = (a+b, a-b, b)$ is a linear transformation, then nullity of $T$ is
(a) 0 (b) 1
(c) 2 (d) None of these

**38.** The only eigen value of the matrix $\begin{bmatrix} 1 & 1 & 0 \\ 0 & 1 & 0 \\ 0 & 0 & 1 \end{bmatrix}$ is
(a) 1 (b) 2
(c) 3 (d) 4

**39.** The eigen values of the triangular matrix $\begin{bmatrix} 1 & 2 & 3 \\ 0 & 2 & 3 \\ 0 & 0 & 3 \end{bmatrix}$ are
(a) 1, 2, 3 (b) 2, 3, 4
(c) 1, 3, 4 (d) None of these

**40.** If $T : R^4 \to R^3$ be the linear transformation defined by $T(x, y, z, w) = (x-y+z+w, x+2z-w, x+y+3z-3w)$, then the dimension of its range is
(a) 3 (b) 2
(c) 1 (d) 0

**41.** Let $T$ be a linear operator on a finite dimensional space $V$ and $C$ is any scalar, then $C$ is characteristic value of $T$ if
(a) the operator $(T - CI)$ is singular
(b) the operator $(T - CI)$ is non-singular
(c) the operator $(T - CI)$ is identity
(d) the operator $(T - CI)$ is zero

**42.** Let $T : V_2(R) \to V_2(R)$ where $T$ be the reflection of the points through the line $y = -x$, then the matrix of $T$ with respect to standard basis is
(a) $\begin{bmatrix} 1 & 0 \\ 0 & -1 \end{bmatrix}$ (b) $\begin{bmatrix} -1 & 0 \\ 0 & 1 \end{bmatrix}$
(c) $\begin{bmatrix} 0 & 1 \\ 1 & 0 \end{bmatrix}$ (d) $\begin{bmatrix} 0 & -1 \\ -1 & 0 \end{bmatrix}$

**43.** Let $M = \begin{bmatrix} 1 & 2 \\ 0 & 0 \end{bmatrix}$ and $T : V \to V$ be the linear map defined by $T(A) = AM$ where $V$ be the vector space of all $2 \times 2$ real matrices. Then, rank and nullity of $T$ respectively
(a) 1, 3 (b) 3, 1
(c) 2, 2 (d) 4, 0

**44.** Let $T : R^n \to R^m$ be a linear transformation and let $A$ be the standard matrix for $T$, then select the correct statement
(I) $T$ maps $R^n$ onto $R^m$ if and only if the columns of $A$ span $R^m$.
(II) $T$ is one-one iff the columns of $A$ are linearly dependent.
(III) $T$ is one-one iff the equation $T(x) = 0$ has only the trivial solution.
(a) Only (I) and (II) (b) Only (I) and (III)
(c) Only (II) and (III) (d) (I), (II) and (III)

**45.** Consider the two linear maps $T_1$ and $T_2$ on $V_3$ defined as $T_1(x_1, x_2, x_3) = (0, x_2, x_1)$ and $T_2(x_1, x_2, x_3) = (x_1, 0, 0)$, then
(a) $T$ is idempotent but $T_2$ is not idempotent
(b) $T_2$ is idempotent but $T_1$ is not idempotent
(c) Both $T_1$ and $T_2$ are idempotent
(d) Neither $T_1$ nor $T_2$ are idempotent

**46.** If the complex field C is the given vector space over the real field R and operator T on C is defined on $T(z) = \bar{z}$, then the matrix of T *wrt* the basis $[1+i, i+2i]$ is
(a) $\begin{bmatrix} 3 & 4 \\ -2 & -3 \end{bmatrix}$ (b) $\begin{bmatrix} 3 & -2 \\ 4 & 3 \end{bmatrix}$
(c) $\begin{bmatrix} 3 & 4 \\ 2 & 3 \end{bmatrix}$ (d) None of these

**47.** The matrix of the linear transformation T on $R^3(R)$ defined as $T(x, y, z) = (2y + z, x - 4y, 3x)$ *wrt* the basis $B = \{(1,1,1), (1,1,0), (1,0,0)\}$ is $[T]_B$ is equal to
(a) $\begin{bmatrix} 3 & 3 & 3 \\ -6 & -6 & -2 \\ 6 & 5 & -1 \end{bmatrix}$ (b) $\begin{bmatrix} 3 & -6 & 6 \\ 3 & -6 & 5 \\ 3 & -2 & -1 \end{bmatrix}$
(c) $\begin{bmatrix} 3 & -6 & 6 \\ -6 & 5 & -2 \\ -1 & 3 & 3 \end{bmatrix}$ (d) None of these

**48.** Let T and S be two linear transformations form $R^3 \to R^3$ such as $T: R^3 \to R^3$ defined as
$S(x, y, z) = (2x, 4x - y, 2x + 3y - z)$
$T(x, y, z) = (x\cos\theta - y\sin\theta,\ x\sin\theta + y\cos\theta, z),$
$0 < \theta < \pi/2$
Then,
(a) S is one-one but T is not
(b) T is one-one but S is not
(c) Both S and T are one-one
(d) Neither S nor T is one-one

**49.** T is non-singular iff
(a) nullity $(T) \neq 0$ (b) nullity $(T) = 0$
(c) nullity $(T) =$ rank T (d) rank $(T) = 0$

**50.** Let C be the vector space of all complex numbers over complex field C and $T: C \to C$ be defined by $T(Z) = \bar{Z}$, $Z \in C$. Then,
(a) T is a linear mapping
(b) T is not linear mapping but a well defined map
(c) T is not well defined
(d) None of the above

**51.** Let $T: R^7 \to R^7$ be a linear transformation such that $T^2 = 0$. Then, the rank of T is
(a) $\leq 3$ (b) $> 3$
(c) $= 5$ (d) $= 6$

**52.** Let a matrix $A_{m\times n}$ represents a linear mapping $T: V_n \to V_m$. Then, range of T is generated by
(a) Rows of A (b) Columns of A
(c) Both (a) and (b) (d) None of these

**53.** Let $T_1$ and $T_2$ be two linear operators on $R^3$ defined by $T_1(x, y, z) = (x, x + y, x - y - z)$,
$T_2(x, y, z) = (x + 2z, y - z, x + y + z)$
Then,
(a) $T_1$ is invertible but not $T_2$
(b) $T_2$ is invertible but not $T_1$
(c) both $T_1$ and $T_2$ are invertible
(d) neither $T_1$ nor $T_2$ is invertible

**54.** Which among the following is not linear?
(a) $F: R^2 \to R^2$ such that $F(x, y) = (2x - y, x)$
(b) $F: R^3 \to R^2$ such that $F(x, y, z) = (z, x + y)$
(c) $F: R \to R^2$ such that $F(x) = (2x, 3x)$
(d) $F: R^3 \to R^2$ such that $F(x, y, z) = (x + 1, y + z)$

**55.** If the linear transformation $T: R^2 \to R^3$ is such that $T(1,0) = (2,3,1)$ and $T(1,1) = (3,0,2)$, then
(a) $T(x, y) = (x + y, 2x + y, 3x - 3y)$
(b) $T(x, y) = (2x + y, 3x - 3y, x + y)$
(c) $T(x, y) = (2x - y, 3x + 3y, x - y)$
(d) $T(x, y) = (x - y, 2x - y, 3x + 3y)$

**56.** The transformation $T: R^3 \to R^2$ defined by $T(x, y, z) = (x + y, y + z)$ is
(a) linear and has zero kernel
(b) linear and has a proper subspace as kernel
(c) neither linear nor one-one
(d) neither linear nor onto

**57.** For a linear transformation $T: R^{12} \to R^6$, the kernel is having dimension 7. Then, the dimension of the range of T is
(a) 5 (b) 6
(c) 4 (d) 2

**58.** Let $T: R^n \to R^m$ be a linear transformation and $A_{m\times n}$ be its matrix representation. Then, choose the incorrect statement
(a) columns of A are LI $\Rightarrow$ T is onto
(b) columns of A span $R^m \Rightarrow$ T is onto
(c) columns of A are LI $\Rightarrow$ T is one-one
(d) T is one-one $\Rightarrow$ columns of A are LI

**59.** If T be a linear operator on a vector space V such that $T^2 - T + I = 0$, then
(a) T is one-one but may not be onto
(b) T is onto but may not be one-one
(c) T is invertible
(d) no such T exists

**60.** Let T be a linear transformation on the vector space $V_2(F)$ defined by $T(a, b) = (a, 0)$, the matrix of T relative to the ordered basis $\{(1,0), (0,1)\}$ of $V_2(F)$ is
(a) $\begin{bmatrix} 1 & 0 \\ 0 & 0 \end{bmatrix}$ (b) $\begin{bmatrix} 0 & 1 \\ 0 & 0 \end{bmatrix}$
(c) $\begin{bmatrix} 0 & 0 \\ 0 & 0 \end{bmatrix}$ (d) $\begin{bmatrix} 0 & 0 \\ 0 & 1 \end{bmatrix}$

**61.** The minimal polynomial of the real matrix $\begin{bmatrix} 0 & 1 \\ 1 & 0 \end{bmatrix}$ is
(a) $x^2 + 1$ (b) $x^2 - 1$
(c) $x + 1$ (d) $x - 1$

62. If $T$ is a linear transformation from a vector space $V$ into a vector space $W$, then the condition for $T^{-1}$ to be a linear transformation from $W$ to $V$ is
   (a) $T$ should be one-one
   (b) $T$ should not onto
   (c) $T$ should be one-one and onto
   (d) None of the above

63. Let $T$ be a linear transformation from a vector space $U(F)$ into a vector space $V(F)$ with $U$ as finite dimensional. The rank of $T$ is the dimension of the
   (a) range of $T$ (b) null space of $T$
   (c) vector space $U$ (d) vector space $V$

64. Let $V$ be the vector space of $2 \times 2$ matrices over $R$ and let $m = \begin{bmatrix} 1 & 2 \\ 3 & 4 \end{bmatrix}$. Let $T$ be the linear operator on $V$ defined by $T(A) = MA$, then the trace of $T$ is
   (a) 5 (b) 10
   (c) 0 (d) None of these

65. Let $U$ be an $n$-dimensional vector space over the field $F$ and let $V$ be an $m$-dimensional vector space over $F$. Then, the vector space $L(U, V)$ of all linear transformation from $U$ into $V$ is finite dimensional and is of dimension.
   (a) $m$ (b) $n$
   (c) $mn$ (d) None of these

66. Let $A = \begin{bmatrix} 1 & 4 \\ 2 & 3 \end{bmatrix}$. The eigen values of $A$ are
   (a) 1, 5 (b) −1, 5
   (c) 1, −5 (d) −1, −5

67. A linear transformation $E$ on $V$ is a projection on some subspace iff
   (a) $E^2 = \hat{0}$ (b) $E^2 = I$
   (c) $E^2 = E$ (d) None of these

68. If the dual basis of the basis set $B = [(1,0,0),(0,1,0),(0,0,1)]$ for $V_3(R)$ is $B' = \{f_1, f_2, f_3\}$, then
   (a) $f_1(a, b, c) = a$, $f_2(a, b, c) = b$, $f_3(a, b, c) = c$
   (b) $f_1(a, b, c) = b$, $f_2(a, b, c) = c$, $f_3(a, b, c) = a$
   (c) $f_1(a, b, c) = c$, $f_2(a, b, c) = a$, $f_3(a, b, c) = b$
   (d) $f_1(a, b, c) = b$, $f_2(a, b, c) = a$, $f_3(a, b, c) = c$

69. Let $V$ be a finite dimensional vector space. The minimal polynomial for the zero operator is
   (a) $-x$ (b) $x$
   (c) $x - 1$ (d) None of these

70. Let $V$ be an $n$-dimensional vector space over the field $F$. The dimension of the dual space of $V$ is
   (a) $n$ (b) $n^2$
   (c) $\frac{1}{2}n$ (d) None of these

71. The characteristic value of the matrix $\begin{bmatrix} 1 & 0 \\ 0 & i \end{bmatrix}$ are
   (a) 1, $i$ (b) 1, $-i$
   (c) −1, $i$ (d) −1, $-i$

72. Let $V$ be a finite dimensional vector space $V(F)$; over the field $F$. If $S$ is any subset of $V$, then $S^{00}$ is equal to
   (a) $S$ (b) $L(S)$
   (c) $[L(S)]^0$ (d) None of these

73. If $V$ is an $n$-dimensional vector space over the field $F$, then the characteristic polynomial of the identify operator on $V$ is
   (a) $x^n$ (b) $(1+x)^n$
   (c) $(1+x)^{2n}$ (d) None of these

74. If $T_1$ and $T_2$ are linear operator on $V$, then
   (a) $(T_1T_2)' = T_1T_2$ (b) $(T_1T_2)' = T_2'T_1'$
   (c) $(T_1T_2)' = T_1'T_2'$ (d) None of these

75. Consider the basis $S = \{v_1, v_2, v_3\}$ for $R^3$ where $v_1 = (1,1,1)$, $v_2 = (1,1,0)$, $v_3 = (1,0,0)$ and let $T: R^3 \to R^2$ be a linear transformation such that $T(v_1) = (1,0)$, $T(v_2) = (2,-1)$, $T(v_3) = (4,3)$. Then, $T(2,-3,5)$ is
   (a) (−1, 5) (b) (3, 4)
   (c) (0, 0) (d) (9, 23)

76. Let $T : C^n \to C^n$ be an linear operator having $n$ distinct eigen values. Then,
   (a) $T$ is invertible
   (b) $T$ is invertible as well as diagonalizable
   (c) $T$ is not diagonalizable
   (d) $T$ is diagonalizable

77. Let $A$ be a non-zero upper triangular matrix all of whose eigen values are 0. Then, $I + A$ is
   (a) invertible (b) singular
   (c) idempotent (d) nilpotent

78. Let $T$ be a linear transformation from $R^3 \to R^2$ defined by $T(x, y, z) = (x + y, y - z)$. Then, the matrix of $T$ with respect to the ordered bases $\{(1,1,1),(1,-1,0),(0,1,0)\}$ and $\{(1,1),(1,0)\}$ is
   (a) $\begin{bmatrix} -2 & 0 & 1 \\ 1 & 1 & -1 \end{bmatrix}$ (b) $\begin{bmatrix} 0 & -1 & 1 \\ 2 & 1 & 0 \end{bmatrix}$
   (c) $\begin{bmatrix} 2 & 1 \\ 0 & -1 \\ 1 & 1 \end{bmatrix}$ (d) $\begin{bmatrix} 0 & 2 \\ -1 & 1 \\ 1 & 0 \end{bmatrix}$

79. Let $V$ be a vector space and $T$ is a linear operator on $V$. If $W$ is a subspace of $V$, then $W$ is invariant under $T$ iff $\alpha \in T \Rightarrow$
   (a) $T(\alpha) = 0$ (b) $T(\alpha) \in W$
   (c) $T(\alpha) = \alpha$ (d) None of these

80. Let $T: R^3 \to R^3$ be the linear transformation which rotates a vector space about the $z$-axis through an angle $\theta$, $T(x, y, z) = (x\cos\theta - y\sin\theta, x\sin\theta + y\cos\theta^z)$. Then, the kernel of $F$ is
   (a) $\{0\}$ (b) $\{(x, 0, 0) : x \in R\}$
   (c) $\{(0, y, 0) : y \in R\}$ (d) $\{(0, 0, z) : z \in R\}$

81. Let $T : R^3 \to R^3$ be the linear transformation defined by $T(x, y, z) = (x + 2y - z, y + z, x - 2z)$. Then, the dimension of the image $U$ of $T$ is
   (a) 0 (b) 1 (c) 2 (d) 3

**82.** Let $T: R^3 \to R^3$ be the linear transformation defined by
$T(x, y, z, t) = (x - y + z + t,\ x + 2z - t,\ x + y + 3z - 3t)$.
Then, the dimension of the image $U$ of $T$ is
(a) 0 (b) 1
(c) 2 (d) 3

**83.** Let $T: R^3 \to R^3$ be the linear transformation defined by $T(x, y, z) = (x + 2y - z, y + z, x - 2z)$. Then, the dimension of the kernel of $T$ is
(a) 0 (b) 1
(c) 2 (d) 3

**84.** Let $T: R^3 \to R^3$ be the linear transformation $T(x, y, z, t) = (x - y + z + t, x + 2z - t, x + y + 3z - 3t)$.
Then, the dimension of the kernel of $T$ is
(a) 0 (b) 1
(c) 2 (d) 3

**85.** The minimal polynomial of $\begin{pmatrix} 1 & 0 & 0 & 0 \\ 1 & 1 & 0 & 0 \\ 0 & 0 & 2 & 0 \\ 0 & 0 & 0 & 2 \end{pmatrix}$ is
(a) $(x-1)^2(x-2)$ (b) $(x-1)(x-2)^2$
(c) $(x-1)(x-2)$ (d) $(x-1)^2(x-2)^2$

**86.** Choose the correct matching from $A, B, C$ and $D$ for the transformation $T_1, T_2$ and $T_3$ (mappings from $R^2$ to $R^3$) as defined in group I with the statements given in group II.

| Group I | Group II |
|---|---|
| P. $T_1(x, y) = (x, x, 0)$ | 1. Liner transformation of rank 2 |
| Q. $T_2(x, y) = (x, x + y, y)$ | 2. Not a linear transformation |
| R. $T_3(x, y) = (x, x + 1, y)$ | 3. Linear transformation of rank 1 |

(a) P – 3, Q – 1, R – 2 (b) P – 1, Q – 2, R – 3
(c) P – 3, Q – 2, R – 1 (b) P – 1, Q – 3, R – 2

**87.** Let $T: V \to V$ be the linear transformation such as $T[f(t)] = t\,f(t)$, where $f(t)$ is a polynomial. Then,
(a) $T$ is singular (b) $T$ is non-singular
(c) $T$ is onto (d) None of these

**88.** Let $T: V \to V$ be the linear transformation such as $T[f(t)] = \dfrac{d^n f}{dt^n}$, (where $n > 0$), then
(a) $T$ is singular (b) $T$ is non-singular
(c) $T$ is one-one (d) None of these

**89.** Let $T: V \to V$ be a non-singular linear transformation, then
(a) $\dim V = \dim(\operatorname{Im} F)$ (b) $\dim V > \dim(\operatorname{Im} F)$
(c) $\dim V < \dim(\operatorname{Im} F)$ (d) None of these

**90.** Let $T: V \to U$ be the linear transformation such that maps independent sets into independent sets, then
(a) $T$ is singular (b) $T$ is non-singular
(c) $\det T = 0$ (d) None of these

**91.** The two transformation $T: R^3 \to R^2$ and $S: R^3 \to R^2$ defined as $T(x, y, z) = (x + 1, y + z)$ and $S(x, y, z) = (|x|, 0)$, then
(a) $T$ and $S$ both are linear
(b) $T$ and $S$ both are not linear
(c) $T$ is linear and $S$ is not linear
(d) $T$ is not linear and $S$ is linear

**92.** Let $T: V \to V$ be a linear operator, then which of the following is/are not correct?
(a) $\{0\}$ is invariant under $T$
(b) $V$ is invariant under $T$
(c) Kernel of $T$ is invariant under $T$
(d) None of the above

**93.** Let $\{V_1, V_2, \ldots, V_{16}\}$ be an ordered basis for $V = C^{16}$. If $T$ is a linear transformation on $V$ defined by $T(V_i) = V_i + 1$ for $1 \le i \le 15$ and $T(V_{16}) = -(V_1 + V_2 + \ldots + V_{16})$, then
(a) $T$ is singular with rational eigen values
(b) $T$ is singular but has no rational eigen values
(c) $T$ is regular (invertible) with rational eigen values
(d) $T$ is regular but has no rational eigen values

**94.** Let $T: R^3 \to R^3$ be a linear transformation defined by $T(x, y, z) = (x + y - z, x + y + z, y - z)$, then the matrix of the linear transformation $T$ with respect to the ordered basis $B = (0, 1, 0), (0, 0, 1), (1, 0, 0)$ of $R^3$ is 0.

(a) $\begin{bmatrix} 1 & 1 & -1 \\ 1 & 1 & 1 \\ 0 & 1 & -1 \end{bmatrix}$ (b) $\begin{bmatrix} 1 & 1 & 0 \\ 1 & 1 & 1 \\ 1 & 0 & -1 \end{bmatrix}$

(c) $\begin{bmatrix} 1 & 1 & 1 \\ 1 & -1 & 0 \\ 1 & -1 & 1 \end{bmatrix}$ (d) $\begin{bmatrix} 1 & -1 & 1 \\ 1 & 1 & 1 \\ 1 & -1 & 0 \end{bmatrix}$

**95.** Let $R^{2\times 2}$ be the real vector space of all $2 \times 2$ real matrices. For $Q = \begin{pmatrix} 1 & -2 \\ -2 & 4 \end{pmatrix}$, define a linear transformation $T$ on $R^{2\times 2}$ as $T(P) = QP$. Then, the rank of $T$ is
(a) 1 (b) 2 (c) 3 (d) 4

**96.** Let $M = \begin{pmatrix} 1 & 3 & 3 \\ 0 & 4 & 5 \\ 0 & 0 & 9 \end{pmatrix}$, then
(a) $M$ is diagonalizable but not $M^2$
(b) $M^2$ is diagonalizable but not $M$
(c) Both $M$ and $M^2$ are diagonalizable
(d) Neither $M$ nor $M^2$ is diagonalizable

**97.** Consider the vector space $R^3$ and the maps $f, g: R^3 \to R^3$ defined by $f(x, y, z) = (x, |y|, z)$ and $g(x, y, z) = (x + 1, y - 1, z)$. Then,
(a) Both $f$ and $g$ are linear
(b) Neither $f$ nor $g$ is linear
(c) $g$ is linear but not $f$
(d) $f$ is linear but not $g$

**98.** Let $S$ and $T$ be two linear operators on $R^3$ defined by $S(x,y,z)=(x,x+y,x-y-z)$, $T(x,y,z)=(x+2z,y-z,x+y+z)$. Then,
(a) $S$ is invertible but not $T$
(b) $T$ is invertible but not $S$
(c) both $S$ and $T$ are invertible
(d) neither $S$ nor $T$ is invertible

**99.** Consider the matrix $M=\begin{pmatrix}0&1&2&0\\1&0&1&0\\2&1&0&2\\0&0&2&0\end{pmatrix}$. Then,
(a) $M$ has no real eigen values
(b) all real eigen values of $M$ are positive
(c) all real eigen values of $M$ are negative
(d) $M$ has both positive and negative real eigen values

**100.** If a square matrix of order 10 has exactly 4 distinct eigen values, then the degree of its minimal polynomial is
(a) atleast 4 (b) atmost 4
(c) atleast 6 (d) atmost 6

**101.** Let $V,W$ and $X$ be three finite dimensional vector spaces such that $\dim V=\dim X$. Suppose, $S:V\to W$ and $T:W\to X$ are two linear maps such that $ToS:V\to X$ is injective, then
(a) $S$ and $T$ are surjective
(b) $S$ is surjective and $T$ is injective
(c) $S$ and $T$ are injective
(d) $S$ is injective and $T$ is surjective

**102.** Let $T:R^3\to R^3$ be the linear transformation defined by $T(x_1,x_2,x_3)=(x_1+3x_2+2x_3, 3x_1+4x_2+x_3, 2x_1+x_2-x_3)$.
The dimension of the null space of $T^2$ is
(a) 0 (b) 1 (c) 2 (d) 3

**103.** Consider the basis $\{u_1,u_2,u_3\}$ of $R^3$, where $u_1=(1,0,0)$, $u_2=(1,1,0)$, $u_3=(1,1,1)$. Let $\{f_1,f_2,f_3\}$ be the dual basis of $\{u_1,u_2,u_3\}$ and $f$ be a linear functional defined by $f(a,b,c)=a+b+c$, $(a,b,c)\in R^3$. If $f=\alpha_1f_1+\alpha_2f_2+\alpha_3f_3$, then $(\alpha_1,\alpha_2,\alpha_3)$ is
(a) (1, 2, 3) (b) (1, 3, 2)
(c) (2, 3, 1) (d) (3, 2, 1)

**104.** Let $T:P_3[0,1]\to P_2[0,1]$ be defined by $(TP)(x)=P''(x)+P'(x)$. Then, the matrix representation of $T$ with respect to the bases $[1,x,x^2,x^3]$ and $[1,x,x^2]$ of $P_3[0,1]$ and $P_2[0,1]$ respectively is

(a) $\begin{bmatrix}0&0&0\\1&0&0\\2&2&0\\0&6&3\end{bmatrix}$ (b) $\begin{bmatrix}0&1&2&0\\0&0&2&6\\0&0&0&3\end{bmatrix}$

(c) $\begin{bmatrix}0&2&1&0\\6&2&0&0\\3&0&0&0\end{bmatrix}$ (d) $\begin{bmatrix}0&0&0\\0&0&1\\0&2&2\\3&6&0\end{bmatrix}$

**105.** Let the linear transformations $S$ and $T:R^3\to R^3$ be defined by
$S(x,y,z)=(2x,4x-y,2x+3y-z)$
$T(x,y,z)=(x\cos\theta-y\sin\theta, \sin\theta+y\cos\theta, z)$
where $0<\theta<\pi/2$, then
(a) $S$ is one to one but not $T$.
(b) $T$ is one to one but not $S$.
(c) both $S$ and $T$ are one to one.
(d) neither $S$ nor $T$ is one to one.

**106.** Let $T$ be a linear transformation such that $T(1,1)=(1,0)$ and $T(5,5)=(0,1)$. Then,
(a) $T$ is one-one
(b) $T$ is isomorphism and rank of $T=2$
(c) $T$ is not one-one and rank $T$ is 1
(d) None of the above

**107.** The characteristic and minimal polynomials of the following matrix $\begin{bmatrix}4&1&0\\0&4&1\\0&0&4\end{bmatrix}$ are
(a) $Ch(\lambda)=(\lambda-4)^3$, $m(\lambda)=(\lambda-4)^3$
(b) $Ch(\lambda)=(\lambda-4)^3$, $m(\lambda)=(\lambda-4)^2$
(c) $Ch(\lambda)=(\lambda-4)^3$, $m(\lambda)=(\lambda-4)$
(d) None of the above

**108.** The minimal polynomial of the matrix
$$A=\begin{bmatrix}4&-2&2\\6&-3&4\\3&-2&3\end{bmatrix}\text{ is}$$
(a) $t^2+3t+2$ (b) $t^2-3t+2$
(c) $t^2+2t+3$ (d) $t^2-2t+3$

**109.** The minimal polynomial of the matrix
$$A=\begin{bmatrix}\alpha&a&0&0\\0&\alpha&a&0\\0&0&\alpha&a\\0&0&0&\alpha\end{bmatrix}\text{ is}$$
(a) $(\lambda-\alpha)$ (b) $(\lambda-\alpha)^2$
(c) $(\lambda-\alpha)^3$ (d) $(\lambda-\alpha)^4$

**110.** The minimal polynomial $m(\lambda)$ of
$$A=\begin{bmatrix}2&8&0&0&0&0&0\\0&2&0&0&0&0&0\\0&0&4&0&0&0&0\\0&0&1&3&0&0&0\\0&0&0&0&0&3&0\\0&0&0&0&0&0&0\\0&0&0&0&0&0&5\end{bmatrix}$$
(a) $t(t-2)(t-5)$
(b) $t^2(t-2)(t-5)$
(c) $t(t-2)^2(t-5)$
(d) $t^2(t-2)^2(t-5)$

**111.** If $\lambda$ is a non-zero eigen value of a linear operator $T$. Then, the following statement is/are correct

(a) $\lambda^n$ is an eigen value of $T^n$ for $n \geq 1$
(b) $\lambda^{-1}$ is an eigen value of $T^{-2}$
(c) $f(\lambda)$ is an eigen value of $f(T^{-1})$ for any polynomial $f(t)$
(d) None of the above

**112.** The linear operator $T$ for which the minimal polynomial $A(\lambda) = \lambda^n + a_{n-1}\lambda^{n-1} + \dots + a_1\lambda + a_0$ is

(a) $\begin{bmatrix} 0 & 0 & \dots & 0 & -a_0 \\ 1 & 0 & \dots & 0 & -a_1 \\ 0 & 1 & \dots & 0 & -a_2 \\ \vdots & \vdots & & \vdots & \vdots \\ 0 & 0 & \dots & 1 & -a_{n-1} \end{bmatrix}$ (b) $\begin{bmatrix} 0 & 0 & \dots & 0 & -a_{n-1} \\ 1 & 0 & \dots & 0 & -a_{n-2} \\ 0 & 1 & \dots & 0 & -a_{n-3} \\ \vdots & \vdots & & \vdots & \vdots \\ 0 & 0 & \dots & 1 & -a_0 \end{bmatrix}$

(c) $\begin{bmatrix} 0 & 0 & \dots & 0 & a_0 \\ 1 & 0 & \dots & 0 & a_1 \\ 0 & 1 & \dots & 0 & a_2 \\ \vdots & \vdots & \dots & \vdots & \vdots \\ 0 & 0 & \dots & 0 & a_{n-1} \end{bmatrix}$ (d) $\begin{bmatrix} 0 & 0 & \dots & 0 & a_{n-1} \\ 1 & 0 & \dots & 0 & a_{n-2} \\ 0 & 1 & \dots & 0 & a_{n-3} \\ \vdots & \vdots & \dots & \vdots & \vdots \\ 0 & 0 & \dots & 1 & a_0 \end{bmatrix}$

**113.** The linear operator $T$ for which the minimal polynomial $m(t) = t^3 - 5t^2 + 6t + 8$ is

(a) $\begin{bmatrix} 0 & 0 & -8 \\ 1 & 0 & -6 \\ 0 & 1 & 5 \end{bmatrix}$ (b) $\begin{bmatrix} 0 & 0 & 8 \\ 1 & 0 & 6 \\ 0 & 1 & 5 \end{bmatrix}$

(c) $\begin{bmatrix} 0 & 0 & 5 \\ 1 & 0 & -6 \\ 0 & 1 & -8 \end{bmatrix}$ (d) $\begin{bmatrix} 0 & 0 & -5 \\ 1 & 0 & 6 \\ 0 & 1 & 8 \end{bmatrix}$

**114.** The linear operator $T$ for which the minimal polynomial $m(t) = t^4 - 5t^3 - 2t^2 + 7t + 4$ is

(a) $\begin{bmatrix} 0 & 0 & 0 & -4 \\ 1 & 0 & 0 & -7 \\ 0 & 1 & 0 & 2 \\ 0 & 0 & 1 & 5 \end{bmatrix}$ (b) $\begin{bmatrix} 0 & 0 & 0 & 5 \\ 1 & 0 & 0 & 2 \\ 0 & 1 & 0 & -7 \\ 0 & 0 & 1 & -4 \end{bmatrix}$

(c) $\begin{bmatrix} 0 & 0 & 0 & -5 \\ 1 & 0 & 0 & -2 \\ 0 & 1 & 0 & 7 \\ 0 & 0 & 1 & 4 \end{bmatrix}$ (d) $\begin{bmatrix} 0 & 0 & 0 & 2 \\ 1 & 0 & 0 & 5 \\ 0 & 1 & 0 & 7 \\ 0 & 0 & 1 & 4 \end{bmatrix}$

**115.** Let $T$ be a linear operator on a finite dimensional vector space $V$. If

$$m(\lambda) = \lambda^r + a_{r-1}\lambda^{r-1} + a_{r-2}t^{r-2} \dots + a_1\lambda + a_0 \quad (a_0 \neq 0)$$

be a minimal polynomial of $T$, then

(a) $T$ is invertible (b) 0 is an eigen value of $T$
(c) $T$ is singular (d) 0 is a root of $m(\lambda)$

**116.** Let $T$ be a linear operator on a finite dimensional vector space $V$. If

$$m(\lambda) = \lambda^r + a_{r-2}\lambda^{r-1} + a_{r-3}\lambda^{r-2} + \dots + a_0\lambda$$

be a minimal polynomial of $T$, then

(a) $T$ is singular (b) $T$ is non-singular
(c) $T$ is invertible (d) 0 is not root of $m(\lambda)$

**117.** The change of basis matrix $P$ from the usual basis $B_1 = \{a_1, a_2, a_3\}$ of $R^3$ to the basis $B_2 = \{(1,1,1),(1,1,0),(1,0,0)\}$ is

(a) $\begin{bmatrix} 1 & 1 & 1 \\ 1 & 1 & 0 \\ 1 & 0 & 0 \end{bmatrix}$ (b) $\begin{bmatrix} 1 & 0 & 0 \\ 0 & 1 & 0 \\ 0 & 0 & 1 \end{bmatrix}$

(c) $\begin{bmatrix} 0 & 0 & 1 \\ 0 & 1 & 0 \\ 1 & 0 & 0 \end{bmatrix}$ (d) $\begin{bmatrix} 1 & 0 & 0 \\ 0 & 1 & 0 \\ 0 & 1 & 1 \end{bmatrix}$

**118.** Let $T$ and $S$ be two linear transformation such that

$$\begin{bmatrix} 1 & 0 & 0 & \dots & 0 \\ 0 & 2 & 0 & \dots & 0 \\ 0 & 0 & 3 & \dots & 0 \\ \vdots & \vdots & \vdots & & \vdots \\ 0 & 0 & 0 & \dots & n \end{bmatrix} \text{ and } S = \begin{bmatrix} 0 & 0 & 0 & \dots & 0 \\ 0 & 1 & 0 & \dots & 0 \\ 0 & 0 & 2 & \dots & 0 \\ \vdots & \vdots & \vdots & & \vdots \\ 0 & 0 & 0 & \dots & n-1 \end{bmatrix}, \text{ then}$$

(a) $T$ and $S$ both are invertible
(b) $T$ and $S$ both are not invertible
(c) $T$ is invertible but $S$ is not invertible
(d) $T$ is invertible but $S$ is not invertible

**119.** Let $T: V_2(R) \to V_2(R)$, where $T$ be the reflection of the points through the line $y = -x$, then (with respect to standard basis)

(a) $T$ must be diagonalizable
(b) $T$ is invertible
(c) minimal polynomial and characteristic polynomial are equal
(d) None of the above

**120.** Let $T: R^n \to R^n$ and $T(x_0) = 0$ for some $x_0 \neq 0, x \in R$, then there exist a matrix $A$ of order $n$ such that

(a) $Tx = Ax$ and $A$ is non singular
(b) $Tx = Ax$ and $A$ is singular
(c) $\ker(T) = \{0\}$
(d) None of the above

**121.** $D: P_n(R) \to P_{n-1}(R)$ and $I: P_{n-1}(R) \to P_n(R)$ defined by differentiation and integration

$D f(x) = f'(x)$, $I\{f(x)\} = \int_0^x f(t)\,dt$, then

(a) $D$ is linear where $I$ is not linear transformation
(b) $D$ is not linear while $I$ is linear transformation
(c) $D$ and $I$ both are not linear transformation
(d) $D$ and $I$ both are linear transformation

**122.** Let $P_2(R)$ be the polynomial space with basis $\{1, x, x^2\}$, then matrix representation of $T: p(x) \to \dfrac{p(x) - p(0)}{x}$ is

(a) $\begin{bmatrix} 1 & 1 & 0 \\ 0 & 0 & 1 \\ 0 & 0 & 0 \end{bmatrix}$ (b) $\begin{bmatrix} 0 & 1 & 0 \\ 0 & 0 & 1 \\ 0 & 0 & 0 \end{bmatrix}$

(c) $\begin{bmatrix} 0 & 1 & 1 \\ 0 & 0 & 0 \\ 0 & 0 & 0 \end{bmatrix}$ (d) $\begin{bmatrix} 1 & 1 & 1 \\ 0 & 0 & 0 \\ 0 & 0 & 0 \end{bmatrix}$

**123.** Let $T, P: (R) \to R^2$ be the linear transformation $T(a+bx) = (a, a+b)$, then which is false?
(a) $T$ is invertible.
(b) $T^{-1} = \begin{bmatrix} 1 & 0 \\ -1 & 1 \end{bmatrix}$ with respect to standard basis.
(c) $\exists$ a trivial subspace of $P$, $(R)$ which is equal to eigen space of $T$.
(d) $y$-axis in two dimensional plane will be eigen vector.

**124.** Let $T$ be any matrix and its characteristic polynomial is $T^2 - T + 1 = 0$, then what about $T$?
(a) $T$ is one-one.
(b) $T$ is not one-one.
(c) may be in some case trace $T \in R$ and in some cases may not.
(d) trace $T \in R$ always.

**125.** Let $T_1$ and $T_2$ be two linear operators on $R^2$ s.t. $T_1(x, y) = (0, x)$ and $T_2(x, y) = (y, 0)$, then
(a) $T_2^2 = T_1^2 = 0$
(b) $(T_1T_2)^2 = T_1T_2$
(c) $T_1 + T_2$ is invertible
(d) $(T_1T_2) \neq 0$

**126.** Let $A$ be a real $4 \times 4$ matrix with characteristic polynomial $P(T) = (T^2 + 1)^2$. Which of the following is true?
(a) $A$ is diagonalizable over complex numbers but not over real numbers
(b) $A$ is nilpotent
(c) $A$ is invertible
(d) There is no such matrix $A$

**127.** If $T: V \to V$ is a linear operator for $\dim V = n$ and $T$ has $n$ distinct eigen values, then
(a) $T$ must be invertible
(b) $T$ must be diagonalizable
(c) $T$ must be invertible as well as diagonalizable
(d) $T$ is not diagonalizable

**128.** Let $V$ be the vector space $R^2$ and let $T$ be the linear transformation on $V$ defined by $T(x, y) = (x + y, y)$. Then, the characteristic polynomial of $T$ is
(a) $1 - 3x + x^2$
(b) $2 - 2x$
(c) $1 - 2x + x^2$
(d) $1 + x^2$

**129.** Let $V$ be the vector space of all linear transformations from $R^3$ to $R^2$ under usual addition and scalar multiplication. Then,
(a) $V$ is a vector space of dimension 5
(b) $V$ is a vector space of dimension 6
(c) $V$ is a vector space of dimension 8
(d) $V$ is a vector space of dimension 9

**130.** Let $A = \begin{bmatrix} 1 & 2 & 2 \\ 2 & 1 & 2 \\ 2 & 2 & 1 \end{bmatrix}$. Then, the minimal polynomial of $A$ is
(a) $\lambda^2 - 4\lambda - 5$
(b) $\lambda^2 + 5\lambda + 4$
(c) $\lambda^3 - 3\lambda^2 - 9\lambda - 5$
(d) $\lambda^3 + 3\lambda^2 - 9\lambda + 5$

**131.** Let $A: R^6 \to R^5$ and $B: R^5 \to R^7$ be two linear transformations. Then, which of the following can be true?
(a) $A$ and $B$ are one-one
(b) $A$ is one-one and $B$ is not one-one
(c) $A$ is onto and $B$ is one-one
(d) $A$ and $B$ both are onto

**132.** Let the minimal polynomial of a linear transformation $T$ from $R^4$ to $R^4$ be $x^2 + x + 1$. Then,
(a) all eigen values of $T$ are real
(b) $T$ has exactly one real eigen values
(c) $T$ has exactly two real eigen values
(d) $T$ has no real eigen values

**133.** Suppose, that the minimal polynomial of a linear map $T: R^5 \to R^5$ is $x^2(x^3 - 1)$. Then,
(a) $T \equiv 0$
(b) $\det(T) = 0$
(c) $\det(T) \neq 0$
(d) $T$ is onto

**134.** Let $W$ be the vector space of all real polynomials of degree atmost 3. Defined $T: W \to W$ by $(TP)(x) = P'(x)$ where $P'$ is the derivative of $P$. The matrix of $T$ in the basis $\{1, x, x^2, x^3\}$ considered as column vectors, is given by
(a) $\begin{pmatrix} 0 & 0 & 0 & 0 \\ 0 & 1 & 0 & 0 \\ 0 & 0 & 2 & 0 \\ 0 & 0 & 0 & 3 \end{pmatrix}$
(b) $\begin{pmatrix} 0 & 0 & 0 & 0 \\ 1 & 0 & 0 & 0 \\ 0 & 2 & 0 & 0 \\ 0 & 0 & 3 & 0 \end{pmatrix}$
(c) $\begin{pmatrix} 0 & 1 & 0 & 0 \\ 0 & 0 & 2 & 0 \\ 0 & 0 & 0 & 3 \\ 0 & 0 & 0 & 0 \end{pmatrix}$
(d) $\begin{pmatrix} 0 & 1 & 2 & 3 \\ 0 & 0 & 0 & 0 \\ 0 & 0 & 0 & 0 \\ 0 & 0 & 0 & 0 \end{pmatrix}$

**135.** Let $T: K^n \to K^n$ s.t. $T(x_1 x_2, \ldots, x_n) = (0, x_1, x_2, \ldots, x_{n-1})$, then
(a) $T$ is diagonalizable
(b) $T$ is invertible
(c) $T$ is nilpotent
(d) Either diagonalizable or nilpotent

**136.** Let $T: R^7 \to R^7$ be a linear transformation such that $T^2 = 0$. Then, the rank of $T$ is
(a) $\leq 3$
(b) $> 3$
(c) $= 5$
(d) $= 6$

**137.** Let $P$ be the transition matrix from a basis $\{e_i\}$ to a basis $\{f_i\}$ in a vector space. Then, for any vector $v \in V_c$
(a) $P[v]_e = [v]_f$
(b) $[v]_e = [v]_f P^{-1}$
(c) $P[v]_f = [v]_e$
(d) $[v]_f = [v]_e P^{-1}$

**138.** Let $V$ be the space of all $n \times n$ matrices and $T: V \to V$ be a linear operator defined by $T(A) = \dfrac{A - A^T}{2}$, then nullity of $T$ is
(a) $2n$
(b) $\dfrac{n^2}{2}$
(c) $\dfrac{n(n+1)}{2}$
(d) $\dfrac{n(n-1)}{2}$

**139.** Let $A$, the matrix representation of a linear transformation $T:R^3 \to R^3$ *wrt* the basis $[5\ 1\ 3]^T, [3\ 2\ 2]^T$ and $[1\ 2\ 1]^T$, be given by

$$A = \begin{bmatrix} 3 & 2 & -2 \\ -1 & 0 & 1 \\ 2 & 1 & -1 \end{bmatrix}, \text{ then } T \text{ is given by}$$

(a) $T(x, y, z)^T = [3x + 2y - 2z, -x + z, 2x + y - z]^T$
(b) $T(x, y, z)^T = [3x - y + 2z, 2x + z, -2x + y - z]^T$
(c) $T(x, y, z)^T = [59x_1 + 16x_2 - 99x_3, 18x_1 + 5x_2 - 30x_3, 37x_1 + 10x_2 - 62x_3]^T$
(d) None of the above

**140.** Let $T:R^3 \to R^3$ be defined by
$T(a, b, c) = (a\cos\theta - b\sin\theta, a\sin\theta + b\cos\theta, c)$.Then,
(a) $T$ is a linear map and dimension of its kernel is 0
(b) $T$ is a linear map and dimension of its kernel is 1
(c) $T$ is not a linear map
(d) None of the above

**141.** The matrix of the linear transformation $T$ on $R^3(R)$ defined as
$T(x, y, z) = (2y + z, x - 4y, 3x)$ *wrt* the basis $B = \{(1,1,1), (1,1,0), (1,0,0)\}$ is $[T]_B$ is equal to

(a) $\begin{bmatrix} 3 & 3 & 3 \\ -6 & -6 & -2 \\ 6 & 5 & -1 \end{bmatrix}$ (b) $\begin{bmatrix} 3 & -6 & 6 \\ 3 & -6 & 5 \\ 3 & -2 & -1 \end{bmatrix}$

(c) $\begin{bmatrix} 3 & -6 & 6 \\ -6 & 5 & -2 \\ -1 & 3 & 3 \end{bmatrix}$ (d) None of these

**142.** Let $\{v_1, v_2, \ldots, v_{16}\}$ be an ordered basis for $V = C^{16}$. If $T$ is a linear transformation on V defined by $T(v_i) = v_i + 1$ for $1 \le i \le 15$ and
$T(v_{16}) = -(v_1 + v_2 + \ldots + v_{16})$. Then,
(a) $T$ is singular with rational eigen values
(b) $T$ is singular but has no rational eigen values
(c) $T$ is regular (invertible) with rational eigen values
(d) $T$ is regular but has no rational eigen values

**143.** Let $C$ be the vector space of all complex numbers over complex field C and $T$: $C \to C$ be defined by $T(z) = \bar{z}, z \in C$. Then,
(a) $T$ is a linear mapping
(b) $T$ is not linear mapping but a well defined map
(c) $T$ is not well defined
(d) None of the above

**144.** Let $R^{2\times2}$ be the real vector space of all $2\times2$ real matrices. For $Q = \begin{bmatrix} 1 & -2 \\ -2 & 4 \end{bmatrix}$, define a linear transformation $T$ on $R^{2\times2}$ as $T(P) = QP$. Then, the nullity of $T$ is
(a) 1 (b) 2
(c) 3 (d) 4

**145.** Let $W$ be the vector space of all polynomials on $R$ upto degree $n$ atmost and $T$ be the differential operator on $W$, then which of the following is not correct?
(a) $T$ is singular
(b) $T$ is nilpotent
(c) If $W$ be subspace of $V$; the vector space of all continuously differentiable function, then $W$ is $T$-invariant subspace of $V$
(d) $T$ is diagonalizable

**146.** Consider the basis $S = (v_1, v_2, v_3)$ for $R^3$ where $v_1 = (1, 1, 1)$, $v_2 = (1, 1, 0)$, $v_3 = (1, 0, 0)$ and let $T:R^3 \to R^2$ be a linear transformation such that $Tv_1 = (1, 0), Tv_2 = (2, -1), Tv_3 = (4, 3)$. Then, $T(2, -3, 5)$ is
(a) $(-1, 5)$ (b) $(3, 4)$
(c) $(0, 0)$ (d) $(9, 23)$

**147.** For the standard basis $\{(1, 0, 0), (0, 1, 0), (0, 0, 1)\}$ of $R^3$, a linear transformation $T$ from $R^3$ to $R^3$ has the matrix representation $\begin{bmatrix} 2 & 1 & -1 \\ 1 & -1 & 1 \\ 3 & 1 & -2 \end{bmatrix}$. Then, the image of $(2, 1, 2)$ under $T$ is
(a) $(11, 0, -1)$ (b) $(11, 3, -5)$
(c) $(7, 3, -5)$ (d) $(7, 3, -1)$

**148.** Let $T$ be a linear operator on a finite dimensional space $V$ and $c$ is any scalar, then $c$ is a characteristic value of $T$, if
(a) the operator $(T - cI)$ is singular
(b) the operator $(T - cI)$ is non-singular
(c) the operator $(T - cI)$ is identity
(d) the operator $(T - cI)$ is zero

**149.** The transformation $T:R^3 \to R^2$ defined by
$$T(x, y, z) = (x + y, y + z) \text{ is}$$
(a) linear and has zero kernel
(b) linear and has a proper subspace as kernel
(c) Neither linear nor one-one
(d) Neither linear nor onto

**150.** Consider the linear map $D$: $C^{(\infty)}(a, b)$, where $C^{(\infty)}(a, b)$ is the set of all real-valued continuously differential functions, defined by $D(f) = f'$, then
(a) $D$ is one-one and onto
(b) $D$ is one-one but not onto
(c) $D$ is onto but not one-one
(d) $D$ is neither one-one nor onto

**151.** If the complex field $C$ is the given vector space over the real field $R$ and operator $T$ on $C$ is defined on $T(z) = \bar{z}$. Then, the matrix of $T$ *wrt* the basis $\{1 + i, 1 + 2i\}$ is

(a) $\begin{bmatrix} 3 & 4 \\ -2 & -3 \end{bmatrix}$ (b) $\begin{bmatrix} 3 & -2 \\ 4 & 3 \end{bmatrix}$

(c) $\begin{bmatrix} 3 & 4 \\ 2 & 3 \end{bmatrix}$ (d) None of these

**152.** Let $V$ be the $l_2$ space of infinite sequences $v = (a_1, a_2, \ldots)$ of real number $a_i$ such that $\Sigma a_i^2$ is convergent, if $T$ be a map defined as $T(a_1, a_2, \ldots) = (0, a_1, a_2, \ldots)$. Then, select the correct statement/statements.

(I) $T$ is linear
(II) $T$ is one-one
(III) $T$ is onto

(a) (I) and (II) only
(b) (I) and (III) only
(c) Only (I)
(d) (I), (II) and (III)

**153.** Let $f, g$ be two non-zero functionals on a real vector space $V$. Then, the function $v \to \langle f(v), g(v) \rangle$ is

(a) also linear
(b) not well defined
(c) linear only if $f$ and $g$ are LD
(d) a quadratic form

**154.** Let $S$ be the parallelogram determined by the vectors $b_1 = \begin{bmatrix} 1 \\ 3 \end{bmatrix}$ and $b_2 = \begin{bmatrix} 5 \\ 1 \end{bmatrix}$, and let $A = \begin{bmatrix} 1 & -1 \\ 0 & 2 \end{bmatrix}$. Then, the area of the image of $S$ under the mapping $x \to Ax$ is

(a) 14
(b) 28
(c) 42
(d) 56

**155.** Consider the vector space $R^3$ and the maps $f, g: R^3 \to R^3$ defined by $f(x, y, z) = (x, |y|, z)$ and $g(x, y, z) = (x+1, y-1, z)$. Then,

(a) both $f$ and $g$ are linear
(b) neither $f$ nor $g$ is linear
(c) $g$ is linear but not $f$
(d) $f$ is linear but not $g$

**156.** Let $A$ be a real $4 \times 4$ matrix with characteristic polynomial $P(T) = (T^2 + 1)^2$. Which of the following is true?

(a) A is diagonalizable over complex numbers but not over real numbers
(b) A is nilpotent
(c) A is invertible
(d) there is no such matrix $A$

**157.** Let $v$ be non-zero vector in $R^3$. Consider the linear transformation $T: R^3 \to R^3$ defined by $T(w) = w - 2\frac{\langle w \bullet v \rangle}{\langle v \bullet v \rangle} v$. Which of the following is false?

(a) $T^2 = \text{identity}$
(b) $\det T = 1$
(c) $T(\mathbf{u}) = -\mathbf{u}$
(d) There is a non-zero vector $w$ such that $Tw = w$

**158.** Let $f: R^n \to R$ be a linear functional defined by $f(x^1, x^2, x^3, x^4) = -x^2$. If $\langle .,. \rangle$ denotes the standard inner product on $R^4$, then the unique vector $v \in R^4$ such that $f(w) = \langle v, w \rangle$ for all $w \in R^4$ is

(a) (0, −1, 0, 0)
(b) (0, 1, 0, 0)
(c) (0, 1, 0, 0)
(d) (1, 0, 1, −1)

**159.** Let the linear transformations $S$ and $T: R^3 \to R^3$ be defined by
$S(x, y, z) = (2x, 4x - y, 2x + 3y - z)$
$T(x, y, z) = (x\cos\theta - y\sin\theta, \sin\theta + y\cos\theta, z)$
where $0 < \theta < \pi/2$. Then,

(a) $S$ is one-to-one but not $T$
(b) $T$ is one-to-one but not $S$
(c) Both $S$ and $T$ are one-to-one
(d) Neither $S$ nor $T$ is one-to-one

**160.** Suppose $T: V \to V$ has characteristics polynomial $C(t) = (t+8)^4 (t-1)^3$ and minimum polynomial $m(t) = (t+8)^3 \ (t-1)^2$. Then,

(a) the geometrical multiplicity of 1 is less than that of −8
(b) the geometrical multiplicity of 1 is greater than that of −8
(c) the geometrical multiplicity of 1 is equal to that of −8
(d) $T$ has 7 LI eigen vectors

**161.** Let $U$ be the set of all invertible linear operators on a space $V$, then $U$ with the operation of composition of mappings

(a) is a group
(b) is not a group as it is not closed *wrt* operation
(c) is not a group as it does not contain null operator
(d) None of the above

**162.** Let a matrix $A_{m \times n}$ represents a linear mapping $T: V_n \to V_m$. Then, range of $T$ is generated by

(a) rows of $A$
(b) columns of $A$
(c) Both (a) and (b)
(d) None of these

**163.** Let $V$ be the space of all $n \times n$ matrices and $T: V \to V$ be a linear operator defined by $T(A) = \frac{A + A^T}{2}$, then nullity of $T$ is

(a) $2n$
(b) $\frac{n^2}{2}$
(c) $\frac{n(n+1)}{2}$
(d) $\frac{n(n-1)}{2}$

**164.** Let $T: C^n \to C^n$ be a linear operator having $n$ distinct eigen values. Then,

(a) $T$ is invertible
(b) $T$ is invertible as well as diagonalizable
(c) $T$ is not diagonalizable
(d) $T$ is diagonalizable

**165.** Let $V, W$ and $X$ be three finite dimensional vector spaces such that $\dim V = \dim X$. Suppose, $S: V \to W$ and $T: W \to X$ are two linear maps such that to $S: V \to X$ is injective. Then,

(a) $S$ and $T$ are surjective
(b) $S$ is surjective and $T$ is injective
(c) $S$ and $T$ are injective
(d) $S$ is injective and $T$ is surjective

**166.** Let $T$ be an arbitrary linear transformation from $R^n$ to $R^n$ which is not one-one. Then,

(a) rank $T > 0$
(b) rank $T = n$
(c) rank $T < n$
(d) rank $T = n - 1$

**167.** Let $T_1$ and $T_2$ be two linear operators on $R^3$ defined by
$T_1(x, y, z) = (x, x + y, x - y - z)$
$T_2(x, y, z) = (x + 2z, y - z, x + y + z)$. Then,

(a) $T_1$ is invertible but not $T_2$
(b) $T_2$ is invertible but not $T_1$
(c) Both $T_1$ and $T_2$ are invertible
(d) Neither $T_1$ nor $T_2$ is invertible

**168.** Consider the following $T:R^2 \to R^2$ such that $T(2,2)=(8,-6)$, $T(5,5)=(3,-2)$, then

(a) $T$ is a linear map and is unique
(b) $T$ is a linear map and they are infinite in number
(c) $T$ is a linear map and they are finitely many in number
(d) $T$ cannot be linear

**169.** If $(f_1, f_2, f_3)$ be the dual basis of the basis set $\{(1,-1,3),(0,1,-1),(0,3,-2)\}$ for $R^3(R)$. Then,

(a) $f_1(x,y,z)=x$
$f_2(x,y,z)=(x-y-3z)$
$f_3(x,y,z)=-2x+y+z$
(b) $f_1(x,y,z)=x$
$f_2(x,y,z)=7x-2y-3z$
$f_3(x,y,z)=-2x+y+z$
(c) $f_1(x,y,z)=x+y-z$
$f_2(x,y,z)=3x-2y-7z$
$f_3(x,y,z)=-2x+y+z$
(d) $f_1(x,y,z)=x$
$f_2(x,y,z)=7x-2y+3z$
$f_3(x,y,z)=-2x-y-z$

**170.** If $W_1=(0,a_2,a_3)$ and $W_2=(b_1,0,b_3)$ are two subspaces of $R^3$, where $R^n$ is a vector space of dim $n$. Then, the subspace $W_1 \cap W_2$ is isomorphic to the vector space

(a) $R$ (b) $R^2$
(c) $R^3$ (d) $2R^3$

**171.** Let $T$ be a linear transformation from $R^3 \to R^2$ defined by $T(x,y,z)=(x+y,y-z)$. Then, the matrix of $T$ with respect to the ordered bases $\{(1,1,1),(1,-1,0),(0,1,0)\}$ and $\{(1,1),(1,0)\}$ is

(a) $\begin{bmatrix}-2 & 0 & 1\\ 1 & 1 & -1\end{bmatrix}$ (b) $\begin{bmatrix}0 & -1 & 1\\ 2 & 1 & 0\end{bmatrix}$

(c) $\begin{bmatrix}2 & 1\\ 0 & -1\\ 1 & 1\end{bmatrix}$ (d) $\begin{bmatrix}0 & 2\\ -1 & 1\\ 1 & 0\end{bmatrix}$

**172.** Which among the following is not linear?

(a) $F:R^2 \to R^2$ such that $F(x,y)=(2x-y,x)$
(b) $F:R^3 \to R^2$ such that $F(x,y,z)=(z,x+y)$
(c) $F:R \to R^2$ such that $F(x)=(2x,3x)$
(d) $F:R^3 \to R^2$ such that $F(x,y,z)=(x+1,y+z)$

**173.** $T$ is non-singular iff

(a) nullity $(T) \neq 0$ (b) nullity $(T)=0$
(c) nullity $(T)=$ rank $(T)$ (d) rank $(T)=0$

**174.** If $T:R^4 \to R^3$ be the linear transformation defined by $T(x,y,z,w)=(x-y+z+w,x+2z-w,x+y+3z-3w)$, then the dimension of its range is

(a) 3 (b) 2
(c) 1 (d) 0

**175.** If the linear transformation $T:R^2 \to R^3$ is such that $T(1,0)=(2,3,1)$ and $T(1,1)=(3,0,2)$, then

(a) $T(x,y)=(x+y,2x+y,3x-3y)$
(b) $T(x,y)=(2x+y,3x-3y,x+y)$
(c) $T(x,y)=(2x-y,3x+3y,x-y)$
(d) $T(x,y)=(x-y,2x-y,3x+3y)$

**176.** Let $T:R^n \to R^m$ be a linear transformation and $A_{m\times n}$ be its matrix, representation. Then, choose the incorrect statement.

(a) Columns of $A$ are LI $\Rightarrow T$ is onto
(b) Columns of $A$ span $R^m \Rightarrow T$ is onto
(c) Columns of $A$ are LI $\Rightarrow T$ is one-one
(d) $T$ is one-one $\Rightarrow$ columns of $A$ are LI

**177.** Let $M=\begin{bmatrix}1 & 2\\ 0 & 0\end{bmatrix}$ and $T:V \to V$ be the linear map defined by $T(A)=AM$ where $V$ be the vector space of all $2\times 2$ real matrices. Then, rank and nullity of $T$, respectively

(a) 1, 3 (b) 3, 1
(c) 2, 2 (d) 4, 0

**178.** Let $T:R^3 \to W$, be the orthogonal projection of $R^3$ on to the xz plane $W$, then

(a) $T(x,y,z)=(x+y,0,y+z)$
(b) $T(x,y,z)=(x-y,0,y-z)$
(c) $T(x,y,z)=(x+y+z,0,z)$
(d) $T(x,y,z)=(x,0,z)$

**179.** Consider the two linear maps $T_1$ and $T_2$ on $V_3$ defined as $T_1(x_1,x_2,x_3)=(0,x_2,x_3)$ and $T_2(x_1,x_2,x_3)=(x_1,0,0)$. Then,

(a) $T_1$ is idempotent but $T_2$ is not idempotent
(b) $T_2$ is idempotent but $T_1$ is not idempotent
(c) Both $T_1$ and $T_2$ are idempotent
(d) Neither $T_1$ nor $T_2$ are idempotent

**180.** For a linear transformation $T:R^{10} \to R^6$, the kernel is having dimension 5. Then, the dimension of the range of $T$ is

(a) 5 (b) 6
(c) 4 (d) 2

**181.** Let $T:R^n \to R^m$ be a linear transformation and let $A$ be the standard matrix for $T$, then select the correct statement

(I) $T$ maps $R^n$ onto $R^m$ if and only if the columns of $A$ span $R^m$.
(II) $T$ is one-one iff the columns of $A$ are linearly independent.
(III) $T$ is one-one iff the equation $T(x)=0$ has only the trivial solution.

(a) only (I) and (II) (b) only (I) and (III)
(c) only (II) and (III) (d) (I), (II) and (III)

**182.** If $T$ be a linear operator on a vector space $V$ such that $T^2-T+I=\hat{0}$, then

(a) $T$ is one-one but may not be onto
(b) $T$ is onto but may not be one-one
(c) $T$ is invertible
(d) no such $T$ exists

**183.** Let $T:V_2(R) \to V_2(R)$ where $T$ be the reflection of the points through the line $y=-x$. Then, the matrix of $T$ with respect to standard basis is

(a) $\begin{bmatrix}1 & 0\\ 0 & -1\end{bmatrix}$ (b) $\begin{bmatrix}-1 & 0\\ 0 & 1\end{bmatrix}$

(c) $\begin{bmatrix}0 & 1\\ 1 & 0\end{bmatrix}$ (d) $\begin{bmatrix}0 & -1\\ -1 & 0\end{bmatrix}$

# Exercise 2 (For Part 'C')

**Directions** (Q. Nos. 1-48) *Questions may have one or more than one correct option.*

**1.** Let $T_1$ and $T_2$ are two linear transforms from $V_3(R)$ to $V_2(R)$, defined by
$T_1(a, b, c) = (2a, b + c)$, $T_2(a, b) = (b, a)$
(a) $T_2 T_1$ is not defined
(b) $T_2 T_1$ is defined
(c) $T_1 T_2$ is not defined
(d) $T_1 T_2$ is defined

**2.** If $V$ is $n$-dimensional vector space and $T$ is a linear transformation on $V$ such that rank and nullity of $T$ are identical
(a) $\dim R(T) = \dim N(T)$
(b) rank $(T)$ + nullity $(T) = \dim V$
(c) $n$ is even number
(d) $n$ is odd number

**3.** If $T_1$ and $T_2$ are two linear operators defined as $T_1(u_1, u_2) = (u_1, 0)$ and $T_2(u_1, u_2) = (u_2, u_1)$
(a) $T_1T_2 = T_2T_1$
(b) $T_1T_2 \neq T_2T_1$
(c) $T_1T_2(u_1, u_2) = (u_1, 0)$
(d) $T_1T_2(u_1, u_2) = (0, u_1)$

**4.** Let $f_1$ and $f_2$ are two lines functionals on vector space $V$ over a set of real numbers, defined as
$f_1(a, b) = a + 2b$ and $f_2(a, b) = 3a - b, a, b \in R$
(a) $(f_1 - f_2)(a, b) = -2a + 3b$
(b) $(f_1 - f_2)(a, b) = 2a + 6b$
(c) $(f_1 - f_2)(a, b) = (a + 2b) - (3a - b)$
(d) $(f_1 - f_2)(a, b) = (a + 3b) - (6a - b)$

**5.** Let $T$ be a linear operator on a finite dimensional vector space such that $N(T) = 0$. Then,
(a) $T$ is non-singular
(b) $T$ is one-one
(c) $T$ is onto
(d) All of these

**6.** Let $T$ be a linear operator on a finite dimensional vector space of dim $n$ such that rank $T = n$. Then,
(a) $T$ is non-singular
(b) $T$ is one-one
(c) $T$ is onto
(d) All of these

**7.** Let $R$ be the field of real numbers and $V$ is a vector space of all functions from $R$ into $R$, which are continuous? If
$(Tf)(x) = \int_0^x f(t)\,dt, f \in V$, then
(a) $T$ is linear transform
(b) $T$ is not a linear transform
(c) $T(cf_1 + f_2)(x) = \int_0^x (cf_1 + f_2)(t)dt$
(d) $T(cf_1 + f_2)(x) = \int_0^x c_1 f_1(t)dx$

**8.** Show that $f(x, y) = (x + 2, y + 2)$ is not linear.
(a) $f$ map zero vector onto zero vector
(b) $f$ does not map zero vector onto zero vector
(c) $f$ is not linear
(d) $f$ is linear

**9.** The product of two linear transformations can be a zero transformation
(a) if both of them are zero transformation
(b) if neither of them is a zero transformation
(c) if one of them is a zero transformation
(d) All of the above statements are true

**10.** Let $X, Y$ and $Z$ be vector spaces over the same field. Let $f: X \to Y$ and $g: y \to Z$ be linear maps.
(a) If $f$ and $g$ are invertible, then $fg$ is invertible
(b) If $f$ and $g$ are invertible, then $fg$ is not invertible
(c) $(fg)(g^{-1}f^{-1}) = (g^{-1}f^{-1})(fg)$
(d) $(fg)(g^{-1}f^{-1}) \neq (g^{-1}f^{-1})(fg)$

**11.** Let $T: \mathbb{R}^5 \to \mathbb{R}^5$ be a linear transformation such that $T^4(x) = 0$. Then,
(a) rank $T = 2$
(b) rank $T = 3$
(c) nullity $T = 2$
(d) nullity $T = 3$

**12.** Let $T: R^4 \to R^3$ be the linear transformation defined by $T(x, y, z, t) = (x - y + z + t, 2x - 2y + 3z + 4t, 3x - 3y + 4z + 5t)$. Then,
(a) $\{(1, 2, 3), (0, 1, 1)\}$ is a basis of rank space of $T$
(b) $\{(1, 2, 3), (2, 4, 6)\}$ is a basis of rank space of $T$
(c) rank $T = 2$
(d) rank $T = 3$

**13.** Let $R$ be the field of real numbers and $V$ is a vector space of all functions from $R$ into $R$, which are continuous. If $(Tf)(x) = \int_0^x f(t)dt, f \in V$
(a) $T$ is linear transform
(b) $T$ is not a linear transform
(c) $T(cf_1 + f_2)x = \int_0^x (cf_1 + f_2)(t)dt$
(d) $T(cf_1 + f_2)x = \int_0^x f_1 f_2(t)dt$

**14.** Given the mapping $f: \mathbb{R}^2 \to \mathbb{R}^2$, such that $f(x, y) = (a_1x + b_1y + c_1, a_2x + b_2y + c_2)$
(a) the mapping $f$ is a vector space isomorphism
(b) the mapping $f$ is not a vector space isomorphism
(c) the mapping $f$ is a linear transformation
(d) the mapping $f$ is one-one onto

**15.** Let $X$ and $Y$ be vector spaces over a field $K$ and let $f: X \to Y$ be an invertible linear map.
(a) $f^{-1}: Y \to X$ is linear
(b) $f^{-1}: Y \to X$ is not linear
(c) $f(x_1 + x_2) = f(x_1) + f(x_2)$
(d) $f(x_1 + x_2) \neq f(x_1) + f(x_2)$

**16.** Let $V$ be a finite dimensional inner product space and let $\mathbb{B} = (\alpha_1, \ldots, \alpha_n)$ be an (ordered) orthonormal basis for $V$.. Let $T$ be a linear operator on $V$ and let $A$ be the matrix of $T$ in the ordered basis $\mathbb{B}$

(a) $A_{kj} \equiv \left(\frac{T_{\alpha j}}{\alpha_k}\right)$ (b) $\alpha = \sum_{k=1}^{n} (\alpha / \alpha_k)\alpha_k$

(c) $\alpha = \sum_{k=1}^{n} (\alpha / \alpha_k)$ (d) $T\alpha_j = \sum_{k=1}^{n} (T\alpha_j / \alpha_k)\alpha_k$

**17.** Let $T: R^4 \to R^3$ be the linear transformation given by $T(x, y, z, t) = (x - y + z + t, x + 2z - t, x + y + 3z - 3t)$. Then,
(a) $\{(1, 1, 1), (0, 1, 2)\}$ form a basis for rank space of $T$
(b) $\{(2, 1, -1, 0), (1, 2, 0, 1)\}$ form a basis of ker $T$
(c) rank $T = 2$
(d) nullity of $T = 2$

**18.** Let $\dim[\hom(V, U)] = 12$. Then, there may exists $V$ and $U$ such that
(a) $\dim V = 3$ and $\dim U = 4$
(b) $\dim V = 6$ and $\dim U = 2$
(c) $\dim V = 1$ and $\dim U = 12$
(d) $\dim V = 4$ and $\dim U = 3$

**19.** A polynomial whose roots are $-3, -1, 4, 5$ is
(a) $(x + 3)(x + 1)(x - 4)(x - 5)$
(b) $(x - 3)(x - 1)(x + 4)(x + 5)$
(c) $x^4 - 5x^3 - 13x^2 + 53x + 60$
(d) $x^4 + 5x^3 + 13x^2 - 53x + 60$

**20.** Let $M_1$ and $M_2$ are complementary subspaces of a linear space $L$, and given the mapping $f$ which assigns to each vector $y$ in $M_2$ the coset $M_1 + y$
(a) $f$ is an isomorphism between $M_2$ and $L / M_1$
(b) $f$ is not an isomorphism between $M_2$ and $L / M_1$
(c) $f$ is one-one
(d) $f$ is onto

**21.** Let $T_1$ and $T_2$ be linear transformations on $\mathbb{R}^2$ defined as follows

$$T_1(x_1, x_2) = (x_2, x_1) \text{ and } T_2(x_1, x_2) = (x_1, 0)$$

(a) $T_1T_2 \neq T_2T_1$ (b) $T_1T_2 = T_2T_1$
(c) $T_1T_2(x_1, x_2) = (0, x_1)$ (d) $T_2T_1(x_1, x_2) = (x_2, 0)$

**22.** Let $V$ be a complex vector space and $f$ a form on $V$ such that $f(\alpha, \alpha)$ is real for every $\alpha$.
(a) $f$ is Hermitian
(b) $f$ is not Hermitian
(c) Let $\alpha, \beta \in V$, then $f(\alpha, \beta) = \overline{f(\beta, \alpha)}$
(d) Let $\alpha, \beta \in V$, then $f(\alpha, \beta) \neq \overline{f(\beta, \alpha)}$

**23.** If $\mathbb{B} = \{\alpha_1, \ldots, \alpha_n\}$ is an ordered basis for $V$ and $\mathbb{B}^* = \{L_1, \ldots, L_n\}$ is the dual basis for $V^*$. Also, given the $n^2$ bilinear forms
$f_{ij}(\alpha, \beta) = L_i(\alpha)L_j(\beta)$, $1 \leq i \leq n$, $1 \leq j \leq n$
(a) it form a basis for the space $L(V, V, F)$
(b) it does not form a basis for the space $L(V, V, F)$
(c) if $\alpha = \Sigma x_i\alpha_i$ and $\beta = \Sigma y_i\alpha_i$, then $f_{ij}(\alpha, \beta) = x_iy_i$
(d) if $\alpha = \Sigma x_i\alpha_i$ and $\beta = \Sigma y_i\alpha_i$, then $f_{ij}(\alpha, \beta) \neq x_iy_i$

**24.** Let $T$ be the linear operator on $R^2$ defined by $T(x, y) = (2x + y, 3x + 2y)$. Then,
(a) $T$ is invertible (b) $T$ is non-singular
(c) $T$ is singular (d) None of these

**25.** Which of the following(s) is/are linear transformation?
(a) $T: R^2 \to R^2$ given by $T(x, y) = (xy, x)$
(b) $T: R^2 \to R^2$ given by $T(x, y) = (x + 3, 2y, x + y)$
(c) $T: R^3 \to R^2$ given by $T(x, y, z) = (|x|, y + z)$
(d) None of the above

**26.** Let $X$ and $Y$ be vector spaces over a field $K$ and let $f: X \to Y$ be a linear map. The mapping $f$ is invertible
(a) if there exists a linear map $g: Y \to X$ such that $fg = id_y$ and $gf = id_x$ and this mapping $g$ is written as $f^{-1}$
(b) if there exists a linear map $g: Y \to X$ such that $fg = id_y$ and $gf = id_x$ and this mapping $g$ is written as $f^{-1}$, then $f$ is invertible.
(c) if $f$ is invertible, then $f$ is onto
(d) if $f$ is invertible, then $f$ is one-one

**27.** Let $P$ be the real linear space of all polynomials $f(x)$ with real coefficients defined on the closed interval $[0, 1]$. Let $D$ and $T$ be two transformations on $P$ defined as for every $f(x) \in P$

$$D[f(x)] = \frac{d}{dx} f(x) \text{ and } T[f(x)] = xf(x)$$

(a) $DT \neq TD$
(b) $DT = TD$
(c) $(DT)[f(x)] = f(x) + x\frac{d}{dx} f(x)$
(d) $(TD)[f(x)] = x\frac{d}{dx} f(x)$

**28.** Which of the following(s) is/are correct?
(a) A square matrix $A$ of order $n$ is invertible, if the corresponding linear operator $f$ (with regard to some fixed basis) is invertible
(b) The linear operator $f$(with regard to some fixed basis) is invertible, if a square matrix of order $n$ is invertible
(c) The linear operator $f$ (with regard to some fixed basis) is invertible, if a square matrix of order $n$ is not invertible
(d) A square matrix $A$ of order $n$ is invertible, if the corresponding linear operator $f$ is not invertible

**29.** Which of the following(s) is/are true?
(a) For the differentiation transformation $D: F[x] \to F[x]$, Im $D = F[x]$, and ker $D$ = Subspace of polynomials of zero degree or scalars.
(b) For the integration transformation $\int : F[x] \to F[x]$, $\ker \int = \{0\}$ and $\text{Im} \int = \{f(x) \in F[x] : f(0) = 0\}$
(c) Either (a) or (b) is true
(d) Neither (a) nor (b) is true

**30.** Let $V$ and $W$ be vector spaces over the field $F$. Let $T$ and $U$ be linear transformations from $V$ into $W$. The function $(T + U)$ is defined as $(T + U)(\alpha) = T\alpha + U\alpha$

If $c$ is any element of $F$, then the function $(cT)$ is defined as $(cT)(\alpha) = c(T\alpha)$

(a) $(T+U)$ is a linear transformation
(b) $(T+U)$ is not a linear transformation
(c) $(cT)$ is a linear transformation
(d) $(cT)$ is not a linear transformation

**31.** Let $L(F)$ be a linear space and $S, T, U$ be linear transformations on $L$. Then,
(a) $S\hat{0} = \hat{0} = \hat{0}S$ (b) $SI = S = IS$
(c) $S(TU) = (ST)U$ (d) $(S+T)U = SU + TU$

**32.** Given $f: X \to Y$ is a linear map
(a) $f$ is one-one $\Rightarrow N(f) = (0)$
(b) $f$ is one-one $\Rightarrow N(f) \neq (0)$
(c) $N(f) = \{0\} \Rightarrow f$ is one-one
(d) $N(f) = \{0\} \Leftrightarrow f$ is one-one

**33.** The following statement(s) is/are true.
(a) A square matrix $A$ of order $n$ is invertible, if the corresponding linear operator $f$ (with regard to some fixed basis) is invertible.
(b) The corresponding linear operator $f$ (with regard to some fixed basis) is invertible, if a square matrix $A$ of order $n$ is invertiable.
(c) A square matrix $A$ of order $n$ is invertible, if the corresponding linear operator $f$ (with regard to some fixed basis) is invertible.
(d) A square matrix $A$ of order $n$ is not invertible, if the corresponding linear operator $f$ (with regard to some fixed basis) is invertible.

**34.** Given the mapping $f: V_3(F) \to V_2(F)$ defined by
$$f(a_1, a_2, a_3) = (a_1, a_2)$$
(a) $f$ is homomorphism of $V_3(F)$ onto $V_2(F)$
(b) $f$ is not a homomorphism of $V_3(F)$ onto $V_2(F)$
(c) $\{(0, 0, a): a \in F\}$ is a kernel of $f$
(d) $\{(0,0,0): a \in F\}$ is not a kernel of $f$

**35.** If $M_1$ and $M_2$ are complementary subspaces of a linear space $L$, then the mapping $f$ which assigns to each vector $y$ in $M_2$ the coset $M_1 + y$ is ... between $M_2$ and $L/M_1$.
(a) onto (b) one-one
(c) linear (d) isomorphism

**36.** Let $T: R^3 \to R^3$ be the linear transformation which rotates a vector about the $z$-axis through an angle $\theta$ $T(x, y, z) = (x\cos\theta - y\sin\theta, x\sin\theta + y\cos\theta, z)$. Then,
(a) $T$ is singular (b) $T$ is non-singular
(c) $T$ is one-one (d) Kernel of $T = \{0\}$

**37.** Let $T: R^2 \to R$ be a linear transformation such that $T(1,1) = 3$ and $T(0,1) = -2$
(a) $T^{-1}(6) = \dfrac{x+5}{6}, \forall x \in R$ (b) $T^{-1}(6) = \dfrac{2x+6}{5}, \forall x \in R$
(c) $T$ is one-one (d) $T$ is not one-one

**38.** If $A$ and $B$ are similar matrices, then
(a) $\text{tr}(A) = \text{tr}(B)$ (b) $|A| = |B|$
(c) $\text{Ch}(A) = \text{Ch}(B)$ (d) None of these

**39.** Let $T$ be a linear operator on a finite dimensional vector space $V$.
If $m(t) = \lambda^r + a_r\lambda^{r-1} + a_{r-3}\lambda^{r-2} + ... + a_2\lambda$ be a minimal polynomial of $T$, then
(a) $T$ is singular (b) $T$ is non-singular
(c) $T$ is invertible (d) 0 is a root of $m(\lambda)$

**40.** Let $T$ be any matrix and its characteristic polynomial is $T^2 - T + 1 = 0$, then what about $T$?
(a) $T$ is one-one.
(b) $T$ is not one-one.
(c) may be in some cases trace $T \in R$ and in some cases may not.
(d) trace $T \in R$ always

**41.** Let $T$ be a linear operator on a finite dimensional vector space $V$. If $m(t) = \lambda^r + a_{r-1}\lambda^{r-1} + a_{r-2}t^{r-2} ... + a_1\lambda + a_0 (a_0 \neq 0)$ be a minimal polynomial of $T$, then
(a) $T$ is invertible
(b) 0 is not an eigen value of $T$
(c) $T$ is not singular
(d) 0 is not a root of $m(\lambda)$

**42.** Let $A = \begin{bmatrix} 7 & 1 & 0 & 0 \\ 0 & 7 & 1 & 0 \\ 0 & 0 & 7 & 1 \\ 0 & 0 & 0 & 7 \end{bmatrix}$ be the Jordan block of order 4, then
(a) characteristic polynomial $= (t-7)^4$
(b) minimal polynomial $= (t-7)^4$
(c) characteristic and minimal, polynomials are not equal
(d) 7 is only eigen value

**43.** Let $T: V \to V$ be a linear operator, then which of the following is/are correct?
(a) $\{0\}$ is invariant under $T$
(b) $V$ is invariant under $T$
(c) Kernel of $T$ is invariant under $T$
(d) image of $T$ is invariant under $T$

**44.** Let $A$ be an $n$ square matrix $A$ of index $r$, then
(a) minimal polynomial $m(t) = t^r$
(b) 0 is an eigen value of $A$
(c) $A$ is singular
(d) $A$ is non-singular

**45.** Let $T: V \to U$ be the linear transformation such that defined by maps independent sets into independent sets, then
(a) $T$ is singular (b) $T$ is non-singular
(c) $\det T \neq 0$ (d) None of these

**46.** Let $T: V \to U$ be a linear transformation such that $V$ has finite dimension and $\dim V = \dim U$. Then, $T$ is an isomorphism if and only if
(a) $T$ is one-one (b) $T$ is onto
(c) $T$ is singular (d) $T$ is non-singular

**47.** If $\lambda$ is a non-zero eigen value of a linear operator $T$. Then, which of the following statement is/are correct?
(a) $\lambda^n$ is an eigen value of $T^n$ for $n \geq 1$
(b) $\lambda^{-1}$ is an eigen value of $T^{-1}$
(c) $f(\lambda)$ is an eigen value of $f(T)$ for any polynomial $f(t)$
(d) None of the above

**48.** Let $T: V \to V$ be the linear transformation such as $T[f(t)] = tf(t)$, where $f(t)$ is a polynomial. Then,
(a) $T$ is singular (b) $T$ is non-singular
(c) $T$ is one-one (d) None of these

# Answers

## Exercise 1

**1.** (b) **2.** (c) **3.** (c) **4.** (d) **5.** (b) **6.** (b) **7.** (c) **8.** (a) **9.** (c) **10.** (d)
**11.** (b) **12.** (d) **13.** (c) **14.** (c) **15.** (c) **16.** (d) **17.** (c) **18.** (c) **19.** (c) **20.** (c)
**21.** (a) **22.** (b) **23.** (a) **24.** (a) **25.** (c) **26.** (c) **27.** (c) **28.** (b) **29.** (c) **30.** (a)
**31.** (a) **32.** (b) **33.** (a) **34.** (a) **35.** (b) **36.** (b) **37.** (a) **38.** (a) **39.** (a) **40.** (b)
**41.** (a) **42.** (d) **43.** (c) **44.** (b) **45.** (b) **46.** (d) **47.** (d) **48.** (c) **49.** (b) **50.** (b)
**51.** (b) **52.** (c) **53.** (a) **54.** (d) **55.** (b) **56.** (b) **57.** (a) **58.** (b) **59.** (c) **60.** (a)
**61.** (b) **62.** (c) **63.** (a) **64.** (b) **65.** (c) **66.** (b) **67.** (c) **68.** (a) **69.** (b) **70.** (a)
**71.** (a) **72.** (b) **73.** (d) **74.** (b) **75.** (d) **76.** (b) **77.** (d) **78.** (b) **79.** (b) **80.** (a)
**81.** (c) **82.** (c) **83.** (b) **84.** (b) **85.** (c) **86.** (a) **87.** (b) **88.** (a) **89.** (a) **90.** (b)
**91.** (b) **92.** (d) **93.** (c) **94.** (c) **95.** (b) **96.** (d) **97.** (c) **98.** (a) **99.** (a) **100.** (a)
**101.** (c) **102.** (b) **103.** (b) **104.** (b) **105.** (c) **106.** (d) **107.** (a) **108.** (b) **109.** (d) **110.** (d)
**111.** (a) **112.** (a) **113.** (a) **114.** (a) **115.** (a) **116.** (a) **117.** (a) **118.** (d) **119.** (b) **120.** (a)
**121.** (a) **122.** (b) **123.** (c) **124.** (a) **125.** (a) **126.** (c) **127.** (c) **128.** (c) **129.** (b) **130.** (a)
**131.** (c) **132.** (d) **133.** (b) **134.** (c) **135.** (c) **136.** (a) **137.** (c) **138.** (c) **139.** (c) **140.** (a)
**141.** (a) **142.** (d) **143.** (b) **144.** (b) **145.** (d) **146.** (d) **147.** (b) **148.** (a) **149.** (b) **150.** (c)
**151.** (a) **152.** (a) **153.** (d) **154.** (b) **155.** (b) **156.** (c) **157.** (b) **158.** (a) **159.** (c) **160.** (c)
**161.** (a) **162.** (c) **163.** (d) **164.** (d) **165.** (d) **166.** (c) **167.** (a) **168.** (d) **169.** (b) **170.** (a)
**171.** (b) **172.** (d) **173.** (b) **174.** (b) **175.** (b) **176.** (a) **177.** (c) **178.** (d) **179.** (c) **180.** (a)
**181.** (c) **182.** (c) **183.** (d)

## Exercise 2

**1.** (b,c) **2.** (a,b,c) **3.** (b,c,d) **4.** (a,c) **5.** (d) **6.** (d) **7.** (a,c) **8.** (b,c) **9.** (d) **10.** (a,c)
**11.** (b,c) **12.** (a,c) **13.** (a,c) **14.** (a,c,d) **15.** (a,c) **16.** (a,b,d) **17.** (a,b,c,d) **18.** (a,b,c,d) **19.** (a,c) **20.** (a,c,d)
**21.** (a,c,d) **22.** (a,c) **23.** (a,c) **24.** (a,b) **25.** (d) **26.** (a,b,c,d) **27.** (a,c,d) **28.** (a,b) **29.** (a,b) **30.** (a,c)
**31.** (a,b,c,d) **32.** (a,c,d) **33.** (a,b,c) **34.** (a,c) **35.** (a,b,c,d) **36.** (b,c,d) **37.** (b,d) **38.** (a,b,c) **39.** (a,d) **40.** (a,d)
**41.** (a,b,c,d) **42.** (a,b,c,d) **43.** (a,b,c,d) **44.** (a,b,c) **45.** (b,c) **46.** (a,b,d) **47.** (a,b,c) **48.** (b,c)

# Hints & Solutions

## Exercise 1

**1.** First we will show that the set $\{(1,0), (1,1)\}$ is a basis of $R^2$.

For linear independent of this set

Let $a(1,0) + b(1,1) = (0,0)$ where $a, b \in R$,

then $(a+b,\ b) = (0,0)$

$\Rightarrow \quad a+b=0,\ b=0$

$\Rightarrow \quad a=0,\ b=0$

Hence, the set $\{(1,0), (1,1)\}$ is linearly independent.

Now, we will show that the set $\{(1,0),(1,1)\}$ space $R^2$.

Let $(x, y) \in R^2$ and let

$(x, y) = a(1,0) + b(1,1)$

$\Rightarrow \quad (x, y) = (a+b,\ b)$

$\Rightarrow \quad a+b = x,\ \ b = y$

$\Rightarrow \quad a = x - b$

$\Rightarrow \quad a = x - y \qquad (\because\ b = y)$

Here, $T(e_1) = (2, 3, 1)$

and $T(e_2) = (3, 0, 2)$

set $(x, y) = ae_1 + be_2$

or $T(x, y) = aT(e_1) + bT(e_2)$

$\leq x - y\,(2, 3, 1) + y\,(3, 0, 2)$

$= (2x - 2y + 3y),\ 3(x-y),\ (x - y + 2y)$

Hence, $T(x, y) = (2x + y,\ 3x - 3y,\ x + y), \forall\ x,\ y \in R^2$

**2.** Here, it is given that

$T : R^3 \to R^2$ be the linear transformation given by

$T(x, y, z) = (x, y),\ \forall\ (x, y, z) \in R^3$

basis $\{(1,0),(1,1)\}$ of $R^2$

$\therefore$ Standard basis of $R^3 = \{(1,0,0),(0,1,0),(0,0,1)\}$
$= \{e_1, e_2, e_3\}$

$\therefore$ $T(1,0,0) = (1,0) = 1(1,0) + 0(1,1)$
$T(0,1,0) = (0,1) = -1(1,0) + 1(1,1)$
$T(0,0,1) = (0,0) = 0(1,0) + 0(1,1)$

Hence, Matrix of $T = \begin{bmatrix} 1 & -1 & 0 \\ 0 & 1 & 0 \end{bmatrix}$

**3.** Here, it is given that
$T : R^3 \to R^3$ be defined by $T(x,y,z) = (x,y,0)$
and $S : R^2 \to R^2$ be defined by $S(x,y) = (2x, 3y)$

$\therefore$ $\ker T = \{(x,y,z) \in R^3 : T(x,y,z) = (0,0,0)\}$
$\ker T = \{(x,y,z) \in R^3 : (x,y,0) = (0,0,0)\}$
*i.e.,* $x = 0,\ y = 0$
$\therefore$ $\ker T = \{(0,0,z)\} \neq \{(0,0,0)\}$,
So, $T$ is singular.

Now, $S(x,y) = (2x, 3y)$
$\therefore$ $\ker S = \{(x,y) \in R^2 : S(x,y) = (0,0)\}$
$\ker S = \{(x,y) \in R^2 : (2x, 3y) = (0,0)$ *i.e.,* $x = 0,\ y = 0$
$\therefore$ $\ker S = \{(0,0)\}$
$S$ is non-singular.

**4.** Here, given linear transformation
$T : R^4 \to R^4$ given by
$T(x,y,z,u) - (x,y,0,0), \forall (x,y,z,u) \in R^4$
$\therefore$ Dimension of $R^4 = 4$
Now, $T(x,y,z,u) = 0\,(x,y,0,0)$
$\therefore$ $\ker T = \{(x,y,z,0) \in R^4 : T(x,y,z,u)\}$
$= \{(0,0,0,0)\}$
$= (x,y,0,0) = (0,0,0,0)$
$x = 0,\ y = 0$
$\therefore$ $\ker T = \{(0,0,z,u)\}$
Now, $(0,0,z,u)$ can be written as
$\{(0,0,z,0) + (0,0,0,0)\}$
*i.e.,* $\{z(0,0,1,0) + (0,0,0,1)u\}$
*i.e.,* $\{(0,0,1,0), (0,0,0,1)\}$ is linearly independent and span $\ker T$. Hence, it is basis for $\ker T$.
$\therefore$ Nullity of $T = 2$
Now, dimension of $R^4$ = Nullity of $T$ + Rank of $T$
$\therefore$ Rank of $T = 4 - 2 = 2$

**5.** Null space or kernel of a linear transformation $T$.
Let $u(F)$ and $v(F)$ be two vector space and let $T$ be a linear transformation from $u$ to $v$, then the null space of $T$ written as $N(T)$ is the set of all vectors $\alpha$ in $u$
such that $T(\alpha) = 0$ (zero vector of $v$)
Thus, $N(T) = \{\alpha \in u : T(\alpha) = 0 \in v\}$
The null space of $T$ is also called the kernel of $T$.
Now, the standard basis for a vector space of all $2 \times 2$ matrix over field $R$ of real number is $\{e_1, e_2, e_3, e_4\}$
where $e_1 = \begin{bmatrix} 1 & 0 \\ 0 & 0 \end{bmatrix},\ e_2 = \begin{bmatrix} 0 & 1 \\ 0 & 0 \end{bmatrix}$

$e_3 = \begin{bmatrix} 0 & 0 \\ 1 & 0 \end{bmatrix},\ e_4 = \begin{bmatrix} 0 & 0 \\ 0 & 1 \end{bmatrix}$

We have, $T(A) = AB - BA$, where $B = \begin{pmatrix} 1 & 2 \\ 0 & 3 \end{pmatrix}$

So, $T(e_1) = \begin{pmatrix} 1 & 0 \\ 0 & 0 \end{pmatrix}\begin{pmatrix} 1 & 2 \\ 0 & 3 \end{pmatrix} - \begin{pmatrix} 1 & 2 \\ 0 & 3 \end{pmatrix}\begin{pmatrix} 1 & 0 \\ 0 & 0 \end{pmatrix}$

Thus, $T(e_1)$, $T(e_2)$, $T(e_3)$, $T(e_4)$ span the range of

Null space $\begin{pmatrix} a & b \\ c & d \end{pmatrix} \in$ Null space of $T$

$\Rightarrow$ $T\left[\begin{pmatrix} a & b \\ c & d \end{pmatrix}\right] = \begin{bmatrix} 0 & 0 \\ 0 & 0 \end{bmatrix}$

$\Rightarrow$ $\begin{pmatrix} a & b \\ c & d \end{pmatrix}\begin{pmatrix} 1 & 2 \\ 0 & 3 \end{pmatrix} - \begin{pmatrix} 1 & 2 \\ 0 & 3 \end{pmatrix}\begin{pmatrix} a & b \\ c & d \end{pmatrix} = \begin{pmatrix} 0 & 0 \\ 0 & 0 \end{pmatrix}$

$\Rightarrow$ $\begin{pmatrix} a & 2a+3b \\ c & 2c+3d \end{pmatrix} - \begin{pmatrix} a+2c & b+2d \\ 3c & 3d \end{pmatrix} = \begin{pmatrix} 0 & 0 \\ 0 & 0 \end{pmatrix}$

$\begin{pmatrix} -2c & 2a+2b-2d \\ -2c & 2c \end{pmatrix} = \begin{pmatrix} 0 & 0 \\ 0 & 0 \end{pmatrix}$

$\Rightarrow$ $2c = 0\ ;$ $\quad 2a + 2b - 2d = 0$

This system of equation have two independent variable, hence it has two independent solution.
$\Rightarrow$ The dimensional of null space is 2.

**6.** Rank let $T$ be a linear transformation from a vector space $V(F)$ into a vector space $V(F)$. The rank of $T$ is denoted by $\rho(T)$ is the dimension of range of $T$ *i.e.,*
$e(T) = \dim R(T)$
Here, the linear transformation $T$ is defined as
$T(x,y,z) = (y,0,z)$
Now, $\{(1,0,0); (0,1,0); (0,0,1)\}$ is a basis for $V_3(R)$, we have
$T(1,0,0) = (0,0,0)$
$T(0,1,0) = (1,0,0)$
$T(0,0,1) = (0,0,1)$
The vector $T(1,0,0); T(0,1,0); T(0,0,1)$ span the range of $T$
$\Rightarrow$ The range of $T$ is the subspace of $V_3(R)$ spanned by the vector $(0,0,0)$, $(1,0,0)$, $(0,0,1)$. Now, the vectors $(1,0,0)$, $(0,0,1) \in V_3(R)$ are linearly independent.
$\Rightarrow$ The vector $(1,0,0)$, $(0,0,1)$ form a basis for range of $T$.
Hence, rank of $T$ = dimension of range of $T$
$= 2$

**7.** $T : C \to C$ be a linear transformation defined as $T(z) = \bar{z}$
Hence, clearly $T$ is one-one and onto.

**8.** Here, it is given that
$T : R^3 \to R^3$ be a linear transformation given by
$T(x,y,z) = (x,y,0)$
$\Rightarrow$ $T(x,y,z) = (x,y,0) = (0,0,0)$
$\Rightarrow$ $x = 0,\ y = 0,\ z$ can be anything.
$\Rightarrow$ $(0,0,1)$ is generator of null space.

**9.** Here, it is given that $T : R^3 \to R^3$ be a linear transformation given by

$$T(x, y, z) = \left(\frac{x}{2}, \frac{y}{2}, 0\right)$$

$$= x\left(\frac{1}{2}, 0, 0\right) + y\left(0, \frac{1}{2}, 0\right)$$

$\therefore$ Rank of $T = 2$

**10.** Here, it is given that

(I) $T : R^3 \to R^2$, $T(x, y, z) = (x+1, y+z)$

$\Rightarrow T(x_1, y_1, z_1) + T(x_2, y_2, z_2)\}$

$\neq T_2\{(x_1, y_1, z_1)(x_2, y_2, z_2)\}$

(II) $T : R^3 \to R$, $T(x, y) = xy$.

$\Rightarrow T\alpha(x, y) \neq \alpha T(x, y)$

(III) $T : R^3 \to R^2$, $T(x, y, z) = (|x|, 0)$

$\Rightarrow T(x_1, y_1, z_1) + T(x_2, y_2, z_2)$

$\neq T\{(x_1, y_1, z_1)(x_2, y_2, z_2)\}$

$\therefore$ None is linear transformation.

**11.** Here, it is given that

$T : R^2 \to R^3$ be defined by

$$T(x, y) = (x+y, x-y)$$

Let $\alpha_1 = (0, 1)$ and $\alpha_2 = (1, 0)$

$\therefore$ By definition of $T$, we have

$$T(\alpha_1) = T(0, 1) = (0+1, 0-1)$$

$\Rightarrow T(0, 1) = (1, -1)$

Now, our aim is to express $(1, -1)$ as a linear combination of the vectors in the basis $\{\alpha_1, \alpha_2\}$

Let $(a, b) = x\alpha_1 + y\alpha_2$

$= x(0, 1) + y(1, 0) = (y, x)$

Then, $a = y$ and $b = x$ ...(i)

Putting $a = 1$, $b = -1$ in Eq. (i), we get

$y = 1$, $x = -1 \Rightarrow T(\alpha_1) = -\alpha_1 + \alpha_2$ ...(ii)

Again $T(\alpha_2) = T(1, 0) = (1, 1)$

Putting $a = 1$, $b = 1$

We get $x = 1$, $y = 1$

$\therefore T(\alpha_2) = \alpha_1 + \alpha_2$ ...(iii)

From the relation (ii) and (iii), we see that the matrix of $T$ relative to the basis $\{\alpha_1, \alpha_2\}$ is

$$= \begin{bmatrix} -1 & 1 \\ 1 & 1 \end{bmatrix}$$

**12.** In given relation

$T : R^2 \to R^2$ be a map defined by

$T(x, y) = (x+y, x-y)$

We can prove that its nullity will be zero

$$W = \{\alpha \in T, T(\alpha) = 0\}$$

**14.** Here, $T(x_1, x_2, x_3, x_4)$

$= (x_1 + x_2 + x_3, x_2 + x_3 + x_4, x_3 + x_4 + x_2)$ (Given)

$T : \mathbb{R}^4 \to \mathbb{R}^4$

$T(1, 0, 0, 0) = (1, 0, 0, 0)$

$T(0, 1, 0, 0) = (1, 1, 0, 1)$

$T(0, 0, 1, 0) = (1, 1, 1, 0)$

and $T(0, 0, 0, 1) = (0, 1, 1, 0)$

$$\therefore \begin{vmatrix} 1 & 0 & 0 & 0 \\ 1 & 1 & 0 & 1 \\ 1 & 1 & 1 & 0 \\ 0 & 1 & 1 & 0 \end{vmatrix} \to \begin{matrix} R_2 = R_2 - R_1 \\ R_3 = R_3 - R_1 \end{matrix}$$

$$= \begin{vmatrix} 1 & 0 & 0 & 0 \\ 0 & 1 & 0 & 1 \\ 0 & 0 & 1 & 0 \\ 0 & 1 & 1 & 0 \end{vmatrix} \to C_4 \to C_4 - C_1$$

$$= \begin{vmatrix} 1 & 0 & 0 & 0 \\ 0 & 1 & 0 & 0 \\ 0 & 0 & 1 & 0 \\ 0 & 1 & 1 & 0 \end{vmatrix} \to R_4 \to R_4 - R_2$$

$$= \begin{vmatrix} 1 & 0 & 0 & 0 \\ 0 & 1 & 0 & 0 \\ 0 & 0 & 1 & 0 \\ 0 & 0 & 1 & 0 \end{vmatrix}$$

$$= \begin{vmatrix} 1 & 0 & 0 & 0 \\ 0 & 1 & 0 & 0 \\ 0 & 0 & 1 & 0 \\ 0 & 0 & 0 & 0 \end{vmatrix} \to R_4 \to R_4 - R_3$$

$\therefore$ Rank $(T) = \dim T(u) = 3$

**15.** Here, it is given that $T(1, 0) = (1, 2)$

and $T(1, 1) = (0, 2)$

Now, we can write it as

$T(1, 0) = (1-0, 2 \cdot 1) = (1, 2)$

and $T(1, 1) = (0, 2 \cdot 1) = (0, 2)$

$\therefore T(a, b) = (a-b, 2 \cdot a) = (a-b, 2a)$

**16.** Here, if $T : V \to V$ is a linear transformation of vector space $V$ and the composite $ToT = 0$, then $T$ will be a non-singular linear transformation.

**18.** If $T$ be a linear transformation from a 3-dimensional. Vector space $V$ into a 2-dimensional vector space $W$. Then, $T$ can be surjective but cannot be injective.

**19.** We can check option (c) as

$$(x_1, x_2) \to (x_1 + 1, x_2)$$

Let $\alpha = (a_1, a_2)$, $\beta = (b_1, b_2) \in \mathbb{R}^2$

Then, $T(\alpha) = (a_1 + 1, a_2)$, $T(\beta) = (b_1 + 1, b_2)$

Also, let $a, b \in R$, then $a\alpha + b\beta \in \mathbb{R}^2$

$$T(a\alpha + b\beta) = T[a(a_1a_2) + b(b_1b_2)]$$

$$= T[aa_1 + bb_1, aa_2 + bb_2]$$

$$= (aa_1 + bb_1 + 1, aa_2 + bb_2)$$

$$\neq aT(\alpha) + bT(\beta)$$

Hence, $T$ is not linear mapping from $\mathbb{R}^2$ in $\mathbb{R}^2$.

**20.** Here, $R$ is the set of real numbers. Let $f_1$ and $f_2$ be the two transformation defined by $f_1(x, y) = (0, y)$ and $f_2(x, y) = (y, x)$

Now, product of mapping $= f_2of_1(x, y)$ (Given)

$= f_2[f_1(x, y)] = f_2(0, y) = (y, 0)$

$\therefore$ The product of the mapping $f_2of_1(x, y)$ gives that projection of the $x$-$y$ plane on the line $y = x$.

**21.** Here, given $T : \mathbb{R}^2 \to \mathbb{R}^3$ as

$$T(x, y) = (-x-y,\ 3x+8y,\ 9x-11y)$$

To find nullity $T$

Let $(x, y) \in n(T)$

$\Rightarrow T(x, y) = (0, 0, 0)$

$\Rightarrow (-x-y,\ 3x+8y,\ 9x-11y) = (0, 0, 0)$

$\Rightarrow \quad x = y = 0$

$\therefore \quad n(T) = \{(0, 0)\}$

$\Rightarrow \quad$ nullity $T = 0$.

$\because$ Rank $T$ + nullity $T$ = dim $R^2$

Rank $T + 0 = 2$

Rank $T = 2$

**22.** First, we shall show that the set $\{(1, 0), (1, 1)\}$ is a basis of $R^2$.

For linear independent of this set.

Then, $\quad (a+b,\ b) = 0, 0$

$\Rightarrow \quad a+b = 0,\ b = 0$

$\Rightarrow \quad a = 0,\ b = 0$

Hence, the set $\{(1, 0), (1, 1)\}$ is linearly independent.

Now, we shall show that the set $\{(1, 0), (1, 1)\}$ spans $R^2$. Let $(x, y) \in R^2$ and let

$(x, y) = a(1+0) + b(1, 1)$

$(x, y) = (a+b,\ b)$

$\Rightarrow \quad a+b = x,\ b = y$

$\Rightarrow \quad a = x - b$

$a = x - y \qquad [\because b = y]$

or here $\quad T(e_1) = (2, 3, 1)$

and $\quad T(e_2) = (3, 0, 2)$

or set $\quad (x, y) = ae_1 + be_2$

$T(x, y) = aT(l_1) + bT(l_2)$

$= x - y(2, 3, 1) + y(3, 0, 2)$

$= (2x - 2y + 3y),\ 3(x-y),\ (x - y + 2y)$

$\therefore \quad T(x, y) = (2x + y,\ 3x - 3y,\ x + y)$

**23.** Here, $\quad T(x, y, z) = (x - y,\ y + 3z,\ x + 2y)$

Now, let $T(x, y, z) = (u\ v\ w)$

then $\quad T^{-1}(u\ v\ w) = (x, y, z)$

So, $\quad T(x, y, z) = (x-y,\ y+3z,\ x+2y) = (u, v, w)$

$\Rightarrow \quad x - y = u \qquad$ ...(i)

$y + 3z = v \qquad$ ...(ii)

$x + 2y = w \qquad$ ...(iii)

Taking Eqs. (i) and (ii), we get

$x - y = u \qquad$ ...(iv)

By subtracting

or $\quad y = -\dfrac{u+w}{3}$

Putting this value in Eq. (i), we get

$$x - \left(\frac{-u+w}{3}\right) = u \text{ or } x + \frac{u-w}{3} = u$$

or $\quad x = u - \dfrac{u-w}{3}$

$$x = \frac{3u - u + w}{3} = \frac{2u+w}{3}$$

and from Eq. (ii)

$$\left(\frac{-u+w}{3}\right) + 3z = v$$

or $\quad 3z = v - \left(\dfrac{-u+w}{3}\right)$

$$3z = \frac{3v + u - w}{3} \quad \therefore z = \frac{3v + u - w}{3 \times 3}$$

$$= \frac{3v}{9} + \frac{u}{9} - \frac{w}{9}$$

$$z = \frac{1}{3}\left(v + \frac{u}{3} - \frac{w}{3}\right)$$

$\therefore \quad T^{-1}(u, v, w) = (x, y, z)$

or $\quad T^{-1}(u, v, w) = \dfrac{1}{3}\left(2u + w,\ -u + w,\ \dfrac{u}{3} + v - \dfrac{w}{3}\right)$

or $\quad T^{-1}(x, y, z) = \dfrac{1}{3}\left(2x + z,\ -x + z,\ \dfrac{x}{3} + y - \dfrac{z}{3}\right)$

**24.** Here, linear mapping is $T : V \to V$, such that

$T(A) = AB - BA$, where

$$B = \begin{bmatrix} 2 & 1 \\ 0 & 3 \end{bmatrix}$$

Let $\quad A = \begin{bmatrix} a & b \\ c & d \end{bmatrix}$

Then, $\quad AB - \begin{bmatrix} a & b \\ c & d \end{bmatrix}\begin{bmatrix} 2 & 1 \\ 0 & 3 \end{bmatrix}$

$$= \begin{bmatrix} 2a & a+3b \\ 2c & c+3d \end{bmatrix}$$

and $\quad BA = \begin{bmatrix} 2a+c & 2b+d \\ 3c & 3d \end{bmatrix}$

Hence, $T(A) = AB - BA$

$$= \begin{bmatrix} 2a & a+3b \\ 2 & c+3b \end{bmatrix} - \begin{bmatrix} 2a+c & 2b+d \\ 3c & 3d \end{bmatrix}$$

$$T(A) = \begin{bmatrix} -c & a+b-d \\ -c & c \end{bmatrix}$$

Here, rank of $T = 1$

Hence, nullity of $T = 2 - 1 = 1$

**25.** Here, matrix of $D$ relative to the basis $\{x_2, 1, x\}$ is equal to

$$\begin{bmatrix} 0 & 0 & 2 \\ 0 & 0 & 0 \\ 0 & 1 & 0 \end{bmatrix}$$

## Exercise 2

**1.** Here, the range of $T_1$ is in the domain of $T_2$

Hence, $T_2T_1 : V_3 \to V_2$ is defined as

$$\begin{aligned} T_2T_1(a, b, c) &= T_2[T_1(a, b, c)] \\ &= T_2[2a, b+c] \\ &= (b+c, 2a) \end{aligned}$$

But the range of $T_2$ is not in the domain of $T_1$

Hence, $T_1T_2$ is not defined.

**2.** Here, $R(T) = N(T)$

$\Rightarrow$ $\dim R(T) = \dim N(T)$

Since, $\text{rank}\,(T) + \text{nullity}\, T = \dim V$

$\Rightarrow$ $\dim R(T) + \dim N(T) = n$

$\Rightarrow$ $2 \dim R(T) = n$

$\Rightarrow$ $2\,\text{rank}\,(T) = n$, an even number

**3.** We have, $T_1T_2(u_1, u_2) = T_1[T_2(u_1, u_2)]$

$$\begin{aligned} &= T_1[u_2, u_1] \\ &= (u_1, 0) \end{aligned}$$

$$\begin{aligned} T_2T_1(u_1, u_2) &= T_2[T_1(u_1, u_2)] \\ &= T_2(u_1, 0) = (0, u_1) \end{aligned}$$

$\Rightarrow$ $T_1T_2 \neq T_2T_1$

**4.** We have, $(f_1 - f_2)(a, b) = f_1(a, b) - f_2(a, b)$

$$\begin{aligned} &= (a+2b) - (3a-b) \\ &= -2a + 3b \end{aligned}$$

**7.** $T$ is a linear transformation from $V$ into $V$.

$$\begin{aligned} T(cf_1 + f_2)(x) &= c(Tf_1)(x) + (Tf_2)(x) \\ &= c\int_0^x f_1(t)\,dt + \int_0^x f_2(t)\,dt \\ &= \int_0^x (cf_1(t) + f_2(t))\,dt \\ &= \int_0^x (cf_1 + f_2)(t)\,dt \end{aligned}$$

**8.** We have, $f(0) = f(0, 0)$

$$\begin{aligned} &= f(0+2, 0+3) \\ f(2, 3) &\neq 0 \end{aligned}$$

$\because$ $f$ does not map zero vector onto zero vector.

Hence, $f$ is not linear.

**9.** Consider the linear transformations $T_1$ and $T_2$ on $\mathbb{R}^2$ defined as

$$T_1(x_1, x_2) = (x_1, 0)$$
$$T_2(x_1, x_2) = (0, x_2)$$

Neither $T_1$ nor $T_2$ are zero transform.

We have,

$$\begin{aligned} (T_1T_2)(x_1, x_2) &= T_1[T_2(x_1, x_2)] \\ &= T_1(0, x_2) = (0, 0) \\ &= \hat{0}(x_1, x_2) \end{aligned}$$

Therefore, $T_1T_2 = \hat{0}$, *i.e.*, $T_1T_2$ is zero transformation. Note that the origin of the linear space $\mathbb{R}^2$ is $(0, 0)$.

**10.** Let $f$ and $g$ have inverses $f^{-1}$ and $g^{-1}$, respectively. We now have

$$ff^{-1} = id_Y,\ f^{-1}f = id_X,\ gg^{-1} = id_Z,\ g^{-1}g = id_Y$$

Further,

$$\begin{aligned} (fg)(g^{-1}f^{-1}) &= f(gg^{-1}f^{-1}) = f(id_Z f^{-1}) \\ &= ff^{-1} = id_Y \end{aligned}$$

and
$$\begin{aligned} (g^{-1}f^{-1})(fg) &= g^{-1}(f^{-1}fg) \\ &= g^{-1}(id_X g) \\ &= g^{-1}g = id_Y \end{aligned}$$

Therefore, $fg$ is invertible.

**13.** $T$ is a linear transformation from $V$ into $V$,

$$\begin{aligned} T(cf_1 + f_2)(x) &= c(Tf_1)(x) + (Tf_2)(x) \\ &= c\int_0^x f_1(t)\,dt + \int_0^x f_2(t)\,dt \\ &= \int_0^x (cf_1(t) + f_2(t))\,dt \\ &= \int_0^x (cf_1 + f_2)(t)\,dt \end{aligned}$$

**14.** Let $\lambda$, $\mu$ be any two scalars of $\mathbb{R}$, then

$$\begin{aligned} f(\lambda x + \mu y) &= f[\lambda(a_1x + b_1y + c_1) + \mu(a_2x + b_2y + c_2)] \\ &= (\lambda a_1 + \mu a_2 x, \lambda b_1 + \mu b_2 y, \lambda c_1 + \mu c_2) \\ &= \lambda(a_1x, b_1y, c_1) + \mu(a_2x, b_2y, c_2) \\ &= \lambda f(x) + \mu f(y) \end{aligned}$$

Hence, $f$ is a linear transformation.

Obviously $f$ is one-one onto mapping.

Hence, $f$ is an isomorphism from $\mathbb{R}^2$ onto $\mathbb{R}^2$.

**15.** Let $y_1, y_2 \in Y$. Let $f^{-1}(y_1) = x_1$

and $f^{-1}(y_2) = x_2 \Rightarrow f(x_1) = y_1$ and $f(x_2) = y_2$

Hence, $y_1 + y_2 = f(x_1) + f(x_2) = f(x_1 + x_2)$, since $f$ is linear.

Hence, $f^{-1}(y_1 + y_2) = x_1 + x_2 = f^{-1}(y_1) + f^{-1}(y_2)$

Also, for $\lambda \in \mathbb{R}$

$$\lambda y_1 = \lambda f(x_1) = f(\lambda x_1)$$

$\Rightarrow$ $f^{-1}(\lambda y_1) = \lambda x_1 = \lambda f^{-1}(y_1)$

Hence, $f^{-1}$ is linear.

**16.** Since, $\mathbb{B}$ is an orthonormal basis, we have

$$\alpha = \sum_{k=1}^{n} (\alpha/\alpha_k)\alpha_k$$

The matrix $A$ is defined by

$$T\alpha_j = \sum_{k=1}^{n} A_{kj}\alpha_k$$

and since $T\alpha_j = \sum_{k=1}^{n} (T\alpha_j/\alpha_k)\alpha_k$

we have $A_{kj} = (T\alpha_j/\alpha_k)\alpha_k$

**19.** Since, $-3, -1, 4$ and $5$ are the roots, the polynomial $f(x)$ is given by

$$\begin{aligned} f(x) &= (x+3)(x+1)(x-4)(x-5) \\ &= x^4 - 5x^3 - 13x^2 + 53x + 60 \end{aligned}$$

**20.** It is given that

$$L = M_1 \oplus M_2$$

and $f : M_2 \to \dfrac{L}{M_1}$

such that $f(y) = M_1 + y, \forall y \in M_2$

We shall show that $f$ is an isomorphism of $M_2$ onto $L/M_1$.

(i) ***f* is one-one.**

If $y_1, y_2 \in M_2$, then

$$f(y_1) = f(y_2) \Rightarrow M_1 + y_1 = M_1 + y_2$$

$$\Rightarrow \quad y_1 - y_2 \in M_1$$

$$\Rightarrow \quad y_1 - y_2 \in M_1 \cap M_2$$

$$[\because y_1 - y_2 \in M_2 \text{ because } M_2 \text{ is a subspace}]$$

$$\Rightarrow \quad y_1 - y_2 = 0 \qquad [\because M_1 \cap M_2 = \{0\}]$$

$$\Rightarrow \quad y_1 = y_2$$

Hence, $f$ is one-one.

(ii) ***f* is onto.**

Let $M_1 + x$ be any coset in $L/M_1$ where $x \in L$.

Since, $L$ is direct sum of $M_1$ and $M_2$, therefore we can write

$$x = z + y, \text{ where } z \in M_1, y \in M_2$$

This gives $z = x - y \in M_1$

Since, $x - y \in M_1$

Therefore, $M_1 + x = M_1 + y$

Now, $\quad f(y) = M_1 + y = M_1 + x$

Thus, $\quad M_1 + x \in \dfrac{L}{M_1} \Rightarrow$ There exists $y \in M_2$

such that $\quad f(y) = M_1 + x$

Therefore, $f$ is onto.

(iii) ***f* is linear.**

Let $\alpha, \beta \in F$ and $y_1, y_2 \in M_2$

$$\begin{aligned} \text{Then, } f(\alpha y_1 + \beta y_2) &= M_1 + (\alpha y_1 + \beta y_2) \\ &= (M_1 + \alpha y_1) + (M_1 + \beta y_2) \\ &= \alpha(M_1 + y_1) + \beta(M_1 + y_2) \\ &= \alpha f(y_1) + \beta f(y_2) \end{aligned}$$

Therefore, $f$ is linear.

Hence, $f$ is an isomorphism between $M_2$ and $L/M_1$.

**21.** We have,

$$\begin{aligned} (T_1T_2)(x_1, x_2) &= T_1[T_2(x_1, x_2)] \\ &= T_1(x_1, 0) \\ &= (0, x_1) \end{aligned}$$

$$\begin{aligned} \text{Also, } (T_2T_1)(x_1, x_2) &= T_2[T_1(x_1, x_2)] \\ &= T_2(x_2, x_1) \\ &= (x_2, 0) \end{aligned}$$

Thus, $(T_1T_2)(x_1, x_2) \neq (T_2T_1), \forall (x_1, x_2)$

$$\forall (x_1, x_2) \in \mathbb{R}^2$$

$$\Rightarrow \quad T_1T_2 \neq T_2T_1$$

**22.** Let $\alpha$ and $\beta$ be vectors in $V$. We must show that

$$f(\alpha, \beta) = f(\overline{\beta}, \alpha)$$

Now,

$$f(\alpha + \beta, \alpha + \beta) = f(\alpha, \beta) + f(\alpha, \beta) + f(\beta, \alpha) + f(\beta, \beta)$$

Since, $f(\alpha + \beta, \alpha + \beta)$, $f(\alpha, \alpha)$ and $f(\beta, \beta)$ are real the number $f(\alpha, \beta) + f(\beta, \alpha)$ is real. Looking at the same argument with $\alpha + i\beta$ instead of $\alpha + \beta$, we see that $-if(\alpha, \beta) + if(\beta, \alpha)$ is real.

Having concluded that two numbers are real, we set them equal to their complex conjugates and obtain

$$f(\alpha, \beta) + f(\beta, \alpha) = \overline{f(\alpha, \beta) + f(\beta, \alpha)} \qquad \text{...(i)}$$

$$-if(\alpha, \beta) + if(\beta, \alpha) = \overline{if(\alpha, \beta) - if(\beta, \alpha)} \qquad \text{...(ii)}$$

If we multiply the Eq. (ii) by $i$ and add the result to the Eq. (i), we obtain

$$2f(\alpha, \beta) = 2\overline{f(\beta, \alpha)}$$

**23.** The dual basis $\{L_1, \ldots, L_n\}$ is essentially defined by the fact that $L_i(\alpha)$ is the $i$th coordinate of $\alpha$ in the ordered basis $\beta$ (for any $\alpha$ in $V$). Now, the functions $f_{ij}$ defined by

$$f_{ij}(\alpha, \beta) = L_i(\alpha)L_j(\beta)$$

are bilinear. If

$$\alpha = x_1\alpha_1 + \ldots + x_n\alpha_n$$

and $\quad \beta = y_1\alpha_1 + \ldots + y_n\alpha_n,$

then $\quad f_{ij}(\alpha, \beta) = x_iy_j$

Let $f$ be any bilinear form on $V$ and let $A$ be the matrix of $f$ in the ordered basis $\mathbb{B}$. Then,

$$f(\alpha, \beta) = \sum_{ij} A_{ij}x_iy_i$$

Which simply says that

$$f = \sum_{ij} A_{ij}f_{ij}$$

It is now clear that the $n^2$ forms $f_{ij}$ comprise a basis for $L(V, V, F)$.

**26.** If $f$ is invertible, then clearly there exists $g = f^{-1}$ with the stated properties.

Conversely, let $f$ and $g$ exist with the property that

$$fg = id_Y \text{ and } gf = id_X$$

Let $\quad x \in N(f)$

Then, $\quad (gf)(x) = id_X(x) = x$

Also, $\quad (gf)(x) = g(f(x)) = g(0) = 0$

Thus, $\quad N(f) = \{0\}$

and hence $f$ is one-one.

Now, let $y \in Y$,

$$\begin{aligned} \text{then} \quad f(g(y)) &= (fg)(y) \\ &= id_Y(y) = y \end{aligned}$$

Put $g(y) = x \in X$

$\Rightarrow \quad \exists x \in X$ such that $f(x) = y$

$\Rightarrow f$ is onto.

$\Rightarrow f$ is invertible.

**27.** We have,

$$\begin{aligned} (DT)[f(x)] &= D[T(f(x))] = D[xf(x)] \\ &= \frac{d}{dx}[xf(x)] \\ &= f(x) + x\frac{d}{dx}f(x) \qquad \text{...(i)} \end{aligned}$$

$$\begin{aligned} \text{Also,} \quad (TD)[f(x)] &= T[D(f(x))] \\ &= T\left[\frac{d}{dx}f(x)\right] \\ &= x\frac{d}{dx}f(x) \qquad \text{...(ii)} \end{aligned}$$

From Eqs. (i) and (ii), we get

$$(DT)(f(x)) \neq (TD)(f(x))$$

$$\Rightarrow \quad DT \neq TD$$

**28.** Let $A$ be invertible. Then, there exists a square matrix $B$ of order $n$ such that $AB = I_n = BA$ where $I_n$ denotes the identity matrix of order $n$. Now, there exists a linear operator $g$ which corresponds to $B$ with regard to the given fixed basis with the property that $fg = I = gf$ where $I$ stands for the identity operator. Therefore, $f$ is invertible.

Conversely, let $f$ be invertible. Then, there exists a linear operator $g$ such that $fg = I = gf$. Let $B$ the matrix associated with $g$ with regard to the given fixed basis. Then, $AB = I_n = BA$. Thus, $A$ is invertible and this completes the proof of the theorem.

**30.** Suppose, $T$ and $U$ are linear transformations from $V$ into $W$ and that we define $(T+U)$ as above. Then,

$$\begin{aligned}(T+U)(c\alpha+\beta) &= T(c\alpha+\beta)+U(c\alpha+\beta)\\ &= c(T\alpha)+T\beta+c(U\alpha)+U\beta\\ &= c(T\alpha+U\alpha)+(T\beta+U\beta)\\ &= c(T+U)(\alpha)+(T+U)(\beta)\end{aligned}$$

which shows that $(T+U)$ is a linear transformation. Similarly,

$$\begin{aligned}(cT)(d\alpha+\beta) &= c[T(d\alpha+\beta)]\\ &= c[d(T\alpha)+T\beta]\\ &= cd(T\alpha)+c(T\beta)\\ &= d[c(T\alpha)+c(T\beta)]\\ &= d[(cT)\alpha]+(cT)\beta\end{aligned}$$

which shows that $(cT)$ is a linear transformation.

**31.** (i) For all $x \in L$, we have

$$\begin{aligned}(S\hat{0})(x) &= S[\hat{0}(x)]\\ &= S(0) = 0 = \hat{0}(x)\end{aligned}$$

Hence, $S\hat{0} = \hat{0}$, by definition of equality of two functions.

Similarly, we can show that $\hat{0}S = \hat{0}$.

(ii) For all $x \in L$

We have, $(SI)(x) = S[I(x)] = S(x)$

Therefore, $SI = S$

Similarly, we can show that

$$IS = S$$

(iii) For all $x \in L$, we have

$$\begin{aligned}[S(TU)](x) &= S[(TU)(x)] = S[T(U(x))]\\ &= (ST)[U(x)] = [(ST)U](x)\end{aligned}$$

Hence, $S(TU) = (ST)U$

(iv) For all $x \in L$, we have

$$\begin{aligned}[S(T+U)](x) &= S[(T+U)(x)]\\ &= S[T(x)+U(x)]\\ &= S[T(x)]+S[U(x)]\\ &= (ST)(x)+(SU)(x)\\ &= (ST+SU)(x)\end{aligned}$$

Hence, $S(T+U) = ST+SU$

(v) For all $x \in L$, we have

$$\begin{aligned}[(S+T)U](x) &= (S+T)[U(x)]\\ &= S[U(x)]+T[U(x)]\\ &= (SU)(x)+(TU)(x)\\ &= (SU+TU)(x)\end{aligned}$$

Hence, $\quad (S+T)U = SU+TU$

**32.** First of all observe that, if $f$ is a linear map, then $f(0) = 0$ and so $0 \in N(f)$. Now, suppose that $f$ is 1–1. Then, $f(x_1) = f(x_2)$ implies $x_1 = x_2$. If $x \in N(f)$, then $f(x) = 0 = f(0)$ and hence $x = 0$.

$$\Rightarrow \quad N(f) = \{0\}$$

Conversely, suppose $\quad N(f) = \{0\}$

Let $\quad f(x_1) = f(x_2)$

Then, $\quad 0 = f(x_1) - f(x_2) = f(x_1 - x_2)$

So, $\quad x_1 - x_2 \in N(f) = \{0\}$

So, $\quad x_1 - x_2 = 0$

i.e., $\quad x_1 = x_2$

$\Rightarrow$ $f$ is one-one.

**33.** Let $A$ be invertible. Then, there exists a square matrix $B$ of order $n$ such that $AB = I_n = BA$ where $I_n$ denotes the identity matrix of order $n$. Now, there exists a linear operator $g$ which corresponds to $B$ with regard to the given fixed basis with the property that $fg = I = gf$ where $I$ stands for the identity operator. Therefore, $f$ is invertible.

Conversely, let $f$ be invertible. Then, there exists a linear operator $g$ such that $fg = I = gf$. Let $B$ the matrix associated with $g$ with regard to the given fixed basis. Then, $AB = I_n = BA$. Thus, $A$ is invertible and this completes the proof of the theorem.

**34.** Let $\alpha = (a_1, a_2, a_3)$ and $\beta = (b_1, b_2, b_3)$ be any two elements of $V_3(V)$.

Let $a, b$ be any two elements of $F$, then

$$\begin{aligned}f(a\alpha+b\beta) &= f[a(a_1, a_2, a_3)+b(b_1, b_2, b_3)]\\ &= f[aa_1+bb_1, aa_2+bb_2, aa_3+bb_3)]\\ &= (aa_1+bb_1, aa_2+bb_2)\\ &= a(a_1, a_2)+b(b_1, b_2)\\ &= af(a_1, a_2, a_3)+bf(b_1, b_2, b_3)\\ &= af(\alpha)+bf(\beta)\end{aligned}$$

Hence, $f$ is a linear transformation.

Let $(a_1, a_2)$ be an element of $V(F)$, then

$(a_1, a_2, 0) \in V_3(F)$ and $f(a_1, a_2, 0) = (a_1, a_2)$

Hence, $f$ is onto.

Thus, $f$ is a homomorphism of $V_3(F)$ onto $V_2(F)$.

If $W$ is the kernel of this homomorphism, then

$$W = \{(0, 0, a) : a \in F\}$$

Thus, $\quad f(0, 0, a) = (0, 0)$

$\quad$ = the zero vector of $V_2(f)$, $\forall\ a \in F$

Also, if $f(a_1, a_2, a_3) = (0, 0)$

Then, $\quad f(a_1, a_2, a_3) = (a_1, a_2) = (0, 0)$

*i.e.*, $a_1 = 0 = a_2$

Hence, $(a_1, a_2, a_3) \in W$

Thus, $W$ is the kernel of $f$.

**35.** It is given that

$$L = M_1 \oplus M_2$$

and $f : M_2 \to \frac{L}{M_1}$

such that $f(y) = M_1 + y, \forall\, y \in M_2$

We shall show that $f$ is an isomorphism of $M_2$ onto $L/M_1$.

(i) ***f* is one-one.**

It $y_1, y_2 \in M_2$, then

$$f(y_1) = f(y_2) \Rightarrow M_1 + y_1 = M_1 + y_2$$

$\Rightarrow \quad y_1 - y_2 \in M_1$

$\Rightarrow \quad y_1 - y_2 \in M_1 \cap M_2$

[$\because y_1 - y_2 \in M_2$ because $M_2$ is a subspace]

$\Rightarrow \quad y_1 - y_2 = 0 \qquad [\because M_1 \cap M_2 = \{0\}]$

$\Rightarrow \quad y_1 = y_2$

Hence, $f$ is one-one.

(ii) ***f* is onto.**

Let $M_1 + x$ be any coset in $L/M_1$ where $x \in L$.

Since, $L$ is direct sum of $M_1$ and $M_2$, therefore we can write

$$x = z + y, \text{ where } z \in M_1, y \in M_2$$

This gives $z = x - y \in M_1$

Since, $\quad x - y \in M_1$

Therefore, $M_1 + x = M_1 + y$

Now, $\quad f(y) = M_1 + y = M_1 + x$

Thus, $\quad M_1 + x \in \frac{L}{M_1} \Rightarrow$ There exists $y \in M_2$

such that $\quad f(y) = M_1 + x$

Therefore, $f$ is onto.

(iii) ***f* is linear.**

Let $\alpha, \beta \in F$ and $y_1, y_2 \in M_2$

Then, $f(\alpha y_1 + \beta y_2) = M_1 + (\alpha y_1 + \beta y_2)$

$$= (M_1 + \alpha y_1) + (M_1 + \beta y_2)$$

$$= \alpha(M_1 + y_1) + \beta(M_1 + y_2)$$

$$= \alpha f(y_1) + \beta f(y_2)$$

Therefore, $f$ is linear.

Hence, $f$ is an isomorphism between $M_2$ and $L/M_1$.

# 10 Quadratic Forms & Inner Product Spaces

## Syllabus

- Canonical Forms
- Diagonal Forms
- Triangular Forms
- Jordan Forms
- Inner Product Space
- Orthonormal Basis
- Quadratic Forms
- Reduction and Classification of Quadratic Forms

## Canonical Forms

### Triangular Form

Let $T : V \to V$ be a linear operator. Then, $V$ has a basis $B$ such that

$$[T]_B = \begin{bmatrix} a_{11} & a_{12} & a_{13} & \dots & a_{1n} \\ 0 & a_{22} & a_{23} & \dots & a_{2n} \\ 0 & 0 & a_{33} & \dots & a_{3n} \\ \vdots & \vdots & \vdots & \dots & \vdots \\ 0 & 0 & 0 & \dots & a_{nn} \end{bmatrix}_{n\times n}$$

This matrix representation is called triangular form.
The characteristic polynomial of the triangular form is

$$\text{Ch}(\lambda) = (\lambda - a_{11})(\lambda - a_{22})\dots(\lambda - a_{nn})$$
$$= \prod_{i=1}^{n} (\lambda - a_{ii})$$

> ***Note*** Let $[A]$ be a square matrix whose $\text{Ch}(\lambda)$ is product of linear factors. Then, matrix is similar to triangular matrix.

### Diagonal Form

Let $T : V \to V$ be a linear operator. Then, $V$ has a basis $B$ such that

$$[T]_B = \begin{bmatrix} a_{11} & 0 & 0 & \dots & 0 \\ 0 & a_{22} & 0 & \dots & 0 \\ 0 & 0 & a_{33} & \dots & 0 \\ \vdots & \vdots & \vdots & \dots & \vdots \\ 0 & 0 & 0 & \dots & a_{nn} \end{bmatrix}_{n\times n}$$

This representation is called diagonal form.
The characteristic polynomial of the diagonal form is

$$\text{ch}(\lambda) = (\lambda - a_{11})(\lambda - a_{22})\dots(\lambda - a_{nm})$$
$$= \prod_{i=1}^{n}(\lambda - a_{ii})$$

> ***Note*** The diagonal entries of the matrix are eigen values for $T$ and the elements of the basis are corresponding eigen vector.

## Jordan Block

The Jordan Block is defined as

$$J = \begin{bmatrix} \lambda & 1 & 0 & \dots & 0 & 0 \\ 0 & \lambda & 1 & \dots & 0 & 0 \\ \vdots & \vdots & \vdots & \dots & \vdots & \vdots \\ 0 & 0 & 0 & \dots & \lambda & 1 \\ 0 & 0 & 0 & \dots & 0 & \lambda \end{bmatrix}_{n \times n}$$

where $\lambda$'s are the eigen values.

## Jordan Matrix

A matrix $A$ is a Jordan matrix, if $A$ is a block diagonal matrix whose diagonal blocks, say, $J_1, J_2, \dots, J_k$ are Jordan blocks.

*e.g.*, The following matrix is a Jordan matrix

$$A = \begin{bmatrix} 2 & 1 & 0 & & & & \\ 0 & 2 & 1 & & & & \\ 0 & 0 & 2 & & & & \\ & & & 7 & 1 & & \\ & & & 0 & 7 & & \\ & & & & & 3 & 1 \\ & & & & & 0 & 3 \end{bmatrix}$$

## Jordan Canonical Form

Let $T : V \to V$ be a linear operator whose characteristic and minimal polynomials are respectively

$$\text{Ch}(\lambda) = (\lambda - a_1)^{n_1} \dots (\lambda - a_r)^{n_r} \text{ and}$$
$$\min(\lambda) = (\lambda - a_1)^{m_1} \dots (\lambda - a_r)^{m_r},$$

where $a_i$ are distinct scalars. Then, $T$ has a unique Jordan matrix representation $A$ with the properties as follows

**(i)** There is atleast one block of order $m_i$; all other blocks are of order $\le m_i$.

**(ii)** The sum of the orders of the blocks corresponding to $a_i$ is $n_i$ *i.e.*, the algebraic multiplicity of $a_i$.

**(iii)** The sum of number of blocks corresponding to $a_i$ is equal to geometric multiplicity of $a_i$.

**(iv)** The number of blocks corresponding to $a_i$ of each possible order is uniquely determined by $T$.

***Theorem*** **Let $A$ be a matrix whose characteristic polynomial Ch($t$) is a product of linear factors. Then, $A$ is a similar to a unique Jordan matrix $A$ with the above four properties.**

---

***Example 1.*** *Let $T : V \to V$ be a linear operator and the characteristic polynomial* $\text{Ch}(t) = (t+6)^4 (t-1)^3$ *and minimal polynomial* $m(t) = (t+6)^3 (t-1)^2$. *Find the Jordan canonical form A of T.*

**Solution.** Since, deg $\text{Ch}(\lambda) = 7$, the order of $A$ is 7. Since, $\text{Ch}(t) = (t+6)^4 (t-1)^3$, $A$ has four $-6$s and three 1s as the diagonal. Also, since $m(t) = (t+6)^3 (t-1)^2$ there must be a block of order 3 belonging to $-6$ and a block of order 2 belonging to 1. Hence, the Jordan canonical form is

$$\begin{bmatrix} -6 & 1 & 0 & & & & \\ 0 & -6 & 1 & & & & \\ 0 & 0 & -6 & & & & \\ & & & 6 & & & \\ & & & & 1 & 1 & \\ & & & & 0 & 1 & \\ & & & & & & 1 \end{bmatrix}$$

## Bilinear Forms

Let $U$ and $V$ be two vector spaces over the same field $F$. A bilinear form on $W = U \oplus V$ is a function $f$ from $W$ into $F$, which assigns to each element $(\alpha, \beta)$ in $W$ a scalar $f(\alpha, \beta)$ in such a way that

$$f(a\alpha_1 + b\alpha_2, \beta) = af(\alpha_1, \beta) + bf(\alpha_2, \beta)$$

and $$f(\alpha, a\beta_1 + b\beta_2) = af(\alpha, \beta_1) + bf(\alpha, \beta_2)$$

***Example 2.*** *Suppose, V is a vector space over the field F. Let $L_1$ and $L_2$ be linear functionals on V. Let f be a function from $V \times V$ into F defined as $f(\alpha, \beta) = L_1(\alpha) L_2(\beta)$. Then, f is bilinear form on V.*

**Solution.** If $\alpha, \beta \in V$, then $L_1(\alpha)$, $L_2(\beta)$ are scalars.

We have,

$$\begin{aligned} f(a\alpha_1 + b\alpha_2, \beta) &= L_1(a\alpha_1 + b\alpha_2) L_2(\beta) \\ &= [aL_1(\alpha_1) + bL_1(\alpha_2)] L_2(\beta) \\ &= aL_1(\alpha_1) L_2(\beta) + bL_1(\alpha_2) L_2(\beta) \\ &= af(\alpha_1, \beta) + bf(\alpha_2, \beta) \end{aligned}$$

and $$\begin{aligned} f(\alpha, a\beta_1 + b\beta_2) &= L_1(\alpha) L_2(a\beta_1 + b\beta_2) \\ &= L_1(\alpha)[aL_2(\beta_1) + bL_2(\beta_2)] \\ &= aL_1(\alpha) L_2(\beta_1) + bL_1(\alpha) L_2(\beta_2) \\ &= af(\alpha, \beta_1) + bf(\alpha, \beta_2) \end{aligned}$$

Hence, $f$ is bilinear form on $V$.

## Matrix of a Bilinear Form

Let $V$ be a finite dimensional vector space and let $B = \{\alpha_1, \alpha_2, \dots, \alpha_n\}$ be an ordered basis for $V$. If $f$ is a bilinear form on $V$, the matrix of $f$ in the ordered basis $B$ is the $n \times n$ matrix $A = [a_{ij}]_{n \times n}$ s.t. $f(\alpha_i, \alpha_j) = a_{ij}$, $i = 1, 2, \dots, n$ and $j = 1, 2, \dots, n$

This matrix $A$ is denoted by $[f]_B$.

## Rank of a Bilinear Form

The rank of a bilinear form is defined as the rank of the matrix of the form in any ordered basis.

## Symmetric Bilinear Form

A bilinear form is said to be symmetric if the corresponding matrix is symmetric.

***Example 3.*** *Let f be the bilinear form on $V_2(R)$ defined by*

$f[(x_1, y_1), (x_2, y_2)] = x_1y_1 + x_2y_2$

*Find the matrix of f in the ordered basis.*

$$B = \{(1, -1), (1, 1)\} \text{ of } V_2(R).$$

**Solution.** Let $B = \{\alpha_1, \alpha_2\}$, where $\alpha_1 = (1, -1), \alpha_2 = (1, 1)$

$$\therefore \quad f(\alpha_1, \alpha_1) = f[(1, -1), (1, -1)] = -1-1 = -2$$
$$f(\alpha_1, \alpha_2) = f[(1, -1), (1, 1)] = -1+1 = 0$$
$$f(\alpha_2, \alpha_1) = f[(1, 1), (1, -1)] = 1-1 = 0$$
$$f(\alpha_2, \alpha_2) = f[(1, 1), (1, 1)] = 1+1 = 2$$
$$\therefore \quad [f]_B = \begin{bmatrix} -2 & 0 \\ 0 & 2 \end{bmatrix}$$

## Bilinear Form Corresponding to a Given Matrix

Let $V_m$ and $V_n$ be two vector spaces over the same field $F$ and let $A = [a_{ij}]_{m \times n}$ be an $m \times n$ matrix over the field $F$.

Let $X = \begin{bmatrix} x_1 \\ x_2 \\ x_3 \\ \vdots \\ x_m \end{bmatrix}$ and $Y = \begin{bmatrix} y_1 \\ y_2 \\ y_3 \\ \vdots \\ y_n \end{bmatrix}$ be any two elements of $V_m$ and $V_n$ respectively, so that

$$X^T = \text{the transpose of the column matrix } X.$$
$$= [x_1\ x_2\ x_3 \ldots x_m]$$
and $$Y^T = [y_1\ y_2\ y_3 \ldots y_n]$$

Then, an expression of the form

$$f(X, Y) = X^T A Y = \sum_{i=1}^{m} \sum_{j=1}^{n} a_{ij} x_i y_j \qquad \ldots\text{(i)}$$

is called a bilinear form over the field $F$ corresponding to the matrix $A$.

> **Note** The matrix $A$ is called the matrix of the bilinear form Eq. (i) and the rank of the matrix $A$ is called the rank of the bilinear form Eq. (i).

***Example 4.*** *Find the matrix A of each of the following bilinear forms $f(X, Y) = X^T AY$.*

(i) $3x_1y_1 + x_1y_2 - 2x_2y_1 + 3x_2y_2 - 3x_1y_3$

(ii) $2x_1y_1 + x_1y_2 - x_1y_3 + 3x_2y_1 - 2x_2y_3 + x_3y_2 - 5x_3y_3$

*Which of the above forms is symmetric?*

**Solution.** (i) The element $a_{ij}$ of the matrix $A$ is the coefficient of $x_iy_j$ in the given bilinear form

$$\therefore \quad A = \begin{bmatrix} 3 & 1 & -3 \\ -2 & 3 & 0 \end{bmatrix}$$

Clearly, the matrix $A$ is not a symmetric matrix. So, the given bilinear form is not symmetric.

(ii) The element $a_{ij}$ of the matrix $A$ which occurs in the $i$th row and the $j$th column is the coefficient of $x_iy_j$ in the given bilinear form

$$\therefore \quad A = \begin{bmatrix} 2 & 1 & 1 \\ 3 & 0 & -2 \\ 0 & 1 & -5 \end{bmatrix}$$

$\Rightarrow$ The matrix $A$ is not symmetric. So, the given bilinear form is not symmetric.

## Quadratic Forms

An expression of the form $\sum_{i=1}^{n} \sum_{j=1}^{n} a_{ij} x_i x_j$, where $a_{ij}$'s are elements of a field $F$, is called a quadratic form in the $n$ variables $x_1, x_2, \ldots, x_n$ over the field $F$.

## Real Quadratic Form

An expression of the form $\sum_{i=1}^{n} \sum_{j=1}^{n} a_{ij} x_i x_j$, where $a_{ij}$'s are all real numbers, is called a real quadratic form in the $n$ variables $x_1, x_2, x_3, \ldots, x_n$.

e.g.,

(i) $3x^2 + 8xy + 11y^2$ is a real quadratic form in the two variables $x$ and $y$.

(ii) $3x^2 - 5y^2 + 3z^2 - 3yz - 5zx + 7xy$ is a real quadratic form in the three variables $x$, $y$ and $z$.

***Theorem*** Every quadratic form over a field $F$ in $n$ variables $x_1, x_2, x_3, \ldots, x_n$ can be expressed in the form $X^TAX$, where $X = \{x_1, x_2, x_3, \ldots, x_n\}^T$ is a column vector and $A$ is a symmetric matrix of order $n$ over the field $F$.

## Matrix of a Quadratic Form

If $\phi = \sum_{i=1}^{n} \sum_{j=1}^{n} a_{ij} x_i x_j$ is a quadratic form in $n$ variables $x_1, x_2, x_3, \ldots, x_n$, then $\exists$ a unique symmetric matrix $A$ of order $n$ such that $\phi = X^T AX$, where $X = \{x_1, x_2, x_3, \ldots, x_n\}^T$. The symmetric matrix $A$ is called the matrix of the quadratic form $\sum_{i=1}^{n} \sum_{j=1}^{n} a_{ij} x_i x_j$.

## Quadratic Form Corresponding to a Symmetric Matrix

Let $A = [a_{ij}]_{n \times n}$ be a symmetric matrix over the field $F$ and let $X = \{x_1, x_2, x_3, \ldots, x_n\}^T$ be a column vector. Then, $X^TAX$ determines a unique quadratic form $\sum_{i=1}^{n} \sum_{j=1}^{n} a_{ij} x_i x_j$ in $n$ variables

$x_1, x_2, x_3, \ldots, x_n$ over the field $F$. We have seen that there exists a one-to-one correspondence between the set of all quadratic forms in $n$ variables over the field $F$ and the set of all $n$ rowed symmetric matrices over $F$.

## Quadratic Form Corresponding to any Given Square Matrix

Let $X = \begin{bmatrix} x_1 \\ x_2 \\ x_3 \\ \vdots \\ x_m \end{bmatrix}$ be any $n$ vector in the vector space $V_n$ over a field $F$, so that $X^T = [x_1, x_2, x_3, \ldots, x_n]$. Let $A = [a_{ij}]_{n \times n}$ be any given square matrix of order $n$ over the field $F$. Then, any polynomial of the form $q(x_1, x_2, x_3, \ldots, x_n) = X^T A X = \sum_{i=1}^{n}\sum_{j=1}^{n} a_{ij}x_i x_j$ is called a quadratic form of order $n$ over $F$ in the $n$ variables $x_1, x_2, x_3, \ldots, x_n$. We can always find a unique symmetric matrix $B = [b_{ij}]_{n \times n}$ of order $n$ s.t. $X^T AX = X^T BX$. We have $b_{ij} = b_{ji} = \frac{1}{2}(a_{ij} + a_{ji})$.

## Non-Singular and Singular Quadratic Forms

By the discriminant of a quadratic form $X^T AX$, it means $\det(A)$. The quadratic form $X^T AX$ is said to be non-singular, if $\det(A) \neq 0$ and if $\det = 0$, then it is said to be singular.

***Example 5.*** *Write down the matrix of each of the following quadratic forms and verify that they can be written as matrix products $X^T AX$.*

(i) $x_1^2 + 2x_2^2 - 5x_3^2 - x_1x_2 + 4x_2x_3 - 3x_3x_1$

(ii) $x_1^2 - 18x_1x_2 + 5x_2^2$

**Solution.** (i) The given quadratic form can be written as

$$x_1x_1 - \frac{1}{2}x_1x_2 - \frac{3}{2}x_1x_3 - \frac{1}{2}x_2x_1 + 2x_2x_2 + 2x_2x_3 - \frac{3}{2}x_3x_1 + 2x_3x_2 - 5x_3x_3$$

Suppose, $A$ is the matrix of this quadratic form. Then,

$$A = \begin{bmatrix} 1 & -1/2 & -3/2 \\ -1/2 & 2 & 2 \\ -3/2 & 2 & -5 \end{bmatrix}$$

Clearly, $A$ is a symmetric matrix.

Suppose, $X = \begin{bmatrix} x_1 \\ x_2 \\ x_3 \end{bmatrix} \Rightarrow X^T = [x_1 \quad x_2 \quad x_3]$

Now, $X^T A = [x_1 \quad x_2 \quad x_3] \begin{bmatrix} 1 & -1/2 & -3/2 \\ -1/2 & 2 & 2 \\ -3/2 & 2 & -5 \end{bmatrix}$

$$= \left[ x_1 - \frac{1}{2}x_2 - \frac{3}{2}x_3 \quad -\frac{1}{2}x_1 + 2x_2 + 2x_3 \quad -\frac{3}{2}x_1 + 2x_2 - 5x_3 \right]$$

$\therefore X'AX$

$$= \left[ x_1 - \frac{1}{2}x_2 - \frac{3}{2}x_3 \quad -\frac{1}{2}x_1 + 2x_2 + 2x_3 \quad -\frac{3}{2}x_1 + 2x_2 - 5x_3 \right] \begin{bmatrix} x_1 \\ x_2 \\ x_3 \end{bmatrix}$$

$$= x_1(x_1 - \frac{1}{2}x_2 - \frac{3}{2}x_3) + x_2(-\frac{1}{2}x_1 + 2x_2 + 2x_3) + x_3(-\frac{3}{2}x_1 + 2x_2 - 5x_3)$$

$$= x_1^2 - \frac{1}{2}x_1x_2 - \frac{3}{2}x_1x_3 - \frac{1}{2}x_2x_1 + 2x_2^2 + 2x_2x_3 - \frac{3}{2}x_3x_1 + 2x_3x_2 - 5x_3^2$$

$$= x_1^2 + 2x_2^2 - 5x_3^2 - x_1x_2 + 4x_2x_3 - 3x_3x_1$$

(ii) The given quadratic form can be written as

$$x_1x_1 - 9x_1x_2 - 9x_2x_1 + 5x_2x_2$$

Suppose, $A$ be the matrix of this quadratic form

$\therefore \quad A = \begin{bmatrix} 1 & -9 \\ -9 & 5 \end{bmatrix}$ and suppose $X = \begin{bmatrix} x_1 \\ x_2 \end{bmatrix} \Rightarrow X^T = [x_1 \quad x_2]$

Now, $X^T A = [x_1 \quad x_2] \begin{bmatrix} 1 & -9 \\ -9 & 5 \end{bmatrix} = [x_1 - 9x_2 \quad -9x_1 + 5x_2]$

$\therefore \quad X^T AX = [x_1 - 9x_2 \quad -9x_1 + 5x_2] \begin{bmatrix} x_1 \\ x_2 \end{bmatrix}$

$$= x_1(x_1 - 9x_2) + x_2(-9x_1 + 5x_2)$$
$$= x_1^2 - 9x_1x_2 - 9x_2x_1 + 5x_2^2$$
$$= x_1^2 - 18x_1x_2 + 5x_2^2$$

## Diagonal and Unit Quadratic Forms

If the matrix of a quadratic form is diagonal, then it is called a diagonal quadratic form.

e.g., $X^T \operatorname{diag}[a_1, a_2, a_3, \ldots, a_n]X = a_1x_1^2 + a_2x_2^2 + a_3x_3^2 + \ldots + a_nx_n^2$ is a diagonal quadratic form. In the diagonal quadratic form some of the $a_i$'s can be zero. If the matrix of a quadratic form is unit, then it is called unit quadratic form.

e.g., $X^T I_n X = x_1^2 + x_2^2 + x_3^2 + \ldots + x_n^2$ is a unit quadratic form.

> ***Note*** If $A$ be any $n$ rowed symmetric matrix of the rank $r$, then there exists a real non-singular matrix $P$ s.t.
>
> $P^T AP = \operatorname{diag} \cdot [1, 1, 1, \ldots 1, -1, -1, -1, \ldots, -1, 0, 0, 0, \ldots, 0]$
>
> so that 1, appears $p$ times and $-1$ appears $r - p$ times.

## Signature and Index of a Real Quadratic Form

Let $y_1^2 + y_2^2 + \ldots + y_p^2 - y_{p+1}^2 - \ldots - y_r^2$ be a normal form of a real quadratic form $X^T AX$ of rank $r$. The number $p$ of positive terms in a normal form of $X^T AX$ is called the index of the quadratic form. The excess of the number of positive terms over the number of negative terms in a normal form of

$$X^T AX \quad i.e., p - (r - p) = 2p - r$$

is called the signature of the quadratic form and is usually denoted by $S$.

Therefore, $\quad S = 2p - r \Rightarrow r = 2p - s$

## Important Theorems on Signature and Index

***Theorem 1*** (Sylvester's Law of Inertia) The signature of a real quadratic form is invariant for all normal reductions.

***Theorem 2*** Two real quadratic forms in $n$ variables are real equivalent if and only if they have the same rank and signature (or same rank and index.)

## Classification of Quadratic Forms

Suppose, $f = X^T AX$ be a real quadratic form in $n$ variables $x_1, x_2, x_3, \dots, x_n$, then the form $f$ is said to be

### (i) Positive Definite (PD)

If $f \geq 0$, for all real values of the variables $x_1, x_2, \dots, x_n$ and $f = 0$ only, if $X = 0$.

*i.e.*, $f = 0 \Rightarrow x_1 = x_2 = x_3 = \dots = x_n = 0$

*e.g.*, The quadratic form $x_1^2 - 4x_1x_2 + 5x_2^2$ in two variables is positive definite because it can be written as $(x_1 - 2x_2)^2 + x_2^2 \geq 0$, $\forall$ real values of $x_1$, $x_2$ and

$$(x_1 - 2x_2)^2 + x_2^2 = 0$$
$$\Rightarrow \quad x_1 - 2x_2 = 0,\ x_2 = 0$$
$$\Rightarrow \quad x_1 = 0,\ x_2 = 0$$

### (ii) Negative Definite (ND)

If $f \leq 0$, for all real values of the variables $x_1, x_2, \dots, x_n$ and $f = 0$ only if $x_1 = x_2 = x_3 = \dots = x_n = 0$.

*e.g.*, $-x_1^2 - x_2^2 - x_3^2$ is a negative definite form in three variables.

### (iii) Positive Semi-Definite (PSD)

If $f \geq 0$, for all real values of the variables $x_1, x_2, \dots, x_n$ and $f = 0$ for some non-zero real vector $X$ *i.e.*, $f = 0$ for some real values of the variables $x_1, x_2, x_3, \dots, x_n$ not all zero.

*e.g.*, the quadratic form $x_1^2 + x_2^2 + 2x_3^2 - 2x_1x_3 - 2x_2x_3$ is positive semi-definite because it can be written in the form $(x_1 - x_3)^2 + (x_2 - x_3)^2$, which is greater than or equal to zero for all real values of $x_1$, $x_2$ and $x_3$ but is zero for non-zero values.

*e.g.*, $x_1 = x_2 = x_3 = 1$

Similarly, the quadratic form $x_1^2 + x_2^2 + 0x_3^2$ in three variables $x_1$, $x_2$ and $x_3$ is positive semi-definite. It is non-negative for all real values of $x_1$, $x_2$ and $x_3$ and it is zero for values $x_1 = 0$, $x_2 = 0$, $x_3 = 2$, which are not all zero.

### (iv) Negative Semi-Definite (NSD)

If $f \leq 0$, for all real values of the variables $x_1, x_2, \dots, x_n$ and $f = 0$ for some values of the variables $x_1, x_2, \dots, x_n$ not all zero.

*e.g.*, the quadratic form $-x_1^2 - x_2^2 - 0x_3^2$ in three variables $x_1$, $x_2$, $x_3$ is negative semi-definite.

### (v) Indefinite (I)

If $f$ takes positive as well as negative values for real values of the variables $x_1, x_2, x_3, \dots, x_n$. *e.g.*, the quadratic form $x_1^2 - x_2^2 + x_3^2$ in three variables is indefinite it takes positive value 1, when $x_1 = 1$, $x_2 = 1$, $x_3 = 1$ and it takes negative value $-1$, when $x_1 = 0$, $x_2 = 1$, $x_3 = 0$.

> ***Note*** **(a)** The above discuss five classes of real quadratic forms are mutually exclusive and are called value classes of real quadratic forms. Every real quadratic form must belong to one and only one value class.
>
> **(b)** A quadratic form which is positive definite or negative definite is called definite and a quadratic form which is positive semi-definite or negative semi-definite is called semi-definite.

## Non-Negative Definite Quadratic Form

A real quadratic form $\phi = X^T AX$ in $n$ variables $x_1, x_2, \dots, x_n$ is said to be non-negative definite, if it takes only non-negative values for all real values of $x_1, x_2, \dots, x_n$.

Thus, $f$ is non-negative definite, if $f \geq 0$, for all real values of $x_1, x_2, \dots, x_n$. A non-negative definite quadratic form may be positive definite or positive semi-definite. If it takes the value 0 only, when $x_1 = x_2 = x_3 = \dots = x_n = 0$, then it is positive definite.

## Criterion for the Value Class of a Real Quadratic Form in Terms of the Eigen Values of its Matrix

Let $f = X^T AX$ is a real quadratic form in $n$ variables. Then, $A$ is a real symmetric matrix of order $n$. Let $r$ be the number of non-zero eigen values of $A$. Then, $r$ = rank of the quadratic form $f$. If $s$ = the number of positive eigen values of $A$ – the number of negative eigen values of $A$, then $s$ = signature of $f$.

***Theorem 1*** A real quadratic form $f = X^T AX$ in $n$ variables is

**(i)** positive definite iff all the eigen values of $A$ are positive.

**(ii)** positive semi-definite iff all the eigen values of $A$ are greater than or equal to zero and atleast one eigen value is zero.

**(iii)** negative definite iff all the eigen values of $A$ are negative.

**(iv)** negative semi-definite iff all the eigen values of $A$ are less than or equal to zero and atleast one eigen value of $A$ is zero.

**(v)** indefinite iff $A$ has positive as well as negative eigen values.

***Theorem 2*** A real symmetric matrix is positive definite iff all its eigen values are positive.

***Theorem 3*** A positive definite real symmetric matrix is non-singular.

## Criterion For Positive Definiteness of a Quadratic Form in Terms of Leading Principal Minors of its Matrix

### Leading Principal Minors of a Matrix

Suppose, $A = [a_{ij}]_{n\times n}$ is a square matrix of order $n$. Then,

$$A_1 = a_{11},\ A_2 = \begin{vmatrix} a_{11} & a_{12} \\ a_{21} & a_{22} \end{vmatrix},\ A_3 = \begin{vmatrix} a_{11} & a_{12} & a_{13} \\ a_{21} & a_{22} & a_{23} \\ a_{31} & a_{32} & a_{33} \end{vmatrix}, \ldots$$

$$\ldots, A_n = \begin{vmatrix} a_{11} & a_{12} & \cdots & a_{1n} \\ a_{21} & a_{22} & \cdots & a_{2n} \\ \vdots & \vdots & \cdots & \vdots \\ a_{n1} & a_{n2} & \cdots & a_{nn} \end{vmatrix}$$

are called the leading principal minors of $A$.

> ***Note*** If $A$ is the matrix of a positive definite form, then $|A| > 0$.

## Some More Criteria to Check the Value Class of a Real Quadratic Form

### Principal Minors of a Matrix

Suppose, $A = [a_{ij}]_{n\times n}$ is a square matrix of order $n$. Any minors of $A$ obtained by deleting the corresponding rows and columns of $A$ are called principal minors of $A$.

Suppose, $A$ be a square matrix given by

$$A = \begin{bmatrix} a_{11} & a_{12} & a_{13} \\ a_{21} & a_{22} & a_{23} \\ a_{31} & a_{32} & a_{33} \end{bmatrix}$$

The principal minors of $A$ of order 1 are $a_{11}, a_{22}, a_{33}$.

The principal minors of $A$ of order 2 are

$$\begin{vmatrix} a_{11} & a_{12} \\ a_{21} & a_{22} \end{vmatrix}, \begin{vmatrix} a_{11} & a_{13} \\ a_{31} & a_{33} \end{vmatrix}, \begin{vmatrix} a_{22} & a_{23} \\ a_{32} & a_{33} \end{vmatrix}$$

These are obtained by omitting the third row and the third column, the second row and the second column and the first row and the first column respectively, the principal minor of $A$ of order 3 is given by

$$\begin{vmatrix} a_{11} & a_{12} & a_{13} \\ a_{21} & a_{22} & a_{23} \\ a_{31} & a_{32} & a_{33} \end{vmatrix}$$

## Important Theorem on Quadratic Form

***Theorem 1*** A real quadratic form $X^TAX$ is positive definite iff all the principal minors of $A$ are positive.

***Theorem 2*** A real quadratic form $X^TAX$ is negative definite iff all the principal minors of $A$ of even order are positive and those of odd order are negative.

***Theorem 3*** A real quadratic form $X^TAX$ is negative semi-definite iff $A$ is singular and all principal minors of even order of $A$ are non-negative while those of odd order are non-positive.

***Theorem 4*** A real quadratic form $X^TAX$ is positive semi-definite iff $A$ is singular and all its principal minors are non-negative.

***Theorem 5*** A real symmetric matrix $A$ is indefinite iff atleast one of the following conditions is satisfied

**(i)** $A$ has a negative principal minor of even order.

**(ii)** $A$ has a positive principal minor of odd order and a negative principal minor of odd order.

***Theorem 6*** A real quadratic form $X^TAX$ is positive semi-definite, if the leading principal minors $A_1, A_2, \ldots, A_{n-1}$ of $A$ are positive and determinant $A = 0$.

---

***Example 6.*** *Write the matrix A of the quadratic form* $6x^2 + 35y^2 + 11z^2 + 4zx$. *Find the eigen values of A and hence, determine the value class of the given quadratic form.*

**Solution.** The matrix $A$ of the given quadratic form is

$$A = \begin{bmatrix} 6 & 0 & 2 \\ 0 & 35 & 0 \\ 2 & 0 & 11 \end{bmatrix}$$

The characteristic equation of $A$ is $|A - \lambda I| = 0$

$\Rightarrow \quad (6-\lambda)(35-\lambda)(11-\lambda) - 2\times 2(35-\lambda) = 0$

$\Rightarrow \quad (35-\lambda)[(6-\lambda)(11-\lambda) - 4] = 0$

$\Rightarrow \quad (35-\lambda)(\lambda^2 - 17\lambda + 62) = 0$

$\Rightarrow \quad (35-\lambda) = 0,\ (\lambda^2 - 17\lambda + 62) = 0$

$\therefore$ The eigen values of $A$ are $35, \dfrac{17 \pm \sqrt{41}}{2}$

$\because$ The eigen values of $A$ are all positive,

$\therefore$ The quadratic form is positive definite.

***Example 7.*** *Prove that the quadratic form* $6x_1^2 + 3x_2^2 + 3x_3^2 - 4x_1x_2 - 2x_2x_3 + 4x_3x_1$ *in three variables is positive definite.*

**Solution.** The matrix $A$ of the given quadratic form is

$$A = \begin{bmatrix} 6 & -2 & 2 \\ -2 & 3 & -1 \\ 2 & 1 & 3 \end{bmatrix}$$

The leading principal minors of $A$ are

$$A_1 = 6 = \text{positive},\ A_2 = \begin{vmatrix} 6 & -2 \\ -2 & 3 \end{vmatrix} = 18 - 4 = 14 = \text{positive}$$

$$A_3 = \begin{vmatrix} 6 & -2 & 2 \\ -2 & 3 & -1 \\ 2 & -1 & 3 \end{vmatrix}$$

$R_2 \to R_2 + R_3, R_1 \to R_1 - 3R_3$

$$= \begin{vmatrix} 0 & 1 & -7 \\ 0 & 2 & 2 \\ 2 & -1 & 3 \end{vmatrix} = 2(2+14) = 32 = \text{positive}$$

$\because$ The leading principal minors of $A$ are all positive. Therefore, the given quadratic form is positive definite.

***Example 8.*** *Determine the value class of the real quadratic form*

$-x_1^2 - 2x_2^2 - 2x_3^2 + 2x_1x_2 + 2x_2x_3$ *in three variables.*

**Solution.** The given quadratic form is

$$q(x_1, x_2, x_3) = -x_1^2 - 2x_2^2 - 2x_3^2 + 2x_1x_2 + 2x_2x_3$$
$$= -x_1x_1 + x_1x_2 + 0x_1x_3 + x_2x_1 - 2x_2x_2 + x_2x_3 + 0x_3x_1 + x_3x_2 - 2x_3x_3$$
$$= X^TAX, \text{ where } A = \begin{bmatrix} -1 & 1 & 0 \\ 1 & -2 & 1 \\ 0 & 1 & -2 \end{bmatrix}$$

is a symmetric matrix.

The leading principal minors of $A$ are

$$A_1 = -1 = \text{negative}, \; A_2 = \begin{vmatrix} -1 & 1 \\ 1 & -2 \end{vmatrix} = 2 - 1 = 1 = \text{positive}$$

$$A_3 = \begin{vmatrix} -1 & 1 & 0 \\ 1 & -2 & 1 \\ 0 & 1 & -2 \end{vmatrix}$$

$C_2 \to C_2 + C_1$

$$= \begin{vmatrix} -1 & 0 & 0 \\ 1 & -1 & 1 \\ 0 & 1 & -2 \end{vmatrix} = -1(2-1) = -1 = \text{negative}$$

We see that $A_1 < 0, A_2 > 0, A_3 < 0$

$\therefore$ The given quadratic form is negative definite.

# Inner Product Space and Orthonormal Basis

## Inner Product

Let $V$ be a vector space. An inner product on $V$ assigns to each ordered pair of vectors $u$ and $v$ in $V$ a scalar (complex, if $V$ is a complex vector space and real, if $V$ is a real vector space) written as $\alpha \cdot \beta$, satisfying the following properties

**(i)** $\alpha \cdot (\beta + \gamma) = \alpha \cdot \beta + \alpha \cdot \gamma, \forall \alpha, \beta, \gamma \in V$

**(ii)** $(a\alpha) \cdot \beta = a(\alpha \cdot \beta), \forall \alpha, \beta \in V$ and all scalars $a$.

**(iii)** $\alpha \cdot \beta = \overline{\beta \cdot \alpha}, \forall \alpha, \beta \in V$

**(iv)** $\alpha \cdot \alpha \geq 0$ and $\alpha \cdot \alpha = 0$ iff $\alpha = 0$.

## Inner Product Space

A vector space $V$ together with an inner product is called an inner product space.

> ***Note*** **(a)** A finite dimensional real inner product space is called an Euclidean space and a finite dimensional complex inner product space is called a unitary space.
>
> **(b)** For a real vector space $V_n(R)$, the inner product is defined as
>
> $$\alpha \cdot \beta = a_1b_1 + a_2b_2 + \ldots + a_nb_n \quad \ldots\text{(i)}$$
>
> and for a complex vector space $V_n(C)$, the inner product is defined as
>
> $$\alpha \cdot \beta = a_1\bar{b}_1 + a_2\bar{b}_2 + \ldots + a_n\bar{b}_n \quad \ldots\text{(ii)}$$
>
> The inner products Eqs. (i) and (ii) are called natural (standard) inner products.
>
> **(c)** If $\alpha$ and $\beta$ are considered column vectors, then $\alpha \cdot \beta$ can also be written as the matrix product $\alpha^T\beta$.
>
> **(d)** If $\alpha$ and $\beta$ are considered row vectors, then $\alpha \cdot \beta$ can also be written as the matrix product $\alpha\beta^T$ norm of vector. The norm of a vector is denoted and defined as
>
> $$||\alpha|| = \sqrt{\alpha \cdot \alpha}$$
>
> and it read as norm of $\alpha$.
>
> **(e)** The norm of the vector $\alpha = (x_1, x_2, \ldots, x_n)$ is defined as $||\alpha|| = [|x_1|^2 + |x_2|^2 + \ldots + |x_n|^2]^{1/2}$

# Important Theorems on Inner Product Space

***Theorem 1*** Let $V$ be an inner product space and $\alpha$, $\beta$ and $\gamma$ be any three vector in $V$ and '$a$' is a scalar. Then,

**(i)** $(\alpha + \beta) \cdot \gamma = \alpha \cdot \gamma + \beta \cdot \gamma$

**(ii)** $\alpha \cdot (a \cdot \beta) = \bar{a}(\alpha \cdot \beta)$

**(iii)** $0 \cdot \alpha = 0 = \alpha \cdot 0$

***Theorem 2*** Let $V$ be an inner product space. Then, for arbitrary vectors $\alpha$ and $\beta$ in $V$ and scalar $a$,

**(i)** $||a\alpha|| = |a| \, ||\alpha||$

**(ii)** $||\alpha|| \geq 0$ and $||\alpha|| = 0$ iff $\alpha = 0$

**(iii)** $|\alpha \cdot \beta| \leq ||\alpha|| \, ||\beta||$ [Schwarz's is inequality]

**(iv)** $||\alpha + \beta|| \leq ||\alpha|| + ||\beta||$ [Triangle inequality]

## Orthogonal Vector

If $\alpha$ and $\beta$ are two vectors in an inner product space $V$, they are said to be orthogonal, if $\alpha \cdot \beta = 0$.

> ***Note*** **(a)** If $\alpha \cdot \beta = 0$, then every scalar multiple of $\alpha$ is orthogonal to $\beta$.
>
> **(b)** The zero vector is orthogonal to every vector.
>
> **(c)** The zero vector is the only vector which is orthogonal to itself.

## Orthogonal Set of Vectors

A set of vectors is said to be orthogonal, if each pair of distinct vectors of the set is orthogonal.

***Theorem Any*** orthogonal set of non-zero vectors in an inner product space is linearly independent.

> **Note** The converse of the above theorem is not true *i.e.*, not every linearly independent set is orthogonal, *e.g.*, the set $\{i, i+j\}$ in $V_2$ is a linearly independent set but the vectors are not orthogonal.

## Angle between Two Vectors

If $\alpha$ and $\beta$ are two vectors in an inner product space $V$, then the angle between $\alpha$ and $\beta$ is given by

$$\cos\theta = \frac{\alpha \cdot \beta}{||\alpha||\,||\beta||}$$

## Projection of One Vector to Another Vector

If $u$ and $v$ belong to an inner product space $V$ and $v \neq 0$, then the vector

$$\frac{\alpha \cdot \beta}{||\alpha||^2}\beta$$

is called the vector projection of $\alpha$ along $\beta$.

## Orthogonal Basis

Let $B = \{\alpha_1, \alpha_2, \ldots, \alpha_n\}$ be any basis of $V_n(K)$, such that $B$ is orthogonal set of vectors. Then, $B$ is called orthogonal basis of $V_n(K)$.

***Theorem*** Every finite dimensional inner product space has an orthogonal basis.

## Normalization

Let $u$ be a non-zero vector. Then, the vector $\dfrac{\alpha}{||\alpha||}$ is called normalizer of $u$.

## Orthonormal Set of Vectors

An orthogonal set of non-zero vectors $\{\alpha_1, \alpha_2, \ldots, \alpha_n\}$ is said to be orthonormal, if $||\alpha_i|| = 1$, $i = 1, 2, \ldots, n$.

*e.g.*, The set $\{\mathbf{i}, \mathbf{j}, \mathbf{k}\}$ is an orthonormal set of vectors in $V_3$.

***Theorem 1*** Every finite dimensional inner product space has an orthonormal basis.

## Gram Schmidt Orthogonalization Process

Suppose, $B = \{\beta_1, \beta_2, \ldots, \beta_n\}$ be a given basis of finite dimensional inner product space $V_n$. Let $\{\alpha_1, \alpha_2, \ldots, \alpha_n\}$ be an orthogonal basis for $V_n$ which we are required to construct from the basis $B$. The vectors $\alpha_1, \alpha_2, \ldots, \alpha_n$, will be obtained in the following way

$$\alpha_1 = \frac{\beta_1}{||\beta_1||}$$

$$\alpha_2 = \frac{\gamma_2}{||\gamma_2||}, \text{ where } \gamma_2 = \beta_2 - (\beta_2 \cdot \alpha_1)\alpha_1$$

$$\alpha_3 = \frac{\gamma_3}{||\gamma_3||}, \text{ where } \gamma_3 = \beta_3 - (\beta_3 \cdot \alpha_1)\alpha_1 - (\beta_3 \cdot \alpha_2)\alpha_2$$

$$\vdots \qquad \vdots$$

$$\alpha_n = \frac{\gamma_n}{||\gamma_n||}, \text{ where } \gamma_n = \beta_n - (\beta_n \cdot \alpha_1)\alpha_1 - (\beta_n \cdot \alpha_2)\alpha_2 \ldots - (\beta_n \cdot \alpha_{n-1})\alpha_{n-1}$$

*e.g.*, We have $B = \{(1, 0, 1), (1, 0, -1), (0, 3, 4)\}$

$$||\beta_1||^2 = \beta_1 \cdot \beta_1 = 1 \cdot 1 + 0 \cdot 0 + 1 \cdot 1 = 2$$

Let $\alpha_1 = \dfrac{\beta_1}{||\beta_1||} = \dfrac{1}{\sqrt{2}}(1, 0, 1) = \left(\dfrac{1}{\sqrt{2}}, 0, \dfrac{1}{\sqrt{2}}\right)$

Now, let $\gamma_2 = \beta_2 - (\beta_2, \alpha_1)\alpha_1$

We have, $\beta_2 \cdot \alpha_1 = 1 \cdot \dfrac{1}{\sqrt{2}} + 0 \cdot 0 + (-1) \cdot \dfrac{1}{\sqrt{2}} = 0$

$\therefore$ $\gamma_2 = (1, 0, -1) - 0\left(\dfrac{1}{\sqrt{2}}, 0, \dfrac{1}{\sqrt{2}}\right) = (1, 0, -1)$

Now, $||\gamma_2||^2 = \gamma_2 \cdot \gamma_2 = 1 \cdot 1 + 0 \cdot 0 + (-1) \cdot (-1) = 2$

Let $\alpha_2 = \dfrac{\gamma_2}{||\gamma_2||} = \dfrac{1}{\sqrt{2}}(1, 0, -1) = \left(\dfrac{1}{\sqrt{2}}, 0, -\dfrac{1}{\sqrt{2}}\right)$

Now, let $\gamma_3 = \beta_3 - (\beta_3, \alpha_1)\alpha_1 - (\beta_3, \alpha_2)\alpha_2$

We have,

$$\beta_3 \cdot \alpha_1 = (0, 3, 4) \cdot \left(\frac{1}{\sqrt{2}}, 0, \frac{1}{\sqrt{2}}\right)$$

$$= 0 \cdot \frac{1}{\sqrt{2}} + 3 \cdot 0 + 4 \cdot \frac{1}{\sqrt{2}} = 2\sqrt{2}$$

Also, $\beta_3 \cdot \alpha_2 = (0, 3, 4) \cdot \left(\dfrac{1}{\sqrt{2}}, 0, -\dfrac{1}{\sqrt{2}}\right) = -2\sqrt{2}$

$$\therefore \quad \gamma_3 = (0, 3, 4) - 2\sqrt{2}\left(\frac{1}{\sqrt{2}}, 0, \frac{1}{\sqrt{2}}\right) + 2\sqrt{2}\left(\frac{1}{\sqrt{2}}, 0, -\frac{1}{\sqrt{2}}\right)$$

$$= (0, 3, 4) - (2, 0, 2) + (2, 0, -2) = (0, 3, 0)$$

Now, $||\gamma_3||^2 = \gamma_3 \cdot \gamma_3 = 0 \cdot 0 + 3 \cdot 3 + 0 \cdot 0 = 9$

Let $\alpha_3 = \dfrac{\gamma_3}{||\gamma_3||} = \dfrac{1}{3}(0, 3, 0) = (0, 1, 0)$

Now, $\{\alpha_1, \alpha_2, \alpha_3\}$

*i.e.*, $\left\{\left(\dfrac{1}{\sqrt{2}}, 0, \dfrac{1}{\sqrt{2}}\right), \left(\dfrac{1}{\sqrt{2}}, 0, -\dfrac{1}{\sqrt{2}}\right), (0, 1, 0)\right\}$ is the required orthonormal basis for $V_3(R)$.

# SOLVED EXAMPLES

## Type I (*Only one correct option*)

**Example 1.** Consider the statements

(I) Let $f : R^n \times R^n \to R$ defined by

$$f(x, y) = \alpha_1\beta_1 + \alpha_2\beta_2 + \ldots + \alpha_n\beta_n$$

where $x = (\alpha_1, \alpha_2, \ldots, \alpha_n)$, $y = (\beta_1, \beta_2, \ldots, \beta_n) \in R^n$

Then, $f$ is a bilinear form on $R^n$.

(II) Let $A = [a_{ij}]_{n \times n}$ be an $n$ square matrix over the field $F$.

Let $f : F^n \times F^n \to F$ defined by

$$f(X, Y) = X^T AY$$

$$= \sum_{i, j=1}^{n} a_{ij} x_i y_j$$

where $X = \begin{bmatrix} x_1 \\ x_2 \\ \vdots \\ x_n \end{bmatrix}$ and $Y = \begin{bmatrix} y_1 \\ y_2 \\ \vdots \\ y_n \end{bmatrix} \in F^n$

Then, $f$ is a bilinear form on $F^n$.

(a) Both (I) and (II) are true
(b) Neither (I) nor (II) is true
(c) (I) is true but (II) is false
(d) (I) is false but (II) is true

**Solution.** (a) (I) Let $a, b \in R$ and $z = (\gamma_1, \gamma_2, \ldots, \gamma_n) \in R^n$

Then,

$$f(ax + bz, y)$$
$$= f((a\alpha_1 + b\gamma_1, a\alpha_2 + b\gamma_2 + \ldots + a\alpha_n + b\gamma_n), (\beta_1, \beta_2, \ldots, \beta_n))$$
$$= (a\alpha_1 + b\gamma_1)\beta_1 + (a\alpha_2 + b\gamma_2)\beta_2 + \ldots + (a\alpha_n + b\gamma_n)\beta_n$$
$$= a(\alpha_1\beta_1 + \alpha_2\beta_2 + \ldots + \alpha_n\beta_n) + b(\gamma_1\beta_1 + \gamma_2\beta_2 + \ldots + \gamma_n\beta_n)$$
$$= af(x, y) + bf(z, y)$$

Hence, $f$ is linear in the first variable.

Similarly, $f$ is linear in the second variable. Hence, $f$ is a bilinear form on $R^n$.

(II) Let $Z = \begin{bmatrix} z_1 \\ z_2 \\ \vdots \\ z_n \end{bmatrix} \in F^n$ and $a, b \in F$

Then,

$$f(aX + bZ, Y) = (aX + bZ)^t AY$$
$$= (aX^t + bZ^t)AY$$
$$= a(X^t AY) + b(Z^t AY)$$
$$= af(X, Y) + bf(Z, Y)$$

Hence, $f$ is linear in the first variable. Similarly, $f$ is linear in the second variable. Hence, $f$ is a bilinear form on $F^n$.

**Example 2.** Let $V$ be a vector space of dimension 3 over a field $F$. Then, $\dim B(V)$ is

(where $B(V)$ denote the set of all bilinear form on $V$)

(a) 3
(b) 8
(c) 9
(d) None of these

**Solution.** (c) Since, $\dim B(V) = n^2$, where $V$ is a vector space of dim $n$.

Hence, $\dim B(V) = 3^2 = 9$

**Example 3.** Let $f$ be the bilinear form on $R^3$ defined by

$$f((x_1, x_2, x_3), (y_1, y_2, y_3))$$
$$= 3x_1y_1 - 2x_1y_2 + 5x_2y_1 + 7x_2y_2 - 8x_2y_3 + 4x_3y_2 - x_3y_3$$

Then, the matrix of $f$ relative to the basis

$\{e_1 = (1, 0, 0), e_2 = (0, 1, 0), e_3 = (0, 0, 1)\}$ is

(a) $\begin{bmatrix} 1 & 0 & 0 \\ 0 & 1 & 0 \\ 0 & 0 & 1 \end{bmatrix}$
(b) $\begin{bmatrix} 3 & -2 & 0 \\ 5 & 7 & -8 \\ 0 & 4 & -1 \end{bmatrix}$
(c) $\begin{bmatrix} 0 & 0 & 1 \\ 0 & 1 & 0 \\ 1 & 0 & 0 \end{bmatrix}$
(d) $\begin{bmatrix} 3 & 2 & 0 \\ 5 & -7 & 8 \\ 0 & -4 & 1 \end{bmatrix}$

**Solution.** (b) Let the matrix $A$ of $f$ relative to the basis

$$\{e_1 = (1, 0, 0), e_2 = (0, 1, 0), e_3 = (0, 0, 1)\}$$

is

$$A = [a_{ij}]_{3\times3}$$

where

$$a_{ij} = f(e_i, e_j), \forall\, i, j = 1, 2, 3$$

$\therefore$ $a_{11} = f(e_1, e_1) = f((1, 0, 0), (1, 0, 0))$
$= 3 \cdot 1 \cdot 1 = 3$
$a_{12} = f(e_1, e_2) = f((1, 0, 0), (0, 1, 0))$
$= -2 \cdot 1 \cdot 1 = -2$
$a_{13} = f(e_1, e_3) = f((1, 0, 0), (0, 0, 1))$
$= 0$

Similarly, $a_{21} = 5$
$a_{22} = 7$
$a_{23} = -8$
$a_{31} = 0$
$a_{32} = 4$
$a_{33} = -1$

Hence, the required matrix is

$$A = \begin{bmatrix} 3 & -2 & 0 \\ 5 & 7 & -8 \\ 0 & 4 & -1 \end{bmatrix}$$

***Example 4.*** *Let f be the bilinear form on $R^3$ defined by*

$$f((x_1, x_2, x_3), (y_1, y_2, y_3)) = 3x_1y_1 - 2x_1y_2 + 5x_2y_1 + 7x_2y_2 - 8x_2y_3 + 4x_3y_2 - x_3y_3$$

*and* $A = \begin{bmatrix} 3 & -2 & 0 \\ 5 & 7 & -8 \\ 0 & 4 & -1 \end{bmatrix}$

*is a matrix of f relative to the basis $\{e_1 = (1, 0, 0), e_2 = (0, 1, 0), e_3 = (0, 0, 1)\}$. Then, the matrix B of f relative to the basis $\{e_1' = (1, 1, 0), e_2' = (1, 0, 1), e_3' = (0, 0, 1)\}$ is*

(a) $\begin{bmatrix} 13 & 0 & -8 \\ 5 & 2 & -1 \\ 4 & -1 & -1 \end{bmatrix}$ (b) $\begin{bmatrix} 13 & 0 & 8 \\ -5 & -2 & 1 \\ -4 & 1 & 1 \end{bmatrix}$

(c) $\begin{bmatrix} 1 & 1 & 0 \\ 0 & 1 & 1 \\ 1 & 1 & 0 \end{bmatrix}$ (d) None of these

**Solution.** (a) We have,

$$e_1' = (1, 1, 0) = 1(1, 0, 0) + 1(0, 1, 0) + 0(0, 0, 1)$$
$$e_2' = (1, 0, 1) = 1(1, 0, 0) + 0(0, 1, 0) + 1(0, 0, 1)$$
$$e_3' = (0, 0, 1) = 0(1, 0, 0) + 0(0, 1, 0) + 1(0, 0, 1)$$

Hence, the transition matrix $p$ from basis $\{e_i\}$ to $\{e_i'\}$ is

$$P = \begin{bmatrix} 1 & 1 & 0 \\ 1 & 0 & 0 \\ 0 & 1 & 1 \end{bmatrix}$$

$$\Rightarrow \quad P^t = \begin{bmatrix} 1 & 1 & 0 \\ 1 & 0 & 1 \\ 0 & 0 & 1 \end{bmatrix}$$

Now, $B = P^tAP$

$$= \begin{bmatrix} 1 & 1 & 0 \\ 1 & 0 & 1 \\ 0 & 0 & 1 \end{bmatrix}\begin{bmatrix} 3 & -2 & 0 \\ 5 & 7 & -8 \\ 0 & 4 & -1 \end{bmatrix}\begin{bmatrix} 1 & 1 & 0 \\ 1 & 0 & 0 \\ 0 & 1 & 1 \end{bmatrix}$$

$$= \begin{bmatrix} 1 & 1 & 0 \\ 1 & 0 & 1 \\ 0 & 0 & 1 \end{bmatrix}\begin{bmatrix} 1 & 3 & 0 \\ 12 & -3 & -8 \\ 4 & -1 & -1 \end{bmatrix}$$

$$= \begin{bmatrix} 13 & 0 & -8 \\ 5 & 2 & -1 \\ 4 & -1 & -1 \end{bmatrix}$$

which is the required matrix

**Alternative method**

Let $B$ be the matrix of $f$ relative to the basis

$\{e_1' = (1, 1, 0), e_2' = (1, 0, 1), e_3' = (0, 0, 1)\}$ is given by

$$B = [b_{ij}]_{3\times3}$$

where

$$b_{ij} = f(e_i', e_j'), \forall\, i, j = 1, 2, 3$$

$$\therefore \quad b_{11} = f(e_1', e_1') = f((1, 1, 0), (1, 1, 0))$$
$$= 3\cdot1\cdot1 - 2\cdot1\cdot1 + 5\cdot1\cdot1 + 7\cdot1\cdot1 - 8\cdot1\cdot0 + 4\cdot0\cdot1 - 0\cdot0$$
$$= 13$$

$$b_{12} = f((1, 1, 0), (1, 0, 1))$$
$$= 3\cdot1\cdot1 - 2\cdot1\cdot0 + 5\cdot1\cdot1 + 7\cdot1\cdot0 - 8\cdot1\cdot1 + 0 + 0$$
$$= 0$$

Similarly,

$$b_{13} = f((1, 1, 0), (0, 0, 1)) = -8\cdot1\cdot1 = -8$$
$$b_{21} = f((1, 0, 1), (1, 1, 0)) = 5$$
$$b_{22} = f((1, 0, 1), (1, 0, 1)) = 2$$
$$b_{23} = f((1, 0, 1), (0, 0, 1)) = -1$$
$$b_{31} = f((0, 0, 1), (1, 1, 0)) = 4$$
$$b_{32} = f((0, 0, 1), (1, 0, 1)) = -1$$
$$b_{33} = f((0, 0, 1), (0, 0, 1)) = -1$$

Hence, the required matrix is

$$B = \begin{bmatrix} 13 & 0 & -8 \\ 5 & 2 & -1 \\ 4 & -1 & -1 \end{bmatrix}$$

***Example 5.*** *The matrix of quadratic form q on $R^3$ given by*

$$q(x_1, x_2, x_3) = x_1^2 - x_3^2 + 3x_1x_2 - 6x_2x_3$$

*is*

(a) $\begin{bmatrix} 1 & 3 & 0 \\ 0 & -1 & -6 \\ 0 & 0 & 0 \end{bmatrix}$ (b) $\begin{bmatrix} 1 & 3/2 & 0 \\ 3/2 & 0 & -3 \\ 0 & -3 & -1 \end{bmatrix}$

(c) $\begin{bmatrix} 1 & 0 & 0 \\ 0 & 1 & 0 \\ 0 & 0 & 1 \end{bmatrix}$ (d) None of these

**Solution.** (b) Let $f$ be the symmetric bilinear form on $R^3$ associated with $q$. Then,

$$f(x, y) = \frac{1}{2}(q(x+y) - q(x) - q(y))$$

where $x = (x_1, x_2, x_3)$

$y = (y_1, y_2, y_3)$

$$\therefore \quad f(x, y) = \frac{1}{2}[(x_1 + y_1)^2 - (x_3 + y_3)^2 + 3(x_1 + y_1)(x_2 + y_2) - 6(x_2 + y_2)(x_3 + y_3) - (x_1^2 - x_3^2 + 3x_1x_2 - 6x_2x_3) - (y_1^2 - y_3^2 + 3y_1y_2 - 6y_2y_3)]$$

$$\Rightarrow \quad f((x_1, x_2, x_3), (y_1, y_2, y_3)) = x_1y_1 - x_3y_3 + \frac{3}{2}y_1x_2 + \frac{3}{2}x_1y_2 - 3x_2y_3 - 3y_2x_3$$

whose matrix relative to standard basis is

$$A = \begin{bmatrix} 1 & 3/2 & 0 \\ 3/2 & 0 & -3 \\ 0 & -3 & -1 \end{bmatrix}$$

***Example 6.*** *The canonical form of quadratic form*

$$q(x, y, z) = x^2 + 5y^2 - 4z^2 + 2xy - 4xz$$

*over the field R is*

(a) $x^2 + 4y^2 - 9z^2$ (b) $x^2 - 4y^2 + 9z^2$

(c) $x^2 - y^2 + z^2$ (d) $x^2 + y^2 + z^2$

**Solution.** (a) The matrix of $q$ relative to the standard basis $\{(1,0,0),(0,1,0),(0,0,1)\}$ of $R^3$ is given by

$$A=\begin{bmatrix}1 & 1 & -2\\ 1 & 5 & 0\\ -2 & 0 & -4\end{bmatrix}$$

Now, the block matrix is

$$[A:I]=\left[\begin{array}{ccc:ccc}1 & 1 & -2 & 1 & 0 & 0\\ 1 & 5 & 0 & 0 & 1 & 0\\ -2 & 0 & -4 & 0 & 0 & 1\end{array}\right]$$

$$\sim\left[\begin{array}{ccc:ccc}1 & 1 & -2 & 1 & 0 & 0\\ 0 & 4 & 2 & -1 & 1 & 0\\ 0 & 2 & -8 & 2 & 0 & 1\end{array}\right]\begin{matrix}R_2\to R_2-R_1\\ R_3\to R_3+2R_1\end{matrix}$$

$$\sim\left[\begin{array}{ccc:ccc}1 & 0 & 0 & 1 & 0 & 0\\ 0 & 4 & 2 & -1 & 1 & 0\\ 0 & 2 & -8 & 2 & 0 & 1\end{array}\right]\begin{matrix}C_2\to C_2-C_1\\ C_3\to C_3+2C_1\end{matrix}$$

$$\sim\left[\begin{array}{ccc:ccc}1 & 0 & 0 & 1 & 0 & 0\\ 0 & 4 & 2 & -1 & 1 & 0\\ 0 & 0 & -9 & \frac{5}{2} & -\frac{1}{2} & 1\end{array}\right]R_3\to R_3-\frac{1}{2}R_2$$

$$\sim\left[\begin{array}{ccc:ccc}1 & 0 & 0 & 1 & 0 & 0\\ 0 & 4 & 0 & -1 & 1 & 0\\ 0 & 0 & -9 & \frac{5}{2} & -\frac{1}{2} & 1\end{array}\right]C_3\to C_3-\frac{1}{2}C_2$$

Therefore, the diagonal form of $A$ is

$$B=\begin{bmatrix}1 & 0 & 0\\ 0 & 4 & 0\\ 0 & 0 & -9\end{bmatrix}$$

Hence, the required normal form is

$$x^2+4y^2-9z^2$$

***Example 7.*** *Let x and y be vectors in an inner product space, then*

(a) $||x+y||^2+||x-y||^2=||x||^2+||y||^2$

(b) $||x+y||^2+||x-y||^2=2(||x||^2+||y||^2)$

(c) $||x+y||^2+||x-y||^2=2||x||\cdot||y||$

(d) None of the above

**Solution.** (b) We have,

$$||x+y||^2=\langle x+y,x+y\rangle$$
$$=||x||^2+\langle x,y\rangle+\langle y,x\rangle+||y||^2 \quad \text{...(i)}$$

and

$$||x-y||^2=\langle x-y,x-y\rangle$$
$$=||x||^2-\langle x,y\rangle-\langle y,x\rangle+||y||^2 \quad \text{...(ii)}$$

Adding Eqs. (i) and (ii), we get

$$||x+y||^2+||x-y||^2=2(||x||^2+||y||^2)$$

***Example 8.*** *Let x and y are two vectors in a real inner product space V, such that x is orthogonal to y, then*

(a) $||x-y||^2>||x||^2+||y||^2$ (b) $||x-y||^2<||x||^2+||y||^2$

(c) $||x-y||^2=||x||^2+||y||^2$ (d) None of these

**Solution.** (c) Let $x$ is orthogonal to $y$, *i.e.*, $x\perp y$. Then,

$$\langle x,y\rangle=\langle y,x\rangle=0 \quad \text{...(i)}$$

Now, $||x-y||^2=\langle x-y,x-y\rangle$

$$=\langle x,x\rangle-\langle x,y\rangle-\langle y,x\rangle+\langle y,y\rangle$$
$$=\langle x,x\rangle+\langle y,y\rangle \quad \text{(by Eq. (i))}$$
$$=||x||^2+||y||^2$$

## Type II (*One or more than one correct option*)

***Example 9.*** *Let f be a bilinear form on V over F. If characteristic of $F\neq 2$ i.e., $1+1\neq 0$ and*

I. $f(u,v)=-f(v,u)$

II. $f(v,v)=0,\forall v\in V$

*Then,*

(a) (I) $\Rightarrow$ (II)

(b) (II) $\Rightarrow$ (I)

(c) (I) $\Leftrightarrow$ (II)

(d) Neither (I) $\Rightarrow$ (II) nor (II) $\Rightarrow$ (I)

**Solution.** (a), (b), (c)

Let characteristic of $F\neq 2$ *i.e.*, $1+1\neq 0$ in $F$.

Now,

(I) $f(u,v)=-f(v,u)$

$\Rightarrow$ $(1+1)f(v,v)=0$

$\Rightarrow$ $f(v,v)=0,\forall v\in V$ (as $1+1\neq 0$ in $F$)

$\Rightarrow$ (II)

Now,

(II) $f(v,v)=0,\forall v\in V$

$\Rightarrow$ $f(x+y,x+y)=0$ $x,y\in V$

$\Rightarrow$ $f(x,x)+f(x,y)+f(y,x)+f(y,y)=0$

$\Rightarrow$ $f(x,y)+f(y,x)=0$ [$\because f(x,x)=0, f(y,y)=0$]

$\Rightarrow$ $f(x,y)=-f(y,x)$

$\Rightarrow$ (I)

Hence, (I) $\Rightarrow$ (II) and (II) $\Rightarrow$ (I) and hence

(I) $\Leftrightarrow$ (II)

***Example 10.*** *Let* $A=\begin{bmatrix}1 & 2 & -3\\ 2 & 5 & -4\\ -3 & -4 & 8\end{bmatrix}$ *be a symmetric matrix.*

*Then,*

(a) the diagonal matrix congruent to $A$ is

$$B=\begin{bmatrix}1 & 0 & 0\\ 0 & 1 & 0\\ 0 & 2 & -5\end{bmatrix}$$

(b) the non-singular matrix $P$ such that $P^tAP = B$ is

$$P = \begin{bmatrix} 1 & -2 & 7 \\ 0 & 1 & -2 \\ 0 & 0 & 1 \end{bmatrix}$$

(c) exactly one of (a) and (b)

(d) Neither (a) nor (b) is true

**Solution.** (a), (b)

Consider the block matrix

$$(A:I) = \left[\begin{array}{ccc:ccc} 1 & 2 & -3 & 1 & 0 & 0 \\ 2 & 5 & -4 & 0 & 1 & 0 \\ -3 & -4 & 8 & 0 & 0 & 1 \end{array}\right]$$

$$\sim \left[\begin{array}{ccc:ccc} 1 & 2 & -3 & 1 & 0 & 0 \\ 0 & 1 & 2 & -2 & 1 & 0 \\ 0 & 2 & -1 & 3 & 0 & 1 \end{array}\right] \begin{matrix} R_2 \to R_2 - 2R_1 \\ R_3 \to R_3 + 3R_1 \end{matrix}$$

$$\sim \left[\begin{array}{ccc:ccc} 1 & 0 & 0 & 1 & 0 & 0 \\ 0 & 1 & 2 & -2 & 1 & 0 \\ 0 & 2 & -1 & 3 & 0 & 1 \end{array}\right] \begin{matrix} C_2 \to C_2 - 2C_1 \\ C_3 \to C_3 + 3C_1 \end{matrix}$$

$$\sim \left[\begin{array}{ccc:ccc} 1 & 0 & 0 & 1 & 0 & 0 \\ 0 & 1 & 2 & -2 & 1 & 0 \\ 0 & 0 & -5 & 7 & -2 & 1 \end{array}\right] R_3 \to R_3 - 2R_2$$

$$\sim \left[\begin{array}{ccc:ccc} 1 & 0 & 0 & 1 & 0 & 0 \\ 0 & 1 & 0 & -2 & 1 & 0 \\ 0 & 0 & -5 & 7 & -2 & 1 \end{array}\right] C_3 \to C_3 - 2C_2$$

Therefore, the required diagonal matrix is

$$B = \begin{bmatrix} 1 & 0 & 0 \\ 0 & 1 & 0 \\ 0 & 2 & -5 \end{bmatrix}$$

and $$P^t = \begin{bmatrix} 1 & 0 & 0 \\ -2 & 1 & 0 \\ 7 & -2 & 1 \end{bmatrix} \Rightarrow P = \begin{bmatrix} 1 & -2 & 7 \\ 0 & 1 & -2 \\ 0 & 0 & 1 \end{bmatrix}$$

***Example 11.*** *Let $V$ be an inner product space. Then,*

(a) $<0, v> = 0, \forall v \in V$

(b) $<u, 0> = 0, \forall u \in V$

(c) $<u, v> = 0, \forall v \in V \Rightarrow u = 0$

(d) $<u, v> = 0, \forall v \in V \Rightarrow u \neq 0$

**Solution.** (a), (b), (c)

We have,

$$<0, v> = <0u, v>$$
$$= 0 <u, v>$$
$$= 0$$

Again,

$$<u, 0> = <u, 0v>$$
$$= \overline{0} <u, v>$$
$$= 0$$

Now, if $<u, v> = 0, \forall v \in V$

Then, $<u, u> = 0$

$\Rightarrow \quad u = 0$

***Example 12.*** *Let $V$ be a finite dimensional inner product space and $S, S_1, S_2$ are subset of $V$.*

Then,

(a) $S_1 \subseteq S_2 \Rightarrow S_2^{\perp} \subseteq S_1^{\perp}$ (b) $S^{\perp} = [S]^{\perp}$

(c) $[S] \subseteq S^{\perp\perp}$ (d) $[S] = S^{\perp\perp}$

**Solution.** (a), (b), (c), (d)

(a) Let $S_1 \subseteq S_2$ and

$v \in S_2^{\perp}$ $\Rightarrow v \perp x, \forall x \in S_2$

$\Rightarrow v \perp x, \forall x \in S_1$ $(\because S_1 \subseteq S_2)$

$\Rightarrow v \in S_1^{\perp}$

$\Rightarrow S_2^{\perp} \subseteq S_1^{\perp}$

Hence, $S_1 \subseteq S_2 \Rightarrow S_2^{\perp} \subseteq S_1^{\perp}$ ...(i)

(b) Since we know that,

$S \subseteq [S]$

$\Rightarrow \quad [S]^{\perp} \subseteq S^{\perp}$ [by Eq. (i)] ...(ii)

Now, let $v \in S^{\perp}$, then

$<v, u> = 0, \forall u \in S$ ...(iii)

If $w \in [S]$, then

$w = \Sigma a_i u_i, \; a_i \in F, u_i \in S$

$\therefore \quad <v, w> = <v, \Sigma a_i u_i>$

$= \sum_i \overline{a}_i <v, u_i>$

$= 0$

$[\because$ by Eq. (iii), $<v, u_i> = 0, \forall u_i \in S]$

$\Rightarrow \quad v \perp W, \forall w \in [S]$

$\Rightarrow \quad v \in [S]^{\perp}$

Hence, $v \in S^{\perp} \Rightarrow v \in [S]^{\perp}$

$\Rightarrow \quad S^{\perp} \subseteq [S]^{\perp}$ ...(iv)

$\therefore$ From Eqs. (ii) and (iv), we have

$S^{\perp} = [S]^{\perp}$

(c) Let $v \in [S]$. Then, $v$ is linear combination of finite number of elements of $S$. If $w \in S^{\perp}$, then $W$ is orthogonal to every vector in $S$ and so $w$ is orthogonal to $v$.

Hence, $v \perp w, \forall w \in S^{\perp}$

$\Rightarrow \quad v \in S^{\perp\perp}$

Hence, $v \in [S] \Rightarrow v \in S^{\perp\perp}$

$\Rightarrow \quad [S] \subseteq S^{\perp\perp}$

(d) Since, $S^{\perp} \subseteq S^{\perp\perp}$

$\Rightarrow \quad [S]^{\perp\perp} = [S]^{\perp\perp}$

$= [S]$

(Since, $W = [S]$ is a subspace of $V$ and $W = W^{\perp\perp}$)

# Exercise 1 (For Part 'B')

**Directions** (Q. Nos. 1-26) *All questions have only one correct option.*

**1.** A real quadratic form in three variables is equivalent to the diagonal form $6y_1^2+3y_2^2+0y_3^2$. Then, the quadratic form is

(a) positive definite
(b) indefinite
(c) positive semi-definite
(d) negative

**2.** A real quadratic form $X^TAX$ in three variables is equivalent to the diagonal form $3y_1^2-4y_2^2+5y_3^2$. Then, the quadratic form $X^TAX$ is

(a) positive definite
(b) negative definite
(c) positive semi-definite
(d) indefinite

**3.** A real quadratic form $X^TAX$ is positive semi definite iff

(a) the eigen values of the matrix $A$ are all $\le 0$
(b) the eigen values of the matrix $A$ are all $> 0$
(c) the eigen values of the matrix $A$ are all $\ge 0$ and atleast one eigen value of $A$ is zero
(d) the eigen values of the matrix $A$ are all negative.

**4.** A real quadratic form $X^TAX$ in three variables is equivalent to the normal form $y_1^2-y_2^2-y_3^2$. If $S$ is the signature of this quadratic form, then

(a) $S=1$ (b) $S=-1$
(c) $S=2$ (d) $S=3$

**5.** If $n$ is the order, $r$ is the rank and $s$ is the signature of a real quadratic form in $n$ variables, then the quadratic form is negative semi-definite if

(a) $s=r=n$ (b) $-s=r=n$
(c) $s=r<n$ (d) $-s=r<n$

**6.** $A$ is $5\times 5$ complex matrix whose characteristic polynomial in $(x+1)^5$ and whose minimal polynomial in $(x+1)^3$. Then,

(a) there is a unique Jordan canonical form for $A$
(b) there are two possible Jordan canonical form for $A$
(c) there are three possible Jordan canonical form for $A$
(d) $A$ does not have a Jordan canonical form

**7.** Let $A$ be a non-null matrix such that $A^k=0$, then choose the incorrect statement

(a) its every eigen value is zero
(b) it is similar to a diagonal matrix
(c) it is nilpotent matrix
(d) None of the above

**8.** Denote the matrix of the quadratic form $(x_1-x_2+2x_3)^2$ by $A$. Then, the trace of $A$ is

(a) 2 (b) 4
(c) 6 (d) 0

**9.** Let $v$ be a non-zero vector in $R^3$. Consider the linear transformation $T:R^3\to R^3$ defined by $T(w)=w-2\frac{<w\cdot v>}{<v\cdot v>}v$. Which of the following is false?

(a) $T^2=$ identity
(b) $\det T=1$
(c) $T(v)=-v$
(d) There is a non-zero vector $w$, such that $Tw=w$

**10.** If $V(F)$ be a vector space of polynomials in $t$ with inner product given by

$$<p,q>=\int_0^1 p(t)q(t)\,dt.$$

Let $P(x)=x+2$, then $||P||^2$ is

(a) $\frac{27}{3}$ (b) $\frac{29}{3}$
(c) $\frac{19}{3}$ (d) $\frac{1}{3}$

**11.** Let $w=\{x,y,z\in R^3 : x+y+z=0\}$ with standard dot product in $R^3$. Then, an orthonormal basis of $w$ is

(a) $\{(1,0,0),(0,1,0),(0,0,1)\}$
(b) $\{\frac{1}{\sqrt{3}}(1,1,1),\frac{1}{\sqrt{2}}(1,0,-1),\frac{1}{\sqrt{2}}(0,1,-1)\}$
(c) $\{\frac{1}{\sqrt{2}}(1,0,-1),\frac{1}{\sqrt{2}}(0,1,-1)\}$
(d) $\{\frac{1}{\sqrt{6}}(1,1,-2),\frac{1}{\sqrt{2}}(1,-1,0)\}$

**12.** Let $T$ be a linear transformation on the real vector space $R^n$ over $R$, such that $T^2=\lambda T$ for some $\lambda\in R$. Then,

(a) $||T_x||=|\lambda|\,||x||$ for all $x\in R^n$
(b) If $||T_x||=||x||$ for some non-zero vector $x\in R^n$, then $\lambda=\pm 2$
(c) $T=\lambda I$, where $I$ is the identity transformation on $R^n$
(d) If $||T_x||>||x||$ for a non-zero vector $x\in R^n$, then $T$ is necessarily singular

**13.** A real quadratic form in three variables $x_1,x_2,x_3$ is equivalent to diagonal form $x_1^2+x_2^2+x_3^2$. Then, the quadratic form is

(a) negative definite
(b) positive definite
(c) semi-positive definite
(d) semi-negative definite

**14.** A real quadratic form in three variables $x_1,x_2,x_3$ is equivalent to diagonal form $-(x_1^2+x_2^2+x_3^2)$. Then, the quadratic form is

(a) positive definite (b) negative definite
(c) semi-positive definite (d) semi-negative definite

**15.** A real quadratic form in three variables is equivalent to the diagonal form $(x_1 - x_2)^2 + x_3^2$. Then, quadratic form is
(a) positive definite
(b) negative definite
(c) semi-positive definite
(d) semi-negative definite

**16.** A real quadratic form in three variables is equivalent to the diagonal form $-(x_1 - x_2)^2 - x_3^2$. Then, the quadratic form is
(a) positive definite
(b) semi-positive definite
(c) negative definite
(d) semi-negative definite

**17.** Consider the inner product space $P([0, 1])$ of all real polynomials on $[0, 1]$ with the inner product
$\langle f \cdot g \rangle = \int_0^1 f(x)g(x)dx$ and $V = \text{span } \{t^2\}$.

Let $h(t) \in V$ be such that
$||(2t - 1)h(t)|| \le ||(2t - 1) - x(t)||$ for $x(t) \in V$.
Then, $h(t)$ is
(a) $\frac{5}{6}t^2$ (b) $\frac{5}{3}t^2$
(c) $\frac{5}{12}t^2$ (d) $\frac{5}{24}t^2$

**18.** Let $M = \begin{pmatrix} 1 & a & b \\ 0 & 2 & c \\ 0 & 0 & 1 \end{pmatrix}$, $a, b, c \in R$, then $M$ is diagonalizable, if and only if
(a) $a = bc$ (b) $b = ac$
(c) $c = ab$ (d) $a = b = c$

**19.** Consider the real inner product space $P[0, 1]$ of all polynomials with the inner product $\langle f, g \rangle = \int_0^1 f(x)g(x)dx$.

Let $M = \text{span } \{1\}$. The orthogonal projection of $x^2$ onto $M$ is
(a) 1 (b) $\frac{1}{2}$
(c) $\frac{1}{3}$ (d) $\frac{1}{4}$

**20.** Denote the matrix of the quadratic form $(x_1 - x_2 + 2x_3)^2$ by $A$. Then, the trace of $A$ is
(a) 2 (b) 4
(c) 6 (d) 0

**21.** In $R^2$, $\langle (x_1, y_1), (x_2, y_2) \rangle = x_1x_2 - \alpha(x_2y_1 + x_1y_2) + y_1y_2$ is an inner product
(a) for all $\alpha \in R$
(b) if and only if $\alpha = 0$
(c) if and only if $\alpha < 1$
(d) if and only if $|\alpha| < 1$

**22.** If $X = AY$. Where $A = \frac{1}{\sqrt{2}}\begin{bmatrix} 1 & -1 \\ -1 & 1 \end{bmatrix}$; $x = (x_1, x_2)^T$ and $y = (y_1, y_2)^T$; then $x_1^2 + x_2^2$ transforms to
(a) $\sqrt{2}(y_1^2 + y_2^2)$
(b) $(y_1 - y_2)^2$
(c) $y_1^2 + y_1y_2 + y_2^2$
(d) $y_1^2 + y_2^2$

**23.** Let $A$ be the matrix of the quadratic form $(x_1 + 2x_2 + 3x_3 + \ldots + nx_n)^2$. Then, the sum of all the entries of $A$ is
(a) $\Sigma n$ (b) $\Sigma n^2$
(c) $\Sigma n^3$ (d) $n\Sigma n$

**24.** If $f(x_1, x_2, \ldots, x_n) = (x_1 + x_2 + \ldots + x_n)^2 - 2\sum_{i \ne j} x_i x_j \ldots$ be a bilinear form then the sum of entries of the matrix associated with the bilinear form is
(a) $\Sigma n$ (b) $n$
(c) $\Sigma(n - 1)$ (d) $-n^2$

**25.** The value of $\cos \theta$ where $\theta$ is the angle between
$A = \begin{bmatrix} 2 & 1 \\ 3 & -1 \end{bmatrix}$ and $B = \begin{bmatrix} 0 & -1 \\ 2 & 3 \end{bmatrix}$
in the vector space of $2 \times 2$ real matrices with inner product defined by $< AB > = \text{tr} < B^T A >$
(a) $\frac{2}{\sqrt{210}}$ (b) $\frac{1}{\sqrt{210}}$
(c) $\frac{1}{\sqrt{105}}$ (d) $\frac{2}{\sqrt{105}}$

**26.** The value of $\cos \theta$ for the angle $\theta$ between $f(t) = 2t - 1$ and $g(t) = t^2$ in the vector space $V$ of polynomial with inner product
$\langle f, g \rangle = \int_0^1 f(t)g(t)dt$ is
(a) $\frac{\sqrt{15}}{4}$ (b) $\frac{\sqrt{15}}{6}$
(c) $\frac{1}{\sqrt{15}}$ (d) $\frac{1}{\sqrt{6}}$

# Exercise 2 (For Part 'C')

**Directions** (Q. Nos. 1-14) *Questions may have one or more than one correct option.*

**1.** Let $f$ be a bilinear form on $V$ over $F$, where characteristic $F \neq 2$. Then,

(a) $f = f_s + f_{ss}$ (b) $f_s = \frac{1}{2}(f(x, y) + f(y, x))$

(c) $f_{ss} = \frac{1}{2}(f(x, y) - f(y, x))$ (d) $f = f_s - f_{ss}$

**2.** Let $A = \begin{bmatrix} 0 & 1 & 1 \\ 1 & -2 & 2 \\ 1 & 2 & -1 \end{bmatrix}$ be a symmetric matrix, then

(a) the diagonal matrix congruent to $A$ is

$$B = \begin{bmatrix} 1 & 0 & 0 \\ 0 & -2 & 0 \\ 0 & 0 & 18 \end{bmatrix}$$

(b) the diagonal matrix congruent to $A$ is

$$B = \begin{bmatrix} -1 & 0 & 0 \\ 0 & 2 & 0 \\ 0 & 0 & -14 \end{bmatrix}$$

(c) the non-singular matrix $P$ such that

$$P^t AP = B \text{ is } P = \begin{bmatrix} 0 & 0 & 2 \\ 0 & 1 & -3 \\ 1 & 1 & -4 \end{bmatrix}$$

(d) All of the above

**3.** Let $u = (1, 3, -4, 2)$, $v = (4, -2, 2, 1)$ and $w = (5, -1, -2, 6)$ in $\mathbb{R}^4$. Then,

(a) $< 3u - 2v, w > = 3 < u, w > -2 < v, w >$
(b) $||u|| = \sqrt{30}$
(c) $||v|| = 5$
(d) None of the above

**4.** Let $f(t) = 3t - 5$ and $g(t) = t^2$ in the polynomial space $P(t)$ with inner product $< f, g > = \int_0^1 f(t)g(t)dt$. Then,

(a) $< f, g > = -\frac{11}{2}$ (b) $< f, g > = 100$

(c) $||f|| = \sqrt{13}$ (d) $||g|| = \sqrt{5}$

**5.** Let $u = (1, 1, 1), v = (1, 2, -3)$ and $w = (1, -4, 3)$ in $\mathbb{R}^3$. Then,

(a) $u$ is orthogonal to $v$ (b) $u$ is orthogonal to $w$
(c) $v$ is orthogonal to $w$ (d) $v$ is not orthogonal to $w$

**6.** The non-zero vector which is orthogonal to $u_1 = (1, 2, 1)$ and $u_2 = (2, 5, 4)$ in $\mathbb{R}^3$ is

(a) (3, 2, −1) (b) (3, −2, 1)
(c) (1, 3, 2) (d) None of these

**7.** Let $u = (1, 3, -4)$. Then, the vector(s) belonging to the basis for the subspace $u^{\perp}$ of $\mathbb{R}^3$ is/ are

(a) (−3, 1, 0) (b) (4, 0, 1)
(c) (a) and (b) both (d) Neither (a) nor (b)

**8.** Let $v$ be the vector space of polynomials $f(t)$ with inner product $< f, g > = \int_{-1}^{1} f(t)\, g(t)dt$. According to Gram-schmidt orthogonal process on $\{1, t, t^2, t^3\}$

(a) $\{1, t, 3t^2 - 1, 5t^3 - 3t\}$ is orthogonal basis
(b) $\{1, t, 3t^2 + 1, 5t^3 + 3t\}$ is orthogonal basis
(c) $\{1, t, \frac{1}{2}(3t^2 - 1), \frac{1}{2}(5t^3 - 3t)\}$ is orthonormal basis
(d) None of the above

**9.** Consider the symmetric matrices $A = \begin{bmatrix} 1 & 3 \\ 3 & 4 \end{bmatrix}$, $B = \begin{bmatrix} 1 & -2 \\ -2 & -3 \end{bmatrix}$, $C = \begin{bmatrix} 1 & -2 \\ -2 & 5 \end{bmatrix}$. Then,

(a) $A$ is not positive definite
(b) $B$ is not positive definite
(c) $C$ is not positive definite
(d) $C$ is positive definite

**10.** Let $\{(1, 1, 0), (1, 2, 3), (1, 3, 5)\}$ be a basis $S$ for Euclidean space $\mathbb{R}^3$. Then, the matrix $A$ that represents the inner product in $\mathbb{R}^3$ relative to the basis $S$ is

(a) $\begin{bmatrix} 2 & 3 & 4 \\ 3 & 14 & 22 \\ 4 & 22 & 35 \end{bmatrix}$ (b) $\begin{bmatrix} -2 & 3 & -4 \\ 3 & -14 & 22 \\ 4 & 22 & -35 \end{bmatrix}$

(c) $\begin{bmatrix} 2 & -3 & 4 \\ -3 & 14 & -22 \\ -4 & 22 & 35 \end{bmatrix}$ (d) None of these

**11.** A real quadratic form is equivalent to the diagonal form $x_1^2 - x_2^2$. Then, quadratic form is

(a) positive definite (b) semi-positive definite
(c) indefinite (d) negative definite

**12.** A real quadratic form $X^T A X$ is indefinite iff

(a) the eigen values of the matrix $A$ are all $\leq 0$
(b) the eigen values of the matrix $A$ are all $\geq 0$
(c) there exists eigen values $\lambda_1, \lambda_2$ of $A$ such that $\lambda_1 \cdot \lambda_2 < 0$
(d) None of the above

**13.** A real quadratic form $X^T AX$, where $A = \begin{bmatrix} 1 & \alpha \\ \beta & 1 \end{bmatrix}$ and $\alpha\beta < 1$. Then, the quadratic form is

(a) positive definite
(b) negative definite
(c) can't be semi-negative
(d) All of the above

**14.** A real quadratic form is equivalent to the diagonal form $f(x_1, x_2, x_3) = (x_1 - 2x_2 + 4x_3 - 5x_4)^2$. Then, $\Sigma a_{ij}$ is

(a) 2 (b) 3
(c) 4 (d) None of these

# Answers

## Exercise 1

**1.** (a) **2.** (d) **3.** (c) **4.** (b) **5.** (d) **6.** (b) **7.** (b) **8.** (c) **9.** (c) **10.** (c)
**11.** (d) **12.** (a) **13.** (b) **14.** (b) **15.** (c) **16.** (d) **17.** (b) **18.** (b) **19.** (c) **20.** (c)
**21.** (b) **22.** (b) **23.** (c) **24.** (b) **25.** (a) **26.** (b)

## Exercise 2

**1.** (a,b,c) **2.** (b,c) **3.** (a,b,c) **4.** (a,c) **5.** (a,b,d) **6.** (b) **7.** (c) **8.** (a,c) **9.** (a,b,d) **10.** (a)
**11.** (c) **12.** (c) **13.** (a,c) **14.** (c)

# Hints & Solutions

## Exercise 1

**1.** We have,

$$f(y_1, y_2, y_3) = 6y_1^2 + 3y_2^2 + 0y_3^2$$
$$= 6y_1^2 + 3y_2^2 > 0, \forall (y_1, y_2, y_3) \in \mathbb{R}^3 - \{0\}$$

Hence, $f$ is positive definite.

**2.** We have,

$$f(y_1, y_2, y_3) = 3y_1^2 - 4y_2^2 + 5y_3^2$$

Let $(y_1, y_2, y_3) = (1, 1, 0)$

Then,

$$f(1, 1, 0) = 3 - 4 + 0 = -1 < 0$$

and let $(y_1, y_2, y_3) = (0, 1, 1)$

then

$$f(0, 1, 1) = 0 - 4 + 5 = 1 > 0.$$

Hence, $f$ is positive indefinite.

**8.** We have,

$$f(x_1, x_2, x_3) = (x_1 - x_2 + 2x_3)^2$$
$$= x_1^2 + x_2^2 + 4x_3^2 + 2(-x_1x_2 - 2x_2x_3 + x_1x_3)$$

Then, $A = \begin{bmatrix} 1 & -1 & -2 \\ -1 & 1 & 1 \\ -2 & 1 & 4 \end{bmatrix}$

Hence, trace $A = 1 + 1 + 4 = 6$

**9.** We have,

$$T(w) = w - 2\frac{<w, v>}{<v, v>}v$$

$$\therefore \quad T(v) = v - 2\frac{<u, v>}{<u, v>}v = v - 2v = -v$$

$$\therefore \quad T(v) = -v$$

**13.** We have,

$$f(x_1, x_2, x_3) = x_1^2 + x_2^2 + x_3^2$$
$$> 0, \forall (x_1, x_2, x_3) \in \mathbb{R}^n - \{0\}.$$

Hence, $f$ is positive definite.

**14.** We have,

$$f(x_1, x_2, x_3) = -(x_1^2 + x_2^2 + x_3^2)$$
$$< 0, \forall (x_1, x_2, x_3) \in \mathbb{R}^3 - \{0\}$$

$\therefore f$ is negative definite.

**15.** We have,

$$f(x_1, x_2, x_3) = (x_1 - x_2)^2 + x_3^2$$
$$\geq 0, \forall (x_1, x_2, x_3) \in \mathbb{R}^3$$

But at (1, 1, 0)

$$f(1, 1, 0) = (1 - 1)^2 + 0^2 = 0$$

Hence, $f$ is semi-positive definite.

**16.** We have,

$$f(x_1, x_2, x_3) = -(x_1 - x_2)^2 - x_3^2$$
$$\leq 0, \forall (x_1, x_2, x_3) \in \mathbb{R}^3$$

But at (1, 1, 0)

$$f(1, 1, 0) = 0$$

Hence, $f$ is semi-negative definite.

## Exercise 2

**1.** We have,

$$f_s(x, y) = \frac{1}{2}(f(x y) + f(y, x))$$

$$\therefore f_s(y, x) = \frac{1}{2}(f(y, x) + f(x, y)) = f_s(x, y)$$

$\therefore$ $f_s$ is symmetric

$$\therefore \; f_s(x, x) = \frac{1}{2}(f(x, x) - f(x, x)) = 0$$

Now,

$$f_{ss}(x, y) = \frac{1}{2}(f(x, y) - f(y, x))$$

$$= -\frac{1}{2}(f(y,x) - f(x,y))$$
$$= -f_{ss}(y,x)$$

$\therefore$ $f_{ss}$ is skew-symmetric.

$\therefore$ $f_s(x,y) + f_{ss}(x,y)$

$$= \frac{1}{2}(f(x,y) + f(y,x)) + \frac{1}{2}(f(x,y) - f(y,x))$$
$$= f(x,y)$$
$$\Rightarrow f_s + f_{ss} = f$$

where

$$f_s = \frac{1}{2}(f(x,y) + f(y,x))$$

and $f_{ss} = \frac{1}{2}(f(x,y) - f(y,x))$

**3.** We have,

$$<u, w> = 5 - 3 + 8 + 12 = 22$$

and $<v, w> = 20 + 2 - 4 + 6 = 24$

Now, $3v - 2v = (-5, 13, -16, 4)$

Hence, $<3u - 2v, w> = -25 - 13 + 32 + 24 = 18$ ...(i)

and $3(u, w) - 2(v, w) = 3(22) - 2(24)$

$= 18$ ...(ii)

From Eqs. (i) and (ii), we have

$$<3u - 2v, w> = 3 <u, w> - 2 <v, w>.$$

Next $||u|| = \sqrt{1 + 9 + 16 + 4} = \sqrt{30}$

and $||v|| = \sqrt{16 + 4 + 4 + 1} = 5$

**4.** Since, $<u, v> = 1 + 2 - 3 = 0$

$<u, w> = 1 - 4 + 3 = 0$

and $<v, w> = 1 - 8 - 9 = -16$

Hence, $u$ is orthogonal to $v$ and $w$, but $v$ and $w$ are not orthogonal.

**5.** Let $w = (x, y, z)$ be the vector orthogonal to $u_1 = (1, 2, 1)$ and $u_2 = (2, 5, 4)$. Then,

$$<u_1, w> = 0 \text{ and } <u_2, w> = 0$$

$\Rightarrow$ $x + 2y + z = 0$ or $x + 2y + z = 0$

$2x + 5y + 4z = 0$ $\quad y + 2z = 0$

Here, $z$ is the only free variable in the echelon system. Let $z = 1$, then $y = -2$ and $x = 3$. Thus, $w = (3, -2, 1)$, which is required vector.

**7.** Since, $u^{\perp}$ consists of all vectors $w = (x, y, z)$ such that $<u, w> = 0 \Rightarrow x + 3y - 4z = 0$. The free variables are $y$ and $z$. Hence, if $y = 1, z = 0 \Rightarrow w = (-3, 1, 0)$, if $y = 0, z = 1$ $\Rightarrow w = (4, 0, 1)$

**8.** Let $f_0 = 1$

Then, $t = \frac{<t, 1>}{<1, 1>}(1) = t - 0 = t$

Let $f_1 = t$

Then, $t^2 - \frac{<t^2, 1>}{<1, 1>}(1) - \frac{<t^2, t>}{<t, t>}(t)$

$$= t^2 - \frac{\frac{2}{3}}{2}(1) + 0(t) = t^2 - \frac{1}{3}$$

multiply by 3 to obtain

$t_2 = 3t^2 - 1$

Then, $t^3 - \frac{<t^3, 1>}{<1, 1>}(1) - \frac{<t^3, t>}{<t, t>}(t) - \frac{<t^3, 3t^2 - 1>}{<3t^3 - 1, 3t^2 - 1>}(3t^2 - 1)$

$$= t^3 - 0(1) - \frac{\frac{2}{5}}{\frac{2}{3}}(t) - 0(3t^2 - 1)$$
$$= t^3 - \frac{3}{5}t$$

Multiply by 5 to obtain $f_3 = 5t^3 - 3t$. Hence, $\{1, t, 3t^2 - 1, 5t^3 - 3t\}$ is the required orthogonal basis.

Hence, $\{1, t, \frac{1}{2}(3t^2 - 1), \frac{1}{2}(5t^3 - 3t)\}$ is orthonormal basis.

**9.** Since, $|A| = 4 - 9 = -5 < 0$. Hence, $A$ is not positive definite. Since, the diagonal entry of matrix $B$ is $-3 < 0$. Hence, $B$ is not positive definite. Since, the diagonal entries of $C$ are 1 and 5 which are positive. Hence, $C$ is positive definite.

**10.** We have,

$<u_1, u_1> = 1 + 1 + 0 = 2$

$<u_1, u_2> = 1 + 2 + 0 = 3$

$<u_1, u_3> = 1 + 3 + 0 = 4$

$<u_2, u_1> = 1 + 2 + 0 = 3$

$<u_2, u_2> = 1 + 4 + 9 = 14$

$<u_2, u_3> = 1 + 6 + 15 = 22$

$<u_3, u_1> = 1 + 3 + 0 = 4$

$<u_3, u_2> = 1 + 6 + 15 = 22$

$<u_3, u_3> = 1 + 9 + 25 = 35$

Hence, the required matrix is $A = \begin{bmatrix} 2 & 3 & 4 \\ 3 & 14 & 22 \\ 4 & 22 & 35 \end{bmatrix}$.

**11.** We have,

$$f(x_1, x_2, x_3) = x_1^2 - x_2^2$$

But at $(1, 0, 0)$

$$f(1, 0, 0) = 1 > 0$$

and at $(0, 1, 0)$

$$f(0, 1, 0) = -1 < 0$$

Hence, $f$ is indefinite.

**13.** We have,

$$A = \begin{bmatrix} 1 & \alpha \\ \beta & 1 \end{bmatrix}$$

$\Rightarrow$ $|A| = 1 - \alpha\beta \neq 0$

$\Rightarrow$ Real quadratic form can't be semi-negative definite and Since $\alpha\beta < 0$. Hence, $1 - \alpha\beta > 0$.

$\Rightarrow$ Real quadratic form is positive definite.

**14.** We have,

$$f(x_1, x_2, x_3) = (x_1 - 2x_2 + 4x_3 - 5x_4)^2$$

Putting $x_1 = x_2 = x_3 = 1$, we get

$$\Sigma a_{ij} = (1 - 2 + 4 - 5)^2$$
$$= (-2)^2$$
$$= 4$$

# 11 Complex Numbers and Analytic Functions

## Syllabus

- Algebra of Complex Number
- The Complex Plane
- Polynomials
- Power Series
- Transcendental Functions such as Exponential, Trigonometric and Hyperbolic Functions
- Analytic Functions Cauchy-Riemann Equations

## Complex Number

Any expression of the form $x + iy$, where $x$ and $y$ are real numbers and $i = \sqrt{-1}$, is called a complex number which is generally denoted by $z$ *i.e.*, $z = x + iy$. $x$ and $y$ are respectively called real part and imaginary part of $z$.

*i.e.*, $\text{Re}(z) = x$, $\text{Im}(z) = y$

> ***Note*** **(a)** $i = \sqrt{-1}$, $i^2 = -1$, $i^3 = -i$, $i^4 = 1 \Rightarrow i^{4n} = 1$
>
> **(b)** $z = x + iy$ is also expressed as an ordered pair $(x, y)$.
>
> **(c)** If $\text{Im}(z) = 0 \Leftrightarrow z$ is purely real and if $\text{Re}(z) = 0 \Leftrightarrow z$ is purely imaginary.
>
> **(d)** Every real number is a complex number.
>
> **(e)** $0 = 0 + i \cdot 0$ is both purely real and purely imaginary number.
>
> **(f)** $z_1 = z_2 \Leftrightarrow \text{Re}(z_1) = \text{Re}(z_2)$ and $\text{Im}(z_1) = \text{Im}(z_2)$. In particular, if $z = 0 \Leftrightarrow \text{Re}(z) = 0$ and $\text{Im}(z) = 0$

## Algebra of Complex Numbers

The sum, difference, product or quotient of any two complex numbers is a complex number.

*i.e.*, for any two given complex numbers $z_1$ and $z_2$,

$z_1 + z_2$, $z_1 - z_2$, $z_1 \cdot z_2$, $\dfrac{z_1}{z_2}$ $(z_2 \neq 0)$ are complex numbers.

### Properties of Complex Numbers

**(i)** $z_1 + z_2 = z_2 + z_1$ (Commutativity in addition)

**(ii)** $z_1 + (z_2 + z_3) = (z_1 + z_2) + z_3$ (Associativity in addition)

**(iii)** $z + 0 = z$ (0 is additive identity)

**(iv)** $z + (-z) = 0$ ($-z$ is additive inverse)

**(v)** $z_1 z_2 = z_2 z_1$ (Commutativity in multiplication)

**(vi)** $z_1(z_2 z_3) = (z_1 z_2) z_3$ (Associativity in multiplication)

**(vii)** $z \cdot 1 = z$ (1 is multiplicative identity)

**(viii)** $z \cdot \dfrac{1}{z} = 1$ ($\dfrac{1}{z}$ multiplicative inverse)

**(ix)** $z_1(z_2 + z_3) = z_1 z_2 + z_1 z_3$ (Dot distribute over addition)

## Conjugate of *z*

Conjugate of $z = x + iy$ is $\bar{z} = \overline{x + iy} = x - iy$

### Properties of Conjugate of *z*

**(i)** $\overline{z_1 \pm z_2} = \bar{z}_1 \pm \bar{z}_2$  **(ii)** $z + \bar{z} = 2\,\text{Re}\,(z)$

**(iii)** $z - \bar{z} = 2i\,\text{Im}(z)$  **(iv)** $\overline{z_1 z_2} = \bar{z}_1 \cdot \bar{z}_2$

**(v)** $\overline{z^n} = (\bar{z})^n$  **(vi)** $\overline{\left(\dfrac{z_1}{z_2}\right)} = \dfrac{\bar{z}_1}{\bar{z}_2} \quad (z_2 \neq 0)$

**(vii)** $\bar{\bar{z}} = z$

## Modulus of *z*

Modulus of $z = x + iy$ is $|z| = |x + iy| = \sqrt{x^2 + y^2}$

### Properties of Modulus of *z*

**(i)** $|z_1 z_2| = |z_1||z_2|$

**(ii)** $|z^n| = |z|^n$

**(iii)** $|z| = |-z| = |\bar{z}| = |-\bar{z}|$

**(iv)** $\left|\dfrac{z_1}{z_2}\right| = \dfrac{|z_1|}{|z_2|} \quad (z_2 \neq 0)$

**(v)** $z\bar{z} = |z|^2$

**(vi)** $||z_1| - |z_2|| \leq |z_1 \pm z_2| \leq |z_1| + |z_2|$

## Argument or Amplitude of *z*

Argument of $z = x + iy$ is denoted by arg $(z)$ and arg $(z) = \tan^{-1}\left|\dfrac{y}{x}\right|$, $\pi - \tan^{-1}\left|\dfrac{y}{x}\right|$, $\tan^{-1}\left|\dfrac{y}{x}\right| - \pi$, $-\tan^{-1}\left|\dfrac{y}{x}\right|$ according as $z = x + iy$ lies in 1st, 2nd, 3rd and 4th quadrants respectively.

### Properties of Argument of *z*

**(i)** $\arg(z_1 z_2) = \arg(z_1) + \arg(z_2)$

**(ii)** $\arg(z^n) = n(\arg z)$

**(iii)** $\arg\left(\dfrac{z_1}{z_2}\right) = \arg(z_1) - \arg(z_2)$

**(iv)** $\arg(\bar{z}) = -\arg(z)$

**(v)** arg (0) is not defined.

## Complex Plane

Corresponding to each complex number $z = x + iy$, there is a unique point $P(x, y)$ in the $xy$-plane which is known as complex plane or argand plane.

$x$-axis is called real axis and $y$-axis is called imaginary axis.

From figure,

**(i)** $|z| = |\overline{OP}| = OP = r = \sqrt{x^2 + y^2}$

**(ii)** $\arg(z) = \theta$

**(iii)** Polar form of $z = r(\cos\theta + i\sin\theta)$

***Example 1.*** *Find real θ such that* $\dfrac{3 + 2i\sin\theta}{1 - 2i\sin\theta}$ *is*

*(i) purely real and* *(ii) purely imaginary*

**Solution.** Let $z = \dfrac{3 + 2i\sin\theta}{1 - 2i\sin\theta} = \dfrac{(3 + 2i\sin\theta)(1 + 2i\sin\theta)}{1 + 4\sin^2\theta}$

$$\Rightarrow \quad z = \frac{3 - 4\sin^2\theta}{1 + 4\sin^2\theta} + i\,\frac{8\sin\theta}{1 + 4\sin^2\theta}$$

(i) $z$ is purely real $\Rightarrow \text{Im}(z) = 0$

$\Rightarrow \sin\theta = 0 \Rightarrow \theta = n\pi$

(ii) $z$ is purely imaginary $\Rightarrow \text{Re}\,(z) = 0$

$\Rightarrow \sin^2\theta = \dfrac{3}{4} = \sin^2\dfrac{\pi}{3} \Rightarrow \theta = n\pi \pm \dfrac{\pi}{3}$

***Example 2.*** *Find modulus and argument of* $\dfrac{1 + i}{1 - \sqrt{3}i}$.

**Solution.** Let

$$z = \frac{1 + i}{1 - \sqrt{3}i} = \frac{(1 + i)(1 + \sqrt{3}i)}{1 + 3} = \frac{(1 - \sqrt{3}) + (1 + \sqrt{3})i}{4}$$

$$|z| = \sqrt{\left(\frac{1 - \sqrt{3}}{4}\right)^2 + \left(\frac{1 + \sqrt{3}}{4}\right)^2} = \frac{\sqrt{8}}{4} = \frac{1}{\sqrt{2}}$$

$$\therefore \quad \tan\theta = \left|\frac{1 + \sqrt{3}}{1 - \sqrt{3}}\right| = \left|\frac{(1 + \sqrt{3})^2}{1 - 3}\right| = 2 + \sqrt{3} = \tan\frac{5\pi}{12}$$

$$\Rightarrow \quad \theta = \frac{5\pi}{12}$$

Here, $z$ lies in 2nd quadrant.

$$\therefore \quad \arg(z) = \pi - \frac{5\pi}{12} = \frac{7\pi}{12}$$

## Stereographic Projection

Let us consider the sphere

$$S = \left\{(x, y, z) \mid x^2 + y^2 + \left(z - \frac{1}{2}\right)^2 = \frac{1}{4}\right\}$$

Let $T = S - \{(0, 0, 1)\}$

$\Rightarrow T \sim S$

but $T \sim \mathbb{C}$ as the point of intersection of line $PN$ and sphere is unique. Hence,

$$S \sim \mathbb{C}$$

The relations which defines the Stereographic projection of the complex plane to sphere are given by

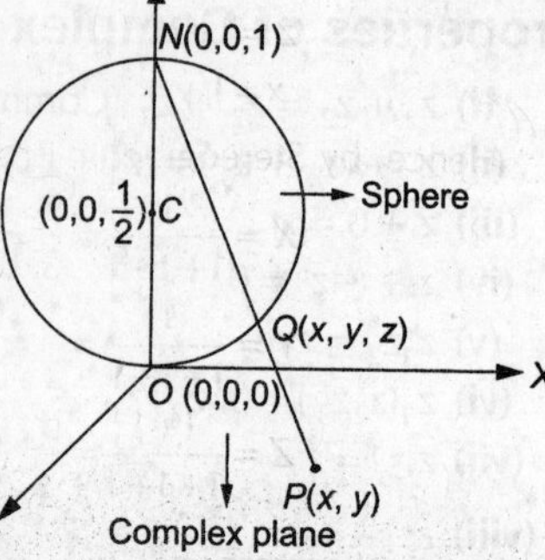


$$X = \frac{x}{1 + x^2 + y^2} = \frac{z + \bar{z}}{2(1 + |z|^2)}$$

$$Y = \frac{y}{1 + x^2 + y^2} = \frac{z - \bar{z}}{2i(1 + |z|^2)}$$

and $Z = \frac{x^2 + y^2}{1 + x^2 + y^2} = \frac{|z|^2}{1 + |z|^2}$

The relations which defines the Stereographic projection of sphere to complex plane are given by

$$x = \frac{X}{1 - Z}, y = \frac{Y}{1 - Z}$$

> **Note** The point in complex plane which correspond to (0, 0, 1) only is define as infinity.

***Example* 3.** *Find the point in sphere which corresponds to $z = 1 + i$.*

**Solution.** We have

$$z = 1 + i$$

$$\therefore \quad x = 1, y = 1$$

$$X = \frac{1}{1+1+1} = \frac{1}{3}$$

$$Y = \frac{1}{1+1+1} = \frac{1}{3}$$

$$Z = \frac{1+1}{1+1+1} = \frac{2}{3}$$

Hence, the required point in sphere is $\left(\frac{1}{3}, \frac{1}{3}, \frac{2}{3}\right)$.

## Chardal Distance

Let the points $z_1, z_2$ in complex plane corresponds to $Z_1, Z_2$ in sphere. Then

$$\chi(z_1, z_2) = d(Z_1, Z_2)$$
$$= \text{distance between } Z_1 \text{ and } Z_2$$

is known as chardal distance between $z_1$ and $z_2$.

In other words, the chardal distance between two complex number is defined as the distance between corresponding points on sphere. This is always less than or equal to the diameter of the sphere.

> **Note** $\chi(z, \infty) = \frac{1}{\sqrt{1 + |z|^2}}$, where $z$ is any complex number.

***Example* 4.** *Find the chardal distance between $1 + i$ and $\infty$.*

**Solution.** We have

$$z = 1 + i$$

$$\therefore \quad x = 1, y = 1$$

Hence, by Stereographic projection

$$X = \frac{1}{1+1+1} = \frac{1}{3}$$

$$Y = \frac{1}{1+1+1} = \frac{1}{3}$$

$$Z = \frac{1+1}{1+1+1} = \frac{2}{3}$$

$\Rightarrow$ $1 + i$ corresponds to $\left(\frac{1}{3}, \frac{1}{3}, \frac{2}{3}\right)$.

Similarly, $\infty$ corresponds to $(0, 0, 1)$. Hence, the chardal distance between $1 + i$ and $\infty$ is

$$\chi(1+i, \infty) = \sqrt{\left(\frac{1}{3} - 0\right)^2 + \left(\frac{1}{3} - 0\right)^2 + \left(\frac{2}{3} - 1\right)^2} = \frac{1}{\sqrt{3}}$$

## Antipodal Points

Two points $z_1, z_2 \in \mathbb{C}$ are said to be antipodal points if their chardal distance is equal to the diameter of sphere.

> **Note** Two points $z_1, z_2$ are antipodal iff
> $$z_1 \bar{z}_2 = -1$$

## Positionally Equal Numbers

Two complex numbers $z_1$ and $z_2$ are said to be positionally equal, if

$$|z_1| = |z_2|$$

and $\arg(z_1) - \arg(z_2) = 2n\pi, n \in \mathbb{Z}$

## Multivalued Function

A complex function $w = f(z)$ is said to be multivalued function if there exists positionally equal points $z_1$ and $z_2$ such that

$$f(z_1) \neq f(z_2)$$

**Definition** Let $w = f(z)$ be a multivalued function, then $z_0$ is said to be a branch point if $\exists \delta > 0$ such that when $z$ moves on $|z - z_0| = r < \varepsilon$, after one complete revolution $f(z)$ does not occupy the same position *i.e.*, $z_1$ and $z_2$ are positionally equal number obtained by revolving around $z_0$ on $|z - z_0| = r - \varepsilon$ and only one revolution is made but $f(z_1) \neq f(z_2)$.

> **Note** The branch points of some special multivalued function are given below:

| Multivalued function | Branch points |
|---|---|
| (i) $f(z) = \sqrt{z}$ | 0 |
| (ii) $f(z) = \log z$ | 0 |
| (iii) $f(z) = \sin^{-1} z$ | $\pm 1$ |
| (iv) $f(z) = \cos^{-1} z$ | $\pm 1$ |
| (v) $f(z) = \tan^{-1} z$ | $\pm i$ |
| (vi) $f(z) = z^2$ | 0 |

***Example* 5.** *Show that*

$$f(z) = \sqrt{z}$$

*is a multivalued function.*

**Solution.** Let $z_1 = re^{i\theta}$ and $z_2 = re^{i(\theta + 2\pi)}$

Then, $z_1$ and $z_2$ are positionally equal points.

Now, $\quad f(z_1) = \sqrt{r} e^{\frac{i\theta}{2}}$

and $\quad f(z_2) = \sqrt{r}e^{i\left(\frac{\theta+2\pi}{2}\right)}$

$$= \sqrt{r}e^{i\frac{\theta}{2}} \cdot e^{\pi i} = -\sqrt{r}e^{i\frac{\theta}{2}}$$

$\Rightarrow \quad f(z_1) \neq f(z_2)$

Hence, $f(z) = \sqrt{z}$ is a multivalued function.

## Monovalent Function

A function $f : \mathbb{C} \to \mathbb{C}$ is said to be monovalent if $f$ is one-one.

***Example 6.*** *In which region $e^z$ is monovalent?*

**Solution.** We have

$$f(z_1) = f(z_2)$$

$\Rightarrow \quad e^{z_1} = e^{z_2}$

$\Rightarrow \quad z_1 - z_2 = 2n\pi i, n \in \mathbb{Z}$

$\therefore$ The required region, is

$$= \{z : |z_1 - z_2| = 2\pi\}$$

## De Moivre's Theorem

**(i)** If $n$ is any integer, then

$$(\cos\theta + i\sin\theta)^n = \cos n\theta + i\sin n\theta$$

**(ii)** If $n$ is any rational number, then one of the value of

$$(\cos\theta + i\sin\theta)^n = \cos n\theta + i\sin n\theta$$

> ***Note*** $n$th roots of unity are $1, \alpha, \alpha^2, \ldots, \alpha^{n-1}$, where $\alpha = e^{i\frac{2\pi}{n}}$ where
> (i) $1 + \alpha + \alpha^2 + \ldots + \alpha^{n-1} = 0$
> (ii) $1 \cdot \alpha \cdot \alpha^2 \cdot \alpha^3 \ldots \alpha^{n-1} = (-1)^{n-1}$

## Geometry of Complex Numbers

**(i)** Distance between $z_1$ and $z_2$ is $|z_1 - z_2|$.

**(ii)** If $z$ divides segment joining $z_1$ and $z_2$ in the ratio $m_1 : m_2$, then

$$z = \frac{m_1 z_2 + m_2 z_1}{m_1 + m_2} \qquad \text{(Internal division)}$$

**(iii)** $\arg\left(\dfrac{z_3 - z_1}{z_2 - z_1}\right) = \theta$

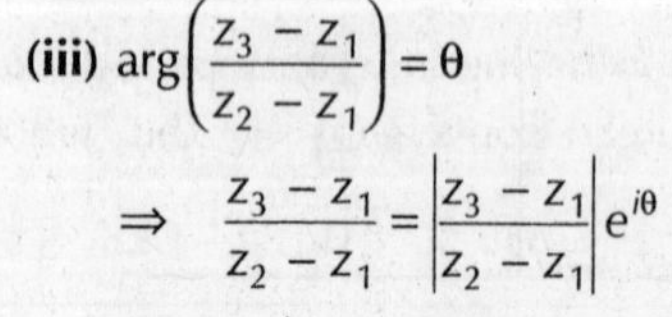

$$\Rightarrow \quad \frac{z_3 - z_1}{z_2 - z_1} = \left|\frac{z_3 - z_1}{z_2 - z_1}\right| e^{i\theta}$$

(From exponential form of z)

C($z_3$)
$\theta$
A($z_1$) B($z_2$)

**(iv)** $\bar{a}z + a\bar{z} = \lambda$ represents equation of a straight line, where a be the complex number (constant) and $\lambda$ be real.

**(v)** $|z - z_0| = r$ represents equation of circle with centre $z_0$ and radius $r$.

**(vi)** $z\bar{z} + a\bar{z} + \bar{a}z + \lambda = 0$ represents a circle with centre $-a$ and radius $\sqrt{|a|^2 - \lambda}$.

**(vii)** $|z - z_1| + |z - z_2| = k$, where $k > |z_1 - z_2|$ represents an ellipse with foci at $z_1$ and $z_2$.

**(viii)** $|z - z_1| - |z - z_2| = k$, where $k < |z_1 - z_2|$ represents hyperbola with foci at $z_1$ and $z_2$.

**(ix)** $\left|\dfrac{z - z_1}{z - z_2}\right| = k$ is a circle, if $k \neq 1$ and straight line, if $k = 1$. (perpendicular bisector of segment joining $z_1$ and $z_2$).

## Polynomials

An expression of the form

$$P_n(z) = a_0 + a_1 z + a_2 z^2 + \ldots\ldots + a_n z^n,$$

where $a_0, a_1, \ldots\ldots, a_n$ are complex numbers and $a_n \neq 0$ is said to be a polynomial of degree $n$.

e.g.,

(i) $5z^4 + 3z^3 + z^2 + z + 1$ is a polynomial of degree 4.

(ii) Every constant is a polynomial of degree 0 which is undefined.

### Properties of Polynomials

**(i)** The order of a zero of a polynomial equals the order of its first non-vanishing derivative.
Suppose, $z = a$ is a zero of order $m$ of polynomial $P(z)$ then, $P(z) = (z - a)^m Q(z)$, $Q(a) \neq 0$
Differentiating both sides successively $m$ times and putting $z = a$, we get
$P'(a) = P''(a) = \ldots = P^{m-1}(a) = 0$ and $P^m(a) \neq 0$.

**(ii)** If all the zeros of a polynomial lie in a half plane, then all the zeros of its derivative also lie in the same half plane (Luca's theorem).

**(iii)** If $S$ is the set of all zeros of a polynomial. Then all the zeros of its derivative lie on convex hall of $S$ (Gauss Theorem).

**(iv)** Let $P(z) = a_0 + a_1 z + a_2 z^2 + \ldots + a_n z^n$, where $n \geq 1$ and $a_n \neq 0$ so that $P(z)$ is a polynomial of degree one or greater, then the equation $P(z) = 0$ has atleast one root (Fundamental theorem of algebra).

## Power Series

A series of the type

$$\sum_{n=0}^{\infty} a_n (z - z_0)^n = a_0 + a_1(z - z_0) + a_2(z - z_0)^2 + \ldots + a_n(z - z_0)^n + \ldots \qquad \ldots\text{(i)}$$

where $z_0, a_0, a_1, a_2, \ldots\ldots, a_n$ are complex constants, called power series. $z_0$ is the centre of series; $a_0, a_1, a_2, \ldots, a_n$ are known as the coefficient of the series.

Eq. (i) is the power series about the point $z_0$, taking $z_0 = 0$, Eq. (i) becomes

$$\sum_{n=0}^{\infty} a_n z^n = a_0 + a_1 z + a_2 z^2 + \ldots + a_n z^n + \ldots$$

## Circle and Radius of Convergence of a Power Series

The circle $|z| = R$ consisting of all the values of $z$ for which the power series $\Sigma a_n z^n$ converges is called the circle of convergence. The radius $R$ of the circle is known as the radius of the convergence. By Cauchy theorem for the power series $\Sigma a_n z^n$, radius of convergence $R$ is given by

**(i)** $\frac{1}{R} = \lim_{n\to\infty} |a_n|^{\frac{1}{n}}$ **(ii)** $\frac{1}{R} = \lim_{n\to\infty} \left|\frac{a_{n+1}}{a_n}\right|$

***Example 7.*** *Find the radius of convergence of the power series.*

(i) $f(z) = \sum_{n=0}^{\infty} \frac{z^n}{n!}$ (ii) $f(z) = \sum_{n=0}^{\infty} \left(1+\frac{1}{n}\right)^{n^2} z^n$

**Solution.** (i) Here, $a_n = \frac{1}{n!} \Rightarrow a_{n+1} = \frac{1}{(n+1)!}$

Now, $R = \lim_{n\to\infty} \left|\frac{a_n}{a_{n+1}}\right| = \lim_{n\to\infty} \frac{(n+1)!}{n!}$

$= \lim_{n\to\infty} (n+1) = \infty$

(ii) Here, $a_n = \left(1+\frac{1}{n}\right)^{n^2} \Rightarrow a_n^{1/n} = \left(1+\frac{1}{n}\right)^n$

Now, $\frac{1}{R} = \lim_{n\to\infty} |a_n|^{\frac{1}{n}} = \lim_{n\to\infty} \left(1+\frac{1}{n}\right)^n = e$

$\Rightarrow R = \frac{1}{e}$

## Region of Convergence

The power series $\Sigma a_n z^n$, either

**(i)** Converges for all values of $z$

**(ii)** Converges only for $z = z_0$

**(iii)** Converges for $z$ in some region in the complex plane.

*i.e.*, The series converges everywhere inside the circle $|z - z_0| = R$ and diverges outside $|z - z_0| = R$ because the terms of the series are unbounded.

***Example 8.*** *Find the domain of convergence of the series* $\Sigma\left(\frac{iz-1}{2+i}\right)^n$.

**Solution.** Here, $u_n = \left(\frac{iz-1}{2+i}\right)^n$, $u_{n+1} = \left(\frac{iz-1}{2+i}\right)^{n+1}$

Now, $\lim_{n\to\infty} \left|\frac{u_{n+1}}{u_n}\right| = \lim_{n\to\infty} \left|\frac{iz-1}{2+i}\right| = \frac{|iz-1|}{\sqrt{5}}$

$\Rightarrow$ The given series is convergent, if

$|iz-1| < \sqrt{5}$

or $|i|\left|z - \frac{1}{i}\right| < \sqrt{5}$

or $|z+i| < \sqrt{5}$

Thus, the given series is convergent for the points which lie inside the circle whose radius is $\sqrt{5}$ and centre is $z = -i$.

***Example 9.*** *The power series* $\sum_{n=0}^{\infty} 2^{-n} \cdot z^{2n}$ *converges, if*

**Solution.** Here, $u_n = 2^{-n} \cdot z^{2n}$,

$u_{n+1} = 2^{-(n+1)} \cdot z^{2(n+1)}$

$\lim_{n\to\infty} \left|\frac{u_{n+1}}{u_n}\right| = \lim_{n\to\infty} \left|\frac{2^{-(n+1)} \cdot z^{2(n+1)}}{2^{-n} \cdot z^{2n}}\right| = \left|\frac{z^2}{2}\right|$

The series $\Sigma u_n$ converges absolutely, if

$\left|\frac{z^2}{2}\right| < 1$

$\Rightarrow |z|^2 < 2 \Rightarrow |z| < \sqrt{2}$

Here, radius of convergence is $\sqrt{2}$ and centre of convergence is 0.

## Complex Function

$f(z)$ is a function of a complex variable $z$ and is denoted by $w$.

$\Rightarrow w = f(z) = u + iv$, where $u$ and $v$ are real functions of $x$ and $y$ and called real and imaginary parts respectively of $f(z)$.

## Transcendental Functions

The function involving trigonometric function, logarithmic function, exponential function and their algebra is known as transcendental function.

### (i) Exponential Function

$$\exp(z) \text{ or } e^z = 1 + \frac{z}{1!} + \frac{z^2}{2!} + \dots\dots\dots + \frac{z^n}{n!} + \dots\dots \infty \qquad \dots(i)$$

### Properties of Exponential Functions

**(a)** $e^z = e^{x+iy} = e^x \cdot e^{iy} = e^x(\cos y + i\sin y)$

$\Rightarrow |e^z| = |e^x| = e^x \qquad (\because e^x > 0)$

and $\arg(e^z) = y$

**(b)** $e^{\bar{z}} = \overline{(e^z)}$

**(c)** $e^z$ is periodic function having imaginary period $2\pi i$.

**(d)** Series (i) is absolutely convergent in the whole complex plane.

**(e)** Exponential form of $z = re^{i\theta}$

### (ii) Trigonometric Functions

All the formula for real trigonometric functions are valid for complex trigonometric functions.

*e.g.*, $\cos z = \frac{e^{iz} + e^{-iz}}{2}$, $\sin z = \frac{e^{iz} - e^{-iz}}{2i}$, $\sin^2 z + \cos^2 z = 1$

$\sin(z_1 + z_2) = \sin z_1 \cos z_2 + \cos z_1 \sin z_2$ and so on.

## (iii) Hyperbolic Functions

Hyperbolic cosine of $z$ is written as $\cosh z$ and is defined as $\frac{e^z + e^{-z}}{2}$,

*i.e.*, $$\cosh z = \frac{e^z + e^{-z}}{2},$$

Similarly, $$\sinh z = \frac{e^z - e^{-z}}{2}$$

### Properties of Hyperbolic Functions

**(a)** $\sinh z$ and $\cosh z$ are periodic functions with imaginary period $2\pi i$.

**(b)** $\cosh z$ is an even function while $\sinh z$ is an odd function.

**(c)** $\sinh 0 = 0, \cosh 0 = 1, \tanh 0 = 0$

**(d)** $\sin(iz) = i\sinh z, \cos(iz) = \cosh z, \tan(iz) = i\tanh z$
Also, $\sinh(iz) = i\sin z, \cosh(iz) = \cos z, \tanh(iz) = i\tan z$

### Important Results on Hyperbolic Functions

**(a)** $\cosh^2 z - \sinh^2 z = 1,\quad \text{sech}^2 z + \tanh^2 z = 1,$
$\coth^2 z - \text{cosech}^2 z = 1$

**(b)** $\sinh(z_1 \pm z_2) = \sinh z_1 \cosh z_2 \pm \cosh z_1 \sinh z_2$

$\cosh(z_1 \pm z_2) = \cosh z_1 \cosh z_2 \pm \sinh z_1 \sinh z_2$

$$\tanh(z_1 \pm z_2) = \frac{\tanh z_1 \pm \tanh z_2}{1 \pm \tanh z_1 \tanh z_2}$$

**(c)** $$\sinh(2z) = 2\sinh z\cosh z = \frac{2\tanh z}{1-\tanh^2 z}$$

$$\cosh(2z) = \cosh^2 z + \sinh^2 z = 2\cosh^2 z - 1$$

$$= 1 + 2\sinh^2 z = \frac{1+\tanh^2 z}{1-\tanh^2 z}$$

$$\tanh(2z) = \frac{2\tanh z}{1+\tanh^2 z}$$

## (iv) Inverse Hyperbolic Functions

If $\sinh w = z$, then $w$ is called the hyperbolic sin inverse of $z$ and is written as $w = \sinh^{-1} z$.

### Important Results on Inverse Hyperbolic Functions

$$\sinh^{-1} z = \log[z + \sqrt{z^2+1}],$$

$$\cosh^{-1} z = \log[z + \sqrt{z^2-1}],\ \tanh^{-1} z = \frac{1}{2}\log\frac{1+z}{1-z}$$

## (v) Logarithmic Function

If $\quad e^w = z \Rightarrow w = \log_e z$

where, $\quad z = x + iy$ and $w = u + iv$ (say)

Since, $\quad e^w = e^{w+2n\pi i} = z$

$\Rightarrow \quad \log z = w + 2n\pi i$

The general value of the logarithm of $z$ is written as $\operatorname{Log} z$.

For $n = 0$

$$\operatorname{Log} z = \log z \text{ (principal value of log of } z)$$

### Formula for log z

Let $$z = x + iy$$

$$\Rightarrow \log_e z = \log_e(x+iy) = \log_e(re^{i\theta})$$
$$= \log_e r + \log_e e^{i\theta}$$
$$= \log_e \sqrt{x^2+y^2} + i\theta$$
$$= \frac{1}{2}\log_e(x^2+y^2) + i\tan^{-1}\left(\frac{y}{x}\right)$$

Put $x = 0, y = 1$, we get

$$\log_e i = \frac{1}{2}\log_e 1 + i\tan^{-1}\infty = 0 + i\frac{\pi}{2}$$

$$\Rightarrow \log_e i = i\frac{\pi}{2}$$

***Example 10.*** *If* $\cosh(u+iv) = x + iy$, *then prove that*

(i) $\dfrac{x^2}{\cosh^2 u} + \dfrac{y^2}{\sinh^2 u} = 1$ *and* (ii) $\dfrac{x^2}{\cos^2 v} - \dfrac{y^2}{\sin^2 v} = 1$

**Solution.** $\cosh(u+iv) = \cosh u\cosh(iv) + \sinh u\sinh(iv)$

$$= \cosh u\cos v + \sinh u(i\sin v)$$
$$= \cosh u\cos v + i\sinh u\sin v$$
$$\Rightarrow x + iy = \cosh u\cos v + i\sinh u\sin v$$

Equating real and imaginary parts from both sides, we get

$$x = \cosh u\cos v,\ y = \sinh u\sin v$$

$$\Rightarrow \frac{x}{\cosh u} = \cos v,\ \frac{y}{\sinh u} = \sin v$$

Since, $\cos^2 v + \sin^2 v = 1$

$$\Rightarrow \frac{x^2}{\cosh^2 u} + \frac{y^2}{\sinh^2 u} = 1$$

Also, $\dfrac{x}{\cos v} = \cosh u,\ \dfrac{y}{\sin v} = \sinh u$

Since, $\cosh^2 u - \sinh^2 u = 1$

$$\Rightarrow \frac{x^2}{\cos^2 v} - \frac{y^2}{\sin^2 v} = 1$$

***Example 11.*** *If* $i^{\alpha+i\beta} = \alpha + i\beta$, *prove that* $\alpha^2 + \beta^2 = e^{-(4n+1)\pi\beta}$

**Solution.** Given, $\quad i^{\alpha+i\beta} = \alpha + i\beta$

$$\Rightarrow (\alpha+i\beta)\log_e i = \log_e(\alpha+i\beta)$$

$$\Rightarrow (\alpha+i\beta)\cdot i\left(\frac{\pi}{2}+2n\pi\right) = \frac{1}{2}\log_e(\alpha^2+\beta^2) + i\left(\tan^{-1}\frac{\beta}{\alpha} + 2n\pi\right)$$

Equating real part from both sides, we get

$$-\beta\left(\frac{\pi}{2}+2n\pi\right) = \frac{1}{2}\log_e(\alpha^2+\beta^2)$$

$$\Rightarrow -\beta(\pi + 4n\pi) = \log_e(\alpha^2+\beta^2)$$

$$\Rightarrow \alpha^2+\beta^2 = e^{-(4n+1)\pi\beta}$$

## Limit of $f(z)$

Let $f: D \to \mathbb{C}$ be any function in a domain $D$ given by

$$w = f(z) = u(x, y) + iv(x, y)$$

Let $l \in \mathbb{C}$ be a limit point of $D$, then $l$ is the limit of $f$ at $z = z_0$ if for any given $\varepsilon > 0$, there exists a $\delta > 0$ such that

$$|f(z) - l| < \varepsilon$$

whenever

$$0 < |z - z_0| < \delta \text{ in } D$$

and we write

$$\lim_{z \to z_0} f(z) = l$$

> **Note** $\lim_{z \to z_0} f(z)$ exists iff
> $\lim_{(x, y) \to (x_0, y_0)} u(x, y)$ and
> $\lim_{(x, y) \to (x_0, y_0)} v(x, y)$ exists

## Continuity of $f(z)$

$f(z)$ is continuous at $z = z_0$

$$\Leftrightarrow \quad \lim_{z \to z_0} f(z) = f(z_0)$$

> **Note** (a) $f(z)$ is a continuous function in a domain $D$, it means $f(z)$ is continuous at every $z \in D$.
> (b) $f(z) = u(x,y) + iv(x,y)$ is a continuous function of $z$. $\Leftrightarrow$ $u$ and $v$ are continuous functions of $x$ and $y$.

## Differentiability of $f(z)$

Let $w = f(z)$ be a single valued function of $z$ defined in a domain $D$. Then, $f(z)$ is said to be differentiable at a point $z_0$ of $D$, if

$$\lim_{\Delta z \to 0} \frac{f(z_0 + \Delta z) - f(z_0)}{\Delta z}$$

or

$$\lim_{z \to z_0} \frac{f(z) - f(z_0)}{z - z_0}$$

exists uniquely and independent of the path along which $\Delta z \to 0$ or $z \to z_0$. It is denoted by $f'(z_0)$ and called derivative of $f(z)$ at $z = z_0$. If the above limit is not unique then $f(z)$ is said to be non-differentiable at $z = z_0$.

> **Note** Every differentiable function is continuous but converse is need not true.

***Example* 12.** *Prove that* $f(z) = |z|^2$ *is continuous everywhere but nowhere differentiable except at origin.*

**Solution.**

$$f'(z) = \lim_{\Delta z \to 0} \frac{f(z + \Delta z) - f(z)}{\Delta z}$$

$$= \lim_{\Delta z \to 0} \frac{|z + \Delta z|^2 - |z|^2}{\Delta z}$$

$$= \lim_{\Delta z \to 0} \frac{(z + \Delta z)(\bar{z} + \Delta \bar{z}) - z\bar{z}}{\Delta z}$$

$$= \lim_{\Delta z \to 0} z\frac{\Delta \bar{z}}{\Delta z} + \bar{z} + \Delta \bar{z}$$

$$= \lim_{\Delta z \to 0} z\frac{\Delta \bar{z}}{\Delta z} + \bar{z} \quad (\because \Delta \bar{z} \to 0, \text{ as } \Delta z \to 0)$$

Let $\quad \Delta z = re^{i\theta} \Rightarrow \Delta \bar{z} = re^{-i\theta}$

$\therefore \quad \frac{\Delta \bar{z}}{\Delta z} = e^{-i2\theta}$, which is not unique as $\Delta z \to 0$.

$\Rightarrow f(z)$ is not differentiable,

At $z = 0$, $f'(z) = 0$ which is differentiable.

Thus, $f(z)$ is not differentiable for any non-zero value of $z$ though it is continuous everywhere.

## Analytic Functions

A single valued function $f(z)$ defined in a domain $D$, which is differentiable at all points of $D$ called an analytic function of $z$ in that domain. An analytic function is also called an holomorphic function.

> **Note** (a) A function $f(z)$ is said to be regular at a point $z_0$, if $f(z)$ is analytic in the deleted neighbourhood of $z_0$ and can be made analytic also at $z_0$ by defining $f(z)$ at $z = z_0$.
> (b) A function which is analytic everywhere in the complex plane is known as an entire function. *e.g.*, polynomial of any degree is an entire function, since derivative of a polynomial exists at every point.
> (c) The point at which $f(z)$ fails to be analytic is called a singular point of the function $f(z)$.

### Properties of Analytic Functions

If $f(z)$ and $g(z)$ are two analytic functions in a domain $D$, then

**(i)** $f(z) \pm g(z)$ **(ii)** $f(z) \cdot g(z)$ **(iii)** $\frac{f(z)}{g(z)}$ $[g(z) \neq 0]$

**(iv)** $kf(z)$ ($k$ is any constant) are also analytic in $D$.

## Cauchy-Riemann Equations

If a function $f(z) = u(x, y) + iv(x, y)$ is differentiable at any point $z = x + iy$, then the partial derivative $\frac{\partial u}{\partial x}, \frac{\partial v}{\partial x}, \frac{\partial u}{\partial y}, \frac{\partial v}{\partial y}$ should exist and satisfy the equations

$$\frac{\partial u}{\partial x} = \frac{\partial v}{\partial y} \quad \text{...(i)}$$

and

$$\frac{\partial u}{\partial y} = -\frac{\partial v}{\partial x} \quad \text{...(ii)}$$

which is the necessary condition for $f(z)$ to be analytic.

Eqs. (i) and (ii) are known as Cauchy-Riemann Equations.

Also, the sufficient condition for $f(z)$ to be analytic in domain $D$ is

**(i)** the four partial derivatives $\frac{\partial u}{\partial x}, \frac{\partial v}{\partial x}, \frac{\partial u}{\partial y}, \frac{\partial v}{\partial y}$ should exist and are continuous and

**(ii)** satisfy Cauchy-Riemann equations at each point of $D$.

***Example 13.*** *Show that $f(z) = xy + iy$ is everywhere continuous but is not analytic.*

**Solution.** Here, $u(x,y) = xy$ and $v(x,y) = y$

Since, $u$ and $v$ are polynomials in $x$ and $y$, therefore they are continuous at each point.

$\Rightarrow$ $f(z)$ is continuous everywhere.

Also, $\frac{\partial u}{\partial x} = y, \quad \frac{\partial u}{\partial y} = x, \frac{\partial v}{\partial x} = 0, \quad \frac{\partial v}{\partial y} = 1$

Clearly, $\frac{\partial u}{\partial x} \neq \frac{\partial v}{\partial y}, \frac{\partial u}{\partial y} \neq -\frac{\partial v}{\partial x}$

$\Rightarrow$ $u$ and $v$ do not satisfy Cauchy-Riemann equations.

$\Rightarrow$ $f(z)$ is not analytic.

> ***Note*** **(a)** $\left(\frac{\partial f}{\partial x}\right)_{(a,b)} = \lim_{h \to 0} \frac{f(a+h,b) - f(a,b)}{h}$
>
> **(b)** $\left(\frac{\partial f}{\partial y}\right)_{(a,b)} = \lim_{k \to 0} \frac{f(a,b+k) - f(a,b)}{k}$
>
> **(c)** In particular, at the origin
>
> $\left(\frac{\partial f}{\partial x}\right)_{(0,0)} = \lim_{h \to 0} \frac{f(h,0) - f(0,0)}{h}$
>
> and $\left(\frac{\partial f}{\partial y}\right)_{(0,0)} = \lim_{k \to 0} \frac{f(0,k) - f(0,0)}{k}$

***Example 14.*** *Show that the function $f(z) = \sqrt{|xy|}$ is not analytic at origin although the Cauchy-Riemann equations are satisfied at that point.*

**Solution.** $f(z) = u(x,y) + iv(x,y) = \sqrt{|xy|}$

$$\Rightarrow \quad u(x,y) = \sqrt{|xy|}$$

$$v(x,y) = 0$$

At the origin, we have

$$\left(\frac{\partial u}{\partial x}\right)_{(0,0)} = \lim_{h \to 0} \frac{u(h,0) - u(0,0)}{h}$$

$$= \lim_{h \to 0} \frac{0-0}{h} = 0$$

$$\left(\frac{\partial u}{\partial y}\right)_{(0,0)} = \lim_{k \to 0} \frac{u(0,k) - u(0,0)}{k}$$

$$= \lim_{k \to 0} \frac{0-0}{k} = 0$$

Similarly, $\left(\frac{\partial v}{\partial x}\right)_{(0,0)} = 0, \left(\frac{\partial v}{\partial y}\right)_{(0,0)} = 0$

Hence, Cauchy-Riemann equations are satisfied at origin.

Now, $f'(0) = \lim_{z \to 0} \frac{f(z) - f(0)}{z - 0}$

$$= \lim_{z \to 0} \frac{\sqrt{|xy|} - 0}{x + iy}$$

Taking $z \to 0$ along $y = mx$, then we have

$$f'(0) = \lim_{x \to 0} \frac{\sqrt{|mx^2|}}{x + imx} = \lim_{x \to 0} \frac{\sqrt{|m|}}{1 + im}$$

which is not independent of $m \Rightarrow f'(0)$ does not exist.

$\Rightarrow$ $f(z)$ is not differentiable at the origin.

Hence, $f(z)$ is not analytic at the origin although the Cauchy-Riemann equations are satisfied at that point.

***Example 15.*** *If $f(z) = \log z$, find $f'(z)$ and determine where $f(z)$ is non-analytic.*

**Solution.** $f'(z) = \lim_{\Delta z \to 0} \frac{f(z + \Delta z) - f(z)}{\Delta z}$

$$= \lim_{\Delta z \to 0} \frac{\log\left(\frac{z + \Delta z}{z}\right)}{\Delta z} = \lim_{\Delta z \to 0} \frac{\log\left(1 + \frac{\Delta z}{z}\right)}{\Delta z}$$

$$= \lim_{\Delta z \to 0} \frac{\log\left(1 + \frac{\Delta z}{z}\right)}{\frac{\Delta z}{z} \cdot z}$$

$$= \frac{1}{z}\left(\because \lim_{x \to 0} \frac{\log(1+x)}{x} = 1, \Delta z \to 0 \Rightarrow \frac{\Delta z}{z} \to 0\right)$$

Therefore, $f(z)$ is differentiable except at $z = 0$

$\Rightarrow$ $f(z)$ is analytic everywhere except at origin.

## Polar Form of Cauchy-Riemann Equations

$$f(z) = u(x,y) + iv(x,y), \text{ where } x = r\cos\theta, y = r\sin\theta$$

$$\Rightarrow \quad x^2 + y^2 = r^2 \quad \text{and} \quad \theta = \tan^{-1}\frac{y}{x}$$

We find

$$\frac{\partial u}{\partial r} = \frac{1}{r}\frac{\partial v}{\partial \theta} \quad \text{...(i)}$$

and

$$\frac{\partial u}{\partial \theta} = -r\frac{\partial v}{\partial r} \quad \text{...(ii)}$$

Eqs. (i) and (ii) are the Cauchy-Riemann equations in polar form.

## Derivative of $f(z)$ in Polar Form

$$f(z) = u(x,y) + iv(x,y)$$

where $x = r\cos\theta, y = r\sin\theta$

$\Rightarrow$ $x^2 + y^2 = r^2$ and $\theta = \tan^{-1}\frac{y}{x}$

we find $f'(z) = (\cos\theta - i\sin\theta)\left(\frac{\partial u}{\partial r} + \frac{\partial v}{\partial r}\right)$

$$\Rightarrow \quad f'(z) = e^{-i\theta}\frac{\partial f}{\partial r}$$

## Harmonic Function

Any function $f(x, y)$ possessing continuous partial derivatives of the first and second orders and satisfying Laplace's equation $\left(\frac{\partial^2 f}{\partial x^2}+\frac{\partial^2 f}{\partial y^2}=0\right)$ is called a harmonic function.

Let $f(z) = u + iv$ be an analytic function, then $u$ and $v$ are both harmonic functions i.e.,

$$\frac{\partial^2 u}{\partial x^2}+\frac{\partial^2 u}{\partial y^2}=0 \text{ and } \frac{\partial^2 v}{\partial x^2}+\frac{\partial^2 v}{\partial y^2}=0$$

## Harmonic Conjugate of a Function

Let $u(x, y)$ be a harmonic function, then a function $v(x, y)$ is said to be a harmonic conjugate of $u(x, y)$, if

**(i)** $v(x, y)$ is harmonic and

**(ii)** $u$ and $v$ satisfy Cauchy-Riemann equations

i.e., $\frac{\partial u}{\partial x}=\frac{\partial v}{\partial y}$ and $\frac{\partial u}{\partial y}=-\frac{\partial v}{\partial x}$

> ***Note*** **(a)** If $f(z) = u + iv$ is analytic in a domain $D$, then $v$ is the harmonic conjugate of $u$. Conversely, if $v$ is the harmonic conjugate of $u$ in a domain $D$, then $f(z) = u + iv$ is analytic in $D$.
>
> **(b)** If $v$ is a harmonic conjugate of $u$ in some domain $D$, then it is always not true that $u$ is also the harmonic conjugate of $v$ in $D$. It can be verified by taking $u = x^2 - y^2$ and $v = 2xy$.
>
> **(c)** Two functions $u(x, y)$ and $v(x, y)$ are harmonic conjugates of each other if and only if they are constants.
>
> **(d)** If $f(z) = u + iv$ be an analytic function of $z = x + iy$, then families of curves $u = c_1, v = c_2$ are orthogonal to each other, where $c_1$ and $c_2$ are constants i.e., $u$ and $v$ satisfy $\frac{\partial u}{\partial x}\cdot\frac{\partial v}{\partial x}+\frac{\partial u}{\partial y}\cdot\frac{\partial v}{\partial y}=0$

***Example 16.*** *Prove that $u = x^2 - y^2$ and $v=\frac{y}{x^2+y^2}$ are harmonic functions of $(x, y)$ but are not harmonic conjugates.*

**Solution.** Given, $u = x^2 - y^2$

$$\Rightarrow \quad \frac{\partial u}{\partial x}=2x, \quad \frac{\partial u}{\partial y}=-2y$$

$$\Rightarrow \quad \frac{\partial^2 u}{\partial x^2}=2, \quad \frac{\partial^2 u}{\partial y^2}=-2$$

$$\Rightarrow \quad \frac{\partial^2 u}{\partial x^2}+\frac{\partial^2 u}{\partial y^2}=0$$

$\Rightarrow$ $u(x, y)$ satisfies Laplace equation, hence, $u(x, y)$ is harmonic.

Again, as given $\quad v=\frac{y}{x^2+y^2}$

$$\frac{\partial v}{\partial x}=-\frac{2xy}{(x^2+y^2)^2}, \quad \frac{\partial v}{\partial y}=\frac{x^2-y^2}{(x^2+y^2)^2},$$

$$\frac{\partial^2 v}{\partial x^2}=\frac{6x^2y-2y^3}{(x^2+y^2)^3}, \quad \frac{\partial^2 v}{\partial y^2}=\frac{-6x^2y+2y^3}{(x^2+y^2)^3}$$

$$\Rightarrow \quad \frac{\partial^2 v}{\partial x^2}+\frac{\partial^2 v}{\partial y^2}=0$$

$\Rightarrow$ $v(x, y)$ also satisfies Laplace equations.

$\Rightarrow$ $v(x, y)$ is also harmonic function.

But $\quad \frac{\partial u}{\partial x}\neq\frac{\partial v}{\partial y}$ and $\frac{\partial u}{\partial y}\neq-\frac{\partial v}{\partial x}$

$\Rightarrow$ $u$ and $v$ are not harmonic conjugates.

## Methods of Constructing an Analytic Function

## (By Milne-Thomson's Method)

### (i) If $u(x, y)$ be given

Let $\quad \frac{\partial u}{\partial x}=\phi_1(x, y), \quad \frac{\partial u}{\partial y}=\phi_2(x, y)$

then, $\quad f(z)=\int \phi_1(z, 0)\,dz - i\int \phi_2(z, 0)\,dz + C$

which is the required analytic function.

### (ii) If $v(x, y)$ be given

Let $\quad \frac{\partial v}{\partial y}=\psi_1(x, y), \quad \frac{\partial v}{\partial x}=\psi_2(x, y)$

then, $\quad f(z)=\int \psi_1(z, 0)\,dz + i\int \psi_2(z, 0)\,dz + C$

which is the required analytic function.

***Example 17.*** *Construct the analytic function $f(z) = u + iv$ where, (i) $u = x^3 - 3xy^2$ (ii) $v = e^x(x\sin y + y\cos y)$*

**Solution.** (i) $\quad \frac{\partial u}{\partial x}=3x^2-3y^2=\phi_1(x, y)$

$$\frac{\partial u}{\partial y}=-6xy=\phi_2(x, y)$$

$$\Rightarrow \quad f(z)=\int \phi_1(z, 0)\,dz - i\int \phi_2(z, 0)\,dz$$

$$=\int 3z^2 dz - i\int 0\cdot dz = z^3 + C$$

which is the analytic function.

Now, $f(z) = z^3 + C = (x + iy)^3 + C$

$$= x^3 + 3x^2(iy) + 3x(iy)^2 + (iy)^3 + C$$

$$= (x^3 - 3xy^2) + i(3x^2y - y^3) + iC'$$

(taking $C = iC'$)

$$\Rightarrow \quad v = 3x^2y - y^3 + C'$$

(ii) $\quad v = e^x(x\sin y + y\cos y)$

$$\frac{\partial v}{\partial y}=e^x[x\cos y + y(-\sin y) + \cos y]$$

$$\Rightarrow \quad \frac{\partial v}{\partial y}=e^x(x\cos y - y\sin y + \cos y)$$

$$=\psi_1(x, y)$$

$$\frac{\partial v}{\partial x}=e^x(\sin y) + e^x(x\sin y + y\cos y)$$

$$\Rightarrow \quad \frac{\partial v}{\partial x} = e^x(\sin y + x\sin y + y\cos y)$$

$$= \psi_2(x,y)$$

$$\therefore \quad f(z) = \int \psi_1(z,0)\,dz + i\int \psi_2(z,0)\,dz$$

$$= \int e^z(z+1)\,dz + i\int 0\cdot dz$$

$$= (z+1)\,e^z - \int e^z dz + C$$

$$= ze^z + C$$

which is the analytic function.

## Important Results on Analytic Functions

**(i)** An analytic function with constant modulus is constant

*i.e.*, if $|f(z)| = C$ (constant)

then, $f(z) = u + iv$ is a constant function.

**(ii)** An analytic function with constant argument is constant

*i.e.*, if $\arg f(z) =$ constant

$\Rightarrow$ $f(z) =$ constant

**(iii)** If $f(z) = u + iv$ be an analytic function in a domain $D$, then $f(z)$ is constant in $D$. If any one of the following conditions hold

(a) $f'(z)$ vanishes identically in $D$

(b) $\text{Re}(f(z)) = u =$ constant

(c) $\text{Im}(f(z)) = v =$ constant

(d) $|f(z)| =$ constant

(e) $\arg f(z) =$ constant

**(iv)** If $f(z) = u + iv$ is analytic function of $z = x + iy$ in any domain $D$, then

(a) $\left(\dfrac{\partial^2}{\partial x^2} + \dfrac{\partial^2}{\partial y^2}\right)|u|^p = p(p-1)|u|^{p-2}|f'(z)|^2$

(b) $\left(\dfrac{\partial^2}{\partial x^2} + \dfrac{\partial^2}{\partial y^2}\right)|f(z)|^p = p^2|f(z)|^{p-2}|f'(z)|^2$

(c) $\left(\dfrac{\partial^2}{\partial x^2} + \dfrac{\partial^2}{\partial y^2}\right)\log|f'(z)| = 0$

**(v)** $|f'(z)|^2 = \dfrac{\partial(u,v)}{\partial(x,y)}$

(Jacobian of $u$ and $v$ with respect to $x$ and $y$)

**(vi)** Let $f(z) = u + iv$ be an analytic function of $z = x + iy$.

If $u$ be a harmonic function, then $\dfrac{\partial^2 u}{\partial z \partial \bar{z}} = 0$

# SOLVED EXAMPLES

## Type I (*Only one correct option*)

***Example 1.*** *The function*

$$f(z) = \frac{z - ib}{z^2 + b^2}$$

*is continuous at*

(a) $ib$ (b) $-ib$

(c) $i^3b$ (d) None of these

**Solution.** (a) We have

$$\lim_{z\to ib} f(z) = \lim_{z\to ib} \frac{z-ib}{z^2+b^2} = -\frac{i}{2b}$$

and $f(ib) = -\dfrac{i}{2b}$

Hence, $f$ is continuous at $z = ib$

***Example 2.*** *The* $\lim_{z\to 0} \dfrac{\bar{z}}{z}$ *is*

(a) 0 (b) 1

(c) $\dfrac{1}{2}$ (d) does not exists

**Solution.** (d) We have

$$f(z) = \frac{\bar{z}}{z} = \frac{x-iy}{x+iy} = \frac{x^2-y^2-2ixy}{x^2+y^2}$$

$$\therefore \quad u(x,y) = \frac{x^2-y^2}{x^2+y^2}$$

and $$v(x,y) = \frac{-2xy}{x^2+y^2}$$

Let us approaching $(0,0)$ along $y = mx$, we get

$$\lim_{x\to 0} u(x,mx) = \lim_{x\to 0} \frac{x^2-m^2x^2}{x^2+m^2x^2} = \lim_{x\to 0} \frac{1-m^2}{1+m^2}$$

which depends on $m$. Hence, $\lim_{(x,y)\to(0,0)} u(x,y)$ does not exist and similarly

$\lim_{(x,y)\to(0,0)} v(x,y)$ does not exists.

Hence, $\lim_{z\to 0} \dfrac{\bar{z}}{z}$ does not exists.

***Example 3.*** *The set of all singular points of the function*

$$f(z) = \begin{cases} 1, & |z| < 1 \\ 2, & 1 \le |z| < 2 \end{cases}$$

*is*

(a) $\{z : |z| \le 1\}$ (b) $\{z : |z| \le 2\}$

(c) $\{z : 1 \le z \le 2\}$ (d) $\{z : |z| = 1\} \cup \{z : |z| = 2\}$

**Solution.** (d) Given that

$$f(z) = \begin{cases} 1, & |z| < 1 \\ 2, & 1 \le |z| < 2 \end{cases}$$

$\therefore$ Domain of $f = D$

$$= \{z : |z| < 2\}$$

The set of regular point of $f(z) = R$

$$= D - \{z : |z| = 1\}$$

$\therefore$ $R' = \{z : |z| \le 2\}$

$\therefore$ The set of singular points of $f(z)$

$$= \{z : |z| = 1\} \cup \{z : |z| = 2\}$$

***Example 4.*** *For given*

$$u(x, y) = x^3 - 3xy^2 + 3x^2 - 3y^2 + 1$$

*The analytic function f(z) is*

(a) $z^3 - 3z^2 + c$ (b) $z^3 + 3z^2 + c$

(c) $z^2 + 2z^3 + c$ (d) $z^2 - 2z^3 + c$

**Solution.** (b) We have

$$u = x^3 - 3xy^2 + 3x^2 - 3y^2 + 1$$

$\therefore$ $u_x = 3x^2 - 3y^2 + 6x$

and $u_y = -6xy - 6y$

$\therefore$ $\phi_1(z, 0) = u_x(z, 0) = 3z^2 + 6z$

and $\phi_2(z, 0) = u_y(z, 0) = 0$

$\therefore$ The analytic function

$$f(z) = \int \{\phi_1(z,0) - i\,\phi_2(z,0)\}\, dz$$

$$= \int \{3z^2 + 6z - i(0)\}\, dz$$

$$= z^3 + 3z^2 + c$$

***Example 5.*** *The radius of convergence of the series* $\sum_{n=1}^{\infty} \frac{z^{2n}}{z^n}$ *is*

(a) 1 (b) $\sqrt{2}$

(c) $\sqrt{3}$ (d) $\sqrt{5}$

**Solution.** (b) Here, $\frac{|u_{n+1}|}{|u_n|}$ does not exists.

Let $u_n = \begin{cases} 0, & n = 2k-1 \\ 2^{-n}, & n = 2k, k = 1, 2, \ldots \end{cases}$

$\therefore$ $\lim_{n\to\infty} \text{Sup} \sqrt[n]{|u_n|} = \lim_{k\to\infty} |2^{-2k}|^{\frac{1}{(2k)}} = \frac{1}{2}$

and $\lim_{n\to\infty} \sqrt[n]{|u_n|} = \lim_{k\to\infty} |u_{2k-1}|^{\frac{1}{2k-1}} = 0$

Hence, $|z|^2 = 2 \Rightarrow k = \sqrt{2}$

## Type II (*One or more than one correct option*)

***Example 6.*** *Which of the following(s) is/are harmonic function(s)?*

(a) $u = \sinh x \cos y$ (b) $u = \frac{1}{2}\log(x^2 + y^2)$

(c) $u = x^2 + y^2$ (d) $u = x^2 - y^2$

**Solution.** (a), (b), (d)

(a) Given that

$$u(x, y) = \sinh x \cos y$$

$\therefore$ $u_x = \cosh x \cos y, u_y = -\sinh x \sin y$

$\therefore$ $u_{xx} = \sinh x \cos y, u_{yy} = -\sinh x \cos y$

$\Rightarrow$ $u_{xx} + u_{yy} = \sinh x \cos y - \sinh x \cos y = 0$

$\Rightarrow$ $u(x, y)$ is harmonic function.

(b) Given that

$$u(x, y) = \frac{1}{2}\log(x^2 + y^2)$$

$\therefore$ $u_x = \frac{1}{2} \cdot \frac{2x}{x^2 + y^2} = \frac{x}{x^2 + y^2}$

$\therefore$ $u_{xx} = \frac{y^2 - x^2}{(x^2 + y^2)^2}$

and $u_y = \frac{y}{(x^2 + y^2)} \Rightarrow u_{yy} = \frac{x^2 - y^2}{(x^2 + y^2)^2}$

$\therefore$ $u_{xx} + u_{yy} = \frac{y^2 - x^2}{(x^2 + y^2)^2} + \frac{x^2 - y^2}{(x^2 + y^2)^2} = 0$

$\Rightarrow$ $u(x, y)$ is harmonic function.

(c) Given that

$$u(x, y) = x^2 + y^2$$

$\therefore$ $u_x = 2x, u_y = 2y$

$u_{xx} = 2, u_{yy} = 2$

$\therefore$ $u_{xx} + u_{yy} = 2 + 2 = 4 \neq 0$

$\Rightarrow$ $u(x, y)$ is not harmonic function.

(d) Given that

$$u(x, y) = x^2 - y^2$$

$\therefore$ $u_x = 2x, u_y = -2y$

$\therefore$ $u_{xx} = 2, u_{yy} = -2$

$\therefore$ $u_{xx} + u_{yy} = 2 - 2 = 0$

$\Rightarrow$ $u(x, y)$ is harmonic function.

***Example 7.*** *Let*

*D = Domain of f(z)*

*R = Set of all regular point of f(z)*

*S = Set of all singular point of f(z)*

*where*

$$f(z) = \cos \frac{1}{\cos \frac{1}{z}}$$

*Then,*

(a) $D = \mathbb{C} - \left\{\dfrac{1}{(2n+1)\pi/2} : n \in \mathbb{Z}\right\}$

(b) $R = D$

(c) $S = \left\{\dfrac{1}{(2n+1)\pi/2} : n \in \mathbb{Z}\right\} \cup \{0\}$

(d) $S = \left\{\dfrac{1}{(2n+1)\pi/2} : n \in \mathbb{Z}\right\}$

**Solution.** (b), (c)

Given that $f(z) = \cos\dfrac{1}{\cos\dfrac{1}{z}}$

Clearly, $f(z)$ is not defined at $z = 0$. Hence,

$$D = \mathbb{C} - \left\{\frac{1}{(2n+1)\pi/2} : n \in \mathbb{Z}\right\} \cup \{0\}$$

$\therefore \quad R = D$

$\therefore \quad R' = \mathbb{C}$

$\therefore \quad S = R' - R = \left\{\dfrac{1}{(2n+1)\pi/2} : n \in \mathbb{Z}\right\} \cup \{0\}$

***Example 8.*** *Consider the function*

$$f(z) = \begin{cases} e^{-\frac{1}{z^4}}, & z \neq 0 \\ 0, & z = 0 \end{cases}$$

*Then*

(a) $f(z)$ is not analytic at $(0, 0)$.

(b) $\lim_{z\to 0} f(z)$ exists.

(c) $\lim_{z\to 0} f(z)$ does not exists.

(d) Cauchy-Riemann equations are satisfied at $(0, 0)$.

**Solution.** (a), (c), (d)

We have

$$\lim_{z\to 0} f(z) = \lim_{z\to 0} e^{-\frac{1}{z^4}}$$

If we approaches $z$ to 0 along $x$-axis, then

$$\lim_{r\to 0} e^{-\frac{1}{r^4}} = \lim_{r\to 0} \frac{1}{e^{\frac{1}{r^4}}} = 0$$

But, if we approaches $z$ to 0 along $y = x$, then

$$\lim_{r\to 0} e^{-\frac{1}{r^4}(e^{\pi i})} = \lim_{r\to 0} e^{\frac{1}{r^4}}$$

$$= \infty$$

$\therefore \quad \lim_{z\to 0} f(z)$ does not exists.

Next, let $\quad f(z) = u + iv$

$\Rightarrow \quad u + iv = e^{-(x+iy)^4}$

$$= e^{-\frac{(x-iy)^4}{(x^2+y^2)^4}}$$

$$= e^{-\left[\frac{x^4+y^4-6x^2y^2-i4xy(x^2-y^2)}{(x^2+y^2)^4}\right]}$$

$$\Rightarrow \quad u(x, y) = e^{\left[-\left\{\frac{x^4+y^4-6x^2y^2}{(x^2+y^2)^4}\right\}\cdot\cos\left\{\frac{4xy(x^2-y^2)}{(x^2+y^2)^4}\right\}\right]}$$

$$v(x, y) = e^{\left[-\left\{\frac{x^4+y^4-6x^2y^2}{(x^2+y^2)^4}\right\}\cdot\sin\left\{\frac{4xy(x^2-y^2)}{(x^2+y^2)^4}\right\}\right]}$$

$$\therefore \quad u_x(0, 0) = \lim_{x\to 0} \frac{u(x, 0) - u(0, 0)}{x}$$

$$= \lim_{x\to 0} \frac{e^{-1/x^4}}{x} = 0$$

$$u_y(0, 0) = \lim_{y\to 0} \frac{u(0, y) - u(0, 0)}{y}$$

$$= \lim_{y\to 0} \frac{e^{-1/y^4}}{y} = 0$$

$$v_x(0, 0) = \lim_{x\to 0} \frac{v(x, 0) - v(0, 0)}{x}$$

$$= \lim_{x\to 0} \frac{e^{-1/x^4}}{x} = 0$$

$$v_y(0, 0) = \lim_{y\to 0} \frac{v(0, y) - v(0, 0)}{y}$$

$$= \lim_{y\to 0} \frac{e^{-1/y^4}}{y} = 0$$

$\therefore \quad u_x(0, 0) = v_y(0, 0)$ and $u_y(0, 0) = -v_x(0, 0)$

$\therefore \quad$ Cauchy- Riemann equation satisfied at origin.

Now, $\quad f'(0) = \lim_{z\to 0} \dfrac{f(z) - f(0)}{z} = \lim_{z\to 0} \dfrac{e^{-1/z^4}}{z}$

Now, $z \to 0$ along $z = re^{\frac{i\pi}{4}}$, then

$$f'(0) = \lim_{r\to 0} \frac{e^{-1/r^4(e^{-\pi i})}}{re^{i\pi/4}} \to \infty$$

$\therefore \quad f'(0)$ does not exists.

Hence, $f(z)$ is not analytic at $(0, 0)$.

***Example 9.*** *If $f(z) = u + iv$, (where $u = u(x, y)$ and $v = v(x, y)$) is an analytic function, then under what condition(s), $u(x, y)$ and $v(x, y)$ cut orthogonally each other?*

(a) $u(x, y) =$ constant and $v(x, y) =$ constant

(b) $u(x, y) =$ variable and $v(x, y) =$ variable

(c) $u(x, y) =$ constant but $v(x, y) =$ variable

(d) $u(x, y) = 2012$, $v(x, y) = 2013$

**Solution.** (a), (d)

We know that $f(z)$ is an analytic function. Hence,

$$u_x = v_y \text{ and } u_y = -v_x$$

Now, if

$$u(x, y) = \text{constant} = C_1 \text{ (say)}$$

$$\Rightarrow \quad u_x dx + u_y dy = 0$$

$$\therefore \quad m_1 = \left(\frac{\partial y}{\partial x}\right)_{C_1} = \frac{-\left(\frac{\partial u}{\partial x}\right)}{\left(\frac{\partial u}{\partial y}\right)} \quad \text{...(i)}$$

Again,

$$v(x, y) = \text{constant} = C_2 \text{ (say)}$$

$$\Rightarrow \quad v_x dx + v_y dy = 0$$

$$\therefore \quad m_2 = \left(\frac{\partial y}{\partial x}\right)_{C_2} = \frac{-\left(\frac{\partial v}{\partial x}\right)}{\left(\frac{\partial v}{\partial y}\right)} \quad \text{...(ii)}$$

Now, from Eqs. (i) and (ii), we get

$$m_1 \cdot m_2 = -1$$

Hence, $u(x, y)$ and $v(x, y)$ are orthogonal. Therefore

$u(x, y) = 2012$ and $v(x, y) = 2013$ are orthogonal.

***Example 10.*** *Consider the function*

$$f(z) = \frac{1}{z^4}, z \neq 0$$

*Then*

(a) $f(z)$ is continuous

(b) Cauchy-Riemann equations are satisfied

(c) $f'(z)$ exists and equal to $-\frac{4}{z^5}$

(d) $f(z)$ is differentiable only at origin

**Solution.** (a), (b), (c)

We have

$$f(z) = \frac{1}{z^4}, z \neq 0$$

$$= r^{-4}(\cos 4\theta - i \sin 4\theta)$$

$$\Rightarrow \quad u(r, \theta) = \frac{\cos 4\theta}{r^4} \text{ and}$$

$$v(r, \theta) = -\frac{\sin 4\theta}{r^4}$$

$$\Rightarrow \quad u_r = -\frac{4 \cos 4\theta}{r^5}, \quad u_\theta = -\frac{4 \sin 4\theta}{r^4}$$

$$\text{and} \quad v_r = \frac{4 \sin 4\theta}{r^5}$$

$$\text{and} \quad v_\theta = -\frac{4 \cos 4\theta}{r^4}$$

$$\therefore \quad u_r = \frac{1}{r} v_\theta$$

$$\text{and} \quad u_\theta = -\frac{1}{r} v_r$$

$\therefore$ Cauchy-Riemann equations are satisfied.

The first partial derivatives of $u$ and $v$ are continuous functions as being rational continuous functions. Thus, $f'(z)$ exists and

$$f'(z) = e^{-i\theta}(u_r + iv_r)$$

$$= e^{-i\theta}\left(-\frac{4 \cos 4\theta}{r^5} + i\frac{4 \sin 4\theta}{r^5}\right)$$

$$= -\frac{4}{(re^{i\theta})^5} = -\frac{4}{z^5}$$

Hence, $f(Z)$ is continuous.

***Example 11.*** *Given power series*

$$\sum_{n=0}^{\infty} \frac{2n!}{(n!)^2}(2 - 3i)^n$$

(a) The radius of convergence of the power series is $\frac{1}{4}$

(b) The power series converges in the open disk $|3 - 3i| < \frac{1}{4}$

(c) The power series converges in the open disk of centre $3i$

(d) The power series is divergent

**Solution.** (a), (b), (c)

The radius of convergence of the power series is

$$\frac{1}{R} = \lim_{n \to \infty}\left|\frac{a_{n+1}}{a_n}\right| = \lim_{n \to \infty}\left|\frac{(2n+2)!}{((n+1)!)^2} \times \frac{(n!)^2}{(2n)!}\right|$$

$$= \lim_{n \to \infty}\left[\frac{(2n+2)(2n+1)}{(n+1)^2}\right] = 4$$

$$\Rightarrow \quad R = \frac{1}{4}$$

Hence, the series converges in the open disk

$$|z - 3i| < \frac{1}{4} \text{ or radius } \frac{1}{4} \text{ and centre } 3i.$$

***Example 12.*** *Given*

$$f(z) = \sin x(\cosh y) + i\cos(\sinh y)$$

(a) $f(z)$ is continuous everywhere

(b) $f(z)$ is discontinuous

(c) $f(z)$ is analytic everywhere

(d) $f(z)$ is not analytic everywhere

**Solution.** (a), (c)

Let $u(x, y) = \sin x(\cosh y)$ and $v(x, y) = \cos x(\sinh y)$. Here, $u$ and $v$ are both rational functions of $x$ and $y$, $u$ and $v$ are both continuous everywhere.

Hence, $f(z)$ is continuous everywhere.

$$\text{Now,} \quad \frac{\partial u}{\partial x} = \cos x(\cosh y)$$

$$\frac{\partial u}{\partial y} = \sin x(\sinh y)$$

and $$\frac{\partial v}{\partial x} = -\sin x(\sinh y)$$

$$\frac{\partial v}{\partial y} = \cos x(\cosh y)$$

Hence, $$\frac{\partial u}{\partial x} = \frac{\partial v}{\partial y}, \frac{\partial v}{\partial x} = -\frac{\partial u}{\partial y}$$

$\Rightarrow$ $u$ and $v$ satisfy Cauchy-Riemann equations and $u_x, u_y, v_x, v_y$ are continuous.

Thus, $f(z)$ is analytic everywhere.

***Example 13.*** *If $f: G \to \mathbb{C}$ is analytic, then*

(a) $f$ is infinitely differentiable

(b) $f$ is not differentiable

(c) $f$ is finitely differentiable

(d) $f$ is everywhere differentiable

**Solution.** (a), (d)

If $f: G \to \mathbb{C}$ is analytic, then for some $a \in G$, we get

$$f(z) = \sum_{n=0}^{\infty} a_n (z-a)^n, \text{ for } |z-a| < R,$$

$$R = d(a, \partial G)$$

$\Rightarrow$ $f(z)$ is infinitely differentiable.

***Example 14.*** *If $f(z) = u + iv$ is an analytic function and $f(z)$ is a constant function in the domains. Then*

(a) $\operatorname{Re} f(z) =$ constant

(b) $\operatorname{Im} f(z) =$ constant

(c) $|f(z)|$ is constant

(d) $|f(z)|$ is not constant

**Solution.** (a), (b), (c)

Since, $f(z) = u + iv$ is analytic in the domain. Therefore, it must satisfy Cauchy-Riemann equations.

Hence, $$\frac{\partial u}{\partial x} = \frac{\partial v}{\partial y}$$

and $$\frac{\partial u}{\partial y} = -\frac{\partial v}{\partial x} \quad \text{...(i)}$$

(a) $\operatorname{Re} f(z) = \text{constant} = u$

$$\Rightarrow \frac{\partial u}{\partial x} = 0 = \frac{\partial u}{\partial y}$$

Now, $$f'(z) = \frac{\partial u}{\partial x} + i\frac{\partial v}{\partial x} = \frac{\partial u}{\partial x} - i\frac{\partial u}{\partial y} \quad \text{[from Eq. (i)]}$$

$$= 0$$

$\Rightarrow$ $f(z)$ is a constant function.

(b) $\operatorname{Im} f(z) = v = \text{constant}$

$$\Rightarrow \frac{\partial v}{\partial x} = 0 = \frac{\partial v}{\partial y} = 0$$

Now, $$f'(z) = \frac{\partial u}{\partial x} + i\frac{\partial v}{\partial x} = \frac{\partial v}{\partial y} + i\frac{\partial v}{\partial x} \quad \text{[from Eq. (i)]}$$

$$= 0$$

$\Rightarrow$ $f(z)$ is a constant function.

(c) $|f(z)| = \text{constant} \Rightarrow u^2 + v^2 = \text{constant}$

$$\Rightarrow u\frac{\partial u}{\partial x} + v\frac{\partial v}{\partial x} = 0 \text{ and } u\frac{\partial u}{\partial y} + v\frac{\partial u}{\partial y} = 0$$

$$\Rightarrow u\frac{\partial u}{\partial x} + v\frac{\partial v}{\partial x} = 0 \text{ and } -u\frac{\partial v}{\partial x} + v\frac{\partial u}{\partial x} = 0$$

$$\Rightarrow \frac{\partial u}{\partial x} = 0 \text{ and } \frac{\partial v}{\partial x} = 0, \text{ provided } u^2 + v^2 \neq 0$$

$\Rightarrow$ If $u^2 + v^2 \neq 0$, $u$ and $v$ are constant and consequently $f(z) = u + iv$ is constant.

If $u^2 + v^2 = 0$ at some point it is constantly zero, *i.e.*, $f'(z) = 0$ hence in either case $f(z)$ is constant.

# Exercise 1 (For Part 'B')

**Directions** (Q. Nos. 1-93) *All questions have only one correct option.*

**1.** The reciprocal of $a+ib$ is equal to

(a) $\dfrac{1}{a^2+b^2}-ib$ (b) $\dfrac{ib}{a+ib}-a$

(c) $\dfrac{a^2}{a^2-b^2}-\dfrac{b^2 i}{a^2+b^2}$ (d) $\dfrac{a}{a^2+b^2}-\dfrac{bi}{a^2+b^2}$

**2.** If $z=x+iy$, then the number of solutions of the equation $z^2=\bar{z}$ is

(a) one (b) two

(c) four (d) infinite

**3.** If $\dfrac{4+3i}{3-4i}=x+iy$, then $\dfrac{x}{y}$ is equal to

(a) 0 (b) 1

(c) $\dfrac{4}{3}$ (d) $\dfrac{4}{5}$

**4.** The value of the Re $f(z)$ at $z=7+2i$ for $f(z)=\dfrac{1}{1-z}$

(a) $-3/20$ (b) $-1/20$

(c) $1/20$ (d) None of these

**5.** The value of $\left(\dfrac{\cos\theta+i\sin\theta}{\cos\theta-i\sin\theta}\right)^4$ is

(a) 1 (b) 0

(c) $\cos 4\theta - i\sin 4\theta$ (d) $\cos 8\theta - i\sin 8\theta$

**6.** If $1, \omega, \omega^2$ are the cube roots of unity, then $(x-y)(x-\omega y)(x-\omega^2 y)$ is equal to

(a) $x-y$ (b) $x^2-y^2$

(c) $x^3-y^3$ (d) $x^3+y^3$

**7.** The real part of the complex number $(1+i)^n$ is

(a) $2^{n/2}\cos\dfrac{n\pi}{4}$ (b) $2^n\cos\dfrac{n\pi}{2}$

(c) $2^{-n/2}\cos n\pi$ (d) $2^{-n}\cos\dfrac{n\pi}{2}$

**8.** Let $z_1$ and $z_2$ are two complex numbers with $\alpha$ and $\beta$ as their principal arguments such that $\alpha+\beta>\pi$, then $\arg(z_1\cdot z_2)$ is given by

(a) $\alpha+\beta$ (b) $\alpha+\beta-\pi$

(c) $\alpha+\beta+\pi$ (d) $\alpha+\beta-2\pi$

**9.** The locus of the complex number satisfying $\arg\left(\dfrac{z-1}{z+1}\right)=\dfrac{\pi}{3}$ is a

(a) straight line (b) circle

(c) parabola (d) hyperbola

**10.** If $\omega$ is an imaginary cube root of unity, $x=a+b$, $y=a\omega+b\omega^2$ and $z=a\omega^2+b\omega$, then $xyz$ equals

(a) $a+b$ (b) $a^2+b^2$

(c) $a^4+b^4$ (d) $a^3+b^3$

**11.** Which of the following is true for complex number $C$?

(a) $\alpha+i\beta=\gamma+i\delta$, if $\alpha=\gamma$ and $\beta=\delta$

(b) $\alpha+i\beta>0+i\beta$, if $\alpha>0$ and $\beta<0$

(c) Transitivity law holds in $C$

(d) Trichotomy law holds in $C$

**12.** Which of the following is false?

(a) $\text{Re}(z_1+z_2)=\text{Re}(z_1)+\text{Re}(z_2)$

(b) $|z_1+z_2|\ge|z_1|+|z_2|$

(c) $|z_1z_2|=|z_1||z_2|$

(d) $\overline{z_1+z_2}=\bar{z}_1+\bar{z}_2$

**13.** If $x=-2-\sqrt{3}\,i$, then the value of $2x^4+5x^3+7x^2+41$ is

(a) $4+\sqrt{3}i$ (b) $4-\sqrt{3}i$

(c) $\sqrt{3}+4i$ (d) $\sqrt{3}-4i$

**14.** The real part of exp (exp $i\theta$) is

(a) $e^{\cos\theta}$ (b) $e^{\cos\theta}\sin(\sin\theta)$

(c) $e^{\cos\theta}\cos(\sin\theta)$ (d) $e^{\cos\theta}\cos(\cos\theta)$

**15.** If $|z|=|z-1|$, then

(a) $\text{Re}(z)=1$ (b) $\text{Re}(z)=\dfrac{1}{2}$

(c) $\text{Im}(z)=1$ (d) $\text{Im}(z)=\dfrac{1}{2}$

**16.** If $\left|\dfrac{z-5i}{z+5i}\right|=1$, then $z=x+iy$ lies on

(a) the real axis

(b) the straight line $x=5$

(c) the straight line $y=5$

(d) a circle passing through origin

**17.** If $\alpha, \beta$ are roots of the equation $x^2-2x+4=0$, $\alpha^n+\beta^n$ is equal to

(a) $2^{n+1}\cos\left(\dfrac{n\pi}{3}\right)$ (b) $2^n\cos\left(\dfrac{n\pi}{3}\right)$

(c) $2^{n+1}\sin\left(\dfrac{n\pi}{3}\right)$ (d) $2^n\sin\left(\dfrac{n\pi}{3}\right)$

**18.** If the imaginary part of $\dfrac{2z+1}{iz+1}$ is $-2$, then the locus of a point representing $z$, is a

(a) circle (b) straight line

(c) parabola (d) None of these

**19.** For complex number $z$, $|z+5|^2+|z-5|^2=75$, represents

(a) a circle (b) an ellipse

(c) a triangle (d) a straight line

**20.** The correct polar form of the complex number $1-i$ is

(a) $\sqrt{2}e^{\frac{\pi}{4}i}$ (b) $e^{-\frac{\pi}{4}i}$

(c) $\sqrt{2}e^{-\frac{\pi}{4}i}$ (d) $e^{\frac{\pi}{4}i}$

**21.** If $1, \omega, \omega^2$ are the cube root of unity, then the roots of $(x-1)^3 + 8 = 0$ are
(a) $-1, -1, -1$ (b) $-1, 1+2\omega, 1+2\omega^2$
(c) $1, \omega, 2\omega$ (d) $-1, 1-2\omega, 1-2\omega^2$

**22.** If $|z-1| = 2$, then the value of $z\bar{z} - z - \bar{z}$ is
(a) 4 (b) 2
(c) 1 (d) 3

**23.** The solution of the equation $|z| - z = 1 + 2i$ is
(a) $1-2i$ (b) $2 - \frac{3}{2}i$
(c) $\frac{3}{2} + 2i$ (d) $\frac{3}{2} - 2i$

**24.** The complex numbers $z_1 = 1+2i, z_2 = 4-2i$ and $z_3 = 1-6i$ form the vertices of a
(a) right angled triangle (b) isosceles triangle
(c) equilateral triangle (d) scalene triangle

**25.** The necessary condition that the points *A*, *B*, *C* representing numbers $z_1, z_2, z_3$ respectively on the Argand plane be the vertices of an equilateral triangle is that
(a) $\frac{1}{z_1 - z_2} = \frac{1}{z_3 - z_1} + \frac{1}{z_2 - z_3}$
(b) $\frac{1}{z_1 - z_2} = \frac{1}{z_1 - z_3} + \frac{1}{z_2 - z_3}$
(c) $\frac{1}{z_1 - z_2} = \frac{1}{z_1 - z_3} + \frac{1}{z_3 - z_2}$
(d) None of the above

**26.** If $2\cos\alpha_1 = a + \frac{1}{a}, 2\cos\alpha_2 = b + \frac{1}{b}$ etc., then $abc + \frac{1}{abc}$.... will be given by
(a) $\cos(2\alpha_1 + 2\alpha_2 + \ldots)$ (b) $2\cos(\alpha_1 + \alpha_2 + \ldots)$
(c) $2\sin(\alpha_1 + \alpha_2 + \ldots)$ (d) $\sin(2\alpha_1 + 2\alpha_2 + \ldots)$

**27.** If $\theta$ is a positive acute angle, then real and imaginary parts of $\cos^{-1}(\cos\theta + i\sin\theta)$ are
(a) $\sin^{-1}(\sqrt{\sin\theta}) + i\log\{\sqrt{1+\sin\theta} - \sqrt{\sin\theta}\}$
(b) $\cos^{-1}(\sqrt{\sin\theta}) + i\log\{\sqrt{1+\cos\theta} - \sqrt{\cos\theta}\}$
(c) $\sin^{-1}(\sqrt{\cos\theta}) + i\log\{\sqrt{1+\sin\theta} - \sqrt{\cos\theta}\}$
(d) None of the above

**28.** If $(1+i\tan\alpha)^{1+i\tan\beta}$ has only real values one of them, is given by
(a) $(\sec\beta)^{\sec^2\alpha}$ (b) $(\sec\alpha)^{\sec\beta}$
(c) $(\sec\alpha)^{\sec^2\beta}$ (d) None of these

**29.** The radius of convergence of the power series $f(z) = \sum \frac{n+1}{(n+2)(n+3)} z^n$ is
(a) 1 (b) 2 (c) 3 (d) 4

**30.** If $\{z_n\}_{n=1}^{\infty}$ converges to $L_1$ and $L_2$, then
(a) $L_1 \neq L_2$ (b) $L_2 = L_2$
(c) $L_1 L_2 = 0$ (d) $\frac{L_1}{L_2} = 1$

**31.** If $\{z_n\}_{n=1}^{\infty}$ converges absolutely, then
(a) $\{z_n\}_{n=1}^{\infty}$ is convergent (b) $\{z_n\}_{n=1}^{\infty}$ is divergent
(c) $\{z_n\}_{n=1}^{\infty}$ is constant (d) None of these

**32.** If *f* is an entire function, then
(a) *f* has a power series expression
(b) *f* has not a power series expression
(c) *f* is constant
(d) None of the above

**33.** Series $\Sigma a_n$ converges absolutely, if
(a) $\Sigma|a_n|$ converges (b) $\Sigma a_n$ converges
(c) $\Sigma|a_n|$ diverges (d) None of these

**34.** The sequence $\left\{\frac{\pi n}{1+3ni}\right\}_{n=1}^{\infty}$ is
(a) divergent (b) constant
(c) unknown (d) convergent

**35.** The series $\sum_{n=0}^{\infty} \frac{(3i)^n \cdot n!}{n^2}$ is
(a) convergent (b) divergent
(c) constant (d) None of these

**36.** The radius of convergence of the power series $\sum_{n=0}^{\infty} (n+2i)^n z^n$ is
(a) 0 (b) one
(c) $\infty$ (d) None of these

**37.** The radius of convergence of $\sum_{n=0}^{\infty} \left(1+\frac{1}{n}\right)^{n^2} z^n$ is
(a) e (b) $\frac{1}{e}$
(c) $e^2$ (d) $\frac{1}{e^2}$

**38.** If the series $\sum_{n=0}^{\infty} n^2 \left(\frac{z^2+1}{1+i}\right)^n$ converges, then
(a) $|z+1| \leq \sqrt{2}$ (b) $|z| \leq \sqrt{2}$
(c) $|z^2+1| < \sqrt{2}$ (d) $|z^2-1| < \sqrt{2}$

**39.** The series $\sum_{n=0}^{\infty} \frac{z^n}{n!}$ converges at
(a) $z = 0$ (b) $z = 1$
(c) $z = 2$ (d) None of these

**40.** The centre of convergence of $\sum_{n=0}^{\infty} (n+2i)^n z^n$ is
(a) 0 (b) 1
(c) 2 (d) 3

**41.** If a function $f(z)$ is continuous at $z_0$, then
(a) $f(z)$ is differentiable at $z_0$
(b) $f(z)$ is not necessarily differentiable at $z_0$
(c) $f(z)$ is analytic at $z_0$
(d) None of the above

**42.** If a function $f(z)$ is analytic at a point $z = z_0$, then which of the following statements is false?
(a) $f$ is differentiable at $z_0$
(b) $f$ is not continuous at $z_0$
(c) $f$ is defined at $z_0$
(d) $f$ is continuous at $z_0$

**43.** If a function $f(z)$ is continuous at $z = z_0$, then which of the following statements does not hold?
(a) $f$ is analytic at $z_0$ (b) $f$ is defined at $z_0$
(c) $\lim_{z \to z_0} f(z)$ exists at $z_0$ (d) None of these

**44.** For the function $f(z) = z^2$, the value of derivative at $z = 4$ is
(a) 2 (b) 5
(c) 8 (d) 6

**45.** The function $f(z) = |z|^2$ is
(a) everywhere analytic (b) nowhere analytic
(c) analytic at $z = 0$ (d) None of these

**46.** The function $f(z) = |z|^2$ is differentiable at
(a) $z = 0$ (b) $z \neq 0$
(c) nowhere (d) None of these

**47.** The function $f(z) = \sec z$ is
(a) analytic for all $z$ (b) analytic for $z = \pi$
(c) not analytic at $z = \frac{\pi}{2}$ (d) None of these

**48.** If an entire function $f(z)$ is bounded in absolute value for all $z$, then
(a) $f(z) =$ constant (b) $f(z) =$ zero
(c) $f(z) = \infty$ (d) None of these

**49.** If $f(z)$ is analytic in a domain $D$, then
(a) $f^{(n)}(z)$ exist in $D$
(b) $f^{(n)}(z)$ does not exist in $D$
(c) $f^{(n)}(z) = 0$ for all $n$ in $D$
(d) None of the above

**50.** A point $z = z_0$ is a singular point of an analytic function $f(z)$, if
(a) at $z = z_0$, $f(z)$ is not analytic
(b) at $z = z_0$, $f(z)$ is analytic
(c) at $z = z_0$, $f(z) = 0$
(d) None of the above

**51.** If $f(z)$ is entire, then
(a) $f(z)$ is analytic for all $z$
(b) $f(z)$ diverges for all $z$
(c) $f(z)$ is not analytic for all $z$
(d) None of the above

**52.** The complement of the unit circle $|z| = 1$ is
(a) open set (b) closed set
(c) semi-open (d) None of these

**53.** An annulus $\rho_1 < |z - a| < \rho_2$ is
(a) connected (b) disconnected
(c) semi-connected (d) None of these

**54.** Half open plane is
(a) connected (b) disconnected
(c) semi-connected (d) None of these

**55.** The complement of the unit circle $|z| = 1$ is
(a) $|z| > 1$ (b) $|z| < 1$
(c) $|z| = 1$ (d) None of these

**56.** The set $S$ is open, then which of the following is true?
(a) $S$ does not contains its boundary points
(b) $S$ contains its boundary points
(c) $S$ have its boundary points
(d) None of the above

**57.** The set $S$ is closed if
(a) it does not contains its boundary points
(b) it has no boundary points
(c) it contains its boundary points
(d) None of the above

**58.** Let $x \in S$ and $x$ be a boundary point of $S$. Also, let $S'$ is the complement of $S$. Then the neighbourhood of $x$ is a set
(a) $\{z : z \in S \cup S'\}$ (b) $\{z : z \notin S \text{ and } z \notin S'\}$
(c) $\{z : z \in S \cap S'\}$ (d) None of these

**59.** The zero of first order is known as
(a) complex zero (b) simple zero
(c) singularity (d) None of these

**60.** For second order zero
(a) $f(z_0) = f'(z_0) = 0$ and $f''(z_0) \neq 0$
(b) $f(z_0) = 0$, $f'(z_0) \neq 0$ and $f''(z_0) \neq 0$
(c) $f(z_0) = f'(z_0) = f''(z_0) = 0$
(d) None of the above

**61.** The only function among the following, that is analytic, is
(a) $f(z) = \text{Re}(z)$ (b) $f(z) = \text{Im}(z)$
(c) $f(z) = \bar{z}$ (d) $f(z) = \sin z$

**62.** The Cauchy-Riemann equations for $f(z) = u(x, y) + iv(x, y)$ to be analytic are
(a) $\frac{\partial^2 u}{\partial x^2} + \frac{\partial^2 u}{\partial y^2} = 0, \frac{\partial^2 v}{\partial x^2} + \frac{\partial^2 v}{\partial y^2} = 0$
(b) $\frac{\partial u}{\partial x} = -\frac{\partial v}{\partial y}, \frac{\partial u}{\partial y} = -\frac{\partial v}{\partial x}$
(c) $\frac{\partial u}{\partial x} = -\frac{\partial v}{\partial y}, \frac{\partial u}{\partial y} = -\frac{\partial v}{\partial x}$
(d) $\frac{\partial u}{\partial x} = -\frac{\partial v}{\partial y}, \frac{\partial u}{\partial y} = \frac{\partial v}{\partial x}$

**63.** Polar form of C-R equations are
(a) $\frac{\partial u}{\partial \theta} = \frac{1}{r}\frac{\partial v}{\partial r}, \frac{\partial u}{\partial r} = r\frac{\partial v}{\partial \theta}$
(b) $\frac{\partial u}{\partial \theta} = r\frac{\partial v}{\partial r}, \frac{\partial u}{\partial r} = \frac{1}{r}\frac{\partial v}{\partial \theta}$
(c) $\frac{\partial u}{\partial r} = \frac{1}{r}\frac{\partial v}{\partial \theta}, \frac{\partial u}{\partial \theta} = -r\frac{\partial v}{\partial r}$
(d) $\frac{\partial u}{\partial r} = r\frac{\partial v}{\partial \theta}, \frac{\partial u}{\partial \theta} = -r\frac{\partial v}{\partial r}$

**64.** Analytic function is
(a) single valued function (b) bounded function
(c) differentiable function (d) All of these

**65.** If $w = f(re^{i\theta})$, then $\frac{dw}{dz}$ is

(a) $(\cos\theta + i\sin\theta)\frac{\partial w}{\partial r}$ (b) $(\cos\theta - i\sin\theta)\frac{\partial w}{\partial r}$

(c) $(\sin\theta + i\cos\theta)\frac{\partial w}{\partial r}$ (d) $(\sin\theta - i\cos\theta)\frac{\partial w}{\partial r}$

**66.** If $w = u(x,y) + iv(x,y)$ is an analytic function of $z = x + iy$, then $\frac{dw}{dz}$ equals

(a) $i\frac{\partial w}{\partial x}$ (b) $-i\frac{\partial w}{\partial x}$

(c) $i\frac{\partial w}{\partial y}$ (d) $-i\frac{\partial w}{\partial y}$

**67.** The curve $u(x,y) = C$ and $v(x,y) = C^1$ are orthogonal, if

(a) $u$ and $v$ are complex functions
(b) $u + iv$ is an analytic function
(c) $u - v$ is an analytic function
(d) $u + v$ is an analytic function

**68.** In order that the function $f(z) = \frac{|z|^2}{z}$, $z \neq 0$ be continuous at $z = 0$, we should define $f(0)$ equal to

(a) 2 (b) −1
(c) 0 (d) 1

**69.** If $f(z)$ is analytic and equal $u(x,y) + iv(x,y)$, then $f'(z)$ equals

(a) $\frac{\partial u}{\partial x} - i\frac{\partial u}{\partial y}$ (b) $\frac{\partial u}{\partial x} - i\frac{\partial v}{\partial x}$

(c) $\frac{\partial u}{\partial y} - i\frac{\partial v}{\partial x}$ (d) None of these

**70.** The value of $m$ so that $2x - x^2 + my^2$ may be harmonic is

(a) 0 (b) 1
(c) 2 (d) 3

**71.** A function is said to be harmonic, if

(a) $\frac{\partial^2 u}{\partial x^2} + \frac{\partial^2 v}{\partial x^2} = 0$ (b) $\frac{\partial^2 u}{\partial x^2} + \frac{\partial^2 u}{\partial y^2} = 0$

(c) $\frac{\partial u}{\partial x} + \frac{\partial u}{\partial y} = 0$ (d) $\frac{\partial v}{\partial x} + \frac{\partial v}{\partial y} = 0$

**72.** $u, v$ are called conjugate harmonic functions, if

(a) $u$, $v$ are harmonic functions and $u + iv$ is analytic function
(b) $u$, $v$ are harmonic functions and $u + iv$ may not be analytic function
(c) $u$, $v$ are harmonic functions
(d) $u + iv$ is analytic function

**73.** If $u + iv$ is analytic function, then $dv$ is equal to

(a) $\frac{\partial v}{\partial x}dx - \frac{\partial v}{\partial y}dy$ (b) $-\frac{\partial u}{\partial y}dx + \frac{\partial u}{\partial x}dy$

(c) $\frac{\partial u}{\partial x}dx - \frac{\partial u}{\partial y}dy$ (d) $\frac{\partial u}{\partial y}dx + \frac{\partial u}{\partial x}dy$

**74.** If $u + iv$ is analytic function, then $v = f(x,y)dx + f(x,y)dy$ is

(a) exact differential equation
(b) linear differential equation
(c) homogeneous differential equation
(d) non-homogeneous differential equation

**75.** If $f: G \to C$ is differentiable with $f'(z) = 0$ for all $z \in G$ and $G$ is open and connected, then

(a) $f$ is constant function
(b) $f$ is increasing function
(c) $f$ is decreasing function
(d) None of these

**76.** A derivative of branch of logarithm function is

(a) $z$ (b) $1/z$
(c) 0 (d) None of these

**77.** The Cauchy-Riemann equations are, if $u = u(x,y)$ and $v(x,y) = v$

(a) $\frac{\partial u}{\partial x} = \frac{\partial v}{\partial y}, \frac{\partial u}{\partial y} = -\frac{\partial v}{\partial x}$ (b) $\frac{\partial^2 u}{\partial x^2} = \frac{\partial^2 v}{\partial y^2}$

(c) $\frac{\partial^3 u}{\partial x^3} = \frac{\partial^2 u}{\partial x^2}$ (d) None of these

**78.** The function $f(z) = u(z) + iv(z)$, $z \in C$ is analytic, iff

(a) $u$, $v$ are harmonic functions
(b) $u$, $v$ are continuous functions
(c) $u$, $v$ are differentiable functions
(d) $u$, $v$ satisfy Cauchy-Riemann equations

**79.** If $G$ is either a whole place $C$ or some open disk. If $u: G \to R$ is harmonic function, then

(a) $u$ has a harmonic conjugate
(b) $u$ has no harmonic conjugate
(c) $u$ is not analytic
(d) None of the above

**80.** An analytic function is

(a) infinitely differentiable
(b) finitely differentiable
(c) not differentiable
(d) None of the above

**81.** If $f$ is analytic function in some domain, then in that domain

(a) $f$ is continuous only
(b) $f$ is differentiable only
(c) $f$ is continuous and differentiable both
(d) None of the above

**82.** If $f$ is a bounded entire function, then

(a) $f$ is constant
(b) $f$ is equal to zero
(c) $f$ is increasing function
(d) $f$ is decreasing function

**83.** If $G \subset C$ and $G$ is open and connected. Also, if $f$ is a branch of $\log z$ on $G$, then the totality of branches of $\log z$ are the functions

(a) $f(z)$ (b) $f(z) + 2n\pi i$
(c) $f(z) +$ constant (d) None of these

**84.** A branch of logarithm function is
(a) continuous function (b) differentiable function
(c) analytic function (d) None of these

**85.** If $f$ and $g$ are analytic functions, then
(a) $f/g$ is always analytic
(b) $f/g$ is analytic, whenever $g(x) \neq 0$
(c) $f/g$ is analytic, whenever $f(x) \neq 0$
(d) None of the above

**86.** A function $f(z+c) = f(z)$, where $c$ is any number, then $f$ is
(a) a periodic function
(b) periodic function with period $c$
(c) periodic function with period $z$
(d) None of the above

**87.** If $G$ is open connected set in $C$ and $f: G \to C$ is a continuous function, then $f$ is a branch of logarithm, if for $z \in G$
(a) $z = \sin f(z)$ (b) $z = \cos f(z)$
(c) $z = \exp f(z)$ (d) $z = f(z)$

**88.** The points which represents the root of the equation $(z+1)^n - z^n = 0$ lie on
(a) a circle (b) a pair of straight lines
(c) a straight line (d) a parabola

**89.** If $z_1, z_2$ are two complex numbers such that
$|z_1 + z_2| = |z_1| + |z_2|$
Then, it is necessary that
(a) $z_1 = z_2$
(b) $z_2 = 0$
(c) $z_1 = \lambda z_2$ for some real number $\lambda$
(d) $z_1 z_2 = 0$ or $z_1 = \lambda z_2$ for some real number $\lambda$

**90.** The function
$f(z) = \log(z^2 + z - 2)$ has branch points at
(a) $z = 1, z = -1$ (b) $z = 2, z = -2$
(c) $z = 1, z = -2$ (d) None of these

**91.** By stereographic projection with South pole at the origin (0, 0, 0) the point (1, 0, 0) goes to the complex number
(a) $z = 1$ (b) $z = 1 + i$
(c) $z = i$ (d) $z = -i$

**92.** Under the stereographic projection of points on the unit sphere $x^2 + y^2 + z^2 = 1$ in $\mathbb{R}^2$ to the extended plane $z = x + iy$ the point $z = x + iy$ corresponds to
(a) $\left(\frac{2x}{x^2+y^2+1}, \frac{2y}{x^2+y^2+1}, \frac{x^2+y^2-1}{x^2+y^2+1}\right)$
(b) $\left(\frac{x^2}{1+x^2+y^2}, \frac{y^2}{1+x^2+y^2}, \frac{1-x^2+y^2}{1+x^2+y^2}\right)$
(c) $\left(\frac{x}{1+x^2+y^2}, \frac{y}{1+x^2+y^2}, \frac{1+x+y}{1+x^2+y^2}\right)$
(d) None of the above

**93.** If the point $z$ on $xy$-plane has projection $\left(\frac{1}{4}, \frac{1}{6}, \frac{1}{2} + \frac{\sqrt{23}}{12}\right)$ on the Riemannian sphere $x^2 + y^2 + \left(z - \frac{1}{2}\right)^2 = \frac{1}{4}$. Then, the projection of $iz$ is
(a) $\left(\frac{1}{4}, \frac{1}{6}, \frac{1}{2} + \frac{\sqrt{23}}{12}\right)$ (b) $\left(\frac{1}{6}, \frac{1}{4}, \frac{1}{2} + \frac{\sqrt{23}}{12}\right)$
(c) $\left(-\frac{1}{6}, \frac{1}{4}, \frac{1}{2} + \frac{\sqrt{23}}{12}\right)$ (d) $\left(-\frac{1}{4}, \frac{1}{6}, \frac{1}{2} + \frac{\sqrt{23}}{12}\right)$

# Exercise 2 (For Part 'C')

**Directions** (Q. Nos. 1-36) *Questions may have one or more than one correct option.*

**1.** The function $f(z) = |z|^2$ is
(a) continuous and differentiable everywhere
(b) continuous at $z = 0$ but not differentiable at $z = 0$
(c) continuous everywhere but nowhere differentiable except at $z = 0$
(d) not analytic except $z = 0$

**2.** Let $f(z) = e^z$, where $z = x + iy$ then
(a) $|f(z)| = e^x$
(b) $\arg(f(z)) = y$
(c) $f(z)$ is an entire function
(d) $f(z)$ is an analytic function

**3.** Which of the following is/are correct?
(a) Real and imaginary parts of an analytic function satisfy Laplace's equation.
(b) Real and imaginary parts of an analytic functions are always harmonic conjugate to each other.
(c) Real and imaginary parts of an analytic function are always orthogonal.
(d) Real and imaginary parts of an analytic function are separately continuous and differentiable in the domain $D$.

**4.** If $f(z) = u + iv$ be an analytic function in a domain $D$ and $f(z)$ is constant in $D$, then
(a) $u =$ constant (b) $v =$ constant
(c) $|f(z)| =$ constant (d) $\arg(f(z)) =$ constant

**5.** Let $u = x^2 - y^2$ and $v = -\frac{y}{x^2 + y^2}$, then
(a) both $u$ and $v$ satisfy Laplace's equation
(b) $u + iv$ is an analytic function of $z$
(c) $u$ is continuous everywhere but $v$ is not continuous at origin.
(d) $u$ is not differentiable at origin

**6.** Which of the following is/are true?

(a) The series $\sum_{n=1}^{\infty} n!z^n$ is convergent only for $z = 0$

(b) The series $\sum_{n=0}^{\infty} z^n$ is convergent for $|z|<1$ and divergent for $|z|\geq 1$

(c) $\sum_{n=0}^{\infty} a_n z^n$ and $\sum_{n=1}^{\infty} n.a_n z^{n-1}$ have the same radius of convergence

(d) The series $\sum_{n=0}^{\infty} a_n z^n$ converges absolutely for all $|z|< R$, where $R$ is the radius of convergence

**7.** For the power series

$$f(z) = \sum_{n=0}^{\infty} \frac{z^n}{2^n + 1}$$

(a) radius of convergence is 2
(b) centre of convergence is 1
(c) $\lim_{z\to 2} (z-2)f(z) = 2$
(d) region of convergence is $|z|< 2$

**8.** Which of the following(s) is/are true?

(a) $\frac{d}{dz}(\sinh z) = \cosh z$ (b) $\frac{d}{dz}(\cosh z) = -\sinh z$
(c) $\sinh^2 z - \cosh^2 z = 1$ (d) $\cosh^2 z - \sinh^2 z = 1$

**9.** If $f(z)$ is analytic in domain $D$, then $f(z)$ is

(a) continuous in $D$
(b) differentiable in $D$
(c) continuous but not necessarily differentiable in $D$
(d) continuous and differentiable both in $D$

**10.** The function $f(z) = \begin{cases} \frac{\text{Im}(z)}{|z|}, & z \neq 0 \\ 0, & z = 0 \end{cases}$ is

(a) continuous at $z = 0$ (b) differentiable at $z = 0$
(c) not analytic at $z = 0$ (d) discontinuous at $z = 0$

**11.** If $i^{i^{\cdots\infty}} = \alpha + i\beta$, then which of the following/s is/are true?

(a) $\frac{\alpha}{\beta} = \tan\frac{\pi\alpha}{2}$ (b) $\alpha^2 + \beta^2 = e^{-\pi\beta}$
(c) $\alpha^2 + \beta^2 = e^{\pi\beta}$ (d) $\frac{\beta}{\alpha} = \tan\frac{\pi\alpha}{2}$

**12.** Let $u + iv = \log \sin(x + iy)$, then

(a) $u = \frac{1}{2}\log\left[\frac{1}{2}(\cosh 2y - \cos 2x)\right]$
(b) $u = -\frac{1}{2}\log\left[\frac{1}{2}(\cosh 2y - \cos 2x)\right]$
(c) $v = \tan^{-1}(\cot x \tanh y)$
(d) $v = \cot^{-1}(\cot x \tanh y)$

**13.** Which of the following is/are true?

(a) The function $e^x \cos y$ is harmonic.
(b) An analytic function with constant imaginary part is constant.
(c) If $u + iv$ is analytic, then $v - iu$ is not analytic.
(d) $f(z) = \text{Re}(z^2)$ is analytic.

**14.** Which of the following function(s) is/are analytic?

(a) $f(z) = \sin z$ (b) $f(z) = \bar{z}$
(c) $f(z) = \text{Im}(z)$ (d) $\text{Re}(iz)$

**15.** Which of the following is/are true?

(a) $\sin ix = i\sinh x$ (b) $\cos ix = \cosh x$
(c) $\sinh ix = i\sin x$ (d) $\cosh ix = \cos x$

**16.** Which of the following(s) is/are correct?

(a) A continuous function of continuous function is continuous
(b) If $f(z)$ is continuous on bounded and closed set $S \subseteq \mathbb{C}$, then maximum of $|f(z)|$ exist in $S$
(c) If $f(z)$ is continuous on bounded and closed set $S \subseteq \mathbb{C}$, then minimum of $|f(z)|$ exist in $S$
(d) $f(z) = z^2$ is uniformly continuous on $|z|< 1$

**17.** The function

$$f(z) = \begin{cases} \frac{1}{z}, & z \neq 0 \\ \infty, & z = 0 \\ 0, & z = \infty \end{cases}$$

is

(a) continuous at every point except origin
(b) continuous only at origin
(c) continuous in the extended complex plane
(d) nowhere continuous

**18.** If $f(z) = u + iv$ is an analytic in $D$, then under what condition(s), $f(z)$ is constant?

(a) $\arg f(z)$ is constant
(b) $\text{Im} f$ is constant
(c) $\text{Re} f$ is constant
(d) $|f(z)|$ is constant

**19.** Let $D$ = Domain of $f(z)$

$R$ = set of all regular points of $f(z)$
$R'$ = set of all limit point of $R$
$S$ = set of all singular point of $f(z)$

where $f(z) = \frac{1}{\sin\frac{1}{z}}$

Then

(a) $S = \left\{\frac{1}{n\pi} : n \in \mathbb{Z} - \{0\}\right\} \cup \{0\}$
(b) $D = \mathbb{C} - \left[\left\{\frac{1}{n\pi} : n \in \mathbb{Z} - \{0\}\right\} \cup \{0\}\right]$
(c) $R = D$
(d) $S = R' - R$

**20.** Let $D$ = Domain of $f(z)$

$R$ = set of all regular point of $f(z)$

$R'$ = set of all limit points of $R$

$S$ = set of all singular points of $f(z)$

where $f(z) = \dfrac{\sin z}{z}$

Then

(a) $D = \mathbb{C} - \{0\}$ (b) $R = \mathbb{C} - \{0\}$

(c) $S = \{0\}$ (d) $S = \mathbb{C} - \{0\}$

**21.** Let $u$ be a harmonic function

(a) harmonic function satisfies the formal differential equation $\dfrac{\partial^2 u}{\partial z \partial \bar{z}} = 0$

(b) $u$ be a harmonic function. Then $u$ will satisfy Laplace's equation

$\therefore \quad \dfrac{\partial^2 u}{\partial x^2} + \dfrac{\partial^2 u}{\partial y^2} = 0$

(c) $\dfrac{\partial u}{\partial \bar{z}} = \dfrac{1}{2}\dfrac{\partial u}{\partial x} - \dfrac{1}{2i}\dfrac{\partial u}{\partial y}$

(d) a harmonic function do not satisfies the formal differential equation $\dfrac{\partial^2 u}{\partial z \partial \bar{z}} \neq 0$

**22.** Given $f(z) = \log(z)$

(a) $\dfrac{df(z)}{dz}$ is not defined for $z = 0$

(b) $\dfrac{df(z)}{dz}$ is defined for $z = 0$

(c) $f(z)$ is analytic at $z = 0$

(d) $f(z)$ is not analytic at $z = 0$

**23.** Given $f(z) = \log z$

(a) $f(z)$ satisfies Cauchy's-Riemann equation

(b) $f(z)$ does not satisfies Cauchy's-Riemann equation

(c) $f(z)$ is analytic

(d) $f(z)$ is not analytic

**24.** Given the function

$$u = x^3 - 3xy^2$$

(a) $u$ is harmonic function

(b) $u$ is not harmonic function

(c) $u$ satisfies Laplace equation

(d) $u$ does not satisfies Laplace equation

**25.** Given function $f(z) = z^n$, where $n$ is a positive integer

(a) $f(z)$ is an analytic function

(b) $f(z)$ is not an analytic function

(c) $f'(z) = nz^{n-1}$

(d) $f'(z) = 0$

**26.** Given $u = \cos x \cosh y$

(a) $u$ is a harmonic function

(b) $u$ is not a harmonic function

(c) $v = -(\sin x \sinh y) + c$ is the harmonic conjugate of $u$

(d) $u$ satisfies Laplace equation

**27.** Given the function $u = \dfrac{1}{2}\log(x^2 + y^2)$

(a) The function $u$ is harmonic

(b) The function $u$ is not harmonic

(c) The harmonic conjugates of $u$ is $\tan^{-1}\dfrac{y}{x} + c$

(d) $u$ satisfies Laplace equation

**28.** Given $f(z) = e^x(\cos y + i \sin y)$

(a) $f(z)$ satisfies Cauchy-Riemann equations

(b) $f(z)$ does not satisfies Cauchy-Riemann equations

(c) $f(z)$ is holomorphic

(d) $f(z)$ is not holomorphic

**29.** Given the function $f(z) = xy + iy$

(a) $f(z)$ is continuous everywhere

(b) $f(z)$ is discontinuous

(c) $f(z)$ is analytic everywhere

(d) $f(z)$ is not analytic

**30.** Let $u - v = (x - y)(x^2 + 4xy + y^2)$ and $f(z) = u + iv$ is an analytic function. Then $f(z)$ in terms of $z$ is

(a) $-iz^3 + d$ (b) $z^2$

(c) $z^2 + 1$ (d) $iz$

**31.** If $f(z) = u + iv$ is an analytic function of $z = x + iy$ and $\psi = \psi(x, y)$, with differential coefficients of first order, then

(a) $\left(\dfrac{\partial \psi}{\partial x}\right)^2 + \left(\dfrac{\partial \psi}{\partial y}\right)^2 - \left\{\left(\dfrac{\partial \psi}{\partial u}\right)^2 + \left(\dfrac{\partial \psi}{\partial v}\right)^2\right\} |f'(z)|^2$

(b) $\dfrac{\partial \psi}{\partial x} = \dfrac{\partial \psi}{\partial u} \cdot \dfrac{\partial u}{\partial x} + \dfrac{\partial \psi}{\partial v} \cdot \dfrac{\partial v}{\partial x}$

(c) $\dfrac{\partial \psi}{\partial x} = \dfrac{\partial \psi}{\partial y}$

(d) $\dfrac{\partial \psi}{\partial x} = -\dfrac{\partial \psi}{\partial y}$

**32.** Given

$u = x^2 - y^2,\ v = -y/(x^2 + y^2)$

(a) $u$ and $v$ satisfies Laplace's equation

(b) $u$ and $v$ does not satisfies Laplace's equation

(c) $u + iv$ is not an analytic function

(d) $u + iv$ does satisfies Cauchy-Riemann equations

**33.** Let $u = \dfrac{\sin 2x}{\cosh 2y + \cos 2x}$,

(a) $\dfrac{\partial u}{\partial x} = \dfrac{2 + 2\cos 2x \cosh 2y}{(\cosh 2y + \cos 2x)^2}$

(b) $\dfrac{\partial u}{\partial y} = -\dfrac{2 \sin 2x \sinh 2y}{(\cosh 2y + \cos 2x)^2}$

(c) corresponding analytic function is $\tan z + c$

(d) corresponding analytic function is $\sin z + c$

**34.** If $f(z)$ is an analytic function of $z$

(a) $\left(\dfrac{\partial^2}{\partial x^2} + \dfrac{\partial^2}{\partial y^2}\right)|\text{Re}\, f(z)|^2 = 2|f'(z)|^2$

(b) $\dfrac{\partial}{\partial x}[\text{Re}\, f(z)]^2 = 0$

(c) $\frac{\partial^2}{\partial x^2}[\text{Re } f(z)]^2 = 0$

(d) $\left(\frac{\partial^2}{\partial x^2} + \frac{\partial^2}{\partial y^2}\right)|\text{Re } f(z)|^2 = 0$

**35.** Let $f(z) = u + iv$ is an analytic function of $z = x + iv$ and $u - v = \dfrac{e^y - \cos x + \sin x}{\cosh y - \cos x}$

(a) $f(z) = \cot\frac{1}{2}z + \frac{c}{1+i}$

(b) $f(z) = \cot\frac{1}{2}z + \frac{1}{2}(1-i)$ given $f(\pi/2) = \frac{3+i}{2}$

(c) $f(z) = \sin z + \pi/2$ given $f(\pi/2) = \frac{3+i}{2}$

(d) $f(z) = 0$

**36.** The following statements are true

(a) Function $u(x, y) = e^x \cos y$ is harmonic

(b) Function $u(x, y) = e^x \cos y$ is not harmonic

(c) $e^x \sin y + c$ is harmonic conjugate

(d) $f(z) = e^z + d$ is the analytic function

# Answers

## Exercise 1

| | | | | | | | | | |
|---|---|---|---|---|---|---|---|---|---|
| **1.** (d) | **2.** (c) | **3.** (a) | **4.** (a) | **5.** (d) | **6.** (c) | **7.** (a) | **8.** (d) | **9.** (b) | **10.** (d) |
| **11.** (a) | **12.** (b) | **13.** (b) | **14.** (c) | **15.** (b) | **16.** (a) | **17.** (a) | **18.** (b) | **19.** (a) | **20.** (c) |
| **21.** (d) | **22.** (d) | **23.** (d) | **24.** (b) | **25.** (c) | **26.** (b) | **27.** (a) | **28.** (b) | **29.** (a) | **30.** (b) |
| **31.** (a) | **32.** (a) | **33.** (a) | **34.** (a) | **35.** (b) | **36.** (a) | **37.** (b) | **38.** (c) | **39.** (a) | **40.** (a) |
| **41.** (b) | **42.** (b) | **43.** (a) | **44.** (c) | **45.** (c) | **46.** (a) | **47.** (c) | **48.** (a) | **49.** (a) | **50.** (a) |
| **51.** (a) | **52.** (a) | **53.** (a) | **54.** (a) | **55.** (a) | **56.** (a) | **57.** (c) | **58.** (a) | **59.** (b) | **60.** (a) |
| **61.** (d) | **62.** (c) | **63.** (c) | **64.** (d) | **65.** (b) | **66.** (d) | **67.** (b) | **68.** (c) | **69.** (c) | **70.** (b) |
| **71.** (b) | **72.** (a) | **73.** (b) | **74.** (a) | **75.** (a) | **76.** (b) | **77.** (a) | **78.** (d) | **79.** (a) | **80.** (a) |
| **81.** (c) | **82.** (a) | **83.** (b) | **84.** (c) | **85.** (b) | **86.** (b) | **87.** (c) | **88.** (b) | **89.** (d) | **90.** (c) |
| **91.** (b) | **92.** (a) | **93.** (c) | | | | | | | |

## Exercise 2

| | | | | | | | | | |
|---|---|---|---|---|---|---|---|---|---|
| **1.** (c,d) | **2.** (a,b,c,d) | **3.** (a,d) | **4.** (a,b,c,d) | **5.** (a,c) | **6.** (a,b,c,d) | **7.** (a,c,d) | **8.** (a,d) | **9.** (a,b,d) | **10.** (c,d) |
| **11.** (b,d) | **12.** (a,c) | **13.** (a,b) | **14.** (a) | **15.** (a,b,c,d) | **16.** (a,b,c,d) | **17.** (c) | **18.** (a,b,c,d) | **19.** (a,b,c,d) | **20.** (a,b,c) |
| **21.** (a,b,c) | **22.** (a,d) | **23.** (a,c) | **24.** (a,c) | **25.** (a,c) | **26.** (a,c,d) | **27.** (a,c,d) | **28.** (a,c) | **29.** (a,d) | **30.** (a) |
| **31.** (a,b) | **32.** (a,c,d) | **33.** (a,b,d) | **34.** (a) | **35.** (a,b) | **36.** (a,c,d) | | | | |

# Hints & Solutions

## Exercise 1

**4.** $f(z) = \dfrac{1}{1-z} = \dfrac{1}{1-7-2i} = \dfrac{1}{-6-2i} \times \dfrac{-6+2i}{-6+2i}$

$$= \frac{-6+2i}{36+4} = -\frac{3}{20} + \frac{i}{20}$$

$$\Rightarrow \quad \text{Re}(f(z)) = -\frac{3}{20}$$

**7.** Put $1 = r\cos\theta,\ 1 = r\sin\theta$

$$\Rightarrow \quad r = \sqrt{2},\ \theta = \frac{\pi}{4}$$

$$\therefore \quad (1+i)^n = r^n(\cos\theta + i\sin\theta)^n = r^n(\cos n\theta + i\sin n\theta)$$

$$\Rightarrow \text{Re}(1+i)^n = r^n \cos n\theta = (\sqrt{2})^n \cos\frac{n\pi}{4} = 2^{\frac{n}{2}}\cos\frac{n\pi}{4}$$

**8.** Since, $-\pi < \arg(z) \le \pi$.

$\therefore$ $\arg(z_1 z_2) = \alpha + \beta$ cannot be greater than $\pi$.

Therefore, $2\pi$ will be subtracted from the $\alpha + \beta$ so that $\arg(z_1 z_2)$ will satisfy the required constraint.

**9.** Put $z = x + iy \Rightarrow \dfrac{z-1}{z+1} = \dfrac{(x-1)+iy}{(x+1)+iy}$

$$\Rightarrow \quad \arg\left(\frac{z-1}{z+1}\right) = \arg(z-1) - \arg(z+1)$$

$$= \arg[(x-1)+iy] - \arg[(x+1)+iy]$$

$$= \tan^{-1}\frac{y}{x-1} - \tan^{-1}\frac{y}{x+1}$$

$$= \tan^{-1}\frac{\frac{y}{x-1}-\frac{y}{x+1}}{1+\frac{y}{x-1}\cdot\frac{y}{x+1}}$$

$\Rightarrow \quad \frac{y(x+1)-y(x-1)}{x^2-1+y^2}=\sqrt{3}$

$\Rightarrow \quad 2y=(x^2+y^2-1)\sqrt{3}$

$\Rightarrow \quad x^2+y^2-\frac{2}{\sqrt{3}}y-1=0$

which is a circle.

**13.** $x=-2-\sqrt{3}i \quad \Rightarrow \quad x+2=-\sqrt{3}i$

$\Rightarrow \quad x^2+4x+4=-3 \quad \Rightarrow \quad x^2+4x+7=0$

Now, $2x^4+5x^3+7x^2+41$

$=2x^2(x^2+4x+7)-3x(x^2+4x+7)+5(x^2+4x+7)+x+6$

$=x+6=4-\sqrt{3}i$

**21.** $(x-1)^3+8=0 \quad \Rightarrow \quad x-1=(-8)^{\frac{1}{3}}$

$=-2,-2\omega,-2\omega^2$

$\Rightarrow \quad x=1-2,\ 1-2\omega,\ 1-2\omega^2$

$\Rightarrow \quad x=-1,\ 1-2\omega,\ 1-2\omega^2$

**22.** Given, $|z-1|=2$

$\Rightarrow \quad |z-1|^2=4 \quad \Rightarrow \quad (z-1)(\bar{z}-1)=4$

$\Rightarrow z\bar{z}-z-\bar{z}+1=4 \quad \Rightarrow \quad z\bar{z}-z-\bar{z}=3$

**23.** Let $z=x+iy$

$\therefore$ From given $|z|-z=1+2i$, we have

$\sqrt{x^2+y^2}-(x+iy)=1+2i$

$\Rightarrow \quad (\sqrt{x^2+y^2}-x)+i(-y)=1+2i$

$\Rightarrow \quad y=-2,\ \sqrt{x^2+y^2}-x=1$

$\Rightarrow \sqrt{x^2+4}=1+x \quad \Rightarrow x^2+4=1+x^2+2x$

$\Rightarrow \quad x=\frac{3}{2}$

$\therefore \quad z=\frac{3}{2}-2i$

**24.** $z_1-z_2=-3+4i,\ z_2-z_3=3+4i$

$z_3-z_1=-8i$

$\Rightarrow \quad |z_1-z_2|=5,\ |z_2-z_3|=5,\ |z_3-z_1|=8$

**25.** In case of equilateral triangle, we have

$$\frac{1}{z_1-z_2}+\frac{1}{z_2-z_3}+\frac{1}{z_3-z_1}=0$$

$\Rightarrow \quad \frac{1}{z_1-z_2}=\frac{1}{z_1-z_3}+\frac{1}{z_3-z_2}$

**26.** From given, it is clear that

$a=e^{i\alpha_1},\ b=e^{i\alpha_2},\ c=e^{i\alpha_3}$, ........

$\Rightarrow \quad abc....=e^{i(\alpha_1+\alpha_2+\alpha_3+......)}$

$\frac{1}{abc.....}=e^{-i(\alpha_1+\alpha_2+\alpha_3+......)}$

$\Rightarrow \quad abc...+\frac{1}{abc....}=2\cos(\alpha_1+\alpha_2+\alpha_3+......)$

**27.** Let $\cos^{-1}(\cos\theta+i\sin\theta)=x+iy$

$\Rightarrow \quad \cos(x+iy)=\cos\theta+i\sin\theta$

$\Rightarrow \quad \cos x\cos iy-\sin x\sin iy=\cos\theta+i\sin\theta$

$\Rightarrow \cos x\cosh y-i\sin x\sinh y=\cos\theta+i\sin\theta$

$(\because \cos ix=\cosh x \text{ and } \sin ix=i\sinh x)$

$\Rightarrow \cos x\cosh y=\cos\theta,\ -\sin x\sinh y=\sin\theta$

Since, $\cosh^2 y-\sinh^2 y=1$

$\Rightarrow \quad \frac{\cos^2\theta}{\cos^2 x}-\frac{\sin^2\theta}{\sin^2 x}=1$

$\Rightarrow \quad \cos^2\theta\sin^2 x-\sin^2\theta\cos^2 x=\cos^2 x\sin^2 x$

$\Rightarrow \quad \cos^2\theta\sin^2 x-\sin^2\theta(1-\sin^2 x)=(1-\sin^2 x)\sin^2 x$

$\Rightarrow \cos^2\theta\sin^2 x-\sin^2\theta+\sin^2\theta\sin^2 x=\sin^2 x-\sin^4 x$

$\Rightarrow \quad \sin^4 x=\sin^2\theta \Rightarrow \sin x=\sqrt{\sin\theta}$

$\Rightarrow \quad x=\sin^{-1}\sqrt{\sin\theta}$

Since, $-\sin x\sinh y=\sin\theta$

$\Rightarrow \quad -\sqrt{\sin\theta}\sinh y=\sin\theta$

$\Rightarrow \quad \sinh y=-\sqrt{\sin\theta}$

$\Rightarrow \quad y=\sinh^{-1}(-\sqrt{\sin\theta})$

$=\log_e[-\sqrt{\sin\theta}+\sqrt{\sin\theta+1}]$

**29.** $a_n=\frac{(n+1)}{(n+2)(n+3)} \quad \Rightarrow a_{n+1}=\frac{(n+2)}{(n+3)(n+4)}$

$\therefore \ R=\lim_{n\to\infty}\left|\frac{a_n}{a_{n+1}}\right|$

$=\lim_{n\to\infty}\left|\frac{(n+1)}{(n+2)(n+3)}\cdot\frac{(n+3)(n+4)}{(n+2)}\right|$

$=\lim_{n\to\infty}\left|\frac{(n+1)(n+4)}{(n+2)^2}\right|=\lim_{n\to\infty}\left|\frac{n^2\left(1+\frac{1}{n}\right)\left(1+\frac{4}{n}\right)}{n^2\left(1+\frac{2}{n}\right)^2}\right|$

$=1$

**34.** $\lim_{n\to\infty}a_n=\lim_{n\to\infty}\frac{n\pi}{1+3ni}=\lim_{n\to\infty}\frac{\pi}{\frac{1}{n}+3i}=\frac{\pi}{3i}\neq 0$

**47.** $f(z)=\sec z=\frac{1}{\cos z}$ which is not defined when $\cos z=0$

$\Rightarrow f(z)$ is not analytic at $z=(2n+1)\frac{\pi}{2},\ n\in I$

**61.** $f(z)=\text{Re}(z)$

$\Rightarrow \quad u+iv=x$

$\Rightarrow \quad u=x,\ v=0$

$\frac{\partial u}{\partial x}=1,\ \frac{\partial u}{\partial y}=0$

$\frac{\partial v}{\partial x}=0,\ \frac{\partial v}{\partial y}=0$

$\because \quad \frac{\partial u}{\partial x}\neq\frac{\partial v}{\partial y}$

$\Rightarrow$ C-R equation is not satisfied.

$\Rightarrow f(z)$ is not analytic.

Similarly, other options can be discussed.

From last option,

$$f(z) = \sin z$$

$$u + iv = \sin(x+iy)$$

$$= \sin x \cos iy + \cos x \sin iy$$

$$= \sin x \cosh y + i \cos x \sinh y$$

$\Rightarrow$ $u = \sin x \cosh y,\ v = \cos x \sinh y$

$$\frac{\partial u}{\partial x} = \cos x \cosh y,\ \frac{\partial v}{\partial x} = -\sin x \sinh y$$

$$\frac{\partial u}{\partial y} = \sin x \sinh y,\ \frac{\partial v}{\partial y} = \cos x \cosh y$$

$\therefore$ $\frac{\partial u}{\partial x} = \frac{\partial v}{\partial y}$ and $\frac{\partial u}{\partial y} = -\frac{\partial v}{\partial x}$

$\Rightarrow$ C-R equation is satisfied.

$\Rightarrow$ $f(z) = \sin z$ is analytic everywhere.

## Exercise 2

**1.** $f(z) = |z|^2$

$\Rightarrow$ $f(0) = 0$

$\therefore$ $\lim_{z \to 0} f(z) = f(0)$

$\Rightarrow$ $f(z)$ is continuous at $z = 0$

Now, $f(z) = u + iv = x^2 + y^2$

for $z = x + iy,\ u = x^2,\ v = y^2$

$\Rightarrow$ $\frac{\partial u}{\partial x} = 2x,\ \frac{\partial u}{\partial y} = 0,\ \frac{\partial v}{\partial x} = 0,\ \frac{\partial v}{\partial y} = 2y$

$\therefore$ $\frac{\partial u}{\partial x} = \frac{\partial v}{\partial y}$ at origin

$\frac{\partial u}{\partial y} = -\frac{\partial v}{\partial x}$ at origin

Hence, C-R equation is satisfied only at origin.

**5.** We have, $\frac{\partial^2 u}{\partial x^2} + \frac{\partial^2 u}{\partial y^2} = 0$

and $\frac{\partial^2 v}{\partial x^2} + \frac{\partial^2 v}{\partial y^2} = 0$

but $u$ and $v$ do not satisfy C-R equation.

$\Rightarrow$ $u + iv$ is not analytic.

Along, $y = mx$

$$\lim_{x \to 0} u(x, mx) = \lim_{x \to 0} x^2 - m^2x^2 = 0$$

$$= u(0,0)$$

$$\lim_{x \to 0} v(x, mx) = \lim_{x \to 0} -\frac{mx}{x^2 + m^2x^2}$$

$$= \infty$$

$\Rightarrow$ $u$ is continuous everywhere but $v$ is not continuous at origin.

Also, $\lim_{x \to 0} \frac{x^2 - m^2x^2}{\sqrt{x^2 + m^2x^2}} = 0$

$\Rightarrow$ $u$ is differentiable at origin.

**70.** Let $u = 2x - x^2 + my^2$

$\Rightarrow$ $\frac{\partial u}{\partial x} = 2 - 2x,\ \frac{\partial^2 u}{\partial x^2} = -2$

$\frac{\partial u}{\partial y} = 2my,\ \frac{\partial^2 u}{\partial y^2} = 2m$

Since, $u$ be given harmonic.

Hence, $\frac{\partial^2 u}{\partial x^2} + \frac{\partial^2 u}{\partial y^2} = 0 \Rightarrow -2 + 2m = 0$

$\Rightarrow$ $2m = 2 \Rightarrow m = 1$

**73.** $dv = \frac{\partial v}{\partial x} dx + \frac{\partial v}{\partial y} dy$

$= -\frac{\partial u}{\partial y} dx + \frac{\partial u}{\partial x} dy$ (by C-R equation)

**10.** $\because$ $f(z) = u + iv$

$\Rightarrow$ $u = \frac{y}{\sqrt{x^2 + y^2}},\ v = 0$ (For $z \neq 0$)

and $u = 0,\ v = 0$ (For $z = 0$)

Along, $y = mx$

$$\lim_{x \to 0} u(x, mx) = \lim_{x \to 0} \frac{mx}{\sqrt{x^2 + m^2x^2}} = \lim_{x \to 0} \frac{m}{\sqrt{1 + m^2}} \neq u(0,0)$$

$\Rightarrow$ $u$ is discontinuous at $z = 0$ but $v$ is continuous.

$\Rightarrow$ $f(z) = u + iv$ is discontinuous at $z = 0$.

**19.** We have

$$D = \mathbb{C} - \left[\left\{\frac{1}{n\pi} : n \in \mathbb{Z} - \{0\}\right\} \cup \{0\}\right]$$

$$R = D,\ R' = \mathbb{C},$$

$$S = \left\{\frac{1}{n\pi} : n \in \mathbb{Z} - \{0\}\right\} \cup \{0\}$$

$$= R' - R$$

**20.** We have

$$D = \mathbb{C} - \{0\}$$

$$R = D = \mathbb{C} - \{0\}$$

$$R' = \mathbb{C}$$

$$S = R' - R$$

**21.** We have

$$z = x + iy \Rightarrow x = \frac{1}{2}(z + \bar{z})$$

and $y = \frac{1}{2i}(z + \bar{z})$

Let $u$ be a harmonic function. Then $u$ will satisfy Laplace's equation.

Hence, $\frac{\partial^2 u}{\partial x^2} + \frac{\partial^2 u}{\partial y^2} = 0$ ...(i)

Now, $\frac{\partial u}{\partial \bar{z}} = \frac{\partial u}{\partial x} \cdot \frac{\partial x}{\partial \bar{z}} + \frac{\partial u}{\partial y} \cdot \frac{\partial y}{\partial \bar{z}} = \frac{1}{2} \frac{\partial u}{\partial x} - \frac{1}{2i} \frac{\partial u}{\partial y}$

$$\Rightarrow \quad \frac{\partial^2 u}{\partial z \partial \bar{z}} = \frac{\partial}{\partial z}\left(\frac{\partial u}{\partial \bar{z}}\right)$$

$$= \frac{1}{2}\frac{\partial^2 u}{\partial x^2}\frac{\partial x}{\partial z} + \frac{1}{2}\frac{\partial^2 u}{\partial y \partial x}\frac{\partial y}{\partial z}$$

$$-\frac{1}{2i}\frac{\partial^2 u}{\partial x \partial y}\frac{\partial x}{\partial z} + \frac{1}{2i}\frac{\partial^2 u}{\partial y^2}\frac{\partial y}{\partial z}$$

$$= \frac{1}{4}\frac{\partial^2 u}{\partial x^2} + \frac{1}{4i}\frac{\partial^2 u}{\partial y \partial x} - \frac{1}{4i}\frac{\partial^2 u}{\partial x \partial y} + \frac{1}{4}\frac{\partial^2 x}{\partial y^2}$$

$$= \frac{1}{4}\left(\frac{\partial^2 u}{\partial x^2} + \frac{\partial^2 u}{\partial y^2}\right) = 0$$

**22.** We have

$$\frac{df(z)}{dz} = \frac{d}{dz}(\log z) = \frac{\partial u}{\partial x} + i\frac{\partial v}{\partial x}$$

$$= \frac{x}{x^2+y^2} + i\frac{-y}{x^2+y^2}$$

$$= \frac{x-iy}{x^2+y^2} = \frac{x-iy}{(x+iy)(x-iy)}$$

$$= \frac{1}{x+iy} = \frac{1}{z} (z \neq 0)$$

$\Rightarrow \frac{df(z)}{dz}$ is not defined at $z = 0$.

**23.** Given that

$$f(z) = u + iv = \log(x+iy)$$

$$= \frac{1}{2}\log(x^2+y^2) + i\tan^{-1}(y/x)$$

$\therefore \quad u = \frac{1}{2}\log(x^2+y^2)$

and $\quad v = \tan^{-1}\left(\frac{y}{x}\right)$

$$\Rightarrow \quad \frac{\partial u}{\partial x} = \frac{x}{x^2+y^2} = \frac{\partial v}{\partial y}$$

and $\quad \frac{\partial u}{\partial y} = \frac{y}{x^2+y^2} = -\frac{\partial v}{\partial x}$

Thus, Cauchy-Riemann equations are satisfied.

**24.** We have $u = x^3 - 3xy^2$

$$\frac{\partial u}{\partial x} = 3x^2 - 3y^2, \frac{\partial^2 u}{\partial x^2} = 6x$$

$$\frac{\partial u}{\partial y} = -6xy \text{ and } \frac{\partial^2 u}{\partial y^2} = -6x$$

Now, $\frac{\partial^2 u}{\partial x^2} + \frac{\partial^2 u}{\partial y^2} = 0$, so that $u$ satisfies Laplace's equation.

Also, since first and second order partial derivatives of $u$ are continuous functions of $x$ and $y$. Hence, $u$ is a harmonic function.

**25.** We have $f(z) = z^n$

Now,

$$f'(z) = \lim_{\Delta z \to 0} \frac{f(z+\Delta z) - f(z)}{\Delta z}$$

$$= \lim_{\Delta z \to 0} \frac{(z+\Delta z)^n - z^n}{\Delta z}$$

$$= \lim_{\Delta z \to 0} \frac{\left[z^n + nz^{n-1}\Delta z + \frac{1}{2}n(n-1) z^{n-2}(\Delta z)^2 + \ldots + \Delta^n z - z^n\right]}{\Delta z}$$

(by binomial theorem)

$$= \lim_{\Delta z \to 0} (nz^{n-1} + \frac{1}{2}n(n-1)z^{n-2}\Delta z + \ldots + \Delta^{n-1} z)$$

$$= nz^{n-1}$$

which exists for all finite values of $z$.

Hence, $f(z)$ is an analytic function.

**26.** Here, $u = \cos x \cosh y$

$$\therefore \quad \frac{\partial u}{\partial x} = -\sin x \cosh y$$

$$\frac{\partial^2 u}{\partial y^2} = -\cos x \cosh y$$

and $\quad \frac{\partial u}{\partial y} = \cos x \sinh y$

and $\quad \frac{\partial^2 u}{\partial y^2} = \cos x \cosh y$

Since, all the first and second order partial derivatives of $u$ are continuous functions.

And $\frac{\partial^2 u}{\partial x^2} + \frac{\partial^2 u}{\partial y^2} = 0 \Rightarrow u$ satisfies Laplace's equation

$\Rightarrow u$ is a harmonic function. Let $v$ be the harmonic conjugate of $u$. Then

We have

$$dv = \frac{\partial v}{\partial x}dx + \frac{\partial v}{\partial y}dy$$

$$= -\frac{\partial u}{\partial y}dx + \frac{\partial u}{\partial x}dy \quad \text{(by Cauchy-Riemann equations)}$$

$$= -\cos x \sinh y \, dx - \sin x \cosh y \, dy$$

$$= -(\cos x \sinh y dx + \sin x \cosh y dy)$$

On integrating, we get

$$v = -(\sin x \sinh y) + C,$$

where C is a real constant.

**27.** We have $\quad u = \frac{1}{2}\log(x^2+y^2)$

$$\Rightarrow \quad \frac{\partial u}{\partial x} = \frac{x}{x^2+y^2}$$

$$\Rightarrow \quad \frac{\partial^2 u}{\partial x^2} = \frac{y^2-x^2}{(x^2+y^2)^2}$$

and $\quad \frac{\partial u}{\partial y} = \frac{y}{x^2+y^2} \Rightarrow \frac{\partial^2 u}{\partial y^2} = \frac{x^2-y^2}{(x^2+y^2)^2}$

Since, all the first and second order partial derivative of $u$ are continuous functions of $x$ and $y$.

Also, $\quad \frac{\partial^2 u}{\partial x^2} + \frac{\partial^2 u}{\partial y^2} = 0$

$\Rightarrow u$ is a harmonic function.

Let $v$ be the harmonic conjugate of $u$. Then

We have

$$dv = \frac{\partial v}{\partial x}dx + \frac{\partial v}{\partial y}dy$$

$$= -\frac{\partial u}{\partial y}dx + \frac{\partial u}{\partial x}dy, \text{ (by Cauchy-Riemann equations)}$$

$$= -\frac{y}{x^2+y^2}dx + \frac{x}{x^2+y^2}dy$$

$$dv = \frac{xdy - ydx}{x^2+y^2}$$

On integrating, we get $v = \tan^{-1}\frac{y}{x} + C$, where $C$ is a real constant.

**28.** Let $f(z) = u + iv = e^x(\cos y + i\sin y)$

Then $u = e^x \cos y, v = e^x \sin y$

$$\Rightarrow \quad \frac{\partial u}{\partial x} = e^x \cos y, \frac{\partial u}{\partial y} = -e^x \sin y$$

and $\frac{\partial v}{\partial x} = e^x \sin y$ and $\frac{\partial v}{\partial y} = e^x \cos y$

Since, $\frac{\partial u}{\partial x} = \frac{\partial v}{\partial y}$ and $\frac{\partial u}{\partial y} = -\frac{\partial v}{\partial x}$, therefore, $f(z)$ satisfies Cauchy-Riemann equations.

Also, $\frac{\partial u}{\partial x}, \frac{\partial u}{\partial y}, \frac{\partial v}{\partial x}$ and $\frac{\partial v}{\partial y}$ are rational functions of $x$ and $y$ with non-zero denominators. Consequently partial derivatives of $u$ and $v$ are continuous functions everywhere. Thus, the function $e^x(\cos y + i\sin y)$ is holomorphic function.

**29.** Let $f(z) = u(x, y) + iv(x, y)$

Then $u(x, y) = xy$ and $v(x, y) = y$

Since, $u$ and $v$ are polynomials in $x$ and $y$, therefore, they are continuous at each point. Hence, $f(z)$ is everywhere continuous.

Here, $\frac{\partial u}{\partial x} = y, \frac{\partial u}{\partial y} = x, \frac{\partial v}{\partial x} = 0, \frac{\partial v}{\partial y} = 1$

and $\frac{\partial u}{\partial x} \neq \frac{\partial v}{\partial y}, \frac{\partial u}{\partial y} \neq -\frac{\partial v}{\partial x}$, so that Cauchy-Riemann equations are not satisfied.

Hence, $f(z)$ is not analytic.

**30.** Given, $f(z) = u + iv$,

then $if(z) = iu - v$

$\Rightarrow \quad (1+i)f(z) = u - v + i(u + v)$

$= U + iV$ (say)

Since, $U = u - v = (x-y)(x^2 + 4xy + y^2)$

$$\Rightarrow \quad \frac{\partial U}{\partial x} = \frac{\partial u}{\partial x} - \frac{\partial v}{\partial x}$$

$$= x^2 + 4xy + y^2 + (x-y)(2x+4y)$$

$$= 3x^2 + 6xy - 3y^2 = \phi_1(x, y)$$

and $\frac{\partial U}{\partial y} = \frac{\partial u}{\partial y} - \frac{\partial v}{\partial y} = -(x^2 + 4xy + y^2) + (x-y)(4x+2y)$

$$= 3x^2 - 6xy - 3y^2 = \phi_2(x, y)$$

Since, $(1+i)f(z)$

$$= \int [\phi_1(z, 0) - i\phi_2(z, 0)]dz + c$$

$$= \int (3z^2 - i3z^2)dz + c$$

$$= \int 3(1-i)z^2 dz + c$$

$$= (1-i)z^3 + c$$

$$\Rightarrow \quad f(z) = \frac{1-i}{1+i}z^3 + \frac{c}{1+i}$$

$$= -iz^3 + d$$

**31.** We have

$$\frac{\partial \psi}{\partial x} = \frac{\partial \psi}{\partial u}\frac{\partial u}{\partial x} + \frac{\partial \psi}{\partial v}\frac{\partial v}{\partial x} \quad \text{...(i)}$$

and $\frac{\partial \psi}{\partial y} = \frac{\partial \psi}{\partial u}\frac{\partial u}{\partial y} + \frac{\partial \psi}{\partial v}\frac{\partial v}{\partial y} = -\frac{\partial \psi}{\partial u}\frac{\partial v}{\partial x} + \frac{\partial \psi}{\partial v}\frac{\partial u}{\partial x}$ ...(ii)

(by Cauchy-Riemann equations)

Squaring and adding Eqs. (i) and (ii), we have

$$\left(\frac{\partial \psi}{\partial x}\right)^2 + \left(\frac{\partial \psi}{\partial y}\right)^2 = \left[\left(\frac{\partial \psi}{\partial u}\right)^2 + \left(\frac{\partial \psi}{\partial v}\right)^2\right]\left[\left(\frac{\partial u}{\partial x}\right)^2 + \left(\frac{\partial v}{\partial x}\right)^2\right]$$

$$= \left[\left(\frac{\partial \psi}{\partial u}\right)^2 + \left(\frac{\partial \psi}{\partial v}\right)^2\right]|f'(z)|^2$$

**32.** We have $u = x^2 - y^2, v = -y/(x^2 + y^2)$

$$\Rightarrow \quad \frac{\partial u}{\partial x} = 2x, \frac{\partial u}{\partial y} = -2y$$

and $\frac{\partial^2 u}{\partial x^2} = 2, \frac{\partial^2 u}{\partial y^2} = -2$

Also, $\frac{\partial v}{\partial x} = \frac{2xy}{(x^2+y^2)^2}, \frac{\partial v}{\partial y} = \frac{y^2 - x^2}{(x^2+y^2)^2}$

and $\frac{\partial^2 v}{\partial x^2} = \frac{2y^3 - 6x^2y}{(x^2+y^2)^3}, \frac{\partial^2 v}{\partial y^2} = \frac{6x^2y - 2y^3}{(x^2+y^2)^3}$

Since, $\frac{\partial^2 u}{\partial x^2} + \frac{\partial^2 u}{\partial y^2} = 0$ and $\frac{\partial^2 v}{\partial x^2} + \frac{\partial^2 v}{\partial y^2} = 0$

$\therefore$ Both $u$ and $v$ satisfy Laplace's equation.

Since, $\frac{\partial u}{\partial x} \neq \frac{\partial v}{\partial y}$ and $\frac{\partial u}{\partial y} \neq -\frac{\partial v}{\partial x}$

Therefore, $u$ and $v$ does not satisfy Cauchy-Riemann equations.

Hence, $u + iv$ is not an analytic function.

**33.** We have

$$u = \frac{\sin 2x}{\cosh 2y + \cos 2x}$$

$$\Rightarrow \quad \frac{\partial u}{\partial x} = \frac{2\cos 2x(\cosh 2y + \cos 2x) - \sin 2x(-2\sin 2x)}{(\cosh 2y + \cos 2x)^2}$$

$$= \frac{2 + 2\cos 2x \cosh 2y}{(\cosh 2y + \cos 2x)^2} = g_1(x, y)$$

and $\frac{\partial u}{\partial y} = \frac{-2\sin 2x \sinh 2y}{(\cosh 2y + \cos 2x)^2} = g_2(x, y)$

The function $f(z)$ is given by

$$f(z)=\int[g_1(z,0)-ig_2(z,0)]\,dz+c$$

$$=\int\left[\frac{2+2\cos 2z}{(1+\cos 2z)^2}-i0\right]dz$$

$$=\int\frac{2dz}{1+\cos 2z}+c=\int\sec^2 z\,dz+c$$

$$=\tan z+c$$

**34.** Let $f(z)=u+iv$, where $z=x+iy$

Then $\operatorname{Re} f(z)=u$

Now, $$\frac{\partial u^2}{\partial x}=2u\frac{\partial u}{\partial x}$$

and $$\frac{\partial^2u^2}{\partial x^2}=2\left(\frac{\partial u}{\partial x}\right)^2+2u\frac{\partial^2 u}{\partial x^2}$$

Also, $$\frac{\partial^2u^2}{\partial y^2}=2\left(\frac{\partial u}{\partial y}\right)^2+2u\frac{\partial^2 u}{\partial y^2}$$

$$\therefore\quad \frac{\partial^2u^2}{\partial x^2}+\frac{\partial^2u^2}{\partial y^2}$$

$$=2\left[\left\{\left(\frac{\partial u}{\partial x}\right)^2+\left(\frac{\partial u}{\partial y}\right)^2\right\}+u\left(\frac{\partial^2 u}{\partial x^2}+\frac{\partial^2 u}{\partial y^2}\right)\right]$$

$$\Rightarrow\left(\frac{\partial^2}{\partial x^2}+\frac{\partial^2}{\partial y^2}\right)u^2=2\left\{\left(\frac{\partial u}{\partial x}\right)^2+\left(\frac{\partial u}{\partial y}\right)^2\right\}+0$$

($u$ is a harmonic function)

$$\Rightarrow\left(\frac{\partial^2}{\partial x^2}+\frac{\partial^2}{\partial y^2}\right)u^2=2\left[\left(\frac{\partial u}{\partial x}\right)^2+\left(\frac{\partial v}{\partial x}\right)^2\right]$$

(By Cauchy-Riemann equations)

$$\left(\frac{\partial^2}{\partial x^2}+\frac{\partial^2}{\partial y^2}\right)|u^2|=2|f'(z)|^2 \qquad \left(\because f'(z)=\frac{\partial u}{\partial x}+i\frac{\partial v}{\partial x}\right)$$

Thus, $$\left(\frac{\partial^2}{\partial x^2}+\frac{\partial^2}{\partial y^2}\right)|\operatorname{Re} f(z)|^2=2|f'(z)|^2$$

**35.** Given, $f(z)=u+iv$, then $if(z)=iu-v$

Adding $f(z)+if(z)$, we have

$f(z)+if(z)=u-v+i(u+v)=uk+iuk$ (say)

Since,

$$U=u-v=\frac{e^y-\cos x+\sin x}{\cosh y-\cos x}$$

$$=\frac{\cosh y+\sinh y-\cos x+\sin x}{\cosh y-\cos x}$$

$$=1+\frac{\sinh y+\sin x}{\cosh y-\cos x}$$

$$\frac{\partial U}{\partial x}=\frac{\cos x(\cosh y-\cos x)-(\sinh y+\sin x)\sin x}{(\cosh y-\cos x)^2}$$

$$=g_1(x,y)$$

$$\Rightarrow\quad g_1(z,0)$$

$$=\frac{\cos z(1-\cos z)-\sin^2 z}{(1-\cos z)^2}$$

$$=\frac{\cos z-1}{(1-\cos z)^2}=\frac{-1}{1-\cos z}$$

$$=-\frac{1}{2}\operatorname{cosec}^2\frac{1}{2}z$$

and $$\frac{\partial U}{\partial y}=\frac{\cosh y(\cosh y-\cos x)-\sinh y(\sinh y+\sin x)}{(\cosh y-\cos x)^2}$$

$$=g_2(x,y)$$

$$\Rightarrow\ \phi_2(z,0)$$

$$=\frac{1-\cos z}{(1-\cos z)^2}$$

$$=\frac{1}{1-\cos z}=-\frac{1}{2}\operatorname{cosec}^2\frac{1}{2}z$$

Since, $(1+i)f(z)$

$$=\int[g_1(z,0)-ig_2(z,0)]dz+c$$

$$=\int\left(-\frac{1}{2}\operatorname{cosec}^2\frac{1}{2}z-i\frac{1}{2}\operatorname{cosec}^2\frac{1}{2}z\right)dz+c$$

$$=-\frac{1}{2}(1+i)\int\operatorname{cosec}^2\frac{1}{2}z\,dz+c$$

$$=(1+i)\cos\frac{1}{2}z+c$$

$$\Rightarrow\quad f(z)=\cot\frac{1}{2}z+\frac{c}{1+i}$$

$$\because\ f\left(\frac{\pi}{2}\right)=\frac{3-i}{2}$$

$$\Rightarrow\ \frac{c}{1+i}=f\left(\frac{\pi}{2}\right)-\cot\frac{\pi}{4}=\frac{3-i}{2}-1=\frac{1-i}{2}$$

which gives $c=\frac{1}{2}(1-i)$

Hence, $f(z)=\cot\frac{1}{2}z+\frac{1}{2}(1-i)$

**36.** Here, $u=e^x\cos y$

$$\Rightarrow\quad \frac{\partial u}{\partial x}=e^x\cos y,\ \frac{\partial u}{\partial y}=-e^x\sin y$$

and $$\frac{\partial^2 u}{\partial x^2}=e^x\cos y,\ \frac{\partial^2 u}{\partial y^2}=-e^x\cos y$$

Now, $\frac{\partial^2 u}{\partial x^2}+\frac{\partial^2 u}{\partial y^2}=0$, so $u$ satisfies Laplace's equation.

Also, first and second order partial derivatives of $u$ are continuous, therefore, $u$ is a harmonic function.

Since, $v$ is the harmonic conjugate of $u$, therefore.

$$dv=\frac{\partial v}{\partial x}dx+\frac{\partial v}{\partial y}dy \qquad [\because v=\phi(x,y)]$$

$$=-\frac{\partial u}{\partial y}dx+\frac{\partial u}{\partial x}dy \quad \text{(by Cauchy-Riemann equations)}$$

$$=e^x\sin y\,dx+e^x\cos y\,dy$$

On integration $v=e^x\sin y+c$,

Hence, $$f(z)=u+iv=e^x\cos y+i(e^x\sin y+c)$$

$$=e^x(\cos y+i\sin y)+ic=e^{x+iy}+d$$

$$=e^z+d$$

# 12 Complex Integration and Calculus of Residues

**Syllabus**

- Contour Integral
- Cauchy's Theorem
- Cauchy's Integral Formula
- Liouville's Theorem
- Maximum Modulus Principle
- Schwarz Lemma
- Open Mapping Theorem
- Taylor Series
- Laurent's Theorem
- Calculus of Residues

## Line Integral

For a real-valued function $f(x)$, definite integral $\int_a^b f(x)\,dx$ is calculated always along the real axis (x-axis), from $x = a$ to $x = b$ *i.e.*, path of integration is always along real-axis.

But for a complex function $f(z)$, the path of the definite integral $\int_a^b f(z)\,dz$ may be along any curve joining $z = a$ to $z = b$. *i.e.*, Value of the integral depends upon the path of integration.

In case the initial point and final point coincide, then curve C, is a closed curve and integral is called **contour integral** and is denoted by $\oint_C f(z)\,dz$.

If $f(z) = u(x, y) + i\,v(x, y)$, where

$$z = x + iy \Rightarrow dz = dx + i\,dy, \text{ then}$$

$$\int_C f(z)dz = \int_C (u + iv)(dx + idy)$$

$$= \int_C (udx - vdy) + i\int_C (vdx + udy)$$

Therefore, definite integral of $f(z)$ is reduced to two line integrals of real functions.

***Example 1.*** *Evaluate* $\int_0^{1+i} (x^2 - iy)\,dz$ *along* $y = x$.

**Solution.** Along the line $y = x$

$\Rightarrow$ $dy = dx$ and $dz = dx(1+i)$

Here, $z = x + iy = x(1+i)$

When $z = 0 \Rightarrow x = 0$ and

when $z = 1 + i \Rightarrow x = 1$

$\therefore$ Given, integral is

$$\int_0^1 (x^2 - ix)(1+i)\,dx$$

$$= (1+i)\left[\int_0^1 x^2 dx - i\int_0^1 x\,dx\right]$$

$$= (1+i)\left[\frac{x^3}{3} - i\frac{x^2}{2}\right]_0^1 = (1+i)\left(\frac{1}{3} - \frac{i}{2}\right) = \frac{5-i}{6}$$

## Complex Line Integral

$\int_L f(z)\,dz$ is called the complex line integral along rectifiable arc $L$ or definite integral of $f(z)$ from $a$ to $b$ along $L$ and

$$\int_L f(z)dz = \lim_{n\to\infty}\sum_{k=1}^{n}(z_k - z_{k-1})f(\zeta_k) \quad (ab - \text{initio method})$$

where, $\zeta_k$ is a point on each arc joining the points $z_{k-1}$ to $z_k$.

> ***Note*** An arc $z = z(t) = x(t) + iy(t), a \le t \le b$ is rectifiable if and only if the functions $x(t)$ and $y(t)$ are of bounded variation in $[a, b]$. Length of arc $l$ is given by
>
> $$l = \int_a^b \sqrt{\{x'(t)\}^2 + \{y'(t)\}^2}\,dt \quad \text{or} \quad l = \int_a^b |z'(t)|dt$$

## Properties of Complex Line Integrals

**(i)** $\int_L \{f(z) + \phi(z)\}\,dz = \int_L f(z)dz + \int_L \phi(z)dz$

We can generalize this property for a finite number of functions.

**(ii)** $\int_L f(z)dz = -\int_{-L} f(z)dz$, where $-L$ is the opposite arc of $L$.

**(iii)** $\int_{L_1+L_2} f(z)dz = \int_{L_1} f(z)dz + \int_{L_2} f(z)dz$,

where the end point of $L_1$ coincides with the initial point of $L_2$.

**(iv)** $\int_L cf(z)dz = c\int_L f(z)dz$, where $c$ is any complex constant.

**(v)** $\int_L [c_1f_1(z) + c_2f_2(z) + \ldots + c_nf_n(z)]\,dz$

$$= c_1\int_L f_1(z)dz + c_2\int_L f_2(z)\,dz + \ldots + c_n\int_L f_n(z)\,dz,$$

where $c_1, c_2 \ldots, c_n$ are complex constants.

**(vi)** $\left|\int_L f(z)\,dz\right| \le \int_L |f(z)||dz|$

**(vii)** If a function $f(z)$ is continuous on a contour $L$ of length $l$ and if $M$ be the upper bound of $f(z)$ on $L$ i.e., $|f(z)| \le M$ on $L$, then

$$\left|\int_L f(z)\,dz\right| \le Ml$$

**(viii)** The line integral $\int p\,dx + qdy$, defined in a domain $D$, depends only on the end points of $\Gamma$ if and only if there exists a function $U(x, y)$ in $D$ such that

$$\frac{\partial U}{\partial x} = p \text{ and } \frac{\partial U}{\partial y} = q$$

***Example 2.*** *Evaluate* $\int_C (z^2 + 3z)dz$ *along the circle* $|z| = 2$ *from* (2, 0) *to* (0, 2).

**Solution.** We have, $z = x + iy\,;\, dz = dx + idy$

$$|z| = 2 \Rightarrow \sqrt{x^2 + y^2} = 2 \Rightarrow x^2 + y^2 = 4$$

Put $\quad x = 2\cos t, y = 2\sin t$

$t$ varies from 0 to $\frac{\pi}{2}$.

$\therefore \quad dx = -2\sin t\,dt, dy = 2\cos t\,dt$

$$z = 2(\cos t + i\sin t) = 2e^{it}$$

$$\Rightarrow \quad dz = (-2\sin t + 2\cos t)\,dt = 2e^{i((\pi/2)+t)}dt$$

$$\therefore \quad \int_C (z^2 + 3z)\,dz = \int_0^{\pi/2}[(2e^{it})^2 + 3\cdot 2e^{it}]2e^{i((\pi/2)+t)}dt$$

$$= 2\int_0^{\pi/2}(4e^{2it} + 6e^{it})\,e^{i((\pi/2)+t)}dt$$

$$= 8\int_0^{\pi/2} e^{i((\pi/2)+3t)} + 12\int_0^{\pi/2} e^{i((\pi/2)+2t)}dt$$

$$= \left[8\cdot\frac{e^{i((\pi/2)+t)}}{3i} + 12\cdot\frac{e^{i((\pi/2)+2t)}}{2i}\right]_0^{\pi/2}$$

$$= \frac{8}{3i}(e^{\pi i} - e^{\pi i/2}) + \frac{12}{2i}(e^{3\pi i/2} - e^{i\pi/2})$$

$$= \frac{8}{3i}(-1 - i) + \frac{6}{i}(-i - i) = -\frac{8}{3i} - \frac{8}{3} - 12$$

$$= -\frac{8i}{3} - \frac{44}{3} = -\left(\frac{44}{3} + \frac{8i}{3}\right)$$

***Example 3.*** *Evaluate* $\int_L \frac{dz}{z-a}$, *where L represents the circle* $|z - a| = r$.

**Solution.** Parametric equation of the circle $|z - a| = r$ is

$$z = a + re^{i\theta}, \text{ where } 0 \le \theta \le 2\pi$$

$$\therefore \quad dz = ire^{i\theta}d\theta$$

Hence, $$\int_L \frac{dz}{z-a} = \int_0^{2\pi}\frac{ir\,e^{i\theta}}{re^{i\theta}}d\theta = i\int_0^{2\pi}d\theta = i[\theta]_0^{2\pi} = 2\pi i$$

***Example 4.*** *Evaluate* $\int_L \frac{z+2}{z}dz$, *where L is the semi-circle* $z = 2e^{it}, 0 \le t \le \pi$.

**Solution.** We have, $\quad z = 2e^{it},\ 0 \le t \le \pi$

$$\Rightarrow \quad dz = 2ie^{it}dt$$

Hence, $$\int_L \frac{z+2}{z}dz = \int_0^{\pi}\frac{(2e^{it} + 2)}{2e^{it}}2i\,e^{it}dt$$

$$= 2i\int_0^{\pi}(1 + e^{-it})\,e^{it}dt$$

$$= 2i\int_0^{\pi}(e^{it} + 1)\,dt = 2i\left[\frac{e^{it}}{i} + t\right]_0^{\pi}$$

$$= 2i\left(\frac{e^{i\pi}}{i} - \frac{1}{i} + \pi\right)$$

$$= 2e^{i\pi} - 2 + 2i\pi = -4 + 2i\pi$$

***Example 5.*** *Evaluate* $\int_C f(z)\,dz$, *where* $f(z) = y - x - 3x^2 i$ *and C*

*(i) is the line segment from* $z = 0$ *to* $z = 1 + i$.

*(ii) consists of two line segments, one from* $z = 0$ *to* $z = i$ *and the other from* $z = i$ *to* $z = 1 + i$.

**Solution.** We have, $f(z) = y - x - 3x^2 i$

(i) Equation of the line joining $z = 0$ and $z = 1 + i$ is

$$y = x.$$

$$\Rightarrow \quad dy = dx$$

$\Rightarrow \quad dz = (1+i)\,dx$ and $x$ varies from 0 to 1.

$$\therefore \int_C f(z)dz = \int_0^1 -3x^2 i(1+i)dx$$

$$= -i(1+i)[x^3]_0^1 = -i(1+i) = 1-i$$

(ii) Along the line $z = 0$, to $z = i$, we have $x = 0, y$ varies from 0 to 1.

$\Rightarrow \quad dx = 0$ and $dz = i\,dy$

$$\therefore \int_C f(z)dz = \int_0^1 y\,dy = i\left[\frac{y^2}{2}\right]_0^1 = \frac{i}{2}$$

Now, along the line $z = i$ to $z = 1+i$, $y = 1$ and $x$ varies from 0 to 1.

$\Rightarrow \quad dy = 0$ and $dz = dx$

$$\therefore \int_C f(z)dz = \int_0^1 (1 - x - 3x^2 i)\,dx = \left[x - \frac{x^2}{2} - x^3 i\right]_0^1$$

$$= \frac{1}{2} - i$$

$$\therefore \int_C f(z)dz = \frac{i}{2} + \frac{1}{2} - i = \frac{1-i}{2}$$

# Important Terms

## (i) Simply Connected Region (or domain)

A connected region or domain ($D$) is said to be a simply connected, if a closed curve $C$, contained in $D$ has its interior contained in $D$, *i.e.*, there is no hole.

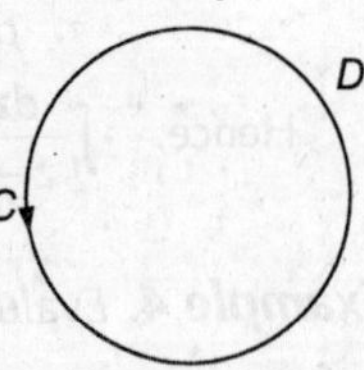


## (ii) Multiple Connected Region

A domain that is not simply connected, *i.e.*, there are some holes called multiple connected region. Multiple connected region is bounded by more than one curve.

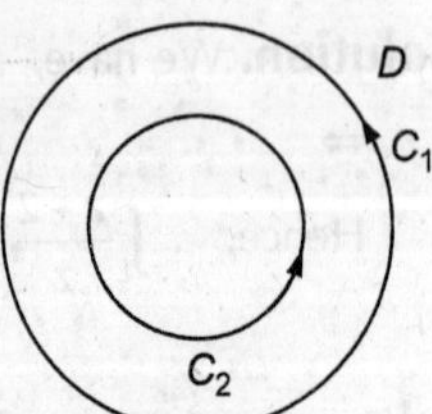


Any multiplically connected region can be reduced to a simply connected region by giving it one or more cuts.

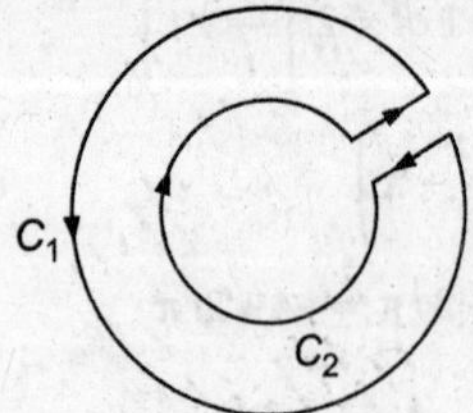


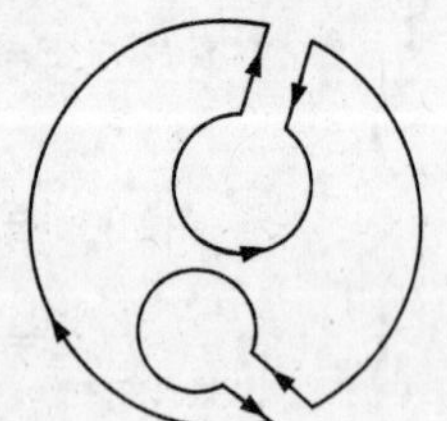

## (iii) Multiple Point

If satisfied by more than one value of the variable in the given range, then the point is called a multiple point of the curve.

## (iv) Jordan Arc

A continuous arc without multiple points is called a Jordan arc.

## (v) Regular Arc

If the derivatives of the given functions are also continuous in the given range, then the arc is said to be a regular arc.

## (vi) Contour

A contour is a Jordan curve consisting of continuous chain of a finite number of regular arc $S$.

The contour is said to be closed if the starting point $A$ coincides with end point $B$.

# Important Theorems

## Cauchy's Theorem

Let $D$ be a simply connected region and let $f(z)$ be a single valued continuously differentiable function on $D$, *i.e.*, $f'(z)$ exists and is continuous at each point of $D$. Then,

$$\int_C f(z)dz = 0,$$

where $C$ is any closed contour contained in $D$.

### Cauchy's Theorem for any Closed Curve

If $f(z)$ is analytic in a simply connected domain $D$ and $C$ is any closed curve, then

$$\int_C f(z)dz = 0$$

### Application of Cauchy's Theorem to Multiple Connected Region

Let $D$ be a doubly connected region bounded by two simple closed curves $C_1$ and $C_2$ such that $C_2$ is contained in $C_1$ and $f(z)$ is analytic in the region between these curves and continuous on $C_1$, then

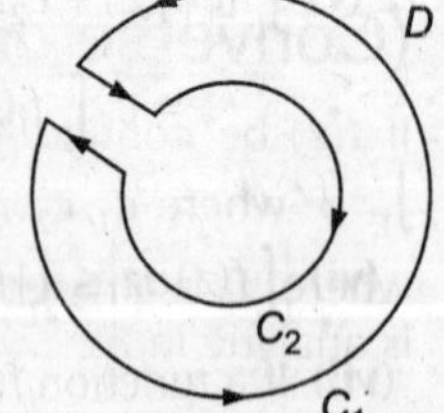


$$\int_{C_1} f(z)dz = \int_{C_2} f(z)dz$$

where, both $C_1$ and $C_2$ are transversed in the positive sense *i.e.*, in anti-clockwise direction.

Similarly, for $n$ curves $C_1, C_2, C_3, \ldots, C_n$

We have,

$$\int_{C_1} f(z)dz = \int_{C_2} f(z)dz + \int_{C_3} f(z)\,dz + \ldots + \int_{C_n} f(z)dz$$

## Cauchy's Integral Formula

Let $f(z)$ be an analytic function in a simply connected domain $D$ enclosed by a rectifiable Jordan Curve $C$ and let $f(z)$ be continuous on $C$. Then,

$$f(z_0) = \frac{1}{2\pi i}\int_C \frac{f(z)}{(z - z_0)}dz$$

where $z_0$ is any point of $C$.

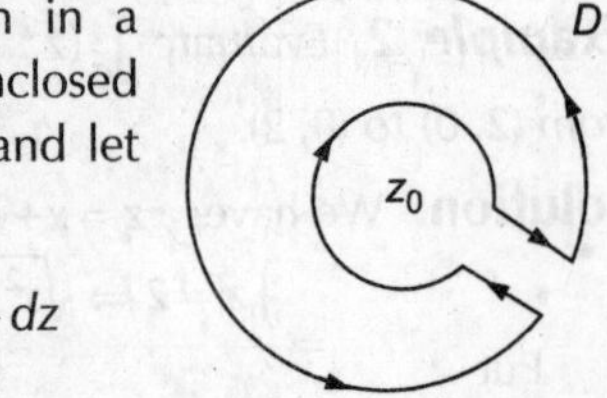

## Derivative Form of Cauchy's Integral Formula

Let $f(z)$ be analytic function within and on the boundary $C$ of a simply connected region $D$ and let $z_0$ be any point within $C$. Then,

$$f^n(z_0) = \frac{n!}{2\pi i}\int_C \frac{f(z)}{(z-z_0)^{n+1}}dz$$

**Proof.** From Cauchy's integral formula,

$$f(z_0) = \frac{1}{2\pi i}\int_C \frac{f(z)}{(z-z_0)}dz \qquad \text{...(i)}$$

Differentiating Eq. (i) both sides w.r.t. '$z_0$', we get

$$f'(z_0) = \frac{1}{2\pi i}\int_C \frac{f(z)}{(z-z_0)^2}dz \qquad \text{...(ii)}$$

Now, differentiating Eq. (ii) both sides w.r.t. '$z_0$', we get

$$f''(z_0) = \frac{2!}{2\pi i}\int_C \frac{f(z)}{(z-z_0)^3}dz \qquad \text{...(iii)}$$

Similarly,

$$f'''(z_0) = \frac{3!}{2\pi i}\int_C \frac{f(z)}{(z-z_0)^4}dz \qquad \text{...(iv)}$$

Proceeding in the same way, we get

$$f^n(z_0) = \frac{n!}{2\pi i}\int_C \frac{f(z)}{(z-z_0)^{n+1}}dz$$

or $$\int_C \frac{f(z)}{(z-z_0)^{n+1}}dz = 2\pi i\frac{f^n(z_0)}{n!}$$

## Morera Theorem (Converse of Cauchy's Theorem)

If $f(z)$ be continuous in a simply connected domain $D$ and $\int_\Gamma f(z)dz = 0$

where, $\Gamma$ is any rectifiable closed Jordon curve in $D$, then $f(z)$ is analytic in $D$.

## Cauchy's Inequality

Let $f(z)$ be analytic in a domain $D$ and let $D$ contain the interior and the boundary of the circle $\gamma$ defined by $|z-z_0| = r$ and if $|f(z)| \le M$ on $\gamma$, then

$$|f^n(z_0)| \le n!\frac{M}{r^n}$$

**Proof.** We have $f^n(z_0) = \dfrac{n!}{2\pi i}\displaystyle\int_\gamma \frac{f(z)}{(z-z_0)^{n+1}}dz$

$$\Rightarrow\ |f^n(z_0)| = \left|\frac{n!}{2\pi i}\int_\gamma \frac{f(z)}{(z-z_0)^{n+1}}dz\right| \le \frac{n!}{2\pi}\int_\gamma \frac{|f(z)|}{|z-z_0|^{n+1}}|dz|$$

$$\le \frac{n!}{2\pi}\cdot\frac{M}{r^{n+1}}\int_\gamma |dz| \qquad [\because |f(z)| \le M]$$

$$= \frac{n!}{2\pi}\cdot\frac{M}{r^{n+1}}2\pi r$$

Hence, $|f^n(z_0)| \le n!\cdot\dfrac{M}{r^n}$

## Liouville's Theorem

If $f(z)$ is an analytic function satisfying the inequality $|f(z)| \le M$ for all values of $z$, where $M$ is a positive constant, then $f(z)$ is constant.

## Maximum Modulus Principle

Let $f(z)$ be analytic within and on a simple closed contour $C$. Then, $|f(z)|$ reaches its maximum value on $C$, unless $f(z)$ is constant. In other words, if $|f(z)| \le M$ on and within $C$, then unless $f$ is a constant, $|f(z)| < M$ for every point within $C$.

## Schwarz Lemma

If $f(z)$ is analytic in a domain $D$ defined by $|z| < R$ and satisfies the conditions $|f(z)| \le M$ for all $z \in D$ and $f(0) = 0$, then $|f(z)| \le \dfrac{M}{R}|z|$.

Also, if the equality occurs for any $z$, then $f(z) = \dfrac{M}{R}ze^{i\alpha}$, where $\alpha$ is a real constant.

or If $D = \{z : |z| < 1\}$ and if $f(z)$ is analytic on $D$ with

(a) $|f(z)| \le 1$ for all $z \in D$

(b) $f(0) = 0$, then

$|f'(0)| \le 1$ and $|f(z)| \le |z|$

for all $z$ in $D$.

In case of equality $f(z) - e^{i\alpha}z$, where $\alpha$ is a real constant. Moreover, if $|f'(0)| = 1$ or $|f(z)| = |z|$ for some $z \ne 0$, then there is a constant $c$, $|c| = 1$, such that $f(w) = cw$ for all $w \in D$.

## The Riemann Mapping Theorem

A region $D$ is conformally equivalent to $C$ if there is analytic function $f : D \to C$ such that $f$ is one-one and $f(D) = C$.

If $D$ is a simple connected region which is not the whole plane and let $z_0 \in D$, then there is a unique analytic function $f : D \to C$, with the property.

(a) $f(z_0) = 0$ and $f'(z_0) > 0$

(b) $f$ is one-one.

(c) $f(D) = \{z : |z| < 1\}$

## The Open Mapping Theorem

Let $D$ be a region and suppose $f$ is a non-constant analytic function on $D$. Then, for any open set $U$ in $D$, $f(U)$ is open.

***Example* 6.** *Evaluate* $\displaystyle\int_C \frac{1}{z(z-1)}dz$, *where* $C$ *is the circle* $|z| = 3$?

**Solution.** $|z| = 3$ is a circle with centre at origin and radius 3.

Now, $z(z-1) = 0$ at $z = 0$ and $z = 1$

*i.e.,* $z = 0$ is at $O(0,0)$ and $z = 1$ is at $A(1,0)$.

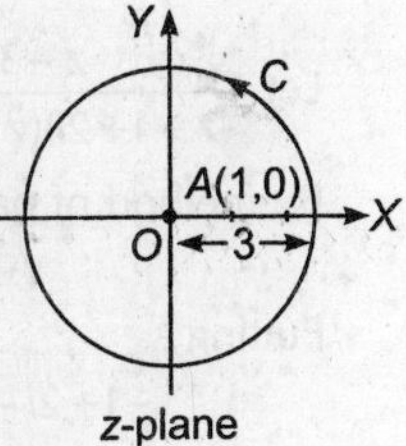

Since, these points are within $C$, we write $f(z)=1$, which is analytic everywhere

and $\dfrac{1}{z(z-1)}=\dfrac{A}{z}+\dfrac{B}{z-1}$

$\therefore$ By the method of partial fractions, we have

$\Rightarrow \quad 1=A(z-1)+Bz$

Putting $z=0$ and $z=1$, we get

$A=-1$ and $B=1$

Hence, $\dfrac{1}{z(z-1)}=\dfrac{1}{z-1}-\dfrac{1}{z}$

$$\therefore \int_C \frac{1}{z(z-1)}dz=\int_C \frac{f(z)}{z(z-1)}dz=\int_C \frac{f(z)}{z-1}dz-\int_C \frac{f(z)}{z}dz \quad \text{...(i)}$$

But by Cauchy's integral formula, we have

$$\int_C \frac{f(z)}{z-1}dz=2\pi i\, f(1) \quad [\because z_0=1]$$

$$=2\pi i \quad [\because f(1)=1]$$

and $\displaystyle\int_C \frac{f(z)}{z}dz=\int_C \frac{f(z)}{z-0}dz=2\pi i\, f(0) \quad [\because z_0=0]$

$$=2\pi i \quad [\because f(0)=1]$$

Hence, from Eq. (i), we have

$$\int_C \frac{1}{z(z-1)}dz=2\pi i-2\pi i=0$$

***Example 7.*** *Evaluate* $\displaystyle\int_C \frac{z-1}{(z+1)^2(z-2)}dz$ *where,* $C:|z-i|=2$.

**Solution.** $|z-i|=2$ is a circle with centre $(0,1)$ and radius 2.

Now, poles are given by putting denominator equal to zero.

$\Rightarrow \quad (z+1)^2(z-2)=0$

$\Rightarrow \quad z=-1,-1,2$

Here, double pole at $z=-1$ and simple pole at $z=2$, out of which only $z=-1$ lies inside contour $C$.

Hence, $\displaystyle\int_C \frac{z-1}{(z+1)^2(z-2)}dz=\int_C \frac{\left(\frac{z-1}{z-2}\right)}{(z+1)^2}dz$

$$=2\pi i\, f'(-1)=\frac{-2\pi i}{9}$$

(from derivative form of Cauchy's integral formula)

where $f(z)=\dfrac{z-1}{z-2}\Rightarrow f'(z)=-\dfrac{1}{(z-2)^2}\Rightarrow f'(-1)=-\dfrac{1}{9}$

***Example 8.*** *Evaluate* $\displaystyle\int_C \frac{z-3}{z^2+2z+5}dz$, *where C is circle*

(i) $|z|=1$ (ii) $|z+1-i|=2$.

**Solution.** (i) Here, $z^2+2z+5=z^2+2z+1+4$

$$=(z+1)^2-(2i)^2=(z+1+2i)(z+1-2i)$$

Let $\dfrac{z-3}{(z+1+2i)(z+1-2i)}=\dfrac{A}{z+1+2i}+\dfrac{B}{z+1-2i}$

By method of partial fractions, we have

$\therefore \quad z-3=A(z+1-2i)+B(z+1+2i)$

Putting $z=-1+2i$, we get

$-1+2i-3=A(0)+B(-1+2i+1+2i)$

$\Rightarrow \quad -4+2i=4iB$

$\Rightarrow \quad B=\dfrac{2i-4}{4i}=\dfrac{1}{2}+i$

Putting $z=-1-2i$, we get

$-1-2i-3=A(-1-2i+1-2i)$

$\Rightarrow \quad -4-2i=-4iA$

$\Rightarrow \quad A=\dfrac{4+2i}{4i}=\dfrac{1}{2}-i$

$$\therefore \quad \frac{z-3}{z^2+2z+5}=\frac{\frac{1}{2}-i}{z+1+2i}+\frac{\frac{1}{2}+i}{z+1-2i}$$

$$\therefore \int_C \frac{z-3}{z^2+2z+5}dz=\left(\frac{1}{2}-i\right)\int_C \frac{1}{z+1+2i}dz+\left(\frac{1}{2}+i\right)\int_C \frac{1}{z+1-2i}dz$$

$f(z)=\dfrac{1}{z+1-2i}$ is analytic within and on the circle $|z|=1$, as the pole $z=-1-2i$ lies outside the circle $|z|=1$.

$$\therefore \int_C \frac{1}{z+1+2i}dz=0, \quad \text{(by Cauchy's integral theorem)}$$

Similarly, $f(z)=\dfrac{1}{z+1-2i}$ is analytic within and on the circle $|z|=1$ as the pole $z=-1+2i$ lies outside the circle $|z|=1$.

$$\therefore \int_C \frac{1}{z+1-2i}dz=0 \quad \text{(by Cauchy's integral theorem)}$$

$$\therefore \int_C \frac{z-3}{z^2+2z+5}dz=0$$

(ii) $|z+1-i|=2$ is the circle with centre $-1+i$ and radius 2. The point $-1-2i$ lies outside the circle $|z+1-i|=2$ and the point $-1+2i$ lies inside the circle $|z+1-i|=2$.

$$\therefore \int_C \frac{1}{z+1+2i}dz=0, \text{ (by Cauchy's integral theorem)}$$

and $\displaystyle\int_C \frac{1}{z+1-2i}dz=2\pi i(1)$,

Since, $f(z)=1\Rightarrow f(-1+2i)=1$

$$=2\pi i$$

$$\therefore \int_C \frac{z-3}{z^2+2z+5}dz=\left(\frac{1}{2}-i\right)0+\left(\frac{1}{2}+i\right)2\pi i$$

$$=\pi i-2\pi=\pi(-2+i)$$

***Example 9.*** *Evaluate the following integrals by using Cauchy's integral formula*

(i) $\displaystyle\int_C \frac{\sin\pi z^2+\cos\pi z^2}{(z-1)(z-2)}dz$ (ii) $\displaystyle\frac{1}{2\pi i}\int_C \frac{e^{zt}}{z^2+1}dz,\ t>0$,

*where C represents the circle* $|z|=3$.

**Solution.** (i) We have, $\dfrac{1}{(z-1)(z-2)}=\dfrac{1}{z-2}-\dfrac{1}{z-1}$

Now, $\displaystyle\int_C \frac{\sin\pi z^2+\cos\pi z^2}{(z-1)(z-2)}dz$

$$=\int_C\left(\frac{1}{z-2}-\frac{1}{z-1}\right)f(z)\,dz,$$

where, $f(z) = \sin \pi z^2 + \cos \pi z^2$ is analytic within and on C

$$= \int_C \frac{f(z)}{z-2} dz - \int_C \frac{f(z)}{z-1} dz$$

$$= 2\pi i\, f(2) - 2\pi i\, f(1)$$

$$= 2\pi i[(\sin \pi \cdot 2^2 + \cos \pi \cdot 2^2) - (\sin \pi \cdot 1^2 + \cos \pi \cdot 1^2)]$$

$$= 2\pi i[1-(-1)] = 4\pi i$$

(ii) We have, $\dfrac{1}{z^2+1} = \dfrac{1}{(z+i)(z-i)} = \dfrac{1}{2i}\left(\dfrac{1}{z-i} - \dfrac{1}{z+i}\right)$

Now, $\dfrac{1}{2\pi i}\displaystyle\int_C \frac{e^{zt}}{z^2+1} dz = \frac{1}{2\pi i}\int_C \frac{1}{2i}\left(\frac{1}{z-i} - \frac{1}{z+i}\right)e^{zt} dz$

$$= \frac{1}{2i}\left[\frac{1}{2\pi i}\int_C \frac{f(z)}{z-i} dz - \frac{1}{2\pi i}\int_C \frac{f(z)}{z+i} dz\right],$$

where, $f(z) = e^{zt}$ is analytic within and on C

$$= \frac{1}{2i}[f(i) - f(-i)]$$

$$= \frac{1}{2i}(e^{it} - e^{-it}) = \sin t$$

***Example 10.*** *Evaluate* $\displaystyle\int_C \frac{e^z}{(z-2)} dz$, *where C is the circle*

(i) $|z| = 3$ (ii) $|z| = 1$.

**Solution.** (i) Let $f(z) = e^z$

$e^z$ is analytic in the z-plane. $a = 2$ lies inside the circle $|z| = 3$.

∴ By Cauchy's integral formula,

$$\frac{1}{2\pi i}\int_C \frac{e^z}{(z-2)} dz = f(2) = e^2 \Rightarrow \int_C \frac{e^z}{z-2} dz = 2\pi i e^2$$

(ii) Let $f(z) = \dfrac{e^z}{z-2}$

∴ $\dfrac{e^z}{z-2}$ is analytic within and on the circle $|z| = 1$ as $z = 2$ lies outside $|z| = 1$.

Hence, from Cauchy's integral theorem, $\displaystyle\int_C \frac{e^z}{z-2} dz = 0.$

***Example 11.*** *Evaluate* $\displaystyle\int_C \frac{z^2-4}{z(z^2+9)} dz$, *where C is the circle* $|z| = 1$

**Solution.** Here, $|z| = 1$ is a circle of unit radius with centre at the origin.

Now, $z(z^2+9) = 0$

$\Rightarrow$ $z = 0$ or $z^2 + 9 = 0$

$\Rightarrow$ $z = 0$ or $z = \pm 3i$

*i.e.*, $z(z^2+9) = 0$ at the points

(i) $z = 0$ or (0, 0) which lies inside C

(ii) $z = \pm 3i$ or (0, 3), (0, −3) which lie outside C.

Y, C, X, O, ←···1···→, z-plane

We have, $f(z) = \dfrac{z^3-4}{z^2+9}$ which is clearly analytic within and on C.

$$\therefore \int_C \frac{z^2-4}{z(z^2+9)} dz = \int_C \frac{f(z)}{z} dz$$

$$= \int_C \frac{f(z)}{z-0} dz = 2\pi i\, f(0)$$

(from Cauchy's integral formula)

But $f(0) = \dfrac{0-4}{0+9} = -\dfrac{4}{9}$

Hence, $\displaystyle\int_C \frac{z^2-4}{z(z^2+9)} dz = 2\pi i\left(-\frac{4}{9}\right) = -\frac{8\pi i}{9}$

***Example 12.*** *Evaluate* $\displaystyle\int \frac{e^{az}}{z^2+1} dz$, *where C is the circle* $|z| = 2$, *where a is measured in radians.*

**Solution.** Here, $|z| = 2$ is a circle with centre at the origin and radius 2.

Now, $z^2 + 1 = 0 \Rightarrow z = \pm i$

∴ $z^2 + 1 = 0$ at the points $z = -i$ and $z = +i$

*i.e.*, at $A(0, -1)$ and $B(0, 1)$.

Let $f(z) = e^{az}$ which is clearly analytic within and on C.

Also, $\dfrac{1}{z^2+1} = \dfrac{1}{(z+i)(z-i)}$

$$= \frac{A}{z+i} + \frac{B}{z-i}$$

Y, B (0, 1), X, O, ←··· 2 ···→, A (0, −1), z-plane

By method of partial fraction, we have

$\Rightarrow$ $1 = A(z-i) + B(z+i)$

Putting $z = i$ and $z = -i$, we get

$$A = -\frac{1}{2i} \text{ and } B = \frac{1}{2i}$$

$$\therefore \frac{1}{z^2+1} = \frac{1}{2i}\cdot\frac{1}{z-i} - \frac{1}{2i}\cdot\frac{1}{z+i}$$

$$\therefore \int_C \frac{e^{az}}{z^2+1} dz = \frac{1}{2i}\int_C \frac{f(z)}{z-i} dz - \frac{1}{2i}\int_C \frac{f(z)}{z+i} dz$$

$$= \frac{1}{2i}\int_C \frac{f(z)}{z+i} dz - \frac{1}{2i}\int_C \frac{f(z)}{z-(-i)} dz$$

$$= \frac{1}{2i} 2\pi i\, f(i) - \frac{1}{2i} 2\pi i\, f(-i) = \pi[f(i) - f(-i)]$$

But $f(i) = e^{ai}$ and $f(-i) = e^{-ai}$

$$\therefore \int_C \frac{e^{az}}{z^2+1} dz = \pi[e^{ai} - e^{-ai}] = 2\pi i \sin a,$$

where a is measured in radians.

***Example 13.*** *Evaluate* $\displaystyle\int_C \frac{e^{2z}}{(z+1)^4} dz$, *where the path of integration C is* $|z| = 3$.

**Solution.** We have, $f(z) = e^{2z}$, which is analytic within and on C. Now applying,

$$f^n(a) = \frac{n!}{2\pi i}\int_C \frac{f(z)}{(z-a)^{n+1}} dz$$

We have, $f^3(-1) = \dfrac{3!}{2\pi i}\displaystyle\int_C \frac{e^{2z}}{(z+1)^{3+1}} dz$

$$\Rightarrow \int_C \frac{e^{2z}}{(z+1)^4}dz = \frac{2\pi i}{6} f^3(-1) = \frac{\pi i}{3}[f^3(z)]_{z=-1}$$

$$= \frac{\pi i}{3}[2^3 e^{2z}]_{z=-1} = \frac{\pi i}{3}\cdot 8e^{-2} = \frac{8\pi i}{3e^2}$$

Hence, $\int_C \frac{e^{2z}}{(z+1)^4}dz = \frac{8\pi i}{3e^2}$

***Example 14.*** *Using Cauchy's integral formula, calculate the following integrals:*

(i) $\int_C \frac{z\,dz}{(9-z^2)(z+i)}$, *where C is the circle* $|z|=2$ *described in positive sense.*

(ii) $\int_C \frac{\cosh(\pi z)dz}{z(z^2+1)}$, *where C is circle* $|z|=2$.

(iii) $\int_C \frac{e^{az}dz}{(z-\pi i)}$, *where C is the ellipse* $|z-2|+|z+2|=6$.

(iv) $\int_C \frac{dz}{z-2}$, *where C is* $|z|=3$.

**Solution.** By Cauchy's integral formula, $f(a) = \frac{1}{2\pi i}\int_C \frac{f(z)\,dz}{z-a}$

or $$\int_C \frac{f(z)}{z-a}dz = 2\pi i\, f(a) \quad \text{...(i)}$$

where $z=a$ is a point inside contour C and $f(z)$ is analytic within and upon C.

(i) Let $I = \int_C \frac{zdz}{(9-z^2)(z+i)}$

Take $f(z) = \frac{z}{9-z^2}$

Here, $f(z)$ is analytic within and upon $C: |z|=2$ and $z=-i$ lies inside C.

Then,

$$I = \int_C \frac{f(z)}{[z-(-i)]} = 2\pi i\, f(-i), \quad \text{[by Eq. (i)]}$$

$$= 2\pi i\left[\frac{-i}{9-(-i)^2}\right] = \frac{2\pi}{9+1} = \frac{\pi}{5}$$

(ii) Let $I = \int_C \frac{\cosh(\pi z)}{z(z^2+1)}dz$

Take $f(z) = \cosh(\pi z)$
$= \cos(i\pi z)$

Then, $I = \int_C \frac{f(z)}{z(z^2+1)}$

$$= \int_C \left[\frac{A}{z} + \frac{B}{z-i} + \frac{C}{z+i}\right] f(z)dz \quad \text{...(ii)}$$

By method of partial fraction, we have

$$\frac{1}{z(z-i)(z+i)} = \frac{A}{z} + \frac{B}{z-i} + \frac{C}{z+i}$$

Then, $A = 1, B = -\frac{1}{2}, C = -\frac{1}{2}$

Here, $z = 0, i, -i$ are points lie inside C.

According to Eqs. (i) and (ii) gives

$$I = 2\pi i[Af(0) + B(f(i) + Cf(-i)]$$

$$= 2\pi i[f(0) - \frac{1}{2}f(i) - \frac{1}{2}f(-i)]$$

$$= 2\pi i[\cos(0) - \frac{1}{2}\cos(i^2\pi) - \frac{1}{2}\cos(-i^2\pi)]$$

$$= 2\pi i[1 + \frac{1}{2} + \frac{1}{2}] = 4\pi i$$

(iii) Let $I = \int_C \frac{e^{az}dz}{z-\pi i}$,

where C is ellipse given by $|z-2|+|z+2|=6$

$\Rightarrow [(x-2)^2+y^2]^{1/2} = 6 - [(x+2)^2+y^2]^{1/2}$

On squaring, we get

$x^2+y^2+4-4x = 36+(x^2+y^2+4+4x) - 12[(x+2)^2+y^2]^{1/2}$

$\Rightarrow 12(x^2+y^2+4+4x)^{1/2} = 36+8x$

$\Rightarrow 3(x^2+y^2+4+4x)^{1/2} = 9+2x$

Again squaring, we get

$$9(x^2+y^2+4+4x) = 81+4x^2+36x$$

$$\Rightarrow 5x^2+9y^2 = 45 \text{ or } \frac{x^2}{9}+\frac{y^2}{5} = 1$$

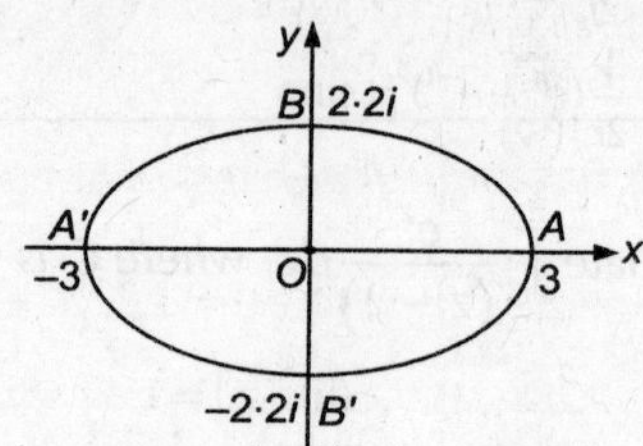


Comparing with $\frac{x^2}{a^2}+\frac{y^2}{b^2} = 1$, we get

$$a^2 = 9,\ b^2 = 5$$

$\therefore$ $a = 3,\ b = \sqrt{5} = 2.2$ (approx)

Evidently, $z = \pi i = 3.14\,i$ lies outside C.

Hence, $\frac{e^{az}}{z-\pi i}$ is analytic within and upon C.

$\therefore$ $I = 0$, by Cauchy's theorem

(iv) Let $$I = \int_C \frac{dz}{z-2} = \int_C \frac{f(z)dz}{z-a} \quad \text{...(ii)}$$

Then, $a=2$, $f(z)=1$. C is circle $|z|=3$ whose centre is at $z=0$ and radius $=3$.

$\therefore$ $a=2$ lies inside C.

According to Eqs. (i) and (ii) gives

$$I = 2\pi i\, f(a) = 2\pi i\, f(2) = 2\pi i(1) = 2\pi i$$

$[\because f(z)=1 \Rightarrow f(2)=1]$

# Expansion of Analytic Functions as Power Series

## Taylor's Theorem

Let $f(z)$ be analytic at all points within a circle $C_0$ with centre $z_0$ and radius $r_0$. Then, for every point $z$ within $C_0$, we have

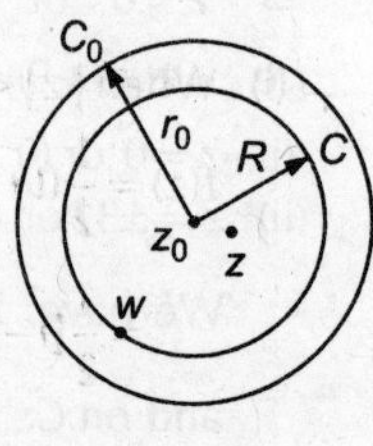


$f(z) = f(z_0) + f'(z_0)(z-z_0)$
$+ \frac{f''(z_0)}{2!}(z-z_0)^2 + \ldots + \frac{f^n(z_0)}{n!}(z-z_0)^n + \ldots$

$$= f(z_0) + \sum_{n=1}^{\infty} \frac{(z-z_0)^n}{n!} f^n(z_0)$$

If we put $z_0 = 0$ in the above series, we get

$f(z) = f(0) + \sum_{n=1}^{\infty} \frac{z^n}{n!} f^n(0)$, which is known as **Maclaurin's series.**

> ***Note*** For the validity of the expansion as a Taylor's series, it is essential that $f(z)$ be analytic at all points inside the circle $C_0$ for then the convergence of Taylor's series for $f(z)$ is assured.
> If $f(z)$ is not analytic at $z = z_0$, then $f(z)$ is expanded about $z = z_0$ by Laurent's method.

## Laurent's Theorem

Let $f(z)$ be analytic in the ring shaped region $D$ bounded by two concentric circles $C_1$ and $C_2$ with centre $z_0$ and radii $r_1$ and $r_2 (r_1 > r_2)$ and let $z$ be any point of $D$. Then,

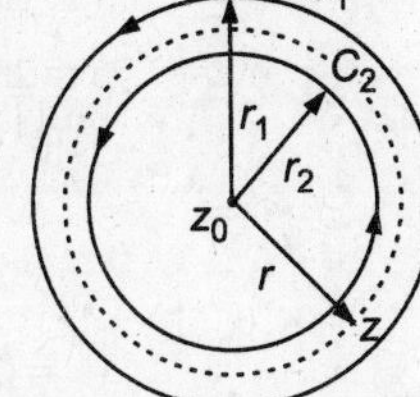


$$f(z) = \sum_{n=0}^{\infty} a_n (z - z_0)^n + \sum_{n=1}^{\infty} b_n (z - z_0)^{-n}$$

where $a_n = \frac{1}{2\pi i} \int_{C_1} \frac{f(w)}{(w - z_0)^{n+1}} dw$

and $b_n = \frac{1}{2\pi i} \int_{C_2} (w - z_0)^{n-1} f(w)\, dw,\ n = 1, 2, 3, \ldots$

> ***Note*** We have, $b_n = a_{-n}$. Therefore, if $C$ is any circle of radius $r$ and centre $z_0$ such that $r_2 < r < r_1$, then since the integrand is analytic in $r_2 < |w - z_0| < r_1$, we can write
>
> $a_n = \frac{1}{2\pi i} \int_C \frac{f(w)}{(w - z_0)^{n+1}} dw$ and
>
> $b_n = a_{-n} = \frac{1}{2\pi i} \int_C (w - z_0)^{n-1} f(w) dw$
>
> In this case the resulting series becomes
>
> $f(z) = \sum_{n=-\infty}^{\infty} a_n (z - z_0)^n$,
>
> where $a_n = \frac{1}{2\pi i} \int \frac{f(w)}{C(w - z_0)^{n+1}} dw$

***Example 15.*** *Expand* $f(z) = \frac{1}{(z+1)(z+3)}$ *in a Laurent's series valid for the regions*

(i) $|z| < 1$ (ii) $1 < |z| < 3$

(iii) $|z| > 3$ (iv) $0 < |z + 1| < 2$

**Solution.** We have, $f(z) = \frac{1}{(z+1)(z+3)}$

Resolving into partial fractions, we get

$$f(z) = \frac{1}{2(z+1)} - \frac{1}{2(z+3)}$$

(i) When $|z| < 1$. Then, we have

$$f(z) = \frac{1}{2}(1+z)^{-1} - \frac{1}{6}\left(1 + \frac{z}{3}\right)^{-1}$$

$$= \frac{1}{2}[1 - z + z^2 - z^3 + \ldots] - \frac{1}{6}\left[1 - \frac{z}{3} + \left(\frac{z}{3}\right)^2 - \left(\frac{z}{3}\right)^3 + \ldots\right]$$

$$= \left(\frac{1}{2} - \frac{1}{6}\right) - \left(\frac{1}{2} - \frac{1}{18}\right)z + \left(\frac{1}{2} - \frac{1}{54}\right)z^2 - \ldots$$

$$= \frac{1}{3} - \frac{4}{9}z + \frac{13}{27}z^2 - \ldots$$

which is the required Laurent's series.

(ii) When $1 < |z| < 3$. Then, we have

$$\frac{1}{|z|} < 1 \text{ and } \frac{|z|}{3} < 1$$

Now, $\frac{1}{2(z+1)} = \frac{1}{2z\left(1 + \frac{1}{z}\right)} = \frac{1}{2z}\left(1 + \frac{1}{z}\right)^{-1}$

$$= \frac{1}{2z}\left(1 - \frac{1}{z} + \frac{1}{z^2} - \frac{1}{z^3} + \ldots\right)$$

$$= \frac{1}{2z} - \frac{1}{2z^2} + \frac{1}{2z^3} - \ldots$$

and $\frac{1}{2(z+3)} = \frac{1}{6\left(1 + \frac{z}{3}\right)}$

$$= \frac{1}{6}\left(1 + \frac{z}{3}\right)^{-1} = \frac{1}{6}\left(1 - \frac{z}{3} + \frac{z^2}{9} - \frac{z^3}{27} + \ldots\right)$$

$$= \frac{1}{6} - \frac{1}{18}z + \frac{1}{54}z^2 - \frac{1}{162}z^3 + \ldots$$

Thus, the Laurent's series valid for the region $1 < |z| < 3$ is

$$f(z) = \ldots + \frac{1}{2z^3} - \frac{1}{2z^2} + \frac{1}{2z} - \frac{1}{6} + \frac{1}{18}z - \frac{1}{54}z^2 + \frac{1}{162}z^3 + \ldots$$

(iii) When $|z| > 3$. Then, we have $(3/|z|) < 1$

$$\therefore \quad f(z) = \frac{1}{2z}\left(1 + \frac{1}{z}\right)^{-1} - \frac{1}{2z}\left(1 + \frac{3}{z}\right)^{-1}$$

$$= \frac{1}{2z}\left(1 - \frac{1}{z} + \frac{1}{z^2} - \frac{1}{z^3} + \ldots\right)$$

$$- \frac{1}{2z}\left[1 - \frac{3}{z} + \left(\frac{3}{z}\right)^2 - \left(\frac{3}{z}\right)^2 + \ldots\right]$$

$$= \frac{1}{z^2} - \frac{4}{z^3} + \frac{13}{z^4} - \frac{40}{z^5} + \ldots$$

Which is the required Laurent's series.

(iv) Given that $0 < |z + 1| < 2$

Let $z + 1 = u$. Then, we have $0 < |u| < 2$

$$\therefore \quad f(z) = \frac{1}{(z+1)(z+3)} = \frac{1}{u(u+2)} = \frac{1}{2u}\left(1 + \frac{u}{2}\right)^{-1}$$

$$= \frac{1}{2u}\left[1 - \frac{u}{2} + \left(\frac{u}{2}\right)^2 - \left(\frac{u}{2}\right)^3 + \ldots\right]$$

$$= \frac{1}{2u} - \frac{1}{4} + \frac{u}{8} - \frac{u^2}{16} + \ldots$$

$$= \frac{1}{2(z+1)} - \frac{1}{4} + \frac{z+1}{8} - \frac{(z+1)^2}{16} + \ldots$$

Which is the required Laurent's series.

***Example 16.*** *Show that when* $0 < |z| < 4$,

$$\frac{1}{4z - z^2} = \sum_{n=0}^{\infty} \frac{z^{n-1}}{4^{n+1}}.$$

**Solution.** We have, $0<|z|<4$, then $\frac{|z|}{4}<1$

$$\therefore \quad \frac{1}{4z-z^2}=\frac{1}{4z(1-z/4)}=\frac{1}{4z}\left(1-\frac{z}{4}\right)^{-1}$$

$$=\frac{1}{4z}\left[1+\frac{z}{4}+\left(\frac{z}{4}\right)^2+\left(\frac{z}{4}\right)^3+\ldots\right]$$

$$=\frac{z^{-1}}{4}+\frac{1}{4^2}+\frac{z}{4^3}+\frac{z^2}{4^4}+\ldots$$

$$=\sum_{n=0}^{\infty}\frac{z^{n-1}}{4^{n+1}}$$

Which is the required series.

***Example 17.*** *Prove that*

$$\frac{1+2z}{z^2+z^3}=\frac{1}{z^2}+\frac{1}{z}-1+z-z^2+z^3\ldots,$$

*where* $0<|z|<1$

**Solution.** Let $f(z)=\frac{1+2z}{z^2+z^3}=\frac{1+2z}{z^2(1+z)}$

Resolving into partial fractions, we get

$$f(z)=\frac{1}{z^2}+\frac{1}{z}-\frac{1}{1+z}=\frac{1}{z^2}+\frac{1}{z}-(1+z)^{-1},\ 0<|z|<1$$

$$=\frac{1}{z^2}+\frac{1}{z}-(1-z+z^2-z^3+\ldots)$$

$$=\frac{1}{z^2}+\frac{1}{z}-1+z-z^2+z^3-\ldots$$

Which is the required series.

***Example 18.*** *Expand* $\frac{1}{z(z^2-3z+2)}$ *for the regions*

(i) $0<|z|<1$ (ii) $1<|z|<2$ (iii) $|z|>2$

**Solution.** Let $f(z)=\frac{1}{z(z^2-3z+2)}=\frac{1}{z(z-1)(z-2)}$

Resolving into partial fractions, we get

$$f(z)=\frac{1}{2z}-\frac{1}{z-1}+\frac{1}{2(z-2)}$$

(i) When $0<|z|<1$. Then, we have

$$f(z)=\frac{1}{2z}+(1-z)^{-1}-\frac{1}{4}\left(1-\frac{z}{2}\right)^{-1}$$

$$=\frac{1}{2z}+(1+z+z^2+z^3+\ldots)$$

$$-\frac{1}{4}\left[1+\frac{z}{2}+\left(\frac{z}{2}\right)^2+\left(\frac{z}{2}\right)^3+\ldots\right]$$

$$=\frac{1}{2z}+\frac{3}{4}+\frac{7}{8}z+\frac{15}{16}z^2+\frac{31}{32}z^3+\ldots.$$

Which is the required Laurent's series.

(ii) When $1<|z|<2$. Then, we have $\frac{1}{|z|}<1$ and $\frac{|z|}{2}<1$

$$\therefore \quad f(z)=\frac{1}{2z}-\frac{1}{z}\left(1-\frac{1}{z}\right)^{-1}-\frac{1}{4}\left(1-\frac{z}{2}\right)^{-1}$$

$$=\frac{1}{2z}-\frac{1}{z}\left(1+\frac{1}{z}+\frac{1}{z^2}+\frac{1}{z^3}+\ldots\right)$$

$$-\frac{1}{4}\left[1+\frac{z}{2}+\left(\frac{z}{2}\right)^2+\left(\frac{z}{2}\right)^3+\ldots\right]$$

$$=\left(-\frac{1}{2z}-\frac{1}{z^2}-\frac{1}{z^3}-\ldots\right)-\frac{1}{4}\left(1+\frac{z}{2}+\frac{z^2}{2^2}+\frac{z^3}{2^3}+\ldots\right)$$

Which is the required Laurent's series.

(iii) When $|z|>2$. Then, we have $\frac{2}{|z|}<1$

$$\therefore \quad f(z)=\frac{1}{2z}-\frac{1}{z}\left(1-\frac{1}{z}\right)^{-1}+\frac{1}{2z}\left(1-\frac{2}{z}\right)^{-1}$$

$$=\frac{1}{2z}-\frac{1}{z}\left(1+\frac{1}{z}+\frac{1}{z^2}+\frac{1}{z^3}+\ldots\right)$$

$$+\frac{1}{2z}\left(1+\frac{2}{z}+\frac{2^2}{z^2}+\frac{2^3}{z^3}+\ldots\right)$$

$$=(2-1)\frac{1}{z^3}+(2^2-1)\frac{1}{z^4}+(2^3-1)\frac{1}{z^5}+\ldots.$$

Which is the required Laurent's series.

***Example 19.*** *Expand* $\frac{(z-2)(z+2)}{(z+1)(z+4)}$ *for*

(i) $|z|<1$ (ii) $1<|z|<4$ (iii) $|z|>4$

**Solution.** Let $f(z)=\frac{(z-2)(z+2)}{(z+1)(z+4)}=1-\frac{5z+8}{(z+1)(z+4)}$

Resolving into partial fractions, we get

$$f(z)=1-\frac{1}{z+1}-\frac{4}{z+4}$$

(i) When $|z|<1$. Then, we have

$$f(z)=1-(1+z)^{-1}-\left(1+\frac{z}{4}\right)^{-1}$$

$$=1-(1-z+z^2-z^3+\ldots)-\left[1-\frac{z}{4}+\left(\frac{z}{4}\right)^2-\left(\frac{z}{4}\right)^3+\ldots\right]$$

$$=-1+\left(1+\frac{1}{4}\right)z+\left(-1-\frac{1}{4^2}\right)z^2+\left(1+\frac{1}{4^3}\right)z^3+\ldots.$$

$$=-1+\frac{5}{4}z-\frac{17}{16}z^2+\frac{65}{64}z^3-\ldots..$$

Which is the required expansion.

(ii) When $1<|z|<4$. Then, we have $\frac{1}{|z|}<1$ and $\frac{|z|}{4}<1$

$$\therefore f(z)=1-\frac{1}{z}\left(1+\frac{1}{z}\right)^{-1}-\left(1+\frac{z}{4}\right)^{-1}$$

$$=1-\frac{1}{z}\left[1-\frac{1}{z}+\frac{1}{z^2}-\frac{1}{z^3}+\ldots\right]-\left[1-\frac{z}{4}+\frac{z^2}{4^2}-\frac{z^3}{4^3}+\ldots\right]$$

$$=\ldots+\frac{1}{z^4}-\frac{1}{z^3}+\frac{1}{z^2}-\frac{1}{z}+\frac{z}{4}-\frac{z^2}{4^2}+\frac{z^3}{4^3}-\ldots$$

Which is the required expansion.

(iii) When $|z|>4$. Then, we have $\frac{4}{|z|}<1$

$$\therefore f(z)=1-\frac{1}{z}\left(1+\frac{1}{z}\right)^{-1}-\frac{4}{z}\left(1+\frac{4}{z}\right)^{-1}$$

$$= 1 - \frac{1}{z}\left(1 - \frac{1}{z} + \frac{1}{z^2} - \frac{1}{z^3} + \ldots\right) - \frac{4}{z}\left(1 - \frac{4}{z} + \frac{4^2}{z^2} - \ldots\right)$$

$$= 1 - \frac{5}{z} + \frac{17}{z^2} - \frac{65}{z^3} + \ldots$$

Which is the required expansion.

***Example 20.*** *Obtain the Taylor's and Laurent's series which represent the function* $f(z) = \dfrac{z^2 - 1}{(z+2)(z+3)}$ *in the regions*

(i) $|z| < 2$ (ii) $2 < |z| < 3$ (iii) $|z| > 3$

**Solution.** Let $f(z) = \dfrac{z^2 - 1}{(z+2)(z+3)} = 1 - \dfrac{5z+7}{(z+2)(z+3)}$

Resolving into partial fractions, we get

$$f(z) = 1 + \frac{3}{z+2} - \frac{8}{z+3}$$

(i) When $|z| < 2$. Then, we have

$$f(z) = 1 + \frac{3}{2}\left(1 + \frac{z}{2}\right)^{-1} - \frac{8}{3}\left(1 + \frac{z}{3}\right)^{-1}$$

$$= 1 + \frac{3}{2}\left(1 - \frac{z}{2} + \frac{z^2}{2^2} - \frac{z^3}{2^3} + \ldots\right) - \frac{8}{3}\left(1 - \frac{z}{3} + \frac{z^2}{3^2} - \frac{z^3}{3^3} + \ldots\right)$$

$$= 1 + \frac{3}{2}\sum_{n=0}^{\infty}(-1)^n\left(\frac{z}{2}\right)^n - \frac{8}{3}\sum_{n=0}^{\infty}(-1)^n\left(\frac{z}{3}\right)^n$$

Which is the required expansion.

(ii) When $2 < |z| < 3$. Then, we have $\dfrac{2}{|z|} < 1$ and $\dfrac{|z|}{3} < 1$

$$\therefore\ f(z) = 1 + \frac{3}{z}\left(1 + \frac{2}{z}\right)^{-1} - \frac{8}{3}\left(1 + \frac{z}{3}\right)^{-1}$$

$$= 1 + \frac{3}{z}\left(1 - \frac{2}{z} + \frac{2^2}{z^2} - \ldots\right) - \frac{8}{3}\left(1 - \frac{z}{3} + \frac{z^2}{3^2} - \frac{z^3}{3^3} + \ldots\right)$$

$$= 1 + \frac{3}{z}\sum_{n=0}^{\infty}(-1)^n\left(\frac{2}{z}\right)^n - \frac{8}{3}\sum_{n=0}^{\infty}(-1)^n\left(\frac{z}{3}\right)^n$$

Which is the required expansion.

(iii) When $|z| > 3$. Then, we have $\dfrac{3}{|z|} < 1$

$$\therefore\ f(z) = 1 + \frac{3}{z}\left(1 + \frac{2}{z}\right)^{-1} - \frac{8}{z}\left(1 + \frac{3}{z}\right)^{-1}$$

$$= 1 + \frac{3}{z}\left[1 - \frac{2}{z} + \left(\frac{2}{z}\right)^2 - \left(\frac{2}{z}\right)^3 + \ldots\right]$$

$$- \frac{8}{3}\left[1 - \frac{3}{z} + \left(\frac{3}{z}\right)^2 - \left(\frac{3}{z}\right)^3 + \ldots\right]$$

$$= 1 + \frac{3}{z}\sum_{n=0}^{\infty}(-1)^n\left(\frac{2}{z}\right)^n - \frac{8}{3}\sum_{n=0}^{\infty}(-1)^n\left(\frac{3}{z}\right)^n$$

Which is the required expansion.

***Example 21.*** *Find two Laurent's series expansions in powers of z of the function*

$$f(z) = \frac{1}{z(1+z^2)}.$$

**Solution.** We have, $f(z) = \dfrac{1}{z(1+z^2)}$

Resolving into partial fractions, we get $f(z) = \dfrac{1}{z} - \dfrac{z}{1+z^2}$.

When, $0 < |z| < 1$. Then, we have

$$f(z) = \frac{1}{z} - z(1+z^2)^{-1} = \frac{1}{z} - z(1 - z^2 + z^4 - z^6 + \ldots)$$

$$= \frac{1}{z} - z + z^3 - z^5 + \ldots$$

When, $|z| > 1$. Then we have

$$f(z) = \frac{1}{z} - \frac{1}{z}\left(1 + \frac{1}{z^2}\right)^{-1} = \frac{1}{z} - \frac{1}{z}\left(1 - \frac{1}{z^2} + \frac{1}{z^4} - \frac{1}{z^6} + \ldots\right)$$

$$= \frac{1}{z^3} - \frac{1}{z^5} + \frac{1}{z^7} - \ldots$$

Which is the required expansion.

***Example 22.*** *Find the Laurent's series of the function* $f(z) = \dfrac{1}{z^2(1-z)}$ *about* $z = 0$.

**Solution.** We have,

$$f(z) = \frac{1}{z^2}(1-z)^{-1} = \frac{1}{z^2}(1 + z + z^2 + \ldots) = \frac{1}{z^2}\sum_{n=0}^{\infty} z^n$$

$$\Rightarrow\ f(z) = \frac{1}{z^2} + \frac{1}{z} + 1 + \sum_{n=1}^{\infty} z^n$$

Which is the required expansion.

***Example 23.*** *Obtain the Taylor's or Laurent's series which represents the function* $f(z) = \dfrac{1}{(1+z^2)(z+2)}$, *when (i)* $|z| < 1$, *(ii)* $1 < |z| < 2$, *(iii)* $|z| > 2$

**Solution.** Resolving $f(z)$ into partial fractions, we obtain

$$f(z) = \frac{1}{5}\left[\frac{1}{z+2} - \frac{z-2}{z^2+1}\right]$$

(i) For $|z| < 1$, $f(z)$ is analytic and so we have,

$$f(z) = \frac{1}{5}\cdot\frac{1}{2}\left(1 + \frac{z}{2}\right)^{-1} - \frac{1}{5}(z-2)(1+z^2)^{-1}$$

$$= \frac{1}{10}\left[1 - \frac{z}{2} + \frac{z^2}{2^2} + \ldots + (-1)^n\frac{z^n}{2^n} + \ldots\right]$$

$$- \frac{(z-2)}{5}[1 - z^2 + z^4 - z^6 + \ldots + (-1)^n z^{2n} + \ldots]$$

$$= \frac{1}{10}\sum_{n=0}^{\infty}(-1)^n\cdot\frac{z^n}{2^n} - \frac{z-2}{5}\sum_{n=0}^{\infty}(-1)^n z^{2n}$$

This series being in the positive powers of z and hence represents Taylor's expansion for $f(z)$.

(ii) When $1 < |z| < 2$, then we have $\dfrac{1}{|z|} < 1$ or $\dfrac{1}{|z|^2} < 1$, so that the binomial expansion of $\left(1 + \dfrac{1}{z^2}\right)^{-1}$ is valid.

$$f(z) = \frac{1}{5}\cdot\frac{1}{2}\left(1 + \frac{1}{2}z\right)^{-1} - \frac{z-2}{5}\cdot\frac{1}{z^2}\left(1 + \frac{1}{z^2}\right)^{-1}$$

$$= \frac{1}{10}\left[1-\frac{z}{2}+\frac{z^2}{2^2}-\frac{z^3}{2^3}+\ldots\right]-\frac{z-2}{5z^2}\left(1-\frac{1}{z^2}+\frac{1}{z^4}-\ldots\right)$$

$$= \frac{1}{10}\sum_{n=0}^{\infty}(-1)^n\frac{z^n}{2^n}-\frac{z-2}{5z^2}\sum_{n=0}^{\infty}(-1)^n\frac{1}{z^{2n}}$$

The above series being in positive and negative powers of $z$ and hence represents Laurent's expansion for $f(z)$ in the region $1<|z|<2$.

(iii) When $|z|>2$, then we have

$$f(z) = \frac{1}{5}\cdot\frac{1}{z}\left(1+\frac{2}{z}\right)^{-1}-\frac{1}{5}(z-2)\cdot\frac{1}{z^2}\left(1+\frac{1}{z^2}\right)^{-1}$$

$$= \frac{1}{5z}\left[1-\frac{2}{z}+\frac{2^2}{z^2}-\frac{2^3}{z^3}+\ldots\right]-\frac{z-2}{5z^2}\left[1-\frac{1}{z^2}+\frac{1}{z^4}-\frac{1}{z^6}+\ldots\right]$$

$$= \frac{1}{5z}\sum_{n=0}^{\infty}(-1)^n\left(\frac{2}{z}\right)^n-\frac{1}{5}\left(\frac{1}{z}-\frac{2}{z^2}\right)\sum_{n=0}^{\infty}\frac{(-1)^n}{z^{2n}}$$

***Example 24.*** *Find the expansion of* $\frac{1}{(z^2+1)(z^2+2)}$ *in powers of z.*

*When, (i)* $|z|<1$ *(ii)* $1<|z|<\sqrt{2}$ *(iii)* $|z|>\sqrt{2}$

**Solution.** Let $f(z) = \frac{1}{(z^2+1)(z^2+2)}$

Resolving into partial fractions, we get

$$f(z) = \frac{1}{z^2+1}-\frac{1}{z^2+2}$$

(i) When $|z|<1$. Then, we have

$$f(z) = (1+z^2)^{-1}-\frac{1}{2}\left(1+\frac{z^2}{2}\right)^{-1}$$

$$= (1-z^2+z^4-z^6+\ldots.)$$

$$-\frac{1}{2}\left[1-\frac{z^2}{2}+\left(\frac{z^2}{2}\right)^2-\left(\frac{z^2}{2}\right)^3+\ldots.\right]$$

$$= \sum_{n=0}^{\infty}(-1)^n z^{2n}-\frac{1}{2}\sum_{n=0}^{\infty}(-1)^n\frac{z^{2n}}{2^n}$$

Which is the required expansion.

(ii) When $1<|z|<\sqrt{2}$, then we have

$$f(z) = \frac{1}{z^2}\left(1+\frac{1}{z^2}\right)^{-1}-\frac{1}{2}\left(1+\frac{z^2}{2}\right)^{-1}$$

$$= \frac{1}{z^2}\left(1-\frac{1}{z^2}+\frac{1}{z^4}-\frac{1}{z^6}+\ldots\right)$$

$$-\frac{1}{2}\left[1-\frac{z^2}{2}+\left(\frac{z^2}{2}\right)^2-\left(\frac{z^2}{2}\right)^3+\ldots\right]$$

$$= \left(\frac{1}{z^2}-\frac{1}{z^4}+\frac{1}{z^6}-\ldots\right)-\left(\frac{1}{2}-\frac{z^2}{2^2}+\frac{z^4}{2^3}-\frac{z^6}{2^4}+\ldots\right)$$

$$= \sum_{n=1}^{\infty}(-1)^{n+1}\frac{1}{z^{2n}}-\sum_{n=0}^{\infty}(-1)^n\frac{z^{2n}}{2^{n+1}}$$

Which is the required expansion.

(iii) When $|z|>\sqrt{2}$, then we have

$$f(z) = \frac{1}{z^2}\left(1+\frac{1}{z^2}\right)^{-1}-\frac{1}{z^2}\left(1+\frac{2}{z^2}\right)^{-1}$$

$$= \frac{1}{z^2}\left(1-\frac{1}{z^2}+\frac{1}{z^4}-\ldots\right)-\frac{1}{z^2}\left(1-\frac{2}{z^2}+\frac{2^2}{z^4}-\ldots\right)$$

$$= (2-1)\frac{1}{z^4}-(2^2-1)\frac{1}{z^6}+(2^3-1)\frac{1}{z^8}-\ldots$$

$$= \sum_{n=1}^{\infty}(-1)^{n+1}(2^n-1)\frac{1}{z^{2n+2}}$$

Which is the required expansion.

***Example 25.*** *If* $0<|z-1|<2$, *then express* $f(z) = \frac{z}{(z-1)(z-3)}$ *in a series of positive and negative powers of* $(z-1)$.

**Solution.** Given that, $f(z) = \frac{z}{(z-1)(z-3)}$.

Resolving into partial fractions, we get

$$f(z) = -\frac{1}{2(z-1)}+\frac{3}{2}\frac{1}{(z-3)}$$

Now, putting $z-1=u$, then we have $0<|u|<2$ and

$$f(z) = -\frac{1}{2u}+\frac{3}{2(u-2)}$$

$$= -\frac{1}{2u}-\frac{3}{4}\left(1-\frac{u}{2}\right)^{-1} = -\frac{1}{2u}-\frac{3}{4}\left(1+\frac{u}{2}+\frac{u^2}{2^2}+\frac{u^3}{2^3}+\ldots.\right)$$

$$= -\frac{1}{2u}-\frac{3}{4}\sum_{n=0}^{\infty}\left(\frac{u}{2}\right)^n = -\frac{1}{2(z-1)}-\frac{3}{4}\sum_{n=0}^{\infty}\left(\frac{z-1}{2}\right)^n$$

Which is the required expansion.

***Example 26.*** *Find different developments of* $\frac{1}{(z-1)(z-3)}$ *in powers of z according to the position of the point in the z-plane. Expand the function in Taylor's series about* $z=2$ *and indicate the circle of convergence.*

**Solution.** Let $f(z) = \frac{1}{(z-1)(z-3)}$

Now, resolving into partial fractions, we get

$$f(z) = -\frac{1}{2(z-1)}+\frac{1}{2(z-3)}$$

Obviously, $f(z)$ is regular everywhere except at $z=1$ and 3.

(i) When $0<|z|<1$, then we have

$$f(z) = \frac{1}{2}(1-z)^{-1}-\frac{1}{6}\left(1-\frac{z}{3}\right)^{-1} = \frac{1}{2}\sum_{n=0}^{\infty}z^n-\frac{1}{6}\sum_{n=0}^{\infty}\left(\frac{z}{3}\right)^n$$

$$= \sum_{n=0}^{\infty}\frac{1}{2}\left(1-\frac{1}{3^{n+1}}\right)z^n$$

which is Taylor's expansion of $f(z)$ in the region $0<|z|<1$.

(ii) When $1<|z|<3$, then we have

$$f(z)=-\frac{1}{2z}\left(1-\frac{1}{z}\right)^{-1}-\frac{1}{6}\left(1-\frac{z}{3}\right)^{-1}$$

$$=-\frac{1}{2z}\sum_{n=0}^{\infty}\frac{1}{z^n}-\frac{1}{6}\sum_{n=0}^{\infty}\left(\frac{z}{3}\right)^n$$

which is Laurent's series in the positive and negative powers of $z$ in the region $1<|z|<3$.

(iii) When $|z|>3$, then we have

$$f(z)=-\frac{1}{2z}\left(1-\frac{1}{z}\right)^{-1}+\frac{1}{2z}\left(1-\frac{3}{z}\right)^{-1}$$

$$=-\frac{1}{2z}\sum_{n=0}^{\infty}\frac{1}{z^n}+\frac{1}{2z}\sum_{n=0}^{\infty}\left(\frac{3}{z}\right)^n=\frac{1}{2}\sum_{n=0}^{\infty}(3^n-1)\frac{1}{z^{n+1}}$$

which is a Laurent's series in the negative powers of $z$ for the region $|z|>3$.

Let us consider a circle with centre at $z=2$. Then, the distance of both the singular points $z=1$ and $z=3$ from the centre of the circle is 1. Hence, if we draw the circle $|z-2|=1$, then the function $f(z)$ is regular within this circle, therefore $f(z)$ can be expanded in a Taylor's series within this circle *i.e.*, in the region $|z-2|<1$. Consequently, $|z-2|=1$ is the circle of convergence.

Hence, $$f(z)=\frac{1}{(z-1)(z-3)}=\frac{1}{z^2-4z+3}=\frac{1}{(z-2)^2-1}$$

$$=-[1-(z-2)^2]^{-1}=-\sum_{n=0}^{\infty}(z-2)^{2n},$$

which is a Taylor's expansion of $f(z)$ about $z=2$.

***Example 27.*** *Represent the function* $f(z)=\dfrac{4z+3}{z(z-3)(z+2)}$ *in Laurent's series*

(*i*) *within* $|z|=1$

(*ii*) *in the annular region between* $|z|=2$ *and* $|z|=3$

(*iii*) *exterior to* $|z|=3$

**Solution.** First of all resolving the given function into partial fractions, we get $f(z)=-\dfrac{1}{2z}+\dfrac{1}{z-3}-\dfrac{1}{2(z+2)}$

The function $f(z)$ is analytic at every point in the z-plane except at $z=-2,0,3$. Thus,

(i) When $0<|z|<1$, then we have

$$f(z)=-\frac{1}{2z}-\frac{1}{3}\left(1-\frac{z}{3}\right)^{-1}-\frac{1}{4}\left(1+\frac{z}{2}\right)^{-1}$$

$$=-\frac{1}{2z}-\frac{1}{3}\sum_{n=0}^{\infty}\left(\frac{z}{3}\right)^n-\frac{1}{4}\sum_{n=0}^{\infty}(-1)^n\left(\frac{z}{2}\right)^n$$

$$=-\frac{1}{2z}-\sum_{n=0}^{\infty}\left[\frac{1}{3^{n+1}}+(-1)^n\frac{1}{2^{n+2}}\right]z^n$$

Which is the required expansion.

(ii) When $2<|z|<3$, then we have

$$f(z)=-\frac{1}{2z}-\frac{1}{3}\left(1-\frac{z}{3}\right)^{-1}-\frac{1}{2z}\left(1+\frac{2}{z}\right)^{-1}$$

$$=-\frac{1}{2z}-\frac{1}{3}\sum_{n=0}^{\infty}\left(\frac{z}{3}\right)^n-\frac{1}{2z}\sum_{n=0}^{\infty}(-1)^n\left(\frac{2}{z}\right)^n$$

$$=-\frac{1}{2z}-\sum_{n=0}^{\infty}\frac{z^n}{3^{n+1}}+\sum_{n=0}^{\infty}(-1)^{n+1}\frac{2^{n-1}}{z^{n+1}}$$

Which is the required expansion.

(iii) When $|z|>3$, then we have

$$f(z)=-\frac{1}{2z}+\frac{1}{z}\left(1-\frac{3}{z}\right)^{-1}-\frac{1}{2z}\left(1+\frac{2}{z}\right)^{-1}$$

$$=-\frac{1}{2z}+\frac{1}{z}\sum_{n=0}^{\infty}\left(\frac{3}{z}\right)^n-\frac{1}{2z}\sum_{n=0}^{\infty}(-1)^n\left(\frac{2}{z}\right)^n$$

$$=-\frac{1}{2z}+\sum_{n=0}^{\infty}\frac{3^n}{z^{n+1}}+\sum_{n=0}^{\infty}(-1)^{n+1}\frac{2^{n-1}}{z^{n+1}}$$

Which is the required expansion.

***Example 28.*** *Expand* $f(z)=\dfrac{z+3}{z(z^2-z-2)}$ *in powers of z, where* (*i*) $|z|<1$ (*ii*) $1<|z|<2$ (*iii*) $|z|>2$

**Solution.** First of all resolving $f(z)$ into partial fractions, we get

$$f(z)=-\frac{3}{2z}+\frac{5}{6(z-2)}+\frac{2}{3(z+1)}$$

(i) When $|z|<1$, then we have

$$f(z)=-\frac{3}{2z}-\frac{5}{12}\left(1-\frac{z}{2}\right)^{-1}+\frac{2}{3}(1+z)^{-1}$$

$$=-\frac{3}{2z}-\frac{5}{12}\sum_{n=0}^{\infty}\left(\frac{z}{2}\right)^n+\frac{2}{3}\sum_{n=0}^{\infty}(-1)^n z^n$$

Which is the required expansion.

(ii) When $1<|z|<2$, then we have

$$f(z)=-\frac{3}{2z}-\frac{5}{12}\left(1-\frac{z}{2}\right)^{-1}+\frac{2}{3z}\left(1+\frac{1}{z}\right)^{-1}$$

$$=-\frac{3}{2z}-\frac{5}{12}\sum_{n=0}^{\infty}\left(\frac{z}{2}\right)^n+\frac{2}{3z}\sum_{n=0}^{\infty}(-1)^n\frac{1}{z^n}$$

Which is the required expansion.

(iii) When $|z|>2$, then we have

$$f(z)=-\frac{3}{2z}+\frac{5}{6z}\left(1-\frac{2}{z}\right)^{-1}+\frac{2}{3z}\left(1+\frac{1}{z}\right)^{-1}$$

$$=-\frac{3}{2z}+\frac{5}{6z}\sum_{n=0}^{\infty}\left(\frac{2}{z}\right)^n+\frac{2}{3z}\sum_{n=0}^{\infty}(-1)^n\frac{1}{z^n}$$

$$=-\frac{3}{2z}+\frac{5}{3}\sum_{n=0}^{\infty}\frac{2^{n-1}}{z^{n+1}}+\frac{2}{3}\sum_{n=0}^{\infty}(-1)^n\frac{1}{z^{n+1}}$$

Which is the required expansion.

***Example 29.*** *Show that*

$$\log z=(z-1)-\frac{(z-1)^2}{2}+\frac{(z-1)^3}{3}-\ldots,\ \text{when } |z-1|<1.$$

**Solution.** Let $f(z)=\log z$, then by Taylor's theorem, we have

$$f(z)=f(z_0)+(z-z_0)f'(z_0)+\frac{(z-z_0)^2}{2!}f''(z_0)+\ldots$$

Taking $z_0 = 1$, we have

$\Rightarrow \quad f(1) = \log 1 = 0 \Rightarrow f'(z) = \frac{1}{z} \Rightarrow f'(1) = 1,$

$\Rightarrow f''(z) = -\frac{1}{z^2} \Rightarrow f''(1) = -1 \Rightarrow f'''(z) = \frac{2}{z^3} \Rightarrow f'''(1) = 2$ and so on.

Substituting these values in Taylor's series (i), we get

$$\log z = f(1) + f'(1)(z-1) + f''(1)\frac{(z-1)^2}{2!} + \dots$$

$$= (z-1) - \frac{1}{2}(z-1)^2 + \frac{1}{3}(z-1)^3 + \dots.$$

**Example 30.** *Prove that* $\tan^{-1} z = z - \frac{z^3}{3} + \frac{z^5}{5} - \dots$, *when* $|z| < 1$.

**Solution.** Let $f(z) = \tan^{-1} z$, then

By Taylor's theorem, we have

$$f(z) = f(z_0) + f'(z_0)(z - z_0) + f''(z_0)\frac{(z-z_0)^2}{2!} + \dots$$

Taking $\quad z_0 = 0$, we have

$$f(z) = f(0) + f'(0)z + \frac{z^2}{2!}f''(0) + \dots \quad \text{...(i)}$$

Now, $\quad f(z) = \tan^{-1} z$, so that $f(0) = \tan^{-1} 0 = 0$

$$\Rightarrow \quad f'(z) = \frac{1}{1+z^2} \Rightarrow f''(z) = -\frac{2z}{(1+z^2)^2},$$

$$\Rightarrow \quad f'''(z) = -\frac{2(1-3z^2)}{(1+z^2)^3} \Rightarrow f^{iv}(z) = \frac{24(-z+z^3)}{(1+z^2)^4},$$

$$\Rightarrow \quad f^{v}(z) = -\frac{24(-1+10z^2-5z^4)}{(1+z^2)^5} \text{ and so on.}$$

$\therefore f'(0) = 1,\ f''(0) = 0,\ f'''(0) = -2,\ f^{iv}(0) = 0,\ f^{v}(0) = 24$ etc.

Substituting all these values in relation (i), we get

$$\tan^{-1} z = z - \frac{1}{3}z^3 + \frac{1}{5}z^5 - \dots.$$

Which is the required series.

**Example 31.** *Expand* $\log(1+z)$ *in a Taylor's series about* $z = 0$ *and determine the region of convergence for the resulting series.*

**Solution.** Let $f(z) = \log(1+z)$, then Taylor's expansion for $f(z)$ about $z = 0$ is given by

$$f(z) = f(0) + zf'(0) + \frac{z^2}{2!}f''(0) + \dots \quad \text{...(i)}$$

We have, $f'(z) = \frac{1}{1+z} \Rightarrow f''(z) = -\frac{1}{(1+z)^2}$

$$\Rightarrow \quad f'''(z) = \frac{2}{(1+z)^3}, \dots \Rightarrow f^n(z) = (-1)^{n-1}\frac{(n-1)!}{(1+z)^n}$$

Hence, $\quad f(0) = 0 \Rightarrow f'(0) = 1 \Rightarrow f''(0) = -1 \Rightarrow f'''(0) = 2, \dots$

$\Rightarrow \quad f^n(0) = (-1)^{n-1}(n-1)!$

Substituting these values in relation (i), we have

$$\log(1+z) = z - \frac{1}{2!}z^2 + \frac{2}{3!}z^3 - \dots + \frac{(-1)^{n-1}(n-1)!\,z^n}{n!} + \dots$$

$$= z - \frac{z^2}{2} + \frac{z^3}{3} - \dots + (-1)^{n-1}\frac{z^n}{n} + \dots.$$

Let $u_n$ be the $n$th term of the series. Then,

$$u_n = (-1)^{n-1}\frac{z^n}{n},\ u_{n+1} = \frac{(-1)^n z^{n+1}}{n+1}$$

Hence, $\lim_{n\to\infty}\left|\frac{u_n}{u_{n+1}}\right| = \lim_{n\to\infty}\left|\frac{n+1}{nz}\right| = \frac{1}{|z|}$

Therefore, by d'Alembert's ratio test the series converges for the region $|z| < 1$.

**Example 32.** *Find Taylor's series expansion of the functions* $f(z) = \frac{z}{z^4+9}$ *around* $z = 0$.

*Find also radius of convergence.*

**Solution.** Given that

$$f(z) = \frac{z}{z^4+9} = \frac{z}{9}\left(1+\frac{z^4}{9}\right)^{-1} = \frac{z}{9}\sum_{n=0}^{\infty}(-1)^n\left(\frac{z^4}{9}\right)^n$$

$$\Rightarrow \quad f(z) = \frac{z}{9}\sum_{n=0}^{\infty}(-1)^n\frac{z^{4n}}{3^{2n}} = \sum_{n=0}^{\infty}(-1)^n\frac{z^{4n+1}}{3^{2n+2}}$$

$$\Rightarrow \quad f(z) = \sum_{n=0}^{\infty}(-1)^n\frac{z^{4n+1}}{3^{2n+2}} \quad \text{...(i)}$$

Which is Taylor's expansion of $f(z)$.

**Second Part.** $\quad$ Let $f(z) = \sum_{n=0}^{\infty}u_n(z) \quad$ ...(ii)

By relations (i) and (ii), we have $u_n(z) = (-1)^n\frac{z^{4n+1}}{3^{2n+2}}$

**Example 33.** *Expand* $f(z) = \frac{z-1}{z+1}$ *as a Taylor's series about*

(*i*) $z = 0$

(*ii*) $z = 1$

(*iii*) *its Laurent's series for the domain* $1 < |z| < \infty$.

**Solution.** (i) Given that,

$$f(z) = \frac{z-1}{z+1} = 1 - \frac{2}{z+1} \text{ or } f(z) = 1 - \frac{2}{z+1} \quad \text{...(i)}$$

$$\Rightarrow \quad f(z) = 1 - 2(1+z)^{-1} = 1 - 2\sum_{n=0}^{\infty}(-1)^n z^n$$

$$\Rightarrow f(z) = 1 - 2\sum_{n=0}^{\infty}(-1)^n z^n$$

Which is Taylor's series about $z = 0$.

(ii) Let $\phi(z) = \frac{1}{z+1} \Rightarrow \phi^{(n)}(z) = \frac{(-1)^n n!}{(z+1)^{n+1}}$

If we write $\quad a_n = \frac{\phi^{(n)}(1)}{n!}$, then $a_n = \frac{(-1)^n}{(1+1)^{n+1}} = \frac{(-1)^n}{2^{n+1}}$

Now, $\quad \phi(z) = \sum_{n=0}^{\infty}a_n(z-1)^n = \sum_{n=0}^{\infty}\frac{(-1)^n(z-1)^n}{2^{n+1}} \quad$ ...(ii)

$$\therefore \quad f(z) = 1 - \sum_{n=0}^{\infty}\frac{(-1)^n(z-1)^n}{2^n}$$

[from relations (i) and (ii)]

Which is Taylor's expansion about $z = 1$.

(iii) We have $f(z) = 1 - \dfrac{2}{z+1} = 1 - \dfrac{2}{z}\left(1+\dfrac{1}{z}\right)^{-1}$

$$\Rightarrow \quad f(z) = 1 - \frac{2}{z}\sum_{n=0}^{\infty}(-1)^n \frac{1}{z^n}$$

Which is the required Laurent's series.

***Example 34.*** *Find Laurent's series of the function* $f(z) = \dfrac{1}{(z^2-4)(z+1)}$ *valid in the region* $1 < |z| < 2$.

**Solution.**

$$f(z) = \frac{1}{(z-2)(z+2)(z+1)} = \frac{1}{12(z-2)} + \frac{1}{4(z+2)} - \frac{1}{3(z+1)}$$

$$= \frac{-1}{24}\left(1-\frac{z}{2}\right)^{-1} + \frac{1}{8}\left(1+\frac{z}{2}\right)^{-1} - \frac{1}{3z}\left(1+\frac{1}{z}\right)^{-1}$$

$$= -\frac{1}{24}\sum_{n=0}^{\infty}\left(\frac{z}{2}\right)^n + \frac{1}{8}\sum_{n=0}^{\infty}(-1)^n\left(\frac{z}{2}\right)^n - \frac{1}{3z}\sum_{n=0}^{\infty}\frac{(-1)^n}{z^n}$$

Which is the required Laurent's series.

***Example 35.*** *Expand* $\sin z$ *in a Taylor's series about* $z = \dfrac{\pi}{4}$.

**Solution.** Let $$f(z) = \sum_{n=0}^{\infty} a_n\left(z - \frac{\pi}{4}\right)^n \qquad \text{...(i)}$$

where, $$a_n = \frac{f^{(n)}\left(\frac{\pi}{4}\right)}{n!} \qquad \text{...(ii)}$$

Now, $$f(z) = \sin z \Rightarrow f^{(n)}(z) = \sin\left(z + \frac{n\pi}{2}\right)$$

$$\Rightarrow \quad f^{(n)}\left(\frac{\pi}{4}\right) = \sin\left(\frac{\pi}{4} + \frac{n\pi}{2}\right)$$

Now, putting these values in relation (i), we get

$$f(z) = \sum_{n=0}^{\infty}\sin\left(\frac{\pi}{4}+\frac{n\pi}{2}\right)\frac{\left(z-\frac{\pi}{4}\right)^n}{n!}$$

Which is the required Taylor's series.

***Example 36.*** *Expand* $\dfrac{1}{z}$ *as a Taylor's series about* $z = 1$.

**Solution.** Given that $f(z) = \dfrac{1}{z}$

For Taylor's expansion about $z = 1$,

Let $$f(z) = \sum_{n=0}^{\infty} a_n (z-1)^n, \text{ where } a_n = \frac{f^{(n)}(1)}{n!}$$

$$f^{(n)}(z) = \frac{(-1)^n n!}{z^{n+1}} \Rightarrow f^{(n)}(1) = \frac{(-1)^n n!}{1^{n+1}}$$

$\therefore$ $$a_n = (-1)^n$$

Hence, $$f(z) = \sum_{n=0}^{\infty}(-1)^n (z-1)^n$$

Which is the required Taylor's series.

# The Zeros of an Analytic Function

The value of $z$ for which the analytic function $f(z)$ becomes zero is said to be the zero of $f(z)$.

If $f(z)$ is analytic in a domain $D$ and $z_0$ is any point of $D$, then we can expand $f(z)$ as Taylor's series about $z = z_0$ given by

$$f(z) = \sum_{n=0}^{\infty} a_n (z - z_0)^n$$

If $a_0 = a_1 = a_2 = \ldots = a_{m-1} = 0$ and $a_m \neq 0$, $f(z)$ is said to have a **zero of order** $m$ at $z = z_0$.

A zero of order one ($m = 1$) is said to be a **simple zero.**

> ***Note*** The zeros are isolated.
>
> *e.g.*, The function $f(z) = \dfrac{z-2}{z^2}\sin\left(\dfrac{1}{z-1}\right)$ has zero at $z = 2$, because at $z = 2$,
>
> $$f(z) = 0$$
>
> Also, zeros are obtained when $\sin\left(\dfrac{1}{z-1}\right) = 0$
>
> $$\Rightarrow \quad \frac{1}{z-1} = n\pi \Rightarrow z - 1 = \frac{1}{n\pi}$$
>
> $$\Rightarrow \quad z = 1 + \frac{1}{n\pi}, \quad n = \pm 1, \pm 2, \ldots$$

# Singular Point or Singularity

A point at which $f(z)$ is not analytic is known as a singular point or singularity of $f(z)$.

For example, $f(z) = \dfrac{1}{z-1}$ has singular point at $z = 1$.

# Isolated and Non-isolated Singularities

If $z_0$ is a singularity of $f(z)$ and if $f(z)$ is analytic at each point in some neighbourhood of $z_0$, then $z_0$ is called an isolated singularity of $f(z)$ otherwise it is called a non-isolated singularity.

*e.g.*, The function $f(z) = \dfrac{z^2+5}{z(z-3)(z^2+1)}$ is analytic at every point except $z = 0, 3, \pm i$. Hence, these are the isolated singular points of $f(z)$.

Let us consider another function $f(z) = \dfrac{1}{\tan(\pi/z)}$. It has infinite number of isolated singularities which lie on the real axis from $z = -1$ to $z = 1$. These isolated singularities are given by $z = \pm\dfrac{1}{n}$, $n = 1, 2, 3, \ldots$ . The origin ($z = 0$) is also a singular point but it is non-isolated, since in every neighbourhood of 0 there are infinite number of other singularities.

## Poles and Removable Singularities

Let $f(z)$ be an analytic function in a domain $D$ except at the point $z = z_0$. Then, there exists a deleted neighbourhood $0 < |z - z_0| < R$ in which $f(z)$ is analytic. In the annulus $0 < |z - z_0| < R$ the Laurent expansion of $f(z)$ is

$$f(z) = \sum_{n=0}^{\infty} a_n(z - z_0)^n + \sum_{n=1}^{\infty} b_n(z - z_0)^{-n}$$

The term $\sum_{n=1}^{\infty} b_n(z - z_0)^{-n}$ of the Laurent's series is called the principal part of $f(z)$ at $z = z_0$.

### Pole

If the principal part of $f(z)$ at $z = z_0$ consists of a finite number of terms, say $m$, then $z = z_0$ is said to be a pole of order $m$ of the function $f(z)$.

For $m = 1$, the point $z = z_0$ is said to be a simple pole. If $z = z_0$ is a pole of order $m$, $f(z)$ has an expansion of the form

$$f(z) = \sum_{n=0}^{\infty} a_n(z - z_0)^n + \frac{b_1}{z - z_0} + \frac{b_2}{(z - z_0)^2} + \ldots + \frac{b_m}{(z - z_0)^m}$$

### Removable Singularity

If all the coefficients $b_n$ are zero *i.e.*, if the principal part of $f(z)$ at $z = z_0$ consists of no terms, then $z_0$ is called removable singularity of $f(z)$.

We can remove this singularity by defining the function $f(z)$ at $z = z_0$ in such a way that it becomes analytic at $z_0$.

*e.g.*, The function $f(z) = \dfrac{\sin(z-1)}{z-1}$ has removable singularity at $z = 1$ because

$$\frac{\sin(z-1)}{z-1} = \frac{1}{z-1}\left[(z-1) - \frac{(z-1)^3}{3!} + \frac{(z-1)^5}{5!} - \ldots\right]$$

$$= 1 - \frac{(z-1)^2}{3!} + \frac{(z-1)^4}{5!} - \ldots$$

contains no negative powers of $(z - 1)$. This singularity can be made to disappear by defining $\dfrac{\sin(z-1)}{z-1} = 1$ at $z = 1$, so that the function becomes analytic at $z = 1$.

> **Note** If $f(z)$ has removable singularity at $z = z_0$, then $\lim_{z \to z_0} (z - z_0) f(z) = 0$
>
> For example, if $f(z) = \dfrac{\sin(z-1)}{z-1}$
>
> $\Rightarrow \lim_{z \to 1} (z-1) f(z) = \lim_{z \to 1} (z-1) \dfrac{\sin(z-1)}{z-1} = 0$

## Isolated Essential Singularity

If there are infinite number of terms in the principal part of $f(z)$ at $z = z_0$, then $z_0$ is called an isolated essential singularity of $f(z)$.

*e.g.*, $\sin\frac{1}{z}$ has an isolated essential singularity at $z = 0$ since,

$\sin\frac{1}{z} = \frac{1}{z} + \frac{1}{3!}\cdot\frac{1}{z^3} + \frac{1}{5!}\frac{1}{z^5} + \ldots$ has infinite number of terms in negative powers of $z$.

> **Note** Limit point of zeros is called isolated essential singularity of $f(z)$.
>
> *e.g.*, $f(z) = \dfrac{z-2}{z^2}\sin\left(\dfrac{1}{z-1}\right)$
>
> Now, $f(z) = 0 \Rightarrow z = 2$ (simple zero)
>
> or $\sin\left(\dfrac{1}{z-1}\right) = 0$
>
> when $\sin\left(\dfrac{1}{z-1}\right) = 0 \Rightarrow \dfrac{1}{z-1} = n\pi$
>
> $\Rightarrow z - 1 = \dfrac{1}{n\pi} \Rightarrow z = 1 + \dfrac{1}{n\pi}$, where $n = \pm 1, \pm 2, \ldots$
>
> and $\lim_{n \to \infty} 1 + \dfrac{1}{n\pi} = 1$
>
> $\Rightarrow z = 1$ is an isolated essential singularity of $f(z)$.

## Non-Isolated Essential Singularity

The limit point of a sequence of poles of a function $f(z)$ is said to be non-isolated essential singularity.

The function $\tan\frac{1}{z}$ has poles at points given by

$$z = \frac{2}{n\pi}, \quad n = \pm 1, \pm 3, \pm 5, \ldots$$

The limit point of this sequence of poles is $z = 0$, which is therefore a non-isolated essential singularity.

***Example 37.*** *Show that the function $e^{1/z}$ actually takes every value except zero an infinite number of times in the neighbourhood of $z = 0$.*

**Solution.** Let $f(z) = e^{1/z}$

To prove the required result, we have to show that $f(z)$ has an isolated essential singularity at $z = 0$.

Now, $f(z) = e^{1/z} = 1 + \dfrac{1}{z} + \dfrac{1}{2!z^2} + \dfrac{1}{3!z^3} + \ldots = 1 + \sum_{n=1}^{\infty} \dfrac{1}{n!}\cdot\dfrac{1}{z^n}$

Since, the principal part of $f(z)$ contains infinite number of terms therefore, $z = 0$ is an isolated essential singularity of $f(z)$.

***Example 38.*** *Show that the function $e^z$ has an isolated essential singularity at $z = \infty$.*

**Solution.** Let $f(z) = e^z$. Then, we have $f(1/w) = e^{1/w}$

The behaviour of $f(z)$ at $z = \infty$ will be the same as that of $f(1/w)$ at $w = 0$.

Now, $f\left(\dfrac{1}{w}\right) = e^{1/w} = 1 + \dfrac{1}{w} + \dfrac{1}{2!}\cdot\dfrac{1}{w^2} + \dfrac{1}{3!}\dfrac{1}{w^3} + \ldots$

We have infinite number of terms in the negative powers of $w$ in the principal part of the expansion of $f(1/w)$, therefore $e^{1/w}$ has an isolated essential singularity at $w = 0$. Hence, $e^z$ has an isolated essential singularity at $z = \infty$.

***Example 39.*** *Show that the function $(z^2 + 4)/e^z$ has an isolated essential singularity at $z = \infty$.*

**Solution.** We have, $f(z) = \dfrac{z^2 + 4}{e^z}$

Putting $z = \dfrac{1}{y}$, we have

$$f\left(\frac{1}{y}\right)=\left(4+\frac{1}{y^2}\right)e^{-1/y}=\left(4+\frac{1}{y^2}\right)\left(1-\frac{1}{y}+\frac{1}{2!}\cdot\frac{1}{y^2}-\frac{1}{3!}\cdot\frac{1}{y^3}+\ldots\right)$$

$$=4+\left[-\frac{4}{y}+(1+2)\frac{1}{y^2}+\left(-1-\frac{2}{3}\right)\frac{1}{y^3}+\left(\frac{1}{2}+\frac{1}{6}\right)\frac{1}{y^4}+\ldots\right]$$

$$=4+\left[-\frac{4}{y}+\frac{3}{y^2}-\frac{5}{3y^3}+\frac{2}{3y^4}-\ldots\right]$$

Since, this series contains an infinite number of terms in the negative powers of $y$ in the principal part of the expansion of $f\left(\frac{1}{y}\right)$, therefore $f\left(\frac{1}{y}\right)$ has an isolated essential singularity at $y=0$.

Hence, $f(z)$ has an isolated essential singularity at $z=\infty$.

***Example 40.*** *What kind of singularity have the following functions.*

(i) $\dfrac{\cot \pi z}{(z-a)^2}$ at $z=0,\ z=\infty$ (ii) $\sin\dfrac{1}{1-z}$ at $z=1$

(iii) $\sin z-\cos z$ at $z=\infty$ (iv) $\operatorname{cosec}\dfrac{1}{z}$ at $z=0$

(v) $\tan\dfrac{1}{z}$ at $z=0$

**Solution.** (i) Let $f(z)=\dfrac{\cot \pi z}{(z-a)^2}=\dfrac{\cos \pi z}{\sin \pi z(z-a)^2}$

Poles of $f(z)$ are obtained by equating to zero the denominator of $f(z)$. Then, we have

$$(z-a)^2 \sin \pi z=0$$

$$\Rightarrow \quad \sin \pi z=0 \text{ or } (z-a)^2=0$$

Now, $\sin \pi z=0 \Rightarrow \pi z=n\pi \Rightarrow z=n$, where $n$ is any integer,

and $(z-a)^2=0 \Rightarrow z=a$

Hence, $z=a$ is a double pole and $z=0,\pm 1,\pm 2,\ldots$, are simple poles.

$z=\infty$ is a limit point of these simple poles, therefore $z=\infty$ is non-isolated essential singularity.

(ii) Let $f(z)=\sin\dfrac{1}{1-z}$, hence zeros of $f(z)$ are given by

$\sin\dfrac{1}{1-z}=0$ or $\dfrac{1}{1-z}=n\pi$ or $z=1-\dfrac{1}{n\pi}$, where $n$ is any integer.

$\therefore$ $z=1$ is a limit point of these zeros, therefore $z=1$ is an isolated essential singularity.

(iii) Let $f(z)=\sin z-\cos z$, hence zeros of $f(z)$ are given by

$$\sin z-\cos z=0 \Rightarrow \sin z=\cos z$$

$$\Rightarrow \quad \tan z=1 \Rightarrow \quad z=n\pi+\frac{\pi}{4},\ n \text{ is any integer.}$$

$z=\infty$ is a limit point of these zeros which is therefore an isolated essential singularity.

(iv) Let $f(z)=\operatorname{cosec}\dfrac{1}{z}=\dfrac{1}{\sin(1/z)}$, hence poles of $f(z)$ are given by

$\sin\dfrac{1}{z}=0 \Rightarrow \dfrac{1}{z}=n\pi,\ z=(1/n\pi)$, where $n$ is any integer.

Since, $z=0$ is a limit point of these poles, therefore $z=0$ is a non-isolated essential singularity.

(v) Let $\quad f(z)=\tan(1/z)=\dfrac{\sin(1/z)}{\cos(1/z)}$

Hence, poles of $f(z)$ are given by

$$\cos(1/z)=0 \quad\Rightarrow\quad \frac{1}{z}=2n\pi\pm\frac{\pi}{2}$$

$$\Rightarrow \quad z=\frac{1}{\left(2n\pm\frac{1}{2}\right)\pi}, \text{ where } n \text{ is any integer.}$$

Since, $z=0$ is a limit point of these poles, therefore $z=0$ is a non-isolated essential singularity.

***Example 41.*** *What kind of singularity have the following functions.*

(i) $\cot z$ at $z=\infty$ (ii) $\sec\dfrac{1}{z}$ at $z=0$

**Solution.** (i) Here, $f(z)=\cot z=\dfrac{\cos z}{\sin z}$, hence

Poles of $f(z)$ are given by $\sin z=0$ or $z=n\pi,\ n\in I$.

Since, $z=\infty$ is a limit point of these poles, therefore $z=\infty$ is a non-isolated essential singularity.

(ii) We have, $f(z)=\sec\dfrac{1}{z}=\dfrac{1}{\cos(1/z)}$, hence

Poles of $f(z)$ are given by $\cos\dfrac{1}{z}=0$

$$\Rightarrow \quad \frac{1}{z}=2n\pi\pm\frac{\pi}{2} \Rightarrow z=\frac{1}{2n\pi\pm\frac{\pi}{2}}=\frac{1}{\left(2n\pm\frac{1}{2}\right)\pi},\ n\in I$$

Since, $z=0$ is a limit point of these poles, therefore $z=0$ is a non-isolated essential singularity.

***Example 42.*** *Specify the nature of singularity at $z=-2$ of $f(z)=(z-3)\sin\dfrac{1}{z+2}$.*

**Solution.** We have zeros of $f(z)$ are given by $f(z)=0$

$$\Rightarrow \quad (z-3)\sin\frac{1}{(z+2)}=0 \Rightarrow z=3 \text{ or } \sin\frac{1}{(z+2)}=0$$

$$\Rightarrow \sin\left(\frac{1}{z+2}\right)=0=\sin n\pi \Rightarrow \frac{1}{z+2}=n\pi$$

$$\Rightarrow \quad z+2=\frac{1}{n\pi} \Rightarrow z=-2+\frac{1}{n\pi}, \text{ where } n=0,1,2,\ldots$$

Limit point of zeros is $-2$.

$\therefore$ $\quad z=-2$ is isolated essential singularity.

***Example 43.*** *(i) Find zeros and poles of $\left(\dfrac{z+1}{z^2+1}\right)^2$.*

*(ii) What kind of singularity has the function $\dfrac{e^z}{z^2+4}$?*

**Solution.** (i) We have, $f(z)=\dfrac{(z+1)^2}{(z^2+1)^2}$, hence

Zeros of $f(z)$ are given by $(z+1)^2=0 \Rightarrow z=-1,-1$

Hence, $z=-1$ is a zero of order 2.

And poles of $f(z)$ are given by

$$(z^2+1)^2=0 \text{ or } (z+i)^2(z-i)^2=0 \Rightarrow z=-i,-i,i,i$$

Hence, $z=i$ and $z=-i$ are poles each of order 2.

(ii) Let $f(z) = \frac{e^z}{z^2+4}$, hence

Poles of $f(z)$ are given by $z^2+4=0$ or $z = \pm 2i$.

Hence, $z = 2i, -2i$ are simple poles.

***Example 44.*** *Find the kind of the singularities of the following functions.*

(i) $\frac{1-e^z}{1+e^z}$ at $z=\infty$ (ii) $\frac{1}{\sin z - \cos z}$ at $z = \frac{\pi}{4}$

(iii) $\sin\frac{1}{z}$ at $z=0$ (iv) $z$ cosec $z$ at $z=\infty$.

**Solution.** (i) Let $f(z) = \frac{1-e^z}{1+e^z}$, hence

Poles of $f(z)$ are obtained by equating to zero the denominator of $f(z)$.

$\therefore \quad 1+e^z = 0 \Rightarrow e^z = -1 = e^{2n\pi i + \pi i}$

$\Rightarrow \quad z = (2n+1)\pi i$, where $n$ is any integer.

Hence, $z = (2n+1)\pi i \, (n \in I)$ are ths simple poles of $f(z)$. and $z = \infty$ is a limit point of these poles, therefore $z = \infty$ is a non-isolated essential singularity.

(ii) Let $f(z) = \frac{1}{\sin z - \cos z}$, hence poles of $f(z)$ are given by

$\sin z - \cos z = 0 \Rightarrow \tan z = 1 \Rightarrow z = n\pi + \frac{\pi}{4}$, $n$ is any integer.

At $n=0, z = \pi/4$ which is a simple pole.

(iii) Let $f(z) = \sin\frac{1}{z}$, hence zeros of $f(z)$ are given by

$\sin\frac{1}{z} = 0$ or $\frac{1}{z} = n\pi$ or $z = \frac{1}{n\pi}, n \in I$.

Obviously, $z=0$ is a limit point of zeros of $f(z)$, hence $z=0$ is an isolated essential singularity of $f(z)$.

(iv) Let $f(z) = z \operatorname{cosec} z = \frac{z}{\sin z}$, hence poles of $f(z)$ are given by $\sin z = 0 \Rightarrow z = n\pi, n \in I$.

Since, $z = \infty$ is a limit point of these poles, therefore $z=\infty$ is a non-isolated essential singularity.

***Example 45.*** *Discuss the nature of singularities of the following functions.*

(i) $\tan z$ (ii) $\frac{1}{z(1-z^2)}$

(iii) $\frac{z}{1+z^4}$ (iv) $\frac{\sin z}{(z-\pi)^2}$

**Solution.** (i) Let $f(z) = \tan z = \frac{\sin z}{\cos z}$, hence to obtain the singularities of $f(z)$ equating to zero the denominator of $f(z)$, we get

$$\cos z = 0 \Rightarrow z = 2n\pi \pm \frac{\pi}{2}, n \in I$$

$$\Rightarrow \quad z = (4n \pm 1)\frac{\pi}{2}, n \in I \Rightarrow z = (2n \pm 1)\frac{\pi}{2}, n \in I$$

Hence, $z = (2n \pm 1)\frac{\pi}{2}, (n \in I)$ give the simple poles of $f(z)$.

and $z = \infty$ is non-isolated singularity.

(ii) Let $f(z) = \frac{1}{z(1-z^2)}$, hence singularities of $f(z)$ are given by $z(1-z^2) = 0 \Rightarrow z = 0, -1, 1$, which are the simple poles.

(iii) Let $f(z) = \frac{z}{1+z^4}$, hence singularities of $f(z)$ are given by

$$1+z^4 = 0 \Rightarrow \quad z = (-1)^{1/4}$$

$$\Rightarrow \quad z = (\cos\pi + i\sin\pi)^{1/4}$$

$$= \{\cos(2n\pi+\pi) + i\sin(2n\pi+\pi)\}^{1/4}$$

$$= \cos(2n+1)\frac{\pi}{4} + i\sin(2n+1)\frac{\pi}{4} = e^{i(2n+1)\frac{\pi}{4}}$$

Now, putting $n = 0, 1, 2, 3$, we get

$$z = e^{i\pi/4}, e^{3\pi i/4}, e^{5\pi i/4}, e^{7\pi i/4}$$

which are the simple poles of $f(z)$.

(iv) Let $f(z) = \frac{\sin z}{(z-\pi)^2}$, hence singularities of $f(z)$ are given by $(z-\pi)^2 = 0$.

Thus, $z = \pi$ is a pole of order two of $f(z)$.

***Example 46.*** *Find the zeros and discuss the nature of singularities of* $f(z) = \frac{z-2}{z^2}\sin\frac{1}{z-1}$.

**Solution.** Zeros of $f(z)$ are obtained by equating to zero its numerator, so that we have,

$$(z-2)\sin\{1/(z-1)\} = 0$$

$z - 2 = 0 \Rightarrow z = 2$ which is a simple zero of $f(z)$,

and $\sin\frac{1}{z-1} = 0 \Rightarrow \frac{1}{z-1} = n\pi \Rightarrow z = 1 + \frac{1}{n\pi}, (n \in I)$, which are also zeros of order one.

Since, $z=1$ is a limit point of the zeros $z = 1 + \frac{1}{n\pi} (n \in I)$, hence, $z=1$ is an isolated essential singularity of $f(z)$.

Again to obtain the poles of $f(z)$ equating to zero its denominator, we get $z^2 = 0$.

Hence, $z = 0$ is a pole of order two.

***Example 47.*** *Show that the function* $e^{-1/z^2}$ *has no singularities.*

**Solution.** Let $f(z) = e^{-1/z^2}$, hence

Zeros of $f(z)$ are given by $e^{-1/z^2} = 0 \Rightarrow z^2 = 0$

$\Rightarrow \quad z = 0$ is a zero of order two.

Since, zeros have no limit point, therefore there is no singularity of $f(z)$.

Now, poles of $f(z)$ are given by $e^{1/z^2} = 0$, which is not possible.

$\therefore$ There exist no poles.

Hence, $e^{-1/z^2}$ has no singularities.

# Residue at a Pole

Let $z = a$ be a pole of order $m$ of a single-valued function $f(z)$ and $\gamma$ be any circle of radius $r$ and centre $z = a$ containing no other singularities except $z = a$. Then, the function $f(z)$ is regular within the region $0<|z-a|<r$, so we can expand $f(z)$ in a Laurent's series in the region $0<|z-a|<r$.

$$\therefore \quad f(z)=\sum_{n=0}^{\infty} a_n(z-a)^n+\sum_{n=1}^{\infty} b_n(z-z_0)^{-n}$$

where $\quad a_n=\dfrac{1}{2\pi i}\displaystyle\int_\gamma \frac{f(z)}{(z-a)^{n+1}}dz$

and $\quad b_n=\dfrac{1}{2\pi i}\displaystyle\int_\gamma (z-a)^{n-1}f(z)dz$

In particular, $b_1=\dfrac{1}{2\pi i}\displaystyle\int_\gamma f(z)dz$

The coefficient $b_1$ is called the residue of $f(z)$ at $z=a$.

## Computation of Residue at a Finite Pole

### (i) Residue at a Simple Pole

If $z=a$ is a simple pole of $f(z)$, then the Laurent's expansion of $f(z)$ is of the form

$$f(z)=\sum_{n=0}^{\infty} a_n(z-a)^n+\frac{b_1}{z-a}$$

$$\therefore \quad b_1=\lim_{z\to a}(z-a)f(z)$$

Hence, the residue at the simple pole $z=a$ is given by

$$\text{Res } f(a)=\lim_{z\to a}(z-a)f(z)$$

**Another form**

If $f(z)=\dfrac{\phi(z)}{\psi(z)}$, where $\psi(z)=(z-a)F(z),\ \ F(a)\neq 0$,

then residue of $f(z)$ at $z=a$ is $\dfrac{\phi(a)}{\Psi'(a)}$

*i.e.*, $\text{Res } f(a)=\dfrac{\phi(a)}{\Psi'(a)}$

### (ii) Residue at a Pole of Order *m*

Let $z=a$ be a pole of order $m$ of $f(z)$ and suppose $f(z)=\dfrac{\phi(z)}{(z-a)^m}$, then residue of $f(z)$ at $z=a$ is given by $\dfrac{\phi^{m-1}(a)}{(m-1)!}$

*i.e.*, $\text{Res } f(a)=\dfrac{\phi^{m-1}(a)}{(m-1)!}$

In particular, if $f(z)=\dfrac{\phi(z)}{(z-a)^2}$, the residue at $z=a$ is $\phi'(a)$ and

if $f(z)=\dfrac{\phi(z)}{(z-a)^3}$, the residue at $z=a$ is $\dfrac{\phi''(a)}{2!}$ etc.

> ***Note*** We have seen that the residue of $f(z)$ at the pole $z=a$ is the coefficient of $\dfrac{1}{(z-a)}$ in the Laurent's expansion of $f(z)$. If we put $z-a=t$ or $z=a+t$, where $t$ is small, then the Laurent's expansion of $f(z)$ becomes
>
> $$f(a+t)=\sum_{n=0}^{\infty} a_n t^n+\frac{b_1}{t}+\frac{b_2}{t^2}+\ldots+\frac{b_m}{t^m}$$
>
> We see that $b_1$ is the coefficient of $1/t$ in the above expansion.
> Hence, to find the residue of $f(z)$ at $z=a$, put $z=a+t$ in $f(z)$ and expand in powers of $t$, where $t$ is small, the coefficient of $1/t$ is the residue at $z=a$.

### (iii) Residue at Infinity

If the function $f(z)$ has an isolated singularity at infinity or is analytic there, then the residue of $f(z)$ at $z=\infty$ is given by

$$-\frac{1}{2\pi i}\int_C f(z)dz$$

Where, C is a large circle containing all the finite singularities of $f(z)$ and integral along C is performed in a anti-clockwise direction provided that this integral has a definite value.

Residue of $f(z)$ at infinity is computed either by finding

(a) $\lim\limits_{z\to\infty}[-z\,f(z)]$ or

(b) coefficient of $-\dfrac{1}{z}$ in the expansion of $f(z)$.

> ***Note*** Residue of $f(z)$ at zero is equal to the coefficient of $\dfrac{1}{z}$ in the expansion of $f(z)$.

***Example 48.*** *Find the residue of* $z\cos\dfrac{1}{z}$ *at* $z=0$.

**Solution.** We have $f(z)=z\cos\dfrac{1}{z}=z\left[1-\dfrac{1}{2!z^2}+\dfrac{1}{4!z^4}-\ldots\right]$

$$=z-\frac{1}{2z}+\frac{1}{24z^3}-\ldots$$

Here, coefficient of $\dfrac{1}{z}=-\dfrac{1}{2}\Rightarrow \text{Res } f(0)=-\dfrac{1}{2}$

***Example 49.*** *Find the residue of* $f(z)=\dfrac{z^3}{z^2-1}$ *at* $z=\infty$.

**Solution.** We have $f(z)=\dfrac{z^3}{z^2-1}=\dfrac{z^3}{z^2\left(1-\dfrac{1}{z^2}\right)}=z\left(1-\dfrac{1}{z^2}\right)^{-1}$

$$=z\left[1+\frac{1}{z^2}+\frac{1}{z^4}+\frac{1}{z^6}+\ldots\right]$$

$$=z+\frac{1}{z}+\frac{1}{z^3}+\frac{1}{z^5}+\ldots$$

$$\Rightarrow \quad \text{Res } f(\infty)=-\text{Coefficient of }\frac{1}{z}=-1$$

***Example 50.*** *Determine the pole and residue at the pole of the function* $f(z)=\dfrac{z}{z-1}$.

**Solution.** The poles of $f(z)$ are given by putting the denominator equal to zero.

$$\Rightarrow \quad z-1=0\Rightarrow \quad z=1$$

$\therefore$ The function $f(z)$ has a simple pole at $z=1$

Now, $\quad \text{res } f(a)=\lim\limits_{z\to 1}(z-1)f(z)$

$$=\lim_{z\to 1}(z-1).\frac{z}{z-1}$$

$$=\lim_{z\to 1} z=1$$

***Example 51.*** *Determine the order of each pole and calculate residue at each of the pole of*

$$f(z)=\frac{1-2z}{z(z-1)(z-2)}$$

**Solution.** Here, $f(z) = \dfrac{1-2z}{z(z-1)(z-2)}$

Poles of $f(z)$ are given by $z(z-1)(z-2) = 0$

$\Rightarrow \quad z = 0, 1, 2$ which are all simple poles.

Now, $\quad \text{res } f(0) = \lim_{z \to 0} z\, f(z)$

$$= \lim_{z \to 0} \frac{1-2z}{(z-1)(z-2)} = \frac{1}{2}$$

$$\text{res } f(1) = \lim_{z \to 1} (z-1) f(z) = \lim_{z \to 1} \frac{1-2z}{z(z-2)} = 1$$

and $\quad \text{res } f(2) = \lim_{z \to 2} (z-2)\, f(z) = \lim_{z \to 2} \dfrac{1-2z}{z(z-1)} = -\dfrac{3}{2}$

***Example 52.*** *Find each pole and its order and calculate residue at each of the pole of* $f(z) = \dfrac{z^2}{(z-1)^2 (z+2)}$.

**Solution.** Poles are given by $(z-1)^2 (z+2) = 0$

$\Rightarrow \quad z = 1$ (pole of order 2)

and $\quad z = -2$ (simple pole)

$\therefore \quad \text{res } f(1) = \phi'(1) = [\phi'(z)]_{z=1}$

where $\quad \phi(z) = \dfrac{z^2}{z+2}$

(by using formula res $f(a) = \dfrac{\phi^{m-1}(a)}{(m-1)!}$ for pole of order $m$)

Now, $\quad \phi'(z) = \dfrac{(z+2) \cdot 2z - z^2 \cdot 1}{(z+2)^2} = \dfrac{z^2 + 4z}{(z+2)^2}$

$\Rightarrow \quad \phi'(1) = \dfrac{5}{9}$

$\therefore \quad \text{res } f(1) = \dfrac{5}{9}$

and $\text{res } f(-2) = \lim_{z \to -2} (z+2)\, f(z) = \lim_{z \to -2} \left(\dfrac{z}{z-1}\right)^2$

$$= \left(\frac{-2}{-3}\right)^2 = \frac{4}{9}$$

***Example 53.*** *Find the residue of* $\dfrac{1}{(z^2+1)^3}$ *at* $z = i$.

**Solution.** We have,

$$f(z) = \frac{1}{(z^2+1)^3} = \frac{1}{(z+i)^3 (z-i)^3} = \frac{\phi(z)}{(z-i)^3},$$

where $\quad \phi(z) = \dfrac{1}{(z+i)^3}$.

Here, $z = i$ is a pole of order 3 of $f(z)$. The residue at this point is $\dfrac{1}{2!} \phi''(i)$.

Now, $\quad \phi'(z) = -\dfrac{3}{(z+i)^4}$ and $\phi''(z) = \dfrac{12}{(z+i)^5}$

$\therefore$ The residue at $z = i$ at $\dfrac{1}{2!}$

$$\phi''(i) = \frac{1}{2} \frac{12}{(i+i)^5} = \frac{3}{16i} = -\frac{3i}{16}$$

***Example 54.*** *Find the residue of* $\dfrac{z^2}{z^2 + a^2}$ *at* $z = ia$.

**Solution.** We have, $f(z) = \dfrac{z^2}{z^2 + a^2} = \dfrac{z^2}{(z+ia)(z-ia)}$

Here, $z = ia$ is a simple pole of $f(z)$.

Residue at $z = ia$ is $\lim_{z \to ia} (z - ia) f(z)$

$$= \lim_{z \to ia} (z - ia) \frac{z^2}{(z-ia)(z+ia)}$$

$$= \lim_{z \to ia} \frac{z^2}{z+ia} = \frac{-a^2}{2ia} = \frac{1}{2} i a$$

***Example 55.*** *Find the residues of the function* $\dfrac{\cot \pi z}{(z-a)^2}$.

**Solution.** We have, $f(z) = \dfrac{\cot \pi z}{(z-a)^2} = \dfrac{\cos \pi z}{\sin \pi z (z-a)^2}$

Poles of $f(z)$ are given by $(z-a)^2 \sin \pi z = 0$

$(z-a)^2 = 0 \Rightarrow z = a$ is a pole of order two

and $\sin \pi z = 0 \Rightarrow \pi z = n\pi \Rightarrow z = n$, where $n \in I$.

$z = n, (n \in I)$ are simple poles of $f(z)$, if $n$ is finite.

$z = \infty$ is the limit point of these poles so $z = \infty$ is the non-isolated essential singularity.

Residue at $z = a$ is $\dfrac{1}{1!} \phi'(a)$, where $\phi(z) = \cot \pi z = -\pi \operatorname{cosec}^2 \pi a$

Residue at $z = n$ is $\left[\dfrac{\phi(z)}{\psi'(z)}\right]_{z=n}$, where $\psi(z) = \sin \pi z$

$$= \left[\frac{\cos \pi z / (z-a)^2}{\pi \cos \pi z}\right]_{z=n} = \frac{1}{\pi (n-a)^2}$$

## Cauchy's Residue Theorem

If $f(z)$ is regular, except at a finite number of poles within a closed contour $C$ and continuous on the boundary of $C$, then $\int_C f(z)\, dz = 2\pi i \Sigma R$,

where $\Sigma R$ is the sum of the residues of $f(z)$ at its poles within $C$.

**Proof.** Let us suppose that $z_1, z_2, \ldots, z_n$ be the $n$ poles within the closed contour $C$. Let $\gamma_1, \gamma_2, \ldots, \gamma_n$ be the circles with centres $z_1, z_2, \ldots, z_n$ respectively and each of radius $r$, so small that all the circles lie entirely within $C$ and do not overlap. Then, $f(z)$ is analytic in the region lying between $C$ and the circles. Then, by Cauchy's theorem, we have

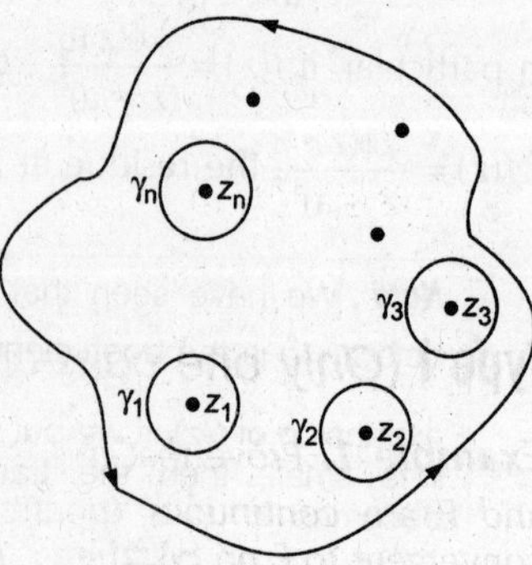


$$\int_C f(z) dz - \sum_{k=1}^{n} \int_{\gamma_k} f(z) dz = 0$$

$$\Rightarrow \quad \int_C f(z) dz = \int_{\gamma_1} f(z) dz + \int_{\gamma_2} f(z) dz + \ldots + \int_{\gamma_n} f(z) dz = 2\pi i \Sigma R$$

***Theorem*** **If an analytic function has singularities at a finite number of points (including that at infinity), then the sum of the residues at these points along with infinity is zero.**

**Proof.** Let C be the circle enclosing within it all the singularities excluding infinity. Then, we have

$\frac{1}{2\pi i}\int_C f(z)dz$ = Sum of the residues at all the finite singular points within C, also the residue at infinity is given by

$$-\frac{1}{2\pi i}\int_C f(z)dz.$$

Hence, the sum of the residues at all the finite poles along with infinity is zero.

***Example 56.*** *Evaluate* $\int_C \frac{z-3}{z^2+2z+5}dz$, *where C is the circle*

(i) $|z|=1$ (ii) $|z+1-i|=2$ (iii) $|z+1+i|=2$

**Solution.** Let $f(z)=\frac{z-3}{z^2+2z+5}$, then poles of $f(z)$ are given by $z^2+2z+5=0 \Rightarrow z=-1\pm 2i$.

(i) The poles $z=-1+2i, -1-2i$ lie outside the circle $|z|=1$, so that $f(z)$ is analytic everywhere within C.

$\therefore$ By Cauchy's theorem, we have

$$\int_C \frac{z-3}{z^2+2z+5}dz=0.$$

(ii) Only one pole $z=-1+2i$ lies inside the circle $|z+1-i|=2$. Thus, $f(z)$ is analytic at every point within C except at $z=-1+2i$.

Now, residue at $z=-1+2i$ is given by

$$\lim_{z\to -1+2i}\{z-(-1+2i)\}f(z)=\lim_{z\to -1+2i}\frac{(z+1-2i)(z-3)}{z^2+2z+5}$$

$$=\lim_{z\to -1+2i}\frac{z-3}{z+1+2i}$$

$$=\frac{-4+2i}{4i}=\frac{1}{2}+i$$

Hence, by residue theorem, we have

$$\int_C f(z)dz = 2\pi i \text{ residue at } (-1+2i)=2\pi i\left(\frac{1}{2}+i\right)=\pi(-2+i)$$

(iii) Only one pole $z=-1-2i$ lies inside the circle C given by $|z+1+i|=2$, so that $f(z)$ is analytic within C except at $z=-1-2i$.

Now, residue at $z=-1-2i$ is given by

$$\lim_{z\to -1-2i}\frac{(z+1+2i)(z-3)}{(z^2+2z+5)}=\lim_{z\to -1-2i}\frac{z-3}{(z+1-2i)}=\frac{-4-2i}{-4i}=\frac{1}{2}-i$$

Hence, by residue theorem, we have

$$\int_C f(z)dz=2\pi i \text{ residue of } f(z) \text{ at } (-1-2i)$$

$$=2\pi i\left(\frac{1}{2}-i\right)=\pi(2+i)$$

***Example 57.*** *Evaluate* $\int_C \frac{\sin \pi z^2+\cos \pi z^2}{(z-1)^2(z-2)}dz$, *where C is the circle* $|z|=3$.

**Solution.** We have, $f(z)=\frac{\sin \pi z^2+\cos \pi z^2}{(z-1)^2(z-2)}$, hence the function $f(z)$ is analytic at every point within C except at the poles $z=1, 2$.

Residue at $z=2$ is given by $\lim_{z\to 2}(z-2)f(z)$

$$=\lim_{z\to 2}\frac{\sin \pi z^2+\cos \pi z^2}{(z-1)^2}=1$$

and residue at $z=1$ is given by $\frac{1}{1!}\left[\frac{d}{dz}(z-1)^2 f(z)\right]_{z=1}$

$$=\left[\frac{d}{dz}\left(\frac{\sin \pi z^2+\cos \pi z^2}{z-2}\right)\right]_{z=1}=2\pi+1$$

Hence, by residue theorem, we have

$$\int_C f(z)dz=2\pi i \text{ [sum of residues at } z=1 \text{ and } z=2]$$

$$=2\pi i[1+(2\pi+1)]=4\pi i(\pi+1)$$

# SOLVED EXAMPLES

## Type I (*Only one correct option*)

***Example 1.*** *Prove that if* $\gamma$ *is a rectifiable curve in* $\mathbb{C}$ *and* $F_n$ *and F are continuous functions on* $\{\gamma\}$. *If* $F_n$ *is uniformly convergent to F on* $\{\gamma\}$, *then*

(a) $\int_\gamma F=\lim\int_\gamma F_n$  (b) $\int_\gamma F\geq\lim\int_\gamma F_n$

(c) $\int_\gamma F\leq\lim\int_\gamma F_n$  (d) $\int_\gamma F=0$

**Solution.** (a) Since, $F_n$ converges uniformly to F, therefore for $\varepsilon>0$, there exist an integer. N such that $|F_n(w)-F(w)|<\varepsilon$, for all w on $\{\gamma\}$ and $n\geq N$.

And, we have

$$\left|\int_\gamma F-\int_\gamma F_n\right|=\left|\int_\gamma (F-F_n)\right|$$

$$\leq\int_\gamma |F(w)-F_n(w)||dw|$$

$$\leq\varepsilon, \text{ whenever } n\geq N$$

$$\Rightarrow \int_\gamma F=\lim\int_\gamma F_n$$

***Example 2.*** *If* $0<|z-1|<2$, *the expansion of* $f(z)=\dfrac{z}{(z-1)(z-3)}$ *is*

(a) $-\dfrac{1}{2(z-1)}-\dfrac{3}{4}\sum_{n=0}^{\infty}\left(\dfrac{z-1}{2}\right)^n$

(b) $\sum_{n=0}^{\infty}\dfrac{2^n-1}{2^n}z^{n-1}$

(c) $\dfrac{1}{2z}-\left(\sum_{n=0}^{\infty}\dfrac{1}{z^{n+1}}\right)-\dfrac{1}{4}\sum_{n=0}^{\infty}\left(\dfrac{z}{2}\right)^n$

(d) No expansion exist

**Solution.** (a) Here, we have

$$f(z)=\frac{z}{(z-1)(z-3)}=-\frac{1}{2(z-1)}+\frac{3}{2}\cdot\frac{1}{(z-3)}$$

On putting $z-1=u$, we have $0<|u|<2$ and

$$f(z)=-\frac{1}{2u}+\frac{3}{2(u-2)}$$

$$=-\frac{1}{2u}-\frac{3}{4}\left(1-\frac{u}{2}\right)^{-1}$$

$$=-\frac{1}{2u}-\frac{3}{4}\left(1+\frac{u}{2}+\frac{u^2}{2^2}+\frac{u^3}{2^3}+\ldots\right)$$

$$=-\frac{1}{2u}-\frac{3}{4}\sum_{n=0}^{\infty}\left(\frac{u}{2}\right)^n$$

$$=-\frac{1}{2(z-1)}-\frac{3}{4}\sum_{n=0}^{\infty}\left(\frac{z-1}{2}\right)^n$$

***Example 3.*** $\int\dfrac{ds}{y}$ *is with respect to the transformation* $Z=\dfrac{az+b}{cz+d}$, *where* $a, b, c, d$ *satisfies* $ad-bc=1$ *and* $ds=\sqrt{(dx^2+dy^2)}$

(a) Invariant

(b) Not invariant

(c) Neither invariant nor not invariant

(d) None of the above

**Solution.** (a) Given $Z=\dfrac{az+b}{cz+d}$, we have

$$z=\frac{b-dZ}{cZ-a} \quad \ldots\text{(i)}$$

On differentiating Eq. (i), we get

$$dz=\frac{(ad-bc)}{(cZ-a)^2}dZ$$

$$\Rightarrow \quad dz=\frac{dZ}{(cZ-a)^2} \quad (\because ad-bc=1)$$

Hence, $ds=\sqrt{(dx^2+dy^2)}=|dz|=\dfrac{|dZ|}{|cZ-a|^2}$

$$=\frac{d\sigma}{|cZ-a|^2} \quad \ldots\text{(ii)}$$

Also, $2iy=z-\bar{z}$

$$=\frac{b-dZ}{cZ-a}-\frac{b-d\bar{Z}}{c\bar{Z}-a}$$

$$=\frac{(ad-bc)(Z-\bar{Z})}{|cZ-a|^2}$$

$$\Rightarrow \quad 2iy=\frac{2iY}{|cZ-a|^2} \quad (\because ad-bc=1, Z=X+iY)$$

$$\Rightarrow \quad \frac{y}{Y}=\frac{1}{|cZ-a|^2}$$

Hence, Eq. (ii) gives,

$$d\sigma=\frac{y}{Y}d\sigma \Rightarrow \int\frac{ds}{y}=\int\frac{d\sigma}{Y}$$

Thus, $\int\dfrac{ds}{y}$ is invariant under the given transformation.

***Example 4.*** *If* $\gamma:[0,1]\to\mathbb{C}$ *is a closed rectifiable curve and* $a\notin\{\gamma\}$, *then*

$$\frac{1}{2\pi i}\int_{\gamma}\frac{dz}{z-a} \text{ is}$$

(a) integer (b) rational number

(c) perfect square (d) irrational number

**Solution.** (a) Define $g:[0,1]\to\mathbb{C}$ such that

$$g(t)=\int_0^t\frac{\gamma'(s)}{\gamma(s)-a}ds$$

$$\Rightarrow \quad g(0)=0 \text{ and } g(1)=\int_{\gamma}\frac{dz}{z-a}$$

Also, we have

$$g'(t)=\frac{\gamma'(t)}{\gamma(t)-a}, 0\le t\le 1$$

$$\Rightarrow \quad \frac{d}{dt}e^{-g}(\gamma-a)$$

$$=e^{-g}\gamma'-g'e^{-g}(\gamma-a)$$

$$=e^{-g}[\gamma'-\gamma'(\gamma-a)^{-1}(\gamma-a)]=0$$

Hence, $e^{-g}(\gamma-a)=$ Constant

and $e^{-g(0)}(\gamma(0)-a)=(\gamma(0)-a)=e^{-g(1)}(\gamma(1)-a)$

Since, $\gamma(1)=\gamma(0)$

$$\Rightarrow \quad e^{-g(1)}=e^{-g(0)}=1 \quad [\because g(0)=1]$$

$$\Rightarrow \quad g(1)=2\pi ik \text{ for some integer } R.$$

***Example 5.*** $\int_C\dfrac{3z^2+z}{z^2-1}dz$

*(where, C is the circle* $|z|=2$*)*

*is*

(a) $4\pi i$ (b) $\pi i$

(c) $2\pi i$ (d) 0

**Solution.** (c) Here, $f(z)=3z^2+z$ is an analytic function. The integrand has singularities at $z^2-1=0$

$$\Rightarrow \quad z=1,-1. \text{ The circle } |z|=2$$

has centre at zero and radius 2. Then, the point $z = 1, -1$ lies inside the circle $|z| = 2$.

Also,
$$\frac{1}{z^2-1} = \frac{1}{(z-1)(z+1)}$$
$$= \frac{1}{2}\left(\frac{1}{z-1} - \frac{1}{z+1}\right)$$

$$\therefore \quad \int_C \frac{3z^2+z}{z^2-1}dz = \int_C \frac{3z^2+z}{(z-1)(z+1)}dz$$
$$= \frac{1}{2}\int_C \frac{3z^2+z}{z-1}dz - \frac{1}{2}\int_C \frac{3z^2+z}{z+1}dz$$

Hence, by Cauchy's integral formula

$$\int_C \frac{3z^2+z}{z^2-1}dz = \frac{1}{2}2\pi i(1) - \frac{1}{2}2\pi i(-1)$$
$$= \pi i(3+1) - \pi i(3-1)$$
$$= 4\pi i - 2\pi i$$
$$= 2\pi i$$

***Example 6.*** Consider

$$I_1 = \int_C \frac{dz}{z-a} = 2\pi i \text{ and}$$
$$I_2 = \int_C (z-a)^n dz = 0, \; n \neq -1$$

*where, C is the circle $|z-a| = r$.*

*Then*

(a) $I_1$ is true but $I_2$ is false (b) $I_1$ is false but $I_2$ is true
(c) both $I_1$ and $I_2$ are true (d) Neither $I_1$ nor $I_2$ is true

**Solution.** (c) We have, circle

$$C : |z-a| = r$$
$$\Rightarrow \quad z - a = re^{i\theta}$$
$$\Rightarrow \quad dz = ire^{i\theta}d\theta$$
$$\therefore \quad I_1 = \int_C \frac{1}{z-a}dz = \int_0^{2\pi} \frac{rie^{i\theta}}{re^{i\theta}}d\theta$$
$$= [i\theta]_0^{2\pi} = 2\pi i$$

Here, $f(z) = (z-a)^n, n \neq -1$ is analytic everywhere within the circle $|z-a| = r$. Hence, by Cauchy's theorem

$$\int_C f(z)dz = 0$$
$$\Rightarrow \quad \int_C (z-a)^n dz = 0, n \neq -1$$

Hence, both $I_1$ and $I_2$ are true.

***Example 7.*** The $\int_C \log z dz$,

*where, C is unit circle, is*

(a) $\pi i$ (b) $2\pi i$
(c) $4\pi i$ (d) 0

**Solution.** (b) Here, $|z| = 1 \Rightarrow z = e^{i\theta}$

$$\Rightarrow \quad dz = ie^{i\theta}d\theta$$

$$\therefore \quad \int_C \log z dz = \int_0^{2\pi} \log e^{i\theta} \cdot ie^{i\theta}d\theta$$
$$= \int_0^{2\pi} i\theta \cdot ie^{i\theta}d\theta$$
$$= -\left[\theta\frac{e^{i\theta}}{i}\right]_0^{2\pi} + \int_0^{2\pi} 1 \cdot \frac{e^{i\theta}}{i}d\theta$$
$$= -\left(\frac{2\pi e^{i2\pi}}{i}\right) + \left[\frac{e^{i\theta}}{i^2}\right]_0^{2\pi}$$
$$= 2\pi i \cdot 1 + \frac{1}{i^2}(e^{2\pi i} - 1)$$
$$= 2\pi i - (1-1) = 2\pi i$$

***Example 8.*** Consider

*$I_1 = \int_C \frac{e^{2z}}{(z-1)^4}dz$, where C is the circle $|z| = 2$ and*

*$I_2 = \int_C \frac{ze^z}{(z-a)^3}dz$, where the point a lies within the closed curve C. Then,*

(a) $I_1 = \frac{8\pi i}{3e^2}, I_2 = 2\pi i e^a \frac{(a+2)}{2}$

(b) $I_1 = 0, I_2 = 2\pi i e^a \frac{(a-2)}{2}$

(c) $I_1 = \frac{8\pi i}{3e^2}, I_2 = 0$

(d) $I_1 = 0, I_2 = 0$

**Solution.** (a) Here, $f(z) = e^{2z}$ is an analytic function, and the integrand has singular point at $z = 1$.

Now, by Cauchy integral formula for derivative, we have

$$f^{(3)}(-1) = \frac{6}{2\pi i}\int_C \frac{e^{2z}}{(z+1)^4}dz \quad \text{...(i)}$$

$$\text{Now,} \quad f(z) = e^{2z}$$
$$\Rightarrow \quad f^{(3)}(z) = 2^3 e^{2z}$$
$$\therefore \quad f^{(3)}(-1) = 8 \cdot e^{-2} = \frac{8}{e^2}$$

Hence, by Eq. (i), we have

$$\frac{8}{e^2} = \frac{3}{\pi i}\int_C \frac{e^{2z}}{(z+1)^4}dz$$
$$\Rightarrow \quad \int_C \frac{e^{2z}}{(z+1)^4}dz = \frac{8\pi i}{3e^2}$$

$$\text{Next,} \quad f(z) = ze^z$$
$$\Rightarrow \quad f'(z) = (z+1)e^z$$
$$\Rightarrow \quad f''(z) = (z+2)e^z$$
$$\text{and} \quad f''(a) = (a+2)e^a$$
$$\therefore \quad \int_C \frac{ze^z}{(z-a)^3}dz = \frac{2\pi i}{2!}(a+2)e^a$$
$$= \frac{2\pi i}{2}(a+2)e^a$$

***Example 9.*** $\int \frac{2z^3 - 5}{(z+2)^2(z^2+4)z^2} dz$ *is*

*(where, c is the square with vertices* $1+i, 2+i, 2+2i, 1+2i$*).*

(a) 0 (b) $\pi i$
(c) $2\pi i$ (d) $4\pi i$

**Solution.** (a) We have,

$$f(z) = \frac{2z^2+5}{(z+2)^2(z^2+4)z^2}$$

Then, $f(z)$ has poles at $z = -2, 0$ of order two at $z = 2i, -2i$ of order one.

y, D (1, 2), C (2, 2), A (1, 1), B (2, 1), O (0, 0), X

Hence, all the poles lie outside the square c. Hence, by Cauchy residue theorem

$$\int_C \frac{2z^2-5}{(z+2)^2(z^2+4)z^2} dz = 2\pi i \times 0 = 0$$

## Type II (*One or more than one correct option*)

***Example 10.*** $f(z) = \int_C \tan z \, dz$ *in the circle* $|z| = 2$.

(a) $\pi/2$ and $-\pi/2$ are two poles inside the circle
(b) no pole exist
(c) $f(z) = -4\pi i$
(d) Residues are $-1, -1$

**Solution.** (a), (c), (d)

Given that, $f(z) = \tan z = \frac{\sin z}{\cos z}$, hence

Poles are given by $\cos z = 0$

$\Rightarrow$ $z = \frac{(2n+1)}{2}\pi$, $n$ is any integer, out of these only $\frac{\pi}{2}$ and $-\frac{\pi}{2}$ are inside circle.

$|z| = 2$ $(\pi = 3.14)$

$$\therefore \quad \text{res } f(\pi/2) = \lim_{z\to\pi/2} \frac{\sin z}{\frac{d}{dz}\cos z}$$

$$= \lim_{z\to\pi/2} \frac{\sin z}{-\sin z} = -1$$

and res $f(-\pi/2) = -1$

By residue theorem,

$$\int_C f(z)dz = 2\pi i[\text{res } f(\pi/2) + \text{res } f(-\pi/2)]$$

$$= 2\pi i(-1-1) = -4\pi i$$

***Example 11.*** *Evaluate* $\int_C \frac{z^2 - z + 1}{z-1} dx$, *where C is the circle.*

(a) when $|z| = 1$, $\int_C \frac{z^2-z+1}{z-1} dz = 2\pi i$

(b) when $|z| = \frac{1}{2}$, $\int_C \frac{z^2-z+1}{z-1} dz = 0$

(c) when $|z| = 1$, $\int_C \frac{z^2-z+1}{z-1} dz = 0$

(d) when $|z| = \frac{1}{2}$, $\int_C \frac{z^2-z+1}{z-1} dz = 2\pi i$

**Solution.** (a), (b)

(i) Since, $\int_C \frac{f(z)dz}{z-a} = \int_C \frac{z^2-z+1}{z-1} dz$

$\Rightarrow$ $f(z) = z^2 - z + 1$ and $a = 1$

Since, $f(z)$ is analytic within and on circle $C : |z| = 1$ and $a = 1$ lies on C.

$\therefore$ By Cauchy's integral formula

$$\frac{1}{2\pi i}\int_C \frac{f(z)}{z-a} dz = f(a) = 1$$

i.e., $\int_C \frac{z^2-z+1}{z-1} dz = 2\pi i$

(ii) Here, $a = 1$ lies outside the circle $C : |z| = 1/2$. So, $(z^2 - z + 1)/(z-1)$ is analytic everywhere within C.

$\therefore$ By Cauchy's theorem $\int_C \frac{z^2-z+1}{z-1} dz = 0$.

***Example 12.*** *Given integral* $\int_C \tan z dz$, *where C is the circle* $|z| = 2$.

(a) The poles are $z = \pi/2$ and $z = -\pi/2$
(b) There is no pole
(c) The value of the integral is $-4\pi i$
(d) The integral does not exist

**Solution.** (a), (c)

Here, the poles of $f(z) = \sin z/\cos z$ are $\cos z = 0$

$\Rightarrow$ $z = (2n+1)\pi/2, n = 0, \pm 1, \pm 2, \ldots$

$z = \pi/2$ and $-\pi/2$ are only poles that are within the given circle.

$$\therefore \quad \text{res } f(\pi/2) = \lim_{z\to\pi/2} \frac{\sin z}{\frac{d}{dz}(\cos z)}$$

$$= \lim_{z\to\pi/2}\left(\frac{\sin z}{-\sin z}\right) = -1$$

and

$$\text{res } f(-\pi/2) = \lim_{z\to-\pi/2} \frac{\sin z}{\frac{d}{dz}(\cos z)} = -1$$

Hence, by residue theorem,

$$\int_C f(z)dz = 2\pi i\{\text{res } f(\pi/2) + \text{res } f(-\pi/2)\}$$

$$= 2\pi i(-1-1) = -4\pi i$$

***Example 13.*** *Given integral*

$$\int_C \frac{\sin \pi z^2 + \cos \pi z^2}{(z-1)^2(z-2)} dz, \text{ where C is the circle } |z| = 3$$

(a) $\dfrac{\sin \pi z^2 + \cos \pi z^2}{(z-1)^2(z-2)}$ is analytic within the circle $|z| = 3$ except at the poles $z = 1$ and $z = 2$

(b) The value of the integral is $4\pi(\pi + 1)i$

(c) The value of the integral is $4\pi$

(d) It has a pole of order 2

**Solution.** (a), (b), (d)

Given that $f(z) = \dfrac{\sin \pi z^2 + \cos \pi z^2}{(z-1)^2(z-2)}$

is analytic within the circle $|z| = 3$ except at the poles $z = 1$ and $z = 2$.

Since, $z = 1$ is a pole of order 2.

Hence, $\text{res } f(1) = \dfrac{1}{1!}\left[\dfrac{d}{dz}[(z-1)^2 f(z)]\right]_{z=1}$

$$= \left[\frac{d}{dz}\left(\frac{\sin \pi z^2 + \cos \pi z^2}{z-2}\right)\right]_{z=1}$$

$$= \left[\frac{(z-2)(2\pi z \cos \pi z^2 - 2\pi z \sin \pi z^2) - (\sin \pi z^2 + \cos \pi z^2)}{(z-2)^2}\right]_{z=1}$$

$$= (-1)(-2\pi) - (-1) = 2\pi + 1$$

and $\text{res } f(2) = \lim\limits_{z \to 2} [(z-2) f(z)]$

$$= \lim_{z \to 2} \frac{\sin \pi z^2 + \cos \pi z^2}{(z-1)^2} = 1$$

Therefore, by residue theorem,

$$\int_C f(z)dz = 2\pi i[\text{res } f(1) + \text{res } f(2)]$$

$$= 2\pi i(2\pi + 1 + 1)$$

$$= 4\pi(\pi + 1)i$$

***Example 14.*** *Given the function*

$$f(z) = \frac{4z+3}{z(z-3)(z+2)}$$

(a) Within $|z| = 1$ the Laurent series is

$$f(z) = -\frac{1}{2z} - \sum_{n=0}^{\infty}\left[\frac{1}{3^{n+1}} + (-1)^n \frac{1}{2^{n+2}}\right] z^n$$

(b) In the angular region between $|z| = 2$ and $|z| = 3$ the Laurent series expansion is

$$f(z) = -\frac{1}{2z} - \sum_{n=0}^{\infty} \frac{z^n}{3^{n+1}} + \sum_{n=0}^{\infty} (-1)^{n+1} \frac{2^{n-1}}{z^{n+1}}$$

(c) Exterior to $|z| = 3$ the Laurent series expansion is

$$f(z) = -\frac{1}{2z} + \sum_{n=0}^{\infty} \frac{3^n}{z^{n+1}} + \sum_{n=0}^{\infty} (-1)^{n+1} \frac{2^{n-1}}{z^{n+1}}$$

(d) The function $f(z)$ is analytic at every point in the z-plane except at $z = -2, 0, 3$

**Solution.** (a), (b), (c), (d)

Given that, $f(z) = \dfrac{4z+3}{z(z-3)(z+2)}$

$$= -\frac{1}{2z} + \frac{1}{z-3} - \frac{1}{2(z+2)}$$

The function $f(z)$ is analytic at every point in the z-plane except at $z = -2, 0, 3$.

(i) When $0 < |z| < 1$, then we have

$$f(z) = -\frac{1}{2z} - \frac{1}{3}\left(1 - \frac{z}{3}\right)^{-1} - \frac{1}{4}\left(1 + \frac{z}{2}\right)^{-1}$$

$$= -\frac{1}{2z} + \frac{1}{3}\sum_{n=0}^{\infty}\left(\frac{z}{3}\right)^n - \frac{1}{4}\sum_{n=0}^{\infty}(-1)^n\left(\frac{z}{2}\right)^n$$

$$= -\frac{1}{2z} - \sum_{n=0}^{\infty}\left[\frac{1}{3^{n+1}} + (-1)^n \frac{1}{2^{n+2}}\right] z^n$$

(ii) When $2 < |z| < 3$, then we have

$$f(z) = -\frac{1}{2z} - \frac{1}{3}\left(1 - \frac{z}{3}\right)^{-1} - \frac{1}{2z}\left(1 + \frac{z}{2}\right)^{-1}$$

$$= -\frac{1}{2z} - \frac{1}{3}\sum_{n=0}^{\infty}\left(\frac{z}{3}\right)^n - \frac{1}{2z}\sum_{n=0}^{\infty}(-1)^n\left(\frac{2}{z}\right)^n$$

$$= -\frac{1}{2z} - \sum_{n=0}^{\infty} \frac{z^n}{3^{n+1}} + \sum_{n=0}^{\infty} (-1)^{n+1} \frac{2^{n-1}}{z^{n+1}}$$

(iii) When $|z| < 3$, then we have

$$f(z) = -\frac{1}{2z} + \frac{1}{z}\left(1 - \frac{3}{z}\right)^{-1} - \frac{1}{2z}\left(1 + \frac{2}{z}\right)^{-1}$$

$$= -\frac{1}{2z} + \frac{1}{z}\sum_{n=0}^{\infty}\left(\frac{3}{z}\right)^n - \frac{1}{2z}\sum_{n=0}^{\infty}(-1)^n\left(\frac{2}{z}\right)^n$$

$$= -\frac{1}{2z} + \sum_{n=0}^{\infty} \frac{3^n}{z^{n+1}} + \sum_{n=0}^{\infty} (-1)^{n+1} \frac{2^{n-1}}{z^{n+1}}$$

***Example 15.*** Given $f(z) = \dfrac{\cot \pi z}{(z-a)^2}$

(a) *$z = 0$ is simple poles*

(b) *$z = \infty$ is non-isolated essential singularity*

(c) *$z = 0$ is not a pole*

(d) *$z = \infty$ is the limit point of the simple pole*

**Solution.** (a), (b), (d)

Given that $f(z) = \dfrac{\cot \pi z}{(z-a)^2}$

$$= \frac{\cos \pi z}{\sin \pi z (z-a)^2}$$

Hence, poles of $f(z)$ are obtained by equating to zero the denominator of $f(z)$.

$$\Rightarrow \qquad (z-a)^2 \sin \pi z = 0$$

$$\Rightarrow \qquad \sin \pi z = 0 \text{ or } (z-a)^2 = 0$$

Now, $\sin \pi z = 0 \Rightarrow \pi z = n\pi \Rightarrow z = n$

where $n$ is any integer,

and $(z-a)^2 = 0 \Rightarrow z = a$

Hence, $z = a$ is a double pole and

$z = 0, \pm 1, \pm 2, \ldots$ are simple poles.

$z = \infty$

is a limit point of these simple poles, therefore $z = \infty$ is non-isolated essential singularity.

***Example 16.*** *If G is a region and $f: G \to \mathbb{C}$ is an analytic function such that there is $a \in G$ with $|f(a)| \geq |f(z)|$ for all $z \in G$, then*

(a) $f$ is constant
(b) $f$ is not constant
(c) $f$ is even function
(d) $f$ is odd function

**Solution.** (a)

Let there is a closed ball $\overline{B}(a; R) \subset G$ and $\gamma(t) = a + re^{it}$ for $0 \leq t \leq 2\pi$, then, we have

$$f(a) = \frac{1}{2\pi i}\int_\gamma \frac{f(w)}{w-a}\,dw = \frac{1}{2\pi}\int_0^{2\pi} f(a+re^{it})\,dt$$

$$\Rightarrow \quad |f(a)| \leq \frac{1}{2\pi}\int_0^{2\pi} |f(a+re^{it})|\,dt \leq |f(a)|$$

Since, $|f(a+re^{it})| \leq |f(a)|$ for all $t$.

$$\Rightarrow \quad \int_0^{2\pi} [\,|f(a)| - |f(a+re^{it})|\,]\,dt = 0$$

Since, the integrand is non-negative, hence we have

$|f(a)| = |f(a+re^{it})|$ for all $t$

Moreover, since $r$ is arbitrary, we have $f$ maps any disk $B(a; R) \subset G$ into circle $|z| = |\alpha|$ where $f(a) = \alpha$. This implies $f$ is constant on $B(a; R)$. In particular $f(z) = \alpha$ for $|z-a| < R$, i.e., $f(z)$ = Constant.

***Example 17.*** *Which of the following statement(s) is/are true?*

(a) If $p(z)$ is a non-constant polynomial, then there is a complex number $a \in \mathbb{C}$ such that $p(a) = 0$.
(b) If $p(z)$ is a non-constant polynomial, then there is a complex number $a \subset \mathbb{C}$ such that $p(a) \neq 0$.
(c) (a) states fundamental theorem of Algebra.
(d) (b) states fundamental theorem of Algebra.

**Solution.** (a), (c)

Suppose, $p(z) \neq 0$ for all $z$ and $f(z) = [p(z)]^{-1}$

Then, $f$ is entire function since $p(z) \neq 0$.

If $p(z)$ is non-constant polynomial, then

$$\lim_{z\to\infty} p(z) = \infty \Rightarrow \lim_{z\to 0} f(z) = 0$$

Hence, there exist $R > 0$ such that $|f(z)| < 1$, if $|z| > 1$.

Since, $f$ is continuous on $\overline{B}(0; R)$, hence there exist $M > 0$ such that $|f(z)| \leq M$ for $|z| \leq R$.

$\Rightarrow f$ is bounded.

By Liouville's theorem, if $f$ is entire function and bounded too, then $f$ is to be constant.

Since, $f$ is constant.

$\Rightarrow \; f(z) = [p(z)]^{-1}$ is also constant, which is a contradiction to our assumption.

Thus, $p(z)$ is a non-constant polynomial, for some $z = a$, $p(a) = 0$.

***Example 18.*** Given $f(z) = \dfrac{z^2}{z^2 + a^2}$

(a) $z = ia$ is a simple pole of $f(z)$
(b) $z = ia$ is not a simple pole of $f(z)$
(c) $\frac{1}{2}ia$ is a residue at $z = ia$ of $f(z)$
(d) $\frac{1}{3}ia$ is a residue at $z = ia$ of $f(z)$

**Solution.** (a), (c)

Given that, $f(z) = \dfrac{z^2}{z^2+a^2} = \dfrac{z^2}{(z+ia)(z-ia)}$

$z = ia$ is a simple pole of $f(z)$.

Now, residue at $z = ia$ is, $\lim\limits_{z\to ia}(z-ia)\,f(z)$

$$= \lim_{z\to ia}(z-ia)\frac{z^2}{(z-ia)(z+ia)}$$

$$= \lim_{z\to ia}\frac{z^2}{z+ia} = \frac{-a^2}{2ia} = \frac{1}{2}ia$$

***Example 19.*** *The roots of the equation $z^4 - z^2 - 2z + 2 = 0$ is/are*

(a) 1
(b) $-1$
(c) $-1+i$
(d) $-1-i$

**Solution.** (a), (b), (c), (d)

Since, by fundamental theorem of algebra every polynomial equation $P(z) = 0$ has atleast one root.

Now, the polynomial equation

$$P(z) = z^4 - z^2 - 2z + 2 = 0$$

has 1 as a root, because

$$P(1) = 1^4 - 1^2 - 2\times 1 + 2 = 0$$

$$\therefore \quad P(2) = (z-1)\,Q(z) = 0$$

where, $Q(z)$ is a polynomial of degree 3.

Now, $$Q(z) = \frac{z^4 - z^2 - 2z + 2}{z-1} = z^3 + z^2 - 2$$

Now, $$Q(1) = 1^3 + 1^2 - 2 = 0$$

$\Rightarrow Q(z)$ has 1 as a root.

$$\therefore \quad Q(z) = (z-1)R(z)$$

where, $R(z)$ is a quadratic polynomial. Thus,

$$R(z) = \frac{z^3 + z^2 - 2}{z-1} = z^2 + 2z + 2$$

Now, $$R(z) = z^2 + 2z + 2 = 0$$

$$\Rightarrow \quad z = \frac{1}{2}[-2 \pm \sqrt{4-8}] = -1 \pm i$$

$\therefore$ The required roots are $\pm 1$ and $-1 \pm i$.

# Exercise 1 (For Part 'B')

**Directions** (Q. Nos. 1-227) *All questions have only one correct option.*

**1.** The complex line integral is
(a) dependent of path
(b) independent of path
(c) independent of end points
(d) None of the above

**2.** If $f(z)$ is analytic in a simple connected domain $D$, then
(a) indefinite integral exist
(b) indefinite integral does not exist
(c) integral of $f(z)$ is dependent of path in $D$
(d) None of the above

**3.** The integral of $\oint_C (z - z_0)^m \, dz$ is equal to
(a) 0 for $m = -1$ (b) $2\pi i$ for $m = -1$
(c) 2 for $m = -1$ (d) $\pi$ for $m = -1$

**4.** The value of $\oint_C \frac{z^3 - 6}{2z - i} dz \; C : |z - i| = 1$ is
(a) $\pi / 8$ (b) $6\pi i$
(c) $(\pi / 8) - 6\pi i$ (d) $-6\pi i - (\pi / 8)$

**5.** The function $f(z) = \cos z$ is
(a) analytic everywhere
(b) singularities at $z = \pm \frac{(n+1)\pi}{2}$
(c) singularities at $z = \frac{n\pi}{2}$
(d) None of the above

**6.** The function $f(z) = \frac{1}{z^n}$ is
(a) analytic for all $z$ (b) singularities at $z = 0$
(c) singularities at $n = 0$ (d) None of these

**7.** If $f(z)$ is continuous in a simple connected domain $D$ and if $\oint_C f(z) dz = 0$ for every closed contour in $D$, then
(a) $f(z)$ is non-analytic in $D$ (b) $f(z)$ is analytic in $D$
(c) $f(z)$ is constant (d) None of these

**8.** The poles of the function $f(z) = \frac{\sin z}{\cos z}$ are at
(a) $\frac{(2\pi + 1)\pi}{2}$, $n$ is any integer
(b) $\frac{2n\pi}{3}$, $n$ is any integer
(c) $n\pi$
(d) None of the above

**9.** If $f(z)$ is analytic in a simply connected domain $D$, then for every closed path $C$ in $D$
(a) $\oint_C f(z) dz = 0$ (b) $\oint_C f(z) dz = 1$
(c) $\oint_C f(z) dz \neq 0$ (d) $\oint_C f(z) dz \neq 1$

**10.** **(A)** Every analytic function can be represented by power series.
**(B)** Taylor series is a power series.
(a) A and B both false
(b) A and B both true
(c) A is true and B is false
(d) A is false and B is true

**11.** If $f(z)$ entire function the Taylor series is
(a) convergent for all $z$ (b) divergent for all $z$
(c) constant (d) None of these

**12.** If $G$ is simply connected, then for every curve $\gamma \in G, \int_\gamma f = 0$
(a) for every function $f$
(b) for every non-analytic function $f$
(c) for every analytic function $f$
(d) None of the above

**13.** If $G$ is simply connected, then $\int_\gamma f = 0$ for
(a) every rectifiable curve
(b) every closed rectifiable curve $\gamma$
(c) every function $f$
(d) None of the above

**14.** If $z = a$ is an isolated singularity of $f$, then a is the pole of $f$, if
(a) $\lim_{z \to a} |f(z)| = 0$ (b) $\lim_{z \to a} |f(z)| = a$
(c) $\lim_{z \to a} |f(z)| = \infty$ (d) None of these

**15.** If $z = a$ is an isolated singularity of $f$ and $f(z) = \sum_{-\infty}^{\infty} a_n (z - a)^n$ is its Laurent Expansion in $ann(a; 0, R)$. Then, $z = a$ is a removable singularity, if
(a) $a_n = 0, n \le -1$ (b) $a_n \neq 0, n \le -1$
(c) $a_n = 0, n \ge -1$ (d) $a_n \neq 0, n \ge -1$

**16.** If $\gamma : [a, b] \to \mathbb{C}$ is of bounded variation and $P$, $Q$ are part of $[a, b]$. If $P \subset Q$, then
(a) $v(\gamma; P) \le v(\gamma; Q)$ (b) $v(\gamma; Q) \le v(\gamma; P)$
(c) $v(\gamma; P) = v(\gamma; Q)$ (d) None of these

**17.** If $\gamma : [a, b] \to \mathbb{C}$ and $P$ is any partition of $[a, b]$. Then, total variation of $\gamma$, $V(\gamma)$ is equal to
(a) Inf $\{v(\gamma; P)\}$ (b) Sup $\{v(\gamma; P)\}$
(c) max $\{v(\gamma; P)\}$ (d) min $\{v(\gamma; P)\}$

**18.** If $\gamma : [a, b] \to \mathbb{C}$ and $\gamma$ is of bounded variation, then total variation $V(\gamma)$ is
(a) $V(\gamma) \le \int_b^i |\gamma'(t)| \, dt$ (b) $V(\gamma) \ge \int_b^i |\gamma'(t)| \, dt$
(c) $V(\gamma) = \int_b^i |\gamma'(t)| \, dt$ (d) None of these

**19.** If $\gamma$ is a rectifiable curve in $\mathbb{C}$ and $F_n$ and $F$ are continuous functions on $\{\gamma\}$, also if $F = u - \lim F_n$ on $\{\gamma\}$, then

(a) $\int_\gamma F = \lim \int_\gamma F_n$ (b) $\int_\gamma F = \int_\gamma F_n$

(c) $\int_\gamma F \neq \lim \int_\gamma F_n$ (d) $\int_\gamma F \neq \int_\gamma F_n$

**20.** If $f: G \to \mathbb{C}$ is analytic and $R = d(a, \partial G)$, then for $a \in G$ and $|z - a| < R$

(a) $f(z) = a_n(z-a)^n$ (b) $f(z) = \sum_{n=0}^{\infty} a_n(z-a)^n$

(c) $f(z) = \sum (z-a)^n$ (d) None of these

**21.** The pole of the function $f(z) = \dfrac{z^2}{(z-1)^2(z+2)}$ is

(a) at $z = -2$ (b) at $z = -1$

(c) at $z = +1$ (d) at $z = +2$

**22.** $G$ is open set in $\mathbb{C}$, $\gamma$ is a closed rectifiable path in $G$ and $f: G \to \mathbb{C}$ is a continuous function, then

(a) $\int_\gamma f(z)dz = 0$ (b) $\int_\gamma f(z)dz > 0$

(c) $\int_\gamma f(z)dz < 0$ (d) None of these

**23.** If $\phi: [a, b] \times [c, d] \to \mathbb{C}$ is a continuous function and $g: [c, d] \to \mathbb{C}$ such that $g(t) = \int_a^b \phi(s, t)ds$, then

(a) $g$ is not a continuous function

(b) $g$ is a continuous function

(c) $g$ is an increasing function

(d) $g$ is not a decreasing function

**24.** If $\gamma$ and $\sigma$ are closed rectifiable curves having same initial points, then for every $a \notin \{\gamma\}$

(a) $n(\gamma; a) = -n(\gamma; a)$ (b) $n(\gamma; a) = n(-\gamma; a)$

(c) $n(\gamma; a) = -n(-\gamma; a)$ (d) None of these

**25.** If $\gamma: [0, 1] \to \mathbb{C}$ is a closed rectifiable curve and $a \notin \{\gamma\}$, then $\dfrac{1}{2\pi i}\int_\gamma \dfrac{dz}{z-a}$ is

(a) an integer (b) rational number

(c) real number (d) complex number

**26.** If $\gamma$ is a closed rectifiable curve in $\mathbb{C}$, then for $a \notin \{\gamma\}$, the index of $\gamma$ with respect to point $a$ is

(a) $n(\gamma; a) = \dfrac{1}{2\pi i}\int_\gamma a dz$ (b) $n(\gamma; a) = \dfrac{1}{2\pi i}\int_\gamma (z-a)^{-1} dz$

(c) $n(\gamma; a) = \dfrac{1}{2\pi i}\int_\gamma a dz$ (d) None of these

**27.** A path in same region is

(a) continuous function

(b) discontinuous function

(c) differentiable function

(d) None of the above

**28.** A path is said to be smooth path, if

(a) it is continuous function

(b) it is a continuous and differentiable function

(c) differentiable function

(d) None of the above

**29.** A path $\gamma$ is piecewise smooth in interval $[a, b]$, if in a partition $P$ of $[a_2, b]$

(a) in each subinterval $\gamma$ is continuous

(b) in each subinterval $\gamma$ is smooth path

(c) in each subinterval $\gamma$ is a path

(d) None of the above

**30.** If $\gamma$ and $\sigma$ are closed rectifiable curves having same initial points, then for every $a \in \{\gamma\} \cup \{\sigma\}$

(a) $m(\gamma + \sigma; a) = n(\gamma; a)$

(b) $m(\gamma + \sigma; a) = n(\sigma; a)$

(c) $m(\gamma + \sigma; a) = n(\gamma; a) + n\{\sigma; a\}$

(d) None of the above

**31.** If $\gamma$ is piecewise smooth and $f: [a, b] \to \mathbb{C}$ is continuous, then

(a) $\int_a^b f\, d\gamma = \int_a^b f(t)\gamma(t)dt$ (b) $\int_a^b f d\gamma = \int_a^b f(t)\gamma(t)dt$

(c) $\int_a^b f d\gamma = \int_a^b f'(t)\gamma(t)dt$ (d) None of these

**32.** If $\gamma$ is a rectifiable curve and $f$ is continuous function on $\{\gamma\}$, then

(a) $\int_\gamma f = -\int_\gamma f$ (b) $\int_\gamma f dt = -\int_{-\gamma} f dt$

(c) $\int_\gamma f dt = \int_\gamma f dt$ (d) $\int_\gamma f dt = -\int_\gamma f dt$

**33.** If $f(z) = \dfrac{1-e^z}{1+e^z}$, then at $z = \infty$, $f(z)$ have

(a) pole (b) removable singularity

(c) isolated singularity (d) non-isolated singularity

**34.** A open set $G$ is simply connected if $G$ is connected and

(a) every curve in $G$ is homotopic to zero

(b) every closed curve in $G$ homotopic to zero

(c) every curve in $G$ is non-homotopic to zero

(d) every closed curve in $G$, $G$ is non-homotopic to zero

**35.** If $z = a$ is an isolated singularity of $f$ and $f(z) = \sum_{-\infty}^{\infty} a_n(z-a)^n$ is its Laurent expansion in $ann(a; 0, R)$. Also, if $a_{-m} \neq 0$ and $a_n = 0$ for $n \leq (m+1)$, then

(a) $z = a$ is a removable singularity

(b) $z = a$ is a pole of order $m$

(c) $z = a$ is an essential singularity

(d) None of the above

**36.** If $G$ is a region and $f$ is non-constant analytic function on $G$. Then, open mapping theorem states, for any open set $U \subset G$

(a) $F(U)$ is closed (b) $F(U)$ is open

(c) $F(U) = U$ (d) None of these

**37.** $f(z) = \dfrac{\sin z}{(z-\pi)^2}$ have the pole of order

(a) 1 (b) 2

(c) 3 (d) 0

**38.** If $\gamma$ is a rectifiable curve and $f$ is a continuous function on $(\gamma)$, then

(a) $\left|\int_\gamma f(z)dz\right| \le \int_\gamma |f(z)||dz|$

(b) $\left|\int_\gamma f(z)dz\right| \ge \int_\gamma |f(z)||dz|$

(c) $\left|\int_\gamma f(z)dz\right| = \int_\gamma |f(z)||dz|$

(d) None of the above

**39.** If $f$ have an isolated singularity at $z = a$ and $f(z) = \sum_{-\infty}^{\infty} a_n(z-a)^n$ is its Laurent expansion about $z = a$. Then, residue of $f$ at $z = a$ is

(a) $a_{-1}$ (b) $a_0$
(c) $a_{-2}$ (d) $a_1$

**40.** $C$ is closed contour $|z| = r$ and $n \neq -1$, then $\int_C z^n dz$ is equal to

(a) $2\pi i$ (b) $2\pi$
(c) $i$ (d) 0

**41.** The value of $\int_C \frac{1}{z} dz$, where $C$ is circle $z = e^{i\theta}$, $0 \le \theta \le \pi$ is

(a) $\pi i$ (b) $-\pi i$
(c) $2\pi i$ (d) 0

**42.** The value of $\frac{1}{2\pi i}\int_{|z|=3} \frac{e^z}{z-2} dz$ is

(a) 0 (b) 1
(c) $e^2$ (d) $e^3$

**43.** If $z = a$ is an isolated singularity of $f$ and $f(z) = \sum_{-\infty}^{\infty} a_n(z-a)^n$ is its Laurent expansion in $ann(a; 0, R)$. Then, $z = a$ is an essential singularity, if

(a) $a_n \neq 0$ for all integers $n$
(b) $a_n = 0$ for all integers $n$
(c) $a_n \neq 0$ for infinitely many negative $n$
(d) $a_n \neq 0$ for many positive $n$

**44.** The value of the integral $\oint_C \frac{e^z}{z-2} dz$ where $C : |z| = 3$ is

(a) $2\pi i e^2$ (b) $2\pi i$
(c) $e^2$ (d) None of these

**45.** If $z = a$ is an isolated singularity of $f$ and $f(z) = \sum_{-\infty}^{\infty} a_n(z-a)^n$ is its Laurent expansion in $ann(a; 0, R)$. Then, if $a_n = 0$ for $n < -1, z = a$ is

(a) a pole of order $m$
(b) an essential singularity
(c) a removable singularity
(d) None of the above

**46.** $f(z) = \sum_{n=0}^{\infty} a_n(z-a)^n$ have radius of convergence $R > 0$, then

(a) for $n \le 0$, $a_n = \frac{1}{n!} f^{(n)}(a)$
(b) for $n \ge 0$, $a_n = 0$
(c) for $n \ge 0$, $a_n = \frac{1}{n!} f^{(n)}(a)$
(d) None of the above

**47.** If $f(z)$ is analytic within and on the circle $C : |z - a| = r$ and $|f(z)| \le M$, then

(a) $|f^n(a)| \le \frac{M}{r^n}$ (b) $|f^n(a)| \le \frac{Mn!}{r^n}$
(c) $|f^n(a)| \ge \frac{Mn!}{r^n}$ (d) $|f^n(a)| \ge \frac{M}{r^n}$

**48.** The sum of the residues of $f(z) = \frac{\sin z}{z \cos z}$ at its poles inside the circle $|z| = 2$, is

(a) 0 (b) 1
(c) $-1$ (d) $\pi$

**49.** If $f$ is analytic in a ball $B(a; R)$ and $|f(z)| \le M$, $\forall$ $a \in B(a; R)$, then

(a) $|f^{(n)}(a)| \le \frac{n!M}{R^n}$ (b) $|f^{(n)}(a)| \ge \frac{n!M}{R^n}$
(c) $|f^{(n)}(a)| = n!M$ (d) None of these

**50.** The value of $\int_C \frac{z dz}{\sin z}$, where $C : |z| = 4$ is

(a) $2\pi i$ (b) 0
(c) $-2\pi i$ (d) $4\pi i$

**51.** The value of $\int_C \tanh z \, dz$, where $C : |z| = 3$ is

(a) 0 (b) $\pi i$
(c) $2\pi i$ (d) $4\pi i$

**52.** If $f$ has a pole of order $m$ at $z = a$ and $g(z) = (z - a)_m f(z)$, then

(a) $\text{res}(f; a) = \frac{1}{(m-1)!} g^{(m-1)}(a)$
(b) $\text{res}(f; a) = g^{(m-1)}(a)$
(c) $\text{res}(f; a) = \frac{1}{(m-1)!} g(a)$
(d) None of the above

**53.** If $\gamma_0$ and $\gamma_1$ are two rectifiable curves in $G$ and $\gamma_0$ and $\gamma_1$ are fixed-end points homotopic, then for any analytic function $f$ in $G$

(a) $\int_{\gamma_0} f - \int_{\gamma} f = 0$ (b) $\int_{\gamma_0} f + \int_{\gamma_1} f = 0$
(c) $\int_{\gamma_0} f \int_{\gamma_1} f = 0$ (d) None of these

**54.** If $f$ and $g$ are continuous functions on $[a, b]$ and $\gamma$ and $\sigma$ are the functions of bounded variation on $[a, b]$. Then,

(a) $\int_a^b (f+g) d\gamma = \int_a^b f \, d\gamma$
(b) $\int_a^b (f+g) d\gamma = \int_a^b g \, d\gamma$
(c) $\int_a^b (f+g) d\gamma = \int_a^b f \, d\gamma + \int_a^b g \, d\gamma$
(d) None of the above

**55.** If $z = a$ is an isolated singularity of $f$ and $f(z) = \sum_{-\infty}^{\infty} a_n(z-a)^n$ is its Laurent expansion in $ann(a;0,R)$. Then, $z = a$ is a pole of order $m$, then

(a) $a_{-m} \neq 0$ and $a_n = 0$ for $n \le -(m+1)$
(b) $a_{-m} = 0$ and $a_n \neq 0$ for $n \le -(m+1)$
(c) $a_{-m} = 0$ and $a_n = 0$ for $m \le -(m+1)$
(d) None of the above

**56.** The value of $\int_C \frac{(3z^2+7z+1)}{z+1} dz$, where C is $|z| = 1/2$ is

(a) $2\pi i$ (b) 0
(c) $\pi i$ (d) $\pi i/2$

**57.** The value of $\int_C \frac{(3z+4)}{z(2z+1)} dz$, where C is the circle $|z| = 1$ is

(a) $2\pi i$ (b) $3\pi i$
(c) 4 (d) $-4$

**58.** The residue of a function can be found, if the pole is an isolated singularity

(a) true (b) false
(c) partially false (d) None of these

**59.** $\int_C f(z)dz$ is equal to

(a) $2\pi i f(a)$ (b) $2\pi i \text{ Im } f(a)$
(c) $2\pi i \text{ res } f(a)$ (d) $-2\pi i \text{ res } f(a)$

**60.** The singularity of the function $\frac{z - \sin z}{z^2}$ is

(a) $z = 0$ (b) $z = 2$
(c) $z = -2$ (d) $z = 4$

**61.** Taylor's expansion of $f(z) = \frac{1}{(z+1)^2}$ about the point $z = -i$ is

(a) $(2i-2) + \frac{1}{z} + \frac{1}{z+1}$
(b) $\frac{i}{2}\left[1 + \sum_{n=1}^{\infty}(-1)^n \frac{(n+1)(z+i)^n}{(1-i)^n}\right]$
(c) $\frac{i}{2}\left[1 - \sum_{n=1}^{\infty}(-1)^n \frac{(n-1)(z+i)^n}{(1-i)^n}\right]$
(d) None of the above

**62.** If $z = a$ is a singularity of $f(z)$ such that $f(z)$ is analytic at each point in its neighbourhood, then $z = a$ is called as

(a) a removable singularity
(b) an isolated singularity
(c) an essential singularity
(d) None of the above

**63.** If $\gamma_0$ and $\gamma_1$ are two closed rectifiable curves in G and $\gamma_0$ is homotopic to $\gamma_1$, then for every analytic function $f$ on G

(a) $\int_{\gamma_0} f \neq \int_{\gamma_1} f$ (b) $\int_{\gamma_0} f = \int_{\gamma_1} f$
(c) $\int_{\gamma_0} f + \int_{\gamma_1} f = 0$ (d) None of these

**64.** If $\gamma$ is a closed rectifiable curve in G and $\gamma$ is homotopic to 0, then for all $\omega \in \mathbb{C} - G$,

(a) $n(\gamma;\omega) = 1$ (b) $n(\gamma;\omega) = 2$
(c) $n(\gamma;\omega) = 0$ (d) $n(\gamma;\omega) = 3$

**65.** If $f$ is analytic in a disk $B(a;R)$ and $\gamma$ is closed rectifiable curve in $P(a;R)$. Then,

(a) $\int_\gamma F = 0$ (b) $\int_\gamma F \neq 0$
(c) $\int_\gamma F = R$ (d) None of these

**66.** For every path between the limits $\int_{-2}^{-2+i} (2+z)^2 dz$ is equal to

(a) $i/3$ (b) $i/2$
(c) $-i/3$ (d) $i/4$

**67.** If $z = a$ is an isolated singularity of $f$ and $f(z) = \sum_{-\infty}^{\infty} a_n(z-a)^n$ is its Laurent expansion in $ann(a;0,R)$. Also, if $a_n \neq 0$ for infinitely many negative integer $n$, then

(a) $z = a$ is a removable singularity
(b) $z = a$ is a pole of order $m$
(c) $z = a$ is an essential singularity
(d) None of the above

**68.** A bounded entire function is constant. This statement is

(a) Cauchy's theorem (b) Liouville's theorem
(c) Morera theorem (d) Schwarz lemma.

**69.** If G is simply connected and $f: G \to \mathbb{C}$ is analytic in G, then

(a) $f$ has a primitive in G (b) $f$ has no primitive in G
(c) $f$ is constant in G (d) None of these

**70.** $\oint_C \frac{\tan z}{z^2 - 1} dz$ has the value around the positive oriented circle $C: |z| = 3/2$

(a) $\tan 1$ (b) $2\pi i \tan 1$
(c) $\frac{\tan 1}{2\pi i}$ (d) None of these

**71.** If function $f(z)$ has an isolated singularities at $z = a$, then $z = a$ has removable singularly, if

(a) $\lim_{z \to a}(z-a) = 0$ (b) $\lim_{z \to a} f(z) = 0$
(c) $\lim_{z \to a}(z-a)f(z) = 0$ (d) None of these

**72.** $\int_L dz$, where $L$ is any rectifiable arc joining the points $z = a$ and $z = b$ is equal to

(a) $z$ (b) $b - a$
(c) $a - b - z$ (d) $z - a - b$

**73.** $\int_L |dz|$, where $L$ is any rectifiable arc joining the points $z = a$ and $z = b$ is equal to

(a) $b - a$ (b) $|b - a|$
(c) arc length of $L$ (d) 0

**74.** If C is circle $|z-a|=r$, then $\int_C \frac{dz}{z-a}$ is

(a) $2\pi i$ (b) $-2\pi i$
(c) $\pi i$ (d) 0

**75.** If $f(z)$ is analytic in a simply connected domain $D$ enclosed by a rectifiable Jordan curve C and $f(z)$ is continuous on C, then for any point $z_0$ in $D$, we have $f(z_0)$ is equal to

(a) $\frac{1}{2\pi}\int_C \frac{f(z)}{z-z_0}dz$ (b) $\frac{1}{2\pi i}\int_C \frac{f(z)}{z-z_0}dz$
(c) $2\pi i\int_C \frac{f(z)}{z-z_0}dz$ (d) $2\pi\int_C \frac{f(z)}{z-z_0}dz$

**76.** Let $f(z)$ be continuous on a contour $L$ of length $l$ and let $|f(z)|\le M$ on $L$, then $\left|\int_L f(z)dz\right|$ is

(a) $\le Ml$ (b) $\ge Ml$
(c) $> Ml$ (d) $< Ml$

**77.** If C is a circle $|z|=1$, then $\int_C \bar{z}dz$ is

(a) $\pi i$ (b) $2\pi i$
(c) 0 (d) None of these

**78.** Which of the following functions does represent the series $\sum_{n=0}^{\infty}\frac{z^n}{n!}$ for $|z|<\infty$?

(a) $\sin z$ (b) $\cos z$
(c) $e^z$ (d) $\log(1+z)$

**79.** When $0<|z|<4$, the expansion of $\frac{1}{4z-z^2}$ is

(a) $\sum_{n=0}^{\infty}\frac{z^{n+1}}{4^{n+1}}$ (b) $\sum_{n=0}^{\infty}\frac{(-1)^n z^{n+1}}{4^{n+1}}$
(c) $\sum_{n=0}^{\infty}\frac{z^{n-1}}{4^{n+1}}$ (d) None of these

**80.** If a function is analytic at all points of a bounded domain except at finitely many points, then these exceptional points are called

(a) zeros (b) singularities
(c) poles (d) simple points

**81.** A function which has poles as its only singularities in the finite part of the plane is said to be

(a) an analytic function
(b) an entire function
(c) a meromorphic function
(d) None of the above

**82.** For the function $f(z)=e^z$, $z=\infty$ is

(a) isolated essential singularity
(b) pole
(c) ordinary point
(d) None of the above

**83.** Number of poles of the function $f(z)=\tan\frac{1}{z}$ is

(a) 2 (b) 4
(c) infinite (d) None of these

**84.** Number of zeros of the function $f(z)=\sin\frac{1}{z}$ is

(a) 3 (b) 4
(c) infinite (d) None of these

**85.** The number of isolated singular points of $f(z)=\frac{z+3}{z^2(z^2+2)}$ is

(a) 1 (b) 2 (c) 3 (d) 4

**86.** If a function $f(z)$ is analytic within a circle C with its centre $z=a$ and radius $R$, then for every point $z$ inside C, $f(z)=\sum_{n=0}^{\infty}a_n(z-a)^n$, where $a_n$ is equal to

(a) $\frac{f^{(n)}(a)}{n}$ (b) $\frac{f^{(n)}(a)}{n!}$
(c) $f^{(n)}(a)$ (d) None of these

**87.** If $f(z)=z^5-3iz^2+2z+i-1$ and C encloses zeros of $f(z)$, then $\int_C \frac{f'(z)}{f(z)}dz$ is

(a) $5\pi i$ (b) 0
(c) $10\pi i$ (d) None of these

**88.** Value of $\frac{2!}{2\pi i}\int_{|z|=3}\frac{z^2+3z+4}{(z-1)^3}dz$ is

(a) 2 (b) 0
(c) $\pi i$ (d) None of these

**89.** The function $f(z)=\frac{\sin\pi z^2+\cos\pi z^2}{(z-1)^2(z-2)}$ have the poles

(a) $m=1,2$ (b) $m=-1,-2$
(c) $m=2$ (d) None of these

**90.** The residue of the function $f(z)=\frac{z^2}{(z-1)^2(z-2)}$ is

(a) res $f(-2)=\frac{9}{4}$ (b) res $f(-2)=\frac{3}{2}$
(c) res $f(-2)=\frac{4}{9}$ (d) res $f(-2)=\frac{2}{3}$

**91.** The series

$$\sum_{n=1}^{\infty}\frac{z^n}{n\sqrt{n+1}}, |z|\le 1 \text{ is}$$

(a) uniformly but not absolutely convergent
(b) uniformly and absolutely convergent
(c) absolutely convergent but not uniformly convergent
(d) convergent but not uniformly

**92.** The radius of convergence of the power series of the function $f(z)=\frac{1}{1-z}$ about $z=\frac{1}{4}$ is

(a) 1 (b) 1/4 (c) 3/4 (d) 0

**93.** If an analytic function $f(z)$ has a zero of $n$th order at $z=\infty$, then the function $f(1/z)$ has such a zero

(a) at $z=\infty$ (b) at each point $z$
(c) at $z=0$ (d) None of these

**94.** The function $f(z) = \tan z$

(a) has poles at $z = (2n+1)\frac{\pi}{2}$, $n \in \mathbb{Z}$

(b) is an entire function

(c) has no zeros in C

(d) has a removable singularity at $z = 0$

**95.** If $F(z, \bar{z})$ be continuous and have continuous partial derivatives in a region $S \in E_2$ and on its boundary $C$, then

$$\oint_C F(z, \bar{z})\,dz = 2i \iint_s (\ldots)\,dA,$$

where $dA$ represents the element of area $dx\,dy$. Here, ... means

(a) $\frac{\partial F}{\partial z}$ (b) $\frac{\partial F}{\partial \bar{z}}$

(c) $\frac{\partial^2 F}{\partial z^2}$ (d) None of these

**96.** For the function $f(z) = \frac{z - \sin z}{z^3}$, the point $z = 0$ is

(a) a pole of order 3 (b) a pole of order 2

(c) an essential singularity (d) a removable singularity

**97.** If $f(z) = z^3$, then it

(a) has an essential singularity at $z = \infty$

(b) has a pole of order 3 at $z = \infty$

(c) has a pole of order 3 at $z = 0$

(d) is analytic at $z = \infty$

**98.** For the function $f(z) = \frac{1 - e^{-z}}{z}$, the point $z = 0$ is

(a) an essential singularity

(b) a pole of order 0

(c) a pole of order one

(d) a removable singularity

**99.** If $A$ be the point $z = a$ and $B$ be the point $z = b$, then $\int_{[a,b]} dz =$

(a) arc $AB$ (b) chord $AB$

(c) any curve $AB$ (d) None of these

**100.** The residue at $z = \infty$ of $f(z) = \frac{z^3}{(z-2)(z-3)(z-5)}$ is

(a) 0 (b) −10

(c) 10 (d) None of these

**101.** For the function $f(z) = \sin\frac{1}{z}$, $z = 0$ is a

(a) removable singularity (b) simple pole

(c) branch point (d) essential singularity

**102.** The value of $\int_{|z|=2} \frac{e^{2z}}{(z+1)}\,dz$ is

(a) $2\pi i e^{-2}$ (b) $\frac{8\pi i}{3} e^{-2}$

(c) $\frac{2\pi i}{3} e^{-2}$ (d) 0

**103.** The value of $\frac{1}{2\pi i}\int_C \frac{e^z\,dz}{(z-2)}$, if C is the circle $|z| = 3$ is

(a) e (b) $e^2$

(c) $e^3$ (d) None of these

**104.** The function $f(z) = \frac{e^{\tan z}}{z^2 + 1}$ has

(a) countable number of essential singularities

(b) only singularity of $f(z)$ are simple poles

(c) uncountable number of essential singularity

(d) None of the above

**105.** $f(z) = e^y(\cos x + i \sin x)$ is

(a) an entire function

(b) analytic in $x^2 + 4y^2 < 24$

(c) nowhere analytic

(d) differentiable everywhere except $z = 0$

**106.** If $f(z)$ is analytic at all points in a region $S \in E_2$ and if C is curve lying in the above region $S$, then along the curve C, the complex function $f(z)$ is

(a) likely to be integrable

(b) not integrable

(c) definitely integrable

(d) None of the above

**107.** The integral $\int_{|z|=2} \frac{\cos z}{z^3}\,dz$ equals

(a) $\pi i$ (b) $-\pi i$

(c) $2\pi i$ (d) $-2\pi i$

**108.** The value of the integral $\int_{-\pi}^{\pi} \frac{dt}{4 + R^2 - 4R\cos(\theta - t)}$ where $-\pi < \theta \le \pi$, $0 < R < 2$ is

(a) $D$ (b) $2\pi R^2(\cos\theta - \sin\theta)$

(c) $\frac{4 - R^2}{2\pi}$ (d) $\frac{2\pi}{R^2 - 4}$

**109.** Let $\Gamma$ denote the boundary of the square whose sides lie along $x = \pm 1$ and $y = \pm 1$, where $\Gamma$ is described in the positive sense. Then, the value of $\int_\Gamma \frac{z^2}{2z+3}\,dz$ is

(a) $\frac{\pi i}{4}$ (b) $2\pi i$

(c) 0 (d) $-2\pi i$

**110.** The value of $\int_0^{2+i} (\bar{z})^2\,dz$ along the line $2y = x$ is

(a) $\frac{5}{3}(2+i)$ (b) $\frac{5}{3}(2-i)$

(c) $(2-i)$ (d) None of these

**111.** If $f(z) = \frac{1}{e^z - 1}$, then

(a) $f$ is an entire function

(b) $f$ has removable singularities at $z = 2n\pi i$, $n \in Z$

(c) $f$ has poles at $z = 2n\pi i$ with residue 1 for $n \in Z$

(d) $f$ has an essential singularity at $z = 0$

**112.** For every path between the limits $\int_{-2}^{-2+i}(2+z)^2\,dz =$

(a) $i/2$ (b) $i/3$
(c) $-i/3$ (d) $-i/2$

**113.** If $f(z) = u + iv$ is analytic and $(u, v)$ lies on a circle of unit radius with centre origin for all values of $z \in \mathbb{C}$, then

(a) $f(z)$ has countably infinite singularity
(b) $f(z)$ is non-constant entire function
(c) $f(z)$ is meromorphic function with non-empty set of singularity
(d) $f(z)$ is constant

**114.** The function $f(z)$ that is holomorphic, with in the unit circle which takes value $\dfrac{a-\cos\theta+i\sin\theta}{a^2-2a\cos\theta+1}$, $|a|>1$, is

(a) $\dfrac{1}{a-z}$ (b) $\dfrac{1}{z-a}$
(c) $\dfrac{1}{z}$ (d) $\dfrac{a}{a-z}$

**115.** If $f(z) = u + iv$ be continuous in a simply connected region $S \in E_2$ and that $u$ and $v$ have continuous partial derivatives and function $\oint_C f(z)\,dz = 0$ around every closed curve $C$ in $S$, then $f(z)$ is

(a) not analytic in $S$
(b) may or may not be analytic in $S$
(c) analytic in $S$
(d) None of the above

**116.** Residue of $f(z) = \dfrac{z^3}{(z-1)^4(z-2)(z-3)}$ at $z = 3$ is

(a) $\dfrac{101}{16}$ (b) $-8$
(c) $\dfrac{27}{16}$ (d) 0

**117.** Residue of $\dfrac{z^3}{z^2-1}$ at $z = \infty$ is

(a) 1 (b) $-1$ (c) 0 (d) $\infty$

**118.** A point $a$ is called an isolated singularity of the function $f(z)$ if in a deleted neighbourhood of $a$ the function $f(z)$ is analytic and at $a$ the function $f(z)$ is

(a) analytic (b) not analytic
(c) may be analytic (d) None of these

**119.** For the function $f(z) = \dfrac{1}{z}\sum_{k=0}^{n}(z+a)^{-k}$, the residue at $z = a$ when $a \neq 0$ and $a \neq 1$

(a) 1 (b) $-n$
(c) $\dfrac{1-a^n}{(1-a)}$ (d) $\dfrac{1-a^n}{a^n(1-a)}$

**120.** Let $f$ be a polynomial function on the entire complex plane, such that $f(z) \neq 0$ for $z$ such that $|z| = 1$. Then, $\dfrac{1}{2\pi i}\displaystyle\int_{|z|=1}\dfrac{f'(z)}{f(z)}\,dz$

(a) can take only integer values
(b) can take any value
(c) is zero
(d) is equal to degree of $f$

**121.** If $f(z)$ is an analytic function and $f'(z)$ is continuous at each point within or on a closed curve $C$, then $\int_C f(z)\,dz =$

(a) $\infty$ (b) 1
(c) 0 (d) None of these

**122.** The integral given below equals $\int_C \dfrac{e^{3z}}{(z-\pi i)}\,dz$, Where $C$ is circle $|z-1| = 6$ is

(a) $-2\pi i$ (b) 0
(c) $\pi i$ (d) $2\pi i$

**123.** If $f(z)$ be an analytic function inside and on the boundary of a triangle, then $\oint_\Delta f(z)\,dz =$

(a) $\infty$ (b) 1
(c) 0 (d) None of these

**124.** Let $I = \int_C \dfrac{\cot(\pi z)}{(z-i)^2}\,dz$, where $C$ is the counter $4x^2 + y^2 = 2$ (counter clockwise). Then, $I$ is equal to

(a) 0 (b) $-2\pi i$
(c) $2\pi i\left(\dfrac{\pi}{\sinh^2\pi} - \dfrac{1}{\pi}\right)$ (d) $-\dfrac{2\pi^2 i}{\sinh^2\pi}$

**125.** It $D$ is the open unit disk in $\mathbb{C}$ and $f:\mathbb{C} \to D$ is analytic with $f(10) = 1/2$, then $f(10+i)$ is

(a) $\dfrac{1+i}{2}$ (b) $\dfrac{1-i}{2}$
(c) $\dfrac{1}{2}$ (d) $\dfrac{i}{2}$

**126.** If $C$ is the curve $y = x^3 - 3x^2 + 4x - 1$, joining the two points (1, 1) and (2, 3). The value of $\int_C (12z^2 - 4iz)\,dz$ is

(a) $-156 + 38i$ (b) $156 - 38i$
(c) $38 + 156i$ (d) $38 - 156i$

**127.** For the function $f(z) = \sin\left(\dfrac{x}{|z|^2} - i\dfrac{y}{|z|^2}\right)$ choose the correct answer.

(a) $f(z)$ has no singularity
(b) $f(z)$ has finite number of singularity with exactly one
(c) all the singularities of $f(z)$ are pole
(d) infinity is simple pole

**128.** If the function $f(z)$ is analytic inside and on a simple closed curve $C$ and if $a$ is a point within $C$ and if $C$ be traversed in the positive sense, then $f(a) =$

(a) $\dfrac{1}{2\pi i}\oint_C f(z)\,dz$ (b) $\dfrac{1}{2\pi i}\oint_C \dfrac{f(z)}{z-a}\,dz$
(c) $\oint_C \dfrac{f(z)}{z-a}\,dz$ (d) None of these

**129.** $\int_C z^2\,dz$, where $C$ is the circle with centre 0 and radius 2 equals

(a) $4\pi^2$ (b) $2\pi i$ (c) 4 (d) 0

**130.** The function $f(z) = e^{-\frac{1}{z^4}}$ at $z = \infty$

(a) limit does not exist
(b) limit exists but $f(z)$ is discontinuous
(c) $f(z)$ is continuous but not differentiable
(d) is differentiable

**131.** If $f(z)$ is analytic within a circle $C$, given by $|z - z_0| = R$ and if $|f(z)| \le M$ on $C$, then $|f^n(z_0)|$

(a) $\ge \frac{n!M}{R^n}$ (b) $> \frac{n!M}{R^n}$
(c) $\le \frac{n!M}{R^n}$ (d) None of these

**132.** The coefficient of $\frac{1}{z}$ in the expansion of $\log\left(\frac{z}{z-1}\right)$, valid in $|z| > 1$ is

(a) $-1$ (b) 1
(c) $-\frac{1}{2}$ (d) $\frac{1}{2}$

**133.** The number of zeros, counting multiplicity, of polynomial $z^5 + 3z^3 + z^2 + 1$ inside the circle $|z| = 2$ is

(a) 0 (b) 2
(c) 3 (d) 5

**134.** Let $\Gamma$ be any circle enclosing the origin an oriented counter-clockwise, then the value of the integral $\int_\Gamma \frac{\cos z}{z^2}\,dz$ is

(a) $2\pi i$ (b) 0
(c) $-2\pi i$ (d) undefined

**135.** The function $f(z) = z^m e^z$ at $z = \infty$ has

(a) non-isolated essential singularity
(b) pole of order $m$
(c) pole of order $m + 1$
(d) isolated essential singularity

**136.** The theorem if for all $z$ in the entire complex plane, the function $f(z)$ is analytic and bounded, then $f(z)$ must be a constant is named after

(a) Morera (b) Cauchy
(c) Jordan (d) Liouville

**137.** The residue of $\frac{\sin z}{z^8}$ at $z = 0$ is

(a) 0 (b) $-\frac{1}{7!}$
(c) $\frac{1}{7!}$ (d) None of these

**138.** If $f(z) = \frac{z^2 + 5z + 6}{z - 2}$ and the path of integration is a circle with originated centre and radius $r$, the Cauchy's theorem is applicable, whenever $r$ equals

(a) 1 (b) 2 (c) 3 (d) 1 and 2

**139.** Laurent's expansion of the function $1/(z^2 - 3z + 2)$ for $|z| > 2$ is

(a) $\sum_{n=0}^{\infty} \frac{2^n - 1}{z^{n+1}}$ (b) $\sum_{n=0}^{\infty} \frac{2^n}{z^{n+1}}$
(c) $\sum_{n=0}^{\infty} \frac{2^n + 1}{z^{n+1}}$ (d) $\sum_{n=0}^{\infty} \frac{2^n}{z^n}$

**140.** The residue of $f(z) = \pi \operatorname{cosec} \pi z$ at $z = n$ is

(a) $(-1)^n n$ (b) $-1$ (c) 1 (d) $(-1)^n$

**141.** Which of the following does give the residue at $z = \infty$ of any function $f(z)$ is/are

(a) $-\text{Res}\,(z = 0) = \frac{1}{z^2} f\left(\frac{1}{z}\right)$
(b) $-\frac{1}{2\pi i}\int_C f(z)\,dz$
(c) negative of the coefficient of $\frac{1}{z}$ in the expansion of $z\,f(z)$ in *nbd* of zero
(d) All of the above

**142.** If the principal part of Laurent's series is zero, then the Laurent's series reduces to

(a) Maclaurin's series (b) Cauchy's series
(c) Taylor's series (d) None of these

**143.** Let $f : C \to C$ s. t. $f(z) = e^z$, then

(a) $f(z)$ is univalent but not onto
(b) $f(z)$ is univalent in $|z| < a$ for $a > \pi$ but not onto
(c) $f(z)$ is univalent in $|z| < \pi$ and onto on $C$
(d) $f(z)$ is univalent in $|z| < \pi$ but not onto therein

**144.** Suppose that a function $f$ is continuous in a domain $D$, then among the following statements

I. $f$ has primitive in $D$
II. The integral of $f(z)$ along any path lying in $D$ between any two fixed points in $D$ is independent of path
III. The integral of $f(z)$ along every closed contour in $D$ is zero.

**Codes**

(a) I implies III but not II
(b) II implies III but not implied by I
(c) I implies II and III but not implied by either of II or III
(d) All the statements are equivalent

**145.** If $f(a) = 0, f'(a) = 0, f''(a) \ne 0$, then at $z = a$ the function $f(z)$ is said to have a zero of

(a) first order (b) second order
(c) third order (d) None of these

**146.** Define a complex function $f(z)$ by $f(z) = \begin{cases} e^{-1/z^2}, & z \ne 0 \\ 0, & z = 0 \end{cases}$, then

(a) at $z = 0$, $f(z)$ is continuous
(b) at $z = 0$, $f(z)$ has removable singularity
(c) at $z = 0$, $f(z)$ has essential singularity
(d) $f(z)$ is analytic at $z = 0$

**147.** The value of $\frac{1}{2\pi i}\int_C \frac{e^z}{z-3}dz$; where $C:(r-4\cos\theta)(r-2\cos\theta)=0$ is

(a) $e^3$ (b) $2e^3$
(c) $\frac{1}{2}e^3$ (d) 0

**148.** The analytical part of Laurent's series is

(a) $\sum_{n=1}^{\infty}\frac{a_{-n}}{(z-a)^n}$ (b) $\sum_{n=0}^{\infty}a_n(z-a)^n$
(c) $\sum_{n=0}^{\infty}a_n(z-a)^{2n}$ (d) None of these

**149.** Function $g$ is defined by $g(z)=z^4\sin\left(\frac{1}{z+1}\right)$ has at infinity

(a) a pole of order 4 (b) a pole of order 3
(c) removable singularity (d) essential singularity

**150.** The residue of $f(z)$ at $z=2$ where $f(z)=\frac{e^{-z}}{(z-2)^4}$

(a) $\frac{1}{6}$ (b) $\frac{e^2}{6}$
(c) $-\frac{1}{6e^2}$ (d) $\frac{1}{6e^2}$

**151.** The third term in the expansion of $\tan z$ with the help of Maclaurin's series is

(a) $\frac{1}{5}z^5$ (b) $\frac{1}{5!}z^5$
(c) $\frac{2}{15}z^5$ (d) None of these

**152.** If $f(z)=\frac{1}{\sinh z}$, then the number of singularities of $f(z)$ on the real line segment $(-n\pi, n\pi)$

(a) $n$ (b) $2n-1$
(c) $2n+1$ (d) 1

**153.** If $f(z)=z^3$. Then, it

(a) has an essential singularity at $z=\infty$
(b) has a pole of order 3 at $z=\infty$
(c) has a pole of order 3 at $z=0$
(d) is analytic at $z=\infty$

**154.** The $\Gamma$ be any circle enclosing the origin and oriented counter clockwise. Then, the value of the integral $\int_\Gamma \frac{\cos z}{z^2}dz$ is

(a) $2\pi$ (b) 0
(c) $-2\pi i$ (d) undefined

**155.** The general term in the expansion of $\cosh z$ with the help of Taylor's series is

(a) $\frac{z^{2n+1}}{(2n+1)!}$ (b) $\frac{z^{2n}}{(2n)!}$
(c) $\frac{z^n}{n!}$ (d) None of these

**156.** If $g(z)$ is analytic at $z=a$ and $f(z)$ has a pole of order $k$ at $z=a$, then $\text{res}_{z=a}\frac{g(z)f'(z)}{f(z)}$ is

(a) $kg(a)$ (b) $\frac{-1}{k'}(a)$
(c) $-kg(a)$ (d) $-k!g(a)$

**157.** Let $f=u+iv$ be analytic in a connected open set $D$ where $u$ and $v$ are real-valued. If $u$ and $v$ satisfies the condition $2u+3v=1$, then

(a) $f(0)=1$ (b) $f(0)=0$
(c) $f(0)=2$ (d) $f(0)=3$

**158.** If $f(z)$ is analytic and has a pole at $z=a$, then $\lim_{z\to a}f(z)=$

(a) 0 (b) any constant
(c) $\infty$ (d) None of these

**159.** Let $a$ be an isolated singularity of $f(z)$ and if $|f(z)|$ is bounded on some neighbourhood of $a$, then $a$ is

(a) removable singularity
(b) essential singularity
(c) isolated singularity
(d) non-isolated essential singularity

**160.** Polynomial $f(z)$ of degree $n$ has a pole of order $n$ at

(a) zero (b) infinity
(c) $|z|=1$ (d) nowhere

**161.** The residue of the function $f(z)=\frac{2z}{(z+4)(z-1)^2}$ at the point $z=1$ is

(a) $\frac{1}{5}$ (b) $\frac{2}{5}$
(c) $\frac{8}{25}$ (d) $\frac{4}{25}$

**162.** If $\sin z=\sum_{n=0}^{\infty}a_n\left(z-\frac{\pi}{4}\right)^n$, then $a_6$ is equal to

(a) 0 (b) $\frac{1}{720}$
(c) $\frac{1}{720\sqrt{2}}$ (d) $\frac{-1}{720\sqrt{2}}$

**163.** For the positively oriented unit circle $\int_{|z|=1}\frac{2\,\text{Re}(z)}{z+2}dz=$

(a) 0 (b) $\pi i$
(c) $2\pi i$ (d) $4\pi i$

**164.** For the function $f(z)=\frac{\log_e(z-2)}{(z^2+2z+2)^4}$, $z=-1-i$ is a pole of order

(a) 1 (b) 2 (c) 3 (d) 4

**165.** Let $\gamma:[0,1]\to C$ be defined by $\gamma(t)=(1+i)(1+t)^2$, then the direction of the tangent at origin is

(a) $\pi/3$ (b) $\pi/6$
(c) $\pi/4$ (d) cannot be determined

**166.** If $f(z)$ has a pole at $z=a$, then as $z\to a$

(a) $|f(z)|\to 0$ (b) $|f(z)|\to a$
(c) $|f(z)|\to\infty$ (d) $|f(z)|\to-\infty$

**167.** The residue at $z = 1$ for $f(z) = \frac{\cos z}{z-1}$

(a) e (b) $e^i$

(c) $\frac{e^i + e^{-i}}{2}$ (d) $\frac{e^i - e^{-i}}{2i}$

**168.** If $f(z)$ has a zero of order $n$ at $z = a$, then $1/[f(z)]$ has a pole of order $n$ at $z$ =

(a) $1/a$ (b) 0

(c) $a$ (d) None of these

**169.** The function $f(z) = e^z - 2i$

(a) has no zeros

(b) has only one zero

(c) has a countable number of zeros

(d) has an uncountable number of zeros

**170.** The function $\frac{1}{z(z-1)^3}$ has a pole of order $p$ and residue $r$ at $z = 1$, then

(a) $p = 1, r = 1$ (b) $p = 3, r = \frac{1}{3}$

(c) $p = 3, r = 1$ (d) $p = 1, r = 1$

**171.** If a single-valued function $f(z)$ is not defined at $z = a$ but $\lim_{z \to a} f(z)$ exists, then $z = a$ is known as

(a) an isolated singularity

(b) an essential singularity

(c) a removable singularity

(d) None of the above

**172.** Let $f$ be an entire function and satisfies the following two equations $f(z+1) = f(z)$, $f(z+i) = f(z)$ for every $z$ in C, then

(a) $f'(z) = f(z)$

(b) $f(z) \in C$

(c) $f \equiv$ constant

(d) $f$ is a non-constant polynomial

**173.** Residue of $\frac{z^2 - 2z}{(z+1)^2 (z^2+4)}$ at double pole as $z = -1$ is

(a) $\frac{4}{25}$ (b) $-\frac{4}{5}$

(c) $-\frac{14}{25}$ (d) $\frac{14}{25}$

**174.** For the function $f(z) = \frac{\pi \cos \pi z}{z^2 \sin \pi z}$ which of the following is true?

(a) $n = 1, 2, 3, \ldots$ are the only simple poles

(b) $z = 0$ is pole of order 2

(c) $z = 0$ is pole of order 3

(d) residue at $z = 0$ is $\frac{\pi^2}{3}$

**175.** Function $f(z) = \frac{1}{(z+1)(z+3)}$ in the domain $|z| > 3$ has a Laurent's expansion given by

(a) $\frac{1}{z^2} - \frac{2}{z^3} + \frac{13}{z^4} - \frac{20}{z^5} + \ldots$

(b) $\frac{1}{z^2} - \frac{8}{z^3} + \frac{13}{z^4} - \frac{40}{z^5} + \ldots$

(c) $\frac{1}{z^2} - \frac{4}{z^3} + \frac{13}{z^4} - \frac{40}{z^5} + \ldots$

(d) $\frac{1}{z^2} - \frac{4}{z^3} + \frac{13}{z^4} - \frac{20}{z^5} + \ldots$

**176.** For the function $f(z) = e^{1/z}$, $z = 0$ is

(a) an essential singularity

(b) a pole

(c) a removable singularity

(d) None of the above

**177.** The origin and the points representing the roots of the equation $z^2 + pz + q = 0$ form an equilateral triangle if

(a) $p = 3q^2$ (b) $p = 3q$

(c) $p^2 = q$ (d) $p^2 = 3q$

**178.** The expansion of $f(z) = \frac{1}{z(z^2 - 3z + 2)}$ for the region $1 < |z| < 2$ is

(a) $\frac{1}{2z} + \sum_0^\infty z^n - \frac{1}{4}\sum_0^\infty \left(\frac{z}{2}\right)^n$

(b) $\frac{1}{2z} + \sum_0^\infty z^n + \frac{1}{4}\sum_0^\infty \left(\frac{z}{2}\right)^n$

(c) $\frac{1}{2z} + \frac{1}{z}\sum_0^\infty z^n + \frac{1}{4}\sum_0^\infty \left(\frac{z}{2}\right)^n$

(d) $\frac{1}{2z} - \frac{1}{z}\sum_0^\infty z^{-n} - \frac{1}{4}\sum_0^\infty \left(\frac{z}{2}\right)^n$

**179.** Which of the following is correct?

(a) Morera's theorem is exact converse of Cauchy's theorem

(b) Morera's theorem is valid for all functions $f(z)$ in a domain for which $\int_C f(z)dz = 0$

(c) Morera's theorem is short of converse of Cauchy's theorem

(d) None of the above

**180.** If C is an arc of the circle $|z| = r$ having $\theta_1 \le \theta \le \theta_2$ and when $r \to \infty$, $zf(z)$ tends uniformly to $A$, then $\lim_{r \to \infty} \int_C f(z)dz =$

(a) $-iA(\theta_2 - \theta_1)$ (b) $iA(\theta_2 - \theta_1)$

(c) $iA(\theta_1 + \theta_2)$ (d) None of these

**181.** The coefficient of $\frac{1}{z}$ in the Laurent series of $\frac{\sin 2z}{z^2}$ is

(a) 0 (b) 2

(c) −1 (d) 1

**182.** For the function $f(z) = (\sin\sqrt{z})/\sqrt{z}$, $z = 0$ is

(a) an essential singularity

(b) a pole

(c) a removable singularity

(d) None of the above

**183.** The value of $\int_C \frac{a^n e^{az}}{z^{n+1} n!} dz$, where $C$ is a closed contour around the origin is

(a) $\frac{2\pi i a^{2n}}{n!}$ (b) $\frac{2\pi i a^n}{n!}$

(c) $2\pi i \left(\frac{a^n}{n!}\right)^2$ (d) $\frac{\pi i}{2n!} a^{2n}$

**184.** The value of the integral $\int_C \frac{\sin \pi z^2 + \cos \pi z^2}{(z-4)(z-2)} dz$, where $C$ is the circle $|z| = 3$ traced anti-clockwise, is

(a) $-2\pi l$ (b) $i\pi$

(c) $-i\pi$ (d) $2i\pi$

**185.** The value of $\int_C \frac{f'(z)}{f(z)} dz$, where $f(z) = \frac{(z^2+1)^2}{(z^2+3z+2)^3}$ and $C$ is the circle $|z| = 3$ with positive sense, is

(a) $2\pi i$ (b) $-2\pi i$

(c) $4\pi i$ (d) $-4\pi i$

**186.** At $z = \infty$, the function $f(z) = \cos z - \sin z$ has

(a) a removable singularity

(b) an essential singularity

(c) a non-essential singularity

(d) None of the above

**187.** The value of $\int_0^{2\pi} \exp(e^{i\theta} - i\theta) d\theta$ is

(a) $2\pi i$ (b) $2\pi$

(c) $\pi$ (d) $i\pi$

**188.** Let $\Gamma$ be a simple closed curve in the complex plane, then the set of all possible values of $\int_\Gamma \frac{dz}{z(1-z^2)}$ is

(a) $\{0, \pm\pi i\}$ (b) $\{0, \pm\pi i, 2\pi i\}$

(c) $\{0, \pm\pi i, \pm 2\pi i\}$ (d) $\{0\}$

**189.** The radius of convergence of the series $1 + z + \frac{z^2}{2} - \frac{z^3}{3!} + \frac{z^4}{2^2} + \frac{z^5}{5!} + \frac{z^6}{2^3} - \frac{z^7}{7!} + \dots$ is given as

(a) 2 (b) $\sqrt{2}$

(c) $\infty$ (d) 0

**190.** The number of roots of the equation $z^8 - 4z^5 + z^2 - 1 = 0$ that lie inside the circle $|z| = 1$ (Using the Rouche's theorem) is

(a) 8 (b) 5

(c) 6 (d) None of these

**191.** Pole is

(a) a removable singularity

(b) an essential singularity

(c) a non-essential singularity

(d) None of the above

**192.** If $I = \int_{|z|=2.5} z^2 \cot \pi z dz$, then $I$ is equal to

(a) $20\pi i$ (b) $20i$

(c) $20\pi^2 i$ (d) $10i$

**193.** Let $f(z) = \frac{e^z}{(z-1)(z+3)^2}$ and $\Gamma$ be the circle $|z| = \frac{3}{2}$ described in the positive sense. Then, $\int_\Gamma f(z)dz$, has the value

(a) 0 (b) $\frac{\pi e i}{8}$

(c) $-\frac{\pi e i}{8}$ (d) $\frac{\pi i(e - 5e^{-3})}{8}$

**194.** The sum of residues of the function $f(z) = z^3 / [(z-1)(z-2)(z-3)]$ at 1, 2, 3 and $\infty$ is

(a) 0 (b) $-1$

(c) 1 (d) None of these

**195.** If $f(z) = z^2 + 2$, then the minimum, value of $|f(z)|$ over the closed region $|z| \leq 1$ is

(a) 0 (b) 1

(c) 3 (d) 2

**196.** Let $\Gamma$ be the curve $\Gamma = 2 + 4\cos\theta$, $(0 \leq \theta \leq 2\pi)$. If $I_1 = \int_\Gamma \frac{dz}{z-1}$ and $I_2 = \int_\Gamma \frac{d_2}{z-3}$. Then,

(a) $I_1 = I_2$ (b) $I_1 = 2I_2$

(c) $2I_1 = I_2$ (d) $I_1 = 0, 2I_2 \neq 0$

**197.** An example of a function with a non-isolated essential singularity at $z = 2$ is

(a) $\tan\frac{1}{z-2}$ (b) $\sin\frac{1}{z-2}$

(c) $e^{-(z-2)}$ (d) $\tan\frac{z-2}{z}$

**198.** The value of $\oint_C \frac{(4-3z)}{z^2 - z} dz$, Where $C$ is a simple closed path (anti-clockwise) enclosing the points $z = 0$ and $z = 1$ is

(a) $-6\pi$ (b) $-6\pi i$

(c) $6\pi i$ (d) None of these

**199.** If $\phi(z) = \text{Re}(z) + f(z)$, where $f(z)$ is meromorphic. Then,

(a) $\phi(z)$ is meromorphic

(b) $\phi(z)$ and $f(z)$ has same number of singularities

(c) $\phi(z)$ is analytic in every closed and bounded region provided it has no poles

(d) $\phi(z)$ has no singularities

**200.** If the function $f(z)$ has a pole of order $m > 1$ at the point $z = a$, then Res $f(a)$ =

(a) $\frac{1}{m!}\lim_{z\to a}\left[\frac{d^m}{dz^m}\{(z-a)^m f(z)\}\right]$

(b) $\frac{1}{(m-1)!}\lim_{z\to a}\left[\frac{d^m}{dz^m}\{f(z)\}\right]$

(c) $\frac{1}{(m-1)!}\lim_{z\to a}\left[\frac{d^{m-1}}{dz^{m-1}}\{(z-a)^m f(z)\}\right]$

(d) None of the above

**201.** Let $h(z)$ is analytic in the whole plane, $h(0) = 3 + 4i$ and $|h(z)| \leq 5$ in $|z| < 1$. Then, choose the incorrect statement

(a) $h(z)$ is bounded
(b) $h(0) = 0$
(c) $h(z)$ is analytic at $z = \infty$
(d) $h(z)$ is non-constant polynomial

**202.** If $f(z)$ is analytic in $D/\{a\}$ and bounded in $0 < |z - a| < r$, then
(a) $f(z)$ has simple pole at $z = a$
(b) $f(z)$ is analytic at $z = a$
(c) $f(z)$ has removable singularity at $z = a$
(d) $f(z)$ is either analytic at $z = a$ or has removable singularity there at

**203.** The residue of the function $f(z)$ at infinity is
(a) $\lim_{z\to\infty}[-f(z)]$ (b) $\lim_{z\to\infty}[-z f(z)]$
(c) $\lim_{z\to\infty}[-z f(1/z)]$ (d) None of these

**204.** The radius of convergence of the series $\sum_{n=1}^{\infty} \frac{z^n}{n^a}, a \in R$
(a) is 1
(b) cannot say unless the value of $a$ is specified
(c) diverges of all value of $a$
(d) diverges only for specified values of $a$

**205.** Let $f(z)$ be defined on the domain $E: |z - 2i| < 3$ and on its boundary $\partial E$. Then, which of the following statements is always true?
(a) If $f(z)$ is analytic on $E$ and $f(z) \neq 0$ for any $z$ in $E$, then $|f|$ attains its maximum on $\partial E$.
(b) If $f(z)$ is analytic on $EU\partial E$, then $|f|$ attains its minimum on $\partial E$.
(c) If $f(z)$ is analytic on $E$ and continuous on $EU\partial E$, then $|f|$ attains its maximum and minimum on $\partial E$.
(d) If $f(z)$ is analytic on $EU\partial E$ and $f(z) \neq 0$ for any $z$ in $EU\partial E$, then $|f|$ attains its minimum on $\partial E$.

**206.** The residue of $f(z) = 1/(z^2 + a^2)^2$ at $z = ai$ is
(a) $1/(8ia^2)$ (b) $1/(4ia^3)$
(c) $1/(2ia^4)$ (d) None of these

**207.** If the radius of convergence of the series $f(z) = \sum_{n=0}^{\infty} a_n (z - z_0)^n$ is finite, then $f(z)$ has atleast one singularity
(a) on the circle of convergence
(b) inside the circle of convergence
(c) outside the circle of convergence
(d) anywhere

**208.** The residue of $f(z) = \tanh z$ at the singular point is
(a) $-i$ (b) 0
(c) 1 (d) $i$

**209.** The infinite product $\Pi(1 + a_n)$ is absolutely convergent if
(a) $\Pi(1 + |a_n|)$ is convergent
(b) $\Pi(a_n)^2$ is convergent
(c) $\Pi(a_n)$ is convergent
(d) None of the above

**210.** If the function $f(z) = \frac{F(z)}{G(z)}$ has a simple pole at $z = a$, then Res $f(a) =$
(a) $\frac{F'(a)}{G(a)}$ (b) $\frac{F(a)}{G'(a)}$
(c) $\frac{F'(a)}{G'(a)}$ (d) None of these

**211.** The radius of convergence of the power series $\sum 5^n z^{3n}$ is
(a) 1 (b) 5
(c) $5^{1/3}$ (d) $5^{-1/3}$

**212.** If $AB$ be the arc $\alpha \le \theta \le \beta$ of the circle $|z| = R$ and $\lim_{z\to\infty} zf(z) = k$, then
(a) $\lim_{R\to\infty} \int_{AB} f(z)dz = i(\beta - \alpha)k$
(b) $\lim_{R\to 0} \int_{AB} f(z)dz = i(\beta - \alpha)k$
(c) $\lim_{R\to\infty} \int_{AB} f(z)dz = (\beta - \alpha)k$
(d) $\lim_{R\to 0} \int_{AB} f(z)dz = (\beta - \alpha)k$

**213.** The residue of $f(z) = \cot z$ is
(a) $i$ (b) $-i$
(c) 1 (d) None of these

**214.** The radius of convergence of the series given as $1 + z + \frac{z^2}{2} - \frac{z^3}{3!} + \frac{z^4}{2^2} + \frac{z^5}{5!} + \frac{z^6}{2^2} - \frac{z^7}{7!} + \ldots$ is
(a) 2 (b) $\sqrt{2}$ (c) $\infty$ (d) 0

**215.** To evaluate $\int_0^{2\pi} \frac{d\theta}{1 - 2a\cos\theta + a^2}$ with the help of Cauchy's Residue Theorem, we should put $z =$
(a) $e^{ai\theta}$ (b) $e^{-i\theta}$
(c) $e^{i\theta}$ (d) None of these

**216.** The series $\sum_{n=1}^{\infty} \frac{z^n}{n\sqrt{n+1}}, |z| \le 1$ is
(a) Uniformly but not absolutely convergent
(b) Uniformly and absolutely convergent
(c) Absolutely convergent but not uniformly convergent
(d) Convergent but not uniformly convergent

**217.** The Jordan's inequality is
(a) $\frac{2}{\pi} < \frac{\sin\theta}{\theta} < 1$ (b) $2\pi < \sin\theta < 0$
(c) $\frac{1}{\pi} < \frac{\theta}{\sin\theta} < 1$ (d) None of these

**218.** Putting $z = e^{i\theta}$, the integral $\int_0^{2\pi} \frac{\sin 3\theta}{5 - 3\cos\theta} d\theta$ reduces to.., where C is the circle $|z| = 1$. Here ... means
(a) $\oint_C \frac{(z^3 - 1)dz}{z^3(z - 3)}$ (b) $\oint_C \frac{(z^6 - 1)dz}{z^3(3z - 1)}$
(c) $\oint_C \frac{(z^6 - 1)dz}{z^3(z - 3)(3z - 1)}$ (d) None of these

**219.** Let $f(z)$ be an entire function such that for some constant $\alpha, |f(z)| \le \alpha |z|^3$ and $|z| \ge 1$ and $f(z) = f(iz)$ for all $z \in \mathbb{C}$, then

(a) $f(z) = \alpha z^3, \forall z \in \mathbb{C}$
(b) $f(z)$ is a constant
(c) $f(z)$ is a quadratic polynomial
(d) No such $f(z)$ exists

**220.** Let $f(z) = u(x, y) + iv(x, y)$ be an entire function having Taylor's series expansion as $\sum_{n=0}^{\infty} a_n z^n$, if $f(x) = u(x, 0)$ and $f(iy) = iv(0, y)$, then

(a) $a_{2n} = 0, \forall n$
(b) $a_0 = a_1 = a_2 = a_3 = 0, a_4 \ne 0$
(c) $a_{2n+1} = 0, \forall n$
(d) $a_0 \ne 0$, but $a_2 = 0$

**221.** Let $f(z)$ be an analytic function with a simple pole at $z = 1$ and a double pole at $z = 2$ with residues 1 and $-2$, respectively. Further if $f(0) = 0, f(3) = \frac{-3}{4}$ and $f$ is bounded as $z \to \infty$, then $f(z)$ must be

(a) $z(z-3) - \frac{1}{4} + \frac{1}{z-1} - \frac{2}{z-1} + \frac{1}{(z-2)^2}$
(b) $-\frac{1}{4} + \frac{1}{z-1} - \frac{2}{z-2} + \frac{1}{(z-2)^2}$
(c) $\frac{1}{z-1} - \frac{2}{z-1} + \frac{5}{(z-2)^2}$
(d) $\frac{15}{4} + \frac{1}{z-1} + \frac{2}{z-2} - \frac{7}{(z-2)^2}$

**222.** The value of the integral $I = \int_C \frac{e^z}{e^z - 1} dz$ is where $C : |z| = 3\pi$

(a) $2\pi i$ (b) $3\pi i$
(c) $6\pi i$ (d) 0

**223.** The value of $\int_C \frac{e^{-z}}{z^2} dz$, where $C$ is the circle $|z| = 1$ is

(a) $-1$ (b) $2\pi i$
(c) $-2\pi i$ (d) None of these

**224.** In the Laurent series expansion of $f(z) = \frac{1}{z-1} - \frac{1}{z-2}$ valid in the region $|z| > 2$, the coefficient of $\frac{1}{z^2}$ is

(a) $-1$ (b) 0
(c) 1 (d) 2

**225.** Given that '$a$' lies inside the closed contour $C$, the value of the integral $\frac{1}{2\pi i} \int_C \frac{ze^z}{(z-a)^3} dz$ is

(a) $e^a(1+a)$ (b) $e^a\left(1+\frac{a}{2}\right)$
(c) $e^a$ (d) $e^a\left(\frac{1+a}{2}\right)$

**226.** The number of roots of the equation $z^5 - 12z^2 + 14 = 0$ that lie in the region $\left\{z \in C : 2 \le |z| < \frac{5}{2}\right\}$ is

(a) 2 (b) 3
(c) 4 (d) 5

**227.** The conjugate (also called symmetric) point of $1+i$ with respect to the circle $|z-1| = 2$ is

(a) $1-i$ (b) $1+4i$
(c) $1+2i$ (d) $-1-i$

# Exercise 2 (For Part 'C')

**Directions** (Q. Nos. 1-69) *Questions may have one or more than one correct option.*

**1.** Let $f(z) = \oint_\gamma \phi(z) dz$, where $\phi(z) = \frac{e^{-z}}{z+1}$ and $\gamma : |z| = \frac{1}{2}$, then

(a) $\phi(z)$ is analytic outside $|z| = \frac{1}{2}$
(b) $\phi(z)$ is analytic on $|z| = \frac{1}{2}$
(c) $\phi(z)$ is analytic in $|z| < \frac{1}{2}, \forall z \in \mathbb{C}$
(d) $f(z) = 0$

**2.** If $f(z)$ is analytic within and on a closed curve $C$ and if $\alpha$ is any point within $C$, then

(a) $\int_C \frac{f(z)}{(z-\alpha)} dz = 2\pi i f(\alpha)$
(b) $\int_C \frac{f(z)}{(z-\alpha)} dz = 2\pi i f'(\alpha)$
(c) $\int_C \frac{f(z)}{(z-\alpha)} dz = \pi i f(\alpha)$
(d) $\int \frac{f(z)}{(z-\alpha)^2} dz = 2\pi i f'(\alpha)$

**3.** If $\int_\gamma \frac{z+4}{z^2+2z+5} dz = 0$, then

(a) $\gamma : |z| = 1$ (b) $\gamma : |z+1| = 1$
(c) $\gamma : |z| = 3$ (d) $\gamma : |z+1| = \frac{1}{2}$

**4.** If $f(a) = \int_\gamma \frac{3z^2 + 7z + 1}{z-a} dz$, where $\gamma : |z| = 2$, then

(a) $f(0) = 2\pi i$ (b) $f'(0) = 14\pi i$
(c) $f''(-1) = 16\pi i$ (d) $f''(-2) = 12\pi i$

**5.** If $f(z)=\dfrac{1}{(z-1)(z-2)}$, then expansion of $f(z)$ is/are

(a) $\sum_{n=1}^{\infty}\left(1-\frac{1}{2^n}\right)z^{n-1}$; $|z|<1$

(b) $\sum_{n=0}^{\infty}\frac{z^{n-1}}{2^n}$; $|z|<1$

(c) $\ldots+7z^{-4}+3z^{-3}+z^{-2}+\ldots$; $|z|>2$

(d) only (a) is true

**6.** Which of the following is/are true?

(a) A polynomial of degree $n$ has no singularities in the finite part of the plane but has a pole of order $n$ at infinity.

(b) A function which has no singularity in the finite part of the plane or at infinity is constant.

(c) A function $f(z)$ is a polynomial of degree $n$ if and only if $f(z)$ has no singularities in the finite part of the plane and has a pole of order $n$ at infinity.

(d) If a function $f(z)$ is analytic for all finite values of $z$ and as $|z|\to\infty, |f(z)|=a|z|^k$, then $f(z)$ is a polynomial of degree $\le k$.

**7.** Which of the following is/are true?

(a) Zeros are isolated.

(b) Poles are isolated.

(c) A zero of order two is called simple zero.

(d) The value of $z$ for which the $f(z)$ fails to be analytic is called zero.

**8.** Let $f(z)=\dfrac{\sin(z-1)}{z-1}$, then

(a) $f(z)$ has simple pole at $z=1$

(b) $f(z)$ has essential singularity at $z=1$

(c) $f(z)$ has removable singularity at $z=1$

(d) Residue of $f(z)$ at $z=0$ is undefined

**9.** Laurent expansion of $f(z)$ is given by $f(z)=\sum_{n=0}^{\infty}a_n(z-z_0)^n+\sum_{n=1}^{\infty}b_n(z-z_0)^{-n}$, where

(a) $a_n=\dfrac{1}{2\pi i}\int_\gamma \dfrac{f(z)}{(z-z_0)^{n+1}}dz$

(b) $b_n=\dfrac{1}{2\pi i}\int_\gamma \dfrac{f(z)}{(z-z_0)^{n+1}}dz$

(c) res $f(z_0)=b_1$

(d) $z_0$ is removable singularity for all $b_n=0$

**10.** Let $f(z)=\dfrac{1}{(z^2+9)^2}$, then

(a) $z=3i$ is a simple pole of $f(z)$

(b) $z=-3i$ is a pole of order two of $f(z)$

(c) $f(z)$ has removable singularity at $z=3i$

(d) Residue of $f(z)$ at $z=3i$ is $=\dfrac{-i}{18}$

**11.** Let $f(z)=e^z\operatorname{cosec}^2 z$, then for $f(z)$

(a) $z=0$ is the pole of order 2

(b) $z=\infty$ is a non-isolated essential singularity

(c) $z=n\pi,\ n\in I$ are the poles of order 2

(d) Residue at $z=0$ is 0

**12.** Let $f(z)=\dfrac{z^2}{(z-a)(z-b)(z-c)}$, then

(a) $\lim_{z\to\infty} f(z)=1$

(b) $\lim_{z\to\infty} zf(z)=-1$

(c) Residue of $f(z)$ at infinity $=1$

(d) $\lim_{z\to\infty} -z\,f(z)=-1$

**13.** Which of the following is/are true?

(a) The order of a zero of a polynomial equals the order of its first non-vanishing derivative.

(b) Zeros are isolated.

(c) Zeros of $f(z)$ are obtained by equating numerator to zero.

(d) Limit points of zero is an essential singularity.

**14.** For the $f(z)=\dfrac{z^3}{(z-1)^4(z-2)(z-3)}$ following hold.

(a) $z=1$ is the pole of order 4

(b) $z=2$ is the simple pole

(c) $z=0$ is the zero of order 3

(d) $z=1,2,3$ are the simple poles

**15.** Following is/are Laurent's power series expansion of $f(z)$.

(a) $f(z)-f(z_0)=\sum_{n=0}^{\infty}\frac{(z-z_0)^n}{n!}f^n(z_0)$

(b) $f(z)-f(z_0)=\sum_{n=1}^{\infty}\frac{(z-z_0)^n}{n!}f^n(z_0)$

(c) $f(z)=\sum_{n=0}^{\infty}a_n(z-z_0)^n+\sum_{n=1}^{\infty}b_n(z-z_0)^{-n}$

(d) $f(z)=\sum_{n=-\infty}^{\infty}a_n(z-z_0)^n$

**16.** Following is/are true.

(a) The limit point of sequence of zero is called non-isolated essential singularity.

(b) The limit point of sequence of pole is called non-isolated essential singularity.

(c) The limit point of sequence of poles are isolated as well as non-isolated essential singularity.

(d) The limit point of sequence of zero is the isolated essential singularity.

**17.** Let $f(z)=e^z$ for which following hold?

(a) $f(z)$ is an entire function.

(b) $f(z)$ has an isolated essential singularity at $z=0$.

(c) $f(z)$ has an isolated essential singularity at $z=\infty$.

(d) $f(z)$ has removable singularity at $z=0$.

**18.** If $f(z)$ is analytic for $|z|<1$ such that $|f(z)|\le 1$, $f(0)=0$, then

(a) $|f(z)|>|z|$ (b) $|f(z)|<|z|$

(c) $|f(z)|=|z|$ (d) $f(z)=z$

**19.** If $f(z)$ is analytic for $|z|<1$ such that $|f(z)|\le|z|$, then

(a) $|f(z)|\le 1$ (b) $f(0)=0$

(c) $|f'(0)|\le 1$ (d) $f(z)=-z$

**20.** If $f(z)$ and $g(z)$ be analytic inside and on a simple closed curve C and let $|g(z)|<|f(z)|$ on C, then $f(z)$ and $h(z)$ have the same number of zeros inside C, where

(a) $h(z)=f(z)g(z)$ (b) $h(z)=\dfrac{f(z)}{g(z)},\ g(z)\neq 0$
(c) $h(z)=f(z)-g(z)$ (d) $h(z)=f(z)+g(z)$

**21.** Let $f(z)$ is meromorphic inside a closed contour C and $O_n$ and $P_n$ are the number of zeros and number of poles inside C, then $\int_C \dfrac{f'(z)}{f(z)}dz = 2\pi ik$, where

(a) $k=O_n+P_n$ (b) $k=O_n-P_n$
(c) $k=O_n\cdot P_n$ (d) $k=\dfrac{P_n}{O_n}$

**22.** Let $f(z)$ be analytic within and on a simple closed contour C, such that $|f(z)|\le 1$, then
(a) $|f(z)|<1$ when $f(z)=$ constant
(b) $|f(z)|\ge 1$ when $f(z)\neq$ constant
(c) $|f(z)|=1$ when $f(z)=$ constant
(d) $|f(z)|<1$ when $f(z)\neq$ constant

**23.** Consider $P(z)=z^{10}-6z^7+3z^3+1$ and $|z|<1$, then
(a) $P(z)$ is analytic on $|z|=1$
(b) $P(z)$ has six zeros inside $|z|=1$
(c) $P(z)$ has seven zeros inside $|z|=1$
(d) only (b) is true

**24.** Let $k_1,k_2,k_3$ be the values of residues of $\dfrac{z^3}{(z-1)(z-2)(z-3)}$ at $z=1,2,3$, then
(a) $k_1=k_2=k_3$ (b) $16k_1+k_2=0$
(c) $6k_1+3k_2+2k_3=0$ (d) $k_1+2k_2+5k_3=0$

**25.** If $\alpha_1,\alpha_2,\alpha_3$ and $\alpha_\infty$ denotes the residues of $\dfrac{z}{(z-1)(z-2)(z-3)}$ at $z=1,2,3$ and $\infty$, then
(a) $\alpha_1+\alpha_2-\alpha_3+\alpha_\infty=0$ (b) $\alpha_1+\alpha_2+\alpha_3-\alpha_\infty=0$
(c) $\alpha_1-\alpha_2+\alpha_3+\alpha_\infty=0$ (d) $\alpha_1+\alpha_2+\alpha_3+\alpha_\infty=0$

**26.** Let $D=\{z\in\mathbb{C}:|z|<1\}$ be the unit disc. Let $f:D\to\mathbb{C}$ be an analytic function satisfying $f\left(\dfrac{1}{n}\right)=\dfrac{2n}{3n+1}$ for $n\ge 1$, then
(a) $f(0)=\dfrac{2}{3}$
(b) $f$ has a simple pole at $z=-3$
(c) $f(3)=\dfrac{1}{3}$
(d) No such $f$ exists

**27.** At $z=0$ the function $f(z)=\dfrac{e^z+1}{e^z-1}$ has
(a) a removable singularity
(b) a pole
(c) an essential singularity
(d) the residue of $f(z)$ at $z=0$ is 2

**28.** Which of the following(s) is/are correct?
(a) If a single-valued function $f(z)$ is not defined at $z=a$, but $\lim_{z\to a} f(z)$ exists, then $z=a$ is known as a removal singularity.
(b) If for the function $f(z)=\dfrac{\sin z}{z}$, $f(0)$ is defined as 2, then $z=0$ is a removable singularity.
(c) Every polynomial of degree $n$ has exactly $n$ roots.
(d) None of the above

**29.** Given $\int_\gamma \dfrac{dz}{z-a}$, where $\gamma$ represents the circle $|z-a|=r$.
(a) The value is $2\pi i$. (b) The value is $\pi$.
(c) The value is zero. (d) The value is one.

**30.** Evaluate $\int_\gamma \dfrac{z+2}{z}dz$, where $\gamma$ is the semi-circle $z=2e^{it}$, $0\le t\le \pi$. Gives
(a) $-2+4i\pi$ (b) $\dfrac{4}{3}i\pi$
(c) $3\pi$ (d) $6\pi/i$

**31.** Prove that if $\gamma$ and $\sigma$ are closed rectifiable curve having the same initial points, then
(a) $n(\gamma;a)=-n(-\gamma;a)$ for every $a\notin\{\gamma\}$
(b) $n(\gamma+\sigma a)=n(\gamma;a)+n(\sigma;a)$, for every $a\notin\{\gamma\}\cup\{\sigma\}$
(c) $n(\gamma:a)-0$
(d) $n(\gamma+\sigma a)=0$

**32.** Which of the following(s) is/are correct?
(a) If $f(z)$ is analytic at all points in a region $S\in E_2$ and C is a curve lying in the above region $S$, then the complex function $f(z)$ is definitely integrable along the curve C.
(b) $\int_{[a,b]} z dz=\dfrac{1}{2}(a^2-b^2)$
(c) $\int_C \bar{z}dz$ from $z=0$ to $z=4+2i$ along the curve C given by $z=t^2+it$ is $(8/3)i$
(d) None of the above

**33.** (I) Given $\int_C \dfrac{e^{2z}dz}{(z-1)(z-2)}$, where C is the circle $|z|=3$.
(II) Given $\int_C \dfrac{\cos \pi z}{z^2-1}dz$ around a rectangle with vertices $2\pm i$, $-2\pm i$.
(a) The value of (I) is $2\pi i(e^4-e^2)$.
(b) The value of (II) is 0.
(c) The value of (I) is 0.
(d) The value of (II) is $2\pi i(e^4-e^2)$.

**34.** If G is an open disk in $\mathbb{C}$ and $\gamma$ is a rectifiable path in G with initial and end points $\alpha$ and $\beta$, respectively. If $f:G\to\mathbb{C}$ is a continuous function with a primitive $F:G\to\mathbb{C}$, then
(a) $\int_\gamma F=F(\beta)-F(\alpha)$ (b) $\int_\gamma F=F(\beta)$
(c) $\int_\gamma F=F(\alpha)$ (d) $\int_\gamma F=0$

**35.** Which of the following(s) is/are correct?

(a) If $F(z,\bar{z})$ be continuous and have continuous partial derivatives in a region $S \in E_2$ and on its boundary $C$, then

$$\oint_C F(z,\bar{z})dz = \int\int_S \frac{\partial F}{\partial \bar{z}} dA$$

where, $dA$ represents the element of area $dxdy$.

(b) Every polynomial equation

$$P(z) = a_0 + a_1 z + a_2 z^2 + ... + a_n z^n = 0$$

where, the degree of $P(z)$ is $n \geq 1$, $a_n \neq 0$, has atleast two roots.

(c) The general term in the expansion of $\cosh z$ in a Taylor's series is $\frac{z^{2n}}{(2n)!}$.

(d) None of the above

**36.** Prove that if $G$ is simply connected and $f: G \to \mathbb{C}$ is analytic in $G$, then $f$ has a primitive in $G$.

(a) If $G$ is simply connected and $f: G \to \mathbb{C}$ is analytic in $G$, then $f$ has a primitive in $G$.

(b) If $G$ is simply connected and $f: G \to \mathbb{C}$ is analytic in $G$, then $f$ has a primitive in $G$.

(c) If $G$ is simple connected and $\gamma_1 - \gamma_2$ is a closed rectifiable curve in $G$, then $\int_{\gamma_1-\gamma_2} f = 0$ for every $f$ an analytic function.

(d) If $G$ is simply connected and $\gamma_1 - \gamma_2$ is closed rectifiable curve in $G$, then $\int_{\gamma_1-\gamma_2} f \neq 0$ for every $f$ an analytic function.

**37.** Given $f(z) = \int_C \frac{z^2 - z + 1}{z-1} dz$, where $C$ is the circle $|z| = 1$.

(a) $f(z)$ is analytic in and on $C$

(b) $\int_C f(z)dz = 2\pi i$

(c) $f(z)$ has simple poles

(d) $f(z)$ is not analytic in and on $C$

**38.** If $G$ is a region and $f: G \to \mathbb{C}$ is continuous function such that $\int_T F = 0$ for every triangular path (closed curve) $T \subset G$.

(a) $f$ is analytic in $G$  (b) $f$ is not analytic in $G$

(c) Both (a) and (b)  (d) None of these

**39.** Which of the following(s) is/are correct?

(a) If $f(z) = u(x,y) + iv(x,y)$ be continuous in a simply connected region $S \in E_2$ and that $u(x,y)$ and $v(x,y)$ have continuous partial derivatives and

$$\oint_C f(z)dz = 0$$

around every closed curve $C$ in $S$, then $f(z)$ is non-analytic in $S$.

(b) The third term in the expansion of $ze^{2z}$ in a Taylor's series about $z = -1$ is $-e^{-2}(z+1)^2$.

(c) If $f(z)$ be continuous in a simply connected region $S \in E_2$, $a$ and $b$ are points in $S$ and $F(z) = \int_a^b f(u)du$, then $F(z)$ is analytic in $S$ and $F'(z) = f(z)$.

(d) None of the above

**40.** Let $G$ be a connected open set and $f: G \to \mathbb{C}$ an analytic function. If $a \in G$ such that $f^{(n)}(a) = 0$, $n \geq 0$, then

(a) $f(a) = 0$  (b) $f(a) =$ constant

(c) $f(a) = 1$  (d) $f(a) = 2$

**41.** Prove that if $f: G \to \mathbb{C}$ is analytic and $\bar{B}(a; r) \subset G$

(a) $f^{(n)}(a) = \frac{n!}{2\pi i}\int_\gamma \frac{f(w)}{(w-a)^{n+1}} dw$, where $\gamma(t) = a + re^{it}$ and $0 \leq t \leq 2\pi$

(b) $f(z) = \frac{1}{2\pi i}\int_\gamma \frac{f(w)}{w-z} dw$, where $\gamma(t) = a + re^{it}$ and $t \in [0, 2\pi]$

(c) $f^{(n)}(a)$ does not exist

(d) $f^{(n)}(a)$ exist

**42.** If $f$ is analytic in open ball $B(a; R)$ and $|f(z)| \leq M$ for all $z \in B(a; R)$.

(a) $|f^{(n)}(a)| \leq \frac{n!M}{r^n}$  (b) $|f^{(n)}(a)| = 0$

(c) $|f^{(n)}(a)| \geq \frac{n!M}{r^n}$  (d) $|f^{(n)}(a)| \approx \frac{n!M}{r^n}$

**43.** Which of the following(s) is/are correct?

(a) If a function $f(z)$ is continuous in a simply connected region $S \in E_2$ and if

$$\oint_C f(z)dz = 0$$

around every simply closed curve $C$ in $S$, then $f(z)$ is analytic in $S$.

(b) If $f(z)$ has a pole at $z = a$, then $\lim_{z \to a} f(z) = 0$.

(c) An analytic function $f(z)$ is said to have a zero of $n$th order at $z = \infty$, if $f(1/2)$ has such a zero at $z = \infty$.

(d) None of the above

**44.** Given $f(z) = \int_C \frac{z^2 - z + 1}{z-1} dz$, where $C$ is the circle $|z| = \frac{1}{4}$

(a) $f(z)$ is analytic everywhere within $C$

(b) $f(z)$ is not analytic

(c) $f(z) = 0$

(d) $f(z)$ has not simple pole

**45.** Given $f(z) = \int_C \frac{z-3}{z^2 - 2z + 5} dz$, where $C$ is a circle $|z| = 1$.

(a) $f$ is analytic everywhere within $C$

(b) $f(z) = 0$

(c) The poles of $f(z)$ lies outside the circle

(d) The poles of $f(z)$ lies inside the circle

**46.** Prove that $\int_0^{2\pi} e^{-\cos\theta}\cos(n\theta + \sin\theta)d\theta = (-1)^n \frac{2\pi}{n!}$, where $n$ is a positive integer.

(a) $\int_0^{2\pi} e^{-\cos\theta} e^{-i(\sin\theta + n\theta)} d\theta = (-1)^n \frac{2n}{n!}$, $n$ is positive integer

(b) $\int_0^{2\pi} e^{-\cos\theta}\cos(n\theta+\sin\theta)d\theta = (-1)^n \frac{2\pi}{n!}$, where $n$ is a positive integer

(c) $\int_0^{2\pi} e^{-\cos\theta} e^{-i(\sin\theta+n\theta)} d\theta = 0$

(d) $\int_0^{2\pi} e^{-\cos\theta}\cos(n\theta+\sin\theta)d\theta = 0$

**47.** Which of the following(s) is/are correct?

(a) The expansion of $\frac{1}{(z^2-3z+2)}$ in a Laurent's series for $0<|z|<1$ is $\sum_{n=0}^{\infty}\left(\frac{z^n}{z^{n+1}}\right)$.

(b) If $f(z)$ has a zero of order $n$ at $z=a$, then $\frac{1}{f(z)}$ has a pole of order $n$ at $z=a$.

(c) The function $f(z)$ is said to be singular at $z=0$ if $f(1/2)$ is singular at $z=0$.

(d) None of the above

**48.** Following statements are true?

(a) If $f$ is bounded function, then $|f(z)|\le M$ for all $z\in\mathbb{C}$.

(b) If $f$ is bounded function, then $|f(z)|\ge M$ for all $z\in\mathbb{C}$.

(c) If $f$ is bounded entire function, then $f$ is constant.

(d) If $f$ is bounded entire function, then $f$ is not constant.

**49.** Given $f(z)=\frac{(z-2)(z+2)}{(z+1)(z+4)}$

(a) For $|z|<1$
$f(z)=-1-\frac{5}{4}z-\frac{17}{16}z^2-\frac{65}{64}z^3-\ldots$

(b) For $|z|<1$
$f(z)=\ldots+\frac{1}{z^4}-\frac{1}{z^3}+\frac{1}{z^2}-\frac{1}{z}+\frac{z}{4}-\frac{z^2}{4^2}+\frac{z^3}{4^3}-\ldots$

(c) For $1<|z|<4$
$f(z)=-1-\frac{5}{4}z-\frac{17}{16}z^2-\frac{65}{64}z^3-\ldots$

(d) For $1<|z|<4$
$F(z)=\ldots+\frac{1}{z^4}-\frac{1}{z^3}+\frac{1}{z^2}-\frac{1}{z}+\frac{z}{4}-\frac{z^2}{4^2}+\frac{z^3}{4^3}-\ldots$

**50.** Which of the following(s) is/are correct?

(a) The zeros of an analytic function $f(z)$ are isolated.

(b) The residue of $f(z)$ at infinity $=\lim_{z\to\infty}[zf(z)]$.

(c) An integral function is the function which is analytic everywhere except at infinity.

(d) None of the above

**51.** Given $f(z)=1/\{(z-1)(z-2)\}$

(a) For $|z|<1$, $f(z)=\frac{1}{2}+\frac{3}{4}z+\frac{7}{8}z^2+\frac{15}{16}z^3+\ldots$

(b) For $1<|z|<2$, $f(z)=\frac{1}{2}+\frac{3}{4}z+\frac{7}{8}z^2+\frac{15}{16}z^3+\ldots$

(c) For $|z|<1$,
$f(z)=\ldots-z^{-4}-z^{-3}-z^{-2}-z^{-1}-\frac{1}{2}-\frac{1}{4}z-\frac{1}{8}z^2-\frac{1}{16}z^3-\ldots$

(d) For $1<|z|<2$,
$f(z)=\ldots-z^{-4}-z^{-3}-z^{-2}-z^{-1}-\frac{1}{2}-\frac{1}{4}z-\frac{1}{8}z^2-\frac{1}{16}z^3-\ldots$

**52.** Given the function $f(z)=\frac{\cot\pi z}{(z-a)^2}$

(a) $z=n$, $(n\in I)$ are simple pole of $f(z)$ if $n$ is finite

(b) $z=\infty$ is the non-isolated essential singularity

(c) Residue at $z=n$ is $\frac{1}{\pi(n-a)^2}$

(d) $z=a$ is the pole of order two

**53.** Which of the following(s) is/are not correct?

(a) If the function $f(z)$ has a simple pole at $z=a$, then res $f(a)=\lim_{z\to a}[(z-a)f(z)]$

(b) If the function $f(z)=\frac{F(z)}{G(z)}$ has a simple pole at $z=a$, then res $f(a)=\frac{F'(a)}{G(a)}$

(c) The function $f(z)=\tan(1/z)$ has a removable singularity at $z=0$

(d) None of the above

**54.** $\log z=(z-1)-\frac{(z-1)^2}{2}+\frac{(z-1)^3}{3}-\ldots$, when $|z-1|<1$

(a) Taylor's theorem expansion is
$f(z)=f(z_0)+(z-z_0)f'(z_0)+\frac{(z-z_0)^2}{2!}f''(z_0)+\ldots$

(b) $\log z=(z-1)-\frac{(z-1)^2}{2}+\frac{(z-1)^3}{3}-\ldots$, when $|z-1|<1$

(c) $\log z=z-\frac{z^2}{2}+\frac{z^3}{3}-\ldots$

(d) $\log z=z^2-\frac{z^4}{4}+\frac{z^6}{6}-\ldots$

**55.** For $0<|z|<4$

(a) $\frac{1}{4z-z^2}=\sum_{n=0}^{\infty}\frac{z^{n-1}}{4^{n+1}}$ (b) $\frac{1}{4z-z^2}=\Sigma z^n$

(c) $\frac{1}{4z-z^2}=\frac{\Sigma z^n}{2i}$ (d) $\frac{1}{4z-z^2}=\Sigma\frac{2i}{z^n}$

**56.** Given $f(z)=\frac{1}{z(z^2-3z+2)}$

(a) For $0<|z|<1$, the expansion of $f(z)$ is
$-\frac{1}{2(z-1)}-\frac{3}{4}\sum_{n=0}^{\infty}\left(\frac{z-1}{2}\right)^n$

(b) For $0<|z|<1$, the expansion of $f(z)$ is
$\sum_{n=0}^{\infty}\frac{2^n-1}{2^n}z^{n-1}$

(c) For $1<|z|<2$, the expansion of $f(z)$ is
$\frac{1}{2z}-\left(\sum_{n=0}^{\infty}\frac{1}{z^{n+1}}\right)-\frac{1}{4}\sum_{n=0}^{\infty}\left(\frac{z}{2}\right)^n$

(d) For $1<|z|<2$, the expansion of $f(z)$ is

$$-\frac{1}{2(z-1)}-\frac{3}{4}\sum_{n=0}^{\infty}\left(\frac{z-1}{2}\right)^n$$

**57.** Given $f(z)=\frac{z-2}{z^2}\sin\frac{1}{z-1}$

(a) $z=0$ is a pole of order one
(b) $z=0$ is a pole of order two
(c) $z=1$ is an isolated essential singularity of $f(z)$
(d) $z=1$ is a limit point of the zeros

**58.** Which of the following(s) is/are correct?

(a) The zeros of an analytic function $f(z)$ are isolated.
(b) A singularity of a function $f(z)$ is a value of $z$ at which the function $f(z)$ causes to be analytic.
(c) A polynomial of $n$th degree has a pole of $n$th order at infinity.
(d) None of the above

**59.** Given $f(z)=\frac{1}{(z+1)(z+3)}$

(a) For $|z|<1$, $f(z)=\frac{1}{3}-\frac{4}{9}z+\frac{13}{27}z^2-\ldots$
(b) For $1<|z|<3$,
$$f(z)=\ldots+\frac{1}{2z^3}-\frac{1}{2z^2}+\frac{1}{2z}+\frac{1}{6}-\frac{1}{18}z+\frac{1}{54}z^2-\frac{1}{162}z^3+\ldots$$
(c) For $|z|<1$, $f(z)=e^z$
(d) For $1<|z|<3$, $f(z)=e^{-z}$

**60.** Given $f(z)=\frac{1}{\sin z-\cos z}$

(a) poles of $f(z)$ are $z=n\pi+\frac{\pi}{4}$, $n\in\mathbb{Z}$
(b) at $n=0$, $z=\frac{\pi}{4}$ is a simple pole
(c) no pole exist
(d) no singularities exist

**61.** Given $f(z)=\frac{z^2}{(z-1)^2(z+2)}$

(a) the function has simple pole at $z=-2$
(b) the function has no pole
(c) the residue of the function is 4/9
(d) the function have no residue

**62.** If $G$ is a region and $f$ is an analytic function with zeros $a_1, a_2, \ldots, a_m$. Also, if $\gamma$ is a closed rectifiable curve in $G$ which does not pass through any point $a_k$ and $\gamma\approx 0$

(a) $\int_\gamma \frac{f'(z)}{f(z)}dz=(2\pi i)\sum_{k=1}^{m} n(\gamma;a_k)$
(b) $\int_\gamma \frac{f'(z)}{f(z)}dz=0$
(c) $\int_\gamma \frac{f'(z)}{f(z)}dz$ does not exist
(d) $\int_\gamma \frac{f'(z)}{f(z)}dz$ exist

**63.** Which of the following(s) is/are correct?

(a) If a function $f(z)$ has a pole of order $n$ at the point $z=a$, then res $f(a)=\frac{1}{(m-1)}\lim_{z\to a}\left[\frac{d^{m-1}}{dz^{m-1}}(z-a)^m f(z)\right]$
(b) the residue of $f(z)$ at infinity is $\lim_{z\to\infty}[zf(z)]$
(c) the residue of $f(z)=\frac{z}{(z-1)(z-2)}$ at $z=\infty$ is 1
(d) None of the above

**64.** When $a_n=\frac{1}{2\pi}\int_0^{2\pi}\cosh n\theta\cosh(2\cos\theta)\,d\theta$

(a) $\cosh\left(z+\frac{1}{z}\right)=a_0$
(b) $\cosh\left(z+\frac{1}{z}\right)=\sum_{n=1}^{\infty}a_n$
(c) $\cosh\left(z+\frac{1}{z}\right)=a_0+\sum_{n=1}^{\infty}a_n\left(z_n+\frac{1}{z_n}\right)$
(d) $\cosh\left(z+\frac{1}{z}\right)=0$

**65.** Given function $e^{-1/z^2}$

(a) zero's of $f(z)$ are $z=0$
(b) zero's of $f(z)$, $z=0$ is of order 2
(c) $f(z)$ has no pole
(d) $f(z)$ has no singularities

**66.** Given $f(z)=z\operatorname{cosec} z$,

(a) the poles of $f(z)$ are $z=n\pi$, $n\in\mathbb{Z}$
(b) $z=\infty$ is a non-isolated essential singularity
(c) the poles of $f(z)$ are $z=0$
(d) $z=\infty$ is the limit point of the poles

**67.** Which of the following(s) is/are correct?

(a) $\int_0^{2\pi}\frac{d\theta}{1-ae^{i\theta}}=0$, if $|a|<1$
(b) Applying calculus of residues, it can be proved that $\int_0^{\pi}\frac{\cos 2\theta}{1-2a\cos\theta+a^2}d\theta=\frac{\pi a^2}{1-a^2}$, where $-1<a<1$
(c) By the method of contour integration, it can be shown that $\int_0^{\infty}\frac{dx}{1+x^2}=\frac{\pi}{2}$
(d) None of the above

**68.** Which of the following(s) is/are correct?

(a) Pole is sometimes known as an essential singularity.
(b) If $f(z)=e^{1/2}$, then $z=0$ is a point of essential singularity.
(c) The function $f(z)=\tan(1/2)$ has a removable singularity at $z=0$
(d) None of the above

**69.** Which of the following(s) is/are correct?

(a) Residue of $f(z)=\frac{1}{(z^2+a^2)^2}$ at $z=ai$ is $4ia^3$.
(b) The residue of $\cot z$ is 1.
(c) The residue of $\tanh z$ is 1.
(d) None of the above

# Answers

## Exercise 1

| | | | | | | | | | |
|---|---|---|---|---|---|---|---|---|---|
| **1.** (a) | **2.** (a) | **3.** (b) | **4.** (c) | **5.** (a) | **6.** (b) | **7.** (b) | **8.** (a) | **9.** (a) | **10.** (b) |
| **11.** (a) | **12.** (c) | **13.** (b) | **14.** (c) | **15.** (a) | **16.** (a) | **17.** (b) | **18.** (c) | **19.** (a) | **20.** (b) |
| **21.** (a) | **22.** (a) | **23.** (c) | **24.** (c) | **25.** (a) | **26.** (d) | **27.** (a) | **28.** (b) | **29.** (b) | **30.** (c) |
| **31.** (a) | **32.** (b) | **33.** (d) | **34.** (b) | **35.** (b) | **36.** (b) | **37.** (b) | **38.** (a) | **39.** (a) | **40.** (d) |
| **41.** (a) | **42.** (c) | **43.** (c) | **44.** (a) | **45.** (c) | **46.** (c) | **47.** (b) | **48.** (a) | **49.** (a) | **50.** (b) |
| **51.** (c) | **52.** (a) | **53.** (a) | **54.** (c) | **55.** (a) | **56.** (b) | **57.** (b) | **58.** (a) | **59.** (c) | **60.** (a) |
| **61.** (b) | **62.** (b) | **63.** (b) | **64.** (c) | **65.** (a) | **66.** (c) | **67.** (c) | **68.** (b) | **69.** (a) | **70.** (b) |
| **71.** (c) | **72.** (b) | **73.** (c) | **74.** (a) | **75.** (b) | **76.** (a) | **77.** (b) | **78.** (c) | **79.** (c) | **80.** (b) |
| **81.** (c) | **82.** (a) | **83.** (c) | **84.** (c) | **85.** (c) | **86.** (b) | **87.** (c) | **88.** (a) | **89.** (a) | **90.** (c) |
| **91.** (b) | **92.** (c) | **93.** (c) | **94.** (a) | **95.** (b) | **96.** (d) | **97.** (b) | **98.** (d) | **99.** (b) | **100.** (b) |
| **101.** (d) | **102.** (a) | **103.** (b) | **104.** (a) | **105.** (c) | **106.** (c) | **107.** (b) | **108.** (d) | **109.** (c) | **110.** (b) |
| **111.** (c) | **112.** (c) | **113.** (d) | **114.** (a) | **115.** (c) | **116.** (b) | **117.** (b) | **118.** (b) | **119.** (d) | **120.** (c) |
| **121.** (c) | **122.** (a) | **123.** (c) | **124.** (c) | **125.** (c) | **126.** (a) | **127.** (b) | **128.** (b) | **129.** (d) | **130.** (a) |
| **131.** (c) | **132.** (b) | **133.** (d) | **134.** (b) | **135.** (d) | **136.** (d) | **137.** (c) | **138.** (a) | **139.** (a) | **140.** (d) |
| **141.** (d) | **142.** (c) | **143.** (d) | **144.** (d) | **145.** (b) | **146.** (c) | **147.** (a) | **148.** (b) | **149.** (b) | **150.** (c) |
| **151.** (c) | **152.** (d) | **153.** (b) | **154.** (b) | **155.** (b) | **156.** (c) | **157.** (b) | **158.** (c) | **159.** (c) | **160.** (b) |
| **161.** (a) | **162.** (d) | **163.** (b) | **164.** (d) | **165.** (c) | **166.** (c) | **167.** (c) | **168.** (c) | **169.** (c) | **170.** (c) |
| **171.** (c) | **172.** (c) | **173.** (c) | **174.** (c) | **175.** (c) | **176.** (a) | **177.** (d) | **178.** (d) | **179.** (c) | **180.** (b) |
| **181.** (b) | **182.** (c) | **183.** (c) | **184.** (c) | **185.** (d) | **186.** (b) | **187.** (b) | **188.** (b) | **189.** (b) | **190.** (b) |
| **191.** (c) | **192.** (b) | **193.** (b) | **194.** (a) | **195.** (b) | **196.** (b) | **197.** (a) | **198.** (b) | **199.** (d) | **200.** (c) |
| **201.** (d) | **202.** (d) | **203.** (b) | **204.** (a) | **205.** (d) | **206.** (b) | **207.** (a) | **208.** (c) | **209.** (a) | **210.** (b) |
| **211.** (d) | **212.** (a) | **213.** (c) | **214.** (b) | **215.** (c) | **216.** (b) | **217.** (a) | **218.** (c) | **219.** (b) | **220.** (a) |
| **221.** (b) | **222.** (c) | **223.** (c) | **224.** (a) | **225.** (b) | **226.** (b) | **227.** (c) | | | |

## Exercise 2

| | | | | | | | | | |
|---|---|---|---|---|---|---|---|---|---|
| **1.** (b,c,d) | **2.** (a,d) | **3.** (a,b,d) | **4.** (a,b,d) | **5.** (a,c) | **6.** (a,b,c,d) | **7.** (a,b) | **8.** (c) | **9.** (a,c,d) | **10.** (b,d) |
| **11.** (a,b,c) | **12.** (d) | **13.** (a,b,c,d) | **14.** (a,b,c) | **15.** (c,d) | **16.** (b,d) | **17.** (a,c,d) | **18.** (b,c,d) | **19.** (a,b,c,d) | **20.** (d) |
| **21.** (b) | **22.** (c,d) | **23.** (a,c) | **24.** (b,c) | **25.** (d) | **26.** (a,b,c) | **27.** (b,d) | **28.** (a,c) | **29.** (a) | **30.** (a) |
| **31.** (a,b) | **32.** (a,c) | **33.** (a,b) | **34.** (a) | **35.** (c) | **36.** (a,c) | **37.** (a,b) | **38.** (a) | **39.** (c) | **40.** (a) |
| **41.** (a,b,d) | **42.** (a) | **43.** (a) | **44.** (a,c) | **45.** (a,b,c) | **46.** (a,b) | **47.** (b) | **48.** (a,c) | **49.** (a,d) | **50.** (a,c) |
| **51.** (a,d) | **52.** (a,b,c,d) | **53.** (b,c) | **54.** (a,b) | **55.** (a) | **56.** (b,c) | **57.** (b,c,d) | **58.** (a,b) | **59.** (a,b) | **60.** (a,b) |
| **61.** (a,c) | **62.** (a,d) | **63.** (a) | **64.** (c) | **65.** (a,b,c,d) | **66.** (a,b,d) | **67.** (b,c) | **68.** (b) | **69.** (b,c) | |

# Hints & Solutions

## Exercise 1

**41.** We have circle

$$z = e^{i\theta},\ 0 \le \theta \le \pi$$

$$\Rightarrow \quad dz = ie^{i\theta}d\theta$$

Hence,

$$\int_C \frac{1}{z}\,dz = \int_0^{\pi} \frac{1}{e^{i\theta}}\,ie^{i\theta}d\theta$$

$$= i\int_0^{\pi} d\theta$$

$$= i[\theta]_0^{\pi} = \pi i$$

**42.** $\dfrac{1}{2\pi i}\displaystyle\int_{|z|=3} \frac{e^z}{z-2}\,dz = f(2) = e^2$ $\qquad [\because f(z) = e^z]$

**44.** $\displaystyle\int \frac{e^z}{z-2}\,dz = 2\pi i f(2)$

$$= 2\pi i e^2 \qquad [\because f(z) = e^2]$$

**56.** Since, $f(z) = \dfrac{3z^2 + 7z + 1}{z+1}$

is analytic within and on $C: |z| = \frac{1}{2}$. Hence, by Cauchy's theorem, we have

$$\int_C \frac{3z^2 + 7z + 1}{z+1}\,dz = 0$$

**57.** We have $f(z) = \dfrac{3z+4}{z(2z+1)}$, then

Poles are given by

$$z(2z+1) = 0$$

$$\Rightarrow \quad z = 0,\ z = -\frac{1}{2}$$

Now, $\dfrac{3z+4}{z(2z+1)} = \dfrac{A}{z} + \dfrac{B}{2z+1}$

By method of partial fraction, we get

$$3z+4 = A(2z+1) + Bz$$

Putting $z = 0$, we get $A = 4$
and

Putting $z = -\frac{1}{2}$, we get $B = -5$

Hence, $\displaystyle\int \frac{3z+4}{z(2z+1)}\,dz = 4\int \frac{1}{z}\,dz - 5\int \frac{1}{2z+1}\,dz$

$\therefore$ By Cauchy's integral formula, we get

$$= 4\cdot 2\pi i - \frac{5}{2}\cdot 2\pi i$$

$$= 8\pi i - 5\pi i = 3\pi i$$

## Exercise 2

**20.** Rouches theorem

**21.** The Argument principle.

**22.** Maximum modulus principle.

**23.** Let $P(z) = z^{10} - 6z^7 + 3z^3 + 1$,
where $f(z) = -6z^7$ and $g(z) = z^{10} + 3z^3 + 1$
Now, $P(z) = f(z) + g(z)$ and both $f(z)$ and $g(z)$ are analytic within and upon $C$

$$\left|\frac{g(z)}{f(z)}\right| = \left|\frac{z^{10} + 3z^3 + 1}{-6z^7}\right| \le \frac{|z|^{10} + 3|z|^3 + 1}{6|z|^7}$$

$$= \frac{1+3+1}{6} = \frac{5}{6} < 1$$

Therefore, by applying Rouche's theorem $P(z)$ and $f(z)$ has same number of zeros inside C.

But $f(z)$ has seven zeros inside C.

Hence, $P(z)$ has seven zeros inside C.

**26.** $f\left(\dfrac{1}{n}\right) = \dfrac{2n}{3n+1}$

Put $\dfrac{1}{n} = w$

$$\Rightarrow \quad f(w) = \frac{\frac{2}{w}}{\frac{3}{w}+1} = \frac{2}{w+3}$$

$$\therefore \quad f(0) = \frac{2}{3},$$

when $w+3 = 0 \quad \Rightarrow \quad w = -3$

$\Rightarrow f$ has a simple pole at $w = -3$

Also, $f(3) = \dfrac{2}{6} = \dfrac{1}{3}$

**60.** $f(z) = \dfrac{z - \sin z}{z^2}$ is singular at $z^2 = 0 \Rightarrow z = 0$

**74.** By Cauchy's integral formula,

$$\int_C \frac{dz}{z-a} = 2\pi i$$

**87.** By using Argument principle,

$$\int_C \frac{f'(z)}{f(z)}\,dz = 2\pi i[O_n - P_n]$$

where, $O_n$ and $P_n$ are number of zeros and poles of $f(z)$.

Here, $\quad O_n = 5$ and $P_n = 0$

$$\Rightarrow \quad \int_C \frac{f'(z)}{f(z)}\,dz = 10\pi i$$

**94.** We have

$$f(z) = \tan z = \frac{\sin z}{\cos z}$$

Now, the poles are given by

$$\cos z = 0$$

$$\Rightarrow \quad z = (2n+1)\frac{\pi}{2},\ n \in \mathbb{Z}.$$

**27.** $\displaystyle\lim_{z\to 0} (z-0)f(z) = \lim_{z\to 0} z\cdot\frac{e^z+1}{e^z-1}$

$$= \lim_{z\to 0} \frac{z}{e^z-1}\cdot e^z + 1$$

$$= 1\times 2 = 2 \ne 0$$

$\Rightarrow z = 0$ is not the removable singularity for $f(z)$.

when $e^z - 1 = 0 \Rightarrow \quad e^z = 1 = e^{2n\pi i}$

$\Rightarrow \quad z = 2n\pi i,\ n = 0, \pm 1, \pm 2, \ldots$

$\Rightarrow z = 0, \pm 2\pi i, \pm 4\pi i, \ldots\ldots$ are the simple poles, which limit points is $\infty$.

$\Rightarrow z = 0$ is not an essential singularity.

Since, $z = 0$ is simple pole.

$$\Rightarrow \quad \text{res } f(0) = \lim_{z\to 0} (z-0)f(z) = 2$$

**29.** Here, for the circle $|z-a| = r$

$z = a + re^{i\theta}$, where $0 \le \theta \le 2\pi$

$\therefore \quad dz = ire^{i\theta}d\theta$

Hence, $\displaystyle\int_\gamma \frac{dz}{z-a} = \int_0^{2\pi} \frac{ire^{i\theta}}{re^{i\theta}}\,d\theta = 2\pi i$

**30.** Here, $\quad z = 2e^{it},\ 0 \le t \le \pi$

$\Rightarrow \quad dz = 2ie^{it}\,dt$

Hence, $\displaystyle\int_\gamma \frac{z+2}{z}\,dz = \int_0^{\pi} \frac{(2e^{it}+2)}{2e^{it}}\,2ie^{it}\,dt$

$$= 2i\int_0^{\pi} (1 + e^{-it})e^{it}\,dt$$

$$= 2i\int_0^{\pi} (e^{it} + 1)\,dt$$

$$= 2i\left[\frac{e^{it}}{i} + t\right]_0^{\pi}$$

$$= 2i\left(\frac{e^{i\pi}}{i} - \frac{1}{i} + \pi\right)$$

$$= 2e^{i\pi} - 2 + 2i\pi$$

$$= -2 + 4i\pi$$

**31.** (a) $\gamma$ is a closed rectifiable curve in $\mathbb{C}$, then for $a \notin \{\gamma\}$

$$n(\gamma; a) = \frac{1}{2\pi i}\int_\gamma (z-a)^{-1}dz$$

$$= \frac{-1}{2\pi i}\int_{-\gamma} (z-a)^{-1}dz$$

$$= -n(-\gamma; a)$$

(b) $$n(\gamma+\sigma; a) = \frac{1}{2\pi i}\int_{\gamma+\sigma}\frac{dz}{z-a}$$

$$= \frac{1}{2\pi i}\int_\gamma \frac{dz}{z-a} + \frac{1}{2\pi i}\int_\sigma \frac{dz}{z-a}$$

$$= n(\gamma; a) + n(\sigma; a)$$

**33.** (I) $f(z) = e^{2z}$ is analytic within the circle $C : |z| = 3$ and the two singular points $a = 1$ and $a = 2$ lie inside $C$.

$$\therefore \int_C \frac{e^{2z}}{(z-1)(z-2)}dz = \int_C e^{2z}\left(\frac{1}{z-2} - \frac{1}{z-1}\right)dz$$

$$= \int_C \frac{e^{2z}}{z-2}dz - \int_C \frac{e^{2z}}{z-1}dz$$

$$= 2\pi i e^4 - 2\pi i e^2 = 2\pi i(e^4 - e^2)$$

(By Cauchy's integral formula)

(II) $f(z) = \cos \pi z$ is analytic in the region bounded by the given rectangle and the two singular points $a = 1$ and $a = -1$ lie inside this rectangle,

y; $-2+i$, $i$, $2+i$; $-2$, $-1$, O, 1, 2, X; $-2-i$, $-i$, $2-i$

$$\therefore \int_C \frac{\cos \pi z}{z^2-1}dz = \frac{1}{2}\int_C\left(\frac{1}{z-1} - \frac{1}{z+1}\right)\cos \pi z\, dz$$

$$= \frac{1}{2}\int_C \frac{\cos \pi z}{z-1}dz - \int_C \frac{\cos \pi z}{z+1}dz$$

$$= \frac{1}{2}[2\pi i \cos \pi(1)] - \frac{1}{2}[2\pi i \cos \pi(-1)]$$

$$= 0$$

**34.** Let $\gamma : [a, b] \to \mathbb{C}$ is piecewise smooth,

Then, $$\int_\gamma F = \int_a^b F(\gamma(t))\gamma'(t)\,dt$$

$$= \int_a^b F'(\gamma(t))\gamma'(t)\,dt$$

$$= \int_a^b (Fo\gamma)'(t)\,dt$$

$$= F(\gamma(b)) - f(\gamma(a)) = F(\beta) - F(\alpha)$$

Let $\gamma : [a, b] \to \mathbb{C}$ is a rectifiable path and since $f$ is a continuous function, then for $\varepsilon > 0$ there is a polygonal path $\Gamma$ in $G$ such that

$$\Gamma(a) = \gamma(a) \text{ and } \Gamma(b) = \gamma(b) \text{ and } \left|\int_\gamma f - \int_\Gamma f\right| < \varepsilon$$

Since, $\Gamma$ is piecewise smooth, from above result proved.

$$\int_\Gamma F = F(\beta) - F(\alpha)$$

$$\Rightarrow \quad \left|\int_\gamma f - [F(\beta) - F(\alpha)]\right| < \varepsilon$$

$\Rightarrow$ Since, $\varepsilon$ is arbitrary

$$\int_\gamma f = F(\beta) - F(\alpha)$$

**36.** Since, $G$ is connected. For some fix point $a \in G$, let $\gamma_1$ and $\gamma_2$ be any two rectifiable curves in $G$ from $a$ to some $z \in G$.

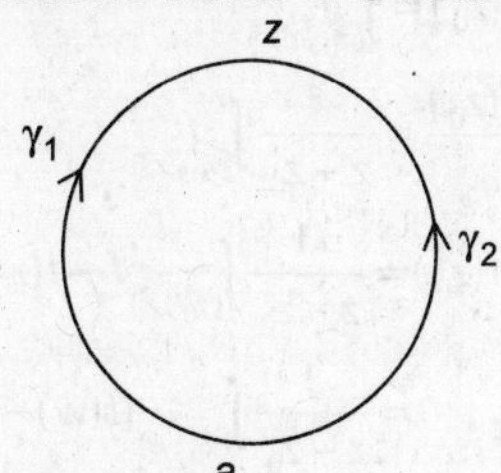


$\therefore \gamma_1 - \gamma_2$ is a curve which goes from $a$ to $z$ and $(-\gamma_2)$ is a curve which then back from $z$ to $a$.

$\therefore \gamma_1 - \gamma_2$ is a closed rectifiable curve.

By Cauchy's theorem, if $G$ is simple connected and $\gamma_1 - \gamma_2$ is a closed rectifiable curve in $G$, then $\int_{\gamma_1 - \gamma_2} f = 0$ for every $f$ an analytic function

$$\Rightarrow \quad \int_{\gamma_1 \gamma_2} f = \int_{\gamma_1} f - \int_{\gamma_2} f = 0$$

Thus, we have an well defined function $F : G \to \mathbb{C}$ such that $F(z) = \int_{\gamma_1} f$, where $\gamma_1$ is a rectifiable curve from $a$ to $z$ in $G$, to prove $F$ is a primitive of $f$.

If $z_0 \in G$ for some $r > 0$, $B(z_0; r) \subset G$, let $\gamma$ be the path from $a$ to $z_0$. For some $z \in B(z_0; r)$ let define $\gamma_z = \gamma + [z_0, z]$, where $[z_0, z]$ is a line segment joining $z_0$ to $z$.

$$\frac{F(z) - F(z_0)}{z - z_0} = \frac{1}{z - z_0}\int_{[z_0, z]} f$$

$$\Rightarrow \quad \frac{F(z) - F(z_0)}{z - z_0} - f(z_0) = \frac{1}{z_0 - z}\int f - f(z_0)$$

$$\Rightarrow \quad \left|\frac{F(z) - F(z_0)}{z - z_0} - f(z_0)\right| \le |f(z) - f(z_0)|$$

$$\Rightarrow \quad \lim_{z \to z_0}\frac{F(z) - F(z_0)}{z - z_0} = f(z_0)$$

$$\Rightarrow \quad \frac{d}{dz}F(z_0) = F(z_0)$$

$$\Rightarrow \quad f = F'$$

**37.** Here, $f(z) = z^2 - z + 1$

and $z_0 = 1$

Since, $f(z)$ is analytic with in and on $C : |z| = 1$ and $z_0$ lies on $C$.

$\therefore$ By Cauchy's integral formula

$$f(z_0) = \frac{1}{2\pi i}\int_C \frac{f(z)}{z-a}dz$$

$$\Rightarrow \int_C \frac{z^2 - z + 1}{z - 1} = 2\pi i f(z_0) = 2\pi i$$

**38.** Here, it is sufficient to prove that $f$ has a primitive.

Let $G$ be open set, *i.e.*, $G = B(a; R)$

For $z \in G$, define $f(z) = \int_{[a,z]} f$

then for some $z_0 \in [a, z]$, we have

$$F(z) = \int_{[a, z_0]} f + \int_{[z_0, z]} f$$

and also $\quad F(z) - F(z_0) = \int_{[a, z_0]} f + \int_{[z_0 - z]} f - \int_{[a, z_0]} f$

$$\Rightarrow \quad F(z) - F(z_0) = \int_{[z_0, z]} f$$

$$\Rightarrow \quad \frac{F(z) - F(z_0)}{z - z_0} = \frac{1}{z - z_0} \int_{[z_0, z]} f$$

or $\quad \dfrac{F(z) - F(z_0)}{z - z_0} - f(z_0) = \dfrac{1}{z - z_0} \displaystyle\int_{[z_0, z]} f - f(z_0)$

$$= \frac{1}{z - z_0} \int_{[z_0, z]} [f(w) - f(z_0) dw]$$

$$\Rightarrow \left| \frac{F(z) - F(z_0)}{z - z_0} - f(z_0) \right| \le |f(z) - f(z_0)|$$

which gives, $\lim\limits_{z \to z_0} \dfrac{F(z) - F(z_0)}{z - z_0} = f(z_0) \Rightarrow \dfrac{d}{dz} F(z_0) = F(z_0)$

*i.e.*, $\quad f(z_0) = F'(z_0)$

**40.** Let $A = \{z \in G : f^{(n)}(a) = 0, n \ge 0\}$

Then, $A \ne \phi$.

Since, $G$ is connected, then only subsets of $G$ which are open and closed both are $\phi$ and $G$. So, here we have to prove $A = G$.

$A$ is closed let $z \in \overline{A}$, closure of $A$ and $z_k$ be a sequence in $A$ such that $z = \lim a_k$. Since, each $f^{(n)}$ is continuous.

$\Rightarrow f^{(n)}(z) = \lim f^{(n)}(z_k) = 0$. So, $z \in A$ and $A$ is closed.

**41.** If $f : G \to \mathbb{C}$ is analytic and there is a closed ball $\overline{B}(a, r) \subset G$, then

$$f(z) = \frac{1}{2\pi i} \int_\gamma \frac{f(w)}{w - z} dw,$$

where $\gamma(t) = a + re^{it}$ and $t \in [0, 2\pi]$.

Differentiating $n$ times *wrt* $z$, we get

$$f^{(n)}(z) = \frac{n!}{2\pi i} \int_\gamma \frac{f(w)}{(w - z)^{n+1}} dw$$

which gives for $z = a$,

$$f^{(n)}(a) = \frac{n!}{2\pi i} \int_\gamma \frac{f(w)}{(w - a)^{n+1}} dw$$

where $\gamma(t) = a + re^{it}$ and $t \in [0, 2\pi]$.

**42.** If $f$ is analytic in a closed ball $\overline{B}(a, r) r < R$, then

$$f^{(n)}(a) = \frac{n!}{2\pi i} \int_\gamma \frac{f(w)}{(w - a)^{n+1}} dw$$

where $\gamma(t) = a + re^{it}$, $0 \le t \le 2\pi$

$$\Rightarrow \quad |f^{(n)}(a)| = \left| \frac{n!}{2\pi i} \cdot \int_{\gamma + a} \frac{f(w)}{w^{n+1}} dw \right|$$

$$\le \frac{n!}{2\pi} \cdot \frac{M}{r^{n+1}} = \frac{n! M}{r^n}$$

Since, $r < R$ for $r \to R$.

**44.** Here, $z_0 = 1$ and it lies outside the circle $C : |z| = \frac{1}{4}$, so

$\dfrac{z^2 - z + 1}{z - 1}$ is analytic everywhere within $C$.

$\therefore$ By Cauchy's theorem $\int_C f(z) dz = 0$

$$\Rightarrow \quad \int_C \frac{z^2 - z + 1}{z - 1} dz = 0$$

**45.** The pole of $f(z) = \dfrac{z - 3}{z^2 + 2z + 5}$ are given by

$$z^2 + 2z + z = 0$$

$$z = \frac{-2 \pm \sqrt{4 - 20}}{2} = -1 \pm 2i$$

Since, both the poles lies outside the circle

$$|z| = 1$$

$\therefore f(z)$ is analytic everywhere within $C$. By Cauchy's theorem $\int_C f(z)\, dz = 0$.

**46.** Let $I = \displaystyle\int_0^{2\pi} e^{-\cos\theta} e^{-i(\sin\theta + n\theta)} d\theta$

$$= \int_0^{2\pi} e^{-(\cos\theta + i\sin\theta)} e^{-in\theta} d\theta$$

$$= \int_0^{2\pi} e^{-e^{i\theta}} e^{-in\theta} d\theta$$

$$= \int_\gamma e^{-z} z^{-n} \frac{dz}{iz}, \text{ putting } z = e^{i\theta}$$

$$= \int_\gamma \frac{e^{-z}}{iz^{n+1}} dz = \int_\gamma f(z) dz, \text{ say}$$

where $\gamma$ is the unit circle, $|z| = 1$, $z = 0$ is the pole of order $(n + 1)$ of $f(z)$.

Residue at $z = 0$ is $\dfrac{1}{n!} \left[ D^n \left( \dfrac{1}{i} e^{-z} \right) \right]_{z=0}$

$$= \frac{(-1)^n}{n!}$$

$$\therefore \quad 1 = 2\pi i \cdot \frac{(-1)^n}{in!} = (-1)^n \frac{2n}{n!}$$

Equating real parts on both sides, we get

$$\int_0^{2\pi} e^{-\cos\theta} \cos(n\theta + \sin\theta) d\theta = (-1)^n \frac{2\pi}{n!}$$

**48.** To prove this theorem, given $f$ a bounded function

$\therefore |f(z)| \le M$ for all $z \in \mathbb{C}$

By Cauchy's estimate theorem, since $f$ is bounded and analytic, we have

$$|f^{(n)}(z)| \le \frac{n! M}{R}$$

$\Rightarrow |f'(z)| \le \dfrac{M}{R}$, Since $R$ is arbitrary, we have

$$|f'(z)| = 0$$

$\therefore f(z)$ is constant.

**49.** Here, $f(z) = \dfrac{(z - 2)(z + 2)}{(z + 1)(z + 4)} = 1 - \dfrac{5z + 8}{(z + 1)(z + 4)}$

$$= 1 - \frac{1}{z + 1} - \frac{4}{z + 4}$$

(i) $|z|<1$. We have

$$f(z)=1-(1+z)^{-1}-\left(1+\frac{z}{4}\right)^{-1}$$

$$=1-(1-z+z^2-z^3+\ldots)-\left[1-\frac{z}{4}+\left(\frac{z}{4}\right)^2-\left(\frac{z}{4}\right)^3+\ldots\right]$$

$$=-1+\left(1+\frac{1}{4}\right)z+\left(-1-\frac{1}{4^2}\right)z^2+\left(1+\frac{1}{4^3}\right)z^3+\ldots$$

$$=-1-\frac{5}{4}z-\frac{17}{16}z^2-\frac{65}{64}z^3-\ldots$$

(ii) $1<|z|<4$. Then, $\frac{1}{|z|}<1$ and $\frac{|z|}{4}<1$.

$$\therefore f(z)=1-\frac{1}{z}\left(1+\frac{1}{z}\right)^{-1}-\left(1+\frac{z}{4}\right)^{-1}$$

$$=1-\frac{1}{z}\left[1-\frac{1}{z}+\frac{1}{z^2}-\frac{1}{z^3}+\ldots\right]-\left[1-\frac{z}{4}+\frac{z^2}{4^2}-\frac{z^3}{4^3}+\ldots\right]$$

$$=\ldots+\frac{1}{z^4}-\frac{1}{z^3}+\frac{1}{z^2}-\frac{1}{z}+\frac{z}{4}-\frac{z^2}{4^2}+\frac{z^3}{4^3}-\ldots$$

**51.** (a) By partial fractions,

$$\frac{1}{(z-1)(z-2)}=\frac{1}{z-2}-\frac{1}{z-1} \quad \ldots\text{(i)}$$

$$=-\frac{1}{2}\left(1-\frac{z}{2}\right)^{-1}+(1-z)^{-1} \quad \ldots\text{(ii)}$$

For $|z|<1$, both $|z/2|$ and $|z|$ are less than 1.

Hence, Eq. (ii) gives on expansion

$$f(z)=-\frac{1}{2}\left(1+\frac{z}{2}+\frac{z^2}{4}+\frac{z^3}{8}+\ldots\right)+(1+z+z^2+z^3+\ldots)$$

$$=\frac{1}{2}+\frac{3}{4}z+\frac{7}{8}z^2+\frac{15}{16}z^3+\ldots$$

(b) For $1<|z|<2$, we have Eq. (i) as

$$f(z)=-\frac{1}{2}\frac{1}{(1-z/2)}-\frac{1}{z(1-z^{-1})} \quad \ldots\text{(iii)}$$

and notice that both $|z/2|$ and $|z^{-1}|$ are less than 1.

Hence, Eq. (iii) gives on expansion

$$f(z)=-\frac{1}{2}\left(1+\frac{z}{2}+\frac{z^2}{4}+\frac{z^3}{8}+\ldots\right)-\frac{1}{z}(1+z^{-1}+z^{-2}+z^{-3}+\ldots)$$

$$=\ldots-z^{-4}-z^{-3}-z^{-2}-z^{-1}-\frac{1}{2}-\frac{1}{4}z-\frac{1}{8}z^2-\frac{1}{16}z^3-\ldots$$

**52.** Here, $f(z)=\frac{\cot\pi z}{(z-a)^2}=\frac{\cos\pi z}{\sin\pi z(z-a)^2}$

Poles of $f(z)$ are given by $(z-a)^2\sin\pi z=0$

so $(z-a)^2=0 \Rightarrow z=a$ is a pole of order two and $\sin\pi z=0 \Rightarrow \pi z=n\pi \Rightarrow z=n$ where $n\in I$.

$z=n$, $(n\in I)$ are simple poles of $f(z)$ if $n$ is finite.

$z=\infty$ is the limit point of these poles so $z=\infty$ is the non-isolated essential singularity.

Residue at $(z=a)$ is $\frac{1}{1!}f'(a)$,

where $f(z)=\cot\pi z=-\pi\,\text{cosec}^2\,\pi a$

Residue at $(z=n)$ is $\left[\frac{f'(z)}{g'(z)}\right]_{z=n}$ [where $g(z)=\sin\pi z$]

$$=\left[\frac{\cos\pi z/(z-a)^2}{\pi\cos\pi z}\right]_{z=n}$$

$$=\frac{1}{\pi(n-a)^2}$$

**54.** Let $f(z)=\log z$

For Taylor's theorem, expansion

$$f(z)=f(z_0)+z-z_0f'(z_0)+\frac{(z-z_0)^2}{2!}f''(z_0)+\ldots \quad \ldots\text{(i)}$$

Taking $z_0=1$

$f(1)=\log 1=0$

$f'(z)=\frac{1}{z}$, $f'(1)=1$

$f''(z)=\frac{1}{z^2}$, $f''(1)=-1$

$f'''(z)=\frac{2}{z^3}$, $f'''(1)=2$ and so on.

Substituting these values in Eq. (i), we get

$$\log z=f(1)+f'(1)(z-1)+f''(1)\frac{(z-1)^2}{2!}+\ldots$$

$$=(z-1)-\frac{1}{2}(z-1)^2+\frac{1}{3}(z-1)^3+\ldots$$

**55.** We have $0<|z|<4 \Rightarrow \frac{|z|}{4}<1$

$$\therefore \frac{1}{4z-z^2}=\frac{1}{4z(1-z/4)}=\frac{1}{4z}\left(1-\frac{z}{4}\right)^{-1}$$

$$=\frac{1}{4z}\left[1+\frac{z}{4}+\left(\frac{z}{4}\right)^2+\left(\frac{z}{4}\right)^3+\ldots\right]$$

$$=\frac{z^{-1}}{4}+\frac{1}{4^2}+\frac{z}{4^3}+\frac{z^2}{4^4}+\ldots=\sum_{n=0}^{\infty}\frac{z^{n-1}}{4^{n+1}}$$

**56.** $f(z)=\frac{1}{z(z^2-3z+2)}$

$$=\frac{1}{z(z-1)(z-2)}$$

$$=\frac{1}{2z}-\frac{1}{z-1}+\frac{1}{2(z-2)}$$

(i) For $0<|z|<1$, we have

$$f(z)=\frac{1}{2z}+(1-z)^{-1}-\frac{1}{4}\left(1-\frac{z}{2}\right)^{-1}$$

$$=\frac{1}{2z}+(1+z+z^2+z^3+\ldots)-\frac{1}{4}\left[1+\frac{z}{2}+\left(\frac{z}{2}\right)^2+\left(\frac{z}{2}\right)^3+\ldots\right]$$

$$=\frac{1}{2z}+\frac{3}{4}+\frac{7}{8}z+\frac{15}{16}z^2+\frac{31}{32}z^3+\ldots$$

$$=\sum_{n=0}^{\infty}\frac{2^n-1}{2^n}z^{n-1}$$

(ii) For $1<|z|<2 \Rightarrow \frac{1}{|z|}<1$ and $\frac{|z|}{2}<1$

$$\therefore\ f(z)=\frac{1}{2z}-\frac{1}{z}\left(1-\frac{1}{z}\right)^{-1}-\frac{1}{4}\left(1-\frac{z}{2}\right)^{-1}$$

$$=\frac{1}{2z}-\frac{1}{z}\left(1+\frac{1}{z}+\frac{1}{z^2}+\frac{1}{z^3}+\ldots\right)$$

$$-\frac{1}{4}\left[1+\frac{z}{2}+\left(\frac{z}{2}\right)^2+\left(\frac{z}{2}\right)^3+\ldots\right]$$

$$=\frac{1}{2z}-\left(\sum_{n=0}^{\infty}\frac{1}{z^{n+1}}\right)-\frac{1}{4}\sum_{n=0}^{\infty}\left(\frac{z}{2}\right)^n$$

**57.** Zeros of $f(z)$ are obtained by equating to zero its numerator *i.e.*,

$$(z-2)\sin\{1/(z-1)\}=0$$

Here, $z-2=0$ gives $z=2$ which is a simple zero of $f(z)$.

and $\quad \sin\frac{1}{z-1}=0$ gives $\frac{1}{z-1}=n\pi$

or $\quad z=1+\frac{1}{n\pi},\ n\in I$

which are also zeros of order one.

Since, $z=1$ is a limit point of the zeros $z=1+\frac{1}{n\pi}(n\in I)$ therefore, $z=1$ is an isolated essential singularity of $f(z)$.

To obtain the poles of $f(z)$ equating to zero its denominator, we get $\quad z^2=0$

Hence, $z=0$ is a pole of order two.

**59.** We have

$$f(z)=\frac{1}{(z+1)(z+3)}$$

Its partial fractions, is

$$f(z)=\frac{1}{2(z+1)}-\frac{1}{2(z+3)}$$

(i) For $|z|<1$, we have

$$f(z)=\frac{1}{2}(1+z)^{-1}-\frac{1}{6}\left(1+\frac{z}{3}\right)^{-1}$$

$$=\frac{1}{2}[1-z+z^2-z^3+\ldots]-\frac{1}{6}\left[1-\frac{z}{3}+\left(\frac{z}{3}\right)^2-\left(\frac{z}{3}\right)^3+\ldots\right]$$

$$=\left(\frac{1}{2}-\frac{1}{6}\right)-\left(\frac{1}{2}-\frac{1}{18}\right)z+\left(\frac{1}{2}-\frac{1}{54}\right)z^2-\ldots$$

$$=\frac{1}{3}-\frac{4}{9}z+\frac{13}{27}z^2-\ldots$$

(ii) For $1<|z|<3$.

Then, we have $\frac{1}{|z|}<1$ and $\frac{|z|}{3}<1$.

$$\frac{1}{2(z+1)}=\frac{1}{2z\left(1+\frac{1}{z}\right)}=\frac{1}{2z}\left(1+\frac{1}{z}\right)^{-1}$$

$$=\frac{1}{2z}\left(1-\frac{1}{z}+\frac{1}{z^2}-\frac{1}{z^3}+\ldots\right)$$

$$=\frac{1}{2z}-\frac{1}{2z^2}+\frac{1}{2z^3}-\ldots$$

and
$$\frac{1}{2(z+3)}=\frac{1}{6\left(1+\frac{z}{3}\right)}=\frac{1}{6}\left(1+\frac{z}{3}\right)^{-1}$$

$$=\frac{1}{6}\left(1-\frac{z}{3}+\frac{z^2}{9}-\frac{z^3}{27}+\ldots\right)$$

$$=\frac{1}{6}-\frac{1}{18}z+\frac{1}{54}z^2-\frac{1}{162}z^3+\ldots$$

Thus, the Laurent's series valid for the region $1<|z|<3$ is

$$f(z)=\ldots+\frac{1}{2z^3}-\frac{1}{2z^2}+\frac{1}{2z}+\frac{1}{6}-\frac{1}{18}z+\frac{1}{54}z^2-\frac{1}{162}z^3+\ldots$$

**60.** Let $f(z)=\frac{1}{\sin z-\cos z}$

Pole of $f(z)$ are given by

$\sin z-\cos z=0$ or $\tan z=1$ or $z=n\pi+\frac{\pi}{4}$, $n$ is any integer.

At $n=0$, $z=\frac{\pi}{4}$ which is a simple pole.

**61.** $\lim_{z\to-2}[f(z)(z+2)]=\lim_{z\to-2}\frac{z^2}{(z-1)^2}=\frac{4}{9}$

which is finite and non-zero.

Thus, the function has a simple pole at $z=-2$ and residue $\text{Re}\,f(-2)=\frac{4}{9}$.

**62.** If analytic function $f(z)$ have zero at $a_1, a_2, \ldots, a_m$, then there is an analytic function $g$

$$f(z)=(z-a_1)(z-a_2)\ldots(z-a_m)\,g(z)$$

which gives,

$$\frac{f'(z)}{f(z)}=\frac{1}{z-a_1}+\frac{1}{z-a_2}+\ldots+\frac{1}{z-a_m}+\frac{g'(z)}{g(z)}$$

If $g(z)\neq0$ then $g'(z)$ is analytic in $G$ and also since $\gamma\approx0$, we have by Cauchy's theorem

$$\int_\gamma\frac{g'(z)dz}{g(z)}=0$$

$$\Rightarrow\quad \int_\gamma\frac{f'(z)}{f(z)}dz=\int_\gamma\frac{1}{z-a_1}dz+\int_\gamma\frac{dz}{z-a_2}+\ldots+\int_\gamma\frac{dz}{z-a_m}$$

$$=2\pi i[n(\gamma;a_1)+n(\gamma;a_2)+\ldots+n(\gamma;a_m)]$$

$$\left(\because n(\gamma;a)=\frac{1}{2\pi i}\int_\gamma\frac{dz}{z-a}\right)$$

$$=2\pi i\left[\sum_{k=1}^{m}n(\gamma;a_k)\right]$$

**64.** The function $\cosh\left(z+\frac{1}{z}\right)$ is analytic everywhere except at $z=0$.

$\therefore$ This function is analytic in the annulus $r\le|z|\le R$, $r<R$. The Laurent series expansion of this function in the annulus $r<|z|<R$ is

$$\cosh\left(z+\frac{1}{z}\right)=\sum_{-\infty}^{\infty}a_nz^n$$

where $$a_n = \frac{1}{2\pi i}\int_\gamma \cosh\left(z+\frac{1}{z}\right)\frac{dz}{z^{n+1}}$$

where $\gamma$ is a circle $|z| = r_1$, $(r < r_1 < R)$

Let $r_1 = 1$, then $|z| = 1$ and $z = e^{i\theta}$

$\Rightarrow dz = ie^{i\theta}d\theta$

$$\therefore\ a_n = \frac{1}{2\pi i}\int_0^{2\pi}\cosh(e^{i\theta}+e^{-i\theta})\frac{ie^{i\theta}d\theta}{e^{i(n+1)\theta}}$$

$$= \frac{1}{2\pi i}\int_0^{2\pi}\cosh(2\cos\theta)e^{-in\theta}d\theta \qquad \left(\because \cos\theta = \frac{e^{i\theta}+e^{-i\theta}}{2}\right)$$

$$= \frac{1}{2\pi i}\int_0^{2\pi}\cosh(2\cos\theta)(\cos n\theta) - i\sin n\theta)\,d\theta$$

$$\left(\because \int_0^{2\pi} f(\theta) = 0, \text{ if } f(2a-\theta) = -f(\theta)\right)$$

$$= \frac{1}{2\pi}\int_0^{2\pi}\cosh(2\cos\theta)\cosh n\theta\, d\theta$$

$$= \frac{1}{2\pi}\int_0^{2\pi}\cosh(2\cos\theta)\cosh(-n\theta)d\theta$$

$$= a_{-n}$$

Also, $\cosh\left(z+\frac{1}{z}\right)$

$$= \sum_{-\infty}^{\infty} a_n z^n = a_0 + \sum_{n=1}^{\infty} a_{-n}z^{-n} + \sum_{n=1}^{\infty} a_n z^n$$

$$= a_0 + \sum_{n=1}^{\infty} a_n\left(z^n + \frac{1}{z^n}\right)$$

Thus, $$\cosh\left(z+\frac{1}{z}\right) = a_0 + \sum_{n=1}^{\infty} a_n\left(z^n + \frac{1}{z^n}\right)$$

where $$a_n = \frac{1}{2\pi}\int_0^{2\pi}\cosh n\theta\cosh(2\cos\theta)d\theta$$

**65.** We have $f(z) = e^{-1/z^2}$

Zeros of $f(z)$ are given by

$$e^{-1/z^2} = 0 \text{ or } z^2 = 0$$

$\therefore$ $z = 0$ is a zero of order two.

Since, zeros have no limit point, therefore there is no singularity of $f(z)$.

Here, the poles of $f(z)$ are given by

$$e^{-1/z^2} = 0, \text{ which is not possible.}$$

$\therefore$ There exist no poles.

Hence, $e^{-1/z^2}$ has no singularities.

**66.** Let $$f(z) = z\operatorname{cosec} z = \frac{z}{\sin z}$$

Poles of $f(z)$ are given by

$$\sin z = 0 \text{ or } z = n\pi,\ n \text{ integer}$$

Since, $z = \infty$ is a limit point of these poles therefore, $z = \infty$ is a non-isolated essential singularity.

# 13 Conformal Mappings

**Syllabus**

- Conformal Mappings
- Mobius Transformations

## Mappings

Let $W = f(z) = u + iv$ is a complex valued function of a complex variable $z$, where $z = x + iy$ and $u = u(x, y), v = v(x, y)$, then we get some correspondence between point $(u, v)$ in the $w$-plane with the point $(x, y)$ in the $z$-plane, called a mapping or transformation of points in z-plane into points of the $w$-plane.

> ***Note*** **(a)** The correspondence is one-one. *i.e.*, for each point of $z$-plane, there corresponds one and only one point of $w$-plane.
>
> **(b)** The corresponding sets of points in the two planes are called images of each other.
>
> **(c)** $\dfrac{\partial(u,v)}{\partial(x,y)} = \begin{vmatrix} \dfrac{\partial u}{\partial x} & \dfrac{\partial u}{\partial y} \\ \dfrac{\partial v}{\partial x} & \dfrac{\partial v}{\partial y} \end{vmatrix} = \dfrac{\partial u}{\partial x}\dfrac{\partial v}{\partial y} - \dfrac{\partial u}{\partial y}\dfrac{\partial v}{\partial x}$, is called the Jacobian of the transformation.

If $u$ and $v$ are continuously differentiable in any region $D$ and if the Jacobian $\dfrac{\partial(u, v)}{\partial(x, y)}$ does not vanish in $D$, then the transformation is one to one.

In particular, if $f(z)$ is an analytic function, then using Cauchy Riemann equations

$$\frac{\partial u}{\partial x} = \frac{\partial v}{\partial y}; \frac{\partial u}{\partial y} = -\frac{\partial v}{\partial x}, \text{ we get}$$

$$\frac{\partial(u, v)}{\partial(x, y)} = \frac{\partial u}{\partial x} \cdot \frac{\partial u}{\partial x} - \frac{\partial u}{\partial y}\left(-\frac{\partial u}{\partial y}\right)$$

$$= \left(\frac{\partial u}{\partial x}\right)^2 + \left(\frac{\partial u}{\partial y}\right)^2 = \left|\frac{\partial u}{\partial x} + i\frac{\partial u}{\partial y}\right|^2 = |f'(z)|^2$$

It follows from above that the transformation is one to one in regions, where $f'(z) \neq 0$.

***Example 1.*** *Consider the transformation $w = z + (1 - i)$ and determine the region $D'$ of the w-plane corresponding to the rectangular region $D$ in the z-plane bounded by $x = 0, y = 0, x = 1$ and $y = 2$.*

**Solution.** We have, $w = z + (1 - i)$

$$\Rightarrow \quad u + iv = x + iy + 1 - i = (x + 1) + i(y - 1)$$

$$\Rightarrow \quad u = x + 1 \text{ and } v = y - 1$$

Hence, the lines $x = 0, y = 0, x = 1$ and $y = 2$ are mapped respectively onto the lines $u = 1, v = -1, u = 2$ and $v = 1$. The two regions are shown in the following figures.

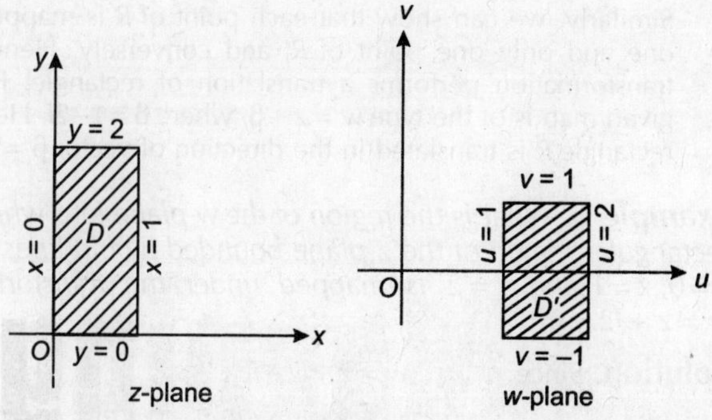


It is clear that there is one and only one point of the region $D'$ corresponding to each point of region $D$ and conversely. Thus, in this case the correspondence is one to one. This transformation accomplishes a translation of the rectangle $D$ in the direction of the vector $1-i$ *i.e.*, each point of $D$ is moved a distance $\sqrt{2}$ parallel to the line $y=-x$, if we consider the transformation in the z-plane only.

***Example 2.*** *Show that $w = iz + i$ maps half plane $x > 0$ onto half plane $v > 1$.*

**Solution.** We have, $w = iz + i$ gives,

$$\Rightarrow \quad u + iv = i(x + iy) + i$$

$$\Rightarrow \quad \left.\begin{array}{l} u = -y \\ v = x+1 \end{array}\right\} \Rightarrow x = v - 1$$

Now, $\quad x > 0 \Rightarrow v - 1 > 0 \Rightarrow v > 1$

Hence, we get the required result.

***Example 3.*** *Show that the transformation $w = iz$ is a rotation of the z-plane through the angle $\frac{\pi}{2}$. Find the image of the infinite strip $0 < x < 1$.*

**Solution.** We have, $w = iz$

$$\Rightarrow \quad |w| = |iz| = |i||z| = |z| \qquad [\because |i| = 1]$$

and $\arg(w) = \arg(iz) = \arg(i) + \arg(z) = \frac{\pi}{2} + \arg(z)$

Hence, the transformation $w = iz$ is a rotation of the z-plane about the origin through an angle $\frac{\pi}{2}$.

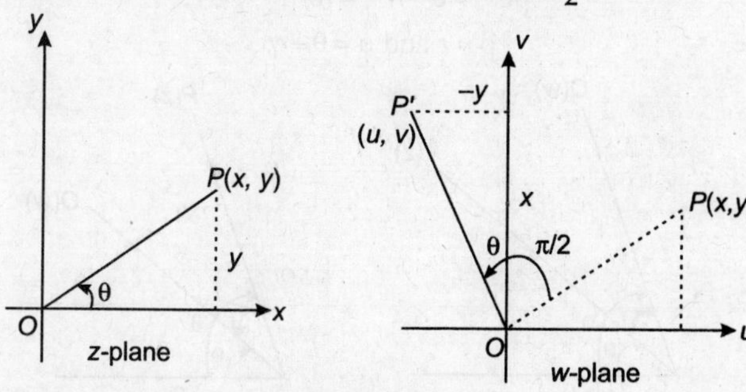


Also, suppose $w = u + iv$, then we have

$$u + iv = i(x + iy) = ix - y$$

$$\Rightarrow \quad u = -y \text{ and } v = x$$

Thus, the region $0 < x < 1$ in the $z$-plane is mapped into the region $0 < v < 1$ in the $w$-plane *i.e.*, an infinite strip parallel to the imaginary axis between $x = 0$ and $x = 1$ in z-plane is mapped into an infinite strip parallel to real axis between $v = 0$ and $v = 1$ in the $w$-plane.

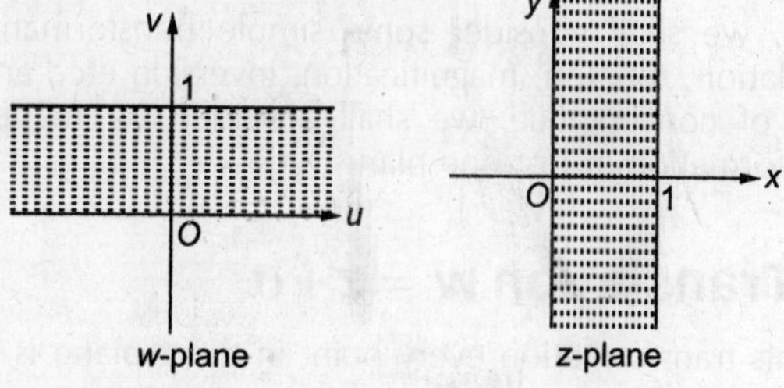


***Example 4.*** *Consider the linear transformation*

$$w = (1 + i)z + 2 - i$$

*and determine the region in the w-plane into which the rectangular region bounded by the lines $x = 0, y = 0, x = 1, y = 2$ in the z-plane is mapped under this transformation.*

**Solution.** We have, $w = (1 + i)z + 2 - i$

$$\Rightarrow \quad u + iv = (1 + i)(x + iy) + 2 - i$$

$$= (x - y + 2) + i(x + y - 1)$$

$$\Rightarrow \quad u = x - y + 2 \text{ and } v = x + y - 1$$

Then, the line $x = 0$ maps into $u = -y + 2, v = y - 1$
*i.e.*, into $u + v = 1$
The line $y = 0$ maps into $u = x + 2, v = x - 1$
*i.e.*, into $u - v = 3$
The line $x = 1$ maps into $u = -y + 3, v = y$
*i.e.*, into $u + v = 3$
The line $y = 2$ maps into $u = x, v = x + 1$
*i.e.*, into $v - u = 1$.

Thus, the rectangular region bounded by the lines $x = 0, y = 0, x = 1, y = 2$ in the z-plane is mapped into the rectangular region bounded by the lines $u + v = 1, u - v = 3, u + v = 3, v - u = 1$ in the w-plane. The two regions are shown in the following figures.

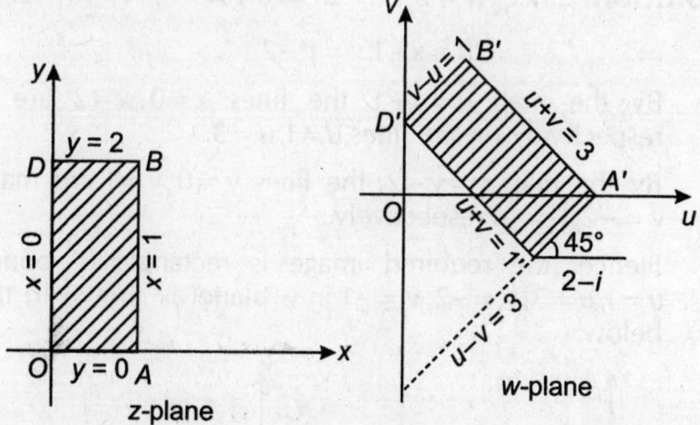


From the above figures it follows that the rectangle in the z-plane is magnified by the factor $|1 + i| = \sqrt{2}$, then rotated through an angle $\arg(1 + i) = \frac{\pi}{4}$ and finally translated in the direction of vector $2 - i$ through a distance $|2 - i| = \sqrt{5}$. Here, the points $A, B$ and $D$ are transformed into the points $A', B'$ and $D'$ and the origin in the z-plane is transformed into the point $2 - i$.

## Some Elementary Transformations

Here, we shall consider some simple transformations e.g., translation, rotation, magnification, inversion etc., and for the sake of convenience, we shall consider the mapping as a transformation in just one plane.

### (i) Translation $w = z + \alpha$

By this transformation every point in the z-plane is displaced or translated in the direction of the vector $\alpha$.

Let $P$ and $A$ be the points $z$ and $\alpha$ where $A$ is the fixed point and $P$ is a variable point. Then, geometrically speaking, the image of the point $P$ under the transformation is the fourth vertex $Q$ of the parallelogram whose adjacent sides are $OP$ and $OA$ as shown in the figure.

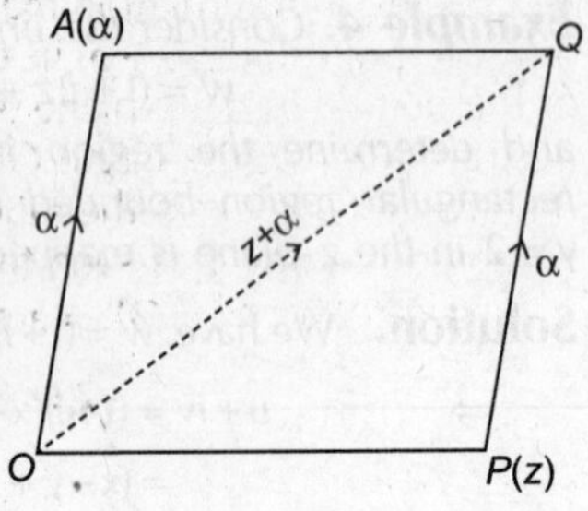


Since, the vector **OP** is represented by $z$ and **OA** is represented by $\alpha$, hence completing the parallelogram $AOPQ$, the sum of the two vectors **OP** and **OA** *i.e.*, **OQ** is represented by $z + \alpha$. In other words the point $Q$ represents the number $w = z + \alpha$.

Thus, $Q$ is obtained from $P$ by moving it a distance equal and parallel to $OA$.

Therefore, by the above transformation the point $P$ is translated along the vector $\alpha$ through a distance $|\alpha|$. Since, it holds for every point in any region of the z-plane, the image of the region is simply a translation of that region. The two regions have the same shape, size and orientation.

***Example 5.*** *Let a rectangular domain R be bounded by $x = 0$, $y = 0$, $x = 2, y = 1$. Determine the region $R'$ of w-plane into which R is mapped under the transformation $w = z + (1 - 2i)$.*

**Solution.** Since, $w = z + (1-2i) \Rightarrow u + iv = x + iy + (1-2i)$

$$\Rightarrow \quad u = x+1, v = y-2$$

By the map $u = x+1$, the lines $x = 0, x = 2$ are mapped respectively on the lines $u = 1, u = 3$.

By the map $v = y-2$, the lines $y = 0, y = 1$ are mapped on $v = -2, v = -1$ respectively.

Hence, the required image is rectangle $R'$ bounded by $u = 1, u = 3, v = -2, v = -1$ in w-plane as shown in the figure below.

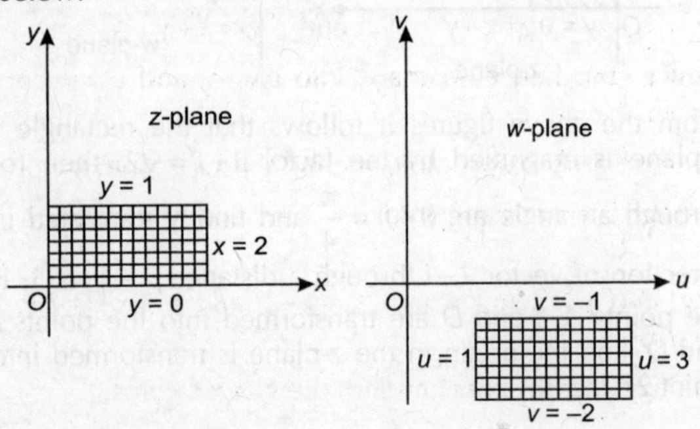


Similarly, we can show that each point of $R$ is mapped into one and only one point of $R'$ and conversely. Hence, the transformation performs a translation of rectangle. For the given map is of the type $w = z + \beta$, where $\beta = 1 - 2i$. Here, the rectangle $R$ is translated in the direction of vector $\beta = 1 - 2i$.

***Example 6.*** *What is the region of the w-plane into which the rectangular region of the z-plane bounded by the lines $x = 0$, $y = 0$, $x = 1$ and $y = 2$ is mapped under the transformation $w = z + (2 - i)$?*

**Solution.** Since, $\quad w = z + (2 - i)$

$$\Rightarrow \quad u + iv = x + iy + (2 - i) = (x + 2) + i(y - 1)$$

$$\Rightarrow \quad u = x + 2, v = y - 1$$

Hence, the lines $x = 0, y = 0, x = 1$ and $y = 2$ are mapped into the lines $u = 2, v = -1, u = 3$ and $v = 1$ respectively. These lines also form a rectangle in the w-plane.

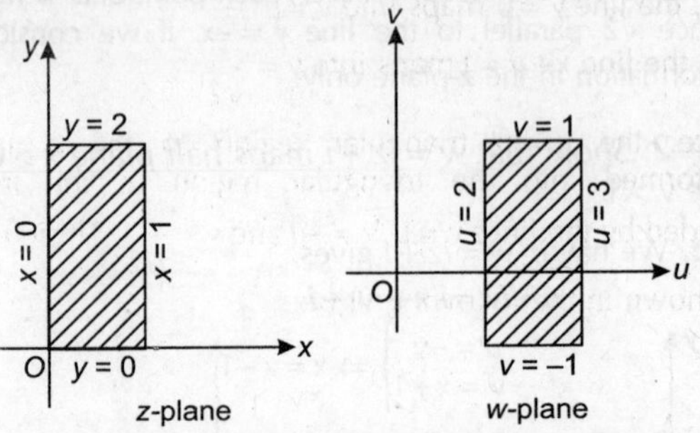


Also, it is clear that there is one and only one point of the region in the w-plane corresponding to each point of the region in the z-plane and conversely. Hence, the correspondence is one-to-one in this case. These regions are shown in the above figures.

### (ii) Rotation $w = e^{i\gamma} z$ ($\gamma$ real)

By this transformation, the image $Q$ of any point $P$ in the z-plane is obtained by rotating the line $OP$ through an angle $\gamma$. If $\gamma > 0$, this rotation is anti-clockwise and if $\gamma < 0$, it is clockwise.

If we write $\quad z = re^{i\theta}$ and $w = \rho e^{i\phi}$, then

$$\rho e^{i\phi} = e^{i\gamma} \cdot re^{i\theta} = re^{i(\theta + \gamma)}$$

$$\Rightarrow \quad \rho = r \text{ and } \phi = \theta + \gamma$$

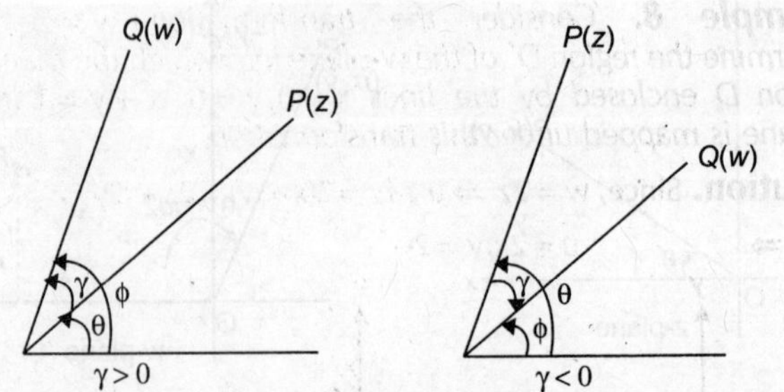


Thus, modulus of $w$ is the same as that of $z$ but the argument of $w$ is increased or decreased by an amount $\gamma$ according as $\gamma > 0$ or $\gamma < 0$. Since, this is true for every point in any region of the z-plane, the image of the region in the z-plane is rotated through an angle $\gamma$. Geometrically, the two regions are exactly the same.

***Example 7.*** *Consider the transformation $w = e^{i\pi/4}z$ and determine the region in the w-plane corresponding to the rectangular region bounded by the lines $x = 0, y = 0$ and $x + y = 1$ in the z-plane.*

**Solution.** Since, $w = e^{i\pi/4}z \Rightarrow u + iv = e^{i\pi/4}(x + iy)$

$$\Rightarrow \quad u + iv = \frac{1}{\sqrt{2}}(1+i)(x+iy) = \frac{1}{\sqrt{2}}[(x-y) + i(x+y)]$$

$$\Rightarrow \quad u = \frac{1}{\sqrt{2}}(x-y) \text{ and } v = \frac{1}{\sqrt{2}}(x+y)$$

When $x = 0, u = -\frac{1}{\sqrt{2}}y$ and $v = \frac{1}{\sqrt{2}}y$

Thus, the line $x = 0$ maps into $v = -u$

When $y = 0, u = \frac{1}{\sqrt{2}}x$ and $v = \frac{1}{\sqrt{2}}x$

Thus, the line $y = 0$ maps into $v = u$

Also, the line $x + y = 1$ maps into $v = \frac{1}{\sqrt{2}}$

Hence, the given triangular region in the z-plane is transformed into the triangular region in the w-plane bounded by the lines $v = u, v = -u$ and $v = \frac{1}{\sqrt{2}}$. These regions are shown in the following figures.

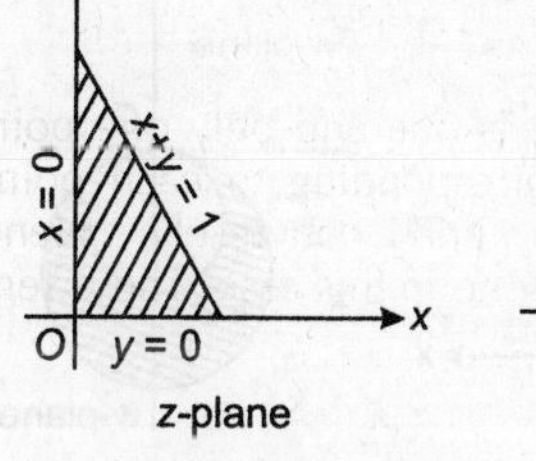


## (iii) Magnification $w = cz\,(c > 0)$

By this transformation, the figure in the z-plane is stretched or contracted according as $c > 1$ or $0 < c < 1$.

The image of a point $P$ in the z-plane is a point $Q$ in $OP$ if $0 < c < 1$ or a point $Q$ in $OP$ produced if $c > 1$ such that $OQ = cOP$.

This transformation is also known as **homothetic transformation.**

***Example 8.*** *Consider the transformation $w = 2z$ and determine the region $D'$ of the w-plane into which the triangular region $D$ enclosed by the lines $x = 0, y = 0, x + y = 1$ in the z-plane is mapped under this transformation.*

**Solution.** Since, $w = 2z \Rightarrow u + iv = 2(x + iy) = 2x + i2y$

$$\Rightarrow \quad u = 2x, v = 2y$$

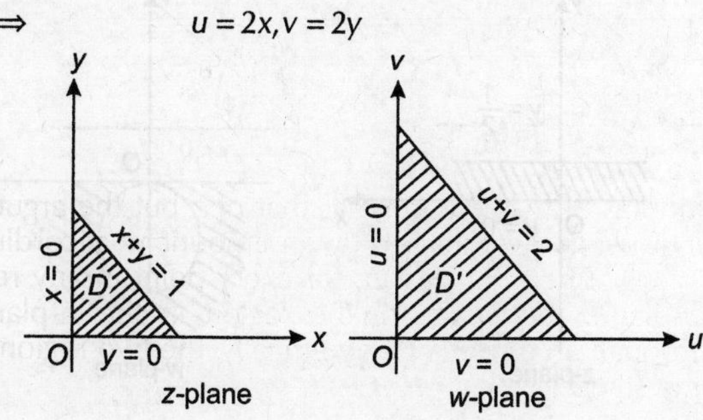


Therefore, the lines $x = 0, y = 0$ and $x + y = 1$ are transformed into the lines $u = 0, v = 0$ and $u + v = 2$ respectively. The two regions are shown in the above figures.

## (iv) Rotation and Magnification $w = \beta z$ ($\beta$ complex)

Let $w = \rho e^{i\phi}, \beta = be^{i\delta}$ and $z = re^{i\theta}$

Then, $w = \beta z \Rightarrow \rho e^{i\phi} = be^{i\delta} re^{i\theta} = bre^{i(\theta+\delta)}$

$\Rightarrow \rho = br, \phi = \theta + \delta$

Hence, the transformation maps the point $P(r, \theta)$ in the z-plane into the point $Q(br, \theta + \delta)$ in the w-plane. Thus, the image $Q$ of the point $P$ in the z-plane is obtained by rotating the radius vector $OP$ about the origin $O$ through an angle $\delta = \arg(\beta)$ and then magnifying $OP$ in the ratio $|\beta| : 1$. In other words, the point $w$ represented by $Q$ is such that

$$\angle QOP = \angle BOX = \arg(\beta) \text{ and } OQ = OB.\,OP$$

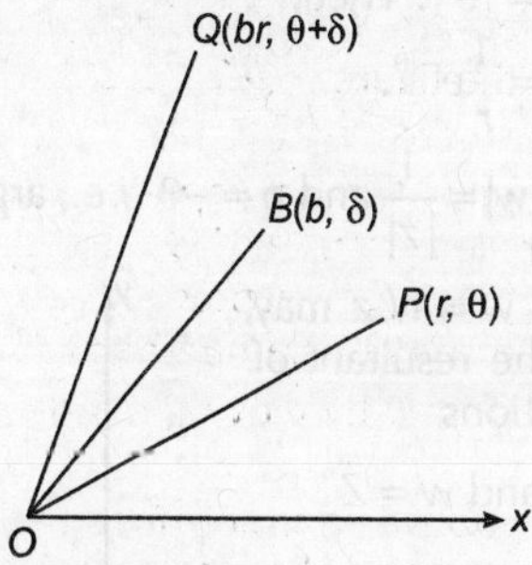


Rotation is anti-clockwise if $\arg(\beta) > 0$ and clockwise if $\arg(\beta) < 0$. Also, magnification is expansion or contraction according as $|\beta| > 1$ or $|\beta| < 1$. The adjoining figure is drawn for $\arg(\beta) > 0$ and $|\beta| > 1$. Thus, we see that the transformation $w = \beta z$ corresponds to a rotation together with a magnification. Ofcourse, there is no magnification if $|\beta| = 1$ and no rotation if $\arg(\beta) = 0$.

***Example 9.*** *Let the rectangular region $D$ in the z-plane be bounded by $x = 0, y = 0, x = 2, y = 3$. Determine the region $D'$ of the w-plane into which $D$ is mapped under the transformation $w = \sqrt{2}e^{i\pi/4}z$.*

**Solution.** Since, $w = \sqrt{2}e^{i\pi/4}z$

$$\Rightarrow \quad u + iv = \sqrt{2}\left(\cos\frac{\pi}{4} + i\sin\frac{\pi}{4}\right)(x + iy)$$

$$= (1+i)(x+iy) = (x-y) + i(x+y)$$

$$\Rightarrow \quad u = x - y \quad \text{and} \quad v = x + y$$

Hence, the line $x = 0$ maps into $u = -y$ and $v = y$ *i.e.*, into $v = -u$.

The line $y = 0$ maps into $u = x$ and $v = x$ *i.e.*, into $v = u$.

The line $x = 2$ maps into $u = 2 - y$ and $v = 2 + y$ *i.e.*, into $u + v = 4$.

The line $y = 3$ maps into $u = x - 3$ and $v = x + 3$ *i.e.*, into $v - u = 6$.

The two regions are shown in the given figures.

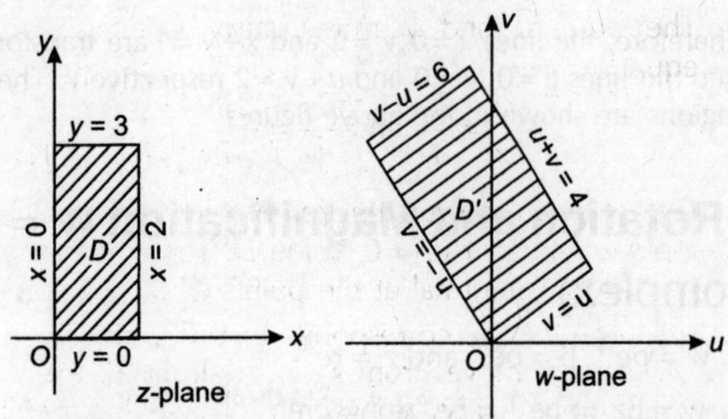


Hence, the given transformation given $D$ a rotation through an angle 45° in anti-clockwise direction and a stretching of length of magnitude $\sqrt{2}$.

## (v) Inversion $w = \dfrac{1}{z}$

Let $w = \rho e^{i\phi}$ and $z = re^{i\theta}$. Then,

$$\rho e^{i\phi} = \frac{1}{r}e^{-i\theta}.$$

$\Rightarrow \quad \rho = \frac{1}{r}$. Hence, $|w| = \frac{1}{|z|}$ and $\phi = -\theta$ *i.e.*, $\arg(w) = -\arg(z)$

The transformation $w = 1/z$ may be considered as the resultant of the two transformations

$$Z = \frac{1}{z} = \frac{1}{r}e^{i\theta} \text{ and } w = \bar{Z}$$

The first gives an inversion in the unit circle $|z| = 1$. It follows that the point $Z$ lies on the radius drawn through the point $z$ and its distance from the centre $O$ is such that

$$|z||Z| = 1$$

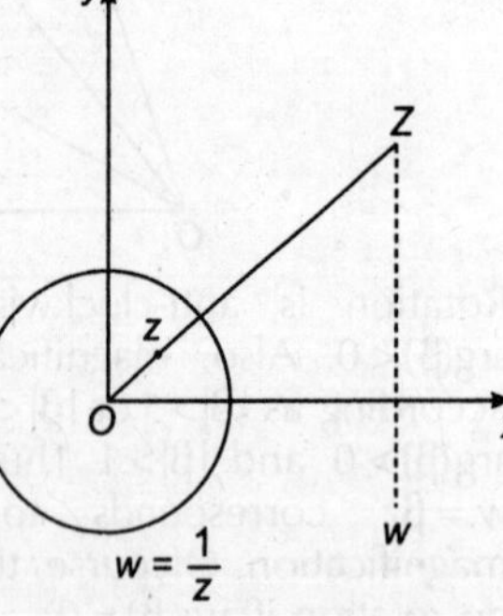


The second transformation $w = \bar{Z}$ gives an inversion (reflection) in the real axis.

Hence, points inside the unit circle are mapped into the points outside the circle and *vice-versa*. The points on the circle are reflected in the real axis.

***Example 10.*** *Find the images of the infinite strips*

(i) $\frac{1}{4} < y < \frac{1}{2}$ (ii) $0 < y < \frac{1}{2}$

*under the transformation* $w = \frac{1}{z}$. *Show the regions graphically.*

**Solution.** Since, $w = \frac{1}{z}$

$$\Rightarrow \quad u + iv = \frac{1}{x+iy} = \frac{x-iy}{x^2+y^2}$$

$$\Rightarrow \quad u = \frac{x}{x^2+y^2} \text{ and } v = -\frac{y}{x^2+y^2}$$

These give $\quad \frac{u}{v} = -\frac{x}{y} \Rightarrow x = -\frac{uy}{v}$

Then, $\quad v = -\dfrac{y}{\dfrac{u^2y^2}{v^2}+y^2} = -\dfrac{v^2}{(u^2+v^2)y}$

$$\Rightarrow \quad -\frac{v}{u^2+v^2} = y$$

(i) If $y = \frac{1}{4}$, then $-\frac{v}{u^2+v^2} = \frac{1}{4}$

$$\Rightarrow u^2 + v^2 + 4v = 0 \Rightarrow u^2 + (v+2)^2 = 4$$

Thus, the line $y = \frac{1}{4}$ is transformed into the circle

$$u^2 + (v+2)^2 = 4$$

If $y = \frac{1}{2}$, then $-\frac{v}{u^2+v^2} = \frac{1}{2} \Rightarrow u^2 + (v+1)^2 = 1$

Thus, the line $y = \frac{1}{2}$ is transformed into the circle

$$u^2 + (v+1)^2 = 1$$

Hence, the infinite strip $\frac{1}{4} < y < \frac{1}{2}$ in the $z$-plane is transformed into the region common to the circles $u^2 + (v+2)^2 = 4$ and $u^2 + (v+1)^2 = 1$ in the $w$-plane. The two regions are shown in the following figures.

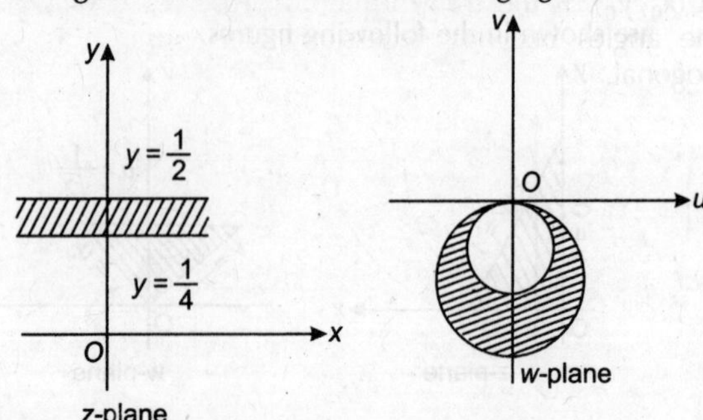


(ii) If $y = 0, v = 0$ and if $y > 0, v < 0$ $\quad \left[\because v = -\frac{y}{x^2+y^2}\right]$

As shown in (i), the line $y = \frac{1}{2}$ is transformed into the circle $u^2 + (v+1)^2 = 1$. Also, it follows from the figure in (i) that the circle gets bigger and bigger as $y$ diminishes from $\frac{1}{2}$ to 0.

Hence, the infinite strip $0 < y < \frac{1}{2}$ in the $z$-plane is transformed into the region outside the circle $u^2 + (v+1)^2 = 1$ in the lower half of $w$-plane. The two regions are shown in the following figures.

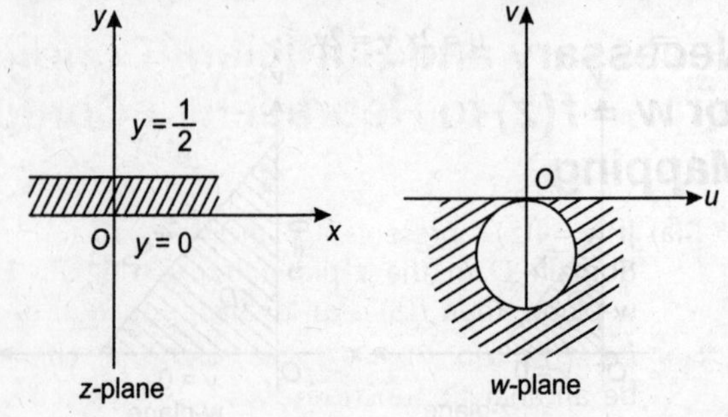

## Linear Transformation

A transformation of the type $w = \alpha z + \beta$, where $\alpha$ and $\beta$ are complex constants is known as a linear transformation. This transformation is the resultant of magnification, rotation and translation.

To obtain the resultant transformation, we first magnify the region in the z-plane by the factor $a = |\alpha|$, then we rotate the region so obtained through an angle $\lambda = \arg(\alpha)$ and finally translate the region so obtained parallel to vector $\beta$ through a distance $|\beta|$.

## Conformal Mapping

Let under the transformation $u = u(x, y)$, $v = v(x, y)$, the point $P(x_0, y_0)$ of the z-plane be mapped into the point $P'(u_0, v_0)$ of the w-plane and let the curves $C_1$ and $C_2$ intersecting at $P(x_0, y_0)$ be mapped respectively into the curves $\Gamma_1$ and $\Gamma_2$ intersecting at $P'(u_0, v_0)$. Then, if the transformation is such that the angle at $P'(x_0, y_0)$ between $C_1$ and $C_2$ is equal to the angle at $(u_0, v_0)$ between $\Gamma_1$ and $\Gamma_2$ both in magnitude and sense, the transformation or mapping is said to be conformal at $(x_0, y_0)$. If the transformation preserves the magnitudes of the angles but not necessarily the sense, it is said to be isogonal.

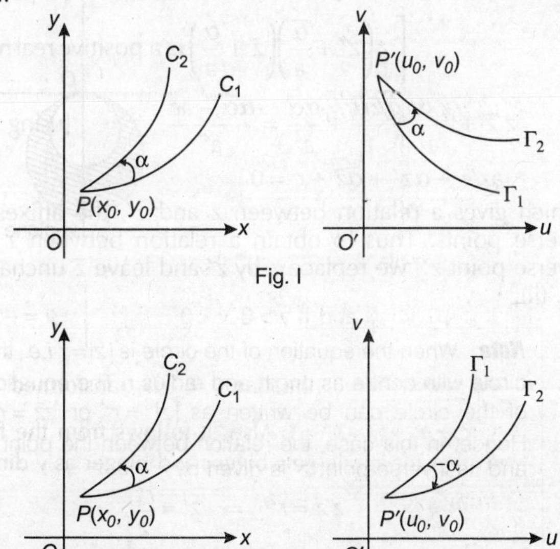


In Fig. I, the transformation is conformal and in Fig. II, it is isogonal.

## Necessary and Sufficient Conditions for $w = f(z)$ to Represent a Conformal Mapping

(a) If $w = f(z)$ represents a conformal transformation of a domain $D$ in the z-plane into a domain $D'$ of the w-plane, then $f(z)$ is an analytic function of $z$ in $D$.

*i.e.*, $f(z) = u(x, y) + iv(x, y)$ is conformal, then $f(z)$ must be an analytic function of $z$.

Therefore, $u$ and $v$ must satisfy Cauchy-Riemann equations

*i.e.*, $$\frac{\partial u}{\partial x} = \frac{\partial v}{\partial y} \text{ and } \frac{\partial u}{\partial y} = -\frac{\partial v}{\partial x}$$

(b) Let $f(z)$ be an analytic function of $z$ in a region $D$ of the z-plane and let $f'(z) \neq 0$ inside $D$. Then, the mapping $w = f(z)$ is conformal at the points of $D$.

**Proof.** Suppose, that $z_0$ corresponds to the point $w_0$ in the w-plane. As a point moves from $z_0$ to $z_1$ along $C_1$, the image point moves from $w_0$ to $w_1$ along $\Gamma_1$ in the w-plane. Similarly, as a point moves from $z_0$ to $z_2$ along $C_2$, the image point moves from $w_0$ to $w_2$ along $\Gamma_2$.

The curve $\Gamma_1$ has a definite tangent at $w_0$ making an angle $\alpha_1 + \theta_0$ with the real axis. Similarly, $\Gamma_2$ has a definite tangent at $w_0$ making an angle $\alpha_2 + \theta_0$ with the real axis. Consequently, the angle between the two curve $\Gamma_1$ and $\Gamma_2$ at $w_0$ is equal $[(\alpha_2 + \theta_0) - (\alpha_1 + \theta_0)] = \alpha_2 - \alpha_1$, which is the same as the angle between $C_1$ and $C_2$ at $z_0$. Also, the angle between $\Gamma_1$ and $\Gamma_2$ has the same sense as the angle between $C_1$ and $C_2$ in the two figures.

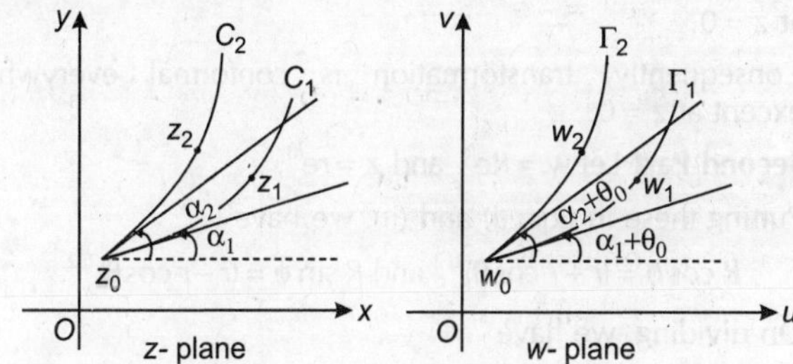


So, the mapping $w = f(z)$ is conformal.

> ***Note*** · If $f(z)$ is analytic at $z_0$ and $f'(z_0) \neq 0$, then under the transformation $w = f(z)$, the tangent at $z_0$ to any curve $C_1$ is rotated through an angle $\theta_0 = \arg\{f'(z_0)\}$. Also, the distance of a point $z_1$ on $C_1$ from the point $z_0$ is magnified by an amount $|f'(z_0)|$.

***Example 11.*** *Prove that the transformation*

$$u = (\sqrt{(x^2 + y^2)} + x)^{1/2} \quad \text{and} \quad v = (\sqrt{(x^2 + y^2)} - x)^{1/2}$$

*satisfies the conditions of a conformal mapping of z-plane to w-plane except at $z = 0$. Prove also that the angles at the origin are doubled in passing from w-plane to z-plane.*

**Solution. First Part** The given transformation is

$$u = (\sqrt{(x^2 + y^2)} + x)^{1/2} \quad \text{...(i)}$$

and $$v = (\sqrt{(x^2 + y^2)} - x)^{1/2} \quad \text{...(ii)}$$

Now, changing to polar system,

$$x = r\cos\theta, y = r\sin\theta$$

We have, $$\left.\begin{aligned} u &= (r + r\cos\theta)^{1/2} \\ v &= (r - r\cos\theta)^{1/2} \end{aligned}\right\} \quad \text{...(iii)}$$

Then, $$u = \sqrt{(2r)}\cos\left(\frac{\theta}{2}\right) \Rightarrow \frac{\partial u}{\partial r} = \frac{\sqrt{2}}{2\sqrt{r}}\cos\left(\frac{\theta}{2}\right)$$

$$\Rightarrow \quad \frac{\partial u}{\partial \theta} = -\frac{1}{2}\sqrt{(2r)}\sin\left(\frac{\theta}{2}\right)$$

$$\frac{\partial u}{\partial r} = \frac{1}{\sqrt{(2r)}}\cos\left(\frac{\theta}{2}\right) \quad \text{...(iv)}$$

and $$\frac{1}{r}\frac{\partial u}{\partial \theta} = -\frac{1}{\sqrt{(2r)}}\sin\left(\frac{\theta}{2}\right) \quad \text{...(v)}$$

Also, $$v = \sqrt{(2r)}\sin\left(\frac{\theta}{2}\right)$$

$$\Rightarrow \frac{\partial v}{\partial r} = \frac{\sqrt{2}}{2\sqrt{r}}\sin\left(\frac{\theta}{2}\right); \frac{\partial v}{\partial \theta} = \frac{\sqrt{(2r)}}{2}\cos\left(\frac{\theta}{2}\right)$$

$$\Rightarrow \frac{\partial v}{\partial r} = \frac{1}{\sqrt{2r}}\sin\left(\frac{\theta}{2}\right) \quad \text{...(vi)}$$

and $$\frac{1}{r}\frac{\partial v}{\partial \theta} = \frac{1}{\sqrt{(2r)}}\cos\left(\frac{\theta}{2}\right) \quad \text{...(vii)}$$

From Eqs. (iv) and (vii), we have $\frac{\partial u}{\partial r} = \frac{1}{r}\frac{\partial v}{\partial \theta}$ if $r \neq 0$

and from Eqs. (v) and (vi), we have $\frac{1}{r}\frac{\partial u}{\partial \theta} = -\frac{\partial v}{\partial r}$ if $r \neq 0$

Hence, $w = u + iv$ is analytic function of $z$ everywhere except at $z = 0$.

Consequently, transformation is conformal everywhere except at $z = 0$.

**Second Part** Let $w = Re^{i\phi}$ and $z = re^{i\theta}$.

Putting these in Eqs. (i) and (ii), we have

$$R\cos\phi = (r + r\cos\theta)^{1/2} \text{ and } R\sin\phi = (r - r\cos\theta)^{1/2}.$$

On dividing, we have

$$\tan\phi = \left(\frac{1-\cos\theta}{1+\cos\theta}\right)^{1/2} = \tan\left(\frac{\theta}{2}\right) \Rightarrow \phi = \frac{\theta}{2} \Rightarrow \theta = 2\phi$$

Hence, the angles are doubled at the origin.

# Inverse Points with Respect to a Circle

Let $\gamma$ be a circle of radius $r$ and centre $C$. Then, the two points $A$ and $B$ collinear with $C$ are said to be inverse points with respect to the circle provided.

$$CA \cdot CB = r^2 \quad \text{...(i)}$$

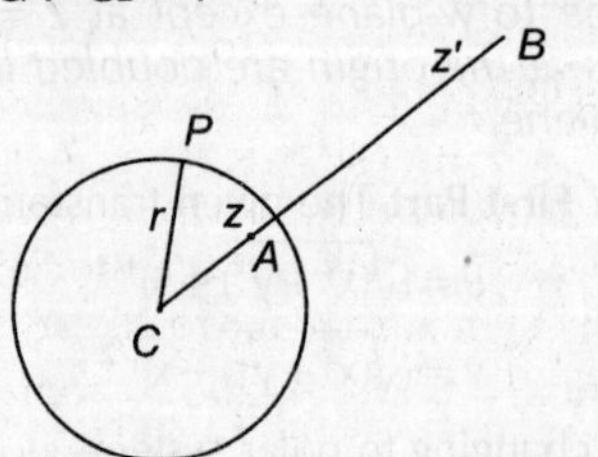


We now find the relation between the inverse points with respect to the circle

$$az\bar{z} + \alpha z + \bar{\alpha}\bar{z} + c = 0 \quad \text{...(ii)}$$

where $a, c$ are real and $\alpha$ is a complex constant.

The centre $C$ of the circle (ii) is $-\frac{\bar{\alpha}}{a}$ and the radius $r$ is given by

$$r^2 = \frac{\alpha\bar{\alpha} - ac}{a^2} \quad \text{...(iii)}$$

Let $A, B$ be the inverse point with respect to the circle with affixes $z$ and $z'$, respectively. The condition (i) in this case becomes

$$\left|z + \frac{\bar{\alpha}}{a}\right| . \left|z' + \frac{\bar{\alpha}}{a}\right| = r^2 \quad \text{...(iv)}$$

Also, the points $C$, $A$, $B$ are collinear, so we have

$$\arg\left(z' + \frac{\bar{\alpha}}{a}\right) = \arg\left(z + \frac{\bar{\alpha}}{a}\right)$$

$$\Rightarrow \arg\left(z' + \frac{\bar{\alpha}}{a}\right) = -\arg\left(\bar{z} + \frac{\alpha}{a}\right)$$

[$\because \arg(z) = -\arg(\bar{z})$ for any complex number $z$]

$$\Rightarrow \arg\left(z' + \frac{\bar{\alpha}}{a}\right)\left(\bar{z} + \frac{\alpha}{a}\right) = 0$$

[$\because \arg(z_1 z_2) = \arg(z_1) + \arg(z_2)$]

$$\Rightarrow \left(z' + \frac{\bar{\alpha}}{a}\right)\left(\bar{z} + \frac{\alpha}{a}\right) \text{ is a positive real number.}$$

Again Eq. (iv) can be written as

$$\left|z' + \frac{\bar{\alpha}}{a}\right| . \left|\bar{z} + \frac{\alpha}{a}\right| = r^2$$

[$\because |z| = |\bar{z}|$ for any complex number $z$]

$$\Rightarrow \left(z' + \frac{\bar{\alpha}}{a}\right)\left(\bar{z} + \frac{\alpha}{a}\right) = r^2$$

$$\left[\because \left(z' + \frac{\bar{\alpha}}{a}\right)\left(\bar{z} + \frac{\alpha}{a}\right) \text{ is a positive real number}\right]$$

$$\Rightarrow z'\bar{z} + \frac{z'\alpha}{a} + \frac{\bar{z}\bar{\alpha}}{a} + \frac{\alpha\bar{\alpha}}{a^2} = \frac{\alpha\bar{\alpha} - ac}{a^2} \quad \text{[using Eq. (iii)]}$$

$$\Rightarrow az'\bar{z} + \alpha z' + \bar{\alpha}\bar{z} + c = 0 \quad \text{...(v)}$$

Which gives a relation between $z$ and $z'$, the affixes of the inverse points. Thus to obtain a relation between $z$ and its inverse point $z'$, we replace $z$ by $z'$ and leave $\bar{z}$ unchanged in Eq. (ii).

> ***Note*** When the equation of the circle is $|z| = r$ *i.e.*, the circle with centre as origin and radius $r$. The equation of the circle can be written as $|z|^2 = r^2$ or $z\bar{z} = r^2$. Hence, in this case, the relation between the point $z$ and its inverse point $z'$ is given by
>
> $$z'\bar{z} = r^2 \Rightarrow z' = \frac{r^2}{\bar{z}}$$
>
> It follows that the inverse of the point $z$ with respect to the circle $|z| = r$ is $\frac{r^2}{\bar{z}}$. If the radius of the circle is unity, then the inverse of the point $z$ is $1/\bar{z}$.

***Example 12.*** *Show that the inverse of a point a with respect to the circle* $|z - c| = R$ *is the point* $c + \frac{R^2}{\bar{a} - \bar{c}}$.

**Solution.** Let $\gamma$ be a circle of radius $R$ and centre $C(c)$. Also, suppose $B(b)$ is the inverse point of $A(a)$ with respect to the circle $\gamma$.

Then, the points $C$, $A$ and $B$ are collinear, so we have

$$\arg(b - c) = \arg(a - c) = -\arg(\bar{a} - \bar{c}) \quad [\because \arg(z) = -\arg(\bar{z})]$$

$$\Rightarrow \arg(b - c) + \arg(\bar{a} - \bar{c}) = 0$$

$$\arg(b - c)(\bar{a} - \bar{c}) = 0 \quad [\because \arg(z_1 z_2) = \arg(z_1) + \arg(z_2)]$$

$\Rightarrow \quad (b-c)(\bar{a}-\bar{c})$ is a positive real number.

Since, $A$ and $B$ are the inverse points with respect to the circle $\gamma$, therefore we have

$$CA \cdot CB = R^2 \Rightarrow |a-c||b-c| = R^2$$

$$\Rightarrow \quad |\bar{a}-\bar{c}||b-c| = R^2 \qquad [\because |z| = |\bar{z}|]$$

$$\Rightarrow \quad |(\bar{a}-\bar{c})(b-c)| = R^2$$

$$\Rightarrow \quad (\bar{a}-\bar{c})(b-c) = R^2$$

[$\because (\bar{a}-\bar{c})(b-c)$ is a positive real number]

$$\Rightarrow \quad b-c = \frac{R^2}{\bar{a}-\bar{c}} \Rightarrow b = c + \frac{R^2}{\bar{a}-\bar{c}}$$

# Mobius Transformations

The transformation $T$ defined by

$$w = T(z) = \frac{az+b}{cz+d}, \qquad \text{...(i)}$$

where $a, b, c, d$ being complex constants and $ad - bc \neq 0$, is called a bilinear transformation or mobius transformation.

The constant $ad - bc$ is called the determinant of the transformation $T$. The transformation $T$ is said to be normalized, if $ad - bc = 1$.

From the transformation Eq. (i) we have

$$cwz + dw - az - b = 0 \qquad \text{...(ii)}$$

Since, Eq. (ii) is linear both in $z$ and $w$, hence it is called a bilinear transformation. It is also called as a Mobius transformation after the name of mathematician Mobius (1770-1868) who first studied the same.

From transformation Eq. (i), we have $z = \dfrac{-dw+b}{cw-a}$

So, the inverse transformation $T^{-1}$ is defined by

$$z = T^{-1}(w) = \frac{-dw+b}{cw-a}$$

The determinant of this transformation is $(-d)(-a) - bc$ $= ad - bc =$ same as the determinant of the transformation $T$.

**Note** **(a)** The elementary transformations *viz.* Translation, Magnification, Rotation and Inversion discussed earlier are special types of bilinear transformations.

**(b)** The transformation (i) sets up a one-to-one correspondence between the points of the closed $z$-plane and the closed $w$-plane.

Now, $w = T(z) = \dfrac{az+b}{cz+d}$, where $a, b, c$ and $d$ are complex constants and $ad - bc \neq 0$. The transformation $T$ associates a unique point of the $w$-plane to each point of the $z$-plane except the point $z = -\dfrac{d}{c}$ when $c \neq 0$. Also, the inverse transformation $T^{-1}$ given by $z = T^{-1}(w) = \dfrac{-dw+b}{cw-a}$ associates a unique point of the $z$-plane to each point of the $w$-plane except the point $w = \dfrac{a}{c}$ when $c \neq 0$. Points $z = -\dfrac{d}{c}$ and $w = \dfrac{a}{c}$ are mapped into the points $w = \infty$ and $z = \infty$ respectively. If the complex plane is closed by the addition of the point infinity, then we can say that every bilinear transformation sets up a one-to-one correspondence between the points of the closed $z$-plane and the closed $w$-plane.

**(c)** The condition $ad - bc \neq 0$ is very much essential for the bilinear transformation $T$ to set up a one-to-one correspondence between the points of the closed $z$-plane and the closed $w$-plane. For if $ad - bc = 0$, then $w$ is either a constant or meaningless as shown below.

Let us suppose $w_1$ and $w_2$ be the points corresponding to $z_1$ and $z_2$ given by Eq. (i). Then,

$$w_1 = \frac{az_1+b}{cz_1+d} \text{ and } w_2 = \frac{az_2+b}{cz_2+d}$$

$$\Rightarrow w_2 - w_1 = \frac{az_2+b}{cz_2+d} - \frac{az_1+b}{cz_1+d}$$

$$= \frac{(ad-bc)(z_2-z_1)}{(cz_1+d)(cz_2+d)} = 0 \qquad [\because ad - bc = 0]$$

$\Rightarrow \quad w_2 = w_1$ *i.e.,* $w$ is constant if $ad - bc = 0$ provided $z_1 \neq -\dfrac{d}{c}$ and $z_2 \neq -\dfrac{d}{c}$.

If $ad - bc = 0$ and if either $z_1 = -\dfrac{d}{c}$ or $z_2 = -\dfrac{d}{c}$, then $w$ becomes meaningless.

# Critical Points

The points where $f'(z) = \dfrac{dw}{dz} = 0$ or $\infty$ are called **critical points.** Also, the points where $\dfrac{dw}{dz} \neq 0$ are called **ordinary points.**

Now, for $\quad w = T(z) = \dfrac{az+b}{cz+d}$

$$\Rightarrow \quad \frac{dw}{dz} = \frac{ad-bc}{(cz+d)^2}$$

If $z = -\dfrac{d}{c}$, then $\dfrac{dw}{dz} = \infty$ and if $z = \infty$, then $\dfrac{dw}{dz} = 0$. The points $z = -d/c$ and $z = \infty$ are the critical points where the conformal property does not hold and these are the only critical points, for Mobius transformation.

We say that a transformation $w = f(z)$ maps the neighbourhood of a point $z_0$ conformally into a neighbourhood of $w = \infty$ if the transformation $\zeta = \dfrac{1}{f(z)}$ maps the neighbourhood of $z_0$ conformally into a neighbourhood of $\zeta = 0$. Again $w = f(z)$ is said to transform the neighbourhood of $z = \infty$ conformally into a neighbourhood of $w_0$ provided $w = \phi(r) = f(1/\tau)$ transforms the neighbourhood of $\tau = 0$ conformally into a neighbourhood of $w_0$. Therefore, $w_0$ may assume the value $\infty$. With the extensions of these definitions, we may now summarize our results as follows.

Every bilinear transformation represents a one-to-one conformal mapping of the whole closed $z$-plane onto the whole closed $w$-plane.

We may, thus say that the transformation is biuniform for the whole planes of $z$ and $w$.

**Note** Since, a bilinear transformation $w = T(z) = \dfrac{az+b}{cz+d}$ represents a conformal mapping, it preserves angles both in magnitude and sense.

## Product of Two Bilinear Transformations

Consider two bilinear transformations $T_1$ and $T_2$ defined by

$$T_1(z) = \frac{a_1 z + b_1}{c_1 z + d_1}, \quad (a_1 d_1 - b_1 c_1 \neq 0)$$

and

$$T_2(z) = \frac{a_2 z + b_2}{c_2 z + d_2}, \quad (a_2 d_2 - b_2 c_2 \neq 0)$$

then,

$$T_2(T_1(z)) = T_2\left(\frac{a_1 z + b_1}{c_1 z + d_1}\right) = \frac{a_2\left(\frac{a_1 z + b_1}{c_1 z + d_1}\right) + b_2}{c_2\left(\frac{a_1 z + b_1}{c_1 z + d_1}\right) + d_2}$$

$$= \frac{(a_2 a_1 + b_2 c_1)z + (a_2 b_1 + b_2 d_1)}{(c_2 a_1 + d_2 c_1)z + (c_2 b_1 + d_1 d_2)}$$

Hence,

$$w = T_2(T_1(z)) = \frac{\alpha z + \beta}{\gamma z + \delta}$$

Where, $\alpha = a_2 a_1 + b_2 c_1, \beta = a_2 b_1 + b_2 d_1,$
$\gamma = c_2 a_1 + d_2 c_1, \delta = c_2 b_1 + d_2 d_1$

The determinant is $\alpha\delta - \beta\gamma$

$$= (a_2 a_1 + b_2 c_1)(c_2 b_1 + d_2 d_1) - (a_2 b_1 + b_2 d_1)(c_2 a_1 + d_2 c_1)$$
$$= a_2 a_1 d_2 d_1 + b_2 b_1 c_2 c_1 - a_2 b_1 d_2 c_1 - b_2 d_1 c_2 a_1$$
$$= (a_1 d_1 - b_1 c_1)(a_2 d_2 - b_2 c_2) \neq 0$$

It follows that the transformation $T_2 T_1$ is also a bilinear transformation and called product of the two transformations $T_1$ and $T_2$.

***Example 13.*** *Consider the transformation* $w = T_1(z) = \frac{z+2}{z+3}$, $w = T_2(z) = \frac{z}{z+1}$ *and find* $T_1^{-1}(w), T_2^{-1}(w), T_2T_1(z), T_1T_2(z)$ *and* $T_2^{-1}T_1(z)$.

**Solution.** Solving $w = \frac{z+2}{z+3}$, we get $z = \frac{2-3w}{w-1}$

$$\therefore \quad T_1^{-1}(w) = \frac{2-3w}{w-1}$$

Again, $w = \frac{z}{z+1}$ given $z = \frac{-w}{w-1}$

$$\therefore \quad T_2^{-1}(w) = -\frac{w}{w-1}$$

Now,

$$T_2T_1(z) = T_2\left(\frac{z+2}{z+3}\right) = \frac{\frac{z+2}{z+3}}{\frac{z+2}{z+3}+1} = \frac{z+2}{2z+5}$$

and

$$T_1T_2(z) = T_1\left(\frac{z}{z+1}\right) = \frac{\frac{z}{z+1}+2}{\frac{z}{z+1}+3} = \frac{3z+2}{4z+3}$$

Also,

$$T_2^{-1}T_1(z) = T_2^{-1}\left(\frac{z+2}{z+3}\right) = -\frac{\frac{z+2}{z+3}}{\frac{z+2}{z+3}-1} = z+2$$

## Important Results on Bilinear Transformation

1. Every bilinear transformation is the resultant of magnification, rotation, inversion and translation.

   We have $w = T(z) = \frac{az+b}{cz+d}$ $(ad - bc \neq 0)$.

   (i) If $c \neq 0$, this transformation can be written as $w = \frac{bc-ad}{c^2\left(z+\frac{d}{c}\right)} + \frac{a}{c}$

   Let us write

   $$Z = z + \frac{d}{c} \quad \text{...(i)}$$

   $$\zeta = \frac{1}{Z} \quad \text{...(ii)}$$

   $$\tau = \frac{bc-ad}{c^2}\zeta \quad \text{...(iii)}$$

   $$w = \tau + \frac{a}{c} \quad \text{...(iv)}$$

   Above relations show that the bilinear transformation is the resultant of a translation given by Eq. (i), inversions in the real axis and unit circle given by Eq. (ii), a rotation and magnification given by Eq. (iii) and then again translation given by Eq. (iv).

   (ii) If $c = 0$, then $w = T(z) = \frac{a}{d}z + \frac{b}{d}$ provided $d \neq 0$

   Let $\zeta = \frac{a}{d}z$. Then, $w = \zeta + \frac{b}{d}$

   It follows that the given transformation is the resultant of magnification, rotation and translation. In this case, inversion falls out and only one translation is needed.

2. Every bilinear transformation can be expressed as the resultant of an even number of inversions.
3. The set of all bilinear transformations forms a non-abelian group under the product of transformations.
4. Every Mobius (bilinear) transformation maps circles or straight lines into circles or straight lines.
5. Every bilinear transformation transforms two points which are inverse points with respect to a circle into two points which are inverse points with respect to the transformed circle.
6. Every bilinear transformation maps the family of circles $\arg\left(\frac{z-z_1}{z-z_2}\right)=\mu\ (\mu \neq 0)$ through the fixed points $z_1$ and $z_2$ onto a similar family in the $w$-plane through two fixed points $w_1$ and $w_2$ which are the transforms of the points $z_1$ and $z_2$ respectively.

***Theorem*** Every bilinear transformation transforms circles or straight lines into circles or straight lines and inverse points into inverse points.

[In the case of a straight line the inverse points become symmetrical about the line.]

***Proof.*** The equation of the family of circles with $z_1, z_2$ as inverse points can be taken as

$$\left|\frac{z-z_1}{z-z_2}\right|=\lambda\ (\lambda>0)$$

Let $w=\dfrac{az+b}{cz+d}$ be any bilinear transformation.

Let $w_1, w_2$ be the transforms of $z_1, z_2$. Then,

$$\frac{w-w_1}{w-w_2}=k\frac{z-z_1}{z-z_2} \quad \text{...(i)}$$

where, $k$ is a constant equal to $\dfrac{cz_2+d}{cz_1+d}$

From Eq. (i), we have $\left|\dfrac{w-w_1}{w-w_2}\right|=|k|\left|\dfrac{z-z_1}{z-z_2}\right|$

It follows that the circles $\left|\dfrac{z-z_1}{z-z_2}\right|=\lambda$ ...(ii)

are transformed into circles $\left|\dfrac{w-w_1}{w-w_2}\right|=|k|\,\lambda$ ...(iii)

with respect to which $w_1, w_2$ (the images of $z_1, z_2$) are the inverse points as required.

**Particular cases**

***Case I*** We have, $w=\dfrac{az+b}{cz+d} \Rightarrow w=\dfrac{a}{c}\,\dfrac{z+\frac{b}{a}}{z+\frac{d}{c}}$

Now, $\left|\dfrac{z+b/a}{z+d/c}\right|=\lambda$ gives a circle in the $z$-plane and it is transformed into $|w|=\lambda\left|\dfrac{a}{c}\right|$ which is a circle in the $w$-plane.

If we give particular values to $a, b, c, d$ and $\lambda$, the boundaries in the $w$-plane corresponding to given boundaries in the $z$-plane can easily be determined.

*e.g.*, Let $\dfrac{b}{a}=i, \dfrac{d}{c}=-i$ and $\lambda=1$, then $\left|\dfrac{z+i}{z-i}\right|=1$ clearly represents the real axis in the $z$-plane and it is transformed into $|w|=\left|\dfrac{a}{c}\right|$ which is a circle in the $w$-plane

In particular, if $|a|=|c|$, this will be a unit circle.

***Case II*** $w=\dfrac{az+b}{cz+d}$, $ad-bc\neq 0$ be the bilinear transformation. The points $w=0$ and $w=\infty$ in the $w$-plane correspond to the points $z=-\dfrac{b}{a}$ and $z=-\dfrac{d}{c}$ in the $z$-plane. Since, $w=0$ and $w=\infty$ are the inverse points w.r.t. circle $|w|=1$, therefore $-\dfrac{b}{a}$ and $-\dfrac{d}{c}$ must be inverse points (symmetrical) w.r.t.

(i) Real axis $[\text{Im}(z)=0]$ and we write $-\dfrac{b}{a}=\alpha$, then $-\dfrac{d}{c}=\bar{\alpha}$.

(ii) Imaginary axis $[\text{Re}(z)=0]$ and we write $-\dfrac{b}{a}=\alpha$, then $-\dfrac{d}{c}=-\bar{\alpha}$.

(iii) Circle $|z|=1$ and we write $-\dfrac{b}{a}=\alpha$, then $-\dfrac{d}{c}=\dfrac{1}{\bar{\alpha}}$.

---

***Example 14.*** *Show that the transformation*

$$w=\frac{iz+2}{4z+i}$$

*maps the real axis in the z-plane into a circle in the w-plane. Find the centre and the radius of the circle and the points in the z-plane which is mapped on the centre of the circle.*

**Solution.** The given transformation is

$$w=\frac{iz+2}{4z+i} \Rightarrow z=\frac{2-iw}{4w-i} \quad \text{...(i)}$$

The equation of the real axis in the $z$-plane is $z-\bar{z}=0$. Substituting for $z$ and $\bar{z}$ the transformed equation is

$$\frac{2-iw}{4w-i}-\frac{2+i\bar{w}}{4\bar{w}+i}=0$$

$$\Rightarrow \quad 8\bar{w}+2i-4iw\bar{w}+w-8w+2i-4iw\bar{w}-\bar{w}=0$$

$$\Rightarrow \quad 8iw\bar{w}+7(w-\bar{w})-4i=0$$

$$\Rightarrow \quad 8i(u^2+v^2)+14iv-4i=0$$

$$\Rightarrow \quad u^2+v^2+\frac{7}{4}v-\frac{1}{2}=0,$$

which is the equation of a circle in the $w$-plane. The centre of the circle is $(0,-\frac{7}{8})$ *i.e.*, the point $w=-\frac{7}{8}i$.

Radius of the circle $= \sqrt{\left(\frac{49}{64}+\frac{1}{2}\right)} = \frac{9}{8}$

For $w = -\frac{7}{8}i$, $z = \dfrac{2-i\left(-\frac{7}{8}i\right)}{4\left(-\frac{7}{8}i\right)-i} = \dfrac{\frac{9}{8}}{-36i} = \frac{1}{4}i$

Hence, the point in the $z$-plane which corresponds to the centre $w = -\frac{7}{8}i$ is $z = \frac{1}{4}i$.

***Example 15.*** *Show that the relation*

$$w = \frac{5-4z}{4z-2}$$

*transforms the circle $|z|=1$ into a circle of radius unity in the w-plane and find the centre of this circle.*

**Solution.** The given transformation is

$$w = \frac{5-4z}{4z-2} \Rightarrow z = \frac{2w+5}{4w+4}$$

The equation of the given circle is $|z|=1 \Rightarrow |z|^2 = 1 \Rightarrow z\bar{z}=1$. Hence, the transformed equation is

$$\frac{2w+5}{4w+4}\cdot\frac{2\bar{w}+5}{4\bar{w}+4}=1$$

$$\Rightarrow \quad 4w\bar{w}+10w+10\bar{w}+25 = 16w\bar{w}+16w+16\bar{w}+16$$

$$\Rightarrow \quad 12w\bar{w}+6(w+\bar{w})-9=0$$

$$\Rightarrow \quad 4w\bar{w}+2(w+\bar{w})-3=0$$

$$\Rightarrow \quad 4(u^2+v^2)+4u-3=0 \text{ or } u^2+v^2+u-\frac{3}{4}=0,$$

which is the equation of a circle in the $w$-plane.

The centre of the circle is $\left(-\frac{1}{2}, 0\right)$ *i.e.*, the point $w = -1/2$.

and Radius of the circle $= \sqrt{\left(\frac{1}{4}+\frac{3}{4}\right)} = 1$

*i.e.*, the transformed circle in the $w$-plane is of radius unity.

***Example 16.*** *Find the image of circle $|z-2|=2$ under the Mobius transformation $w = \dfrac{z}{z+1}$*

**Solution.** Given that $w = \dfrac{z}{z+1} \Rightarrow wz + w = z$

$$\Rightarrow \quad z(w-1) = -w \Rightarrow z = \frac{w}{1-w} \quad \text{...(i)}$$

Now, $\quad |z-2| = 2 \Rightarrow (z-2)(\bar{z}-2) = 2^2 \quad$ ...(ii)

From Eq. (i), we have $z-2 = \dfrac{w}{1-w}-2 = \dfrac{3w-2}{1-w}$

$$\Rightarrow \quad \bar{z}-2 = \frac{\bar{w}}{1-\bar{w}}-2 = \frac{3\bar{w}-2}{1-\bar{w}}$$

Putting these values in Eq. (ii), we have

$$\frac{(3w-2)(3\bar{w}-2)}{(1-w)(1-\bar{w})} = 4$$

$$\Rightarrow \quad 9w\bar{w}+4-6(w+\bar{w}) = 4[1+w\bar{w}-(w+\bar{w})]$$

$$\Rightarrow \quad 5w\bar{w}-2(w+\bar{w}) = 0$$

$$\Rightarrow \quad 5(u^2+v^2)-2(2u)=0$$

$$\Rightarrow \quad u^2+v^2-\frac{4}{5}u=0$$

Which is a circle with centre $(-g,-f) = \left(\frac{2}{5},0\right)$

and radius $= (g^2+f^2-c)^{1/2} = \frac{2}{5}$

Hence, image is a circle with centre $\left(\frac{2}{5},0\right)$ and radius $= \frac{2}{5}$ in $w$-plane.

***Example 17.*** *Show that the transformation*

$$w = \frac{2z+3}{z-4}$$

*maps the circle $x^2+y^2-4x=0$ onto the straight line $4u+3=0$ and explain why the curve obtained is not a circle.*

**Solution.** The given transformation is

$$w = \frac{2z+3}{z-4} \text{ gives } z = \frac{4w+3}{w-2}$$

The equation of the given circle is

$$x^2+y^2-4x=0 \text{ or } z\bar{z}-2(z+\bar{z})=0$$

Hence, the transformed equation is

$$\frac{4w+3}{w-2}\cdot\frac{4\bar{w}+3}{\bar{w}-2}-2\left(\frac{4w+3}{w-2}+\frac{4\bar{w}+3}{\bar{w}-2}\right)=0$$

$$\Rightarrow \quad 16w\bar{w}+12w+12\bar{w}+9-2(4w\bar{w}-8w+3\bar{w}-6 + 4w\bar{w}+3w-8\bar{w}-6)=0$$

$$\Rightarrow \quad 22(w+\bar{w})+33=0 \text{ or } 4u+3=0,$$

Which is the equation of a straight line in the $w$-plane.

> ***Remark*** Here, circle is transformed into a straight line which is possible under a bilinear transformation, since we consider a straight line as a particular case of a circle.
>
> The equation $a\ w\bar{w}+\bar{b}w+b\bar{w}+c=0$, where $c$ is real, represents a circle and if $a=0$, then it represents a straight line.

***Example 18.*** *Find the Mobius transformation which maps the circle $|z|\le 1$ conformally onto $|w-1|\le 1$ and makes the points $z=0$, $1$ correspond to $w=\frac{1}{2}$, $0$ respectively. Is the transformation uniquely determined by the data?*

**Solution.** Let $\quad w = \dfrac{az+b}{cz+d}$, $ad-bc \ne 0 \quad$ ...(i)

be the required Mobius transformation. The points $w=1$ and $w=\infty$ correspond to the points

$$z = -\frac{b-d}{a-c} \text{ and } z = -\frac{d}{c} \text{ respectively.}$$

Since, $w=1$ and $w=\infty$ are inverse points with respect to the circle $|w-1|=1$, the points $-\dfrac{b-d}{a-c}$ and $-\dfrac{d}{c}$ must be the inverse points with respect to the circle $|z|=1$.

Thus,

$$\frac{b-d}{a-c} = \alpha \text{ and } \frac{d}{c} = \frac{1}{\bar{\alpha}}$$

Now, from Eq. (i) we have

$$w-1=\frac{(a-c)z+b-d}{cz+d}=\frac{a-c}{c}\,\frac{z+\frac{b-d}{a-c}}{z+\frac{d}{c}}$$

$$\Rightarrow \quad w-1=\frac{a-c}{c}\frac{z-\alpha}{z-\frac{1}{\bar{\alpha}}}=\frac{(a-c)\bar{\alpha}}{c}\frac{z-\alpha}{\bar{\alpha}z-1} \qquad ...(ii)$$

To find the value of $\frac{(a-c)\bar{\alpha}}{c}$ we use the condition that $|w-1|=1$ when $|z|=1$ *i.e.*, when $z\bar{z}=1$.

Hence, $$1=|w-1|=\left|\frac{(a-c)\bar{\alpha}}{c}\right|\left|\frac{z-\alpha}{\bar{\alpha}z-1}\right|=\left|\frac{(a-c)\bar{\alpha}}{c}\right|\left|\frac{z-\alpha}{\bar{\alpha}z-z\bar{z}}\right|$$

$$=\left|\frac{(a-c)\bar{\alpha}}{c}\right|\left|\frac{z-\alpha}{z(\bar{\alpha}-\bar{z})}\right|=\left|\frac{(a-c)\bar{\alpha}}{c}\right|$$

$$[\because |z-\alpha|=|\bar{\alpha}-\bar{z}| \text{ and } |z|=1]$$

Hence, $\left|\frac{(a-c)\bar{\alpha}}{c}\right|=1$, so that we may take $\frac{(a-c)\bar{\alpha}}{c}=e^{i\lambda}$, where $\lambda$ is real.

Consequently, the general transformation which maps $|z|\le 1$ onto $|w-1|\le 1$ is

$$w-1=e^{i\lambda}\frac{z-\alpha}{\bar{\alpha}z-1} \qquad ...(iii)$$

We can easily verify that the interiors correspond.

If the points $z=0, 1$ correspond to $w=\frac{1}{2}$, 0 respectively, then

$$-\frac{1}{2}=e^{i\lambda}\frac{0-\alpha}{0-1} \text{ and } -1=e^{i\lambda}\frac{1-\alpha}{\bar{\alpha}-1}$$

$$\Rightarrow \quad \frac{1-\alpha}{\bar{\alpha}-1}\cdot\frac{1}{2\alpha}=1$$

$$\Rightarrow \quad 2\alpha\bar{\alpha}-\alpha-1=0$$

$$\Rightarrow \quad 2(a_1^2+a_2^2)-(a_1+ia_2)-1=0 \qquad [\text{Take } \alpha=a_1+ia_2].$$

$$\Rightarrow \quad a_2=0,\ 2(a_1^2+a_2^2)-a_1-1=0$$

$$\Rightarrow \quad 2a_1^2-a_1-1=0$$

$$\Rightarrow \quad (2a_1+1)(a_1-1)=0 \Rightarrow a_1=-\frac{1}{2}, 1$$

$$\therefore \quad \alpha=-\frac{1}{2} \text{ or } 1$$

Taking $\alpha=1$, Eq. (iii) becomes $w-1=e^{i\lambda}$ which is not a bilinear transformation.

When, $\alpha=-\frac{1}{2}, e^{i\lambda}=1$. Then Eq. (iii) becomes

$$w-1=\frac{z+\frac{1}{2}}{-\frac{1}{2}z-1}=-\frac{2z+1}{z+2}$$

$$\Rightarrow \quad w=1-\frac{2z+1}{z+2}=\frac{1-z}{z+2}$$

Hence, the required Mobius transformation is $w=\frac{1-z}{z+2}$. It is clear that this transformation is uniquely determined.

***Example 19.*** *Discuss the application of the transformation*

$$w=\frac{iz+1}{z+i}$$

*to the areas in the z-plane which are respectively inside and outside the unit circle with its centre at the origin.*

**Solution.** The given transformation is

$$w=\frac{iz+1}{z+i} \Rightarrow z=\frac{1-iw}{w-i}$$

The equation of the unit circle with centre as origin in the z-plane is given by $|z|=1$.

Let $|z|=r$. Then, we get $z\bar{z}=r^2$

$$\Rightarrow \quad \left(\frac{1-iw}{w-i}\right)\left(\frac{1+i\bar{w}}{\bar{w}+i}\right)=r^2$$

$$\Rightarrow \quad (1-iw)(1+i\bar{w})=r^2(w-i)(\bar{w}+i)$$

$$1-i(w-\bar{w})+w\bar{w}=r^2[w\bar{w}+i(w-\bar{w})+1]$$

$$\Rightarrow \quad (1-r^2)(w\bar{w}+1)-(1+r^2)i(w-\bar{w})=0$$

$$\Rightarrow \quad (1-r^2)(u^2+v^2+1)-(1+r^2)i(2iv)=0$$

$$\Rightarrow \quad (1-r^2)(u^2+v^2+1)+2v(1+r^2)=0$$

$$\Rightarrow \quad 2v=\frac{r^2-1}{r^2+1}(u^2+v^2+1)$$

When $r=1, v=0$ *i.e.*, the circle $|z|=1$ is transformed into the real axis of the *w*-plane. When $r<1$ or $>1$, $v<0$ or $>0$. It follows that the interior and the exterior of the circle $|z|=1$ are transformed respectively into the lower and the upper half of the *w*-plane.

**Alternative method** Let $z=re^{i\theta}$. Then,

$$w=\frac{ire^{i\theta}+1}{re^{i\theta}+i}=\frac{(ire^{i\theta}+1)(re^{-i\theta}-i)}{(re^{i\theta}+i)(re^{-i\theta}-i)}$$

$$=\frac{i(r^2-1)+r(e^{i\theta}+e^{-i\theta})}{r^2-ir(e^{i\theta}-e^{-i\theta})+1}$$

$$=\frac{2r\cos\theta+i(r^2-1)}{r^2-ir(2i\sin\theta)+1}$$

$$\Rightarrow \quad u+iv=\frac{2r\cos\theta+i(r^2-1)}{r^2+2r\sin\theta+1}$$

$$\Rightarrow \quad u=\frac{2r\cos\theta}{r^2+2r\sin\theta+1} \text{ and } v=\frac{r^2-1}{r^2+2r\sin\theta+1}$$

If $|z|=r=1$, then $v=0$. Therefore, the circle $|z|=1$ is transformed into the real axis $v=0$ of the *w*-plane. Also, when $|z|=r<1, v<0$ and when $|z|=>1, v>0$. Hence, the interior and the exterior of the circle $|z|=1$ are transformed respectively into the lower half and the upper half of the *w*-plane.

We now examine the boundaries in some detail.

When $|z|=r=1$, we have

$$u=\frac{\cos\theta}{1+\sin\theta}=\frac{\sin\left(\frac{\pi}{2}-\theta\right)}{1+\cos\left(\frac{\pi}{2}-\theta\right)}$$

$$= \frac{2\sin\left(\frac{\pi}{4}-\frac{\theta}{2}\right)\cos\left(\frac{\pi}{4}-\frac{\theta}{2}\right)}{2\cos^2\left(\frac{\pi}{4}-\frac{\theta}{2}\right)} = \tan\left(\frac{\pi}{4}-\frac{\theta}{2}\right)$$

Hence, for $-\frac{\pi}{2} \le \theta \le \frac{\pi}{2}$, we have $u \ge 0$

and for $\frac{\pi}{2} \le \theta \le \frac{3\pi}{2}$ we have $u \le 0$

It follows that the right half arc of the circle $|z|=1$ is transformed into the positive part of the real axis and the left half arc into the negative part of the real axis.

***Example 20.*** *Show that the transformation*

$$w = i\frac{1-z}{1+z}$$

*transforms the circle $|z|=1$ onto the real axis of the w-plane and the interior of the circle into the upper half of the w-plane.*

**Solution.** Let $z = re^{i\theta}$. Then,

$$w = i\frac{1-re^{i\theta}}{1+re^{i\theta}} = i\frac{(1-re^{i\theta})(1+re^{-i\theta})}{(1+re^{i\theta})(1+re^{-i\theta})}$$

$$= i\frac{1-r(e^{i\theta}-e^{-i\theta})-r^2}{1+r(e^{i\theta}+e^{-i\theta})+r^2} = i\frac{1-2ir\sin\theta-r^2}{1+2r\cos\theta+r^2}$$

$$\Rightarrow \quad u+iv = \frac{2r\sin\theta+i(1-r^2)}{1+2r\cos\theta+r^2}$$

$$\Rightarrow \quad u = \frac{2r\sin\theta}{1+2r\cos\theta+r^2} \text{ and } v = \frac{1-r^2}{1+2r\cos\theta+r^2}$$

When, $|z|=r=1, v=1$. Therefore, the boundary of the circle $|z|=1$ is transformed into the real axis $v=0$ of the w-plane. Also, when $|z|=r<1, v>0$.

Hence, the interior of the circle $|z|=1$ is transformed into the upper half of the w-plane. If $|z|=r>1, v<0$, so that the exterior of the circle $|z|=1$ is transformed into the lower half of the w-plane.

We now examine the boundaries more closely. When, $|z|=r=1$, we have

$$v=0 \text{ and } u = \frac{\sin\theta}{1+\cos\theta} = \frac{2\sin\frac{\theta}{2}\cos\frac{\theta}{2}}{2\cos^2\frac{\theta}{2}} = \tan\frac{\theta}{2}$$

Thus, for $0 \le \theta \le \pi, u \ge 0$ and for $\pi \le \theta \le 2\pi$, $u \le 0$. It follows that the upper half arc of the circle $|z|=1$ is transformed into the positive part of the real axis and the lower half arc into the negative part of the real axis.

***Example 21.*** *Prove that the transformation*

$$w = \frac{i(z-i)}{(z+i)}$$

*maps the upper half of the z-plane into the interior of the unit circle in the w-plane.*

**Solution.** The given bilinear transformation is

$$w = \frac{i(z-i)}{z+i} \qquad \text{...(i)}$$

$$\Rightarrow \quad z = \frac{1-iw}{w-i} \Rightarrow x+iy = \frac{(1-iw)(w+i)}{(w-i)(w+i)}$$

$$= \frac{2w+i(1-w^2)}{w^2+1}$$

$$\Rightarrow \quad y = \frac{1-w^2}{1+w^2} \qquad \text{...(ii)}$$

Since, the upper half of the z-plane is defined by

$$y>0 \text{ i.e., } \text{Im}(z)>0,$$

therefore $y>0$ in the z-plane is mapped into the region $\frac{1-w^2}{1+w^2}>0$ in the w-plane.

$$y>0 \quad \Rightarrow 1-w^2>0 \Rightarrow w^2<1 \qquad \text{...(iii)}$$

Now, $w^2 = |w|^2 = |u+iv|^2$, where $w = u+iv$

$$= u^2+v^2$$

∴ From Eq. (iii), we have

$$u^2+v^2<1,$$

Which clearly represents the points inside the unit circle $|w|=1$ in the w-plane.

Hence, the upper half of the z-plane is mapped into the interior of the unit circle in the w-plane.

***Example 22.*** *Show that both the transformations $w = \frac{z+i}{z-i}$ and $w = \frac{i+z}{i-z}$ transform $|w| \le 1$ into the lower half plane $I(z) \le 0$.*

**Solution.** Here, $\quad w = \frac{z+i}{z-i} \Rightarrow \overline{w} = \frac{\overline{z}-i}{\overline{z}+i}$

$$\therefore \quad w\overline{w}-1 = \left(\frac{z+i}{z-i}\right)\left(\frac{\overline{z}-i}{\overline{z}+i}\right)-1$$

$$= \frac{(z+i)(\overline{z}-i)-(z-i)(\overline{z}+i)}{(z-i)(\overline{z}+i)}$$

$$= \frac{-2i(z-\overline{z})}{|z-i|^2} = \frac{4I(z)}{|z-i|^2} \qquad [\because z-\overline{z} = 2iI(z)]$$

Also, if we take $w = \frac{i+z}{i-z}$, then we get the same expression for $w\overline{w}-1$.

Hence, for both the transformations $|w|^2-1 \le 0$

*i.e.,* $|w| \le 1$ gives $I(z) \le 0$.

Thus, the boundary of the circle $|w|=1$ corresponds to the real axis in the z-plane and the interior of the circle transforms into the lower half z-plane.

***Example 23.*** *Show that both the transformations $w = \frac{z-i}{z+i}$ and $w = \frac{i-z}{i+z}$ transform $|w| \le 1$ into the upper half plane $I(z) \ge 0$.*

**Solution.** Here, for both the transformations

$$w\overline{w}-1 = |w|^2-1 = \frac{-4I(z)}{|z+i|^2}$$

Hence, $\quad |w|^2-1 \le 0 \Rightarrow |w| \le 1 \Rightarrow I(z) \ge 0$

**Example 24.** *Show that both the transformations* $w=\dfrac{1-z}{1+z}$ *and* $w=\dfrac{z-1}{z+1}$ *transform* $|w|\le 1$ *into the right half plane* $R(z)\ge 0$.

**Solution.** Here, for both the transformations

$$w\overline{w}-1=|w|^2-1=\frac{-4R(z)}{|z+1|^2}$$

Hence, $\quad |w|^2-1\le 0 \Rightarrow |w|\le 1 \Rightarrow R(z)\ge 0$

**Example 25.** *Find the condition that the transformation* $w=\dfrac{az+b}{cz+d}$ *transforms a straight line of z-plane into the unit circle of w-plane.*

**Solution.** In the z-plane a straight line is given by

$$\left|\frac{z-p}{z-q}\right|=1 \qquad \text{...(i)}$$

In the w-plane a unit circle is given by $|w|=1$ ...(ii)

The given transformation is

$$w=\frac{az+b}{cz+d}=\frac{a\left(z+\dfrac{b}{a}\right)}{c\left(z+\dfrac{d}{c}\right)}=\frac{a(z-p)}{c(z-q)} \qquad \text{...(iii)}$$

The transformation Eq. (iii) maps the straight line Eq. (i) in a curve of w-plane namely $|w|=\left|\dfrac{a}{c}\right|\left|\dfrac{z-p}{z-q}\right|=\left|\dfrac{a}{c}\right|$ which will be $|w|=1$ if $|a|=|c|$.

**Example 26.** *Find the radius and centre of the circle in the w-plane which corresponds to the real axis in the z-plane, where* $w=\dfrac{ze^{\alpha}-i}{z-ie^{\alpha}}$, *α being a real constant.*

**Solution.** The given transformation is

$$w=\frac{ze^{\alpha}-i}{z-ie^{\alpha}}$$

$$\Rightarrow \qquad z=\frac{i(we^{\alpha}-1)}{w-e^{\alpha}}$$

The equation of the real axis in the z-plane is $y=0$ or $2iy=0$ or $z-\overline{z}=0$. This transforms in the w-plane to the curve is given by

$$\frac{i(we^{\alpha}-1)}{w-e^{\alpha}}+\frac{i(\overline{w}e^{\alpha}-1)}{\overline{w}-e^{\alpha}}=0$$

$$\Rightarrow \quad (we^{\alpha}-1)(\overline{w}-e^{\alpha})+(w-e^{\alpha})(\overline{w}e^{\alpha}-1)=0$$

$$\Rightarrow 2w\overline{w}e^{\alpha}-(w+\overline{w})e^{2\alpha}-(w+\overline{w})+2e^{\alpha}=0 \qquad [\because w=u+iv]$$

$$\Rightarrow \qquad 2(u^2+v^2)e^{\alpha}-2ue^{2\alpha}-2u+2e^{\alpha}=0$$

$$\Rightarrow \qquad u^2+v^2-ue^{\alpha}-ue^{\alpha}-ue^{-\alpha}+1=0$$

$$\Rightarrow \qquad u^2+v^2-2u\cosh\alpha+1=0, \qquad \left[\because \cosh\alpha=\frac{e^{\alpha}+e^{-\alpha}}{2}\right]$$

Which represents a circle with its centre $(\cosh\alpha,\ 0)$ *i.e.*, $w=\cosh\alpha$ and radius $=\sqrt{(\cosh^2\alpha+0-1)}=\sinh\alpha$.

**Example 27.** *To find all the bilinear transformations which transform the half-plane* $I(z)\ge 0$ *onto the unit circular disc* $|w|\le 1$.

**Solution.** Let $\quad w=\dfrac{az+b}{cz+d}, ad-bc\ne 0$ ...(i)

be the required bilinear transformation. Now, $c\ne 0$ otherwise the points at infinity will correspond. The points $w=0$ and $w=\infty$ in the w-plane correspond to the points $z=-\dfrac{b}{a}$ and $z=-\dfrac{d}{c}$ in the z-plane. Since, $w=0$ and $w=\infty$ are the inverse points with respect to the unit circle $|w|=1$, therefore $-b/a$ and $-d/c$ must be the inverse points (conjugate points in this case) with respect to the real axis $I(z)=0$. Thus, we may write $-\dfrac{b}{a}=\alpha$ and $-\dfrac{d}{c}=\overline{\alpha}$.

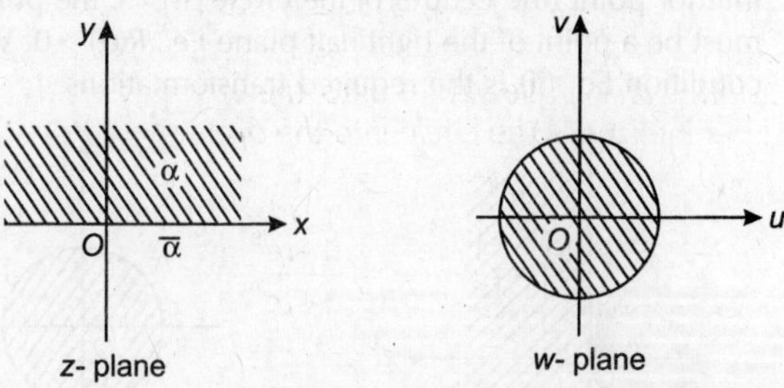


Then, from Eq. (i) we have

$$w=\frac{a}{c}\cdot\frac{z-\alpha}{z-\overline{\alpha}}$$

To find the value of $a/c$, we use the condition that the point $z=0$ (which is a point on $I(z)=0$) must correspond to a point on $|w|=1$. Since, the real axis $I(z)=0$ is to be transformed into the unit circle $|w|=1$.

$$\therefore \qquad \left|\frac{a}{c}\right|\left|\frac{0-\alpha}{0-\overline{\alpha}}\right|=|w|=1\Rightarrow\left|\frac{a}{c}\right|=1$$

Thus, we may take $\dfrac{a}{c}=e^{i\lambda}$, where λ is real.

Consequently, the required transformation is

$$w=e^{i\lambda}\,\frac{z-\alpha}{z-\overline{\alpha}} \qquad \text{...(ii)}$$

Since, $z=\alpha$ gives $w=0$ which is the centre of the circle $|w|=1$, α must be a point of the upper half plane. *i.e.*, $I(\alpha)>0$. With this the condition (ii) is the required transformation.

**Example 28.** *To find all the bilinear transformations which transform the half plane* $R(z)\ge 0$ *onto the unit circular disc* $|w|\le 1$.

**Solution.** Let $\quad w=\dfrac{az+b}{cz+d},\ ad-bc\ne 0$ ...(i)

be the required bilinear transformation. We first note that $c\ne 0$ otherwise the points at infinity will correspond. The points $w=0$ and $w=\infty$ in the w-plane correspond to the points $z=-\dfrac{b}{a}$ and $z=-\dfrac{d}{c}$ in the z-plane. Since, $w=0$ and $w=\infty$ are the inverse points with respect to the unit circle $|w|=1$, hence $-b/a$ and $-d/c$ must be the inverse points (symmetrical) with respect to the imaginary axis $R(z)=0$. Therefore, we may write $-\dfrac{b}{a}=\alpha$ and $-\dfrac{d}{c}=-\overline{\alpha}$.

Then, from Eq. (i) we have $w = \frac{a}{c} \cdot \frac{z - \alpha}{z + \bar{\alpha}}$

To find the value of $a/c$, we use the condition that any point on $R(z) = 0$ (in particular $z = 0$) must correspond to a point on $|w| = 1$.

Hence, $\left|\frac{a}{c}\right| \left|\frac{0 - \alpha}{0 + \bar{\alpha}}\right| = |w| = 1 \Rightarrow \left|\frac{a}{c}\right| = 1$

Thus, we may take $\frac{a}{c} = e^{i\lambda}$, where $\lambda$ is real. Consequently, the required transformation is

$$w = e^{i\lambda} \cdot \frac{z - \alpha}{z + \bar{\alpha}} \quad \text{...(ii)}$$

Note that, since $z = \alpha$ corresponds to $w = 0$ which is an interior point (the centre) of the circle $|w| = 1$, the point $z = \alpha$ must be a point of the right half plane *i.e.*, $R(\alpha) > 0$. With this condition Eq. (ii) is the required transformations.

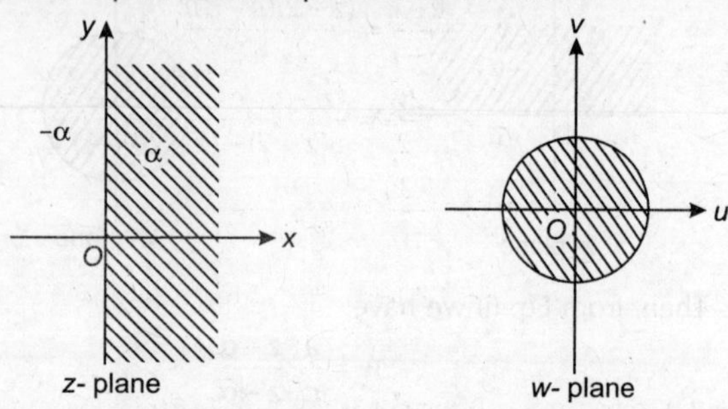


***Example 29.*** *To find the general bilinear transformation which transforms the unit circular disc $|z| \le 1$ onto the unit circular disc $|w| \le 1$.*

**Solution.** Let $w = \frac{az + b}{cz + d}$, $ad - bc \ne 0$ ...(i)

be the required transformation. The points $w = 0$ and $w = \infty$ correspond to $z = -b/a$ and $z = -d/c$ respectively. Since 0, $\infty$ are the inverse points with respect to the circle $|w| = 1$, the points $-b/a, -d/c$ must be the inverse points with respect to the circle $|z| = 1$. Thus, we have

$$-\frac{b}{a} = \alpha \quad \text{and} \quad -\frac{d}{c} = \frac{1}{\bar{\alpha}}$$

Then, from Eq. (i) we have

$$w = \frac{a}{c} \cdot \frac{z - \alpha}{z - \frac{1}{\bar{\alpha}}} = \frac{a\bar{\alpha}}{c} \cdot \frac{z - \alpha}{z\bar{\alpha} - 1}$$

To find the value of $a/c$, we use the condition that any point on $|z| = 1$ (in particular $z = 1$) must correspond to a point on $|w| = 1$.

$$\therefore \quad \left|\frac{a\bar{\alpha}}{c}\right| \left|\frac{1 - \alpha}{\bar{\alpha} - 1}\right| = |w| = 1$$

$$\Rightarrow \quad \left|\frac{a\bar{\alpha}}{c}\right| = 1 \quad [\because |1 - \alpha| = |\bar{\alpha} - 1|]$$

Hence, we may take $\frac{a\bar{\alpha}}{c} = e^{i\lambda}$, where $\lambda$ is real.

Consequently, the required transformation is

$$w = e^{i\lambda} \frac{z - \alpha}{z\bar{\alpha} - 1} \quad \text{...(ii)}$$

Since, $z = \alpha$ gives $w = 0$ which is an interior point (the centre) of the circle $|w| = 1$, the point $\alpha$ must be an interior point of the circle $|z| = 1$ *i.e.*, $|\alpha| < 1$. With this condition (ii) is the required transformation.

**Particular cases** If $z = 0$ corresponds to $w = 0$, then

$$0 = e^{i\lambda} \frac{0 - \alpha}{0 - 1} = e^{i\lambda}\alpha$$

Hence, $\alpha = 0$ and the transformation becomes $w = -ze^{i\lambda}$.

If further $\frac{dw}{dz} = 1$ at $z = 0$, then $\frac{dw}{dz} = -e^{i\lambda} = 1$

So that in this case the transformation reduces to the identity mapping.

***Example 30.*** *To find the bilinear transformation which maps the circular disc $|z| \le \rho$ onto the circular disc $|w| \le \rho'$.*

**Solution.** Let $w = \frac{az + b}{cz + d}$, $ad - bc \ne 0$ ...(i)

be the required transformation. The points $w = 0$ and $w = \infty$ which are the inverse points with respect to the circle $|w| = \rho'$ correspond to $z = -b/a$ and $z = -d/c$ respectively.

Therefore, $-b/a$ and $-d/c$ must be the inverse points with respect to the circle $|z| = \rho$.

Thus, we have $-\frac{b}{a} = \alpha$ and $-\frac{d}{c} = \frac{\rho^2}{\bar{\alpha}}$, where $|\alpha| < \rho$.

Then from Eq. (i) we have

$$w = \frac{a}{c} \cdot \frac{z - \alpha}{z - \rho^2/\bar{\alpha}} = \frac{a\bar{\alpha}}{c} \cdot \frac{z - \alpha}{\bar{\alpha}z - \rho^2}.$$

To find the value of $a/c$ we use the condition that $|w| = \rho'$ when $|z| = \rho$ *i.e.*, $z\bar{z} = \rho^2$.

$$\therefore \quad \rho' = |w| = \left|\frac{a\bar{\alpha}}{c}\right| \left|\frac{z - \alpha}{\bar{\alpha}z - z\bar{z}}\right| = \left|\frac{a\bar{\alpha}}{c}\right| \left|\frac{z - \alpha}{\bar{\alpha} - \bar{z}}\right| \left|\frac{1}{z}\right| = \left|\frac{a\bar{\alpha}}{c}\right| \frac{1}{\rho}$$

$$\Rightarrow \quad \left|\frac{a\bar{\alpha}}{c}\right| = \rho\rho'.$$

Thus, we have $\frac{a\bar{\alpha}}{c} = \rho\rho' e^{i\lambda}$, where $\lambda$ is real.

Consequently, the required transformation is

$$w = \rho\rho' e^{i\lambda} \frac{z - \alpha}{\bar{\alpha}z - \rho^2}, \; |\alpha| < \rho \quad \text{...(ii)}$$

# Equation of a Circle Through Three Given Points

Equation of a circle passing through three given points $z_1$, $z_2$ and $z_3$ is given by

$$\frac{(z - z_1)(z_3 - z_2)}{(z - z_2)(z_3 - z_1)} = \frac{(\bar{z} - \bar{z}_1)(\bar{z}_3 - \bar{z}_2)}{(\bar{z} - \bar{z}_2)(\bar{z}_3 - \bar{z}_1)}$$

where $z$ is any complex variable lies on circle.

***Theorem*** The four points $z_1, z_2, z_3$ and $z_4$ are concyclic, if $\frac{(z_4 - z_1)(z_3 - z_2)}{(z_4 - z_2)(z_3 - z_1)}$ is purely real.

## Cross Ratio

If $z_1, z_2, z_3$ and $z_4$ are distinct complex numbers, then the quantity $\dfrac{(z_1-z_2)(z_3-z_4)}{(z_2-z_3)(z_4-z_1)}$ is called the cross ratio of $z_1, z_2, z_3$ and $z_4$ taken in order and is denoted by $(z_1, z_2, z_3, z_4)$.

Four points $z_1, z_2, z_3$ and $z_4$ can be arranged among themselves in 4! *i.e.,* 24 ways but only six different arrangements (cross ratios) satisfy the above definition.

> ***Note*** Consider the bilinear transformation
>
> $$w = T(z) = \frac{(z-z_2)(z_3-z_4)}{(z_2-z_3)(z_4-z)} \quad \text{...(i)}$$
>
> where $z_2, z_3$ and $z_4$ are any three distinct points in the extended complex plane and none of these points is $\infty$.
>
> The images of $z_2, z_3$ and $z_4$ are $0, 1, \infty$ respectively under the transformation (i). Also, the point $z_1$ transforms to
>
> $$\frac{(z_1-z_2)(z_3-z_4)}{(z_2-z_3)(z_4-z_1)}$$
>
> Which is the cross ratio of the four points $z_1, z_2, z_3$ and $z_4$ as defined earlier.
>
> Thus, the cross ratio $(z_1, z_2, z_3, z_4)$ of the four points $z_1, z_2, z_3, z_4$ is the image of $z_1$ under the bilinear transformation (i) which carries $z_2, z_3, z_4$ into $0, 1, \infty$ respectively.
>
> The transformation (i) reduces to
>
> $$\frac{z_3-z_4}{z-z_4}, \frac{z-z_2}{z-z_4}, \frac{z-z_2}{z_3-z_2} \text{ if } z_2, z_3 \text{ or } z_4 = \infty$$
>
> respectively.

## Important Result on Cross Ratios

Let $w_1, w_2, w_3$ and $w_4$ be the images of the four distinct points $z_1, z_2, z_3$ and $z_4$ in the $z$-plane under a bilinear transformation. Then, $(w_1, w_2, w_3, w_4) = (z_1, z_2, z_3, z_4)$.

The bilinear transformation which transforms $z_1, z_2, z_3$ respectively into $w_1, w_2, w_3$ is given by

$$\frac{(w-w_1)(w_2-w_3)}{(w_1-w_2)(w_3-w)} = \frac{(z-z_1)(z_2-z_3)}{(z_1-z_2)(z_3-z)}$$

$$\Rightarrow \quad (w_1, w_2, w_3, w) = (z_1, z_2, z_3, z)$$

$$\therefore \quad (w_1, w_2, w_3, w_4) = (z_1, z_2, z_3, z_4)$$

The cross ratio $(z_1, z_2, z_3, z_4)$ is real if and only if the four points $z_1, z_2, z_3, z_4$ lie on a circle or on a straight line.

We have,

$$(z_1, z_2, z_3, z_4) = \left(\frac{z_1-z_2}{z_2-z_3}\right) \Big/ \left(\frac{z_4-z_1}{z_3-z_4}\right)$$

$$\therefore \quad \arg(z_1, z_2, z_3, z_4) = \arg\left(\frac{z_1-z_2}{z_2-z_3}\right) - \arg\left(\frac{z_4-z_1}{z_3-z_4}\right). \quad \text{...(i)}$$

Hence, the difference of the angle on the right hand side of (i) is 0 or $\pm\pi$ depending on the relative position of the points $z_1, z_2, z_3$ and $z_4$ if and only if these points lie on a circle and consequently, the cross ratio $(z_1, z_2, z_3, z_4)$ is real if and only if the four points lie on a circle.

***Example 31.*** *Find the bilinear transformation which maps the points $z_1 = 2, z_2 = i$ and $z_3 = -2$ into the points $w_1 = 1, w_2 = i$ and $w_3 = -1$ respectively.*

**Solution.** The bilinear transformation which transforms $z_1, z_2, z_3$ respectively into $w_1, w_2, w_3$ is given by

$$\frac{(w-w_1)(w_2-w_3)}{(w_1-w_2)(w_3-w)} = \frac{(z-z_1)(z_2-z_3)}{(z_1-z_2)(z_3-z)}$$

Substituting

$z_1 = 2,\ z_2 = i,\ z_3 = -2;\ w_1 = 1, w_2 = i, w_3 = -1$, we get

$$\frac{(w-1)(i+1)}{(1-i)(-1-w)} = \frac{(z-2)(i+2)}{(2-i)(-2-z)}.$$

$$\Rightarrow \quad -\frac{(w-1)(1+i)^2}{(w+1)(1-i)(1+i)} = -\frac{(z-2)(2+i)^2}{(z+2)(2-i)(2+i)}$$

$$\Rightarrow \quad \frac{(w-1)2i}{(w+1)2} = \frac{(z-2)(3+4i)}{(z+2)\cdot 5}$$

$$\Rightarrow \quad \frac{w-1}{w+1} = \frac{(z-2)(4-3i)}{5(z+2)}$$

$$\Rightarrow \quad \frac{2w}{2} = \frac{(z-2)(4-3i)+5(z+2)}{5(z+2)-(z-2)(4-3i)}$$

$$\Rightarrow w = \frac{3(3-i)z+2(1+3i)}{(1+3i)z+6(3-i)} = \frac{3z+[2(1+3i)/(3-i)]}{[(1+3i)/(3-i)]z+6}$$

$\Rightarrow \quad w = \dfrac{3z+2i}{iz+6}$, which is the required bilinear transformation.

**Alternative method** Let the bilinear transformation be

$$w = \frac{az+b}{cz+d} \quad \text{...(i)}$$

Putting $z_1 = 2, w_1 = 1;\ z_2 = i, w_2 = i$ and $z_3 = -2, w_3 = -1$, in pairs in Eq. (i), we get

$$1 = \frac{2a+b}{2c+d} \Rightarrow 2a+b-2c-d = 0 \quad \text{...(ii)}$$

$$i = \frac{ai+b}{ci+d} \Rightarrow ai+b+c-di = 0 \quad \text{...(iii)}$$

and

$$-1 = \frac{-2a+b}{-2c+d} \Rightarrow 2a-b+2c-d = 0 \quad \text{...(iv)}$$

Adding Eqs. (ii) and (iv), we get

$$4a-2d = 0 \Rightarrow 2a = d$$

Subtracting Eq. (iv) from Eq. (ii), we get

$$2b-4c = 0 \Rightarrow b = 2c$$

Now, Eq. (iii) becomes $ai+2c+c-2ai = 0 \Rightarrow ai = 3c$

Thus, $\quad 2a = d,\ b = 2c, ai = 3c$

$$\Rightarrow \quad a = \frac{d}{2} = \frac{3c}{i} = \frac{3b}{2i} \Rightarrow \frac{a}{1} = \frac{d}{2} = \frac{c}{i/3} = \frac{b}{2i/3}$$

Putting these values in Eq. (i), we get

$$w = \frac{z+(2i/3)}{(i/3)z+2} = \frac{3z+2i}{iz+6}, \text{ as earlier.}$$

***Example 32.*** *Find a bilinear transformation which transforms the unit circle $|z| = 1$ into the real axis in such a way that the point $z_1 = 1$ is mapped into $w_1 = 0$, the point $z_2 = i$ is mapped into $w_2 = 1$ and the point $z_3 = -1$ is mapped into $w_3 = \infty$. Into what regions the interior and exterior of the circle are mapped?*

**Solution.** Obviously, the points $z_1 = 1, z_2 = i$ and $z_3 = -1$ lie on the circle $|z| = 1$ in the z-plane and the points $w_1 = 0, w_2 = 1, w_3 = \infty$ lie on the real axis of the w-plane. The required transformation can be obtained by substituting the values of $z_1, z_2, z_3; w_1, w_2, w_3$ in

$$\frac{(w-w_1)(w_2-w_3)}{(w_1-w_2)(w_3-w)} = \frac{(z-z_1)(z_2-z_3)}{(z_1-z_2)(z_3-z)}$$

Hence, the transformation is

$$\frac{(w-0)(1-\infty)}{(0-1)(\infty-w)} = \frac{(z-1)(i+1)}{(1-i)(-1-z)}$$

$$\Rightarrow \quad w = -\frac{(z-1)(1+i)^2}{(z+1)(1+i)(1-i)} = -\frac{(z-1)2i}{(z+1)2}$$

$$\Rightarrow \quad w = \frac{i(1-z)}{1+z}$$

The inverse transformation is given by

$$z = -\frac{w-i}{w+i} \Rightarrow |z| = \left|\frac{w-i}{w+i}\right|$$

Hence, $|z| = 1$ is transformed into $\left|\frac{w-i}{w+i}\right| = 1$ *i.e.,* into $|w-i| = |w+i|$ which is the real axis of the w-plane being the locus of the points equidistant from $w = i$ and $w = -i$. The point $z = 0$, centre of the circle $|z| = 1$ is transformed into the point $w = i$ of the w-plane. It follows that the interior of the circle $|z| = 1$ is mapped into the upper half of the w-plane. Also, since $w = -i$ corresponds to $z = \infty$ hence, the region exterior to the circle $|z| = 1$ is mapped into the lower half of the w-plane.

***Example 33.*** *Find the transformation which maps outside $|z| = 1$, on the half plane $R(w) \geq 0$ so that the points $z = 1, -i, -1$ correspond to $w = i, 0, -i$ respectively.*

**Solution.** Let $z_1 = 1, z_2 = -i, z_3 = -1, w_1 = i, w_2 = 0, w_3 = -i.$

Since, cross ratio is preserved under a bilinear transformation and so

$$\frac{(w-w_1)(w_2-w_3)}{(w_1-w_2)(w_3-w)} = \frac{(z-z_1)(z_2-z_3)}{(z_1-z_2)(z_3-z)}$$

Putting the values, we get

$$\frac{(w-i)(0+i)}{(i-0)(-i-w)} = \frac{(z-1)(-i+1)}{(1+i)(-1-z)}$$

$$\Rightarrow \quad \frac{w-i}{w+i} = -i\left(\frac{z-1}{z+1}\right) = \frac{-iz+i}{z+1} \quad \left[\because \frac{1-i}{1+i} = -i\right]$$

$$\Rightarrow \quad \frac{(w-i)+(w+i)}{(w-i)-(w+i)} = \frac{-iz+i+z+1}{-iz+i-(z+1)}$$

$$\Rightarrow \quad \frac{2w}{-2i} = \frac{z(1-i)+(1+i)}{-z(1+i)-(1-i)}$$

$$\Rightarrow \quad w = i\left(\frac{1-i}{1+i}\right)\left[\frac{z+\left(\frac{1+i}{1-i}\right)}{z+\left(\frac{1-i}{1+i}\right)}\right] = i(-i)\left(\frac{z+i}{z-i}\right)$$

$$\Rightarrow \quad w = \frac{z+i}{z-i} \quad \text{...(i)}$$

Which is the required transformation.

From Eq.(i), $\quad w(z-i) = z+i \Rightarrow z = i\left(\frac{w+1}{w-1}\right) \quad$ ...(ii)

$|z| \geq 1$ is transformed into $\left|\frac{w+1}{w-1}\right| . |i| \geq 1$

$$\Rightarrow \quad |w+1|^2 \geq |w-1|^2 \Rightarrow (u+1)^2 + v^2 \geq (u-1)^2 + v^2$$

$$\Rightarrow \quad R(w) = u \geq 0.$$

Thus, exterior of the circle $|z| = 1$ is transformed into half plane $R(w) \geq 0$.

***Example 34.*** *Find the bilinear transformation that maps the points $z_1 = \infty$, $z_2 = i$ and $z_3 = 0$ into the points $w_1 = 0, w_2 = i$ and $w_3 = \infty$.*

**Solution.** Substituting these values in

$$\frac{(w-w_1)(w_2-w_3)}{(w_1-w_2)(w_3-w)} = \frac{(z-z_1)(z_2-z_3)}{(z_1-z_2)(z_3-z)}$$

We get the required transformation as

$$\frac{(w-0)(i-\infty)}{(0-i)(\infty-w)} = \frac{(z-\infty)(i-0)}{(\infty-i)(0-z)}$$

$$\Rightarrow \quad \frac{1}{i}w = \frac{i}{z}$$

$$\Rightarrow \quad w = -\frac{1}{z}$$

***Example 35.*** *Find the bilinear transformation which transforms the points $z = 2, 1, 0$ into $w = 1, 0, i$ respectively.*

**Solution.** Substituting the given values in

$$\frac{(w-w_1)(w_2-w_3)}{(w_1-w_2)(w_3-w)} = \frac{(z-z_1)(z_2-z_3)}{(z_1-z_2)(z_3-z)}$$

We get the required transformation as

$$\frac{(w-1)(0-i)}{(1-0)(i-w)} = \frac{(z-2)(1-0)}{(2-1)(0-z)}$$

$$\Rightarrow \quad \frac{(iw-i)}{(w-i)} = \frac{z-2}{-z}$$

$$\Rightarrow \quad -z(iw-i) = (z-2)(w-i)$$

$$\Rightarrow \quad w\{(z-2)+iz\} = i(z-2)+iz$$

$$\Rightarrow \quad w = \frac{2i(z-1)}{(1+i)z-2}$$

***Example 36.*** *Find the bilinear transformation that maps the points $0, -i, -1$ into the points $i, 1, 0$.*

**Solution.** Substituting the given values in

$$\frac{(w-w_1)(w_2-w_3)}{(w_1-w_2)(w_3-w)} = \frac{(z-z_1)(z_2-z_3)}{(z_1-z_2)(z_3-z)},$$

we get the required transformation as

$$\frac{(w-i)(1-0)}{(i-1)(0-w)} = \frac{(z-0)(-i+1)}{(0+i)(-1-z)}$$

$$\Rightarrow \quad \frac{w-i}{w-wi} = \frac{z-zi}{-i-iz}$$

$$\Rightarrow \quad -wi-wzi-1-z = wz-wzi-wzi-wz$$

$$\Rightarrow \quad wi(z-1) = 1+z$$

$$\Rightarrow \quad w = \frac{1+z}{i(z-1)} = -i\frac{(1+z)}{(z-1)} = i\left(\frac{1+z}{1-z}\right).$$

## Fixed Points or Invariant Points of a Bilinear Transformation

The points which coincide with their transforms under a bilinear transformation are called fixed points or invariant points of the transformation.

Consider any bilinear transformation

$$w = \frac{az+b}{cz+d}, \ (ad-bc \neq 0) \quad \text{...(i)}$$

Then, the fixed points of this transformation are obtained by putting $w = z$ *i.e.*,

$$z = \frac{az+b}{cz+d} \Rightarrow cz^2 + (d-a)z - b = 0 \quad \text{...(ii)}$$

Now, there are two cases.

***Case I.*** Let $c \neq 0$. Then, the roots of the quadratic Eq. (ii) are given by

$$z = \frac{(a-d) \pm \sqrt{[(d-a)^2 + 4bc]}}{2c}$$

Thus, one or two finite fixed points according as $(d-a)^2 + 4bc = 0$ or $\neq 0$.

***Case II.*** Let $c = 0$ and $d \neq 0$.

In this case the transformation Eq. (i) becomes $w = \frac{a}{d}z + \frac{b}{d}$

For this transformation one of the fixed points is easily seen to be $\infty$ while the other fixed point is given by

$$z = \frac{a}{d}z + \frac{b}{d} \text{ or } (a-d)z + b = 0$$

Hence, if $a - d \neq 0$, the transformation has two fixed points $\infty$ and $\frac{b}{d-a}$ but it has only one fixed point $\infty$ if $a - d - 0$.

Hence, we conclude that the transformation (i) has

(i) only one finite fixed point if $c \neq 0$ and $(d-a)^2 + 4bc = 0$

(ii) two finite fixed points if $c \neq 0$ and $(d-a)^2 + 4bc \neq 0$

(iii) one finite and other infinite fixed points if $c = 0$ and $a - d \neq 0$

(iv) only one infinite fixed point if $c = 0$ and $a - d = 0$

### Important Results on Fixed Point

(i) Every bilinear transformation with two finite fixed points $\alpha, \beta$ can be put in the form

$$\frac{w-\alpha}{w-\beta} = \lambda \frac{z-\alpha}{z-\beta}$$

(a) If $|\lambda| = 1$, then transformation is elliptic.

(b) If $\lambda > 0 \ (\neq 1)$, then transformation is hyperbolic.

(ii) Every bilinear transformation which has only one finite fixed point $\alpha$ can be put in the form

$$\frac{1}{w-\alpha} = \frac{1}{z-\alpha} + \lambda$$

In this case transformation is parabolic.

***Example 37.*** *Find the fixed points and the normal form of the following bilinear transformations.*

(i) $w = \frac{z}{2-z}$ (ii) $w = \frac{3z-4}{z-1}$ (iii) $w = \frac{z-1}{z+1}$

(iv) $w = \frac{3iz+1}{z+i}$ (v) $w = \frac{(2+i)z-2}{z+i}$

*Discuss the nature of these transformations (hyperbolic, elliptic or parabolic).*

**Solution.** (i) The fixed points are given by

$$z = \frac{z}{2-z} \Rightarrow z(z-1) = 0 \Rightarrow z = 0, 1$$

Hence, 0 and 1 are the two fixed points in this case. To obtain the normal form, we have

$$w = \frac{z}{2-z} \Rightarrow w - 1 = \frac{2z-2}{2-z}$$

$$\therefore \quad \frac{w}{w-1} = \frac{z}{2z-2} = \frac{1}{2} \cdot \frac{z}{z-1},$$

which is the required normal form.

Here, $\lambda = \frac{1}{2}$, which is real. Hence, the transformation is hyperbolic.

(ii) The fixed points are given by

$$z = \frac{3z-4}{z-1} \Rightarrow z^2 - 4z + 4 = 0 \Rightarrow (z-2)^2 = 0$$

Hence, $z = 2$ is the only fixed point in this case.

To obtain the normal form, we have

$$w = \frac{3z-4}{z-1} \Rightarrow wz - w = 3z - 4$$

$$\Rightarrow \quad (w-2)(z-2) + 2z + 2w - w - 3z = 0$$

$$\Rightarrow \quad (w-2)(z-2) - (z-2) + (w-2) = 0$$

$$\Rightarrow \quad 1 - \frac{1}{w-2} + \frac{1}{z-2} = 0 \text{ or } \frac{1}{w-2} = \frac{1}{z-2} + 1,$$

Which is the required normal form.

Here, the transformation is parabolic.

(iii) The fixed points are given by

$$z = \frac{z-1}{z+1} \Rightarrow z^2 + 1 = 0 \Rightarrow z = \pm i$$

Hence, $i$ and $-i$ are the two fixed points in this case. To obtain the normal form, we have

$$w = \frac{z-1}{z+1}$$

$$\Rightarrow \quad w - i = \frac{z-1}{z+1} - i \text{ and } w + i = \frac{z-1}{z+1} + i$$

$$\Rightarrow \quad \frac{w-i}{w+i} = \frac{z-1-iz-i}{z-1+iz+i} = \frac{(1-i)(z-i)}{(1+i)(z+i)}$$

$$\Rightarrow \quad \frac{w-i}{w+i} = \frac{(1-i)^2(z-i)}{(1+i)(1-i)(z+i)} = -i\frac{z-i}{z+i},$$

which is the required normal form.

Here, $\lambda = -i \Rightarrow |\lambda| = 1$. Hence, the transformation is elliptic.

(iv) The fixed points are given by

$$z = \frac{3iz+1}{z+i} \Rightarrow z^2 - 2iz - 1 = 0 \Rightarrow (z-i)^2 = 0$$

Hence, $z = i$ is the only fixed point in this case and consequently the transformation is parabolic.

To obtain the normal form, we have

$$w = \frac{3iz+1}{z+i} \Rightarrow wz + iw - 3iz - 1 = 0$$

$$\Rightarrow \quad (w-i)(z-i) + iz + iw + iw - 3iz = 0$$

$$\Rightarrow \quad (w-i)(z-i) + 2i(w-i) - 2i(z-i) = 0$$

$$\Rightarrow \quad 1 + \frac{2i}{z-i} - \frac{2i}{w-i} = 0$$

or

$$\frac{1}{w-i} = \frac{1}{z-i} + \frac{1}{2i}$$

$$\Rightarrow \quad \frac{1}{w-i} = \frac{1}{z-i} - \frac{i}{2},$$

which is the required normal form.

(v) The fixed points are given by

$$z = \frac{(2+i)z-2}{z+i} \Rightarrow z^2 - 2z + 2 = 0$$

$$\therefore \quad z = \frac{2 \pm \sqrt{(4-8)}}{2} = 1 \pm i$$

Hence, $1+i$ and $1-i$ are the two fixed points in this case. To obtain the normal form, we have

$$w = \frac{(2+i)z-2}{z+i}$$

$$\therefore \quad w-(1+i) = \frac{(2+i)z-2}{z+i} - (1+i)$$

$$= \frac{2z+iz-2-z-iz-i+1}{z+i} = \frac{z-(1+i)}{z+i}$$

$$\text{and } w-(1-i) = \frac{(2+i)z-2}{z+i} - (1-i)$$

$$= \frac{2z+iz-2-z+iz-i-1}{z+i}$$

$$= \frac{z-(1-i)+2iz-2-2i}{z+i}$$

$$= \frac{z-(1-i)+2i(z+i-1)}{z+i}$$

$$= \frac{(1+2i)[z-(1-i)]}{z+i}$$

$$\Rightarrow \quad \frac{w-(1+i)}{w-(1-i)} = \frac{z-(1+i)}{(1+2i)[z-(1-i)]} = \frac{1-2i}{5} \cdot \frac{z-(1+i)}{z-(1-i)},$$

which is the required normal form.

Here, $\lambda = \frac{1-2i}{5}$. Neither $\lambda$ is real nor $|\lambda| = 1$.

Hence, the transformation is loxodromic in this case.

# SOLVED EXAMPLES

## Type I (*Only one correct option*)

***Example 1.*** *The image of the unit circle $|z| = 1$ under the transformation $w = 2z + z^2$ is*

(a) circle (b) straight line
(c) parabola (d) cardiod

**Solution.** (d) We have,

$$w = 2z + z^2$$

$$\Rightarrow \quad w + 1 = (z+1)^2$$

Let $\quad w + 1 = \rho e^{i\phi}$

Then,

$$|z| = 1 \text{ i.e., } z = e^{i\theta}$$

is transformed into the curve

$$\rho e^{i\phi} = (e^{i\theta} + 1)^2$$

$$= [(1+\cos\theta) + i\sin\theta]^2$$

$$= 2(1+\cos\theta)e^{i\theta}$$

Hence, $\quad \rho = 2(1+\cos\theta), \ \phi = \theta$

Eliminating $\theta$, we get

$$\rho = 2(1+\cos\phi)$$

as the equation of the image curve, which is cardiod.

***Example 2.*** *The bilinear transformation $w(z) = i\frac{1-z}{1+z}$ maps*

(a) $i, 1, -1$ onto $1, 0, \infty$
(b) $-1, 0, 1$ onto $0, i, 3i$
(c) Both (a) and (b) are true
(d) Neither (a) nor (b) is true

**Solution.** (a) We have,

$$w(i) = i\frac{1-i}{1+i} = \frac{i(1+i^2-2i)}{1+1} = \frac{-2i^2}{2} = 1$$

$$w(1) = i\frac{1-1}{1+1} = 0$$

$$w(-1) = i\frac{1+1}{1-1} = \infty$$

But $\quad w(-1) = i\frac{1+1}{1-1} = \infty$

Hence, only (a) is true.

***Example 3.*** *The set of all bilinear transformations which map the right half plane $\text{Re}(z) > 0$ onto the open disc $|w| < 1$ and the boundary $\text{Re}(z) = 0$ onto the boundary $|w| = 1$ is*

(a) $e^{i\alpha}\frac{iz+z_0}{iz-\bar{z}_0}, \ \text{Im}(z_0) > 0, \alpha \in \mathbb{R}$

(b) $e^{i\alpha}\frac{iz-z_0}{iz+\bar{z}_0}, \ \text{Im}(z_0) < 0, \alpha \in \mathbb{R}$

(c) $e^{i\alpha}\frac{iz-z_0}{iz-\bar{z}_0}, \ \text{Im}(z_0) > 0, \alpha \in \mathbb{R}$

(d) $e^{i\alpha}\frac{iz+z_0}{iz+\bar{z}_0}, \ \text{Im}(z_0) > 0, \alpha \in \mathbb{R}$

**Solution.** (c) The right half plane

$$\text{Re}(z) > 0$$

and $\quad \text{Re}(z) = 0$

are rotated by $\frac{\pi}{2}$ to get the upper half plane with boundary as $\text{Im}(z) = 0$. This transformation is

$$f(z) = iz, \ \text{Re}(z) \geq 0$$

The bilinear transformations which map $\text{Im}(z) \geq 0$, onto $|w| \leq 1$ are given by $g(z) = e^{i\alpha} \frac{z - z_0}{z - \bar{z}_0}$. $\text{Im}(z_0) > 0$, $\alpha \in \mathbb{R}$.

Hence, the required transformations $g(f(z))$ are of the form

$$g(f(z)) = g(iz) = e^{i\alpha} \frac{iz - z_0}{iz - \bar{z}_0}, \ \text{Im}(z_0) > 0, \alpha \in \mathbb{R}$$

We have, $\alpha = \pi$, $\text{Im}(z_0) = 1 > 0$

Hence, the bilinear transformation maps $y \geq 0$ onto $|w| \leq 1$, *i.e.*, $\text{Im}(z) \geq 0$ onto $|w| \leq 1$.

***Example 4.*** *Consider the transformation* $w = \frac{i - z}{i + z}$. *Then,*

(a) $w$ maps $\text{Im}(z) \geq 0$ onto $|w| \geq 1$
(b) $w$ maps $\text{Im}(z) \geq 0$ onto $|w| \leq 1$
(c) Both (a) and (b) are true
(d) Neither (a) nor (b) is true

**Solution.** (b) Let us write the transformation $w = \frac{i - z}{i + z}$ in the form

$$w = e^{i\pi} \cdot \frac{z - i}{z + i}$$

Comparing with $w = e^{i\alpha} \frac{z - z_0}{z - \bar{z}_0}$, $\text{Im}(z_0) > 0, \alpha \in \mathbb{R}$

***Example 5.*** *The set of all bilinear transformations which have fixed points as* $-1$ *and* $1$ *is*

(a) $\left\{ T(z) = \frac{az + b}{bz + a}; \ a^2 - b^2 = 0 \right\}$

(b) $\left\{ T(z) = \frac{az + b}{bz + a}; \ a^2 - b^2 \neq 0 \right\}$

(c) $\left\{ T(z) = \frac{az + b}{bz + a}; \ a^2 + b^2 = 0 \right\}$

(d) $\left\{ T(z) = \frac{az + b}{bz + a}; \ a^2 + b^2 \neq 0 \right\}$

**Solution.** (b) Let $T(z) = \frac{az + b}{cz + d}$, then we have,

$$T(1) = 1 \ \Rightarrow a + b = c + d$$
$$\Rightarrow a + b - c - d = 0 \quad \text{...(i)}$$
$$T(-1) = -1 \ \Rightarrow -a + b = -(-c + d)$$
$$\Rightarrow -a + b - c + d = 0 \quad \text{...(ii)}$$

On solving Eqs. (i) and (ii), we get

$$a = d, \ b = c$$

Hence, the required set of bilinear transformation is

$$T(z) = \frac{az + b}{bz + a}, \ a^2 - b^2 \neq 0$$

## Type II (*One or more than one correct option*)

***Example 6.*** *Consider the map*

$$w = \frac{1}{z},$$

*then*

(a) a circle not passing through origin in $z$-plane is mapped on a circle in $w$-plane not passing through origin
(b) a circle passing through origin in $z$-plane is mapped on a line in $w$-plane not passing through origin
(c) a line not passing through origin in $z$-plane is mapped on a circle in $w$-plane passing through origin
(d) a line passing through origin in $z$-plane is mapped on a line in a $w$-plane passing through origin

**Solution.** (a), (b), (c), (d)

Let $a$, $b$, $c$ and $d$ be real numbers such that $b^2 + c^2 > 4ad$.

Then,

$$a(x^2 + y^2) + bx + cy + d = 0 \quad \text{...(i)}$$

represents the equation of a circle in the $z$-plane.

Now, putting $w = u + iv$ and $z = x + iy$ in $w = \frac{1}{z}$, we get

$$u = \frac{x}{x^2 + y^2}, v = -\frac{y}{x^2 + y^2} \quad \text{...(ii)}$$

and

$$x = \frac{u}{u^2 + v^2}, y = -\frac{v}{u^2 + v^2} \quad \text{...(iii)}$$

Now, using Eq. (iii) in Eq. (i), we get

$$d(u^2 + v^2) + bu - cv + a = 0 \quad \text{...(iv)}$$

which is a circle or a line in $w$-plane depending on the nature of real numbers.

Thus, from Eqs. (i) and (iv), we have

(a) a circle not passing through origin $(a \neq 0, d \neq 0)$ in $z$-plane is mapped on a circle in $w$-plane not passing through origin.
(b) a circle passing through origin $(a \neq 0, d = 0)$ in $z$-plane is mapped on a line in $w$-plane not passing through origin.
(c) a line not passing through origin $(a = 0, d \neq 0)$ in $z$-plane is mapped on a circle in $w$-plane passing through origin.
(d) a line passing through origin $(a = 0, d = 0)$ in $z$-plane is mapped on a line in $w$-plane passing through origin.

***Example 7.*** *Consider the bilinear transformation*

$$w = \frac{iz + 2}{4z + i}$$

*Then,*

(a) the line $3y = x$ is mapped onto a straight line

(b) the line $3y = x$ is mapped onto the circle

(c) the line $3y = x$ is mapped onto the circle with centre at $\left(-\frac{3}{8}, -\frac{7}{8}\right)$

(d) the line $3y = x$ is mapped onto the circle with radius $\left(\frac{3}{4}\right)\sqrt{\frac{5}{2}}$

**Solution.** (b), (c), (d)

We have,

$$w = \frac{iz+2}{4z+i}$$

$$\Rightarrow \quad 4zw + iw = iz + 2$$

$$\Rightarrow \quad (4w - i)z = 2 - iw$$

$$\Rightarrow \quad z = \frac{2-iw}{4w-i}$$

Putting $z = x + iy$ and $w = u + iv$, we have

$$x + iy = \frac{v + 2 - iu}{4u + i(4v-1)}$$

$$= \frac{(v+2-iu)[4u - i(4v-1)]}{16u^2 + (4v-1)^2}$$

$$= \frac{9u - i(4u^2 + 4v^2 + 7v - 2)}{16u^2 + (4v-1)^2}$$

On comparing, we get

$$x = \frac{9u}{16u^2 + (4v-1)^2}, \; y = -\frac{4u^2 + 4v^2 + 7u - 2}{16u^2 + (4v-1)^2}$$

Putting these values of $x$ and $y$ in $3y = x$, we get

$$\frac{9u}{16u^2 + (4v-1)^2} = -\frac{3(4u^2 + 4v^2 + 7u - 2)}{16u^2 + (4v-1)^2}$$

$$\Rightarrow \quad u^2 + v^2 + \frac{3}{4}u + \frac{7}{4}v - \frac{1}{2} = 0$$

which is a equation of circle with centre $\left(-\frac{3}{8}, -\frac{7}{8}\right)$ and radius $\left(\frac{3}{4}\right)\sqrt{\frac{5}{2}}$.

***Example 8.*** *Every bilinear transformation maps*

(a) circles into circles
(b) circles into lines
(c) lines into lines
(d) lines into circles

**Solution.** (a), (b), (c), (d)

Let $T(z) = \dfrac{az+b}{cz+d}$, $ad - bc \neq c$, be any bilinear transformation.

If $c = 0$, then

$$T(z) = \frac{a}{d}z + \frac{b}{d} = Az + B,$$

where $A = \frac{a}{d}, B = \frac{b}{d}$

Clearly, $Az + B$, being linear, maps circles and lines into circles and lines (a line is a circle with infinite radius)

If $c \neq 0$, then

$$T(z) = \frac{a(z + d/c)}{c(z + d/c)} + \frac{b}{cz+d} - \frac{ad}{c(cz+d)}$$

$$= \frac{a}{c} + \frac{bc - ad}{c(cz+d)}$$

$$= \frac{a}{c} + \frac{bc - ad}{c^2} \cdot \frac{1}{z + d/c}$$

Putting $z_1 = z + \frac{d}{c}, z_2 = \frac{1}{z_1}$,

$$z_3 = \frac{bc - ad}{c^2} z_2,$$

we get

$$T(z) = \frac{a}{c} + z_3$$

which is of the form

$$w_1 = z + \alpha, w_2 = \frac{1}{z}, w_3 = \beta z$$

which shows that every bilinear transformation is the resultant of bilinear transformations with simple geometric imports. Thus, a bilinear transformation maps circle and lines into circles and lines.

***Example 9.*** *Consider the transformation from $\mathbb{C}_\infty \to \mathbb{C}$ given by*

$$T(z) = \begin{cases} \infty, z = \infty, c = 0 \\ a/c, \; z = \infty, c \neq 0 \\ \infty, \; z = -\dfrac{d}{c}, c \neq 0 \\ \dfrac{dz+b}{cz+d} \quad otherwise \end{cases}$$

*Then, which of the following(s) is/are true?*

(a) $T^{-1}$ is a bilinear transformation

(b) $T^{-1}$ is not a bilinear transformation

(c) $T^{-1}(z) = \dfrac{-dw+b}{cw-a}$

(d) None of the above

**Solution.** (a), (c)

Clearly, $T(z)$ is one-one and onto mapping from $\mathbb{C}_\infty$ to $\mathbb{C}$. Hence, $T^{-1}$ exists and is given by

$$w = T(z) \Leftrightarrow z = T^{-1}(w)$$

Solving $w = \dfrac{az+b}{cz+d}$

for $z$, we get

$$z = \frac{-dw+b}{cw-a}, \; ad - bc \neq 0$$

$$\therefore \quad T^{-1}(w) = \frac{-dw+b}{cw-a}$$

Again, for $T^{-1}(w)$, $ad - bc \neq 0$

Hence, $T^{-1}$ is bilinear transformation,

and $ad - bc \neq 0$

# Exercise 1 (For Part 'B')

**Directions** (Q. Nos. 1-65) *All questions have only one correct option.*

**1.** If $w = f(z)$ represents a conformal mapping of a domain $D$, then $f(z)$ is
(a) analytic in $D$
(b) not necessarily analytic in $D$
(c) not analytic in $D$
(d) None of the above

**2.** A translation of the type $w = \alpha z + \beta$, where $\alpha$ and $\beta$ are complex constants, is known as a
(a) translation (b) magnification
(c) linear transformation (d) bilinear transformation

**3.** The angle through which a curve drawn from the point $z_0 = i$ is rotated under the mapping $w = z^2$ is
(a) $\frac{\pi}{2}$ (b) $\pi$
(c) $\frac{\pi}{4}$ (d) None of these

**4.** Which of the following is a bilinear transformation?
(a) $w = \frac{2z+1}{4z+2}$ (b) $w = \frac{(2+3i)z+i}{-13iz+(2-3i)}$
(c) $w = z$ (d) $w = \frac{(1+i)z+1}{2z+(1-i)}$

**5.** The set of all bilinear transformations under the product of transformations forms
(a) a semi group (b) an abelian group
(c) a non-abelian group (d) None of these

**6.** The inverse of the point $z$ with respect to the circle $|z| = r$ is
(a) $\frac{r^2}{z}$ (b) $\frac{r^2}{\bar{z}}$
(c) $\frac{r}{\bar{z}}$ (d) None of these

**7.** By the transformation $w = ze^{i\pi/4}$, the line $x = 0$ is transformed into the line
(a) $v = -u$ (b) $v = u$
(c) $u + v = 1$ (d) $v = 0$

**8.** Under the transformation $w = z + 1 - i$, the image of the line $y = 0$ in the z-plane is
(a) $v = 1$ (b) $v = -1$
(c) $u = 1$ (d) $u = 0$

**9.** Critical points of $w = \frac{\alpha z + \beta}{\gamma z + \delta}, \alpha\delta - \beta\gamma \neq 0$ are
(a) $-\frac{\delta}{\gamma}$ (b) $-\frac{\delta}{\gamma}$ and $\infty$
(c) $-\frac{\delta}{\gamma}$ and 0 (d) None of these

**10.** The bilinear transformation which maps the points $z = 1, z = 0, z = -1$ of z-plane into $w = i, w = 0, w = -i$ of w-plane respectively is
(a) $w = iz$ (b) $w = z$
(c) $w = i(z+1)$ (d) None of these

**11.** Under the transformation $w = (1+i)z + 2 - i$, the line $x = 0$ is mapped into the line
(a) $u + v = 1$ (b) $v - u = 1$
(c) $u + 2v = 1$ (d) None of these

**12.** Under the transformation $w = \frac{1}{z}$, the image of the line $y = \frac{1}{4}$ in z-plane is
(a) circle $u^2 + v^2 + 4v = 0$
(b) circle $u^2 + v^2 = 4$
(c) circle $u^2 + v^2 = 2$
(d) None of the above

**13.** The analytic function which maps the annular region $0 \le \theta \le \pi/4$ onto the upper half plane is
(a) $z^2$ (b) $4z$
(c) $z^n$ (d) $2z$

**14.** An annular domain in the complex plane is defined by $0 <$ amp $(z) < \pi/4$. The mapping which maps this region onto the left half plane is
(a) $w = z^4$ (b) $w = iz^4$
(c) $w = -z^4$ (d) $w = -iz^4$

**15.** The mapping $w = z^2 - 2z - 3$ is
(a) conformal within $|z| = 1$
(b) not conformal at $z = 1$
(c) not conformal at $z = -1$ and $z = 3$
(d) conformal everywhere

**16.** If $z = re^{i\theta}$, then the image of $\theta$ = constant under the mapping $w(z) = Re^{i\phi} = iz^3$ is
(a) $\phi = 3\theta$ (b) $\phi = 3\theta + \pi/2$
(c) $\phi = 3\theta - \pi/2$ (d) $\phi = \theta^3$

**17.** The fixed points of the mapping $w = (5z+4)/(z+5)$ are
(a) 2, 2 (b) 2, $-2$
(c) $-2$, $-2$ (d) $-4/5$, 5

**18.** If $T_1(z) = \frac{z+2}{z+3}$ and $T_2(z) = \frac{z}{z+1}$, then $T_2T_1(z)$ is
(a) $z + 2$ (b) $\frac{2}{2z+5}$
(c) $\frac{z+2}{2z+5}$ (d) None of these

**19.** Point at which $f'(z) = 0$ is called as
(a) critical point of the transformation
(b) laplace transformation
(c) joukowski's transformation
(d) None of the above

**20.** The invariant points of the transformation $w = \frac{(z-1)}{(z+1)}$ are
(a) $z = i$ (b) $z = \pm i$
(c) $z = i/2$ (d) $z = -i/2$

**21.** If $\omega' = T_1(z) = \frac{z+2}{z+3}$, then $T_1^{-1}(z)$ is
(a) $\frac{2-3z}{z+1}$ (b) $\frac{2-3z}{z-1}$
(c) $\frac{1}{z+3}$ (d) None of these

**22.** The Mobius transformation maps the points $1-2i, 2+i, 2+3i$, respectively into $2+2i, 1+3i, 4$ is
(a) $\omega = \frac{i(1-z)}{1+z}$
(b) $\omega = \frac{1-z}{1+z}$
(c) $\omega = \frac{(20+18i)-(32+12i)z}{(29+17i)-(11-3i)z}$
(d) $\omega = \frac{(20+18i)+(32-12i)z}{(29+17i)-(11+3i)z}$

**23.** If $t_1, t_2, t_3, t_4$ be any four numbers, then their cross ratio is
(a) $\frac{(t_1-t_2)(t_3-t_4)}{(t_1-t_4)(t_3-t_2)}$ (b) $\frac{(t_1-t_2)(t_2-t_3)}{(t_3-t_4)(t_4-t_1)}$
(c) $\frac{(t_2-t_1)(t_4-t_1)}{(t_3-t_1)(t_1-t_2)}$ (d) $\frac{(t_3-t_1)(t_4-t_2)}{(t_3-t_2)(t_1-t_2)}$

**24.** A Mobius transformation maps circles into
(a) circles (b) hyperbola
(c) parabola (d) straight line

**25.** Condition of a conformal mapping is
(a) $J\left(\frac{u, v}{x, y}\right) = 0$ (b) $J\left(\frac{x, y}{u, v}\right) \neq 0$
(c) $J\left(\frac{u, v}{x, y}\right) \neq 0$ (d) $J\left(\frac{x, y}{u, v}\right) \neq 0$

**26.** If $T_1(z) = \frac{z+2}{z+3}$ and $T_2(z) = \frac{z}{z+1}$, then $T_2^{-1}T_1(z)$ is
(a) $z+3$ (b) $z+2$
(c) $z+6$ (d) $z-3$

**27.** If $T_1(z) = \frac{z+2}{z+3}$ and $T_2(z) = \frac{z}{z+1}$, then $T_1T_2(z)$ is equal to
(a) $\frac{3z+2}{4z+2}$ (b) $\frac{2}{2z+1}$
(c) $\frac{3z}{4z-2}$ (d) None of these

**28.** The Mobius transform takes
(a) circles into line (b) circle into line
(c) circle into square (d) None of these

**29.** For any point $z_1$, if $z_2, z_3, z_4$ are distinct points and $T$ is any Mobius transformation, then the cross ratio $(z_1, z_2, z_3, z_4)$ is equal to
(a) $(T_{z_2}, T_{z_2, z_3, z_4})$ (b) $(T_{z_2}, T_{z_2}, T_{z_3, z_4})$
(c) $(T_{z_2}, T_{z_2}, T_{z_3}, T_{z_4})$ (d) None of these

**30.** If $z_1 \neq z_2 \neq z_3 \neq z_4$ in $C_\infty$. Then, cross ratio $(z_1, z_2, z_3, z_4)$ is a real number if $z_1, z_2, z_3, z_4$ lies on
(a) triangle (b) a parabola
(c) a circle (d) a hyperbola

**31.** If $(z_1, z_2, z_3)$ is an orientation of $\Gamma$, then right side of $\Gamma$ with respect to $(z_1, z_2, z_3)$ is
(a) $\{z : \text{Im}(z, z_1, z_2, z_3) < 0\}$
(b) $\{z : \text{Im}(z, z_1, z_2, z_3) > 0\}$
(c) $\{z : \text{Re}(z, z_1, z_2, z_3) < 0\}$
(d) None of the above

**32.** If $(1, 0, \infty)$ is the orientation of R, then the cross ratio is
(a) $(z, 1, 0, \infty) = 1$ (b) $(z, 1, 0, \infty) = 0$
(c) $(z, 1, 0, \infty) = \infty$ (d) $(z, 1, 0, \infty) = z$

**33.** A mapping $S(z)$ is called linear functional transformation if
(a) $S(z) = \frac{az}{cz}$ (b) $S(z) = az$
(c) $S(z) = \frac{az+b}{cz+d}$ (d) None of these

**34.** $\Gamma$ is a circle through points $z_2, z_3$ and $z_4$. The points $z, z^* \in C_\infty$ are symmetric with respect to $\Gamma$, if
(a) $(z^*, z_2, z_3, z_4) = (z_1, z_2, z_3, z_4)$
(b) $(z^*, z_2, z_3, z_4) = (z, z_2, z_3, z_4)$
(c) $z^*, z_2 = z, z_3$
(d) None of the above

**35.** The transformation which maps the semi-infinite strip in the *w*-plane into the upper half of the *z*-plane is
(a) $z = \cosh \frac{\pi w}{b}$ (b) $z = \sinh \frac{\pi w}{a}$
(c) $z = \text{sech} \frac{\pi w}{b}$ (d) $z = \text{cosech} \frac{\pi w}{a}$

**36.** The mapping $f(z) = \bar{z}$ is
(a) conformal
(b) isogonal
(c) neither conformal nor isogonal
(d) analytic

**37.** The transformation $w = \frac{az+b}{cz+d}$ is said to be normalized, if $ad - bc$ is equal to
(a) 0 (b) 1
(c) 2 (d) 3

**38.** Under the mapping $w = z + 2 - i$, the image of line $y = 0$ is
(a) $\text{Im}(w) = 1$ (b) $\text{Im}(w) = -1$
(c) $\text{Re}(w) = 1$ (d) $\text{Re}(w) = -1$

**39.** The angle through which a curve drawn from the point $1+i$ is rotated under the mapping $f(z) = z^2$ is
(a) $\frac{\pi}{6}$ (b) $\frac{\pi}{4}$
(c) $\frac{\pi}{3}$ (d) $\frac{\pi}{2}$

**40.** By the transformation $w = ze^{i\frac{\pi}{3}}$, the line $y = 0$ in the z-plane is transformed into the line
(a) $v = \sqrt{3}u$ (b) $u = \sqrt{3}v$
(c) $u + \sqrt{3}v = 0$ (d) $v + \sqrt{3}u = 0$

**41.** Let $f = u(x, y) + iv(x, y)$ and $g = u(x, y) + iv(x, y)$ be non-zero analytic functions on $|z| < 1$. Then, it follows that
(a) $f' \equiv 0$ (b) $f$ is conformal on $|z| < 1$
(c) $f \equiv kg$ for some real $k$ (d) $f$ is one-to-one

**42.** The function $f(z) = z^2$ maps the first quadrant onto
(a) itself (b) upper half plane
(c) third quadrant (d) right half plane

**43.** An example of a map which is conformal in the whole of its domain of definition is
(a) $f(z) = z^2$ (b) $f(z) = e^{z+2}$
(c) $f(z) = \cos z$ (d) $f(z) = e^{z^2}$

**44.** The bilinear transformation $w = 2z/(z-2)$ maps $\{z : |z-1| < 1\}$ onto
(a) $\{w : \text{Re}(w) < 0\}$ (b) $\{w : \text{Im}(w) > 0\}$
(c) $\{w : \text{Re}(w) > 0\}$ (d) $\{w : |w+2| < 1\}$

**45.** If $f(z) = (z-2)^3 g(z)$, where $g(z)$ is analytic in $|z-2| < r$ and $g(2) \neq 0$, if angle at the vertex $z = 2$ is $\pi/3$, then the angle at $f(2)$ is
(a) $\frac{2\pi}{3}$ (b) $\pi$
(c) $\frac{\pi}{2}$ (d) $\frac{\pi}{3}$

**46.** The transformation $\omega = e^{i\theta}\left(\frac{z-p}{\bar{p}z-1}\right)$ where $p$ is a constant, maps, $|z| < 1$ onto
(a) $|\omega| < 1$, if $|p| < 1$ (b) $|\omega| > 1$, if $|p| > 1$
(c) $|\omega| = 1$, if $|p| = 1$ (d) $|\omega| = 3$, if $|p| = 0$

**47.** The cross ratio of the four points $(z_1, z_2, z_3, z_4)$ is real if and only if the four points, lie on a
(a) circle
(b) straight line
(c) circle and on a straight line
(d) circle or on a straight line

**48.** The fixed points of $f(z) = \frac{2iz+5}{z-2i}$ are
(a) $1 \pm i$ (b) $1 \pm 2i$
(c) $2i \pm 1$ (d) $i \pm 1$

**49.** A Mobius transformation which transforms the upper half plane onto the lower half plane is
(a) $w = \bar{z}$ (b) $w = \frac{z-i}{z+i}$
(c) $w = \frac{1}{z}$ (d) $w = \frac{z+i}{z-i}$

**50.** Bilinear transformation, which maps the half plane $\text{Im}(z) \geq 0$ onto the circular disc $|w| \leq 1$, is
(a) $w = e^{i\lambda}\left(\frac{z-\alpha}{z-\bar{\alpha}}\right)$ (b) $w = e^{i\lambda}\left(\frac{z-\alpha}{z+\bar{\alpha}}\right)$
(c) $w = e^{i\lambda}\left(\frac{z-\alpha}{\bar{\alpha}z-1}\right)$ (d) None of these

**51.** The image of $x$ = constant under the transformation $w = \sin z$ is
(a) a parabola (b) a hyperbola
(c) a circle (d) an ellipse

**52.** A bilinear transformation $w = \frac{az+b}{cz+d}$ having only one fixed point is called
(a) loxodromic (b) elliptic
(c) parabolic (d) hyperbolic

**53.** If the cross ratio $(z_1, z_2, z_3, z_4)$ is real. Then,
(a) $z_1, z_2$ and $z_3$ are collinear
(b) $z_1, z_2$ and $z_3$ are concyclic
(c) $z_1, z_2$ and $z_3$ are collinear, when atleast one $z_1, z_2$ or $z_3$ is real
(d) $z_1, z_2$ and $z_3$ are concyclic, when atleast one of $z_1, z_2$ or $z_3$ is real

**54.** Transformation $w = \frac{az+b}{cz+d}$ transforms the unit circle in the $w$-plane into straight line in the z-plane, if
(a) $\frac{az+b}{cz+d}$ (b) $|a| = |c|$
(c) $bc + ad = 0$ (d) $bc - ad = 0$

**55.** The magnification factor of the conformal mapping $w = \sqrt{2}e^{\pi i/4}z + (1-2i)$ is
(a) 1 (b) 2
(c) 3 (d) $\sqrt{2}$

**56.** If a bilinear transformation $w = \frac{az+b}{cz+d}$ which has one fixed point at $\alpha$ and the other fixed point $\infty$, has the form $w - \alpha = \lambda(z-\alpha)$, then $\lambda$ equal to
(a) $\frac{d}{a}$ (b) $\frac{c}{b}$
(c) $\frac{a}{d}$ (d) $\frac{b}{c}$

**57.** Let $f(z) = (z-z_0)^{100}e^z$, then the mapping $w = f(z)$ magnifies the angle at the vertex $z_0$ by the factor $k$, where $k$ is
(a) 1 (b) 100
(c) 101 (d) 0

**58.** A linear transformation which takes the triangle $\Delta(z) = (0, 1, i)$ in the z-plane into the triangle $\Delta(w) = (-1, -i, i)$ in the w-plane is

(a) $W = (1-i)z - 1$ (b) $W = (1+i)z - 1$
(c) $W = (1-i)z + 1$ (d) $W = (1+i)z + 1$

**59.** Which of the following transformation is not conformal in a unit disc centered at origin

(a) $e^{\sin z}$ (b) $e^{\log z}$
(c) $e^{\sin z^2}$ (d) $e^{\tan z}$

**60.** The non-constant transformation $w = \bar{z}$ is

(a) both isogonal and conformal
(b) isogonal but not conformal
(c) conformal but not isogonal
(d) neither isogonal nor conformal

**61.** A transformation $w = \dfrac{5-4z}{4z-2}$ transforms the circle $|z| = 1$ into a circle (in w-plane) whose centre is

(a) $\left(\frac{1}{2}, 0\right)$ (b) $\left(-\frac{1}{2}, \frac{1}{2}\right)$
(c) $\left(-\frac{1}{2}, 0\right)$ (d) $\left(\frac{1}{2}, -\frac{1}{2}\right)$

**62.** The bilinear transformation that maps the points $z_1 = 2, z_2 = i, z_3 = -2$ into the points $w_1 = 1, w_2 = i, w_3 = -1$ is

(a) $w = \dfrac{3z - 2i}{iz - 6}$ (b) $w = \dfrac{3z - 2i}{iz + 6}$
(c) $w = \dfrac{3z + 2i}{iz - 6}$ (d) $w = \dfrac{3z + 2i}{iz + 6}$

**63.** Transformation $w = z^{1/\alpha}$ maps

(a) half planes into circles
(b) wedges or sectors into half planes
(c) half planes into confocal hyperbolas
(d) None of the above

**64.** Critical points of the transformation $w = \dfrac{1}{2}\left(z + \dfrac{1}{z}\right)$ are

(a) $-\infty, 0$ (b) $0, \infty$
(c) $\pm 1$ (d) $\pm\infty$

**65.** Which of the following is not correct, if $f(z)$ is conformal at $z_0$?

(a) $f(z)$ is analytic at $z_0$
(b) $f(z)$ has local inverse at $z_0$
(c) $z_0$ is critical point of $f(z)$
(d) None of the above

# Exercise 2 (For Part 'C')

**Directions** (Q. Nos. 1-23) *Questions may have one or more than one correct option.*

**1.** Mobius transformation is also called

(a) bilinear transformation
(b) linear transformation
(c) linear fractional transformation
(d) bilinear fractional transformation

**2.** Let the transformation $f(z) = u(x, y) + iv(x, y)$ is conformal, then

(a) $|f'(z)| \neq 0$
(b) $\left|\dfrac{\partial(u, v)}{\partial(x, y)}\right| = 0$
(c) $\left|\dfrac{\partial(u, v)}{\partial(x, y)}\right| \neq 0$
(d) $f(z)$ is not necessarily analytic

**3.** Transformation $f(z) = \dfrac{1}{z}$ maps

(a) $|z| < 1$ onto $|f(z)| > 1$ (b) $|z| < 1$ onto $|f(z)| < 1$
(c) $|z| > 1$ onto $|f(z)| > 1$ (d) $|z| > 1$ onto $|f(z)| < 1$

**4.** Transformation $f(z) = \dfrac{1}{z}$

(a) always maps a circle into a circle
(b) always maps a circle into straight line
(c) maps circle into straight line if circle in z-plane passes through origin
(d) maps straight line into circle

**5.** Consider transformation

$$f(x + iy) = (x + iy)^2 = u + iv,$$

then following/s is/are hold,

(a) $f$ maps $x > 0$ to $u > 0$ (b) $f$ maps $y > 0$ to $v > 0$
(c) $f$ maps $y > 0$ to $u < 0$ (d) under the mapping $f$, angles at the origin are doubled

**6.** Any linear transformation maps

(a) straight lines to straight lines
(b) straight lines to circle
(c) circles to circles
(d) circles to straight lines

**7.** Consider any bilinear transformation

$$w = \frac{az + b}{cz + d} (ad - bc \neq 0), \quad \text{where } \Delta = (d - a)^2 + 4bc,$$

then

(a) only one finite fixed point, if $c \neq 0$ and $\Delta \neq 0$
(b) two finite fixed point, if $c \neq 0$ and $\Delta \neq 0$
(c) one finite and other infinite fixed points, if $c \neq 0$ and $a \neq d$
(d) only one infinite fixed point, if $c = 0$ and $a \neq d$

**8.** For the transformation $w = \dfrac{z}{2 - z}$

(a) fixed points are 0 and 2
(b) fixed points are 0 and 1
(c) transformation is parabolic
(d) transformation is hyperbolic

**9.** Which of the following(s) is/are true?

(a) Every bilinear transformation can be expressed as the resultant of translation, dialation and rotation.

(b) Every bilinear transformation can be expressed as the resultant of an even number of inversions.

(c) The set of all bilinear transformations forms a abelian group under the product of transformation.

(d) The set of all bilinear transformations forms a non-abelian group under the product of transformations.

**10.** Let $w_i = T(z_i) = \dfrac{(z_i - z_2)(z_3 - z_4)}{(z_2 - z_3)(z_4 - z_i)}$ and $(z_1, z_2, z_3, z_4)$ denotes the cross ratio of four distinct points $z_1, z_2, z_3$ and $z_4$, then which of the following(s) is/are true?

(a) $T(z_1) = (z_1, z_2, z_3, z_4)$

(b) $(z_1, z_2, z_3, z_4) = (w_1, w_2, w_3, w_4)$

(c) $T(z_1)$ is real, then $z_1, z_2, z_3, z_4$ are concyclic

(d) $z_1$ is real, then $w_1, w_2, w_3, w_4$ are concyclic

**11.** Define

$$H^+ = \{z \in C : y > 0\}$$
$$H^- = \{z \in C : y < 0\}$$
$$L^+ = \{z \in C : x > 0\}$$
$$L^- = \{z \in C : x < 0\}$$

the function $f(z) = \dfrac{z}{3z+1}$

(a) maps $H^+$ onto $H^+$ and $H^-$ onto $H^-$

(b) maps $H^+$ onto $H^-$ and $H^-$ onto $H^+$

(c) maps $H^+$ onto $L^+$ and $H^-$ onto $L^-$

(d) maps $H^+$ onto $L^-$ and $H^-$ onto $L^+$

**12.** If $w_1, w_2, w_3$ and $w_4$ is the images of the four distinct points $z_1, z_2, z_3$ and $z_4$ in the z-plane under a bilinear transformation, then

(a) $(w_1, w_2, w_3, w_4) = (z_1, z_2, z_3, z_4)$

(b) $(w_1, w_2, w_3, w_4) = (z_1, z_3, z_4, z_2)$

(c) $\dfrac{(w_1 - w_2)(w_3 - w_4)}{(w_2 - w_3)(w_4 - w_1)} = \dfrac{(z_1 - z_2)(z_3 - z_4)}{(z_2 - z_3)(z_4 - z_1)}$

(d) $(w_1, w_2, w_3, w_4) = (0, 0, 0, 0)$

**13.** Given, the transformation $w = \dfrac{iz+2}{4z+i}$

(a) it maps the real axis in the z-plane into a circle in the w-plane

(b) it does not maps the real axis in the z-plane into a circle in the w-plane

(c) it maps the real axis in the z-plane into a parabola in the w-plane

(d) it maps the real axis in the z-plane into a square in the w-plane

**14.** Given, $w = \dfrac{5-4z}{4z-2}$

(a) it transform circle $|z| = 1$ into circle of radius unity in w-plane

(b) it transform circle $|z| = 1$ into parabola in w-plane

(c) it transform circle $|z| = 1$ into square in w-plane

(d) it transform circle $|z| = 1$ into rectangle in w-plane

**15.** Which of the following statement(s) is/are true?

(a) the transformations $w = \dfrac{z+i}{z-i}$ transform $|w| \le 1$ into lower half of the plane $I(z) \le 0$

(b) the transformations $w = \dfrac{i+z}{i-z}$ transform $|w| \le 1$ into lower half of the plane $I(z) \le 0$

(c) the transformations $w = \dfrac{z+i}{z-i}$ and $w = \dfrac{i+z}{i-z}$ transform $|w| \le 1$ into the lower half plane $I(z) \le 0$

(d) for the transformation $w = \dfrac{z+i}{z-i}$ and $w = \dfrac{i+z}{i-z}$, $|w|^2 - 1 \le 0$

**16.** Consider the bilinear transformation from $\mathbb{C}_\infty$ to $\mathbb{C}$

$$T(z) = \begin{cases} \infty, \; z = \infty, \; c = 0 \\ \dfrac{a}{c}, \; z = \infty, \; c \neq 0 \\ \infty, \; z = -\dfrac{d}{c}, \; c \neq 0 \\ \dfrac{(az+b)}{(cz+d)}, \quad \text{otherwise} \end{cases}$$

Then,

(a) $T$ is one-one

(b) $T$ is onto

(c) Inverse of $T$ i.e., $T^{-1}$ is a bilinear transformation

(d) None of the above

**17.** Consider the transformation $w = \sin z$. Then,

(a) the rectangle $-\pi < x < \pi$, $c < y < d$ maps onto the elliptic ring cut along the negative v-axis

(b) the straight lines $x =$ constant map onto confocal hyperbola

(c) Both (a) and (b) is true

(d) Neither (a) nor (b) is true

**18.** Consider the transformation $w = f(z) = \dfrac{e^z - i}{e^z + i}$. Then,

(a) $w$ is one-one conformal mapping of the horizontal strip $0 < y < \pi$ onto the disc $|w| < 1$

(b) x-axis is mapped onto the lower semi-circle bounding the disc

(c) the line $y = \pi$ is mapped onto the upper semi-circle

(d) None of the above

**19.** Which of the following(s) is/are true?

(a) composite of two bilinear transformations is bilinear

(b) every bilinear transformation (except identity map) has at most two fixed points

(c) Both (a) and (b) are true

(d) Neither (a) nor (b) is true

**20.** Which of the following(s) is/are correct?

(a) The cross ratio is invarient under bilinear transformation

(b) The bilinear transformation, which maps $-1, 0, 1$ onto $0, i, 3i$ is $w = -\frac{3i(z+1)}{z-3}$

(c) Both (a) and (b) are true

(d) Neither (a) nor (b) is true

**21.** The bilinear transformation which maps the points $z_1 = 2, z_2 = i$ and $z_3 = -2$ into the points $w_1 = 1, w_2 = i$ and $w_3 = -1$ respectively, is

(a) $w = \frac{3z+2i}{iz+6}$

(b) $w = 0$

(c) $w = iz$

(d) $w = z^2/2$

**22.** The bilinear transformation which maps the points $z = 1, i, -1$ onto the points $w = i, 0, -i$ is

(a) $z = i\frac{1-w}{1+w}$ (b) $z = i\frac{1+w}{1-w}$

(c) $z = i^2$ (d) $z = 1-w$

**23.** Which of the following(s) is/are correct?

(a) The bilinear transformation $w = \frac{-iz+4i}{z}$ maps the crescent-shaped region that lies inside the circle $|z-2|<2$ and outside the circle $|z-1|>1$ onto a horizontal strip in the upper half plane

(b) The transformation $w = \frac{z-1}{z+1}$ maps $x>0$ and the boundary $x=0$ on $|w|\le 1$

(c) Let $w = \frac{i(1-z)}{1+z}$, then $\text{Im}(z)<1 \Rightarrow \text{Im}(w)>0$

(d) None of the above

# Answers

## Exercise 1

| | | | | | | | | | |
|---|---|---|---|---|---|---|---|---|---|
| **1.** (a) | **2.** (c) | **3.** (a) | **4.** (c) | **5.** (c) | **6.** (b) | **7.** (a) | **8.** (b) | **9.** (b) | **10.** (a) |
| **11.** (a) | **12.** (a) | **13.** (c) | **14.** (b) | **15.** (b) | **16.** (b) | **17.** (b) | **18.** (c) | **19.** (a) | **20.** (b) |
| **21.** (b) | **22.** (c) | **23.** (a) | **24.** (a) | **25.** (c) | **26.** (b) | **27.** (a) | **28.** (b) | **29.** (c) | **30.** (c) |
| **31.** (b) | **32.** (d) | **33.** (c) | **34.** (b) | **35.** (a) | **36.** (b) | **37.** (b) | **38.** (b) | **39.** (b) | **40.** (a) |
| **41.** (a) | **42.** (b) | **43.** (b) | **44.** (a) | **45.** (b) | **46.** (a) | **47.** (d) | **48.** (c) | **49.** (c) | **50.** (a) |
| **51.** (b) | **52.** (c) | **53.** (a) | **54.** (b) | **55.** (b) | **56.** (c) | **57.** (b) | **58.** (a) | **59.** (c) | **60.** (b) |
| **61.** (c) | **62.** (d) | **63.** (b) | **64.** (c) | **65.** (c) | | | | | |

## Exercise 2

| | | | | | | | | | |
|---|---|---|---|---|---|---|---|---|---|
| **1.** (a,c) | **2.** (a,c) | **3.** (a,d) | **4.** (a,c) | **5.** (a,c,d) | **6.** (a,b,c) | **7.** (b) | **8.** (b,d) | **9.** (a,b,d) | **10.** (a,b,c) |
| **11.** (a) | **12.** (a,c) | **13.** (a) | **14.** (a) | **15.** (a,b,c,d) | **16.** (a,b,c) | **17.** (a,b,c) | **18.** (a,b,c) | **19.** (a,b,c) | **20.** (a,b,c) |
| **21.** (a) | **22.** (a) | **23.** (a,b,c) | | | | | | | |

# Hints & Solutions

## Exercise 1

**7.** Given, $w = ze^{i\pi/4} \Rightarrow z = we^{-i\pi/4}$

$$\Rightarrow \quad x+iy = (u+iv)\left(\frac{1-i}{\sqrt{2}}\right)$$

$$= \frac{1}{\sqrt{2}}(u-iu+iv+v)$$

$$= \frac{1}{\sqrt{2}}[(u+v)+i(v-u)]$$

Equating real and imaginary parts from both sides, we get

$$x = \frac{u+v}{\sqrt{2}}$$

Now, $x = 0 \Rightarrow u+v=0 \Rightarrow v=-u$

**9.** We have, $w = \frac{\alpha z+\beta}{\gamma z+\delta}$

$$\Rightarrow \quad \frac{dw}{dz} = \frac{(\gamma z+\delta).\alpha-(\alpha z+\beta).\gamma}{(\gamma z+\delta)^2}$$

$$\Rightarrow \quad \frac{dw}{dz} = \frac{\alpha\delta-\beta\gamma}{(\gamma z+\delta)^2}$$

Now, critical points are those values of $z$ for which either $\frac{dw}{dz} = 0$ or $\infty$

$$\Rightarrow \quad z=\infty \text{ or } z = -\frac{\delta}{\gamma}$$

**10.** Required transformation is given by

$$\frac{(w-w_1)(w_2-w_3)}{(w_1-w_2)(w_3-w)}=\frac{(z-z_1)(z_2-z_3)}{(z_1-z_2)(z_3-z)}$$

$$\Rightarrow \quad \frac{(w-i)(0+i)}{(i-0)(-i-w)}=\frac{(z-1)(0+1)}{(1-0)(-1-z)}$$

$$\Rightarrow \quad \frac{w-i}{-w-i}=\frac{z-1}{-z-1}$$

$$\Rightarrow \quad \frac{w-i}{w+i}=\frac{z-1}{z+1}$$

Using componendo and dividendo, we get

$$\frac{w-i+w+i}{w-i-w-i}=\frac{z-1+z+1}{z-1-z-1}$$

$$\Rightarrow \quad \frac{2w}{-2i}=\frac{2z}{-2} \quad \Rightarrow \quad iw=-z$$

$$\Rightarrow \quad w=-\frac{1}{i}z \quad \Rightarrow \quad w=iz$$

**13.** $f(z)=z^n$ maps annular region $0\le \arg(z)\le \frac{\pi}{n}$ onto upper half plane and $f(z)=iz^n$ maps onto lower half plane.

**15.** $$\frac{dw}{dz}=2z-2=0 \quad \Rightarrow \quad z=1$$

For conformal mapping $\frac{dw}{dz}\neq 0$

$$\Rightarrow \quad z=1$$

## Exercise 2

**3.** Transformation $f(z)=\frac{1}{z}$ maps interior of circle in z-plane onto exterior of circle in $f(z)$-plane and exterior of circle in z-plane onto interior of circle in $f(z)$-plane.

**4.** Transformation $f(z)=\frac{1}{z}$ always maps a circle into a circle and into straight line as a particular case.

**5.** We have, $(re^{i\theta})^2=Re^{i\phi} \quad \Rightarrow \quad r^2=R,\ e^{i2\theta}=e^{i\phi}$

$$r^2e^{i2\theta}=R\cos\phi+iR\sin\phi$$

$$\Rightarrow \quad x=r^2\cos 2\theta,\quad u=R\cos\phi=R\cos 2\theta$$

$$\Rightarrow \quad y=r^2\sin 2\theta$$

**8.** For fixed point, $\frac{z}{2-z}=z$

$$\Rightarrow \quad z=2z-z^2$$

$$\Rightarrow \quad z^2-z=0 \quad \Rightarrow \quad z(z-1)=0$$

$$\Rightarrow \quad z=0,1$$

$\therefore$ Fixed points are 0 and 1.

Since, fixed points are both finite and distinct, therefore transformation is hyperbola.

**10.** Since, $\frac{(z_1-z_2)(z_3-z_4)}{(z_2-z_3)(z_4-z_1)}$ is the cross ratio of four distinct points $z_1$, $z_2$, $z_3$ and $z_4$

$$\Rightarrow \quad T(z_1)=(z_1,z_2,z_3,z_4)$$

Also, from preservance of cross ratio under bilinear transformation

$$(z_1,z_2,z_3,z_4)=(w_1,w_2,w_3,w_4)$$

**16.** We have,

$$Re^{i\phi}=iz^3=ir^3e^{i3\theta}=e^{i\pi/2}\cdot r^3\cdot e^{i3\theta}=r^3e^{i(3\theta+\pi/2)}$$

$$\Rightarrow \quad \phi=3\theta+\frac{\pi}{2}$$

**17.** For, fixed points $f(z)=z$

$$\Rightarrow \quad \frac{5z+4}{z+5}=z \quad \Rightarrow \quad 5z+4=z^2+5z$$

$$\Rightarrow \quad z^2=4 \quad \Rightarrow \quad z=\pm 2$$

**18.** We have, $$T_2T_1(z)=T_2\left(\frac{z+2}{z+3}\right)=\frac{\frac{z+2}{z+3}}{\frac{z+2}{z+3}+1}=\frac{z+2}{2z+5}$$

**21.** We have, $$w=\frac{z+2}{z+3}=T(z)$$

$$\Rightarrow \quad z+2=wz+3w$$

$$\Rightarrow \quad z(1-w)=3w-2$$

$$\Rightarrow \quad z=\frac{3w-2}{1-w}=\frac{2-3w}{w-1}$$

$$\Rightarrow \quad T^{-1}(w)=\frac{2-3w}{w-1} \Rightarrow T^{-1}(z)=\frac{2-3z}{z-1}$$

**30.** Cross ratio is a real, if points lies on circle or straight line.

**36.** $f(z)=\bar{z}$ preserves the magnitude of the angles only not the sense, hence it is isogonal.

**11.** Let $z=x+iy$

$$\Rightarrow \quad f(z)=\frac{z}{3z+1}=\frac{x+iy}{3x+1+3iy}$$

$$=\frac{(x+iy)(3x+1-i3y)}{(3x+1)^2+9y^2}$$

$$=\frac{3x^2+x+3y^2+i3xy+iy-i3xy}{(3x+1)^2+9y^2}$$

$$=\frac{3x^2+3y^2+x}{(3x+1)^2+9y^2}+i\frac{y}{(3x+1)^2+9y^2}$$

$$=u+iv$$

Clearly, $u>0$ for all $x, y\in R-\{0\}$ and $v>0$ or $<0$ as $y>0$ or $<0$ respectively.

$\Rightarrow$ $f(z)$ maps $H^+$ onto $H^+$ and $H^-$ onto $H^-$.

**12.** Let the bilinear transformation be

$$w=T(z)=\frac{az+b}{cz+d}\ (ad-bc\neq 0) \quad \text{...(i)}$$

Since, $w_1, w_2, w_3, w_4$ are the images of $z_1, z_2, z_3, z_4$ respectively, we have

$$w_1=\frac{az_1+b}{cz_1+d},\ w_2=\frac{az_2+b}{cz_2+d}$$

$$\Rightarrow \quad w_1-w_2=\frac{(ad-bc)(z_1-z_2)}{(cz_1+d)(cz_2+d)}$$

Similarly, we have

$$w_2 - w_3 = \frac{(ad-bc)(z_2-z_3)}{(cz_2+d)(cz_3+d)}$$

$$w_3 - w_4 = \frac{(ad-bc)(z_3-z_4)}{(cz_3+d)(cz_4+d)}$$

$$w_4 - w_1 = \frac{(ad-bc)(z_4-z_1)}{(cz_4+d)(cz_1+d)}$$

$$\Rightarrow \frac{(w_1-w_2)(w_3-w_4)}{(w_2-w_3)(w_4-w_1)} = \frac{(z_1-z_2)(z_3-z_4)}{(z_2-z_3)(z_4-z_1)}$$

$$\Rightarrow (w_1, w_2, w_3, w_4) = (z_1, z_2, z_3, z_4)$$

**13.** The given transformation

$$w = \frac{iz+2}{4z+i} \Rightarrow z = \frac{2-iw}{4w-i}$$

The equation of the real axis in the $z$-plane is $z-\bar{z}=0$. substituting for $z$ and $\bar{z}$ the transformed equation is

$$\frac{2-iw}{4w-i} - \frac{2-i\bar{w}}{4\bar{w}+i} = 0$$

$$\Rightarrow 8\bar{w}+2i-4iw\bar{w}+w-8w+2i-4iw\bar{w}-\bar{w}=0$$

$$\Rightarrow 8iw\bar{w}+7(w-\bar{w})-4i=0$$

$$\Rightarrow 8i(u^2+v^2)+14iv-4i=0$$

$$\Rightarrow u^2+v^2+\frac{7}{4}v-\frac{1}{2}=0$$

which is the equation of a circle in the $w$-plane.

**14.** The given transformation is

$$w = \frac{5-4z}{4z-2} \Rightarrow z = \frac{2w+5}{4w+4}$$

The equation of the circle is $|z|=1$

$$\Rightarrow z\bar{z}=1$$

Hence, the transformed equation is

$$\Rightarrow \frac{2w+5}{4w+4}\cdot\frac{2\bar{w}+5}{4\bar{w}+4}=1$$

$$\Rightarrow 4w\bar{w}+10w+10\bar{w}+25=16w\bar{w}+16w+16\bar{w}+16$$

$$\Rightarrow 12w\bar{w}+6(w+\bar{w})-9=0$$

$$\Rightarrow 4w\bar{w}+2(w+\bar{w})-3=0$$

$$\Rightarrow 4(u^2+v^2)+4u-3=0$$

$$\Rightarrow u^2+v^2+u-\frac{3}{4}=0$$

which is the equation of a circle in the $w$-plane.

**15.** Here,

$$w = \frac{z+i}{z-i} \Rightarrow \bar{w} = \frac{\bar{z}-i}{\bar{z}+i}$$

$$\therefore \quad w\bar{w}-1 = \frac{z+i}{z-i}\cdot\frac{\bar{z}-i}{\bar{z}+i}-1$$

$$= \frac{(z+i)(\bar{z}-i)-(z-i)(\bar{z}+i)}{(z-i)(\bar{z}+i)}$$

$$= \frac{-2i(z-\bar{z})}{|z-i|^2} = \frac{4I(z)}{|z-i|^2} \qquad [\because z-\bar{z}=2iI(z)]$$

Taking $w = \dfrac{i+z}{i-z}$, we have $w = \bar{w}-1$

Hence, for both the transformations

$|w|^2-1 \le 0$ *i.e.*, $|w| \le 1$ gives $I(z) \le 0$

*i.e.*, the boundary of the circle $|w|=1$ corresponds to the real axis in the $z$-plane and the interior of the circle transforms into the lower half $z$-plane.

**19.** Let $T(z)$ and $S(z)$ be two bilinear transformations defined by

$$T(z) = \frac{az+b}{cz+d}, \; ad-bc \ne 0$$

and
$$S(z) = \frac{pz+q}{rz+s}, \; ps-qr \ne 0$$

Consider the composition

$$(ST)(z) = S(T(z)) = S\left(\frac{az+b}{cz+d}\right)$$

$$= \frac{p[(az+b)/(cz+d)]+q}{r[(az+b)/(cz+d)]+s}$$

$$= \frac{paz+bp+qcz+qd}{raz+rb+scz+sd}$$

$$= \frac{(pa+qc)z+bp+dq}{(ar+cs)z+br+ds}$$

Now,

$$(pa+qc)(br+ds)-(bp+dq)(ar+cs)$$

$$=(ad-bc)ps-(ad-bc)rq$$

$$=(ad-bc)(ps-qr)\ne 0$$

Therefore, $(ST)$ is a bilinear transformation. Similarly, $(TS)$ is also bilinear transformation.

Hence, the composition of two linear fractional transformations in either way is bilinear transformation.

Next, if $T(z)$ has a fixed point $z$.

Then,
$$T(z)=z$$

$$\Rightarrow \frac{az+b}{cz+d}=z$$

$$\Rightarrow cz^2+dz=az+b$$

$$\Rightarrow cz^2-(a-d)z-b=0$$

which is quadratic equation in $z$ and hence can have atmost two roots. Hence, every bilinear transformation has atmost two fixed points.

**20.** Let $w=T(z)$ be a bilinear transformation given by

$$w=T(z)=\frac{az+b}{cz+d}, \; ad-bc=1$$

such that

$$w_k = T(z_k), \; k=1,2,3$$

Then, we have to show that

$$(T(z), T(z_1), T(z_2), T(z_3)) = (z, z_1, z_2, z_3) \qquad \text{...(i)}$$

Since, $z_k$ corresponds to $w_k$, assuming $ad-bc=1$, we have

$$w-w_k = \frac{z-z_k}{(cz_k+d)(cz+d)}$$

Hence, for any pair of $(z, w)$

$$w-w_1 = \frac{z-z_1}{(cz_1+d)(cz+d)}, \; w-w_3 = \frac{z-z_3}{(cz_3+d)(cz+d)} \qquad \text{...(ii)}$$

Replacing $w$ by $w_2$ and $z$ by $z_2$, we have

$$w_2-w_1 = \frac{z_2-z_1}{(cz_1+d)(cz_2+d)},$$

$$w_2 - w_3 = \frac{z_2 - z_3}{(cz_3 + d)(cz_2 + d)} \quad \text{...(iii)}$$

From Eqs. (ii) and (iii), we have

$$\left(\frac{w - w_1}{w_2 - w_3}\right)\left(\frac{w_1 - w_2}{w_3 - w}\right) = \left(\frac{z - z_1}{z_2 - z_3}\right)\left(\frac{z_1 - z_2}{z_3 - z}\right)$$

$$\Rightarrow \quad (w, w_1, w_2, w_3) = (z, z_1, z_2, z_3)$$

$$\Rightarrow (T(z), T(z_1), T(z_2), T(z_3)) = (z, z_1, z_2, z_3)$$

Hence, the cross ratio is invariant under the bilinear transformation.

Next, we have

$$\frac{(w - 0)(i - 3i)}{(0 - i)(3i - w)} = \frac{(z + 1)(0 - 1)}{(-1 - 0)(1 - z)}$$

$$\Rightarrow \quad w = -\frac{3i(z + 1)}{z - 3}$$

which is required bilinear transformation.

**21.** The bilinear transformation which transforms $z_1, z_2, z_3$, respectively into $w_1, w_2, w_3$ is given by

$$\frac{(w - w_1)(w_2 - w_3)}{(w_1 - w_2)(w_3 - w)} = \frac{(z - z_1)(z_2 - z_3)}{(z_1 - z_2)(z_3 - z)}$$

Substituting $z_1 = 2$, $z_2 = i$, $z_3 = -2$; $w_1 = 1$, $w_2 = i$, $w_3 = -1$, we have

$$\frac{(w - 1)(i + 1)}{(1 - i)(-1 - w)} = \frac{(z - 2)(i + 2)}{(2 - i)(-2 - z)}$$

$$\Rightarrow \quad -\frac{(w - 1)(1 + i)^2}{(w + 1)(1 - i)(1 + i)} = -\frac{(z - 2)(2 + i)^2}{(z + 2)(2 - i)(2 + i)}$$

$$\Rightarrow \quad \frac{(w - 1)\cdot 2i}{(w + 1)\cdot 2} = \frac{(z - 2)(3 + 4i)}{(z + 2)\cdot 5}$$

$$\Rightarrow \quad \frac{w - 1}{w + 1} = \frac{(z - 2)(4 - 3i)}{5(z + 2)}$$

$$\Rightarrow \quad \frac{2w}{2} = \frac{(z - 2)(4 - 3i) + 5(z + 2)}{5(z + 2) - (z - 2)(4 - 3i)}$$

$$\Rightarrow \quad w = \frac{3(3 - i)z + 2(1 + 3i)}{(1 + 3i)z + 6(3 - i)} = \frac{3z + [2(1 + 3i)/(3 - i)]}{[(1 + 3i)/(3 - i)]z + 6}$$

$$\Rightarrow \quad w = \frac{3z + 2i}{iz + 6}$$

The required transformation.

**22.** Let the points $z_1 = 1$, $z_2 = i$, $z_3 = -1$ and $z_4 = z$ map onto the points $w_1 = i$, $w_2 = 0$, $w_3 = -i$ and $w_4 = w$.

Since, the cross ratio remains unchanged under a bilinear transformation.

$$\therefore \quad \frac{(1 - i)(-1 - z)}{(1 - z)(-1 - i)} = \frac{(i - 0)(-i - w)}{(i - w)(-i - 0)}$$

$$\Rightarrow \quad \frac{w + i}{w - i} = \frac{(z + 1)(1 - i)}{(z - 1)(1 + i)}$$

By componendo and dividendo, we get

$$\frac{2w}{2i} = \frac{(z + 1)(1 - i) + (z - 1)(1 + i)}{(z + 1)(1 - i) - (z - 1)(1 + i)}$$

$$\Rightarrow \quad w = \frac{1 + iz}{1 - iz}$$

which is the required bilinear transformation.

# 14 Combinatorics

**Syllabus**

- Permutations
- Combinations
- Pigeonhole Principle
- Inclusion-Exclusion Principle
- Derangement
- Fundamental Theorem of Arithmetic
- Divisibility in Z
- Congruences
- Chinese Remainder Theorem
- Euler's j-Function
- Primitive Roots

## Factorial

For any natural number $n$, we define factorial of $n$ ($n!$ or $\underline{|n}$) as follows

$$n\,! = n(n-1)(n-2).....3 \cdot 2 \cdot 1$$

$$\therefore \quad 1! = 1,\ 2! = 2 \times 1 = 2,\ 3! = 3 \times 2 \times 1 = 6 \text{ and so on.}$$

> ***Note*** **(a)** $n! = n(n-1)! = n(n-1)(n-2)! = ...$
>
> **(b)** $0! = 1$
>
> **(c)** $(-k)! = \infty,\ (k \in Z^+)$
>
> *e.g.*, $(-2)! = \infty \Rightarrow \dfrac{1}{(-2)!} = \dfrac{1}{\infty} = 0$

## Exponent of Prime $p$, in $n!$

Let $p$ be a prime number and $n$ be a positive integer, then the last integer amongst $1, 2, 3, ...., (n-1), n$ which is divisible by $p$ is $\left[\dfrac{n}{p}\right]p$, where $\left[\dfrac{n}{p}\right]$ denotes the greatest integer less than or equal to $\dfrac{n}{p}$. *e.g.*, $\left[\dfrac{10}{3}\right] = 3$, $\left[\dfrac{12}{5}\right] = 2$ etc.

Let $E_p(n!)$ denote the exponent of the prime $p$ in the positive integer $n$, then

$$E_p(n!) = \left[\frac{n}{p}\right] + \left[\frac{n}{p^2}\right] + \left[\frac{n}{p^3}\right] + \left[\frac{n}{p^4}\right] + ... + \left[\frac{n}{p^s}\right]$$

where $s$ is the largest positive integer, such that $p^s \le n < p^{s+1}$.

***Example 1.*** *Find the exponent of 3 in 100!.*

**Solution.** In terms of prime factors 100! can be written as $2^a \cdot 3^b \cdot 5^c \cdot 7^d ...$

$$\Rightarrow \quad E_3(100!) = \left[\frac{100}{3}\right] + \left[\frac{100}{3^2}\right] + \left[\frac{100}{3^3}\right] + \left[\frac{100}{3^4}\right]$$

$$= 33 + 11 + 3 + 1 = 48$$

***Example 2.*** *Find the number of zeros at the end of 100!.*

**Solution.** $100! = 2^a \cdot 3^b \cdot 5^c \cdot 7^d ....$

$$E_2(100!) = \left[\frac{100}{2}\right] + \left[\frac{100}{2^2}\right] + \left[\frac{100}{2^3}\right] + \left[\frac{100}{2^4}\right] + \left[\frac{100}{2^5}\right] + \left[\frac{100}{2^6}\right]$$

$$= 50 + 25 + 12 + 6 + 3 + 1 = 97$$

and

$$E_5(100!) = \left[\frac{100}{5}\right] + \left[\frac{100}{5^2}\right]$$

$$= 20 + 4 = 24$$

$\therefore \quad 100! = 2^{97} \cdot 3^b \cdot 5^{24} \cdot 7^d \ldots$

$= 2^{73} \cdot 3^b \cdot (10)^{24} \cdot 7^d \ldots$

$\Rightarrow$ Number of zeros at the end of 100! is 24.

# Permutations

Each of the different arrangements which can be made by taking some or all of a number of things is called a permutation. The number of permutations of $n$ different objects taken $r$ at a time $(0 \le r \le n)$ is denoted by ${}^nP_r$ or $P(n, r)$ and its value is given by $n(n-1)(n-2)\ldots\ldots(n-r+1)$, when repetition of object is not allowed.

*i.e.*, $\quad {}^nP_r = n(n-1)(n-2)\ldots..(n-r+1)$

$$= \frac{n!}{(n-r)!}$$

If repetition of object is allowed, then ${}^nP_r = n^r$

> **Note** (a) ${}^nP_0 = 1$
> (b) ${}^nP_n = n!$

***Example 3.*** *How many four digit numbers can be made from digits 1, 2, 3, 4, 5, 6 with no two digits common or repeated?*

**Solution.** Required number of numbers is equal to permutations of 6 different digits taken 4 at a time.

6ways 5ways 4ways 3ways

$$= {}^6P_4 = \frac{6!}{(6-4)!} = \frac{6!}{2!}$$

$$= 6 \times 5 \times 4 \times 3 = 360$$

Or

Total number of numbers in which four vacant places can be filled by six different digits

$$= {}^6P_4$$

$$= 6 \times 5 \times 4 \times 3 = 360$$

(Since, here there is no restriction on either of any extreme right as well as extreme left places.)

***Example 4.*** *Find the number of 4 digit numbers with no two digits common.*

**Solution.** Here, 4 digit numbers are to be formed with the digits 0, 1, 2, ..., 9 (Total 10 digits) but here 0 cannot occupy thousands place.

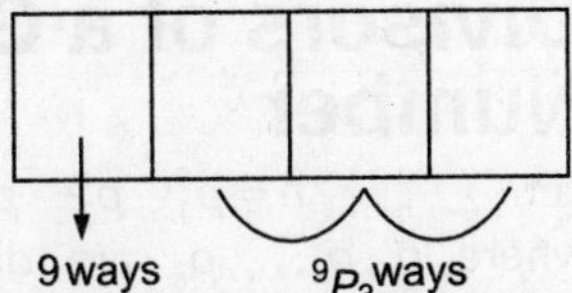


$\therefore$ Thousand place is filled by 9 ways and the remaining three places can be filled simultaneously is ${}^9P_3$ ways.

$\Rightarrow$ Total number of numbers $= 9 \times {}^9P_3 = 9 \times 9 \times 8 \times 7$

$$= 4536$$

***Example 5.*** *There are 4 candidates for the post of a lecturer in Mathematics and one is to be selected by votes of 5 men. Find the number of ways in which the votes can be given.*

**Solution.** Each man can vote for one of the 4 candidates and this can be done in 4 ways.

Similar is the case with every other man.

[$\because$ Repetition is allowed]

Hence, 5 men can vote in $4^5$ *i.e.*, 1024 ways.

***Example 6.*** *Find the number of ways in which n different prizes can be distributed among m(< n) persons, if each is entitled to receive at most n − 1 prizes.*

**Solution.** Total number of ways

$$= m \times m \times \ldots\ldots \text{ to } n \text{ times} = m^n.$$

The number of ways in which one gets all the prizes $= m$.

$\therefore$ The required number of ways $= m^n - m$

# Permutations of Objects not All Distinct

The number of permutations of $n$ things taken all at a time, when $p$ are alike of one kind, $q$ are alike of second kind and $r$ are alike of a third kind and the rest $n-(p+q+r)$ are all different is $\dfrac{n!}{p!\,q!\,r!}$.

***Example 7.*** *How may words can be formed with the letters of the word 'PATALIPUTRA'?*

**Solution.** The word 'PATALIPUTRA' has 11 letters, in which P occurs 2 times, A occurs 3 times, T occurs 2 times and remaining all letters occur 1 time.

$\therefore$ Required number of words $= \dfrac{11!}{2!3!2!}$

# Important Results on Permutations

1. The sum of the digits in the unit place of all numbers formed with the help of $a_1, a_2, a_3, \ldots, a_n$ taken all at a time is $= (n-1)!\,(a_1 + a_2 + \ldots\ldots + a_n)$ (repetition of digits not allowed).
2. The sum of all digit numbers that can be formed using the digits $a_1, a_2, \ldots, a_n$ taken all at a time is $= (n-1)!(a_1 + a_2 + \ldots..+a_n)\left(\dfrac{10^n - 1}{9}\right)$

   (repetition of digits not allowed)

***Example 8.*** *Find the sum of the digits in the unit place of all numbers formed with the help of 3, 4, 5, 6 taken all at a time. Find also sum of all these numbers.*

**Solution.** Sum of the digits in the unit place

$$= (4-1)!(3+4+5+6)$$

$$= 6 \times 18 = 108$$

and sum of all these numbers

$$= (4-1)!(3+4+5+6)\left(\frac{10^4-1}{9}\right)$$

$$= 108 \times 111 = 11988$$

## Circular Permutations

The number of circular permutations of $n$ different things taken all at a time is

$$= (n-1)!$$

(If clockwise and anti-clockwise orders of arrangement are taken as different)

$$= \frac{(n-1)!}{2}$$

(If clockwise and anti-clockwise arrangements are same)

***Example 9.*** *In how many ways 20 persons can be seated around a circular table?*

**Solution.** Required number of ways $= (20-1)! = 19!$

***Example 10.*** *How many number of ways in which 12 different beads can be arranged to form a necklace?*

**Solution.** Required number of ways $= \frac{(12-1)!}{2} = \frac{11!}{2}$

## Combinations

The number of combinations (selections) of $n$ different things taken $r$ at a time is denoted by ${}^nC_r$ or $C(n, r)$ or $\binom{n}{r}$ and its value is given by $\frac{n!}{r!(n-r)!}$

i.e., $${}^nC_r = \frac{n!}{r!(n-r)!} \qquad (0 \le r \le n)$$

Clearly, $${}^nC_r = \frac{{}^nP_r}{r!}$$

## Important Properties of Combinations

(i) ${}^nC_0 = {}^nC_n = 1$, ${}^nC_1 = n$

(ii) ${}^nC_r = {}^nC_{n-r}$ e.g., ${}^{10}C_8 = {}^{10}C_{10-8} = {}^{10}C_2$

(iii) ${}^nC_r + {}^nC_{r-1} = {}^{n+1}C_r$

(iv) ${}^nC_x = {}^nC_y \Leftrightarrow x = y$ or $x + y = n$

(v) $\frac{{}^nC_r}{{}^nC_{r-1}} = \frac{n-r+1}{r}$

(vi) ${}^nC_0 + {}^nC_1 + {}^nC_2 + \ldots\ldots + {}^nC_n = 2^n$

(vii) ${}^nC_0 + {}^nC_2 + {}^nC_4 + \ldots\ldots = {}^nC_1 + {}^nC_3 + {}^nC_5 + \ldots\ldots = 2^{n-1}$

***Example 11.*** *A box containing 2 white balls, 3 red balls and 4 green balls. In how many ways three balls of (i) same colour (ii) different colours can be selected.*

**Solution.** (i) ${}^3C_3 + {}^4C_3 = 1 + 4 = 5$ ways

(ii) ${}^2C_1 \times {}^3C_1 \times {}^4C_1 = 2 \times 3 \times 4 = 24$ ways

## Important Results on Combinations

1. Out of $n$ non-concurrent and non-parallel straight lines, points of intersection are ${}^nC_2$
2. Out of '$n$' points, the number of straight lines are (when no three are collinear) ${}^nC_2$.
3. If out of $n$ points $m$ are collinear, then Number of straight lines $= {}^nC_2 - {}^mC_2 + 1$
4. In a polygon, the total number of diagonals out of $n$ points (no three are collinear) $= \frac{n(n-3)}{2}$
5. Number of triangles formed from $n$ points ${}^nC_3$. (when no three points are collinear)
6. Number of triangles out of $n$ points in which $m$ are collinear ${}^nC_3 - {}^mC_3$.
7. Number of triangles that can be formed out of $n$ points (when none of the side is common to the sides of polygon).
$${}^nC_3 - {}^nC_1 - {}^nC_1 \cdot {}^{n-4}C_1$$
8. Number of parallelograms in two systems of parallel lines (when 1st set contains $m$ parallel lines and 2nd set contains $n$ parallel lines)
$$= {}^nC_2 \times {}^mC_2$$
9. Number of squares in two systems of perpendicular parallel lines (when 1st set contains $m$ parallel lines and 2nd set contains $n$ parallel lines).
$$= \sum_{r=1}^{m-1} (m-r)(n-r); (m < n)$$

## Selection of One or More Objects

### (i) Selection from Different Items

The number of ways of selecting one or more items from a group of $n$ distinct items is $2^n - 1$.

### (ii) Selection from Identical and Distinct Objects

The total number of ways of selecting one or more items from $p$ identical items of one kind, $q$ identical items of second kind, $r$ identical items of third kind and $n$ different items is

$$(p+1)(q+1)(r+1)2^n - 1$$

## The Number and the Sum of the Divisors of a Given Natural Number

Let $$n = p_1^{n_1} \cdot p_2^{n_2} \cdot p_3^{n_3} \ldots\ldots p_k^{n_k} \qquad \ldots(i)$$

where $p_1, p_2, \ldots, p_k$ are distinct prime numbers and $n_1, n_2, \ldots, n_k$ are positive integers.

Clearly, any divisor of $n$ is of the form

$$d = p_1^{m_1} \cdot p_2^{m_2} \cdot p_3^{m_3} \ldots\ldots p_k^{m_k} \qquad \ldots(ii)$$

where $m_1, m_2, \ldots, m_k$ are natural numbers, such that

$$0 \le m_i \le n_i, i = 1, 2, 3, \ldots\ldots, k.$$

Therefore, the total number of divisors of Eq. (i) will be equal to the number of selecting atleast one from $n_1$ identical primes $p_1$, $n_2$ identical primes $p_2$ and so on, finally $n_k$ identical primes $p_k$. The number of such ways is

$$(n_1+1)(n_2+1)......(n_k+1)$$

Hence, the total number of divisors of

$$n = p_1^{n_1} p_2^{n_2} p_3^{n_3}......p_k^{n_k} \text{ is}$$

$$(n_1+1)(n_2+1)(n_3+1)......(n_k+1).$$

This includes 1 and $n$ as divisors. Therefore, number of divisors other than 1 and $n$ is

$$(n_1+1)(n_2+1)(n_3+1).....(n_k+1)-2.$$

The sum of all divisors of Eq. (i) is given by

$$\sum_{r_1=0}^{n_1}\sum_{r_2=0}^{n_2}\sum_{r_3=0}^{n_3}...\sum_{r_k=0}^{n_k} p_1^{r_1}\cdot p_2^{r_2}\cdot p_3^{r_3}....p_k^{r_k}$$

$$=\left\{\frac{p_1^{n_1+1}-1}{p_1-1}\right\}\left\{\frac{p_2^{n_2+1}-1}{p_2-1}\right\}\left\{\frac{p_3^{n_3+1}-1}{p_3-1}\right\}.....\left\{\frac{p_k^{n_k+1}-1}{p_k-1}\right\}$$

***Example 12.*** *Find the total number of divisors of number 38808 excluding 1 and the number itself.*

**Solution.** Factorizing the given number, we have

$$38808 = 2^3\cdot 3^2\cdot 7^2\cdot 11$$

Therefore, the total number of divisors

$$=(3+1)(2+1)(2+1)(1+1)-2$$
$$=70$$

## Important Results on Divisors

1. The number of ways in which $n$ can be resolved as a product of two factors is $\frac{1}{2}(n_1+1)(n_2+1)...(n_k+1)$, if $n$ is not a perfect square and $\frac{1}{2}[(n_1+1)(n_2+1).....(n_k+1)+1]$, if $n$ is a perfect square.
2. The number of ways in which a composite number $n$ can be resolved into two factors, which are relatively prime (or coprime) to each other is equal to $2^{t-1}$, where $t$ is the number of different factors in $n$.
   *e.g.*, $n = 18900 = 2^2\cdot 3^3\cdot 5^2\cdot 7^1$
   Here, $t = 4$ (number of different factors is $n$)
   Hence, number of ways in which composite numbers *i.e.*, 18900 can be resolved into two relatively primes factor is $2^{4-1} = 2^3 = 8$.

## Pigeonhole Principle

1. If $n$ pigeons are assigned to $m$ pigeonholes and $m < n$, then atleast one pigeonhole contains two or more pigeons (atleast two pigeons).
2. If $n$ pigeons are assigned to $m$ pigeonholes and $m < n$, then one of the pigeonholes must contain atleast $\left[\frac{(n-1)}{m}\right]+1$ pigeons.
   (Here [.] is the greatest integer function)

> ***Note*** To use the pigeonhole principle, we must identify pigeons (objects) and pigeonholes (categories of the desired characteristic) and be able to count the number of pigeons and the number of pigeonholes.

***Example 13.*** *Show that if 30 dictionaries in a library contain a total of 61327 pages, then one of the dictionaries must have atleast 2045 pages.*

**Solution.** Here, $n = 61327$, $m = 30$

$\therefore$ Required number of pages

$$=\left[\frac{(n-1)}{m}\right]+1=\left[\frac{61326}{30}\right]+1$$

$$=2044+1=2045$$

***Example 14.*** *If 13 people are assembled in a room, show that atleast 2 of them must have their birthday in the same month.*

**Solution.** Here, $n = 13$ (number of people)

$m = 12$ (number of months)

Now, $\left[\frac{n-1}{m}\right]+1=\left[\frac{13-1}{12}\right]+1=1+1=2$

# Inclusion-Exclusion Principle

Let $A_1, A_2, ....., A_n$ be $n$ finite sets. Then,

$$|A_1\cup A_2\cup A_3\cup...\cup A_n| = \sum_{i=1}^{n}|A_i| - \sum_{1\le i<j\le n}|A_i\cap A_j|$$
$$+\sum_{1\le i<j<k\le n}|A_i\cap A_j\cap A_k|.....$$
$$.....+(-1)^{n-1}|A_1\cap A_2\cap.....\cap A_n|$$

(Here, $|A|$ is the cardinal number, *i.e.*, number of elements in set $A$)

In particular, for any two finite sets $A$ and $B$, we have

$$|A\cup B| = |A|+|B|-|A\cap B|$$

and for any three finite sets $A$, $B$ and $C$, we have

$$|A\cup B\cup C| = |A|+|B|+|C|-|A\cap B|-|A\cap C|$$
$$-|B\cap C|+|A\cap B\cap C|$$

***Example 15.*** *Find the number of integers between 1 and 1000 that are divisible by 2 or 3.*

**Solution.** Let $A$: Set of integers between 1 and 1000 that are divisible by 2.

$B$: Set of integers between 1 and 1000 that are divisible by 3.

$A\cap B$: Set of integers between 1 and 1000 that are divisible by both 2 and 3 *i.e.*, (LCM of 2 and 3) 6.

Now, $|A| = \left[\frac{1000}{2}\right] = 500$, $|B| = \left[\frac{1000}{3}\right] = 333$

$$|A\cap B| = \left[\frac{1000}{6}\right] = 166$$

$\therefore$ $|A\cup B| = |A|+|B|-|A\cap B| = 500+333-166 = 667$

(Here, [.] denotes the greatest integer function)

*Example 16. Find number of integers between 1 and 250 that are divisible by any of the integers 2, 3 and 7.*

**Solution.** Similarly, as above

$$|A|=\left[\frac{250}{2}\right]=125, |B|=\left[\frac{250}{3}\right]=83$$

$$|C|=\left[\frac{250}{7}\right]=35$$

$$|A\cap B|=\left[\frac{250}{6}\right]=41, |A\cap C|=\left[\frac{250}{14}\right]=17,$$

$$|B\cap C|=\left[\frac{250}{21}\right]=11, |A\cap B\cap C|=\left[\frac{250}{42}\right]=5$$

$$\therefore |A\cup B\cup C|=|A|+|B|+|C|-|A\cap B|-|A\cap C|-|B\cap C|+|A\cap B\cap C|$$

$$=125+83+35-41-17-11+5=179$$

## Derangements

If $n$ things are arranged in a row, then number of ways in which they can be deranged, so that none of them occupies its original place is

$$D_n=n!\left(\frac{1}{2!}-\frac{1}{3!}+\dots+(-1)^n\cdot\frac{1}{n!}\right)$$

> **Note** If $r$ things out of $n$ things goes to wrong place, then $(n-r)$ things goes to original place and in this case total derangement is equal to ${}^nC_{n-r}\,D_r$.
> where, $D_r=r!\left(\frac{1}{2!}-\frac{1}{3!}+\dots+(-1)^r\cdot\frac{1}{r!}\right)$

*Example 17. A person writes letters to six friends and addresses the corresponding envelopes. In how many ways can the letters be placed in the envelopes, so that*

*(i) all the letters are in the wrong envelopes*

*(ii) exactly two letters are in correct places*

*(iii) atleast two letters are in the wrong envelopes.*

**Solution.** (i) Required number of ways $=D_6$

$$=6!\left(\frac{1}{2!}-\frac{1}{3!}+\frac{1}{4!}-\frac{1}{5!}+\frac{1}{6!}\right)$$

$$=720\left(\frac{1}{2}-\frac{1}{6}+\frac{1}{24}-\frac{1}{120}+\frac{1}{720}\right)$$

$$=360-120+30-6+1=265$$

(ii) Required number of ways

$$={}^6C_2\cdot D_4={}^6C_2\cdot 4!\left(\frac{1}{2!}-\frac{1}{3!}+\frac{1}{4!}\right)$$

$$=15(12-4+1)=135$$

(iii) Required number of ways

$$={}^6C_4\cdot D_2+{}^6C_3\cdot D_3+{}^6C_2\cdot D_4+{}^6C_1\cdot D_5+{}^6C_0\cdot D_6$$

$$={}^6C_4\cdot 2!\left(\frac{1}{2!}\right)+{}^6C_3\cdot 3!\left(\frac{1}{2!}-\frac{1}{3!}\right)+{}^6C_2\cdot 4!\left(\frac{1}{2!}-\frac{1}{3!}+\frac{1}{4!}\right)$$

$$+{}^6C_1\cdot 5!\left(\frac{1}{2!}-\frac{1}{3!}+\frac{1}{4!}-\frac{1}{5!}\right)$$

$$+6!\left(\frac{1}{2!}-\frac{1}{3!}+\frac{1}{4!}-\frac{1}{5!}+\frac{1}{6!}\right)$$

$$=15+40+135+264+265$$

$$=719$$

## Two Important Algorithm

***Theorem 1*** **Division Algorithm** Let $a$ and $b$ $(\geq 1)$ be integers, then $\exists$ unique integers $q$ and $r$ such that $a=bq+r$ with $0\leq r<b$.

**Corollary** If $a$ and $b$ be two integers with $b\neq 0$, then $\exists$ unique integers $q$ and $r$, such that

$$a=bq+r, \text{ where } 0\leq r<|b|$$

***Theorem 2*** **Euclid's Algorithm** Let $a$ and $b$ be any two integers with $b>0$, then $\exists$ unique integers $q$ and $r$, such that $a=bq+r$, where $0\leq r<b$.

## Divisibility in Z (Set of Integers)

Let $a$ and $b$ be two integers such that $a\neq 0$. If there exists integers $c$ such that $b=ac$, then a is said to divide $b$ or a is said to be a divisor of $b$ and we write it as $a|b$.

The notation $a\nmid b$ means that a does not divide $b$.

Clearly, $1|a$ and if $b\neq 0$, then $b|0$ and $b|b$.

### Important Properties on Divisibility

Let $a, b, c$ be integers such that $a\neq 0, b\neq 0$.

**(i)** If $a|b$, $b|c$ then $a|c$.

**(ii)** If $b|a$, then $cb|ca$.

**(iii)** If $a|b$ and $a|c$, then $a|(bx+cy)$ for any integer $x, y$.

**(iv)** If $a|b$ and $b|a$, then $a=\pm b$.

### Prime Number

An integer $p>1$ is called a prime number or simply a prime if the only positive divisors of $p$ are 1 and $p$. An integer $q>1$ which is not a prime is called composite.

> **Note** **(a)** An integer $p>1$ is a prime number if and only if
> $$p|ab \Rightarrow \text{either } p|a \text{ or } p|b$$
> where $a, b$ are any two integers.
> **(b)** Two integers $m$ and $n$ are said to be relatively prime if $\gcd(m,n)=1$.
> **(c)** Let $m$ and $n$ be two integers and both are not zero, then $m$ and $n$ are relatively prime, if $1=rm+tn$ for some $r$ and $t$.

### Common Divisor

An integer $d>0$ is said to be a common divisor of integers $m$ and $n$, if $d|m$ and $d|n$.

### Greatest Common Divisor (GCD or gcd)

An integer $d>0$ is said to be a greatest common divisor (gcd) of integers $m$ and $n$, if

(i) $d$ is a common divisor of $m$ and $n$ and

(ii) if $c$ is a common divisor of $m$ and $n$, then $c$ is a divisor of $d$ *i.e.*, $c|d$. The greatest common divisor of $m$ and $n$ is denoted by gcd $(m, n)$ or simply $(m, n)$.

## Common Multiple

An integer $l > 0$ is said to be a common multiple of integers $m$ and $n$, if $m|l$ and $n|l$.

## Least Common Multiple (LCM or lcm)

An integer $l > 0$ is said to be the least common multiple (lcm) of integers $m$ and $n$ and

(i) $l$ is a common multiple of $m$ and $n$ and

(ii) if $l'$ is a common multiple of $m$ and $n$, then $l|l'$.

The least common multiple of $m$ and $n$ is denoted by lcm $(m, n)$ or simply $[m, n]$.

> **Note** The gcd $(m,n)$ and lcm $(m,n)$ of any two given integers $m$ and $n$ may not exist. However, if they exist, then they are unique.
>
> *e.g.*, If $d_1 = \gcd(m,n)$ and $d_2 = \gcd(m,n)$, then we have $d_1|d_2$ and $d_2|d_1$.
>
> $\Rightarrow \quad d_1 = \pm d_2$
>
> But both $d_1, d_2$ are greater than zero
>
> $\therefore \quad d_1 = d_2$.

## Important Results on GCD and LCM

1. Let $m$ and $n$ be integers, not both zero. Then gcd $(m, n)$ exist and if $d = \gcd(m, n)$, then there exist integers $s$ and $t$ such that
$$d = sm + tn.$$
2. If $m$ and $n$ are two positive integers and $m = qn + r$, $0 \le r < n$, then
$$\gcd(m, n) = \gcd(n, r)$$
3. $\gcd(m, n) = \gcd(m, -n) = \gcd(-m, n) = \gcd(-m, -n)$
4. If $a$, $b$ and $c$ are integers such that $\gcd(a, b) = 1$ and $\gcd(a, c) = 1$, then $\gcd(a, bc) = \gcd(ac, b)$
5. For any positive integers $a$ and $b$,
$\gcd(a^2, b^2) = (\gcd(a, b))^2$
6. If $m$ and $n$ be integers not both zero and $\gcd(m, n) = d$, then $\gcd\left(\dfrac{m}{d}, \dfrac{n}{d}\right) = 1$
7. $\gcd(ka, kb) = |k| \gcd(a, b)$
where, $k$ is any non-zero integer.

***Example 18.*** *Find the gcd (475,120) and put it in the form gcd $(a, b) = sa + tb$ for some $s, t \in Z$.*

**Solution.** Since,
$$475 = 3(120) + 115$$
$$120 = 1(115) + 5$$
$$115 = 23(5) + 0$$

Hence, $\gcd(475, 120) = 5$

Now,
$$5 = 120 - 1(115)$$
$$= 120 - 1[475 - 3(120)]$$
$$= 120 + 3(120) + (-1)(475)$$
$$5 = (-1)\,475 + (4)\,120$$

***Example 19.*** *If $m, n, p$ and $q$ are positive integers such that $m|p$ and $n|q$, then prove that gcd $(m,n)$ divides gcd $(p,q)$.*

**Solution.** Let $\gcd(m,n) = d_1$ and $\gcd(p,q) = d_2$

To show that $d_1|d_2$

Since, $\gcd(m,n) = d_1 \Rightarrow d_1|m$ and $d_1|n$

Now, $d_1|m$ and $m|p \Rightarrow d_1|p$

Also, $d_1|n$ and $n|q \Rightarrow d_1|q$

Thus, $d_1|p$ and $d_1|q \Rightarrow d_1|\gcd(p,q)$ *i.e.*, $d_1|d_2$

***Example 20.*** *For any integer $n$, show that $2n+1$ and $13n+6$ are relatively prime.*

**Solution.** Now,
$$13n + 6 = 6(2n+1) + n$$
$$2n + 1 = 2 \cdot n + 1$$
$$n = 1 \cdot n + 0$$

$\therefore \quad \gcd(13n+6, 2n+1) = 1$

Also,
$$1 = (2n+1) - 2n$$
$$= (2n+1) - 2\{(13n+6) - 6(2n+1)\}$$
$$1 = 13(2n+1) - 2(13n+6)$$
$$1 = r(2n+1) + s(13n+6),$$

where, $r = 13, s = -2$

***Example 21.*** *Let $a$, $b$ and $c$ be three consecutive integers. Show that 3 divides one of these.*

**Solution.** Since $a$, $b$ and $c$ are consecutive integers.

$\therefore$ $\exists$ an integer $n$ such that
$$a = n-1, b = n \text{ and } c = n+1$$

By division algorithm,

$\exists$ integers $q$ and $r$, such that
$$n = 3q + r, \text{ where } 0 \le r < 3$$

If $r = 0$, then $b = 3q$ and hence $3|b$

If $r = 1$, then $a = 3q$ and hence $3|a$

If $r = 2$, then $c = 3q + 2 + 1 = 3(q+1)$ and hence $3|c$

So, we find that 3 divides one of $a, b, c$.

***Example 22.*** *For any integer $n$, show that $3n+1$ and $13n+4$ are relatively prime.*

**Solution.** Let $\gcd(3n+1, 13n+4) = d$. Then,

$d|3n+1$ and $d|13n+4$

Now, $13n + 4 = 4(3n+1) + n$

$\Rightarrow \quad n = (13n+4) - 4(3n+1)$

As, $d|3n+1$ and $d|13n+4$

$\Rightarrow \quad d|(13n+4) - 4(3n+1) \Rightarrow d|n$

Again, $d|3n+1$ and $d|n$

$\Rightarrow \quad d|(3n+1) - 3 \cdot n) \Rightarrow d|1$

$\therefore \quad d = 1$

Hence, $3n+1$ and $13n+4$ are relatively prime.

## Fundamental Theorem of Arithmetic

**(i)** Every integer $n \geq 2$ can be expressed uniquely as a product of (one or more) primes, upto the order of factors. More precisely, any integer $n \geq 2$ can be expressed as $n = p_1 p_2 \ldots\ldots p_r$, where $p_1, p_2, \ldots, p_r$ are primes. Moreover, if $n = p_1 p_2 \ldots p_r$ and $n = q_1 q_2 \ldots \ldots q_t$ be two factorization of $n$ as a product of primes, then $r = t$ and the primes $q_j$ can be relabelled so that $p_i = q_i$ for all $i = 1, 2, \ldots, r$.

**(ii)** Let $a$ and $b$ be positive integers with prime factorizations

$a = p_1^{a_1} p_2^{a_2} \ldots\ldots p_n^{a_n}$ and $b = p_1^{b_1} p_2^{b_2} \ldots\ldots p_n^{b_n}$,

where $a_i \geq 0$ and $b_i \geq 0$ for all $i$ (allowing use of the same prime factors).

For each $i$, let $d_i = \min\{a_i, b_i\}$ and let $m_i = \max\{a_i, b_i\}$. Then,

(a) $\gcd(a, b) = p_1^{d_1} p_2^{d_2} \ldots\ldots p_n^{d_n}$

(b) $\text{lcm}\,[a, b] = p_1^{m_1} p_2^{m_2} \ldots\ldots p_n^{m_n}$

*e.g.,* we take $a = 108$ and $b = 225$

Now, $a = 2^2 \cdot 3^3 \cdot 5^0$, $b = 2^0 \cdot 3^2 \cdot 5^2$, then

$(a, b) = 2^0 \cdot 3^2 \cdot 5^0 = 9$

and $[a, b] = 2^2 \cdot 3^3 \cdot 5^2 = 2700$

**(iii)** Every positive integer $n > 1$ is either a prime or product of primes in an unique way as

$$n = p_1^{n_1} \cdot p_2^{n_2} \cdot p_3^{n_3} \ldots\ldots p_r^{n_r}$$

where $p_1 < p_2 < \ldots < p_r$ are primes and $n_1, n_2, \ldots, n_r$ are positive integers.

> ***Note*** **(a)** If $a$ and $b$ are positive integers, then $(a,b)[a,b] = ab$
>
> **(b)** There exist infinitely many prime numbers. (Euclid theorem)

## Congruences

Let $n$ be a positive integer, then for all $a, b \in \mathbb{Z}$; $a \equiv b \pmod n \Leftrightarrow n \mid (a - b)$

*i.e.,* $a - b = nk$ for some $k \in \mathbb{Z}$ and for $n \nmid (a - b)$, then we write $a \not\equiv b \pmod n$

> ***Note*** $a \equiv b \pmod n$ is called "a is congruent to b modulo n" and similarly, $a \not\equiv b \pmod n$ is called "a is not congruent to b modulo n".

## Important Properties of Congruences

**1.** Let $a, b, c \in \mathbb{Z}$ and $n$ be a fixed positive integer, then

(i) $a \equiv a \pmod n$ for all $a \in \mathbb{Z}$

(ii) $a \equiv b \pmod n \Rightarrow b \equiv a \pmod n$

(iii) $a \equiv b \pmod n$, $b \equiv c \pmod n$

$\Rightarrow a \equiv c \pmod n$

Therefore, congruence relation $\equiv$ on integers is an equivalence relation.

**2.** Let $a, b, c, d \in \mathbb{Z}$ and $n$ a fixed positive integer, then if $a \equiv b \pmod n$ and $c \equiv d \pmod n$, then

(i) $a + c \equiv b + d \pmod n$

(ii) $ac \equiv bd \pmod n$

(iii) $ax + cy \equiv bx + dy \pmod n$, where $x$ and $y$ are any integers.

**3.** If $a \equiv b \pmod n$, then for any integer $k$, we have

(i) $a + k \equiv b + k \pmod n$

(ii) $ak \equiv bk \pmod n$

**4.** Two integers $a$ and $b$ are congruent modulo a positive integer $n$, if and only if $a$ and $b$ leave the same remainder when divided by $n$.

**5.** If $a \equiv b \pmod n$ and $0 \leq |a - b| < n$, then $a = b$.

**6.** Let $a, b, c$ be integers and $n$ be a positive integer, then

$ab \equiv ac \pmod n \Leftrightarrow b \equiv c \left(\bmod \dfrac{n}{(a, n)}\right)$ and if $(a, n) = 1$,

then $ab \equiv ac \pmod n \Leftrightarrow b \equiv c \pmod n$

**7.** If $ax \equiv 1 \pmod n$ and $ay \equiv 1 \pmod n$, then $x \equiv y \pmod n$

**8.** Let $a$ and $n > 1$ be integers, such that $(a, n) = 1$, then $\exists$ integer $b$ such that $ab \equiv 1 \pmod n$

**9.** If $ax \equiv b \pmod n$ and $(a, n) = 1$, then

$$x \equiv \frac{b}{a} \pmod n \equiv \frac{b + nq}{a} \pmod n \equiv r \pmod n,$$

where, $q$ is chosen, so that $\dfrac{b + nq}{a} = r$

> ***Note*** $ax \equiv b \pmod n$ is solvable only when $\gcd(a,n) \mid b$.

***Example 23.*** *Find the solution, if any*

*(i)* $12x \equiv 5 \pmod{16}$

*(ii)* $7x \equiv 2 \pmod{31}$

**Solution.** (i) $\gcd(12,16) = 4 \nmid 5$

$\therefore$ There is no solution.

(ii) $\gcd(7,31) = 1/2$

$\therefore$ Its solution exist.

Now, $7x \equiv 2 \pmod{31}$

$\Rightarrow x \equiv \dfrac{2}{7} \pmod{31}$

$\Rightarrow x \equiv \dfrac{2 + 4 \times 31}{7} \pmod{31}$

$\Rightarrow x \equiv 18 \pmod{31}$

$\Rightarrow x = 18, 49, 80, \ldots$

## Chinese Remainder Theorem

**(i)** Let $m$ and $n$ be positive integers, with $(m, n) = 1$. Then the system of congruences

$$x \equiv a \pmod n,\ x \equiv b \pmod n$$

has a solution which is unique modulo $mn$.

**(ii)** Suppose $(m_i, m_j) = 1$ for $1 \leq i < j \leq t$ and let $a_1, a_2, \ldots\ldots, a_t \in \mathbb{Z}$, then the system of congruences $x \equiv a_1 \pmod{m_1}$,

$x \equiv a_2 \pmod{m_2}, \ldots\ldots\; x \equiv a_t \pmod{m_t}$ has solution which is unique modulo $m_1 m_2 \ldots\ldots m_t$.

(Generalised form)

The common solution $x_0$ of the congruences is given by, $\sum_{j=1}^{t} \frac{m}{m_j} c_j a_j \pmod{m}$, where $\frac{m}{m_j}$ is an integer such that $\left(\frac{m}{m_j}, m_j\right) = 1$ and $\left(\frac{m}{m_j}\right) c_j \equiv 1 \pmod{m_j}$

***Example 24.*** *Solve $x \equiv 2 \pmod 3$, $x \equiv 3 \pmod 4$, $x \equiv 4 \pmod 5$.*

**Solution.** Since here $m_1 = 3, m_2 = 4, m_3 = 5$ are such that

$$(m_1, m_2) = (m_1, m_3) = (m_2, m_3) = 1$$

$\therefore$ By Generalised form of Chinese Remainder Theorem

Let $\quad m = m_1 m_2 m_3 = 3 \cdot 4 \cdot 5 = 60$

Then $c_1, c_2$ and $c_3$ are determined by the congruences

$20\, c_1 \equiv 1 \pmod 3$, $15\, c_2 \equiv 1 \pmod 4$, $12\, c_3 \equiv 1 \pmod 5$

$\Rightarrow \quad c_1 \equiv -1 \pmod 3$; $c_2 \equiv -1 \pmod 4$ and $c_3 \equiv 3 \pmod 5$

$\therefore \quad x_0 \equiv [20 \cdot (-1) \cdot 2 + 15 \cdot (-1) \cdot 3 + 12 \cdot (3) \cdot 4] \pmod{60}$

$\equiv 59 \pmod{60} \equiv -1 \pmod{60}$

$\Rightarrow \quad x_0 = -1, 59, 119, \ldots$

are the common solution of given congruences.

# Euler's φ-Function

The Euler's φ-function is the function $\varphi : z^+ \to z^+$ defined as follows

(i) $\varphi(1) = 1$

(ii) for $n (> 1) \in z^+$, $\varphi(n) =$ the number of positive integers less than $n$ and relatively prime to $n$,

thus $\varphi(2) = 1$

($\because$ The only positive integer less than 2 and relatively prime to 2 is 1)

Similarly, $\quad \varphi(3) = 2$, $\varphi(4) = 2$, $\varphi(5) = 4$ and so on.

In particular, $\varphi(p) = p - 1$, where $p$ is a prime.

e.g., $\quad \varphi(5) = 5 - 1 = 4$, $\varphi(7) = 7 - 1 = 6$ and so on.

# Important Results on Euler's φ-Function

1. If $m$ and $n$ are positive integers such that $\gcd(m, n) = 1$, then $\varphi(mn) = \varphi(m)\varphi(n)$

   e.g., $\varphi(12) = \varphi(4 \times 3) = \varphi(4) \cdot \varphi(3)$

   $= 2 \times 2 = 4 \qquad (\because \gcd(4, 3) = 1)$

2. If $n = p_1^{n_1} \cdot p_2^{n_2} \ldots p_t^{n_t}$ be any positive integer, where $p_1, p_2, \ldots, p_t$ are distinct primes. Then,

$$\varphi(n) = n\left(1 - \frac{1}{p_1}\right)\left(1 - \frac{1}{p_2}\right) \ldots\ldots \left(1 - \frac{1}{p^t}\right).$$

3. Let $(a, n) = 1$, then $a^{\varphi(n)} \equiv 1 \pmod n$ (Euler's theorem)

4. If $p$ is a prime and $p \nmid a$, then $a^p \equiv a \pmod p$ or

   $a^{p-1} \equiv 1 \pmod p$ (Euler's-Fermat theorem)

5. If $p$ is a prime, then $(p - 1)! \equiv -1 \pmod p$

   e.g., Let $p = 3$, then $(3 - 1)! \equiv -1 \pmod 3 \Rightarrow 2 \equiv -1 \pmod 3$

***Example 25.*** *How many positive integers which are less than 108 and prime to 108?*

**Solution.** Since, $\quad 108 = 2^2 \times 3^3$

$$\Rightarrow \quad \varphi(108) = \varphi(2^2 \times 3^3) = 108\left(1 - \frac{1}{2}\right)\left(1 - \frac{1}{3}\right)$$

$$= 108 \times \frac{1}{2} \times \frac{2}{3} = 36$$

***Example 26.*** *Show that $2^{48} \equiv 1 \pmod{105}$.*

**Solution.** Since, $105 = 3 \times 5 \times 7$ and $2^{48} = 16^2 \cdot 16^4 \cdot 16^6$

By Fermat's theorem

$16^2 \equiv 1 \pmod 3$, $16^4 \equiv 1 \pmod 5$, $16^6 \equiv 1 \pmod 7$

Hence, $2^{48} = 16^2 \cdot 16^4 \cdot 16^6 \equiv 1 \cdot 1 \cdot 1 \pmod{105}$

$\Rightarrow \quad 2^{48} \equiv 1 \pmod{105}$

***Example 27.*** *If a, b are two integers, such that a and b are relatively prime, then prove that $a^2$ and $b^2$ are relatively prime.*

**Solution.** Since, $a, b$ are relatively prime.

$\therefore \quad \gcd(a, b) = 1$

Since $\gcd(a^2, b^2) = \{\gcd(a, b)\}^2 = (1)^2 = 1$

$\Rightarrow \quad a^2, b^2$ are relatively prime.

***Example 28.*** *List all integers x in the range $1 \le x \le 10$ that satisfy $x \equiv 7 \pmod{17}$.*

**Solution.** Since, $\quad x \equiv 7 \pmod{17}$

$\Rightarrow \quad x = 17y + 7$, where $y \in \mathbb{Z}^+$

Putting $\quad y = 0, 1, 2, 3, 4, 5$, we get

$x = 7, 24, 41, 58, 75, 92. \qquad [\because 1 \le x \le 100]$

***Example 29.*** *Evaluate $\varphi(m)$ for $m = 1, 2, 3, \ldots, 12$.*

**Solution.** By definition $\varphi(1) = 1$, $\varphi(2) = 1$;

$\varphi(3) = 2$, $\quad$ Since $(1, 3) = 1, (2, 3) = 1$

$\varphi(4) = 2$, $\quad$ Since $(1, 4) = 1, (3, 4) = 1$

$\varphi(5) = 4$, $\quad$ Since $(1, 5) = 1, (2, 5) = 1, (3, 5) = 1, (4, 5) = 1$

$\varphi(6) = 2$, $\quad$ Since $(1, 6) = 1, (5, 6) = 1$

$\varphi(7) = 6$, $\quad$ Since $(1, 7) = 1, (2, 7) = 1, (3, 7) = 1, (4, 7) = 1, (5, 7) = 1, (6, 7) = 1$,

$\varphi(8) = 4$ $\quad$ Since $(1, 8) = 1, (3, 8), = 1, (5, 8) = 1, (7, 8) = 1$

Similarly, $\varphi(9) = 6$; $\varphi(10) = 4$; $\varphi(11) = 10$; $\varphi(12) = 4$

***Example 30.*** *Show that $\varphi(12) = \varphi(4)\,\varphi(3) \neq \varphi(6)\,\varphi(2)$.*

**Solution.** Here, $\quad 12 = 2^2 \times 3^1$

$$\Rightarrow \quad \varphi(12) = 12\left(1 - \frac{1}{2}\right)\left(1 - \frac{1}{3}\right) = 12 \cdot \frac{1}{2} \cdot \frac{2}{3} = 4$$

and $4 = 2^2$

$\Rightarrow \varphi(4) = 4\left(1-\frac{1}{2}\right) = 4\cdot\frac{1}{2} = 2$

and $3 = 3^1$

$\Rightarrow \varphi(3) = 3\left(1-\frac{1}{3}\right) = 3\cdot\frac{2}{3} = 2$

and $6 = 2^1 \times 3^1 \Rightarrow \varphi(6) = 6\cdot\left(1-\frac{1}{2}\right)\left(1-\frac{1}{3}\right) = 6\cdot\frac{1}{2}\cdot\frac{2}{3} = 2$

and $2 = 2^1 \quad \Rightarrow \varphi(2) = 2\cdot\left(1-\frac{1}{2}\right) = 2\cdot\frac{1}{2} = 1$

Clearly, $4 = \varphi(12) = 2\times 2 = \varphi(4)\,\varphi(3)$

But $\varphi(6)\,\varphi(2) = 2\times 1 = 2 \neq \varphi(12) = 4$

Thus, $\varphi(12) = \varphi(4)\,\varphi(3) \neq \varphi(6)\,\varphi(2)$.

***Example 31.*** *Find all solutions of $\varphi(x) = 24$.*

**Solution.** Here, $24 = 2\times 12, 4\times 6, 4\times 6, 8\times 3, 24\times 1$

Now, $2\times 12 = \varphi(3)\,\varphi(13) = \varphi(39)$, so $x = 39$

Also, $2\times 12 = \varphi(4)\,\varphi(13) = \varphi(52)$, so $x = 52$

Again, $\varphi(6) = 2$ and so $x = 13\times 6 = 78$

Thus, $\varphi(x) = 24 \Rightarrow x = 39, 52, 78$

Now, $\varphi(7) = 6$ but $\varphi(5) = 4$, $\varphi(8) = 4$,

$\varphi(10) = 4$, $\varphi(12) = 4$

Hence, $\varphi(x) = 4\times 6 \Rightarrow x = 35, 56, 70, 84.$

***Example 32.*** *If a and b be positive integers, then (a, b) [a, b] = ab.*

**Solution.** Since, we know that

$(a, b) = p_1^{\max\{a_1, b_1\}}\cdot p_2^{\max\{a_2, b_2\}}\ldots.p_n^{\max\{a_n, b_n\}}$ and

$= p_1^{d_1} p_2^{d_2}\ldots\ldots p_n^{d_n}$, where $d_i = \min\{a_i, b_i\}$

and $[a, b] = p_1^{\max\{a_1, b_1\}}\cdot p_2^{\max\{a_2, b_2\}}\ldots p_n^{\max\{a_n, b_n\}}$

$= p_1^{m_1} p_2^{m_2}\ldots.p_n^{m_n}$, where $m_i = \max\{a_i, b_i\}$

$\therefore \quad (a, b)[a, b] = p_1^{d_1+m_1} p_2^{d_2+m_2}\ldots.p_n^{d_n+m_n}$

$= p_1^{a_1+b_1} p_2^{a_2+b_2}\ldots\ldots p_n^{a_n+b_n}$

$[\because \min\{x, y\} + \max\{x, y\} = x + y]$

$= (p_1^{a_1} p_2^{a_2}\ldots p_n^{a_n})(p_1^{b_1} p_2^{b_2}\ldots p_n^{b_n})$

$= ab$

***Example 33.*** *Show that $(a+b)^p \equiv a^p + b^p \pmod p$. Where p is any prime.*

**Solution.** Since, $(a+b)^p = a^p + {}^pC_1 a^{p-1}b + {}^pC_2 a^{p-2}b^2 + \ldots + {}^pC_{p-1}\, ab^{p-1} + b^p$

$= a^p + pa^{p-1}b + \frac{p(p-1)}{2!}a^{p-2}b^2 + \ldots + pab^{p-1} + b^p$

$= a^p + b^p + p\left(a^{p-1}b + \frac{p-1}{2!}a^{p-2}b^2 + \ldots + ab^{p-1}\right)$

$\equiv a^p + b^p \pmod p$

***Example 34.*** *Prove that, there exist infinitely many prime numbers.*

**Solution.** If possible, let there be finite number of primes.

$$P = \{p_1, p_2, p_3, \ldots, p_m\}$$

where $m$ denote the total number of primes and $p_1, p_2, \ldots$ are listed in increasing order s.t.

$$p_1 = 2, p_2 = 3, p_3 = 5, \ldots \text{ upto } p_m$$

the last (and the largest ) prime.

Let us now construct the positive integer.

$$n = p_1 p_2 p_3\ldots\ldots p_m + 1$$

In view of fundamental theorem of arithmetic, $n$ can be factorized into primes.

Let $n = q_1 q_2\ldots\ldots q_k$, where $q_1, q_2, \ldots, q_k \in P$, with $k > 1$ (for if $k = 1$, then $n = q_1 > p_m$, contrary to the definition of $p_m$ as greatest prime)

Since, $q_1 | n$ and $q_1 \in P$

$\Rightarrow \quad q_1 = p_r$, for some $1 \le r \le m$

$\Rightarrow \quad q_1 | p_1 p_2\ldots\ldots p_m$, also $q_1 | n$

$\Rightarrow \quad q_1 | n - (p_1 p_2\ldots\ldots p_m)$

*i.e.,* $\quad q_1 | 1 \Rightarrow q_1 = 1$, which is not a prime number.

$\therefore$ we arrive at a contradiction.

Hence, there are infinite many prime numbers.

***Example 35.*** *If $n = p_1^{a_1} p_2^{a_2}\ldots p_t^{a_t}$ be any positive integer, where $p_1, p_2, \ldots, p_t$ are distinct primes. Then prove that*

$$\varphi(n) = n\left(1-\frac{1}{p_1}\right)\left(1-\frac{1}{p_2}\right)\ldots\ldots\left(1-\frac{1}{p_t}\right)$$

**Solution.** Since, $n = p_1^{a_1} p_2^{a_2}\ldots p_t^{a_t}$

$\therefore \quad \varphi(n) = \varphi(p_1^{a_1} p_2^{a_2}\ldots p_t^{a_t})$

$= \varphi(p_1^{a_1})\varphi(p_2^{a_2})\ldots\varphi(p_t^{a_t})$

$= [p_1^{a_1} - p_1^{a_1-1}][p_2^{a_2} - p_2^{a_2-1}]\ldots[p_t^{a_t} - p_t^{a_t-1}]$

$= \left[p_1^{a_1}\left(1-\frac{1}{p_1}\right)\right]\left[p_2^{a_2}\left(1-\frac{1}{p_2}\right)\right]\ldots\left[p_t^{a_t}\left(1-\frac{1}{p_t}\right)\right]$

$= p_1^{a_1} p_2^{a_2}\ldots p_t^{a_t}\left(1-\frac{1}{p_1}\right)\left(1-\frac{1}{p_2}\right)\ldots\left(1-\frac{1}{p_t}\right)$

$= n\left(1-\frac{1}{p_1}\right)\left(1-\frac{1}{p_2}\right)\ldots\ldots\left(1-\frac{1}{p_t}\right)$

***Example 36.*** *Find the number of elements in the set $\{m : 1 \le m \le 1000$, m and 1000 are relatively prime$\}$.*

**Solution.** $1000 = 10\times 10\times 10 = 2\times 5\times 2\times 5\times 2\times 5 = 2^3\times 5^3$

$\therefore \quad \varphi(1000) = 1000\left(1-\frac{1}{2}\right)\left(1-\frac{1}{5}\right)$

$= 1000\times\frac{1}{2}\times\frac{4}{5}$

$= 400$

**Remark** $\varphi(n) = \{x : 1 \le x \le n, \gcd(x, n) = 1\}$

***Example 37.*** *Find the unit digit of* $2^{100}$.

**Solution.** $2^{100} = (2^4)^{25} = 16^{25} = .....6$

***Example 38.*** *If m and n are positive integers such that* $\gcd(m,n) = 1$, *then prove that*

$$\varphi(mn) = \varphi(m)\varphi(n).$$

**Solution.** Let the integers 1, 2, 3, ..... upto $mn$ as follows

$$\begin{array}{llllll} 1, & 2 & ,......, & r & ,......, & m \\ m+1, & m+2 & ,......, & m+r & ,......, & 2m, \\ 2m+1, & 2m+2 & ,......, & 2m+r & ,......, & 3m, \\ ...... & ...... & ...... & ...... & ...... & ...... \\ ...... & ...... & ...... & ...... & ...... & ...... \\ (n-1)m+1 & (n-1)m+2 & ...... & (n-1)m+r & ...... & nm \end{array}$$

Now, $\varphi(mn)$ is the number of the above which are relatively prime to $mn$ *i.e.*, relatively prime to both $m$ and $n$.

Consider the $r$th column

(i) If $\gcd(r,m) = 1$, then all the numbers in that column are relatively prime to $m$ as $\gcd(km+r, m) = \gcd(r,m) = 1$

(ii) It $\gcd(r,m) \neq 1$, then all the numbers in that column are not relatively prime to $m$.
So, $\varphi(m)$ is the number of columns in which all numbers are relatively prime to $m$.
But $r, m+r, ......, (n-1)m+r$ form a complete set mod $n$, as $\gcd(m,n) = 1$.
So, the number of integers in the $r$th column which are relatively prime to $n$ is $\varphi(n)$.
Hence, $\varphi(m)\varphi(n)$ in the total number of integers in the table which are relatively prime to $m$ and $n$
Hence, $\varphi(mn) - \varphi(m)\varphi(n)$.

***Example 39.*** *Solve the congruences.*

(i) $3x \equiv -2 \pmod 7$

(ii) $15x \equiv 6 \pmod{21}$

(iii) $36x \equiv 7 \pmod{157}$

(iv) $17x \equiv 11 \pmod{43}$

(v) $42x \equiv 50 \pmod{76}$

**Solution.** (i) Here, $(a,m) = (3,7) = 1$ which divide $b = -2$ and hence, the solution of given congruence exists.

Now, $3x \equiv -2 \pmod 7 \equiv 12 \pmod 7$

$\Rightarrow \quad x \equiv 4 \pmod 7$

(ii) Here, $(a,m) = (15,21) = 3$ which divide 6
Hence, the given congruence is equivalent to
$5x \equiv 2 \pmod 7$, where $(5,7) = 1$

$\therefore \quad x \equiv \dfrac{2}{5} \pmod 7$

$= \dfrac{2 \pmod 7}{5} \equiv \dfrac{(28+2)}{5} \pmod 7 \equiv 6 \pmod 7$

$\therefore \quad x \equiv 6 \pmod 7$ and so $x \equiv 6, 13, 20 \pmod{21}$

(iii) Here, $(36,157) = 1$ which divide 7

$\therefore \quad 36 \equiv 7 \pmod{157}$

$\Rightarrow \quad 12x \equiv \dfrac{7}{3} \pmod{157} = \dfrac{7-157}{3} \pmod{157}$

$= -\dfrac{150}{3} \pmod{157}$

$12x \equiv -50 \pmod{157}$

$\therefore \quad x \equiv -\dfrac{50}{12} \pmod{157} \equiv -\dfrac{25}{6} \pmod{157}$

$= \dfrac{157-25}{6} \pmod{157}$

$\equiv \dfrac{132}{6} \pmod{157} \equiv 22 \pmod{157}$

(iv) Here, $(17,43) = 1$ which divide 11

$\therefore \quad 17x \equiv 11 \pmod{43}$

$x \equiv \dfrac{11}{17} \pmod{43} = \dfrac{11+12\times 43}{17} \pmod{43}$

$\equiv \dfrac{11+516}{17} \pmod{43} = \dfrac{527}{17} \pmod{43}$

$\equiv 31 \pmod{43}$

$\therefore \quad x \equiv 22 \pmod{157}$

(v) Here, $(42,76) = 2$, which divide 50 and hence the solution of given congruence exists.
The given congruence is equivalent to

$21x \equiv 25 \pmod{38}$

$\Rightarrow \quad x \equiv \dfrac{25}{21} \pmod{38} = \dfrac{(25+38)}{21} \pmod{38}$

$\equiv 3 \pmod{38}$

Hence, $x \equiv 3, 41 \pmod{76}$

***Example 40.*** *Solve* $x \equiv 7 \pmod{18}$, $x \equiv 10 \pmod{15}$, $x \equiv 1 \pmod{14}$.

**Solution.** Here,

$(18,15) \equiv 3|1-10, (18,14) = 2|7-1, (15,14) = 1|10-1$

$\therefore$ The solution exists.

$\therefore \quad x \equiv 7 \pmod{18}$

$\Rightarrow \quad x = 7 + 18\lambda$, for some integer $\lambda$

$\Rightarrow \quad 7 + 18\lambda \equiv 10 \pmod{15}$ *i.e.*, $18\lambda \equiv 3 \pmod{15}$

$\Rightarrow \quad \lambda \equiv 1 \pmod{15}$

Remember $90 = [18, 15]$

Hence, substituting $7 + 18 + 90\mu$ in $x \equiv 1 \pmod{14}$, we have

$90\mu \equiv -24 \pmod{14} \Rightarrow \mu \equiv 3 \pmod{14}$

$\therefore$ The common solution is

$x \equiv (7 + 18 + 90.3) \pmod{630}$

$\equiv 295 \pmod{630}$, where $630 = [18, 15, 14]$

***Example 41.*** *Solve the set of congruences.*

$x \equiv 1 \pmod 4$, $x \equiv 0 \pmod 3$, $x \equiv 5 \pmod 7$

**Solution.** Here, $(m_1, m_2) = (4,3) = 1, (m_1, m_3) = (4,7) = 1,$
$(m_2, m_3) = (3,7) = 1$

$\therefore \quad x \equiv 1 \pmod 4 \Rightarrow x = 1 + 4\lambda$ for same integer $\lambda$

$\therefore \quad x \equiv 0 \pmod 3 \Rightarrow 1 + 4\lambda \equiv 0 \pmod 3$

$\Rightarrow 4\lambda \equiv -1 \pmod 3$

$\Rightarrow \lambda \equiv -1 \pmod 3$

$\Rightarrow \lambda = -1 + 3\mu$, for some integer $\mu$

$\therefore \quad x = 1 + 4\lambda = 1 + 4(-1 + 3\mu) = -3 + 12\mu \pmod{12}$

Since, $\text{lcm}\{3, 4\} = 12$

Now, $x = -3 + 12\mu$ reduces the congruence $x \equiv 5 \pmod 7$ to $-3 + 12\mu \equiv 5 \pmod 7$

$\Rightarrow \quad 12\mu \equiv 8 \pmod 7$

$\Rightarrow \quad 5\mu \equiv 1 \pmod 7$

$\Rightarrow \quad \mu \equiv 3 \pmod 7$

Hence, the common solution is

$$x \equiv -3 + 12\mu = -3 + 36 \equiv 33 \pmod 8,$$

where $84 = [3, 4, 7]$

# SOLVED EXAMPLES

## Type I (*Only one correct option*)

***Example 1.*** *The sum of all the 4 digits numbers that can be formed with the digits 1, 2, 2 and 3 is*

(a) 22264 (b) 122234
(c) 26664 (d) None of these

**Solution.** (c) Here, the number of digits = 4 out of which 2 occurs twice and the number of numbers of 4 digits $= \dfrac{^4P_4}{2!}$

$$= \frac{4 \times 3 \times 2 \times 1}{2}$$

$$= 12$$

$$\text{Hence, The required sum} = \frac{\text{number of numbers formed}}{\text{number of digits}} \times (\text{sum of digits}) \times (1 + 10 + 100 + 1000)$$

$$= \frac{12}{4}(1 + 2 + 2 + 3)(1111)$$

$$= 3 \times 8 \times (1111)$$

$$= 24 \times 1111$$

$$= 26664$$

***Example 2.*** *The highest power of 3 in $^{50}C_{10}$ is*

(a) 0 (b) 1 (c) 2 (d) 3

**Solution.** (a) We have

$$^{50}C_{10} = \frac{50!}{10!\,40!}$$

$$\therefore \quad H_3(50!) = \left[\frac{50}{3}\right] + \left[\frac{50}{9}\right] + \left[\frac{50}{27}\right] + \left[\frac{50}{81}\right]$$

$$= 16 + 5 + 1 + 0 = 22$$

$$H_3(40!) = \left[\frac{40}{3}\right] + \left[\frac{40}{9}\right] + \left[\frac{40}{27}\right] + \left[\frac{40}{81}\right]$$

$$= 13 + 4 + 1 + 0 = 18$$

$$\text{and } H_3(10!) = \left[\frac{10}{3}\right] + \left[\frac{10}{9}\right] + \left[\frac{10}{27}\right] + \left[\frac{50}{81}\right]$$

$$= 3 + 1 + 0$$

$$= 4$$

$$\therefore \quad H_3(^{50}C_{10}) = H_3(50!) - H_3(40!) - H_3(10!)$$

$$= 22 - 18 - 4$$

$$= 0$$

***Example 3.*** *The largest integer $n$ such that $33!$ is divisible by $2^n$ is*

(a) 15 (b) 20 (c) 30 (d) 31

**Solution.** (d) Here, $n = 33, p = 2$

Since, $\quad 2^5 < 33 < 2^6$

$\therefore \quad S = 5$

$$\text{So, } E_2(33!) = \left[\frac{33}{2}\right] + \left[\frac{33}{2^2}\right] + \left[\frac{33}{2^3}\right] + \left[\frac{33}{2^4}\right] + \left[\frac{33}{2^5}\right]$$

$$= 16 + 8 + 4 + 2 + 1$$

$$= 31$$

Hence, the exponent of 2 in $33!$ is 31 *i.e.*, $33!$ is divisible by $2^{31}$. Hence, the largest integer $n$ such that $33!$ is divisible by $2^n$ is 31.

***Example 4.*** *The number of zeros at the end of 75! is*

(a) 75 (b) 10 (c) 20 (d) 18

**Solution.** (d) We have,

$$E_2(75!) = \left[\frac{75}{2}\right] + \left[\frac{75}{2^2}\right] + \left[\frac{75}{2^3}\right] + \left[\frac{75}{2^4}\right] + \left[\frac{75}{2^5}\right] + \left[\frac{75}{2^6}\right] + \ldots$$

$$= 27 + 18 + 9 + 4 + 2 + 1 + \ldots = 71$$

$$\text{and } E_5(75!) = \left[\frac{75}{5}\right] + \left[\frac{75}{5^2}\right] + \left[\frac{75}{5^3}\right] + \ldots$$

$$= 15 + 3 + 0 = 18$$

Hence, the number of zeros at the end of $75! = \min(71, 18)$ $= 18$

***Example 5.*** *The positive number of solutions of $x + y + z + w = 20$ including zero values is*

(a) 1991 (b) 2001 (c) 1771 (d) 2011

**Solution.** (c) Since, $x \geq 0, y \geq 0, z \geq 0$ and $w \geq 0$.

and $x + y + z + w = 20$. Hence,

Total number of solutions

= The number of non-negative integral solution

$$= {}^{20+4-1}C_{4-1}$$

$$= {}^{20}C_3$$

$$= 1771$$

## Type II (*One or more than one correct option*)

***Example 6.*** *If $\alpha = 10800$, then*

(a) total number of divisor of $\alpha$ is 60

(b) the number of even divisor of $\alpha$ is 48

(c) the number of divisor of $\alpha$ of the form $4m+2$ is 12

(d) the number of divisor of $\alpha$ which are multiple of 15 is 30

**Solution.** (a), (b), (c), (d)

We have,

$$\alpha = 10800 = 2^4 \cdot 2^3 \cdot 5^2$$

(a) Total number of divisors

$$= (4+1)(3+1)(2+1) = 60$$

(b) Since, divisor to be even. We must have atleast one 2 out of four 2's any number of 3's and 5's.

So, the total number of even divisor $= 4(3+1)(2+1)$

$$= 48$$

(c) Since, $4m+2 = 2(2m+1)$. In any divisor of the form $4m+2, m$ should be exactly 1. So, number of divisors of the form $4m+2 = 1(3+1)(2+1)$

$$= 12$$

(d) A divisor of $\alpha$ will be multiple of 15. If it contains atleast one 3 out of three 3's and atleast one 5 out of two 5's.

So, number of divisors $= (4+1) \times 3 \times 2$

$$= 30$$

***Example 7.*** *If p is a prime number and b any integer.*

(a) $b^p \equiv b(mod\ p)$ (b) $b^p \not\equiv b(mod\ p)$

(c) $b^{p-1} \equiv 1(mod\ p)$ (d) $b^{p-1} \not\equiv 1(mod\ p)$

**Solution.** (a), (c)

If $p \mid b, b \equiv 0(\text{mod}\ p)$ and so is,

$$b^p \equiv 0(\text{mod}\ p)$$

$\therefore$ $b^p \equiv b(\text{mod}\ p)$

If $p \chi b, (b, p) = 1$

$\Rightarrow$ $b^{\phi(p)} \equiv 1(\text{mod}\ p)$ (by Euler's theorem)

But $\phi(p) = p-1$

Hence, $b^{p-1} \equiv 1(\text{mod}\ p)$

or $b^p = b(\text{mod}\ p)$

***Example 8.*** *If p is a prime integer and if a, b are any integers such that $p \mid ab$,*

(a) either $p \mid a$ or $p \mid b$ (b) $p \mid a$ and $p \mid b$

(c) $p \not| a$ and $p \not| b$ (d) either $p \not| a$ or $p \not| b$

**Solution.** (a)

When $a = 0$ and $b = 0$, the results holds. When $a \neq 0$ and $b \neq 0$.

Let us assume that $p \mid (ab)$ and $p$ does not divide $a$.

Now, since $p$ is prime and $p$ does not divide $a$,

$\Rightarrow$ The greatest common divisor of $a$ and $p$ is 1.

And, therefore there exist integers $m$ and $n$ such that

$$1 = am + pn \quad \text{...(i)}$$

Multiplication $b$ on both sides of Eq. (i) gives

$$b = (ab)m + p(nb) \quad \text{...(ii)}$$

$\Rightarrow$ $p \mid ab \Rightarrow$ There exist some integer $c$ such that $ab = pc$.

This on substitution in Eq. (ii) gives,

$$b = p(cm) + p(nb)$$

$\Rightarrow$ $b = p[cm + nb]$

$\Rightarrow$ $p \mid b$

Thus $p \mid ab$; $p$ is not a divisor of $a \Rightarrow p \mid b$.

Similarly, $p \mid ab$, $p$ is not a divisor of $b \Rightarrow p \mid a$.

# Exercise 1 (For Part 'B')

**Directions** (Q. Nos. 1-32) *All questions have only one correct option.*

**1.** If $a, b \in D$, $D$ is an ordered set, then which of the following is true?

(a) $a > b \Rightarrow -a > -b$ (b) $a > 0 \Rightarrow ab > ac \Rightarrow b < c$
(c) $a > b \Rightarrow -a < -b$ (d) $a \geq |a|$

**2.** If any 11 numbers are chosen from the set $\{1, 2, \ldots, 20\}$, then

(a) two of them will be a multiple of another
(b) one of them will be a multiple of another
(c) three of them will be multiple of another
(d) None of the above

**3.** If 30 dictionaries in a library contain a total of 61327 pages, then one of the dictionaries must have atleast .... pages

(a) 1045 pages (b) 945 pages
(c) 2045 pages (d) 1065 pages

**4.** If $n$ pigeons are assigned to $m$ pigeonholes, then one of the pigeonholes must contain atleast ... pigeons

(a) $\left(\frac{n-1}{m}\right)$ (b) $\left(\frac{n-1}{m}\right)+1$
(c) $\left(\frac{n}{m}-1\right)$ (d) $\left(\frac{n+1}{m}\right)-1$

**5.** If $A$ and $B$ are finite sets, then

(a) $|A \cup B| = |A| + |B| - |A \cap B|$
(b) $|A \cap B| = |A| + |B| - |A \cup B|$
(c) $|A \cap B| = |A \cup B| - |A| + |B|$
(d) $|A \cup B| = |A| - |B| + |A \cap B|$

**6.** If $A$ and $B$ are disjoint sets, then

(a) $A \cap B = 0$ (b) $A \cap B = \phi$
(c) $A \cup B = \phi$ (d) $A \cup B = 0$

**7.** If $A$, $B$ and $C$ are finite sets, then

$|A \cup B \cup C|$ is equal to

(a) $|A| + |B| - |C| + |A \cap B| + |B \cap C| - |A \cap B \cap C|$
(b) $|A| + |B| + |C| - |A \cap B| - |B \cap C| - |A \cap C| + |A \cap B \cap C|$
(c) $|A| - |B| - |C| + |A \cap B| - |B \cap C| - |A \cap C| - |A \cap B \cap C|$
(d) $|A| - |B| - |C| - |A \cap B| - |B \cap C| - |A \cap C| + |A \cap B \cap C|$

**8.** Numbers between 5000 and 10000 can be formed from the digits 1, 2, 3, 4, 5, 6, 7, 8, 9 each digit not appearing more than once in each number.

(a) 1080 (b) 1680
(c) 336 (d) 1008

**9.** If $n$ is a positive integer and a is any integer relatively prime to $n$, then

(a) $a^{\phi(n)} \equiv 1 \pmod{n}$ (b) $a^{\phi(n)} \equiv 0 \pmod{n}$
(c) $a^{\phi(n)} \equiv 2 \pmod{n}$ (d) $a^{\phi(n)} \equiv n + 1 \pmod{n}$

**10.** For Euler $\phi$-function $\phi(6)$ is equal to

(a) 3 (b) 2
(c) 4 (d) 6

**11.** The number of derangements of a set with $n$ elements is given by the formula

(a) $D_n = n(D_n - D_{n+1})$ (b) $D_n = (n+1)D_{n+1}$
(c) $D_{n+1} = n(D_{n+1} - D_n)$ (d) $D_{n+1} = n(D_n + D_{n-1})$

**12.** For 5 elements, there are

(a) 44 derangements (b) 54 derangements
(c) 64 derangements (d) 24 derangements

**13.** There are 35 microcomputers in a computer centre. Each microcomputer has 18 ports. How many different ports are there in the centre?

(a) 620 ports (b) 630 ports
(c) 650 ports (d) 690 ports

**14.** Eleven papers are set for the engineering examination of which two are in Mathematics. Number of ways can the papers be arranged if the two Mathematics papers do not come together.

(a) $8! \times 9!$ (b) $9! \times 11!$
(c) $8! \times 11!$ (d) $9! \times 10!$

**15.** In how many ways can 6 different beads be strung together to form a necklace?

(a) 60 ways (b) 80 ways
(c) 25 ways (d) 30 ways

**16.** The sum of all numbers of four digits can be formed with the digits 1, 2, 3.

(a) 162 (b) 179982
(c) 17982 (d) 199982

**17.** How many different words can be made out of the letters, which form the word ALLAHABAD?

(a) $\frac{4!}{9!\,2!}$ (b) $\frac{2!}{4!\,9!}$
(c) $\frac{9!}{4!\,2!}$ (d) $\frac{4!\,2!}{9!}$

**18.** I have 4 friends, in how many ways can I invite them for dinner?

(a) 15 (b) 11
(c) 16 (d) 20

**19.** The unit digit of $2^{100}$ is

(a) 2 (b) 4
(c) 6 (d) 8

**20.** The number of elements in the set

$\{m : 1 \leq m \leq 1000,\ m \text{ and } 1000 \text{ are relatively prime}\}$ is

(a) 100 (b) 250
(c) 300 (d) 400

**21.** The number of 4 digit number with no two digits common is
(a) 4536 (b) 3024
(c) 5040 (d) 4823

**22.** gcd (56, 72) is
(a) 2 (b) 4
(c) 6 (d) 8

**23.** Let gcd $(a, b) = 1$, then
gcd $(a + b, a^2 - ab + b^2)$ is
(a) 0 or 1 (b) 1 or 2
(c) 1 or 3 (d) 2 or 3

**24.** The remainder when $2^{50}$ is divided by 7 is
(a) 1 (b) 2
(c) 3 (d) 4

**25.** The remainder when $\sum_{r=1}^{100} r!$ is divided by 12 is
(a) 5 (b) 7 (c) 9 (d) 11

**26.** Number of integers, which are less than 108 and prime to 108 is
(a) 15 (b) 17 (c) 18 (d) 36

**27.** For prime $p$, if $a^{p-1} \equiv 1 \pmod p$, then $(a, p)$ equals to
(a) 1 (b) 2 (c) 3 (d) 4

**28.** If $(a, 7) = 1$, then $a^{12} - 1$ is divisible by $k$, where $k$ is
(a) 3 (b) 5 (c) 7 (d) 8

**29.** One of the solution for the equation $15x \equiv 6 \pmod{21}$ is
(a) 5 (b) 6
(c) 7 (d) 8

**30.** If $a^2 \equiv b^2 \pmod n$, then which of the following is correct?
(a) $a \equiv b \pmod n$ always hold
(b) $a \equiv b \pmod n$ never hold
(c) $a \equiv b \pmod n$ need not hold
(d) None of the above

**31.** If integers $a, b > 1$; then the set of all integer of the form $ma + nb (m, n \in Z)$ includes
(a) Both their gcd and lcm
(b) their gcd but not lcm
(c) their lcm but not gcd
(d) Neither their lcm nor gcd

**32.** Select the correct statement/statements
I. If $d = (c, m)$, then $ca \equiv cb \pmod m$
$\Rightarrow a \equiv b \pmod{m/d}$
II. $ca \equiv cb \pmod p \{p \text{ is prime}\}$
$\Rightarrow a \equiv b \pmod p$
III. $a \equiv b \pmod p \Rightarrow \gcd(a, m) = \gcd(b, m)$

**Codes**
(a) I and II (b) I and III
(c) II and III (d) I, II and III

# Exercise 2 (For Part 'C')

**Directions** (Q. Nos. 1-48) *Questions may have one or more than one correct option.*

**1.** Let $a, b$ be integers not both zero, then which of the following(s) is/are true?
(a) If gcd $(a, b) = 1$, then gcd$(a + b, a - b) = 1$ or 2
(b) If gcd $(a, 4) = 2 =$ gcd $(b, 4)$, then gcd$(a + b, 4) = 4$
(c) gcd $(a, b) =$ gcd $(a, b + ac)$ for any integer $c$
(d) gcd $(a^2, b^2) =$ gcd $(a, b)$

**2.** If $d$ is a positive integers such that $d | 13n + 6$, $d | 12n + 5$ for some integer $n$, then
(a) $d = 1$ (b) $d = 3$
(c) $d = 5$ (d) $d = 7$

**3.** Which of the following(s) is/are true for two relatively prime integers $a$ and $b$?
(a) gcd$(a, b) = 1$
(b) $ax + by = 1$ for any integers $x$ and $y$
(c) $ax = by$ for any integers $x$ and $y$
(d) gcd $(a^n b^n) = 1$, where $n$ is any positive integer

**4.** Let $n = 2^3 \cdot 3^2 \cdot 7^2 \cdot 11$, then which of the following(s) is/are true?
(a) Total number of divisors of $n$ (excluding 1 and $n$) is 70.
(b) Total number of divisors of $n$ (including 1 and $n$) is 71.
(c) The number of ways in which $n$ can be resolved as a product of two factors is 35.
(d) The number of ways in which $n$ can be resolved as a product of two factors is 36.

**5.** Which of the following(s) is\are true?
(a) $5^6 \equiv 1 \pmod 7$ (b) $5^{\varphi(7)} \equiv 1 \pmod 7$
(c) $5^7 \equiv 5 \pmod 7$ (d) $5^{\varphi(7)} \equiv 5 \pmod 7$

**6.** Let $x$ and $y$ are the values of remainder when $2^{100}$ is divided by 11 and $2^{105}$ is divided by 11 respectively, then which of the following is/are true?
(a) $\varphi(x + y) = 10$ (b) $\varphi(xy) = 6$
(c) $\varphi(xy) = 4$ (d) $\varphi(x + y) = \varphi(x)\varphi(y)$

**7.** For any integer $a$, satisfying $a^3 \equiv x \pmod 9$, then $x$ is/are
(a) 2 (b) 1
(c) 0 (d) 8

**8.** If a is a whole number and $p$ is a prime number, then according to Fermat's theorem
(a) $2^p - 2$ is divisible by $p$
(b) $2^p - 1$ is divisible by $p$
(c) $2^{p-1} - 1$ is divisible by $p$
(d) $2^{p-1} - 2$ is divisible by $p$

**9.** For positive integers $a$ and $b$ satisfying $\text{lcm}\{a, b\} = 10$ and $\gcd\{a, b\} = 100$ simultaneously, then
(a) $a = 10, b = 100$ (b) $a = 20, b = 100$
(c) $a = 100, b = 10$ (d) $a = 100, b = 20$

**10.** Which of the following(s) is/are true for prime number $p$?
(a) $2^{p-1} - 1 \equiv (\text{mod } p)$ (b) $2^p - 1 \equiv (\text{mod } p)$
(c) $(p-1)! \equiv -1 \pmod p$ (d) $p! \equiv -1 \pmod p$

**11.** If $a$ is not divisible by $p$ and if $n \equiv m \bmod (p-1)$,
(a) $a^n \equiv a^m \bmod p$
(b) $a^n \not\equiv a^m \bmod p$
(c) $p - 1 | n - m$
(d) $p - 1 \nmid n - m$

**12.** For any integer $n > 1$,
(a) Euler function $\phi(n) = n - 1$, if $n$ is prime
(b) Euler function $\phi(n) = n - 1$, if $n$ is not prime
(c) If $n$ is prime, then Euler function $\phi(n) = n - 1$
(d) If $n$ is prime, then Euler function $\phi(n) \neq n - 1$

**13.** Which of the following statement(s) are true?
(a) Euler's criterion. Let $p$ be an odd prime. Then, for all $n$, we have
$$(n|p) \equiv n^{(p-1)/2} \pmod p$$
(b) Euler's criterion: Let $p$ be an odd prime. Then, for all $n$ we have
$$(n|p) \not\equiv n^{(p-1)/2} \pmod p$$
(c) Suppose that $(n|p) = 1$. Then, there is an $x$ such that $x^2 \equiv n \pmod p$ and we have $n^{(p-1)/2} \equiv (x^2)^{(p-1)/2} = x^{p-1} \equiv 1 = (n|p) \pmod p$
(d) Suppose $(n|p) = 1$. There does not exist $x$ such that $x^2 \equiv n \pmod p$

**14.** For any two integers, if atleast one of them is non-zero
(a) there exist integers $x$ and $y$ such that $(a, b) = ax + by$
(b) there does not exist integers $x$ and $y$ such that $(a, b) = ax + by$
(c) if $c | a$ and $c | b$, then $c | ax + by$
(d) if $c | a$ and $c | b$, then $c | ax + by$

**15.** For every odd prime $p$,
(a) $(2|p) = (-1)^{(p^2-1)/8}$
(b) $((p-1)/2)! \not\equiv 0 \pmod p$
(c) $((p-1)/2)! \equiv 0 \pmod p$
(d) $(2|p) \neq (-1)^{(p^2-1)/8}$

**16.** Prove that if $p$ is a prime and $b$ an integer coprime to $p$. Then, the linear congruence $bx \equiv y \pmod p$ has a solution $(x_0, y_0)$ such that
(a) $0 < |x_0| < \sqrt{p}$ (b) $0 < |y_0| < \sqrt{p}$
(c) $\sqrt{p} < |x_0| < 0$ (d) $\sqrt{p} < |y_0| < 0$

**17.** Which of the following statement(s) is/are true?
(a) The greatest common divisor of 169 and −962 is 13
(b) The greatest common divisor of 169 and −962 is 69
(c) $(169, -962) = (169)(-17) + (-962)(-3)$
(d) $(169, -962) = (169)(6) + (-962)(13)$

**18.** Which of the following statement(s) is/are true?
(a) If $p$ is a prime number and $k$ any positive integer, then $\phi(p^k) = p^k - p^{k-1} = p^k\left(1 - \frac{1}{p}\right)$
(b) If $p$ is a prime number and $k$ any positive integer, then $\phi(p^k) \neq p^k\left(1 - \frac{1}{p}\right)$
(c) Both (a) and (b)
(d) None of the above

**19.** If $ac \equiv bc \pmod m$ and $d = (m, c)$
(a) $a \equiv b\left(\text{mod } \frac{m}{d}\right)$ (b) $a \equiv \text{mod}\left(\frac{m}{d}\right)$
(c) $a \equiv m \bmod b$ (d) $a \equiv m \,\text{mod}\left(\frac{b}{a}\right)$

**20.** Which of the following statement(s) is/are true?
(a) $7 = 21.1547 - 58.560$ (b) $7 = 21.427 - 16.560$
(c) $7 = 28 - 1.21$ (d) $7 = 5.28 - 1.133$

**21.** Let $k$ be any integer and $a, b$ any integers atleast one of which is non-zero, then
(a) $(ka, kb) = |k|(a, b)$ (b) $(a, b) \neq |k|(a, b)$
(c) $(a, b) < |k|(a, b)$ (d) $(a, b) > |k|(a, b)$

**22.** Let $p \equiv 1 \pmod 4$, it can be expressed as sum of two squares.
(a) $p$ can be expressed as sum of two squares
(b) $p$ cannot be expressed as sum of two squares
(c) $p = x^2 + y^2$ for some $x, y$
(d) $p \neq x^2 + y^2$ for some $x, y$

**23.** If $a_1, a_2, \ldots, a_k$ form a reduced residue system (mod $m$)
(a) $k = \phi(m)$
(b) $k \neq \phi(m)$
(c) For every $i$, $1 \le i \le k (a_i, m) = 1$
(d) For every $i$, $1 \le i \le k (a_i, m) \neq 1$

**24.** Let $p$ be an odd prime with $p \equiv 3 \pmod 4$.
(a) $\left[\left(\frac{p-1}{2}\right)!\right]^2 \equiv 1 \pmod p$
(b) If $\left(\frac{p-1}{2!}\right)$ is a solution of $x^2 \equiv -1 \pmod p$, then $-1 \equiv (p-1)!$
(c) $\left(\left(\frac{p-1}{2}\right)!\right)^2 \not\equiv 1 \pmod p$
(d) If $\left(\frac{p-1}{2!}\right)$ is a solution of $x^2 \equiv -1 \pmod p$, then $-1 \not\equiv (p-1)!$

**25.** If $b^{\frac{p-1}{2}} \equiv 1 \pmod p$

(a) then $b$ is a quadratic residue (mod $p$)

(b) then $b$ is not a quadratic residue (mod $p$)

(c) $p-1 \mid \frac{k(p-1)}{2}$

(d) $p-1 \nmid \frac{k(p-1)}{2}$

**26.** Which of the following statement(s) is/are true?

(a) gcd $(1547, 560) = 7$ (b) $1547 = 2.560 + 427$

(c) $427 = 3.133 + 28$ (d) $28 = 1.21 + 9$

**27.** For any integers a and b, if $d = (a, b)$

(a) $\left(\frac{a}{d}, \frac{b}{d}\right) = 1$ (b) $\left(\frac{a}{d}, \frac{b}{d}\right) = 2$

(c) $d\left(\frac{a}{d}, \frac{b}{d}\right) = d$ (d) $\left(\frac{a}{d}, \frac{b}{d}\right) = 4$

**28.** Which of the following statement(s) is/are true?

(a) Any integer $b$ is a quadratic residue (mod $p$), then $b^{\frac{p-1}{2}} \equiv 1 \pmod p$

(b) Any integer $b$ is not a quadratic residue (mod $p$), then $b^{\frac{p-1}{2}} \equiv 1 \pmod p$

(c) If any integer $b$ is a quadratic residue (mod $p$), then $x^2 \equiv b \pmod p$ has a solution

(d) If any integer $b$ is quadratic residue (mod $p$). Then, $x^2 \equiv b \pmod p$, has no solution

**29.** Let if integers $m, n > 1$ and every prime divisor of $n$ is a prime divisor of $m$. Then,

(a) $\phi(mn) = n\phi(m)$ (b) $\phi(n^2) = n\phi(n)$

(c) $\phi(mn) = n$ (d) $\phi(n^2) = n^2$

**30.** Which of the following statement(s) is/are true?

(a) An integer $b$ coprime to $p$ is a quadratic residue or quadratic non-residue (mod $p$). If $b^{\frac{p-1}{2}} \equiv 1 \pmod p$

(b) An integer $b$ coprime to $p$ is a not quadratic residue or quadratic non-residue (mod $p$), if $b^{p-1/2} \equiv 1 \pmod p$

(c) Fermat little theorem is $a^{p-1} \equiv 1 \pmod p$

(d) If $b$ is a quadratic residue (mod $p$), then $b^{\frac{p-1}{2}} \equiv 1 \pmod p$

**31.** Let $p$ be any odd prime.

(a) Congruence $x^2 \equiv -1 \pmod p$ has a solution, if $p \equiv 1 \pmod 4$

(b) Congruence $x^2 \equiv -1 \pmod p$ has no solution, if $p \equiv 1 \pmod 4$

(c) If $p \equiv 1 \pmod 4$, then congruence $x^2 \equiv -1 \pmod p$ has a solution

(d) If $p \equiv 1 \pmod 4$, then $x^2 \equiv -1 \pmod p$ has no solution

**32.** Let $a = 8316$ and $b = 10920$. Let $d = \gcd(a, b)$.

I. The greatest common divisor of $a$ and $b$ is 84.

II. Find integers $m$ and $n$ such that $d = ma + nb$.

(a) $d = 84$

(b) $d = 65$

(c) There exist no integer $m, n$ such $d = ma + nb$

(d) For integer 4 and 3, $d = 4a + 3b$

**33.** Which of the following statement(s) is/are true?

(a) For any integer $n > 2$, Euler's function $\phi(n)$ is even

(b) For any integer $n > 2$, Euler's function $\phi(n)$ is odd

(c) For any integer $n > 2$, Euler's function $\phi(n)$ is rational number

(d) For any integer $n > 2$, Euler's function $\phi(n)$ is zero

**34.** Which of the following statement(s) is/are true?

(a) 6 is the integral root of $x^7 + x + 2 \equiv 0 \pmod 7$

(b) 6 is not the integral root of $x^7 + x + 2 \equiv 0 \pmod 7$

(c) $6^7 \equiv 6 \pmod 7$

(d) $6^7 \not\equiv 6 \pmod 7$

**35.** Which of the following statement(s) is/are true?

(a) There exists no rational number whose square is 2

(b) There exists a rational number whose square is 2

(c) $p$ is even, then $p^2$ is even

(d) $p^2$ is even, then $p$ is even

**36.** Which of the following statement(s) is/are true?

(a) $\sin 10°$ is rational

(b) $\sin 10°$ is not rational

(c) $\sin 30°$ is rational

(d) $\sin 30°$ is not rational

**37.** Which of the following statement(s) is/are true?

(a) There exist a positive integer less than one

(b) There exist a positive integer less than zero

(c) There does not exist a positive integer less than one

(d) $n \in Z$ and $n$ is positive integer, then $n \geq 1$

**38.** Which of the following statement(s) is/are true?

(a) Between two integers there exists no integer

(b) Between two integers there exists an integer

(c) Between two rational numbers there exists a rational numbers

(d) Between two rational numbers there exists no rational numbers

**39.** Which of the following statement(s) is/are true?

(a) The repeating decimal represents a rational number

(b) The repeating decimal does not represents a rational number

(c) The repeating decimal represents an irrational number

(d) The repeating decimal represents integers

**40.** Which of the following(s) is/are correct?
(a) The product of two negative integers is positive
(b) The product of two negative integers is negative
(c) The product of two negative rational numbers is positive
(d) The product of two negative rational number is negative

**41.** Show that the product of two positive rational numbers is positive.
(a) Square of any integer is positive
(b) Product of two positive integer is positive
(c) Product of two positive rational numbers is positive
(d) Product of two positive rational numbers is negative

**42.** Which of the following statement(s) is/are true?
(a) Every integer greater than 1 has a prime factor
(b) Every integer greater than 1 has no prime factor
(c) Both (a) and (b)
(d) None of the above

**43.** Expressing the number as the sum of square.
(a) $10 = 3^2 + 1^2$ (b) $10 = 6^2 + 1^2$
(c) $153 = 12^2 + 3^2$ (d) $153 = 12^2 + 6^2$

**44.** Which of the following statement(s) is/are true?
(a) $|a \pm b| \le |a| + |b|$
(b) $|a \pm b| \ge |a| + |b|$
(c) $|a \pm b| \le \sqrt{(a+b)^2}$
(d) $|a \pm b| \ge 0$

**45.** Which of the following statement(s) is/are true?
(a) Every integer $n$ of the form $4k + 3$ is the sum of two squares
(b) Every integer $n$ of the form $4k + 3$ is not the sum of two squares
(c) No integer $n$ of the form $4k + 3$ is the sum of two squares
(d) Every integer $n$ of the form $4k + 3$ is the sum of squares

**46.** Which of the following statement(s) is/are true?
(a) The product of two positive integers is equal to the product of their lowest common multiple and greatest common divisor
(b) The product of two positive integers is not equal to the product of lowest common multiple and greatest common divisor
(c) The product of two positive integers is equal to there lowest common multiple
(d) The product of two positive integers is equal to there greatest common divisor

**47.** Which of the following statement(s) is/are true?
(a) Every integer $n > 1$ is either a prime number or a product of prime numbers
(b) Every integer $n > 1$ is a prime number
(c) Every integer $n > 1$ is a product of prime numbers
(d) Every integer is a product of prime numbers but not a prime number

**48.** Which of the following statement(s) is/are true?
(a) Lowest common multiple of two integers is unique
(b) LCM of two integers can be distinct
(c) Both (a) and (b)
(d) None of the above

# Answers

## Exercise 1

| | | | | | | | | | |
|---|---|---|---|---|---|---|---|---|---|
| **1.** (c) | **2.** (b) | **3.** (c) | **4.** (b) | **5.** (a) | **6.** (b) | **7.** (b) | **8.** (b) | **9.** (a) | **10.** (b) |
| **11.** (d) | **12.** (a) | **13.** (b) | **14.** (d) | **15.** (a) | **16.** (b) | **17.** (c) | **18.** (a) | **19.** (c) | **20.** (d) |
| **21.** (a) | **22.** (d) | **23.** (c) | **24.** (d) | **25.** (c) | **26.** (c) | **27.** (a) | **28.** (c) | **29.** (b) | **30.** (c) |
| **31.** (a) | **32.** (b) | | | | | | | | |

## Exercise 2

| | | | | | | | | | |
|---|---|---|---|---|---|---|---|---|---|
| **1.** (a,b,c) | **2.** (a,d) | **3.** (a,b,d) | **4.** (a,d) | **5.** (a,b) | **6.** (a,c) | **7.** (b,c,d) | **8.** (a,c) | **9.** (a,c) | **10.** (a,c) |
| **11.** (a,c) | **12.** (a,c) | **13.** (a,c) | **14.** (a,c) | **15.** (a,b) | **16.** (a,b) | **17.** (a,c) | **18.** (a) | **19.** (a) | **20.** (a,b,c,d) |
| **21.** (a) | **22.** (a,c) | **23.** (a,c) | **24.** (a,b) | **25.** (a,c) | **26.** (a,b,c) | **27.** (a,c) | **28.** (a,c) | **29.** (a,b) | **30.** (a,c,d) |
| **31.** (a,c) | **32.** (a,d) | **33.** (a) | **34.** (a,c) | **35.** (a,c,d) | **36.** (b,d) | **37.** (c,d) | **38.** (a,c) | **39.** (a) | **40.** (a,c) |
| **41.** (a,b,c) | **42.** (a) | **43.** (a,c) | **44.** (a,c,d) | **45.** (b,c) | **46.** (a) | **47.** (a) | **48.** (a) | | |

# Hints & Solutions

## Exercise 1

**8.** Numbers between 5000 and 10000 will be of four digits.

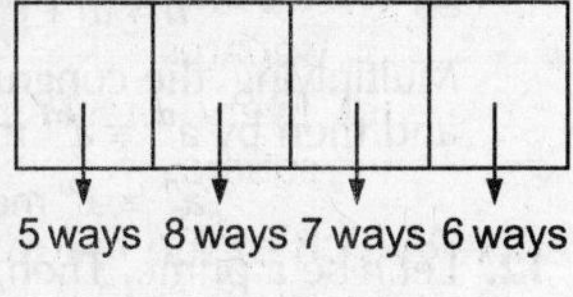


Since, number is greater than 5000 therefore, thousands place will be filled either 5 or 6 or 7 or 8 or 9 (total 5) ways.

$\therefore$ Required number of numbers $= 5 \times 8 \times 7 \times 6 = 1680$

**10.** $6 = 2^1 \times 3^1$

$$\Rightarrow \quad \varphi(6) = 6\left(1 - \frac{1}{2}\right)\left(1 - \frac{1}{3}\right)$$

$$= 6 \times \frac{1}{2} \times \frac{2}{3} = 2$$

**11.** For $n = 4$

$$n(D_n + D_{n-1}) = 4(D_4 + D_3)$$

$$D_4 = 4!\left(\frac{1}{2!} - \frac{1}{3!} + \frac{1}{4!}\right) = 12 - 4 + 1 = 9$$

$$D_3 = 3!\left(\frac{1}{2!} - \frac{1}{3!}\right) = 3 - 1 = 2$$

$$\Rightarrow \quad 4(D_4 + D_3) = 4 \times 11 = 44$$

Now, $\quad D_{n+1} = D_5 = 5!\left(\frac{1}{2!} - \frac{1}{3!} + \frac{1}{4!} - \frac{1}{5!}\right)$

$$= 60 - 20 + 5 - 1 = 44$$

**15.** Required number of ways $= \frac{5!}{2} = \frac{120}{2} = 60$

**18.** $2^4 - 1 = 15$

**19.** $2^{100} = (2^4)^{25} = 16^{25}$

**20.** $\varphi(1000) = \varphi(2^3 \times 5^3)$

$$= 1000\left(1 - \frac{1}{2}\right)\left(1 - \frac{1}{5}\right)$$

$$= 1000 \times \frac{1}{2} \times \frac{4}{5} = 400$$

**21.** Required number $= 9 \times 9 \times 8 \times 7 = 4536$

**22.** $72 = 1 \times 56 + 16$

$56 = 16 \times 3 + 8$

$16 = 8 \times 2 + 0$

Since, last non-zero remainder is 8.

**23.** Let $\gcd(a + b, a^2 - ab + b^2) = d$

$\Rightarrow \quad d \mid a + b, \; d \mid a^2 - ab + b^2$

$\Rightarrow \quad d \mid (a + b)^2 = a^2 + b^2 + 2ab, \; d \mid a^2 - ab + b^2$

$\Rightarrow \quad d \mid 3ab$

Let $\quad \gcd(d \cdot a) = e$

Then, $e \mid d \mid a + b \Rightarrow \; e \mid a + b \mid$ and $e \mid a$

$\Rightarrow \quad e \mid a + b - a = b$

So, $e \mid \gcd(a, b) = 1 \;\Rightarrow\; e = 1$

$\Rightarrow \quad \gcd(d \cdot a) = 1$

Similarly, $\gcd(d, b) = 1$

Hence, $\quad d/3 \;\Rightarrow\; d = 1$ or $3$

**24.** Since, $\quad 2^3 \equiv 1 \pmod 7$

$\Rightarrow \quad (2^3)^{16} \equiv 1^{16} \equiv 1 \pmod 7$

$\Rightarrow \quad 2^{48} \equiv 1 \pmod 7$

$\Rightarrow \quad 2^{48} \times 2^2 \equiv 2^2 \pmod 7$

$\quad 2^{50} \equiv 4 \pmod 7$

Hence, 4 is the remainder as required.

**25.** Since, $1! + 2! + 3! + 4! + \ldots + 100!$

$\equiv 1! + 2! + 3! + 0 + \ldots + 0 \pmod{12}$

$\Rightarrow \quad 1! + 2! + 3! + 4! + \ldots + 100! \equiv 9 \pmod{12}$

$\Rightarrow \quad 9$ is the required remainder.

**27.** $a$ and $p$ must be relatively prime to each other, from Euler's. Fermat theorem.

**28.** Given $(a, 7) = 1$

Hence, by Euler's-Fermat theorem,

$a^{\varphi(7)} \equiv 1 \pmod 7$

$\Rightarrow \quad a^6 \equiv 1 \pmod 7 \qquad [\because \varphi(7) = 6]$

$\Rightarrow \quad (a^6)^2 \equiv 1^2 \pmod 7$

$\Rightarrow \quad a^{12} \equiv 1 \pmod 7$

$\Rightarrow \quad a^{12} - 1 \equiv 0 \pmod 7$

$\Rightarrow \quad a^{12} - 1$ is divisible by 7.

**29.** Here, $(15, 21) = 3$ which divide 6.

Hence, the given congruence is equivalent to

$5x \equiv 2 \pmod 7$, where $(5, 7) = 1$

Hence, $\quad x \equiv \frac{2}{5} \pmod 7$

$$\equiv \frac{2 + 4 \times 7}{5} \bmod (7)$$

$$\equiv 6 \bmod (7)$$

$\Rightarrow \quad x = 6, 13, 20 \pmod{21}$

## Exercise 2

**1.** (a) Let $\gcd(a + b, a - b) = d$

$\Rightarrow \quad d \mid a + b$ and $d \mid a - b$

$\Rightarrow \quad d \mid (a + b) \pm (a - b)$

$\Rightarrow \quad d \mid 2a$ and $d \mid 2b$

$\Rightarrow \quad d \mid \gcd(2a, 2b)$

But $\gcd(2a, 2b) = 2 \cdot \gcd(a, b) = 2 \cdot 1 = 2$

$\therefore \quad d \mid 2 \Rightarrow d = 1$ or $2$

(b) Since, $\gcd(a, 4) = 2$

$\Rightarrow \quad a = 2k_1$, where $k_1$ is odd integer.

Also, $\gcd(b, 4) = 2$

$\Rightarrow \quad b = 2k_2$, where $k_2$ is odd integer.

Hence, $\quad a + b = 2k_1 + 2k_2 = 2(k_1 + k_2) = 2(2k_3) = 4k_3$,

where $k_1 + k_2 = 2k_3$, for some $k_3 \in Z$

$\Rightarrow \gcd(a + b, 4) = 4$

(c) Let $\gcd(a, b) = d_1$, and $\gcd(a, b + ac) = d_2$

To show that, $d_1 = d_2$

Now, $d_2 = \gcd(a, b + ac)$

$\Rightarrow d_2 | a$ and $d_2 | b + ac$

$\Rightarrow d_2 | ac$ and $d_2 | b + ac$

$\Rightarrow d_2 | (b + ac) - (ac)$ i.e., $d_2 | b$

Hence, $d_2 | a$ and $d_2 | b \Rightarrow d_2 | \gcd(a, b)$ i.e., $d_2 | d_1$ ...(i)

Again, $\quad \gcd(a, b) = d_1$

$\Rightarrow d_1 | a$ and $d_1 | b$

$\Rightarrow d_1 | ac$ and $d_1 | b \Rightarrow d_1 | b + ac$

Hence, $d_1 | a$ and $d_1 | b + ac$

$\Rightarrow d_1 | \gcd(a, b + ac)$ i.e., $d_1 | d_2$ ...(ii)

$\therefore$ From Eqs. (i) and (ii), we get

$$d_1 = d_2$$

i.e., $\quad \gcd(a, b) = \gcd(a, b + ac)$

**2.** $d | 13n + 6$ and $d | 12n + 5$

$\Rightarrow d | (13n + 6) - (12n + 5)$ i.e., $d | n + 1$

Now, $d | n + 1$ and $d | 13n + 6 \Rightarrow d | 13(n + 1) - (13n + 6)$

$\Rightarrow d | 7$

But 7 is a prime number

Hence, $\quad d = 1$ or $7$

**4.** Total number of divisors of $n$ including 1 and $n$ is

$= (3 + 1)(2 + 1)(2 + 1)(1 + 1)$

$= 4 \times 3 \times 3 \times 2$

$= 72$

$\Rightarrow$ Total number of divisors excluding 1 and

$n = 72 - 2 = 70$

Since, $n$ is not a perfect square.

$\therefore$ Number of ways in, which $n$ can be resolved as a product of two factors is

$$= \frac{1}{2}(3 + 1)(2 + 1)(2 + 1)(1 + 1) = 36$$

**5.** From Euler's-Fermat theorem,

$(a, p) = 1$, then $a^{\varphi(p)} \equiv 1 \pmod p$

or $\quad a^{p-1} \equiv 1 \pmod p$, which is equivalent to

$a^p \equiv a \pmod p$

Here, $(5, 7) = 1 \Rightarrow 5^{\varphi(7)} \equiv 1 \pmod 7$

$\Rightarrow 5^6 \equiv 1 \pmod 7 \quad [\because \varphi(7) = 6]$

**6.** Here, $2^{100} = (2^{10})^{10}$ and by using Fermat theorem, we have

$2^{10} \equiv 1 \pmod{11}$

$\Rightarrow (2^{10})^{10} \equiv 1^{10} \pmod{11} \Rightarrow 2^{100} \equiv 1 \pmod{11}$

$\Rightarrow \quad x = 1$

Also, $2^{105} = 2^{100} \cdot 2^5 \equiv 32 \pmod{11}$

$\Rightarrow \quad 2^{105} \equiv 10 \pmod{11}$

Hence, $\quad y = 10$

**11.** If $n > m$, since $p - 1 | n - m$

$\Rightarrow \quad n - m = c(p - 1)$

for some positive integer $c$.

$\Rightarrow \quad n = m + c(p - 1)$

Multiplying the congruence $a^{p-1} \equiv 1 \mod m$ by itself $c$ times and then by $a^m \equiv a^m \mod p$, we have

$$a^n \equiv a^m \mod p.$$

**12.** Let $n$ be a prime. Then, $1, 2, 3, \ldots, n - 1$ are all integers $\leq n$ and are coprime to $n$.

Therefore, $\phi(n) = n - 1$.

Conversely, if $n$ has a divisor $d$ and $1 < d < n$, then

$$\phi(n) \leq n - 2 < n - 1$$

Hence, $n$ has no divisor $d$ and $1 < d < n$ or the only divisors of $n$ are 1 and $n$. Thus, $n$ is a prime.

**13.** Euler's criterion. Let $p$ be an odd prime. Then, for all $n$, we have

$$(n | p) \equiv n^{(p-1)/2} \pmod p$$

**Proof** ***Case 1*** If $n \equiv 0 \pmod p$ the result is trivial, since both members are congruent to 0 mod $p$.

***Case 2*** Suppose that $(n | p) = 1$. Then, there is an $x$ such that $x^2 \equiv n \pmod p$ and we have

$$n^{(p-1)/2} \equiv (x^2)^{(p-1)/2} = x^{p-1} \equiv 1 = (n | p) \pmod p$$

***Case 3*** Suppose that $(n | p) = -1$, consider the polynomial

$$f(x) = x^{(p-1)/2} - 1$$

Since, $f(x)$ has degree $(p - 1)/2$ the congruence

$$f(x) \equiv 0 \pmod p$$

has most $(p - 1)/2$ solutions.

But since $(p - 1)/2$ quadratic residues mod $p$ are solutions so the non-residues are not the solutions. Hence,

$$n^{(p-1)/2} \not\equiv 1 \pmod p, \text{ if } (n | p) = -1$$

But $\quad n^{(p-1)/2} \equiv \pm 1 \pmod p$

So, $\quad n^{(p-1)/2} \equiv -1 \equiv (n | p) \pmod p$

**14.** Let $d = (a, b)$ and define a set $S$, such that

$S = \{au + bv \mid au + bv > 0, u, v \text{ integers}\}$

Since, atleast one of $a$ or $b$ is non-zero, therefore either $|a| \in S$ or $|b| \in S$.

By well ordering principle, $S$ has a least $d = ax + by$ (say) such that $d \leq |a|$ and $d \leq |b|$.

By division algorithm,

$$|a| = dq + r, \text{ where } 0 \leq r \leq d$$

$\Rightarrow \quad r = |a| - dq$

$= \pm a - q(ax + by)$

$= a(\pm 1 - xq) + (-y)b \geq 0$ and $r \in S$.

Choose $d$, such that $r = 0$, we have

$$|a| = dq \Rightarrow d \,|\, |a| \Rightarrow d | a$$

Similarly, $d | b$

If $c | a$ and $c | b$, then $c | ax + by$

$\Rightarrow \quad c | d$

Hence, $\quad d = (a, b) = ax + by$

**15.** Since,

$$p-1 \equiv 1(-1)^1 \pmod p$$
$$2 \equiv 2(-1)^2 \pmod p$$
$$p-3 \equiv 3(-1)^3 \pmod p$$
$$4 \equiv 4(-1)^4 \pmod p$$
$$\vdots \quad \vdots$$
$$r \equiv \frac{p-1}{2}(-1)^{(p-1)/2} \pmod p$$

where $r$ is either $p-(p-1)/2$ or $(p-1)/2$

Multiplying $p-\frac{(p-1)}{2}$ and $\frac{p-1}{2}$

we have $\left(p-\frac{(p-1)}{2}\right)\left(\frac{p-1}{2}\right)=\left(\frac{p-1}{4}\right)$ which is the even integer. Therefore, we have

$$2\cdot 4\cdot 6\ldots(p-1) \equiv \left(\frac{p-1}{2}\right)!(-1)^{1+2+\ldots+(p-1)/2} \pmod p$$

Which gives

$$2^{(p-1)/2}\left(\frac{p-1}{2}\right)! \equiv \left(\frac{p-1}{2}\right)!(-1)^{(p^2-1)/8} \pmod p$$

Since, $\left(\frac{p-1}{2}\right)! \not\equiv 0 \pmod p$

$$\Rightarrow \quad 2^{(p-1)/2} \equiv (-1)^{(p^2-1)/8} \pmod p$$

**16.** Let $n = 1+[\sqrt{p}]$. Then, $n^2 > p$

Then, set $S = \{ax \quad y \mid 0 \le x \le n \quad 1, 0 \le y \le n \quad 1\}$ contains $n^2$ elements. Since, $ax-y$ can take atmost $p$ values (mod $p$), hence there exist integers $(x_1, y_1)$ and $(x_2, y_2)$ such that

$$bx_1 - y_1 \equiv bx_2 - y_2 \pmod p$$

with $\quad x_1 \ne x_2$ and $y_1 \ne y_2$

Let $\quad x_0 = x_1 - x_2$

and $\quad y_0 = y_1 - y_2$

Then, $\quad x_0 \ne 0, y_0 \ne 0$

and $\quad 0 < |x_0| = |x_1 - x_2| \le n-1$

$$= [\sqrt{p}] < \sqrt{p}$$

$$0 < |y_0| = |y_1 - y_2| \le n-1$$
$$= [\sqrt{p}] < \sqrt{p}$$

Hence, $(x_0, y_0)$ is the required solution.

**17.** Since, $\quad -962 = 169\times(-6)+52$

$$169 = 52\times 3 + 13$$
$$52 = 13\times 4$$

Thus, $\quad 13 = (52, 13)$

$$= (169, 52)$$
$$= (-962, 169)$$

Also,

$$(169, -962) = 169 - 52\times 3$$
$$= 169 - \{-962 - 169\times(-6)\times 3\}$$
$$= 169\times(-17) + (-962)\times(-3)$$
$$= 169m + (-962)n,$$

where $m = -17$ and $n = -3$

**18.** We have,

$\phi(p^k)$ = number of integers $\le p^k$ that are coprime to $p^k$

= all the integers in the set $S$

$S = [1, 2, \ldots, p, \ldots, p^k]$ that are not divisible by $p$.

But the integers that are not divisible by $p$ are those that are not multiples of $p$.

Hence to count their number, it is enough to count the number of integers in $S$ that are multiples of $p$.

And the integers in the set $S$ that are multiples of $p$ are

$p, 2p, \ldots, (p-1)p, p\cdot p = p^2$; (count upto be $p$)

$(p+1)p, (p+2)p, \ldots, (p+(p-1))p, 2p\cdot p = 2p^2$; (count upto be $p$)

$\vdots \qquad \vdots$

$(2p+1)p, (2p+2)p, \ldots, (2p+(p-1))p, 3p\cdot p = 3p^2$; (count upto be $p$)

$\vdots \qquad \vdots$

$(p-1)(p+1)p, (p(p-1)+2)p, \ldots, (p(p-1)+p)p = p^3$; (count upto by $p$)

$\ldots p^{k-1}\cdot p = p^k$

and total is $p^{k-1}$ in number.

Hence, $\quad \phi(p^k) = p^k - p^{k-1}$

$$= p^k\left(1-\frac{1}{p}\right)$$

**19.** Since, $d = (m, c)$

Therefore, there exist integer $r, s : (r, s) = 1$

and $\quad c = rd, m = sd$

Here, $\quad ac \equiv bc \pmod m$

$\Rightarrow \quad m \mid ac - bc = ard - brd$

$$= (a-b)rd$$

$\Rightarrow \quad \left(\frac{m}{d}\right) \mid (a-b)r$

$\Rightarrow \quad s \mid (a-b)r$

Since, $\quad (r, s) = -1$

$\therefore \quad s \mid (b-a) \quad$ (by Euclid's lemma)

$\Rightarrow \quad a \equiv b \pmod s$

or $\quad a \equiv b\left(\bmod \frac{m}{d}\right)$

**20.** Since, $7 = 28 - 1.21$

$$= 28 - 1(133 - 4.28)$$
$$= 5.28 - 1.133$$
$$= 5(425 - 3.133) - 1.133$$
$$= 5.427 - 16.133$$
$$= 5.427 - 16(560 - 1427)$$
$$= 21.427 - 16.560$$
$$= 21(1547 - 2.560) - 16.560$$
$$= 21.1547 - 58.560$$

**21.** Let $d = (a, b)$ and $t = (ka, kb)$

It is enough to take $k$ as positive, since

$$(a, b) = (|a|, |b|)$$

Since, $d = (a, b)$ there exist integers $u$ and $v$, such that

$$d = ua + vb$$

$$\therefore \quad dk = u(ka) + v(kb)$$

$$= t \cdot r$$

$$\Rightarrow \quad t \mid dk \quad \text{...(i)}$$

Also, $d \mid a \Rightarrow dk \mid ka$ and $d \mid b \Rightarrow dk \mid db$

Therefore, $dk$ is a common divisor of $ka$ and $kb$ and $dk \mid t$ ...(ii)

Since, $dk$ and $t$ are both positive, by Eqs. (i) and (ii), we get

$$t = dk$$

or $(ka, kb) = k(a, b)$

**22.** Since,

$$p \equiv 1 \pmod 4$$

The quadratic congruence

$$x^2 \equiv -1 \pmod p$$

has a solution, $a$ (say)

$$\Rightarrow \quad a^2 \equiv -1 \pmod p$$

$$\Rightarrow \quad (a, p) = 1$$

$\Rightarrow$ The linear congruence

$$ax = y \pmod p$$

has solution $(x_0, y_0)$ such that

$$0 < |x_0| < \sqrt{p} \text{ and } 0 < |y_0| < \sqrt{p} \quad \text{...(i)}$$

Now, $a^2 \equiv -1 \pmod p$

$$\Rightarrow \quad a^2 x_0^2 \equiv -x_0^2 \pmod p$$

$$\Rightarrow \quad y_0^2 \equiv -x_0^2 \pmod p \quad [\because a^2x_0^2 \equiv y_0^2 \pmod p]$$

$$\Rightarrow \quad x_0^2 + y_0^2 \equiv 0 \pmod p$$

$\Rightarrow$ There exist an integer $k$ such that $x_0^2 + y_0^2 = kp$ and $k > 0$

and $kp = x_0^2 + y_0^2$

$$< (\sqrt{p})^2 + (\sqrt{p})^2 \quad \text{[by Eq. (i)]}$$

$$\Rightarrow \quad 0 < kp < 2p$$

$$\Rightarrow \quad 0 < k < 2$$

But $k$ is an integer $\Rightarrow k = 1$

Hence, $p = x_0^2 + y_0^2$

**23.** Suppose,

$$t_i \equiv t_j \pmod m, \quad 1 \le t_i, t_j < m$$

Hence, $m \mid t_i - t_j$ ...(i)

But $1 \le t_i, t_j < m$

$$\Rightarrow \quad t_i - t_j < m,$$

Hence, Eq. (i) cannot be possible unless $t_i - t_j = 0$

$$\Rightarrow \quad t_i = t_j$$

Let $n$ be an integer such that $(n, m) = 1$. By division algorithm

$$n = qm + r, 0 \le r < m$$

and the quotient $q = 0$, if $n < m$ and $q \ge 1$, if $n > m$.

Since, $(r, m) = 1$

$\Rightarrow$ $r = t_i$ for some $i$, $1 \le i \le \phi(m)$

and $n \equiv r \equiv t_i \pmod m$

Since, for every $i$, $1 \le i \le k$, $(a_i, m) = 1$, there exist a unique $l$, $1 \le l \le \phi(m)$ in $a_i \equiv t_l \pmod m$

$$\Rightarrow \quad k \le \phi(m).$$

Similarly, $\phi(m) \le k$

$$\Rightarrow \quad k = \phi(m)$$

**24.** We have $\left(\dfrac{p-1}{2!}\right)$ is a solution of $x^2 \equiv -1 \pmod p$

$$\Rightarrow \quad -1 \equiv (p-1)!$$

$$\equiv (-1)^{\frac{p-1}{2}} \left[\left(\frac{p-1}{2}\right)!\right]^2 \pmod p$$

$$\equiv (-1)^{2k-1} \left[\left(\frac{p-1}{2}\right)!\right]^2 \pmod p$$

$$\equiv -\left[\left(\frac{p-1}{2}\right)!\right]^2 \pmod p$$

$$\Rightarrow \left[\left(\frac{p-1}{2}\right)!\right]^2 \equiv 1 \pmod p$$

**25.** Given, $b^{\frac{p-1}{2}} \equiv 1 \pmod p$

If $r$ is a primitive root $(\text{mod}\, p)$, then $1, r, r^2, \dots, r^{p-2}$ form a reduced residue system $(\text{mod}\, p)$

*i.e.*, $b \equiv r^k \pmod p$ for some integer $k$, $1 \le k \le p-2$

Now, $1 \equiv b^{\frac{p-1}{2}} \equiv (r^k)^{\frac{p-1}{2}} \equiv r^{\frac{k(p-1)}{2}} \pmod p$

Since, $r$ is a primitive root $(\text{mod}\, p)$, $r$ has exponent $p - 1 \pmod p$

$\Rightarrow p - 1 \mid \dfrac{k(p-1)}{2} \Rightarrow k = 2t$, an even integer

Hence, $b \equiv r^{2t} \pmod p$

$\Rightarrow r^t$ is a solution of $x^2 \equiv b \pmod p$

**26.** Since, $1547 = 2.560 + 427$

$$560 = 1.427 + 133$$

$$427 = 3.133 + 28$$

$$133 = 4.28 + 21$$

$$28 = 1.21 + 7$$

Since, $7 \mid 21$

Hence, gcd $(1547, 560) = 7$

**27.** Since, $d = (a, b)$; $\dfrac{a}{d}$ and $\dfrac{b}{d}$ are both integers. Also,

$$d = (a, b)$$

$$= \left(d\frac{a}{b}, d\frac{b}{d}\right)$$

$$= d\left(\frac{a}{d}, \frac{b}{d}\right)$$

$$\Rightarrow \left(\frac{a}{d}, \frac{b}{d}\right) = 1$$

**28.** Suppose that $b$ is a quadratic residue $(\text{mod}\, p)$. Then, $x^2 \equiv b \pmod p$ has a solution $x_0$.

$$\Rightarrow \quad x_0^2 \equiv a \pmod p$$

$$\Rightarrow \quad (x_0, p) = 1 \quad \text{...(i)}$$

By Fermat littles theorem

$$x_0^{p-1} \equiv 1 \pmod p \quad \text{... (ii)}$$

Hence, $a^{\frac{p-1}{2}} \equiv (x_0^2)^{\frac{p-1}{2}} \equiv x_0^{p-1} \pmod p$

$$\equiv 1 \pmod p$$

**29.** (i) Since every prime divisor of $n$ is also a prime divisor of $m$, $n$ and $m$ can be expressed as

$$n = p_1^{r_1} p_2^{r_2} \ldots p_k^{r_k}$$

and $m = p_1^{s_1} p_2^{s_2} \ldots p_k^{s_k} p_{k+1}^{s_{k+1}} \ldots p_t^{s_t}$, where $p_i$ being prime numbers and $r_i, s_i > 1$ are integers and also $t > k$.

$$\therefore \phi(mn) = \phi(p_1^{r_1+s_1} p_2^{r_2+s_2} \ldots p_k^{r_k+s_k} p_{k+1}^{s_{k+1}} \ldots p_t^{s_t})$$

$$= \phi(p_1^{r_1+s_1})\phi(p_2^{r_2+s_2})\ldots\phi(p_k^{r_k+s_k})\phi(p_{k+1}^{s_{k+1}})\ldots\phi_t(p_t^{s_t})$$

$$= (p_1^{r_1+s_1} - p_1^{r_1+s_1-1})(p_2^{r_2-s_2} - p_2^{r_2+s_2-1}) \ldots (p_k^{r_k+s_k} - p_k^{r_k+s_k-1})\phi(p_{k+1}^{s_{k+1}})\ldots\phi(p_t^{s_t})$$

$$= p_1^{r_1} p_2^{r_2} \ldots p_k^{r_k}(p_1^{s_1} - p_1^{s_1-1})(p_2^{s_2} - p_2^{s_2-1})\ldots(p_k^{s_k} - p_k^{s_k-1}) \phi(p_{k+1}^{s_{k+1}})\ldots\phi(p_t^{s_t})$$

$$= m \cdot \phi(p_1^{s_1})\phi p_2^{s_2})\ldots\phi(p_1^{s_t})$$

$$= m \cdot \phi(n)$$

(ii) Taking $m = n$, we have

$$\phi(n^2) = n\phi(n)$$

**30.** By Fermat little theorem

$$a^{p-1} \equiv 1 \pmod p$$

$$\Rightarrow \quad 0 \equiv a^{p-1} - 1$$

$$\equiv (a^{\frac{p-1}{2}} - 1)(a^{\frac{p-1}{2}} + 1) \pmod p$$

If $b$ is a quadratic residue (mod $p$), then

$$b^{\frac{p-1}{2}} \equiv 1 \pmod p$$

$\Rightarrow b$ is a quadratic non-residue, if

$$b^{\frac{p+1}{2}} \equiv -1 \pmod p$$

**31.** Suppose, $x^2 \equiv -1 \pmod p$ has a solution, say $a$

$$\Rightarrow \quad a^2 = -1 \pmod p \text{ and } (a, p) = 1$$

By Fermat little theorem, we have

$$a^{p-1} \equiv 1 \pmod p$$

Hence, $1 \equiv a^{p-1} \equiv (a^2)\frac{p-1}{2} \pmod p$

Since, $p$ is odd, $\frac{p-1}{2}$ is an integer

and $\quad a^2 \equiv -1 \pmod p$

$$\Rightarrow \quad 1 \equiv (-1)^{\frac{p-1}{2}} \pmod p \quad \text{...(i)}$$

It is true only when $\frac{p-1}{2} = 2k$ (an even number) and $p = 4k+1$

$$\Rightarrow \quad p \equiv 1 \pmod 4$$

Conversely,

Suppose, $p \equiv 1 \pmod 4$, then

$p = 4k+1$ for some integer k,

By Wilson's theorem

$$(p-1)! = -1 \pmod p$$

$$\Rightarrow \quad 1 \cdot 2 \ldots \frac{p-1}{2} \cdot \frac{p+1}{2} \cdot \frac{p+3}{2} \ldots$$

$$(p-1) \equiv -1 \pmod p \quad \text{... (ii)}$$

Since, 
$$\left.\begin{aligned} \frac{p+1}{2} &\equiv -\frac{p-1}{2} \pmod p \\ \frac{p+3}{2} &\equiv -\frac{p-3}{2} \pmod p \\ &\vdots \\ p-1 &= \;\; 1 \pmod p \end{aligned}\right\} \quad \text{.... (iii)}$$

Using Eq. (iii) in Eq. (ii), we have

$$(-1)^{\frac{p-1}{2}}\left[1 \cdot 2 \ldots \frac{(p-1)}{2}\right]^2 \equiv -1 \pmod p$$

$$\Rightarrow \quad (-1)^{2k}\left[\left(\frac{p-1}{2}\right)!\right]^2 \equiv -1 \pmod p$$

$$\Rightarrow \quad \left[\left(\frac{p-1}{2}\right)!\right]^2 \equiv -1 \pmod p$$

$$\Rightarrow \quad \left(\frac{p-1}{2}\right)! \text{ is a solution of } x^2 \equiv -1 \pmod p$$

**32.** Since,

(a) $\quad 10920 = 8316.1 + 2604$

$8316 = 2604.3 + 504$

$2604 = 504.5 + 84$

$504 = 84.6 \Rightarrow 841504$

$\therefore$ gcd (10920, 8316) = 84

(b) To find $m$ and $n$ such that

$$84 = 8316m + 10920n$$

We have,

$$2604 = 504.5 + 84$$

$$\Rightarrow \quad 84 = 2604 - 504.5 \quad \text{...(i)}$$

Since, $8316 = 2604.3 + 504$

$$\Rightarrow \quad 504 = 8316 - 2604.3 \quad \text{...(ii)}$$

Hence, by Eqs. (i) and (ii), we get

$$84 = 2604 - (8316 - 2604.3) \quad \text{...(iii)}$$

Since, $10920 = 8316.1 + 2604$

$$\Rightarrow \quad 2604 = 10920 - 8316.1 \quad \text{...(iv)}$$

By Eqs. (iii) and (iv), we get

$$84 = 2604 - (8316 - 2604.3)$$

$$= 2604.4 - 8316$$

$$= (10920 - 8316).4 - 8316$$

$$= 10920.4 - 8316.3$$

$$= 2604.3$$

**33.** By fundamental theorem of arithmetic any number $n$ can be expressed as product of primes

Hence, $\quad n = 2^{k_0} p_1^{k_1} p_2^{k_2} \ldots p_r^{k_r}$,

where $p_i$ distinct odd primes and integers

$$k_i \geq 0, 0 \leq i \leq r$$

If $k_i \geq 1$ atleast for one $i$, then

$$\phi(p_i^{k_i}) = p_i^{k_i} - p_i^{k_i-1} = \text{even integer} \quad \text{...(i)}$$

Since, $\phi(n) = \phi(2^{k_0})\phi(p_1^{k_1})....\phi(p_r^{k_r})$

$= (2^{k_0} - 2^{k_0-1})(p_1^{k_1} - p_1^{k_1-1})....(p_r^{k_r} - p_r^{k_r-1})$ [by Eq. (i)]

and $n > 2$, either $k_0 \geq 2$ or atleast on $k_i \geq 1$;

$\Rightarrow$ Euler's function $\phi(n)$ is even.

**34.** By Fermat's little theorem, we have

$$6^7 \equiv 6 \pmod 7$$

or $\quad 6^7 + 6 + 2 \equiv 6 + 6 + 2 \equiv 0 \pmod 7$

$\Rightarrow$ 6 is a root of the given congruence.

**35.** Let, if possible $\sqrt{2}$ be a rational number.

Then, for some integers $p$ and $q \neq 0$, we have

$$\frac{p}{q} = \sqrt{2}$$

$\Rightarrow \quad p^2 = 2q^2 \quad \Rightarrow \quad p^2$ is even

We then claim that $p$ is even for, if $p$ is not even, then it is of the form $p = 2n+1$ for some integer $n$ and therefore, $p^2 = (2n+1)^2 = 4n^2 + 4n + 1$, which is not even, contradicting the hypothesis that $p^2$ is even.

Thus, $p^2$ is even $\Rightarrow p$ is even

Let $p = 2n$ for some integer $n$.

Then, $\quad p = 2n$

$\Rightarrow \quad p^2 = 4n^2$

$\Rightarrow \quad 2q^2 = 4n^2 \quad [\because p^2 = 2q^2]$

$\Rightarrow \quad q^2 = 2n^2$

$\Rightarrow q^2$ is even.

$\Rightarrow q$ is even.

Thus, we conclude that $p$ and $q$ have 2 as a common factor, contradicting the hypothesis that $p$ and $q$ have no common factor.

Hence, $\sqrt{2}$ is not rational.

**36.** $\sin 30° = \sin 3(10°) = 3\sin 10° - 4\sin^3 10°$

Let $\sin 10° = x$

Then, $\quad \frac{1}{2} = 3x - 4x^3$

$\Rightarrow \quad 8x^3 - 6x + 1 = 0$

$\Rightarrow (2x)^3 - 3(2x) + 1 = 0$

$\Rightarrow \quad y^3 - 3y + 1 = 0$, where $y = 2x$

Since, no rational number satisfies this equation, so $x = \sin 10°$ is not rational.

Hence, $\sin 30°$ is not rational.

**37.** Suppose there does exist a positive integer less than 1. By the wellordering principle, there exists a least positive integer a such that

$$0 < a < 1$$

Multiplying the inequality by the positive integer a we obtain

$$0 < a^2 < a$$

Therefore, $a^2$ is a positive integer less than $a$ which is also less than 1. This contradicts $a$'s property of being the least positive integer less than 1.Thus, there exists no positive integer less than 1.

**38.** Let $x$ and $y$ are two distinct rational number and $x < y$.

$\Rightarrow \quad x + x < x + y$ and $x + y < y + y$ (compatibility)

$\Rightarrow \quad 2x < x + y$ and $x + y < 2y$

$\Rightarrow \quad \left(\frac{1}{2} \times 2x\right) < \frac{1}{2}(x+y)$

and $\quad \frac{1}{2}(x+y) < \frac{1}{2} \times 2y$ (compatibility)

$\Rightarrow \quad x < \frac{1}{2}(x+y)$ and $\frac{i}{2}(x+y) < y$

$\Rightarrow \quad x < \frac{1}{2}(x+y) < y$ (by transitivity)

Hence, $\quad z = \frac{1}{2}(x+y)$ is a rational number such that $x < z < y$

**39.** Let $p_0 \cdot p_1 p_2 p_3 p_4 p_5 p_3 p_4 p_5 ....$ be the repeating decimal representation of a given number.

Then,

$p_0 \cdot p_1 p_2 p_3 p_4 p_5 p_3 p_4 p_5 ....$

$= (p_0 \cdot p_1 p_2) + (0.00 p_3 p_4 p_5) + (0.00000 p_3 p_4 p_5) + ...$

$= (p_0 \cdot p_1 p_2) + (0.00 p_3 p_4 p_5)$
$+ (0.00000 p_3 p_4 p_5) + ...]$

$= (p_0 \cdot p_1 p_2) + \frac{0.00 p_3 p_4 p_5}{1 - 0.001}$ [sum of a GP]

$= p_0 \cdot p_1 p_2 + \frac{0.00 p_3 p_4 p_5}{0.999}$

$= p_0 \cdot p_1 p_2 + \frac{p_3 p_4 p_5}{99900}$ which is a rational number.

**40.** Let $x = \frac{a}{b}$ and $y = \frac{c}{d}$ be any two negative rational numbers, where $a, b, c, d$ are integers and $ab < 0$, $cd < 0$.

Now, $xy = \frac{a}{b} \cdot \frac{c}{d} = \frac{ac}{bd} = \frac{ac}{bd} \cdot \frac{b}{b} = \frac{abc}{b^2 d}$

$= \frac{ab \cdot cd}{b^2 d^2}$

($\because ab \cdot cd > 0$ product of two negative integers is positive and square of any integer is positive.)

Hence, $\frac{ac}{bd} > 0 \Rightarrow xy > 0$,

whenever $x < 0$ and $y < 0$.

**41.** Let $x = \frac{a}{b}$ and $y = \frac{c}{d}$ be any two positive rational numbers, where $a, b, c, d$ are integers and $ab > 0$, $cd > 0$

Now, $\quad xy = \frac{a}{b} \frac{c}{d}$

$= \frac{abc}{b^2 d} = \frac{abcd}{b^2 d^2} > 0$

$= \frac{a}{b} \cdot \frac{c}{d}$

(Since, $ab > 0$, $cd > 0$ and product of two positive integers is positive and square of any integer is positive)

$\Rightarrow \quad xy > 0$, when every $x > 0, y > 0$

**42.** Let $\alpha$ be an integer greater than 1.

Let $Z = \{x \in N : x | \alpha\}$

Then, $Z$ is non-empty, since $a | a \Rightarrow a \in Z$

By well ordering principle $Z$ has a least element $l$.

If $l$ is not prime, then $\exists Z \in N$ such that $1 < Z < l$ and $Z | l$.

Now $Z | l$ and $l | a \Rightarrow Z | a \Rightarrow Z \in Z$,

which is a contradiction, since $l$ is the least member of $K$ and $1 < k < l$.

Hence, $l$ is prime.

**43.** (A) We have, $10 = 2.5$

$$= (1^2 + 1^2)(2^2 + 1^2)$$

$$= (2 \cdot 1 + 1 \cdot 1)^2 (1 \cdot 1 - 1 \cdot 2)^2 = 3^2 + 1^2$$

(C) We have, $153 = 3^2 \cdot 17$

$$= 3^2(4^2 + 1^2) = 12^2 + 3^2$$

**44.** Since, $ab \le |ab| = |a|\,|b|$ and so $2ab \le 2|a|\,|b|$. Hence,

$$(a+b)^2 = a^2 + 2ab + b^2 \le |a|^2 + 2|a||b| + |b|^2$$

$$= (|a| + |b|)^2$$

But $\sqrt{(a+b)^2} = |a+b|$. Thus, the square root of the above yields $|a+b| \le |a| + |b|$. Also,

$$|a-b| = |a + (-b)| \le |a| + |-b| = |a| + |b|$$

**45.** Every integer $n$ can be written as

$n = 4n + r$, where $r = 0, 1, 2$ or $3$

$\Rightarrow$ $n \equiv 0$ or $1$ or $2$ or $3 \pmod 4$

and $n^2 \equiv 0$ or $1 \pmod 4$

Assume $m$ is an integer of the form $4k+3$ for some $k$

and $m = a^2 + b^2$

Hence, $m \equiv a^2 + b^2 \pmod 4$

$\Rightarrow$ $3 \equiv a^2 + b^2 \pmod 4$

But $a^2 + b^2$ is either 0 or 1 or 2 (mod 4) and never 3

$\Rightarrow$ $a^2 + b^2 \equiv 3 \pmod 4$ never holds.

Hence, $m \ne a^2 + b^2$

and no integer of the form $4k+3$ is the sum of two squares.

**46.** Let $x$ and $y$ be any two positive integers. Let $d$ be the greatest common divisor and $l$ be lowest common multiple.

Let $x = pd$ and $y = qd$ ...(i)

Then, $xy = d[pqd]$ ...(ii)

(a) If $(p, q) \ne 1$

$\Rightarrow$ $\exists$ some $t \in \mathbb{N}$ such that $t | p$ and $t | q$

$\Rightarrow$ $p = th$ and $q = tk$ for some $h, k \in \mathbb{N}$

$\Rightarrow$ $x = thd$ and $y = tkd$ [$\because x = pd$ and $y = qd$]

$\Rightarrow$ $x = t(hd)$ and $y = k(td)$

$\Rightarrow$ $td > d$ is a common factor of $x$ and $y$.

and this contradicts the fact that $d$ is the greatest common divisor of $x$ and $y$.

Hence, $(p, q) = 1$

(b) Let $m$ be any common multiple of $x$ and $y$

Then, $m = ax = by$ for some $a, b \in N$ and, therefore,

$m = apd = bqd$ ...(iii)

Now, $(p, q) = 1$

$\Rightarrow \exists\, r$ and $s$ such that $1 = rp + sq$

$\Rightarrow$ $m = rpm + sqm$

$\Rightarrow$ $m - rp(bqd) + sq(apd)$ [using Eq. (iii)]

$\Rightarrow$ $m = pqd(rb + sa)$

$\Rightarrow$ $(pqd) | m$

Thus, $pqd$ divides every common multiple of $x$ and $y$.

So, $l = pqd$ ...(iv)

By eqs. (iv) and (ii), we have

$$xy = ld$$

**47.** By induction

For $n = 2$, the statement is true.

For $n - 3$, the statement is also true.

$\vdots$

Assume it is true for every integer $p < n$.

If $n$ is not a prime, it has a positive divisor $d \ne 1$ and $d \ne n$

Hence, $n = cd$, where $c \ne n$

Since, $c < n$ and $d < n$ (also $c > 1, d > 1$)

$\Rightarrow$ $c$ and $d$ are product of prime.

Hence, $n = cd$ is also a product of prime.

**48.** Let $l_1$ and $l_2$ be the lowest common multiple of integers $x$ and $y$, then $l_1$ is LCM of $x$ and $y$ and $l_2$ is a multiple of $x$ and $y$.

$\Rightarrow$ $l_1 | l_2$

Again, $l_2$ is LCM of $x$ and $y$ and $l_1$ is a multiple of $x$ and $y$.

$\Rightarrow$ $l_2 | l_1$

Now, $l_1 | l_2$ and $l_2 | l_1 \Rightarrow l_1 = l_2$ (since $l_1$ and $l_2$ are both positive)

# 15 Group Theory

**Syllabus**

- Groups
- Subgroups
- Normal Subgroups
- Quotient Groups
- Homomorphism
- Cyclic Groups
- Permutation Groups
- Cauchy's Theorem
- Claus Equations
- Sylow Theorem

## Algebraic Structure

A non-empty set with one or more binary operations defined over it and satisfying certain laws of binary operations is called, algebraic structure or an algebraic system.

### Groupoid

Let $G$ be any non-empty set and $*$ is a binary operation, then the structure $(G, *)$ is called a Groupoid or quasi-group, if $a * b \in G, \forall\ a, b \in G$. *i.e.*, $G$ is closed for the binary operation.

If the binary operation $*$ in the set $G$ satisfies the commutative property is

$$a * b = b * a, \forall\ a, b \in G$$

then, the structure $(G, *)$ is said to be a commutative groupoid.

e.g.,

(i) The structures $(N,+), (N, .), (Z,+), (Z, .), (Q,+), (Q, .), (R,+), (R, .), (C, +), (C, .)$ are all commutative groupoids.

(ii) The set $N$ is not a groupoid with respect to the operation '–'. Since, if $a, b \in N$, then $a - b$ is not always a natural number.

### Semi-group

Let G be a non-empty set and $*$ be a binary operation defined on it, then the structure $(G, *)$ is said to be a semi-group, if

$$a * (b * c) = (a * b) * c, \forall\ a, b, c \in G$$

e.g.,

(i) The structures $(N, +), (N, \cdot)(Z,+), (Z, .), (Q,+), (Q, .), (R, +), (R, .), (C,+), (C, .)$ are commutative semi-group.

(ii) The structures $(Z, -), (Q, -), (R, -), (C, -)$ are not semi-groups, since associative law is not satisfied.

### Monoid

Let $G$ a non-empty set and $*$ be a binary operation defined on it. Then, the structure $(G, *)$ is said to be a monoid, if the following axioms are satisfied.

(i) **Associative law**

$$a * (b * c) = (a * b) * c, \forall\ a, b, c \in G$$

(ii) **Existence of identity** There exist an element, denoted by e and called the identity, in $G$ such that

$$a * e = a = e * a, \forall\ a \in G$$

e.g.,

(i) The structures $(Z,+), (Z, .), (Q,+), (Q, .), (R,+), (R, .), (C,+), (C, .)$ are monoids.

(ii) The structures $(N,+)$ is a semi-group, but not a monoid, since the additive identity (*i.e.*, 0) does not exists in $N$.

## Group

" Let $G$ be a non-empty set and $*$ be a binary operation defined on it, then the structure $(G, *)$ is said to be a group, if the following axioms are satisfied.

(i) **Closure property** $a * b \in G, \forall\ a, b \in G$

(ii) **Associativity** The operation $*$ is associative on $G$. *i.e.*,

$$a * (b * c) = (a * b) * c,\ \forall\ a, b, c \in G.$$

(iii) **Existence of identity** There exists an element $e \in G$, such that

$$a * e = a = e * a,\ \forall\ a \in G$$

$e$ is called identity of $*$ in $G$.

(iv) **Existence of inverse** For each element $a \in G$, there exist an element $b \in G$ such that

$$a * b = e = b * a$$

The element $b$ is called the inverse of element a with respect to $*$ and we write

$$b = a^{-1}$$

## Abelian Group

A group $(G, *)$ is said to be abelian or commutative, if $a * b = b * a,\ \forall\ a, b \in G$.

> ***Note*** **(a)** A group is not simply a set, but it is an algebraic structure.
> **(b)** The smallest group for a given composition is the set $\{e\}$, containing identity elements.
> **(c)** A group consisting of the identity element only, is called a trivial group, others are called non-trivial groups.
> **(d)** If a group contains a finite number of elements, it is called a finite group.
> **(e)** If the number of elements in a group is infinite, it is called an infinite group.

## Order of a Group

The number of elements in a finite group is called the order of the group. It is denoted by $O(G)$.
An infinite group is called a group of infinite order.
*e.g.*,

(i) The set $Z$ of integers is an infinite abelian group with respect to the operation of addition but $Z$ is not a group with respect to the multiplication.

(ii) Let $G = \{1\}$, then $G$ is an abelian group of order 1 with respect to multiplication.

(iii) Let $G = \{0\}$, then $G$ is an abelian group of order 1 with respect to addition.

(iv) Let $G = \{1, -1\}$, then $G$ is an abelian group of order 2 with respect to multiplication.

## Properties of Groups

Let $(G, *)$ be a group, then

1. The identity element '$e$' is unique.
2. There exists unique inverse in $G$. *i.e.*, $a^{-1} \in G,\ \forall\ a \in G$.

Also, $(a^{-1})^{-1} = a, \forall a \in G$ and $(a * b)^{-1} = b^{-1} * a^{-1}, \forall a, b \in G$
In general, if $a_1, a_2, \ldots.. a_n$, are elements of a group $G$, then

$$(a_1 * a_2 * \ldots * a_n)^{-1} = a_n^{-1} * a_{n-1}^{-1} * \ldots * a_2^{-1} * a_1^{-1}.$$

3. (i) $a * c = b * c \Rightarrow a = b$ (Right cancellation law)
   (ii) $c * a = c * b \Rightarrow a = b$ (Left cancellation law)
   Where, $a, b, c \in G$
4. The left identity is also the right identity.
   *i.e.*, $ea = a$ and $ae = a$
5. The left inverse of an element is also its right inverse
   *i.e.*, $a^{-1}a = e$ and $aa^{-1} = e$
6. The equations $a * x = b$ and $y * a = b$, where $a, b \in G$ have unique solutions in $G$, which are $x = a^{-1} * b \in G$ and $y = b * a^{-1} \in G$, respectively.

> ***Note*** **(a)** With the help of the above theorem, we can define the group alternatively as follows
> **(b)** "A set $G$ with a binary composition $*$ is a group iff"
> (i) The composition $*$ is associative.
> (ii) The equations $ax = b$ and $ya = b$ have unique solutions in $G$.
> or (ii) Left identity and left inverse exist in group.
> or (ii) Right identity and right inverse exist in group.
> **(c)** or A finite set $G$, with a binary operation $*$ which is associative, is a group iff the cancellation laws hold.
> **(d)** The result of the above theorem may not hold when $G$ is an infinite group.
> *e.g.*, In the set $N$ of natural numbers, for the binary operation +, associative and cancellation laws also hold. But $(N,+)$ is not a group.

**Example 1.** *Show that the set Z of all integers form a group with respect to binary operation $*$ defined by*

$$a * b = a + b + 1, \forall\ a, b \in Z$$

*is an abelian group.*

**Solution.** (i) **Closure property** Let $a, b \in Z$

$\Rightarrow\ a + b + 1 \in Z \Rightarrow a * b \in Z$
$\Rightarrow$ $Z$ is closed with respect to $*$.

(ii) **Associativity** If $a, b, c \in Z$, then

$$(a * b) * c = (a + b + 1) * c = (a + b + 1) + c + 1$$
$$= a + b + c + 2$$

Also, $a * (b * c) = a * (b + c + 1) = a + \{b + (+1) + 1\}$
$$= a + b + c + 2$$
$$\Rightarrow \quad (a * b) * c = a * (b * c), \forall a, b, c \in Z$$

(iii) **Existence of identity** An element $e \in Z$ will be the identity, if $e * a = a, \forall a \in Z$.

Now, $e * a = e + a + 1$
$e + a + 1 = a \Rightarrow e = -1$
Since, $-1 \in Z$ and we have for any $a \in Z$
$(-1) * a = -1 + a + 1 = a$
$\Rightarrow$ $-1$ is the identity element.

(iv) **Existence of inverse** If $a \in Z$, then $b \in Z$ will be the inverse of a, if $b * a = -1$ ($\because -1$ is the identity element)

Now,
$b * a = -1 \Rightarrow b + a + 1 = -1 \Rightarrow b = -2 - a$
Also, $a \in Z \Rightarrow -2 - a \in Z$

and $(-2-a) * a = (-2-a) + a + 1 = -1$, identity element

$\therefore (-2-a)$ is the inverse of $a$.

(v) **Commutativity** Since,

$$a * b = a + b + 1 = b + a + 1 = b * a$$

$\Rightarrow$ Commutativity satisfied.

Hence, $Z$ is an infinite abelian group under the given composition.

***Example 2.*** *Show that the set $\{1, -1, i, -i\}$ is an abelian finite group of order 4 under multiplication.*

**Solution.** (i) **Closure property** Closure property is satisfied as

$1(-1) = -1, 1 \cdot i = i, i(-i) = 1, i(-1) = -i$, etc.

(ii) **Associativity** Associative property is satisfied as

$(1 \cdot i)(-i) = 1 \cdot \{i(-i)\} = 1, \{1 \cdot i\} \cdot (-1) = 1, \{i(-1)\} = -i$, etc.

(iii) **Existence of identity** Axioms on identity is satisfied, 1 being the multiplicative identity.

(iv) **Existence of inverse** Axiom on inverse is satisfied, since the inverse of each element of the set exists.

$1 \cdot 1 = e = 1, (-1)(-1) = e = 1, i(-i) = e = 1, (-i)(i) = e = 1$

(v) **Commutativity** The commutative law is also satisfied as

$$1(-1) = (-1) \cdot 1, (-1)\, i = i\,(-1), \text{ etc.}$$

Since, there are four elements in the given set, hence it is a group of order 4.

## Order of an Element of a Group

Let $G$ be a group under multiplication. Let e be the identity element in $G$. Suppose, $a$ is any element of $G$, then the least positive integer $n$, if exist, such that $a^n = e$ is said to be order of an element $a \in G$, and can be written as

$$o(a) = n$$

In case, such a positive integer $n$ does not exist, we say that the element a is of infinite or zero order.

> ***Note*** **(a)** If $G$ is an additive group, we write $na$ in place of $a^n$.
>
> **(b)** If $m$ is a positive integer such that $a^m = e$, then $o(a) \le m$.
>
> **(c)** Identity element $e$ in a group $G$, is the only element whose order is one.
>
> **(d)** The order of an element of an infinite group may be finite or infinite.

e.g.,

(i) Consider the multiplicative group

$G = \{1, -1, i, -i\}$ of fourth roots of unity

$$(1)^1 = 1 \Rightarrow o(1) = 1$$
$$(-1)^2 = 1 \Rightarrow o(-1) = 2$$
$$(i)^4 = 1 \Rightarrow o(i) = 4$$
$$(-i)^4 = 1 \Rightarrow o(-i) = 4$$

(ii) Consider the additive group

$$Z = \{\ldots, -3, -2, -1, 0, 1, 2, 3, \ldots\}$$

$1 \cdot 0 = 0 \Rightarrow$ order of zero is one (finite)

but $na \ne 0$ for any non-zero integers $a$.

$\Rightarrow o(a)$ is infinite.

(iii) Let $Q_0 = Q - \{0\}$ be the multiplicative group of non-zero rational numbers, then

$1, -1 \in Q_0$ such that

$o(1) = 1$ and $o(-1) = 2$, and the order of any other element of this group is infinite.

### Important Results on Order

1. The order of every element of a finite group is finite.
2. If the element '$a$' of a group $G$ is of order $n$, then $a^m = e \Leftrightarrow n$ is a divisor of $m$.

   *i.e.*, $a^m = e \Rightarrow m = nq$ for $q \in Z^+$ and also if $m = nq$, then $a^m = a^{nq} = (a^n)^q = e^q = e$
3. $o(a) = o(a^{-1})$ for any element $a \in G$.
4. $o(a^r) \le o(a)$ for any element $a \in G$. *i.e.*, order of any integral power of an element '$a$' cannot exceed the order of $a$. Also, $o(a^r)$ is a divisor of $o(a)$.
5. $o(a) = o(b^{-1}ab)$

   where $a$ and $b$ are any two elements of a group $G$.
6. $o(ab) = o(ba)$ for any two elements $a, b \in G$.
7. $o(a) / o(G), \forall\, a \in G$.
8. If $o(G) = n$, then $a^n = e, a \in G$.
9. If $o(a) = n$, then $o(a^p) = n$, where $p$ is prime to $n$.
10. If every element of a group has its own inverse, then group must be abelian.
11. If number of elements in a group is less than or equal to 4, then group is abelian.
12. If $o(a) = o(b) = o(ab) = 2$

    Then, $ab = ba$ *i.e.*, group $G$ is abelian.
13. If $G$ is a group such that $(ab)^m = a^m b^m$ for three consecutive integers $m, \forall\, a, b \in G$, then $G$ is abelian.
14. Group $G$ is abelian iff

    $(ab)^{-1} = a^{-1}b^{-1}, \forall\, a, b \in G$

15. If in a group G,

$$a^5 = e, \quad aba^{-1} = b^2$$

For $a, b \in G$, then

$o(b) = 1$, if $b = e$ and $o(b) = 31$, if $b \neq e$

where '$e$' is an identity element of group.

16. A group of even order has atleast one element of order 2.

17. Let $G = \{a + b\sqrt{2}\,;\, a, b \in Q\}$, then G is an infinite abelian group *wrt* binary operation '+'.

18. $G = \left\{\begin{bmatrix} a & b \\ -b & a \end{bmatrix};\, a, b \in R \text{ such that } a^2 + b^2 \neq 0\right\}$

Form an infinite abelian group under the operation of matrix multiplication.

***Example 3.*** *Show that if G is an abelian group, then for all a, b ∈ G and all integers n*

$$(ab)^n = a^n b^n$$

**Solution.** (i) Let $n = 0$

Then, $(ab)^0 = e$

Also, $a^0 b^0 = e \cdot e = e$

$\therefore$ $(ab)^0 = a^0 b^0$

(ii) Let $n > 0$

If $n = 1$, then $(ab)^1 = ab = a^1 b^1$.

Let us suppose our result is true for $n = r$

*i.e.*, $(ab)^r = a^r b^r$.

Then, $(ab)^{r+1} = (ab)^r \cdot ab = a^r b^r ab = a^r ab^r b$ $\quad (\because ab^r = b^r a)$

$= a^{r+1} b^{r+1}$

Then, by mathematical induction for all $n > 0$,

$$(ab)^n = a^n \cdot b^n$$

(iii) Let $n < 0$

Let $n = -r$, where $r$ is a positive integer.

Then, $(ab)^n = (ab)^{-r} = [(ab)^r]^{-1} = [a^r b^r]^{-1}$

$= [b^r a^r]^{-1}$ $\quad (\because a^m b^m = b^m a^m)$

$= [a^r]^{-1} [b^r]^{-1}$ $\quad [\because (ab)^{-1} = b^{-1} a^{-1}]$

$= a^{-r} b^{-r} = a^n b^n$

***Example 4.*** *For any two elements a and b of a group G, show that G is abelian iff* $(ab)^2 = a^2 b^2$.

**Solution.** Let us first suppose that, G is abelian.

So that $ab = ba, \forall\, a, b \in G$

Consider $(ab)^2 = (ab)(ab) = a(ba)b$ (by associativity)

$= a(ab)b$ (by commutativity)

$= (aa)(bb)$ (by associativity)

$= a^2 \cdot b^2$

Thus, $(ab)^2 = a^2 b^2, \forall\, a, b \in G$

**Conversely,** Let $(ab)^2 = a^2 b^2, \forall\, a, b \in G$

To show $ab = ba$

Consider $(ab)^2 = a^2 b^2 \Rightarrow (ab)(ab) = (aa)(bb)$

$\Rightarrow$ $a(ba)b = a(ab)b$, (by associativity)

$\Rightarrow$ $ba = ab$ (by left and right cancellation law)

Thus, we have $ab = ba, \forall\, a, b \in G$

Hence, G is abelian.

## Modulo System

Let $n$ be a fixed positive integer and $a$ and $b$ are two integers, we define $a \equiv b \pmod{n}$, if $n \mid (a - b)$ and read as "a is congruent to b modulo n".

## Addition Modulo *m*

Let a and $b$ are any two integers and $m$ is a fixed positive integers, then

$$a +_m b = r, \; 0 \leq r < m$$

where $r$ is the least non-negative remainder, when $a + b$ is divide by $m$.

e.g., $8 +_3 8 = 1$

Since, $8 + 8 = 16 - 3(5) + 1$, *i.e.*, 1 is the least non-negative remainder, when $8 + 8$ is divided by 3.

## Multiplication Modulo *p*

The multiplication modulo $p$ is written as $a \times_p b$, where $a$ and $b$ are any integers and $p$ is a fixed.

Then, by definition, we have

$$a \times_p b = r, \; 0 \leq r < p$$

where $r$ is the least non-negative remainder, when $a \cdot b$ is divided by $p$.

e.g., $4 \times_3 5 = 2$

Since, $4 \times 5 = 20 = 3(6) + 2$

e.g.,

(i) The set $\{0, 1, 2, \ldots, (n-1)\}$ of $n$ elements is a finite abelian group under addition modulo $n$.

(ii) If $p$ is a prime number, then the set $\{1, 2, 3, \ldots, (p-1)\}$ is a finite abelian group under multiplication modulo $p$.

***Note*** **(a)** The relation, congruence modulo $n$, is an equivalence relation on the set of integer.

**(b)** Also, this equivalence relation has $n$ distinct equivalence classes.

Let the equivalence class under the equivalence relation of congruence modulo $n$ of $k \in Z$ be denoted by $[k]$, then $[k] = \{a \in Z : a \equiv k \pmod{n}\}$.

Thus, $[k]$ is the set of integers which are congruent to $k$ modulo $n$, we call it the congruence class (mod $n$) of $k$.

Now, let $a$ be any integer, then by division algorithm $a = qn + r$ where $0 \le r < n$. Then, $a - r = qn$ and hence $a \equiv r(\text{mod} n)$. Since, $0 \le r < n$, it follows that every integer is congruent modulo $n$ to some one of the $n$ integers $0, 1, 2, \ldots, n-1$. Moreover, since each of these integers is less than $n$, no two of them can be congruent to each other modulo $n$. Furthermore $a \equiv r$ (mod $n$) implies that $a \in [r]$ and so $[a] = [r]$. Consequently, then there are exactly $n$ distinct congruence classes (mod $n$), namely

$$[0], [1], [2], \ldots, [n-1]$$

## Residue Classes Modulo *n*

The equivalence relation $\equiv$ (mod $n$), *i.e.*, congruence modulo $n$ decomposes the set $Z$ into disjoint classes, called equivalence classes. These equivalence classes are called residue classes modulo $n$. The set of all these equivalence classes is called the quotient set of $Z$ and is denoted by $Z_n$.

Thus, $\quad Z_n = \{[0], [1], [2], \ldots, [n-1]\}$.

## Addition of Residue Classes

The addition of residue classes is defined by

$$[a] + [b] = \begin{cases} [a+b], & \text{if } a+b < m \\ [r], & \text{if } a+b \ge m, \end{cases}$$

where, $r$ is the least non-negative remainder when $a + b$ is divided by $m$.

e.g., If [1], [2], ...., [5], [6], [7] are residue classes modulo 8. Then

(i) $[2] + [5] = [7]$ for $2 + 5 = 7 < 8$

(ii) $[1] + [5] = [6]$ for $1 + 5 = 6 < 8$

(iii) $[6] + [7] = [5]$ for $6 + 7 > 8$ and $6 + 7 = 13 = 1 \times 8 + 5$

## Multiplication of Residue Classes

The multiplication of residue classes is defined by

$$[a] \cdot [b] = \begin{cases} [ab], & \text{if } ab < m \\ [r], & \text{if } ab \ge m \end{cases}$$

where $r$ is the least non-negative remainder when $ab$ is divided by $m$.

e.g.,

(i) If [1], [2], ..., [6], [7] are residue classes modulo 8, then

(i) $[2] \cdot [5] = [2]$ for $2 \times 5 > 8$ and $2 \times 5 = 10 = 1 \times 8 + 2$

(ii) $[1] \cdot [5] = [5]$ for $1 \times 5 < 8$.

(ii) The set $G = \{[0], [1], [2], \ldots, [n-1]\}$ of residue classes modulo $n$ form a finite abelian group under the operation addition of residue classes modulo $n$.

(iii) The set $G = \{[1], [2], \ldots, [p-1]\}$, of residue classes modulo $p$ (where $p$ is prime number) form a finite abelian group under the operation multiplication of residue classes modulo $p$.

***Example 5.*** *Show that the set $G = \{1, 2, 3, 4, 5, 6\}$ is a finite abelian group of order 6 with respect to multiplication modulo 7.*

**Solution.** Let us prepare the composition table as follows

| $\times_7$ | 1 | 2 | 3 | 4 | 5 | 6 |
|---|---|---|---|---|---|---|
| 1 | 1 | 2 | 3 | 4 | 5 | 6 |
| 2 | 2 | 4 | 6 | 1 | 3 | 5 |
| 3 | 3 | 6 | 2 | 5 | 1 | 4 |
| 4 | 4 | 1 | 5 | 2 | 6 | 3 |
| 5 | 5 | 3 | 1 | 6 | 4 | 2 |
| 6 | 6 | 5 | 4 | 3 | 2 | 1 |

Here, we have the following observation

(i) **Closure property** We see that all the entries in the composition table are elements of the set G. Therefore, G is closed with respect to multiplication modulo 7.

(ii) **Associativity** Associative law always hold in modulo system.

(iii) **Existence of identity** We have $1 \in G$. Let $a \in G$. Then, from the composition table we see that

$$1 \times_7 a = a = a \times_7 1$$

$\therefore$ 1 is the identity element.

(iv) **Existence of inverse** From table we have that the inverses of 1, 2, 3, 4, 5, 6 are 1, 4, 5, 2, 3, 6, respectively.

(v) **Commutativity** Since, each row is identical to corresponding column, therefore, the composition is commutative.

Also, the set G has six element $\Rightarrow$ $o(G) = 6$.

Hence, $(G, \times_7)$ is a finite abelian group of order 6.

# Permutation Groups

A one-one mapping $f$ of a finite non-empty set $S$ onto itself is called a permutation.

If the set $S$ consists of $n$ distinct elements, then a one-one mapping of $S$ onto itself is called a permutation of degree $n$.

Let $\quad S = \{a_1, a_2, \ldots, a_n\}$.

Then, we denote a permutation $f$ on the set $S$ in a two-rowed notation.

$$f = \begin{pmatrix} a_1, a_2, \ldots, a_i, \ldots, a_n \\ b_1, b_2, \ldots, b_i, \ldots, b_n \end{pmatrix}.$$

So that in the first row all the elements of $S$ are written in a certain order and

$f(a_1) = b_1, f(a_2) = b_2 \ldots, f(a_i) = b_i, \ldots, f(a_n) = b_n$,

where $b_i$s are $a_i$'s.

> ***Note*** Interchange of columns does not change the permutation.
>
> *e.g.,* $\begin{pmatrix} 1 & 2 & 3 & 4 \\ 2 & 3 & 4 & 1 \end{pmatrix} = \begin{pmatrix} 2 & 1 & 3 & 4 \\ 3 & 2 & 4 & 1 \end{pmatrix} = \begin{pmatrix} 1 & 4 & 3 & 2 \\ 2 & 1 & 4 & 3 \end{pmatrix}$

## Types of Permutations

### Equality of Permutations

Two permutations $f$ and $g$ of a set $S$ are said to be equal, if $f(a) = g(a), \forall a \in S$.

e.g., If $f = \begin{pmatrix} 1 & 2 & 3 \\ 3 & 1 & 2 \end{pmatrix}$ and $g = \begin{pmatrix} 2 & 3 & 1 \\ 1 & 2 & 3 \end{pmatrix}$ are two permutation of degree 3, then we have

$f = g$ since, $f(1) = g(1) = 3$, $f(2) = g(2) = 1$, $f(3) = g(3) = 2$.

### Identity Permutation

A permutation on the set $S$ is called the identity permutation, if it maps each element of $S$ onto itself.

It is usually denoted by the symbol $I$.

Thus, $\quad I(a) = a, \forall a \in S$

e.g., $I = \begin{pmatrix} 1\,2\,3\ldots n \\ 1\,2\,3\ldots n \end{pmatrix}$ is the identity permutation of degree $n$.

### Inverse Permutations

Since, a permutation is a one-one onto mapping and hence, it is invertible, *i.e.*, every permutation $f$ on a set $P = \{a_1, a_2, \ldots, a_n\}$ has a unique inverse permutation denoted by $f^{-1}$.

e.g., If $\quad f = \begin{pmatrix} a_1 & a_2 \ldots a_n \\ b_1 & b_2 \ldots b_n \end{pmatrix}$

Then, $\quad f^{-1} = \begin{pmatrix} b_1 & b_2 \ldots b_n \\ a_1 & a_2 \ldots a_n \end{pmatrix}$

## Product or Composition of Permutations

The product or composite of two permutations $f$ and $g$ of the same degree, denoted by $f \cdot g$ is obtained by first carrying out the operation defined by mapping $f$ and then by mapping $g$.

Let, $f, g \in P_n$, so that

$$f = \begin{pmatrix} a_1 & a_2 \ldots a_n \\ b_1 & b_2 \ldots b_n \end{pmatrix}, \; g = \begin{pmatrix} b_1 & b_2 \ldots b_n \\ c_1 & c_2 \ldots c_n \end{pmatrix}$$

where, $a_i, b_i, c_i \in S$, $i = 1, 2, \ldots, n$

Then,

$$fg = \begin{pmatrix} a_1 & a_2 \ldots a_n \\ b_1 & b_2 \ldots b_n \end{pmatrix}\begin{pmatrix} b_1 & b_2 \ldots b_n \\ c_1 & c_2 \ldots c_n \end{pmatrix} = \begin{pmatrix} a_1 & a_2 \ldots a_n \\ c_1 & c_2 \ldots c_n \end{pmatrix} \in P_n$$

e.g., Let $\quad f = \begin{pmatrix} 1 & 2 & 3 & 4 \\ 2 & 3 & 4 & 1 \end{pmatrix}, g = \begin{pmatrix} 1 & 2 & 3 & 4 \\ 3 & 4 & 2 & 1 \end{pmatrix}$

be two permutations of degree 4. Then,

$$fg = \begin{pmatrix} 1 & 2 & 3 & 4 \\ 2 & 3 & 4 & 1 \end{pmatrix}\begin{pmatrix} 1 & 2 & 3 & 4 \\ 3 & 4 & 2 & 1 \end{pmatrix}$$

$$= \begin{pmatrix} 1 & 2 & 3 & 4 \\ 2 & 3 & 4 & 1 \end{pmatrix}\begin{pmatrix} 2 & 3 & 4 & 1 \\ 4 & 2 & 1 & 3 \end{pmatrix} = \begin{pmatrix} 1 & 2 & 3 & 4 \\ 4 & 2 & 1 & 3 \end{pmatrix}$$

and $\quad gf = \begin{pmatrix} 1 & 2 & 3 & 4 \\ 3 & 4 & 2 & 1 \end{pmatrix}\begin{pmatrix} 1 & 2 & 3 & 4 \\ 2 & 3 & 4 & 1 \end{pmatrix}$

$$= \begin{pmatrix} 1 & 2 & 3 & 4 \\ 3 & 4 & 2 & 1 \end{pmatrix}\begin{pmatrix} 3 & 4 & 3 & 1 \\ 4 & 1 & 3 & 2 \end{pmatrix} = \begin{pmatrix} 1 & 2 & 3 & 4 \\ 4 & 1 & 3 & 2 \end{pmatrix}$$

Here, we observe that $fg \neq gf$. Thus, the product of permutations is not commutative.

## Permutation Group (Symmetric Group)

Let $A(S)$ denote the set of all permutation on a non-empty set $S$.

Then, $A(S)$ form a group under the composition of maps. Moreover, if $S$ contain $n$ elements, then the permutation group $A(S)$ contains $n!$ elements. The group of $n!$ permutations of a set of $n$ elements is called symmetric group $(S_n)$ of degree $n$.

***Example 6.*** *Write down all the elements of the permutation group (or symmetric group) $S_3$ on three elements* 1, 2 *and* 3.

**Solution.** Let $S = \{1, 2, 3\}$

Then, there are $3! = 6$ elements in $S_3$.

$$\Rightarrow S_3 = \left\{\begin{pmatrix} 1 & 2 & 3 \\ 1 & 2 & 3 \end{pmatrix}, \begin{pmatrix} 1 & 2 & 3 \\ 2 & 1 & 3 \end{pmatrix}, \begin{pmatrix} 1 & 2 & 3 \\ 3 & 2 & 1 \end{pmatrix}, \begin{pmatrix} 1 & 2 & 3 \\ 1 & 3 & 2 \end{pmatrix},\right.$$

$$\left.\begin{pmatrix} 1 & 2 & 3 \\ 2 & 3 & 1 \end{pmatrix}, \begin{pmatrix} 1 & 2 & 3 \\ 3 & 1 & 2 \end{pmatrix}\right\}$$

which can be written as

$$S_3 = \{I, (1\;\;2), (1\;\;3), (2\;\;3), (1\;\;2\;\;3), (1\;\;3\;\;2)\}.$$

## Cyclic Permutation (Cycle)

A permutation $f$ on a set $S$ is called a cyclic permutation of length $l$, if there exist $x_1, x_2, \ldots, x_l \in S$ such that $f(x_1) = x_2, f(x_2) = x_3, \ldots, f(x_{l-1}) = f(x_l)$, $f(x_l) = x_1$ and $f(x) = x$, $\forall x \in S$, if $x \neq x_1, x_2, \ldots, x_l$.

*e.g.*,

(i) $\begin{pmatrix} 1 & 2 & 3 \\ 2 & 3 & 1 \end{pmatrix}$ is a cyclic permutation of length 3.

(ii) $\begin{pmatrix} 1 & 2 & 3 & 4 & 5 \\ 2 & 3 & 4 & 5 & 1 \end{pmatrix}$ is a cyclic permutation of length 5.

(iii) We denote the cyclic permutation

$\begin{pmatrix} x_1 & x_2 \ldots & x_l \\ x_2 & x_3 \ldots & x_1 \end{pmatrix}$ by the symbols $(x_1 . x_2 \ldots x_l)$.

Thus, cyclic permutation $\begin{pmatrix} 1 & 2 & 3 & 4 & 5 & 6 \\ 2 & 3 & 4 & 5 & 6 & 1 \end{pmatrix}$ is expressed as $(1\;\;2\;\;3\;\;4\;\;5\;\;6)$.

**Note** (a) Permutation $\begin{pmatrix} 1 & 2 & 3 & 4 & 5 & 6 \\ 1 & 2 & 3 & 5 & 6 & 4 \end{pmatrix}$ is expressed as (456). Here, degree of permutation is 6 and length of cycle is 3.
(b) A cycle does not change by changing the places of its elements in cyclic order.
Thus, (1 2 3 4) = (2 3 4 1) = (3 4 1 2)
(c) The number of distinct objects permuted by a cycle is known as the length of the cycle.
(d) A cyclic permutation of length $l$ is also called $l$-cycle.
(e) A cycle of length 1 is the identity permutation and cycle of length 2 is called transposition.
(f) Two cycles are said to be disjoint, if they have no elements in common. e.g., (1 2) and (3 4) are disjoint cycles.
(g) Every permutations can be expressed as a product of disjoint cycles.
(h) Every permutation can be expressed as a product of transpositions.
e.g., $(a_1 a_2 \dots a_n) = (a_1 a_2)(a_1 a_3)\dots(a_1 a_n)$,
i.e., for $n = 1$, $(a_1) = (a_1 a_2)(a_2 a_1)$ for $n = 3$,
$(a_1 a_2 a_3) = (a_1 a_2)(a_1 a_3)$
(i) In $S_n$, the number of distinct cycles of length $r (r \le n)$ is $\frac{1}{r} \cdot \frac{n!}{(n-r)!}$
e.g., Number of distinct 3-cycles of $S_4 = \frac{1}{3} \cdot \frac{4!}{(4-3)!} = 8$

## Even and Odd Permutation

A permutation is said to be even or odd according as it can be expressed as a product of even or odd number of transpositions, respectively.

Let $f = \begin{pmatrix} 1 & 2 & 3 & 4 & 5 & 6 \\ 2 & 4 & 5 & 1 & 3 & 6 \end{pmatrix}$ be a permutation on the set $S = \{1, 2, 3, 4, 5, 6\}$.

Then, $f = (1\ 2\ 4)(3\ 5) = (1\ 2)(1\ 4)(3\ 5)$

Since, $f$ is product of 3 (odd number of) transposition, therefore, $f$ is an odd permutation.

**Note** (a) Every transposition is always an odd permutations.
(b) Identity permutation is an even permutation.
(c) The product of two odd permutation is an even permutation.
(d) The product of two even permutation is an even permutations.
(e) The product of an odd and an even permutation is an odd permutation.
(f) The inverse of an even permutation is even.
(g) The inverse of an odd permutation is odd.
(h) A cycle of length $n$ is expressible as the product of $(n-1)$ transpositions.
(i) A permutation cannot be both odd and even.
(j) In the symmetric group $S_n$ of degree $n (> 1)$, half of the permutations are even and the other half are odd.
i.e., $\frac{n!}{2}$ permutations in $S_n$ are even and $\frac{n!}{2}$ permutations are odd.

## Alternating Set ($A_n$)

Let $S_n$ denote the symmetric group of degree $n$. Then, the subset of $S_n$ consisting of all even permutations is called alternating set of permutations of degree $n$.

**Note** (a) The set $A_n$ of all even permutations of degree $n$ forms a finite non-abelian group of order $\frac{n!}{2}$ with respect to permutation multiplication as composition.
(b) If $n > 1$, then the subset $A_n$ of $S_n$ consisting of all even permutations is a normal subgroup of index 2.

## Subgroup

A non-empty subset $H$ of a group $(G, *)$ is said to be a subgroup of $G$, if $(H, *)$ is itself a group.

**Note** (a) Every group $G$ has atleast two subgroups, viz, $\{e\}$ and $G$ itself. These two subgroups are called trivial or improper subgroups.
(b) Any non-empty subset $H$ of $G$ is called a complex of the group $G$.

e.g.,

(i) $[\{1, -1\}, \cdot]$ is a subgroup of $[\{1, -1, i, -i\}, \cdot]$
(ii) $(Z, +)$ is a subgroup of $(Q, +)$.
(iii) $(Q, +)$ is a subgroup of $(R, +)$.
(iv) The set of all non-singular matrices with real elements whose determinants are 1, is a subgroup of multiplicative group of all non-singular $n \times n$ matrices.

## Criterion for a Subset to be a Subgroup

1. A non-empty subset $H$ of a group $G$ is a subgroup of $G$ if and only if
   (i) $a, b \in H \Rightarrow ab \in H$
   (ii) $a \in H \Rightarrow a^{-1} \in H$,
   where $a^{-1}$ is the inverse of $a \in G$.
2. A non-empty subset $H$ of a finite group is a subgroup of $G$ iff $ab \in H, \forall a, b \in H$.

**Note** In case of additive notation, the above results can be stated as a non-empty subset $H$ of a group $G$ is a subgroup iff
(i) $a + b \in H, \forall a, b \in H$
(ii) $-a \in H, \forall a \in H$,
which can be combined to a single condition $a - b \in H, \forall a, b \in H$
(iii) Let $H$ be a non-empty subset of a group $G$. Then, $H$ is a subgroup of $G$ iff $a, b \in H \Rightarrow ab^{-1} \in H$, where $b^{-1}$ is the inverse of $b$ in $G$.

## Important Results on Subgroups

1. The intersection of an arbitrary collection of subgroups of a group is again a subgroup of the group. In particular, if $H$ and $K$ be two subgroups of a group $G$, then $H \cap K$ is also a subgroup of $G$.
2. The union of two subgroups of a group is a subgroup iff one is contained in the other *i.e.*, $H \cup K$ is a subgroup $\Leftrightarrow H \subseteq K$ or $K \subseteq H$.
3. Let $H$ be a subgroup of $G$. Then,
   (i) Identity of $H$ is same as that of $G$.
   (ii) The inverse of an element $a \in H$ is the same as the inverse of the same element regard as an element of the group $G$.
   (iii) The order of an element $a \in H$ is the same order of the same element regarded as an element of the group $G$.

## Product of Two Subgroups

Let $H$ and $K$ be two subgroups of a group $G$, then the set $HK$ defined by $HK = \{hk : h \in H,\ k \in K\}$ is called the product of the subgroups $H$ and $K$.

**Note** (a) The product $HK$ of two subgroups of a group $G$ may or may not be a subgroup of $G$.
*e.g.*,
Let $H = \{I, (1\,2)\}$ and $K = \{I, (1\,3)\}$ be two subgroups of the symmetric group $S_3$ on three elements 1, 2, 3.
But $HK = \{I, (1\,2)(1\,3), (1\,2)(1\,3)\} = \{I, (1\,2), (1\,3), (1\,2\,3)\}$
So, $HK$ is not a subgroup of $S_3$, for $(1\,2\,3) \in HK$ and $(1\,2\,3)\,(1\,2\,3) = (1\,3\,2) \notin HK$
**(b)** If $H$ and $K$ are two subgroups of a group $G$, then $HK$ is a subgroup of $G$ iff $HK = KH$.
**(c)** If $H$ and $K$ are two abelian subgroups of a group $G$, then $HK$ need not be a subgroup of $G$.
*e.g.*, Let $H = \{I, (1\,2)\}$ and $K = \{I, (1\,3)\}$; be two abelian subgroups of symmetric group $S_3$ on three elements 1, 2, 3. But $HK$ is not a subgroup of $G$.
**(d)** If $H$ and $K$ are subgroups of an abelian group $G$, then $HK$ is a subgroup of $G$.
**(e)** If $H$ and $K$ are finite subgroups of a group $G$, then
$$o(HK) = \frac{o(H) \cdot o(K)}{o(H \cap K)}$$

## Inverse of a Subset of a Group

Let $H$ be a subset of a group $G$, then the inverse of $H$ is $H^{-1}$ and is defined as
$$H^{-1} = \{h^{-1} : h \in H\}$$

## Important (Theorems) on Inverse

1. A non-empty subset $H$ of a group $G$ is a subgroup iff any one holds from the followings
   (i) $H^{-1} = H$ (ii) $HH = H$ (iii) $HH^{-1} = H$
2. If $H$ and $K$ be any two subsets of a group $G$, then $(HK)^{-1} = K^{-1}H^{-1}$.

**Note** The subgroup defined in above example is known as centre of the group. Thus, "If $G$ is a group, then the subgroup $Z$, defined by
$$Z = \{xz = zx : x \in G, z \in Z\}$$
is said to be centre of the group.

***Example 7.*** *If a is any element of a group G, then $\{a^n : n \in Z\}$ is a subgroup of G.*

**Solution.** Let a be any arbitrary element of a group $G$. Define
$$H = [a^n : n \in Z].$$

**To show $H$ is a subgroup of $G$.**
For any $h_1, h_2 \in H \Rightarrow h_1 = a^x,\ h_2 = a^y$, where, $x, y \in Z$.
$\Rightarrow\ h_1h_2^{-1} = a^{x-y}$, where $x - y \in Z$
$\Rightarrow\ h_1h_2^{-1} \in H$
$\Rightarrow\ H$ is a subgroup of $G$.

***Example 8.*** *If G is a group, then the set Z, defined by*
$$Z = \{z \in G : zx = xz,\ \forall\ x \in G\}$$
*Prove that Z is a subgroup of G.*

**Solution.** Let $z_1, z_2 \in Z$, then
$$z_1x = xz_1,\ z_2x = xz_2, \forall x \in G \qquad \text{...(i)}$$
Now, $xz_1 = z_1x = z_1(z_2^{-1}z_2x), \forall x \in G$
$= z_1z_2^{-1}(z_2x) = z_1z_2^{-1}(xz_2)$ [from Eq. (i)]
$\therefore\ (xz_1)z_2^{-1} = z_1z_2^{-1}(xz_2)z_2^{-1}$
or $x(z_1z_2^{-1}) = z_1z_2^{-1}x(z_2z_2^{-1}) = (z_1z_2^{-1})x, \forall\ x \in G$
Therefore, $z_1z_2^{-1} \in Z \Rightarrow Z$ is a subgroup of $G$.

***Example 9.*** *If a is a fixed element of a group G, then prove that the set*
$N(a) = \{x \in G : xa = ax\}$ *is a subgroup of G.*

**Solution.** Let $x, y \in N(a)$, then $xa = ax, ya = ay$
Now, $ya = ay \Rightarrow y^{-1}(ya)y^{-1} = y^{-1}(ay)y^{-1}$
$\Rightarrow ay^{-1} = y^{-1}a$ ...(i)
$\Rightarrow y^{-1} \in N(a)$
Also, $(xy^{-1})a = x(y^{-1}a) = x(ay^{-1})$ [by Eq. (i)]
$= (xa)y^{-1} = (ax)y^{-1} = a(xy^{-1})$
$\Rightarrow\ xy^{-1} \in N(a)$, whenever $x, y \in N(a)$
Hence, $N(a)$ is a subgroup of $G$.

**Note** The subgroup defined above is called the Normalizer $N(a)$ of an element $a \in G$ *i.e.*, $N(a) = \{x \in G : xa = ax\}$.

## Cosets

Let $H$ be a subgroup of a group $(G, \bullet)$. Let $a \in G$ be arbitrary. We define

$$aH = \{ah : h \in H\} \text{ and } Ha = \{ha : h \in H\}$$

then, $aH$ is called left coset of $H$ in $G$ generated by $a$, and $Ha$ is called right coset of $H$ in $G$ generated by $a$.

> ***Note*** **(a)** Since, $He = H = eH$, hence $H$ itself is right as well as left cosets.
>
> **(b)** If the group $(G, \bullet)$ is abelian, then $ah = ha, \forall h \in H$, so that $aH = Ha, \forall a \in H$
>
> **(c)** If the composition in $G$ is additive, then the coset of $H$ in $G$ generated by $a$ is defined as
>
> $H + a = \{h + a : h \in H\}$ (Right coset)
>
> and $a + H = \{a + h : h \in H\}$. (Left coset)

## Index of a Subgroup in a Group

If $H$ is a subgroup of a group $G$, then number of distinct right (or left) cosets of $H$ in $G$ is called index of $H$ in $G$ and is denoted by $[G:H]$ or by $i_G(H) = o(G)/o(H)$.

## Important (Theorems) on Coset

**(i)** $a \equiv b \pmod H$ iff $ab^{-1} \in H$ or $Ha = Hb$

**(ii)** $a \in Hb \Leftrightarrow ab^{-1} \in H \Leftrightarrow Ha = Hb$.

**(iii)** Let $a \in G$ be arbitrary and let $H$ be a subgroup of a group $G$. Then, $Ha = H = aH \Leftrightarrow a \in H$.

**(iv)** $Ha = Hb \Leftrightarrow ab^{-1} \in H$

$aH = bH \Leftrightarrow a^{-1}b \in H$

**(v)** $aH \cap bH = \phi$ or $aH = bH$

and $Ha \cap Hb = \phi$ or $Ha = Hb$

**(vi)** A group $G$ is equal to the union of all right cosets of $H$ in $G$

*i.e.*, $G = H \cup Ha \cup Hb \cup Hc \cup \ldots$

**(vii)** $f: H \to aH$ is one-one and onto. Also, $f: H \to Ha$ is one-one and onto.

**(viii)** If $H$ is a subgroup of $G$, then there exists one-one correspondence between the set of left cosets of $H$ in $G$ and the set of right cosets of $H$ in $G$.

This theorem can also be stated as follows

"If $H$ is a subgroup of $G$, then the number of distinct left cosets of $H$ in $G$ is equal to the number of distinct right cosets of $H$ in $G$."

**(ix)** $(Ha)^{-1} = a^{-1}H$, where $a \in G$.

## Lagrange's Theorem

The order of each subgroup of a finite group is a divisor of the divisor of group.

*i.e.*, Let $H$ be a subgroup of a finite group $G$ and let

$o(G) = n$ and $o(H) = m$, then

$m \mid n$ ($m$ divides $n$)

Since, $f: H \to aH$ and $f: H \to Ha$ is one-one and onto.

$\Rightarrow \quad o(H) = o(Ha) = m$

Now, $\quad G = H \cup Ha \cup Hb \cup Hc \cup \ldots$, where, $a, b, c, \ldots \in G$

$\Rightarrow \quad o(G) = o(H) + o(Ha) + o(Hb) + \ldots$

$\Rightarrow \quad n = m + m + m + \ldots +$ upto $p$ terms (say)

$\Rightarrow \quad n = mp$

$\Rightarrow$ Order of the subgroup of a finite group is a divisor of the order of the group.

> ***Note*** The converse of the Lagrange's theorem is not true, *i.e.*, if $G$ is a finite group of order $n$ and $m$ is any divisor of $n$, then it is not necessary that $G$ must have a subgroup of order $m$.
>
> *e.g.*, Consider the symmetric group $P_4$ of permutation of degree 4. Then, $o(P_4) = 4! = 24$. Let $A_4$ be the alternating group of even permutation of degree 4. Then, $o(A_4) = \frac{24}{2} = 12$. There exist no subgroup $H$ of $A_4$, such that $o(H) = 6$, though 6 is a divisor of 12.
>
> The Lagrange's theorem has important applications in group theory. If $G$ is a group of order 8, then there will not exist subgroup of $G$ of order 3, 5, 6, 7. The only subgroup of $G$ may be of order 2 and 4. Since, 2 and 4 are divisors of 8.

## Cayley Theorem

Every finite group $G$ is isomorphic to its permutation group.

**Proof.** Let $G$ be a finite group of order $n$ such that $G = \{a_1, a_2, \ldots, a_n\}$

Let $a \in G$. Define a map $f_a: G \to G$ given by

$$f_a(x) = ax, \forall x \in G. \quad \ldots(i)$$

**$f_a$ is one-one**

Let $f_a(x_1) = f_a(x_2) : x_1, x_2 \in G \Rightarrow ax_1 = ax_2 \Rightarrow x_1 = x_2$

**$f_a$ is onto**

$f_a: G \to G$ is one-one and $G$ is finite $\Rightarrow f_a$ is onto. Thus, $f_a$ is one-one map of a finite set $G$ onto itself. It means that $f_a$ is a permutation of degree $n$. Here,

$$f_a = \begin{pmatrix} a_1 & a_2 \ldots a_n \\ aa_1 & aa_2 \ldots aa_n \end{pmatrix}$$

The elements $aa_1, aa_2, \ldots, aa_n$ are all distinct elements of $G$. Write $G' = \{f_a : a \in G\}$, then $G'$ is a set of permutations of degree $n$.

Now, we claim that $(G', \bullet)$ is a group, where $(\bullet)$ denotes permutations multiplication.

Let $a, b, c \in G$ be arbitrary and $e$ be the identity in $G$.

Let $a^{-1}$ denote inverse of $a$ in $G$.

So that $\quad a^{-1}a = aa^{-1} = e$.

and then we can prove $(G, \bullet) \cong (G', \bullet)$

> ***Note*** Cayley's theorem can also be stated as "Any finite group of order $n$ is homomorphic to a subgroup of the symmetric group $S_n$."

## Cyclic Group

If a group $G$ contains an element $a$ such that every element $x \in G$ is of the form $a^m$, where $m \in Z$, then $G$ is said to be cyclic group and $G$ is generated by $a$.

*i.e.*, $a$ is the generator of $G$, and we write,

$$G = \langle a \rangle = \{a^k : k \in Z\}$$

> **Note** If $a$ is a generator of a cyclic group $G$, then $a^{-1}$ is also a generator of $G$.

e.g.,

(i) The multiplicative group $G = \{1, -1, i, -i\}$ is a cyclic group with generator $i$,

$\because$ $(i)^1 = i, (i)^2 = -1, (i)^3 = -i$ and $(i)^4 = 1$

$\Rightarrow$ Each element of $G$ can be expressed as some integral power of $i$.

$\Rightarrow$ $G$ is cyclic, generated by $i$.

In general, multiplicative group of $n$th roots of unity is cyclic group with generator $e^{2\pi i/n}$.

(ii) The group $Z$ of integers under addition is an infinite cyclic group generated by 1 and –1.

Since, each $n \in Z$ can be written as $n = n \cdot 1$

(iii) The group $G = \{(0, 1, 2, 3, 4, 5), +_6\}$ is a cyclic group under the operation addition modulo 6.

Since,
$$0 = 0(1)$$
$$1 = 1(1)$$
$$2 = 1 +_6 1 = 2(1)$$
$$3 = 1 +_6 1 +_6 1 = 3(1)$$
$$4 = 1 +_6 1 +_6 1 +_6 1 = 4(1)$$
$$5 = 1 +_6 1 +_6 1 +_6 1 +_6 1 = 5(1)$$

$\Rightarrow$ Every element $n$ of $G$ is written as $n = n(1)$.

$\Rightarrow$ $G$ is a cyclic group with generator 1.

## Important Results on Cyclic Group

1. Every cyclic group is abelian but abelian group need not be cyclic.
   *e.g.*, $(Q, +)$ be the group of rational numbers under addition is an abelian group but not cyclic group.
2. Let $G$ be a finite group of order $n$. If $G$ contains an element of order $n$, then $G$ must be cyclic.
3. Every subgroup of a cyclic group is cyclic but the group $G$ need not be cyclic if every subgroup of a group $G$ are cyclic.
   *e.g.*, Consider the group,
   $$S_3 = \{I, (1\ 2), (1\ 3), (2\ 3), (1\ 2\ 3), (1\ 3\ 2)\}$$
   then, all the subgroups of $S_3$ are
   $$H_1 = \{I, (1\ 2)\} = \langle (1\ 2) \rangle$$
   $$H_2 = \{I, (1\ 3)\} = \langle (1\ 3) \rangle$$
   $$H_3 = \{I, (2\ 3)\} = \langle (2\ 3) \rangle$$
   $$H_4 = \{I, (1\ 2\ 3), (1\ 3\ 2)\} = \langle (1\ 2\ 3) \rangle$$
   which are cyclic, but the group $S_3$ is not cyclic, as there exist no element $a \in G$, such that $o(a) = 6 = o(G)$.
4. The number of generators of a finite cyclic group of order $n$ is $\varphi(n)$, where $\varphi(n)$ is the number of integers less than $n$ and coprime to $n$.
   *e.g.*, Total number of generators of a cyclic group of order 28 is 12 as
   $$\varphi(28) = \varphi(2^2 \times 7) = 28\left(1 - \frac{1}{2}\right)\left(1 - \frac{1}{7}\right) = 28 \times \frac{1}{2} \times \frac{6}{7} = 12$$
5. The order of a cyclic group is equal to the order of any generator of the group.
6. If cyclic group $G$ is generated by an element $a$ of order $n$, then $a^m$ is a generator of $G$ iff $(m, n) = 1$, *i.e.*, the greatest common divisor of $m$ and $n$ is 1.
   *e.g.*, Suppose that the cyclic group $G$ of order 8 is generated by an element $a$, then $o(a) = 8$.
   Clearly, $G = \{a, a^2, a^3, a^4, a^5, a^6, a^7, a^8 = e\}$
   Now, from theorem an element $a^m$ is also a generator of $G$, if $m$ is less than 8 and relatively prime to 8.
   Such numbers are 1, 3, 5 and 7.
   Hence, $a, a^3, a^5$ and $a^7$ are generators of $G$.
7. Every group of prime order is cyclic.
8. An infinite cyclic group has precisely two generators.
9. Cyclic group is infinite it means that order of its generator is infinite.
10. If $G$ be cyclic group of order $n$, then for any divisor $m$ of $n$ there exist a unique subgroup of $G$ of order $m$. or converse of lagrange's theorem holds for cyclic groups.
11. A cyclic group $G$ with a generator of finite order $n$, is isomorphic to the multiplicative group of $n$, $n$th roots of unity.
12. Every isomorphic image of a cyclic group is cyclic. *i.e.*, if $\langle a \rangle$ is cyclic, then $\langle f(a) \rangle$ is also cyclic.
13. Every infinite group is isomorphic to the additive group of integers.
14. A cyclic group of finite order $n$ is isomorphic to the additive group of residue classes modulo $n$.

## Normal Subgroups

A subgroup $H$ of a group $G$ is called a normal subgroup of $G$, if every left coset of $H$ in $G$ is equal to the corresponding right coset of $H$ in $G$.

i.e., $aH = Ha, \forall a \in G$

In addition composition, $H$ will be normal subgroup of $G$ iff

$$a + H = H + a, \forall a \in G$$

if $H$ is a normal subgroup of $G$, then it is expressed as $H \triangleleft G$.

> ***Note*** **(a)** When $G$ is an abelian group, then every subgroup $H$ of $G$ is a normal subgroup, for $aH = Ha, \forall a \in G$
> **(b)** The subgroups $\{e\}$ and $G$ of any group $G$ are always normal subgroups of $G$. These are called trivial normal subgroups.
> **(c)** A normal subgroup is also called as an invariant subgroup or a self conjugate subgroup or a normal divisor of the group.
> **(d)** A group $G \neq \{e\}$ is known as simple group, if it has no proper normal subgroup.
> **(e)** A non-abelian group, each of whose subgroups is normal, is said to be Hamiltonian group.
> **(f)** The centre $Z$ of group $G$ is a normal subgroup of $G$.

***Example 10.*** *If G is a group and H is a subgroup of index 2 in G, show that H is a normal subgroup of G.*

**Solution.** Since, index of $H$ in $G$ is 2, there are two distinct left (right) cosets of $H$ in $G$. Also, we have $H = eH = He$, so, $H$ is itself a left as well as right cosets of $H$ in $G$.

Let $a \in G$. If $a \in H$, then

$$aH = Ha = H$$

Again, for an $a \in G, a \notin H$, the left cosets $aH$ is different from $H$ and likewise the right coset $Ha$ is different from $H$. Since, there are only two distinct left (right) cosets of $H$ in $G$, the decomposition of $G$ into left cosets with respect to $H$ consist of $H$ and $aH$ for an $a \in G, a \notin H$, therefore

$$G = H \cup aH$$

Also, decomposing $G$ into right cosets with respect to $H$, we have

$$G = H \cup Ha$$

Now, the left cosets $H$ and $aH$ as well as the right cosets $H$ and $Ha$ have no element in common (since they are disjoint), it follows from the above relation, we must have

$$Ha = aH$$

Now, since $a$ is arbitrary, therefore every left cosets of $H$ is also a right coset of $H$. Hence, $H$ is a normal subgroup of $G$.

***Example 11.*** *Let $G = S_3$, the symmetric group on three numbers 1, 2, 3, then show that the subgroup $H = \{I, (1\ 2\ 3), (1\ 3\ 2)\}$ is a normal subgroup of G but the subgroup $K = \{I, (1\ 2)\}$ is not a normal subgroup of G.*

**Solution.** Since, we know that

$$Ha = H = aH, \text{ if } a \in H$$

Since, $I, (1\ 2\ 3), (1\ 3\ 2) \in H$

$\therefore$ $IH = HI$

$(1\ 2\ 3)H = H(1\ 2\ 3)$

$(1\ 3\ 2)H = H(1\ 3\ 2)$

Given, $G = S_3 = \{I, (1\ 2), (1\ 3), (2\ 3), (1\ 2\ 3), (1\ 3\ 2)\}$

Now, $(1\ 2)H = \{(1\ 2)I, (1\ 2)(1\ 2\ 3), (1\ 2)(1\ 3\ 2)\}$
$= \{(1\ 2), (1\ 3), (2\ 3)\}$

$H(1\ 2) = \{I(1\ 2), (1\ 2\ 3)(1\ 2), (1\ 3\ 2)(1\ 2)\}$
$= \{(1\ 2), (2\ 3), (1\ 3)\}$

$\therefore$ $(1\ 2)H = H(1\ 2)$

Similarly,

$(1\ 3)H = H(1\ 3)$

$(2\ 3)H = H(2\ 3)$

$\Rightarrow$ $xH = Hx, \forall x \in G (= S_3)$

$\Rightarrow$ $H$ is a normal subgroup of $S_3$.

Again, $(1\ 3)K = \{(1\ 3)I, (1\ 3)(1\ 2)\}$
$= \{(1\ 3), (1\ 3\ 2)\}$

and $K(1\ 3) = \{I(1\ 3), (1\ 2)(1\ 3)\}$
$= \{(1\ 3), (1\ 2\ 3)\}$

$\Rightarrow$ $(1\ 3)K \neq K(1\ 3)$

Hence, $K$ is not a normal subgroup of $G$.

## Important Theorems on Normal Subgroup

***Theorem 1*** A subgroup $H$ of a group $G$ is normal iff $ghg^{-1} \in H$ for all $h \in H, g \in G$.

***Theorem 2*** A subgroup $H$ of a group $G$ is normal iff

$$gHg^{-1} = H, \forall\ g \in G$$

***Theorem 3*** A subgroup $H$ of a group $G$ is a normal subgroup of $G$ if and only if the product of two right cosets of $H$ in $G$ is again a right coset of $H$ in $G$.

***Proof.*** Let $H$ be a normal subgroup of a group $G$, and $x, y$ be any two elements of $G$.

$\Rightarrow Hx, Hy$ are any two right cosets of $H$ in $G$.

We have

$$\begin{aligned}(Hx)(Hy) &= H(xH)y && \text{(by associativity)}\\ &= H(Hx)y && (\because H \text{ is normal} \Rightarrow Hx = xH)\\ &= (HH)xy && \text{(by associativity)}\\ &= Hxy && (\because HH = H)\end{aligned}$$

$x, y \in G \Rightarrow xy \in G \Rightarrow Hxy$ is a right coset of $H$ is $G$, thus the product of two right cosets $Hx$ and $Hy$ is the right coset $Hxy$.

***Theorem 4*** If $H$ and $K$ are normal subgroup of $G$, then $H \cap K$ is also a normal subgroup of $G$.

***Proof.*** Let $H$ be a subgroup of an abelian group $G$ so that $H$ is abelian and hence, $H$ is a normal subgroup of $G$.

**To show $G/H$ is abelian**

Let $Ha, Hb \in G/H$, then

$(Ha)(Hb) = Hab = Hba \quad (\because ab = ba \ \forall \ a, b \in G)$
$= (Hb)(Ha)$

$\Rightarrow \quad (Ha)(Hb) = (Hb)(Ha)$

$\Rightarrow \quad G/H$ is abelian.

---

***Example 12.*** *If $G = \{a\}$ is a cyclic group of order 8, then find the quotient groups corresponding to the subgroups generated by $a^2$ and $a^4$, respectively.*

**Solution.** Let $\quad G = \{a, a^2, a^3, a^4, a^5, a^6, a^7, a^8 = e\}$

and $\quad H_1 = \{a^2, a^4, a^6, a^8 = e\}$

$H_2 = \{a^4, a^8 = e\}$

Since, $G$ is abelian, therefore, the subgroups $H_1$ and $H_2$ are normal in $G$.

$$o(G/H_1) = \frac{8}{4} = 2, \ o(G/H_2) = \frac{8}{2} = 4$$

## Conjugate Element

Let $G$ be a group. An element $a \in G$ is called conjugate to an element $b \in G$, if and only if $a = x^{-1}bx$ for some $x \in G$.

## Normalizer

The normalizer of an element $a \in G$ is the set of all those elements of $G$ which commutes with $a$ and is denoted by $N(a)$. i.e.

$$N(a) = \{x \in G \ : \ ax = xa\}$$

> ***Note*** **(a)** $N(a)$ is a subgroup of $G$
> **(b)** In general, $N(a)$ is not a normal subgroup of $G$
> **(c)** $N(e) = G \quad (\because ex = xe, \forall x \in G)$
> **(d)** $N(a) = G$ iff $G$ is abelian

## Conjugate Class

Since, an equivalence relation defined on a set decomposes the set into mutually disjoint equivalence classes, hence the relation of conjugacy, defined on a group $G$ decomposes $G$ into mutually disjoint equivalence classes known as classes of conjugate element.

Let $C_a$ denote the equivalence class determined by an element $a \in G$, then

$$C_a = \{x \in G : x \approx a\} = \{x \in G : x \approx y^{-1}ay \text{ for some } y \in G\}$$
$$= \{y^{-1}ay : y \in G\}.$$

Here, $C_a$ is defined as conjugate class of a in $G$. Also, $C_a$ is the class element conjugate to a.

## Self Conjugate

An element a of a group $G$ is called self conjugate element iff

$$C_a \ \{a\}$$

i.e., iff $C_a$ consists of the single element a.

i.e., iff $\quad x^{-1}ax = a \ \forall \ x \in G$

$\Rightarrow$ iff $\quad ax = xa \ \forall \ x \in G$

# Important Theorems

***Theorem 1*** The normalizer $N(a)$ of $a \in G$ is a subgroup of $G$.

***Theorem 2*** Let $G$ be a finite group and $a \in G$. Let $N(a)$ denotes the normalizer of $a$ in $G$ and $C_a$ the conjugate class of $a$ in $G$. Then, $o(C_a) = \dfrac{o(G)}{o(N(a))}$, *i.e.*, number of distinct elements conjugate to $a$ in $G$ is the index of the normalizer of $a$ in $G$.

***Proof.*** Let $G$ be a finite group and $a \in G$.

To show $\quad o(C_a) = \dfrac{o(G)}{o(N(a))}$

By definition, we have

$$N(a) = \{x \in G : ax = xa\}$$

and $\quad C_a = \{x^{-1}ax : x \in G\}$

Write $\quad M = \{N(a)x : x \in G\}$
= set of right cosets of $N(a)$ in G.

Define a map $f : M \to C_a$, such that $f[N(a) \cdot x] = x^{-1}ax$, $\forall \ x \in G$, obviously, $f$ is well defined.

To show $f$ is one-one and onto.

$f$ is one-one

Consider $\quad f[N(a) \cdot x] = f[N(a) \cdot y]; \ x, y \in G$

$\Rightarrow \quad x^{-1}ax = y^{-1}ay$

$\Rightarrow \quad x(x^{-1}ax)y^{-1} = x(y^{-1}ay)y^{-1}$

$\Rightarrow \quad (xx^{-1})(axy^{-1}) = (xy^{-1}a)(yy^{-1})$

$\Rightarrow \quad e(axy^{-1}) = (xy^{-1}a)e$

$\Rightarrow \quad axy^{-1} = xy^{-1}a \Rightarrow a(xy^{-1}) = (xy^{-1})a$

$\Rightarrow \quad xy^{-1} \in N(a) \Rightarrow N(a)xy^{-1} = N(a)$

$\Rightarrow \quad N(a) \cdot x = N(a) \cdot y$

$\Rightarrow \quad f$ is one-one.

$f$ is onto.

For given any $x^{-1}ax \in C_a \ \exists \ N(a) \cdot x \in M$, such that

$$f[N(a) \cdot x] = x^{-1}ax$$

$\Rightarrow \quad f$ is onto.

Hence, $o(C_a) = o(M) =$ Number of distinct right cosets of $N(a)$ in $G$

= index of $N(a)$ in G

$= \dfrac{o(G)}{o(N(a))}$, by definition of index.

***Theorem 3*** If $G$ is a finite group, then $o(G) = \sum \dfrac{o(G)}{o(N(a))}$

where this sum is taken over one element of each conjugate class.

***Proof.*** Since, we know that, the relation of conjugacy is an equivalence relation on the set $G$.

$\Rightarrow$ This relation partitions $G$ into disjoint equivalence classes.

Let $C_a, C_b, C_c$ respectively denote conjugate classes of elements $a, b, c \in G$. Also, let

$$o(C_a) = C_a, o(C_b) = C_b, o(C_c) = C_c$$

Then, $G = C_a \cup C_b \cup C_c \cdots$

$\Rightarrow$ $o(G) = oC_a + o(C_b) + o(C_c) + \ldots$

($\because C_a, C_b, C_c$ are mutually disjoint)

$= \sum C_a$, where the sum runs over each elements of conjugate class.

But $C_a = \dfrac{o(G)}{o(N(a))}$

$\therefore$ $o(G) = \sum \dfrac{o(G)}{oN(a)}$

This relation is called class equation of $G$.

***Theorem 4*** Let $Z$ denote the centre of a group $G$, then $a \in Z \Leftrightarrow N(a) = G$ and also if $G$ is finite, then $a \in Z \Leftrightarrow o(N(a)) = o(G)$.

***Theorem 5*** If $G$ is a finite group and $Z$ is its centre, then class equation of $G$ is expressible as

$$o(G) = o(Z) + \sum_{a \notin Z} \left\{\frac{o(G)}{o(N(a))}\right\}$$

where the summation runs over one element $a$ in each conjugate class.

***Proof.*** Let $a$ be an element of a conjugate class. The class equation of $G$ is

$$o(G) = \sum \frac{o(G)}{o(N(a))} \quad \ldots\text{(i)}$$

We know that

$$a \in Z \Leftrightarrow o(N(a)) = o(G) \Rightarrow \frac{o(G)}{o(N(a))} = 1$$

or $a \in Z \Rightarrow \dfrac{o(G)}{o(N(a))} = 1$

Now Eq. (i) becomes

$$o(G) = o(Z) + \sum_{a \notin Z} \frac{o(G)}{o(N(a))}$$

***Theorem 6*** If $o(G) = p^n$, where $p$ is a prime number, then centre $Z \neq \{e\}$, *i.e.*, group of prime power order must have a non-trivial centre.

If $n = 3$

*i.e.*, $o(G) = p^3$, then $o(Z) = p$

If $n = 2$

*i.e.*, $o(G) = p^2$, then $G$ is an abelian group.

# Quotient Group

If $G$ is a group and $H$ is a normal subgroup of $G$, then the set $G/H$ of all cosets of $H$ in $G$ is a group with respect to multiplication of cosets, is called quotient group or factor group of $G$ by $H$.

*i.e.*, $\dfrac{G}{H} = \{Ha : a \in G\}$

In other words, if $H$ is a normal subgroup of a group $G$, then the group $\dfrac{G}{H}$ of all the right cosets of $H$ in $G$ under the composition $(Ha)(Hb) = Hab$ is called a quotient group or a factor group.

If the composition in $\dfrac{G}{H}$ is addition, then $\dfrac{G}{H}$ is defined by

$$(H + a) + (H + b) = H + (a + b)$$

> ***Note*** If $H$ is a normal subgroup of a finite group $G$, then $\dfrac{G}{H}$ form a group of order $\dfrac{o(G)}{o(H)}$.
>
> $\Rightarrow \dfrac{o(G)}{o(H)}$ = The number of distinct right cosets of $H$ in $G$.

# Important Theorem on Quotient Group

***Theorem 1*** A subgroup $H$ of a group $G$ is normal iff the set $G/H$ of all its left cosets is closed under multiplication.

*i.e.*, for $aH, bH \in \dfrac{G}{H} \Rightarrow (ab)H \in \dfrac{G}{H}$

Subgroup $H$ of $G$ is normal.

***Theorem 2*** Every quotient group of a cyclic group is cyclic, but converse is not true.

***Theorem 3*** Every quotient group of an abelian group $G$ is abelian but converse is not true.

# Homomorphism and Isomorphism of Groups

## Homomorphism

Let $(G, o)$ and $(G', *)$ be two groups. Then, a mapping $f: G \to G'$ is called a homomorphism if

$$f(x \, o \, y) = f(x) * f(y), \forall\ x, y \in G$$

The homomorphism $f$ is called

(i) isomorphism, if $f$ is ono-one and onto.

(ii) monomorphism, if $f$ is one-one.

(iii) epimorphism, if $f$ is onto.

If $f$ is a homomorphic mapping of a group $G$ onto the group $G'$, so that $f(G) = G'$, then the group $G'$ is called a homomorphic image of the group $G$.

## Isomorphism of Groups

Let $(G, o)$ and $(G', *)$ be any two groups.

"A one-one onto map $f: G \to G'$ is called an isomorphism iff

$$f(a \, o \, b) = f(a) * f(b), \forall\ a, b \in G$$

Here, we say that $G$ is isomorphic to $G'$ and can be written as

$$G \cong G'$$

We also say that $G$ is isomorphically mapped onto $G'$; or $G$ and $G'$ are isomorphic groups.

e.g., If $R$ is the additive group of real numbers and $R^+$ is the multiplicative group of positive real numbers, then the mapping $f: R \to R^+$ defined by $f(x) = e^x, \forall\, x \in R$ is an isomorphism.

## Endomorphism

A homomorphism of a group $G$ into itself is called an endomorphism.

## Automorphism

An isomorphism of a group onto itself is called an automorphism of the group.

In other words, we can say that "A one-one map $f: G \to G$ is called an automorphism of the group $(G, *)$, if

$$f(x * y) = f(x) * f(y), \forall\, x, y \in G$$

e.g., Let $(G, *)$ be a group.

Then, a mapping $f: G \to G$ given by $f(x) = x, \forall\, x \in G$ is an automorphism of $G$.

## Inner Automorphism

Let $(G, *)$ be a group and $a \in G$ be arbitrary but fixed. A mapping $f_a: G \to G$ given by $f_a(x) = a^{-1}xa, \forall\, x \in G$ is an automorphism of $G$, where $a^{-1}$ is the inverse of $a$. This automorphism is called inner automorphism of $G$ induced by the element $a$.

## Natural Homomorphism

Let $H$ be a normal subgroup of group $G$, then the map $f: G \to G/H$ such that $f(x) = Hx$ is a homomorphism. This homomorphism is called natural or canonical homomorphism.

e.g.,

(i) If $f(x) = e, \forall\, x \in G$, this is homomorphism.

(ii) If $G$ be a group of all real numbers under addition, i.e., $a * b$ for $a, b \in G$ is the real number $a + b$ and $G'$ be the multiplicative group of non-zero real numbers and $f: G \to G'$ defined by $f(a) = 2^a$ is a homomorphism. $[\because f(a+b) = 2^{a+b} = 2^a \cdot 2^b = f(a) \cdot f(b)]$

(iii) If $G$ be the group of integers under addition and $G' = G$ and let $f(x) = 2x, \forall\, x \in G$, then

$$f(x+y) = 2(x+y) = 2x + 2y = f(x) + f(y)$$

$\Rightarrow$ $f$ is a homomorphism.

(iv) If $G$ be the group of integers under addition and $G'_n$ be the group of integers under addition modulo $n$ and let $f$ be defined as $f(x) =$ remainder of $x$ on division by $n$, then it is a homomorphism.

## Kernel of a Homomorphism

If $f$ is a homomorphism of a group $G$ into a group $G'$, then kernel of $f$, is defined as

$$\ker f = \{x \in G : f(x) = e'\}$$

where, $e'$ is the identity element of $G'$.

# Important Theorems on Homomorphism and Isomorphism

***Theorem 1*** If $f: G \to G'$ be a homomorphism of groups and $e, e'$ be the identities in $G$ and $G'$, respectively. Then,

(i) $f(e) = e'$

(ii) $f(a^{-1}) = [f(a)]^{-1}$, where $a \in G$.

***Proof.*** (i) We have

$$f(a)e' = f(a) = f(ae) \qquad (\because a = ae)$$
$$= f(a) \cdot f(e)$$
$$\Rightarrow \quad e' = f(e)$$

(ii) If $a \in G$, then $aa^{-1} = a^{-1}a = e$

Thus, $f(a^{-1})f(a) = f(a^{-1}a) = f(e) = e'$

and $f(a)f(a^{-1}) = f(aa^{-1}) = f(e) = e'$

$$f(a^{-1}) = [f(a)]^{-1}$$

***Theorem 2*** A homomorphism $f$ of a group $G$ into a group $G'$ is an isomorphism iff $\ker f = \{e\}$.

***Proof.*** Let $f$ be a homomorphism of a group $G$ into a group $G'$, suppose $f$ is one-one.

Let $x \in \ker(f)$

Then, $f(x) = e'$ (where $e'$ is the identity of $G'$)

Also, $f(e) = e'$

$\Rightarrow$ $f(x) = f(e) \Rightarrow x = e$

$\therefore$ $\text{Ker } f = [e]$

Conversely, let $\ker f = [e]$

Let $x, y \in G$ be such that $f(x) = f(y)$

Then, $f(x)f(y)^{-1} = e' \Rightarrow f(xy^{-1}) = f(x)f(y^{-1}) = e'$

$\Rightarrow xy^{-1} \in \ker f = [e]$

$\Rightarrow xy^{-1} = e \Rightarrow x = y$

Hence, $f$ is one-one $\Rightarrow f$ is an isomorphism.

***Theorem 3*** If $f$ is a homomorphism of group $G$ into a group $G'$ with kernel $K$, then $K$ is a normal subgroup of $G$.

***Theorem 4*** If $f$ is a homomorphism of a group $G$ into a group $G'$ with kernel $K$. Let $a \in G$ be such that $f(a) = a' \in G'$. Then, the set of all those elements of $G$, which have the image $a'$ in $G'$ is the coset $Ka$ of $K$ in $G$.

***Theorem 5*** Let $G$ be a group and $N$ is a normal subgroup of $G$. Let $f$ be a mapping from $G$ to $G/N$ defined by

$$f(x) = Nx, \forall\, x \in G$$

Then, $f$ is a homomorphism of $G$ onto $G/N$ and kernel $f = N$.

***Theorem 6*** (Fundamental theorem on homomorphism of groups) Every homomorphic image of a group $G$ is isomorphic to some quotient group of $G$.

If $G'$ be a homomorphic image of $G$ and $f$ be the homomorphism of $G$ onto $G'$.

Let $K = \text{Ker } f$

If $a \in G$, then $Ka \in G/K$ and $f(a) \in G'$.

Define a mapping

$\phi : G/K \to G'$ such that $\phi(Ka) = f(a),\ \forall\ a \in G$

Then, $\phi$ is one-one and onto and hence $\frac{G}{K} \cong G'$

> **Note** For any normal subgroup $N$ of $G$, $\frac{G}{N}$ is a homomorphic image of $G$.

***Theorem 7*** (First theorem on isomorphism) Let $f$ be a homomorphism of a group $G$ onto a group $G'$ and

$H = \text{Ker } f$, $K'$ is any normal subgroup of $G'$ and

$K = \{x \in G : f(x) \in K'\} = f^{-1}(K')$,

then $K$ is a normal subgroup of $G$ containing $H$ and $G/K \cong G'/K'$.

***Theorem 8*** (Second law of isomorphism) If $H$ be a normal subgroup of a group $G$ and $K$ be a normal subgroup of $G$ containing $H$, then $G/K \cong \frac{(G/H)}{(K/H)}$.

***Theorem 9*** (Third law of isomorphism) Let $G$ be a group and $H$ be any subgroup of $G$. If $N$ is any normal subgroup of $G$, then

$$HN/N \cong H/(H \cap N).$$

***Theorem 10*** If $f : G \to G'$ is an isomorphism of groups, then $o(a) = o(f(a)),\ \forall\ a \in G$.

***Theorem 11*** The relation of isomorphism in the set of groups is an equivalence relation.

---

***Example 13.*** *If $R$ be the additive group of real numbers and $R^+$ the multiplicative group of positive real numbers show that the following mapping are isomorphism.*

(i) $f : R \to R^+$ s.t., $f(x) = e^x,\ \ x \in R$.

(ii) $f : R^+ \to R$ s.t., $f(x) = \log x,\ \ x \in R^+$.

**Solution.** (i) Since, $x \neq y \Rightarrow e^x \neq e^y,\ \forall x, y \in R \Rightarrow f$ is one-one.

Now, to every positive real number $x \in R^+$, there is a real number $\log x \in R$, such that $f(\log x) = e^{\log x} = x$

$\Rightarrow$ $f$ is onto.

Also, $f(x+y) = e^{x+y} = e^x \cdot e^y = f(x) \cdot f(y)$

Hence, $f$ is an isomorphism of $R$ onto $R^+$.

(ii) Since, any two distinct real positive numbers have two different logarithms as real numbers.

$\Rightarrow f$ is one-one.

Also, every real number has a unique anti-logarithms as a positive real number *i.e.*

$a \neq b \ \Rightarrow \log a \neq \log b,\ \forall\ a,\ b \in R^+$

and $\forall\ x \in R, x = \log e^x = f(e^x)$, where $e^x \in R^+$

$\Rightarrow$ $f$ is onto.

Also, for all $xy \in R^+$

$$f(xy) = \log(xy) = \log x + \log y = f(x) + f(y)$$

Hence, $f$ is an isomorphism.

***Example 14.*** *Show that the multiplicative group $G$ of $n$, $n$th roots of unity is isomorphic to the group $G' = (\{0, 1, 2, \ldots, n-1\}\ +_n)$.*

**Solution.** Let the element of $G$ are $e^{2r\pi i/n}$,

where, $r = 0, 1, 2, \ldots, n-1$

Define a map $f : G \to G'$ such that $f(e^{2r\pi i/n}) = r$

(i) **$f$ is one-one** If $0 \leq r_1 \leq n-1$ and $0 \leq r_2 \leq n-1$, then $f(e^{2r_1\pi i/n}) = r_1$ and $f(e^{2r_2\pi i/n}) = r_2$

We have $f(e^{2r_1\pi i/n}) = f(e^{2r_2\pi i/n})$

$\Rightarrow \qquad r_1 = r_2$

$\Rightarrow \qquad e^{2r_1\pi i/n} = e^{2r_2\pi i/n}$

$\Rightarrow f$ is one-one.

(ii) **$f$ is onto** Since, the number of elements in $G$ is equal to the number of elements in $G'$, therefore

$f$ is one-one $\Rightarrow f$ is onto.

(iii) **Structure preserving property** Consider

$f(e^{2r_1\pi i/n} \cdot e^{2r_2\pi i/n}) = f[e^{2(r_1+r_2)\pi i/n}] = f[e^{2q\pi i/n}]$

(where, $q$ is least non-negative remainder when $r_1 + r_2$ is divided by $n$)

$$= q = r_1 +_n r_2 = f(e^{2r_1\pi i/n}) +_n f(e^{2r_2\pi i/n})$$

$\Rightarrow \qquad f$ preserves composition.

Hence, $\qquad G \cong G'$.

***Example 15.*** *Let $G$ be a group and $e$ be the identity element of $G$. Then, show that the mapping $f : G \to G$ defined by $f(a) = e,\ \forall a \in G$ is an endomorphism of $G$.*

**Solution.** Let $a$ and $b$ be any two elements of $G$, then

$f(a) = e = f(b)$

Now, $\ f(ab) = e = ee = f(a) \cdot f(b)$

$\Rightarrow f$ is a homomorphism of $G$ into $G$. Therefore, $f$ is an endomorphism of $G$.

***Example 16.*** *Show that $\frac{4\mathbb{Z}}{1} \cong \mathbb{Z}_3$*

*where $\mathbb{Z}_3 = (\{[0], [1], [2], +_3\})$ be the additive group of residue classes modulo 3.*

**Solution.** Define the map $f : 4\mathbb{Z} \to \mathbb{Z}_3$ by $f(4n) = [n],\ \forall\ n \in \mathbb{Z}$

Clearly, $f$ is surjective and

$$f(4n + 4m) = f(4(n+m)) = [n+m] = [n] + [m]$$

$\therefore f$ is homomorphism.

$\therefore$ By first theorem on homomorphism,

$$\frac{4\mathbb{Z}}{\ker f} \cong \mathbb{Z}_3$$

Now, $\quad \ker f = \{4n \in 4\mathbb{Z} : f(4n) = [0]\}$

$\qquad = \{4n \in 4\mathbb{Z} :\ [n] = [0]\}$

$= \{4n \in 4\mathbb{Z} : n = 3k, k \in \mathbb{Z}\}$
$= 12\mathbb{Z}$

Hence, $\frac{4\mathbb{Z}}{12\mathbb{Z}} \cong \mathbb{Z}_3$

***Example 17.*** *Find all subgroups of* $\frac{\mathbb{Z}}{21\mathbb{Z}}$.

**Solution.** Let $K$ be subgroup of $\frac{\mathbb{Z}}{21\mathbb{Z}}$, then $K = \frac{H}{21\mathbb{Z}}$ for some subgroup $H$ of $\mathbb{Z}$, such that $21\mathbb{Z} \subseteq H$, then $\frac{H}{21\mathbb{Z}}$ is a subgroup of $\frac{\mathbb{Z}}{21\mathbb{Z}}$. So, we have to determine all subgroups of $\mathbb{Z}$ that contain $21\mathbb{Z}$. Now, $1, 3, 7, 21$ are the only positive divisors of 21.

Hence, $\mathbb{Z}, 3\mathbb{Z}, 7\mathbb{Z}$ and $21\mathbb{Z}$ are the only subgroups of $\mathbb{Z}$ that contain $21\mathbb{Z}$.

$\Rightarrow \frac{\mathbb{Z}}{21\mathbb{Z}}, \frac{3\mathbb{Z}}{21\mathbb{Z}}, \frac{7\mathbb{Z}}{21\mathbb{Z}}$ and $\frac{21\mathbb{Z}}{21\mathbb{Z}} = \{e\}$ are $\phi$ the subgroups of $\frac{\mathbb{Z}}{21\mathbb{Z}}$.

# Sylow Package

## Cauchy's Theorem for Abelian Groups

Let $G$ be a finite abelian group and a prime $p \mid o(G)$, then there exists an element $a \neq e$ in $G$ such that $o(a) = p$.

## Sylow $p$-subgroups

Let $o(G) = p^m n$, where $p$ is the prime and $m$, $n$ the positive integers such that $p \nmid n$. Then, a subgroup $H$ of $G$ is said to be a sylow p-subgroup of $G$, if $o(H) = p^m$ and $o(H)$ is the highest power of $p$ that divides $o(G)$.

## Sylow's First Theorem

Let $G$ be a finite group such that $p^m \mid o(G)$ and $p^{m+1} \nmid o(G)$, where $p$ is a prime number and $m$ is a positive integer. Then, $G$ has subgroups of order $p, p^2, p^3, \ldots, p^m$.

## Sylow's Second Theorem

Let $G$ be a finite group and $p$ be a prime number such that $p \mid o(G)$. Then, any two sylow $p$-subgroups of $G$ are conjugate.

***Theorem*** Let $p \mid o(G)$, where $G$ is a finite group and $p$ is any prime number. Then, a sylow $p$-subgroup $H$ of $G$ is normal, if $H$ is unique sylow $p$-subgroup of $G$.

## Sylow's Third Theorem

The number of sylow $p$-subgroups in $G$ for a given prime $p$, is of the form $1 + kp$, where $k$ is some non-negative integer and $(1 + kp) \mid o(G)$.

***Example 18.*** *Prove that a group of order 45 is abelian.*

**Solution.** Let $o(G) = 45$ and since $45 = 3^2 \times 5$, then $G$ has a 3-sylow subgroup $H$ of order 9 and a 5-sylow subgroup $K$ of order 5. Let $H$ have $n$ conjugates, then $n = 1 + 3r$ $(r \geq 0)$ and $n \mid 45$ and so, we conclude easily that as the factors of 45 are 1, 3, 5, 9, 15, 45, therefore $n = 1$ and $H$ is normal in $G$ because it is unique 3-sylow subgroup in $G$.

Similarly, $K$ is normal in $G$.

Now, $|HK| = |HK||H \cap K| = |H||K|$ $\quad [\because H \cap K = \{e\}]$
$= 9 \times 5 = 45$

$\therefore$ $G = HK$ and thus $G$ is isomorphic to the direct product $H \times K$. But $H$ is abelian and $K$ is cyclic and this $G$ is abelian.

***Example 19.*** *Let $G$ be a finite group and let $H$ be a p-sylow subgroup of $G$. If $N$ is a normal subgroup of $G$, prove that $N \cap H$ is a p-sylow subgroup of $N$.*

**Solution.** Since, $H$ is a $p$-sylow subgroup of the groups $HN$ and $G$, so we may write $|HN| = |H| m_1$, $|G| = |H| m_1 m_2$, where $m_1, m_2$ are the integers not divisible by $p$. Then,

$$|N| = \frac{|H||N|}{|H|} = \frac{|HN||H \cap N|}{|H|} = |H \cap N| m_1$$

Hence, $H \cap N$, being a $p$-subgroup of $N$ of highest possible order is a $p$-sylow subgroup of $N$.

***Example 20.*** *Show that if $H$ is a sylow $p$-subgroup of a finite group $G$, then for an arbitrary $x \in G$, $x^{-1}Hx$ Is also a $p$-subgroup of $G$.*

**Solution.** Let $G$ be a finite group of order $p^m n$, where $p$ is not a divisor of $n$ and let $H$ be a sylow $p$-subgroup of $G$, so that $o(H) = p^m$.

Let $x$ be an arbitrary element of $G$ and let $x^{-1}h_1x$ and $x^{-1}h_2x$ be any two elements of $x^{-1}Hx$, then

$(x^{-1}h_1x)(x^{-1}h_2x)^{-1} = (x^{-1}h_1x)(x^{-1}h_2^{-1}x)$
$= x^{-1}h_1(xx^{-1})h_2^{-1}x = x^{-1}h_1h_2^{-1}x$ $\quad [\because xx^{-1} = e]$

Since, $h_1, h_2 \in H \Rightarrow h_1h_2^{-1} \in H \Rightarrow x^{-1}h_1h_2^{-1}x \in x^{-1}Hx$

$\therefore$ $(x^{-1}h_1x)(x^{-1}h_2x)^{-1} \in x^{-1}Hx$

Thus, $x^{-1}Hx$ is a subgroup of $G$.

Since, $G$ is finite, so that

$$o(x^{-1}Hx) = o(H) = p^m$$

Hence, $x^{-1}Hx$ is a $p$-subgroup of $G$.

***Example 21.*** *Prove that there is no simple group of order 120.*

**Solution.** Let $G$ be a group of order 120. Then, $o(G) = 120 = 2^3 \cdot 3 \cdot 5$.

The number of sylow 2-subgroups of $G$ is of the form $1+2k$ such that $1+2k|\, o(G)$, *i.e.,* $1+2k|15$ as $1+2k$ is relatively prime to 2.

The factor of 15 are 1,3,5,15, then $1+2k$ is 1,3 or 15.

If $1+2K=1$, then there is a unique sylow 2-subgroup of $G$ of order 8. Thus, it is normal in $G$.

If $1+2k=3$, then there are 3 sylow 2-subgroups of $G$ each of order 8, let $H_1, H_2$ and $H_3$ be these subgroups. Since, $o(H_1)=o(H_2)=o(H_3)=2^3$.

Thus, the centre of either $H_1, H_2$ or $H_3$ will have 2 elements and then centre of a group is normal subgroup. Thus, each $H_1, H_2$ and $H_3$ contains a normal subgroup of order 2.

If $1+2k=15$, there are 15 sylow 2-subgroups each of order 8. By the same argument, each subgroup will contain a normal subgroup.

Thus, $G$ has a proper normal subgroup. Hence, $G$ is not simple.

***Example 22.*** *Let G be a group of order 108. Show that there exists a normal subgroup of order 27 or 9.*

**Solution.** Since, $o(G)=108=2^2\cdot 3^3$

The number of sylow 3-subgroups of $G$ is of the form $1+3k$ such that $1+3k|\, o(G)$ *i.e.,* $1+3k|2^2\cdot 3^3$

Since, $1+3k$ is relatively prime to 3, so that $1+3k|2^2$. Now, the factor of 4 are 1,2,4, therefore $1+3k=1$ or 4.

If $1+3k=1$, then there is a unique sylow 3-subgroup of order 27, which is normal in $G$.

If $1+3k=4$, there are four sylow 3-subgroups each of order 27. Let $H$ and $K$ be two such distinct sylow 3-subgroup. Then, we have

$$o(HK)=\frac{o(H)o(K)}{o(H\cap K)}=\frac{27\times 27}{o(H\cap K)}$$

But $\quad o(HK)\le o(G)=108$

$$\therefore \quad \frac{27\times 27}{o(H\cap K)}\le 108 \Rightarrow o(H\cap K)>\frac{27\times 27}{108}$$

$$\Rightarrow \quad o(H\cap K)\ge\frac{27}{4}$$

Since, $\quad o(H)=o(K)=27$, so $o(H\cap K)=9$.

Also, $H\cap K\subseteq H$ and $H\cap K\subseteq K$, so that $H\cap K$ is a subgroup of $H$ as well of $K$. Thus, $H\cap K$ is a normal subgroup of $H$ as well as of $K$, because subgroups of order $p^{n-1}$ are normal in a group of order $p^n$.

Since, $H\cap K$ is normal in $H$ as well as in $K$, so that $H\subset N(H\cap K)$ and $K\subset N(H\cap K)$, then $HK\subset N(H\cap K)$, where $N(H\cap K)$ is normalizer of $H\cap K$.

Also, $\quad o(HK)=\dfrac{o(H)o(K)}{o(H\cap K)}=\dfrac{27\times 27}{9}=81$

and $N(H\cap K)$ is a subgroup of $G$, $o(N(H\cap K))=108$

Thus, $N(H\cap K)=G$. Hence, $H\cap K$ is a normal subgroup of $G$ of order 9.

# SOLVED EXAMPLES

## Type I (*Only one correct option*)

***Example 1.*** *Let*

$$S=\left\{\begin{bmatrix} a & a\\ a & a\end{bmatrix}: a\in R-\{0\}\right\}$$

*is a group with respect to matrix multiplication. Then, inverse of*

$$A=\begin{bmatrix} 3 & 3\\ 3 & 3\end{bmatrix} \text{ is}$$

(a) $\begin{bmatrix} \frac{1}{4} & \frac{1}{4}\\ \frac{1}{4} & \frac{1}{4}\end{bmatrix}$ (b) $\begin{bmatrix} 3 & 3\\ 3 & 3\end{bmatrix}$

(c) $\begin{bmatrix} \frac{1}{12} & \frac{1}{12}\\ \frac{1}{12} & \frac{1}{12}\end{bmatrix}$ (d) None of these

**Solution.** (c) Let $A'=\begin{bmatrix} a & a\\ a & a\end{bmatrix}$ be inverse of $A$, then

$$A'A=AA'=I$$

where $I=\begin{bmatrix} \frac{1}{2} & \frac{1}{2}\\ \frac{1}{2} & \frac{1}{2}\end{bmatrix}$ is multiplicative identity of $S$. Then,

$$\begin{bmatrix} 3 & 3\\ 3 & 3\end{bmatrix}\begin{bmatrix} a & a\\ a & a\end{bmatrix}=\begin{bmatrix} \frac{1}{2} & \frac{1}{2}\\ \frac{1}{2} & \frac{1}{2}\end{bmatrix}$$

$$\Rightarrow \quad \begin{bmatrix} 6a & 6a\\ 6a & 6a\end{bmatrix}=\begin{bmatrix} \frac{1}{2} & \frac{1}{2}\\ \frac{1}{2} & \frac{1}{2}\end{bmatrix}$$

$$\Rightarrow \quad 6a=\frac{1}{2} \Rightarrow a=\frac{1}{12}$$

$$\therefore \quad A'=\begin{bmatrix} \frac{1}{12} & \frac{1}{12}\\ \frac{1}{12} & \frac{1}{12}\end{bmatrix} \text{ is inverse of } A.$$

***Example 2.*** *Let $G = \{f_1, f_2, f_3, f_4\}$ with respect to composition of mapping be a group, where*

$$f_1(x) = x,\ f_2(x) = -x$$

$$f_3(x) = \frac{1}{x},\ f_4(x) = \frac{1}{4}$$

*Then, inverse of $f_3$ is*

(a) $f_1$ (b) $f_2$

(c) $f_4$ (d) self invertible

**Solution.** (d) Since, $f_1(x) = x$ is identity of the group G. Hence,

$$(f_3 o f_3)(x) = f_3(f_3(x))$$
$$= f_3\left(\frac{1}{x}\right)$$
$$= x$$
$$= f_1(x)$$

$\Rightarrow$ $f_3$ is self invertible.

***Example 3.*** *The number of cosets of H in G, where $G = (\mathbb{Z}, +)$ and $H = (4\mathbb{Z}, +)$ is*

(a) 0 (b) 1 (c) 2 (d) 4

**Solution.** (d) We have

$$G = \{\ldots -3, -2, -1, 0, 1, 2, 3, \ldots\}$$

and $\quad H = 4\mathbb{Z} = \{\ldots, -12, -8, -4, 0, 4, 8, 12, \ldots\}$

Then, the coset of $H$ by 0 is

$$H_0 = \{h + 0 : h \in H\}$$
$$= \{\ldots, -12, -8, -4, 0, 4, 8, 12, \ldots\}$$
$$= H$$

The coset of $H$ by 1 is

$$H_1 = \{h + 1 : h \in H\}$$
$$= \{\ldots, -7, -3, 1, 5, 9, \ldots\}$$

The coset of $H$ by 2 is

$$H_2 = \{h + 2 : h \in H\}$$
$$= \{\ldots, -6, -2, 2, 6, 10, \ldots\}$$

The coset of $H$ by 3 is

$$H_3 = \{h + 3 : h \in H\}$$
$$= \{\ldots, -5, -1, 3, 7, 11, \ldots\}$$

Hence, these are the four different cosets of $H$ in $G$.

Further, the coset of $H$ by 4 is

$$H_4 = \{h + 4 : h \in H\}$$
$$= \{\ldots, -4, 0, 4, \ldots\}$$

which $H_0$, so we cannot find fifth coset different from above cosets.

***Example 4.*** *The number of homomorphism f from $(\mathbb{Z}, +)$ to $(Q^*, \cdot)$ such that $f(2) = \frac{1}{3}$, is*

(a) 0 (b) 1 (c) 2 (d) 3

**Solution.** (a) If $f(1) = r \Rightarrow f(2) = r^2 = \frac{1}{3}$

Since, there is no rational number $r$ such that $r^2 = 1/3$.. It follows that there is no such homomorphism $f$ from $(\mathbb{Z}, +)$ to $(Q^*, \cdot)$.

***Example 5.*** *The number of permutations conjugate to the permutation* $\begin{pmatrix} 1 & 2 & 3 & 4 & 5 & 6 & 7 & 8 & 9 \\ 6 & 3 & 4 & 5 & 2 & 7 & 1 & 9 & 8 \end{pmatrix}$

(a) 40320 (b) 5040

(c) 15120 (d) None of these

**Solution.** (c) Given permutation is

$$\begin{pmatrix} 1 & 2 & 3 & 4 & 5 & 6 & 7 & 8 & 9 \\ 6 & 3 & 4 & 5 & 2 & 7 & 1 & 9 & 8 \end{pmatrix}$$
$$= \begin{pmatrix} 1 & 6 & 7 \\ 6 & 7 & 1 \end{pmatrix}\begin{pmatrix} 2 & 3 & 4 & 5 \\ 3 & 4 & 5 & 2 \end{pmatrix}\begin{pmatrix} 8 & 9 \\ 9 & 8 \end{pmatrix}$$

which is product of three disjoint cycles (1 6 7)(2 3 4 5)(8 9).

Hence, the number of permutation conjugate to the given permutation is

$$= \frac{9!}{2^1 \times 3^1 \times 4^1 \times 1! \times 1! \times 1!} = 15120$$

***Example 6.*** *In the group $GL(2, Z_7)$, the inverse of $A = \begin{bmatrix} 4 & 5 \\ 6 & 3 \end{bmatrix}$ is*

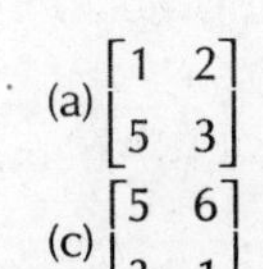

(a) $\begin{bmatrix} 1 & 2 \\ 5 & 3 \end{bmatrix}$ (b) $\begin{bmatrix} 1 & 3 \\ 5 & 6 \end{bmatrix}$

(c) $\begin{bmatrix} 5 & 6 \\ 3 & 1 \end{bmatrix}$ (d) None of these

**Solution.** (b) We have

$$A = \begin{bmatrix} 4 & 5 \\ 6 & 3 \end{bmatrix}$$

$$\Rightarrow \quad |A| = 4 \times 3 - 5 \times 6 = 12 - 30 = -18$$
$$= 3 \pmod 7$$

and the inverse of 3 is 5 as $3.5 = 1 \pmod 7$.

Hence, the inverse of $A = \begin{bmatrix} 4 & 5 \\ 6 & 3 \end{bmatrix}$ is

$$\begin{bmatrix} 3.5 & 2.5 \\ 1.5 & 4.5 \end{bmatrix} \begin{bmatrix} 1 & 3 \\ 5 & 6 \end{bmatrix}$$

***Example 7.*** *In the group U(15), the order of 7 is*

(a) 1 (b) 2 (c) 3 (d) 4

**Solution.** (d) Since,

$$7^1 = 7, 7^2 = 49 = 4 \pmod{15}$$
$$7^3 = 343 = 13 \pmod{15}$$
$$7^4 = 2401 = 1 \pmod{15}$$

Hence, order of 7 in $U(15)$ is 4.

***Example 8.*** *The number of element of order 10 in $\mathbb{Z}_{30}$ is*

(a) 2 (b) 3 (c) 4 (d) 5

**Solution.** (c) Since, the number of elements of order $d$ in a cyclic group of order $n$ is $\phi(d)$, where $d$ is positive divisor of $n$. Hence, the number of elements of order 10 in $\mathbb{Z}_{30}$ is

$$\phi(10) = \phi(2) \cdot \phi(5)$$
$$= (2 - 2^0)(5 - 5^0) = 1 \cdot 4 = 4$$

***Example 9.*** *Which of the following pair of groups is isomorphic to each other?*

(a) $U(10)$ and $U(5)$ (b) $U(10)$ and $U(12)$
(c) $(Q, +)$ and $(Q^*, \cdot)$ (d) None of these

**Solution.** (a) Since, $U(10)$ and $U(5)$ are cyclic group of order 4.

Hence, $U(10) \cong U(5)$

Next, $x^2 = 1, \forall\, x \in U(12)$.

Now, suppose that $\phi$ is an isomorphism from $U(10)$ onto $U(12)$. Then,

$$\phi(9) = \phi(3 \cdot 3) = \phi(3) \cdot \phi(3) = 1$$

and $$\phi(1) = \phi(1 \cdot 1) = \phi(1) \cdot \phi(1) = 1$$

Thus, $\phi(9) = \phi(1)$ but $9 \neq 1$

Which contradict the fact that $\phi$ is one-one. Hence,

$$U(10) \not\cong U(12)$$

Next, if $\phi$ is an isomorphism between $(Q, +)$ to $(Q^*, \cdot)$, then there would be a rational number a such that $\phi(a) = -1$.

But, then

$$-1 = \phi(a) = \phi\left(\frac{1}{2}a + \frac{1}{2}a\right)$$

$$= \phi\left(\frac{1}{2}a\right)\phi\left(\frac{1}{2}a\right)$$

$$= \left[\phi\left(\frac{1}{2}a\right)\right]^2$$

However, no rational number squared is $-1$. Hence,

$$(Q, +) \not\cong (Q^*, \cdot)$$

***Example 10.*** *The number of element of order 5 in the group* $\mathbb{Z}_{25} \oplus \mathbb{Z}_5$ *is*

(a) 5 (b) 10
(c) 24 (d) 25

**Solution.** (c) We may count the number of elements $(a, b)$ in $\mathbb{Z}_{25} \oplus \mathbb{Z}_5$ with the property that $5 = \text{order}\,(a, b)$

$$= \text{lcm}\,(|a|, |b|)$$

$\Rightarrow$ Either $|a| = 5$ and $|b| = 1$ or

$|b| = 5$ and $|a| = 1$ or 5

Now, we consider three mutually exclusive cases.

**Case I** $|a| = 5$ and $|b| = 1$. In this case, there are four choices for a and only one for b. This gives four elements of order 5.

**Case II** $|a| = 5$ and $|b| = 5$. In this case, there are four choices of *a viz.* 5, 10, 15, 20; and four choices for b. This gives 16 elements of order 5.

**Case III** $|a| = 1$ and $|b| = 5$. In this case, there is one choice for a and there are four choices for b, so we obtain four more elements of order 5.

Hence, $\mathbb{Z}_{25} \oplus \mathbb{Z}_5$ has 24 elements of order 5.

***Example 11.*** *The order of subgroup* $<5> \oplus <3>$ *in* $\mathbb{Z}_{30} \oplus \mathbb{Z}_{12}$ *is*

(a) 6 (b) 12
(c) 24 (d) 30

**Solution.** (c) Since, 5 has order 6 in $\mathbb{Z}_{30}$ and 3 has order 4 in $\mathbb{Z}_{12}$. Hence, $<5> \oplus <3>$ is a subgroup of order 24 in $\mathbb{Z}_{30} \oplus \mathbb{Z}_{12}$.

***Example 12.*** *The group* $U(105)$ *is isomorphic to the group*

(a) $\mathbb{Z}_2$ (b) $\mathbb{Z}_2 \oplus \mathbb{Z}_4$
(c) $\mathbb{Z}_2 \oplus \mathbb{Z}_4 \oplus \mathbb{Z}_6$ (d) None of these

**Solution.** (c) We have

$$U(105) = U(3 \cdot 5 \cdot 7)$$
$$\cong U(3) \oplus U(5) \oplus U(7)$$
$$\cong \mathbb{Z}_2 \oplus \mathbb{Z}_4 \oplus \mathbb{Z}_6$$

## Type II (*One or more than one correct option*)

***Example 13.*** *The generator(s) of the group* $\mathbb{Z}_{30}$ *is/are*

(a) 3 (b) 7 (c) 5 (d) 11

**Solution.** (a), (d)

Since, 7 and 11 are coprime to 30. Hence, 7 and 11 are generator of $\mathbb{Z}_{30}$.

***Example 14.*** *Consider the symmetric group* $S_5$. *Then,*

(a) the number of distinct cycles of length 3 in $S_5$ is 20
(b) the number of distinct cycle of length 2 is 10
(c) the number of elements of order 6 in $S_5$ is 20
(d) the number of element of order 6 in $S_5$ is 10

**Solution.** (a), (b), (c)

The number of distinct cycles of length 3 in $S_5$ is $\frac{1}{3} \cdot \frac{5!}{(5-3)!} = 20$.

The number of distinct cycles of length of 2 in $S_5$ is $\frac{1}{2} \cdot \frac{5!}{(5-2)!} = 10$.

Now, an element of $S_5$ is of order 6 if and only if it is product of two disjoint cycles of one of length 2 and another of length 3. Further, once a cycle of length 3 the disjoint transposition is uniquely determined. Hence, the number of element of 6 in $S_5$ is 20.

***Example 15.*** *Which of the following(s) pair of groups has no non-trivial homomorphism?*

(a) $(Q, +)$ to $(\mathbb{Z}, +)$ (b) $(Q, +)$ to $(\mathbb{Z}_m, \oplus)$
(c) $(Q, +)$ to $(Q^*, \cdot)$ (d) None of these

**Solution.** (a), (b), (c)

Any homomorphism from $(Q, +)$ to $(\mathbb{Z}, +)$ can be viewed as a homomorphism from $(Q, +)$ to $(Q, +)$ such that the image is contained in $\mathbb{Z}$. Such homomorphism is multiplication by a rational number. Thus, (a) follows if we note that there is no non-zero rational number such that all multiplies of that rational numbers are integers. For (b), let $f$ be a homomorphism from $(Q, +)$ to $(\mathbb{Z}_m, \oplus)$. Let $r \in Q$, then $f(r) = m \cdot f\left(\frac{r}{m}\right) = m\bar{u} = \overline{mu} = \bar{0}$. Hence, $f$ is homomorphism.

For (c), let $f$ be a homomorphism from $(Q,+)$ to $(Q^*,\cdot)$.

Hence, $f\left(\frac{r}{m}\right) = f(r)^{1/m} \in Q^*, \forall\, m \in Q$.

Since, there is no rational number except 1 all of whose roots are rationals, it follows that

$$f(r) = 1, \forall r \in Q$$

***Example 16.*** *Which of the following(s) is/are correct?*

(a) End $(\mathbb{Z}_m, \oplus) \cong (\mathbb{Z}_m, *)$ as a semi-group

(b) End $(\mathbb{Z}, +) \cong (\mathbb{Z}, \cdot)$ as a semi-group

(c) Aut $(\mathbb{Z}, +) \cong (\{1, -1\}, \cdot)$

(d) None of the above

**Solution.** (a), (b), (c)

(a) Define a map $\eta$ from end $(\mathbb{Z}_m, \oplus)$ to $\mathbb{Z}_m$ by $\eta(f) = f(\bar{1})$. Suppose that $\eta(f) = \eta(g)$. Then,

$$f(\bar{1}) = g(\bar{1})$$

Now, $f(\bar{r}) = f(\underbrace{\bar{1} \oplus \bar{1} \oplus \bar{1} \oplus \ldots \oplus \bar{1}}_{r\text{-times}})$

$$= g(\underbrace{\bar{1} \oplus \bar{1} \oplus \bar{1} \oplus \ldots \oplus \bar{1}}_{r\text{-times}})$$

$$= g(\bar{r})$$

Hence, $f = g \Rightarrow \eta$ is injective. Now, let $\bar{r} \in \mathbb{Z}_m$. Define a map $f$ from $\mathbb{Z}_m$ to $\mathbb{Z}_m$ by $f(\bar{a}) = \bar{r} \cdot \bar{a}$. Then, $f \in$ End $(\mathbb{Z}_m, \oplus)$ and $\eta(f) = \bar{r} \Rightarrow \eta$ is surjective. Now,

$$\eta(gof) = (gof)(\bar{1})$$
$$= gf(\bar{1})$$
$$= g(\bar{1}) * f(\bar{1})$$
$$= \eta(g) * \eta(f)$$

$\Rightarrow \eta$ is an isomorphism.

$\Rightarrow$ End $(\mathbb{Z}_m, \oplus) \cong (\mathbb{Z}_m, *)$ as a semi-group.

(b) Define $\eta$; End $(\mathbb{Z},+)$ to $\mathbb{Z}$ by

$$\eta(f) = f(1)$$

Clearly, $\eta$ is bijective.

And, $\eta(gof) = (gof)(1) = g(f(1))$

$$= g(1) \cdot f(1)$$
$$= \eta(g) \cdot \eta(f)$$

$\Rightarrow \eta$ is an isomorphism.

$\Rightarrow$ End $(\mathbb{Z}, +) \cong (\mathbb{Z}, \cdot)$ as a semi-group.

(c) Let $f \in$ Aut $(\mathbb{Z}, +)$. Then,

$$f(a) = a \cdot f(1)$$

$\Rightarrow f$ is bijective and $f(1) = \pm 1$

Thus, $\eta$ defined in (b) when restricted to Aut $(\mathbb{Z},+)$ defines an isomorphism from Aut $(\mathbb{Z},+)$ to the group $(\{1, -1\}, \cdot)$.

***Example 17.*** *Which of the following(s) is/are correct?*

(a) Hom $(\mathbb{Z}_2, \mathbb{Z}_3) \cong \mathbb{Z}$

(b) Hom $(\mathbb{Z}_4, \mathbb{Z}_6) \cong \mathbb{Z}_2$

(c) The number of homomorphism from $\mathbb{Z}_2$ to $\mathbb{Z}_3$ is 1

(d) The number of homomorphism from $\mathbb{Z}_4$ to $\mathbb{Z}_6$ is 2

**Solution.** (a), (b), (c), (d)

Since, we know that

$$\text{Hom}(\mathbb{Z}_m, \mathbb{Z}_n) \cong \mathbb{Z}_d$$

where $d$ is gcd of $m$ and $n$, which is the number of Hom from $\mathbb{Z}_m$ to $\mathbb{Z}_n$. Hence, Hom $(\mathbb{Z}_2, \mathbb{Z}_3) \cong \mathbb{Z}$, hence number of homomorphism from $\mathbb{Z}_2$ to $\mathbb{Z}_3$ is 1.

Similarly,

$$\text{Hom}(\mathbb{Z}_4, \mathbb{Z}_6) \cong \mathbb{Z}_2$$

$\Rightarrow$ Number of homomorphism from $\mathbb{Z}_4$ to $\mathbb{Z}_6$ is 2.

***Example 18.*** *Non-trivial proper subgroups of the quaternion group $Q_8$ is/are*

(a) $\{1, -1\}$ (b) $\{\pm 1, \pm i\}$

(c) $\{\pm 1, \pm j\}$ (d) $\{\pm 1, \pm k\}$

**Solution.** (a), (b), (c), (d)

Non-trivial proper subgroups of quaternion group $Q_8$ are $\{1, -1\}$, $\{\pm 1, \pm i\}$, $\{\pm 1, \pm j\}$ and $\{\pm 1, \pm k\}$.

***Example 19.*** *Which of the following(s) is/are correct?*

(a) $\mathbb{R}/\mathbb{Z} \cong$ circle group $S^1$

(b) $Q/\mathbb{Z} \cong$ group of roots of unity $P$

(c) Exactly one of (a) and (b)

(d) Neither (a) nor (b) is correct

**Solution.** (a), (b)

(a) Let $f : \mathbb{R} \to S^1$ be a map defined by

$$f(a) = e^{2\pi i a}$$

Now, let $a, b \in \mathbb{R}$, then

$$f(a+b) = e^{2\pi i(a+b)}$$
$$= e^{2\pi i a} \cdot e^{2\pi i b}$$
$$= f(a) \cdot f(b)$$

$\Rightarrow f$ is homomorphism.

Further, $a \in \ker f$

$\Rightarrow \quad f(a) = 1$

$\Rightarrow \quad e^{2\pi i a} = 1$

$\Rightarrow \quad a \in \mathbb{Z}$

Hence, $\ker f = \mathbb{Z}$.

Hence, by fundamental theorem of homomorphism.

$$\mathbb{R}/\mathbb{Z} \cong S^1$$

(b) $e^{2\pi i a} \in P \Leftrightarrow \exists\, n \in \mathbb{Z}$ such that

$$(e^{2\pi i a})^n = e^{2\pi i a} = 1$$

$\Rightarrow \quad a \in Q$

Hence, we have a surjective homomorphism $f$ from $Q$ to $P$, given by $f(a) = e^{2\pi i a}$ whose kernel is $\mathbb{Z}$. Hence, by fundamental theorem of homomorphism

$$Q/\mathbb{Z} \cong P$$

# Exercise 1 (For Part 'B')

**Directions** (Q. Nos. 1-82) *All questions have only one correct option.*

1. If $G$ is a finite group of order $n$, then for every $a \in G$, we have
   (a) $a^n = e$, an identity element
   (b) $a^n = a^{-1}$
   (c) $a^n = a$
   (d) None of the above

2. If $H_1$ and $H_2$ are two subgroups of $G$, then following is also a subgroup of $G$
   (a) $H_1 \cap H_2$ (b) $H_1 \cup H_2$
   (c) $H_1 H_2$ (d) None of these

3. The set $M$ of square matrices (of same order), with respect to matrix multiplication is
   (a) group (b) semi-group
   (c) monoid (d) quasi-group

4. If $(G, *)$ is a group and for all $a, b \in G$, $b^{-1} * a^{-1} * b * a = e$, then $G$ is
   (a) abelian group
   (b) non-group
   (c) ring
   (d) field

5. If $G$ is a group such that $a^2 = e, \forall a \in G$, then $G$ is
   (a) abelian group
   (b) non-abelian group
   (c) ring
   (d) field

6. If $f = (2\ 3)$ and $g = (4\ 5)$ are two permutations on $1, 2, 3, 4, 5$, then $fg$ is
   (a) $\begin{pmatrix} 1 & 2 & 3 & 4 & 5 \\ 1 & 3 & 2 & 5 & 4 \end{pmatrix}$ (b) $\begin{pmatrix} 1 & 2 & 3 & 4 & 5 \\ 1 & 2 & 2 & 5 & 6 \end{pmatrix}$
   (c) $\begin{pmatrix} 1 & 2 & 3 & 4 & 5 \\ 1 & 2 & 4 & 5 & 6 \end{pmatrix}$ (d) $\begin{pmatrix} 1 & 2 & 3 & 4 & 5 \\ 1 & 2 & 3 & 4 & 5 \end{pmatrix}$

7. If $n$ is the order of element $a$ of group $G$, then $a^m = e$, an identity element iff
   (a) $m \mid n$ (b) $n \mid m$
   (c) $m \nmid n$ (d) $n \nmid m$

8. If $H$ is a subgroup of finite group $G$ and order of $H$ and $G$ are respectively, $m$ and $n$, then
   (a) $m \mid n$ (b) $n \mid m$
   (c) $m \nmid n$ (d) None of these

9. If $G$ is a group, then for all $a, b \in G$
   (a) $(ab)^{-1} = a^{-1}b^{-1}$ (b) $(ab)^{-1} = b^{-1}a^{-1}$
   (c) $(ab)^{-1} = ab$ (d) $(ab)^{-1} = ba$

10. If $G$ is a set of integers and $a \cdot b \equiv a - b$, then $G$ is
    (a) quasi-group (b) semi-group
    (c) monoid (d) group

11. In a group $G$, for each element $a \in G$, there is
    (a) no inverse
    (b) a unique inverse $a^{-1} \in G$
    (c) more than one inverse
    (d) None of the above

12. If $a, b \in G$, a group, then $b$ is conjugate to $a$, if there exist $c \in G$, such that
    (a) $b = c^{-1}ac$ (b) $a = cb$
    (c) $b = ac^{-1}$ (d) $b = cc^{-1}a$

13. If $G$ is a group and $a \in G$, such that $a^2 = a$, then $a$ is equal to
    (a) identity element (b) inverse
    (c) zero element (d) None of these

14. The generators of a group $G = \{a, a^2, a^3, a^4, a^5, a^6 = e\}$ are
    (a) $a$ and $a^5$ (b) $a^2$ and $a^4$
    (c) $a^3$ and $a^5$ (d) $a^2$ and $a^3$

15. If $G = \{1, -1, i, -i\}$ is a multiplicative group, then order of $-i$ is
    (a) one (b) two
    (c) three (d) four

16. If $G = \{(0, 1, 2, 3, 4), +_5\}$, the order of 2 is
    (a) one (b) two
    (c) four (d) five

17. If $G$ is a group of even order, $\forall\ a \neq e$, if $a^2 = e$, then $G$ is
    (a) abelian group (b) sub-group
    (c) normal group (d) None of these

18. In a group $G$, we have $ab = a$ or $ba = a \Rightarrow$
    (a) $a = e$ (b) $a^2 = e$
    (c) $b = e$ (d) $b^2 = e$

19. Order of the permutation $\begin{pmatrix} 1 & 2 & 3 & 4 \\ 1 & 3 & 4 & 2 \end{pmatrix}$ is
    (a) 3 (b) 4
    (c) 5 (d) 6

20. Check the correct statement.
    (a) The identity of a subgroup is the same as that of the group.
    (b) The inverse of any element of a subgroup is the same as the inverse of the same regarded as an element of the group.
    (c) The order of any element of a subgroup is the same as the order of the element regarded as a member of the group.
    (d) All of the above

**21.** The multiplicative group $\{1, -1\}$ is a subgroup of the multiplicative group
(a) $\{1, i, -i\}$ (b) $\{1, -1, i, -i\}$
(c) $\{1, 0, -1, i\}$ (d) $\{-1, i, -i\}$

**22.** If $H, K$ are two subgroups of a group $G$, then $HK$ is a subgroup of $G$, iff
(a) $HK = 1$ (b) $HK = KH$
(c) $HK = H^{-1}K^{-1}$ (d) None of these

**23.** A necessary and sufficient condition for a non-empty subset $H$ of a finite group $G$ to be a subgroup is that
(a) $a \in H,\ b \notin H \Rightarrow a, b \notin H$
(b) $a \in H,\ b \in H \Rightarrow (a + b) \in H$
(c) $a \in H,\ b \in H \Rightarrow ab \in H$
(d) $a \in H,\ b \in H \Rightarrow (a - b) \in H$

**24.** Four fourth roots of unity namely $1, -1, i, -i$ form a group with respect to
(a) addition
(b) subtraction
(c) multiplication
(d) division

**25.** Set of all $n$, $n$th roots of unity form a finite abelian group of order $n$ with respect to
(a) addition (b) subtraction
(c) multiplication (d) division

**26.** Set of rational numbers of the form $\dfrac{m}{2^n}$ ($m, n$ integers) is a group under
(a) addition (b) subtraction
(c) multiplication (d) division

**27.** A set $G$ with a binary composition denoted multiplicatively is a group, if
(a) the composition is associative
(b) for every pair of elements $a, b \in G$, the equations $ax = b$ and $ya = b$ have solutions in $G$
(c) Both (a) and (b)
(d) None of the above

**28.** Set $\{1, 2, 3, 4\}$ is a finite abelian group of order... under multiplication modulo.......as composition.
(a) 3, 4 (b) 4, 5
(c) 1, 2 (d) 2, 3

**29.** Given, $axa = b$ in $G$, then $x$ is equal to
(a) $a^{-1}b$ (b) $a^{-1}b^{-1}$
(c) $a^{-1}b^{-1}b^{-1}$ (d) $a^{-1}ba^{-1}$

**30.** If $G$ is a group, such that $(ab)^m = a^m b^m$ for three consecutive integers $m$ for all $a, b \in G$, then $G$ is
(a) abelian (b) non-abelian
(c) cyclic (d) additive group

**31.** Let $Z$ be a set of integers, then under ordinary multiplication $(Z, \cdot)$ is
(a) monoid (b) semi-group
(c) quasi-group (d) group

**32.** If $N$ is a set of natural numbers, then under binary operation $a \cdot b = a + b$, $(N, \cdot)$ is
(a) quasi-group (b) semi-group
(c) monoid (d) group

**33.** If $G$ is a finite group and order of group is $m$, then $\forall\, a \in G$
(a) $a^m = e$, an identity (b) $a^m \neq e$
(c) $a^m = a$ (d) $a^m = a^{-1}$

**34.** $HK$ is a sub-group of $G$ iff
(a) $HK = KH$ (b) $HK \subset KH$
(c) $HK \supset KH$ (d) $HK \neq KH$

**35.** Number of elements of the cyclic group of order 6 can be used as generators of the group are
(a) 3 (b) 5
(c) 2 (d) 4

**36.** The number of generators in cyclic group of order 10 are
(a) 3 (b) 1
(c) 2 (d) 4

**37.** Check the correct statement.
(a) Every subgroup of a cyclic group is cyclic.
(b) If $G$ is an infinite cyclic group, then $G$ has exactly two generators and $G$ is isomorphic to the additive group of integers.
(c) Every finite group of composite order possesses proper subgroups.
(d) All of the above

**38.** Algebraic structure $(G, \bullet)$ is a group, if the binary operation $\bullet$ satisfies the following postulates
(a) closure property
(b) associativity
(c) existence of identity and existence of inverse
(d) All of the above

**39.** For abelian group, the additional postulate is
(a) closure property (b) associativity
(c) commutativity (d) None of these

**40.** The set of all positive rational numbers forms an abelian group under the composition defined by
(a) $a * b = (ab)/2$ (b) $a * b = \dfrac{(a+b)}{2}$
(c) $a * b = \dfrac{2(a)}{b}$ (d) $a * b = \dfrac{(a-b)}{2}$

**41.** If $b$ and $c$ are the inverse of some element $a \in G$, then
(a) $b = c$
(b) $b \neq c$
(c) $b = \alpha c$, for same $\alpha$
(d) None of the above

**42.** In the additive group of integers, the order of every element $a \neq 0$ is
(a) infinity (b) one
(c) zero (d) None of these

**43.** If $G$ is a finite group of order $n, a \in G$ and order of $a$ is $m$, if $G$ is cyclic, then
(a) $m = n$ (b) $m > n$
(c) $m < n$ (d) None of these

**44.** If $a \in G$ is a generator of a cyclic group and order of $a$ is $n < \infty$, then order of a cyclic group $m$ is
(a) infinity (b) $m = n$
(c) $m > n$ (d) $m < n$

**45.** If $e_1$ and $e_2$ are two identity elements of a group $G$, then
(a) $e_1 = e_2$ (b) $e_1 \neq e_2$
(c) $e_1 = ce_2$, for some $c$ (d) None of these

**46.** The idempotent element in a group are
(a) inverse elements of a group
(b) identity elements of a group
(c) any element of a group
(d) None of the above

**47.** Let $G = \{1, -1\}$, then under ordinary multiplication $(G, \cdot)$ is
(a) monoid (b) semi-group
(c) quasi-group (d) group

**48.** Let $Q$ be a set of rational numbers, then under ordinary addition $(Q, +)$ is
(a) monoid (b) semi-group
(c) quasi-group (d) group

**49.** Let $G$ be a group of square matrices of same order with respect to matrix multiplication, then it is not a
(a) quasi-group (b) abelian group
(c) semi-group (d) None of these

**50.** If $G$ is a finite group, then for every $a \in G$, the order of $a$ is
(a) finite (b) infinite
(c) zero (d) None of these

**51.** In the additive group of integers, the order of identity element is
(a) zero (b) one
(c) infinity (d) None of these

**52.** In the additive group $G$ of integers, the order of inverse element $a^{-1}$, $\forall\, a \in G$ is
(a) zero (b) one
(c) infinity (d) None of these

**53.** The permutation $\begin{pmatrix} 1 & 2 & 5 & 3 & 4 \\ 3 & 4 & 1 & 5 & 2 \end{pmatrix}$ is equal to
(a) (1 3)(1 5)(2 4) (b) (1)(2)(3)
(c) (1 3 5)(5 6) (d) (1 4 2)(5 3)

**54.** Given, the permutation $c = (1\ 2\ 3\ 4\ 5\ 6\ 7)$, then $c^3$ is
(a) (1 3 5 7 2 4) (b) (1 4 7 3 6 2 5)
(c) (1 7 6 5 4 3 2) (d) $I$

**55.** If $c = (1\ 2\ 3\ 4)$, then $c^2$ is
(a) (1 3)(2 4) (b) (1 3)
(c) (2 4) (d) (2 3)(3 1)

**56.** **Statement A** All cyclic groups are abelian.
**Statement B** The order of cyclic group is same as the order of its generator.
(a) A and B are false (b) A is true, B is false
(c) B is true, A is false (d) A and B are true

**57.** **Statement A** Every isomorphic image of a cyclic group is cyclic.
**Statement B** Every homomorphic image of a cyclic group is cyclic.
(a) Both A and B are true
(b) Both A and B are false
(c) A is true only
(d) B is true only

**58.** A element $a^p$ of a finite cyclic group $G$ of order $n$ is a generator of $G$ iff $0 < p < n$ and also
(a) $p$ is prime to $n$ (b) $p$ is the multiple of $n$
(c) $n$ is the multiple of $n$ (d) None of these

**59.** If $f = (2\ 3)$ and $g = (4\ 5)$ be two permutation on five symbols 1, 2, 3, 4, 5, then $gf$ is
(a) $\begin{pmatrix} 1 & 2 & 3 & 4 & 5 \\ 1 & 3 & 5 & 4 & 2 \end{pmatrix}$ (b) $\begin{pmatrix} 1 & 2 & 3 & 5 & 6 \\ 1 & 4 & 6 & 5 & 4 \end{pmatrix}$
(c) $\begin{pmatrix} 1 & 2 & 3 & 5 & 7 \\ 1 & 4 & 6 & 4 & 1 \end{pmatrix}$ (d) $\begin{pmatrix} 1 & 2 & 3 & 4 & 5 \\ 1 & 3 & 2 & 5 & 4 \end{pmatrix}$

**60.** Given, permutation $\begin{pmatrix} 1 & 2 & 3 & 4 & 5 & 6 \\ 6 & 1 & 2 & 5 & 4 & 3 \end{pmatrix}$ is equivalent to
(a) (1 6 3 2)(2 1) (b) (1 6 3 2)(1 1)
(c) (1 6 3 2)(4 5) (d) (1 6 3 2)(5 4)

**61.** If given permutations are
$A = \begin{pmatrix} 1 & 2 & 3 & 4 & 5 \\ 2 & 3 & 1 & 5 & 4 \end{pmatrix}$
$B = \begin{pmatrix} 1 & 2 & 3 & 4 & 5 \\ 1 & 3 & 4 & 5 & 2 \end{pmatrix}$, $BA$ is equal to
(a) $\begin{pmatrix} 1 & 2 & 3 & 4 & 5 \\ 2 & 1 & 5 & 4 & 3 \end{pmatrix}$ (b) $\begin{pmatrix} 2 & 1 & 5 & 3 & 5 \\ 1 & 6 & 4 & 2 & 1 \end{pmatrix}$
(c) $\begin{pmatrix} 1 & 2 & 3 & 4 & 5 \\ 1 & 2 & 5 & 4 & 1 \end{pmatrix}$ (d) $\begin{pmatrix} 1 & 2 & 3 & 4 & 5 \\ 1 & 2 & 3 & 4 & 5 \end{pmatrix}$

**62.** If number of left cosets of $H$ in $G$ are $n$ and the number of right cosets of $H$ in $G$ are $m$, then
(a) $m = n$ (b) $m \geq n$
(c) $m \leq n$ (d) None of these

**63.** Every group of prime order is
(a) cyclic (b) abelian
(c) sub-group (d) normal group

**64.** If $H_1$ and $H_2$ are two right coset sets of subgroup $H$, then
(a) $H_1 \cap H_2 = \phi$ or $H_1 = H_2$
(b) $H_1 \cap H_2 \neq \phi$
(c) $H_1 \cup H_2 = \phi$
(d) $H_1 \neq H_2$ and $H_1 \cap H_2 \neq \phi$

**65.** The number of elements in a group is
(a) identity of group (b) order of group
(c) inverse of group (d) None of these

**66.** A one-one mapping of a finite group onto itself is
(a) isomorphism (b) homomorphism
(c) automorphism (d) None of these

**67.** If in a group $G, \forall a \in G$
(a) $(a^{-1})^{-1} = a$ (b) $(a^{-1})^{-1} = a^{-1}$
(c) $(a^{-1})^{-1} = a^2$ (d) None of these

**68.** If $p$ is prime number and $p | o(G)$, then $a \in G$
(a) $a^p \in G$ (b) $a^p \notin G$
(c) $a^p \subset G$ (d) $a^p \supset G$

**69.** If $G$ is a group of order $n$, then order of identity element is
(a) one (b) greater than one
(c) $n$ (d) None of these

**70.** If $a \in G$ is of order $n$ and $p$ is prime to $n$, then the order of $a^p$ is
(a) $n$ (b) one
(c) less than $n$ (d) greater than $n$.

**71.** If the orders of elements $a, a^{-1} \in G$ are $m$ and $n$ respectively, then
(a) $m = n$ (b) $m \neq n$
(c) $m = n = 0$ (d) None of these

**72.** If in a group $G$, $a \in G$, the order of $a$ is $n$ and order of $a^p$ is $m$, then
(a) $m \leq n$ (b) $m \geq n$
(c) $m = 0$ (d) None of these

**73.** The set $S$ of square matrices of same order with respect to matrix addition, is a
(a) quasi-group (b) semi-group
(c) group (d) abelian group

**74.** The set of square matrices of order 2, with respect to matrix multiplication is a
(a) quasi-group (b) semi-group
(c) monoid (d) group

**75.** The set of all non-singular square matrices of same order with respect to matrix multiplication is
(a) quasi-group (b) monoid
(c) group (d) abelian group

**76.** If order of group $G$ is $p^2$, where $p$ is prime, then
(a) $G$ is abelian (b) $G$ is not abelian
(c) $G$ is ring (d) None of these

**77.** If $G$ is a group, for $a \in G$, $N(a)$ is the normalizer of $a$, then $\forall\ x \in N(a)$
(a) $xa = ax$ (b) $xa = e$
(c) $ax = e$ (d) $xa \neq ax$

**78.** If $a_1^{-1}$ and $a_2^{-1}$ are two multiplicative inverse of non-zero elements $a \in F$, a field then
(a) $a_1^{-1} \neq a_2^{-1}$ (b) $a_1^{-1} = a_2^{-1}$
(c) $a_1^{-1} < a_2^{-1}$ (d) None of these

**79.** If $a, b \in G$, a group of order $m$, then order of $ab$ and $ba$ are
(a) same (b) equal to $m$
(c) unequal (d) None of these

**80.** If $G = \{1, -1\}$ is a group, then order of 1 is
(a) one (b) two
(c) zero (d) None of these

**81.** The product of permutations $(1\ 2\ 3)\cdot(2\ 4\ 3)\cdot(1\ 3\ 4)$ is equal to
(a) $I$ (b) $\begin{pmatrix} 1 & 2 & 3 & 4 \\ 5 & 6 & 2 & 1 \end{pmatrix}$
(c) $\begin{pmatrix} 1 & 2 & 5 & 1 \\ 1 & 6 & 5 & 1 \end{pmatrix}$ (d) $\begin{pmatrix} 1 & 2 & 5 & 3 \\ 1 & 2 & 3 & 4 \end{pmatrix}$

**82.** The generators of the group $G = \{a, a^2, a^3, a^4 = e\}$ are
(a) $a$ only (b) $a$ and $a^2$
(c) $a$ and $a^3$ (d) $a$ and $a^4$

**83.** Which of the following is an even permutation?
(a) $f = (1\ 2\ 3)(1\ 2)$
(b) $g = (1\ 2\ 3\ 4\ 5)\ (1\ 2\ 3)\ (4\ 5)$
(c) $h = (1\ 2)\ (1\ 3)\ (1\ 4)\ (2\ 5)$
(d) None of the above

**84.** The order of the group $S_4$ (symmetric group) is
(a) 24 (b) 12
(c) 16 (d) 20

**85.** 'Every finite group $G$ is isomorphic to a permutation group.' This statement is
(a) cayley's theorem (b) lagrange's theorem
(c) liouville's theorem (d) None of these

**86.** The identity permutation is
(a) even permutation (b) odd permutation
(c) neither even nor odd (d) None of these

**87.** The product of even permutation is
(a) even permutation (b) odd permutation
(c) neither even nor odd (d) None of these

**88.** The inverse of an even permutation is
(a) odd permutation
(b) even permutation
(c) even or odd permutation
(d) None of the above

**89.** The product of $(1\ 2\ 4\ 5)\ (3\ 2\ 1\ 5\ 4)$ is
(a) $(2\ 3)$ (b) $(1\ 5)$
(c) $(3\ 4\ 1)$ (d) $(1\ 5\ 3\ 1)$

**90.** The inverse of an odd permutation is
(a) odd permutation
(b) even permutation
(c) even or odd permutation
(d) None of the above

**91.** Two permutations $f$ and $g$ of degree $n$ are said to be equal, if we have
(a) $f(a) + g(a) = 1,\ \forall\ a \in S$ (b) $f(a) - g(a) = 1,\ \forall\ a \in S$
(c) $f(a) = g(a),\ \forall\ a \in S$ (d) None of these

**92.** The group $P_n$ of all permutations of degree $n$ is called
(a) the symmetric group
(b) the non-symmetric group
(c) transposition
(d) abelian group

**93.** A cycle of length two is called
(a) transposition (b) remainder
(c) disjoint cycle (d) non-abelian

**94.** $f = (1\ 2\ 3)\ (1\ 2)$ is
(a) odd permutation (b) even permutation
(c) Both (a) and (b) (d) None of these

**95.** The multiplicative group $\{1, \omega, \omega^2\}$ is
(a) abelian (b) non-abelian
(c) cyclic (d) irreducible

**96.** The number of generators in group $(\{1, 2, 3, 4, 5, 6\}, \times_7)$ are
(a) 4 (b) 3
(c) 2 (d) 5

**97.** The order of identity element in a group $G$ is
(a) one (b) zero
(c) order of group (d) less than order of group

**98.** If $G = \{1, -1\}$ is a group with ordinary multiplication the order of $-1$ is
(a) one (b) two
(c) zero (d) None of these

**99.** Which one is true?
(a) Every quotient group of a cyclic group is cyclic and the converse is also true.
(b) Every quotient group of a group is abelian and the converse is not true.
(c) Every quotient group of a cyclic group is cyclic and the converse is not true.
(d) None of the above

**100.** If $N_1$ and $N_2$ are the normal subgroups of $G$, then $G/N_1 = G/N_2$ if and only if
(a) $N_1 \subseteq N_2$ (b) $N_2 \subseteq N_1$
(c) $N_1 = N_2$ (d) $N_1N_2 \subseteq N_1$

**101.** Let $Z$ be the centre of the groups $G$. If $G/Z$ is cyclic, then
(a) $G$ is group (b) $G$ is abelian
(c) $G$ is cyclic (d) $G$ is not a group

**102.** If $p$ is a prime number and $G$ is a non-abelian group of order $p^3$, then the centre of $G$ has
(a) exactly $p - 1$ elements (b) exactly $p$ elements
(c) exactly $p^3$ elements (d) None of the above

**103.** If $H$ and $K$ are normal subgroups of $G$, then which one is true?
(a) $H \cap K$ and $HK$ are normal in $G$.
(b) $HK$ and $H \cup K$ are normal in $G$.
(c) $H \cap K$ is normal but $HK$ is not normal.
(d) $H \cup K$ is normal but $HK$ is not normal.

**104.** If $H$ and $K$ are two subgroups of $G$ of orders 6 and 8, then order of $HK$ is 16 if
(a) order of $H \cap K$ is 3 (b) order of $H \cap K$ is 4
(c) order of $H \cap K$ is 5 (d) None of these

**105.** Let $H$ and $K$ are the subgroups of order 3 and 5, respectively. If $o(G) = 4$, then
(a) $H \cap K = \{e\}$ (b) $H \cap K \neq \{e\}$
(c) $H \cup K = \{e\}$ (d) None of these

**106.** If $H \subseteq K$ are two subgroups of $G$ and if $[G:H] = 8$ and $[G:K] = 4$, then $[K:H]$ is
(a) 2 (b) 3
(c) 5 (d) None of these

**107.** Let $G$ be a group of order 49, then
(a) $G$ is abelian (b) $G$ is cyclic
(c) $G$ is non-abelian (d) Centre of $G$ has order 7

**108.** Let $S_3$ be the group of all permutations on three symbols, with the identity element e, then the number of elements in $S_3$ that satisfy the equation $x^2 = e$ is
(a) 1 (b) 2
(c) 3 (d) 4

**109.** If $H$ and $K$ are subgroups of $G$, then
(a) $HK$ is a subgroup but $H \cap K$ may not be a subgroup
(b) $H \cap K$ is a subgroup but $HK$ may not be a subgroup
(c) Either (a) or (b)
(d) None of the above

**110.** If $G = \{1, \omega, \omega^2\}$, then there may be
(a) 2 subgroups (b) 3 subgroups
(c) 4 subgroups (d) No subgroup possible

**111.** If $H$ is a subgroup of $G$, then number of left cosets of $H$ in $G$ and number of right cosets of $H$ in $G$ are
(a) equal (b) not equal
(c) Either (a) or (b) (d) None of these

**112.** Choose the correct answers: If $H$ is a normal subgroup of $G$ and $K$ is a normal subgroup of $H$, then
(a) $K$ is a normal subgroup of $G$
(b) $K$ is not a normal subgroup of $G$
(c) $K$ is a subgroup of $G$
(d) $K$ is a subgroup of $G$

**113.** If $G$ is a group and $H$ is a subgroup of index 2 in $G$, then choose the correct statement.
(a) $H$ is a normal subgroup of $G$
(b) $H$ is not a normal subgroup of $G$
(c) $H$ is a subgroup of $G$
(d) None of the above

**114.** Pick up the correct statement
(a) group $\{1, -1\}$ is a simple group
(b) group $\{1, -1, i, i\}$ is a simple group
(c) $\{1, \omega, \omega^2\}$ is not a simple group
(d) Any group of prime order is simple

**115.** Following are the orders of some proper subgroups of a groups, which subgroup is necessarily normal?

(a) 2 (b) 3
(c) 4 (d) 5

**116.** Let $H = Z_2 \times Z_6$ and $K = Z_2 \times Z_4$, then

(a) $H$ is isomorphic to $K$, since both are cyclic
(b) $H$ is isomorphic to $K$, since 2 divides 6 and $\gcd(3,4) = 1$
(c) $H$ is not isomorphic to $K$, since $K$ is cyclic whereas $H$ is number
(d) $H$ is not isomorphic to $K$, since there is no homomorphism from $H$ to $K$

**117.** Let $G$ be a group of order 15. Then, the number of sylow subgroup of $G$ of order 3 is

(a) 0 (b) 1
(c) 3 (d) 5

**118.** In the group $(Z, +)$ the subgroup generated by 2 and 7 is

(a) $Z$ (b) $5Z$
(c) $9Z$ (d) $14Z$

**119.** The cardinality of the centre of $Z_{12}$ is

(a) 1 (b) 2
(c) 3 (d) 12

**120.** Let $G$ and $H$ be two groups. The groups $G \times H$ and $H \times G$ are isomorphic

(a) for any $G$ and any $H$
(b) only if one of them is cyclic
(c) only if one of them is abelian
(d) only if $G$ and $H$ are isomorphic

**121.** Pick up the correct answer.

If $H$ be a subgroup of $G$, then $H$ is normal in $G$, if

(a) $H$ is a subgroup of index 2 in $G$
(b) $H$ is a subgroup of index 3 in $G$
(c) $H$ is a subgroup of index 4 in $G$
(d) None of the above

**122.** If $N$ is normal subgroup of $G$ and $H$ is any subgroup of $G$, then which answer is correct?

(a) $NH$ is a subgroup of $G$
(b) $NH$ is normal subgroup of $G$
(c) Either (a) or (b)
(d) None of the above

**123.** If $G$ is a group and $H \leq G$, then $G/H$ is quotient group, when

(a) $H$ is a subgroup of $G$
(b) $H$ is a normal subgroup of $G$
(c) $H$ is a complex of $G$
(d) None of the above

**124.** Let $I$ be the additive group of integers. Let $H = \{3x / x \in I\}$ normal subgroup of $I$, the elements of $I/H$ are

(a) $\{H, H+1, H+2\}$ (b) $\{H+1, H+2, H+3, H)$
(c) $\{H, H+1, H+3\}$ (d) $\{H, H+1, H+4\}$

**125.** If $G$ is a finite group and $H$ is a normal subgroup of $G$, then $o(G/H)$ is

(a) $\frac{o(H)}{o(G)}$ (b) $\frac{o(G)}{o(H)}$
(c) $o(G) \cdot o(H)$ (d) None of these

**126.** Every quotient group of an abelian group is

(a) non-abelian
(b) abelian
(c) complex
(d) cyclic

**127.** Which one is true?

(a) Every quotient group of a group is abelian and its converse is also true.
(b) Every quotient group of a group is abelian but its converse is not true.
(c) Every quotient group of an abelian group is abelian and its converse is also true.
(d) Every quotient group of an abelian group is abelian but the converse is not true.

**128.** Let $(Z, +)$ denote the group of all integers under addition, then the number of all automorphisms of $(Z, +)$ is

(a) 1 (b) 2
(c) 3 (d) 4

**129.** Let $G$ be a finite group of order 200, then the number of subgroups of $G$ of order 25 is

(a) 1 (b) 4
(c) 5 (d) 10

**130.** If $F$ is a homomorphism of a group $G$ into a group $G'$ with kernal $K$, then

(a) $K$ is a complex of $G$
(b) $K$ is a subgroup of $G$ but not a normal subgroup of $G$
(c) $K$ is a normal subgroup of $G$
(d) None of the above

**131.** Suppose, $G$ is a group and $N$ is a normal subgroup of $G$. Let $F: G \to G/N$ defined by

$$F(x) = Nx, \forall x \in G$$

Then,

(a) $F$ is a homomorphism of $G$ into $G/N$ with $\ker F \neq N$
(b) $F$ is a homomorphism of $G$ onto $G/N$ with $\ker F \neq N$
(c) $F$ is a homomorphism of $G$ into $G/N$ with $\ker F = N$
(d) $F$ is a homomorphism of $G$ onto $G/N$ with $\ker F = N$

**132.** Let $F$ be a homomorphic mapping of a group $G$ into a group $G'$. Let $F(G)$ be the homomorphic image of $G$ in $G'$. Then,

(a) $F(G)$ is a complex of $G'$
(b) $F(G) = G'$
(c) $F(G)$ is a subgroup of $G'$
(d) $F(G)$ is a normal subgroup of $G$

**133.** A homomorphism from a simple group is
(a) trivial but not one to one
(b) non-trivial but one to one
(c) either trivial or one to one
(d) None of the above

**134.** If $a$ and $a^2$ are both generators of a cyclic group of order $n$, then
(a) $n$ must be odd (b) $n$ must be even
(c) $n$ must be prime (d) $n$ must not be a prime

**135.** Let $G$ be a cyclic group of order 6. Then, the number of elements $g \in G$ such that $G = \langle g \rangle$ is
(a) 5 (b) 3
(c) 4 (d) 2

**136.** Let $G$ be a group of order 30. Let $A$ and $B$ be normal subgroup of order 2 and 5, respectively.
Then, the order of the group $G/AB$ is
(a) 10 (b) 3
(c) 2 (d) 5

**137.** The number of elements of order 5 in the symmetric group $S_5$ is
(a) 5 (b) 20
(c) 24 (d) 12

**138.** Consider a group $G$. Let $Z(G)$ be its centre, *i.e.*, $Z(G) = \{g \in G : gh = hg \text{ for all } h \in G\}$. For $n \in N$, the set of positive integers, define

$J_n = \{(g_1, \ldots, g_n) \in Z(G) \times \ldots \times Z(G) : g_1 \ldots g_n = e\}$

As a subset of the direct product group $Gx\ldots xG$ ($n$ times direct product of the group $G$), $J_n$ is
(a) not necessarily a subgroup
(b) a subgroup but not necessarily a normal subgroup
(c) a normal subgroup
(d) isomorphic to the direct product $Z(G) \times \ldots \times Z(G)((n-1)$ time)

**139.** Let $G$ be a group of order 77. Then, the centre of $G$ is isomorphic to
(a) $Z_{(1)}$ (b) $Z_{(7)}$
(c) $Z_{(11)}$ (d) $Z_{(77)}$

**140.** Given, permutation $\begin{pmatrix} 1 & 2 & 3 & 4 & 5 & 6 \\ 6 & 1 & 2 & 5 & 4 & 6 \end{pmatrix}$ is equivalent to
(a) (1 6 3 2)(2 1) (b) (1 6 3 2)(1 1)
(c) (1 6 3 2)(4 5) (d) (1 6 3 2)(5 4)

**141.** If $G = \{1, -1\}$ is a group with ordinary multiplication the order of $-1$ is
(a) one (b) two
(c) zero (d) None of these

**142.** The generators of a group $G = \{a, a^2, a^3, a^4, a^5, a^6 = e\}$ are
(a) $a$ and $a^5$ (b) $a^2$ and $a^4$
(c) $a^3$ and $a^5$ (d) $a^2$ and $a^3$

**143.** If $G$ is a group of even order, $\forall\, a \neq e$ if $a^2 = e$, then $G$ is
(a) abelian group (b) subgroup
(c) normal group (d) None of these

**144.** If given permutations are $A = \begin{pmatrix} 1 & 2 & 3 & 4 & 5 \\ 2 & 3 & 1 & 5 & 4 \end{pmatrix}$, $B = \begin{pmatrix} 1 & 2 & 3 & 4 & 5 \\ 1 & 3 & 4 & 5 & 2 \end{pmatrix}$, find $BA$.
(a) $\begin{pmatrix} 1 & 2 & 3 & 4 & 5 \\ 2 & 1 & 5 & 4 & 3 \end{pmatrix}$ (b) $\begin{pmatrix} 2 & 1 & 5 & 3 & 5 \\ 1 & 6 & 4 & 2 & 1 \end{pmatrix}$
(c) $\begin{pmatrix} 1 & 2 & 3 & 4 & 5 \\ 1 & 2 & 5 & 4 & 1 \end{pmatrix}$ (d) $\begin{pmatrix} 1 & 2 & 3 & 4 & 5 \\ 1 & 2 & 3 & 4 & 5 \end{pmatrix}$

**145.** If $f = (2\ 3)$ and $g = (4\ 5)$ be two permutation on five symbols 1, 2, 3, 4, 5, then $gf$ is
(a) $\begin{pmatrix} 1 & 2 & 3 & 4 & 5 \\ 1 & 3 & 5 & 4 & 2 \end{pmatrix}$ (b) $\begin{pmatrix} 1 & 2 & 3 & 5 & 6 \\ 1 & 4 & 6 & 5 & 4 \end{pmatrix}$
(c) $\begin{pmatrix} 1 & 2 & 3 & 5 & 7 \\ 1 & 4 & 6 & 4 & 1 \end{pmatrix}$ (d) $\begin{pmatrix} 1 & 2 & 3 & 4 & 5 \\ 1 & 3 & 2 & 5 & 4 \end{pmatrix}$

**146.** If $f = (2\ 3)$ and $g = (4\ 5)$ are two permutations on 1, 2, 3, 4, 5, then $fg$ is
(a) $\begin{pmatrix} 1 & 2 & 3 & 4 & 5 \\ 1 & 3 & 2 & 5 & 4 \end{pmatrix}$ (b) $\begin{pmatrix} 1 & 2 & 3 & 4 & 5 \\ 1 & 2 & 2 & 5 & 6 \end{pmatrix}$
(c) $\begin{pmatrix} 1 & 2 & 3 & 4 & 5 \\ 1 & 2 & 4 & 5 & 6 \end{pmatrix}$ (d) $\begin{pmatrix} 1 & 2 & 3 & 4 & 5 \\ 1 & 2 & 3 & 4 & 5 \end{pmatrix}$

**147.** If $(G, *)$ is a group and $\forall\, a, b \in G\ b^{-1} * a^{-1} * b * a = e$, then $G$ is
(a) abelian group
(b) non-abelian
(c) ring
(d) field

**148.** If $G$ is a group and $a \in G$ such that $a^2 = a$, then $a$ is equal to
(a) identity element (b) inverse
(c) zero element (d) None of these

**149.** If $G$ is a group such that $a^2 = e$, $\forall\, a \in G$, then $G$ is
(a) abelian group (b) non-abelian group
(c) ring (d) field

**150.** If $G = \{1, -1, i, -i\}$ is a multiplicative group, then order of $-i$ is
(a) one (b) two
(c) three (d) four

**151.** The set $M$ of square matrices (of same order), with respect to matrix multiplication is
(a) group (b) semi-group
(c) monoid (d) quasi-group

**152.** The generators of the group $G = \{a, a^2, a^3, a^4 = e\}$ are
(a) $a$ only (b) $a$ and $a^2$
(c) $a$ and $a^3$ (d) $a$ and $a^4$

**153.** The product of permutations $(1\ 2\ 3)\cdot(2\ 4\ 3)\cdot(1\ 3\ 4)$ is equal to

(a) $I$ (b) $\begin{pmatrix}1 & 2 & 3 & 4\\5 & 6 & 2 & 1\end{pmatrix}$

(c) $\begin{pmatrix}1 & 2 & 5 & 1\\1 & 6 & 5 & 1\end{pmatrix}$ (d) $\begin{pmatrix}1 & 2 & 5 & 3\\1 & 2 & 3 & 4\end{pmatrix}$

**154.** If $c = (1\ 2\ 3\ 4)$, then $c^2$ is

(a) $(1\ 3)(2\ 4)$ (b) $(1\ 3)$
(c) $(2\ 4)$ (d) $(2\ 3)(3\ 1)$

**155.** The number of 5-*SSG* in $A_5$

(a) 1 (b) 5
(c) 6 (d) 12

**156.** $S_5$ be the permutation group on 5 symbols. Then, number of element in $S_5$ s.t. $a^5 = a^2$ are

(a) 10 (b) 15
(c) 20 (d) 30

**157.** Let $G$ be permutation group on a set $A$ of 6 symbols. Then, the order of proper normal subgroup of $G$ is

(a) 120 (b) 240
(c) 360 (d) 720

**158.** The alternating group $A_4$ on 4 symbols has a normal subgroup of order

(a) 2 (b) 3
(c) 4 (d) 6

**159.** $G$ be the set of all permutation with signature 1 on a set of *n*-symbols ($n \geq 5$) and $H$ be a normal subgroup of $G$ containing a cycle of length 3. Then, $H$ is isomorphic to

(a) $S_n$ (b) $A_n$
(c) a trivial group $\{0\}$ (d) None of these

**160.** Let $S$ be a set and $P(S)$ be the power set of $S$. Then, $\{P(S), \cup\}$ is not a group because

(a) $P(S)$ is not closed *wrt* $\cup$
(b) $\cup$ is not associative
(c) inverse does not exist
(d) the identity element does not exist

**161.** Let $G = \{a, b, c, d\}$ be a set with four elements define a binary operation on $G$ by the following table with the help of table choose the incorrect statement

| | a | b | c | d |
|---|---|---|---|---|
| a | a | b | c | d |
| b | b | c | c | d |
| c | c | d | d | a |
| d | d | b | d | c |

(a) binary operation is not associative
(b) binary operation is not commutative
(c) absence of identity element
(d) None of the above

**162.** Define $T : Z_{12} \to Z_{12}$, then find the number of inner automorphisms

(a) 1 (b) 12
(c) 4 (d) 6

**163.** Let the set $\frac{Z}{nZ}$ denote the ring of integers modulo $n$ under addition and multiplication modulo $n$. Then, $\frac{Z}{9Z}$ is not a subring of $\frac{Z}{12Z}$ because

(a) $Z/9Z$ is not a subset of $Z/12Z$
(b) $\gcd(9, 12) = 3 \neq 1$
(c) 12 is not a power of 3
(d) 9 does not divide 12

**164.** If $a$ and $a^2$ both are generator of a cyclic group, then the order of the group

$\gcd(2, n) = 1$

$\Rightarrow n =$ odd positive integer $> 1$

(a) cannot be prime
(b) only prime
(c) any odd positive integer $> 1$
(d) only even integer

**165.** Let $(Z, +)$ denote the group of all integers under addition. Then, the number of automorphisms on $(Z, +)$ is

(a) 1 (b) 2
(c) 3 (d) 4

**166.** Let $G = \left\{\begin{bmatrix}x & y\\x & y\end{bmatrix} : x, y \in R, \text{s.t. } x + y \neq 0\right\}$

Then $(G, *)$ (where $*$ denotes matrix multiplication on $G$) is

(a) not a group as identity element does not exist
(b) not a group as closure property failed
(c) group but not abelian
(d) abelian group

**167.** The order of the element $(\bar{2}, \bar{2})$ in $Z_4 \times Z_6$ is

(a) 2 (b) 6
(c) 4 (d) 12

**168.** Match the following

**Name**

(A) Fermat's theorem
(B) Fermat's little theorem
(C) Euler's theorem
(D) Wilson's theorem

**Theorem**

(i) $(p-1)! \equiv 1 \pmod p$; $p$ is prime
(ii) $a^{\phi(n)} \equiv 1 \pmod p$
(iii) $a^p \equiv a \pmod p$; $p$ is prime
(iv) $a^{p-1} \equiv 1 \pmod p$; $p$ is prime

| | A | B | C | D |
|---|---|---|---|---|
| (a) | (iii) | (iv) | (ii) | (i) |
| (b) | (iv) | (iii) | (ii) | (i) |
| (c) | (i) | (iv) | (ii) | (iii) |
| (d) | (iii) | (iv) | (i) | (ii) |

**169.** The pairs $p = (a, b)$ of complex number where $b \neq 0$ under composition rule $(a, b)*(c, d) = (a + bc, bd)$ from a group. The inverse of the element $(a, b)$ is

(a) $\left(-\frac{1}{a}, \frac{1}{b}\right)$ (b) $\left(-\frac{a}{b}, \frac{1}{b}\right)$

(c) $\left(\frac{a}{b}, -\frac{1}{b}\right)$ (d) $\left(\frac{1}{a}, \frac{-1}{b}\right)$

**170.** The mapping from $R$ under addition to itself given by $\phi(x) = x^3$ is

(a) homomorphism but not isomorphism
(b) isomorphism
(c) not isomorphism as not 1 – 1
(d) not preserved

**171.** Let $D_8$ denote the group of symmetries of square (dihedral group). The minimal number of generators for $D_8$ is

(a) 1 (b) 2
(c) 4 (d) 8

**172.** Let $G = \{x \in R : 0 \leq x < 1\}$ and for $x, y \in G$, let $x * y$ be the fractional part of $x + y$ *i.e.*, $x * y = x + y - [x + y]$ (where [a] is the greatest integer less than or equal to a). Then, select the incorrect statement

(a) $G$ is monoid *wrt* the given operation
(b) the identity of the algebraic structure $(G, *)$ is 0
(c) the inverse of $a \in G$ is $1 - a$
(d) the structure is non-abelian group

**173.** Number of elements of order $p$ in $Zp^2q$, where $p$ is prime and $p$ and $q$ are distinct, is

(a) $p$ (b) $p + 1$
(c) $p + 2$ (d) $p - 1$

**174.** The number of elements of order 2 in a cyclic group of even order is

(a) 1 (b) 2
(c) 4 (d) None of these

**175.** If a cyclic group has only 3 subgroups $\{e\}$, a subgroup of order 7 and the group itself. Then, the order of group is

(a) 7
(b) 14
(c) 49
(d) Cannot be determined

**176.** The number of homomorphism from $Z_{12}$ to $Z_{30}$ are

(a) 4 (b) 20
(c) 120 (d) 6

**177. Assertion (A)** A group can be isomorphic to its proper subgroup

**Reason (R)** The additive group $Z$ of integer is isomorphic to $(H, +)$ where

$H = \{mx : x \in Z \text{ and } 0 \neq m \in Z\}$

(a) Both A and R are true and R is the correct explanation of A
(b) Both A and R are true but R is not the correct explanation of A
(c) A is true, but R is false
(d) A is false but R is true

**178.** If $G$ is a group of even order, then it has element of order two

(a) atleast one (b) atleast two
(c) exactly two (d) atmost two

**179.** Let $G$ be the additive group of integers and $G'$ be the multiplicative group of the fourth roots of unity. Let $f : G \to G'$ be a homomorphism mapping given by $f(n) = (i)^n$ where $i = \sqrt{-1}$. Then, the kernel of $f$ is

(a) $\{0\}$ (b) $\{4m : m \in I\}$
(c) $\{(2m)^2 + 1 : m \in I\}$ (d) $\{2m + 1 : m \in I\}$

**180.** Consider $A = \{3n : n \in Z\}$, $B = \{4n : n \in Z\}$ the subgroup of the additive group $Z$ is

(a) $\{A \cup B, +\}$ (b) $\{A \cap B, +\}$
(c) $\{A \cup B, \bullet\}$ (d) $\{A \cap B, \bullet\}$

**181.** The following table defines a cyclic group

| | A | B | C | D |
|---|---|---|---|---|
| A | C | A | D | B |
| B | A | B | C | D |
| C | D | C | B | A |
| D | B | D | A | C |

It's generators are

(a) A, B (b) D, B
(c) C, D (d) D, A

**182.** Let $D_4 = \begin{cases} x^2 = e \\ y^4 = e \\ \text{and } xy, xy^2, xy^3 \end{cases}$

be the dihedral group of order 8. Then, $y^{-42}$ is equal to

(a) $y$ (b) $y^2$
(c) $y^3$ (d) e

**183.** A finitely generated subgroup $G$ of additive group $Q$ of rational numbers satisfies the condition

(a) $G$ is isomorphic to $Q$
(b) $G$ is trivial
(c) $G$ is cyclic
(d) $G$ is finite

**184.** In an infinite cyclic group $G$ the number of automorphism is

(a) $\infty$ (b) two
(c) zero (d) one

**185.** The set of four rotations of a square in its plane about a normal passing through the centre of the plane form a

(a) group but not abelian
(b) abelian group but not cyclic
(c) cyclic group
(d) symmetric group

**186.** If $G_1$ and $G_2$ are commutator subgroup and centre of the dihedral group $D_4$ respectively, then select the incorrect statement

(a) $G_1 \cap G_2 \neq \{e\}$ (b) $o(G_1) | o(G_2)$
(c) $o(G_1) = 2$ (d) None of these

**187.** If in a group $a^5 = e$, $aba^{-1} = b^2$ for $a, b \in G$, then $o(b)$ is

(a) 30 (b) 31
(c) 32 (d) 33

**188.** Let $G$ be a group of order $p^q$ where $p$ and $q$ are prime numbers. Such that $p > q$. Then, $G$ can have

(a) atmost one subgroup of order $p$
(b) atleast one subgroup of order $q$
(c) atleast one subgroup of order $p$
(d) atleast one subgroup of order $q$

**189.** Let $\sigma$ and $\tau$ be the permutations defined by

$$\sigma = \begin{pmatrix} 1 & 2 & 3 & 4 & 5 & 6 & 7 & 8 & 9 \\ 1 & 3 & 5 & 7 & 9 & 6 & 4 & 8 & 2 \end{pmatrix} \text{ and}$$

$$\tau = \begin{pmatrix} 1 & 2 & 3 & 4 & 5 & 6 & 7 & 8 & 9 \\ 7 & 8 & 3 & 4 & 9 & 6 & 5 & 2 & 1 \end{pmatrix}$$

Then,

(a) $\sigma$ and $\tau$ generate the group of permutations on (1, 2, 3, 4, 5, 6, 7, 8, 9)
(b) $\sigma$ is contained in the group generated by $\tau$
(c) $\tau$ is contained in the group generated by $\sigma$
(d) $\sigma$ and $\tau$ are in the same conjugacy class

**190.** The number of abelian groups of order 20 upto isomorphism is

(a) 1 (b) 2
(c) 8 (d) 6

**191.** The set of complex numbers $Z$ with $|z| = 1$ under the operation $*$ denoted by $z_1 * z_2 = |z_1| \cdot z_2$

(a) group but not abelian
(b) group but not cyclic
(c) cyclic group
(d) None of the above

**192.** For any integer $n > 2$ how many elements in $U(n)$ that satisfy $x^2 = 1$

(a) only one element
(b) exactly two elements
(c) atleast two elements
(d) there exist no element in $U(n)$ which satisfy $x^2 = 1$

**193.** Suppose that $o(a) = 24$, then the a generator for $< a^{21} > \cap < a^{10} >$ are

(a) $a^6, a^{18}$ (b) $a^5, a^7$
(c) $a^3, a^2$ (d) $a^9, a^{15}$

**194.** Find the smallest subgroup of $Z$ containing 8 and 13 the notation for this $< 8, 13 >$

(a) 8Z (b) Z
(c) 13Z (d) 104Z

**195.** $U(n)$ is cyclic for

(a) any $n$
(b) only for odd prime
(c) only when $n = P^n$
(d) None of the above

**196.** Select the incorrect statement

(a) $S_n$, $\forall\, n \in N$ has atleast one self inverse element
(b) $A_n$, $\forall\, n > 3$ has atleast one self inverse element
(c) every element of a finite ordered group is of finite order
(d) the order of every non-identity element in any infinite group is infinite

**197.** The number of elements of order 5 in a non-abelian group of order 10 is

(a) 1 (b) 5
(c) 4 (d) 8

**198.** Two permutations in the symmetric group $S_n$ are conjugate iff

(a) they fix the same number of elements
(b) they have the same cycle decomposition
(c) they have the same order
(d) they are odd powers of each other

**199.** Let $G$ be group of order 1225, then $G$ is

(a) abelian but not cyclic group
(b) cyclic group
(c) simple group
(d) None of the above

**200.** The number of elements of order 11 in a group of order 33 are

(a) 0 (b) 10
(c) 20 (d) 30

**201.** In the symmetric group $S_n$ of degree $n$, $n > 2$ the set of all 3-cycles generates a subgroup of order

(a) 3 (b) $3n$
(c) $\frac{n!}{2}$ (d) $n!$

**202.** Let $G$ be a group of permutation of 5 symbols. Then, the number of distinct cycles of length '3' is

(a) 10 (b) 15
(c) 20 (d) 30

**203.** The number of conjugate classes of a non-abelian group of order 125 are

(a) 29 (b) 25
(c) 125 (d) 1

**204.** The cardinality of the centre of $D_{12}$ is

(a) 1 (b) 2
(c) 3 (d) 12

**205.** What is the maximum order of any element in $A_{10}$

(a) 25 (b) 24
(c) 21 (d) 20

**206.** If $G$ be a non-cyclic group in which every non-identity element is of same order $p$ where $p$ is prime, then select the incorrect

(a) $G$ is inner direct product (IDP) of two cyclic group
(b) $G$ is isomorphic to an abelian group
(c) every subgroup of $G$ is normal
(d) $G$ is non-abelian

**207.** Let $f$ be a homomorphism from $(Z, +)$ to $(R^+, \bullet)$, if $f(2) = \frac{1}{3}$, then value of $f(6)$ is

(a) 1/27 (b) 27
(c) 81 (d) 1/81

**208.** In $S_4$ how many element satisfying the equation $x^2 = e$ are

(a) 8 (b) 9
(c) 10 (d) 11

**209.** In which one of the following cases, given $*$ is a binary operation on the set $S$?

(a) $S = \{1, 2, 3, 6, 18\}, a * b = ab$
(b) $S = \{1, -2, 3, 2, -4\}, a * b = |b|$
(c) $S = Z, a * b = a + b^2$
(d) $S = N, a * b = a - b$

**210.** If $O(G) = 1001$, then about $G$ correct statements is/are ($SSG$ = Sylow subgroup)

I. Only 13-$SSG$ is normal
II. 11-$SSG$ and 13-$SSG$ are normal
III. All $SSG$ are normal
IV. $G$ is non-cyclic

(a) I and IV (b) III
(c) II and IV (d) All are correct

**211.** Let $G$ be the group with the generators $a$ and $b$ given by

$$G = \langle a, b : a^4 = b^2 = 1, ba = a^{-1}b \rangle$$

If $Z(G)$ denotes the centre of $G$, then $G/Z(G)$ is isomorphic to

(a) the trivial group
(b) $C_2$, the cyclic group of order 2
(c) $C_2 \times C_2$
(d) $C_4$

**212.** Let $G$ be any group of order 224 and $a \in G$ be an element of order 56. Then, order of $a^4$ is

(a) 4 (b) 7
(c) 14 (d) 56

**213.** Let $C$ and $R$ be the group of complex numbers and real numbers respectively under addition. Define a map $f : C \to R$ s.t.

$$f(x + iy) = x$$

Then, ker $f$ is

(a) $\{x : x \in R\}$
(b) $\{0\}$
(c) $\{iy : y \in R\}$
(d) $\{x + iy : x$ and $y$ are non-zero$\}$

**214.** The number of idempotent elements in a group is

(a) always even
(b) always odd greater than one
(c) always an odd prime
(d) only one

**215.** The number of cyclic subgroups of order 10 in $Z_{100} \oplus Z_5$ are

(a) 6 (b) 10
(c) 24 (d) 4

**216.** If $Q_1$ stands for the set of rational numbers except 1 and operation is defined as $a * b = a + b - ab$. Then, $(Q_1, *)$ is a group. Now, for $a \in Q_1$, $a^{-1}$ is

(a) $a - 1$ (b) $a + 1$
(c) $\frac{a}{a-1}$ (d) $\frac{2a}{a-1}$

**217.** If $Z$ is the centre of $G$ and $H$ is any subgroup of $G$ not contained in $Z$. Then,

I. $Z \cap H$ is normal subgroup of $G$.
II. $Z \cap H$ is normal subgroup of $H$.
III. $Z \cap H$ is normal subgroup of $Z$.
IV. $HZ$ is subgroup of $G$.

(a) Only I and II are correct
(b) Only III and IV are correct
(c) II, III and IV are correct
(d) All are correct

**218.** The number of subgroups of $\frac{Z}{48Z}$ is

(a) 2 (b) 8
(c) 10 (d) 24

**219.** The smallest odd order for non-abelian group is

(a) 9 (b) 15
(c) 21 (d) 23

**220.** Let $G = GL(2, R)$ and

$H = \{A \in G \mid \det(A) = 3^k, k \in Z\}$, then

(a) $H$ is abelian subgroup
(b) $H$ is cyclic subgroup
(c) $H$ is normal subgroup
(d) None of the above

**221.** Let $ABCD$ be a square. The four rotation of the square about the centre in the anti-clockwise direction through $0°, 90°, 180°, 270°$, be represented by $R_0, R_1, R_2, R_3$. Then, the set $\{R_0, R_1, R_2, R_3\}$ is

(a) a non-abelian group
(b) non-cyclic abelian group
(c) cyclic group
(d) not a group

**222.** $G = \{x : x \in N$ and gcd of $(x, n) = 1\}$ where $2 < n \in N$ and $H = \{y \in G : y^2 = e\}$ in $\{G, \times_n\}$ choose correct?

(a) $|H|$ is even
(b) $|H|$ is odd
(c) $|H|$ is even if $n$ is even
(d) $|H|$ is odd if $n$ is odd

223. Number of elements of order 20 in $U(100)$ are
(a) 8 (b) 12
(c) 16 (d) 20

224. Which of the following statements about the permutation group on $\{1, 2, 3, ..., n\}$ is false
(a) every element is a product of transpositions
(b) the elements (12)(13) and (12)(34) are conjugate
(c) every element is a product of disjoint cycles
(d) the group is generated by (12) and $(12...n)$

225. The number of quotient groups of $S_4$ (the symmetric group of 4 symbols) up to isomorphism is/are
(a) 1 (b) 2
(c) 3 (d) 4

226. For any two real number $a, b \in R$ define a mapping $f_{ab} : R \to R$ as
$f_{ab}(x) = ax + b, \forall x \in R$
Let $G = \{f_{ab} : a \neq 0\}$, then
(a) $G$ is not a group as identity does not exist
(b) $G$ is not a group as inverse does not exist
(c) $G$ is not a group as it is not closed
(d) $G$ is a group

227. Let $S_{10}$ denote the group of permutations on ten symbols (1, 2,..., 10), the number of elements of $S_{10}$ commuting the element $\sigma = (1\,3\,5\,7\,9)$ are
(a) 5! (b) $5 \cdot 5!$
(c) 5!5! (d) $\frac{10!}{5!}$

228. The number of non-isomorphic groups of order 6 is
(a) 2 (b) 6
(c) 3 (d) 1

229. In a non-abelian group the element $a$ has order 108. Then, the order of $a^{42}$ is
(a) 54 (b) 27
(c) 18 (d) 9

230. Which of the following is false?
(a) Each element of an abelian group is self conjugate
(b) All the self conjugate elements of a group form a subgroup
(c) If $H$ is a subgroup of $G$ and all the subgroups conjugate to $H$ in $G$ are equal to $H$, then $H$ is normal
(d) None of the above

231. Any subgroup of $Q$ (the group of rational numbers under addition) is
(a) cyclic and finitely generated but not abelian and normal
(b) cyclic and abelian but not finitely generated and normal
(c) normal, cyclic and finitely generated
(d) finitely generated and normal but not cyclic and abelian

232. The order of Aut $(G)$, where $G$ is a group with 65 elements is/are
(a) 1 (b) 64
(c) 48 (d) 24

233. If $A \in GL(2, Z_7)$ s.t. $A = \begin{bmatrix} 4 & 5 \\ 6 & 3 \end{bmatrix}$, then $A^{-1}$ is
(a) $\begin{bmatrix} 4 & 5 \\ 6 & 3 \end{bmatrix}$ (b) $\begin{bmatrix} 4 & 5 \\ 3 & 6 \end{bmatrix}$
(c) $\begin{bmatrix} 1 & 3 \\ 5 & 6 \end{bmatrix}$ (d) $\begin{bmatrix} 5 & 6 \\ 1 & 3 \end{bmatrix}$

234. If $a$ be a fixed non-identity element of a group $G$ and if
$H = \{x \in G : xa^2 = a^2 x\}$
$K = \{x \in G : xa = ax\}$
(a) Both $H$ and $K$ are subgroup of $G$ and $H$ is contained in $K$
(b) Both $H$ and $K$ are subgroup of $G$ and $K$ is contained in $H$
(c) $K$ is subgroup of $G$ but not $H$
(d) $H \cap K$ is trivial subgroup of $G$

235. Select the incorrect statement among the followings
(a) if $G$ is infinite cyclic group, then Aut $(G) \cong Z_2$
(b) group of automorphisms over non-isomorphic groups can be isomorphic
(c) Aut $(G)$ is abelian whenever $G$ is cyclic
(d) there are exactly 4 homomorphism from $Z_{20}$ to $Z_{10}$

236. $U(2^n)$ where $n \geq 3$ is
(a) cyclic (b) abelian
(c) abelian but not cyclic (d) None of these

237. Suppose that $\phi$ is an automorphism of $U(36)$, $\ker \phi = \{1, 13, 25\}$ and $\phi(5) = 17$. Determine all the elements that map to 17 in that order
(a) {5, 29, 17} (b) {7, 31, 13}
(c) {7, 13, 31} (d) None of these

238. In $U(40)$ how many cyclic subgroup of order 4
(a) there is 4 cyclic subgroup of order 4
(b) only one
(c) atmost equal to order of the group
(d) exactly two

239. The smallest order for a group to have a non-abelian proper subgroup
(a) 8 (b) 12
(c) 24 (d) 120

240. Select the incorrect statement about the groups $Z$ and $Z \times Z_2$
(a) $Z$ and $Z \times Z_2$ are not isomorphic as there cannot be 1 − 1 and onto map between them
(b) $Z$ and $Z \times Z_2$ are not isomorphic as the identity of $Z$ cannot be mapped to the identity of $Z \times Z_2$
(c) $Z$ and $Z \times Z_2$ are not isomorphic as $Z$ is cyclic but $Z \times Z_2$ is not
(d) $Z$ and $Z \times Z_2$ are isomorphic

**241.** If order $o(G) = 2p, p$ is prime number, then $G$ has a subgroup of order $p$, this subgroup
(a) need not to be cyclic (b) is non-abelian
(c) normal (d) None of these

**242.** The number of non-abelian groups of order 12 upto isomorphism is
(a) 0 (b) 1
(c) 3 (d) 4

**243.** If $G$ is a group of order 91, then which statement is false?
(a) $G$ has one subgroup of order 7
(b) $G$ has two subgroups of order 13
(c) $G$ has a subgroups of order 7 and 13
(d) None of the above

**244.** Let $R^+$ be multiplicative group of all positive reals and $R$ be a additive group of all reals and $f : R^+ \to R$ be a map given by $f(x) = \log x, \forall x \in R^+$
(a) $f$ is not preserves the composition
(b) $f$ is an isomorphism
(c) $f$ is homomorphism but not onto
(d) $f$ is homomorphism but not one-one

**245.** Let $G$ be a finite group of order 200. Then the number of subgroup of $G$ of order 25 is
(a) 1 (b) 4
(c) 5 (d) 10

**246.** Let $U(n)$ be the set of all positive integers less than $n$ and relatively prime to $n$. Then, $U(n)$ is a group under multiplication modulo $n$. For $n = 248$, the number of elements in $U(n)$ is
(a) 60 (b) 120
(c) 180 (d) 240

**247.** Let $G$ and $G'$ be any two groups such that $o(G) = 12$, $o(G') = 16$ and $f : G \to G'$ be an homomorphism such that $o(f(a)) = 4$. Then, what are the possibilities for order of $a$?
(a) $\{3, 4, 6, 12\}$ (b) $\{4, 12\}$
(c) $\{4, 6, 12\}$ (d) $\{4\}$

**248.** Let $G$ be a group of even order and $H = \{x \in G : x^2 \neq e\}$. Then, number of element in $H$ is
(a) odd prime (b) prime
(c) odd (d) even

**249.** Let $G$ be a group of order 15. Then, the number of 3-sylow subgroups of $G$ is
(a) 0 (b) 1
(c) 3 (d) 5

**250. Assertion (A)** $A_4$ has a subgroup of order 2 but not of order 6.
**Reason (R)** The group $A_4$ has 3-sylow subgroup but not normal
**Codes**
(a) A and R both are correct and R explain A correctly
(b) A and R both are correct but R does not explain A correctly
(c) A is correct but R is incorrect
(d) R is correct but A is incorrect

**251.** Let $G$ be a finite abelian group of odd order let $H = \{x^2 \mid x \in G\}$, then
(a) $H$ is a subgroup of $G$ only if $G$ is cyclic
(b) $H$ is a proper subgroup of $G$
(c) $H = G$
(d) $H$ may not be subgroup of $G$

**252.** Determine how many homomorphisms are there from $Z_{20}$ onto $Z_{10}$ and how many are there to $Z_{10}$?
(a) 4 onto, 10 to (b) 20 onto, 10 to
(c) 8 onto, 10 to (d) 10 onto, 20 to

**253.** Consider the following statements
$S$ Every non-abelian group has a non-trivial abelian subgroup
$T$ Every non-trivial abelian group has a cyclic subgroup
(a) Both $S$ and $T$ are false
(b) $S$ is true and $T$ is false
(c) $T$ is true and $S$ is false
(d) Both $S$ and $T$ are true

**254.** A homomorphism from a simple group is
(a) trivial but not one-to-one
(b) non-trivial but one-to-one
(c) either trivial or one-to-one
(d) None of the above

**255.** Find the order of the normalizer of $\sigma = (12)(34)$ in $S_6$
(a) 8 (b) 16
(c) 24 (d) 4

**256.** The order 2-sylow subgroup of $A_4$ is
(a) 4 (b) 6
(c) 2 (d) None of these

**257.** If $G$ is non-cyclic abelian group of order $n$ and $m$ be the largest order of any element of group can possess, then select the correct statement about $G$
(a) there is only one pair of elements of order $m$
(b) the order of every element divides $m$
(c) this is unique element of any such group
(d) there is atleast one element in $G$ whose order does not divide $m$

**258.** Given, $H$ is subgroup of $Z$. If $H$ contains exactly three elements of the set $\{p, p+q, pq, p^q, q^p\}$ where $p$ and $q$ are primes. Then, which of the following are the three elements in $H$?
(a) $pq, p^q, q^p$ (b) $p+q, pq, p^q$
(c) $p, p+q, pq$ (d) $p, pq, p^q$

**259.** Let $GL(2, Z_3)$ is a group [of course! of the type $\begin{bmatrix} a & b \\ c & d \end{bmatrix}$ under matrix multiplication with entries from the field $Z_3$ and $(ad - bc \neq 0)$]. Then, the order of $GL(2, Z_3)$ is
(a) 81 (b) 27
(c) 24 (d) 48

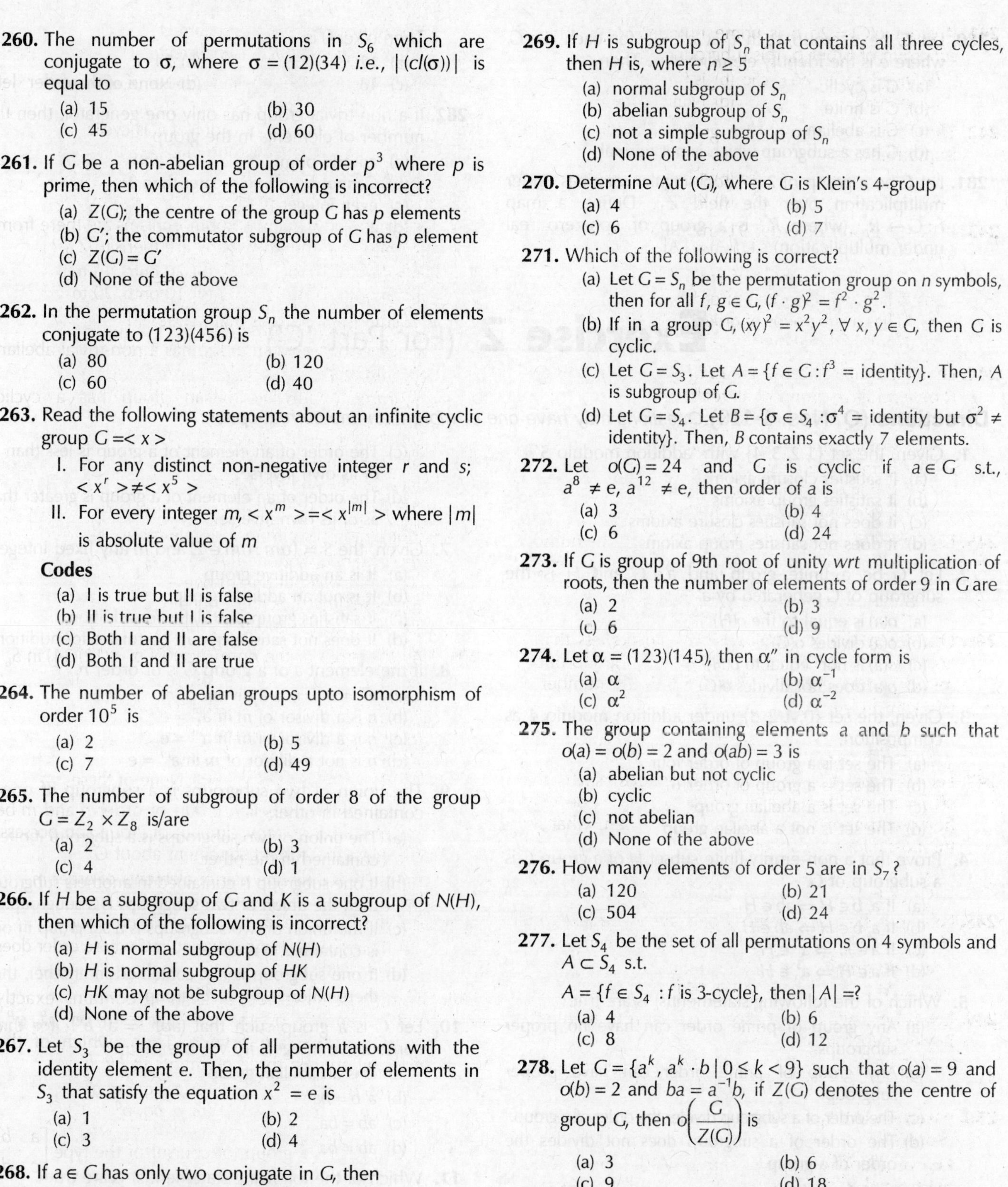

**260.** The number of permutations in $S_6$ which are conjugate to $\sigma$, where $\sigma = (12)(34)$ *i.e.*, $|(cl(\sigma))|$ is equal to

(a) 15 (b) 30
(c) 45 (d) 60

**261.** If $G$ be a non-abelian group of order $p^3$ where $p$ is prime, then which of the following is incorrect?

(a) $Z(G)$; the centre of the group $G$ has $p$ elements
(b) $G'$; the commutator subgroup of $G$ has $p$ element
(c) $Z(G) = G'$
(d) None of the above

**262.** In the permutation group $S_n$ the number of elements conjugate to (123)(456) is

(a) 80 (b) 120
(c) 60 (d) 40

**263.** Read the following statements about an infinite cyclic group $G = < x >$

I. For any distinct non-negative integer $r$ and $s$; $< x^r > \neq < x^5 >$

II. For every integer $m, < x^m > = < x^{|m|} >$ where $|m|$ is absolute value of $m$

**Codes**

(a) I is true but II is false
(b) II is true but I is false
(c) Both I and II are false
(d) Both I and II are true

**264.** The number of abelian groups upto isomorphism of order $10^5$ is

(a) 2 (b) 5
(c) 7 (d) 49

**265.** The number of subgroup of order 8 of the group $G = Z_2 \times Z_8$ is/are

(a) 2 (b) 3
(c) 4 (d) 1

**266.** If $H$ be a subgroup of $G$ and $K$ is a subgroup of $N(H)$, then which of the following is incorrect?

(a) $H$ is normal subgroup of $N(H)$
(b) $H$ is normal subgroup of $HK$
(c) $HK$ may not be subgroup of $N(H)$
(d) None of the above

**267.** Let $S_3$ be the group of all permutations with the identity element e. Then, the number of elements in $S_3$ that satisfy the equation $x^2 = e$ is

(a) 1 (b) 2
(c) 3 (d) 4

**268.** If $a \in G$ has only two conjugate in $G$, then

(a) $N(a)$ has only two conjugate subgroups in $G$
(b) $N(a)$ has atleast two conjugate in $G$
(c) $N(a)$ has atmost two conjugate in $G$
(d) $N(a)$ is self conjugate

**269.** If $H$ is subgroup of $S_n$ that contains all three cycles, then $H$ is, where $n \geq 5$

(a) normal subgroup of $S_n$
(b) abelian subgroup of $S_n$
(c) not a simple subgroup of $S_n$
(d) None of the above

**270.** Determine Aut $(G)$, where $G$ is Klein's 4-group

(a) 4 (b) 5
(c) 6 (d) 7

**271.** Which of the following is correct?

(a) Let $G = S_n$ be the permutation group on $n$ symbols, then for all $f, g \in G, (f \cdot g)^2 = f^2 \cdot g^2$.
(b) If in a group $G, (xy)^2 = x^2y^2, \forall\, x, y \in G$, then $G$ is cyclic.
(c) Let $G = S_3$. Let $A = \{f \in G : f^3 = \text{identity}\}$. Then, $A$ is subgroup of $G$.
(d) Let $G = S_4$. Let $B = \{\sigma \in S_4 : \sigma^4 = \text{identity but } \sigma^2 \neq \text{identity}\}$. Then, $B$ contains exactly 7 elements.

**272.** Let $o(G) = 24$ and $G$ is cyclic if $a \in G$ s.t., $a^8 \neq e, a^{12} \neq e$, then order of a is

(a) 3 (b) 4
(c) 6 (d) 24

**273.** If $G$ is group of 9th root of unity *wrt* multiplication of roots, then the number of elements of order 9 in $G$ are

(a) 2 (b) 3
(c) 6 (d) 9

**274.** Let $\alpha = (123)(145)$, then $\alpha''$ in cycle form is

(a) $\alpha$ (b) $\alpha^{-1}$
(c) $\alpha^2$ (d) $\alpha^{-2}$

**275.** The group containing elements $a$ and $b$ such that $o(a) = o(b) = 2$ and $o(ab) = 3$ is

(a) abelian but not cyclic
(b) cyclic
(c) not abelian
(d) None of the above

**276.** How many elements of order 5 are in $S_7$?

(a) 120 (b) 21
(c) 504 (d) 24

**277.** Let $S_4$ be the set of all permutations on 4 symbols and $A \subset S_4$ s.t.

$A = \{f \in S_4 : f \text{ is 3-cycle}\}$, then $|A| = ?$

(a) 4 (b) 6
(c) 8 (d) 12

**278.** Let $G = \{a^k, a^k \cdot b \mid 0 \leq k < 9\}$ such that $o(a) = 9$ and $o(b) = 2$ and $ba = a^{-1}b$, if $Z(G)$ denotes the centre of group $G$, then $o\left(\dfrac{G}{Z(G)}\right)$ is

(a) 3 (b) 6
(c) 9 (d) 18

**279.** In the group $(Z, +)$ the subgroup generated by 2 and 7 is

(a) $Z$ (b) $5Z$
(c) $9Z$ (d) $14Z$

**280.** Let $G$ be a group such that $a^2 = e$ for each $a \in G$, where e is the identity element of $G$. Then,
(a) $G$ is cyclic
(b) $G$ is finite
(c) $G$ is abelian
(d) $G$ has a subgroup which is not normal

**281.** Let G be a group of $2 \times 2$ non-singular matrices under multiplication over the field $Z_3$. Define a map $f: G \to R^*$ (where $R^*$ is a group of non-zero real under multiplication) s.t. $f(A) = |A|$

Then $o(\ker f)$ is
(a) 12 (b) 24
(c) 48 (d) None of these

**282.** If a non-trivial group has only one generator, then the number of elements in the group
(a) an odd prime
(b) Cannot be prime greater than 2
(c) even integer
(d) 2

# Exercise 2 (For Part 'C')

**Directions** (Q. Nos. 1-110) *Questions may have one or more than one correct option.*

1. Given, the set {1, 2, 3, 4} with 'addition modulo 5'
(a) it satisfies closure axioms
(b) it satisfies group axioms
(c) it does not satisfies closure axioms
(d) it does not satisfies group axioms

2. Let $G$ be a finite group and $a \in G$ and $H$ is the subgroup of $G$ generated by a.
(a) $o(a)$ is equal to the $o(H)$
(b) $o(a)$ divides $o(G)$
(c) $o(a)$ is not equal to $o(H)$
(d) $o(a)$ does not divides $o(G)$

3. Given, the set {0, 1, 2, 3} under addition modulo 4 as composition.
(a) The set is a group of order four
(b) The set is a group of order 6
(c) The set is a abelian group
(d) The set is not a abelian group

4. Prove that a non-empty finite subset $H$ of a group $G$ is a subgroup of $G$.
(a) If $a, b \in H \Rightarrow ab \in H$
(b) If $a, b \in H \not\Rightarrow ab \in H$
(c) If $a \in H \Rightarrow a^2 \in H$
(d) If $a \in H \Rightarrow a^3 \in H$

5. Which of the following statement(s) is/are true?
(a) Any group of prime order can have no proper subgroups.
(b) Any group of prime order can have proper subgroup.
(c) The order of a subgroup divides the order of a group.
(d) The order of a subgroup does not divides the order of a group.

6. Which of the following statement(s) is/are true?
(a) The order of an element of a group is the same as that of its inverse.
(b) The order of an element of a group is not same as of its own inverse.
(c) The order of an element of a group is less than as of its own inverse.
(d) The order of an element of a group is greater than as of its own inverse.

7. Given, the $S = \{\alpha m : \alpha m \in \mathbb{Z}$ and $m$ any fixed integer$\}$
(a) It is an additive group
(b) It is not an additive group
(c) It satisfies group postulates for addition
(d) It does not satisfies group postulates for addition

8. If the element a of a group G is of order $n$.
(a) $a^m = e$, if $n$ is a divisor of $m$
(b) $n$ is a divisor of $m$ iff $a^m = e$
(c) $n$ is a divisor of $m$ iff $a^m = e$
(d) $n$ is not a divisor of $m$ iff $a^m = e$

9. The union of two subgroups is a subgroup iff one is contained in other.
(a) The union of two subgroups is a subgroup if one is contained in the other.
(b) If one subgroup is contained in anothers subgroup, then the union of two subgroups is a subgroup.
(c) If the union of two subgroups is a subgroup iff one is contained in another.
(d) If one subgroup is not contained in another, then there union is not a subgroup.

10. Let $G$ is a group such that $(ab)^m = a^m b^m$, for three consecutive integers $m$, $\forall\, a, b \in G$.
(a) $G$ is an abelian group
(b) $a^n b = ba^n$
(c) $ab = ba$
(d) $ab \neq ba$

11. Which of the following statement(s) is/are true?
(a) In a group G, for $a \in G$, if $a^2 = a$, then $a = e$
(b) In a group G, for $a \in G$, if $a^2 = a$, then $a \neq e$
(c) In a group G, for $a, b \in G$, $a \cdot b = b \cdot a$
(d) In a group G, for $a, b \in G$, $a \cdot b \neq b \cdot a$

12. Which of the following statement(s) is/are true?
(a) $(1\ 2\ 3\ldots n)^{-1} = (n, n-1\ldots 2\ 1)$
(b) $(1\ 2\ 3\ldots n)^{-1} \neq (n, n-1\ldots 2\ 1)$
(c) Both (a) and (b)
(d) Neither (a) nor (b)

13. Which of the following statement(s) is/are true?
(a) The order of the power of an element a in group cannot be greater than the order of a.
(b) The order of the power of an element a in group is greater than the order of a.
(c) The order of the power of an element a in group is always equal to be order of a.
(d) The order of the power of an element a in group is less than or equal to the order of a.

14. Which of the following statement(s) is/are true?
(a) The order of every element of a finite group $G$ is finite.
(b) The order of every element of a finite group is infinite.
(c) The order of every element of a finite group is rational.
(d) The order of every element of a finite group is an integer.

15. Let $H$ be a non-empty subset of a group $G$
(a) $H$ is a subgroup if $a, b \in H \Rightarrow aob^{-1} \in H$
(b) if $a, b \in H \Rightarrow aob^{-1} \in H$, then $H$ is a subgroup
(c) $H$ is a subgroup iff $a, b \in H \Rightarrow a\, ob^{-1} \in H$
(d) $H$ is not a subgroup if $a, b \in H \Rightarrow a\, ob^{-1} \in H$

16. If $n$ is the order of the element $a$, then
$a^m = e$ (the identity element) iff $m = np$
(a) $a^m = e$ (an identity element) $\Rightarrow m = np$
(b) $a^m \neq e$ (an identity element) $\Rightarrow m = np$
(c) $m = np \Rightarrow a^m = e$
(d) $m = np \Leftrightarrow a^m = e$

17. If $a, b$ are any two elements of a group $G$ and $H$ is any subgroup of $G$.
(a) $a \in Hb \Rightarrow Ha = Hb$
(b) $Ha = Hb \Rightarrow a \in Hb$
(c) $Ha = Hb \Leftrightarrow a \in Hb$
(d) $Ha \neq Hb \Leftrightarrow a \in Hb$

18. If $G$ is a group and for $a, b \in G$
(a) $(a \cdot b)^2 = a^2 \cdot b^2$ if $G$ be Abelian
(b) If $G$ is abelian, if $(a \cdot b)^2 = a^2 \cdot b^2$
(c) $G$ is abelian iff $(a \cdot b)^2 = a^2 \cdot b^2$
(d) $G$ is not abelian iff $(a \cdot b)^2 = a^2 \cdot b^2$

19. Which of the following statement(s) is/are true?
(a) If finite group $G$ contains an element of even order, then order of $G$ is even.
(b) If finite group $G$ contains an element of even order, the order of $G$ is odd.
(c) If finite group $G$ contains an element of even order, then order of $G$ is not even.
(d) If finite group $G$ contains an element of even order, the order of $G$ is a prime number.

20. Given, the group $\{I_4, +_4\}$ where $I$ is the set of non-negative integers.
(a) The order of $\{0\}$ is one
(b) The order of $\{1\}$ is six
(c) The order of $\{2\}$ is two
(d) The order of $\{3\}$ is one

21. Which of the following statement(s) is/are true?
(a) The set $\mathbb{C}$ of complex numbers is ordered
(b) The set $\mathbb{C}$ of complex numbers is not ordered
(c) Both (a) and (b)
(d) Neither (a) nor (b)

22. Given, the set $\{1, 2, 3, 4\}$ with 'multiplication modulo 5'.
(a) There exist an identify element
(b) It forms an abelian group
(c) It forms an abelian group of order 4
(d) It forms an finite abelian group

23. If $a$ is of order $n$ and $p$ is prime to $n$.
(a) The order of $a^p$ is also $n$
(b) The order of $a^p$ is $n+1$
(c) The order of $a^p$ is less than $n$
(d) The order of $a^p$ is greater than $n$

24. Which of the following statement(s) is/are true?
(a) The identity element in a group is of order one.
(b) The identity element in a group is of order two.
(c) The identity element is the only element in the group that is of order one.
(d) The identity element is the only element in the group that is of order two.

25. Given, the set of $n$th roots of unity,
(a) this set forms a multiplicative group
(b) the set does not form a multiplicative group
(c) the set satisfies associativity with respect to multiplication
(d) the set does not satisfy associativity with respect to multiplication

26. Given, the group $\{0, 1, 2, 3, 4, 5\}$ with the composition being addition modulo 6.
(a) Order of (5) is 6
(b) Order of (4) is 3
(c) Order of (0) is 0
(d) Order of (2) is 3

27. Prove that intersection of two subgroups is again a subgroup.
(a) The intersection of two subgroups is a group
(b) The intersection of two subgroups is not a group
(c) Both (a) and (b) are true
(d) Neither (a) nor (b) is true

28. If $a, b$ are any two elements of a group
(a) $a$ and $b^{-1}ab$ are of same order
(b) $a$ and $b^{-1}ab$ are of different order
(c) The order of $a$ is less than order of $b^{-1}ab$
(d) The order of $a$ is more than order of $b^{-1}ab$

**29.** Let $S$ be a set of all vectors.
(a) $(S, \cdot)$ is a group (b) $(S, \cdot)$ is not a group
(c) $(S, \times)$ is a group (d) $(S, \times)$ is not a group

**30.** Which of the following statement(s) is/are true?
(a) The four fourth roots of unity forms multiplicative group.
(b) The four fourth roots of unity does not forms multiplicative group.
(c) The four fourth roots of unity with multiplicative satisfies associativity.
(d) The four fourth roots of unity with multiplication does not satisfies associativity.

**31.** In a group $G$ and $a \in G$,
(a) for any positive integer $k$, $o(a^k) \le o(a)$
(b) $o(a^{-1}) = o(a)$
(c) $o(a^k) > o(a)$, for any positive integer $k$
(d) $o(a^{-1}) \ne o(a)$

**32.** The order of (3) in the multiplicative group of integers modulo 5 is
(a) 1 (b) 2
(c) 3 (d) 4

**33.** Which of the following statement(s) is/are true?
(a) A normal subgroup of a group is commutative with every complex of the group.
(b) A normal subgroup of a group is not commutative with every complex of the group.
(c) Both (a) and (b)
(d) Neither (a) nor (b)

**34.** Let $H$ be a subgroup of group $G$ and $K$ is a subset of $G$ such that $K = \{x \in G : xH = Hx\}$.
(a) $x_1x_2^{-1} \in K$, $x_1, x_2 \in K$
(b) $x_2^{-1} \in K$, $x_2 \in K$
(c) $K$ is a subgroup of $G$
(d) $K$ is not a subgroup of $G$

**35.** Let $H$ is the only subgroup of finite order of group $G$, $H$ is normal in $G$.
(a) $H$ is normal in $G$ (b) $H$ is not normal in $G$
(c) $o(xHx^{-1}) = o(H)$, $x \in H$ (d) $o(xH^{-1}) \ne o(H)$, $x \in H$

**36.** Given, the set of integer $Z$ with binary operation $a \cdot b = a - b$, $\forall\, a, b \in Z$
(a) $Z$ is a group on defined operation
(b) $Z$ is not a group on defined operation
(c) $\forall\, a, b, c \in Z$, $(a - b) - c = a - (b - c)$
(d) $\forall\, a, b, c \in Z$, $(a - b) - c \ne a - (b - c)$

**37.** Which of the following statement(s) is/are true?
(a) If every element of a group $(G, *)$ is its own inverse, then $(G, *)$ is abelian.
(b) If group $(G, *)$ is commutative, then $(G, *)$ is abelian.
(c) If every element of a group $(G, *)$ is not its own inverse, then $(G, *)$ is abelian.
(d) If group $(G, *)$ is not commutative, then $(G, *)$ is abelian.

**38.** In the additive group of integers,
(a) order of 0 is 0.
(b) order of 0 is infinite.
(c) order of every element $a(\ne 0)$ is infinite.
(d) order of every element is infinite.

**39.** Given, singleton $S = \{0\}$, with 0 as its only element,
(a) it forms as additive group
(b) it does not form additive group
(c) it is associative with addition
(d) it is closure with addition

**40.** Given, $(G, *)$ a group.
(a) $(G, *)$ is commutative $\Rightarrow$ $(a * b)^{-1} = a^{-1} * b^{-1}, \forall\, a, b \in G$
(b) $(a * b)^{-1} = a^{-1} * b^{-1}, \forall\, a, b \in G \Rightarrow (G, *)$ is commutative.
(c) $(a * b)^{-1} = a^{-1} * b^{-1}, \forall\, a, b \in G \Leftrightarrow (G, *)$ is commutative.
(d) $(a * b)^{-1} = a^{-1} * b^{-1}, \forall\, a, b \in G \not\Rightarrow (G, *)$ is not commutative.

**41.** Let order of a group $G$ be prime number $p$, then
(a) $G$ does not possess proper sub groups
(b) $G$ possess proper sub group
(c) $p$ is a prime number, its divisors are only $\pm 1$ and $\pm p$
(d) $p$ is prime it is divisible by 2

**42.** Given, set $S = \{-2, -1, 1, 2\}$
(a) $S$ forms a group with respect to addition
(b) $S$ does not forms a group with respect to addition
(c) $S$ satisfies closure with respect to multiplication
(d) $S$ does not satisfies closure with respect to multiplication

**43.** If $G = \{1, -1\}$ is a group $(G, \cdot)$,
(a) the order of 1 is 1 (b) the order of 1 is 2
(c) the order of $-1$ is 1 (d) the order of $-1$ is 2

**44.** Let finite group $G$ contains an element of even order,
(a) the order of $G$ is even
(b) the order of $G$ is odd
(c) the order of $G$ is prime number
(d) the order of $G$ is irrational number

**45.** Prove that if $G$ is a group such that $(ab)^2 = a^2b^2$ for all $a, b \in G$
(a) $a \cdot b = b \cdot a$, $\forall\, a, b \in G$
(b) $a \cdot b \ne b \cdot a$, $\forall a, b \in G$
(c) $G$ is an abelian group
(d) $G$ is not an abelian group

**46.** In any group
(a) $e^n = e$, for any integer (b) $e^n = 0$, for any integer
(c) $e^n = 1$, for any integer (d) $e^n \ne e$, for any integer

**47.** The set $G = \{1, -1, i, -i\}$ which is a group under multiplication is a cyclic group.
(a) The order of $G$ is 4
(b) $i$ is the generator of $G$
(c) 1 is the identity element of $G$
(d) There is no identity element in $G$

**48.** Which of the following statement(s) is/are true?
(a) Finite group cannot be expressed as the union of two of its proper sub groups.
(b) Finite group can be expressed as the union of two of its proper sub groups.
(c) Both (a) and (b)
(d) Neither (a) nor (b)

**49.** Which of the following statement(s) is/are true?
(a) Any group of prime order can have no proper subgroup.
(b) Any group of prime order can have a proper subgroup.
(c) Both (a) and (b)
(d) Neither (a) nor (b)

**50.** Let $H$ be a subgroup of group $G$ and $K$ is a subset of $G$ such that $K = \{x \in G : xH = Hx\}$.
(a) $K$ is a subgroup of $G$
(b) $K$ is not a subgroup of $G$
(c) $x_1, x_2 \in K, x_1x_2^{-1} \in K$
(d) $x_1 \in K \Rightarrow x^{-1} \in K$

**51.** Which of the following statement(s) is/are true?
(a) Two right cosets $Ha$ and $Hb$ are distinct iff two left cosets $a^{-1}H$ and $b^{-1}H$ are distinct.
(b) Two right cosets $Ha$ and $Hb$ are distinct $\Rightarrow$ two left cosets $a^{-1}H$ and $b^{-1}H$ are distinct.
(c) Two left cosets $a^{-1}H$ and $b^{-1}H$ are distinct $\Rightarrow$ two right cosets $Ha$ and $Hb$ are distinct.
(d) Two left cosets $a^{-1}H$ and $b^{-1}H$ are distinct, then two right coset $aH$ and $bH$ are same.

**52.** If $a$ and $b$ are two distinct element of a group $G$ and $H$ is a subgroup of $G$,
(a) $Ha = Hb \Rightarrow ab^{-1} \in H$ (b) $ab^{-1} \in H \Rightarrow Ha = Hb$
(c) $Ha \neq Hb \Rightarrow ab^{-1} \in H$ (d) $ab^{-1} \in H \Rightarrow Ha \neq Hb$

**53.** Which of the following statement(s) is/are true?
(a) Left cosets of a subgroup are neither disjoint nor identical.
(b) Left cosets of a subgroup are either disjoint or identical.
(c) Left cosets of a subgroup are always disjoint.
(d) Left cosets of a subgroup are always identical.

**54.** Let $f$ be a homomorphism from $G$ into $\overline{G}$ with the kernel $K_f$
(a) $a \in G$ and $k \in K_f \Rightarrow aka^{-1} \in K_f$
(b) $a \notin G$ and $k \in K_f \Rightarrow ak^{-1}a \notin K_f$
(c) $K_j$ is a normal subgroup of $G$
(d) $K_j$ is not a normal subgroup of $G$.

**55.** If $a$ and $b$ are two distinct element of a group $G$ and $H$ is a subgroup of $G$,
(a) $Ha = Hb$ iff $ab^{-1} \in H$
(b) $ab^{-1} \in H \Rightarrow Ha = Hb$
(c) $a^{-1}b \in H \Leftrightarrow Ha = Hb$
(d) $a^{-1}b \in H \Leftrightarrow Ha \neq Hb$

**56.** The regular permutation group isomorphic to the group $G = [\{1, \omega, \omega^2\}, \cdot]$ are
(a) $I$ (b) $(1\ \omega\ \omega^2)$
(c) $(\omega^2\ \omega\ 1)$ (d) $(1\ 0\ 0)$

**57.** $H \subseteq K$ be two subgroup of a finite group $G$,
(a) $[G:H] = [G:K][K:H]$
(b) $H$ is a subgroup of $K$
(c) $[G:H] = [G:K][G:H]$
(d) $H$ is not a subgroup of $K$.

**58.** Let $H$ and $K$ be two subgroups of a group $G$.
(a) Any right coset relative to $H \cap K$ is the intersection of a right coset relative to $H$ with a right coset relative to $K$
(b) $(H \cap K)a \neq Ha \cap Ka, a \in G$
(c) $(H \cap K)a = aH \cap Ka, a \in G$
(d) $(H \cap K)a = aH \cap aK, a \in G$

**59.** Let $G$ be a group and $H$ be a subgroup of $G$. Let for $x \in G$

$$xHx^{-1} = \{xax^{-1} : a \in H\}$$

(a) $xHx^{-1}$ is a subgroup of $G$
(b) $xHx^{-1}$ is not a subgroup of $G$
(c) Both (a) and (b) are true
(d) Neither (a) nor (b) is true

**60.** If $I$ is an additive group of integers and $E$ the additive group of even integers with zero and map $f : I \to E$ given by $f(x) = 2x$, where $x \in I$
(a) $f$ is one-one
(b) $f$ is onto
(c) $f$ preserves the group composition
(d) $f$ is isomorphism

**61.** Let $G$ be the group of all real numbers under addition and $G'$ be the group of all non-zero real numbers under multiplication. Given, the mapping $\phi : G \to G'$ such that $\phi(x) = 2^x$, $x \in G$,
(a) $\phi$ is homomorphism
(b) $\phi$ is not homomorphism
(c) If $m \in G$, then $\phi(m) = 2^m$
(d) If $n \in G$, then $\phi(n) = 2^n$

**62.** Which of the following statement(s) is/are true?
(a) The centre of a group is always a normal subgroup of the group.
(b) The centre of a group is not always a normal subgroup of the group.
(c) The centre of a group is subgroup of the group.
(d) The centre of a group is not a subgroup of the group.

**63.** If $H$ is a subgroup of $G$,
(a) $H^{-1} = H$ (b) $h \in H \Rightarrow h^{-1} \in H$
(c) $H^{-1} \neq H$ (d) $h^{-1} \in H^{-1}$ then $h \in H$

**64.** Which of the following statement(s) is/are true?
(a) The normalizer of any element of a group is always a subgroup of the same.

(b) The normalizer of any element of a group is not always a subgroup of the same.
(c) Both (a) and (b) are true
(d) Neither (a) nor (b)

**65.** If $H$ and $K$ are two subgroups of a groups $G$,
(a) $HK$ is a subgroup, if $HK = KH$
(b) $HK = KH$, if $HK$ is a subgroup
(c) $HK$ is a subgroup iff $HK = KH$
(d) $HK$ is not a subgroup iff $HK \neq KH$

**66.** Let $f$ be a homomorphism from $G$ into $\overline{G}$.
(a) $f(e) = \overline{e}$ where $\overline{e}$ is the unit element of $\overline{G}$
(b) $f(a^{-1}) = f(a)^{-1}$ for each $a \in G$
(c) $f(e) = e$
(d) $f(a^{-1}) \neq f(a)^{-1}, \forall\, a \in G$

**67.** Given additive group
$G = \{..., -3, -2, -1, 0, 1, 2, 3, ...\}$ and additive group $G' = \{..., -3m, -2m, -m, 0, m, 2m, ...\}$
for any given integer $m$
Let $f: G \to G'$
(a) $f$ is one-one
(b) $f$ is onto
(c) $f$ is an isomorphic mapping
(d) $f$ preserves group composition

**68.** Let $a$ and $b$ be any elements of a group $G$,
(a) $(bab^{-1})^n = ba^nb^{-1}$, for any integer $n$
(b) $(bab^{-1}) \neq ba^nb^{-1}$, for any integer $n$
(c) if e is an identity element, then $(bab^{-1}) = e$
(d) if e is an identity element, then $(bab^{-1}) \neq e$

**69.** The relation of isomorphism in the set of all groups
(a) it an equivalence relation
(b) it satisfies reflexivity
(c) it satisfies anti-symmetrically
(d) it satisfies transitivity

**70.** Let $G$ be a group, $H$ a subgroup of $G$. Let for $x \in G$ such that
$xHx^{-1} = \{xax^{-1} : a \in H\}$
(a) $xHx^{-1}$ is a subgroup of $G$
(b) $xHx^{-1}$ is not a subgroup of $G$
(c) $xHx^{-1}$ is a group
(d) $xHx^{-1}$ is not a group

**71.** Which of the following(s) is/are true?
(a) Every cyclic group is abelian group.
(b) The order of a cyclic group is same as that of its generator.
(c) Every cyclic group is not abelian.
(d) The order of a cyclic group is not same as that of its generator.

**72.** Given, a non-empty subset $H$ of a group $G$
(a) $H$ is a subgroup of $G \Rightarrow HH^{-1} \subseteq H$
(b) $HH^{-1} \subseteq H \Rightarrow H$ is a subgroup of $G$
(c) $HH^{-1} \subseteq H \Leftrightarrow H$ is a subgroup of $G$
(d) $H$ is a subgroup of $G \Leftrightarrow HH^{-1} \supseteq H$

**73.** If $f = \begin{pmatrix} 1 & 2 & 3 & 4 & 5 \\ 1 & 5 & 3 & 2 & 4 \end{pmatrix}$ and $g = \begin{pmatrix} 1 & 2 & 3 & 4 & 5 \\ 2 & 3 & 1 & 5 & 4 \end{pmatrix}$

Then, show that $f^{-1}og^{-1} \neq g^{-1}of^{-1}$
(a) $f^{-1}og^{-1} \neq g^{-1}of^{-1}$
(b) $f^{-1}og^{-1} = g^{-1}of^{-1}$
(c) $f^{-1}og^{-1} = \begin{pmatrix} 1 & 2 & 3 & 4 & 5 \\ 3 & 5 & 2 & 4 & 1 \end{pmatrix}$
(d) $g^{-1}of^{-1} = \begin{pmatrix} 1 & 2 & 3 & 4 & 5 \\ 3 & 5 & 2 & 4 & 1 \end{pmatrix}$

**74.** Let $f = \begin{pmatrix} 1 & 2 & 3 & 4 & 5 \\ 1 & 5 & 3 & 2 & 4 \end{pmatrix}$ and $g = \begin{pmatrix} 1 & 2 & 3 & 4 & 5 \\ 2 & 3 & 1 & 5 & 4 \end{pmatrix}$,
(a) $(fog) = \begin{pmatrix} 1 & 2 & 3 & 4 & 5 \\ 2 & 4 & 1 & 3 & 5 \end{pmatrix}$
(b) $fog = \begin{pmatrix} 1 & 2 & 3 & 4 & 5 \\ 2 & 4 & 1 & 5 & 3 \end{pmatrix}$
(c) $gof = \begin{pmatrix} 1 & 2 & 3 & 4 & 5 \\ 5 & 3 & 1 & 4 & 2 \end{pmatrix}$
(d) $fog = gof$

**75.** If $A_1 = \begin{pmatrix} 1 & 2 & 3 \\ 3 & 1 & 2 \end{pmatrix} A_2 = \begin{pmatrix} 1 & 2 & 3 \\ 2 & 3 & 1 \end{pmatrix} A_3 = \begin{pmatrix} 1 & 2 & 3 \\ 3 & 2 & 1 \end{pmatrix}$
(a) $(A_1oA_2)^{-1} = I$
(b) $(A_2oA_3)^{-1} = (1, 2)$
(c) $(A_3oA_1)^{-1} = (1, 2)$
(d) $(A_3oA_1)^{-1} = (A_1oA_2)^{-1}$

**76.** Let $f = (1\ 2\ 5)$ and $g = (3\ 4\ 6)$ be the permutations of degree six.
(a) $fg = gf$
(b) $fg \neq gf$
(c) The product of $f$ and $g$ is commutative
(d) The product of $f$ and $g$ is not commutative

**77.** If $A = (1\ 2\ 3\ 4\ 5)$, $B = (2\ 3)(4\ 5)$, then
(a) $AoB = (1\ 3\ 5)$
(b) $AoB = I$
(c) $AoB = (1\ 2\ 3)$
(d) $AoB = (1\ 6\ 5)$

**78.** Given, $C = \begin{pmatrix} 1 & 2 & 3 & 4 \\ 1 & 3 & 4 & 2 \end{pmatrix}$
(a) $C^3 = \begin{pmatrix} 1 & 2 & 3 & 4 \\ 1 & 4 & 2 & 3 \end{pmatrix}$
(b) $C^3 = \begin{pmatrix} 1 & 2 & 3 & 4 \\ 1 & 2 & 3 & 4 \end{pmatrix}$
(c) $C^2 = C^3$
(d) $C = C^2$

**79.** Given, the permutation $\begin{pmatrix} 1 & 2 & 3 & 4 \\ 1 & 3 & 4 & 2 \end{pmatrix}$
(a) The inverse of the permutation is $\begin{pmatrix} 1 & 3 & 4 & 2 \\ 1 & 2 & 3 & 4 \end{pmatrix}$
(b) The inverse of the permutation is $\begin{pmatrix} 1 & 2 & 3 & 4 \\ 1 & 2 & 3 & 4 \end{pmatrix}$
(c) No inverse of the permutation exist
(d) The inverse of the permutation exist

**80.** Given, permutation $\begin{pmatrix} 1 & 2 & 3 & 4 \\ 1 & 3 & 4 & 2 \end{pmatrix}$

(a) Order of permutation is 1
(b) Order of permutation is 2
(c) Order of permutation is 3
(d) Order of permutation is 4

**81.** Given, the symmetric group $S_4$ on four symbols.

(a) The cyclic group of order 2 is $\{(1\ 2), (1)\ (2)\ (3)\ (4) = 1\}$
(b) The cyclic group of order 3 is $\{(2\ 3\ 4), (2, 4, 3), (1)\ (2)\ (3)\ (4) = I\}$
(c) The cyclic group of order 4 is $\{(1\ 3\ 2\ 4), (1\ 2)(3\ 4), (1\ 4\ 2\ 3), (1)\ (2)\ (3)\ (4) = I\}$
(d) No cyclic group exist

**82.** The permutation $\begin{pmatrix} 1 & 2 & 3 & 4 \\ 2 & 4 & 3 & 1 \end{pmatrix}$ is even and $(1\ 2)(5\ 4\ 3)(6\ 7\ 8)$ is odd.

(a) The permutation $\begin{pmatrix} 1 & 2 & 3 & 4 \\ 2 & 4 & 3 & 1 \end{pmatrix}$ is even
(b) The permutation $\begin{pmatrix} 1 & 2 & 3 & 4 \\ 2 & 4 & 3 & 1 \end{pmatrix}$ is odd
(c) The permutation $(1\ 2)(5\ 4\ 6)(6\ 7\ 8)$ is odd
(d) The permutation $(1\ 2)(5\ 4\ 6)(6\ 7\ 8)$ is even

**83.** If $f = (2\ 3)$ and $g = (4\ 5)$ be the two permutations on five symbols 1, 2, 3, 4, 5,

(a) $fg = \begin{pmatrix} 1 & 2 & 3 & 4 & 5 \\ 1 & 3 & 2 & 5 & 4 \end{pmatrix}$
(b) $gf = \begin{pmatrix} 1 & 2 & 3 & 4 & 5 \\ 1 & 3 & 2 & 5 & 4 \end{pmatrix}$
(c) $fg = gf$
(d) $fg \neq gf$

**84.** Given, $(1\ 2)o(1\ 3)o(1\ 4)o...o(1\ n)$

(a) $(1\ 2\ 3\ 4 \ldots n)$
(b) $(1, 3, 5, \ldots, n)$
(c) $(1, 2, 4, \ldots, n)$
(d) $(1\ 2\ 6\ 8\ 9 \ldots n)$

**85.** Let a binary operation $*$ is defined on set of positive rational numbers, $Q^+$ such that $a * b = \dfrac{ab}{2}, \forall\, a, b \in Q^+$, then

(a) 2 is the identity element of $(Q^+, *)$
(b) 2 is the inverse of 2
(c) 4 is the inverse of 1
(d) $(Q^+, *)$ is not an abelian group

**86.** Which of the following(s) is/are groupoid?

(a) $(N, +)$
(b) $(Z, +)$
(c) $(\{1, 3, 5\}, +)$
(d) $(G, +)$, where $G = \{-5, -3, -1, 1, 3, 5\}$

**87.** Which of the following(s) is/are groups?

(a) Set of all even integers (including zero) under addition.
(b) Set of all non-zero rational numbers with respect to binary operation of multiplication.
(c) The set of all real numbers with respect to addition.
(d) The set $C$ of all non-zero complex numbers with respect to multiplication.

**88.** Which of the following(s) is/are true? For $G$ to be an abelian group?

(a) $a^2 = e, \forall a \in G$
(b) $o(a) = 2, \forall a \in G$
(c) $ab = ba, \forall a, b \in G$
(d) $(ab)^{-1} = (b^{-1}a^{-1}), \forall a, b \in G$

**89.** If $G$ is an abelian group, then which of the following(s) is/are hold/s?

(a) $(ab)^{-1} = a^{-1}b^{-1}, \forall\, a, b \in G.$
(b) $(ab)^n = a^n b^n, \forall\, a, b \in G$ for any three consecutive integers $n$.
(c) $(bab^{-1})^n = ba^n b^{-1}, \forall a, b \in G$ and $n \in Z$.
(d) Number of elements in a group $G$ is less than or equal to four.

**90.** If in a group $G$, $a^5 = e$, $aba^{-1} = b^2$ for $a, b \in G$, then

(a) $b^4 = a^2 ba^{-2}$
(b) $b^{16} = a^8 ba^{-8}$
(c) $o(b) = 31, b \neq e$
(d) $o(b) = 32, b \neq e$

**91.** Let $Z$ be the group of all integers under addition. Let $G = \{2^n : n \in Z\}$ be a group under multiplication. Define a map, $f : Z \to G$ by $f(n) = 2^n, \forall\, n \in Z$, then

(a) $f$ is a homomorphism
(b) $f$ is an isomorphism
(c) $f$ is a homomorphism but not an isomorphism
(d) $\text{Ker } f = \{0\}$

**92.** Let a mapping $f : G \to G$ defined by $f(x) = x^{-1}$, then which of the following/s is/are correct?

(a) $f$ is one-one.
(b) $f$ is onto.
(c) $f$ is homomorphism as well as automorphism.
(d) $G$ is a non-abelian group.

**93.** If $G$ is a group and $a \in G$. Let the set $H = \{a^n : n \in Z\}$, then

(a) $H$ is a non-empty subset of $G$
(b) $H$ is not a subgroup of $G$
(c) $H$ is a subgroup of $G$
(d) $H$ is the smallest subgroup of $G$, which contains the element '$a$'

**94.** Let $G = \left\{ I = \begin{bmatrix} 1 & 0 \\ 0 & 1 \end{bmatrix}, A = \begin{bmatrix} -1 & 0 \\ 0 & 1 \end{bmatrix}, B = \begin{bmatrix} 1 & 0 \\ 0 & -1 \end{bmatrix}, C = \begin{bmatrix} -1 & 0 \\ 0 & -1 \end{bmatrix} \right\}$ be a multiplicative group of matrices, then

(a) $o(A) = o(B) = o(C) = 2$
(b) $G$ is a cyclic group of order 4
(c) $G$ is an abelian group of order 4
(d) $G$ is a non-abelian group of order 4

**95.** Let cyclic group $G = \{a, a^2, a^3, ..., a^n = e\}$ and group $G' = \{x : x$ is a solution of $x^n = 1\}$, then which of the following/s holds/s?
(a) Both $G$ and $G'$ are abelian group
(b) $G'$ is not a cyclic group
(c) $f : G \rightarrow G'$ is one-one and onto
(d) $f$ is an isomorphism.

**96.** Consider the cyclic group
$G = \{a, a^2, a^3, a^4, a^5, a^6 = e\}$, then which of the following/s is/are correct?
(a) Atleast two generators of $G$.
(b) Exactly two generators of $G$.
(c) $o(a^2) = o(a^4)$
(d) $o(a^3) = o(a^5)$

**97.** If $H$ and $K$ are normal subgroups of $G$, then which of the following/s are correct?
(a) $HK$ is normal subgroup of $G$.
(b) $KH$ is not a normal subgroup of $G$.
(c) $H \cap K$ is normal subgroup of $G$.
(d) If $H \cap K = \{e\}$, then $hk = kh, \forall h \in H, k \in K$

**98.** Let $G = \{e, a, a^2, a^3, b, ab, a^2b, a^3b\}$ with $a^4 = e$, $b^2 = e$, $ab = a^{-1}b$ and $H = \{e, a^2, ab, a^3b\}$, $K = \{e, a^3b\}$, then
(a) $H$ is normal subgroup of $G$
(b) $K$ is normal subgroup of $G$
(c) $K$ is normal subgroup of $H$
(d) $[G : H][H : K] = 4$

**99.** Let $Z$ be the centre of group $G$ of order 27, then
(a) $G$ has non-trivial centre
(b) $G = \{e\}$
(c) $o(Z) = 3$
(d) $o(Z) = 27$

**100.** Let $G$ be a group of order $pq$, where $p$ and $q$ are distinct primes and $p > q$. Then,
(a) $G$ has a normal cyclic subgroup of order $p$
(b) $G$ is a simple group
(c) If $q$ does not divide $(p - 1)$, then $G$ is cyclic
(d) $G$ is a cyclic group

**101.** Which statement(s) is/are true?
(a) Every cyclic group is abelian.
(b) Every group of prime order is cyclic.
(c) Every group of composite order is cyclic.
(d) Every abelian group is cyclic.

**102.** Which of the following(s) is/are true?
(a) Every group of order 2 is cyclic.
(b) Every group of order 3 is cyclic.
(c) Every group of order 4 is cyclic.
(d) Every group of order 6 is cyclic.

**103.** If $H$ is normal subgroup of $G$, then which of the following(s) is/are true?
(a) $aH = Ha, \forall a \in G$
(b) $a^{-1}Ha = H, \forall a \in G$
(c) $a^{-1}ha = H, \forall a \in G$ and $h \in H$
(d) order of $H$ is 2

**104.** Which of the following(s) is/are true?
(a) Group $\{1, -1\}$ is a simple group.
(b) Group $\{1, -1, -i, i\}$ is a simple group.
(c) $\{1, \omega, \omega^2\}$ is not a simple group.
(d) Any group of prime order is simple.

**105.** Let $S_3$ be the symmetric group on three numbers 1, 2 and 3 and $N(a)$ and $Z(G)$ are respectively normalizer of element $a$ and centre of $G$, then which of the following/s is/are true?
(a) $N(12) = \{I, (12)\}$ (b) $N(13) \neq \{I, (13)\}$
(c) $Z(G) = \{I\}$ (d) $N(I) = S_3$

**106.** Let $S_n$ be symmetric group on $n$ symbols and $A_n$ be the alternating subgroup of $S_n$, then
(a) $A_n$ is normal subgroup of $S_n$
(b) $[S_n : A_n] = 2$
(c) order of $A_n$ is $n!$
(d) $A_n$ is the set of all odd permutations of $S_n$

**107.** Let $S_3 = \{I, (1\ 2), (1\ 3), (2\ 3), (1\ 2\ 3), (1\ 3\ 2)\}$ be a symmetric group on three numbers 1, 2 and 3, then
(a) $S_3$ has 2 sylow 2-subgroups of $G$
(b) $S_3$ has 3 sylow 2-subgroups of $G$
(c) $S_3$ has 1 sylow 3-subgroups of $G$
(d) $S_3$ has 2 sylow 3-subgroups of $G$

**108.** Consider a group $G$ with order 28, *i.e.*, $o(G) = 28$, then
(a) there exists exactly one 7-sylow subgroup of $G$
(b) there exists exactly two 7-sylow subgroups of order 7
(c) $G$ is a simple group
(d) $G$ is not a simple group

**109.** Consider any group $G$ of order 15, then
(a) there exists exactly one 3-sylow subgroup of $G$
(b) there exists exactly two 3-sylow subgroup of $G$
(c) group given in (a) is normal subgroup of $G$
(d) group given in (a) in cyclic

**110.** Let $G$ be a group of order 225, then which of the following(s) is/are correct?
(a) There exists exactly one 5-sylow subgroup of $G$
(b) There exists exactly three 3-sylow subgroup of $G$
(c) Group given in (a) is normal in $G$
(d) 3-sylow subgroup of $G$ is abelian

# Answers

## Exercise 1

**1.** (a) **2.** (a) **3.** (c) **4.** (a) **5.** (a) **6.** (a) **7.** (b) **8.** (a) **9.** (b) **10.** (a)

**11.** (b) **12.** (a) **13.** (a) **14.** (a) **15.** (d) **16.** (d) **17.** (a) **18.** (c) **19.** (a) **20.** (d)

**21.** (b) **22.** (b) **23.** (c) **24.** (c) **25.** (c) **26.** (a) **27.** (c) **28.** (b) **29.** (d) **30.** (a)

**31.** (a) **32.** (b) **33.** (a) **34.** (a) **35.** (c) **36.** (d) **37.** (d) **38.** (d) **39.** (c) **40.** (a)

**41.** (a) **42.** (a) **43.** (a) **44.** (b) **45.** (a) **46.** (b) **47.** (d) **48.** (a) **49.** (b) **50.** (a)

**51.** (b) **52.** (c) **53.** (a) **54.** (b) **55.** (a) **56.** (d) **57.** (a) **58.** (a) **59.** (d) **60.** (c)

**61.** (a) **62.** (a) **63.** (a) **64.** (a) **65.** (b) **66.** (c) **67.** (a) **68.** (a) **69.** (a) **70.** (a)

**71.** (a) **72.** (a) **73.** (d) **74.** (b) **75.** (c) **76.** (a) **77.** (a) **78.** (b) **79.** (a) **80.** (a)

**81.** (a) **82.** (c) **83.** (c) **84.** (a) **85.** (a) **86.** (a) **87.** (a) **88.** (b) **89.** (a) **90.** (a)

**91.** (c) **92.** (a) **93.** (a) **94.** (a) **95.** (c) **96.** (c) **97.** (a) **98.** (b) **99.** (c) **100.** (c)

**101.** (b) **102.** (b) **103.** (a) **104.** (a) **105.** (b) **106.** (a) **107.** (a) **108.** (c) **109.** (b) **110.** (a)

**111.** (a) **112.** (b) **113.** (a) **114.** (a) **115.** (a) **116.** (c) **117.** (b) **118.** (d) **119.** (c) **120.** (d)

**121.** (a) **122.** (a) **123.** (b) **124.** (a) **125.** (b) **126.** (b) **127.** (d) **128.** (b) **129.** (a) **130.** (c)

**131.** (d) **132.** (c) **133.** (c) **134.** (a) **135.** (d) **136.** (b) **137.** (c) **138.** (c) **139.** (c) **140.** (c)

**141.** (b) **142.** (a) **143.** (a) **144.** (a) **145.** (d) **146.** (a) **147.** (a) **148.** (a) **149.** (a) **150.** (d)

**151.** (c) **152.** (c) **153.** (a) **154.** (a) **155.** (c) **156.** (c) **157.** (c) **158.** (c) **159.** (b) **160.** (c)

**161.** (d) **162.** (a) **163.** (d) **164.** (c) **165.** (b) **166.** (a) **167.** (b) **168.** (a) **169.** (b) **170.** (d)

**171.** (b) **172.** (d) **173.** (d) **174.** (a) **175.** (c) **176.** (d) **177.** (a) **178.** (a) **179.** (b) **180.** (b)

**181.** (d) **182.** (b) **183.** (c) **184.** (b) **185.** (c) **186.** (d) **187.** (b) **188.** (c) **189.** (d) **190.** (b)

**191.** (d) **192.** (c) **193.** (a) **194.** (b) **195.** (d) **196.** (d) **197.** (c) **198.** (b) **199.** (b) **200.** (b)

**201.** (c) **202.** (c) **203.** (a) **204.** (b) **205.** (c) **206.** (d) **207.** (a) **208.** (c) **209.** (c) **210.** (b)

**211.** (c) **212.** (c) **213.** (c) **214.** (d) **215.** (a) **216.** (c) **217.** (d) **218.** (c) **219.** (c) **220.** (c)

**221.** (c) **222.** (a) **223.** (c) **224.** (d) **225.** (c) **226.** (d) **227.** (b) **228.** (a) **229.** (c) **230.** (d)

**231.** (c) **232.** (c) **233.** (c) **234.** (b) **235.** (d) **236.** (c) **237.** (a) **238.** (b) **239.** (c) **240.** (c)

**241.** (c) **242.** (c) **243.** (b) **244.** (b) **245.** (a) **246.** (b) **247.** (b) **248.** (d) **249.** (b) **250.** (a)

**251.** (c) **252.** (a) **253.** (d) **254.** (c) **255.** (b) **256.** (a) **257.** (b) **258.** (b) **259.** (d) **260.** (c)

**261.** (d) **262.** (d) **263.** (d) **264.** (d) **265.** (b) **266.** (c) **267.** (d) **268.** (d) **269.** (a) **270.** (c)

**271.** (c) **272.** (d) **273.** (c) **274.** (b) **275.** (c) **276.** (c) **277.** (c) **278.** (d) **279.** (a) **280.** (c)

**281.** (b) **282.** (d)

## Exercise 2

**1.** (c,d) **2.** (a,b) **3.** (a,c) **4.** (a,c,d) **5.** (a,c) **6.** (a) **7.** (a,c) **8.** (a,b,c) **9.** (a,b,c) **10.** (a,b,c)

**11.** (a,d) **12.** (a) **13.** (a,d) **14.** (a,d) **15.** (a,b,c) **16.** (a,c,d) **17.** (a,b,c) **18.** (a,b,c) **19.** (a) **20.** (a,c)

**21.** (b) **22.** (a,b,c,d) **23.** (a) **24.** (a,c) **25.** (a,c) **26.** (a,b,d) **27.** (a) **28.** (a) **29.** (b,d) **30.** (a,c)

**31.** (a,b) **32.** (d) **33.** (a) **34.** (a,b,c) **35.** (a,c) **36.** (b,d) **37.** (a,b) **38.** (a,c) **39.** (a,c,d) **40.** (a,b,c)

**41.** (a,c) **42.** (a,c) **43.** (a,d) **44.** (a) **45.** (a,c) **46.** (a) **47.** (a,b,c) **48.** (a) **49.** (a) **50.** (a,c,d)

**51.** (a,b,c) **52.** (a,b) **53.** (b) **54.** (a,c) **55.** (a,b,c) **56.** (a,b,c) **57.** (a,b) **58.** (a) **59.** (a) **60.** (a,b,c,d)

**61.** (a,c,d) **62.** (a,c) **63.** (a,b,d) **64.** (a) **65.** (a,b,c) **66.** (a,b) **67.** (a,b,c,d) **68.** (a,c) **69.** (a,b,c) **70.** (a,c)

**71.** (a,b) **72.** (a,b,c) **73.** (a,c) **74.** (a,c) **75.** (a,b,c) **76.** (a,c) **77.** (a) **78.** (a,b) **79.** (a,d) **80.** (a)

**81.** (c) **82.** (a,b,c) **83.** (a,c) **84.** (a) **85.** (a,b,c) **86.** (a,b) **87.** (a,b,c,d) **88.** (a,c) **89.** (a,b,c,d) **90.** (a,c)

**91.** (a,b,d) **92.** (a,b,c) **93.** (a,c,d) **94.** (a,c) **95.** (a,c,d) **96.** (b,c) **97.** (a,c,d) **98.** (a,c,d) **99.** (a,c) **100.** (a,c)

**101.** (a,b) **102.** (a,b) **103.** (a,b,d) **104.** (a,d) **105.** (a,c,d) **106.** (a,b) **107.** (a,c) **108.** (a,d) **109.** (a,c,d) **110.** (a,c,d)

# Hints & Solutions

## Exercise 1

**6.** $fg = (2\ \ 3)(4\ \ 5)$

$$= \begin{pmatrix} 2 & 3 \\ 3 & 2 \end{pmatrix}\begin{pmatrix} 4 & 5 \\ 5 & 4 \end{pmatrix}$$

$$= \begin{pmatrix} 1 & 2 & 3 & 4 & 5 \\ 1 & 3 & 2 & 4 & 5 \end{pmatrix}\begin{pmatrix} 1 & 2 & 3 & 4 & 5 \\ 1 & 2 & 3 & 5 & 4 \end{pmatrix}$$

$$= \begin{pmatrix} 1 & 2 & 3 & 4 & 5 \\ 1 & 3 & 2 & 5 & 4 \end{pmatrix}$$

**14.** $o(G) = 6$ and prime to 6 are 1 and 5.

**16.** 0 is the identity element of $G$ and $2 +_5 2 +_5 2 +_5 2 +_5 2 = 0$

**32.** Identity element does not exist.

**35.** $6 = 2 \times 3$

$$\varphi(6) = 6\left(1 - \frac{1}{2}\right)\left(1 - \frac{1}{3}\right) = 6 \times \frac{1}{2} \times \frac{2}{3} = 2$$

**53.** $\begin{pmatrix} 1 & 2 & 5 & 3 & 4 \\ 3 & 4 & 1 & 5 & 2 \end{pmatrix} = (1\ \ 3\ \ 5)(2\ \ 4)$

$= (1\ \ 3)(1\ \ 5)(2\ \ 4)$

**54.** $C = (1\ 2\ 3\ 4\ 5\ 6\ 7)$

$$= \begin{pmatrix} 1 & 2 & 3 & 4 & 5 & 6 & 7 \\ 2 & 3 & 4 & 5 & 6 & 7 & 1 \end{pmatrix}$$

$$\Rightarrow \quad C^2 = \begin{pmatrix} 1 & 2 & 3 & 4 & 5 & 6 & 7 \\ 3 & 4 & 5 & 6 & 7 & 1 & 2 \end{pmatrix}$$

$$\Rightarrow \quad C^3 = \begin{pmatrix} 1 & 2 & 3 & 4 & 5 & 6 & 7 \\ 4 & 5 & 6 & 7 & 1 & 2 & 3 \end{pmatrix}$$

$= (1\ 4\ 7\ 3\ 6\ 2\ 5)$

**61.** $BA = \begin{pmatrix} 1 & 2 & 3 & 4 & 5 \\ 1 & 3 & 4 & 5 & 2 \end{pmatrix}\begin{pmatrix} 1 & 2 & 3 & 4 & 5 \\ 2 & 3 & 1 & 5 & 4 \end{pmatrix} = \begin{pmatrix} 1 & 2 & 3 & 4 & 5 \\ 2 & 1 & 5 & 4 & 3 \end{pmatrix}$

**94.** $(1\ 2\ 3)\ (1\ 2) = (1\ 2)\ (1\ 3)\ (1\ 2)$

which is a product of odd number of transpositions.

**104.** $$o(HK) = \frac{o(H)\,o(K)}{o(H \cap K)}$$

$$\Rightarrow \quad 16 = \frac{6 \times 8}{o(H \cap K)}$$

$$\Rightarrow \quad o(H \cap K) = 3$$

**107.** Group of order $p^2$ ($p$ is prime) is abelian.

**117.** To find number of sylow subgroup of G of order 3.

$15 = 5 \times 3$, by a known theorem.

Number of 3-sylow subgroup $= 3K + 1$

Now, $(3K + 1)$ must divide $15, (3K + 1)$ being prime to 3 should divide 5.

Thus, is true only for $K = 0$

Thus, $\quad 3K + 1 = 1$

$\therefore$ Number of 3-sylow subgroup = 1

**136.** $$o(AB) = \frac{o(A)o(B)}{o(A \cap B)} = \frac{2 \times 5}{1} = 10$$

$$\Rightarrow \quad o\left(\frac{G}{AB}\right) = \frac{o(G)}{o(AB)} = \frac{30}{10} = 3$$

**137.** Since, number of elements of order $r$ in the symmetric group $S_n$ is $\frac{^nP_r}{r}$.

$$\Rightarrow \quad \frac{^5P_5}{5} = \frac{5!}{5} = 24$$

**138.** Since, centre of $G$, *i.e.*, $Z(G)$ is normal subgroup of $G$.

**139.** $o(G) = 77 = 11 \times 7 \quad (11 > 7)$

centre of $G$ is isomorphic to largest order subgroup of $G$. Which is only normal subgroup of $G$.

**140.** $\begin{pmatrix} 1 & 2 & 3 & 4 & 5 & 6 \\ 6 & 1 & 2 & 5 & 4 & 3 \end{pmatrix} = \begin{pmatrix} 1 & 6 & 3 & 2 & 4 & 5 \\ 6 & 3 & 2 & 1 & 5 & 4 \end{pmatrix} = (1\ 6\ 3\ 2)(4\ 5)$

**141.** Here, 1 is an identity element,

also, $\quad (-1)^2 = 1$

$\therefore \quad o(-1) = 2$

$\because \quad o(a) = p$

$\Rightarrow p$ is the least positive integer : $a^p = e$, an identity.

**142.** Here, $a$ is one generator of the group

The order of $G$ is 6.

$a^p$ is a generator of $G$ of order $n$ iff $p$ is prime to $n$, *i.e.*,

$(n, p) = 1$

Here, $\quad (6, 5) = 1$

$\therefore \quad p = 5 \quad$ and $\quad a^5$ is also a generator.

**143.** $a, b \in G \Rightarrow ab \in G, \ \forall, \ a, b \in G$

$\Rightarrow \quad (ab)^2 = e \ \Rightarrow \ (ab)(ab) = e$

$\Rightarrow \quad (ab)^{-1} = ab$

$\Rightarrow \quad b^{-1}a^{-1} = ab \quad$ ...(i)

But $\quad a^2 = e \ \Rightarrow \quad a \cdot a = e$

$\Rightarrow \quad a^{-1} = a \quad$ ...(ii)

and $\quad b^2 = e$

$\Rightarrow \quad b^{-1} = b \quad$ ...(iii)

$\therefore$ By Eqs. (ii), (iii) and (i), we have

$ab = ba$

$\therefore$ G is abelian group.

**144.** $BA = \begin{pmatrix} 1 & 2 & 3 & 4 & 5 \\ 1 & 3 & 4 & 5 & 2 \end{pmatrix}\begin{pmatrix} 1 & 2 & 3 & 4 & 5 \\ 2 & 3 & 1 & 5 & 4 \end{pmatrix}$

$$= \begin{pmatrix} 1 & 2 & 3 & 4 & 5 \\ 1 & 3 & 4 & 5 & 2 \end{pmatrix}\begin{pmatrix} 1 & 3 & 4 & 5 & 2 \\ 2 & 1 & 5 & 4 & 3 \end{pmatrix}$$

$$= \begin{pmatrix} 1 & 2 & 3 & 4 & 5 \\ 2 & 1 & 5 & 4 & 3 \end{pmatrix}$$

**145.** $gf = \begin{pmatrix} 1 & 2 & 3 & 4 & 5 \\ 1 & 2 & 3 & 5 & 4 \end{pmatrix}\begin{pmatrix} 1 & 2 & 3 & 4 & 5 \\ 1 & 3 & 2 & 4 & 5 \end{pmatrix}$

$= \begin{pmatrix} 1 & 2 & 3 & 4 & 5 \\ 1 & 2 & 3 & 5 & 4 \end{pmatrix}\begin{pmatrix} 1 & 2 & 3 & 5 & 4 \\ 1 & 3 & 2 & 5 & 4 \end{pmatrix}$

$= \begin{pmatrix} 1 & 2 & 3 & 4 & 5 \\ 1 & 3 & 2 & 5 & 4 \end{pmatrix}$

**146.** $fg = \begin{pmatrix} 1 & 2 & 3 & 4 & 5 \\ 1 & 3 & 2 & 4 & 5 \end{pmatrix}\begin{pmatrix} 1 & 2 & 3 & 4 & 5 \\ 1 & 2 & 3 & 5 & 4 \end{pmatrix}$

$= \begin{pmatrix} 1 & 2 & 3 & 4 & 5 \\ 1 & 3 & 2 & 4 & 5 \end{pmatrix}\begin{pmatrix} 1 & 3 & 2 & 4 & 5 \\ 1 & 3 & 2 & 5 & 4 \end{pmatrix}$

$= \begin{pmatrix} 1 & 2 & 3 & 4 & 5 \\ 1 & 3 & 2 & 5 & 4 \end{pmatrix}$

**147.** We have

$a * b = a * b * e$

$= a * b * (b^{-1} * a^{-1} * b * a)$

$(\because b^{-1} * a^{-1} * b * a = e)$

$= a * (b * b^{-1}) * a^{-1} * b * a$

$= a * e * a^{-1} * b * a$

$= (a * a)^{-1} * b * a$

$= e * b * a$

$= b * a$

**148.** $a^2 = a$

$\Rightarrow \quad a \cdot a = e$

$\Rightarrow \quad (a \cdot a) a^{-1} = a \cdot a^{-1}$

$\Rightarrow \quad a \cdot (a \cdot a^{-1}) = e$

$\Rightarrow \quad a \cdot e = e \Rightarrow \quad a = e$

**149.** $\forall \ a \in G$

$a^2 = e \Rightarrow a \cdot a = a \cdot a^{-1} = e$

$\Rightarrow \quad a = a^{-1}$

$\therefore \quad \forall a \cdot b \in G,$

$ab = (ab)^{-1}$

$\Rightarrow \quad a \cdot b = b^{-1} a^{-1}$

$= b \cdot a \qquad (\because a = a^{-1}, \ b = b^{-1})$

Hence, $G$ is abelian group.

**150.** Here, 1 is an identity.

as $\quad (-i)^4 = 1$

$\Rightarrow \quad 0(-i) = 4$

$\because \quad 0\ (a) = p$

$\Rightarrow$ $p$ is the least positive integer.

$a^p = e$, an identity.

**151.** a is one of the generator.

$a^p$ is generator of $G$ of order $n$ iff $(n, p) = 1, 1 < p < n$

Here, $\quad n = 4$

and $\quad (4, 3) = 1$

$\therefore$ $a^3$ is also a generator of $G$.

**153.** $(1\ 2\ 3) \cdot (2\ 4\ 3) \cdot (1\ 3\ 4)$

$= \begin{pmatrix} 1 & 2 & 3 & 4 \\ 2 & 3 & 1 & 4 \end{pmatrix}\begin{pmatrix} 1 & 2 & 4 & 3 \\ 1 & 4 & 3 & 2 \end{pmatrix}\begin{pmatrix} 1 & 2 & 3 & 4 \\ 3 & 2 & 4 & 1 \end{pmatrix}$

$= \begin{pmatrix} 1 & 2 & 3 & 4 \\ 2 & 3 & 1 & 4 \end{pmatrix}\begin{pmatrix} 2 & 3 & 1 & 4 \\ 4 & 2 & 1 & 3 \end{pmatrix}\begin{pmatrix} 1 & 2 & 3 & 4 \\ 3 & 2 & 4 & 1 \end{pmatrix}$

$= \begin{pmatrix} 1 & 2 & 3 & 4 \\ 4 & 2 & 1 & 3 \end{pmatrix}\begin{pmatrix} 4 & 2 & 1 & 3 \\ 1 & 2 & 3 & 4 \end{pmatrix}$

$= \begin{pmatrix} 1 & 2 & 3 & 4 \\ 1 & 2 & 3 & 4 \end{pmatrix}$

**154.** $c^2 = c \cdot c = \begin{pmatrix} 1 & 2 & 3 & 4 \\ 2 & 3 & 4 & 1 \end{pmatrix}\begin{pmatrix} 1 & 2 & 3 & 4 \\ 2 & 3 & 4 & 1 \end{pmatrix}$

$= \begin{pmatrix} 1 & 2 & 3 & 4 \\ 2 & 3 & 4 & 1 \end{pmatrix}\begin{pmatrix} 2 & 3 & 4 & 1 \\ 3 & 4 & 1 & 2 \end{pmatrix} = \begin{pmatrix} 1 & 2 & 3 & 4 \\ 3 & 4 & 1 & 2 \end{pmatrix}$

$= (1\ \ 3)(2\ \ 4)$

## Exercise 2

**1.** Under 'addition modulo 5' the composition table is

| $+_5$ | 1 | 2 | 3 | 4 |
|---|---|---|---|---|
| 1 | 2 | 3 | 4 | 0 |
| 2 | 3 | 4 | 0 | 1 |
| 3 | 4 | 0 | 1 | 2 |
| 4 | 0 | 1 | 2 | 3 |

$P_1$ : The above table shows that the sum of any two elements of the given set does not belong to the set e.g., $2 +_5 3 = 0$, which does not belong to the set $(1, 2, 3, 4)$. Hence, under the given operation the given set is not closed and so the given set does not form a group.

**2.** The subgroup $H$ of $G$ generated by a is given by

$H = \{a^r : r \in I\}$

where $I$ is the set of integers.

Let $\quad o(H) = m$

We can show that $H$ has exactly $m$ distinct elements $a, a^2, a^3, \ldots, a^m$ and that every element of $H$ is equal to one of these $m$ elements.

So, $\quad o(H) = o(a) = m$

By Lagrange's theorem

$o(H) | o(G)$

Hence, $\quad o(a) | o(G)$

**3.** The composition table is

| $+_4$ | 0 | 1 | 2 | 3 |
|---|---|---|---|---|
| 0 | 0 | 1 | 2 | 3 |
| 1 | 1 | 2 | 3 | 0 |
| 2 | 2 | 3 | 0 | 1 |
| 3 | 3 | 0 | 1 | 2 |

**Closure property** The above table shows that the sum of any two elements of the given set belongs to the set and therefore under the given operation the set is closed.

**Associative law** $(a + b) + c$ and $a + (b + c)$ both denote zero or the least non-negative integer obtained on dividing the ordinary sum of $a, b$ and $c$ by 4, *i.e.*, the composition is associative.

**Existence of identity** From the table it is evident that 0 is the identity.

**Existence of inverse** The inverses of 0, 1, 2, 3 are 0, 3, 2, 1 s

Since, $0+0=0$

$1+3=4\equiv 0 \pmod 4$

$2+2=4\equiv 0 \pmod 4$

$3+1=4\equiv 0 \pmod 4$

and which is also evident from the table.

**Commutativity law** $a+b=b+a$ for any two elements $a, b$ in the given set.

Hence, all the group postulates are satisfied and so the given is a finite abelian group of order 4 under the given composition.

**4.** The non-empty subset $H$ of $G$ is a subgroup of $G$ if it satisfies group axioms.

**Closure property** Closure property is already given because of the given condition.

$$a, b \in H \Rightarrow ab \in H$$

**Associative law** Since, $H$ is a subset of the group $G$, the associative law holds for all elements of $H$.

**Existence of inverse and identity** To prove existence of identity and inverse

Let $a \in H$, then by closure law, we have

$$a^2 \in H, a^3 \in H, \dots, a^n \in H, \dots \text{ i.e., } a, a^2, a^3, \dots, a^n, \dots \in H.$$

Since, $H$ is a finite subset of $G$, there must be repetitions in the elements stated above otherwise $H$ will become infinite.

Let $a^r = a^s$ for $r \neq s$ and $r > s > 0$

then $a^{r-s} = e$ (by cancellation law)

Also $a^{r-s} \in H$

$\therefore$ e, the identity element $\in H$

Clearly, $r-s \geq 1$

Therefore, $r-s-1 \geq 0$

Hence, $a^{r-s-1} \in H$

$\Rightarrow$ $a^{r-s} o\, a^{-1} \in H$

$\Rightarrow$ $e\, o\, a^{-1} \in H$

$\Rightarrow$ $a^{-1} \in H$ $\quad$ ($\because a^{r-s} = e$ already proved)

All the axioms of a group are satisfied and $H \subset G$ is a subgroup of $G$.

**5.** Let $o(G) = p$, where $p$ is a prime number.

Let $H$ be a subgroup of $G$ and let $o(H) = m$.

By Lagrange's theorem we know $o(H) | o(G)$

Hence, $m$ is a divisor of $p$.

Also, $p$ being prime, we find that either

$$m = 1 \text{ or } m = p$$

Now, $m = 1 \Rightarrow o(H) = 1 \Rightarrow H = \{e\}$

and $m = p \Rightarrow o(H) = o(G)$

$\Rightarrow H = G$

Hence, either $H = \{e\}$ or $H = G$

*i.e.,* $H$ is not a proper subgroup of $G$.

Hence, any group of prime order can have no proper subgroups.

**6.** Let $a \in G$ and let $n$ and $m$ be the orders of $a$ and $a^{-1}$, respectively.

Therefore, $a^n = e, (a^{-1})^m = e$ ...(i)

Now, $a^n = e \Rightarrow (a^n)^{-1} = e^{-1}$

$\Rightarrow (a^{-1})^n = e$

$\Rightarrow m \leq n$ (as $m$ is order of $a^{-1}$)

Again, $(a^{-1})^m = e \Rightarrow (a^m)^{-1} = e$

$\Rightarrow a^m = e$ $\quad [\because x^{-1} = e \Rightarrow x = e]$

$\Rightarrow n \leq m$ (as $n$ in order of $a$)

Thus, $m \leq n$ and $n \leq m \Rightarrow m = n$

**7.** Here,

$S = \{\alpha m : m \text{ fixed integer}, \alpha \in \mathbb{Z}\}$

$= \{\dots, -3m, -2m, -m, 0, m, 2m, 3m, \dots\}$

To prove that $S$ is a group it satisfies group postulate.

**Closure property** If $am$ and $bm$ be any two elements of $S$, where $a, b \in \mathbb{Z}$, then we get $am + bm = (a+b)m \in S$.

($\because a + b \in \mathbb{Z}$)

**Associativity law** $\forall\, abc \in \mathbb{Z}$, we get

$$am + (bm + cm) = am + (b + c)m$$
$$= (a + b + c)m \quad \text{...(i)}$$

and $(am + bm) + cm = (a + b)m + cm$

$= (a + b + c)m$

...(ii)

$\therefore$ From Eqs. (i) and (ii), we find that

$$am + (bm + cm) = (am + bm) + cm$$

Hence, the operation of addition is associative in $S$.

**Existence of identity** Since,

$$0 + \alpha m = \alpha m = \alpha m + 0, \forall\ \alpha m \in S$$

So, 0 is the identity of $S$ for addition.

**Existence of inverse** $\alpha m \in S$ is the inverse of $\alpha m \in S$. Since,

$$(\alpha m) + (\alpha m) = 0 = (\alpha m) + (-\alpha m)$$

Hence, the inverse of each elements of $S$ exists.

Since, all group postulates are satisfied and so the set $S$ forms a group under addition.

**8.** Let $n$ be a divisor of $m$.

Then, there exists an integer $q$ such that

$$nq = m$$

Now, $a^m = a^{nq} = (a^n)^q = e^q = e$

Conversely, let $a^m = e$

Since, $m$ is an integer and $n$ is a positive integer, therefore, by division algorithm there exists integers $q$ and $r$ such that

$$m = nq + r \text{ where } 0 \leq r < n$$

Now, $a^m = a^{nq+r} = a^{nq}\, a^r$

$= (a^n)^q \cdot a^r$

$= e^q \cdot a^r = a^r$

Hence, $a^m = e \Rightarrow a^r = e$

Since, $0 \leq r < n$, $a^r = e \Rightarrow r$ should be equal to zero because otherwise order of $a$ will not be equal to $n$. If order of $a$ is $n$, then there will exist no positive integer $r < n$ such that $a^r = e$.

Therefore, $m = nq \Rightarrow n$ is divisor of $m$.

**9.** Let $H_1$ and $H_2$ are two subgroups of a group.

(i) Let $H_1 \subseteq H_2$

or $H_2 \subseteq H_1$

Then, $H_1 \cup H_2 = H_2$ or $H_1$

Hence, $H_1 \cup H_2$ is a subgroup as $H_1$, $H_2$ are subgroups.

(ii) Suppose, $H_1 \cup H_2$ is a subgroup.

If possible let us assume that $H_1$ is not contained in $H$ or $H_2$ is not contained in $H_1$.

If $H_1$ is not contained in $H_2$

$\Rightarrow \quad a \in H_1$, and $a \notin H_2$ ...(i)

and $H_2$ is not contained in $H_1$

$\Rightarrow \quad b \in H_2$, and $b \notin H_1$ ...(ii)

Hence, from Eqs. (i) and (ii), we get

$$a \in H_1 \cup H_2 \text{ and } b \in H_1 \cup H_2$$

As $H_1 \cup H_2$ is a subgroup so $ab$ is also an element of $H_1 \cup H_2$.

But $\quad ab \in H_1 \cup H_2$

$\Rightarrow \quad ab \in H_1$

or $\quad ab \in H_2$

Let $ab \in H_1$, then $a^{-1}ab \in H_1$ as $a \in H_1$ and $H_1$ is a subgroup. So that $a^{-1}ab = b \in H_1$, which is a contradiction of the assumption that

$$b \notin H_1$$

Hence, either

$$H_1 \subseteq H_2 \text{ or } H_2 \subseteq H_1$$

**10.** Let the three consecutive integral values of $m$ be $n-1$, $n$ and $n+1$, then for

$$\forall\ a, b \in G$$

$$(ab)^{n-1} = a^{n-1}b^{n-1}$$

$$(ab)^n = a^n b^n$$

and $\quad (ab)^{n+1} = a^{n+1}b^{n+1}$

Now, $\quad (ab)^{n+1} = (ab)^n(ab)$

$\Rightarrow \quad a^{n+1}b^{n+1} = a^n b^n (ab)$

$(\because (ab)^m = a^m b^m$, for $m = n, n+1)$

$\Rightarrow \quad a^n ab^n b = a^n b^n ab$

$\Rightarrow \quad ab^n b = b^n ab$, (by left cancellation law)

$\Rightarrow \quad ab^n = b^n a$, (by right cancellation law)

$\Rightarrow \quad a^{n-1}(ab^n) = a^{n-1}(b^n a)$,

(multiplying both sides by $a^{n-1}$ on left)

$\Rightarrow \quad (a^{n-1}a)b^n = a^{n-1}(b^{n-1}ba)$ (by associative law)

$\Rightarrow \quad a^n b^n = a^{n-1}b^{n-1}(ba)$

$\Rightarrow \quad (ab)^n = (ab)^{n-1}(ba)$,

$(\because (ab)^m = a^m b^m$, for $m = n, n-1)$

$\Rightarrow \quad (ab)^{n-1}(ab) = (ab)^{n-1}(ba)$

$\Rightarrow \quad ab = ba$ (by left cancellation law)

Hence, $G$ is an abelian group.

**11.** We have, $\quad a^2 = a \Rightarrow \quad a \cdot a = a$

$\Rightarrow \quad (a \cdot a) \cdot a^{-1} = a \cdot a^{-1}$

(multiplying both sides by $a^{-1}$ on the right)

$\Rightarrow \quad a(a \cdot a^{-1}) = e^{-1}$ (by associative law and as $a \cdot a^{-1} = e$, the identity element)

$\Rightarrow \quad a \cdot e = e \Rightarrow a = e \quad (\because a \cdot e = a, \forall a \in G)$

**12.** We have,

$$(1\ 2\ 3 \ldots n) = \begin{pmatrix} 1 & 2 & 3 \ldots n-1 & n \\ 2 & 3 & 4 \ldots n & 1 \end{pmatrix}$$

and $(n\ n-1 \ldots 2\ 1) = \begin{pmatrix} n & n-1 & \ldots & 3 & 2 & 1 \\ n-1 & n-2 & \ldots & 2 & 1 & n \end{pmatrix}$

Hence, $(1\ 2\ 3 \quad n) o (n\ n-1 \quad 2\ 1)$

$$= \begin{pmatrix} 1 & 2 & \ldots & n-1 & n \\ 2 & 3 & \ldots & n & 1 \end{pmatrix} o \begin{pmatrix} n & n-1 & \ldots & 3 & 2 & 1 \\ n-1 & n-2 & \ldots & 2 & 1 & n \end{pmatrix}$$

$$= \begin{pmatrix} 1 & 2 & \ldots & n-1 & n \\ 2 & 3 & \ldots & n & 1 \end{pmatrix} o \begin{pmatrix} 2 & 3 & \ldots & n & 1 \\ 1 & 2 & \ldots & n-1 & n \end{pmatrix}$$

(rearranging columns of second permutation)

$$= \begin{pmatrix} 1 & 2 & \ldots & n-1 & n \\ 1 & 2 & \ldots & n-1 & n \end{pmatrix} = I$$

Hence, we have $(1\ 2\ 3 \ldots n)^{-1} = (n\ n-1 \ldots 2\ 1)$

**13.** Let the order of $a$.

$$o(a) = m$$

and $\quad o(a^p) = n$

Then, $\quad a^m = e$, the identity element

$\Rightarrow \quad (a^m)^p = e^p = e$

$\Rightarrow \quad a^{mp} = e$

$\Rightarrow \quad (a^p)^m = e$

$\Rightarrow \quad$ Order of $a^p$ is less than or equal to $m$.

Hence, the order of $a^p$ cannot be greater than $m$, the order of $a$.

**14.** Let $o(G) = n$ and let $a \in G$ be arbitrary. The elements $e$, $a, a^2, \ldots, a^n$ are $(n+1)$ in number and $o(G) = n$, and hence they are not all distinct. In other words, there exists $r, s$ with $1 \le r \le s \le n$ such that $a^r = a^s$.

Hence, $\quad e = a^r a^{-r} = a^{sa-r} = a^{s-r} = a^k$

where $k = s - r$, $1 \le k \le n$.

Therefore, $o(a)$ is finite.

**15.** Suppose, $H$ is a subgroup of $G$ and let

$$a \in H,\ b \in H$$

Now, each element of $H$ must possess inverse because $H$ itself is a group (assumption).

$$b \in H \Rightarrow b^{-1} \in H$$

Also, $H$ is closed under the composition ($o$ say) in $G$. Therefore,

$$a \in H,\ b^{-1} \in H \Rightarrow a\, o\, b^{-1} \in H$$

Let $\quad a \in H,\ b \in H \Rightarrow a\, o\, b^{-1} \in H$

then to show that $H$ is a subgroup it has to satisfy group postulate.

(i) **Closure property** Let $a, b \in H$, then

$$b \in H \Rightarrow b^{-1} \in H$$

Therefore, by the given condition

$$a \in H,\ b^{-1} \in H \Rightarrow a\, o\, (b^{-1})^{-1} \in H$$

$$\Rightarrow aob \in H$$

Thus, $H$ is closed with respect to the composition in $G$.

(ii) **Associativity law** Since, the elements of $H$ are also the elements of $G$, the composition is associative in $H$.

(iii) **Existence of identity** Since,

$$a \in H,\ a^{-1} \in H \Rightarrow aoa^{-1} \in H$$

$\Rightarrow$ $e \in H$

Identity element $e \in H$

(iv) **Existence of inverse** Let $a \in H$, then

$$e \in H,\ a \in H \Rightarrow eoa^{-1} \in H$$

$\Rightarrow$ $a^{-1} \in H$

Each element of $H$ possesses inverse.

Hence, $H$ itself is a group for the composition $o$ in group $G$.

**16.** We have, $m > n$

So let $m = np + r$

where $0 \le r < n$

If $a^m = e$

then $a^{np+n} = e$

or $(a^n)^p \cdot a^r = e$

or $a^r = e$

Since, $a^n = e$

*i.e.*, the order of $a$ is $n$.

But the order of $a$ is $n$ and $r$ is less than $n$ so it is not possible.

Hence, $r = 0$ and so $m = np$.

**17.** We have, $a \in Hb$

$\Rightarrow$ $ab^{-1} \in Hbb^{-1}$

$\Rightarrow$ $ab^{-1} \in He$ $(\because bb^{-1} = e)$

$\Rightarrow$ $ab^{-1} \in H$ $(\because He = H)$

$\Rightarrow$ $Hab^{-1} = H$

$\Rightarrow$ $Hab^{-1}b = Hb$

(multiplying both sides on the left by $b$)

$\Rightarrow$ $Hae = Hb$ $(\because b^{-1}b = e)$

$\Rightarrow$ $Ha = Hb$ $(\because ae = a)$

Conversely, let $Ha = Hb$

Since, $a \in Ha$

therefore, $a \in Hb$

**18.** Let $(a \cdot b)^2 = a^2 \cdot b^2$

$\Rightarrow$ $(a \cdot b) \cdot (a \cdot b) = (a \cdot a) \cdot (b \cdot b)$

$\Rightarrow$ $a \cdot (b \cdot a) \cdot b = a(a \cdot b) \cdot b$ (by associative law)

$\Rightarrow$ $a \cdot (b \cdot a) = a \cdot (a \cdot b)$ (by right cancellation law)

$\Rightarrow$ $b \cdot a = a \cdot b$ (by left cancellation law)

Hence, $G$ is abelian.

Conversely,

Let $G$ is abelian.

$\Rightarrow$ $b \cdot a = a \cdot b,\ \forall\ a, b \in G$

$\Rightarrow$ $a \cdot (b \cdot a) = a \cdot (a \cdot b)$,

(multiplying both sides on the left by $a$)

$\Rightarrow$ $a \cdot (b \cdot a) \cdot b = a \cdot (a \cdot b) \cdot b$,

(multiplying both sides on the right by $b$)

$\Rightarrow$ $(a \cdot b) \cdot (a \cdot b) = (a \cdot a) \cdot (b \cdot b)$, (by associative law)

$\Rightarrow$ $(a \cdot b)^2 = a^2 \cdot b^2$

Hence, $(a \cdot b)^2 = a^2 \cdot b^2,\ \forall\ a, b \in G$

iff $G$ is abelian.

**19.** Let $o(G) = n$

Let $a \in G$ and $o(a) = m$, $m$ is even

Let $H = \{a^r : r \text{ any integer}\}$

be a subgroup of $G$ generated by $a$.

Then, $o(H) = o(a) = m$

Hence, by Lagrange's theorem

$$o(H) \mid o(G) = m \mid n \text{ as } m \text{ is even}$$

Hence, $n$ must be even, *i.e.*, $o(G)$ is to be even.

**20.** We have $I_4 = \{\{0\}, \{1\}, \{2\}, \{3\}\}$

The identity element of $\{I_4, +_4\}$ is $\{0\}$

Also, $\{0\} = \{0\}$

Hence, $\{0\}$ has order one.

$$\{1\} +_4 \{1\} = \{2\} \ne \{0\}$$

$$\{1\} +_4 \{1\} +_4 \{1\} = \{2\} +_4 \{1\} = \{3\} \ne \{0\}$$

But $\{1\} +_4 \{1\} +_4 \{1\} +_4 \{1\} = 3 +_4 \{1\} = \{0\}$,

$[\because 3 + 1 \equiv 0 \pmod 4]$

Hence, order of $\{1\}$ is 4.

Again, $\{2\} +_4 \{2\} = \{0\}$, as $2 + 2 \equiv (\text{mod} 4)$

Hence, order of $\{2\}$ is 2.

And $\{3\} +_4 \{3\} +_4 \{3\} +_4 \{3\} = \{0\}$

as $3 + 3 + 3 + 3 = 0 \pmod 4$

Hence, order of $\{3\}$ is 4.

**21.** Suppose that $\mathbb{C}$ be ordered, *i.e.*, the non-zero elements of $\mathbb{C}$ can be divided into two subsets $\mathbb{C}_+$ and $\mathbb{C}_-$ satisfying the conditions of ordered integral domain.

For every $i \in \mathbb{C} \Rightarrow i \ne 0$ and $i = \sqrt{-1}$.

Hence, $i \in \mathbb{C}$ and $i \in \mathbb{C}_-$

$i \in \mathbb{C}_+ \Rightarrow i \cdot i = -1 \in \mathbb{C}_+$

But $\mathbb{C}$ has the multiplicative identity 1 and as such $1 \in \mathbb{C}_+$.

Also, $1 \in \mathbb{C}_+ \Rightarrow -1 \in \mathbb{C}_-$

Thus, $i \in \mathbb{C}_+ \Rightarrow -1 \in \mathbb{C}_+$ and $-1 \in \mathbb{C}_-$

which is impossible.

Hence, $i \notin \mathbb{C}_+$.

Now, $i \in \mathbb{C}_- \Rightarrow i \cdot i = -1 \in \mathbb{C}_+$

which also, as argued above, is impossible.

Thus, $i \notin \mathbb{C}_-$

Hence, we conclude that if $\mathbb{C}$ is ordered, then neither $i$ is in $\mathbb{C}_+$ nor in $\mathbb{C}_-$, which is absurd.

Therefore, our assumption is wrong and consequently $\mathbb{C}$ is not ordered.

**22.** Under 'multiplication modulo 5', the composition table is

| $\bullet_5$ | 1 | 2 | 3 | 4 |
|---|---|---|---|---|
| 1 | 1 | 2 | 3 | 4 |
| 2 | 2 | 4 | 1 | 3 |
| 3 | 3 | 1 | 4 | 2 |
| 4 | 4 | 3 | 2 | 1 |

**Closure property** This table shows that the product of any two elements of the given set under multiplication modulo

5 as composition belongs to the set and therefore, under the given operation the set is closed.

**Associative law** $(a\cdot b)\cdot c$ and $a\cdot(b\cdot c)$ both denote zero or the least non-negative integer obtained on dividing the ordinary multiplication of $a, b$ and $c$ by 5, *i.e.*, the composition is associative.

**Existence of identity** From the table it is evident that 1 is the identity.

**Existence of inverse** The inverse of 1, 2, 3 and 4 are 1, 3, 2 and 4 respectively, because $1\cdot 1=1, 2\cdot 3=6\equiv 1 \pmod 5$, $3\cdot 2\equiv 1 \pmod 5$ and $4\cdot 4=1 \pmod 5$. This is also evident from the composition table.

**Commutative law** $a\cdot b=b\cdot a$

for any two elements $a, b$ in the given set.

Hence, all the group postulates are satisfied and so the given set is a finite abelian group of order 4 under multiplication.

**23.** Let $n'$ be the order of $a^p$.

Then, we have $n'\le n$ ...(i)

Again, $p$ is prime to $n$, so there exist integers $\alpha$ and $\beta$ such that

$$\alpha n+\beta n=1$$

Hence, we can write

$$a=a'=a^{\alpha n+\beta n}=a^{\alpha p}\cdot a^{\beta n}$$
$$=a^{\alpha p}$$

as $a^n=e$, then identity element

$$=(a^p)^\alpha.$$

Hence, $a$ is a power of $a^p$, hence, we have

$$n\le n' \quad \text{...(ii)}$$

$\Rightarrow$ From Eqs. (i) and (ii), we have

$$n'=n$$

**24.** Let e be the identity element of the group.

If possible let $a\ne e$ be an element of order one of this group. Then, by the definition of order of an element of a group, we have

$$a^{-1}=e \text{ or } a=e$$

which is the contradiction to assumption that

$$a\ne e.$$

Hence, the identity element e is the only element of order one in any group.

**25.** The set of $n$th roots of unity be given by

$$S=\{e^{2r\pi i/n}, r=0,1,2,\ldots(n-1)\}$$

$S$ is multiplication group if it satisfies group axioms.

**Closure property** Let

$$a, b\in S$$

and $a=e^{2r_1\pi i/n}, r_1\le(n-1)$

$b=e^{2r_2\pi i/n}, r_2\le(n-1)$

Thus, $ab=e^{2(r_1+r_2)\pi i/n}\in S$

If $r_1+r_2\le(n-1)$

But, if $r_1+r_2>(n-1)$,

then let $r_1+r_2=n+\lambda, \lambda\le(n-2)$

Then, $ab=e^{2(r_1+r_2)\pi i/n}$

$$=e^{2(n+\lambda)\pi i/n}$$
$$=e^{2\lambda\pi i/n} \quad (\because e^{2ni}=1)$$

or $ab\in S$ as $\lambda\le(n-2)$

Thus, the multiplication is a binary operation in $S$.

**Associativity law** Also, the elements of $S$ are complex numbers and the multiplication of complex numbers is associative.

**Existence of identity** The identity for multiplication exists and is

$$e^{2\cdot 0\cdot\pi i/n}=1$$

**Existence of inverse** The inverse of any element $e^{2\pi i/n}$ is $e^{2\pi i(n-r)^n}$, since

$$e^{2\pi i}=1$$

Hence, $S$ form a group.

**26.** The identity element in this group

$$e=0$$

Hence, order of $(0)=1$

Here, $2(1)=1+_6 1=2$

$3(1)=1+_6 1+_6 1=1+_6 2(1)$

$=1+_6 2=3$

$4(1)=1+_6 3(1)$

$=1+_6 3=4$

$5(1)=1+_6 4(1)$

$=1+_6 4=5$

and $6=(1)=1+_6 5(1)$

$=1+_6 5=0=e$

Hence, $o(1)=6$

Proceeding in similar way, we have

$\because$ $3(2)=2+_6 2+_6 2=0$

$\Rightarrow$ Order of $(2)=3$

$\because$ $2(3)=3+_6 3=0$

$\Rightarrow$ $(3)=2$

$\because$ $3(4)=4+_6 4=0$

$\Rightarrow$ Order of $(4)=3$

$\because$ $6(5)=5+_6 5+_6 5+_6 5+_6 5+_6 5$

$=0$

$\Rightarrow$ Order of $(5)=6$

**27.** Let $H_1$ and $H_2$ are two subgroups of group $G$.

Let $a\in H_1\cap H_2$ and $b\in H_1\cap H_2$

Then, $a\in H_1\cap H_2$, $b\in H_1\cap H_2$

$\Rightarrow$ $a\in H_1$, $a\in H_2$ and $b\in H_1$, $b\in H_2$

$\Rightarrow$ $a\in H_1$, $b\in H_1$ and $a\in H_2$, $b\in H_2$

$\Rightarrow$ $ab^{-1}\in H_1$ and $ab^{-1}\in H_2$

($\because$ $H_1$ and $H_2$ are subgroups)

$\Rightarrow$ $ab^{-1}\in H_1\cap H_2$

Hence, $H_1\cap H_2$ is a subgroup.

**28.** Let the order of a be $n$, then $a^n=e$.

Now, $(b^{-1}ab)^2=(b^{-1}ab)(b^{-1}ab)$

$=b^{-1}a(bb^{-1})ab$

$=b^{-1}aeab=b^{-1}a^2b$

In general, we have

$$(b^{-1}ab)^r = (b^{-1}ab)(b^{-1}ab)\ldots(b^{-1}ab) \text{ (r factors)}$$
$$= b^{-1}a(bb^{-1})a(bb^{-1})\ldots(bb^{-1})ab$$
$$= b^{-1}a^r b \neq e.$$

For $0 < r < n$

Also, $(b^{-1}ab)^n = b^{-1}a^n b$

$$= b^{-1}eb = b^{-1}b = e$$

Thus, $n$ is the least positive integer such that

$$(b^{-1}ab)^n = e$$

Hence, order of $(b^{-1}ab)$ is same as the order of $a$.

**29.** (a) For scalar product: If $\bar{a}, \bar{b} \in S$

$\Rightarrow$ $\bar{a}\cdot\bar{b} = ab \notin S$, an scalar,

*i.e.*, scalar product of two vectors is a scalar.

Since, closure property is dissatisfied.

Thus, for scalar product $S$ is not a group.

(b) For vector product:

$$\bar{a}, \bar{b}, \bar{c} \in S$$
$$(\bar{a}\times\bar{b})\times\bar{c} = \bar{a}\times(\bar{b}\times\bar{c})$$

Associativity is not satisfied, $(S, \times)$ is not a group.

**30.** The fourth roots of units are $(1, -1, i, -i)$ and there composition table is

| | +1 | −1 | +i | −i |
|---|---|---|---|---|
| +1 | 1 | −1 | +i | −i |
| −1 | −1 | 1 | −i | +i |
| +i | +i | −i | −1 | +1 |
| −i | −i | +i | +1 | −1 |

They forms a multiplicative group if they satisfy group axioms.

**Closure property** Composition table shows that the product of any two elements of the given set under multiplication belongs to the set, and therefore, the given set is closed under multiplication.

**Associativity law** The multiplication of complex numbers is associative *e.g.*,

$$(1\cdot i) : (-i) = i\cdot(-i) = +1$$

and $1\cdot[(i)\cdot(-i)] = 1\cdot(+1) = +1$

$\therefore$ $(1\cdot i)(-i) = 1[(i)\cdot(-i)]$

*i.e.*, the associative law holds.

**Existence of identity** From the table it is evident that +1 is the identity.

**Existence of inverse** From the table the inverse of $1, -1, +i$ and $-i$ are $1, -1, -i$ and $+i$ respectively, since

$$1\cdot 1 = 1$$
$$(-1)\cdot(-1) = 1$$
$$(+i)\cdot(-i) = 1$$
$$(-i)\cdot(+i) = 1$$

**Commutativity law**

$$x\cdot y = y\cdot x, \ \forall\ x, y \text{ belonging to the given set.}$$

Hence, all the group postulates are satisfied.

Therefore, given set is a finite abelian group under multiplication.

**31.** (i) Let $o(a) = n$

and $o(a^k) = m$

Therefore, $a^n = e$ and $(a^k)^m = e$

So, $(a^k)^n = (a^n)^k$

$$= e^k$$
$$= e$$

But $m$ is the smallest positive integer for which

$$(a^k)m = e$$

So, $m \le n$

(ii) Let $o(a) = n$ and $o(a^{-1}) = m$

Now, $(a^{-1})^n = a^{-n}$

$$= (a^n)^{-1} = e^{-1}$$
$$= e$$

Hence, $m \le n$

Similarly, $a^m = ((a^{-1})^{-1})^m$

$$= (a^{-1})^m = e^{-1}$$
$$= e$$

and so $n \le m$

Therefore, $m = n$ and this completes the proof.

**32.** The identity of the multiplicative group of integers modulo 5 is $\{1\}$.

Here, $\{3\}._5\{3\} = 4$

$$\neq \{1\} \qquad [\because 3\cdot 3 \equiv 4 \pmod 5)]$$

Hence, $\{3\}._5\{3\}._5\{3\} = \{4\}._5\{3\}$

$$= \{2\} \neq \{1\} \qquad [\because 4\cdot 3 \equiv 2 \pmod 5)]$$

$\Rightarrow$ $\{3\}._5\{3\}._5\{3\}._5\{3\} = \{2\}._5\{3\}$

$$= \{1\} \qquad [\because 2\cdot 3 \equiv (\text{mod } 5)]$$

Hence, the order of $\{3\}$ is 4.

**33.** Let $H$ be the normal subgroup of a group $G$ and $K$ be any complex of the group. Let $hk$ be an arbitrary element of $HK$ so that $e \in H$ and $k \in K$.

Also, $hk = kk^{-1}hk = (k^{-1}hk)$ ...(i)

Now, $k \in K,\ h \in H$

$\Rightarrow$ $k \in G,\ h \in H$

$\Rightarrow$ $k^{-1} \in G, h \in H$

$\Rightarrow$ $k^{-1}h(k^{-1})^{-1} \in H$ (since, $H$ is normal in $G$)

$\Rightarrow$ $k^{-1}hk \in H$ [by Eq. (i)]

$hk = k(k^{-1}hk) \in KH$ [$\because$ $k \in K$ and $k^{-1}hk \in H$]

Thus, $hk \in HK$

$\Rightarrow$ $hk \in KH$

$\Rightarrow$ $HK \subseteq KH$ ...(ii)

Again, let $kh \in KH$ such that $k \in K$ and $h \in H$.

Also, $kh = khk^{-1}k = (khk^{-1})k$ ...(iii)

But $k \in K,\ h \in H$

$\Rightarrow$ $khk^{-1} \in H$ [$\because$ $H$ is normal in $G$]

Hence, from Eq. (iii),

$$kh = (khk^{-1})k \in HK$$

[$\because$ $khk^{-1} \in H$ and $k \in K$]

Thus, $kh \in KH$

$\Rightarrow$ $kh \in HK$ ...(iv)

Hence, from Eqs. (ii) and (iv), we get

$$HK = KH$$

**34.** Let $x_1, x_2$ be the two arbitrary elements of $K$.

Then, $x_1H = Hx_1$

and $x_2H = Hx_2$ ...(i)

We shall first show that

$$x_2^{-1} \in K$$

Here, $x_2H = Hx_2$

$\Rightarrow$ $x_2^{-1}(x_2H)x_2^{-1} = x_2^{-1}(Hx_2)x_2^{-1}$

$\Rightarrow$ $Hx_2^{-1} = x_2^{-1}H$ ...(ii)

$\Rightarrow$ $x_2^{-1} \in K$

Now, we shall show that

$$x_1x_2^{-1} \in K$$

Here, $(x_1x_2^{-1})H = x_1(x_2^{-1}H)$ (by associative law)

$= x_1(Hx_2^{-1})$ [from Eq. (ii)]

$= (x_1H)x_2^{-1}$ (by associative law)

$= (Hx_1)x_2^{-1}$ [from Eq. (i)]

$= H(x_1x_2^{-1})$ (by associative law)

$\Rightarrow$ $x_1x_2^{-1} \in K$

$\Rightarrow$ $x_1, x_2 \in K$

$\Rightarrow$ $x_1x_2^{-1} \in K$

Hence, $K$ is a subgroup of $G$.

**35.** Let $m$ be order of $H$, the only subgroup of finite order of a group $G$.

Let $x \in G$, then $xH^{-1}$ is a subgroup.

Suppose $H = \{h_1, h_2, \ldots, h_m\}$

Hence, $xI\,Ix^{-1} = \{xh_1x^{-1}, xh_2x^{-1}, \ldots, xh_mx^{-1}\}$

The elements in $xH^{-1}$ are distinct because if not, then

$$xh_ix^{-1} = xh_jx^{-1}$$

$\Rightarrow$ $h_i = h_j$ (by cancellation)

for $i \neq j$

which is contradictory to the fact that

$$h_i \neq h_j \text{ in } Hf \text{ for } i \neq j$$

Thus, $o(xH^{-1}) = o(H) = m$

But $H$ is the only subgroup of finite order in $G$, hence

$$xHx^{-1} = H$$

Therefore, $H$ is normal in $G$.

**36.** (a) **Closure property** $a - b \in Z, \forall\ a, b \in Z$

(b) **Associativity law** $a, b, c \in Z$

$$(a-b)-c \neq a-(b-c)$$

Hence, set of integers $Z$ is not a group on defined operation.

**37.** If $a, b \in G \Rightarrow a^{-1}, b^{-1} \in G$

and as $(a*b) \in G \Rightarrow (a*b)^{-1} \in G$

For $a = a^{-1}$ and $b = b^{-1}$ and

$$(a*b) = (a*b)^{-1} = b^{-1}*a^{-1} = (b*a)$$

Hence, $(G, *)$ is an abelian group.

**38.** For additive group of integers, 0 is an identity element and $o(0) = 1$ as $0' = 0$

There exist no positive integer $n$ which gives

$$na = 0 \text{ for } (a \neq 0).$$

Hence, order of every element except 0 is infinite.

**39.** $(\{0\}, +)$ is a group as

(a) **Closure property** $0 + 0 = 0 \in S$

(b) **Associativity law** $(0+0)+0 = 0+(0+0)$

(c) **Existence of identity '0'** $0+0 = 0 \in S$

(d) **Existence of inverse '0'** $0+0 = 0 \in S$

**40.** $(G, *)$ is commutative, $a^{-1}, b^{-1} \in G$

$\Rightarrow$ $a^{-1}*b^{-1} = b^{-1}*a^{-1}$ ...(i)

and $(a*b)^{-1} = b^{-1}*a^{-1}$ ...(ii)

By Eqs. (i) and (ii), we get

$$(a*b)^{-1} = a^{-1}*b^{-1}$$

Conversely, let

$(a*b)^{-1} = a^{-1}*b^{-1}, \forall\, a, b \in G$ ...(iii)

By Eqs. (ii) and (iii), we have

$$a^{-1}*b^{-1} = b^{-1}*a^{-1}, \forall\, a, b \in G$$

$\Rightarrow$ $*$ is commutative.

$\Rightarrow$ The group $(G, *)$ is abelian.

**41.** $p$ is a prime number, its divisors are only $\pm 1$ and $\pm p$.

Let $H$ be a subgroup of $G$, by Lagrange's theorem $o(H) \cdot o(G)$ is a divisor of $p$.

$\Rightarrow$ $o(H) = p$ or 1

$\Rightarrow$ $H = G$ or $H = \{e\}$

$\Rightarrow$ $H$ is not a subgroup of $G$ in either case.

Hence, $G$ does not possess proper subgroup.

**42.** $(-2)\cdot(2) = -4 \notin S$, closure property not satisfied.

Hence, $S$ is not a group.

**43.** $G$ have an identity element 1

$$(1)^1 = 1 \Rightarrow o(1) = 1$$

and $(-1)^2 = 1 \Rightarrow o(-1) = 2$

Thus, order of 1 is 1 and $(-1)$ is 2.

**44.** Let $o(G) = n$

Let $a \in G$ and $o(a) = m$, $m$ is even

Let $H = \{a^r : r \text{ any integer}\}$

be a subgroup of $G$ generated by $a$.

Then, $o(H) = o(a) = m$

Hence, by Lagrange's theorem

$$o(H) \mid o(G) = m \mid n \text{ as } m \text{ is even}$$

$\Rightarrow$ $n$ must be even, i.e., $o(G)$ is to be even.

**45.** For all $a, b \in G$, we have

$$(ab)^2 = a^2b^2$$

i.e., $(ab)(ab) = (aa)(bb)$

i.e., $a(ba)b = a(ab)b$

i.e., $a(ba) = a(ab)$ (by right cancellation)

i.e., $ba = ab$ (by left cancellation)

Therefore, $G$ is abelian.

**46.** (i) Let $n=0$

If $n=0$, then $e^n = e^0 = e$

(ii) Let $n>0$, (*i.e.*, $n$ is a positive integer)

Let $e^n = e$ be true for $n=m$ *i.e.*, $e^m = e$

Now, $e^{m+1} = e^m \cdot e^1 = e^m \cdot e = e \cdot e$ $(\because e^m = e)$

or $e^{m+1} = e$ $(\because a \cdot e = a, \forall a \in G)$

This shows that $e^n = e$ is true for $n=m+1$, if it is true for $n=m$.

Obviously, $e^1 = e$ *i.e.*, $e^n = e$ is true for $n=1$.

Hence, it is true for $n=1+1$ *i.e.*, 2 if it is true for $n=1$ and proceeding in this way we can show that it is true for $n=3, 4$ etc.

Hence, $e^n = e$ is true fo all positive integral values of $n$.

(iii) Let $n<0$ (*i.e.*, $n$ is a negative integer)

Let $n=-k$, where $k$ is a positive integer.

Then, $e^n = e^{-k} = (e^k)^{-1} = (e)^{-1}$ $(\because e^k = e)$

For $k>0 = e^{-1} = e$

Hence, in any group $e^n = e$ for any integer $n$.

**47.** $G$ is a cyclic group, if there exist $a \in G : o(a) = o(G) = 4$.

Since, 1 is an identity element of $G$.

$$i^1 = i, i^2 = -1, i^3 = -1, i^4 = 1$$

Hence, $o(i) = 4 = o(G)$

Hence, the given set $G$ forms a cyclic group and $i$ is its generator.

Hence, $G$ is also expressible as $\{i, i^2, i^3, i^4\}$.

Also, $-i^1 = -i, (-i)^2 = -1, (-i)^3 = i, (-i)^4 = 1$

$\Rightarrow$ $o(i) = 4 = o(G)$

$(-i)$ is also a generator and $G$ is expressible as $\{(-i)^4, (-i)^3, (-i)^2, -i\}$.

**48.** Let $o(G) = n$, $G$ is a finite group.

Let $G$ be a union of two of its proper subgroups $H_1$ and $H_2$, *i.e.*, $G = H_1 \cup H_2$

Since, $e \in H_1$ and $e \in H_2$ and $G = H_1 \cup H_2$, therefore, atleast one of $H_1$ and $H_2$ must contain more than half the elements of $G$. Let it be $H_1$.

Then, $o(H_1) = m, \frac{n}{2} < m < n$

Now, as $\frac{n}{2} < m < n, \; m \nmid n$

But by Lagrange theorem $o(H_1) | o(G)$ *i.e.*, $m | n$ which is a contradiction.

Thus, $G \neq H_1 \cup H_2$.

**49.** Let $o(G) = p$, $p$ is a prime number.

Let $H$ be a subgroup of $G$ and let $o(H) = m$.

By Lagrange's theorem $o(H) | o(G) \Rightarrow m | p$

Since, $p$ is a prime number.

Hence, $m = 1$ or $p$

If $m = 1 \Rightarrow o(H) = 1 \Rightarrow H = \{e\}$

If $m = p \Rightarrow o(H) = o(G) \Rightarrow H = G$

$\Rightarrow$ Either $H = \{e\}$ or $H = G$,

*i.e.*, $H$ is not a proper subgroup of $G$.

Hence, any group of prime order can have no proper subgroup.

**50.** Let $x_1, x_2$ be two arbitrary elements of $K$.

Then, $x_1H = Hx_1$

and $x_2H = Hx_2$ ...(i)

We shall first show that

$$x_2^{-1} \in K$$

Here, $x_2H = Hx_2$

$\Rightarrow$ $x_2^{-1}(x_2H)x_2^{-1} = x_2^{-1}(Hx_2)x_2^{-1}$

$\Rightarrow$ $Hx_2^{-1} = x_2^{-1}H$ ...(ii)

$\Rightarrow$ $x_2^{-1} \in K$

Now, we shall show that

$$x_1x_2^{-1} \in K$$

Here, $(x_1x_2^{-1})H = x_1(x_2^{-1}H)$ (by associative law)

$= x_1(Hx_2^{-1})$ [from Eq. (ii)]

$= (x_1H)x_2^{-1}$ (by associative law)

$= (Hx_1)x_2^{-1}$ [from Eq. (i)]

$= H(x_1x_2^{-1})$ (by associative law)

$\Rightarrow$ $x_1x_2^{-1} \in K$

$\Rightarrow$ $x_1, x_2 \in K$

$\Rightarrow$ $x_1x_2^{-1} \in K$

Here, $K$ is a subgroup of $G$.

**51.** Let $a^{-1}H = b^{-1}H$, then

$a^{-1}H = b^{-1}H \Leftrightarrow (b^{-1})^{-1}a^{-1} \in H$

$\Leftrightarrow ba^{-1} \in H$

$\Leftrightarrow (ba^{-1})^{-1} \in H$

$\Leftrightarrow (a^{-1})^{-1}b^{-1} \in H$

$\Leftrightarrow ab^{-1} \in H$

$\Leftrightarrow Ha = Hb$

Since, $Ha = Hb \Leftrightarrow ab^{-1} \in H$

which is a contradiction.

Hence, $Ha \neq Hb \Rightarrow a^{-1}H \neq b^{-1}H$

Similarly, $a^{-1}H \neq b^{-1}H \Rightarrow Ha \neq Hb$

Hence, $Ha \neq Hb \Leftrightarrow a^{-1}H \neq b^{-1}H$

**52.** Let $H$ be a subgroup of the group $G$ and $a, b$ be any two arbitrary elements of $G$ such that

$$Ha = Hb.$$

Now, if e be the identity element, then

$$e \in H \Rightarrow ea \in Ha \Rightarrow a \in Ha$$

$\Rightarrow$ $Ha = Hb \Rightarrow a \in Hb$

Since, $a \in Ha$ and $Ha = Hb$

$\Rightarrow$ $ab^{-1} \in (Hb)b^{-1}$

$\Rightarrow$ $ab^{-1} \in H(bb^{-1})$ (by associative law)

$\Rightarrow$ $ab^{-1} \in He$ $(\because bb^{-1} = e)$

$\Rightarrow$ $ab^{-1} \in H$ $(\because He = H)$ ...(i)

Conversely, let $H$ be a subgroup of the group $G$ and $a, b$ be any two arbitrary element of $G$ such that

$$ab^{-1} \in H$$

Then, we are to prove that $Ha = Hb$

Now, $ab^{-1} \in H \Rightarrow Hab^{-1} = H$ $(\because h \in H$, then $Hh = H)$

$\Rightarrow$ $Hab^{-1}b = Hb$ (multiplying both sides on the left by $b$)

$\Rightarrow$ $Hae = Hb$ $(\because b^{-1}b = e)$

$\Rightarrow \quad Ha = Hb \quad (\because ae = a) \quad ...(ii)$

Hence, from Eqs. (i) and (ii), we get

$$Ha = Hb \Leftrightarrow ab^{-1} \in H$$

**53.** Let $H$ be a subgroup of a group $G$ and $a, b \in G$.

If there is no element common to $aH$ and $bH$,

then $\quad aH \cap bH = \phi$, then null set.

i.e., $\quad aH$ and $bH$ are disjoint.

If there is an element $c$ (say) common to $aH$ and $bH$, then we have

$$c = ah_1, h_1 \in H$$
$$c = bh_2, h_2 \in H$$

Hence, $\quad ah_1 = bh_2$

$\Rightarrow \quad (ah_1)h_2^{-1} = (bh_2)h_2^{-1}$

$\Rightarrow \quad a(h_1h_2^{-1}) = b(h_2h_2^{-1})$

$\Rightarrow \quad a(h_1h_2^{-1}) = b$

$\Rightarrow \quad a^{-1}a(h_1h_2^{-1}) = a^{-1}b$

$\Rightarrow \quad (a^{-1}a)(h_1h_2^{-1}) = a^{-1}b$

$\Rightarrow \quad h_1h_2^{-1} = a^{-1}b$

Hence, $\quad a^{-1}b \in H$, since $h_1h_2^{-1} \in H$

Hence, $\quad aH = bH$

Hence, two left cosets which are not disjoint are identical.

**54.** First of all note that

$$K_f \neq \phi$$

Since, $\quad e \in K_f$

We now check that $K_f < G$

For this purpose, let $a, b \in K_f$

Then, $\quad f(a) = \bar{e}$

and $\quad f(b) = \bar{e}$

Now, $\quad f(ab^{-1}) = f(a)f(b^{-1})$

$\quad = \bar{e}f(b)^{-1}$

$\quad = \bar{e}\bar{e}^{-1}$

$\quad = \bar{e}$

Hence $\quad ab^{-1} \in K_f$

and thus $\quad K_f < G$

For the normality of $K_f$, we have to show that for every

$$a \in G$$

and $\quad k \in K_f$

$$aka^{-1} \in K_f$$

Now, let $\quad a \in G$

and $\quad k \in K_f$

Then $\quad f(aka^{-1}) = f(a)f(k)f(a^{-1})$

$\quad = f(a)\bar{e}f(a)^{-1}$

$\quad = f(a)f(a)^{-1}$

$\quad = \bar{e}$

**55.** Let $H$ be a subgroup of the group $G$ and $a, b$ be any two arbitrary elements of $G$ such that $Ha = Hb$.

Now, if $e$ be the identity element, then

$$e \in H \Rightarrow ea \in Ha \Rightarrow a \in Ha$$

Hence, $Ha = Hb \Rightarrow a \in Hb$

Since, $\quad a \in Ha$ and $Ha = Hb$

$\Rightarrow \quad ab^{-1} \in (Hb)b^{-1}$

$\Rightarrow \quad ab^{-1} \in H(bb^{-1})$, (by associative law)

$\Rightarrow \quad ab^{-1} \in He \quad (\because bb^{-1} = e)$

$\Rightarrow \quad ab^{-1} \in H \quad (\because He = H) \quad ...(i)$

Conversely, let $H$ be a subgroup of the group $G$ and $a, b$ are any two arbitrary element of $G$ such that $ab^{-1} \in H$.

Then, we are to prove that $Ha = Hb$

Now, $ab^{-1} \in H \Rightarrow Hab^{-1} = H \quad (\because h \in H$, then $Hh = H)$

$\Rightarrow \quad Hab^{-1} = Hb$, (Multiplying both sides on the left by $b$)

$\Rightarrow \quad Hae = Hb \quad (\because b^{-1}b = e)$

$\Rightarrow \quad Ha = Hb \quad (\because ae = a) \quad ...(ii)$

$\therefore$ From Eqs. (i) and (ii), we get

$$Ha = Hb \Leftrightarrow ab^{-1} \in H$$

**56.** By Cayley's theorem the possible permutations are

$$P_1 = \begin{pmatrix} 1 & \omega & \omega^2 \\ 1\cdot 1 & 1\cdot\omega & 1\cdot\omega^2 \end{pmatrix}$$

$$= \begin{pmatrix} 1 & \omega & \omega^2 \\ 1 & \omega & \omega^2 \end{pmatrix} = 1$$

$$P_2 = \begin{pmatrix} 1 & \omega & \omega^2 \\ \omega\cdot 1 & \omega\cdot\omega & \omega\cdot\omega^2 \end{pmatrix}$$

$$= \begin{pmatrix} 1 & \omega & \omega^2 \\ \omega & \omega^2 & 1 \end{pmatrix} \quad (\because \omega^3 = 1)$$

$$= (1 \;\; \omega \;\; \omega^2)$$

$$P_3 = \begin{pmatrix} 1 & \omega & \omega^2 \\ \omega^2\cdot 1 & \omega^2\cdot\omega & \omega^2\cdot\omega^2 \end{pmatrix}$$

$$= \begin{pmatrix} 1 & \omega & \omega^2 \\ \omega^2 & 1 & \omega \end{pmatrix} \quad (\because \omega^3 = 1)$$

$$= \begin{pmatrix} \omega^2 & \omega & 1 \\ \omega & 1 & \omega^2 \end{pmatrix} = (\omega^2 \;\; \omega \;\; 1)$$

Hence, the regular permutation group isomorphic to the group $G$ is

$$G_1 = \{1, (1 \;\; \omega \;\; \omega^2), (\omega^2 \;\; \omega \;\; 1)\}$$

**57.** $\because \; H \subseteq K$ are subgroups of a group $G$.

Hence, $H$ is also a subgroup of $K$.

Since, $H$ is a subgroup of finite group $G$.

By Lagrange's theorem

$$[G:H] = \frac{o(G)}{o(H)} = \frac{o(G)}{o(K)} \cdot \frac{o(K)}{o(H)}$$
$$= [G:K][K:H]$$

**58.** Let $a \in G$

Then, $\quad H \cap K \subseteq H$

$\Rightarrow \quad (H \cap K)a \subseteq Ha$

and $\quad H \cap K \subseteq K$

$\Rightarrow \quad (H \cap K)a \subseteq Ka$

Hence, $\quad (H \cap K)a \subseteq Ha \cap Ka \quad ...(i)$

Again, if $x$ is any element of $Ha \cap Ka$, then $x \in Ha$ and $x \in Ka$

So $\quad x = ha = ka$ for some $h \in H, k \in K$

$\Rightarrow \quad xa^{-1} = h = k$

$\Rightarrow \quad xa^{-1} \in H \cap K$

$\Rightarrow \quad (xa^{-1})a \in (H \cap K)a$

$\Rightarrow \quad x \in (H \cap K)a$

$\Rightarrow \quad Ha \cap Ka \subseteq (H \cap K)a$ ...(ii)

From Eqs. (i) and (ii), we have

$$(H \cap K)a = Ha \cap Ka$$

**59.** Let $xa_1x^{-1}$ and $xa_2x^{-1}$ be any two elements of $xHx^{-1}$, then $a_1, a_2 \in H$.

Now, we have

$$(xa_1x^{-1})(xa_2x^{-1}) = (xa_1x^{-1})(xa_2^{-1}x^{-1})$$
$$= xa_1(x^{-1}x)a_2^{-1}x^{-1}$$
$$= xa_1ea_2^{-1}x^{-1}$$
$$= xa_1a_2^{-1}x^{-1}$$
$$= xax^{-1}, \text{ if } a = a_1a_2^{-1} \in H$$

Evidently, $xax^{-1} \in xHx^{-1}$

Hence, $Hx^{-1}$ is a subgroup of $G$.

**60.** Let $m, n \in I$, then $f(m) = f(n)$

$\Rightarrow \quad 2m = 2n$

$\Rightarrow \quad m = n$

*i.e.*, mapping $f$ is one-one.

Let $Z \in E, \exists x \in I : x = \dfrac{Z}{2}$, $Z$ even,

*i.e.*, mapping $f$ is onto.

Again, $f(m+n) = 2(m+n)$

$$= 2m + 2n$$
$$= f(m) + f(n)$$

Hence, the mapping $f$ preserves the group composition and hence the mapping $f$ is an isomorphism.

**61.** Let $m, n \in G$, then $\phi(m) = 2^m$

$$\phi(n) = 2^n$$

Since, $\phi(x) = 2^x, x \in G$

Now, $\phi(m+n) = 2^{m+n} = 2^m \cdot 2^n$

$$= \phi(m)\phi(n)$$

*i.e.*, $\phi(m+n) = \phi(m)\phi(n)$

Hence, the mapping $\phi$ is a homomorphism.

**62.** Let $Z$ be the centre of $G$ so that

$Z = \{z \in G : zx = xz, \forall x \in G\}$

Let $z_1, z_2 \in Z$, then

$z_1, z_2 \in Z \Rightarrow z_1x = xz_1$ and $z_2x = xz_2, \forall x \in G$

Now, $z_2x = xz_2, \forall x \in G$

$\Rightarrow \quad z_2^{-1}z_2xz_2^{-1} = z_2^{-1}xz_2z_2^{-1}, \forall x \in G$

$\Rightarrow \quad xz_2^{-1} = z_2^{-1}x, \forall x \in G$

But $(z_1z_2^{-1})x = z_2(z_2^{-1}x)$ (associativity)

$= z_1(xz_2^{-1})$ $(\because z_2^{-1}x = xz_2^{-1})$

$= (z_1x)z_2^{-1}$ (associativity)

$= (xz_1)z_2^{-1}$ $(\because z_1x = xz_1)$

$= x(z_1z_2^{-1}), \forall x \in G$

Hence, $z_1z_2^{-1} \in Z$

Hence, $z_1 \in Z, z_2 \in Z \Rightarrow z_1z_2^{-1} \in Z$.

and therefore, $Z$ is a subgroup of $G$.

Again, let $x \in G$ and $z \in Z$, then

$xzx^{-1} = (xz)x^{-1}$ (associativity)

$= (zx)x^{-1}$ $(\because xz = zx)$

$= z(xx^{-1})$ (associativity)

$= ze = z \in Z$

Hence, $xzx^{-1} \in Z, \forall x \in G$ and $z \in Z$

Hence, $Z$ is a normal in $G$. Thus, $Z$ is a normal subgroup of $G$.

**63.** Let $h^{-1} \in H^{-1}$, then $h \in H$

Since, $H$ is a subgroup of $G$.

$h \in H \Rightarrow h^{-1} \in H$ (by inverse axiom)

Therefore, $h^{-1} \in H^{-1} \Rightarrow h^{-1} \in H$

Hence, $H^{-1} \subseteq H$ ...(i)

Again, $h \in H \Rightarrow h^{-1} \in H$ [$\because$ $H$ itself is a group]

$\Rightarrow \quad (h^{-1})^{-1} \in H^{-1}$

$\Rightarrow \quad h \in H^{-1}$

Hence, $H \subseteq H^{-1}$

Hence, from Eqs. (i) and (ii), we get

$$H^{-1} = H$$ ...(ii)

**64.** Let $G$ be any group and $N(a)$ the normalizer of $a (\in G)$ in $G$. Let $x, y \in N(a)$, then

$x \in N(a)$ and $z \in N(a)$

$\Rightarrow \quad ax = xa$ and $ay = ya$

Now, $ay = ya \Rightarrow y^{-1}ayy^{-1} = y^{-1}yay^{-1}$

$\Rightarrow \quad y^{-1}a = ay^{-1}$

$y^{-1}a = ay^{-1}$

and therefore,

$$a(xy^{-1}) = (ax)y^{-1} = (xa)y^{-1} = x(ay^{-1})$$
$$= x(y^{-1}a) = (xy^{-1})a$$

which shows that $xy^{-1} \in N(a)$.

Hence, $N(a)$ is a subgroup of $G$.

**65.** Suppose that $HK$ is a subgroup, then

$(HK)^{-1} = HK$

$\Rightarrow \quad K^{-1}H^{-1} = HK$

$\Rightarrow \quad KH = HK$ [$\because$ $H$ is subgroup $\Rightarrow H^{-1} = H$ and $K$ is a subgroup $\Rightarrow K^{-1} = K$]

Let $HK = KH$ then, we have to prove that $HK$ is a subgroup of $G$. For this it is sufficient to prove

$(HK)(HK)^{-1} = HK$

Now, $(HK)(HK)^{-1} = HK(K^{-1}H^{-1})$ (reversal law)

$= H(KK^{-1})H^{-1}$ (associativity)

$= (HK)H^{-1}$ [$\because$ $K$ is a subgroup $\therefore KK^{-1} = K$]

$= (KH)H^{-1}$ [$\because HK = KH$]

$= K(HH^{-1})$

$= KH$ [$\because$ $H$ is a subgroup $\therefore HH^{-1} = H$]

Hence, $HK = KH$

$\Rightarrow \quad HK$ is a subgroup.

**66.** (i) For each $a \in G$

$$f(a)\bar{e} = f(a) = f(ae) = f(a)f(e)$$

and hence $f(e) = \bar{e}$

(ii) For each $a \in G$

$$f(a)f(a^{-1}) = f(aa^{-1}) = f(e) = \bar{e}$$
$$= f(a)f(a)^{-1}$$

and hence $f(a^{-1}) = f(a)^{-1}$

**67.** Let $f: G \to G'$ defined as $f(a) = ma$, $a \in G$ and $ma \in G'$. Then,

***f* is one-one** Let $a, b \in G$

then $f(a) = f(b)$

$\Rightarrow \quad am = bm$

$\Rightarrow \quad a = b$

***f* is onto** Let $Z \in G'$, $\exists\, x \in G : x = \dfrac{Z}{m}, Z = xm.$

***f* preserves group composition**

$$f(a+b) = m(a+b)$$
$$= ma + mb$$
$$= f(a) + f(b) \qquad \text{(additivity)}$$

Hence, $f$ is an isomorphic mapping of $G$ onto $G'$.

**68.** (i) Let $n = 0$

If $e$ be the identity element, then by definition, we have $(bab^{-1})^0 = e$

Also, $\quad ba^0b^{-1} = beb^{-1} = bb^{-1} = e$

$\therefore \quad (bab^{-1})^0 = ba^0b^{-1}$

(ii) Let $\quad n > 0$

Here, we get

$$(bab^{-1})^1 = bab^{-1} = ba^1b^{-1} \qquad (\because a^1 = a)$$

$\Rightarrow \quad (bab^{-1})^n = ba^nb^{-1}$ is true for $n = 1$

Let us now suppose that this result is true for $n = k$, i.e., suppose

$$(bab^{-1})^k = ba^kb^{-1} \qquad \text{...(i)}$$

Then, $\quad (bab^{-1})^{k+1} = (bab^{-1})^k(bab^{-1})^1$

$$= (ba^kb^{-1})(bab^{-1}), \qquad \text{[from Eq. (i)]}$$
$$= ba^kb^{-1}bab^{-1} = ba^keab^{-1}$$
$$= ba^kab^{-1}$$
$$= ba^{k+1}b^{-1}$$

Hence, the result is true for $n = k+1$ also if it is true for $n = k$. Also, the result is true for $n = 1$.

Hence, by mathematical induction it is true for all values of $n > 0$.

(iii) Let $\quad n < 0$

Let $n = -k$, where $k > 0$

Then, $\quad (bab^{-1})^n = (bab^{-1})^{-k} = [(bab^{-1})^k]^{-1}$

$$= [ba^kb^{-1}]^{-1}$$
$$= (b^{-1})^{-1}(a^k)^{-1}(b)^{-1} \qquad \text{(by reversal rule)}$$
$$= ba^{-k}b^{-1}$$
$$= ba^nb^{-1} \qquad (\because -k = n)$$

Hence, $\quad (bab^{-1})^n = ba^nb^{-1}$, for any integer $n$.

**69.** If $G$ and $\overline{G}$ are isomorphic

i.e., $\quad G \approx \overline{G}$

The $G \approx \overline{G}$ is a equivalence a relation if it satisfies the following axioms

(i) $G \approx G$ (reflexivity)

(ii) $G \approx \overline{G}$ implies $\overline{G} \approx G$ (symmetry)

(iii) $G \approx G$, $\overline{G} \approx \overline{\overline{G}}$ implies $\overline{G} \approx \overline{\overline{G}}$ (transitivity)

For each $x \in G$ define $f: G - G$ by $f(x) = x$.

Then, $f$ is an isomorphism of $G$ onto itself and hence $G \approx G$.

Let $G \approx \overline{G}$. Then, there exists an isomorphism $f$ from $G$ onto $\overline{G}$. Since $f$ is 1–1 and onto, the map $f^{-1}: \overline{G} \to G$ exists and is 1–1 and onto.

Let $\quad a, b \in \overline{G}$ and let $f(x) = a$

$$f(y) = b \text{ for } x, y \in G$$

Now, $\quad x = f^{-1}(a), y = f^{-1}(b)$

$$f(xy) = f(x)f(y) = ab$$

and so $\quad f^{-1}(ab) = xy = f^{-1}(a)f^{-1}(b)$

Then, $f^{-1}$ is also a homomorphism and so $\overline{G} \approx G$.

Let $G \approx \overline{G}$ and $\overline{G} \approx \overline{\overline{G}}$. Thus, there exist isomorphisms $f$ and $g$ from $G$ onto $\overline{G}$ and from $\overline{G}$ onto $\overline{\overline{G}}$, respectively. Since, $f$ and

$g$ are one-one and onto, the composition $gof: G \to \overline{\overline{G}}$ is 1–1 and onto.

Further from $x, y \in G$

$$(gof)(xy) = g(f(xy))$$
$$= g(f(x)f(y))$$
$$= g(f(x))g(f(y))$$

Thus, $gof$ is a homomorphism and hence $G \approx \overline{\overline{G}}$.

**70.** Let $xa_1x^{-1}$ and $xa_2x^{-1}$ be any two elements of $xHx^{-1}$, then $a_1, a_2 \in H$

Now, we have

$$(xa_1x^{-1})(xa_2x^{-1})^{-1} = (xa_1x^{-1})(xa_2^{-1}x^{-1})$$
$$= xa_1(x^{-1}x)a_2^{-1}x^{-1}$$
$$= xa_1a_2^{-1}x^{-1}$$
$$= xax^{-1}, \text{ if } a = a_1a_2^{-1} \in H$$

Evidently, $xax^{-1} \in xHx^{-1}$

Hence, $xHx^{-1}$ is a subgroup of $G$.

**71.** (i) Let $G = (a) = \{e, a, a^2, a^3, \ldots\}$

be a cyclic group with $a$ as the generator. Then, for any

$$m, n \in Z, a^m, a^n \in G$$

and $\quad a^ma^n = a^{m+n} = a^{n+m}$

$$= a^na^m$$

and hence, $G$ is abelian.

In the additive notation, we write

$$G = \{1, a, 2a, 3a, \ldots\}$$

In this case,

$$ma + na = (m+n)a = (n+m)a$$
$$= na + ma$$

and thus $G$ is abelian.

(ii) Let $G$ be a cyclic group with a generator

$$a \in G$$

Let $\quad o(a) = n$

i.e., $\quad a^n = e$ and $a^m \neq e$ for $0 < m < n$

If $\quad m > n$ let $m = qn + r$

$$0 \le r < n$$

So, $a^m = a^{qn+r} = a^{qn} \cdot a^r = (a^n)^q \cdot a^r$
$= e^q \cdot a^r = e \cdot a^r = a^r$

Therefore, there are exactly $n$ elements in the group and they are

$$\{e, a, a^2, \ldots, a^{n-1}\} \Rightarrow o(G) = n$$

**72.** Let $H$ is a subgroup of $G$.

Let $ab^{-1}$ be any element of $HH^{-1}$

Then, $a \in H$ and $b \in H$

Also, $b \in H \Rightarrow b^{-1} \in H$ as $H$ is a subgroup.

Thus, $a \in H, b^{-1} \in H, \Rightarrow ab^{-1} \in H$ (by closure property)

Hence, $ab^{-1} \in HH^{-1} \Rightarrow ab^{-1} \in H$

Hence, $HH^{-1} \subseteq H$

Let $HH^{-1} \subseteq H$

Let $a \in H, b \subseteq H$, then $ab^{-1} \in HH^{-1}$

Since, $HH^{-1} \subseteq H$ so $ab^{-1} \in HH^{-1}$

$\Rightarrow$ $ab^{-1} \in H$

*i.e.*, $a \in H, b \in H \Rightarrow ab^{-1} \in H$

Hence, $H$ is a subgroup of $G$.

**73.** Here,

$$f^{-1} = \begin{pmatrix} 1 & 5 & 3 & 2 & 4 \\ 1 & 2 & 3 & 4 & 5 \end{pmatrix}$$

and $$g^{-1} = \begin{pmatrix} 2 & 3 & 1 & 5 & 4 \\ 1 & 2 & 3 & 4 & 5 \end{pmatrix}$$

Hence, $$f^{-1}og^{-1} = \begin{pmatrix} 1 & 5 & 3 & 2 & 4 \\ 1 & 2 & 3 & 4 & 5 \end{pmatrix} o \begin{pmatrix} 2 & 3 & 1 & 5 & 4 \\ 1 & 2 & 3 & 4 & 5 \end{pmatrix}$$

$$= \begin{pmatrix} 1 & 5 & 3 & 2 & 4 \\ 1 & 2 & 3 & 4 & 5 \end{pmatrix} o \begin{pmatrix} 1 & 2 & 3 & 4 & 5 \\ 3 & 1 & 2 & 5 & 4 \end{pmatrix}$$

(rearranging columns)

$$= \begin{pmatrix} 1 & 5 & 3 & 2 & 4 \\ 3 & 1 & 2 & 5 & 4 \end{pmatrix}$$

$$= \begin{pmatrix} 1 & 2 & 3 & 4 & 5 \\ 3 & 5 & 2 & 4 & 1 \end{pmatrix} \quad \ldots\text{(i)}$$

$$g^{-1}of^{-1} = \begin{pmatrix} 2 & 3 & 1 & 5 & 4 \\ 1 & 2 & 3 & 4 & 5 \end{pmatrix} o \begin{pmatrix} 1 & 5 & 3 & 2 & 4 \\ 1 & 2 & 3 & 4 & 5 \end{pmatrix}$$

$$= \begin{pmatrix} 2 & 3 & 1 & 5 & 4 \\ 1 & 2 & 3 & 4 & 5 \end{pmatrix} o \begin{pmatrix} 1 & 2 & 3 & 4 & 5 \\ 1 & 4 & 3 & 5 & 2 \end{pmatrix}$$

(rearranging columns)

$$= \begin{pmatrix} 2 & 3 & 1 & 5 & 4 \\ 1 & 4 & 3 & 5 & 2 \end{pmatrix}$$

$$= \begin{pmatrix} 1 & 2 & 3 & 4 & 5 \\ 3 & 1 & 4 & 2 & 5 \end{pmatrix} \quad \ldots\text{(ii)}$$

By Eqs. (i) and (ii), $f^{-1}og^{-1} \neq g^{-1}of^{-1}$

**74.** $$fog = \begin{pmatrix} 1 & 2 & 3 & 4 & 5 \\ 1 & 5 & 3 & 2 & 4 \end{pmatrix} o \begin{pmatrix} 1 & 2 & 3 & 4 & 5 \\ 2 & 3 & 1 & 5 & 4 \end{pmatrix}$$

$$= \begin{pmatrix} 1 & 2 & 3 & 4 & 5 \\ 1 & 5 & 3 & 2 & 4 \end{pmatrix} o \begin{pmatrix} 1 & 5 & 3 & 2 & 4 \\ 2 & 4 & 1 & 3 & 5 \end{pmatrix}$$

(rearranging columns)

$$= \begin{pmatrix} 1 & 2 & 3 & 4 & 5 \\ 2 & 4 & 1 & 3 & 5 \end{pmatrix}$$

$$gof = \begin{pmatrix} 1 & 2 & 3 & 4 & 5 \\ 2 & 3 & 1 & 5 & 4 \end{pmatrix} o \begin{pmatrix} 1 & 2 & 3 & 4 & 5 \\ 1 & 5 & 3 & 2 & 4 \end{pmatrix}$$

$$= \begin{pmatrix} 1 & 2 & 3 & 4 & 5 \\ 2 & 3 & 1 & 5 & 4 \end{pmatrix} o \begin{pmatrix} 2 & 3 & 1 & 5 & 4 \\ 5 & 3 & 1 & 4 & 2 \end{pmatrix}$$

(rearranging columns)

$$= \begin{pmatrix} 1 & 2 & 3 & 4 & 5 \\ 5 & 3 & 1 & 4 & 2 \end{pmatrix}$$

**75.** For the given permutations, we have

$$A_1oA_2 = \begin{pmatrix} 1 & 2 & 3 \\ 3 & 1 & 2 \end{pmatrix} o \begin{pmatrix} 1 & 2 & 3 \\ 2 & 3 & 1 \end{pmatrix}$$

$$= \begin{pmatrix} 1 & 2 & 3 \\ 3 & 1 & 2 \end{pmatrix} o \begin{pmatrix} 3 & 1 & 2 \\ 1 & 2 & 3 \end{pmatrix} \quad \text{(rearranging columns)}$$

or $$A_1oA_2 = \begin{pmatrix} 1 & 3 \\ 1 & 2 & 3 \end{pmatrix};$$

$$A_2oA_3 = \begin{pmatrix} 1 & 2 & 3 \\ 2 & 3 & 1 \end{pmatrix} o \begin{pmatrix} 1 & 2 & 3 \\ 3 & 2 & 1 \end{pmatrix}$$

$$= \begin{pmatrix} 1 & 2 & 3 \\ 2 & 3 & 1 \end{pmatrix} o \begin{pmatrix} 2 & 3 & 1 \\ 2 & 1 & 3 \end{pmatrix} \quad \text{(rearranging columns)}$$

$$= \begin{pmatrix} 1 & 2 & 3 \\ 2 & 1 & 3 \end{pmatrix};$$

$$A_3oA_1 = \begin{pmatrix} 1 & 2 & 3 \\ 3 & 2 & 1 \end{pmatrix} o \begin{pmatrix} 1 & 2 & 3 \\ 3 & 1 & 2 \end{pmatrix}$$

$$= \begin{pmatrix} 1 & 2 & 3 \\ 3 & 2 & 1 \end{pmatrix} o \begin{pmatrix} 3 & 2 & 1 \\ 2 & 1 & 3 \end{pmatrix} \quad \text{(rearranging columns)}$$

$$= \begin{pmatrix} 1 & 2 & 3 \\ 2 & 1 & 3 \end{pmatrix}$$

If $A^{-1}$ be the inverse of the permutation $A$, then $A^{-1}oA = I$

Hence, $(A_1oA_2)^{-1} = \text{Inverse of} \begin{pmatrix} 1 & 2 & 3 \\ 1 & 2 & 3 \end{pmatrix}$

$$= \begin{pmatrix} 1 & 2 & 3 \\ 1 & 2 & 3 \end{pmatrix} = I$$

$$(A_2oA_3)^{-1} = \text{Inverse of} \begin{pmatrix} 1 & 2 & 3 \\ 2 & 1 & 3 \end{pmatrix}$$

$$= \begin{pmatrix} 2 & 1 & 3 \\ 1 & 2 & 3 \end{pmatrix}$$

$$= \begin{pmatrix} 1 & 2 & 3 \\ 2 & 1 & 3 \end{pmatrix} = (1\ 2)$$

$$(A_2oA_1)^{-1} = \text{Inverse of} \begin{pmatrix} 1 & 2 & 3 \\ & 2 & 3 \end{pmatrix}$$

$$= \begin{pmatrix} 2 & 1 & 3 \\ 1 & 2 & 3 \end{pmatrix} = \begin{pmatrix} 1 & 2 & 3 \\ 2 & 1 & 3 \end{pmatrix}$$

$$= (1\ 2)$$

**76.** Here,

$$fg = (1\ 2\ 5)(3\ 4\ 5)$$

$$= \begin{pmatrix} 1 & 2 & 5 & 3 & 4 & 6 \\ 2 & 5 & 1 & 3 & 4 & 6 \end{pmatrix}\begin{pmatrix} 3 & 4 & 6 & 1 & 2 & 5 \\ 4 & 6 & 3 & 1 & 2 & 5 \end{pmatrix}$$

$$= \begin{pmatrix} 1 & 2 & 3 & 4 & 5 & 6 \\ 2 & 5 & 3 & 4 & 1 & 6 \end{pmatrix}\begin{pmatrix} 2 & 5 & 3 & 4 & 1 & 6 \\ 2 & 5 & 4 & 6 & 1 & 3 \end{pmatrix}$$

$$= \begin{pmatrix} 1 & 2 & 3 & 4 & 5 & 6 \\ 2 & 5 & 4 & 6 & 1 & 3 \end{pmatrix}$$

Also, $gf = (3\ 4\ 6)(1\ 2\ 5)$

$$= \begin{pmatrix} 3 & 4 & 6 & 1 & 2 & 5 \\ 4 & 6 & 3 & 1 & 2 & 5 \end{pmatrix}\begin{pmatrix} 1 & 2 & 5 & 5 & 4 & 6 \\ 2 & 5 & 1 & 3 & 4 & 6 \end{pmatrix}$$

$$= \begin{pmatrix} 1 & 2 & 3 & 4 & 5 & 6 \\ 1 & 2 & 4 & 6 & 5 & 3 \end{pmatrix}\begin{pmatrix} 1 & 2 & 4 & 6 & 5 & 3 \\ 2 & 5 & 4 & 6 & 1 & 3 \end{pmatrix}$$

$$= \begin{pmatrix} 1 & 2 & 3 & 4 & 5 & 6 \\ 2 & 5 & 4 & 6 & 1 & 3 \end{pmatrix}$$

$\Rightarrow \quad fg = gf$

**77.** Given,

$$A = \begin{pmatrix} 1 & 2 & 3 & 4 & 5 \\ 2 & 3 & 4 & 5 & 1 \end{pmatrix}$$

$$B = \begin{pmatrix} 1 & 2 & 3 & 4 & 5 \\ 1 & 3 & 2 & 5 & 4 \end{pmatrix}$$

Hence, $AoB = \begin{pmatrix} 1 & 2 & 3 & 4 & 5 \\ 2 & 3 & 4 & 5 & 1 \end{pmatrix} o \begin{pmatrix} 1 & 2 & 3 & 4 & 5 \\ 1 & 3 & 2 & 5 & 4 \end{pmatrix}$

$$= \begin{pmatrix} 1 & 2 & 3 & 4 & 5 \\ 2 & 3 & 4 & 5 & 1 \end{pmatrix} o \begin{pmatrix} 2 & 3 & 4 & 5 & 1 \\ 3 & 2 & 5 & 4 & 1 \end{pmatrix}$$

(rearranging columns of $B$)

$$= \begin{pmatrix} 1 & 2 & 3 & 4 & 5 \\ 3 & 2 & 5 & 4 & 1 \end{pmatrix} = (1\ 3\ 5)$$

**78.** Let $\quad C = \begin{pmatrix} 1 & 2 & 3 & 4 \\ 1 & 3 & 4 & 2 \end{pmatrix}$

Then, $\quad C^2 = CC$

$$= \begin{pmatrix} 1 & 2 & 3 & 4 \\ 1 & 3 & 4 & 2 \end{pmatrix}\begin{pmatrix} 1 & 2 & 3 & 4 \\ 1 & 3 & 4 & 2 \end{pmatrix}$$

$$= \begin{pmatrix} 1 & 2 & 3 & 4 \\ 1 & 3 & 4 & 2 \end{pmatrix}\begin{pmatrix} 1 & 3 & 4 & 2 \\ 1 & 4 & 3 & 2 \end{pmatrix}$$

(rearranging columns)

$$= \begin{pmatrix} 1 & 2 & 3 & 4 \\ 1 & 4 & 2 & 3 \end{pmatrix} \quad \text{...(i)}$$

and $\quad C^3 = C^2C$

$$= \begin{pmatrix} 1 & 2 & 3 & 4 \\ 1 & 4 & 2 & 3 \end{pmatrix}\begin{pmatrix} 1 & 2 & 3 & 4 \\ 1 & 3 & 4 & 2 \end{pmatrix} \quad \text{[from Eq. (i)]}$$

$$= \begin{pmatrix} 1 & 2 & 3 & 4 \\ 1 & 4 & 2 & 3 \end{pmatrix}\begin{pmatrix} 1 & 4 & 2 & 3 \\ 1 & 2 & 3 & 4 \end{pmatrix}$$

(rearranging columns)

$$= \begin{pmatrix} 1 & 2 & 3 & 4 \\ 1 & 2 & 3 & 4 \end{pmatrix}$$

**79.** Let the required inverse be

$$\begin{pmatrix} 1 & 2 & 3 & 4 \\ a & b & c & d \end{pmatrix}$$

we have to determine $a, b, c, d$. Then,

$$\begin{pmatrix} 1 & 2 & 3 & 4 \\ 1 & 3 & 4 & 2 \end{pmatrix}\begin{pmatrix} 1 & 2 & 3 & 4 \\ a & b & c & d \end{pmatrix} = \begin{pmatrix} 1 & 2 & 3 & 4 \\ 1 & 2 & 3 & 4 \end{pmatrix},$$

$$\Rightarrow \begin{pmatrix} 1 & 2 & 3 & 4 \\ 1 & 3 & 4 & 2 \end{pmatrix}\begin{pmatrix} 1 & 3 & 4 & 2 \\ a & b & c & d \end{pmatrix} = \begin{pmatrix} 1 & 2 & 3 & 4 \\ 1 & 2 & 3 & 4 \end{pmatrix},$$

(rearranging columns on LHS)

$$\Rightarrow \begin{pmatrix} 1 & 2 & 3 & 4 \\ a & c & d & b \end{pmatrix} = \begin{pmatrix} 1 & 3 & 3 & 4 \\ 1 & 2 & 3 & 4 \end{pmatrix}$$

On comparing these, we have

$$a = 1, c = 2, d = 3, b = 4$$

Hence, the required inverse is

$$\begin{pmatrix} 1 & 2 & 3 & 4 \\ a & b & c & d \end{pmatrix} = \begin{pmatrix} 1 & 2 & 3 & 4 \\ 1 & 4 & 2 & 3 \end{pmatrix} = \begin{pmatrix} 1 & 3 & 4 & 2 \\ 1 & 2 & 3 & 4 \end{pmatrix}$$

**80.** $(1\ 2\ 3) o (2\ 4\ 3) o (1\ 3\ 4)$

$$= \begin{pmatrix} 1 & 2 & 3 & 4 \\ 2 & 3 & 1 & 4 \end{pmatrix} o \begin{pmatrix} 1 & 2 & 4 & 3 \\ 1 & 4 & 3 & 2 \end{pmatrix} o \begin{pmatrix} 1 & 2 & 3 & 4 \\ 3 & 2 & 4 & 1 \end{pmatrix}$$

$$= \begin{pmatrix} 1 & 2 & 3 & 4 \\ 2 & 3 & 1 & 4 \end{pmatrix} o \begin{pmatrix} 2 & 3 & 1 & 4 \\ 4 & 2 & 1 & 3 \end{pmatrix} o \begin{pmatrix} 1 & 2 & 3 & 4 \\ 3 & 2 & 4 & 1 \end{pmatrix}$$

$$= \begin{pmatrix} 1 & 2 & 3 & 4 \\ 4 & 2 & 1 & 3 \end{pmatrix} o \begin{pmatrix} 1 & 2 & 3 & 4 \\ 3 & 2 & 4 & 1 \end{pmatrix}$$

$$= \begin{pmatrix} 1 & 2 & 3 & 4 \\ 4 & 2 & 1 & 3 \end{pmatrix} o \begin{pmatrix} 4 & 2 & 1 & 3 \\ 1 & 2 & 3 & 4 \end{pmatrix}$$

$$= \begin{pmatrix} 1 & 2 & 3 & 4 \\ 1 & 2 & 3 & 4 \end{pmatrix} = I$$

**81.** Let $P_4$ be the symmetric group of all permutations on the set $S = \{1, 2, 3, 4\}$.

The identity of this group is the identity permutation

$$\begin{pmatrix} 1 & 2 & 3 & 4 \\ 1 & 2 & 3 & 4 \end{pmatrix}$$

Let $P$ denote the given permutation $\begin{pmatrix} 1 & 2 & 3 & 4 \\ 1 & 3 & 4 & 2 \end{pmatrix}$

Then, $\quad P^1 = P,$

$$P^2 = PoP = \begin{pmatrix} 1 & 2 & 3 & 4 \\ 1 & 3 & 4 & 2 \end{pmatrix} o \begin{pmatrix} 1 & 2 & 3 & 4 \\ 1 & 3 & 4 & 2 \end{pmatrix}$$

$$= \begin{pmatrix} 1 & 2 & 3 & 4 \\ 1 & 3 & 4 & 2 \end{pmatrix} o \begin{pmatrix} 1 & 3 & 4 & 2 \\ 1 & 4 & 2 & 3 \end{pmatrix}$$

(rearranging columns)

$$= \begin{pmatrix} 1 & 2 & 3 & 4 \\ 1 & 4 & 2 & 3 \end{pmatrix}$$

$$P^3 = PoPoP = P^2 oP$$

$$= \begin{pmatrix} 1 & 2 & 3 & 4 \\ 1 & 4 & 2 & 3 \end{pmatrix} o \begin{pmatrix} 1 & 2 & 3 & 4 \\ 1 & 3 & 4 & 2 \end{pmatrix}$$

$$= \begin{pmatrix} 1 & 2 & 3 & 4 \\ 1 & 4 & 2 & 3 \end{pmatrix} o \begin{pmatrix} 1 & 4 & 2 & 3 \\ 1 & 2 & 3 & 4 \end{pmatrix}$$

(rearranging columns)

$$=\begin{pmatrix}1 & 2 & 3 & 4\\ 1 & 2 & 3 & 4\end{pmatrix}$$

= The identity of the group $P_4$

Hence, order of $P$ is 3.

**82.** The required cyclic groups of order 2 are

$H_1 = \{(1\ 2), (1)(2)(3)(4) = I\}$

Here, if $\alpha = (1, 2)$, then

$\alpha^2 = (1)(2)(3)(4)$

$H_2 = \{(1\ 3), (1)(2)(3)(4) = I\}$

$H_3 = \{(1\ 4), (1)(2)(3)(4) = I\}$

$H_4 = \{(2\ 3), (1)(2)(3)(4) = I\}$

$H_5 = \{(2\ 4), (1)(2)(3)(4) = I\}$

$H_6 = \{(3\ 4), (1)(2)(3)(4) = I\}$

The required cyclic groups of order 3 are

$H_1' = \{(1\ 2\ 3), (1\ 3\ 2), (1)(2)(3)(4) = I\}$

If $\alpha = (1\ 2\ 3)$, then $\alpha^2 = (1\ 3\ 2)$ and $\alpha^3 = I$

$H_2' = \{(1\ 2\ 4), (1\ 4\ 2), (1)(2)(3)(4) = I\}$

$H_3' = \{(1\ 3\ 4), (1\ 4\ 3), (1)(2)(3)(4) = I\}$

$H_4' = \{(2\ 3\ 4), (2\ 4\ 3), (1)(2)(3)(4) = I\}$

and the required cyclic group of order 4 are

$H_1'' = \{(1\,2\,3\,4), (1\,3)(2\ 4), (1\,4\,3\,2), (1)(2)(3)(4) = I\}$

($\because$ If $\alpha = (1\ 2\ 3\ 4)$, then $\alpha^2 = (1\ 3)(2\ 4)$,

$\alpha^3 = (1\ 4\ 3\ 2)$ and $\alpha^4 = I$)

$H_2'' = \{(1\,2\,4\,3), (1\,4)(2\ 3), (1\,3\,4\,2), (1)(2)(3)(4) = I\}$

$H_3'' = \{(1\,3\,2\,4), (1\,2)(3\ 4), (1\,4\,2\,3), (1)(2)(3)(4) = I\}$

**83.** $\begin{pmatrix}1 & 2 & 3 & 4\\ 2 & 4 & 3 & 1\end{pmatrix} = (1\ 2\ 4)(3) = (1\ 2\ 4) = (1\ 2)(1\ 4)$

The given permutation is the product of two transposes, so it is even permutation.

$(1\ 2)(5\ 4\ 3)(6\ 7\ 8) = (1\ 2)(5\ 4)(5\ 3)(6\ 7)(6\ 8)$

*i.e.*, the given permutation is the product of five transpose, so it is odd permutation.

**84.** $(1\ 2)o(1\ 3) = \begin{pmatrix}1 & 2 & 3 & 4 & 5 & \dots & n\\ 2 & 1 & 3 & 4 & 5 & \dots & n\end{pmatrix} o \begin{pmatrix}1 & 2 & 3 & 4 & \dots & n\\ 3 & 2 & 1 & 4 & \dots & n\end{pmatrix}$

$$= \begin{pmatrix}1 & 2 & 3 & \dots & n\\ 2 & 1 & 3 & \dots & n\end{pmatrix} o \begin{pmatrix}2 & 1 & 3 & 4 & \dots & n\\ 2 & 3 & 1 & 4 & \dots & n\end{pmatrix},$$

(Rearranging columns of second permutation)

$$= \begin{pmatrix}1 & 2 & 3 & 4 & \dots & n\\ 2 & 3 & 1 & 4 & \dots & n\end{pmatrix}$$

Now, $(1\ 2)o(1\ 3)o(1\ 4)$

$$= \begin{pmatrix}1 & 2 & 3 & 4 & \dots & n\\ 2 & 3 & 1 & 4 & \dots & n\end{pmatrix} o \begin{pmatrix}1 & 2 & 3 & 4 & \dots & n\\ 4 & 2 & 3 & 1 & \dots & n\end{pmatrix}$$

$$\left[\because (1\ 4) = \begin{pmatrix}1 & 2 & 3 & 4 & \dots & n\\ 4 & 2 & 3 & 1 & \dots & n\end{pmatrix}\right]$$

$$= \begin{pmatrix}1 & 2 & 3 & 4 & \dots & n\\ 2 & 3 & 1 & 4 & \dots & n\end{pmatrix} o \begin{pmatrix}2 & 3 & 1 & 4 & \dots & n\\ 2 & 3 & 4 & 1 & \dots & n\end{pmatrix}$$

$$= \begin{pmatrix}1 & 2 & 3 & 4 & 5 & \dots & n\\ 2 & 3 & 4 & 1 & 5 & \dots & n\end{pmatrix}$$

Similarly, we get $(1\ 2)o(1\ 3)o(1\ 4)o(1\ 5)$

$$= \begin{pmatrix}1 & 2 & 3 & 4 & 5 & 6 & \dots & n\\ 2 & 3 & 4 & 5 & 1 & 6 & \dots & n\end{pmatrix}$$

Proceeding in similar way, we have

$(1\ 2)o(1\ 3)o(1\ 4)o \dots o(1\ n)$

$$= \begin{pmatrix}1 & 2 & 3 & 4 & 5 & \dots & n-1 & n\\ 2 & 3 & 4 & 5 & 6 & \dots & n & 1\end{pmatrix}$$

$$= (1\ 2\ 3\ 4\ 5\ \dots\ n)$$

**85.** Let $Q^+$ denote the set of all positive rational numbers to show $(Q^+, *)$ is a group.

(i) **Closure property** For every $a, b \in Q^+$, $ab/2 \in Q^+$

$\Rightarrow$ $Q^+$ is closed under the composition*.

(ii) **Associativity law** Let $a, b, c \in Q^+$, then

$$(a * b) * c = \left(\frac{ab}{2}\right) * c = \frac{[(ab)/2]\cdot c}{2} = \frac{a[(bc)/2]}{2}$$

$$= a * \left(\frac{bc}{2}\right) = a * (b * c)$$

(iii) **Existence of identity** An element $e$ will be the identity element, if $e \in Q^+$ and if

$$e * a = a = a * e,\ \forall\ a \in Q^+$$

Now, $e * a = a \dfrac{(ea)}{2} = a \Rightarrow \left(\dfrac{a}{2}\right)(e-2) = 0$

$\Rightarrow$ $e = 2$

Since, $a \in Q^+ \Rightarrow a \neq 0$

$2 \in Q^+$ and we have

$$2 * a = (2a)/2 = a = a * 2,\ \forall\ a \in Q^+$$

$\Rightarrow$ 2 is the identity element.

(iv) **Existence of inverse** Let $a \in Q^+$, $b$ is the inverse of $a$, then we must have

$$b * a = e = 2$$

$\Rightarrow$ $\dfrac{(ba)}{2} = 2 \Rightarrow b = \dfrac{4}{a}$

Now, $a \in Q^+ \Rightarrow 4/a \in Q^+$

We have, $(4/a) * a = \{(4/a)\cdot a\}/2 = 2 = a * (4/a)$

$\Rightarrow$ $4/a$ is the inverse of $a$.

$\Rightarrow$ Inverse of each element of $Q^+$ exist.

(v) **Commutativity law** Let $a, b \in Q^+$

$\Rightarrow$ $a * b = (ab)/2 = (ba)/2 = b * a$

Hence, $(Q^+, *)$ is an abelian group.

**93.** Clearly, $H$ is non-empty subset of $G$.

Let $x, y \in H$, then $x = a^p, y = a^q$, where $p, q \in Z$.

Therefore, $xy^{-1} = (a^p)(a^q)^{-1} = a^p a^{-q} = a^{p-q} \in H$

($\because p - q \in Z$)

$\Rightarrow$ $H$ is a non-empty subset of $G$ and $x, y \in H \Rightarrow xy^{-1} \in H$.

Therefore, $H$ is a subgroup of $G$.

Now, if $K$ is any subgroup of $G$ which contain $a$, then by closure property in $K$, $a^n \in K$ for every integer $n$. Also,

$$a^0 = e \in K \text{ and } a^{-n} = (a^n)^{-1} \in K$$

$\Rightarrow$ Every integral power of a belong to $K$, *i.e.*, $H \subseteq K$. Hence, $H$ is the smallest subgroup of $G$ which contain a.

**95.** Since, we know that, if G be a cyclic group with a generator of finite order n, then G contains exactly n distinct elements namely

$$a, a^2, a^3, \dots, a^n = e$$

How, let G′ be the multiplicative group of n, nth roots of unity so that

$$G' = \{x : x \text{ is a solution of } x^n = 1\}$$
$$= \{x : x \text{ is a solution of } x^{1/n} = e^{2\pi i/n}\}$$
$$= \{e^{2\pi ri/n} : r = 0, 1, 2, \dots, (n-1)\}.$$

Also, $G = \{a^r : r = 1, 2, 3, \dots, n\} = \{a^r : r = 0, 1, 2, 3, \dots, (n-1)\}$.

For $a^n = e = a^0$, by definition of e.

Consider the map $f : G \to G'$, such that

$$f(a^r) = e^{2\pi ri/n}, \ \forall a^r \in G.$$

Now, $f(a^r) = f(a^s) \Rightarrow e^{2\pi ir/n} = e^{2\pi si/n}$

$\Rightarrow \quad r = s \Rightarrow a^r = a^s$

⇒ f is one-one.

Further, $o(G) = n = o(G')$

⇒ f is onto.

Now,

$$f(a^r \cdot a^s) = f(a^{r+s}) = e^{2\pi(r+s)i/n} = e^{2\pi ri/n} \cdot e^{2\pi si/n} = f(a^r) \cdot f(a^s)$$

i.e., $\quad f(a^r . a^s) = f(a^r) f(a^s), \ \forall a^r, a^s \in G,$

⇒ f preserves composition in G and G′.

⇒ f is an isomorphism.

Hence, $\quad (G, \bullet) \cong (G', \bullet)$.

**98.** Clearly, H and K are subgroups of H.

Also, $\quad [G:H] = \dfrac{o(G)}{o(H)} = \dfrac{8}{4} = 2$

and $\quad [H:K] = \dfrac{o(H)}{o(k)} = \dfrac{4}{2} = 2$

Hence, H is normal subgroup of G and K is normal subgroup of H.

But K is not normal subgroup of G.

Since, $a^3 b \in K$ and $b \in G$.

We have, $\quad b(a^3 b) b^{-1} = ba^3 \notin K$

**100.** (i) Since, $o(G) = pq$ with $p > q$.

Let $t = 1 + kp$ be the number of sylow p-subgroups of G such that $t \mid o(G)$ i.e., $t \mid pq$. Since, t is relatively prime to p so $t \mid q$. But $p > q$, therefore, $t = 1$. Thus, there is a unique sylow p-subgroup H of G of order p. Hence, H is normal in G and also cyclic, since, $o(H) = p$, the prime.

Consequently, G has a normal subgroup of order p. Hence, G is not simple.

(ii) The number of sylow q-subgroups in G is of the form $1 + kq$, such that $1 + kq \mid o(G)$.

Since, $1 + kq$ is relatively prime to q so that $1 + kq \mid p$. But $q \nmid p - 1$, i.e., $1 + kq \neq p$. Thus, there is only one sylow q-subgroup of order q.

Let it be K and it is normal in G. Also, $o(K) = q$, the prime, so K is cyclic.

But G has a normal cyclic sylow p-subgroup H. Let $H = (a)$ and $K = (b)$. Then, $H \cap K = \{1\}$.

Since, H and K are normal, so that

$$aba^{-1}b^{-1} \in H \cap K$$

$\Rightarrow \quad aba^{-1}b^{-1} = 1 \Rightarrow ab = ba$

Thus, $\quad o(ab) = pq = o(G)$ as p and q are distinct primes.

Hence, G is generated by ab, so it is cyclic.

**109.** Let $o\{G\} = 15 = 3 \times 5$.

By first sylow theorem, G has sylow 3-subgroups and sylow 5-subgroups. The number $(n_3)$ of 3-$SSG_3$ is given by

$$n_3 = 1 + 3k \qquad (k = 0, 1, 2, \dots)$$

Where $\quad n_3 \mid o(G) = 15$

$\Rightarrow \quad k = 0$ only $\Rightarrow n_3 = 1$

Thus, there exists exactly one 3-SSG say A, $o(A) = 3$ and so $A \lhd G$. Furthermore, A is cyclic. Let

$$A = \langle a \rangle, a^3 = e$$

The number $(n_5)$ of 5-SSGs is given by

$$n_5 = 1 + 5k (k = 0, 1, 2, \dots) \text{ and } n_5 \mid o(G) = 15$$

$\Rightarrow \quad k = 0$, only $\Rightarrow n_5 = 1$

Thus, there exists exactly one 5-SSG say B. $o(B) = 5$ and so $B \lhd G$. Also, B is cyclic. Let $B = \langle b \rangle, b^5 = e$.

We have $\quad A \cap B = (e)$.

Since, $A \lhd G$, $B \lhd G$ and $A \cap B = (e)$, therefore

$$xy = yx, \forall x \in A, y \in B$$

In particular, $\quad ab = ba \quad$ ...(i)

Further $\quad (o(a), o(b)) = (3, 5) = 1 \quad$ ...(ii)

By virtue of conditions Eqs. (i) and (ii), we have

$$o(ab) = o(a)\, o(b) = 3 \times 5 = 15$$

Hence, $\quad G = \langle ab \rangle (ab)^{15} = e$, i.e., G is cyclic.

**110.** $\quad o(G) = 225 = 3^2 \cdot 5^2$

The number $(n_5)$ of 5-SSGs of G is given by

$$n_5 = 1 + 5k (k = 0, 1, 2 \dots);$$

where, $\quad n_5 \mid o(G) = 225$

$\Rightarrow \quad k = 0$ only $\Rightarrow n_5 = 1$

Hence, there exists exactly one 5-SSG, of G and so it must be normal in G.

The number $(n_3)$ of 3-SSGs of G is given by

$$n_3 = 1 + 3k (k = 0, 1, 2, \dots);$$

where, $\quad n_3 \mid o(G) = 225$

For $k = 0$, $\quad n_3 = 1$ and $n_3 \mid o(G) = 225$

For $k = 8$, $\quad n_5 = 25$ and $n_3 \mid o(G) = 225$

Hence, G has 1 or 25 sylow 3-subgroups each of order $3^2$ and they are abelian, since any group of order $p^2$ (p prime) is abelian.

# 16 Ring Theory

## Syllabus

- Rings
- Ideals
- Prime and Maximal Ideals
- Quotient Rings
- Unique Factorization Domain
- Principal Ideal Domain
- Euclidean Domain
- Polynomial Rings and Irreducibility Criteria
- Fields
- Finite Fields
- Field Extensions
- Galois Theory

## Ring

Let $R$ be a non-empty set. An algebraic structure $(R, +, \cdot)$ together with two binary operations addition and multiplication for all $a, b \in R$ is called a ring, if this structure satisfies following properties

(i) **Closed under addition**

$$a + b \in R, \forall a, b \in R$$

(ii) **Associative under addition**

$$a + (b + c) = (a + b) + c, \forall a, b, c \in R$$

(iii) **Existence of identity**

$$0 + a = a = a + 0, \forall a \in R$$

Then, 0 is an additive identity of $R$.

(iv) **Existence of inverse**

There exists an element $-a \in R$, such that

$$-a + a = 0 = a + (-a), \forall a \in R$$

Then, $-a$ is an additive inverse of $a$.

(v) **Commutative under addition**

$$a + b = b + a, \forall a, b \in R$$

(vi) **Closed under multiplication**

$$a \cdot b \in R, \forall a, b \in R$$

(vii) **Associative under multiplication**

$$a \cdot (b \cdot c) = (a \cdot b) \cdot c, \forall a, b \in R$$

(viii) **Distributive laws** (Distribution of '$\cdot$' over '+'), $\forall a, b, c \in R$

$$a \cdot (b + c) = a \cdot b + a \cdot c \quad \text{(left distributive)}$$

and $$(b + c) \cdot a = b \cdot a + c \cdot a \quad \text{(right distributive)}$$

or

An algebraic structure $(R, +, \cdot)$ is said to be a ring, if it satisfies following properties

**(i)** $(R, '+')$ is an abelian group.

**(ii)** Multiplication is closed.

**(iii)** Multiplication is associative.

**(iv)** Multiplication is distributive over addition.

## Ring with Unity

A ring $R$ is said to be a ring with unity, if the multiplicative identity. *i.e.*, $1 \in R$ such that

$$1 \cdot a = a = a \cdot 1, \forall a \in R$$

## Commutative Ring

A ring $R$ is said to be a commutative ring, if

$$a \cdot b = b \cdot a, \ \forall \ a, b \in R.$$

> **Note** (a) A set $R$ having a single element 0 with two binary operations addition and multiplication defined by $0+0=0$ and $0 \cdot 0 = 0$ is called a null ring.
>
> (b) A ring $R$ is called finite or infinite ring according as it contains finite or infinite number of elements.
>
> (c) A ring R is called boolean, if $a^2 = a, \forall a \in R$, e.g., $Z_2 = \{0,1\}$ is a boolean ring, since $0^2 = 0$ and $1^2 = 1$ in $Z_2$.
>
> (d) A ring $R$ is called $p$ ring, if $a^p = a$ and $pa = 0$, $\forall$ $a \in R$.

e.g.,

(i) The set $Z = \{....-3, -2, -1, 0, 1, 2, 3, ....\}$ of integers is a commutative ring under the usual addition and multiplication of integers. Here, 0 is the additive identity. Since, $a + 0 = 0 + a = a, \ \forall \ a \in Z$. $-a$ is the additive inverse of $a \in Z$. Since, $a + (-a) = 0 = (-a) + a$.

Also, $1 \in Z$ is the unit element. Since, $a.1 = 1.a = a, \forall a \in Z$.

Therefore, $Z$ is a commutative ring with unity.

(ii) Set of natural numbers,

$N = \{1, 2, 3, ....\}$ is not a ring. Since, additive identity of $a \in N$ does not exist in $N$.

(iii) The set $E = \{....,-4, -2, 0, 2, 4, ....\}$ of all even integers is a commutative ring without unit element.

(iv) The sets R (all real numbers) and $Q$ (all rational numbers) are commutative rings with unity with respect to usual addition and multiplication.

(v) The set M of all matrices of order $n \times n$ whose elements as integers, real, complex number forms a non-commutative ring with or without unit element under matrix addition and matrix multiplication, is called a ring of matrices.

(vi) $(Z_n, \oplus, \otimes)$ is a commutative ring with respect to addition and multiplication modulo $n$, denoted as $\oplus_n$ and $\otimes_n$, respectively. e.g., $Z_6 = \{0, 1, 2, 3, 4, 5\}$ is a ring of integers modulo 6.

Here, $2 \oplus_6 3 = 5$ , $3 \oplus_6 4 = 1$ , $4 \oplus_6 5 = 3, 2 \otimes_6 3 = 0$, $4 \otimes_6 5 = 2$

(vii) $z[i] = \{m + ni : m, n \text{ are integers}, i = \sqrt{-1}\}$ is a commutative ring with unity with respect to the usual addition and multiplication of complex numbers called ring of Gaussian integers.

## Ring with Zero Divisors

A ring $R$ is said to be ring with zero divisor, if there exists elements $a$, $b$ in $R$, such that $ab = 0 \ \Rightarrow a \neq 0, \ b \neq 0$.

e.g.,

(i) The set $M$ of all matrices of order $2 \times 2$ having their elements as integers forms a ring with zero divisors under addition and multiplication of matrices.

i.e.,

If $A = \begin{bmatrix} 1 & 1 \\ 1 & 1 \end{bmatrix}, B = \begin{bmatrix} -1 & -1 \\ 1 & 1 \end{bmatrix}, O = \begin{bmatrix} 0 & 0 \\ 0 & 0 \end{bmatrix}$, then $AB = O$

but $A \neq O$ and $B \neq O$.

(ii) $(\{0, 1, 2, 3, 4, 5\} +_6, \times_6)$ is a ring and $2 \times_6 3 = 0$. However, $2 \neq 0$, $3 \neq 0$. Hence, this ring is a ring with zero divisors.

## Ring without Zero Divisors

A ring $R$ is said to be ring without zero divisor, if $ab = 0$ $\Rightarrow$ Either $a = 0$ or $b = 0$

e.g., The ring of integers is a ring without zero divisors.

> **Note** A ring $R$ is without zero divisors if and only if the cancellations laws holds in $R$.
>
> Let $R$ be a ring and $a, b, c \in R$, such that $a \neq 0$.
>
> Now, $ab = ac$
>
> $\Rightarrow$ $a(b - c) = 0$
>
> $\Rightarrow$ $a(b - c) = 0$
>
> Since, $R$ is ring without zero divisors,
>
> then $a(b - c) - 0 \rightarrow a = 0$ or $b - c = 0$
>
> but $a \neq 0$
>
> $\therefore$ $b - c = 0 \ \Rightarrow b = c$
>
> Similarly, $ba - ca \rightarrow b - c$

## Some Definitions

**(i)** An element a in a ring $R$ is called idempotent, if $a^2 = a$.

**(ii)** An element a in a ring $R$ is called nilpotent, if $a^n = 0$ for some positive integer $n$.

e.g., In the ring $Z_4 = \{0, 1, 2, 3\}$ of integers modulo 4; 0 and 1 are idempotent elements, since $0^2 = 0$, $1^2 = 1$. 0 and 2 are nilpotent elements, since $2^2 = 0$.

***Example 1.*** *Show that the set $R = \{0, 1, 2, 3, 4, 5\}$ forms a commutative ring with respect to binary operations '$+_6$' and '$\times_6$'.*

**Solution.** First we shall prove that $(R, '+_6')$ is an abelian group.

Now, forming a composition table for '$+_6$'

| $+_6$ | 0 | 1 | 2 | 3 | 4 | 5 |
|---|---|---|---|---|---|---|
| 0 | 0 | 1 | 2 | 3 | 4 | 5 |
| 1 | 1 | 2 | 3 | 4 | 5 | 0 |
| 2 | 2 | 3 | 4 | 5 | 0 | 1 |
| 3 | 3 | 4 | 5 | 0 | 1 | 2 |
| 4 | 4 | 5 | 0 | 1 | 2 | 3 |
| 5 | 5 | 0 | 1 | 2 | 3 | 4 |

From composition table it is clear that R is closed under '$+_6$'.

**Associativity law** If $a, b, c \in R$, then we have to show that

$a +_6 (b +_6 c) = (a +_6 b) +_6 c$

$a +_6 (b +_6 c)$ = a remainder when $a + (b + c)$ is divided by 6
= a remainder when $(a + b) + c$ is divided by 6
$= (a +_6 b) +_6 c$

**Existence of identity** Since, $0 \in R$, then

$$0 +_6 a = a = a +_6 0, \forall a \in R$$

Thus, 0 is the identity which exists in R.

**Existence of inverse** From composition table it is observed that $1 +_6 5 = 0, 2 +_6 4 = 0, 3 +_6 3 = 0$. Hence, inverse of every element exists in R.

**Commutativity law** If $a, b \in R$, then we have to show that

$a +_6 b = b +_6 a$

$a +_6 b$ = a remainder when $(a + b)$ is divide by 6
= a remainder when $(b + a)$ is divided by 6
$= b +_6 a$

Thus, $(R, '+_6')$ is an abelian group.

Next we form a composition table for $'\times_6'$ as follows

| $\times_6$ | 0 | 1 | 2 | 3 | 4 | 5 |
|---|---|---|---|---|---|---|
| 0 | 0 | 0 | 0 | 0 | 0 | 0 |
| 1 | 0 | 1 | 2 | 3 | 4 | 5 |
| 2 | 0 | 2 | 4 | 0 | 2 | 4 |
| 3 | 0 | 3 | 0 | 3 | 0 | 3 |
| 4 | 0 | 4 | 2 | 0 | 4 | 2 |
| 5 | 0 | 5 | 4 | 3 | 2 | 1 |

From this composition table it is observed that R is closed under $'\times_6'$. Also, $'\times_6'$ is associative. For this, we have

$$a \times_6 (b \times_6 c) = (a \times_6 b) \times_6 c, \forall a, b, c \in R$$

Now,

$a \times_6 (b \times_6 c)$ = a remainder when $a \times (b \times c)$ is divided by 6
= a remainder when $(a \times b) \times c$ is divided by 6
$= (a \times_6 b) \times_6 c$

$\therefore \quad a \times_6 (b \times_6 c) = (a \times_6 b) \times_6 c$.

**Distributive laws** If $a, b, c \in R$, then

$a \times_6 (b +_6 c) = (a \times_6 b) +_6 (a \times_6 c)$

and $(b +_6 c) \times_6 a = (b \times_6 a) +_6 (c \times_6 a)$

Now,

$a \times_6 (b +_6 c)$ = a remainder when $a(b + c)$ is divided by 6
= a remainder when $ab + ac$ is divided by 6
$= (a \times_6 b) +_6 (a \times_6 c)$

Similarly, $(b +_6 c) \times_6 a = (b \times_6 a) +_6 (c \times_6 a)$

**Commutativity under** $\times_6$ If $a, b \in R$, then

$$(a \times_6 b) = (b \times_6 a)$$

Now, $a \times_6 b$ = a remainder when $a \times b$ is divided by 6
= a remainder when $b \times a$ is divided by 6
$= b \times_6 a$

$\therefore \quad a \times_6 b = b \times_6 a$

Hence, $(R, '+_6', '\times_6')$ is a commutative ring.

# Integral Domain

A commutative ring R with unit element having no zero divisors is called an integral domain. *e.g.*,

(i) The ring Z of integers $(Z, +, \cdot)$ is an integral domain.
Since, Z is a commutative ring with identity element and for any two integers a and b, $ab = 0 \Rightarrow a = 0$ or $b = 0$.

(ii) The commutative ring $Z_6 = \{0, 1, 2, 3, 4, 5\}$ is not an integral domain.
Since, $2 \otimes_6 3 = 0$ but $2 \neq 0$ and $3 \neq 0$ in $Z_6$.

(iii) $Z_5 = \{0, 1, 2, 3, 4\}$ is an integral domain, since, $\forall$ $a, b \in Z_5$, $a \otimes_5 b \neq 0$ and $a \neq 0$, $b \neq 0$.

# Division Ring (Skew-field)

A ring R with unit element having atleast two elements is called a division ring or a skew-field, if every non-zero elements of R possesses their multiplicative inverse.

# Field

A commutative ring R with unit element having atleast two elements is called a field, if every non-zero elements of R possesses their multiplicative inverse.

or

A commutative division ring is called a field.

> **Note** If R is a field, then $a \neq 0 \in R \Rightarrow a^{-1} \in R$.

*e.g.*,

(i) The set $C = \{a + ib : a, b \in R\}$ of complex number is a field under usual addition and multiplication of complex numbers.

(ii) $(Q, +, \cdot)$ is a field, where Q is set of all rational numbers.

(iii) For any prime p, $Z_p = \{0, 1, 2, \ldots, p-1\}$ is a field with respect to addition and multiplication modulo p.

(iv) $(Z_6, \oplus_6, \otimes_6)$ is not a field.
Since, $2 \neq 0 \in Z_6$ has no multiplicative inverse in $Z_6$.

## Important Results on Integral Domain and Field

1. Let $R$ be a commutative ring. Then, $R$ is an integral domain if and only if $ab = ac \Rightarrow b = c$ where $a, b, c \in R$ and $a \neq 0$.
2. Every field is an integral domain but every integral domain is not a filed. e.g., the set of integers $Z$ is an integral domain but not field. Since, $a \neq 0 \in Z$ does not have the multiplicative inverse in $Z$.
3. Every finite integral domain is a field.
4. Let $R$ be a ring, such that the equation $ax = b$ has a solution for all $a \neq 0 \in R$ and for all $b \in R$, then $R$ is a division ring.
5. A field has no zero divisors.
6. A finite commutative ring without zero divisors is a field.
7. Every field is skew-field, but converse is not true. e.g., let $M$ be the set of all matrices of order $2 \times 2$ of the form $\begin{bmatrix} a+ib & c+id \\ -c+id & a-ib \end{bmatrix}$, then it is not a field because $AB = BA$ does not hold in $M$.

***Example 2.*** *Show that the set of numbers of the form $a + b\sqrt{2}$, where a and b are rational numbers is a field with respect to addition and multiplication.*

**Solution.** Let $R = \{a + b\sqrt{2}: a, b \in Q\}$. First we shall show that $(R, '+')$ is an abelian group.

**Closure property** Let $a_1 + b_1\sqrt{2}, a_2 + b_2\sqrt{2} \in R$

Now, $(a_1 + b_1\sqrt{2}) + (a_2 + b_2\sqrt{2}) = (a_1 + a_2) + (b_1 + b_2)\sqrt{2}$ (by associative law)

Since, $a_1, a_2 \in Q \Rightarrow a_1 + a_2 \in Q$ and $b_1, b_2 \in Q \Rightarrow b_1 + b_2 \in Q$

$\therefore \quad (a_1 + a_2) + (b_1 + b_2)\sqrt{2} \in R$

Thus, $R$ is closed under addition.

**Associative law** Since, $a + b\sqrt{2}$ is real number and addition in real numbers is associative, so associative law holds in $R$.

**Existence of identity** Since, $0 \in Q$, then $0 + 0 \cdot \sqrt{2} \in R$

Now, $(a + b\sqrt{2}) + (0 + 0 \cdot \sqrt{2}) = (a + 0) + (b + 0)\sqrt{2}$

$$= a + b\sqrt{2} \quad \left(\because \begin{matrix} a + 0 = a \\ b + 0 = b \end{matrix}\right)$$

Thus, 0 is an additive identity of $R$.

**Existence of inverse** Since, $a \in Q \Rightarrow -a \in Q$

If $a + b\sqrt{2} \in R$, then $(-a) + (-b)\sqrt{2} \in R$, we have

$(a + b\sqrt{2}) + [(-a) + (-b)\sqrt{2}] = (a - a) + (b - b)\sqrt{2} = 0 + 0 \cdot \sqrt{2}$

Thus, $(-a) + (-b)\sqrt{2}$ is an additive inverse of $a + b\sqrt{2}$ in $R$.

**Addition is always commutative**

Hence, $(R, '+')$ is an abelian group.

**Closed under multiplication**

If $a_1 + b_1\sqrt{2}, \; a_2 + b_2\sqrt{2} \in R$, then

$(a_1 + b_1\sqrt{2}) \cdot (a_2 + b_2\sqrt{2}) = (a_1a_2 + 2b_1b_2) + (a_1b_2 + b_1a_2)\sqrt{2}$

Since, $a_1, a_2, b_1, b_2 \in Q$, then $a_1a_2 + 2b_1b_2 \in Q$ and $a_1b_2 + b_1a_2 \in Q$

Thus, $(a_1a_2 + 2b_1b_2) + (a_1b_2 + b_1a_2)\sqrt{2} \in R$. Hence, $R$ is closed under multiplication.

Multiplication is always distributive over addition.

**Multiplication is always commutative**

Hence, $(R, '+', '\bullet')$ is an abelian ring. Now, in order to prove that $R$ is a field, we have to prove that unity belong to $R$ and every non-zero elements of $R$ possesses its multiplicative inverse. For this purpose, we have

$$1 \in Q, \text{ then } 1 + 0 \cdot \sqrt{2} \in R, \text{ then}$$

$$(a + b\sqrt{2}) \cdot (1 + 0 \cdot \sqrt{2}) = a + b\sqrt{2}$$

Thus, $1 + 0 \cdot \sqrt{2} = 1 \in R$ is a multiplicative identity. Further let

$$a + b\sqrt{2} \neq 0 \text{ and } a + b\sqrt{2} \in R$$

$\Rightarrow \quad$ Either $a \neq 0$ or $b \neq 0$.

Then, we have

$$\frac{1}{a + b\sqrt{2}} = \frac{a - b\sqrt{2}}{a^2 - 2b^2} = \left(\frac{a}{a^2 - 2b^2}\right) + \left(\frac{-b}{a^2 - 2b^2}\right)\sqrt{2}$$

Since, $a, b \in Q$, then we can have that $a^2 = 2b^2$ only if $a = 0$ and $b = 0$ but this is not possible because either $a \neq 0$ or $b \neq 0$. Thus, $\frac{a}{a^2 - 2b^2}$ and $-\frac{b}{a^2 - 2b^2}$ are both rational numbers and hence, we have

$$\frac{1}{a + b\sqrt{2}} \in R \text{ and } (a + b\sqrt{2}) \cdot \frac{1}{a + b\sqrt{2}} = 1 = 1 + 0 \cdot \sqrt{2}$$

Hence, $\frac{1}{a + b\sqrt{2}}$ is a multiplicative inverse of non-zero element $a + b\sqrt{2}$. Consequently, $(R, '+', '\bullet')$ is a field.

# Subrings

Let $(R, +, \cdot)$ be a ring. A non-empty subset $S$ of $R$ is called a subring of $R$, if $(S, +, \cdot)$ is a ring. e.g.,

(i) The ring of rational numbers is a subring of the ring of real numbers.

(ii) The set $S = \{0, 2\}$ is a subring of $Z_4 = \{0, 1, 2, 3\}$ of integers modulo 4, under addition and multiplication modulo 4.

***Note*** **(a)** $\{0\}$ and $R$ itself are the subrings of $R$, called improper or trivial subrings.

**(b)** All subrings of $R$ except $\{0\}$ and $R$ called proper subrings.

## Important Results on Subrings

1. The necessary and sufficient condition for a non-empty subset $S$ of a ring $R$ to be a subring, if
   (i) $a \in S,\ b \in S \Rightarrow a - b \in S$ (ii) $a \in S,\ b \in S \Rightarrow ab \in S$
2. The intersection of two subrings is again a subring.
3. An arbitrary intersection of subrings is a subring.
4. The union of two subrings of $R$ need not be a subring of $R$. The union of two subrings is a subring if and only if one is contained in the other.
5. The centre of a ring $R$, is a subring of R *i.e.*, $Z(R) = \{a \in R: xa = ax, \forall\, x \in R\}$ is a subring of $R$.
6. The centre of a division ring (or skew-field) is a field. *i.e.*, if $R$ be a division ring, then $Z(R)$ is a field.
7. The sum of two subrings of a ring $R$ may not be a subring of $R$.

# Subfield

Let $(F, +, \cdot)$ be a field. A non-empty subset $K$ of $F$ is called a subfield of $F$, if $(K, +, \cdot)$ is a field. *e.g.,*

(i) The field of real numbers is a subfield of the field of complex numbers.

(ii) The field of rational numbers is a subfield of the field of real numbers.

### Important Result on Subfield

The necessary and sufficient condition for a non-empty subset $K$ of a field $F$ to be a subfield of $F$ are

(i) $a \in K,\ b \in K \Rightarrow a - b \in K$

(ii) $a \in K,\ b \in K \Rightarrow ab^{-1} \in K$

# Characteristic of a Ring

Let $R$ be a ring with zero element '0' and suppose there exists a positive integer $n$, such that

$na = a + a + a + \ldots + a$ (upto $n$ terms) $= 0,\ \forall\, a \in R.$

Then, the smallest such positive integer $n$ is called the characteristic of a ring. If there does not exist such positive integer $n$ such that $na = 0, \forall\ a \in R$ and $a \neq 0$, then the ring $R$ is said to be of characteristic zero or infinite. e. g.,

(i) Char $(Z) = 0$, Char $(Q) = 0$, Char $(R) = 0$. Here, $Z, Q$ and $R$ are the rings of integers, rationals and reals, respectively.

(ii) Char $(Z_2) = 2$

Here, $Z_2 = \{0, 1\}$

Clearly, 2 is the smallest positive integers, such that $2 \otimes_2 0 = 0$ and $2 \otimes_2 1 = 0$. In general, Char $(Z_n) = n$.

**Note** Characteristic of any integral domain is either zero or a prime number.

# Theorem on Characteristic of a Ring

***Theorem 1*** The characteristic of a field is either zero or a prime number.

***Theorem 2*** Order of a finite field $F$ is $p^n$, for some prime $p$ and some positive integer $n$.

***Theorem 3*** If $R$ is a finite (non-zero) integral domain, then $O(R) = p^n$.

e. g.,

(i) Let $R$ be a non-zero ring, such that $x^2 = x,\ \forall\, x \in R$, then $R$ is commutative ring of characteristic 2.

Since, $x + x \in R$, so $(x + x)^2 = x + x$

$\Rightarrow \quad x^2 + x^2 + x^2 + x^2 = x + x$

$\Rightarrow \quad x + x + x + x = x + x$

$\Rightarrow \quad 2x = 0$

$\Rightarrow \quad$ Char $(R) = 2$

(ii) If $R$ be a commutative ring of characteristic 2, then $(a + b)^2 = (a - b)^2 = a^2 + b^2,\ \forall\ a, b \in R.$

(iii) If $F$ is a field of characteristic $p$, (prime number), then $(a + b)^p = a^p + b^p,\ \forall\ a,\ b \in F.$

(iv) Let $R$ be a ring with characteristic $n$. Suppose, $ma = 0$, $\forall\ a \in R$ and for some positive integer $m$, then $n/m$.

(v) If $F$ is a finite field, its characteristic must be a prime number $p$ and $F$ contains $p^n$ elements for some integer $n$. Further, if $a \in F$, then $a^{p^n} = a$.

# Ordered Integral Domain

Let $(R, +, \cdot)$ be an integral domain. This integral domain is said to be ordered, if $R$ contains a subset $R_+$ (the set of positive elements of $R$), such that

**(i)** $R_+$ is closed under addition and multiplication as define on $R$.

**(ii)** There is one and only one $a = 0$, $a \in R_+, -a \in R_+$, $\forall\ a \in R$ holds.

e.g., The integral domain of integers is ordered.

## Ordered Field

A field $F$ is said to be ordered, if it is ordered as an integral domain.

**Note (a)** The set of complex numbers is not ordered integral domain.

**(b)** The field $Z_p = \{0, 1, 2, \ldots, p - 1\}$, where $p$ is a prime number is not ordered.

# Ideals

**Definition** A non-empty subset $S$ of a ring $R$ is called an ideal or a two sided ideal of $R$, if

**(i)** $(S,+)$ is a subgroup of $(R,+)$ *i.e.,*
$a \in S$ and
$b \in S \Rightarrow a-b \in S$

**(ii)** $a \in S$ and $r \in R \Rightarrow ra \in S$ and $ar \in S$. In other words, a non-empty subset $S$ of a ring $R$ is an ideal of $R$, if $S$ is both a left and right ideal of $R$.

## Left Ideal

A non-empty subset $S$ of a ring $R$ is called a left ideal of $R$, if

**(i)** $(S,+)$ is a subgroup of $(R,+)$ *i.e.,*
$a \in S$ and $b \in S \Rightarrow a-b \in S$

**(ii)** $a \in S$ and $r \in R \Rightarrow ra \in S$.

## Right Ideal

A non-empty subset $S$ of a ring $R$ is called a right ideal of $R$, if

**(i)** $(S,+)$ is a subgroup of $(R,+)$ *i.e.,*
$a \in S$ and $b \in S \Rightarrow a-b \in S$

**(ii)** $a \in S$ and $r \in R \Rightarrow ar \in S$

> ***Note*** **(a)** $(2) = \{...-4, -2, 0, 2, 4, ...\}$
> **(b)** $(3) = \{...-6, -3, 0, 3, 6, ...\}$ etc., are ideals in $Z$.

*e.g.,*

(i) If $Z$ be the ring of integers and $n$ be any integers, then $(n) = \{nx : x \in Z\}$ is an ideal of $Z$.

Since, for $a, b \in (n) \Rightarrow a-b \in (n)$ and for any integer $r \in (n)$,

$$ra \in (n) \text{ and } ar \in (n)$$

(ii) If $S$ be an ideal of a ring $R$ and $1 \in S$, then $S = R$

Since, for any $r \in R$, $1r \in S$

($\because$ $S$ is an ideal of $R$ and $1 \in S$)

$\therefore$ $R \subseteq S$

Obviously, $S \subseteq R$

Hence, $S = R$

## Important Results on Ideals

1. The intersection of any two ideals of a ring $R$ is again an ideal of $R$.
2. The union of two ideals of a ring $R$ need not be an ideal of $R$. $A \cup B$ will be ideal $\Leftrightarrow A \subseteq B$ or $B \subseteq A$.
3. The sum of two ideals of a ring $R$ is an ideal of $R$.
4. Product of two ideals of a ring $R$ is an ideal of $R$.
5. If $A$ is a left ideal and $B$ is a right ideal of a ring $R$, then $AB$ is a two sided ideal of $R$.
6. If $A$ and $B$ are two ideals of a ring $R$, then
   (i) $AB \subseteq A \cap B$
   (ii) $AB \subseteq A + B$
7. If $S$ is any ideal of a ring $R$ and $T$ any subring of $R$, then $S$ is an ideal of $S + T$.
8. The intersection of all ideals of a ring $R$ containing a non-empty subset $M$ of $R$ is the smallest ideal of $R$ containing $M$.
9. If $R$ is a commutative ring and $a \in R$, then the set $Ra = \{ra : r \in R\}$ is an ideal of $R$.
10. Let $R$ be a commutative ring with unit element whose only ideals are $\{0\}$ and $R$ itself, then $R$ is a field.
11. A field has no proper ideals.

***Example* 3.** *Let $R$ be the ring of all matrices of order $2 \times 2$ over integers and let $S$ be the set of all $2 \times 2$ matrices of the form $\begin{pmatrix} a & 0 \\ b & 0 \end{pmatrix}$, where $a$, $b$ are integers, then $S$ is a left ideal but not right ideal of $R$.*

**Solution.** Let $A, B \in S$, then

$$A = \begin{pmatrix} a_1 & 0 \\ b_1 & 0 \end{pmatrix}, B = \begin{pmatrix} a_2 & 0 \\ b_2 & 0 \end{pmatrix}$$

$$\text{Now, } A - B = \begin{pmatrix} a_1 & 0 \\ b_1 & 0 \end{pmatrix} - \begin{pmatrix} a_2 & 0 \\ b_2 & 0 \end{pmatrix} = \begin{pmatrix} a_1 - a_2 & 0 \\ b_1 - b_2 & 0 \end{pmatrix} \in S$$

($\because$ $a_1, a_2, b_1, b_2$ are integers so are $a_1 - a_2$ and $b_1 - b_2$)

Moreover, if $X = \begin{pmatrix} a & b \\ c & d \end{pmatrix}$ be an arbitrary element of $R$ and let $A = \begin{pmatrix} p & 0 \\ q & 0 \end{pmatrix}$ be any element of $S$, then

$$XA = \begin{pmatrix} a & b \\ c & d \end{pmatrix}\begin{pmatrix} p & 0 \\ q & 0 \end{pmatrix} = \begin{pmatrix} ap + bq & 0 \\ cp + dq & 0 \end{pmatrix} \in S$$

($\because$ $ap + bq$, $cp + dq$ are integers)

$\therefore$ $A \in S$, $X \in R \Rightarrow XA \in S$

Hence, $S$ is a left ideal of $R$.

Also, if $A = \begin{pmatrix} 1 & 0 \\ 1 & 0 \end{pmatrix} \in S$ and $X = \begin{pmatrix} 1 & 3 \\ 0 & 1 \end{pmatrix} \in R$, then $AX = \begin{pmatrix} 1 & 0 \\ 1 & 0 \end{pmatrix}\begin{pmatrix} 1 & 3 \\ 0 & 1 \end{pmatrix} = \begin{pmatrix} 1 & 3 \\ 1 & 3 \end{pmatrix} \notin S$

Thus, $AX \in S$. Hence, $S$ is not a right ideal of $R$.

***Example 4.*** *If $S$ is an ideal of $R$. Let $r(S) = \{x \in R : xa = 0, \forall a \in S\}$. Prove that $r(S)$ is an ideal of $R$.*

**Solution.** Since, $0 \in R$, such that $0a = 0$, it follows that $0 \in r(S)$. Thus, $r(S)$ is non-empty. Now, if $u, v$ are any elements of $r(S)$, then, $ua = 0$ and $va = 0$, where, $a \in S$, then

$$(u - v)a = ua - va = 0 - 0 = 0, \forall a \in S.$$

Thus, $u - v \in r(S)$. Hence, $r(S)$ is an additive subgroup of $R$.

Let $r_1$ be any arbitrary element of $R$ and $u \in r(S)$, then $ua = 0, \forall a \in S$. Since, $S$ being an ideal of $R$, therefore,

$$a \in S, r_1 \in R \Rightarrow ar_1 \in S \text{ and } r_1 a \in S$$

Then, $(r_1 u)a = r_1(ua) = r_1 0 = 0$

*i.e.,* $r_1 u \in r(S)$

Also, $(ur_1)a = u(r_1 a) = 0$ ($\because u \in r(S)$ and $r_1 a \in S$ so $u(r_1 a) = 0$)

*i.e.,* $ur_1 \in r(S)$

Thus, $r(S)$ is an additive subgroup of $R$ and $r_1 u \in r(S)$ and $ur_1 \in r(S)$. Hence, $r(S)$ is an ideal of $R$.

***Example 5.*** *Let $R$ be the ring of all real-valued, continuous functions on $[0,1]$. Show that the set $S = \{f \in R : f\left(\frac{1}{2}\right) = 0\}$ is an ideal of $R$.*

**Solution.** Let $f, g \in S \Rightarrow f\left(\frac{1}{2}\right) = 0 = g\left(\frac{1}{2}\right)$

$\Rightarrow (f - g)\left(\frac{1}{2}\right) = 0 \Rightarrow f - g \in S$

Also, Let $f \in S$ and $h \in R$

$$fh\left(\frac{1}{2}\right) = f\left(\frac{1}{2}\right) h\left(\frac{1}{2}\right) = 0 = hf\left(\frac{1}{2}\right)$$

$\Rightarrow S$ is an ideal of $R$.

> ***Note*** **(a)** Let $S$ be any subset of a ring $R$. An ideal $A$ of $R$ is said to be generated by $S$, if
> **(b)** $S \subseteq A$
> **(c)** If $I$ is any ideal of $R$, such that $S \subseteq I$, then $A \subseteq I$. We denote it by $A = \langle S \rangle$, and $\langle S \rangle$ is the smallest ideal containing $S$
> *e.g.,* let $A$ and $B$ be any two ideals of a ring $R$, then $A + B$ is an ideal of $R$ generated by $A \cup B$ *i.e.,* $A + B = \langle A \cup B \rangle$

# Homomorphism of Ring

Let $R$ and $R'$ be two rings with two binary operations addition and multiplication, then a mapping $\phi$ from the ring $R$ into the ring $R'$ is said to be a homomorphism, if

**(i)** $\phi(a + b) = \phi(a) + \phi(b)$

**(ii)** $\phi(ab) = \phi(a)\phi(b)$,

$\forall\ a, b \in R$.

> ***Note*** **(a)** Here, both rings have same binary operations, in case both have the operations as $(R, '+', '\cdot')$ and $(R', '*', 'O')$, then above conditions (i) and (ii) can be written as
> (i) $\phi(a + b) = \phi(a) * \phi(b)$
> (ii) $\phi(ab) = \phi(a) O \phi(b)$

e.g.,

(i) If $R$ is a ring, then the mapping $f : R \to R$ defined as $f(x) = x, \forall x \in R$ is a homomorphism.

Since, for any $x, y \in R$, we find that

$$f(x + y) = x + y = f(x) + f(y) \text{ and}$$
$$f(xy) = xy = f(x)f(y)$$

(ii) $f : Z_2 \to Z_2$ defined by $f(n) = n^2 - n$ is a ring homomorphism, where $Z_2 = \{0, 1\}$. Since, $\forall\ n, m \in Z_2$, we get

$$f(n + m) = f(n) + f(m) \qquad (\because 2nm = 0 \text{ in } Z_2)$$

and $f(nm) = f(n)f(m)$

## Important Results on Homomorphism

1. If $\phi$ is a homomorphism of $R$ into $R'$, then
   (i) $\phi(0) = 0'$, $0 \in R$, $0' \in R'$
   (ii) $\phi(-a) = -\phi(a)$, $\forall\ a \in R$
2. The homomorphic image of a commutative ring is a commutative ring. The converse need not be true *i.e.*, if $\phi : R \to R'$ be a homomorphism from a commutative ring $R$ onto a ring $R'$ then $R'$ is a commutative ring.
3. If $\phi : R \to R'$ is a homomorphism of a ring $R$ into a ring $R'$, then $\phi(R)$ is a subring of $R'$.

# Kernel of a Ring Homomorphism

Let $R$ and $R'$ be two rings and $\phi$ be a homomorphism from a ring $R$ into a ring $R$, then the set of all those elements of $R$ which are mapped onto the zero element of $R'$, is said to be kernel of $\phi$ and is usually denoted by ker ($\phi$).

*i.e.,* If $0'$ be the zero element of $R'$, then

$$\ker(\phi) = \{a \in R : \phi(a) = 0'\}.$$

## Important Results on Kernel

1. If $\phi$ is a homomorphism of a ring $R$ into a ring $R'$ with kernel $S$, then $S$ is an ideal of $R$.
2. If $\phi$ is homomorphism of a ring $R$ into a ring $R'$ and let $S$ be an ideal of $R$, then $\phi(S)$ is an ideal of $\phi(R)$.

# Isomorphism of a Ring

A mapping $\phi : R \to R'$ is called an isomorphism, if

**(i)** $\phi$ is a homomorphism.

**(ii)** $\phi$ is one-one.

**(iii)** $\phi$ is onto.

### Important Results on Isomorphism

1. If $f: R \to R'$ is a homomorphism, then $\ker(f) = \{0\}$, if and only if $f$ is one-to-one.
2. If $f: F \to R$ be a homomorphism, where $F$ be a field and $R$ be a ring, then $f$ is an isomorphism or takes each element into 0.
3. (i) Every isomorphic image of an integral domain is an integral domain.
   (ii) Every isomorphic image of a field is a field.
   (iii) Every isomorphic image of a division ring is a division ring.

# Quotient Rings

Let $R$ be a ring and $S$ be any ideal of $R$, then

$$\frac{R}{S} = \{a + S : a \in R\}$$

is called quotient ring of $R$ with respect to ideal $S$. When $(a + S) + (b + S) = (a + b) + S$ and $(a + S)(b + S) = ab + S$, $\forall a, b \in R$.

> **Note** (a) Zero element of $\frac{R}{S}$ is $S$.
> (b) Unit element of $\frac{R}{S}$ is $S + 1$.
> (c) If $S + a = S + b \Rightarrow a - b \in S$
> (d) The quotient ring is also known as residue class ring.

### Important Results on Quotient Rings

1. Let $S$ be an ideal of a ring $R$, then quotient ring $\frac{R}{S}$ is a homomorphic image of $R$ with kernel $S$ i.e., $f: R \to \frac{R}{S}$ is a homomorphism, where $\ker(f) = S$ = ideal of $R$.
2. Let $f: R \to R'$ be a homomorphism of a ring $R$ onto a ring $R'$, then $\frac{R}{\ker(f)} \equiv R'$, which is called fundamental theorem of homomorphism.
3. If $S$ and $T$ are two ideals of a ring $R$, then
   (i) $\frac{S+T}{T} \equiv \frac{S}{S \cap T}$
   (ii) $\frac{S+T}{S} \equiv \frac{T}{S \cap T}$
   (iii) $\frac{R}{S} \equiv \frac{R/T}{S/T}$ $(T \subseteq S)$

# Principal Ideal

An ideal $S$ of a ring $R$ is said to be principal ideal, if it is generated by a single element of $S$, *i.e.*, if $a \in S$, then $S = (a)$.

If $R$ is a ring with unity, then the ideal generated by 1, *i.e.*, (1) is the ring $R$ itself, because $r \cdot 1 = r$, $\forall\, r \in R$. Therefore, the ring $R$ itself is called the unit ideal.

Also, the ideal generated by the zero element of $R$. *i.e.*, (0) is called null ideal, because (0) consists of the zero element alone.

> **Note** (a) Every ring $R$ has atleast one principal ideal, namely (0).
> (b) Every ring with unit element has atleast two principal ideals, namely (0) and (1).
> (c) If $a$ is an element in a commutative ring $R$ with unity, then the set $S = \{ra : r \in R\}$ is a principal ideal of $R$ generated by the element $a$. *i.e.*, $S = (a)$.
> (d) A commutative ring $R$ with unity having no zero divisor is called a principal ideal ring, if every ideal of $R$ is a principal ideal.
> (e) The ring of integers is a principal ideal ring.
> (f) Every field is a principal ideal ring.

## Important Definitions

### Units

Let $R$ be a commutative ring with unity *i.e.*, $1 \in R$. Then, an element $a$ of $R$ is said to be unit in $R$, if there exists an element $b \in R$, such that $ab = 1$.

In other words, we can say that units of $R$ are those elements of $R$ which possess as multiplicative inverse.

*e.g.*, Every non-zero element in a field is a unit.

It is obvious that, if $a$ is a unit in a ring $R$, then $a^{-1}$ is also a unit in $R$. Also, the product of two units is again a unit, as if, $a$, $b$ are units of $R$, then $(ab)^{-1} = b^{-1}a^{-1} \in R$.

### Associates

Let $R$ be a commutative ring with unity. Then, an element $a$ of $R$ is said to be an associate of $b \in R$, if $a = ub$ for some unit $u$ of $R$.

If $a$ is an associate of $b$, then it can be denoted by $a \sim b$.

*e.g.*, The units of Gaussian integers $J[i]$ are $1, -1, i$ and $-i$. Therefore, if $a + ib$ be any non-zero element of $J[i]$, then it has exactly four associates namely,

$1 \cdot (a + ib) = a + ib$, $-1 \cdot (a + ib) = -a - ib$, $i(a + ib) = -b + ai$ and $(-i)(a + ib) = b - ai$.

> **Note** Let $D$ be an integral domain with unity 1. Two non-zero elements $a, b \in D$ are associates if and only if $a / b$ and $b / a$.

# Prime Ideals

Let $R$ be a commutative ring, then an ideal $S \neq R$ is said to be prime ideal, if

$ab \in S \Rightarrow$ either $a \in S$ or $b \in S$, $\forall\, a, b \in R$

e.g.,

(i) The ideal $\{0\}$ in $Z$ (ring of integers) is a prime ideal.
(ii) For any prime $p$, $(p) = \{px : x \in Z\}$ is a prime ideal of Z.

(iii) The ideal $(4)=\{....,-12,-8,-4,0,4,8,12,....\}$ is not a prime ideal of $Z$. Since, $2\cdot 6=12\in(4)$ but $2\notin(4)$ and $6\notin(4)$.

## Important Results on Prime Ideals

1. Let $R$ be a commutative ring with unity and let $S\neq R$ be an ideal of $R$. Then, $S$ is a prime ideal if and only if $\frac{R}{S}$ is an integral domain.
2. Let $R$ be a commutative ring and $S$ an ideal of $R$. Then, $S$ is a prime ideal of $R$ if and only if for any two ideals $A$ and $B$ of $R$. $AB\subseteq S \Rightarrow A\subseteq S$ or $B\subseteq S$.
3. Intersection of two prime ideals of a ring $R$ may not be a prime ideal of $R$. If $S_1$ and $S_2$ be prime ideals of $R$, then $S_1\cap S_2$ is a prime ideal of $R$, if $S_1\subseteq S_2$ or $S_2\subseteq S_1$.
4. Let $R$ be commutative ring with unit element in which every ideal is a prime ideal, then $R$ is a field.
5. Let $R$ be a commutative ring. Let $I$ be an ideal of $R$ and $S$ a prime ideal of $I$, then $S$ is an ideal of $R$.

# Maximal Ideals

An ideal $M\neq R$ of a ring $R$ is called a maximal ideal of $R$, if for any ideal $U$ of $R$, such that $M\subset U\subset R$, then either $M=U$ or $U=R$. In other words, an ideal $M\neq R$ is a maximal ideal of $R$, if there does not exist any proper ideal between $M$ and $R$.

e.g.,

(i) $\{0,2\}$ is a maximal ideal of the ring $Z_4=\{0,1,2,3\}$ modulo 4, because there is no proper ideal between $\{0,2\}$ and $Z_4$.

(ii) Proper ideals of $Z_8=\{0,1,2,3,4,5,6,7\}$ modulo 8 are

$(2)=\{0,2,4,6\}$

$(4)=\{0,4\}$

Now, $\{0,4\}$ is an ideal of $Z_8$ but is not a maximal ideal. Since, $\{0,4\}\subset\{0,2,4,6\}\subset Z_8$ *i.e.*, a proper ideal exist between $\{0,4\}$ and $Z_8$. Clearly, $\{0,3\}$ and $\{0,2,4,6\}$ are maximal ideals of the ring $Z_8$.

## Important Results on Maximal Ideals

1. If $M$ be an ideal of a ring $Z$ of all integers. Then, $M$ is maximal if and only if it is generated by some prime integer.
2. If $R$ is a commutative ring with unity, then an ideal $M$ of $R$ is maximal if and only if $\frac{R}{M}$ is a field.
3. $\{0\}$ is the only maximal ideal of a field.
4. Let $R$ be a commutative ring with unity. Then, every maximal ideal of $R$ is a prime ideal.
5. If $R$ is a finite commutative ring with unity, then every prime ideal of $R$ is a maximal ideal of $R$.
6. If $R$ is a finite commutative ring with unity, then an ideal is maximal if and only if it is a prime ideal in $R$.
7. If $f$ is a homomorphism from a ring $R$ onto a field $F$, then ker($f$) is a maximal ideal of $R$.
8. Intersection of two maximal ideals of a ring $R$ may not be a maximal ideal of $R$.
9. Let $S$ be a proper ideal of a ring $R$. Then, $S$ is contained in a maximal ideal of $R$.

***Example 6.*** *If $Z_{12}$ is a ring under addition and multiplication modulo 12, then find its all prime ideals and maximal ideals.*

**Solution.** Since, $Z_{12}=\{0,1,2,3,4,5,6,7,8,9,10,11\}$, it is commutative ring with unity.

Let $S_1=\{0,2,4,6,8,10\}$ and $S_2=\{0,3,6,9\}$ be two subsets of $Z_{12}$. Obviously, $S_1$ and $S_2$ are both ideals of $Z_{12}$.

For $S_1$, if $ab\in S_1$, then either $a\in S_1$ or $b\in S_1$

*i.e.*, $10\in S_1\Rightarrow 2\cdot 5\in S_1\Rightarrow 2\in S_1$

$8\in S_1\Rightarrow 2\cdot 4\in S_1\Rightarrow 2\in S_1$ and $4\in S_1$

$6\in S_1\Rightarrow 2\cdot 3\in S_1\Rightarrow 2\in S_1$

$4\in S_1\Rightarrow 2\cdot 2\in S_1\Rightarrow 2\in S_1$

$2\in S_1\Rightarrow 2\cdot 1\in S_1\Rightarrow 2\in S_1$

$0\in S_1\Rightarrow 0\cdot 0\in S_1\Rightarrow 0\in S_1$

Thus, $S_1$ is a prime ideal of $Z_{12}$.

For $S_2$, if $ab\in S_2\Rightarrow$ either $a\in S_2$ or $b\in S_2$

*i.e.* $9\in S_2\Rightarrow 3\cdot 3\in S_2\Rightarrow 3\in S_2$

$6\in S_2\Rightarrow 2\cdot 3\in S_2\Rightarrow 3\in S_2$

$3\in S_2\Rightarrow 3\cdot 1\in S_2\Rightarrow 3\in S_2$

$0\in S_2\Rightarrow 0\cdot 0\in S_2\Rightarrow 0\in S_2$

Thus, $S_2$ is a prime ideal of $Z_{12}$.

Further, since $Z_{12}$ is commutative ring with unity, so that $S_1, S_2$ are also maximal ideals.

***Example 7.*** *If E is a ring of even integers, then show that an ideal (4), generated by 4 is a maximal ideal of E.*

**Solution.** Let $S=(4)$ and let $T$ be an ideal of $E$, such that $S\subseteq T$. Then, there exists an element $a\in T$, such that $a\notin(4)=S$ implying that a is an even integer not divisible by 4.

So, that we have

$$a=4m+2 \text{ for some integer } m$$

Now, $2=a-4m\in T$ because $4m\in(4)=S$ and $S\subseteq T\Rightarrow 4m\in T$ and $a\in T$. Thus, $T$ has every even integral multiple of 2. Hence, $T=E$, consequently, $S=(4)$ is maximal ideal of $E$.

***Example 8.*** *Let R be the ring of all real-valued continuous functions on the closed interval [0, 1]. Let $M=\left\{f\in R: f\left(\frac{1}{3}\right)=0\right\}$, show that M is a maximal ideal of R.*

**Solution.** First we will show that $M$ is an ideal of $R$. Since, the continuous functions $\omega(x)=0, \forall x\in[0,1]$ belongs to $M$, so that $M$ is non-empty.

Let $f(x), g(x)\in M$, then $f\left(\frac{1}{3}\right)=0$, $g\left(\frac{1}{3}\right)=0$, now consider

$$h(x)=f(x)-g(x), \text{ then}$$

$$h\left(\frac{1}{3}\right)=f\left(\frac{1}{3}\right)-g\left(\frac{1}{3}\right)=0-0=0$$

$\therefore$ Thus, $M$ is an additive subgroup of $R$.

Let $r(x)$ be any arbitrary element of $R$ and $f(x) \in M$, such that $f\left(\frac{1}{3}\right)=0$, then suppose $t(x)=r(x)\,f(x)$.

$$\Rightarrow \quad t\left(\frac{1}{3}\right)=r\left(\frac{1}{3}\right)f\left(\frac{1}{3}\right)=r\left(\frac{1}{3}\right)\cdot 0=0$$

$\therefore \quad t(x) \in M$ i.e., $r(x)f(x) \in M$

Similarly, $f(x)\,r(x) \in M$. Hence, $M$ is an ideal of $R$. Now, we will show that $M$ is maximal. Obviously, $M \neq R$ because $i(x) \in R$ given by $i(x)=1$, which does not belong to $M$.

Let $N$ be an ideal of $R$ such that $M \subseteq N$, then there exists $\lambda(x) \in N$ and $\lambda(x) \notin M$, therefore, $\lambda\left(\frac{1}{3}\right) \neq 0$ so assumes $\lambda\left(\frac{1}{3}\right)=c$, where $c \neq 0$. Now, consider $\mu(x) \in R$ given by $\mu(x)=\lambda(x)-\beta(x)$, where $\beta(x)=c$, $\forall\, x \in [0,1]$. Then,

$$\mu\left(\frac{1}{3}\right)=\lambda\left(\frac{1}{3}\right)-\beta\left(\frac{1}{3}\right)=c-c=0$$

$\therefore \quad \mu(x) \in M$

$\Rightarrow \quad \mu(x) \in N$

$\therefore \quad \beta(x)=\lambda(x)-\mu(x) \in N \qquad (\because M \subseteq N)$

Let us define $\gamma(x) \in R$ by $\gamma(x)=\frac{1}{c}$, $\forall\, x \in [0, 1]$ and $N$ is an ideal of $R$, then $\beta(x) \in N, \gamma(x) \in R$

$\Rightarrow \quad \beta(x)\;\gamma(x) \in N$

$\Rightarrow \quad c\cdot\frac{1}{c} \in N$

$\Rightarrow \quad 1 \in N$

$\Rightarrow \quad i(x) \in N \qquad (\because i(x)=1)$

But $i(x)$ is the unit of $R$. Hence, $N=R$. Consequently, $M$ is a maximal ideal.

***Example 9.*** *Show that in a boolean ring $R$, every prime ideal $S \neq R$ is maximal.*

**Solution.** Let $T$ be any ideal of $R$, such that $S \subset T \subset R$, where $S \neq T$. We will prove that $T=R$. Since, $S \subset T$ and $S \neq T$, then there exists some $x \in T$, such that $x \notin S$. Since, $R$ is a boolean ring. So, $x^2=x \Rightarrow x^2r=xr, \forall r \in R$.

$\Rightarrow x(xr-r)=0 \in S$, since $S$ is an ideal of $R$.

$\Rightarrow x \in S$ or $xr-r \in S$. Since, $S$ is a prime ideal of $R$.

$\Rightarrow xr-r \in S$, since $x \notin S$. Let $xr-r=s$, where $s \in S$. Then,

$r=xr-s$. Since, $T$ is an ideal of $R$, so $x \in T$ and

$r \in R \Rightarrow xr \in T$

Also, $s \in S \subset T \Rightarrow S \in T$

$\therefore xr-s \in T$, since $T$ is an ideal of $R$.

$\Rightarrow \quad r \in T, \forall r \in R$

$\Rightarrow \quad R \subseteq T \Rightarrow T=R$

Hence, $S$ is a maximal ideal of $R$.

***Example 10.*** *Let $R$ be a commutative ring with unity and let $M$ be a maximal ideal of $R$, such that $M^2=\{0\}$. Show that if $N$ is any other maximal ideal of $R$, then $N=M$.*

**Solution.** $M^2=\{ab\colon a \in M,\ b \in M\}$

Since, $N$ is a maximal ideal of a commutative ring $R$ with unity

$\Rightarrow \quad \frac{R}{N}$ is a field.

$\Rightarrow \quad \frac{R}{N}$ is an integral domain.

$\Rightarrow \quad N$ is a prime ideal of $R$.

Let $m \in m$ be arbitrary.

Then, $\quad m^2=m\cdot m \in M^2=\{0\}$

$\Rightarrow \quad m^2=0 \Rightarrow m^2 \in N$, since $N$ is an ideal of $R$.

$\Rightarrow \quad m\cdot m \in N \Rightarrow m \in N$, since $N$ is a prime ideal of $R$.

Thus, $\quad M \subseteq N \subseteq R$

Since, $M$ is a maximal ideal of $R$, either $N=M$ or $N=R$

Hence, $\quad N=M$.

# Embedding Mapping

Let $R$ and $R'$ be two rings. A monomorphism (or one-one homomorphism) $\phi$ from $R$ into $R'$ is called an embedding (or imbedding) mapping and the ring $R'$ itself is called an extension of $R$.

***Example 11.*** *An integral domain can be embedded into a field.*

**Solution.** Let $D$ be an integral domain and let,

$$S=\{(a, b) \mid a,\ b \in D,\ b \neq 0\}$$

Now, define a relation $\sim$ on $S$ by

$$(a, b) \sim (c, d) \Leftrightarrow ad=bc$$

It is easy to check that $\sim$ is an equivalence relation on $S$. Thus, this relation partitions $S$ into disjoint equivalence classes. Let the equivalence class of $(a, b)$ be denoted by $[a, b]$. Let $F$ be the set of all these equivalence classes. Define addition and multiplication on $F$ as follows

$$[a, b]+[c, d]=[ad+bc,\ bd]$$

and $\quad [a, b]\cdot[c, d]=[ac,\ bd]$

Now, we shall show that $F$ forms a field under these operations.

First of all we shall show that the operations of addition and multiplication are well defined.

Let $\quad [a, b]=[a_1, b_1]$ and $[c, d]=[c_1, d_1]$

Then, $(a, b) \sim (a_1, b_1)$ and $(c, d) \sim (c_1, d_1)$

$\Rightarrow \quad ab_1=ba_1$ and $cd_1=dc_1$

$\Rightarrow \quad (ab_1)dd_1=(ba_1)dd_1$ and $(cd_1)bb_1=(dc_1)bb_1$

$\Rightarrow \quad ab_1dd_1+cd_1bb_1=ba_1dd_1+dc_1bb_1 \qquad \ldots(i)$

Now, we show that

$$[ad+bc,\ bd]=[a_1d_1+b_1c_1,\ b_1d_1]$$

This equality will hold, if

$$(ad+bc,\ bd) \sim (a_1d_1+b_1c_1,\ b_1d_1)$$

or $\quad (ad+bc)b_1d_1 = bd(a_1d_1+b_1c_1)$

or $\quad adb_1d_1 + bcb_1d_1 = bda_1d_1 + bdb_1c_1$

This is true by Eq. (i).

Hence, addition is well defined.

Next, Let $[a, b]=[a_1, b_1]$ and $[c, d]=[c_1, d_1]$,

then $\quad ab_1 = ba_1$ and $cd_1 = dc_1$

or $\quad ab_1cd_1 = ba_1dc_1 \quad$ ...(ii)

Now, $[a, b].[c, d]=[a_1, b_1]\cdot[c_1, d_1]$ will hold

if $\quad [ac, bd]=[a_1c_1, b_1d_1]$

or $\quad (ac, bd)\sim(a_1c_1, b_1d_1)$

or $\quad acb_1d_1 = bda_1c_1$

This is true by Eq. (ii).

Hence, multiplication is well defined.

**Associative law** Let $[a, b],[c, d]$ and $[e, f]\in F$. Then,

$$\begin{aligned}[a, b]+([c, d]+[e, f]) &= [a, b]+[cf+de, df]\\ &= [a(df)+b(cf+de), b(df)]\\ &= [(ad)f+(bc)f+(bd)e, (bd)f]\\ &= [(ad+bc)f+(bd)e, (bd)f]\\ &= [ad+bc, bd]+[e, f]\\ &= ([a, b]+[c, d])+[e, f]\end{aligned}$$

$\therefore$ Addition is associative in $F$.

**Commutative law** Let $[a, b],[c, d]\in F$, then

$$\begin{aligned}[a, b]+[c, d] &= [ad+bc, bd]\\ &= [bc+ad, db]=[cb+da, db]\\ &= [c, d]+[a, b]\ \forall\ [a, b],[c, d]\in F\end{aligned}$$

$\therefore$ Addition is commutative in $F$.

**Existence of additive identity** Let $[a, b]\in F$, then

$$\begin{aligned}[a, b]+[0, b] &= [ab+b.0, b^2]=[ab, b^2]\\ &= [a, b] \text{ as } (ab, b^2)\sim(a, b).\end{aligned}$$

Thus, $[0, b]$ the additive identity, since $[0, x]=[0, y]$

For any non-zero element $x, y\in D$.

**Existence of additive inverse** Let $[a, b]\in F$ be any element, then $[-a, b]\in F$

Also, $$\begin{aligned}[a, b]+[-a, b] &= [ab+b(-a), b^2]\\ &= [ab-ba, b^2]=[0, b^2]\\ &= [0, b] \quad [\because (0, b^2)\sim(0, b)]\end{aligned}$$

Thus, $[-a, b]$ is the additive inverse of $[a, b]$.

Therefore, $\{F, '+'\}$ forms an abelian group.

Now, we shall verify that multiplication is commutative, associative and is distributive over addition.

**Associative law** Let $[a, b],[c, d]$ and $[e, f]$ be any three elements of $F$.

Then, we have $$\begin{aligned}[a, b]\cdot([c, d]\cdot[e, f]) &= [a, b]\cdot[ce, df]\\ &= [a(ce), b(df)]\\ &= [(ac)e, (bd)f]\\ &= [ac, bd]\cdot[e, f]\\ &= ([a, b]\cdot[c, d])\cdot[e, f]\end{aligned}$$

Thus, multiplication is associative in $F$.

**Commutative law** Let $[a, b]$, $[c, d]$ be any two elements of $F$, then we have

$$\begin{aligned}[a, b]\cdot[c, d] &= [ac, bd]\\ &= [ca, db]=[c, d]\cdot[a, b].\end{aligned}$$

Thus, multiplication is commutative in $F$.

**Existence of multiplicative identity** Let $x$ be any non-zero element of $D$ and let $[a, b]\in F$, then we have

$[a, b]\cdot[x, x]=[ax, bx]=[a, b]$ as $(ax, bx)\sim(a, b)$

Thus, $[x, x]$ acts as a multiplicative identity.

**Existence of multiplicative inverse**

Let $[a, b]$ be any non-zero element of $F$, then $a\neq 0$ and $b\neq 0$.

Therefore, $\quad [b, a]\in F$.

Also, $[a, b]\cdot[b, a]=[ab, ba]=[x, x]$ as $(ab, ab)\sim(x, x)$.

$\therefore$ Every non-zero element possesses multiplicative inverse.

Hence, $\{F, +, \cdot\}$ is a field.

We now show that $D$ can be embedded into $F$ as follows

Define a mapping,

$$\theta : D\to F$$

by $\theta(a)=[ax, x]$, where $x$ is a non-zero element of $D$.

First we show that $\theta$ is well defined.

Let $a, b\in D$ and if $a=b$, then

$$ax=bx \quad (\because x\neq 0)$$

$\Rightarrow \quad xax=xbx \Rightarrow axx=xbx$

$\Rightarrow \quad [ax, x]=[bx, x]\Rightarrow\theta(a)=\theta(b)$

Now, to show that $\theta$ is one-one.

Let $\theta(a)=\theta(b)$ for $a, b\in D$, then

$$[ax, x]=[bx, x]$$

$\Rightarrow \quad (ax, x)\sim(bx, x) \Rightarrow axx=xbx$

$\Rightarrow \quad xxa=xxb\Rightarrow x^2a=x^2b$

$\Rightarrow x^2(a-b)=0$

$\Rightarrow \quad a-b=0 \quad (\because x^2\neq 0$ as $x\neq 0)$

$\Rightarrow \quad a=b$

$\therefore$ $\theta$ is one-one mapping.

Clearly, $\quad \theta(a+b)=\theta(a)+\theta(b), \forall\ a, b\in D$

and $\quad \theta(ab)=\theta(a)\ \theta(b)$

$\Rightarrow$ $\theta$ is homomorphism.

$\Rightarrow\theta$ is isomorphism of $D$ into $F$. $\theta$ is the required mapping which embedds the integral domain $D$ to a field $F$.

## Quotient Field

Since, $f: D\to F$ is an isomorphism of $D$ (integral domain) into $F$ (field), the field $F=\{[a, b]: a, b\in D \text{ and } b\neq 0\}$ is called field of quotients or quotient field of the integral domain $D$. The quotient field of an integral domain $D$ may be defined as a pair $(F, f)$ such that each $x\in F$ is expressible as the equivalence class $[f(a), f(b)]$ or $\dfrac{f(a)}{f(b)}$ for some $a, b\in D$ and $b\neq 0$.

e.g., The field of quotients of the integral domain $Z$ of integers is $Q$ (all rational numbers).

***Example 12.*** *Find the field of quotients of the integral domain* $J[i] = \{a + ib | a, b \in I\}$.

**Solution.** Let $F$ be the field of quotients of $J[i]$. Then, by definition

$$F = \left\{\frac{a+ib}{c+id} | a, b, c, d \in I \text{ and } c+id \neq 0\right\}$$

$$= \left\{\frac{(a+ib)(c-id)}{c^2+d^2} | a, b, c, d \in I\right\}$$

$$= \left\{\left(\frac{ac+bd}{c^2+d^2} + i\frac{bc-ad}{c^2+d^2}\right) | a, b, c, d \in I\right\}$$

$\therefore$ $F \subseteq F_1$, where $F_1 = \{x + iy | x, y \in Q\}$.

Now, let $x + iy$ be any element of $F_1$, then $x, y \in Q$, then we have,

$$x + iy = \frac{p_1}{q_1} + i\frac{p_2}{q_2},$$

with $p_1, p_2, q_1, q_2 \in I$ and $q_1 \neq 0$, $q_2 \neq 0$.

$$= \frac{p_1q_2 + ip_2q_1}{q_1q_2}$$

$$= \frac{p_1q_2 + ip_2q_1}{q_1q_2 + i \cdot 0} \in F \text{ as}$$

$$(p_1q_2 + ip_2q_1) \text{ and } (q_1q_2 + i \cdot 0) \in J[i]$$

$\therefore$ $(x + iy) \in F_1 \Rightarrow x + iy \in F$

$\therefore$ $F_1 \subseteq F_2$

Thus, $F = F_1$. Now, define a mapping

$$\theta : J[i] \rightarrow F_1$$

by $\theta(a + ib) = a + ib$

This mapping will be the embedding mapping.

Hence, $F_1 = \{x + iy | x, y \in Q\}$ is the field of quotients of $J[i]$.

# Principal Ideal Domain

An integral domain with unity is called a principal ideal domain (PID), if each ideal $A$ of $R$ is a principal ideal *i.e.*, $A = (a) = \{ar : r \in R\}$ for some $a \in A$.

*e.g.*,

(i) Ring of integers $Z$ is a PID.

(ii) For any prime $p$, the ring $Z_p$ of integers modulo $p$, is a PID.

## Important Results on Principal Ideal Domain

**1.** Every field is a PID but the converse is not true.

**2.** Any two non-zero elements $a$, $b$ in a PID have a gcd. Further, if $d \in R$ is a gcd of $a$ and $b$, then $d = xa + yb$ for some $x, y \in R$.

If $a$ and $b$ are relatively prime or coprime *i.e.*, $(a, b) = 1$, then $d$ is unit.

$\Rightarrow$ $xa + yb = 1$

**3.** In a PID an element is prime if and only if it is irreducible.

**4.** Let $R$ be a commutative ring with unity. A non-zero, non-unit element $p \in R$ is called an irreducible element, if $p = ab \Rightarrow$ either $a$ or $b$ is unit, $a, b \in R$.

**5.** Let $R$ be a PID, which is not a field, then an ideal $A = (a)$ is a maximal ideal if and only if '$a$' is an irreducible element of $R$.

# Euclidean Domain (ED)

An integral domain $R$ is called a Euclidean domain (or Euclidean ring), if for each $a \neq 0 \in R$, there exists a non-negative integer $d(a)$, such that

**(i)** $d(a) \leq d(ab)$, $\forall\ a \neq 0$, $b \neq 0 \in R$.

**(ii)** for each $a, b \in R$ with $b \neq 0$ $\exists$ $q, r \in R$, such that $a = bq + r$, where either $r = 0$ or $d(r) < d(b)$.

> ***Note*** **(a)** $d$ is called the Euclidean valuation on $R$ or Euclidean norm function.
> **(b)** $d(0)$ is not defined.
> **(c)** $d(b) \leq d(ab)$ also holds in above definition of Euclidean domain.

*e.g.*,

(i) The ring $Z$ of integers is a Euclidean domain.

(ii) Every field $F$ is a Euclidean domain.

(iii) The field $Q$ of rational numbers with $d(a) = 1$, $\forall\ a \neq 0 \in Q$ is a Euclidean domain but $d(a) = |a|$ is not an Euclidean domain.

(iv) The ring of Gaussian integers *i.e.*, $z\{i\} = \{m + ni : m, n \in Z\}$ is a Euclidean domain.

(v) $Z[\sqrt{2}] = \{m + n\sqrt{2} : m, n \in Z\}$ is a Euclidean domain.

(vi) Every Euclidean domain is a principal ideal domain. *i.e.*, ED $\Rightarrow$ PID.

(vii) If $d(a) = d(ab) \Leftrightarrow b$ is a unit and $d(a) < d(ab) \Leftrightarrow b$ is not a unit.

(viii) Let $D$ be a Euclidean domain with unit element 1, then $d(1) < d(x)$, then $x$ is not unit in $D$, if $d(1) = d(x)$, then $x$ is unit in $D$.

(ix) Let $R$ be a Euclidean domain,then
 (i) $d(a) = d(-a)$, $\forall\ a \neq 0 \in R$.
 (ii) If $d(a) = 0$ for $a \neq 0 \in R$, then a is unit in $R$.

(x) Let $a$ and $b$ be two non-zero elements of a Euclidean domain $R$, then if $a$ and $b$ are associates, then $d(a) = d(b)$ but converse is not true.

(xi) If $(m)$ be ideal of ED, then $d(m)$ is minimal.

# Unique Factorization Domain (UFD)

An integral domain $R$ with unity is called a unique factorization domain (UFD), if it satisfies the following conditions.

**(i)** Each non-zero element of $R$ is either a unit or can be expressed as a product of finite number of irreducible elements of $R$.

**(ii)** The above decomposition is unique upto the order and associates of the irreducible elements. It means if a non-zero, non-unit element $a \in R$ is expressible as $a = p_1 p_2 \dots p_r$ and $a = q_1 q_2 \dots q_s$, where $p_i's$ and $q_i's$ are irreducible elements of $R$, then $\exists$ a one-to-one correspondence between $p_i's$ and $q_i's$, such that the corresponding elements are associates. In particular, $r = s$.

**(iii)** Every irreducible element of $R$ is prime.

e.g.,

(i) Every field $F$ is a UFD.

(ii) The ring $Z$ of integers is a UFD.

(iii) Every Euclidean domain is a UFD.

(iv) $Z[i]$, $Z[\sqrt{2}]$, $F[x]$ are UFD.

## Important Results on UFD

**1.** An element in a UFD is prime if and only if it is irreducible.

**2.** Every Euclidean domain is a UFD.

**3.** Every principal ideal domain is a UFD.

**4.** ED $\Rightarrow$ PID $\Rightarrow$ UFD

# Polynomial Rings

Let $R$ be a ring and $x$ be an indeterminate which does not belong to $R$. Then, a polynomial of the form

$$f(x) = a_0 + a_1x + a_2x^2 + \dots + a_nx^n, \ a_n \neq 0$$

Where, $a_0, a_1, a_2 \dots, a_n, \dots$ all are in $R$ with finite and non-zero is called a polynomial over a ring $R$.

Set of all polynomials $f(x)$ of a ring $R$ is called polynomial ring and denoted by $R[x]$.

## Zero Polynomial

A polynomial over a ring $R$ of the type $a_0 + a_1x + a_2x^2 + \dots + a_nx^n + \dots$ is called a zero polynomial, if $a_n = 0, \ \forall \ n$.

## Degree of a Polynomial

Let $f(x) \in R[x]$ is of the form

$$f(x) = a_0 + a_1x + a_2x^2 + \dots + a_nx^n + \dots$$

Then, the degree of $f(x)$ is $n$ if and only if $a_n \neq 0$ and $a_m = 0$, $\forall \ m > n$.

**Definition** If a polynomial $f(x)$ is of degree $n$, then the term $a_nx^n$ is called the leading term and $a_n$ is called the leading coefficient and $a_0$ is called the constant term.

## Equality, Sum and Product of Polynomial

### Equality

Let $R$ be a ring and let, $f(x) = a_0 + a_1x + a_2x^2 + \dots$

and $g(x) = b_0 + b_1x + b_2x^2 + \dots$

be two polynomials over R. Then, they are said to be equal, if $a_n = b_n, \forall \ n$.

### Sum of Polynomials

Let $R$ be a ring and $x$ be indeterminate and let

$$f(x) = a_0 + a_1x + a_2x^2 + \dots$$

and $g(x) = b_0 + b_1x + b_2x^2 + \dots$ be two polynomials over $R$, *i.e.* $f(x), g(x) \in R[x]$. Then, $f(x) + g(x) = c_0 + c_1x + c_2x^2 + \dots$ is said to be the sum of $f(x)$ and $g(x)$, if $c_n = a_n + b_n, \forall \ n$.

### Product of Polynomials

Let $R$ be a ring and $x$ be an indeterminate and let $f(x), g(x) \in R[x]$, where,

$$f(x) = a_0 + a_1x + a_2x^2 + \dots$$

and $g(x) = b_0 + b_1x + b_2x^2 + \dots$

Then, the polynomial $f(x)g(x) = c_0 + c_1x + c_2x^2 + \dots$

Where, $c_n = a_0b_n + a_1b_{n-1} + \dots + a_nb_0$.

***Theorem*** The set $R[x]$ of all polynomial over an arbitrary ring $R$ forms a ring with respect to addition and multiplication of polynomials.

**Proof.** Since, by the definition of addition (sum) and multiplication (product) of polynomials $f(x), g(x) \in R[x]$. We have that $R[x]$ is closed under addition and multiplication.

**Associativity law** Let $f(x), g(x), h(x) \in R[x]$. *i.e.*,

$$f(x) = a_0 + a_1x + a_2x^2 + \dots = \sum_{k=0} a_kx^k$$

$$g(x) = b_0 + b_1x + b_2x^2 + \dots = \sum_{k=0} b_kx^k$$

and $h(x) = c_0 + c_1x + c_2x^2 + \dots = \sum_{k=0} c_kx^k$

We have that

$$\begin{aligned} f(x) + [g(x) + h(x)] &= \sum_{k=0} a_kx^k + \sum_{k=0} (b_k + c_k)x^k \\ &= \sum_{k=0} [a_k + (b_k + c_k)]x^k \\ &= \sum_{k=0} [(a_k + b_k) + c_k)]x^k \\ &= \sum_{k=0} (a_k + b_k)x^k + \sum_{k=0} c_kx^k \\ &= [f(x) + g(x)] + h(x) \end{aligned}$$

**Existence of identity** Let $0(x)$ be the zero polynomial of $R[x]$ that is, $0(x) = 0 + 0 \cdot x + 0 \cdot x^2 + \dots$

Let $f(x) = a_0 + a_1x + a_2x^2 + \dots \in R[x]$, we have

$$f(x)+0(x)=(a_0+0)+(a_1+0)x+(a_2+0)x^2+\dots$$
$$=a_0+a_1x+a_2x^2+\dots=f(x)$$

$\therefore$ $0(x)$ is the additive identity of $R[x]$.

**Existence of additive inverse** Let $f(x)\in R[x]$ and let $-f(x)$ be a polynomial of $R[x]$ defined as
$-f(x)=(-a_0)+(-a_1)x+(-a_2)x^2+\dots$. Then, we have

$$-f(x)+f(x)=(-a_0+a_0)+(-a_1+a_1)x+(-a_2+a_2)x^2+\dots$$
$$=0+0\cdot x+0\cdot x^2+\dots=0(x)$$

$\therefore -f(x)$ is the additive inverse of $f(x)$ and exists in $R\{x\}$.

**Commutativity for addition** Let $f(x), g(x)\in R[x]$

*i.e.*, $\quad f(x)=a_0+a_1x+a_2x^2+\dots$

and $\quad g(x)=b_0+b_1x+b_2x^2+\dots$

We have,

$$f(x)+g(x)=(a_0+b_0)+(a_1+b_1)x+(a_2+b_2)x^2+\dots$$
$$=(b_0+a_0)+(b_1+a_1)x+(b_2+a_2)x^2+\dots$$
$$=g(x)+f(x)$$

Thus, $(R[x],+)$ is an abelian group.

**Associativity for multiplication**

Let $f(x), g(x), h(x)\in R[x]$ *i.e.*,

$$f(x)=a_0+a_1x+a_2x^2+\dots=\sum_{i=0}a_ix^i$$

$$g(x)=b_0+b_1x+b_2x^2+\dots=\sum_{j=0}b_jx^j$$

and $$h(x)=c_0+c_1x+c_2x^2+\dots=\sum_{k=0}c_kx^k$$

We have,

$$f(x)[g(x)h(x)]=\sum_{i=0}a_ix^i\left[\sum_{j=0}b_jx^j.\sum_{k=0}c_kx^k\right]$$

$$=\sum_{i=0}a_ix^i[\sum_{l=0}d_lx^l],\text{ Where } d_l=\sum_{j+k=l}b_jc_k$$

$$=\sum_{m=0}e_mx^m,\quad \text{Where } e_m=\sum_{i+l=m}a_id_l$$

$\therefore e_m$ is the coefficient of $x^m$ in $f(x)[g(x)h(x)]$.

*i.e.*, $$e_m=\sum_{i+l=m}a_id_l$$

$$=\sum_{i+l=m}a_i[\sum_{j+k=l}b_jc_k]=\sum_{i+j+k=m}a_ib_jc_k$$

Similarly, we have the coefficient of $x^m$ in $[f(x)g(x)]h(x)$ is $e_m$, which is equal to

$$\sum_{i+j+k=m}a_ib_jc_k$$

Thus, $\quad f(x)[g(x)h(x)]=[f(x)g(x)]h(x)$

**Distributivity of multiplication over addition**

Let $$f(x)=\sum_{i=0}a_ix^i$$

$$g(x)=\sum_{j=0}b_jx^j\ \text{ and }\ h(x)=\sum_{k=0}c_kx^k$$

be the elements of $R[x]$, we have

$$f(x)[g(x)+h(x)]=\sum_{i=0}a_ix^i\left[\sum_{j=0}b_jx^j+\sum_{k=0}c_kx^k\right]$$

$$=\sum_{i=0}a_ix^i\left[\sum_{l=0}d_lx^l\right],\text{ where } d_l=b_l+c_l$$

$$=\sum_{m=0}e_mx^m,\text{ where } l_m=\sum_{i+l=m}a_id_l$$

$\therefore$ $l_m$ is the coefficient of $x^m$ in $f(x)\cdot[g(x)+h(x)]$

*i.e.*, $$l_m=\sum_{i+l-m}a_id_l=\sum_{i+l-m}a_i(b_l+c_l)$$

or $$l_m=\sum_{i+l=m}a_ib_l+\sum_{i+l=m}a_ic_l$$

$=$ Coefficient of $x^m$ in $[f(x)g(x)]$

$+$ Coefficient of $x^m$ in $[f(x)h(x)]$

$=$ Coefficient of $x^m$ in $[f(x)g(x)+f(x)h(x)]$

$\therefore$ $f(x)[g(x)+h(x)]=f(x)g(x)+f(x)h(x)$

Similarly, we can prove that

$$[g(x)+h(x)]f(x)=g(x)f(x)+h(x)f(x)$$

Hence, $R[x]$ forms a ring. This ring is called polynomial ring.

## Important Results on Polynomial Ring

1. If $R$ is commutative ring with unity, then $R[x]$ is also commutative ring with unity.
2. If $F$ is field, then $F[x]$ is commutative ring with unity. However, $F(x)$ is not a field.
3. If $R$ is an integral domain, then $R[x]$ is an integral domain.
4. If $F$ is a field, then $F[x]$ is an integral domain.
5. Units of $R$ and $R[x]$ are same.
6. Let $f(x), g(x)\in R(x)$, then
   (i) If $f(x)+g(x)\neq 0$, then deg $(f(x)+g(x))\leq$ max (deg $f(x)$, deg $g(x)$).
   (ii) If $f(x)\cdot g(x)\neq 0$, then deg $(f(x)g(x))\leq$ deg $f(x)+$ deg $g(x)$ equality holds, when $R[x]$ is an integral domain.
7. If $F$ is a field, then
   (i) $F(x)$ is an Euclidean domain.
   (ii) $F(x)$ is a principal ideal domain.
   (iii) $F(x)$ is a unique factorization domain.
8. If $R$ is a UFD, then $R[x]$ is a UFD.

## Division Algorithm

If $f(x)$ and $g(x)$ are two non-zero polynomials in $F(x)$, ($F$ being a field), then there exist two polynomials $r(x)$ and $s(x)$ in $F(x)$, such that

$$f(x) = r(x)\,g(x) + s(x)$$

where, $s(x) = 0$ or $\deg(s(x)) < \deg(g(x))$

**Content** Let $R$ be a UFD and let $f(x) = a_0 + a_1x + a_2x^2 + \ldots + a_nx^n$ be any non-zero polynomial in $R[x]$. Then, content of $f(x)$ i.e., $c(f) = \gcd$ of $a_0, a_1, a_2, \ldots, a_n$.

**Primitive** If $c(f) = 1$, then $f(x)$ is said to be primitive polynomial in $R[x]$.

e.g.,

(i) Let $f(x) = 1 + 2x + 6x^2 \in Z[x]$

$$a_0 = 1, a_1 = 2, a_2 = 6$$

Now, $c(f) = \gcd(1, 2, 6) = 1$

$\Rightarrow$ Content of $f(x)$ is 1.

$\Rightarrow$ $f(x)$ is primitive polynomial in $Z[x]$.

(ii) Let $f(x) = 4 + 2x + 6x^2 \in Z[x]$

$c(f) = \gcd(4, 2, 6) = 2$

$\Rightarrow$ $f(x)$ is not a primitive polynomial in $Z[x]$.

## Monic Polynomial

Let $f(x) = a_0 + a_1x + a_2x^2 + \ldots + a_nx^n$ be any non-zero polynomial in $R[x]$, such that $a_n = 1$, then $f(x)$ is called monic polynomial. e.g., $x^3 + 4x^2 + 6$ is monic polynomial whereas $2x^2 - 5$ is not monic polynomial.

## Important Results on Division Algorithm

1. Let $R$ be a UFD and $0 \neq f(x) \in R[x]$. Then, $f(x) = a f_1(x)$, where $a = c(f)$ and $f_1(x) \in R[x]$ is primitive.
2. If $R$ is a UFD and $f(x)$ and $g(x)$ are two polynomials in $R[x]$, then $f(x)$ and $g(x)$ are primitive polynomial in $R[x]$ $\Leftrightarrow$ $f(x)g(x)$ is primitive polynomial in $R[x]$.
   Also, $c(fg) = c(f) \cdot c(g)$

## Irreducible Polynomial

Let $R$ be an integral domain with unity. A polynomial $f(x) \in R[x]$ is said to be irreducible over $R$, if whenever $f(x) = g(x)h(x)$, where $g(x), h(x) \in R[x]$, then either $\deg(g(x)) = 0$ or $\deg(h(x)) = 0$ i.e., either $g(x)$ or $h(x)$ is a constant polynomial.

Further, $f(x) \in R[x]$ is said to be reducible over $R$, if it is not irreducible over $R$ i.e., $f(x)$ can be written as $f(x) = g(x)h(x)$, for some $g(x), h(x) \in R[x]$, where $\deg(g(x)) > 0$ and $\deg(h(x)) > 0$.

e.g.,

(i) The polynomial $x^2 + 1$ is irreducible over the field of real numbers.

(ii) The polynomial $x^2 - 2$ is irreducible over $Q$ (all rationals).

> ***Note*** **(a)** If $p$ is prime, then $1 + x + x^2 + \ldots + x^{p-1}$ is irreducible over $Q$ e.g.,
> For $p = 5$, $1 + x + x^2 + x^3 + x^4$ is irreducible over $Q$.
> **(b)** It may be observed that any ideal I of $F(x)$ is expressible as $I = \langle p(x) \rangle$, for some $p(x) \in I$ i.e.,
> $I = \langle p(x) \rangle = \{p(x)f(x) : f(x) \in F[x]\}$
> In particular, $\langle x \rangle = \{xf(x) : f(x) \in F(x)\}$

## Important Results on Irreducible Polynomial

1. The ideal $I = \langle p(x) \rangle$ in $F(x)$ is maximal ideal if and only if $p(x)$ is an irreducible element of $F[x]$.
2. $\dfrac{F[x]}{\langle p(x) \rangle}$ is a field if and only if $p(x)$ is an irreducible element of $F(x)$.

   e.g., $\langle x^2 + 1 \rangle$ is maximal ideal of $Q[x] \Rightarrow \dfrac{Q[x]}{\langle x^2 + 1 \rangle}$ is a field.
3. If $R$ is a ring, then $\dfrac{R[x]}{\langle x \rangle} \equiv R$, where $\langle x \rangle$ is the ideal generated by x.
4. Let $F$ be a field. The ideal $I = \langle p(x) \rangle = \{p(x)f(x) : f(x) \in F[x]\}$ in $F[x]$ is a maximal ideal if and only if $p(x)$ is an irreducible polynomial over $F$.
   Further, $\dfrac{F(x)}{\langle p(x) \rangle}$ is a field.
5. Let $f(x) \in R[x]$ be a primitive polynomial in $R[x]$ and an irreducible polynomial in $F[x]$. Then, $f(x)$ is an irreducible polynomial in $R[x]$.

***Example 13.*** *Show that $x^2 + 1$ is irreducible over the integer mod 7.*

**Solution.** We have,

$$F = Z_7 = \{0, 1, 2, 3, 4, 5, 6\}$$

Let $x^2 + 1 = (x + a)(x + b)$, $a, b \in F$

$\Rightarrow$ $a + b = 0$ ...(i)

$ab = 1$ ...(ii)

Eq. (i) is satisfied, when

$(a, b) = (0, 0), (1, 6), (2, 5), (3, 4), (4, 3), (5, 2), (6, 1)$

For these values of a and b,

$$ab = 0, 6, 3, 5, 5, 3, 6$$

Thus, Eq. (ii) is not satisfied and so $x^2 + 1$ is irreducible over Q.

***Example 14.*** *Factorize $x^2 + x + 5$ in F[x], where F is the field of integers mod 11.*

**Solution.** We have, $F = Z_{11} = \{0, 1, 2, 3, 4, 5, 6, 7, 8, 9, 10\}$.

Let $\quad x^2 + x + 5 = (x + a)(x + b),\ a, b \in F.$

Comparing the coefficients of x and constant terms on both the sides, we get

$$1 = a + b \quad \text{...(i)}$$

$$5 = ab \quad \text{...(ii)}$$

Eq. (i) is satisfied, when

$(a, b) = (1, 0), (2, 10), (3, 9), (4, 8), (5, 7), (6, 6)$

Consequently, $ab = 0, 9, 5, 10, 2, 3.$

We see that, both Eqs. (i) and (ii) are satisfied, when $a = 3,\ b = 9$.

Hence, $x^2 + x + 5 = (x + 3)(x + 9)$ in $Z_{11}$.

***Example 15.*** *Prove that $x^3 - 9$ is reducible over the integers mod 11.*

**Solution.** $F = Z_{11} = \{0, 1, 2, 3, 4, 5, 6, 7, 8, 9, 10\}$.

Since, $9 + 2 = 0$ in $Z_{11}$, so $-9 = 2$ in $Z_{11}$.

Let $x^3 - 9 = x^3 + 2 = (x + a)(x^2 + bx + c)$, where $a, b, c \in F$.

Comparing the coefficients of $x^2$, x and constant terms on both sides, we get

$$0 = a + b,$$

$$0 = ab + c,$$

$$2 = ac$$

The above equations are all satisfied, if $a = 7$, $b = 4$ and $c = 5 \in F$.

Hence, $x^3 - 9$ is reducible over $Z_{11}$ and

$$x^3 - 9 = x^3 + 2 = (x + 7)(x^2 + 4x + 5)$$

***Example 16.*** *If f(x) is in F[x], where F is the field of integers mod p, p a prime, and f(x) is irreducible over F of degree n, prove that $\frac{F[x]}{\langle f(x)\rangle}$ is a field with $p^n$ elements.*

**Solution.** Since, f(x) is irreducible over $F = Z_p$, $\frac{F[x]}{\langle f(x)\rangle}$ is a field.

Any element of this field is $a(x) + \langle f(x)\rangle$, where $a(x) \in F[x]$. By division algorithm in F[x], there exist $t(x), r(x) \in F[x]$, such that $a(x) = f(x)t(x) + r(x)$, ...(i)

where, $\quad r(x) = 0$ or $\deg r(x) < \deg f(x) = n$.

We take $r(x) = a_0 + a_1x + a_2x^2 + \ldots + a_{n-1}x^{n-1} \in F[x]$

From Eq. (i), $a(x) + \langle f(x)\rangle = r(x) + \langle f(x)\rangle$.

Since, $f(x)t(x) \in \langle f(x)\rangle$.

$\therefore\ a(x) + \langle f(x)\rangle = a_0 + a_1x + \ldots + a_{n-1}x^{n-1} + \langle f(x)\rangle$ ...(ii)

Where, $a_0, a_1, \ldots, a_{n-1} \in F = Z_p, o(Z_p) = p$.

Since, each of $a_0, a_1, \ldots, a_{n-1}$ (which are n in number) can be selected in p ways, so by Eq. (i), the number of elements of $\frac{F[x]}{\langle f(x)\rangle}$ is $p^n$.

***Example 17.*** *Prove that $x^2 + x + 4$ is irreducible over F, the field of integers mod 11. Also, prove that $\frac{F[x]}{< x^2 + x + 4 >}$ is a field having 121 elements.*

**Solution.** We have,

$$F = Z_{11} = \{0, 1, 2, 3, 4, 5, 6, 7, 8, 9, 10\}.$$

We observe that $f(x) = x^2 + x + 4$ is not satisfied by the elements of F (*i.e.*, $f(\alpha) \neq 0$ for each $\alpha \in F$). Consequently, $x^2 + x + 4$ is not expressible as a product of two linear factors in F[x]. Hence, $x^2 + x + 4$ is irreducible over F. By Theorem 3, $\frac{F[x]}{(x^2 + x + 4)}$ is a field. Any element of this field is of the form $f(x) + (x^2 + x + 4)$, where $f(x) \in F[x]$.

By Division algorithm in F[x], there exist $t(x), r(x) \in F[x]$, such that

$$f(x) = t(x)(x^2 + x + 4) + r(x), \text{ where}$$

$$r(x) = 0 \text{ or } \deg r(x) < \deg (x^2 + x + 4) = 2.$$

We may take $r(x) = \alpha x + \beta \in F[x]$

Since, $t(x)(x^2 + x + 4) \in \langle x^2 + x + 4\rangle$, therefore

$$f(x) + \langle x^2 + x + 4\rangle = r(x) + \langle x^2 + x + 4\rangle$$

$$= \alpha x + \beta + < x^2 + x + 4 > \quad \text{...(i)}$$

In the above expression $\alpha, \beta \in F = Z_{11}$ and $o(Z)_{11} = 11$. Consequently, each of $\alpha$ and $\beta$ can be selected in 11 ways. Hence, by Eq. (i), the number of elements of the field $\frac{F[x]}{\langle x^2 + x + 4\rangle}$ is $11^2 = 121$.

***Example 18.*** *If $f(x) \in R[x]$ is both primitive and irreducible polynomial in R[x], then f(x) is an irreducible polynomial in F[x].*

**Solution.** Let, if possible, f(x) be a reducible polynomial in F[x]. Then,

$$f(x) = g(x)h(x) \quad \text{...(i)}$$

where, $g(x), h(x) \in F[x]$, $\deg g(x) > 0$ and $\deg h(x) > 0$

$\therefore$ We can write

$$g(x) = \frac{g_0(x)}{a},\ h(x) = \frac{h_0(x)}{b}, \quad \text{...(ii)}$$

where $a, b \in R$ and $g_0(x) \in R[x]$, $h_0(x) \in R[x]$.

We can write

$$g_0(x) = \alpha\, g_1(x),\ h_0(x) = \beta h_1(x), \quad \text{...(iii)}$$

where, $\alpha = c(g_0)$, $\beta = c(h_0)$; $g_1(x)$ and $h_1(x)$ are primitive in R[x].

From Eqs. (i), (ii) and (iii), we obtain

$$f(x) = \frac{\alpha\beta}{ab} g_1(x)h_1(x) \text{ or } abf(x) = \alpha\beta g_1(x)\, h_1(x) \quad \text{...(iv)}$$

Since, $f(x)$ is primitive in $R[x]$,

$c$ ( LHS of Eq. (iv)) $= ab$.

Since, $g_1(x)\,h_1(x)$ is primitive in $R[x]$ (by Gauss's Lemma),

$c$ (RHS of Eq. (iv)) $= \alpha\beta$.

It follows that $ab = \alpha\beta$ and so by Eq. (iv), we have

$$f(x) = g_1(x)h_1(x)$$

where, $g_1(x), h_1(x) \in R[x]$ and

$$\deg g_1 = \deg g_0 = \deg g > 0$$

and $\deg h_1 = \deg h_0 = \deg h > 0$.

This means that $f(x)$ is reducible in $R[x]$, which is contrary to the given hypothesis.

Hence, $f(x)$ is an irreducible polynomial in $F[x]$.

**Example 19.** *If R is a UFD and if p(x) is a primitive polynomial in R[x], then, p(x) can be factored in a unique way as the product of irreducible elements (polynomials) in R[x].*

**Solution.** Let $F$ be a quotient field of $R$. We can consider $R[x]$ to be a subring of $F[x]$ and so $p(x) \in F[x]$. Since, $F$ is a field, $F[x]$ is a Euclidean domain $\Rightarrow F[x]$ is a UFD. Consequently, $p(x) \in F[x]$ can be written as

$$p(x) = p_1(x)p_2(x)\dots p_n[x] \qquad \text{...(i)}$$

Where, each $p_i(x) \in F[x]$ is an irreducible polynomial over $F$. Then, for each $i$, $1 \le i \le n$, we can write

$$p_i(x) = \frac{f_i(x)}{a_i},\ a_i \in R,\ f_i(x) \in R[x] \qquad \text{...(ii)}$$

Also, we can write

$$f_i(x) = b_i q_i(x), \qquad \text{...(iii)}$$

where $b_i = c(f_i)$ and $q_i(x) \in R[x]$ is primitive in $R[x]$.

From Eqs. (i), (ii) and (iii), we obtain

$$p(x) = \frac{1}{a_1a_2\dots a_n} f_1(x)f_2(x)\dots f_n(x)$$

$$= \frac{b_1b_2\dots b_n}{a_1a_2\dots a_n} q_1(x)q_2(x)\dots q_n(x)$$

$$\therefore\ a_1a_2\dots a_n p(x) = b_1b_2\dots b_n q_1(x)q_2(x)\dots q_n(x). \qquad \text{...(iv)}$$

Since, $p(x)$ is primitive in $R[x]$,

$c$ (LHS of Eq. (iv)) $= a_1a_2\dots a_n$

By Gauss's Lemma, $q_1(x)q_2(x)\dots q_n(x)$ is primitive in $R[x]$ and so

$c$(RHS of Eq. (iv)) $= b_1b_2\dots b_n$

If follows that $a_1a_2\dots a_n = b_1b_2\dots b_n$.

Hence, by Eq. (iv),

$$p(x) = q_1(x)q_2(x)\dots q_n(x) \qquad \text{...(v)}$$

We now show that, each $q_i(x)$ in Eq. (v) is irreducible in $R[x]$. Since, $p(x)$ is primitive in $R[x]$, so by Eq. (i), each $p_i(x)$ is necessarily primitive in $R[x]$. Further, each $p_i(x) \in F[x]$ is an irreducible polynomial in $F[x]$. Therefore, each $p_i(x)$ is an irreducible polynomial in $R[x] \Rightarrow$ each $f_i(x)$ is irreducible in $R[x]$, by Eq. (ii).

Thus, each $q_i(x)$ is irreducible in $R[x]$.

Lastly, we prove the uniqueness of Eq. (v).

Let $p(x) = t_1(x)\,t_2(x)\dots t_m(x)$, ...(vi)

where, each $t_i(x)$ is irreducible in $R[x]$.

Since, $p(x)$ is primitive in $R[x]$, each $t_i(x)$ is necessarily primitive in $R[x]$. Hence, each $t_i(x)$ is irreducible in $F[x]$. Similarly, in Eq. (v), each $q_i(x)$ is irreducible in $F[x]$.

Since, $F[x]$ is a UFD, $m = n$ and $q_i(x)$, $t_i(x)$ are associates in $F[x]$ for each $i$.

$$\therefore\quad q_i(x) = u_it_i(x), \qquad \text{...(vii)}$$

where, $u_i$ is a unit in $F[x]$ *i.e.*, $u_i$ is a unit in $F$. Let

$$u_i = \frac{a_i}{b_i},\ a_i, b_i \ne 0 \in R.$$

$$\therefore\quad b_iq_i(x) = a_it_i(x). \qquad \text{...(viii)}$$

Since, $q_i(x)$ and $t_i(x)$ are primitive in $R[x]$, therefore

$c$ (LHS of Eq. (viii)) $= b_i$, $c$ (RHS of Eq. (viii)) $= a_i$.

Since, the content of a polynomial is unique upto associates, So $a_i$ and $b_i$ are associates in $R$. *i.e.*, $b_i = ua_i$, for some unit $u \in R$.

$$\Rightarrow\quad \frac{a_i}{b_i} = u^{-1} \Rightarrow u_i = u^{-1} \cdot u^{-1} \text{ is a unit in } R.$$

Putting in Eq. (vii), $q_i(x) = u^{-1}t_i(x)$, $u^{-1}$ is a unit in $R$ and hence in $R[x]$. This shows that $q_i(x)$ and $t_i(x)$ are associates in $R[x]$. For each $i$ and $m = n$. Hence, $p(x)$ has a unique factorization as a product of irreducible polynomials in $R[x]$.

**Example 20.** *If R is a UFD, then R[x] is a UFD.*

**Solution.** Let $f(x)$ be any non-zero, non-unit element of $R[x]$, we have

$$f(x) = af_1(x), \qquad \text{...(i)}$$

where $a = c(f)$ and $f_1(x)$ is primitive in $R[x]$. By Theorem, we can write

$$f_1(x) = q_1(x)q_2(x)\dots q_n(x), \qquad \text{...(ii)}$$

where each $q_i(x)$ is irreducible in $R[x]$ and further this representation is unique upto associates.

Since, $a \in R$ and $R$ is a UFD. We can write $a$ is an unique way as a finite product of irreducible elements of $R$, say

$$a = d_1d_2\dots d_m \qquad \text{...(iii)}$$

Since, $R$ is a UFD, any irreducible element of $R$ is an irreducible element of $R[x]$. So, each $d_i$ is an irreducible element of $R[x]$.

From Eqs. (i), (ii) and (iii), we see that

$$f(x) = d_1d_2\dots d_m q_1(x)q_2(x)\dots q_n(x),$$

which is a unique representation of $f(x)$ as a product of irreducible elements in $R[x]$.

Hence, $R[x]$ is a UFD.

**Example 21.** *Prove that every field is an Euclidean ring.*

**Solution.** Let $F$ be an arbitrary field. Then, we shall show that $F$ is an Euclidean ring. Define a mapping

$d: F \to N$ (the set of all non-negative integer)

given by $d(a) = 0$, $\forall$ all non-zero $a \in F$.

Thus, we assign every non-zero element of $F$ to integer zero.

(i) If $a$ and $b$ are any two non-zero elements of $F$, then $ab$ is also a non-zero element of $F$, therefore

$$d(a) = 0 \text{ and } d(ab) = 0$$

So, $d(a) \le d(ab)$

(ii) If $a$ and $b$ are any elements of $F$ with $b \neq 0$, then we can write

$$a = a(b^{-1}b) \qquad (\because a = a \cdot 1)$$

or $\quad a = a(b^{-1}b) + 0$ or $a = (ab^{-1})\, b + r$, where, $r = 0$

or $\quad a = qb + r$, where, $r = 0$ and $q = ab^{-1}$.

Hence, $F$ is an Euclidean ring.

***Example 22.*** *Prove that the ring of polynomials over a field of reals is a Euclidean ring.*

**Solution.** Let $F[x]$ be the ring of polynomials over a field $F$. Then, we shall show that $F[x]$ is Euclidean ring.

Define a mapping.

$$d : F[x] \to N \text{ ( Set of all non-negative integers)}$$

by $d[f(x)] = \deg f(x)$, $\forall$ all non-zero $f(x) \in F(x)$

(i) Let $f(x)$ and $g(x)$ be any two non-zero polynomials of $F[x]$. Then, we have

$d[f(x)g(x)] = \deg\ [f(x)g(x)] = \deg f(x) + \deg\ g(x)$

Now, $\deg f(x) + \deg g(x) \geq \deg f(x) \quad (\because \deg g(x) \geq 0)$

$\therefore \quad d[f(x)g(x)] \geq \deg f(x) = d[f(x)]$

(ii) Let $f(x)$ and $g(x)$ be any two non-zero polynomials of $F[x]$ with $g(x) \neq 0$, then there exist $q(x)$ and $r(x)$, such that $\quad f(x) = q(x)g(x) + r(x) \quad$ (By division algorithm)

where, either $r(x) = 0$ or $\deg r(x) < \deg g(x)$

or either $r(x) = 0$ or $d[r(x)] < d[g(x)]$.

Thus, the mapping $d$ is an Euclidean evaluation.

Therefore, $F[x]$ is an Euclidean ring.

***Example 23.*** *Prove that every Euclidean ring is a principal ideal ring.*

**Solution.** Let $R$ be a Euclidean ring. Then, we shall show that every ideal of $R$ is a principal ideal.

Let $S$ be an arbitrary ideal of $R$. If $S$ just consists of the zero element *i.e.*, $S$ is a null ideal or $S = (0)$ so it is generated by 0, thus $S$ is a principal ideal.

Now, we may assume that $S \neq 0$, therefore there exists a non-zero element in $S$. Let $b$ be a non-zero element in $S$, such that $d(b)$ is minimal, this implies that there is no element $c$ in $S$, such that $d(a) < d(b)$. We shall show that $S$ is generated by $b$, *i.e.*, $S = (b)$.

Let $a$ be any element of $S$ and $S$ is a Euclidean ring; therefore, there exist $q$ and $r$ in $R$, such that

$$a = bq + r$$

where, either $r = 0$ or $d(r) < d(b)$.

Since, $S$ is an ideal so that,

$$q \in R \text{ and } b \in S \Rightarrow bq \in S$$

Also, $\quad a \in S$ and $bq \in S \Rightarrow a - bq \in S \Rightarrow r \in S$.

But we have either $r = 0$ or $d(r) < d(b)$, therefore, $d(r) < d(b)$ contradicts that $d(b)$ is minimal, thus we must have $r = 0$.

$\therefore \quad a = bq$

This shows that every element of $S$ can be expressed as the multiple of $b$. Thus, $S$ is generated by $b$ *i.e.*, $S = (b)$, so that $S$ is a principal ideal and since, $S$ is an arbitrary ideal of $R$. Hence, $R$ is a principal ideal ring.

• ***Example 24.*** *Prove that this ring $I$ of all integers is an Euclidean ring.*

**Solution.** Define a mapping $d$ from a set of all integers $I$ into the set $N$ of all non-negative integers as $d : I \to N$, given by

$$d(a) = |a|,\ \forall\ a \in I \text{ with } a \neq 0.$$

Since, $a \neq 0$ is any element of $I$, then $|a|$ is also a non-negative integer, thus the mapping $d$ assigns every non-zero integer to a non-negative of $I$.

(i) If $a$ and $b$ are any two non-zero elements of $I$, then

$$d(ab) = |ab| = |a||b| \geq |a|$$

$[\because |b| \geq 1$ for all non-zero $b \in I]$

$\Rightarrow \quad d(ab) \geq d(a)$

$\therefore \quad d(a) \leq d(ab), \qquad \forall\ a, b \in I$

(ii) If $a$ and $b$ are any two non-zero elements of $I$, then by division algorithm there exist $q, r \in I$, such that

$$a = bq + r \text{ where, } 0 \leq r < |b|$$

So that $\quad 0 \leq r < |b|$

$\Rightarrow \quad$ either $r = 0$ or $0 < r < |b|$

$\Rightarrow \quad$ either $r = 0$ or $|r| < |b| \qquad (\because 0 < r \Rightarrow |r| = r)$

$\Rightarrow \quad$ either $r = 0$ or $d(r) < d(b)$

Hence, the mapping $d$ is a Euclidean valuation on $I$ and accordingly $I$ is a Euclidean ring.

## Finite Fields

Field with finite number of elements is called finite fields.

Also, if order of an element of a field is finite, then field is called finite fields.

*e.g.*, $\quad F = \{Z_p, \oplus_p, \otimes_p\}$ is a finite field, where $p$ is any prime.

## Subfield

A subset $F$ of a field $(F, +, \cdot)$ is called a subfield, if $F$ is itself a field under addition and multiplication.

*e.g.*, (i) $(Q, +, \cdot)$ is a subfield of $(C, +, \cdot)$.

(ii) $(IR, +, \cdot)$ is a subfield of $(C, +, \cdot)$

## Prime Field

A field is called prime field if it has no proper subfield.

*e.g.*, (i) The set $F$ of residue classes modulo $p$, where $p$ is a prime number is a prime field if the characteristic of $F$ is $p$.

(ii) The field $(Q, +, \cdot)$ is prime field as $q$ has no proper subfield.

## Modular Field

Field with zero characteristic is called modular field.

*e.g.*, Field of rational numbers is a modular field for its characteristic is zero.

## Ordered Field

A field is said to be ordered when it is ordered as an integral domain.

[An ordered field is a field which contains subset of positive elements satisfying the additive and multiplicative closure and trichotomy].

**Explanation** Let $(F, +, \cdot)$ be a field. Let $F_+$ be the set of all positive elements of $F$. If the elements of $F_+$ satisfy.

**(i)** $F_+$ is closed under addition and multiplication. *i.e.*, $a \in F_+, b \in F_+, \Rightarrow a + b \in F_+$ and $a, b \in F_+$.

**(ii)** Law of Trichotomy is satisfied.

That is, $\forall$ $a \in F$ only are condition is satisfied $a = 0$, $a \in F_+ - a \in F_+$.

*e.g.*, $(Q, +, \cdot)$ and $(R, +, \cdot)$ are ordered field $Q$ and $R$ stand for rational and real numbers set.

## Field Extensions

Let $F$ be a field. A field $K$ is said to be an extension of $F$, if $F$ is a subfield of $K$.

Or

A field extension of a field $F$ is an ordered pair $(K, \phi)$, where $K$ is a field and $\phi$ is a monomorphism of $F$ into $K$.

Suppose, $K$ is a field and $F$ is a subfield of $K$. The injection mapping $i : F \to K$ defined by $i(x) = x$, $\forall$ $x \in F$ is a monomorphism. Hence, $(K, i)$ is a field extension of $F$.

> ***Note*** **(a)** If field $K$ is extension of field $F$, then $K$ is a vector space over $F$.
>
> **(b)** If $K$ is an extension of $F$, then the degree of $K$ over $F$ is defined as the dimension of $K$ as a vector space over $F$. It is denoted by $[K: F]$. Thus, $[K: F] = \dim_F K$.
>
> **(c)** If $[K: F]$ is finite *i.e.*, if $K$ is a finite-dimensional vector space over $F$, we say that $K$ is a finite extension of $F$.

*e.g.*,

(i) Every field $F$ is an extension of $F$ and $[F : F] = 1$, since, $\{1\}$ is a basis of $F$ over $F$.

(ii) Since, $\{1, i\}$ is a basis of $c$ (field of complex numbers) over $R$ (field of real numbers )
$\Rightarrow$ $[c : R] = 2$

(iii) $Q[\sqrt{2}] = \{a + b\sqrt{2} : a, b \in Q\}$ is a field extension of $Q$. The subset $\{1, \sqrt{2}\}$ forms a basis of $Q[\sqrt{2}]$ over $Q$. Hence, $[Q[\sqrt{2}] : Q] = 2$.

(iv) If $[K : F] = 1 \Leftrightarrow K = F$

### Important Results on Field Extension

1. Let $K$ be a finite extension of $F$ and $L$ a finite extension of $K$. Then, $L$ is a finite extension of $F$ and
$$[L : F] = [L : K][K : F]$$
2. Let $L$ be a finite extension of $F$ and $K$ a subfield of $L$ which contains $F$. Then, $[K: F]$ divides $[L : F]$.
3. If $K$ is an extension of $F$ and $[K: F]$ is a prime number $p$ there is no field $L$, such that $F \subset L \subset K$.

## Important Definitions

1. An extension $K$ of a field $F$ is called a simple extension of $F$, if $K = F(a)$, where, $a \in K$. This element $a$ is known as primitive element of $K$ over $F$.
*e.g.*, $Q(\sqrt{2})$ is a simple extension of the field $Q$ of all rational numbers.
2. $F(a)$ is the smallest subfield of $K$ containing both $F$ and $a$. $F(a)$ is read as the subfield obtained by adjoining a to $F$.
3. Let $K$ be an extension of a field $F$. An element $a \in K$ is said to be algebraic over $F$, if there exists a non-zero polynomial $f(x) \in F[x]$, such that $f(a) = 0$. Otherwise, a is called a transcendental element.
*e.g.*
(i) $\sqrt{2} \in Q(\sqrt{2})$ is algebraic over $Q$, since $\sqrt{2}$ satisfies the polynomial $f(x) = x^2 - 2 \in Q[x]$.
(ii) $\sqrt{2} + \sqrt{3}$ is algebraic over $Q$.
Let $a = \sqrt{2} + \sqrt{3}$. Then, $a^2 = 5 + 2\sqrt{6}$ and
$a^4 = 49 + 20\sqrt{6} = 10(5 + 2\sqrt{6}) - 1 = 10a^2 - 1$
*i.e.*, $a^4 - 10a^2 + 1 = 0$. Thus, $a = \sqrt{2} + \sqrt{3}$ satisfies the polynomial $x^4 - 10x^2 + 1 \in Q[x]$ and so $\sqrt{2} + \sqrt{3}$ is algebraic over $Q$.
(iii) $\pi$ and $e \in R$ are not algebraic over $Q$.
4. An extension $K$ of a field $F$ is called an algebraic extension, if every element of $K$ is algebraic over $F$.
*e.g.*,
(i) $Q(\sqrt{2})$ is an algebraic extension of $Q$, since, $[Q(\sqrt{2}) : Q] = 2$ (finite) and every finite extension is algebraic.
(ii) The field $C$ of complex numbers is an algebraic extension of the field $R$ of real numbers.
(iii) $Q(\sqrt{2}, \sqrt{3})$ is an algebraic extension of $Q$.
(iv) $R$ is not an algebraic extension of $Q$, since $\pi$, $e \in R$ are not algebraic over $Q$.
5. A non-zero polynomial $f(x) \in F[x]$ is said to be a monic polynomial over $F$, if the coefficient of the highest power of $x$ in $f(x)$ is equal to 1.
6. Let $K$ be an extension of a field $F$. If an element $a \in K$ is algebraic over $F$, then a monic polynomial of smallest degree over $F$ satisfied by a, is called the minimal polynomial of a over $F$.
If the degree of the minimal polynomial of a is $n$, then $a \in K$ is said to be algebraic over $F$ of degree $n$.

***Example 25.*** *$\sqrt[3]{2}$ is algebraic of degree 3 over $Q$.*

**Solution.** Let $x = 2^{1/3} \Rightarrow x^3 - 2 = 0$

$\Rightarrow x^3 - 2$ is the minimal polynomial of $\sqrt[3]{2}$ over $Q$.

Hence, $\sqrt[3]{2}$ is algebraic of degree 3 over $Q$.

7. A complex number is said to be an algebraic number, if it is algebraic over $Q$ (rationals). e.g., (i) $1+i$ is an algebraic number, since $x = 1+i$ satisfies, the polynomial $x^2 - 2x + 2 \in Q[x]$.

> **Note** (a) $1+i$ is also an algebraic integer.
> (b) $\sin 1°$ is an algebraic number.

# Important Theorems an Field Extension

***Theorem 1*** Every finite extension of a field $F$ is an algebraic extension. But the converse is not true.

***Theorem 2*** Let $K$ be an extension of $F$ and let $a \in K$ be algebraic over $F$. Then,

**(i)** There exists a unique monic irreducible polynomial $f(x) \in F(x)$ of least positive degree, such that $f(a) = 0$.

**(ii)** If $g(x) \in F(x)$ is such that $g(a) = 0$ , then $f(x)$ divides $g(x)$.

***Theorem 3*** Let $a \in K$ be algebraic over $F$ and let $f(x)$ be a minimal polynomial over $F$, then $f(x)$ is irreducible over $F$.

***Theorem 4*** Let $a \in K$ be algebraic over $F$. Then, any two minimal monic polynomials over $F$ are equal.

***Theorem 5*** Let $K$ be an extension of a field $F$ and $a \in K$ be algebraic over $F$. Then,

$F[a] = F(a)$, where $F[a] = \{f(a): f(x) \in F[x]\}$

***Theorem 6*** Let $K$ be an extension of a field $F$. An element $a \in K$ is algebraic over $F$ if and only if $[F(a)]: F]$ is finite.

> **Note** $[F(a): F]$ = degree of the unique monic irreducible polynomial over $F$ satisfied by $a$.

***Theorem 7*** If $\alpha, \beta \in K$ are algebraic over $F$, then $\alpha \pm \beta$, $\alpha\beta$ and $\alpha / \beta (\beta \neq 0)$ are all algebraic over $F$. In other words, the elements in $K$ which are algebraic over $F$ form a subfield of $K$.

***Theorem 8*** Let $F$ be a finite field and $K$ be subfield of $F$, then $\frac{F}{K}$ is algebraic.

***Theorem 9*** If $a \in K$ is algebraic over $F$ of odd degrees, then $F(a) = F(a^2)$.

***Theorem 10*** Let $K$ be an extension of a field $F$ and let $f(x) \in F[x]$ and $a \in K$. Then, there exists $g(x) \in K[x]$ such that $f(x) = (x-a)g(x) + f(a)$, where $\deg(g(x) = \deg(f(x)) - 1$.

If $f(a) = 0$ *i.e.*,

If $a \in K$ is a root of $f(x) \in F[x]$, then $(x-a)$ divides $f(x)$ in $K[x]$.

*i.e.*, $f(x) = (x-a)g(x)$

***Theorem 11*** A polynomial of degree $n \geq 1$ over a field can have atmost $n$ roots in any extension field of $F$.

***Theorem 12*** Let $f(x)$ be any polynomial of positive degree in $F[x]$. Then, there exists an extension $K$ of $F$ in which $f(x)$ has a root in $K$ and $[K: F] \leq \deg(f(x))$

If $f(x)$ is irreducible polynomial, then equality holds

*i.e.*, $[K: F] = \deg(f(x))$

***Theorem 13*** Let $f(x) \in F[x]$ be a polynomial of positive degree $n$ over a field $F$, then there exists a finite extension $K$ of $F$ of degree atmost $n!$ *i.e.*, $[K: F] \leq n!$ and $f(x)$ has atmost $n$ roots in $K$.

# Splitting Field

Let $f(x)$ be any polynomial of degree $n \geq 1$ over a field $F$. A field extension $K$ of $F$ is called a splitting field of $f(x)$, if

**(i)** $f(x)$ can be factored into $n$ linear factors over $K$, and

**(ii)** $f(x)$ cannot be factored into $n$ linear factors over any subfield of $K$ containing $F$.

In other words, $K$ is a splitting field of $f(x) \in F[x]$ with $\deg f(x) = n \geq 1$, if $K$ contains the $n$ roots $a_1, a_2, \ldots, a_n$ of $f(x)$ and $K = F(a_1, a_2, \ldots, a_n)$, the smallest field containing $F$ and $n$ roots $a_1, a_2, \ldots, a_n$ of $f(x)$ in $K$.

> **Note** (a) There exists a splitting field for every polynomial $f(x) \in F[x]$ with $\deg f(x) \geq 1$.
> **(b)** Any two splitting fields of a polynomial $f(x) \in F[x]$ with $\deg f(x) \geq 1$ are isomorphic. More specifically, if $K$ and $K'$ are any two splitting fields of a polynomial $f(x)$ of degree $n \geq 1$ over a field $F$, then there exists are isomorphism $\psi$ of $K$ onto $K'$, such that $\psi(\alpha) = \alpha$, for all $\alpha \in F$.

***Example 26.*** *Show that* $[Q(\sqrt{2}): Q] = 2$.

**Solution.** We know that $Q(\sqrt{2})$ is the smallest field containing $Q$ and $\sqrt{2}$ and so $Q(\sqrt{2})$ is an extension of $Q$. Further, $\{1, \sqrt{2}\}$ is a basis of $Q(\sqrt{2})$ over $Q$ .Hence, $[Q(\sqrt{2}):Q] = 2$.

***Example 27.*** *Find a basic of* $Q(\sqrt{2}, \sqrt{3})$ *over* $Q$. *Hence, find* $[Q(\sqrt{2}, \sqrt{3}): Q]$.

**Solution.** $Q(\sqrt{2}, \sqrt{3})$ is the smallest field containing $Q$, $\sqrt{2}$ and $\sqrt{3}$. Any element of $Q(\sqrt{2}, \sqrt{3})$ is of the form

$$a + b\sqrt{2} + c\sqrt{3} + d\sqrt{2}\sqrt{3}, \text{ where } a, b, c, d \in Q.$$

If follows that $\{1, \sqrt{2}, \sqrt{3}, \sqrt{2}\ \sqrt{3}\}$ is a basic of $Q(\sqrt{2}, \sqrt{3})$ over $Q$.

Hence, $[Q(\sqrt{2}, \sqrt{3}): Q] = 4$.

***Example 28.*** *(i) Prove that $\sqrt{3}$ and $\sqrt{5}$ are both algebraic over Q.*

*(ii) What is the degree of $\sqrt{3}+\sqrt{5}$ over Q*

*(iii) What is a basic of $Q(\sqrt{3},\sqrt{5})$ over Q*

**Solution.** (i) $\sqrt{3}$ and $\sqrt{5}$ are both algebraic over Q, since they satisfy the polynomials $x^2-3$ and $x^2-5$, respectively over Q.

(ii) We have,

$$[Q(\sqrt{3}):Q]=\deg(x^2-3)=2,$$

and $[(Q(\sqrt{3}))(\sqrt{5})], Q(\sqrt{3})] = [Q(\sqrt{3},\sqrt{5}):Q(\sqrt{3})]$

$$=\deg(x^2-5)=2$$

$\therefore \quad [Q(\sqrt{3},\sqrt{5}):Q)]=[Q(\sqrt{3},\sqrt{5}): Q(\sqrt{3})][Q(\sqrt{3}):Q]$

$$=2\times 2=4$$

or $\quad [Q(\sqrt{3}+\sqrt{5}):Q]=4$

Since, $\quad Q(\sqrt{3},\sqrt{5})=Q(\sqrt{3}+\sqrt{5})$ (Verify)

Hence, the degree of $\sqrt{3}+\sqrt{5}$ over Q is 4.

(iii) $Q(\sqrt{3},\sqrt{5})$ is the smallest field containing Q, $\sqrt{3}$ and $\sqrt{5}$.

Any element of $Q(\sqrt{3},\sqrt{5})$ is of the form

$$a+b\sqrt{3}+c\sqrt{5}+d\sqrt{3}\sqrt{5}:\ a,b,c,d\in Q$$

Hence, $\{1,\sqrt{3},\sqrt{5},\sqrt{3}\sqrt{5}\}$ is a basis of $Q(\sqrt{3},\sqrt{5})$ over Q.

***Example 29.*** *Determine the degrees of the following extensions by finding bases for them*

*(i) $Q(\sqrt[3]{2},\sqrt{2})$ over $Q(\sqrt[3]{2})$, over $Q(\sqrt{2})$, over Q.*

*(ii) $Q\left(\cos\frac{2\pi}{3}\right)$, $Q\left(\sin\frac{2\pi}{3}\right)$, $Q\left(\cos\frac{2\pi}{5}\right)$ over Q.*

**Solution.** (i) $Q(\sqrt[3]{2},\sqrt{2})$ is an extension of $Q(\sqrt[3]{2})$ and $Q(\sqrt[3]{2})$ of Q.

Then, by transitivity of extensions, we have

$$[Q(\sqrt[3]{2},\sqrt{2}):Q]=[Q(\sqrt[3]{2},\sqrt{2}):Q(\sqrt{2})][(Q\sqrt{2}):Q]$$

$$=[Q(\sqrt[3]{2},\sqrt{2}):Q(\sqrt[3]{2})][Q(\sqrt[3]{2}):Q]$$

This shows that $[Q(\sqrt[3]{2},\sqrt{2}):Q]$ is a multiple of 2 and 3, so it is a multiple of 6. As $\sqrt[3]{2}$ is algebraic of degree $\leq 3$ over every field containing Q, we have

$$[Q(\sqrt[3]{2},\sqrt{2}):Q]=[Q(\sqrt[3]{2},\sqrt{2}):Q(\sqrt{2})][Q(\sqrt{2}):Q]\leq 6.$$

$\therefore \quad [Q(\sqrt[3]{2},\sqrt{2}):Q]=6$

Consequently, $[Q(\sqrt[3]{2},\sqrt{2}):Q(\sqrt{2})]=3$

and $\quad [Q(\sqrt[3]{2},\sqrt{2}):Q(\sqrt[3]{2})]=2$

A basis of $Q(\sqrt[3]{2},\sqrt{2})$ over Q can be obtained from the bases $\{1,\sqrt[3]{2},\sqrt[3]{4}\}$ of $Q(\sqrt[3]{2})$ over Q and $\{1,\sqrt{2}\}$ of $Q(\sqrt[3]{2},\sqrt{2})$ over $Q(\sqrt[3]{2})$. We therefore obtain

$$\{1,\sqrt[3]{2},\sqrt[3]{4},\sqrt{2},2^{5/6}\ 2^{7/6}\}.$$

As, $\quad 2^{7/6}=2\times 2^{1/6}$, a simple basis is given by

$$\{2^{k/6}: 0\leq k\leq 5\}$$

Hence, $\quad Q(\sqrt[3]{2},\sqrt{2})=Q(\sqrt[6]{2})$.

(ii) Since, we have

$$Q\left(\cos\frac{2\pi}{3}\right)=Q\left(-\frac{1}{2}\right)=Q$$

and $\quad Q\left(\sin\frac{2\pi}{3}\right)=Q\left(\frac{\sqrt{3}}{2}\right)=Q(\sqrt{3})$

Let $\xi=e^{2\pi i/5}$, and $\xi$ is a root of the polynomial $x^4+x^3+x^2+x+1$, which is irreducible over Q, so x is algebraic of degree is over Q.

If we set $y=2\cos\frac{2\pi}{5}=\xi+\xi^4$, then

$$y^2=(\xi+\xi^4)^2$$

$$y^2=\xi^2+\xi^2+2 \qquad (\because \xi^4+\xi^3+\xi^2+\xi+1=0)$$

$$=-y+1$$

$\therefore$ Thus, y is a root of $x^2+x-1$, so $y=\frac{-1\pm\sqrt{5}}{2}$

As $\cos\left(\frac{2\pi}{5}\right)>0$, then $\cos\left(\frac{2\pi}{5}\right)=\frac{-1+\sqrt{5}}{4}$, so that

$Q\left(\cos\frac{2\pi}{5}\right)=Q(\sqrt{5})$. As $2\cos\left(\frac{2\pi}{5}\right)=\xi+\xi^4$, we have

$Q\left(\cos\frac{2\pi}{5}\right)\subseteq Q(\xi)$ and $\left[Q(\xi):Q\left(\cos\frac{2\pi}{5}\right)\right]=2.$

***Example 30.*** *Obtain the splitting field and its degree over Q for $f(x)=x^4-5x^2+6\in Q[x]$.*

**Solution.** We have

$f(x)=(x^2-3)(x^2-2)=(x-\sqrt{3})(x+\sqrt{3})(x-\sqrt{2})(x+\sqrt{2})$. Thus, the roots of $f(x)$ are $\pm\sqrt{2}$ and $\pm\sqrt{3}$. Hence, $Q(\sqrt{2},\sqrt{3})$ is the splitting field of $f(x)$ over Q. We have

$$[Q(\sqrt{2}):Q]=\deg(x^2-2)=2,$$

Since, $x^2-2$ is the irreducible polynomial over Q of degree 2, satisfied by $\sqrt{2}$. Again, $x^2-3$ is an irreducible polynomial of degree 2 over $Q\subset Q(\sqrt{2})$, which is satisfied by $\sqrt{3}$. Consequently,

$$[(Q(\sqrt{2}))(\sqrt{3}): Q(\sqrt{2})]=\deg(x^2-3)=2$$

*i.e.*, $[Q(\sqrt{2},\sqrt{3}): Q(\sqrt{2})]=2$

Hence, $\quad [Q(\sqrt{2},\sqrt{3}):Q]=[Q(\sqrt{2},\sqrt{3}):Q(\sqrt{2})][Q(\sqrt{2}):Q]$

$$=2\times 2=4$$

***Example 31.*** *Obtain the splitting field and its degree over Q for $f(x)=x^4-8x^2+15\in Q[x]$.*

**Solution.** $K=Q(\sqrt{3},\sqrt{5})$ is the splitting field of $f(x)$ over Q and $[K:Q]=4$.

***Example 32.*** *Find the degree of the splitting field of $x^4+1$ over Q.*

**Solution.** We have $x^4+1=0\Rightarrow x=(-1)^{1/4}$

$$\therefore \quad x=(\cos\pi+i\sin\pi)^{1/4}$$

By De Moivre's Theorem, we get

$$x=\cos\frac{2k\pi+\pi}{4}+i\sin\frac{2k\pi+\pi}{4},\ k=0,1,2,3$$

or $\quad x=\frac{1}{\sqrt{2}}+\frac{i}{\sqrt{2}},-\frac{1}{\sqrt{2}}+\frac{i}{\sqrt{2}},\ -\frac{1}{\sqrt{2}}-\frac{i}{\sqrt{2}},\frac{1}{\sqrt{2}}-\frac{i}{\sqrt{2}}, i=\sqrt{-1}$

The smallest field containing Q and the above roots is $Q(\sqrt{2},i)$. Hence, $Q(\sqrt{2},i)$ is the splitting field of $x^4+1$ over Q. We see that

$$Q\subset Q(\sqrt{2})\subset Q(\sqrt{2},i).$$

Since, $x^2-2$ is the irreducible polynomial over Q of degree 2, satisfied by $\sqrt{2}$.

$$[Q(\sqrt{2}):Q]=\deg(x^2-2)=2$$

***Example 33.*** *If a is any algebraic number, prove that there exists a positive integer n, such that na is an algebraic integer.*

**Solution.** Since, $a$ is an algebraic number, there exists a non-zero polynomial $f(x)\in Q[x]$, such that $f(a)=0$.

Let $f(x)=x^r+\alpha_1x^{r-1}+\alpha_2x^{r-2}+\ldots+\alpha_r,\ \alpha_i\in Q$.

We can write $\alpha_i=\frac{m_i}{n_i}$, $m_i$, $n_i$ are integers and $n_i>0$.

Since, $f(a)=0$, $a^r+\frac{m_1}{n_1}a^{r-1}+\frac{m_2}{n_2}a^{r-2}+\ldots+\frac{m_r}{n_r}=0$ ...(i)

Let $n=n_1n_2\ldots n_r$, which is a positive integer.

From Eq. (i), we get

$$na^r+m_1n_2\ldots n_ra^{r-1}+m_2n_1n_3\ldots n_ra^{r-2}+m_rn_1n_2\ldots n_{r-1}=0$$

Multiplying throughout by $n^{r-1}$, we get

$$n^ra^r+m_1n_2\ldots n_rn^{r-1}a^{r-1}+m_2n_1n_3\ldots n_rn.n^{r-2}a^{r-2}+\ldots+m_rn_1n_2\ldots n_{r-1}n^{r-1}=0$$

We see that $na$ satisfies the integer monic polynomial

$$x^r+m_1n_2\ldots n_rx^{r-1}+\ldots+m_rn_1n_2\ldots n_{r-1}n^{r-1}$$

Hence, $na$ is an algebraic integer, where, $n=n_1n_2\ldots n_r$ is a positive integer.

***Example 34.*** *Let $\alpha,\beta\in K$ be algebraic over F of degree m and n respectively, and let m and n be relatively prime. Show that $F(\alpha,\beta)$ is of degree mn over F.*

**Solution.** Since, we have

$$[F(\alpha):F]=m \text{ and } [F(\beta):F]=n$$

Then, we show that $[F(\alpha,\beta):F]=mn$

Let $[F(\alpha,\beta):F]=K$, then we show that $K=mn$

Now, $[F(\alpha,\beta):F]=[F(\alpha,\beta):F(\alpha)][F(\alpha):F]$

$\Rightarrow$ $k=[F(\alpha,\beta):F(\alpha)]m\Rightarrow m|k$

Also, $[F(\alpha,\beta):F]=[F(\alpha,\beta):F(\beta)][F(\beta):F]$

$\Rightarrow$ $k=[F(\alpha,\beta):F(\beta)]n\Rightarrow n|k$

But $m$ and $n$ are relative prime so that $m|k$ and $n|k$

$\Rightarrow$ $mn|k\Rightarrow k\geq mn$ ...(i)

Again, we have

$$[F(\alpha,\beta):F]\leq[F(\alpha):F][F(\beta):F]$$

$\Rightarrow$ $k\leq mn$ ...(ii)

From Eqs. (i) and (ii), we get

$$k=mn$$

Hence, $F(\alpha,\beta)$ is algebraic extension of degree $mn$ over $F$.

***Example 35.*** *Show that an element $\alpha\in K$, the finite extension of a field F generates the whole extension, iff $[K:F]\,[\alpha:F]$ = degree of $\alpha$ over F.*

**Solution.** Since, we know that

$$[F(\alpha):F]=\text{degree of }\alpha\text{ over }F=[\alpha:F] \quad ...(i)$$

Suppose, $\alpha$ generates the whole extension $K$, then we have $K=F(\alpha)$

$\therefore$ $[K:F]=[F(\alpha):F]=[\alpha:F]$ [Using Eq. (i)]

Conversely, suppose $[K:F]=[\alpha:F]$, then we shall prove that $\alpha$ generates the whole extension $K$, *i.e.*, $K=F(\alpha)$.

By transitivity of extensions, we have

$$[K:F]=[K:F(\alpha)][F(\alpha):F]$$

$\Rightarrow$ $[K:F]=[K:F(\alpha)][\alpha:F]$ [Using Eq. (i)]

$\Rightarrow$ $[K:F]=[K:F(\alpha)][K:F]$ ($\because [K:F]=[\alpha:F]$)

$\Rightarrow$ $1=[K:F(\alpha)]\Rightarrow K=F(\alpha)$

Hence the result.

***Example 36.*** *Let K be an extension of a field F. Let $\alpha$ be an algebraic element of odd degree over F. Show that $\alpha^2$ is algebraic over F and that $F(\alpha)=F(\alpha^2)$.*

**Solution.** Since, $\alpha$ is an algebraic element of odd degree over $F$, so $F(\alpha)$ is the extension of $F$ of odd degree.

$F(\alpha)$ is a field, so $\alpha\in F(\alpha)$ implies that $\alpha^2\in F(\alpha)$, thus $\alpha^2$ is algebraic over $F$ and $F(\alpha^2)\subseteq F(\alpha)$.

As $\alpha$ is a root of the polynomial $x^2-\alpha^2$ with coefficients in $F(\alpha^2)$, so $\alpha$ is algebraic of degree at most 2 over $F(\alpha^2)$ *i.e.*, $[F(\alpha):F(\alpha^2)]\leq 2$. Moreover,

$$[F(\alpha):F]=[F(\alpha):F(\alpha^2)][F(\alpha^2):F]$$

$\Rightarrow$ $[F(\alpha):F(\alpha^2)]\,|\,[F(\alpha):F]$.

But $[F(\alpha):F(\alpha^2)]\leq 2$ and $[F(\alpha):F]$ is odd, then we must have $[F(\alpha):F(\alpha^2)]=1$.

***Example 37.*** *If K is an extension of F of prime degree, then prove that any element in K but not in F generates the whole extension K.*

**Solution.** Suppose, $[K:F]=p$, where $p$ is a prime.

Let $\alpha\in K$, such that $\alpha\notin K$, then we shall prove that

$$K=F(\alpha)$$

Since, $[K:F]=[K:F(\alpha)][F(\alpha):F]$

$\Rightarrow$ $[K:F(\alpha)][F(\alpha):F]=p$ ...(i)

As $\alpha\notin F$, so that $[F(\alpha):F]\neq 1$ so that $[F(\alpha):F]>1$. But $p$ is a prime number, then Eq. (i) gives that one of the factor must be 1 and the other must be $p$. Also, $[F(\alpha):F]>1$ so that $[K:F(\alpha)]=1$.

$\Rightarrow$ $K=F(\alpha)$

***Example 38.*** *Show that every quadratic extension of $\alpha$ is of the form $Q(\sqrt{a})$, where a is a square free relative integer.*

**Solution.** A quadratic extension of Q is an extension by a number of the form $(x\pm\sqrt{y})/2$ with $x,y$ relations, thus it is an extension of the form $Q(\sqrt{y})$. If $y=\frac{m}{n}$ with $m$ and $n$ rational, then

$$Q(\sqrt{y})=Q\left(\sqrt{\frac{m}{n}}\right)=Q\left(\sqrt{\frac{mn}{n}}\right)=Q(\sqrt{mn})$$

If $mn=k^2a$, for a square free integer $a$, then

$$Q(\sqrt{mn})=Q(k\sqrt{a})+Q(\sqrt{a}).$$

***Example 39.*** *Let K be an extension of a field F and let $\alpha \in K$ algebraic over F. Then, $F(\alpha)$ is isomorphic of $F[x] / V$, where V is an ideal of $F[x]$, generated by minimal polynomial for $\alpha$ over F.*

**Solution.** Let $p(x)$ be the minimal polynomial for $\alpha$ over $F$.

Then, $p(x)$ is irreducible over $F$.

$\therefore \quad V = \{q(x) \in F[x] : q(\alpha) = 0\}$ ...(i)

Clearly, $V$ is an ideal of $F[x]$ generated by the minimal polynomial for $\alpha$ over $F$.

Evidently $p(x) \in V$ is of lowest degree so that $V$ is an ideal generated by $p(x)$, *i.e.*, $V = (p(x))$.

Moreover, $p(x)$ is irreducible, so that $V$ is maximal ideal of $F[x]$. Hence, $F[x]/V$ is a field.

Now, define a map $\phi : F[x] \to F[\alpha]$, such that

$$\phi(f(x)) = f(\alpha), \quad \forall f(x) \in F[x]$$

Then, $\phi(f(x) + g(x)) = f(\alpha) + g(\alpha) = \phi(f(x)) + \phi(g(x))$.

$\therefore$ $\phi$ is homomorphism. Obviously, $\phi$ is onto.

Thus, $\ker \phi = \{q(x) \in F[x] : \phi(q(x)) = 0\}$

$= \{q(x) \in F[x] : q(\alpha) = 0\} = V$ [Using Eq. (i)]

Hence, by fundamental theorem of homomorphism.

$$F(\alpha) \cong F[x]/V.$$

## Galois Theory

### Definitions

1. Let $K$ be an extension of a field $F$. Then, the group of automorphism of $K$ relative to $F$ denoted by $G(K, F)$, is the set of all automorphism of $K$, which leaves every element of $F$ fixed.
2. Let $G$ be a subgroup of the automorphism group of a field $F$. Let $F_0$ be the subset of $F$ consisting of those elements of $F$ which are left fixed by every automorphism in $G$. *i.e.*,
$$F_0 = \{a \in F : \sigma(a) = a, \ \forall \sigma \in G\}$$
then, $F_0$ is called fixed field of $G$.
3. Let $K$ be a finite extension of a field $F$. Then, $K$ is said to be normal extension of $F$, if the fixed field of $G(K, F)$ is $F$.
4. Let $K$ be a finite normal extension of a field $F$. Then, the group $G(K, F)$ of all $F$-automorphisms of $K$ is called the Galois group of $K$ over $F$ and $K$ is called Galois extension of $F$.
5. Let $K$ be a finite extension of a field $F$, then two elements $\alpha$ and $\beta$ of a field $K$ are said to be conjugate over $F$, if they have the same minimal polynomial over $F$.
6. Let $K$ be a separable normal extension of finite degree over a subfield $F$, then $\exists$ a one-one correspondence between the family of subfields of $K$ containing $F$ and the family of all subgroups of $G(K, F)$. Further, if $E$ is any subfield of $K$, such that $F \subset E \subset K$, then
   (i) $[K : E] = o(G(K, E))$
   and $[E : F] =$ index of $G(K, E)$ in $G(K, F)$.
   (ii) $E$ is a normal extension of $F$ if and only if $G(K, E)$ is a normal subgroup of $G(K, F)$.
   (iii) If $E$ is a normal extension of $F$, then
   $$G(E, F) \cong G(K, F) / G(K, E)$$
   Which is called Fundamental theorem of Galois Theory.
7. A finite field is also called Galois field.

### Important Results on Galois Theory

1. $K$ is a normal extension of $F$ if and only if $K$ is the splitting field of some polynomial over $F$.
2. An element of $K$ which remains invariant under each member of the Galois group $G(K, F)$ of $K$ over $F$ is necessarily a member of $F$.
3. $o(G(K, F)) = o([K : F])$
4. Let $K$ be a finite separable normal extension of a field $F$ of characteristic zero, then the fixed field of Galois group $G(K, F)$ is $F$ itself.
5. A field is called prime, if it has no proper subfield.
   *e.g.*, $Q$ and $\frac{Z}{(p)}$, where $p$ is prime, are prime fields.
6. The characteristic of a finite field is necessarily non-zero but the converse is not true.
7. The number of elements in finite field of characteristic $p$ is of the form $p^n$, where $n$ being some positive integer.
8. Each element of a finite field $F$ with $p^n$ elements satisfies the equation $x^{p^n} = x$.
9. If a finite field $F$ has $p^n$ elements, then $F$ is the splitting field of the polynomial
   $$f(x) = x^{p^n} - x.$$
10. The multiplicative group of a Galois field (finite field) is cyclic.

## Number Theory

**Definition** A map $f$ from $N$ to $\mathbb{C}$ the field of complex numbers is called an arithmetic function.

*e.g.*, The exponential function $n \to e^n$, the log function $n \to \log(n)$, the factorial function $n \to n!$, the fraction $n \to \sqrt{n}$, the function $n \to 1 + \frac{1}{2} + \frac{1}{3} + \ldots + \frac{1}{n} - \log n$ are some examples of some arithmetic functions.

**Definition** The function $\tau$ from $N$ to $N$ defined by $\tau(n)$ = The number of divisors of $n$ is called the divisor function.

**Definition** The function $\sigma$ from $N$ to $N$ defined by

$$\sigma(n) = \sum_{d/n} d$$

where the notation $d/n$ stands for the statement "$d$ divides $n$" is called the sum of divisors function. Thus, $\sigma(n)$ is the sum of divisors of $n$.

**Definition** The function $\mu$ from $N$ to $Z$ defined by $\mu(1) = 1$, $\mu(n) = 0$, if $n$ is divisible by $a^2$ for some $a > 1$ and $\mu(n) = (-1)^r$ if $n = p_1, p_2, \ldots, p_r$, where $p_1, p_2, \ldots, p_r$ are distinct primes, is called the mobius function.

**Definition** An arithmetic function $f$ from $N$ to $C$ is called multiplicative if $f$ is not identically zero and

$$(m, n) = 1 \Rightarrow f(mn) = f(m)f(n)$$

It is said to be absolutely multiplicative if

$$f(mn) = f(m)f(n), \forall m, n \in N$$

> ***Note*** If $f$ is multiplicative non-zero function, then $f(1) = 1$ for, $(m, 1) = 1$ and so $f(m) = f(m)f(1)$, $\forall m \in N$.

# Quadratic Residue

**Definition** Let $m \in N$, $m \geq 2$. Let $a \in Z$ be such that $(a, m) = 1$. We say that $a$ is a quadratic residue mod $m$ if

$$x^2 \equiv a (\text{mod } m)$$

is solvable.

# Theorems on Quadratic Residue

***Theorem 1*** Let $m = p_1^{\alpha_1}, p_2^{\alpha_2}, \ldots, p_r^{\alpha_r}$, where $p_1, p_2, \ldots, p_r$ are distinct primes and $\alpha_i \geq 1, \forall i$. Then, $a$ is a quadratic residue mod $p$ if and only if $a$ is quadratic residue mod $p_i^{\alpha_i}, \forall i$.

***Theorem 2*** Let $p$ be odd prime and $a$ an integer coprime to $p$. Then, $a$ is a quadratic residue modulo $p^m$, $m \geq 1$ if and only if $a$ is quadratic residue modulo $p$. Further, then there are only two distinct solutions modulo $p^m$ of

$$X^2 \equiv a (\text{mod } p^m)$$

***Theorem 3*** Let $a$ be an odd integer. Then,

**(i)** $X^2 \equiv a (\text{mod } 2)$ has unique mod 2 solution.

**(ii)** $X^2 \equiv a (\text{mod } 4)$ has a solution if and only if $a \equiv 1 (\text{mod } 4)$ and then it has exactly 2 distinct mod 4 solutions.

**(iii)** $X^2 \equiv a (\text{mod } 2^m)$, $m \geq 3$ has a solution if and only if $a \equiv 1 (\text{mod } 8)$ and then it has exactly 4 distinct solutions.

***Theorem 4*** (Euler's Criterion) Let $p$ be an odd prime and $a$ an integer such that $p$ does not divide $a$. Then, $a$ is quadratic residue modulo $p$ iff

$$a^{\frac{p-1}{2}} \equiv 1 (\text{mod } p)$$

# SOLVED EXAMPLES

## Type I (*Only one correct option*)

***Example 1.*** *The set*

$$R = \{(a_{ij})_{2\times 2} : a_{ij} \in \mathbb{Z}\}$$

*is a ring with respect to '+' and '·' defined by*

$$(a_{ij})_{2\times 2} + (b_{ij})_{2\times 2} = (a_{ij} + b_{ij})_{2\times 2}$$

*and* $\quad (a_{ij})_{2\times 2} \cdot (b_{ij})_{2\times 2} = (a_{ij} \cdot b_{ij})_{2\times 2}$

*Then, the number of units in R is*

(a) 2 (b) 4
(c) 6 (d) 8

**Solution.** (d) Let $\begin{pmatrix} a & b \\ c & d \end{pmatrix}$ be units of $R$.

Then, $\begin{pmatrix} a & b \\ c & d \end{pmatrix}^{-1} = \begin{pmatrix} a & b \\ c & d \end{pmatrix}$

$\Rightarrow \quad a = \pm 1, b = \pm 1, c = \pm 1, d = \pm 1$

Hence, the number of units in $R$ is 8.

***Example 2.*** *The characteristic of the ring* $\mathbb{Z}_2 \times \mathbb{Z}_4 \times \mathbb{Z}_6$ *is*

(a) 2 (b) 4 (c) 6 (d) 12

**Solution.** (d) The characteristic of the ring $\mathbb{Z}_2 \times \mathbb{Z}_4 \times \mathbb{Z}_6$ is LCM of 2, 4, 6 which is 12.

***Example 3.*** *The cardinality of an finite integral domain can not be*

(a) 2 (b) 3 (c) 5 (d) 6

**Solution.** (d) Since, the cardinality of finite integral domain cannot be multiple of two distinct prime.

Hence, there is no integral domain of cardinality 6.

***Example 4.*** *The number of prime ideal of* $\mathbb{Z}_{10^5}$ *is*

(a) 2 (b) 5 (c) 10 (d) 10000

**Solution.** (a) Since, $10^5$ has 2 distinct prime divisor *viz.*, 2 and 5. Hence, number of prime ideal in $\mathbb{Z}_m$ is 2.

***Example 5.*** *Which of the following is not a field?*

(a) $\frac{\mathbb{Z}}{2\mathbb{Z}}$ (b) $\frac{\mathbb{Z}}{3\mathbb{Z}}$ (c) $\frac{\mathbb{Z}}{4\mathbb{Z}}$ (d) $\frac{\mathbb{Z}}{5\mathbb{Z}}$

**Solution.** (c) Since, $\frac{\mathbb{Z}}{p\mathbb{Z}}$ is field iff $p$ is prime.

Hence, $\frac{\mathbb{Z}}{4\mathbb{Z}}$ is not a field.

***Example 6.*** *Which of the following is irreducible over $\mathbb{Z}$?*

(a) $x^2-5x+6$ (b) $x^2-7x+12$
(c) $x^2-9x+20$ (d) None of these

**Solution.** (d) Since,

$$x^2-5x+6=(x-2)(x-3) \text{ in } \mathbb{Z}$$
$$x^2-7x+12=(x-3)(x-4) \text{ in } \mathbb{Z}$$

and $x^2-9x+20=(x-4)(x-5)$ in $\mathbb{Z}$

Hence, all three are not irreducible in $\mathbb{Z}$.

***Example 7.*** *The number of elements in the field $\frac{\mathbb{Z}_{11}[x]}{<x^2+1>}$ is*

(a) 11 (b) 121
(c) 22 (d) None of these

**Solution.** (b) If $F$ is a finite field and $p(x)$ is an irreducible polynomial over $F$, then the field $\frac{F[x]}{<p(x)>}$ has $|F|^{\deg p(x)}$ elements.

Hence, $\frac{\mathbb{Z}_{11}[x]}{<x^2+1>}$ has $11^2=121$ elements.

***Example 8.*** *The idempotent element of $\mathbb{Z}_6$ is*

(a) $\overline{3}$ (b) $\overline{4}$
(c) $\overline{5}$ (d) None of these

**Solution.** (a) Since, $\overline{3}*\overline{3}=\overline{9}=\overline{3}$ in $\mathbb{Z}_6$.

Hence, $\overline{3}$ is idempotent in $\mathbb{Z}_6$.

***Example 9.*** *Let $(D,+,\cdot)$ be a division ring containing q elements. Then,*

(a) $a^q=0, \forall\, a\in D$ (b) $a^q=a, \forall\, a\in D$
(c) $a^q=a-1, \forall\, a\in D$ (d) None of these

**Solution.** (b) If $a=0$, then there is nothing to do. Suppose that $a\neq 0$. Then, $a\in D^*$ and since $D^*$ is a group with respect to the induced multiplication which contains $q-1$ elements it follows that $a^{q-1}=1$ and so $a^q=a$

***Example 10.*** *If R is a finite field of characteristic p, then given any $b\in R$, $\exists\, a\in R$ such that*

(a) $a^p=b$ (b) $a^p=b-1$
(c) $a^p=b^{-1}$ (d) None of these

**Solution.** (a) Suppose that $a^p=b^p$. Then, $(a-b)^p=a^p-b^p=0$. Now, since $R$ is an integral domain, $a-b=0$ and so $a=b$. Hence, the map $a\sim a^p$ is an injective map. Since, $R$ is finite it is surjective. Hence, given any $b\in R$, $\exists\, a\in R$ such that $b=a^p$.

## Type II (*One or more than one correct option*)

***Example 11.*** *Which of the following(s) is/are prime ideal of $\mathbb{Z}$?*

(a) $4\mathbb{Z}$ (b) $6\mathbb{Z}$ (c) $3\mathbb{Z}$ (d) $5\mathbb{Z}$

**Solution.** (c), (d)

Since, $2\cdot 2\in 4\mathbb{Z}$ but $2\notin 4\mathbb{Z}$. Hence, $4\mathbb{Z}$ is not prime ideal of $\mathbb{Z}$. Similarly, $2\cdot 3\in 6\mathbb{Z}$ but $2\notin 6\mathbb{Z}$ and $3\notin 6\mathbb{Z}$. Hence, $6\mathbb{Z}$ is not prime ideal of $\mathbb{Z}$.

Now, $3\mathbb{Z}$ and $5\mathbb{Z}$ are prime ideal of $\mathbb{Z}$ as 3 and 5 are prime number.

***Example 12.*** *Which of the following(s) is/are subfield of other?*

(a) $F_2$ (b) $F_4$ (c) $F_8$ (d) $F_{16}$

**Solution.** (a), (b), (c)

If $|F|=p^n$, $p$ is prime and $|k|=p^r$, $r\leq n$ then $k$ is subfield of $F$.

Hence, $F_2, F_4, F_8$ are subfield of $F_{16}$.

***Example 13.*** *Let $(R,+,\cdot)$ be a ring such that $a^2=a, \forall\, a\in R$. Then*

(a) $R$ is commutative (b) $R$ is not commutative
(c) $a+a=0, \forall\, a\in R$ (d) $a+a\neq 0, \forall\, a\in R$

**Solution.** (a), (c)

$$(a+a)=(a+a)^2=(a+a)\cdot(a+a)$$
$$=a^2+a^2+a^2+a^2=a+a+a+a, \forall\, a\in R$$

Hence, by cancellation law

$$a+a=0, \forall\, a\in R$$

Now,

$$(a+b)=(a+b)^2=(a+b)(a+b)$$
$$=a^2+ab+ba+b^2=a+ab+ba+b$$

Hence, by cancellation law

$$ab+ba=0$$

and so $ab+ba=0=ab+ab$

Hence, by cancellation law

$$ab=ba$$

***Example 14.*** *Which of the following(s) is/are not integral domain?*

(a) $\mathbb{Z}_6$ (b) $\mathbb{Z}_7$
(c) $M_n(\mathbb{Z})$ (d) None of these

**Solution.** (a), (c)

In $\mathbb{Z}_6, \overline{2}$ is a left as well as right zero divisor for, $\overline{2}*\overline{3}=\overline{0}=\overline{3}*\overline{2}$ whereas $\overline{3}\neq\overline{0}$. Hence, $\mathbb{Z}_6$ is not integral domain. Whereas $\mathbb{Z}_7$ is an integral domain as 7 is prime number.

Now, in $M_n(\mathbb{Z})$ the matrix $e^1_{ij}, i\neq j$ all of whose entries except $i$th row $j$th column entry is zero and the $i$th row $j$th column entry is 1 is a zero divisor for $(e^1_{ij})^2$ is the zero matrix.

# Exercise 1 (For Part 'B')

**Directions** (Q. Nos. 1-153) *All questions have only one correct option.*

**1.** A field is a
(a) vector space
(b) integral domain
(c) division ring
(d) commutative division ring

**2.** An integral domain $D$ is of finite characteristic, if $\forall\, a \in D$, there exist $m$ a positive integer such that
(a) $ma = 1$ (b) $ma = 0$
(c) $ma = a$ (d) None of these

**3.** $I$ is the set of integers and define $a \oplus b = a + b + 1$ and $a \odot b = a + b + ab$. Then, the ring $\{I, \oplus, \odot\}$ is
(a) commutative ring (b) integral domain
(c) field (d) None of these

**4.** If in a ring with unity $(xy)^2 = x^2y^2$, $\forall\, x, y \in R$, then
(a) $R$ is a commutative ring
(b) $R$ is an integral domain
(c) $R$ is field
(d) None of the above

**5.** Every non-zero nilpotent element of the ring $R$ is
(a) zero divisor (b) non-zero divisor
(c) unity (d) None of these

**6.** $A = \begin{bmatrix} 1 & 1 \\ 1 & 1 \end{bmatrix}$ and $B = \begin{bmatrix} 1 & 0 \\ -1 & 0 \end{bmatrix}$ are
(a) zero divisors (b) non-zero divisors
(c) $A = 0$ or $B = 0$ (d) $AB \neq 0$

**7.** If $I$ is a ideal in ring $R$, then
(a) $R/I$ is a ring (b) $RI$ is a ring
(c) $R + I$ is a ring (d) None of these

**8.** If the ring $R$ has unities $e_1$ and $e_2$, then
(a) $e_1 = e_2$ (b) $e_1 = me_2$
(c) $e_1 \neq e_2$ (d) None of these

**9.** A ring $(R, +, \cdot)$ is said to have zero divisor, if
(a) $a, b \in R,\ a \cdot b = 0 \Rightarrow a \neq 0$ or $b \neq 0$
(b) $a, b \in R,\ a \cdot b = 0 \Rightarrow a \neq 0$ and $b \neq 0$
(c) $a, b \in R,\ a \cdot b = 0 \Rightarrow a = 0$ or $b = 0$
(d) $a, b \in R,\ a \cdot b = 0 \Rightarrow a = 0$ and $b = 0$

**10.** If $R$ is commutative ring with unit element, $M$ is an ideal of $R$ and $R/M$ is finite integral domain, then
(a) $M$ is a maximal ideal of $R$
(b) $M$ is not a maximal ideal of $R$
(c) $M$ is minimal ideal of $R$
(d) None of the above

**11.** If $R$ is an Euclidean ring and $a, b \in R$. If $b \neq 0$ is not a unit in $R$, then
(a) $d(a) < d(ab)$ (b) $d(a) > d(ab)$
(c) $d(a) = d(ab)$ (d) None of these

**12.** If $\pi$ is prime element in Euclidean ring $R$ and $\pi / ab$, $a, b \in R$, then
(a) $\pi \nmid a$ or $\pi \nmid b$
(b) $\pi \nmid a$ and $\pi \nmid b$
(c) $ab \neq m\pi$, for some $m \in R$
(d) None of the above

**13.** If $f(x)$ and $g(x)$ are two polynomials, then
(a) $\deg(f(x)\,g(x)) \leq \deg f(x),\ g(x) \neq 0$
(b) $\deg(f(x)\,g(x)) \geq \deg f(x),\ g(x) \neq 0$
(c) $\deg(f(x)\,g(x)) = \deg f(x) \cdot \deg g(x),\ g(x) \neq 0$
(d) $\deg(f(x)\ g(x)) = \deg f(x) - \deg g(x),\ g(x) \neq 0$

**14.** Given, a polynomial $f(x) = a_0 + a_1x + \ldots + a_nx^n$, where $a$'s are integer, then content of $f(x)$ is
(a) gcd of integers $a_0, \ldots, a_n$
(b) mean of integers $a_0, \ldots, a_n$
(c) mode of integers $a_0, \ldots, a_n$
(d) None of the above

**15.** If $R$ is a commutative ring, with unit element, then
(a) every maximal ideal is prime ideal
(b) every prime ideal is maximal ideal
(c) every ideal is prime ideal
(d) every ideal is maximal ideal

**16.** A ring $(R, +, \cdot)$ is said to have a ring without zero divisor, if
(a) $a, b \in R,\ a \cdot b = 0 \Rightarrow a \neq 0$ or $b \neq 0$
(b) $a, b \in R,\ a \cdot b = 0 \Rightarrow a \neq 0$ and $b \neq 0$
(c) $a, b \in R,\ a \cdot b = 0 \Rightarrow a = 0$ or $b = 0$ or both are zero
(d) $a, b \in R,\ a \cdot b = 0 \Rightarrow a = 0$ and $b \neq 0$

**17.** If integral domain $I$ is of finite characteristic, then
(a) $I$ is finite only (b) $I$ is infinite only
(c) $I$ is finite or infinite (d) None of these

**18.** $A$ : $F$ is a field
$B$ : $F$ is an integral domain
(a) $A \Rightarrow B$ (b) $B \Rightarrow A$
(c) $A \Leftrightarrow B$ (d) $A \Leftrightarrow B$

**19.** A commutative division ring is
(a) vector space (b) group
(c) integral domain (d) field

**20.** $I$ is an ordered integral domain and $a, b \in I$, if $a > b$, then
(a) $a + c \geq b + c,\ \forall\, c \in I$ (b) $a + c \leq b + c,\ \forall\, c \in I$
(c) $a + c < b + c,\ \forall\, c \in I$ (d) $a + c > b + c,\ \forall\, c \in I$

**21.** If $R$ is a ring in which $a^4 = a,\ \forall\, a \in R$, then
(a) $R$ is commutative
(b) $R$ is not commutative
(c) $R$ is zero ring
(d) None of the above

**22.** If the ring $R$ is such that $(ab)^2 = a^2b^2$, $a, b \in R$, then
(a) $R$ is commutative (b) $R$ is non-commutative
(c) $R$ is zero ring (d) None of these

**23.** Given, the polynomial $p(x) = a_0 + a_1x + ... + a_mx^m$, its degree is $m$, if
(a) $a_m = 0$ (b) $a_m \neq 0$
(c) $a_{m-1} = 0$ (d) $a_{m-1} \neq 0$

**24.** The element $a \neq 0 \in R$, the commutative ring is an integral domain, if
(a) $ab = 0$, $b \in R$ and $b = 0$
(b) $ab = 0$, $b \in R$ and $b \neq 0$
(c) $ab \neq 0$, $b \in R$ and $b = 0$
(d) $ab = 0$, $b \in R$ and $b = 0$

**25.** A ring $R$ is an integral domain, if
(a) $R$ is commutative ring
(b) $R$ is skew-field
(c) $R$ has no non-zero divisor
(d) None of the above

**26.** A ring $R$ with binary operation addition is an Abelian group. It with binary operation multiplication, $\forall\, a, b \in R$, $a \cdot b = b \cdot a$, then $R$ is
(a) commutative ring (b) integral domain
(c) field (d) null ring

**27.** An integral domain $D$ is of characteristic zero, if
(a) $ma = 0$, $a \neq 0 \in D \Rightarrow m = 0$
(b) $ma = 0$, $a \neq 0 \in D \Rightarrow m \neq 0$
(c) $ma = 0$, $a \neq 0 \in D \Rightarrow m = a$
(d) $ma = 0$, $a \neq 0 \in D \Rightarrow m \neq a$

**28.** If $R$ is an integral domain with unit element, then
(a) $R[x]$ is not a commutative ring
(b) $R[x]$ have a unit element
(c) any unit in $R[x]$ is unit in $R$
(d) any unit in $R[x]$ is not an unit in $R$

**29.** If $K$ is an extension of $F$, then degree of $K$ over $F$ is
(a) dimension of $K$ as vector space over $F$
(b) $e^k$
(c) $e^{k+1}$
(d) None of the above

**30.** If the ring $R$ has left identity $e_1$ and right identity $e_2$, then
(a) $e_1 = e_2$ (b) $e_1 \neq e_2$
(c) $e_1 = me_2$ (d) None of these

**31.** If a ring $R \neq \{0\}$ has the multiplicative identity $I$, then
(a) $I > 0$ (b) $I = 0$
(c) $I \neq 0$ (d) None of these

**32.** The non-zero elements $a$ and $b$ of a ring $(R, +, \cdot)$ are called zero divisors, if
(a) $a \cdot b = 0$ (b) $a \cdot b = 1$
(c) $a \cdot b \neq 0$ (d) $a \cdot b \neq 1$

**33.** A skew-field have
(a) non-zero divisors
(b) zero divisors
(c) $a, b : a \cdot b = 0 : a \neq 0,\ b \neq 0$
(d) None of the above

**34.** If $f$ is an isomorphism of a ring $(R_1, +, \cdot)$ onto a ring $(R'_1, +', \bullet')$
A: Isomorphic image of a field is a field
B: Isomorphic image of a division ring is a division ring
C: Isomorphic image of a ring with unity is a ring with unity
then
(a) A, B, C are true (b) A and B are false
(c) B and C are false (d) A is false

**35.** A field having no proper subfield is
(a) prime field (b) division ring
(c) integral domain (d) None of these

**36.** Every finite integral of domain is
(a) of finite characteristic
(b) of not finite characteristic
(c) not a field
(d) None of the above

**37.** Let $(D, +, \cdot)$ is an integral domain, $D$ is a field, if
(a) for $\forall\ a \in D$, there exist $a^{-1} \in D : a \cdot a^{-1} = 1$
(b) for $\forall\ a \in D$, there exist $a^{-1} \in D : a + a^{-1} = 0$
(c) for $\forall\ a \in D$, there exist $b \in D : ab = 0$
(d) None of the above

**38.** Let $R$ be a ring, $U \neq \phi \subset R$ is ideal of $R$, then
A: $U$ is a subgroup of $R$ under addition
B: $\forall\ u \in U$ and $r \in R$; $ur$, $ru \in U$
(a) A and B Both are true
(b) Only A is true
(c) Only B is true
(d) Both A and B are false

**39.** If $U$ is an ideal of ring $R$, then
(a) $U/R$ is a ring (b) $R/U$ is a ring
(c) $RU$ is a ring (d) None of these

**40.** An integer monic polynomial is a
(a) primitive polynomial
(b) non-primitive polynomial
(c) polynomial with lowest coefficient as 1
(d) polynomial without lowest coefficient as 1

**41.** $E$ is the set of even integers under ordinary addition and multiplication, then $E$ is a ring, $E$ is also a
(a) commutative ring (b) integral domain
(c) field (d) None of these

**42.** A commutative division ring is
(a) finite integral domain
(b) integral domain
(c) zero ring
(d) None of these

**43.** If $R$ is a commutative ring with unit element, $M$ is maximum ideal of $R$ iff
(a) $R/M$ is a field (b) $M/R$ is a field
(c) $RM$ is a field (d) None of these

**44.** If $F$ is a field, then its only ideals are
A : $F$, a field itself
B : (0)
(a) A and B are true
(b) A is true, B is false
(c) A is false, B is true
(d) A and B false

**45.** The ring of complex numbers $C = \{x + iy : x, y$ are real numbers, $i = \sqrt{-1}\}$ is
(a) not an integral domain
(b) an integral domain
(c) ordered set
(d) None of the above

**46.** If $I$ is an integral domain and $a \neq 0 \in I$, then
(a) $a^2 = 0$ (b) $a^2 \geq 0$
(c) $a^2 \neq 0$ (d) None of these

**47.** The singleton {0} with binary operations addition and multiplication is ring and it is called
(a) zero ring (b) division ring
(c) singleton ring (d) None of these

**48.** The polynomial $f(x) = a_0 + a_1x + a_2x + ... + a_nx^n$, where $a_0, a_1, a_2, ..., a_n$ are integers, is primitive polynomial, if
(a) gcd of $(a_0, ...., a_n) = 0$
(b) gcd of $(a_0, ...., a_n) = 1$
(c) gcd of $(a_0, ...., a_n) - 2$
(d) gcd of $(a_0, ...., a_n) =$ prime number

**49.** A polynomial is said to be integer monic, if
(a) its coefficients are integers and highest coefficient is 1
(b) its coefficients are real numbers
(c) its coefficients are real numbers and highest coefficient is 0
(d) its coefficients are integers and highest coefficient is 2

**50.** If $f(x) = 2x^4 + 3x^3 + 2$ and $g(x) = 3x^5 + 4x^3 + 2x + 3$ be two polynomials over the field $Z_5 = (\{0, 1, 2, 3, 4\}, +_5, \times_5)$, then $\frac{d}{dx} f(x)$ is
(a) $3x^* + 4x^3$ (b) $3x^3 + 4x^2$
(c) $3x^3 + 4x^4$ (d) $4x^3 + 3x^2$

**51.** $f(x) = x^2 + 8x - 2$ is irreducible over
(a) $Z$ (b) $Q$
(c) $N$ (d) None of these

**52.** If $f(x) \in F(x)$ and $a \in F$, for a field $F$, then $x - a$ divides $f(x)$ if and only if
(a) $f(a) = 0$ (b) $f(a) \neq 0$
(c) $f(a) = 1$ (d) $f(a) = \infty$

**53.** Ring of polynomials over a field is a
(a) prime field
(b) group
(c) unique factorization domain
(d) irreducible

**54.** An integral domain $R$, with unity element 1 is a unique factorization domain, if
(a) any non-zero element in $R$ is either a unit or can be written as the product of a finite number of irreducible (prime) elements of $R$.
(b) any non-zero element in $R$ is either a unity or can be written as the sum of a finite number of irreducible (prime) element of $R$.
(c) any non-zero element in $R$ is either a unit or can be written as the difference of finite number of irreducible (prime) elements of $R$.
(d) None of the above

**55.** Check the correct statement
(a) The polynomial $x^2 - 2$ is irreducible over the field of rational numbers while it is irreducible over the field of real numbers.
(b) The polynomial $x^2 - 2$ is irreducible over the field of rational numbers. While it is reducible over the field of real numbers.
(c) The polynomial $x^2 + 1$ is reducible over the field of real numbers.
(d) The polynomial $x^2 + 1$ is irreducible over the field of complex numbers.

**56.** A polynomial domain $F(x)$ over a field $F$ is a
(a) group
(b) principal ideal ring
(c) unique factorization domain
(d) None of the above

**57.** Check the correct statement.
(a) The ring of integers is a Euclidean ring.
(b) The ring of polynomials over a field is a Euclidean ring.
(c) The ring of Gaussian integers is a Euclidean ring.
(d) All of the above

**58.** Let $R$ be a Euclidean ring and $a$ and $b$ be any two elements in $R$, not both of which are zero. Then, $a$ and $b$ have a greatest common divisor $d$, which can be expressed in the form
(a) $d = \frac{\lambda a}{\mu b}$ for some $\lambda, \mu \in R$
(b) $d = \lambda a + \mu b$ for some $\lambda, \mu \in R$
(c) $d = \lambda a - \mu b$ for some $\lambda, \mu \in R$
(d) $d = (\lambda a)(\lambda b)$ for some $\lambda, \mu \in R$

**59.** If $R$ be a Euclidean ring and $a$ and $b$ be two non-zero elements in $R$. Then,
(a) if $b$ is a unit in $R$, $d(ab) = d(a)$
(b) if $b$ is not a unit in $R$, $d(ab) > d(a)$
(c) Both (a) and (b)
(d) None of the above

**60.** If $R$ is an integral domain (not necessarily a unique factorization domain) and $F$ is its field of quotients, then any element $f(x)$ in $F(x)$ can be written as
(a) $f(x) = \frac{f_0(x)}{a}$, where $f_0(x) \in R[x]$ and where $a \in R$
(b) $f(x) = a f_0(x)$, where $f_0(x) \in R[x]$ and $a \in R$
(c) $f(x) = a - f_0(x)$, where $f_0(x) \in R[x]$ and $a \in R$
(d) None of the above

**61.** Let $R$ and $R'$ be two arbitrary rings, $\phi: R \to R'$ defined as $\phi(a) = 0$ for all $a \in R$, then.
(a) $\phi$ is homomorphism (b) $\phi$ is automorphism
(c) $\phi$ is isomorphism (d) None of these

**62.** The homomorphism $\phi$ of rings $R$ into $R'$ is an isomorphism iff the kernel $I(\phi)$ is
(a) $I(\phi) = (0)$ (b) $I(\phi) = R$
(c) $I(\phi) = R'$ (d) None of these

**63.** A ring with no zero divisors is
(a) quotient ring (b) principal ideal domain
(c) maximum ideals (d) None of these

**64.** The converse of statement
Every principal ideal domain is a unique factorization domain, is
(a) true (b) false
(c) partially true (d) not possible

**65.** Every Euclidean ring is a
(a) principal ideal domain
(b) quotient ring
(c) maximum ideals
(d) None of the above

**66.** An ideal $M \neq R$ in a ring $R$ is maximal ideal of $R$, if $U$ is an ideal of $R$ and $M \subset U \subseteq R$, then
(a) either $M = U$ or $R = U$
(b) $M = U = R$
(c) $M = U \neq R$
(d) $M \neq U \neq R$

**67.** The set of all even integers is ring it is also a
(a) commutative ring (b) integral domain
(c) field (d) None of these

**68.** Every integral domain is not a
(a) field
(b) commutative ring
(c) ring
(d) abelian group with respect to addition

**69.** Which of the following statement is false?
(a) Every field is an integral domain.
(b) Every finite integral domain is a field.
(c) Every field is a ring.
(d) Every integral domain is a field.

**70.** A field is defined as
(a) division ring (b) commutative ring
(c) integral domain (d) finite integral domain

**71.** A commutative ring $R$ with unity is called integral domain if $a, b \in R$
(a) $ab = 0 \Rightarrow a \neq 0, b \neq 0$ (b) $ab = 0 \Rightarrow a = 0, b = 0$
(c) $ab = 0 \Rightarrow a = b$ (d) None of these

**72.** If $f(x)$ and $g(x)$ are two non-zero polynomials of $f[x]$, then
(a) $\deg(f(x)\ g(x)) = \deg(f(x) \cdot \deg\ g(x))$
(b) $\deg(f(x)\ g(x)) = \deg f(x) + \deg\ g(x)$
(c) $\deg(f(x)\ g(x)) = \deg f(x) - \deg\ g(x)$
(d) $\deg(f(x)\ g(x)) = \deg f(x) \div \deg\ g(x)$

**73.** If $F$ is a finite field and $\alpha \neq 0$, $\beta \neq 0$ are two elements of $F$, then we can find elements $a$ and $b$ in $F$, such that
(a) $1 + \alpha a + \beta b = 0$ (b) $1 + \alpha a^2 + \beta b^2 = 0$
(c) $1 + \alpha a + \beta b \neq 0$ (d) $1 + \alpha a^2 + \beta b^2 \neq 0$

**74.** The set $C$ of complex number of the form $x + iy$ is a field with respect to ordinary addition and multiplication, then the unit and zero elements are respectively
(a) $1 + i0$ and $0 + i0$ (b) $0 + i$ and $1 + i0$
(c) 0 and 1 (d) $i$ and $-i$

**75.** If $C = \{x + iy : x, y \in R, i = \sqrt{-1}\}$ is a field with respect to ordinary addition and multiplication, then the multiplicative inverse of non-zero element of $a + ib \in C$ is
(a) $a + b$ (b) $\left(\frac{a}{a^2 + b^2}\right) + i\left(\frac{-b}{a^2 + b^2}\right)$
(c) $\frac{a^2 + ib}{a^2 + b^2}$ (d) None of these

**76.** If integral domain $D$ is of finite characteristic, then its characteristic is
(a) odd number (b) even number
(c) prime number (d) natural number

**77.** A mapping $f$ from a ring $R$ into a ring $R'$ is said to be a homomorphism of $R$ into $R'$, if
(a) $f(a - b) = f(a) - f(b) + f(ab)$, $\forall\ a, b \in R$
(b) $f(a + b) = f(a) + f(b)$, $\forall\ a, b \in R$
(c) $f(ab) = f(a)f(b)$, $\forall\ a, b \in R$
(d) Both (a) and (b)

**78.** If $f$ is a homomorphism of a ring $R$ into a ring $R'$, then
(a) $f(0) = 0'$, where 0 is the zero element of the ring $R$ and $0'$ is the zero element of $R'$
(b) $f(-a) = -f(a)$, $\forall\ a \in R$
(c) Both (a) and (b)
(d) $f(a) = f(-a)$

**79.** Kernel of a ring homomorphism is
(a) if $f$ is a homomorphism of a ring $R$ into a ring $R'$, then the set $S$ of all those elements of $R$ which are mapped onto the zero element of $R'$ is called the kernel of the homomorphism $f$.
(b) the homomorphism of a ring $R$ onto a ring $R'$, then the set $S$ of all those elements of $R$ which are mapped into the zero element of $R'$ is called the kernel of the homomorphism $f$.
(c) if $f$ is a homomorphism of $R$ onto $R'$, then $S$ is the kernel of $f$, if $S = \{x \in R : f(x) = 0'$, where $0'$ is the zero element of $R'\}$
(d) None of the above

**80.** Check the correct statement.
(a) The homomorphism $\phi$ of a ring $R$ into a ring $R'$, is an isomorphism of $R$ into $R'$ if and only if $I(\phi) = 0$, where $I(\phi)$ denotes the kernel of $\phi$.
(b) Suppose, $R$ is a ring, $S$ is an ideal of $R$. Let $f$ be a mapping from $R$ to $R/S$ defined by $f(a) = S + a$, $\forall\ a \in R$. Then, $f$ is a homomorphism of $R$ onto $R/S$.

(c) If $f$ is a homomorphism of a ring $R$ into a ring $R'$ with kernel $S$, then $S$ is an ideal of $R$.
(d) All of the above

**81.** If the ring $R$ is finite and commutative with unit element, then
(a) every prime ideal is a maximal ideal
(b) every ideal is maximal ideal
(c) every maximal ideal is prime ideal
(d) Both (a) and (c) are true

**82.** Theorems related to the unique factorization theorem are
(a) let $f(x)$, $g(x)$ and $h(x)$ be polynomials in $F(x)$ for a field $F$. If $f(x)| g(x)h(x)$ and the greatest common divisor of $f(x)$ and $g(x)$ is 1, then $f(x)| h(x)$.
(b) if $f(x)$ is an irreducible polynomial in $F(x)$ for a field $F$ and $g(x)| g(x)h(x)$, where $g(x), h(x) \in F[x]$, then $f(x)$ divides atleast one of $g(x)$ or $h(x)$.
(c) Both (a) and (b)
(d) None of the above

**83.** If $U$ is an ideal of ring $R$ and $1 \in U$, then
(a) $U$ is a proper subset of $R$
(b) $U$ is equal to $R$
(c) $U$ is a super set of $R$
(d) $U = \phi$

**84.** Let $R$ is a commutative ring with unit element whose only ideals are (0) and $R$ itself, then
(a) $R$ is finite integral domain
(b) $R$ is integral domain
(c) division ring
(d) None of the above

**85.** Let $R$ is a commutative ring with unit element whose only ideals are (0) and $R$ itself, then
(a) $R$ is integral domain (b) $R$ is field
(c) division ring (d) None of these

**86.** Which of the following statements is false?
(a) $F[x]$ is an integral domain
(b) $F[x]$ is Euclidean ring
(c) $F[x]$ is principal ideal ring
(d) $F[x]$ is not a group

**87.** A polynomials $f(x)$ and $g(x)$ are primitive polynomials, then
(a) $f(x)\,g(x)$ is a primitive polynomial
(b) $f(x) + g(x)$ is a primitive polynomial
(c) $f(x) - g(x)$ is a primitive polynomial
(d) $f(x)/g(x)$ is a primitive polynomial

**88.** If the ring $R$ is an integral domain, then
(a) $R[x]$ is an integral domain
(b) $R[x]$ is not an integral domain
(c) $R[x]$ is a field
(d) $R[x]$ is a commutative division ring

**89.** Let $I_1$ be the ideal generated by $x^4 + 3x^2 + 2$ and $I_2$ be the ideal generated by $x^3 + 1$ in $Q[x]$. If $F_1 = \dfrac{Q[x]^2}{I_1}$ and $F_2 = \dfrac{Q[x]}{I_2}$, then
(a) $F_1$ and $F_2$ are fields
(b) $F_1$ is a field, but $F_2$ is not a field
(c) $F_1$ is not a field while $F_2$ is a field
(d) Neither $F_1$ nor $F_2$ is a field

**90.** If $K$ is a extension of field $F$ and $a \in K$ is algebraic of degree $n$ over $F$, then
(a) $[F(a):F] = n$ (b) $[F(a):K] = n$
(c) $[K:F(a)] = n$ (d) $[F:F(a)] = n$

**91.** The extension $K$ of field $F$ is an algebraic extension of $F$
(a) every element $a \in K$ is algebraic over $F$
(b) for some $a \in K$ is algebraic over $F$
(c) zero element is algebraic over $F$
(d) None of the above

**92.** Transitivity of algebraic extension is
(a) if $L$ is an algebraic extension of $K$ and $K$ is an algebraic extension of $F$, then $L$ is an algebraic extension of $F$.
(b) if $K$ be an extension of a field $F$, then the elements in $K$ which are algebraic over $F$ form a subfield of $K$.
(c) every finite extension $K$ of a field $F$ is algebraic.
(d) if $K$ be an extension of a field $F$ and let $a \in K$ be algebraic of degree $n$ over $F$. Then, $[F(a):F] = n$

**93.** Check the correct statement.
(a) If $F$ is any field, so degree of $F$ over $F$ is two.
(b) If $L$ is a finite extension of $K$ and if $K$ is a finite extension of $F$, then $L$ is a finite extension of $F$.
(c) If $K$ be an extension of the field $F$, then $K$ is said to be a finite extension of $F$, if the degree of $K$ over $F$ is finite.
(d) Both (b) and (c)

**94.** If $K$ be an extension of a field $F$. Then, the element $a \in K$ is algebraic over $F$ if and only if
(a) $F(a)$ is a infinite extension of $F$
(b) $F(a)$ is a finite extension of $F$
(c) $F(a)$ is non-algebraic over $F$
(d) None of the above

**95.** If $K$ be an extension of a field $F$, then mapping $\phi: F[x] \to F(a)$ defined by $h(x) = h(a)$ is
(a) isomorphism (b) homomorphism
(c) Both (a) and (b) (d) None of these

**96.** Degree of $Q(\sqrt{2}, \sqrt{3})$ over $Q$, where $Q$ is the field of rational numbers is
(a) 4 (b) 3
(c) 1 (d) 2

**97.** The relation between the fields $Q(\sqrt{2})$ and $Q(3+\sqrt{2})$, where $Q$ is the field of rational numbers is
(a) $Q(\sqrt{2}) + Q(3+\sqrt{2}) = 0$
(b) $Q(\sqrt{2}) = Q(3+\sqrt{2})$
(c) $Q(\sqrt{2}) \times Q(3+\sqrt{2}) = 0$
(d) $\dfrac{Q\sqrt{2}}{Q(3+\sqrt{2})} = 0$

**98.** If $L$ is a finite extension of $K$ and $K$ is a finite extension of field $F$, then
(a) $F$ is a finite extension of $L$
(b) $L$ is a finite extension of $F$
(c) $K$ is a subfield of $F$
(d) $L$ is subfield of $K$

**99.** If $L$ is a finite extension of $F$ and $K$ is a subfield of $L$ which contains $F$, then
(a) $[L:F] \mid [K:F]$ (b) $[K:F] \mid [L:F]$
(c) $[K:F] \mid [F:L]$ (d) $[F:K] \mid [L:F]$

**100.** If $K$ is an extension of $F$ and $a \in K$, $F(a)$ is a finite extension, then
(a) $a$ is algebraic over $F$
(b) $a$ is not algebraic over $F$
(c) $F(a)$ is the largest subfield of $K$
(d) None of the above

**101.** If a and b in $K$ (where $K$ is an extension of field $F$) are algebraic over $F$ of degree $m$ and $n$, respectively the following is false
(a) $ab$ is algebraic over $F$
(b) $a+b$ is algebraic over $F$
(c) $a-b$ is algebraic over $F$
(d) None of the above

**102.** If $F$ is a subfield of $L$ and $K$ is a subfield of $L$ which contains $F$. Then,
(a) $[K:F] \mid [L:F]$ (b) $[K:F] \nmid [L:F]$
(c) $[F:K] \mid [F:L]$ (d) $[F:K] \nmid [F:L]$

**103.** An element $a \in K$ is algebraic over field $F$, if for $\alpha_0, \ldots, \alpha_n \in F$ all not zero
(a) $\alpha_0 a^n + \alpha_1 a^{n-1} + \ldots + \alpha_n \neq 0$
(b) $\alpha_0 a^n + \alpha_1 a^{n-1} + \ldots + \alpha_n a^{n-1} = 0$
(c) $\alpha_0 a^n + \alpha_1 a^{n-1} + \ldots + \alpha_n = 0$
(d) None of the above

**104.** If $K$ is an extension of field $F$ and $a \in K$ is algebraic over $F$, if
(a) $F(a)$ is an extension of $F$
(b) $F(a)$ is a subfield of $F$
(c) $F(a)$ is finite extension of $F$
(d) None of the above

**105.** A complex number is algebraic number, if
(a) it is algebraic over real numbers
(b) it is algebraic over rational numbers
(c) it is algebraic over integers
(d) it is algebraic over natural numbers

**106.** If $f(x) \in F[x]$, then there is a finite extension $E$ of $F$, such that
(a) $[E:F] \leq \deg f(x)$ (b) $[E:F] \geq \deg f(x)$
(c) $[F:E] \geq \deg f(x)$ (d) $[F:E] \leq \deg f(x)$

**107.** If $a, b, c$ are the roots of $x^3 + px^2 + qx + r$, then the value of $\Sigma \frac{b^2+c^2}{bc}$ is
(a) $\frac{pq}{r} - 3$ (b) $\frac{p}{r}$
(c) $\frac{pq}{3}$ (d) $pq - r$

**108.** If $f$ and $g$ are multiplicative,
(a) The Dirichlet product $f * g$ is multiplicative
(b) The Dirichlet product $f * g$ is not multiplicative
(c) Both (a) and (b)
(d) Neither (a) nor (b)

**109.** If $x$ is any real number
(a) $\left[\frac{[x]}{m}\right] = \left[\frac{x}{m}\right]$, if $m$ is a positive integer
(b) $\left[\frac{[x]}{m}\right] \neq \left[\frac{x}{m}\right]$, if $m$ is a positive integer
(c) Both (a) and (b)
(d) Neither (a) nor (b)

**110.** If $f$ and $g$ are two arithmetic functions and

$$g(n) = \sum_{d/n} \mu(d) f\left(\frac{n}{d}\right) = \sum_{d/n} \mu\left(\frac{n}{d}\right) f(d)$$

(a) $f(n) = \sum_{d/n} g(d)$ (b) $f(n) \neq \sum_{d/n} g(d)$
(c) $f(n) = 0$ (d) $f(n) = g(n)$

**111.** If $f$ and $g$ are two arithmetic functions and

(I) $f(n) = \sum_{d/n} g(d)$

(II) $g(n) = \sum_{d/n} \mu(d) f\left(\frac{n}{d}\right)$

$$= \sum_{d/n} \mu\left(\frac{n}{d}\right) f(d)$$

(a) if $f$ and $g$ satisfy either (I), then it also satisfies (II)
(b) if $f$ and $g$ satisfy (I), then they also satisfy (II)
(c) Both (a) and (b)
(d) Neither (a) nor (b)

**112.** If $F$ is a field of characteristics 3, then $\forall\, a, b \in F$; $(a+b)^3$ is equal to
(a) $a+b$ (b) $a^3 + b^3$
(c) $a+b+ab$ (d) 0

**113.** Number of prime ideals of $Z_{10}$ is
(a) 1 (b) 0
(c) 2 (d) 5

**114.** The number of nilpotent element in ring $(Z_{30}, +_{30}, \times_{30})$ is/are
(a) 0 (b) 1
(c) 2 (d) 3

**115.** The number of idempotent and nilpotent elements in $Z_4$, respectively
(a) 1, 3 (b) 3, 1
(c) 2, 2 (d) 0, 1

**116.** Consider the following statements
(I) Every principal ideal domain is a Euclidean domain.
(II) The group of units in the ring $Z/37Z$ is cyclic.
(III) There is a field with $6^5$ elements.

**Codes**
(a) (I) is true but (II) and (III) are false
(b) (II) is true but (I) and (III) are false
(c) (III) is true but (I) and (II) are false
(d) All three statements above are false

**117.** Let $F$ be a field of the complex numbers and consider the ideal of $F[x]$ as $M = <x+2>F[x] + <x^2+8x+16> F[x]$. Then, $M$ is
(a) a prime ideal of $F[x]$
(b) a proper but not prime ideal of $F[x]$
(c) $M = F[x]$
(d) None of the above

**118.** A non-zero element of a ring $R$ is said to be nilpotent if $a^n = 0$, for some integer $n$. In the ring of integers (mod 8), all the nilpotent elements are
(a) 2, 4 and 6 (b) 2 and 4
(c) 4 (d) 0, 2, 4, 6

**119.** Which of the following statements is true about $S = Z[x]$?
(a) $S$ is an Euclidean domain since all its ideals are principal.
(b) $S$ is an Euclidean domain since $Z$ is an Euclidean domain.
(c) $S$ is not an Euclidean domain since $S$ is not an integral domain.
(d) $S$ is not an Euclidean domain since it has non-principal ideals.

**120.** Let $R$ be an integral domain with unity '1', in which $20.1 = 0$ and $12.1 = 0$. Then, characteristics of $R$ is
(a) 2 (b) 4
(c) 20 (d) 12

**121.** Let $I_1 = <x^2 - 3>$ and $I_2$ be two ideals of $Z_{11}[x]$ where $I_2 = \{f(x) \in Z_{11}[x] : f(2) = 0\}$, then
(a) $I_1$ and $I_2$ both are maximal
(b) $I_1$ is maximal but $I_2$ is not
(c) $I_2$ is maximal but $I_1$ is not
(d) $I_1$ and $I_2$ both are not maximal

**122.** Consider $Z_5$ as a field modulo 5 and let $f(x) = x^5 + 4x^4 + 4x^3 + 4x^2 + x + 1$
Then, the zeros of $f(x)$ over $Z_5$ are 1 and 3 with respective multiplicity
(a) 1 and 4 (b) 2 and 3
(c) 2 and 2 (d) 1 and 2

**123.** A subring $S$ of $R$ has the following axioms
(a) $S$ is closed under addition and multiplication
(b) $S$ is closed under addition only
(c) $S$ is closed under multiplication only
(d) $S$ is a ring under the operation defined in $R$

**124.** Let $Q$ be the field of rational numbers and consider $Z_2$ as a field modulo 2. Let $f(x) = x^3 - 9x^2 + 9x + 3$. Then, $f(x)$ is
(a) irreducible over $Q$ but reducible over $Z_2$
(b) irreducible over both $Q$ and $Z_2$
(c) reducible over $Q$ but irreducible over $Z_2$
(d) reducible over both $Q$ and $Z_2$

**125.** The number of element in the field $\frac{Z[i]}{<2+i>}$ is
(a) 2 (b) 3
(c) 5 (d) $\infty$

**126.** If $S$ is a finite commutative ring with unity 1, then
(a) each prime ideal is a maximal ideal
(b) $S$ may have a prime ideal which is not maximal
(c) $S$ has no non-trivial maximal ideals
(d) $S$ is a field

**127.** Let $(E, +, \cdot)$ be the ring of even integers and $H_4 = \{4n : n \in Z\}$, then which is/are correct
(I) $H_4$ is an ideal
(II) $H_4$ is prime ideal
(III) $H_4$ is maximal ideal
(a) Only (I) (b) (I) and (II)
(c) (I) and (III) (d) (I), (II) and (III)

**128.** If $f : R[x] \to \mathbb{C}$ as $f(p(x)) = p(i)$, where $R[x]$ is polynomial ring over $R$ set of real number, then
(a) $f$ is not homomorphism
(b) $f$ is homomorphism and $\ker f = <x-1>$
(c) $f$ is homomorphism and $\ker f = <x^2+1>$
(d) $f$ is homomorphism and $\ker f = <x^2-1>$

**129.** $x^2 + 1$ irreducible over $F$ the field of integers modulo 11. The number of elements in $\frac{F[x]}{<x^2+1>}$ is
(a) 11 (b) 121
(c) 1331 (d) None of these

**130.** The ring $M$ of $2 \times 2$ matrices with elements in $R$, is
(a) commutative ring with zero divisors, without unity
(b) non-commutative ring with zero divisors, with unity
(c) commutative ring with unity
(d) field

**131.** Let $f(x) \in Q[x]$ where $Q$ be the field of rationals, define $I = \{f(x) \in Q[x] : f(x) = 0\}$, then
(a) $I$ is not ideal but subring of $Q[x]$
(b) $I$ is an ideal but not principal
(c) $I$ is principal ideal but not maximal
(d) $I$ is principal as well as maximal

**132.** Let $m$ and $n$ be coprime natural number then the kernel of the ring homomorphism $\phi : Z \to Z_m \times Z_n$ defined by $\phi(x) = (\bar{x}, \bar{x})$ is (where $\bar{x}$ is reduced mod $m$ when abscissa and reduced mod $n$ when ordinate)
(a) $mZ$ (b) $mnZ$
(c) $nZ$ (d) $Z$

**133.** Let $R$ be a $CRU$ and $M$ be a maximal ideal of $R$ such that $M^2 = \{0\}$, if $N$ is any ideal of $R$, then
(a) $N \subset M$ i.e., $N$ is properly contained in $M$
(b) if $N$ is also maximal then $N = M$
(c) $N$ is properly contained in $M$ if $N$ is prime
(d) None of the above

**134.** The number of associates of $2 + 3i$ (including this) in the Euclidean domain of Gaussian integer is
(a) 1 (b) 2
(c) 3 (d) 4

**135.** The polynomial $f(x) = x^5 + 5$ is
(a) irreducible over $C$
(b) irreducible over $R$
(c) irreducible over $Q$
(d) not irreducible over $Q$
(where $Q$ denote the field of rational number)

**136.** The integral domain of which cardinality is not possible
(a) 5 (b) 6 (c) 7 (d) 8

**137.** Let $F$ be a finite field. If $f : F \to F$, given by $f(x) = x^3$ is a ring homomorphism, then
(a) $F = Z/3Z$
(b) $F = Z/2Z$ or characteristic of $F = 3$
(c) $F = Z/2Z$ or $Z/3Z$
(d) characteristic of $F$ is 3

**138.** What is the characteristic of the ring of even integer
(a) 2 (b) 1
(c) 0 (d) None of these

**139.** Which one is not a subring of the given ring
(a) $(I, +, \cdot)$ of the ring $(R, +, \cdot)$ ($R$ is a set of reals)
(b) $(E, +, \cdot)$ of $(I, +, \cdot)$; ($E$ is set of even integers)
(c) $(Q, +, \cdot)$ of $(R, +, \cdot)$
(d) $(O, +, \cdot)$ of $(I, +, \cdot)$ ($O$ stands for odd integers)

**140.** Find out which algebraic structure is a field
(a) $(\{a\sqrt{2} : a \in I\}, +, \cdot)$ (b) $(\{a\sqrt{2} : a \in Q\}, +, \cdot)$
(c) $(\{a\sqrt{2} : a \in R\}, +, \cdot)$ (d) None of these

**141.** Let $R[x]$ be the polynomial ring in $x$ with real coefficients and let $I = \langle x^2 + 1 \rangle$ be the ideal generated by the polynomial $x^2 + 1$ in $R[x]$. Then,
(a) $I$ is a maximal ideal
(b) $I$ is a prime ideal but not a maximal ideal
(c) $I$ is not a prime ideal
(d) $R[x]/I$ has zero divisors

**142.** As in the above if $I = \{f(x) \in Q[x] : f(4) = 0\}$, then
(a) $I$ is not ideal but subring of $Q[x]$
(b) $I$ is an ideal but not principal
(c) $I$ is principal ideal but not maximal
(d) $I$ is principal as well as maximal

**143.** Consider, $Z_5$ and $Z_{20}$ as rings modulo 5 and 20, respectively. Then, the number of homomorphism $\varphi : Z_5 \to Z_{20}$ is
(a) 1 (b) 2 (c) 4 (d) 5

**144.** Let $F_4$, $F_8$ and $F_{16}$ be finite fields of 4, 8 and 16 elements, respectively. Then,
(a) $F_4$ is isomorphic to a subfield of $F_8$
(b) $F_8$ is isomorphic to a subfield of $F_{16}$
(c) $F_4$ isomorphic to a subfield of $F_{16}$
(d) None of the above

**145.** Let $I$ be any ideal in the ring $Z$ on integers. Then,
(a) can be generated by one element
(b) $I = \langle 0 \rangle$ or $I = Z$
(c) there is an ideal $I'$ such that $I \oplus I' = Z$
(d) $I$ is generated by a prime number

**146.** For any two non-zero polynomials
$f = a_0 + a_1x + a_2x^2 + \ldots + a_nx^n$,
$g = b_0 + b_1x + b_2x^2 + \ldots + b_nx^n$ over $R$, select the correct statement
(a) $\deg(f + g) = \max(m, n)$ for any ring $R$
(b) $\deg(f \cdot g) = m + n$ iff $R$ is field
(c) $\deg(f \cdot g) = m + n$ iff $R$ is integral domain
(d) $\deg(f + g)$ can never be zero if any of $f$ and $g$ is non-zero polynomial

**147.** Let $PID$, $ED$, $UFD$ denote the set of all principal ideal domains, Euclidean domains, unique factorization domains, respectively. Then,
(a) $UFD \subset ED \subset PID$
(b) $PID \subset ED \subset UFD$
(c) $ED \subset PID \subset UFD$
(d) $PID \subset UFD \subset ED$

**148.** Let $I$ denote the ideal generated by $x^4 + x^3 + x^2 + x + 1$ in $Z_2[x]$ and $F = Z_2[x]/I$. Then,
(a) $F$ is an infinite field
(b) $F$ is a finite field of 4 elements
(c) $F$ is a finite field of 8 elements
(d) $F$ is a finite field of 16 elements

**149.** The set of all matrices of the form $\begin{pmatrix} 0 & x \\ 0 & y \end{pmatrix}$; $x, y \in Q$ under the two operations matrix addition and matrix multiplication is
(a) a ring with unity
(b) commutative ring
(c) non-commutative ring with zero divisors
(d) a ring without zero divisors but with unity

**150.** Let $R[x]$ be the polynomial ring in $x$ with real coefficients and let $I = \langle x^2 + 1 \rangle$ be the ideal generated by the polynomial $x^2 + 1$ in $R[x]$. Then,
(a) $I$ is a maximal ideal
(b) $I$ is a prime ideal but not a maximal ideal
(c) $I$ is not a prime ideal
(d) $R[x]/I$ has zero divisors

**151.** Let $R = \left\{\frac{a}{b}; a, b \in Z, b \text{ odd}\right\}$. Then, $R$ is a ring such that
(a) $R$ has unique maximal ideal $I = \left\{\frac{a}{b} \in R : a \text{ even}\right\}$
(b) $R$ has infinitely many maximal ideals
(c) $R$ has finitely many, but more than one maximal ideals
(d) $R$ has no maximal ideal

**152.** Which one is not a ring?
(a) Set of all $2 \times 2$ matrices whose elements are in $Q$.
(b) Set of all $2 \times 2$ matrices whose elements are in $C$.
(c) Set of all $2 \times 2$ matrices whose elements are in $I$.
(d) All $2 \times 2$ matrices whose elements are in $R^+$ and determinant of the artrices is zero. ($R^+$ represents the set of positive real numbers).

**153.** Consider, $S = C[x^5]$, complex polynomials is $x^5$, as a subset of $T = C[x]$, the ring of all complex polynomials. Then,

(a) $S$ is neither an ideal nor a subring of $T$
(b) $S$ is an ideal, but not a subring of $T$
(c) $S$ is a subring but not an ideal of $T$
(d) $S$ is both a subring and an ideal of $T$

# Exercise 2 (For Part 'C')

**Directions** (Q. Nos. 1-90) *Questions may have one or more than one correct option.*

**1.** A commutative ring $R$ with unit (identity) element is an integral domain, if, $\forall a, b \in R$

(a) $ab = 0 \Rightarrow a = 0$ but $b \neq 0$
(b) $ab = 0 \Rightarrow a \neq 0$ but $b = 0$
(c) $ab \neq 0 \Rightarrow a = 0$ or $b = 0$
(d) $ab \neq 0 \Rightarrow a \neq 0$ and $b \neq 0$

**2.** Let $Z_6 = \{0, 1, 2, 3, 4, 5\}$ is a ring of integers modulo 6, then following(s) is/are true.

(a) $Z_6$ is a ring without zero divisor.
(b) $Z_6$ is a ring with zero divisor.
(c) 3 is an idempotent element in $Z_6$.
(d) $Z_6$ is an integral domain.

**3.** Which of the following(s) is/are correct?

(a) An integral domain is a field.
(b) A field is an integral domain.
(c) A field has no zero divisors.
(d) A field has zero divisor.

**4.** Which of the following(s) is/are true?

(a) Every integral domain is a field.
(b) A field has no zero divisors.
(c) A skew-field has zero divisors.
(d) A finite commutative ring without zero divisors is a field.

**5.** Which of the following(s) is/are correct?

(a) Every integral domain is a field.
(b) Every field is an integral domain.
(c) Finite integral domain is a field.
(d) Integral domain has zero divisors.

**6.** Let $M$ be the set of $2 \times 2$ matrices over the field of real numbers, then following hold

(a) $(M, +, \cdot)$ is a commutative ring
(b) $(M, +, \cdot)$ possesses zero divisors
(c) $AB = 0 \Rightarrow A = 0$ or $B = 0$, where 0 be the null matrix and $A, B \in M$
(d) $(M, +, \cdot)$ is an integral domain

**7.** Which of the following(s) is/are field?

(a) The ring of integers $(Z, +, \cdot)$.
(b) The ring of rational numbers $(Q, +, \cdot)$.
(c) $(Z_5, +, \cdot)$, where $Z_5 = \{0, 1, 2, 3, 4\}$.
(d) $(Z_6, +, \cdot)$, where $Z_6 = \{0, 1, 2, 3, 4, 5\}$.

**8.** If $S$ is any ideal of a ring $R$ and $T$ be any subring of $R$, then

(a) $S + T$ is a subring of $R$
(b) $S + T$ is an ideal of $R$
(c) $S$ is a subring of $S + T$
(d) $S$ is an ideal of $S + T$

**9.** Let $I_1$ and $I_2$ are any two ideals of a ring $R$, then which of the following is/are correct?

(a) $I_1 \cup I_2$ is an ideal of $R$.
(b) $I_1 \cap I_2$ is an ideal of $R$.
(c) $I_1 + I_2$ is an ideal of $R$.
(d) $I_1 I_2$ is an ideal of $R$.

**10.** Let $F$ be an field, then

(a) $F$ has no zero divisors
(b) $F$ has no proper ideals
(c) only ideals of $F$ are $\{0\}$ and $F$ itself
(d) $F$ has only proper ideals

**11.** Let $f : F \rightarrow R$ be a homomorphism of a field $F$ into a ring $R$, then

(a) ker($f$) is an ideal of $R$
(b) ker($f$) is an ideal of $F$
(c) if ker($f$) $= \{0\}$, then $f$ is isomorphism
(d) if ker($f$) $= F \rightarrow f(x) = 0, \ \forall \ x \in F$

**12.** If $S$ and $T$ are two ideals of a ring $R$, then

(a) $\dfrac{S+T}{S} \equiv \dfrac{S}{S \cap T}$ (b) $\dfrac{S+T}{S} \equiv \dfrac{T}{S \cap T}$

(c) $\dfrac{S+T}{T} \equiv \dfrac{T}{S \cap T}$ (d) $\dfrac{R}{S} \equiv \dfrac{R/T}{S/T}$, if $T \subseteq S$

**13.** Choose the correct option/s.

(a) Quotient field $F$ of an integral domain $D$ is the smallest field containing $D$.
(b) The field of quotients of the integral domain, $Z$ of integers is $Q$ (set of all rational numbers).
(c) Every integral domain can be imbedded in a field.
(d) Every integral domain can be imbedded in its quotient field.

**14.** Which of the following/s is/are correct?

(a) Field of quotients of a finite integral domain $D$ is $D$ itself.
(b) The quotient field $F$ of an integral domain $D$ is the largest field containing $D$.
(c) Quotient field of the integral domain $Z_5 = \{0, 1, 2, 3, 4\}$ of integers modulo 5 is $Z_5$.
(d) The field of quotients of the integral domain $Z$ of integers is $R$ (set of all real numbers).

**15.** Let ring $R$ is defined as $R = \{f | f : [0, 1] \to R$ is continuous on $[0, 1]\}$, then, which of the following/s is/are maximal ideal of $R$?

(a) $\left[f \in R : f\left(\frac{1}{3}\right) = 0\right]$ (b) $\left[f \in R : f\left(\frac{1}{5}\right) = 0\right]$

(c) $\left[f \in R : f\left(\frac{5}{2}\right) = 0\right]$ (d) $\left[f \in R : f\left(\frac{2}{3}\right) = 0\right]$

**16.** Let $R$ is a commutative ring with unity and $I$ be any ideal of $R$, then

(a) if $I$ is maximal, then $\frac{R}{I}$ is a field

(b) if $I$ is maximal, then $\frac{R}{I}$ is an integral domain

(c) if $I$ is prime ideal, then $\frac{R}{I}$ is an integral domain

(d) if $I$ is prime ideal, then $\frac{R}{I}$ is field

**17.** If $R$ is a finite commutative ring with unity, then which of the following/s is/are true?

(a) Every prime ideal of $R$ is a maximal ideal of $R$.
(b) Every maximal ideal of $R$ is a prime ideal of $R$.
(c) If every ideal of $R$ is a prime ideal, then $R$ is a field.
(d) If $P$ be prime ideal of $R$, then $\frac{R}{P}$ is a field.

**18.** Let $R$ be a commutative ring with unity such that $\{0\}$ is a prime ideal of $R$, then

(a) $R$ has zero divisors
(b) $R$ is an integral domain
(c) $R$ is a field
(d) $\{0\}$ is a maximal ideal of $R$

**19.** Let $f(x) = 3 + 4x + 2x^2$ and $g(x) = 1 + 3x + 4x^2 + 2x^3$ are two polynomials over the ring $(Z_5, +_5, \times_5)$, then

(a) $f(x) + g(x) = 4 + 7x + 6x^2 + 2x^3$
(b) $f(x)g(x) = 3 + 3x + x^2 + 3x^3 + x^4 + 4x^5$
(c) $f(x) + g(x) = 4 + 2x + x^2 + 2x^3$
(d) $f(x)\ g(x) = 3 + 13x + 26x^2 + 28x^3 + 16x^4 + 4x^5$

**20.** Let $F$ be a field, then

(a) $F$ has only ideal is $\{0\}$
(b) $F$ has only two ideals $\{0\}$ and $F$ itself
(c) $\{0\}$ and $F$ are maximal ideals of $F$
(d) $\{0\}$ is the only maximal ideal of $F$

**21.** Let $I$ and $J$ are any two ideals of $Z$ (ring of integers), such that $I \subset J \subset Z$, then $I$ will be maximal ideal of $Z$, if

(a) $I = Z$ (b) $I = J$
(c) $J = Z$ (d) $I \neq J$

**22.** Which of the following(s) is/are true for ring of integers $Z$?

(a) $Z$ is a field.
(b) $Z$ is a Euclidean domain.
(c) $Z$ is not a principal ideal domain.
(d) $Z$ is a unique factorization domain.

**23.** Let $F$ be a field, then choose the correct options.

(a) $F$ is a Euclidean domain.
(b) $F$ is a principal ideal domain.
(c) $F$ is a unique factorization domain.
(d) $F$ is not unique factorization domain.

**24.** Let $R[x]$ be the polynomial ring of commutative ring $R$, then

(a) $R$ is an integral domain, then $R[x]$ is an integral domain
(b) $R$ is a field, then $R[x]$ is a field
(c) $R$ is a Euclidean domain, then $R[x]$ is a Euclidean domain
(d) $R$ is a principal ideal domain, then $R[x]$ is a principal ideal domain

**25.** Let $K$ be a field, $L$ a finite extension of $K$ and $M$ a finite extension of $L$. Then,

(a) $[M : K] = [M : L] + [L : K]$
(b) $[M : K] = [M : L][L : K]$
(c) $[M : L]$ divides $[M : K]$
(d) $[L : K]$ divides $[M : K]$

**26.** Let $Q$ be the field of rational numbers, then

(a) $\sqrt{2}$ and $\sqrt{3}$ are both algebraic over $Q$
(b) $[Q(\sqrt{2}, \sqrt{3}) : Q(\sqrt{2})] = 2$
(c) $[Q(\sqrt{2}, \sqrt{3}) : Q(\sqrt{3})] = 3$
(d) $[Q(\sqrt{2}, \sqrt{3}) : Q] = 4$

**27.** If a, b belongs to a ring $R$ and $(a + b)^2 = a^2 + 2ab + b^2$. Then

(a) $R$ is a commutative ring
(b) $R$ is not a commutative ring
(c) $ab = ba$
(d) $ab + ba = 2ab$

**28.** The set of Gaussian integers which is an commutative ring with unity,

$S = \{x : x = a + ib,\ a, b \in I\}$, where $I$ the set of integers. Then

(a) $S$ is without zero divisors
(b) $S$ is with zero divisors
(c) $(S, +, \cdot)$ is an integral domain
(d) $(S, +, \cdot)$ is not an integral domain

**29.** Let $M$, the set of $2 \times 2$ matrices of form $\begin{bmatrix} a+bi & c+di \\ -c+di & a-bi \end{bmatrix}$, $i = \sqrt{-1}$, where $a, b, c, d$ are real numbers. Then

(a) $M$ is a ring with unity under matrix addition and multiplication.
(b) $M$ is a division ring.
(c) $M$ is not a division ring.
(d) $\begin{bmatrix} 1 & 0 \\ 0 & 1 \end{bmatrix}$ is the identity element.

**30.** If a non-zero element $x$ of a ring $R$ with unity has a multiplicative inverse, then

(a) $x$ is a zero divisor
(b) $x$ cannot be a zero divisor
(c) Both (a) and (b)
(d) None of the above

**31.** Let $F$ be a field and let $p(x)$ and $g(x) \neq 0$ be any two polynomials in $F[x]$. Then, there exist two polynomials $t(x)$ and $r(x)$ in $F[x]$ such that $p(x) = t(x)q(x) + r(x)$, then
(a) Here, $r(x) = 0$ or deg $r(x) <$ deg $q(x)$
(b) Here, $r(x) \neq 0$ neither deg $r(x) <$ deg $q(x)$
(c) Here, $r(x) = 0$ or deg $r(x) >$ deg $q(x)$
(d) Here, $r(x) \neq 0$ or deg $r(x) >$ deg $q(x)$

**32.** Let $p(x) \in F[x]$. Let $E$ be an extension of $F$ and let $b \in E$.
(a) $p(x) = (x - b)q(x) + p(b)$ where $q(x) \in E[x]$
(b) deg $q(x) =$ deg $p(x) - 1$
(c) degree of $q(x)$ is one less than degree of $p(x)$
(d) degree of $q(x)$ is one more than degree of $p(x)$

**33.** If any field
(a) $\frac{a}{b} - \frac{c}{d} = \frac{ad - bc}{bd}$ (b) $(-a)^{-1} = -(a^{-1})$
(c) $\frac{(-a)}{(-b)} = \frac{a}{b}$ (d) $\frac{-a}{-b} \neq \frac{a}{b}$

**34.** Given set $C$ of complex numbers, which is a commutative ring with addition and multiplication, then
(a) $C$ is a field
(b) $C$ is not a field
(c) $1 + i0$ is unit element
(d) $0 + i \cdot 0$ is zero element

**35.** Let $I$ be an ideal of a ring $R$ with unity $1 \in I$. Then
(a) $I = R$ (b) $I \neq R$
(c) $a \in R \Rightarrow a \in I$ (d) $a \in R \Rightarrow a \notin I$

**36.** Which of the following statement(s) is/are true?
(a) Any field containing the integral domain $I$ contains a subfield isomorphic to the quotient field of $I$.
(b) Any field containing the integral domain $I$ does not contains a subfield isomorphic to the quotient field of $I$.
(c) Both (a) and (b)
(d) None of the above

**37.** Let $R$ be a system satisfying all the conditions of a ring except commutativity of addition. If there exists an element $x \in R$ which can be right cancelled in the sense $ax = bx \Rightarrow a = b$, then
(a) In $R$ commutative law for addition also holds
(b) In $R$ commutative law for addition does not holds
(c) $R$ is a ring
(d) $R$ is not a ring

**38.** Given field $F$ and the set $M$ of all $2 \times 2$ matrices of the form $\begin{bmatrix} a & b \\ 0 & 0 \end{bmatrix}$ for $a, b \in F$, then
(a) $M$ is a subring of $F$
(b) $M$ is right ideal in $F$
(c) $M$ is left ideal in $F$
(d) $M$ is right ideal but not left ideal in $F$

**39.** The set of all rational numbers with respect to ordinary addition and multiplication is
(a) $A$ set is a ring with respect to addition and multiplication
(b) is not ring
(c) $A$ set is a abelian group with respect to addition
(d) $A$ set is a semi-group with respect to multiplication

**40.** If $S$ is any ideal of ring $R$ and $T$ any subring of $R$, then
(a) $S$ is ideal of $S + T$
(b) $S$ is not ideal of $S + T$
(c) $S + T$ is a subring of $R$
(d) $S + T$ is not a subring of $R$

**41.** Given, set $C$ of complex numbers, which is a commutative ring with addition and multiplication, then
(a) $C$ is a field
(b) $C$ is not a field
(c) $1 + i0$ is unit element
(d) $\left(\frac{a}{a^2 + b^2}\right) + i\left(\frac{-b}{a^2 + b^2}\right)$ is the multiplicative inverse of $a + ib$

**42.** Which of the following statement(s) is/are true?
(a) The set of natural number is not a ring with respect to addition and multiplication.
(b) The set of natural numbers is not a ring with respect to addition and multiplication.
(c) The set of natural number is an additive group.
(d) The set of natural number is not an additive group.

**43.** Given the mapping $I \to I(n)$ defined by $f(a) = \{a\}$ when $I$ being the set of all integers and $I(n)$ is the set of residue classes modulo $n$. Then
(a) $\forall\ a \in I$ is a homomorphism of $I$ onto $I(n)$
(b) $\forall\ a \in I$ is not homomorphism of $I$ onto $I(n)$
(c) Both (a) and (b)
(d) Neither (a) nor (b)

**44.** Given, the set $M$ of all $2 \times 2$ matrices of the form $\begin{bmatrix} 0 & a \\ 0 & b \end{bmatrix}$.
Here, $M$ is the subset of $\mathbb{R}$ consisting of those elements whose first column contains only zero. Then
(a) For the integer $a, b$ set $M$ is left ideal in $\mathbb{R}$.
(b) For the integer $a, b$ set $M$ is right ideal in $\mathbb{R}$.
(c) For the integer $a, b$ set $M$ is left ideal but not right ideal in $\mathbb{R}$.
(d) For the integer $a, b$ set $M$ is right ideal but not left ideal in $\mathbb{R}$.

**45.** If $R$ is an integral domain. Then
(a) $R[x]$ is also an integral domain
(b) $R[x]$ is not a field
(c) $R[x]$ is not an integral domain
(d) $R[x]$ is a field

**46.** If $R$ be commutative ring with unity and $I$ an ideal in $R$, then
(a) $R/I$ is a field if $I$ is a maximal ideal in $R$
(b) $R/I$ is not a field if $I$ is a maximal ideal in $R$
(c) $I$ is maximal ideal in $R$ if $R/I$ is a field
(d) $I$ is not a maximal ideal in $R$ if $R/I$ is a field

**47.** If $R$ is a Boolean ring, then
(a) $a+a=0$, for every $a \in R$
(b) $a+b=0$, implies $a=b$
(c) $a+a \neq 0$ for every $a \in R$
(d) $a+a=0 \Rightarrow a \neq b$

**48.** If $R$ is a commutative ring and $a \in R$, then
(a) $Ra=\{ra : r \in R\}$ is an ideal of $R$
(b) $Ra=\{ra : r \in R\}$ is a subring of $R$
(c) $Ra$ is not an ideal of $R$
(d) $Ra$ is not a subring of $R$

**49.** $I$ being the set of all integers and $I(n)$ is the set of residue classes modulo $n$. Given mapping $I \to I(n)$ defined by $f(a)=\{a\}$, $\forall\, a \in I$. Then
(a) $I$ is a homomorphism of $I$ onto $I(n)$
(b) $I$ is not a homomorphism of $I$ onto $I(n)$
(c) $x, y \in I \Rightarrow x+y \in I$
(d) $x, y \in I \Rightarrow xy \in I$

**50.** If $E$ is finite extension of $F$ and $L$ is a finite extension of $E$. Then
(a) $L$ is the finite extension of $F$
(b) $[L:F]=[L:E][E:F]$
(c) $[L:F] \neq [L:E][E:F]$
(d) $L$ is not the finite

**51.** If $E$ is finite extension of $F$ and $L$ is a finite extension of $E$, then
(a) $L$ is a finite extension of $F$
(b) $[L:F]=[L:E][E:F]$
(c) $L$ is not a finite extension of $F$
(d) $[L:F] \neq [L:E][E:F]$

**52.** Consider the commutative integral domain $\mathbb{Z}[\sqrt{-5}]$ with identity 1. Then,
(a) the group $U(\mathbb{Z}[\sqrt{-5}])$, units of $\mathbb{Z}[\sqrt{-5}]$ is a cyclic group of order 2
(b) the associate of $a+b\sqrt{-5}$ are $\pm(a+b\sqrt{-5})$
(c) 2 is not irreducible in $\mathbb{Z}[\sqrt{-5}]$
(d) $1+\sqrt{-5}$ and $1-\sqrt{-5}$ both are irreducible in $\mathbb{Z}[\sqrt{-5}]$

**53.** Which of the following(s) is/are correct?
(a) $\mathbb{Z}$ is prime element in $\mathbb{Z}[\sqrt{-5}]$.
(b) $1+\sqrt{-5}$ and $1-\sqrt{-5}$ both are not prime element in $\mathbb{Z}[\sqrt{-5}]$.
(c) Every irreducible element in $\mathbb{Z}[\sqrt{-5}]$ need not be prime element.
(d) The gcd of 6 and $2(1+\sqrt{-5})$ does not exists in $\mathbb{Z}[\sqrt{-5}]$.

**54.** Which of the following(s) is/are commutative integral domain?
(a) $\mathbb{Z}[i]$ (b) $\mathbb{Z}[\sqrt{-5}]$
(c) $\mathbb{Z}[\sqrt{-2}]$ (d) None of these

**55.** Consider the commutative integral domain with identity $\mathbb{Z}[i]$. Then,
(a) the group $U(\mathbb{Z}[i])$, group of units of $\mathbb{Z}[i]$ is a cyclic group of order 4
(b) $2+3i$ divides $-1+5i$ in $\mathbb{Z}[i]$
(c) $2+3i$ does not divide $-1+4i$ in $\mathbb{Z}[i]$
(d) 2 is not irreducible in $\mathbb{Z}[i]$ but irreducible in $\mathbb{Z}$

**56.** Consider the commutative integral domain with identity $\mathbb{Z}[i]$. Then,
(a) every prime element is an irreducible element in $\mathbb{Z}[i]$
(b) every irreducible element is a prime element in $\mathbb{Z}[i]$
(c) $1+i$ is an irreducible element in $\mathbb{Z}[i]$
(d) the lcm of any two element of $\mathbb{Z}[i]$ exists but gcd does not exists.

**57.** Consider the commutative integral domain with identity $\mathbb{Z}[\sqrt{-5}]$. Then,
(a) gcd of 2 and $1+\sqrt{-5}$ is 1
(b) lcm of 2 and $1+\sqrt{-5}$ does not exists
(c) in $\mathbb{Z}[\sqrt{-5}]$, a pair of elements may have gcd but no lcm
(d) only one of the above is correct

**58.** Let $f(x)=a_0+a_1x+\ldots+a_nx^n$ be a polynomial over the set of integers. If $\frac{p}{q}$ a rational number is a root of $f(x)$.
(a) $\frac{p}{a_n}$
(b) $\frac{q}{a_n}$
(c) $p$ and $q$ are relatively prime
(d) $p$ and $q$ are not relatively prime

**59.** Which of the following statement(s) is/are true?
(a) Legendre's symbol $(n \mid p)$ is completely multiplicative function of $n$.
(b) Legendre's symbol $(n \mid p)$ is not completely multiplicative function of $n$.
(c) If $p \mid m$ or $p \mid n$, then $(mn \mid p=(m \mid p)(n \mid p))$.
(d) If $p \nmid m$ and $p \nmid n$ then $p \nmid mn$.

**60.** Which of the following statement(s) is/are true?
(a) If $\alpha$ is a root of $x^n-1$, then $\alpha^r$ is also a root of $x^n-1$ where $r$ is a positive integer.
(b) If $m$ and $n$ are relatively prime, then the polynomials $x^n-1$ and $x^m-1$ not have any common root except 1.
(c) If $\alpha$ is a root of $x^n-1$, then $\alpha^r$ is not a root of $x^n-1$, where $r$ is positive integer.
(d) If $m$ and $n$ are relatively prime, then the polynomials $x^n-1$ and $x^m-1$ have many common root.

**61.** If one root of $x^4+2x^3-5x^2+6x+2$ is $-2+\sqrt{3}$, then
(a) irrational roots occurs in pair
(b) irrational roots does not occurs in pair
(c) $1 \pm i$ is also one root
(d) if $-2+\sqrt{3}$ is a root, therefore $-2-\sqrt{3}$ is also a root

**62.** Let $R$ is a Euclidean ring and $b \in R$ is not a unit, then
(a) $d(a) < d(ab)$, $\forall\, a \in R$
(b) $d(a) > d(ab)$, $\forall\, a \in R$
(c) $d(a) \neq d(ab)$, $\forall\, a \in R$
(d) $d(a)=d(ab)$, $\forall\, a \in R$

**63.** Let $f(x)$ be a polynomial with rational coefficients, then
(a) if irrational roots occurs in pair
(b) if irrational roots does not occurs in pair
(c) if $a+\sqrt{b}$ is a irrational root, then $a+\sqrt{b}$ is also the irrational root
(d) No irrational root occurs

**64.** If a polynomial $f(x)$ with real coefficients has $\alpha + i\beta$ as one of the roots, then
(a) $\alpha - i\beta$ is the another root
(b) $\alpha - i\beta$ is not the root
(c) if $\alpha + i\beta$ is the root than $f(\alpha - i\beta) = 0$
(d) if $\alpha + i\beta$ is the root than $f(\alpha - i\beta) \neq 0$

**65.** Let $f(x) = a_0 + a_1x + \ldots + a_nx^n$ be a polynomial over the set of integers. If $\frac{p}{q}$ a rational number is a root of $f(x)$, then
(a) $p / a_n$ (b) $q / a_n$
(c) $p \nmid a_n$ (d) $q \nmid a_n$

**66.** If $f(x) = x^3 - 2x^2 + 3x - 7$ and $g(x) = x^2 + 2$
$d(x) = a(x)f(x) + b(x)g(x)$, then
(a) The gcd of $f(x)$ and $g(x)$, $d(x)$ is 1
(b) The gcd of $f(x)$ and $g(x)$, $d(x) = 2$
(c) The expression $d(x) = a(x)f(x) + b(x)g(x)$ is
$$1 = \left(\frac{2}{11}x^2 + \frac{1}{11}x - \frac{4}{11}\right)(x^2+2) + \left(\frac{1}{11}x - \frac{3}{11}\right)(x^3 - 2x^2 + 3x - 7)$$
(d) The expression $d(x) = a(x)f(x) + b(x)g(x)$ is $2 = 6x^2 + 7x^3 + 2x$

**67.** If sum of two roots of $x^3 + px^2 + qx + r$ is equal to the third root, then
(a) $p^3 - 4pq + 8r = 0$
(b) $p^3 - 4pq + 4r \neq 0$
(c) $(4q - p^2)(-p) = -8r$
(d) $(4q - p^2)(-p) \neq -8r$

**68.** A polynomial whose roots are $-3, -1, 4, 5$ is
(a) $(x+3)(x+1)(x-4)(x-5)$
(b) $x^4 - 5x^3 - 13x^2 + 53x + 60$
(c) $(x-3)(x-1)(x+4)(x+5)$
(d) $x^4 + x^3 + 6x + 7$

**69.** If the sum of the roots of $2x^3 - 3x^2 + kx - 1$ is 1. And $\alpha_1, \alpha_2, \alpha_3$ be the roots. Then
(a) $\alpha_1 + \alpha_2 + \alpha_3 = 3/2$
(b) $\alpha_1\alpha_2\alpha_3 = 1/2$
(c) The value of $k$ is 3
(d) The value of $k$ is 6

**70.** Which of the following statement(s) is/are true?
(a) Euclid's theorem states the number of positive prime is infinite.
(b) Euclid's theorem states that number of positive prime is finite.
(c) Every integer greater than one has a prime factor.
(d) Every integer greater than one has no prime factor.

**71.** If $n \geq 1$, then
(a) Euler totient function is
$$\varphi(n) = \sum_{d|n} \mu(d)\frac{n}{d}$$
(b) Euler's totient function is
$$\varphi(n) = \sum_{d|n} \sum_{q=1}^{n|d} \mu(d)$$
(c) Euler's totient function is
$$\varphi(n) = \sum_{k=1}^{n}\left[\frac{1}{(n,k)}\right]$$
(d) Euler's totient function is
$$\varphi(n) = \prod_{k=1}^{n}\left[\frac{1}{(n,k)}\right]$$

**72.** Which of the following statement(s) is/are true?
(a) $(n, \phi)$ is a Mobius pair
(b) $n = \sum_{d|n} \phi(d)$
(c) Euler function $\phi(n) = n\left(\sum_{d|n} \mu\right)$
(d) Euler's function $\phi(n) = n\left(\sum_{d|n} \frac{\mu(d)}{d}\right)$

**73.** Let $f(n) = \prod_{d|n} g(d)$, then
(a) $g(n) = \prod_{d|n} (f(d))^{\mu\left(\frac{n}{d}\right)}$ (b) $g(n) = \sum_{d|n} (f(d))^{\mu\left(\frac{n}{d}\right)}$
(c) $\log f(n) = \sum_{d|n} \log g(d)$ (d) $\log f(n) = \prod_{d|n} \log g(d)$

**74.** If $n \geq 1$, then
(a) $\sum_{d|n} \mu(d) = \frac{1}{n}$ (b) $\sum_{d|n} \mu(d) = 1$, if $n = 1$
(c) $\sum_{d|n} \mu(d) = 0$, if $n > 1$ (d) $\sum_{d|n} \mu(d) \neq \frac{1}{n}$

**75.** For integer $n \geq 1$,
(a) $\sum_{d|n} \mu(d) = 1$, if $n = 1$ (b) $\sum_{d|n} \mu(d) = 0$, if $n = 1$
(c) $\sum_{d|n} \mu(d) = 1$, if $n > 1$ (d) $\sum_{d|n} \mu(d) = 0$, if $n > 1$

**76.** Let for any integer $n > 1$, $\tau(n)$ is odd iff $n$ is a perfect square. Then
(a) For any $n > 1$, $\tau(n)$ is odd if $n$ is a perfect square.
(b) For any $n > 1$, $\tau(n)$ is even if $n$ is a perfect square.
(c) For any $n > 1$, if $n$ is a perfect square, then $\tau(n)$ is odd.
(d) For any $n > 1$, if $n$ is a perfect square, then $\tau(n)$ is even.

**77.** Which of the following statement(s) is/are true?

(a) For an integer $n > 1$,

$$\prod_{d|n} d = n^{\frac{\tau(n)}{2}}$$

(b) Since, $d$ is an integer and $d \mid n$,
$\therefore$ There exists an integer $d'$ such that
$n = dd'$

(c) If $\tau(n)$ is even, $\frac{\tau(n)}{2}$ is an integer

(d) If $\tau(n)$ is even, $\frac{\tau(n)}{2}$ is not an integer

**78.** For any integer $n > 1$,

(a) $\sigma(n)$ is odd if $n$ is a perfect square or twice a perfect square

(b) $\sigma(n)$ is even if $n$ is a perfect square or twice a perfect square

(c) If $n$ is perfect square or twice a perfect square then $\sigma(n)$ is even

(d) If $n$ is perfect square or twice a perfect square then $\sigma(n)$ is odd

**79.** If $f$ is a multiplicative arithmetic function and $g(n) = \sum_{d|n} f(d)$, then

(a) $g(n)$ is multiplicative arithmetic function

(b) $g(n)$ is not a multiplicative arithmetic function

(c) $g(mn) = g(m)g(n)$ where $m, n$ are two coprime integers

(d) $g(mn) \neq g(m)g(n)$ where $m, n$ are two coprime integers

**80.** If both $g$ and $f * g$ are multiplicative, then

(a) $f$ is multiplicative

(b) $f$ is not multiplicative

(c) If $f$ is not multiplicative, then there exist positive integer $m$ and $n$, $(m, n) = 1$ and $f(mn) \neq f(m)f(n)$

(d) If $f$ is not multiplicative, then there exist positive integer $m$ and $n$, $(m, n) = 1$ and $f(m, n) = f(m)f(n)$

**81.** If $f$ is multiplicative, then

(a) $f$ is completely multiplicative, if $f^{-1}(n) = \mu(n)f(n)$ for all $n \geq 1$

(b) $f$ is completely multiplicative, if $f^{-1}(n) = \mu(n)$, $n \geq 1$

(c) If $f^{-1}(n) = \mu(n)f(n)$ for all $n \geq 1$, then $f$ is completely multiplicative

(d) If $f^{-1}(n) = \mu(n)$, $n \geq 1$, then $f$ is completely multiplicative

**82.** Which of the following statement(s) is/are true?

(a) $\sigma$ is multiplicative.

(b) $\mu$ is multiplicative.

(c) $\sigma(mn) = \sigma(m)\sigma(n)$

(d) $\mu(mn) = \mu(m)\mu(n)$

**83.** Which of the following statement(s) is/are true?

(a) Functions $\phi$ and $\tau$ are multiplicative arithmetic functions.

(b) Functions $\phi$ and $\tau$ are not multiplicative arithmetic functions.

(c) $\phi(mn) = \phi(m)\phi(n)$

(d) $\tau(mn) = \tau(m)\tau(n)$

**84.** Which of the following statement(s) is/are true?

(a) If $a / bc$ and $(a, b) = 1$, then $a / c$.

(b) If $a \nmid bc$ and $(a, b) = 1$, then $a / c$.

(c) Euclid's theorem if $a / bc$ and $(a, b) = 1$, then $a / c$.

(d) Euclid's theorem if $a \nmid bc$ and $(a, b) = 1$, then $a / c$.

**85.** Given, two numbers 12277 and $399 + 20i$.

(a) $-132 + 178i = (2i)(89 + 66i)$

(b) $-132 + 178i \neq (2i)(89 + 66i)$

(c) $\gcd(12277, 399 + 20i) = 89 + 66i$

(d) $\gcd(12277, 399 + 20i) = 86 + 7i$

**86.** Which of the following statement(s) is/are true?

(a) All positive divisors of 18 are 1, 2, 3, 6, 9, 18.

(b) All positive divisors of 256 are 1, 2, 4, 8, 16, 32, 64, 128, 256.

(c) All positive divisors of 392 are 1, 2, 4, 8, 7, 14, 28, 56, 49, 98, 196, 392.

(d) $392 = 2^3 \cdot 7^2$.

**87.** Let $p$ be the odd prime, then

(a) every reduced residue system mod $p$ contains exactly $(p - 1)/2$ quadratic residue

(b) every reduced residue system mod $p$ contains exactly $(p - 1)/2$ quadratic non-residues mod $p$

(c) the quadratic residues belong to the residue classes containing the numbers

$$1^2, 2^2, 3^2, \ldots, \left(\frac{p-1}{2}\right)^2$$

(d) $1^2, 2^2, \ldots, \left(\frac{p-1}{2}\right)^2$ are distinct mod $p$

**88.** Which of the following statement(s) is/are true?

(a) $219 = 3 \times 73$

(b) $(219 \mid 383) = 1$

(c) 219 is quadratic residue mod 383.

(d) 219 is not quadratic residue mod 383.

**89.** Which of the following statement(s) is/are true?

(a) If $a$ is a quadratic residue modulo $p$, then $x^2 \equiv a \pmod p$ has two solutions.

(b) If $a$ is a quadratic residue $(\bmod\, p)$, then $a \equiv t^2 \pmod p$ for some $t$, $1 \leq t \leq p - 1$.

(c) If $a$ is a quadratic residue modulo $p$, then $x^2 \equiv a \pmod p$ has no solution.

(d) If $a$ is a quadratic residue $(\bmod\, p)$, then $a^2 \not\equiv t^2 \pmod p$ for some $t$, $1 \leq t \leq p - 1$.

**90.** Which of the following statement(s) is/are true?

(a) The quadratic residue mod 11 are 1, 3, 4, 5, 9.

(b) The non-quadratic residue mod are 2, 6, 7, 8, 10.

(c) The quadratic residue mod 11 are 2, 6, 7, 8, 10.

(d) The non-quadratic residue mod are 1, 3, 4, 5, 9.

# Answers

## Exercise 1

| | | | | | | | | | |
|---|---|---|---|---|---|---|---|---|---|
| **1.** (d) | **2.** (b) | **3.** (b) | **4.** (a) | **5.** (c) | **6.** (a) | **7.** (a) | **8.** (a) | **9.** (b) | **10.** (a) |
| **11.** (a) | **12.** (a) | **13.** (b) | **14.** (a) | **15.** (b) | **16.** (c) | **17.** (c) | **18.** (a) | **19.** (d) | **20.** (d) |
| **21.** (a) | **22.** (a) | **23.** (b) | **24.** (b) | **25.** (c) | **26.** (a) | **27.** (a) | **28.** (c) | **29.** (a) | **30.** (a) |
| **31.** (c) | **32.** (a) | **33.** (a) | **34.** (a) | **35.** (a) | **36.** (a) | **37.** (a) | **38.** (a) | **39.** (b) | **40.** (a) |
| **41.** (a) | **42.** (a) | **43.** (a) | **44.** (a) | **45.** (b) | **46.** (c) | **47.** (a) | **48.** (b) | **49.** (a) | **50.** (b) |
| **51.** (b) | **52.** (a) | **53.** (c) | **54.** (a) | **55.** (b) | **56.** (b) | **57.** (d) | **58.** (b) | **59.** (c) | **60.** (a) |
| **61.** (a) | **62.** (a) | **63.** (b) | **64.** (b) | **65.** (a) | **66.** (a) | **67.** (a) | **68.** (a) | **69.** (d) | **70.** (d) |
| **71.** (b) | **72.** (b) | **73.** (b) | **74.** (a) | **75.** (b) | **76.** (c) | **77.** (d) | **78.** (c) | **79.** (a) | **80.** (d) |
| **81.** (d) | **82.** (c) | **83.** (b) | **84.** (a) | **85.** (b) | **86.** (d) | **87.** (a) | **88.** (a) | **89.** (b) | **90.** (a) |
| **91.** (a) | **92.** (a) | **93.** (d) | **94.** (b) | **95.** (b) | **96.** (a) | **97.** (b) | **98.** (b) | **99.** (b) | **100.** (a) |
| **101.** (d) | **102.** (a) | **103.** (c) | **104.** (c) | **105.** (b) | **106.** (a) | **107.** (a) | **108.** (a) | **109.** (a) | **110.** (a) |
| **111.** (a) | **112.** (b) | **113.** (c) | **114.** (b) | **115.** (c) | **116.** (a) | **117.** (c) | **118.** (a) | **119.** (d) | **120.** (a) |
| **121.** (c) | **122.** (d) | **123.** (d) | **124.** (a) | **125.** (c) | **126.** (a) | **127.** (c) | **128.** (c) | **129.** (b) | **130.** (b) |
| **131.** (d) | **132.** (b) | **133.** (b) | **134.** (d) | **135.** (d) | **136.** (b) | **137.** (d) | **138.** (c) | **139.** (d) | **140.** (c) |
| **141.** (a) | **142.** (d) | **143.** (b) | **144.** (c) | **145.** (a) | **146.** (c) | **147.** (a) | **148.** (d) | **149.** (c) | **150.** (a) |
| **151.** (a) | **152.** (d) | **153.** (c) | | | | | | | |

## Exercise 2

| | | | | | | | | | |
|---|---|---|---|---|---|---|---|---|---|
| **1.** (a,b,d) | **2.** (b,c) | **3.** (b,c) | **4.** (b,d) | **5.** (b,c) | **6.** (b) | **7.** (b,c) | **8.** (a,d) | **9.** (b,c,d) | **10.** (a,c) |
| **11.** (b,c,d) | **12.** (b,d) | **13.** (a,b,c,d) | **14.** (a,c) | **15.** (a,b,d) | **16.** (a,b,c) | **17.** (a,b,c) | **18.** (b) | **19.** (b,c) | **20.** (b,d) |
| **21.** (b,c) | **22.** (b,d) | **23.** (a,b,c) | **24.** (a) | **25.** (b,c,d) | **26.** (a,b,d) | **27.** (a,c d) | **28.** (a,c) | **29.** (a,b,d) | **30.** (b) |
| **31.** (a) | **32.** (a,b,c) | **33.** (a,b,c) | **34.** (a,c,d) | **35.** (a,c) | **36.** (a) | **37.** (a,c) | **38.** (a,b,d) | **39.** (a,c,d) | **40.** (a,c) |
| **41.** (a,c,d) | **42.** (a,d) | **43.** (a) | **44.** (a,c) | **45.** (a,b) | **46.** (a,c) | **47.** (a,b) | **48.** (a,c) | **49.** (a,c,d) | **50.** (a,b) |
| **51.** (a,b) | **52.** (a,b,d) | **53.** (b,c,d) | **54.** (a,b,c) | **55.** (a,b,c,d) | **56.** (a,b,c) | **57.** (a,b,c) | **58.** (a,b,c) | **59.** (a,b,c,d) | **60.** (a,b) |
| **61.** (a,c,d) | **62.** (a,c) | **63.** (a,c) | **64.** (a,c) | **65.** (a,b) | **66.** (a,c) | **67.** (a,c) | **68.** (a,b) | **69.** (a,b,c) | **70.** (a,c) |
| **71.** (a,b,c) | **72.** (a,b,d) | **73.** (a,c) | **74.** (a,b,c) | **75.** (a,d) | **76.** (a,c) | **77.** (a,b,c) | **78.** (a,d) | **79.** (a,c) | **80.** (a,c) |
| **81.** (a,c) | **82.** (a,b,c,d) | **83.** (a,c,d) | **84.** (a,c) | **85.** (a,c) | **86.** (a,b,c,d) | **87.** (a,b,c,d) | **88.** (a,b,c) | **89.** (a,b) | **90.** (a,b) |

# Hints & Solutions

## Exercise 1

**4.** Given, $(xy)^2 = x^2y^2, \ \forall \ x, y \in R$

Replacing $y$ by $y + 1 \in R$, we get

$$[x(y+1)]^2 = x^2(y+1)^2$$

$$\Rightarrow \quad (xy + x)^2 = x^2(y^2 + 2y + 1)$$

$$\Rightarrow \quad (xy)^2 + (xy)x + x(xy) + x^2 = x^2y^2 + 2x^2y + x^2$$

Using cancellation law.

$$x(yx) + x^2y = 2x^2y$$

$$\Rightarrow \quad x(yx) = x^2y = x(xy)$$

$$\Rightarrow \quad yx = xy$$

**59.** Since, $R$ is a Euclidean ring. So, by the definition of Euclidean ring, we must have

$$d(a) \le d(ab) \qquad \text{...(i)}$$

for two non-zero elements of $R$.

(i) If $b$ is a unit in $R$, then by definition it has multiplicative inverse. Therefore, $b^{-1}$ exists in $R$, then

$$d(a) = d[a(bb^{-1})] \qquad (\because bb^{-1} = 1)$$

$$= d[(ab)b^{-1}] \qquad \text{(by associative law)}$$

Since, $d[(ab)b^{-1}] \ge d(ab)$

$$\therefore \quad d(a) \ge d(ab) \qquad \text{...(ii)}$$

From Eqs. (i) and (ii), we have

$$d(ab) = d(a)$$

(ii) If $b$ is not a unit in $R$, therefore, we have

$$0 \ne a \in R, \ 0 \ne b \in R \Rightarrow 0 \ne ab \in R$$

Since, $R$ is a Euclidean ring so that for two non-zero elements $a$ and $ab$ in $R$ there exist $q$ and $r$ in $R$, such that

$$a = q(ab) + r$$

where, either $r=0$ or $d(r)<d(ab)$

Now, if $r=0$, then

$$a=q(ab) \Rightarrow a-q(ab)=0$$

$$\Rightarrow \quad a(1-qb)=0$$

$$\Rightarrow \quad 1-qb=0$$

($\because a\neq 0$, $1-qb \in R$ and $R$ is without zero divisors)

$$qb=1$$

$\Rightarrow$ $b$ has a multiplicative inverse in $R$.

$\Rightarrow$ $b$ is a unit in $R$.

But, by given hypothesis that $b$ is not a unit in $R$, so we must have $r\neq 0$.

Consequently, we must have

$$d(r)<d(ab) \Rightarrow d[a-q(ab)]<d(ab)$$

$$\Rightarrow \quad d[a(1-qb)]<d(ab)$$

$$\Rightarrow \quad d(a)\leq d[a(1-qb)]<d(ab) \Rightarrow d(a)<d(ab).$$

**83.** Since, $1\in U$

$\Rightarrow$ For any $r\in R$; $1r\in U$,

as $U$ is an ideal of $R$.

Thus, $r\in U, \forall r\in R$

$\Rightarrow$ $R\subseteq U$, obviously, $U\subseteq R$

$\Rightarrow$ $U=R$

**89.** Since, $x^4+3x^2+2$ is irreducible over $Q[x]$, but $x^3+1$ is not irreducible over $Q[x]$.

**96.** $[Q(\sqrt{2},\sqrt{3}):Q]=[Q(\sqrt{2},\sqrt{3}):Q(\sqrt{2})][Q(\sqrt{2}):Q]$

$$=2\times 2=4$$

**97.** Both $\sqrt{2}$ and $3+\sqrt{2}$ satisfies the irreducible monic polynomial of degree 2.

**107.** Since, $a$, $b$ and $c$ are the roots of $x^3+px^2+qx+r$, we have

$$\Sigma a=-p$$

$$\Sigma ab=q$$

$$abc=-r$$

Now, $\Sigma \dfrac{b^2+c^2}{bc}=\dfrac{\Sigma a^2 b}{abc}$

Again, $\Sigma a \Sigma ab=\Sigma a^2 b+3abc$

Therefore, $\Sigma \dfrac{b^2+c^2}{bc}=\dfrac{\Sigma a\Sigma ab-3abc}{abc}$

$$=\frac{-pq+3r}{-r}$$

$$=\frac{pq}{r}-3$$

**108.** Let $h=f*g$ and choose relatively prime integers $m$ and $n$. Then, we have

$$h(mn)=\sum_{c\mid mn} f(c)g\left(\frac{mn}{c}\right).$$

Now, every divisor $c$ of $mn$ can be expressed in the form $c=ab$ where $a\mid m$ and $b\mid n$.

Moreover, $(a,b)=1$, $(m\mid a, n\mid b)=1$, and there is a one-to-one correspondence between the set of products $ab$ and the divisors $c$ of $mn$. Hence,

$$h(mn)=\sum_{\substack{a\mid m\\ b\mid n}} f(ab)g\left(\frac{mn}{ab}\right)$$

$$=\sum_{\substack{a\mid m\\ b\mid n}} f(a)f(b)g\left(\frac{m}{a}\right)g\left(\frac{n}{b}\right)$$

$$=\sum_{a\mid m} f(a)g\left(\frac{m}{a}\right)\sum_{b\mid n} f(b)g\left(\frac{n}{b}\right)$$

$$=h(m)h(n)$$

**109.** By division algorithm

$$[x]=mq+r, 0\leq r<m$$

Also, $x=[x]+\theta$,

$$\therefore \left[\frac{x}{m}\right]=\left[\frac{[x]+\theta}{m}\right]=\left[\frac{mq+r+\theta}{m}\right]$$

Since, $r<m \Rightarrow r\leq m-1$

$\Rightarrow$ $r+\theta<m$

$$\therefore \left[\frac{x}{m}\right]=q$$

Also, $\left[\dfrac{[x]}{m}\right]=\left[q+\dfrac{r}{m}\right]=q$

**110.** We known

$$\sum_{d\mid n} g(d)=\sum_{d\mid n} g\left(\frac{n}{d}\right) \quad (\because \text{If } d \text{ runs over all divisors of } n \text{ so does } \tfrac{n}{d})$$

$$=\sum_{d\mid n}\left(\sum_{d\mid n\mid d}\mu\left(\frac{n}{cd}\right)f(c)\right) \quad \left(\because g(n)=\sum_{d\mid n}\mu(d)f\left(\frac{n}{d}\right)\right)$$

$$=\sum_{d\mid n}\sum_{cd\mid n}\mu\left(\frac{n}{cd}\right)f(c)$$

$$=\sum_{c\mid n}\left(\sum_{d\mid n/c}\mu\left(\frac{n}{cd}\right)f(c)\right)$$

$$=\sum_{c\mid n}\left(\sum_{d\mid n/c}\mu(d')f(c)\right) \quad \left(\because \text{If } \frac{n}{c}=dd' \Rightarrow d'=\frac{n}{cd}\right)$$

By Merten's lemma, we get

$$\sum_{d\mid n/c}\mu(d')=\begin{cases}1, \text{ if } \frac{n}{c}=1\\ 0, \text{ if } \frac{n}{c}>1\end{cases}$$

$$\therefore \sum_{d\mid n} g(d)=\sum_{\substack{c\mid n\\ n=c}} 1\cdot f(c) \quad \left(\because \frac{n}{c}=1 \Rightarrow n=c\right)$$

$$=f(n).$$

**111.** Suppose, $f$ and $g$ satisfy (I). Then,

$$\sum_{d\mid n}\mu(d)f\left(\frac{n}{d}\right)=\sum_{d\mid n}\mu(d)\sum_{e\mid\left(\frac{n}{d}\right)} g(e)$$

$$=\sum_{e\mid n}\sum_{d\mid\left(\frac{n}{e}\right)}\mu(d)g(e)=\sum_{e\mid n}\left(\sum_{d\mid\frac{n}{e}}\mu(d)\right)g(e)$$

By Merten's lemma,

$$\sum_{d\mid\frac{n}{e}}\mu(d)=\begin{cases}1, \text{ if } n/e=1\\ 0, \text{ otherwise}\end{cases}=\begin{cases}1, \text{ if } n=e\\ 0, \text{ if } n\neq e\end{cases}$$

$$\therefore \sum_{d\mid n}\mu(d)f\left(\frac{n}{d}\right)=g(n) \quad \text{...(i)}$$

which shows (II) holds.

## Exercise 2

**6.** (i) **Closure property** Let $A, B \in M$. Then, $A+B \in M$ and $AB \in M$, therefore $M$ is closed with respect to addition and multiplication of matrices.

(ii) **Associative law** Let $A, B, C \in M$. Then,

$$A+(B+C)=(A+B)+C, \forall\ A, B, C \in M$$

and $$A(BC)=(AB)C, \ \forall\ A, B, C \in M$$

Thus, both addition and multiplication of matrices are associative.

(iii) **Additive identity** Let $O=\begin{bmatrix}0 & 0\\0 & 0\end{bmatrix}$ be a null matrix of order $2\times 2$, then $O \in M$ and

$$O+A=A+O=A, \forall\ A \in M.$$

$\therefore$ $O$ is the additive identity of $M$.

(iv) **Additive inverse** If $A \in M$, then $-A$ will be a matrix of order $2\times 2$, so that $-A \in M$ also,

$$A+(-A)=O, \forall\ A \in M$$

$\therefore$ $-A$ is the additive inverse of $A$.

(v) **Commutative law** Let $A, B \in M$, then

$$A+B=B+A, \forall\ A, B \in M.$$

$\therefore$ Addition is commutative in $M$.

(vi) **Distributive property** Let $A, B, C \in M$, then

$$A(B+C)=AB+AC$$

and $$(B+C)A=BA+CA, \forall\ A, B, C \in M$$

$\therefore$ Multiplication of matrices is distributive over addition.

Hence, $M$ forms a ring with respect to the given compositions.

If $I$ is the unit matrix of order $2\times 2$ *i.e.*,

$$I=\begin{bmatrix}1 & 0\\0 & 1\end{bmatrix}$$

then, $I \in M$ and also, $AI=A=IA, \forall\ A \in M$.

$\therefore$ $M$ has unit element.

But multiplication of matrices is not in general a commutative composition.

*e.g.*, $A=\begin{bmatrix}1 & 2\\-1 & 3\end{bmatrix}, B=\begin{bmatrix}2 & -1\\-1 & 2\end{bmatrix}$,

then, $AB=\begin{bmatrix}0 & 3\\-5 & 7\end{bmatrix}$ and $BA=\begin{bmatrix}3 & 1\\-3 & 4\end{bmatrix}$

$\therefore$ $AB \neq BA$.

Therefore, $M$ is non-commutative ring but has unity. The zero element of $M$ is the null matrix $O$. The ring possesses zero divisors, because the product of two non-zero elements of the ring is equal to the zero element of the ring.

*e.g.*, If $A=\begin{bmatrix}0 & 1\\0 & 2\end{bmatrix}, B=\begin{bmatrix}2 & 3\\0 & 0\end{bmatrix}$,

then $AB=\begin{bmatrix}0 & 1\\0 & 2\end{bmatrix}\begin{bmatrix}2 & 3\\0 & 0\end{bmatrix}=\begin{bmatrix}0 & 0\\0 & 0\end{bmatrix}=O$

**8.** Since, $S$ is an ideal of $R$, so that

$$a \in S,\ b \in S \Rightarrow a-b \in S$$

and $$a \in S,\ b \in R \Rightarrow ab \in S$$

Now, first we shall show that $S+T$ is a subring of $R$.

Let $a+\alpha$ and $b+\beta$ be any two elements of the set $S+T$. *i.e.*,

$$a+\alpha \in S+T \Rightarrow a \in S \text{ and } \alpha \in T$$

and $$b+\beta \in S+T \Rightarrow b \in S \text{ and } \beta \in T$$

But $T$ is a subring of $R$, so that

$$\alpha \in T,\ \beta \in T \Rightarrow \alpha-\beta \in T$$

and $$\alpha \in T,\ \beta \in T \Rightarrow \alpha\beta \in T$$

Hence, $$(a+\alpha)-(b+\beta)=(a-b)+(\alpha-\beta) \in S+T$$

$$(\because a-b \in S \text{ and } \alpha-\beta \in T)$$

and $$(a+\alpha)(b+\beta)=(a+\alpha)b+(a+\alpha)\beta = ab+\alpha b+a\beta+\alpha\beta$$

Further, since $S$ is an ideal of $R$, therefore

$$b \in S,\ \alpha \in R \Rightarrow \alpha b \in S$$

and $$a \in S,\ \beta \in R \Rightarrow \alpha\beta \in S$$

so that $ab+\alpha b+a\beta+\alpha\beta \in S$ ($\because$ $S$ is closed under addition)

Hence, $(a+\alpha)(b+\beta) \in S+T$

Hence, $S+T$ is a subring of $R$.

Next, since $S$ is an ideal of $R$ so that for $a \in S$, we have

$$a=a+0$$

Hence, $$a=a+0 \in S+T \quad (\because 0 \in T)$$

$\Rightarrow$ $a \in S+T$

$\Rightarrow$ $S \subseteq S+T$

But $S+T$ is contained in $R$. Hence, $S$ is an ideal of $S+T$.

**11.** Since, $f: F \to R$ is a homomorphism.

$\Rightarrow$ $\ker(f)$ is an ideal of $F$

Since, the only ideals of a field $F$ are $\{0\}$ and $F$ itself.

Hence, $\ker(f)=0$ or $F$

If $\ker(f)=0 \Rightarrow f$ is one-to-one

$\Rightarrow f$ is an isomorphism

and if $\ker(f)=F$

$\Rightarrow$ $x \in \ker(f), \forall\ x \in F$

*i.e.*, $f(x)=0, \forall\ x \in F$

**15.** If $x \in [0, 1]$, then $\{f \in R : f(x)=0\}$ is a maximal ideal.

**16.** $\frac{R}{I}$ is a field and every field is an integral domain.

Also, if $I$ is prime ideal, then $\frac{R}{I}$ is an integral domain.

**19.** We have $f(x)=3+4x+2x^2,\ g(x)=1+3x+4x^2+2x^3$

$$f(x)+g(x)=3+4x+2x^2+1+3x+4x^2+2x^3$$
$$=4+7x+6x^2+2x^3$$
$$=4+2x+x^2+2x^3 \ [\because 7\equiv 2 \pmod 5, 6\equiv 1 \pmod 5]$$

and $$f(x)g(x)=(3+4x+2x^2)(1+3x+4x^2+2x^3)$$
$$=3+13x+26x^2+28x^3+16x^4+4x^5$$
$$=3+3x+x^2+3x^3+x^4+4x^5$$
$$[\because 13\equiv 3 \pmod 5, 28\equiv 3 \pmod 5, 16\equiv 1 \pmod 5]$$

**24.** If $R$ is a field, then $R[x]$ is an integral domain not field.
In order to $R[x]$ be ED and PID $R$ must be field.
Now, if $R$ is ID or PID, then it is not necessarily that $R$ is a field.
Since, every field is ID or PID but converse is not true.
As ring of integers $Z$ is ID as well as PID but not field.

**25.** From transitivity of finite extension

$$[M:K]=[M:L][L:K]$$

$\Rightarrow$ $[M:L]$ divides $[M:K]$
and $[L:K]$ also divides $[M:K]$

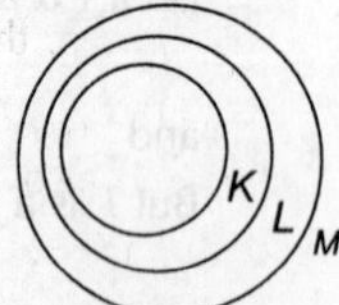


**26.** Since, $\sqrt{2}$ and $\sqrt{3}$ satisfy polynomial $x^2-2$ and $x^2-3$, respectively over $Q$.
$\Rightarrow$ $\sqrt{2}$ and $\sqrt{3}$ are algebraic over $Q$.
Hence, $\sqrt{2}$ is algebraic of degree 2 over $Q$.
$\Rightarrow$ $[Q(\sqrt{2}):Q]=2$
Also, $\sqrt{3}$ is algebraic of degree 2 over $Q$.
$\Rightarrow$ $[Q(\sqrt{3}):Q]=2$
Since, $\sqrt{3}$ satisfy $x^2-3$ which is irreducible over $Q(\sqrt{2})$
$\Rightarrow$ $[Q(\sqrt{2},\sqrt{3}):Q(\sqrt{2})]=2$
Similarly, $[Q(\sqrt{2},\sqrt{3}):Q(\sqrt{3})]=2$
Now, $[Q(\sqrt{2},\sqrt{3}):Q]=[Q(\sqrt{2},\sqrt{3}):Q(\sqrt{2})]\times[Q(\sqrt{2}):Q]$
$=2\times 2=4$

**27.**
$$(a+b)^2=(a+b)\cdot(a+b)$$
$$=a\cdot(a+b)+b\cdot(a+b)$$
$$=a\cdot a+a\cdot b+b\cdot a+b\cdot b$$
$$=a^2+ab+ba+b^2 \quad \text{...(i)}$$
Given, $(a+b)^2=a^2+2ab+b^2$ ...(ii)
By Eqs. (i) and (ii), we conclude
$$ab+ba=2ab$$
$\Rightarrow$ $ba=ab$
*i.e.*, $R$ is a commutative ring.

**28.** If $x=a+ib$ and $y=c+id$ belongs to $S$ and $\alpha\in I$, then $\alpha x=\alpha y$
$\Rightarrow$ $\alpha(a+ib)=\alpha(c+id)$
$\Rightarrow$ $\alpha a+i\alpha b=\alpha c+i\alpha d$
$\Rightarrow$ $\alpha a=\alpha c,\ \alpha b=\alpha d$
$\Rightarrow$ $a=c,\ b=d$
$\Rightarrow$ $x=y$
Hence, cancellation law hold in $S$.
$\Rightarrow$ $S$ is without zero divisors.
$\Rightarrow$ $(S,+,\cdot)$ is an integral domain.

**29.** $I=\begin{bmatrix}1&0\\0&1\end{bmatrix}$, $M$ is a ring with unity under matrix addition and multiplication.
Let $A$ is non-zero matrix in $M$ and let
$$A=\begin{bmatrix}a+bi & c+di\\ -c+di & a-bi\end{bmatrix}$$
where $a$, $b$, $c$ and $d$ are not all zero.
Consider
$$B=\begin{bmatrix}\dfrac{a-bi}{a^2+b^2+c^2+d^2} & \dfrac{c+di}{a^2+b^2+c^2+d^2}\\ \dfrac{c-di}{a^2+b^2+c^2+d^2} & \dfrac{a+bi}{a^2+b^2+c^2+d^2}\end{bmatrix}$$
Evidently $B\in M$ and $AB=BA=\begin{bmatrix}1&0\\0&1\end{bmatrix}$

**30.** Given, $x\neq 0$ and $x^{-1}$ exists.
Also, let $y\neq 0$ but $xy=0$
So, $xy=0$
$\Rightarrow$ $x^{-1}(xy)=x^{-1}(0)$
$\Rightarrow$ $(x^{-1}x)y=0$
$\Rightarrow$ $1\cdot y=0$ $\quad$ ($\because xx^{-1}=1$ an unity)
$\Rightarrow$ $y=0$
Thus, $x\neq 0$, $xy=0\Rightarrow y=0$, which is against our assumptions that $y=0$.
Hence, $x$ cannot be a zero divisor.

**31.** If $\deg p(x)<\deg q(x)$, then take $r(x)=0$ and $r(x)=p(x)$. Then, we have $p(x)=0q(x)+p(x)$ where $p(x)=0$ or $\deg p(x)<\deg q(x)$ and this completes the proof. Now, assume that $\deg p(x)\geq\deg q(x)$. More precisely, let $p(x)=a_0+a_1x+\ldots+a_mx^m$, $q(x)=b_0+b_1x+\ldots+b_nx^n$, $a_m\neq 0$, $b_n\neq 0$, $m\geq n$. Since, $F$ is field and $b_n\in F$, $b_n^{-1}\in F$.
Put $p_1(x)=p(x)-a_mb_n^{-1}x^{m-n}q(x)$
Then, $\deg p_1(x)\leq m-1$. By mathematical induction on the degree of $p(x)$, we assume that
$$p_1(x)=t_1(x)q(x)+r(x)$$
where $r(x)=0$ or $\deg r(x)<\deg q(x)$
Then, $p(x)=a_mb_n^{-1}x^{m-n}q(x)+t_1(x)q(x)+r(x)$
Put $t(x)=a_mb_n^{-1}x^{m-n}+t_1(x)$. Then, we have
$$p(x)=t(x)q(x)+r(x)$$
where $r(x)=0$ or $\deg r(x)<\deg q(x)$

**32.** Since, $F\subset E$, $F[x]\subset E[x]$ and hence we can consider $p(x)$ to lie in $E[x]$. By applying division algorithm for polynomials in $E[x]$, we get
$$p(x)=(x-b)q(x)+r$$
where $q(x)\in E[x]$ and $r=0$ or $\deg r<\deg(x-b)=1$. Thus, either $r=0$ or $\deg r=0$, so in either case $r$ is an element of $E$. Now, $p(b)=(b-b)q(x)+r=0+r=r$.
$\therefore$ $p(x)=(x-b)q(x)+r$
where $q(x)\in E(x)$ and $\deg q(x)$ is one less than $\deg p(x)$ and this completes the proof.

**33.** (a) We have $\dfrac{a}{b}-\dfrac{c}{d}$
$=ab^{-1}-cd^{-1}$
$=b^{-1}a-cd^{-1}$ $\quad$ ($\because$ commutative law holds)
$=b^{-1}add^{-1}-b^{-1}bcd^{-1}$ $\quad$ ($\because b^{-1}b=1=dd^{-1}$)
$=(b^{-1}ad-b^{-1}bc)d^{-1}$ ($\because$ right distributive law holds)
$=b^{-1}(ad-bc)d^{-1}$ ($\because$ left distributive law holds)
$=\dfrac{ad-bc}{bd}$

(b) Let $(-a)^{-1}=x$
$\Rightarrow$ $(-a)x=1$, $\quad$ (unit element of the field)

$\Rightarrow \quad ax = -1$

$\Rightarrow \quad x = a^{-1}\cdot(-1)$

($a^{-1}$ is the multiplicative inverse of $a$)

$\Rightarrow \quad x = -(a^{-1}\cdot 1) = -(a^{-1})$

$\because \quad a^{-1}\cdot 1 = a^{-1}$

$\Rightarrow \quad (-a)^{-1} = -(a^{-1}).$

(c) $\dfrac{(-a)}{(-b)} = (-a)\cdot(-b)^{-1}$

$= (-a)[(-b^{-1})] = ab^{-1} = \dfrac{a}{b}$

**34.** $C = \{x + iy : x, y \in Q$, the set of rational numbers$\}$

The unit element is $1 + i0$ and zero element is $0 + i\cdot 0$.

The multiplicative inverse of non-zero element $a + ib \in C$ is

$$\frac{1}{a+ib} = \frac{a-ib}{(a+ib)(a-ib)} = \frac{a-ib}{a^2+b^2}$$

$$= \left(\frac{a}{a^2+b^2}\right) + i\left(\frac{-b}{a^2+b^2}\right)$$

which is also of the form $x + iy$.

Hence, $C$ is a field with respect to ordinary addition and multiplication.

**35.** Let $a$ be any arbitrary element of $R$.

Then, $\quad 1 \in I$

$a \in R$

$\Rightarrow \quad a \in I, \forall a \in R$

Hence, $\quad a \in R$

$\Rightarrow \quad a \in I$

*i.e.,* $\quad R \subseteq I \quad$ ...(i)

Again, if $I$ is an ideal of the ring $R$, then by definition

$I \subseteq R \quad$ ...(ii)

Hence, from Eqs. (i) and (ii), we conclude that $I = R$.

**36.** Let $F$ be the field containing the integral domain $I$ and $F'$ be the quotient field of $I$.

If $a$ and $b$, where $b \neq 0$ belong to $I$ then $ab^{-1} \in F$.

Let $F_1$ be the subfield of $F$ and let $F_1$ contain elements of the type $ab^{-1}$. Then, the mapping $f : F' \to F_1$, given by

$$f\left(\frac{a}{b}\right) = ab^{-1}$$

where $\quad \dfrac{a}{b} \in F'$

can be easily proved to be one-one and onto mapping.

Also, if $\quad f\left(\dfrac{a}{b}\right) = ab^{-1}$

$f\left(\dfrac{c}{d}\right) = cd^{-1}$

Then, $f\left(\dfrac{a}{b} + \dfrac{c}{d}\right) = f\left(\dfrac{ad+bc}{bd}\right)$

$= (ad+bc)(bd)^{-1}, \; bd \neq 0$

$= (ad+bc)\cdot b^{-1}d^{-1} \quad [\because (bd)^{-1} = b^{-1}d^{-1}]$

$= adb^{-1}d^{-1} + bcb^{-1}d^{-1}$

$= ab^{-1}dd^{-1} + cd^{-1}bb^{-1}$

$= ab^{-1} + cd^{-1}$

Again, $f\left(\dfrac{a}{b}\cdot\dfrac{c}{d}\right) = f\left(\dfrac{ac}{bd}\right)$

$= (ac)(bd)^{-1}$

$= (ac)(b^{-1}d^{-1})$

$= (ab^{-1}\cdot cd^{-1})$

Also, $b, d$ (where $b \neq 0, d \neq 0$) being elements of $F$ are the elements of an Abelian multiplicative group.

Hence, the subfield $F_1$ is isomorphic to the quotient field $F$.

**37.** Here, $\quad (a+b)\cdot(x+x) = (a+b)\cdot x + (a+b)\cdot x$

and also

$(a+b)\cdot(x+x) = a\cdot x + b\cdot x + a\cdot x + b\cdot x$

Hence, $\quad a\cdot x + b\cdot x + a\cdot x + b\cdot x = a\cdot x + a\cdot x + b\cdot x + b\cdot x$

$\Rightarrow \quad b\cdot x + a\cdot x = a\cdot x + b\cdot x$

$\Rightarrow \quad (b+a)\cdot x = (a+b)\cdot x$

$\Rightarrow \quad b + a = a + b \quad (\because a\cdot x = b\cdot x \Rightarrow a = b)$

Hence, commutative law of addition also holds in $R$ besides the other conditions of a ring.

Hence, $(R, +, \cdot)$ is a ring.

**38.** Let any two elements of the set $M$ be

$$A = \begin{bmatrix} a_1 & b_1 \\ 0 & 0 \end{bmatrix}$$

and $\quad B = \begin{bmatrix} a_2 & b_2 \\ 0 & 0 \end{bmatrix}$

where $a_1, a_2, b_1, b_2 \in F$

Then, $A - B = \begin{bmatrix} a_1 & b_1 \\ 0 & 0 \end{bmatrix}\begin{bmatrix} a_2 & b_2 \\ 0 & 0 \end{bmatrix}$

$= \begin{bmatrix} a_1 - a_2 & b_1 - b_2 \\ 0 & 0 \end{bmatrix}$

$\in M$, as $a_1 - a_2 \in F$ and $b_1 - b_2 \in F$

Also, $A + B = \begin{bmatrix} a_1 & b_1 \\ 0 & 0 \end{bmatrix}\begin{bmatrix} a_2 & b_2 \\ 0 & 0 \end{bmatrix}$

$= \begin{bmatrix} a_1a_2 & a_1b_2 \\ 0 & 0 \end{bmatrix}$

$\in M$, as $a_1a_2 \in F$ and $a_1b_2 \in F$

Hence, $M$ is a subring of $F$.

Again, let $N = \begin{bmatrix} c & d \\ e & f \end{bmatrix}$ be any element of $F$

and $\quad S = \begin{bmatrix} x & y \\ 0 & 0 \end{bmatrix}$ be any element of $M$

Then, $\quad NS = \begin{bmatrix} c & d \\ e & f \end{bmatrix}\begin{bmatrix} x & y \\ 0 & 0 \end{bmatrix}$

$= \begin{bmatrix} cx & cy \\ ex & ey \end{bmatrix} \notin M$

*i.e.,* $\quad N \in F$

and $\quad S \in M$

$\Rightarrow \quad NS \notin M$

Hence, $M$ is not a left ideal in $F$.

Again, $SN = \begin{bmatrix} x & y \\ 0 & 0 \end{bmatrix} \begin{bmatrix} c & d \\ e & f \end{bmatrix}$

$$= \begin{bmatrix} xc + ye & xd + yf \\ 0 & 0 \end{bmatrix}$$

or $SN \in M$ as $xc + ye \in F$

and $xd + yf \in F$

*i.e.*, $S \in M$ and $N \in F$

$\Rightarrow$ $SN \in M$

Hence, $M$ is a right ideal in $F$.

**39.** Let $Q$ be the set of all rational numbers.

(I) $(Q, +)$ is Abelian.

**Closure property** Let $a, b \in Q$

then $a + b \in Q$

because sum of two rational numbers is a rational number.

**Associativity law** Let $a, b, c \in Q$

then $(a + b) + c = a + (b + c)$

because associative law for addition holds.

**Existence of identity**

$$0 \in Q$$

and $0 + a = a + 0$

$$= a, \forall a \in Q$$

*i.e.*, 0 is additive identity in $Q$.

**Existence of inverse**

$$\forall a \in Q, -a \in Q$$

and $a + (-a) = 0$

Hence, additive inverse in $Q$ exists for each element in $Q$.

**Commutative law**

Let $a, b \in Q$

Then $a + b = b + a$

because addition is commutative for rationals.

(II) $(Q, \cdot)$ is a semi-group.

**Closure property** Since, the product of two rational numbers is a rational number

$$a, b \in Q$$

$\Rightarrow$ $a \cdot b \in Q$

**Associativity law** Multiplication in $Q$ is associative.

(II) Multiplication is left as well as right distributive over addition in the set of rational numbers, *i.e.*,

$$a \cdot (b + c) = a \cdot b + a \cdot c$$

$$(b + c) \cdot a = b \cdot a + c \cdot a \text{ for } a, b, c \in Q$$

Hence, $(Q, +, \cdot)$ is a ring.

**40.** If $a, b \in S$ and $\alpha, \beta \in T$

$\Rightarrow$ $a + \alpha \in S + T$ and $b + \beta \in S + T$

Also, $(a + \alpha)(b + \beta) \equiv ab + a\beta + \alpha b + \alpha\beta$

$\Rightarrow (a + \alpha)(b + \beta) - \alpha\beta = ab + a\beta + \alpha b \in S$

$S$ being an ideal, we get

$$ab \in S, \alpha b \in S \text{ and } a\beta \in S$$

Also, $\alpha\beta \in T$

Hence, $(a + \alpha)(b + \beta) \in S + T$

Again, $(a + \alpha) - (b + \beta) = (a - b) + (\alpha - \beta) \in S + T$

Hence, $S + T$ is a subring of $R$.

Also, we have

$$S \subset S + T \subset R$$

Hence, $S$ is an ideal of $S + T$.

**41.** $C = \{x + iy : x, y \in Q$, the set of rational numbers$\}$

The unit element is $1 + i0$ and zero element is $0 + i \cdot 0$.

The multiplicative inverse of non-zero element $a + ib \in C$ is

$$\frac{1}{a + ib} = \frac{a - ib}{(a + ib)(a - ib)} = \frac{a - ib}{a^2 + b^2}$$

$$= \left(\frac{a}{a^2 + b^2}\right) + i\left(\frac{-b}{a^2 + b^2}\right)$$

which is also of the form $x + iy$.

Hence, $C$ is a field with respect to ordinary addition and multiplication.

**42.** If $(N, +, \cdot)$ is a ring, then $(N, +)$ must be a group.

But there exist no identity element $e \in N$ such that $a + e = e + a = a, \forall a \in N$

Thus, $(N, +)$ is not an additive group and consequently the set $N$ is not a ring.

**43.** Let $x, y$ be any two elements of $I$, then

$x + y \in I$ and $xy \in I$ and we have

$$f(a + b) = (a + b) \qquad (\because f(a) = \{a\}, \forall a \in I)$$

$$= \{a\} +_n \{b\}$$

*i.e.*, $f(a + b) = f(a) +_n f(b)$ ...(i)

and $f(a \cdot b) = \{a \cdot b\}$, $(\because f(a) = \{a\}, \forall a \in I)$

$$= \{a\} \cdot_n \{b\}$$

or $f(a \cdot b) = f(a) \cdot_n \{b\}$ ...(ii)

Hence, from Eqs. (i) and (ii), we conclude that the mapping $f$ is a homomorphism of $I$ onto $I(n)$, as $\forall \{a\} \in I(n)$ there exists an element $a \in I$ such that

$$f(a) = \{a\}$$

**44.** Let any two elements of the set $M$ be

$$A = \begin{bmatrix} 0 & a_1 \\ 0 & b_1 \end{bmatrix} \text{ and } B = \begin{bmatrix} 0 & a_2 \\ 0 & b_2 \end{bmatrix}$$

where $a_1, b_1, a_2, b_2$ are integers.

Then, $A - B = \begin{bmatrix} 0 & a_1 \\ 0 & b_1 \end{bmatrix} - \begin{bmatrix} 0 & a_2 \\ 0 & b_2 \end{bmatrix}$

$$= \begin{bmatrix} 0 & a_1 - a_2 \\ 0 & b_1 - b_2 \end{bmatrix} \in M$$

Since, $(a_1 - a_2), (b_1 - b_2)$ are integers.

Hence, $A \in M, B \in M$

$\Rightarrow$ $A - B \in M$

Now, let $N = \begin{bmatrix} c & d \\ e & f \end{bmatrix}$ be any element of $\mathbb{R}$

and $S = \begin{bmatrix} 0 & x \\ 0 & y \end{bmatrix}$ be any element of $M$

Then, $NS = \begin{bmatrix} c & d \\ e & f \end{bmatrix} \begin{bmatrix} 0 & x \\ 0 & y \end{bmatrix}$

$$= \begin{bmatrix} c\cdot 0+d\cdot 0 & c\cdot x+d\cdot y \\ e\cdot 0+f\cdot 0 & e\cdot x+f\cdot y \end{bmatrix}$$

$$= \begin{bmatrix} 0 & cx+dy \\ 0 & ex+fy \end{bmatrix} \in M$$

i.e., $S \in M, N \in E$

$\Rightarrow$ $NS \in M$

Hence, that set $M$ is a left ideal in $\mathbb{R}$.

Also, $SN = \begin{bmatrix} 0 & x \\ 0 & y \end{bmatrix}\begin{bmatrix} c & d \\ e & f \end{bmatrix}$

$$= \begin{bmatrix} 0\cdot c+x\cdot e & 0\cdot d+x\cdot f \\ 0\cdot c+y\cdot e & 0\cdot d+y\cdot f \end{bmatrix}$$

$$= \begin{bmatrix} xe & xf \\ ye & yf \end{bmatrix} \notin M$$

i.e., $S \in M$

$N \in \mathbb{R}$ does not imply.

$SN \in M$

Hence, the set $M$ is not a right ideal in $\mathbb{R}$.

**45.** (I) Let $R$ be an integer domain and let $p(x) \neq 0$ and $q(x) \neq 0$ be in $R[x]$. Since, $R$ is an integral domain, we have

$$\deg(p(x)q(x)) = \deg p(x) + \deg q(x).$$

Now, it is impossible to have $p(x)q(x) = 0$ and therefore, $R[x]$ is an integral domain.

(II) Let $p(x) \in R[x]$ and $\deg p(x) > 0$. Since, degree of the identity polynomial 1 is 0, there exists no $q(x) \in R[x]$ such that $\deg p(x) + \deg q(x) = \deg 1 = 0$. Thus, no polynomial of non-zero degree has a multiplicative inverse and thus $R[x]$ is not a field.

**46.** Let $I$ be a maximal ideal in $R$.

Then, $I \subset R$ and $R/I$ is a commutative ring with unity.

Let $x$ be any element of $R/I$ and let us consider a subset $S$ of $R$ where

$$S = \{a + xb : a \in I, b \in I\}$$

Now, $y \in R$

$a + xb \in S$

$\Rightarrow$ $(a + xb)y \in S$

$\Rightarrow$ $a \cdot y + x(b \cdot y) \in S$

Similarly, $y(a + xb) \in S$

Hence, $S$ is an ideal in $R$.

Also, as $I \subset S$ so $S = R$.

Hence, any element $z \in R$ can be written as

$$z = a + xc, \text{ where } c \in R$$

Let $e$ be the unity in $R$ and $e = a + x$, $d$, where $d \in R$

Again, as $e + I = (a + I) + (xc + I)$

$= (a + I) + (x + I)\cdot(c + I)$

$= (x + I)\cdot(c + I)$

So, $(c + I)$ is the multiplicative inverse of $(x + I)$.

Hence, the ring of cosets $R/I$ is a field as $x$ is any element of $R/I$.

On the contrary assume let $R/I$ is a field and suppose $I$ is not maximal in $R$.

Let $I'$ be another ideal in $R$ such that

$$I \subset I' \subset R$$

Let $z$ be any element of $R$ and let

$$q \in I' - I$$

Then if, we define

$$(q + I)^{-1}\cdot(z + I) = (p + I)$$

we get $(z + I) = (q + I)\cdot(p + I)$

Now, as $z - q, p \in I'$ and $I \subset I'$ so $z - q \cdot p \in I$

But $p \in I'$, so $z \in I'$. Also $z \in R$

Hence, $I' = R$, which contradicts the fact $I' \subset R$.

Hence, our supposition is wrong and so $I$ is a maximal in $R$.

**47.** (I) For every $a \in R, a + a \in R$.

Since, $R$ is a Boolean ring, we have

$(a + a) + 0 = (a + a)$

$= (a + a)^2$

$= (a + a)(a + a)$

$= (a^2 + a^2) + (a^2 + a^2)$

$= (a + a) + (a + a)$

By cancellation law, we have

$$a + a = 0$$

(II) Let $a, b \in R$ be such that $a + b = 0$. But, since $R$ is a Boolean ring $a + a = 0$

Therefore, $a + a = 0 = a + b$

and by cancellation law it follows that

$$a = b$$

**48.** If $x, y$ be any two arbitrary elements of $Ra$,

then $x = r_1a$ and $y = r_2a$

for some $r_1, r_2 \in R$

Hence, $x - y = r_1a - r_2a = (r_1 - r_2)a \in Ra$

(Since, $r_1 - r_2 \in R$ as $r_1, r_2 \in R$)

$\Rightarrow$ $x \in Ra, y \in Ra \Rightarrow x - y \in Ra$ ...(i)

Again, $x - y = (r_1a)\cdot(r_2a) = (r_1r_2a)a \in Ra$,

(Since, $r_1r_2a \in R$ as $r_1, r_2 \in R$)

$\Rightarrow$ $x \in Ra, y \in Ra \Rightarrow x \cdot y \in Ra$ ...(ii)

From Eqs. (i) and (ii), we conclude that $Ra$ is a subring of $R$.

Again, if $u \in R$,

then $ux = u(r_1a) = (ur_1)a \in Ra$ (Since, $ur_1 \in R$ as $ur_1 \in R$)

Similarly, we can prove that

$xa = (r_1a)u$

$= u(r_1 \cdot a)$ as $R$ is a commutative ring.

$= (ur_1)a \in Ra$, as above

Thus, we find that $Ra$ is a subring of $R$ and for each element $x \in Ra$ and $u \in R$, we find that $ux \in Ra$ and $xu \in Ra$.

$\Rightarrow$ $Ra$ is an ideal.

**49.** Let $x, y$ be any two elements of $I$, then

$x + y \in I$ and $xy \in I$ and we have

$f(a + b) = \{a + b\}$ $(\because f(a) = \{a\}, \forall\, a \in I)$

$= \{a\} +_n \{b\}$

i.e., $f(a + b) = f(a) +_n f(b)$ ...(i)

and $\quad f(a\cdot b)=\{a\cdot b\}, \qquad (\because f(a)=\{a\},\ \forall\, a\in I)$

$$=\{a\}\cdot_n\{b\}$$

or $\quad f(a\cdot b)=f(a)\cdot_n f(b) \qquad \text{...(ii)}$

Hence, from Eqs. (i) and (ii), we conclude that the mapping $f$ is a homomorphism of $I$ onto $I(n)$, as $\forall\{a\}\in I(n)$ there exists an element $a\in I$ such that

$$f(a)=\{a\}$$

**50.** Let $\alpha_1,\alpha_2,\ldots,\alpha_n$ be a basis for $E$ over $F$ and $\beta_1,\beta_2,\ldots,\beta_m$ a basis for $L$ over $E$. Then, we claim that the $mn$ element $\alpha_i\beta_j$ form a basis of $L$ over $F$.

Let $\alpha$ be any element of $L$. Then, since $\beta_1,\beta_2,\ldots,\beta_m$ is a basis for $L$ over $E$, we can find elements $k_1,k_2,\ldots,k_m$ in $E$ such that

$$\alpha=k_1\beta_1+k_2\beta_2+\ldots+k_m\beta_m$$

Again, since $\alpha_1,\alpha_2,\ldots,\alpha_n$ is a basis for $E$ over $F$, for each $k_i$ we can find elements $f_{i1},f_{i2},\ldots,f_{in}$ in $F$, such that

$$k_i=f_{i1}\alpha_1+f_{i2}\alpha_2+\ldots+f_{in}\alpha_n$$

So, $\quad \alpha=\sum_{i=1}^{m}k_i\beta_i$

$$=\sum_{i=1}^{m}(f_{i1}\alpha_1+f_{i2}\alpha_2+\ldots+f_{in}\alpha_n)\beta_i$$

$$=\sum_{i=1}^{m}\sum_{j=1}^{m}f_{ij}\alpha_j\beta_i$$

Further it is left to the reader as an exercise to prove that the $mn$ elements $\alpha_i\beta_j$ are linearly independent. Hence, $L$ is a finite extension of $F$ and

$$[L:F]=mn=[L:E][E:F]$$

**51.** Let $\alpha_1,\alpha_2,\ldots,\alpha_n$ be a basis for $E$ over $F$ and $\beta_1,\beta_2,\ldots,\beta_m$ a basis for $L$ over $E$. Then, we claim that the $mn$ element $\alpha_i\beta_j$ form a basis of $L$ over $F$.

Let $\alpha$ be any element of $L$. Then, since $\beta_1,\beta_2,\ldots,\beta_m$ is a basis for $L$ over $E$, we can find elements $k_1,k_2,\ldots,k_m$ in $E$ such that

$$\alpha=k_1\beta_1+k_2\beta_2+\ldots+k_m\beta_m$$

Again, since $\alpha_1,\alpha_2,\ldots,\alpha_n$ is a basis for $E$ over $F$, for each $k_i$ we can find elements $f_{i1},f_{i2},\ldots,f_{in}$ in $F$, such that

$$k_i=f_{i1}\alpha_1+f_{i2}\alpha_2+\ldots+f_{in}\alpha_n$$

So, $\quad \alpha=\sum_{i=1}^{m}k_i\beta_i$

$$=\sum_{i=1}^{m}(f_{i1}\alpha_1+f_{i2}\alpha_2+\ldots+f_{in}\alpha_n)\beta_i$$

$$=\sum_{i=1}^{m}\sum_{j=1}^{n}f_{ij}\alpha_j\beta_i$$

Further it is left to the reader as an exercise to prove that the $mn$ elements $\alpha_i\beta_j$ are linearly independent. Hence, $L$ is a finite extension of $F$ and

$$[L:F]=mn=[L:E][E:F]$$

**58.** If $\dfrac{p}{q}$ is a root of $f(x)$, then

$$a_0+a_1\left(\frac{p}{q}\right)+\ldots+a_n\left(\frac{p}{q}\right)^n=0$$

or $\quad a_0q^n+a_1pq^{n-1}+\ldots+a_np^n=0$

or $\quad a_0q^n=-a_1pq^{n-1}-\ldots-a_np^n$

$$=p(-a_1p^{n-1}-\ldots-a_{n-1}p^{n-2}-a_np^{n-1})$$

Thus, $p/a_0q^n$ and since $p$ and $q$ are relatively prime $p/a_0$. Also, we have

$$a_np^n=-a_0p^n-a_1pq^{n-1}-\ldots-a_{n-1}p^{n-1}q$$

$$=q(-a_0q^{n-1}-a_1pq^{n-2}-\ldots-a_{n-1}p^{n-1})$$

Thus, $q/a_np^n$ since $p$ and $q$ are relatively prime $q/a_n$.

**59.** If $p\mid m$ or $p\mid n$, then $p\mid mn$ so $(mn\mid p)=0$ and either $(m\mid p)=0$ or $(n\mid p)=0$

***Case I*** If $p\mid m$ or $p\mid n$, then $(mn\mid p)=(m\mid p)(n\mid p)$

***Case II*** If $p\nmid m$ and $p\nmid n$, then $p\nmid mn$ then

$$(mn\mid n)\equiv(mn)^{(p-1)/2}=m^{(p-1)/2}n^{(p-1)/2}\equiv(m\mid p)(n\mid p)(\text{mod }p)$$

But each of $(mn\mid p),(m\mid p)$ and $(n\mid p)$ is 1 or $-1$ so $(mn\mid p)-(m\mid p)(n\mid p)=0,2$ or $-2$

Since, this difference is divisible by $p$ it must be 0.

**60.** (I) Since, $\alpha$ is a root of $x^n-1$, we have

$$\alpha^n=1$$

Therefore, $(\alpha^r)^n=(\alpha^n)^r=1^r=1$

and hence $\alpha^r$ is a root of $x^n-1$.

(II) Since, $m$ and $n$ are relatively prime we can choose integers $a$ and $b$ such that $mb-na=\pm1$.

Assume that $\alpha$ is a root of both the polynomials $x^n-1$ and $x^m-1$. Then,

$$\alpha^m=1 \text{ and } \alpha^n=1$$

By (I) we have $\alpha^{mb}=1$ and $\alpha^{ma}=1$

Therefore, $\alpha^{mb-na}=1$

*i.e.*, $\quad \alpha^{\pm1}=1 \quad$ *i.e.*, $\alpha=1$

**61.** Since, irrational roots occur in pair and since $-2+\sqrt{3}$ is a root, $-2-\sqrt{3}$ is another root. Therefore, $(x+2+\sqrt{3})(x+2-\sqrt{3})=x^2+4x+1$ is a factor of the given polynomial. Dividing the given polynomial by $x^2+4x+1$, we get $x^2-2x+2$. Hence, the other roots are the roots of $x^2-2x+2$ and they are

$$\frac{2\pm\sqrt{4-8}}{2}=1\pm i$$

**62.** Let

$$a(\neq0)\in R$$

Consider the ideal $U=(a)$. By the definition of Euclidean ring $d(a)\le d(xa)$ for any non-zero $x\in R$.

Also, $\quad ab\in U$

and if $\quad d(a)=d(ad)$

then $\quad (a)=(ab)=U$

*i.e.*, every element of $U$ is a multiple of $ab$. In particular, $a$ is also a multiple of $ab$, *i.e.*,

$$a=abx \text{ for some } x \text{ in } R$$

Now, $\quad a=abx$

$\Rightarrow \quad a\cdot1=abx\Rightarrow 1=bx \qquad (\because a\neq0)$

$\Rightarrow$ $b$ is a unit in $R$.

Thus, if $b$ is not unit in $R$, then

$$d(a)\neq d(ab)$$

and hence we conclude that

$$d(a)<d(ab)$$

**63.** Le $f(x)$ be a polynomial of degree $n$ over the field $Q$ of rational numbers. Let $a+\sqrt{b}$ be an irrational root of $f(x)$.

Observe that

$$(x-a-\sqrt{b})(x-a+\sqrt{b})=(x-a)^2-b$$

Divide $f(x)$ by $(x-a)^2-b$

Let $f(x)=\{(x-a)^2-b\}\,\phi(x)+k_1x+k_2$

where $k_1$ and $k_2$ are rationals.

Since, $a+\sqrt{b}$ is a root of $f(x)$, we have

$$\begin{aligned}0&=f(a+\sqrt{b})\\&=\{(a+\sqrt{b}-a)^2-b\}\,\phi(a+\sqrt{b})+k_1(a+\sqrt{b})+k_2\\&=k_1(a+\sqrt{b})+k_2\\&=(k_1a+k_2)+k_1\sqrt{b}\end{aligned}$$

Hence, $k_1a+k_2=0$ and $k_1=0$

Consequently,

$$k_2=0$$

Thus, $f(x)=\{(x-a)^2-b\}\,\phi(x)$

$$=[\{x-(a+\sqrt{b})\}\{x-(a-\sqrt{b})\}]\,\phi(x)$$

Therefore, $a-\sqrt{b}$ is also a roots of $f(x)$.

**64.** Let $f(x)\in R[x]$ be of degree $n$ and let $\alpha+i\beta$ be a root of $f(x)$, *i.e.*, $f(\alpha+i\beta)=0$.

Observe that

$$\begin{aligned}\{x-(\alpha+i\beta)\}\{x-(\alpha-i\beta)\}\\=(x-\alpha)^2+\beta^2\end{aligned}$$

Now, divide $f(x)$ by $\{(x-\alpha)^2+\beta^2\}$.

By division algorithm, we obtain

$$f(x)=\{(x-\alpha)^2+\beta^2\}\,\phi(x)+(k_1x+k_2)$$

where $\phi(x)$ is a polynomial over $R$ of degree $(n-2)$ and $k_1$, $k_2$ are two real constants. Now,

$\alpha\times i\beta$ is a root of $f(x)$, *i.e.*, $f(\alpha+I\beta)=0$

Therefore,

$$\begin{aligned}0&=\{(\alpha+i\beta-\alpha)^2+\beta^2\}\,\phi(\alpha+i\beta)+k_1(\alpha+i\beta)+k_2\\&=(-\beta^2+\beta^2)\,\phi(\alpha+i\beta)+k_1(\alpha+i\beta)+k_2\\&=k_1(\alpha+i\beta)+i\beta k_1\end{aligned}$$

Consequently,

$$k_1\alpha+k_2=0$$

and $\quad k_1\beta=0$ where $\beta\neq 0$

Therefore, $k_1=0$ and so $k_2=0$

Hence, $\quad f(x)=\{(x-\alpha)^2+\beta^2\}\,\phi(x)$

$$=\{x-(\alpha+i\beta)\}\,\{x-(\alpha-i\beta)\}\,\phi(x)$$

Now, since $\{x-(\alpha-i\beta)\}$ is also a factor of $f(x)$ this shows that $(\alpha-i\beta)$ is also a root of $f(x)$.

**65.** If $\dfrac{p}{q}$ is a root of $f(x)$, then

$$a_0+a_1\left(\frac{p}{q}\right)+\ldots+a_n\left(\frac{p}{q}\right)^n=0$$

$$\Rightarrow\quad a_0q^n+a_1pq^{n-1}+\ldots+a_np^n=0$$

$$\begin{aligned}\Rightarrow\quad a_0q^n&=-a_1pq^{n-1}-\ldots-a_np^n\\&=p(-ap^{n-1}-\ldots-a_{n-1}p^{n-2}-a_np^{n-1})\end{aligned}$$

Thus, $p/a_0q^n$ and since $p$ and $q$ are relatively prime $p/a_0$.

Also, we have

$$\begin{aligned}a_np^n&=-a_0p^n-a_1pq^{n-1}-\ldots-a_{n-1}p^{n-1}q\\&=q(a_0q^{n-1}-a_1pq^{n-2}-\ldots-a_n-{}_1p^{n-1})\end{aligned}$$

Thus, $q/a_np^n$ since $p$ and $q$ are relatively prime $q/a_n$.

**66.** By the division algorithm,

$$(x^3-2x^2+3x-7)=(x-2)(x^2+2)+(x-3)\quad\ldots\text{(i)}$$

$$x^2+2=(x+3)(x-3)+11\quad\ldots\text{(ii)}$$

$$x-3=\left(\frac{x}{11}-\frac{3}{11}\right)11+0\quad\ldots\text{(iii)}$$

The constant polynomial 11, divides both $f(x)$ and $g(x)$. Therefore, $d(x)=$ the gcd of $f(x)$ and $g(x)=1$. From Eq. (ii), we get

$$11=(x^2+2)-(x+3)(x-3)\quad\ldots\text{(iv)}$$

From Eqs. (i) and (iv), we get

$$\begin{aligned}11&=(x^2+2)-(x+3)[(x^3-2x^2+3x-7)-(x-2)(x^2+2)]\\&=(x^2+2)(x+3)(x^3-2x^2+3x-7)+(x^2-x-6)(x^2+2)\\&=(2x^2+x-4)(x^2+2)+(-x-3)x(x^3-2x^2+3x-7)\end{aligned}$$

Therefore,

$$1=\left(\frac{2}{11}x^2+\frac{1}{11}x-\frac{4}{11}\right)(x^2+2)+\left(-\frac{1}{11}x-\frac{3}{11}\right)(x^3-2x^2+3x-7)$$

**67.** Let $\alpha_1,\alpha_2,\alpha_3$ be the roots of $x^3+px^2+qx+r$ and let $\alpha_1+\alpha_2=\alpha_3$

We have

$$\alpha_1+\alpha_2+\alpha_3=-p\quad\ldots\text{(i)}$$

$$\alpha_1\alpha_2+\alpha_2\alpha_3+\alpha_3\alpha_1=q\quad\ldots\text{(ii)}$$

$$\alpha_1\alpha_2\alpha_3=-r\quad\ldots\text{(iii)}$$

Since, $\alpha_1+\alpha_2=\alpha_3$ from Eq. (i), we get

$$\alpha_3=-\frac{p}{2}$$

From Eq. (ii), it follows that

$$\alpha_1\alpha_2+(\alpha_1+\alpha_2)\alpha_3=q$$

$$\Rightarrow\quad\alpha_1\alpha_2+\alpha_3^2=q$$

$$\Rightarrow\quad\alpha_1\alpha_2+\frac{p^2}{4}=q$$

$$\Rightarrow\quad\alpha_1\alpha_2=q-\frac{p^2}{4}$$

From Eq. (iii), we get

$$\left(q-\frac{p^2}{4}\right)\left(-\frac{p}{2}\right)=-r$$

$$\Rightarrow\quad(4q-p^2)(-p)=-8r$$

$$\Rightarrow\quad p^3-4pq+8r=0$$

**68.** Since, $-3,-1,4$ and 5 are the roots, the polynomial $f(x)$ is given by

$$\begin{aligned}f(x)&=(x+3)(x+1)(x-4)(x-5)\\&=x^4-5x^3-13x^2+53x+60\end{aligned}$$

**69.** Let $\alpha_1,\alpha_2,\alpha_3$ be the roots of $2x^3-3x^2-kx-1$.

Now, $\quad\alpha_1+\alpha_2+\alpha_3=\dfrac{3}{2}\quad\ldots\text{(i)}$

$$\alpha_1\alpha_2+\alpha_2\alpha_3+\alpha_3\alpha_1=\frac{k}{2} \quad ...(ii)$$

$$\alpha_1\alpha_2\alpha_3=\frac{1}{2} \quad ...(iii)$$

$$\alpha_1+\alpha_2=1 \quad ...(iv)$$

From Eqs. (i) and (ii), we get

$$\alpha_3=\frac{3}{2}-1=\frac{1}{2}$$

From Eq. (iii), $\alpha_1\alpha_2=1$ ...(v)

From Eqs. (iv) and (v), we get

$$(\alpha_1-\alpha_2)^2=(\alpha_1+\alpha_2)^2-4\alpha_1\alpha_2=1-4=-3$$

Thus, $\alpha_1-\alpha_3=\pm\sqrt{3}i$

Therefore, $\alpha_1$, $\alpha_2$ and $\alpha_3$ are respectively

$$\frac{1}{2},\frac{1}{2}(1+\sqrt{3}i),\frac{1}{2}(1-\sqrt{3}i)$$

and $\alpha_1\alpha_2+\alpha_3(\alpha_1+\alpha_2)=\frac{k}{2}$ or $1+\frac{1}{2}=\frac{k}{2}$

or $k=3$

**70.** Assume there are finite number of all positive primes which, when arranged, in the ascending order of magnitude are $p_1, p_2, \ldots, p_m$.

Let $a=p_1\cdot p_2 \ldots p_m$

Then, $(a+1)=(p_1\cdot p_2\cdot p_3\ldots p_m)+1$, which is clearly greater than 1.

Since, every integer greater than 1 has a prime factor, so $(a+1)$ has some prime factor $p$.

Assume that $p_1 \mid (a+1)$, then

$p_1 \mid (a+1)$ and clearly, $p_1 \mid a$, together imply that

$p_1 \mid (a+1-a) \Rightarrow p_1 \mid 1$

which is not possible, since $p_1$ is a positive prime.

So, the assumption that $p_1 \mid (a+1)$ is wrong.

Similarly, none of $p_2, p_3, \ldots, p_m$ divides $(a+1)$.

Consequently, $p$ is a positive prime different from each one of $p_1, p_2, \ldots, p_m$.

Thus, we can always produce a new positive prime corresponding to any finite collection of positive primes.

Hence, the number of positive primes and, therefore, of all primes is infinite.

**71.** The Euler's totient function can be expressed as

$$\varphi(n)=\sum_{k=1}^{n}\left[\frac{1}{(n,k)}\right]$$

Since, for $n\geq 1$,

$$\sum_{d\mid n}\mu(d)=\left[\frac{1}{n}\right]=\begin{cases}1, & \text{if } n=1\\ 0, & \text{if } n>1\end{cases}$$

Replacing $n$ by $(n, k)$, we have

$$\varphi(n)=\sum_{k=1}^{n}\sum_{d\mid(n,k)}\mu(d)=\sum_{k=1}^{n}\sum_{\substack{d\mid n\\ d\mid k}}\mu(d)$$

If $k=qd$, then $1\leq k\leq n$ if and only if $1\leq q\leq n\mid d$.

Hence, $$\varphi(n)=\sum_{d\mid n}\sum_{q=1}^{n\mid d}\mu(d)=\sum_{d\mid n}\mu(d)\sum_{q=1}^{n\mid d}1=\sum_{d\mid n}\mu(d)\frac{n}{d}$$

**72.** We know that $(n, \phi)$ is a Möbius pair and

$$n=\sum_{d\mid n}\phi(d)$$

Hence, by inversion formula,

$$\phi(n)=\sum_{d\mid n}\mu(d)\frac{n}{d}$$

$$\Rightarrow \quad \phi(n)=n\sum_{d\mid n}\frac{\mu(d)}{n}\frac{n}{d}=n\sum_{d\mid n}\frac{\mu(d)}{d}$$

**73.** We have

$$f(n)=\prod_{d\mid n}g(d)$$

Taking log of both sides, we get

$$\log f(n)=\sum_{d\mid n}\log g(d)$$

and by inversion formula

$$\log g(n)=\sum_{d\mid n}\mu\left(\frac{n}{d}\right)\log f(d)$$

$$=\sum_{d\mid n}\log f(d)^{\mu\left(\frac{n}{d}\right)}$$

$$=\log\prod_{d\mid n}f(d)\mu\left(\frac{n}{d}\right)$$

On taking antilogs, we get

$$g(n)=\prod_{d\mid n}(f(d))^{\mu\left(\frac{n}{4}\right)}$$

**74.** For $n=1$, the formula is true.

For $n>1$,

Let $n=p_1^{a_1}\ldots p_k^{a_k}$. Then, in the sum $\sum_{d\mid n}\mu(d)$ the only non-zero terms come from $d=1$ and from those divisors of $n$ which are products of distinct primes.

Hence, $$\sum_{d\mid n}\mu(d)=\mu(1)+\mu(p_1)+\ldots+\mu(p_k)+\mu(p_1p_2)+\ldots$$

$$+\mu(p_{k-1}p_k)+\ldots+\mu(p_1p_2\ldots p_k)$$

$$=1+\binom{k}{1}(-1)+\binom{k}{2}(-1)^2+\ldots+\binom{k}{k}(-1)^k$$

$$=(1-1)^k=0$$

**75.** By mathematical induction, if $n=1$, $\sum_{d\mid n}\mu(1)=\mu(1)=1$ (by definition)

Let $n\geq 2$

By fundamental theorem of arithmetic. Let

$$n=p_1^{k_1}p_2^{k_2}\ldots p_r^{k_r},$$

where $p_i$ distinct primes and integers $k_i\geq 1$.

Hence, $$\sum_{d\mid n}\mu(d)=\mu(1)+\sum_{i=1}^{r}\mu(p_i)+\sum_{\substack{i<j\\ i,j=1}}^{r}\mu(p_ip_j)+\ldots+\mu(p_1p_2\ldots p_r)+0+\ldots+0;$$

(the remaining all terms vanish since they contain square factors)

$$\Rightarrow \sum_{d\mid n}\mu(d)=1+r(-1)+\binom{r}{2}(-1)^2+\ldots+(-1)^r$$

$$=1+\binom{r}{2}(-1)+\binom{r}{2}(-1)^2+\ldots+(-1)^r$$

$$=(1-1)^r=0$$

**76.** By fundamental theorem of arithmetic, we have

$$n=p_1^{k_1}\cdot p_2^{k_2}\ldots.p_r^{k_r}$$

where $p_i$ distinct primes and integers $k_i \geq 1$.

Hence, $\tau(n)=(k_1+1)(k_2+1)\ldots(k_r+1)$

$\Rightarrow$ $\tau(n)$ is odd.

$\Leftrightarrow$ $(k_1+1)(k_2+1)\ldots(k_n+1)$ is odd.

$\Leftrightarrow$ $k_i+1$ odd $\quad\forall i=1,2,\ldots,r$

$\Leftrightarrow$ $k_i$ is even $\quad\forall i=1,2,\ldots,r$

Assume $k_i=2m_i$ for $i=1,2,\ldots,n$. Then

$$n=p_1^{2m_1}p_2^{2m_2}\ldots p_r^{2m_r}$$

$$=(p_1^{m_1})^2(p_2^{m_2})^2\ldots(p_r^{m_r})^2 \quad \text{(a prefect square)}$$

Hence, $\tau(n)$ is odd $\Leftrightarrow$ $n$ is a perfect square.

**77.** Since, $d$ is an integer and $d\mid n$.

Hence, there exist an integer $d'$ such that

$$n=dd'$$

$$\Rightarrow d'\mid n \text{ and } d'=\frac{n}{d}$$

Thus, divisors $d$ of $n$ are in pairs $\left(d,\frac{n}{d}\right)$.

$\Rightarrow$ Product of all divisors of

$$n=\left(\prod_{d\mid n} d\right)^2=n^{\tau(n)} \quad\text{or}\quad \prod_{d\mid n} d=n^{\frac{\tau(n)}{2}}$$

where $\tau(n)$ is the number of divisors of $n$.

If $\tau(n)$ is even, $\frac{\tau(n)}{2}$ is an integer.

Hence, $n^{\frac{\tau(n)}{2}}$ is an integer and if $\tau(n)$ is odd, $n$ is a perfect square.

$$\Rightarrow \quad n^{\frac{\tau(n)}{2}}=(n^{1/2})^{\tau(n)} \text{ is again an integer.}$$

$$\Rightarrow \quad \prod_{d\mid n} d=n^{\frac{\tau(n)}{2}}$$

**78.** For $n=p_1^{k_1},p_2^{k_2},\ldots,p_r^{k_r}$, where $p_i$ are distinct primes and integers $k_i>1$, we have

$$\sigma(n)=\frac{p_1^{k_1+1}-1}{p_1-1}\cdot\frac{p_2^{k_2+1}-1}{p_2-1}\ldots\frac{p_r^{k_r+1}-1}{p_r-1}$$

$$=(1+p_1+\ldots+p_1^{k_1})(1+p_2+\ldots+p_2^{k_2})$$

$$(1+p_r+p_r^2+\ldots+p_r^{k_r})$$

Hence, $\sigma(n)$ is odd.

$\Leftrightarrow$ $(1+p_1+\ldots+p_1^{k_1})(1+p_2+\ldots+p_2^{k_2})\ldots(1+p_r+p_r^2+\ldots+p_r^{k_r})$ is odd.

$\Leftrightarrow$ $1+p_i+\ldots+p_i^{k_i}$ is odd for every $i=1,2,\ldots,r$.

$\Leftrightarrow$ $k_i$ is even for every $i$, if all $p_i$ are odd and if one of $p_i$ say $p_1=2$ then $k_i$ is even for every $i=2,3,\ldots,r$.

$\Leftrightarrow$ $k_i=2m_i$ for some integer $m_i$ for every $i=1,2,\ldots,r$.

or $k_i=2m_i'$ of some integer $m_i'$ for every $i=2,3,\ldots,r$ and $k_i$ is any integer $\geq 1$.

$$\Leftrightarrow \quad n=(p_1^{m_1}\ldots p_r^{m_r})^2 \quad\text{or}\quad n=2^{k_i}(p_1^{m_2'}\ldots p_r^{m_r'})^2$$

If $k_i$ is even, then

$$n=\left(2^{\frac{k_1}{2}}p_2^{m_1'}\ldots p_r^{m_r'}\right)^2 \quad \text{(a perfect square)}$$

If $k_i$ is odd

$$k_1=2^{m_1'}+1, \text{ then}$$

$$n=2\cdot(2m_i'p_2^{m_2'}\ldots p_r^{m_r'})^2, \text{ (twice a perfect square)}$$

Hence, $\sigma(n)$ is odd iff $n$ is a perfect square or twice a perfect square.

**79.** Let $m$, $n$ be any two coprime integers. Then, every divisor $d_1$ of $m$ and every divisor $d_2$ of $n$ are also coprime.

$$\text{Thus, } g(mn)=\sum_{d\mid mn}f(d)=\sum_{\substack{d_1\mid m\\ d_2\mid n\\ (d_1,d_2)=1}}f(d_1d_2)=\sum_{\substack{d_1\mid m\\ d_2\mid n\\ (d_1,d_2)=1}}f(d_1)f(d_2)$$

$$=\left(\sum_{d_1\mid m}f(d_1)\right)\left(\sum_{d_2\mid n}f(d_2)\right)=g(m)g(n)$$

**80.** On the contrary we assume that $f$ is not multiplicative. Let $h=f*g$. Since, $f$ is not multiplicative there exist positive integers $m$ and $n$ with $(m,n)=1$, such that

$$f(mn)\neq f(m)f(n)$$

choose $m$, $n$ such that $mn$ is as small as possible.

**Case I** If $mn=1$, then $f(1)\neq f(1)f(1)$ so $f(1)\neq 1$. Since, $h(1)=f(1)g(1)=f(1)\neq 1$, that $h$ is not multiplicative.

**Case II** If $mn>1$, then we have $f(ab)=f(a)f(b)$ for all positive integers $a$ and $b$ with $(a,b)=1$ and $ab<mn$. Let $h=f*g$ and choose relative prime integers $m$ and $n$, then

$$h(mn)=\sum_{\substack{a\mid m\\ b\mid n\\ ab<mn}}f(ab)g\left(\frac{mn}{ab}\right)+f(mn)\,g(1)$$

$$=\sum_{\substack{a\mid m\\ b\mid n\\ ab<mn}}f(a)f(b)g\left(\frac{m}{a}\right)g\left(\frac{n}{b}\right)+f(mn)$$

$$=\sum_{a\mid m}f(a)g\left(\frac{m}{a}\right)\sum_{b\mid n}f(b)g\left(\frac{n}{b}\right)-f(m)f(n)+f(mn)$$

$$=h(m)h(n)-f(m)f(n)+f(mn)$$

Since, $f(mn)\neq f(m)f(n)$ this shows that $h(mn)\neq h(m)h(n)$ so $h$ is not multiplicative, which is the contradiction.

**81.** Let $g(n)=\mu(n)f(n)$. If $f$ is completely multiplicative, then

$$(g*f)(n)=\sum_{d\mid n}\mu(d)f(d)f\left(\frac{n}{d}\right)$$

$$=f(n)\sum_{d\mid n}\mu(d)=f(n)I(n)=I(n)$$

Since, $\quad f(1)=1$ and $I(n)=0$ for $n>1$.

Hence, $\quad g=f^{-1}$.

Conversely, assume $f^{-1}(n) = \mu(n)f(n)$.

$\Rightarrow \sum_{d|n} \mu(d)f(d)f\left(\frac{n}{d}\right) = 0$ for all $n > 1$.

Taking $n = p^a$, we have

$\mu(1)f(1)f(p)^a + \mu(p)f(p)f(p^{a-1}) = 0$

$\Rightarrow f(p^a) = f(p)f(p^{a-1})$

This implies $f(p^a) = f(p)^a$, so $f$ is completely multiplicative.

**82.** Let $m > 1$ and $n > 1$ be two coprime integers and $m = p_1^{\alpha_1} p_2^{\alpha_2} \dots p_r^{\alpha_r}$

and $\quad n = q_1^{\beta_1} q_2^{\beta_2} \dots q_t^{\beta_t}$

be their unique factorization in to primes.

Since, $(m, n) = 1$, $p_1, p_2, \dots, p_r, q_1, q_2, \dots, q_t$ are all distinct primes

and $mn = p_1^{\alpha_1} p_2^{\alpha_2} \dots p_r^{\alpha_r} q_1^{\beta_1} q_2^{\beta_2} \dots q_t^{\beta_t}$

$$\sigma(mn) = \frac{p_1^{\alpha_1+1} - 1}{p_1 - 1} \cdot \frac{p_2^{\alpha_2+1} - 1}{p_2 - 1} \cdots \frac{p_r^{\alpha_r+1} - 1}{p_r - 1}$$

$$\frac{q_1^{\beta_1+1} - 1}{q_1 - 1} \cdot \frac{q_2^{\beta_2+1} - 1}{q_2 - 1} \cdots \frac{q_t^{\beta_t+1} - 1}{q_t - 1}$$

$$= \sigma(m)\sigma(n);$$

$$\text{and } \mu(mn) = \begin{cases} (-1)^{r+t} & \text{if } \alpha_i = \beta_j = 1, \forall\, i = 1, 2, \dots, r,\ j = 1, 2, \dots, t \\ 0 & \text{if } \alpha_i \beta_j > 1 \text{ for atleast one } i \text{ or } j \end{cases}$$

$$= \mu(m)\mu(n).$$

Thus, by definition of multiplicative arithmetic functions 0 and $\mu$ are multiplicative.

**83.** Let $m > 1$ and $n > 1$ be two coprime integers and

$m = p_1^{\alpha_1} p_2^{\alpha_2} \dots p_r^{\alpha_r}$ and $n = q_1^{\beta_1} q_2^{\beta_2} \dots q_t^{\beta_t}$

be their unique factorizations into primes.

Since, $(m, n) = 1$ and $p_1, p_2, \dots, p_r, q_1, q_2, \dots, q_t$ are all distinct primes

and $\quad mn = p_1^{\alpha_1} p_2^{\alpha_2} \dots p_r^{\alpha_r} q_1^{\beta_1} q_2^{\beta_2} \dots q_t^{\beta_t}$

Hence, $\phi(mn) = \phi(p_1^{\alpha_1})\phi(p_2^{\alpha_2}) \dots \phi(p_r^{\alpha_r})\phi(q_1^{\beta_1})\phi(q_2^{\beta_2}) \dots \phi(q_t^{\beta_t})$

$= \phi(m)\phi(n);$

$\tau(mn) = (\alpha_1 + 1)(\alpha_2 + 1) \dots (\alpha_r + 1)(\beta_1 + 1)(\beta_2 + 1) \dots (\beta_t + 1)$

$= \tau(m)\tau(n)$

Thus, $\phi$ and $\tau$ are multiplicative arithmetic functions.

**84.** Since, $(a, b) = 1$

$\Rightarrow$ There exist integers $u$ and $v$ such that

$1 = au + bv$

$\therefore \quad c = c \cdot 1 = cau + cbv$

Now, $a | bc$ and $a | ca \Rightarrow a | c$

**85.** We have, $12277 = (31 - 2i)(399 + 20i) + (-132 + 178i)$

$399 + 20i = (-1 - i)(-132 + 178i) + 89 + 66i$

$-132 + 178i = (2i)(89 + 66i)$

$\Rightarrow \gcd(12277, 399 + 20i) = 89 + 66i$

**86.** (I) The all positive divisors of 18 are

1, 2, 3, 6, 9, 18

(II) Since, 2 is a prime, the positive divisors of $256 = 2^8$ are

$2^0, 2^1, 2^2, 2^3, 2^4, 2^5, 2^6, 2^7, 2^8$

$\Rightarrow$ 1, 2, 4, 8, 16, 32, 64, 128, 256

(III) Since, 2 and 7 are prime, the positive divisors of $392 = 2^3 \cdot 7^2$ are products of lower powers of 2 times lower powers of 7. i.e.,

$2^0 \cdot 7^0, 2^1 \cdot 7^0, 2^2 \cdot 7^0, 2^3 \cdot 7^0, 2^0 \cdot 7^1, 2^1 \cdot 7^1,$
$2^2 \cdot 7^1, 2^3 \cdot 7^1, 2^0 \cdot 7^2, 2^1 \cdot 7^2, 2^2 \cdot 7^2, 2^3 \cdot 7^2.$

$\Rightarrow$ 1, 2, 4, 8, 7, 14, 28, 56, 49, 98, 196, 392.

**87.** The numbers $1^2, 2^2, \dots, \left(\frac{p-1}{2}\right)^2$ are distinct mod $p$. And if $x^2 \equiv y^2 \pmod p$ with $1 \le x \le (p-1)/2$ and $1 \le y \le (p-1)/2$, then

$(x - y)(x + y) \equiv 0 \pmod p$

But $1 < x + y < p$ so $x - y \equiv 0 \pmod p$, hence $x = y$. Since,

$(p - k)^2 \equiv k^2 \pmod p$

every quadratic residue is congruent mod $p$ to exactly one of the numbers $1^2, 2^2, \dots, \left(\frac{p-1}{2}\right)^2$.

**88.** Since,

$219 = 3.73,$

By multiplicative property

$(219 | 383) = (3 | 383)(73 | 383)$

By reciprocity law and periodicity, we have

$(3 | 383) = (383 | 3)(-1)^{(383-1)(3-1)/4}$

$= -(-1 | 3)$

$= -(-1)^{(3-1)/2} = 1$

and $\quad (73 | 383) = (383 | 73)(-1)^{(383-1)(73-1)/4}$

$= (18 | 73)$

$= (2 | 73)(9 | 73)$

$= (-1)^{(73^2-1)/8} = 1$

Hence, $(219 | 383) = 1$

Hence, 219 is a quadratic residue mod 383.

**89.** (I) Since, $a$ is a quadratic residue (mod $p$), $x^2 \equiv a \pmod p$ has a solution say $x_0$

Hence, $\quad x_0^2 \equiv a \pmod p$

Now, since $(p - x_0)^2 \equiv (-x_0)^2 \pmod p$

$= a \pmod p$

Hence, $p - x_0$ satisfies the congruence.

$\Rightarrow x_0$ and $p - x_0$ are two solutions of $x^2 \equiv a \pmod p$.

(II) If $a$ is a quadratic residue (mod $p$) and $x_0$ is a solution of the congruence

$x^2 \equiv a \pmod p$

$\Rightarrow \quad x_0^2 \equiv a \pmod p$

$\Rightarrow (x_0, p) = 1$

But then any integer (mod $p$) is 0, 1, 2, ...

or $p - 1 \Rightarrow x_0 \equiv t \pmod p$ for some $t$, $1 \le t \le p - 1$

Hence, $a \equiv t^2 \pmod p$ for some $t$, $1 \le t \le p - 1$.

**90.** To find the quadratic residues modulo 11, squaring the numbers 1, 2, ..., 10 and reduce mod 11, we have

$1^2 \equiv 1, 2^2 \equiv 4, 3^2 \equiv 9, 4^2 \equiv 5, 5^2 \equiv 3 \pmod{11}$

$6^2 \equiv (-5)^2 \equiv 3, 7^2 \equiv (-4)^2 \equiv 5, \dots, 10^2 \equiv (-1)^2 \equiv 1 \pmod{11}$

Consequently, the quadratic residues mod 11 are 1, 3, 4, 5, 9 and the non-residues are 2, 6, 7, 8, 10.

# 17 Topology

## Syllabus

- Basis
- Dense Sets
- Subspace
- Product Topology
- Separation Axioms
- Connectedness
- Compactness

## Definitions

**1.** Let $X \neq \phi$. The power set $P(X)$ is the family of all subsets of $X$. Conventionally, $\phi \in P(X), X \in P(X)$.

A sub-family $\Im$ of $P(X)$ having the properties listed below

(i) $\phi \in \Im, X \in \Im$.

(ii) $A \in \Im, B \in \Im \Rightarrow A \cap B \in \Im$.

(iii) $A_\alpha \in \Im, \forall \alpha \in \Delta \Rightarrow \bigcup_{\alpha \in \Delta} A_\alpha \in \Im$, $\Delta$ being an indexed set.

is called a Topology on $X$.

And a set $X$, together with a topology $\Im$ defined on it is called topological space and denoted by $(X, \Im)$.

Elements of $X$ are referred to as points, whereas elements of $\Im$ are referred to as $\Im$-open sets (or simply open sets).

The same set $X$ may have different topologies. Let $\Im_1$ and $\Im_2$ be any two topologies on the same set $X$. If $\Im_1 \subset \Im_2$, then $\Im_1$ is called smaller or weaker or coarser topology than $\Im_2$. If $\Im_1 \subset \Im_2$, then we also say that $\Im_2$ is longer or finer or stronger or larger than $\Im_1$.

**2.** $\Im_1$ is said to be strictly finer than $\Im_2$ if $\Im_1$ is finer than $\Im_2$ and $\Im_1 \neq \Im_2$, *i.e.*, if $\Im_2 \subset \Im_1$ and $\Im_1 \neq \Im_2$, $\Im_1$ and $\Im_2$ are the topologies on the same set $X$.

The topologies $\Im_1$ and $\Im_2$ are said to be comparable if $\Im_1 \subset \Im_2$ or $\Im_2 \subset \Im_1$.

$\Im_1$ and $\Im_2$ are said to be not comparable if neither $\Im_1 \subset \Im_2$ nor $\Im_2 \subset \Im_1$. $\Im_1$ and $\Im_2$ being topologies on the same set $X$.

**3.** Whatever the set $X$ may be, the family $\{\phi, X\}$ is always a topology on $X$ and is called indiscrete or trivial topology. This topology is smaller than any other topology defined for $X$. The set $X$ together with indiscrete topology is called an indiscrete topological space or indiscrete space.

The family $P(X)$ is always a topology on $X$ and is called discrete topology on $X$. This topology is longer than any other topology defined for $X$, so that $P(X)$ is the strongest topology on $X$. The set $X$ together with discrete topology is called a discrete topological space or simply a discrete space. In a discrete space $(X, \Im)$, every subset of $X$ is an open set.

*e.g.*,

(i) If $X = \phi$, then $P(X) = \{X\} = \Im$. Here, all the postualates of a topology are trivially satisfied.

(ii) Let $X = \{a\}$. Then, $P(X) = \Im = \{\phi, X\}$ is the only topology on $X$.

(iii) Let $X = \{a, b\}$.

Then, $P(X) = \{\phi, X, \{a\}, \{b\}\}$.

If we take

(1) $\Im = \{\phi, X\}$ (2) $\Im = P(X)$ (3) $\Im = \{\phi, X, \{a\}\}$ (4) $\Im = \{\phi, X, \{b\}\}$

the result is always a topology. If we take

(1) $\Im = \{\phi, \{a\}, \{b\}\}$

(2) $\Im = \{X, \{a\}, \{b\}\}$

(3) $\Im = \{\phi, \{a\}\}$ the result is not a topology.

(iv) Let $X$ be an infinite set. Let $\Im$ be the family consisting of $\phi$, $X$ and complements of finite subsets of $X$. This topology is defined as confinite topology or $\Im_1$-topology or finite complement topology.

(v) Let $(X, \rho)$ be metric space. $G \subset X$ is called an open set if $\exists r \in R^+$ s.t. $S_{r(X)} \subset G$. Let $\Im$ be the family of subsets of $X$ which are open in the above sense. Then, $\Im$ is a topology on $X$ and is called usual topology on $X$ or metric topology on $X$.

Whenever we consider a metric space as a topological space, then its topology is the usual topology provided nothing contradictory is stated. Furthermore, the topologies on $R$ and $R^2$ are taken to be the usual topologies provided nothing contradictory is stated.

(vi) The topology generated by the family of intervals of the form $(a, \infty) = \{x \in R : x > a\}$ is called right hand topology.

(vii) The topology generated by the family of intervals of the form $(-\infty, a) = \{x \in R : x < a\}$ is called left hand topology.

(viii) If $X = (0, 1)$, then $\Im = \{\phi, X, \{0\}\}$ is topology on $X$. This topological space is called Sier Pinski space.

***Example 1.*** *Let* $X = \{1, 2, 3, 4, 5\}$,

$\Im_1 = \{X, \phi, \{1, 2, 3\}, \{2, 3, 5\}, \{1, 5\}\}$

$\Im_2 = \{X, \phi, \{1\}, \{2\}, \{1, 2\}, \{4, 5\}, \{1, 2, 4, 5\}, \{1, 4, 5\}, \{2, 4, 5\}\}$,

*then show that* $\Im_2$ *is topology on* $X$ *but* $\Im_1$ *is not.*

**Solution.** Here, $\phi, X \in \Im_1 \cap \Im_2$

For each $A, B \in \Im_2$ we find $A \cup B \in \Im_2$ and $A \cap B \in \Im_2$

$\Rightarrow$ $\Im_2$ is topology on $X$.

But $\Im_1$ is not topology on $X$

as $\{1, 2, 3\}, \{2, 3, 5\} \in \Im_1$

and $\{1, 2, 3\} \cap \{2, 3, 5\} = \{2, 3\} \notin \Im_1$

## Open Sets and Closed Sets

Let $(X, \Im)$ be a topological space.

Any set $A \in \Im$ is called an open subset of $X$ or simply a open set and $X - A$ is called a closed subset of $X$.

A topological space $(X, \Im)$ is said to be a door space if every subset of $X$ is either $\Im$-open or $\Im$-closed.

e.g., Let $X = \{1, 2, 3\}$,

and $\Im = \{\phi, \{1, 2\}, \{2, 3\}, \{2\}, X\}$

Then, $\Im$-closed sets are $X, \{3\}, \{1\}, \{1, 3\}, \phi$.

From this it follows that every subset of $X$ is either $\Im$-open or $\Im$-closed. Hence $(X, T)$ is door space.

## Neighbourhood

Let $(X, \Im)$ be a topological space. $A \subset X$ is called a neighbourhood of a point $x \in X$ if $\exists G \in \Im$ with $x \in G$ s.t. $G \subset A$. The word neighbourhood is , in short, written as 'nbd'.

Any open set $G \subset X$ with $x \in G$ is also nbd of a point $x \in X$.

If $A$ is a nbd of a point $x \in X$, then $A - \{x\}$ is called deleted neighbourhood of $x$.

> ***Note*** **(a)** In any topological space, nbd of a point need not be an open set. On the other hand, every open set is nbd of each of its points.
>
> **(b)** Such a nbd of a point is called open neighbourhood of that point.
>
> **(c)** From this definition, it is clear that nbd of a point $x$ is superset of some open set containing $x$.
>
> **(d)** A set $N \subset X$ is called a nbd of a set $A \subset X$ if $\exists G \in \Im$ s.t. $A \subset G \subset N$.

***Example 2.*** *Let* $\Im = \{\phi, X, \{b\}, \{a, b\}, \{a, b, d\}\}$, *be a topology on* $X = \{a, b, c, d\}$. *Find* $\Im$*-nbd of*

(i) *a* (ii) *b* *and* (iii) *c*

**Solution.** (i) $\Im$-open sets containing a are $X, \{a, b\}, \{a, b, d\}$.

Supersets of $X$ is $X$.

Supersets of $\{a, b\}$ are $\{a, b\}, \{a, b, c\}, \{a, b, d\}, X$.

Supersets of $\{a, b, d\}$ are $\{a, b, d\}, X$.

$\Im$-nbds of a are $\{a, b\}, \{a, b, c\}, \{a, b, d\}, X$.

(ii) $\Im$-open sets containing $b$ are $\{b\}, \{a, b\}, \{a, b, d\}, X$.

Supersets of $\{a, b\}$ are $\{a, b\}, \{a, b, c\}, \{a, b, d\}, X$.

Supersets of $\{a, b, d\}$ are $\{a, b, d\}, X$.

Supersets of $\{b\}$ are $\{b\}, \{a, b\}, \{b, c\}, \{b, d\}, \{a, b, c\}, \{b, c, d\}, \{a, b, d\}, X$.

$\Im$-nbd of $b$ are $\{b\}, \{a, b\}, \{b, c\}, \{b, d\}, \{a, b, c\}, \{a, b, d\}, \{b, c, d\}, X$.

(iii) $\Im$-open set containing c is $X$.

Hence, $\Im$-nbd of c is $X$.

***Example 3.*** *Give an example of a non-trivial topological space in which open sets are exactly same as closed sets.*

**Solution.** In every discrete topological space $(X, D)$ consisting more than one element, every proper subset of $X$ is both open and closed. Consider the following topological spaces in which every proper subset of $X$ is both open and closed.

e.g., (i) $X = \{a, b, c\}, \Im = \{\phi, X, \{a\}, \{b, c\}\}$.

Then, $(X, \Im)$ is a topological space. Evidently, $\{a\}$, $\{b, c\}$ are $\Im$-open sets, so that

$X - \{a\}$, $X - \{b, c\}$ are $\Im$ closed set *i.e.*, $\{b, c\}$, $\{a\}$ are closed sets.

$\therefore$ $\{a\}, \{b, c\}$ are both open sets as well as closed sets.

(ii) Suppose, $X = \{a, b, c\}$ and

$\Im = \{\phi, X, \{a\}, \{b\}, \{c\}, \{a, b\}, \{b, c\}, \{c, a\}\}$.

Then, $\Im$ is a topology on $X$. Also, each proper subset of $X$ is open as well as closed.

**Example 4.** *Prove that in a topological space, an arbitrary union of open sets is open and a finite intersection of open sets is open.*

**Solution.** Let $(X, \Im)$ be a topological space.

Let $G_i \in \Im, \forall i \in N$

Let $G = \bigcup_{i=1}^{\infty} G_i,\ H = \bigcap_{i=1}^{n} G_i$

To prove that $G$ and $H$ are open subsets of $X$.

By definition of topology,

(i) $G_i \in \Im, \forall i \in N \Rightarrow \bigcup_{i=1}^{\infty} G_i \in \Im \Rightarrow G \in \Im$

(ii) $G_i \in \Im, \forall i \in N \Rightarrow G_1 \cap G_2 \in \Im$

An application of this rule shows that

$G_1 \cap G_2 \in \Im, G_3 \in \Im \Rightarrow G_1 \cap G_2 \cap G_3 \in \Im$

By induction, it follows that $\bigcap_{i=1}^{n} G_i = H \in \Im$

**Example 5.** *In a topological space $(X, \Im)$, prove that an arbitrary intersection of closed sets is closed and finite union of closed sets is closed.*

**Solution.** Let $(X, \Im)$ be a topological space.

Let $F_i \subset X$ be closed, $\forall\ i \in N$.

Let $H = \bigcap_{i=1}^{\infty} F_i,\ F = \bigcup_{i=1}^{n} F_i$

To prove that $F$ and $H$ are closed sets.

$F_i$ is closed, $\forall i \in N \Rightarrow X - F_i$ is open, $\forall i \in N$.

$\Rightarrow \quad \bigcup_{i=1}^{\infty}(X - F_i);\ \bigcap_{i=1}^{n}(X - F_i)$ are open sets,

$\Rightarrow \quad X - \bigcap_{i=1}^{\infty} F_i,\ X - \bigcup_{i=1}^{n} F_i$ are open sets,

(by De-Morgan's law)

$\Rightarrow \quad \bigcap_{i=1}^{\infty} F_i, \bigcup_{i=1}^{n} F_i$ are closed sets.

(by definition of closed sets)

$\Rightarrow \quad H$, and $F$ are closed sets.

This completes the proof.

**Example 6.** *Give an example to show that the union of an infinite collection of closed sets in a topological space is not necessarily closed.*

**Solution.** Let $\Im$ denote the usual topology on $R$. Let

$$F_n = \left[0, \frac{n}{n+1}\right], \forall\ n \in N$$

Then, $F_n$ is a closed set

$$\bigcup_{n=1}^{\infty} F_n = \left[0, \frac{1}{2}\right] \cup \left[0, \frac{2}{3}\right] \ldots \cup [0, 1)$$

$= [0, 1)$ – semi open set $\neq$ A closed set.

$\therefore \bigcup_{n=1}^{\infty} F_n$ is not a closed set, though each $F_n$ is a closed set.

# Closure

Let $(X, \Im)$ be a topological space and $A \subset X$. The closure of $A$ is defined as the intersection of all closed sets which contains $A$ and is denoted by the symbol $\bar{A}$.

Symbolically, $\bar{A} = \cap\{F \subset X : F \text{ is closed}, F \supset A\}$

Evidently,

**(i)** $\bar{A}$ is closed. For an arbitrary intersection of closed sets is closed.

**(ii)** $A \subset \bar{A}$.

We also define $\bar{A} = \cap F_i$, where $F_i$'s are closed super sets of $A$.

**(iii)** $\bar{A}$ is the smallest closed set which contain $A$.

> ***Note*** A point $x \in \bar{A}$ is called a point of closure.

# Interior

Let $(X, \Im)$ be a topological space and $A \subset X$. A point $x \in A$ is called an interior point of $A$, iff $\exists$ open set $G \in \Im$ with $x \in G$ s.t. $G \subset A$.

The interior of $A$ is defined as the set of all interior points of $A$ and is denoted by $A°$ or by int $(A)$.

Alternatively, we define

$$A° = \text{int}(A) = \cup\{G \in \Im : G \subset A\}$$

Evidently,

**(i)** $A°$ is open. For an arbitrary union of open sets is open.

**(ii)** $A° \subset A$.

**(iii)** $A°$ is the largest open subset of $A$.

# Limit Point

Let $(X, \Im)$ be a topological space and $A \subset X$. A point $x \in X$ is called a limit point of $A$ if every open set $G$ containing $x$ contains a point of $A$ other than $x$.

Symbolically, $x \in X$ is called a limit point of $A$ if for every $G \in \Im$ with $x \in G$.

$$(G - \{x\}) \cap A \neq \phi$$

The following have the same meaning

Limit point, accumulation point, cluster point.

The set of all accumulation points of $A$ is called the derived set of $A$ and is denoted by $D(A)$.

> ***Note*** **(a)** $x \in D(A) \Rightarrow x$ is a limit of point of $A$
> $\Rightarrow$ for every $G \in \Im$ with $x \in G$, $(G - \{x\}) \cap A \neq \phi$
>
> **(b)** $x \notin D(A) \Rightarrow x$ is not a limit point of $A$.
> $\Rightarrow$ for every $G \in \Im$ with $x \in G$,
> $(G - \{x\}) \cap A = \phi$
> $\Rightarrow$ for every $G \in \Im$ with $x \in G$, $G \cap A = \phi$ or $\{x\}$

# Adherent Point

A point $x \in X$ is called an adherent point (or contact point) of $A \subset X$ iff every nbd of $x$ contains atleast one point of $A$. That is to say, $x \in X$ is called adherent point of $A$ iff $\exists$ nbd $N$ of $x$ s.t. $N \cap A \neq \phi$. The set of all adherent points of $A$ is denoted by adh($A$).

> ***Note*** From the above it is clear that every limit point is an adherent point of $A$ but conversely every adherent point need not a limit point.

## Isolated Point

Let $(X, \Im)$ be a topological space and $A \subset X$. An adherent point $x \in A$ is called isolated point of $A$ if $x$ is not a limit point of $A$. In other words, $\exists$ nbd $G$ of $x$ s.t. $(G - \{x\}) \cap A = \phi$ or $G \cap A = \{x\}$. If every point of a set $A$ is an isolated point of $A$, then the set $A$ is called isolated set.

> ***Note*** **(a)** Let $(X, \Im)$ be a topological space and $A \subset X$.
>
> **(b)** $A$ is dense in itself if $A \subset D(A)$.
>
> **(c)** $A$ is said to be dense or everywhere dense in $X$ if $\overline{A} = X$.
>
> **(d)** $A$ is said to be dense in a set $B \subset X$ if $B \subset \overline{A}$.
>
> **(e)** $A$ is said to be somewhere dense if $(\overline{A})^\circ \neq \phi$, *i.e.*, closure of $A$ contains some open sets.
>
> **(f)** $A$ is said to be nowhere dense if it is not somewhere dense.
> *i.e.*, $A$ is said to be nowhere dense or non-dense set in $X$ if $(\overline{A})^\circ = \phi$.
>
> **(g)** $X$ is said to be separable if $\exists A \subset X$ s.t. $A$ is countable and $\overline{A} = X$.
>
> **(h)** The boundary set of $A$ is the set of all those points which belong neither to the interior of $A$ nor to the interior of its complement and is denoted by $b(A)$.
>
> **(i)** Symbolically, $b(A) = X - A^\circ \cup (X - A)^\circ$.
>
> **(j)** Elements of $b(A)$ are called boundary points of $A$. Boundary points are sometimes called frontier points.
>
> **(k)** The exterior of $A$ is defined as the set $(X - A)^\circ$ and is denoted by ext $(A)$.
>
> **(l)** Symbolically, ext $(A) = (X - A)^\circ$.
>
> **(m)** Elements of ext $(A)$ are called exterior points of $A$.
>
> *e.g.*,
> (i) If $A = (a,b)$ or $[a,b)$ or $(a, b]$ or $[a,b]$, then
> $\overline{A} = [a,b]$, $A^\circ = (a,b)$, $b(A) = \{a,b\}$
>
> (ii) If $A$ = rational points in (0, 1), then $b(A) = \{0, 1\}$,
> Since, every sub-interval of (0, 1) contains rationals as well as irrationals
> int $(\overline{A})$ = int ([0, 1]) = $\phi$
> $\therefore$ $A$ is nowhere dense in $R$.

## Important Results

1. A subset $A$ of a topological space $(X, \Im)$ is closed iff $\overline{A} = A$.
2. A subset $A$ of a topological space $(X, \Im)$ is open iff $A^\circ = A$.
3. $A^\circ$ is the largest open subset of $A$.
4. Let $(X, \Im)$ be a topological space and $A \subset X$. Then, $A$ is $\Im$-open $\Leftrightarrow$ $A$ contains $\Im$-nbds of each of its points.
5. Let $(X, \Im)$ be a topological space and $A \subset X$. $A$ is called a perfect set if $A = D(A)$.
6. A set $G$ in a topological space $X$ is open iff $G$ is a nbd of each of its point.
7. Any finite subset of $R$ is closed set for the usual topology $U$ on $R$.
8. Let $X$ be a topological space and $A \subset X$. If $x$ is limit point of $A$, then $x$ is also limit point of $A - \{x\}$.
9. Let $(X, \Im)$ be a topological space and $A \subset X$, then $A$ is closed iff $D(A) \subset A$.
10. Let $(X, \Im)$ be a topological space and let $A, B$ be non-empty subsets of $X$. Then,
    (i) $D(\phi) = \phi$ (ii) $x \in D(A) \Rightarrow x \in D(A - \{x\})$
    (iii) $A \subset B \Rightarrow D(A) \subset D(B)$ (iv) $D(A \cup B) = D(A) \cup D(B)$
    (v) $D(A \cap B) \subset D(A) \cap D(B)$
11. A subset $A$ of a topological space is closed iff it contains each of its limit points.
12. Let $(X, \Im)$ be a topological space and $A \subset X$, then
    (i) $D(A)$ is a closed set (ii) $A \cup D(A)$ is a closed set (iii) $\overline{A} = A \cup D(A)$
13. Let $(X, \Im)$ be a topological space and let $A, B$ be any subsets of $X$. Then,
    (i) $\overline{\phi} = \phi$ (ii) $A \subset \overline{A}$ (iii) $A \subset B \Rightarrow \overline{A} \subset \overline{B}$
    (iv) $\overline{A \cup B} = \overline{A} \cup \overline{B}$ (v) $\overline{A \cap B} \subset \overline{A} \cap \overline{B}$ (vi) $\overline{\overline{A}} = \overline{A}$
14. Let $(X, \Im)$ be a topological space and $A_r \subset X$, then $\overline{\left(\bigcup_{r=1}^{n} A_r\right)} = \bigcup_{r=1}^{n} \overline{A_r}$
15. Let $(X, \Im)$ be a topological space and $A \subset X$. A point $x$ of $A$ is an interior point of $A$ iff it is not a limit point of $X - A$.
16. Let $(X, \Im)$ be a topological space and $A, B \subset X$. Then,
    (i) $\phi^\circ = \phi$ (ii) $X^\circ = X$ (iii) $A \subset B \Rightarrow A^\circ \subset B^\circ$

(iv) $(A^o)^o = A^o$ (v) $(A \cap B)^o = A^o \cap B^o$ (vi) $A^o \cup B^o \subsetneq (A \cup B)^o$

**17.** Every non-empty subset of an indiscrete space is dense in $X$.
*i.e.*, Let $(X, \Im)$ be an indiscrete space. Let $A \subset X$ be non-empty set, then $\overline{A} = X$.

**18.** If $\Im_1$, $\Im_2$ are two topologies defined on the same set $X$, then $\Im_1 \cap \Im_2$ is also a topology on $X$ but $\Im_1 \cup \Im_2$ is not a topology on $X$.

**19.** Family of all open subsets of a metric space defines a topology on it.
or Every metric space is a topological space.

## Base

Let $(X, \Im)$ be a topological space.
Let $B \subset \Im$ s.t. $B \neq \phi$.
$B$ is said to be a base or open base or basis for the topology $\Im$ on $X$ if given any non-empty set $G \in \Im \Rightarrow \exists B_1 \subset B$ s.t. $G = \cup\{B : B \in B_1\}$.

**Another definition** $B$ is said to be a base for the topology $\Im$ on $X$ if $x \in G \in \Im \Rightarrow \exists\, B \in B$ s.t. $x \in B \subset G$.

The elements of $B$ are referred to as basic open sets.

Later on, we shall show that both definitions of bases are equivalent.

*e.g.*,

(i) The set of all open intervals in $R$ form a base for the usual topology on $R$.

(ii) The set of all open circular discs (*i.e.*, not containing the points on circumference) in $R^2$ forms a base for the usual topology on $R^2$.

(iii) The set of all open intervals $(r, s)$ with $r$ and $s$ as rationals forms a base for the usual topology on $R$.

(iv) The set of all circular discs (not containing points on the circumference) with centres and radii as rationals forms a base for the usual topology on $R$.

## Sub-base

Let $(X, \Im)$ be a topological space. Let

$$S \subset \Im \text{ s.t. } S \neq \phi$$

$S$ is said to be a sub-base or open sub-base for the topology $\Im$ on $X$ if finite intersections of the members of $S$ form a base for the topology $\Im$ on $X$. *i.e.*, the unions of the members of $S$ give all the members of $\Im$. The elements of $S$ are referred to as sub-basic open sets.

*e.g.*, Let $a, b \in R$ be arbitrary s.t. $a < b$. Evidently,

$$(-\infty, b) \cap (a, \infty) = (a, b)$$

The open intervals $(a, b)$ form a base for the usual topology on $R$. Hence, by definition, the family of infinite open intervals forms a sub-base for the usual topology on $R$.

## Local-base

Let $(X, \Im)$ be a topological space. A family $B_x$ of open subsets of $X$ is said to be a local-base at $x \in X$ for the topology $\Im$ on $X$ if

(i) any $B \in B_x \Rightarrow x \in B$

(ii) any $G \in \Im$ with $y \in G \Rightarrow \exists\, B \in B_x$ s.t. $y \in B \subset G$

*e.g.*, Let $x \in R$ be arbitrary.

Write $A_n = \left(x - \dfrac{1}{n}, x + \dfrac{1}{n}\right), \forall\, n \in N.$

Take $B_x = \{A_n : n \in N\}$

Evidently, $B_x$ is a local-base at $x \in X$ for the usual topology on $R$.

## First Countable Space

Let $(X, \Im)$ be a topological space. The space $X$ is said to satisfy the first axiom of countability if $X$ has a countable local base at each $x \in X$. The space $X$, in this case, is called first countable or first axiom space.

## Second Countable Space

Let $(X, \Im)$ be a topological space. The space $X$ is said to satisfy the second axiom of countability if $\exists$ a countable base for $\Im$ on $X$.

In this case, the space $X$ is called second countable or second axiom space.

A second countable space is also called 'completely separable space'.

*e.g.*, The set of all open intervals $(r, s)$ with $r$ and $s$ as rational numbers forms a base, say, $B$ for the usual topology $U$ of $R$. Since, $Q$, $Q \times Q$ are countable sets and so $B$ is a countable base for $U$ on $R$.

$\therefore$ $(R, U)$ is second countable.

> **Note** Let $(X, \Im)$ be a topological space. A property $P$ of $X$ is said to be hereditary if the property is possessed by every subspace of $X$ *e.g.*, first countable, second countable are hereditary properties, whereas closed sets, open sets, are not hereditary properties.

## Important Results

1. Let $(X, \Im)$ be a topological space. A subcollection $B$ of $\Im$ is a base for $\Im$ iff ever $\Im$-open set can be expressed as union of members of $B$.

   **An alternative statement.** If $\Im$ be a topology on $X$ and $B \subset \Im$, then following conditions are equivalent

   (i) Each $G \in \Im$ is the union of members of $B$.

   (ii) For any $x$ belonging to an open set $G$, $\exists\ B \in B$ with $x \in B \subset G$

2. A second countable space is always first countable space

   OR

   Second axiom of countability $\Rightarrow$ first axiom of countability.

3. First countable space doesn't imply second countable space.
4. Property of a space being first countable is hereditary.
5. Property of a space being second countable is hereditary.

   OR

   Every subspace of a second countable space is second countable.

6. Let $X$ be an arbitrary set and $B$ a non-empty subset of the power set $P(X)$ of $X$. $B$ is a base for some topology on $X$ iff

   (i) $\cup \{B : B \in B\} = X$,

   (ii) $x \in B_1 \in B, x \in B_2 \in B \Rightarrow \exists\ B_3 \in B$ s.t. $x \in B_3 \subset B_1 \cap B_2$

   OR

   Let $X$ be any non-empty set, and let $S$ be an arbitrary class of subsets of $X$. Prove that $S$ can serve as an open sub-base for a topology on $X$.

   OR

   Given, a non-empty family $S$ of subsets of a set $X$, show that $\exists$ weakest topology $\Im$ on $X$ in which all the members of $S$ are open sets and $S$ is a sub-base for $\Im$.

7. Let $S$ be a non-empty collection of subsets of a non-empty set $X$. Then, $S$ is a sub-base for a unique topology $\Im$ for $X$, *i.e.*, finite intersections of members of $\boldsymbol{S}$ form a base for $\Im$.
8. A second countable space is always separable but converse is not true.
9. Every second axiom space is hereditarily separable.
10. Any open subspace of a separable space is separable.
11. A metric space is second countable iff it is separable.

## Important Theorems

***Theorem 1*** A metric space is first countable.

***Proof.*** Let $(X,\rho)$ be a metric space. Let $\Im$ be metric topology on $X$, corresponding to the metric $\rho$ on $X$. Let $p \in X$ be arbitrary.

To prove that $(X, \Im)$ is first countable, it suffices to show that $\exists$ a countable local-base at $p$ for the topology $\Im$ on $X$.

Write $\quad L_p = \{S_{(p,r)} : r \in Q^+\}$

$Q$ is enumerable and hence its subset $Q^+$,

$Q^+$ is enumerable $\Rightarrow L_p$ is enumerable.

Let $G \in \Im$ be arbitrary s.t. $p \in G$.

Then, by definition of an open set.

$$\exists\ s \in R^+ \text{ s.t. } S_{(p,s)} \subset G$$

Choose a positive rational number $r$ s.t. $r < s$.

Then, $\quad S_{(p,r)} \subset S_{(p,s)} \subset G \quad$ or $\quad S_{(p,r)} \subset G$

Given, any $G \in \Im$ with $p \in G, \exists\ r \in Q^+$ s.t. $S_{(p,r)} \subset G$.

Now, $L_p$ has the following properties

(i) Every member of $L_p$ is an open set containing $p$.

$\because\quad$ Each open sphere forms an open set.

(ii) $L_p$ is enumerable set.

(iii) Given, any $G \in \Im$ with $p \in G$, $\exists\ r \in Q^+$ s.t.

$$S_{(p,r)} \subset G$$

From what has been done it follows that $L_p$ is an enumerable local-base at $p$ for the topology $\Im$ on $X$.

***Theorem 2*** Every metric space is not second countable.

***Proof.*** Let $R$ be set of real numbers and $d$ be a discrete metric on $R$. Then,

$$d(x, y) = \begin{cases} 1, & \text{if } x \neq y \\ 0, & \text{if } x = y \end{cases}$$

Let $x \in R$ be arbitrary, then $B_x = \{\{x\}\}$ is a local base at $x$. So, $(R, d)$ is first countable. But the family $B$ of subsets of $R$ will form a base for open sets iff $B$ contains all singleton subsets of $R$. Since, $R$ is uncountable and so base $B$ is uncountable base.

Here, there does not exist a countable base for all open subsets of $R$.

Hence, $(R,d)$ is first countable but it is not second countable.

***Theorem 3*** Let $(X,d)$ be a metric space and $B$ be the collection of all open spheres $S_r(x)$, where $r$ is any positive number and $x \in X$, then $B$ is a base for some topology $\Im$ on $X$.

***Proof.*** Recall that $B$ is base for $\Im$ on $X$ iff the following conditions are satisfied

(i) $X = \cup\{B : B \in B\}$

(ii) $x \in B_1 \in B, x \in B_2 \in B \Rightarrow \exists\ B_3 \in B$ s.t.
$x \in B_3 \subset B_1 \cap B_2$

Evidently, (i) is satisfied. To prove (ii).

Let $u \in Sr_1(x) \in B,\ u \in Sr_2(y) \in B$

Then, $d(u,x) < r_1, d(u,y) < r_2$

This$\Rightarrow$ $r_1 - d(u,x) > 0, r_2 - d(u,y) > 0$

Let $r = \min\{r_1 - d(u,x), r_2 - d(u,y)\}$

Then, $r \le r_1 - d(u,x), r \le r_2 - d(u,y)$

Evidently, $r > 0$ and $r + d(u,x) \le r_1,\ r + d(u,y) \le r_2$

We claim $S_r(u) \subset Sr_1(x) \cap Sr_2(y)$

Let $v \in S_r(u)$, then $d(u,v) < r$

$$d(x,v) \le d(x,u) + d(u,v) < d(x,u) + r \le r_1$$

or $d(x,v) \le r_1$ or $v \in Sr_1(x)$

Similarly, we can show that $v \in Sr_2(y)$.

Now, $v \in Sr_2(y),\ v \in Sr_1(x)$

so that $v \in Sr_1(x) \cap Sr_2(y)$

$\therefore$ any $v \in S_r(u) \Rightarrow v \in Sr_1(x) \cap Sr_2(y)$

This $\Rightarrow$ $S_r(u) \subset Sr_1(x) \cap Sr_2(y)$

This proves the result (ii). Hence, $B$ the collection of all open spheres forms a base for a topology $\Im$ on $X$. Such a topology $\Im$ is called metric topology on $X$ as this is induced by the metric $d$.

***Theorem 4*** If $d$ is a usual metric on $R^n$, then $(R^n, d)$ is called Euclidean space and $d$ is called Euclidean metric. If $\Im$ is a topology on $R^n$ induced by $d$, then $\Im$ is called Euclidean topology on $R^n$.

*e.g.*, The usual metric $d(x,y) = |x - y|$ induces the usual topology $U$ on $R$.

$$\begin{aligned} S_r(x_0) &= \{y : d(x_0, y) < r\} \\ &= \{y : |x_0 - y| < r\} \\ &= \{y : -r < x_0 - y < r\} \\ &= \{y : y \in (x_0 - r, x_0 + r)\} \\ &= (x_0 - r, x_0 + r). \end{aligned}$$

Hence, $U$ open sets or $d$-open sets means open intervals.

***Example 7.*** *Prove that $(R, U)$ is second axiom space (second countable).*

**Solution.** We know that $Q$ is a countable subset of $R$. If we write $B = \{(a,b) : a < b \text{ and } a, b \in Q\}$

Then, $B$ forms a countable base for the usual topology $U$ on $R$, so that $R$ is second countable.

***Example 8.*** *Prove that $(R^2, U)$ is second countable.*

**Solution.** If we write $B = \{S_r(x) : x, r \in Q\}$,

then $B$ forms a countable base for the usual topology $U$ on $R^2$. Hence, $(R^2, U)$ is second countable space.

***Example 9.*** *Let $X = \{1,2,3,4\}$. Let $A = \{\{1,2\},\{2,4\},\{3\}\}$. Determine the topology on $X$ generated by the elements of $A$ and hence determine the base for this topology.*

**Solution.** Let $X = \{1,2,3,4\}$

and $A = \{\{1,2\},\{2,4\},\{3\}\}$

Finite intersections of the members of $A$ form the class $B$ given by

$$B = \{\{1,2\},\{3\},\{2,4\},\phi,\{2\},X\}$$

The unions of the members of $B$ form the class $\Im$ given by

$$\Im = \{\{1,2\},\{3\},\{2,4\},\phi,\{2\},X,\{1,2,3\},\{1,2,3\},\{1,2,4\},\{3,2,4\},\{3,2\}\}$$

It can be easily verified that $B$ is base for the topology $\Im$ on $X$.

***Example 10.*** *Let $(X,\Im)$ be a discrete space. Let $B = \{\{x\} : x \in X\}$. Show that any family $B^*$ of subsets of $X$ is a base for $\Im$ on $X$ iff it is a superset of $B$.*

**Solution.** Let $(X,\Im)$ be a discrete space.

Let $B = \{\{x\} : x \in X\}$. Let $B^*$ be a family of all subsets of $X$ s.t. $B \subset B^*$.

To prove that $B^*$ is a base for the topology $\Im$ on $X$.

Since, $X$ is a discrete space and therefore $A$ is an open subset of $X\ \forall\ A \subset X$.

In particular, $\{x\}$ is open in $X, \forall\, x \in X$.

We can write $A = \cup\{\{x\} : x \in A\}$. Also, $B = \{\{x\} : x \in X\}$.

This means that every non-empty open set is expressible as a union of some members of $B$. Hence, by definition, $B$ is a base for the topology $\Im$ on $X$.

Furthermore, $\phi \ne G \in \Im \Rightarrow \exists\, B_1 \subset B$ s.t. $G = \cup\{B : B \in B_1\}$
$\Rightarrow \exists\, B_1 \subset B^*$ s.t. $G = \cup\{B : B \in B_1\}$

For $B \subset B^*$

Finally, $\phi \ne G \in \Im \Rightarrow \exists\, B_1 \subset B^*$ s.t. $G = \cup\{B : B \in B_1\}$.

This $\Rightarrow B^*$ is a base for the topology $\Im$ on $X$.

Conversely, suppose that $B^*$ is a base for the discrete topology $\Im$ on $X$.

Also suppose $B = \{\{x\} : x \in X\}$

To prove that $B \subset B^*$

Let $\{x\} \in B$ be arbitrary, so that $\{x\}$ is a non-empty open subset of $X$. Since, $B^*$ is a base for the topology $\Im$ on $X$ and hence $\{x\}$ must be expressed as a union of some members of $B^*$. Since, any singleton set is a union of itself or itself with the set $\phi$, showing thereby $\{x\} \in B^*$.

$\therefore$ any $\{x\} \in B \Rightarrow \{x\} \in B^*$

This, $\Rightarrow B \subset B^*$

***Example 11.*** *Find out a sub-base $S$ for the discrete topology $\Im$ on $X = \{a, b, c\}$ s.t. $S$ does not contain any singleton set.*

**Solution.** Let $X = \{a, b, c\}$. Let $\Im$ be the discrete topology on $X$.

If we write $B = \{\{x\} : x \in X\}$, then $B$ is a base for the topology $\Im$ on $X$. Any family $B^*$ of subsets of $X$. $S$ does not contain any singleton set. Hence, $S$ is the required sub-base.

## Continuous Functions

1. Let $(X, \Im)$ and $(Y, U)$ be any two topological spaces.

   Let $f : (X, \Im) \to (Y, U)$ be a map.

   The map $f$ is said to be continuous at $x_0 \in X$ if given any $U$-open set $H$ containing $f(x_0)$, $\exists$ a $\Im$-open set $G$ containing $x_0$ s.t. $f(G) \subset H$.

   If the map is continuous at each $x \in X$, then the map is called a continuous map.

   **Definition.** Continuity on a set. A function

   $$f : (X, \Im) \to (Y, U)$$

   is said to be continuous on a set $A \subset X$ iff it is continuous at each point of $A$.

> ***Note*** The following have the same meaning
> (i) $f$ is a continuous map.
> (ii) $f$ is continuous relative to $\Im$ and $U$.
> (iii) $f$ is $\Im$-$U$ continuous map.

2. Let $(X, d)$ and $(Y, \rho)$ be metric spaces. A map $f : (X, d) \to (Y, \rho)$ is said to be continuous at $x_0 \in X$ iff given $\varepsilon > 0$, $\exists\ \delta > 0$ s.t. $d(x, x_0) < \delta \Rightarrow \rho[f(x), f(x_0)] < \varepsilon$.

   or equivalently, $f$ is continuous at $x_0$ iff to each open sphere $S_\varepsilon(f(x_0))$, $\exists$ open sphere

   $$S(x_0, \delta) \text{ s.t. } f[S(x_0, \delta)] \subset S_\varepsilon(f(x_0))$$

   $f$ is continuous on $X$ iff it is continuous at every point of $X$.

3. Let $f : (X, \Im) \to (Y, U)$ be a map.

   $f$ is sequentially continuous at $x_0 \in X$ if for every sequence

   $$< x_n \in X : n \in N >$$

   converging to $x_0$, the sequence $< f(x_n) \in Y : n \in N >$ converges to $f(x_0)$, *i.e.*, if

   $$x_n \to x_0 \Rightarrow f(x_n) \to f(x_0)$$

4. A map $f : (X, \Im) \to (Y, U)$ is said to be homeomorphism or topological mapping if

   (i) $f$ is one-one onto.

   (ii) $f$ and $f^{-1}$ are continuous.

   In this case, the spaces $X$ and $Y$ are said to be homeomorphic or topological equivalent to one another and $Y$ is called the homeomorphic image of $X$.

   *e.g.*, Let $\Im$ denote the usual topology on $R$ and $a$ any non-zero real number.

   Then, each of the following maps is a homeomorphism.

   (i) $f : (R, \Im) \to (R, \Im)$ s.t. $f(x) = a + x$

   (ii) $f : (R, \Im) \to (R, \Im)$ s.t. $f(x) = ax$

   (iii) $f : (R, \Im) \to (R, \Im)$ s.t. $f(x) = x^3$, where $x \in R$

5. A map $f$ is called a bicontinuous map if $f$ and $f^{-1}$ both are continuous maps.

6. A map $f : (X, \Im) \to (Y, U)$ is called an open or interior map if it maps open sets onto open sets, *i.e.*, if

   any $\quad G \in \Im \Rightarrow f(G) \in U$

7. A map $f : (X, \Im) \to (Y, U)$ is called a closed map if any $\Im$-closed set $F \Rightarrow f(F)$ is $U$-closed set.

   *e.g.*, (i) Let $\Im$ denote the usual topology on $R$. Let $a$ be any non-zero real number. Then, each of the following map is open as well as closed.

   (a) $f : (R, \Im) \to (R, \Im)$ s.t. $f(x) = a + x$

   (b) $f : (R, \Im) \to (R, \Im)$ s.t. $f(x) = ax$

   In this case, if $a = 0$, then this map is closed but not open.

   (ii) The identity map $f : (X, \Im) \to (X, \Im)$ is open and as well as closed.

   (iii) A map from an indiscrete space into a topological space is open as well as closed.

   (iv) A map from a topological space into a discrete space is open as well as closed.

***Theorem*** The function $f : (X, \Im) \to (Y, U)$ is continuous iff $f^{-1}(V)$ is open in $X$ for every open set $V$ in $Y$.

***Proof.*** Let $f : (X, \Im) \to (Y, U)$ be a map.

(i) Suppose, $f$ is continuous. Let $G$ be an open subset of $Y$.

To prove that $f^{-1}(G)$ is open in $X$.

If $f^{-1}(G) = \phi$, then $f^{-1}(G) \in \Im$

If $f^{-1}(G) \neq \phi$, then $\exists\ x \in f^{-1}(G)$, so that $f(x) \in G$.

Continuity of $f \Rightarrow f$ is continuous at $x$

$\Rightarrow \exists H \in \Im$ s.t. $x \in H$ and $f(H) \subset G$

$\Rightarrow x \in H \subset f^{-1}(G), H \in \Im$

Thus, we have shown that $f^{-1}(G)$ is a nbd of each of its points and so $f^{-1}(G)$ is $\Im$-open.

Conversely, suppose that $f : (X, \Im) \to (Y, U)$ is a map such that $f^{-1}(V)$ is open in $X$ for each open set $V \subset Y$.

To prove that $f$ is continuous.

Let $V \in U$ be arbitrary.

Then, by assumption, $f^{-1}(V)$ is open in $X$.

Take $\quad U = f^{-1}(V)$, so that $U \in \Im$.

*i.e.*, $\quad f(U) = f(f^{-1}(V)) \subset V$, or $f(U) \subset V$

given any $V \in U, \exists U \in \Im$ s.t. $f(U) \subset V$

This proves that $f$ is a continuous map.

## Important Results on Continuous Maps

1. If $f$ and $g$ are continuous real or complex functions defined on a topological space $X$, then $f+g, \alpha f$ and $fg$ are also continuous. Furthermore, if $f$ and $g$ are real, then $f \vee g$ and $f \wedge g$ are continuous.
2. Let $(X, \Im)$ be a topological space and let $\langle f_n(x) \rangle$ be a sequence of real or complex functions defined on $X$ which converges uniformly to a function $f$ defined on $X$. If all $f_n$'s are continuous, then $f$ is also continuous.
3. The function $f:(X,\Im) \to (Y,U)$ is continuous iff $f^{-1}(C)$ is closed in $X$ for every closed set $C \subset Y$.
4. Let $(X, \Im)$ and $(Y, U)$ be topological spaces. Let $f:(X,\Im) \to (Y,U)$ be a map. Then, $f$ is continuous iff $f^{-1}(B)$ is open for every $B \in B$, $B$ being a base for $U$ on $Y$.

   OR

   $f$ is continuous iff the inverse image of each basic open set is open.
5. A mapping $f: X \to Y$ is continuous iff $\overline{f^{-1}(B)} \subset f^{-1}(\overline{B})$ for any set $B \subset Y$.
6. Let $f:(X,\Im) \to (Y,U)$ be a map. Then, $f$ is a continuous map iff $f(\overline{A}) \subset \overline{f(A)}$ for any set $A \subset X$.

   OR

   A map $f:(X,d) \to (Y,\rho)$ be continuous iff $f(\overline{A}) \subseteq \overline{f(A)}$, $\forall A \subset X$.
7. A one-one map $f:(X,\Im) \xrightarrow{\text{onto}} (Y,U)$ is a homeomorphism iff $f(\overline{A}) = \overline{f(A)}$ for any $A \subset X$.
8. A one-one onto continuous map $f:(X,\Im) \to (Y,V)$ is a homeomorphism if $f$ is either open or closed.
9. A map $f:(X,\Im) \to (Y,V)$ is closed iff $\overline{f(A)} \subset f(\overline{A})$ for every $A \subset X$.
10. A function $f:(X,\Im) \to (Y,V)$ is continuous iff $f^{-1}(B^\circ) \subset [f^{-1}(B)]^\circ$ for every $B \subset Y$.
11. A function $f:(X,\Im) \to (Y,V)$ is open iff $f(A^\circ) \subset [f(A)]^\circ$ for every $A \subset X$.
12. A one-one onto map $f:(X,\Im) \to (Y,V)$ is a homeomorphism iff $f(A^\circ) = [f(A)]^\circ$ for every $A \subset X$.
13. A homeomorphic image of a second countable space is second countable

    *i.e.,* Let $f:(X,\Im) \to (Y,V)$

    be homeomorphism such that $(X,\Im)$ be second countable, then $(Y,V)$ will also be second countable.
14. A homeomorphic image of a first countable space is a first countable.
15. In a topological space

    (i) if $f: A \to B$ and $g: B \to C$ are continuous $\Rightarrow$ $gof: A \to C$ is continuous.

    (ii) An identity mapping is a continuous map.

## Separation Axioms

1. A topological space $(X, \Im)$ is said to satisfy the $T_0$-axiom of separation if given a pair of distinct points $x, y \in X$, either

   $\exists\ G \in \Im$ s.t. $x \in G, y \notin G$.

   or $\exists\ H \in \Im$ s.t. $y \in H, x \notin H$

   In this case, the space $(X, \Im)$ is called a $T_0$-space.

   e.g.,

   (i) Every discrete space is $T_0$-space.

   (ii) An indiscrete space containing only one point is a $T_0$-space.

   (iii) If $(X, \Im)$ is cofinite topological space, then it is $T_0$-space.

   (iv) Every metric space is $T_0$-space.
2. **$T_1$-Axiom or Frechet Axiom of Separation** A topological space $(X, \Im)$ is said to satisfy the $T_1$-axiom of separation if given a pair of distinct points $x, y \in X$.

   $\exists\ G, H \in \Im$ s.t. $x \in G, y \notin G; y \in H, x \notin H$

   In this case, the space $(X, \Im)$ is called $T_1$- space or Frechet space.

   e.g.,

   (i) Every metric space is $T_1$-space.

   (ii) If $(X, \Im)$ is cofinite topological space, then it is $T_1$-space.
3. **$T_2$-Axiom of Separation** A topological space $(X, \Im)$ is said to satisfy the $T_2$-axiom or separation if given a pair of distinct points $x, y \in X$,

   $\exists\ G, H \in \Im$ s.t. $x \in G, y \in H, G \cap H = \phi$

   In this case, the space $(X, \Im)$ is called a $T_2$-space or Hausdorff space or separated space.

   e.g.,

   (i) A discrete topological space is a $T_2$-space.

   (ii) Every metric space is $T_2$-space.
4. **Normal Space** A topological space $(X, \Im)$ is said to be a normal space if given a pair of disjoint closed sets $C_1, C_2 \subset X$.

   $\exists$ disjoint open sets $G_1, G_2 \subset X$ s.t. $C_1 \subset G_1, C_2 \subset G_2$.
5. **Regular Space** A topological space $(X, \Im)$ is said to be a regular space if given an element $x \in X$ and closed set $F \subset X$ s.t. $x \notin F$,

   $\exists$ disjoint open sets $G_1, G_2 \subset X$ s.t. $x \in G_1, F \subset G_2$

A regular $T_1$-space is called a $T_3$-space.
A normal $T_1$-space is called a $T_4$-space.

e.g.,

(i) Every discrete space is regular.
(ii) Every indiscrete space is regular.
(iii) The space of real or complex numbers with usual topology of open sets is regular.
(iv) A metric space is a regular space.

6. **Completely Regular Space** A topological space $(X, \mathfrak{I})$ is called a completely regular space if given a closed set $F \subset X$ and a point $x \in X$ s.t. $x \notin F$,
$\exists$ a continuous map $f: X \to [0, 1]$ with the property,
$$f(x) = 0, f(F) = \{1\}$$
7. **Tychonoff-Space** A completely regular $T_1$-space is called a Tychonoff space. Tychonoff space is also called $T3\frac{1}{2}$ space.
8. Two sets $A$ and $B$ are separated sets if
$$A \neq \phi, B \neq \phi, \bar{A} \cap B = \phi, A \cap \bar{B} = \phi$$
9. **Completely Normal** Let $A$ and $B$ be separated sets in a topological space $(X, \mathfrak{I})$. Then, $X$ is said to be completely normal iff
given a pair of separated sets, there are disjoint open sets $U$ and $V$ s.t. $A \subset U$, $B \subset V$.
It can be shown that Completely normal $\Rightarrow$ normal.
10. **$T_5$-Space** A topological space $(X, \mathfrak{I})$ is a $T_5$-space iff it is a $T_1$-space and completely normal.

***Example 12.*** *If $X = \{a, b\}$ and $\mathfrak{I} = \{\phi, \{a\}, X\}$. Is the space $(X, \mathfrak{I})$ a $T_0$-space or a $T_1$-space.*

**Solution.** (i) $(X, \mathfrak{I})$ is $T_0$-space.

For given $a, b \in X, \exists \{a\} \in \mathfrak{I}$ s.t. $a \in \{a\}, b \notin \{a\}$

(ii) $(X, \mathfrak{I})$ is not $T_1$-space. For given $a, b \in X, \exists \{a\}$ and $X \in \mathfrak{I}$ s.t. $a \in \{a\}, b \notin \{a\}$ and $b \in X, a \in X$.

***Example 13.*** *Prove that $(R, \mathfrak{I})$ is a Hausdorff space.*

**Solution.** Let $a, b \in R$ be arbitrary s.t. $|a - b| = \varepsilon > 0$.

Write $G = \left(a - \frac{\varepsilon}{3}, a + \frac{\varepsilon}{3}\right), H = \left(b - \frac{\varepsilon}{3}, b + \frac{\varepsilon}{3}\right)$

Let $\mathfrak{I}$ be the usual topology on $R$.

Then, $G, H \in \mathfrak{I}$ s.t. $a \in G, b \in H, G \cap H = \phi$

By definition this implies that $(R, \mathfrak{I})$ is a Hausdorff space.

***Example 14.*** *Show that every discrete space is a Hausdorff space.*

**Solution.** Let $(X, \mathfrak{I})$ be a discrete space and $x, y \in X$ be arbitrary s.t. $x \neq y$.

By definition of discrete space, $\{x\}$ and $\{y\}$ are $\mathfrak{I}$-open sets.

Obviously, $\{x\} \cap \{y\} = \phi, x \in \{x\}, y \in \{y\}$

Thus, $\exists$ disjoint open sets $\{x\}$ and $\{y\}$ containing $x$ and $y$, respectively. Consequently, $(X, \mathfrak{I})$ is a Hausdorff space.

## Important Results on Separation Axioms

1. Every Hausdorff space is a $T_1$-space but converse is not true.
2. Every $T_1$-space is $T_0$-space but converse is not true.
3. A topological space $(X, \mathfrak{I})$ is a $T_0$-space iff for any distinct arbitrary points $x, y$ of $X$, the closures of $\{x\}$ and $\{y\}$ are distinct.
4. A topological space $(X, \mathfrak{I})$ is a $T_1$-space iff $\{x\}$ is closed for each $x \in X$.
In a topological space, $T_1$-space $\Leftrightarrow$ each point is a closed set.
5. A normal space ($T_4$-space) is a regular space ($T_3$-space).
6. If $(X, \mathfrak{I})$ is a $T_0$-space and $\mathfrak{I}_1$ is finer than $\mathfrak{I}$, then $(X, \mathfrak{I}_1)$ is also $T_0$-space.
7. A finite subset of a $T_1$-space has no cluster point.
8. $(X, \mathfrak{I})$ is a $T_3$-space $\Rightarrow (X, \mathfrak{I})$ is a $T_2$-space.
9. $(X, \mathfrak{I})$ is a $T_4$-space $\Rightarrow (X, \mathfrak{I})$ is a $T_2$-space.
10. A Tychonoff space is a $T_3$-space
OR
A completely regular space is regular.
11. In a topological space
(i) Every subspace of a $T_0$-space is a $T_0$-space.
(ii) Every subspace of a $T_1$-space is a $T_1$-space.
(iii) Every subspace of a $T_2$-space is a $T_2$-space.
(iv) Every subspace of a $T_3$-space is a $T_3$-space.
(v) Every subspace of a $T_4$-space is a $T_4$-space.
(vi) Every subspace of a $T_5$-space is a $T_5$-space.
12. A topological space $(X, \mathfrak{I})$ is completely normal iff every subspace is normal.
13. In a topological space, homeomorphic image of
(i) $T_0$-space is $T_0$-space.
(ii) $T_1$-space is $T_1$-space.
(iii) $T_2$-space is $T_2$-space.
(iv) regular space is regular.
(v) normal space is normal.
(vi) completely regular space is completely regular.

14. If a sequence in a Hausdorff space converges, then it converges to a unique limit.
15. Let $(X, \Im)$ be any topological space and $(Y, U)$ a Hausdorff space. Let $f$ and $g$ be continuous mapping of $X$ into $Y$. Then, the set $\{x \in X : f(x) = g(x)\}$ is closed.
16. If $f$ and $g$ are continuous functions on a topological space $X$ with values in Hausdorff space $Y$, then set of all points $x$ in $X$ such that $f(x) = g(x)$ is closed and if $f$ and $g$ agree on a dense subset on $X$, then $f = g$ on the whole $X$.
17. If $f:(X, \Im) \to (X, \Im)$ is a continuous map and $(X, \Im)$ is a Hausdorff space, then $A = \{x \in X: f(x) = x\}$ is closed.
18. Let $f : (X, \Im) \to (Y, U)$ be a continuous map such that $(Y, U)$ is a Hausdorff space, then $(X, \Im)$ is a Hausdorff space.
19. Consider the set R with usual topology, where $R = \{x \in R : 0 \le x \le 1\}$. A topological space $(X, \Im)$ is normal iff given a pair of disjoint closed sets $A, B \subset X$ there is a continuous function $f: X \to R$ s.t. $f(A) = \{0\}$ and $f(B) = \{1\}$
20. Every metric space is a
    (i) $T_1$-space (ii) $T_2$-space (iii) normal space
    (iv) regular space (v) $T_3$-space (vi) $T_4$-space
    (vii) completely normal

# Compactness

1. Let $(X, \Im)$ be a topological space and $A \subset X$. Let $G$ denote a family of subsets of $X$. $G$ is called a cover (or covering) of $A$ if $A \subset \cup\{G : G \in G\}$.
   (i) If every member of $G$ is an open set, then the cover $G$ is called an open cover.
   (ii) If there exist $G_1 \subset G$ s.t. $G_1$ is a finite set and cover of $A$, then $G_1$ is called a finite subcover of $G$.
2. Let $(X, \Im)$ be a topological space and $A \subset X$. If $\exists$ finite subcover of a cover $G$ of $A$, then the cover $G$ of $A$ is said to be reducible (to a finite subcover).
3. Let $(X, \Im)$ be a topological space and $A \subset X$. $A$ is said to be a compact set if every open covering of $A$ is reducible to finite subcovering.
4. Let $(X, \Im)$ be a topological space. Let $G$ denote a family of open subsets of $X$. Then, $G$ is called an open cover of $X$, if $X = \cup\{G : G \in G\}$.
5. Let $(X, \Im)$ be a topological space. Let $F$ denote a family of subsets of $X$. Then, $F$ is said to have finite intersection property, if $\exists F_1 \subset F$ s.t. $F_1$ is finite $\cap\{F : F \in F_1\} \ne \phi$.
6. For a closed and bounded subset of $R$, every open covering admits a finite subcovering.
   **Another statement** A closed and bounded subset of $R$ is compact. (Heine Borel Theorem)
7. A topological space $(X, \Im)$ is called Lindel of space if every open cover of $X$ is reducible to a countable cover.
   If follows from the above definition that every compact space is Lindel of space. But the converse is not true. For example, $(X, D)$ is Lindel of space, where $X$ is any infinite countable set but it is not compact.
   Lindel of theorem. Let $(X, \Im)$ be a second countable space. Let $G$ be an open cover of a set $A \subset X$, then $G$ is reducible to a countable cover.
8. Let $(X, \Im)$ be a topological space and let $x \in X$ be arbitrary. Then, $X$ is said to be locally compact at $x$ if the closure of any neighbourhood of $x$ is compact.
   $X$ is called locally compact if it is compact at each of its points, but need not be compact as a whole.

**Alternative definition** A topological space $(X, \Im)$ is locally compact, if each element $x \in X$ has a compact neighbourhood.

> ***Note*** Locally compact need not be compact.

9. A closed and bounded infinite subset of $R$ contains a limit point. (Bolzano Weierstrass Theorem)
10. A metric space $(X, d)$ is said to sequentially compact if every sequence in $X$ has a convergent subsequence e.g., the set of all real numbers in (0, 1) is not sequentially compact. For the sequence $\left\langle \frac{1}{2}, \frac{1}{3}, \frac{1}{4}, \ldots \right\rangle$ in (0, 1) converges to $0 \notin (0, 1)$, on the other hand [0, 1] is sequentially compact.
    A sequence $\langle x_n \in X : n \in N \rangle$ is said to be convergent if
    $$x_n \to x_0 \in X$$
11. If $(X, d)$ be a metric space and $A \subset X$, then the statement that $A$ is compact, $A$ is countably compact and $A$ is sequentially compact are equivalent.
12. A topological space $(X, \Im)$ is said to be countably compact iff every countable $\Im$-open cover of $X$ has a finite subcover. Obviously,
    Compact $\Rightarrow$ Countably compact
13. A metric space $(X, d)$ is said to have the Bolzano Weierstrass property if every infinite subset of $X$ has a limit point.
    In brief, the phrase 'Bolzano Weierstrass Property' is written as BWP. A space with BWP is also called Frechet compact space.
14. Let $(X, d)$ be a metric space. Let $\varepsilon > 0$ be any given real number. A set $A \subset X$ is called an $\varepsilon$-net if
    (i) A is finite set.
    (ii) $X = \cup\{S_{\varepsilon(a)} : a \in A\}$
    The metric space $(X, d)$ is said to be totally bounded if it contains an $\varepsilon$-net for every $\varepsilon > 0$.
    Here, (ii) $\Rightarrow$ given any point $p \in X$, $\exists$ atleast one point $a \in A$ s.t. $d(p, a) < \varepsilon$.
15. Let $\{G_i : i \in \Delta\}$ be an open cover for a metric space $(X, d)$. A real number $\delta > 0$ is called a Lebesgue number for the

cover if any $A \subset X$ s.t. $d(A) < \delta \Rightarrow A \subset G_{i0}$ for atleast one index $i_0 \in \Delta$.

**Lebesgue covering lemma** Every open covering of a sequentially compact space has a Lebesgue number.

**16.** Let $(X, \Im)$ be a topological space and $A \subset X$. An open cover $G$ of $A$ is called basic open cover if all the open sets of the cover are contained in some given base.

An open cover $G$ of $A$ is called sub-basic open cover if all the open sets of the cover are contained in some given open sub-base.

**17.** A topological space $(Y, U)$ is said to be embedded in a topological space $(X, \Im)$ if $(Y, U)$ is a homeomorphic subspace of $(X, \Im)$.

Furthermore, if $(X, \Im)$ is compact, then $Y$ is called compactification of $X$.

**18.** Let $(X, \Im)$ be a topological space. Let $G$ and $G_1$ be two open covers of $X$. Then, $G$ is said to be a refinement of $G_1$ iff any $G \in G \Rightarrow \exists\, G_1 \in G_1$ s.t. $G \subset G_1$.

A space $X$ is said to be para compact iff every open cover of $X$ has a locally finite open refinement, *i.e.*, a refinement, which is locally finite open cover of $X$.

*e.g.*,

(i) Every indiscrete space is compact.

Let $(X, \Im)$ be an indiscrete space. Then, $\Im = \{\phi, X\}$. Consequently, the only open cover of $X$ is $\{X\}$ which is finite cover. Since, it consists of only one member $X$. Hence, $X$ is compact.

(ii) Any infinite subset of a discrete topological space is not compact, for

Let $(X, \Im)$ be a discrete topological space. Let $A \subset X$ be an infinite set. To prove that $A$ is not a compact set. By definition of discrete topology, every finite subset of $X$ is open and hence $\{a\}$ is open, $\forall a \in X$.

Write $$A = \{\{a\} : a \in A\}...$$

Clearly, $A$ is an open cover of $A$. Evidently, $A$ is an infinite set. Hence, any finite subfamily of $A$ is not a cover of $A$, showing thereby $A$ is not compact.

(iii) Every topological space $(X, \Im)$ is compact, if $X$ is finite.

(iv) $(R, I)$ is compact and $(R, D)$ is not compact, where *I and D are respectively indiscrete and discrete topology.*

(v) $(R, U)$ is not compact where $U$ being the usual topology on $R$.

(vi) Any open interval is not compact.

## Important Results on Compactness

**1.** A closed subset of a compact space is compact. *i.e.*, if $(X, \Im)$ be a compact space and $A \subset X$ be closed, then A is compact.

**2.** Let $(A, U)$ be a subspace of $\{X, \Im)$, then A is compact with respect to the topology $U$ iff A is compact with respect to the topology $\Im$ on $X$.

**3.** Every cofinite topological space $(X, \Im)$ is compact.

**4.** A countably compact topological space has a BWP.

**5.** A closed subset of a countably compact space is countably compact.

**6.** If $(X, \Im)$ is a compact topological space, then every basic open cover of it is reducible to a finite subcover.

**7.** A topological space is compact if every basic open cover has a finite subcover.

**8.** A continuous image of a sequentially compact set is sequentially compact.

**9.** $(X, \Im)$ is compact $\Leftrightarrow$ each family of closed sets with finite intersection property has a non-empty intersection.

**10.** A topological space is compact $\Leftrightarrow$ Every class of closed sets which has empty intersection, has a finite subclass with empty intersection.

**11.** Suppose, $A$ is a compact set in a regular space $(X, \Im)$ and $G \subset X$ is a neighbourhood of $A$. Then, $\exists$ a neighbourhood $V \subset X$ of $A$ s.t. $\overline{V} \subset G$.

**12.** Let $A$ be a compact subset of a regular $(X, \Im)$. If $G$ is an open subset containing $A$, then $\exists$ a closed set $H$ containing $A$ s.t. $A \subset H \subset G$.

**13.** Every compact regular space is normal.

**14.** A compact Hausdorff space is normal.

OR

If $A$ and $B$ be disjoint compact subsets of a Hausdorff space $X$, then there exist open sets $G$ and $H$ s.t. $A \subset G, B \subset H$.

**15.** A compact Hausdorff space is regular.

**16.** A compact subset of a Hausdorff space is closed.

**17.** Let $A$ and $B$ be disjoint compact subsets of a Hausdorff space $(X, \Im)$, then there exist disjoint open sets $G$ and $H$ such that $A \subset G, B \subset H$

OR

A topological space $(X, \Im)$ is a Hausdorff space iff disjoint compact subsets of $X$ can be separated by disjoint open sets.

**18.** A continuous image of a compact space is compact.

**19.** Compactness is a topological property.
*i.e.*, if $f:(X,\Im)\to(Y,U)$ is a continuous map, then any compact set $A\subset X \Rightarrow f(A)\subset Y$ is compact.

**20.** (i) A closed and bounded subset (subspace) of $R$ is compact.
(ii) Every closed interval $[a,b]$ is compact.
(iii) Cantor's set is compact. Cantor's set is given by

$$\Gamma=\bigcap_{n=1}^{\infty}F_n \text{ where}$$

$$F_0=[0,1],\ F_1=\left[0,\frac{1}{3}\right]\cup\left[\frac{2}{3},1\right]$$

$$F_2=\left[0,\frac{1}{9}\right]\cup\left[\frac{2}{9},\frac{1}{3}\right]\cup\left[\frac{2}{3},\frac{7}{9}\right]\cup\left[\frac{8}{9},1\right] \text{ and so on.}$$

*i.e.*, $F_n$ is the union of 2nd disjoint closed intervals each of length $\frac{1}{3^n}$. Being finite union of closed sets, $F_n$ is closed also $\Gamma$ is bounded as $\Gamma\subset[0,1]$

**21.** A subspace $(Y,U_1)$ of $(R,U)$ is compact iff $Y$ is bounded and $U$-closed.

**22.** A continuous real-valued function, whose domain is closed and bounded interval of $R$, attains its supremum and infimum.

OR

A continuous real map of a compact space into any metric space is bounded.

**23.** A compact metric space is separable.

**24.** If a metric space $(X,d)$ is totally bounded, then $X$ is bounded.

**25.** Every totally bounded metric space is separable.

**26.** A metric space is sequentially compact iff it has the BWP.

**27.** Every compact metric space has the BWP.

**28.** A countably compact topological space has BWP.

**29.** Every open cover of sequentially compact metric space has a Lebesgue number.

**30.** Every sequentially compact metric space is totally bounded.

**31.** Every compact subset of a metric space is closed and bounded.

**32.** A metric space $X$ is compact $\Leftrightarrow$ metric space $X$ is sequentially compact.

**33.** A metric space is Lindel of space iff it is second countable.

**34.** A metric space is compact iff it is totally bounded and complete.

**35.** Every compact metric space is complete.

**36.** A metric space $(X,d)$ is said to be complete if every Cauchy sequence in $X$ is convergent at some point in $X$.

***Example 15.*** *Let $(X,\Im)$ and $(Y,U)$ be topological spaces. Let $f:(X,\Im)\to(Y,U)$ be a continuous map and $A$ a compact subset of $X$. Show that $f(A)$ is compact.*

OR

*Show that compactness is a topological invariant.*

**Solution.** Let $f:(X,\Im)\to(Y,U)$ be a continuous map and let $A$ be a compact subset of $X$.

To prove that $f(A)$, is compact.

Let $\{G_\alpha:\alpha\in\Delta\}$ be an open cover of $f(A)$,

$$f(A)\subset\bigcup_{\alpha\in\Delta}G_\alpha \qquad \text{...(i)}$$

From which

$$A\subset f^{-1}(f(A))\subset f^{-1}\left(\bigcup_{\alpha\in\Delta}G_\alpha\right)=\bigcup_{\alpha\in\Delta}f^{-1}(G_\alpha),$$

*i.e.*, $$A\subset\bigcup_{\alpha\in\Delta}f^{-1}(G_\alpha)$$

Taking $$f^{-1}(G_\alpha)=O_\alpha,\ A\subset\bigcup_{\alpha\in\Delta}O_\alpha \qquad \text{...(ii)}$$

Therefore, since $f$ is continuous, $f^{-1}(G_\alpha)=O_\alpha$ is open in $X$. Then, Eq. (ii) shows that $\{O_a:\alpha\in\Delta\}$ is an open cover of $A$ which is known to be compact and hence this cover must be reducible to a finite subcover, say, $\{O_{\alpha_i}:1\le i\le n\}$. Clearly,

$$A\subset\bigcup_{i=1}^{n}O_{\alpha i}$$

From which $$f(A)\subset\bigcup_{i=1}^{n}f(O_{\alpha_i})$$

*i.e.*, $$f(A)\subset\bigcup_{i=1}^{n}f(O_{\alpha_i}) \qquad \text{...(iii)}$$

$$f(O_\alpha)=f(f^{-1}(G_\alpha))\subset G_\alpha$$

*i.e.*, $$f(O_\alpha)\subset G_\alpha \quad \therefore \bigcup_{i=1}^{n}f(O_{\alpha_i})\subset\bigcup_{i=1}^{n}G_{\alpha_i}$$

Making use of Eq. (iii), we get $f(A)\subset\bigcup_{i=1}^{n}G_{\alpha_i}$

This proves that $\{G_{\alpha_i} : 1 \le i \le n\}$ is an open cover of $f(A)$. Thus, an arbitrary open cover $\{G_\alpha : \alpha \in A\}$ of $f(A)$ is reducible to a finite subcover $\{G_{\alpha_i} : 1 \le i \le n\}$ showing thereby $f(A)$ is compact.

***Example 16.*** *A one-one continuous map of a compact space onto Hausdorff space is a homeomorphism.*

**Solution.** Let $(X, \Im)$ be a compact topological space and $(Y, U)$ a Hausdorff space. Let $\exists$ a one-one continuous map

$$f : X \xrightarrow{\text{onto}} Y.$$

To prove that $f$ is a homeomorphism, it is enough to show that

(i) $f$ is one-one onto, (ii) $f$ is continuous,

(iii) $f^{-1}$ is continuous.

The results (i) and (ii) immediately follow from our initial assumption. Remains to prove (iii).

*i.e.*, to prove that $f^{-1}$ is continuous.

For this we must show that $f(F)$ is closed in $Y$ for any closed set $F \subset X$.

Let $F \subset X$ be an arbitrary closed set.

Being a closed subset of a compact set $X, F$ is compact.

$f(F)$ is compact, being a continuous image of a compact set.

Furthermore $f(F)$ is a compact subset of a Hausdorff space $(Y, U)$ and hence $f(F)$ is closed in $Y$,

Thus, we have shown that

any $F \subset X$ is closed $\Rightarrow f(F) \subset Y$ is closed.

This $\Rightarrow f^{-1}$ is continuous.

## Connectedness

1. Let $(X, \Im)$ be a topological space. $X$ is said to be disconnected iff $\exists\ G, H \in \Im$ s.t.

   (i) $G \neq \phi, H \neq \phi, G \cap H = \phi$

   (ii) $X = G \cup H$

   $X$ is said to be connected iff it is not disconnected.

   e.g.,

   (i) Every indiscrete space is connected.

   (ii) Every discrete space is disconnected if the space contains more than one point.

   (iii) If $X = \{a, b, c, d\}$ and $\Im = \{\phi, X, \{a, b\}\}$, then the topological space $(X, \Im)$ is connected.

   (iv) The empty set $\phi$ and the singleton sets $\{x\}$ are assumed to be connected.

   (v) The set $R$ with usual topology is connected.

   (vi) If $X$ is disconnected, then $G \cup H$ is not a unique representation of $X$, *i.e.*, there may be many representation of this type.

   (vii) If $(X, \Im)$ disconnected, then $\exists$ non-empty disjoint open sets $G, H \subset X$ s.t. $X = G \cup H$.

   $G \cap H = \phi \Rightarrow G = X - H \Rightarrow G$ is closed [$\because H$ is open]

   Similarly, $G \cap H = \phi \Rightarrow H = X - G \Rightarrow H$ is closed [$\because G$ is open]

   $\therefore$ If $(X, \Im)$ is disconnected, then $\exists$ non-empty disjoint closed sets $G, H \subset X$ s.t. $X = G \cup H$.

2. A topological space is totally disconnected if given any pair of distinct points $x, y \in X$, then $\exists$ a disconnection $G \cup H$ of $X$ with $x \in G, y \in H$.

   By the property of a Hausdorff space,

   totally disconnected $\Leftrightarrow$ Hausdorff space,

   $\Leftrightarrow$ disconnected space provided the space has more than one point.

   A one point space is connected as well as totally disconnected.

3. Let $(X, \Im)$ be a topological space and $A \subset X$. Then, the set $A$ is called a maximal connected subset of $X$ if

   (i) $A$ is connected.

   (ii) $A$ is not a proper subset of any connected subset of $X$.

4. A subset $B$ of a topological space $(X, \Im)$ is called a component of $X$ if it is maximal connected subset of $X$.

   e.g.,

   (i) Every indiscrete space has only one component, namely, the space itself.

   (ii) Let $(X, \Im)$ be a discrete space. Let $x \in X$ be arbitrary, then $\{x\}$ is a connected subset of $X$ and also $\{x\}$ is not a proper subset of any connected subset of $X$. Hence, by definition, $\{x\}$ is a component of $X$. From this it follows that each point of a discrete space $(X, \Im)$ is a component of $X$.

5. Let $(X, \Im)$ be a topological space and $A \subset X$. $A$ is called arcwise connected if for any two points $a, b \in A$, there is a path $f : I \to X$, from $a$ to $b$ s.t. $f(I) \subset A$.

6. Let $(X, \Im)$ be a topological space and $x \in X$ be arbitrary. Then, $X$ is locally connected iff for every open nbd $G$ of $x$, there exists connected open nbd $H$ of $x$ s.t. $x \in H \subset G$. That is to say, $X$ is locally connected iff the collection of all connected open nbds of $x$ forms a local base at $x$.

7. The union of two disjoint open intervals on the real line is a space which is locally connected but not connected. Similarly, there are topological space which are connected but they are not locally connected. That is to say, locally connected does not imply connectedness.

8. Let $(X, \Im)$ be a discrete topological space containing more than one point. Then, $X$ is disconnected.

   For each $x \in X$, $\{x\}$ is an open connected set containing $x$ and $\{x\}$ is contained in every open set containing $x$. Thus, $X$ is locally connected but not connected.

9. Let $(X, \Im)$ be a topological space. Let $I$ be the set of all real numbers belonging to the closed interval $[0, 1]$ with usual topology.

   Let $a, b \in X$ be arbitrary.

   A continuous map $f : I \to X$ with the properties

   $$f(0) = a,\ f(1) = b,$$

   is called a path from the point $a$ to the point $b$. In this case, $a$ is called the initial point and $b$ is called the terminal or final point of the path.

   A map $f : I \to X$ defined as $f(x) = p,\ \forall\ x \in I$ is called a constant path at $p$.

   For $f$ is a constant map and hence $f$ is always continuous.

## Important Results on Connectedness

1. Two closed subsets of a topological space are separated iff they are disjoint.
2. Two open subsets of a topological space are separated iff they are disjoint.
3. Suppose, $A$ and $B$ are separated subsets of a topological space $(X, \Im)$. Suppose, $C$ and $D$ are non-empty subsets of $X$ s.t. $C \subset A, D \subset B$. Then, $C$ and $D$ are separated sets.
4. A topological space $X$ is disconnected $\Leftrightarrow$ there exists a continuous map of $X$ onto the discrete two point space $\{0, 1\}$.

   OR

   A metric space $X$ is connected iff every continuous function $f$ from $X$ to two point discrete metric space is constant.
5. Let $(X, \Im)$ be a topological space. Then, $X$ is disconnected iff $\exists$ a non-empty proper subset of $X$ which is both open and closed.
6. A topological space $(X, \Im)$ is connected iff the only non-empty subset which is both open and closed in $X$ is $X$ itself.
7. A subspace of a real line is connected iff it is an interval.

   OR

   A subset $A$ of the real line $R$ containing atleast two points is connected iff $A$ is an interval.
8. The set $R$ of real numbers with usual metric is a connected space.

   OR

   The set of real numbers with the usual topology is connected.
9. Let $(X, \Im)$ be a topological space and $A \subset X$. $A$ is disconnected iff it is a union of two separated sets.
10. Let $(X, \Im)$ be a topological space and $A$ be a connected subset of $X$ such that $A \subset B \subset \overline{A}$, then $B$ is connected and hence $\overline{A}$ is connected.
11. Let $(X, \Im)$ be a topological space and $A \subset X$, if $A$ is connected, then $\overline{A}$ is connected.

    OR

    The closure of connected set is connected.
12. (i) A continuous image of connected space is a connected space.
    (ii) The range of a continuous real-valued function defined on a connected space is an interval.
    (iii) If $f: X \to R$ is a continuous map, then $f(X)$ is an interval where $X$ be a connected space.
13. Let $\{A_\alpha : \alpha \in \Delta\}$ be a family of connected subsets of $(X, \Im)$ s.t. $\cap \{A_\alpha : \alpha \in \Delta\} \neq \phi$. Then, $\cup \{A_\alpha : \alpha \in \Delta\}$ is a connected set.

    OR

    Let $A = \{A_i\}$ be a class of connected subsets of a space $X$ such that no two members of $A$ are separated. Then, $B = \bigcup_i A_i$ is connected.
14. Let $\{A_\alpha\}$ be a family of connected subsets of a topological space $(X, \Im)$ s.t. one member of the system intersects every other member. Then, $\bigcup_{\alpha \in \Delta} A_\alpha$ is connected.
15. The components of a totally disconnected set $X$ are singleton sets in $X$.

    OR

    The components of a totally disconnected space are its points.

***Example 17.*** *Suppose, $(X, \Im)$ is a topological space and $E \subset X$. If any two points of $E$ are contained in some connected subset of $E$, then show that $E$ is a connected set.*

**Solution.** Suppose, $(X, \Im)$ is a topological space and $E \subset X$. If any two points of $E$ are contained in some connected subset of $E$.

We claim $E$ is connected.

Suppose not. Then, $E$ is expressible as union of two non-empty subsets $G, H \subset X$ s.t.

$$E = G \cup H, \overline{G} \cap H = \phi, G \cap \overline{H} = \phi, G \cap H = \phi \quad \text{...(i)}$$

$G, H \neq \phi \Rightarrow \exists p \in G, q \in H$

$\Rightarrow p, q \in E$. For $E = G \cup H$

$\Rightarrow \exists F \subset E$ s.t. $F$ is connected and $p, q \in F$, by initial assumption

$$E = G \cup H, F \subset E \Rightarrow F \subset G \cup H$$

Now, $F \subset G \cup H$; $F$ is connected; $G, H$ are separated sets,

$\Rightarrow F \subset G$ or $F \subset H$ (theorem)

$\Rightarrow p, q \in G$ or $p, q \in H$. Also, $p \in G, q \in H$

$\Rightarrow G \cap H \neq \phi$

Contrary to the fact that $G \cap H = \phi$

Hence, our assumption "$E$ is disconnected" is wrong, so that connected.

**Remark** This problem can also be expressed as A topological space $X$ is connected iff for every two points in $X$, there is some connected subspace of $X$ which contains both.

***Example 18.*** *Prove that the union of two non-empty separated subsets of a topological space is disconnected.*

*OR*

*Prove that a set $A$ is connected iff $A$ is not union of two separated sets.*

**Solution.** Let $A$ and $B$ be separated subsets of a topological space $(X, \Im)$.

To prove that $A \cup B$ is disconnected.

Our assumption implies that

(i) $A \neq \phi, B \neq \phi$

(ii) $\overline{A} \cap B = \phi, A \cap \overline{B} = \phi$

(iii) $\Rightarrow A \cap B = \phi$ ...(i)

write $X - \overline{A} = G, X - \overline{B} = H$

$\because$ $\overline{A}$ and $\overline{B}$ are non-empty closed subsets of $X \Rightarrow G$ and $H$ are non-empty open subsets of $X$.

$$G \cup H = (X - \overline{A}) \cup (X - \overline{B}) = \overline{X} - \overline{A} \cap \overline{B}$$

$$(A \cup B) \cap G = (A \cup B) \cap (X - \overline{A})$$
$$= [A \cap (X - \overline{A})] \cup [B \cap (X - \overline{A})]$$
$$= \phi \cup B = B$$

$\therefore$ $(A \cup B) \cap G = B$

Similarly, $(A \cup B) \cap H = A$ ...(ii)

For $\overline{A} \cap B = \phi \Rightarrow B \subset X - \overline{A}$

$B \cap (X - \overline{A}) = B$

and $A \subset \overline{A} \Rightarrow X - \overline{A} \subset X - A$

$\Rightarrow A \cap (X - \overline{A}) \subset A \cap (X - A)$

$\Rightarrow A \cap (X - \overline{A}) \subset \phi \Rightarrow A \cap (X - \overline{A}) = \phi$

Now, $A \neq \phi \neq B \Rightarrow (A \cup B) \cap G \neq \phi, (A \cup B) \cap H \neq \phi$.

According to Eq. (ii),

$[(A \cup B) \cap G] \cap [(A \cup B) \cap H] = A \cap B = \phi$ [by Eqs. (i) and (ii)]

$[(A \cup B) \cap G] \cup [(A \cup B) \cap H] = A \cup B$ [by Eq. (ii)]

Finally, we have shown that $\exists\, G, H \in \Im$ s.t.

$$(A \cup B) \cap G \neq \phi, (A \cup B) \cap H \neq \phi,$$
$$[(A \cup B) \cap G] \cap [(A \cup B) \cap H] = \phi,$$
$$[(A \cup B) \cap G] \cup [(A \cup B) \cap H] = A \cup B$$

By definition, this proves that $G \cup H$ is a disconnection of $A \cup B$ and hence $A \cup B$ is disconnected.

***Example 19.*** *Let $(X, \Im)$ be a topological space and $A \subset X$. Let $G \cup H$ be a disconnection of $A$. Then, show that $A \cap G$, $A \cap H$ are separated sets.*

**Solution.** Let $G \cup H$ be a disconnection of a subset $A$ of a topological space $(X, \Im)$.

To prove $A \cap G, A \cap H$ are separated sets.

For this we must show that

(i) $(A \cap G), (A \cap H) \neq \phi$

(ii) $[D(A \cap G)] \cap (A \cap H) = \phi$

(iii) $(A \cap G) \cap [D(A \cap H)] = \phi$

Our assumption implies that $G, H \in \Im$ s.t.

(iv) $A \cap G \neq \phi, A \cap H \neq \phi$

(v) $(A \cap G) \cap (A \cap H) = \phi$

(vi) $(A \cap G) \cup (A \cap H) = A$

Evidently, (v) $\Rightarrow$ (i)

To prove (ii)

Suppose not

This $\Rightarrow [D(A \cap G)] \cap (A \cap H) \neq \phi$

$\Rightarrow \exists\, x \in [D(A \cap G) \cap (A \cap H)]$

$\Rightarrow x \in D(A \cap G)$ and $x \in A, x \in H$

$\Rightarrow H$ is an open set containing $x$ s.t. $x$ is limit point of $A \cap G$

$\Rightarrow H$ contains points of $A \cap G$ other than $x$

$\Rightarrow (A \cap G) \cap H \neq \phi$

$\Rightarrow [(A \cap A) \cap G] \cap H \neq \phi$

$\Rightarrow (A \cap G) \cap (A \cap H) \neq \phi$. Contrary to (v)

Hence, the result (ii).

Similarly, we can prove (iii).

***Example 20.*** *Let $(X, \Im)$ be a topological space and $Y \subset X$. If $Y$ is connected, then so is $\overline{Y}$.*

***An Alternate Statement*** *The closure of connected set is connected.*

**Solution.** This theorem is a particular case of the previous theorem, since $Y \subset \overline{Y} \subset \overline{Y}$. But due to its importance, we shall give an independent proof here.

Let $Y$ be a connected subset of a topological space $(X, \Im)$.

To prove that $\overline{Y}$ is connected.

Suppose contrary. Then, $\overline{Y}$ is disconnected. It follows that $\exists$ non-empty sets

$$A, B \subset X \text{ s.t. } \overline{A} \cap B = \phi, A \cap \overline{B} = \phi, \overline{Y} = A \cup B$$
$$A \cup B = \overline{Y} \supset Y, Y \text{ is connected.}$$

This $\Rightarrow Y \subset A \cup B, Y$ is connected

$\Rightarrow Y \subset A$ or $Y \subset B$,

$$Y \subset A \Rightarrow \overline{Y} \subset \overline{A} \Rightarrow \overline{Y} \cap B \subset \overline{A} \cap B = \phi$$

$\Rightarrow$ $\overline{Y} \cap B \subset \phi \Rightarrow \overline{Y} \cap B = \phi$ ...(i)

$$\overline{Y} = A \cup B \Rightarrow B \subset \overline{Y} \Rightarrow \overline{Y} \cap B = B$$

$\Rightarrow$ $B = \phi$. For $\overline{Y} \cap B = \phi$, [by Eq. (i)]

A contradiction. For $B \neq \phi$

Similarly, $Y \subset B \Rightarrow A = \phi$

Again, we get a contradiction.

Hence, the required result follows.

***Example 21.*** *Show that a totally disconnected space is a $T_2$-space.*

**Solution.** Let $(X, \Im)$ be a totally disconnected set so that given a pair of distinct points $x, y \in X, \exists$ disjoint open sets $G, H \subset X$ s.t. $X = G \cup H, x \in G, y \in H$.

By definition this proves that $X$ is a $T_2$-space.

***Example 22.*** *Show that a totally disconnected space is a $T_1$-space.*

**Solution.** Since, $(X, T)$ is a totally disconnected space and so given a pair of distinct points $x, y \in X, \exists$ disjoint open sets $G, H \subset X$

s.t. $X = G \cup H, x \in G, y \in H$

By definition, this $\Rightarrow X$ is $T_2$-space.

Now, $x \in G, G \cap H = \phi \Rightarrow x \notin H$

$y \in H, G \cap H = \phi \Rightarrow y \notin G$

Thus, we get

$x \in G, y \notin G$

and $y \in H, x \notin H$

From this it follows that $X$ is $T_1$-space.

# Product Spaces

1. Let $\{(X_i, T_i);\ i = 1, 2, \ldots, n\}$ be a finite collection of $n$ topological spaces. Then, the collection
$$B = \{G_1 \times G_2 \ldots \times G_n : G_i \in \mathfrak{I}_i \text{ for } 1 \le i \le n\}$$
is a base for some topology on $X = X_1 \times \ldots \times X_n$.
Then, the topology $\mathfrak{I}$ generated by the base $B$ is called product topology for $X$ and $(X, T)$ is called product topological space of the given spaces.
The mapping $\pi_i; X \to X_i$ s.t. $\pi_i(x) = x_i$ is called projection on the $i$th coordinate space, where $x = (x_1, \ldots, x_n)$.
2. Let $\{A_\alpha : \alpha \in \Delta\}$ be an arbitrary family of indexed sets. Also, let $A = \times\{A_\alpha : \alpha \in \Delta\}$.
Then, any $a \in A$ is expressible as $a = (a_1, a_2, \ldots, a_n)$.
The mapping $\pi_a : A \to A_\alpha$ s.t. $\pi_a(a) = a_\alpha$ is called projection map of $A$ into the $\alpha$th coordinate space $A_\alpha$.
The mapping $\pi_\alpha$ is also called evaluation map.

***Note*** **(a)** If $A_\alpha = \phi$ for some $\alpha$, then product of $A = \phi$.
**(b)** If $A_\alpha = A, \forall_\alpha$, then product of $\{A_\alpha : \alpha \in \Delta\} = A^\Delta$.

3. Let $\{(X_\alpha, \mathfrak{I}_\alpha) : \alpha \in \Delta\}$ be arbitrary collection of topological spaces and let
$$X = \text{product of } \{X_\alpha : \alpha \in \Delta\}$$
Then, the topology $\mathfrak{I}$ on $X$ which has subbase the collection.
$$B = \{\pi_a^{-1}(G_a);\ G_\alpha \in \mathfrak{I}_a, \forall \alpha \in \Delta\}$$
is called product topology or Tychonoff topology for $X$. The space $(X, \mathfrak{I})$ is called Tychonoff space of the given spaces.
Since, $G_\alpha \in \mathfrak{I}_\alpha \Rightarrow \pi_\alpha^{-1}(G_\alpha) \in B \subset \mathfrak{I} \Rightarrow \pi_\alpha^{-1}(G_\alpha) \in \mathfrak{I}$
This proves that $\pi_\alpha$ is a continuous map.
Thus, the projection maps $\pi_\alpha$ are continuous.
4. The mappings,
$$\pi_x; X \times Y \to X \text{ s.t. } \pi_x(x, y) = x,\ \forall (x, y) \in X \times Y$$
$$\pi_y; X \times Y \to Y \text{ s.t. } \pi_y(x, y) - y,\ \forall (x, y) \in X \times Y$$
are called projection maps of $X \times Y$ onto $X$ and $Y$ spaces, respectively.

## Important Results on Product Space

1. If $(X_1, \mathfrak{I}_1)$ and $(X_2, \mathfrak{I}_2)$ are any two topological spaces, then the collection
$B = \{G_1 \times G_2 : G_1 \in \mathfrak{I}_1, G_2 \in \mathfrak{I}_2\}$
is a base for some topology on $X = X_1 \times X_2$
2. Let $(X_1, \mathfrak{I}_1)$ and $(X_2, \mathfrak{I}_2)$ be two topological spaces and let $B_1, B_2$ be bases for $\mathfrak{I}_1$ and $\mathfrak{I}_2$, respectively. Let $X = X_1 \times X_2$. Then, $B = \{B_1 \times B_2 : B_1 \in B_1, B_2 \in B_2\}$ is a base for the product topology $\mathfrak{I}$ on $X$.
3. Let $(X, \mathfrak{I}_1)$ and $(Y, V)$ be two topological spaces and let $L$ and $M$ be sub-bases for $\mathfrak{I}_1$ and $V$, respectively. Then, the collection $A$ of all subsets of the form $L \times Y$ and $X \times M$, is a sub-base for the product topology $\mathfrak{I}$ on $X \times Y$, where $L \in \mathbf{L}, M \in \mathbf{M}$.
4. If $(X, \mathfrak{I})$ is the product space of topological spaces $(X_1, \mathfrak{I}_1)$ and $(X_2, T_2)$, then the projection maps $\pi_1$ and $\pi_2$ are continuous and open.
5. Let $(X, \mathfrak{I})$ be the product topological space of $(X_1, \mathfrak{I}_1)$ and $(X_2, \mathfrak{I}_2)$.
Let $\pi_1 : X \to X_1, \pi_2 : X \to X_2$
be the projection maps on the first and second coordinate spaces, respectively.
Let $f : Y \to X$ be another map, where $Y$ is another topological space. Show that $f$ is continuous iff $\pi_1 o f$ and $\pi_2 o f$ are continuous maps.
6. The product topology is the coarser (weak) topology for which projections are continuous.
7. The product space $X_1 \times X_2$ is connected iff both $X_1$ and $X_2$ are connected.
8. Let $(Z, \mathfrak{I})$ be the product topological space of topological spaces $(X, \mathfrak{I}_1)$ and $(Y, \mathfrak{I}_2)$ . Then, $Z$ is compact iff $X$ and $Y$ both are compact.
9. **Tychonoff Theorem** Let $\{(X_\lambda, T_\lambda) : \lambda \in \Delta\}$ be a collection of topological spaces and let $X = \times\{X_\lambda : \lambda \in \Delta\}$. Then, $X$ is compact relative to product topology iff each space $X_\lambda$ is compact.
10. A subset of $R^n$ is closed and bounded iff it is compact.
11. The product of two second countable spaces is a second countable space.

**12.** The product space of two Hausdorff spaces is Hausdorff space.
**13.** The product of any non-empty class of Hausdorff spaces is a Hausdorff space.
**14.** The product topology $\Im$ is the coarsest topology for $X$ for which the projections are continuous.
**15.** The product space $X = \times\{X_\alpha : \alpha \in \Delta\}$ is $T_1$-space iff each coordinate space is $T_1$-space.
**16.** Let $s$ be a sequence in a product space $X = \times\{X_\alpha : \alpha \in \Delta\}$. Then, $s$ converges to a point $x$ iff $\pi_\alpha o s$ converges to $\pi_\alpha(x) = x_\alpha$ for each $\alpha \in \Delta$.
**17.** Let $f$ be a map of a space $Y$ into a product space $X = \times\{X_\alpha : \alpha \in \Delta\}$. Then, $f$ is continuous iff the composition map $\pi_\lambda\, o\, f : Y \to X_\lambda$ continuous.

OR

Let $f$ be a map of $X$ into a product space $P_i X_i$, then show that $f$ is continuous $\Leftrightarrow \pi_i f$ is continuous for each projection $\pi_i$.

**Example 23.** Let $\Im_1 = \{\phi, \{1\}, X_1\}$ be a topology on $X_1 = \{1, 2, 3\}$
*and* $\Im_2 = \{\phi, X_2, \{a\}, \{b\}, \{a, b\}, \{c, d\}, \{a, c, d\}, \{b, c, d\}\}$
*be a topology for* $X_2 = \{a, b, c, d\}$
*Find a base for the product topology* $\Im$.

**Solution.** Let $\boldsymbol{B}_1$ be a base for $\Im_1$ and $\boldsymbol{B}_2$ be a base for $\Im_2$.

Then, $\boldsymbol{B} = \{B_1 \times B_2 : B_1 \in \boldsymbol{B}_1, B_2 \in \boldsymbol{B}_2\}$
is a base for the product topology $\Im$.
We can take $\boldsymbol{B}_1 = \{\{1\}, X_1\}$

$$\boldsymbol{B}_2 = \{\{a\}, \{b\}, \{c, d\}\}$$

The elements of $\boldsymbol{B}$ are

$$\{1\} \times \{a\}, \{1\} \times \{b\}, \{1\} \times \{c, d\},$$
$$\{1, 2, 3\} \times \{a\}, \{1, 2, 3\} \times \{b\}, \{1, 2, 3\} \times \{c, d\}.$$

That is to say,

$$B = \begin{Bmatrix} \{(1, a)\}, \{(1, b)\}, \{(1, c), (1, d)\}, \\ \{(1, a), (2, a), (3, a)\}, \{(1, b), (2, b), (3, b)\} \\ \{(1, c), (2, c), (3, c), (1, d), (2, d), (3, d)\} \end{Bmatrix}$$

is a base for $\Im$.

# Homotopy

If $f$ and $f'$ are continuous map of the space $X$ into space $Y$, then $f$ is homotopic to $f'$ ($f = f'$) if there is one continuous map $F : X \times [0, 1] \to Y$ such that $F(x, 0) = f(x)$ and $F(x, 1) = f'(x)$ for each $x \in X$.
The map $F$ is called a homotopy between $f$ and $f'$.

## Path Homotopic

Two paths $f$ and $f'$, mapping the interval [0, 1] into $X$ are said to be path homotopic $f =_p f'$ if they have the same initial $x_0$ and same final path $x_1$ and if there is continuous map $F : [0, 1] \times [0, 1] \to X$ such that

$$f(s, 0) = f(s) \text{ and } F(s, 1) = f(s)$$

$$F(0, t) = x_0 \text{ and } F(1, t) = x_1.$$

for each $s \in I$ and each $t \in [0, 1]$. The map $F$ is called path homotopy between $f$ and $f'$.

## Straight Line Homotopy

If $f, g : x \to R^2$ such that the map $F(x, t) - (1 - t)f(x) + tg(x)$ is a homotopy between $f$ and $g$. Then, $F$ is called straight line homotopy.

## Contractible

A space is contractible if the identity map $i_X : X \to X$ is homotopic a constant map.

## Composition

If $f$ is a path in $X$ from $x_0$ to $x_1$ and $g$ is a path in $X$ from $x_1$ to $x_2$, then composition $f * g$ of $f$ and $g$ is a path $h$ given by

$$h(s) = \begin{cases} f(2s) & , \text{if } s \in \left[0, \frac{1}{2}\right] \\ g(2s - 1), & \text{if } s \in \left[\frac{1}{2}, 1\right] \end{cases}$$

## Simply Connected Space

In simply connected space $X$, any two paths having the same initial and final points are path homotopic.

## Homeomorphism induced by *h*

Let $h : (X, x_0) \to (Y, y_0)$ be a continuous map and map $h^* : \pi_1(X, x_0) \to \pi_1(Y, y_0)$ is such that $h*([f]) = (hof)$.
The map $h*$ is called homeomorphism induced by $h$, relative to the base point $x_0$.

## Zero Homeomorphism

Let $A \subset R^n, h : (A, a_0) \to (Y, y_0)$. If $h$ is extandable to a continuous map of $R^n$ into $Y$. Then, $h*$ is zero homeomorphism.

# Fundamental Group (First Homotopy Group)

Let $X$ be a topological space; let $x_0 \in X$. The path in $X$, that begins and ends at $x_0$ is called a loop based at $x_0$, with the operation * is called fundamental group $\Pi_1(X, x_0)$ of $X$ relative to the base point $x_0$.

## Important Theorems on Fundamental Group

1. If $X$ is path connected and $x_0, x_1 \in X$, then $\pi_1(X, x_0)$ is isomorphic to $\pi_1(X, x_1)$.
2. In a simply connected space $X$ any two paths having the same initial and final points are path homotopic.
3. If $h:(X, x_0) \to (Y, y_0)$, $k:(Y, y_0) \to (Z, z_0)$, then $(koh)_* = k_* o h_*$
4. If $i:(X, x_0) \to (X, x_0)$ is identity map, then $i_*$ is the identity homeomorphism.
5. If $h:(X, x_0) \to (Y, y_0)$ is homeomorphism of $X$ with $Y$, then $h_*$ is an isomorphism of $\pi_1(X, x_0)$ with $\pi_1(Y, y_0)$.

# SOLVED EXAMPLES

## Type I (*Only one correct option*)

***Example 1.*** *Let $X = \{1, 2, 3, 4, 5\}$. Then, which of the following is topology on X?*

(a) $T_1 = \{X, \phi, \{1, 2, 3\}, \{2, 3, 5\}, \{1, 5\}\}$ is topology on $X$.

(b) $T_2 = \{X, \phi, \{1\}, \{2\}, \{1, 2\}, \{4, 5\}, \{1, 2, 4, 5\}, \{1, 4, 5\}$ $\{2, 4, 5\}\}$

(c) $T_3 = \{X, \phi, \{1, 2, 3\}, \{1, 2, 4\}, \{1, 3, 5\}\}$

(d) None of the above

**Solution.** (b) Here, $\phi, X \in T_1 \cap T_2 \cap T_3$

Now, for each $G_1, G_2 \in T_2$, we find $G_1 \cup G_2 \in T_2$ and $G_1 \cap G_2 \in T_2$. Hence, $T_2$ is topology on $X$ but $T_1$ and $T_3$ are not topology on $X$ as

$$\{1, 2, 3\}, \{2, 3, 5\} \in T_1 \text{ but}$$
$$\{1, 2, 3\} \cap \{2, 3, 5\} = \{2, 3\} \notin T_1$$

and $\{1, 2, 3\}, \{1, 2, 4\} \in T_3$ but

$$\{1, 2, 3\} \cap \{1, 2, 4\} = \{1, 2\} \notin T_3$$

***Example 2.*** *Let $(X, T)$ be a topological space, where $X = \{1, 2, 3, 4, 5\}$ and $T = \{X, \phi, \{1\}, \{2\}, \{1, 2\}, \{4, 5\}, \{1, 2, 4, 5\}, \{1, 4, 5\}, \{2, 4, 5\}\}$ Then, which of the following is neighbourhood of 2?*

(a) $\{1, 3\}$ (b) $\{3, 4, 5\}$

(c) $\{1, 2, 4, 5\}$ (d) None of these

**Solution.** (c) Since, $\{1, 2, 3, 5\} \in T$. Hence, $\{1, 2, 3, 5\}$ is open set. Hence, $\{1, 2, 3, 5\}$ is neighbourhood of each of element belonging to $\{1, 2, 3, 5\}$. Hence, $\{1, 2, 3, 5\}$ is *nbd* of 2.

## Type II (*One or more than one correct option*)

***Example 3.*** *Which of the following(s) is/are true?*

(a) The collection $S = \{\pi_1^{-1}(U) | U \text{ open in } X\} \cup \{\pi_2^{-1}(V) | V \text{ open in } Y\}$ is a sub-basis for the product topology on $X \times Y$.

(b) If $\mathbb{B}$ is a basis for the topology of $X$, then
$$B_Y = \{B \cap Y | B \in \mathbb{B}\}$$
is a basis for the subspace topology on $Y$.

(c) If $Y$ is a subspace of $X$. If $U$ is open in $Y$ and $Y$ is open in $X$, then $U$ is open in $X$.

(d) None of the above

**Solution.** (a), (b), (c)

(a) Let $T$ denote the product topology on $X \times Y$. Let $T'$ be the topology generated by $S$. Since, every element of $S$ belongs to $T$, so do arbitrary unions of finite intersections of elements of $S$. Thus, $T' \subset T$. On the other hand, every basis element $U \times V$ for the topology $T$ is a finite intersection of elements of $S$, since.
$$U \times V = \pi_1^{-1}(U) \cap \pi_2^{-1}(V)$$
Hence, $U \times V \in T'$, hence $T \subset T^1$
Hence, $S$ is a sub-basis for product topology on $X \times Y$.

(b) Given, $U$ open in $X$ and given $y \in U \cap Y$, we can choose an element $B$ of $\mathbb{B}$ such that $y \in B \subset U$. Then,
$$y \in B \cap Y \subset U \cap Y$$
Hence, $\mathbb{B}_Y$ is a basis for subspace topology on $Y$.

(c) Since, $U$ is open in $Y, U = Y \cap V$ for some set $V$ open in $X$. Since, $Y$ and $V$ are both open in $X$, so is $Y \cap V$.

***Example 4.*** *Which of the following(s) is/are true?*

(a) The subset $[a, b]$ of $\mathbb{R}$ is closed.

(b) In the plane $\mathbb{R}^2$, the set $\{x \times y | x \geq 0 \text{ and } y \geq 0\}$ is closed.

(c) In the discrete topology on the set $X$, every set is open.

(d) None of the above

**Solution.** (a), (b), (c)

(a) Since, $\mathbb{R} - [a, b] = (-\infty, a) \cup (b, \infty)$ is open. Hence, $[a, b]$ is closed in $\mathbb{R}$.

(b) Since, the complement of $\{x \times y \mid x \geq 0 \text{ and } y \geq 0\}$ in $\mathbb{R}^2$ is the union of the two sets $(-\infty, 0) \times \mathbb{R}$ and $\mathbb{R} \times (-\infty, 0)$, each of which is a product of open set of $\mathbb{R}$ and is therefore, open in $\mathbb{R}^2$.

(c) Obviously, in the discrete topology on the set $X$, every set is open.

***Example 5.*** *Let X be the real line* $\mathbb{R}$. *If* $A = (0, 1]$, *then*

(a) $\overline{A} = (0, 1]$ (b) $\overline{A} = (0, 1)$
(c) $\overline{A} = [0, 1]$ (d) $\overline{A} = [0, 1)$

**Solution.** (c) Since, every neighbourhood of 0 intersects $A$, while every point outside $[0, 1]$ has a neighbourhood disjoint from $A$. Hence,

$$\overline{A} = [0, 1]$$

***Example 6.*** *Let* $f : A \to X \times Y$ *be given by the equation*

$$f(a) = (f_1(a), f_2(a))$$

*and f is continuous, then*

(a) $f_1 : A \to X$ is continuous.

(b) $f_1 : A \to X$ need not be continuous.

(c) $f_2 : A \to X$ is continuous.

(d) $f_2 : A \to X$ need not be continuous.

**Solution.** (a), (c)

Let $\pi_1 : X \times Y \to X$ and $\pi_2 : X \times Y \to Y$ be projections onto the first and second factors, respectively. These maps are continuous. Note that for each $a \in A$.

$$f_1(a) = \pi_1(f(a)) \text{ and } f_2(a) = \pi_2(f(a))$$

It $f$ is continuous, then $f_1$ and $f_2$ are composites of continuous functions and therefore continuous.

***Example 7.*** *Which of the following(s) is/are correct?*

(a) If $A$ be a connected subspace of $X$ and $A \subset B \subset \overline{A}$, then $B$ is also connected.

(b) The union of a collection of connected subspaces of $X$ that have a point in common is connected.

(c) The image of a connected space under a continuous map is connected.

(d) None of the above

**Solution.** (a), (b), (c)

(a) Let $A$ be connected and $A \subset B \subset \overline{B}$. Suppose that, $B = C \cup D$ is separation of $B$. Hence, the set $A$ must lie entirely in $C$ or in $D$. Suppose that, $A \subset C$. Then, $A \subset \overline{C}$; since $\overline{C}$ and $D$ are disjoint, $B$ cannot intersect $D$. This contradict the fact that $D$ is a non-empty subset of $B$. Hence, $B$ is also connected.

(b) Let $\{A_\alpha\}$ be a collection of connected subspace of a space $X$. Let $p \in \cap A_\alpha$. We prove that the space $Y = UA_\alpha$ is connected. Suppose that, $Y = C \cup D$ is a separation of $Y$. The point $p$ is in one of the sets $C$ or $D$; suppose $p \in C$. Since, $A_\alpha$ is connected, it must lie entirely in either $C$ or $D$ and it cannot lie in $D$ as it contains the point $p$ of $C$. Therefore, $A_\alpha \subset C, \forall \alpha$. Hence, $UA_\alpha \subset C$, which contradict the fact that $D$ is non-empty. Hence, $Y$ is connected. Hence, arbitrary union of connected set is connected.

(c) Let $f : X \to Y$ be a continuous map and $X$ be connected. Since, the map obtained from $f$ by restricting its range to the space $Z$ is also continuous, it suffices to consider the case of a continuous surjective map $g : X \to Z$.

Suppose that, $Z = A \cup B$ is a separation of $Z$ into two disjoint non-empty sets, open in $Z$. Then, $g^{-1}(A)$ and $g^{-1}(B)$ are disjoint sets, whose union is $X$; they are open in $X$ because $g$ is continuous and non-empty because $g$ is surjective. Hence, they form a separation of $X$, which contradict the assumption that $X$ is connected. Hence, image of a connected space under a continuous map is connected.

# Exercise 1 (For Part 'B')

**Directions** (Q. Nos. 1-239) *All questions have only one correct option.*

**1.** If $X = \{a, b\}, P(X) = \{\phi, X, \{a\}, \{b\}\}$, then which one of the following is a topology?
(a) $T = \{\phi, \{a\}, \{b\}\}$ (b) $T = \{X, \{a\}, \{b\}\}$
(c) $T = \{\phi, \{a\}\}$ (d) $T = \{\phi, X\}$

**2.** If $X = \{a, b\}$, $P(X) = \{\phi, X, \{a\}, \{b\}\}$, then which one of the following is not a topology?
(a) $T = \{\phi, X\}$ (b) $T = \{\phi, X, \{a\}\}$
(c) $T = \{\phi, X, \{b\}\}$ (d) $T = \{\phi, \{a\}, \{b\}\}$

**3.** Which of the following is a topology on $X = \{1, 2, 3, 4\}$?
(a) $T = \{\phi, \{1\}, \{2\}, \{1, 2\}\}$ (b) $T = \{\phi, X, \{1\}, \{2\}\}$
(c) $T = \{X, \{1\}, \{1, 2\}\}$ (d) $T = \{\phi, X, \{1\}\}$

**4.** Which of the following is not correct for topological space $(X, P(X))$?
(a) Every function on $(X, P(X))$ is continuous.
(b) $P(X)$ is the strongest topology on $X$.
(c) Every subset of $X$ is open and closed.
(d) $\bar{A} \neq A, \forall\ A \subset X$

**5.** Which of the following is a topology on $X = \{1, 2, 3, 4\}$?
(a) $T = \{\phi, X, \{1\}, \{2\}\}$
(b) $T = \{\phi, X, \{1\}, \{2\}, \{1, 2\}, \{3\}\}$
(c) $T = \{\phi, \{1\}, \{2\}, \{1, 2\}\}$
(d) $T = \{\phi, X, \{1\}, \{2\}, \{1, 2\}\}$

**6.** Which one of the following is not true?
(a) A second countable space is always first countable.
(b) First countable space always implies second countable space.
(c) Every subspace of a second countable space is second countable.
(d) A second countable space is always separable.

**7.** Which of the following is always true?
(a) An open subspace of a separable space need not separable.
(b) Every metric space is separable.
(c) Every metric space is first countable.
(d) Every metric space is second countable.

**8.** If $f$ is a continuous function from a topological space $X$ into a topological space $Y$, then
(a) $f^{-1}(A)$ is closed if $A$ is closed subset of $Y$
(b) $f^{-1}(A)$ is compact if $A$ is compact subset of $Y$
(c) $\overline{f(A)} \subset f(\bar{A}), \forall\ A \subset X$
(d) None of the above

**9.** Which one of the following is correct?
(a) Every discrete space is a Hausdorff space.
(b) If $T$ is a cofinite topology on an infinite set $X$, then $(X, T)$ is a Hausdorff space.
(c) If $T$ is a cofinite topology on an infinite set $X$, then $(X, T)$ is not $T_1$-space.
(d) None of the above

**10.** Let $(X, T)$ be a $T_3$-space, then which one is true?
(a) $X$ is a $T_2$-space
(b) $X$ is a $T_1$-space
(c) $X$ is a $T_4$-space
(d) None of the above

**11.** Every topological space $(X, \Im)$ is compact if
(a) $X$ is not finite
(b) $\Im$ is not finite
(c) every open cover of $X$ is reducible to finite subcover
(d) None of the above

**12.** Which of the following is not true?
(a) A closed subset of a compact space is compact.
(b) An infinite discrete space is compact.
(c) Every cofinite topological space is infinite.
(d) A closed and bounded subset of $R$ is compact.

**13.** Which one of the following is incorrect?
(a) An infinite subset $A$ is discrete topological space is compact.
(b) Every indiscrete space is compact.
(c) Every topological space $(X, \Im)$ is compact if $X$ is finite.
(d) None of the above

**14.** A one to one continuous map of a compact space $X$ onto a Hausdorff space $Y$ is
(a) open map
(b) not an open map
(c) not an homeomorphism
(d) None of the above

**15.** Which of the following is incorrect in $(X, \Im)$?
(a) A subset $A$ of compact space $X$ is compact.
(b) Continuous image of a compact space is compact.
(c) If $X = R$ and $T$ is usual topology, then $A = (0, 1)$ is not compact.
(d) Closed subset of compact space is compact.

**16.** Which of the following is not true?
(a) Every sequentially compact metric space is compact.
(b) Every sequentially compact metric space is totally bounded.
(c) Every sequentially compact metric space has the Bolzano Weierstrass property.
(d) Every sequentially compact metric space is not separable.

**17.** Let $A = (X, \Im)$ where $\Im = \{\phi, X\}$, then
(a) $A$ is not compact.
(b) $A$ is disconnected.
(c) $A$ is connected but not compact.
(d) $A$ is compact and connected both.

**18.** If $X = \{a, b, c\}$, $\Im = \{\phi, X, \{a, c\}, \{b\}\}$, then topological space $(X, \Im)$ is
(a) not a connected space
(b) a connected space
(c) not compact
(d) not a Hausdorff space

**19.** Every metric space is not a
(a) $T_2$-space (b) $T_3$-space
(c) $T_4$-space (d) $T_5$-space

**20.** Let $(X, \Im)$ and $(Y, U)$ be two topological spaces such that $f:(X, \Im) \to (Y, U)$ is a homeomorphism, then
(a) $f$ is not one-one and onto
(b) $f$ is not onto
(c) $f$ is not continuous
(d) $f^{-1}$ is continuous

**21.** If $(X, T)$ is a topological space and $A \subset X$, then the set $A$ is said to be disconnected subset of $X$, if there exist $G, H \in T$ s.t.
(a) $A \cap G, A \cap H = \phi$
(b) $(A \cap G) \cap (A \cap H) \neq \phi$
(c) $A \neq (A \cap G) \cup (A \cap H)$
(d) None of the above

**22.** Two sets $A$ and $B$ are not separated sets if
(a) $A = \{2, 3\}$ and $B = \{3, 4\}$
(b) $A = \{2, 3\}$ and $B = \{4, 5\}$
(c) $A = \{3, 4\}$ and $B = \{4, 5\}$
(d) None of the above

**23.** If $X$ is a topological space, which of the following is incorrect?
(a) Intersection of non-empty class of connected subspaces of $X$ is non-empty.
(b) The components of totally disconnected space are points.
(c) Each component of locally connected space is closed.
(d) Every compact Hausdorff space is normal.

**24.** Which of the following subset is connected?
(a) $\{(x, y): |x^2 - y^2| \geq 4\}$ of $R^2$
(b) $A = \{a, d, e\}$ subset of a topological space $(X, T)$ where $X = \{a, b, c, d, e\}$.
(c) Real line $R$, with usual topology.
(d) $A = \{x \in R: |x| > 2\}$ as a subset of real line with usual topology.

**25.** Let $f: X \to Y$ be bijective continuous function. If $X$ is compact and $Y$ is Hausdorff, then
(a) $f$ is automorphism
(b) $f$ is isomeomorphism
(c) $f$ is homeomorphism
(d) None of the above

**26.** An $m$-manifold is
(a) hausdorff space with a uncountable basis such that some point $x \in X$, has a neighbourhood that is homeomorphic with an open subset of $R^m$.
(b) hausdorff space with a uncountable basis such that each point $x \in X$, has a neighbourhood that is homeomorphic with an closed subset of $R^m$.
(c) hausdorff space with a countable basis such that each point $x \in X$, has a neighbourhood that is homeomorphic with an open subset of $R^m$.
(d) hausdorff space with a uncountable basis such that some point $x \in X$, has a neighbourhood that is homeomorphic with an closed subset of $R^m$.

**27.** Let $X$ be a topological space. If every collection $G$ of closed sets in $X$, satisfy finite intersection condition the intersection $\cap_{C \in G} C \neq \phi$. Then, $X$ is
(a) compact space
(b) hausdorff space
(c) null set
(d) None of the above

**28.** The ........ operations are continuous function from $R \times R$ into $R$ and quotient operation is continuous function from $R \times (R - \{0\}$ into $R$.
(a) addition (b) subtraction
(c) multiplication (d) All of these

**29.** If $X$ is a topological space and if $f, g: X \to R$ are continuous functions, then
(a) $f/g$ is continuous
(b) if $g(x) \neq 0$ for all $x$, then $f/g$ is continuous
(c) if $g(x) = 0$ for all $x$, then $f/g$ is continuous
(d) None of the above

**30.** Let $X$ be a simply ordered set having the least upper bound property. In the order topology, each closed interval in $X$ is
(a) compact space (b) hausdorff space
(c) null set (d) None of these

**31.** Uniform limit theorem states: Let $f_n: X \to Y$ be a sequence of continuous functions from the topological space $X$ into the metric space $Y$.
(a) If $\{f_n\}$ converges uniformly to $f$, then $f$ is continuous.
(b) If $\{f_n\}$ diverges uniformly to $f$, then $f$ is continuous.
(c) If $\{f_n\}$ converges uniformly to $f$, then $f$ is discontinuous.
(d) None of the above

**32.** If $X$ is a topological space and if $f, g: X \to R$ are continuous functions, then ....... are continuous functions.
(a) $f + g$ (b) $f - g$
(c) $fg$ (d) All of these

**33.** The product of finitely many compact spaces is
(a) compact space (b) open set
(c) null set (d) None of these

**34.** If $B$ is the collection of all intervals in the real line $(a, b) = \{x | a < x < b|\}$, the topology generated by $B$ is called the
(a) standard topology on the real line
(b) discrete topology on real line
(c) hausdorff topology on real line
(d) None of the above

**35.** A collection $G$ of subsets of topological space satisfies finite intersection condition, if for every finite subcollection $\{C_1, C_2, ..., C_n\}$ of $G$, the intersection $\bigcap_{i=1}^{n} C_i$
(a) is a null set (b) is not a null set
(c) is a set $G$ (d) None of these

**36.** If $X$ and $Y$ are topological space. Let $f : X \to Y$ and $X$ be metrizable. The function $f$ is continuous iff
(a) for every divergent sequence $x_n \to x$ in $X$, the sequence $f(x_n)$ divergent to $f(x)$
(b) for every divergent sequence $x_n \to x$ in $X$, the sequence $f(x_n)$ converges to $f(x)$
(c) for every convergent sequence $x_n \to x$ in $X$, the sequence $f(x_n)$ converges to $f(x)$
(d) for every convergent sequence $x_n \to x$ in $X$, the sequence $f(x_n)$ diverges to $f(x)$

**37.** A topological space $X$ is connected in kleinen at $x$, if
(a) for every neighbourhood $U$ of $x$, there is a disconnected subset $Y$ of $U$ that contains a neighbourhood of $x$.
(b) for every neighbourhood $U$ of $x$, there is a connected subset $Y$ of $U$ that contains a neighbourhood of $x$.
(c) for every neighbourhood $U$ of $x$, there is a connected subset $Y$of $U$ that does not contains a neighbourhood of $x$.
(d) None of the above

**38.** A topological space $X$ is compact, if every open covering $a$ of $X$ contains
(a) a finite subcollection that covers $X$
(b) a infinite subcollection that covers $X$
(c) a finite subcollection that does not covers $X$
(d) None of the above

**39.** If $f, g : X \to R^2$ such that the map $F(x, t) = (1-t)f(x) + tg(x)$, is a homotopy between $f$ and $g$.
(a) Then, $F$ is called straight line homotopy
(b) Then, $F$ is called path homotopy
(c) Both (a) and (b)
(d) None of the above

**40.** Sequence lemma states: Let $X$ be a topological space and $A \subset X$.
(a) If there is a sequence of points of $A$ converging to $x$, then $x \in \bar{A}$;
(b) The converse holds, if $X$ is metrizable
(c) Both (a) and (b)
(d) None of the above

**41.** A collection $B$ of subsets of topological space $X$ is countably locally finite
(a) if $B$ can be written as uncountable union of collection $B_n$, each of which is locally finite.
(b) if $B$ can be written as countable intersection of collection $B_n$, each of which is locally finite.
(c) if $B$ can be written as countable union of collection $B_n$, each of which is locally finite.
(d) None of the above

**42.** The image of a compact topological space under continuous map is
(a) continuous (b) discontinuous
(c) constant (d) None of these

**43.** If set $B$ is formed by adjoining to the connected set $A$ of topological space $X$, some or all its limit points, then $B$ is
(a) connected (b) separable
(c) disconnected (d) None of these

**44.** Let $a$ be a collection of subsets of the space $X$. A collection $B$ of subsets of $X$ is called refinement of $a$ (refine $a$)
(a) if for some $\mathbb{B} \in B$, there is $\mathbb{A} \in a$ such that $\mathbb{B} = \mathbb{A}$
(b) if for each $\mathbb{B} \in B$, there is $\mathbb{A} \in a$ such that $\mathbb{B} \subset \mathbb{A}$
(c) if for each $\mathbb{B} \in B$, there is $\mathbb{A} \in a$ such that $\mathbb{B} = \subset \mathbb{A}$
(d) None of the above

**45.** Let $X$ be a topological space. A collection $a$ of subsets of $X$ are locally finite
(a) if every point of $X$ has a neighbourhood that intersect only finitely many elements of $a$
(b) if some point of $X$ has a neighbourhood that intersect infinitely many elements of $a$
(c) if every point of $X$ has a neighbourhood that intersect infinitely many elements of $a$
(d) None of the above

**46.** A topological space $X$ is Para compact space, if it is hausdorff space and
(a) every open covering $a$ of $X$ has a locally infinite open refinement $B$ that covers $X$
(b) every open covering $a$ of $X$ has a locally finite open refinement $B$ that covers $X$
(c) every closed covering $a$ of $X$ has a locally infinite open refinement $B$ that covers $X$
(d) None of the above

**47.** Let $A$ be a connected subset of topological space $X$. If $A \subset B \subset \bar{A}$, then $B$ is
(a) connected (b) separable
(c) disconnected (d) None of these

**48.** Let $X$ be a regular space with basis $B$ that is countably locally finite. Then,
(a) $X$ is metrizable only
(b) $X$ is normal only
(c) $X$ is metrizable and normal both
(d) None of the above

**49.** Let $X$ be a topological space. Given, an equivalence relation on $X$ such that $x \sim y$ if there is a path in $X$ from $x$ to $y$. Then,
(a) equivalence classes are called the path components of $X$
(b) equivalence classes are called the separation of $X$
(c) equivalence classes are called the compact of $X$
(d) None of the above

**50.** If $Y$ is a compact subset of the Hausdorff space $X$ and $x_0 \notin Y$, then
(a) there exist disjoint open sets $U$ and $V$ of $X$, such that $x_0 \in U$ and $Y \subset V$
(b) there exist overlapping open sets $U$ and $V$ of $X$, such that $x_0 \in U$ and $Y \subset V$
(c) there exist disjoint closed sets $U$ and $V$ of $X$, such that $x_0 \in U$ and $Y \subset V$
(d) None of the above

**51.** The union of a collection of connected sets that have a point in common is
(a) connected (b) separable
(c) disconnected (d) None of these

**52.** Nagata-Smirnov metrization theorem of $G_\delta$ set states: A subset $A$ of topological space $X$ is $G_\delta$ set in $X$
(a) if it is equals to the union of a countable collection of open subsets of $X$
(b) if it is equals to the intersection of a countable collection of open subsets of $X$
(c) if it is equals to the union of a uncountable collection of open subsets of $X$
(d) None of the above

**53.** A compactification of a space $X$
(a) is hausdorff space $Y$ containing $X$ such that $X$ is dense in $Y$
(b) is compact hausdorff space $Y$ containing $X$ such that $X$ is dense in $Y$
(c) is compact hausdorff space $Y$ not containing $X$
(d) None of the above

**54.** Every compact subset of hausdorff space is
(a) closed set (b) open set
(c) null set (d) None of these

**55.** If sets $C$ and $D$ from a separation of topological space $X$ and if $Y$ is a connected subset of $X$, then
(a) $Y$ lies entirely within $C$
(b) $Y$ lies entirely within $D$
(c) $Y$ lies entirely within either $C$ or $D$
(d) $Y$ lies entirely within $C$ and $D$

**56.** A countable product of first countable spaces is
(a) first countable (b) second countable
(c) third countable (d) fourth countable

**57.** Every hausdorff topological group is
(a) normal (b) regular
(c) completely regular (d) None of these

**58.** Every closed subset of a compact space is
(a) compact space (b) open set
(c) null set (d) None of these

**59.** Let $Y$ be a subspace of topological space $X$. Then, $Y$ is compact iff
(a) every covering of $Y$ by sets open in $X$ contains a finite subcollection covering $Y$
(b) every covering of $Y$ by sets closed in $X$ does not contain a finite subcollection covering $Y$
(c) every covering of $Y$ by sets open in $X$ does not contain a infinite subcollection covering $Y$
(d) None of the above

**60.** Let a be a locally finite collection of subsets of $X$. Then
(a) any subcollection of a is locally finite
(b) the collection $B = \{\bar{A}\}_{A \in a}$ of closures of the elements of a is locally finite
(c) $\overline{U_{A\in a} A} = U_{A \in a} \bar{A}$
(d) All of the above

**61.** A subbasis $\zeta$ for a topology on $X$ is a collection of subsets of $X$
(a) whose union equals $X$
(b) whose union is subset of $X$
(c) whose union superset of $X$
(d) None of the above

**62.** If $Y$ is a subspace of topological space $X$
(a) $Y$ is connected, if there exist no separation of $Y$
(b) $Y$ is connected, if there exist atleast one separation of $Y$
(c) $Y$ is connected, if there exists separation of $Y$
(d) None of the above

**63.** A topological space $X$ is locally path connected at $x$, if
(a) for every neighbourhood $U$ of $x$, there is a path connected neighbourhood $V$ of $x$, $V \subset U$
(b) for every neighbourhood $U$ of $x$, there is a path connected neighbourhood $V$ of $x$, $V = U$
(c) for every neighbourhood $U$ of $x$, there is a disconnected neighbourhood $V$ of $x$
(d) None of the above

**64.** A subspace of a first countable space is
(a) first countable
(b) second countable
(c) third countable
(d) fourth countable

**65.** A topological space $X$ is locally connected at $x$, if
(a) for every neighbourhood $U$ of $x$, there is a connected neighbourhood $V$ of $x$, $V \subset U$
(b) for every neighbourhood $U$ of $x$, there is a connected neighbourhood $V$ of $x$, $V = U$
(c) for every neighbourhood $U$ of $x$, there is a disconnected neighbourhood $V$ of $x$
(d) None of the above

**66.** If $Y$ is a subspace of topological space $X$, a separation of $Y$ is a pair of disjoint non-empty sets $A$ and $B$ whose union is $Y$, and

(a) neither of which contains a limit point of the other
(b) each of which contains a limit point of the other
(c) one of which contains a limit point of the other
(d) None of the above

**67.** Topology generated by the subbasis $\zeta$ is defined as

(a) the collection $T$ of all unions of any intersections of elements of $\zeta$
(b) the collection $T$ of all unions of finite intersections of elements of $\zeta$
(c) the collection $T$ of all intersection of any intersections of elements of $\zeta$
(d) None of the above

**68.** Let $X$ be a topological space satisfy first countability axiom, if

(a) the function $f: X \to Y$ is continuous iff for every diverding sequence $\{x_n\}$ in $X$, converging to $x$ the sequence $\{f(x_n)\}$ converges to $f(x)$
(b) the function $f: X \to Y$ is continuous iff for every convergent sequence $\{x_n\}$ in $X$, converging to $x$ the sequence $\{f(x_n)\}$ converges to $f(x)$
(c) the function $f: X \to Y$ is continuous iff for every convergent sequence $\{x_n\}$ in $X$, converging to $x$ the sequence $\{f(x_n)\}$ diverges to $f(x)$
(d) None of the above

**69.** Let $f: X \to Y$ also $X$ and $Y$ be metrizable with metrics $d_X$ and $d_Y$, respectively. Then, $f$ is continuous, if

(a) to given $x \in X$ and $\varepsilon > 0$, there exist $\delta > 0$ such that $d_X(x, y) < \delta \Rightarrow d_Y(f(x), f(y)) < \varepsilon$
(b) to given $x \in X$ and $\varepsilon > 0$, there does not exist $\delta > 0$ such that $d_X(x, y) < \delta \Rightarrow d_Y(f(x), f(y)) < \varepsilon$
(c) to given $x \in X$ and $\varepsilon > 0$, there exist $\delta > 0$ such that $d_X(x, y) = \delta \Rightarrow d_Y(f(x), f(y)) = \varepsilon$
(d) None of the above

**70.** Let $X$, $Y$ and $Z$ be topological spaces. If $f: X \to Y$ and $g: Y \to Z$ are continuous, then

(a) composite $(gof): X \to Z$ is continuous
(b) composite $(gof): X \to Z$ is discontinuous
(c) composite $(fog): X \to Z$ is continuous
(d) None of the above

**71.** Let $X$ be a set for which a topology $T$ is defined, then

(a) only $X$ is in $T$ (b) only $X$ is not in $T$
(c) $\phi$ and $X$ are in $T$ (d) None of these

**72.** Let $X$ be a locally compact Hausdorff space which is not compact. Let $Y$ be the one point compactification of $X$. Then,

(a) $X$ is subspace of $Y$
(b) the set $Y - X$ consists of a single point
(c) $\overline{X} = Y$
(d) All of the above

**73.** Let $\overline{d}(a, b) = \min\{|a - b|\}$ be the standard metric on $R$. If $x$ and $y$ are two points of $R^\omega$, define

$$D(\overline{x}, \overline{y}) = \text{lub}\left[\frac{\overline{d}(x_i, y_i)}{i}\right]. \text{ Then,}$$

(a) $D$ is not a metric that induces the product topology on $R^\omega$
(b) $D$ is a metric that induces the product topology on $R^\omega$
(c) $D$ is a metric that does not induces the product topology on $R^\omega$
(d) None of the above

**74.** Let $X$ and $Y$ be topological spaces and $f: X \to Y$. If $f$ is continuous, then

(a) for every closed set $B \subset Y$, set $f^{-1}(B)$ is closed in $X$
(b) for every open set $B \subset Y$, set $f^{-1}(B)$ is closed in $X$
(c) for every closed set $B \subset Y$, set $f^{1}(B)$ is open in $X$
(d) None of the above

**75.** If $B$ is a basis for a topology on $X$, the topology $T$ generated by $B$ is defined as

(a) subset $U \subset X$ is closed in $(X, T)$, if for each $x \in U$, there is a basis element $\mathbb{B} \in B$ such that $x \in \mathbb{B}$ and $\mathbb{B} \subset U$
(b) subset $U \subset X$ is open in $(X, T)$, if for each $x \in U$, there is a basis element $\mathbb{B} \in B$ such that $x \in \mathbb{B}$ and $\mathbb{B} \subset U$
(c) subset $U \subset X$ is open in $(X, T)$, if for some $x \in U$, there is a basis element $\mathbb{B} \in B$ such that $x \in \mathbb{B}$ and $\mathbb{B} = U$
(d) None of the above

**76.** Let $X$ be a topological space satisfy first countability axiom, if

(a) the point $x \in \overline{A}$, closure of $A \subset X$ iff there is a sequence of points of $A$ converging to $x$
(b) the point $x \in \overline{A}$, closure of $A \subset X$ iff there is a sequence of points of $A$ diverging to $x$
(c) the point $x \in \overline{A}$, closure of $A \subset X$ iff there is a sequence of points of $A$ converging to 0
(d) None of the above

**77.** The uniform topology on $R^3$ is finer than the product topology and

(a) they are same, if $J$ is infinite
(b) they are different, if $J$ is infinite
(c) they are different, if $J$ is finite
(d) None of the above

**78.** Let $X$ and $Y$ are topological spaces. A function $f: X \to Y$ is continuous at $x \in X$

(a) if for every neighbourhood $N$ of $f(x)$, there is a neighbourhood $M$ of $x$ such that $f(N) = M$
(b) if for every neighbourhood $N$ of $f(x)$, there is a neighbourhood $M$ of $x$ such that $f(N) \subset M$
(c) if for some neighbourhood $N$ of $f(x)$, there is a neighbourhood $M$ of $x$ such that $f(N) = M$
(d) None of the above

**79.** Let $(X, T)$ is a topological space, $U \subset X$ is open set

(a) $U$ is a subset of $T$ (b) $U$ is an element of $T$
(c) $U$ is a superset of $T$ (d) None of these

**80.** The product of completely regular spaces is

(a) normal (b) regular
(c) completely regular (d) None of these

**81.** Let $X$ and $Y$ are topological space. A map $h : X \to Y$ is inessential map

(a) if $h$ is homotopic to a constant map
(b) if $h$ is homotopic to a non-constant map
(c) if $h$ is not homotopic to a constant map
(d) None of the above

**82.** Let $X$ and $Y$ be topological spaces. A map $f : X \to Y$ is closed map, if

(a) for every closed set $A$ of $X$, the set $f(A)$ is closed in $Y$
(b) for every closed set $U$ of $X$, the set $f(U)$ is open in $Y$
(c) for every open set $U$ of $X$, the set $f(U)$ is closed in $Y$
(d) None of the above

**83.** Let $X$ be a set for which a topology $T$ is defined, then

(a) the intersection of the elements of any finite subcollection of $T$ is in $T$
(b) the intersection of the elements of any subcollection of $T$ is in $T$
(c) the intersection of the elements of any finite subcollection of $T$ is not in $T$
(d) None of the above

**84.** Let $X$ be a topological space. Given, an equivalence relation on $X$ such that $x \sim y$, if there is a connected subset of $X$ containing both $x$ and $y$

(a) Then, equivalence classes are called the connected components of $X$
(b) Then, equivalence classes are called the separation of $X$
(c) Then, equivalence classes are called the compact of $X$
(d) None of the above

**85.** Let $f : X \to Y$ also $X$ and $Y$ be metrizable with metrics $d_X$ and $d_Y$, respectively. If given $x \in X$ and $\varepsilon > 0$, there exist $\delta > 0$, such that $d_X(x, y) < \delta \Rightarrow d_Y(f(x), f(y)) < \varepsilon$, then

(a) $f$ is continuous (b) $f$ is discontinuous
(c) $f$ is constant (d) None of these

**86.** Let $X$ be a topological space. A covering of $X$ is called open covering, if

(a) its elements are closed subsets of $X$
(b) its elements are open subsets of $X$
(c) its elements are null sets
(d) None of the above

**87.** Let $X$ be a set for which a topology $T$ is defined, then

(a) the union of the elements of finite subcollection of $T$ is in $T$
(b) the union of the elements of any subcollection of $T$ is in $T$
(c) the union of the elements of any subcollection of $T$ is not in $T$
(d) None of the above

**88.** A subspace of a completely regular space is

(a) normal (b) regular
(c) completely regular (d) None of these

**89.** A topological space $X$ that has a countable basis at each of its points is said to satisfy

(a) the first countability axiom
(b) the second countability axiom
(c) the third countability axiom
(d) the fourth countability axiom

**90.** Every closed interval of real line $R$ is

(a) uncountable (b) countable
(c) disjoint (d) None of these

**91.** Let $X$ and $Y$ are topological spaces. A function $f : X \to Y$ is a continuous function,

(a) if for each open subset $V$ of $Y$, the set $f^{-1}(V)$ is an closed subset of $X$
(b) if for each closed subset $V$ of $Y$, the set $f^{-1}(V)$ is an open subset of $X$
(c) if for each open subset $V$ of $Y$, the set $f^{-1}(V)$ is an open subset of $X$
(d) None of the above

**92.** A topological space $X$ have a countable basis at the point $x$

(a) if there is a countable collection $\{U_n\}_{n \in z}$, of neighbourhood of $x$ such that any neighbourhood $U$ of $x$ contains atleast one of the sets $U_n$
(b) if there is a uncountable collection $\{U_n\}_{n \in z}$, of neighbourhood of $x$ such that any neighbourhood $U$ of $x$ contains none of the sets $U_n$
(c) if there is a countable collection $\{U_n\}_{n \in z}$, of neighbourhood of $x$ such that any neighbourhood $U$ of $x$ contains none of the sets $U_n$
(d) None of the above

**93.** A topological space $X$ is locally path connected iff

(a) for every closed set $U$ of $X$, each path component of $U$ is open in $X$
(b) for every open set $U$ of $X$, each path component of $U$ is open in $X$
(c) for every open set $U$ of $X$, each path component of $U$ is closed in $X$
(d) None of the above

**94.** Two paths $f$ and $f'$, mapping the interval $[0, 1]$ into $X$ are said to be.......$f =_p f'$, if they have the same initial $x_0$ and same final path $x_1$ and if there is continuous map $F : [0, 1] \times [0, 1] \to X$ such that $F(s, 0) = f(s)$ and $F(s, 1) = f'(s)$, $F(0, t) = x_0$ and $F(1, t) = x_1$, for each $s \in I$ and each $t \in [0, 1]$.

(a) homotopic (b) homomorphic
(c) path homotopic (d) None of these

**95.** A subspace of a Hausdorff space is a
(a) hausdorff space (b) closed set
(c) discrete space (d) None of these

**96.** A sequence $\{x_m\}$ of points of $X$ is convergences to a point $x \in X$
(a) if for every neighbourhood $U$ of $x$, there exists positive integer $N$ such that $x_n \in U$ for all $n \geq N$
(b) if for every neighbourhood $U$ of $x$, there exists positive integer $N$ such that $x_n \in U$ for all $n < N$
(c) if for every neighbourhood $U$ of $x$, there exists positive integer $N$ such that $x_n \in U$ for all $n = N$
(d) None of the above

**97.** Let $X$ be a topological space. Suppose that, collection $C$ is a collection of open sets of $X$ such that each $x \in X$ and each open set $U$ of $X$, there is an element $\mathbb{C} \in C$ such that $x \in C \subset U$.
(a) Then, $\mathbb{C}$ is a not a basis for the topology of $X$
(b) Then, $\mathbb{C}$ is a basis for the topology of $X$
(c) Then, $\mathbb{C}$ is a sub-basis for the topology of $X$
(d) None of the above

**98.** A topological space $X$ is locally connected iff
(a) for every open set $U$ of $X$, each component of $U$ is closed in $X$
(b) for every closed set $U$ of $X$, each component of $U$ is open in $X$
(c) for every open set $U$ of $X$, each component of $U$ is open in $X$
(d) None of the above

**99.** If $f$ and $f'$ are continuous map of the space $X$ into space $Y$, then $f$......to is $f'(f = f')$, if there is one continuous map $F : X \times [0, 1] \to Y$ such that $F(x, 0) = f(x)$ and $F(x, 1) = f'(x)$ for each $x \in X$.
(a) homotopic (b) homomorphic
(c) path homotopic (d) None of these

**100.** Let $X$ be a Hausdorff space. Then, $X$ is locally compact at $x$ iff
(a) for every neighbourhood $U$ of $x$, there is a neighbourhood $V$ of $x$, such that $\overline{V}$ is compact and $\overline{V} \subset \overline{U}*$
(b) for some neighbourhood $U$ of $x$, there is a neighbourhood $V$ of $x$, such that $\overline{V}$ is compact and $\overline{V} = \overline{U}$
(c) for some neighbourhood $U$ of $x$, there is a neighbourhood $V$ of $x$, such that $\overline{V}$ is compact and $\overline{V} \subset U$
(d) None of the above

**101.** If $X$ is an ordered set in the order topology and if $Y$ is an interval or a ray in $X$,
(a) then the subspace topology and order topology on $Y$ are same
(b) then the subspace topology and order topology on $Y$ are different
(c) then the subspace topology and order topology on $Y$ are open
(d) None of the above

**102.** If $X$ is a topological space and $A$ is a set, if $p : X \to A$ is surjective map, then there exists exactly one topology $T$ on $A$ relative to which $p$ is a quotient map and this topology is called
(a) quotient topology induced by $p$
(b) hausdorff topology
(c) discrete topology
(d) None of the above

**103.** Given, an index set $J$ and $\bar{x} = (x_\alpha)_{\alpha \in J}$ and $\bar{y} = (y_\alpha)_{\alpha \in J}$ of $R^J$, $\bar{d}(x_\alpha, y_\alpha) = \min\{d(x_\alpha, y_\alpha), 1\}$ the standard bounded metric on $R$. The uniform metric on $R^J$ is defined as
(a) $\bar{\rho}(\bar{x}, \bar{y}) = \{\bar{d}(x_\alpha, y_\alpha), \alpha \in J\}$
(b) $\bar{\rho}(\bar{x}, \bar{y}) = \text{lub}\{\bar{d}(x_\alpha, y_\alpha), \alpha \in J\}$
(c) $\bar{\rho}(\bar{x}, \bar{y}) = \text{glb}\{\bar{d}(x_\alpha, y_\alpha), \alpha \in J\}$
(d) None of the above

**104.** Let $X$ be the union of two open sets $U$ and $V$. Suppose that, $U \cap V$ can be written as the union of two disjoint open sets $A$ and $B$. Let $a \in A$ and $b \in B$ and $a$ and $b$ are joined by paths in $U$ and in $V$, then
(a) $\pi_i(X, a)$ is not zero (b) $\pi_i(X, a)$ is zero
(c) $\pi_i(X, a)$ is positive (d) None of these

**105.** Let $B$ and $B'$ be basis for the topologies $T$ and $T'$, respectively on $X$. Then, $T'$ is finer than $T$ is equivalent to
(a) for each $x \in X$ and each basis element $\mathbb{B} \in B$ containing $x$, there is a basis element $\mathbb{B}' \in B'$ such that $x \in \mathbb{B}' \subset B$.
(b) for some $x \in X$ and some basis element $\mathbb{B} \in B$ containing $x$, there is a basis element $\mathbb{B}' \in B'$ such that $x \in \mathbb{B}' \subset B$
(c) for $x \in X$ and basis element $\mathbb{B} \in B$ containing $x$, there is a basis element $\mathbb{B}' \in B'$ such that $x \in \mathbb{B}' \subset B$
(d) None of the above

**106.** A topological space $X$ is normal
(a) if for each pair $A, B, A \cap B = \phi$ of open sets of $X$, there exist disjoint open sets $O_1$ and $O_2$, $O_1 \cap O_2 \neq \phi$, such that $A \subset O_1$ and $B \subset O_2$
(b) if for each pair $A, B, A \cap B \neq \phi$ of closed sets of $X$, there exist disjoint open sets $O_1$ and $O_2$, $O_1 \cap O_2 \neq \phi$, such that $A \subset O_1$ and $B \subset O_2$
(c) if for each pair $A, B, A \cap B = \phi$ of closed sets of $X$, there exist non-disjoint open sets $O_1$ and $O_2$, $O_1 \cap O_2 = \phi$, such that $A \subset O_1$ and $B \subset O_2$
(d) None of the above

**107.** Let $X = U \cup V$, $U$ and $V$ are open in $X$ and $U \cap V$ is path connected. Let $x_0 \in U \cap V$. If both inclusions $i : (U, x_0) \to (X, x_0)$ and $j : (V_0, x_0) \to (X, x_0)$ induce zero homeomorphisms of fundamental groups, then $\pi_1(X, x_0) = 0$.
(a) Locally metrizable theorem
(b) Smirnov metrization theorem
(c) Special van Kampen theorem
(d) None of the above

**108.** Let $X$ be a locally compact Hausdorff space which is not compact. Let $Y$ be the one point compactification of $X$. Then,

(a) $Y$ is compact Hausdorff space
(b) $X$ is subspace of $Y$
(c) the set $Y$-$X$ consists of a single point
(d) All of the above

**109.** The cartesian product of connected topological space is

(a) connected (b) separable
(c) disconnected (d) None of these

**110.** Let $X$ and $Y$ be topological spaces. A map $f : X \to Y$ is open map, if

(a) for every open set $U$ of $X$, the set $f(U)$ is open in $Y$
(b) for every closed set $U$ of $X$, the set $f(U)$ is open in $Y$
(c) for every open set $U$ of $X$, the set $f(U)$ is closed in $Y$
(d) None of the above

**111.** Standard bounded metric (corresponding to $d$) is defined as

(a) let $X$ be a metric space with metric $d$ and $\overline{d} : X \times X \to R$ and $\overline{d}(x, y) = \max\{d(x, y), 1\}$
(b) let $X$ be a metric space with metric $d$ and $\overline{d} : X \times X \to R$ and $\overline{d}(x, y) = \{d(x, y), 1\}$
(c) let $X$ be a metric space with metric $d$ and $\overline{d} : X \times X \to R$ and $\overline{d}(x, y) = \min\{d(x, y), 1\}$
(d) None of the above

**112.** Brouwer theorem on invariance of domain for $R^2$ states

(a) if $U$ is an closed subset of $R^2$ and $f : U \to R^2$ is continuous and injective, then $f(U)$ is open in $R^2$
(b) if $U$ is an open subset of $R^2$ and $f : U \to R^2$ is discontinuous and injective, then $f(U)$ is open in $R^2$
(c) if $U$ is open subset of $R^2$ and $f : U \to R^2$ is continuous and injective, then $f(U)$ is open in $R^2$
(d) None of the above

**113.** If $(X, T)$ is a topological space. Then,

(a) $X$ is open
(b) $X$ is discrete
(c) $X$ is closed
(d) None of the above

**114.** If one point sets are closed in topological space $X$. Then, $X$ is regular, if

(a) for each pair consisting of a point $x$ and a closed set $B$ disjoint from $x$, there exist disjoint open sets containing $x$ and $B$ respectively
(b) for each pair consisting of a point $x$ and a open set $B$ disjoint from $x$, there exist disjoint closed sets containing $x$ and $B$ respectively
(c) for each pair consisting of a point $x$ and a open set $B$ disjoint from $x$, there exist disjoint closed sets not containing $x$ and $B$ respectively
(d) None of the above

**115.** A space $X$ is metrizable iff it is para compact and locally metrizable.

(a) Locally metrizable theorem
(b) Smirnov metrization theorem
(c) Special van Kampen theorem
(d) None of the above

**116.** The path components of topological space $X$ are path connected disjoint subsets of $X$, whose

(a) intersection is $X$, such that each path connected subset of $X$ intersects only one of them
(b) union is $X$, such that each path connected subset of $X$ intersects all of them
(c) union is $X$, such that each path connected subset of $X$ intersects only one of them
(d) None of the above

**117.** If $Y$ is a subspace of $X$. Then, set $A$ is closed in $Y$ iff

(a) it is equal to the intersection of a open set of $X$ with $Y$
(b) it is equal to the union of a closed set of $X$ with $Y$
(c) it is equal to the intersection of a closed set of $X$ with $Y$
(d) None of the above

**118.** The product of two Hausdorff spaces is a

(a) Hausdorff space (b) closed set
(c) discrete space (d) None of these

**119.** Let $\overline{x} \in R^n$, the square metric $\rho$ is defined as

(a) $\rho(\overline{x}, \overline{y}) = \min\{|x_1 - y_1|, \ldots, |x_n - y_n|\}$
(b) $\rho(\overline{x}, \overline{y}) = \max\{|x_1 - y_1|, \ldots, |x_n - y_n|\}$
(c) $\rho(\overline{x}, \overline{y}) = \{|x_1 - y_1|, \ldots, |x_n - y_n|\}$
(d) None of the above

**120.** Borsuk theorem states

(a) Let $X$ be a compact subset of $R^2$. If 0 does not lies in a bounded component $C$ of $R^2 - X$, then the inclusion map $j : X \to R^2 - 0$ is essential (and conversely).
(b) Let $X$ be a compact subset of $R^2$. If 0 lies in a bounded component $C$ of $R^2 - X$, then the inclusion map $j : X \to R^2 - 0$ is essential (and conversely).
(c) Let $X$ be a compact subset of $R^2$. If 0 lies in a bounded component $C$ of $R^2 - X$, then the inclusion map $j : X \to R^2 - 0$ is not essential (and conversely).
(d) None of the above

**121.** If $B$ is a basis for the topology of $X$ and $C$ is a basis for the topology of $Y$, then

(a) the collection $D = \{\mathbb{B} \times C \mid \mathbb{B} \in B \text{ and } \mathbb{C} \in C\}$ is a basis for the topology of $X \times Y$
(b) the collection $D = \{\mathbb{B} \times C \mid \mathbb{B} \in B \text{ and } \mathbb{C} \in C\}$ is not a basis for the topology of $X \times Y$
(c) the collection $D = \{\mathbb{B} \times C \mid \mathbb{B} \in B \text{ and } \mathbb{C} \in C\}$ is not a basis for the topology of $X \times X$.
(d) None of the above

**122.** Neighbourhood of $x$ is
(a) an open set $U$ containing $x$
(b) a null set
(c) a closed set $U$ containing $x$
(d) None of the above

**123.** Which of the following is true?
(a) If $p : X \to Y$ is a quotient map and if $Z$ is a locally compact Hausdorff space, then the map $\pi = p \times t_2 : X \times Z \to Y \times Z$ is a quotient map.
(b) Let $p : A \to B$ and $q : C \to D$ be quotient maps. If $B$ and $C$ are locally compact Hausdorff spaces, then $p \times q : A \times C \to B \times D$ is a quotient map.
(c) Both (a) and (b)
(d) None of the above

**124.** $X$ is locally compact,
(a) if topological space $X$ is locally compact at each $x \in X$
(b) if topological space $X$ is locally compact at some $x \in X$
(c) if topological space $X$ is locally compact at none $x \in X$
(d) None of the above

**125.** Let $X$ be a topological space $A, B \subset X$, $f : X \to [0, 1]$ a continuous function such that $f(A) = \{0\}$ and $f(B) = \{1\}$, then
(a) sets $A$ and $B$ are separated by continuous function
(b) sets $A$ and $B$ are separated by discontinuous function
(c) sets $A$ and $B$ are separated by step function
(d) None of the above

**126.** Every simple ordered set is a Hausdorff space in the
(a) order topology
(b) discrete topology
(c) non-ordered topology
(d) None of the above

**127.** The Euclidean metric $d$ on $R^n$ is defined as
(a) $d(\bar{x}, \bar{y}) = [(x_1 - y_1)^2 + (x_2 - y_2)^2 + \ldots + (x_n - y_n)^2]$
(b) $d(\bar{x}, \bar{y}) = [(x_1 - y_1)^2 + (x_2 - y_2)^2 + \ldots + (x_n - y_n)^2]^2$
(c) $d(\bar{x}, \bar{y}) = [(x_1 - y_1)^2 + (x_2 - y_2)^2 + \ldots + (x_n - y_n)^2]^{1/2}$
(d) None of the above

**128.** Homotopy existence lemma states
(a) Let $X$ and $X \times [0, 1]$ be normal, let $A$ be a closed subset of $X$. If $f : A \to R^2 - 0$ is continuous map and $f$ is inessential, then $f$ can be extended to a continuous map $g : X \to R^2 - 0$.
(b) Let $X$ and $X \times [0, 1]$ be normal, let $A$ be a open subset of $X$. If $f : A \to R^2 - 0$ is discontinuous map and $f$ is inessential, then $f$ can be extended to a continuous map $g : X \to R^2 - 0$.
(c) Let $X$ and $X \times [0, 1]$ be normal, let $A$ be a closed subset of $X$. If $f : A \to R^2 - 0$ is continuous map and $f$ is inessential, then $f$ cannot be extended to a continuous map $g : X \to R^2 - 0$.
(d) None of the above

**129.** A topological space $X$ is sequentially compact,
(a) if every sequence in a topological space has a convergent subsequence
(b) if some sequence in a topological space has a convergent subsequence
(c) if no sequence in a topological space has a convergent subsequence
(d) None of the above

**130.** Let $(X, T)$ is a given topological space, $A \subset X$, then closure of $A$
(a) is the intersection of all closed sets containing $A$
(b) is the union of all closed sets containing $A$
(c) is the intersection of all open sets containing $A$
(d) None of the above

**131.** A topological space $X$ is called path connected, if
(a) each pair of points of $X$ can be joined by a path in $X$
(b) some pair of points of $X$ can be joined by a path in $X$
(c) some pair of points of $X$ cannot be joined by a path in $X$
(d) None of the above

**132.** Bing metrization theorem states
(a) A space $X$ is metrizable iff it is regular and has a basis that is countably locally discrete.
(b) A space $X$ is metrizable iff it is non-regular and has a basis that is not countably locally discrete.
(c) Every para compact space $X$ is normal.
(d) Every closed subspace of a para compact space is para compact.

**133.** A product of regular spaces is
(a) Hausdorff
(b) disjoint
(c) regular
(d) None of these

**134.** Let $X$ be a Hausdorff space, $A \subset X$. Then, a point $x$ is a limit point of $A$ iff
(a) every neighbourhood of $x$ contains infinitely many points of $A$
(b) every neighbourhood of $x$ contains finitely many points of $A$
(c) every neighbourhood of $x$ contains no points of $A$
(d) None of the above

**135.** Given, $\bar{x} \in R^n$, then norm of $\bar{x}$ is
(a) $|\bar{x}| = (x_1^2 + x_2^2 + \ldots + x_n^2)^{1/2}$
(b) $|\bar{x}| = (x_1^2 + x_2^2 + \ldots + x_n^2)^2$
(c) $|\bar{x}| = (x_1^2 + x_2^2 + \ldots + x_n^2)$
(d) None of the above

**136.** Let $A$ and $B$ be closed connected subsets of $S^2$, whose intersection consists of precisely two points.
(a) Then, $A \cup B$ separates $S^2$
(b) Then, $A \cap B$ separates $S^2$
(c) Then, $A - B$ separates $S^2$
(d) None of the above

**137.** Every metrizable space is
(a) Hausdorff (b) disjoint
(c) normal (d) None of these

**138.** Let $(X, T)$ is a given topological space, $A \subset X$, then interior of $A$
(a) is the union of all open sets contained in $A$
(b) is the intersection of all open sets contained in $A$
(c) is the union of all closed sets contained in $A$
(d) None of the above

**139.** Let $X$ be a topological space and $x, y \in X$. The path in $X$ from $x$ to $y$ is
(a) a continuous map $f:[a, b] \to X$ of some open interval $(a, b)$ in the real line into $X$, such that $f(a) = x$ and $f(b) = y$
(b) a discontinuous map $f:[a, b] \to X$ of some closed interval $(a, b)$ in the real line into $X$, such that $f(a) = f(b)$
(c) a continuous map $f:[a, b] \to X$ of some closed interval $[a, b]$ in the real line into $X$, such that $f(a) = x$ and $f(b) = y$
(d) a continuous map $f:[a, b] \to X$ of some open interval $(a, b)$ in the real line into $X$, such that $f(a) = x$ and $f(b) = y$

**140.** Let $X$ be metrizable space. Then, $X$ has a basis that is
(a) countable locally finite
(b) uncountable locally finite
(c) countable locally infinite
(d) uncountable locally infinite

**141.** A topological space $X$ is limit point compact,
(a) if every disjoint subset of $X$ has a limit point
(b) if every infinite subset of $X$ has a limit point
(c) if every finite subset of $X$ has a limit point
(d) None of the above

**142.** A subset of a topological space is closed iff
(a) it contains none of its limit points
(b) it contains all its limit points
(c) it contains some of its limit points
(d) None of the above

**143.** A topological space $X$ is totally disconnected, if
(a) its only connected subsets are one-point set
(b) its only connected subsets are empty set
(c) its only connected subsets are set $X$ itself
(d) its only connected subsets are empty set and set $X$ itself

**144.** Jordan separation theorem states
(a) Let $C$ be a simple closed curve in $S^2$. Then, $S^2 - C$ is not connected
(b) Let $C$ be a simple closed curve in $S^2$. Then, $S^2 - C$ is connected
(c) Let $C$ be a simple open curve in $S^2$. Then, $S^2 - C$ is not connected.
(d) None of the above

**145.** Every compact Hausdorff space is
(a) Hausdorff (b) disjoint
(c) normal (d) None of these

**146.** A subset $A$ of topological space $X$ is closed set, if
(a) $(X - A)$ is open (b) $A$ is closed
(c) $A$ is open (d) None of these

**147.** Which of the following statement is true?
(a) The product of two quotient map need not be a quotient map.
(b) The product of two quotient map is a quotient map.
(c) The product of one quotient map need not be a quotient map.
(d) None of the above

**148.** Let $X$ be a metrizable space. If a is an open covering of $X$, then there is a collection $D$ of subsets of $X$ such that
(a) $D$ is an open covering of $X$
(b) $D$ is countably locally finite
(c) $D$ is a refinement of a
(d) All of the above

**149.** A subspace of regular space is
(a) Hausdorff (b) disjoint
(c) regular (d) None of these

**150.** Let $A$ be a subset of topological space $X$ and $A'$ be the set of all limit points. Then, closure of $A$
(a) $\overline{A} = A \cup A$ (b) $\overline{A} = A \cap \overline{A}'$
(c) $\overline{A} = A - \overline{A}'$ (d) None of these

**151.** Let $X$ be a topological space. A space $X$ is connected iff
(a) the only subset of $X$ that are both open and closed in $X$ are empty set and $X$ itself
(b) the only subset of $X$ that are both open but not closed in $X$ are empty set and $X$ itself
(c) the only subset of $X$ that are closed in $X$ are empty set only
(d) the only subset of $X$ that are both open and closed in $X$ are $X$ itself only

**152.** Brouwer theorem on invariance of domain for $R^2$ states
(a) If $U$ is a closed subset of $R^2$ and $f: U \to R^2$ is continuous and injective, then $f(U)$ is open in $R^2$ and $f$ is an imbedding
(b) If $U$ is an open subset of $R^2$ and $f: U \to R^2$ is discontinuous and injective, then $f(U)$ is open in $R^2$ and $f$ is an imbedding
(c) If $U$ is an open subset of $R^2$ and $f: U \to R^2$ is continuous and injective, then $f(U)$ is open in $R^2$ and $f$ is an imbedding
(d) None of the above

**153.** The components of topological space $X$ are connected disjoint subsets of $X$, whose
(a) intersection is $X$ such that each connected subset of $X$ intersects only one of them

(b) union is $X$ such that each connected subset of $X$ intersects all of them

(c) union is $X$ such that each connected subset of $X$ intersects only one of them

(d) None of the above

**154.** If $X$ is a topological space with topology $T$ and $Y \subset X$, the collection $T_y = \{Y \cap U | U \in T\}$ is a topology on $Y$. Then, $(Y, T_y)$ is called ..... of $(X, T)$.

(a) subspace topology (b) discrete topology
(c) super space topology (d) None of these

**155.** Let $X$ and $Y$ be topological spaces, $p : X \to Y$ be a surjective map. The map $p$ is said to be a quotient map

(a) provided a subset $U \subset Y$ is closed in $Y$ iff $p^{-1}(U)$ is open in $X$

(b) provided a subset $U \subset Y$ is open in $Y$ iff $p^{-1}(U)$ is closed in $X$

(c) provided a subset $U \subset Y$ is open in $Y$ iff $p^{-1}(U)$ is open in $X$

(d) None of the above

**156.** A collection $B$ is countably locally discrete (σ-locally discrete), if

(a) it is equal to a countable intersection of locally discrete collections

(b) it is equal to a countable union of locally discrete collections

(c) it is equal to a uncountable union of locally discrete collections

(d) None of the above

**157.** A subspace of normal space is

(a) need not normal (b) Hausdorff
(c) Normal (d) need not Hausdorff

**158.** If $A$ is a subset of topological space, $X$. Let $x \in \overline{A}$, closure of $A$ in $X$ if

(a) every open set $U$ containing $x$, intersects $A$

(b) every open set $U$ that does not contain $x$, intersects $A$

(c) every closed set $U$ containing $x$, intersects $A$

(d) None of the above

**159.** Let $X$ be a topological space. The space $X$ is called connected,

(a) if there does not exist a separation of $X$

(b) if there exist a separation of $X$

(c) if there exist some separation of $X$

(d) None of the above

**160.** Let $a, b \in S^2$ and $A$ be a compact space. Let $f : A \to S^2 - a - b$ be continuous map. Then, $f$ is inessential.

(a) If $a$ and $b$ lie in same component of $S^2 - f(A)$.

(b) If $a$ and $b$ lie in different component of $S^2 - f(A)$.

(c) If $a$ and $b$ does not lie in same component of $S^2 - f(A)$.

(d) None of the above

**161. Weierstrass M-test** Let $f_n : X \to R$ be a sequence of functions from topological space $X$ into $R$ and $s_n(x) = \sum_{i=1}^{n} f_i(x)$. The sequence $\{s_n\}$ converges uniformly to a function $s$, if

(a) $|f_i(x)| \leq b_i$ for all $x \in X$ and all $i = 1, ..., n$

(b) the series $\Sigma b_i$ is convergent

(c) both (a) and (b)

(d) None of the above

**162.** If $A$ is a subspace of topological space $X$, the inclusion function $j : A \to X$ is

(a) continuous function (b) discontinuous function
(c) inverse function (d) None of these

**163.** $X$ is locally compact Hausdorff iff

(a) a space $X$ is homeomorphic to an open subset of a compact Hausdorff space

(b) a space $X$ is homeomorphic to an closed subset of a compact Hausdorff space

(c) a space $X$ is homeomorphic to a null subset of a compact Hausdorff space

(d) None of the above

**164.** A collection $a$ of subsets of topological space $X$ is locally discrete,

(a) if each point of $X$ has neighbourhood that intersects atmost one element of $a$

(b) if each point of $X$ has neighbourhood that intersects at all element of $a$

(c) if each point of $X$ has neighbourhood that intersects no one element of $a$

(d) None of the above

**165.** Product of normal spaces is

(a) need not normal (b) Hausdorff
(c) normal (d) need not Hausdorff

**166.** If $X$ and $Y$ are topological spaces. The product topology on $X \times Y$ is

(a) topology having as basis the collection $B$ of all sets of the form $U \times V$, where $U$ is a closed subset of $X$ and $V$ is a closed subset of $Y$

(b) topology having as basis the collection $B$ of all sets of the form $U \times V$, where $U$ is an open subset of $X$ and $V$ is an open subset of $Y$

(c) topology having as basis the collection $B$ of all sets of the form $U \times V$, where $U$ and $V$ are null sets

(d) None of the above

**167.** Let $X$ be a topological space. A separation of $X$

(a) is a pair $U$, $V$ of disjoint non-empty open subsets of $X$, whose union is $X$

(b) is a pair $U$, $V$ of non-disjoint empty open subsets of $X$, whose union is $X$

(c) is a pair $U$, $V$ of disjoint empty closed subsets of $X$, whose union is $X$

(d) is a pair $U$, $V$ of non-empty closed subsets of $X$, whose intersection is $X$

**168.** A simple closed curve is
(a) a space homeomorphic to the circle $S'$
(b) not space homeomorphic to the circle $S'$
(c) both (a) and (b)
(d) Neither (a) nor (b)

**169.** Every regular space with countable basis is
(a) Hausdorff (b) disjoint
(c) normal (d) None of these

**170.** If $A$ is a subset of topological space $X$. Suppose, $B$ is a basis for $X$, then $x \in \bar{A}$ iff
(a) every basis element $\mathbb{B} \in B$, containing $x$ does not intersects $A$
(b) every basis element $\mathbb{B} \in B$, containing $x$ intersects $A$
(c) every basis element $\mathbb{B} \in B$, containing $x$ is disjoint to $A$
(d) None of the above

**171.** A subset C of a topological space $X$ is saturated (with respect to the surjective map $p: X \to Y$), if
(a) C contains every set $p^{-1}(\{y\})$ that it intersects
(b) C contains some set $p^{-1}(\{y\})$ that it intersects
(c) C contains every set $p^{-1}(\{y\})$ that it does not intersects
(d) None of the above

**172.** Let $A \subset X$ a topological space and $f: A \to Z$ be a continuous map of $A$ into Hausdorff space $Z$.
(a) there is atmost one extension of $f$ to a continuous function $g: \bar{A} \to Z$
(b) there is at no extension of $f$ to a continuous function $g: \bar{A} \to Z$
(c) every continuous real-valued function of X can be uniquely extended to real valued function of $\beta(X)$
(d) every bounded real valued function of X can be uniquely extended to real-valued function of $\beta(X)$

**173.** Product of Hausdorff space is
(a) Hausdorff (b) disjoint
(c) normal (d) None of these

**174.** Let $X$ be a set; let $B$ be a basis for a topology $T$ on $X$. Then, $T$ is equal to
(a) the collection of all intersection of elements of $B$
(b) the collection of all unions of elements of $B$
(c) the collection of all sum of elements of $B$
(d) None of the above

**175.** Let $f: X \to Y$ be continuous, $f(x_0) = y_0$. If $f$ is homotopy equivalence, then
(a) $f: \pi_i(X, x_0) \to \pi i(Y, y_0)$ is
(b) zero homoeomorphism
(c) isomorphism
(d) homeomorphism

**176.** The uniform topology on $R^3$ is ..... than the product topology. They are different if $J$ is infinite.
(a) finer (b) strictly finer
(c) not finer (d) None of these

**177.** Let $X$ be a topological space. Given, an equivalence relation on $X$ such that $x \sim y$, if there is a connected subset of $X$ containing both $x$ and $y$.
(a) Then, equivalence classes are called the components of $X$.
(b) Then, equivalence classes are called the separation of $X$.
(c) Then, equivalence classes are called the compact of $X$.
(d) None of the above

**178.** Let $X$ be a set with order relation. The collection $B$ is a basis for topology on $X$ and is called order topology. If $B$ basis for $X$ is a collection of all sets of the form
(a) all open intervals $(a, b) \in X$
(b) all intervals of the form $[a_0, b]$, $a_0$ is the smallest element (if any) of $X$
(c) all intervals of the form $(a, b_0]$, $b_0$ is the largest element (if any) of $X$
(d) All of the above

**179.** Which one of the statement is true?
(a) A subspace of a topological space having a countable dense subset need not have a countable dense subset.
(b) A subspace of a topological space having a countable dense subset have a countable dense subset.
(c) Both (a) and (b)
(d) Neither (a) nor (b)

**180.** Let $X$ be completely regular, $\beta(X)$ be its Stone-Cech compactification. Then,
(a) every continuous real-valued function of $X$ can be uniquely extended to real-valued function of $\beta(X)$
(b) every bounded real-valued function of $X$ can be uniquely extended to real-valued function of $\beta(X)$
(c) every bounded continuous real-valued function of $X$ can be uniquely extended to continuous real-valued function of $\beta(X)$
(d) None of the above

**181.** A topological space $X$ is completely regular,
(a) if one point sets are open in $X$ and if every $a \in X$, every open set $\mathbb{B}$, $a \in B$, there exists a continuous function $f: X \to [0, 1]$ such that $f(a) = f(B) = \{1\}$
(b) if one point sets are closed in $X$ and if every $a \in X$, every closed set $\mathbb{B}$, $a \in B$, there exists a continuous function $f: X \to [0, 1]$, such that $f(a) = 0$ and $f(B) = \{1\}$
(c) if one point sets are closed in $X$ and if every $a \in X$, every closed set $\mathbb{B}$, $a \in B$, there exists a discontinuous function $f: X \to [0, 1]$ such that $f(a) = f(B)$
(d) None of the above

**182.** Urysohn metrization theorem states
(a) Let $A$ and $B$ closed disjoint subsets of the normal space $X$. There exists a continuous function $f: X \to [0, 1]$ such that $f^{-1}(\{0\}) = A$ and $f(B) = \{1\}$ iff $A$ is a $G_\delta$ set in $X$.

(b) Any continuous map of $A$ into the closed interval $[a, b]$ of $R$ may be extended to a continuous map of all of $X$ into $[a, b]$.
(c) Every regular space $X$ with countable basis is metrizable.
(d) None of the above

**183.** Let $h: X \to Y$ and $h(x_0) = y_0$. If $h$ is homotopic to a constant map, then
(a) $h$ is the zero homeomorphism
(b) $h$ is the isomorphism
(c) $h$ is the homeomorphism
(d) None of the above

**184.** The topologies on $R^n$ induced by the euclidean metric $d$ and the square metric $\rho$ are ... as the product topology on $R^n$.
(a) same (b) dissimilar
(c) different (d) None of these

**185.** If $X$ is a topological space and locally path connected, then
(a) the components and the path components of $X$ are different
(b) the components and the path components of $X$ are the same
(c) the components and the path components of $X$ are the disjoint
(d) None of the above

**186.** If $X$ is any set, $T$ is a collection of all subsets of $X$, then topology $(X, T)$ is
(a) a discrete topology
(b) trivial topology
(c) indiscrete topology
(d) None of the above

**187.** If topological space has a countable basis. Then,
(a) every open covering of $X$ contains a countable subcollection covering $X$
(b) there exist a countable subset of $X$, which is dense in $X$
(c) both (a) and (b)
(d) either (a) or (b)

**188.** Compactification $Y_1$ and $Y_2$ of topological space $X$ are equivalent,
(a) if there is a homeomorphism $h: Y_1 \to Y_2$ such that $h(x) = x$ for every $x \in X$
(b) if there is a homeomorphism $h: Y_1 \to Y_2$ such that $h(x) = x$ for some $x \in X$
(c) if there is a homeomorphism $h: Y_1 \to Y_2$ such that $h(x) =$ constant $x$ for every $x \in X$
(d) None of the above

**189.** Let $X$ be a topological space. Let one point sets in $X$ be closed. $X$ is .... iff given a closed set $A$ and open set $U$, $A \subset U$, there is an open set $V$, $A \subset V$ such that $\overline{V} \subset U$.
(a) regular (b) disjoint
(c) normal (d) None of these

**190.** If $(X, T)$ is a topological space. Then,
(a) arbitrary intersections of closed sets are open
(b) arbitrary intersections of closed sets are closed
(c) arbitrary intersections of open sets are closed
(d) None of the above

**191.** Let $h, k: X \to Y$, $h(x_0) = y_0$ and $k(x_0) = y_1$. If $h$ and $k$ are homotopic, then there is a path $\alpha \in Y$ from $y_0$ to $y_1$ such that $k = \hat{\alpha} oh$. If $y_0 = y_1$ and if the base point $x_0$ remains fixed during the homotopy, then
(a) $h$ is equal to $k$ (b) $h$ is not equal to $k$
(c) $h$ is equal to $k - 1$ (d) None of these

**192.** Let $d$ and $d'$ be two metrics on the set $X$ and let $T$ and $T'$ be the topologies they induce, respectively. Then, $T$ is ..... than $T$ iff for each $x \in X$ and each $\varepsilon > 0$, there exist $\delta > 0$, such that $B_d(x, \delta) \subset B_d(x, \varepsilon)$.
(a) finer (b) strictly finer
(c) not finer (d) None of these

**193.** A space $X$ is locally metrizable, if every $x \in X$ has a neighbourhood $U$ that is metrizable in the subspace topology.
(a) Locally metrizable theorem
(b) Smirnov metrizable theorem
(c) Special van kampen theorem
(d) None of the above

**194.** A topological space $X$ is Hausdorff space, if for each pair $x_1 \neq x_2 \in X$,
(a) there exist neighbourhoods $U_1$ and $U_2$ of $x_1$ and $x_2$, respectively such that $U_1$ and $U_2$ are disjoint
(b) there exist neighbourhoods $U_1$ and $U_2$ of $x_1$ and $x_2$, respectively such that $U_1$ and $U_2$ are not disjoint
(c) there exist no neighbourhoods $U_1$ and $U_2$ of $x_1$ and $x_2$, respectively such that $U_1$ and $U_2$ are not disjoint
(d) None of the above

**195.** Separable space
(a) A topological space having a countable dense subset
(b) A topological space having a countable non-dense subset
(c) A topological space having a uncountable dense subset
(d) None of the above

**196.** A space $X$ is completely regular iff
(a) one-point sets are closed in $X$
(b) for each $x_0 \in X$ and each closed set $A$, $x_0 \notin A$, there is a continuous function $f: X \to [0, 1]$ such that $f(x_0) = 1$ and $f(A) = \{0\}$
(c) both (a) and (b)
(d) either (a) or (b)

**197.** A subspace of Hausdorff space is
(a) Hausdorff (b) regular
(c) normal (d) None of these

**198.** If $(X, T)$ is a topological space. Then,
(a) $\phi$ is open (b) $\phi$ is discrete
(c) $\phi$ is closed (d) None of these

**199.** Let continuous map $f: X \to Y$ is homotopy equivalence and if there is a continuous map $g: Y \to X$ such that *gof* is homotopic to the identity map $i_x$ of $X$ and *fog* is homotopic to the identity map $i_y$ of $Y$.
(a) The map $g$ is homotopy inverse for the map $f$
(b) The map $g$ is not homotopy inverse for the map $f$
(c) The map $g$ is equal to map $f$
(d) None of the above

**200.** Strong form of Urysohn lemma states
(a) Let $A$ and $B$ closed disjoint subsets of the normal space $X$. There exists a continuous function $f: X \to [0, 1]$ such that $f^{-1}(\{0\}) = A$ and $f(B) = \{1\}$ iff $A$ is a $G_\delta$ set in $X$.
(b) Any continuous map of $A$ into the closed interval $[a, b]$ of $R$ may be extended to a continuous map of all of $X$ into $[a, b]$.
(c) Every regular space $X$ with countable basis is metrizable
(d) None of the above

**201.** Let $X$ be a regular space. Every open convering of $X$ has a refinement. If
(a) an open covering of $X$ and countably locally finite
(b) an open covering of $X$ and locally finite
(c) a closed covering of $X$ and locally finite
(d) All of the above

**202.** If $Y$ is a subspace of $X$, $A \subset Y$ and $\overline{A}$ is a closure of $A$ in $X$. Then, closure of $A$ in $Y$
(a) is equal to $A \cap Y$ (b) is equal to $Y$
(c) is equal to $A \cup Y$ (d) None of these

**203.** A subset $Y$ of topological space $X$ is dense in $X$, if
(a) $\overline{Y} = X$ (b) $\overline{Y} \not\subset X$
(c) $Y = X$ (d) None of these

**204.** Tychonoff theorem states
(a) Any arbitrary product of compact spaces is compact in the product topology.
(b) A topological space for which every open covering contains a countable subcovering.
(c) Path connected topological space is connected but converse is not true.
(d) None of the above

**205.** Let $X$ be a topological space. Let one point sets in $X$ be closed. $X$ is ...... iff given a point $x \in X$ and neighbourhood $U$ of $x$, there is a neighbourhood $V$ of $x$ such that $\overline{V} \subset U$.
(a) regular (b) disjoint
(c) normal (d) None of these

**206.** Let $X$ and $Y$ be topological spaces. The constant function $f: X \to Y$, is
(a) continuous function
(b) inverse function
(c) discontinuous function
(d) None of the above

**207.** A continuous map $f: X \to Y$ is homotopy equivalence,
(a) if there is a continuous map $g: Y \to X$ such that *gof* is homotopic to the identity map $i_x$ of $X$ and *fog* is homotopic to the identity map $i_y$ of $Y$.
(b) if there is a discontinuous map $g: Y \to X$ such that *gof* is homotopic to the identity map $i_x$ of $X$ and *fog* is homotopic to the identity map $i_y$ of $Y$.
(c) if there is a constant map $g: Y \to X$ such that *gof* is homotopic to the identity map $i_x$ of $X$ and *fog* is homotopic to the identity map $i_y$ of $Y$.
(d) None of the above

**208.** Set $A$ is a $G_\delta$ set in $X$, if
(a) set $A$ is the intersection of a countable collection of open sets of $X$
(b) set $A$ is the union of a countable collection of open sets of $X$
(c) set $A$ is the intersection of a uncountable collection of closed sets of $X$
(d) set $A$ is the union of a countable collection of closed sets of $X$

**209.** Which of the following is false?
(a) Every para compact space $X$ is normal.
(b) Every closed subspace of a para compact space is para compact.
(c) An arbitrary subspace of a para compact space and product of para compact spaces need not be para compact.
(d) Every metrizable space need not be para compact.

**210.** If $X$ is any set, $T = \{\phi, X\}$, then topology $(X, T)$
(a) a discrete topology (b) trivial topology
(c) indiscrete topology (d) Both (a) and (b)

**211.** A topological space $X$ satisfies .... countability axiom, if $X$ has a countable basis for its topology.
(a) first (b) third
(c) second (d) fourth

**212.** A topological space $X$ is locally compact at $x$,
(a) if there is some compact subspace, $C$ of $X$ that contains a neighbourhood of $x$
(b) if there is some compact subspace, $C$ of $X$ that does not contains a neighbourhood of $x$
(c) if there is no compact subspace, $C$ of $X$ that does not contains a neighbourhood of $x$
(d) None of the above

**213.** Maximum and minimum value theorem states
(a) Let $f: X \to Y$ be continuous, where $Y$ is an ordered set in the order topology. If $X$ is compact, then there $c, d \in X$ such that $f(c) \le f(x) \le f(d)$ for every $x \in X$.
(b) Let $f: X \to Y$ be continuous, where $Y$ is an ordered set in the order topology. If $X$ is compact, then there $c, d \in X$ such that $f(c) = f(x) = f(d)$ for every $x \in X$.

(c) Let $f: X \to Y$ be discontinuous, where $Y$ is unordered set in the order topology. If $X$ is compact, then there $c, d \in X$ such that $f(c) \leq f(x) \leq f(d)$ for every $x \in X$.
(d) None of the above

**214.** If $A$ is a subspace of $X$ and $B$ is a subspace of $Y$, then
(a) product topology on $A \times B$ is the same as the topology $A \times B$ inherits as a subspace of $X \times Y$
(b) product topology on $A \times B$ is the different as the topology $A \times B$ inherits as a subspace of $X \times Y$
(c) product topology on $A \times B$ is the same as the topology $A \times B$
(d) None of the above

**215.** Brouwer theorem on invariance of domain for $R^2$ states
(a) If $U$ is an closed subset of $R^2$ and $f: U \to R^2$ is continuous and injective, then $f$ is an imbedding.
(b) If $U$ is an open subset of $R^2$ and $f: U \to R^2$ is discontinuous and injective, then $f$ is an imbedding.
(c) If $U$ is an open subset of $R^2$ and $f: U \to R^2$ is continuous and injective, then $f$ is an imbedding.
(d) None of the above

**216.** Tietze extension theorem states

Then, Let $X$ be a normal space. Let $A$ be a closed subset of $X$. Then,
(a) any continuous map of $A$ into closed interval $[a, b]$ of $R$ may be extended to a continuous map of all of $X$ into $[a, b]$
(b) any continuous map of $A$ into $R$ may be extended to a continuous map of $X$ into $R$
(c) both (a) and (b)
(d) None of the above

**217.** Let $X$ be a regular space. Every open covering of $X$ has a refinement. If
(a) an open covering of $X$ and countably locally finite
(b) a covering of $X$ and locally finite
(c) a closed covering of $X$ and locally finite
(d) All of the above

**218.** If $(X, T)$ is a topological space. Then,
(a) finite unions of closed sets are closed
(b) finite unions of closed sets are open
(c) finite unions of open sets are closed
(d) None of the above

**219.** A topological space has a countable basis at each of its points is called.... countability axiom.
(a) first (b) third
(c) second (d) fourth

**220.** Let $X$ be a locally compact Hausdorff space which is not compact. Let $Y$ be the one point compactification of $X$. Then,
(a) $Y$ is compact Hausdorff space
(b) the set $Y - X$ consists of a single
(c) $\bar{X} = Y$
(d) All of the above

**221.** Let $X$ be a (non-empty) compact Hausdorff space. If every point of $X$ is a limit point of $X$, then
(a) $X$ is uncountable (b) $X$ is disjoint
(c) $X$ is countable (d) None of these

**222.** Given, $(X, T)$ a topological space and $A \subset X$, a point $x \in X$ is a limit point of $A$,
(a) if every neighbourhood of $x$ intersects $A$ in some point other than $x$
(b) if every neighbourhood of $x$ intersects $A$ in all point other than $x$
(c) if every neighbourhood of $x$ intersects $A$ in some point including $x$
(d) None of the above

**223.** Jordan curve theorem states

Let $C$ be a simple closed curve in $S^2$,
(a) then $S^2 - C$ has precisely two components $W_1$ and $W_2$ of which $C$ is not the common boundary
(b) then $S^2 - C$ has precisely two components $W_1$ and $W_2$ of which $C$ is the common boundary
(c) then $S^2 - C$ has no components $W_1$ and $W_2$ of which $C$ is the common boundary
(d) None of the above

**224.** Urysohn lemma states
(a) Let $X$ be a normal space; $A$ and $B$ are disjoint closed subsets of $X$ and $[a, b]$ closed interval of $R$. Then, there exist a continuous map $f: X \to [a, b]$ such that for every $x \in A$, $f(x) = a$ and for every $x \in B$, $f(x) = b$
(b) Let $X$ be a normal space; $A$ and $B$ are open subsets of $X$ and $[a, b]$ closed interval of $R$. Then, there exist a discontinuous map $f: X \to [a, b]$ such that for every $x \in A$, $f(x) = a$ and for every $x \in B$, $f(x) = b$
(c) Let $X$ be a normal space; $A$ and $B$ are disjoint open subsets of $X$ and $[a, b]$ closed interval of $R$. Then, there exist a discontinuous map $f: X \to [a, b]$ such that for every $x \in A$, $f(x) = a$ and for every $x \in B$, $f(x) = b$
(d) None of the above

**225.** Let $X$ be topological space. An indexed family $\{A_\alpha\}_{\alpha \in J}$ of subsets of $X$ is locally finite indexed family,
(a) if some point of $X$ has a neighbourhood that intersects $A_\alpha$ for infinitely many values of $\alpha$
(b) if each point of $X$ has a neighbourhood that intersects $A_\alpha$ for infinitely many values of $\alpha$
(c) if each point of $X$ has a neighbourhood that intersects $A_\alpha$ for only finitely many values of $\alpha$
(d) None of the above

**226.** If $B$ is a basis for the topology of $X$, then
(a) the collection $B_Y = \{B \cap Y \mid B \in B\}$ is not a basis for the subspace topology on $X$
(b) the collection $B_Y = \{B \cap Y \mid B \in B\}$ is a basis for the subspace topology on $X$
(c) the collection $B_Y = \{B \cap Y \mid B \in B\}$ is a basis for the topology on $X$
(d) None of the above

**227.** A topological space $X$ have a countable basis at $x$,

(a) if there is a countable collection $B$ of neighbourhoods of $x$, such that each neighbourhood of $x$ contains atleast one of the elements of $B$

(b) if there is a collection $B$ of neighbourhood of $x$, such that some neighbourhood of $x$ contains all of the elements of $B$

(c) if there is a countable collection $B$ of neighbourhoods of $x$, such that each neighbourhood of $x$ contains all of the elements of $B$

(d) None of the above

**228.** Uniform continuity theorem states $f$ is uniformly continuous on topological space $X$ and $Y$.

(a) If $f: X \to Y$ is a continuous map of the compact metric space $(X, d_X)$ to the metric space $(Y, d_Y)$.

(b) If $f: X \to Y$ is a discontinuous map of the compact metric space $(X, d_X)$ to the metric space $(Y, d_Y)$.

(c) If $f: X \to Y$ is a continuous map of the non-compact metric space $(X, d_X)$ to the metric space $(Y, d_Y)$.

(d) None of the above

**229.** A subset $A \subset R^n$ is compact iff

(a) it is closed in the Euclidean metric $d$ or square metric $\rho$

(b) is bounded in the Euclidean metric $d$ or square metric $\rho$

(c) Both (a) and (b)

(d) None of the above

**230.** If $Y$ is a subspace of $X$. If $A$ is closed in $Y$ and $Y$ is closed in $X$, then

(a) $A$ is semi-closed in $X$

(b) $A$ is not closed in $X$

(c) $A$ is open in $X$

(d) None of the above

**231.** Non-separation theorem states

(a) Let $A$ be an are in $S^2$. Then, $S^2 - A$ is disconnected.

(b) Let $A$ be an are in $S^2$. Then, $S^2 - A$ is connected.

(c) Let $A$ be an are in $S^2$. Then, $S^2 - A$ is separable.

(d) None of the above

**232.** A topological space $X$ is completely regular,

(a) if one point sets are open in $X$ and if every $a \in X$, every open set $B$, $a \notin B$, there exists a continuous function $f: X \to [0, 1]$ such that $f(a) = 0$ and $f(B) = \{1\}$

(b) if one point sets are closed in $X$ and if every $a \in X$, every closed set $B$, $a \notin B$, there exists a continuous function $f: X \to [0, 1]$ such that $f(a) = 0$ and $f(B) = \{1\}$

(c) if one point sets are closed in $X$ and if every $a \in X$, every closed set $B$, $a \in B$, there exists a discontinuous function $f: X \to [0, 1]$ such that $f(a) = 0$ and $f(B) = \{1\}$

(d) None of the above

**233.** An indexed collection $\{A_\alpha\}$ of subsets of $X$ is point-finite indexed family,

(a) if some $x \in X \Rightarrow x \in A_\alpha$ for infinitely many values of $\alpha$

(b) if each $x \in X \Rightarrow x \in A_\alpha$ for only finitely many values of $\alpha$

(c) if each $x \in X \Rightarrow x \in A_\alpha$ for infinite many values of $\alpha$

(d) if some $x \in X \Rightarrow x \in A_\alpha$ for only finitely many values of $\alpha$

**234.** Let $Y$ be a subspace of $X$. If $U$ is open in $Y$ and $Y$ is open in $X$, then

(a) $U$ is open in $X$

(b) $U$ is null set in $X$

(c) $U$ is closed in $X$

(d) None of the above

**235.** Let $X$ be locally compact Hausdorff space and $Y$ be a subspace of $X$. $Y$ is locally compact,

(a) if $Y$ is closed in $X$

(b) if $Y$ is open in $X$

(c) both (a) and (b)

(d) either (a) or (b)

**236.** A topological space $X$ is countably compact,

(a) if every countable open covering of $X$ contains a infinite subcollection covering $X$

(b) if every countable open covering of $X$ contains a finite subcollection covering $X$

(c) if every countable open covering of $X$ contains no subcollection covering $X$

(d) None of the above

**237.** Every closed interval in real line $R$ is

(a) compact space (b) Hausdorff space

(c) null set (d) None of these

**238.** The lower limit topology $T'$ on real line $R$

(a) is strictly finer than the standard topology $T$

(b) is inferior than the standard topology $T$

(c) is finer than the standard topology $T$

(d) None of the above

**239.** Let $X = U \cup V$, where $U$ and $V$ are open set and $U \cap V = A \cup A' \cup B$, where $A$, $B$, $A'$ are disjoint open sets. Let $a \in A$, $a' \in A'$ and $b \in B$. Suppose that $a$, $a'$ and $b$ are joined by paths in $U$ and in $V$. Then,

(a) $\pi_i(X, a)$ is not cyclic

(b) $\pi_i(X, a)$ is not infinite cyclic

(c) $\pi_i(X, a)$ is infinite cyclic

(d) None of the above

# Exercise 2 (For Part 'C')

**Directions** (Q. Nos. 1-35) *Questions may have one or more than one correct option.*

**1.** Let $a, b, c$ be arbitrary distinct points of the set $R$.

Let $X = \{a, b, c\}$ and $\Im = \{\phi, X, \{a\}, \{b, c\}\}$, then which of the following/s is/are true?

(a) $(X, \Im)$ is a topological space
(b) $(X, \Im)$ is a $T_1$-space
(c) $(X, \Im)$ is a regular space
(d) $(X, \Im)$ is a normal space

**2.** Define topology $\Im$ on $N$ s.t.

(i) $\phi, N \in \Im$
(ii) $A_n \in \Im$, $\forall\, n \in N$, where $A_n = \{1, 2, 3, \ldots, n\}$, then $(N, \Im)$ is

(a) $T_0$-space (b) $T_1$-space
(c) $T_0$ and $T_1$-space (d) Neither $T_0$ nor $T_1$-space

**3.** Let $\{X, \Im\}$ be a finite Hausdorff space and $A \subset X$, then

(a) $A$ is open subset of $X$
(b) $A$ is closed subset of $X$
(c) $A$ is indiscrete space
(d) $A$ is discrete space

**4.** Which of the following/s is/are true?

(a) The real line $R$ with usual topology is a Hausdorff space.
(b) Every discrete space is a Hausdorff space.
(c) Every finite Hausdorff space is discrete space.
(d) Every Hausdorff space is discrete space.

**5.** Which of the following/s is/are correct?

(a) Singleton subset of $T_1$-space is closed.
(b) Every metric space is a Hausdorff space.
(c) Every metric space is normal.
(d) Every metric space is compact Hausdorff space.

**6.** Which of the following/s is/are true?

(a) Every indiscrete space is not connected.
(b) Every indiscrete space is compact.
(c) Every discrete space is connected.
(d) Every discrete space is not compact.

**7.** Let $X = \{a, b, c\}$, $\Im = \{\phi, \{a\}, \{a, b\}, X\}$, then $(X, \Im)$ is a

(a) compact space (b) hausdorff space
(c) connected space (d) disconnected space

**8.** Let $(X, \Im)$ be a product topological space of topological spaces $(X, \Im_1)$ and $(X, \Im_2)$, then

(a) $X_1 \times X_2$ is connected iff both $X_1$ and $X_2$ are connected
(b) $X_1 \times X_2$ is compact iff both $X_1$ and $X_2$ are compact
(c) $X_1 \times X_2$ is second countable space if $X_1$ and $X_2$ are second countable
(d) $X_1 \times X_2$ is a Hausdorff space if $X_1$ and $X_2$ are Hausdorff space

**9.** Let $X$ and $Y$ be topological spaces and $f : X \to Y$ is continuous. Then,

(a) for every subset $A$ of $X$, one has $f(\overline{A}) \subseteq \overline{f(A)}$
(b) for every closed set $B$ of $Y$, the set $f^{-1}(B)$ is closed in $X$
(c) for each $x \in X$ and each neighbourhood $V$ of $f(x)$, there is a neighbourhood $U$ of $x$ such that $f(U) \subset V$
(d) None of the above

**10.** Which of the following(s) is/are correct?

(a) The function $f : \mathbb{R} \to \mathbb{R}$ defined by $f(x) = 3x + 1$ is a homeomorphism.
(b) The function $f : (-1, 1) \to \mathbb{R}$ defined by $f(x) = \dfrac{x}{1 - x^2}$ is a homeomorphism.
(c) A bijective function $f : X \to Y$ can be continuous without being a homeomorphism.
(d) None of the above

**11.** Let $X$, $Y$ and $Z$ be topological spaces, then

(a) if $f : X \to Y$ maps all of $X$ into the single point $y_0$ of $Y$, then $f$ is continuous
(b) if $A$ is a subspace of $X$, the inclusion function $j : A \to X$ is continuous
(c) if $f : X \to Y$ and $g : Y \to Z$ are continuous, then $gof : X \to Z$ is continuous
(d) None of the above

**12.** Let $X$, $Y$ and $Z$ be topological spaces. Then,

(a) if $f : X \to Y$ is continuous and if $A$ is a subspace of $X$, then the restricted function $f/A : A \to Y$ is continuous
(b) the map $f : X \to Y$ is continuous, if $X$ can be written as the union of open sets $U_\alpha$ such that $f/U_\alpha$ is continuous for each $\alpha$
(c) Both (a) and (b) are true
(d) Neither (a) nor (b) is true

**13.** Which of the following(s) is/are correct?

(a) Let $A_\alpha$ be a subspace of $X_\alpha$, for each $\alpha \in J$. Then, $\pi A_\alpha$ is a subspace of $\pi X_\alpha$, if both products are given the box topology or if both products are given the product topology.
(b) If each space $X_\alpha$ is a Hausdorff space, then $\pi X_\alpha$ is a Hausdorff space in both the box and product topologies.
(c) Let $\{X_\alpha\}$ be an indexed family of spaces. Let $A_\alpha \subset X_\alpha$ for each $\alpha$. If $\pi X_\alpha$ is given either the product or the box topology, then

$$\pi \overline{A_\alpha} = \overline{\pi A_\alpha}$$

(d) None of the above

**14.** If $X$ is a topological space and if $f, g : X \to R$ are continuous functions. Then,
(a) $f + g$ is continuous
(b) $f - g$ is continuous
(c) $f \cdot g$ is continuous
(d) $\frac{f}{g}$ is continuous provided $g(x) \neq 0, \forall x$

**15.** Let $\pi_1 : \mathbb{R} \times \mathbb{R} \to \mathbb{R}$ be projection onto the first coordinate. Then,
(a) $\pi_1$ is continuous (b) $\pi_1$ is surjective
(c) $\pi_1$ is open (d) $\pi_1$ is closed

**16.** Let $X$ be the subspace $[0, 1] \cup [2, 3]$ of $\mathbb{R}$ and let $Y$ be the subspace $[0, 2]$ of $\mathbb{R}$. The map $p : X \to Y$ given by

$$p(x) = \begin{cases} x & , x \in [0, 1] \\ x - 1, & x \in [2, 3] \end{cases}$$

Then,
(a) $p$ is surjective map
(b) $p$ is continuous map
(c) $p$ is quotient map
(d) $p$ is closed map

**17.** Which of the following(s) is/are topological group?
(a) $(\mathbb{Z}, +)$
(b) $(\mathbb{R}, +)$
(c) $(\mathbb{R}_+, \bullet)$
(d) $(S^1, \bullet)$, where $S^1$ to be the space of all complex numbers $z$ for which $|z| = 1$

**18.** Which of the following(s) is/are connected?
(a) The subspace $[-1, 1]$ of the real line $\mathbb{R}$.
(b) The subspace Q of rational of real line $\mathbb{R}$.
(c) The subspace $X = \{x \times y \mid y = 0\} \cup \{x \times y \mid x > 0 \text{ and } y = \frac{1}{x}\}$ of plane $\mathbb{R}^2$.
(d) None of the above

**19.** Which of the following(s) is/are true?
(a) The unit space $S^{n-1}$ in $\mathbb{R}^n$ given by $S^{n-1} = \{x \mid \|x\| = 1\}$, if $n > 1$, is path connected.
(b) The ordered square $I_0^2$ is connected but not path connected.
(c) The subset $S = \{x \times \sin(1/x) \mid 0 < x \leq 1\}$ is connected.
(d) None of the above

**20.** Which of the following(s) pairs of topological space is/are homeomorphic?
(a) $(0, 1)$ and $(0, 1]$ (b) $(0, 1)$ and $[0, 1]$
(c) $(0, 1]$ and $[0, 1]$ (d) None of these

**21.** Let $X$ be a topological space. Then,
(a) $X$ is locally connected implies for every open set $U$ of $X$, each component of $U$ is open in $X$
(b) if for every open set $U$ of $X$, each component of $U$ is open in $X$, then $X$ is locally connected
(c) exactly only one of above
(d) neither (a) nor (b) is true

**22.** Let $X$ be a topological space. Then,
(a) $X$ is locally path connected if for every open set $U$ of $X$, each path component of $U$ is open in $X$
(b) $X$ is locally path connected implies for every open set $U$ of $X$, each path component of $U$ is open in $X$
(c) exactly only one of (a) and (b) is true
(d) either (a) or (b) is true

**23.** Which of the following(s) is/are compact?
(a) The real line $\mathbb{R}$.
(b) The subspace $X = \{0\} \cup \{1/n \mid n \in \mathbb{Z}_+\}$ of $\mathbb{R}$.
(c) The interval $(0, 1]$.
(d) None of the above

**24.** Which of the following(s) is/are true?
(a) $(0, 1)$ is compact.
(b) Every closed subspace of compact space is compact.
(c) Every compact subspace of a Hausdorff space is closed.
(d) None of the above

**25.** Which of the following(s) is/are true?
(a) The image of a compact space under a continuous map is compact.
(b) Let $f : X \to Y$ be a bijective continuous function. If $X$ is compact and $Y$ is Hausdorff, then $f$ is a homeomorphism.
(c) The product of finitely many compact space is compact.
(d) None of the above

**26.** Let $X$ be a metrizable space. Then,
(a) $X$ is compact
(b) $X$ is limit point of compact
(c) $X$ is sequentially compact
(d) None of the above

**27.** Let $X$ has a countable basis. Then,
(a) every open covering of $X$ contains a countable subcollection covering $X$
(b) there exists a countable subset of $X$ that is dense in $X$
(c) Either (a) or (b) is true
(d) Neither (a) nor (b) is true

**28.** Let $X$ be a topological space. Let one point sets in $X$ be closed. Then,
(a) $X$ is regular implies given a point $x$ of $X$ and a neighbourhood $U$ of $x$, there is a neighbourhood $V$ of $x$ such that $\overline{V} \subset U$
(b) $X$ is regular if it given a point $x$ of $X$ and a neighbourhood $U$ of $x$, there is a neighbourhood $V$ of $x$ such that $\overline{V} \subset U$
(c) $X$ is normal if given a closed set $A$ and an open set $U$ containing $A$, there is an open set $V$ containing $A$ such that $\overline{V} \subset U$
(d) $X$ is normal implies given a closed set $A$ and an open set $U$ containing $A$, there is an open set $V$ containing $A$ such that $\overline{V} \subset U$

**29.** Which of the following(s) is/are true?
(a) A subspace of a Hausdorff space is Hausdorff.
(b) A product of Hausdorff space is Hausdorff.
(c) A subspace of a regular space is regular.
(d) A product of regular space is regular.

**30.** Let $p: X \to Y$ be a closed continuous surjective map such that $p^{-1}(\{y\})$ is compact for each $y \in Y$. Then,
(a) if $X$ is Hausdorff, then $Y$ is also Hausdorff
(b) if $X$ is regular, then $Y$ is also regular
(c) if $X$ is locally compact, then $Y$ is also locally compact
(d) if $X$ is second countable, then $Y$ is also second countable

**31.** Which of the following(s) is/are true?
(a) Every metrizable space is normal.
(b) Every compact Hausdorff space is normal.
(c) Every well ordered set $X$ is normal in the order topology.
(d) None of the above

**32.** Which of the following(s) mapping is/are homeomorphism?
(a) $f:(1, \infty) \to (0, 1)$, given by
$$f(x) = \frac{1}{x}$$
(b) $f:(1, \infty) \to (a, \infty)$, given by
$$f(x) = ax,\ a > 0$$
(c) $f:(a, \infty) \to (-\infty, -a)$, given by
$$f(x) = -x$$
(d) None of the above

**33.** Which of the following(s) mapping is/are homeomorphism?
(a) $f: R \to \left(-\frac{\pi}{2}, \frac{\pi}{2}\right)$ given by
$$f(x) = \arctan x$$
(b) $f:(a, b) \to (0, 1)$ given by
$$f(x) = \frac{x-a}{x-b},\ a < b$$
(c) $f:[a, b] \to [0, 1]$ given by
$$f(x) = \frac{x-a}{x-b},\ a < b$$
(d) None of the above

**34.** Let $Y$ be a subspace of a space $X$ and let $A$ be a set in $Y$. Then,
(a) $Cl_Y(A) = Cl_X A \cap Y$
(b) $D_Y(A) = D_X(A) \cap Y$
(c) $\text{Int}_Y(A) \supseteq \text{Int}_X A \cap Y$
(d) $Bd_Y A \subset Bd_X A \cap Y$

**35.** Which of the following(s) is/are true?
(a) A subspace of a metric space is a metric space.
(b) A subspace of a second countable space.
(c) A subspace of a first countable space is a first countable space.
(d) None of the above

# Answers

## Exercise 1

| | | | | | | | | | |
|---|---|---|---|---|---|---|---|---|---|
| **1.** (d) | **2.** (d) | **3.** (d) | **4.** (a) | **5.** (d) | **6.** (b) | **7.** (c) | **8.** (a) | **9.** (a) | **10.** (b) |
| **11.** (c) | **12.** (b) | **13.** (a) | **14.** (d) | **15.** (a) | **16.** (d) | **17.** (d) | **18.** (a) | **19.** (d) | **20.** (d) |
| **21.** (d) | **22.** (c) | **23.** (c) | **24.** (c) | **25.** (c) | **26.** (c) | **27.** (a) | **28.** (d) | **29.** (b) | **30.** (a) |
| **31.** (a) | **32.** (d) | **33.** (a) | **34.** (a) | **35.** (b) | **36.** (c) | **37.** (b) | **38.** (a) | **39.** (a) | **40.** (c) |
| **41.** (c) | **42.** (a) | **43.** (a) | **44.** (b) | **45.** (a) | **46.** (b) | **47.** (a) | **48.** (c) | **49.** (a) | **50.** (a) |
| **51.** (a) | **52.** (b) | **53.** (b) | **54.** (a) | **55.** (c) | **56.** (a) | **57.** (c) | **58.** (a) | **59.** (a) | **60.** (d) |
| **61.** (a) | **62.** (a) | **63.** (a) | **64.** (a) | **65.** (a) | **66.** (a) | **67.** (b) | **68.** (b) | **69.** (a) | **70.** (a) |
| **71.** (c) | **72.** (d) | **73.** (a) | **74.** (a) | **75.** (b) | **76.** (a) | **77.** (b) | **78.** (b) | **79.** (a) | **80.** (c) |
| **81.** (a) | **82.** (a) | **83.** (a) | **84.** (a) | **85.** (a) | **86.** (b) | **87.** (b) | **88.** (c) | **89.** (a) | **90.** (a) |
| **91.** (c) | **92.** (a) | **93.** (b) | **94.** (c) | **95.** (a) | **96.** (a) | **97.** (b) | **98.** (c) | **99.** (a) | **100.** (a) |
| **101.** (a) | **102.** (a) | **103.** (b) | **104.** (a) | **105.** (a) | **106.** (b) | **107.** (c) | **108.** (d) | **109.** (a) | **110.** (a) |
| **111.** (c) | **112.** (c) | **113.** (c) | **114.** (a) | **115.** (b) | **116.** (c) | **117.** (c) | **118.** (a) | **119.** (b) | **120.** (b) |
| **121.** (a) | **122.** (a) | **123.** (c) | **124.** (a) | **125.** (a) | **126.** (a) | **127.** (c) | **128.** (a) | **129.** (a) | **130.** (a) |
| **131.** (a) | **132.** (a) | **133.** (c) | **134.** (a) | **135.** (a) | **136.** (a) | **137.** (c) | **138.** (a) | **139.** (c) | **140.** (a) |
| **141.** (b) | **142.** (b) | **143.** (a) | **144.** (a) | **145.** (c) | **146.** (a) | **147.** (a) | **148.** (d) | **149.** (c) | **150.** (a) |
| **151.** (a) | **152.** (c) | **153.** (c) | **154.** (a) | **155.** (c) | **156.** (b) | **157.** (a) | **158.** (a) | **159.** (a) | **160.** (a) |
| **161.** (c) | **162.** (a) | **163.** (a) | **164.** (a) | **165.** (a) | **166.** (b) | **167.** (a) | **168.** (a) | **169.** (c) | **170.** (b) |
| **171.** (a) | **172.** (a) | **173.** (a) | **174.** (b) | **175.** (c) | **176.** (a) | **177.** (a) | **178.** (d) | **179.** (a) | **180.** (c) |
| **181.** (b) | **182.** (c) | **183.** (a) | **184.** (a) | **185.** (b) | **186.** (a) | **187.** (c) | **188.** (a) | **189.** (c) | **190.** (b) |
| **191.** (a) | **192.** (a) | **193.** (b) | **194.** (a) | **195.** (a) | **196.** (c) | **197.** (a) | **198.** (c) | **199.** (a) | **200.** (a) |
| **201.** (d) | **202.** (a) | **203.** (a) | **204.** (a) | **205.** (a) | **206.** (a) | **207.** (a) | **208.** (a) | **209.** (d) | **210.** (c) |
| **211.** (c) | **212.** (a) | **213.** (a) | **214.** (a) | **215.** (c) | **216.** (c) | **217.** (d) | **218.** (a) | **219.** (a) | **220.** (d) |
| **221.** (a) | **222.** (a) | **223.** (b) | **224.** (a) | **225.** (c) | **226.** (b) | **227.** (a) | **228.** (a) | **229.** (c) | **230.** (a) |
| **231.** (b) | **232.** (b) | **233.** (b) | **234.** (a) | **235.** (d) | **236.** (b) | **237.** (a) | **238.** (a) | **239.** (b) | |

## Exercise 2

| | | | | | | | | | |
|---|---|---|---|---|---|---|---|---|---|
| **1.** (a,c,d) | **2.** (a) | **3.** (a,b,d) | **4.** (a,b,c) | **5.** (a,b,c) | **6.** (b,d) | **7.** (a,c) | **8.** (a,b,c,d) | **9.** (a,b,c) | **10.** (a,b,c) |
| **11.** (a,b,c) | **12.** (a,b,c) | **13.** (a,b,c) | **14.** (a,b,c,d) | **15.** (a,b,c) | **16.** (a,b,c) | **17.** (a,b,c,d) | **18.** (a) | **19.** (a,b,c) | **20.** (d) |
| **21.** (a,b) | **22.** (a,b) | **23.** (b) | **24.** (a,b,c) | **25.** (a,b,c) | **26.** (a,b,c) | **27.** (a,b) | **28.** (a,b,c,d) | **29.** (a,b,c,d) | **30.** (a,b,c,d) |
| **31.** (a,b,c) | **32.** (a,b,c) | **33.** (a,b,c) | **34.** (a,b,c,d) | **35.** (a,b,c) | | | | | |

# Hints & Solutions

## Exercise 1

**1.** $\phi$ and $X$ must belong to $T$

**5.** $A, B \in T \Rightarrow A \cup B \in T$ and $A \cap B \in T$ must be satisfied.

**17.** Every indiscrete space is compact and connected.

**18.** $\{a, c\} \cap \{b\} = \phi$

and $\{a, c\} \cup \{b\} = \{a, b, c\} = X$

$\Rightarrow$ $(X, \Im)$ is disconnected.

## Exercise 2

**1.** $a, b, c$ be arbitrary distinct points of the set $R$ and

$$X = (a, b, c) \text{ and } \Im = \{\phi, X, \{a\}, \{b, c\}\}.$$

Then, $(X, \Im)$ is a topological space.

Evidently, $\{a\}, \{b, c\}$ are $\Im$-open sets.

$\therefore$ $X - \{a\}, X - \{b, c\}$ are $\Im$-closed sets.

*i.e.,* $\{b, c\}, \{a\}$ are $\Im$-closed sets.

Thus, $\{a\}$ and $\{b, c\}$ are $\Im$-open sets as well as $\Im$-closed sets.

Consider a pair of distinct elements $b, c \in X$. Then, the only open sets containing either of the elements $b, c$ are $X, \{b, c\}$ s.t. $b \in X, b \in \{b, c\}$; $c \in X, c \in \{b, c\}$.

This proves that $(X, \Im)$ is not a $T_1$-space.

Given, a pair of disjoint closed sets $\{a\}, \{b, c\} \subset X$, we can find a pair of disjoint open sets $\{a\}, \{b, c\} \subset X$ s.t.

closed set $\{a\} \subset$ open set $\{a\}$.

closed set $\{b, c\} \subset$ open set $\{b, c\}$.

This proves that $(X, \Im)$ is a normal space.

Repeating the same arguments we can show that $(X, \Im)$ is a regular space.

From this example, it is clear that a regular space need not be a $T_1$-space as well as a normal space need not be a $T_1$-space.

**2.** Consider $2, 4 \in N$

$A_2 \in \Im$, $2 \in A_2$ and $4 \notin A_2$.

Given, two distinct numbers $2, 4$, $\exists$ open set $A_2$ s.t. $2 \in A_2$ but $4 \notin A_2$.

$\therefore$ $(N, \Im)$ is $T_0$-space.

$A_4 \in \Im$, $2 \in A_4$, $4 \in A_4$.

Hence, $\exists$ no open set which contains 4 but not 2.

Thus, $(N, \Im)$ is not $T_1$-space.

**7.** Since, every topological space $(X, \Im)$ is compact if $X$ is finite

Also, $\{a\} \cap \{a, b\} = \{a\}$

$\neq \phi$

$\{a\} \cup \{a, b\} = \{a, b\}$

$\neq X$

$\Rightarrow$ $(X, \Im)$ is connected.

**9.** Assume that $f$ is continuous. Let $A$ be a subset of $X$. We show that, if $x \in \overline{A}$, then $f(x) \in f(A)$. Let $V$ be a neighbourhood of $f(x)$. Then, $f^{-1}(V)$ is an open set of $X$ containing $x$; it must intersect $A$ in some point $y$. Then, $V$ intersects $f(A)$ in the point $f(y)$. Hence, $f(x) \in \overline{f(A)}$

Hence, $f(\overline{A}) \subseteq \overline{f(A)}$

Now, let $B$ be closed set in $Y$ and let $A = f^{-1}(B)$. We wish to prove that $A$ is closed in $X$.

We show that $\overline{A} = A$, by elementary set theory, we have

$$f(A) = f(f^{-1}(B)) \subset B$$

Therefore, if $x \in \overline{A}$

$$f(x) \in f(\overline{A}) \subset \overline{f(A)} \subset \overline{B} = B$$

$\Rightarrow$ $x \in f^{-1}(B) = A$

Hence, $\overline{A} \subset A \Rightarrow \overline{A} = A$

Hence, $f^{-1}(B)$ is closed in $X$.

Now, let $x \in X$ and $V$ be a neighbourhood of $f(x)$. Then, the set $U = f^{-1}(V)$ is a neighbourhood of $x$ such that $f(U) \subset V$.

**11.** (a) Let $f(x) = y_0$, $\forall x \in X$. Let $V$ be open in $Y$. The set $f^{-1}(V)$ equal to $X$ or $\phi$, depending on wherther $V$ contains $y_0$ or not. In either case, it is open. Hence, $f$ is continuous.

(b) Let $U$ be open set in $X$, then $j^{-1}(U) = U \cap A$, which is open in $A$ by definition of subspace topology.

(c) Let $U$ be open set in $Z$, then $g^{-1}(U)$ is open in $Y$ and $f^{-1}(g^{-1}(U))$ is open in $X$. But

$$f^{-1}(g^{-1}(U)) = (gof)^{-1}(U).$$

Hence, $gof$ is continuous.

**12.** The function $f/A$ equals the composite of the inclusion map $j: A \to X$ and the map $f: X \to Y$ both of which are continuous.

Next, by Hypothesis, we can write $X$ as a union of open sets $U_\alpha$, such that $f/U_\alpha$ is continuous for each $\alpha$. Let $V$ be an open set in $Y$. Then,

$$f^{-1}(V) \cap U_\alpha = (f/U_\alpha)^{-1}(V)$$

because both expressions represent the set of those points $x$ lying in $U_\alpha$ for which $f(x) \in V$. Since, $f/U_\alpha$ is continuous, this set is open in $U_\alpha$ and hence open in $X$. But

$$f^{-1}(V) = U_\alpha(f^{-1}(V) \cap U_\alpha)$$

Hence, $f^{-1}(V)$ is also open in $X$.

**14.** The map $h: \mathbb{R} \times \mathbb{R}$ given by

$$h(x) = f(x) \times g(x)$$

is continuous. The function $f + g$ equals the composite of $h$ and the addition operation $f: \mathbb{R} \times \mathbb{R} \to \mathbb{R}$; therefore $f + g$ is continuous. Similarly, $f - g$, $f \cdot g$ and $f/g$ are continuous maps.

**18.** (a) The sets $[-1, 0]$ and $(0, 1]$ are disjoint and non-empty but they do not form a separation of $X$ because the first set is not open in $[-1, 1]$. Hence, the subspace $[-1, 1]$ of real line $\mathbb{R}$ is connected.

(b) Let $Y$ be a subspace of $Q$ containing two points $p$ and $q$, one can choose an irrational number $a$ lying between $p$ and $q$, and write $Y$ as the union of the open sets

$$Y \cap (-\infty, a) \text{ and } Y \cap (a, \infty)$$

Hence, $Q$ is disconnected.

(c) $X$ is not connected as the two indicated sets form a separation of $X$ because neither contains a limit point of other shown in the following figure.

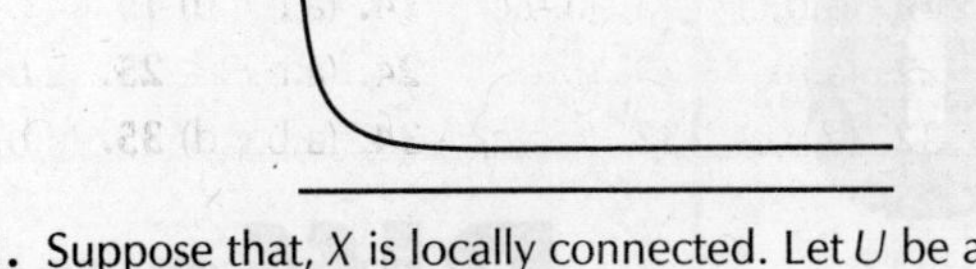

**21.** Suppose that, $X$ is locally connected. Let $U$ be an open set in $X$. Let $C$ be a component of $U$. If $x$ is a point of $C$, we can choose a connected neighbourhood $V$ of $x$ such that $V \subset U$. Since, $V$ is connected, it must lie entirely in the component $C$ of $U$. Hence, $C$ is open in $X$.

Next, suppose that, components of open sets in $X$ are open. Given, a point $x$ of $X$ and a neighbourhood $U$ of $x$, let $C$ be the component of $U$ containing $x$. Now, $C$ is connected.

Since, it is open in $X$ by hypothesis. Hence, $X$ is locally connected at $x$.

**23.** (a) The real line $\mathbb{R}$ is not compact, for the covering of $\mathbb{R}$ of open intervals

$$A = \{(n, n+2) \mid n \in \mathbb{Z}\}$$

Contains no finite subcollection that covers $\mathbb{R}$.

(b) Given, an open covering $A$ of $X$, there is an element $U$ of $A$ containing 0. The set $U$contains all but finitely many of the points $1/n$; choose, for each point of $X$ not in $U$, an element of $A$ containing it. The collection consisting of these elements of $A$, along with the element $U$, is a finite subcollection of $A$ that covers $X$.

(c) The open covering

$$A = \{(1/n, 1] \mid n \in \mathbb{Z}_+\}$$

Contains no finite subcollection covering $(0, 1]$.

# 18 Differential Equations

## Ordinary Differential Equations

An equation which involves differential coefficient is called a differential equation.

e.g.,

(i) $\frac{dy}{dx} = \frac{1+x^2}{1-y^2}$ (ii) $\frac{d^2y}{dx^2} + 2\frac{dy}{dx} - 8y = 0$

(iii) $\left[1+\left(\frac{dy}{dx}\right)^2\right]^{3/2} = k\frac{d^2y}{dx^2}$

## Order and Degree of Differential Equations

The order of a differential equation is the order of the highest differential coefficient present in the equation. Consider the differential equation

**(i)** $L\frac{d^2q}{dt^2} + R\frac{dq}{dt} + \frac{q}{c} = E\sin wt$ **(ii)** $\cos x\frac{d^2y}{dx^2} + \sin x\left(\frac{dy}{dx}\right)^2 + 8y = \tan x$

**(iii)** $\left[1+\left(\frac{dy}{dx}\right)^2\right]^3 = \left(\frac{d^2y}{dx^2}\right)^2$

The order of all of the above equations is 2.

The degree of a differential equation is the degree of the highest derivative after removing the radical sign and fraction.

The degree of the equations (i) and (ii) is 1 while the degree of the equation (iii) is 2.

***Example 1.*** *Form the differential equation by eliminating arbitrary constants, in the following cases and also write down the order of the differential equations obtained.*

(i) $y = Ax + A^2$ (ii) $y = A\cos x + B\sin x$ (iii) $y^2 = Ax^2 + Bx + C$

**Solution.** (i) We have $y = Ax + A^2$ ...(i)

On differentiation, $\frac{dy}{dx} = A$

On putting the value of $A$ in Eq. (i), we get $y = x\frac{dy}{dx} + \left(\frac{dy}{dx}\right)^2$

On eliminating constant $A$, we get the differential equation of order 1.

(ii) We have $y = A\cos x + B\sin x$

On differentiation, $\frac{dy}{dx} = -A\sin x + B\cos x$

**Syllabus**

- Ordinary Differential Equations (ODEs)
- Existence and Uniqueness of Solutions of Initial Value Problems for First Order Ordinary Differential Equations
- Singular Solutions of First Order ODEs
- System of First Order ODEs
- General Theory of Homogeneous and Non-Homogeneous Linear ODEs
- Variation of Parameters
- Sturm-Liouville
- Boundary Value Problem
- Green's Function
- Partial Differential Equations (PDEs)
- Lagrange and Charpit Methods for Solving First Order PDEs, Cauchy Problem for First Order PDEs.
- Classification of Second Order PDEs
- General Solution of Higher Order PDEs with Constant Coefficients
- Method of Separation of Variables for Laplace, Heat and Wave Equations

Again on differentiating, we set

$$\frac{d^2y}{dx^2} = -A\cos x - B\sin x$$

$$\Rightarrow \quad \frac{d^2y}{dx^2} = -(A\cos x + B\sin x)$$

$$\Rightarrow \quad \frac{d^2y}{dx^2} = -y \Rightarrow \frac{d^2y}{dx^2} + y = 0$$

This is differential equation of order 2 obtained by eliminating two constants $A$ and $B$.

(iii) We have $y^2 = Ax^2 + Bx + C$

On differentiation, $2y\frac{dy}{dx} = 2Ax + B$

Again differentiating, $2y\frac{d^2y}{dx^2} + 2\left(\frac{dy}{dx}\right)^2 = 2A$

On differentiating again

$$y\frac{d^3y}{dx^3} + \frac{dy}{dx}\frac{d^2y}{dx^2} + 2\frac{dy}{dx}\frac{d^2y}{dx^2} = 0$$

$$\Rightarrow \quad y\frac{d^3y}{dx^3} + 3\frac{dy}{dx}\frac{d^2y}{dx^2} = 0$$

This is the differential equation of order 3, obtained by eliminating three constants $A$, $B$, and $C$

# Types of Solutions of Differential Equations

## (i) General Solution

The solution which contains the number of arbitrary independent constants equal to the order of the differential equation is called the general solution or the complete primitive of the equation.

## (ii) Particular Solution

The solution obtained from the general solution by assigning particular values to one or more of the arbitrary constants is called particular solution.

## (iii) Singular Solution

Solution of the differential equation which does not contain any arbitrary constant called singular solution.

From Abel's formula, we have

$$r(x_1)w(y_1(x_1)y_2(x_1)) = \text{a constant } (k)$$

$\Rightarrow \quad k < 0$ as $r(x_1) > 0, w < 0$

$\Rightarrow \quad y_1(x_1) > 0$

$\Rightarrow \quad r(x_2)w(y_1(x_2)y_2(x_2)) < 0$

$\Rightarrow \quad y_2(x_2) < 0$ as $r(x_2) > 0$

$\Rightarrow \quad y_1(x_1) > 0,\ y_2(x_2) < 0$

and $y_2(x)$ is continuous.

$\Rightarrow$ By Bolzano theorem,

$y_2(x)$ must have atleast one zero in $(x_1\ x_2)$.

(iv) By using method of variation of parameter.

(v) If IVP satisfies Lipschitz condition, then it must have a unique solution.

e.g., Solution of differential equation

$$y = x\frac{dy}{dx} + \frac{a}{\frac{dy}{dx}}$$

is $y^2 = 4ax$ which does not contain any arbitrary constant.

# Linear Differential Equations

If the degree of the dependent variable and all its derivatives is one and they do not occur together with multiple operation called linear differential equation.

e.g., (i) $\frac{d^2y}{dx^2} - x\frac{dy}{dx} + y = 0$

(ii) $\frac{dy}{dx} = x + y + 1$

OR

A differential equation is linear, if it can be expressed as

$$a_0\frac{d^ny}{dx^n} + a_1\frac{d^{n-1}y}{dx^{n-1}} + a_2\frac{d^{n-2}y}{dx^{n-2}} + \ldots + a_ny = b$$

where, $a_0, a_1, a_2, \ldots, a_n$ and $b$ are constants or functions of $x$. Clearly, this differential equation is of $n$th order and degree one.

# Non-Linear Differential Equations

A differential equation which is not linear is called a non-linear differential equation.

Thus, a differential equation will be non-linear iff

**(a)** its degree is more than one

**(b)** exponent of the dependent variable is more than one

**(c)** any of the differential coefficient has exponent more than one.

**(d)** products containing dependent variable and its derivative are present.

e.g.,

(i) $\frac{d^3y}{dx^3} - \left(\frac{dy}{dx}\right)^2 + y = x^2$ (ii) $\frac{dy}{dx} = \frac{x}{y}$

# Differential Equations of the First Order and First Degree

General ordinary differential equation of the $n$th order is

$$F\left(x, y, \frac{dy}{dx}, \frac{d^2y}{dx^2}, \ldots, \frac{d^ny}{dx^n}\right) = 0$$

or

$$F(x, y, y', y'', \ldots, y^{(n)}) = 0$$

The simplest differential equations is

$$F(x, y, y') = 0 \quad \text{or} \quad y' = f(x, y)$$

which is the first order differential equation.

Differential equations of the first order and the first degree cannot be solved in every case. They can be solved if they belong to some standard form, which are given below:

## (i) Variable Separable Equation

If a differential equation is written in the form $f(x)dx = \phi(y)dy$, then we say that variables are separable.

***Example 2.*** *Solve*

(i) $(x + 1)\frac{dy}{dx} = x(y^2 + 1)$

(ii) $(xy^2 + x)dx + (yx^2 + y)dy = 0$

**Solution.** (i) We have $(x+1)\frac{dy}{dx} = x(y^2+1)$

$$\Rightarrow \quad (x+1)dy = x(y^2+1)\,dx$$

$$\Rightarrow \quad \frac{dy}{y^2+1} = \frac{xdx}{x+1}$$

$$\Rightarrow \quad \frac{1}{1+y^2}dy = \left(1 - \frac{1}{x+1}\right)dx$$

On integrating, we get $\int \frac{1}{1+y^2}dy = \int dx - \int \frac{1}{x+1}dx + C$

$$\Rightarrow \quad \tan^{-1} y = x - \log(1+x) + C$$

(ii) We have $(xy^2 + x)\,dx + (yx^2 + y)\,dy = 0$

$$\Rightarrow \quad (y^2+1)\,xdx = -(x^2+1)\,y\,dy$$

$$\Rightarrow \quad \frac{ydy}{y^2+1} = -\frac{x}{x^2+1}dx$$

$$\Rightarrow \quad \frac{1}{2}\int \frac{2y}{y^2+1}dy = -\frac{1}{2}\int \frac{2x}{x^2+1}dx + \frac{1}{2}C$$

$$\Rightarrow \quad \frac{1}{2}\log(y^2+1) = -\frac{1}{2}\log(x^2+1) + \frac{1}{2}C$$

$$\Rightarrow \quad \log(y^2+1) + \log(x^2+1) = \log C'$$

$$\Rightarrow \quad (y^2+1)(x^2+1) = C'$$

***Example 3.*** *Solve* $\frac{dy}{dx} = \frac{x(2\log x + 1)}{\sin y + y\cos y}$

**Solution.** We have,

$$\frac{dy}{dx} = \frac{x(2\log x+1)}{\sin y + y\cos y}$$

$$\Rightarrow \quad (\sin y + y\cos y)dy = \{x(2\log x + 1)\}dx$$

On integrating both the sides, we get

$$\int (\sin y + y\cos y)dy = \int \{x(2\log x + 1)\}dx + C$$

$$-\cos y + y\sin y - \int (1)\cdot \sin y\,dy = 2\int \log x \cdot x dx + \int x dx + C$$

$$\Rightarrow \quad -\cos y + y\sin y + \cos y = 2\left[\log x \cdot \frac{x^2}{2} - \int \frac{1}{x}\cdot\frac{x^2}{2}dx\right] + \frac{x^2}{2} + C$$

$$\Rightarrow \quad y\sin y = 2\log x \cdot \frac{x^2}{2} - \int x dx + \frac{x^2}{2} + C$$

$$\Rightarrow \quad y\sin y = 2\log x \cdot \frac{x^2}{2} - \frac{x^2}{2} + \frac{x^2}{2} + C$$

$$\Rightarrow \quad y\sin y = x^2\log x + C$$

***Example 4.*** *Find the solution of the differential equation* $\frac{dy}{dx} - x\tan(y - x) = 1$

**Solution.** We have $\frac{dy}{dx} - x\tan(y - x) = 1$ ...(i)

On putting, $y - x = t$ so that $\frac{dy}{dx} - 1 = \frac{dt}{dx}$ in Eq. (i), we get

$$\left(1 + \frac{dt}{dx}\right) - x\tan t = 1, \quad \frac{dt}{dx} = x\tan t \Rightarrow \cot t\,dt = xdx$$

On integrating, we have $\log \sin t = \frac{x^2}{2} + C$

$$\Rightarrow \quad \log\sin(y - x) = \frac{x^2}{2} + C$$

***Example 5.*** *Solve the equation*

$$(2x^2 + 3y^2 - 7)\,x\,dx - (3x^2 + 2y^2 - 8)\,y\,dy = 0$$

**Solution.** We have,

$$(2x^2 + 3y^2 - 7)xdx - (3x^2 + 2y^2 - 8)y\,dy = 0 \quad \text{...(i)}$$

Rearranging Eq. (i), we get

$$\frac{x\,dx}{y\,dy} = \frac{3x^2 + 2y^2 - 8}{2x^2 + 3y^2 - 7}$$

Applying componendo and dividendo rule, we get

$$\frac{xdx + y\,dy}{xdx - y\,dy} = \frac{5x^2 + 5y^2 - 15}{x^2 - y^2 - 1}$$

$$\Rightarrow \quad \frac{xdx + y\,dy}{x^2 + y^2 - 3} = 5\left(\frac{xdx - y\,dy}{x^2 - y^2 - 1}\right)$$

Multiplying by 2 both sides, we get

$$\Rightarrow \quad \left(\frac{2xdx + 2y\,dy}{x^2 + y^2 - 3}\right) = 5\left(\frac{2xdx - 2y\,dy}{x^2 - y^2 - 1}\right)$$

On integrating both sides, we get

$$\log(x^2 + y^2 - 3) = 5\log(x^2 - y^2 - 1) + \log C$$

$$\Rightarrow \quad x^2 + y^2 - 3 = C(x^2 - y^2 - 1)^5$$

where C is arbitrary constant of integration.

## (ii) Homogeneous Differential Equations

A differential equation of the form

$$\frac{dy}{dx} = \frac{f(x, y)}{\phi(x, y)}$$

is called a homogeneous equation, if each term of $f(x, y)$ and $\phi(x, y)$ are hamogeneous equation of the same degree.

e.g., $$\frac{dy}{dx}=\frac{2xy}{x^2+y^2}$$

In such cases, we put $y = vx$

$$\Rightarrow \quad \frac{dy}{dx}=v+x\frac{dv}{dx}$$

and equation is reduced to variable separable.

***Example 6.*** *Solve* $x^2dy + y(x+y)\,dx = 0$

**Solution.** We have $x^2dy + y(x+y)\,dx = 0$

$$\Rightarrow \quad \frac{dy}{dx}=-\frac{xy+y^2}{x^2}$$

Put $y = vx$, then $\frac{dy}{dx}=v+x\frac{dv}{dx}$

The given equation becomes, on substitution,

$$v+x\frac{dv}{dx}=-\frac{vx^2+v^2x^2}{x^2}=-\frac{v+v^2}{1}$$

$$\Rightarrow \quad x\frac{dv}{dx}=-2v-v^2$$

Separating the variables, we get

$$\frac{dv}{v^2+2v}=-\frac{dx}{x}$$

$$\Rightarrow \quad \frac{1}{2}\int\frac{dv}{v}-\frac{1}{2}\int\frac{dv}{v+2}=-\int\frac{dx}{x}+C$$

$$\Rightarrow \quad \frac{1}{2}\log v-\frac{1}{2}\log(v+2)=-\log x+C$$

$$\log v-\log(v+2)=-2\log x+2C$$

$$\log\frac{v}{v+2}+\log x^2=2C$$

$$\Rightarrow \quad \log\frac{vx^2}{v+2}=\log a \quad\Rightarrow\quad \frac{vx^2}{v+2}=a$$

$$\Rightarrow \quad \frac{\frac{y}{x}.x^2}{\frac{y}{x}+2}=a, \quad\Rightarrow\quad \frac{x^2y}{2x+y}=a$$

$$\Rightarrow \quad x^2y=a(2x+y)$$

***Example 7.*** *Solve the equation*

$$\frac{dy}{dx}=\frac{y}{x}+x\sin\frac{y}{x}$$

**Solution.** We have $\frac{dy}{dx}=\frac{y}{x}+x\sin\frac{y}{x}$ ...(i)

Put $y = vx$ in Eq. (i), so that $\frac{dy}{dx}=v+x\frac{dv}{dx}$

$$\Rightarrow \quad v+x\frac{dv}{dx}=v+x\sin v$$

$$\Rightarrow \quad x\frac{dv}{dx}=x\sin v \quad\Rightarrow\quad \frac{dv}{dx}=\sin v$$

$$\Rightarrow \quad \frac{dv}{\sin v}=dx$$

$$\Rightarrow \quad \int \operatorname{cosec} v\,dv=\int dx+C$$

$$\log\tan\frac{v}{2}=x+C$$

$$\Rightarrow \quad \log\tan\frac{y}{2x}=x+C$$

***Example 8.*** *Solve* $(x+2y)(dx-dy)=dx+dy$

**Solution.** We have $$\frac{dy}{dx}=\frac{x+2y-1}{x+2y+1} \quad ...(i)$$

Put $x+2y=z$

$$\Rightarrow \quad 1+2\frac{dy}{dx}=\frac{dz}{dx}$$

$\therefore$ Eq. (i) becomes

$$\frac{1}{2}\left(\frac{dz}{dx}-1\right)=\frac{z-1}{z+1}$$

$$\Rightarrow \quad \frac{dz}{dx}=\frac{2z-2}{z+1}+1=\frac{3z-1}{z+1}$$

$$\Rightarrow \quad \frac{z+1}{3z-1}dz=dx \quad\Rightarrow\quad \left(\frac{1}{3}+\frac{4}{3}\cdot\frac{1}{3z-1}\right)dz=dx$$

On integrating, we get $\frac{z}{3}+\frac{4}{9}\log(3z-1)=x+C$

$$\Rightarrow \quad 3z+4\log(3z-1)=9x+9C$$

$$\Rightarrow \quad 3(x+2y)+4\log(3x+6y-1)=9x+9C$$

$$3x-3y+a=2\log(3x+6y-1)$$

***Example 9.*** *Solve* $\frac{dy}{dx}=\frac{x+2y-3}{2x+y-3}$

**Solution.** Put $x = X+h, \quad y=Y+k$

The given equation reduces to

$$\frac{dY}{dX}=\frac{(X+h)+2(Y+k)-3}{2(X+h)+(Y+k)-3}$$

$$=\frac{X+2Y+(h+2k-3)}{2X+Y+(2h+k-3)}$$

Now, choose $h$ and $k$, so that $h+2k-3=0$, $2h+k-3=0$

Solving these equations, we get $h=k=1$

$$\frac{dY}{dX}=\frac{X+2Y}{2X+Y} \quad ...(i)$$

Put $Y = vX$, so that $\frac{dY}{dX}=v+X\frac{dv}{dX}$

The Eq. (i) is transformed as

$$v+X\frac{dv}{dX}=\frac{X+2vX}{2X+vX}=\frac{1+2v}{2+v}$$

$$X\frac{dv}{dX}=\frac{1+2v}{2+v}-v=\frac{1-v^2}{2+v}$$

$$\Rightarrow \quad \left(\frac{2+v}{1-v^2}\right)dv=\frac{dX}{X}$$

$$\Rightarrow \quad \frac{1}{2}\cdot\frac{1}{(1+v)}dv+\frac{3}{2}\cdot\frac{1}{1-v}dv=\frac{dX}{X}$$

On integrating, we have

$$\frac{1}{2}\log(1+v)-3/2\log(1-v)=\log X+\log C$$

$$\Rightarrow \quad \log \frac{1+v}{(1-v)^3} = \log C^2X^2$$

$$\Rightarrow \quad \frac{1+v}{(1-v)^3} = C^2X^2$$

$$\frac{1+\frac{Y}{X}}{\left(1-\frac{Y}{X}\right)^3} = C^2X^2$$

$$\Rightarrow \quad \frac{X+Y}{(X-Y)^3} = C^2$$

or $\quad X+Y = C^2(X-Y)^3$

Put $X = x-1$ and $Y = y-1$,

$$x+y-2 = a(x-y)^3$$

## (iii) Linear Differential Equations

A differential equation of the form

$$\frac{dy}{dx} + Py = Q \quad \text{...(i)}$$

Where $P$ and $Q$ are functions of $x$ or constants is called a linear differential equation.

To solve Eq. (i), we multiply both sides of Eq. (i) by $e^{\int Pdx}$ (called integrating factor) so that Eq. (i) reduces to

$$\frac{d}{dx}\left[y \cdot e^{\int Pdx}\right] = Q \cdot e^{\int Pdx}$$

On integrating both sides, we get

$$y \cdot e^{\int Pdx} = \int \left(Q \cdot e^{\int Pdx}\right) dx + C$$

$$\Rightarrow \quad y \times \text{IF} = \int (Q \times \text{IF})\, dx + C$$

where $\quad \text{IF} = e^{\int Pdx}$

***Example 10.*** *Solve* $x(x-1)\frac{dy}{dx} - (x-2)y = x^2(2x-1)$

**Solution.** We have $\frac{dy}{dx} - \frac{x-2}{x(x-1)}y = \frac{x^2(2x-1)}{x(x-1)}$

Hence, the integrating factor is

$$\text{IF} = e^{-\int \frac{x-2}{x(x-1)}dx} = e^{\int\left(\frac{1}{x-1} - \frac{2}{x}\right)dx}$$

$$= e^{\log(x-1) - 2\log x} = e^{\log\frac{x-1}{x^2}} = \frac{x-1}{x^2}$$

Hence, the solution is

$$y \cdot \frac{x-1}{x^2} = \int \frac{x^2(2x-1)}{x(x-1)} \cdot \frac{x-1}{x^2}\, dx + C = \int \frac{2x-1}{x}\, dx + C$$

$$= \int \left(2 - \frac{1}{x}\right) dx + C = 2x - \log x + C$$

***Example 11.*** *If* $\frac{dy}{dx} + 2y\tan x = \sin x$ *and* $y\left(\frac{\pi}{3}\right) = 0$, *then find maximum value of* $y(x)$.

**Solution.** We have $\frac{dy}{dx} + 2y\tan x = \sin x$

$$\text{IF} = e^{2\int \tan x\, dx} = e^{2\log \sec x} = e^{\log \sec^2 x} = \sec^2 x$$

Hence, solution is

$$y \cdot \sec^2 x = \int \sec^2 x \cdot \sin x\, dx + C = \int \tan x \sec x\, dx + C$$

$$= \sec x + C \quad \text{...(i)}$$

Put $x = \frac{\pi}{3}, y = 0$ in Eq. (i),

$$0 \times \sec^2 \frac{\pi}{3} = \sec\frac{\pi}{3} + C$$

$$0 = 2 + C \text{ or } C = -2$$

Substituting $C = -2$ in Eq. (i), we get

$$y\sec^2 x = \sec x - 2$$

$$y = \cos x - 2\cos^2 x,$$

$$\frac{dy}{dx} = -\sin x + 4\cos x \sin x$$

For maxima or minima, we have

$$0 = -\sin x + 4\sin x\cos x$$

$$\Rightarrow \quad -\sin x(1 - 4\cos x) = 0$$

$$\Rightarrow \quad \sin x = 0 \text{ or } \cos x = \frac{1}{4}$$

Now, $\quad \frac{d^2y}{dx^2} = -\cos x - 4\sin^2 x + 4\cos^2 x$

If $\cos x = \frac{1}{4}$, then

$$\frac{d^2y}{dx^2} = -\frac{1}{4} - 4\sqrt{1 - \frac{1}{16}} + 4\left(\frac{1}{16}\right) = -\sqrt{15}$$

So, $y$ is maximum if $\cos x = \frac{1}{4}$, Maximum value of

$$y = \frac{1}{4} - \frac{2}{16} = \frac{1}{8}$$

***Example 12.*** *Solve* $x^2dy + y(x+y)dx = 0$

**Solution.** We have, $\quad x^2dy + y(x+y)dx = 0$

$$\Rightarrow \quad \frac{dy}{dx} + \frac{y}{x} = -\frac{y^2}{x^2} \quad \Rightarrow \quad \frac{1}{y^2}\frac{dy}{dx} + \frac{1}{xy} = -\frac{1}{x^2}$$

Put $\quad -\frac{1}{y} = z \quad$ so that $\quad \frac{1}{y^2}\frac{dy}{dx} = \frac{dz}{dx}$

The given equation reduces to a linear differential equation in $z$, as

$$\frac{dz}{dx} - \frac{z}{x} = -\frac{1}{x^2}$$

Hence, $\quad \text{IF} = e^{-\int 1/x\, dx} = e^{-\log x} = e^{\log 1/x} = \frac{1}{x}$

Hence, the solution is

$$z \cdot \frac{1}{x} = \int -\frac{1}{x^2} \cdot \frac{1}{x}\, dx + C \Rightarrow \frac{z}{x} = \int -x^{-3}dx + C$$

$$\Rightarrow \quad -\frac{1}{xy} = -\frac{x^{-2}}{-2} + C \Rightarrow \frac{1}{xy} = -\frac{1}{2x^2} - C$$

***Example 13.*** *Solve*

$$(\sec x \tan x \tan y - e^x)dx + \sec x \sec^2 y\, dy = 0$$

**Solution.** We have $\sec x \tan x \tan y - e^x + \sec x \sec^2 y \dfrac{dy}{dx} = 0$

$$\Rightarrow \quad \sec^2 y \frac{dy}{dx} + \tan x \tan y = e^x \cos x$$

Put $\tan y = z, \Rightarrow \sec^2 y \dfrac{dy}{dx} = \dfrac{dz}{dx}$

$$\Rightarrow \quad \frac{dz}{dx} + z \tan x = e^x \cos x$$

$$\text{IF} = e^{\int \tan x\, dx} = e^{\log \sec x} = \sec x$$

Hence, the solution is $z \sec x = \int e^x \cos x \sec x\, dx + C$

$$\Rightarrow \quad z \sec x = \int e^x dx + C$$

$$\Rightarrow \quad \tan y \sec x = e^x + C$$

## (iv) Exact Differential Equation

A differential equation of the form

$$Mdx + Ndy = 0$$

is said to be an exact differential equation, if it satisfies the condition $\dfrac{\partial M}{\partial y} = \dfrac{\partial N}{\partial x}$

and the solution of above differential equation is

$$\underbrace{\int M\, dx}_{y\, =\, \text{constant}} + \underbrace{\int N\, dy}_{\text{Terms of } N \text{ free from } x} = C$$

***Example 14.*** *Solve*

$$xdx + ydy = \frac{a^2(xdy - ydx)}{x^2 + y^2}$$

**Solution.** Given, differential equation can be written as

$$\left(x + \frac{a^2 y}{x^2 + y^2}\right)dx + \left(y - \frac{a^2 x}{x^2 + y^2}\right)dy = 0$$

Here, $\quad M = x + \dfrac{a^2 y}{x^2 + y^2}$

and $\quad N = y - \dfrac{a^2 x}{x^2 + y^2}$

Now, $\quad \dfrac{\partial M}{\partial y} = \dfrac{a^2(x^2 - y^2)}{(x^2 + y^2)^2} = \dfrac{\partial N}{\partial x}$

Hence, given, differential equation is exact. Hence, required solution is

$$\underbrace{\int \left(x + \frac{a^2 y}{x^2 + y^2}\right)dx}_{y\, =\, \text{constant}} + \underbrace{\int \left(y - \frac{a^2 x}{x^2 + y^2}\right)dy}_{\text{Terms free from } x} = C$$

$$\Rightarrow \quad \int x dx + a^2 y \int \frac{dx}{x^2 + y^2} + \int y dy = C$$

$$\Rightarrow \quad \frac{x^2}{2} + a^2 y \cdot \frac{1}{y} \tan^{-1}\left(\frac{x}{y}\right) + \frac{y^2}{2} = C$$

$$\Rightarrow \quad \left(\frac{x^2 + y^2}{2}\right) + a^2 \tan^{-1}\left(\frac{x}{y}\right) = C$$

## Integrating Factor

Sometimes a differential equation which is not exact may become so, on multiplying a suitable function known as the integrating factor.

**1.** If $\dfrac{\dfrac{\partial M}{\partial y} - \dfrac{\partial N}{\partial x}}{N}$ is a function of $x$ alone, say $f(x)$,

then $\text{IF} = e^{\int f(x) dx}$

***Example 15.*** *Solve* $(2x \log x - xy)dy + 2ydx = 0$

**Solution.** Here, $M = 2y$ and $N = 2x \log x - xy$

Hence, $\quad \dfrac{\partial M}{\partial y} = 2$ and $\dfrac{\partial N}{\partial x} = 2(1 + \log x) - y$

Here, $\quad \dfrac{\dfrac{\partial M}{\partial y} - \dfrac{\partial N}{\partial x}}{N} = \dfrac{-2 \log x + y}{2x \log x - xy} = -\dfrac{1}{x} = f(x)$

Now, $\quad \text{IF} = e^{\int f(x) dx} = e^{\int -\frac{1}{x} dx} = e^{-\log x} = e^{\log x^{-1}} = x^{-1} = \dfrac{1}{x}$

On multiplying the given differential equation by $\dfrac{1}{x}$, we get

$$\frac{2y}{x} dx + (2 \log x - y)dy = 0 \;\Rightarrow\; \int \frac{2y}{x} dx + \int -y dy = C$$

$$\Rightarrow \quad 2y \log x - \frac{1}{2} y^2 = C$$

**2.** If $\dfrac{\dfrac{\partial N}{\partial x} - \dfrac{\partial M}{\partial y}}{M}$ is a function of $y$ alone, say $f(y)$, then

$$\text{IF} = e^{\int f(y) dy}$$

***Example 16.*** *Solve* $(y^4 + 2y)dx + (xy^3 + 2y^4 - 4x)dy = 0$

**Solution.** Here, $M = y^4 + 2y$ and $N = xy^3 + 2y^4 - 4x$

$$\therefore \quad \frac{\partial M}{\partial y} = 4y^3 + 2 \text{ and } \frac{\partial N}{\partial x} = y^3 - 4$$

$$\therefore \quad \frac{\dfrac{\partial N}{\partial x} - \dfrac{\partial M}{\partial y}}{M} = \frac{(y^3 - 4) - (4y^3 + 2)}{y^4 + 2y} = \frac{-3(y^3 + 2)}{y(y^3 + 2)} = -\frac{3}{y} = f(y)$$

$$\text{IF} = e^{\int f(y) dy} = e^{\int -\frac{3}{y} dy} = e^{-3 \log y}$$

$$= e^{\log y^{-3}} = y^{-3} = \frac{1}{y^3}$$

On multiplying the given Eq. (i) by $\dfrac{1}{y^3}$, we get the exact differential equation as

$$\left(y + \frac{2}{y^2}\right)dx + \left(x + 2y - \frac{4x}{y^3}\right)dy = 0$$

$$\Rightarrow \quad \int \left(y + \frac{2}{y^2}\right)dx + \int 2y dy = C$$

$$\Rightarrow \quad x\left(y + \frac{2}{y^2}\right) + y^2 = C$$

**3.** If the given equation $Mdx + Ndy = 0$ is homogeneous such that $Mx + Ny \neq 0$, then $\frac{1}{Mx + Ny}$ is an integrating factor.

***Example 17.*** *Solve* $\frac{dy}{dx} = \frac{x^2 + y^2}{xy}$

**Solution.** We have $\quad (x^2 + y^2)dx - (xy)dy = 0 \qquad$ ...(i)

Hence, $\quad M = x^2 + y^2 \quad$ and $\quad N = -xy$

$$Mx + Ny = x^3 + xy^2 - xy^2 = x^3 \neq 0$$

Hence, $\quad \text{IF} = \frac{1}{x^3}$

Multiplying Eq. (i) both sides by $\frac{1}{x^3}$, we get

$$\left(\frac{1}{x} + \frac{y^2}{x^3}\right)dx - \left(\frac{y}{x^2}\right)dy = 0$$

which is an exact differential equation.

Hence, Solution is $\underbrace{\int \left(\frac{1}{x} + \frac{y^2}{x^3}\right)d}_{y\,=\,\text{constant}} - \underbrace{\int \frac{y}{x^2}dy}_{\text{Terms free from } x} = C$

y = constant Terms free from x

$$\Rightarrow \quad \int \frac{dx}{x} + y^2 \int \frac{dx}{x^3} - \int 0 \cdot dy = C$$

$$\Rightarrow \quad \log x - \frac{y^2}{2x^2} = C$$

**4.** If the differential equation $Mdx + Ndy = 0$ is not exact, then it can be made exact by multiplying $x^\alpha y^\beta$ both sides.

$\alpha$ and $\beta$ are found out from $\frac{\partial M}{\partial y} = \frac{\partial N}{\partial x}$

***Example 18.*** *Solve* $(y^3 - 2x^2y)dx + (2xy^2 - x^3)dy = 0$

**Solution.** Here, $M = y^3 - 2x^2y \quad$ and $\quad N = 2xy^2 - x^3$

$$\frac{\partial M}{\partial y} = 3y^2 - 2x^2 \quad \text{and} \quad \frac{\partial N}{\partial x} = 2y^2 - 3x^2$$

Clearly, $\quad \frac{\partial M}{\partial y} \neq \frac{\partial N}{\partial x}$

Multiplying both sides the above differential equation by, $x^\alpha y^\beta$, so that it reduces in the form of $M_1dx + N_1dy = 0$

where, $\quad M_1 = x^\alpha y^{\beta+3} - 2x^{\alpha+2}y^{\beta+1}$,

and $\quad N_1 = 2x^{\alpha+1}y^{\beta+2} - x^{\alpha+3}y^\beta$

Now, $\quad \frac{\partial M_1}{\partial y} = \frac{\partial N_1}{\partial x}$

$$\Rightarrow \quad x^\alpha \cdot (\beta+3)y^{\beta+2} - 2x^{\alpha+2}(\beta+1)y^\beta$$
$$= 2y^{\beta+2} \cdot (\alpha+1)x^\alpha - y^\beta \cdot (\alpha+3)x^{\alpha+2}$$

Dividing both sides by $x^\alpha y^\beta$, we get

$$\Rightarrow \quad (\beta+3)y^2 - 2(\beta+1)x^2 = 2(\alpha+1)y^2 - (\alpha+3)x^2$$

$$\Rightarrow \quad (\alpha + 3 - 2\beta - 2)x^2 + (\beta + 3 - 2\alpha - 2)y^2 = 0$$

$$\Rightarrow \quad \alpha - 2\beta + 1 = 0, \quad 2\alpha - \beta - 1 = 0$$

$$\Rightarrow \quad \alpha = 1, \quad \beta = 1$$

Hence, $\quad \text{IF} = xy$

Hence, required solution is

$$\underbrace{\int M_1 dx}_{y\,=\,\text{constant}} + \underbrace{\int N_1 dy}_{\text{Terms free from } x} = C$$

$$\Rightarrow \quad \int (xy^4 - 2x^3y^2)dx + \int (2x^2y^3 - x^4y)dy = C$$

y = constant Terms free from x

$$\Rightarrow \quad y^4 \int x dx - 2y^2 \int x^3 dx + \int 0 \cdot dy = C$$

$$\Rightarrow \quad \frac{x^2y^4}{2} - \frac{x^4y^2}{2} = C$$

$$\Rightarrow \quad x^2y^4 - x^4y^2 = C'$$

## Differential Equation of the Form $f(x, y, p) = 0$, where $p = \frac{dy}{dx}$

***Example 19.*** *Solve* $\quad y^2 = 1 + p^2$

**Solution.** We have $\quad p^2 = y^2 - 1$

$$\Rightarrow \quad p = \pm\sqrt{y^2 - 1}$$

$$\Rightarrow \quad \frac{dy}{dx} = \pm\sqrt{y^2 - 1}$$

$$\Rightarrow \quad \frac{dy}{\sqrt{y^2 - 1}} = \pm dx$$

$$\Rightarrow \quad \log(y + \sqrt{y^2 - 1}) = \pm x + C$$

***Example 20.*** *Solve* $y = xp - p^2$

**Solution.** We have $y = xp - p^2$

Differentiating both sides *wrt x*, we get

$$\frac{dy}{dx} = x\frac{dp}{dx} + p - 2p\frac{dp}{dx}$$

$$\Rightarrow \quad \frac{dp}{dx}(x - 2p) = 0 \quad \Rightarrow p = C$$

Hence, required solution is $y = Cx - C^2$

## Singular Solution

The equation of the form

$$y = px + f(p) \qquad \text{...(i)}$$

where, $p = \frac{dy}{dx}$ and $f(p)$ is a function of $p$ is called as Clairaut's equation.

Differentiating Eq. (i) *wrt x* both sides after simplification, we get

$$[x+f'(p)]\frac{dp}{dx}=0$$

$\Rightarrow$ Either $\frac{dp}{dx}=0$ ...(ii)

or $x+f'(p)=0$ ...(iii)

Eq. (ii) gives $p=C$

Putting the value of $p$ into Eq. (i), we get

$$y=Cx+f(C) \quad \text{...(iv)}$$

which is called the general or complete solution of the given equation.

Eliminating $p$ from Eqs. (i) and (iii) we get relation between $x$ and $y$ called singular solution of the differential equation. Singular solution is not contained into general solution given by Eq. (iv) nor can it be derived from it. Also, singular solution does not contain any arbitrary constant.

> ***Note*** **(a)** $y=cx+f(c)$ represents a family of straight lines for different values of $c$.
>
> **(b)** Process of eliminating $p$ from $y=px+f(p)$ and $x+f'(p)=0$ is same as that of eliminating $c$ between $y=cx+f(c)$ and $x+f'(c)=0$
>
> **(c)** Eliminating $c$ between $y=cx+f(c)$ and $x+f'(c)=0$ amounts to finding envelope of the line $y=cx+f(c)$ for different values of $c$.
> Thus, singular solution represents the envelope of the family of straight lines represented by the complete solution.
>
> **(d)** If in particular $f(c)$ is a quadratic in $c$, then eliminating $c$ between $y=cx+f(c)$ and $x+f'(c)=0$ amounts to finding the condition that the two roots of the quadratic equation $f(c)+cx-y=0$ are equal.

**Example 21.** *Solve* $y=px+\frac{a}{p}$ *and find singular solution.*

**Solution.** The given equation is in Clairant's form. Hence, its general solution is

$$y=cx+\frac{a}{c} \quad \text{..(i)}$$

$$\Rightarrow \quad c^2x-cy+a=0$$

$$D=0$$

$$\Rightarrow \quad y^2-4ax=0$$

which is the singular solution.

## Lipschitz Condition

A function $f(x,y)$ is said to satisfy a Lipschitz condition in a region $D$ in $xy$-plane, if $\exists$ a positive constant $K$ such that

$$|f(x,y_1)-f(x,y_2)|\le K|y_1-y_2|$$

whenever the points $(x,y_1)$ and $(x,y_2)$ both lie in $D$. The constant $K$ is called a Lipschitz constant for the function $f(x,y)$.

## Existence and Uniqueness Theorem

1. Let $f(x,y)$ be continuous in a domain $D$ of the $(x,y)$ plane and let $M$ be a constant such that

$$|f(x,y)|\le M \text{ in } D \quad \text{...(i)}$$

Let $f(x,y)$ satisfy the Lipschitz condition in $y$ in $D$ namely

$$|f(x,y_1)-f(x,y_2)|\le K|y_1-y_2|, \quad \text{...(ii)}$$

where the constant $K$ is independent of $x, y_1, y_2$.

Let the rectangle $R$, defined by

$$|x-x_0|\le h, \qquad |y-y_0|\le k, \quad \text{...(iii)}$$

lie in $D$, where $Mh<k$. Then, for $|x-x_0|\le h$, the differential equation $dy/dx=f(x,y)$ has a unique solution $y=y(x)$ for which $y(x_0)=y_0$

2. If $S$ in either a rectangle $|x-x_0|\le h, |y-y_0|\le k, (h,k>0)$ or a strip $|x-x_0|\le h, |y|<\infty\,(h>0)$, and if $f(x,y)$ is a real valued function defined on $S$ such that $\partial f/\partial y$ exists, is continuous on $S$, and $\left|\frac{\partial}{\partial y}f(x,y)\right|\le K, (x,y)\in S$ for a positive constant $K$, then $f(x,y)$ satisfies a Lipschitz condition on $S$ with Lipschitz constant $K$.

**Proof.** Now,

$$|f(x,y_1)-f(x,y_2)|=\left|\int_{y_1}^{y_2}\frac{\partial}{\partial y}f(x,y)dy\right|$$

$$=\int_{y_1}^{y_2}\left|\frac{\partial}{\partial y}f(x,y)\right||dx|\le K\int_{y_1}^{y_2}|dy|$$

Thus, $|f(x,y_1)-f(x,y_2)|=K|y_1-y_2|$ for $(x,y_1),(x,y_2)\in S$ showing that $f(x,y)$ satisfies Lipschitz condition on $S$ with Lipschitz constant $K$.

***Example* 22.** *Prove that the continuity of $f(x,y)$ is not enough to guarantee the uniqueness of the solution of the initial value problem*

$$\frac{dy}{dx}=f(x,y)=\sqrt{|y|},y(0)=0$$

*OR*

*Show that the solution of the initial value problem $dy/dx=f(x,y)$, $y(x_0)=y_0$ may not be unique although $f(x,y)$ is continuous.*

**Solution.** Consider the initial value problem

$$\frac{dy}{dx}=\sqrt{|y|},y(0)=0 \quad \text{...(i)}$$

Clearly, $f(x,y)=\sqrt{|y|}$ is continuous for all $y$ and Eq. (i) has the following two solutions

$$y\equiv 0 \text{ and } y=\begin{cases} x^2/4, & \text{when } x\ge 0 \\ -x^2/4, & \text{when } x<0\end{cases}$$

We now show that Lipschitz condition

$$\frac{|f(x,y_2)-f(x,y_1)|}{|y_2-y_1|}\le K \quad \text{...(ii)}$$

does not hold good in any region which includes the line $y=0$. e.g., when $y_1=0$ and $y_2$ is positive, then

$$\frac{|f(x,y_2)-f(x,y_1)|}{|y_2-y_1|}=\frac{\sqrt{y_2}}{y_2}=\frac{1}{\sqrt{y_2}}, \text{ as } \sqrt{y_2}>0$$

showing that quantity on LHS of Eq. (ii) can be made as large as we please by choosing $y_2$ sufficiently small. This violates Eq. (ii) because the quantity on LHS of Eq. (ii) should not exceed a fixed constant $K$.

***Example 23.*** *Illustrate by an example that a continuous function may not satisfy a Lipschitz condition on a rectangle.*

**Solution.** Consider the function $f(x,y) = y^{2/3}$ on

the rectangle $S : |x| \le 1,\ |y| \le 1$ ...(i)

Clearly, $f(x,y)$ is continuous in the rectangle $S$.

Here, $\left|\frac{\partial}{\partial y} f(x,y)\right| = \left|\frac{2}{3y^{1/3}}\right| \to \infty$, when, $y \to 0$ ...(ii)

Since, $y = 0$ is a point of the rectangle $S$, Eq. (ii) shows that the Lipschitz condition is not satisfied by the function $f(x,y) = y^{2/3}$ on the rectangle $S$.

***Example 24.*** *Show that* $f(x,y) = 4x^2 + y^2$ *on* $R: |x| \le 1, |y| \le 1$ *satisfies Lipschitz condition.*

**Solution.** Since, $|\partial f/\partial y| = |2y| \le 2$, for each $(x,y) \in R$.

Hence, $f(x,y)$ satisfies the Lipschitz condition with Lipschitz constant 2.

***Example 25.*** *Consider* $f(x,y) = x^3|y|$. *Prove that f satisfies a Lipschitz condition on* $R: |x| \le 2,\ |y| \le 2$ *even though* $\frac{\partial f}{\partial y}$ *does not exist at* $(x, 0)$, *if* $x \ne 0$.

**Solution.** We have $\left(\frac{\partial f}{\partial y}\right)_{(x,\,0)} = \lim_{k \to 0} \frac{f(x,k) - f(x,0)}{k}$

$$= \lim_{k \to 0} \frac{x^3|k|}{k}$$

which does not exist.

Now, $|f(x, y_1) - f(x, y_2)| = |x^3|y_1| - x^3|y_2|| = |x^3|\,||y_1| - |y_2||$

$$\le |x^3||y_1 - y_2|$$

$$\le 8|y_1 - y_2| \qquad (\because |x| \le 2)$$

$\Rightarrow$ $f(x, y)$ satisfies Lipschitz condition on $R$ with Lipschitz constant 8.

***Example 26.*** *Show that* $f(x, y) = xy^2$ *satisfies the Lipschitz condition on the rectangle* $|x| \le 1,\ |y| \le 1$ *but does not satisfy a Lipschitz condition on the strip* $|x| \le 1,\ |y| < \infty$.

**Solution.** We have $|f(x, y_1) - f(x, y_2)|$

$$= |xy_1^2 - xy_2^2| = |x||y_1 + y_2||y_1 - y_2|$$

$$\le |x|(|y_1| + |y_2|)|y_1 - y_2|$$

$$\le 1(1+1)|y_1 - y_2|$$

$$= 2|y_1 - y_2|$$

$\Rightarrow$ $f(x,y)$ satisfies Lipschitz condition on the given rectangle $|x| \le 1, |y| \le 1$

**Alternate Method**

Given, $f(x,y) = xy^2$

$\Rightarrow$ $\frac{\partial f}{\partial y} = 2xy$

$\Rightarrow$ $\left|\frac{\partial f}{\partial y}\right| = |2xy|$

$$= 2|x||y| \le 2 \cdot 1 \cdot 1 = 2$$

$\Rightarrow$ Lipschitz condition holds for $|x| \le 1, |y| \le 1$

but when $|x| \le 1, |y| < \infty$

$$\left|\frac{\partial f}{\partial y}\right| = 2|x||y| < \infty$$

$\Rightarrow$ $\left|\frac{\partial f}{\partial y}\right|$ is unbounded.

*i.e.*, Lipschitz condition is not satisfied.

# Homogeneous and Non-Homogeneous Linear Differential Equations

A linear differential equation of order $n$ and degree one is of the form

$$y^n + p_{n-1}(x)y^{n-1} + p_{n-2}(x)y^{n-2} + \ldots + p_0(x)y = r(x) \qquad \text{...(i)}$$

where $y^n = \frac{d^n y}{dx^n}$

If $r(x) = 0$, then Eq. (i) is homogeneous, otherwise non-homogeneous.

For $r(x) = 0$, Eq. (i) is

$$y^n + p_{n-1}(x)y^{n-1} + p_{n-2}(x)y^{n-2} + \ldots + p_0(x) = 0 \qquad \text{...(ii)}$$

1. If $y_1, y_2, \ldots, y_n$ be $n$ independent solutions of Eq. (ii), then $y = C_1y_1 + C_2y_2 + \ldots + C_ny_n$ is also a solution of Eq. (ii); where $C_1, C_2, \ldots, C_n$ are arbitrary constants. *i.e.*, $y_1, y_2, \ldots, y_n$ forms a basis of solutions of Eq. (ii).
2. $y = C_1y_1 + C_2y_2 + \ldots + C_ny_n$ is the general solution of Eq. (ii).
3. A solution obtained from general solution by giving particular values to constants $C_1, C_2, \ldots, C_n$ called particular solution.
4. Let $u$ be any solution of Eq. (i) and $v$ be complete solution (general solution) of Eq. (ii), then solution of Eq. (i) is $y = u + v$.
5. If $p_0(x), \ldots, p_{n-1}(x)$ are continuous function on some open interval $I$, $x_0 \in I$, then initial value problem
$$y^n + p_{n-1}(x)y^{n-1} + \ldots + p_0(x)y = 0$$
$$y(x_0) = k_0,\ y'(x_0) = k_1, \ldots, y^{n-1}(x_0) = k_{n-1}$$
has a unique solution $y(x)$ on $I$.
6. The wronskion of $y_1, y_2, \ldots, y_n$ is given by
$$W(y_1, \ldots, y_n) = \begin{vmatrix} y_1 & y_2 & \cdots & y_n \\ y_1' & y_2' & \cdots & y_n' \\ \vdots & & & \\ y_1^{(n-1)} & y_2^{(n-1)} & \cdots & y_n^{(n-1)} \end{vmatrix}$$
If the coefficients $p_0(x), \ldots, p_{n-1}(x)$ of $n$-order homogeneous linear differential equation,
$$p_0(x)y^{(n-1)} + p_1(x)y^{(n-1)} + \ldots + p_{n-1}(x)y = 0$$
are continuous on some open interval $I$. Then, $n$ solutions $y_1, y_2, \ldots, y_n$ on interval $I$ are
(i) linearly independent iff their Wronskion $W = 0$ for some $x_0 \in I$. Furthermore, if $W = 0$ for $x = x_0$, then $W \equiv 0$ on $I$.
(ii) linearly dependent, if for all $x \in I$, $W \ne 0$.

***Example 27.*** *Show that functions 1, x, $x^2$ are the basis of a differential equation. Also, find the differential equation.*

**Solution.** Here, $y_1(x)=1$, $y_2(x)=x$, $y_3(x)=x^2$

$$\text{Now,}\quad W(y_1,y_2,y_3)=\begin{vmatrix} y_1 & y_2 & y_3 \\ y_1' & y_2' & y_3' \\ y_1'' & y_2'' & y_3'' \end{vmatrix}$$

$$=\begin{vmatrix} 1 & x & x^2 \\ 0 & 1 & 2x \\ 0 & 0 & 2 \end{vmatrix}=2\neq 0$$

$\Rightarrow$ $y_1, y_2$ and $y_3$ are linearly independent and hence these are the basis of a differential equation.

The general solution is

$$y=C_1(1)+C_2(x)+C_3(x^2)$$

$$\Rightarrow\quad y'=C_2+C_3(2x),\ y''=2C_3,\ y'''=0$$

$\therefore$ Required differential equation is

$$\frac{d^3y}{dx^3}=0$$

***Example 28.*** *Show that the function $y=cx^2+x+3$ is not a unique solution of the initial value problem*

$$x^2y''-2xy'+2y=6 \text{ with } y(0)=3,\ y'(0)=1 \text{ on } (-\infty,\infty)$$

**Solution.** Given, $\quad y=cx^2+x+3$

$$\Rightarrow\quad y'=2cx+1,\ y''=2c$$

$$\text{Now,}\quad x^2y''-2xy'+2y=x^2(2c)-2x(2cx+1)+2y$$

$$=2cx^2-4cx^2-2x+2y$$

$$=-2cx^2-2x+2y$$

$$=2(y-cx^2-x)=6$$

$\Rightarrow$ $y=cx^2+x+3$ is a solution of given IVP.

Given, IVP can be written as

$$y''-\frac{2}{x}y'+\frac{2}{x^2}y=\frac{6}{x^2}$$

Here, $p_0(x)=\dfrac{2}{x^2}$, $p_1(x)=-\dfrac{2}{x^2}$, $r(x)=\dfrac{6}{x^2}$

which are not continuous at $x=0\in(-\infty,\infty)$.

Hence, given IVP does not have a unique solution.

# Linear Differential Equations with Constant Coefficients

Linear differential equation with constant coefficient is given by

$$y^n+a_{n-1}y^{n-1}+a_{n-2}y^{n-2}+\ldots+a_0y=r(x),\ r(x)\neq 0 \quad \ldots\text{(i)}$$

where $a_0, a_1, a_2, \ldots, a_n$ are constants.

Eq. (i) is non-homogeneous.

If $r(x)=0$, then Eq. (i) becomes homogeneous

$$\text{i.e.,}\quad y^n+a_{n-1}y^{n-1}+a_{n-2}y^{n-2}+\ldots+a_0y=0 \quad \ldots\text{(ii)}$$

Denoting $y^n=D^n(y)$, then

From Eq. (i)

$$(D^n+a_{n-1}D^{n-1}+a_{n-2}D^{n-2}+\ldots+a_0)y=r(x)$$

$$\Rightarrow\quad f(D)y=r(x) \quad \ldots\text{(iii)}$$

where, $\quad f(D)=D^n+a_{n-1}D^{n-1}+a_{n-2}D^{n-2}+\ldots+a_0$

Now, the general solution of Eq. (i) is given by

$$y=y_c+y_p$$

where $y_c=c_1y_1+c_2y_2+\ldots+c_ny_n$ is the general solution of Eq. (ii) is called complementary function (CF) of Eq. (iii) and $y_p=\dfrac{1}{f(D)}r(x)$ is called particular integral (PI).

## Method of Finding CF of Eq. (iii)

From Eq. (ii), we have

$$f(D)y=0$$

$\therefore$ Auxiliary Equation (AE) is

$$f(D)=0$$

$$\Rightarrow\quad f(m)=0 \quad \ldots\text{(iv)}$$

**(i)** If $m_1, m_2, \ldots, m_n$ be the different roots of the AE Eq. (iv), then CF of Eq. (iii) is given by

$$y=C_1e^{m_1x}+C_2e^{m_2x}+\ldots+C_ne^{m_nx}$$

where $C_1, C_2, \ldots, C_n$ are constants equal in number to the order of equation.

***Example 29.*** *Solve* $\dfrac{d^3y}{dx^3}-6\dfrac{d^2y}{dx^2}+11\dfrac{dy}{dx}-6y=0$

**Solution.** Here, AE is

$$m^3-6m^2+11m-6=0$$

$$\Rightarrow\quad m=1,2,3$$

Hence, General solution is $y=C_1e^x+C_2e^{2x}+C_3e^{3x}$

**(ii)** If all roots of $f(m)=0$ are equal, then CF is given by

$$y=(C_1+C_2x+C_3x^2+\ldots+C_nx^{n-1})e^{mx}$$

***Example 30.*** *Solve* $\dfrac{d^2y}{dx^2}-6\dfrac{dy}{dx}+9y=0$

**Solution.** Here AE is $m^2-6m+9=0$

$$\Rightarrow\quad m=3,3$$

Hence, General solution is

$$y=(C_1+C_2x)\,e^{3x}$$

**(iii)** If $\alpha\pm i\beta$ be roots of $f(m)=0$, then CF is given by

$$y=e^{\alpha x}(C_1\cos\beta x+C_2\sin\beta x)$$

***Example 31.*** *Solve* $\dfrac{d^3y}{dx^3}-8y=0$

**Solution.** Here, AE is $\quad m^3-8=0$

$$\Rightarrow\quad m=2,\ -1\pm\sqrt{3}i$$

Hence, General solution is

$$y=C_1e^{2x}+e^{-x}(C_2\cos\sqrt{3}x+C_3\sin\sqrt{3}x)$$

**(iv)** When the roots $\alpha\pm i\beta$ are each repeated $r$ times, then CF is

$$y=e^{\alpha x}[(C_1+C_2x+C_3x^2+\ldots+C_rx^{r-1})\cos\beta x$$
$$+(d_1+d_2x+d_3x^2+\ldots+d_rx^{r-1})\sin\beta x]$$

***Example 32.*** *Solve* $\frac{d^4y}{dx^4}+4\frac{d^2y}{dx^2}+4y=0$

**Solution.** Here, AE is $m^4+4m^2+4=0$

$\Rightarrow \quad (m^2+2)^2=0$

$\Rightarrow \quad m=\pm\sqrt{2}i,\ \pm\sqrt{2}i$

Hence, General solution is

$y=e^{0\cdot x}[(C_1+C_2x)\cos\sqrt{2}x+(C_3+C_4x)\sin\sqrt{2}x]$

$\Rightarrow \quad y=(C_1+C_2x)\cos\sqrt{2}x+(C_3+C_4x)\sin\sqrt{2}x$

## Method of Finding PI of Eq. (iii)

PI of differntial Eq. (iii) is $y_p=\frac{1}{f(D)}r(x)$

> ***Note*** **(a)** $Df(x)\equiv$ Differential of $f(x)$
>
> **(b)** $\frac{1}{D}f(x)\equiv$ Integral of $f(x)$

**(i)** $\frac{1}{f(D)}x^m=\{f(D)\}^{-1}x^m$

Expanding $\{f(D)\}^{-1}$ in ascending powers of $D$ by using binomial theorem.

***Example 33.*** *Find PI of* $\frac{d^2y}{dx^2}-4\frac{dy}{dx}+4y=x^2$

**Solution.** We have $(D^2-4D+4)y=x^2$

Hence, $\quad \text{PI}=\frac{1}{D^2-4D+4}x^2$

$$=\frac{1}{(D-2)^2}x^2=\frac{1}{4\left(1-\frac{D}{2}\right)^2}x^2$$

$$=\frac{1}{4}\left(1-\frac{D}{2}\right)^{-2}x^2$$

$$=\frac{1}{4}\left[1+2\cdot\left(\frac{D}{2}\right)+3\left(\frac{D}{2}\right)^2+\ldots\right]x^2$$

$$=\frac{1}{4}\left[x^2+2x+\frac{3}{2}\right]$$

> ***Remark*** AE of the above equation is
>
> $m^2-4m+4=0\Rightarrow m=2,2$
>
> $\therefore$ CF is $y_c=(C_1+C_2x)e^{2x}$
>
> $\therefore$ Complete solution of the above equation is
>
> $y=\text{CF}+\text{PI}$
>
> $\Rightarrow \quad y=(C_1+C_2x)e^{2x}+\frac{1}{4}x^2+\frac{x}{2}+\frac{3}{8}$

**(ii)** $\frac{1}{f(D^2)}(\sin ax)=\frac{1}{f(-a^2)}\sin ax$

and $\quad \frac{1}{f(D^2)}(\cos ax)=\frac{1}{f(-a^2)}\cos ax$

If $f(-a^2)=0$, then

$$\frac{1}{f(D^2)}(\sin ax)=x\cdot\frac{1}{f'(-a^2)}(\sin ax)$$

Similar results for $\cos ax$.

If $f'(-a^2)=0$, then

$$\frac{1}{f(D^2)}(\sin ax)=x^2\cdot\frac{1}{f''(-a^2)}(\sin ax)\ \text{and so on.}$$

Similar results for $\cos ax$.

***Example 34.*** *Find PI for* $(D^2+D+1)y=\cos 2x$

**Solution.** We have $\text{PI}=\frac{1}{D^2+D+1}(\cos 2x)$

$$=\frac{1}{-2^2+D+1}(\cos 2x)=\frac{1}{D-3}(\cos 2x)$$

$$=\frac{D+3}{D^2-9}(\cos 2x)=\frac{D+3}{-2^2-9}(\cos 2x)$$

$$=-\frac{1}{13}(-2\sin 2x+3\cos 2x)$$

***Example 35.*** *Find PI for* $(D^2+4)y=\sin 2x$

**Solution.** We have $\text{PI}=\frac{1}{D^2+4}(\sin 2x)$

$$=x.\frac{1}{2D}(\sin 2x) \quad (\because -2^2+4=0)$$

$$=\frac{x}{2}\left(-\frac{\cos 2x}{2}\right)$$

$$=-\frac{x\cos 2x}{4}$$

**(iii)** $\frac{1}{f(D)}e^{ax}=\frac{1}{f(a)}e^{ax}, \quad$ if $\quad f(a)\neq 0$

$=x\cdot\frac{1}{f'(a)}e^{ax}, \quad$ if $\quad f(a)=0$

$=x^2\cdot\frac{1}{f''(a)}e^{ax}, \quad$ if $\quad f'(a)=0$

OR

$\frac{1}{f(D)}e^{ax}=e^{ax}\cdot\frac{1}{f(D+a)}\cdot 1, \quad$ if $\quad f(a)=0$

***Example 36.*** *Find PI of* $(D^2+3D+2)y=e^{2x}$

**Solution.** We have $\text{PI}=\frac{1}{D^2+3D+2}(e^{2x})=\frac{1}{2^2+3\times 2+2}e^{2x}$

$$=\frac{1}{4+6+2}e^{2x}=\frac{e^{2x}}{12}$$

***Example 37.*** *Find PI of* $(D^2-6D+9)y=6e^{3x}$

**Solution.** We have $\text{PI}=\frac{1}{D^2-6D+9}6e^{3x}=x\cdot\frac{1}{2D-6}6e^{3x}$ $\quad [\because f(a)=0]$

$$=\frac{x^2}{2}6e^{3x} \quad [\because f'(a)=0]$$

$$=3x^2e^{3x}$$

OR

We have $PI = 6e^{3x}\cdot\frac{1}{(D+3)^2-6(D+3)+9}\cdot 1$

$= 6e^{3x}\cdot\frac{1}{D^2+6D+9-6D-18+9}\cdot 1$

$= 6e^{3x}\cdot\frac{1}{D^2}(1) = 6e^{3x}\cdot\frac{x^2}{2} = 3x^2e^{3x}$

**(iv)** $\frac{1}{f(D)}[e^{ax}\phi(x)] = e^{ax}\cdot\frac{1}{f(D+a)}\phi(x)$

***Example 38.*** *Find PI for* $(D^2-4D+4)y = xe^{2x}$

**Solution.** We have $PI = \frac{1}{D^2-4D+4}xe^{2x} = \frac{1}{(D-2)^2}xe^{2x}$

$= e^{2x}\cdot\frac{1}{(D+2-2)^2}x = e^{2x}\cdot\frac{1}{D^2}(x)$

$= \frac{x^3\cdot e^{2x}}{6}$

**(v)** $\frac{1}{D-a}\phi(x) = e^{ax}\int e^{-ax}\phi(x)\,dx$

***Example 39.*** *Find PI for* $(D^2+9)y = \sec 3x$

**Solution.** We have $PI = \frac{1}{D^2+9}\cdot\sec 3x = \frac{1}{(D+3i)(D-3i)}\cdot\sec 3x$

$= \frac{1}{6i}\left[\frac{1}{D-3i}-\frac{1}{D+3i}\right]\cdot\sec 3x$

$= \frac{1}{6i}\cdot\frac{1}{D-3i}\cdot\sec 3x - \frac{1}{6i}\cdot\frac{1}{D+3i}\cdot\sec 3x$ ...(i)

Now, $\frac{1}{D-3i}\cdot\sec 3x = e^{3ix}\int e^{-3ix}\sec 3x\,dx$

$= e^{3ix}\int\frac{\cos 3x - i\sin 3x}{\cos 3x}dx$

$= e^{3ix}\int(1-i\tan 3x)\,dx$

$= e^{3ix}\left(x+\frac{i}{3}\log\cos 3x\right)$

Changing $i$ to $-i$, we have

$\frac{1}{D+3i}\sec 3x = e^{-3ix}\left(x-\frac{i}{3}\log\cos 3x\right)$

Putting these values in Eq. (i), we get

$PI = \frac{1}{6i}\left[e^{3ix}\left(x+\frac{i}{3}\log\cos 3x\right) - e^{-3ix}\left(x-\frac{i}{3}\log\cos 3x\right)\right]$

$= \frac{x}{6i}e^{3ix} + \frac{e^{3ix}\log\cos 3x}{18} - \frac{xe^{-3ix}}{6i} + \frac{e^{-3ix}}{18}\log\cos 3x$

$= \frac{x}{3}\cdot\frac{e^{3ix}-e^{-3ix}}{2i} + \frac{1}{9}\cdot\frac{e^{3ix}+e^{-3ix}}{2}\log\cos 3x$

$= \frac{x}{3}\cdot\frac{e^{3ix}-e^{3ix}}{2i} + \frac{1}{9}\cdot\frac{e^{3ix}-e^{-3ix}}{2}\log\cos 3x$

$= \frac{x}{3}\sin 3x + \frac{1}{9}\cos 3x\cdot\log\cos 3x$

***Example 40.*** *Solve* $(D^2+4)y = \cos 2x$

**Solution.** We have $(D^2+4)y = \cos 2x$

Hence, Auxiliary equation is $D^2+4=0$

$\Rightarrow D = \pm 2i$ $\therefore$ $CF = A\cos 2x + B\sin 2x$

Now $PI = \frac{1}{D^2+4}\cos 2x$

$= x\cdot\frac{1}{2D}\cos 2x = \frac{x}{2}\left(\frac{1}{2}\sin 2x\right) = \frac{x}{4}\sin 2x$

Complete solution is $y = A\cos 2x + B\sin 2x + \frac{x}{4}\sin 2x$

***Example 41.*** *Solve* $(D^2-5D+6)y = e^x\cos 2x$

**Solution.** We have $(D^2-5D+6)y = e^x\cos 2x$

$\therefore$ AE is $D^2-5D+6=0$

$(D-2)(D-3)=0$, or $D = 2, 3$

$CF = C_1e^{2x}+C_2e^{3x}$

Now, $PI = \frac{1}{D^2-5D+6}e^x\cos 2x$

$= e^x\cdot\frac{1}{(D+1)^2-5(D+1)+6}\cos 2x$

$= e^x\cdot\frac{1}{D^2-3D+2}\cos 2x = e^x\cdot\frac{1}{-4-3D+2}\cos 2x$

$= -e^x\cdot\frac{1}{3D+2}\cos 2x = -e^x\cdot\frac{3D-2}{9D^2-4}\cos 2x$

$= -e^x\cdot\frac{3D-2}{9(-4)-4}\cos 2x = \frac{e^x}{40}(3D-2)\cos 2x$

$= \frac{e^x}{40}(-6\sin 2x - 2\cos 2x) = -\frac{e^x}{20}(3\sin 2x+\cos 2x)$

Hence, The complete solution is

$y = C_1e^{2x}+C_2e^{3x} - \frac{e^x}{20}(3\sin 2x+\cos 2x)$

***Example 42.*** *Solve* $\frac{d^3y}{dx^3} - 3\frac{d^2y}{dx^2} + 4\frac{dy}{dx} - 2y = e^x + \cos x$

**Solution.** Given, $(D^3-3D^2+4D-2)y = e^x+\cos x$

$\therefore$ AE is $m^3-3m^2+4m-2=0$

$\Rightarrow$ $(m-1)(m^2-2m+2)=0$ *i.e.*, $m = 1, 1\pm i$

$\therefore$ $CF = C_1e^x + e^x(C_2\cos x + C_3\sin x)$

Now, $PI = \frac{1}{(D-1)(D^2-2D+2)}e^x + \frac{1}{D^3-3D^2+4D-2}\cos x$

$= \frac{1}{(D-1)(1-2+2)}e^x + \frac{1}{(-1)D-3(-1)+4D-2}\cos x$

$= \frac{1}{(D-1)}e^x + \frac{1}{3D+1}\cos x$

$= e^x\frac{1}{D+1-1}\cdot 1 + \frac{3D-1}{9D^2-1}\cos x$

$= e^x\frac{1}{D}\cdot 1 + \frac{(-3\sin x-\cos x)}{-9-1}$

$= e^x\cdot x + \frac{1}{10}(3\sin x+\cos x)$

Hence, complete solution is

$y = C_1e^x + e^x(C_2\cos x + C_3\sin x) + xe^x + \frac{1}{10}(3\sin x+\cos x)$

***Example 43.*** *Solve the following simultaneous equations*

$$\frac{dx}{dt}+\frac{dy}{dt}+2x+y=0$$

$$\frac{dy}{dt}+5x+3y=0$$

**Solution.** We have $\frac{dx}{dt}+\frac{dy}{dt}+2x+y=0$

$$\frac{dy}{dt}+5x+3y=0$$

$$(D+2)x+(D+1)y=0 \quad \text{...(i)}$$

$$5x+(D+3)y=0 \quad \text{...(ii)}$$

Multiplying Eq. (i) by 5 and Eq. (ii) by $(D+2)$, we get

$$5(D+2)x+5(D+1)y=0 \quad \text{...(iii)}$$

$$5(D+2)x+(D+2)(D+3)y=0 \quad \text{...(iv)}$$

Subtracting Eq. (iii) from Eq. (iv), we get

$$(D+2)(D+3)y-5(D+1)y=0$$

$$(D^2+5D+6-5D-5)y=0$$

$$\Rightarrow \quad (D^2+1)y=0 \ \Rightarrow \ D^2+1=0,\ D=\pm i$$

$$y=C_1\cos t+C_2\sin t$$

$$\frac{dy}{dt}=-C_1\sin t+C_2\cos t$$

Putting the values of $Dy$ and $y$ in Eq. (ii), we get

$$5x-C_1\sin t+C_2\cos t+3C_1\cos t+3C_2\sin t=0$$

$$\Rightarrow \quad 5x=C_1\sin t-3C_2\sin t-3C_1\cos t-C_2\cos t$$

$$x=\frac{1}{5}(C_1-3C_2)\sin t-\frac{1}{5}(3C_1+C_2)\cos t$$

# Variation of Parameters

Consider second order linear differential equation

$$y''+a_1y'+a_0y=r(x),\quad r(x)\neq 0$$

then the complete solution of above differential equation by method of variation of parameter is given by

$$y=C_1y_1+C_2y_2+uy_1+vy_2$$

where $$u=\int -\frac{y_2}{W(y_1,y_2)}r(x)\,dx,$$

$$v=\int \frac{y_1}{W(y_1,y_2)}r(x)\,dx$$

$y_1$ and $y_2$ are two linearly independent solution of

$$y''+a_1y'+a_0y=0$$

> ***Note*** In the above solution $C_1y_1+C_2y_2$ is the CF and $uy_1+vy_2$ is the PI of the differential equation.
> $$y''+a_1y'+a_0y=r(x)$$

***Example 44.*** *By using variation of parameters method, solve* $y''+y=\sec x$

**Solution.** Here, AE is $m^2+1=0 \quad \Rightarrow m=\pm i$

CF is $y_c=C_1\cos x+C_2\sin x$

Here, two linearly independent solutions of $y''+y=0$ are

$$y_1=\cos x \text{ and } y_2=\sin x$$

$$W(y_1\ y_2)=\begin{vmatrix} y_1 & y_2\\ y_1' & y_2'\end{vmatrix}=\begin{vmatrix}\cos x & \sin x\\ -\sin x & \cos x\end{vmatrix}$$

$$=\cos^2 x+\sin^2 x=1$$

$$r(x)=\sec x$$

$$\therefore \quad u=\int -\frac{y_2}{W(y_1,y_2)}r(x)\,dx=\int -\frac{\sin x}{1}\sec x\,dx$$

$$=-\int \tan x\,dx=\log\cos x$$

and $$v=\int \frac{y_1}{W(y_1,y_2)}r(x)\,dx=\int \frac{\cos x}{1}\sec x\,dx$$

$$=\int dx=x$$

Hence, PI is $y_p=uy_1+vy_2=(\log\cos x)\cos x+(x)\sin x$

$\Rightarrow$ Complete solution is

$$y=y_c+y_p$$

$$=C_1\cos x+C_2\sin x+(\log\cos x)\cos x+x\sin x$$

# Self-Adjoint Equation

If the coefficients $a_0(x), a_1(x)$ and $a_2(x)$ in the differential equation $a_0(x)y''+a_1(x)y'+a_2(x)y=0$ are continuous on $a\le x\le b$ and $a_0(x)\neq 0$ on $a\le x\le b$.

Then, above differential equation can be transformed into the equivalent self-adjoint equation

$$[r(x)y']'+p(x)y=0$$

where, $r(x)=e^{\int\frac{a_1(x)}{a_0(x)}dx},\ p(x)=\frac{a_2(x)}{a_0(x)}r(x)$

> ***Note*** **(a)** $a_0(x)$ has a continuous second order derivative.
> **(b)** $a_1(x)$ has continuous first order derivative and
> **(c)** $a_2(x)$ is continuous on $x\in[a,b]$
> **(d)** $a_0(x)\neq 0$, then
> The necessary and sufficient condition that above equation be self-adjoint is
> $$a_0'(x)=a_1(x) \text{ on } x\in[a,b]$$
> and in that case differential equation may be written in a form $[a_0(x)y']'+a_2(x)y=0$

***Example 45.*** *Transform* $x^2y''-2xy'+2y=0$ *into an self-adjoint equation.*

**Solution.** Here, $a_0(x)=x^2,\ a_1(x)=-2x,\ a_2(x)=2$

and $a_0'(x)\neq a_1(x)$

$$r(x)=e^{\int\frac{a_1(x)}{a_0(x)}dx}=e^{\int -\frac{2x}{x^2}dx}$$

$$=e^{-2\int\frac{dx}{x}}=e^{-2\log x}=e^{\log x^{-2}}=\frac{1}{x^2}$$

$$p(x)=\frac{a_2(x)}{a_0(x)}r(x)=\frac{2}{x^2}\frac{1}{x^2}=\frac{2}{x^4}$$

⇒ Required self-adjoint equation is

$$[r(x)y']' + p(x)y = 0$$

⇒ $$\left[\frac{1}{x^2}y'\right]' + \frac{2}{x^4}y = 0$$

***Example 46.*** *Show that equation* $x^3y'' + 3x^2y' + y = 0$ *is self-adjoint and also write the equation.*

**Solution.** Here, $a_0(x) = x^3$, $a_1(x) = 3x^2$, $a_2(x) = 1$

$$a_0'(x) = a_1(x)$$

∴ Required self-adjoint equation is

$$[a_0(x)y']' + a_2(x)y = 0$$

⇒ $$[x^3y']' + y = 0$$

# Strum-Liouville Problem (S-L-P)

A second order Strum-Liouville problem is a homogeneous boundary-value problem of the form

$$[r(x)y']' + [q(x) + \lambda p(x)]y = 0 \quad ...(i)$$

with the following boundary conditions.

$$\left.\begin{aligned}\alpha_1 y(a) + \alpha_2 y'(a) = 0\\ \beta_1 y(b) + \beta_2 y'(b) = 0\end{aligned}\right\} \quad ...(ii)$$

Here, $p(x)$, $q(x)$, $r(x)$, $r'(x)$ in Eq. (i) are continuous on $[a, b]$ and $p(x) > 0$. $\lambda$ is a parameter. Any two out of $\alpha_1$, $\alpha_2$, $\beta_1$, $\beta_2$ are non-zero. $y = 0$ always a solution of S-L-P for any $\lambda$, called trivial solution.

The non-zero solutions of the S-L-P given by Eq. (i) and Eq. (ii) are called eigen functions of the S-L-P and the values of $\lambda$ for which such solutions exist are called eigen values of the S-L-P.

## Properties of Sturm-Liouville Problem

**(i)** The eigen values of a S-L-P are real and non-negative.

**(ii)** Eigen values follow

$$\lambda_1 < \lambda_2 < \lambda_3 < \ldots$$

such that $\lim_{n\to\infty} \lambda_n = \infty$

**(iii)** For each $\lambda_i$ in S-L-P, there exist one and only one linearly independent eigen function.

**(iv)** The set of eigen functions $\{y_i(x)\}$ of S-L-P are orthogonal with respect to weight function $p(x)$

i.e., $\int_a^b p(x)y_m(x)y_n(x)\,dx = 0 \quad (m \neq n)$

e.g., (i) $y'' + \lambda y = 0$ where $y(a) = y(b) = 0$ is the simplest form of S-L-P.

(ii) $(xy')' + \{(x^2 + 1) + \lambda e^x\}y = 0$;

$y(1) + 2y'(1) = 0$

$y(2) - 3y'(2) = 0$ is a S-L-P.

Here, $r(x) = x$, $q(x) = x^2 + 1$, $p(x) = e^x$ and $r(x), q(x)$ and $p(x)$ are all continuous in [1, 2] and also $p(x) = e^x > 0$, $\forall\ x \in [a, b]$.

***Example 47.*** *Find the eigen values and eigen functions of the Strum-Liouville Problem.*

$$y'' + \lambda y = 0;\ y(0) = 0,\ y'(1) = 0$$

**Solution.** ***Case I*** Let $\lambda = 0$, then

S-L equation becomes $y'' = 0$

⇒ $$y(x) = ax + b$$

$$y'(x) = a$$

By using boundary conditions, we get

$$y(0) = 0 \Rightarrow a \times 0 + b = 0$$

⇒ $$b = 0$$

and $$y'(1) = 0$$

⇒ $$a = 0$$

∴ Solution $y = ax + b$ reduces to $y = 0$ which is a trivial solution of S-L-P.

⇒ There is no eigen function corresponding to $\lambda = 0$.

***Case II*** Let $\lambda = k^2 \quad (k \neq 0)$

Then, given equation is

$$y'' + k^2y = 0$$

AE is $m^2 + k^2 = 0 \Rightarrow m = \pm ki$

∴ Solution is

$$y(x) = a\cos kx + b\sin kx$$

⇒ $$y'(x) = -ak\sin kx + bk\cos kx$$

From boundary conditions,

$$y(0) = 0,\ y'(1) = 0$$

⇒ $$a = 0,\ bk\cos k = 0$$

⇒ $$a = 0,\ b\cos k = 0 \quad (\because k \neq 0)$$

If $b = 0$, then with $a = 0$, $y(x) = 0$ which is not an eigen function, so $b \neq 0$ for the existence of eigen functions.

Now, $b \neq 0 \Rightarrow \cos k = 0$

⇒ $$k = (2n+1)\frac{\pi}{2}, n = 0, 1, 2, \ldots$$

∴ Eigen values are

$$\lambda = k^2 = (2n+1)^2\frac{\pi^2}{4}, n = 0, 1, 2, \ldots$$

and the corresponding eigen functions are

$$y(x) = b\sin(2n+1)\frac{\pi}{2}x$$

So, required eigen functions $y_n(x)$ with corresponding eigen values $\lambda_n$ are $y_n(x) = b_n\sin(2n+1)\frac{\pi x}{2}$, where $n = 0, 1, 2, \ldots$

***Case III*** Let $\lambda = -k^2 \quad (k \neq 0)$

Then, equation is

$$y'' - k^2y = 0$$

AE is $m^2 - k^2 = 0 \Rightarrow m = \pm k$

∴ Solution is $y(x) = C_1e^{kx} + C_2e^{-kx}$

⇒ $$y'(x) = kC_1e^{kx} - kC_2e^{-kx}$$

From boundary conditions, we get

$$y(0) = 0,\ y'(1) = 0$$

⇒ $$C_1 + C_2 = 0,\ k(C_1e^k - C_2e^{-k}) = 0$$

⇒ $$C_1 = 0,\ C_2 = 0 \quad (\because k \neq 0)$$

⇒ $$y(x) = 0$$

⇒ No eigen function exist.

## Green's Function

Consider a linear homogeneous differential equation of order $n$, i.e.,

$$L[y]=0 \quad \text{...(i)}$$

where $L$ is the differential operator

i.e., $$L=p_0(x)\frac{d^n}{dx^n}+p_1(x)\frac{d^{n-1}}{dx^{n-1}}+\ldots+p_n(x) \quad \text{...(ii)}$$

where the functions $p_0(x), p_1(x), \ldots, p_n(x)$ are continuous on $[a, b]$, $p_0(x)\neq 0$ on $[a, b]$ and the boundary conditions are

$$B_k(y)=0 \qquad (k=1,2,\ldots,n) \quad \text{...(iii)}$$

$$B_k(y)=\sum \alpha_k^{n-1}y^{n-1}(a)+\sum \beta_k^{n-1}y^{n-1}(b) \quad \text{...(iv)}$$

where the linear forms $B_1, B_2, \ldots, B_n$ in $y(a), y'(a), y''(a), \ldots, y^{n-1}(a); y(b), y'(b), \ldots, y^{n-1}(b)$ are linearly independent.

If the homogeneous boundary value problem given by Eq. (i) to Eq. (iv) has only a trivial solution $y(x)=0$, then the Green's function $G(x, t)$ constructed for any point $a<t<b$ for BVP Eq. (i) to Eq. (iv) which has the following four properties.

**(i)** In each of the interval $[a, t)$ and $[t, b]$ the function $G(x, t)$ considered as a function of $x$ is a solution of Eq. (i) i.e., $L[G]=0$

**(ii)** $G(x, t)$ is continuous in $x$ for fixed $t$ and has continuous derivative with respect to $x$ upto order $(n-2)$ inclusive for $a\leq x\leq b$.

**(iii)** $(n-1)$ th derivative of $G(x, t)$ with respect to $x$ at $x=t$ has the discontinuity of the first kind, the jump being equal to $-\dfrac{1}{p_0(t)}$,

i.e., $$\left[\frac{\partial^{n-1}}{\partial x^{n-1}}G(x, t)\right]_{x=t+0}-\left[\frac{\partial^{n-1}}{\partial x^{n-1}}G(x, t)\right]_{x=t-0}=-\frac{1}{p_0(t)}$$

**(iv)** $G(x, t)$ satisfies boundary conditions

i.e., $$B_k(G)=0,\ k=1, 2, \ldots, n$$

### A Particular Case

Consider the second order linear differential equation

$$L[y]+\phi(x)=0$$

where $$L\equiv\frac{d}{dx}\left(p\frac{d}{dx}\right)+q$$

together with homogeneous boundary condition

$$\alpha y+\beta\frac{dy}{dx}=0$$

Then, the constructed Green's function for any point $t$; $a<t<b$ having following properties. Assuming $G(x, t)=G_1(x, t)$ when $x<t$ and $G(x, t)=G_2(x, t)$ when $x>t$

**I.** $G_1$ and $G_2$ satisfy $L[G]=0$

i.e., $$L[G_1]=0 \quad x<t$$

and $$L[G_2]=0 \quad x>t$$

**II.** $G(x, t)$ is continuous at $x=t$

i.e., $$G_1(x, t)\big|_{x=t-0}=G_2(x, t)\big|_{x=t+0}$$

**III.** $$G_2'(x, t)\big|_{x=t+0}-G_1'(x, t)\big|_{x=t-0}=\frac{-1}{p(t)}$$

**IV.** $G_1$ and $G_2$ satisfy boundary conditions at the end points $G(x, t)$ as defined called the Green's function.

If $G(x, t)$ exists, then the solution of the given problem can be transformed into integral equation

$$y(x)=\int_a^b G(x, t)y(t)\,dt+F(x)$$

which is a Fredholm homogeneous integral equation of the second kind.

> ***Note*** **(a)** The Green's function $G(x, t)$ is called one dimensional, because one of the two arguments $x$ and $t$ as the independent variable and the other is a parameter.
>
> **(b)** The use of Green's function enables the conversion of a self-adjoint eigen value problem to a Fredholm integral equation of second kind.

## Method of Constructing Green's Function

Consider a second order differential equation

$$[p(x)y'(x)]'+q(x)y(x)+r(x)=0$$

which is in the form of

$$L[y(x)]+\phi(x)=0$$

Green's function is constructed only when trivial solution $y(x)=0$ exist for the given differential equation with the help of given boundary condition and the Green function is given by

$$G(x, t)=\begin{cases}-\dfrac{y_1(x)y_2(t)}{C}; & x<t\\ -\dfrac{y_2(x)y_1(t)}{C}; & x>t\end{cases}$$

where, $$C=p(t)W(y_1(t), y_2(t))$$

Here, $y_1(x)$ and $y_2(x)$ are two independent solutions of

$$L[y(x)]=0$$

by using given boundary conditions.

***Example 48.*** *Construct Green's function for the BVP*

$$u''-u=x;\quad u(0)=u(1)=0$$

**Solution.** Given equation is

$$u''-u-x=0$$

Comparing with $L[u(x)]+\phi(x)=0$

$$L[u(x)]=u''-u \text{ and } \phi(x)=-x$$

The associated BVP is given by

$$L[u(x)]=0$$

$$\Rightarrow \quad u''-u=0$$

$$\Rightarrow \quad (D^2-1)u=0 \quad \text{...(i)}$$

with boundary conditions

$$u(0)=0,\ u(1)=0 \quad \text{...(ii)}$$

The general solution of Eq. (i) is given by

$$u(x)=a\cosh x+b\sinh x$$

By using Eq. (ii), $\quad a=0$

and $\quad b\sinh 1=0 \Rightarrow b=0 \qquad (\because \sinh 1\neq 0)$

Therefore, only the trivial solution $u(x)=0$ exist for the given BVP (i) subject to the boundary conditions Eq. (ii) and therefore, Green's function exist

When, $u(0)=0 \Rightarrow a=0$

Hence, $u(x)=b\sinh x$

For $b=1$, $u_1(x)=\sinh x$

and when $u(1)=0$

$\Rightarrow a\cosh 1+b\sinh 1=0$

$$\Rightarrow \quad b=-a\frac{\cosh 1}{\sinh 1}$$

Hence,
$$u(x)=a\cosh x-a\frac{\cosh 1}{\sinh 1}\sinh x$$
$$=a\left[\frac{\cosh x\sinh 1-\sinh x\cosh 1}{\sinh 1}\right]$$
$$=-\frac{a\sinh(x-1)}{\sinh 1}$$

For $a=-\sinh 1$

$$u_2(x)=\sinh(x-1)$$
$$W(u_1(t),u_2(t))=\begin{vmatrix}u_1(t) & u_2(t)\\ u_1'(t) & u_2'(t)\end{vmatrix}$$
$$=\begin{vmatrix}\sinh t & \sinh(t-1)\\ \cosh t & \cosh(t-1)\end{vmatrix}$$
$$=\sinh t\cosh(t-1)-\cosh t\sinh(t-1)$$
$$=\sin[ht-h(t-1)]=\sinh 1$$
$$p(x)=1 \Rightarrow p(t)=1$$

Hence, $C=p(t)W(u_1(t),u_2(t))=\sinh 1$

Therefore, Green's function is

$$G(x,t)=\begin{cases}-\dfrac{u_1(x)u_2(t)}{C}; & 0\le x<t\\[2mm] -\dfrac{u_2(x)u_1(t)}{C}; & t<x\le 1\end{cases}$$

$$=\begin{cases}-\dfrac{\sinh x\sinh(t-1)}{\sinh 1}; & 0\le x<t\\[2mm] -\dfrac{\sinh(x-1)\sinh t}{\sinh 1}; & t<x\le 1\end{cases}$$

***Example 49.*** *Construct the Green's function for BVP*

$$u''+\lambda u=x;\quad u(0)=u\left(\frac{\pi}{2}\right)=0$$

**Solution.** Given, equation is

$$u''(x)+\lambda u(x)=x$$
$$\Rightarrow \quad u''(x)+\lambda u(x)-x=0$$

For sake of simplicity we take associated BVP

$$L[u(x)]=u''(x)$$

and $\phi(x)=\lambda u(x)-x$, so that

$$L[u(x)]+\phi(x)=0$$

Now, $L[u(x)]=0 \Rightarrow u''(x)=0$

$$\Rightarrow \quad u(x)=ax+b$$

When $u(0)=0$, $u\left(\frac{\pi}{2}\right)=0 \Rightarrow u(x)=0$

Hence, Green's function exist.

For $u(0)=0$, $b=0$

$$\Rightarrow \quad u(x)=ax$$

For $a=1$, $u_1(x)=x$

For $u\left(\frac{\pi}{2}\right)=0 \Rightarrow a\frac{\pi}{2}+b=0$

$$\Rightarrow \quad a\frac{\pi}{2}=-b \Rightarrow a=-\frac{2b}{\pi}$$

$$\Rightarrow \quad u(x)=-\frac{2b}{\pi}x+b=\left(1-\frac{2}{\pi}x\right)b$$

For $b=1$

$$u_2(x)=\frac{\pi-2x}{\pi}$$
$$W(u_1(t),u_2(t))=\begin{vmatrix}u_1(t) & u_2(t)\\ u_1'(t) & u_2'(t)\end{vmatrix}=\begin{vmatrix}t & 1-\frac{2}{\pi}t\\ 1 & -\frac{2}{\pi}\end{vmatrix}$$
$$=-\frac{2t}{\pi}-\left(1-\frac{2t}{\pi}\right)=-1$$
$$p(t)=1$$
$$\Rightarrow \quad C=-1$$

Hence,
$$G(x,t)=\begin{cases}x\left(1-\dfrac{2t}{\pi}\right); & 0\le x<t\\[2mm] \left(1-\dfrac{2x}{\pi}t\right); & t<x\le\dfrac{\pi}{2}\end{cases}$$

# Partial Differential Equations

Let $z=f(x,y)$ be a function of two independent variables $x$ and $y$. Then, partial derivative of $z$ with respect to $x$ keeping $y$ constant is $\frac{\partial z}{\partial x}$ and partial derivative of $z$ with respect to $y$ keeping $x$ constant is $\frac{\partial z}{\partial y}$.

**Notations** $p=\frac{\partial z}{\partial x}$, $q=\frac{\partial z}{\partial y}$,

$$r=\frac{\partial^2 z}{\partial x^2},\; s=\frac{\partial^2 z}{\partial x\partial y} \text{ and } t=\frac{\partial^2 z}{\partial y^2}$$

In case of $u=f(x,y)$

$$p=\frac{\partial u}{\partial x},\; q=\frac{\partial u}{\partial y}$$
$$r=\frac{\partial^2 u}{\partial x^2},\; s=\frac{\partial^2 u}{\partial x\partial y} \text{ and } t=\frac{\partial^2 u}{\partial y^2}$$

**Definition** An equation involving partial derivatives is called a partial differential equation (PDE).

e.g.,

(i) $\frac{\partial z}{\partial x}=a$

(ii) $\frac{\partial z}{\partial x}+\frac{\partial z}{\partial y}-z=xy$

(iii) $$x\frac{\partial z}{\partial x}+y\frac{\partial z}{\partial y}=\left(\frac{\partial z}{\partial y}\right)^2$$

> ***Note*** Order and degree of PDE are defined in same way as order and degree of ODE are defined.

## Linear and Non-Linear PDE

A partial differential equation is said to be linear, if the dependent variable and its partial derivative occur only in the first degree and are not multiplied.

e.g., (i) $\frac{\partial z}{\partial x}+\frac{\partial z}{\partial y}=xyz$

(ii) $x\frac{\partial z}{\partial x}+y\frac{\partial z}{\partial y}=z$

A partial differential equation is not linear called non-linear PDE.

e.g., (i) $\left(\frac{\partial z}{\partial x}\right)^2+\frac{\partial^3 z}{\partial y^3}=x\left(\frac{\partial z}{\partial x}\right)$ (ii) $\left(\frac{\partial z}{\partial x}\right)^2+\left(\frac{\partial z}{\partial y}\right)^2=1$

# Formation of PDEs

***Example 50.*** *Form PDE by eliminating arbitrary constants a and b from equation*

$$z = ax + by + ab$$

**Solution.** We have $\frac{\partial z}{\partial x}=a,\ \frac{\partial z}{\partial y}=b$

Putting the values of $a$ and $b$ in given equation, we get the required PDE

$$z=x\frac{\partial z}{\partial x}+y\frac{\partial z}{\partial y}+\left(\frac{\partial z}{\partial x}\right)\left(\frac{\partial z}{\partial y}\right)$$

***Example 51.*** *Form the partial differential equation from* $z = f(x^2-y^2)$

**Solution.** We have $z=f(x^2-y^2)$ ...(i)

$$\Rightarrow \quad p=\frac{\partial z}{\partial x}=f'(x^2-y^2)\,2x \quad \text{...(ii)}$$

and $$q=\frac{\partial z}{\partial y}=f'(x^2-y^2)(-2y) \quad \text{...(iii)}$$

Dividing Eq. (ii) by Eq. (iii), we get

$$\frac{p}{q}=-\frac{x}{y} \text{ or } py=-qx$$

$$\Rightarrow \quad yp+xq=0$$

> ***Note*** By eliminating $F$, from the equation $F(u, v) = 0$ where $u$ and $v$ are functions of $x$, $y$ and $z$, PDE can be derived by method given below
> $$\frac{\partial(u,v)}{\partial(y,z)}p+\frac{\partial(u,v)}{\partial(z,x)}q=\frac{\partial(u,v)}{\partial(x,y)}$$

***Example 52.*** *Form PDE from* $F(x+y+z,\ x^2+y^2-z^2)=0$

**Solution.** Here, $u=x+y+z,\ v=x^2+y^2-z^2$

$$\Rightarrow \quad \frac{\partial u}{\partial x}=1,\quad \frac{\partial v}{\partial x}=2x$$

$$\frac{\partial u}{\partial y}=1,\quad \frac{\partial v}{\partial y}=2y$$

and $$\frac{\partial u}{\partial z}=1,\quad \frac{\partial v}{\partial z}=-2z$$

Now, $$\frac{\partial(u,v)}{\partial(y,z)}=\begin{vmatrix}\frac{\partial u}{\partial y} & \frac{\partial u}{\partial z}\\ \frac{\partial v}{\partial y} & \frac{\partial v}{\partial z}\end{vmatrix}=\begin{vmatrix}1 & 1\\ 2y & -2z\end{vmatrix}=-2(y+z)$$

Similarly, $\frac{\partial(u,v)}{\partial(z,x)}=2(x+z)$ and $\frac{\partial(u,v)}{\partial(x,y)}=2(y-x)$

$\therefore$ PDE is $(y+z)p-(x+z)q=(x-y)$

# Solution of PDE by Direct Integration

***Example 53.*** *Solve* $\frac{\partial^2 z}{\partial x\partial y}=xy^2$

**Solution.** On integrating *wrt* $x$, we get

$$\frac{\partial z}{\partial y}=y^2\left(\frac{x^2}{2}\right)+f(y)$$

On integrating *wrt* $y$, we get

$$z=\frac{x^2}{2}\left(\frac{y^3}{3}\right)+\int f(y)\,dy+g(x)$$

$$\Rightarrow \quad z=\frac{x^2y^3}{6}+F(y)+g(x)$$

***Example 54.*** *Solve the PDE*

$$x\frac{\partial^2 z}{\partial x^2}=\frac{\partial z}{\partial x}$$

**Solution.** Given PDE can be written as

$$\frac{\frac{\partial^2 z}{\partial x^2}}{\frac{\partial z}{\partial x}}=\frac{1}{x}$$

On integrating *wrt* $x$, we get

$$\log\left(\frac{\partial z}{\partial x}\right)=\log x+\log f(y)$$

$$\Rightarrow \quad \frac{\partial z}{\partial x}=xf(y)$$

On integrating *wrt* $x$, we get

$$z=f(y)\left(\frac{x^2}{2}\right)+g(y)$$

which is the required solution of given PDE.

**Example 55.** *Solve $xys - qy = x^2$*

**Solution.** Given PDE is

$$xy\frac{\partial^2 z}{\partial x \partial y} - \frac{\partial z}{\partial y}\cdot y = x^2$$

$$\Rightarrow \quad xy\frac{\partial}{\partial x}\left(\frac{\partial z}{\partial y}\right) - \left(\frac{\partial z}{\partial y}\right)y = x^2$$

$$\Rightarrow \quad xy\frac{\partial q}{\partial x} - qy = x^2$$

$$\frac{\partial q}{\partial x} - \frac{q}{x} = \frac{x}{y}$$

$$\text{IF} = e^{\int -\frac{1}{x}dx} = e^{-\log x} = \frac{1}{x}$$

$\Rightarrow$ Required solution is

$$q\left(\frac{1}{x}\right) = \int \frac{1}{y}dx + f(y)$$

$$\Rightarrow \quad \frac{q}{x} = \frac{x}{y} + f(y) \Rightarrow q = \frac{x^2}{y} + xf(y)$$

$$\Rightarrow \quad \frac{\partial z}{\partial y} = \frac{x^2}{y} + xf(y)$$

On integrating *wrt* $y$, we get

$$z = x^2 \log y + x\int f(y)\,dy + g(x)$$

$$\Rightarrow \quad z = x^2 \log y + xF(y) + g(x)$$

**Example 56.** *If the complete solution of $z = px + qy - 2\sqrt{pq}$ is $z = ax + by - 2\sqrt{ab}$ where, a and b are arbitrary constants. Find the general solution and singular solution of*

$$z = px + qy - 2\sqrt{pq}$$

**Solution.** Complete solution is

$$z = ax + by - 2\sqrt{ab} \quad \text{...(i)}$$

General solution

Put $b = \phi(a)$ in Eq. (i), we get

$$z = ax + \phi(a)y - 2\sqrt{a\phi(a)} \quad \text{...(ii)}$$

Differentiating Eq. (ii) partially *wrt* '$a$', we get

$$0 = x + y\phi'(a) - \frac{a\phi'(a) + \phi(a)}{\sqrt{a\phi(a)}} \quad \text{...(iii)}$$

The general integral is obtained by eliminating '$a$' between Eqs. (ii) and (iii).

**Singular Solution**

Differentiating Eq. (i) partially *wrt* '$a$' and '$b$', we get

$$0 = x - \frac{b}{\sqrt{ab}} \Rightarrow x = \sqrt{\frac{b}{a}} \quad \text{...(iv)}$$

and

$$0 = y - \frac{a}{\sqrt{ab}} \Rightarrow y = \sqrt{\frac{a}{b}} \quad \text{...(v)}$$

Eliminating $a$ and $b$ from Eqs. (iv) and (v), we get

$xy = 1$, which is the required singular solution.

## Types of Solutions of PDE

For the PDE $f(x, y, z, p, q) = 0$

1. The complete solution is given by

$$z = F(x, y, a, b)$$

or

$$F_1(x, y, z, a, b) = 0 \quad \text{...(i)}$$

Since, it involves two arbitrary parameters, it belongs to a double infinite system of surfaces or to a single infinite system of family of surfaces.

2. The general solution is obtained by eliminating '$a$' between Eq. (i),

$$b = \phi(a) \quad \text{...(ii)}$$

and

$$\frac{\partial F_1}{\partial a} + \frac{\partial F_1}{\partial b}\phi'(a) = 0 \quad \text{...(iii)}$$

where, $\phi$ is an arbitrary function.

The general solution represents the envelope of a one parameter family of surfaces.

3. The singular solution is obtained by eliminating '$a$' and '$b$' between Eq. (i),

$$\frac{\partial F_1}{\partial a} = 0 \quad \text{...(iv)}$$

and

$$\frac{\partial F_1}{\partial b} = 0 \quad \text{...(v)}$$

The singular solution represents the envelope of the two parameter family of surfaces or general envelope of all surfaces included in the complete solution.

## Linear PDEs of Order One

### Lagrange's Equation

A quasi-linear partial differential equation of order one is of the form $Pp + Qq = R$, where $P$, $Q$ and $R$ are functions of $x$, $y$, $z$. Such form of PDE is called Lagrange equation.

For example, $xyp + yzq = zx$ is a Lagrange equation.

### Lagrange's Method to Solve PDE of the Form $Pp + Qq = R$

**Step 1** Writing the given PDE in the form of

$$Pp + Qq = R \quad \text{...(i)}$$

**Step 2** Writing auxiliary equations for Eq. (i) as

$$\frac{dx}{P} = \frac{dy}{Q} = \frac{dz}{R} \quad \text{...(ii)}$$

**Step 3** Solve the above auxiliary equations.

Let the two independent solutions of Eq. (ii) be $u(x, y, z) = C_1$ and $v(x, y, z) = C_2$

**Step 4** $F(u, v) = 0$ is the required solution of Eq. (i) which is equivalent to $u = f(v)$ or $v = g(u)$

> ***Note*** Eq. (ii) is called Lagrange's auxiliary (or subsidiary) equation for Eq. (i)

***Example 57.*** *Solve* $y^2p - xyq = x(z-2y)$

**Solution.** We have $y^2p - xyq = x(z-2y)$

The auxiliary equations are

$$\frac{dx}{y^2} = \frac{dy}{-xy} = \frac{dz}{x(z-2y)} \quad \text{...(i)}$$

Considering first two members of the equations

$$\frac{dx}{y} = \frac{dy}{-x} \Rightarrow xdx = -ydy$$

On integrating, we get $\frac{x^2}{2} = -\frac{y^2}{2} + \frac{C_1}{2}$

$$\Rightarrow \quad x^2 + y^2 = C_1 \quad \text{...(ii)}$$

From last two members of Eq. (i), we have

$$-\frac{dy}{y} = \frac{dz}{z-2y}$$

$$\Rightarrow \quad -zdy + 2ydy = ydz$$

or $\quad 2y\,dy = y\,dz + z\,dz$

On integration, we get

$$y^2 = yz + C_2$$

$$y^2 - yz = C_2 \quad \text{...(iii)}$$

From Eqs. (ii) and (iii), we get

$$x^2 + y^2 = f(y^2 - yz)$$

which is the required solution.

Above solution can also be expressed as

$$F(x^2+y^2, y^2-yz) = 0$$

***Example 58.*** *Solve* $(y+z)p - (x+z)q = x - y$

**Solution.** We have $(y+z)p - (x+z)q = x - y \quad \text{...(i)}$

∴ The auxiliary equations are

$$\frac{dx}{y+z} = \frac{dy}{-(x+z)} = \frac{dz}{x-y} \quad \text{...(ii)}$$

$$\Rightarrow \quad \frac{dx}{y+z} = \frac{dy}{-(x+z)} = \frac{dz}{x-y} = \frac{dx+dy+dz}{y+z-(x+z)+x-y}$$

$$\Rightarrow \quad \frac{dx}{y+z} = \frac{dy}{-(x+z)} = \frac{dz}{x-y} = \frac{dx+dy+dz}{0}$$

Thus, we have $\quad dx + dy + dz = 0$

which on integration gives

$$x + y + z = C_1 \quad \text{...(iii)}$$

Let us use multipliers $(x, y, -z)$ for Eq. (ii)

$$\frac{dx}{y+z} = \frac{dy}{-(x+z)} = \frac{dz}{x-y} = \frac{xdx + ydy - zdz}{x(y+z) - y(x+z) - z(x-y)}$$

$$\Rightarrow \quad \frac{dx}{y+z} = \frac{dy}{-(x+z)} = \frac{dz}{x-y} = \frac{xdx + ydy - zdz}{0}$$

On integrating $xdx + ydy - zdz = 0$, we get

$$\frac{x^2}{2} + \frac{y^2}{2} - \frac{z^2}{2} = C_2$$

$$\Rightarrow \quad x^2 + y^2 - z^2 = 2C_2 \quad \text{...(iv)}$$

From Eqs. (iii) and (iv), we get the required solution

$$f(x+y+z, x^2+y^2-z^2) = 0$$

***Example 59.*** *Solve*

$$(mz - ny)\frac{\partial z}{\partial x} + (nx - lz)\frac{\partial z}{\partial y} = ly - mx$$

**Solution.** We have $(mz - ny)\frac{\partial z}{\partial x} + (nx - lz)\frac{\partial z}{\partial y} = ly - mx$

Here, the auxiliary equations are

$$\frac{dx}{mz - ny} = \frac{dy}{nx - lz} = \frac{dz}{ly - mx}$$

Using multipliers $x$, $y$ and $z$, we get

$$\text{Each fraction} = \frac{xdx + ydy + zdz}{x(mz-ny) + y(nx-lz) + z(ly-mx)} = \frac{xdx + ydy + zdz}{0}$$

Hence, $\quad xdx + ydy + zdz = 0$

which on integration gives

$$x^2 + y^2 + z^2 = C_1 \quad \text{...(i)}$$

Again, using multipliers $l, m$ and $n$, we get

$$\text{Each fraction} = \frac{ldx + mdy + ndz}{l(mz-ny) + m(nx-lz) + n(ly-mx)} = \frac{ldx + mdy + ndz}{0}$$

Hence, $ldx + mdy + ndz = 0$

which on integration gives

$$lx + my + nz = C_2 \quad \text{...(ii)}$$

Hence, from Eqs. (i) and (ii), the required solution is

$$x^2 + y^2 + z^2 = f(lx + my + nz)$$

***Example 60.*** *Solve* $(x^2 + 2y^2)p - xyq = xz$

**Solution.** Auxiliary equations are

$$\frac{dx}{x^2 + 2y^2} = \frac{dy}{-xy} = \frac{dz}{xz} \quad \text{...(i)}$$

From last two members of Eq. (i), we get

$$\frac{dy}{y} + \frac{dz}{z} = 0 \Rightarrow \int \frac{dy}{y} + \int \frac{dz}{z} = \int 0$$

$$\Rightarrow \quad \log y + \log z = \log C_1$$

$$\Rightarrow \quad yz = C_1 \quad \text{...(ii)}$$

From first two members of Eq. (i), we get

$$\frac{dx}{dy} = \frac{x^2 + 2y^2}{-xy} = -\frac{x}{y} - 2\frac{y}{x} \quad \text{...(iii)}$$

Put $x = vy$

$$\Rightarrow \quad \frac{dx}{dy} = v + y\frac{dv}{dy}$$

From Eq. (iii),

$$v + y\frac{dv}{dy} = -v - \frac{2}{v} \Rightarrow 2v + y\frac{dv}{dy} = -\frac{2}{v}$$

$$\Rightarrow \quad y\frac{dv}{dy} = -\frac{2}{v} - 2v = \frac{-2 - 2v^2}{v}$$

$$\Rightarrow \quad -\frac{vdv}{2 + 2v^2} = \frac{dy}{y}$$

$$\Rightarrow \quad 2\frac{dy}{y}+\frac{v\,dv}{1+v^2}=0$$

$$\Rightarrow \quad 2\int\frac{dy}{y}+\frac{1}{2}\int\frac{2v\,dv}{1+v^2}=\int 0$$

$$\Rightarrow \quad 2\log y+\frac{1}{2}\log(1+v^2)=\log C_2$$

$$\Rightarrow \quad y^2\sqrt{1+v^2}=C_2$$

$$\Rightarrow \quad y^2\sqrt{1+\frac{x^2}{y^2}}=C_2$$

$$\Rightarrow \quad y\sqrt{x^2+y^2}=C_2 \quad \text{or} \quad y^2(x^2+y^2)=C_2'' \qquad \text{...(iv)}$$

From Eqs. (ii) and (iv),

Complete solution is

$$F(yz,\, y^2(x^2+y^2))=0$$

# Non-Linear PDE

## Charpit's Method

Let the PDE is

$$f(x,\,y,\,z,\,p,\,q)=0 \qquad \text{...(i)}$$

Since, $\quad dz=\frac{\partial z}{\partial x}dx+\frac{\partial z}{\partial y}dy$

$$\Rightarrow \quad dz=p\,dx+q\,dy \qquad \text{...(ii)}$$

We find another relation between the variables $x,\ y,\ z,\ p$ and $q$.

i.e., $\quad F(x,\,y,\,z,\,p,\,q)=0 \qquad \text{...(iii)}$

On solving Eqs. (i) and (iii), we get the values of $p$ and $q$.

By putting these values of $p$ and $q$ in Eq. (ii), it becomes integrable and hence complete integral is found out.

Eq. (iii) is obtained by following equations.

$$\frac{dp}{\frac{\partial f}{\partial x}+p\frac{\partial f}{\partial z}}=\frac{dq}{\frac{\partial f}{\partial y}+q\frac{\partial f}{\partial z}}=\frac{dz}{-p\frac{\partial f}{\partial p}-q\frac{\partial f}{\partial q}}=\frac{dx}{-\frac{\partial f}{\partial p}}$$

$$=\frac{dy}{-\frac{\partial f}{\partial q}}=\frac{dF}{0}$$

which is known as Charpit's auxiliary equation.

***Example 61.*** *Find the complete solution of the equation*

$$z=px+qy+p^2+q^2$$

**Solution.** Given equation $f(x,\,y,\,z,\,p,\,q)=0$ is

$$px+qy-z+p^2+q^2=0 \qquad \text{...(i)}$$

$$\Rightarrow \quad \frac{\partial f}{\partial x}=p,\ \frac{\partial f}{\partial y}=q,\ \frac{\partial f}{\partial z}=-1$$

$$\frac{\partial f}{\partial p}=x+2p,\ \frac{\partial f}{\partial q}=y+2q$$

The Charpit's auxiliary equation is

$$\frac{dp}{\frac{\partial f}{\partial x}+p\frac{\partial f}{\partial z}}=\frac{dq}{\frac{\partial f}{\partial y}+q\frac{\partial f}{\partial z}}=\frac{dz}{-p\frac{\partial f}{\partial p}-q\frac{\partial f}{\partial q}}$$

$$=\frac{dx}{-\frac{\partial f}{\partial p}}=\frac{dy}{-\frac{\partial f}{\partial q}}$$

$$\Rightarrow \quad \frac{dp}{0}=\frac{dq}{0}=\frac{dz}{-p(x+2p)-q(y+2q)}$$

$$=\frac{dx}{-(x+2p)}=\frac{dy}{-(y+2q)} \qquad \text{...(ii)}$$

From first two members of Eq. (ii), we get

$$dp=0 \text{ and } dq=0$$

$$\Rightarrow \quad p=a \text{ and } q=b$$

Substituting these values of $p$ and $q$ in Eq. (i). The complete solution is

$$z=ax+by+a^2+b^2$$

***Example 62.*** *Solve $xp+yq=pq$*

**Solution.** We have $\ f(x,\,y,\,z,\,p,\,q)=0$ is

$$xp+yq-pq=0 \qquad \text{...(i)}$$

$$\therefore \quad \frac{\partial f}{\partial x}=p,\ \frac{\partial f}{\partial y}=q,\ \frac{\partial f}{\partial z}=0$$

$$\frac{\partial f}{\partial p}=x-q,\ \frac{\partial f}{\partial q}=y-p$$

Charpit's auxiliary equations are

$$\frac{dp}{\frac{\partial f}{\partial x}+p\frac{\partial f}{\partial z}}=\frac{dq}{\frac{\partial f}{\partial y}+q\frac{\partial f}{\partial z}}=\frac{dz}{-p\frac{\partial f}{\partial p}-q\frac{\partial f}{\partial q}}=\frac{dx}{-\frac{\partial f}{\partial p}}=\frac{dy}{-\frac{\partial f}{\partial q}}$$

$$\Rightarrow \quad \frac{dp}{p}=\frac{dq}{q}=\frac{dz}{-p(x-q)-q(y-p)}$$

$$=\frac{dx}{-(x-q)}=\frac{dy}{-(y-p)} \qquad \text{...(ii)}$$

From first two members of Eq. (i), we get

$$\int\frac{dp}{p}=\int\frac{dq}{q}$$

$$\Rightarrow \quad \log p=\log q+\log a$$

$$\Rightarrow \quad p=aq$$

Putting for $p$ in the given Eq. (i), we get

$$q(ax+y)=aq^2 \qquad \therefore\ q=\frac{y+ax}{a}$$

$$\therefore \quad p=aq=y+ax$$

Now, $\quad dz=p\,dx+q\,dy \qquad \text{...(iii)}$

Putting for $p$ and $q$ in Eq. (iii), we get

$$dz=(y+ax)\,dx+\frac{y+ax}{a}dy$$

$$a\,dz=(y+ax)\,dx+(y+ax)\,dy$$

$$a\,dz=(y+ax)(a\,dx+dy)$$

On integrating, we get $\quad az=\frac{(y+ax)^2}{2}+b$

## Application of Charpit's Method

### (i) Equation of the Type $f(p,\,q)=0$

Let solution be $\quad z=ax+by+c$

where, $\quad f(a,\,b)=0$

$\Rightarrow \quad b = \phi(a)$

$\therefore$ Complete solution is

$$z = ax + \phi(a)y + C$$

***Example 63.*** *Solve* $\sqrt{p} + \sqrt{q} = 1$

**Solution.** Let solution be $z = ax + by + c$

Where, $\sqrt{a} + \sqrt{b} = 1$

$\therefore$ Complete solution is

$$z = ax + (1 - \sqrt{a})^2 y + C$$

### (ii) Equation of the Type $z = px + qy + f(p, q)$

Whose solution is given by

$$z = ax + by + f(a, b)$$

***Example 64.*** *Solve* $z = px + qy + pq$

**Solution.** Solution is

$$z = ax + by + ab$$

### (iii) Equation of the Type $f(z, p, q) = 0$

Let $z$ be a function of $u$, where $u = x + ay$

From which we get $q = ap$, where $p = \dfrac{dz}{du}$

***Example 65.*** *Solve* $z^2(p^2 + q^2 + 1) = 1$

**Solution.** We have, $z^2(p^2 + q^2 + 1) = 1$

$$u = x + ay \text{ and } q = ap \quad \text{...(i)}$$

From Eq. (i), we get

$$z^2(p^2 + a^2p^2 + 1) = 1$$

$$\Rightarrow \quad p^2(1 + a^2) + 1 = \frac{1}{z^2}$$

$$\Rightarrow \quad p^2(1 + a^2) = \frac{1}{z^2} - 1 = \frac{1 - z^2}{z^2}$$

$$\Rightarrow \quad p^2 = \frac{1 - z^2}{z^2} \cdot \frac{1}{1 + a^2}$$

$$\Rightarrow \quad \frac{dz}{du} = \frac{\sqrt{1 - z^2}}{z} \cdot \frac{1}{\sqrt{1 + a^2}}$$

$$\Rightarrow \quad \frac{z\,dz}{\sqrt{1 - z^2}} = \frac{du}{\sqrt{1 + a^2}}$$

$$\Rightarrow \quad -\frac{1}{2}\int \frac{-2z}{\sqrt{1 - z^2}}dz = \frac{1}{\sqrt{1 + a^2}}\int du$$

$$\Rightarrow \quad -\frac{1}{2}\sqrt{1 - z^2} = \frac{1}{\sqrt{1 + a^2}}u + C$$

$$\Rightarrow \quad \sqrt{1 - z^2} = -\frac{2(x + ay)}{\sqrt{1 + a^2}} + C'$$

### (iv) Equation of the Type $f(x, p) = g(y, q)$

Let $f(x, p) = g(y, q) = a$

Finding $p$ and $q$ and from $dz = p\,dx + q\,dy$, complete solution is found out.

***Example 66.*** *Solve* $p^2 - q^2 = x - y$

**Solution.** Let $\quad p^2 - x = q^2 - y = a$

$$\Rightarrow \quad p^2 = a + x, \; q^2 = a + y$$

$$\Rightarrow \quad p = \sqrt{a + x}, \; q = \sqrt{a + y}$$

Now, $\quad dz = p\,dx + q\,dy$

$$\Rightarrow \quad dz = \sqrt{a + x}\,dx + \sqrt{a + y}\,dy$$

$$\Rightarrow \quad z = \frac{2}{3}(a + x)^{3/2} + \frac{2}{3}(a + y)^{3/2} + C$$

## Cauchy Problem for First Order PDEs

If

**(i)** $x_0(\lambda)$, $y_0(\lambda)$ and $z_0(\lambda)$ are functions which together with their first derivatives, are continuous in the interval I defined by $\lambda_1 < \lambda < \lambda_2$.

**(ii)** $f(x, y, z, p, q)$ is a continuous function of $x, y, z, p$ and $q$ in a certain region $D$ of the $xyzpq$ space with the existence of a function $\phi(x, y)$ such that

(a) $\phi(x, y)$, $\phi_x(x, y)$, $\phi_y(x, y)$ are continuous in a region $R$ of $xy$-space.

(b) $\{x, y, \phi, \phi_x, \phi_y\}$ lies in $\dfrac{D}{x}$ and

$$f(x, y, \phi, \phi_x, \phi_y) = 0, \quad \forall \; x, y \in R.$$

(c) Point $(x_0, y_0) \in R$ and $\phi(x_0, y_0) = z_0$

Then, there exists a surface $z = \phi(x, y)$ passes through the curve

$C : x = x_0(\lambda)$, $y = y_0(\lambda)$, $z = z_0(\lambda)$ and at every point of which the direction ratio of normal $(p, q, -1)$ is such that $f(x, y, z, p, q) = 0$

***Example 67.*** *Solve the Cauchy problem for* $z\dfrac{\partial z}{\partial x} + \dfrac{\partial z}{\partial y} = 1$ *with initial conditions* $x_0 = \lambda$, $y_0 = \lambda$, $z_0 = \dfrac{\lambda}{2}$, $\; 0 \le \lambda \le 1$

**Solution.** Given $f(x, y, z, p, q) \equiv zp + q - 1 = 0 \quad$ ...(i)

$$\frac{\partial f}{\partial p} = z, \; \frac{\partial f}{\partial q} = 1$$

$$\frac{dx_0}{d\lambda} = 1, \; \frac{dy_0}{d\lambda} = 1$$

$$\frac{\partial f}{\partial q} \cdot \frac{dx_0}{d\lambda} - \frac{\partial f}{\partial p} \cdot \frac{dy_0}{d\lambda} = 1 - z = 1 - \frac{\lambda}{2} \ne 0 \text{ for } 0 \le \lambda \le 1$$

Now, we get following ordinary differential equations

$$\frac{dx}{dt} = \frac{\partial f}{\partial p}, \; \frac{dy}{dt} = \frac{\partial f}{\partial q}$$

$$\Rightarrow \quad \frac{dx}{dt} = z \quad \text{...(ii)}$$

$$\frac{dy}{dt} = 1 \quad \text{...(iii)}$$

Since, $\quad dz = \dfrac{\partial z}{\partial x}dx + \dfrac{\partial z}{\partial y}dy$

$$\Rightarrow \quad \frac{dz}{dt} = \frac{\partial z}{\partial x} \cdot \frac{dx}{dt} + \frac{\partial z}{\partial y} \cdot \frac{dy}{dt}$$

$$\Rightarrow \quad \frac{dz}{dt} = pz + q = 1 \qquad \text{...(iv)}$$

On integrating Eqs. (iii) and (iv), we get

$$y = t + C_1 \text{ and } z = t + C_2$$

From given initial conditions

$$C_1 = \lambda \text{ and } C_2 = \frac{\lambda}{2}$$

$$\therefore \quad y = t + \lambda \qquad \text{...(v)}$$

$$\text{and} \quad z = t + \frac{\lambda}{2} \qquad \text{...(vi)}$$

From Eq. (ii),

$$\frac{dx}{dt} = t + \frac{\lambda}{2} \Rightarrow dx = (t + \frac{\lambda}{2})\, dt$$

$$\Rightarrow \quad \int dx = \int \left(t + \frac{\lambda}{2}\right) dt$$

$$\Rightarrow \quad x = \frac{t^2}{2} + \frac{\lambda}{2} t + C_3$$

From initial condition $C_3 = \lambda$

$$\text{Hence,} \quad x = \frac{t^2}{2} + \frac{\lambda}{2} t + \lambda \qquad \text{...(vii)}$$

From Eqs. (v) and (vii), we get

$$x = \frac{t^2}{2} + \frac{t}{2}(y - t) + (y - t)$$

$$\Rightarrow \quad x = \frac{yt}{2} + y - t$$

$$\Rightarrow \quad x - y = t\left(\frac{y}{2} - 1\right)$$

$$\Rightarrow \quad t = \frac{x - y}{\frac{y}{2} - 1}$$

Now, from Eq. (v), we get

$$\lambda = y - t = y - \frac{x - y}{\frac{y}{2} - 1}$$

$$= \frac{\frac{y^2}{2} - y - x + y}{\frac{y}{2} - 1} = \frac{\frac{y^2}{2} - x}{\frac{y}{2} - 1}$$

Hence, from Eq. (vi),

$$z = \frac{x - y}{\frac{y}{2} - 1} + \frac{1}{z}\left(\frac{\frac{y^2}{2} - x}{\frac{y}{2} - 1}\right)$$

which is the required solution.

# Classification of Second Order PDEs

Let $z$ be a function of two independent variables $x$ and $y$. Consider a general partial differential equation of second order in the form

$$Rr + Ss + Tt + f(x, y, z, p, q) = 0 \qquad \text{...(i)}$$

where, $R, S$ and $T$ are continuous functions of $x$ and $y$ and possessing partial derivatives defined in some domain $D$ on the $xy$-plane.

Then, Eq. (i) is said to be

**(i)** Elliptic at a point $(x, y)$ in $D$, if

$$S^2 - 4RT < 0$$

**(ii)** Parabolic at a point $(x, y)$ in $D$, if

$$S^2 - 4RT = 0$$

**(iii)** Hyperbolic at a point $(x, y)$ in $D$, if

$$S^2 - 4RT > 0$$

***Note*** If we write $u$ in place of $z$, then all symbols will change accordingly.

*e.g.*, $r = \frac{\partial^2 u}{\partial x^2}$, $s = \frac{\partial^2 u}{\partial x \partial y}$, $t = \frac{\partial^2 u}{\partial y^2}$

Here, $u$ be a function of $x$ and $y$.

***Example 68.*** *Classify the following PDEs*

(i) $2u_{xx} + 4u_{xy} + 3u_{yy} = 2$

(ii) $xyr - (x^2 - y^2)s - xyt + py - qx = 2(x^2 - y^2)$

(iii) $u_{xx} + 4u_{xy} + 4u_{yy} = 0$

**Solution.** (i) Given equation can be written as

$$2r + 4s + 3t - 2 = 0$$

Here, $R = 2, S = 4, T = 3$

$$\therefore S^2 - 4RT = 16 - 4 \times 2 \times 3 = 16 - 24 = -8 < 0$$

$\Rightarrow$ Given equation is elliptic at all points.

(ii) Given equation is

$$xyr - (x^2 - y^2)s - xyt + py - qx - 2(x^2 - y^2) = 0$$

Here, $R = xy$, $S = -(x^2 - y^2)$, $T = -xy$

$$\therefore \quad S^2 - 4RT = (x^2 - y^2)^2 + 4x^2y^2 > 0$$

$\Rightarrow$ Given equation is hyperbolic at all points.

(iii) Given equation is

$$r + 4s + 4t = 0$$

Here, $R = 1, S = 4, T = 4$

$$\therefore \quad S^2 - 4RT = 16 - 16 = 0$$

$\Rightarrow$ Given equation is parabolic at all points.

# Classification of PDEs if $u = \phi(x, y, z)$

We find matrix $A$ as below

$$A = \begin{bmatrix} c_{xx} & c_{xy} & c_{xz} \\ c_{yx} & c_{yy} & c_{yz} \\ c_{zx} & c_{zy} & c_{zz} \end{bmatrix}$$

Where $c_{xx}$ = Coefficient of $u_{xx}$ and so on.

**(i)** If $|A| = 0$, then equation is parabolic.

**(ii)** If $|A| \neq 0$ and all coefficients are positive, then equation is elliptic.

**(iii)** If $|A| \neq 0$ and coefficients are positive as well as negative, then equation is hyperbolic.

***Example 69.*** *Classify* $u_{xx} + u_{yy} = u_{zz}$

**Solution.** Given equation is

$$u_{xx} + u_{yy} - u_{zz} = 0$$

$$\therefore \text{ Matrix } A = \begin{bmatrix} 1 & 0 & 0 \\ 0 & 1 & 0 \\ 0 & 0 & -1 \end{bmatrix} \Rightarrow |A| = \begin{vmatrix} 1 & 0 & 0 \\ 0 & 1 & 0 \\ 0 & 0 & -1 \end{vmatrix} = -1 \neq 0$$

and coefficients are positive as well as negative.

$\Rightarrow$ Given, equation is hyperbolic type.

## Characteristic Equation and Characteristic Curves of the Second Order PDEs

Consider the second order PDE

$$Rr + Ss + Tt + f(x, y, z, p, q) = 0 \quad \text{...(i)}$$

Then, quadratic equation in $\lambda$ for Eq. (i) is given by

$$R\lambda^2 + S\lambda + T = 0 \quad \text{...(ii)}$$

For $S^2 - 4RT \geq 0$ Eq. (ii) has real roots. Then, the ordinary differential equations

$$\frac{dy}{dx} + \lambda = 0 \quad \text{...(iii)}$$

are called the characteristic equations. The solutions of Eq. (iii) are known as characteristic curves or characteristic of the second order PDEs.

**Case I** If $\quad S^2 - 4RT > 0$

*i.e.*, if Eq. (i) is hyperbolic, then Eq. (ii) has two distinct roots $\lambda_1, \lambda_2$ (say) and corresponding to which we get two characteristic equations

$$\frac{dy}{dx} + \lambda_1 = 0$$

and $\quad \dfrac{dy}{dx} + \lambda_2 = 0$

solving these we get two distinct families of characteristics.

**Case II** If $\quad S^2 - 4RT = 0$

*i.e.*, if Eq. (i) is parabolic and we get characteristic equation $\dfrac{dy}{dx} + \lambda = 0$. Solving it we get only one family of characteristic.

**Case III** If $\quad S^2 - 4RT < 0$

*i.e.*, Eq. (i) is elliptic, then Eq. (ii) has complex roots. Hence, there are no real characteristics.

We get two families of complex characteristics.

***Example 70.*** *Find the characteristics of*

$$4u_{xx} + 5u_{xy} + u_{yy} + u_x + u_y = 2$$

**Solution.** Here, $\quad R = 4, S = 5, T = 1$

$$S^2 - 4RT = 25 - 16 = 9 > 0$$

$\lambda$-quadratic equation is

$$R\lambda^2 + S\lambda + T = 0$$

$$\Rightarrow \quad 4\lambda^2 + 5\lambda + 1 = 0$$

$$\Rightarrow \quad 4\lambda^2 + 4\lambda + \lambda + 1 = 0$$

$$\Rightarrow \quad 4\lambda(\lambda + 1) + (\lambda + 1) = 0$$

$$\Rightarrow \quad (\lambda + 1)(4\lambda + 1) = 0$$

$$\Rightarrow \quad \lambda = -1, -\frac{1}{4}$$

$$\Rightarrow \quad \lambda_1 = -1, \lambda_2 = -\frac{1}{4}$$

Hence, characteristic equations are

$$\frac{dy}{dx} + \lambda_1 = 0, \quad \frac{dy}{dx} + \lambda_2 = 0$$

$$\Rightarrow \quad \frac{dy}{dx} - 1 = 0, \quad \frac{dy}{dx} - \frac{1}{4} = 0$$

$$\Rightarrow \quad \int dy = \int dx, \quad 4\int dy = \int dx$$

$$\Rightarrow \quad y = x + C_1, \quad 4y = x + C_2$$

Hence, characteristic curves are

$$y - x = C_1, \quad 4y - x = C_2$$

## PDEs with Constant Coefficients

Consider the PDE

$$a_0 \frac{\partial^n z}{\partial x^n} + a_1 \frac{\partial^n z}{\partial x^{n-1} \partial y} + \ldots + a_n \frac{\partial^n z}{\partial y^n} = f(x, y) \quad \text{...(i)}$$

or $\quad (a_0 D^n + a_1 D^{n-1} D' + \ldots + a_n D'^n) z = f(x, y) \quad$ ...(ii)

or $\quad F(D, D') z = f(x, y) \quad$ ...(iii)

where $D = \dfrac{\partial z}{\partial x}, \quad D' = \dfrac{\partial z}{\partial x}$, $a_0, a_1, a_2, \ldots, a_n$ are all constants.

The Eq. (i) or Eq. (ii) or Eq. (iii) is called linear PDE with constant coefficients.

If $F(D, D')$ is homogeneous in $D$ and $D'$, then above equation is a homogeneous PDE.

And if $F(D, D')$ is not homogeneous in $D$ and $D'$, then above PDE is non-homogeneous.

*e.g.*,

(i) $\quad \dfrac{\partial^2 z}{\partial x^2} + \dfrac{\partial^2 z}{\partial y^2} = x + y$

or $\quad D^2 + D'^2 = x + y \quad$ (Homogeneous PDE)

(ii) $\quad \dfrac{\partial^2 z}{\partial x^2} + \dfrac{\partial^2 z}{\partial y^2} + \dfrac{\partial z}{\partial x} = xy$

or $\quad D^2 + D'^2 + D = xy \quad$ (Non-Homogeneous PDE)

## Method of Finding CF of PDEs

Let PDE be

$$(a_0 D^n + a_1 D^{n-1} D' + a_2 D^{n-2} D'^2 + \ldots + a_n D'^n) z = f(x, y) \quad \text{...(i)}$$

CF of Eq. (i) is the general solution of

$$(a_0 D^n + a_1 D^{n-1} D' + a_2 D^{n-2} D'^2 + \ldots + a_n D'^n) z = 0 \quad \text{...(ii)}$$

Then, put $D = m$; $D' = 1$ in Eq. (ii), we get an equation of the form

$$a_0 m^n + a_1 m^{n-1} + a_2 m^{n-2} + \ldots + a_n = 0 \quad \text{...(iii)}$$

which is called auxiliary equation of PDE (ii).

**Case I** Let $m_1, m_2, \ldots, m_n$ be distinct roots of Eq. (iii).

Then, general solution of Eq. (ii) or CF of Eq. (i) is given by

$$\phi_1(y+m_1x)+\phi_2(y+m_2x)+\ldots+\phi_n(y+m_nx)$$

where $\phi_1, \phi_2, \ldots, \phi_n$ are arbitrary functions.

**Case II** Let root $m$ be repeated '$r$' times, then corresponding part of CF is

$$\phi_1(y+mx)+x\,\phi_2(y+mx)+x^2\,\phi_3(y+mx)+\ldots+x^{r-1}\phi_r(y+mx)$$

> ***Note*** We can find auxiliary equation by putting $D=m$ and $D'=1$ only when $D'$ is not a factor of $F(D, D')$. If it is so, then we will take $D'$ common and then put $D'=1$ in the remaining factor of $F(D, D')$. Now, we will find out CF by method given below.
>
> **1.** (i) If $D$ is the only factor, part of CF is $\phi(y)$.
> (ii) If $D$ is repeated $r$ times, part of CF is
> $\phi_1(y)+x\phi_2(y)+x^2\phi_3(y)+\ldots+x^{r-1}\phi_r(y)$
>
> **2.** (i) If $D'$ is the only factor, part of CF is $\phi(x)$
> (ii) If $D'$ is repeated $r$ times, part of CF is
> $\phi_1(x)+y\phi_2(x)+y^2\phi_3(x)+\ldots+y^{r-1}\phi_r(x)$

***Example 71.*** *Solve* $(2D^2+5DD'+2D'^2)z=0$

**Solution.** Here, AE is $2m^2+5m+2=0$

$$\Rightarrow \quad 2m^2+4m+m+2=0$$
$$\Rightarrow \quad 2m(m+2)+1(m+2)=0$$
$$\Rightarrow \quad (2m+1)(m+2)=0$$
$$\Rightarrow \quad m=-2, -\frac{1}{2}$$

Hence, General solution is

$$z=\phi_1(y-2x)+\phi_2\left(y-\frac{x}{2}\right)$$

or $$z=\phi_1(y-2x)+\phi_2(2y-x)$$

***Example 72.*** *Solve* $r+t+2s=0$

**Solution.** Given equation is

$$(D^2+D'^2+2DD')z=0$$

It's auxiliary equation is

$$m^2+1+2m=0$$
$$\Rightarrow \quad (m+1)^2=0$$
$$\Rightarrow \quad m=-1, -1$$

Hence, General solution is

$$z=\phi_1(y-x)+x\phi_2(y-x)$$

***Example 73.*** *Solve* $(D^4+D'^2-2D^2D'^2)z=0$

**Solution.** Here, AE is $m^4+1-2m^2=0$

$$\Rightarrow \quad (m^2-1)^2=0$$
$$\Rightarrow \quad m^2=1 \text{ twice}$$
$$\Rightarrow \quad m=1, 1, -1, -1$$

Hence, General solution is

$$z=\phi_1(y+x)+x\phi_2(y+x)+\phi_3(y-x)+x\phi_4(y-x)$$

***Example 74.*** *Solve* $(D^4-2D^3D'+2DD'^3-D'^4)z=0$

**Solution.** Here, AE is $m^4-2m^3+2m-1=0$

$$\Rightarrow \quad (m^4-1)-2m(m^2-1)=0$$
$$\Rightarrow \quad (m^2+1)(m^2-1)-2m(m^2-1)=0$$
$$\Rightarrow \quad (m^2-1)(m^2+1-2m)=0$$
$$\Rightarrow \quad (m^2-1)(m-1)^2=0$$
$$\Rightarrow \quad m=-1, 1, 1, 1$$

Hence, General solution is

$$z=\phi_1(y-x)+\phi_2(y+x)+x\phi_3(y+x)+x^2\phi_4(y+x)$$

***Example 75.*** *Solve* $(D^3D'^2+D^2D'^3)z=0$

**Solution.** Given, equation can be written as

$$D^2D'^2(D+D')z=0$$

Now, part of CF for $D^2=0$ is $\phi_1(y)+x\phi_2(y)$

part of CF for $D'^2=0$ is $\phi_3(x)+y\,\phi_4(x)$

Put $D=m,\ D'=1$ in $D+D'=0$

$$\Rightarrow \quad m+1=0 \quad \Rightarrow \quad m=-1$$

Part of CF for $D+D'=0$ is $\phi_5(y-x)$

Hence, General solution is

$$z=\phi_1(y)+x\phi_2(y)+\phi_3(x)+y\,\phi_4(x)+\phi_5(y-x)$$

> ***Note*** In case of non-homogeneous PDEs, part of CF corresponding to equation $D-aD'-b=0$ is given by
> $$e^{bx}\phi(y+ax)$$

***Example 76.*** *Solve* $(D^2-D'^2+D-D')z=0$

**Solution.** Given, equation is non-homogeneous PDE, which can be written as

$$(D-D')(D+D'+1)z=0$$

Part of CF for $D-D'=0$ is $\phi_1(y+x)$

and part of CF for $D+D'+1=0$ is $e^{-x}\phi_2(y-x)$

Hence, General solution is $\phi_1(y+x)+e^{-x}\phi_2(y-x)$

## Method of Finding PI

Given, PDE is

$$F(D, D')z=f(x, y)$$

Then, $$\text{PI}=\frac{1}{F(D, D')}f(x, y)$$

**(i)** $$\frac{1}{F(D, D')}x^my^n=[F(D, D')]^{-1}x^my^n$$

*i.e.*, expanding $[F(D, D')]^{-1}$ by using binomial theorem in ascending powers of $D$ or $D'$ and then operate $x^my^n$ term by term.

> ***Note*** $\frac{1}{D-\lambda D'}f(x, y)=\int f(x, c-\lambda x)dx$
> where $c$ is replaced by $y+\lambda x$ after integration.

**(ii)** $$\frac{1}{F(D, D')}e^{ax+by}=\frac{e^{ax+by}}{F(a, b)};\ F(a, b)\neq 0$$

$$=x\cdot\frac{e^{ax+by}}{F'(a, b)};\quad \text{if } F(a, b)=0$$

$$= x^2 \cdot \frac{e^{ax+by}}{F''(a, b)}; \text{ if } F'(a, b) = 0 \text{ and so on.}$$

OR

$$\frac{1}{F(D, D')} e^{ax+by} = e^{ax+by} \frac{1}{F(D+a, D'+b)} \cdot 1$$

In general,

$$\frac{1}{F(D, D')} f(x, y) e^{ax+by} = e^{ax+by} \cdot \frac{1}{F(D+a, D'+b)} f(x, y)$$

**(iii)** $\dfrac{1}{F(D^2, DD', D'^2)} \sin(ax + by)$

$$= \frac{1}{F(-a^2, -ab, -b^2)} \sin(ax+by)$$

provided that $F(-a^2, -ab, -b^2) \neq 0$

If $F(-a^2, -ab, -b^2) = 0$, then similar method given in (ii) will follow.

> ***Note*** Similar results hold in case of cos $(ax + by)$.

***Example 77.*** *Solve* $(D^2 + DD' - 6D'^2)z = x + y$

**Solution.** Here, AE is $m^2 + m - 6 = 0$

$\Rightarrow \quad m = -3, 2$

$CF = \phi_1(y - 3x) + \phi_2(y + 2x)$

Now, $PI = \dfrac{1}{D^2 + DD' - 6D'^2}(x + y)$

$$= \frac{1}{D^2}\left(1 + \frac{D'}{D} - \frac{6D'^2}{D^2}\right)^{-1}(x+y) = \frac{1}{D^2}\left[1 - \frac{D'}{D} + \dots\right](x+y)$$

$$= \frac{1}{D^2}\left[x + y - \frac{1}{D}(1)\right] = \frac{1}{D^2}(x + y - x) = \frac{1}{D^2} y = \frac{yx^2}{2}$$

Hence, complete solution is

$$z = \phi_1(y - 3x) + \phi_2(y + 2x) + \frac{x^2 y}{2}$$

***Example 78.*** *Solve* $\dfrac{\partial^3 z}{\partial x^3} - 3\dfrac{\partial^3 z}{\partial x^2 \partial y} + 4\dfrac{\partial^3 z}{\partial y^3} = e^{x+2y}$

**Solution.** Given equation can be written as

$$(D^3 - D^2 D' + 4D'^3)z = e^{x+2y}$$

Its AE is $\quad m^3 - 3m^2 + 4 = 0 \Rightarrow m = -1, 2, 2$

$\therefore \quad CF = \phi_1(y - x) + \phi_2(y + 2x) + x\phi_3(y + 2x)$

Now, $PI = \dfrac{1}{D^3 - 3D^2 D' + 4D'^3} e^{x+2y}$

Put $D = 1, D' = 2 \quad = \dfrac{1}{1 - 6 + 32} e^{x+2y} = \dfrac{e^{x+2y}}{27}$

Hence, complete solution is

$$z = \phi_1(y - x) + \phi_2(y + 2x) + x\phi_3(y + 2x) + \frac{e^{x+2y}}{27}$$

***Example 79.*** *Solve* $(D^2 + 2DD' + D'^2)z = \sin(2x + 3y)$

**Solution.** Here, AE is $m^2 + 2m + 1 = 0$

$\Rightarrow \quad (m + 1)^2 = 0 \Rightarrow m = -1, -1$

$\therefore \quad CF = \phi_1(y - x) + x\phi_2(y - x)$

Now, $\quad PI = \dfrac{1}{D^2 + 2DD' + D'^2} \sin(2x + 3y)$

$$= \frac{1}{-2^2 + 2(-2 \times 3) + (-3)^2} \sin(2x + 3y)$$

$$= \frac{1}{-4 - 12 - 9} \sin(2x + 3y)$$

$$= -\frac{\sin(2x + 3y)}{25}$$

Hence, complete solution is

$$\phi_1(y - x) + x\phi_2(y - x) - \frac{\sin(2x + 3y)}{25}$$

***Example 80.*** *Solve* $\dfrac{\partial^2 z}{\partial x^2} + \dfrac{\partial^2 z}{\partial x \partial y} - 6\dfrac{\partial^2 z}{\partial y^2} = y\cos x$

**Solution.** We have $\dfrac{\partial^2 z}{\partial x^2} + \dfrac{\partial^2 z}{\partial x \partial y} - 6\dfrac{\partial^2 z}{\partial y^2} = y\cos x$

$$(D^2 + DD' - 6D'^2) = y\cos x$$

Its auxiliary equation is

$$m^2 + m - 6 = 0 \Rightarrow (m + 3)(m - 2) = 0$$

$\Rightarrow \quad m = 2, \ 3$

$\therefore \quad CF = \phi_1(y + 2x) + \phi_2(y - 3x)$

Now, $\quad PI = \dfrac{1}{D^2 + DD' - 6D'^2} y\cos x$

$= \dfrac{1}{(D - 2D')(D + 3D')} y\cos x$

$= \dfrac{1}{D - 2D'} \int (c + 3x)\cos x\, dx \qquad$ (put $y = c + 3x$)

$= \dfrac{1}{D - 2D'} [(c + 3x)\sin x + 3\cos x]$

$= \dfrac{1}{D - 2D'} [y\sin x + 3\cos x] \qquad$ (put $c + 3x = y$)

$= \int [(c - 2x)\sin x + 3\cos x]dx \qquad$ (put $y = c - 2x$)

$= (c - 2x)(-\cos x) - 2\sin x + 3\sin x$

$= -y\cos x + \sin x \qquad$ (put $c - 2x = y$)

Hence, the complete solution is

$$z = \phi_1(y + 2x) + \phi_2(y - 3x) + \sin x - y\cos x$$

***Example 81.*** *Solve* $(4D^2 - 4DD' + D'^2)z = e^{x+2y}$

**Solution.** We have $\quad CF = \phi_1(2y + x) + x\phi_2(2y + x)$

Now, $\quad PI = \dfrac{1}{F(D, D')} e^{x+2y} \qquad$ (here, $a = 1, b = 2$)

$$F(D, D') = 4D^2 - 4DD' + D'^2$$

$$F(1, 2) = 4 - 8 + 4 = 0$$

$$F'(D, D') = 8D - 4D'$$

$$F'(1, 2) = 8 \times 1 - 4 \times 2 = 0$$

$$F''(D, D') = 8 \Rightarrow F''(1, 2) = 8 \neq 0$$

$\therefore \quad PI = \dfrac{x^2}{F''(1, 2)} e^{x+2y} = \dfrac{x^2}{8} e^{x+2y}$

Hence, complete solution is = CF + PI

*Example 82.* *Solve* $(D^3 - 4D^2D' + 4DD'^2)z = \cos(2x + y)$

**Solution.** We have CF $= \phi_1(y) + \phi_2(y + 2x) + x\phi_3(y + 2x)$

$$\text{Now, PI} = \frac{1}{D^3 - 4D^2D' + 4DD'^2}\cos(2x+y)$$

$$= \frac{1}{D(-2^2) - 4D(-2\times 1) + 4D'(-2\times 1)}\cos(2x+y)$$

$$= \frac{1}{-4D + 8D - 8D'}\cos(2x+y)$$

$$= \frac{1}{4D - 8D'}\cos(2x+y)$$

For $D = 2, D' = 1, 4D - 8D' = 0$

$$= \frac{x}{4}\cos(2x+y) \quad \text{(On differentiating)}$$

Hence, complete solution = CF + PI

*Example 83.* *Solve* $(D^2 - 5DD' + 4D'^2)z = \sin(4x + y)$

**Solution.** We have CF $= \phi_1(y + x) + \phi_2(y + 4x)$

$$\text{Now, PI} = \frac{1}{D^2 - 5DD' + 4D'^2}\sin(4x+y)$$

Here, $F(D^2, DD', D'^2) = D^2 - 5DD' + 4D'^2$

$$a = 4,\ b = 1$$

$$\Rightarrow F(-4^2, -4\times 1, -1^2) = -4^2 - 5(-4\times 1) + 4(-1^2)$$

$$= -16 + 20 - 4 = 0$$

$$\therefore \quad \text{PI} = \frac{x}{2D - 5D'}\sin(4x+y)$$

$$= \frac{x\cdot D}{2D^2 - 5DD'}\sin(4x+y)$$

$$= \frac{x}{2(-4^2) - 5(-4\times 1)}D\sin(4x+y)$$

$$= \frac{x}{-32+20}\cdot 4\cos(4x+y) = -\frac{x}{3}\cos(4x+y)$$

Hence, complete solution = CF + PI

*Example 84.* *Solve* $(D^2 - D'^2 + D - D')z = e^{2x+3y}$

**Solution.** The given equation can be written as

$$[(D - D')(D + D') + (D - D')]z = e^{2x+3y}$$

$$\Rightarrow \quad (D - D')(D + D' + 1)z = e^{2x+3y}$$

Part of CF for $D - D' = 0$ is obtained by putting

$$D = m,\ D' = 1 \Rightarrow m - 1 = 0$$

$$\Rightarrow \quad m = 1$$

Hence, part of CF is $\phi_1(y + x)$.

Part of CF for $D + D' + 1 = 0$ is obtained by using the method $D - aD' - b = 0$ for which CF is given by $e^{bx}\phi(y + ax)$.

Here, $a = -1,\ b = -1$

Hence, part of CF is $e^{-x}\phi_2(y - x)$.

$$\Rightarrow \quad \text{CF} = \phi_1(y + x) + e^{-x}\phi_2(y - x)$$

$$\text{PI} = \frac{1}{D^2 - D'^2 + D - D'}e^{2x+3y} = \frac{1}{2^2 - 3^2 + 2 - 3}e^{2x+3y}$$

$$= \frac{1}{-6}e^{2x+3y}$$

Hence, complete solution = CF + PI

# Application of PDEs

## Method of Separation of Variables

*Example 85. By using the method of separation of variables solve* $3u_x + 2u_y = 0$, $u(x, 0) = 4e^{-x}$

**Solution.** Given, PDE is $3\dfrac{\partial u}{\partial x} + 2\dfrac{\partial u}{\partial y} = 0$

Here, $u$ is function of $x$ and $y$.

$\therefore$ Let solution be

$$u(x, y) = X(x)\,Y(y)$$

$$\Rightarrow \quad u_x = X'Y,\ u_y = XY'$$

Now, from given equation, we get

$$3X'Y + 2XY' = 0$$

$$\Rightarrow \quad 3\frac{X'}{X} + 2\frac{Y'}{Y} = 0$$

$$\Rightarrow \quad 3\frac{X'}{X} = -2\frac{Y'}{Y} = k \text{ (say)}$$

On integration, we get

$$\log X = \frac{k}{3}x + \log C_1,\quad \log Y = -\frac{k}{2}y + \log C_2$$

$$\Rightarrow \quad X = C_1e^{\frac{k}{3}x},\quad Y = C_2e^{-\frac{k}{2}y}$$

$$\therefore \quad u(x, y) = XY = C_1C_2e^{k\left(\frac{x}{3} - \frac{y}{2}\right)}$$

From given,

$$u(x, 0) = 4e^{-x}$$

$$\Rightarrow \quad 4e^{-x} = C_1C_2e^{k\frac{x}{3}}$$

$$\therefore \quad C_1C_2 = 4,\ k = -3$$

$$\Rightarrow \quad u(x, y) = 4e^{-3\left(\frac{x}{3} - \frac{y}{2}\right)} = 4e^{\left(-x + \frac{3y}{2}\right)}$$

which is the required solution .

*Example 86. By using method of separation of variables solve one dimensional wave equation*

$$\frac{\partial^2 u}{\partial t^2} = c^2\frac{\partial^2 u}{\partial x^2}$$

**Solution.** Given equation is

$$\frac{\partial^2 u}{\partial t^2} = c^2\frac{\partial^2 u}{\partial x^2} \quad \text{...(i)}$$

Assume the solution of Eq. (i) is of the form

$$u(x, t) = X(x)\cdot T(t) \quad \text{...(ii)}$$

$$\Rightarrow \quad u_{tt} = XT'',\ u_{xx} = X''T$$

From Eq. (i),

$$XT'' = c^2X''T$$

$$\text{i.e.,} \quad \frac{X''}{X} = \frac{1}{C^2}\cdot\frac{T''}{T} = \lambda \text{ (say)}$$

$$\Rightarrow \quad X'' - \lambda X = 0 \quad \text{...(iii)}$$

$$\text{and} \quad T'' - \lambda c^2T = 0 \quad \text{...(iv)}$$

**Case I** When $\lambda = 0$

The general solution of Eqs. (iii) and (iv) are $X = a_1x + a_2$, $T = a_3t + a_4$, respectively.

Now, by using Eq. (ii) solution of Eq. (i) is

$$u(x, t) = (a_1x + a_2)(a_3t + a_4) \quad \text{...(v)}$$

**Case II** When $\lambda$ is positive.

Let $\lambda = \mu^2$. Then, general solution of Eqs. (iii) and (iv) are respectively

$$X = b_1e^{\mu x} + b_2e^{-\mu t}; \quad T = b_3e^{c\mu t} + b_4e^{-c\mu t}$$

$\therefore$ Solution of Eq. (i) in this case is

$$u(x, t) = (b_1e^{\mu x} + b_2e^{-\mu x})(b_3e^{c\mu x} + b_4e^{-c\mu x}) \quad \text{...(vi)}$$

**Case III** Where $\lambda$ is negative.

Let $\lambda = -\mu^2$. Then, general solution of Eqs. (iii) and (iv) are respectively

$$X = C_1 \cos\mu x + C_2 \sin\mu x$$
$$T = C_3 \cos c\mu t + C_4 \sin c\mu t$$

$\therefore$ Solution of Eq. (i) in this case is

$$u(x, t) = (C_1 \cos\mu x + C_2 \sin\mu x)(C_3 \cos\mu t + C_4 \sin\mu t) \quad \text{...(vii)}$$

Thus, the various possible solutions of wave Eq. (i) are given, by Eqs. (v), (vi) and (vii) of these three solutions, we will select that solution which is suitable as per nature of problem.

> ***Note*** **(a)** Two dimensional wave equation is given by
>
> $$\frac{\partial^2 u}{\partial t^2} = c^2\left(\frac{\partial^2 u}{\partial x^2} + \frac{\partial^2 u}{\partial y^2}\right)$$
>
> **(b)** Two dimensional heat equation is given by
>
> $$\frac{\partial u}{\partial t} = k\left(\frac{\partial^2 u}{\partial x^2} + \frac{\partial^2 u}{\partial y^2}\right)$$
>
> **(c)** In polar coordinates $(r, \theta)$ Laplace's equation
>
> $$\frac{\partial^2 u}{\partial x^2} + \frac{\partial^2 u}{\partial y^2} = 0 \text{ changes to } \frac{\partial^2 u}{\partial r^2} + \frac{1}{r}\frac{\partial u}{\partial r} + \frac{1}{r^2}\frac{\partial^2 u}{\partial \theta^2} = 0$$

***Example 87.*** *By using method of separable of variables solve one dimensional heat equation*

$$\frac{\partial u}{\partial t} = k\frac{\partial^2 u}{\partial x^2}$$

**Solution.** We have $\dfrac{\partial u}{\partial t} = k\dfrac{\partial^2 u}{\partial x^2}$ ...(i)

Let solution be of the form

$$u(x, t) = X(x)T(t) \quad \text{...(ii)}$$

$\Rightarrow$ $u_t = XT'$, $u_{xx} = X''T$

$\Rightarrow$ Given equation is

$$XT' = kX''T$$

$\Rightarrow$ $\dfrac{X''}{X} = \dfrac{T'}{kT} = \lambda$ (say)

$\Rightarrow$ $X'' - \lambda X = 0$ ...(iii)

and $T' - \lambda kT = 0$ ...(iv)

**Case I** When $\lambda = 0$

Then, $X = a_1x + a_2$, $T = a_3$

$\Rightarrow$ $u(x, t) = (a_1x + a_2)a_3 = A_1x + A_2$ ...(v)

**Case II** Let $\lambda$ be positive *i.e.*, $\mu^2$ (say)

Then, $X = b_1e^{\mu x} + b_2e^{-\mu x}$ and $T = b_3e^{\mu^2 kt}$

$\Rightarrow$ $u(x, t) = (B_1e^{\mu x} + B_2e^{-\mu x})e^{\mu^2 kt}$ ...(vi)

**Case III** Let $\lambda$ be negative *i.e.*, $-\mu^2$ (say)

Then, $X = C_1 \cos\mu x + C_2 \sin\mu x$ and $T = C_3e^{-\mu^2 kt}$

$\Rightarrow$ $u(x, t) = (C_1 \cos\mu x + C_2 \sin\mu x)e^{-\mu^2 kt}$ ...(vii)

Therefore, Eqs. (v), (vi) and (vii) are the required solutions of heat Eq. (i).

***Example 88.*** *By using method of separation of variables solve two dimensional Laplace equation.*

$$\frac{\partial^2 u}{\partial x^2} + \frac{\partial^2 u}{\partial y^2} = 0$$

**Solution.** We have $\dfrac{\partial^2 u}{\partial x^2} + \dfrac{\partial^2 u}{\partial y^2} = 0$ ...(i)

Let solution of Eq. (i) be

$$u(x, y) = X(x)Y(y) \quad \text{...(ii)}$$

$\Rightarrow$ $u_{xx} = X''Y$, $u_{yy} = XY''$

$\therefore$ From Eq. (i),

$$X''Y + XY'' = 0$$

$\Rightarrow$ $X''Y = -XY''$

$\Rightarrow$ $\dfrac{X''}{X} = -\dfrac{Y''}{Y} = \lambda$ (say)

$\Rightarrow$ $X'' - \lambda X = 0$ ...(iii)

and $Y'' + \lambda Y = 0$ ...(iv)

**Case I** When $\lambda = 0$

Then, $X = a_1x + a_2$, $Y = a_3y + a_4$

$\Rightarrow$ $u(x, y) = (a_1x + a_2)(a_3y + a_4)$ ...(v)

**Case II** When $\lambda = \mu^2 > 0$, then

$$X = b_1e^{\mu x} + b_2e^{-\mu x}$$
$$Y = b_3 \cos\mu y + b_4 \sin\mu y$$

$\Rightarrow$ $u(x, y) = (b_1e^{\mu x} + b_2e^{-\mu x})(b_3 \cos\mu y + b_4 \sin\mu y)$ ...(vi)

**Case III** When $\lambda = -\mu^2 < 0$, then

$$X = C_1 \cos\mu x + C_2 \sin\mu x, \quad Y = C_3e^{\mu y} + C_4e^{-\mu y}$$

$\Rightarrow$ $u(x, y) = (C_1 \cos\mu x + C_2 \sin\mu x)(C_3e^{\mu y} + C_4e^{-\mu y})$ ...(vii)

Therefore, Eqs. (v), (vi) and (vii) are solutions of Laplace Eq. (i).

# SOLVED EXAMPLES

## Type I (*Only one correct option*)

***Example 1.*** *The solution of differential equation*

$$y(x^2+y^2+1)\,dy+[2x(x^2+y^2)-1]\,dx=0 \text{ is}$$

(a) $2x^2+y^2+3\log(x^2+y^2-2)=C$

(b) $2x^2-y^2-3\log(x^2+y^2-2)=C$

(c) $2x^2+y^2+3\log(x^2+y^2+2)=C$

(d) $2x^2-y^2-3\log(x^2+y^2+2)=C$

**Solution.** (a) Let $x^2+y^2=t$

Differentiating *wrt* *x*, we get

$$2x+2y\frac{dy}{dx}=\frac{dt}{dx}$$

$$\Rightarrow \quad \frac{y}{x}\frac{dy}{dx}=\frac{1}{2x}\frac{dt}{dx}-1$$

Therefore, the given equation becomes

$$\frac{1}{2x}\frac{dt}{dx}-1+\frac{2t-1}{t+1}=0$$

$$\Rightarrow \quad \frac{1}{2x}\frac{dt}{dx}=1-\frac{2t-1}{t+1}$$

$$=\frac{2-t}{t+1}$$

$$\Rightarrow \quad 2x\,dx=\frac{t+1}{2-t}\,dt$$

$$\Rightarrow \quad 2x\,dx+\left(1+\frac{3}{t-2}\right)dt=0$$

On integration, we get

$$x^2+t+3\log(t-2)=C$$

$$\Rightarrow \quad 2x^2+y^2+3\log(x^2+y^2-2)=C$$

which is the required solution.

***Example 2.*** *Solution of* $(1+y^2)\,dx=(\tan^{-1}y-x)\,dy$ *is*

(a) $x=\tan^{-1}y-1+ce^{-\tan^{-1}y}$

(b) $y=\tan^{-1}x-1+ce^{-\tan^{-1}x}$

(c) $x=\tan^{-1}y+ce^{-\tan^{-1}y}$

(d) $y=\tan^{-1}x+ce^{\tan^{-1}x}$

**Solution.** (a) Given, differential equation is

$$(1+y^2)\,dx=(\tan^{-1}y-x)\,dy$$

which contains $y^2$ and $\tan^{-1}y$ and is therefore not a linear in $y$ but since only $x$ occurs, we have $(1+y^2)\dfrac{dx}{dy}=\tan^{-1}y-x$

$$\Rightarrow \quad \frac{dx}{dy}+\frac{x}{1+y^2}=\frac{\tan^{-1}y}{1+y^2}$$

which is linear differential equation.

Hence, Integrating factor is

$$\text{IF}=e^{\int p(y)\,dy}=e^{\int\frac{1}{1+y^2}dy}=e^{\tan^{-1}y}$$

Hence, the solution is

$$x\cdot(\text{IF})=\int\frac{\tan^{-1}y}{1+y^2}(\text{IF})\,dy+C$$

$$\Rightarrow \quad xe^{\tan^{-1}y}=\int\frac{\tan^{-1}y}{1+y^2}e^{\tan^{-1}y}dy+C$$

Let $\tan^{-1}y=t$

$$\Rightarrow \quad \frac{dy}{1+y^2}=dt$$

$$=\int te^t\,dt+C$$

$$=te^t-\int 1\cdot e^t\,dt+C$$

$$=te^t-e^t+C$$

$$=(\tan^{-1}y-1)\,e^{\tan^{-1}y}+C$$

$$\Rightarrow \quad x=\tan^{-1}y-1+ce^{-\tan^{-1}y}$$

which is the required solution.

***Example 3.*** *The particular integral of* $(D^2-2D+4)\,y=e^x\cos x$ *is*

(a) $\cos x$ (b) $\sin x$

(c) $\dfrac{1}{2}e^x\cos x$ (d) $\dfrac{1}{2}e^x\sin x$

**Solution.** (c) Particular integral

$$=\left(\frac{1}{D^2-2D+4}\right)(e^x\cos x)$$

$$=e^x\frac{1}{(D+1)^2-2(D+1)+4}\cos x$$

$$=e^x\frac{1}{D^2+3}\cos x$$

$$=e^x\frac{1}{-1+3}\cos x$$

$$=\frac{1}{2}e^x\cos x$$

***Example 4.*** *Solution of* $\frac{\partial^2 z}{\partial x^2} + z = 0$

*with* $x = 0,\ z = e^y$ *and* $\frac{\partial z}{\partial x} = 1$ *is*

(a) $z = \cos x + e^y \sin x$ (b) $z = \sin x + e^y \cos x$

(c) $z = \cos x - e^x \sin y$ (d) $z = \sin x - e^x \cos y$

**Solution.** (b) If $z$ were function of $x$ alone, the solution would have been $z = A \sin x + B \cos x$

where $A$ and $B$ are constants. Since, $z$ is a function of $x$ and $y$, $A$ and $B$ can be arbitrary functions of $y$. Hence, the solution of given eqation is $z = f(y) \sin x + \phi(y) \cos x$

$$\Rightarrow \quad \frac{\partial z}{\partial x} = f(y) \cos x - \phi(y) \sin x$$

If $x = 0;\ z = e^y$

Then, $e^y = f(y)$

If $x = 0,\ \frac{\partial z}{\partial x} = 1$, then $f(y) = 1$

Hence, the required solution is $z = \sin x + e^y \cos x$

***Example 5.*** *Solution of* $p^2 + q^2 = x + y$ *is*

(a) $z = (a + x)^{3/2} + \frac{3}{2}(y - a)^{3/2} + b$

(b) $z = \frac{2}{3}(a + x)^{3/2} + \frac{2}{3}(y - a)^{3/2} + b$

(c) $z = \frac{3}{2}(a + x)^{3/2} + \frac{3}{2}(y - a)^{3/2} + b$

(d) None of the above

**Solution.** (b) Given that $p^2 + q^2 = x + y$

$$\Rightarrow \quad p^2 - x = y - q^2 = a \text{ (say)}$$

$$\Rightarrow \quad p^2 - x = a \Rightarrow p = \sqrt{a + x}$$

and $y - q^2 = a \Rightarrow q = \sqrt{y - a}$

Hence, we have $dz = p\,dx + q\,dy$

$$\Rightarrow \quad dz = \sqrt{a + x}\,dx + \sqrt{y - a}\,dy$$

On integration, we get

$$z = \frac{2}{3}(a + x)^{3/2} + \frac{2}{3}(y - a)^{3/2} + b$$

***Example 6.*** *Solution of* $r - 4s + 4t = e^{2x + y}$ *is*

(a) $z = f_1(y + 2x) + x f_2(y + 2x) + \frac{1}{2} x^2 e^{2x + y}$

(b) $z = f_1(y + 2x) + f_2(y + 2x) + e^{2x + y}$

(c) $z = f_1(y - 2x) + f_2(y - 2x) + e^{2x - y}$

(d) None of the above

**Solution.** (a) Given that $r - 4s + 4t = e^{2x + y}$

$$\Rightarrow \quad \frac{\partial^2 z}{\partial x^2} - 4\frac{\partial^2 z}{\partial x \partial y} + 4\frac{\partial^2 z}{\partial y^2} = e^{2x + y}$$

$$\Rightarrow \quad (D^2 - 4DD' + 4D'^2)\, z = e^{2x + y}$$

Hence, Auxiliary equation is

$$(\lambda - 2)^2 = 0 \Rightarrow \lambda = 2, 2$$

Hence, complement any function is

$$CF = f_1(y + 2x) + x f_2(y + 2x)$$

Now, particular integral is

$$PI = \frac{1}{(D - 2D')} e^{2x + y}$$

The usual rule fails because

$$(D - 2D')^z = 0 \text{ for } D = 2, D' = 1$$

Now, we find

$$(D - 2D')\, u = e^{2x + y}$$

$$u = \int F(x, C - mn)\, dx$$

$$= \int e^{2x} + (C - 2x)\, dx = xe^c = xe^{2x + y}$$

and from $(D - 2D')\, z = u = xe^{2x + y}$,

The solution is $z = \int x e^{2x + (c - 2x)}\, dy = \frac{1}{2} x^2 e^c = \frac{1}{2} x^2 e^{2x + y}$

Hence, the complete solution is

$$z = f_1(y + 2x) + x f_2(y + 2x) + \frac{1}{2} x^2 e^{2x + y}$$

***Example 7.*** *Solution of* $\frac{\partial u}{\partial x} = 2\frac{\partial u}{\partial t} + 4$ *where* $u(x, 0) = 6e^{-3x}$ *is*

(a) $u = e^{3x - 2t}$ (b) $u = 3^{3x + 2t}$

(c) $u = 6e^{3x + 2t}$ (d) $u = 6e^{-(3x + 2t)}$

**Solution.** (d) Let $u(x, t) = X(x)\, T(t)$ be the solution of

$$\frac{\partial u}{\partial x} = 2\frac{\partial u}{\partial t} + u$$

Then, we have $X'T = 2XT' + XT$

$$\Rightarrow \quad (X' - X)\, T = 2XT'$$

$$\Rightarrow \quad \frac{X' - X}{2X} = \frac{T'}{T} = k \text{ (say)}$$

$$\therefore \quad X' - X - 2kX = 0 \Rightarrow \frac{X'}{X} = 1 + 2k \quad \ldots\text{(i)}$$

and $\frac{T'}{T} = k$ ...(ii)

Solving Eq. (i), we get

$$\log X = (1 + 2k)x + \log C$$

$$\Rightarrow \quad X = Ce^{(1 + 2k)x}$$

and solving Eq. (ii), we get

$$\log T = kt + \log C'$$

$$\Rightarrow \quad T = C' e^{kt}$$

Hence, we have

$$u(x, t) = X(x)\, T(t)$$

$$= CC' e^{(1 + 2k)x} e^{kt} \quad \ldots\text{(iii)}$$

Now, $6e^{-3x} = u(x, 0) = CC' e^{(1 + 2k)x}$

$$\Rightarrow \quad CC' = 6 \text{ and } 1 + 2k = -3 \Rightarrow k = -2$$

On putting these values in Eq. (iii), we get the desired solution

$$u(x, t) = 6e^{-3x} e^{-2t} = 6e^{-(3x + 2t)}$$

## Type II (*One or more than one correct option*)

***Example 8.*** *Given*

$$2xz - \left(\frac{\partial z}{\partial x}\right)x^2 - 2\left(\frac{\partial z}{\partial y}\right)xy + \left(\frac{\partial z}{\partial x}\right)\left(\frac{\partial z}{\partial y}\right) = 0 \quad ...(i)$$

(a) Using charpit's method, we have $\frac{dx}{x^2 - q} = \frac{dy}{2xy - p}$

(b) Using charpits method, we have

$$\frac{dz}{px^2 + 2xyq - 2pq} = \frac{dp}{2z - 2qy}$$

(c) Complete integral is $z = ay + b(x^2 - a^2)$

(d) No solution exist

**Solution.** (a), (b), (c)

By Charpit's method, the subsidiary equations of $F(x, y, z, p, q) = 0$

$$\frac{dx}{-\frac{\partial F}{\partial p}} = \frac{dy}{-\frac{\partial F}{\partial q}}$$

$$= \frac{dz}{-p\frac{\partial F}{\partial p} - q\frac{\partial F}{\partial q}}$$

$$= \frac{dp}{\frac{\partial F}{\partial x} + p\frac{\partial F}{\partial z}}$$

$$= \frac{dq}{\frac{\partial F}{\partial y} + q\frac{\partial F}{\partial z}} = \frac{\partial f}{0}$$

We take $\quad \frac{dx}{x^2 - q} = \frac{dy}{2xy - p}$

$$= \frac{dz}{px^2 + 2xyq - 2pq}$$

$$= \frac{dp}{2z - 2qy} = \frac{dp}{0} = \frac{df}{0}$$

On integrating, we get $\quad q = a \quad ...(ii)$

Eqs. (i) and (ii) gives,

$$p = \frac{2x(z - ay)}{x^2 - a}$$

Hence, $\quad dz = pdx + qdy$

$$= \frac{2x(z - ay)\,dx}{x^2 - a} + ady$$

$$\Rightarrow \quad \frac{dz - ady}{z - ay} = \frac{2xdx}{x^2 - a^2}$$

$$\Rightarrow \quad z = ay + b(x^2 - a^2)$$

***Example 9.*** *Given* $u_{xx} - 2\sin x u_{xy} - \cos^2 x uyy - \cos x u_y = 0$

(a) Given partial equation is hyperbolic

(b) Given partial equation is parabolic

(c) Solution of the given partial equation is $u(x, y) = \psi(y - x - \cos x) + g(y + x - \cos x)$

(d) No solution exist

**Solution.** (a), (c)

Comparing with the general second order partial differential equation, we have

$$A = 1, B = -2\sin x, C = -\cos^2 x,$$
$$D = 0, E = -\cos x, F = 0, G = 0$$

The discriminant $\quad B^2 - 4AC = 4(\sin^2 x + \cos^2 x) = 4 > 0.$

Hence, the given partial differential equation is hyperbolic.

The characteristic equations are

$$\frac{dy}{dx} = \frac{B - \sqrt{B^2 - 4AC}}{2A} = -\sin x - 1$$

and $\quad \frac{dy}{dx} = \frac{B + \sqrt{B^2 - 4AC}}{2A}$

$$= 1 - \sin x$$

$\Rightarrow \quad y = \cos x - x + C_1$

and $\quad y = \cos x + x + C_2$

$\Rightarrow \quad \xi = x + y - \cos x = C_1$

$\quad \eta = -x + y - \cos x = C_2$

On Integrating with respect to $\xi$, we obtain $u_\eta = f(\eta)$

where $f$ is arbitrary. Integrating once again with respect to $n$, we have

$$u - \int f(\eta)\,d\eta + g(\xi)$$

$$\Rightarrow \quad u = \psi(\eta) + g(\xi)$$

Where $g(\xi)$ is an arbitrary function. Returning to the old variables $x$ and $y$ the solution of the given partial differential equation is

$$u(x, y) = \psi(y - x - \cos x) + g(y + x - \cos x)$$

***Example 10.*** *Given,* $yu_{xx} + (x + y)u_{xy} + xu_{yy} = 0$

(a) The canonical equation for the given partial differential equation is $-2(x - y)^2 u_{\xi\eta} + 2(x - y)u_\eta = 0$

(b) No canonical form of the given equation exist

(c) The general solution of the equation is

$$u = \frac{1}{y - x}\int f(y^2 - x^2)\,d(y^2 - x^2) + g(y - x)$$

(d) No general solution exist

**Solution.** (a), (c)

Here, $A = y, B = x + y, C = x$

$B^2 - 4AC = (x + y)^2 - 4xy = (x - y)^2 > 0$

Hence, the given partial differential equation is hyperbolic everywhere except along the line $y = x$; whereas on the line $y = x$, it is parabolic.

When $y \neq x$, the characteristics equations are

$$\frac{dy}{dx} = \frac{B \mp \sqrt{B^2 - 4AC}}{2A}$$

$$= \frac{(x + y) \mp (x + y)}{2y}$$

Hence, $\frac{dy}{dx} = 1$ and $\frac{dy}{dx} = \frac{x}{y}$

$\Rightarrow \quad y = x + C_1$ and $y^2 = x^2 + C_2$

The characteristic equations are

$$\xi = y - x \text{ and } \eta = y^2 - x^2$$

The canonical form can be obtained by computing

$$\overline{A} = A\xi_x^2 + B\xi_x\xi_y + C\xi_y^2$$

$$= y - x - y + x = 0$$

$$\overline{B} = -2(x-y)^2$$

$$\overline{C} = 0, \overline{D} = 0, \overline{E} = 2(x-y), \overline{F} = \overline{G} = 0$$

Thus, the canonical equation for the given partial differential equation is

$$-2(x-y)^2 u_{\xi\eta} + 2(x-y) u_\eta = 0$$

$$\Rightarrow \quad 2\xi^2 u_{\xi\eta} + 2(-\xi) u_\eta = 0$$

$$\Rightarrow \quad \xi u_{\xi\eta} + u_\eta = 0$$

$$\frac{\partial}{\partial\xi}\left(\xi\frac{\partial u}{\partial\eta}\right) = 0$$

On integrating, we get

$$\xi\frac{\partial u}{\partial\eta} = f(\eta)$$

Again, integrating with respect to $\eta$, we have

$$u = \frac{1}{\xi}\int f(\eta)\, d\eta + g(\xi)$$

$$\Rightarrow \quad u = \frac{1}{y-x}\int f(y^2 - x^2)\, d(y^2 - x^2) + g(y-x)$$

which is the required general solution.

***Example 11.*** *Given, the wave equation $u_{tt} = c^2 u_{xx}$*

*Also,*

I. $u(0,t) = u(2,t) = 0$

II. $u(x,0) = \sin^3 \pi x/2$

III. $u_t(x,0) = 0$

(a) The possible solution is $u(x,t) = (c_1 \cos \lambda x + c_2 \sin \lambda x)[c_3 \cos(c\lambda t) + c_4 \sin(c\lambda t)]$

(b) The required solution is

$$u(x,t) = \frac{3}{4}\sin\frac{\pi x}{2}\cos\frac{\pi ct}{2} - \frac{1}{4}\sin\frac{3\pi x}{2}\cos\frac{3\pi ct}{2}$$

(c) No solution exist

(d) Solution exist

**Solution.** (a), (b), (d)

The possible solution is

$$u(x,t) = (c_1 \cos \lambda x + c_2 \sin \lambda x)[c_3 \cos(c\lambda t) + c_4 \sin(c\lambda t)]$$

Using the condition $u(0,t) = 0$, we obtain $c_1 = 0$. Also, condition III $\Rightarrow c_4 = 0$. The condition $u(2,t) = 0$ gives

$$\sin 2\lambda = 0$$

$$\Rightarrow \quad \lambda = n\pi/2, n = 1, 2 \ldots$$

Hence, the solution is

$$u(x,t) = \sum_{n=1}^{\infty} A_n \sin\frac{n\pi x}{2}\cos\frac{n\pi ct}{2}$$

Using condition II, we have

$$\sum_{n=1}^{\infty} A_n \sin\frac{n\pi x}{2} = \sin^3\frac{\pi x}{2}$$

$$= \frac{3}{4}\sin\frac{\pi x}{2} - \frac{1}{4}\sin\frac{3\pi x}{2}$$

Which gives $A_1 = 3/4$, $A_3 = -1/4$, while all other $A_n'$s are zero. Hence, the required solution is

$$u(x,t) = \frac{3}{4}\sin\frac{\pi x}{2}\cos\frac{\pi ct}{2} - \frac{1}{4}\sin\frac{3\pi x}{2}\cos\frac{3\pi ct}{2}$$

***Example 12.*** *Given,* $\frac{\partial u}{\partial t} = c^2\frac{\partial^2 u}{\partial x^2}$

*Boundary conditions* $u(0,t) = 0 = u(l,t), t > 0$

*Initial conditions* $u(x,0) = \frac{100}{l}x$

(a) The general solution is

$$u(x,t) = \sum_{n=1}^{\infty} b_n \sin\frac{n\pi x}{l} e^{-c^2n^2\pi^2t/l^2}$$

(b) No general solution exist

(c) The solution is $u(x,t) = \frac{200}{\pi}\sum_{n=1}^{\infty}\frac{(-1)^{n+1}}{n}\sin\frac{n\pi x}{l}e^{-(cn\pi/l)^2 t}$

(d) No solution exist

**Solution.** (a), (c)

The solution of partial differential equation is

$$u(x,t) = (c_1 \cos px + c_2 \sin px)\, e^{-c^2p^2t} \quad \ldots(i)$$

By $u(0,t) = 0$, we have

$$u(0,t) = c_1 e^{-c^2p^2t} = 0, t > 0$$

Hence, $c_1 = 0$ and Eq. (i) reduces to

$$u(x,t) = c_2 \sin px \cdot e^{-c^2p^2t} \quad \ldots(ii)$$

Since, $u(l,t) = 0$ we have

$$u(l,t) = c_2 \sin pl \cdot e^{-c^2p^2t} = 0, t > 0$$

Hence, $\sin pl = 0 \Rightarrow pl = n\pi$ as $c_2 \neq 0$

$\Rightarrow \quad p = n\pi/l$, ($n$ is integer)

Hence, Eq. (ii) reduces to

$$u(x,t) = b_n \sin\frac{n\pi x}{l}\cdot e^{-c^2n^2\pi^2t/l^2}$$

Where $b_n = c_2$

Hence, the general solution is

$$u(x,t) = \sum_{n=1}^{\infty} b_n \sin\frac{n\pi x}{l} e^{-c^2n^2\pi^2t/l^2} \quad \ldots(iii)$$

Putting $t = 0$, $u(x,0) = \sum_{n=1}^{\infty} b_n \sin\frac{n\pi x}{l}$

Hence, $u(x,0) = \frac{100}{l}x$, we have

$$\frac{100x}{l} = \sum_{n=1}^{\infty} b_n \sin\frac{n\pi x}{l}$$

where $b_n = \frac{2}{l}\int_0^l \frac{100x}{l}\cdot \sin\frac{n\pi x}{l}\,dx$

$$= \frac{200}{l^2}\left[x\left\{-\frac{\cos(n\pi x/l)}{(n\pi/l)}\right\} - (1)\left\{-\frac{\sin(n\pi x/l)}{(n\pi/l)^2}\right\}\right]_0^l$$

$$= \frac{200}{l^2}\left(-\frac{l^2}{n\pi}\cos n\pi\right)$$

$$= \frac{200}{n\pi}(-1)^{n+1}$$

$$\Rightarrow \quad u(x,t) = \frac{200}{\pi}\sum_{n=1}^{\infty}\frac{(-1)^{n+1}}{n}\sin\frac{n\pi x}{l}\,e^{-(cn\pi/l)^2 t}$$

which is the required solution.

***Example 13.*** *Given, the problem partial differential equation*

$$u_t = au_{xx},\ 0 \le x \le L, t > 0$$

*Boundary conditions*

$$u(0,t) = u(L,t) = 0, t > 0$$

*Initial conditions*

$$u(x,0) = f(x)\ 0 \le x \le L$$

(a) The Green's function of the given equation is

$$G(x,y,t) = \frac{2}{L}\sum_{n=1}^{\infty}\exp(-\alpha\lambda_n^2 t)\sin\lambda_n y\sin\lambda_n x$$

for $0 \le x, y \le L$ and $t > 0$

(b) No Green's function of the given equation exist

(c) The given partial differential equation is equivalent to

$$u(x,t) = (A\cos\lambda x + B\sin\lambda x)\,e^{-\alpha\lambda^2 t}$$

(d) The given partial differential equation is equivalent to

$$u(x,t) = \frac{A\cos x}{B\sin x} + 2$$

**Solution.** (a), (c)

By the separation of variable method, the solution of partial differential equation

$$\frac{\partial u}{\partial t} = \alpha\frac{\partial^2 u}{x^2} \text{ is}$$

$$u(x,t) = (A\cos\lambda x + B\sin\lambda x)\,e^{-\alpha\lambda^2 t}$$

Using boundary condition,

$$u(0,t) = 0, t > 0, \text{ we have}$$

$$u(0,t) = A\cos(\lambda, 0) = 0 \Rightarrow A = 0$$

Hence, $u(x,t) = B\sin\lambda x\,e^{-\alpha\lambda^2 t}$

Applying the Boundary conditions; $u(0,l) = u(L,t) = 0$

we get $u(L,t) = Be^{-\alpha\lambda^2 t}\sin\lambda L = 0$

$$\Rightarrow \quad \sin\lambda L = 0$$

$$\Rightarrow \quad \lambda = n\pi/L, n = 1, 2\ldots$$

Using the superposition principle, we have

$$u(x,t) = \sum_{n=1}^{\infty} C_n\exp(-\alpha\lambda_n^2 t)\sin\lambda_n x,$$

$$\lambda_n = n\pi/L \qquad \ldots\text{(i)}$$

Now, using the Initial conditions $u(x,0) = f(x)$, we get

$$f(x) = \sum_{n=1}^{\infty} C_n\sin\lambda_n x,$$

which is a half-range Fourier sine series.

Therefore,

$$C_n = \frac{2}{L}\int_0^L f(y)\sin\lambda_n y\,dy \qquad \ldots\text{(ii)}$$

Now, by Eqs. (i) and (ii), we have

$$u(x,t) = \int_0^L\left[\frac{2}{L}\sum_{n=1}^{\infty}\exp(-\alpha\lambda_n^2 t)\sin\lambda_n y\sin\lambda_n x\right]f(y)\,dy \quad \ldots\text{(iii)}$$

The Eq. (iii) can be expressed as

$$u(x,t) = \int_0^l G(x,y,t)\,f(y)\,dy \qquad (\text{for } 0 \le x \le L, t \ge 0)$$

where $G(x,y,t)$ is the Green's function defined as

$$G(x,y,t) = \frac{2}{L}\sum_{n=1}^{\infty}\exp(-\alpha\lambda_n^2 t)\sin\lambda_n y\sin\lambda_n x$$

for $0 \le x, y \le L$ and $t > 0$.

# Exercise 1 (For Part 'B')

**Directions** (Q. Nos. 1-292) *All questions have only one correct option.*

**1.** The *c*-discriminant does not contain one of the following.
(a) The envelope (b) The tac-locus
(c) The cusp-locus (d) The node-locus

**2.** The *c*-discriminant when equated to zero includes nodal locus
(a) once (b) twice
(c) thrice (d) None of these

**3.** The *c*-discriminant and *p*-discriminant both contain
(a) envelope (b) tac-locus once
(c) node-locus (d) None of these

**4.** The *c*-discriminant of the equation $(y-c)^2 = x(x-a)^2$ is
(a) $x(x-a^2)=0$ (b) $x-a^2=0$
(c) $x=a$ (d) None of these

**5.** The *p*-discriminant of the equation $y = px + \frac{1}{p}$ is
(a) $y^2 = x$ (b) $y = x$
(c) $y^2 = 4x$ (d) None of these

**6.** Which one of the following is the solution of differential equation?
(a) Envelope (b) Cusp-locus
(c) Node-locus (d) Tac-locus

**7.** **A** The solution of ordinary differential equation of order *n* have *n* arbitrary constants.
**B** The solution of partial differential equation of order *n* have *n* arbitrary functions.
(a) A is true, B is false (b) A is false, B is true
(c) Both A and B are true (d) Both A and B are false

**8.** The solution of ordinary differential equation of *n* order contains
(a) *n*-arbitrary constants
(b) more than *n*-arbitrary constants
(c) no arbitrary constants
(d) None of the above

**9.** The nodes have a double point
(a) with distinct tangent
(b) with coincident tangent
(c) same tangent
(d) None of the above

**10.** For a given differential equation
(a) an envelope gives a singular solution
(b) node-locus gives a solution
(c) cusp-locus gives a solution
(d) (a), (b) and (c) are false

**11.** The *p*-discriminant does not contain one of the following.
(a) The envelope (b) The tac-locus
(c) The cusp-locus (d) The node-locus

**12.** If $\phi(x, y) = 0$ is a singular solution, then $\phi(x, y)$ is a factor of
(a) *p*-discriminant only
(b) *c*-discriminant only
(c) Both *p*-and *c*-discriminant
(d) None of the above

**13.** What is the order and degree of a differential equation?
$$\frac{d^2y}{dx^2} + \sqrt{1+\left(\frac{dy}{dx}\right)^3} = 0$$
(a) First order, second degree
(b) First order, first degree
(c) Second degree, first order
(d) Second order, first degree

**14.** The *n*th order ordinary linear homogeneous differential equation have
(a) *n*-singular solutions (b) no singular solution
(c) one singular solution (d) None of these

**15.** The homogeneous differential equation $M(x, y)dx + N(x, y)dy = 0$ can be reduced to a differential equation. In which the variable are separated, by the substitution
(a) $y = vx$ (b) $xy = v$
(c) $x + y = v$ (d) $x - y = v$

**16.** The solution of
$$\frac{dy}{dx} + \frac{y\cos x + \sin y + y}{\sin x + x\cos y + x} = 0 \text{ is}$$
(a) $y\sin x + (\sin y + y)x = C$ (b) $y\sin x + (\sin x + x) = C$
(c) $y = \sin x + y\sin y + C$ (d) None of these

**17.** $\frac{d^2y}{dx^2} + \frac{dy}{dx} - 2y = 0$, has the solution
(a) $y = C_1e^{-2x} + C_2e^x$
(b) $y = Ce^{-2x}$
(c) $y = C_1e^{-2x} + C_2e^{-x} + C_3$
(d) None of the above

**18.** A differential equation of first order and first degree is homogeneous, if
(a) $\frac{dy}{dx} = \phi\left(\frac{y}{x}\right)$ (b) $\frac{dy}{dx} = \text{constant}$
(c) $\frac{dy}{dx} = \phi(x)$ (d) None of these

**19.** The equation $\frac{dy}{dx}+Py=Q$ is linear differential equation of first order, if
(a) $P, Q$ are functions of $x$ only
(b) $P, Q$ are functions of $y$ only
(c) $P, Q$ are functions of $x$ and $y$
(d) None of the above

**20.** General solution of $\frac{dy}{dx}+2xy=2e^{-x^2}$ is
(a) $y=(2x+c)e^{-x^2}$ (b) $y=2xe^{-x}$
(c) $y=e^{-x}$ (d) None of these

**21.** General solution of $2\frac{d^2y}{dx^2}+5\frac{dy}{dx}+2y=0$, is
(a) $y=Ae^{-2x}$ (b) $y=Be^{\frac{1}{2}x}$
(c) $y=Ae^{-2x}+Be^{-\frac{1}{2}x}$ (d) None of these

**22.** The differential equation $\frac{dy}{dx}+Py=Q$, $P$ and $Q$ are functions of $x$ only, have the integrating factor
(a) $e^{\int Pdx}$ (b) $e^{\int Qdy}$ (c) $e^{\int Pdy}$ (d) $e^{\int Qdx}$

**23.** A solution of a differential equation which contains no arbitrary constants is
(a) particular solution (b) general solution
(c) primitive (d) None of these

**24.** A general solution of a linear differential equation with constant coefficients is
(a) sum of particular solution and complementary function
(b) product of particular solution and complementary function
(c) quotient of particular solution and complementary function
(d) None of the above

**25.** The integrating factor for the differential equation $(x+1)\frac{dy}{dx}-y=e^{3x}(x+1)^2$, is
(a) $\frac{1}{x+1}$ (b) $x+1$
(c) $\frac{1}{x^2+1}$ (d) $x^2+1$

**26.** The necessary condition for the equation $M(x,y)dx+N(x,y)dy=0$, to be exact is
(a) $\frac{\partial N}{\partial y}=\frac{\partial M}{\partial x}$ (b) $\frac{\partial N}{\partial y}=-\frac{\partial M}{\partial x}$
(c) $\frac{\partial M}{\partial y}=\frac{\partial N}{\partial x}$ (d) $\frac{\partial M}{\partial y}=-\frac{\partial N}{\partial x}$

**27.** The equation $y\,dx+xdy=0$, is
(a) exact differential equation
(b) not-exact differential equation
(c) partial differential equation
(d) None of the above

**28.** The solution of differential equation contains as many as arbitrary constants as the order of a differential equation, then the solution is said to be
(a) particular solution (b) complete primitive
(c) singular solution (d) None of these

**29.** The solution derived from complete primitive by giving particular values to arbitrary constants is
(a) singular solution (b) particular integral
(c) complete solution (d) None of these

**30.** The number of arbitrary constants complete primitive of differential equation $\frac{d^5y}{dx^5}+2\frac{d^4y}{dx^4}=0$ contains
(a) 5 (b) 4
(c) 1 (d) None of these

**31.** Any equation contains $n$-arbitrary constants, then the order of differential equation derived from it is
(a) $n$ (b) $n-1$ (c) 2 (d) $n+1$

**32.** The differential equation, derived from $y=Ae^{2x}+Be^{-2x}$ have the order, where $A$, $B$ are constants
(a) 3 (b) 2
(c) 1 (d) None of these

**33.** In linear ordinary differential equation, the dependent variable and its differential coefficients are not multiplied together and occurs only in
(a) first degree (b) second degree
(c) third degree (d) fourth degree

**34.** The solution of the differential equation
$$\frac{dy}{dx}=\frac{3x^2y^4+2xy}{x^2-2x^3y^3}$$ is
(a) $x^3y^2+\frac{x^2}{y}=\frac{x}{y}$ (b) $x^3y^2+\frac{x^2}{y^2}=x$
(c) $x^3y^2+\frac{x^2}{y}=C$ (d) None of these

**35.** The equation $y=Ae^{3x}+Be^{5x}$ can be represented as
(a) $y''-8y+15y=0$ (b) $y''+8y'=0$
(c) $y'+8y'=0$ (d) $y''+8y'+15y=0$

**36.** The equation $x=A\cos(pt-\alpha)$ can be expressed as
(a) $\frac{d^2x}{dt^2}=x$ (b) $\frac{d^2x}{dt^2}=-p^2x$
(c) $\frac{d^2x}{dt^2}=0$ (d) None of these

**37.** The solution of the differential equation $\left(x\sin\left(\frac{y}{x}\right)\right)dx-\left(y\sin\left(\frac{y}{x}\right)-x\right)dx=0$ is
(a) $\cos\left(\frac{y}{x}\right)=0$
(b) $\sin\left(\frac{y}{x}\right)=0$

(c) $\cos\left(\frac{y}{x}\right) - \log x = \text{constant}$

(d) $\sin\left(\frac{y}{x}\right) - \log x = \text{constant}$

**38.** The *n*-order differential linear equation with constant coefficient, $y^{(n)} + a_{n-1}y^{(n-1)} + \ldots + a_1y' + a_0y = 0$, $a_1, \ldots, a_n$ are constant and characteristic equation $\lambda^n + a_{n-1}\lambda^{n-1} + \ldots + a_1\lambda + \alpha_0 = 0$ has a solution iff all *n*-roots of characteristic equations are

(a) all distinct (b) all same
(c) partially distinct (d) None of these

**39.** The difference of two solutions of non-homogeneous *n*-order ordinary differential equation is a solution of corresponding homogeneous equation. The statement is

(a) always true (b) always false
(c) partially true (d) partially false

**40.** If $M(x, y)dx + N(x, y)dy = 0$ and $\frac{\partial M}{\partial y} = \frac{\partial N}{\partial x}$, then

(a) the equation is exact (b) not exact
(c) linear (d) non-linear

**41.** If an equation $Mdx + Ndy = 0$ is not exact, let $F(x, y)$ be such that $FMdx + FNdy = 0$ is exact, then the function $F$ is called

(a) differentiable function (b) arbitrary function
(c) integrating factor (d) None of these

**42.** For the equation $y' + p(x)y = r(x)$ to be homogeneous

(a) $r(x) \neq 0$ (b) $r(x) = 0$
(c) $r(x) = p(x)$ (d) $p(x) = 0$

**43.** For non-homogeneous equation $y' + p(x)y = r(x)$, if $y_1$ and $y_2$ are its solutions, then the solution of homogeneous equation $y' + p(x)y = 0$ is

(a) $y = y_1 - y_2$ (b) $y = \frac{y_1}{y_2}$
(c) $y = \frac{y_2}{y_1}$ (d) None of these

**44.** The linearity principle for ordinary differential equation holds for

(a) non-homogeneous equation
(b) non-linear equation
(c) linear differential equation
(d) None of the above

**45.** For homogeneous linear ordinary differential equation, the linear combination of two solutions is again a solution of the equation the statement is

(a) true (b) false
(c) neither true nor false (d) Can't say

**46.** If $y_1$ and $y_2$ are two solutions of $y'' + p(x)y' + q(x)y = 0$, then for general solution of this given equation, $y_1$ and $y_2$ are

(a) linearly dependent (b) linearly independent
(c) proportional (d) None of these

**47.** If $y_1$ and $y_2$ are two solutions of initial value problem $y'' + p(x)y' + q(x)y = 0$, $y(x_0) = y_0$, $y'(x_0) = y_0$ and the Wronskion $W(y_1, y_2) = 0$, then $y_1$ and $y_2$ are

(a) linearly dependent (b) linearly independent
(c) proportional (d) None of these

**48.** The *n*th order homogeneous linear differential equation $y^{(n)} + p_0y^{(n-1)} + \ldots + p_ny = 0$ has general solution if the coefficients $p_0(x), \ldots, p_n(x)$ on some interval $I$ are

(a) continuous
(b) discontinuous
(c) discontinuous and differentiable
(d) None of the above

**49.** Solving by variation of parameter $y'' - 2y' + y = e^x \log x$, the value of Wronskion $W$ is

(a) $e^{2x}$ (b) 2
(c) $e^{-2x}$ (d) None of these

**50.** Singular solution of differential equation contains

I. arbitrary constant
II. can be obtained from general
III. do not contain arbitrary constant
IV. cannot be obtained from general solution

(a) I, II are true (b) III, IV are true
(c) I, IV are true (d) II, IV are true

**51.** **A.** Singular solution contains no arbitrary constants.
**B.** Singular solution can be obtained from complete primitive.

(a) A is true, B is false
(b) Both A and B are true
(c) Both A and B are false
(d) None of the above

**52.** For $\frac{d^2y}{dx^2} + 4y = \tan 2x$ solving by variation of parameters. The value of Wronskion $W$ is

(a) 1 (b) 2
(c) 3 (d) 4

**53.** The value of Wronskion $W(x, x^2, x^3)$ is

(a) $2x^4$ (b) $2x^2$
(c) $2x^3$ (d) None of these

**54.** Solving by variation of parameter for the equation $y'' + y = \sec x$, the value of Wronskion is

(a) 1 (b) 2
(c) 3 (d) 4

**55.** $\frac{d^3z}{dx^3} + \frac{d^2y}{dx^2} + 4\frac{dy}{dx} + 4 = 0$, has the solution

(a) $y = C_1e^{-x} + xC_2e^{-x} + x^2C_3e^{-x}$
(b) $y = C_1\cos 2x + C_2\sin 2x$
(c) $y = C_1e^{-x} + C_2\cos 2x + C_3\sin 2x$
(d) None of the above

**56.** The particular solution of $\frac{d^3y}{dx^2}+y=\cos(2x-1)$ is

(a) $\frac{1}{65}[\cos(2x-1)-8]$

(b) $\frac{1}{65}[\cos(2x-1)-8\sin(2x-1)]$

(c) $\frac{1}{65}[\cos(2x+1)+8]$

(d) None of the above

**57.** The complementary function of $(D^4-a^4)y=0$ is

(a) $y=C_1e^{ax}+C_2e^{-ax}$

(b) $y=C_1e^{ax}+C_2e^{-ax}+C_3\cos ax+C_4\sin ax$

(c) $y=C_1e^{-ax}+C_2e^{ax}+C_3\sin ax+C_4\cos ax$

(d) None of the above

**58.** $e^{-x}(C_1\cos\sqrt{3}x+C_2\sin\sqrt{3}x)+C_3e^{2x}$ is the general solution of

(a) $d^3y/dx^3+4y=0$

(b) $d^3y/dx^3-8y=0$

(c) $d^3y/dx^3+8y=0$

(d) $d^3y/dx^3-2d^2y/dx^2+dy/dx-2=0$

**59.** PI of $\frac{d^2y}{dx^2}+\frac{dy}{dx}=x^2+2x+4$ is

(a) $\frac{x^2}{3}+4x$ (b) $\frac{x^3}{3}+4$

(c) $\frac{x^3}{3}+4x$ (d) $\frac{x^3}{3}+4x^2$

**60.** The PI of the differential equation

$(D^3-D)y=e^x+e^{-x}, D=\frac{d}{dx}$ is

(a) $\frac{1}{2}(e^x+e^{-x})$ (b) $\frac{1}{2}x(e^x+e^{-x})$

(c) $\frac{1}{2}x^2(e^x+e^{-x})$ (d) $\frac{1}{2}x^2(e^x-e^{-x})$

**61.** The CF of $x^2y''-xy'+2y=x\log x$ is

(a) $x[C_1\cos(\log x)+C_2\sin(\log x)]$

(b) $x[C_1\sin(\log x)+C_2\cos(\log x)]$

(c) $x[C_1\cos(\log x)-C_2\sin(\log x)]$

(d) $x[C_1\sin(\log x)-C_2\cos(\log x)]$

**62.** Given, an equation $\frac{d^3y}{dx^3}=\frac{dy}{dx}$ and a solution of it is $y=a_0+a_1\sinh x+a_2\cosh x$, where $a_0, a_1, a_2$ are arbitrary constants, then this solution is

(a) particular solution (b) complete primitive

(c) singular solution (d) None of these

**63.** General solution of

$\frac{d^3y}{dx^3}=-6\frac{d^2y}{dx^2}+11\frac{dy}{dx}-6y=0$ is

(a) $y=Ae^x+Be^{2x}+Ce^{3x}$ (b) $y=3e^x$

(c) $y=A+Be^{2x}$ (d) None of these

**64.** The differential equation $y''+6y'+9y=50e^{2x}$ have particular integral

(a) $\frac{2e^{2x}}{3}$ (b) $2e^{2x}$

(c) $e^{2x}$ (d) None of these

**65.** Solution of differential equation $\frac{d^2y}{dx^2}+n^2y=\sec nx$ is

(a) $y=C_1\sin nx+C_2\cos nx+\frac{1}{n^2}\sin nx\log\cos nx+\frac{x}{n}\sin nx$

(b) $y=C_1\cos nx+C_2\sin nx+\frac{1}{n^2}\cos nx\log\sin nx+\frac{x}{n}\cos nx$

(c) $y=C_1\cos nx+C_2\sin nx+\frac{1}{n^2}\cos nx\log\cos nx+\frac{x}{n}\sin nx$

(d) None of the above

**66.** Solution of differential equation $\frac{d^2y}{dx^2}+y=\operatorname{cosec} x$ is

(a) $y=C_1\cos x+C_2\sin x-x\cos x+\sin x\log\sin x$

(b) $y=C_1\sin x+C_2\cos x-x\sin x+\sin x\log\cos x$

(c) $y=C_1\cos x+C_2\sin x-x\sin x+\cos x\log\sin x$

(d) None of the above

**67.** Solution of $x\frac{d^2y}{dx^2}-(2x-1)\frac{dy}{dx}+(x-1)y=0$ is

(a) $y=e^x(C_1\log x+C_2\sin x)$

(b) $y=e^x(C_1\log x+C_2)$

(c) $y=e^x(C_1\log x+C_2\cos x)$

(d) $y=-e^x(C_1\log x-C_2\sin x)$

**68.** Solution of $\frac{d^2y}{dx^2}-\frac{2}{x}\frac{dy}{dx}+\left(1+\frac{2}{x^2}\right)y=xe^x$ is

(a) $y=x(C_1\cos x+C_2\log x+\frac{1}{2}e^x)$

(b) $y=x(C_1\cos x+C_2\sin x)$

(c) $y=-x(C_1\cos x+C_2\sin x)$

(d) $y=x(C_1\cos x+C_2\sin x+\frac{1}{2}e^x)$

**69.** Solution of $\frac{d^2y}{dx^2}+\cot x\frac{dy}{dx}+4y\operatorname{cosec}^2x=0$, is

(a) $y=k_1\cos\left(2\log\tan\frac{x}{2}+k_2\right)$

(b) $y=k_1\sin\left(\log\tan\frac{x}{2}-k_2\right)$

(c) $y=k_1\cos\left(\log\tan\frac{x}{2}-k_2\right)$

(d) $y=k_1\sin\left(-\log\tan\frac{x}{2}+k_2\right)$

**70.** If $y_1(x)$ and $y_2(x)$ are solutions of $y'' + x^2 y' + (1-x)y = 0$ such that

$$y_1(0) = 0, y_1'(0) = 1$$
$$y_2'(0) = 1, y_2(0) = 1$$

then the Wronskian $W(y_1, y_2)$ on R

(a) 0 (b) 1
(c) −1 (d) 2

**71.** A function $f(t) = \frac{d}{dt}\left\{\frac{dx}{1-\cos t \cos x}\right\}$ satisfies the differential equation

(a) $\frac{df}{dt} + 2f(t)\cos t = 0$ (b) $\frac{df}{dt} - 2f(t)\cos t = 0$
(c) $\frac{df}{dt} + 2f(t)\sin t = 0$ (d) $\frac{df}{dt} - 2f(t)\sin t = 0$

**72.** The largest value of $c$ such that there exists a function $h(x)$ for $-c < x < c$ that is a solution $\frac{dy}{dx} = 1 + y^2$ with $h(0) = 0$ is given by

(a) $\frac{\pi}{3}$ (b) $\frac{\pi}{2}$
(c) $\frac{\pi}{4}$ (d) $\pi$

**73.** Which of the following transformation reduce the differential equation $\frac{dz}{dx} + \frac{z}{x}\log z = \frac{z}{x^2}(\log z)^2$ into the form $\frac{du}{dx} + P(x)(u) = Q(x)$

(a) $u = \log z$ (b) $u = \frac{1}{\log z}$
(c) $u = e^z$ (d) $u = (\log z)^2$

**74.** For the differential equation $xy' - y = 0$ which of the following function is not an integrating factor.

(a) $\frac{1}{x^2}$ (b) $\frac{1}{y^2}$
(c) $\frac{1}{xy}$ (d) $\frac{1}{x+y}$

**75.** The differential equation

$(3a^2x^2 + by\cos x)dx + (2\sin x - 4ay^3)dy = 0$ is exact for

(a) $a$ be any value, but $b \neq 2$
(b) $a$ be any value, but $b = 2$
(c) $b$ be any value, but $a = 2$
(d) $a$ and $b$ may be any value

**76.** If $Mdx + Ndy = 0$ is a differential equation and is $\frac{1}{M}\left(\frac{\partial N}{\partial x} - \frac{\partial M}{\partial y}\right)$ is a function of $y$ alone, say $f(y)$, then integrating factor is

(a) $e^x$ (b) $e^{x+y}$
(c) $e^{\int f(y)dy}$ (d) None of these

**77.** In equation $Mdx + Ndy = 0$ has the form $f_1(x, y)ydx + f_2(x, y)xdy = 0$ and $Mx - Ny = 0$ an integrating factor is

(a) $Mx - Ny$ (b) $My - Nx$
(c) $\frac{1}{Mx - Ny}$ (d) None of these

**78.** Which of the following is not an integrating factor of $xdy - ydx = 0$?

(a) $\frac{1}{x^2}$ (b) $\frac{1}{x^2 + y^2}$
(c) $\frac{1}{xy}$ (d) $\frac{x}{y}$

**79.** General solution of differential equation $\frac{dy}{dx} + \tan x \tan y = \cos x \sec y$

(a) $\sin y = (x + c)\cos x$ (b) $\sin y = (x + c)\sin y$
(c) $\sin x = (x + c)\sin y$ (d) $\cos y = (x + c)\sin x$

**80.** The equation of the envelope of the family of curves represented by the general solution of the differential equation is called

(a) complementary solution
(b) particular solution
(c) singular solution
(d) None of the above

**81.** Integrating factor of $(x^7y^2 + 3y)dx + (3x^8y - x)dy = 0$ is $x^m y^n$, then

(a) $m = -7, n = 2$ (b) $m = -1, n = 7$
(c) $m = -7, n = 1$ (d) $m = -7, n = -2$

**82.** The equation $\frac{\partial z}{\partial x}e^y = \frac{\partial z}{\partial y}e^x$ gives the general solution

(a) $z = ae^x - be^x$ (b) $z = e^x + e^y$
(c) $z = a(e^x + e^y) + b$ (d) None of these

**83.** The complete solution of $z = px + qy + p^2 + q^2$ is

(a) $z = ax + by + a^2 + b^2$ (b) $z = ax + by$
(c) $z = a^2x^2 + z^2 + by^2$ (d) $z = ax^2 + by^2 + z^2$

**84.** $\frac{\partial^2 z}{\partial x^2} - \frac{\partial^2 z}{\partial y^2} + \frac{\partial z}{\partial x} - \frac{\partial z}{\partial y} = 0$, has the solution

(a) $z = f_1(y - x) + e^{-x}f_2(y - x)$
(b) $z = f_1(y + x) + f_2(y - x)$
(c) $z = e^{-x}f(y - x)$
(d) $z = f_1(y + x) + e^{-x}f_2(y - x)$

**85.** The solution of the equation $\frac{\partial^2 z}{\partial x \partial y}\left(\frac{\partial z}{\partial x} - 2\frac{\partial z}{\partial y} - 3\right) = 0$, is

(a) $z = f_1(y) + f_2(x)$
(b) $z = e^{2x}f_1(y + 3x)$
(c) $z = f_1(y) + e^{2x}f_2(y + 3x)$
(d) $z = f_1(y) + f_2(x) + e^{3x}f_3(y + 3x)$

**86.** $\frac{\partial^2 z}{\partial x^2} - \frac{\partial^2 z}{\partial x^2} + \frac{\partial z}{\partial x} = 1$, has the solution

(a) $z = f_1(y) + e^{-x} f_2(y + x) + x$
(b) $z = f_1(y) + e^{-x} f_2(y + x)$
(c) $z = x$
(d) None of the above

**87.** $\frac{\partial^2 z}{\partial x^2} + 2\frac{\partial^2 z}{\partial x \partial y} + \frac{\partial^2 z}{\partial y^2} + 2\left(\frac{\partial z}{\partial x} + \frac{\partial z}{\partial y}\right) + z = 0$

(a) $z = 2e^{-x} f_1(y + x)$
(b) $z = e^{-x} f_1(y - x) + xe^{-x} f_2(y - x)$
(c) $z = f_1(y - x) + xf_2(y - x)$
(d) None of the above

**88.** The relation $z = (x + a)(y + b)$ represents the partial differential equation

(a) $z = \frac{p}{q}$ (b) $z = pq$
(c) $z = p - q$ (d) None of these

**89.** General solution of $\frac{\partial^2 u}{\partial x^2} + \frac{\partial^2 u}{\partial y^2} = 0$ is of the form,

(a) $u = f(x + iy) + g(x - iy)$
(b) $u = f(x - iy) + g(x + iy)$
(c) $u = f(x + iy) - g(x - iy)$
(d) $u = f(x - iy) - g(x - iy)$

**90.** Solution of $x^2\frac{\partial^2 z}{\partial x^2} + 2xy\frac{\partial^2 z}{\partial x \partial y} + y^2\frac{\partial^2 z}{\partial y^2} = 0$ is

(a) $z = f_1\left(\log\frac{y}{x}\right) + xf_2\left(\log\frac{y}{x}\right)$
(b) $z = f_1\left(\log\frac{x}{y}\right) + xf_2\left(\log\frac{y}{x}\right)$
(c) $z = f_1\left(\log\frac{x}{y}\right) \times f_2\left(\log\frac{y}{x}\right)$
(d) None of the above

**91.** A solution of $u_{xx} = 0$ is of the form

(a) $u = \int f(y)dy + \phi(x)$
(b) $u = \int f'(y)dy + f(y)dx$
(c) $u = \int f(y)dx$
(d) $u = \int f(x)dx + f(y)dy$

**92.** The solution of $xp + yq = z$ is

(a) $f(x^2, y^2) = 0$ (b) $f(xy, yz)$
(c) $f(x, y) = 0$ (d) $f\left(\frac{x}{y}, \frac{y}{z}\right) = 0$

**93.** The solution of $(y - z)p + (z - x)q = x - y$, is

(a) $f(x^2 + y^2 + z^2) = xyz$
(b) $f(x + y + z) = xyz$
(c) $f(x + y + z) = x^2 + y^2 + z^2$
(d) $f(x^2 + y^2 + z^2, xyz) = 0$

**94.** $4\frac{\partial^2 z}{\partial x^2} - 4\frac{\partial^2 z}{\partial x \partial y^2} + \frac{\partial^2 z}{\partial y^2} = 16\log(x + 2y)$ has the solution

(a) $z = f_1(2y + x) + xf_2(2y + x) + 2x^2\log(x + 2y)$
(b) $z = 2x^2\log(x + 2y)$
(c) $z = 2f_1(2y + x) + 2x^2\log(x + 2y)$
(d) None of the above

**95.** The solution of

$\frac{\partial^2 z}{\partial x^2} - 5\frac{\partial^2 z}{\partial x \partial y} + \frac{4\partial^2 z}{\partial y^2} = \sin(4x + y)$, is

(a) $z = \frac{1}{3}x\cos(4x + y)$
(b) $z = f_1(y + x) + f_2(y + 4x)$
(c) $z = f(y + x) - \frac{1}{3}x\cos(4x + y)$
(d) $z = f_1(y + x) + f_2(y + 4x) - \frac{1}{3}x\cos(4x + 3y)$

**96.** The solution of $p + q = z$ is

(a) $f(xy, y\log z) = 0$ (b) $f(x + y, y + \log z) = 0$
(c) $f(x - y, y - \log z) = 0$ (d) None of these

**97.** Particular integral of $(2D^2 - 3DD' + D'^2)z = e^{x+2y}$ is

(a) $\frac{1}{2}e^{x+2y}$ (b) $-\frac{x}{2}e^{x+2y}$
(c) $xe^{x+2y}$ (d) $x^2e^{x+2y}$

**98.** The solution of $\frac{\partial^3 z}{\partial x^3} = 0$, is

(a) $z = (1 + x + x^2)f(y)$
(b) $z = (1 + y + y^2)f(x)$
(c) $z = f_1(x) + yf_2(x) + y^2f_3(x)$
(d) $z = f_1(y) + xf_2(y) + x^2f_3(y)$

**99.** Particular integral of $(D^2 - D'^2)z = \cos(x + y)$ is

(a) $x\cos(x + y)$ (b) $\frac{x}{2}\cos(x + y)$
(c) $x\sin(x + y)$ (d) $\frac{x}{2}\sin(x + y)$

**100.** Solution of $(mz - ny)p + (nx - lz)q = ly - mx$, is

(a) $f(lx + my + nz, x^2 + y^2 + z^2) = 0$
(b) $f(lx - my - nz, x^2 + y^2 + z^2) = 0$
(c) $f(mz - nx + ny) = 0$
(d) None of the above

**101.** Surface whose tangent planes cut off an intercept of constant length $k$ from the axis of $z$ is

(a) $f\left(\frac{x}{y}, \frac{x - k}{y}\right) = 0$ (b) $f\left(\frac{y}{x}, \frac{z - k}{y}\right) = 0$
(c) $f\left(\frac{y}{x}, \frac{z - k}{x}\right) = 0$ (d) $f\left(\frac{x}{y}, \frac{z - k}{y}\right) = 0$

**102.** Solution of equation $(y^2 + z^2)p - xyq = -3x$, is

(a) $\phi(y/z, x^2 + y^2 + z^2) = 0$
(b) $\phi(y/z, x^2 - y^2 + z^2) = 0$
(c) $\phi(x/y, x^2 + y^2 + z^2) = 0$
(d) None of the above

**103.** The complete integral of $(y-x)(qy-px)=(p-q)^2$, is
(a) $x=a^2(y+x)+bxy+c$ (b) $z=b^2(y+x)+bxy-c$
(c) $z=c^2(x+y)-bxy+a$ (d) $z=a^2(x+y)+b^2xy+ca$

**104.** Solution of equation $2zx-px^2-2qxy+pq=0$, is
(a) $z=ay+b(x^2-a)$ (b) $z=by-a(x^2+a)$
(c) $z=cy+b(x-a)$ (d) $z=ay-b(x^2+a)$

**105.** Solution of equation $z=pq$, is
(a) $z=\sqrt{ax}+\frac{1}{\sqrt{a}}y-b$ (b) $z=\sqrt{ax}-\frac{y}{\sqrt{a}}+b$
(c) $z=\sqrt{ax}+\frac{y}{2\sqrt{a}}+b$ (d) $2\sqrt{z}=\sqrt{ax}+\frac{1}{\sqrt{a}}y+b$

**106.** The partial differential equation formed by eliminating arbitrary functions from the relation $z=f(x+at)+g(x-at)$ is
(a) $\frac{\partial^2 z}{\partial t^2}-a^2\frac{\partial^2 z}{\partial x^2}=0$ (b) $a^2\frac{\partial z}{\partial t}+\frac{\partial z}{\partial x}=0$
(c) $a\frac{\partial^2 z}{\partial t^2}+\frac{\partial^2 z}{\partial x^2}=0$ (d) None of these

**107.** Solution of $(D^2-D'^2+D-D')z=0$ is
(a) $z=f_1(y+x)+e^{-x}f_2(y-x)$
(b) $z=f_1(y-x)+e^{x}f_2(y+x)$
(c) $z=f_1(y-x)+e^{-x}f_2(y-x)$
(d) $z=f_1(x-y)+e^{-x}f_2(x-y)$

**108.** Solution of $s+p-q=z+xy$, is
(a) $z=e^xf_1(y)+xy-y+x+1$
(b) $z=e^{-x}f_2(y)+x-y+xy+1$
(c) $z=e^xf_1(y)+e^{-y}f_2(x)-xy-y+x+1$
(d) $z=e^xf_1(y)+e^{-x}f_2(y)$

**109.** A surface passing through the two lines $z=x=0, z-1=x-y=0$, satisfying $r-4s+4t=0$, is
(a) $z=\frac{2x}{3x+y}$ (b) $z=x\cdot\frac{3}{2x+y}$
(c) $z=\frac{x+y}{3x\ y}$ (d) $z=x\cdot\frac{2}{3x+2y}$

**110.** A surface satisfying $t=6x^3y$, containing the two lines, $y=0=z, y=1=z$ is
(a) $y=z^2y^2+x(1-y^2)$ (b) $z=x^2y^3+y(1-x^2)$
(c) $z=x^3y^2-y(1+x^2)$ (d) $z=x^2y^3+y(1-x^2)$

**111.** $\frac{\partial^3 z}{\partial x^3}-4\frac{\partial^3 z}{\partial x^2\partial y}+4\frac{\partial^3 z}{\partial x\partial y^2}=0$ has the solution
(a) $z=\phi(y)+f_1(y+2x)+f_2(y-2x)$
(b) $z=\phi(y)+2f_1(y+2x)$
(c) $z=\phi(y)+f_1(y+2x)+xf_2(y+2x)$
(d) None of the above

**112.** Elimination of a function $f$ from $z=f\left(\frac{y}{x}\right)$ gives a partial differential equation
(a) $x\frac{\partial z}{\partial x}+\frac{\partial z}{\partial y}=0$ (b) $\frac{\partial z}{\partial x}+\frac{\partial z}{\partial y}=0$
(c) $\frac{\partial z}{\partial x}+y\frac{\partial z}{\partial y}=0$ (d) $x\frac{\partial z}{\partial x}+y\frac{\partial z}{\partial y}=0$

**113.** $x\frac{\partial u}{\partial x}+y\frac{\partial u}{\partial y}+z\frac{\partial u}{\partial z}=0$, gives the general solution
(a) $f\left(\frac{x}{y},\frac{y}{z},xyz-3u\right)=0$ (b) $f\left(xyz-3u,\frac{y}{z}\right)=0$
(c) $f\left(xyz-3u,\frac{x}{y}\right)=0$ (d) $f(xyz-3u)=0$

**114.** The general integral of $\frac{\partial z}{\partial y}=3\left(\frac{\partial z}{\partial x}\right)^2$, is
(a) $z=ax+3ay+c$ (b) $z=ax+3a^2y+c$
(c) $z=ax^2+3ay+c$ (d) None of these

**115.** The partial differential equation $y^2z\frac{\partial z}{\partial x}+zx^2\frac{\partial z}{\partial y}=xy^2$, has the general solution
(a) $f(x^3+y^3,x^2+y^2)=0$ (b) $f(x^3-y^3,x^2-y^2)=0$
(c) $f(x^2+y,x-y)=0$ (d) None of these

**116.** The general integral of the partial differential equation $\frac{\partial z}{\partial x}+3\frac{\partial z}{\partial y}=5z+\tan(y-3x)$ is
(a) $y-3x=f(e^{-5x}\{5z+\tan(y-3x)\})=0$
(b) $y-3x=f(e^{-5x}\{5z+\tan x\})=0$
(c) $y-3x=f(\tan(y-3x))=5z$
(d) None of the above

**117.** One dimensional wave equation is
(a) $\frac{\partial^2 u}{\partial y^2}=\frac{1}{c^2}\cdot\frac{\partial^2 u}{\partial x^2}$ (b) $\frac{\partial^2 u}{\partial t^2}=\frac{1}{c^2}\cdot\frac{\partial^2 u}{\partial x^2}$
(c) $\frac{\partial^2 u}{\partial t^2}=c^2\cdot\frac{\partial^2 u}{\partial x^2}$ (d) $\frac{\partial^2 u}{\partial x^2}=\frac{1}{c^2}\cdot\frac{\partial^2 u}{\partial t^2}$

**118.** Two dimensional wave equation is
(a) $\frac{\partial^2 u}{\partial t^2}=c^2\left(\frac{\partial^2 u}{\partial x^2}+\frac{\partial^2 u}{\partial y^2}\right)$ (b) $\frac{\partial^2 u}{\partial x^2}=c^2\left(\frac{\partial^2 u}{\partial y^2}+\frac{\partial^2 u}{\partial z^2}\right)$
(c) $\frac{\partial^2 u}{\partial z^2}=c^2\left(\frac{\partial^2 u}{\partial x^2}+\frac{\partial^2 u}{\partial y^2}\right)$ (d) None of these

**119.** Heat equation is
(a) $\frac{\partial u}{\partial x}=c^2\nabla^2x^2$ (b) $\frac{\partial u}{\partial y}=\frac{1}{c^2}\nabla^2t^2$
(c) $\frac{\partial u}{\partial t}=c^2\nabla^2u$ (d) $\frac{\partial u}{\partial t}=c^2\nabla^2y^2$

**120.** Laplace's equation is
(a) $u_{xx}+u_{yy}-u_z=0$
(b) $u_{xx}+u_{yy}+u_z^2=0$
(c) $u_{xx}+u_{yy}-u_{zz}=0$
(d) $u_{xx}+u_{yy}+u_{zz}=0$

**121.** PDE of second order in canonical forms $Rr+Ss+Tt+f(x,y,z,p,q)=0$, then $S^2-4RT>0$ represent
(a) hyperbola (b) parabola
(c) ellipse (d) straight line

**122.** Complete integral for the PDE $z = px + qy - \sin pq$, is
(a) $z = ax + qy - \sin aq$
(b) $z = ax + by - \sin ab$
(c) $z = ax - by + \sin ab$
(d) $z = bx + ay + \sin ab$

**123.** The solution of $\partial^2 z/\partial x^2 = \partial^2 z/\partial y^2$, is
(a) $z = f_1(y + x) + f_2(y - x)$
(b) $z = f_1(y + x) + f_1(y - x)$
(c) $z = f(x^2 - y^2)$
(d) $z = f(x^2 + y^2)$

**124.** The general solution of $u_{xx} = xy$, is
(a) $u = \frac{1}{6}x^3y + xf(y) + \phi(y)$ (b) $u = \frac{1}{3}x^2y - xf(y) + \phi(y)$
(c) $u = \frac{1}{6}xy^3 + xf(y) + \phi(y)$ (d) $u = xy^3 - \frac{1}{3}xf(y) + \phi(y)$

**125.** The partial differential equation representing variable heat flow in three dimensions, is
(a) $\frac{\partial u}{\partial t} = c^2\left(\frac{\partial u}{\partial x} + \frac{\partial u}{\partial y} + \frac{\partial u}{\partial z}\right)$
(b) $\frac{\partial u}{\partial t} = c^2\left(\frac{\partial^2 u}{\partial x^2} + \frac{\partial^2 u}{\partial y^2} + \frac{\partial^2 u}{\partial z^2}\right)$
(c) $\frac{\partial^2 u}{\partial t^2} = c^2\left(\frac{\partial u}{\partial x} \times \frac{\partial u}{\partial y} \times \frac{\partial u}{\partial z}\right)$
(d) None of the above

**126.** The differential equation $f_{xx} + 2f_{xy} + 4f_{yy} = 0$, is classified as
(a) elliptic (b) hyperbolic
(c) parabolic (d) None of these

**127.** Classify the equation
$$\frac{\partial^2 u}{\partial t^2} - 4\frac{\partial^2 u}{\partial x \partial t} + 4\frac{\partial^2 u}{\partial x^2}$$
(a) elliptic (b) hyperbolic
(c) parabolic (d) None of these

**128.** Classify the equation
$$\frac{\partial^2 u}{\partial x^2} + \frac{\partial^2 u}{\partial y^2} + \frac{\partial^2 u}{\partial z^2} = 0$$
(a) elliptic (b) hyperbolic
(c) parabolic (d) None of these

**129.** Classify the wave equation
$$\frac{\partial^2 u}{\partial x^2} + \frac{\partial^2 u}{\partial y^2} + \frac{\partial^2 u}{\partial z^2} + = \frac{1}{c^2} \cdot \frac{\partial^2 u}{\partial t^2}$$
(a) elliptic (b) hyperbolic
(c) parabolic (d) None of these

**130.** Classify the heat equation
$$\frac{\partial^2 u}{\partial x^2} + \frac{\partial^2 u}{\partial y^2} + \frac{\partial^2 u}{\partial z^2} = \frac{1}{c^2} \cdot \frac{\partial u}{\partial t}$$
(a) elliptic (b) hyperbolic
(c) parabolic (d) None of these

**131.** The partial differential equation of the transverse vibrations of a string is
(a) $\frac{\partial^2 y}{\partial t^2} = c^2\frac{\partial^2 y}{\partial x^2}$ (b) $\frac{\partial^2 y}{\partial t^2} = c\frac{\partial y}{\partial x}$
(c) $\frac{\partial^2 y}{\partial x^2} = \frac{1}{c^4} \cdot \frac{\partial^2 y}{\partial t^2}$ (d) None of these

**132.** The equation $u_t = c^2 u_{xx}$ is classified as
(a) elliptic (b) hyperbolic
(c) parabolic (d) None of these

**133.** In two dimensional heat flow, the temperature along the normal to the *xy*-plane is
(a) zero (b) infinity
(c) finite (d) $100K$

**134.** Solution of $\frac{\partial u}{\partial x} = 4\frac{\partial u}{\partial y}$, given $u(0, y) = 8e^{-3y}$, is
(a) $u = e^{-12x+3y}$ (b) $u = 8e^{-12x-3y}$
(c) $u = 8e^{12x-3y}$ (d) $u = -8e^{-12x+3y}$

**135.** Solution of $\frac{\partial z}{\partial x} + 4z = \frac{\partial z}{\partial t}$, given $z(x, 0) = 4e^{-3x}$ is
(a) $z = 4e^{3x+t}$ (b) $z = 3e^{4x+t}$
(c) $z = e^{3x+t}$ (d) $z = 4e^{-3x+t}$

**136.** Solution of $\frac{\partial^2 u}{\partial t^2} = c^2\frac{\partial^2 u}{\partial x^2}$, where $u(0,t) = 0, u(1,t) = 0$ and $u(x,0) = A\sin\pi x, \left(\frac{\partial u}{\partial t}\right)_{t=0} = 0$, is
(a) $u(x,t) = A\sin 2\pi ct \cos \pi x$
(b) $u(x,t) = A\cos c\pi t \sin \pi x$
(c) $u(x,t) = A\sin 2\pi ct \sin \pi x$
(d) None of the above

**137.** Solution of one dimensional wave equation is
(a) $u_n(x, t) = \left(C_n \cos\frac{n\pi ct}{l} + D_n \sin\frac{n\pi ct}{l}\right)\sin\frac{n\pi x}{l}$
(b) $u_n(x, t) = \left(C_n \cos^2\frac{n\pi ct}{l} + D_n \sin^2\frac{n\pi ct}{l}\right)\cos\frac{n\pi x}{l}$
(c) $u_n(x, t) = \left(C_n \cos\frac{n\pi ct}{l} - D_n \sin\frac{n\pi ct}{l}\right)\sin\frac{n\pi x}{l}$
(d) None of the above

**138.** Value of constant $C_n$ in solution of one dimensional wave equation is
(a) $C_n = \frac{1}{l}\int_0^l f(x)\sin\frac{n\pi x}{l}\,dx$
(b) $C_n = \frac{2}{l}\int_0^l f(x)\sin\frac{n\pi x}{l}\,dx$
(c) $C_n = \frac{1}{l}\int_0^l f'(x)\cos\frac{n\pi x}{l}\,dx$
(d) None of the above

**139.** $\lambda_n = \frac{cn\pi}{l}$ in solution of one dimensional wave equation is
(a) eigen functions (b) eigen values
(c) set of spectrum (d) fourier functions

**140.** d'Alembert's solution of the wave equation is
(a) $u(x, t) = \phi(x+ct) - \psi(x-ct)$
(b) $u(x, t) = \phi(x+ct) + \psi(x-ct)$
(c) $u(x, t) = \phi'(x+ct) - \psi'(x-ct)$
(d) $u(x, t) = \phi(x-ct) + \psi(x+ct)$

**141.** Elimination of $a$ and $b$ from $z = ae^{bt}\sin bx$ gives the partial differential equation
(a) $\frac{\partial^2 z}{\partial x^2} - \frac{\partial^2 z}{\partial t^2} = 0$ (b) $\frac{\partial z}{\partial x} - \frac{\partial z}{\partial t} = 0$
(c) $\frac{\partial z}{\partial x} + z = 0$ (d) None of these

**142.** Solution of $p^2 + px + py + xy = 0$, $\left(p = \frac{\partial y}{\partial x}\right)$ is
(a) $(2y + x^2 + c_1)(x + \log y) = 0$
(b) $(2y + x^2 - c_1)(x + \log y - c_2) = 0$
(c) $(2y + x^2 + c_1) = 0$
(d) None of the above

**143.** The solution of the given partial differential equation $\frac{\partial^4 z}{\partial x^4} - 2\frac{\partial^4 z}{\partial x^3 \partial y} + 2\frac{\partial^4 z}{\partial x \partial y^3} - \frac{\partial^4 z}{\partial y^4} = 0$
(a) $z = f_1(y-x) + f_2(y+x) + xf_3(y+x) + x^2 f_4(y+x)$
(b) $z = f(x)$
(c) $z = f_2(z)$
(d) None of the above

**144.** $\frac{\partial^2 z}{\partial x^2} + \frac{\partial^2 z}{\partial y^2} = 12(x+y)$ has the solution
(a) $z = f_1(y+ix) + f_2(y-ix)$
(b) $z = f_1(y+ix) + f_2(y-ix) + (x+y)^3$
(c) $z = (x+y)^3$
(d) None of the above

**145.** The solution of the given partial differential equation $\frac{\partial^2 z}{\partial x^2} - a^2\frac{\partial^2 z}{\partial y^2} = 0$, is
(a) $z = f_1(y+ax) + f_2(y-ax)$
(b) $z = 2f_1(y+ax)$
(c) $z = f_1(y+ax) + f_2(y)$
(d) None of the above

**146.** The solution of the given partial differential equation $\frac{\partial^4 z}{\partial x^4} - \frac{\partial^4 z}{\partial y^4} = 0$, is
(a) $f_1(y+x) + f_2(y-x) + f_3(y+ix) + f_4(y-ix)$
(b) $f_1(y+x) + f_2(y-x)$
(c) $f_1(y+ix) + f_2(y-ix)$
(d) None of the above

**147.** The solution of the following partial differential equations $2\frac{\partial^2 z}{\partial x^2} + 5\frac{\partial^2 z}{\partial x \partial y} + 2\frac{\partial^2 z}{\partial y^2} = 0$, is
(a) $z = \phi(2y-x)$
(b) $z = \psi(y-2x)$
(c) $z = \phi(2y-x) + \psi(y-2x)$
(d) $z = \phi(y-x) + \psi(y+x)$

**148.** The relation $2z = \frac{x^2}{a^2} + \frac{y^2}{b^2}$ represents the partial differential equation
(a) $z = p + q$ (b) $z = p - q$
(c) $2z = xp + yq$ (d) $2z = xp/yq$

**149.** The partial differential equation formed by eliminating arbitrary functions from the equation $z = f(x^2 - y^2)$, is
(a) $xp + yq = 0$ (b) $xq + yp = 0$
(c) $\frac{x}{y} = p$ (d) $\frac{x}{y} = q$

**150.** The solution of $\frac{\partial^2 z}{\partial x^2} + \frac{\partial^2 z}{\partial y^2} = \frac{z}{a}$, is
(a) $z = e^{y/a} f(x-y)$ (b) $z = e^{y/a} f(x)$
(c) $z = e^y f(y)$ (d) $z = e^a f(x+y)$

**151.** The general integral of $yzp + zxq = xy$, is
(a) $f(x+y, y+z) = 0$ (b) $f(x^2 - y^2, x^2 - z^2) = 0$
(c) $f(x^2 + y^2, x^2 + z^2) = 0$ (d) None of these

**152.** $y = px - 2p^2$ find its singular solution
(a) $8y = x^2$ (b) $x^2 - 4y = 0$
(c) $x^2 = 2y$ (d) $x^2 = y$

**153.** If $e^{ax}u(x)$ is a PI of $\frac{d^2y}{dx^2} - 2a\frac{dy}{dx} + a^2 y = f(x)$ where $a$ is a constant, then $\frac{d^2u}{dx^2}$ is equal to
(a) $f(x)$ (b) $f(x)e^{ax}$
(c) $f(x)e^{-ax}$ (d) $f(x)(e^{ax} + e^{-ax})$

**154.** The solution of the differential equation $x^2\frac{d^2y}{dx^2} - 4x\frac{dy}{dx} + 6y = x$ is
(a) $y = c_1 x + c_2 x^2 + \frac{x}{2}$ (b) $y = c_1 x + c_2 x^3 + \frac{x^2}{2}$
(c) $y = c_1 x^2 + c_2 x^3 + \frac{x}{2}$ (d) $y = c_1 x^2 + c_2 x^3 + \frac{x^2}{2}$

**155.** The interval for $x$, over which the solution of IVP exists IVP $dy(2 + x^2 + y^2) - dx(1 + 2x + 3y) = 0$, $y(0) = 0$, $R: |x| \le 2, |y| \le 1$
(a) $-2 \le x \le 2$ (b) $-1 \le x \le 1$
(c) $-\frac{1}{4} \le x \le \frac{1}{4}$ (d) $-\frac{1}{2} \le x \le \frac{1}{2}$

**156.** An integrating factor for $(\cos y \sin 2x)dx + (\cos^2 y - \cos^2 x)dy = 0$ is
(a) $\sec^2 y + \sec y \tan y$ (b) $\tan^2 y + \sec y \tan y$
(c) $1/(\sec^2 y + \sec y \tan y)$ (d) $1/(\tan^2 y + \sec y \tan y)$

**157.** $(a_1 x + b_1 y + c_1)dx + (a_2 x + b_2 y + c_2)dy = 0$, where $a_1 b_1 - a_2 b_2 = 0$ is
I. homogeneous first order, first degree differentiation equation.

II. non-homogeneouse first order, first degree differential equation

III. homogeneous and reduced by $a_1x + b_1y = t$

IV. non-homogeneous and reduced by $a_1x + b_1y = t$

(a) I is true only (b) I and III are true

(c) II and IV are true (d) None of these

**158.** The solution of the differential equation, $\frac{d^2y}{dx^2} - 3\frac{dy}{dx} + 2y = e^x, y = 3$ and $\frac{dy}{dx} = 3$, when $x = 0$ is

(a) $y = 2e^x + e^{-2x} - xe^{-x}$ (b) $y = 2e^x + e^{2x} - xe^x$

(c) $y = e^x + 2e^{2x} - x^2e^x$ (d) $y = e^x - e^{2x} + xe^x$

**159.** Integrating factor of the DE $(y^2 + 2x^2y)dx + (2x^3 - xy)dy = 0$ is

(a) $x^{1/2}y^{-5/2}$ (b) $\frac{x^{3/2}}{y^{5/2}}$

(c) $x^{-5/2}y^{-1/2}$ (d) $x^{-5/2}y^{-5/2}$

**160.** The coordinate at a moving point $P$ satisfying the equtions $\frac{dx}{dt} = \tan x : \frac{dy}{dt} = -\sin^2 x : t \geq 0$ of the curve passes through the point $(\pi/2, 0)$. When $t = 0$, then the equation of the curve in rectangles coordinates is

(a) $y = \frac{1}{2}\cos^2 x$ (b) $y = \sin 2x$

(c) $y = \cos 2x + 1$ (d) $y = \sin^2 x - 1$

**161.** If $2x(1 - y) = K$ and $g(x, y) = L$ are orthogonal families of curves where $K$ and $L$ constants, then $g(x, y)$ is

(a) $x^2 + 2y - y^2$ (b) $2\{y + 2(y + (1 - x))\}$

(c) $x^2 + 2x - y^2$ (d) $x^2 - 2y + y^2$

**162.** Consider a general first order linear non-homogeneous ordinary differential equation with $y = \varphi(x)$ as its solution. Let $\Psi(x)$ be the solution of the associated homogeneous equation and $C$ an arbitrary constant. Then, the general equation has the following solution.

(a) $y = C\varphi(x)$ (b) $y = C\varphi(x) + \psi(x)$

(c) $y = C\psi(x) + \varphi(x)$ (d) $y = C\psi(x)$

**163.** Order and degree of the differential equation $e^{y'''} - xy'' + y = 0$ are respectively

(a) 3, 1

(b) 3, not defined

(c) not defined, 1

(d) both order and degree are not defined

**164.** Let $y$ be a function of $x$ satisfying $\frac{dy}{dx} = 2x^3\sqrt{y} - 4xy$ of $y(0) = 0$, then $y(1)$ is

(a) $\frac{1}{4e^2}$ (b) $\frac{1}{e}$

(c) $e^{1/2}$ (d) $e^{3/2}$

**165.** Solution of the differential equation $(a^2 - 2xy - y^2)dx = (x + y)^2 dy$ is

(a) $3a^2x - 3x^2y - 3xy^2 - y^3 = C$

(b) $a^2x^2 - 3y^2xz - 3xy - y^3 = C$

(c) $3a^2x - 3xy - 3x^2y^2 - y^3 = C$

(d) None of the above

**166.** The solution of the differential equation $\frac{d^2y}{dx^2} - y = 1$, which vanishes when $x = 0$ and tends to a finite limit as $x \to -\infty$ is

(a) $y = e^{-x} + 1$ (b) $2y = e^{-x} + 1$

(c) $y = e^x - 1$ (d) $y = e^{-x} - 1$

**167.** The ordinary differential equation $x\frac{dy}{dx} - y = 2x^2$ with initial conditions $y(0) = 0$, has

(a) no solution (b) a unique solution

(c) two distinct solution (d) an infinity of solutions

**168.** The singular solution of $\sqrt{x}dy + \sqrt{y}dx = 0$ is

(a) only $x = 0$ (b) only $y = 0$

(c) both $x = 0$ and $y = 0$ (d) None of these

**169.** The solution of $\frac{dy}{dx} = y^2, y(0) = 1$, exists for all

(a) $x \in (-\infty, 1)$ (b) $x \in [0, a]$ where $a > 1$

(c) $x \in (-\infty, \infty)$ (d) $x \in [1, a]$ where $a > 1$

**170.** A particular solution of

$$x^2\frac{d^2y}{dx^2} + 2x\frac{dy}{dx} + \frac{y}{4} = \frac{1}{\sqrt{x}} \text{ is}$$

(a) $\frac{1}{2\sqrt{x}}$ (b) $\frac{\log x}{2\sqrt{x}}$

(c) $\frac{(\log x)^2}{2\sqrt{x}}$ (d) $\frac{(\log x)\sqrt{x}}{2}$

**171.** Particular Integral of the following differential equation $(D^2 - 4D + 4)y = \frac{e^{2x}\log x}{x}$ is obtain by integrating

(a) $\frac{x\log x}{2}$ (b) $\frac{x(\log x)^2}{2}$

(c) $\frac{(\log x)^2}{2}$ (d) $\left(\frac{x\log x}{2}\right)^2$

**172.** If $y_1$ and $y_2$ are linearly independent solutions of the homogeneous equation $L(y) = y'' + p_1(x)y' + p_2(x)y = 0$. Then, $p_1(x)$ and $p_2(x)$ are given by

(a) $p_1(x) = \frac{y_1y_2'' - y_1''y_2}{w(x)}$ $p_2(x) = \frac{y_1'y_2'' - y_1'y_2'}{w(x)}$

(b) $p_1(x) = \left[\frac{y_1y_2'' - y''_1y_2}{w(x)}\right]$ $p_2(x) = \frac{y_1''y_2' - y_1''y_2'}{w(x)}$

(c) $p_1(x) = \frac{y_1y_2' - y_1'y_2}{w(x)}$ $p_2(x) = \left[\frac{y_1'y_2' - y_1''y_2}{w(x)}\right]$

(d) $p_1(x) = -\left[\frac{y_1y_2' - y_1'y_2}{w(x)}\right]$ $p_2(x) = -\left[\frac{y_1'y_2' - y_1'y_2''}{w(x)}\right]$

**173.** An integrating factor for $y\,dx - x\,dy = 0$

(a) $\frac{x}{y}$ (b) $\frac{y}{x}$

(c) $\frac{1}{x^2+y^2}$ (d) $\frac{1}{x^2+y}$

**174.** Solve $\frac{dy}{dt} = \sqrt{|y|}$, for $0 < y < 10$ and $y(0) = 0$

(a) has unique solution
(b) has no solution
(c) has two independent solution
(d) has infinite solution

**175.** The solution of the differential equation $\frac{d^3y}{dx^3} - 2\frac{d^2y}{dx^2} - 5\frac{dy}{dx} + 6y = e^{3x}$ is

(a) $y = Ae^x + Be^{3x} + Ce^{-2x} + \frac{e^{3x}}{10}$
(b) $y = Ae^x + Be^{-3x} + Ce^{-2x} + \frac{e^{3x}}{10}$
(c) $y = Ae^x + Be^{3x} + Ce^{-2x} + \frac{xe^{3x}}{10}$
(d) $y = Ae^x + Be^{-3x} + Ce^{-2x} - \frac{xe^{3x}}{10}$

**176.** The general solution of the system of differential equations $\frac{dX}{dt} = MX + b$, where $X = \begin{bmatrix} x_1(t) \\ x_2(t) \end{bmatrix}$ M. a. $2\times2$ matrix $\begin{bmatrix} 0 & 1 \\ 1 & 0 \end{bmatrix}$ and a $2\times2$ constant vector $\begin{bmatrix} 1 \\ 1 \end{bmatrix}$ is given by

(a) $e^{Mt}c + b$ (b) $e^{mt}c + bt$
(c) $e^{Mt}c - b$ (d) $e^{Mt}c - bt$

(where c is any $2\times1$ constant vector)

**177.** The initial value problem $x\frac{dy}{dx} = y$, $y(0) = 0$, $x \geq 0$ has

(a) no solution
(b) a unique solution
(c) exactly two solution
(d) uncountable many solution

**178.** Consider the following statement for IVP $\frac{dy}{dx} = x^2 + y$, $y(0) = 1$, $D: |x| \leq 1 |y-1| \leq 1$

I. It has a solution whcih exists for all $n$.

II. The local interval for which the solution exists uniquely is $|x| \leq \frac{1}{3}$.

III. It has no solution in the interval $|x| \leq 3$.

Then select the correct code

(a) Only II is true (b) II and III are true
(c) I and II are true (d) All are true

**179.** If $y_1(x) = x$ and $y_2(x) = xe^x$ are two linearly independent solutions of

$$x^2\frac{d^2y}{dx^2} - x(x+2)\frac{dy}{dx} + (x+2)y = 0,$$

ther the interval on which they form a fundamental set of solutions is

(a) $x > 0$ or $x < 0$ (b) $-1 < x < \infty$
(c) $-1 < x < 2$ (d) $-\infty < x < \infty$

**180.** Consider the following differential equations

I. $x^2(y'')^6 + y^{-2/3}\{1 + (y''')^2\}^{1/2} + \frac{d^2}{dx^2}\{(y'')^{-2/3}\} = 0$

II. $y' - 6x = \{ay + bxy'\}^{-3/2}$, $b \neq 0$

Sum of order of 1st differential equation and degree of second differential equation is,

(a) 6 (b) 7
(c) 8 (d) 9

**181.** The solution of the differential equation $y\frac{dy}{dx} + (1+y^2)\sin x = 0$, $y(0) = 0$ exists in the open interval $(-a, a)$ then '$a$' equals to

(a) $2\cos^{-1}\left(\frac{1}{2}\sqrt{\ln 2}\right)$ (b) $2\tan^{-1}\left(\frac{1}{2}\sqrt{\ln 2}\right)$

(c) $2\sin^{-1}\left(\frac{1}{2}\sqrt{\ln 2}\right)$ (d) $2\cot^{-1}\left(\frac{1}{2}\sqrt{\ln 2}\right)$

**182.** Using the method of variation of paramiters for the particular solution to the differential equation

$$y'' + 4y = \frac{3}{\sin 2x}, \quad 0 < x < \pi/2$$

(a) $\frac{3}{4}\sin 2x \log\cos 2x - \frac{3}{4}\cos 2x$
(b) $\frac{3}{2}\sin 2x \log\cos 2x - \frac{3}{4}\cos 2x$
(c) $\frac{3}{2}\sin 2x \log\sin 2x - \frac{3}{2}x\cos 2x$
(d) $\frac{3}{4}\sin 2x \log\sin 2x - \frac{3}{2}x\cos 2x$

**183.** The solution of the differential equation $(x^3y^3 + xy)\frac{dy}{dx} = 1$ is

(a) $\frac{1}{x} = 2 - y^2 + Ae^{y^2/2}$ (b) $x = 2 - y^2 + Ae^{y^2/2}$

(c) $\frac{1}{x} = 2 - y^2 + Ae^{-y^2/2}$ (d) $x = 2 + y^2 + Ae^{-y^2/2}$

**184.** The solution of $\frac{dy}{dx} = \frac{(1-x)}{y}$ represents

(a) a family of circle centre at (1, 0)
(b) a family of circle centre at (0, 0)
(c) a family of circle centre at (–1, 0)
(d) a family of straight line with slope –1

**185.** For the initial value problem

$$y' = f(x, y) \text{ with } y(0) = 0,$$

which of the following statements is true?

(a) $f(x, y) = \sqrt{xy}$ satisfies Lipschitz's condition and IVP has unique solution.

(b) $f(x, y) = \sqrt{xy}$ does not satisfy Lipschitz's condition and IVP has no solution

(c) $f(x, y) = |y|$ satisfies Lipschitz condition and IVP has unique solution

(d) $f(x, y) = |y|$ does not satisfy Lipschitz condition.

**186.** The solution of the differential equation

$$x\left\{y\frac{d^2y}{dx^2} + \left(\frac{dy}{dx}\right)^2\right\} + y\frac{dy}{dx} = 0 \text{ is}$$

(a) $ax + by = C$ (b) $ax^2 + by = 0$

(c) $ax^2 + by^2 = 1$ (d) $ax + by^2 = 0$

**187.** For the ordinary differential equation

$$(x-1)\frac{d^2y}{dx^2} + (\cot \pi x)\frac{dy}{dx} + (\text{cosec}^2 \pi x)y = 0$$

which of the following statement is true?

(a) 0 is regular and 1 is irregular.

(b) 0 is irregular and 1 is regular.

(c) Both 0 and 1 are regular.

(d) Both 0 and 1 are irregular.

**188.** Complete integral for the partial differential equation $z = px + qy - \sin(pq)$ is

(a) $z = ax + by + \sin ab$ (b) $z = ax + by - \sin ab$

(c) $z = ax + y + \sin b$ (d) $z = x + by - \sin a$

**189.** The solution of the differential equation

$$y = px + \sqrt{4 + p^2} \text{ is}$$

(a) $(y - Cx)^2 - C^2 = 4$ (b) $(y - Cx)^2 - 4C^2 = 0$

(c) $(y - Cx)^2 + C^2 = 0$ (d) $(y - Cx)^2 + 4C^2 = 0$

**190.** The differential equation whose linearly independent solutions are $\cos 2x$, $\sin 2x$ and $e^{-x}$ is

(a) $(D^3 + D^2 + 4D)y = 0$

(b) $(D^3 - D^2 + 4D - 4)y = 0$

(c) $(D^3 + D^2 - 4D - 4)y = 0$

(d) $(D^3 - D^2 - 4D + 4)y = 0$

**191.** Let $y(x)$ be a non-trivial solution of the 2nd order linear differential equation

$$\frac{d^2y}{dx^2} + 2C\frac{dy}{dx} + Ky = 0$$

where $C < 0$; $K > 0$ and $C^2 > K$, then

(a) $|y(x)| \to \infty$ as $x \to \infty$

(b) $|y(x)| \to 0$ as $x \to \infty$

(c) $\lim_{x \to \pm\infty} |y(x)|$ exists and is finite

(d) None of the above

**192.** The orthogonal trajectory of the family $x^2 - y^2 = C_2$ are given by

(a) $x^2 + y^2 = C_2$ (b) $xy = C_2$

(c) $y = C_2$ (d) $x = 0$

**193.** The solution of the differential equation

$$\frac{dy}{dx} = \frac{x + y + 1}{x + y - 1} \text{ for } y\left(\frac{2}{3}\right) = \frac{1}{3} \text{ is}$$

(a) $y = x + \log(x + y) - \frac{1}{3}$

(b) $y = x - \log(x + y) + \frac{2}{3}$

(c) $y = x - \log(x + y) + \frac{2}{3}$

(d) $2y = x - \log(x + y) + 1$

**194.** $\left(D^2 - \frac{3}{x}D + \frac{3}{x^2}\right)y = (x - 1)e^x$ one solution of this differential equation is

(a) $x$ (b) $xe^x$

(c) $e^x$ (d) $e^x + x$

**195.** Let $y_1(x)$ and $y_2(x)$ be two solutions of $(1 - x)^2\frac{d^2y}{dx^2} - 2x\frac{dy}{dx} + (\sec x)y = 0$ with Wronskian $W(x)$. If $y_1(0) = 1$, $\left(\frac{dy_1}{dx}\right)_{x=0} = 0$ and $W\left(\frac{1}{2}\right) = \frac{1}{3}$, then $\left(\frac{dy_2}{dx}\right)_{x=0}$ equals

(a) 1/4 (b) 1 (c) 3/4 (d) 4/3

**196.** The degree of differential equation satisfying the relation

$$\sqrt{1 + x^2} + \sqrt{1 + y^3} = \lambda(x\sqrt{1 + y^2} - y\sqrt{1 + x^2}) \text{ is}$$

(a) 1 (b) 2

(c) 3 (d) None of these

**197.** Which of the follmowing is/are integrating factor of the differential equation $xdx + ydy = 0$

(a) $\frac{1}{x^2 + y^2}$ (b) $\frac{1}{(x^2 + y^2)^2}$

(c) $\frac{1}{(x^2 + y^2)^n}$ (d) All of these

**198.** The general solution $\frac{d^4y}{dx^4} + y = 0$ is

(a) $y = \exp\left(\frac{x}{\sqrt{2}}\right)\left[C_1 \cos\frac{x}{\sqrt{2}} + C_2\frac{x}{\sqrt{2}}\right] + \exp\left(\frac{-x}{\sqrt{2}}\right)\left[C_3 \cos\frac{x}{\sqrt{2}} + C_4 \sin\frac{x}{\sqrt{2}}\right]$

(b) $y = C_1 \sin x + C_2 \cos x + C_3 \sinh x + C_4 \cosh x$

(c) $y = C_1 e^x + C_2 e^{-x} + C_3 e^{-2x} + C_4 e^{2x}$

(d) $y = C_1 \sin 2x + C_2 \cos 2x + C_3 \sinh 2x + C_4 \cosh x$

**199.** $\frac{dy}{dx} = 1 + y^2$, $y(0) = 0$ in the domain $R : |x| < 5$, $|y| < 3$ the equation has

(a) no solution

(b) unique solution for $|x| < 0.3$

(c) has infinite number of solution

(d) nothing about solution can be concluded

**200.** Solve $(D+1)x+(D-1)y=e^t$, $(D^2+D+1)x+(D^2-D+1)y=t^2$ where $D=\frac{d}{dt}$

(a) $y=\frac{1}{3}(3t+t^2-2e^t)$ (b) $y=\frac{1}{4}(2t+t^3-3e^t)$
(c) $y=\frac{1}{2}(2t+t^2-2e^t)$ (d) $y=\frac{1}{2}(2t+t^2-3e^t)$

**201.** The solution of the differential equation $x\,dy-y\,dx=\sqrt{x^2+y^2}\,dx$ is

(a) $y+\sqrt{x^2+y^2}=xc$ (b) $y+\sqrt{x^2+y^2}=x^2c$
(c) $y-\sqrt{x^2+y^2}=xc^2$ (d) $y-\sqrt{x^2+y^2}=cx^3$

**202.** Consider the following statements

I. A singular solution of differential equation satisfies the differential equation but is not a particular solution of the equation.
II. If $T(x, y)=0$ is the equation of the tac-locus, then $T(x, y)$ is a factor of the $P$-discriminant.
III. $T(x, y)$ is a factor of a $c$-discriminant.
IV. Cusp-locus has two distinct tangent.

Choose the correct answer.

(a) Only I is true (b) I, II and IV are true
(c) All are true (d) No one is true

**203.** Let $a, b\in R$. Let $y=(y_1, y_2)^T$ be a solution of the system of equations

$y_1'=y_2', y_2=ay_1+by_2$

Every solution $y(x)\to 0$ as $x\to\infty$ if

(a) $a<0, b<0$ (b) $a<0, b>0$
(c) $a>0, b>0$ (d) $a>0, b<0$

**204.** Let $n$ be a non-negative integer. The eigen values of the Sturm-Lioville problem $\frac{d^2y}{dx^2}+\lambda y=0$ with boundary condtion $y(0)=y(2\pi)$, $\frac{dy}{dx}(0)=\frac{dy}{dx}(2\pi)$ are

(a) $n$ (b) $n^2\pi^2$
(c) $n\pi$ (d) $n^2$

**205.** The singular solution of the differential equation $p^3+px-y=0$ is

(a) $4x^3+27y^2=0$ (b) $27x^3+4y^2=0$
(c) $4x^2+27y^2=0$ (d) $4x^3+27y^3=0$

**206.** Order and degree of the differential equation $\frac{d^2\rho}{d\theta^2}=\left(\rho+\left(\frac{d\rho}{d\theta}\right)^2\right)^{1/4}$ are respectively

(a) 2, 1 (b) 1, 1
(c) 2, 2 (d) 2, 4

**207.** Differential equation $|y'|+|y|=0$ has

(a) GS solution exists
(b) GS solution exists but no arbitrary constant
(c) it has particular solution which is bounded
(d) None of the above

**208.** For the sturm-Liouville problem $(1+x^2)y''+2xy'+\lambda x^2y=0$ with $y'(1)=0$ and $y'(10)=0$ the eigen values, $\lambda$ satisfy

(a) $\lambda\geq 0$ (b) $\lambda<0$ (c) $\lambda\neq 0$ (d) $\lambda\leq 0$

**209.** The solution of the differential equation $(2ax+by)y\,dx+(ax+2by)x\,dy=0$ is

(a) $axy^2+bxy=c$ (b) $ax^2y^2+bxy=c$
(c) $ayx^2+bxy^2=c$ (d) $axy+by^2=c$

**210.** For IVP

$y'=2y^{1/2}, y(0)=0$

Which one is correct in a nbd of $\theta$?

(a) It has unique solution
(b) It has no solution
(c) Solution exist but not uniquely
(d) None of the above

**211.** Let $y_1$ and $y_2$ be two linearly independent solutions of

$y''+(\sin x)y=0, 0\leq x\leq 1$

Let $g(x)=W(y_1, y_2)(x)$ be the Wronskian of $y_1$ and $y_2$. Then,

(a) $g'>0$ on $[0, 1]$
(b) $g'<0$ on $[0, 1]$
(c) $g'$ vanishes at only one point of $[0, 1]$
(d) $g'$ vanishes at all points of $[0, 1]$

**212.** Particular solution of differential equation $r+s-6t=y\cos x$ is

(a) $y\sin x+\cos x$ (b) $\sin x+y\cos x$
(c) $y\sin x-\cos x$ (d) $\sin x-y\cos x$

**213.** The singular solution of the diffential equation $(xp-y^2)=p^2-1$ is

(a) $x^2+y^2=1$ (b) $y^2-x^2=1$
(c) $x^2+2y^2=1$ (d) $x^2-y^2=1$

**214.** Let $y_1$ and $y_2$ be solution of Bessel's equation $t^2y''+ty'+(t^2-n^2)y=0$ on the interval $0<t<\infty$ with $y_1(1)=1$, $y_1'(1)=0$, $y_2(1)=0$ and $y_2'(1)=1$, then value of $W[y_1, y_2](t)$ is

(a) $1/t^2$ (b) $1/t$ (c) $\frac{(\log t)^2}{t}$ (d) 0

**215.** A particular integral of $y''-(a+b)y'+aby=Q(x)$ is,

(a) $e^{ax}\int\{e^{(a-b)x}(\int Qe^{bx}dx)\}dx$
(b) $e^{ax}\int\{e^{(b-a)x}(\int Qe^{-bx}dx)\}dx$
(c) $e^{-ax}\int\{e^{(a-b)x}\int Qe^{bx}dx\}dx$
(d) $e^{ax}\int e^{(a-b)x}x\{\int Qe^{bx}dx\}dx$

**216.** All real solutions of the differential equation $y''+2ay'+by=\cos x$ (where $a$ and $b$ are real constants) are periodic if

(a) $a=1$ and $b=0$ (b) $a=0$ and $b=1$
(c) $a=1$ and $b\neq 0$ (d) $a=0$ and $b\neq 1$

**217.** If $e^{-x}$, $xe^{-x}$ are solution of $y''+ay'+by=0$, then

(a) $a=0, b=1$ (b) $a=1, b=2$
(c) $a=2, b=1$ (d) $a=-1, b=0$

**218.** Let $y_1(x)$ and $y_2(x)$ be two linearly independent solution of the differential equation $x\frac{d^2y}{dx^2} - 2x^2\frac{dy}{dx} + e^x y = 0$ satisfying $y_1(0) = 1$, $y_2(0) = -1$, $y_1'(0) = 1$ and $y_2'(0) = 1$. Then, the Wronskian of $y_1(x)$ and $y_2(x)$ at $x = 2$ *i.e.*, $W(y_1, y_2)|_{x=2}$ is equal to

(a) $2e^{-1}$ (b) $2e^2$ (c) $2e^4$ (d) $2e^{-4}$

**219.** The general solution $\frac{dy}{dx} + y = f(x)$,

where $f(x) = \begin{cases} x, & 0 \le x \le 1 \\ 0, & x \ge 1 \end{cases}$ and $y(0) = 0$ is

(a) $y = \begin{cases} 2(1 - e^{-x}), & 0 \le x \le 1 \\ 2e^{-x}(e - 1), & x \ge 1 \end{cases}$

(b) $y = \begin{cases} 2(e^{-x} - 1), & 0 \le x \le 1 \\ 2e^{-x}(e - 1), & x \ge 1 \end{cases}$

(c) $y = \begin{cases} 2(1 - e^{-x}), & 0 \le x \le 1 \\ 2e^{-x}(1 - e), & x \ge 1 \end{cases}$

(d) None of the above

**220.** Suppose $y_p(x) = x\cos(2x)$ is a particular solution of $y'' + \alpha y = -4\sin(2x)$

Then, the constant *a* equals

(a) $-4$ (b) $-2$ (c) 2 (d) 4

**221.** The solution of $(x + 1)\frac{dy}{dx} = 1 - e^{-y}$ is

(a) $(x + 1)e^y = x + C$ (b) $(x + 1)(1 + e^y) = C$

(c) $\frac{x + 1}{(1 + e^y)} = C$ (d) $\frac{x + 1}{(1 - e^y)} = C$

**222.** The initial value problem $(x^2 - x)\frac{dy}{dx} = (2x - 1)y$, $y(x_0) = y_0$ has a unique solution, if $(x_0, y_0)$ equals

(a) (2, 1) (b) (1, 1) (c) (0, 0) (d) (0, 1)

**223.** The CF for the differential equation $(D^4 + D^2 + 1)y = ax^2 - be^{-x}\sin^{2x}$

(a) $e^x + e^{-x}$

(b) $e^{x/2}\left(C_1\cos\frac{\sqrt{3}}{2}x + C_2\sin\frac{\sqrt{3}}{2}x\right) + e^{-x/2}\left(C_3\cos\frac{\sqrt{3}}{2}x + C_4\sin\frac{\sqrt{3}}{2}x\right)$

(c) $e^x\left(C_1\cos\frac{\sqrt{3}}{2}x + C_2\sin\frac{\sqrt{3}}{2}x\right) + e^{-x}\left(C_3\cos\frac{\sqrt{3}}{2}x + C_4\sin\frac{\sqrt{3}}{2}x\right)$

(d) None of the above

**224.** If $\phi_1(x)$ is a particular integral of

$$L(y) = \frac{d^2y}{dx^2} - a\frac{dy}{dx} + by = a^{ax} + f(x)$$

and $\phi_2(x)$ is a particular integral of $L(y) = e^{ax} - f(x)$, *a*, *b* being constants, then a PI of $L(y) = 2be^{ax}$ is

(a) $b\phi_1(x) + \phi_2(x)$ (b) $\phi_1(x) - b\phi_2(x)$

(c) $a\phi_1(x) + b\phi_2(x)$ (d) $b[\phi_1(x) + \phi_2(x)]$

**225.** The solution of the equation $(x + y - 2)\frac{dy}{dx} = (x + y)$ is

(a) $(y + x) = \log(y - x + 1) + C$

(b) $(y - x) = \log(x + y - 1) + C$

(c) $y - 2x = \log(x + y - 1) + C$

(d) $y + 2x = \log(x + y + 1) + C$

**226.** The initial value problem

$$x\frac{d^2y}{dx^2} + \frac{dy}{dx} + xy = 0;\ y(0) = 1, \left(\frac{dy}{dx}\right)_{x=0} = 0 \text{ has}$$

(a) a unique solution

(b) no solution

(c) infinitely many solutions

(d) two linearly independent solution

**227.** General solution of equation $(\sin x - x\cos x)y'' - (x\sin x)y' + (\sin x)y = 0$, given that $y = \sin x$ is a solution

(a) $C_1\sin x + C_2 x\sin x$ (b) $C_1 x\sin x + C_2\cos x$

(c) $C_1\sin x + C_2 x^2$ (d) $C_1 x + C_2\sin x$

**228.** The eigen values for the boundary value problem $x'' + \lambda x = 0; x(0) = 0, x(\pi) + x'(\pi) = 0$ satisfy

(a) $\lambda + \tan\lambda\pi = 0$ (b) $\sqrt{\lambda} - \tan\lambda\pi = 0$

(c) $\sqrt{\lambda} + \tan\sqrt{\lambda}\pi = 0$ (d) $\lambda + \tan\sqrt{\lambda}\pi - 0$

**229.** If $y' - x \ne 0$, a solution of the differential equation $y'(y' + y) = x(x + y)$ is given, if $y(0) = 0$

(a) $1 - x - e^{-x}$ (b) $1 - x + e^x$

(c) $1 + x + e^{-x}$ (d) $1 + x + e^x$

**230.** If $y_1(x)$ and $y_2(x)$ are solution of $y'' + x^2y' = (1 - x)y = 0$ such that $y_1(0) = 0$, $y_1'(0) = -1$ and $y_2(0) = -1$, $y_2'(0) = 1$, then the Wronskian $W(y_1, y_2)$ on *R*

(a) is never zero

(b) is identically zero

(c) is zero only at finite number of points

(d) is zero at countable infinite number of points

**231.** Let $y = e^x$ be a solution of

$$x\frac{d^2y}{dx^2} - \frac{dy}{dx} + (1 - x)y = 0$$

Then, the second linearly independent solution of this ODE is

(a) $xe^{-x} + \frac{1}{2}$ (b) $\frac{1}{2}\left(x - \frac{1}{2}\right)e^{-x}$

(c) $-\frac{1}{2}\left(x + \frac{1}{2}\right)e^{-x}$ (d) $xe^{-x} - \frac{1}{2}$

**232.** The solution of $y'' + ay' + by = 0$ where $a$ and $b$ are constants, approaches to zero as $x \to \infty$, then

(a) $a > 0, b > 0$ (b) $a > 0, b < 0$
(c) $a < 0, b < 0$ (d) $a < 0, b > 0$

**233.** If the integrating factor of $(x^7y^2 + 3y)\,dx + (3x^8y - x)\,dy = 0$ is $x^m y^n$, then

(a) $m = -7, n = 1$ (b) $m = 1, n = -7$
(c) $m = n = 0$ (d) $m = n = 1$

**234.** If $y_1(x)$, $y_2(x)$ are solutions of $y'' + xy' + (1 - x^2)y = \sin x$, then which of the following is also its solution?

(a) $y_1(x) + y_2(x)$ (b) $y_1(x) - y_2(x)$
(c) $2y_1(x) - y_2(x)$ (d) $y_1(x) - 2y_2(x)$

**235.** General solution of the equation

$$(\cos x - \sin x)\frac{d^2y}{dx^2} + 2\sin x\frac{dy}{dx} - (\cos x + \sin x)\,y = 0$$

Given that $y = \sin x$ is a solution

(a) $C_1\cos x + C_2 x\sin x$ (b) $C_1\sin x + C_2 x\sin x$
(c) $C_1\sin x + C_2 e^x$ (d) $C_1\sin x + C_2 x$

**236.** The orthogonal trajectory to the family of circles $x^2 + y^2 = 2cx$ ($c$ arbitrary) is describe by the differential equation,

(a) $(x^2 + y^2)y' = 2xy$ (b) $(x^2 - y^2)y' = 2xy$
(c) $(y^2 - x^2)y' = xy$ (d) $(y^2 - x^2)y' = 2xy$

**237.** The differential equation $\frac{dy}{dx} = k(a - y)(b - y)$ when solved with the conditon $y(0) = 0$, yields the result.

(a) $\frac{b(a-y)}{a(b-y)} = e^{(a-b)kx}$ (b) $\frac{a(b-y)}{b(a-y)} = e^{(a-b)kx}$
(c) $\frac{b(a-x)}{a(b-x)} = e^{(b-a)k}$ (d) $xy = kC$

**238.** Which of the following pair of function are linear independent

I. $y_1 = \begin{cases} x^2, & x \ge 0 \\ 0, & x < 0 \end{cases}, \; y_2 = \begin{cases} 0, & x \ge 0 \\ x^2, & x < 0 \end{cases}$

II. $y_1 = x^2, y_2 = x|x|, |x| \le 1$

III. $y_1 = x^3, y_2 = x^2|x|, |x| \le 1$

IV. $y_1 = \begin{cases} (x-1)^2, & 0 \le x \le 1 \\ 0, & 1 < x < 2 \end{cases}, \; y_2 = \begin{cases} 0, & 0 \le x \le 1 \\ (x-1)^2, & 1 \le x \le 2 \end{cases}$

Select the correct code

(a) Only I is true (b) Only II is true
(c) I and III are true (d) All are true

**239.** All non-trivial solution of $x^2y'' + xy' + 4xy = 0, x > 0$ are

(a) bounded and non-periodic
(b) unbounded and non-periodic
(c) bounded and periodic
(d) unbounded and periodic

**240.** The solution of the equation $y'\sin x = y\log y$ satisfying the initial condition $y\left(\frac{\pi}{2}\right) = e$ is

(a) $e^{\tan x/2}$ (b) $e^{\cot x/2}$
(c) $\log\tan\left(\frac{x}{2}\right)$ (d) $\log\cot\left(\frac{x}{2}\right)$

**241.** The integrating factor of the DE $(2xy^4e^y + 2xy^3 + y)\,dx + (x^2y^4e^y - x^2y^2 - 3x)\,dy = 0$

(a) $\frac{1}{x^4}$ (b) $\frac{y^2}{x^4}$
(c) $\frac{1}{y^4}$ (d) None of these

**242.** $Ly = xe^x \ln x$ $(x > 0)$ when $L = \left(\frac{d^2}{dx^2} + P\frac{d}{dx} + Q\right)$ the two LI solution of $Ly = 0$ are $xe^x$ and $e^x$, then PI is

(a) $xe^x\left[\frac{x}{2}\ln\frac{x - x^2}{4}\right] + e^{-x}\left[\frac{-x^3}{3}\ln\frac{x^3}{9}\right]$

(b) $x^2e^x\left[\frac{x^2}{2}\ln\frac{x - x^2}{4}\right] + e^x\left[\frac{-x^2}{2}\ln\frac{x + x^3}{9}\right]$

(c) $x^2e^x\left[\frac{x^2}{2}\ln\frac{x - x^2}{4}\right] + e^x\left[\frac{-x^3}{3}\ln\frac{x + x^3}{9}\right]$

(d) None of the above

**243.** The primitive of the differntial equation $(2xy^4e^y = 2xy^3 + y)\,dx + (x^2y^4e^y - x^2y^2 - 3x)\,dy = 0$ is

(a) $x^2e^y + \frac{x^2}{y} + \frac{x}{y^3} = C$ (b) $x^2e^y - \frac{x^2}{y} + \frac{x}{y^3} = C$
(c) $x^2e^y + \frac{x^2}{y} - \frac{x}{y^3} = C$ (d) $x^2e^y - \frac{x^2}{y} - \frac{x}{y^3} = C$

**244.** The differential equation $(3a^2x^2 + by\cos x)\,dx + (2\sin x - 4ay')\,dy = 0$ is exact for

(a) $a = 3, b = 2$ (b) $a = 2, b = 3$
(c) $a = 3, b = 4$ (d) $a = 2, b = 5$

**245.** Consider the following statement about the following PDE $p + q - pq = 0$

I. It has no singular solutions

II. $z = \frac{ax}{a-1} + ay + b$ is a solution

III. $z = ax + \frac{a}{a-1}y + b$ is a solution

IV. It is a first order non-linear PDE

Then, choose the correct code

(a) Only I and II are true
(b) Only II and IV are true
(c) II, III and IV are true
(d) All are true

**246.** Which of the following is elliptic?
(a) Laplace equation (b) Wave equation
(c) Heat equation (d) $u_{xx} + 2u_{xy} - 4u_{xy} = 0$

**247.** Find the general solution of
$$ayp^2 + (2x - b)p - y = 0, a > 0$$
(a) $ac^2 + 2(2x - b)c - 4y^2 = 0$
(b) $ayc^2 + 2(2x - b)c - y = 0$
(c) $ay + (2x - b)c - yc^2 = 0$
(d) None of the above

**248.** CF of the following PDE
$(bD - aD' - c)(bD - aD' - c)z = 0$ is
(a) $z = e^{c/a^x}[\phi_1(by + ax) + y\phi_2(by + ax)]$, if $b \neq 0$
(b) $z = e^{\left(\frac{c}{b}\right)^x}[\phi_1(by + ax) + x\phi_2(by + ax)]$, if $b \neq 0$
(c) $z = e^{\frac{c}{a}y}[\psi_1(by + ax) + x\psi_2(by + ax)]$, if $a \neq 0$
(d) None of the above

**249.** Find a complete integral of
$$Z(p^2 - q^2) = (x - y)$$
(a) $Z^{3/2} = (x + a)^{3/2} + (y + b)^{3/2} + c$
(b) $Z^{3/2} = (x + a)^{3/2} + (y + b)^{3/2} + b$
(c) $Z^{3/2} = (a - x)^{3/2} + (b - y)^{3/2} + c$
(d) $Z^{3/2} = (a - x)^{3/2} + (b - y)^{3/2} + b$

**250.** The complete integral of the differential equation $y(1 + x^2)p^2 - qx^2 = 0$
(a) $z = \pm\frac{a}{2}(1 + x)^{\frac{1}{2}} + \frac{a^2y^2}{2} + C$
(b) $z = \pm a(1 + x^2)^{1/2} + \frac{a^2y^2}{2} + C$
(c) $z = \pm\frac{3}{2}a(1 + 2x^2)^{1/2} + \frac{a^2y^2}{2} + C$
(d) $z = \pm\frac{a}{\sqrt{1 + x^2}} + a^2y^2 + C$

**251.** Find the complete integral of the PDE
$$\left(\frac{\partial z'}{\partial x}\right)\left(\frac{\partial z}{\partial y}\right)z = \left(\frac{\partial z}{\partial x}\right)^2\left[x\frac{\partial z}{\partial y} + \left(\frac{\partial z}{\partial x}\right)^2\right] + \left(\frac{\partial z}{\partial y}\right)^2\left[y\left(\frac{\partial z}{\partial x}\right) + \left(\frac{\partial z}{\partial y}\right)^2\right]$$
(a) $z = ax + by + \frac{a^3 + b^3}{a + b}$
(b) $z = ax + by + \frac{a^4 + b^4}{a + b}$
(c) $z = -ax - by + \frac{a^4 + b^4}{ab}$
(d) $z = -ax - by - \frac{a^4 + b^4}{a \cdot b}$

**252.** Complete integral of $z^2(p^2 + q^2) = x^2 + y^2$ is
(a) $z^2 = x^2\sqrt{a^2 + x^2} + a^2 \log[x + \sqrt{x^2 + a^2}]$
$+ y\sqrt{(y^2 + a^2)} - a^2 \log\{y + \sqrt{y^2 + a^2}\} + b$
(b) $z^{3/2} = (x + a)^{3/2} + (y + b)^{3/2} + b$
(c) $z^2 = x^2\sqrt{a^2 - x^2} - a^2 \log[x + \sqrt{x^2 + a^2}]$
$- y\sqrt{y^2 - a^2} + a^2 \log\{y + \sqrt{y^2 - a^2}\} + b$
(d) None of the above

**253.** Pick the region in which the following differential equation is hyperbolic
$$yu_{xx} + 2xyu_{xy} + xu_{yy} = u_x + u_y$$
(a) $xy \neq 1$ (b) $xy \neq 0$
(c) $xy > 1$ (d) $xy > 0$

**254.** General solution of the partial differential equation given below is $(y^2 + z^2 - x^2)p - 2xyq + 2xz = 0$
(a) $\phi\left[\frac{y}{z}, \frac{x^2 + y^2 + z^2}{z}\right]$
(b) $\phi\left[\frac{x}{z}, \frac{x^2 + y^2 + z^2}{y}\right] = 0$
(c) $\phi\left[\frac{y}{z}, \frac{x^2 - y^2 + z^2}{z}\right] = 0$
(d) $\phi\left[\frac{x}{z}, \frac{x^2 - y^2 + z^2}{z}\right] = 0$

**255.** For PDE $p^2x + q^2y = z$, correct code is/are
I. it can be reduced to $P^2 + Q^2 = 1$ from by some suitable transformation
II. it has solution
$2\sqrt{z} = 2a\sqrt{x} + 2\sqrt{y}\sqrt{1 - a^2} + b$; $a, b$ are constant
III. it has no singular solution
IV. it has a solution which passes through origin
(a) I, II III and IV are correct
(b) II, III and IV are correct
(c) I, II and IV are correct
(d) I, III and IV are correct

**256.** The complete integral of
$q(p - \cos x) = \cos y$ is
(a) $z = ax + \cos x + \frac{\cos y}{a} + b$
(b) $z = ax + \sin x + \frac{\sin y}{a} + b$
(c) $z = ax + \sin x + \frac{\cos y}{a} + b$
(d) $z = ax + \cos x + \frac{\sin y}{a} + b$

**257.** The characteristic of the partial differential equation
$$\frac{\partial u}{\partial x} + \frac{\partial u}{\partial y} = u \text{ are}$$

(a) exponential curves along which $u$ remains constant
(b) exponential curves along which $u$ varies linearly with $x$
(c) straight lines along which $u$ remains constant
(d) straight lines along which $u$ varies exponentially with $x$

**258.** The complete integral of $z = pq$ is
(a) $2\sqrt{y} = x\sqrt{a} + z/\sqrt{b} + \sqrt{a}$
(b) $2\sqrt{z} = \sqrt{a} + x\sqrt{b} + \sqrt{b}$
(c) $2\sqrt{z} = x\sqrt{a} + \left(\frac{1}{\sqrt{a}}\right)y + b$
(d) None of the above

**259.** Integral surface of
$(2xy - 1)p + (z - 2x^2)q = 2(x - yz)$ passing through the line $x_0(s) = 1, y_0(s) = 0, z_0(s) = s$
(a) $x^2 + y^2 - yz - x + z = 1$
(b) $x^2 + y^2 - xz - y + z = 1$
(c) $x^2 + y^2 - xy - x + z = 1$
(d) $y^2 + z^2 - xy + z - x = 1$

**260.** The general integral of the partial differntial equation
$(y + zx)z_x - (x + yz)z_y = x^2 - y^2$ is
(a) $F(x^2 + y^2 + z^2, xy + z) = 0$
(b) $F(x^2 + y^2 - z^2, xy + z) = 0$
(c) $F(x^2 - y^2 - z^2, xy + z) = 0$
(d) $F(x^2 + y^2 + z^2, xy - z) = 0$
where $F$ is an arbitrary function.

**261.** For obtaining the complete integral of the non-linear partial differential equation $pq(x^4 + y^3) = p + q$, the required forms of $p = \frac{\partial z}{\partial x}$ and $q = \frac{\partial z}{\partial y}$ involving an arbitrary constant a, are
(a) $p = (x^4 + a)^{-1}, q = (y^3 - a)^{-1}$
(b) $p = (2x^{-1} + a)^{-1}, q = (3y^3 - a)^{-1}$
(c) $p = (-2x^4 + a)^{-1}, q = (-3y^3 - a)^{-1}$
(d) $p = (x^4 - a)^{-1}, q = (y^3 - a)^{-1}$

**262.** The solution of $\left(\frac{\partial^2 z}{\partial x^2}\right) + \left(\frac{\partial^2 z}{\partial z^2}\right) = x + y$ is
(a) $z = \frac{2}{3}[(x + a)^{3/2} + (y - a)^{3/2}] + b$
(b) $z = \frac{2}{3}[(x + a) + (y - a)] + b$
(c) $z = \frac{2}{3}[(x + a)^2 + (y - a)^2] + b$
(d) $z = \frac{2}{3}[(x + a)^3 + (y - a)^3] + b$

**263.** The variable $\xi$ and $\eta$ which reduce the differential equation $\frac{\partial^2 u}{\partial x^2} - x^2\frac{\partial^2 u}{\partial y^2} = 0$ to the canonical form, are
(a) $\xi = y^2 + \frac{1}{2}x, \eta = y^2 - \frac{1}{2}x$
(b) $\xi = y + \frac{1}{2}x^2, \eta = y - \frac{1}{2}x^2$
(c) $\xi = y + x^2, \eta = y - x^2$
(d) $\eta = y^2 + x, \eta = y^2 - x$

**264.** If $u_1, u_2, u_3$ are solutions of the equation
$$\frac{d^3y}{dx^3} + \sin^2 x\frac{d^2y}{dx^2} + e^{2x}\frac{dy}{dx} + (\log x)y = x^5,$$
then $2u_1 + au_2 + bu_3$ and $au_1 + bu_2 + u_3$ are also solutions of given differential equation, then the value of a and b are
(a) $a = -1, b = 1$ (b) $a = -2, b = 2$
(c) $a = 2, b = -3$ (d) No such solution exists

**265.** The general solution of the partial differential equation $(D + D' - 2)(D - D')Z = 0$, where $D \equiv \frac{\partial}{\partial x}$ and $D' \equiv \frac{\partial}{\partial y}$ is
(a) $f_1(x + y) + e^{2x}f_2(x - y)$
(b) $e^{2x}f_1(x + y) + f_2(x - y)$
(c) $e^{-2x}f_1(x + y) + f_2(x - y)$
(d) $f_1(x + y) + e^{-2x}f_2(x - y)$

**266.** The complete integral of $(p + q)(z - xp - yq) = 1$
(a) $z = ax + by + a + b$ (b) $z + ax + by = \frac{1}{a + b}$
(c) $z = ax - by + \frac{1}{a + b}$ (d) $z = ax + by + \frac{1}{a + b}$

**267.** The complete integral of the partial differential equation $6z\frac{\partial z}{\partial x}\cdot\frac{\partial z}{\partial y} = 3\left(\frac{\partial z}{\partial x}\right)^2\cdot$
$$\left(3\left(\frac{\partial z}{\partial x}\right)^3 + 2x\left(\frac{\partial z}{\partial y}\right)\right) + 2\left(\frac{\partial z}{\partial y}\right)^2\left(\cdot 2\left(\frac{\partial z}{\partial y}\right)^3 + 3y\left(\frac{\partial z}{\partial x}\right)\right)$$
is
(a) $z = 2ax + 3y + 9\frac{a^4}{b} + 4\frac{b^4}{a}$
(b) $z = ax + by + 4\frac{b^4}{a} + 9\frac{a^4}{b}$
(c) $z = ax + by + \frac{3}{2}\frac{a^4}{b} + \frac{2}{3}\frac{b^3}{a}$
(d) $z = \frac{2}{3}ax + \frac{1}{3}by + \frac{3}{2}\frac{a^4}{b} + \frac{2}{3}\frac{b^4}{a}$

**268.** If $f(x)$ and $g(y)$ are arbitrary functions, then the general solution of the partial differntial equation
$$u\frac{\partial^2 u}{\partial x\partial y} - \frac{\partial u}{\partial x}\frac{\partial u}{\partial y} = 0$$
is given by
(a) $u(x, y) = f(x) + g(y)$
(b) $u(x, y) = f(x + y) + g(x - y)$
(c) $u(x, y) = f(x)g(y)$
(d) $u(x, y) = xg(y) + yf(x)$

**269.** The characteristics curves of the equation $x^2u_{xx} - y^2u_{yy} = x^2y^2 + x; x > 0, u = u(x, y)$ are

(a) rectangular hyperbopla (b) parabola
(c) circle (d) straight line

**270.** $\frac{\partial^2 z}{\partial x^2} - \frac{\partial^2 z}{\partial y \partial z} + \frac{\partial z}{\partial x} = 1$ has the solution

(a) $Z = f_1(y) + e^{-x} f_2(y + x) + x$
(b) $Z = f_1(y) + e^{-x} f(y + x) + x^2$
(c) $Z = x^2$
(d) None of the above

**271.** Let $PQRS$ be a rectangle in the first quadrant whose adjacent sides $PQ$ and $QR$ have slopes 1 and $-1$, respectively.

If $u(x, t)$ is a solution of $\frac{\partial^2 u}{\partial t^2} - \frac{\partial^2 u}{\partial x^2} = 0$ and $u(P) = 1$,

$u(Q) = -\frac{1}{2}$, $u(R) = \frac{1}{2}$, then $u(S)$ equals

(a) 2 (b) 1
(c) $\frac{1}{2}$ (d) $-\frac{1}{2}$

**272.** The complete integral of the following PDE is $p^2x^2 + q^2y^2 = z^2$

(a) $z^2 = cx^2y\sqrt{1-a^2}$ (b) $z = cx^2y\sqrt{1-a^2}$
(c) $z = c(xy)^a$ (d) $z = c(x + y)^a$

**273.** Solve $\frac{dx}{\cos(x+y)} = \frac{dy}{\sin(x+y)} = \frac{dz}{z}$

(a) $z^{\sqrt{2}} \cot\frac{1}{2}\left(x + y + \frac{\pi}{4}\right) = C_1$

$[\cos(x+y) + \sin(x+y)]\, e^{y-x} = C_2$

(b) $z^2 \cot\frac{1}{2}\left(x + y + \frac{\pi}{4}\right) = C_1$

$[\cos(x+y) + \sin(x+y)]\, e^{y-x} = C_2$

(c) $z^2 \cot\frac{1}{2}\left(x + y + \frac{\pi}{4}\right) = C_1$

$[\cos(x+y) + \sin(x+y)]\, e^{x-y} = C_2$

(d) None of the above

**274.** The complete integral of PDE $x(1+y)p = y(1+x)q$ is

(a) $Z = a(\log xy + x + y) + b$
(b) $Z = a(\log xy + x) + b$
(c) $Z = a(1+x) + (1+y)$
(d) $Z = ax + by + (a+b)xy$

**275.** Solve the differential equations $r + 5s + 6t = (y - 2x)^{-1}$ is

(a) $\phi_1(y + 2x) + \phi_2(y + 3x) + \log(y + 2x)$
(b) $\phi_1(y - 2x) + \phi_2(y + 3x) + x\log(y - 2x)$
(c) $\phi_1(y - 2x) + \phi_2(y - 3x) + x\log(2x + y)$
(d) $\phi_1(y - 2x) + \phi_2(y - 3x) + x\log(y - 2x)$

**276.** In the region $x > 0$, $y > 0$, the partial differntial equation

$$(x^2 - y^2)\frac{\partial^2 u}{\partial x^2} + 2(x^2 + y^2)\frac{\partial^2 u}{\partial x \partial y} + (x^2 - y^2)\frac{\partial^2 u}{\partial y^2} = 0$$

(a) changes type (b) is elliptic
(c) is parabolic (d) is hyperbolic

**277.** The general integral of $\frac{dx}{x^3(y^3 - z^3)} = \frac{dy}{y^3(z^3 - x^3)} = \frac{dz}{z^2(x^3 - y^3)}$ is

(a) $\phi\left(\frac{1}{x} + \frac{1}{y} + \frac{1}{z}, x^2 + y^2 + z^2\right) = 0$
(b) $\phi\left(\frac{1}{x} + \frac{1}{y} + \frac{1}{z}, x + y + z\right) = 0$
(c) $\phi(x + y + z, x^2 + y^2 + z^2) = 0$
(d) None of the above

**278.** The complete integral of PDE $x^2p^2 + y^2q^2 - 4 = 0$ is

(a) $z = a\log x + \sqrt{4 - a^2}\log y + b$
(b) $z^2 = ax^2 + \sqrt{4 - a^2}y^2 + b$
(c) $z = ax^2 + by^2 + c$
(d) $z = a\log x^2 \sqrt{(4 - a^2)}\log y^2 + b$

**279.** Let $u(x, y)$ be the solution to the Cauchy problem $xu_x + u_y = 1$, $u(x, 0) = 2\ln(x)$, $x > 1$

Then, $u(e, 1) =$

(a) $-1$ (b) 0 (c) 1 (d) e

**280.** The initial value problem $u_x + u_y = 1$, $u(s, s) = \sin s$, $0 \le s \le 1$, has

(a) two solutions
(b) a unique solution
(c) no solution
(d) infinitely many solutions

**281.** The equation $x^2(y - 1)z_{xx} - x(y^2 - 1)z_{xy} + y(y^2 - 1)z_{yy} + z_x = 0$ is hyperbolic in the entire $xy$-plane except along

(a) $x$-axis
(b) $y$-axis
(c) a line parallel to $y$-axis
(d) a line parallel to $x$-axis

**282.** The complete integrals of the PDE is $p^2q^2 + x^2y^2 = x^2q^2(x^2 + y^2)$ is

(a) $z = \frac{1}{3}(x^2 + a^2)^{1/2} + (y^2 - a^2)^{3/2} + b$
(b) $z = \frac{1}{3}(x^2 + a^2)^{3/2} + (y^2 - a^2)^{1/2} + b$
(c) $z = \frac{1}{3}(x^2 + a^2)^{1/2} + (y^2 - a^2)^{1/2} + b$
(d) $z = \frac{1}{3}(x^2 + a^2)^{3/2} + (y^2 - a^2)^{3/2} + b$

**283.** Solution of PDE

$r + s - 2t = (2x + y)^{1/2}$ is

(a) $\phi_1(x - y) + \phi_2(2x - y) + \frac{1}{15}(2x + y)^{3/2}$

(b) $\phi_1(x + y) + \phi_2(y - 2x) + \frac{1}{15}(2x + y)^{3/2}$

(c) $\phi_1(x + y) + \phi_2(y - 2x) + \frac{1}{15}(2x + y)^{5/2}$

(d) None of the above

**284.** The characteristic curve of $2yu_x + (2x + y^2)u_y = 0$ passing through (0, 0) is

(a) $y^2 = 2(e^x + x - 1)$ (b) $y^2 = 2(e^x - x + 1)$

(c) $y^2 = 2(e^x - x - 1)$ (d) $y^2 = 2(e^x + x + 1)$

**285.** The general solution of the partial differential equation

$$(D^2 - D'^2 - 2D - 2D')Z = 0,$$

where $D = \frac{\partial}{\partial x}$ and $D' = \frac{\partial}{\partial y}$

(a) $f(y + x) + e^{2x}g(y - x)$

(b) $e^{2x}f(y + x) + g(y - x)$

(c) $e^{2x}f(y + x) + g(y - x)$

(d) $f(y + x) + e^{-2x}(y - x)$

**286.** Integral surface of PDE $x^2p + y^2q = -z^2$ which passes through hyperbola $xy = x + y$, $z = 1$ is given by

(a) $xy + 2yz + xz = 3xyz$ (b) $yz + 2xy + xz = 3xyz$

(c) $xz + 2zx + xy = 3xyz$ (d) None of these

**287.** The general solution of $\frac{\partial^2 u}{\partial x^2} + \frac{\partial^2 u}{\partial y^2} = 0$ is of the form

(a) $u = f(x + iy) + g(x - iy)$

(b) $u = f(x + y) + g(x - y)$

(c) $u = cf(x - iy)$

(d) $u = g(x + y)$

**288.** The solution of $xu_x + yu_y = 0$ is of the form

(a) $f\left(\frac{y}{x}\right)$ (b) $f(x + y)$

(c) $f(x - y)$ (d) $f(xy)$

**289.** The characteristic curves for the equation $xz_y - yz_x = z$ are

(a) straight line passing through origin

(b) circle with centre at origin

(c) parabola with vertex at origin

(d) rectangular hyperbola

**290.** Consider the $4xyz = pq + 2px^2y + 2qxy^2$

I. It can be reduced to Clairaut form by some suitable transformation

II. $z = ax + by + a \cdot b$ is complete integral

III. $z = -x^2y^2$ is singular soluton

Choose correct code

(a) Only I and II are correct

(b) Only II and III are correct

(c) I and III are correct

(d) All the correct

**291.** The solution of

$(2D + D' - 1)(D + 2D' - 2)z = 0$ is

(a) $z = e^{x/2}\phi(x - 2y) + e^{-2x}\phi(2x - y)$

(b) $z = e^y\phi(x - 2y) + e^y\phi(2x - y)$

(c) $z = e^{x/2}\phi(2x - y) + e^{+2y}\phi(x - 2y)$

(d) None of the above

**292.** The integral curves of the equation $p + 2q = 5z + \cos h(2x - y)$ are given by the intersection of the surface

(a) $2x - y = C_1$; $[5z + \cos h(2x - y)]e^{-5x} = C_2$

(b) $x - 2y = C_3$; $[5z + \cos h(x - 2y)]e^{-5x} = C_4$

(c) $2x - y = C_5$; $[z + \cos h(2x - y)]e^{-x} = C_6$

(d) $x - 2y = C_7$; $[z + \cos h(2x - y)]e^{-x} = C_8$

# Exercise 2 (For Part 'C')

**Directions** (Q. Nos. 1-58) *Questions may have one or more than one correct option.*

**1.** Let $y_1(x)$ and $y_2(x)$ be two solutions of $[r(x)y']' + p(x)y = 0$ such that $y_1(x)$ and $y_2(x)$ have a common zero on $x \in [a, b]$. Then, which of the following/s is/are true?

(a) $y_1(x)$ and $y_2(x)$ are linearly independent on $a \le x \le b$.

(b) $y_1(x)$ and $y_2(x)$ are linearly dependent on $a \le x \le b$.

(c) $W(y_1, y_2) \ne 0$

(d) $W(y_1, y_2) = 0$

**2.** Let $y_1(x)$ and $y_2(x)$ be two linearly independent solutions of

$[r(x)y']' + p(x)y = 0$; $x \in [a, b]$, then

(a) $y_1(x_0) = y_2(x_0) = 0$, where $a \le x_0 \le b$

(b) between two consecutive zeros of $y_1(x)$, there is exactly one zero of $y_2(x)$

(c) between two consecutive zeros of $y_2(x)$ there is exactly one zero of $y_1(x)$

(d) between two consecutive zeros of $y_1(x)$ (or $y_2(x)$) there are infinitely many zeros of $y_2(x)$ (or $y_1(x)$)

**3.** Let $y(x)$ is a non-trivial solution of $y''(x) + p(x)y = 0$ in $[a, b]$, then

(a) $y(x_0) = 0, y'(x_0) = 0$, when $a \le x_0 \le b$

(b) $y(x_0) = 0, y'(x_0) \ne 0$, when $a \le x_0 \le b$

(c) $y(x)$ has atmost one zero, when $p(x) \neq 0$ for $a \leq x \leq b$

(d) $y(x)$ has atmost finite number of zeros on $[a, b]$ when $p(x) > 0$

**4.** General solution of differential equation

$$\frac{d^2y}{dx^2} + y = \operatorname{cosec} x \text{ is given by}$$

$$y = A\cos x + B\sin x + y_1 \cos x + y_2 \sin x,$$

then

(a) $y_1 = x,\ y_2 = \sin x$ (b) $y_1 = -x,\ y_2 = \log\cos x$

(c) $y_1 = -x,\ y_2 = \log\sin x$ (d) $W(y_1, y_2) = 1$

**5.** Which of the following informations are true for the differential equation?

$$E : (x^3 + y^3)dx - (xy^2)dy = 0$$

(a) $E = 0$ is an exact differential equation

(b) Integrating factor of $E = 0$ is $x^{-4}$

(c) Solution of $E = 0$ is $\log x - \frac{y^3}{3x^3} = C$

(d) Solution of $E = 0$ is $\log y - \frac{x^3}{3y^3} = C$

**6.** For the initial value problem (IVP)

$$\frac{dy}{dx} = f(x, y) \text{ with } y(0) = 0, \text{ which of the}$$

following/s is/are true?

(a) If $f(x, y)$ satisfies Lipschitz's condition, then IVP has unique solution.

(b) IVP may not be unique although $f(x, y)$ is continuous.

(c) IVP does not satisfy Lipschitz's condition still IVP has unique solution

(d) IVP does not satisfy Lipschitz's condition and so, IVP has no solution

**7.** In a Strum-Liouville problem

$$[r(x)y']' + [q(x) + \lambda p(x)]y = 0;$$

$\alpha y(a) + \beta y'(a) = 0$ and $\gamma y(b) + \delta y'(b) = 0$ which of the following/s is/are true for $x \in [a, b]$?

(a) $r'(x)$ is continuous and $p(x) > 0$

(b) Atleast two from $\alpha, \beta, \gamma, \delta$ must be non-zero.

(c) Atleast one from $\alpha, \beta$ is non-zero and atleast one from $\gamma, \delta$ is non-zero.

(d) $\int_a^b p(x) y_m(x) y_n(x) dx = 0$, where $y_m(x)$ and $y_n(x)$ are two eigen functions.

**8.** Which of the following/s is/are true about Strum-Liouville problem (SLP)?

(a) All eigen values of SLP are real and non-negative.

(b) Eigen functions corresponding to different eigen values are orthogonal with respect to weight function.

(c) SLP has always an eigen function.

(d) For each eigen value of a SLP there exists only one linearly independent eigen function.

**9.** Green's function of the boundary value problem $y'' = 0;\ y(0) = y(1) = 0$ given by

(a) $G(x, t) = x(1 - t);\ 0 \leq x < t$

(b) $G(x, t) = t(1 - x);\ t < x \leq 1$

(c) $G(x, t) = x^2(1 - t);\ 0 \leq x < t$

(d) $G(x, t) = x(1 - t^2);\ t < x \leq 1$

**10.** Let Green's function $G(x,t)$ is defined for the differential equation

$$y'' + y = x;\quad y(0) = y\left(\frac{\pi}{2}\right) = 0, \text{ then}$$

(a) $G'(x, t)\big|_{x=t+0} - G'(x, t)\big|_{x=t-0} = -1$

(b) $G'(x, t)\big|_{x=t+0} - G'(x, t)\big|_{x=t-0} = 1$

(c) $G(0, t) = 0, G\left(\frac{\pi}{2}, t\right) \neq 0$

(d) $G(0, t) = G\left(\frac{\pi}{2}, t\right) = 0$

**11.** General solution of PDE $(y + z)p + (z + x)q = x + y$, is/are

(a) $\phi\left[(x - y)^2(x + y + z), \left(\frac{x - y}{y - z}\right)\right] = 0$

(b) $\frac{x - y}{y - z} = f[(x - y)^2(x + y + z)]$

(c) $(x - y)^2(x + y + z) = F\left(\frac{x - y}{y - z}\right)$

(d) $\psi\left[(y - z)^2(x + y + z), \left(\frac{y - z}{z - x}\right)\right] = 0$

**12.** For PDE $(p^2 + q^2)y = qz$

(a) no singular solution exist

(b) $z = x^2 y$ is the singular solution

(c) $z = 0$ is the singular solution

(d) $z^2 = (ax + b)^2 + a^2y^2$ is the complete solution

**13.** Consider the PDE,

$$z = px + qy + \log(pq)$$

then which of the following/s is/are true?

(a) Complete solution of PDE is $z = ax + by + \log(ab)$

(b) Singular solution of PDE is $(x - y)(y - z) = 1$

(c) Singular solution does not exist

(d) Singular solution is $(x - z)(y - z) = 1$

**14.** For the PDE $r - 2s + t = \cos(2x + 3y)$

(a) CF is $\phi_1(y + x) + \phi_2(y - x)$

(b) CF is $\phi_1(y + x) + x\,\phi_2(y + x)$

(c) PI is $-\cos(2x + 3y)$

(d) PI is $\cos(2x + 3y)$

**15.** Consider a general PDE of second order of the form

$$Rr + Ss + Tt + f = 0,$$

where $R, S, T$ are continuous functions of $x$ and $y$, then PDE at a point $(x, y)$

(a) parabolic, if $S^2 - 4RT = 0$

(b) hyperbolic, if $S^2 - 4RT < 0$

(c) elliptical, if $S^2 - 4RT > 0$

(d) hyperbolic or elliptic, when $S^2 - 4RT \neq 0$

**16.** Consider PDE $\frac{\partial^2 u}{\partial x^2} = x^2 \frac{\partial^2 u}{\partial y^2}$, then select the correct option/s.

(a) PDE is elliptic for $x \neq 0$
(b) PDE is parabolic for $x = 0$
(c) characteristic equations are $dy \pm x^2 dx = 0$
(d) characteristic curves are $y = c \pm \frac{x^2}{2}$

**17.** Consider the PDE

$$x^2 r - y^2 t + px - qy = x^2,$$

select the correct option/s.

(a) PDE is hyperbolic for $(x, y) \neq (0, 0)$
(b) $xy = C_1$ and $\frac{x}{y} = C_2$ are the characteristic curves
(c) $x^2 y = C_1$ and $\frac{x}{y^2} = C_2$ are the characteristic curves
(d) Canonical form of PDE is $4\frac{\partial^2 z}{\partial u \partial v} = 1$ where, $u = xy$, $v = \frac{x}{y}$

**18.** Which of the following/s is/are true?

(a) Two dimensional Laplace's equation is elliptic.
(b) One dimensional wave equation is hyperbolic.
(c) One dimensional heat equation is parabolic.
(d) Canonical form of one-dimensional wave equation is of the form $\frac{\partial^2 z}{\partial u \partial v} = 0$

**19.** Which of the following/s is/are true?

(a) Canonical form of hyperbolic PDE is of the form $\frac{\partial^2 z}{\partial u \partial v} = \phi(u, v, z, z_u, z_v)$
(b) Canonical form of parabolic PDE is of the form $\frac{\partial^2 z}{\partial v^2} = \phi(u, v, z, z_u, z_v)$
(c) Canonical form of elliptic PDE does not exist
(d) Canonical form of elliptic PDE is of the form $\frac{\partial^2 z}{\partial \alpha^2} + \frac{\partial^2 z}{\partial \beta^2} = \phi(\alpha, \beta, z, z_\alpha, z_\beta)$

**20.** For the PDE

$$\frac{\partial^2 z}{\partial x^2} + 2\frac{\partial^2 z}{\partial x \partial y} + \frac{\partial^2 z}{\partial y^2} = 0$$

(a) general solution is $z = \phi_1(y - x) + x\,\phi_2(y - x)$
(b) general solution is $z = (x + y)\phi_1(x - y) + \phi_2(x - y)$
(c) characteristic curves are orthogonal
(d) canonical form is $\frac{\partial^2 z}{\partial v^2} = 0$

**21.** Consider PDE

$$\frac{\partial^2 u}{\partial t^2} = c^2 \frac{\partial^2 u}{\partial x^2} \quad (c > 0)$$

such that $u(x, 0) = f(x)$ and $u_t(x, 0) = g(x)$, then

(a) if $g(x) = 0$, then $u(x, t) = \frac{1}{2}[f(x - ct) + f(x + ct)]$
(b) if $f(x) = \sin x$, $g(x) = 0$, then $u(x, t) = \sin x \cos ct$
(c) if $g(x) = 1$, then $u(x, t) = f(x, t) + t$
(d) canonical form of PDE is $\frac{\partial^2 z}{\partial u \partial v} = 0$

**22.** Given, $\frac{dy}{dx} = 2xy$

Solving the above equation, then

(a) $\frac{dy}{y} = 2x dx$ (b) $\log y = x^2 + \log a$
(c) $\log y = \frac{x}{\log a}$ (d) $y = a^{e^{x^2}}$

**23.** Given, the equation $x = A\cos(pt - \alpha)$, then

(a) $\frac{d^2 x}{dt^2} = -p^2 x$
(b) $\frac{d^3 x}{dt^3} = -p^2 \frac{dx}{dt}$
(c) $\frac{d^2 x}{dt^2} = px^2$
(d) Eliminate $A$, $p$ and $x$ gives $x\frac{d^3 x}{dt^3} - \frac{dx}{dt} \cdot \frac{d^2 x}{dt^2} = 0$

**24.** Given, $\frac{dx}{x} = \tan y \, dy$

Solving the above equation gives

(a) $\log x = -\log \cos y + C$ (b) $\log(x \cos y) = C$
(c) $\log(x \sin y) = C$ (d) $x \cos y = e^C$

**25.** Given $\frac{d^2 y}{dx^2} - 6\frac{dy}{dx} + 13y = 0$, then

(a) auxiliary equation is $m^2 - 6m + 13 = 0$
(b) auxiliary equation is $m^2 + 6m - 13 = 0$
(c) general solution is $y = e^{ax} + A\cos x + Bx$
(d) general solution $y = Ae^{(3+2i)x} + Be^{(3-2i)x}$

**26.** Given, $\frac{d^2 y}{dx^2} - 2\frac{dy}{dx} + 4y = 50e^{2x}$, then

(a) $(D - 2)^2 y = 50\, e^{2x}$
(b) $(D + 2)^2 y = e^{5x}$
(c) general solution is $y = 25x^2 e^{2x} + (A + Bx)e^{2x}$
(d) No solution exist

**27.** Given, continuous function $f(x, y) = y^{2/3}$ on rectangle $|x| \leq 1, |y| \leq 1$.

(a) This function satisfies Lipschitz condition on a rectangle
(b) This function does not satisfies Lipschitz conditions a rectangle
(c) $\left|\frac{\partial f}{\partial y}\right| \leq$ Constant for $y = 0$
(d) $\left|\frac{\partial f}{\partial y}\right| \nleq$ Constant for $y = 0$

**28.** Given, $f(x, y) = xy^2$ satisfies the Lipschitz condition on the rectangle $|x| \le 1, |y| \le 1$ but does not satisfy a Lipschitz condition on the strip $|x| \le 1, |y| < \infty$.

(a) It satisfies Lipschitz condition on the rectangle $|x| \le 1, |y| \le 1$

(b) It does not satisfies Lipschitz condition of the rectangle $|x| \le 1, |y| \le 1$

(c) It satisfies Lipschitz condition on strip $|x| \le 1, |y| < \infty$

(d) It does not satisfies Lipschitz condition strip $|x| \le 1, |y| < \infty$

**29.** Given, $(x + c)^2 + y^2 = r^2$, then

(a) This equation is equivalent to $(x + c) = \pm \sqrt{r^2 - y^2}$

(b) This equation is equivalent to $x + c = r^2 - y^2$

(c) The $p$-discriminant is $y^2 (y^2 - r^2) = 0$

(d) The $p$-discriminant is $y (y - r) = 0$

**30.** Given, $cy = c^2 x + 1$, then

(a) Elimination of $c$ gives $y = \pm 2\sqrt{x}$

(b) Elimination of $c$ gives $y^2 = 4x$

(c) Elimination of $c$ gives $y = 4x$

(d) Elimination of $c$ gives $y = 3x + 2$

**31.** Show that if $S$ is either a rectangle $|x - x_0| \le a, |y - y_0| \le b\ (a, b > 0)$ or strip $|x - x_0| \le a, |y| < \infty\ (a > 0)$ and if $f$ is real valued continuous function defined on $S$ and $\frac{\partial f}{\partial y}$ exist and

also, $\left| \frac{\partial}{\partial y} f(x, y) \right| \le k, (x, y) \in S$ for a positive constant $k$.

(a) $f$ satisfies Lipschitz condition on $S$ with Lipschitz constant $k$

(b) $f$ does not satisfies Lipschitz condition on $S$ with Lipschitz constant $k$

(c) Both (a) and (b) are true

(d) None of the above

**32.** For the equation $\frac{dy}{dx} + 3y = e^{2x}$

(a) Integrating factor is $e^{3x}$

(b) Integrating factor is $\cos x$

(c) Solution of the equation is $y = \frac{1}{5} e^{2x} + Ce^{-3x}$

(d) Solution of the equation is $y = e^x + \frac{1}{x}$

**33.** Given, $y = px \pm \sqrt{(p^2 + m^2)}$, then

(a) The $c$-discriminant is
$$4x^2 y^2 - 4(x^2 - 1)(y^2 - m^2) = 0$$

(b) The $x$-discrimininant is $4xy + 6x^2 + 2y = 0$

(c) The singular solution is $y^2 - m^2 x^2 = m^2$

(d) no singular solution exist

**34.** For the equation $\frac{d^2 v}{dr^2} + \frac{2}{r}\frac{dv}{dr} = 0$

(a) $v = \frac{A}{r} + B$ is a solution of given equation

(b) $v = \frac{A}{r} + B$ is not a solution of given equation

(c) $\frac{dv}{dr} = -\frac{A}{r^2}$ is a solution of given equation

(d) $\frac{dv}{dr} = -\frac{A}{r^2}$ is not a solution of given equation

**35.** The differential equation satisfied by the system of parabolas, $y^2 = 4a(x + a)$ is

(a) $y\left(\frac{dy}{dx}\right)^2 - y + 2x\frac{dy}{dx} = 0$

(b) $y\left(\frac{dy}{dx}\right)^2 + 2x\frac{dy}{dx} - y = 0$

(c) No such equation exist

(d) Differentiating with respect to $x$ we have
$$2y\frac{dy}{dx} = 4a$$

**36.** Given, $\sin x$, $\cos x$, $\sin 2x$, then

(a) the wronskion of given equation is $3 \sin 2x$

(b) the wronskion of given equation is zero

(c) the variables are linearly independent

(d) the variables are linearly dependent

**37.** For Strum-Liouville problem,
$$y'' + \lambda y = 0 \text{ and } y(0) = 0 = y(\pi),\ 0 \le \pi \le \pi.$$

(a) The eigen values of the problem are
$$\lambda = n^2,\ n = 1, 2, \ldots$$

(b) The eigen values of the problem are
$$\lambda = -n,\ n = 1, 2, \ldots$$

(c) The eigen functions are
$$y(x) = \sin nx,\ n = 1, 2, \ldots$$

(d) The eigen functions are
$$y(x) = \cos nx,\ n = -1, -2, \ldots$$

**38.** Given, the initial value problem
$$\frac{dy}{dx} = y^2,\ y(1) = -1, \text{ then}$$

(a) there exist atleast one solution

(b) there does not exist any solution

(c) the initial value problem has no unique solution

(d) the given problem possesses a unique solution when $|x - 1| < \frac{1}{4}$.

**39.** Given,
$$z = a(x + y) + b(x - y) + abt + c, \text{ then}$$

(a) $\frac{\partial z}{\partial x} = a + b$

(b) $\frac{\partial z}{\partial y} = a - b$

(c) $\frac{\partial z}{\partial t} = ab$

(d) Elimination of arbitrary constant given
$$\left(\frac{\partial z}{\partial x}\right)^2 - \left(\frac{\partial z}{\partial y}\right)^2 = 4\frac{\partial z}{\partial t}$$

**40.** Given, one dimensional diffusion equation satisyfing the following boundary condtions, then

I. $T$ is bounded at $t \to \infty$

II. $\left.\frac{\partial T}{\partial x}\right|_{x=0} = 0$ for all $t$

III. $\left.\frac{\partial T}{\partial x}\right|_{x=a} = 0$ for all $t$

IV. $T(x, 0) = x(a - x),\ 0 < x < a$

(a) The possible solution is
$$T(x, t) = \exp(-a\lambda^2 t)(A\cos\lambda x + B\sin\lambda x)$$

(b) $\frac{\partial T}{\partial x} = \exp(-a\lambda^2 t)(-A\lambda\sin\lambda x + B\lambda\cos\lambda x)$

(c) The required solution is
$$T(x, t) = \frac{a^2}{6} - \frac{4a^2}{\pi^2}\sum_{n=2,4,\ldots \text{even}}^{\infty}\frac{1}{n^2}\cos\left(\frac{n\pi}{a}\right)x\exp\left[-\alpha\left(\frac{n\pi}{a}\right)^2 t\right]$$

(d) No solution exist

**41.** Given, $\frac{\partial u}{\partial t} = \alpha^2\frac{\partial^2 u}{\partial x^2}$ subject to

I. $u$ is not infinite for $t \to \infty$

II. $\frac{\partial u}{\partial x} = 0$ for $x = 0$ and $x = l$

III. $u = lx - x^2$ for $t = 0$, between $x = 0$ and $x = l$, then

(a) The general solution is
$$u = a_0 + \Sigma a_n\cos\left(\frac{n\pi x}{l}\right)e^{-n^2\pi^2\alpha^2 t/l^2}$$

(b) No general solution exist

(c) The solution is
$$u = \frac{l^2}{6} - \frac{l^2}{\pi^2}\sum_{m=1}^{\infty}\frac{1}{m^2}\cos\left(\frac{2m\pi x}{l}\right)e^{-4m^2\pi^2\alpha^2 t/l^2}$$

(d) No solution exist

**42.** Given, partial differential equation
$$h\frac{\partial^2}{\partial h^2}(hv) + \frac{\partial}{\partial x}\left\{(1-x)^2\frac{\partial v}{\partial x}\right\} = 0, \text{ then}$$

(a) $(1 - 2xh + h^2)^{-3/2}$ is a solution of given partial differential equation

(b) $(1 - 2xh + h^2)^{-3/2}$ is not a solution of given partial differential equation

(c) Both (a) and (b) are true

(d) None of the above

**43.** Given, the equation
$$u_{xx} + \frac{2N}{x}u_x = \frac{1}{a^2}u_{tt}$$
where $N$ and $a$ are constants, then

(a) The given partial differential equation is hyperbolic

(b) The given partial differential equation is parabolic

(c) The canonical form is
$$\mu_{\xi\eta} + \frac{N}{\xi + \eta}(u_\xi + u_\eta) = 0$$

(d) $\mu_{\xi\eta} = 0$ is the canonical form

**44.** Given, the equation
$$(\sin^2 x)u_{xx} + (\sin 2x)u_{xy} + (\cos^2 x)u_{yy} = x, \text{ then}$$

(a) The equation is parabolic

(b) The equation is hyperbolic

(c) The canonical equation is
$$(\cos^2 x)u_{\eta\eta} + u\xi = x$$

(d) The canonical equation is
$$u_{\eta\eta} = \frac{\sin^{-1}(e^{\eta-\xi}) - u_\xi}{1 - 2^{2(\eta-\xi)}}$$

**45.** The surface passing through the parabolas $u = 0$, $y^2 - 4ax$ and $u = 1$, $y^2 = -4ax$ and satisyfing the equation is
$$x\frac{\partial^2 u}{\partial x^2} + 2\frac{\partial u}{\partial x} = 0$$

(a) $u = -\frac{y^2}{8ax} + \frac{1}{2}$
(b) No such surface exist
(c) $u = -y^2 + \cos x$
(d) $u = y^2\sin x$

**46.** Solving (by the method of separation of variables)
$$\frac{\partial^2 z}{\partial x^2} - 2\frac{\partial z}{\partial x} + \frac{\partial z}{\partial y} = 0$$

(a) If $z = X(x)Y(y)$, then the given equation is
$$X''Y - 2X'Y + XY' = 0$$

(b) If $z = X(x)Y(x)$, then the given equation is
$$X'' + Y'' + XY = 0$$

(c) The solution is
$$z = \{k_1 e^{\{1+\sqrt{1+a}\}x} + k_2 e^{(1-\sqrt{1+a})x}\}e^{-ay}$$

(d) No solution exist

**47.** Given, partial differential equation
$$\frac{\partial\theta}{\partial t} = \alpha\frac{\partial^2\theta}{\partial x^2},\ 0 \le x \le L,\ t > 0$$

Boundary conditions
$$\theta(0, t) = 0,\ t \ge 0, \quad \frac{\partial\theta}{\partial x}(L, t) = 0,\ t > 0$$

Initial conditions
$$\theta(x, 0) = \theta_0,\ 0 \le x \le L, \text{ then}$$

(a) By separation of variable, the possible solution is
$$\theta(x, t) = e^{-a\lambda^2}(A\cos\lambda x + B\sin\lambda x)$$

(b) The required solution is
$$\theta(x, t) = \sum_{n=0}^{\infty}\frac{4\theta_0}{(2n+1)\pi}\exp[-\alpha\{(2n+1)/2L\}^2\pi^2 t]\sin\left(\frac{2n+1}{2L}\pi x\right)$$

(c) No solution exist

(d) Solution exist

**48.** Given, $\frac{\partial u}{\partial x}=2\frac{\partial u}{\partial t}+u$

where $u(x, 0)=6e^{-3x}$, then

(a) $u=6e^{-3x}e^{-2t}$ is a solution

(b) $u=6e^{-(3x+2t)}$ is a solution

(c) No solution exist

(d) Solution exist

**49.** Given, $y=f(x-at)+F(x+at)$, then

(a) $\frac{\partial y}{\partial x}=f'(x-at)+F'(x+at)$

(b) $\frac{\partial y}{dt}=-af'(x-at)+aF'(x+at)$

(c) $\frac{\partial^2 y}{\partial x^2}=\frac{1}{a^2}\frac{\partial^2 y}{\partial t^2}$

(d) Elimination of arbitrary functions gives partial differention equation of second order.

**50.** Given, $y^2u_{xx}-2xy\,u_{xy}+x^2u_{yy}=\frac{y^2}{x}u_x+\frac{x^2}{y}u_y$, then

(a) The canonical equation is $4x^2y^2u_{\eta\eta}=0$

(b) The canonical equation is $u_{\eta\eta}=0$

(c) The solution is $u=y^2f(x^2+y^2)+g(x^2+y^2)$

(d) No solution exist

**51.** Given, the equation

$(1+x^2)u_{xx}+(1+y^2)u_{yy}+xu_x+yu_y=0$, then

(a) The discriminant of the given partial differential equation is $B^2-4AC=-4(1+x^2)(1+y^2)<0$

(b) The given partial differential equation is an elliptic type

(c) The characteristic equation are $\frac{dy}{dx}=\pm i\sqrt{\frac{1+y^2}{1+x^2}}$

(d) Canonical equation for the given partial differential equation is $u_{\alpha\alpha}+u_{\beta\beta}=0$

**52.** Given, partial differential equation $\frac{\partial^2 y}{\partial t^2}=c^2\frac{\partial^2 y}{\partial x^2}$

Boundary conditions $y(0, t)=0=y(l, t)$

Initial conditions $y(x, 0)=0$

$\left(\frac{\partial y}{\partial t}\right)_{t=0}=v_0\sin^3\frac{\pi x}{l}$, then

(a) The general solution of the given equation is $y(x,t)=\sum_{n=1}^{\infty}b_n\sin\frac{n\pi x}{l}\sin\frac{cn\pi t}{l}$

(b) $\frac{\partial y}{\partial t}=\sum_{n=1}^{\infty}b_n\sin\frac{n\pi x}{l}\cdot\frac{cn\pi}{l}\cos\frac{cn\pi t}{l}$

(c) The solution of the given equation is

$$y=\frac{lv_0}{12c\pi}\left(9\sin\frac{\pi x}{l}\sin\frac{c\pi t}{l}-\sin\frac{3\pi x}{l}\sin\frac{3c\pi t}{l}\right)$$

(d) No solution exist

**53.** Given, partial differential equation $\frac{\partial u}{\partial t}=c^2\frac{\partial^2 u}{\partial x^2}$ with boundary condition $\frac{\partial u}{\partial x}(0,t)=0=\frac{\partial u}{\partial x}(l,t), t>0$ and initial conditions $u(x, 0)=x$, $0<x<l$, then

(a) The solution of partial differential equation by method of separation of variable is of the form $u(x,t)=(C_1\cos px+C_2\sin px)e^{c^2p^2t}$

(b) $\frac{\partial u}{\partial x}=(-C_1p\sin px+C_2p\cos px)e^{-c^2p^2t}$

(c) $u(x,t)=\frac{l}{2}-\sum_{n=1,3}^{\infty}\frac{4l}{n^2\pi^2}\cos\frac{n\pi x}{l}e^{-c^2n^2\pi^2t/l^2}$

$=\frac{l}{2}-\frac{4l}{\pi^2}\sum_{1}^{\infty}\frac{1}{(2n-1)^2}\cos\frac{(2n-1)\pi x}{l}e^{-c^2(2n-1)^2\pi^2t/l^2}$

is the required solution

(d) No solution exist

**54.** Given, the partial differential equation with boundary conditions

$$\frac{\partial^2 y}{\partial x^2}+\frac{\partial^2 u}{\partial y^2}=0$$

where $u(0,y)=0=u(\pi,y), y>0$

$u(x,\infty)=0, 0<x<\pi.$

$u(x,0)=u_0, 0<x<\pi$, then

(a) This is the Neumann problem for the rectangle

(b) This is the Neumann problem for the circle

(c) The solution is $u(x,y)=\frac{4u_0}{\pi}\left[e^{-y}\sin x+\frac{1}{3}e^{-3y}\sin 3x+\frac{1}{5}e^{-5y}\sin 5x+\ldots\right]$

(d) No solution exist

**55.** Given, the wave equation $\frac{\partial^2 y}{\partial t^2}=c^2\frac{\partial^2 y}{\partial x^2}$, then

(a) The general solution of the wave equation is $y(x,t)=\phi(x+ct)+\psi(x-ct)$

(b) No general solution exist

(c) The d' Alembert's solution of the given equation is $y(x,t)=f(x+ct)+f(x-ct)$

(d) No d' Alembert's solution exist

**56.** The surface satisfying $\frac{\partial^2 u}{\partial y^2}=\sigma x^3y$ containing two lines $y=0=u$ and $y=1=u$ is

(a) $u=x^3y^3+y(1-x^3)$ (b) No such surface exist

(c) $u=-\frac{y^2}{8ax}+1$ (d) $u=\sin x\cos y$

**57.** Given, the partial differential equation

$$\frac{\partial^2 y}{dt^2}=c^2\frac{\partial^2 y}{dx^2}$$

Boundary conditions $y(0,t)=y(l,t)=0, t>0$

Initial conditions $y(x, 0) = a \sin (px/l)$

$$\left(\frac{\partial y}{\partial t}\right)_{t=0} = 0, \text{ then}$$

(a) A expected solution for the given equation is $y(x, t) = (C_1 \cos px + C_2 \sin px)(C_3 \cos cpt + C_4 \sin cpt)$

(b) The expected solution for the given equation is $y(x, t) = C_2 \sin px\,(C_3 \cos cpt + C_4 \sin cpt)$

(c) Hence, required solution is $y(x, t) = a \sin \frac{\pi x}{l} \cos \frac{\pi ct}{l}$

(d) No solution exist

**58.** Given, the one-dimensional diffusion equation in the region $0 \le x \le \pi$, $t \ge 0$, subject to the conditions

I. $T$ is finite as $t \to \infty$.

II. $T = 0$, if $x = 0$ and $\pi$ for all $t$.

III. At $t = 0$, $T = \begin{cases} x, & 0 \le x \le \pi/2 \\ \pi - x, & \frac{\pi}{2} \le x \le \pi \end{cases}$

then

(a) The solution is of the form $T(x, t) = ce^{-\alpha n^2 t} \sin nx$

(b) The solution is a heat conduction equation

(c) The solution is $T(x, t) = \frac{4}{\pi} \sum_{n=1}^{\infty} \frac{e^{-\alpha n^2 t} \sin (n\pi/2)}{n^2} \sin nx.$

(d) No solution exists

# Answers

## Exercise 1

| | | | | | | | | | |
|---|---|---|---|---|---|---|---|---|---|
| **1.** (b) | **2.** (b) | **3.** (a) | **4.** (a) | **5.** (c) | **6.** (a) | **7.** (c) | **8.** (a) | **9.** (a) | **10.** (a) |
| **11.** (d) | **12.** (c) | **13.** (d) | **14.** (b) | **15.** (a) | **16.** (a) | **17.** (a) | **18.** (a) | **19.** (a) | **20.** (a) |
| **21.** (c) | **22.** (a) | **23.** (a) | **24.** (a) | **25.** (a) | **26.** (c) | **27.** (a) | **28.** (b) | **29.** (b) | **30.** (a) |
| **31.** (a) | **32.** (b) | **33.** (a) | **34.** (c) | **35.** (a) | **36.** (b) | **37.** (c) | **38.** (a) | **39.** (a) | **40.** (a) |
| **41.** (c) | **42.** (b) | **43.** (a) | **44.** (c) | **45.** (a) | **46.** (b) | **47.** (a) | **48.** (a) | **49.** (a) | **50.** (b) |
| **51.** (b) | **52.** (b) | **53.** (c) | **54.** (a) | **55.** (c) | **56.** (b) | **57.** (b) | **58.** (b) | **59.** (c) | **60.** (b) |
| **61.** (a) | **62.** (b) | **63.** (a) | **64.** (b) | **65.** (c) | **66.** (a) | **67.** (b) | **68.** (d) | **69.** (a) | **70.** (c) |
| **71.** (c) | **72.** (b) | **73.** (b) | **74.** (d) | **75.** (b) | **76.** (c) | **77.** (c) | **78.** (d) | **79.** (a) | **80.** (c) |
| **81.** (c) | **82.** (c) | **83.** (a) | **84.** (d) | **85.** (d) | **86.** (a) | **87.** (b) | **88.** (b) | **89.** (a) | **90.** (a) |
| **91.** (a) | **92.** (d) | **93.** (c) | **94.** (a) | **95.** (d) | **96.** (c) | **97.** (b) | **98.** (d) | **99.** (d) | **100.** (a) |
| **101.** (c) | **102.** (a) | **103.** (b) | **104.** (a) | **105.** (d) | **106.** (a) | **107.** (a) | **108.** (c) | **109.** (b) | **110.** (b) |
| **111.** (c) | **112.** (d) | **113.** (a) | **114.** (b) | **115.** (b) | **116.** (a) | **117.** (c) | **118.** (a) | **119.** (c) | **120.** (d) |
| **121.** (a) | **122.** (b) | **123.** (a) | **124.** (a) | **125.** (b) | **126.** (a) | **127.** (b) | **128.** (a) | **129.** (b) | **130.** (c) |
| **131.** (a) | **132.** (c) | **133.** (a) | **134.** (b) | **135.** (a) | **136.** (b) | **137.** (a) | **138.** (a) | **139.** (b) | **140.** (b) |
| **141.** (a) | **142.** (b) | **143.** (a) | **144.** (b) | **145.** (a) | **146.** (a) | **147.** (c) | **148.** (c) | **149.** (b) | **150.** (a) |
| **151.** (c) | **152.** (a) | **153.** (c) | **154.** (c) | **155.** (c) | **156.** (c) | **157.** (b) | **158.** (b) | **159.** (c) | **160.** (a) |
| **161.** (a) | **162.** (c) | **163.** (b) | **164.** (a) | **165.** (a) | **166.** (c) | **167.** (d) | **168.** (d) | **169.** (a) | **170.** (c) |
| **171.** (c) | **172.** (b) | **173.** (c) | **174.** (a) | **175.** (c) | **176.** (c) | **177.** (d) | **178.** (c) | **179.** (a) | **180.** (d) |
| **181.** (c) | **182.** (d) | **183.** (c) | **184.** (a) | **185.** (c) | **186.** (c) | **187.** (a) | **188.** (b) | **189.** (a) | **190.** (b) |
| **191.** (a) | **192.** (b) | **193.** (a) | **194.** (b) | **195.** (a) | **196.** (a) | **197.** (b) | **198.** (a) | **199.** (b) | **200.** (d) |
| **201.** (b) | **202.** (b) | **203.** (a) | **204.** (d) | **205.** (a) | **206.** (d) | **207.** (c) | **208.** (a) | **209.** (c) | **210.** (c) |
| **211.** (d) | **212.** (d) | **213.** (d) | **214.** (b) | **215.** (b) | **216.** (b) | **217.** (c) | **218.** (c) | **219.** (d) | **220.** (d) |
| **221.** (c) | **222.** (a) | **223.** (b) | **224.** (d) | **225.** (b) | **226.** (a) | **227.** (d) | **228.** (c) | **229.** (a) | **230.** (a) |
| **231.** (c) | **232.** (a) | **233.** (a) | **234.** (c) | **235.** (c) | **236.** (d) | **237.** (a) | **238.** (d) | **239.** (a) | **240.** (a) |
| **241.** (c) | **242.** (d) | **243.** (a) | **244.** (a) | **245.** (d) | **246.** (a) | **247.** (a) | **248.** (b) | **249.** (b) | **250.** (b) |
| **251.** (c) | **252.** (d) | **253.** (c) | **254.** (a) | **255.** (a) | **256.** (b) | **257.** (d) | **258.** (c) | **259.** (b) | **260.** (b) |
| **261.** (a) | **262.** (a) | **263.** (b) | **264.** (d) | **265.** (a) | **266.** (d) | **267.** (c) | **268.** (c) | **269.** (a) | **270.** (a) |
| **271.** (a) | **272.** (b) | **273.** (a) | **274.** (a) | **275.** (d) | **276.** (b) | **277.** (a) | **278.** (a) | **279.** (c) | **280.** (d) |
| **281.** (b) | **282.** (b) | **283.** (c) | **284.** (c) | **285.** (a) | **286.** (b) | **287.** (a) | **288.** (a) | **289.** (b) | **290.** (c) |
| **291.** (b) | **292.** (a) | | | | | | | | |

## Exercise 2

1. (b,d) 2. (b,c) 3. (b,d) 4. (c,d) 5. (b,c) 6. (a,b,d) 7. (a,c,d) 8. (a,b,d) 9. (a,b) 10. (a,d)
11. (a,b,c) 12. (c,d) 13. (a,d) 14. (b,c) 15. (a,d) 16. (b,d) 17. (a,b,d) 18. (a,b,c,d) 19. (a,b,d) 20. (a,b,c,d)
21. (a,b,c,d) 22. (a,b,d) 23. (a,b,d) 24. (a,b,d) 25. (a,d) 26. (a,c) 27. (b,d) 28. (a,c) 29. (a,c) 30. (a,b)
31. (a) 32. (a,c) 33. (a,c) 34. (a,c) 35. (a,b,d) 36. (a,c) 37. (a,c) 38. (a,d) 39. (a,b,c,d) 40. (a,b,c)
41. (a,c) 42. (a) 43. (a,c) 44. (a,d) 45. (a) 46. (a,c) 47. (a,b,d) 48. (a,b,d) 49. (a,b,c,d) 50. (a,b,d)
51. (a,b,c,d) 52. (a,b,c) 53. (a,b,c) 54. (a,c) 55. (a,c) 56. (a) 57. (a,b,c) 58. (a,b,c)

# Hints & Solutions

## Exercise 1

**1.** The c-discriminant equated to zero may include the envelope ($E$) once, the cusp-locus ($C$) thrice and nodal locus ($N$) twice

$$\Rightarrow \quad EC^3N^2$$

**3.** The $p$-discriminant equated to zero may include the envelope ($E$) once, the cusp-locus ($C$) once and tac-locus ($T$) twice

$$\Rightarrow \quad ECT^2$$

**4.** Given, equation is

$$(y-c)^2 = x(x-a)^2$$
$$\Rightarrow \quad y^2+c^2-2cy = x(x-a)^2$$
$$\Rightarrow \quad c^2-2cy+y^2-x(x-a)^2=0$$
$$c\text{-discriminant} = 0$$
$$\Rightarrow \quad 4y^2-4[y^2-x(x-a)^2]=0$$
$$\Rightarrow \quad 4x(x-a)^2=0$$
$$\Rightarrow \quad x(x-a)^2=0$$

**5.** Given, equation is

$$y = px+\frac{1}{p}$$
$$\Rightarrow \quad p^2x-py+1=0$$
$$p\text{-discriminant} = 0$$
$$\Rightarrow \quad (-y)^2-4\cdot x\cdot 1=0$$
$$\Rightarrow \quad y^2=4x$$

**17.** Here, AE is $\quad m^2+m-2=0$

$$\Rightarrow \quad m^2+2m-m-2=0$$
$$\Rightarrow \quad m(m+2)-(m-2)=0$$
$$\Rightarrow \quad (m+2)(m-1)=0$$
$$\Rightarrow \quad m=-2,\ m=1$$

Hence General solution is $y = C_1e^{-2x}+C_2e^{x}$

**20.** We have $\quad \text{IF} = e^{\int 2x\,dx} = e^{x^2}$

Hence, solution is

$$ye^{x^2} = \int 2e^{-x^2}e^{x^2}\,dx = 2\int dx$$
$$\Rightarrow \quad ye^{x^2} = 2x+C$$
$$\Rightarrow \quad y=(2x+C)e^{-x^2}$$

**49.** AE for given differential equation is

$$m^2-2m+1=0$$
$$\Rightarrow \quad (m-1)^2=0 \Rightarrow m=1,1$$

Hence, CF is $\quad y_c=(C_1+xC_2)e^x$

$$\Rightarrow \quad y_1=e^x,\ y_2=xe^x$$

are two linearly independent solutions of given differential equation.

Now, $\quad W(y_1,y_2)=\begin{vmatrix} y_1 & y_2 \\ y_1' & y_2' \end{vmatrix} = \begin{vmatrix} e^x & xe^x \\ e^x & xe^x+e^x \end{vmatrix}$

$$= xe^{2x}+e^{2x}-xe^{2x}=e^{2x}$$

**56.** We have $\text{PI} = \dfrac{1}{D^3+1}\cos(2x-1)$

$$= \frac{1}{D(-2^2)+1}\cos(2x-1) = \frac{1}{-4D+1}\cos(2x-1)$$
$$= \frac{1+4D}{1-16D^2}\cos(2x-1) = \frac{1+4D}{1-16(-2)^2}\cos(2x-1)$$
$$= \frac{1}{65}[\cos(2x-1)+4D\cos(2x-1)]$$
$$= \frac{1}{65}[\cos(2x-1)-8\sin(2x-1)]$$

**64.** We have $\text{PI} = \dfrac{1}{D^2+6D+9}50e^{2x} = \dfrac{50e^{2x}}{2^2+6\times 2+9} = 2e^{2x}$

**70.** We have $W(y_1,y_2)=\begin{vmatrix} y_1(0) & y_2(0) \\ y_1'(0) & y_2'(0) \end{vmatrix} = \begin{vmatrix} 0 & 1 \\ 1 & 1 \end{vmatrix} = -1$

**82.** Lagrange's auxiliary equation is

$$\frac{dx}{e^y}=\frac{dy}{-e^x}=\frac{dz}{0}$$

From first two members, we get

$$e^xdx+e^ydy=0 \Rightarrow e^x+e^y=C_1$$

By using $\dfrac{dz}{0}$, we get $\quad z=C_2$

Hence, required solution is $f(e^x+e^y, z)=0$

or $\quad z=\phi(e^x+e^y)$

**84.** Differential equation can be written as

$$(D^2 - D'^2 + D - D')z = 0$$

AE is $D^2 - D'^2 + D - D' = 0$

$\Rightarrow$ $(D - D')(D + D' + 1) = 0$

**88.** $z = (x + a)(y + b)$

$\Rightarrow$ $\frac{\partial z}{\partial x} = (y + b), \quad \frac{\partial z}{\partial y} = (x + a)$

$\Rightarrow$ $p = (y + b), \quad q = (x + a)$

**89.** Here, AE is $m^2 + 1 = 0$

$\Rightarrow$ $m = \pm i$

Hence, General solution is

$$u = f(x + iy) + g(x - iy)$$

**95.** Hre, AE is $m^2 - 5m + 4 = 0$

$\Rightarrow$ $(m - 1)(m - 4) = 0 \Rightarrow m = 1, 4$

$$CF = f_1(y + x) + f_2(y + 4x)$$

and $\quad PI = -\frac{x}{3}\cos(4x + 3)$

**109.** PDE is $r - 4s + 4t = 0$

Hence, AE is $m^2 - 4m + 4 = 0$

$\Rightarrow$ $(m - 2)^2 = 0 \Rightarrow m = 2, 2$

Hence, General solution is $z = \phi_1(y + 2x) + x\phi_2(y + 2x)$

As per given options, option (b) is written as function of $(y + 2x)$.

**112.** Euler's equation

$$x\frac{\partial u}{\partial x} + y\frac{\partial u}{\partial y} = nu$$

**126.** We have $S^2 - 4RT = 4 - 4 \times 4 = 4 - 16 = -12 < 0$

**127.** Here, $|A| \neq 0$ and coefficients are with positive and negative signs.

## Exercise 2

**1.** Since, $y_1(x_0) = y_2(x_0) = 0$

$\Rightarrow$ $W(y_1, y_2) = 0$

$\Rightarrow$ $y_1$ and $y_2$ are linearly dependent.

**2.** Since, $y_1$ and $y_2$ are two linearly independent solutions of given differential equation.

$\Rightarrow$ They cannot have a common zero.

Assuming $y_1(x) > 0$ where $x \in (x_1, x_2)$

where, $y_1(x_1) = y_1(x_2) = 0$ on $[a, b]$

and $y_1'(x_1) > 0$ and $y_1'(x_2) < 0$

We may assume $y_2(x_1) > 0$

**9.** $$G(x, t) = \begin{cases} -\dfrac{y_1(x)y_2(t)}{c} & x < t \\ -\dfrac{y_2(x)y_1(t)}{c} & x > t \end{cases}$$

Where, $c = p(t)W[y_1(t), y_2(t)]$

**14.** Here, AE is $m^2 - 2m + 1 = 0$

$\Rightarrow$ $m = 1, 1$

$CF = \phi_1(y + x) + x\phi_2(y + x)$

and $\quad PI = \frac{1}{D^2 - 2DD' + D'^2}\cos(2x + 3y)$

(using $D^2 = -2^2, DD' = -2 \times 3, D'^2 = -3^2$)

$= -\cos(2x + 3y)$

**22.** $\frac{dy}{y} = 2x\,dx$

$\Rightarrow$ $\log y = x^2 + \log a$

$\Rightarrow$ $y = a e^{x^2}$

**23.** $\frac{dx}{dt} = -pA\sin(pt - \alpha)$

$$\frac{d^2x}{dt^2} = -p^2 A\cos(pt - \alpha) = -p^2 x$$

$$\frac{d^3x}{dt^3} = -p^2\frac{dx}{dt}$$

$\Rightarrow$ $\frac{d^3x}{dt^3} / \frac{dx}{dt} = -p^2 = \frac{d^2x}{dt^2} / x$

$\Rightarrow$ $x\frac{d^3x}{dt^3} = \frac{dx}{dt} \cdot \frac{d^2x}{dt^2}$

**24.** $\log x = -\log\cos y + c$

$\Rightarrow$ $\log(x\cos y) = c$

$\Rightarrow$ $x\cos y = e^c = a$ (say)

**25.** Auxiliary equation is

$$m^2 - 6m + 13 = 0$$

$\Rightarrow$ $m = 3 \pm 2i$

Hence, General solution is

$$y = Ae^{(3 + 2i)x} + Be^{(3 - 2i)x}$$

**26.** We have $(D^2 - 2D + 4)y = 50e^{2x}$

$\Rightarrow$ $(D - 2)^2 y = 50e^{2x}$

AE $\quad (m - 2)^2 = 0 \Rightarrow m = +2, +2$

CF $\quad y = (A + Bx)e^{2x}$

PI $\quad \frac{1}{(D - 2)^2} \cdot 50e^{2x} = 50e^{2x}, \frac{1}{D^2} = 50e^{2x} \cdot \frac{1}{2}x^2 = 25x^2 e^{2x}$

Hence, General solution $y = 25x^2e^{2x} + (A + Bx)e^{2x}$

**27.** Here, $f(x, y) = y^{2/3}$ is continuous but

$$\left|\frac{\partial}{\partial y} f(x, y)\right| = \left|\frac{2}{3y^{1/3}}\right| \nleq k > 0$$

for $y = 0$ which is a point of the rectangle.

Hence, Lipschitz condition is not satisfied on the rectangle.

**28.** Given, $f(x, y) = xy^2$ and $\left|\frac{\partial}{\partial y} f(x, y)\right| = |2xy| \leq 2$ for $(x, y)$ on rectangle $|x| \leq 1, |y| \leq 1$.

Hence, $\frac{\partial f}{\partial y}$ exists and is continuous and bounded in the rectangle $|x| \leq 1, |y| \leq 1$

Thus, Lipschitz condition is satisfied on

$$|x| \le 1, |y| \le 1.$$

On strip $|x| \le 1, |y| < \infty$, there does not exist any positive constant $k > 0$, such that

$$\left|\frac{\partial}{\partial y} f(x, y)\right| = |2xy| \le k$$

Hence, Lipschitz condition not satisfied.

**29.** We have $(x + c)^2 + y^2 = r^2$

$$\Rightarrow \quad x + c = \pm\sqrt{r^2 - y^2}$$

or $$1 = \mp yp/\sqrt{r^2 - y^2}$$

$$\Rightarrow \quad y^2p^2 + y^2 - r^2 = 0$$

The $p$-discriminant of $y^2p^2 + y^2 - r^2 = 0$ is

$$0 - 4(y^2)(y^2 - r^2) = 0$$

$$\Rightarrow \quad 4y^2(y^2 - r^2) = 0$$

$$\Rightarrow \quad y^2(y^2 - r^2) = 0$$

**30.** We have $f(x, y, c) = 0$

$$\Rightarrow \quad cy = c^2x + 1 = 0$$

$$\Rightarrow \quad y - cx - \frac{1}{c} = 0 \quad \ldots(i)$$

and $$\frac{\partial f}{\partial c} = 0$$

$$\Rightarrow \quad -x + \frac{1}{c^2} = 0$$

$$\Rightarrow \quad c = \pm\frac{1}{\sqrt{x}} \quad \ldots(ii)$$

Substituting $c$ in Eq. (i), gives

$$y = \pm 2\sqrt{x}$$

or $$y^2 = 4x$$

**31.** By fundamental theorem of calculus,

$$f(x, y_2) - f(x, y_1) = \int_{y_1}^{y_2} \frac{\partial}{\partial y} f(x, y)\, dy$$

$$\Rightarrow \quad |f(x, y_2) - f(x, y_1)| = \left|\int_{y_1}^{y_2} \frac{\partial}{\partial y} f(x, y)\, dy\right|$$

$$\le \int_{y_1}^{y_2} \left|\frac{\partial}{\partial y} f(x, y)\right| |dy|$$

$$\le k\int_{y_1}^{y_2} |dy|$$

$$\Rightarrow \quad |f(x, y_2) - f(x, y_1)| \le k|y_2 - y_1|$$

for all $(x, y_1), (x, y_2) \in S$

$\Rightarrow$ $f(x, y)$ satisfy Lipschitz condition on $S$, where $k$ is Lipschitz constant.

**32.** We have $\int p\,dx = 3x$

Hence, integrating factor is $e^{3x}$

$$\Rightarrow \quad e^{3x}\frac{dy}{dx} + 3e^{3x}y = e^{5x}$$

$$\Rightarrow \quad \frac{d}{dx}(ye^{3x}) = e^{5x}$$

$$\Rightarrow \quad ye^{3x} = \frac{1}{5}e^{5x} + C$$

$$\Rightarrow \quad y = \frac{1}{5}e^{2x} + Ce^{-3x}$$

**33.** The Clairaut's form

$$y = px + f(p)$$

$$\Rightarrow \quad y = cx \pm \sqrt{(c^2 + m^2)}$$

$$\Rightarrow \quad (y^2 - cx)^2 = (c^2 + m^2)$$

$$\Rightarrow \quad c^2(x^2 - 1) - 2xyc + (y^2 - m^2) = 0$$

The $c$-discriminant is

$$4x^2y^2 - 4(x^2 - 1)(y^2 - m^2) = 0$$

$$\Rightarrow \quad y^2 - m^2x^2 = m^2$$

which is the singular solution.

**34.** Differentiating $v = \frac{A}{r} + B$ twice with respect to $r$

$$\frac{dv}{dr} = -\frac{A}{r^2}$$

and $$\frac{d^2v}{dr^2} = \frac{2A}{r^3}$$

Hence, $$\left(\frac{d^2v}{dr^2}\right) \Big/ \left(\frac{dv}{dr}\right) = \frac{2A}{r^3} \times \frac{r^2}{-A} = \frac{-2}{r}$$

$$\Rightarrow \quad \frac{d^2v}{dr^2} = -\frac{2}{r}\frac{dv}{dr}$$

$$\Rightarrow \quad \frac{d^2v}{dr^2} + \frac{2}{r}\cdot\frac{dv}{dr} = 0$$

**35.** Differentiating

$$y^2 = 4a(x + a) \quad \ldots(i)$$

With respect to $x$, we get

$$2y\frac{dy}{dx} = 4a \quad \ldots(ii)$$

Dividing Eq. (i) by Eq. (ii), we get

$$\frac{y^2}{2\left(\frac{dy}{dx}\right)} = x + a$$

$$\Rightarrow \quad a = \frac{y^2}{2\left(\frac{dy}{dx}\right)} - x$$

Substituting this value of 'a' in Eq. (ii), a is eliminated and we get

$$y\left(\frac{dy}{dx}\right) = 2\left(\frac{y}{2\left(\frac{dy}{dx}\right)} - x\right)$$

$$\Rightarrow \quad y\left(\frac{dy}{dx}\right)^2 - y + 2x\frac{dy}{dx} = 0$$

$$\Rightarrow \quad y\left(\frac{dy}{dx}\right)^2 + 2x\frac{dy}{dx} - y = 0$$

**36.** The Wronskion of the given variables, is

$$W(x)=\begin{vmatrix} \sin x & \cos x & \sin 2x \\ \cos x & -\sin x & 2\cos 2x \\ -\sin x & -\cos x & -4\sin 2x \end{vmatrix}$$

$$=\sin x\begin{vmatrix} -\sin x & 2\cos 2x \\ -\cos x & -4\sin 2x \end{vmatrix} - \cos x\begin{vmatrix} \cos x & \sin 2x \\ -\cos x & -4\sin 2x \end{vmatrix} - \sin x\begin{vmatrix} \cos x & \sin 2x \\ -\sin x & -2\cos 2x \end{vmatrix}$$

$$=\sin x\,(4\sin 2x\sin x + 2\cos 2x\cos x)$$
$$-\cos x\,(-4\sin 2x\cos x + \sin 2x\cos x)$$
$$-\sin x\,(2\cos x\cos 2x + \sin x\sin 2x)$$
$$=3\sin^2 x\sin 2x + 3\cos^2 x\sin 2x + 2\sin x\cos x\cos 2x$$
$$-2\sin 2x\cos x\cos 2x$$
$$=3\sin 2x \neq 0$$

Since, the Wronskion is not zero; they are linear independent.

**37.** Here, $r=1, q=0, p=1$ in Sturm-Liouville equation

$$a=0,\ b=\pi,\ k_1=l_1=1 \text{ and } k_2=l_2=0$$

For negative $\lambda=-n^2$, a general solution of the equation is $y(x)=C_1e^{px}+C_2e^{-px}$ using condition $y(0)=0=y(\pi)$ $C_1=C_2=0$. Hence, $y\equiv 0$ is not an eigen function.

For $\lambda=+n^2$, the general solution is

$$y(x)=A\cos nx + B\sin nx$$
$$y(0)=0 \text{ gives } A=0$$

and $\quad y(\pi)=B\sin n\pi=0 \Rightarrow n=0,\pm 1,\pm 2,\ldots$

For $\quad n=0$ we have $y\equiv 0$

For $\quad \lambda=n^2=1, 4, 9, 16, \ldots$ and $B=1$

We have $y(x)=\sin nx$

Hence, the eigen values of the problem are $\lambda=n^2, n=1, 2\ldots$ and corresponding eigen functions are $y(x)=\sin nx$.

**38. The existence** Given,

$$f(x,y)=\frac{dy}{dx}=y^2 \text{ and } y(1)=-1$$

Here, $\frac{\partial f}{\partial x}=2y$, so $f$ and $\frac{\partial f}{\partial y}$ are both continuous for all $(x, y)$.

Consider the rectangle $R: |x-1|<a, |y+1|\leq b$ about $(1,-1)$.

Then, $|f(x, y_2)-f(x, y_1)|$

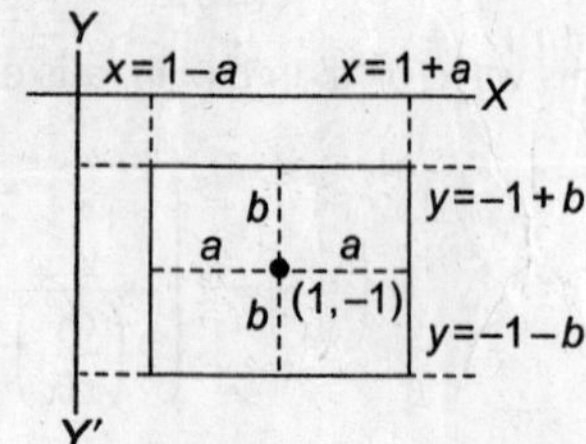


$$=|y_2^2-y_1^2|$$
$$=|y_2+y_1||y_2-y_1|$$
$$\leq (2+2b)|y_2-y_1|$$

and Lipschitz condition is satisfied in the rectangle $R$.

Thus, by existence theorem, there exist atleast one solution.

**To uniqueness** Now, let

$$M=\max|f(x,y)| \text{ for } x, y\in R \text{ and}$$
$$m=\min(a, b/M)$$

then $\quad M=\max|f(x,y)^2|$
$$=\max|y^2|$$
$$=|(-1-b)^2|$$
$$=(1+b)^2$$

and $\quad m=\min(a, b/M)$
$$=\min\left\{a, \frac{b}{(1+b)^2}\right\}$$

For maximum or minimum of

$$\frac{b}{(1+b)^2}=\phi(b)$$

$$\phi'(b)=\frac{1-b}{(1+b)^3} \text{ and } \phi''(b)=\frac{2b-4}{(1+b)^4}$$

$\Rightarrow$ when $b=1$, $\phi'(1)=0$ and $\phi''(1)=\frac{-2}{2^4}<0$.

Hence, $\phi(b)$ is max at $b=1$ and $\phi(1)=\frac{1}{4}$

$\therefore$ If $\quad a<\frac{1}{4}, m<\frac{1}{4}$

If $\quad a\geq\frac{1}{4}, m\leq\frac{1}{4}$

and thus $\quad m=\min\left(a, \frac{b}{M}\right)$
$$=\min\left\{a, \frac{1}{4}\right\}=\frac{1}{4} \text{ for } b=1$$

Hence, the given problem possesses a unique solution $|x-1|<\frac{1}{4}$.

**39.** We have $\frac{\partial z}{\partial x}=a+b$

$$\frac{\partial z}{\partial y}=a-b$$
$$\frac{\partial z}{\partial t}=ab$$

Since, $\quad (a+b)^2-(a-b)^2=4ab$

Hence, $\quad \left(\frac{\partial z}{\partial x}\right)^2-\left(\frac{\partial z}{\partial y}\right)^2=4\frac{\partial z}{\partial t}$

**40.** The possible solution is

$$T(x,t)=\exp(-a\lambda^2 t)(A\cos\lambda x + B\sin\lambda x)$$

and $\quad \frac{\partial T}{\partial x}=\exp(-a\lambda^2 t)(-A\lambda\sin\lambda x + B\lambda\cos\lambda x) \quad \ldots\text{(i)}$

Using boundary conditions II, Eq. (i) gives $B=0$ and boundary condtions III into Eq. (i) gives

$$\sin\lambda a=0 \text{ implying } \lambda a=n\pi,\ \pi=0, 1, 2, \ldots$$

By the principle of superposition, we have

$$T(x,t)=\Sigma A_n\exp(-a\lambda^2 t)\cos\lambda x$$
$$=\sum_{n=0}^{\infty} A_n\exp\left[-\alpha\left(\frac{n\pi}{\alpha}\right)^2 t\right]\cos\left(\frac{n\pi}{\alpha}\right)x$$

The boundary condtion IV gives

$$T(x, 0) = x(a - x)$$

$$= A_0 + \sum_{n=1}^{\infty} A_n \exp\left[-\alpha\left(\frac{n\pi}{a}\right)^2 t\right]\cos\left(\frac{n\pi}{a}\right)x$$

where $A_0 = \frac{2}{a}\int_0^a (ax - x^2)\,dx = \frac{a^2}{6}$

$$A_n = \frac{2}{a}\int_0^a (ax - x)^2 \cos\left(\frac{n\pi}{\alpha}x\right)dx$$

$$= \frac{2a^2}{n^2\pi^2}(1 + \cos n\pi) = \frac{2a^2}{n^2\pi^2}[1 + (-1)^n]$$

Hence, $A_n = \begin{cases} -\frac{4a^2}{n^2\pi^2}, & \text{for } n \text{ even} \\ 0, & \text{for } n \text{ odd} \end{cases}$

The required solution is

$$T(x, t) = \frac{a^2}{6} - \frac{4a^2}{\pi^2}\sum_{n=2,4\ldots\text{even}}^{\infty}\frac{1}{n^2}$$

$$\cos\left(\frac{n\pi}{a}\right)x \exp\left[-\alpha\left(\frac{nx}{a}\right)^2 t\right]$$

**41.** Let $u = X(x)T(t)$, we have partial differential equation

$$XT' = \alpha^2 X'' T \text{ i.e., } \frac{X''}{X} = \frac{T'}{\alpha^2 T} = -k^2$$

Hence, $\frac{d^2X}{dx^2} + k^2 X = 0$ and $\frac{dT}{dt} + k^2\alpha^2 T = 0$ ...(i)

which gives $X = C_1 \cos kx + C_2 \sin kx$,

$$T = C_3 e^{-k^2\alpha^2 t} \quad \text{...(ii)}$$

If $k^2$ is changed to $-k^2$, we have

$$X = C_4 e^{kx} + C_5 e^{-kx}$$

$$T = C_6 e^{k^2\alpha^2 t} \quad \text{...(iii)}$$

If $k^2 = 0, X = C_7 x + C_8, T = C_9$ ...(iv)

In Eq. (iii), $T \to \infty$ for $t \to \infty$, therefore, $u$ also $\to \infty$ i.e., the given condition I is not satisfied, so Eq. (iii) is not a solution.

Applying the condition II to IV, we get

$$C_7 = 0$$

Hence, $u = XT = C_8 C_9 = a_0$ (say) ...(v)

From Eq. (ii),

$$\frac{\partial u}{\partial x} = (-C_1 \sin kx + C_2 \cos kx)\,kC_3\, e^{-k^2\alpha^2 t}$$

Applying the condition II, we get $C_2 = 0$ and

$$-C_1 \sin kl + C_2 \cos kl = 0$$

i.e., $C_2 = 0$ and $kl = n\pi$ (n is integer)

Since, $u = C_1 \cos kx \cdot C_3\, e^{-k^2\alpha^2 t}$

$$= a_n \cos\left(\frac{n\pi x}{l}\right)\frac{e^{-n^2\pi^2\alpha^2 t}}{l^2} \quad \text{...(vi)}$$

Thus, the general solution being the sum of Eqs. (v) and (vi), is

$$u = a_0 + \Sigma a_n \cos(n\pi l/l)\, e^{-n^2\pi^2\alpha^2 t/l^2} \quad \text{...(vii)}$$

Now, using the condition III, we get

$$lx - x^2 = a_0 + \Sigma a_n \cos\left(\frac{n\pi x}{l}\right)$$

This being the expansion of $lx - x^2$ as a half-range cosine series in $(0, l)$, we get

$$a_0 = \frac{1}{l}\int_0^l (lx - x^2)\,dx$$

$$= \frac{1}{l}\left|\frac{lx^2}{2} - \frac{x^3}{3}\right|_0^l = \frac{l^2}{6}$$

and $a_n = \frac{2}{l}\int_0^l (lx - x^2)\cos\frac{n\pi x}{l}\,dx$

$$= \frac{2}{l}\left[(lx - x^2)\left(\frac{l}{n\pi}\sin\frac{n\pi x}{l}\right) - (l - 2x)\right.$$

$$\left.\left(-\frac{l^2}{n^2\pi^2}\cos\frac{n\pi x}{l}\right) + (-2)\left(-\frac{l^3}{n^3\pi^3}\sin\frac{n\pi x}{l}\right)\right]_0^l$$

$$= \frac{2}{l}\left\{0 - \frac{l^3}{n^2\pi^2}(\cos n\pi + 1) + 0\right\}$$

$$a_n = \begin{cases} -\frac{4l^2}{n^2\pi^2}, & \text{if } n \text{ is even} \\ 0, & \text{if } n \text{ is odd} \end{cases}$$

Hence, taking $n = 2m$, the required solution is

$$u = \frac{l^2}{6} - \frac{l^2}{\pi^2}\sum_{m=1}^{\infty}\frac{1}{m^2}\cos\left(\frac{2m\pi x}{l}\right)e^{-4m^2\pi^2\alpha^2 t/l^2}$$

**42.** Since, we have

$$(1 - 2xh + h^2)^{-3/2} = \sum_{n=0}^{\infty} h^n P_n(x) = v \text{ (say)}$$

then $vh = \sum_{n=0}^{\infty} h^{n+1} P_n(x)$

$$\Rightarrow \quad h\frac{\partial^2}{\partial h^2}(vh) - \sum_{n=0}^{\infty}(n+1)nh^n P_n(x) \quad \text{...(i)}$$

and $\frac{\partial v}{\partial x} = \sum_{n=0}^{\infty} h^n P_n'(x)$

Hence, $\frac{\partial}{\partial x}\left\{(1 - x^2)\frac{\partial v}{\partial x}\right\} = \frac{\partial}{\partial x}\left\{(1 - x^2)\sum_{n=0}^{\infty} h^n P'_n(x)\right\}$

$$= (1 - x^2)\sum_{n=0}^{\infty} h^n P_n''(x) - 2x\sum_{n=0}^{\infty} h^n P_n'(x) \quad \text{...(ii)}$$

By adding Eqs. (i) and (ii), we get

$$h\frac{\partial^2}{\partial h^2}(hv) + \frac{\partial}{\partial x}\left\{(1 - x^2)\frac{\partial v}{\partial x}\right\}$$

$$= \sum_{n=0}^{\infty}(n+1)nh^n P_n(x)$$

$$+ (1 - x^2)\sum_{n=0}^{\infty} h^n P_n''(x) - 2x\sum_{n=0}^{\infty} h^n P_n'(x)$$

$$= \sum_{n=0}^{\infty} h^n\{(1 - x^2)P_n''(x) - 2xP_n'(x) + n(n+1)P_n(x)\}$$

$$= 0$$

Hence, $P_n(x)$ is the solution of Ledendre's equation.

**43.** Comparing with the general partial differential equation here $A = 1$, $B = 0$, $C = -\frac{1}{a^2}$, $D = \frac{2N}{x}$ and $E = F = G = 0$.

The discriminant $B^2 - 4AC = \frac{4}{a^2} > 0$.

Hence, the given partial differential equation is hyperbolic. The characteristic equations are

$$\frac{dt}{dx}=\frac{B\mp\sqrt{B^2-4AC}}{2A}=\mp\frac{\sqrt{4/a^2}}{2}$$

$$=\mp\frac{1}{a}$$

Hence, $\frac{dt}{dx}=-\frac{1}{a}$ and $\frac{dt}{dx}=\frac{1}{a}$

Integration gives,

$$t=-\frac{x}{a}+C_1 \text{ and } t=\frac{x}{a}+C_2$$

Here, the characteristic equations are

$$\xi=x+at \text{ and } \eta=x-at$$

$$\Rightarrow \quad 2x=\xi+\eta$$

To obtain, canonical form, computing

$$\bar{A}=A\xi_x^2+B\xi_x\xi_t+C\xi_t^2=0$$

$$\bar{B}=2A\xi_x\eta_x+B(\xi_x\eta_t+\xi_t\eta_x)+2C\xi_t\eta_t=4$$

$$\bar{C}=0,\ \bar{D}=D\xi_x+E\xi_t=\frac{2N}{x}$$

$$\bar{E}=D\eta_x+E\eta_t=\frac{2N}{x}$$

The canonical equation for the given PDE is

$$4u_{\xi\eta}+\frac{2N}{x}(u_\xi+u_\eta)=0$$

Substituting the value of $x$, the required canonical equation is

$$4u_{\xi\eta}+\frac{4N}{\xi+\eta}(u_\xi+u_\eta)=0$$

or $$u_{\xi\eta}+\frac{N}{\xi+\eta}(u_\xi+u_\eta)=0$$

**44.** Here, $A=\sin^2 x$, $B=\sin 2x$, $C=\cos^2 x$, $D=E=F=0$ and $G=x$.

The discrminant of the given partial differential equation is

$$B^2-4AC=\sin^2 2x-4\sin^2 x\cos^2 x=0$$

Hence, the given equation is of parabolic type.

The characteristic equation is

$$\frac{dy}{dx}=\frac{B}{2A}=\cot x$$

$$\Rightarrow \quad y=\ln\sin x+C_1$$

Hence, the characteristic equations are

$$\xi=y-\ln\sin x \text{ and } \eta=y$$

$\eta$ is chosen in such a way that the Jacobian of the transformation is non-zero. To compute the canonical form. Here,

$$\bar{A}=0,\ \bar{B}=0,\bar{C}=\cos^2 x,\ \bar{D}=1$$

$$\bar{E}=0,\ \bar{F}=0,\ \bar{G}=x$$

$\therefore$ The canonical equation is

$$(\cos^2 x)u_{\eta\eta}+u_\xi=x$$

or $$u_{\eta\eta}=\frac{\sin^{-1}(e^{\eta-\xi})-u_\xi}{1-e^{2(\eta-\xi)}}$$

**45.** Here,

$$x\frac{\partial^2 u}{\partial x^2}+2\frac{\partial u}{\partial x}=0$$

$$\Rightarrow \quad x^2\frac{\partial^2 u}{\partial x^2}+2x\frac{\partial u}{\partial x}=0$$

$$\Rightarrow \quad \frac{\partial}{\partial x}\left(x^2\frac{\partial u}{\partial x}\right)=0$$

On integrating *wrt* $x$, we have

$$x^2\frac{\partial u}{\partial x}=\phi(y)$$

or $$\frac{\partial u}{\partial x}=\frac{\phi(y)}{x^2}$$

Again, on integrating *wrt* $x$, we have

$$u=-\frac{1}{x}\phi(y)+\psi(y) \quad \text{...(i)}$$

Since, $u=0$, $y^2=4ax$

$\therefore$ We have by Eq. (i)

$$-\frac{4a}{y^2}\phi(y)+\psi(y)=0 \quad \text{...(ii)}$$

and $u=1$, $y^2=-4ax$, we have by Eq. (i)

$$1=\frac{4a}{y^2}\phi(y)+\psi(y) \quad \text{...(iii)}$$

Now, adding Eq. (ii) and (iii), we have

$$2\psi(y)=1 \Rightarrow \psi(y)=\frac{1}{2}$$

Putting $\psi(y)=\frac{1}{2}$ in Eq. (ii), we get $\phi(y)=\frac{y^2}{8a}$

Now, Eqs. (i) gives

$$u=-\frac{y^2}{8ax}+\frac{1}{2}$$

**46.** Assume the trial solution

$$z=X(x)Y(y) \quad \text{...(i)}$$

Substituting this value of $z$ in the given equation, we have

$$X''Y-2X'Y+XY'=0$$

Now, separating the variables, we get

$$\frac{X''-2X'}{X}=-\frac{Y'}{Y} \quad \text{...(ii)}$$

Since, $x$ and $y$ are independent variables, therefore, Eq. (ii) can only be true, if each side is equal to the same constant, a (say).

Hence, $\frac{X''-2X'}{X}=a$ *i.e.*, $X''-2X'-aX=0$ ...(iii)

and $-Y''/Y'=a$ *i.e.*, $Y'+aY=0$ ...(iv)

To solve the ordinary linear equation (iii), the auxiliary equation is

$$m^2-2m-a=0, \text{ when } m=1\pm\sqrt{1+a}$$

Hence, the solution of Eq. (iii) is

$$X=c_1e^{(1+\sqrt{1+a})x}+c_2e^{(1-\sqrt{1+a})x}$$

and the solution of Eq. (iv) is

$$Y=c_3e^{-ay}$$

Substituting these values of $X$ and $Y$ in Eq. (i), we have

$$z = \{c_1 e^{\{1+\sqrt{1+a}\}x} + c_2 e^{\{1-\sqrt{1+a}\}x}\} c_3 e^{-ay}$$

$$\Rightarrow \quad z = \{k_1 e^{\{1+\sqrt{1+a}\}x} + k_2 e^{\{1-\sqrt{1+a}\}x}\} e^{-ay}$$

which is the required complete solution.

**47.** By separation of variable, the possible solution is

$$\theta(x, t) = e^{-a\lambda^2 t}(A\cos\lambda x + B\sin\lambda x)$$

Using the first boundary condition $\theta(0,t) = 0, t \geq 0$, we have $A = 0$ and

$$\theta = Be^{-a\lambda^2 t}\sin\lambda x$$

$$\frac{\partial\theta}{dx} = \lambda Be^{-a\lambda^2 t}\cos\lambda x$$

Now, using boundary condition $\frac{\partial\theta}{\partial x}(L, t) = 0$, we have

$$0 = \lambda Be^{-a\lambda^2 t}\cos\lambda L$$

$$\Rightarrow \quad \cos\lambda L = 0$$

Therefore, the eigen values and the corresponding eigen functions are

$$\lambda_n = \frac{(2n+1)}{2L}\pi, \qquad n = 0, 1, 2\ldots$$

and the acceptable solution is of the form

$$\theta = B_n \exp[-\alpha\{(2n+1)/2L\}^2 \pi^2 t]\sin\left(\frac{2n+1}{2L}\right)\pi x$$

By the principle of superposition, we have

$$\theta(x,t) = \sum_{n=0}^{\infty} B_n \exp[-\alpha\{(2n+1)/2L\}^2\pi^2 t]\sin\left(\frac{2n+1}{2L}\pi x\right)$$

By initial condition $\theta(x, 0) = \theta_0$, we have

$$\theta_0 = \sum_{n=0}^{\infty} B_n \sin\left(\frac{2n+1}{2L}\pi x\right)$$

Which is half range Fourier sine series and

$$B_n = \frac{2}{L}\int_0^L \theta_0 \sin\left(\frac{2n+1}{2L}\pi x\right)dx$$

$$B_n = \frac{2}{L}\left[-\theta_0 \frac{2L}{(2n+1)\pi}\left\{\cos\left(\frac{2n+1}{2L}\pi x\right)\right\}_0^L\right]$$

$$= -\frac{4\theta_0}{(2n+1)\pi}[\cos\{(2n+1)\pi/2\} - \cos 0]$$

$$= \frac{4\theta_0}{(2n+1)\pi}$$

Thus, the required solution is

$$\theta(x, t) = \sum_{n=0}^{\infty} \frac{4\theta_0}{(2n+1)\pi}\exp[-\alpha\{(2n+1)/2L\}^2\pi^2 t] \sin\left(\frac{2n+1}{2L}\pi x\right)$$

**48.** Let the solution be

$$u(x, t) = X(x)T(t)$$

Substituting in the given partial differential equation, we have

$$X'T = 2XT' + XT$$

$$\Rightarrow \quad (X' - X)T = 2XT'$$

$$\Rightarrow \quad \frac{X' - X}{2X} = \frac{T'}{T} = k \text{ (say)}$$

Hence, $\quad X' - X - 2kX = 0$

or $\quad \frac{X'}{X} = 1 + 2k \quad \ldots\text{(i)}$

and $\quad \frac{T'}{T} = k \quad \ldots\text{(ii)}$

Solving Eq. (i), we have

$$\log X = (1 + 2k)x + \log c$$

$$\Rightarrow \quad X = ce^{(1+2k)x}$$

From Eq. (ii), we have

$$\log T = kt + \log c' \text{ or } T = c'e^{kt}$$

Hence, $\quad u(x, t) = XT = cc' e^{(1+2k)x}e^{kt}$

Since, $\quad 6e^{-3x} = u(x, 0) = cc' e^{(1+2k)x} \quad \ldots\text{(iii)}$

Hence, $cc' = 6$ and $1 + 2k = -3 \Rightarrow k = -2$

Substituting these values in Eq. (iii), we get

$$u = 6e^{-3x}e^{-2t} \Rightarrow u = 6e^{-(3x+2t)}$$

Which is the required solution.

**49.** $\frac{\partial y}{\partial x} = f'(x - at) + F'(x + at)$

and $\quad \frac{\partial^2 y}{\partial x^2} = f''(x - at) + F''(x + at) \quad \ldots\text{(i)}$

Similarly,

$$\frac{\partial y}{\partial t} = -af'(x - at) + aF'(x + at)$$

$$\frac{\partial^2 y}{\partial t^2} - a^2 f''(x - at) + a^2 F''(x + at) \quad \ldots\text{(ii)}$$

By Eqs. (i) and (ii), we get

$$\frac{\partial^2 y}{\partial x^2} = \frac{1}{a^2} = \frac{\partial^2 y}{\partial t^2}$$

A partial differential equation of second order.

**50.** The discriminant of the given partial differential equation is

$$B^2 \text{ 4 } AC = 4x^2y^2 - 4x^2y^2 = 0$$

Hence, the given equation is of a parabolic type.

The characteristic equation is

$$\frac{dy}{dx} = \frac{B}{2A} = \frac{-2xy}{2y^2} = -\frac{x}{y}$$

$\Rightarrow x^2 + y^2 = c_1$ and $\xi = x^2 + y^2$ satisfies the characteristic equation.

The $\eta$-coordinate can be chosen arbitrarily so that it is not parallel to $\xi$, *i.e.*, the Jacobian of the transformation is not zero.

Choose, $\xi = x^2 + y^2, \eta = y^2$

To compute the canonical equation.

$$\bar{A} = A\xi^2{}_x + B\xi_x\xi_y + C\xi^2{}_y$$

$$= 4x^2y^2 - 8x^2y^2 + 4x^2y^2 = 0$$

$$\bar{B} = 0, \bar{C} = 4x^2y^2,$$

$$\bar{D} = \bar{E} = \bar{F} = \bar{G} = 0$$

The required canonical equation is

$$4x^2y^2u_{\eta\eta} = 0 \text{ or } u_{\eta\eta} = 0$$

Integrating twice *wrt* $\eta$

$$u_\eta = f(\xi),\ u = f(\xi)\eta + g(\xi)$$

where $f(\xi)$ and $g(\xi)$ are arbitrary functions of $\xi$.

The required solution is

$$u = y^2 f(x^2 + y^2) + g(x^2 + y^2)$$

**51.** Here, $A = 1 + x^2,\ B = 0,\ C = 1 + y^2$

$D = x,\ E = y,\ F = 0,\ G = 0$

The discriminant of the given partial differential equation is

$$B^2 - 4AC = -4(1 + x^2)(1 + y^2) < 0$$

Hence, the given partial differential equation is an elliptic type.

The characteristic equations are

$$\frac{dy}{dx} = \frac{B - \sqrt{B^2 - 4AC}}{2A} = -\frac{\sqrt{-4(1+x^2)(1+y^2)}}{2(1+x^2)} = -i\sqrt{\frac{1+y^2}{1+x^2}}$$

$$\frac{dy}{dx} = \frac{B + \sqrt{B^2 - 4AC}}{2A} = i\sqrt{\frac{1+y^2}{1+x^2}}$$

Integration gives,

$$\xi = \ln(x + \sqrt{(x^2+1)}) - i\ln(y + \sqrt{y^2+1}) = c_1$$

$$\eta = \ln(x + \sqrt{x^2+1}) + i\ln(y + \sqrt{y^2+1}) = c_2$$

Let $\alpha = \dfrac{\xi + \eta}{2},\ \beta = \dfrac{\eta - \xi}{2i}$

We have $\alpha = \ln(x + \sqrt{x^2+1})$

$$\beta = \ln(y + \sqrt{y^2+1})$$

Computing

$$\overline{A} = A\alpha_x^2 + B\alpha_x\alpha_y + C\alpha_y^2 = 1,$$

$$\overline{B} = 0,\ \overline{C} = 1,\ \overline{D} = \overline{E} = \overline{F} = \overline{G} = 0$$

The canonical equation for the given partial differential equation is

$$u_{\alpha\alpha} + u_{\beta\beta} = 0$$

**52.** The solution of partial differential equation is

$$y(x,t) = (c_1\cos px + c_2\sin px)(c_3\cos cpt + c_4\sin cpt)$$

By $u(0,t) = 0$, we have

$$y(0,t) = c_1(c_3\cos cpt + c_4\sin cpt) = 0$$

$\Rightarrow \quad c_1 = 0$

Hence, $y(x,t) = c_2\sin px\,(c_3\cos cpt + c_4\sin cpt)$

Also, $y(l,t) = c_2\sin pl\,(c_3\cos cpt + c_4\sin cpt) = 0,\ t > 0$

$\Rightarrow \quad pl = n\pi$ or $p = \dfrac{n\pi}{l}$,

Hence, $y(x,t) = c_2\sin\dfrac{n\pi x}{l}\left(c_3\cos\dfrac{cn\pi}{l}t + c_4\sin\dfrac{cn\pi}{l}t\right)$

By $y(x,0) = 0$, we have

$$0 = c_2c_3\sin\frac{n\pi x}{l}$$

for all $x \Rightarrow c_2c_3 = 0$

Hence, $y(x,t) = b_n\sin\dfrac{nc\pi}{l}\sin\dfrac{cn\pi t}{l}$

where $b_n = c_2c_4$

The general solution of partial differential equation is

$$y(x,t) = \sum_{n=1}^{\infty} b_n\sin\frac{n\pi x}{l}\sin\frac{cn\pi t}{l} \quad \text{...(i)}$$

and
$$\frac{\partial y}{\partial t} = \sum_{n=1}^{\infty} b_n\sin\frac{n\pi x}{l}\cdot\frac{cn\pi}{l}\cos\frac{nc\pi t}{l}$$

Since, $\left(\dfrac{\partial y}{\partial t}\right)_{t=0} = v_0\dfrac{\sin^3\pi x}{l}$

Hence, $v_0\sin^3\dfrac{\pi x}{l} = \left(\dfrac{\partial y}{\partial t}\right)_{t=0} = \displaystyle\sum_{n=1}^{\infty}\frac{cn\pi}{l}b_n\sin\frac{n\pi x}{l}$

$$\Rightarrow \quad \frac{v_0}{4}\left(3\sin\frac{\pi x}{l} - \sin\frac{3\pi x}{l}\right) = \sum_{n=1}^{\infty}\frac{cn\pi}{l}b_n\sin\frac{n\pi x}{l}$$

$$= \frac{c\pi}{l}b_1\sin\frac{\pi x}{l} + \frac{2c\pi}{l}b_2\sin\frac{2\pi x}{l} + \frac{3c\pi}{l}b_3\sin\frac{3\pi x}{l} + \ldots$$

Equating the coefficients from both sides, we get

$$\frac{3v_0}{4} = \frac{c\pi}{l}b_1,\ 0 = \frac{2c\pi}{l}b_2,\ \frac{-v_0}{u} = \frac{3c\pi}{l}b_3,\ldots$$

Hence,
$$b_1 = \frac{3lv_0}{4c\pi},\ b_3 = -\frac{lv_0}{12c\pi},$$

$$b_2 = b_4 = b_3 = \ldots = 0$$

Substituting in Eq. (i) we have

$$y = \frac{lv_0}{12c\pi}\left(9\sin\frac{\pi x}{l}\sin\frac{c\pi t}{l} - \sin\frac{3\pi x}{l}\sin\frac{3c\pi t}{l}\right)$$

**53.** The solution of partial differential equation by method of separation of variable is of the form

$$u(x,t) = (C_1\cos px + C_2\sin px)\,e^{-C^2p^2t} \quad \text{...(i)}$$

and
$$\frac{\partial u}{\partial x} = (-C_1 p\sin px + C_2 p\cos px)\,e^{-C^2p^2t} \quad \text{...(ii)}$$

By boundary condition,

$$\left(\frac{\partial u}{\partial x}\right)_{x=0} = 0, \text{ Eq. (ii) gives}$$

$$\left(\frac{\partial u}{\partial x}\right)_0 = C_2pe^{-c^2p^2t} = 0,\ t > 0$$

Hence, $C_2 = 0$

By boundary condition,

$$\left(\frac{\partial u}{\partial x}\right)_{x=l} = 0, \text{ Eq. (ii) gives}$$

$$\left(\frac{\partial u}{\partial x}\right)_0 = -C_1 p\sin ple^{-c^2p^2t},\ t > 0$$

$\Rightarrow \quad C_1p\sin pl = 0$ i.e., $C_1 = 0$ or $\sin pl = 0$

When $C_1 = 0$, gives $u(x,t) = 0$, which is a trivial solution, therefore, $\sin pl = 0$

$\Rightarrow \quad pl = n\pi \Rightarrow p = n\pi/l, \quad n = 0, 1, 2, \ldots$

Hence, Eq. (ii) becomes

$$u(x,t) = C_1\cos\frac{n\pi x}{l}\,e^{-C^2n^2\pi^2t/l^2}$$

Hence, the most general solution of partial differential equation satisfying the boundary conditions is

$$u(x,t)=\sum_{n=0}^{\infty} A_n \cos\frac{n\pi x}{l}\, e^{-c^2n^2\pi^2t/l^2}$$

$$= A_0 + \sum_{n=1}^{\infty} A_n \cos\frac{n\pi x}{l}\, e^{-c^2n^2\pi^2t/l^2}$$

(where $A_n = c_1$) ...(iii)

By initial condition $u(x,0)=0$ Eq. (iii) gives

$$u(x,0)=A_0+\sum_{n=1}^{\infty} A_n\cos\frac{n\pi x}{l}=x$$

This requires the expansion of $x$ into a half range cosine series in $(0, l)$

Hence, $x=\frac{a_0}{2}+\sum_{n=1}^{\infty} a_n\cos\frac{n\pi x}{l}$

where, $a_0=\frac{2}{l}\int_0^l x\,dx = l$

and $a_n=\frac{2}{l}\int_0^l x\cos\frac{n\pi x}{l}\,dx$

$$=\frac{2l}{n^2\pi^2}(\cos n\pi - 1)$$

$$=\begin{cases}0, & \text{when } n \text{ is even}\\ -\frac{4l}{n^2\pi^2}, & \text{when } n \text{ is odd}\end{cases}$$

Hence, $A_0=\frac{a_0}{2}=\frac{l}{2}$ and $A_n=a_n=\begin{cases}0, & \text{for } n \text{ is even}\\ -\frac{4l}{n^2\pi^2}, & \text{for } n \text{ is odd}\end{cases}$

Hence, Eq. (iii) takes the form

$$u(x,t)=\frac{l}{2}-\sum_{n=1,3}^{\infty}\frac{4l}{n^2\pi^2}\cos\frac{n\pi x}{l}\, e^{-c^2n^2\pi^2t/l^2}$$

$$=\frac{l}{2}-\frac{4l}{\pi^2}\sum_{1}^{\infty}\frac{1}{(2n-1)^2}\cos\frac{(2n-1)\pi x}{l}\, e^{-c^2(2n-1)^2\pi^2t/l^2}$$

Which is the required solution.

**54.** This is the Neumann problem for a rectangle, one of the possible solution is of the form

$$u(x,y)=(c_1\cos px + c_2\sin px)(c_3 e^{py}+c_4 e^{-py})$$

Using boundary condition $u(0,y)=0$, we have

$$u(0,y)=c_1(c_3e^{py}+c_4e^{-py})=0,\ y>0$$

Hence, $c_1=0$ and we have

$$u(x,y)=c_2\sin p\pi\,(c_3e^{py}+c_4e^{-py})$$

Using, $u(\pi,y)=0,\ y>0$, we have

$$u(\pi,y)=c_2\sin p\pi\,(c_3e^{py}+c_4e^{-py})=0,\ y=0$$

Hence, $\sin p\pi=0$, *i.e.*, $p\pi=n\pi$ as $c_2\neq 0$

$\Rightarrow$ $p=n$,

as $u(x,\infty)=0,\ 0<x<\pi$ gives $u=0$ as $y\to\infty$,

$c_3=0$.

Hence, the general solution

$$u(x,y)=\sum_{n=1}^{\infty} b_n\sin nx\cdot e^{-ny}$$

where, $b_n=c_2c_4$

Putting $y=0$,

$$u(x,0)=\sum_{n=1}^{\infty} b_n\sin nx$$

Since, $u(x,0)=u_0,\ 0<x<\pi$,

Hence, $u_0=\sum_{n=1}^{\infty} b_n\sin nx$

where, $b_n=\frac{2}{\pi}\int_0^{\pi}u_0\sin nx\,dx=\frac{2u_0}{n\pi}[1-(-1)^n]$

$$\Rightarrow\quad b_n=\begin{cases}0, & \text{if } n \text{ is even}\\ \frac{4u_0}{n\pi}, & \text{if } n \text{ is odd}\end{cases}$$

Hence,

$$u(x,y)=\frac{4u_0}{\pi}\left[e^{-y}\sin x+\frac{1}{3}e^{-3y}\sin 3x+\frac{1}{5}e^{-5y}\sin 5x+\ldots\right]$$

**55.** Given, the wave equation

$$\frac{\partial^2 y}{\partial t^2}=c^2\frac{\partial^2 y}{\partial x^2} \quad \text{...(i)}$$

Let $u=x+ct$ and $v=x-ct$ so that $y$ becomes function of $u$ and $v$ and $\frac{\partial y}{\partial x}=\frac{\partial y}{\partial u}+\frac{\partial y}{\partial v}$

Also,

$$\frac{\partial^2 y}{\partial x^2}=\frac{\partial}{\partial x}\left(\frac{\partial y}{\partial u}+\frac{\partial y}{\partial v}\right)$$

$$=\frac{\partial}{\partial u}\left(\frac{\partial y}{\partial u}+\frac{\partial y}{\partial v}\right)+\frac{\partial}{\partial v}\left(\frac{\partial y}{\partial u}+\frac{\partial y}{\partial v}\right)$$

$$=\frac{\partial^2 y}{\partial u^2}+2\frac{\partial^2 y}{\partial u\partial v}+\frac{\partial^2 y}{\partial v^2}$$

and

$$\frac{\partial^2 y}{\partial t^2}=c^2\left(\frac{\partial^2 y}{\partial u^2}-2\frac{\partial^2 y}{\partial u\partial v}+\frac{\partial^2 y}{\partial v^2}\right)$$

Substituting in Eq. (i), we get

$$\frac{\partial^2 y}{\partial u\partial v}=0 \quad \text{...(II)}$$

On integrating Eq. (ii) *wrt* $v$, we have

$$\frac{\partial y}{\partial u}=f(u) \quad \text{...(iii)}$$

where $f(u)$ is an arbitrary function of $u$. Integrating Eq. (iii) *wrt* $u$, gives

$$y=\int f(u)\,du+\psi(v)$$

where $\psi(v)$ is an arbitrary function of $v$. Since, the integral is a function of $u$ alone. Thus,

$$y=\phi(u)+\psi(v)$$

$$\Rightarrow\quad y(x,t)=\phi(x+ct)+\psi(x-ct) \quad \text{...(iv)}$$

This is the general solution of the wave Eq. (i).

To determine $\phi$ and $\psi$, suppose initially $y(x,0)=f(x)$ and $\partial y(x,0)/\partial t=0$.

Differentiating Eq. (iv) *wrt* $t$, we have

$$\frac{\partial y}{\partial t}=c\phi'(x+ct)-c\psi'(x-ct)$$

At $t=0$, $\quad \phi'(x)=\psi'(x)$ ...(v)

and $\quad y(x,0)=\phi(x)+\psi(x)=f(x)$ ...(vi)

Eq. (v) gives, $\phi(x)=\psi(x)+k$

Hence, Eq. (vi) becomes $2\psi(x)+k=f(x)$

or $\psi(x)=\frac{1}{2}[f(x)-k]$

and $\phi(x)=\frac{1}{2}[f(x)+k]$

Hence, the solution of Eq. (iv) takes the form

$$y(x,t)=\frac{1}{2}[f(x+ct)+k]+\frac{1}{2}[f(x-ct)-k]$$

$$=f(x+ct)+f(x-ct) \quad \text{...(vii)}$$

The required d'Alembert's solution of the wave Eq. (i).

**56.** Here, $\frac{\partial^2 u}{\partial y^2}=\sigma x^3 y$

Integrating *wrt* $y$, we get

$$\frac{\partial u}{\partial y}=3x^3y^2+\phi(x)$$

Again, on integrating *wrt* $y$, we get

$$u=x^3y^3+y\phi(x)+\psi(x) \quad \text{...(i)}$$

Since, Eq. (i) contains the line $y=0=u$ and $y=1=u$, thus $0=\psi(x)$ and

$$1=x^3+\phi(x)+\psi(x)$$

or $\phi(x)=1-x^3$

Hence, the required surface is

$$u=x^3y^3+y(1-x^3)$$

**57.** The expected solution of given partial differential equation is

$$y(x,t)=(C_1\cos px+C_2\sin px)(C_3\cos cpt+C_4\sin cpt)$$

$$y(0,t)=C_1(C_3\cos cpt+C_4\sin cpt)=0$$

$\Rightarrow$ $C_1=0$

Hence,

$$y(x,t)=C_2\sin px\,(C_3\cos cpt+C_4\sin cpt) \quad \text{...(i)}$$

and $\frac{\partial y}{\partial t}=C_2\sin px\,\{C_3(-cp\cdot\sin cpt)+C_4(cp\cdot\cos cpt)\}$

Since, $\left(\frac{\partial y}{\partial t}\right)_{t=0}=0$

Hence, $\left(\frac{\partial y}{\partial t}\right)_{t=0}=C_2\sin px\cdot(C_4\,cp)=0,$

$\Rightarrow$ $C_2C_4\,cp=0$

If $C_2=0$ Eq. (i) will lead to the trivial solution $y(x,t)=0$.

Hence, $C_4=0$

Thus, Eq. (i) becomes

$$y(x,t)=C_2\,C_3\sin px\cos cpt \quad \text{...(ii)}$$

Since, $y(l,t)=0$

$$y(l,t)=C_2\,C_3\sin pl\cos cpt=0, t>0$$

Since, $C_2$ and $C_3\neq 0$.

Hence, $\sin pl=0$

$\Rightarrow$ $pl=n\pi$, *i.e.*, $p=n\pi/l$

Now, partial differential Eq. (ii) reduces to

$$y(x,t)=C_2C_3\sin\frac{n\pi x}{l}\cos\frac{n\pi ct}{l}$$

By $y(x,0)=a\sin(\pi x/l)$, we have

$$y(x,0)=C_2\,C_3\sin\frac{n\pi x}{l}=a\sin\frac{\pi x}{l}$$

which will be satisfied by taking

$$C_2C_3=a \text{ and } n=1$$

Hence, the required solution is

$$y(x,t)=a\sin\frac{\pi x}{l}\cos\frac{\pi ct}{l}$$

**58.** The three possible solutions are

$$T(x,t)=(C_1e^{\lambda x}+C_2e^{-\lambda x})e^{a\lambda^2 t}$$

$$T(x,t)=(C_1\cos\lambda x+C_2\sin\lambda x)e^{-a\lambda^2 t}$$

$$T(x,t)=(C_1x+C_2)$$

(i) The first condition demands the $T$ should remain finite as $t\to\infty$. We therefore, reject the first solution.

(ii) Using *BC* Eq. (ii), the third solution gives

$$0=C_1\cdot 0+C_2, 0=C_1\cdot\pi+C_2$$

$$\Rightarrow C_1=C_2=0\Rightarrow T=0$$

This is a trivial solution.

(iii) Thus, the only possible solution satisfying the first condition is

$$T(x,t)=(C_1\cos\lambda x+C_2\sin\lambda x)e^{-\alpha\lambda^2 t}$$

Using the boundary condition Eq. (ii), we have

$$0=(C_1\cos\lambda x+C_2\sin\lambda x)/_{x=0} \Rightarrow C_1=0$$

The possible solution is now, is

$$T(x,t)=C_2e^{-\alpha\lambda^2 t}\sin\lambda x$$

Applying the boundary condition $T=0$ when $x=\pi$, we have

$$\sin\lambda\pi=0\Rightarrow\lambda\pi=n\pi \Rightarrow \lambda=n$$

Hence, the solution is to be of the form

$$T(x,t)=ce^{-\alpha n^2 t}\sin nx$$

Since, the heat conduction equation is linear, its most general solution is obtained by applying the principle of superposition, *i.e.*,

$$T(x,t)=\sum_{n=1}^{\infty}c_n\,e^{-\alpha n^2 t}\sin nx$$

Applying third condition, we have

$$T(x,0)=\sum_{n=1}^{\infty}C_n\sin nx$$

Which is a half range fourier sine series and,

$$C_n=\frac{2}{\pi}\int_0^{\pi}T(x,0)\sin nx\,dx$$

$$=\frac{2}{\pi}\left[\int_0^{\pi/2}x\sin nx\,dx+\int_{\pi/2}^{\pi}(\pi-x)\sin nx\,dx\right]$$

or $C_n=\frac{2}{\pi}\left[\left(-x\frac{\cos nx}{n}+\frac{\sin nx}{n^2}\right)_0^{\pi/2}+\left\{-(\pi-x)\frac{\cos nx}{n}-\frac{\sin nx}{n^2}\right\}_{\pi/2}^{\pi}\right]$

$\Rightarrow$ $C_n=\frac{4\sin(n\pi/2)}{n^2\pi}$

Hence, the required solution is

$$T(x,t)=\frac{4}{\pi}\sum_{n=1}^{\infty}\frac{e^{-\alpha n^2 t}+\sin(n\pi/2)}{n^2}\sin nx$$

# 19 Numerical Analysis

## Syllabus

- Numerical Solutions of Algebraic Equations
- Method of Iteration and Newton-Raphson Method
- Rate of Convergence
- Solution of System of Linear Algebraic Equations Using Gauss Eliminations and Gauss Seidel Method
- Finite Differences
- Lagrange, Hermite and Spline Interpolation
- Numerical Differentiation and Integration
- Numerical Solutions of DEs using Picard, Euler, Modified Euler and Runge-Kutta Methods

## Numerical Solutions of Algebraic Equations

An equation of the form $a_0x^n + a_1x^{n-1} + a_2x^{n-2} + \ldots + a_n = 0$ where $a_0 (\neq 0), a_1, a_2, \ldots, a_n$ are constants and $n$ is a positive integer called an algebraic equation of degree $n$.

If $\quad f(x) = a_0x^n + a_1x^{n-1} + a_2x^{n-2} + \ldots + a_n$, then above equation becomes

$f(x) = 0$

If $f(x_0) = 0$ for $x = x_0$, then $x_0$ is called a root of $f(x) = 0$.

There are various numerical methods to solve algebraic equations.

## 1. Method of Iteration

To find the roots of equation

$$f(x) = 0 \quad \ldots(i)$$

by successive approximations, we rewrite Eq.(i) in the form

$$x = \phi(x) \quad \ldots(ii)$$

e.g., $x^3 + x^2 - 1 = 0$ can be written as

(i) $x^3 = 1 - x^2 \Rightarrow x = (1 - x^2)^{1/3}$

(ii) $x^2 = 1 - x^3 \Rightarrow x = (1 - x^3)^{1/2}$

(iii) $x^2(1 + x) = 1 \Rightarrow x = (1 + x)^{-1/2}$

Let $x = x_0$ be an initial approximation of the desired root $\alpha$. Then, the first approximation $x_1$ is given by $x_1 = \phi(x_0)$

Second approximation $x_2$ is given by $x_2 = \phi(x_1)$

Proceeding in this way, the $n$th approximation is given by $x_n = \phi(x_{n-1})$

> ***Note*** **(a)** The roots of $f(x) = 0$ are same as the point of intersection of the straight line $y = x$ and $y = \phi(x)$.
>
> **(b)** The form $x = \phi(x)$ can be chosen in many ways. We choose $\phi(x)$ in such a way that
>
> $$|\phi'(x)| < 1, \forall\, x = x_0, x_1, x_2, \ldots$$
>
> **(c)** Sequence $\{x_n\}$ converge to the root $\alpha$.
>
> **(d)** The rate of convergence is more, if the value of $\phi'(x)$ is smaller.
>
> **(e)** This method is useful for finding the real roots of an equation given in the form of an infinite series.
>
> **(f)** Type of convergence is linear.

***Example 1.*** *Using method of iteration convert the equation $x^3+x^2-1=0$ into $x=\phi(x)$ assuming initial approximation of root is $x_0=0.80$.*

**Solution.** Given equation $x^3+x^2-1=0$ can be written as

(i) $$x=(1-x^2)^{\frac{1}{3}}$$

$$\Rightarrow \quad \phi(x)=(1-x^2)^{\frac{1}{3}}$$

$$\Rightarrow \quad \phi'(x)=\frac{1}{3}(1-x^2)^{-\frac{2}{3}}\cdot(-2x)$$

$$\Rightarrow \quad |\phi'(x)|=\frac{2}{3}\left|\frac{x}{(1-x^2)^{2/3}}\right|>1, \quad \text{for } x=x_0=0.80$$

(ii) $$x=(1-x^3)^{1/2}$$

$$\Rightarrow \quad \phi(x)=(1-x^3)^{1/2}$$

$$\Rightarrow \quad \phi'(x)=\frac{1}{2}(1-x^3)^{-1/2}\cdot(-3x^2)]$$

$|\phi'(x)|>1$ for $x=x_0=0.80$

(iii) $$x^3+x^2-1=0$$

$$\Rightarrow \quad x^2(x+1)=1$$

$$\Rightarrow \quad x^2=(1+x)^{-1}$$

$$\Rightarrow \quad x=(1+x)^{-1/2}$$

$$\phi(x)=(1+x)^{-1/2}$$

$$\phi'(x)=-\frac{1}{2}(1+x)^{-3/2}$$

$|\phi'(x)|<1$ for $x=x_0=0.80$

$\therefore$ Required form $x=\phi(x)$ is

$$x=(1+x)^{-1/2}$$

## 2. Newton-Raphson Method

Let $x_0$ be an approximate root of the equation $f(x)=0$. If $x_1=x_0+h$, such that $f(x_0+h)=0$

$$\Rightarrow \quad f(x_0)+hf'(x_0)+\frac{h^2}{2!}f''(x_0)+\ldots=0$$

(Expanding $f(x_0+h)$ by Taylor's series)

$$\Rightarrow \quad f(x_0)+hf'(x_0)=0$$

(By neglecting $h^2$ and higher powers of $h$. Since, $h$ is small)

$$\Rightarrow \quad h=-\frac{f(x_0)}{f'(x_0)}$$

$$\therefore \quad x_1=x_0-\frac{f(x_0)}{f'(x_0)}$$

Similarly, $$x_2=x_1-\frac{f(x_1)}{f'(x_1)}$$

In general

$$x_n=x_{n-1}-\frac{f(x_{n-1})}{f'(x_{n-1})}, \quad n=1,2,3,\ldots$$

Here, $x_i$ is better approximation than $x_{i-1}$.

***Note*** **(a)** This method is useful in case of large value of $f'(x)$. For large $f'(x)$, $h$ will be small. If $f'(x)$ is small, $h$ will be large and computation of the root is slow or not possible. Therefore, this method is not suitable in those cases, where graph of $f(x)$ is nearly horizontal while crossing the $x$-axis.

**(b)** Newton's formula converges provided $x_0$ is chosen sufficiently close to the root. Comparing with the iteration method, we get

$$\phi(x)=x-\frac{f(x)}{f'(x)},\ \phi'(x)=\frac{f(x)f''(x)}{(f'(x))^2}$$

Since, $|\phi'(x)|<1$

$\Rightarrow$ $|f(x)f''(x)|<|f'(x)|^2$

**(c)** This formula converges rapidly, if $x_0$ is very near to the root $\alpha$.

**(d)** Convergence is of quadratic order. or order of convergence of Newton-Raphson method is 2.

**(e)** Rate of convergence $=\left|\dfrac{f''(\alpha)}{2f'(\alpha)}\right|$

**(f)** If $x_0$ is not given, then we take two numbers $a$ and $b$, such that

$$f(a)f(b)<0,$$

then the root $\alpha$ lies between $a$ and $b$.
Now, $x_0=a$, if $f(a)$ is nearer to zero than $f(b)$.
or $x_0=b$, if $f(b)$ is nearer to zero than $f(a)$.

***Example 2.*** *Find first approximate root of equation $x^3-3x-5=0$, where $x_0=3$.*

**Solution.** $f(x)=x^3-3x-5$, $f'(x)=3x^2-3$

$$f(x_0)=f(3)=3^3-3\times3-5=27-9-5=13$$

$$f'(x_0)=f'(3)=3\times3^2-3=27-3=24$$

$$\Rightarrow \quad x_1=x_0-\frac{f(x_0)}{f'(x_0)}=3-\frac{13}{24}=3-0.5417=2.4583$$

***Example 3.*** *Find $x_1$ and $x_2$ for equation $x^3-5x+3=0$ by using Newton's-Raphson method.*

**Solution.** Here, $x_0$ is not given.

$$f(x)=x^3-5x+3,\ f'(x)=3x^2-5$$

$$f(0)=3,\quad f(1)=-1$$

$\Rightarrow$ $f(0)f(1)<0$,

then root lies between $(0, 1)$.

Here, $f(1)=-1$ is nearer to zero,

then $f(0)=3$

$\Rightarrow$ $x_0=1$

Now, $f(x_0)=f(1)=1^3-5\times1+3=1-5+3=-1$

$$f'(x_0)=f'(1)=3\times1^2-5=3-5=-2$$

$$\therefore \quad x_1=x_0-\frac{f(x_0)}{f'(x_0)}=1-\frac{-1}{-2}=1-\frac{1}{2}=0.5$$

Now, $$f(x_1)=f(0.5)=(0.5)^3-5(0.5)+3$$

$$=0.125-2.5+3=0.625$$

$$f'(0.5)=3(0.5)^2-5=-4.25$$

$$\therefore \quad x_2 = x_1 - \frac{f(x_1)}{f'(x_1)} = 0.5 - \frac{0.625}{-4.25}$$
$$= 0.5 + 0.1471 = 0.6471$$

***Example 4.*** *Using Newton's-Raphson method, find an iterative formula to compute the reciprocal of a natural number N.*

**Solution.** Let $x = \frac{1}{N}$

$$\Rightarrow \quad N - \frac{1}{x} = 0$$
$$f(x) = N - \frac{1}{x} = 0$$
$$f'(x) = \frac{1}{x^2}$$

Using Newton's-Raphson formula

$$x_{n+1} = x_n - \frac{f(x_n)}{f'(x_n)}$$
$$= x_n - \frac{N - \frac{1}{x_n}}{\frac{1}{x_n^2}}$$
$$= x_n - N \cdot x_n^2 + x_n$$
$$= x_n(2 - N \cdot x_n)$$

which is the required iterative formula to find $\frac{1}{N}$.

**Remark** We can derive the following results by using Newton's-Raphson method, similarly as above.

(i) To find $\sqrt{N}$, iterative formula is $x_{n+1} = \frac{1}{2}\left(x_n + \frac{N}{x_n}\right)$.

(ii) To find $\frac{1}{\sqrt{N}}$, iterative formula is

$$x_{n+1} = \frac{1}{2}\left(x_n + \frac{1}{N \cdot x_n}\right)$$

(iii) To find $\sqrt[3]{N}$, iterative formula is

$$x_{n+1} = \frac{1}{3}\left(2x_n + \frac{N}{x_n^2}\right)$$

In general,

(iv) To find $\sqrt[k]{N}$, iterative formula is given by

$$x_{n+1} = \frac{1}{k}\left[(k-1)x_n + \frac{N}{x_n^{k-1}}\right]$$

***Example 5.*** *Obtain extended formula for the root of equation $f(x) = 0$ by using Newton's-Raphson method.*

**Solution.** $f(x) = f[x_0 + (x - x_0)]$

$$\Rightarrow \quad f(x) = f(x_0) + (x - x_0) f'(x_0) \quad \ldots(i)$$

(By Taylor's series)

Also, $$f(x) = f(x_0) + (x - x_0) f'(x_0) + \frac{(x - x_0)^2}{2!} f''(x_0) \quad \ldots(ii)$$

But $f(x) = 0$

From Eq. (i), $x = x_0 - \frac{f(x_0)}{f'(x_0)}$

From Eq. (ii), we get

$$0 = f(x_0) + (x - x_0) f'(x_0) + \frac{1}{2}\left(-\frac{f(x_0)}{f'(x_0)}\right)^2 f''(x_0)$$
$$\Rightarrow \quad (x - x_0) f'(x_0) = -f(x_0) - \frac{1}{2}\left(\frac{f(x_0)}{f'(x_0)}\right)^2 f''(x_0)$$
$$\Rightarrow \quad x - x_0 = -\frac{f(x_0)}{f'(x_0)} - \frac{1}{2}\left(\frac{f(x_0)}{f'(x_0)}\right)^2 f''(x_0)$$
$$\Rightarrow \quad x = x_0 - \frac{f(x_0)}{f'(x_0)} - \frac{1}{2}\left(\frac{f(x_0)}{f'(x_0)}\right)^2 f''(x_0)$$

which is the required extended formula.

# Solution of System of Linear Algebraic Equations

## 1. Gauss Elimination Method

It is a direct method to solve systems of linear algebraic equations. In this method, the unknowns are eliminated successively and the system is reduced to an upper triangular system. The unknowns are obtained by back substitution.

Consider the equations

$$\left.\begin{aligned} a_{11}x + a_{12}y + a_{13}z &= b_1 \quad \ldots(i) \\ a_{21}x + a_{22}y + a_{23}z &= b_2 \quad \ldots(ii) \\ a_{31}x + a_{32}y + a_{33}z &= b_3 \quad \ldots(iii) \end{aligned}\right\} \quad \ldots(1)$$

## Method to Solve System of Eq. (1)

**Step 1** Assuming $a_{11} \neq 0$. We eliminate $x$ from Eqs. (ii) and (iii) with the help of Eq. (i) and then, we get new system.

$$\left.\begin{aligned} a_{11}x + a_{12}y + a_{13}z &= b_1 \quad \ldots(iv) \\ a'_{22}\,y + a'_{23}\,z &= b'_2 \quad \ldots(v) \\ a'_{32}\,y + a'_{33}\,z &= b'_3 \quad \ldots(vi) \end{aligned}\right\} \quad \ldots(2)$$

Here, the first Eq. (iv) is called the pivotal equation and $a_{11}$ is called the first pivot.

**Step 2** Assuming $a'_{22} \neq 0$, we eliminate $y$ from Eq. (vi) with the help of Eq. (v).

Now, we get the new system

$$\left.\begin{aligned} a_{11}x + a_{12}y + a_{13}z &= b_1 \quad \ldots(vii) \\ a'_{22}\,y + a'_{23}\,z &= b'_2 \quad \ldots(viii) \\ a'_{33}\,z &= b''_3 \quad \ldots(ix) \end{aligned}\right\} \quad \ldots(3)$$

Here, second Eq. (viii) is pivotal and $a'_{22}$ is the new pivot.

**Step 3** The values of $x$, $y$ and $z$ are found from system of Eq. (3) by back substitution.

> ***Note*** Solving system of Eq. (1) by above method is equivalent to solve the matrix equation, $AX = B$
>
> i.e., $$\begin{bmatrix} a_{11} & a_{12} & a_{13} \\ a_{21} & a_{22} & a_{23} \\ a_{31} & a_{32} & a_{33} \end{bmatrix}\begin{bmatrix} x \\ y \\ z \end{bmatrix} = \begin{bmatrix} b_1 \\ b_2 \\ b_3 \end{bmatrix}$$
>
> by converting coefficient matrix $A$ to upper triangular matrix by elementary row transformations.
> This method fail, if any one of the pivots $a_{11}, a'_{22}$ or $a''_{33}$ becomes zero.
> In such cases, we rewrite the equations in a different order, so that the pivots are non-zero.

***Example 6.*** *By using Gauss-elimination method, solve the equations*

$$2x + 4y + z = 3$$
$$3x + 2y - 2z = -2$$
$$x - y + z = 6$$

**Solution.** Given system of equations can be written as

$$x - y + z = 6 \quad \text{...(i)}$$
$$2x + 4y + z = 3 \quad \text{...(ii)}$$
$$3x + 2y - 2z = -2 \quad \text{...(iii)}$$

**Step 1** To eliminate $x$ from Eqs. (ii) and (iii) with the help of Eq. (i).
From Eq. (ii) −2 Eq. (i) and Eq. (iii) − 3 Eq. (i), we get

$$x - y + z = 6 \quad \text{...(iv)}$$
$$6y - z = -9 \quad \text{...(v)}$$
$$5y - 5z = -20 \quad \text{...(vi)}$$

**Step 2** To eliminate $y$ from Eq. (vi) with the help of Eq. (v) by $\frac{6}{5}$ Eq. (vi) — Eq. (v), we get

$$x - y + z = 6 \quad \text{...(vii)}$$
$$6y - z = -9 \quad \text{...(viii)}$$
$$-5z = -15 \quad \text{...(ix)}$$

**Step 3** Finding $x$, $y$ and $z$ by back substitution

From Eq. (ix), $z = 3$
From Eq. (viii), $6y = z - 9 = 3 - 9 = -6 \Rightarrow y = -1$
From Eq. (vii), $x = y - z + 6 = -1 - 3 + 6 = 2$
Hence, $x = 2,\ y = -1,\ z = 3$

**Alternative Method** From given equations, we have

$$\begin{bmatrix} 1 & -1 & 1 \\ 2 & 4 & 1 \\ 3 & 2 & -2 \end{bmatrix}\begin{bmatrix} x \\ y \\ z \end{bmatrix} = \begin{bmatrix} 6 \\ 3 \\ -2 \end{bmatrix}$$

$R_2 - 2R_1,\ R_3 - 3R_1$

$$\begin{bmatrix} 1 & -1 & 1 \\ 0 & 6 & -1 \\ 0 & 5 & -5 \end{bmatrix}\begin{bmatrix} x \\ y \\ z \end{bmatrix} = \begin{bmatrix} 6 \\ -9 \\ 20 \end{bmatrix}$$

$\frac{6}{5}R_3 - R_2$

$$\begin{bmatrix} 1 & -1 & 1 \\ 0 & 6 & -1 \\ 0 & 0 & -5 \end{bmatrix}\begin{bmatrix} x \\ y \\ z \end{bmatrix} = \begin{bmatrix} 6 \\ -9 \\ -15 \end{bmatrix}$$

Here, coefficient matrix in upper triangular form.

Thus, we have $-5z = -15 \Rightarrow z = 3$

$6y - z = -9 \Rightarrow 6y = z - 9 = 3 - 9 = -6$

$\Rightarrow y = -1$

and $x - y + z = 6 \Rightarrow x = y - z + 6$

$\Rightarrow x = -1 - 3 + 6 = 2$

$\Rightarrow \quad x = 2,\ y = -1,\ z = 3.$

***Example 7.*** *Using Gauss-elimination method, solve the equations*

$$x + 2y + 3z - u = 10$$
$$2x + 3y - 3z - u = 1$$
$$2x - y + 2z + 3u = 7$$
$$3x + 2y - 4z + 3u = 2$$

**Solution.** Writing the given system of equation in matrix form $AX = B$, we have

$$\begin{bmatrix} 1 & 2 & 3 & -1 \\ 2 & 3 & -3 & -1 \\ 2 & -1 & 2 & 3 \\ 3 & 2 & -4 & 3 \end{bmatrix}\begin{bmatrix} x \\ y \\ z \\ u \end{bmatrix} = \begin{bmatrix} 10 \\ 1 \\ 7 \\ 2 \end{bmatrix}$$

$(R_2 - 2R_1,\ R_3 - 2R_1,\ R_4 - 3R_1)$

$$\begin{bmatrix} 1 & 2 & 3 & -1 \\ 0 & -1 & -9 & 1 \\ 0 & -5 & -4 & 5 \\ 0 & -4 & -13 & 6 \end{bmatrix}\begin{bmatrix} x \\ y \\ z \\ u \end{bmatrix} = \begin{bmatrix} 10 \\ -19 \\ -13 \\ -28 \end{bmatrix}$$

$(R_3 - 5R_2,\ R_4 - 4R_2)$

$$\begin{bmatrix} 1 & 2 & 3 & -1 \\ 0 & -1 & -9 & 1 \\ 0 & 0 & 41 & 0 \\ 0 & 0 & 23 & 2 \end{bmatrix}\begin{bmatrix} x \\ y \\ z \\ u \end{bmatrix} = \begin{bmatrix} 10 \\ -19 \\ 82 \\ 48 \end{bmatrix}$$

$\left(R_4 - \frac{23}{41}R_3\right)$

$$\begin{bmatrix} 1 & 2 & 3 & -1 \\ 0 & -1 & -9 & 1 \\ 0 & 0 & 41 & 0 \\ 0 & 0 & 0 & 2 \end{bmatrix}\begin{bmatrix} x \\ y \\ z \\ u \end{bmatrix} = \begin{bmatrix} 10 \\ -19 \\ 82 \\ 2 \end{bmatrix}$$

Now, the coefficient matrix in the upper triangular form.
Now, from backward substitution, we get

$2u = 2 \Rightarrow u = 1$

$41z = 82 \Rightarrow z = 2$

$-y - 9z + u = -19 \Rightarrow y = -9z + u + 19$

$\Rightarrow y = -18 + 1 + 19 = 2$

$x + 2y + 3z - u = 10 \Rightarrow x = -2y - 3z + u + 10$

$\Rightarrow x = -4 - 6 + 1 + 10 = 1$

Hence, $x = 1,\ y = 2,\ z = 2,\ u = 1$

## 2. Gauss-Seidel Method

It is an iterative method of solving system of linear algebraic equations.

Consider, the system of equations

$$\left.\begin{aligned} a_{11}x+a_{12}y+a_{13}z=b_1 \quad &\ldots(i)\\ a_{21}x+a_{22}y+a_{23}z=b_2 \quad &\ldots(ii)\\ a_{31}x+a_{32}y+a_{33}z=b_3 \quad &\ldots(iii)\end{aligned}\right\} \quad \ldots(1)$$

Now, Eq. (1) can be written as

$$\left.\begin{aligned} x=\frac{1}{a_{11}}(b_1-a_{12}y-a_{13}z) \quad &\ldots(iv)\\ y=\frac{1}{a_{22}}(b_2-a_{21}x-a_{23}z) \quad &\ldots(v)\\ z=\frac{1}{a_{33}}(b_3-a_{31}x-a_{32}y) \quad &\ldots(vi)\end{aligned}\right\} \quad \ldots(2)$$

Assuming initial approximations for $x, y, z$ are $x_0, y_0, z_0$ respectively.

(We may take $x_0=0$, $y_0=0$, $z_0=0$ as initial approximation, if it is not given in problem).

### First iteration

Putting $y=y_0$, $z=z_0$ in Eq. (iv), we get

$$x_1=\frac{1}{a_{11}}(b_1-a_{12}y_0-a_{13}z_0)$$

Putting $x=x_1$, $z=z_0$ in Eq. (v), we get

$$y_1=\frac{1}{a_{22}}(b_2-a_{21}x_1-a_{23}z_0)$$

Putting $x=x_1$, $y=y_1$ in Eq. (vi), we get

$$z_1=\frac{1}{a_{33}}(b_3-a_{31}x_1-a_{32}y_1)$$

Similarly, we find second iteration, third and so on to get the values of $x$, $y$ and $z$ with desired degree of accuracy.

> ***Note*** **(a)** We can stop the iteration, when we get nearly same values of $x$, $y$ and $z$ for two consecutive iteration.
> OR, we can stop the iteration, when we get to the nearest of exact values of $x$, $y$ and $z$.
>
> **(b)** The convergence in the Gauss-seidel method is twice as fast as in Jacobi's method.
>
> **(c)** Gauss-seidel method converges for any choice of the initial approximations, if in each equation of the system, the absolute value of the largest coefficient is almost equal to the sum of the absolute values of all the remaining coefficients.
> OR, In atleast one equation, the absolute value of the largest coefficient is greater than the sum of the absolute values of all the remaining coefficients.

***Example 8.*** *Solve by Gauss-Seidel method*

$$\begin{aligned}6x+y+z&=105\\ 4x+8y+3z&=155\\ 5x+4y-10z&=65\end{aligned}$$

**Solution.** Given equations can be written as

$$x=\frac{35}{2}-\frac{1}{6}y-\frac{1}{6}z \quad \ldots(i)$$

$$y=\frac{155}{8}-\frac{1}{2}x-\frac{3}{8}z \quad \ldots(ii)$$

$$z=-\frac{13}{2}+\frac{1}{2}x+\frac{2}{5}y \quad \ldots(iii)$$

### First iteration

Putting $y=y_0=0$, $z=z_0=0$ in Eq. (i), we get

$$x_1=\frac{35}{2}$$

Putting $x=x_1=\frac{35}{2}$, $z=z_0=0$ in Eq. (ii), we get

$$y_1=\frac{155}{8}-\frac{35}{4}=\frac{85}{8}$$

Putting $x=x_1=\frac{35}{2}$, $y=y_1=\frac{85}{8}$ in Eq. (iii), we get

$$z_1=-\frac{13}{2}+\frac{35}{4}+\frac{17}{4}=\frac{13}{2}=6.5$$

### Second iteration

Putting $y=y_1$, $z=z_1$ in Eq. (i), we get

$$x_2=\frac{35}{2}-\frac{1}{6}y_1-\frac{1}{6}z_1=14.64$$

Putting $x=x_2$, $z=z_1$ in Eq. (ii), we get

$$y_2=\frac{155}{8}-\frac{1}{2}x_2-\frac{3}{8}z_1=9.62$$

Putting $x=x_2$, $y=y_2$ in Eq. (iii), we get

$$z_2=-\frac{13}{2}+\frac{1}{2}x_2+\frac{2}{5}y_2=4.67$$

Similarly, we can find third iteration, fourth iteration and so on.

***Example 9.*** *Apply Gauss-seidal method to solve the system of equations*

$$\begin{aligned}20x+y-2z&=17\\ 3x+20y-z&=-18\\ 2x-3y+20z&=25\end{aligned}$$

**Solution.** We write the given equations in the form

$$x=\frac{1}{20}(17-y+2z) \quad \ldots(i)$$

$$y=\frac{1}{20}(-18-3x+z) \quad \ldots(ii)$$

$$z=\frac{1}{20}(25-2x+3y) \quad \ldots(iii)$$

### First iteration

Putting $y=y_0=0$, $z=z_0=0$ in Eq. (i), we get

$$x_1=\frac{1}{20}(17-y_0+2z_0)=0.85$$

Putting $x=x_1$, $z=z_0$ in Eq. (ii), we get

$$y_1=\frac{1}{20}(-18-3x_1+z_0)=-1.0275$$

Putting $x=x_1$, $y=y_1$ in Eq. (iii), we get

$$z_1=\frac{1}{20}(25-2x_1+3y_1)=1.0109$$

**Second iteration**

Putting $y = y_1$, $z = z_1$ in Eq. (i), we get

$$x_2 = \frac{1}{20}(17 - y_1 + 2z_1) = 1.0025$$

Putting $x = x_2$, $z = z_1$ in Eq. (ii), we get

$$y_2 = \frac{1}{20}(-18 - 3x_2 + z_1) = -0.9998$$

Putting $x = x_2$, $y = y_2$ in Eq. (iii), we get

$$z_2 = \frac{1}{20}(25 - 2x_2 + 3y_2) = 0.9998$$

**Third iteration**

$$x_3 = \frac{1}{20}(17 - y_2 + 2z_2) = 1.0000$$

$$y_3 = \frac{1}{20}(-18 - 3x_3 + z_2) = -1.0000$$

$$z_3 = \frac{1}{20}(25 - 2x_3 + 3y_3) = 1.0000$$

The values in the second and third iterations are nearly same, we can stop. Hence, the solution is $x = 1$, $y = -1$, $z = 1$.

# Finite Differences

Let $y = f(x)$ is tabulated for the equally spaced values of $x = x_0, x_1, x_2, \ldots, x_n$, where $x_i = x_0 + ih$, $i = 0, 1, 2, \ldots, n$

$\Rightarrow \quad x_1 = x_0 + h,\ x_2 = x_0 + 2h, \ldots,\ x_n = x_0 + nh.$

we now define the following operators.

## 1. The Shift Operator

We have, $\quad E f(x_i) = f(x_i + h)$

or $\quad Ey_i = y_{i+1}$ or $Ef_i = f_{i+1}$

For $i = 0$, $\quad E f(x_0) = f(x_0 + h) = f(x_1)$

For $i = 1$, $\quad Ef(x_1) = f(x_1 + h) = f(x_0 + 2h) = f(x_2)$

For $i = 2$, $\quad Ef(x_2) = f(x_2 + h) = f(x_0 + 3h) = f(x_3)$

... ... ... ... ... ...

For $i = n$, $\quad Ef(x_n) = f(x_{n+1})$

Also, $\quad E^2 f(x_i) = E[E f(x_i)] = E[f(x_i + h)] = f(x_i + 2h)$

$\Rightarrow \quad E^n f(x_i) = f(x_i + nh)$

## 2. The Forward Difference Operator

We have, $\quad \Delta f(x_i) = f(x_i + h) - f(x_i)$

or $\quad \Delta y_i = y_{i+1} - y_i$ or $\Delta f_i = f_{i+1} - f_i$

For $i = 0$, $\quad \Delta f(x_0) = f(x_0 + h) - f(x_0)$

For $i = 1$, $\quad \Delta f(x_1) = f(x_1 + h) - f(x_1)$

$$= f(x_0 + 2h) - f(x_0 + h)$$

For $i = 2$, $\quad \Delta f(x_2) = f(x_2 + h) - f(x_2)$

$$= f(x_0 + 3h) - f(x_0 + 2h)$$

... ... ... ... ... ...

For $i = n$, $\quad \Delta f(x_n) = f(x_n + h) - f(x_n)$

$$= f(x_0 + \overline{n+1}\,h) - f(x_0 + nh)$$

Also, $\quad \Delta^2 f(x_i) = \Delta(\Delta f(x_i))$

$$= \Delta[f(x_i + h) - f(x_i)]$$
$$= \Delta f(x_i + h) - \Delta f(x_i)$$
$$= \{f(x_i + 2h) - f(x_i + h)\} - \{f(x_i + h) - f(x_i)\}$$
$$= f(x_i + 2h) - 2f(x_i + h) + f(x_i)$$

In general $\quad \Delta^n f(x_i) = \sum_{k=0}^{n} (-1)^k \cdot {}^nC_k \cdot f_{i+n-k}$

## 3. The Backward Difference Operator

We have, $\quad \nabla f(x_i) = f(x_i) - f(x_i - h)$

or $\quad \nabla y_i = y_i - y_{i-1}$ or $\nabla f_i = f_i - f_{i-1}$

For $i = 0$, $\quad \nabla f(x_0) = f(x_0) - f(x_0 - h)$

For $i = 1$, $\quad \nabla f(x_1) = f(x_1) - f(x_1 - h)$

$$= f(x_0 + h) - f(x_0)$$

For $i = 2$, $\quad \nabla f(x_2) = f(x_2) - f(x_2 - h)$

$$= f(x_0 + 2h) - f(x_0 + h)$$

Also, $\quad \nabla^2 f(x_i) = \nabla(\nabla f(x_i))$

$$= \nabla(f(x_i) - f(x_i - h))$$
$$= \nabla f(x_i) - \nabla f(x_i - h)$$
$$= \{f(x_i) - f(x_i - h)\} - \{f(x_i - h) - f(x_i - 2h)\}$$
$$= f(x_i) - 2f(x_i - h) + f(x_i - 2h)$$

In general

$$\nabla^n f(x_i) = \sum_{k=0}^{n} (-1)^k \cdot {}^nC_k \cdot f_{i-k}$$

## 4. The Central Difference Operator

We have, $\quad \delta f(x_i) = f\left(x_i + \frac{h}{2}\right) - f\left(x_i - \frac{h}{2}\right)$

or $\quad \delta y_i = y_{i+\frac{1}{2}} - y_{i-\frac{1}{2}}$ or $\delta f_i = f_{i+\frac{1}{2}} - f_{i-\frac{1}{2}}$

For $i = 0$, $\quad \delta f(x_0) = f\left(x_0 + \frac{h}{2}\right) - f\left(x_0 - \frac{h}{2}\right)$

or $\quad \delta y_0 = y_{\frac{1}{2}} - y_{\frac{1}{2}}$

For $i = 1$, $\quad \delta f(x_1) = f\left(x_1 + \frac{h}{2}\right) - f\left(x_1 - \frac{h}{2}\right)$

$$= f\left(x_0 + \frac{3h}{2}\right) - f\left(x_0 + \frac{h}{2}\right)$$

or, $\quad \delta y_1 = y_{\frac{3}{2}} - y_{\frac{1}{2}}$

Also, $\quad \delta^2 f(x_i) = \delta(\delta f(x_i))$

$$= \delta\left(f\left(x_i + \frac{h}{2}\right) - f\left(x_i - \frac{h}{2}\right)\right)$$

$$= \delta f\left(x_i + \frac{h}{2}\right) - \delta f\left(x_i - \frac{h}{2}\right)$$
$$= \{f(x_i + h) - f(x_i)\} - \{f(x_i) - f(x_i - h)\}$$
$$= f(x_i + h) - 2f(x_i) + f(x_i - h)$$

In general

$$\delta^n f(x_i) = \sum_{k=0}^{n} (-1)^k . {}^nC_k . f_{i+\frac{n}{2}-k}$$

## 5. The Average Operator

We have, $\mu f(x_i) = \frac{1}{2}\left[f\left(x_i + \frac{h}{2}\right) + f\left(x_i - \frac{h}{2}\right)\right]$

or $\mu y_i = \frac{1}{2}\left(y_{i+\frac{1}{2}} + y_{i-\frac{1}{2}}\right)$ or $\mu f_i = \frac{1}{2}\left(f_{i+\frac{1}{2}} + f_{i-\frac{1}{2}}\right)$

For $i = 0$, $\mu f(x_0) = \frac{1}{2}\left[f\left(x_0 + \frac{h}{2}\right) + f\left(x_0 - \frac{h}{2}\right)\right]$

or $\mu y_0 = \frac{1}{2}\left(y_{\frac{1}{2}} + y_{-\frac{1}{2}}\right)$

For $i = 1$, $\mu f(x_1) = \frac{1}{2}\left[f\left(x_1 + \frac{h}{2}\right) + f\left(x_1 - \frac{h}{2}\right)\right]$

$$= \frac{1}{2}\left[f\left(x_0 + \frac{3h}{2}\right) + f\left(x_0 + \frac{h}{2}\right)\right]$$

or $\mu y_1 = \frac{1}{2}\left(y_{\frac{3}{2}} + y_{\frac{1}{2}}\right)$

## Important Relations on Operators

1. $E = \Delta + 1$
2. $E^{-1} = 1 - \nabla$
3. $E\nabla = \nabla E = \Delta$
4. $\delta = \nabla(1-\nabla)^{-\frac{1}{2}}$
5. $\mu = \left(1 + \frac{\delta^2}{4}\right)^{\frac{1}{2}}$
6. $\mu\delta = \frac{1}{2}(\Delta + \nabla)$
7. $hD = \log(1+\Delta) = -\log(1-\nabla) = \sinh^{-1}(\mu\delta)$, where $D$ is the differential operator.
8. $\delta = E^{\frac{1}{2}} - E^{-\frac{1}{2}}$
9. $\mu = \frac{1}{2}\left(E^{\frac{1}{2}} + E^{-\frac{1}{2}}\right)$
10. $E\Delta = \Delta E$

## Important Properties on Operators

1. $\Delta[f(x) + g(x)] = \Delta f(x) + \Delta g(x)$
2. $E[f(x) + g(x)] = Ef(x) + Eg(x)$
3. $\Delta^m \Delta^n f(x) = \Delta^{m+n} f(x)$
4. $E^m E^n f(x) = E^{m+n} f(x)$
5. $\Delta k = 0$ and $Ek = k$ where $k$ is any constant.
6. $\Delta(cf(x)) = c\Delta f(x)$ and $E(cf(x)) = cEf(x)$, where $c$ is any constant.

## Important Results on Finite Differences

1. $\Delta(f(x)g(x)) = f(x+h)\Delta g(x) + \Delta f(x)g(x)$
2. $\Delta\left(\frac{f(x)}{g(x)}\right) = \frac{\Delta f(x)\cdot g(x) - f(x)\Delta g(x)}{g(x+h)g(x)}$
3. The value of $\Delta^n x^m$ at $x = 0$, *i.e.*, $(\Delta^n x^m)_{x=0} = n^m - {}^nC_1(n-1)^m + {}^nC_2(n-2)^m - \ldots$, where $m > n$.
   The value $= 0$, if $m < n$.

***Example 10.*** *Find $\Delta^2 x^3$ at $x = 0$.*

**Solution.** Here, $n = 2$, $m = 3$ $(m > n)$

$$\therefore\ (\Delta^2 x^3)_{x=0} = 2^3 - {}^2C_1(2-1)^3 + {}^2C_2(2-2)^3 - \ldots$$
$$= 8 - 2 + 0 = 6$$

***Example 11.*** *Find $\Delta^3 x^2$ at $x = 0$.*

**Solution.** $(\Delta^3 x^2)_{x=0} = 0$. Since, $m < n$.

4. $\Delta x^{(n)} = nx^{(n-1)}$, where $x^{(n)} = x(x-h)(x-2h)\ldots(x - \overline{n-1}h)$
5. $\frac{1}{\Delta}x^{(n)} = \frac{x^{(n+1)}}{n+1}$

***Example 12.*** *Evaluate $\Delta \tan^{-1}\left(\frac{n-1}{n}\right)$.*

**Solution.** Let $h = 1$

$$\therefore\ \Delta\tan^{-1}\left(\frac{n-1}{n}\right) = \tan^{-1}\left(\frac{n+1-1}{n+1}\right) - \tan^{-1}\left(\frac{n-1}{n}\right)$$
$$= \tan^{-1}\left(\frac{n}{n+1}\right) - \tan^{-1}\left(\frac{n-1}{n}\right)$$
$$= \tan^{-1}\left(\frac{\frac{n}{n+1} - \frac{n-1}{n}}{1 + \frac{n}{n+1}\cdot\frac{n-1}{n}}\right)$$
$$= \tan^{-1}\left(\frac{n^2 - (n^2-1)}{n^2 + n + n^2 - n}\right) = \tan^{-1}\left(\frac{1}{2n^2}\right)$$

***Example 13.*** *Evaluate $\Delta^2 \cos 2x$.*

**Solution.** $\Delta^2 \cos 2x = \Delta\{\cos 2(x+h) - \cos 2x\}$

$$= \Delta\cos 2(x+h) - \Delta\cos 2x$$
$$= [\cos 2(x+2h) - \cos 2(x+h)] - [\cos 2(x+h) - \cos 2x]$$
$$= -2\sin(2x+3h)\sin h + 2\sin(2x+h)\sin h$$
$$= -2\sin h[\sin(2x+3h) - \sin(2x+h)]$$
$$= -2\sin h[2\cos(2x+2h)\sin h]$$
$$= -4\sin^2 h\cos(2x+2h)$$

***Example 14.*** *Evaluate $\Delta^2\left(\frac{5x+12}{x^2+5x+6}\right)$ interval of differencing being unity.*

**Solution.** $\Delta^2\left(\frac{5x+12}{x^2+5x+6}\right)=\Delta^2\left(\frac{5x+12}{(x+2)(x+3)}\right)$

$$=\Delta^2\left\{\frac{2}{x+2}+\frac{3}{x+3}\right\}$$

$$=\Delta\left\{\Delta\left(\frac{2}{x+2}\right)+\Delta\left(\frac{3}{x+3}\right)\right\}$$

$$=\Delta\left\{2\left(\frac{1}{x+3}-\frac{1}{x+2}\right)+3\left(\frac{1}{x+4}-\frac{1}{x+3}\right)\right\}$$

$$=-2\Delta\left\{\frac{1}{(x+2)(x+3)}\right\}-3\Delta\left\{\frac{1}{(x+3)(x+4)}\right\}$$

$$=-2\left\{\frac{1}{(x+3)(x+4)}-\frac{1}{(x+2)(x+3)}\right\}$$

$$-3\left\{\frac{1}{(x+4)(x+5)}-\frac{1}{(x+3)(x+4)}\right\}$$

$$=\frac{4}{(x+2)(x+3)(x+4)}+\frac{6}{(x+3)(x+4)(x+5)}$$

$$=\frac{2(5x+16)}{(x+2)(x+3)(x+4)(x+5)}.$$

***Example 15.*** *Prove that* $\left(\frac{\Delta^2}{E}\right)e^x\cdot\frac{Ee^x}{\Delta^2 e^x}=e^x$, *the interval of differencing being h.*

**Solution.** $\left(\frac{\Delta^2}{E}\right)e^x=\frac{(E-1)^2}{E}e^x=\left(\frac{E^2-2E+1}{E}\right)e^x$

$$=(E-2+E^{-1})e^x=e^{x+h}-2e^x+e^{x-h} \quad \text{...(i)}$$

$$\frac{Ee^x}{\Delta^2 e^x}=\frac{e^{x+h}}{(E-1)^2e^x}=\frac{e^{x+h}}{(E^2-2E+1)e^x}$$

$$=\frac{e^{x+h}}{e^{x+2h}-2e^{x+h}+e^x}=\frac{e^x}{e^{x+h}-2e^x+e^{x-h}} \quad \text{...(ii)}$$

From Eqs. (i) and (ii), we get

$$\left(\frac{\Delta^2}{E}\right)e^x.\frac{Ee^x}{\Delta^2e^x}=\frac{(e^{x+h}-2e^x+e^{x-h})e^x}{(e^{x+h}-2e^x+e^{x-h})}=e^x$$

***Example 16.*** Evaluate $\Delta(e^{ax}\log bx)$.

**Solution.** Let $f(x)=e^{ax}$, $g(x)=\log bx$

Using $\Delta\{f(x)g(x)\}=f(x+h)\Delta g(x)+\Delta f(x)\cdot g(x)$

$$\Delta(e^{ax}\log bx)=e^{a(x+h)}(\Delta\log bx)+(\Delta e^{ax})\log bx$$

$$=e^{a(x+h)}\{\log b(x+h)-\log bx\}$$

$$+\{e^{a(x+h)}-e^{ax}\}\log bx$$

$$=e^{a(x+h)}\cdot\log\left(1+\frac{h}{x}\right)+e^{ax}(e^{ah}-1)\log bx$$

***Example 17.*** Evaluate $\Delta\left(\frac{x^2}{\cos 2x}\right)$.

**Solution.** Take $f(x)=x^2$ and $g(x)=\cos 2x$

$\therefore$ $\Delta f(x)=f(x+h)-f(x)=(x+h)^2-x^2=h(2x+h)$

and $\Delta g(x)=g(x+h)-g(x)=\cos 2(x+h)-\cos 2x$

$$=-2\sin(2x+h)\sinh$$

We know that, $\Delta\left[\frac{f(x)}{g(x)}\right]=\frac{g(x)\,\Delta f(x)-f(x)\,\Delta g(x)}{g(x+h)g(x)}$

Putting the values of $f(x)$ and $g(x)$, we have

$$\Delta\left[\frac{f(x)}{g(x)}\right]=\frac{(\cos 2x)\,h\,(2x+h)-x^2[-2\sinh\sin(2x+h)]}{\cos(2x+2h)\cos 2x}$$

$$=\frac{h(2x+h)\cos 2x+2x^2\sinh\sin(2x+h)}{\cos(2x+2h)\cos 2x}$$

***Example 18.*** Evaluate $\Delta^n\left(\frac{1}{x}\right)$.

**Solution.** Now, $\Delta\left(\frac{1}{x}\right)=\frac{1}{x+1}-\frac{1}{x}=-\frac{1}{x(x+1)}$

$$\Delta^2\left(\frac{1}{x}\right)=\Delta\left[-\frac{1}{x(x+1)}\right]=-\left[\frac{1}{(x+1)(x+2)}-\frac{1}{x(x+1)}\right]$$

$$=-\frac{x-(x+2)}{x(x+1)(x+2)}$$

Again,

$$\Delta^2\left(\frac{1}{x}\right)=\frac{(-1)^2 2!}{x(x+1)(x+2)} \text{ and so on,}$$

.......................................................................

$$\therefore \quad \Delta^n\left(\frac{1}{x}\right)=\frac{(-1)^n n!}{x(x+1)(x+2)\dots(x+n)}.$$

***Example 19.*** *If* $\Delta^3 u_x=0$, *prove that*

$$u_{x+1/2}=\frac{1}{2}(u_x+u_{x+1})-\frac{1}{16}(\Delta^2u_{x+1}+\Delta^2u_x).$$

**Solution.** $u_{x+1/2}=E^{1/2}u_x=(1+\Delta)^{1/2}u_x$

$$=\left(1+\frac{1}{2}\Delta-\frac{1}{8}\Delta^2+\dots\right)u_x$$

(Expanding up to $\Delta^2$ only, since $\Delta^3 u_x=0$, etc.)

$$=u_x+\frac{1}{2}\Delta u_x-\frac{1}{8}\Delta^2u_x+\dots$$

$$=u_x+\frac{1}{2}[u_{x+1}-u_x]-\frac{1}{16}\Delta^2u_x-\frac{1}{16}\Delta^2u_x+\dots$$

$$\left[\begin{aligned}\Delta^3u_x&=\Delta^2u_{x+1}-\Delta^2u_x\\0&=\Delta^2u_{x+1}-\Delta^2u_x\\\Delta^2u_{x+1}&=\Delta^2u_x\end{aligned}\right]$$

$$=u_x+\frac{1}{2}u_{x+1}-\frac{1}{2}u_x-\frac{1}{16}\Delta^2u_x-\frac{1}{16}\Delta^2u_{x+1}+\dots$$

$$=\frac{1}{2}(u_x+u_{x+1})-\frac{1}{16}[\Delta^2u_x+\Delta^2u_{x+1}]+\dots$$

***Example 20.*** Evaluate $\Delta^3(1-x)(1-2x)(1-3x)$, *the interval of difference being unity.*

**Solution.** $f(x)=(1-x)(1-2x)(1-3x)$

$$=-6x^3+11x^2-6x+1$$

$$\Rightarrow \quad \Delta^3f(x)=-6\Delta^3x^3+11\Delta^3x^2-6\Delta^3x+\Delta^3(1)$$

$$=(-6)(3!)+11(0)-6(0)+0 \quad \left(\begin{aligned}\Delta^nx^m&=n!,\text{ if } m=n\\&=0,\text{ if } n>m\end{aligned}\right)$$

$$=-36.$$

***Example 21.*** *If $f(x) = x(x-1)(x-2)(x-3)$. Then, find $\Delta f(x)$.*

**Solution.** As we know that

$$x^{(1)} = x,\ x^{(2)} = x(x-1),\ x^{(3)} = x(x-1)(x-2),$$
$$x^{(4)} = x(x-1)(x-2)(x-3)$$

and $\Delta x^{(n)} = nx^{(n-1)}$

$\Rightarrow \quad \Delta f(x) = \Delta x^{(4)} = 4x^{(3)} = 4x(x-1)(x-2)$

***Example 22.*** *If $f(x) = 2x^3 - 3x^2 + 3x - 10$. Then, show that $\Delta^3 f(x) = 12$.*

**Solution.** Let $f(x) = ax^{(3)} + bx^{(2)} + cx^{(1)} + d$.

By synthetic division method,

| | $x^3$ | $x^2$ | $x$ | |
|---|---|---|---|---|
| 1 | 2 | −3 | 3 | $-10 = d$ |
| | 0 | 2 | −1 | |
| 2 | 2 | −1 | $2 = c$ | |
| | 0 | 4 | | |
| | $2 = a$ | $3 = b$ | | |

$\Rightarrow \quad f(x) = 2x^{(3)} + 3x^{(2)} + 2x^{(1)} - 10$

$\Rightarrow \quad \Delta f(x) = 6x^{(2)} + 6x^{(1)} + 2$

$$\left(\because \ \Delta x^{(1)} = \Delta x = x + 1 - x = 1 \text{ and } \Delta(k) = 0\right)$$

$\Rightarrow \quad \Delta^2 f(x) = 12x^{(1)} + 6$

$\Rightarrow \quad \Delta^3 f(x) = 12$

***Example 23.*** *Find the function $f(x)$, whose first difference is $9x^2 + 11x + 5$.*

**Solution.** Given, $\Delta f(x) = 9x^2 + 11x + 5$

Let $9x^2 + 11x + 5 = ax^{(2)} + bx^{(1)} + c$

Now,

| | $x^2$ | $x$ | |
|---|---|---|---|
| 1 | 9 | 11 | $5 = c$ |
| | 0 | 9 | |
| | $9 = a$ | $20 = b$ | |

$\Rightarrow \quad \Delta f(x) = 9x^{(2)} + 20x^{(1)} + 5$

$\Rightarrow \quad f(x) = \dfrac{9x^{(3)}}{3} + \dfrac{20x^{(2)}}{2} + \dfrac{5x^{(1)}}{1} + k$

(After integration)

$\Rightarrow \quad f(x) = 3x^{(3)} + 10x^{(2)} + 5x^{(1)} + k$

$= 3x(x-1)(x-2) + 10x(x-1) + 5x + k$

$= 3(x^3 - 3x^2 + 2x) + 10(x^2 - x) + 5x + k$

$= 3x^3 - 9x^2 + 6x + 10x^2 - 10x + 5x + k$

$= 3x^3 + x^2 + x + k$

***Example 24.*** *Construct a forward difference table for*

$$f(1) = 1,\ f(2) = 3,\ f(3) = 8,\ f(4) = 15,\ f(5) = 25$$

*and hence find $\Delta^4 f(1)$.*

**Solution.**

| $x$ | $f(x)$ | $\Delta f(x)$ | $\Delta^2 f(x)$ | $\Delta^3 f(x)$ | $\Delta^4 f(x)$ |
|---|---|---|---|---|---|
| 1 | 1 | | | | |
| | | 2 | | | |
| 2 | 3 | | 3 | | |
| | | 5 | | −1 | |
| 3 | 8 | | 2 | | 2 |
| | | 7 | | 1 | |
| 4 | 15 | | 3 | | |
| | | 10 | | | |
| 5 | 25 | | | | |

From, the table, $f(1) = 1, \Delta f(1) = 2$,

$\Delta^2 f(1) = 3, \Delta^3 f(1) = -1, \Delta^4 f(1) = 2$

***Example 25.*** *Find the missing term in the following table*

| $x$ | 0 | 1 | 2 | 3 | 4 |
|---|---|---|---|---|---|
| $f(x)$ | 1 | 3 | 9 | — | 81 |

**Solution.** Here, given $f(0) = 1,\ f(1) = 3,\ f(2) = 9,\ f(3) = k$ (say), $f(4) = 81$

Here, four values of $f(x)$ are given, so we can assume $f(x)$ to be a polynomial of degree three.

Hence, $\Delta^4 f(x) = 0$

$\Rightarrow \quad (E-1)^4 f(x) = 0$

$\Rightarrow \quad (E^4 - 4E^3 + 6E^2 - 4E + 1)f(x) = 0$

$\Rightarrow \quad E^4 f(x) - 4E^3 f(x) + 6E^2 f(x) - 4Ef(x) + f(x) = 0$

$\Rightarrow \quad f(x+4) - 4f(x+3) + 6f(x+2) - 4f(x+1) + f(x) - 0$

(Since, $E^n f(x) = f(x + nh)$. Here, we have taken $h = 1$)

Put $x = 0$, we get

$f(4) - 4f(3) + 6f(2) - 4f(1) + f(0) = 0$

$\Rightarrow \quad 81 - 4k + 54 - 12 + 1 = 0$

$\Rightarrow \quad 4k = 124 \Rightarrow k = 31$

***Example 26.*** *Construct a central difference table for $f(0) = 8,\ f(1) = 12,\ f(2) = 20,\ f(3) = 34,\ f(4) = 60$ and hence, find $\delta^4 f(2)$.*

**Solution.**

| $x$ | $f(x)$ | Ist diff. $\delta f$ | IInd diff. $\delta^2 f$ | IIIrd diff. $\delta^3 f$ | IVth diff. $\delta^4 f$ |
|---|---|---|---|---|---|
| 0 | $8 = f_0$ | | | | |
| | | $4 = \delta f_{\frac{1}{2}}$ | | | |
| 1 | $12 = f_1$ | | $4 = \delta^2 f_1$ | | |
| | | $8 = \delta f_{\frac{3}{2}}$ | | $2 = \delta^3 f_{\frac{3}{2}}$ | |
| 2 | $20 = f_2$ | | $6 = \delta^2 f_2$ | | $4 = \delta^4 f_2$ |
| | | $14 = \delta f_{\frac{5}{2}}$ | | $6 = \delta^3 f_{\frac{5}{2}}$ | |
| 3 | $34 = f_3$ | | $12 = \delta^2 f_3$ | | |
| | | $26 = \delta f_{\frac{7}{2}}$ | | | |
| 4 | $60 = f_4$ | | | | |

From table, $\delta^4 f_2 = 4 \Rightarrow \delta^4 f(2) = 4$.

## Divided Differences

If $(x_0, y_0), (x_1, y_1), (x_2, y_2), \ldots$ be given points, then the first divided difference for $x_0, x_1$ is defined by the relation

$$f[x_0, x_1] = \frac{y_1 - y_0}{x_1 - x_0}$$

$$\Rightarrow \quad f[x_0, x_1] = \frac{f(x_1) - f(x_0)}{x_1 - x_0}$$

Similarly, $f[x_1, x_2] = \dfrac{f(x_2) - f(x_1)}{x_2 - x_1}$

$f[x_2, x_3] = \dfrac{f(x_3) - f(x_2)}{x_3 - x_2}$ and so on.

The second divided difference for $x_0, x_1, x_2$ is defined as

$$f[x_0, x_1, x_2] = \frac{f[x_1, x_2] - f[x_0, x_1]}{x_2 - x_0}$$

The third divided difference for $x_0, x_1, x_2, x_3$ is defined as

$$f[x_0, x_1, x_2, x_3] = \frac{f[x_1, x_2, x_3] - f[x_0, x_1, x_2]}{x_3 - x_0}$$

and so on.

> ***Note*** **(a)** $f[x_0, x_1] = f[x_1, x_0]$
>
> **(b)** $f[x_0, x_1, x_2] = f[x_1, x_2, x_0]$
> $= f\{x_2, x_0, x_1\}$ and so on.
>
> **(c)** $f[x_0, x_1] = \dfrac{f(x_1) - f(x_0)}{x_1 - x_0} = \dfrac{f(x_0 + h) - f(x_0)}{h} = \dfrac{\Delta f(x_0)}{h}$
>
> Similarly, $f[x_0, x_1, x_2] = \dfrac{\Delta^2 f(x_0)}{2! h^2}$
>
> In general, $f[x_0, x_1, x_2, \ldots, x_n] = \dfrac{\Delta^n f(x_0)}{n! h^n}$

***Example 27.*** *Find second divided difference of $x^2$.*

**Solution.** Here, $f(x) = x^2$

Assuming $x_0 = 0$, and $h = 1$.

Now, second divided difference is given by

$$\frac{\Delta^2 f(x_0)}{2h^2} = \frac{(E-1)^2 f(0)}{2}$$

$$= \frac{E^2 f(0) - 2Ef(0) + f(0)}{2}$$

$$= \frac{f(2) - 2f(1) + f(0)}{2}$$

$$= \frac{4 - 2 + 0}{2} = 1$$

***Example 28.*** *Construct divided difference table for the following*

| $x$ | 2 | 4 | 9 | 10 |
|---|---|---|---|---|
| $f(x)$ | 4 | 56 | 711 | 980 |

*and hence, find third divided difference.*

**Solution.**

| $x$ | $f(x)$ | Ist diff. $f[x_0, x_1]$ | IInd diff. $f[x_0, x_1, x_2]$ | IIIrd diff. $f[x_0, x_1, x_2, x_3]$ |
|---|---|---|---|---|
| 2 | 4 | | | |
| | | $\frac{56-4}{4-2} = 26$ | | |
| 4 | 56 | | $\frac{131-26}{9-2} = 15$ | |
| | | $\frac{711-56}{9-4} = 131$ | | $\frac{23-15}{10-2} = 1$ |
| 9 | 711 | $\frac{980-711}{10-9} = 269$ | $\frac{269-131}{10-4} = 23$ | |
| 10 | 980 | | | |

and therefore, third divided difference is 1.

## Interpolation and Numerical Differentiation

Let $y = f(x)$ be a function of $x$. The corresponding values of $y$ for $x_0, x_0 + h, x_0 + 2h, \ldots, x_0 + nh$ are given as
$y_0 = f(x_0), y_1 = f(x_0 + h), y_2 = f(x_0 + 2h), \ldots, y_n = f(x_0 + nh)$.
Interpolation is the process of finding the values of $y$ for any $x \in [x_0, x_0 + nh]$ under the following assumptions

**(i)** The function is a polynomial function.

**(ii)** There is no sudden jump or fall in the value of $y$ for given $x$.

**(iii)** The function is one-one.

### 1. Gregory-Newton Forward Difference Interpolation Formula

$$\because \quad f(x_0 + ph) = E^p f(x_0) \Rightarrow f(x_0 + ph) = (1 + \Delta)^p f(x_0)$$

$$\Rightarrow \quad y_p = (1 + \Delta)^p y_0$$

$$= \left\{1 + p\Delta + \frac{p(p-1)}{2!}\Delta^2 + \frac{p(p-1)(p-2)}{3!}\Delta^3 + \ldots + \frac{p(p-1)(p-2)\ldots p-n-1}{n!}\Delta^n\right\} y_0$$

(Using Binomial Theorem)

$$\Rightarrow \quad y_p = y_0 + p\,\Delta y_0 + \frac{p(p-1)}{2!}\Delta^2 y_0 + \frac{p(p-1)(p-2)}{3!}\Delta^3 y_0 + \ldots + \frac{p(p-1)(p-2)\ldots(p-n-1)}{n!}\Delta^n y_0 \quad \ldots\text{(i)}$$

Another form of Eq. (i)

Let $x_0 + ph = x$

$$\Rightarrow \qquad p = \frac{x - x_0}{h} = X \qquad \text{(say)}$$

Then, from Eq. (i), we get

$$f(x) = y = y_0 + X\,\Delta y_0 + \frac{X(X-1)}{2!}\Delta^2 y_0 + \ldots$$

## Differentiation

$$\frac{dy}{dx} = \frac{dy}{dp}\cdot\frac{dp}{dx} = \frac{1}{h}\cdot\frac{dy}{dp} \qquad \ldots\text{(i)}$$

$$\left(\text{Since, } x = x_0 + ph \Rightarrow \frac{dx}{dp} = h\right)$$

and

$$\frac{d^2y}{dx^2} = \frac{d}{dx}\left(\frac{dy}{dx}\right) = \frac{d}{dx}\left(\frac{1}{h}\frac{dy}{dp}\right)$$

$$= \frac{1}{h}\cdot\frac{d}{dx}\left(\frac{dy}{dp}\right) = \frac{1}{h}\cdot\frac{d}{dp}\left(\frac{dy}{dp}\right)\cdot\frac{dp}{dx}$$

$$= \frac{1}{h}\cdot\frac{d^2y}{dp^2}\cdot\frac{1}{h}$$

$$= \frac{1}{h^2}\cdot\frac{d^2y}{dp^2} \qquad \ldots\text{(ii)}$$

Differentiating Eq. (i) both sides, *wrt* $p$, we get

$$\frac{dy}{dp} = \Delta y_0 + \frac{2p-1}{2!}\Delta^2 y_0 + \frac{3p^2 - 6p + 2}{3!}\Delta^3 y_0 + \ldots \qquad \ldots\text{(iii)}$$

From Eqs. (i) and (iii), we get

$$\Rightarrow \quad \frac{dy}{dx} = \frac{1}{h}\left[\Delta y_0 + \frac{2p-1}{2!}\Delta^2 y_0 + \frac{3p^2 - 6p + 2}{3!}\Delta^3 y_0 + \ldots\right] \qquad \ldots\text{(iv)}$$

In particular, if $p = 0$, (At $x = x_0$)

Then,

$$\frac{dy}{dx} = \frac{1}{h}\left[\Delta y_0 - \frac{\Delta^2 y_0}{2} + \frac{1}{3}\Delta^3 y_0 - \ldots\right] \qquad \ldots\text{(v)}$$

Differentiating Eq. (iii) both sides *wrt p*, we get

$$\frac{d^2y}{dp^2} = \Delta^2 y_0 + (p-1)\Delta^3 y_0 + \ldots \qquad \ldots\text{(vi)}$$

From Eqs. (ii) and (vi), we get

$$\frac{d^2y}{dx^2} = \frac{1}{h^2}[\Delta^2 y_0 + (p-1)\Delta^3 y_0 + \ldots]$$

In particular, for $p = 0$, (At $x = x_0$)

$$\frac{d^2y}{dx^2} = \frac{1}{h^2}[\Delta^2 y_0 - \Delta^3 y_0 + \ldots]$$

## 2. Gregory-Newton Backward Difference Formula

$$y_p = f(x_n + ph) = E^p f(x_n) = (1-\nabla)^{-p} y_n \; [\because E^{-1} = 1 - \nabla]$$

$$= \left[1 + p\nabla + \frac{p(p+1)}{2!}\nabla^2 + \frac{p(p+1)(p+2)}{3!}\nabla^3 + \ldots\right] y_n$$

[Using binomial theorem]

*i.e.*,

$$y_p = y_n + p\nabla y_n + \frac{p(p+1)}{2!}\nabla^2 y_n + \frac{p(p+1)(p+2)}{3!}\nabla^3 y_n + \ldots$$

which is the required formula.

## Differentiation

**(i)** $$\frac{dy}{dx} = \frac{1}{h}\left[\nabla y_n + \frac{2p+1}{2!}\nabla^2 y_n + \frac{3p^2 + 6p + 2}{3!}\nabla^3 y_n + \ldots\right]$$

**(ii)** $$\frac{d^2y}{dx^2} = \frac{1}{h^2}[\nabla^2 y_n + (p+1)\nabla^3 y_n + \ldots]$$

***Note*** Particular cases are obtained, when $p = 0$ *i.e.*, for $x = x_n$.

## 3. Stirling's Formula

It is a central difference interpolation formula, which is used for interpolation near the middle value of the table. It is given by

$$y_p = y_0 + p\left(\frac{\Delta y_0 + \Delta y_{-1}}{2}\right) + \frac{p^2}{2!}\Delta^2 y_{-1} + \frac{p(p^2-1)}{3!}\left(\frac{\Delta^3 y_{-1} + \Delta^3 y_{-2}}{2}\right) + \frac{p^2(p^2-1)}{4!}\Delta^4 y_{-2} + \ldots$$

which is called Stirling's formula.

***Note*** Since, $$\frac{\Delta y_0 + \Delta y_{-1}}{2} = \frac{\delta y_{\frac{1}{2}} + \delta y_{-\frac{1}{2}}}{2} = \mu\delta y_0$$

$$\Delta^2 y_{-1} = \delta^2 y_0, \; \Delta^4 y_{-2} = \delta^4 y_0$$

and $$\frac{\Delta^3 y_{-1} + \Delta^3 y_{-2}}{2} = \frac{\delta^3 y_{\frac{1}{2}} + \delta^3 y_{-\frac{1}{2}}}{2} = \mu\delta^3 y_0 \text{ and so on.}$$

$\therefore$ Stirling's formula can also be written as

$$y_p = y_0 + p(\mu\delta y_0) + \frac{p^2}{2!}(\delta^2 y_0) + \frac{p(p^2-1)}{3!}(\mu\delta^3 y_0) + \frac{p^2(p^2-1)}{4!}\delta^4 y_0 + \ldots$$

## Differentiation

**(i)** $$\frac{dy}{dx} = \frac{1}{h}\left[\left(\frac{\Delta y_0 + \Delta y_{-1}}{2}\right) + p(\Delta^2 y_{-1}) + \frac{3p^2 - 1}{6}\left(\frac{\Delta^3 y_{-1} + \Delta^3 y_{-2}}{2}\right) + \ldots\right.$$

**(ii)** $$\frac{d^2y}{dx^2} = \frac{1}{h^2}\left[\Delta^2 y_{-1} + p\left(\frac{\Delta^3 y_{-1} + \Delta^3 y_{-2}}{2}\right) + \ldots\right]$$

***Note*** Particular cases are obtained, when $p = 0$ *i.e.*, for $x = x_0$.

***Example 29.*** *Find the cubic polynomial, which takes the following values*

| $x$ | 0 | 1 | 2 | 3 |
|---|---|---|---|---|
| $f(x)$ | 1 | 2 | 1 | 10 |

*Hence, or otherwise evaluate $f(4)$.*

**Solution.** The difference table is

| $x$ | $f(x)$ | $\Delta f(x)$ | $\Delta^2 f(x)$ | $\Delta^3 f(x)$ |
|---|---|---|---|---|
| 0 | **1** | | | |
| | | **1** | | |
| 1 | 2 | | **−2** | |
| | | −1 | | **12** |
| 2 | 1 | | **10** | |
| | | **9** | | |
| 3 | **10** | | | |

We take $x_0 = 0$ and $p = \frac{x-0}{h} = x$ $\quad [\because h = 1]$

$\therefore$ Using Newton's forward interpolation formula, we get

$$f(x) = f(0) + \frac{x}{1}\Delta f(0) + \frac{x(x-1)}{1\cdot 2}\Delta^2 f(0) + \frac{x(x-1)(x-2)}{1\cdot 2\cdot 3}\Delta^3 f(0)$$

$$= 1 + x(1) + \frac{x(x-1)}{2}(-2) + \frac{x(x-1)(x-2)}{6}(12)$$

$$= 2x^3 - 7x^2 + 6x + 1,$$

which is the required polynomial.

$$\Rightarrow \quad f(4) = 2(4)^3 - 7(4)^2 + 6(4) + 1$$

$$= 128 - 112 + 24 + 1 = 41$$

***Example 30.*** *By using Stirling's formula, find $f(35)$ from the following table.*

| $x$ | 20 | 30 | 40 | 50 |
|---|---|---|---|---|
| $f(x)$ | 512 | 439 | 346 | 243 |

**Solution.** Here, $x_0 + ph = 35 \Rightarrow 30 + p(10) = 35 \Rightarrow p = 0.5$

| $x$ | $f(x)$ | $\delta$ | $\delta^2$ | $\delta^3$ |
|---|---|---|---|---|
| 20 | 512 | | | |
| | | −73 | | |
| 30 | 439 | | −20 | |
| | | −93 | | 10 |
| 40 | 346 | | −10 | |
| | | −103 | | |
| 50 | 243 | | | |

By Stirling's formula

$$y_p = y_0 + p(\mu\delta y_0) + \frac{p^2}{2!}(\delta^2 y_0) + \frac{p(p^2-1)}{3!}(\mu\delta^3 y_0) + \ldots$$

$$\Rightarrow y(35) = 439 + 0.5\left(\frac{-73-93}{2}\right) + \frac{(0.5)^2}{2}(-20)$$

$$\Rightarrow f(35) = 395$$

***Example 31.*** *Consider the table*

| $x$ | 1.5 | 2 | 2.5 | 3 | 3.5 | 4 |
|---|---|---|---|---|---|---|
| $f(x)$ | 3.375 | 7 | 13.625 | 24 | 38.875 | 59 |

*Find $f'(x)$ and $f''(x)$ at $x = 1.5$.*

**Solution.**

| $x$ | $f(x)$ | $\Delta f(x)$ | $\Delta^2 f(x)$ | $\Delta^3 f(x)$ | $\Delta^4 f(x)$ |
|---|---|---|---|---|---|
| 1.5 | 3.375 | | | | |
| | | 3.625 | | | |
| 2 | 7 | | 3 | | |
| | | 6.625 | | 0.75 | |
| 2.5 | 13.625 | | 3.75 | | 0 |
| | | 10.375 | | 0.75 | |
| 3 | 24 | | 4.50 | | 0 |
| | | 14.875 | | 0.75 | |
| 3.5 | 38.875 | | 5.25 | | |
| | | 20.125 | | | |
| 4 | 59 | | | | |

$$x_0 + ph = 1.5$$

$$\Rightarrow \quad 1.5 + p(0.5) = 1.5 \quad \Rightarrow \quad p = 0$$

$\therefore$ From derivative formula of Newton's forward difference interpolation, we get

$$f'(x_0) = \frac{1}{h}\left[\Delta f(x_0) - \frac{1}{2}\Delta^2 f(x_0) + \frac{1}{3}\Delta^3 f(x_0) + \ldots\right]$$

and $\quad f''(x_0) = \frac{1}{h^2}[\Delta^2 f(x_0) - \Delta^3 f(x_0) + \ldots]$

$$\Rightarrow \quad f'(1.5) = \frac{1}{0.5}\left[3.625 - \frac{1}{2}(3) + \frac{1}{3}(0.75)\right] = 4.75$$

and $\quad f''(1.5) = \frac{1}{(0.5)^2}[3 - 0.75] = 9$

***Example 32.*** *From the table given below*

| $x$ | 1 | 2 | 3 | 4 | 5 |
|---|---|---|---|---|---|
| $y$ | 0 | 1 | 5 | 6 | 8 |

*Find $\frac{dy}{dx}$ and $\frac{d^2y}{dx^2}$ at $x = 1.2$.*

**Solution.**

| $x$ | $y$ | $\Delta y$ | $\Delta^2 y$ | $\Delta^3 y$ | $\Delta^4 y$ |
|---|---|---|---|---|---|
| 1 | 0 | | | | |
| | | 1 | | | |
| 2 | 1 | | 3 | | |
| | | 4 | | −6 | |
| 3 | 5 | | −3 | | 10 |
| | | 1 | | 4 | |
| 4 | 6 | | 1 | | |
| | | 2 | | | |
| 5 | 8 | | | | |

$$x_0 + ph = 1.2 \Rightarrow 1 + p(1) = 1.2 \Rightarrow p = 0.2$$

Since, $f'(x) = \frac{1}{h}\left[\Delta y_0 + \frac{2p-1}{2}\Delta^2 y_0 + \frac{3p^2-6p+2}{6}\Delta^3 y_0 + \frac{4p^3-18p^2+22p-6}{24}\Delta^4 y_0 + \ldots\right]$

and $f''(x) = \frac{1}{h^2}\left[\Delta^2 y_0 + (p-1)\Delta^3 y_0 + \frac{6p^2-18p+11}{12}\Delta^4 y_0 + \ldots\right]$

Putting $h=1$, $p=0.2$,

$$\Delta y_0 = 1,\ \Delta^2 y_0 = 3,\ \Delta^3 y_0 = -6,\ \Delta^4 y_0 = 10,$$

we get

$$f'(1.2) = -1.77$$

and $$f''(1.2) = 14.16$$

***Example 33.*** *A slider in a machine moves along a fixed straight rod. Its distance x cm along the rod is given below for various values of the time t seconds. Find the velocity of the slider and its acceleration when t = 0.3 s.*

| $t$ | 0 | 0.1 | 0.2 | 0.3 | 0.4 | 0.5 | 0.6 |
|---|---|---|---|---|---|---|---|
| $x$ | 30.13 | 31.62 | 32.87 | 33.64 | 33.95 | 33.81 | 33.24 |

**Solution.** The difference table is

| $t$ | $x$ | $\delta$ | $\delta^2$ | $\delta^3$ | $\delta^4$ | $\delta^5$ | $\delta^6$ |
|---|---|---|---|---|---|---|---|
| 0 | 30.13 | | | | | | |
| | | 1.49 | | | | | |
| 0.1 | 31.62 | | −0.24 | | | | |
| | | 1.25 | | −0.24 | | | |
| 0.2 | 32.87 | | −0.48 | | 0.26 | | |
| | | 0.77 | | 0.02 | | 0.27 | |
| 0.3→ | 33.64 | | −0.46 | | −0.01 | | 0.29 |
| | | 0.31 | | 0.01 | | 0.02 | |
| 0.4 | 33.95 | | −0.45 | | 0.01 | | |
| | | −0.14 | | 0.02 | | | |
| 0.5 | 33.81 | | −0.43 | | | | |
| | | −0.57 | | | | | |
| 0.6 | 33.24 | | | | | | |

As the derivatives are required near the middle of the table, we use Stirling's formulae

$$f'(a) = \frac{1}{h}\left[\mu\delta f(a) - \frac{1}{6}\mu\delta^3 f(a) + \frac{1}{30}\mu\delta^5 f(a) - \ldots\right],$$

$$f''(a) = \frac{1}{h^2}\left[\delta^2 f(a) - \frac{1}{12}\delta^4 f(a) + \frac{1}{90}\delta^6 f(a) - \ldots\right]$$

Here, $h = 0.1,\ a = 0.3,\ \mu\delta f(0.3) = \frac{1}{2}(0.77 + 0.31) = 0.54,$

$$\mu\delta^3 f(0.3) = \frac{1}{2}(0.02 + 0.01) = 0.015,$$

$$\mu\delta^5 f(0.3) = \frac{1}{2}(-0.\ 27 + 0.02) = -0.125$$

$$\therefore\quad f'(0.3) = \frac{1}{0.1}\left[0.54 - \frac{1}{6}(0.015) + \frac{1}{30}(-0.125)\right] = 5.34$$

Also,

$$f''(0.3) = \frac{1}{(0.1)^2}\left[-0.46 - \frac{1}{12}(-0.01) + \frac{1}{90}(0.29)\right] = -45.6$$

Hence, the required velocity is 5.34 cm/s and acceleration is $-45.6\ \text{cm/s}^2$.

## 4. Lagrange's Interpolation Formula

This formula is used for unequal intervals.

If $y = f(x)$ takes the value $y_0, y_1, y_2, \ldots, y_n$ corresponding to $x = x_0, x_1, x_2, \ldots, x_n$, then

$$f(x) = \frac{(x-x_1)(x-x_2)\ldots(x-x_n)}{(x_0-x_1)(x_0-x_2)\ldots(x_0-x_n)}y_0 + \frac{(x-x_0)(x-x_2)\ldots(x-x_n)}{(x_1-x_0)(x_1-x_2)\ldots(x_1-x_n)}y_1 + \ldots + \frac{(x-x_0)(x-x_1)\ldots(x-x_{n-1})}{(x_n-x_0)(x_n-x_1)\ldots(x_n-x_{n-1})}y_n \quad \ldots\text{(i)}$$

This is known as Lagrange's interpolation formula for unequal intervals.

### Differentiations

We find $f(x)$ from Eq. (i) and then differentiating it *wrt* $x$.

***Example 34.*** *Find f(3) and f′(3) from following table.*

| $x$ | 0 | 1 | 2 | 5 |
|---|---|---|---|---|
| $f(x)$ | 2 | 3 | 12 | 147 |

**Solution.** Here, $x_0 = 0,\ x_1 = 1,\ x_2 = 2,\ x_3 = 5$

and $y_0 = 2,\ y_1 = 3,\ y_2 = 12,\ y_3 = 147$

Lagrange's formula is

$$y = \frac{(x-x_1)(x-x_2)(x-x_3)}{(x_0-x_1)(x_0-x_2)(x_0-x_3)}y_0 + \frac{(x-x_0)(x-x_2)(x-x_3)}{(x_1-x_0)(x_1-x_2)(x_1-x_3)}y_1 + \frac{(x-x_0)(x-x_1)(x-x_3)}{(x_2-x_0)(x_2-x_1)(x_2-x_3)}y_2 + \frac{(x-x_0)(x-x_1)(x-x_2)}{(x_3-x_0)(x_3-x_1)(x_3-x_2)}y_3$$

$$= \frac{(x-1)(x-2)(x-5)}{(0-1)(0-2)(0-5)}(2) + \frac{(x-0)(x-2)(x-5)}{(1-0)(1-2)(1-5)}(3) + \frac{(x-0)(x-1)(x-5)}{(2-0)(2-1)(2-5)}(12) + \frac{(x-0)(x-1)(x-2)}{(5-0)(5-1)(5-2)}(147)$$

Hence, $f(x) = x^3 + x^2 - x + 2$ and $f'(x) = 3x^2 + 2x - 1$

$\Rightarrow\quad f(3) = 27 + 9 - 3 + 2 = 35$

and $\quad f'(3) = 27 + 6 - 1 = 32$

## 5. Newton's Divided Difference Interpolation Formula

This formula is used for unequal intervals. The interpolation formula is given by

$$f(x) = f(x_0) + (x - x_0)f[x_0, x_1] + (x - x_0)(x - x_1)f[x_0, x_1, x_2]$$
$$+(x - x_0)(x - x_1)(x - x_2)f[x_0, x_1, x_2, x_3] + \ldots,$$

where $f[x_0, x_1, x_2, \ldots, x_{r-1}]$ is the $r$th divided difference.

### Differentiations

Finding $f(x)$ from above formula and then differentiating *wrt* $x$.

***Example 35.*** *Find f(2) and f′(2) from following table.*

| $x$ | −1 | 0 | 1 | 3 |
|---|---|---|---|---|
| $f(x)$ | 2 | 1 | 0 | −1 |

**Solution.** Newton's divided difference table is as below

| $x$ | $f(x)$ | $f[x_0, x_1]$ | $f[x_0, x_1, x_2]$ | $[x_0, x_1, x_2, x_3]$ |
|---|---|---|---|---|
| −1 | 2 | | | |
| | | $\frac{1-2}{0+1} = -1$ | | |
| 0 | 1 | | $\frac{-1+1}{1+1} = 0$ | |
| | | $\frac{0-1}{1-0} = -1$ | | $\frac{\frac{1}{6}-0}{3+1} = \frac{1}{24}$ |
| 1 | 0 | | $\frac{-0.5+1}{3-0} = \frac{1}{6}$ | |
| | | $\frac{-1-0}{3-1} = -0.5$ | | |
| 3 | −1 | | | |

Now, from Newton's divided difference interpolation formula

$$f(x) = f(x_0) + (x - x_0)f[x_0, x_1]$$
$$+(x - x_0)(x - x_1)f[x_0, x_1, x_2]$$
$$+(x - x_0)(x - x_1)(x - x_2)f[x_0, x_1, x_2, x_3]$$
$$= 2 + (x+1)(-1) + (x+1)(x-0)(0)$$
$$+(x+1)(x-0)(x-1)\left(\frac{1}{24}\right)$$

$$\Rightarrow \quad f(x) = 2 - x - 1 + x^2 + x + \frac{1}{24}(x^3 - x)$$
$$= \frac{x^3}{24} + x^2 - \frac{x}{24} + 1$$

and $\quad f'(x) = \frac{x^2}{8} + 2x - \frac{1}{24}$

$$\therefore \quad f(2) = \frac{8}{24} + 4 - \frac{2}{24} + 1 = \frac{1}{3} - \frac{1}{12} + 5 = \frac{63}{12}$$

and $\quad f'(2) = \frac{4}{8} + 4 - \frac{1}{24} = \frac{1}{2} + 4 - \frac{1}{24} = \frac{107}{24}$

## 6. Hermite's Interpolation Formula

The Hermite interpolating polynomial interpolates $f(x)$ as well as its derivative (depends on given set of tabular points). Hermite interpolation formula is given by

$$P(x) = \sum_{i=0}^{n} [1 - 2(x - x_i)L_i'(x_i)][L_i(x)]^2 y(x_i)$$
$$+ \sum_{i=0}^{n} (x - x_i)[L_i(x)]^2 y'(x_i) \quad \ldots(i)$$

Where, $L_i(x) = \dfrac{(x - x_0)(x - x_1)\ldots(x - x_{i-1})(x - x_{i+1})\ldots(x - x_n)}{(x_i - x_0)(x_i - x_1)\ldots(x_i - x_{i-1})(x_i - x_{i+1})\ldots(x_i - x_n)}$

***Note*** **(a)** From Eq. (i) $P(x)$ is in the form of sum of two polynomials.
*i.e.*, $P(x) = \sum_{i=0}^{n} F_i(x)y(x_i) + \sum_{i=0}^{n} G_i(x)y'(x_i)$

**(b)** Polynomial $P(x)$, satisfying
$P(x_i) = y(x_i)$ and
$P'(x_i) = y'(x_i), \; i = 0, 1, 2, 3, \ldots, n$
Since, there are $2n + 2$ conditions to be satisfied, $P(x)$ must be a polynomial of degree less than or equal to $2n + 1$.

**(c)** (i) $F_i(x_j) = 0, \; i \neq j$
$= 1, i = j$
(ii) $G_i'(x_j) = 0, \; i \neq j$
$= 1, i = j$
(iii) $F_i'(x_j) = 0, \forall \; i$ and $j$
(iv) $G_i(x_j) = 0, \; \forall \; i$ and $j$

**(d)** $F_i(x)$ and $G_i(x)$ are both linear functions.

### Differentiations

Finding the polynomial $P(x)$ and then differentiating *wrt* $x$.

***Example 36.*** *Determine the Hermite polynomial of degree 4, which fits the following data.*

| $x$ | 0 | 1 | 2 |
|---|---|---|---|
| $f(x)$ | 0 | 1 | 0 |
| $y'(x)$ | 0 | 0 | 0 |

**Solution.** Here,
$x_0 = 0, \; x_1 = 1, \; x_2 = 2, y(x_0) = 0, \; y(x_1) = 1, y(x_2) = 0$ and
$y'(x_0) = 0, \; y'(x_1) = 0, \; y'(x_2) = 0$

Hermite's formula in this case is

$$P(x) = [1 - 2L_0'(x_0)(x - x_0)][L_0(x)]^2 y(x_0) + (x - x_0)[L_0(x)]^2 y'(x_0)$$
$$+ [1 - 2L_1'(x_1)(x - x_1)][L_1(x)]^2 \times y(x_1) + (x - x_1)[L_1(x)]^2 y'(x_1)$$
$$+ [1 - 2L_2'(x_2)(x - x_2)] \times [L_2(x)]^2 y(x_2) + (x - x_2)[L_2(x)]^2 y'(x_2)$$

Substituting the above values in $P(x)$, we get

$$P(x) = [1 - 2L_1'(x_1)(x - 1)][L_1(x)]^2$$

Where, $L_1(x) = \dfrac{(x - x_0)(x - x_2)}{(x_1 - x_0)(x_1 - x_2)} = 2x - x^2$ and

$$L_1'(x_1) = (2 - 2x)_{x=1} = 0$$

Hence, $\quad P(x) = [L_1(x)]^2 = (2x - x^2)^2$

**_Example 37._** *For the following data*

| $x$ | $f(x)$ | $f'(x)$ |
|---|---|---|
| 0.5 | 4 | −16 |
| 1 | 1 | −2 |

*Find the Hermite interpolating polynomial.*

**Solution.** We have,

$$x_0 = 0.5,\ x_1 = 1,\ y(x_0) = 4,\ y(x_1) = 1;$$
$$y'(x_0) = -16,\ y'(x_1) = -2$$

Also, $L(x_0) = \dfrac{x-x_1}{x_0-x_1} = \dfrac{x-1}{-0.5} = -2(x-1);\ L'(x_0) = -2$

$$L(x_1) = \frac{x-x_0}{x_1-x_0} = \frac{x-0.5}{1-0.5} = 2x-1;\ L'(x_1) = 2$$

Hermite's interpolation formula in this case, is

$$P(x) = [1-2(x-x_0)L'x_0][L(x_0)]^2y(x_0)$$
$$+(x-x_0)[L(x_0)]^2y'(x_0) + [1-2(x-x_1)L'(x_1)]$$
$$[L(x_1)]^2y(x_1) + (x-x_1)[L(x_1)]^2y'(x_1)$$
$$= [1-2(x-0.5)(-2)][-2(x-1)]^2(4)$$
$$+(x-0.5)[-2(x-1)]^2(-16)+$$
$$[1-2(x-1)(2)](2x-1)^2(1) + (x-1)(2x-1)^2(-2)$$
$$= 16[1+4(x-0.5)](x^2-2x+1)$$
$$-164(x-0.5)(x^2-2x+1) + [1-4(x-1)]$$
$$(4x^2-4x+1) - 2(x-1)(4x^2-4x+1)$$

Hence, $P(x) = -24x^3 + 324x^2 - 130x + 23.$

## 7. Spline Interpolation

### Cubic Spline Interpolation

A cubic spline satisfies the following conditions.

**(i)** $f(x)$ is linear polynomial outside the interval $[x_0, x_n]$.

**(ii)** On each subinterval $[x_{i-1}, x_i]$, $1 \le i \le n$, $f(x)$ is a third degree polynomial.

**(iii)** $f(x)$, $f'(x)$ and $f''(x)$ are continuous on $(x_0, x_n)$ cubic spline interpolation formula is given by

$$f(x) = \frac{(x_{i+1}-x)^3}{6h}M_i + \frac{(x-x_i)^3}{6h}M_{i+1}$$
$$+\frac{x_{i+1}-x}{h}\left(y_i - \frac{h^2}{6}M_i\right) + \frac{x-x_i}{h}\left(y_{i+1} - \frac{h^2}{6}M_{i+1}\right)$$

Where, $M_i$ and $M_{i+1}$ are found out by solving the relations.

$$M_{i-1} + 4M_i + M_{i+1} = \frac{6}{h^2}(y_{i-1} - 2y_i + y_{i+1}) \quad i = 1, 2, \ldots, (n-1)$$

and $\qquad M_0 = M_n = 0$

### Differentiations

Finding $f(x)$ and differentiating *wrt x*.

**_Example 38._** *The following values of x and y are given*

| $x$ | 1 | 2 | 3 | 4 |
|---|---|---|---|---|
| $y$ | 1 | 2 | 5 | 11 |

*Find the cubic splines and evaluate y(3) and y′(3).*

**Solution.** Here, $h = 1, x = 3$

Using $M_{i-1} + 4M_i + M_{i+1} = \dfrac{6}{h^2}(y_{i-1} - 2y_i + y_{i+1}) \qquad i = 1, 2, \ldots$

and $\qquad M_0 = M_3 = 0$

$$\Rightarrow \quad M_0 + 4M_1 + M_2 = 6(y_0 - 2y_1 + y_2) = 6(1-4+5) = 12$$
$$\Rightarrow \quad 4M_1 + M_2 = 12 \qquad \ldots\text{(i)}$$

Also, $M_1 + 4M_2 + M_3 = 6(y_1 - 2y_2 + y_3)$
$$= 6(2-10+11) = 18$$
$$\Rightarrow \quad M_1 + 4M_2 = 18 \qquad \ldots\text{(ii)}$$

Solving Eqs. (i) and (ii), we get
$$M_1 = 2, M_2 = 4$$

Now, cubic spline in $[x_i, x_{i+1}]$ is
$$f(x) = \frac{1}{6}[(x_{i+1}-x)^3M_i + (x-x_i)^3M_{i+1}]$$
$$+(x_{i+1}-x)\left(y_i - \frac{M_i}{6}\right) + (x-x_i)\left(y_{i+1} - \frac{M_{i+1}}{6}\right) \qquad \ldots\text{(iii)}$$

Taking $i = 0, 1, 2$ in Eq. (iii) and using
$$M_0 = 0, M_1 = 2, M_2 = 4, M_3 = 0$$

We find cubic splines as

$$f(x) = \begin{cases} \dfrac{1}{3}(x^3 - 3x^2 + 5x)\ ; & x \in [1, 2] \\ \dfrac{1}{3}(x^3 - 3x^2 + 5x)\ ; & x \in [2, 3] \\ \dfrac{1}{3}(-2x^3 + 24x^2 - 76x + 81)\ ; & x \in [3, 4] \end{cases}$$

For $x \in [2, 3]$, $y(x) = \dfrac{1}{3}(x^3 - 3x^2 + 5x)$

$$\Rightarrow \quad y(3) = \frac{1}{3}(27 - 27 + 15) = 5$$

We get the same value when, we use $f(x)$ for $x \in [3, 4]$.

Also, for $x \in [2, 3]$
$$y'(x) = \frac{1}{3}(3x^2 - 6x + 5)$$
$$\Rightarrow \quad y'(3) = \frac{1}{3}(27 - 18 + 5) = \frac{14}{3}$$

We get the same value when, we use $y'(x)$ for $x \in [3, 4]$.

# Numerical Integration

The process of evaluating a definite integral from a set of tabulated values of the $f(x)$ is called numerical integration or quadrature.

Let the interval $[a, b]$ be divided into $n$ equal subintervals, such that $a = x_0 < x_1 < x_2 < \ldots < x_n = b$. Where, $x_n = x_0 + nh$.

Hence, the definite integral is

$$\int_{x_0}^{x_0+nh} f(x)\,dx = \int_{x_0}^{x_0+nh} y\,dx$$

## 1. Trapezoidal Rule

Formula for this rule is given by

$$\int_{x_0}^{x_0+nh} y\,dx = \frac{h}{2}[(y_0 + y_n) + 2(y_1 + y_2 + y_3 + \ldots + y_{n-1})]$$

Where, $n \in N$.

> ***Note*** **(a)** Geometrically, this formula is the area of a trapezium.
>
> **(b)** It is obtained by taking $n = 1$ in Newton-cotes quadrature formula. Here, curve is linear through $(x_0, y_0)$ and $(x_1, y_1)$.
>
> **(c)** Total error in trapezoidal rule is given by
>
> $$E = -\frac{h^3}{12}(y_0'' + y_1'' + \ldots + y_{n-1}'') \qquad \ldots(i)$$
>
> If $y''$ is constant, $\forall\, x$ in $[a, b]$ or $y''(\eta)$ is maximum of the $n$ quantities $y_0'', y_1'', \ldots, y_{n-1}''$.
>
> *i.e.*, $y''(\eta) = \max\limits_{a \le x \le b} |y''(x)|$, where $a < \eta < b$, then
>
> Eq. (i) becomes
>
> $$|E| \le \frac{h^3}{12} \cdot n \cdot y''(\eta)$$
>
> Since, $h = \dfrac{b-a}{n}$, we get
>
> $$|E| \le \frac{(b-a)}{12} h^2 y''(\eta) \qquad \ldots(ii)$$
>
> **(d)** From Eq. (ii), error in the trapezoidal rule is of the order $h^2$.

## 2. Simpson's One-Third Rule

Formula for this rule is given by

$$\int_{x_0}^{x_0+nh} y\,dx = \frac{h}{3}[(y_0 + y_n) + 4(y_1 + y_3 + \ldots + y_{n-1}) + 2(y_2 + y_4 + \ldots + y_{n-2})]$$

where $n$ is even.

> ***Note*** **(a)** It is obtained by putting $n = 2$ in Newton-cotes formula.
>
> **(b)** Curve is a parabola through $(x_0, y_0)$, $(x_1, y_1)$ and $(x_2, y_2)$.
>
> **(c)** Geometrically, by this formula we find area of two strips at a time, hence, the given interval is divided into even number of equal sub intervals.
>
> **(d)** Total error is given by
>
> $$|E| \le \frac{(b-a)}{180} h^4 y^{iv}(\eta)$$
>
> Where, $E = -\dfrac{h^5}{90}(y_0^{iv} + y_2^{iv} + \ldots + y_{2(n-1)}^{iv})$
>
> and $y^{iv}(\eta) = \max\limits_{a \le x \le b} |y^{iv}(x)|$, $a < \eta < b$.
>
> **(e)** The error in Simpson's $\frac{1}{3}$rd rule is of the order $h^4$

## 3. Simpson's Three-Eight Rule

Formula for this rule is given by

$$\int_{x_0}^{x_0+nh} y\,dx = \frac{3h}{8}[(y_0 + y_n) + 3(y_1 + y_2 + y_4 + y_6 + \ldots + y_{n-1}) + 2(y_3 + y_6 + \ldots + y_{n-3})]$$

Where $n$ is a multiple of 3.

> ***Note*** **(a)** It is obtained by putting $n = 3$ in Newton's-cotes formula.
>
> **(b)** Geometrically, by this rule we find area of three strips at a time, hence the given interval is divided into multiple of 3 subdivision while using this rule.
>
> **(c)** The curve passes through $(x_0, y_0)$, $(x_1, y_1)$, $(x_2, y_2)$ and $(x_3, y_3)$.
>
> **(d)** The principal part of error in the interval $[x_0, x_3]$ $= -\dfrac{3h^5}{80} y_0^{iv}$ and total error is same as that of total error in Simpson's $\frac{1}{3}$rd rule.
>
> **(e)** The error in the Simpson's $\frac{1}{3}$rd rule is of the order $h^4$.

## 4. Weddle's Rule

Formula for this is given by

$$\int_{x_0}^{x_0+nh} y\,dx = \frac{3h}{10}(y_0 + 5y_1 + y_2 + 6y_3 + y_4 + 5y_5 + 2y_6 + 5y_7 + y_8 + \ldots)$$

Where, $n$ is a multiple of 6.

> ***Note*** **(a)** It is obtained by putting $n = 6$ in Newton-cotes formula.
>
> **(b)** Curve is passing through $(x_i, y_i)$ for $i = 0, 1, 2, \ldots, 6$.
>
> **(c)** Principal part error in interval $[x_0, x_6]$ is $= -\dfrac{h^7}{140} y_0^{iv}$ and total error is given by
>
> $$|E| \le \frac{b-a}{840} h^6 y^{iv}(\eta)$$
>
> **(d)** Order of error is $h^6$.

***Example 39.*** *Use trapezoidal rule to evaluate* $\int_0^1 x^2\,dx$ *by taking five subintervals.*

**Solution.** Here, $a = 0, b = 1, n = 5$

Now, $nh = b - a \Rightarrow 5h = 1 - 0 = 1$

$$\Rightarrow h = \frac{1}{5} = 0.2$$

The values of $f(x) = x^2$ are given below

| $x$ | 0 | 0.2 | 0.4 | 0.6 | 0.8 | 1 |
|---|---|---|---|---|---|---|
| $f(x)$ | $0 = f_0$ | $0.04 = f_1$ | $0.16 = f_2$ | $0.36 = f_3$ | $0.64 = f_4$ | $1 = f_5$ |

From table,

$$f_0 = f(0) = 0,\ f_1 = f(0.2) = 0.04,\ f_2 = f(0.4) = 0.16,$$

$f_3 = f(0.6) = 0.36, f_4 = f(0.8) = 0.64, f_5 = f(1) = 1$

By using trapezoidal rule, we get

$$\int_0^1 x^2 dx = \frac{h}{2}[(f_0 + f_5) + 2(f_1 + f_2 + f_3 + f_4)]$$
$$= 0.1[(0+1) + 2(0.04 + 0.16 + 0.36 + 0.64)]$$
$$= 0.1(1 + 1.20) = 0.1 \times 2.20 = 0.22$$

***Example 40.*** *Evaluate* $\int_0^6 \frac{dx}{1+x^2}$ *by using*

(i) *Trapezoidal rule,*

(ii) *Simpson's 1/3 rule*

(iii) *Simpson's 3/8 rule*

(iv) *Weddle's rule and compare the result with its actual value.*

**Solution.** Divide the interval (0, 6) into six parts each of width $h = 1$. The values of $f(x) = \frac{1}{1+x^2}$ are given below

| $x$ | 0 | 1 | 2 | 3 | 4 | 5 | 6 |
|---|---|---|---|---|---|---|---|
| $f(x)$ | 1<br>$y_0$ | 0.5<br>$y_1$ | 0.2<br>$y_2$ | 0.1<br>$y_3$ | 0.0588<br>$y_4$ | 0.0385<br>$y_5$ | 0.027<br>$y_6$ |

(i) By Trapezoidal rule,

$$\int_0^6 \frac{dx}{1+x^2} = \frac{h}{2}[(y_0 + y_6) + 2(y_1 + y_2 + y_3 + y_4 + y_5)]$$
$$= \frac{1}{2}[(1 + 0.027) + 2(0.5 + 0.2 + 0.1 + 0.0588 + 0.0385)] = 1.4108$$

(ii) By Simpson's 1/3 rule,

$$\int_0^6 \frac{dx}{1+x^2} = \frac{h}{3}[(y_0 + y_6) + 4(y_1 + y_3 + y_5) + 2(y_2 + y_4)]$$
$$= \frac{1}{3}[(1 + 0.027) + 4(0.5 + 0.1 + 0.0385) + 2(0.2 + 0.0588)] = 1.3662$$

(iii) By Simpson's 3/8 rule,

$$\int_0^6 \frac{dx}{1+x^2} = \frac{3h}{8}[(y_0 + y_6) + 3(y_1 + y_2 + y_4 + y_5) + 2y_3]$$
$$= \frac{3}{8}[(1 + 0.027) + 3(0.5 + 0.2 + 0.0588 + 0.0385) + 2(0.1)] = 1.3571$$

(iv) By Weddle's rule,

$$\int_0^6 \frac{dx}{1+x^2} = \frac{3h}{10}[(y_0 + 5y_1 + y_2 + 6y_3 + y_4 + 5y_5 + y_6)]$$
$$= 0.3[1 + 5(0.5) + 0.2 + 6(0.1) + 0.0588 + 5(0.0385) + 0.027] = 1.3735$$

Also, $\int_0^6 \frac{dx}{1+x^2} = |\tan^{-1} x|_0^6 = \tan^{-1} 6 = 1.4056$

This shows that the value of the integral found by Weddle's rule is the nearest to the actual value followed by its value given by Simpson's 1/3 rule.

***Example 41.*** *The velocity (v) of a car which starts from rest, is given at fixed intervals of time (t) as follows.*

| $t$ | 2 | 4 | 6 | 8 | 10 | 12 | 14 | 16 | 18 | 20 |
|---|---|---|---|---|---|---|---|---|---|---|
| $v$ | 10 | 18 | 25 | 29 | 32 | 20 | 11 | 5 | 2 | 0 |

*Estimate approximately the distance covered by car in 20 units of time.*

**Solution.** Here, initial velocity $v_0 = 0$ and final velocity $v_{10} = 0$.

$\Rightarrow \quad v_0 = 0, v_1 = 10, v_2 = 18, v_3 = 25, \dots, v_{10} = 0$

Here, $n = 10, h = 2$

Therefore, Simpson's $\frac{1}{3}$rd rule can be used.

$\because \quad ds = v\,dt$

$\Rightarrow$ Total distance $= \int_0^{20} v\,dt$

$$= \frac{h}{3}[(v_0 + v_{10}) + 4(v_1 + v_3 + v_5 + v_7 + v_9) + 2(v_2 + v_4 + v_6 + v_8)]$$
$$= \frac{2}{3}[(0+0) + 4(10 + 25 + 32 + 11 + 2) + 2(18 + 29 + 20 + 5)]$$
$$= \frac{2}{3}(0 + 4 \times 80 + 2 \times 72) = \frac{928}{3} \text{ units}$$

# Numerical Solutions of ODEs

## 1. Picard's Method

Let us consider the first order differential equation.

$$\frac{dy}{dx} = f(x, y) \quad \dots(i)$$

and $\quad y(x_0) = y_0$

then from Picard's method, $n$th approximation $y_n$ to the solution of IVP Eq. (i) is

$$y_n = y_0 + \int_{x_0}^{x_1} f(x, y_{n-1})dx$$

***Example 42.*** *Use Picard's method to solve* $\frac{dy}{dx} = -xy$ *upto the fourth approximation, when* $y(0) = 1$.

**Solution.** $\int_{y_0}^{y} dy = -\int_{x_0}^{x} xy\,dx$

$$y_1 = y_0 - \int_{x_0}^{x} xy_0 dx \quad \dots(i)$$

$$y_1 = 1 - \int_0^x x(1)\,dx = 1 - \int_0^x x\,dx = 1 - \frac{x^2}{2}$$

$$y_2 = y_0 - \int_0^x xy_1 dx \quad \dots(ii)$$

Now, putting the value of $y_1$ in Eq. (ii), we get

$$y_2 = 1 - \int_0^x x\left(1 - \frac{x^2}{2}\right)dx = 1 - \int_0^x \left(x - \frac{x^3}{2}\right)dx = 1 - \frac{x^2}{2} + \frac{x^4}{8}$$

$$y_3 = 1 - \int_0^x xy_2 dx \quad \dots(iii)$$

Putting the value of $y_2$ in Eq. (iii), we get

$$y_3 = 1 - \int_0^x x\left(1 - \frac{x^2}{2} + \frac{x^4}{8}\right)dx = 1 - \int_0^x \left(x - \frac{x^3}{2} + \frac{x^5}{8}\right)dx$$
$$= 1 - \frac{x^2}{2} + \frac{x^4}{8} - \frac{x^6}{48}$$

Repeating once again, we shall obtain

$$y_4 = 1 - \frac{x^2}{2} + \frac{x^4}{8} - \frac{x^6}{48} + \frac{x^8}{384}$$

***Example 43.*** *Using Picard's method, find a solution of* $\frac{dy}{dx} = 1 + xy$ *upto the third approximation, when* $x_0 = 0, y_0 = 0$.

**Solution.**
$$\frac{dy}{dx} = 1 + xy \quad \text{...(i)}$$

On Integrating Eq. (i) *wrt* $x$ between the limits 0 and $x$, we get

$$\int_{y_0}^{y} dy = \int_{x_0}^{x} (1 + xy_0)dx \text{ or } y - y_0 = \int_0^x (1 + xy_0)dx$$

$$\Rightarrow \quad y_1 = \int_0^x (1 + xy_0)\,dx \quad \text{...(ii)}$$

On putting $y_0 = 0$ on RHS of Eq. (ii), we get

$$y_1 = \int_0^x (1 + 0)dx \Rightarrow \quad y_1 = x$$

$$y_2 = \int_0^x (1 + xy_1)dx \quad \text{...(iii)}$$

On substituting $y_1 = x$ on RHS of Eq. (iii), we obtain

$$y_2 = \int_0^x (1 + x^2)dx = x + \frac{x^3}{3}$$

$$y_3 = \int_0^x (1 + xy_2)dx \quad \text{...(iv)}$$

On putting $y_2 = x + \frac{x^3}{3}$ on RHS of Eq. (iv), we get

$$y_3 = \int_0^x \left[1 + x\left(x + \frac{x^3}{3}\right)\right]dx = \int_0^x \left[1 + x^2 + \frac{x^4}{3}\right]dx$$

$$\Rightarrow \quad y_3 = x + \frac{x^3}{3} + \frac{x^5}{15}$$

***Example 44.*** *Using Picard's method, solve* $\frac{dy}{dx} = x + z$, $\frac{dz}{dx} = x - y^2$ *upto the third approximation, when* $y_0 = 2, z_0 = 1$.

**Solution.** Here, $y_0 = 2, z_0 = 1$

$$\frac{dy}{dx} = f(x, y, z) = x + z$$

and
$$\frac{dz}{dx} = \phi(x, y, z) = x - y^2$$

$$\therefore \quad y = y_0 + \int_{x_0}^{x} f(x, y, z)dx$$

and
$$z = z_0 + \int_{x_0}^{x} \phi(x, y, z)dx$$

First approximations

$$y_1 = y_0 + \int_{x_0}^{x} f(x, y_0, z_0)dx$$

$$= 2 + \int_0^x (x + 1)dx = 2 + x + \frac{1}{2}x^2$$

$$z_1 = z_0 + \int_{x_0}^{x} \phi(x, y_0, z_0)dx$$

$$= 1 + \int_0^x (x - 4)dx = 1 - 4x + \frac{1}{2}x^2$$

Second approximations

$$y_2 = y_0 + \int_{x_0}^{x} f(x, y_1, z_1)dx$$

$$= 2 + \int_0^x (x + 1 - 4x + \frac{1}{2}x^2)dx = 2 + x - \frac{3}{2}x^2 + \frac{x^3}{6}$$

$$z_2 = z_0 + \int_{x_0}^{x} \phi(x, y_1, z_1)dx$$

$$= 1 + \int_{x_0}^{x} [x - (2 + x + \frac{1}{2}x^2)^2]dx$$

$$= 1 - 4x + \frac{3}{2}x^2 - x^3 - \frac{x^4}{4} - \frac{x^5}{20}$$

Third approximations

$$y_3 = y_0 + \int_{x_0}^{x} f(x, y_2, z_2)dx$$

$$= 2 + x - \frac{3}{2}x^2 - \frac{1}{2}x^3 - \frac{1}{4}x^4 - \frac{1}{20}x^5 - \frac{1}{120}x^6$$

$$z_3 = z_0 + \int_{x_0}^{x} \phi(x, y_2, z_2)dx$$

$$= 1 - 4x - \frac{3}{2}x^2 + \frac{5}{3}x^3 + \frac{7}{12}x^4 - \frac{31}{60}x^5 + \frac{1}{12}x^6 - \frac{1}{252}x^7$$

## 2. Euler's Method

Formula for finding $n$th approximate solution $(y_n)$ of IVP $\frac{dy}{dx} = f(x, y),\ y(x_0) = y_0$ is $y_n = y_{n-1} + hf(x_{n-1}, y_{n-1})$

Where, $x_{n-1} = x_0 + (n-1)h$

> ***Note*** The truncation error in Euler's method is $\frac{1}{2}h^2 y_n''$. *i.e.*, of order $h^2$.

***Example 45.*** *Using Euler's method solve in three steps* $\frac{dy}{dx} = x + y,\ y_0 = 0$ *with* $h = 0.2$

**Solution.** Here, $f(x, y) = x + y$

$$\Rightarrow \quad f(x_{n-1}, y_{n-1}) = x_{n-1} + y_{n-1} = x_0 + (n-1)h + y_{n-1}$$

$$\Rightarrow \quad f(x_0, y_0) = x_0 + (1-1)h + y_0$$

$$= 0 + 0 \times h + 0 = 0 \qquad (\because x_0 = 0)$$

Now, by Euler's method

$$y_1 = y_0 + hf(x_0, y_0) = 0 + h \times 0 = 0$$

$$f(x_1, y_1) = x_1 + y_1 = x_0 + h + 0 = 0 + 0.2 + 0 = 0.2$$

$$\Rightarrow \quad y_2 = y_1 + hf(x_1, y_1) = 0 + 0.2 \times 0.2 = 0.04$$

$$f(x_2, y_2) = x_2 + y_2 = x_0 + 2h + y_2$$

$$= 0 + 2 \times 0.2 + 0.04 = 0.4 + 0.04 = 0.44$$

$$\Rightarrow \quad y_3 = y_2 + hf(x_2, y_2)$$

$$= 0.04 + 0.2 \times 0.44 = 0.04 + 0.088 = 0.128$$

## 3. Modified Euler's Method

Formula for this method upto $n$th approximation to solution of IVP is

$$y_n = y_{n-1} + \frac{h}{2}[f(x_{n-1}, y_{n-1}) + f(x_n, \bar{y}_n)]$$

Where, $\bar{y}_n$ is calculated by using Euler's method

*i.e.*, $\bar{y}_n = y_{n-1} + hf(x_{n-1}, y_{n-1})$.

***Example 46.*** *Use Euler's modified method to compute y for* $x = 2$. *Given that* $\frac{dy}{dx} = x + y,\ x_0 = 0, y_0 = 1$ *with* $h = 1$.

**Solution.** $f(x, y) = x + y$

Since, Euler's formula is $y_n = y_{n-1} + hf(x_{n-1}, y_{n-1})$

Here, we write $\bar{y}_n$ in place of $y_n$

*i.e.*, $\bar{y}_n = y_{n-1} + hf(x_{n-1}, y_{n-1})$

$\Rightarrow$ $\bar{y}_n = y_{n-1} + x_{n-1} + y_{n-1} = x_{n-1} + 2y_{n-1}$ $\quad (\because h = 1)$

Value of $y(1)$

$$\bar{y}_1 = x_0 + 2y_0 = 0 + 2 = 2$$

$$\Rightarrow \quad y_1 = y_0 + \frac{1}{2}[f(x_0, y_0) + f(x_1, \bar{y}_1)]$$

$$= 1 + \frac{1}{2}[x_0 + y_0 + x_1 + \bar{y}_1]$$

$$= 1 + \frac{1}{2}[0 + 1 + 1 + 2] = 1 + 2 = 3$$

$$(\because x_1 = x_0 + h = 0 + 1 = 1)$$

Value of $y(2)$ $\bar{y}_2 = x_1 + 2y_1 = 1 + 6 = 7$

$$\Rightarrow \quad y_2 = y_1 + \frac{1}{2}[f(x_1, y_1) + f(x_2, \bar{y}_2)]$$

$$= 3 + \frac{1}{2}[x_1 + y_1 + x_2 + \bar{y}_2]$$

$$= 3 + \frac{1}{2}[1 + 3 + 2 + 7] = 3 + \frac{13}{2} = \frac{19}{2}$$

## 4. Runge-Kutta Method

### (i) First Order R-K Method

Euler's method is the Runge-Kutta method of the first order.

### (ii) Second Order R-K Method

Modified Euler's method is the Runge-Kutta method of the second order.

### (iii) Third Order R-K Method

$$y_1 = y_0 + \frac{1}{6}(k_1 + 4k_2 + k_3)$$

Where, $k_1 = hf(x_0, y_0),\ k_2 = hf(x_0 + \frac{h}{2}, y_0 + \frac{k_1}{2})$,

and $k_3 = hf(x_0 + h, y_0 + k')$, where $k' = hf(x_0 + h, y_0 + k_1)$.

### (iv) Fourth Order R-K Method

This method is most commonly used and is generally called as Runge-Kutta method only.

In the initial value problem

$$\frac{dy}{dx} = f(x, y),\ y(x_0) = y_0$$

Approximate value of $y$ is given as

$$y_1 = y_0 + k$$

Where, $k = \frac{1}{6}(k_1 + 2k_2 + 2k_3 + k_4)$ in which

$$k_1 = hf(x_0, y_0),\ k_2 = hf\left(x_0 + \frac{h}{2}, y_0 + \frac{k_1}{2}\right),$$

$$k_3 = hf\left(x_0 + \frac{h}{2}, y_0 + \frac{k_2}{2}\right),\ k_4 = hf(x_0 + h, y_0 + k_3)$$

***Example 47.*** *Apply Runge-Kutta method to find an approximate value of y, when* $x = 0.1$ *given that* $\frac{dy}{dx} = x + y, y = 1$, *when* $x = 0$, *with* $h = 0.1$

**Solution.** Here, $x_0 = 0,\ y_0 = 1,\ f(x, y) = x + y$

Now, $k_1 = hf(x_0, y_0) = 0.1(0 + 1) = 0.1$

$$k_2 = hf\left(x_0 + \frac{h}{2}, y_0 + \frac{k_1}{2}\right) = 0.1\ f(0 + 0.05, 1 + 0.05)$$

$$= 0.1[0.05 + 1.05] = 0.11$$

$$k_3 = hf\left(x_0 + \frac{h}{2}, y_0 + \frac{k_2}{2}\right)$$

$$= 0.1\ f(0 + 0.05, 1 + 0.055) = 0.1(0.05 + 1.055)$$

$$= 0.1105$$

$$k_4 = hf(x_0 + h, y_0 + k_3) = 0.1 f(0 + 0.1, 1 + 0.1105)$$

$$= 0.1\ f(0.1, 1.1105) = 0.1(0.1 + 1.1105)$$

$$= 0.12105$$

According to Runge-Kutta (Fourth order) formula

$$y = y_0 + \frac{1}{6}[k_1 + 2k_2 + 2k_3 + k_4]$$

$$y_{0.1} = 1 + \frac{1}{6}(0.1 + 0.22 + 0.221 + 0.12105)$$

$$= 1 + \frac{1}{6}(0.66205) = 1.11034$$

# SOLVED EXAMPLES

## Type I (*Only one correct option*)

***Example 1.*** *The real roots of the equation $x \sin x = -\cos x$ between (2, 3) by using bisection method is*

(a) 2.796875 (b) 2.847313
(c) 2.98755 (d) None of these

**Solution.** (a)

Let $f(x) = x \sin x + \cos x$

**Step 1** We have, $f(2) = 2 \sin 2 + \cos 2 = 1.4024$

and $f(3) = 3 \sin 3 + \cos 3 = -0.5666$

$\therefore f(2)$ and $f(3)$ are both positive and negative. So, roots lie between 2 and 3.

So, first approximation of the root is $x_1 = \dfrac{2+3}{2} = 2.5$

**Step 2** $\because f(2.5) = 2.5 \sin 2.5 + \cos 2.5 = 0.6950 =$ positive

$\because$ $f(2.5)$ is positive and $f(3)$ is negative.

So, root must lie between 2.5 and 3.

So, second approximation of roots is

$$x_2 = \frac{2.5+3}{2} = 2.75$$

**Step 3** $\because$ $f(2.75) = 2.75 \sin 2.75 + \cos 2.75$

$= 0.6950 =$ positive

$\because$ $f(2.75)$ is positive and $f(3)$ is negative. So, third approximation of roots lie between 2.75 and 3.

So, third approximation of roots is

$$x_3 = \frac{2.75+3}{2} = 2.875$$

**Step 4** $\because$ $f(2.875) = 2.875 \sin(2.875) + \cos(2.875)$

$= -0.2073 =$ negative

$\because$ $f(2.75)$ is positive and $f(2.875)$ is negative. So, fourth approximation of roots lie between 2.75 and 2.875

So, $x_4 = \dfrac{2.75+2.875}{2} = 2.8125$

**Step 5** $\because$ $f(2.8125) = 2.8125 \sin(2.8125) + \cos(2.8125)$

$= -0.0374 =$ negative

$\because$ $f(2.75)$ and $f(2.8125)$ are positive and negative, respectively. So, fifth approximation of roots lie between 2.75 and 2.8125.

Hence, $x_5 = \dfrac{2.75+2.8125}{2} = 2.78125$

**Step 6** $\because$ $f(2.78125)$

$= 2.78125 \sin(2.78125) + \cos(2.78125)$

$= 0.0449 =$ positive

$\because$ $f(2.78125)$ and $f(2.8125)$ are positive and negative, respectively. So, sixth approximation of roots lie between 2.78125 and 2.8125.

So, $x_6 = \dfrac{2.78125+2.8125}{2} = 2.796875$

**Step 7** $\because$ $f(2.796875) = 2.796875 \sin(2.796875)$

$+ \cos(2.796875) = 0.004$

$\therefore$ This is nearly to zero.

So, the root of given equation is 2.796875.

***Example 2.*** *In the solution of the following set of linear equations by Gauss elimination use partial pivoting*

$$5x + y + 2z = 34,\ 4y - 3z = 12,\ 10x - 2y + z = -4$$

*The pivots for elimination of x and y are*

(a) 10, 4 (b) 10, 2
(c) 5, 4 (d) 5, −4

**Solution.** (a) The given equation can be written as

$$5x + y + 2z = 34 \quad \text{...(i)}$$
$$4y - 3z = 12 \quad \text{...(ii)}$$
$$10x - 2y + z = -4 \quad \text{...(iii)}$$

On putting above equations in augmented matrix form

$$[A:B] = \left[\begin{array}{ccc|c} 5 & 1 & 2 & 34 \\ 0 & 4 & -3 & 12 \\ 10 & -2 & 1 & -4 \end{array}\right]$$

Operating $R_1 \leftrightarrow R_3$

$$= \left[\begin{array}{ccc|c} 10 & -2 & 1 & -4 \\ 0 & 4 & -3 & 12 \\ 5 & 1 & 2 & 34 \end{array}\right]$$

$\because$ The first column has absolute value 10, so the pivot for element $x$ is $a_{11} = 10$.

Now, to eliminate $y$, we need to compare the elements in second column at and below the diagonal element.

$\because$ $a_{22} = 4$ is already larger in absolute values of IInd column, so the pivot for $y$ is $a_{22} = 4$.

Hence, the pivots for $x$ and $y$ are 10 and 4.

***Example 3.*** *The Newton-Raphson algorithm for the function will be*

(a) $x_{k+1} = \dfrac{1}{2}\left(x_k + \dfrac{a}{x_k}\right)$ (b) $x_{k+1} = x_k + \dfrac{a}{2} x_k^2$

(c) $x_{k+1} = 2x_k - a x_k^2$ (d) $x_{k+1} = x_k - \dfrac{a}{2} x_k^2$

**Solution.** (c) To calculate $\dfrac{1}{a}$ by Newton-Raphson method.

Let $x = \dfrac{1}{a} \Rightarrow \dfrac{1}{x} - a = 0$

*i.e.*, $f(x) = \dfrac{1}{x} - a = 0$

$$f'(x) = -\frac{1}{x^2},\ f''(x) = \frac{2}{x^3}, \ldots$$

Now, $f'(x_k) = \frac{1}{x_k} - a$

$\Rightarrow$ $f'(x_k) = -\frac{1}{x_k^2}$

For Newton-Raphson method,

$$x_{k+1} = x_k - \frac{f(x_k)}{f'(x_k)}$$

$$x_{k+1} = x_k - \frac{\frac{1}{x_k} - a}{-\frac{1}{x_k^2}}$$

$$\Rightarrow \quad x_{k+1} = 2x_k - ax_k^2$$

***Example 4.*** *Consider the series* $x_{n+1} = \frac{x_n}{2} + \frac{9}{8x_n}, x_0 = 0.5$ *obtained from the Newton-Raphson method. The series converges to*

(a) 1.5 (b) $\sqrt{2}$
(c) 1.6 (d) 1.4

**Solution.** (a)

$\because$ $x_{n+1} = \frac{x_n}{2} + \frac{9}{8x_n}, x_0 = 0.5$

$\because$ $n \to \infty$, then series is converging.

So, $x_{n+1} = x_n = \alpha$ = root of equation

So, $\alpha = \frac{\alpha}{2} + \frac{9}{8\alpha}$

$\Rightarrow$ $8\alpha^2 = 4\alpha^2 + 9$

$\Rightarrow$ $\alpha^2 = \frac{9}{4}$

$\Rightarrow$ $\alpha = \frac{3}{2} = 1.5$

***Example 5.*** *The values of a function f(x) are tabulated below.*

| $x$ | $f(x)$ |
|---|---|
| 0 | 1 |
| 1 | 2 |
| 2 | 1 |
| 3 | 10 |

*Using Newton's forward difference formula, the cubic polynomial that can be fitted to the above data, is*

(a) $2x^3 + 7x^2 - 6x + 2$
(b) $2x^3 - 7x^2 + 6x - 2$
(c) $x^3 - 7x^2 - 6x + 1$
(d) $2x^3 - 7x^2 + 6x + 1$

**Solution.** (d) Given,

| $x$ | 0 | 1 | 2 | 3 |
|---|---|---|---|---|
| $f(x)$ | 1 | 2 | 1 | 10 |

Difference table

| $x$ | $f(x)$ | $\Delta f(x)$ | $\Delta^2 f(x)$ | $\Delta^3 f(x)$ |
|---|---|---|---|---|
| 0 | 1 | | | |
| | | 1 | | |
| 1 | 2 | | −2 | |
| | | −1 | | 12 |
| 2 | 1 | | 10 | |
| | | 9 | | |
| 3 | 10 | | | |

We get, $x_0 = 0, P = \frac{x - 0}{k} = x$ $[\because k = 1]$

Using Newton's forward interpolation formula, we get

$$f(x) = f(0) + \frac{x}{1}\Delta f(0) + \frac{x(x-1)}{1 \times 2}\Delta^2 f(0) + \frac{x(x-1)(x-2)}{1 \times 2 \times 3}\Delta^3 f(0)$$

$$= 1 + x(1) + \frac{x(x-1)}{2}(-2) + \frac{x(x-1)(x-2)(12)}{6}$$

$$= 1 + x + x - x^2 + 2x(x^2 - 3x - 2)$$

$$= 1 + x + x - x^2 + 2x^3 - 6x^2 + 4x$$

$$= 2x^3 - 7x^2 + 6x + 1$$

***Example 6.*** *The value of* $\int_0^1 \frac{dx}{1+x^2}$ *by using Simpson's* $\frac{3}{8}$*th rule is*

(a) 0.539785 (b) 0.785395
(c) 1.00314 (d) None of these

**Solution.** (b)

Here, $h = \frac{1-0}{6} = \frac{1}{6}$

So,

| $x$ | $y = \frac{1}{1+x^2}$ | |
|---|---|---|
| 0 | 1.0000 | $y_0$ |
| 1/6 | 0.97297 | $y_1$ |
| 2/6 | 0.90000 | $y_2$ |
| 3/6 | 0.80000 | $y_3$ |
| 4/6 | 0.69231 | $y_4$ |
| 5/6 | 0.59016 | $y_5$ |
| 10 | 0.50000 | $y_6$ |

We have, from Simpson's three-eighth rule

$$\int y\,dx = \frac{3h}{8}[(y_0 + y_n) + 3(y_1 + y_2 + y_4 + y_5 + \ldots + y_{n-1}) + 2(y_3 + y_6 + y_9 + \ldots + y_{n-3})]$$

$$= \frac{3h}{8}[(y_0 + y_6) + 3(y_1 + y_2 + y_4 + y_5) + 2y_3]$$

$$= \frac{3}{8} \times \frac{1}{6} [(1 + 0.5) + 3(0.97297 + 0.9000 + 0.69231 + 0.59016) + 2 \times 0.80000]$$

$$= \frac{1}{16}[12.56632] = 0.785395$$

***Example 7.*** *The minimum number of equal length subintervals needed to approximate $\int_1^2 xe^x dx$ to an accuracy of atleast $\frac{1}{3} \times 10^{-6}$ using the trapezoidal rule is*

(a) 1000 e (b) 1000 (c) 100 e (d) 100

**Solution.** (a)

$\because$ The given function is $f(x) = xe^x$

On differentiating above *wrt* '*x*'

$$f'(x) = xe^x + e^x = e^x(x+1)$$

Again differentiating,

$$f''(x) = e^x(x+2)$$

$\because$ Both $e^x$ and $x$ are increasing functions of $x$. So, maximum value of $f''(\eta)$ in interval $1 \le \eta \le 2$ occurs at $\eta = 2$.

So, $\text{Max}|f''(\eta)| = e^2(2+2) = 4e^2$

So, truncation error for trapezoidal rule $T_E$ (bound)

$$= \frac{h^3}{12} \text{Max}|f''(\eta)| N_i$$

where, $N_i = \frac{b-a}{h}$ = number of subintervals

So, $$T_{E(\text{bound})} = \frac{h^3}{12} \text{Max}|f''(\eta)| \times \frac{b-a}{h}$$

$$= \frac{h^2}{12}(b-a)\text{Max}|f''(\eta)|, 1 \le \eta \le 2$$

$$= \frac{h^2}{12} \times 4e^2 = \frac{h^2}{3} e^2$$

Now, putting $T_{E(\text{bound})} = \frac{1}{3} \times 10^{-6}$

Hence, $$\frac{h^2}{2} e^2 = \frac{1}{3} \times 10^{-6}$$

$$\Rightarrow \quad h^2 = \frac{10^{-6}}{e^2} \Rightarrow h = \frac{10^{-3}}{e}$$

Now, number of intervals $= N_i$

$$= \frac{b-a}{h} = \frac{2-1}{10^{-3}/e} = 1000\ e$$

***Example 8.*** *Use Euler's modified method to compute y for $x = 0.05$. Given that, $\frac{dy}{dx} = x + y$ with initial conditions $x_0 = 0$, $y_0 = 1$, so that result correct upto three decimal places*

(a) 1.0525 (b) 1.5025 (c) 1.00255 (d) 1.0565

**Solution.** (a)

$$\because \quad \frac{dy}{dx} = x + y \Rightarrow f(x, y) = x + y$$

$$x_0 = 0, y_0 = 1 \text{ and } h = 0.01$$

Then, by Euler's modified formula

$$y_{n+1} = y_n + \frac{h}{2}[f(x_n, y_n) + f(x_{n+1}, y_{n+1})]$$

$$y(0.01) = y_0 + \frac{0.01}{2}[(0+1) + (0.01 + 1.01)]$$

$$= 1 + 0.005(1 + 1.02) = 1.0101$$

Now, value at (0.02)

$$y(0.02) = y_{0.01} + \frac{h}{2}[f(x_n, y_n) + f(x_{n+1} + y_{n+1})]$$

$$= 1.0101 + \frac{0.01}{2}[(0.01 + 1.0101) + (0.02 + 1.0203)]$$

$$= 1.0101 + 0.005(1.0201 + 1.0403) = 1.0204$$

$$\text{Value of } y(0.03) = y(0.02) + \frac{0.01}{2}[(0.02 + 1.0204) + (0.03 + 1.0308)]$$

$$= 1.0204 + 0.005(1.0404 + 1.0608) = 1.0309$$

$$\text{Value of } y(0.04) = y(0.03) + \frac{0.01}{2}[(0.03 + 1.0309) + (0.04 + 1.0415)]$$

$$= 1.0309 + 0.005(1.0609 + 1.0815) = 1.0416$$

$$\text{Value of } y(0.05) = y(0.04) + \frac{0.01}{2}[(0.04 + 1.0416) + (0.05 + 1.0524)]$$

$$= 1.0416 + 0.005(2.1840) = 1.0525$$

***Example 9.*** *Using Runge's formula (third order), solve the differential equation $\frac{dy}{dx} = x - y$ subject to $y = 1$ when $x = 1$. Find $y(1.1)$.*

(a) 1.004833 (b) 1.048331

(c) 1.009433 (d) None of these

**Solution.** (a) $f(x, y) = x - y$

Here, $h = 0.1, x_0 = 1, y_0 = 1$

$$k_1 = hf(x_0, y_0) = 0.1(x - y) = 0.1(1-1) = 0$$

$$k_2 = hf\left[x_0 + \frac{h}{2}, y_0 + \frac{k_1}{2}\right]$$

$$= (0.1) f\left[1 + \frac{0.1}{2}, 1 + \frac{0}{2}\right] = (0.1) f(1.05, 1)$$

$$= 0.1(1.05 - 1) = 0.005$$

$$k_3 = hf(x_0 + h, y_0 + 2k_2 - k_1)$$

$$= (0.1) f[1 + 0.1, 1 + 2(0.005) - 0]$$

$$= 0.1 f(1.1, 1.01)$$

$$= 0.1(1.1 - 1.01) = 0.009$$

$$y_1 = y_0 + \frac{1}{6}[k_1 + 4k_2 + k_3]$$

$$y_{1.0} = 1 + \frac{1}{6}[0 + 4(0.005) + 0.009]$$

$$= 1 + \frac{1}{6}[0.02 + 0.009]$$

$$= 1 + \frac{1}{6}(0.029) = 1.004833$$

Hence, $y$ at $x = 1.1$ is 1.004833

## Type II (*One or more than one correct option*)

***Example 10.*** *For the given data*

| $x$ | 1.0 | 1.1 | 1.2 | 1.3 | 1.4 | 1.5 | 1.6 |
|---|---|---|---|---|---|---|---|
| $y$ | 7.989 | 8.403 | 8.781 | 9.129 | 9.451 | 9.750 | 10.031 |

(a) $\frac{dy}{dx} = 3.941$ at $x = 1.1$ (b) $\frac{dy}{dx} = 2.732$ at $x = 1.6$

(c) $\frac{d^2y}{dx^2} = -3.3167$ at $x = 1.1$ (d) $\frac{d^2y}{dx^2} = -1.475$ at $x = 1.6$

**Solution.** (a), (b), (c), (d)

The difference table is

| $x$ | $y$ | $\Delta$ | $\Delta^2$ | $\Delta^3$ | $\Delta^4$ | $\Delta^5$ | $\Delta^6$ |
|---|---|---|---|---|---|---|---|
| 1.0 | 7.989 | | | | | | |
| | | 0.414 | | | | | |
| 1.1 | 8.403 | | – 0.036 | | | | |
| | | 0.378 | | 0.006 | | | |
| 1.2 | 8.781 | | – 0.030 | | – 0.002 | | |
| | | 0.348 | | 0.004 | | 0.002 | |
| 1.3 | 9.129 | | – 0.026 | | 0.000 | | – 0.003 |
| | | 0.322 | | 0.004 | | – 0.001 | |
| 1.4 | 9.451 | | – 0.023 | | – 0.001 | | |
| | | 0.299 | | 0.005 | | | |
| 1.5 | 9.750 | | – 0.018 | | | | |
| | | 0.281 | | | | | |
| 1.6 | 10.031 | | | | | | |

(a,c) We know that

$$\left(\frac{dy}{dx}\right)_{x_0} = \frac{1}{h}\left[\Delta y_0 - \frac{1}{2}\Delta^2 y_0 + \frac{1}{3}\Delta^3 y_0 - \frac{1}{4}\Delta^4 y_0 + \ldots\right] \quad \ldots\text{(i)}$$

and

$$\left(\frac{d^2y}{dx^2}\right)_{x_0} = \frac{1}{h^2}\left[\Delta^2 y_0 - \Delta^3 y_0 + \frac{11}{12}\Delta^4 y_0 - \frac{5}{6}\Delta^5 y_0 + \ldots\right] \quad \ldots\text{(ii)}$$

Here, $h = 0.1, x_0 = 1.1, \Delta y_0 = 0.378,$

$\Delta^2 y_0 = -0.03$

Putting these values in Eqs. (i) and (ii), we get

$$\left(\frac{dy}{dx}\right)_{1.1} = \frac{1}{0.1}\left[0.378 - \frac{1}{2}(-0.03) + \frac{1}{3}(0.004) - \frac{1}{4}(0) + \frac{1}{5}(-0.001)\right]$$

$$= 3.941$$

$$\left(\frac{d^2y}{dx^2}\right)_{1.1} = \frac{1}{(0.1)^2}\left[-0.03 - (0.004) + + \frac{11}{12}(0) - \frac{5}{6}(-0.001)\right]$$

$$= -3.3167$$

(b,d) We know that

$$\left(\frac{dy}{dx}\right)_{x_n} = \frac{1}{h}\left[\nabla y_n + \frac{1}{2}\nabla^2 y_n + \frac{1}{3}\nabla^3 y_n + \frac{1}{4}\nabla^4 y_n + \ldots\right] \quad \ldots\text{(iii)}$$

and

$$\left(\frac{d^2y}{dx^2}\right)_{x_n} = \frac{1}{h^2}\left[\nabla^2 y_n + \nabla^3 y_n + \frac{11}{12}\nabla^4 y_n + \frac{5}{6}\Delta^5 y_n + \ldots\right] \quad \ldots\text{(iv)}$$

Here, $h = 0.1, x_n = 1.6, \nabla y_n = 0.281$

$\nabla^2 y_n = -0.018$ by the above table.

Putting these values in Eqs. (iii) and (iv), we get

$$\left(\frac{dy}{dx}\right)_{1.6} = \frac{1}{0.1}\left[0.281 + \frac{1}{2}(-0.018) + \frac{1}{3}(0.005) + \frac{1}{4}(-0.001) + \frac{1}{5}(-0.001)\right]$$

$$= 2.732$$

$$\left(\frac{d^2y}{dx^2}\right)_{1.6} = \frac{1}{(0.1)^2}\left[-0.018 + 0.005 + \frac{11}{15}(-0.001) + \frac{5}{6}(-0.001)\right]$$

$$= -1.475$$

The values of $\frac{dy}{dx}$ at $x = 1.1$ is 3.941 and at $x = 1.6$ is 2.732

The value of $\frac{d^2y}{dx^2}$ at $x = 1.1$ is $-3.3167$ and at $x = 1.6$ is $-1.475$.

***Example 11.*** *Given the equation $x^4 - x - 10 = 0$. By Newton-Raphson method*

(a) the root of the given equation lies between 1 and 2

(b) the roots of the equation is 1.855

(c) no root exist

(d) the root of equation lies between 0 and 1

**Solution.** (a), (b)

We have,

$$f(x) = x^4 - x - 10 = 0 \quad \ldots\text{(i)}$$

and

$$f'(x) = 4x^3 - 1$$

By Newton-Raphson formula, we get

$$x_{i+1} = x_i - \frac{f(x_i)}{f'(x_i)} = x_i - \frac{x_i^4 - x_i - 10}{4x_i^3 - 1}$$

$$\Rightarrow \quad x_{i+1} = \frac{4x_i^4 - x_i - x_i^4 + x_i + 10}{4x_i^3 - 1}$$

$$= \frac{3x_i^4 + 10}{4x_i^3 - 1} \quad \ldots\text{(ii)}$$

Also, from Eq. (i), we have

$f(1) = 1 - 1 - 10 = -10 =$ negative

$f(2) = 2^4 - 1 - 10 = 16 - 2 - 10 = 4 =$ positive

Hence, The root of the given equation lies between 1 and 2.

Also, $f(1.5) = (1.5)^4 - 1.5 - 10 =$ negative

$f(1.8) = (1.8)^4 - 1.8 - 10$

$= 10.5 - 1.8 - 10 =$ negative

$f(1.9) = (1.9)^4 - (1.9) - 10$

$= 13.032 - 1.9 - 10 =$ positive

$\therefore$ The root of (1) lies between 1.8 and 1.9.

**First approximation** Let $i = 0$, so $x_i = x_0 = 1.8$ (say)

Then, from Eq. (ii), we get

$$x_1 = \frac{3x_0^4 + 10}{4x_0^3 - 1} = \frac{3(1.8)^4 + 10}{4(1.8)^3 - 1}$$

$$= \frac{3(10.498) + 10}{4(5.832) - 1} = \frac{41.494}{22.328} = 1.858$$

**Second approximation** Let $i = 1$, so $x_i = x_1 = 1.858$

Then, from Eq. (ii), we get

$$x_2 = \frac{3(x_1^4) + 10}{4x_1^3 - 1} = \frac{3(1.858)^4 + 10}{4(1.858)^3 - 1}$$

$$\Rightarrow \quad x_2 = \frac{3(11.9174) + 10}{4(6.414) - 1} = \frac{45.7522}{24.656}$$

**Third approximation**

Let $i = 2$, so, $x_i = x_2 = 1.8556$

Then, from Eq. (ii), we get

$$x_3 = \frac{3(x_2)^4 + 10}{4x_2^3 - 1} = \frac{3(1.8556)^4 + 10}{4(1.8556)^3 - 1}$$

$$= \frac{3(11.856) + 10}{4(6.3893) - 1} = \frac{45.568}{24.557}$$

$$= 1.855602$$

Hence, the root of the equation is 1.855.

***Example 12.*** *Let $x = s$ be a solution of $x = g(x)$ and suppose that g has a continuous derivative in some interval I containing s. If $|g'(x)| \le k < 1$ in J the iteration process defined by $x_n = g(x_{n-1})$ converges for any $x_0 \in J$*

(a) If $|g'(x)| \le k < 1$ in $J$, the iteration process defined by $x_n = g(x_{n-1})$ converges for any $x_0 \in J$

(b) If $|g'(x)| \le k < 1$ in $J$, the iteration process defined by $x_n = g(x_{n-1})$ diverges for any $x_0 \in J$

(c) $g'(t) = \dfrac{g(x) - g(s)}{x - s} (s \in I)$

(d) $g'(x) \ne \dfrac{g(x) - g(s)}{x - s} 1 (s \in I)$

**Solution.** (a), (c)

Since, $g$ has a continuous derivative in interval $I$ by mean value theorem,

$$g'(t) = \frac{g(x) - g(s)}{x - s} \; (s \in I)$$

$$\Rightarrow \quad g(x) - g(s) = g'(t)(x - s) \; (s \in I)$$

Here, $g(s) = s$

and $x_1 = g(x_0),\ x_2 = g(x_1), \ldots$

We have,
$$|x_n - s| = |g(x_{n-1}) - g(s)|$$
$$= |g'(t)||x_{n-1} - s|$$
$$\le k|x_{n-1} - s| = k|g(x_{n-2}) - g(s)|$$
$$= k|g'(t^*)||x_{n-2} - s| \le k^2|x_{n-2} - s|$$
$$\vdots$$
$$\le k^n|x_0 - S|$$

Since, $k < 1$, we have $k^n \to 0 \Rightarrow |x_n - s| \to 0$ as $n \to \infty$.

Hence, The iteration process defined by $x_n = g(x_{n-1})$ converges to $x_0 \in J$.

***Example 13.*** *Given the system of equations,*

$$3x + 2y + 7z = 4$$
$$2x + 3y + z = 5$$
$$3x + 4y + z = 7, \text{ then}$$

(a) The given system can be represented as

$$\begin{bmatrix} 3 & 2 & 7 \\ 2 & 3 & 1 \\ 3 & 4 & 1 \end{bmatrix} \begin{bmatrix} x \\ y \\ z \end{bmatrix} = \begin{bmatrix} 4 \\ 5 \\ 7 \end{bmatrix}$$

(b) The given system can be represented as

$$\begin{bmatrix} 3 & 2 & 7 \\ 0 & \frac{5}{3} & -\frac{11}{3} \\ 0 & 0 & -\frac{8}{5} \end{bmatrix} \begin{bmatrix} x \\ y \\ z \end{bmatrix} = \begin{bmatrix} 4 \\ \frac{7}{3} \\ \frac{1}{5} \end{bmatrix}$$

(c) The solution of the given system of equation is

$$x = \frac{7}{8}, y = \frac{9}{8}, z = -\frac{1}{8}$$

(d) No solution exist of the given system of equations

**Solution.** (a), (b), (c)

We have,

$$\begin{bmatrix} 3 & 2 & 7 \\ 2 & 3 & 1 \\ 3 & 4 & 1 \end{bmatrix} \begin{bmatrix} x \\ y \\ z \end{bmatrix} = \begin{bmatrix} 4 \\ 5 \\ 7 \end{bmatrix}$$

Let $A = LU$, then

$$\begin{bmatrix} 1 & 0 & 0 \\ l_{21} & 1 & 0 \\ l_{31} & l_{32} & 1 \end{bmatrix} \begin{bmatrix} u_{11} & u_{12} & u_{13} \\ 0 & u_{22} & u_{23} \\ 0 & 0 & u_{33} \end{bmatrix} = \begin{bmatrix} 3 & 2 & 7 \\ 2 & 3 & 1 \\ 3 & 4 & 1 \end{bmatrix}$$

So that, $u_{11} = 3, u_{12} = 2, u_{13} = 7$

$$l_{21}u_{11} = 2, \quad \therefore \quad l_{21} = \frac{2}{3}$$
$$l_{31}u_{11} = 3, \quad \therefore \quad l_{31} = 1$$
$$l_{21}u_{12} + u_{22} = 3 \quad \therefore \quad u_{22} = \frac{5}{3}$$
$$l_{21}u_{13} + u_{23} = 1 \quad \therefore \quad u_{23} = -\frac{11}{3}$$
$$l_{31}u_{12} + l_{32}u_{22} = 4 \quad \therefore \quad l_{32} = \frac{6}{5}$$
$$l_{31}u_{13} + l_{32}u_{23} + u_{33} = 1, \quad \therefore \quad u_{33} = \frac{8}{5}$$

Thus,
$$A = \begin{bmatrix} 1 & 0 & 0 \\ \frac{2}{3} & 1 & 0 \\ 1 & \frac{6}{5} & 1 \end{bmatrix} \begin{bmatrix} 3 & 2 & 7 \\ 0 & \frac{5}{3} & -\frac{11}{3} \\ 0 & 0 & -\frac{8}{5} \end{bmatrix}$$

Writing $UX = V$, the given system becomes

$$\begin{bmatrix} 1 & 0 & 0 \\ 2/3 & 1 & 0 \\ 1 & 6/5 & 1 \end{bmatrix}\begin{bmatrix} v_1 \\ v_2 \\ v_2 \end{bmatrix} = \begin{bmatrix} 4 \\ 5 \\ 7 \end{bmatrix}$$

Solving this system, we have $v_1 = 4$,

$$\frac{2}{3}v_1 + v_2 = 5 \Rightarrow v_2 = \frac{7}{3}$$

$$v_1 + \frac{6}{5}v_2 + v_3 = 7 \Rightarrow v_3 = \frac{1}{5}$$

Hence, the original system becomes

$$\begin{bmatrix} 3 & 2 & 7 \\ 0 & \frac{5}{3} & \frac{11}{3} \\ 0 & 0 & -\frac{8}{5} \end{bmatrix}\begin{bmatrix} x \\ y \\ z \end{bmatrix} = \begin{bmatrix} 4 \\ \frac{7}{3} \\ \frac{1}{5} \end{bmatrix}$$

$$\Rightarrow \quad 3x + 2y + 7z = 4$$

$$\frac{5}{3}y - \frac{11}{3}z = \frac{7}{3}$$

$$-\frac{8}{5}z = \frac{1}{5}$$

By back substitution, we have

$$z = -\frac{1}{8}, y = \frac{9}{8} \text{ and } x = \frac{7}{8}$$

***Example 14.*** *Given* $\frac{dy}{dx} = \frac{1}{x+y}$ *for* $x - 0.5$ *use Runge-Kutta method with* $x_0 = 0$, $y(x_0) = 1$, *taking* $h = 0.5$

(a) $k_1 = 1$

(b) $k_2 = 0.333$

(c) $k - 0.357$

(d) the $y = 1.357$, when $x = 0.5$

**Solution.** (a), (b), (c), (d)

Given, $x_0 = 0, y_2 = 1, h = 0.5$ ...(i)

and $f(x, y) = \frac{1}{(x+y)}$ ...(ii)

Hence $f(x_0, y_0) = \frac{1}{(x_0 + y_0)} = \frac{1}{(0+1)} = 1$

Here, $k_1 = hf(x_0, y_0) = (0.5)(1) = 0.5$ ...(iii)

$$k_2 = hf\left(x_0 + \frac{1}{2}h, y_0 + \frac{1}{2}k_1\right)$$

$$= (0.5) f(0 + 0.25, 1 + 0.25)$$

$$= (0.5) f(0.25, 1.25)$$

$$= (0.5)\left[\frac{1}{(1.50)}\right] = 0.333 \quad \text{...(iv)}$$

$$k_3 = hf\left(x_0 + \frac{1}{2}h, y_0 + \frac{1}{2}k_2\right)$$

$$= (0.5) f(0.25, 1.167)$$

$$= (0.5)\left[\frac{1}{(0.25 + 1.167)}\right]$$

$$= (0.5)\left[\frac{1}{1.417}\right]$$

$$= 0.353 \quad \text{...(v)}$$

and $k_4 = hf(x_0 + h, y_0 + k_3)$

$$= (0.5) f(0.5, 1.353)$$

$$= (0.5)\left[\frac{1}{(0.5 + 1.353)}\right]$$

$$= (0.5)\left[\frac{1}{(1.853)}\right]$$

$$= 0.270 \quad \text{...(vi)}$$

Hence, $k = \frac{1}{6}(k_1 + 2k_2 + 2k_3 + k_4)$

$$k = \frac{1}{6}[0.5 + 2(0.333) + 2(0.353) + 0.27]$$

Hence, from Eqs. (iii), (iv), (v) and (vi), we get

$$k = \frac{1}{6}[0.5 + 0.666 + 0.706 + 0.27]$$

$$= \frac{1}{6}[2.142] = 0.357$$

Hence, $y_{n+1} = y_n + k$

$\Rightarrow$ $y_1 = y_0 + k = 1 + 0.357 = 1.357$

Thus, the required value of $y$, when $x = 0.5$ is 1.357.

***Example 15.*** *If fourth and higher differences are zero*

$$U_4 = U_0 + 4\Delta U_0 + 6U^2U_{-1} + 10\Delta^3 U_{-1}$$

(a) If fourth and higher differences are zero.

$U_4 = U_0 + 4\Delta U_0 + 6U^2U_{-1} + 10\Delta^3 U_{-1}$

(b) $u_4 = E^5 U_{-1}$

(c) $E^5 = (1 + \Delta)^5$

(d) $E^5 = (1 + \Delta)^5$

**Solution.** (a), (b), (c)

$$U_4 = E^5 U_{-1} = (1 + \Delta)^5 U_{-1}$$

$$= U_{-1} + 5\Delta U_{-1} + 10\Delta^2 U_{-1} + 10\Delta^3 U_{-1}$$

$$= (U_{-1} + \Delta U_{-1}) + 4(\Delta U_{-1} + \Delta^2 U_{-1}) + 6\Delta^2 U_{-1} + 10\Delta^3 U_{-1}$$

$$= U_0 + 4\Delta U_0 + 6\Delta^2 U_{-1} + 10\Delta^2 U_{-1}$$

***Example 16.*** *Evaluating* $\int_0^6 \frac{dx}{1+x^2}$ *by*

(a) Trapezoidal rule gives 1.4108

(b) Simpson's 1/3 rule gives 1.3662

(c) Simpson's 3/8 rule gives 1.3571

(d) The value find by Trapezoidal rule is more nearer to actual value

**Solution.** (a), (b), (c), (d)

Divide the interval (0, 6) into six parts each of width $h = 1$. The values of

$$f(x) = \frac{1}{1+x^2}$$

are given below

| 6x | 0 | 1 | 2 | 3 | 4 | 5 | 6 |
|---|---|---|---|---|---|---|---|
| 6y | 1 | 0.5 | 0.2 | 0.1 | 0.588 | 0.0385 | 0.027 |

(i) By trapezoidal rule, we have

$$\int_0^6 \frac{dx}{1+x^2} = \frac{h}{2}[(y_0 + y_6) + 2(y_1 + y_2 + y_3 + y_4 + y_5)]$$

$$= \frac{1}{2}[(1 + 0.027) + 2(0.5 + 0.2 + 0.1 + 0.0588 + 0.0385) = 1.4108$$

(ii) By Simpson's 1/3 rule, we have

$$\int_0^6 \frac{dx}{1+x^2} = \frac{h}{3}[(y_0 + y_6) + 4(y_1 + y_3 + y_5) + 2(y_2 + y_4)]$$

$$= \frac{1}{3}[(1 + 0.027) + 4(0.5 + 0.1 + 0.0385) + 2(0.2 + 0.0588)]$$

$$= 1.3662$$

(iii) By simpson's 3/8 rule, we have

$$\int_0^6 \frac{dx}{1+x^2} = \frac{3h}{8}[(y_0 + y_6) + 3(y_1 + y_2 + y_4 + y_5) + 2y_3]$$

$$= \frac{3}{8}[(1 + 0.027) + 3(0.5 + 0.2) + 0.0588 + 0.0385 + 2(0.1)]$$

$$= 1.3571$$

(iv) The actual value

$$\int_0^6 \frac{dx}{1+x^2} = |\tan^{-1} x|_0^6 = \tan^{-1} 6 = 1.4056$$

Here, the value find by Trapezoidal rule is more nearer to actual value.

***Example 17.*** *Given*

| $x$ | –4 | –1 | 0 | 2 | 5 |
|---|---|---|---|---|---|
| $f(x)$ | 1245 | 33 | 5 | 9 | 1335 |

(a) The Newton's divided difference formula

$$f(x) = f(x_0) + (x - x_0)[x_0, x_1] + (x - x_0)(x - x_1)[x_0, x_1, x_2] + \ldots$$

(b) By using Newton's divided difference formula

$$f(x) = 3x^4 - 5x^3 + 6x^2 - 14x + 5$$

(c) By using Newton's divided difference formula

$$f(x) = \sin x \cos x + 6x^2 + 6$$

(d) None of the above

**Solution.** (a), (b)

The divided differences table is

| $x$ | $y$ | $\Delta$ | $\Delta^2$ | $\Delta^3$ | $\Delta^4$ |
|---|---|---|---|---|---|
| –4 | 1245 | | | | |
| | | – 404 | | | |
| –1 | 33 | | 94 | | |
| | | – 28 | | – 14 | |
| 0 | 5 | | 10 | | 3 |
| | | 2 | | 13 | |
| 2 | 9 | | 88 | | |
| | | 442 | | | |
| 5 | 1335 | | | | |

By Newton's divided difference formula

$$f(x) = f(x_0) + (x - x_0)[x_0, x_1] + (x - x_0)(x - x_1)[x_0, x_1, x_2] + \ldots$$

$$= 1245 + (x + 4)(-404) + (x + 4)(x + 1)(94) + (x + 4)(x + 1)(x - 0)(-14) + (x + 4)(x + 1)x(x - 2)(3)$$

$$= 3x^4 - 5x^3 + 6x^2 - 14x + 5$$

***Example 18.*** *By Euler's method to initial value problem* $\frac{dy}{dx} = x + y$, $y = 0$ *when* $x = 0$ *in the range* $x = 0$ *to* $x = 0.04$ *taking* $h = 0.2$.

(a) $y_1 = 0$ (b) $y_2 = 0.04$ (c) $y_3 = 0.128$ (d) $y_1 = y_2 = y_3$

**Solution.** (a), (b) (c)

Taking $h = 0.2$ split up the interval (0, 1) into subintervals of width 0.2 each with the help of $x_n = 0 + nh$, so that the points of division are given by

$x_0 = 0$, $x_1 = 0.2$, $x_2 = 0.4$, $x_3 = 0.6$, $x_4 = 0.8$, $x_5 = 1.0$

Let us write

$$f(x, y) = x + y \quad \ldots(i)$$

Here, $x_0 = 0$, $y = 0$ and $h = 0.2$ ...(ii)

and we have to calculate $y_5$

Hence $f(x_0, y_0) = x_0 + y_0$, from Eq. (i)

$$= 0 + 0 = 0 \quad (\because x_0 = 0 = y_0)$$

Now $y_1 = y_0 + hf(x_0, y_0)$

$\Rightarrow$ $y_1 = 0 + (0.2)(0) = 0$

$\Rightarrow$ $y_1 = 0$ ...(iii)

Hence, $f(x_1, y_1) = x_1 + y_1$, [from Eq. (i)]

$$= 0.2 + 0 = 0.2$$

Now, $y_2 = y_1 + hf(x_1, y_1)$,

$$= 0 + (0.2)(0.2), \quad \text{[from Eq. (iv)]}$$

or $y_2 = 0.04$]

Hence, $f(x_2, y_2) = x_2 + y_2$ [from Eq. (i)]

$$= 0.4 + 0.04 = 0.44$$

Now, $y_3 = y_2 + hf(x_2, y_2)$

$$= (0.04) + (0.2)(0.44) = 0.128$$

Thus, we have $y_1 = 0$, $y_2 = 0.04$ and $y_3 = 0.128$

***Example 19.*** *Given that*

| $x$ | 1 | 2 | 3 | 4 | 5 |
|---|---|---|---|---|---|
| $u$ | 2 | 5 | 10 | 20 | 30 |

(a) $\nabla \equiv \Delta E^{-1}$ (b) $\Delta \equiv E - 1$

(c) $\nabla^2 u_4 = u_4 - 2u_3 + u_2$ (d) $\nabla^2 u_4 = 5$

**Solution.** (a), (b), (c), (d)

$$\nabla^2 u_4 = (\Delta E^{-1})^2 u_4, \quad (\because \nabla = \Delta E^{-1})$$

$$= \Delta^2 E^{-2} u_4$$

$$= \Delta^2 u_2 \quad (\because E^{-2} = u_4 = u_2)$$

$$= (E - 1)^2 u_2 \quad (\because \Delta \equiv E - 1)$$

$$= (E^2 - 2E + 1)u_2$$

$$= E^2 u_2 - 2Eu_2 + u_2 = u_4 - 2u_3 + u_2$$

$$= 20 - 2(10) + 5 \quad (\because u_4 = 20, u_3 = 10, u_2 = 5)$$

$$= 5$$

***Example 20.*** *Evaluate the missing terms*

| Years | 1945 | 1950 | 1955 | 1960 | 1965 | 1970 | 1975 |
|---|---|---|---|---|---|---|---|
| Production | $200 y_0$ | $220 y_1$ | $260 y_2$ | $*y_3$ | $350 y_4$ | $*y_5$ | $430 y_6$ |

(a) $y_3 = 306$ (b) $y_5 = 390$ (c) $y_3 = 400$ (d) $y_5 = 555$

**Solution.** (a), (b)

Since, five figures are known, we can assume that all the differences or order fifth are zero. As, there are two figures unknown, we need two equations to determine them

Hence, $\Delta^5 y_0 = 0$

and $\Delta^5 y_1 = 0$

$$\Rightarrow \begin{cases} (E-1)^5 y_0 = 0 \\ (E-1)^5 y_1 = 0 \end{cases}$$

$$\Rightarrow \begin{cases} y_5 - 5y_4 + 10y_3 - 10y_2 + 5y_1 - y_0 = 0 \\ y_6 - 5y_5 + 10y_4 - 10y_3 - 5y_2 - y_1 = 0 \end{cases}$$

Substituting the values of known $y_i'$ s, we get

$$\Rightarrow \begin{cases} y_5 - 5\times 350 + 10y_3 - 10\times 260 + 5\times 220 - 200 = 0 \\ 430 - 5y_5 + 10\times 350 - 10y_3 + 5\times 260 - 220 = 0 \end{cases}$$

$$\Rightarrow \begin{cases} y_5 - 1750 + 10y_3 - 2600 + 1100 - 260 = 0 \\ 430 - 5y_5 + 3500 - 10y_3 + 1300 - 220 = 0 \end{cases}$$

$$\Rightarrow \begin{cases} y_5 + 10y_3 = 3450 & \ldots\text{(i)} \\ -5y_5 - 10y_3 = -5010 & \ldots\text{(ii)} \end{cases}$$

Adding Eqs. (i) and (ii), we get

$$-4y_5 = -1560$$

$$y_5 = 390$$

Substituting the value $y_5$ in Eq. (i), we get

$$390 + 10y_3 = 3450$$

$$10y_3 = 3450 - 390 = 3060$$

Hence, $y_3 = 306$

# Exercise 1 (For Part 'B')

**Directions** (Q. Nos. 1-139) *All questions have only one correct option.*

**1.** Newton-Raphson iteration formula for finding $\sqrt[3]{c}$, where $c > 0$ is

(a) $x_{n+1} = \dfrac{2x_n^3 + \sqrt[3]{c}}{2x_n^2}$ (b) $x_{n+1} = \dfrac{3x_n^3 - \sqrt[3]{c}}{3x_n^2}$

(c) $x_{n+1} = \dfrac{2x_n^3 + c}{3x_n^2}$ (d) $x_{n+1} = \dfrac{2x_n^3 - c}{3x_n^2}$

**2.** The following table gives the values of $x$ and $y$

| $x$ | 30 | 35 | 40 | 45 | 50 |
|---|---|---|---|---|---|
| $y$ | 15.9 | 14.9 | 14.1 | 13.3 | 12.5 |

Find the value of $x$ corresponding to $y = 13.6$

(a) 43.1 (b) 43.0

(c) 43.2 (d) None of these

**3.** Certain corresponding values of $x$ and $\log_{10} x$ are (300, 2.4771), (304, 2.4829), (305, 2.4843) and (307, 2.4871) $\log_{10} 301$ will be

(a) 1.4786 (b) 2.4786 (c) 3.4786 (d) 4.4786

**4.** The order of convergence in Newton-Raphson method is

(a) 2 (b) 3

(c) 0 (d) None of these

**5.** The value of $\int_0^1 \dfrac{dx}{1+x}$ by simpson's rule is

(a) 0.96315 (b) 0.63915 (c) 0.69315 (d) 0.69351

**6.** As soon as a new value of a variable is found by iteration, it is used immediately in the following equations, this method is called

(a) Gauss-Jordan method (b) Gauss-Seidal method

(c) Jacobi method (d) Relaxation method

**7.** With the help of trapezoidal rule for numerical integration and the following table

| $x$ | 0 | 0.25 | 0.50 | 0.75 | 1 |
|---|---|---|---|---|---|
| $f(x)$ | 0 | 0.0625 | 0.2500 | 0.5625 | 1 |

the value $\int_0^1 f(x)dx$ is

(a) 0.33334 (b) 0.34375 (c) 0.034457 (d) 0.35342

**8.** The population of a town in the decimal census was as given below

| **Year : x** | 1891 | 1901 | 1911 | 1921 | 1931 |
|---|---|---|---|---|---|
| **Population : y (in lacs)** | 46 | 66 | 81 | 93 | 101 |

Estimate the population for the year 1895.

(a) 34.75 lacs (b) 54.85 lacs

(c) 74.32 lacs (d) 50.32 lacs

**9.** Sum of the series $1.2\Delta x^n - 2.3\Delta^2 x^n + 3.4\Delta^3 x^n - \dots$ to $n$ terms is

(a) $2[(x-2)^n - (x-3)^n]$ (b) $2[(x-3)^n - 1]$

(c) $2[(x-1)^n - (x-4)^n]$ (d) $2[(x-1)^n - (x-3)^n]$

**10.** Which one of the following result is incorrect?

(a) $\Delta x^n = nx^{n-1}$ (b) $\Delta x^{n-1} = nx^{(n-1)}$

(c) $\Delta^n e^x = e^x$ (d) $\Delta \cos x = -\sin x$

**11.** The Newton-Raphson method is used to find the root of the equation $x^2 - 2 = 0$. If the iterations are started from $-1$, the iterations will

(a) converge to $-1$ (b) converge to $\sqrt{2}$

(c) converge to $-\sqrt{2}$ (d) not converge

**12.** Simpson's rule for integration gives exact result, when $f(x)$ is a polynomial of degree

(a) 1 (b) 2

(c) 3 (d) All of these

**13.** $\Delta^2 \cos 2x$ with $h$ interval is equal to

(a) $\cos 2(x+h)$ (b) $2\sin^2 h \cos 2(x+h)$

(c) $\sin 2h \cos 2(x+h)$ (d) None of these

**14.** A second degree polynomial passes through (0, 3), (1, 6), (2, 11), (3, 18), and (4, 27). The polynomial is

(a) $x^2 + x + 1$ (b) $x^2 + 2x + 3$

(c) $x^2 + 2x + 1$ (d) $x^2 + x + 2$

**15.** A second degree polynomial passes through (0, 1), (1, 3), (2, 7) and (3, 13). The polynomial is

(a) $x^2 + 5x + 4$ (b) $x^2 + 2x + 1$

(c) $x^2 + x + 1$ (d) None of these

**16.** The pressure $P$ of wind corresponding to velocity $V$ is given by the following data

| $V$ | 10 | 20 | 30 | 40 |
|---|---|---|---|---|
| $P$ | 1.1 | 2.0 | 4.4 | 7.9 |

Value of $P$ when $V$ is equal to 25 is

(a) 3 (b) 3.0375 (c) 3.3075 (d) 3.5

**17.** The first term of the series whose second and subsequent terms are 8, 3, 0, – 1, 0 is

(a) 5 (b) 10 (c) 15 (d) 20

**18.** Let $\left\{0, \dfrac{1}{2}, 1\right\}$ be three distinct points on [0, 1]. Let $p$ be the unique interpolating polynomial of suitable degree on [0, 1], such that

$p(0) = 0,\ p\left(\dfrac{1}{2}\right) = 0,\ p(1) = 1$, then $p\left(\dfrac{1}{4}\right)$ is equal to

(a) – 1/8 (b) – 1/2

(c) 2/5 (d) None of these

**19.** From the following table, using trapezoidal rule, the area bounded by the curve, the x-axis and the lines $x = 7.47$, $x = 7.52$ is

| $x$ | 7.47 | 7.48 | 7.49 | 7.50 | 7.51 | 7.52 |
|---|---|---|---|---|---|---|
| $f(x)$ | 1.93 | 1.95 | 1.98 | 2.01 | 2.03 | 2.06 |

(a) 0.0996 (b) 0.0896
(c) 0.1096 (d) 0.0776

**20.** In simpson's one-third rule the curve $y = f(x)$ is assumed to be a

(a) circle (b) parabola
(c) hyperbola (d) None of these

**21.** Trapezoidal rule for evaluation of $\int_a^b f(x)dx$ requires the interval $(a, b)$ to be divided into

(a) $2n$ subintervals of equal width
(b) $2n + 1$ subintervals of equal width
(c) any number of subintervals of equal width
(d) $3n$ subintervals of equal width

**22.** In the Gauss elimination method for solving a system of linear algebraic equations, triangularization leads to

(a) diagonal matrix
(b) lower triangular matrix
(c) upper triangular matrix
(d) singular matrix

**23.** Considering four subintervals, the value of $\int_0^1 \frac{1}{1+x}dx$ by Trapezoidal rule is

(a) 0.6870 (b) 0.6677
(c) 0.6970 (d) 0.3597

**24.** By simpson's $\frac{1}{3}$ rule, the value of $\int_1^7 \frac{dx}{x}$ is

(a) 1.358 (b) 1.958 (c) 1.625 (d) 1.458

**25.** The quadrature formulae

$$\int_{-1}^{1} f(x)dx = \frac{1}{3}[f(-1) + 4f(0) + f(1)]$$

with step length $h = 1.0$ is exact for polynomials of degree less than or equal to

(a) two (b) three
(c) four (d) None of these

**26.** The quadrature formulae

$$\int_{-1}^{1} f(x)dx = \frac{1}{9}\left[5f\left(-\sqrt{\frac{3}{5}}\right) + 8f(0) + 5f\left(\sqrt{\frac{3}{5}}\right)\right]$$

is exact for polynomials of degree less than are equal to

(a) 3 (b) 4 (c) 5 (d) 6

**27.** Let $p$ be the unique polynomial of suitable degree, such that $p(1) = 2$, $p'(1) = 3$, $p(2) = 6$, $p'(2) = 7$, $p''(2) = 8$, then $p(0)$ is

(a) $-8$ (b) 0
(c) 16 (d) None of these

**28.** Simpson's one-third rule for evaluation of $\int_a^b f(x)dx$ requires the interval $[a, b]$ to be divided into

(a) an even number of subintervals of equal width
(b) an odd number of subintervals of equal width
(c) any number of subintervals of equal width
(d) any number of subintervals

**29.** The value of $f(x)$ given only at $x = 0, \frac{1}{3}, \frac{2}{3}$ and 1. Which of the following can be used to evaluate $\int_0^1 f(x)dx$ approximately

(a) trapezoidal rule
(b) simpson's rule
(c) trapezoidal as well as Simpson rule
(d) None of the above

**30.** The accuracy of simpson's rule quadrature for a step size $h$ is

(a) $O(h^2)$ (b) $O(h^3)$
(c) $O(h^4)$ (d) $O(h^5)$

**31.** For cubic polynomial which takes the following values $y(0) = 1$, $y(1) = 0$, $y(2) = 1$ and $y(3) = 10$, $y(4) = ...$

(a) 24 (b) 33
(c) 36 (d) 42

**32.** The value of $\Delta^n(a^x)$ is

(a) $(a^h + 1)^n a^x$ (b) $(a^h - 1)^n a^x$
(c) $(a^{nh} - 1)a^x$ (d) $(a^{nh} + 1)a^x$

**33.** Expression of the function $x^3 + x^2 - 5x + 2$ in factorial notation is

(a) $x^{(3)} + 4x^{(2)} - 3x^{(1)} + 2$
(b) $x^{(3)} - 4x^{(2)} - 3x^{(1)} + 2$
(c) $x^{(3)} - 4x^{(2)} + 3x^{(1)} + 2$
(d) $x^{(3)} + 4x^{(2)} - 3x^{(1)} - 2$

**34.** Which of the following relation in false?

(a) $E = 1 + \Delta$
(b) $E^{-1} = 1 - \nabla$
(c) $\nabla.\nabla = 1 - 2E^{-1} + E^{-2}$
(d) None of the above

**35.** The value of $E^2x^2$, when the value of $x$ vary by a constant increment of 2 is

(a) $x^2 - 4x + 4$ (b) $x^2 + 2$
(c) $x^2 + 8x + 16$ (d) None of these

**36.** If $y_1 = 4$, $y_3 = 12$, $y_4 = 19$ and $y_x = 7$, then $x$ will be

(a) 1.42 (b) 1.68
(c) 1.86 (d) 1.98

**37.** If for $n = 4$, the value of integral $\int_1^9 x^2 dx$ by Trapezoidal rule is $2\left[\frac{1}{2}(1+9^2) + \alpha^2 + \beta^2 + 7^2\right]$, then

(a) $\alpha = 1, \beta = 3$ (b) $\alpha = 2, \beta = 4$
(c) $\alpha = 3, \beta = 5$ (d) $\alpha = 4, \beta = 6$

**38.** The Taylor series for $y(x) = \log(1+x)$ is

(a) $1+x+\frac{1}{2}x^2+\frac{1}{6}x^3+\ldots+\frac{1}{n!}x^n$

(b) $x-\frac{1}{2}x^2+\frac{1}{3}x^3-\frac{1}{4}x^4+\ldots$

(c) $x-\frac{1}{2}x^2-\frac{1}{3}x^3+\frac{1}{4}x^4+\ldots$

(d) $1-x-\frac{1}{2}x^2-\frac{1}{6}x^3-\ldots-\frac{1}{n!}x^n$

**39.** The value of $f(3)$ from the following table using the Lagrange's formula is

| $x$ | 0 | 1 | 2 | 4 | 5 | 6 |
|---|---|---|---|---|---|---|
| $f(x)$ | 1 | 14 | 15 | 5 | 6 | 19 |

(a) 10 (b) 10.5 (c) 11 (d) 11.5

**40.** Value of $\frac{\Delta^2}{E}(x^3)$ is

(a) $6x$ (b) $3x$
(c) $2x$ (d) None of these

**41.** If $h$ is the interval of differencing, then $(\Delta - \nabla)x^2$ equals to

(a) $2h$ (b) $2h^2$
(c) $2h^3$ (d) None of these

**42.** The value of $\frac{\Delta^2}{E}\sin x$ is

(a) $2\sin x(\sinh + 1)$ (b) $2\sin x(\sinh - 1)$
(c) $2\sin x(\cosh + 1)$ (d) $2\sin x(\cosh - 1)$

**43.** If $y = a2^x + b2^x$ and $h = 1$, then $(\Delta^2 - 2\Delta + 1)y$ equals to

(a) 0 (b) 1
(c) 2 (d) None of these

**44.** Let $f(0) = 1$, $f(1) = 2.72$, then the Trapezoidal rule gives approximate value of $\int_0^1 f(x)dx$ is

(a) 3.72 (b) 1.86 (c) 1.72 (d) 0.86

**45.** Using Newton's forward Interpolation formula find the value of $f(1.6)$. If

| $x$ | 1 | 1.4 | 1.8 | 2.2 |
|---|---|---|---|---|
| $y$ | 3.49 | 4.82 | 5.96 | 6.5 |

(a) 5.54 (b) 4.45
(c) 5.35 (d) None of these

**46.** Find the number of students who obtained less than 45 marks, from the following data

| Marks | 30–40 | 40–50 | 50–60 | 60–70 | 70–80 |
|---|---|---|---|---|---|
| No. of Students | 31 | 42 | 51 | 35 | 31 |

(a) 45 (b) 75 (c) 105 (d) 52

**47.** If $y(1) = -3$, $y(3) = 9$, $y(4) = 30$ and $y(6) = 132$, find the four point Lagrange Interpolation polynomial that takes the same values as the function $y$ at the given points

(a) $x^3 + 2x^2 - 7x + 13$ (b) $x^3 - 3x^2 + 5x - 6$
(c) $x^3 - 3x^2 - 7x + 6$ (d) None of these

**48.** For the following values of $x$ and $y$, the first derivative at $x = 4$ is

| $x$ | 1 | 2 | 4 | 8 | 10 |
|---|---|---|---|---|---|
| $y$ | 0 | 1 | 5 | 21 | 27 |

(a) 0.28326 (b) 20.8326
(c) 2.8326 (d) 283.826

**49.** The order of error in the Simpson's rule for numerical integration with a step size $h$ is

(a) $h$ (b) $h^2$
(c) $h^3$ (d) $h^4$

**50.** We wish to solve $x^2 - 2 = 0$ by Newton-Raphson technique. Let the initial guess by $x_0 = 1.0$ subsequent estimate of $x$ (*i.e.*, $x_1$) will be

(a) 1.414 (b) 1.5
(c) 2.0 (d) None of these

**51.** The root of equation $x^3 + x - 3 = 0$, lies in the interval [1, 2]. After second iteration by false position method. It will be in

(a) (1.178, 2.00) (b) (1.25, 1.75)
(c) (1.125, 1.375) (d) (1.825, 2.00)

**52.** Newton-Raphson formula of successive approximation to find the approximate value of a root of the equation $f(x) = 0$ is

(a) $x_{n+1} = x_n - \frac{f(x_n)}{f'(x_n)}$ (b) $x_{n+1} = x_n - \frac{f'(x_n)}{f(x_n)}$

(c) $x_{n+1} = x_n + \frac{f(x_n)}{f'(x_n)}$ (d) $x_{n+1} = x_n + \frac{f'(x_n)}{f(x_n)}$

**53.** If 3 is taken as an approximate root of the equation $x^3 - 30 = 0$, then a better approximation by Newton-Raphson method is

(a) $\frac{10}{3}$ (b) $\frac{28}{9}$

(c) $\frac{8}{3}$ (d) $\frac{26}{9}$

**54.** If one root of the equation $f(x) = 0$ is near to $x_0$, then the first approximation of this root as calculated by Newton-Raphson method is the abscissa of the point, where the following straight line intersects the $x$-axis

(a) normal to the curve $y = f(x)$ at the point $(x_0, y = f(x_0))$

(b) tangent to the curve $y = f(x)$ at the point $(x_0, y = f(x_0))$

(c) the straight line through the point $(x_0, y = f(x_0))$ having the gradient $\frac{1}{f'(x_0)}$

(d) passing through the point $(x, f(x_0))$

**55.** The equation $x^3 - 15x + 4 = 0$ has a root close to 0.3, then value of this root upto 4 decimal places using inverse interpolation is

(a) 0.2679 (b) 2.0679
(c) 2.6790 (d) 267.90

**56.** If $f(1.15)=1.07723$, $f(1.20)=1.0954$, $f(1.25)=1.1180$ and $f(1.30)=1.1401$, then value of $f(1.28)$ is

(a) 113.12 (b) 11.312 (c) 1.1312 (d) 0.11312

**57.** $\sum_{x=1}^{n} x(x+2)(x+4)$ is equal to

(a) $\frac{n(n+1)(n+4)}{3}$ (b) $\frac{n(n+1)(n+4)(n+5)}{4}$

(c) $\frac{n(n-1)(n+4)}{4}$ (d) $\frac{n(n+1)(n+2)(n+3)}{4}$

**58.** Starting with $x_0 = 1$, the next approximation $x_1$ to $(2)^{1/3}$ obtained by Newton's method is

(a) $\frac{5}{3}$ (b) $\frac{4}{3}$ (c) $\frac{5}{4}$ (d) $\frac{5}{6}$

**59.** The Newton-Raphson method converges fast, if $f'(\alpha)$ is ($\alpha$ is the exact value of root)

(a) small (b) large

(c) zero (d) None of these

**60.** The estimated positive root of the function $f(x) = x^4 - 2x^2 - 4$ from an initial guess of $x_0 = 2$ with one iteration of Newton's method is equal to

(a) 1.81 (b) 1.82

(c) 1.83 (d) 1.84

**61.** If one root of the equation $x^3 + x^2 - 1 = 0$ is near to 1.0, then by Newton-Raphson method, the first calculated approximate value of this root is

(a) 0.9 (b) 0.6 (c) 1.2 (d) 0.8

**62.** If $a$ and $a+h$ are two consecutive approximate roots of the equation $f(x)=0$ as obtained by Newton's method, then $h$ is equal to

(a) $\frac{f(a)}{f'(a)}$ (b) $\frac{f'(a)}{f(a)}$ (c) $-\frac{f'(a)}{f(a)}$ (d) $-\frac{f(a)}{f'(a)}$

**63.** Newton-Raphson method is used to calculate $\sqrt[3]{65}$ by solving $x^3 = 65$. If $x_0 = 4$ is taken as initial approximation, then the first approximation $x_1$ is

(a) $\frac{65}{16}$ (b) $\frac{131}{32}$ (c) $\frac{191}{48}$ (d) $\frac{193}{48}$

**64.** The value of $\sqrt{12}$ correct to 3 decimal places by Newton-Raphson method is given by

(a) 3.463 (b) 3.462

(c) 3.467 (d) None of these

**65.** After second iteration of Newton-Raphson method the positive root of equation $x^2 = 3$ is (taking initial approximation $\frac{3}{2}$).

(a) $\frac{7}{4}$ (b) $\frac{97}{56}$ (c) $\frac{3}{2}$ (d) $\frac{347}{200}$

**66.** The value of the root nearest to the 2 after first iteration of the equation $x^4 - x - 10 = 0$ by Newton-Raphson method is

(a) 2.321 (b) 2.125

(c) 1.983 (d) 1.871

**67.** By Simpson's rule, the value of $\int_1^7 \frac{dx}{x}$ is

(a) 1.358 (b) 1.958

(c) 1.625 (d) 1.458

**68.** If (2, 6) is divided into four intervals of equal length, then the approximate value of $\int_2^6 \frac{1}{x^2 - x} dx$ using Simpson's rule is

(a) 0.3222 (b) 0.2333

(c) 0.5222 (d) 0.2555

**69.** Root of the equation $x^4 - 12x + 7 = 0$ which is approximately equal to 2, is

(a) 2.05 (b) 1.95

(c) 2.15 (d) None of these

**70.** By Simpson's rule taking $n = 4$, the value of the integral $\int_2^1 \frac{1}{1+x^2} dx$ is equal to

(a) 0.785 (b) 0.788

(c) 0.781 (d) None of these

**71.** Taking $n = 4$, by Trapezoidal rule, the value of $\int_0^2 \frac{dx}{1+x}$ is

(a) 1.1167 (b) 1.1176

(c) 1.118 (d) None of these

**72.** The values of a function $f(x)$ are tabulated below

| $x$ | 0 | 1 | 2 | 3 |
|---|---|---|---|---|
| $f(x)$ | 1 | 2 | 1 | 10 |

Using Newton's forward difference formula, the cubic polynomial that can be fitted to the above data is

(a) $2x^3 + 7x^2 - 6x + 2$ (b) $2x^3 - 7x^2 + 6x - 2$

(c) $x^3 - 7x^2 - 6x + 1$ (d) $2x^3 - 7x^2 + 6x + 1$

**73.** A river is 80 m wide. The depth $d$ in metres at a distance x metres from one bank is given by the following table

| $x$ | 0 | 10 | 20 | 30 | 40 | 50 | 60 | 70 | 80 |
|---|---|---|---|---|---|---|---|---|---|
| $d$ | 0 | 4 | 7 | 9 | 12 | 15 | 14 | 8 | 3 |

The area of the cross-section by Simpson's one–third rule is

(a) 710 sq m (b) 800 sq m

(c) 600 sq m (d) 510 sq m

**74.** The population of a town in the decennial census is given below. Estimate the population for the year 1893.

| Year | 1950 | 1960 | 1970 | 1980 | 1990 |
|---|---|---|---|---|---|
| Population (in thousands) | 45 | 66 | 81 | 93 | 101 |

(a) 96.837 (b) 100.27

(c) 86.4 (d) 79.3

**75.** If $f(x)$ has an isolated zero of multiplicity 3 at $x = \xi$ and the iteration

$$x_{n+1} = x_n - \frac{3f(x_n)}{f'(x_n)}, n = 0, 1, 2, \ldots$$

Converges to $\xi$, then the rate of convergent is
(a) linear
(b) faster than one but slower than two
(c) quadratic
(d) cubic

**76.** For finding root of $f(x) = 0$, the iteration scheme

$$x_{n+1} = x_n - \frac{(x_n - x_{n-1})}{f(x_n) - f(x_{n-1})} f(x_n)$$

(a) bracket the root at each iteration
(b) bracket the roof at each iteration, if $f(x_n)f(x_{n-1}) < 0$
(c) bracket the roof at each iteration, if $f(x_n)f(x_{n-1}) > 0$
(d) None of the above

**77.** To find the positive square root of $a > 0$ by solving $x^2 - a = 0$ by the Newton-Raphson method, if $x_n$ denotes the $n^{th}$ iterate with $x_0 > 0$, $x_0 \neq \sqrt{a}$, then the sequence $\{x_n, n \geq 1\}$ is
(a) strictly decreasing
(b) strictly increasing
(c) constant
(d) may be increasing or decreasing

**78.** The Trapezoidal rule for integration gives the exact result when the integrant is a polynomial of degree
(a) one (b) two
(c) three (d) None of these

**79.** Which of following method always converges to root of equation $f(x) = 0$?
(a) Newton's-Raphson method
(b) Regula false mathed
(c) Secant method
(d) All of the above

**80.** If permissible error $|\epsilon| \leq 10^{-5}$ for finding root of $\cos x - e^{-x} = 0$ in interval [3, 4] using interval halving mehtod. Then, there will be
(a) atleast 17 iteration required
(b) atleast 14 iteration required
(c) atleast 12 iteration required
(d) method not applicable

**81.** In solving the ordinary differential equation $y' = 2x$, $y(0) = 0$ using Euler's method, the iterates $y_n$, $n \in N$ satisfy
(a) $y_n = x_n^2$ (b) $y_n = 2x_n$
(c) $y_n = x_n x_{n-1}$ (d) $y_n = x_n + x_{n-1}$

**82.** Simpson's rule for integration gives exact results when $f(x)$ is a polynomial of degree
(a) 1 (b) 2
(c) 3 (d) All of these

**83.** The least squares approximation of first degree to the function $f(x) = \sin x$ over the interval $\left[-\frac{\pi}{2}, \frac{\pi}{2}\right]$ is
(a) $\frac{24x}{\pi^3}$ (b) $\frac{24x}{\pi^2}$
(c) $\frac{24x}{\pi}$ (d) $24x$

**84.** The number of iteration for finding root of $\cos x - e^{-x} = 0$ by bisection method in interval $\left[-\frac{1}{2}, \frac{1}{2}\right]$ is if $|\text{error}| < 10^{-4}$
(a) atleast 10 (b) atleast 14
(c) atleast 17 (d) None of these

**85.** The order of the difference equation $u_{n+2} + u_{n+1} + 3u_n = 0$ is
(a) 1 (b) 2
(c) 3 (d) does not exist

**86.** The Newton-Raphson method is used to find the roots of the equation $x^2 - 2 = 0$. If the iterations are started from $-1$, the iteration will
(a) converge to $-1$ (b) converge to $\sqrt{2}$
(c) converge to $-\sqrt{2}$ (d) not Converge

**87.** Which of the following statement is correct?
(a) The number of positive real roots of $P_n(x) = 0$ cannot exceed the number of changes of sign of $P_n(x)$
(b) The number of negative real roots of cannot exceed the number of changes of sign of $P_n(-x)$
(c) Both are true
(d) None of the above

**88.** In Simpson's one-third rule the curve $y = f(x)$ is assumed to be a
(a) circle (b) parabola
(c) hyperbola (d) None of these

**89.** The value of constant $\alpha$ in the third order Runge-kutta method

$$u_{j+1} = u_j + \frac{1}{8}(2k_1 + \alpha k_2 + 3k_1) \text{ is}$$

(a) 3 (b) 4
(c) 2 (d) 1

**90.** The value of $f(x)$ given only at $x = 0$, 1/3, 2/3, 1. Which of the following can be used to evaluate $\int_0^1 f(x)\,dx$ approximately.
(a) Trapezoidal rule
(b) Simpson's rule
(c) Trapezoidal as well as Simpson's rule
(d) None of the above

**91.** The conditions on the matrix $A$ for the cholesky method applicable
(a) $A$ is symmetric (b) positive definite
(c) Both 'a' and 'b' (d) for any matrix $A$

**92.** The third divided difference of $\frac{1}{x}$ based on the points $x_0, x_1, x_2, x_3$ is

(a) $-\frac{1}{x_0x_1x_2x_3}$ (b) $\frac{1}{x_0x_1x_2x_3}$

(c) $-\frac{1}{x_0x_1x_2}$ (d) $\frac{1}{x_0x_1x_2}$

**93.** The truncation error of the following method

$$u_{j+1} = u_j + \frac{1}{6}(k_1 + 2k_2 + 2k_3 + k_4)$$

is of order

(a) 3 (b) 4
(c) 5 (d) 6

**94.** The condition for convergence of the Newton-Raphson method to a root α is

(a) $\frac{1f'(\alpha)}{2f''(\alpha)} < 1$ (b) $\frac{f'(\alpha)}{f''(\alpha)} < 1$

(c) $\frac{f'(\alpha)}{f''(\alpha)} > 1$ (d) None of these

**95.** $\int_{-1}^{1} f(x)\,dx = \lambda_0 f(x_0) + \lambda_1 f(x_1)$

In above quadrature formula the values of $\lambda_0, \lambda_1, x_0, x_1$ are

(a) $1, 1, \frac{-1}{\sqrt{3}}, \frac{1}{\sqrt{3}}$ (b) $1, \frac{-1}{\sqrt{3}}, \frac{1}{\sqrt{3}}, 1$

(c) $1, \frac{1}{\sqrt{3}}, \frac{1}{\sqrt{3}}, 1$ (d) $1, \frac{1}{\sqrt{3}}, \frac{-1}{\sqrt{3}}, 1$

**96.** The remainder of the following rule

$$\int_{x_0}^{x_1} f(x)\,dx = \frac{3h}{8}(f(x_0) + 3f(x_1) + 3f(x_2) + f(x_3))$$

is of order

(Here, all points are equally spaced).

(a) four (b) six
(c) does not exist (d) None of these

**97.** The Gauss-Seidal method gives results faster when the pivotal element are

(a) smaller than other coefficients
(b) larger than other coefficients
(c) equal to other coefficients
(d) None of the above

**98.** For the matrix $\begin{bmatrix} 0 & 1 & -1 & 1 \\ 1 & 0 & 0 & 2 \\ -1 & 0 & 0 & 0 \\ 1 & 2 & 0 & 0 \end{bmatrix}$ the bounded for the eigen values predicted by Gershgorin's theorem is

(a) 3 (b) 1
(c) 2 (d) 4

**99.** The iterative scheme based on Newton's – Raphson method for finding $p^{\text{th}}$ root at a number $N$ is

(a) $\frac{1}{p}\left\{(p-1)x_n + \frac{N}{x_n^p}\right\}$ (b) $\frac{1}{p-1}\left\{px_n - \frac{N}{x_n^{p-1}}\right\}$

(c) $\frac{1}{p}\left\{(p-1)x_n - \frac{N}{x_n^{p-1}}\right\}$ (d) None of these

**100.** If $x = \xi$ be multiple root of $f(x)$ with multiplicity $m \neq 1$, then rate of convergent of iterative scheme

$$x_{n+x} = x_n - \left(\frac{p}{m}\right)\frac{f(x_n)}{f'(x_n)} \text{ is}$$

(a) linear, if $p \neq m$ (b) quadratic, if $p = m$
(c) linear, if $p = m$ (d) linear if, $p = m^2$

**101.** The Newton divided difference polynomial which interpolate the data $f(0) = 1$, $f(1) = 3$, $f(3) = 55$ is

(a) $8x^2 + 6x + 1$ (b) $8x^2 - 6x + 1$
(c) $8x^2 - 6x - 1$ (d) $8x^2 + 6x - 1$

**102.** The fourth divided difference of the polynomial $3x^3 + 11x^2 + 5x + 11$ over the points $x = 0, 1, 4, 6$ and 7 is

(a) 18 (b) 11
(c) 3 (d) 0

**103.** By the application of Simpson's one-third rule for numerical integration, with two subintervals, the value of $\int_0^1 \frac{dx}{1+x}$ is

(a) $\frac{17}{24}$ (b) $\frac{17}{36}$

(c) $\frac{25}{36}$ (d) $\frac{17}{25}$

**104.** If $x = \xi$ be multiple root of $f(x)$ with multiplicity $m$ and iterative scheme $x_{n+1} = x_n - \left(\frac{16}{m}\right)\frac{f(x_n)}{f'(x_n)}$ converges to $x = \xi$ with second order rate of convergent, then

(a) $m = 3$ (b) $m = 4$
(c) $m = 2$ (d) None of these

**105.** Corresponding value of $x = (0, 1, 2, 3, 4)$ the sequence of value of $f(x)$ are $(0, 0, \varepsilon, 0, 0)$ where ε is error, then

(a) the error increases in magnitude as the order of differences is incorrect
(b) the error decrease in magnitude as the order of differences is incorrect
(c) the error remain same as the order of differences is incorrect
(d) can't say

**106.** The second order Runge-Kutta method is applied to the initial value problem $y' = -y$, $y(0) = y_0$, with step size $h$. Then, $y(h)$ is

(a) $y_0(h-1)^2$ (b) $\frac{y_0}{2}(h^2 - 2h + 2)$

(c) $\frac{y_0}{6}(h^2 - 2h + 2)$ (d) $y_0\left(1 - h + \frac{h}{2} + \frac{h^3}{6}\right)$

**107.** After second interaction of Newton-Raphson method the positive root of equation $x^2 = 3$ is, (taking initial approximation $\frac{3}{2}$)

(a) $\frac{3}{2}$ (b) $\frac{7}{4}$

(c) $\frac{97}{56}$ (d) $\frac{347}{200}$

**108.** If $x = \xi$ be isolated zero of $f(x)$ with multiplicity '$m$', then difference between rate of convergent of iterative scheme

$$x_{n+1} = x_n - \frac{pf(x_n)}{f'(x_n)}$$

and $x_{n+1} = x_n - \frac{f(x_n)}{f'(x_n)}$. If $p = m \neq 1$, then

(a) zero (b) one

(c) two (d) None of these

**109.** If $E_1$ be the error for a linear interpolation of the equispaced data

$$x : x_0, x_1$$

$$f(x) : f(x_0), f(x_1), \text{ then}$$

(a) $|E_1| \leq \frac{1}{2}$ (b) $|E_1| \leq \frac{1}{4}$

(c) $|E_1| \leq \frac{1}{8}$ (d) $|E_1| \geq \frac{1}{8}$

**110.** The maximum step size $h$ such that the error in linear interpolation for the function $y = \sin x$ in $[0, \pi]$ is less than $5 \times 10^{-5}$ is

(a) 0.02 (b) 0.002

(c) 0.04 (d) 0.06

**111.** If one of the equation $f(x) = 0$ is near to $x_0$, then the first approximation of this root as calculated by Newton-Raphson method is the abscissa of the point where the following straight line intersects the $x$-axis

(a) normal to the curve $y = f(x)$ at the point $[x_0, f(x_0)]$

(b) tangent to the curve $y = f(x)$ at the point $[x_0, f(x_0)]$

(c) the straight line through the point $[x_0, f(x_0)]$ having the gradient $\frac{1}{f'(x_0)}$

(d) the ordinate through the point $[x_0, f(x_0)]$

**112.** Find the necessary condition on $k$, so that the Jacobi method converges for the following system of equations $AX = b$, where $A = \begin{pmatrix} 1 & 0 & k \\ 2 & 1 & 3 \\ k & 0 & 1 \end{pmatrix}$, $b$ is arbitrary

(a) $|k| < 1$ (b) $|k| > 1$

(c) $|k| = 1$ (d) None of these

**113.** The values of $a, b, c$ respectively for which the formula

$$\int_0^b f(x)\,dx = h\left\{af(0) + bf\left(\frac{h}{3}\right) + cf(h)\right\}$$

is exact for polynomials of as higher order as possible are

(a) 0, 1/4, 3/4 (b) 3/4, 0, 1/4

(c) 0, 3/4, 1/4 (d) 1/4, 0, 3/4

**114.** The interactive scheme

$x_{n+1} - \frac{x_n}{2}\left(1 + \frac{a}{x_n^2}\right)$ converges to $\sqrt{a}$ the convergence is

(a) linear (b) quadratic

(c) cubic (d) biquadratic

**115.** An iterative method to find the $n^{th}$ root ($n \in N$) of a positive number $a$ is given by $x_{k+1} = \frac{1}{2}\left[x_k + \frac{a}{x_k^{n-1}}\right]$, A value of $n$ for which this iterative method fails to converge is

(a) 1 (b) 2

(c) 3 (d) 8

**116.** The rate of convergence of the method is given in previous question is

(a) $v = -\log_{10} \rho(H)$ (b) $v = -\ln \rho(H)$

(c) Either 'a' or 'b' (d) None of these

**117.** The approximate value of integral $\int_0^1 \frac{\sin x}{x}\,dx$ by using mid-point method is

(a) $\frac{1}{2}\sin(2)$ (b) $2\sin\left(\frac{1}{2}\right)$

(c) $\frac{1}{2}\sin\left(\frac{1}{2}\right)$ (d) $2\sin(2)$

**118.** The Jacobi's iteration method for the set of equations

$x_1 + ax_2 = 2$, $ax_1 + x_2 = 7$, $\left(a \neq \frac{1}{\sqrt{2}}\right)$ converges for

(a) All values of a (b) $a = 1$

(c) $|a| < \frac{1}{\sqrt{2}}$ (d) $\frac{1}{\sqrt{2}} < a < \sqrt{\frac{3}{2}}$

**119.** The necessary and sufficient condition for the convergence of the iterative method $x^{(k+1)} = Hx^{(k)} + c$ is that the eigen values of the iteration method satisfy

(a) $|\lambda i(H)| < 1$ (b) $|\lambda i(H)| > 1$

(c) $|\lambda i(H)| = 1$ (d) $|\lambda i(H)| \geq 1$

**120.** Let $h(x)$ be a twice continuously differentiable function on [1, 2] with fixed point $a$. Then, the sequence of iterates $x_{n+1} = h(x_n)$ converges to a quadratically, provided

(a) $\frac{dh}{dx}(a) \neq 0$ (b) $\frac{dh}{dx}(a) \neq 0, \frac{d^2h}{dx^2}(a) = 0$

(c) $\frac{dh}{dx}(a) \neq 0, \frac{d^2h}{dx^2}(a) \neq 0$ (d) $\frac{dh}{dx}(a) = 0, \frac{d^2h}{dx^2}(a) \neq 0$

**121.** Backward Euler method for solving differential equation $\frac{dy}{dx} = f(x, y)$ is

(a) $y_{n+1} = y_n + hf(x_n, y_n)$
(b) $y_{n+1} = y_n + hf(x_{n+1}, y_{n+1})$
(c) $y_{n+1} = y_{n-1} + 2hf(x_n, y_n)$
(d) $y_{n+1} = (1+h) f(x_{n+1}, y_{n+1})$

**122.** The interpolating polynomial of highest degree which corresponds to function values

$$f(-1) - 9,\ f(0) = 5,\ f(2) = 3,\ f(5) = 15 \text{ is}$$

(a) $x^3 + x^2 + 2x + 5$ (b) $x^2 - 3x + 5$
(c) $x^4 + 4x^3 + 5x^2 + 5$ (d) $x + 5$

**123.** Consider the initial values problem

$$\frac{dy}{dx} = f(x, y(x)), y(x_0) y = 0$$

Let $y_1 = y_0 + w_1 k_1 + 3k_2$ approximate the solution of the above IVP at $x_1 = x_0 + h$ with

$k_1 = hf(x_0, y_0)$, $k_2 = hf(x_0 + ah, y_0 + bk_1)$ and $h$ being the step-size, if the formula for $y_1$ yields a second order method, then the value of $w_1$, $a$, $b$ are

(a) $-1, 1/6, 1/6$ (b) $-2, 1/3, 1/3$
(c) $-2, 1/6, 1/6$ (d) $3, 1/3, 1/3$

**124.** If the matrix $A$ is diagonally dominant matrix, the Jacobin iteration scheme

(a) convgerges for any initial starting vector
(b) convergent for non-negative initial starting vector
(c) converges for certain initial starting vectors
(d) can't say

**125.** Suppose the matrix $M = \begin{pmatrix} 2 & a & -1 \\ a & 2 & 1 \\ -1 & 1 & 4 \end{pmatrix}$ has a unique Cholesky decomposition of the form $M = LL^T$, where $L$ is a lower triangular matrix. The range of values of a is

(a) $-2 < a < 2$ (b) $a > 2$
(c) $-2 < a < \frac{3}{2}$ (d) $\frac{3}{2} < a < 2$

**126.** If $\Delta$ and $\nabla$ are the forward and the backward difference operators respectively, then $\Delta - \nabla$ is equal to

(a) $-\Delta\nabla$ (b) $\Delta\nabla$
(c) $\Delta + \nabla$ (d) $\frac{\Delta}{\nabla}$

**127.** The polynomial of 4[th] degree which interpolated the following data is

$u_0 = 1, u_1 = 1, u_2 = 11, u_3 = 61, u_4 = 205, u_5 = 521$

(a) $u_x = 1 - 2x + 3x^2 - 4x^3 + 5x^4$
(b) $u_x = 1 + x - x^2 + x^3 - x^4$
(c) $u_x = 1 - x + x^2 - x^3 + x^4$
(d) None of the above

**128.** If $x = \xi$ be isolated zero of $f(x)$ with multiplicity '$m$', then difference between rate of convergent of iterative scheme

$$x_{n+1} = x_n - \frac{pf(x_n)}{f'(x_n)} \text{ and } x_{n+1} = x_n - \frac{f(x_n)}{f'(x_n)}$$

If $p \neq m \neq 1$, then

(a) zero (b) one
(c) two (d) None of these

**129.** Let $M$ be the length of the initial interval $[a_0, b_0]$ containing a solution of $f(x) = 0$, let $\{x_0, x_1, x_2, \ldots\}$ represent the successive points generated by the bisection method, then the minimum number of iterations required to guarantee an approximation to the solution with an accuracy of $\varepsilon$ is given by

(a) $-2 - \frac{\log\left(\frac{\varepsilon}{M}\right)}{\log 2}$ (b) $-2 + \frac{\log\left(\frac{\varepsilon}{M}\right)}{\log 2}$
(c) $-2 + \frac{\log(M\varepsilon)}{\log 2}$ (d) $-2 - \frac{\log\left(\frac{\varepsilon}{M}\right)}{(\log 2)^2}$

**130.** One root of the equation $e^x - 3x^2 = 0$ lies in the interval (3, 4), the least number of iterations of the bisection method, so that $|\text{error}| \leq 10^3$ are

(a) 10 (b) 8
(c) 6 (d) 4

**131.** Total number of divisions and multiplications required for solving a system of 5 equations using Gauss elimination method are

(a) 113 (b) 208
(c) 65 (d) 45

**132.** If $x = \xi$ be isolated zero of $f(x)$ with multiplicity $m \neq 1$, then rate of convergent of Newton's-Raphson method for findng simple root is

(a) linear (b) quadratic
(c) linear if, $m = 2$ (d) quadratic if, $m = 2$

**133.** An iterative scheme is given by

$$x_{n+1} = \frac{1}{5}\left(16 - \frac{12}{x_n}\right), n \in N \cup \{0\}$$

Such a scheme, with suitable $x_0$, will

(a) not converge (b) converge to 1.6
(c) converge to 1.8 (d) converge to 2

**134.** Choose correct

(a) $\nabla = 1 - E^{-1}$ (b) $\nabla = 1 + E^{-1}$
(c) $\nabla = -1 + E^{-1}$ (d) $\nabla = -1 - E^{-1}$

**135.** Trapezoidal rule for evaluation of $\int_a^b f(x)\, dx$ requires the interval $(a, b)$ to be divided into

(a) $2n$ sub intervals of equal width
(b) $2n + 1$ sub intervals of equal width
(c) any number of subintervals of equal width
(d) $3n$ subintervals of equal width

**136.** Consider the following statements.

I. The convergence rate of secant method is 1.61.

II. Convergence of regular falsi method is linear.

III. Bisection method is based upon the repeated application of intermediate value theorem

Which one of the following is correct?

(a) Only I and II are true
(b) Only I and III are true
(c) Only II and III are true
(d) All three I, II and III are true

**137.** Newton-Raphson method is applicable only when

(a) $f(x) \neq 0$ in the *nbd* of actual root $x = \alpha$
(b) $f'(x) \neq 0$ in the *nbd* of actual root $x = \alpha$
(c) $f'(x) = 0$ in the *nbd* of actual root $x = \alpha$
(d) None of the above

**138.** Simpson's one-third rule for evaluation of $\int_a^b f(x)\,dx$ requires the interval $[a, b]$ to be divided into

(a) an even number of subintervals of equal width
(b) an odd number of subintervals of equal width
(c) any number of subintervals of equal width
(d) any number of subintervals

**139.** Consider the quadrature formula

$$\int_0^h f(x)\,dx = \left\{af(0) + bf\left(\frac{3h}{4}\right) + c\,f(h)\right\} h$$

the values of $a, b, c$ for which this is exact for polynomial of as high degree as possible are

(a) $a = \frac{5}{18}, b = \frac{8}{9}, c = -\frac{1}{6}$ (b) $a = \frac{1}{2}, b = -\frac{1}{4}, c = \frac{3}{4}$
(c) $a = 0, b = 1, c = -\frac{1}{4}$ (d) $a = 1, b = 2, c = 3$

# Exercise 2 (For Part 'C')

**Directions** (Q. Nos. 1-34) *Questions may have one or more than one correct option.*

**1.** Which of the following/s is/are equivalent to $\Delta \log f(x)$?

(a) $\log\left(\frac{\Delta f(x)}{f(x)}\right)$ (b) $\log\left(\frac{Ef(x)}{f(x)}\right)$
(c) $\log\left\{\frac{(1-\nabla)^{-1} f(x)}{f(x)}\right\}$ (d) $\log\left(1 + \frac{\Delta f(x)}{f(x)}\right)$

**2.** The value/s of $\Delta\{f(x) \cdot \phi(x)\}$ is/are equal to

(a) $f(x) \cdot \Delta\phi(x) + \Delta f(x) \cdot \phi(x)$
(b) $f(x+1) \cdot \phi(x+1) + \Delta f(x) \cdot \phi(x)$
(c) $f(x+1)\Delta\phi(x) + \phi(x)\Delta f(x)$
(d) $f(x)\Delta\phi(x) + \Delta f(x) \cdot \phi(x+1)$

**3.** Which of the following(s) is/are true about Newton-Raphson method to find approximate roots of an algebraic equation?

(a) Newton-Raphson formula is $x_n = x_{n-1} - \frac{f(x_{n-1})}{f'(x_{n-1})}$, where $n = 1, 2, \ldots$
(b) Formula given in (a) converges, if $f(x)$ satisfies $|f'(x)|^2 < f(x) f''(x)$
(c) Formula (a) is useful in case of a large value of $f'(x)$
(d) Order of convergence of formula (a) is two

**4.** If $x^{(n)} = x(x-1)(x-2)\ldots(x-n+1)$ and $f(x) = 2x^4 - 9x^3 + 4$, then

(a) $f(x) = 2x^{(4)} + 3x^{(3)} + 13x^{(2)} - 7x^{(1)} + 4$
(b) $f(x) = 2x^{(4)} + 3x^{(3)} + 13x^{(2)} + 7x^{(1)} + 4$
(c) $f(x) = 2x^{(4)} + 3x^{(3)} - 13x^{(2)} - 7x^{(1)} + 4$
(d) $\Delta^4 f(x) = 48$

**5.** For the following table

| $x$ | 1 | 3 | −4 |
|---|---|---|---|
| $f(x)$ | 3 | −5 | 4 |

Select the correct option/s

(a) $f(x)$ is only an increasing function in $R$
(b) $f(x)$ is maximum at $x = -\frac{41}{26}$
(c) $f(x)$ is minimum at $x = -\frac{41}{26}$
(d) $f''(x) = -\frac{13}{5}$

**6.** Which of the following(s) is/are true about Trapezoidal rule?

(a) $\int_{x_{n-1}}^{x_n} y\,dx = \frac{h}{2}[y_{n-1} + y_n]$
(b) It gives exact results while integrating polynomials upto degree one
(c) It is more accurate than any other method while integrating polynomials upto degree 3
(d) The error in this rule is of order $h^2$

**7.** From the following table

| $x$ | −1 | 0 | 2 | 3 | 7 | 10 |
|---|---|---|---|---|---|---|
| $f(x)$ | −11 | 1 | 1 | 1 | 141 | 561 |

Select correct option/s

(a) $f(0) = 1$ (b) $f''(x)$ is increasing in $R$
(c) $f''(6) = 26$ (d) $f'''(6) = 3$

**8.** Which of the following(s) is/are true?

(a) Simpson's $\frac{1}{3}$rd rule requires the division of the whole range into an even number of subintervals

(b) Simpson's $\frac{3}{8}$ rule is more accurate than Simpson's $\frac{1}{3}$rd rule

(c) The accuracy of Simpson's rule is of order $h^5$

(d) The error in Simpson's rule is of order $h^4$

**9.** A second degree polynomial, $f(x)$ has values of 1, 4 and 15 at $x = 0$, 1 and 2, respectively. The integral $\int_0^2 f(x)dx$ is to be estimated by applying the trapezoidal rule to this data. Then, which of the following(s) is/are correct?

(a) $\int_0^2 f(x)dx = 10$ (b) $f(x) = 4x^2 - x + 1$

(c) Error $= \frac{4}{3}$ (d) Error $= -\frac{4}{3}$

**10.** By applying Runge-Kutta method to find an approximate value of $y$ when $x = 0.2$ for IVP $\frac{dy}{dx} = x + y,\ y(0) = 1$. Which of the following/s is/are true?

(a) $k_1 = 0.2$ (b) $k_2 = 0.24$

(c) $k_3 = 0.2440$ (d) $k_4 = 0.2888$

**11.** Solve the following equation $f(x) \equiv x^3 - 25 = 0$ by Newton-Raphson's method to three decimal places.

(a) $f'(x) \equiv 3x^2$

(b) By Newton-Raphson formula $x_{i+1} = \frac{2x_i^3 + 25}{3x_i^2}$

(c) The roots of $f(x) = 0$ lies between 2 and 3

(d) The solution is (approximately) 2.9

**12.** If $u_4 = u_3 + \Delta u_2 + \Delta^2 u_1 + \Delta^3 u_1$, then

(a) $\Delta u_2 = u_3 - u_2$

(b) $\Delta u_1 = u_2 - u_1$

(c) $u_4 = u_3 + \Delta u_2 + \Delta^2 u_1 + \Delta^3 u_1$

(d) $\Delta u_x = u_{x+h} - u_x$

**13.** In the table below, the values of $y$ are consecutive terms of a series of which 52.8 is the 8th term.

| $x$ | 3 | 4 | 5 | 6 | 7 | 8 | 9 |
|---|---|---|---|---|---|---|---|
| $y$ | 4.8 | 8.4 | 14.5 | 23.6 | 36.2 | 52.8 | 73.9 |

(a) The first term is 3.1

(b) The tenth term is 100

(c) The first and tenth term are equal

(d) The first term is zero and the tenth term is non-zero

**14.** Given the values

| $x_i$ | 5 | 7 | 11 | 13 | 17 |
|---|---|---|---|---|---|
| $y_i$ | 150 | 392 | 1452 | 2366 | 5202 |

Then,

(a) By Lagrange's formula $f(9) = 810$

(b) By Newton's divided difference formula $f(9) = 810$

(c) The Newton's divided difference formula is

$$f(x) = y_0 + (x - x_0)f(x_0, x_1) + (x - x_0)(x - x_1)f(x_0, x_1, x_2) + (x - x_0)(x - x_1)(x - x_2)f(x_0, x_1, x_2, x_3)$$

(d) $f(9) = 825$

**15.** Which of the following(s) is/are true?

(a) $\frac{\Delta^2}{E}x^2 = h$

(b) $\Delta(\sin x \cos 3x) = \cos x \sin x$

(c) $\frac{\Delta^2}{E}x^2 = 2h^2$

(d) $\Delta(\sin x \cos 3x) = (\sin h)[2\cos(4x + 2h)\cos h - \cos(2x + h)]$

**16.** Using Picard's method solve $\frac{dy}{dx} = 1 - 2xy$, given $y = 0$ at $x = 0$

(a) First approximation $y_1 = x$

(b) Second approximation $y_2 = x - \frac{2}{3}x^3$

(c) Third approximation $y_3 = x - \frac{2}{3}x^3 - \frac{4}{15}x^5$

(d) $y_n = y_0 + \int_{x_0}^{x} f(x, y_{n-1})dx$

**17.** The sum of first $n$-terms of $1 \cdot 2\Delta x^n - 2 \cdot 3\Delta^2 x^n + 3 \cdot 4\Delta^3 x^n - 4 \cdot 5\Delta^4 x^n + \ldots 2\{(x-2)^n - (x-3)^n\}$ is/are

(a) The sum of first $n$-terms of $1 \cdot 2\Delta x^n - 2 \cdot 3\Delta^2 x^n + 3 \cdot 4\Delta^3 x^n - 4 \cdot 5\Delta^4 x^n + \ldots + 2\{(x-2)^n - (x-3)^n\}$

(b) $E^{-3}\Delta x^n = \Delta E^3 x^n$

(c) $E^{-3}x^n = \Delta(x-3)^n$

(d) $E^{-3}x^n = \Delta(x+3)^n$

**18.** Given the table

| $x$ | 0 | 1 | 2 | 3 | 4 |
|---|---|---|---|---|---|
| $y$ | 1 | 3 | 9 | ... | 81 |

Then,

(a) $u_3 = 31$

(b) $u_3 = 62$

(c) $\Delta^4 u_x = (E-1)^4 u_x$

(d) $\Delta^4 u_x = u_4 - 4u_3 + 6u_2 - 4u_1 + u_0$

**19.** Solving the transcendental equation $3x - \cos x - 2 = 0$ by fixed point iteration method, correct upto five decimal places. Given, $x_0 = 0.5$

(a) $x_1 = 0.9999873$

(b) $x_2 = 0.9999493$

(c) $x_3 = 0.9999493$

(d) the required root is 0.99995

**20.** Which of the following(s) is/are true?

(a) $\Delta\sqrt{u_x} = \sqrt{u_{x+h}} - \sqrt{u_x}$ (b) $\Delta\sqrt{u_x} = \sqrt{u_x} - \sqrt{u_{x+h}}$

(c) $\Delta\sqrt{u_x} = \nabla\sqrt{u_x}$ (d) $\Delta\sqrt{u_x} = \dfrac{\Delta u_x}{\sqrt{u_x} + \sqrt{u_{x+h}}}$

**21.** Given,

$$3x + y + 2z = 3$$
$$2x - 3y - z = -3$$
$$x - 2y + z = 4, \text{ then}$$

(a) The system in $AX = D$ can be represented as

$$\begin{bmatrix} 3 & 1 & 2 \\ 2 & -3 & -1 \\ 1 & -2 & 1 \end{bmatrix}\begin{bmatrix} x \\ y \\ z \end{bmatrix} = \begin{bmatrix} 3 \\ -3 \\ 4 \end{bmatrix}$$

(b) $\begin{bmatrix} x \\ y \\ z \end{bmatrix} = \dfrac{1}{8}\begin{bmatrix} -1 & 3 & 5 \\ -3 & 1 & 7 \\ 7 & -5 & 11 \end{bmatrix}\begin{bmatrix} 3 \\ -3 \\ 4 \end{bmatrix}$

(c) $\begin{bmatrix} x \\ y \\ z \end{bmatrix} = \begin{bmatrix} 1 \\ 2 \\ -1 \end{bmatrix}$

(d) $\begin{bmatrix} x \\ y \\ z \end{bmatrix} = \begin{bmatrix} 1 \\ 2 \\ 3 \end{bmatrix}$

**22.** Which of the following(s) is/are true?

(a) $\Delta \log f(x) = \log f(x+h) - \log f(x)$

(b) $\log(f(x+h)) = \log(Ef(x))$

(c) $\log(Ef(x)) = \log(\Delta + 1)f(x)$

(d) $\Delta \log f(x) = \log\left[1 + \dfrac{\Delta f(x)}{f(x)}\right]$

**23.** By using Runge-Kutta method, when $x = 1.1$ and given

$$y(x_0) = 1.2, \quad x_0 = 1$$

and $\dfrac{dy}{dx} = 3x + y^2$, then

(a) $k_1 = 0.444$

(b) $k_2 = 0.517$

(c) $k = 0.527$

(d) The required value of y when $x = 1.1$ is 1.727

**24.** Which of the following(s) is/are true?

(a) $\Delta\left(\dfrac{x^2}{\cos 2x}\right) = \dfrac{(2hx + h^2)\cos 2x + 2x^2 \sin h \sin(2x+h)}{\cos 2(x+h)\cos 2x}$

(b) $\Delta^2 \cos 2x = -4\sin^2 h \cos(2x + 2h)$

(c) $\Delta\left(\dfrac{x^2}{\cos 2x}\right) = -4\sin^2 h\cos(2x + 2h)$

(d) $\Delta^2 \cos 2x = \dfrac{(2hx + h^2)\cos 2x + 2x^2 \sin h \sin(2x+h)}{\cos 2(x+h)\cos 2x}$

**25.** Make the best estimate of the missing values of y from the following data

| $x$ | 0 | 0.1 | 0.2 | 0.3 | 0.4 | 0.5 | 0.6 |
|---|---|---|---|---|---|---|---|
| $y_x$ | 0.135 | ? | 0.111 | 0.100 | ? | 0.082 | 0.074 |

(a) $y_{0.1} = 0.123$ (b) $y_{0.4} = 0.090$

(c) $y_{0.1} = 0.263$ (d) $y_{0.4} = 0.276$

**26.** When interval of differencing is unity, then

(a) $\Delta\left(\dfrac{2}{x+2}\right) = 2\left\{\left(\dfrac{1}{x+3}\right) - \left(\dfrac{1}{x+2}\right)\right\}$

(b) $\Delta\left(\dfrac{3}{x+3}\right) = 3\left\{\dfrac{1}{x+4} - \dfrac{1}{x+3}\right\}$

(c) $\Delta^2\left(\dfrac{5x+12}{x^2+5x+6}\right) = \dfrac{2(5x+16)}{(x+2)(x+3)(x+4)(x+5)}$

(d) $\Delta^2 x = x(\Delta x)$

**27.** If $u_x = u_{x-1} + \Delta u_{x-2} + \Delta^2 u_{x-3} + \ldots + \Delta^{n-1} u_{x-n+1} + \Delta^n u_{x-n}$,

then

(a) $E^n u_x = u_{x+nh}$

(b) $E = 1 + \Delta$

(c) $u_x = u_{x-1} + \Delta u_{x-2} + \Delta^2 u_{x-3} + \ldots + \Delta^{n-1} u_{x-n+1} + \Delta^n u_{x-n}$

(d) $E = 1 - \Delta$

**28.** Which of the following (s) is/are true?

$U_0 + U_1 + U_2 + \ldots + U_n = {}^{n+1}C_1 U_0 + {}^{n+1}C_2 \Delta U_0 + \ldots + {}^{n+1}C_{n+1}\Delta^n U_0$

(a) $U_0 + U_1 + U_2 + \ldots + U_n = U_0 + EU_0 + E^2 U_0 + \ldots + E^n U_0$

(b) $U_0 + U_1 + \ldots + U_n = (1 + E + E^2 + \ldots + E^n)U_0$

(c) $U_0 + U_1 + U_2 + \ldots + U_n = {}^{n+1}C_1 U_0 + {}^{n+1}C_2 \Delta U_0 + \ldots + {}^{n+1}C_{n+1}\Delta^n U_0$

(d) $\dfrac{E^{n+1} - 1}{\Delta} = \dfrac{1 - E^{n+1}}{1 - E}$

**29.** Using Picard's method of successive approximation obtain a solution upto second approximation to the differential equation.

$\dfrac{dy}{dx} = 2 - \dfrac{y}{x}$, where $y = 2$ when $x = 1$

(a) The $n$th approximation is given by

$$y_n = y_0 + \int_{x_0}^{x} f(x, y_{n-1})\,dx$$

(b) $y_1 = 2x - 2\log x$

(c) $y_2 = 2 + 2\displaystyle\int_1^x \frac{1}{x}(\log x)\,dx$

(d) $y_2 = 2 + (\log x)^2$

**30.** Solve

$$10x - 7y + 3z + 5u = 6$$
$$-6x + 8y - z - 4u = 5$$
$$3x + y + 4z + 11u = 2$$
$$5x - 9y - 2z + 4u = 7$$

by Crout's triangularization method.

(a) The following system of equation can be represented as

$$\begin{bmatrix}10 & -7 & 3 & 5\\ -6 & 8 & -1 & -4\\ 3 & 1 & 4 & 11\\ 5 & -9 & -2 & 4\end{bmatrix}\begin{bmatrix}x\\ y\\ z\\ u\end{bmatrix}=\begin{bmatrix}6\\ 5\\ 2\\ 7\end{bmatrix}$$

(b) The following system of equation can be

$$\begin{bmatrix}10 & -7 & 3 & 5\\ 0 & 3.8 & 0.8 & -1\\ 0 & 0 & 2.447 & 10.315\\ 0 & 0 & 0 & 9.924\end{bmatrix}\begin{bmatrix}x\\ y\\ z\\ u\end{bmatrix}=\begin{bmatrix}6\\ 8.6\\ -6.815\\ 9.924\end{bmatrix}$$

(c) The solution for the given system of equation is $u = 1$, $z = -7$, $y = 4$ and $x = 5$

(d) No solution exist for the following system of equation

**31.** Which of the following(s) is/are true

(a) $y' = \frac{1}{h}\left[\nabla y + \frac{1}{2}\nabla^2 y + \frac{1}{3}\nabla^3 y + ...\right]$

(b) $y'' = \frac{1}{h^2}\left[\nabla^2 y + \nabla^3 y + \frac{11}{12}\nabla^4 y + ...\right]$

(c) $e^{-hD} = 1 - \nabla$

(d) $E = e^{hD}$

**32.** Given the table

| Marks | 30-40 | 40-50 | 50-60 | 60-70 | 70-80 |
|---|---|---|---|---|---|
| No. of students | 31 | 42 | 51 | 35 | 31 |

(a) the number of students with marks less than 45 is 47.87 *i.e.,* 48

(b) the number of students with marks less than 40 is 31

(c) the number of students getting marks between 40 and 45 = 48 − 31 = 17

(d) the number of students getting marks less than 45 is 98

**33.** Which of the following(s) is/are true?

(a) $\nabla = \frac{E-1}{E}$ (b) $\nabla E = \Delta$

(c) $(1+\Delta)(1-\nabla) = 1$ (d) $\nabla E = E\nabla$

**34.** The value of $\left(\frac{1}{35}\right)$ correct by the fixed point iteration formula $x_{n+1} = x_n, [2 - 35x_n]$ is/are

(a) $x_1 = 0.026$

(b) $x_2 = 0.02834$

(c) $x_3 = 0.0285695$

(d) $x_4 = 0.285713$

# Answers

## Exercise 1

| | | | | | | | | | |
|---|---|---|---|---|---|---|---|---|---|
| **1.** (c) | **2.** (a) | **3.** (b) | **4.** (a) | **5.** (c) | **6.** (b) | **7.** (b) | **8.** (b) | **9.** (a) | **10.** (b) |
| **11.** (c) | **12.** (d) | **13.** (d) | **14.** (b) | **15.** (c) | **16.** (b) | **17.** (c) | **18.** (a) | **19.** (a) | **20.** (b) |
| **21.** (c) | **22.** (c) | **23.** (c) | **24.** (b) | **25.** (b) | **26.** (a) | **27.** (a) | **28.** (a) | **29.** (c) | **30.** (d) |
| **31.** (b) | **32.** (b) | **33.** (a) | **34.** (c) | **35.** (c) | **36.** (c) | **37.** (b) | **38.** (b) | **39.** (a) | **40.** (a) |
| **41.** (b) | **42.** (d) | **43.** (a) | **44.** (b) | **45.** (a) | **46.** (d) | **47.** (b) | **48.** (c) | **49.** (b) | **50.** (b) |
| **51.** (a) | **52.** (a) | **53.** (b) | **54.** (b) | **55.** (a) | **56.** (c) | **57.** (b) | **58.** (b) | **59.** (b) | **60.** (c) |
| **61.** (d) | **62.** (d) | **63.** (b) | **64.** (d) | **65.** (b) | **66.** (d) | **67.** (b) | **68.** (c) | **69.** (a) | **70.** (a) |
| **71.** (a) | **72.** (d) | **73.** (a) | **74.** (a) | **75.** (c) | **76.** (b) | **77.** (b) | **78.** (a) | **79.** (b) | **80.** (d) |
| **81.** (c) | **82.** (d) | **83.** (a) | **84.** (b) | **85.** (b) | **86.** (b) | **87.** (b) | **88.** (b) | **89.** (a) | **90.** (c) |
| **91.** (c) | **92.** (a) | **93.** (c) | **94.** (c) | **95.** (a) | **96.** (a) | **97.** (b) | **98.** (a) | **99.** (c) | **100.** (c) |
| **101.** (b) | **102.** (b) | **103.** (c) | **104.** (b) | **105.** (a) | **106.** (b) | **107.** (c) | **108.** (b) | **109.** (c) | **110.** (a) |
| **111.** (b) | **112.** (a) | **113.** (c) | **114.** (b) | **115.** (d) | **116.** (a) | **117.** (b) | **118.** (c) | **119.** (a) | **120.** (d) |
| **121.** (b) | **122.** (b) | **123.** (c) | **124.** (a) | **125.** (a) | **126.** (c) | **127.** (c) | **128.** (a) | **129.** (a) | **130.** (a) |
| **131.** (b) | **132.** (a) | **133.** (d) | **134.** (a) | **135.** (c) | **136.** (d) | **137.** (b) | **138.** (a) | **139.** (a) | |

## Exercise 2

| | | | | | | | | | |
|---|---|---|---|---|---|---|---|---|---|
| **1.** (b,c,d) | **2.** (c,d) | **3.** (a,c,d) | **4.** (c,d) | **5.** (a,b,d) | **6.** (a,b,d) | **7.** (a,b,c) | **8.** (a,c,d) | **9.** (b,d) | **10.** (a,b,c,d) |
| **11.** (a,b,c,d) | **12.** (a,b,c,d) | **13.** (a,b) | **14.** (a,b,c) | **15.** (c,d) | **16.** (a,b,c,d) | **17.** (a,b,c) | **18.** (a,b,c,d) | **19.** (a,b,c,d) | **20.** (a,d) |
| **21.** (a,b,c) | **22.** (a,b,c,d) | **23.** (a,b,c,d) | **24.** (a,b) | **25.** (a,b) | **26.** (a,b,c) | **27.** (a,b,c) | **28.** (a,b,c,d) | **29.** (a,b,c,d) | **30.** (a,b,c) |
| **31.** (a,b,c,d) | **32.** (a,b,c) | **33.** (a,b,c,d) | **34.** (a,b,c,d) | | | | | | |

# Hints & Solutions

## Exercise 1

**1.** $x = \sqrt[3]{c} = c^{1/3} \quad \Rightarrow \quad x^3 = c$

Let $f(x) = x^3 - c = 0$

$\Rightarrow f'(x) = 3x^2$

$$x_{n+1} = x_n - \frac{f(x_n)}{f'(x_n)} = x_n - \frac{x_n^3 - c}{3x_n^2}$$

$$\Rightarrow \quad x_{n+1} = \frac{2x_n^3 + c}{3x_n^2}.$$

**9.** Put $n = 1$

LHS $= 2\Delta x = 2 \times 1 = 2$

and also for $n = 1$

$$2[(x-2)^n - (x-3)^n] = 2[(x-2)-(x-3)] = 2$$

**13.** $\Delta^2 \cos 2x = (E-1)^2 \cos 2x \qquad [\because E = 1 + \Delta]$

$$\begin{aligned}
&= (E^2 - 2E + 1)\cos 2x \\
&= E^2(\cos 2x) - 2E(\cos 2x) + \cos 2x \\
&= \cos 2(x+2h) - 2[\cos 2(x+h)] + \cos 2x \\
&= \cos(2x+4h) + \cos 2x - 2[\cos 2(x+h)] \\
&= 2\cos\frac{x+4h+2x}{2}\cos\frac{2x+4h-2x}{2} - 2\cos 2(x+h) \\
&= 2\cos 2(x+h)\cos 2h - 2\cos 2(x+h) \\
&= 2\cos 2(x+h)[\cos 2h - 1] = 4\sin^2 h \cos 2(x+h)
\end{aligned}$$

**14.** The difference table is given below

| $x$ | $y$ | $\Delta y$ | $\Delta^2 y$ | $\Delta^3 y$ |
|---|---|---|---|---|
| 0 | 3 | | | |
| | | 3 | | |
| 1 | 6 | | 2 | |
| | | 5 | | 0 |
| 2 | 11 | | 2 | |
| | | 7 | | 0 |
| 3 | 18 | | 2 | |
| | | 9 | | |
| 4 | 27 | | | |

In Newton's formula for interpolation $a = 0, h = 1$; $f(a + hx) = f(x)$

$$\therefore \; y = f(x) = 3 + x(3) + \frac{x(x-1)}{2}(2) + \frac{x(x-1)(x-2)}{6}(0) + \dots$$

or $y = 3 + 3x + x(x-1) = x^2 + 2x + 3$

**15.** The difference table is given below

| $x$ | $y$ | $\Delta y$ | $\Delta^2 y$ | $\Delta^3 y$ |
|---|---|---|---|---|
| 0 | 1 | | | |
| | | 2 | | |
| 1 | 3 | | 2 | |
| | | 4 | | 0 |
| 2 | 7 | | 2 | |
| | | 6 | | |
| 3 | 13 | | | |

In Newton's formula for interpolation

$$a = 0, h = 1; f(a + hx) = f(x)$$

Hence, $y = f(x) = 1 + x(2) + \dfrac{x(x-1)}{2}(2) + \dfrac{x(x-1)(x-2)}{6}(0) + \dots$

$$= 1 + 2x + x(x-1) = x^2 + x + 1$$

**16.** The difference table is as under

| $V$ | $P$ | $\Delta P$ | $\Delta^2 P$ | $\Delta^3 P$ |
|---|---|---|---|---|
| 10 | 1.1 | | | |
| | | 0.9 | | |
| 20 | 2.0 | | 1.5 | |
| | | 2.4 | | −0.4 |
| 30 | 4.4 | | 1.1 | |
| | | 3.5 | | |
| 40 | 7.9 | | | |

To calculate $P$, when $V = 25$, we use forward interpolation formula for which

$$n = \frac{x-a}{h} = \frac{25-10}{10} = 1.5$$

$$P(25) = 1.1 + 1.5 \times 0.9 + \frac{1.5 \times 0.5}{2} \times 1.5 + \frac{1.5 \times 0.5 \times 0.5}{6} \times 0.4$$

$$= 1.1 + 1.35 + 0.5625 + 0.0250 = 3.0375$$

**17.** The difference table is as under

| $x$ | $y$ | $\Delta y$ | $\Delta^2 y$ | $\Delta^3 y$ |
|---|---|---|---|---|
| 1 | | | | |
| | 8 | | | |
| 2 | | −5 | | |
| | 3 | | 2 | |
| 3 | | −3 | | 0 |
| | 0 | | 2 | |
| 4 | | −1 | | 0 |
| | −1 | | 2 | |
| 5 | | 1 | | |
| | 0 | | | |
| 6 | | | | |

Obviously, the first value of $\Delta y$ is $-7$ and hence the first term of the series is $8 - (-7) = 15$.

**18.** The difference table is as under

| $x$ | $y$ | $\Delta y$ | $\Delta^2 y$ |
|---|---|---|---|
| 0 | 0 | | |
| | | 0 | |
| 1/2 | 0 | | 1 |
| | | 1 | |
| 1 | 1 | | |

Here, $\quad a = 0, h = 1/2$

Also, for $x = \dfrac{1}{4}$, $n = \dfrac{x-a}{h} = \dfrac{1/4 - 0}{1/2} = \dfrac{1}{2}$

∴ Using formula, we get

$$f(a+nh)=f(a)+n\Delta f(a)+\frac{n(n-1)}{2}\Delta^2 f(a)+\ldots$$

Here, $a=0$ and $nh=\frac{1}{4}$ where $n=\frac{1}{2}$

Hence, $f\left(\frac{1}{4}\right)=0+\frac{1}{2}(0)+\frac{\frac{1}{2}\left(\frac{1}{2}-1\right)}{2}(1)=-\frac{1}{8}$

**19.** Since, the area bounded by the x-axis is given by $\int_{x_1}^{x_2} f(x)dx$, according to the table

$$\int_{7.47}^{7.52} f(x)dx=\frac{h}{2}[y_0+2(y_1+y_2+y_3+y_4)+y_5]$$

$$=\frac{(0.01)}{2}[1.93+2(1.95+1.98+2.01+2.03)+2.06]$$

$$=\frac{(0.01)}{2}[1.93+15.94+2.06]=0.0996$$

**23.** Here, $n=4$, $\Delta x=h=\frac{b-a}{n}=\frac{1-0}{4}=0.25$

The values of x and y are tabulated below,

Where $y=f(x)=\frac{1}{1+x}$

| x | 0 | 0.25 | 0.50 | 0.75 | 1.00 |
|---|---|---|---|---|---|
| y | 1 | 0.8000 | 0.6667 | 0.5714 | 0.5 |
| | $(y_0)$ | $(y_1)$ | $(y_2)$ | $(y_3)$ | $(y_4)$ |

Trapezoidal rule gives

$$\int_0^1 \frac{1}{1+x}dx=\frac{h}{2}\{y_0+2(y_1+y_2+y_3)+y_4\}$$

$$=\frac{0.25}{2}\{1+2(0.8+0.6667+0.5714)+0.5\}$$

$$=0.6977$$

**24.** The value of x and y are tabulated below, where

$$y=f(x)=\frac{1}{x}$$

| x | 1 | 2 | 3 | 4 | 5 | 6 | 7 |
|---|---|---|---|---|---|---|---|
| y | 1 | 0.5 | 0.34 | 0.25 | 0.167 | 0.167 | 0.147 |
| | $y_0$ | $y_1$ | $y_2$ | $y_3$ | $y_4$ | $y_5$ | $y_6$ |

Substituting the values is Simpson's $\frac{1}{3}$ formula, we get

$$\int_1^7 \frac{dx}{x}=\frac{1}{3}\{y_0+4(y_1+y_3+y_5)+2(y_2+y_4)+y_6\}$$

$$=\frac{1}{3}\{1+4(0.5+0.25+0.167)+2(0.34+0.20)+0.142\}$$

$$\cong 1.958$$

**25.** Given quadrature formula is Simpson's one-third formula as $h=1$.

The degree of precision's one-third formula is 3.

**27.** Let $p(x)=Ax^4+Bx^3+Cx^2+Dx+E$

$p(1)=A+B+C+D+E=2$ ...(i)

$p'(1)=4A+3B+2C+D=3$ ...(ii)

$p(2)=16A+8B+4C+2D+E=6$ ...(iii)

$p'(2)=32A+12B+4C+D=7$ ...(iv)

$p''(2)=48A+12B+2C=8$ ...(v)

Solving all these equations, we get

$$A=-1, B=8, C=-20, D=23, E=-8$$

Hence, The polynomial is

$$p(x)=-x^4+8x^3-20x^2+23x-5$$

$\Rightarrow$ $p(0)=-8$

**32.** Here, $y=a^x$

So, $\Delta y=a^{x+h}-a^x=a^x(a^h-1)$

$\Delta^2 y=(a^h-1)\Delta a^x=(a^h-1)^2 a^x$

... ... ... ...

$\Delta^n y=(a^h-1)^n a^x$

**33.** Let $x^3+x^2-5x+2$

$=Ax^{(3)}+Bx^{(2)}+Cx^{(1)}+D$

$=Ax(x-1)(x-2)+Bx(x-1)+Cx+D$ ...(i)

Putting $x=0$ on both sides of Eq. (i), we get $D=2$.

Again, putting $x=1$, we get $C+D=1$, which gives $C=-3$

Next, putting $x=2$ on both sides of Eq. (i), we get

$2B+2C+D=4$, giving $B=4$

Again, equating the coefficient of $x^3$, we get $A=1$.

Hence, $x^3+x^2-5x+2=x^{(3)}+4x^{(2)}-3x^{(1)}+2$

**35.** Here; $E^2x^2=E(Ex^2)=E(x+2)^2$

$=(x+2+2)^2=(x+4)^2=x^2+8x+16$

**40.** We have, $\frac{\Delta^2}{E}(x^3)=(E-2+E^{-1})(x^3)$

$=E(x^3)-2(x^3)+E^{-1}(x^3)$

$=(x+1)^3-2x^3+(x-1)^3$

$=(x^3+3x^2+3x+1)-2x^3+(x^3-3x^2+3x-1)$

$=6x$

**41.** Here, $(\Delta-\nabla)x^2=\Delta x^2-\nabla x^2$

$=(x+h)^2-x^2-x^2+(x-h)^2$

$=x^2+2xh+h^2-2x^2+x^2-2xh+h^2$

$=2h^2$

**42.** We have, $\frac{\Delta^2}{E}(\sin x)=(E-2+E^{-1})(\sin x)$

$=\sin(x+h)-2\sin x+\sin(x-h)$

$=\sin(x+h)+\sin(x-h)-2\sin x$

$=2\sin\frac{(x+h)+(x-h)}{2}\cos\frac{(x+h)-(x-h)}{2}-2\sin x$

$=2\sin x\cos h-2\sin x=2\sin x(\cos h-1)$

**43.** We have, $\Delta^2-2\Delta+1=(\Delta-1)^2=(E-2)^2$ $[\because E=1+\Delta]$

$=E^2-4E+4$

Hence, $(\Delta^2-2\Delta+1)y=(E^2-4E+4)(a2^x+bx2^x)$

$=E^2(a2^x+bx2^x)-4E(a2^x+bx2^x)+4(a2^x+bx2^x)$

$=a2^{x+2}+b(x+2)2^{x+2}-4[a2^{x+1}+b(x+1)2^{x+1}]+4(a2^x+bx2^x)$

$=a2^{x+2}+2bx2^{x+1}+4b2^{x+1}-2a2^{x+2}-4bx2^{x+1}-4b2^{x+1}+a2^{x+2}+2bx2^{x+1}$

$=0$

**73.** Here, $h = 10$,

Hence using Simpson's one-third rule, the approximate area of the cross-section

$$= \int_0^{80} y dx$$

$$= \int_0^{0+8h} d\, dx$$

$$= \frac{1}{3} h[y_0 + 4(y_1 + y_3 + y_5 + y_7) + 2(y_2 + y_4 + y_6 + y_8)]$$

$$= \frac{1}{3}(10)[0 + 4(4 + 9 + 15 + 8) + 2(7 + 12 + 14) + 3],$$

(from table)

$$= \frac{1}{3}(10)[4(36) + 2(33) + 3]$$

$$= \frac{1}{3}(10)(144 + 66 + 3)$$

$$= 10(48 + 22 + 1)$$

$$= 710 \text{ sq m}$$

**74.** Here, $a = 1950$, $h = 10$ and $a + hu = 1985$

Hence, $a + hu = 1985$

$\Rightarrow$ $1990 + 10u = 1985$

$\Rightarrow$ $10u = 34$

$\Rightarrow$ $u = 3.4$

For the given data, we have the following difference table

| Year | $x$ | Population ($y_x$) | $\Delta y_x$ | $\Delta^2 y_x$ | $\Delta^3 y_x$ | $\Delta^4 y_x$ |
|---|---|---|---|---|---|---|
| 1950 | 0 | $46 = y_0$ | | | | |
| | | | $20 = y_0$ | | | |
| 1960 | 1 | 66 | | $-5 = \Delta^2 y_0$ | | |
| | | | 15 | | $2 = \Delta^3 y_0$ | |
| 1970 | 2 | 81 | | $-3$ | | $-3 = \Delta^4 y_0$ |
| | | | 12 | | $-1$ | |
| 1980 | 3 | 93 | | $-4$ | | |
| | | | 8 | | | |
| 1990 | 4 | 101 | | | | |

Now from Newton Gregory's formula, we have

$$y_{3.4} = y_2 + \frac{u^{(1)}}{1!}\Delta y_0 + \frac{u^{(2)}}{2!}\Delta^2 y_0 + \frac{u^{(3)}}{3!}\Delta^3 y_0 + \frac{u^{(4)}}{4!}\Delta^4 y_0$$

$$= 46 + \frac{(3.4)}{1}(20) + \frac{(3.4)(3.4-1)}{2!}(-5) + \frac{3.4(3.4-1)(3.4-2)}{3!}(2) + \frac{3.4(3.4-1)(3.4-2)(3.4-3)}{4!}(-3)$$

$$= 46 + 68 - \frac{(3.4)(2.4)(5)}{2}(2) - \frac{(3.4)(2.4)(1.4)}{6}(2) - \frac{(3.4)(2.4)(1.4)(0.4)}{24}(3)$$

$$= 46 + 68 - 20.4 + 3.808 - 0.571 = 96.837$$

Hence, the required population for the year 1985 is 96.837 thousands.

## Exercise 2

**1.** We have, $\Delta \log f(x) = \log f(x+h) - \log f(x)$

$$= \log \frac{f(x+h)}{f(x)} = \log \frac{Ef(x)}{f(x)} \quad \text{...(i)}$$

Since, $E = (1-\nabla)^{-1}$

and $E = 1 + \Delta$

Hence, from Eq. (i), we get

$$\Delta \log f(x) = \log\left\{\frac{[(1-\Delta)^{-1} f(x)]}{f(x)}\right\}$$

Also, from Eq. (i), we get

$$\Delta \log f(x) = \log \frac{(1+\Delta)f(x)}{f(x)} = \log\left(1 + \frac{\Delta f(x)}{f(x)}\right)$$

**9.** We have, $f(0) = 1$, $f(1) = 4$, $f(2) = 15$

$$\Rightarrow \int_0^2 f(x)dx = \frac{h}{2}[f_1 + 2f_2 + f_3]$$

$$= \frac{1}{2}(1 + 2 \times 4 + 15) = 12$$

Also, $f(x) = 4x^2 - x + 1$

Hence, Error = Exact − Approximate

$$= \frac{32}{3} - 12 = -\frac{4}{3}$$

**10.** Here, $x_0 = 0, y_0 = 1, h = 0.2$

$\Rightarrow$ $f(x_0, y_0) = x_0 + y_0 = 0 + 1 = 1$

$\Rightarrow$ $k_1 = hf(x_0, y_0) = 0.2 \times 1 = 0.2$

$$k_2 = hf\left(x_0 + \frac{h}{2}, y_0 + \frac{k_1}{2}\right)$$

$$= 0.2 f(0.1, 1.1) = 0.2 \times 1.2$$

$$= 0.240$$

Similarly, $k_3 = 0.2440$ and $k_4 = 0.2888$

**11.** Here, $f(x) \equiv x^3 - 25 = 0$ ...(i)

Then, $f'(x) \equiv 3x^2$

Hence, by Newton-Raphson formula

$$x_{i+1} = x_i - \frac{f(x_i)}{f'(x_i)}$$

$$= x_i - \frac{x_i^3 - 25}{3x_i^2} = \frac{3x_i^3 - x_i^3 + 25}{3x_i^2}$$

$$\Rightarrow \quad x_{i+1} = \frac{2x_i^3 + 25}{3x_i^2} \quad \text{...(ii)}$$

From Eq. (i) $f(2) = 2^3 - 25 = -17$ = negative

and $f(3) = 3^3 - 25 = 27 - 25$

$= 2$ = positive

Hence, the root of Eq. (i) lies between 2 and 3.

Again from Eq. (i), we have

$$f(2.8) = (2.8)^3 - 25$$
$$= 21.952 - 25 = \text{negative}$$
$$f(2.9) = (2.9)^3 - 25$$
$$= 24.389 - 25 = \text{negative}$$
$$f(3) = (3)^3 - 25 = 27 - 25$$
$$= 2 = \text{positive}$$

Therefore, the root of Eq. (i) lies between 2.9 and 3.

**For a first approximation** Let $i = 0$ and $x_0 = 2.9$

Then, $$x_1 = \frac{(2x_0^3 + 25)}{3x_0^2} = \frac{[2(2.9)^3 + 55]}{3(2.9)^2}$$
$$= \frac{2(24.389) + 25}{3(8.41)} = \frac{73.778}{25.23}$$
$$= 2.92$$

**For a second approximation** Let $i = 1$, then $x_i = x_1 = 2.92$

Then, $$x_2 = \frac{2(2.92)^3 + 25}{3(2.92)^2}$$
$$= \frac{2(24.897) + 25}{3(8.526)} = \frac{74.794}{25.579}$$
$$= 2.924$$

**For a third approximation** Let $i = 2$, then $x_i = x_2 = 2.924$

Then, $$x_3 = \frac{2(2.924)^3 + 25}{3(2.924)^2} = \frac{2(24.9995) + 25}{3(8.55)} = \frac{74.999}{25.65}$$
$$= 2.9239 = 2.924$$

Hence, the solution (approximate) is $x = 2.924$

**12.** We know,

$$\Delta u_x = u_{x+h} - u_x$$

Hence, $u_4 - u_3 = \Delta u_3$
$$u_3 - u_2 = \Delta u_2$$
$$u_2 - u_1 = \Delta u_1$$

Hence, $$u_4 = u_3 + \Delta u_3$$
$$= u_3 + \Delta(u_2 + \Delta u_2) \qquad (\because u_3 - u_2 = \Delta u_2)$$
$$= u_3 + \Delta u_2 + \Delta^2 u_2$$
$$= u_3 + \Delta u_2 + \Delta^2(u_1 + \Delta u_1) \qquad (\because \Delta u_1 = u_2 - u_1)$$
$$= u_3 + \Delta u_2 + \Delta^2 u_1 + \Delta^3 u_1$$

**13.** The difference table is

| $x$ | $y$ | $\Delta y$ | $\Delta^2 y$ | $\Delta^3 y$ | $\Delta^4 y$ |
|---|---|---|---|---|---|
| 3 | 4.8 | | | | |
| | | 3.6 | | | |
| 4 | 8.4 | | 2.5 | | |
| | | 6.1 | | 0.5 | |
| 5 | 14.5 | | 3.0 | | 0 |
| | | 9.1 | | 0.5 | |
| 6 | 23.6 | | 3.5 | | 0 |
| | | 12.6 | | 0.5 | |
| 7 | 36.2 | | 4.0 | | 0 |
| | | 16.6 | | 0.5 | |
| 8 | 52.8 | | 4.5 | | |
| | | 21.1 | | | |
| 9 | 73.9 | | | | |

**The first term** By Newton's forward interpolation formula with $x_0 = 3$, $x = 1$, $h = 1$ and $p = -2$. We have,

$$y(1) = 4.8 + \frac{(-2)}{1} \times 3.6 + \frac{(-2)(-3)}{1 \cdot 2} \times 25 + \frac{(-2)(-3)(-4)}{1 \cdot 2 \cdot 3} \times 0.5$$
$$= 3.1$$

**The tenth term** By Newton's backward interpolation formula with $x_n = 9$, $x = 10$, $h = 1$ and $p = 1$. We have,

$$y(10) = 73.9 + \frac{1}{1} \times 21.1 + \frac{1(2)}{1 \cdot 2} \times 4 \cdot 5 + \frac{1(2)(3)}{1 \cdot 2 \cdot 3} \times 0.5$$
$$= 100$$

**14.** (i) Here, $x_0 = 5$, $x_1 = 7$, $x_2 = 11$, $x_3 = 13$, $x_4 = 17$ and $y_0 = 150$, $y_1 = 392$, $y_2 = 1452$, $y_3 = 2366$, $y_4 = 5202$ and the Lagrange interpolation formula is given by

$$f(x) = \sum_{k=0}^{n} \left( \prod_{\substack{j=0 \\ j \neq k}}^{n} \frac{(x - x_j)}{(x_k - x_j)} \right) y_k$$

Putting $x = 9$ and substituting the above values in Lagrange's formula, we get

$$f(9) = \frac{(9-7)(9-11)(9-13)(9-17)}{(5-7)(5-11)(5-13)(5-17)} \times 150$$
$$+ \frac{(9-5)(9-11)(9-13)(9-17)}{(7-5)(7-11)(7-13)(7-17)} \times 392$$
$$+ \frac{(9-5)(9-7)(9-13)(9-17)}{(11-15)(11-7)(11-13)(11-17)} \times 1452$$
$$+ \frac{(9-5)(9-7)(9-11)(9-17)}{(13-5)(13-7)(13-11)(13-17)} \times 2366$$
$$+ \frac{(9-5)(9-7)(9-11)(9-13)}{(17-5)(17-7)(17-11)(17-13)} \times 5202$$
$$= -\frac{50}{3} + \frac{3136}{15} + \frac{3872}{3} - \frac{2366}{3} + \frac{578}{5}$$
$$= 810$$

(ii) The divided difference table is given by

| $x$ | $f(x)$ | $\Delta$ | $\Delta^2$ | $\Delta^3$ |
|---|---|---|---|---|
| 5 | 150 | | | |
| | | 121 | | |
| 7 | 392 | | 24 | |
| | | 265 | | 1 |
| 11 | 1452 | | 32 | |
| | | 457 | | 1 |
| 13 | 2366 | | 42 | |
| | | 709 | | |
| 17 | 5202 | | | |

The Newton's divided difference formula is given by

$$f(x) = y_0 + (x - x_0) f(x_0, x_1) + (x - x_0)(x - x_1) f(x_0, x_1, x_2)$$
$$+ (x - x_0)(x - x_1)(x - x_2) f(x_0, x_1, x_2, x_3)$$

Taking $x = 9$ in the Newton's divided difference, we obtain

$$f(9) = 150 + (9-5) \times 121 + (9-5)(9-7) \times 24$$
$$+ (9-5)(9-7)(9-11) \times 1$$
$$= 150 + 484 + 192 - 16$$
$$= 810$$

**15.** We have, $\frac{\Delta^2}{E}x^2 = \Delta^2 E^{-1}x^2$

$= \Delta^2(x-h)^2 \qquad (\because E^n y_x = y_{x+nh})$

$= \Delta[\Delta(x-h)^2]$

$= \Delta[\{(x+h)-h\}^2 - \{x-h\}^2] \quad (\because \Delta y_x = y_{x+h} - y_x)$

$= \Delta[x^2 - (x-h)^2]$

$= \Delta[x^2 - (x^2 - 2xh + h^2)]$

$= \Delta(2xh - h^2)$

$= [\{2(x+h)h - h^2\} - \{2xh - h^2\}] (\because \Delta y_x = y_{x+h} - y_x)$

$= \{2xh + 2h^2 - h^2\} - \{2xh - h^2\}$

$= 2h^2$

(b) We have, $\Delta(\sin x \cos 3x)$

$= \Delta\left[\frac{1}{2}(2\sin x \cos 3x)\right]$

$= \Delta\left[\frac{1}{2}(\sin 4x - \sin 2x)\right]$

$= \frac{1}{2}[\Delta(\sin 4x) - \Delta(\sin 2x)]$

$= \frac{1}{2}[\{\sin 4(x+h) - \sin 4x\} - \{\sin 2(x+h) - \sin 2x\}]$

$= \frac{1}{2}[2\cos(4x+2h)\sin 2h - 2\cos(2x+h)\sin h]$

$= \cos(4x+2h)\sin 2h - \cos(2x+h)\sin h$

$= (\sin h)[2\cos(4x+2h)\cos h - \cos(2x+h)]$

**16.** Here, $y_0 = 0$

Integrating the given equation between the limits gives

$$[dy]_{y=0}^{y} = \int_{x=0}^{x} (1-2xy)\,dx$$

$$\Rightarrow \quad y = \int_0^x (1-2xy)\,dx \qquad \ldots(i)$$

$$y_n = y_0 + \int_{x_0}^{x} f(x, y_{n-1})\,dx$$

First approximation $y_1$ Replace $y$ by 0 in $(1-2xy)$ from Eq. (i)

$$y_1 = \int_0^{\infty} (1)\,dx = x \qquad \ldots(ii)$$

**Second approximation $y_2$** Replace $y$ by $y_1$ in $(1-2xy)$ from Eq. (i)

$$y_2 = \int_0^x (1-2xy_1)\,dx$$

$$= \int_0^x (1-2x^2)\,dx, \qquad \text{[from Eq. (ii)]}$$

$$= \left(x - \frac{2}{3}x^3\right)_0^x$$

$$= x - \frac{2}{3}x^3 \qquad \ldots(iii)$$

**Third approximation $y_3$** Replace $y$ by $y_2$ in $(1-2xy)$ from Eq. (i)

$$y_3 = \int_0^x (1-2xy_2)\,dx$$

$$= \int_0^x \left[1 - 2x\left(x - \frac{2}{3}x^3\right)\right]dx \quad \text{[from Eq. (iii)]}$$

or $$y_3 = \int_0^x \left(1 - 2x^2 + \frac{4}{3}x^4\right)dx$$

$$= x - \frac{2}{3}x^3 - \frac{4}{15}x^5$$

Thus, the solution of the given equation upto third approximation are

$$y_1 = x$$

$$y_2 = x - \frac{2}{3}x^3$$

$$y_3 = x - \frac{2}{3}x^3 - \frac{4}{15}x^5$$

**17.** Since, $x^n$ is a polynomial of degree $n$, therefore, $\Delta^{n+k}x^n = 0$ for $k \geq 1$. In this series the $n$th term is $n(n+1)\Delta^n x^n$. Hence, sum to $n$ terms will be same as sum to infinity.

Hence, required sum is

$= (1\cdot 2\Delta - 2\cdot 3\Delta^2 + 3\cdot 4\Delta^3 - 4\cdot 5\Delta^4 + \ldots)x^n$

$= 2(1 - 3\Delta + 6\Delta^2 - 10\Delta^3 + \ldots)\Delta x^n$

$= 2(1+\Delta)^{-3}\Delta x^n = 2E^{-3}\Delta x^n$

$= 2\Delta E^{-3}x^n = 2\Delta(x-3)^n$

$= 2\{(x-2)^n - (x-3)^n\}$

**18.** For the given data we have the following difference table

| $x$ | 0 | 1 | 2 | 3 | 4 |
|---|---|---|---|---|---|
| $y = u_x$ | 1 | 3 | 9 | | 81 |

Also as four values are given we assume $u_x$ to be a polynomial of third degree, so that

$$\Delta^4 u_x = 0$$

Now, $\quad \Delta^4 u_x = (E-1)^4 u_x \qquad (\because E \equiv 1 + \Delta)$

$\Rightarrow \quad \Delta^4 u_x = (E^4 - 4E^3 + 6E^2 - 4E + 1)u_x$

Putting $x = 0$, we get

$\Delta^4 u_x = E^4 u_0 - 4E^3 u_0 + 6E^2 u_0 - 4Eu_0 + u_0$

$= u_4 - 4u_3 + 6u_2 - 4u_1 + u_0 \qquad (\because E^n u_0 = u_n)$

$\Rightarrow \quad 0 = 81 - 4u_3 + 6(9) - 4(3) + (1)$, (from the table)

$\Rightarrow \quad 4u_3 = 81 + 54 - 12 + 1$

$= 136 - 12$

$= 124$

$\Rightarrow \quad u_3 = 31$

Hence, the missing term is $u_3 = 31$.

**19.** The given equation

$$f(x) = 3x - \cos x - 2 = 0$$

can be rewritten as

$$x = \frac{1}{3}[2 + \cos x] = g(x)$$

$$\Rightarrow \quad g'(x) = -\frac{1}{3}\sin x$$

$$\Rightarrow \quad g'(0.4) = -\frac{1}{3}\sin(0.5)$$

$$= -\frac{1}{3}(0.0087) < 1$$

Hence, by iteration formula

$$x_{n+1} = \frac{1}{3}[2 + \cos\{x_n\}] \qquad \ldots(i)$$

Putting $n=0$ in Eq. (i), we get

$$x_1 = \frac{1}{3}[2+\cos(x_0)]$$

$$= \frac{1}{3}[2+\cos(0.5)] \quad \text{Putting } x_0 = 0.5$$

$$= \frac{1}{3}[2+0.999962]$$

$$= 0.9999873 \quad \ldots\text{(ii)}$$

Putting $n=1$ in Eq. (i), we get

$$x_2 = \frac{1}{3}[2+\cos(x_1)]$$

$$= \frac{1}{3}[2+\cos(0.9999873)]$$

$$= \frac{1}{3}[2+0.999848]$$

$$= 0.9999493 \quad \ldots\text{(iii)}$$

Putting $n=2$ in Eq. (i), we get

$$x_3 = \frac{1}{3}[2+\cos(x_2)]$$

$$= \frac{1}{3}[2+\cos(0.9999493)]$$

$$= \frac{1}{3}[2+0.9999848]$$

$$= 0.9999493 \quad \ldots\text{(iv)}$$

From Eqs. (iii) and (iv), the required root, correct to five places of decimal, is 0.99995.

**20.** We have, $\Delta\sqrt{u_x} = \sqrt{u_{x+h}} - \sqrt{u_x}$

By definition of $\Delta$

$$= \frac{(\sqrt{u_{x+h}} - \sqrt{u_x})(\sqrt{u_{x+h}} + \sqrt{u_x})}{(\sqrt{u_{x+h}} + \sqrt{u_x})}$$

$$= \frac{u_{x+h} - u_x}{\sqrt{u_x} + \sqrt{u_{x+h}}} = \frac{\Delta u_x}{\sqrt{u_x} + \sqrt{u_{x+h}}}$$

**21.** We have, $\begin{bmatrix} 3 & 1 & 2 \\ 2 & -3 & -1 \\ 1 & -2 & 1 \end{bmatrix}\begin{bmatrix} x \\ y \\ z \end{bmatrix} = \begin{bmatrix} 3 \\ -3 \\ 4 \end{bmatrix}$

$\Leftrightarrow \quad AX = D$

Hence, $X = \dfrac{1}{|A|}\begin{bmatrix} A_1 & A_2 & A_3 \\ B_1 & B_2 & B_3 \\ C_1 & C_2 & C_3 \end{bmatrix}\begin{bmatrix} d_1 \\ d_2 \\ d_3 \end{bmatrix}$

where $A_1, B_1 \ldots$ are cofactors of $a_1, b_1 \ldots$ in the determinant $|A|$.

Hence, $\begin{bmatrix} x \\ y \\ z \end{bmatrix} = \dfrac{1}{8}\begin{bmatrix} -1 & 3 & 5 \\ -3 & 1 & 7 \\ 7 & -5 & 11 \end{bmatrix}\begin{bmatrix} 3 \\ -3 \\ 4 \end{bmatrix} = \begin{bmatrix} 1 \\ 2 \\ -1 \end{bmatrix}$

Thus, $x=1$, $y=2$ and $z=-1$

**22.** We have, $\Delta \log f(x) = \log f(x+h) - \log f(x)$

By definition of $\Delta = \log\left[\dfrac{f(x+h)}{f(x)}\right]$

$$= \log\left[\frac{Ef(x)}{f(x)}\right] \quad (\because Eu_x = u_{x+h})$$

$$= \log\left[\frac{(\Delta+1)f(x)}{f(x)}\right] \quad (\because E = \Delta + 1)$$

$$= \log\left[\frac{\Delta f(x) + f(x)}{f(x)}\right]$$

$$= \log\left[\frac{f(x)}{f(x)} + \frac{\Delta f(x)}{f(x)}\right]$$

$$= \log\left[1 + \frac{\Delta f(x)}{f(x)}\right]$$

**23.** Given, $x_0 = 1, y_0 = 1.2, h = 0.1$ ...(i)

and $f(x, y) = 3x + y^2$ ...(ii)

Hence, $f(x_0, y_0) = 3x_0 + y_0^2$

$$= 3(1) + (1.2)^2$$

$$= 3 + 1.44$$

$$= 4.44$$

Here, $k_1 = hf(x_0, y_0)$

$$= (0.1)(4.44) = 0.444 \quad \ldots\text{(iii)}$$

$$k_2 = hf\left(x_0 + \frac{1}{2}h, y_0 + \frac{1}{2}k_1\right)$$

$$= (0.1) f(1.05, 1.422)$$

$$= (0.1)(3.15 + 2.022)$$

$$= (0.1)(5.172) = 0.517 \quad \ldots\text{(iv)}$$

$$k_3 = hf\left(x_0 + \frac{1}{2}h, y_0 + \frac{1}{2}k_2\right)$$

$$= (0.1) f(1.05, 1.459)$$

$$= (0.1)[3.15 + 2.129]$$

$$= (0.1)(5.279) = 0.528 \quad \ldots\text{(v)}$$

and $k_4 = hf(x_0 + h, y_0 + k_3)$

$$= (0.1) f(1.1, 1.728)$$

$$= (0.1)(3.3 + 2.986)$$

$$= (0.1)(6.286) = 0.629 \quad \ldots\text{(vi)}$$

Hence, $k = \dfrac{1}{6}(k_1 + 2k_2 + 2k_3 + k_4)$

$$= \frac{1}{6}[0.444 + 2(0.517) + 2(0.528) + 0.629]$$

$$= \frac{1}{6}[3.163] = 0.527$$

Therefore, $y_{n+1} = y_n + k$

$\Rightarrow \quad y_1 = y_0 + k$

$$= 1.2 + 0.527 = 1.727$$

Thus, the required value of $y$ when $x = 1.1$ is 1.727.

**24.** (a) We have, $\Delta\left(\dfrac{x^2}{\cos 2x}\right) = \dfrac{(x+h)^2}{\cos 2(x+h)} - \dfrac{x^2}{\cos 2x}$

$$= \frac{(x+h)^2 \cos 2x - x^2 \cos 2(x+h)}{\cos 2(x+h)\cos 2x}$$

$$= \frac{[(x+h)^2 - x^2]\cos 2x + x^2[\cos 2x - \cos 2(x+h)]}{\cos 2(x+h)\cos 2x}$$

$$= \frac{(2hx + h^2)\cos 2x + 2x^2 \sin h \sin(2x+h)}{\cos 2(x+h)\cos 2x}$$

(b) We have, $\Delta^2 \cos 2x$

$$= \Delta [\cos 2(x+h) - \cos 2x]$$
$$= \Delta \cos 2(x+h) - \Delta \cos 2x$$
$$= [\cos 2(x+2h) - \cos 2(x+h)] - [\cos 2(x+h) - \cos 2x]$$
$$= -2\sin(2x+3h)\sin h + 2\sin(2x+h)\sin h$$
$$= -2\sin h[\sin(2x+3h) - \sin(2x+h)]$$
$$= -2\sin h[2\cos(2x+2h)\sin h]$$
$$= -4\sin^2 h \cos(2x+2h)$$

**25.** Since, five values of $y$ are known, we can assume that $y_x$ can be represented by a polynomial of degree four.

Hence, $\Delta^4 y_x = \text{constant}$

and $\Delta^{4+k} y_x = 0$, for $k \geq 1$

Thus, in particular, we get

$$\Delta^5 y_x = 0$$

$\Rightarrow \quad \Delta^5 y_0 = 0 \quad \text{and} \quad \Delta^5 y_1 = 0$

Here, the interval of differencing being 0.1.

Now, from the two equations

$$\Delta^5 y_0 = 0 \quad \text{and} \quad \Delta^5 y_1 = 0$$

To evaluate the missing term

$$\Delta^5 y_0 = 0$$

$$\Rightarrow (E-1)^5 y_0 = (E^5 - 5E^4 + 10E^3 - 10E^2 + 5E - 1) y_0 = 0$$

$$\Rightarrow \quad y_{0.5} - 5y_{0.4} + 10y_{0.3} - 10y_{0.2} + 5y_{0.1} - y_0 = 0$$

$$\Rightarrow \quad 0.082 - 5y_{0.4} + 10(0.100) - 10(0.111) + 5y_{0.1} - 0.135 = 0$$

$$\Rightarrow \quad 5y_{0.4} - 5y_{0.1} = -0.163 \qquad \ldots(i)$$

Similarly, $\Delta^5 y_{0.1} = 0$ gives

$$10y_{0.4} - y_{0.1} = 0.781 \qquad \ldots(ii)$$

Solving Eqs. (i) and (ii) for $y_{0.4}$ and $y_{0.1}$, we have

$$y_{0.1} = 0.123$$

and $y_{0.4} = 0.090$

**26.** We have, $\Delta^2 \left(\dfrac{5x+12}{x^2+5x+6}\right)$

$$= \Delta^2 \left\{\frac{5x+12}{(x+2)(x+3)}\right\}$$
$$= \Delta^2 \left\{\frac{2}{x+2} + \frac{3}{x+3}\right\}$$
$$= \Delta \left\{\Delta\left(\frac{2}{x+2}\right) + \Delta\left(\frac{3}{x+3}\right)\right\}$$
$$= \Delta \left\{2\left(\frac{1}{x+3} - \frac{1}{x+2}\right) + 3\left(\frac{1}{x+4} - \frac{1}{x+3}\right)\right\}$$
$$= -2\Delta \left\{\frac{1}{(x+2)(x+3)}\right\} - 3\Delta \left\{\frac{1}{(x+3)(x+4)}\right\}$$
$$= -2\left\{\frac{1}{(x+3)(x+4)} - \frac{1}{(x+2)(x+3)}\right\} - 3\left\{\frac{1}{(x+4)(x+5)} - \frac{1}{(x+3)(x+4)}\right\}$$
$$= \frac{4}{(x+2)(x+3)(x+4)} + \frac{6}{(x+3)(x+4)(x+5)}$$
$$= \frac{2(5x+16)}{(x+2)(x+3)(x+4)(x+5)}$$

**27.** We know,

$$E^n u_x = u_{x+nh}, \text{ we have}$$
$$E^{-m} u_x = u_{x-mh}$$

Hence, $\text{RHS} = E^{-1} u_x + \Delta E^{-2} u_x + \Delta^2 E^{-3} u_x + \ldots$

$$= (E^{-1} + \Delta E^{-2} + \Delta^2 E^{-3} + \ldots) u_x$$
$$= E^{-1}(1 + \Delta E^{-1} + \Delta^2 E^{-2} + \ldots) u_x$$
$$= E^{-1}(1 - \Delta E^{-1})^{-1} u_x$$
$$[\because (1-y)^{-1} = 1 + y + y^2 + \ldots]$$
$$= \left(\frac{E^{-1}}{1 - \Delta E^{-1}}\right) u_x = \left(\frac{1}{E - \Delta}\right) u_x$$
$$= \frac{1}{(1 + \Delta - \Delta)} u_x \qquad (\because E = 1 + \Delta)$$
$$= u_x = \text{LHS}$$

**28.** Here, $\text{LHS} = U_0 + EU_0 + E^2 U_0 + \ldots + E^n U_0$

$$= (1 + E + E^2 + \ldots + E^n) U_0$$
$$= \left(\frac{1 - E^{n+1}}{1 - E}\right) U_0$$
$$= \left(\frac{E^{n+1} - 1}{\Delta}\right) U_0$$
$$= \frac{1}{\Delta}\{(1+\Delta)^{n+1} - 1\} U_0$$
$$= \frac{1}{\Delta}\{1 + {}^{n+1}C_1 \Delta + {}^{n+1}C_2 \Delta^2 + \ldots + {}^{n+1}C_{n+1} \Delta^{n+1} - 1\} U_0$$
$$= {}^{n-1}C_1 U_0 + {}^{n+1}C_2 \Delta U_0 + \ldots + {}^{n+1}C_{n+1} \Delta^n U_0$$
$$= \text{RHS}$$

**29.** Here, integrating the given equation between limits, we have

$$\int_{y=0}^{y} dy = \int_{x=1}^{x} \left(2 - \frac{y}{x}\right) dx$$

$$\Rightarrow \quad y = 2 + \int_1^x \left(2 - \frac{y}{x}\right) dx \qquad \ldots(i)$$

The $n$th approximation is

$$y_n = y_0 + \int_{x_0}^{x} f(x, y_{n-1})\, dx$$

**First approximation $y_1$** Replacing $y$ by 2 in $\left[2 - \left(\dfrac{y}{x}\right)\right]$ from Eq. (i), we get

$$y_1 = 2 + \int_1^x \left(2 - \frac{2}{x}\right) dx$$
$$= 2 + [2x - 2\log x]_0^x$$
$$= 2 + [(2x - 2\log x) - (2 - 2\log 1)]$$
$$= 2x - 2\log x \qquad \ldots(ii)$$

**Second approximation $y_2$** Replacing $y$ by $y_1$ in $\left[2-\left(\frac{y}{x}\right)\right]$ from Eq. (i), we get

$$y_2 = 2 + \int_1^x \left(2 - \frac{y_1}{x}\right) dx$$

$$= 2 + \int_1^x \left[2e - \left\{2 - \frac{2}{x}\log x\right\}\right] dx \quad \text{[from Eq. (ii)]}$$

$$= 2 + 2\int_1^x \frac{1}{x}(\log x)\, dx \quad \ldots\text{(iii)}$$

Now let $\int_1^x \left(\frac{1}{x}\right) \log x\, dx = I$, then integrating by parts, we have

$$I = \left[\{(\log x)(\log x)\}_1^x - \int_1^x \frac{1}{x}\cdot(\log x)\, dx\right]$$

Taking log $x$ as first function

$$\Rightarrow \quad I = (\log x)^2 - I$$

$$\text{or} \quad 2I = (\log x)^2$$

$$\text{or} \quad I = \frac{1}{2}(\log x)^2$$

Then from Eq. (iii), we have

$$y_2 = 2 + 2I$$

$$= 2 + (\log x)^2 \quad \ldots\text{(iv)}$$

The first and second approximation of given equation gives the soluton

$$y_1 = 2(x - \log x)$$

and $$y_2 = 2 + (\log x)^2$$

**30.** Here, $$\begin{bmatrix} 10 & -7 & 3 & 5 \\ -6 & 8 & -1 & -4 \\ 3 & 1 & 4 & 11 \\ 5 & -9 & -2 & 4 \end{bmatrix}\begin{bmatrix} x \\ y \\ z \\ u \end{bmatrix} = \begin{bmatrix} 6 \\ 5 \\ 2 \\ 7 \end{bmatrix}$$

and $A = LU$

$$\Rightarrow \begin{bmatrix} 1 & 0 & 0 & 0 \\ l_{21} & 1 & 0 & 0 \\ l_{31} & l_{32} & 1 & 0 \\ l_{41} & l_{42} & l_{43} & 1 \end{bmatrix}\begin{bmatrix} u_{11} & u_{12} & u_{13} & u_{23} \\ 0 & u_{22} & u_{23} & u_{24} \\ 0 & 0 & u_{33} & u_{34} \\ 0 & 0 & 0 & u_{44} \end{bmatrix}$$

$$= \begin{bmatrix} 10 & -7 & 3 & 5 \\ -6 & 8 & -1 & -4 \\ 3 & 1 & 4 & 11 \\ 5 & -9 & -2 & 4 \end{bmatrix}$$

Therefore,

$R_1$ of $U$ : $u_{11} = 10, u_{12} = -7, u_{13} = 3, u_{14} = 5$

$C_1$ of $L$ : $l_{21} = -0.6, l_{31} = 0.3, l_{41} = 0.5$

$R_2$ of $U$ : $u_{22} = 3.8, u_{23} = 0.8, u_{24} = -1$

$C_2$ of $L$ : $l_{32} = 0.815, l_{42} = -1.447$

$R_3$ of $U$ : $u_{33} = 2.447, u_{34} = 10.315$

$C_3$ of $L$ : $l_{43} = -0.956$

$R_4$ of $U$ : $u_{44} = 9.924$

Thus, $$A = \begin{bmatrix} 1 & 0 & 0 & 0 \\ -0.6 & 1 & 0 & 0 \\ 0.3 & 0.815 & 1 & 0 \\ 0.5 & -1.447 & -0.956 & 1 \end{bmatrix}\begin{bmatrix} 10 & -7 & 3 & 5 \\ 0 & 3.8 & 0.8 & -1 \\ 0 & 0 & 2.447 & 10.315 \\ 0 & 0 & 0 & 9.924 \end{bmatrix}$$

Writing $UX = V$, the given system becomes

$$\begin{bmatrix} 1 & 0 & 0 & 0 \\ -0.6 & 1 & 0 & 0 \\ 0.3 & 0.815 & 1 & 0 \\ 0.5 & -1.447 & -0.956 & 1 \end{bmatrix}\begin{bmatrix} V_1 \\ V_2 \\ V_3 \\ V_4 \end{bmatrix} = \begin{bmatrix} 6 \\ 5 \\ 2 \\ 7 \end{bmatrix}$$

Solving this system, we have

$$V_1 = 6, V_2 = 8.6, V_3 = -6.815, V_4 = 9.924$$

Hence, the original system becomes

$$\begin{bmatrix} 10 & -7 & 3 & 5 \\ 0 & 3.8 & 0.8 & -1 \\ 0 & 0 & 2.447 & 10.315 \\ 0 & 0 & 0 & 9.924 \end{bmatrix}\begin{bmatrix} x \\ y \\ z \\ u \end{bmatrix} = \begin{bmatrix} 6 \\ 8.6 \\ -6.815 \\ 9.924 \end{bmatrix}$$

$$10x - 7y + 3z + 5u = 6,\ 3.8y + 0.8z - u = 8.6$$

$$2.447z + 10.315u = -6.815u = 1$$

So, by back substitution, we get

$$u = 1, z = -7, y = 4 \text{ and } x = 5$$

**31.** We know that

$$\nabla = 1 - E^{-1}$$

$$= 1 - e^{-hD} \quad (\because E = e^{hD})$$

$$\Rightarrow \quad e^{-hD} = 1 - \nabla$$

$$\Rightarrow \quad -hD = \log(1 - \nabla)$$

$$= -\left[\nabla + \frac{\nabla^2}{2} + \frac{\nabla^3}{3} + \ldots\right]$$

$$\Rightarrow \quad D = \frac{1}{h}\left[\nabla + \frac{1}{2}\nabla^2 + \frac{1}{3}\nabla^3 + \ldots\right] \quad \ldots\text{(i)}$$

Operating this on $y$, we get

$$y' = Dy$$

$$= \frac{1}{h}\left[\nabla y + \frac{1}{2}\nabla^2 y + \frac{1}{3}\nabla^3 y + \frac{1}{4}\nabla^4 y + \ldots\right]$$

Now, squaring Eq. (i), we get

$$D^2 = \frac{1}{h^2}\left[\nabla + \frac{1}{2}\nabla^2 + \frac{1}{3}\nabla^3 + \ldots\right]^2$$

$$\Rightarrow \quad D^2 = \frac{1}{h^2}\left[\nabla^2 + \nabla^3 + \frac{11}{12}\nabla^4 + \ldots\right]$$

Operating this on $y$, we have

$$y'' = D^2 y$$

$$= \frac{1}{h^2}\left[\nabla^2 y + \nabla^3 y + \frac{11}{12}\nabla^4 y + \ldots\right]$$

**32.** The cumulative frequency table is given by

| Marks less than ($x$) | 40 | 50 | 60 | 70 | 80 |
|---|---|---|---|---|---|
| No. of students ($y_x$) | 31 | 73 | 124 | 159 | 190 |

The difference table is

| $x$ | $y$ | $\Delta y_x$ | $\Delta^2 y_x$ | $\Delta^3 y_x$ | $\Delta^4 y_x$ |
|---|---|---|---|---|---|
| 40 | 31 | | | | |
| | | 42 | | | |
| 50 | 73 | | 9 | | |
| | | 51 | | −25 | |
| 60 | 124 | | −16 | | 37 |
| | | 35 | | 12 | |
| 70 | 159 | | −4 | | |
| | | 31 | | | |
| 80 | 190 | | | | |

The number of students whose marks are less than 45 is $y_{45}$

Taking $\quad x_0 = 40$

$x = 45$

We have, $\quad p = \dfrac{x - x_0}{h} = \dfrac{5}{10} = 0.5$

where $\quad h = 10$

$\therefore$ Using Newton's forward interpolation formula, we get

$$y_{45} = y_{40} + p\Delta y_{40} + \frac{p(p-1)}{2}\Delta^2 y_{40} + \frac{p(p-1)(p-2)}{1\cdot 2\cdot 3}\Delta^3 y_{40} + \ldots$$

$$= 31 + 0.5 \times 42 + \frac{0.5(-0.5)}{2} \times 9 + \frac{0.5(0.5)(-1.5)}{6} \times (-25) + \frac{0.5(-0.5)(-1.5(-2.5)}{24} \times 37$$

$$= 47.87$$

Hence, the number of students with marks less than 45 is $47.87 \cong 48$.

But the number of students with marks less than 40 is 31. Therefore, the number of students getting marks between 40 and 45 is

$$= 48 - 31 = 17$$

**33.** (a) We have, $\left(\dfrac{E-1}{E}\right) y_x = (1 - E^{-1}) y_x$

$$= y_x - E^{-1} y_x$$

$$= y_x - y_{x-h} \qquad (\because E^n y_x = y_{x+nh})$$

$$= \Delta y_x$$

$$\Rightarrow \quad \frac{(E-1)}{E} = \nabla$$

(b) We have, $\nabla E y_x = \nabla(E y_x) = \nabla y_{x+h}$

$$= y_{x+h} - y_{x+h-h} \qquad (\because \nabla y_x = y_x - y_{x-h})$$

$$= y_{x+h} - y_x$$

$$= \Delta y_x$$

Hence, $\quad \nabla E = \Delta$

Again, $\quad E\nabla y_x = E(\nabla y_x) = E(y_x - y_{x-h})$

$$= E y_x - E y_{x-h}$$

$$= y_{x+h} - y_{x-h+h} = y_{x+h} - y_x$$

$$= \Delta y_x$$

Hence, $\quad E\nabla = \Delta$

(c) $(1+\Delta)(1-\nabla) = E(1-\nabla) \qquad (\because E = 1+\Delta)$

$$= E - E\nabla = E - \Delta$$

$$= (1+\Delta) - \Delta$$

$$= 1$$

**34.** Given, iteration formula

$$x_{n+1} = x_n\,[2 - 35x_n] \qquad \ldots(i)$$

Putting $n = 0$, $x_1 = x_0\,[2 - 35x^{(0)}]$ ...(ii)

Let $x_0$ *i.e.*, $\quad x_0 = \dfrac{1}{35} = 0.02$ approximate

Then, from Eq. (ii), we have

$$x_1 = (0.02)[2 - 35(0.02)]$$

$$x_1 = (0.02)[2 - 0.7]$$

$$= (0.02)(1.3)$$

$$= 0.026 \qquad \ldots(iii)$$

Putting $n = 1$ in Eq. (i), we get

$$x_2 = x_1\,[2 - 35x^{(1)}]$$

$$= (0.026)[2 - 35(0.026)], \qquad \text{[from Eq. (ii)]}$$

$$= (0.02834)[2 - 0.9919]$$

$$= (0.026)[2 - 0.9]$$

$$= (0.026)[1.09]$$

$$= 0.02834 \qquad \ldots(iv)$$

Putting $n = 2$ in Eq. (i), we get

$$x_3 = x_2\,[2 - 35x^{(2)}]$$

$$= (0.02834)[2 - 35(0.02834)] \qquad \text{[from Eq. (iv)]}$$

$$= (0.02834)[2 - 0.9919]$$

$$= (0.02834)(1.0081)$$

$$= 0.0285695 \qquad \ldots(v)$$

Putting $n = 3$ in Eq. (i), we get

$$x_4 = x_3\,[2 - 35x^{(3)}],$$

$$= (0.0285695)[2 - 35(0.0285695)] \qquad \text{[from Eq. (v)]}$$

$$= (0.0285695)[2 - 0.9999343]$$

$$= (0.0285695)(1.0000657)$$

$$= 0.0285713 \qquad \ldots(vi)$$

Hence, from Eqs. (v) and (vi), the approximate value of $\dfrac{1}{35}$ correct to decimal place is 0.0285.

# 20 Calculus of Variations and Linear Integral Equations

## Calculus of Variations

One of the main problem of the calculus of variation is to determine that curve connecting two given points which either maximizes or minimizes some given integral. Consider the curve $y = y(x)$, where $y(x_1) = y_1$ and $y(x_2) = y_2$ such that for some given known function $F(x, y, y')$ of variables $x, y, y'$ the integral

$$I[y(x)] = \int_{x_1}^{x_2} F(x, y, y')dx \quad \text{...(i)}$$

is either maximum or minimum, also called an extremum or stationary values. A curve $y = y(x)$ which satisfies this property is called an extremal.

An integral such as Eq. (i) which assumes a numerical value for some class of functions $y(x)$ is said to be functional.

It is assumed that the function $y(x)$ is taken from a class of functions on which the functional $I[y(x)]$ is defined.

**Syllabus**

- Variation of a Function
- Euler-Lagrange Equation
- Necessary and Sufficient Conditions for Extreme
- Variational Method for Boundary Value Problems in Ordinary and Partial Differential Equations
- Linear Integral Equation of the First and Second Kind of Fredholm and Volterra Type
- Solutions with Separable Kernels
- Characteristic Numbers and Eigen Functions
- Resolvent Kernel

## Linear Functional

A linear functional is a functional $L[y(x)]$ if it satisfies that following two conditions.

**(i)** $L[Cy(x)] = CL[y(x)]$, $C$ being an arbitrary constant.

**(ii)** $L[y_1(x) + y_2(x)] = L[y_1(x)] + L[y_2(x)]$

e.g., The functional $I[y(x)] = \int_a^b \{y'(x) + y(x)\}dx$ is linear in the class $C'[a, b]$ but the functional

$$I[y(x)] = \int_a^b [p(x)\{y'(x)\}^2 + q(x)\{y(x)\}^2]dx$$

is non-linear. Here, $C'[a, b]$ denotes the set of all functions having continuous first order derivatives in $[a, b]$.

***Theorem 1*** If a functional $I[y(x)]$ having a variation attains a maximum or minimum on $y = y_0(x)$. Where, $y(x)$ is an interior point of the domain of definition of the functional, then at $y = y_0(x)$, $\delta I = 0$.

> ***Note*** **(a)** Problems which investigate extrema of functionals are known as variational problems.
> **(b)** Calculus of variation deals with variational problems of functionals.

***Theorem 2*** If for every continuous function $\eta(x), \int_{x_1}^{x_2} \phi(x)\eta(x)dx = 0$, where the function $\phi(x)$ is continuous on the interval $[x_1, x_2]$, then $\phi(x) \equiv 0$ on that interval.

## Euler-Lagrange Equation

A necessary condition for

$$I[y(x)] = \int_{x_1}^{x_2} F(x, y(x), y'(x))dx \quad \text{...(i)}$$

to be an extremum is that

$$\frac{\partial F}{\partial y} - \frac{d}{dx}\left(\frac{\partial F}{\partial y'}\right) = 0 \quad \text{...(ii)}$$

which is called Euler's equation or Euler-Lagrange equation.

> ***Note*** **(a)** We assume that given function $F(x, y(x), y'(x))$ or $F(x, y, y')$ is twice differentiable with respect to any combination of its arguments.
> **(b)** Let $\phi(x)$ be the curve which extremizes the functional Eq. (i), then $\phi(x)$ is twice differentiable and satisfies the boundary conditions $\phi(x_1) = \phi_1$ and $\phi(x_2) = \phi_2$.

## Other Forms of Euler's Equation

Since, $F$ is a function of $x, y, y'$

$$\Rightarrow \quad \frac{dF}{dx} = \frac{\partial F}{\partial x} + \frac{\partial F}{\partial y}\frac{dy}{dx} + \frac{\partial F}{\partial y'}\frac{dy'}{dx}$$

$$\Rightarrow \quad \frac{dF}{dx} = \frac{\partial F}{\partial x} + \frac{\partial F}{\partial y}y' + \frac{\partial F}{\partial y'}y'' \quad \text{...(i)}$$

and

$$\frac{d}{dx}\left(y'\frac{\partial F}{\partial y'}\right) = y'\frac{d}{dx}\left(\frac{\partial F}{\partial y'}\right) + \frac{\partial F}{\partial y'}y'' \quad \text{...(ii)}$$

On subtracting Eq. (i) from Eq. (ii), we get

$$\frac{d}{dx}\left(y'\frac{\partial F}{\partial y'}\right) - \frac{dF}{dx} = y'\frac{d}{dx}\left(\frac{\partial F}{\partial y'}\right) - \frac{\partial F}{\partial x} - \frac{\partial F}{\partial y}y'$$

$$\Rightarrow \quad \frac{d}{dx}\left(y'\frac{\partial F}{\partial y'} - F\right) = y'\frac{\partial F}{\partial y} - \frac{\partial F}{\partial x} - \frac{\partial F}{\partial y}y'$$

[from Eulers' Eq. (ii)]

$$\Rightarrow \quad \frac{\partial F}{\partial x} + \frac{d}{dx}\left(y'\frac{\partial F}{\partial y'} - F\right) = 0$$

$$\Rightarrow \quad \frac{\partial F}{\partial x} - \frac{d}{dx}\left(F - y'\frac{\partial F}{\partial y'}\right) = 0 \quad \text{...(iii)}$$

which is another form of Eq. (ii).

Now, let $\phi = \frac{\partial F}{\partial y'}$, then $\phi$ is also a function of $x, y, y'$.

*i.e.,* $\quad \phi = \phi(x, y, y')$

$$\therefore \quad \frac{d\phi}{dx} = \frac{\partial \phi}{\partial x} + \frac{\partial \phi}{\partial y}\frac{dy}{dx} + \frac{\partial \phi}{\partial y'}\frac{dy'}{dx}$$

$$\Rightarrow \quad \frac{d}{dx}\left(\frac{\partial F}{\partial y'}\right) = \frac{\partial}{\partial x}\left(\frac{\partial F}{\partial y'}\right) + \frac{\partial}{\partial y}\left(\frac{\partial F}{\partial y'}\right)y' + \frac{\partial}{\partial y'}\left(\frac{\partial F}{\partial y'}\right)y''$$

Putting this value of $\frac{d}{dx}\left(\frac{\partial F}{\partial y'}\right)$ in Eq (ii), we get

$$\frac{\partial F}{\partial y} - \frac{\partial}{\partial x}\left(\frac{\partial F}{\partial y'}\right) - \frac{\partial}{\partial y}\left(\frac{\partial F}{\partial y'}\right)y' - \frac{\partial}{\partial y'}\left(\frac{\partial F}{\partial y'}\right)y'' = 0$$

$$\Rightarrow \quad \frac{\partial F}{\partial y} - \frac{\partial^2 F}{\partial x \partial y'} - y'\frac{\partial^2 F}{\partial y \partial y'} - y''\frac{\partial^2 F}{\partial y'^2} = 0 \quad \text{...(iv)}$$

which is an extended form of Eq (ii).

Now, following cases may be discussed.

***Case I*** When $F$ is independent of $x$

$$\Rightarrow \quad \frac{\partial F}{\partial x} = 0$$

From Eq. (iii), we get

$$\frac{d}{dx}\left(F - y'\frac{\partial F}{\partial y'}\right) = 0$$

$$\Rightarrow \quad F - y'\frac{\partial F}{\partial y'} = C \quad \text{(a constant)}$$

***Case II*** When $F$ is independent of $y$

$$\Rightarrow \quad \frac{\partial F}{\partial y} = 0$$

From Eq. (ii), we get

$$\frac{d}{dx}\left(\frac{\partial F}{\partial y'}\right) = 0$$

$$\Rightarrow \quad \frac{\partial F}{\partial y'} = C \quad \text{(a constant)}$$

***Case III*** When $F$ is independent of $y'$

$$\Rightarrow \quad \frac{\partial F}{\partial y'} = 0, \text{ then from Eq. (ii), we get}$$

$$\frac{\partial F}{\partial y} = 0$$

***Case IV*** When $F$ independent of $x$ and $y$

*i.e.,* $\quad \frac{\partial F}{\partial x} = 0, \ \frac{\partial F}{\partial y} = 0$

Then, from Eq. (iv), we get

$$y''\frac{\partial^2 F}{\partial y'^2} = 0$$

If $\frac{\partial^2 F}{\partial y'^2} \neq 0$, it reduces to $y'' = 0$ which gives a solution of the form $y = C_1x + C_2$ where $C_1$ and $C_2$ are constants.

***Example 1.*** *Find the extremal of the functional* $\int_0^{\frac{\pi}{2}} (y'^2 - y^2 + 2xy)dx$ *that satisfy the boundary conditions* $y(0) = 0,\ y(\pi/2) = 0$

**Solution.** Here, $F(x, y, y') = y'^2 - y^2 + 2xy$

$$\Rightarrow \quad \frac{\partial F}{\partial y} = 0 - 2y + 2x = 2(x - y)$$

$$\frac{\partial F}{\partial y'} = 2y' - 0 + 0 = 2y'$$

Since, Euler's-Lagrange equation is

$$\frac{\partial F}{\partial y} - \frac{d}{dx}\left(\frac{\partial F}{\partial y'}\right) = 0$$

$$\Rightarrow \quad 2(x - y) - \frac{d}{dx}(2y') = 0$$

$$\Rightarrow \quad x - y - y'' = 0$$

$$\Rightarrow \quad y'' + y = x$$

AE is $\quad m^2 + 1 = 0 \Rightarrow m = \pm i$

$\therefore \quad CF = C_1 \cos x + C_2 \sin x$

$$PI = \frac{1}{D^2 + 1}(x) = (1 + D^2)^{-1} x = (1 - D^2 + \ldots)x$$

$$= x$$

Thus, $y = C_1 \cos x + C_2 \sin x + x$

From boundary conditions

$$y(0) = 0,\ y(\pi/2) = 0$$

$$\Rightarrow \quad 0 = C_1 + 0 + 0,\ 0 = 0 + C_2 + \frac{\pi}{2}$$

$$\Rightarrow \quad C_1 = 0,\ C_2 = -\frac{\pi}{2}$$

Hence, required extremal is

$$y = -\frac{\pi}{2}\sin x + x$$

or

$$y = x - \frac{\pi}{2}\sin x$$

***Example 2.*** *Find the extremal of the functional* $\int_0^1 (y^2 + y'^2)dx$, *where* $y(0) = 0,\ y(1) = 1$.

**Solution.** Here, $F(x, y, y') = y^2 + y'^2$

$$\Rightarrow \quad \frac{\partial F}{\partial y} = 2y + 0 = 2y$$

$$\frac{\partial F}{\partial y'} = 0 + 2y' = 2y'$$

From Euler's equation, we get

$$2y - 2y'' = 0$$

$$\Rightarrow \quad y'' - y = 0 \qquad \ldots\text{(i)}$$

Alternatively, here $x$ is absent in $F$

$$\Rightarrow \quad \frac{d}{dx}\left(F - y'\frac{\partial F}{\partial y'}\right) = 0$$

$$\Rightarrow \quad \frac{d}{dx}(y^2 + y'^2 - 2y'^2) = 0$$

$$\Rightarrow \quad \frac{d}{dx}(y^2 - y'^2) = 0$$

$$\Rightarrow \quad 2yy' - 2y'y'' = 0$$

$$\Rightarrow \quad y'' - y = 0 \qquad (\because y' \neq 0)$$

AE is $\quad m^2 - 1 = 0 \Rightarrow m = \pm 1$

$\therefore$ Solution of Eq. (i) is

$$y = C_1 \cosh x + C_2 \sinh x$$

Where $C_1$ and $C_2$ are arbitrary constants.

From given boundary conditions

$$y(0) = 0,\ y(1) = 1$$

$$\Rightarrow \quad C_1 = 0,\quad 1 = C_1 \cosh 1 + C_2 \sinh 1$$

$$\Rightarrow \quad C_1 = 0,\ C_2 = \frac{1}{\sinh 1}$$

$\therefore$ Required extremal is

$$y = \frac{\sinh x}{\sinh 1}$$

***Example 3.*** *Find the extremals of the functional* $\int_{x_0}^{x_1} \frac{y'^2}{x^3} dx$.

**Solution.** $F(x, y, y') = \frac{y'^2}{x^3}$

$$\Rightarrow \quad \frac{\partial F}{\partial y} = 0,\ \frac{\partial F}{\partial y'} = \frac{2y'}{x^3}$$

Here, $y$ is absent.

$$\therefore \quad \frac{\partial F}{\partial y'} = \text{constant}$$

$$\Rightarrow \quad \frac{2y'}{x^3} = \text{constant}$$

$$\Rightarrow \quad y' = Cx^3$$

$$\Rightarrow \quad dy = Cx^3 dx$$

On integrating both sides, we get

$$y = C\frac{x^4}{4} + C'$$

Hence, $y = k_1 x^4 + k_2$ is the required extremal, where $k_1$ and $k_2$ are constants.

***Example 4.*** *Find the extremal of the functional* $\int_1^3 y(3x - y)dx$ *that satisfy the boundary conditions* $y(1) = 1,\ y(3) = \frac{9}{2}$.

**Solution.** $F(x, y, y') = 3xy - y^2$

$$\frac{\partial F}{\partial y} = 3x - 2y,\ \frac{\partial F}{\partial y'} = 0$$

$\therefore$ From Euler's equation

$$\frac{\partial F}{\partial y} - \frac{d}{dx}\left(\frac{\partial F}{\partial y'}\right) = 0$$

$$\Rightarrow \quad (3x-2y)-\frac{d}{dx}(0)=0$$

$$\Rightarrow \quad 3x-2y=0$$

which is the only extremal of the given functional.

Given, $\quad y(1)=1 \Rightarrow 3\times 1-2\times 1=0$

$$\Rightarrow \quad 1=0$$

which is absurd. Hence, the given functional has no extremal.

***Example 5.*** *Show that the shortest distance between two fixed points in a plane is a straight line.*

**Solution.** Let $PA = s$ and $AB = ds$

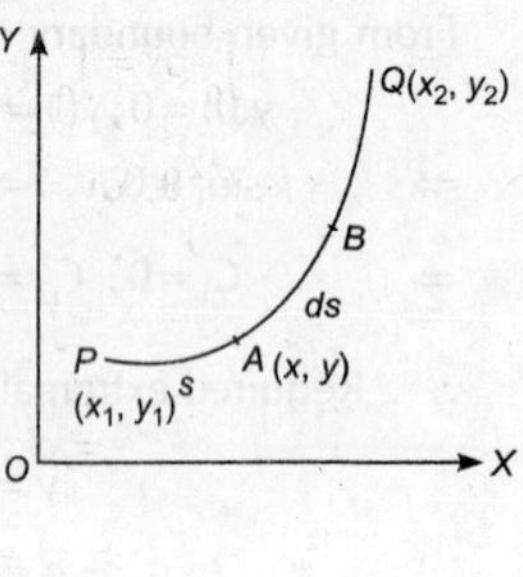


Then, arc length

$$PQ=\int_{x_1}^{x_2} ds$$

$$=\int_{x_1}^{x_2}\sqrt{(dx)^2+(dy)^2}$$

$$=\int_{x_1}^{x_2}\sqrt{1+\left(\frac{dy}{dx}\right)^2}\cdot dx$$

$$=\int_{x_1}^{x_2}(1+y'^2)^{\frac{1}{2}}dx$$

$$F(x,y,y')=(1+y'^2)^{\frac{1}{2}}$$

Here, $F$ is independent of $x$ and $y$

$$\Rightarrow \quad y''\frac{\partial^2 F}{\partial y'^2}=0$$

but $\quad \frac{\partial^2 F}{\partial y'^2}\neq 0$

$$\Rightarrow \quad y''=0$$

On integration giving

$y = C_1x + C_2$ which is a straight line joining $P$ and $Q$.

$\Rightarrow$ Shortest distance between two fixed points in a plane is a straight line.

***Example 6.*** *Find the path on which a particle will take minimum time in sliding from a point $(x_1, y_1)$ to another point $(x_2, y_2)$, if its rate of motion $\upsilon\left(=\frac{dx}{dt}\right)$ is equal to $x$.*

*It is known as the problem of Brachistochrone (shortest time) in horizontal plane.*

**Solution.** Since, $ds=(1+y'^2)^{1/2}dx$

Given, $\quad \upsilon=\frac{ds}{dt}=x$

$$\Rightarrow \quad dt=\frac{ds}{x}$$

$$\Rightarrow \quad t[y(x)]=\int_{x_1}^{x_2}\frac{(1+y'^2)^{1/2}}{x}dx \quad \text{...(i)}$$

where $t[y(x)]$ is the time taken in sliding from $(x_1, y_1)$ to $(x_2, y_2)$.

Here, $\quad F=\frac{(1+y'^2)^{1/2}}{x}$

$$\frac{\partial F}{\partial y'}=\frac{y'}{x(1+y'^2)^{1/2}}$$

Here, $y$ is absent.

$$\Rightarrow \quad \frac{\partial F}{\partial y'}=C$$

$$\Rightarrow \quad \frac{m}{x(1+m^2)^{1/2}}=C \quad \text{(Put } y'=m\text{)}$$

$$\Rightarrow \quad m^2=x^2(1+m^2)C^2=x^2C^2+x^2m^2C^2$$

$$\Rightarrow \quad m^2(1-C^2x^2)=x^2C^2$$

$$\Rightarrow \quad m=\frac{Cx}{\sqrt{1-C^2x^2}} \quad \text{(taking } m>0\text{)}$$

$$\Rightarrow \quad y=\int\frac{x}{\sqrt{\frac{1}{C^2}-x^2}}dx=\int\frac{xdx}{\sqrt{k^2-x^2}} \quad \left(\because k=\frac{1}{C}\right)$$

Put $\quad x=k\sin\theta \quad$ ...(ii)

$$\Rightarrow \quad dx=k\cos\theta\, d\theta$$

$$\therefore \quad y=\int\frac{k^2\sin\theta\cos\theta\, d\theta}{k\cos\theta}=k\int\sin\theta\, d\theta$$

$$=-k\cos\theta+k'$$

$$\Rightarrow \quad y-k'=-k\cos\theta$$

$$\Rightarrow \quad (y-k')^2=k^2-k^2\sin^2\theta=k^2-x^2 \quad \text{[from Eq. (ii)]}$$

$$\Rightarrow \quad x^2+(y-k')^2=k^2$$

which is a family of circles with centre on $y$-axis.

Hence, required path is circle so that particle takes minimum time in sliding from a point $(x_1, y_1)$ to $(x_2, y_2)$.

***Example 7.*** *Find the curve passing through the points $(x_1, y_1)$ and $(x_2, y_2)$ which when rotated about the x-axis gives a minimum surface area.*

**Solution.** Surface area $=2\pi\int_{x_1}^{x_2}y\, ds$

$$\Rightarrow \quad S[y(x)]=2\pi\int_{x_1}^{x_2}y\sqrt{1+y'^2}\,dx$$

Here, $\quad F=y\sqrt{1+y'^2}$

$$\Rightarrow \quad \frac{\partial F}{\partial y}=\sqrt{1+y'^2},\ \frac{\partial F}{\partial y'}=\frac{yy'}{\sqrt{1+y'^2}}$$

Since, $x$ is absent,

$$\therefore \quad F-y'\frac{\partial F}{\partial y'}=\text{constant}$$

$$\Rightarrow \quad y\sqrt{1+y'^2}-\frac{yy'^2}{\sqrt{1+y'^2}}=C$$

$$\Rightarrow \quad \frac{y}{\sqrt{1+y'^2}}=C$$

$$\Rightarrow \quad y^2=C^2(1+y'^2)$$

$$\Rightarrow \quad \frac{y^2-C^2}{C^2}=y'^2$$

$$\Rightarrow \quad y'=\frac{\sqrt{y^2-C^2}}{C}$$

$$\Rightarrow \quad dy = \frac{\sqrt{y^2 - C^2}}{C}\, dx$$

$$\Rightarrow \quad \frac{dy}{\sqrt{y^2 - C^2}} = \frac{dx}{C}$$

On integrating both sides, we get

$$\cosh^{-1}\left(\frac{y}{C}\right) = \frac{1}{C}x + D = \frac{x + B}{C}$$

$$\Rightarrow \quad \frac{y}{C} = \cosh\left(\frac{x + B}{C}\right)$$

$$\Rightarrow \quad y = C\cosh\left(\frac{x + B}{C}\right) \qquad \text{...(i)}$$

which is a catenary, where $B$ and $C$ are two arbitrary constants Eq. (i) is the family of catenaries of two parameter having one, two or no solution.

***Example 8.*** *Find the curve joining two given points P and Q which is traversed by a particle sliding from P to Q in the shortest time (friction and resistance of the medium are neglected).*

**Solution.** Let $P$ be taken as origin and $Q$ be $(x_1, y_1)$. It is required to minimize the time in order to slide from $P$ to $Q$. Let the position of the particle at $R$ at any time $t$.

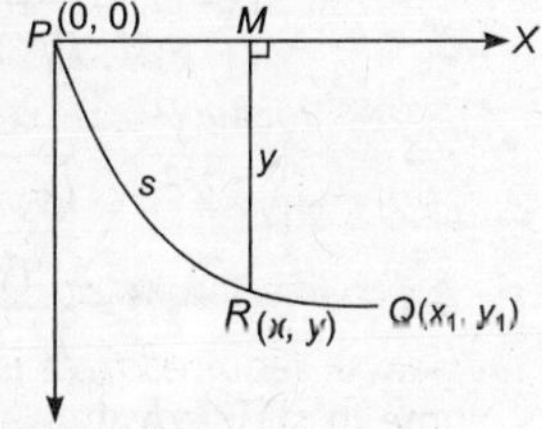


By using Work-Energy theorem, we get

kinetic energy at $R$ – kinetic energy at $P$

= work done in moving the particle from $P$ to $R$.

$$\Rightarrow \quad \frac{1}{2}mv^2 - 0 = mgy$$

$$\Rightarrow \quad v^2 = 2gy \Rightarrow v = \sqrt{2gy}$$

$$\Rightarrow \quad \frac{ds}{dt} = \sqrt{2gy}$$

$$\Rightarrow \quad dt = \frac{ds}{\sqrt{2gy}} = \frac{\sqrt{1 + y'^2}}{\sqrt{2g}\sqrt{y}}\, dx$$

$$\Rightarrow \quad t[y(x)] = \frac{1}{\sqrt{2g}} \int_0^{x_1} \frac{\sqrt{1 + y'^2}}{\sqrt{y}}\, dx$$

Here, $F = \dfrac{\sqrt{1 + y'^2}}{\sqrt{y}}$

Since, $F$ is independent of $x$.

$$\therefore \quad F - y'\frac{\partial F}{\partial y'} = C$$

$$\Rightarrow \quad \frac{\sqrt{1 + y'^2}}{\sqrt{y}} - y' \cdot \frac{1}{\sqrt{y}} \cdot \frac{1}{2\sqrt{1 + y'^2}} \cdot 2y' = C$$

$$\Rightarrow \quad \frac{(1 + y'^2) - y'^2}{\sqrt{y}\sqrt{1 + y'^2}} = C$$

$$\Rightarrow \quad \frac{1}{y(1 + y'^2)} = C^2$$

$$\Rightarrow \quad C^2 y(1 + y'^2) = 1 \Rightarrow y(1 + y'^2) = k$$

$$\Rightarrow \quad 1 + y'^2 = \frac{k}{y} \Rightarrow \qquad y'^2 = \frac{k - y}{y}$$

$$\Rightarrow \quad y' = \sqrt{\frac{k - y}{y}}\, dx$$

$$\Rightarrow \quad dy = \sqrt{\frac{k - y}{y}}\, dx$$

$$\Rightarrow \quad dx = \sqrt{\frac{y}{k - y}}\, dy$$

$$\Rightarrow \quad \int_0^x dx = \int_0^y \sqrt{\frac{y}{k - y}}\, dy$$

Put $y = k\sin^2\theta$, $dy = 2k\sin\theta\cos\theta\, d\theta$

$$\Rightarrow \quad x = \int_0^\theta \sqrt{\frac{k\sin^2\theta}{k\cos^2\theta}} \cdot 2k\sin\theta\cos\theta\, d\theta$$

$$= k\int_0^\theta 2\sin^2\theta\, d\theta = k\int_0^\theta (1 - \cos 2\theta)\, d\theta$$

$$= k\left(\theta - \frac{\sin 2\theta}{2}\right) = \frac{k}{2}(2\theta - \sin 2\theta)$$

Writing $\dfrac{k}{2} = A$ and $2\theta = \phi$, we get

$$x = A(\phi - \sin\phi)$$

$$\because \quad y = k\sin^2\theta = k\left(\frac{1 - \cos 2\theta}{2}\right) = A(1 - \cos\phi)$$

Thus, required curve is

$$x = A(\phi - \sin\phi),\ y = A(1 - \cos\phi)$$

which is a cycloid.

The constant $A$ is found from the fact that curve goes through the point $Q(x_1, y_1)$.

## Geodesics

A geodesics on a surface is a curve along which the distance between two points on the surface is a minimum.

To find the geodesics on a surface is a variational problem involving the conditional extremum.

**(i)** Geodesics on a plane are straight lines.

**(ii)** Geodesics on a sphere of fixed radius are its great circles.

**(iii)** Geodesics on a circular cylinder of fixed radius are circular helix.

## Isoperimetric Problems

Isoperimetric problems includes finding extremals of

$$I[y(x)] = \int_{x_1}^{x_2} F(x, y, y')\, dx$$

when another functional

$$I[y(x)] = \int_{x_1}^{x_2} G(x, y, y')\, dx = \text{constant}$$

such problems are generally solved by method of Lagrange multipliers.

***Example* 9.** *Find the extremal of the functional* $\int_0^2 y'^2 dx$ *under the constraint* $\int_0^2 y\,dx = 1$, *given* $y(0) = 0$ *and* $y(2) = 1$

**Solution.** Let $$I = \int_0^2 y'^2 dx \quad \text{...(i)}$$

and $$J = \int_0^2 y\,dx = 1 \quad \text{...(ii)}$$

Here, $F = y'^2$ and $G = y$

Let $$H = F + \lambda G = y'^2 + \lambda y \quad \text{...(iii)}$$

where $\lambda$ is Lagrange multiplier.

Now, $H$ satisfies Euler's equation, *i.e.*,

$$\frac{\partial H}{\partial y} - \frac{d}{dx}\left(\frac{\partial H}{\partial y'}\right) = 0$$

$$\Rightarrow \quad \lambda - \frac{d}{dx}(2y') = 0 \quad \Rightarrow \lambda - 2y'' = 0$$

$$\Rightarrow \quad y'' = \frac{\lambda}{2}$$

On integrating twice, we get

$$y = \frac{\lambda}{4}x^2 + C_1 x + C_2 \quad \text{...(iv)}$$

where $C_1$ and $C_2$ are arbitrary constants.

Using boundary conditions, *i.e.*,

$y(0) = 0$ and $y(2) = 1$, we get

$C_2 = 0$ and $\lambda + 2C_1 = 1$

$$\Rightarrow \quad C_1 = \frac{1-\lambda}{2}, C_2 = 0$$

$\therefore$ From Eq. (iv), we get

$$y = \frac{\lambda}{4}x^2 + \left(\frac{1-\lambda}{2}\right)x$$

Now, from Eq. (ii), we get

$$\left(\frac{\lambda}{12}x^3 + \frac{1-\lambda}{4}x^2\right)_0^2 = 1$$

$$\Rightarrow \quad \frac{8\lambda}{12} + 1 - \lambda = 1 \Rightarrow \lambda = 0$$

$$\therefore \quad C_1 = \frac{1}{2}$$

$\therefore$ From Eq. (iv) required extremal is $y = \frac{x}{2}$.

***Example* 10.** *Find the curve of length l which passes through the points (0, 0) and (1, 0) and for which the area between the curve and the x-axis is a maximum.*

**Solution.** Here, $l$ is the fixed perimeter of a plane curve passing through two given points $O(0, 0)$ and $A(1, 0)$. Let $S$ be the area enclosed by that plane curve and x-axis. Then, we are to maximinze.

$$S[y(x)] = \int_0^1 y\,dx$$

subject to the constraint.

$$L[y(x)] = \int_0^1 (1+y'^2)^{\frac{1}{2}} dx = l$$

and the boundary conditions

$$y(0) = 0 \text{ and } y(1) = 0$$



Here, $F = y$ and $G = \sqrt{1+y'^2}$

Let $H = F + \lambda G = y + \lambda\sqrt{1+y'^2}$

Now, $H$ satisfies Euler's equation *i.e.*,

$$\frac{\partial H}{\partial y} - \frac{d}{dx}\left(\frac{\partial H}{\partial y'}\right) = 0$$

$$\Rightarrow \quad 1 - \frac{d}{dx}\left(\frac{\lambda y'}{\sqrt{1+y'^2}}\right) = 0$$

Integrating *wrt x*, we get

$$x - \frac{\lambda y'}{\sqrt{1+y'^2}} = c$$

$$\Rightarrow \quad (x-c)^2 = \frac{\lambda^2 y'^2}{(1+y'^2)}$$

$$\Rightarrow \quad \frac{1+y'^2}{y'^2} = \frac{\lambda^2}{(x-c)^2}$$

$$\Rightarrow \quad y'^2 = \frac{(x-c)^2}{\lambda^2 - (x-c)^2}$$

$$\Rightarrow \quad \frac{dy}{dx} = \frac{(x-c)}{\sqrt{\lambda^2 - (x-c)^2}} \quad \text{(with positive sign)}$$

$$\Rightarrow \quad dy = \frac{(x-c)}{\sqrt{\lambda^2 - (x-c)^2}}dx$$

Integrating, we get

$$y = -\sqrt{\lambda^2 - (x-c)^2} + c'$$

$$\Rightarrow \quad (y-c')^2 = \lambda^2 - (x-c)^2$$

$$\Rightarrow \quad (x+c)^2 + (y-c')^2 = \lambda^2$$

which is a circle.

## System of Euler's Equations

We now extend the variational problem to a problem with several variables as function of a single independent variable.

Consider the functional

$$I[y_1, y_2, \ldots, y_n] = \int_{x_1}^{x_2} F(x, y_1, y_2, \ldots, y_n, y_1', y_2', \ldots, y_n')dx \quad \text{...(i)}$$

where boundary conditions of all functions $y_1, y_2, \ldots, y_n$ are given.

A necessary condition for Eq. (i) to be an extremum is that

$$\frac{\partial F}{\partial y_i} - \frac{d}{dx}\left(\frac{\partial F}{\partial y_i'}\right) = 0, \; i = 1, 2, \ldots, n$$

which is the system of $n$ Euler's equations corresponding to $n$ variables $y_1, y_2, \ldots, y_n$.

***Example 11.*** *Find the extremals of the functional* $I[y(x), z(x)] = \int_0^{\frac{\pi}{2}} (y'^2 + z'^2 + 2yz)dx$, *satisfying* $y(0) = 0$, $y\left(\frac{\pi}{2}\right) = 1$, $z(0) = 0$, $z\left(\frac{\pi}{2}\right) = -1$.

**Solution.** Here, $F(x, y, z, y', z') = y'^2 + z'^2 + 2yz$

The system of Euler's equations is given by

$$\frac{\partial F}{\partial y} - \frac{d}{dx}\left(\frac{\partial F}{\partial y'}\right) = 0 \text{ and } \frac{\partial F}{\partial z} - \frac{d}{dz}\left(\frac{\partial F}{\partial z'}\right) = 0$$

$$\Rightarrow \quad 2z - \frac{d}{dx}(2y') = 0 \text{ and } 2y - \frac{d}{dx}(2z') = 0$$

$$\Rightarrow \quad z - y'' = 0 \quad \text{and} \quad y - z'' = 0$$

$$\Rightarrow \quad y'' = z \qquad \text{...(i)}$$

$$\text{and} \quad z'' = y \qquad \text{...(ii)}$$

Differentiating Eq. (i) *wrt* $x$ twice, we get

$$y^{iv} = z''$$

$$\Rightarrow \quad y^{iv} = y \qquad \text{[from Eq. (ii)]}$$

$$\Rightarrow \quad \frac{d^4y}{dx^4} - y = 0 \qquad \text{...(iii)}$$

$$\text{AE is} \quad m^4 - 1 = 0$$

$$\Rightarrow \quad m^4 = 1$$

$$\Rightarrow \quad m = \pm 1, \pm i$$

Hence, general solution of Eq. (iii) is

$$y = c_1e^x + c_2e^{-x} + c_3\cos x + c_4 \sin x \qquad \text{...(iv)}$$

$$\Rightarrow \quad z = y'' = c_1e^x + c_2e^{-x} - c_3\cos x - c_4\sin x \qquad \text{...(v)}$$

From given boundary conditions

$$y(0) = 0, y\left(\frac{\pi}{2}\right) = 1 \text{ and } z(0) = 0, z\left(\frac{\pi}{2}\right) = -1$$

From Eq. (iv), we get

$$c_1 + c_2 + c_3 = 0$$

$$\text{and} \quad c_1e^{\frac{\pi}{2}} + c_2e^{-\frac{\pi}{2}} + c_4 = 1$$

From Eq. (v), we get

$$c_1 + c_2 - c_3 = 0 \text{ and } c_1e^{\frac{\pi}{2}} + c_2e^{-\frac{\pi}{2}} - c_4 = -1$$

$$\Rightarrow \quad c_1 = c_2 = c_3 = 0, c_4 = 1$$

Hence, required extremals are

$$y = \sin x \text{ and } z = -\sin x$$

# Euler's Equation for Higher Order Derivatives

A necessary condition for the functional

$$I[y(x)] = \int_{x_1}^{x_2} F(x, y, y', y'', \ldots, y^{(n)})dx$$

to be extremum is

$$\frac{\partial F}{\partial y} - \frac{d}{dx}\left(\frac{\partial F}{\partial y'}\right) + \frac{d^2}{dx^2}\left(\frac{\partial F}{\partial y''}\right) - \ldots + (-1)^n\frac{d^n}{dx^n}\left(\frac{\partial F}{\partial y^{(n)}}\right) = 0$$

In particular for $n = 2$, we get

$$\frac{\partial F}{\partial y} - \frac{d}{dx}\left(\frac{\partial F}{\partial y'}\right) + \frac{d^2}{dx^2}\left(\frac{\partial F}{\partial y''}\right) = 0$$

***Example 12.*** *Find the curve which extremizes the functional* $\int_0^{\frac{\pi}{4}} (y''^2 - y^2 + x^2)dx$ *under the conditions* $y(0) = 0$, $y'(0) = 1$, $y\left(\frac{\pi}{4}\right) = y'\left(\frac{\pi}{4}\right) = \frac{1}{\sqrt{2}}$.

**Solution.** Here, $\quad F = y''^2 - y^2 + x^2$

The Euler's equation is

$$\frac{\partial F}{\partial y} - \frac{d}{dx}\left(\frac{\partial F}{\partial y'}\right) + \frac{d^2}{dx^2}\left(\frac{\partial F}{\partial y''}\right) = 0$$

$$\Rightarrow \quad -2y - \frac{d}{dx}(0) + \frac{d^2}{dx^2}(2y'') = 0$$

$$\Rightarrow \quad -2y + 2y^{iv} = 0$$

$$\Rightarrow \quad y^{iv} - y = 0$$

$$\Rightarrow \quad \frac{d^4y}{dx^4} - y = 0 \qquad \text{...(i)}$$

$$\text{AE is} \quad m^4 - 1 = 0$$

$$\Rightarrow \quad m^4 = 1$$

$$\Rightarrow \quad m = \pm 1, \pm i$$

$\therefore$ General solution of Eq. (i) is

$$y = c_1e^x + c_2e^{-x} + c_3\cos x + c_4\sin x \qquad \text{...(ii)}$$

$$\Rightarrow \quad y' = c_1e^x - c_2e^{-x} - c_3\sin x + c_4\cos x \qquad \text{...(iii)}$$

From boundary conditions

$$y(0) = 0, y'(0) = 1, y\left(\frac{\pi}{4}\right) = y'\left(\frac{\pi}{4}\right) = \frac{1}{\sqrt{2}}$$

We get

$$c_1 + c_2 + c_3 = 0$$

$$c_1 - c_2 + c_4 = 1$$

$$\text{and} \quad c_1e^{\frac{\pi}{4}} + c_2e^{-\frac{\pi}{4}} + c_3\cdot\frac{1}{\sqrt{2}} + c_4\cdot\frac{1}{\sqrt{2}} = \frac{1}{\sqrt{2}}$$

$$c_1e^{\frac{\pi}{4}} - c_2e^{-\frac{\pi}{4}} - c_3\cdot\frac{1}{\sqrt{2}} + c_4\cdot\frac{1}{\sqrt{2}} = \frac{1}{\sqrt{2}}$$

solving these, we get $c_1 = c_2 = c_3 = 0, c_4 = 1$

Hence, the required curve is $y = \sin x$.

***Example 13.*** *Find the extremal of the functional* $\int_0^1 (1 + y''^2)dx$ *which satisfy* $y(0) = 0$, $y'(0) = 1$, $y(1) = 1$, $y'(1) = 1$.

**Solution.** Here, $F = 1 + y''^2$

From Euler's equation for higher derivative

$$\frac{\partial F}{\partial y} - \frac{d}{dx}\left(\frac{\partial F}{\partial y'}\right) + \frac{d^2}{dx^2}\left(\frac{\partial F}{\partial y''}\right) = 0$$

$$\Rightarrow \quad 0 - 0 + \frac{d^2}{dx^2}(2y'') = 0$$

$$\Rightarrow \quad 2y^{iv} = 0 \Rightarrow y^{iv} = 0$$

$$\Rightarrow \quad \frac{d^4y}{dx^4} = 0$$

By integrating successively four times, we get

$$y = c_1x^3 + c_2x^2 + c_3x + c_4$$

$$\Rightarrow \quad y' = 3c_1x^2 + 2c_2x + c_3$$

From boundary conditions

$$y(0) = 0, y'(0) = 1, y(1) = 1,$$

$$y'(1) = 1$$

We get

$$c_4 = 0, c_3 = 1, c_1 + c_2 + c_3 + c_4 = 1,$$

$$3c_1 + 2c_2 + c_3 = 1$$

$$\Rightarrow \quad c_1 = c_2 = c_4 = 0, c_3 = 1$$

Hence, required extremal is $y = x$.

# Sufficient Conditions for Extrema

## Proper Field

A family of curves $y = y(x, c)$ is said to form a proper field in a given region $D$ of the $xy$-plane if one and only one curve of the family passes through every point of the region $D$. *e.g.*, inside the circle $x^2 + y^2 = 1$, the family of parallel lines $y = x + c$ ($c$ being an arbitrary constant) forms a proper field, since through any point of the above circle there passes one and only one straight line of the family as shown in Fig. (i). On the other hand, the family of parabolas $(x - c)^2 = y + 1$ inside the same circle $x^2 + y^2 = 1$ does not form a proper field, since the parabolas of this family intersect inside the circle as shown in Fig. (ii).

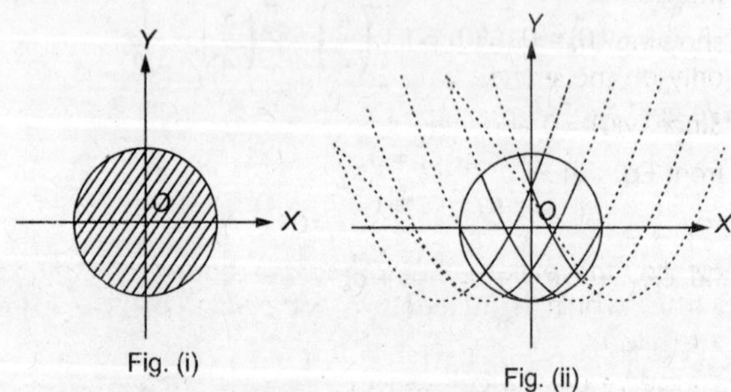


Fig. (i) Fig. (ii)

## Central Field

If all the curves of the family $y = y(x, c)$ pass through a certain point $(x_0, y_0)$, *i.e.*, if they form a pencil of curves, then they do not form a proper field in the region $D$, if the centre of the pencil $(x_0, y_0)$ belongs to $D$. However, if the curves of the pencil cover the entire region $D$ and do not intersect anywhere in this region, with the exception of the centre of the pencil $(x_0, y_0)$, then the family $y = y(x, c)$ is said to form a central field as shown in Fig. (iii).

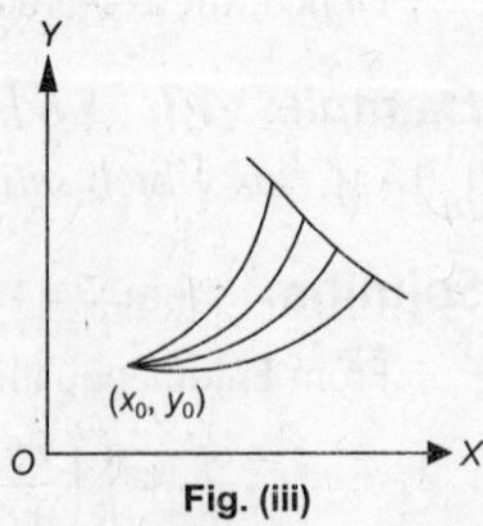


Fig. (iii)

For example, the pencil of curve $y = c \sin x$ for $0 \le x \le a$, $a < \pi$ forms a central field (Fig. (iv)). But the pencil of curves forms a proper field in a sufficiently small neighbourhood of the segment of $x$-axis for $\delta \le x \le a$, where $\delta > 0$, $a < \pi$.

Pencil of curves does not form a proper field in a neighbourhood of the segment of the $x$-axis, for $0 \le x \le a_1$, $a_1 > \pi$.

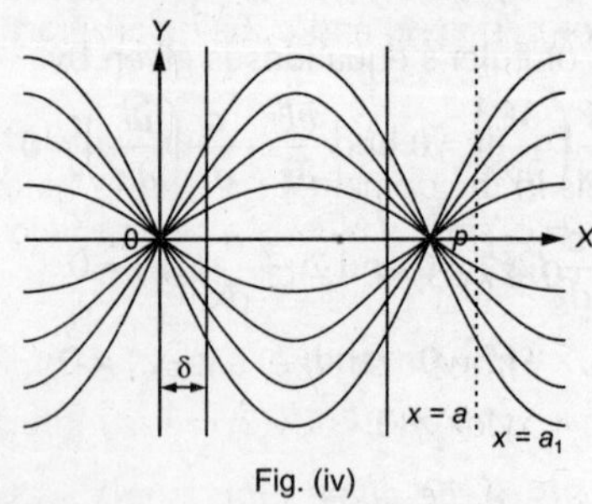


Fig. (iv)

## Extremal Field

If a proper field or a central field is formed by a family of extremals of a given variational problem, then it is called an extremal field.

***Example 14.*** *Discuss the extremal field for the functional*

$$I[y(x)] = \int_0^a (y'^2 - y^2)dx, \; y(0) = 0, \; y(a) = 0.$$

**Solution.** $F = y'^2 - y^2$

Euler's equation is

$$\frac{\partial F}{\partial y} - \frac{d}{dx}\left(\frac{\partial F}{\partial y'}\right) = 0$$

$$\Rightarrow \quad -2y - \frac{d}{dx}(2y') = 0$$

$$\Rightarrow \quad y'' + y = 0$$

$$\Rightarrow \quad (D^2 + 1)y = 0 \qquad \text{...(i)}$$

The general solution of Eq. (i) is

$$y = c_1 \cos x + c_2 \sin x \qquad \text{...(ii)}$$

Since, the required extremal passes through $(0, 0)$

$\therefore$ From Eq. (ii), we get

$$0 = c_1 + 0 \Rightarrow c_1 = 0$$

$\therefore$ Eq. (ii) reduces to

$$y = c_2 \sin x \qquad \text{...(iii)}$$

which pencil curves form as central field on $0 \le a \le x$, $a < \pi$ including, for $c_2 = 0$, the extremal is $y = 0$.

For $a \ge \pi$, the family of extremals Eq. (iii) does not form an extremal field.

***Example 15.*** *Find the proper and central fields of extremals for the functional* $\int_0^{\pi/4} (y'^2 - y^2 + 2x^2 + 4)\, dx$.

**Solution.** $F(x, y, y') = y'^2 - y^2 + 2x^2 + 4$

$$\therefore \quad \text{Euler's equation} \quad \frac{\partial F}{\partial y} - \frac{d}{dx}\left(\frac{\partial F}{\partial y'}\right) = 0$$

$$\Rightarrow \quad -2y - \frac{d}{dx}(2y') = 0$$

$$\frac{d^2y}{dx^2} + y = 0 \quad \text{or} \quad (D^2+1)y = 0 \qquad \text{...(i)}$$

Auxiliary equation of Eq. (i) is $D^2+1=0$, so that $D = \pm i$ and hence solution of Eq. (i) is given by

$y = c_1 \cos x + c_2 \sin x$, $c_1$ and $c_2$ being arbitrary constants ...(ii)

For $c_2 = 0$, Eq. (ii) yields $y = c_1 \cos x$, which is a proper field of extremals in the domain $0 \le x \le \pi/4$. Again, for $c_1 = 0$, Eq. (ii) yields $y = c_2 \sin x$, which is a central field of extremals in the domain $0 \le x \le \pi/4$.

***Example 16.*** *Show that the extremal of the variational problem* $\int_0^2 (y'^2 + x^2)dx$, $y(0) = 1$, $y(2) = 3$ *is included in a proper field of extremals of the given functional.*

**Solution.** Here, $F = y'^2 + x^2$

$\therefore$ Euler's equation is

$$\frac{\partial F}{\partial y} - \frac{d}{dx}\left(\frac{\partial F}{\partial y'}\right) = 0$$

$$\Rightarrow 0 - \frac{d}{dx}(2y') = 0$$

$$\Rightarrow \quad \frac{dy'}{dx} = 0$$

$$\Rightarrow \quad y' = c_1$$

$$\Rightarrow \quad y = c_1 x + c_2 \quad \text{...(i)}$$

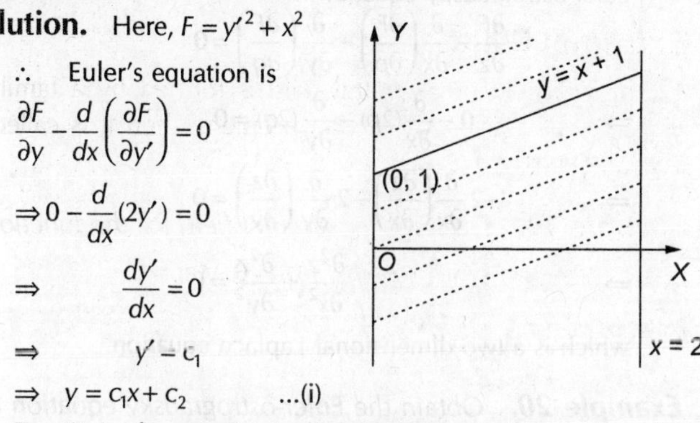


Eq. (i) is the equation of the extremals. Using the given boundary condition $y(0) = 1$ and $y(2) = 3$, Eq. (i) yields $c_2 = 1$ and $2c_1 + c_2 = 3$ so that $c_1 = c_2 = 1$.

Hence, Eq. (i) $\Rightarrow y = x + 1$, which is the extremal of the given variational problem.

For $c_1 = 1$, Eq. (i) reduces to $y = x + c_2$, which is a proper field of the extremals in the domain $0 \le x \le 2$. For $c_2 = 1, y = x + c_2$, yields $y = x + 1$, showing that the extremal $y = x + 1$ is included in the proper field of extremals $y = x + c_2$.

## Working Rule for Testing for a Weak Minimum/Weak Maximum and Strong Minimum/Strong Maximum of an Extremal of a given Functional with help of Legendre Condition

**Legendre Condition** Let $I[y(x)] = \int_{x_1}^{x_2} F(x, y, y')dx$ ...(i)

be a functional with fixed boundaries $P_1(x_1, y_1)$ and $P_2(x_2, y_2)$. Let $F(x, y, y')$ possess a continuous paritial derivative $F_{y',y'}$, *i.e.*, $\frac{\partial^2 F}{\partial y' \partial y'}$. Let C be the curve of the extremal of the given functional which passes thorough $P_1$ and $P_2$. Also, assume that the extremal of the curve C is included in a field of extremals. Then, the following table provides the sufficient conditions for the nature of the extremal of the given functional.

| S.No. | Nature of the extremal of the given functional | Sufficient conditions |
|---|---|---|
| 1. | For a weak minimum to be attained on the extremal on the curve C | $F_{y'y'} > 0$ on C |
| 2. | For a weak maximum to be attained on the extremal on the curve C | $F_{y'y'} < 0$ on C |
| 3. | For a strong minimum to be attained on the extremal on the curve C | $F_{y'y'} \ge 0$ at points close to C and also for arbitrary values of $y'$ |
| 4. | For a strong maximum to be attained on the extremal on the curve C | $F_{y'y'} \le 0$ at points close to C and also for arbitrary values of $y'$ |

***Example 17.*** *Test for an extremum the functional* $I[y(x)] = \int_0^2 (e^{y'} + 3)dx$, $y(0) = 0$, $y(2) = 1$.

**Solution.** Here, $\quad F(x, y, y') = e^{y'} + 3 \qquad$ ...(i)

Euler's equation is

$$\frac{\partial F}{\partial y} - \frac{d}{dx}\left(\frac{\partial F}{\partial y'}\right) = 0 \qquad \text{...(ii)}$$

From Eq. (i), $\frac{\partial F}{\partial y} = 0, \ \frac{\partial F}{\partial y'} = e^{y'}$ so that

$$\frac{d}{dx}\left(\frac{\partial F}{\partial y'}\right) = \frac{de^{y'}}{dx} = e^{y'}y''$$

With these values, Eq. (ii) gives $0 - e^{y'}y'' = 0$ or $y'' = 0$

Integrating it, $y' = C_1$ so that $y = C_1 x + C_2$ ...(iii)

showing that an extremal of the given functional is attained only on the straight lines Eq. (iii).

Since, $y(0) = 0$ and $y(2) = 1$,

from Eq. (iii) $\Rightarrow \quad 0 = C_2$ and $1 = 2C_1$

$$\Rightarrow \quad C_1 = 1/2, C_2 = 0$$

Hence, the extremal satisfying the boundary condition is $y = x/2$ which is included in the central field of extremals $y = C_1 x$.

Since, $F(x, y, y')$ is three times differentiable with respect to $y'$ for any $y'$ and $F_{y'y'} = e^{y'} > 0$ for any value of $y'$, it follows by (Legendre condition) that on the straight line $y = x/2$ a strong minimum is attained.

***Example 18.*** *Test for an extremum the functional* $I[y(x)] = \int_0^a (y'^2 - y^2)\,dx$, $a > 0$; $y(0) = 0$, $y(a) = 0$.

**Solution.** Comparing the given functional with $\int_0^a F(x, y, y')\,dx$,

$$F(x, y, y') = y'^2 - y^2 \qquad \text{...(i)}$$

Euler's equation is

$$\frac{\partial F}{\partial y} - \frac{d}{dx}\left(\frac{\partial F}{\partial y'}\right) = 0 \qquad \text{...(ii)}$$

From Eq. (i), $\frac{\partial F}{\partial y} = -2y, \frac{\partial F}{\partial y'} = 2y'$ and

$$\frac{d}{dx}\left(\frac{\partial F}{\partial y'}\right) = \frac{d(2y')}{dx} = 2y''$$

Using these values, Eq. (ii) reduces to

$$-2y - 2y'' = 0 \text{ or } (D^2 + 1)y = 0, \quad \text{...(iii)}$$

The general solution of Eq. (iii) is $y = c_1 \cos x + c_2 \sin x$ ...(iv)

where $c_1$ and $c_2$ are arbitrary constants.

Since, $y(0) = 0$ and $y(a) = 0$, Eq. (iv) gives $0 = c_1$ and $0 = c_2 \sin a$, if $a \neq n\pi$ where $n$ is an integer, then $c_1 = 0$ and $c_2 = 0$. Thus, for $a \neq n\pi$ an extremum may be attained only on the straight line $y = 0$. If $a < \pi$, then the pencil of extremals $y = c_2 \sin x$ with centre at $(0, 0)$ forms a central field.

For $a > \pi$ extremals $y = c_2 \sin x$ neither forms proper field nor central field.

Now, $F_{y'y'} = 2 > 0, \ \forall y'$

$\Rightarrow$ A strong minimum is attained on $y = 0$ for $a < \pi$.

But for $a > \pi$, minimum is not attained on $y = 0$.

## Euler-ostrogradsky Equation

**1.** Consider the functional dependent on the functions of several independent variables, *i.e.*,

$$I[z(x, y)] = \iint_D F(x, y, z, p, q)\, dx\, dy$$

where $p = \frac{\partial z}{\partial x}, q = \frac{\partial z}{\partial y}$ ...(i)

We assume that $F$ is thrice differentiable. The values of $z(x, y)$ are given on the boundary of the some closed region (Domain) $D$.

The functional Eq. (i) has an extremum or on the extremizing surface $z = z(x, y)$ we must have

$$\frac{\partial z}{\partial z} - \frac{\partial}{\partial x}\left(\frac{\partial F}{\partial p}\right) - \frac{\partial}{\partial y}\left(\frac{\partial F}{\partial q}\right) = 0 \quad \text{...(ii)}$$

which is known as Euler-ostrogradsky equation.

**2.** System of Euler-ostrogradsky equation for extremizing the functional

$$I[z(x_1, x_2, \ldots, x_n)] = \iint \ldots \int_D F(x_1, x_2, \ldots, x_n, z_1, p_1, p_2, \ldots, p_n) dx_1, dx_2, \ldots, dx_n$$

where $p_i = \frac{\partial z}{\partial x_i}$ is given by

$$\frac{\partial F}{\partial z} - \sum_{i=1}^{n} \frac{\partial}{\partial x_i}\left(\frac{\partial F}{\partial p_i}\right) = 0 \quad \text{...(iii)}$$

**3.** Euler-ostrogradsky equation for extremizing the functional containing higher order derivative *i.e.*,

$I[z(x, y)] = \iint_D F(x, y, z, p, q, r, s, t)\, dx\, dy$ is given by

$$\frac{\partial F}{\partial z} - \frac{\partial}{\partial x}\left(\frac{\partial F}{\partial p}\right) - \frac{\partial}{\partial y}\left(\frac{\partial F}{\partial q}\right) + \frac{\partial^2}{\partial x^2}\left(\frac{\partial F}{\partial r}\right) + \frac{\partial^2}{\partial x \partial y}\left(\frac{\partial F}{\partial z}\right) + \frac{\partial^2}{\partial y^2}\left(\frac{\partial F}{\partial t}\right) = 0 \quad \text{...(iv)}$$

where $p = \frac{\partial z}{\partial x}, q = \frac{\partial z}{\partial y}, r = \frac{\partial^2 z}{\partial x^2}, s = \frac{\partial^2 z}{\partial x \partial y}, t = \frac{\partial^2 z}{\partial y^2}$

***Example 19.*** *Obtain the Euler-ostrogradsky equation for* $I[z(x, y)] = \iint_D (p^2 + q^2)\, dx\, dy$, *where the values of z are prescribed on the boundary C of the domain D.*

**Solution.** Here, $F(x, y, z, p, q) = p^2 + q^2$

$$\Rightarrow \quad \frac{\partial F}{\partial z} = 0, \frac{\partial F}{\partial p} = 2p, \frac{\partial F}{\partial q} = 2q$$

Euler-ostrogradsky equation is

$$\frac{\partial F}{\partial z} - \frac{\partial}{\partial x}\left(\frac{\partial F}{\partial p}\right) - \frac{\partial}{\partial y}\left(\frac{\partial F}{\partial q}\right) = 0$$

$$\Rightarrow \quad 0 - \frac{\partial}{\partial x}(2p) - \frac{\partial}{\partial y}(2q) = 0$$

$$\Rightarrow \quad -2\frac{\partial}{\partial x}\left(\frac{\partial z}{\partial x}\right) - 2\frac{\partial}{\partial y}\left(\frac{\partial z}{\partial y}\right) = 0$$

$$\Rightarrow \quad \frac{\partial^2 z}{\partial x^2} + \frac{\partial^2 z}{\partial y^2} = 0$$

which is a two dimensional Laplace equation.

***Example 20.*** *Obtain the Euler-ostrogradsky equation for*

$$I[z(x, y)] = \iint_D \{p^2 + q^2 + 2z\, f(x, y)\}\, dx\, dy,$$

*where the values of z are prescribed on the boundary C of the domain D.*

**Solution.** Here, $F(x, y, z, p, q) = p^2 + q^2 + 2z\, f(x, y)$

$$\Rightarrow \quad \frac{\partial F}{\partial z} = 2f(x, y), \frac{\partial F}{\partial p} = 2p, \frac{\partial F}{\partial q} = 2q$$

Now, Euler-ostrogradsky equation is

$$\frac{\partial F}{\partial z} - \frac{\partial}{\partial x}\left(\frac{\partial F}{\partial p}\right) - \frac{\partial}{\partial y}\left(\frac{\partial F}{\partial q}\right) = 0$$

$$\Rightarrow \quad 2f(x, y) - \frac{\partial}{\partial x}(2p) - \frac{\partial}{\partial y}(2q) = 0$$

$$\Rightarrow \quad \frac{\partial^2 z}{\partial x^2} + \frac{\partial^2 z}{\partial y^2} = f(x, y)$$

which is well known Poisson's equation.

***Example 21.*** *Obtain the Euler-ostrogradsky equation for* $I[u(x, y, z)] = \iiint_D \{(\partial u/\partial x)^2 + (\partial u/\partial y)^2 + (\partial u/\partial z)^2\}\, dx\, dy\, dz$ *where the values of u are prescribed on the boundary C of the domain D.*

**Solution.** Let $p_1 = \partial u/\partial x, p_2 = \partial u/\partial y, p_3 = \partial u/\partial z$. Then, the given functional can be rewritten as

$$I[u(x, y, z)] = \iiint_D (p_1^2 + p_2^2 + p_3^2)\, dx\, dy\, dz \quad \text{...(i)}$$

Comparing Eq. (i) with $\iiint_D F(x,y,z,u,p_1,p_2,p_3)\,dx\,dy\,dz$, we get

$$F(x,y,z,u,p_1,p_2,p_3) = p_1^2 + p_2^2 + p_3^2 \quad \text{...(ii)}$$

Now, by using system of Euler-ostrogradsky equation, we have

$$\frac{\partial F}{\partial u} - \frac{\partial}{\partial x}\left(\frac{\partial F}{\partial p_1}\right) - \frac{\partial}{\partial y}\left(\frac{\partial F}{\partial p_2}\right) - \frac{\partial}{\partial z}\left(\frac{\partial F}{\partial p_3}\right) = 0$$

$$\Rightarrow\ 0 - \frac{\partial}{\partial x}(2p_1) - \frac{\partial}{\partial y}(2p_2) - \frac{\partial}{\partial z}(2p_3) = 0, \quad \text{[using Eq. (ii)]}$$

or
$$\frac{\partial}{\partial x}\left(\frac{\partial u}{\partial x}\right) + \frac{\partial}{\partial y}\left(\frac{\partial u}{\partial y}\right) + \frac{\partial}{\partial z}\left(\frac{\partial u}{\partial z}\right) = 0$$

or
$$\frac{\partial^2 u}{\partial x^2} + \frac{\partial^2 u}{\partial y^2} + \frac{\partial^2 u}{\partial z^2} = 0$$

***Example* 22.** *Find the fourth order partial differential equation satisfied by the function extremizing the functional $I[z(x,y)] = \iint_D (r^2 + t^2 + 2s^2)\,dx\,dy$, where the values of z are prescribed on the boundary C of the domain D.*

**Solution.** Here, $F(x,y,z,p,q,r,s,t) = r^2 + t^2 + 2s^2$

By using Euler-ostrogradsky for extremizing the higher order derivative functional is

$$\frac{\partial F}{\partial z} - \frac{\partial}{\partial x}\left(\frac{\partial F}{\partial p}\right) - \frac{\partial}{\partial y}\left(\frac{\partial F}{\partial q}\right) + \frac{\partial^2}{\partial x^2}\left(\frac{\partial F}{\partial r}\right) + \frac{\partial^2}{\partial x \partial y}\left(\frac{\partial F}{\partial s}\right) + \frac{\partial^2}{\partial y^2}\left(\frac{\partial F}{\partial t}\right) = 0$$

$$\Rightarrow\quad 0 - 0 - 0 + \frac{\partial^2}{\partial x^2}(2r) + \frac{\partial^2}{\partial x \partial y}(4s) + \frac{\partial^2}{\partial y^2}(2t) = 0$$

$$\Rightarrow\quad 2\frac{\partial^2}{\partial x^2}\left(\frac{\partial^2 z}{\partial x^2}\right) + 4\frac{\partial^2}{\partial x \partial y}\left(\frac{\partial^2 z}{\partial x \partial y}\right) + 2\frac{\partial^2}{\partial y^2}\left(\frac{\partial^2 z}{\partial y^2}\right) = 0$$

$$\Rightarrow\quad \frac{\partial^4 z}{\partial x^4} + 2\frac{\partial^4 z}{\partial x^2 \partial y^2} + \frac{\partial^4 z}{\partial y^4} = 0$$

which is a biharmonic equation.

# Variational Problems with Natural Boundary Conditions

In a variational problem, if one or both the boundary conditions are not prescribed, then added condition is called natural boundary condition.

**1.** Let the problem of optimizing the functional

$$I[y(x)] = \int_{x_1}^{x_2} F(x,y,y')\,dx \quad \text{...(i)}$$

and $y(x_1)$ and $y(x_2)$ may or may not be prescribed. Then, for the extremizing functional Eq. (i). Euler's equation is $\frac{\partial F}{\partial y} - \frac{d}{dx}\left(\frac{\partial F}{\partial y'}\right) = 0$ and the natural boundary condition

$$\left.\frac{\partial F}{\partial y'}\right|_{x_1} = 0; \text{ if } y(x_1) \text{ is not prescribed.}$$

and $$\left.\frac{\partial F}{\partial y'}\right|_{x_2} = 0, \text{ if } y(x_2) \text{ is not prescribed.}$$

**2.** For the extremizing functional

$$I[y(x), z(x)] = \int_{x_1}^{x_2} F(x,y,z,y',z')\,dx$$

Euler's equations are

$$\frac{\partial F}{\partial y} - \frac{d}{dx}\left(\frac{\partial F}{\partial y'}\right) = 0,$$

$$\frac{\partial F}{\partial z} - \frac{d}{dx}\left(\frac{\partial F}{\partial z'}\right) = 0$$

and natural boundary conditions are $\frac{\partial F}{\partial y'} = 0$, if $y(x)$ is not prescribed at an end point and $\frac{\partial F}{\partial z'} = 0$, if $z(x)$ is not prescribed at an end point.

**3.** For extremizing the functional

$$I[y(x)] = \int_{x_1}^{x_2} F(x,y,y',y'')\,dx$$

Euler's equation is

$$\frac{\partial F}{\partial y} - \frac{d}{dx}\left(\frac{\partial F}{\partial y'}\right) + \frac{d^2}{dx^2}\left(\frac{\partial F}{\partial y''}\right) = 0$$

and the natural boundary conditions are

$\frac{\partial F}{\partial y} - \frac{d}{dx}\left(\frac{\partial F}{\partial y'}\right) = 0$, if $y(x)$ is not prescribed at an end point and

$\frac{\partial F}{\partial y''} = 0$, if $y'(x)$ is not prescribed at an end point.

***Example* 23.** *Find the extremals of the functional $I[y(x)] = \int_0^1 (y'^2 - y^2)\,dx$ subject to the following boundary conditions*

*(i)* $y(0) = 0, y(1) = 1$

*(ii)* $y(0) = 0$

*(iii)* $y(1) = 1$

*(iv) Neither $y(0)$ nor $y(1)$ is specified.*

**Solution.** Here, $F = y'^2 - y^2$

From Euler's equation, we have

$$\frac{\partial F}{\partial y} - \frac{d}{dx}\left(\frac{\partial F}{\partial y'}\right) = 0$$

$$\Rightarrow\quad -2y - \frac{d}{dx}(2y') = 0 \Rightarrow y'' + y = 0$$

$$\Rightarrow\quad (D^2 + 1)y = 0$$

$$\Rightarrow\quad y = c_1 \cos x + c_2 \sin x$$

(i) $y(0) = 0, y(1) = 1$

$$\Rightarrow c_1 = 0, c_2 \sin 1 = 1 \Rightarrow c_1 = 0, c_2 = \frac{1}{\sin 1}$$

$$\therefore \text{ The extremal is } y(x) = \frac{\sin x}{\sin 1}$$

(ii) $y(0) = 0 \Rightarrow c_1 = 0$

Here, $y(x_2)$ is not prescribed.

$$\Rightarrow \left.\frac{\partial F}{\partial y'}\right|_{x_2} = 0 \Rightarrow 2y'(x_2) = 0$$

$$\Rightarrow y'(x_2) = 0 \Rightarrow y'(1) = 0$$

$$\Rightarrow (-c_1 \sin x + c_2 \cos x)_{x=1} = 0 \qquad (\because x_2 = 1)$$

$$\Rightarrow c_2 \cos 1 = 0 \qquad (\because c_1 = 0)$$

$$\Rightarrow c_2 = 0 \qquad (\text{since } \cos 1 \neq 0)$$

$\therefore$ Required extremal is $y(x) = 0$

(iii) $y(1) = 1$

$$\Rightarrow c_1 \cos 1 + c_2 \sin 1 = 1 \qquad \text{...(i)}$$

Here, $y(x_1)$ is not prescribed.

$$\therefore \left.\frac{\partial F}{\partial y'}\right|_{x_1} = 0 \Rightarrow y'(x_1) = 0$$

$$\Rightarrow y'(0) = 0 \qquad (\because x_1 = 0)$$

$$\Rightarrow (-c_1 \sin x + c_2 \cos x)_{x=0} = 0$$

$$\Rightarrow c_2 = 0$$

From Eq. (i), $c_1 = \dfrac{1}{\cos 1}$

$\therefore$ Extremal is $y(x) = \dfrac{\cos x}{\cos 1}$

(iv) Neither $y(x_1)$ nor $y(x_2)$ is given

$$\Rightarrow \left.\frac{\partial F}{\partial y'}\right|_{x_1} = 0 \text{ and } \left.\frac{\partial F}{\partial y'}\right|_{x_2} = 0$$

$$\Rightarrow y'(x_1) = 0, \; y'(x_2) = 0$$

$$\Rightarrow y'(0) = 0, \; y'(1) = 0$$

$$\Rightarrow c_2 = 0, \; -c_1 \sin 1 = 0$$

$$\Rightarrow c_2 = 0, \; c_1 = 0 \qquad (\because \sin 1 \neq 0)$$

$\therefore$ Extremal is $y(x) = 0$

## Variational Problems with Moving Boundaries and Transversality Conditions

Let the functional $I[y(x)] = \int_{x_1}^{x_2} F(x, y, y')\, dx$ ...(i)

in which the boundary points are not specified, but are to be determined along the unknown function.

*i.e.*, $x_1$ and $x_2$ are not specified but $(x_1, y_1)$ and $(x_2, y_2)$ lie on the curves.

Let $F$ does not involve $x$ and $y$.

Suppose, the boundary point $(x_2, y_2)$ moves along the curve $y = \psi(x)$. Then, the sufficient condition to determine the extremals of the pencil $y = y(x, c)$ on which functional (i) attains extremum is given by

$$F + (\psi' - y')\frac{\partial F}{\partial y'} = 0 \text{ at } x = x_2 \qquad \text{...(ii)}$$

which is known as transversality condition.

If the boundary point $(x_1, y_1)$ moves along the curve $y = \phi(x)$, then as above transversality condition is

$$F + (\phi' - y')\frac{\partial F}{\partial y'} = 0 \text{ at } x = x_1 \qquad \text{...(iii)}$$

### Particular Case

There is a particular situation when the transversality condition Eq. (ii) reduces to the orthogonality condition. Suppose, the function $F(x, y, y')$ in Eq. (i) is given by

$$F(x, y, y') = A(x, y) \cdot (1 + y'^2)^{1/2}$$

where $A(x, y) \neq 0$ at the movable boundary point $(x_2, y_2)$. In this case the transversality condition takes the form

$$A(x, y) \cdot (1 + y'^2)^{1/2} + \frac{A(x, y)y'}{(1 + y'^2)^{1/2}} \cdot (\psi' - y') = 0$$

$$\Rightarrow \frac{A(x, y)(1 + \psi' y')}{(1 + y'^2)^{1/2}} = 0$$

$$\Rightarrow 1 + \psi' y' = 0 \qquad [\text{since } A(x, y) \neq 0]$$

$$\Rightarrow \psi' = -\frac{1}{y'} \text{ at } x = x_2$$

***Example 24.*** *Find the shortest distance between the point* (1, 0) *and the ellipse* $4x^2 + 9y^2 = 36$.

**Solution.** We have to find the shortest distance $P_1(1, 0)$ and $P_2(x_2, y_2)$, where $P_2$ lies on the ellipse $4x^2 + 9y^2 = 36$ ...(i)

The arc length $P_1P_2$ of the minimizing curve $y = y(x)$ is given by

$$I[y(x)] = \int_1^{x_2} (1 + y'^2)^{1/2} dx \qquad \text{...(ii)}$$

where the end point $P_1(1, 0)$ is fixed while the end $P_2(x_2, y_2)$ lies on Eq. (i).

Here, $F = (1 + y'^2)^{1/2}$

Since, $F$ is independent of $x$ and $y$.

Euler's equation (extended form) reduces to

$$y'' \frac{\partial^2 F}{\partial y'^2} = 0$$

$$\Rightarrow y'' = 0 \qquad \left(\because \frac{\partial^2 F}{\partial y'^2} \neq 0\right)$$

$$\Rightarrow y = c_1 x + c_2 \qquad \text{...(iii)}$$

which is a straight line along which the required shortest distance is attained.

$\therefore$ Eq. (iii) must pass through $P_1(1, 0)$.

$$\Rightarrow c_1 + c_2 = 0 \Rightarrow c_2 = -c_1$$

$\Rightarrow$ Eq. (iii) becomes $y(x) = c_1 x - c_1 = c_1(x - 1)$

Also, it must pass through $(x_2, y_2)$.

$$\Rightarrow y_2 = c_1(x_2 - 1) \qquad \text{...(iv)}$$

Now, from Eq. (i) $y = \dfrac{2}{3}\sqrt{9 - x^2} = \psi(x)$ (say) ...(v)

Here, the end $P_2(x_2, y_2)$ lies on Eq. (i) *i.e.*,

$$4x_2^2 + 9y_2^2 = 36 \qquad ...(vi)$$

Now, by using transversality condition for $\psi(x)$, we get

$$[F + (\psi' - y')F_{y'}]_{x=x_2} = 0$$

$$\Rightarrow \left[\sqrt{1+y'^2} + \left(\frac{2}{3}\cdot\frac{1}{2}\cdot\frac{-2x}{\sqrt{9-x^2}} - y'\right)\cdot\frac{1}{2}\cdot\frac{2y'}{\sqrt{1+y'^2}}\right]_{x=x_2} = 0$$

$$\Rightarrow \quad 1 + c_1^2 - \frac{2x_2c_1}{-3\sqrt{9-x_2^2}} - c_1^2 = 0 \qquad (\because y' = c_1)$$

$$\Rightarrow \quad 3\sqrt{9-x_2^2} = 2x_2c_1$$

$$\Rightarrow \quad 9(9-x_2^2) = 4x_2^2c_1^2 \qquad ...(vii)$$

From Eqs. (iv) and (vi), we get

$$4x_2^2 + 9c_1^2(x_2-1)^2 = 36$$

$$\Rightarrow \quad 4(9-x_2^2) = 9c_1^2(x_2-1)^2 \qquad ...(viii)$$

Dividing Eq. (vii) by Eq. (viii), we get

$$\frac{9}{4} = \frac{4}{9}\frac{x_2^2}{(x_2-1)^2} \Rightarrow \frac{x_2}{x_2-1} = \frac{9}{4}$$

$$\Rightarrow 9x_2 - 9 = 4x_2 \quad \Rightarrow \quad 5x_2 = 9$$

$$\Rightarrow \quad x_2 = \frac{9}{5}$$

From Eq. (vii), we get

$$3\sqrt{9-\frac{81}{25}} = 2\times\frac{9}{5}\times c_1 \Rightarrow 3\times\frac{12}{5} = 2\times\frac{9}{5}\times c_1$$

$$\Rightarrow \quad c_1 = 2$$

$\therefore$ From Eq. (iv), we get

$$y_2 = 2\left(\frac{9}{5}-1\right) = 2\times\frac{4}{5} = \frac{8}{5}$$

$$\Rightarrow \quad P_2(x_2, y_2) \equiv P_2\left(\frac{9}{5}, \frac{8}{5}\right)$$

$\therefore$ Required shortest distance

$$= \sqrt{\left(\frac{9}{5}-1\right)^2 + \left(\frac{8}{5}-0\right)^2} = \sqrt{\frac{16}{25}+\frac{64}{25}}$$

$$= \sqrt{\frac{80}{25}} = \frac{4\sqrt{5}}{5}$$

***Example 25.*** *Find the shortest distance between the parabola $y = x^2$ and the straight line $y = x - 5$.*

**Solution.** Let $P_1(x_1, y_1)$ lies on straight line

$$y = x - 5 = \phi(x) \text{ (say)} \qquad ...(i)$$

and $P_2(x_2, y_2)$ lies on parabola

$$y = x^2 = \psi(x) \text{ (say)} \qquad ...(ii)$$

$$\Rightarrow \quad y_1 = x_1 - 5,\ y_2 = x_2^2$$

The arc length $P_1P_2$ for the minimizing curve $y = y(x)$ is given by

$$I[y(x)] = \int_{x_1}^{x_2} (1+y'^2)^{\frac{1}{2}} dx$$

for which, we get

$$y = c_1x + c_2 \qquad ...(iii)$$

Since, $P_1$ and $P_2$ lie on Eq. (iii), we get

$$y_1 = c_1x_1 + c_2 \text{ and } y_2 = c_1x_2 + c_2$$

From transversality conditions

$$[F + (\phi' - y')F_{y'}]_{x=x_1} = 0$$

and $$[F + (\psi' - y')F_{y'}]_{x=x_2} = 0$$

$$\Rightarrow \quad \sqrt{1+c_1^2} + (1-c_1)\cdot\frac{c_1}{\sqrt{1+c_1^2}} = 0$$

$$\Rightarrow \quad c_1 = -1$$

and $$\sqrt{1+c_1^2} + (2x_2 - c_1)\cdot\frac{c_1}{\sqrt{1+c_1^2}} = 0$$

$$\Rightarrow \quad 1 + 2x_2c_1 = 0$$

$$\Rightarrow \quad x_2 = -\frac{1}{2c_1} = \frac{1}{2}$$

$$\therefore \quad y_2 = \frac{1}{4}$$

$$\because \quad y_2 = c_1x_2 + c_2 \quad \Rightarrow \quad \frac{1}{4} = -1\times\frac{1}{2} + c_2$$

$$\Rightarrow \quad c_2 = \frac{3}{4}$$

$\Rightarrow$ From Eq. (iii) required extremal is

$$y = -x + \frac{3}{4}$$

Since, $$y_1 = c_1x_1 + c_2 = -x_1 + \frac{3}{4}$$

but $$y_1 = x_1 - 5$$

$$\Rightarrow \quad x_1 - 5 = -x_1 + \frac{3}{4}$$

$$\Rightarrow \quad 2x_1 = \frac{23}{4}$$

$$\Rightarrow \quad x_1 = \frac{23}{8}$$

$$\therefore \quad y_1 = \frac{23}{8} - 5 = -\frac{17}{8}$$

$$\Rightarrow \quad P_1P_2 = \sqrt{\left(\frac{23}{8}-\frac{1}{2}\right)^2 + \left(-\frac{17}{8}-\frac{1}{4}\right)^2}$$

$$= \sqrt{\left(\frac{19}{8}\right)^2 + \left(\frac{19}{8}\right)^2} = \frac{19\sqrt{2}}{8}$$

# Boundary value Problems (Rayleigh-Ritz Method)

The solution of Euler's differential equation along with boundary conditions amounts to extremising a certain definite integral. This fact provides a technique of solving a boundary value problem approximately by assuming a trial solution satisfying the given boundary conditions and then extremising the integral whose integrand is found from the given differential equation.

To solve a boundary value problem by Rayleigh-Ritz method, we try to write the given differential equation as the Euler's equation of some variational problem. Then, we reduce this variational problem to a minimizing problem, assuming an approximate solution in the form

$$\bar{y}(x) = y_0(x) + \Sigma c_i\phi_i(x) \quad \text{...(i)}$$

where the trial functions $\phi_i(x)$ satisfy the boundary conditions and $\phi_i(x) = 0$ on the boundary $C$ of its region $R$.

Let the functional which is to be extremised is

$$I = \int_a^b F(x, y, y')\,dx \quad \text{...(ii)}$$

such that $y(a) = \alpha$ and $y(b) = \beta$. Replacing $y$ by $\bar{y}$ in Eq. (ii) and then putting the value of $\bar{y}(x)$ from Eq. (i) into Eq. (ii) giving $I$ as a function of the unknown $c_i$ which is determined by the relation $\frac{dI}{dc_i} = 0$ (condition for extremising $I$)

$$i = 1, 2, \ldots$$

solving these equations, we get the values of $c_i$.

Now, from Eq. (i), we get the desired solution.

***Example 26.*** *Solve the BVP*

$$y'' - y + x = 0 \quad (0 \le x \le 1),$$
$$y(0) = y(1) = 0$$

*by Rayleigh-Ritz method.*

**Solution.** Given, differential equation is $y''-y+x=0$ which solution is equivalent to extremising the integral

$$I = \int_0^1 F(x, y, y')\,dx \quad \text{...(i)}$$

where $F(x, y, y') = 2xy - y^2 - y'^2$

for which Euler's equation

$$\frac{\partial F}{\partial y} - \frac{d}{dx}\left(\frac{\partial F}{\partial y'}\right) = 0$$

gives the differential equation $y'' - y + x = 0$.

Assume that the trial function is

$$\bar{y}(x) = c_0 + c_1x + c_2x^2$$

Given, $y(0) = y(1) = 0$

$$\Rightarrow \quad c_0 = 0, c_2 = -c_1$$

$$\Rightarrow \quad \bar{y}(x) = c_1x(1-x), \bar{y}'(x) = c_1(1-2x)$$

Now, Eq. (i) becomes

$$I = \int_0^1 [2x\bar{y} - (\bar{y})^2 - (\bar{y}')^2]dx$$

$$= \int_0^1 [2xc_1x(1-x) - c_1^2x^2(1-x)^2 - c_1^2(1-2x)^2]dx$$

$$= \int_0^1 [2c_1(x^2 - x^3) - c_1^2(x^2 - 2x^3 + x^4) - c_1^2(1 - 4x + 4x^2)]dx$$

$$= 2c_1\left(\frac{1}{3} - \frac{1}{4}\right) - c_1^2\left(\frac{1}{3} - \frac{1}{2} + \frac{1}{5}\right) - c_1^2\left(1 - 2 + \frac{4}{3}\right)$$

$$\Rightarrow \quad I = \frac{c_1}{6} - \frac{11}{30}c_1^2$$

Now, $\frac{dI}{dc_1} = 0$ (For extremum)

$$\Rightarrow \quad \frac{1}{6} - \frac{11}{15}c_1 = 0$$

$$\Rightarrow \quad c_1 = \frac{5}{22}$$

Thus, the approximate solution is

$$\bar{y}(x) = \frac{5}{22}x(1-x)$$

***Example 27.*** *Find an approximate solution of $y'' + y = -x$, $y(0) = y(1) = 0$ with the integrand $F(x, y, y') = y'^2 - y^2 - 2xy$.*

**Solution.** Here, $I = \int_0^1 (y'^2 - y^2 - 2xy)\,dx$ ...(i)

The given equation $y'' + y = -x$ is the Euler's equation of the variational problem of extremising the integral Eq. (i).

Let approximate solution of $y'' + y = -x$ is

$$y(x) = cx(1-x) = c(x - x^2)$$

$$\Rightarrow \quad y'(x) = c(1-2x)$$

Now, from Eq. (i)

$$I = \int_0^1 [c^2(1-2x)^2 - c^2(x-x^2)^2 - 2xc(x-x^2)]dx$$

$$= \int_0^1 [c^2(1 - 4x + 4x^2 - x^2 + 2x^3 - x^4) - 2c(x^2 - x^3)]dx$$

$$= \frac{3}{10}c^2 - \frac{c}{6}$$

Now, $\frac{dI}{dc} = 0 \Rightarrow \frac{3}{5}c - \frac{1}{6} = 0 \Rightarrow c = \frac{5}{18}$

$$\therefore \quad y(x) = \frac{5}{18}(x - x^2)$$

> ***Note*** Selection of approximate solution may be done from solution
> $$y(x) = (c_1 + c_2x + c_3x^2 + \ldots + c_nx^n)(x - x^2)$$
> one term approximation
> $$y(x) = c_1(x - x^2)$$
> two term approximation
> $$y(x) = (c_1 + c_2x)(x - x^2)$$
> which gives better approximation.
> Evidently, approximate solutions of *ODE* are linearly independent.

***Example 28.*** *Find the approximate solution of $y'' + xy = -x$, $y(0) = y(1) = 0$ and $F(x, y, y') = y'^2 - xy^2 - 2xy$.*

**Solution.** Here, $I = \int_0^1 (y'^2 - xy^2 - 2xy)\,dx$

Let solution is $y(x) = c(x - x^2)$

$$\Rightarrow \quad y'(x) = c(1-2x)$$

$$\therefore \quad I = \int_0^1 [c^2(1-2x)^2 - c^2(x-x^2)^2x - 2cx(x-x^2)]dx$$

$$\frac{dI}{dc} = 0$$

$$\Rightarrow \quad \int_0^1 [c\{(1-2x)^2 - x(x-x^2)^2\} - x(x-x^2)]dx = 0$$

$$\therefore \quad 19c = 5 \text{ or } c = \frac{5}{19}$$

The approximate solution is

$$y(x) = \frac{5}{19}(x - x^2)$$

Better approximation is

$$y(x) = (c_1 + c_2 x)(x - x^2)$$

***Example 29.*** *Find the approximate the smallest eigen value $\lambda$ of $y'' + \lambda y = 0$, $y(0) = y(1) = 0$ and $F(x, y, y') = y'^2 - \lambda y^2$.*

**Solution.** Let solution be $y = c(x - x^2)$

$$\Rightarrow \quad I = \int_0^1 [c^2(1-2x)^2 - \lambda c^2 (x - x^2)^2] dx$$

$$\therefore \quad \frac{dI}{dc} = 0$$

$$\Rightarrow \quad \int_0^1 [2c(1-2x)^2 - \lambda 2c(x-x^2)^2] dx = 0$$

$$\Rightarrow \quad \int_0^1 (1-2x)^2 dx = \lambda \int_0^1 (x - x^2)^2 dx$$

$$\Rightarrow \quad \int_0^1 (1 - 4x + 4x^2)\, dx = \lambda \int_0^1 (x^2 - 2x^3 + x^4)\, dx$$

$$\Rightarrow \quad \left(x - 2x^2 + \frac{4}{3}x^3\right)_0^1 = \lambda \left(\frac{x^3}{3} - \frac{x^4}{2} + \frac{x^5}{5}\right)_0^1$$

$$\Rightarrow \quad \left(1 - 2 + \frac{4}{3}\right) = \lambda \left(\frac{1}{3} - \frac{1}{2} + \frac{1}{5}\right)$$

$$\Rightarrow \quad \frac{3 - 6 + 4}{3} = \lambda \times \frac{10 - 15 + 6}{30} \quad \Rightarrow \lambda = 10$$

which is the least approximate eigen value of the given differential equation.

> ***Note*** From the Strum-Liouville problem it is known that eigen values are given by
> $$\lambda_n = n^2 \pi^2$$
> and smallest one is obtained for $n = 1$
> *i.e.*, $\quad \lambda_1 = \pi^2 = 9.870$

***Example 30.*** *Find the least eigen value of $y'' + \lambda y = 0$, $y'(0) = 0$, $y(1) = 0$ and $F(x, y, y') = y'^2 - \lambda y^2$.*

**Solution.** Here, $\quad I = \int_0^1 (y'^2 - \lambda y^2)\, dx$

Choosing solution in one term approximately

$$y(x) = c(x - 1)$$

$$I = \int_0^1 [c^2 - \lambda c^2 (x-1)^2] dx$$

$$\therefore \quad \frac{dI}{dc} = 0$$

$$\Rightarrow \quad \lambda = \frac{1}{\int_0^1 (x-1)^2 dx} = 3$$

To improve the estimate,

Choosing solution in two term approximately

$$y(x) = (x - 1)(c_1 + c_2 x)$$

$$I = \int_0^1 [(c_1 - c_2)^2 + c_1 c_2^2 x^2 + c_1 c_2 (c_1 - c_2) x - \lambda$$

$$\{c_1^2 + (c_1 - c_2)^2 x^2 + c_2^2 x^4 - 2c_1(c_1 - c_2)x + 2c_2$$

$$(c_1 - c_2)x^3 - 2c_1 c_2 x^3\}] dx$$

$$= (c_1 - c_2)^2 + \frac{4c_2^2}{3} + 2c_2(c_1 - c_2) - \lambda$$

$$\left[c_1^2 + \frac{(c_1 - c_2)^2}{3} + \frac{c_2^2}{5} - c_1(c_1 - c_2) + \frac{c_2}{2}(c_1 - c_2) - 2\frac{c_1 c_2}{3}\right]$$

Now, $\dfrac{dI}{dc_1} = 0, \dfrac{dI}{dc_2} = 0$ gives

$$\frac{2}{3}(3 - \lambda)c_1 - \frac{\lambda}{6}c_2 = 0$$

$$-\frac{\lambda}{6}c_1 + \frac{20 - \lambda}{30}c_2 = 0$$

For non-trivial solution

$$\begin{vmatrix} \frac{2}{3}(3-\lambda) & -\frac{\lambda}{6} \\ -\frac{\lambda}{6} & \frac{20-\lambda}{30} \end{vmatrix} = 0 \Rightarrow \lambda^2 + 92\lambda - 240 = 0$$

$$\Rightarrow \quad \lambda = \frac{-92 + \sqrt{92^2 + 4 \times 240}}{2} > 0$$

$$= -46 + \sqrt{2256} = 2.539$$

which is nearly equal to true value

$$\frac{\pi^2}{4} = 2.467$$

# Partial Differential Equations (By Rayleigh-Ritz Method)

Let the boundary value problem

$$u_{xx} + u_{yy} + qu = r$$

in the region $R$ bounded by the closed curve C.

Let $u(x)$ be prescribed on C.

The corresponding variational problem is to optimize the functional.

$$\iint_R (u_x^2 + u_y^2 - qu^2 + 2ru)\, dx\, dy$$

selecting the trial function such that it satisfies the given condition.

***Example 31.*** *Solve $u_{xx} + u_{yy} = 0$,*

$$|x| \le 1, |y| \le 1;\ u = 0 \text{ on } |x| = 1, u = 1 - x^2 \text{ on } |y| = 1.$$

**Solution.** Let solution be

$$u(x, y) = (1 - x^2)[1 + c(1 - y^2)] \quad \text{...(i)}$$

The required functional is

$$I = \int_{-1}^1 \int_{-1}^1 (u_x^2 + u_y^2)\, dx\, dy \quad \text{...(ii)}$$

From Eq. (i), we get

$$u_x = -2x[1 + c(1 - y^2)]$$

and $\quad u_y = -2yc(1 - x^2)$

$\therefore$ Eq. (ii) becomes

$$I = \int_{-1}^1 \int_{-1}^1 [4x^2\{1 + 2c(1-y^2) + c^2(1-y^2)^2\}$$

$$+ 4y^2 c^2 (1 - 2x^2 + x^4)]\, dx\, dy$$

Now, $\frac{dI}{dc} = 0$

$\Rightarrow \int_{-1}^{1}\int_{-1}^{1}[8x^2(1-y^2) + 8x^2c(1-y^2)^2 + 8y^2c(1-x^2)^2]dxdy = 0$

$\Rightarrow$ Evaluating the integral, we get

$$c = -\frac{5}{8}$$

$$\therefore \quad u(x, y) = (1-x^2)\left[1 - \frac{5}{8}(1-y^2)\right]$$

***Example 32.*** *Solve poisson's equation in a square*

$u_{xx} + u_{yy} = -1, |x| \le 1, |y| \le 1; u = 0$ *at* $x = \pm 1$ *and at* $y = \pm 1$.

**Solution.** Let $u(x, y) = c(1-x^2)(1-y^2)$ the functional is

$$I = \iint_R (u_x^2 + u_y^2 - 2u)\, dxdy$$

$$= \int_{-1}^{1}\int_{-1}^{1} [4c^2x^2(1-y^2)^2 + 4c^2y^2(1-x^2)^2 - 2c(1-x^2)(1-y^2)]dxdy$$

$$= \frac{32}{45}(8c^2 - 5c)$$

$$\frac{dI}{dc} = 0 \Rightarrow c = \frac{5}{16}$$

The approximate solution is

$$u(x, y) = \frac{5}{16}(1-x^2)(1-y^2)$$

***Example 33.*** *Find an estimate of the least eigen value of* $u_{xx} + u_{yy} + \lambda u = 0$ *in the region R bounded by* $x^2 + y^2 = 1$ *and* $u = 0$ *on its boundary.*

**Solution.** Let solution be

$$u(x, y) = c(1 - x^2 - y^2)$$

and functional $I = \iint_R (u_x^2 + u_y^2 - \lambda u^2)dxdy$

$$\Rightarrow \quad I = \iint_R [4c^2x^2 + 4c^2y^2 - \lambda c^2(1-x^2-y^2)^2]dxdy$$

$$\frac{dI}{dc} = 0$$

$$\Rightarrow \quad \iint_R (8cx^2 + 8cy^2 - 2\lambda c(1-x^2-y^2)^2]dxdy = 0$$

$$\Rightarrow \quad \lambda = \frac{4\iint_R (x^2+y^2)dxdy}{\iint_R (1-x^2-y^2)^2 dxdy}$$

Putting $x = r\cos\theta, y = r\sin\theta$ and

$\Rightarrow \quad dxdy = rdrd\theta$ with limit $r = 0$ to $1$, $\theta = 0$ to $2\pi$

$$\Rightarrow \quad \lambda = \frac{4\int_0^{2\pi}\int_0^1 r^2 \cdot r\, drd\theta}{\int_0^{2\pi}\int_0^1 (1+r^2)^2 .\, rdr\, d\theta}$$

$$= \frac{4 \times \frac{1}{4}\int_0^{2\pi} d\theta}{\int_0^{2\pi}\left(\frac{1}{2} - \frac{1}{2} + \frac{1}{6}\right)d\theta} = \frac{2\pi}{\frac{2\pi}{6}} = 6$$

# Linear Integral Equations

The most general type of linear integral equation is of the form

$$v(x) \cdot u(x) = f(x) + \lambda \int_a k(x, t)u(t)\,dt \qquad \text{...(i)}$$

where the upper limit may be either variable $x$ or fixed. The functions $f(x)$, $v(x)$ and $k(x, t)$ are known while $u(x)$ is unknown. $\lambda$ is a non-zero real or complex parameter. The function $k(x, t)$ is known as kernel of the integral Eq. (i).

## Types of the Linear Integral Equation

**(i)** If $v(x) \ne 0$, then Eq. (i) is known as linear integral equation of the third kind.

**(ii)** When $v(x) = 0$, then Eq. (i) reduces to

$$f(x) + \lambda \int_a k(x, t)\,u(t)\,dt = 0$$

which is known as linear integral equation of the first kind.

**(iii)** When $v(x) = 1$, then Eq. (i) reduces to

$$u(x) = f(x) + \lambda \int_a k(x, t)u(t)dt$$

which is known as linear integral equation of the second kind.

## 1. Fredholm Integral Equation

A linear integral equation of the form

$$v(x) \cdot u(x) = f(x) + \lambda \int_a^b k(x, t)\,u(t)dt \qquad \text{...(i)}$$

where $a$ and $b$ both are constants, is called Fredholm integral equation.

### (i) Fredholm Integral Equation of the Third Kind

If $v(x) \ne 0$ in Eq. (i), then Eq. (i) is called Fredholm integral equation of the third kind.

### (ii) Fredholm Integral Equation of the Second Kind

Put $v(x) = 1$ in Eq. (i), then integral equation of the form

$$u(x) = f(x) + \lambda \int_a^b k(x, t)u(t)\,dt \qquad \text{...(ii)}$$

is called Fredholm integral equation of the second kind.

Putting $f(x) = 0$ in Eq. (ii), we get

$$u(x) = \lambda \int_a^b k(x, t)u(t)\,dt \qquad \text{...(iii)}$$

which is called homogeneous Fredholm integral equation of the second kind.

### (iii) Fredholm Integral Equation of the First Kind

Put $v(x) = 0$ in Eq. (i), then integral equation of the form

$$f(x) + \lambda \int_a^b k(x, t)u(t)\,dt = 0 \quad \text{...(iv)}$$

is called Fredholm integral equation of the first kind.

## 2. Volterra Integral Equation

A linear integral equation of the form

$$v(x) \cdot u(x) = f(x) + \lambda \int_a^x k(x, t)u(t)\,dt \quad \text{...(i)}$$

where $a$ is fixed (constant) and $x$ is variable which is called Volterra integral equation.

### (i) Volterra Integral Equation of the Third Kind

If $v(x) \neq 0$ in Eq. (i), then Eq. (i) is called Volterra integral equation of the third kind.

### (ii) Volterra Integral Equation of the Second Kind

Put $v(x) = 1$ in Eq. (i), then Eq. (i) takes the form

$$u(x) = f(x) + \lambda \int_a^x k(x, t)u(t)\,dt \quad \text{...(ii)}$$

which is called Volterra integral equation of the second kind. Putting $f(x) = 0$ in Eq. (ii), we get

$$u(x) = \lambda \int_a^x k(x, t)u(t)\,dt \quad \text{...(iii)}$$

which is called homogeneous Volterra integral equation of the second kind.

### (iii) Volterra Integral Equation of the First Kind

Put $v(x) = 0$ in Eq. (i), then Eq. (i) reduces to

$$f(x) + \lambda \int_a^x k(x, t)u(t)\,dt = 0 \quad \text{...(iv)}$$

which is called Volterra integral equation of the first kind.

# Verification of Solutions of Integral Equations

***Example 34.*** *Verify that $u(x) = 1$ is a solution of the Fredholm integral equation*

$$u(x) + \int_0^1 x(e^{xt} - 1)\, u(t)\,dt = e^x - x.$$

**Solution.** Given, $u(x) = 1 \Rightarrow u(t) = 1$

LHS of the given integral equation

$$= 1 + \int_0^1 x(e^{xt} - 1)\,dt = 1 + x\left(\frac{1}{x}e^{xt} - t\right)_0^1$$

$$= 1 + x\left(\frac{1}{x}e^x - 1 - \frac{1}{x}\right) = e^x - x$$

$$= \text{RHS}$$

Hence, $u(x) = 1$ is the solution of given integral equation.

***Example 35.*** *Show that the function $u(x) = e^x\left(2x - \frac{2}{3}\right)$ is the solution of Fredholm integral equation*

$$u(x) + 2\int_0^1 e^{x-t}u(t)\,dt = 2xe^x$$

**Solution.** The given integral equation is

$$u(x) + 2\int_0^1 e^{x-t}u(t)\,dt = 2xe^x \quad \text{...(i)}$$

Given,

$$u(x) = e^x\left(2x - \frac{2}{3}\right) \Rightarrow u(t) = e^t\left(2t - \frac{2}{3}\right)$$

Then, LHS of Eq. (i) is

$$= e^x\left(2x - \frac{2}{3}\right) + 2\int_0^1 e^{x-t}e^t\left(2t - \frac{2}{3}\right)dt$$

$$= e^x\left(2x - \frac{2}{3}\right) + 2e^x\int_0^1 \left(2t - \frac{2}{3}\right)dt$$

$$= e^x\left(2x - \frac{2}{3}\right) + 2e^x\left[t^2 - \frac{2}{3}t\right]_0^1$$

$$= 2xe^x - \frac{2}{3}e^x + \frac{2}{3}e^x = 2xe^x$$

$$= \text{RHS}$$

Hence, $u(x) = e^x\left(2x - \frac{2}{3}\right)$ is the solution of the given integral equation.

***Example 36.*** *Show that the function $u(x) = 1 - x$ is a solution of the Volterra integral equation*

$$\int_0^x e^{x-t}u(t)\,dt = x$$

**Solution.** The given integral equation is

$$\int_0^x e^{x-t}u(t)\,dt = x \quad \text{...(i)}$$

Given that $u(x) = 1 - x \Rightarrow u(t) = 1 - t$

Then, LHS of Eq. (i) is

$$= \int_0^x e^{x-t}(1 - t)\,dt$$

$$= e^x\int_0^x e^{-t}\,dt - e^x\int_0^x te^{-t}dt$$

$$= e^x[-e^{-t}]_0^x + e^x[te^{-t} + e^{-t}]_0^x$$

$$= e^x(1 - e^{-x}) + e^x(xe^{-x} + e^{-x} - 1)$$

$$= x = \text{RHS}$$

Hence, $u(x) = 1 - x$ is the solution of the given integral equation.

***Example 37.*** *Verify that $u(x) = xe^x$ is a solution of the volterra integral equation*

$$u(x) = \sin x + 2\int_0^x \cos(x - t)\, u(t)\,dt$$

**Solution.** The given integral equation is

$$u(x) = \sin x + 2\int_0^x \cos(x-t)\, u(t)\, dt \quad \text{...(i)}$$

$\because$ $u(x) = xe^x \Rightarrow u(t) = te^t$

Then, RHS of Eq. (i) is

$$= \sin x + 2\int_0^x t[e^t \cos(x-t)]dt$$

$$= \sin x + 2\int_0^x t[e^t \cos(t-x)]dt$$

$$= \sin x + 2\left\{\left[t\frac{e^t}{2}\{\cos(t-x)+\sin(t-x)\}\right]_0^x - \int_0^x 1\cdot\frac{e^t}{2}\{\cos(t-x)+\sin(t-x)\}\,dt\right\}$$

[By using $\int e^{ax}\cos(bx+c)\,dx = \frac{e^{ax}}{a^2+b^2}[a\cos(bx+c)+b\sin(bx+c)]$ and on integrating by parts]

$$= \sin x + xe^x - \int_0^x e^t\cos(t-x)\,dt - \int_0^x e^t \sin(t-x)\,dt$$

$$= \sin x + xe^x - \left[\frac{e^t}{2}\{\cos(t-x)+\sin(t-x)\}\right]_0^x - \left[\frac{e^t}{2}\{\sin(t-x)-\cos(t-x)\}\right]_0^x$$

$$= \sin x + xe^x - \left[\frac{e^x}{2} - \frac{1}{2}(\cos x - \sin x)\right] - \left[-\frac{e^x}{2} - \frac{1}{2}(-\sin x - \cos x)\right]$$

$$= xe^x = u(x)$$

Hence, $u(x) = xe^x$ is the solution of the given integral equation.

***Example 38.*** *Verify that the given function $u(x) = \frac{1}{2}$ is the solution of the integral equation*

$$\int_0^x \frac{u(t)}{\sqrt{x-t}}\,dt = \sqrt{x}$$

**Solution.** Here, the given integral equation is

$$\int_0^x \frac{u(t)}{\sqrt{x-t}}\,dt = \sqrt{x}$$

Put $u(x) = \frac{1}{2}$ in the given equation, we get

$$\frac{1}{2}\int_0^x \frac{dt}{\sqrt{x-t}} = \sqrt{x}$$

$\Rightarrow$ $\frac{1}{2}[-2\sqrt{x-t}]_0^x = \sqrt{x}$

$\Rightarrow$ $[\sqrt{x-x}\ \sqrt{x-0}] = \sqrt{x}$

$\Rightarrow$ $\sqrt{x} = \sqrt{x}$ which is an identity.

$\Rightarrow$ $u(x) = \frac{1}{2}$ is the solution of the given integral equation.

# Conversion of a Linear Differential Equation into an Integral Equation

To make this transformation, we use the following formula

$$\int_a^x \int_a^x \dots \int_a^x f(x)dx^n = \frac{1}{(n-1)!}\int_a^x (x-t)^{n-1} f(t)\,dt$$

In particular

$$\int_a^x \int_a^x f(x)\,dx dx = \int_a^x (x-t) f(t)\,dt$$

***Example 39.*** *Convert the differential equation*

$$y''(x) - 3y'(x) + 2y(x) = 5\sin x;\ y(0) = 1,\ y'(0) = -2$$

*into an integral equation.*

**Solution.** Given, integral equation is

$$y''(x) - 3y'(x) + 2y(x) = 5\sin x \quad \text{...(i)}$$

Integrating Eq. (i) both sides *wrt* $x$ from 0 to $x$, we get

$$[y'(x) - y'(0)] - 3[y(x) - y(0)] + 2\int_0^x y(t)\,dt = 5(1-\cos x) \quad \text{...(ii)}$$

Given, $y(0) = 1, y'(0) = -2$

Now, Eq. (ii) becomes

$$y'(x) + 2 - 3(y(x) - 1) + 2\int_0^x y(t)\,dt = 5(1-\cos x)$$

$\Rightarrow$ $$y'(x) - 3y(x) + 2\int_0^x y(t)\,dt = -5\cos x \quad \text{...(iii)}$$

Integrating Eq. (iii) *wrt* $x$ from 0 to $x$, we get

$$\{y(x) - y(0)\} - 3\int_0^x y(t)\,dt + 2\int_0^x\int_0^x y(x)\,dx^2 = -5\sin x$$

$\Rightarrow$ $$y(x) - 1 - 3\int_0^x y(t)\,dt + 2\int_0^x (x-t)\,y(t)\,dt = -5\sin x$$

$\Rightarrow$ $$y(x) + \int_0^x \{2(x-t) - 3\}y(t)\,dt = 1 - 5\sin x$$

which is the required integral equation.

***Example 40.*** *Form an integral equation corresponding to the differential equation given by*

$$\frac{d^2y}{dx^2} - 2x\frac{dy}{dx} - 3y = 0$$

*with initial conditions $y(0) = 1, y'(0) = 0$.*

**Solution.** Here, the given differential equation is

$$\frac{d^2y}{dx^2} - 2x\frac{dy}{dx} - 3y = 0 \quad \text{...(i)}$$

such that $y(0) = 1$ and $y'(0) = 0$ ...(ii)

Let us suppose

$$\frac{d^2y}{dx^2} = u(x) \quad \text{...(iii)}$$

By integrating *wrt* to $x$ from 0 to $x$, we get

$$\left[\frac{dy}{dx}\right]_0^x = \int_0^x u(x)\,dx \Rightarrow \frac{dy}{dx} - y'(0) = \int_0^x u(x)\,dx$$

$\Rightarrow$ $$\frac{dy}{dx} = \int_0^x u(x)\,dx \quad [\because y'(0) = 0]$$

or $$\frac{dy}{dx} = \int_0^x u(t)\,dt \quad ...(iv)$$

Integrating Eq. (iv) *wrt* x, we get

$$y(x) - y(0) = \int_0^x \int_0^x u(x)\,dx^2$$

$$\Rightarrow \quad y(x) = 1 + \int_0^x (x-t)\,u(t)\,dt \quad ...(v)$$

Now, putting the value of $\frac{d^2y}{dx^2}$, $\frac{dy}{dx}$ and $y(x)$ from Eqs. (iii), (iv) and (v) in Eq. (i), we get

$$u(x) - 2x\int_0^x u(t)\,dt - 3\left[1 + \int_0^x (x-t)\,u(t)\,dt\right] = 0$$

$$\Rightarrow \quad u(x) - 3 - \int_0^x (2x)\,u(t)\,dt - \int_0^x 3(x-t)\,u(t)\,dt = 0$$

$$\Rightarrow \quad u(x) = 3 + \int_0^x (5x-3t)\,u(t)\,dt$$

which is the required Volterra integral equation of second kind.

# Conversion of Integral Equation into Linear Differential Equation

## Differentiation Under the Sign of Integration (Leibnitz's Rule)

Let $F(x, t)$ and $\frac{\partial F}{\partial x}$ be continuous functions of both x and t and let $\phi'(x)$ and $\psi'(x)$ be continuous. Then,

$$\frac{d}{dx}\int_{\phi(x)}^{\psi(x)} F(x,t)\,dt = \int_{\phi(x)}^{\psi(x)} \frac{\partial F}{\partial x}\,dt + F(x, \psi(x))\psi'(x) - F(x, \phi(x))\phi'(x)$$

**Note** If $\phi(x)$ and $\psi(x)$ are constants, then above result reduces to

$$\frac{d}{dx}\int_{\phi}^{\psi} F(x,t)\,dt = \int_{\phi}^{\psi} \frac{\partial F}{\partial x}\,dt$$

***Example 41.*** *Show that the integral equation*

$$y(x) = \frac{1}{2}x^2 + \int_0^x t(t-x)y(t)\,dt$$

*is equivalent to the differential equation* $\frac{d^2y}{dx^2} + xy = 1$ *with the conditions* $y(0) = y'(0) = 0$.

**Solution.** Given, integral equation is

$$y(x) = \frac{1}{2}x^2 + \int_0^x t(t-x)y(t)\,dt \quad ...(i)$$

Differentiating Eq. (i) both sides *wrt* x, we get

$$\frac{dy}{dx} = x + \int_0^x \frac{\partial}{\partial x}[t(t-x)y(t)]\,dt + x(x-x)y(x)\frac{d}{dx}(x) - 0(0-x)y(0)\frac{d}{dx}(0)$$

$$\Rightarrow \quad \frac{dy}{dx} = x + \int_0^x -ty(t)\,dt$$

$$\Rightarrow \quad \frac{dy}{dx} = x - \int_0^x ty(t)\,dt \quad ...(ii)$$

Differentiating Eq. (ii) *wrt* x, we get

$$\frac{d^2y}{dx^2} = 1 - \left[\int_0^x \frac{\partial}{\partial x}(ty(t))\,dt + xy(x)\frac{d}{dx}(x) - 0\cdot y(0)\frac{d}{dx}(0)\right]$$

$$\Rightarrow \quad \frac{d^2y}{dx^2} = 1 - \left[\int_0^x 0\cdot dt + xy(x) - 0\right]$$

$$\Rightarrow \quad \frac{d^2y}{dx^2} = 1 - xy(x)$$

$$\Rightarrow \quad \frac{d^2y}{dx^2} + xy = 1$$

Put $x = 0$ in Eq. (i), we get $y(0) = 0$ and put $x = 0$ in Eq. (ii), we get $y'(0) = 0$.

***Example 42.*** *Convert* $\frac{d^2y}{dx^2} + xy = 1$, $y(0) = 0$, $y(1) = 1$ *into an integral equation.*

**Solution.** Here, the given differential equation is

$$y''(x) + xy(x) = 1 \quad ...(i)$$

Integrating Eq. (i) *wrt* x from 0 to x, we get

$$y'(x) - y'(0) + \int_0^x xy(x)\,dx = x$$

$$\Rightarrow \quad y'(x) = x + c - \int_0^x xy(x)\,dx \quad ...(ii)$$

(Let $y'(0) = c$)

Integrating Eq. (ii) *wrt* x from 0 to x, we get

$$y(x) - y(0) = \frac{x^2}{2} + cx - \int_0^x \int_0^x xy(x)\,dx^2$$

$$\Rightarrow \quad y(x) = \frac{x^2}{2} + cx - \int_0^x t(x-t)y(t)\,dt \quad ...(iii)$$

Put $x = 1$ in Eq. (iii), we get

$$y(1) = \frac{1}{2} + c - \int_0^1 t(1-t)\,y(t)\,dt$$

$$\Rightarrow \quad 1 = \frac{1}{2} + c - \int_0^1 t(1-t)\,y(t)\,dt$$

$$\Rightarrow \quad c = \frac{1}{2} + \int_0^1 t(1-t)y(t)\,dt$$

Putting this value of c into Eq. (iii), we get

$$y(x) = x\left[\frac{1}{2} + \int_0^1 (1-t)\,t\,y(t)\,dt\right] + \frac{1}{2}x^2 - \int_0^x (x-t)\,t\,y(t)\,dt$$

$$= \frac{1}{2}x(1+x) + \int_0^1 xt(1-t)\,y(t)\,dt - \int_0^x t(x-t)\,y(t)\,dt$$

$$= \frac{1}{2}x(1+x) + \int_0^x xt(1-t)\,y(t)\,dt + \int_x^1 xt(1-t)\,y(t)\,dt - \int_0^x t(x-t)\,y(t)\,dt$$

$$= \frac{1}{2}x(1+x) + \int_0^x ty(t)\{x - xt - x + t\}\,dt + \int_x^1 xt(1-t)y(t)\,dt$$

$$= \frac{1}{2}x(1+x) + \int_0^x t^2(1-x)y(t)\,dt + \int_x^1 xt(1-t)\,y(t)\,dt$$

$$= \frac{1}{2}x(1+x) + \int_0^1 k(x,t)y(t)\,dt$$

where, $k(x,t) = \begin{cases} t^2(1-x); & 0 < t < x \\ xt(1-t); & x < t < 1 \end{cases}$

# Important Definitions

## 1. Kernel

The function $k(x, t)$ is known as kernel of the integral equation.

### (i) Symmetric Kernel

A kernel $k(x, t)$ is said to be symmetric or hermitian, if

$$k(x,t) = \bar{k}(t,x)$$

where $\bar{k}$ stands for complex conjugate of $k$.

In case of real symmetric kernel $k(x, t)$,

$$k(x,t) = k(t,x)$$

e.g., $x^2 + t^2$, $(x-t)^2$, $\sin(x+t)$ etc., are all symmetric kernels.

$xt^2$ is not a symmetric kernel.

> ***Note*** **(a)** The eigen values of a symmetric kernel are real.
> **(b)** The eigen functions of a symmetric kernel, corresponding to different eigen values are orthogonal.
> **(c)** All iterated kernels of a symmetric kernel are also symmetric.
> **(d)** Every symmetric kernel with a norm $\neq 0$ has at least one eigen value.

### (ii) Separable or Degenerate Kernel

A kernel $k(x, t)$ is called separable or degenerate, if it can be expressed as the sum of a finite number of terms, each of which is the product of a function of $x$ and a function of $t$ i.e.,

$$k(x,t) = \sum_{i=1}^{n} f_i(x) g_i(t)$$

where $n$ is finite and $f_i$, $g_i$ are linearly independent sets of functions.

> ***Note*** **(a)** A degenerate kernel has a finite number of characteristic values (eigen values).
> **(b)** A degenerate or separable kernel is mainly used to solve Fredholm equation.

### (iii) Iterated Kernels

(a) Consider Fredholm integral equation of the second kind

$$u(x) = f(x) + \lambda \int_a^b k(x,t)u(t)\,dt$$

Then, the iterated kernels $k_n(x, t)$, $n = 1, 2, 3, \ldots$ are defined as follows

$$k_1(x,t) = k(x,t)$$

and $$k_n(x,t) = \int_a^b k(x,s)k_{n-1}(s,t)\,ds, \quad n = 2, 3, \ldots$$

(b) Consider Volterra integral equation of the second kind

$$u(x) = f(x) + \lambda \int_a^x k(x,t)\,u(t)\,dt$$

Then, the iterated kernels $k_n(x, t)$, $n = 1, 2, 3, \ldots$ are defined as follows

$$k_1(x,t) = k(x,t)$$

and $$k_n(x,t) = \int_t^x k(x,s)k_{n-1}(s,t)\,ds, \; n = 2, 3, \ldots$$

### (iv) Resolvent Kernel or Reciprocal Kernel

Consider the integral equations

$$u(x) = f(x) + \lambda \int_a^b k(x,t)u(t)\,dt \quad \ldots\text{(i)}$$

and $$u(x) = f(x) + \lambda \int_a^x k(x,t)u(t)\,dt \quad \ldots\text{(ii)}$$

Let the solution of Eqs. (i) and (ii) are, respectively given by

$$u(x) = f(x) + \lambda \int_a^b R(x,t;\lambda)f(t)\,dt \quad \ldots\text{(iii)}$$

and $$u(x) = f(x) + \lambda \int_a^x R(x,t;\lambda)f(t)\,dt \quad \ldots\text{(iv)}$$

Then, $R(x, t; \lambda)$ is called the resolvent kernel or reciprocal kernel.

## 2. Eigen Values and Eigen Functions

Consider the homogeneous Fredholm integral equation

$$u(x) = \lambda \int_a^b k(x,t)u(t)\,dt \quad \ldots\text{(i)}$$

Then, for $\lambda = 0$, Eq. (i) reduces to $u(x) = 0$ which is a solution of Eq. (i) called zero or trivial solution of Eq. (i).

The values of parameter $\lambda$ for which Eq. (i) has a non-zero solution i.e., $u(x) \neq 0$ are called eigen values of Eq. (i), and every non-zero solution of Eq. (i) is called an eigen function corresponding to eigen value $\lambda$.

Clearly, for Eq. (i) $\lambda = 0$ is not an eigen value.

> ***Note*** **(a)** For a given value of $\lambda$, if $u(x)$ is an eigen function of Eq. (i), then $cu(x)$ is also an eigen function of Eq. (i) where $c$ is any arbitrary constant.
> **(b)** Generally a homogeneous Fredholm integral equation of the second kind have no eigen value and eigen function.

## 3. $L_2$-Function

A given function $y(x)$ is said to be $L_2$-function or square integrable function, if

$$\int_a^b |y(x)|^2\,dx < \infty$$

$k(x, t)$ is an $L_2$-function, if for each set of values of $x, t$ in the square $a \leq x \leq b$, $a \leq t \leq b$

**(i)** $\int_a^b |k(x,t)|^2\,dx < \infty$

**(ii)** $\int_a^b |k(x,t)|^2\,dt < \infty$

**(iii)** $\int_a^b \int_a^b |k(x,t)|^2\,dx\,dt < \infty$

## Solution of Fredholm Integral Equation of the Second Kind

### (I) With Separable Kernel

#### Homogeneous Equation

Consider a homogeneous Fredholm integral equation of the second kind

$$u(x) = \lambda \int_a^b k(x, t)\, u(t)\, dt \qquad \text{...(i)}$$

Here, we have assumed that $k(x, t)$ is separable, therefore we can take

$$k(x, t) = \sum_{i=1}^{n} f_i(x) g_i(t) \qquad \text{...(ii)}$$

Put this value of $k(x, t)$ in Eq. (i), we get

$$u(x) = \lambda \int_a^b \left[\sum_{i=1}^{n} f_i(x) g_i(t)\right] u(t)\, dt = \lambda \sum_{i=1}^{n} \int_a^b f_i(x) g_i(t) u(t)\, dt$$

$$= \lambda \sum_{i=1}^{n} f_i(x) \int_a^b g_i(t) u(t)\, dt \qquad \text{...(iii)}$$

Assume that

$$\int_a^b g_i(t)\, u(t)\, dt = C_i \qquad (i = 1, 2, 3, \dots, n) \quad \text{...(iv)}$$

Then, Eq. (iii) gives

$$u(x) = \lambda \sum_{i=1}^{n} C_i f_i(x) \qquad \text{...(v)}$$

Now, we want to evaluate the constants $C_i$.

Multiplying both sides of Eq. (v) successively by $g_1(x)$, $g_2(x)$, ..., $g_n(x)$ and integrating over the range of $[a, b]$, we get

$$\int_a^b g_1(x) u(x)\, dx = \lambda \sum_{i=1}^{n} C_i \int_a^b g_1(x) f_i(x)\, dx \qquad \text{...(vi)}$$

$$\int_a^b g_2(x) u(x)\, dx = \lambda \sum_{i=1}^{n} C_i \int_a^b g_2(x) f_i(x)\, dx \qquad \text{...(vii)}$$

$$\dots \quad \dots \quad \dots \quad \dots$$

$$\int_a^b g_n(x) u(x)\, dx = \lambda \sum_{i=1}^{n} C_i \int_a^b g_n(x) f_i(x)\, dx \qquad \text{...(viii)}$$

Let us define

$$\alpha_{ji} = \int_a^b g_j(x) f_i(x) \qquad [i, j \in N] \quad \text{...(ix)}$$

Using the value of $\alpha_{ji}$ in Eq. (vi) and using Eq. (iv), we get

$$C_1 = \lambda \sum_{i=1}^{n} C_i \alpha_{1i}$$

$$= \lambda (C_1\alpha_{11} + C_2\alpha_{12} + \dots + C_n\alpha_{1n})$$

$$\Rightarrow \quad (1 - \lambda\alpha_{11})C_1 - \lambda\alpha_{12}C_2 - \dots - \lambda\alpha_{1n}C_n = 0$$

Similarly, we can simplify Eq. (vii),...,(viii). Then, we get a system of homogeneous linear equation to find the value of $C_i$.

$$\left.\begin{aligned} (1 - \lambda\alpha_{11})C_1 - \lambda\alpha_{12}C_2 - \dots - \lambda\alpha_{1n}C_n &= 0 \\ -\lambda\alpha_{21}C_1 + (1 - \lambda\alpha_{22})C_2 - \dots - \lambda\alpha_{2n}C_n &= 0 \\ \dots \quad \dots \quad \dots \quad \dots \quad \dots \quad \dots & \\ \dots \quad \dots \quad \dots \quad \dots \quad \dots \quad \dots & \\ -\lambda\alpha_{n1}C_1 - \lambda\alpha_{n2}C_2 - \dots + (1 - \lambda\alpha_{nn})C_n &= 0 \end{aligned}\right\} \quad \text{...(x)}$$

The determinant of Eq. (x), *i.e.*, $D(\lambda)$, can be written as

$$D(\lambda) = \begin{vmatrix} (1 - \lambda\alpha_{11}) & -\lambda\alpha_{12} & \dots & -\lambda\alpha_{1n} \\ -\lambda\alpha_{21} & 1 - \lambda\alpha_{22} & \dots & -\lambda\alpha_{2n} \\ \vdots & \vdots & & \vdots \\ -\lambda\alpha_{n1} & -\lambda\alpha_{n2} & \dots & 1 - \lambda\alpha_{nn} \end{vmatrix} \quad \text{...(xi)}$$

The values of $\lambda$ for which $D(\lambda) = 0$ are called eigen values of integral Eq. (i)

***Case I*** If $D(\lambda) \neq 0$, then system of Eq. (x) has only trivial solution

$$\Rightarrow \qquad C_1 = C_2 = C_3 = \dots = C_n = 0$$

$\therefore$ From Eq. (v), $u(x) = 0$ which is zero or trivial solution of integral Eq. (i).

***Case II*** When $D(\lambda) = 0$, then atleast one of the $C_i$s can be fixed and the remaining can be determined accordingly.

$\Rightarrow$ From Eq. (v) infinitely many $C_i f_i(x)$ is possible and hence integral Eq. (i) has infinitely many solutions.

***Example 43.*** *Find the eigen values and eigen functions of the Integral equation* $u(x) = \lambda \int_0^1 e^{x+t} u(t)\, dt$.

**Solution.** The given equation can be written as

$$u(x) = \lambda e^x \int_0^1 e^t u(t)\, dt \qquad \text{...(i)}$$

Assume that $C = \int_0^1 e^t u(t)\, dt$ ...(ii)

Then, from Eq. (i), we have

$$u(x) = \lambda C e^x \qquad \text{...(iii)}$$

$$\Rightarrow \qquad u(t) = \lambda C e^t \qquad \text{...(iv)}$$

Putting this value in Eq. (ii), we get

$$C = \int_0^1 e^t (\lambda C e^t)\, dt = \lambda C \left[\frac{e^{2t}}{2}\right]_0^1 = \frac{\lambda C}{2}(e^2 - 1)$$

$$\Rightarrow \qquad C\left[1 - \frac{\lambda}{2}(e^2 - 1)\right] = 0 \qquad \text{...(v)}$$

If $C = 0$, then Eq. (iii) gives $u(x) = 0$. We, therefore assume that for non-zero solution of Eq. (i), $C \neq 0$, then Eq. (v) gives

$$1 - \frac{\lambda}{2}(e^2 - 1) = 0 \Rightarrow \lambda = \frac{2}{e^2 - 1} \qquad \text{...(vi)}$$

which is an eigen value of Eq. (i).

To find the corresponding eigen function, putting the value of $\lambda$ [from Eq. (vi)] in Eq. (iii), we get

$$u(x) = \frac{2C}{e^2 - 1} \cdot e^x$$

Taking $\dfrac{2C}{e^2 - 1} = 1$, the eigen function is $e^x$.

***Example 44.*** *Find the eigen values and corresponding eigen functions of the integral equation*

$$y(x) = \lambda \int_0^{2\pi} \sin x \cos t \, y(t)\, dt$$

**Solution.** $y(x) = \lambda \sin x \int_0^{2\pi} \cos t \, y(t)\, dt$

$$\Rightarrow \quad y(x) = (\lambda \sin x) C \quad \text{...(i)}$$

where $C = \int_0^{2\pi} \cos t \, y(t)\, dt$ ...(ii)

Using Eq. (i) into Eq. (ii), we get

$$C = \int_0^{2\pi} \cos t(\lambda \sin t C)\, dt = \lambda C \int_0^{2\pi} \sin t \cos t \, dt$$

$$\Rightarrow \quad C = \lambda C \times 0 = 0$$

(Since, $\int_0^{2\pi} \sin t \cos t \, dt = \int_0^{2\pi} \sin(2\pi - t) \cos(2\pi - t)\, dt$

$$= -\int_0^{2\pi} \sin t \cos t \, dt$$

$$\Rightarrow \quad 2\int_0^{2\pi} \sin t \cos t \, dt = 0$$

$$\Rightarrow \quad \int_0^{2\pi} \sin t \cos t \, dt = 0)$$

$\therefore$ From Eq. (i), $y(x) = 0$

$\Rightarrow$ Given integral equation has no eigen value and has trivial solution.

***Example 45.*** *Solve the homogeneous Fredholm integral equation of the second kind*

$$u(x) = \lambda \int_0^{2\pi} \sin(x + t) u(t) dt$$

**Solution.** Here, the given integral equation can be written as

$$u(x) = \lambda \int_0^{2\pi} (\sin x \cos t + \cos x \sin t)\, u(t)\, dt$$

$$= \lambda \sin x \int_0^{2\pi} \cos t \, u(t)\, dt + \lambda \cos x \int_0^{2\pi} \sin t \, u(t)\, dt \quad \text{...(i)}$$

Let us assume

$$C_1 = \int_0^{2\pi} \cos t \, u(t)\, dt \quad \text{...(ii)}$$

and $C_2 = \int_0^{2\pi} \sin t \, u(t)\, dt$ ...(iii)

Using Eqs. (ii) and (iii), Eq. (i) reduces to

$$u(x) = \lambda C_1 \sin x + \lambda C_2 \cos x \quad \text{...(iv)}$$

$$\Rightarrow u(t) = \lambda C_1 \sin t + \lambda C_2 \cos t \quad \text{...(v)}$$

Putting the value of $u(t)$, from Eq. (v) in Eq. (ii), we get

$$C_1 = \int_0^{2\pi} \cos t(\lambda C_1 \sin t + \lambda C_2 \cos t)\, dt$$

$$= \frac{\lambda C_1}{2} \int_0^{2\pi} \sin 2t \, dt + \frac{\lambda C_2}{2} \int_0^{2\pi} (1 + \cos 2t)\, dt$$

$$= \frac{\lambda C_1}{2}\left[-\frac{\cos 2t}{2}\right]_0^{2\pi} + \frac{\lambda C_2}{2}\left[t + \frac{\sin 2t}{2}\right]_0^{2\pi}$$

or $C_1 = 0 + \lambda C_2 \pi$ or $C_1 - \lambda \pi C_2 = 0$ ...(vi)

Similarly, from Eq. (iii), we get

$$C_2 = \int_0^{2\pi} \sin t(\lambda C_1 \sin t + \lambda C_2 \cos t)\, dt$$

$$= \frac{\lambda C_1}{2} \int_0^{2\pi} (1 - \cos 2t)\, dt + \frac{\lambda C_2}{2} \int_0^{2\pi} \sin 2t \, dt$$

$$= \frac{\lambda C_1}{2}\left[t - \frac{\sin 2t}{2}\right]_0^{2\pi} + \frac{\lambda C_2}{2}\left[-\frac{\cos 2t}{2}\right]_0^{2\pi}$$

or $C_2 = \lambda C_1 \pi$ or $\lambda \pi C_1 - C_2 = 0$ ...(vii)

Eqs. (vi) and (vii) gives the system of linear homogeneous equations for determination of $C_1$ and $C_2$. For non-zero solution, we must have

$$\begin{vmatrix} 1 & -\lambda\pi \\ \lambda\pi & -1 \end{vmatrix} = 0$$

$$\Rightarrow \quad -1 + \lambda^2\pi^2 = 0 \Rightarrow \lambda = \pm\frac{1}{\pi} \quad \text{...(viii)}$$

Therefore, the required eigen value are given by $\lambda_1 = \frac{1}{\pi}$ and

$$\lambda_2 = -\frac{1}{\pi}$$

Determination of eigen function

Eq. (i) For $\lambda = \lambda_1 = \frac{1}{\pi}$

Putting $\lambda = \frac{1}{\pi}$ in Eqs. (vi) and (vii), we get

$$C_1 - C_2 = 0 \quad \text{...(ix)}$$

$$C_1 - C_2 = 0 \quad \text{...(x)}$$

which implies, $C_1 = C_2$. Therefore, from Eq. (iv), we have

$$u(x) = \frac{1}{\pi} C_1 \sin x + \frac{1}{\pi} C_1 \cos x = \frac{C_1}{\pi}(\sin x + \cos x)$$

Let $\frac{C_1}{\pi} = 1$. Hence, the required eigen function is given by

$$u_1(x) = (\sin x + \cos x) \quad \text{...(xi)}$$

Eq. (ii) For $\lambda = \lambda_2 = -\frac{1}{\pi}$

Putting $\lambda = -\frac{1}{\pi}$ in Eqs. (vi) and (vii), we get

$$C_1 + C_2 = 0 \quad \text{...(xii)}$$

and $C_1 + C_2 = 0$ ...(xiii)

which implies, $C_1 = -C_2$. Therefore, from Eq. (iv), we have

$$u(x) = -\frac{1}{\pi} C_1 \sin x + \left(-\frac{1}{\pi}\right)(-C_1) \cos x = \left(-\frac{C_1}{\pi}\right)(\sin x - \cos x)$$

Taking $\left(-\frac{C_1}{\pi}\right) = 1$, the required eigen function is given by

$$u_2(x) = \sin x - \cos x$$

## Non-Homogeneous Equation

Consider the Fredholm integral equation of second kind is given by

$$u(x) = F(x) + \lambda \int_a^b k(x, t) u(t) dt \quad \text{...(i)}$$

The separable kernel $k(x, t)$ can be written as

$$k(x, t) = \sum_{i=1}^{n} f_i(x) g_i(t) \quad \text{...(ii)}$$

Put this value in Eq. (i), we get

$$u(x) = F(x) + \lambda \int_a^b \left[ \sum_{i=1}^{n} f_i(x) g_i(t) \right] u(t)\, dt$$

$$= F(x) + \lambda \sum_{i=1}^{n} f_i(x) \int_a^b g_i(t) u(t)\, dt \qquad \text{...(iii)}$$

Let us assume

$$\int_a^b g_i(t) u(t)\, dt = C_i \qquad i \in N \qquad \text{...(iv)}$$

Then, from Eq. (iii), we have

$$u(x) = F(x) + \lambda \sum_{i=1}^{n} C_i f_i(x) \qquad \text{...(v)}$$

To find the solution of the given Eq. (i), in the form of Eq. (v), we should find the value of constants $C_i$.

Now, multiplying Eq. (v) successively by $g_1(x), g_2(x), \ldots, g_n(x)$ and integrating over $(a, b)$, we get

$$\int_a^b g_1(x) u(x)\, dx = \int_a^b g_1(x) F(x)\, dx + \lambda \sum_{i=1}^{n} C_i \int_a^b g_1(x) f_i(x)\, dx \qquad \text{...(vi)}$$

$$\int_a^b g_2(x) u(x)\, dx = \int_a^b g_2(x) F(x)\, dx + \lambda \sum_{i=1}^{n} C_i \int_a^b g_2(x) f_i(x)\, dx \qquad \text{...(vii)}$$

$$\ldots \quad \ldots \quad \ldots \quad \ldots \quad \ldots \quad \ldots$$

$$\ldots \quad \ldots \quad \ldots \quad \ldots \quad \ldots \quad \ldots$$

$$\int_a^b g_n(x) u(x)\, dx = \int_a^b g_n(x) F(x)\, dx + \lambda \sum_{i=1}^{n} C_i \int_a^b g_n(x) f_i(x)\, dx \qquad \text{...(viii)}$$

Define

$$\alpha_{ji} = \int_a^b g_j(x) f_i(x)\, dx \qquad (i, j \in N) \qquad \text{...(ix)}$$

$$\beta_j = \int_a^b g_j(x) F(x)\, dx \qquad (j \in N) \qquad \text{...(x)}$$

Putting these values in Eq. (vi), we get

$$C_1 = \beta_1 + \lambda \sum_{i=1}^{n} C_i \alpha_{1i} = \beta_1 + \lambda [C_1 \alpha_{11} + C_2 \alpha_{12} + \ldots + C_n \alpha_{1n}]$$

$$\Rightarrow \quad (1 - \lambda\alpha_{11}) C_1 - \lambda\alpha_{12} C_2 - \ldots - \lambda\alpha_{1n} C_n = \beta_1$$

Similarly, we can solve Eqs. (vii) and (viii).

Therefore, we get the following system of linear equations.

$$(1 - \lambda\alpha_{11}) C_1 - \lambda\alpha_{12} C_2 - \ldots - \lambda\alpha_{1n} C_n = \beta_1 \qquad \text{...(xi)}$$

$$-\lambda\alpha_{21} C_1 + (1 - \lambda\alpha_{22}) C_2 - \ldots - \lambda\alpha_{2n} C_n = \beta_2 \qquad \text{...(xii)}$$

$$\ldots \quad \ldots \quad \ldots \quad \ldots$$

$$\ldots \quad \ldots \quad \ldots \quad \ldots$$

$$-\lambda\alpha_{n1} C_1 - \lambda\alpha_{n2} C_2 - \ldots (1 - \lambda\alpha_{nn}) C_n = \beta_n \qquad \text{...(xiii)}$$

Therefore, the determinant of $D(\lambda)$ of this system is given by

$$D(\lambda) = \begin{vmatrix} 1 - \lambda\alpha_{11} & -\lambda\alpha_{12} & \ldots & -\lambda\alpha_{1n} \\ -\lambda\alpha_{21} & 1 - \lambda\alpha_{22} & \ldots & -\lambda\alpha_{2n} \\ \vdots & \vdots & \ldots & \vdots \\ -\lambda\alpha_{n1} & -\lambda\alpha_{n2} & \ldots & (1 - \lambda\alpha_{nn}) \end{vmatrix} \qquad \text{...(xiv)}$$

which is a polynomial in $\lambda$ of degree $n$.

Now, there are following cases

**Case I** When atleast one right member of the system Eq. (xi)...(xiii) is non-zero.

Here, we have the following two situations

**(i)** If $D(\lambda) \neq 0$, In this case, a unique non-zero solution of the system Eq. (xi)...(xiii) exists and therefore Eq. (i) has a unique non-zero solution given by Eq. (v).

**(ii)** If $D(\lambda) = 0$, Then, the above equations have either no solution or they possess infinite solution and hence Eq. (i) has no solution or infinite solutions.

**Case II** When $F(x) = 0$.

Here, we have the following two situations

**(i)** If $D(\lambda) \neq 0$ In this case, a unique zero solution $C_1 = C_2 = C_3 = \ldots = C_n = 0$ of the system Eq. (xi)... (xiii) exists and therefore, Eq. (i) has only unique zero solution $u(x) = 0$.

**(ii)** If $D(\lambda) = 0$ In this case the above system possesses infinite non-zero solutions and therefore Eq. (i) has infinite non-zero solutions.

**Case III** When $F(x) \neq 0$ and $F(x)$ is orthogonal to all $g_n(t)$.

In this case Eq. (xi) gives

$$\beta_1 = 0, \beta_2 = 0, \ldots, \beta_n = 0.$$

and therefore the Eq. (xi)...(xiii) reduce to a system of homogeneous linear equations.

Now, following situations may arise

**(i)** If $D(\lambda) \neq 0$, In this case, a unique zero solution $C_1 = C_2 = C_3 = \ldots = C_n = 0$ exists and therefore Eq. (i) has only one solution $u(x) = F(x)$.

**(ii)** If $D(\lambda) = 0$, In this case the above system have infinite non-zero solutions and therefore Eq. (i) has infinite non-zero solutions.

> ***Note*** **(a)** The determinant $D(\lambda)$, given by Eq. (xiv) is not identically zero, since when $\lambda = 0$, then $D(\lambda) = 1$.
> **(b)** Case II is discussed in Eq. (i) solution of homogeneous Fredholm integral equation of second kind.

***Example 46.*** *Solve* $u(x) = e^x + \lambda \int_0^1 2e^{x+t} u(t)\, dt$.

**Solution.** Here, the given equation can be written as

$$u(x) = e^x + 2\lambda e^x \int_0^1 e^t \cdot u(t)\, dt \qquad \text{...(i)}$$

Let $$C = \int_0^1 e^t u(t)\, dt \qquad \text{...(ii)}$$

From Eqs. (i) and (ii), we have

$$u(x) = e^x + 2\lambda C e^x = e^x (1 + 2C\lambda) \qquad \text{...(iii)}$$

$$\Rightarrow \qquad u(t) = e^t (1 + 2C\lambda) \qquad \text{...(iv)}$$

Therefore, From Eq. (ii), we have

$$C = \int_0^1 [e^t \cdot e^t (1 + 2C\lambda)]\, dt$$

$$= (1 + 2C\lambda) \left[ \frac{e^{2t}}{2} \right]_0^1 = (1 + 2\lambda C) \frac{1}{2} (e^2 - 1)$$

*i.e.,* $C[1 - \lambda(e^2 - 1)] = \frac{1}{2}(e^2 - 1)$

$$\Rightarrow \quad C = \frac{e^2 - 1}{2[1 - \lambda(e^2 - 1)]}$$

where $\lambda \neq \frac{1}{e^2 - 1}$

Putting this value in Eq. (iii), we obtained the solution of integral Eq. (i) given by

$$u(x) = e^x\left[1 + 2\lambda\frac{e^2 - 1}{2[1 - \lambda(e^2 - 1)]}\right]$$

$$= e^x\left[\frac{1 - \lambda(e^2 - 1) + \lambda(e^2 - 1)}{1 - \lambda(e^2 - 1)}\right]$$

$$\Rightarrow \quad u(x) = \frac{e^x}{1 - \lambda(e^2 - 1)}, \text{ where } \lambda \neq \frac{1}{e^2 - 1}$$

***Example 47.*** *Solve the integral equation*

$$u(x) = x + \lambda\int_0^1 (x + t)u(t)\,dt.$$

**Solution.**

$$u(x) = x + \lambda x\int_0^1 u(t)\,dt + \lambda\int_0^1 tu(t)\,dt \qquad \text{...(i)}$$

$$\Rightarrow \quad u(x) = x + \lambda x C_1 + \lambda C_2 \qquad \text{...(ii)}$$

where $C_1 = \int_0^1 u(t)\,dt$ and $C_2 = \int_0^1 tu(t)\,dt$ ...(iii)

Using Eq. (ii) in Eq. (iii), we get

$$C_1 = \int_0^1 (t + \lambda t C_1 + \lambda C_2)\,dt = \frac{1}{2} + \frac{\lambda C_1}{2} + \lambda C_2$$

$$\Rightarrow \quad C_1(2 - \lambda) - 2\lambda C_2 = 1 \qquad \text{...(iv)}$$

and $C_2 = \int_0^1 t(t + \lambda t C_1 + \lambda C_2)\,dt = \frac{1}{3} + \frac{\lambda C_1}{3} + \frac{\lambda C_2}{2}$

$$\Rightarrow \quad 2\lambda C_1 + (3\lambda - 6)C_2 = -2 \qquad \text{...(v)}$$

Now, the determinant $D(\lambda)$ of the system of linear Eqs. (iv) and (v) is

$$D(\lambda) = \begin{vmatrix} 2 - \lambda & -2\lambda \\ 2\lambda & 3\lambda - 6 \end{vmatrix} = (2 - \lambda)(3\lambda - 6) + 4\lambda^2$$

$$= 6\lambda - 12 - 3\lambda^2 + 6\lambda + 4\lambda^2$$

$$= \lambda^2 + 12\lambda - 12$$

If $D(\lambda) = 0$

$$\Rightarrow \quad \lambda^2 + 12\lambda - 12 = 0$$

$$\Rightarrow \quad \lambda = \frac{-12 \pm \sqrt{192}}{2} = -6 \pm 4\sqrt{3}$$

Hence, a unique solution of the system Eqs. (iii) and (iv) exists if and only if $D(\lambda) \neq 0$ *i.e.*, $\lambda \neq -6 \pm 4\sqrt{3}$

Now, solving Eqs. (iv) and (v) for $C_1$ and $C_2$, we get

$$C_1 = \frac{4\lambda^2 - \lambda - 6}{4\lambda^2 + 3\lambda - 6} \cdot \frac{1}{(2 - \lambda)},$$

$$C_2 = -\frac{2}{4\lambda^2 + 3\lambda - 6}$$

Putting these value of $C_1$ and $C_2$ in Eq. (ii), we get required unique solution.

$$u(x) = x + \frac{\lambda(4\lambda^2 - \lambda - 6)}{(2 - \lambda)(4\lambda^2 + 3\lambda - 6)}x - \frac{2\lambda}{4\lambda^2 + 3\lambda - 6}$$

***Example 48.*** *Solve the integral equation*

$$u(x) = \cos x + \lambda\int_0^x \sin(x - t)\,u(t)\,dt$$

**Solution.** The given equation can be written as

$$u(x) = \cos x + \lambda\int_0^\pi (\sin x\cos t - \cos x\sin t)\,u(t)\,dt$$

$$= \cos x + \lambda\sin x\int_0^x \cos t\,u(t)\,dt - \lambda\cos x\int_0^\pi \sin t\,u(t)\,dt \qquad \text{...(i)}$$

Let $C_1 = \int_0^\pi \cos u(t)\,dt$ ...(ii)

and $C_2 = \int_0^\pi \sin t\,u(t)\,dt$ ...(iii)

Putting these values in Eq. (i), we get

$$u(x) = \cos x + \lambda C_1\sin x - \lambda C_2\cos x \qquad \text{...(iv)}$$

$$\Rightarrow \quad u(t) = \cos t + \lambda C_1\sin t - \lambda C_2\cos t \qquad \text{...(v)}$$

Putting this value in Eq. (ii), we get

$$C_1 = \int_0^\pi \cos(\cos t + \lambda C_1\sin t - \lambda C_2\cos t)\,dt$$

$$\Rightarrow \quad C_1 = \frac{1 - \lambda C_2}{2}\pi \quad \Rightarrow \quad 2C_1 + \lambda\pi C_2 = \pi \qquad \text{...(vi)}$$

and $C_2 = \frac{\lambda C_1\pi}{2} \quad \Rightarrow \quad \lambda\pi C_1 - 2C_2 = 0$ ...(vii)

$$D(\lambda) = \begin{vmatrix} 2 & \lambda\pi \\ \lambda\pi & -2 \end{vmatrix} = -4 - \lambda^2\pi^2 \neq 0 \text{ for any real } \lambda$$

∴ System of Eqs. (vi) and (vii) will have

On solving Eqs. (vi) and (vii) for $C_1$ and $C_2$, we get

$$C_1 = \frac{2\pi}{4 + \lambda^2\pi^2}, C_2 = \frac{\lambda\pi^2}{4 + \lambda^2\pi^2}$$

Hence, the required solution of integral Eq. (i) is given by

$$u(x) = \cos x + \frac{2\pi\lambda\sin x}{4 + \lambda^2\pi^2} - \frac{\lambda^2\pi^2\cos x}{4 + \lambda^2\pi^2}$$

$$= \cos x\left[1 - \frac{\lambda^2\pi^2}{4 + \lambda^2\pi^2}\right] + \frac{2\pi\lambda\sin x}{4 + \lambda^2\pi^2}$$

$$\Rightarrow \quad u(x) = \frac{4\cos x + 2\pi\lambda\sin x}{4 + \lambda^2\pi^2}$$

***Example 49.*** *Solve the integral equation*

$$u(x) = f(x) + \lambda\int_{-1}^1 (xt + x^2t^2)\,u(t)\,dt$$

*Also, find its resolvent kernel.*

**Solution.** The given equation can be written as

$$u(x) = f(x) + \lambda x\int_{-1}^1 t\,u(t)\,dt + \lambda x^2\int_{-1}^1 t^2u(t)\,dt \qquad \text{...(i)}$$

Let us assume

$$C_1 = \int_{-1}^1 t\,u(t)\,dt \qquad \text{...(ii)}$$

and $C_2 = \int_{-1}^1 t^2\,u(t)\,dt$ ...(iii)

Putting these values in Eq. (i), we get

$$u(x) = f(x) + \lambda C_1 x + \lambda C_2 x^2 \qquad \text{...(iv)}$$

$$\Rightarrow \quad u(t) = f(t) + \lambda C_1 t + \lambda C_2 t^2 \qquad \text{...(v)}$$

Putting the value of $u(t)$ in Eq. (ii), we get

$$C_1 = \int_{-1}^{1} t[f(t) + \lambda C_1 t + \lambda C_2 t^2]dt$$

$$= \int_{-1}^{1} t \cdot f(t)\,dt + \lambda C_1\left[\frac{t^3}{3}\right]_{-1}^{1} + \lambda C_2\left[\frac{t^4}{4}\right]_{-1}^{1}$$

$$= \int_{-1}^{1} t \cdot f(t)\,dt + \frac{2\lambda C_1}{3}$$

$$\Rightarrow \quad C_1\left(1 - \frac{2\lambda}{3}\right) = \int_{-1}^{1} t\, f(t)\,dt$$

i.e., $$C_1 = \frac{3}{3 - 2\lambda}\int_{-1}^{1} f(t)\,dt \quad \text{...(vi)}$$

Similarly, putting the value of $u(t)$ in Eq. (iii), we get

$$C_2 = \int_{-1}^{1} t^2[f(t) + \lambda C_1 t + \lambda C_2 t^2]dt$$

$$= \int_{-1}^{1} t^2 f(t)\,dt + \lambda C_1\left[\frac{t^4}{4}\right]_{-1}^{1} + \lambda C_2\left[\frac{t^5}{5}\right]_{-1}^{1}$$

$$= \int_{-1}^{1} t^2 f(t)\,dt + \frac{2\lambda C_2}{5}$$

$$\Rightarrow \quad C_2 = \frac{5}{5 - 2\lambda}\int_{-1}^{1} t^2 f(t)\,dt \quad \text{...(vii)}$$

Putting the values of $C_1$ and $C_2$ in Eq. (iv), we get

$$u(x) = f(x) + \frac{3\lambda x}{3 - 2\lambda}\int_{-1}^{1} t f(t)\,dt + \frac{5\lambda x^2}{5 - 2\lambda}\int_{-1}^{1} t^2 f(t)\,dt$$

$$= f(x) + \lambda\int_{-1}^{1}\left\{\frac{3xt}{3 - 2\lambda} + \frac{5x^2t^2}{5 - 2\lambda}\right\} f(t)\,dt \quad \text{...(viii)}$$

which is the required solution of the given integral equation.

The resolvent kernel $R(x, t; \lambda)$ is given by

$$R(x, t; \lambda) = \frac{3xt}{3 - 2\lambda} + \frac{5x^2t^2}{5 - 2\lambda}$$

> ***Note*** As we know that, if $R(x, t; \lambda)$ be the resolvent kernel of the integral equation
>
> $$u(x) = f(x) + \lambda\int_{-1}^{1} k(x, t)u(t)dt \quad \text{...(i)}$$
>
> Then, solution of Eq. (i) is given by
>
> $$u(x) = f(x) + \lambda\int_{-1}^{1} R(x, t; \lambda) f(t)dt$$

***Example 50.*** *Solve* $u(x) = f(x) + \lambda\int_0^1 (1 - 3xt)\,u(t)\,dt$ *with separable kernel and discuss all possible cases.*

**Solution.** The given equation can be written as

$$u(x) = f(x) + \lambda[C_1 - 3C_2 x] \quad \text{...(i)}$$

where, $$C_1 = \int_0^1 u(t)\,dt,\; C_2 = \int_0^1 t\,u(t)\,dt \quad \text{...(ii)}$$

Putting the value of $u(t)$ from Eq. (i) in Eq. (ii), we get

$$C_1 = \int_0^1 [f(t) + \lambda C_1 - 3C_2\lambda t]dt$$

and $$C_2 = \int_0^1 t\,[f(t) + \lambda C_1 - 3C_2\lambda t]dt$$

$$\Rightarrow \quad C_1(1 - \lambda) + \frac{3}{2}\lambda C_2 = \int_0^1 f(t)\,dt \quad \text{...(iii)}$$

and $$-\frac{1}{2}C_1\lambda + (1 - \lambda)C_2 = \int_0^1 t\, f(t)\,dt \quad \text{...(iv)}$$

The determinant of this system is given by

$$D(\lambda) = \begin{vmatrix} 1-\lambda & \frac{3}{2}\lambda \\ -\frac{1}{2}\lambda & 1-\lambda \end{vmatrix} = 1 - \frac{\lambda^2}{4},$$

***Case* I** When $f(x) = 0$, then integral Eq. (i) reduces to homogeneous equation. Then, for

**(i)** $D(\lambda) \neq 0$, *i.e.*, $\lambda \neq \pm 2$, Eq. (i) has only trivial solution $u(x) = 0$ (Since, $C_1 = C_2 = 0$)

**(ii)** $D(\lambda) = 0$, *i.e.*, $\lambda = \pm 2$, Eq. (i) has non-trivial solution given by

$$u(x) = \pm 2(C_1 - 3C_2 x)$$

where $C_1$ and $C_2$ are found out by system of Eqs. (iii) and (iv). For $\lambda = 2$ eigen function is $u(x) = 6C_2(1 - x)$ and for $\lambda = -2$, eigen function is $u(x) = -2C_2(1 - 3x)$.

***Case* II** When $f(x) \neq 0$

**(i)** When $D(\lambda) \neq 0$, *i.e.*, $\lambda \neq \pm 2$, Eq. (i) possesses an unique solution.

**(ii)** When $\lambda = 2$, then no solution exists unless $f(x)$ is orthogonal to eigen function corresponding to $\lambda = 2$ over the interval (0, 1).

Let $f(x)$ is orthogonal to $6C_2(1 - x)$.

$$\Rightarrow \quad \int_0^1 6C_2(1 - x) f(x)\,dx = 0$$

then infinitely many solutions exist for the system of Eqs. (iii) and (iv) and consequently integral Eq. (i) will have infinitely many solution.

From Eq. (iii), for $\lambda = 2$, we get

$$-C_1 + 3C_2 = \int_0^1 f(t)dt$$

$$\Rightarrow \quad C_1 = 3C_2 - \int_0^1 f(t)\,dt$$

From Eq. (i), we get

$$u(x) = f(x) + 2\left[3C_2 - \int_0^1 f(t)\,dt\right] - 6C_2 x$$

$$\Rightarrow \quad u(x) = f(x) - 2\int_0^1 f(t)dt + 6C_2(1 - x) \quad \text{...(v)}$$

Thus, for $\lambda = 2$, Eq. (i) possesses infinitely many solution given by Eq. (v)

**(iii)** When $\lambda = -2$, then similarly as above we find Eq. (i) possesses infinitely many solution given by

$$u(x) = f(x) - \frac{2}{3}\int_0^1 f(t)\,dt - 2C_2(1 - 3x) \quad \text{...(vi)}$$

where $$\int_0^1 -2C_2(1 - 3x) f(x)\,dx = 0$$

## (II) With the Help of Resolvent Kernel

1. Consider the Fredholm integral equation of the second kind

$$u(x) = f(x) + \lambda\int_a^b k(x, t)u(t)dt \quad \text{...(i)}$$

Suppose that

**(i)** Kernel $k(x, t) \neq 0$ is real and continuous in a rectangle $R\ (a \le x \le b,\ a \le t \le b)$.

Also, $k(x, t)$ is boundded by $M$ in $R$, i.e., $|k(x, t)| \le M$ in $R$.

**(ii)** $f(x) \ne 0$ is real and continuous in the interval $I$, for which $a \le x \le b$.

Also, let $|f(x)| \le N$ in $I$.

**(iii)** $\lambda$ is a constant such that $|\lambda| < \dfrac{1}{M(b-a)}$

Then, Eq. (i) has a unique continuous solution in $I$, which is given by

$$u(x) = f(x) + \lambda \int_a^b k(x, t) f(t)\, dt$$

$$+\lambda^2 \int_a^b k(x, t) \int_a^b k(t, t_1) f(t_1)\, dt_1 dt + \dots \quad \text{...(ii)}$$

> ***Note*** **(a)** Series in RHS of Eq. (ii) is absolutely and uniformly convergent.
> **(b)** The above method of finding solution of Fredholm integral equation of second kind is known as method of substitution.

2. Consider Fredholm integral equation of the second kind

$$u(x) = f(x) + \lambda \int_a^b k(x, t) u(t)\, dt \quad \text{...(i)}$$

Let $u_n(x)$ be the $n$th order approximations of solution of $u(x)$ of Eq. (i) such that $u_0(x) = f(x)$, then with the help of iterated kernels, we obtain

$$u_n(x) = f(x) + \sum_{m=1}^{n} \lambda^m \int_a^b k_m(x, t) f(t)\, dt \quad \text{...(ii)}$$

Taking limit $n \to \infty$, we get

$$u(x) = f(x) + \sum_{m=1}^{n} \lambda^m \int_a^b k_m(x, t) f(t)\, dt \quad \text{...(iii)}$$

$$\Rightarrow \quad u(x) = f(x) + \lambda \int_a^b \left[ \sum_{m=1}^{\infty} \lambda^{m-1} k_m(x, t) \right] f(t)\, dt$$

$$\Rightarrow \quad u(x) = f(x) + \lambda \int_a^b R(x, t; \lambda) f(t)\, dt \quad \text{...(iv)}$$

Here, $R(x, t; \lambda) = \sum_{m=1}^{\infty} \lambda^{m-1} k_m(x, t)$

Eq. (iv) gives the solution of integral Eq. (i).

> ***Note*** **(a)** The above method of finding solution of Eq.(i) is called successive approximation method or iterative method or resolvent kernel method.
> **(b)** Series in RHS of Eq. (iii) is called Neumann series, which is uniformly convergent, if $|\lambda| B < 1$
> where $B = \left[ \int_a^b \int_a^b |k(x, t)|^2\, dx\, dt \right]^{1/2}$
> **(c)** The series for the resolvent kernel $R(x, t; \lambda) = \sum_{m=1}^{\infty} \lambda^{m-1} k_m(x, t)$ is absolutely and uniformly convergent for all $x$ and $t$ in the region $|\lambda| < \dfrac{1}{B}$ (interior of circle $|\lambda| = \dfrac{1}{B}$) where $B$ is the expression mentioned in Eq. (ii).
> **(d)** To each $L_2$-kernel $k(x, t)$, there corresponds a unique resolvent kernel $R(x, t; \lambda)$ which is analytic in the region $|\lambda| < \dfrac{1}{B}$.
> **(e)** Furthermore, if $f(x)$ is also an $L_2$-function, then the unique $L_2$-solution of $u(x) = f(x) + \lambda \int_a^b k(x, t) u(t) dt$ valid in $|\lambda| < \dfrac{1}{B}$ is given by
> $$u(x) = f(x) + \lambda \int_a^b R(x, t; \lambda) f(t)\, dt$$
> **(f)** The resolvent kernel satisfies the integral equation
> $$R(x, t; \lambda) = k(x, t) + \lambda \int_a^b k(x, z) R(z, t; \lambda)\, dz$$
> **(g)** The $m$th iterated kernel $k_m(x, t)$ satisfies the relation
> $$k_m(x, t) = \int_a^b k_r(x, y) k_{m-r}(y, t)\, dy$$
> where $r$ is any positive integer less than $m$.

***Example 51.*** *Solve* $u(x) = x + \int_0^{1/2} u(t)\, dt$

**Solution.** Here, $\lambda = 1, k(x, t) = 1$

**Step 1** Finding resolvent kernel $R(x, t; \lambda)$ by using iterated kernel.

Let $k_m(x, t)$ be the $m$th iterated kernel. Then, we have

$$k_1(x, t) = k(x, t) = 1$$

and $\quad k_m(x, t) = \int_0^{1/2} k(x, z) k_{m-1}(z, t)\, dz$

$$\therefore \quad k_2(x, t) = \int_0^{1/2} k(x, z) k_1(z, t)\, dz$$

$$= \int_0^{1/2} 1 \times 1 dz = \int_0^{1/2} dz = \frac{1}{2}$$

$$k_3(x, t) = \int_0^{1/2} k(x, z) k_2(z, t)\, dz = \int_0^{1/2} 1 \times \frac{1}{2} dz$$

$$= \frac{1}{2} \int_0^{1/2} dz = \frac{1}{2^2} \text{ and so on.}$$

$$\Rightarrow \quad k_m(x, t) = \frac{1}{2^{m-1}}$$

$$\therefore \quad R(x, t; \lambda) = \sum_{m=1}^{\infty} \lambda^{m-1} k_m(x, t) = \sum_{m=1}^{\infty} \frac{1}{2^{m-1}}$$

$$= 1 + \frac{1}{2} + \frac{1}{2^2} + \dots + \infty = \frac{1}{1 - \frac{1}{2}} = 2$$

**Step 2** Required solution is given by

$$u(x) = f(x) + \lambda \int_a^b R(x, t; \lambda) f(t)\, dt$$

$$\Rightarrow \quad u(x) = x + \int_0^{1/2} 2t\, dt = x + [t^2]_0^{1/2} = x + \frac{1}{4}$$

***Example 52.*** *Solve* $y(x) = x + \lambda \int_0^1 xt y(t)\, dt.$

**Solution.** Here, $k(x, t) = xt$

$$\Rightarrow \quad k_1(x, t) = k(x, t) = xt$$

$$k_2(x, t) = \int_0^1 k(x, z) k_1(z, t)\, dz = \int_0^1 (xz)(zt)\, dz$$

$$= xt \int_0^1 z^2 dz = \frac{1}{3}(xt)$$

Similarly, $k_3(x,t) = \frac{1}{3^2}(xt)$

$k_4(x,t) = \frac{1}{3^3}(xt)$ and so on.

We get $k_m(x,t) = \frac{1}{3^{m-1}}(xt)$

$$\therefore \quad R(x,t;\lambda) = \sum_{m=1}^{\infty} \lambda^{m-1} k_m(x,t)$$

$$= \sum_{m=1}^{\infty} \lambda^{m-1} \cdot \frac{1}{3^{m-1}}(xt)$$

$$= xt \sum_{m=1}^{\infty} \left(\frac{\lambda}{3}\right)^{m-1}$$

$$= xt \cdot \frac{1}{1-\frac{\lambda}{3}}, \quad \text{where } \left|\frac{\lambda}{3}\right| < 1$$

$$= \frac{3xt}{3-\lambda} \quad \Rightarrow \quad |\lambda| < 3$$

Now, required solution is

$$y(x) = x + \lambda \int_0^1 R(x,t;\lambda) t\, dt$$

$$= x + \lambda \int_0^1 \frac{3xt}{3-\lambda} t\, dt$$

$$= x + \frac{3\lambda x}{3-\lambda} \int_0^1 t^2 dt = x + \frac{\lambda x}{3-\lambda}$$

$$= \frac{3x}{3-\lambda}$$

***Example 53.*** *Solve* $\phi(x) = f(x) + \lambda \int_0^1 e^{x-t} \phi(t)\, dt$.

**Solution.** Here, $k_1(x,t) = k(x,t) = e^{x-t}$

$$k_2(x,t) = \int_0^1 k(x,z) k_1(z,t)\, dz$$

$$= \int_0^1 e^{x-z} \cdot e^{z-t} dz = \int_0^1 e^{x-t} dt = e^{x-t}$$

Similarly, $k_3(x,t) = k_4(x,t) = \ldots = k_m(x,t) = e^{x-t}$

$$R(x,t;\lambda) = \sum_{m=1}^{\infty} \lambda^{m-1} k_m(x,t) = \sum_{m=1}^{\infty} \lambda^{m-1} e^{x-t}$$

$$= e^{x-t} \cdot \frac{1}{1-\lambda} \quad \text{where } |\lambda| < 1$$

$\therefore$ Required solution is

$$\phi(x) = f(x) + \lambda \int_0^1 e^{x-t} \cdot \frac{1}{1-\lambda} f(t)\, dt$$

$$= f(x) + \frac{\lambda e^x}{1-\lambda} \int_0^1 e^{-t} \cdot f(t)\, dt \quad \text{where } |\lambda| < 1$$

***Example 54.*** *Solve* $u(x) = 1 + \lambda \int_0^{\pi} \sin(x+t) u(t)\, dt$.

**Solution.** Here, $k(x,t) = \sin(x+t)$

$$\Rightarrow \quad k_1(x,t) = k(x,t) = \sin(x+t)$$

$$k_2(x,t) = \int_0^{\pi} k(x,s) k_1(s,t)\, ds = \int_0^{\pi} \sin(x+s) \sin(s+t)\, ds$$

$$= \frac{1}{2} \int_0^{\pi} [\cos(x-t) - \cos(2s+x+t)]\, ds$$

$$[\because 2\sin A \sin B = \cos(A-B) - \cos(A+B)]$$

$$= \frac{1}{2}\left[ s\cos(x-t) - \frac{1}{2}\sin(2s+x+t) \right]_0^{\pi}$$

$$= \frac{1}{2}\left[ \pi\cos(x-t) - \frac{1}{2}\sin(x+t) + \frac{1}{2}\sin(x+t) \right]$$

$$= \frac{\pi}{2}\cos(x-t)$$

Similarly,

$$k_3(x,t) = \int_0^{\pi} k(x,s) k_2(s,t)\, ds$$

$$= \int_0^{\pi} \sin(x+s) \frac{\pi}{2} \cos(s-t)\, ds$$

$$= \frac{\pi}{4} \int_0^{\pi} [\sin(2s+x-t) + \cos(x+t)] ds$$

$$= \frac{\pi}{4}\left[ -\frac{1}{2}\cos(2s+x-t) + s\cdot\sin(x+t) \right]_0^{\pi}$$

$$= \frac{\pi}{4}\left[ -\frac{1}{2}\cos(x-t) + \frac{1}{2}\cos(x-t) + \pi\sin(x+t) \right]$$

$$= \left(\frac{\pi}{2}\right)^2 \sin(x+t)$$

Similarly, we may get

$$k_4(x,t) = \left(\frac{\pi}{2}\right)^3 \cos(x-t); \quad k_5(x,t) = \left(\frac{\pi}{2}\right)^4 \sin(x+t)$$

$$k_6(x,t) = \left(\frac{\pi}{2}\right)^5 \cos(x-t) \text{ and so on.}$$

Now, $R(x,t;\lambda) = \sum_{m=1}^{\infty} \lambda^{m-1} k_m(x,t)$

$$= k_1(x,t) + \lambda k_2(x,t) + \lambda^2 k_3(x,t) + \lambda^3 k_4(x,t) + \ldots$$

$$= k_1(x,t) + \lambda^2 k_3(x,t) + \lambda^4 k_5(x,t) + \ldots$$

$$+ \lambda[k_2(x,t) + \lambda^2 k_4(x,t) + \lambda^4 k_6(x,t) + \ldots]$$

$$= \sin(x+t)\left\{1 + \left(\frac{\lambda\pi}{2}\right)^2 + \left(\frac{\lambda\pi}{2}\right)^4 + \ldots\right\}$$

$$+ \frac{\lambda\pi}{2}\cos(x-t)\left\{1 + \left(\frac{\lambda\pi}{2}\right)^2 + \left(\frac{\lambda\pi}{2}\right)^4 + \ldots\right\}$$

$$= \left\{\sin(x+t) + \frac{\lambda\pi}{2}\cos(x-t)\right\}\left\{1 + \left(\frac{\lambda\pi}{2}\right)^2 + \left(\frac{\lambda\pi}{2}\right)^4 + \ldots\right\}$$

$$= \left\{\sin(x+t) + \frac{\lambda\pi}{2}\cos(x-t)\right\} \frac{1}{1-\left(\frac{\lambda\pi}{2}\right)^2}, \text{ provided } |\lambda| < \frac{2}{\pi}$$

$$= \frac{2}{4-\lambda^2\pi^2}\{2\sin(x+t) + \lambda\pi\cos(x-t)\}$$

Hence, the required solution of the given integral equation is

$$u(x) = f(x) + \lambda \int_0^{\pi} R(x,t;\lambda) f(t)\, dt$$

$$= 1 + \frac{2\lambda}{4 - \lambda^2\pi^2}\int_0^{\pi}\{2\sin(x+t) + \lambda\pi\cos(x-t)\}\,dt$$

$$= 1 + \frac{2\lambda}{4 - \lambda^2\pi^2}[-2\cos(x+t) - \lambda\pi\sin(x-t)]_0^{\pi}$$

$$= 1 + \frac{2\lambda}{4 - \lambda^2\pi^2}\{-2\cos(\pi + x) - \lambda\pi\sin(x-\pi) + 2\cos x + \lambda\pi\sin x\}$$

$$= 1 + \frac{2\lambda}{4 - \lambda^2\pi^2}[4\cos x + 2\lambda\pi\sin x]$$

$$\Rightarrow \quad u(x) = 1 + \frac{4\lambda}{4 - \lambda^2\pi^2}[2\cos x + \lambda\pi\sin x]$$

## (III) By Assuming $u_0(x)$

This method is used when resolved kernel cannot be obtained in closed form *i.e.*, the sum of infinite series occurring in the formula of the resolvent kernel cannot be determined. In such cases we assume $u_0(x)$ (initial approximate solution of $u(x)$) and then we find the solution by successive approximations.

***Example 55.*** *Solve* $u(x) = 2x + \lambda\int_0^1 (x+t)\,u(t)\,dt$ *by taking* $u_0(x) = 1$.

**Solution.** If $u_n(x)$ denotes the $n$th approximation, then

$$u_n(x) = 2x + \lambda\int_0^1 (x+t)u_{n-1}(t)\,dt$$

$$\Rightarrow \quad u_1(x) = 2x + \lambda\int_0^1 (x+t)\,u_0(t)\,dt = 2x + \lambda\int_0^1 (x+t)\cdot 1\,dt$$

$$= 2x + \lambda\left[tx + \frac{t^2}{2}\right]_0^1 = 2x + \lambda\left(x + \frac{1}{2}\right)$$

$$u_2(x) = 2x + \lambda\int_0^1 (x+t)\,u_1(t)\,dt$$

$$= 2x + \lambda\int_0^1 (x+t)\left\{2t + \lambda\left(t + \frac{1}{2}\right)\right\}dt$$

$$= 2x + \lambda\int_0^1 (x+t)\left\{\frac{\lambda}{2} + t(2+\lambda)\right\}dt$$

$$= 2x + \lambda\int_0^1 \left\{\frac{x\lambda}{2} + t\left(\frac{\lambda}{2} + 2x + x\right) + t^2(2+\lambda)\right\}dt$$

$$= 2x + \lambda\left[\frac{x\lambda t}{2} + \frac{t^2}{2}\left(\frac{\lambda}{2} + 2x + x\lambda\right) + \frac{t^3}{3}(2+\lambda)\right]_0^1$$

$$= 2x + \lambda\left[\frac{x\lambda}{2} + \frac{1}{2}\left(\frac{\lambda}{2} + 2x + x\lambda\right) + \frac{1}{3}(2+\lambda)\right]$$

$$= 2x + \lambda\left(x + \frac{2}{3}\right) + \lambda^2\left(x + \frac{7}{12}\right)$$

Similarly,

$$u_3(x) = 2x + \lambda\int_0^1 (x+t)u_2(t)\,dt$$

$$= 2x + \lambda\int_0^1 (x+t)\left\{2t + \lambda\left(t + \frac{2}{3}\right) + \lambda^2\left(t + \frac{7}{12}\right)\right\}dt$$

$$= 2x + \lambda\int_0^1\left[\left\{x\left(\frac{2\lambda}{3} + \frac{7\lambda^2}{12}\right) + t\left(\frac{2\lambda}{3} + \frac{7\lambda^2}{12} + 2x + x\lambda + x\lambda^2\right) + t^2(2 + \lambda + \lambda^2\right\}dt$$

$$= 2x + \lambda\left\{xt\left(\frac{2\lambda}{3} + \frac{7\lambda^2}{12}\right) + \frac{t^2}{2}\left(\frac{2\lambda}{3} + \frac{7\lambda^2}{12} + 2x + x\lambda + x\lambda^2\right) + \frac{t^3}{3}(2 + \lambda + \lambda^2)\right\}_0^1$$

$$= 2x + \lambda\left(x + \frac{2}{3}\right) + \lambda^2\left(\frac{7}{6}x + \frac{2}{3}\right) + \lambda^3\left(\frac{13}{12}x + \frac{5}{8}\right)$$

Proceeding in the same way, we may get the other approximations $u_4(x), u_5(x), \ldots$ and so on.

# Solution of Volterra Integral Equation of the Second kind

## (I) With the Help of Resolvent Kernel

**1.** Consider the Volterra integral equation of the second kind

$$u(x) = f(x) + \lambda\int_a^x k(x, t)u(t)\,dt \quad \ldots(i)$$

Also, suppose that

(i) Kernel $k(x, t) \neq 0$ is real and continuous in a rectangle $R$ $(a \leq x \leq b,\ a \leq t \leq b)$.

Also, $k(x, t) \leq M$ on $R$, *i.e.*, $k(x, t)$ is bounded by $M$ on $R$

(ii) $f(x) \neq 0$ is real and continuous in the interval $I(a \leq x \leq b)$.

Also, let $|f(x)| \leq N$ in $I$.

(ii) $\lambda$ is a constant.

Then, given integral Eq. (i) has a unique continuous solution in $I$, which is given by the absolutely and uniformly series

$$u(x) = f(x) + \lambda\int_a^x k(x, t)f(t)\,dt + \lambda^2\int_a^x k(x, t)\int_a^t k(t, t_1)f(t_1)\,dt_1\,dt + \ldots \quad \ldots(ii)$$

> ***Note*** The above method to find solution of Eq. (i) is called method of substitution.

**2.** Consider volterra integral equation of the second kind

$$u(x) = f(x) + \lambda\int_a^x k(x, t)u(t)\,dt \quad \ldots(i)$$

where $\quad u_0(x) = f(x)$

Then, by the method of iterated kernel $n$th order approximate solution of Eq. (i) is

$$u_n(x) = f(x) + \sum_{m=1}^{n}\lambda^m\int_a^x k_m(x, t)f(t)\,dt \quad \ldots(ii)$$

Taking limit $n \to \infty$, we get

$$u(x) = f(x) + \sum_{m=1}^{\infty}\lambda^m\int_a^x k_m(x, t)f(t)\,dt \quad \ldots(iii)$$

$$\Rightarrow \quad u(x) = f(x) + \lambda \int_a^x \left[ \sum_{m=1}^{\infty} \lambda^{m-1} k_m(x,t) \right] f(t)\, dt$$

$$\Rightarrow \quad u(x) = f(x) + \lambda \int_a^x R(x, t; \lambda) f(t)\, dt \qquad \text{...(iv)}$$

here, $$R(x, t; \lambda) = \sum_{m=1}^{\infty} \lambda^{m-1} k_m(x, t) \qquad \text{...(v)}$$

Eq. (iv) gives the solution of integral Eq. (i).

> ***Note*** **(a)** The above method of finding solution of Eq. (i) is successive approximation method or iterative method or resolvent kernel method.
>
> **(b)** Neumann series Eq. (iii) and resolvent kernel series Eq. (v) converges absolutely and uniformly, when $k(x, t)$ is continuous in $R$.

***Example 56.*** *Find the resolvent kernel of the volterra integral equation with kernel*

(i) $k(x, t) = 1$

(ii) $k(x, t) = e^{x-t}$

(iii) $k(x, t) = \dfrac{2 + \cos x}{2 + \cos t}$

(iv) $k(x, t) = \dfrac{1 + x^2}{1 + t^2}$

(v) $k(x, t) = e^{x^2 - t^2}$

(vi) $k(x, t) = t - x \qquad (\lambda = 1)$

(vii) $k(x, t) = x - t \qquad (\lambda = 1)$

**Solution.** (i) Here, we have $k(x, t) = 1$

*i.e.,* $k_1(x, t) = k(x, t) = 1$

and $k_2(x, t) = \int_t^x k(x, z) k_1(z, t)\, dz = \int_t^x dz = x - t$

Also $k_3(x, t) = \int_t^x k(x, z) k_2(z, t)\, dz = \int_t^x 1 \cdot (z - t)\, dz$

$$= \left[ \frac{(z-t)^2}{2} \right]_t^x = \frac{(x-t)^2}{2!}$$

Similarly,

$$k_4(x, t) = \int_t^x k(x, z) k_3(z, t)\, dz$$

$$= \int_t^x 1 \cdot \frac{(z-t)^2}{2!} = \frac{1}{2!} \left[ \frac{(z-t)^3}{3} \right]_t^x = \frac{(x-t)^3}{3!} \text{ and so on.}$$

$$\Rightarrow \quad k_n(x, t) = \frac{(x-t)^{n-1}}{(n-1)!}$$

$$\therefore \quad R(x, t; \lambda) \sum_{m=1}^{\infty} \lambda^{m-1} k_m(x, t)$$

$$= k_1(x, t) + \lambda k_2(x, t) + \lambda^2 k_3(x, t) + \ldots$$

$$= 1 + \frac{\lambda(x-t)}{1!} = \frac{[\lambda(x-t)]^2}{2!} + \frac{[\lambda(x-t)]^2}{3!} + \ldots = e^{\lambda(x-t)}$$

(ii) Here, $k(x, t) = e^{x-t}$

$$\Rightarrow \quad k_1(x, t) = k(x, t) = e^{x-t}$$

and $k_2(x, t) = \int_t^x k(x, z) k_1(z, t)\, dz$

$$= \int_t^x e^{x-z} e^{z-t}\, dz = e^{x-t} \int_t^x dz = e^{x-t}(x - t)$$

Similarly,

$$k_3(x, t) = \int_t^x k(x, z) k_2(z, t)\, dz$$

$$= \int_t^x e^{x-z} e^{z-t} (z - t)\, dz = e^{x-t} \int_t^x (z - t)\, dz$$

$$= e^{x-t} \left[ \frac{(z-t)^2}{2} \right]_t^x = e^{x-t} \frac{(x-t)^2}{2!}$$

and $$k_4(x, t) = \int_t^x e^{x-z} e^{z-t} \frac{(z-t)^2}{2!}\, dz = \frac{e^{x-t}}{2!} \int_t^x (z-t)^2\, dz$$

$$= e^{x-t} \frac{(x-t)^3}{3!} \text{ and so on.}$$

In general

$$k_n(x, t) = e^{x-t} \frac{(x-t)^{n-1}}{(n-1)!}, \quad n \in N$$

$$\therefore \quad R(x, t; \lambda) = \sum_{m=1}^{\infty} \lambda^{m-1} \cdot k_m(x, t)$$

$$= k_1(x, t) + \lambda k_2(x, t) + \lambda^2 k_3(x, t) + \ldots$$

$$= e^{x-t} + e^{x-t} \frac{\lambda \cdot (x-t)}{1!} + e^{x-t} \frac{[\lambda(x-t)]^2}{2!} + \ldots$$

$$= e^{x-t} \left[ 1 + \frac{\lambda \cdot (x-t)}{1!} + \frac{[\lambda(x-t)]^2}{2!} + \ldots \right]$$

$$= e^{x-t} \cdot e^{\lambda(x-t)} = e^{(x-t)(1+\lambda)}$$

(iii) Here,

$$k_1(x, t) = k(x, t) = \frac{2 + \cos x}{2 + \cos t}$$

Also, $k_2(x, t) = \int_t^x k(x, z) k_1(z, t)\, dz$

$$= \int_t^x \frac{2 + \cos x}{2 + \cos z} \cdot \frac{2 + \cos z}{2 + \cos t}\, dz$$

$$= \frac{2 + \cos x}{2 + \cos t} \int_t^x dz = \frac{2 + \cos x}{2 + \cos t}(x - t)$$

Similarly,

$$k_3(x, t) = \int_t^x k(x, z) k_2(z, t)\, dz$$

$$= \int_t^x \frac{2 + \cos x}{2 + \cos z} \cdot \frac{2 + \cos z}{2 + \cos t}(z - t)\, dz$$

$$= \frac{2 + \cos x}{2 + \cos t} \left( \frac{(x-t)^2}{2!} \right)$$

Again, $k_4(x, t) = \int_t^x k(x, z) k_3(z, t)\, dz$

$$= \int_t^x \frac{2 + \cos x}{2 + \cos z} \cdot \frac{2 + \cos z}{2 + \cos t} \cdot \frac{(z-t)^2}{2!}\, dz$$

$$= \frac{2 + \cos x}{2 + \cos t} \cdot \frac{1}{2!} \left[ \frac{(z-t)^3}{3} \right]_t^x = \frac{2 + \cos x}{2 + \cos t} \frac{(x-t)^3}{3!}$$

and so on.

In general, we get

$$k_n(x, t) = \frac{2 + \cos x}{2 + \cos t} \frac{(x-t)^{n-1}}{(n-1)!}$$

$$\therefore \quad R(x,t;\lambda) = \sum_{m=1}^{\infty} \lambda^{m-1} k_m(x,t)$$

$$= k_1(x,t) + \lambda k_2(x,t) + \lambda^2 k_3(x,t) + \ldots$$

$$= \frac{2+\cos x}{2+\cos t} + \frac{2+\cos x}{2+\cos t} \cdot \frac{\lambda(x-t)}{1!} + \frac{2+\cos x}{2+\cos t} \cdot \frac{\{\lambda(x-t)\}^2}{2!} + \ldots$$

$$= \frac{2+\cos x}{2+\cos t}\left[1 + \frac{\lambda(x-t)}{1!} + \frac{\{\lambda(x-t)\}^2}{2!} + \ldots\right]$$

$$= \frac{2+\cos x}{2+\cos t} \cdot e^{\lambda(x-t)}$$

Now, similarly as above

(iv) $R(x,t;\lambda) = \dfrac{1+x^2}{1+t^2} e^{\lambda(x-t)}$

(v) $R(x,t;\lambda) = e^{x^2-t^2} e^{\lambda(x-t)}$

(vi) $R(x,t;\lambda) = \sin(t-x)$ (Here, $\lambda = 1$)

(vii) $R(x,t;\lambda) = \sinh(x-t)$ (Here, $\lambda = 1$)

***Example 57.*** *Solve* $u(x) = 1 + \int_0^x u(t)\,dt$.

**Solution.** Here, $\lambda = 1$, $k(x,t) = 1$

$$\Rightarrow \quad R(x,t;\lambda) = e^{\lambda(x-t)} = e^{(x-t)}$$

Now, the required solution of given integral equation is given by

$$u(x) = f(x) + \lambda\int_0^x R(x,t;\lambda) f(t)\,dt$$

$$\Rightarrow \quad u(x) = 1 + \int_0^x e^{x-t} dt = 1 + e^x \int_0^x e^{-t} dt = 1 + e^x[-e^{-t}]_0^x$$

$$= 1 - e^x(e^{-x} - 1) = e^x$$

***Example 58.*** *Find the solution of the integral equation* $u(x) = e^{x^2} + \int_0^x e^{x^2-t^2} u(t)\,dt$ *with the help of resolvent kernel.*

**Solution.** Comparing the given equation with

$$u(x) = f(x) + \int_0^x k(x,t) u(t)\,dt$$

we get, $f(x) = e^{x^2}$, $\lambda = 1$, $k(x,t) = e^{x^2-t^2}$

$$\therefore \quad R(x,t;\lambda) = e^{x^2-t^2} \cdot e^{\lambda(x-t)} = e^{x^2-t^2} \cdot e^{(x-t)}$$

Here, the required solution of the given integral equation is given by

$$u(x) = f(x) + \lambda\int_0^x R(x,t;\lambda) f(t)dt$$

$$= e^{x^2} + \int_0^x e^{x^2-t^2} e^{x-t} \cdot e^{t^2} dt$$

$$= e^{x^2} + e^{x^2+x}\int_0^x e^{-t} dt = e^{x^2} + e^{x^2+x}[-e^{-t}]_0^x$$

$$= e^{x^2} - e^{x^2} + e^{x^2+x} \quad \Rightarrow \quad u(x) = e^{x^2+x}$$

***Example 59.*** *Solve* $u(x) = x + \int_0^x (t-x)\,u(t)\,dt$.

**Solution.** Comparing the given equation with

$$u(x) = f(x) + \lambda\int_0^x k(x,t) u(t)\,dt$$

we get, $f(x) = x, \lambda = 1, k(x,t) = t - x$

Now, $k_1(x,t) = k(x,t) = t - x$

$\therefore$ $R(x,t;\lambda) = \sin(t-x)$

Hence, the required solution is given by

$$u(x) = f(x) + \lambda\int_u^x R(x,t;\lambda) f(t)\,dt$$

$$= x + \int_0^x \sin(t-x) t\,dt$$

$$= x + [t\{-\cos(t-x)\}]_0^x - \int_0^x 1 \cdot \{-\cos(t-x)\}dt$$

$$= x - x + [\sin(t-x)]_0^x = \sin x$$

## (II) With the Help of Resolvent Kernel When $k(x,t)$ is in Some Particular Form

**(1)** When $k(x,t)$ is a polynomial of degree $(n-1)$ in $x$.

*i.e.,* $k(x,t) = A_0(x) + A_1(x)(x-t) + A_2(x)\dfrac{(x-t)^2}{2!} + \ldots + A_{n-1}(x)\dfrac{(x-t)^{n-1}}{(n-1)!}$ ...(i)

Then, the resolvent kernel $R(x,t;\lambda)$ is given by

$$R(x,t;\lambda) = \frac{1}{\lambda} \cdot \frac{d^n \phi(x,t;\lambda)}{dx^n}$$

where, $\phi(x,t;\lambda)$ is a solution of the differential equation.

$$\frac{d^n\phi}{dx^n} - \lambda\left[A_0(x)\frac{d^{n-1}\phi}{dx^{n-1}} + A_1(x)\frac{d^{n-2}\phi}{dx^{n-2}} + \ldots + A_{n-1}(x)\phi\right] = 0$$

with conditions

$$\phi = \frac{d\phi}{dx} = \frac{d^2\phi}{dx^2} = \ldots = \frac{d^{n-2}\phi}{dx^{n-2}} = 0 \quad \text{when } x = t$$

and $\dfrac{d^{n-1}\phi}{dx^{n-1}} = 1$ when $x = t$

**(2)** Assume that $k(x,t)$ is a polynomial of degree $(n-1)$ in $t$

*i.e.,* $k(x,t) = B_0(t) + B_1(t)(t-x) + B_2(t)\dfrac{(t-x)^2}{2!} + \ldots + B_{n-1}(t)\dfrac{(t-x)^{n-1}}{(n-1)!}$

Then, $R(x,t;\lambda) = -\dfrac{1}{\lambda}\dfrac{d^n\psi(x,t;\lambda)}{dt^n}$

where $\psi(x,t;\lambda)$ is a solution of the differential equation

$$\frac{d^n\psi}{dt^n} + \lambda\left[B_0(t)\frac{d^{n-1}\psi}{dt^{n-1}} + B_1(t)\frac{d^{n-2}\psi}{dt^{n-2}} + \ldots + B_{n-1}(t)\psi\right] = 0$$

Satisfying the conditions

$$\psi = \frac{d\psi}{dt} = \frac{d^2\psi}{dt^2} = \ldots = \frac{d^{n-2}\psi}{dt^{n-2}} = 0 \quad \text{when } t = x$$

and $\dfrac{d^{n-1}\psi}{dt^{n-1}} = 1$ when $t = x$

***Example 60.*** *Solve* $u(x) = 29 + 6x + \int_0^x [5 - 6(x - t)]u(t)\,dt.$

**Solution.** Here, we have

$$f(x) = 29 + 6x, \lambda = 1, k(x, t) = 5 - 6(x - t)$$

Let $\quad k(x, t) = A_0(x) + A_1(x)(x - t)$

Then, we have $A_0(x) = 5, A_1(x) = -6$

The resolvent kernel $R(x, t; \lambda)$ is given by

$$R(x, t; \lambda) = \frac{d^2\phi(x, t; \lambda)}{dx^2}$$

i.e., $\quad R(x, t; 1) = \frac{d^2\phi(x, t; 1)}{dx^2} = \frac{d^2\phi}{dx^2}$

where $\phi(x, t; 1)$ satisfies the differential equation

$$\frac{d^2\phi}{dx^2} - \lambda\left[A_0(x)\frac{d\phi}{dx} + A_1(x)\phi\right] = 0$$

$$\Rightarrow \quad \frac{d^2\phi}{dx^2} - 5\frac{d\phi}{dx} + 6\phi = 0$$

$$\Rightarrow \quad (D^2 - 5D + 6)\phi = 0 \quad \text{...(i)}$$

with conditions

$$\phi = 0, \text{ when } x = t$$

$$\frac{d\phi}{dx} = 1, \text{ when } x = t \quad \text{...(ii)}$$

Auxiliary equation of Eq. (i) is given by

$$m^2 - 5m + 6 = 0 \quad \Rightarrow \quad m = 3, 2$$

$\Rightarrow$ The general solution of Eq. (i) is given by

$$\phi = Ae^{3x} + Be^{2x} \quad \text{...(iii)}$$

$$\Rightarrow \quad \frac{d\phi}{dx} = 3Ae^{3x} + 2Be^{2x}$$

Using Eq. (ii), we get

$$0 = Ae^{3t} + Be^{2t} \text{ and } 1 = 3Ae^{3t} + 2Be^{2t}$$

On solving, we get

$$A = e^{-3t}, B = -e^{-2t}$$

Then, Eq. (iii) gives

$$\phi = \phi(x, t; \lambda) = e^{3(x-t)} - e^{2(x-t)}$$

$$\Rightarrow \frac{d\phi}{dx} = 3e^{3(x-t)} - 2e^{2(x-t)} \text{ and } \frac{d^2\phi}{dx^2} = 9e^{3(x-t)} - 4e^{2(x-t)}$$

Thus, the resolvent kernel $R(x, t; \lambda)$ is given by

$$R(x, t; \lambda) = \frac{d^2\phi}{dx^2} = 9e^{3(x-t)} - 4e^{2(x-t)}$$

Hence, the required solution is

$$u(x) = f(x) + \lambda\int_0^x R(x, t; \lambda)f(t)\,dt$$

$$= 29 + 6x + \int_0^x R(x, t; 1)(29 + 6t)\,dt$$

$$= 29 + 6x + \int_0^x [9e^{3(x-t)} - 4e^{2(x-t)}][29 + 6t]\,dt$$

$$= 29 + 6x + [(29 + 6t)\{-3e^{3(x-t)} + 2e^{2(x-t)}\}]$$

$$-\int_0^x 6\{-3e^{3(x-t)} + 2e^{2(x-t)}\}\,dt$$

$$= 29 + 6x - 29x - 6x - 29(-3e^{3x} + 2e^{2x})$$

$$-6[0 - (e^{3x} - e^{2x})]$$

$$= 93e^{3x} - 64e^{2x}$$

***Example 61.*** *Solve* $u(x) = \cos x - x - 2 + \int_0^x (t - x)u(t)\,dt.$

**Solution.** We have,

$$u(x) = \cos x - x - 2 + \int_0^x (t - x)\,u(t)\,dt \quad \text{...(i)}$$

On comparing with the standard equation, we get

$$f(x) = \cos x - x - 2, \lambda = 1, k(x, t) = t - x$$

Let us assume $k(x, t) = B_0(t) + B_1(t)[t - x]$.

which gives $B_0(t) = 0, B_1(t) = 1$.

Therefore, the resolvent kernel $R(x, t; \lambda)$ is given by

$$R(x, t; \lambda) = -\frac{1}{\lambda}\cdot\frac{d^2\psi(x, t; \lambda)}{dt^2}$$

i.e., $\quad R(x, t; 1) = -\frac{d^2\psi(x, t; 1)}{dt^2} = -\frac{d^2\psi}{dt^2}$

where $\psi$ satisfies

$$\frac{d^2\psi}{dt^2} + \lambda\left[B_0(t)\frac{d\psi}{dt} + B_1(t)\psi\right] = 0$$

i.e., $\quad \frac{d^2\psi}{dt^2} + \psi = 0 \Rightarrow (D^2 + 1)\psi = 0 \quad \text{...(ii)}$

With conditions

$$\psi = 0 \text{ at } t = x \text{ and } \frac{d\psi}{dt} = 1 \text{ at } t = x$$

Now, general solution of Eq. (ii) is

$$\psi = a\cos t + b\sin t$$

$$\Rightarrow \quad \frac{d\psi}{dt} = -a\sin t + b\cos t$$

Using given conditions, we get

$$a = -\sin x \text{ and } b = \cos x$$

$$\therefore \quad \psi = -\sin x\cos t + \cos x\sin t$$

$$= -\sin(x - t) = \sin(t - x)$$

$$\Rightarrow \quad \frac{d\psi}{dt} = \cos(t - x) \text{ and } \frac{d^2\psi}{dt^2} = -\sin(t - x)$$

$$\therefore R(x, t; \lambda) = -\frac{d^2\psi}{dt^2} = \sin(t - x)$$

Hence, the required solution is given by

$$u(x) = f(x) + \lambda\int_0^x R(x, t; \lambda)f(t)\,dt$$

$$= \cos x - x - 2 + \int_0^x \sin(t - x)(\cos t - t - 2)\,dt$$

$$= \cos x - x - 2 + \int_0^x \sin(t - x)\cos t\,dt$$

$$+ \int_0^x (-t - 2)\sin(t - x)\,dt$$

After simplification, we get

$$u(x) = \cos x - x - 2 + \frac{1}{2}\left[-\frac{\cos(2t - x)}{2} - t\sin x\right]_0^x + (x + 2)$$

$$-2\cos x - [\sin(t - x)]_0^x$$

$$= -\cos x + \frac{1}{2}\left[-\frac{\cos x}{2} - x\sin x + \frac{\cos x}{2}\right] + \sin(-x)$$

$$= -\cos x - \sin x - \frac{1}{2}x\sin x$$

## (III) By Assuming $u_0(x)$

If $u(x) = f(x) + \lambda \int_0^x k(x,t)u(t)\,dt$ be the given equation, then use the following formula

$$u_n(x) = f(x) + \lambda \int_0^x k(x,t)u_{n-1}(t)\,dt$$

and $$u(x) = \lim_{n\to\infty} u_n(x)$$

***Example* 62.** *Solve* $u(x) = 1 + \int_0^x (x-t)\,u(t)\,dt$ *by assuming* $u_0(x) = 0$.

**Solution.** Here, $f(x) = 1, \lambda = 1, k(x,t) = x - t$

$n$th approximation of $u(x)$ is

$$u_n(x) = f(x) + \lambda \int_0^x k(x,t)u_{n-1}(t)\,dt$$

$$\Rightarrow \quad u_1(x) = 1 + \int_0^x (x-t)u_0(t)\,dt = 1 + \int_0^x 0\,dt = 1$$

$$u_2(x) = 1 + \int_0^x (x-t)u_1(t)\,dt = 1 + \int_0^x (x-t)\,dt$$

$$= 1 + \left[xt - \frac{t^2}{2}\right]_0^x$$

$$= 1 + x^2 - \frac{x^2}{2} = 1 + \frac{x^2}{2}$$

$$= 1 + \frac{x^2}{2!}$$

Similarly, $u_3(x) = 1 + \frac{x^2}{2!} + \frac{x^4}{4!}$ and so on.

$$\therefore \quad u(x) = \lim_{n\to\infty} u_n(x)$$

$$= 1 + \frac{x^2}{2!} + \frac{x^4}{4!} + \ldots$$

$$\Rightarrow \quad u(x) = \cosh x$$

## (IV) By Reducing to Differential Equation

***Example* 63.** *Solve*

$$u(x) = 1 - 2x - 4x^2 + \int_0^x [3 + 6(x-t) - 4(x-t)^2]u(t)\,dt.$$

**Solution.** By using Leibnitz rule differentiating both sides of given equation *wrt* $x$, we get

$$u'(x) = -2 - 8x + \int_0^x [6 - 8(x-t)]u(t)\,dt + 3u(x) \quad \ldots\text{(i)}$$

$$u''(x) = -8 - 8\int_0^x u(t)\,dt + 6u(x) + 3u'(x) \quad \ldots\text{(ii)}$$

and $u'''(x) = -8u(x) + 6u''(x) + 3u''$

$\Rightarrow \quad u'''(x) - 9u''(x) + 8u(x) = 0$

which general solution is

$$u(x) = ae^x + be^{4x} + ce^{-2x} \quad \ldots\text{(iii)}$$

$$\Rightarrow \quad u'(x) = ae^x + 4be^{4x} - 2ce^{-2x} \quad \ldots\text{(iv)}$$

$$u''(x) = ae^x + 16be^{4x} + 4ce^{-2x} \quad \ldots\text{(v)}$$

Since, $u(0) = 1$ (From given integral equation)

$u'(0) = -2 + 3u(0) = -2 + 3 = 1$ [From Eq. (i)]

$u''(0) = -8 + 6u(0) + 3u'(0)$

$= -8 + 6 + 3 = 1$ [From Eq. (i)]

Now, From Eqs. (iii), (iv) and (v)

$$a + b + c = 0,\ a + 4b - 2c = 0,\ a + 16b + 4c = 0$$

$$\Rightarrow \quad a = 1, b = 0, c = 0$$

$\therefore$ From Eq. (iii), required solution is $u(x) = e^x$

## (V) By Using Laplace Transformation Integral Equation of Convolution Type

The integral equation

$$u(x) = f(x) + \int_0^x k(x-t)u(t)\,dt$$

in which the kernel $k(x-t)$ is a function of the difference $x - t$ only, is known as integral equation of the convolution type and can be written as

$$u(x) = f(x) + k(x) * u(x)$$

Taking Laplace transform of both sides

$$\Rightarrow \quad L[u(x)] = L[f(x)] + L[k(x)] \cdot L[u(x)]$$

$$\Rightarrow \quad L[u(x)] = \frac{L[f(x)]}{1 - L[k(x)]}$$

$$\Rightarrow \quad u(x) = L^{-1}\frac{L[f(x)]}{1 - L[k(x)]}$$

which is the required solution.

***Example* 64.** *Solve* $u(x) = x + 2\int_0^x \cos(x-t)u(t)\,dt$

**Solution.** The given equation can be written as

$$u(x) = x + (2\cos x) * (u(x))$$

$$\Rightarrow \quad L[u(x)] = L[x] + 2L[\cos x] \cdot L[u(x)]$$

$$= \frac{1}{s^2} + 2 \cdot \frac{s}{s^2+1} \cdot L[u(x)]$$

$$\Rightarrow \quad u(s)\left[1 - \frac{2s}{s^2+1}\right] = \frac{1}{s^2} \quad \text{where } L[u(x)] = u(s)$$

$$\Rightarrow \quad u(s) = \frac{s^2+1}{s^2(s-1)^2} = \frac{1}{s^2} + \frac{2}{s} - \frac{2}{s-1} + \frac{2}{(s-1)^2}$$

Taking inverse Laplace transformation, we get

$$u(x) = L^{-1}\left[\frac{1}{s^2} + \frac{2}{s} - \frac{2}{s-1} + \frac{2}{(s-1)^2}\right]$$

$$\Rightarrow \quad u(x) = x + 2 - 2e^x + 2xe^x$$

which is the required solution.

## Solution of Volterra Equation of First Kind

***Example 65.*** *Solve* $f(x) = \int_0^x e^{x-t} u(t)\, dt.$

**Solution.** Using Leibnitzs' rule of differentiation, we get

$$f'(x) = \int_0^x \frac{\partial}{\partial x}[e^{x-t} \cdot u(t)]\, dt + e^{x-x} u(x) \cdot 1 - 0$$

$$\Rightarrow \quad f'(x) = \int_0^x e^{x-t} u(t)\, dt + u(x)$$

$$\Rightarrow \quad u(x) = f'(x) - \int_0^x e^{x-t} u(t)\, dt$$

which is a volterra integral equation of second kind.

Here, $\lambda = 1,\ k(x, t) = e^{x-t}$

$\Rightarrow \quad R(x, t; \lambda) = e^{(1+\lambda)(x-t)} = e^0 = 1$

$\therefore$ Required solution is

$$u(x) = f'(x) - \int_0^x f'(t)\, dt = f' x - [f(t)]_0^x$$

$$= f'(x) - [f(x) - f(0)] = f'(x) - f(x)$$

## Important Properties of Eigen Values and Eigen Functions

1. If a kernel is symmetric, then all its iterated kernels are also symmetric.
2. If the kernel $k(x, t)$ is symmetrical and not identically equal to zero, then it has atleast one eigen value.

   OR

   Every symmetric kernel with a norm not equal to zero has atleast one eigen value. (Hilbert Theorem)
3. The eigen values of a symmetric kernel are real.
4. The eigen functions of a symmetric kernel, corresponding to different eigen values are orthogonal.
5. The multiplicity of any non-zero eigen value is finite for every symmetric kernel for which $\int_a^b \int_a^b |k(x, t)|^2\, dx\, dt$ is finite.
6. The sequence of eigen functions of a symmetric kernel can be made orthonormal.
7. The eigen values of a symmetric $L_2$-kernel form a finite or infinite sequence $\{\lambda_i\}$ with no finite limit point.
8. The set of eigen values of the second iterated kernel coincide with the set of squares of the eigen values of the given kernel.
9. Let $\{\phi_i(x)\}$ be the sequence of all eigen functions of a symmetric $L_2$-kernel with $\{\lambda_i\}$ as the sequence of corresponding eigen values. Then, the series $\sum_{i=1}^{\infty} \frac{|\phi_i(x)|^2}{\lambda_i^2}$ converges and its sum is bounded by $C_1^2$ which is an upper bound of the integral $\int_a^b |k(x, t)|^2\, dt$

   Also, the truncated kernel

   $$k^{n+1}(x, t) = k(x, t) - \sum_{i=1}^{n} \frac{\phi_i(x)\bar{\phi}_i(t)}{\lambda_i}$$

   has the eigen values $\lambda_{n+1}, \lambda_{n+2}, \ldots$ and corresponding eigen functions $\phi_{n+1}(x), \phi_{n+2}(x), \ldots$

   The kernel $k^{n+1}(x, t)$ has no other eigen values or eigen functions.
10. A necessary and sufficient condition for a symmetric $L_2$-kernel to be separable is that it must possess a finite number of eigen values.
11. If $$f(x) = \int_a^b k(x, t) h(t)\, dt \quad \ldots\text{(i)}$$

    where $k(x, t)$ is a symmetric $L_2$-kernel and $h(t)$ is an $L_2$-function. Then, $f(x)$ can be expanded in an absolutely and uniformly convergent Fourier series with respect to orthonormal sequence of eigen functions $\{\phi_i(x)\}$ of $k(x, t)$ *i.e.,*

    $$f(x) = \sum_{i=1}^{\infty} f_i\, \phi_i(x)$$

    where $f_i = (f, \phi_i)$

    Also, $$f_i = \frac{h_i}{\lambda_i} \text{ and } h_i = (h, \phi_i)$$

    where $\lambda_i$ are the eigen values of $k(x, t)$

    (Hilbert-Schmidt Theorem)
12. A symmetric $L_2$-kernel $k(x, t)$ is said to be
    (i) Non-negative definite, if
    $$(k\phi, \phi) \geq 0, \ \forall \ L_2\text{-function } \phi$$
    (ii) Positive definite, if
    $$(k\phi, \phi) \geq 0 \text{ and } (k\phi, \phi) = 0 \ \Rightarrow \ \phi \text{ is null}$$
    (iii) Non-positive definite, if
    $$(k\phi, \phi) \leq 0, \ \forall \ L_2\text{-function } \phi$$
    (iv) Negative definite, if
    $$(k\phi, \phi) \leq 0 \text{ and } (k\phi, \phi) = 0 \ \Rightarrow \ \phi \text{ is null.}$$

## Hilbert-Schmidt Method of Solving Non-Homogeneous Fredholm Integral Equation of the Second Kind

Consider the non-homogeneous Fredholm integral equation of second kind

$$u(x) = f(x) + \lambda \int_a^b k(x, t) u(t)\, dt \quad \ldots\text{(i)}$$

where $k(x, t)$ is continuous, real and symmetric and $\lambda$ is a constant (not an eigen value) method of solution of Eq. (i) is given below.

**Step 1** Determining eigen values and the corresponding normalized eigen functions of

$$u(x) = \lambda \int_a^b k(x, t) u(t)\, dt$$

Let $\phi_1(x)$ and $\phi_2(x)$ are eigen functions corresponding to eigen values $\lambda_1$ and $\lambda_2$ respectively, then normalized eigen functions are

$$\phi_1(x) = \frac{u_1(x)}{\left[\int_a^b \{u_1(x)\}^2\right]^{\frac{1}{2}}} = \frac{u_1(x)}{||u_1(x)||}$$

and $$\phi_2(x) = \frac{u_2(x)}{\left[\int_a^b \{u_2(x)\}^2\right]^{\frac{1}{2}}} = \frac{u_2(x)}{||u_2(x)||}$$

**Step 2** Finding $f_1 = \int_a^b f(x)\phi_1(x)\,dx$

and $$f_2 = \int_a^b f(x)\phi_2(x)\,dx$$

**Step 3**

(i) If $\lambda \neq \lambda_1$ and $\lambda \neq \lambda_2$, then Eq. (i) will have unique solution given by

$$u(x) = f(x) + \lambda \sum_{m=1}^{2} \frac{f_m}{\lambda_m - \lambda} \phi_m(x)$$

(ii) Eq. (i) will have no solution, if

$\lambda = \lambda_1$ but $f_1 \neq 0$

or $\lambda = \lambda_2$ but $f_2 \neq 0$

(iii) Eq. (i) will have infinitely many solutions, if $\lambda = \lambda_1$ and $f_1 = 0$ and solution is given by

$$u(x) = f(x) + A\phi_1(x) + \frac{\lambda}{\lambda_2 - \lambda} f_2\phi_2(x).$$

where, $A$ is an arbitrary constant.

OR

$\lambda = \lambda_2$ and $f_2 = 0$ and solution is given by

$$u(x) = f(x) + B\phi_2(x) + \frac{\lambda}{\lambda_1 - \lambda} f_1\phi_1(x)$$

where, $B$ is an arbitrary constant.

***Example 66.*** *Solve* $u(x) = 1 + \lambda \int_0^{\pi} \cos(x - t)\, u(t)\, dt$ *and discuss the cases.*

**Solution. Step 1** Determining eigen values and the corresponding normalized eigen functions of

$$u(x) = \lambda \int_0^{\pi} \cos(x + t)\, u(t)\, dt \quad \text{...(i)}$$

Eq. (i) can be written as

$$u(x) = \lambda C_1 \cos x - \lambda C_2 \sin x \quad \text{...(ii)}$$

where $$C_1 = \int_0^{\pi} \cos t\, u(t)\, dt \quad \text{...(iii)}$$

and $$C_2 = \int_0^{\pi} \sin t\, u(t)\, dt \quad \text{...(iv)}$$

Using Eq. (ii) in Eqs. (iii) and (iv), we get after simplification

$$(2 - \lambda\pi)C_1 + 0 \cdot C_2 = 0 \quad \text{...(v)}$$

and $$0 \cdot C_1 + (2 + \lambda\pi)C_2 = 0 \quad \text{...(vi)}$$

For non-trivial solution of Eqs. (v) and (vi), we get

If $$D(\lambda) = \begin{vmatrix} 2 - \lambda\pi & 0 \\ 0 & 2 + \lambda\pi \end{vmatrix} = 0 \Rightarrow \lambda = \pm\frac{2}{\pi}$$

For $\lambda = \lambda_1 = \frac{2}{\pi}$ we get from Eqs. (v) and (vi), we get

$C_2 = 0$ and $C_1$ is arbitrary

From Eq. (ii) $u_1(x) = \frac{2}{\pi} C_1 \cos x$

Putting $\frac{2}{\pi} C_1 = 1 \Rightarrow u_1(x) = \cos x$

$$\therefore \quad ||u_1(x)|| = \left[\int_0^{\pi} \{u_1(x)\}^2 dx\right]^{\frac{1}{2}}$$

$$= \left[\int_0^{\pi} \cos^2 x\, dx\right]^{\frac{1}{2}} = \left(\frac{\pi}{2}\right)^{\frac{1}{2}}$$

$$\therefore \quad \phi_1(x) = \frac{u_1(x)}{||u_1(x)||} = \left(\frac{2}{\pi}\right)^{\frac{1}{2}} \cos x$$

Similarly, for $\lambda = \lambda_2 = -\frac{2}{\pi}$ we can find

$$\phi_2(x) = \left(\frac{2}{\pi}\right)^{\frac{1}{2}} \sin x$$

Also, $$f_1 = \int_0^{\pi} f(x)\phi_1(x)\, dx$$

$$= \left(\frac{2}{\pi}\right)^{\frac{1}{2}} \int_0^{\pi} \cos x\, dx = 0$$

Similarly, $$f_2 = \int_0^{\pi} f(x)\phi_2(x)\, dx = 2\left(\frac{2}{\pi}\right)^{\frac{1}{2}}$$

Now, following cases arise

(i) Let $\lambda \neq \lambda_1$ and $\lambda \neq \lambda_2$, then given integral equation $u(x) = 1 + \lambda \int_0^{\pi} \cos(x + t)\, u(t)\, dt$ will possess unique solution given by

$$u(x) = 1 + \frac{\lambda}{\lambda_1 - \lambda} f_1\phi_1(x) + \frac{\lambda}{\lambda_2 - \lambda} f_2\phi_2(x)$$

$$= 1 + 0 + \frac{\lambda}{-\frac{2}{\pi} - \lambda} \cdot 2\left(\frac{2}{\pi}\right)^{\frac{1}{2}} \cdot \left(\frac{2}{\pi}\right)^{\frac{1}{2}} \sin x$$

$$= 1 - \frac{4\lambda \sin x}{2 + \lambda\pi}$$

(ii) Let $\lambda = \lambda_1 = \frac{2}{\pi}$. Since, $f_1 = 0$

$\Rightarrow$ Integral equation will have infinitely many solution given by

$$u(x) = 1 + A\phi_1(x) + \frac{\lambda}{\lambda_2 - \lambda} f_2\phi_2(x)$$

$$= 1 + A\left(\frac{2}{\pi}\right)^{\frac{1}{2}} \cos x + \frac{\frac{2}{\pi}}{-\frac{2}{\pi} - \frac{2}{\pi}} 2\left(\frac{2}{\pi}\right)^{\frac{1}{2}} \cdot \left(\frac{2}{\pi}\right)^{\frac{1}{2}} \sin x$$

$$= 1 + C \cos x - \frac{2}{\pi} \sin x$$

where $C = \frac{4\sqrt{2}}{\sqrt{\pi}}$ is an arbitrary constant.

(iii) Let $\lambda = \lambda_2 = -\frac{2}{\pi}$, then given integral equation will have no solution, since $f_2 \neq 0$.

# Solved Examples

## Type I (*Only one correct option*)

***Example 1.*** *On what curves can the function* $I=\int_0^1\left[\left(\frac{dy}{dx}\right)^2+12xy\right]dx$ *with* $y(0)=0$ *and* $y(1)=1$ *be extremized?*

(a) $y=x$ (b) $y=x^2$

(c) $y=x^3$ (d) None of these

**Solution.** (c) We have, $F(x,y,y')=y'^2+12xy$

$$\Rightarrow \frac{\partial f}{\partial y}=12x,\ \frac{\partial F}{\partial y'}=2y'$$

Hence, Euler's equation is

$$\frac{\partial F}{\partial y}-\frac{d}{dx}\left(\frac{\partial F}{\partial y'}\right)=0$$

$$\Rightarrow 12x-\frac{d}{dx}(xy')=0$$

$$\Rightarrow \frac{d}{dx}(2y')=12x$$

On integration, we get

$$\Rightarrow 2y'=\frac{12x^2}{2}+C$$

$$\Rightarrow y'=3x^2+C_1,\ C_1=\frac{C}{2}$$

On integration, we get

$$y(x)=x^3+C_1x+C_2$$

Using boundary conditions, we get

$$y(0)=C_2=0$$

$$y(1)=1+C_1+C_2=1$$

$$\Rightarrow C_1=0$$

Hence, $y=x^3$

***Example 2.*** *The extremal for the functional*

$$I=\int_0^{\pi/2}(y'^2-y^2)\,dx$$

*with* $y(0)=0,\ y\left(\frac{\pi}{2}\right)=1$ *is*

(a) $y=x$ (b) $y=\frac{x}{2}$

(c) $y=-\frac{x}{2}$ (d) Problem is meaningless

**Solution.** (d) We have, $F(x,y,y')=xy+y^2-2y^2y'$

$$\Rightarrow \frac{\partial F}{\partial y}=x+2y-4yy'$$

and $$\frac{\partial F}{\partial y'}=0-2y^2$$

Hence, Euler's equation is $\frac{\partial F}{\partial y}-\frac{d}{dx}\left(\frac{\partial F}{\partial y'}\right)=0$

$$\Rightarrow x+2y-4yy'+\frac{d}{dx}(2y^2)=0$$

$$\Rightarrow x+2y-4yy'+4yy'=0$$

$$\Rightarrow x=-2y \Rightarrow y(x)=-\frac{x}{2}$$

But $y(0)=-\frac{0}{2}=0,\ y(1)=-\frac{1}{2}$

Hence the curve $y=-\frac{x}{2}$ does not satisfies given conditions, so the variational problem become meaningless.

***Example 3.*** *The integral equation of the initial value problem*

$$\phi''(x)+\lambda\phi(x)=F(x)$$

*with* $\phi(0)=1,\ \phi'(0)=0$ *is*

(a) $\phi(x)=x+\int_0^x(x-\xi)\{F(\xi)-\lambda\phi(\xi)\}\,d\xi$

(b) $\phi(x)=1+\int_0^x(x-\xi)\{F(\xi)-\lambda\phi(\xi)\}d\xi$

(c) $\phi(x)=\int_0^x(x-\xi)\{F(\xi)-\lambda\phi(\xi)\}d\xi$

(d) None of the above

**Solution.** (b) Given differential equation is

$$\phi''(x)+\lambda\phi(x)=F(x)$$

$$\Rightarrow \phi''(x)=F(x)-\lambda\phi(x)$$

On integrating *wrt x*, we get

$$\int_0^x\phi''(x)\,dx=\int_0^x\{F(x)-\lambda\phi(x)\}\,dx$$

$$\Rightarrow [\phi'(x)]_0^x=\int_0^x\{F(x)-\lambda\phi(x)\}\,dx$$

$$\Rightarrow \phi'(x)-\phi'(0)=\int_0^x\{F(x)-\lambda\phi(x)\}\,dx$$

Using initial condition, we have

$$\Rightarrow \phi'(x)=\int_0^x\{F(x)-\lambda\phi(x)\}\,dx$$

Again on integrating *wrt x*, we get

$$\int_0^x\phi'(x)\,dx=\int_0^x\int_0^x\{F(x)-\lambda\phi(x)\}\,dx\,dx$$

$$\Rightarrow [\phi(x)]_0^x=\int_0^x(x-\xi)\{F(x)-\lambda\phi(x)\}\,dx$$

$$\Rightarrow \phi(x)-\phi(0)=\int_0^x(x-\xi)\{F(x)-\lambda\phi(x)\}\,dx$$

$$\Rightarrow \phi(x)-\phi(0)=\int_0^x(x-\xi)\{F(x)-\lambda\phi(x)\}\,dx$$

Using initial condition, we have

$$\Rightarrow \phi(x)=1+\int_0^x(x-\xi)\{F(x)-\lambda\phi(x)\}\,dx$$

which is the required integral equation.

***Example 4.*** *The kernel, corresponding to the boundary value problem*

$$\frac{d^2\phi(x)}{dx^2} + \lambda\phi(x) = x \text{ with } \phi(0) = 0.\ \phi'(0) = 0 \text{ is}$$

(a) $K(x, \xi) = \begin{cases} x, & x > \xi \\ \xi, & x < \xi \end{cases}$ (b) $K(x, \xi) = \begin{cases} x, & x < \xi \\ \xi, & x > \xi \end{cases}$

(c) $K(x, \xi) = \begin{cases} x, & x > \xi \\ 0, & x < \xi \end{cases}$ (d) None of these

**Solution.** (a) Given differential equation is

$$\frac{d^2\phi}{dx^2} = x - \lambda\phi$$

On integrating *wrt* x, we get

$$\int_0^x \frac{d^2\phi}{dx^2} dx = \int_0^x x\,dx - \lambda\int_0^x \phi(x)\,dx$$

$$\Rightarrow \quad \phi'(x) - \phi'(0) = \frac{1}{2}x^2 - \lambda\int_0^x \phi(\xi)\,d\xi$$

Again on integrating *wrt* x, we get

$$\phi(x) - \phi(0) = cx + \frac{1}{6}x^3 - \lambda\int_0^x\int_0^x \phi(\xi)\,d\xi\,d\xi$$

$$\Rightarrow \quad \phi(x) = cx + \frac{1}{6}x^3 - \lambda\int_0^x (x-\xi)\,d\xi\,d\xi$$

Using boundary Condition,

$$\phi'(1) = 0 \Rightarrow \phi'(1) = c + \frac{1}{2} - \lambda\int_0^1 \phi(\xi)\,d\xi$$

$$\Rightarrow \quad c = -\frac{1}{2} + \lambda\int_0^1 x\phi(\xi)\,d\xi$$

$$\Rightarrow \quad \phi(x) = -\left(\frac{1}{2}\right)x + \left(\frac{1}{6}\right)x^3 + \lambda\int_0^1 \phi(\xi)\,d\xi - \lambda\int_0^x (x-\xi)\,\phi(\xi)\,d\xi$$

$$\Rightarrow \quad \phi(x) = -\left(\frac{1}{2}\right)x + \left(\frac{1}{6}\right)x^3 + \lambda\left\{\int_0^x x\phi(x)\,d\xi + \int_0^1 x\,\phi(\xi)\,d\xi\right\}$$

$$-\lambda\int_0^x (x-\xi)\,\phi(\xi)\,d\xi$$

$$\Rightarrow \quad \phi(x) = \left(\frac{1}{6}\right)(x^3 - 3x) + \lambda\left\{\int_0^x \xi\phi(\xi)\,d\xi + \int_x^1 x\phi(\xi)\,d\xi\right\}$$

$$\Rightarrow \quad \phi(x) = \left(\frac{1}{6}\right)(x^3 - 3x) + \lambda\int_0^1 K(x, \xi)\,\phi(\xi)$$

where, $K(x, \xi) = \begin{cases} x, & x > \xi \\ \xi, & x < \xi \end{cases}$

which is the required kernel.

***Example 5.*** *The solution of the integral equation*

$$\phi(x) = x + \int_0^x (\xi - x)\,\phi(\xi)\,d\xi \text{ is}$$

(a) $\sin x$ (b) $\cos x$

(c) $\tan x$ (d) None of these

**Solution.** (a) We have, $K_1(x, \xi) = K(x, \xi) = \xi - x$

and $K_n(x, \xi) = \int_\xi^x K(x, z)\,K_{n-1}(z, \xi)\,dz$

Putting $n = 2, 3, 4, \ldots\ldots$, We get

$$K_2(x, \xi) = \int_\xi^x K(n, z)\,K_1(z, \xi)\,dz$$

$$= \int_\xi^x (x - z)(\xi - z)\,dz$$

$$= -\frac{1}{3!}(\xi - x)^3$$

$$K_3(x, \xi) = \int_\xi^x K(x, z)\,K_2(z, \xi)\,dz$$

$$= \int_\xi^x (x - z)\left\{-\frac{1}{3!}(\xi - z)^2\right\}dz$$

$$= \frac{1}{5!}(\xi - x)^5$$

By mathematical induction, we get

$$K_n(x, \xi) = (-1)^{n-1}\frac{1}{(2n-1)!}(\xi - x)^{2n-1},\ n = 1, 2, 3, \ldots$$

Henece, the resolvent kernel is $R(x, \xi; \lambda) = \sum_{n=1}^{\infty} \lambda^{n-1}K_n(x, \xi)$

$$= \sum_{n=1}^{\infty} K_n(x, \xi) \quad (\because \lambda = 1)$$

$$= \frac{(\xi - 1)}{1!} - \frac{(\xi - x)^3}{3!} + \frac{(\xi - x)^5}{5!} + \ldots$$

$$= \sin(\xi - x)$$

Hence, the solution of the integral equation is

$$\phi(x) = f(x) + \lambda\int_0^x R(x, \xi; \lambda)\,\phi(\xi)\,d\xi$$

$$= x + \int_0^x \xi\sin(\xi - x)\,d\xi$$

$$= \sin x$$

$\Rightarrow$ $\phi(x) = \sin x$, which is the required solution.

***Example 6.*** *The eigen values of the homogeneous integral equation* $\phi(x) = \lambda\int_0^\pi \{\cos^2 x\cos 2\xi + \cos 3x\cos^3 \xi\}\phi(\xi)\,d\xi$ *are*

(a) $\frac{\pi}{4}, \frac{\pi}{8}$ (b) $\frac{4}{\pi}, \frac{8}{\pi}$

(c) $\frac{4}{\pi}, \frac{\pi}{8}$ (d) $\frac{\pi}{4}, \frac{8}{\pi}$

**Solution.** (b) Given integral equation can be written as

$$\phi(x) = \lambda[\cos^2 x\int_0^\pi \cos 2\xi\phi(\xi)\,d\xi + \cos 3x\int_0^\pi \cos^2\xi\phi(\xi)\,d\xi]$$

$$= \lambda[C_1\cos^2 x + C_2\cos 3x] \quad \ldots\text{(i)}$$

where, $C_1 = \int_0^\pi \cos 2\xi\phi(\xi)\,d\xi,\ C_2 = \int_0^\pi \cos^3\xi\phi(\xi)\,d\xi$ ...(ii)

Substituting the Eq. (i) into Eq. (ii), we get

$$C_1 = \int_0^\pi \cos 2\xi[\lambda C_1\cos^2\xi + \lambda C_2\cos 3\xi]\,d\xi$$

$$C_2 = \int_0^\pi \cos^3\xi[\lambda C_1\cos^2\xi + \lambda_2 C_2\cos 3\lambda]\,d\xi$$

or $C_1[1 - \lambda\int_0^\pi \cos 2\xi\cos^2\xi\,d\xi] - c_2\lambda\int_0^\pi \cos 2\xi\cos 3\xi\,d\xi = 0$

$$-C_1\lambda\int_0^\pi \cos^5\xi\,d\xi + c_2[1 - \lambda\int_0^\pi \cos^3\xi\cos 3\xi\,d\xi] = 0$$

By evaluating the integrals, we obtain a linear system of homogeneous equation

$$\left(1 - \frac{\lambda\pi}{4}\right)C_1 = 0,\ \left(1 - \frac{\lambda\pi}{8}\right)C_2 = 0 \quad \ldots\text{(iii)}$$

Hence for non-trivial solution of homogeneous Eq. (iii), we have

$$\begin{vmatrix} 1-\dfrac{\lambda\pi}{4} & 0 \\ 0 & 1-\dfrac{\lambda\pi}{8} \end{vmatrix} = 0$$

$$\Rightarrow \quad \lambda_1 = \frac{4}{\pi} \text{ and } \lambda_2 = \frac{8}{\pi}$$

which are required eigen values.

***Example 7.*** *Solution of the integral equation*

$$\phi(x) = x + \lambda \int_{-\pi}^{\pi} (x\cos\xi + \xi^2 \sin x + \cos x \sin\xi)\,\phi(\xi)\,d\xi \text{ is}$$

(a) $\phi(x) = x + \dfrac{2\lambda\pi}{1+2\lambda^2\pi^2}[\lambda\pi x - 4\lambda\pi \sin x + \cos x]$

(b) $\phi(x) = \dfrac{2\lambda\pi}{1+2\lambda^2\pi^2}[\lambda\pi x - 4\lambda\pi \sin x + \cos x]$

(c) $\phi(x) = \dfrac{2\lambda\pi}{1+2\lambda^2\pi^2}$

(d) None of the above

**Solution.** (a) We have,

$$\phi(x) = x + \lambda \int_{-\pi}^{\pi} (x\cos\xi + \xi^2 \sin x + \cos x \sin\xi)\,\phi(\xi)\,d\xi$$

$$= x + \lambda\left[x \int_{-\pi}^{\pi} \cos\xi\,\phi(\xi)\,d\xi + \sin x \int_{-\pi}^{\pi} \xi^2\,\phi(\xi)\,d\xi + \cos x \int_{-\pi}^{\pi} \sin\xi\,\phi(\xi)\,d\xi\right]$$

$$\Rightarrow \quad \phi(x) = x + \lambda\,[C_1 x + C_2 \sin x + C_3 \cos x] \quad \text{...(i)}$$

Where, $C_1 = \int_{-\pi}^{\pi} \cos\xi\,\phi(\xi)\,d\xi$, $C_2 = \int_{-\pi}^{\pi} \xi^2\,\phi(\xi)\,d\xi$

and $C_3 = \int_{-\pi}^{\pi} \sin\xi\,\phi(\xi)\,d\xi$ ...(ii)

Substituting expression Eq. (i) into Eq. (ii), we get

$$C_1 = \int_{-\pi}^{\pi} \cos\xi\,[\xi + C_1\lambda\xi + C_2\lambda \sin\xi + C_3\lambda\cos\xi]\,d\xi$$

$$C_2 = \int_{-\pi}^{\pi} \xi^2\,[\xi + C_1\lambda\xi + C_2\lambda \sin\xi + C_3\lambda\cos\xi]\,d\xi$$

$$C_3 = \int_{-\pi}^{\pi} \sin\xi\,[\xi + C_1\lambda\xi + C_2\lambda \sin\xi + C_3\lambda\cos\xi]\,d\xi$$

or $C_1\left[1 - \lambda\int_{-\pi}^{\pi} \xi\cos\xi\,d\xi\right] - C_2\lambda\int_{-\pi}^{\pi} \sin\xi\cos\xi\,d\xi$

$$- C_3\lambda\int_{-\pi}^{\pi} \cos^2\xi\,d\xi = \int_{-\pi}^{\pi} \cos\xi\,d\xi$$

$$- C_1\lambda\int_{-\pi}^{\pi} \xi^3\,d\xi + C_2\left[1 - \lambda\int_{-\pi}^{\pi} \xi^2\sin\xi\,d\xi\right]$$

$$- C_3\lambda\int_{-\pi}^{\pi} \xi^2\cos\xi\,d\xi = \int_{-\pi}^{\pi} \xi^2\,d\xi$$

$$- C_1\lambda\int_{-\pi}^{\pi} \xi\sin\xi\,d\xi - C_2\lambda\int_{-\pi}^{\pi} \sin^2\xi\,d\xi$$

$$+ C_3\left[1 - \lambda\int_{-\pi}^{\pi} \cos\xi\sin\xi\,d\xi\right]$$

$$= \int_{-\pi}^{\pi} \xi\sin\xi\,d\xi$$

By evaluating integrals, we obtain a system of algebraic equations

$$\left.\begin{aligned} C_1 + 0\cdot C_2 - \lambda\pi C_3 &= 0 \\ 0\cdot C_1 + C_2 + 4\lambda\pi C_3 &= 0 \\ -2\lambda\pi C_1 - \lambda\pi C_2 + C_3 &= 2\pi \end{aligned}\right\} \quad \text{...(iii)}$$

For, non-trivial solution of system of non-homogeneous Eq. (iii), we have

$$\partial(\lambda) = \begin{vmatrix} 1 & 0 & -\lambda\pi \\ 0 & 1 & 4\lambda\pi \\ -2\lambda\pi & -\lambda\pi & 1 \end{vmatrix}$$

$$= 1 + 2\lambda^2\pi^2 \neq 0$$

Hence, the system (iii) has unique solution

$$C_1 = \frac{2\lambda\pi^2}{1+2\lambda^2\pi^2},\quad C_2 = \frac{-8\lambda\pi^2}{1+2\lambda^2\pi^2},\quad C_3 = \frac{2\pi}{1+2\lambda^2\pi^2}$$

Putting the values of $C_1, C_2$ and $C_3$ in Eq. (i), We get

$$\phi(x) = x + \frac{2\lambda\pi}{1+2\lambda^2\pi^2}[\lambda\pi x - 4\lambda\pi \sin x + \cos x]$$

which is the required solution.

***Example 8.*** *The integral equation*

$$\phi(x) = \lambda \int_0^1 [\sqrt{(x)}\xi - \sqrt{(\xi)}x]\,\phi(\xi)\,d\xi \text{ has}$$

(a) real eigen values (b) has real eigen vector

(c) imaginary eigen vector (d) None of these

**Solution.** (c) We have,

$$\phi(x) = \lambda\left[\sqrt{(x)}\int_0^1 \xi\,\phi(\xi)\,d\xi - x\int_0^1 \sqrt{(\xi)}\,\phi(\xi)\,d\xi\right]$$

$$\Rightarrow \quad \phi(x) = \lambda\,[C_1\sqrt{(x)} - C_2 x] \quad \text{...(i)}$$

where, $C_1 = \int_0^1 \xi\,\phi(\xi)\,d\xi$, $C_2 = \int_0^1 \sqrt{(\xi)}\,\phi(\xi)\,d\xi$ ...(ii)

Substituting expression Eq. (i) into Eq. (ii), we get

$$C_1 = \int_0^1 \lambda\xi\,(C_1\sqrt{\xi} - C_2\xi)\,d\xi$$

$$C_2 = \int_0^1 \lambda\sqrt{\xi}\,(C_1\sqrt{\xi} - C_2\xi)\,d\xi$$

or $\left[1 - \lambda\int_0^1 \xi^{3/2}\,d\xi\right] + \left[\lambda\int_0^1 \xi^2\,d\xi\right]C_2 = 0$

and $\left[-\lambda\int_0^1 \xi\,d\xi\right]C_1 + \left[1 + \lambda\int_0^1 \xi^{3/2}\,d\xi\right]C_2 = 0$

By evaluating integral, we obtain

$$\left.\begin{aligned} \left(1 - \frac{2\lambda}{5}\right)C_1 + \frac{\lambda}{3}C_2 &= 0 \\ -\frac{\lambda}{2}C_1 + \left(1 + \frac{2\lambda}{5}\right)C_2 &= 0 \end{aligned}\right\} \quad \text{...(iii)}$$

For non-trivial solution, we have

$$D(\lambda) = \begin{vmatrix} 1 - \dfrac{2\lambda}{5} & \dfrac{\lambda}{3} \\ -\dfrac{\lambda}{2} & 1 + \dfrac{2\lambda}{5} \end{vmatrix} = 1 + \frac{\lambda^2}{150}$$

Which is not vanish for real $\lambda$. So, from Eq. (iii), we have

$$C_1 = 0 \text{ and } C_2 = 0$$

Which implies that the algebraic equations contain only one solution for all real $\lambda$, *i.e.*, the trivial solution $\phi(x) = 0$, therefore the integral equation does not have real characteristic numbers of characters functions.

## Type II (One or more than one correct option)

***Example 9.*** *The curve joining two points along which a particle falling from rest under the influence of gravity travels from higher to the lower point in the minimum time is*

(a) $y^2\left(\frac{1}{C}-x\right)=x$ (b) $y^2\left(\frac{x}{C}-x^2\right)=x^2$

(c) $\frac{y^2}{C}=x(1+y^2)$ (d) $y^2=x$

**Solution.** (a), (b), (c),

Let $H$ and $L$ be the highest and lowest point of the curve and $v$ is the speed of the particle along the curve; then in traversing $ds$ portion of the curve, time spent will be $ds/v$, so that total time taken by the particle in moving from highest point $H$ to the lowest point $L$ will be

$$t_{HL}=\int_H^L \frac{ds}{v}$$

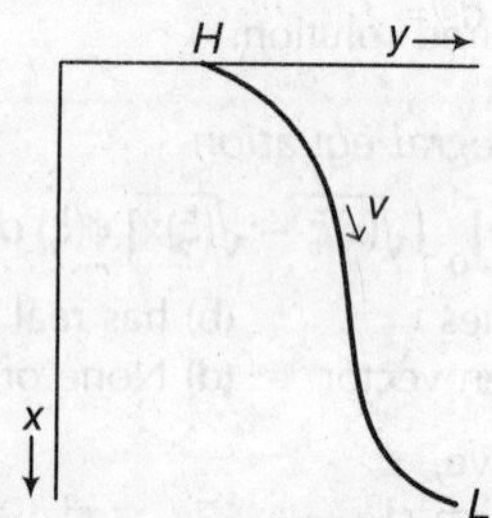


Suppose, vertical distance of fall upto the point $L$ be $x$, then from the conservation principle for the energy of the particle, we find that

$$\frac{1}{2}mv^2=mgx$$

$$\Rightarrow \quad v=\sqrt{(2gx)}$$

Hence, $$t_{HL}=\int_H^L \frac{\sqrt{(dx^2+dy^2)}}{\sqrt{(2gx)}}=\int_H^L \frac{\sqrt{(1+y'^2)}}{\sqrt{(2gx)}}\,dx$$

$$=\int_H^L f\,dx, \text{ where } F=\left(\frac{1+y'^2}{2gx}\right)^{1/2}$$

For $t_{HL}$ to be minimum, the Euler-Lagrange equation is given by

$$\frac{d}{dx}\left(\frac{\partial F}{\partial y'}\right)-\frac{\partial F}{\partial y}=0$$

must be satisfied. From the expression for $f$, we have

$$\frac{\partial F}{\partial y}=0$$

$$\Rightarrow \quad \frac{\partial F}{\partial y'}=\frac{y'}{\sqrt{(2gx)}\sqrt{(1+y'^2)}}$$

So that above equation becomes

$$\frac{d}{dx}\left(\frac{y'}{\sqrt{(2gx)}\sqrt{(1+y'^2)}}\right)=0 \Rightarrow \frac{y'^2}{x(1+y'^2)}=C$$

where C is a constant. On rearranging the above equation, we get

$$\frac{y'^2}{C}=x(1+y'^2)$$

$$\Rightarrow \quad y'^2\left(\frac{1}{C}-x\right)=x$$

$$\Rightarrow \quad y'^2\left(\frac{x}{C}-x^2\right)=x^2$$

$$\Rightarrow \quad y'=\frac{x}{\left(\frac{x}{C}-x^2\right)^{1/2}}$$

Let us put $\frac{1}{C}=2a$,

On integration, we get

$$y=a\cos^{-1}\left(1-\frac{x}{a}\right)-(2ax-x^2)^{1/2}+C'$$

where $C'$ is the constant of integration, which represents an inverted cycloid with its base along $y$-axis and cusp at the origin.

***Example 10.*** *A surface is generated by revolving the curve y(x) along the axis of X. By variational principle choose the curve y(x), which passes through two fixed points $(x_1, y_1)$ and $(x_2, y_2)$, so that the area of the resulting surface is minimum. This curve is*

(a) $y=c_1\cosh\left(\frac{x}{c_1}+c_2\right)$

(b) the catenary of revolution of catenoid pass through points $(x_1, y_1)-(x_2, y_2)$

(c) $y=c_1\cosh^{-1}\left(\frac{x}{c_2}\right)$

(d) $y=c_1\sinh\left(\frac{x}{c_1}+c_2\right)$

**Solution.** (a), (b)

Let the function $y(x)$ be revolved about $X$-axis, so that the surface is generated.

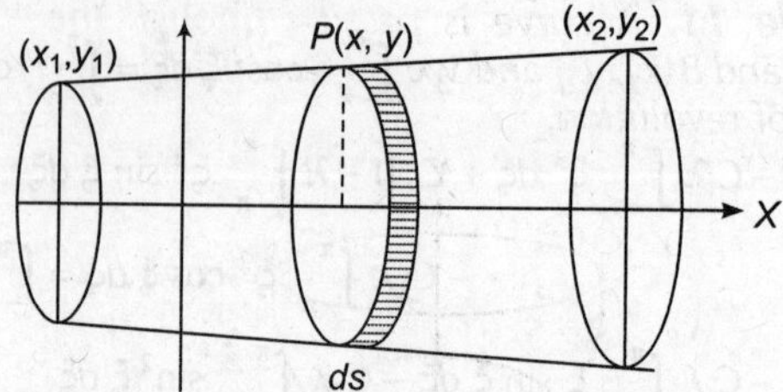


An element of the surface in the neighbourhood of a point $P(x, y)$ have

$$\text{area}=2\pi y\,ds=2\pi y\,(dx^2+dy^2)^{1/2}$$

$$=2\pi y\left[1+\left(\frac{dy}{dx}\right)^2\right]^{1/2}dx$$

Hence, the surface generated between fixed points $(x_1, y_1)$ and $(x_2, y_2)$ have area

$$I = \int_{x_1}^{x_2} 2\pi y \left[1+\left(\frac{dy}{dx}\right)^2\right]^{1/2} dx \quad \text{...(i)}$$

Here, $$f = 2\pi y \left[1+\left(\frac{dy}{dx}\right)^2\right]^{1/2} \quad \text{...(ii)}$$

$$\Rightarrow \quad \frac{\partial f}{\partial x} = 0$$

Hence from Eq. (ii), we get

$$\frac{\partial f}{\partial y'} = \frac{2\pi y y'}{(1+y'^2)^{1/2}}, \text{ where } y' = \frac{dy}{dx}$$

On integrating, we get

$$2\pi y\, [1+y'^2]^{1/2} - \frac{2\pi y y'^2}{(1+y'^2)^{1/2}} = C$$

where c is constant of integration

$$\Rightarrow \quad y\,(1+y'^2)^{1/2} - \frac{yy'^2}{(1+y'^2)^{1/2}} = \frac{C}{2\pi} = C_1 \text{ (say)}$$

$$\Rightarrow \quad \frac{y}{(1+y'^2)^{1/2}} = C_1$$

On squaring, we get

$$\frac{y^2}{1+y'^2} = C_1^2$$

$$\Rightarrow \quad y^2 = C_1^2 + C_1^2 y'^2$$

$$\Rightarrow \quad y'^2 = \frac{y^2 - C_1^2}{C_1^2} \Rightarrow y' = \frac{\sqrt{(y^2 - C_1^2)}}{C_1}$$

$$\Rightarrow \quad dy = \frac{\sqrt{(y^2 - C_1^2)}}{C_1} dx \Rightarrow \frac{dy}{\sqrt{(y^2 - C_1^2)}} = \frac{dx}{C_1}$$

On integrating, we get

$$y = C_1 \cosh\left(\frac{x}{C_1} + C_2\right) \quad \text{...(iii)}$$

where $C_2$ is the constant of integration, Eq. (iii) represent the curve that and is known as catenary of revolution of catenoid pass through the points $(x_1, y_1)$ and $(x_2, y_2)$.

***Example 11.*** *A curve is passing through the fixed points $A(x_1, y_1)$ and $B(x_2, y_2)$ and we revolve it about Y-axis to form a surface of revolution.*

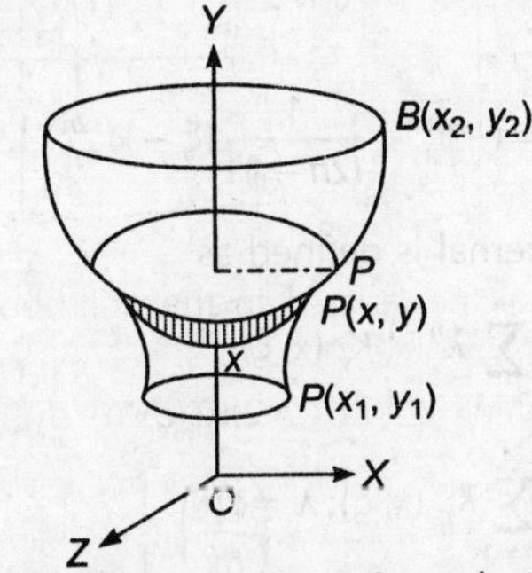

Minimum surface of revolution

(a) The total area of revolution is $S = 2\pi \int_A^B x\sqrt{1+y^2}\, dx$

(b) The total area of revolution is $S = 2\pi \int_A^B xy\, dx$

(c) $x = a \cosh \frac{yb}{a}$ is the required equation of the curve for which the ssurface of revolution is minimum

(d) $x = a \sinh \frac{y-b}{a}$ is the required equation of the curve for which the surface revolution is minimum

**Solution.** (a), (c)

Let $AB$ be the curve which passes through the fixed points $A(x_1, y_1)$ and $B(x_2, y_2)$.

The curve $AB$ has been revolved about $Y$-axis to generate a surface. Consider a strip of the surface whose radius is $x$ and breadth is $PP' = ds$ given by

$$ds^2 = dx^2 + dy^2$$

$$\Rightarrow \quad ds = \sqrt{1+y'^2}\, dx$$

Circular strip of are $2\pi x dx$

Area of the strip $= 2\pi x\, ds = 2\pi x \sqrt{1-y'^2}\, dx$

Here, total area of revolution

$$S = 2\pi \int_A^B x\sqrt{1+y'^2}\, dx \quad \text{...(i)}$$

This area will be minimum, if $\delta S = 0$, for which Euler characteristic equation is satisfied,

Hence, $$\frac{\partial F}{\partial y} - \frac{d}{dx}\left(\frac{\partial F}{\partial y}\right) = 0 \quad \text{...(ii)}$$

where $F = x\sqrt{1+y'^2}$

$$\Rightarrow \quad \frac{\partial F}{\partial y} = 0, \frac{\partial F}{\partial y'} = \frac{xy'}{\sqrt{1+y'^2}}$$

Substituting in Eq. (ii), we have

$$\frac{d}{dx} \cdot \frac{xy'}{\sqrt{1+y'^2}} = 0$$

$$\Rightarrow \quad \frac{xy'}{\sqrt{1+y'^2}} = a \quad \text{...(iii)}$$

where $a$ is constant of integration. On squaring Eq. (iii), we get

$$x^2 y'^2 = a^2 + a^2 y'^2$$

$$\Rightarrow \quad y' = \frac{dy}{dx} = \frac{a}{\sqrt{x^2 - a^2}}$$

Hence $$y = \int \frac{a}{\sqrt{x^2 - a}} dx$$

$$= a \cosh^{-1} \frac{x}{a} + b \quad \text{...(iv)}$$

where $b$ is constant of integration.

From Eq. (iv), we have

$$\cosh^{-1}\frac{x}{a}=\frac{y-b}{a} \Rightarrow x=a\cosh\frac{y-b}{a} \quad ...(v)$$

This is the required equation of the curve for which the surface of revolution is minimum.

***Example 12.*** *Given the differential equation* $y''(x)-3y'(x)+2y(x)=5\sin x,\ y(0)=1,\ y'(0)=-2.$

(a) Equivalent equation is Volterra integrral equation of first kind

(b) Equivalent equation is Volterra integral equation of the second kind

(c) The equivalent integer equation is

$$y(x)+\int_0^x[2(x-t)-3]\,y(t)\,dt=1-5\sin x$$

(d) $y(x)=1-5\sin x$

**Solution.** (b), (c)

Given differential equation is

$$y''(x)-3y'(x)+2y(x)=5\sin x,\ y(0)=1,\ y'(0)=-2.$$

Integrating both side of the given differential equation, we get

$$[y'(x)-y'(0)]-3[y(x)-y(0)]+2\int_0^x y(t)\,dt=(1-\cos x) \quad ...(i)$$

Substituting $y'(0)=-2$ and $y(0)=1$ in Eq. (i), we get

$$y'(x)+2-3y(x)+3+2\int_0^x y(t)\,dt=5-5\cos x$$

$$\Rightarrow \quad y'(x)-3y'(x)+2\int_0^x y(t)\,dt=-5\cos x \quad ...(ii)$$

On integrating both sides of Eq. (ii), we get

$$[y(x)-y(0)]-3\int_0^x y(t)\,dt+2\int_0^x\int_0^x y(t)\,dt=-5\sin x$$

$$\Rightarrow \quad y(x)-1-3\int_0^x y(t)\,dt+2\int_0^x (x-t)\,y(t)\,dt=-5\sin x$$

$$\Rightarrow \quad y(t)+\int_0^x[2(x-t)-3]\,y(t)\,dt=1-5\sin x$$

Which is the required integral equation.

***Example 13.*** *Given an integral equation*

$$\phi(x)=\int_0^x(x+\xi)\,\phi(\xi)\,d\xi$$

(a) $\phi'(x)=\int_0^x\phi(\xi)\,d\xi+2x\,\phi(x)$

(b) $\phi''(x)-2x\phi'(x)-3\phi(x)=0$ is the equivalent differential equation

(c) $\phi(0)=0$ and $\phi'(0)=0$ are the initial condition for the equivalent differential equations

(d) A volterra integral equation

**Solution.** (a), (b), (c), (d)

Given integral equation is

$$\phi(x)=\int_0^x(x+\xi)\,\phi(\xi)\,d\xi \quad ...(i)$$

Differentiating it *wrt* $x$, we have

$$\phi'(x)=\frac{d}{dx}\int_0^x(x+\xi)\,\phi(\xi)\,d\xi$$

$$\Rightarrow \quad \phi'(x)=\int_0^x\frac{\partial}{\partial x}(x+\xi)\,\phi(\xi)\,d\xi$$

$$\Rightarrow \quad \phi'(x)=\int_0^x\phi(\xi)\,d\xi+2x\,\phi(x) \quad ...(ii)$$

Again differentiating Eq. (ii) *wrt* $x$, we get

$$\phi''(x)=\frac{d}{dx}\int_0^x\phi(\xi)\,d\xi+2\{x\phi'(x)+\phi(x)\}$$

$$\Rightarrow \quad \phi''(x)=\phi(x)+2x\phi'(x)+2\phi(x)=0$$

$$\Rightarrow \quad \phi''(x)-2x\phi'(x)-3\phi(x)=0$$

which is the required differential equation

Also from Eq. (i) and Eq. (ii), for $x=0$, we have

$$\phi(0)=0 \text{ and } \phi'(0)=0$$

Which is the required initial conditions.

***Example 14.*** *Given the integral equations*

$$\phi(x)=x+\int_0^x(\xi-x)\,\phi(\xi)\,d\xi$$

(a) $K_2(x,\xi)=-\frac{1}{3!}(\xi-x)^3$

(b) $K_3(x,\xi)=\frac{1}{5!}(\xi-x)^5$

(c) The resolvent kernel is $R(x,\xi:\lambda)=\sin(\xi-x)$

(d) The solution is $\phi(x)=\sin x$

**Solution.** (a), (b), (c), (d)

We have,

$$K_1(x,\xi)=K(x,\xi)=\xi-x \quad ...(i)$$

and

$$K_n(x,\xi)=\int_\xi^x K(x,z)K_{n-1}(z,\xi)\,dz \quad ...(ii)$$

Substituting $n=2,3,4,\ldots$ in the relation Eq. (ii), we have

$$K_2(x,\xi)=\int_\xi^x K(x,z)\,K_1(z,\xi)\,dz$$

$$\Rightarrow \quad K_2(x,\xi)=\int_\xi^x(z-x)(\xi-z)\,dz$$

$$=-\frac{1}{3!}(\xi-x)^3$$

and $\quad K_3(x,\xi)=\int_\xi^x K(x,z)\,K_2(z,\xi)\,dz$

$$\Rightarrow \quad K_3(x,\xi)=\int_\xi^x(z-x)\left\{-\frac{1}{3!}(\xi-z)^3\right\}dz$$

$$=\frac{1}{5!}(\xi-x)^5$$

The $n$th term is

$$K_n(x,\xi)=(-1)^{n-1}\frac{1}{(2n-1)!}(\xi-x)^{2n-1}, \quad v=1,2,3,\ldots$$

Now resolvent kernal is defined as

$$R(x,\xi;\lambda)=\sum_{n=1}^{\infty}\lambda^{n-1}K_v(x,\xi)$$

$$=\sum_{n=1}^{\infty}K_n(x,\xi);\ \lambda=1$$

$$\Rightarrow \quad R(x, \xi; \lambda) = \frac{(\xi - x)}{1!} - \frac{(\xi - x)^3}{3!} + \frac{(\xi - x)^5}{5!} - \ldots$$

$$\Rightarrow \quad R(x, \xi; \lambda) = \sin(\xi - x)$$

The solution of the integral equation is determinad as

$$\phi(x) = f(x) + \lambda \int_0^x R(x, \xi; \lambda)\, f(\xi)\, d\xi$$

$$\Rightarrow \quad \phi(x) = x + \int_0^x \xi \sin(\xi - x)\, d\xi$$

$$\Rightarrow \quad \phi(x) = \sin x$$

***Example 15.*** *Given the homogeneous integral equation*

$$y(x) = \lambda \int_0^1 (2xt - 4x^2)\, y(t)\, dt$$

*with degenerate kernel.*

(a) The eigen values are – 3, – 3
(b) The eigen values are – 4, – 4
(c) The eigen function is $y(x) = x - 2x^2$
(d) The eigen function is $y(x) = \sin x - \cos x$

**Solution.** (a), (b)

Given equation may be written as

$$y(x) = \lambda \{2x \int_0^1 ty(t)\, dt - 4x^2 \int_0^1 y(t)\, dt\}$$

$$\Rightarrow \quad y(x) = (2\lambda x)\, C_1 - (4\lambda x^2)\, C_2 \qquad \ldots(i)$$

where $C_1 = \int_0^1 ty(t)\, dt$

$$C_2 = \int_0^1 y(t)\, dt$$

Substituting $y(x)$ in $C_1, C_2$, we get

$$C_1 = \int_0^1 t\, \{(2\lambda t)\, C_1 - (4\lambda t^2)\, C_2\}\, dt$$

$$C_2 = \int_0^1 \{(2\lambda t)\, C_1 - (4\lambda t^2)\, C_2\}\, dt$$

or $$C_1 \{1 - 2\lambda \int_0^1 t^2\, dt\} + C_2 \{4\lambda \int_0^1 t^3\, dt\} = 0$$

$$C_1 \{-2\lambda \int_0^1 t\,dt\} + C_2 \{1 + 4\lambda \int_0^1 t^2 dt\} = 0$$

or $$C_1 \left(1 - \frac{2\lambda}{3}\right) + \lambda C_2 = 0;$$

$$-\lambda C_1 + C_2 \left(1 + \frac{4\lambda}{3}\right) = 0 \qquad \ldots(ii)$$

∴ The determinant of eigen values will be

$$\begin{vmatrix} 1 - 2\lambda/3 & \lambda \\ -\lambda & 1 + 4\lambda/3 \end{vmatrix} = 0$$

or $$(\lambda + 3)^2 = 0$$

∴ The eigen values are $\lambda_1 = -3, \lambda_2 = -3$

For $\lambda_1 = \lambda_2 = -3$, the Eq. (ii) reduce to

$3C_1 - 3C_2 = 0; 3C_1 - 3C_2 = 0$, *i.e.*, $C_1 = C_2$

∴ From Eq. (i) $y(x) = -6C_1(x - 2x^2) = x - 2x^2$, if $C_1 = -\frac{1}{6}$

Hence, the eigen function corresponding to $\lambda_1 = \lambda_2 = -3$, is

$$y(x) = x - 2x^2$$

***Example 16.*** *Given the kernel*

$$K(x, \xi) = 2e^x e^\xi;\ a = 0,\ b = 1$$

(a) $D(\lambda) = 1 - (e^2 - 1)\lambda$
(b) $D(x, \xi; \lambda) = 2e^x e^\xi$
(c) $D(\lambda) = e^\lambda$
(d) $(D, \xi, \lambda) = 1 - e^\lambda$

**Solution.** (a), (b)

We have,

$$B_0(x, \xi) = C_0 K(x, \xi) = 2e^x, e^\xi$$

or $$B_1(x, \xi) = \int_0^1 \begin{vmatrix} 2e^x \cdot e^\xi & 2e^x \cdot e^{\xi_1} \\ 2e^{\xi_1} \cdot e^\xi & 2e^{2\xi_1} \end{vmatrix} d\xi_1 = 0$$

and $$B_2(x, \xi) = B_3(x, \xi) = \ldots = 0$$

and $$C_1 = \int_0^1 2e^{2\xi_1}\, d^{\xi_1}\, 5 = e^2 - 1$$

or $$C_2 = \int_0^1 \int_0^1 \begin{vmatrix} 2e^{2\xi_1} & 2e^{\xi_1} e^{\xi_2} \\ 2e^{\xi} 2e^{\xi_2} & 2e^{2\xi_2} \end{vmatrix} d\xi_1\, d\xi_2 = 0$$

$$C_3 = C_4 = \ldots = 0$$

Thus, the recursive relations reduce to

$$D(\lambda) = 1 + \sum_{m=1}^{\infty} \frac{(-\lambda)^m}{m!} C_m = 1 - (e^2 - 1)\lambda$$

and $$D(x, \xi, \lambda) = K(x, \xi) + \sum_{m=1}^{\infty} \frac{(-\lambda)^m}{m!} B_m(x, \xi) = 2e^x e^\xi$$

***Example 17.*** *Then, function $\phi(x) = 1 + \lambda x$ is a solution of the integral equation*

$$x = \int_0^x e^{x - \xi}\, \phi(\xi)\, d\xi,\ \textit{if}$$

(a) $\lambda = -1$
(b) $\lambda = \frac{x+1}{e^x} \neq 0$
(c) $\lambda = -2$
(d) $\lambda = -3$

**Solution.** (a), (b)

Given integral equation is

$$x = \int_0^x e^{x - \xi}\, \phi(\xi)\, d\xi \qquad \ldots(i)$$

If the function $\phi(x) = 1 + \lambda x$ satisfies the integral Eq. (i), then

$$x = \int_0^x e^{x - \xi}\, (1 + \lambda\xi)\, d\xi$$

$$\Rightarrow \quad x = e^x \int_0^x e^{-\xi}\, (1 + \lambda\xi)\, d\xi$$

$$\Rightarrow \quad x = -e^x\, (e^{-\xi} + \lambda\, (\xi e^{-\xi} + e^{-\xi})\}_0^x$$

$$\Rightarrow \quad x = -e^x\, \{e^{-x} + \lambda e^{-x}(x + 1) - (1 + \lambda)\lambda\}$$

$$\Rightarrow \quad x = -1\{1 + \lambda\,(x + 1) - \lambda\,(\lambda + 1)\, e^x\}$$

$$\Rightarrow \quad (\lambda + 1)\, \{(x + 1) - \lambda e^x\} = 0$$

$$\Rightarrow \quad \lambda + 1 = 0 \text{ or } \{(x + 1) - \lambda e^x\} = 0$$

$$\Rightarrow \quad \lambda = -1 \text{ or } \lambda = \frac{x+1}{e^x} \neq 0$$

Thus, the function $\phi(x) = 1 + \lambda x$ is a solution of the integral equation for $\lambda = -1$.

***Example 18.*** *Given boundary value problem*

$$\frac{d^2u}{dx^2} - u(x) = 0;\ u(0) = u(1) = 0$$

(a) A general solution of the differential equation is $u(x) = 0$

(b) The only trivial solution $u(x) = 0$

(c) The fundamental system of solutions for the differential equation is given as $u_1(x) = \sinh x$ which satisfies the boundary condition $u(0) = 0$, $u_2(x) = \sinh(x-1)$ satisfies the boundary condition $u(1) = 0$

(d) The Green's function is of the form

$$G(x, \xi) = \begin{cases} \dfrac{\sinh x \sinh(\xi - 1)}{\sinh 1}, & 0 \le x \le \xi \\ \dfrac{\sinh \xi \sinh(x-1)}{\sinh 1}, & \xi \le x \le 1 \end{cases}$$

**Solution.** (a), (c), (d)

Given differential equation is

$$\frac{d^2u}{dx^2} - u(x) = 0 \qquad \text{...(i)}$$

with $\quad u(0) = u(1) = 0 \qquad$ ...(ii)

The general solution of the differential equation

$$u(x) = Ae^x + Be^{-x}$$

$$u(0) = 0 \Rightarrow A + B = 0 \Rightarrow A = B = 0$$

$$u(1) = 0 \Rightarrow Ae + Be^{-1} = 0$$

These conditions have only a trivial solution $u(x) \equiv 0$, hence we can construct a unique Green's function.

The fundamental system of solutions for the differential Eq. (i) is given as $u_1(x) = \sinh x$ which satisfies the boundary condition $u(0) = 0$

$u_2(x) = \sinh(x-1)$ satisfies the boundary condition $u(1) = 0$

The solution are linearly independent. The value of the Wronskian for sin hx andsin h (x – 1) at the point $x = \xi$ is

$$W(\xi) = \begin{vmatrix} \sinh \xi & \sinh(\xi - 1) \\ \cosh \xi & \cosh(\xi - 1) \end{vmatrix}$$

$$\Rightarrow \quad W(\xi) = \sinh \xi \cosh(\xi - 1) - \cosh \xi \sinh(\xi - 1) = \sinh 1$$

Here, $\quad p(x) = 1$

$\therefore$ The Green's function is

$$G(x, \xi) = \begin{cases} \dfrac{\sinh x \sinh(\xi - 1)}{\sinh 1}, & 0 \le x \le \xi \\ \dfrac{\sin \xi \sinh(x-1)}{\sinh 1}, & \xi \le x \le 1 \end{cases}$$

***Example 19.*** *Given the kernels*

$$K(x, \xi) = (1 + x)(1 - \xi);\ a = -1,\ b = 0.$$

(a) A resolvent kernel is given by

$$R(x, \xi, \lambda) = \sum_{n=1}^{\infty} \lambda^{n-1} K_n(x, \xi)$$

(b) A resolvent kernel is $R(x, \xi, \lambda) = \dfrac{3(1+x)(1+\xi)}{3 - 2\lambda}$

Where, $\quad |\lambda| < \dfrac{3}{2}$

(c) $K_n(x, \xi) = \int_a^b K_m(x, z) K_{n-m}(z, \xi)\, dz \ (m = 1, \dots, n-1)$

(d) $K_n(x, \xi) = \left(\dfrac{2}{3}\right)^{n-1} (1 + x)(1 - \xi)$

**Solution.** (a), (b), (c), (d)

Here,

$$K_n(x, \xi) = \int_a^b {}_{k_m}(x, z) K_{n-m}(z, \xi)\, dz \ (m = 1, \dots, n-1)$$

where, $\quad K_1(x, \xi) = K(1 + x)(1 - \xi)$

Hence, $\quad K_2(x, \xi) = \int_{-1}^{0} (1 + x)(1 - z)(1 + z)(1 - \xi)\, dz$

$$\Rightarrow \quad K_2(x, \xi) = \frac{2}{3}(1 - x)(1 - \xi)$$

$$K_3(x, \xi) = \frac{2}{3}\int_{-1}^{0} (1 + x)(1 - z)\cdot(1 + z)(1 - \xi)\, dz$$

$$\Rightarrow \quad K_3(x, \xi) = \frac{2}{3} K_2(x, \xi) = \left(\frac{2}{3}\right)^2 (1 + x)(1 - \xi)$$

Hence, we have

$$K_n(x, \xi) = \left(\frac{2}{3}\right)^{n-1} (1 + x)(1 - \xi)$$

Hence, the resolvent kernel is

$$R(x, \xi, \lambda) = \sum_{n=1}^{\infty} \lambda^{n-1} K_n(x, \xi)$$

$$= (1 + x)(1 - \xi) \sum_{n=1}^{\infty} \left(\frac{2\lambda}{3}\right)^{n-1}$$

$$\Rightarrow \quad R(x, \xi, \lambda) = \frac{3(1 + x)(1 - \xi)}{3 - 2\lambda}$$

where $\quad |\lambda| < \dfrac{3}{2}$

***Example 20.*** *Given an integral equation*

$$y(x) = 1 + x + \int_0^x (x - t) y(t)\, dt$$

(a) A Volterra integral equation

(b) A Fredholm integral equation

(c) A solution by successive approximations is $y(x) = e^x$

(d) A solution by successive approximation is

$$y(x) = 1 + \frac{x}{1!} + \frac{x^2}{2!} + \frac{x^3}{3!} + \dots \infty$$

**Solution** (a), (c), (d)

Given Volterra integral equation

$$y(x) = 1 + x + \int_0^x (x - t) y(t)\, dt \qquad \text{...(i)}$$

Take initial approximation $y_1(x) = 1 + x$, then

Hence, from Eq. (i), we get

$$y_1(x) = 1 + x + \int_0^x (x - t)(1 + t)\, dt$$

$$= 1 + x + x\left(x + \frac{x^2}{2}\right) - \left(\frac{x^2}{2} + \frac{x^3}{3}\right)$$

$$= 1 + x + \frac{x^2}{2} + \frac{x^3}{6}$$

On substituting $y_1(x)$ in Eq. (i), we get

$$y_2(x) = 1 + x + \int_0^x (x - t)\left(1 + t + \frac{t^2}{2} + \frac{t^3}{6}\right) dt$$

$$= 1 + x + x\left(x + \frac{x^2}{2} + \frac{x^3}{6} + \frac{x^4}{24}\right) - \left(\frac{x^2}{2} + \frac{x^3}{3} + \frac{x^4}{8} + \frac{x^5}{30}\right)$$

$$= 1 + x + \frac{x^2}{2} + \frac{x^3}{6} + \frac{x^4}{24} + \frac{x^5}{120}$$

Successively proceeding in this manner, we get

$$y_n(x) = 1 + \frac{x}{1!} + \frac{x^2}{2!} + \frac{x^3}{3!} + \frac{x^4}{4!} + \frac{x^5}{5!} + \ldots + \frac{x^n}{n!}$$

As $n \to \infty$ the exact solution of Eq. (i) is

$$y(x) = \lim_{n\to\infty}\left(1 + \frac{x}{1!} + \frac{x^2}{2!} + \frac{x^3}{3!} + \ldots + \frac{x^n}{n!}\right)$$

$$1 + \frac{x}{1!} + \frac{x^2}{2!} + \frac{x^3}{3!} + \ldots \infty = e^x$$

***Example 21.*** *Given integral equation*

$$\phi(x) = \frac{1}{e^2 - 1}\int_0^1 2e^x e^\xi \phi(\xi)\, d\xi$$

(a) The solution of the equation is $\phi(x) = 0$

(b) The solution of the equation is $\phi(x) = \cos x$

(c) The equation is freedholm integral equation

(d) The equation is Volterra integral equation

**Solution** (a), (c)

Given that

$$\phi(x) = \frac{1}{e^2 - 1}\int_0^1 2e^x e^\xi \phi(\xi)\, d\xi \quad \text{...(i)}$$

$$= \frac{2e^x}{e^2 - 1}\int_0^1 e^\xi \phi(\xi)\, d\xi$$

$$= \frac{1}{e^2 - 1} = C \quad \text{...(ii)}$$

where $$C = \int_0^1 e^\xi \phi(\xi)\, dx\xi \quad \text{...(iii)}$$

Hence, from the Eqs. (ii) and (iii) we get

$$C = \frac{2C}{e^2 - 1}\int_0^1 e^\xi\, d\xi$$

$$\Rightarrow \quad C\left[1 - \frac{1}{e^2 - 1}\int_0^1 e^{2\xi}\, d\xi\right] = 0$$

$$\Rightarrow \quad C = 0 \quad \text{...(iv)}$$

Hence, the required solution is $\phi(x) \equiv 0$.

# Exercise 1 (For Part 'B')

**Directions** (Q. Nos. 1-198) *All questions have only one correct option.*

**1.** For $F[y(x)] = \int_a^b f[x, y(x), y'(x)]dx$, $F$ is called
(a) functional (b) range
(c) arc length (d) None of these

**2.** Euler-lagrange Equation is
(a) $\frac{\partial f}{\partial x'} - \frac{d}{dx}\left(\frac{\partial f}{\partial x}\right) = 0$ (b) $\frac{\partial f}{\partial x} - \frac{d}{dx}\left(\frac{\partial f}{\partial y}\right) = 0$
(c) $\frac{\partial f}{\partial x} - \frac{d}{dx}\left(\frac{\partial f}{\partial x'}\right) = 0$ (d) $\frac{\partial f}{\partial x} - \frac{d}{dy}\left(\frac{\partial f}{\partial x'}\right) = 0$

**3.** The minimizing curve must satisfy a differential equation, called as
(a) Lagrange's equation
(b) Euler-Lagrange equation
(c) Gauss equation
(d) None of the above

**4.** If $P$ and $Q$ be two points in the $xy$-plane and $P$ and $Q$ be two points and $y(x)$ be a curve with $P = (a, y(a))$ and $Q = (b, y(b))$. The arc length of the curve $y(x)$ is given by the integral
(a) $\int_b^a \sqrt{(1+y(x))^2}\, dx$ (b) $\int_a^b \sqrt{1+[y'(x)]^2}\, dx$
(c) $\int_b^a \sqrt{1+[y'(x)]^2}\, dx$ (d) $\int_a^b \sqrt{1+[y(x)]^2}\, dx$

**5.** Shortest path between two points is
(a) a straight line (b) a zigzag line
(c) a circle (d) None of these

**6.** Rayleigh-Ritz method is used to
(a) find maxima
(b) find minima
(c) solve boundary value problems
(d) None of the above

**7.** Solution to $0 = \frac{y''(x)}{\{1+[y'(x)]\}^{3/2}}$ is
(a) a straight line (b) a hyperbola
(c) a circle (d) None of these

**8.** If $F[y(x)] = \int_a^b \sqrt{1+[y'(x)]^2}\, dx$, then the Euler-Lagrange Equation is given by
(a) $\frac{y'(x)}{[1+(y'(x))]^{3/2}} = 0$ (b) $\frac{y''(x)}{[1+(y'(x))]^{3/2}} = 0$
(c) $\frac{y'(x)}{[1+(y'(x))]^{3/2}} = 0$ (d) None of these

**9.** The simplification of the Euler-Lagrange equation is known as
(a) Beltrami Identity (b) Hamiltons' Identity
(c) Liouville's Identity (d) None of these

**10.** The______curve is the path of a fixed point on the rim of a wheel as the wheel is rotated along a straight line
(a) ellipsoid (b) straight line
(c) cycloid (d) zigzag

**11.** The necessary condition for the integral $\int_{x_1}^{x_2} H\, dx$ to be an extremum is
(a) $\frac{\partial H}{\partial y} - \frac{\partial}{\partial x}\left(\frac{\partial H}{\partial y'}\right) = 0$ (b) $\frac{\partial H}{\partial x} - \frac{\partial}{\partial y}\left(\frac{\partial H}{\partial \dot{x}}\right) = 0$
(c) $\frac{\partial H}{\partial y'} - \frac{\partial}{\partial x}\left(\frac{\partial H}{\partial y}\right) = 0$ (d) $\frac{\partial H}{\partial y'} - \frac{d}{dx}\left(\frac{\partial H}{\partial \dot{x}}\right) = 0$

**12.** $f(x, y, \dot{y})$, is not functional because
(a) its range is $R$ (b) its range is not $R$
(c) its range is infinity (d) None of these

**13.** Necessary condition for $I = \int_{t_1}^{t_2} F(t, x, \dot{x}, \ddot{x})dt$ to be an extremum is that
(a) $\frac{\partial f}{\partial x} - \frac{d}{dx}\left(\frac{\partial F}{\partial \dot{x}}\right) = 0$
(b) $\frac{\partial f}{\partial x} - \frac{d}{dt}\left(\frac{\partial F}{\partial \dot{x}}\right) + \frac{d^2}{dt^2}\left(\frac{\partial F}{\partial \ddot{x}}\right) = 0$
(c) $\frac{\partial f}{\partial \dot{x}} - \frac{d}{dt}\left(\frac{\partial F}{\partial \dot{x}}\right) + \frac{d^2}{dt^2}\left(\frac{\partial F}{\partial \ddot{x}}\right) = 0$
(d) $\frac{\partial f}{\partial x} - \frac{\partial f}{\partial t}\left(\frac{\partial F}{\partial \dot{x}}\right) = 0$

**14.** A fixed volume of water is rotating in a cylinder with constant angular velocity $\omega$. The curve of the water surface that will minimize the total potential energy of the water in the combined gravitational centrifugal force field is
(a) parabola (b) cycloid (c) catenary (d) ellipse

**15.** The solution of variational problem
$\delta \int_1^2 [x^2(y')^2 + 2y(x+y)]dx = 0$, given $y(1) = y(2) = 0$ is
(a) $y = \frac{1}{21}\{8 \log 2(x^2 - x^{-1}) + 7x \log x\}$
(b) $y = \frac{1}{21}\{8 \log 3(x^{-2} - x) + 7x \log x^2\}$
(c) $y = \frac{1}{21}\{8 \log 2(x^{-2} - x) + 7x \log x\}$
(d) None of the above

**16.** A rectangular parallelopiped is inscribed in an ellipsoid of semi-axes $a$, $b$ and $c$. The ratio of the maximum volume to the volume of the ellipsoid is

(a) $\frac{2\pi}{\sqrt{3}}$ (b) $2/\pi\sqrt{3}$
(c) $2\sqrt{3}\pi$ (d) $\frac{2\pi^2}{\sqrt{3}}$

**17.** Solid figure of revolution which, for a given surface area, has maximum volume is
(a) a circle (b) a sphere
(c) an ellipse (d) a parabola

**18.** Curve on which the functional $\int_0^1 [(y')^2 + 12xy]dx$ with $y(0) = 0$ and $y(1) = 1$ can be extremised is
(a) $y = x^3$ (b) $y = x^2$
(c) $y = x$ (d) $y = x^4$

**19.** Extremals of the isoperimetric problem $v[y(x)] = \int_{x_0}^{x_1} y'^2\, dx$ given that $\int_{x_0}^{x_1} y\,dx = C$, a constant is
(a) $y = \lambda x^2 + ax + b$ (b) $y = \lambda x + b$
(c) $y = b$ (d) $y = \lambda x + bx^2$

**20.** The extremals of the functional $\int_{-a}^{a} (\lambda y + \frac{1}{2}\mu y''^2)\,dx$ which satisfies the boundary conditions $y(-a) = 0$, $y'(-a) = 0$, $y(a) = 0$, $y'(a) = 0$ is
(a) $y = -\frac{\lambda}{\mu}(x^2 - a^2)$ (b) $y = \frac{\lambda}{24\mu}(x^2 - a^2)^2$
(c) $y = \frac{\lambda}{24\mu}(a^2 - x^2)^2$ (d) $y = \frac{-\lambda}{24\mu}(x^2 - a^2)$

**21.** A perfectly flexible rope of uniform density per unit length is suspended with its end points fixed. It assumes the shape of a
(a) cycloid (b) catenary
(c) parabola (d) None of these

**22.** Of all the parabolas which pass through (0, 0) and (1, 1), the one, which when rotated about the x-axis, generates a solid of revolution with least possible volume between $x = 0$ and $x = 1$ is
(a) $y = 5x^2 - 3x$ (b) $y = \frac{1}{2}(5x^2 - 3x)$
(c) $y = 3x^2 - 5x$ (d) $y = \frac{1}{2}(3x^2 - 5x)$

**23.** The extremals of the functional $\int_0^{\pi/2} (y''^2 - y^2 + x^2)\,dx$ that satisfies the conditions $y(0) = 1$, $y'(0) = 0$, $y(\pi/2) = 0$, $y'(\pi/2) = -1$, is
(a) $y = \cos x$ (b) $y = \sin x$
(c) $y = \tan x$ (d) $y = \sec x$

**24.** A particle is moving with a force perpendicular to and proportional to its distance from the line of zero velocity. The path of quickest descent (brachistochrone) is
(a) a parabola
(b) straight line
(c) a circle
(d) a hyperbola

**25.** Equation of the curve which gives minimum surface of revolution about any axis say y-axis is
(a) $y = c\cosh\frac{x-b}{c}$ (b) $x = c\cos h\frac{y-b}{c}$
(c) $y = x\cosh\frac{x-a}{b}$ (d) $x = y\cosh\frac{y-a}{b}$

**26.** In the brachitischrone problem, if the particle is given an initial velocity $v_0 = 0$, the path of minimum time is
(a) parabola (b) cycloid
(c) catenary (d) ellipse

**27.** In the equation $H = f + \lambda g$, where $\int_1^2 H\,dx$ to be an extremum, $\lambda$ is called as
(a) Isoperimetric constant (b) Kernels
(c) Lagrange multiplier (d) Green's function

**28.** Plane curve of fixed perimeter and maximum area is a
(a) circle (b) parabola
(c) straight line (d) hyperbola

**29.** Extremal of the isoperimetric problem $v[y(x)] = \int_1^4 y_2' dx$, $y(1) = 3$, $y(4) = 24$ subject to the condition $\int_1^4 y dx = 36$ is
(a) a parabola (b) straight line
(c) a circle (d) a hyperbola

**30.** The curve made by a cable of fixed length suspended from two fixed points for minimum gravitational potential energy is
(a) circular (b) parabolic
(c) hyperbolic (d) catenary

**31.** Function $y(x)$ for which $\int_0^1 (x^2 + y'^2)dx$ is stationary, given that $\int_0^1 y^2\,dx = 2$; $y(0) = 0$, is
(a) $y = \sin m\pi x$ (b) $y = \pm 2\sin m\pi x$
(c) $y = 4\sin m\pi x$ (d) $y = \pm 3\sin m\pi x$

**32.** Curve on which the functional $\int_0^{\pi/2} (y'^2 - y^2 + 2xy)dy$ with $y(0) = 0$ and $y(\pi/2) = 0$, be extremized is
(a) $y = \frac{\pi}{2}\sin x$ (b) $y = x - \frac{\pi}{2}\sin x$
(c) $y = x^2 - \frac{\pi}{2}\sin x$ (d) $y = \frac{\pi}{2}\sin x$

**33.** Mark the correct statement.
(a) A geodesic on a surface is a curve along which the distance between any two points of the surface is a minimum.
(b) A geodesic on a surface is a curve along which the distance between any two points of the surface is a maximum.
(c) A geodesic on a surface is a curve along which the two points tends to infinity.
(d) None of the above

**34.** Geodesics on a plane are
(a) parabola (b) straight lines
(c) ellipse (d) cycloid

**35.** The approximate solution of the boundary value problem $\frac{d}{dx}\left(x\frac{dy}{dx}\right)+y=x, y(0)=0, y(1)=1$, in the form $\bar{y}(x)=x+x(1-x)(c_1+c_2x)$, is
(a) $c_1=1.27, c_2=2.69$
(b) $c_1=3.27, c_2=-2.69$
(c) $c_1=4.27, c_2=-1.69$
(d) $c_1=c_2=2.54$

**36.** Solution of boundary value problem $y''=3x+4y; y(0)=0, y(1)=1$ is
(a) $\bar{y}=\frac{x}{2}(5x-4)$ (b) $\bar{y}=\frac{x}{4}(5x-1)$
(c) $\bar{y}=\frac{x}{3}(5x-1)$ (d) $\bar{y}=\frac{x}{4}(5x+1)$

**37.** An approximate solution of the problem $y''-y+4xe^x=0, y'(0)-y(0)=1, y'(1)+y(1)=-e$ is
(a) $\bar{y}=1.58+0.27x$ (b) $\bar{y}=1.58+0.27x$
(c) $\bar{y}=-1.58-0.27x$ (d) $\bar{y}=0.58+0.27x$

**38.** For the boundary value problem $y''+\pi^2y=x$, $y(0)=1, y(1)=-0.9$, value of $y(0.5)$ is, if trial solution is $y=1-1.9x+c_1x(1-x)+c_2x^2(1-x)$
(a) 0.05 (b) 0.005
(c) 0.50 (d) 0.55

**39.** A function $y(x)$ such that $\int_0^{\pi}y^2\,dx=1$ which makes $\int_0^{\pi}y''^2\,dx$ a minimum, if
$y(0)=0=y(\pi)y''(0)=0=y''(\pi)$ is
(a) $y=a_n\cos nx, n=0,1,2,3,\ldots$
(b) $y=a_n\sin mx, m=0,1,2,3,\ldots$
(c) $y=a_n\sin nx, n=0,1,2,3,\ldots$
(d) $y=\frac{a_n}{\sin nx}, n=0,1,2,3,\ldots$

**40.** The solutions of Euler-Poisson equation are called as
(a) trial solution (b) extremals
(c) stationary solution (d) functional

**41.** Equation $\frac{d}{dx}\left\{f-y'\frac{\partial f}{\partial y'}\right\}-\frac{\partial f}{\partial x}$ is
(a) Hamilton's equation
(b) Euler's equation
(c) Liouville's equation
(d) Bessel's equation

**42.** The solution of integral equation
$y(x)=3x^2+\int_0^x y(t)\sin(x-t)\,dt$
(a) $y=3x^2+x^4$ (b) $y=3x^2+\frac{x^4}{4}$
(c) $y=4x^2+x^3$ (d) $y=3x^4+x^3$

**43.** The solution of integral equation
$y(x)=x+2\int_0^x\cos(x-t)y(t)\,dt$ is
(a) $y=x+2+2(x-1)e^x$ (b) $y=2+x+x^2+e^x$
(c) $y=x+2+3(x-1)e^x$ (d) $y=x^2+2+3(x-1)e^x$

**44.** The solution of integral equation $\int_0^x\frac{y(t)}{\sqrt{x-t}}dt=1$ is
(a) $y(x)=\frac{1}{\pi\sqrt{x}}$ (b) $y(x)=\frac{x}{\sqrt{\pi}}$
(c) $y(x)=\frac{\pi}{\sqrt{x}}$ (d) $y(x)=\frac{\pi}{\sqrt{x^3}}$

**45.** The solution of integral equation $\int_0^x\frac{y(t)}{(x-t)}dt=\sqrt{x}$ is
(a) $y(x)=1/2$ (b) $y(x)=1$
(c) $y(x)=3/2$ (d) $y(x)=3/4$

**46.** The solution of integral equation
$y'(x)=\int_0^x y(t)\cos(x-t)\,dt, y(0)=1$ is
(a) $y(x)=1+x^2$ (b) $y(x)=1+\frac{x^2}{2}$
(c) $y(x)=2+x^2$ (d) $y(x)=1-x^2$

**47.** $y(x)=\lambda\int_0^1(3x-2)t\cdot y(t)\,dt$ has
(a) eigen value $\lambda=1$, eigen function $y=x^2$
(b) eigen value $\lambda=1/4$, eigen function $y(x)=x^2+1/2$
(c) no eigen values and eigen functions
(d) None of the above

**48.** The eigen values and eigen functions of integral equation $y(x)=\lambda\int_{-1}^{1}(5xt^3+4x^2t+3xt)y(t)\,dt$ are
(a) eigen value $\lambda=1/4$, eigen function is $y(x)=x^2+3x/2$
(b) eigen value $\lambda=1$, eigen function is $y(x)=x^2+1/2$
(c) eigen value $\lambda=1/2$, eigen function is $y(x)=5x^2+3x$
(d) None of the above

**49.** The solution of integral equation
$y(x)=1-\lambda\int_0^x xt\,y(t)\,dt$ is
(a) $y(x)=1-\frac{2\lambda x}{(1+\lambda)}$
(b) $y(x)=1-\frac{3\lambda x}{2(3+\lambda)}, (\lambda\neq-3)$
(c) $y(x)=1+\frac{3\lambda x}{2(3-\lambda)}, (\lambda\neq-3)$
(d) None of the above

**50.** The solution of integral equation
$y(x)=1+\int_0^x y(t)\,dt$ is
(a) $y=e^x$ (b) $y=e^{-x}$
(c) $y=e^{x^2}$ (d) $y=e^{-x^2}$

**51.** The function $k(x,t)$ is called as
(a) constant of the integral equation
(b) kernel of the integral equation
(c) functional of the integral equation
(d) None of the above

**52.** Equation in which an unknown function appears under the integral sign is called as
(a) Linear differential equation
(b) Partial integral equation
(c) Linear integral equation
(d) Gauss integral equation

**53.** In linear integral equation

$$y(x) = F(x) + \lambda \int_a^b k(x, t) y(t)\, dt$$

If $a$ and $b$ are constants. The equation is known as
(a) Fredholm integral equation
(b) Volterra integral equation
(c) Green's integral equation
(d) Markov integral equation

**54.** The solution of Fredholm integral equation $y(x) + \int_0^1 e^{x-t} y(t)\, dt = 2xe^x$ is
(a) $y(x) = e^x(1 - x^2)$ (b) $y(x) = e^x\left(2x - \frac{2}{3}\right)$
(c) $y(x) = e^x\left(x - \frac{2x}{3}\right)$ (d) None of these

**55.** A kernel $k(x, t)$ of Fredholm integral equation is said to be ....... if it can be expressed as the sum of a finite number of terms, each of which is the product of a function of $x$ alone and a function of $t$ alone.
(a) non-degenerate (b) separable
(c) non-separable (d) Abel

**56.** Solution of integral equation

$$y(x) = \lambda \int_a^b k(x, t) \cdot y(t)\, dt + F(x) \text{ is}$$

(a) $y(x) = \lambda \sum_{n=1}^{m} C_n f_n(x) + F(x)$
(b) $y(x) = \lambda + \sum_{n=1}^{m} C_n f_n(x) + F'(x)$
(c) $y(x) = \lambda - \sum_{n=1}^{m} C_n f_n(x) + F(x)$
(d) $y(x) = \lambda + \sum_{n=1}^{m} f_n(x) + C_n$

**57.** Starting with the initial approximation $y^{(0)}(x) = 1$, for the solution of the integral equation.

$$y(x) = 1 + \int_0^x (x + t) y(t)\, dt, \text{ then } y^{(3)}(x) \text{ is}$$

(a) $1 + \frac{x^2}{2} + \frac{3x^3}{4} + \frac{7x^4}{8} + \frac{70x^5}{80}$
(b) $1 + \frac{x^3}{3} + \frac{2x^4}{4} + \frac{3x^5}{5}$
(c) $1 + \frac{3x^2}{2} + \frac{7x^4}{8} + \frac{77x^6}{240}$
(d) None of the above

**58.** Any non-trivial solution of the homogeneous integral equation for a certain value of $\lambda$ is called
(a) eigen values (b) eigen functions
(c) kernels (d) constants

**59.** Choosing the initial approximation $y^{(0)}(x) = 0$, for the solution of the integral equation $y(x) = \int_0^x t(t - x) y(t)\, dt + \frac{x^2}{2}$. The $y^{(2)}(x)$ is
(a) $\frac{x^2}{1} - \frac{x^4}{20} + \ldots$ (b) $\frac{x^2}{2} - \frac{x^5}{40}$
(c) $\frac{x^2}{2} - \frac{x^4}{40}$ (d) $\frac{x^2}{2} - \frac{x^3}{40}$

**60.** The values of $\lambda$ for which determinant $\Delta = 0$ are known as
(a) eigen values (b) eigen functions
(c) kernels (d) separable kernel

**61.** The solution of Volterra integral equation

$$y(x) = 1 + x + \int_0^x (x - t) y(t)\, dt \text{ is}$$

(a) $y = e^{-x}$ (b) $y = e^x$
(c) $y = e^{x^2}$ (d) $y = e^{-x^2}$

**62.** The solution of Volterra integral equation

$$y(x) = 1 + \int_0^x y(t)\, dt \text{ is}$$

(a) $y = e^x$ (b) $y = e^{-x}$
(c) $y = \frac{e^x}{2!}$ (d) $y = 1 + e^x$

**63.** Integral equation for boundary value problem $y'' + xy' + y = 0$, given that $y(0) = 1$, $y'(0) = 0$ is
(a) $y(x) = \int_0^x (5 - 6x + 6t) y(t)\, dt$
(b) $y(x) = -\int_0^5 (5 - 6x + 6t)\, dt$
(c) $y(x) = 6x - 5 + \int_0^x (5 - 6x + 6t) y(t)\, dt$
(d) $y(x) = 6x + 5 + \int_0^x (5 - 6x + 6t)\, dt$

**64.** The differential equation corresponding to integral equation $y(x) = \int_0^x (x + t) y(t)\, dt - 1$ is
(a) $y''(x) - y(x) + 3\sin x = 0$, $y(0) = 3$, $y'(0) = 0$
(b) $y''(x) + 6y(x) = 0$, $y(0) = 4$, $y'(0) = -3$, $y''(0) = 2$
(c) $y''(x) - y'(x) + 4\cos x = 0$, $y(0) = 2$, $y'(0) = 1$
(d) $y''(x) - 2xy'(x) - 3y(x) = 0$, $y(0) = 1$, $y'(0) = 1$

**65.** For Fredholm equation $y(x) = F(x) = \lambda \int_a^b k(x, t) y(t)\, dt$ will have a continuous solution, when
(a) $|\lambda| = \frac{1}{m(b - a)}$ (b) $|\lambda| < \frac{1}{m(b - a)}$
(c) $|\lambda| = \frac{1}{m(a - b)}$ (d) $|\lambda| > \frac{1}{m(b - a)}$

**66.** The solutions corresponding to eigen values of $\lambda$ can be expressed as
(a) sum of eigen functions
(b) difference of eigen functions
(c) arbitrary multiples of eigen functions
(d) None of the above

**67.** Integral equation for boundary value problem $\frac{d^3y}{dx^3} + y = \cos x$, given that $y = 0,\ y' = 1, y'' = 2$ at $x = 0$ is

(a) $y(x) = \cos x - \frac{1}{2}x^2 - \frac{1}{3}x^3 - \frac{1}{2}\int_0^x (x-t)^2 y(t)\,dt$

(b) $y(x) = \sin x - \frac{1}{2} + \int_0^x \left\{\frac{1}{2}x(x-t)^2 - 1\right\} y(t)\,dt$

(c) $y(x) = \frac{x^5}{20} - \frac{5x^3}{6} + x - 3$

(d) None of the above

**68.** Given the integral equation $\phi(x) + \int_0^1 x(e^{x\xi} - 1)y(\xi)d\xi = e^x - x$, then

(a) the solution is $y(x) = 1$
(b) the solution is $y(x) \neq 1$
(c) the Volterra integral equation
(d) the Fredholm integral equation

**69.** The plane curve of fixed perimeter and maximum area is

(a) a circle (b) a rectangle
(c) a square (d) an ovel

**70.** Which of the following statement is true?

(a) The shortest distance between two points in a plane is a straight line
(b) The shortest distance between two points in a plane is a semi-circle
(c) The shortest distance between two points in a plane is a free curve
(d) The shortest distance between the two points in a plane is not a straight line

**71.** The curve on which the functional $\int_0^1 [(y')^2 + 12xy]dx$ with $y(0) = 0$ and $y(1) = 1$ can be extremised?

(a) $y = x^3$ (b) $y = \cos x$
(c) $y = \frac{\sin x}{2}$ (d) $y = \sin x \cos x$

**72.** Given boundary value problem $y'' - y + x = 0$ $(0 \le x \le 1)$, $y(0) = y(1) = 0$, then

(a) The approximate solution is $\bar{y}(x) = \frac{5}{22}x(1-x)$
(b) The solution is $y(x) = \sin x \cos x$
(c) The solution is $y(x) = \tan x \cot x$
(d) The solution is $y(x) = c_1 \sin x + c_2$

**73.** Given the functional

$$\int_{x_0}^{x_1} \left(\frac{y'^2}{x^3}\right) dx, \text{ then}$$

(a) the extremal is $y = \frac{x^4}{4} + c_2$
(b) the extremal is $y = cx^2 + c_1$
(c) the extremal is $y = \sin x$
(d) the extremal is $y = \cos x$

**74.** Given the integral equation

$$f(x) = \int_a^x \frac{\phi(\xi)}{(\cos\xi - \cos x)^{1/2}} d\xi,\ 0 \le a < x < b \le \pi. \text{ Then,}$$

(a) $\phi(\xi) = \frac{1}{\pi}\frac{d}{d\xi}\left\{\int_0^\xi \frac{\sin u\, f(u)\,du}{(\cos u - \cos\xi)^{1/2}}\right\}$ where $a < \xi < b$ is the required solution
(b) no solution exist
(c) $\phi(\xi) = 0$ is the required solution
(d) $\phi(\xi) = \frac{1}{\pi}\int_0^\xi \cos u\, du$ is the required solution

**75.** The curve ....... extremizes the functional

$$I = \int_0^{\pi/4} (y''^2 - y^2 + x^2)dx$$

under the conditions

$y(0) = 0,\ y'(0) = 1,\ y(\pi/4) = y'(\pi/4) = 1/\sqrt{2}$ is

(a) $y = \sin x$ (b) $y = \cos x$
(c) $y = \sin x \cos x$ (d) $y = \cot x$

**76.** Given the functional

$$\int_0^{\pi/2} \left\{2xy + \left(\frac{dx}{dt}\right)^2 + \left(\frac{dy}{dt}\right)^2\right\} dt \text{ such that}$$

$x(0) = 0,\ x(\pi/2) = -1,\ y(0) = 0,\ y(\pi/2) = 1$, then

(a) it is stationary for $x = -\sin t,\ y = \sin t$
(b) it is non-stationary for $x = -\sin t,\ y = \sin t$
(c) it is stationary for $x = -\cos t,\ y = \cos t$
(d) it is stationary for $x = -\cos t,\ y = \sin t$

**77.** Given the integral equation

$$f(x) = \int_x^b \frac{\phi(\xi)}{(\cos x - \cos\xi)^{1/2}} d\xi,\ 0 \le a < x < b < \pi, \text{ then}$$

(a) $\phi(\xi) = -\frac{1}{\pi}\frac{d}{d\xi}\left\{\int_\xi^b \frac{\sin(u) f(u)\,du}{(\cos\xi - \cos u)^{1/2}}\right\}$ where $a < \xi$ is the required solution
(b) $\phi(\xi) = \frac{1}{\pi}\frac{d}{d\xi}\left\{\int_a^\xi \frac{\sin u\, f(u)\,du}{(\cos u - \cos\xi)^{1/2}}\right\}$ where $a < \xi < b$ is the required solution
(c) is the required solution
(d) no solution exist

**78.** The curve on which functional $\int_0^{\pi/2} (y'^2 - y^2 + 2xy)dy$ with $y(0) = 0$ and $y\left(\frac{\pi}{2}\right) = 0$, be extremized?

(a) $y = x - \frac{\pi}{2}\sin x$ (b) $y = x - \pi \sin x$
(c) $y = 2x \cos x$ (d) $y = 2x \sin x$

**79.** The extremals of the functional

$$I[y(x), z(x)] = \int_0^{\pi/2} (y'^2 + z'^2 + 2yz)dx$$

$y(0) = 0,\ y(\pi/2) = 1;\ z(0) = 0,\ z(\pi/2) = -1$ occurs on the curves is

(a) $y = \cos x,\ z = \sin x$ (b) $y = \sin x,\ z = -\sin x$
(c) $y = \cos x,\ z = \cos x$ (d) $y = \cos x,\ z = -\sin x$

**80.** The functional $\int_0^1 (y'^2 + x^2)dx$ given $y(1) = 1$, achieves its
(a) weak maximum on all its extremals
(b) weak minimum on all its extremals
(c) weak maximum on some, but not on all of its extremals
(d) weak minimum on some, but not on all of its extremals

**81.** Euler's equations for the functional $\int_1^2 (y'^2 + z^2 + z'^2)dx$ are given by
(a) $y'' = 0, z'' - z = 0$
(b) $y'' - y = 0, z'' = 0$
(c) $y'' + y = 0, z'' + z = 0$
(d) None of the above

**82.** The extremum of the functional $I[y(x)] = \int_0^1 \left[\left(\frac{dy}{dx}\right)^2 + 12xy\right]dx$ satisfying the condition $y(0) = 0$ and $y(1) = 1$ is
(a) $y = \sin^2 \frac{\pi x}{2}$ (b) $y = \frac{\sin \pi x}{2}$
(c) $y = x^3$ (d) $y = \frac{1}{2}\left[x^3 + \frac{\sin \pi x}{2}\right]$

**83.** The possible values of $\alpha$ for which the variational problem $J[y(x)] = \int_0^1 (3y^2 + 2x^3 y')dx, \quad y(\alpha) = 1$ has extremals are
(a) $-1, 0$ (b) $0, 1$ (c) $-1, 1$ (d) $-1, 0, 1$

**84.** Extremals of the functional $I[y(x)] = \int_{x_0}^{x_1} (2xy + y'''^2)dx$ lies on the
(a) five parameter family of curves
(b) six parameter family of curves
(c) seven parameter family of curves
(d) None of the above

**85.** Extremal for the functional $I = \int_1^2 (y'^2 + z^2 + z'^2)dx$ satisfying the conditions $y(1) = 1$, $y(2) = 2$, $z(1) = 0$ and $z(2) = 1$ is
(a) $y(x) = x,\ z(x) = \frac{\sinh(x-1)}{\sinh(1)}$
(b) $y(x) = x,\ z(x) = \frac{\sin(x-1)}{\sin 1}$
(c) $y(x) = x,\ z(x) = \frac{\cosh(x-1)}{\cosh(1)}$
(d) None of the above

**86.** The extremum for the variational problem $I[y(x)] = \int_0^{\pi/8} (y'^2 + 2yy' - 16y^2)dx$ $y(0) = 0$, $y(\pi/8) = 1$. Occurs for the curve is
(a) $y = \sin 4x$ (b) $y = \sqrt{2}\sin 2x$
(c) $y = 1 - \cos 4x$ (d) $y = \frac{1 - \cos 8x}{2}$

**87.** In which situation the variational problem $\int_{x_1}^{x_2} f(x, y, y')dx;\quad y(x_1) = y_1,\quad y(x_2) = y_2$ becomes meaningless
(a) when Euler's equation reduces into identity
(b) when $y(x)$ exists but it not satisfies the given boundary condition
(c) when $f(x, y, y') = M(x, y) + N(x, y)$
(d) All of the above

**88.** The Euler's equation for a functional of the form $\int_a^b F(x, y)dx$ is
(a) $F_{y'} = c_1$ (b) $F_y - y'F_{y'} = c_1$
(c) $F_y = c_1$ (d) None of these

**89.** The extremum value of the variational problem $\int_0^{\pi/2} (y'^2 - y^2)dx,\ y(0) = 0,\ y\left(\frac{\pi}{2}\right) = 1$ is
(a) $\frac{1}{5}$ (b) 2 (c) 1 (d) 0

**90.** Solution of the poisson's equation in the square $u_{xx} + u_{yy} = -1$, $|x| \le 1$, $|y| \le 1$; $u = 0$ at $x = \pm 1$ and $y = \pm 1$ is
(a) $u(x, y) = \frac{1}{16}(1 - x^2)(1 - y^2)$
(b) $u(x, y) = \frac{5}{16}(1 - x^2)(1 - y^2)$
(c) $u(x, y) = \frac{5}{16}(1 + x^2)(1 + y^2)$
(d) None of the above

**91.** The number of extremals of the functional $\int_0^{\pi} (2yz - 2y^2 + y'^2 - z'^2)dx$ satisfying the conditions $y(0) = 0$, $y(\pi) = 1$, $z(0) = 0$, $z(\pi) = -1$ is
(a) 1 (b) 2 (c) 0 (d) infinite

**92.** The extremals of the functional $I[y(x), z(x)] = \int_0^{\pi/2} (y'^2 + z'^2 + 2yz)dx$ are the solution of simultaneous differential equation
(a) $y'' - z = 0, z'' - y = 0$ (b) $y'' + z = 0, z'' + y = 0$
(c) $y'' - z = 0, z'' + y = 0$ (d) $y'' + z = 0, z'' - y = 0$

**93.** The functional $V[y(x)] = \int_0^2 [y'^2 + 6xy + x^3]dx,\ y(0) = 0,\ y(2) = 2$ can be extremised on the curve
(a) $y = x$ (b) $2y = x^3$
(c) $y = x^3 - 6x$ (d) $2y = x^3 - 2x$

**94.** The Extremal for the functional $V[y(x)] = \int_{x_0}^{x_1} (xy' + y'^2)dx$ are given by the following family of curve.
(a) $y = c_1 + c_2 x + \frac{x^2}{4}$ (b) $y = 1 + c_1 x + c_2\left(\frac{x^2}{4}\right)$
(c) $y = c_1 + x + c_2\left(\frac{x^2}{4}\right)$ (d) $y = c_1 + c_2 x - \left(\frac{x^2}{4}\right)$

**95.** The corresponding variational problem of BVP $y'' + \lambda^2 y = 0, y(-1) = 0 = y(1)$ is

(a) $I[y(x)] = \int_0^1 [y'^2 - \lambda^2 y^2] dx$

(b) $I[y(x)] = \int_0^1 [y'' - \lambda^2 y^2] dx$

(c) $I[y(x)] = \int_0^1 [y'^2 + \lambda^2 y^2] dx$

(d) None of the above

**96.** The extremum of the functional $\int_1^e (xy'^2 + yy')dx$ satisfying the conditions $y(1) = 0, y(e) = 1$ is attained on

(a) $y = \log x$ (b) $y = e^x$

(c) $y = \log\left(\frac{1}{x}\right)$ (d) None of these

**97.** The functional $J[y(x)] = \int_a^b (y'^2 + 12xy)dx$; $y(0) = 0$ and $y(1) = 1$ can be extrematsed on the curve

(a) $y(x) = x$ (b) $y = x^3$

(c) $y(x) = x^2 + x$ (d) $y(x) = x^3 - 1$

**98.** Let $J[y(x)]$ be the functional defined by

$$J[y(x)] = \int_0^{\pi/2} \left[\left(\frac{dy}{dx}\right)^2 - y^2\right] dx, \quad y(0) = 0, \quad y\left(\frac{\pi}{2}\right) = 1$$

where the unknown function $y(x)$ possesses two derivatives every where in $\left(0, \frac{\pi}{2}\right)$, then

(a) the functional has an extremum which cannot be achieved in the class of continuous function

(b) the corresponding Euler's equation does not have a unique solution satisfying the given BC

(c) $J$ is non-linear

(d) $J$ is linear

**99.** An approximately the smallest eigen value of BVP $y'' + \lambda y = 0, y(0) = y(1) = 0$ is

(a) $\lambda = 5$ (b) $\lambda = 10$

(c) $\lambda = 15$ (d) None of these

**100.** For the functional $\int_0^\pi (y'^2 - y^2)dx$; $y(0) = 0$, $y(\pi) = 0$ the number of extremals are

(a) 1 (b) 2

(c) 0 (d) infinite

**101.** The approximate solution of the functional $I[y(x)] = \int_0^1 (2xy + y^2 - y'^2)dx$; $y(0) = y(1) = 0$ is

(a) $\frac{5}{8}(x + x^2)$ (b) $\frac{5}{8}(x - x^2)$

(c) $\frac{5}{8}(x + x^3)$ (d) $\frac{5}{8}(1 - x^3)$

**102.** $I[y(x)] = \int_0^1 f(x, y, y')dx$ satisfying $y(0) = 0$, $y(1) = 1$, where $F$ has continuous second order derivatives with respect to its argument and the unknown function $y(x)$ possess two derivatives everywhere in $(0, 1)$ If $F = F(x, y')$, then Euler's equation is an ODE in $y$, which is in general is

(a) first order linear (b) first order non-linear

(c) second order linear (d) second order non-linear

**103.** Extremal of the functional $I[y(x)] = \int_1^2 \frac{x^3}{y'^2} dx$, $y(1) = 0$ and $y(2) = 3$ is

(a) $y = x^2 - 1$ (b) $y = x^3 - 1$

(c) $y = x - 1$ (d) $y = x^3 - x$

**104.** For the functional $\int_0^{\pi/2} (y'^2 - y^2)dx$; $y(0) = 0$, $y(\pi/2) = 1$. The number of extremals is

(a) 1 (b) 2

(c) 0 (d) infinite

**105.** The approximate and exact solutions of boundary values problem $y''(x) = 1, y(0) = y(1) = 0$ are

(a) $y(x) = \frac{1}{2}(x^2 - x)$; $y(x) = \frac{1}{2}(x^2 - x)$

(b) $y(x) = (x^2 + x)$; $y(x) = \frac{1}{2}(x^2 - x)$

(c) $y(x) = \frac{1}{2}(x^2 + x)$; $y(x) = \frac{1}{2}(x^2 + x)$

(d) None of the above

**106.** Extremal $y = y(x)$ for the variational problem $V[y(x)] = \int_0^1 (y + y')^2 dx$ satisfies the differential equation

(a) $y'' + y = 0$ (b) $y'' - y = 0$

(c) $y'' + y' = 0$ (d) $y' + y = 0$

**107.** The shortest distance between two points in a plane is given by the equation

(a) $(x - h)^2 + (y - k)^2 = r^2$ (b) $y = mx + c$

(c) $y = ax^2 + b$ (d) $y = x^3$

**108.** Extremals of the functional $\int_{x_1}^{x_2} y\sqrt{1 + y'^2}\, dx$ is attained on the

(a) catenary (b) parabola

(c) circle (d) sphere

**109.** The number of extremals for the functional $\int_0^\pi (4y \cos x + y'^2 - y^2)dx$, $y(0) = 0$, $y(\pi) = 0$ is

(a) one

(b) two

(c) more than two but finite

(d) infinite

**110.** An extremal of the functional $I[y(x)] = \int_a^b \left(x, y, \frac{dy}{dx}\right)dx$; $y(a) = y_1$, $y(b) = y_2$ satisfies Euler's equation which in general

(a) is a second order linear ordinary differential equation

(b) is a non-linear ODE of order greater than two

(c) admits a unique solution satisfying the conditions $y(a) = y_1$, $y(b) = y_2$

(d) may not admits a solution satisfy the conditions $y(a) = y_1$; $y(b) = y_2$

**111.** The functional $I[y(x)] = \int_0^1 (1 + y'')dx$ defined on the set of functions $C^2([0, 1])$ satisfying $y(0) = 1$, $y(1) = 1$, $y'(0) = 0$ and $y'(1) = -1$ has
(a) only one extremal
(b) exactly two extremals
(c) infinite number of extremals
(d) no extremals

**112.** Extremal of the functional $I[y(x)] = \int_0^4 (y'^2 + 4y^2)dx$; $y(0) = e^2$, $y(1) = 1$ lies on the curve
(a) $y = e^{2+2x}$ (b) $y = 2^{2-2x}$
(c) $y = e^{2x}$ (d) None of these

**113.** For the functional $J[y(x)] = \int_a^b (x - y)^2\, dx$ the extremal is a
(a) straight line (b) parabola
(c) circle (d) catenary

**114.** Extremal for the variational problem $V[y(x)] = \int_1^2 (y^2 + x^2 y'^2)dx$ satisfies the differential equation
(a) $x^2y'' + 2xy' - y = 0$ (b) $xy'' - 2xy' + y = 0$
(c) $2xy' - y = 0$ (d) $x^2y'' - y = 0$

**115.** If $F(x, y, y')$ is independent of $x$, then Euler's equation for the functional $\int_{x_1}^{x_2} F(x, y, y')dx$ reduces to
(a) $F_{y'} = c_1$ (b) $F - y'F_{y'} = c$
(c) $F + y'F_{y'} = c$ (d) None of these

**116.** The functional $I[y(x)] = \int_0^{\pi/2} \left[\left(\frac{dy}{dx}\right)^2 - y^2\right]dx$; $y(0) = 0$, $y(\pi/2) = 1$ has
(a) unique extremal (b) two extremal
(c) no extremal (d) infinite extremal

**117.** Which one of the following is linear functional?
(a) $J[y(x)] = \int_a^b (y' + 2y^2)dx$ (b) $J[y(x)] = \int_a^b (y'^2 + 2y^2)dx$
(c) $J[y(x)] = \int_a^b (y'^2 + 2y)dx$ (d) $J[y(x)] = \int_a^b (y' + 2y)dx$

**118.** The functional $\int_0^1 (1 + x)(y')^2\, dx$, $y(0) = 0$, $y(1) = 1$ possess
(a) strong maxima
(b) strong minima
(c) weak minima but not a strong maxima
(d) weak maxima but not a strong minima

**119.** If $F(x, y, y')$ is a function of $y'$ alone, then the extremal of the functional $\int_{x_1}^{x_2} F(x, y, y')dx$ is
(a) parabola (b) hyperbola
(c) circle (d) straight line

**120.** The functional $I[y(x)] = \int_0^1 [xy + y^2 - 2y^2y']dx$; $y(0) = 1$, $y(1) = 2$ has
(a) one extremal
(b) no extremal
(c) infinite extremal
(d) more than one but finite extremal

**121.** Closseness of the curves $y(x) = \frac{\sin nx}{n^2}$ and $y_1(x) = 0$ on $[0, \pi]$ is
(a) first order proximity (b) second order proximity
(c) third order proximity (d) fourth order proximity

**122.** The extremum value of the function $\int_0^1 (y'^2 + 12xy)dx$, $y(0) = 0$, $y(1) = 1$ is
(a) $\frac{1}{5}$ (b) $\frac{2l}{5}$
(c) 5 (d) 25

**123.** The extremal of the functional $\int_0^2 \frac{y'^2}{x} dx$ with $y(0) = \alpha$, $y(2) = \beta$ is parabola passing through origin, then $\alpha$ and $\beta$ are
(a) $\alpha = 0, \beta = 1$ (b) $\alpha = 1, \beta = 2$
(c) $\alpha = -1, \beta = 2$ (d) None of these

**124.** The extremal of the function $J = \int_a^b \frac{\sqrt{1 + y'^2}}{x} dx$ is
(a) family of catenary (b) family of parabolas
(c) a family of circle (d) None of these

**125.** The distance between the curves $y_1(x) = x$ and $y_2(x) = x^2$ on the interval $[0, 1]$ is
(a) $\frac{1}{4}$ (b) $\frac{1}{2}$ (c) $\frac{3}{4}$ (d) 1

**126.** Extremal of the isoperimetric problem $\int_{x_0}^{x_1} y'^2\, dx$ subject to $\int_{x_0}^{x_1} y\, dx = c$ is
(a) $y = \lambda x^2 + ax + b$ (b) $y = \lambda x^3 + ax + b$
(c) $ax + b$ (d) None of these

**127.** When $F(x, y, y')$ is independent of $y'$, then in general Euler's equation of the variational problem $\int_{x_1}^{x_2} F(x, y, y')dx$ reduces to
(a) a linear differential equation of first order
(b) a linear differential equation of second order
(c) finite equation
(d) None of the above

**128.** For the functional $\int_a^b (y^2 + 2xyy')dx$; $y(a) = y_a$, $y(b) = y_b$. The number of extremals equals to
(a) 1 (b) 0
(c) 2 (d) infinite

**129.** Extremal for the variational problem $I[y(x)] = \int_0^{\pi/2} [e^{-x}y'^2 - e^x y^2]dx$ satisfies the differential equation.
(a) $y'' + y' + e^{2x}y = 0$ (b) $y'' - y' + e^{2x}y = 0$
(c) $y'' + y' + e^x y = 0$ (d) $y'' + y' + e^{-x}y = 0$

**130.** Euler's equation for the functional $I[z(x, y)] = \iint_R \left[\left(\frac{\partial z}{\partial x}\right)^2 - \left(\frac{\partial z}{\partial y}\right)^2\right] dxdy$ is

(a) $\frac{\partial^2 z}{\partial y^2} - \frac{\partial^2 z}{\partial x^2} = 0$ (b) $\frac{\partial^2 z}{\partial y^2} + \frac{\partial^2 z}{\partial x^2} = 0$

(c) $\frac{\partial^2 z}{\partial y^2} = 0$ (d) $\frac{\partial^3 z}{\partial y^3} + \frac{\partial^3 z}{\partial x^3} = 0$

**131.** The extremal problem $J[y(x)] = \int_0^{\pi} \left\{\left(\frac{dy}{dx}\right)^2 - y^2\right\} dx$, $y(0) = 1$, $y(\pi) = \alpha$, has

(a) a unique extremal, if $\alpha = 1$
(b) infinite many extremal, if $\alpha = 1$
(c) a unique extremal, if $\alpha = -1$
(d) infinite many extremal, if $\alpha = -1$

**132.** Extremal $y = y(x)$ for the variational problem $J = \int_0^1 (1 + y''^2) dx$ satisfies the ODE is

(a) homogeneous linear differential equation of fourth order
(b) non-homogeneous linear differential equation of fourth order
(c) homogeneous non-linear differential equation of fourth order
(d) homogeneous linear differential equation of order more than fourth order

**133.** Euler's equation for the functional $\int_{x_1}^{x_2} [a(x)y'^2 + 2b(x)yy' + c(x)y^2] dx$

(a) first order linear differential equation
(b) second order linear differential equation
(c) second order non-linear differential equation
(d) a linear differential equation of order more than two

**134.** The functional $I[y(x)] = \int_0^1 \left(x + 2y + \frac{1}{2}y'^2\right) dx$, $y(0) = 0$, $y(1) = 0$ has

(a) weak minimum on the function $y = x^2 - x$
(b) strong minimum on the function $y = x^2 - x$
(c) weak maximum on the function $y = x^2 - x$
(d) strong maximum on the function $y = x^2 - x$

**135.** Extremal for the variational problem $V[y(x)] = \int_{x_0}^{x_1} y'(1 + x^2 y') dx$ is solution of differential equation

(a) $y'' + 2y' = 0$ (b) $xy'' + y' = 0$
(c) $xy'' + 2y' = 0$ (d) $y'' + 2xy' = 0$

**136.** Extremals of the functional $\int_0^{\pi/2} (y''^2 - y^2 + x^2) dx$ are

(a) one parameter family of curves
(b) two parameter family of curves
(c) three parameter family of curves
(d) four parameter family of curves

**137.** A necessary condition for functional $I[y(x)] = \int_a^b f(x, y, y') dx$ to be an extremum is

(a) $\frac{\partial f}{\partial y} - \frac{d}{dx}\left(\frac{\partial f}{\partial y'}\right) = 0$ (b) $\frac{\partial f}{\partial y} + \frac{d}{dx}\left(\frac{\partial f}{\partial y'}\right) = 0$

(c) $\frac{\partial f}{\partial y'} - \frac{d}{dx}\left(\frac{\partial f}{\partial y}\right) = 0$ (d) $\frac{\partial f}{\partial y'} + \frac{d}{dx}\left(\frac{\partial f}{\partial y}\right) = 0$

**138.** The weak minimum of the functional $I[y(x)] = \int_1^2 \frac{x^3}{y'^2} dx$, $y(1) = 1$, $y(2) = 4$ attained on the curve

(a) $y = x^3$ (b) $y = x^2$
(c) $y = x^3 - x$ (d) None of these

**139.** The integral equation

$$y(x) = \lambda \int_0^{2\pi} \sin(x + t)\, y(t) dt \text{ has}$$

(a) no solution for any value of $\lambda$
(b) unique solution for every value of $\lambda$
(c) infinite many solution for only one value of $\lambda$
(d) infinite many solution for two values of $\lambda$

**140.** The value $\lambda$ of for which the integral equation $y(x) = \lambda \int_0^1 (6x - t)\, y(t)\, dt$ has a non-trivial solution are roots of the equation

(a) $(3\lambda - 1(2 + \lambda) - \lambda^2 = 0$
(b) $(3\lambda - 1)(2 + \lambda) + 2 = 0$
(c) $(3\lambda - 1)(2 + \lambda) - 4\lambda^2 = 0$
(d) $(3\lambda - 1)(2 + \lambda) + \lambda^3 = 0$

**141.** The value of $\lambda$ for which the solution of IE $\phi(x) = 1 + \lambda \int_0^1 (1 - 3xt)\, \phi(t)\, dt$ does not exists

(a) $|\lambda| < 2$ (b) $|\lambda| < 1$
(c) $|\lambda| > 2$ (d) None of these

**142.** The integral equation $y(x) = x + \int_0^1 xt(1 - t)\, y(t) - \int_0^x t(x - t)\, y(t) dt$ in equivalent to BVP

(a) $y'' + xy = 0, \quad y(0) = 0, \quad y(1) = 1$
(b) $y'' - xy = 0, \quad y(0) = 0, \quad y(1) = 0$
(c) $y'' + xy = 0, \quad y(0) = 1, \quad y(1)) = 0$
(d) None of the above

**143.** The volterra's integral equation of first kind can be converted into a

(a) non-homogeneous volterra's integral equation of IInd kind
(b) homogeneous volterra's IE of IInd kind
(c) non-homogeneous volterra's IE of Ist kind
(d) non-homogeneous Fredholm IE of Ist kind

**144.** The iterated kernel for the integral equation

$$\phi(x) = \left(e^x - \frac{1}{2}e + \frac{1}{2}\right) + \frac{1}{2}\int_0^1 \phi(t)\, dt, \text{ is}$$

(a) 1 (b) 0
(c) $-1$ (d) 1/2

**145.** The resolvent kernel of integral equation with kernel $k(x, t) = 2x$, $(\lambda = 1)$ is

(a) $2e^{x^2 - t^2}$ (b) $2xe^{x^2 - t^2}$
(c) $2xe^{x-t}$ (d) $(x - t)$

**146.** Given that the eigen value of integral equation $y(x) = \lambda \int_0^{2\pi} \cos(x + t)\, y(t)\, dt$ are $\frac{1}{\pi}$ and $-\frac{1}{\pi}$ with respective eigen functions cos x and sin x, then the integral equation

$y(x) = \sin x + \cos x + \lambda \int_0^{2\pi} \cos(x + t)\, y(t)$ has

(a) unique solution for $\lambda = \frac{1}{\pi}$
(b) unique solution for $\lambda = -\frac{1}{\pi}$
(c) unique solution for $\lambda = \pi$
(d) no solution for $\lambda = -\pi$

**147.** Solution of integro differential equation

$y''(x) + 2y'(x) - 2\int_0^x \sin(x - t)\, y'(t)\, dt = \cos x$,

$y(0) = y'(0) = 0$ is

(a) $1 - e^{-x} - xe^{-x}$ (b) $1 + e^{-x} + xe^{-x}$
(c) $1 - e^{x}$ (d) $1 + e^{x}$

**148.** The solution of Integral equation

$f(x) = \int_0^x e^{x-t} y(t)\, dt$. $f(0) = 0$ is

(a) $y(x) = f'(x) - \int_0^x f(t)\, y(t)\, dt$
(b) $y(x) = f'(x) = \int_0^x t(t)\, dt$
(c) $y(x) = f(x) - \int_0^x f(t)\, dt$
(d) None of the above

**149.** The solution of integral equation $\int_0^x e^{x-t} \phi(t)\, dt = \sinh x$ is

(a) $\phi(x) = e^{-x}$ (b) $\phi(x) = e^{x}$
(c) $\phi(x) = \sinh x$ (d) $\phi(x) = \cosh x$

**150.** The eigen value $\lambda$ of the integral equation $y(x) = \lambda \int_0^{2\pi} \sin(x + t)\, y(t)\, dt$ are

(a) $\frac{1}{2\pi}, -\frac{1}{2\pi}$ (b) $\frac{1}{\pi}, -\frac{1}{\pi}$
(c) $\pi, -\pi$ (d) $2\pi, -2\pi$

**151.** The initial value problem

$\frac{d^2y}{dx^2} + \alpha_1(x)\frac{dy}{dx} + \alpha_2(x)y = F(x), 0 \le x \le 1, \; y(0) = C_0,$
$y'(0) = C_1$

(where $\alpha_1(x)$, $\alpha_2(x)$ and $F(x)$ are continuous functions on [0, 1]). In general reduced to

(a) Fredholm integral equation of first kind
(b) Volterra's integral equation of first kind
(c) Fredholm integral equation of second kind
(d) Volterra's integral equation of second kind

**152.** Suppose, $y(x) = \lambda \int_0^{2\pi} y(t) \sin(x + t)$, $y(t)\, dt$, $x \in [0, 2\pi]$ has eigen values $\lambda = \frac{1}{\pi}$ and $\lambda = -\frac{1}{\pi}$ with corresponding eigen functions $y_1(x) = \sin x + \cos x$ and $y_2(x) = \sin x - \cos x$ respectively, then the integral equation. $y(x) = f(x) + \frac{1}{\pi}\int_0^x y(t) \sin(x + t)\, dt$, $x \in [0, 2\pi]$ has a solution when $f(x)$ is equal to

(a) 1 (b) cos x
(c) sin x (d) 1 + sin x + cos x

**153.** The integral equation $y(x) = (1 + x) + \int_0^x (x - t)\, y(t)\, dt$, is solved by the method of successive approximation with initial approximation $y_n(x) = 1$, then the $n_{th}$ approximation converges to a limit $y(x)$, then $y(x)$ is

(a) $y(x) = e^x$ (b) $y(x) = \sin x$
(c) $y(x) = 1$ (d) $y(x) = \cos x$

**154.** For the kernel $K(x, t) = (1 + x)(1 - t)$; $a = -1$, $b = 0$. The third iterated kernel $k_3(x, t)$ is

(a) $(1 + x)(1 - t)$
(b) $\frac{2}{3}(1 + x)(1 - t)$
(c) $\left(\frac{2}{3}\right)^2 (1 + x)(1 - t)$
(d) None of the above

**155.** Eigen values of the homogeneous integral equation $g(s) = \lambda \int_1^2 \left(st + \frac{1}{st}\right) g(t)\, dt$ are solution of equation

(a) $\lambda^2 + 17\lambda + 6 = 0$ (b) $\lambda^2 - 17\lambda + 6 = 0$
(c) $\lambda^2 + 6\lambda + 6 = 0$ (d) None of these

**156.** Which of the following function is a solution of volterra's type integral equation $f(x) = x + \int_0^x \sin(x - t)\, f(t)\, dt$

(a) $x + \frac{x^3}{3}$ (b) $x - \frac{x^3}{3}$
(c) $x + \frac{x^3}{6}$ (d) $x - \frac{x^3}{6}$

**157.** The integral equation $y(x) = 1 + \int_0^x (x - t)\, y(t)$ is solved by the method of successive approximation, with initial approximation $y_0(x) = 0$, then third approximation, $y_3(x)$ is given by

(a) $y_3(x) = x + \frac{x^3}{3!} + \frac{x^5}{5!}$ (b) $y_3(x) = 1 + \frac{x^2}{2!} + \frac{x^4}{4!}$
(c) $y_3(x) = x - \frac{x^3}{3!} + \frac{x^5}{5!}$ (d) $y_3(x) = 1 - \frac{x^2}{2!} + \frac{x^4}{4!}$

**158.** The resolvent kernel of Volterra's integral equation $y(x) = f(x) + \lambda \int_0^x k(x, t), y(t)\, dt$ with kernel $k(x, t) = 1$ is

(a) $e^{\lambda(x-t)}$ (b) $e^{\lambda(x+t)}$
(c) $-1$ (d) 1

**159.** Integral equation $g(s) = \lambda \int_a^b k(x, t)\, g(t)\, dt$ where $k(x, t) = \sum_{r=1}^{n} a_r(x) b_r(t)$ has

(a) atleast $n$-eigen values
(b) atmost $n$-eigen values
(c) exactly $n$-eigen values
(d) None of the above

**160.** The integral equation $y(x) = x - \int_0^x (x - t)\, y(t)\, dt$ is solved by the method of successive approximation, with initial approximation $y_0(x) = x$, then the second approximation is given by

(a) $y_2(x) = x + \frac{x^3}{3!} + \frac{x^5}{5!}$ (b) $y_2(x) = x + \frac{x^3}{3!}$
(c) $y_2(x) = x - \frac{x^3}{3!}$ (d) $y_2(x) = x - \frac{x^3}{3!} + \frac{x^5}{5!}$

**161.** The resolvent kernel of integral equation $\phi(x) = x + \int_0^x (t - x)\, \phi(t)\, dt$ is

(a) $\sin(t + x)$ (b) $\sin(t - x)$ (c) $\cos(t + x)$ (d) $\cos(t - x)$

**162.** The resolvent kernel of integral equation $\phi(x) = \sin x + 2 \int_0^x e^{x-t} \phi(t)\, dt$ is

(a) $e^{3(x-t)}$ (b) $e^{2(x-t)}$
(c) $e^{3(x+t)}$ (d) $e^{(x-t)}$

**163.** The resolvent kernel of IE $g(s) = f(s) + \int_{-1}^{1} (st + s^2t^2)\, g(t)\, dt$ is

(a) $3st - 5s^2t^2$
(b) $3st + 5s^2t^2$
(c) $st + s^2t^2$
(d) None of the above

**164.** The solution of integral equation $\phi(x) = x + \int_0^x (t - x)\, \phi(t)\, dt$ is

(a) $\phi(x) = \sin x$ (b) $\phi(x) = \cos x$
(c) $\phi(x) = e^x$ (d) $\phi(x) = e^{-x}$

**165.** The solution of integral equation $y(x) = x + \int_0^{1/2} y(t)\, dt$ is of the form

(a) $y(x) = x + A$ (b) $y(x) = e^x + A$
(c) $y(x) = e^{-x} + A$ (d) None of these

**166.** The integral equation $y(x) = \int_0^x (x - t)\, y(t)\, dt - x \int_0^1 (1 - t)\, y(t)\, dt$ is equivalent to

(a) $y'' - y = 0, y(0) = 0, y(1) = 0$
(b) $y'' - y = 0, y(0) = 0, y'(0) = 0$
(c) $y'' + y = 0, y(0) = 0, y(1) = 0$
(d) $y'' + y = 0, y(0) = 0, y'(0) = 0$

**167.** If $y(x) = 1 + \int_0^x y(t)\, dt$, then $y(x)$ at $x = \frac{1}{2}$ is

(a) $e$ (b) $e^2$
(c) $\sqrt{e}$ (d) None of these

**168.** The solution of integral equation $\phi(x) = 1 + \int_0^x (t - x)\, \phi(t)\, dx$, is

(a) $\phi(x) = \sin x$ (b) $\phi(x) = \cos x$
(c) $\phi(x) = \tan x$ (d) $\phi(x) = e^x$

**169.** Which of the following function is solution of $y(x) = x + \int_0^1 xt\, y(t)\, dt$

(a) $\frac{2}{3}x$ (b) $\frac{3}{2}x$
(c) $\frac{3}{4}x$ (d) $\frac{4}{3}x$

**170.** Integral equation corresponding to initial value problem $y'' + y = 0, y(0) = y'(0) = 0$ is

(a) $y(x) = x - \int_0^x (x - t)\, y(t)\, dt$
(b) $y(x) = -\int_0^x (x - t)\, y(t)\, dt$
(c) $y(x) = x^2 + \int_0^x (x - t)\, y(t)\, dt$
(d) $y(x) = 1 - \int_0^x (x - t)\, y(t)\, dt$

**171.** The solution of integral equation. $g(x) = x + \int_0^1 xt^2 g(t)\, dt$ given by

(a) $g(x) = \frac{3x}{4}$ (b) $g(x) = \frac{4x}{3}$
(c) $g(x) = \frac{2x}{3}$ (d) $g(x) = \frac{3x}{2}$

**172.** Solution of integral equation
$y(x) = 1 - 2x - 4x^2 + \int_0^x [3 + 6(x - t) - 4(x - t)^2]\, y(t)\, dt$ is

(a) $y(x) = e^x$ (b) $y(x) = e^{x^2}$
(c) $y(x) = e^{-x}$ (d) None of these

**173.** Solution of I.E $\int_0^x 3^{x-t} y(t)\, dt - x$ is

(a) $y(x) = 1 + x \log e^3$ (b) $y(x) = 1 - x \log e^3$
(c) $y(x) = x + x^2 \log e^3$ (d) None of these

**174.** The boundary value problem $y''(x) + A(x)\, y' + B(x)\, y = f(x)$,

$$y(a) = y_0 \cdot y(b) = y_1$$

(where $A$, $B$ and $f$ are continuous functions on $[a, b]$) may be reduced, in general to a solution of some linear

(a) Volterra's IE of Ist kind
(b) Volterra's IE of IInd kind
(c) Fredholm IE of Ist kind
(d) Fredholm IE of IInd kind

**175.** The initial value problem corresponding to integral equation $y(x) = 1 + \int_0^x y(t)\, dt$ is

(a) $y' + y = 0, y(0) = 0$
(b) $y' - y = 0, y(0) = 1$
(c) $y' - y = 0, y(0) = 0$
(d) $y' + y = 0, y(0) = 1$

**176.** Which of the following is not a symmetric Kernel?

(a) $K(x, t) = \sin(x + t)$ (b) $K(x, t) = xt + x^2t^2$

(c) $K(x, t) = xt^2 + x^3t$ (d) $K(x, t) = \begin{cases} x(1-t), & x < t \\ (1-x)t, & x > t \end{cases}$

**177.** Solution of integral equation is $3 \sin 2x = y(x) + \int_0^x (x - t)\, y(t)\, dt$

(a) $2 \sin x - \sin 2x$ (b) $\sin x + \sin 2x$

(c) $\sin x + \sin^2 x$ (d) None of these

**178.** The integral equation

$x(t) - \int_0^1 [\cos t \sec s\, x(s)]\, ds = \sinh t,\ 0 \le t \le 1$ has

(a) no solution

(b) a unique solution

(c) more than one but finitely many solution

(d) infinitely many solutions

**179.** Solution of integral equation $y + \int_0^x y dt = 1 - e^{-t}$ is

(a) $te^t$ (b) $te^{-t}$

(c) $e^t$ (d) $e^{-t}$

**180.** The value of $\lambda$ for which the function $\phi(x) = 1 + x$ is a solution of integral equation

$x = \int_0^x e^{x-t} \phi(t)\, dt$

(a) $\lambda = 1$ (b) $\lambda = -1$

(c) $\lambda = 2$ (d) $\lambda = 3$

**181.** The Kernel $K(x, t)$ is separable or degenerate, if

(a) $K(x, t) = \sum_{i=1}^{\infty} g_i(x)\, h_i(t)$

(b) $K(x, t) = \sum_{i=1}^{n} g_i(x)\, h_i(t)$

(c) $K(x, t) = \sum_{i=1}^{\infty} g_i(x, t)\, h_i(x, t)$

(d) $K(x, t) = \sum_{i=1}^{n} g_i(x, t)\, h_i(x, t)$

**182.** The integral equation,

$x(t) = \sin t + \lambda \int_0^t (s^2 t + e^{x^2 + t^2})\, x(s)\, ds,$

$0 \le t \le 1,\ \lambda \in R,\ \lambda \ne 0$

(a) all non-zero values of $\lambda$

(b) no value of $\lambda$

(c) only countable many positive value of $\lambda$

(d) only countable many negative value of $\lambda$

**183.** Solution of integral equation

$\int_0^x y(x)\, y(x - t)\, dt = 16 \sin 4x$ is

(a) $J_0(4x)$ (b) $J_1(4x)$

(c) $8J_0(4x)$ (d) $4J_0(8x)$

**184.** Integral equation corresponding to differential equation $\frac{dy}{dx} - y = 0,\ y(0) = 1$ is

(a) $y(x) = 1 + \int_0^x y(t)\, dt$

(b) $y(x) = 1 + x - \int_0^x \sin(x + t)\, y(t)\, dt$

(c) $y(x) = 2 - \int_0^x y(t)\, dt$

(d) None of the above

**185.** Which of the following is solution of Integral Equation $\int_0^x e^{x-t} \phi(t)\, dt = x$?

(a) $\phi(x) = 1 + x$ (b) $\phi(x) = 1 - x$

(c) $\phi(x) = 1 + x^2$ (d) $\phi(x) = 1 - x^2$

**186.** Which of the following is not a linear integral equation?

(a) $\phi(x) = x - \int_0^x \sinh(x - t)\, \phi(t)\, dt$

(b) $\phi(x) = x + \int_0^x (x - t)^2\, \phi(t)\, dt$

(c) $\phi(x) = 1 + \int_0^x e^{(x-t)}\, \phi(t)\, dt$

(d) $\phi(x) = 1 + \int_0^x \sinh(x + t)\, \phi^2(t)\, dt$

**187.** If $y(x) = x + x \int_0^1 ty(t)\, dt$, then $y(x)$ at $x = 2$ is

(a) $\frac{3}{2}$ (b) 3

(c) $\frac{3}{4}$ (d) 1

**188.** If $\bar{y}(p)$ denotes the Laplace transform of $y(x)$, then for the integral equation $y(x) = x^2 + \int_0^x \sin(x - t)\, y(t)\, dt$, $\bar{y}(p)$ is given by

(a) $\frac{2(1 + p^2)}{p^5}$ (b) $\frac{2(1 - p^2)}{p^5}$

(c) $\frac{2(1 + p)}{p^3}$ (d) None of these

**189.** Which of the following function is solution of Fredholm type integral equation

$y(x) + \int_0^1 x(e^{st} - 1)\, y(t)\, dt = e^x - x$ ?

(a) $y(x) = 1$ (b) $y(x) = -1$

(c) $y(x) = 2$ (d) $y(x) = -2$

**190.** The integral equation

$y(x) = 1 + \frac{1}{\pi} \int_0^{2\pi} \sin(x + t)\, y(t)\, dt$ has

(a) infinite solution (b) no solution

(c) unique solution (d) None of these

**191.** Solution of initial value problem $\frac{d^2y}{dx^2} + p(x)\, y = 0;$

$0 \le x \le 1,\ y(0) = a,\ \left(\frac{dy}{dx}\right)_{x=0} = b$

(where $p(x)$ is continuous on $[0, 1]$) is reduced to a solution of linear

(a) non-homogeneous Fredholm IE of Ist kind

(b) homogeneous Volterra's IE of Ist kind

(c) non-homogeneous Fredholm IE of Second kind

(d) non-homogeneous Volterras' IE of second kind

**192.** If $\bar{\phi}(p)$ denotes the Laplace transform of $\phi(x)$, then for the integral equation of convolution type

$\phi(x) = 1 + 2\int_0^x \cos(x-t)\,\phi(t)\,dt$, $\bar{\phi}(p)$ is given by

(a) $\dfrac{p^2+1}{(p-1)^2}$ (b) $\dfrac{p^2+1}{(p+1)^2}$

(c) $\dfrac{(p^2+1)}{p(p-1)^2}$ (d) $\dfrac{p^2+1}{p(p+1)^2}$

**193.** Solution of initial value problem $y''(x) = 0$, $0 \le x \le 1$

$y(0) = C_0,\ y'(0) = C_1$

may be reduced, in general solution of some linear

(a) homogeneous Fredholm IE of Ist kind
(b) non-homogeneous Fredholm IE of IInd kind
(c) homogeneous Volterra's IE of IInd kind
(d) non-homogeneous Volterra's IE Ist kind

**194.** The value of $\alpha$ for which the integral equation $u(x) = \alpha\int_0^1 e^{x-t}u(t)\,dt$ has trivial solution

(a) $-2$ (b) $-1$ (c) 1 (d) 2

**195.** If $L\{y(x)\} = \bar{y}(p)$, then for integral equation

$y(x) = e^{-x} - 2\int_0^x y(t)\cos(x-t)\,dt$, $\bar{y}(p)$ is given by

(a) $\dfrac{p^3+1}{(p+1)^3}$ (b) $\dfrac{p^2+1}{(p+1)^3}$

(c) $\dfrac{p^2-1}{(p+1)^3}$ (d) $\dfrac{p^2+1}{(p-1)^3}$

**196.** Which of the following is solution of integral equation $\int_0^x \dfrac{\phi(t)}{\sqrt{x-t}}\,dt = \sqrt{x}$?

(a) $\phi(x) = \dfrac{1}{2}$ (b) $\phi(x) = -\dfrac{1}{2}$

(c) $\phi(x) = 1$ (d) $\phi(x) = -1$

**197.** Solution of initial value problem

$$\frac{d^2y}{dx^2} + \alpha_1(x)\frac{dy}{dx} + \alpha_2(x) \qquad y = 0,\ 0 \le x \le 1$$

$y(0) = C_0,\ y'(0) = C_1$

(where $\alpha_1(x)$ and $\alpha_2(x)$ are continuous function on [0, 1]) may be reduced in general to a solution of some linear

(a) homogeneous Volterra's IE of Ist kind
(b) non-homogeneous Volterra's IE of the first kind
(c) homogeneous volterra's IE of IInd kind
(d) non-homogeneous Volterra's IE of IInd kind

**198.** Let $k(x,t) = \begin{cases} x+t, & 0 \le t \le x \\ 0, & \text{otherwise} \end{cases}$

Then, the integral equation

$$y(x) = 1 + \lambda\int_0^1 y(t)\,k(x,t)\,dt \text{ has}$$

(a) a unique solution for every value of $\lambda$
(b) no solution for any value of $\lambda$
(c) a unique solution for infinite many values of only $\lambda$
(d) infinite many solutions for infinite many values of $\lambda$

# Exercise 2 (For Part 'C')

**Directions** (Q. Nos. 1-59) *Questions may have one or more than one correct option.*

**1.** A necessary condition for $I[y(x)] = \int_{x_1}^{x_2} f(x, y, y')\,dx$ to be an extremum is/are

(a) $\dfrac{\partial f}{\partial x} - \dfrac{d}{dy}\left(\dfrac{\partial f}{\partial x'}\right) = 0$

(b) $\dfrac{\partial f}{\partial y} - \dfrac{d}{dx}\left(\dfrac{\partial f}{\partial y'}\right) = 0$

(c) $\dfrac{\partial f}{\partial x} - \dfrac{d}{dx}\left(f - y'\dfrac{\partial f}{\partial y'}\right) = 0$

(d) $\dfrac{\partial f}{\partial y} - \dfrac{\partial^2 f}{\partial x\partial y'} - y'\dfrac{\partial^2 f}{\partial y\partial y'} - y''\dfrac{\partial^2 f}{\partial y'^2} = 0$

**2.** Consider the functional $v[y(x)] = \int_{x_1}^{x_2} \dfrac{(1+y'^2)^{1/2}}{x}\,dx$,

then following/s is/are valid; if $F = \dfrac{(1+y'^2)^{1/2}}{x}$,

(a) $\dfrac{\partial F}{\partial y'} = \text{constant}$

(b) $F - y'\dfrac{\partial F}{\partial y'} = \text{constant}$

(c) extremal of the given functional is a circle
(d) extremal is a straight line

**3.** Consider the functional $I = \int_0^1 (2x + x'^2 + y'^2)\,dt$ such that $x(0) = 1$, $y(0) = 1$, $x(1) = 1.5$, $y(1) = 1$. Assuming $F = 2x + x'^2 + y'^2$. Then,

(a) for extremum of $I$

$$\frac{\partial F}{\partial x} - \frac{d}{dt}\left(\frac{\partial F}{\partial x'}\right) = 0 \text{ and } \frac{\partial F}{\partial y} - \frac{d}{dt}\left(\frac{\partial F}{\partial y'}\right) = 0$$

(b) $x'' = 0,\ y'' = 1$
(c) $x'' = 1,\ y'' = 0$
(d) $x = 1 + \dfrac{t^2}{2},\ y = 1$

**4.** Let $I = \int_0^1 (y'^2 - y^2)\,dx$. Then, select the correct option/s

(a) if $y(0) = 0, y(1) = 0$, then extremal is $y(x) = \sin x$
(b) if $y(0) = 0$, then extremal is $y(x) = 1$
(c) if $y(1) = 1$, then extremal is $y(x) = \dfrac{\cos x}{\cos 1}$
(d) extremal is $y(x) = 0$, if end conditions are not specified

**5.** Consider the variational problem $I[y(x)] = \int_0^2 (y'^3 + \sin^2 x)\,dx,\ y(0) = 0,\ y(2) = 6$. Which of the following/s is/are true?

(a) Extremal of $I[y(x)]$ is $y = 3x$
(b) Central field of extremals of $I[y(x)]$ is $y = ax, 0 \le x \le 2$
(c) Extremal of $I[y(x)]$ is included in a proper field of extremals of $I[y(x)]$
(d) Given variational problem has no proper field

**6.** Let $\phi(x) = 1 + x^2 + \int_0^x \dfrac{1+x^2}{1+t^2}\phi(t)\,dt$. Then,

(a) $k_2(x,t) = (x-t)\dfrac{1+x^2}{1+t^2}$ (b) $R(x,t;1) = \dfrac{1+x^2}{1+t^2}e^{x-t}$
(c) $\phi(x) = x(1+e^x)$ (d) $\phi(x) = e^x(1+x^2)$

**7.** Consider the integral equation $y(x) = \lambda \int_0^1 (2xt - 4x^2)y(t)\,dt$. Then,

(a) integral equation has no solution for $\lambda = 2$
(b) integral equation has zero (trivial) solution for $\lambda = 3$
(c) integral equation has an unique solution for $\lambda = -3$
(d) integral equation has infinitely many solution for $\lambda = -3$

**8.** For the integral equation $u(x) = \cos x + \lambda \int_0^{\pi} \sin(x-t)u(t)\,dt$. Which of the following/s is/are true?

(a) Integral equation has unique solution for any real $\lambda$.
(b) Integral equation has infinitely many solution for any $\lambda$.
(c) Unique solution given by $u(x) = \dfrac{\sin x + \cos x}{2}$ for $\lambda = \dfrac{2}{\pi}$
(d) Unique solution given by $u(x) = \dfrac{\cos x - \sin x}{2}$ for $\lambda = -\dfrac{2}{\pi}$

**9.** Let $y(x) = 1 + \lambda \int_0^{\pi} \cos(x+t)y(t)\,dt$, then which of the following is/are true?

(a) For $\lambda \ne \dfrac{2}{\pi}$ integral equation has an unique solution
(b) For $\lambda \ne -\dfrac{2}{\pi}$ integral equation has an unique solution
(c) For $\lambda = \dfrac{2}{\pi}$ integral equation has infinitely many solution
(d) For $\lambda = -\dfrac{2}{\pi}$ integral equation has no solution

**10.** Given that the eigen values of the integral equation $y(x) = \lambda \int_0^{2\pi} \cos(x+t)y(t)\,dt$ are $\dfrac{1}{\pi}$ and $-\dfrac{1}{\pi}$ with respect to eigen functions $\cos x$ and $\sin x$. Then, the integral equation

$y(x) = \sin x + \cos x + \lambda \int_0^{2\pi} \cos(x+t)y(t)\,dt$ has

(a) unique solution for $\lambda = \dfrac{1}{\pi}$
(b) unique solution for $\lambda = -\dfrac{1}{\pi}$
(c) unique solution for $\lambda = \pi$
(d) no solution for $\lambda = -\pi$

**11.** Which of the following statements are true?

(a) The geodesics on a sphere of radius are its great circles
(b) The geodesics on a sphere of radius are not its great circles
(c) For a spherical surface, the geodesics are greatest circles
(d) For a spherical surface, the geodesies are not greatest circles

**12.** Given $y(x) = x + 2\int_0^x \cos(x-t)\,y(t)\,dt$, is

(a) Volterra equation
(b) Fredholm equation
(c) A solution is $y = 2 + x - 2e^x + 2xe^x$
(d) A solution is $y = x + 2 + 2(x-1)e^x$

**13.** Given integral equation $y(x) = \int_0^x (x+t)\,y(t)\,dt + 1$ is

(a) A Fredholm integral equation
(b) A Volterra's integral equation
(c) The required differential equation is

$$\frac{d^2y}{dx^2} - 2x\frac{dy}{dx} - 3y = 0$$

(d) The initial equation of required differential equation is $y(0) = 1, y'(0) = 0$

**14.** Given, $\dfrac{d^2y}{dx^2} - \sin x\dfrac{dy}{dx} + e^x y = x$ with the initial conditions $y(0) = 1, y'(0) = -1$. Then,

(a) the equivalent integral equation is $y(x) = [x - \sin x + e^x(x-1)] + \int_0^x [\sin x - e^x(x-\xi)]\,y(\xi)\,d\xi$
(b) the Volterra's integral equation of first find
(c) the Volterra's integral equation of second kind
(d) the Fredholm integral equation of first kind

**15.** Given the integral equation

$$y(x) = \int_0^{\pi} t(t-x)\,y(t)\,dt + \frac{1}{2}x^2 \text{ is}$$

(a) a Volterra integral equation
(b) a Fredholm integral equation
(c) the equivalent differential equation is $\frac{d^2y}{dx^2} + xy = 1$ with $y(0) = 0 = y'(0)$
(d) the equivalent differential equation is $y'' + xy = 1$ with $y(0) = y'(0) = 1$

**16.** Given kernel $K(x, \xi) = 1$; $a = 0$ $b = 1$, then
(a) $D(\lambda) = 1 - \lambda$ (b) $D(x, \xi; \lambda) = 1$
(c) $D(\lambda) = \frac{\lambda}{3}$ (d) $D(x, \xi; \lambda) = 0$

**17.** Given the integral equation $\phi(x) = x + 2\int_0^x \cos(x-\xi)\,\phi(\xi)\,d\xi$, then
(a) $\phi(x) = 2e^x(x-1) + x + 2$ is a solution to
(b) $\phi(x) = \sin x \cos x$ is a solution to given problem
(c) a Volterra integral equation
(d) a Fredholm integral equation

**18.** Given an integral equation $\phi(x) = (1 - x - 4\sin x) + \int_0^x [3 - 2(x-\xi)]\,\phi(\xi)\,d\xi$, then
(a) $\phi'(x) = -1 - 4\cos x + 3\phi(x) - 2\int_0^x \phi(\xi)\,d\xi$
(b) $\phi''(x) - 3\phi'(x) + 2\phi(x) = 4\sin x$ is the equivalent differential equation
(c) $\phi(0) = 1$, $\phi'(0) = 2$ are initial condition for differential equation
(d) $\phi''(x) - \phi(x) = \cos x$ is the equivalent differential equation

**19.** Given the integral equation

$$\phi(x) = -\frac{1}{2}x + \frac{1}{6}x^3 + \lambda\int_0^1 x\,\phi(\xi)\,d\xi - \lambda\int_0^1 (x-\xi)\,\phi(\xi)\,d\xi.$$

Then,
(a) $\phi'(x) = -\frac{1}{2} + \frac{1}{2}x^2 + \lambda\int_0^1 \phi(\xi)\,d\xi - \lambda\int_0^x \phi(\xi)\,d\xi$
(b) $\phi''(x) = x - \lambda\phi(x)$
(c) $\phi(0) = \phi'(1) = 0$ are the boundary conditions fo required differential equation
(d) No differential equation exist

**20.** Given kernal $K(x, \xi) = x\xi$ $a = 0$, $b = 10$, then
(a) $D(\lambda) = 1 - \frac{10^3}{3}\lambda$ (b) $D(\lambda) = e^{\lambda} + 6g$
(c) $D(x, \xi; \lambda) = x\xi$ (d) $D(x, \xi; \lambda) = x + \cos\xi$

**21.** Find the solution of Volterra equation of the second kind.
(a) $\phi(x) = \lambda\int_0^x e^{x-y}\,\phi(y)\,dy = f(x)$ is the Volterra integral equation of second type
(b) $H(x, y; \lambda) = -e^{(1+\lambda)(x-y)}$ is the resolvent kernel for this Volterra integral equation
(c) $\phi(x) = f(x) + \lambda\int_0^1 e^{(1+\lambda)(x-y)} f(y)\,dy$ is the solution of this Volterra integral equation
(d) $J(x, y) = e^x e^{-y}$ is the kernel for Volterra integral equation

**22.** Given differential equation $\frac{d^3y}{dx^3} + x\frac{d^2y}{dx^2} + (x^2 - x)y = xe^x + 1$ with initial conditions $y(0) = 1 = y'(0)$, $y''(0) = 0$, then
(a) the equivalent integral equation is Volterra integral equation
(b) the equivalent integral equation is Fredholm integral equation
(c) the equivalent integral equation is

$$y(x) = xe^x + 1 - x(x^2 - 1) - \int_0^x \left[x + \frac{1}{2}(x^2 - x)(x-\xi)^2\right] y(\xi)\,d\xi$$

(d) the equivalent integral equation is

$$\phi(x) = \frac{1}{6}x^3 + \lambda\int_0^1 xp(\xi)\,d\xi$$

**23.** Given the integral equation $\phi(x) = 1 + \int_0^x \phi(\xi)\,d\xi$, then
(a) $\phi(x) = e^x$ is the solution of the given integral equation
(b) $\phi(x) = 1 + x + \frac{1}{2!}x^2 + \frac{1}{3!}x^3 + \ldots$ is the solution of the given integral equation
(c) a Volterra integral equation
(d) a Fredholm integral equation

**24.** Given the integral equation

$$\phi(x) = \lambda\int_0^1 [\sqrt{(x)}\xi - \sqrt{(\xi)}x]\,\phi(\xi)\,d\xi, \text{ then}$$

(a) the integral have no real characteristic numbers
(b) the integral have real characteristic number
(c) it have a trivial solution $\phi(x) = 0$
(d) a Fredholm integral equation

**25.** Given the integral equation

$$f(x) = \int_0^x \frac{\phi(\xi)}{(x^2 - \xi^2)^{\alpha}}\,d\xi,\ 0 < \alpha < 1,\ a < x < b, \text{ then}$$

(a) $\phi(\xi) = \frac{2\sin\alpha\pi}{\pi}\frac{d}{d\xi}\left\{\int_a^{\xi}\frac{u\,f(u)\,du}{(\xi^2 - u^2)^{1-\alpha}}\right\}$ is a solution of the given integral equation
(b) Abel's integral equation is

$$f(x) = \int_a^x \frac{\phi(\xi)}{[h(x) - h(\xi)]^{\alpha}}\,d\xi,\ 0 < \alpha < 1, \text{ where } h(\xi) = \xi^2$$

is a strictly monotonically increasing function in the interval $(a, b)$ and $h'(\xi) \neq 0$ in this interval
(c) a Volterra integral equation
(d) a Fredholm integral equation

**26.** Given the kernel $K(x, \xi) = 1$, then

(a) $K_4(x, \xi) = \int_\xi^x 1 \cdot \frac{(z-\xi)^2}{2!} dz = \frac{1}{3!}(x-\xi)^3$

(b) $K_\nu(x, \xi) = \int_\xi^x 1 \cdot K_{\nu-1}(z, \xi) dz$

(c) $K_\nu(x, \xi) = \frac{1}{(\nu-1)!}(x-\xi)^{\nu-1}$

(d) $R(x, \xi; \lambda) = \sum_{\nu=0}^{\infty} \frac{\lambda^\nu (x, \xi)^\nu}{\nu!} = e^{\lambda(x-\xi)}$

**27.** Given the integral equation $\sin x = \int_0^x J_0(x, \xi)\, \phi(\xi)\, d\xi$, then

(a) a Volterra integral equation

(b) a Fredholm integral equation

(c) $\phi(x) = J_0(x)$ is a solution

(d) $\phi(x) = J_1(x)$ is a solution

**28.** Given the integral equation $\phi(x) = (1 + x) + \int_0^x (x - \xi)\, \phi(\xi)\, d\xi$. $\phi_0(x) = 1$, then

(a) a Volterra integral equation of first kind

(b) a Volterra integral eqution of second kind

(c) the solution is $\phi(x) = 1 + x + \frac{x^2}{2!} + \frac{x^3}{3!} + \frac{x^4}{4!} + \ldots$

(d) the solution is $\phi(x) = e^x$

**29.** Given $\frac{dy}{dx} + 3y + 2\int_0^x y dx = x$, with $y(0) = 1$. then

(a) the solution is $y = \frac{1}{2} - 2e^{-x} + \frac{5}{2}e^{-2x}$

(b) the solution is $y = \frac{1}{2} - e^x + (e^x + 5)$

(c) the Volterra integral equation

(d) the Fredholm integral equation

**30.** Given integral equation $\phi(x) = \sec^2 x + \lambda \int_0^1 \phi(\xi)\, d\xi$ is

(a) The Volterra integral equation

(b) The Fredholm integral equation

(c) The solution is $\phi(x) = \sec^2 x + \frac{\lambda}{1+\lambda} \tan 1$

(d) The solution is $\phi(x) = \sec^2 x + \tan x$

**31.** Given the integral equation $y(x) = 3x^2 + \int_0^x y(t) \sin(x - t)\, dt$, then

(a) the solution is $y = 3x^2 + x^4/4$

(b) the solution is $y(x) = \sin x \cos x$

(c) the Volterra integral equation

(d) fredholm integral equation

**32.** Given the differential equation $\frac{d^2\phi}{dx^2} - 2x\frac{d\phi}{dx} - 3\phi = 0$ with initial conditions $\phi(0) = 0$, $\phi'(0) = 0$, is

(a) equivalent integral equation is Volterra equation of first kind

(b) equivalent integral equation is Volterra equation of second kind

(c) the equivalent integral equation is

$$\phi(x) = \int_0^x (x + \xi)\, \phi(\xi)\, d\xi$$

(d) the equivalent integral equation is

$$\phi(x) = \int_0^x \sin(x + \xi)\, \phi(\xi)$$

**33.** Given the kernel $K(x, \xi) = e^{x+\xi}$; $a = 0, b = 1$, then

(a) $K_n(x, \xi) = \int_a^b K_m(x, z) K_{n-m}(z, \xi)\, dz$
$m = 1, 2, \ldots, n-1$

(b) $K_n(x, \xi) = \left(\frac{e^2 - 1}{2}\right)^{n-1} e^{x+\xi}$

(c) The resolvent kernel is $R(x, \xi; \lambda) = \frac{2e^{x+\xi}}{2 - \lambda(e^2 - 1)}$, where $|\lambda| < \frac{2}{e^2 - 1}$

(d) The resolvent kernel is $R(x, \xi, \lambda) = \frac{2e^{x+\xi}}{\lambda}$, where $|\lambda| \le \frac{1}{e^2}$

**34.** Given the integral equation

$$\int_0^x y(t)\, y(x - t)\, dt = 4 \sin 9x, \text{ then}$$

(a) Volterra equation

(b) Fredholm equation

(c) $y = 6J_0(9x)$ is a solution

(d) $y = -6J_0(9x)$ is a solution

**35.** Given the boundary value problem

$u''(x) + \mu^2 u = 0; u(0) = u(1) = 0$, then

(a) the solution $u_1(x) = \sin(x)$ and $u_2(x) = \sin\mu(x - 1)$ are linearly independent

(b) the solution $u_1(x) = \sin x$ and $u_2(x) = \sin\mu(x - 1)$ are linearly dependent

(c) the Green's function is

$$G(x, \xi) = \begin{cases} \frac{\sin\mu(\xi - 1)\sin\mu x}{\mu \sin\mu}, & 0 \le x < \xi \\ \frac{\sin\mu\xi \sin\mu(x - 1)}{\mu \sin\mu}, & \xi < x \le 1 \end{cases}$$

(d) The Wronskian is

$$W(\xi) = \mu\,[\sin\mu\xi \cos\mu(\xi - 1) - \cos\mu\xi \sin\mu(\xi - 1)] = \mu \sin\mu$$

**36.** Given the differential equation $\phi''(x) - 3\phi'(x) + 2\phi(x) = 4\sin x$ with initial conditions $\phi(0) = 1$, $\phi'(0) = -2$, then

(a) $\phi''(x) = 4\sin x - 2\phi(x) + 3\phi'(x)$

(b) $\phi(x) = (1 - x - 4\sin x) + \int_0^x [3 - 2(x - \xi)]\, \phi(\xi) d\xi$

(c) equivalent integral equation is Volterra equation

(d) equivalent integral equation is Fredholm equation

**37.** Given integral equation

$$y(x) = \cos x + \lambda \int_0^\pi \sin(x - t) y(t)\, dt, \text{ then}$$

(a) a Volterra integral equation

(b) a Fredholm integral equation

(c) an equation can be rewritten as
$$y(x)=\cos x+\lambda\,\{\sin x\int_0^{\pi}\cos t\,y(t)\,dt - \cos x\int_0^{\pi}\sin t\,y(t)\,dt\}$$

(d) the solution of the equation is
$$y(x)=\frac{2}{4+\lambda^2\pi^2}(2\cos x+\pi\lambda\sin x)$$

**38.** Given $\frac{d^2y}{dx^2}+x\frac{dy}{dx}+y=0,\ y(0)=1, y'(0)=0$, then

(a) the equivalent integral equation is a Volterra equation of first kind

(b) the equivalent integral equation is Fredholm equation

(c) $y(x)=-1-\int_0^x(2x-\xi)y(\xi)d\xi$ is the equivalent integral equation

(d) the equivalent integral equation is a Volterra equation of second kind

**39.** Given the integral equation
$$\frac{1}{1+x^2}-\int_0^x\frac{\xi}{1+x^2}y(\xi)\,d\xi=\frac{1}{(1+x^2)^{3/2}},\text{ then}$$

(a) a Volterra equation

(b) a Fredholm equation

(c) the solution is $y(x)=\frac{1}{(1+x^2)}$

(d) the solution is $y(x)=(1+x^2)^{-3/2}$

**40.** Given the differential equation
$$\frac{d^2y}{dx^2}-5\frac{dy}{dx}+6y=0$$
$y(0)=0, y'(0)=-1$, then

(a) equivalent integral equation is Volterra equation of first kind

(b) equivalent integral equation is Volterra equation of second kind

(c) $y(x)=(6x-5)+\int_0^x(5-6x+6\xi)y(\xi)d\xi$ is the equivalent integral equation

(d) equivalent equation is a Fredholm equation

**41.** Given the boundary value problem $y''(x)+\lambda y(x)=0, y(0)=y(1)=0$, then

(a) an equivalent integral equation is Volterra equation

(b) an equivalent integral equation is Fredholm equation

(c) an equivalent integral equation is
$$y(x)=\lambda\int_0^1K(x,t)y(t)\,dt$$
where $K(x,t)=\begin{cases}t(1-x)\text{ when }t<x\\ x(1-t)\text{ when }t>x\end{cases}$

(d) equivalent integral equation exist

**42.** Given the differential equation
$$\frac{d^2y}{dx^2}-2x\frac{dy}{dx}-3y=0,$$
with initial condition $y(0)=1, y'(0)=0$. Then,

(a) equivalent equation is Volterra equation

(b) equivalent equation is Fredholm equation

(c) $\phi(x)=3+\int_0^x(5x-3\xi)\phi(\xi)d\xi$ is the equivalent integral equation

(d) $\frac{dy}{dx}=\int_0^x\phi(\xi)d\xi$

**43.** Given the integral equation
$$\phi(x)=e^{-x}-2\int_0^1\cos(x-\xi)\phi(\xi)\,d\xi\text{ is}$$

(a) Volterra integral equation

(b) Fredholm integral equation

(c) $\phi(x)=e^{-x}(1-2x+x^2)$ is a solution of given integral equation

(d) $\phi(x)=e^{x}\sin x\cot x$ is a solution of given integral equation

**44.** Given the integral equation
$$y(x)=\sin x+2\int_0^x\cos(x-t)y(t)dt,\text{ then}$$

(a) $y(x)=xe^x$ is a solution of given integral equation

(b) $y(x)=e^x$ is a solution of given integral equation

(c) a Volterra integral equation

(d) a Fredholm integral equation

**45.** Given the boundary value problem
$$\frac{d^2\phi}{dx^2}+\lambda\phi=x;\ \phi(0)=0,\ \phi'(1)=0\text{ is}$$

(a) An equivalent integral equation is
$$\phi(x)=\frac{1}{6}(x^3-3x)+\lambda\int_0^1K(x,\xi)\phi(\xi)d\xi$$
where $K(x,\xi)=\begin{cases}x, x>\xi\\ \xi, x>\xi\end{cases}$

(b) the equivalent integral equation is Fredholm integral equation of first kind

(c) the equivalent integral equation's Fredholm integral equation of second kind

(d) the equivalent integral equation is Volterra integral equation

**46.** Given integral equation, $y(x)=1+\lambda\int_0^1xt\,y(t)dt$, then

(a) the solution is
$$y(x)=1+\frac{3\lambda x}{2(3-\lambda)},\ \lambda<3$$

(b) the solution is
$$y(x)=1+\frac{\lambda x}{2}\left(1+\frac{\lambda}{3}+\left(\frac{\lambda}{3}\right)^2+\left(\frac{\lambda}{3}\right)^3+\ldots+\infty\right)$$

(c) if initial approximation $y_1(x)=1$, then $y_1(x)=1+\frac{\lambda x}{2}$

(d) if initial approximation, $y_1(x)=1$, then $y_2(x)=1+\frac{\lambda x}{2}+\frac{\lambda^2x}{6}$

**47.** Given a differential equation $\frac{d^2y}{dx^2} + y = \cos x;\ y(0) = 0,$ $y'(0) = 1$ form an integral equation.

(a) The equivalent integral equation is Volterra integral equation of first kind

(b) The equivalent integral equation is Volterra integral equation of second kind

(c) The equivalent integral equation is $y(x) = (\cos x - x) - \int_0^x (x - \xi)\, y(\xi)\, d\xi$

(d) The equivalent integral equation is Fredholm integral equation

**48.** Given the homogeneous integral equation

$\phi(x) = \lambda \int_1^2 \left( x\xi + \frac{1}{x\xi} \right) \phi(\xi)\, d\xi$, then

(a) the non-trivial solution of the system can be obtained only, if the determinant

$$\begin{vmatrix} 1-\left(\frac{7}{3}\right)\lambda & -\lambda \\ -\lambda & 1-\left(\frac{1}{2}\right)\lambda \end{vmatrix} = \frac{1}{6}(\lambda^2 - 17\lambda + 6) \text{ Vanishes}$$

(b) the required eigen values are

$$\lambda_1 = \frac{1}{2}[17 + \sqrt{(265)}] \simeq 6.639$$

$$\lambda_2 = \frac{1}{2}[17 - \sqrt{(265)}] \simeq 0.3606$$

(c) the eigen functions corresponding to the eigen values $\lambda_1, \lambda_2$ are given by

$\left[x - 2.2732\frac{1}{x}\right]$, if $\lambda_1 \simeq 6.639$

and $\left[x + 0.4399\frac{1}{x}\right]$, $\lambda_2 \simeq 0.3606$

(d) a Fredholm integral equation

**49.** Given the integral equation

$$\int_0^x e^{x-\xi}\, y(\xi)\, d\xi = x, \text{ then}$$

(a) a Volterra integral equation

(b) a Fredholm integral equation

(c) $y(x) = 1 - x$ is a solution of integral equation

(d) $y(x) = 1 - x$ is not a solution of integral equation

**50.** Given the kernel

$K(x, \xi) = (x - \xi)^2;\ a = -1,\ b = 1$, then

(a) $K_2(x, \xi) = \int_{-1}^{1} K_m\, (x - z)^2\, (z, \xi)^2\, dz$

(b) $K_3(x, \xi) = \frac{56}{45}(x^2 + \xi^2) + \frac{8}{3}x^2\xi^2 - \frac{32}{9}z\xi + \frac{8}{15}$

(c) $K_n(x, \xi) = \int_a^b K_m\, (x - z)\, K_{n-m}\, (z, \xi)\, dz$

$$m = 1, 2, \ldots, n-1$$

(d) $K_1(x, \xi) = (x - \xi)^2$

**51.** Given the integral equation

$$\phi(x) = 1 + \int_0^x \phi(\xi)\, d\xi;\ \phi_0(x) = 0 \text{ is}$$

(a) a Volterra integral equation of first kind

(b) a Volterra integral equation of second kind

(c) $\phi(x) = e^x$ is a solution

(d) $\phi(x) = 0$ is a solution

**52.** Given the equation

$\frac{dy}{dx} = 3\int_0^x \cos 2\,(x - t)\, y(t)\, dt + 2$, given $y(0) = 1$ is

(a) a Volterra integral equation

(b) a Fredholm integral equation

(c) the solution is

$$y = 4 + 8x - 3\cos x - 6\sin x$$

(d) the solution is

$$y = 4x + 3\sin x + 2\cos x$$

**53.** Given a differential equation $\frac{d^3y}{dx^3} - 2xy = 0$ with initial conditions

$$y(0) = \frac{1}{2},\ y'(0) = 1 = y''(0)$$

The integral equation is

(a) the Volterra integral equation

(b) the Fredholm integral equation

(c) the solution is $\phi(x) = \sec^2 x + \frac{\lambda}{1+\lambda}\tan 1$

(d) the solution is $\phi(x) = \sec^2 x + \tan x$

**54.** Given the integral equation

$\int_0^x \frac{y(t)}{\sqrt{(x-t)}}\, dt = 1 + 2x - x^2$ is

(a) the Volterra integral equation

(b) the fredholm integral equation

(c) the solution is

$$y = \frac{1}{3\pi\sqrt{x}}(3 + 12x - 8x^3)$$

(d) the solution is

$$y = \frac{1}{3\pi}(\sqrt{x} + 2)$$

**55.** Given the integral equation

$\int_0^x e^{x-t}\, y(t)\, dt = e^x + x + t$, then

(a) $y(t) = 2 - t$ is the solution

(b) $y(t) = 2 + t$ is the solution

(c) Volterra integral equation

(d) Fredholm integral equation

**56.** Given the homogeneous integral equation $y(x) = \frac{1}{e^2 - 1}\int_0^1 e^{x+t}\, y(t)\, dt$ with degenerate kernel, then

(a) has no trivial solution

(b) has only trivial solution

(c) it does not contains any eigen value or eigen function

(d) it contains eigen value of eigen function

**57.** Given linear integral equation

$$\phi(x) = x + \int_0^{1/2} \phi(\xi)\, d\xi \text{ is}$$

(a) Volterra integral equation of first kind
(b) Volterra integral equation of second kind
(c) $K_3(x, \xi) = \frac{1}{2}\int_0^{1/2} dz = \left(\frac{1}{2}\right)^2$
(d) the solution is
$$\phi(x) = x + \int_0^{1/2} 2\xi\, d\xi = x + \frac{1}{4}$$

**58.** Given the integral equation,

$$\int_0^x \frac{y(\xi)}{\sqrt{(x-\xi)}}\, d\xi = 1 \text{ is}$$

(a) Volterra integral equation of first kind
(b) Volterra integral equation of second kind
(c) Fredholm integral equation
(d) the solution of the equation is
$$y(x) = \frac{1}{\pi\sqrt{x}}$$

**59.** Given the integral equation

$$x = \int_0^x e^{x-\xi}\, \phi(\xi)\, d\xi \text{ is}$$

(a) a Volterra equation
(b) a Fredholm equation
(c) the solution is $\phi(x) = 1 - x$
(d) the solution is $\phi(x) = \frac{1}{1-x}$

# Answers

## Exercise 1

**1.** (a) **2.** (d) **3.** (b) **4.** (b) **5.** (a) **6.** (c) **7.** (a) **8.** (b) **9.** (a) **10.** (c)
**11.** (a) **12.** (b) **13.** (b) **14.** (a) **15.** (c) **16.** (b) **17.** (b) **18.** (a) **19.** (a) **20.** (b)
**21.** (b) **22.** (b) **23.** (a) **24.** (c) **25.** (b) **26.** (b) **27.** (c) **28.** (a) **29.** (a) **30.** (d)
**31.** (b) **32.** (b) **33.** (a) **34.** (b) **35.** (b) **36.** (b) **37.** (d) **38.** (a) **39.** (c) **40.** (b)
**41.** (b) **42.** (b) **43.** (a) **44.** (c) **45.** (a) **46.** (a) **47.** (b) **48.** (a) **49.** (b) **50.** (a)
**51.** (b) **52.** (c) **53.** (a) **54.** (a) **55.** (b) **56.** (a) **57.** (c) **58.** (b) **59.** (b) **60.** (a)
**61.** (b) **62.** (a) **63.** (c) **64.** (d) **65.** (b) **66.** (c) **67.** (a) **68.** (a) **69.** (a) **70.** (a)
**71.** (a) **72.** (a) **73.** (a) **74.** (a) **75.** (a) **76.** (a) **77.** (a) **78.** (a) **79.** (b) **80.** (b)
**81.** (a) **82.** (c) **83.** (c) **84.** (b) **85.** (a) **86.** (a) **87.** (d) **88.** (d) **89.** (c) **90.** (b)
**91.** (d) **92.** (a) **93.** (d) **94.** (d) **95.** (a) **96.** (a) **97.** (b) **98.** (c) **99.** (b) **100.** (b)
**101.** (b) **102.** (c) **103.** (a) **104.** (a) **105.** (a) **106.** (b) **107.** (b) **108.** (a) **109.** (d) **110.** (d
**111.** (d) **112.** (b) **113.** (a) **114.** (a) **115.** (b) **116.** (a) **117.** (d) **118.** (b) **119.** (d) **120.** (b)
**121.** (a) **122.** (b) **123.** (a) **124.** (c) **125.** (a) **126.** (a) **127.** (c) **128.** (b) **129.** (b) **130.** (a)
**131.** (c) **132.** (a) **133.** (b) **134.** (b) **135.** (c) **136.** (d) **137.** (a) **138.** (b) **139.** (d) **140.** (c)
**141.** (c) **142.** (a) **143.** (a) **144.** (a) **145.** (b) **146.** (c) **147.** (a) **148.** (b) **149.** (b) **150.** (b)
**151.** (d) **152.** (a) **153.** (a) **154.** (c) **155.** (b) **156.** (b) **157.** (b) **158.** (a) **159.** (b) **160.** (d)
**161.** (b) **162.** (a) **163.** (b) **164.** (a) **165.** (a) **166.** (a) **167.** (c) **168.** (b) **169.** (b) **170.** (b)
**171.** (b) **172.** (a) **173.** (b) **174.** (d) **175.** (b) **176.** (c) **177.** (c) **178.** (a) **179.** (b) **180.** (b)
**181.** (b) **182.** (a) **183.** (c) **184.** (a) **185.** (b) **186.** (d) **187.** (b) **188.** (a) **189.** (a) **190.** (a)
**191.** (d) **192.** (c) **193.** (c) **194.** (c) **195.** (b) **196.** (a) **197.** (d) **198.** (a)

## Exercise 2

**1.** (b,c,d) **2.** (a,c) **3.** (a,c,d) **4.** (c,d) **5.** (a,b,d) **6.** (a,b,d) **7.** (b,d) **8.** (a,c,d) **9.** (a,b,c,d) **10.** (c)
**11.** (a,c) **12.** (a,c,d) **13.** (b,c,d) **14.** (a,c,) **15.** (a,c,d) **16.** (a,b) **17.** (a,c) **18.** (a,b,c) **19.** (a,b,c) **20.** (a,c)
**21.** (a,b,c,d) **22.** (a,c) **23.** (a,b,c) **24.** (a,c,d) **25.** (a,b,c) **26.** (a,b,c,d) **27.** (a,c) **28.** (b,c,d) **29.** (a,c) **30.** (a,c)
**31.** (a,c) **32.** (b,c) **33.** (a,b,c) **34.** (a,c,d) **35.** (a,c,d) **36.** (a,b,c) **37.** (a,b,c,d) **38.** (c,d) **39.** (a,d) **40.** (b,c))
**41.** (a,c) **42.** (a,c,d) **43.** (a,c) **44.** (a,c) **45.** (a,c) **46.** (a,b,c,d) **47.** (b,c) **48.** (a,b,c,d) **49.** (a,c) **50.** (a,b,c,d)
**51.** (a,c) **52.** (a,c) **53.** (a,c) **54.** (a,c) **55.** (a,c) **56.** (b,c) **57.** (c,d) **58.** (a,d) **59.** (a,c)

# Hints & Solutions

## Exercise 1

**42.** By using laplace transformation, we get

*i.e.,* $$L[y(x)] = 3L[x^2] + L[y(x)]\cdot L[\sin x]$$

$$\Rightarrow \quad \bar{y}(s) = 3\times\frac{2}{s^3} + \bar{y}(s)\cdot\frac{1}{s^2+1}$$

$$\Rightarrow \quad \bar{y}(s)\left[1-\frac{1}{s^2+1}\right] = \frac{6}{s^3}$$

$$\Rightarrow \quad \bar{y}(s) = \frac{6(s^2+1)}{s^5} = 6\left(\frac{1}{s^3}+\frac{1}{s^5}\right)$$

Hence, $$y(x) = 6L^{-1}\left(\frac{1}{s^3}\right) + 6L^{-1}\left(\frac{1}{s^5}\right)$$

$$= 6\times\frac{x^2}{2} + 6\times\frac{x^4}{24}$$

$$= 3x^2 + \frac{x^4}{4}$$

Since, $$L(x^n) = \frac{n!}{s^{n+1}}$$

and $$L^{-1}\left(\frac{1}{s^n+1}\right) = \frac{x^n}{n!}$$

**49.** For $k(x,t) = xt;\quad a = 0,\ b = 1$

$$R(x,t;\lambda) = \frac{3xt}{3-\lambda} \qquad \lambda \neq 3$$

$$\Rightarrow \quad R(x,t;-\lambda) = \frac{3xt}{3+\lambda} \qquad \lambda \neq -3$$

$\therefore$ Solution is

$$y(x) = 1 - \lambda\int_0^1 \frac{3xt}{3+\lambda}\,dt$$

$$= 1 - \lambda\,\frac{3x}{3+\lambda}\int_0^1 t\,dt$$

$$= 1 - \frac{3\lambda x}{2(3+\lambda)}$$

**57.** Using

$$y_n(x) = 1 + \int_0^x (x+t)y_{n-1}(t)dt$$

Putting $n = 1$

$$y^{(1)}(x) = 1 + \int_0^x (x+t)\,dt$$

$$= 1 + \left(xt + \frac{t^2}{2}\right)_0^x = 1 + \frac{3x^2}{2}$$

Similarly,

$$y^{(2)}(x) = 1 + \frac{3x^2}{2} + \frac{7x^4}{8}$$

and $$y^{(3)}(x) = 1 + \frac{3x^2}{2} + \frac{7x^4}{8} + \frac{77x^6}{240}$$

**68.** Substituting the function $y(x) = 1$ is the given equation, we have

$$= 1 + \int_0^1 x\,(e^{x\xi} - 1)\,d\xi = 1 + (e^{x\xi} - x\xi)_0^1$$

$$= 1 + (e^x - x - 1) = e^x - x = \text{RHS}$$

Thus, $y(x) = 1$ is a solution of the given integral equation.

**69.** Let $l$ be the fixed perimeter of a plane curve between the points with abscissae $x_1$ and $x_2$.

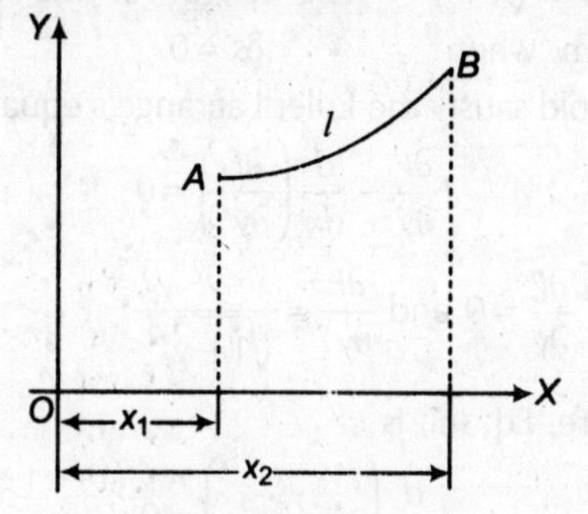


Then, $$l = \int_{x_1}^{x_2} \sqrt{(1+y'^2)}\,dx \qquad \ldots\text{(i)}$$

The area between the curve and the x-axis is

$$A = \int_{x_1}^{x_2} y\,dx \qquad \ldots\text{(ii)}$$

Here, $$F = y + \lambda\sqrt{(1+y'^2)}$$

Now, $F$ must satisfy the Euler's equation

$$\frac{\partial F}{\partial y} - \frac{d}{dx}\left(\frac{\partial F}{\partial y'}\right) = 0$$

$$\Rightarrow \quad 1 - \frac{d}{dx}\left[\frac{\lambda y'}{\sqrt{(1+y'^2)}}\right] = 0$$

On integrating *wrt* $x$, we have

$$x - \lambda y'/\sqrt{(1+y'^2)} = 0$$

Solving for $y'$, we get

$$y' = \frac{x-a}{\sqrt{[\lambda^2 - (x-a)^2]}}$$

On integrating again, we get

$$y = \sqrt{[\lambda^2 - (x-a)^2]} + b$$

$$\Rightarrow \quad (x-a)^2 + (y-b)^2 = \lambda^2$$

which represent a circle.

**70.** Let $A(x_1, y_1)$ and $B(x_2, y_2)$ are two points in $XY$-plane. An element of length $ds$ of any curve, say $AP'B$, passing through $A$ and $B$ points is given by

$$ds^2 = dx^2 + dy^2$$

$$\Rightarrow \quad ds = \sqrt{1 - y'^2}\,dx = 0 \qquad \ldots\text{(i)}$$

Total length of the curve from point $A$ to the point $B$ is given by

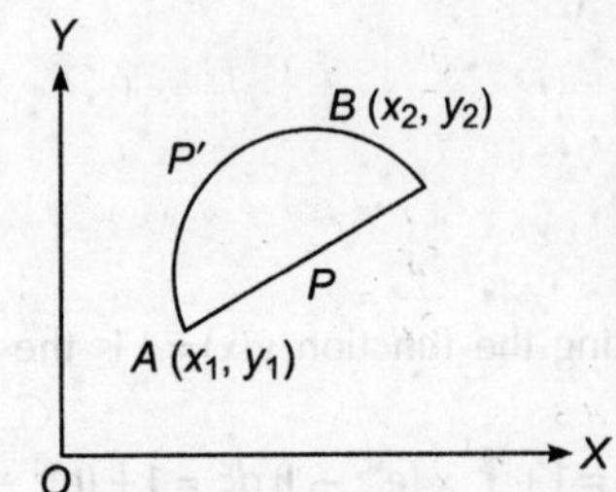


Shortest distance between two points in a plane

$$s = \int_A^B \sqrt{1+y'^2}\, dx = \int_A^B F dx \qquad \text{...(ii)}$$

where $F = \sqrt{1+y'^2}$. The length of the curve $s$ will be minimum, when $\delta s = 0$.

$\Rightarrow F$ should satisfy the Euler Lagrange's equation *i.e.*,

$$\frac{\partial F}{\partial y} - \frac{d}{dx}\left(\frac{\partial F}{\partial y'}\right) = 0 \qquad \text{...(iii)}$$

Here, $\frac{\partial F}{\partial y} = 0$ and $\frac{\partial F}{\partial y'} = \frac{y'}{\sqrt{1+y'^2}}$

Therefore, Eq. (iii) is

$$\frac{d}{dx}\left(\frac{y'}{\sqrt{1+y'^2}}\right) = 0$$

$$\Rightarrow \frac{y'}{\sqrt{1+y'^2}} = C \text{ (a constant)}$$

On squaring, we get

$$y'^2 = C^2(1+y'^2)$$

$$\Rightarrow y'^2(1-C^2) = C^2$$

$$\Rightarrow y' = \frac{C}{\sqrt{1-C^2}} = a \text{ (constant)}$$

$$\Rightarrow \frac{dy}{dx} = a \qquad \text{...(iv)}$$

On integrating, we get

$$y = ax + b \qquad \text{...(v)}$$

where $b$ is a constant of integration, which represents a straight line. Therefore, the shortest distance between any two points in a plane is a straight line.

**71.** We have,

$$F = y'^2 + 12xy$$

Hence, $\frac{\partial F}{\partial y} = 12x$; $\frac{\partial F}{\partial y'} = 2y'$; $\frac{d}{dx}\left(\frac{\partial F}{\partial y'}\right) = 2y''$

Hence, the Euler's equation $\frac{\partial F}{\partial y} - \frac{d}{dx}\left(\frac{\partial F}{\partial y'}\right) = 0$ becomes

$$12x - 2y'' = 0, \text{ i.e., } y'' = 6x \qquad \text{...(i)}$$

On integrating Eq. (i), we get

$$y' = 3x^2 + C \qquad \text{...(ii)}$$

and $$y = x^3 + Cx + C' \qquad \text{...(iii)}$$

Using the boundary conditions, when $x = 0$, $y = 0$ Eq (iii) gives $C' = 0$.

When $x = 1$, $y = 1$, Eq (iii) again, gives $C = 0$.

Hence, Eq. (iii) reduces to $y = x^3$ which is the only curve on which extremum can be attained.

**72.** Given, differential equation is

$$y'' - y + x = 0 \qquad \text{...(i)}$$

Its solution is equivalent to extremising the integral

$$I = \int_0^1 F(x, y, y')\, dx$$

where $$F(x, y, y') = 2xy - y^2 - y'^2, \qquad \text{...(ii)}$$

Since, the Euler's equation is given by

$$\frac{\partial F}{\partial y} - \frac{d}{dx}\left(\frac{\partial F}{\partial y'}\right) = 0, \text{ gives Eq. (i),}$$

Assume that the trial function is

$$\bar{y}(x) = c_0 + c_1x + c_2x^2 \qquad \text{...(iii)}$$

To satisfy boundary condition

$y(0) = 0$, $y(1) = 0$, we require

$$c_0 = 0, c_2 = -c_1$$

Therefore, Eq. (iii) becomes $\bar{y}(x) = c_1(1-x)$ ...(iv)

Substituting $\bar{y}$ and $\bar{y}'$ in $I$, we have

$$I = \int_0^1 [2x\bar{y} - \bar{y}^2 - (\bar{y}')^2]\, dx$$

$$= \int_0^1 [2c_1(x^2 - x^3) - c_1^2(x - x^2)^2 - c_1^2(1-x)^2]\, dx$$

$$= \frac{1}{6}c_1 - \frac{11}{30}c_1^2$$

Its stationary values are given by $dI/dc_1 = 0$

Hence, $\frac{1}{6} - \frac{11}{15}c_1 = 0$, *i.e*, $c_1 = \frac{5}{22}$

Thus, the approximate solution is

$$\bar{y}(x) = \frac{5}{22}x(1-x)$$

**73.** Here, $F(x, y, y') = \frac{y'^2}{x^3}$

$$\frac{\partial F}{\partial y} = 0 \text{ and } \left(\frac{\partial F}{\partial y'}\right) = \frac{2y'}{x^3}$$

Hence, $$\frac{\partial F}{\partial y} - \frac{d}{dx}\left(\frac{\partial F}{\partial y'}\right) = 0$$

$$\Rightarrow \frac{d}{dx}\left(\frac{2y'}{x^3}\right) = 2\frac{x^3y'' - y'3x^2}{x^6}$$

$$= \frac{2}{x^4}(xy'' - 3y') = 0$$

$$\Rightarrow \frac{y''}{y'} = \frac{3}{x}$$

On integrating both sides, we get

$$\int \frac{y''}{y'}dx = 3\int \frac{dx}{x} + \log c$$

$$\Rightarrow \log y' = 3\log x + \log c$$

$$\Rightarrow y' = cx^3 \Rightarrow dy = cx^3dx$$

$$\Rightarrow y = \frac{cx^4}{4} + c_2 \text{ which is the required extremal.}$$

**74.** Given, the integral equation,

$$f(x)=\int_a^x \frac{\phi(\xi)}{(\cos\xi-\cos x)^{1/2}}\,d\xi \qquad \ldots(i)$$

This equation can be rewritten as,

$$f(x)=\int_a^x \frac{\phi(\xi)\,d\xi}{[(1-\cos x)-(1-\cos\xi)]^{1/2}} \qquad \ldots(ii)$$

Comparing. Eq (ii) with general form of Abel's integral equation

$$f(x)=\int_a^x \frac{\phi(\xi)}{[h(x)-h(\xi)]\alpha},\ 0<\alpha<1$$

Here, $\alpha=\frac{1}{2},\ h(\xi)=1-\cos\xi.$

where $h(\xi)$ is a strictly monotonically increasing function in the interval $(0,\pi)$. The solution of the given equation be

$$\phi(\xi)=\frac{\sin\alpha\pi}{\pi}\frac{d}{d\xi}\left\{\int_a^\xi \frac{h'(u)\,f(u)\,du}{[h(\xi)-h(u)]^{1-\alpha}}\right\} \qquad \ldots(iii)$$

Substituting $\alpha=\frac{1}{2},\ h(\xi)=1-\cos\xi,$

$h(u)=1-\cos u$ and $h'(u)=\sin u$ in Eq. (iii), we have

$$\phi(\xi)=\frac{\sin(\pi/2)}{\pi}\frac{d}{d\xi}$$

$$\left\{\int_a^\xi \frac{\sin u\,f(u)}{[(1-\cos\xi)-(1-\cos u)]^{1/2}}\,du\right\}$$

$$\phi(\xi)=\frac{1}{\pi}\frac{d}{d\xi}\left\{\int_a^\xi \frac{\sin u\,f(u)\,du}{(\cos u-\cos\xi)^{1/2}}\right\} \quad \text{where } a<\xi<b$$

The required solution.

**75.** The Euler-Poisson equation is

$$\frac{\partial f}{\partial y}-\frac{d}{dx}\left(\frac{\partial f}{\partial y'}\right)+\frac{d^2}{dx^2}\left(\frac{\partial f}{\partial y''}\right)=0 \qquad \ldots(i)$$

Here, $f=(y'')^2-y^2+x^2,\ \frac{\partial f}{\partial y}=-2y,\ \frac{\partial f}{\partial y'}=0,\ \frac{\partial f}{\partial y''}=2y''$

Therefore, Eq. (i) becomes

$$-2y+\frac{d^2}{dx^2}(2y'')=0 \text{ or } y^{iv}-y=0$$

$$(D^4-1)\,y=0$$

Its solution is

$$y(x)=c_1e^x+c_2e^{-x}+c_3\cos x+c_4\sin x \qquad \ldots(ii)$$

$$\Rightarrow \quad y'(x)=c_1e^x-c_2e^{-x}-c_3\sin x+c_4\cos x \qquad \ldots(iii)$$

Applying the given boundary conditions to Eqs. (ii) and (iii), we get

$$\left.\begin{aligned}&0=y(0)=c_1+c_2+c_3,\ 1=y'(0)=c_1-c_2+c_4\\ &\frac{1}{\sqrt2}=y\left(\frac{\pi}{4}\right)=c_1e^{\pi/4}+c_2e^{-\pi/4}+\frac{1}{\sqrt2}c_3+\frac{1}{\sqrt2}c_4\\ &\frac{1}{\sqrt2}=y'\left(\frac{\pi}{4}\right)=c_1e^{\pi/4}+c_2e^{-\pi/4}-\frac{1}{\sqrt2}c_3+\frac{1}{\sqrt2}c_4\end{aligned}\right\} \ldots(iv)$$

On solving the Eq. (iv), we get

$$c_1=c_2=c_3=0,\ c_4=1$$

Substituting these values in eq (ii), the required curve is $y=\sin x$

**76.** Euler's equations are

$$\frac{\partial F}{\partial x}-\frac{d}{dx}\left(\frac{\partial F}{\partial x'}\right)=0 \qquad \ldots(i)$$

$$\frac{\partial F}{\partial y}-\frac{d}{dt}\left(\frac{\partial F}{\partial y'}\right)=0 \qquad \ldots(ii)$$

Here, $F=2xy+x'^2+y'^2$

Hence, $\frac{\partial F}{\partial x}=2y,\ \frac{\partial F}{\partial x'}=2x',\ \frac{\partial F}{\partial y'}=2x,\ \frac{\partial F}{\partial y'}=2y'$

Eq. (i), gives

$$2y-\frac{d}{dt}(2x')=0,\ i.e.,\ 2y-2\frac{d^2x}{dt^2}=0$$

or $$\frac{d^2x}{dt^2}=y \qquad \ldots(iii)$$

Eq. (ii), gives $2x-\frac{d}{dt}(2y')=0,$

*i.e.,* $$2x-2\frac{d^2y}{dt^2}=0$$

$$\frac{d^2y}{dt^2}=x \qquad \ldots(iv)$$

To solve these simultaneous differential equations, differentiate Eq. (iii) twice, gives

$$\frac{d^4x}{dt^4}=\frac{d^2y}{dt^2}=x \qquad \text{[by Eq. (iv)]}$$

or $$(D^4-1)\,x=0$$

which is a linear equation with constant coefficients.

Its solution is

$$x=c_1e^x+c_2e^{-x}+c_3\cos x+c_4\sin x \qquad \ldots(v)$$

From Eq. (iii), we have

$$y=x''=c_1e^x+c_2e^{-x}-c_3\cos x-c_4\sin x \qquad \ldots(vi)$$

Since, $x=0$ when $t=0$

Hence $0=c_1+c_2+c_3$ ...(vii)

Now, $y=0$ when $t=0$

Hence, $0=c_1+c_2-c_3$ ...(viii)

Also $x=-1$ when $t=\pi/2$

Hence, $-1=c_1e^{\pi/2}+c_2e^{-\pi/2}+c_4$ ...(ix)

$y=1$, when $t=\pi/2$

Hence, $1=c_1e^{\pi/2}+c_2e^{-\pi/2}-c_4$ ...(x)

On adding Eqs. (vii) and (viii), we get

$$c_1+c_2=0$$

On adding Eqs (ix) and (x), we get

$$c_1e^{\pi/2}+c_2e^{-\pi/2}=0$$

On solving these equations, we get

$$c_1=c_2=0$$

From Eq. (viii), we get

$$c_3=c_1+c_2=0$$

From Eq. (ix),we get

$$c_4=-1$$

Hence, from Eq. (v), we get

$x=-\sin x$ and from Eq. (vi), $\quad y=\sin x$

**77.** Given, the integral equation,

$$f(x) = \int_x^b \frac{\phi(\xi)}{(\cos x - \cos \xi)^{1/2}} d\xi \quad \ldots\text{(i)}$$

This equation can be rewritten as,

$$f(x) = \int_x^b \frac{\phi(\xi)}{[(1-\cos \xi)-(1-\cos x)]^{1/2}} d\xi \quad \ldots\text{(ii)}$$

Comparing the equation with the general form of Abel's integral equation

$$f(x) = \int_x^b \frac{\phi(\xi)}{[h(\xi)-h(x)]^{\alpha}} d\xi, \; 0 < \alpha < 1$$

We have $\alpha = \frac{1}{2}, h(\xi) = 1-\cos \xi$.

where $h(\xi)$ is a strictly monotonically increasing function in the interval $(0, \pi)$. The solution of the integral equation is,

$$\phi(\xi) = -\frac{\sin \alpha\pi}{\pi} \frac{d}{d\xi}\left\{\int_\xi^b \frac{h'(u) f(u)\, du}{[h(u)-h(\xi)]^{1-\alpha}}\right\} \quad \ldots\text{(iii)}$$

Substituting $\alpha = \frac{1}{2}, h'(\xi) = 1-\cos \xi$,

$h(u) = 1-\cos u$ and $h'(u) = \sin u$ in Eq. (iii), we have

$$\phi(\xi) = -\frac{\sin(\pi/2)}{\pi} \frac{d}{d\xi}\left\{\int_\xi^b \frac{\sin(u) f(u)\, du}{[(1-\cos u)-(1-\cos \xi)]^{1/2}}\right\}$$

$$\phi(\xi) = -\frac{1}{\pi} \frac{d}{d\xi}\left\{\int_\xi^b \frac{\sin(u) f(u)\, du}{(\cos \xi - \cos u)^{1/2}}\right\},$$

where $a < \xi$

The required solution.

**78.** Let $F = y'^2 - y^2 + 2xy$

So that $\frac{\partial F}{\partial y} = 0 - 2y + 2x$

and $\frac{d}{dx}\left(\frac{\partial F}{\partial y'}\right) = \frac{d}{dx}(2y') = 2y''$

$\therefore$ Euler's equation $\frac{\partial F}{\partial y} - \frac{d}{dx}\left(\frac{\partial F}{\partial y'}\right) = 0$ becomes

$$-2y + 2x - 2y'' = 0$$

$$\Rightarrow \quad y'' + y = x$$

$$\Rightarrow \quad (D^2+1)y = x$$

The auxiliary equation is

$$D^2 + 1 = 0 \text{ gives } D = \pm i$$

Hence, $\quad CF = c_1 \cos x + c_2 \sin x$

and $\quad PI = \frac{1}{D^2+1} x = (1+D^2)^{-1} x$

$$= (1-D^2)x = x$$

Thus, $\quad y = c_1 \cos x + c_2 \sin x + x \quad \ldots\text{(i)}$

Using boundary conditions,

when $x = 0, y = 0$ Eq (i) gives $c_1 = 0$

when $x = \pi/2, y = 0$, Eq. (i) gives $0 = c_2 + \pi/2$,

*i.e.*, $\quad c_2 = -\pi/2$

Hence, Eq. (i) reduces to $y = x - \frac{\pi}{2} \sin x$, which is the only curve on which the given functional can be extremized.

## Exercise 2

**2.** Since, $F$ is independent of y

$$\Rightarrow \quad \frac{\partial F}{\partial y} = 0$$

Then, by Euler's formula

$$-\frac{d}{dx}\left(\frac{\partial H}{\partial y'}\right) = 0 \;\Rightarrow\; \frac{\partial F}{\partial y'} = \text{Constant}$$

**5.** Comparing the given functional with $\int_0^2 F(x, y, y')\,dx$,

$F(x, y, y') = y'^3 + \sin^2 x$

$\therefore$ Euler's equation $\frac{\partial F}{\partial y} - \frac{d}{dx}\left(\frac{\partial F}{\partial y'}\right) = 0 \Rightarrow 0 - \frac{d(3y'^2)}{dx} = 0$

On integrating it, $y'^2 = c_1^2$ or $y' = dy/dx = c_1$ so that

$$y = c_1 x + c_2 \quad \ldots\text{(i)}$$

where $c_1$ and $c_2$ are arbitrary constants.

Eq. (i) is the equation of the extremals. Using the given boundary conditions $y(0) = 0$ and $y(2) = 6$, Eq. (i) gives $0 = c_2$ and $6 = 2c_1 + c_2$ so that $c_1 = 3$ and $c_2 = 0$.

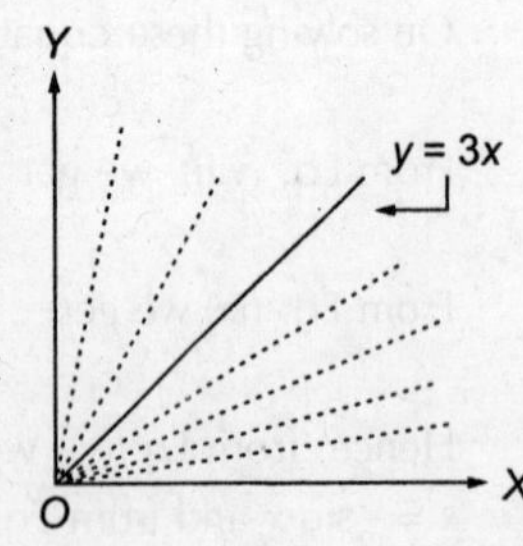


Therefore, on putting the value of $c_1$ and $c_2$ in Eq. (i), we get $\Rightarrow y = 3x$,

which is the extremal of the given variational problem.

For $c_2 = 0$, Eq. (i) yields $y = c_1 x$, which is a central field of extremals in the domain $0 \le x \le 2$ with centre at $(0, 0)$. For $c_1 = 3, y = c_1 x$ reduces, to $y = 3x$, showing that the extremal $y = 3x$ is included in the central field of extremals $y = c_1 x$.

**7.** $D(\lambda) = \begin{vmatrix} 1-\frac{2\lambda}{3} & \lambda \\ -\lambda & 1+\frac{4\lambda}{3} \end{vmatrix} = (\lambda+3)^2$

For trivial solution $D(\lambda) \neq 0$

and for infinitely many solutions for $D(\lambda) = 0$

**8.** $D(\lambda) = \begin{vmatrix} 1 & \frac{\lambda\pi}{2} \\ -\frac{\lambda\pi}{2} & 1 \end{vmatrix} = 1 + \frac{\lambda^2\pi^2}{4}$

and $\quad u(x) = \frac{2}{4+\lambda^2\pi^2}(2\cos x + \pi\lambda \sin x)$

which is using solution for any $\lambda$.

**9.** $D(\lambda)=\begin{vmatrix}2-\lambda\pi & 0\\ 0 & 2+\lambda\pi\end{vmatrix}=4-\lambda^2\pi^2$

for the equation $y(x)=\lambda\int_0^{\pi}\cos(x+t)y(t)dt$

for unique solution $D(\lambda)\neq 0 \Rightarrow \lambda \neq \pm\frac{2}{\pi}$

for $\lambda=\lambda_1=\frac{2}{\pi}$ and $f_1=0$

for $\lambda=\lambda_2=-\frac{2}{\pi}$ and $f_2\neq 0$

(By using Hilbert-Schmidt theorem)

**10.** $\lambda=\pm\frac{1}{\pi}$ are eigen values. Then,

either there is no solution or there exist infinitely many solutions,

$\lambda=-\pi$ is not an eigen value.

$\Rightarrow$ unique solution exist for $\lambda=-\pi$

Since, for $\lambda=-\pi, D(\lambda)\neq 0$

**11.** In spherical coordinates, the element of arc on the surface of a sphere of radius a is given by

$$ds^2=dr^2+(rd\theta)^2+(r\sin\theta\, d\phi)^2$$

$$=a^2\,d\theta^2+(a\sin\theta)^2\,d\phi^2 \qquad (\because r=a \text{ and } dr=0)$$

and $\frac{ds}{d\theta}=a\sqrt{[1+\sin^2\theta\,(d\phi/d\theta)^2]}$

Hence $s=a\int_{\theta_1}^{\theta_2}\sqrt{(1+\sin^2\theta\cdot\phi'^2)}\,d\theta$

Here, $F=a\sqrt{(1+\sin^2\theta\cdot\phi'^2)}$, is a function of $\theta$ and $\phi'$ only.

So, Euler's equation reduces to

$$\partial F/\partial\phi'=\text{Constant}$$

$$\Rightarrow \frac{\partial F}{\partial\phi'}=\frac{a\sin^2\theta\cdot\phi'}{\sqrt{(1+\sin^2\theta\cdot\phi')}}=\text{Constant}$$

$$\Rightarrow \frac{\sin^2\theta\cdot\phi'}{\sqrt{(1+\sin^2\theta\cdot\phi'^2)}}=c\text{ (say)}$$

$$\Rightarrow \sin^2\theta\,(\sin^2\theta-c^2)\,\phi'^2=c^2$$

$$\Rightarrow \frac{d\phi}{d\theta}=\frac{c}{\sin\theta\sqrt{(\sin^2\theta-c^2)}}$$

$$=\frac{c\,\text{cosec}^2\,\theta}{\sqrt{(1-c^2\,\text{cosec}^2\,\theta)}}$$

On integrating, we get

$$\phi=\int\frac{c\,\text{cosec}^2\,\theta\cdot d\theta}{\sqrt{[(1-c^2)-(c\cot\theta)^2]}}+c'$$

$$=-\sin^{-1}\left\{\frac{c\cot\theta}{\sqrt{(1-c^2)}}\right\}+c$$

$$\Rightarrow \cot\theta=A\cos\phi+B\sin\phi$$

$$\Rightarrow a\cos\theta=Aa\sin\theta\cos\phi+Ba\sin\theta\sin\phi$$

$$\Rightarrow z=Ax+By \text{ in cartesian coordinates}$$

This is a plane through the centre (0, 0, 0) of the sphere which cut, the sphere along a great circle. Hence, the required geodesics are the area of the great circle.

**12.** Given, the integral equation

$$y(x)=x+2\int_0^x\cos(x-t)\,y(t)\,dt$$

It can be rewritten as

$$y(x)=x+2\cos(x)*y(x)$$

Taking Laplace transform of both sides, we get

$$\bar{y}(s)=\frac{1}{s^2}+2\frac{s}{s^2+1}\cdot\bar{y}(s)$$

$$\Rightarrow \bar{y}\left(1-\frac{2s}{s^2+1}\right)=\frac{1}{s^2}$$

$$\Rightarrow \bar{y}=\frac{s^2+1}{s^2(s-1)^2}=\frac{2}{s}+\frac{1}{s^2}-\frac{2}{s-1}+\frac{2}{(s-1)^2}$$

On inversion, we get

$$y=2+x-2e^x+2xe^x$$

$$\Rightarrow y=x+2+2(x-1)e^x$$

**13.** Given, an integral equation

$$y(x)=\int_0^x(x+t)\,y(t)\,dt+1 \qquad \text{...(i)}$$

Differentiating Eq. (i) *wrt x* two times, we get

$$\frac{dy}{dx}=\int_0^x\frac{\partial}{\partial x}(x+t)\,y(t)\,dt+(x+x)\,y(x)\frac{d}{dx}(x)$$

$$-(x+0)\,y(0)\frac{d}{dx}(0)$$

$$=\int_0^x y(t)\,dt+2x\,y(x)$$

$$=\int_0^x y(x)\,dx+2x\,y(x) \qquad \text{...(ii)}$$

and $\frac{d^2y}{dx^2}=y(x)+2[xy'(x)+1\cdot y(x)]$

$$=2xy'(x)+3y(x)$$

$$\Rightarrow \frac{d^2y}{dx^2}-2x\frac{dy}{dx}-3y(x)=0 \qquad \text{...(iii)}$$

Also, putting $x=0$ in Eq. (i) we get

$y(0)=\int_0^0(x+t)\,y(t)\,dt+1 \Rightarrow y(0)=1$ and putting $x=0$ in Eq. (ii), we get $y'(0)=0$

Hence, the required differential equation is

$$\frac{d^2y}{dx^2}-2x\frac{dy}{dx}-3y=0$$

with initial condition

$$y(0)=1 \text{ and } y'(0)=0.$$

**14.** Let

$$\frac{d^2y}{dx^2}=y(x) \qquad \text{...(i)}$$

Then, $\frac{dy}{dx}=\int_0^x y(\xi)\,d\xi-1 \qquad \text{...(ii)}$

and $y=\int_0^x(x-\xi)\,y(\xi)\,d\xi-x+1 \qquad \text{...(iii)}$

Substituting $\frac{d^2y}{dx^2}, \frac{dy}{dx}$ and $y$ in the given differential equation, we have

$$y(x) - \sin x\left[\int_0^x y(\xi)\,d\xi - 1\right] + e^x\left[\int_0^x (x-\xi)\,y(\xi)\,d\xi - x + 1\right] = x$$

$$\Rightarrow \quad y(x) = [x - \sin x + e^x(x-1)] + \int_0^x [\sin x - e^x(x-\xi)]\,y(\xi)\,d\xi$$

A Volterra's integral equation of second kind.

**15.** Given, an integral equation

$$y(x) = \int_0^x t(t-x)\,y(t)\,dt + \frac{1}{2}x^2 \quad \ldots(i)$$

Differentiating Eq. (i) *wrt* $x$ twice, we get

$$\frac{dy}{dx} = \int_0^\pi \frac{\partial}{\partial x}[t(t-x)]\,y(t)\,dt + [t(t-x)\,y(t)]_{t=x}\cdot 1 + x - [t(t-x)\,y(t)]_{t=0}\cdot 0$$

$$= \int_0^\pi t(-1)\,y(t)\,dt + x$$

$$= x - \int_0^x t y(t)\,dt \quad \ldots(ii)$$

and $$\frac{d^2y}{dx^2} = 1 - \left\{\int_0^x \frac{\partial}{\partial x}[t\,y(t)]\,dt - [ty(t)]_{t=0}\cdot 0 + [ty(t)]_{t=x}\cdot 1\right\}$$

$$= 1 - xy(x)$$

$$\Rightarrow \quad \frac{d^2y}{dx^2} + xy = 1$$

Also, putting $x=0$ in Eq. (i), we get $y(0)=0$ and putting $x=0$ in Eq. (ii), we get $y'(0)=0$

Hence, the equivalent differential equation is

$$\frac{d^2y}{dx^2} + xy = 1$$

with $$y(0) = 0 = y'(0)$$

**16.** Here,

$$B_0(x,\xi) = K(x,\xi) = 1$$

and $$B_1(x,\xi) = B_2(x,\xi) = \ldots = 0$$

Also, $$C_1 = \int_0^1 K(\xi_1,\xi_1)\,d\xi_1 = \int_0^1 d\xi_1 = 1$$

and $C_2 = C_3 = \ldots = 0$

The recursive relations for $D(\lambda)$ and $D(x,\xi;\lambda)$ are given by

$$D(\lambda) = 1 + \sum_{m=1}^{\infty}\frac{(-\lambda)^m}{m!}C_m = 1 - \lambda,$$

and $$D(x,\xi;\lambda) = K(x,\xi) + \sum_{m=1}^{\infty}\frac{(-\lambda)^m}{m!}B_m(x,\xi) = 1$$

**17.** The integral equation is given by

$$\phi(x) = x + 2\int_0^x \cos(x-\xi)\,\phi(\xi)\,d\xi \quad \ldots(i)$$

By convolution theorem, the integral Eq. (i) can be written as

$$\phi(x) = x + 2\,\phi(x) * \cos x$$

Taking the Laplace transform of the above, we have

$$L\{\phi(x)\} = L(x) + 2L\{\phi(x)\}\cdot L(\cos x)$$

$$\Rightarrow \quad L\{\phi(x)\} = \frac{1}{p^2} + \frac{2p}{p^2+1}L\{\phi(x)\}$$

$$\Rightarrow \quad \left(1 - \frac{2p}{p^2+1}\right)L\{\phi(x)\} = \frac{1}{p^2}$$

$$\Rightarrow \quad L\{\phi(x)\} = \frac{p^2+1}{p^2(p-1)^2} = \frac{1}{(p-1)^2} + \frac{1}{p^2(p-1)^2}$$

Taking inverse Laplace transform, we get

$$\phi(x) = L^{-1}\left(\frac{1}{(p-1)^2}\right) + L^{-1}\left(\frac{1}{p^2(p-1)^2}\right)$$

$$\Rightarrow \quad \phi(x) = xe^x + (x-2)e^x + x + 2$$

$$= 2e^x(x-1) + x + 2$$

which is the required solution.

**18.** The given integral equation is

$$\phi(x) = (1 - x - 4\sin x) + \int_0^x [3 - 2(x-\xi)]\,\phi(\xi)\,d\xi \quad \ldots(i)$$

Differentiating Eq. (i) *wrt* $x$, we get

$$\phi'(x) = -1 - 4\cos x + \frac{d}{dx}\int_0^x [3 - 2(x-\xi)]\,\phi(\xi)\,d\xi$$

$$\Rightarrow \quad \phi'(x) = -1 - 4\cos x + \int_0^x \frac{\partial}{\partial x}[3 - 2(x-\xi)]\,\phi(\xi)\,d\xi + [3 - 2(x-x)]\,\phi(x)\cdot 1$$

$$\Rightarrow \quad \phi'(x) = -1 - 4\cos x + 3\phi(x) - 2\int_0^x \phi(\xi)\,d\xi \quad \ldots(ii)$$

Differentiating Eq. (ii) both the sides with regard to $x$, we have

$$\Rightarrow \quad \phi''(x) = 4\sin x + 3\phi'(x) - 2\frac{d}{dx}\int_0^x \phi(\xi)\,d\xi$$

$$\Rightarrow \quad \phi''(x) = 4\sin x + 3\phi'(x) - 2\,\phi(x)$$

$$\Rightarrow \quad \phi''(x) - 3\phi'(x) + 2\,\phi(x) = 4\sin x$$

Which is the required given differential equation. Putting $x=0$ in the Eqs. (i) and (ii), we have the initial conditions.

$$\phi(0) = 1,\ \phi'(0) = -2$$

**19.** Given, an integral equation

$$\phi(x) = -\frac{1}{2}x + \frac{1}{6}x^3 + \lambda\int_0^1 x\,\phi(\xi)\,d\xi - \lambda\int_0^x (x-\xi)\,\phi(\xi)\,d\xi \quad \ldots(i)$$

Differentiating Eq. (i) with regard to $x$, we get

$$\phi'(x) = -\frac{1}{2} + \frac{1}{2}x^2 + \lambda\frac{d}{dx}\int_0^1 x\phi(\xi)\,d\xi - \lambda\frac{d}{dx}\int_0^x (x-\xi)\,\phi(\xi)\,d\xi$$

$$\Rightarrow \quad \phi'(x) = -\frac{1}{2} + \frac{1}{2}x^2 + \lambda\int_0^1 \phi(\xi)\,d\xi - \lambda\int_0^x \phi(\xi)\,d\xi \quad \ldots(ii)$$

Differentiating again with regard to $x$, we get

$$\phi''(x) = x + \lambda\frac{d}{dx}\int_0^1 \phi(\xi)\,d\xi - \lambda\frac{d}{dx}\int_0^x \phi(\xi)\,d\xi$$

$$\Rightarrow \phi''(x) = x + \lambda\int_0^1 \frac{\partial}{\partial x}\{\phi(\xi)\}\,d\xi - \lambda\int_0^x \frac{\partial}{\partial x}\{\phi(\xi)\}\,d\xi - \lambda\phi(x)$$

$$\Rightarrow \qquad \phi''(x) = x - \lambda\phi(x)$$

$$\Rightarrow \qquad \phi''(x) + \lambda\phi(x) = x \qquad \text{...(iii)}$$

From Eqs. (i) and (ii) for $x = 0$ and $x = 1$ respectively, we have

$$\phi(0) = 0 \text{ and } \phi'(1) = -\frac{1}{2} + \frac{1}{2} = 0 \qquad \text{...(iv)}$$

Thus, the required differential equation together with the boundary conditions is given by

$$\phi''(x) + \lambda\phi(x) = x;\ \phi(0) = 0,\ \phi'(1) = 0$$

**20.** Here, $B_0(x, \xi) = K(x, \xi) = x\xi$

$$\Rightarrow \qquad B_1(x, \xi) = \int_0^{10} \begin{vmatrix} x\xi & x\xi_1 \\ \xi_1\xi & \xi_1^2 \end{vmatrix} d\xi_1 = 0$$

and $\quad B_2(x, \xi) = B_3(x, \xi) = \ldots = 0$

Also, $\quad C_1 = \int_0^{10} K(\xi_1, \xi_1)\, d\xi_1$

$$= \int_0^{10} \xi_1^2\, d\xi_1 = (10^3/3)$$

and $\quad C_2 = \int_0^{10}\int_0^{10} \begin{vmatrix} \xi_1^2 & \xi_1\xi_2 \\ \xi_2\xi_1 & \xi_2^2 \end{vmatrix} d\xi_1\, d\xi_2 = 0$

and $\quad C_3 = C_4 = \ldots = 0$

Thus, the recursive relations reduce to

$$D(\lambda) = 1 + \sum_{m=1}^{\infty} \frac{(-\lambda)^m}{m!} C_m = 1 - \frac{10^3}{3}\lambda,$$

and $\quad D(x, \xi; \lambda) = K(x, \xi) + \sum_{m=1}^{\infty} \frac{(-\lambda)^m}{m!} B_m(x, \xi)$

$$= x\xi$$

**21.** Given, the Volterra equation of second kind

$$\phi(x) - \lambda\int_0^x e^{x-y}\phi(y)\, dy = f(x) \qquad \text{...(i)}$$

Here, the kernel

$$K(x, y) = e^{x-y} = e^x e^{-y}$$

So, $\quad K_2(x, y) = \int_y^x e^{x-z} e^{z-y}\, dz$

$$= e^{x-y}\int_y^x dz = e^{x-y}(x - y)$$

$$K_3(x, y) = \int_y^x e^{x-z} e^{z-y}(z - y)\, dz$$

$$= e^{x-y}\int_y^x (z - y)\, dz$$

$$= e^{x-y}\frac{(x-y)^2}{2}$$

$$\vdots$$

$$K_{n+1}(x, y) = e^{x-y}\frac{(x-y)^n}{n!},\ n = 0, 1, 2, \ldots$$

So, the resolvent kernel is given by

$$H(x, y; \lambda) = -\sum_{n=0}^{\infty} \lambda^n K_{n+1}(x, y)$$

$$= -e^{x-y}\sum_{n=0}^{\infty}\frac{[\lambda(x-y)]^n}{n!}$$

$$= -e^{(1+\lambda)(x-y)}$$

and the solution to Eq. (i) is given by

$$\phi(x) = f(x) + \lambda\int_0^1 e^{(1+\lambda)(x-y)} f(y)\, dy$$

**22.** Let $\dfrac{d^3y}{dx^3} = y(x)$

Then, $\quad \dfrac{d^2y}{dx^2} = \int_0^x y(\xi)\, d\xi \qquad \text{...(i)}$

$$\frac{dy}{dx} = \int_0^x (x - \xi)\, y(\xi)\, d\xi + 1$$

and $\quad y = \dfrac{1}{2!}\int_0^x (x - \xi)^2\, y(\xi)\, d\xi + x + 1 \qquad \text{...(ii)}$

Substituting $\dfrac{d^2y}{dx^2}, \dfrac{dy}{dx}$ and $y$ in the given differential equation, we have

$$y(x) + x\left[\int_0^x y(\xi)\, d\xi\right] + (x^2 - x)\left[\frac{1}{2}\int_0^x (x, \xi)^2\, y(\xi)\, d\xi + x + 1\right],$$

$$= xe^x + 1$$

$$\Rightarrow \qquad y(x) = xe^x + 1 - x(x^2 - 1) - \int_0^x \left[x + \frac{1}{2}(x^2 - x)(x - \xi)^2\right] y(\xi)\, d\xi$$

Which is a Volterra's integral equation of second kind.

**23.** Assume, $\phi(x) = \phi_0(x) + \lambda\phi_1(x) + \lambda^2\phi_2(x) + \ldots + \lambda^n\phi_n(x) + \ldots$

Here, $\quad f(x) = 1;\ K(x, \xi) = 1,\ \lambda = 1$

Equating the coefficients of like powers of $\lambda$, we get

$$\phi_0(x) = 1$$

$$\phi_1(x) = \int_0^x d\xi = x$$

$$\phi_2(x) = \int_0^x \xi\, d\xi = \frac{1}{2}x^2$$

$$\phi_3(x) = \frac{1}{2}\int_0^x \xi^2 d\xi = \frac{1}{3!}x^3$$

$$\vdots$$

Thus, the solution of the integral equation is

$$\phi(x) = 1 + x + \frac{1}{2!}x^2 + \frac{1}{3!}x^3 + \ldots = e^x$$

**24.** Expanding the given integral equation, we have

$$\phi(x) = \lambda\left[\sqrt{(x)}\int_0^1 \xi\phi(\xi)\, d\xi - x\int_0^1 \sqrt{(\xi)}\,\phi(\xi)\, d\xi\right]$$

$$\Rightarrow \qquad \phi(x) = \lambda\,[C_1\sqrt{(x)} - C_2 x] \qquad \text{...(i)}$$

where $\quad C_1 = \int_0^1 \xi\phi(\xi)\, d\xi$

and $\quad C_2 = \int_0^1 \sqrt{(\xi)}\,\phi(\xi)\, d\xi \qquad \text{...(ii)}$

Using Eq. (i) into Eq. (ii), we get

$$C_1 = \int_0^1 \lambda\,\xi\,(C_1\sqrt{\xi} - C_2, \xi)\, d\xi$$

and $\quad C_2 = \int_0^1 \lambda\sqrt{\xi}\,(C_1\sqrt{\xi} - C_2, \xi)\, d\xi$

or $\quad \left[1 - \lambda\int_0^1 \xi^{3/2} d\xi\right]C_1 + \left[\lambda\int_0^1 \xi^2 d\xi\right]C_2 = 0$

and $\quad \left[-\lambda\int_0^1 \xi d\xi\right]C_1 + \left[1 + \lambda\int_0^1 \xi^{3/2} d\xi\right]C_2 = 0$

$$\left(1 - \frac{2\lambda}{5}\right)C_1 + \frac{\lambda}{3}C_2 = 0$$

$$-\frac{\lambda}{2}C_1+\left(1+\frac{2\lambda}{5}\right)C_2=0 \qquad \text{...(iii)}$$

The determinant of the system is

$$D(\lambda)=\begin{vmatrix}1-\frac{2\lambda}{5} & \frac{\lambda}{3}\\ -\frac{\lambda}{2} & 1+\frac{2\lambda}{5}\end{vmatrix}=1+\frac{\lambda^2}{150}$$

This does not vanish for real $\lambda$, so from Eq. (iii), we get

$$C_1=0 \text{ and } C_2=0$$

$\Rightarrow$ That the algebraic equations contain only one solution for all real $\lambda$, *i.e.*, the trivial solution $\phi(x)=0$, therefore, the integral equation does not have real characteristic numbers of characters functions.

**25.** Given, the integral equation $f(x)=\int_a^x \frac{\phi(\xi)}{(x^2-\xi^2)^\alpha}d\xi$ ...(i)

Comparing the equation with general form of abel's integral equation, we have

$$f(x)=\int_a^x \frac{\phi(\xi)}{[h(x)-h(\xi)]^\alpha}d\xi,\ 0<\alpha<1 \qquad \text{...(ii)}$$

where $h(\xi)=\xi^2$ is a strictly monotonically increasing function in the interval $(a, b)$ and $h'(\xi)\neq 0$ in this interval.

The solution of the Eq. (ii) is

$$\phi(\xi)=\frac{\sin\alpha\pi}{\pi}\frac{d}{d\xi}\left\{\int_a^\xi \frac{h'(u)f(u)}{[h(\xi)-h(u)]^{1-\alpha}}du\right\} \qquad \text{...(iii)}$$

Substituting $h(\xi)=\xi^2$, $h(u)=u^2$ and $h'(u)=2u$ in Eq. (iii), we get

$$\phi(\xi)=\frac{\sin\alpha\pi}{\pi}\frac{d}{d\xi}\left\{\int_a^\xi \frac{2u\,f(u)}{(\xi^2-u^2)^{1-a}}du\right\},\ a<\xi<b \qquad \text{...(iv)}$$

This equation remains valid when $a\to 0$, then the solution of the integral equation

$$f(x)=\int_0^x \frac{\phi(\xi)}{(x^2-\xi^2)^\alpha},\ 0<\alpha<1$$

gives $$\phi(\xi)=\frac{2\sin\alpha\pi}{\pi}\frac{d}{d\xi}\left\{\int_a^\xi \frac{u\,f(u)\,du}{(\xi^2-u^2)^{1-\alpha}}\right\}$$

Which is the required solution,

**26.** We know that

$k_1(x,\xi)=k(x,\xi)=1$

By the iterated kernels, we get

$$K_2(x,\xi)=\int_\xi^x K(x,z)K_1(z,\xi)\,dz$$

$$\Rightarrow \quad K_2(x,\xi)=\int_\xi^x dz=(z)_\xi^x=(x-\xi)$$

$$\Rightarrow \quad K_3(x,\xi)=\int_\xi^x 1\cdot(z-\xi)\,dz=\frac{1}{2!}(x,\xi)^2$$

$$\Rightarrow \quad K_4(x,\xi)=\int_\xi^x 1\cdot\frac{(z-\xi)^2}{2!}dz=\frac{1}{3!}(x-\xi)^3$$

$\vdots$

$$\Rightarrow \quad K_\nu(x,\xi)=\int_\xi^x 1\cdot K_{\nu-1}(z,\xi)\,dz$$

$$\Rightarrow \quad K_\nu(x,\xi)=\int_\xi^x 1\cdot\frac{(z-\xi)^{\nu-2}}{(\nu-2)!}dz=\frac{1}{(\nu-1)!}(x-\xi)^{\nu-1}$$

Hence, the resolvent kernel is determined as

$$R(x,\xi;\lambda)=\sum_{\nu=0}^{\infty}\lambda^\nu K_{\nu+1}(x,\xi)$$

$$\Rightarrow \quad R(x,\xi;\lambda)=\sum_{\nu=0}^{\infty}\frac{\lambda^\nu(x,\xi)^\nu}{\nu!}=e^{\lambda(x-\xi)}$$

**27.** The given integral equation may be expressed as

$$\sin x=\phi(x)*J_0(x) \qquad \text{...(i)}$$

Taking the Laplace transform of Eq. (i), we have

$$L(\sin x)=L\{\phi(x)\cdot L\{J_0(x)\}$$

$$\Rightarrow \quad \frac{1}{p^2+1}=L\{\phi(x)\}\cdot\frac{1}{\sqrt{p^2+1}}$$

$$\Rightarrow \quad L\{\phi(x)\}=\frac{1}{\sqrt{p^2+1}}$$

Taking the inverse Laplace transform, we get

$$\phi(x)=L^{-1}\left(\frac{1}{\sqrt{p^2+1}}\right)=J_0(x)$$

which is the required solution.

**28.** The integral equation $\phi(x)=(1+x)+\int_0^x(x-\xi)\,\phi(\xi)\,d\xi;\ \phi_0(x)=1$ is Volterra integral equation of second kind.

Here, $f(x)=1+x$, $K(x,\xi)=x-\xi$ and $\lambda=1$.

The $\nu$th order approximation is given by

$$\phi_\nu(x)=f(x)+\lambda\int_0^x K(x-\xi)\,\phi_{\nu-1}(\xi)\,d\xi$$

or $$\phi_\nu(x)=(1+x)+\lambda\int_0^x(x-\xi)\,\phi_{\nu-1}(\xi)\,d\xi$$

Substituting $\nu=1,2,3,\ldots$, we get

$$\phi_1(x)=(1+x)+\int_0^x(x-\xi)\,\phi_0(\xi)\,d\xi$$

$$\Rightarrow \quad \phi_1(x)=(1+x)+\int_0^x(x-\xi)\,d\xi$$

$$=1+x+\frac{x^2}{2!}$$

or $$\phi_2(x)=(1+x)+\int_0^x(x-\xi)\,\phi_1(\xi)\,d\xi$$

$$\Rightarrow \quad \phi_2(x)=(1+x)+\int_0^x(x-\xi)\left\{1+\xi+\frac{x^2}{2!}\right\}d\xi$$

$$\Rightarrow \phi_2(x)=(1+x)+\left[\left(x\xi-\frac{\xi^2}{2}\right)+\left(x\frac{\xi^2}{2}-\frac{\xi^3}{3}\right)+\left(x\frac{\xi^3}{6}-\frac{\xi^4}{8}\right)\right]_0^x$$

$$\Rightarrow \phi_2(x)=(1+x)+\left(x^2-\frac{x^2}{2}\right)+\left(\frac{x^3}{2}-\frac{x^3}{3}\right)+\left(\frac{x^4}{6}-\frac{x^4}{8}\right)$$

$$\Rightarrow \phi_2(x)=1+x+\frac{x^2}{2!}+\frac{x^3}{3!}+\frac{x^4}{4!}$$

$\vdots$

In general, we have

$$\phi_\nu(x)=1+x+\frac{x^2}{2!}+\frac{x^3}{4!}+\ldots+\frac{x^\nu}{\nu!}$$

Hence, the solution of the integral equation is

$$\phi(x)=\lim_{\nu\to\infty}\phi_\nu(x)=1+x+\frac{x^2}{2!}+\frac{x^3}{3!}+\frac{x^4}{4!}+\ldots+\frac{x^\nu}{\nu!}=e^x$$

**29.** Given, $y(x) + 3y(x) + 2\int_0^x y\,dx = x$

Taking Laplace transform of both sides, we get

$$L[y'(x)] + 3L[y(x)] + 2L\left\{\int_0^x y(x)\,dx\right\} = L(x)$$

$$\Rightarrow \quad \{s\bar{y}(s) - y(0)\} + 3\bar{y}(s) + 2\,\frac{1}{s}\bar{y}(s) = \frac{1}{s^2}$$

$$\Rightarrow \quad s\bar{y} + 3\bar{y} + 2\,\frac{1}{s}\bar{y} = 1 + \frac{1}{s^2} \qquad [\because y(0) = 1]$$

$$\Rightarrow \quad \bar{y} = \frac{1 + s^2}{s(s^2 + 3s + 2)} = \frac{1 + s^2}{s(s+1)(s+2)}$$

$$= \frac{1}{2s} - \frac{2}{s+1} + \frac{5}{2(s+2)}$$

On inversion, we get

$$y = \frac{1}{2}L^{-1}\left(\frac{1}{s}\right) - 2L^{-1}\left(\frac{1}{s+1}\right) + \frac{5}{2}L^{-1}\left(\frac{1}{s+2}\right)$$

$$\Rightarrow \quad y = \frac{1}{2} - 2e^{-x} + \frac{5}{2}e^{-2x}$$

**30.** We have $\phi(x) = \sec^2 x + \lambda\int_0^1 \phi(\xi)\,d\xi$

Here, $K(x, \xi) = 1$, $f(x) = \sec^2 x$

The resolvent kernel of the kernel $K(x, \xi)$ is obtained as

$$R(x, \xi; \lambda) = \frac{D(x, \xi, \lambda)}{D(\lambda)} = \frac{1}{1 - \lambda}$$

Thus, the solution of the integral equation is given by

$$\phi(x) = f(x) + \lambda\int_a^b R(x, \xi; \lambda) f(\xi)\,d\xi$$

$$\Rightarrow \quad \phi(x) = \sec^2 x + \frac{\lambda}{1+\lambda}\int_0^1 \sec^2\xi\,d\xi$$

$$\Rightarrow \quad \phi(x) = \sec^2 x + \frac{\lambda}{1+\lambda}\tan 1$$

**31.** Given, $y(x) = 3x^2 + \int_0^x y(t)\sin(x - t)\,dt$ ...(i)

It can be rewritten as,

$$y(x) = 3x^2 + y(x) * \sin(x - t)$$

Taking Laplace transform of both sides and by the convolution theorem, we get

$$\bar{y} = \frac{6}{s^3} + \bar{y}\cdot\frac{s}{s^2+1}$$

$$\Rightarrow \quad \bar{y} = \frac{6(s^2+1)}{s^5} = 6\left(\frac{1}{s^3} + \frac{1}{s^5}\right)$$

On inversion, we get

$$y = 6\left(\frac{x^2}{2!} + \frac{x^4}{4!}\right) = 3x^2 + x^4/4$$

which is the required solution of Eq. (i).

**32.** Given, a differential equation

$$\frac{d^2\phi}{dx^2} = 2x\frac{d\phi}{dx} + 3\phi$$

On integrating *wrt* $x$, gives

$$\left(\frac{d\phi}{dx}\right)_0^x = 2\int_0^x x\,\frac{d\phi}{dx}\,dx + 3\int_0^x \phi\,dx$$

$$\Rightarrow \quad \frac{d\phi}{dx} = 2\left\{x(\phi)_0^x - \int_0^x \phi\,dx\right\} + 3\int_0^x \phi\,dx$$

$$\Rightarrow \quad \frac{d\phi}{dx} = 2x\,\phi(x) - 2\int_0^x \phi\,dx + 3\int_0^x \phi\,dx$$

$$\Rightarrow \quad \frac{d\phi}{dx} = 2x\,\phi(x) + \int_0^x \phi\,dx$$

On integrating again with regard to $x$, we get

$$(\phi)_0^x = 2\int_0^x x\phi(x)\,dx + \int_0^x \phi\,dx^2$$

$$\Rightarrow \quad \phi(x) = 2\int_0^x \xi\phi(\xi)\,d\xi + \int_0^x \phi\,d\xi^2$$

$$\Rightarrow \quad \phi(x) = 2\int_0^x \xi\,\phi(\xi)\,d\xi + \int_0^x (x - \xi)\,\phi(\xi)\,d\xi$$

$$\Rightarrow \quad \phi(x) = \int_0^x (x + \xi)\,\phi(\xi)\,d\xi \qquad \text{...(i)}$$

Which is the Volterra's integral equation of first kind.

**33.** We have,

$$K_n(x, \xi) = \int_a^b K_m(x, z)\,K_{n-m}(z, \xi)\,dz$$

$$m = 1, 2, \ldots, n-1$$

and $\quad K_1(x, \xi) = K(x, \xi) = e^{x+\xi}$

$$\Rightarrow \quad K_2(x, \xi) = \int_0^1 e^{x+z}\cdot e^{x+\xi}\,dz$$

$$\Rightarrow \quad K_2(x, \xi) = e^{x+\xi}\left(\frac{e^2 - 1}{2}\right)$$

$$K_3(x, \xi) = \frac{e^2 - 1}{2}\int_0^1 e^{x+z}\cdot e^{z+\xi}\,dz$$

$$\Rightarrow \quad K_3(x, \xi) = \frac{e^2 - 1}{2}K_2(x, \xi)$$

$$= \left(\frac{e^2 - 1}{2}\right)^2 e^{x+\xi}$$

In general, we get

$$K_n(x, \xi) = \left(\frac{e^2 - 1}{2}\right)^{n-1} e^{x+\xi}$$

Hence, the resolvent kernel is

$$R(x, \xi; \lambda) = \sum_{n=1}^{\infty} \lambda^{n-1} K_n(x, \xi)$$

$$= e^{x+\xi}\sum_{n=1}^{\infty} \lambda^{n-1}\left(\frac{e^2 - 1}{2}\right)^{n-1}$$

$$R(x, \xi; \lambda) = \frac{2e^{x+\xi}}{2 - \lambda(e^2 - 1)}$$

where $\quad |\lambda| < \dfrac{2}{e^2 - 1}$

**34.** Given, the integral equation

$$\int_0^x y(t)\,y(x - t)\,dt = 4\sin 9x \qquad \text{...(i)}$$

$$\Rightarrow \quad y(x) * y(x) = 4\sin 9x$$

Taking Laplace transform of both sides and using the convolution theorem, we get

$$\{\bar{y}(s)\}^2 = \frac{36}{s^2+81} \Rightarrow \bar{y} = \pm\frac{6}{\sqrt{s^2+81}}$$

On inversion and noting that

$$L^{-1}\frac{1}{\sqrt{(s^2+a^2)}} = J_0(ax)$$

we get $$y = \pm 6L^{-1}\left\{\frac{1}{\sqrt{(s^2+9^2)}}\right\}$$

$$= \pm 6J_0(9x)$$

Thus, $y = 6J_0(9x)$ and $y = -6J_0(9x)$ are both solutions of Eq. (i).

**35.** Given, the differential equation

with $u(0) = u(1) = 0$

The fundamental system of solutions for the differential Eq. (i) is given by

$$u_1(x) = \sin \mu x$$

which satisfies the boundary condition $u_1(0) = 0$

$$u_2(x) = \sin \mu(x-1)$$

which satisfies the boundary condition $u_2(1) = 0$

The solutions are linearly independent.

Hence, the Wronskian $W(\xi)$ is,

$$W(\xi) = \begin{vmatrix} \sin \mu\xi & \sin\mu(\xi-1) \\ \mu\cos\mu\xi & \mu\cos\mu(\xi-1)\end{vmatrix}$$

or $$W(\xi) = \mu[\sin\mu\xi\cos\mu(\xi-1) - \cos\mu\xi\sin\mu(\xi-1)]$$

$$= \mu \sin \mu$$

Here, $p(x) = 1$,

$\therefore$ The green's function is given by

$$G(x,\xi) = \begin{cases} \dfrac{\sin\mu(\xi-1)\sin\mu x}{\mu\sin\mu}, & 0 \le x \le \xi \\ \dfrac{\sin\mu\xi\sin\mu(x-1)}{\mu\sin\mu}, & \xi < x \le 1 \end{cases}$$

**36.** Given, a differential equation

$$\phi''(x) = 4\sin x - 2\phi(x) + 3\phi'(x) \quad \text{...(i)}$$

On integrating with regard to $x$, both the sides, we get

$$\int_0^x \phi''(x)\,dx = 4\int_0^x \sin x\,dx - 2\int_0^x \phi(x)\,dx + 3\int_0^x \phi'(x)\,dx$$

$$\Rightarrow \quad [\phi'(x)]_0^x = -4(\cos x)_0^x - 2\int_0^x \phi(x)\,dx + 3[\phi(x)]_0^x$$

$$\Rightarrow \quad \phi'(x) - \phi'(0) = -4(\cos x - 1) - 2\int_0^x \phi(x)\,dx + 3\{\phi(x) - 1\}$$

$$\Rightarrow \quad \phi'(x) = -2 - 4(\cos x - 1) + 3[\phi(x) - 1] - 2\int_0^x \phi(x)\,dx$$

$$\Rightarrow \quad \phi'(x) = -1 - 4\cos x + 3\phi(x) - 2\int_0^x \phi(x)\,dx \quad \text{...(ii)}$$

On integrating again with regard to $x$, both the sides, we get

$$\int_0^x \phi'(x)\,dx = -\int_0^x dx - 4\int_0^x \cos x\,dx$$

$$+ 3\int_0^x \phi(x)\,dx - 2\int_0^x \phi(x)\,dx^2$$

$$\Rightarrow \quad [\phi(x)]_0^x = -x - 4\sin x + 3\int_0^x \phi(x)\,dx - 2\int_0^x \phi(x)\,dx^2$$

$$\Rightarrow \quad \phi(x) - \phi(0) = -x - 4\sin x + 3\int_0^x \phi(\xi)\,d\xi - 2\int_0^x \phi(\xi)\,d\xi^2$$

$$\Rightarrow \quad \phi(x) - 1 = -x - 4\sin x + 3\int_0^x \phi(\xi)\,d\xi$$

$$-2\int_0^x (x-\xi)\phi(\xi)\,d\xi$$

$$\Rightarrow \phi(x) = (1 - x - 4\sin x) + \int_0^x [3 - 2(x-\xi)]\phi(\xi)\,d\xi \quad \text{...(iii)}$$

Which is the non-homogeneous Volterra's integral equation of second kind.

**37.** Given, the integral equation is

$$y(x) = \cos x + \lambda\int_0^\pi \sin(x-t)\,y(t)\,dt \quad \text{...(i)}$$

rewriting the given equation, we get

$$y(x) = \cos x + \lambda$$

$$\{\sin x\int_0^\pi \cos t\,y(t)\,dt - \cos x\int_0^\pi \sin t\,y(t)\,dt\}$$

$$\Rightarrow \quad y(x) = \cos x + (\lambda\sin x)C_1 - (\lambda\cos x)C_2 \quad \text{...(ii)}$$

where $C_1 = \int_0^\pi \cos t\cdot y(t)\,dt$, $C_2 = \int_0^\pi \sin t\cdot y(t)\,dt$

Substituting $y(x)$ in $C_1$ and $C_2$, we get

$$C_1 = \int_0^\pi \cos t\{\cos t + (\lambda\sin t)C_1 - (\lambda\cos t)C_2\}\,dt$$

$$C_2 = \int_0^\pi \sin t\{\cos t + (\lambda\sin t)C_1 - (\lambda\cos t)C_2\}\,dt$$

or $$C_1\{1 - \lambda\int_0^\pi \cos t\sin t\,dt\}$$

$$C_2(\lambda\int_0^\pi \cos^2 t\,dt) = \int_0^\pi \cos^2 t\,dt$$

$$C_1\{-\lambda\int_0^\pi \sin^2 t\,dt\} + C_2 \quad \text{...(iii)}$$

$$\left\{1 + \lambda\int_0^\pi \sin t\cos t\,dt\right\} = \int_0^\pi \sin t\cos t\,dt$$

By evaluating each of the integrals in Eq. (ii), we get

$$C_1 + \frac{1}{2}C_2\lambda\pi = \frac{1}{2}\pi; \; -\frac{1}{2}C_1\lambda\pi + C_2 = 0 \quad \text{...(iv)}$$

The determinant of the Eq. (iv) is

$$\begin{vmatrix} 1 & \frac{1}{2}\lambda\pi \\ -\frac{1}{2}\lambda\pi & 1 \end{vmatrix} = 1 + \frac{1}{4}\lambda^2\pi^2 \ne 0$$

and the Eq. (iv) have a unique solution

$$C_1 = \frac{2\pi}{4+\lambda^2\pi^2};\; C_2 = \frac{\lambda\pi^2}{4+\lambda^2\pi^2}$$

Substituting these values of $C_1$ and $C_2$ in Eq. (ii), we have

$$y(x) = \cos x + \frac{\lambda}{4+\lambda^2\pi^2}(2\pi\sin x - \lambda\pi^2\cos x)$$

$$\Rightarrow \quad y(x) = \frac{2}{4+\lambda^2\pi^2}(2\cos x + \pi\lambda\sin x)$$

**38.** Let $\dfrac{d^2y}{dx^2} = y(x)$ ...(i)

Then, $$\frac{dy}{dx} = \int_0^x y(\xi)\,d\xi + A$$

$$= \int_0^x y(\xi)\,d\xi, \text{ since } y'(0) = 0 \quad \text{...(ii)}$$

and $$y = \int_0^x (x-\xi)\,\phi(\xi)\,d\xi + B$$

or $\quad y = \int_0^x (x-\xi)\,\phi(\xi)\,d\xi + 1$

Since, $y(0)=1$ ...(iii)

From the relations Eqs. (i), (ii) and (iii) the given differential equation reduces to

$$y(x) + x\int_0^x \phi(\xi)\,d\xi + \{\int_0^x (x-\xi)\,y(\xi)\,d\xi + 1\} = 0$$

$$\Rightarrow \quad y(x) = -1 - \int_0^x (2x-\xi)\,y(\xi)\,d\xi$$

Which is a Volterra's integral equations of second kind.

**39.** Substituting the function

$$y(x) = (1+x^2)^{-3/2}$$

in the given equation, we get

$$\frac{1}{1+x^2} - \int_0^x \frac{\xi}{1+x^2}\cdot\frac{1}{(1+\xi^2)^{3/2}}\,d\xi$$

$$= \frac{1}{1+x^2} + \frac{1}{1+x^2}\left[\frac{1}{(1+\xi^2)^{1/2}}\right]_0^x$$

$$= \frac{1}{1+x^2} + \frac{1}{(1+x^2)^{3/2}} - \frac{1}{1+x^2}$$

$$= \frac{1}{(1+x^2)^{3/2}} = \phi(x)$$

The substitution of $\phi(x)$ reduces the given equation to an identity with respect to x, thus $y(x)\ (1+x^2)^{-3/2}$ is a solution of the integral equation.

**40.** Given, the differential equation is

$$\frac{d^2y}{dx^2} - 5\frac{dy}{dx} + 6y = 0 \quad \text{...(i)}$$

Let $\quad \frac{d^2y}{dx^2} = y(x)$ ...(ii)

On integrating with regard to x, we get

$$\frac{dy}{dx} = \int_0^x y(\xi)\,d\xi + A$$

$$= \int_0^x y(\xi)\,d\xi - 1, \text{ since } y''(0) = -1 \quad \text{...(iii)}$$

and $\quad y = \int_0^x y(\xi)\,d\xi^2 - x + B$, since $y(0)=0$

$$\Rightarrow \quad y = \int_0^x (x-\xi)\,y(\xi)\,d\xi - x \quad \text{...(iv)}$$

Substituting Eqs. (ii), (iii) and (iv) in Eq. (i) we get,

$$y(x) - 5\{\int_0^x \phi(\xi)\,d\xi - 1\}$$

$$+ 6\{\int_0^x (x-\xi)\,y(\xi)\,d\xi - x\} = 0$$

$$\Rightarrow \quad y(x) = (6x-5) + \int_0^x (5-6x+6\xi)\,y(\xi)\,d\xi$$

Which a Volterra's integral equation of second kind.

**41.** Given differential equation is

$$y''(x) + \lambda y(x) = 0 \text{ and } y(0) = 0 = y \quad \text{...(i)}$$

On integrating both sides of Eq. (i) over (0, x) we get

$$y'(x) - y'(0) + \lambda\int_0^x y(x)\,dx = 0$$

$$\Rightarrow \quad y'(x) = c - \lambda\int_0^x y(x)\,dx \quad \text{...(ii)}$$

taking $y'(0) = c$

Again, integrating Eq. (ii) *wrt* x in (0, x), we obtain

$$y(x) - y(0) = cx - \lambda\int_0^x\int_0^x y(x)\,dx$$

$$y(x) = cx - \lambda\int_0^x (x-t)\,y(t)\,dt \quad \text{...(iii)}$$

Putting x = 1 in Eq. (iii), we get

$$y(1) = c - \lambda\int_0^1 (1-t)\,y(t)\,dt \quad [\because y(1)=0]$$

Hence $\quad c = \lambda\int_0^1 (1-t)\,y(t)\,dt$ ...(iv)

Substituting the value of c from Eq. (iv) in (iii), we get

$$y(x) = \lambda x\int_0^1 (1-t)\,y(t)\,dt - \lambda\int_0^x (x-t)\,y(t)dt$$

$$= \lambda x\{\int_0^x (1-t)\,y(t)\,dt + \int_x^1 (1-t)\,y(t)\,dt\}$$

$$- \lambda\int_0^x (x-t)\,y(t)\,dt$$

$$= \lambda\int_0^x t(1-x)\,y(t)dt + \lambda\int_x^1 (1-t)\,y(t)\,dt$$

$$= \lambda\{\int_0^x K(x,t)\,y(t)\,dt + \int_x^1 (x,t)\,y(t)\,dt\}$$

where $\quad K(x,t) = \begin{cases} t(1-x), & \text{when } t < x \\ x(1-t), & \text{when } t > x \end{cases}$ ...(v)

Hence, $\quad y(x) = \lambda\int_0^1 K(x,t)\,y(t)\,dt$

which is a Fredholm integral equation with a symmetric kernel $K(x,t)$ given by (v).

**42.** Let $\quad \frac{d^2y}{dx^2} = \phi(x)$ ...(i)

On integrating with regard to x both sides, we get

$$\left(\frac{dy}{dx}\right)_0^x = \int_0^x \phi(\xi)\,d\xi$$

$$\frac{dy}{dx} = \int_0^x \phi(\xi)\,d\xi, \text{ as } y'(0) = 0 \quad \text{...(ii)}$$

On integrating again with regard to x both the sides, we get

$$(y)_0^x = \int_0^x \phi(\xi)\,d\xi^2$$

$$\Rightarrow \quad y(x) - y(0) = \int_0^x \phi(\xi)\,d\xi^2 \text{ as } y(0) = 1$$

$$\Rightarrow \quad y(x) = 1 + \int_0^x (x-\xi)\,\phi(\xi)\,d\xi \quad \text{...(iii)}$$

Substituting $\frac{d^2y}{dx^2}, \frac{dy}{dx}$ and $y$ in the given differential equation, we get

$$\phi(x) - 2x\{\int_0^x \phi(\xi)\} - 3\{1 + \int_0^x (x-\xi)\,\phi(\xi)\,d\xi\} = 0$$

$$\Rightarrow \quad \phi(x) = 3 + \int_0^x (5x - 3\xi)\,\phi(\xi)\,d\xi$$

A non-homogeneous Volterra's integral equation of second kind.

**43.** Given, the integral equations is

$$\phi(x) = e^{-x} - 2\int_0^1 \cos(x-\xi)\,\phi(\xi)\,d\xi \quad \text{...(i)}$$

By using convolution threorem, the Eq. (i) can be rewritten as

$$\phi(x) = e^{-x} - 2\phi(x) * \cos x \quad \text{...(ii)}$$

Taking the Laplace transform of the relation (ii), we get

$$L\{\phi(x)\} = L(e^{-x}) - 2L\{\phi(x) * \cos x\}$$

$$\Rightarrow \quad L\{\phi(x)\} = \frac{1}{p+1} - 2L\{\phi(x)\}\frac{p}{p^2+1}$$

$$\Rightarrow \quad \left(1+\frac{2p}{p^2+1}\right)L\{\phi(x)\} = \frac{1}{p+1}$$

$$\Rightarrow \quad L\{\phi(x)\} = \frac{p^2+1}{(p+1)^3} = \frac{[(p+1)-1]^2+1}{(p+1)^3}$$

Taking the inverse Laplace transform, we get

$$\phi(x) = L^{-1}\left[\frac{[(p+1)-1]^2+1}{(p+1)^3}\right]$$

By using first shifting property, we get

$$\Rightarrow \quad \phi(x) = e^{-x} L^{-1}\left[\frac{(p-1)^2+1}{p^3}\right]$$

$$\Rightarrow \quad \phi(x) = e^{-x} L^{-1}\left[\frac{p^2-2p+2}{p^3}\right]$$

$$= e^{-x} L^{-1}\left[\frac{1}{p} - \frac{2}{p^2} + \frac{2}{p^3}\right]$$

$$\Rightarrow \quad \phi(x) = e^{-x}\left[1-2x+2\cdot\frac{x^2}{2!}\right]$$

$$\Rightarrow \quad \phi(x) = e^{-x}(1-2x+x^2)$$

**44.** Given, the function is

$$y(x) = \sin x + 2\int_0^x \cos(x-t)\,y(t)\,dt \qquad \ldots(i)$$

Since, $y(x) = xe^x$ is a solution of Eq. (i).

Substituting $y(x) = xe^x$ in the RHS of Eq. (i), we have

$$\sin x + 2\int_0^x \cos(x-t)\cdot te^t\,dt$$

$$= \sin x + 2\left\{\cos x \int_0^x t\cdot e^t \cos t\,dt + \sin x \int_0^x te^t \sin t\,dt\right\}$$

(integrating by parts)

$$= \sin x + 2\cos x\left\{\frac{1}{2}|t\cdot e^t(\cos t+\sin t)|_0^x - \frac{1}{2}\int_0^x e^t(\cos t+\sin t)\,dt\right\} + 2\sin x$$

$$\left\{\frac{1}{2}|t\cdot e^t(\sin t-\cos t)|_0^x - \frac{1}{2}\int_0^x e^t(\sin t-\cos t)\,dt\right\}$$

$$= \sin x + xe^x(\cos^2 x + \cos x\sin x + \sin^2 x - \sin x\cos x) - \cos x\int_0^x e^t(\cos t+\sin t)\,dt$$

$$- \sin x\int_0^x t(\sin t - \cos t)\,dt$$

$$= \sin x + xe^x - \cos x\,|e^t \sin t|_0^x + \sin x\,|e^t\cos t|_0^x$$

$$= \sin x + xe^x - e^x\cos x\sin x + e^t \sin x\cos x - \sin x$$

$$= xe^x$$

Hence, $y(x) = xe^x$ is a solution of the integral Eq (i).

**45.** Given, differential equation is $\dfrac{d^2\phi}{dx^2} = x - \lambda\phi$

On integrating *wrt* $x$, we get

$$\int_0^x \frac{d^2\phi}{dx^2}\,dx = \int_0^x x\,dx - \lambda\int_0^x \phi(x)\,dx$$

$$\Rightarrow \quad \phi(x) - \phi(0) = \frac{1}{2}x^2 - \lambda\int_0^x \phi(\xi)\,d\xi$$

Let $\phi'(0) = C$, then we get

$$\phi'(x) = C + \frac{1}{2}x^2 - \lambda\int_0^x \phi(\xi)\,d\xi$$

On integrating with regard to $x$, we get

$$\phi(x) - \phi(0) = Cx + \left(\frac{1}{6}\right)x^3 - \lambda\int_0^x \phi(\xi)\,d\xi^2$$

$$\Rightarrow \quad \phi(x) = Cx + \left(\frac{1}{6}\right)x^3 - \lambda\int_0^x \phi(\xi)d\xi^2$$

$$\Rightarrow \quad \phi(x) = Cx + \left(\frac{1}{6}\right)x^3 - \lambda\int_0^x (x-\xi)\,\phi(\xi)\,d\xi$$

Since, $\phi'(1) = 0 \Rightarrow \phi'(1) = C + \dfrac{1}{2} - \lambda\displaystyle\int_0^1 \phi(\xi)\,d\xi$

$$\Rightarrow \quad C = -\frac{1}{2} + \lambda\int_0^1 \phi(\xi)\,d\xi$$

$$\Rightarrow \phi(x) = -\frac{1}{2}x + \frac{1}{6}x^3 + \lambda\int_0^1 x\,\phi(\xi)\,d\xi - \lambda\int_0^x (x-\xi)\,\phi(\xi)\,d\xi$$

$$\Rightarrow \phi(x) = -\frac{1}{2}x + \frac{1}{6}x^3 + \lambda\left\{\int_0^1 x\,\phi(x)\,d\xi + \int_0^1 x\,\phi(\xi)\,d\xi\right\} - \lambda\int_0^x (x-\xi)\,\phi(\xi)\,\delta\xi$$

$$\Rightarrow \phi(x) = \frac{1}{6}(x^3-3x) + \lambda\left\{\int_0^x \xi\phi(\xi)d\xi + \int_x^1 x\,\phi(\xi)\,d\xi\right\}$$

$$\phi(x) = \frac{1}{6}(x^3-3x) + \lambda\int_0^1 K(x,\xi)\,\phi(\xi)\,d\xi \qquad \ldots(i)$$

where, $K(x,\xi) = \begin{cases} x, & x > \xi \\ \xi, & x > \xi \end{cases}$

Which is the non-homogeneous Fredholm integral equation of second kind.

**46.** Given, the integral equation is

$$y(x) = 1 + \lambda\int_0^1 xt\,y(t)\,dt \qquad \ldots(i)$$

Taking the initial approximation $y_1(x) = 1$ by Eq. (i), we get

$$y_1(x) = 1 + \lambda\int_0^1 xt\cdot 1\,dt = 1 + \lambda x\left|\frac{t^2}{2}\right|_0^1 = 1 + \frac{\lambda x}{2}$$

Substitution of $y_1(x)$ in Eq. (i), we get

$$y_2(x) = 1 + \lambda\int_0^1 xt\left(1+\lambda\frac{t}{2}\right)dt$$

$$= 1 + \lambda x\int_0^1 \left(t + \frac{\lambda t^2}{2}\right)dt$$

$$= 1 + \lambda x\left|\frac{t^2}{2} + \frac{\lambda}{2}\cdot\frac{t^3}{3}\right|_0^1 = 1 + \frac{\lambda x}{2} + \frac{\lambda^2 x}{6}$$

Substitution of $y_2(x)$ in Eq. (i), we get

$$y_3(x) = 1 + \lambda\int_0^1 xt\left(1 + \frac{\lambda t}{2} + \frac{\lambda^2 t}{6}\right)dt$$

$$= 1 + \lambda x \left| \frac{t^2}{2} + \left(\frac{\lambda}{2} + \frac{\lambda^2}{6}\right)\frac{t^3}{3} \right|_0^1$$

$$= 1 + \frac{\lambda x}{2} + \frac{\lambda^2 x}{6} + \frac{\lambda^3 x}{18}$$

$$= 1 + \frac{\lambda x}{2}\left(1 + \frac{\lambda}{3} + \frac{\lambda^2}{3^2} + \ldots\right)$$

Successive iteration gives

$$y(x) = 1 + \frac{\lambda x}{2}\left(1 + \frac{\lambda}{3} + \left(\frac{\lambda}{3}\right)^2 + \left(\frac{\lambda}{3}\right)^3 + \ldots \infty\right)$$

$$= 1 + \frac{\lambda x}{2}\left(\frac{1}{1 - \lambda/3}\right), \text{ (GP)}$$

$$\Rightarrow \quad y(x) = 1 + \frac{3\lambda x}{2(3 - \lambda)} \text{ only if } \lambda < 3$$

Which is the required solution.

**47.** Let $\quad \dfrac{d^2y}{dx^2} = y(x)$ ...(i)

Then, $\quad \dfrac{dy}{dx} = \int_0^x y(\xi)\, d\xi + 1$

and $\quad y = \int_0^x (x - \xi)\, y(\xi)\, d\xi + x$ ...(ii)

Substituting $\dfrac{d^2y}{dx^2}, \dfrac{dy}{dx}$ and $y$ in the given differential equation, we have

$$y(x) = \int_0^x (x - \xi)\, y(\xi)\, d\xi + x = \cos x$$

$$\Rightarrow \quad y(x) = (\cos x - x) - \int_0^x (x - \xi)\, y(\xi)\, d\xi$$

Which is a Volterra's integral equation of second kind.

**48.** The equation is a homogeneous Freodholm integral equation is

$$\phi(x) = \lambda \int_1^2 \left(x\xi + \frac{1}{x\xi}\right)\phi(\xi)\, d\xi \quad \text{...(i)}$$

$$\phi(x) = \lambda\left[x \int_1^2 \xi\phi(\xi)\, d\xi + \frac{1}{x}\int_1^2 \frac{1}{\xi}\,\phi(\xi)\, d\xi\right]$$

$$\phi(x) = \lambda\left[C_1 x + \frac{C_2}{x}\right] \quad \text{...(ii)}$$

where $\quad C_1 = \int_1^2 \xi\phi(\xi)\, d\xi$

and $\quad C_2 = \int_1^2 \frac{1}{\xi}\,\phi(\xi)\, d\xi$ ...(iii)

Hence, from the relations Eqs. (i) and (iii), we have

$$C_1 = \lambda \int_1^2 \xi\left(C_1\xi + \frac{C_2}{\xi}\right) d\xi = \lambda\left(\frac{7}{3}C_1 + C_2\right)$$

$$C_2 = \lambda \int_1^2 \frac{1}{\xi}\left(C_1\xi + \frac{C_2}{\xi}\right) d\xi = \lambda\left(C_1 + \frac{1}{2}C_2\right)$$

or $\quad \left(1 - \dfrac{7\lambda}{3}\right)C_1 - \lambda C_2 = 0$

and $\quad -\lambda C_1 + \left(1 - \dfrac{1}{2}\lambda\right)C_2 = 0$

The non-trivial solution of the system can be obtained only, if the determinant

$$\begin{vmatrix} 1 - \left(\frac{7}{3}\right)\lambda & -\lambda \\ -\lambda & 1 - \left(\frac{1}{2}\right)\lambda \end{vmatrix} = \frac{1}{6}(\lambda^2 - 17\lambda + 6)$$

vanishes. Thus, the required eigen values are given by

$$\lambda_1 = \frac{1}{2}[17 + \sqrt{(265)}] \simeq 6.639$$

$$\lambda_2 = \frac{1}{2}[17 - \sqrt{(265)}] \simeq 0.3606$$

The eigen functions corresponding to the eigen values $\lambda_1, \lambda_2$ are

$$\left[x - 2.2732\frac{1}{x}\right], \text{ if } \lambda_1 \simeq 6.639$$

and $\quad \left[x + 0.4399\dfrac{1}{x}\right], \lambda_2 \simeq 0.3606$

**49.** Substituting the function $y(x) = 1 - x$ in the given equation, we get

$$\int_0^x e^{x-\xi}(1 - \xi)\, d\xi = e^x \int_0^x e^{-\xi}\, d\xi - e^x \int_0^x \xi e^{-\xi}\, d\xi$$

$$= -e^x (e^{-\xi})_0^x + e^x (\xi e^{-\xi} + e^{-\xi})_0^x$$

$$= e^x (1 - e^{-x}) + e^x (xe^{-x} + e^{-x} - 1) = x$$

Hence, $y(x) = 1 - x$ is a solution of the integral equation.

**50.** We have,

$$K_n(x, \xi) = \int_a^b K_m(x - z)\, K_{n-m}(z, \xi)\, dz, \quad m = 1, 2, \ldots, n - 1$$

where, $\quad K_1(x, \xi) = K(x, \xi) = (x - \xi)^2$

Hence, $\quad K_2(x, \xi) = \int_a^b K(x, z)\, K_1(z, \xi)\, dz$

$$\Rightarrow \quad K_2(x, \xi) = \int_{-1}^1 K_m (x - z)^2 (z, \xi)^2\, dz$$

$$\Rightarrow \quad K_2(x, \xi) = \frac{2}{3}(x + \xi)^2 + 2x^2\xi^2 + \frac{4}{3}x\xi + \frac{2}{5}$$

$$K_3(x, \xi) = \int_a^b K(x, z)\, K_2(z, \xi)\, dz$$

$$\Rightarrow \quad K_3(x, \xi) = \int_{-1}^1 (x - z)^2$$

$$\left|\frac{2}{3}(z + \xi)^2 + 2z^2\xi^2 + \frac{4}{3}z\xi + \frac{2}{5}\right| dz$$

$$\Rightarrow \quad K_3(x, \xi) = \frac{56}{45}(x^2 + \xi^2) + \frac{8}{3}x^2\xi^2 - \frac{32}{9}z\xi + \frac{8}{15}$$

**51.** The integral equation $\phi(x) = 1 + \int_0^x \phi(\xi)\, d\xi$ with $\phi_0(x) = 0$ is Volterra integral equation of second kind.

Here, $\quad f(x) = 1, K(x, \xi) = 1, \lambda = 1$

The vth order approximation is

$$\phi_v(x) = f(x) + \lambda \int_0^x K(x, \xi)\, \phi_{v-1}(\xi)\, d\xi$$

$$\Rightarrow \quad \phi_v(x) = 1 + \int_0^x \phi_{v-1}(\xi)\, d\xi$$

Substituting $v = 1, 2, 3, \ldots,$ we get

$$\phi_1(x) = 1 + \int_0^x \phi_0(\xi)\, d\xi = 1$$

$$\Rightarrow \quad \phi_2(x) = 1 + \int_0^x \phi_1(\xi)\, d\xi = 1 + \int_0^x d\xi = 1 + x$$

$$\Rightarrow \quad \phi_3(x) = 1 + \int_0^x \phi_2(\xi)\, d\xi = 1 + \int_0^x (1+\xi)\, d\xi$$

$$= 1 + x + \frac{x^2}{2!}$$

In general, we get

$$\phi_v(x) = 1 + x + \frac{x^2}{2!} + \frac{x^3}{3!} + \ldots + \frac{x^{v-1}}{(v-1)!} + \ldots$$

Hence, the solution of the integral equation is

$$\phi(x) = \lim_{v \to \infty} \phi_v(x)$$

$$\phi(x) = 1 + x + \frac{x^2}{2!} + \frac{x^3}{3!} + \ldots + \frac{x^{v-1}}{(v-1)!} = e^x$$

**52.** The given equation in convolution form can be written as

$$y'(x) = 3\cos 2x * y(x) + 2$$

Taking Laplace transform of both sides, we get

$$L[y'(x)] = 3L(\cos 2x) \cdot \bar{y}(s) + \frac{2}{s}$$

$$\Rightarrow \quad s\bar{y}(s) - y(0) = \frac{3s\bar{y}(s)}{s^2+4} + \frac{2}{s}$$

$$\Rightarrow \quad \bar{y} = \frac{(s+2)(s^4+4)}{s^2(s^2+1)} \qquad [\because y(0) = 1]$$

$$= \frac{4}{s} + \frac{8}{s^2} + 3\frac{s}{s^2+1} - 6\frac{1}{s^2+1}$$

On inversion, we get

$$y = 4 + 8x - 3\cos x - 6\sin x$$

**53.** Let $\dfrac{d^3y}{dx^3} = \phi(x)$

$$\Rightarrow \quad \frac{d^2y}{dx^2} = \int_0^x y(\xi)\, d\xi + 1 \qquad \ldots\text{(i)}$$

$$\Rightarrow \quad \frac{dy}{dx} = \int_0^x (x-\xi)\, y(\xi) d\xi + x + 1$$

$$\Rightarrow \quad y = \frac{1}{2!}\int_0^x (x-\xi)^2\, y(\xi)\, d\xi + \frac{1}{2}x^2 + x + \frac{1}{2} \qquad \ldots\text{(ii)}$$

Substituting $\dfrac{d^2y}{dx^2}, \dfrac{dy}{dx}$ and $y$ into the given differential equation, we get

$$y(x) - 2x\left[\frac{1}{2}\int_0^x (x-\xi)^2 y(\xi)\, d\xi + \frac{1}{2}x^2 + x + \frac{1}{2}\right] = 0$$

$$y(x) = x(x+1)^2 + \int_0^x x(x-\xi)^2\, y(\xi)\, d\xi$$

Which is a Volterra's integral equation of second kind.

**54.** Given equation

$$\int_0^x \frac{y(t)}{\sqrt{x-t}}\, dt = 1 + 2x - x^2$$

is an Abel's equation

$$\Rightarrow y(x) * x^{-1/2} = 1 + 2x - x^2$$

Taking the Laplace transform of both sides, we get

$$\bar{y} \cdot L(x^{-1/2}) = L(1 + 2x - x^2)$$

$$\Rightarrow \quad \bar{y} \cdot \frac{\Gamma(1/2)}{s^{1/2}} = \frac{1}{s} + \frac{2}{s^2} - \frac{2}{s^3}$$

$$\Rightarrow \quad \bar{y} = \frac{1}{\Gamma(1/2)}\left(\frac{1}{s^{1/2}} + 2\cdot\frac{1}{s^{3/2}} - 2\frac{1}{s^{5/2}}\right)$$

which on inversion gives,

$$y = \frac{1}{\Gamma\left(\frac{1}{2}\right)}\frac{x^{-1/2}}{\Gamma\left(\frac{1}{2}\right)} + 2\cdot\frac{x^{1/2}}{\Gamma\left(\frac{3}{2}\right)} - 2\frac{x^{3/2}}{\Gamma\left(\frac{5}{2}\right)}$$

$$= \frac{1}{\pi}\left(x^{-1/2} + 4x^{1/2} - \frac{8}{3}x^{3/2}\right)$$

$$\Rightarrow \quad y = \frac{1}{3\pi\sqrt{x}}(3 + 12x - 8x^3)$$

**55.** Given integral equation is

$$\int_0^x e^{x-t}\, y(t)\, dt = e^x + x - 1 \qquad \ldots\text{(i)}$$

and since $y(t) = 2 - t$ is one of the solution

Hence, $\displaystyle\int_0^x e^{x-t}\, y(t)\, dt = \int_0^x e^{x-t}(2-t)\, dt$

$$= 2e^x \int_0^x e^{-t}\, dt - e^x \int_0^x te^{-t}\, dt$$

$$= 2e^x \left| -e^{-t} \right|_0^x - e^x \left\{ \left| t\cdot(-e^{-t}) \right|_0^x - \int_0^x 1\cdot(-e^{-t})\, dt \right\}$$

$$= 2e^x(-e^{-x} + 1) + e^x(xe^{-x}) - e^x \left| -e^{-t} \right|_0^x$$

$$= -2 + 2e^x + x + e^x(e^{-x} - 1)$$

$$= e^x + x - 1$$

Thus Eq. (i) is identically satisfied by $y(x) = 2 - x$. Hence, $y(x) = 2 - x$ is the requred solution.

**56.** Given the integral equation is

$$y(x) = \frac{1}{e^2-1}\int_0^1 e^{x+t}\, y(t)\, dt \qquad \ldots\text{(i)}$$

$$\Rightarrow \quad y(x) = \frac{e^x}{e^2-1}\int_0^1 e^t \cdot y(t)\, dt$$

$$= \frac{e^x}{e^2-1} C,$$

when $\quad C = \displaystyle\int_0^1 e^t . y(t)\, dt$

Substituting the value of $y(t)$ from Eq. (i) in C, we get

$$C = \int_0^1 e^t \left(\frac{e^t C}{e^2-1}\right) dt$$

$$= \frac{C}{e^2-1}\int_0^1 e^{t^2}\, dt$$

$$\Rightarrow \quad C\left[1 - \frac{1}{e^2-1}\int_0^1 e^2\, dt\right] = 0, \text{ i.e., } C = 0$$

Hence, from Eq. (i), $y(x) = 0$

Which shows that the given integral equation has only trivial solution.

Thus, it does not contain any eigen values or eigen functions.

**57.** Here, $K(x, \xi) = 1$, $\lambda = 1$ and $F(x) = x$. But we know that

$$K_n(x, \xi) = \int_a^b K_m(x, z) K_{n-m}(z, \xi) dz \quad m = 1, 2, \ldots, n-1$$

when $\quad K_1(x, \xi) = K(x, \xi) = 1$

Hence, $K_2(x, \xi) = \int_0^{1/2} dz = \frac{1}{2}$

$\Rightarrow \quad K_3(x, \xi) = \frac{1}{2}\int_0^{1/2} dz = \left(\frac{1}{2}\right)^2$

$\vdots$

$K_n(x, \xi) = \left(\frac{1}{2}\right)^{n-1}$

Thus, the resolvent kernel is

$$R(x, \xi; \lambda) = \sum_{n=1}^{\infty}\left(\frac{\lambda}{2}\right)^{n-1} = \frac{2}{2-\lambda}$$

$\Rightarrow \quad R(x, \xi; 1) = 2$, as $\lambda = 1$.

Hence, the solution of the integral equation is

$$\phi(x) = F(x) + \lambda\int_a^b R(x, \xi; \lambda) F(\xi)\, d\xi$$

$$\Rightarrow \quad \phi(x) = x + \int_0^{1/2} 2\xi\, d\xi = x + \frac{1}{4}$$

$$= x + \text{ constant.}$$

**58.** Substituting the function $y(x) = \frac{1}{\pi}\sqrt{x}$ in the given equation, we have

$$\frac{1}{\pi}\int_0^x \frac{1}{\sqrt{(\xi x - \xi^2)}}\, d\xi = \frac{1}{\pi}\int_0^x \frac{1}{\sqrt{\left[\frac{x^2}{4} - \left(\xi - \frac{x}{2}\right)^2\right]}}\, d\xi$$

$$= \frac{1}{2}\left[\sin^{-1}\frac{\left(\xi - \frac{x}{2}\right)}{\left(\frac{x}{2}\right)}\right]_0^x = \frac{1}{\pi}\left(\frac{\pi}{2} + \frac{\pi}{2}\right) = 1$$

Thus, $y(x) = 1/\pi\sqrt{x}$ is a solution of the integral equation.

**59.** The integral may be expressed as

$$x = \phi(x) * e \qquad \text{...(i)}$$

Taking the Laplace transform of both the sides of Eq. (i), we have

$$L(x) = L\{\phi(x)\} * L(e^x)$$

$$\Rightarrow \quad \frac{1}{p^2} = L\{\phi(x)\}\frac{1}{p-1}$$

$$\Rightarrow \quad L\{\phi(x)\} = \frac{p-1}{p^2} = \frac{1}{p} - \frac{1}{p^2} \qquad \text{...(ii)}$$

Taking inverse Laplace transform of Eq. (ii), we get

$$\phi(x) = L^{-1}\left(\frac{1}{p}\right) - L^{-1}\left(\frac{1}{p^2}\right)$$

$$\Rightarrow \quad \phi(x) = 1 - x$$

# 21 Classical Mechanics

**Syllabus**

- Generalized Coordinates
- Lagrange's Equation
- Hamilton's Canonical Equation
- Hamilton's Principle and Principle of Least Action
- Two Dimensional Motion of Rigid Bodies
- Euler's Dynamical Equation for Motion of a Rigid Body about an Axis
- Theory of Small Oscillations

## Transformation Equations

In three dimensions the spherical coordinates $(r, \theta, \phi)$ of the position of a particle is related to the cartesian coordinates $(x, y, z)$ as follows

$$x = r\sin\theta\cos\phi, \quad y = r\sin\theta\sin\phi, \quad z = r\cos\theta\,;$$

$$r = (x^2 + y^2 + z^2)^{1/2}, \quad \theta = \tan^{-1}\frac{\sqrt{x^2+y^2}}{z}, \quad \phi = \tan^{-1}\frac{y}{x}$$

We may represent, the relationships for spherical and cartesian coordinates as follows

$$x = x(r, \theta, \phi), \quad y = y(r, \theta, \phi), \quad z = z(r, \theta)$$

$$\Rightarrow \qquad \mathbf{r} = \mathbf{r}(r, \theta, \phi)$$

If the time variable is included, then

$$\mathbf{r} = \mathbf{r}(r, \theta, \phi, t)$$



We may represent the coordinates by $q_1, q_2$ and $q_3$ having the relationships with the cartesian coordinates as

$$x = x(q_1, q_2, q_3, t),$$

$$y = y(q_1, q_2, q_3, t),$$

$$z = z(q_1, q_2, q_3, t)$$

or $$\mathbf{r} = \mathbf{r}(q_1, q_2, q_3, t)$$

In general, if $x_i$, $y_i$ and $z_i$ are the cartesian coordinates of the $i$th particle, then its position vector $\mathbf{r}_i$ is given by $\mathbf{r}_i = \mathbf{r}_i(q_1, q_2, \ldots, q_n, t)$ which gives the transformation equations.

## Degree of Freedom

The minimum number of independent variables or coordinates required to specify the position of a dynamical system, consisting of one or more particles, is called the number of degrees of freedom of the system.

e.g., the motion of a particle, moving freely in space, can be described by a set of three coordinates, e.g., $(x, y, z)$ and hence the number of degrees of freedom, possessed by the particle, is three. A system of two particles, moving freely in space, requires two sets of three coordinates [e.g., $(x_1, y_1, z_1)$ and $(x_2, y_2, z_2)$] i.e., six coordinates to specify its position. Thus, the system has six degrees of freedom. If a system consists of $N$ particles, moving freely in space, we need $3N$ independent coordinates to describe its position. Hence, the number of degrees of freedom of the system is $3N$.

The configuration of the system of $N$ particles, moving freely in space, may be represented by the position of a single point in $3N$ dimensional space, which is called configuration space of the system. The configuration space for a system of one freely moving particle is 3-dimensional and for a system of two freely moving particles, it is six dimensional. In the later case, the configuration of the system of the two particles can be represented by the position of a single point with six coordinates in six dimensional space. This system has six degrees of freedom and its configuration space is six dimensional.

The number of coordinates, needed to specify a dynamical system, becomes smaller, when the constraints (which we describe below) are present in the system. Hence, the degrees of freedom of a dynamical system is defined as the minimum number of independent coordinates (or variables) required to specify the system compatible with the constraints.

Limitations imposed on the motion of a particle or system of particles is called constraints. Constraints limit the motion of a system and therefore the number of independent coordinates, needed to describe the motion, is reduced. For example, if a particle moves on a circle, then only one coordinate $q_1 = \theta$ is sufficient to describe the motion, because the radius (a) of the circle remains the same, hence the degree of freedom of the system is 1. If $\mathbf{r}$ is the position vector of the particle at angle $\theta$ relative to centre of circle, then

$$|\mathbf{r}| = a$$

or

$$r = a \qquad \text{...(i)}$$

Eq. (i) expresses the constraint for a particle in circular motion, which is called holonomic constraint. Similarly, in case of particle moving on the surface of sphere. Two independent coordinates $q_1 = \theta$ and $q_2 = \phi$ are required to describe the motion, since radius (a) is constant, hence degree of freedom of the system is 2.

Let the constraints are present in the system of $N$ particles, then holonomic constraints (Equation form of constraints) is

$$f(\mathbf{r}_1, \mathbf{r}_2, \dots, t) = 0 \qquad \text{...(ii)}$$

Let there be $m$ number of such equations to describe the constraints in the $N$ particle system. Then, by using Eq. (ii) we may eliminate $m$ of the $3N$ coordinates, thereby leaving $3N - m$ independent coordinates with $3N - m$ degrees of freedom of the system.

Let $3N - m = n$ (say). Then, degrees of freedom of the system is $n$. Thus, we have $n$ independent variables $q_1, q_2, \dots, q_n$ in terms of which the coordinates $\mathbf{r}_1, \mathbf{r}_2, \dots, \mathbf{r}_N$ can be expressed as

$$\left.\begin{aligned} \mathbf{r}_1 &= \mathbf{r}_1(q_1, q_2, \dots, q_n, t) \\ \mathbf{r}_2 &= \mathbf{r}_2(q_1, q_2, \dots, q_n, t) \\ &\vdots \\ \mathbf{r}_N &= \mathbf{r}_N(q_1, q_2, \dots, q_n, t) \end{aligned}\right\} \qquad \text{...(iii)}$$

## Generalized Coordinates

The name generalized coordinates is given to a set of independent coordinates sufficient in number to describe completely the state of configuration of a dynamical system.

In Eq. (iii), $q_1, q_2, \dots, q_n$ are the generalized coordinates.

The generalized coordinates of the functions of $N$ variables $r_1, r_2, \dots, r_N$ and one time variable $t$ are given by

$$q_i = q_i(r_1, r_2, \dots, r_N, t)$$

where, $i = 1, 2, \dots, k$.

where, $q_k = q_k(r_1, r_2, \dots, r_N, t)$ is the coordinates of a point in a $k$-dimensional space which may represent the configuration of the system and hence called configuration space of the system. Here, $q_1, q_2, \dots, q_k$ are independent of each other.

## Non-holonomic Constraints

The constraints which are neither expressible in the form of Eq. (i) nor Eq. (ii) called non-holonomic constraints.

For example, the motion of a particle placed on the surface of a sphere of radius a is described by

$$|\mathbf{r}| \geq a \quad \text{or} \quad r - a \geq 0$$

The particle will first slide down the surface and then fall off.

Constraint for the motion of gas molecule contained in spherical shape container is

$$|\mathbf{r}| \leq a \quad \text{or} \quad r \leq a$$

In a non-holonomic system, all the coordinates cannot vary independently and hence the number of degrees of freedom of the system is less than the minimum number of coordinates needed to specify the configuration of the system.

Constraints are further described as (i) rheonomous and (ii) scleronomous. In the former, the equations of constraint contain the time as an explicit variable, while in the later they are not explicitly dependent on time. Constraints may also be classified as (i) conservative and (ii) dissipative. In case of conservative constraints, total mechanical energy of the system is conserved during the constrained motion and the constraint forces do not do any work. In dissipative constraints, the constraint forces do work and the total mechanical energy is not conserved. Time dependent or rheonomic constraints are generally dissipative.

***Note*** **(a)** In case of the motion of a rigid body, the distance between any two particles of the body remains fixed and do not change with time. The constraint is holonomic and scleronomic.

**(b)** Motion of a simple pendulum with rigid support is also an example of holonomic and scleronomic constraint.

**(c)** Motion of rolling disc on a rough horizontal $x$-$y$ plane is an example of non-holonomic constraint.

**(d)** Holonomic system has integrable differential equations of constraints. But in case of non-holonomic system it is not so.

**(e)** Constraints are always related to forces which restrict the motion of the system. These forces are called Forces of Constraint. It acts in a direction perpendicular to the surface of constraints.

*e.g*, constraint force in a simple pendulum is the tension in the string.

The total force $F_i$ on the $i$th particle can be expressed as

$$\mathbf{F}_i = \mathbf{F}_i^a + \mathbf{f}_i$$

where $\mathbf{F}_i^a$ is the applied force and $\mathbf{f}_i$ is the force of constraint.

Suppose, the system is in equilibrium, then the total force on any particle is zero *i.e.*,

$$\mathbf{F}_i = 0, \qquad i = 1, 2, \dots, N$$

The virtual work of the force $\mathbf{F}_i$ in the virtual displacement $\delta\mathbf{r}_i$ will also be zero *i.e.*,

$$\delta W_i = \mathbf{F}_i \cdot \delta \mathbf{r}_i = 0$$

where, $\delta \mathbf{r}_i = \delta \mathbf{r}_i(q_1, q_2, ..., q_n)$

Similarly, the sum of virtual work for all the particles must vanish *i.e.*,

$$\delta W = \sum_{i=1}^{N} \mathbf{F}_i \cdot \delta \mathbf{r}_i = 0$$

This result represents the principle of virtual work which states that the work done is zero in the case of an arbitrary virtual displacement of a system from a position of equilibrium.

**(f)** Work done by constraint force in a rigid body is zero and hence constraint is conservative.

**(g)** For the system of $N$ particles

we have, $\sum_{i=1}^{N} (\mathbf{F}_i - \dot{\mathbf{p}}_i) \cdot \delta \mathbf{r}_i = 0$

which is called d'Alembert's principle.

Here, $\mathbf{F}_i \to$ Actual force acting on the $i$th particle

$\dot{\mathbf{p}}_i \to$ Reversed effective force

and $\delta \mathbf{r}_i \to$ Virtual displacement

# Lagrange's Equations

Consider a system of $N$ particles. The transformation equations for the position vectors of the particles are

$$\mathbf{r}_i = \mathbf{r}_i(q_1, q_2, ..., q_k, ..., q_n, t) \quad i = 1, 2, ..., N \qquad ...(i)$$

where $t$ is the time and $q_k (k = 1, 2, ..., n)$ are the generalized coordinates.

Differentiating Eq. (i) *wrt* $t$, we obtain the velocity of the $i$th particle, *i.e.*,

$$\frac{d\mathbf{r}_i}{dt} = \frac{\partial \mathbf{r}_i}{\partial q_1}\frac{dq_1}{dt} + \frac{d\mathbf{r}_i}{\partial q_2}\frac{dq_2}{dt} + ... + \frac{\partial \mathbf{r}_i}{\partial q_k}\frac{dq_k}{dt} + ... + \frac{d\mathbf{r}_i}{\partial q_n}\frac{dq_n}{dt} + \frac{\partial \mathbf{r}_i}{\partial t}$$

or

$$\mathbf{v}_i = \dot{\mathbf{r}}_i = \sum_{k=1}^{n} \frac{\partial \mathbf{r}_i}{\partial q_k}\dot{q}_k + \frac{\partial \mathbf{r}_i}{\partial t} \qquad ...(ii)$$

where $\dot{q}_k$ are the generalized velocities.

The virtual displacement is given by

$$\delta \mathbf{r}_i = \frac{\partial \mathbf{r}_i}{\partial q_1}\delta q_1 + \frac{\partial \mathbf{r}_i}{\partial q_2}\delta q_2 + ... + \frac{\partial \mathbf{r}_i}{\partial q_k}\delta q_k + ... + \frac{\partial \mathbf{r}_i}{\partial q_n}\delta q_n$$

or

$$\delta \mathbf{r}_i = \sum_{k=1}^{N} \frac{\partial \mathbf{r}_i}{\partial q_k}\delta q_k \qquad ...(iii)$$

since by definition the virtual displacements do not depend on time.

According to d'Alembert's principle,

$$\sum_{i=1}^{N} (\mathbf{F}_i - \dot{\mathbf{p}}_i) \cdot \delta \mathbf{r}_i = 0 \qquad ...(iv)$$

Here,

$$\sum_{i=1}^{N} \mathbf{F}_i \cdot \delta \mathbf{r}_i = \sum_{i=1}^{N} \mathbf{F}_i \cdot \sum_{k=1}^{n} \frac{\partial \mathbf{r}_i}{\partial q_k}\delta q_k = \sum_{k=1}^{n}\sum_{i=1}^{N}\left[\mathbf{F}_i \cdot \frac{\partial \mathbf{r}_i}{\partial q_k}\right]\delta q_k$$

$$= \sum_{k=1}^{n} G_k \delta q_k \qquad ...(v)$$

where

$$G_k = \sum_{i=1}^{N} \mathbf{F}_i \cdot \frac{\partial \mathbf{r}_i}{\partial q_k}$$

are called the components of generalized force associated with the generalized coordinates $q_k$.

and

$$\sum_{i=1}^{N} \dot{\mathbf{p}}_i \cdot \delta \mathbf{r}_i = \sum_{k=1}^{n}\left[\frac{d}{dt}\left(\frac{\partial T}{\partial \dot{q}_k}\right) - \frac{\partial T}{\partial \dot{q}_k}\right]\delta q_k \qquad ...(vi)$$

where, $T = \sum_{i=1}^{N} \frac{1}{2} m_i v_i^2$ is the kinetic energy of the system.

$\frac{\partial T}{\partial \dot{q}_k}$ is defined to be generalized momentum associated with $q_k$.

Using Eqs. (v) and (vi) in Eq. (iv), we get

$$\sum_{k=1}^{n}\left[\left\{\frac{d}{dt}\left(\frac{\partial T}{\partial \dot{q}_k}\right) - \frac{\partial T}{\partial q_k}\right\} - G_k\right]\delta q_k = 0 \qquad ...(vii)$$

As the constraints are holonomic,

$$\Rightarrow \quad \frac{d}{dt}\left(\frac{\partial T}{\partial \dot{q}_k}\right) - \frac{\partial T}{\partial q_k} - G_k = 0$$

or

$$\frac{d}{dt}\left(\frac{\partial T}{\partial \dot{q}_k}\right) - \frac{\partial T}{\partial q_k} = G_k \qquad ...(viii)$$

This represents the general form of Lagrange's equations for holonomic dynamical system. For a conservative system, the force is derivable from a scalar potential $V$

$$G_k = -\frac{\partial V}{\partial q_k} \qquad ...(ix)$$

Thus, Eq. (viii) becomes

$$\frac{d}{dt}\left(\frac{\partial T}{\partial \dot{q}_k}\right) - \frac{\partial T}{\partial q_k} = -\frac{\partial V}{\partial q_k}$$

$$\Rightarrow \quad \frac{d}{dt}\left(\frac{\partial T}{\partial \dot{q}_k}\right) - \frac{\partial (T - V)}{\partial q_k} = 0 \qquad ...(x)$$

Since, the scalar potential $V$ is the function of generalized coordinates $q_k$ only not depending on generalized velocities, we can write Eq. (x) as

$$\frac{d}{dt}\left[\frac{\partial (T - V)}{\partial \dot{q}_k}\right] - \frac{\partial (T - V)}{\partial q_k} = 0 \qquad ...(xi)$$

We define a new function given by

$$L = T - V$$

which is called the Lagrangian of the system.

Thus, Eq. (xi) changes to

$$\frac{d}{dt}\left(\frac{\partial L}{\partial \dot{q}_k}\right) - \frac{\partial L}{\partial q_k} = 0 \qquad ...(xii)$$

for $k = 1, 2, 3, ..., n$

which are known as Lagrange's equations for conservative system.

**Note** **(a)** Total number of equations in Eq. (xii) is $n$.

**(b)** $p_k = \frac{\partial T}{\partial \dot{q}_k}$ is defined to be the generalized (or conjugate) momentum associated with generalized coordinates $q_k$.

In case of conservative system , we have

$$L = T - V$$

or

$$T = L + V$$

$$\Rightarrow \quad \frac{\partial T}{\partial \dot{q}_k} = \frac{\partial L}{\partial \dot{q}_k} + \frac{\partial V}{\partial \dot{q}_k} = \frac{\partial L}{\partial \dot{q}_k}$$

Since, potential energy (V) of the system is independent from $\dot{q}_k$

i.e.,

$$\frac{\partial V}{\partial \dot{q}_k} = 0$$

$$\therefore \quad p_k = \frac{\partial L}{\partial \dot{q}_k}$$

**(c)** In case of presence of non-conservative force, for example, frictional force acting on the system, then Eq. (xii) takes the form

$$\frac{d}{dt}\left(\frac{\partial L}{\partial \dot{q}_k}\right) - \frac{\partial L}{\partial q_k} = -\frac{\partial R}{\partial \dot{q}_k}$$

where $R = \frac{1}{2}\sum_i k_i v_i^2$ is known as Rayleigh's dissipation function.

$v_i$ is the velocity of the $i^{th}$ particle and $k_i$ is the constant of proportionality.

***Example 1.*** *A bead slides on a smooth rod which is rotating about one end in a vertical plane with uniform angular velocity ω. Find equation of motion.*

**Solution.** Let '$m$' be the mass of bead.

At time position of the bead is $(r, \theta)$ on XY-plane.

Total kinetic energy

$$T = \frac{1}{2}mv^2 + \frac{1}{2}I\omega^2$$

$$= \frac{1}{2}m\dot{r}^2 + \frac{1}{2}mr^2 \cdot \dot{\theta}^2$$

$$= \frac{1}{2}m(\dot{r}^2 + r^2\dot{\theta}^2)$$

and potential energy

$$V = mgr \sin\theta$$

$$\therefore \quad L = T - V$$

$$= \frac{1}{2}m(\dot{r}^2 + r^2\dot{\theta}^2) - mgr \sin\theta$$

By using Lagrange's equation, we get

$$\frac{\partial L}{\partial r} - \frac{d}{dt}\left(\frac{\partial L}{\partial \dot{r}}\right) = 0$$

$$\Rightarrow \quad (mr\dot{\theta}^2 - mg \sin\theta) - \frac{d}{dt}(m\dot{r}) = 0$$

$$\Rightarrow \quad r\dot{\theta}^2 - g \sin\theta - \ddot{r} = 0$$

which is the required equation of motion.

Putting $\dot{\theta} = \omega$ and $\theta = \omega t$ equation becomes

$$\ddot{r} + g \sin\omega t = r\omega^2$$

***Example 2.*** *Obtain the equation of motion of a simple pendulum by using Lagrangian method and hence deduce the formula for its time period for small amplitude oscillations.*

**Solution.** Let θ be the angular displacement of the simple pendulum from the equilibrium position. If $l$ be the effective length of the pendulum and $m$ be the mass of the bob, then the displacement along arc $OA = s$ is given by

$$s = l\theta$$

Kinetic energy

$$T = \frac{1}{2}mv^2 = \frac{1}{2}ml^2\dot{\theta}^2$$

$$\left[\because \; v = \frac{ds}{dt} = \frac{d(l\theta)}{dt} = \frac{l\,d\theta}{dt} = l\dot{\theta}\right]$$

If the potential energy of the system, when the bob is at $O$, is zero, then the potential energy, when the bob is at $A$, is given by

$$V = mg(OB) = mg(OC - BC)$$

$$= mg(l - l\cos\theta) = mgl(1 - \cos\theta)$$

Hence,

$$L = T - V,$$

$$\Rightarrow \quad L = \frac{1}{2}ml^2\dot{\theta}^2 - mgl(1 - \cos\theta)$$

Now,

$$\frac{\partial L}{\partial \theta} = -mgl \sin\theta \quad \text{and} \quad \frac{\partial L}{\partial \dot{\theta}} = ml^2\dot{\theta}$$

From Lagrange's equation,

$$\frac{d}{dt}\left(\frac{\partial L}{\partial \dot{\theta}}\right) - \frac{\partial L}{\partial \theta} = 0$$

(Here, there is only generalized coordinate $q_1 = \theta$)

$$\Rightarrow \quad \frac{d}{dt}[ml^2\dot{\theta}] + mgl \sin\theta = 0$$

$$\Rightarrow \quad ml^2\ddot{\theta} + mgl \sin\theta = 0$$

$$\Rightarrow \quad \ddot{\theta} + \frac{g}{l}\sin\theta = 0$$

This represents the equation of motion of a simples pendulum.

For small amplitude oscillations, $\sin\theta \cong \theta$, and therefore the equation of motion of a simple pendulum is

$$\ddot{\theta} + \frac{g}{l}\theta = 0$$

This represents a simple harmonic motion of period, given by

$$T = 2\pi\sqrt{\frac{l}{g}}$$

***Example 3.*** *Use Lagrange's equations to find the equation of motion of a compound pendulum in a vertical plane about a fixed horizontal axis. Hence, find the period of small amplitude oscillations of the compound pendulum.*

**Solution.** Let the compound pendulum be suspended from $S$ with $C$ as centre of mass. It is oscillating in the vertical plane which is the plane of paper.

Moment of inertia of the pendulum about the axis of rotation through $S$ is given by

$$I = I_C + Ml^2 = M(K^2 + l^2)$$

where $M$ is the mass of the pendulum,

$$I_C = MK^2$$

($K$ = radius of gyration) about a parallel axis through $C$ and $l$ the distance between centre of suspension and centre of mass. If $\theta$ is the instantaneous angle which $SC$ makes with the vertical axis through $O$, then the kinetic energy of the oscillating system is

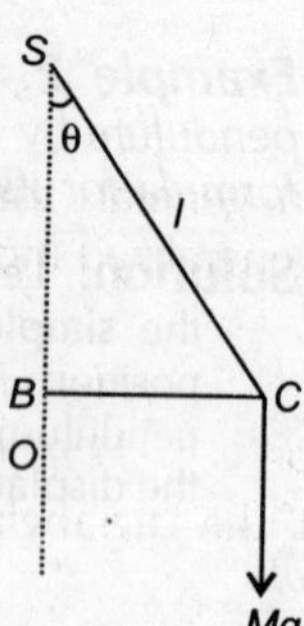


$$T = \frac{1}{2} I \dot{\theta}^2 = \frac{1}{2} M(K^2 + l^2)\dot{\theta}^2$$

Potential energy with respect to horizontal plane through $S$ is

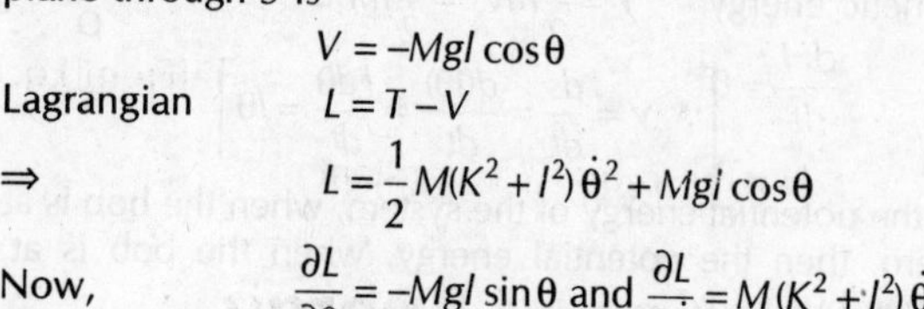

$$V = -Mgl \cos\theta$$

Lagrangian $\quad L = T - V$

$$\Rightarrow \qquad L = \frac{1}{2} M(K^2 + l^2)\dot{\theta}^2 + Mgl\cos\theta$$

Now, $\quad \dfrac{\partial L}{\partial \theta} = -Mgl\sin\theta$ and $\dfrac{\partial L}{\partial \dot{\theta}} = M(K^2 + l^2)\dot{\theta}$

Lagrange's equation in $\theta$ coordinate is

$$\frac{d}{dt}\left(\frac{\partial L}{\partial \dot{\theta}}\right) - \frac{\partial L}{\partial \theta} = 0$$

Therefore, $\quad \dfrac{1}{2} M(K^2 + l^2)\ddot{\theta} + Mgl\sin\theta = 0$

$$\Rightarrow \qquad \ddot{\theta} + \frac{gl}{K^2 + l^2}\sin\theta = 0$$

This is the equation of motion of the compound pendulum. If $\theta$ is small, $\sin\theta \cong \theta$ and then

$$\ddot{\theta} + \frac{gl}{K^2 + l^2}\theta = 0$$

This equation represents a simple harmonic motion whose period is given by

$$T = 2\pi\sqrt{\frac{K^2 + l^2}{lg}} = 2\pi\sqrt{\frac{\frac{K^2}{l} + l}{g}}$$

***Example 4.*** *A mass, suspended at the end of a light spring having spring constant $k$, is set into vertical motion. Use Lagrange's equation, to find the equation of motion of the mass.*

**Solution.** At any time $t$, let the displacement of $m$ from the equilibrium position $O$ be $x$. Then, the kinetic energy of $P$ is

$$T = \frac{1}{2} m\left(\frac{dx}{dt}\right)^2 = \frac{1}{2} m\dot{x}^2$$

Also, the work done during its fall from $O$ to $P$ is

$$W = \int_0^x (mg - kx)\,dx = mgx - \frac{1}{2}kx^2$$

If $V$ is the potential energy of the mass at $P$, then

$$V = -W = \frac{1}{2}kx^2 - mgx$$

Hence, Lagrangian $L = T - V$

$$= \frac{1}{2} m\dot{x}^2 + mgx - \frac{1}{2}kx^2$$

Thus, the Lagrange's equation is

$$\frac{\partial L}{\partial x} - \frac{d}{dt}\left(\frac{\partial L}{\partial \dot{x}}\right) = 0$$

becomes $(mg - kx) - \dfrac{d}{dt}(m\dot{x}) = 0$

$$\Rightarrow \qquad m\frac{d^2x}{dt^2} = mg - kx$$

which is the required equation of motion.

# Lagrange's Equations of Motions for Non-holonomic Systems

Lagrange's equations of motions for non-holonomic system are given by

$$\frac{\partial L}{\partial q_k} - \frac{d}{dt}\left(\frac{\partial L}{\partial \dot{q}_k}\right) = -\sum_{l=1}^{m} \lambda_l a_{lk} \qquad \text{...(i)}$$

where $k = 1, 2, \ldots, n$, $\lambda_l (l = 1, 2, \ldots, m)$ are undetermined quantities.

Eq. (i) represents $n$ equations, but there are $n + m$ unknowns, $n$ coordinates, $q_k$ and $m$ Lagrange's mutipliers. The remaining $m$ unknown $q_k$'s are determined from $m$ first order differential equations

$$\sum_k a_{lk}\dot{q}_k + a_{lt} = 0$$

which is the equations of constraints.

# Hamilton's Principle

Hamilton's principle states that "the time integral of the difference between the kinetic and potential energies of a dynamical system is stationary" *i.e.*, from time $t_1$ to time $t_2$

$$S = \int_{t_1}^{t_2} (T - V)\,dt$$

has stationary (extremum) value on actual path of motion.

$$\Rightarrow \qquad S = \int_{t_1}^{t_2} L\,dt \text{ has stationary value } (\because L = T - V)$$

The quantity $S$ is called as Hamilton's variational principle function.

Since, $S$ is stationary

$$\Rightarrow \qquad \delta S = 0$$

$$\Rightarrow \qquad \delta\int_{t_1}^{t_2} L\,dt = 0$$

***Note* (a)** By Hamilton's principle, the system moves so that $\int_{t_1}^{t_2} L\,dt$ is stationary.

$\therefore$ Euler's equation must hold good, *i.e.*,

$$\frac{\partial L}{\partial q_k} - \frac{d}{dt}\left(\frac{\partial L}{\partial \dot{q}_k}\right) = 0, k = 1, 2, \ldots, n.$$

These are Lagrange's equations which determine the motion of the system.

***Example 5.*** *Use Hamilton's principle to find the equation of motion of one-dimensional harmonic oscillator.*

**Solution** The kinetic energy of harmonic oscillator is $T = \frac{1}{2}m\dot{x}^2$

and the potential energy

$$V = -\int_0^x F\,dx = \int_0^x kx\,dx$$

$$\Rightarrow \quad V = \frac{1}{2}kx^2 \qquad (\because F = -kx)$$

$\therefore$ Lagrangian of the system is

$$L = T - V = \frac{1}{2}m\dot{x}^2 - \frac{1}{2}kx^2$$

$$\Rightarrow \quad L = L(x, \dot{x}, t) = \frac{1}{2}m\dot{x}^2 - \frac{1}{2}kx^2$$

From Hamilton's principle $\int_{t_1}^{t_2} L\,dt$ is stationary

$$\Rightarrow \quad \frac{\partial L}{\partial q_1} - \frac{d}{dt}\left(\frac{\partial L}{\partial \dot{q}_1}\right) = 0 \qquad (\text{here, } q_1 = x)$$

$$\Rightarrow \quad \frac{\partial L}{\partial x} - \frac{d}{dt}\left(\frac{\partial L}{\partial \dot{x}}\right) = 0$$

$$\Rightarrow \quad -kx - \frac{d}{dt}(m\dot{x}) = 0 \Rightarrow m\ddot{x} + kx = 0$$

which is the required equation of motion.

## Hamiltonian Function ($H$)

Consider a general Lagrangian $L$ of a system given by

$$L = L(q_1, q_2, \ldots, q_k, \ldots, q_k, \dot{q}_1, \dot{q}_2, \ldots, \dot{q}_k, \ldots, \dot{q}_n, t)$$

We denote it for convenience by

$$L = L(q_k, \dot{q}_k, t), \quad k = 1, 2, \ldots, n$$

$$\Rightarrow \quad \frac{dL}{dt} = \sum_k \frac{\partial L}{\partial q_k}\frac{dq_k}{dt} + \sum_k \frac{\partial L}{\partial \dot{q}_k}\frac{d\dot{q}_k}{dt} + \frac{\partial L}{\partial t} \qquad \text{...(i)}$$

From Lagrangian equations, we have

$$\frac{\partial L}{\partial q_k} = \frac{d}{dt}\left(\frac{\partial L}{\partial \dot{q}_k}\right) \qquad \text{...(ii)}$$

Using Eq. (ii) in Eq. (i), we get

$$\frac{dL}{dt} = \sum_k \frac{d}{dt}\left(\frac{\partial L}{\partial \dot{q}_k}\right)\dot{q}_k + \sum_k \frac{\partial L}{\partial \dot{q}_k}\frac{\partial \dot{q}_k}{\partial t} + \frac{\partial L}{\partial t}$$

$$\Rightarrow \quad \frac{dL}{dt} = \sum_k \frac{d}{dt}\left(\dot{q}_k \frac{\partial L}{\partial \dot{q}_k}\right) + \frac{\partial L}{\partial t}$$

$$\Rightarrow \quad \frac{d}{dt}\left(\sum_k \dot{q}_k \frac{\partial L}{\partial \dot{q}_k} - L\right) = -\frac{\partial L}{\partial t} \qquad \text{...(iii)}$$

But $$\frac{\partial L}{\partial \dot{q}_k} = p_k$$

$\Rightarrow$ Eq. (iii) becomes

$$\frac{d}{dt}\left(\sum_k p_k\dot{q}_k - L\right) = -\frac{\partial L}{\partial t} \qquad \text{...(iv)}$$

The quantity in the bracket is called the Hamiltonian function $H$, i.e.,

$$H = \sum_k p_k\dot{q}_k - L$$

In general, the Hamiltonian function $H$ is the function of generalized momenta $p_k$, generalized coordinates $q_k$ and time $t$, i.e.,

$$H = H(p_1, p_2, \ldots, p_k, \ldots, p_n, q_1, q_2, \ldots, q_k, \ldots, q_n, t)$$

or $$H = H(p_k, q_k, t)$$

If the Lagrangian $L$ does not depend on time $t$ explicitly, then $\frac{\partial L}{\partial t} = 0$

$$\Rightarrow \quad \frac{dH}{dt} = 0 \qquad [\text{From Eq. (iv)}]$$

or $$H = \sum_k p_k\dot{q}_k - L = \text{constant} \qquad \text{...(v)}$$

## Conservation of Energy

Consider transformation equations not containing time explicitly *i.e.*,

$$\mathbf{r}_i = \mathbf{r}_i(q_1, q_2, \ldots, q_k, \ldots, q_n)$$

For a conservative system

$$\frac{\partial V}{\partial \dot{q}_k} = 0$$

$$p_k = \frac{\partial L}{\partial \dot{q}_k} = \frac{\partial}{\partial \dot{q}_k}(T - V) = \frac{\partial T}{\partial \dot{q}_k}$$

Hence, $$H = \sum_k p_k\dot{q}_k - L = \sum_k \frac{\partial T}{\partial \dot{q}_k}\dot{q}_k - L \qquad \text{...(i)}$$

Since, $r_i$ does not depend on time $t$ explicitly.

$\Rightarrow$ Kinetic energy $T$ is a homogeneous quadratic function.

Then, it is derived that

$$\sum_k \frac{\partial T}{\partial \dot{q}_k}\dot{q}_k = 2T$$

$\therefore$ From Eq. (i), we get

$$H = 2T - L = 2T - (T - V)$$

$$\Rightarrow \quad H = T + V = \text{constant } (E)$$

Thus, the Hamiltonian $H$ represents the total energy of the system $E$ and is conserved, provided the system is conservative and $T$ is a homogeneous quadratic function.

## Principle of Least Action

According to the principle of least action for a conservative system

$$\Delta \int_{t_1}^{t_2} \sum_k p_k\dot{q}_k\,dt = 0 \qquad \text{...(i)}$$

where Eq. (i) quantity

$$\int_{t_1}^{t_2} \sum_k p_k\dot{q}_k\,dt = W$$

is called action and also known as Hamilton's characteristic function.

Hence, Eq. (i) can be written as

$$\Delta W = \Delta \int_{t_1}^{t_2} \sum_k p_k \dot{q}_k dt = 0$$

but $$\Delta = \delta + \Delta t \frac{d}{dt}$$

i.e., The $\Delta$-variation of any function $f = f(q_k, \dot{q}_k, t)$ is given by

$$\Delta f = \delta f + \Delta t \frac{df}{dt}.$$

Therefore, principle of least action is

$$\Delta W = 0 \Rightarrow \delta W + \Delta t \frac{dW}{dt} = 0$$

**Other Form of (i)**

For a conservative system, the Hamiltonian is constant and the potential energy is independent of time. So that

$$p_k = \frac{\partial L}{\partial \dot{q}_k} = \frac{\partial (T - V)}{\partial \dot{q}_k} = \frac{\partial T}{\partial \dot{q}_k}$$

Therefore, $$\sum_k p_k \dot{q}_k = \sum_k \frac{\partial T}{\partial \dot{q}_k} \dot{q}_k = 2T$$

Therefore, the principle of least action (i) becomes

$$\Delta \int_{t_1}^{t_2} 2T \, dt = 0 \quad \text{or} \quad \Delta \int_{t_1}^{t_2} T \, dt = 0$$

This is another form of principle of least action.

> ***Note*** **(a)** Principle of least action in terms of path length $dp$ is given by
>
> $$\Delta \int_{t_1}^{t_2} \sqrt{2(H - V)} \, dp = 0$$
>
> which is also known as Jacobi's form of the principle of least action.
>
> Here, $H = T + V$,
>
> total energy is constant for conservative system.
>
> **(b)** Principle of least action in terms of arc length $ds$ of the particle trajectory is given by
>
> $$\Delta \int_{t_1}^{t_2} \sqrt{2m(H - V)} \, ds = 0$$
>
> where, $m$ is the mass of a particle in the system.

## Hamilton's Canonical Equations

The Hamiltonian, in general, is a function of generalized coordinates $q_k$, generalized momenta $p_k$ and time $t$, *i.e.*, $H = H(q_1, q_2, \ldots, q_k, \ldots, q_n, p_1, p_2, \ldots, p_k, \ldots, p_n, t)$

$$\Rightarrow \quad dH = \sum_k \frac{\partial H}{\partial q_k} dq_k + \sum_k \frac{\partial H}{\partial p_k} dp_k + \frac{\partial H}{\partial t} dt \quad \text{...(i)}$$

But Hamiltonian function $H$ is defined as

$$H = \sum_k p_k \dot{q}_k - L$$

$$\Rightarrow \quad dH = \sum_k \dot{q}_k dp_k + \sum_k p_k d\dot{q}_k - dL$$

$$dL = \sum_k \dot{q}_k dp_k + \sum_k p_k d\dot{q}_k - dH \quad \text{...(ii)}$$

Also,

$$L = L(q_1, q_2, \ldots, q_k, \ldots, q_n, \dot{q}_1, \dot{q}_2, \ldots, \dot{q}_k, \ldots, \dot{q}_n, t)$$

$$\Rightarrow \quad dL = \sum_k \frac{\partial L}{\partial q_k} dq_k + \sum_k \frac{\partial L}{\partial \dot{q}_k} d\dot{q}_k + \frac{\partial L}{\partial t} dt \quad \text{...(iii)}$$

Since, the generalized momentum corresponding to the generalized coordinate $q_k$ is

$$p_k = \frac{\partial L}{\partial \dot{q}_k}$$

From Lagrange's equations (For conservative holonomic system)

$$\frac{\partial L}{\partial q_k} - \frac{d}{dt}\left(\frac{\partial L}{\partial \dot{q}_k}\right) = 0$$

$$\Rightarrow \quad \frac{\partial L}{\partial q_k} - \frac{d}{dt}(p_k) = 0$$

$$\Rightarrow \quad \frac{\partial L}{\partial q_k} = \dot{p}_k$$

Now, from Eq. (iii), we get

$$dL = \sum_k \dot{p}_k dq_k + \sum_k p_k d\dot{q}_k + \frac{\partial L}{\partial t} dt \quad \text{...(iv)}$$

From Eqs. (ii) and (iv), we get

$$\sum_k \dot{q}_k dp_k - dH = \sum_k \dot{p}_k dq_k + \frac{\partial L}{\partial t} dt$$

$$\Rightarrow \quad dH = \sum_k \dot{q}_k dp_k - \sum_k \dot{p}_k dq_k - \frac{\partial L}{\partial t} dt \quad \text{...(v)}$$

Now, Eqs. (i) and (v) are identical

$$\therefore \quad \frac{\partial H}{\partial p_k} = \dot{q}_k \quad \text{...(vi)}$$

$$\frac{\partial H}{\partial q_k} = -\dot{p}_k \quad \text{...(vii)}$$

and $$\frac{\partial H}{\partial t} = -\frac{\partial L}{\partial t} \quad \text{...(viii)}$$

Eqs. (vi), (vii) and (viii) giving total of $2n + 1$ equations, [ $n$ equations each for Eqs. (vi) and (vii), 1 for Eq. (viii)] are called Hamilton's canonical equations of motion.

> ***Note*** **(a)** If any coordinate $q_k$ is cyclic *i.e.*, not contained in $H$, then
>
> $$\frac{\partial H}{\partial q_k} = 0 \Rightarrow \dot{p}_k = 0$$
>
> $\Rightarrow \quad p_k = \text{constant}$ [from Eq. (vii)]
>
> $\therefore$ From Eq. (i), we get
>
> $$dH = \frac{\partial H}{\partial t} dt$$
>
> $\Rightarrow \quad \dfrac{dH}{dt} = \dfrac{\partial H}{\partial t} = -\dfrac{\partial L}{\partial t}$ [from Eq. (viii)]
>
> **(b)** If $H$ does not contain $H$ explicitly, then Hamilton's canonical equations of motion reduces to
>
> $$\frac{\partial H}{\partial p_k} = \dot{q}_k \quad \text{and} \quad \frac{\partial H}{\partial q_k} = -\dot{p}_k$$

***Example 6.*** *Write Hamilton's equations of motion in cartesian coordinates.*

**Solution.** Kinetic energy of the particle is

$$T = \frac{1}{2} m(\dot{x}^2 + \dot{y}^2 + \dot{z}^2)$$

Potential energy of the particle is

$$V = V(x, y, z)$$

$\therefore$ Lagrangian $L = T - V = \frac{1}{2}m(\dot{x}^2 + \dot{y}^2 + \dot{z}^2) - V(x, y, z)$

Here, generalized coordinates are

$$q_1 = x,\ q_2 = y \text{ and } q_3 = z$$

Generalized momentum

$$p_k = \frac{\partial L}{\partial \dot{q}_k}, \quad k = 1, 2, 3, \ldots.$$

$$\Rightarrow \quad p_1 = \frac{\partial L}{\partial \dot{q}_1} = \frac{\partial L}{\partial \dot{x}} \quad (\because q_1 = x)$$

$$\Rightarrow \quad p_1 = m\dot{x}$$

$$\Rightarrow \quad \dot{x} = \frac{p_1}{m}$$

Similarly, $\dot{y} = \frac{p_2}{m}$

and $\dot{z} = \frac{p_3}{m}$

$\therefore$ Hamiltonian $H = \sum_k p_k \dot{q}_k - L,$ for $k = 1, 2, 3$

$$H = p_1\dot{q}_1 + p_2\dot{q}_2 + p_3\dot{q}_3 - L$$
$$= p_1\dot{x} + p_2\dot{y} + p_3\dot{z} - L$$
$$= \frac{p_1^2}{m} + \frac{p_2^2}{m} + \frac{p_3^2}{m} - L$$
$$= \frac{1}{m}(p_1^2 + p_2^2 + p_3^2) - L$$

Since, $L = \frac{1}{2}m(\dot{x}^2 + \dot{y}^2 + \dot{z}^2) - V(x, y, z)$

$$\Rightarrow \quad L = \frac{1}{2}m\left(\frac{p_1^2}{m^2} + \frac{p_2^2}{m^2} + \frac{p_3^2}{m^2}\right) - V(x, y, z)$$
$$= \frac{1}{2m}(p_1^2 + p_2^2 + p_3^2) - V(x, y, z)$$

$$\therefore \quad H = \frac{1}{2m}(p_1^2 + p_2^2 + p_3^2) + V(x, y, z)$$

Now, Hamilton's equations are

$$\frac{\partial H}{\partial p_k} = \dot{q}_k \text{ and } \frac{\partial H}{\partial q_k} = -\dot{p}_k$$

For $k = 1$, we get

$$\frac{\partial H}{\partial p_1} = \dot{q}_1 \text{ and } \frac{\partial H}{\partial q_1} = -\dot{p}_1$$

$$\Rightarrow \quad \frac{p_1}{m} = \dot{x} \text{ and } \frac{\partial H}{\partial x} = -\dot{p}_1$$

but $\frac{\partial H}{\partial x} = \frac{\partial V}{\partial x}$ and $\dot{p}_1 = m\ddot{x}$

$$\Rightarrow \quad \frac{\partial V}{\partial x} = -m\ddot{x} \quad \text{...(i)}$$

Similarly, for $k = 2$

$$\frac{\partial V}{\partial y} = -m\ddot{y} \quad \text{...(ii)}$$

and for $k = 3$

$$\frac{\partial V}{\partial z} = -m\ddot{z} \quad \text{...(iii)}$$

Eqs. (i), (ii) and (iii) are the required Hamiltons canonical equation of motion in cartesian coordinate.

***Example 7.*** *Write Hamilton's equations in polar coordinates.*

**Solution.** If $r$, $\theta$ are the polar coordinates of a particle of mass $m$, then

$$x = r\cos\theta,\ y = r\sin\theta$$

$$\Rightarrow \quad \dot{x} = \dot{r}\cos\theta - r\dot{\theta}\sin\theta,\ \dot{y} = \dot{r}\sin\theta + r\dot{\theta}\cos\theta$$

Kinetic energy,

$$T = \frac{1}{2}m(\dot{x}^2 + \dot{y}^2) = \frac{1}{2}m(\dot{r}^2 + r^2\dot{\theta}^2)$$

Potential energy $= V(r, \theta)$

$$\therefore \quad L = T - V = \frac{1}{2}m(\dot{r}^2 + r^2\dot{\theta}^2) - V(r, \theta)$$

Here, $q_1 = r, \quad q_2 = \theta$

$\therefore$ Generalised momenta are

$$p_1 = \frac{\partial L}{\partial \dot{q}_1} \Rightarrow p_r = \frac{\partial L}{\partial \dot{r}} = m\dot{r}$$

$$p_2 = \frac{\partial L}{\partial \dot{q}_2} \Rightarrow p_\theta = \frac{\partial L}{\partial \dot{\theta}} = mr^2\dot{\theta}$$

$$\therefore \quad \dot{r} = \frac{p_r}{m}, \quad \dot{\theta} = \frac{p_\theta}{mr^2}$$

Thus, $H = \sum_k p_k \dot{q}_k - L$

$$= p_r\dot{r} + p_\theta\dot{\theta} - \frac{1}{2}m(\dot{r}^2 + r^2\dot{\theta}^2) + V(r, \theta)$$

$$\Rightarrow \quad H = \frac{1}{2m}\left(p_r^2 + \frac{p_\theta^2}{r^2}\right) + V(r, \theta)$$

$\therefore$ Hamilton's equations are

$$\frac{\partial H}{\partial p_k} = \dot{q}_k \text{ and } \frac{\partial H}{\partial q_k} = -\dot{p}_k$$

For $k = 1$

$$\Rightarrow \quad \frac{\partial H}{\partial p_1} = \dot{q}_1 \text{ and } \frac{\partial H}{\partial q_1} = -\dot{p}_1$$

$$\Rightarrow \quad \frac{\partial H}{\partial p_r} = \dot{r} \text{ and } \frac{\partial H}{\partial r} = -\dot{p}_r$$

$$\Rightarrow \quad \frac{p_r}{m} = \dot{r} \text{ and } \frac{p_\theta^2}{mr^3} + \frac{\partial V}{\partial r} = -\dot{p}_r$$

$$\Rightarrow \quad \frac{p_r}{m} = \dot{r} \text{ and } \frac{p_\theta^2}{mr^3} - \frac{\partial V}{\partial r} = \dot{p}_r \quad \text{...(i)}$$

Similarly, for $k = 2$

$$\frac{p_\theta}{mr^2} = \dot{\theta} \text{ and } -\frac{\partial V}{\partial \theta} = \dot{p}_\theta \quad \text{...(ii)}$$

Eqs. (i) and (ii) are the required Hamilton's equation of motion in polar coordinates.

***Example 8.*** *Write the Hamiltonian for a simple pendulum and deduce its equations of motion.*

**Solution.** Since, in simple pendulum, Lagrangian

$$L = T - V = \frac{1}{2}ml^2\dot{\theta}^2 - mgl(1 - \cos\theta)$$

$$\therefore \quad \frac{\partial L}{\partial \theta} = ml^2\dot{\theta} \Rightarrow \quad p_\theta = ml^2\dot{\theta}$$

Now, Hamiltonian $\quad H = \sum_k p_k \dot{q}_k - L$

Here, $k = 1 \quad (q_1 = \theta)$

$$H = p_1\dot{q}_1 - L = p_\theta\dot{\theta} - L$$

$$\Rightarrow \quad H = ml^2\dot{\theta}^2 - \frac{1}{2}ml^2\dot{\theta}^2 + mgl(1-\cos\theta)$$

$$= \frac{1}{2}ml^2\dot{\theta}^2 + mgl(1-\cos\theta)$$

$$= \frac{1}{2}ml^2\left(\frac{p_\theta}{ml^2}\right)^2 + mgl(1-\cos\theta)$$

Now, Hamilton's equation is

$$\frac{\partial H}{\partial p_\theta} = \dot{\theta} \quad \text{and} \quad \frac{\partial H}{\partial \theta} = -\dot{p}_\theta$$

$$\Rightarrow \quad \dot{\theta} = \frac{p_\theta}{ml^2} \text{ and } mgl\sin\theta = -\dot{p}_\theta$$

$$\Rightarrow \quad ml^2\ddot{\theta} = \dot{p}_\theta = -mgl\sin\theta$$

$$\Rightarrow \quad l\ddot{\theta} = -g\sin\theta$$

$$\Rightarrow \quad l\ddot{\theta} = -g\theta \quad \text{(For small angle } \sin\theta \cong \theta)$$

$$\Rightarrow \quad \ddot{\theta} + \frac{g}{l}\theta = 0$$

which is equation of motion of simple pendulum.

***Example 9.*** *Describe the Hamiltonian and Hamilton's equations for an ideal spring mass arrangement.*

**Solution.** $\quad L = \frac{1}{2}m\dot{x}^2 - \frac{1}{2}kx^2$

where $k$ is the force constant of the spring.

$$p_x = \frac{\partial L}{\partial \dot{x}} = m\dot{x} \quad \text{or} \quad \dot{x} = \frac{p_x}{m}$$

$$H = \sum_k p_k\dot{q}_k - L = p_x\dot{x} - \left[\frac{1}{2}m\dot{x}^2 - \frac{1}{2}kx^2\right] = \frac{1}{2}m\dot{x}^2 + \frac{1}{2}kx^2$$

$$\Rightarrow \quad H = \frac{p_x^2}{2m} + \frac{1}{2}kx^2$$

Hamilton's equations are

$$\dot{x} = \frac{\partial H}{\partial p_x} = \frac{p_x}{m} \text{ and } \dot{p}_x = -\frac{\partial H}{\partial x} = -kx$$

Thus, the equation of motion of spring-mass system is

$$m\ddot{x} = -kx \quad \Rightarrow \quad \ddot{x} + \frac{k}{m}x = 0$$

***Example 10.*** *Using Hamilton's equations of motion, show that the Hamiltonian*

$$H = \frac{p^2}{2m}e^{-rt} + \frac{1}{2}m\omega^2x^2e^{rt}$$

*leads to the equation of motion of a damped harmonic oscillator*

$$\ddot{x} + r\dot{x} + \omega^2x = 0$$

**Solution.** Equations of motion are

$$\dot{q} = \frac{\partial H}{\partial p} \quad \text{and} \quad \dot{p} = -\frac{\partial H}{\partial q}$$

For $q = x$,

$$\dot{x} = \frac{\partial H}{\partial p} \quad \text{and} \quad \dot{p} = -\frac{\partial H}{\partial x}$$

Here, $\quad \dot{x} = \frac{p}{m}e^{-rt}$ and $\dot{p} = -m\omega^2xe^{rt}$

whence $\quad p = m\dot{x}e^{rt}$ and $\dot{p} = m\ddot{x}e^{rt} + mr\dot{x}e^{rt}$

Substituting for $\dot{p}$ in Eq. (i), we get

$$m\ddot{x}e^{rt} + mr\dot{x}e^{rt} = -m\omega^2xe^{rt}$$

$$\Rightarrow \quad \ddot{x} + r\dot{x} + \omega^2x = 0$$

which is the desired equation of damped harmonic oscillator.

***Example 11.*** *Write Hamilton's equations of motion for a particle moving in the XY-plane under the influence of a central force with inverse square law.*

**Solution.** Kinetic energy

$$T = \frac{1}{2}m(\dot{r}^2 + r^2\dot{\theta}^2)$$

Potential energy $= V(r)$

$$\left(\text{Since, } F \propto \frac{1}{r^2} \text{ and } F = -\frac{dV}{dr} = -\frac{\partial V}{\partial r}\right)$$

$$\therefore \quad L = T - V = \frac{1}{2}m(\dot{r}^2 + r^2\dot{\theta}^2) - V(r)$$

Here, $\quad q_1 = r,\ q_2 = \theta$

$\therefore$ Generalized momenta are

$$p_1 = \frac{\partial L}{\partial \dot{q}_1} \quad \Rightarrow \quad p_r = \frac{\partial L}{\partial \dot{r}} = m\dot{r}$$

$$p_2 = \frac{\partial L}{\partial \dot{q}_2}, \quad \Rightarrow \quad p_\theta = \frac{\partial L}{\partial \dot{\theta}} = mr^2\dot{\theta}$$

$$\therefore \quad \dot{r} = \frac{p_r}{m} \quad \text{and} \quad \dot{\theta} = \frac{p_\theta}{mr^2}$$

Hence, $\quad H = T + V$

$$= \frac{1}{2}m\left[\frac{p_r^2}{m^2} + r^2\frac{p_\theta^2}{m^2r^4}\right] + V(r)$$

$$= \frac{1}{2m}\left[p_r^2 + \frac{p_\theta^2}{r^2}\right] + V(r)$$

The Hamilton's equations are

For $k = 1$

$$\frac{\partial H}{\partial p_1} = \dot{q}_1 \quad \text{and} \quad \frac{\partial H}{\partial q_1} = -\dot{p}_1$$

$$\Rightarrow \quad \frac{\partial H}{\partial p_r} = \dot{r} \quad \text{and} \quad \frac{\partial H}{\partial r} = -\dot{p}_r$$

$$\Rightarrow \quad \frac{p_r}{m} = \dot{r} \quad \text{and} \quad -\frac{p_\theta^2}{mr^3} + \frac{\partial V}{\partial r} = -\dot{p}_r$$

$$\Rightarrow \quad \frac{p_\theta^2}{mr^3} - \frac{\partial V}{\partial r} = m\ddot{r} \quad \text{...(i)}$$

For $k = 2$

$$\frac{\partial H}{\partial p_2} = \dot{q}_2 \quad \text{and} \quad \frac{\partial H}{\partial q_2} = -\dot{p}_2$$

$$\Rightarrow \quad \frac{\partial H}{\partial p_\theta} = \dot{\theta} \quad \text{and} \quad \frac{\partial H}{\partial \theta} = -\dot{p}_\theta$$

$$\Rightarrow \quad \frac{p_\theta}{mr^2} = \dot{\theta} \quad \text{and} \quad 0 = -\dot{p}_\theta$$

$$\Rightarrow \quad p_\theta = mr^2\dot{\theta} \quad \text{and} \quad p_\theta = \text{constant}$$

$$\Rightarrow \quad mr^2\dot{\theta} = \text{constant} \qquad \text{...(ii)}$$

Eqs. (i) and (ii) are the required equation of motions.

# Motion of a Rigid Body

A rigid body is defined as a system of particles in which the distance between any two particles remains fixed throughout the motion. Thus, a system of $N$ particles is said to be a rigid body, if it is subjected to holonomic constraints of the form

$r_{ij} = C_{ij}$

where, $r_{ij}$ is the distance between $i$th and $j$th particles and $C_{ij}$ is the constant.

Number of degrees of freedom for the general motion of a rigid body is six. *i.e.*, six independent coordinates are needed to specify the motion.

Consider three non-collinear particles $P_1$, $P_2$ and $P_3$ in a rigid body.

As each particle has three degrees of freedom, subjected to three equations of constraints *i.e.*, $r_{12}$, $r_{23}$, $r_{13}$.

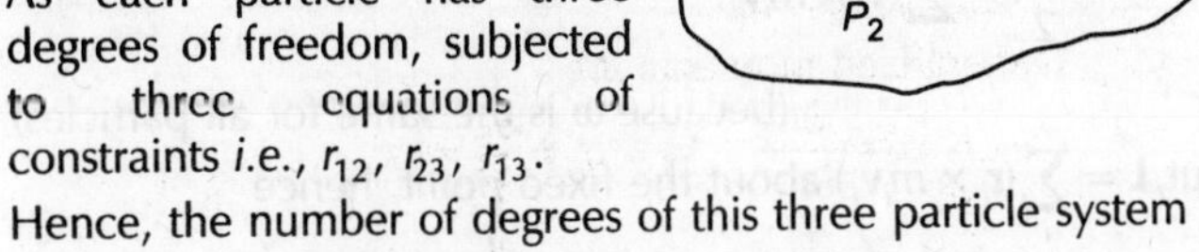

Hence, the number of degrees of this three particle system is

$$= 9 - 3 = 6$$

We may describe the motion of a rigid body by using two coordinate systems.

## 1. Space Coordinate System

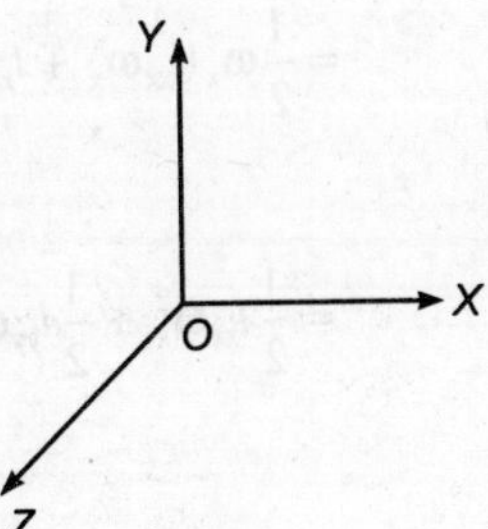


The axes of such a coordinate system are fixed in the space are called space set of axes.

In figure $XYZ$ represents the space reference system with origin $O$.

## 2. Body Coordinate System

A coordinate system, fixed in the rigid body is called a body coordinate system and its axes are called body set of axes.

In figure $X'Y'Z'$ represents the body coordinate system, fixed in the rigid body with origin $O'$. We choose the origin $O'$ of the body set of axes such that it coincide with the centre of mass of the rigid body. Clearly, three coordinates are required to specify $O'$ relative to $O$. Also, for the general motion of the rigid body three angles relative to $O$ are required and hence six independent coordinates which provide complete configuration of the rigid body in motion at any instant of time.

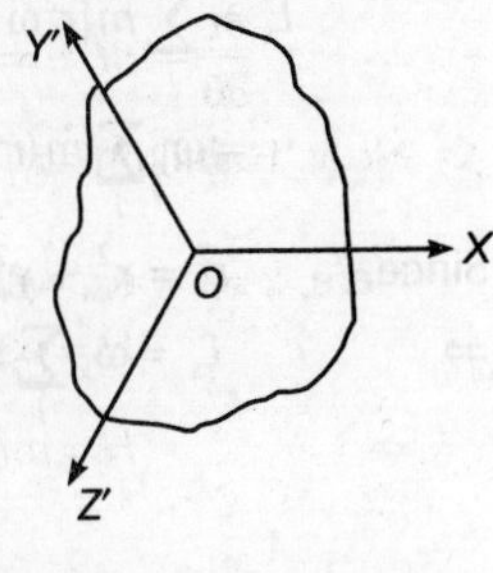


These angles may be chosen in various ways, but the most commonly used set of three angles are the Euler's angles, represented by $\phi$ (First rotation), $\theta$ (second rotation) and $\psi$ (third rotation).

$\phi$, $\theta$ and $\psi$ are respectively called precession angle, nutation angle and body angle.

If $\phi$, $\theta$ and $\psi$ represent the Euler's angles, then the time derivatives $\dot{\phi}$, $\dot{\theta}$ and $\dot{\psi}$ represent the angular speeds about the space $Z$-axis, line of nodes (intersection of two XY-plane as a result of second rotation ($\theta$)) and body $Z'$-axis, respectively. We denote these three angular speeds by $\omega_\phi$, $\omega_\theta$ and $\omega_\psi$ as a three components of the angular velocity. But the rigid body describes the motion in terms of body coordinate system. The angular velocity components $\omega_{x'}(=\omega_1)$, $\omega_{y'}(=\omega_2)$, $\omega_{z'}(=\omega_3)$ along the body set of axes are as follows.

$$\omega_1 = \dot{\phi}\sin\theta\sin\psi + \dot{\theta}\cos\psi$$

$$\omega_2 = \dot{\phi}\sin\theta\cos\psi - \dot{\theta}\sin\psi$$

$$\omega_3 = \dot{\phi}\cos\theta + \dot{\psi}$$

These equations are known as Euler's geometrical equations.

Now, motion of a rigid body is described in the following terms.

### (i) Angular Momentum ($L$)

Let rigid body rotates about a fixed point $O$ in the body with angular velocity $\omega$.

A particle $P$ of the body with position vector $\mathbf{r}_i$ with respect to $O$ and has an linear velocity $\mathbf{v}_i$, then

$$\mathbf{v}_i = \omega \times \mathbf{r}_i$$

$(\mathbf{r}_i = x_i\mathbf{i} + y_i\mathbf{j} + z_i\mathbf{k})$

Let $OXYZ$ be the body set of axes fixed in the body. The angular velocity $\omega$ has components $\omega_x$, $\omega_y$, $\omega_z$ along $X$, $Y$, $Z$ axes, respectively and is given by

$$\omega = \omega_x\mathbf{i} + \omega_y\mathbf{j} + \omega_z\mathbf{k}$$

The angular momentum of the particle at $P$ about the point $O$ is given by

$$\mathbf{L}_P = \mathbf{r}_i \times m_i\mathbf{v}_i$$

where, $m_i$ is the mass of the particle at $P$.

Hence, the angular momentum $\mathbf{L}$ of the entire body about the point $O$ is

$$\mathbf{L} = \sum_i \mathbf{r}_i \times m_i\mathbf{v}_i = \sum_i m_i\mathbf{r}_i \times (\omega \times \mathbf{r}_i)$$

$$= \sum_i m_i[(\mathbf{r}_i \cdot \mathbf{r}_i)\omega - (\mathbf{r}_i \cdot \omega)\mathbf{r}_i]$$

$$= \sum_i m_i[r_i^2\omega - (\mathbf{r}_i \cdot \omega)\mathbf{r}_i]$$

If $L_x$, $L_y$ and $L_z$ are the components of $L$ along $X$, $Y$ and $Z$-axes respectively, then

$$L_x = \sum_i m_i[r_i^2\omega_x - (x_i\omega_x + y_i\omega_y + z_i\omega_z)x_i]$$

$$= \omega_x \sum_i m_i(r_i^2 - x_i^2) - \omega_Z \sum_i m_i x_i y_i - \omega_z \sum_i m_i x_i z_i$$

Since, $r_i^2 = x_i^2 + y_i^2 + z_i^2$

$$\Rightarrow \quad L_x = \omega_x \sum_i m_i(y_i^2 + z_i^2) - \omega_y \sum_i m_i x_i y_i - \omega_z \sum_i m_i x_i z_i \quad \text{...(i)}$$

Taking $I_{xx} = \sum_i m_i(y_i^2 + z_i^2)$ as the moment of inertia of the body about $X$-axis.

$$I_{xy} = -\sum_i m_i x_i y_i = I_{yx}$$

and $I_{xz} = -\sum_i m_i x_i z_i = I_{zx}$

as the product of inertia, then Eq. (i) becomes

$$L_x = I_{xx}\,\omega_x + I_{xy}\,\omega_y + I_{xz}\,\omega_z \quad \text{...(ii)}$$

By symmetry, we can write

$$L_y = I_{yx}\,\omega_x + I_{yy}\,\omega_y + I_{yz}\,\omega_z \quad \text{...(iii)}$$

$$L_z = I_{zx}\,\omega_x + I_{zy}\,\omega_y + I_{zz}\,\omega_z \quad \text{...(iv)}$$

In matrix form Eqs. (ii), (iii) and (iv) may be written as

$$\begin{pmatrix} L_x \\ L_y \\ L_z \end{pmatrix} = \begin{pmatrix} I_{xx} & I_{xy} & I_{xz} \\ I_{yx} & I_{yy} & I_{yz} \\ I_{zx} & I_{zy} & I_{zz} \end{pmatrix} \begin{pmatrix} \omega_x \\ \omega_y \\ \omega_z \end{pmatrix} \quad \text{...(v)}$$

or $\qquad \mathbf{L} = I\omega \qquad$ ...(vi)

where, matrix $I$ is called inertia tensor.

### (ii) Principal Moments of Inertia

If we choose the axes of the coordinate system fixed in the body with respect to which off diagonal elements disappear and only the diagonal elements remain in the inertia tensor, then such axes are called the principal axes of the body and the corresponding moments of inertia as the principal moments of inertia. In general, the directions of the principal axes are different to those of arbitrary axes fixed in the body. If we denote the principal axes by $X'$, $Y'$, $Z'$, then Eq. (v) becomes

$$\begin{pmatrix} L_1 \\ L_2 \\ L_3 \end{pmatrix} = \begin{pmatrix} I_1 & 0 & 0 \\ 0 & I_2 & 0 \\ 0 & 0 & I_3 \end{pmatrix} \begin{pmatrix} \omega_1 \\ \omega_2 \\ \omega_3 \end{pmatrix}$$

or $\qquad L_1 = I_1\,\omega_1, \; L_2 = I_2\omega_2$ and $L_3 = I_3\omega_3$

Thus, in general, if a rigid body rotates about a principal axis, $L$ and $\omega$ are directed along any of the principal axes, then from Eq. (vi)

$$\mathbf{L} = I\omega$$

We can write

$$L_x\mathbf{i} + L_y\mathbf{j} + L_z\mathbf{k} = I(\omega_x\mathbf{i} + \omega_y\mathbf{j} + \omega_z\mathbf{k})$$

$$\Rightarrow \quad L_x = I\omega_x, \; L_y = I\omega_y, \; L_z = I\omega_z$$

and then Eq. (v) changes to

$$\begin{pmatrix} I_{xx} - I & I_{xy} & I_{xz} \\ I_{yx} & I_{yy} - I & I_{yz} \\ I_{zx} & I_{zy} & I_{zz} - I \end{pmatrix} \begin{pmatrix} \omega_x \\ \omega_y \\ \omega_z \end{pmatrix} = 0 \quad \text{...(vii)}$$

For non-trivial solutions of Eq. (vii), we get

$$\begin{vmatrix} I_{xx} - I & I_{xy} & I_{xz} \\ I_{yx} & I_{yy} - I & I_{yz} \\ I_{zx} & I_{zy} & I_{zz} - I \end{vmatrix} = 0 \quad \text{...(viii)}$$

which is called secular or characteristic equation and its solutions are called eigen values. Eq. (viii) is a cubic in $I$ giving three solutions $I_1$, $I_2$, $I_3$ are the three principal moments of inertia.

### (iii) Rotational Kinetic Energy

Total kinetic energy of the entire body is given by

$$T = \sum_i \frac{1}{2} m_i v_i^2 = \sum_i \frac{1}{2} m_i \mathbf{v}_i \cdot \mathbf{v}_i = \frac{1}{2} \sum \mathbf{v}_i \cdot m_i \mathbf{v}_i$$

$$= \frac{1}{2} \sum_i (\omega \times \mathbf{r}_i) \cdot m_i \mathbf{v}_i$$

$$= \frac{1}{2} \sum_i \omega \cdot (\mathbf{r}_i \times m_i \mathbf{v}_i) \quad [\because (A \times B) \cdot C = A \cdot (B \times C)]$$

$$= \frac{1}{2} \omega \cdot \sum_i (\mathbf{r}_i \times m_i \mathbf{v}_i)$$

(because $\omega$ is the same for all particles)

But, $\mathbf{L} = \sum_i (\mathbf{r}_i \times m_i \mathbf{v}_i)$ about the fixed point, hence

$$T = \frac{1}{2} \omega \cdot \mathbf{L} \quad \text{...(i)}$$

Which is a scalar Eq. (i) can also be written as

$$T = \frac{1}{2}\omega_x L_x + \frac{1}{2}\omega_y L_y + \frac{1}{2}\omega_z L_z$$

$$= \frac{1}{2}\omega_x(I_{xx}\omega_x + I_{xy}\omega_y + I_{xz}\omega_z) + \frac{1}{2}\omega_y(I_{yx}\omega_x + I_{yy}\omega_y + I_{yz}\omega_z) + \frac{1}{2}\omega_z(I_{zx}\omega_x + I_{zy}\omega_y + I_{zz}\omega_z)$$

$$= \frac{1}{2} I_{xx}\omega_x^2 + \frac{1}{2} I_{yy}\omega_y^2 + \frac{1}{2} I_{zz}\omega_z^2 + I_{xy}\omega_x\omega_y + I_{yz}\omega_y\omega_z + I_{zz}\omega_z\omega_x \quad \text{...(ii)}$$

(Since, $I_{xy} = I_{yx}$, $I_{yz} = I_{zy}$, $I_{xz} = I_{zx}$)

In terms of $I_1$, $I_2$ and $I_3$ rotational kinetic energy in principal axes coordinate system is

$$T = \frac{1}{2}\omega \cdot \mathbf{L} = \frac{1}{2}\omega_1 L_1 + \frac{1}{2}\omega_2 L_2 + \frac{1}{2}\omega_3 L_3$$

$$= \frac{1}{2} I_1\omega_1^2 + \frac{1}{2} I_2\omega_2^2 + \frac{1}{2} I_3\omega_3^2$$

## Euler's Equations of Motion for a Rigid Body

If a rigid body is rotating under the action of a torque $\tau$ with one point fixed, then the torque is given by

$$\tau = \frac{d\mathbf{L}}{dt} + \omega \times \mathbf{L} \qquad ...(i)$$

where, $\omega$ is the angular velocity and $\mathbf{L}$ is the angular momentum of the rigid body in body coordinate system.

If $I_1$, $I_2$ and $I_3$ are the principal moments of inertia, then

$$\mathbf{L} = I_1\omega_1\mathbf{i} + I_2\omega_2\mathbf{j} + I_3\omega_3\mathbf{k}$$

where, $\omega_1$, $\omega_2$ and $\omega_3$ are the components of $\omega$ along the principal axes.

Since, principal moments of inertia are constants

$$\therefore \quad \frac{d\mathbf{L}}{dt} = I_1\dot{\omega}_1\mathbf{i} + I_2\dot{\omega}_2\mathbf{j} + I_3\dot{\omega}_3\mathbf{k}$$

Now, from Eq. (i), we get

$$\tau = I_1\dot{\omega}_1\mathbf{i} + I_2\dot{\omega}_2\mathbf{j} + I_3\dot{\omega}_3\mathbf{k} + (\omega_1\mathbf{i} + \omega_2\mathbf{j} + \omega_3\mathbf{k}) \times (I_1\omega_1\mathbf{i} + I_2\omega_2\mathbf{j} + I_3\omega_3\mathbf{k})$$

For $\tau = \tau_1\mathbf{i} + \tau_2\mathbf{j} + \tau_3\mathbf{k}$, we obtain

$$\tau_1 = I_1\dot{\omega}_1 - (I_2 - I_3)\omega_2\omega_3 \qquad ...(ii)$$

$$\tau_2 = I_2\dot{\omega}_2 - (I_3 - I_1)\omega_3\omega_1 \qquad ...(iii)$$

$$\tau_3 = I_3\dot{\omega}_3 - (I_1 - I_2)\omega_1\omega_2 \qquad ...(iv)$$

Eqs, (ii), (iii) and (iv) are known as Euler's equations for the motion of a rigid body with one point fixed under the action of a torque.

***Case* I** In case a rigid body is rotating about a fixed axis, say principal $Z$-axis, then

$$\omega_1 = \omega_2 = 0 \text{ and } \omega_3 = \omega$$

and equations of motions reduces to

$$\tau_1 = \tau_2 = 0$$

and $\quad \tau_3 = I_3\dot{\omega}_3$

$$\Rightarrow \quad \tau = I\dot{\omega}$$

(Here, we have put $\tau_3 = \tau$ and $I_3 = I$ corresponding to $Z$-axis)

Also, angular momentum about $Z$-axis is

$$L_3 = I_3\omega_3$$

$$\Rightarrow \quad L = I\omega$$

and rotational kinetic energy (instantaneous) is

$$T = \frac{1}{2}I_3\omega_3^2 = \frac{1}{2}I\omega^2$$

***Case* II** When a rigid body is not subjected to any net torque *i.e.*,

$$\tau_1 = \tau_2 = \tau_3 = 0$$

$\therefore$ Euler's equations of motion becomes

$$I_1\dot{\omega}_1 = (I_2 - I_3)\omega_2\omega_3 \qquad ...(i)$$

$$I_2\dot{\omega}_2 = (I_3 - I_1)\omega_3\omega_1 \qquad ...(ii)$$

$$I_3\dot{\omega}_3 = (I_1 - I_2)\omega_1\omega_2 \qquad ...(iii)$$

Multiplying Eqs. (i), (ii) and (iii) by $\omega_1$, $\omega_2$ and $\omega_3$, respectively and adding, we get

$$I_1\omega_1\dot{\omega}_1 + I_2\omega_2\dot{\omega}_2 + I_3\omega_3\dot{\omega}_3 = (I_2 - I_3 + I_3 - I_1 + I_1 - I_2)\,\omega_1\omega_2\omega_3 = 0$$

$$\Rightarrow \quad \frac{d}{dt}\left(\frac{1}{2}I_1\omega_1^2 + \frac{1}{2}I_2\omega_2^2 + \frac{1}{2}I_3\omega_3^2\right) = 0$$

$$\Rightarrow \quad \frac{1}{2}I_1\omega_1^2 + \frac{1}{2}I_2\omega_2^2 + \frac{1}{2}I_3\omega_3^2 = \frac{1}{2}\omega \cdot \mathbf{L} = \text{constant}$$

which is the principle of conservation of total rotational kinetic energy in absence of external torque.

Also, $\quad \tau = \dfrac{d\mathbf{L}}{dt} = 0$

$$\Rightarrow \quad \mathbf{L} = I_1\omega_1\mathbf{i} + I_2\omega_2\mathbf{j} + I_3\omega_3\mathbf{k} = \text{constant}$$

which is the principle of conservation of angular momentum.

***Case* III** In case of force free motion of a symmetrical rigid body *i.e.*, a symmetrical top, for which $I_1 = I_2$ and the third principal axis ($Z$-axis) is the axis of symmetry of the body. In such a case Euler's equations becomes

$$I_1\dot{\omega}_1 = (I_1 - I_3)\omega_2\omega_3 \qquad ...(i)$$

$$I_1\dot{\omega}_2 = (I_3 - I_1)\omega_3\omega_1 \qquad ...(ii)$$

$$\dot{\omega}_3 = 0 \qquad ...(iii)$$

From Eq. (iii), we get

$$\omega_3 = \text{constant} \qquad ...(iv)$$

Multiplying Eqs. (i) and (ii) by $\omega_1$ and $\omega_2$, respectively and adding, we get

$$I_1\dot{\omega}_1\omega_1 + I_1\dot{\omega}_2\omega_2 = (I_1 - I_3 + I_3 - I_1)\omega_1\omega_2\omega_3 = 0$$

$$\Rightarrow \quad \omega_1\dot{\omega}_1 + \omega_2\dot{\omega}_2 = 0$$

$$\Rightarrow \quad \frac{1}{2}\frac{d}{dt}(\omega_1^2 + \omega_2^2) = 0$$

$$\Rightarrow \quad \omega_1^2 + \omega_2^2 = \text{constant} = \omega_c^2 \qquad ...(v)$$

It is an equation of a circle with radius $\omega_c$.

Hence, the total angular velocity is given by

$$\omega = \omega_1\mathbf{i} + \omega_2\mathbf{j} + \omega_3\mathbf{k}$$

$$\Rightarrow \quad |\omega| = \sqrt{\omega_1^2 + \omega_2^2 + \omega_3^2} = \text{constant}$$

[from Eqs. (iv) and (v)]

$$\Rightarrow \quad \omega = \text{constant}$$

> ***Note*** **(a)** Kinetic energy $T = \frac{1}{2}I_1\omega_c^2 + \frac{1}{2}I_3\omega_3^2$
>
> **(b)** Angular momentum $L^2 = I_1^2\omega_c^2 + I_3^2\omega_3^2$

***Case* IV** If we put $\alpha = \dfrac{I_3 - I_1}{I_1} = \omega_3 = \text{constant}$

In first two equations of Euler's equations of motion in case of Case III, we get

$$\dot{\omega}_1 = \left(\frac{I_1 - I_3}{I_1}\omega_3\right)\omega_2 = -\alpha\omega_2 \qquad ...(i)$$

and $\quad \dot{\omega}_2 = \left(\dfrac{I_3 - I_1}{I_1}\omega_3\right)\omega_1 = \alpha\omega_1 \qquad ...(ii)$

From Eq. (i), we get

$$\ddot{\omega}_1 = -\alpha\dot{\omega}_2$$

$$\Rightarrow \quad \ddot{\omega}_1 = -\alpha(\alpha\omega_1) \qquad \text{[from Eq. (ii)]}$$

$$\Rightarrow \quad \ddot{\omega}_1 = -\alpha^2\omega_1$$

$$\Rightarrow \quad \ddot{\omega}_1 + \alpha^2\omega_1 = 0$$

$$\Rightarrow \quad \omega_1 = a\cos\alpha t + b\sin\alpha t = \sqrt{a^2 + b^2}\sin(\alpha t + \beta) = c\sin(\alpha t + \beta)$$

At $t = 0$, $\omega_1 = 0$

$$\Rightarrow \quad \beta = 0$$

$$\therefore \quad \omega_1 = c\sin\alpha t$$

Taking $c = \omega_c$, we get

$$\omega_1 = \omega_c\sin\alpha\, t$$

From Eq. (i), $\dot{\omega}_1 = -\alpha\omega_2$

$\Rightarrow \quad \alpha\omega_c \cos\alpha t = -\alpha\omega_2$

$\Rightarrow \quad \omega_2 = -\omega_c \cos\alpha t$

$\therefore \quad \omega_1^2 + \omega_2^2 = \omega_c^2$

Hence, $\omega_1$ and $\omega_2$ satisfy simple harmonic equations.

> ***Note*** Frequency and period of precession of angular velocity $\omega$ about the axis of symmetry (Z-axis) are respectively given by
>
> $$f = \frac{\alpha}{2\pi} \Rightarrow f = \frac{\omega_3}{2\pi}\frac{I_3 - I_1}{I_1}$$
>
> and $$T = \frac{2\pi}{\omega_3}\frac{I_1}{I_3 - I_1}$$

***Example 12.*** *A body under the action of no forces moves so that the resolved part of its angular velocity about one of the principal axes at the centre of gravity is constant. Show that the angular velocity of the body must be constant.*

**Solution.** Let $\omega_1$, $\omega_2$ and $\omega_3$ are the angular velocities about the CG axes and $I_1, I_2$ and $I_3$ are the principal moments of inertia at the CG, then Euler's equations of motion under no forces are

$$I_1\dot{\omega}_1 = (I_2 - I_3)\,\omega_2\omega_3 \quad \text{...(i)}$$

$$I_2\dot{\omega}_2 = (I_3 - I_1)\,\omega_3\omega_1 \quad \text{...(ii)}$$

$$I_3\dot{\omega}_3 = (I_1 - I_2)\,\omega_1\omega_2 \quad \text{...(iii)}$$

Multiplying Eqs. (i), (ii) and (iii) by $\omega_1, \omega_2$ and $\omega_3$, respectively and adding, we get

$$I_1\omega_1\dot{\omega}_1 + I_2\omega_2\dot{\omega}_2 + I_3\omega_3\dot{\omega}_3 = 0$$

After integration it becomes

$$I_1\omega_1^2 + I_2\omega_2^2 + I_3\omega_3^2 = \text{constant} \quad \text{...(iv)}$$

Now, from given problem, it is given that one angular velocity is constant.

$\therefore$ Let $\omega_1$ = constant. Now, two cases arise

**Case I** When $I_2 = I_3$. Then, from Eq. (iv),

$$\omega_2^2 + \omega_3^2 = \text{constant}$$

$\Rightarrow \quad \omega_1^2 + \omega_2^2 + \omega_3^2 = \text{constant}$

$\Rightarrow \quad |\omega| = \text{constant} \quad (\text{Since, } \omega_1 = \text{constant})$

**Case II** When $I_2 \neq I_3$. Then, from Eq. (i)

$$\omega_2\omega_3 = 0 \qquad (\text{Since, } \dot{\omega}_1 = 0)$$

$\therefore$ Either $\omega_2 = 0$ or $\omega_3 = 0$

If $\omega_2 = 0$, then from Eq. (iii),

$$\omega_3 = \text{constant}$$

$\Rightarrow \quad \omega_1^2 + \omega_2^2 + \omega_3^2 = \text{constant}$

and if $\omega_3 = 0$, then from Eq. (ii),

$$\omega_2 = \text{constant}$$

$\Rightarrow \quad \omega_1^2 + \omega_2^2 + \omega_3^2 = \text{constant}$

$\Rightarrow \quad |\omega| = \text{constant}$

Therefore, angular velocity of the body must be constant.

***Example 13.*** *A body moves about a point O under no forces, the principal moments of inertia at O being 3A, 5A and 6A. Initially angular velocity has components $\omega_1 = n$, $\omega_2 = 0$, $\omega_3 = n$ about the corresponding principal axes. Show that any time t, $\omega_2 = \frac{3n}{\sqrt{5}}\tanh\left(\frac{nt}{\sqrt{5}}\right)$ and the body ultimately rotates about its mean axis.*

**Solution.** Euler's equations of motion under no forces are

$$I_1\dot{\omega}_1 - (I_2 - I_3)\,\omega_2\omega_3 = 0 \quad \text{...(i)}$$

$$I_2\dot{\omega}_2 - (I_3 - I_1)\,\omega_3\omega_1 = 0 \quad \text{...(ii)}$$

and $$I_3\dot{\omega}_3 - (I_1 - I_2)\,\omega_1\omega_2 = 0 \quad \text{...(iii)}$$

Given, $I_1 = 3A$, $I_2 = 5A$ and $I_3 = 6A$

From Eq. (i), we have

$$3A\dot{\omega}_1 - (5A - 6A)\,\omega_2\omega_3 = 0$$

$\Rightarrow \quad 3A\dot{\omega}_1 + A\omega_2\omega_3 = 0$

$\Rightarrow \quad 3\dot{\omega}_1 = -\omega_2\omega_3 \quad \text{...(iv)}$

From Eq. (ii), we have

$$5A\dot{\omega}_2 - (6A - 3A)\,\omega_3\omega_1 = 0$$

$\Rightarrow \quad 5A\dot{\omega}_2 - 3A\omega_3\omega_1 = 0$

$\Rightarrow \quad 5\dot{\omega}_2 = 3\omega_3\omega_1 \quad \text{...(v)}$

From Eq. (iii), we have

$$6A\dot{\omega}_3 - (3A - 5A)\,\omega_1\omega_2 = 0$$

$\Rightarrow \quad 6A\dot{\omega}_3 + 2A\omega_1\omega_2 = 0$

$\Rightarrow \quad 3\dot{\omega}_3 = -\omega_1\omega_2 \quad \text{...(vi)}$

Multiplying Eq. (iv) by $3\omega_1$ and Eq. (v) by $\omega_2$ and adding, we get

$$9\omega_1\dot{\omega}_1 + 5\omega_2\dot{\omega}_2 = 0$$

which on integration gives

$$9\omega_1^2 + 5\omega_2^2 = \text{constant} = a \text{ (say)} \quad \text{...(vii)}$$

From given,

$$\omega_1 = n \text{ and } \omega_2 = 0$$

From Eq. (vii), $\quad 9n^2 = a \Rightarrow a = 9n^2$

Eq. (vii) becomes

$$9\omega_1^2 + 5\omega_2^2 = 9n^2 \quad \text{...(vii a)}$$

From Eq. (iv) and (vi), we get

$$3\omega_1\dot{\omega}_1 - 3\omega_3\dot{\omega}_3 = 0$$

which on integration gives

$$\omega_1^2 - \omega_3^2 = \text{constant} = b \text{ (say)} \quad \text{...(viii)}$$

From given, $\quad \omega_1 = n, \ \omega_3 = n$

From Eq. (viii), we get

$$0 = b \Rightarrow b = 0$$

Eq. (viii) becomes

$$\omega_1^2 = \omega_3^2 \quad \text{...(viii a)}$$

From Eq. (5), we get

$$5\dot{\omega}_2 = 3\omega_3\omega_1 = 3\omega_1^2$$

$\Rightarrow \quad 5\frac{d\omega_2}{dt} = (9n^2 - 5\omega_2^2) \times \frac{1}{3}$

$\Rightarrow \quad \frac{5}{(9n^2 - 5\omega_2^2)}\,d\omega_2 = \frac{dt}{3}$

$\Rightarrow \quad dt = \frac{3}{\left(\frac{9}{5}n^2 - \omega_2^2\right)}\,d\omega_2$

which on integration gives

$$t = 3\times\frac{1}{2\times\frac{3n}{\sqrt{5}}}\log\frac{\frac{3}{\sqrt{5}}n+\omega_2}{\frac{3}{\sqrt{5}}n-\omega_2}+C$$

At $t=0,\ \omega_2=0 \Rightarrow C=0$

$$\therefore \qquad t=\frac{\sqrt{5}}{2n}\log\frac{\frac{3}{\sqrt{5}}n+\omega_2}{\frac{3}{\sqrt{5}}n-\omega_2}$$

when $t\to\infty$, then $\omega_2\to\frac{3n}{\sqrt{5}}$

and from Eq. (vii a), we get $\omega_1=0$

and from Eq. (viii a), we get $\omega_3=0$

*i.e.*, the rotation ultimately is about the mean axis.

# Theory of Small Oscillations

The potential energy of a conservative system, specified by $n$ generalized coordinates $q_1, q_2, \ldots, q_n$, is represented as

$$V=(q_1, q_2, \ldots, q_n) \qquad \ldots(i)$$

We are interested in the motion of the system, when the displacements of the particles are small from the position of stable equilibrium. We denote the displacements of the generalized coordinates from equilibrium position by $u_i$, *i.e.*,

$$q_i = q_i^0 + u_i \qquad \ldots(ii)$$

Since, $q_i^0$ is fixed, $u_i$ may be taken as new generalized coordinates of the motion. Expanding the potential energy about the position of equilibrium, we obtain

$$V(q_1,\ldots,q_n)=V(q_1^0, q_2^0,\ldots,q_n^0)+\sum_{i=1}^{n}\left[\frac{\partial V}{\partial q_i}\right]_0 (q_i-q_i^0)$$

$$+\frac{1}{2!}\sum_{i=1}^{n}\sum_{j=1}^{n}\left[\frac{\partial^2 V}{\partial q_i\,\partial q_j}\right]_0 (q_i-q_i^0)(q_j-q_j^0)+\ldots \qquad \ldots(iii)$$

In consequence of equilibrium, $\left(\frac{\partial V}{\partial q_i}\right)_0=0$. First term in the expansion represents the potential energy in the equilibrium position and is constant for the system. Assuming the potential energy in the equilibrium to be zero and writing $u_i=q_i-q_i^0$ and $u_j=q_j-q_j^0$, we get

$$V=\frac{1}{2}\sum_{i=1}^{n}\sum_{j=1}^{n}V_{ij}\,u_i u_j \qquad \ldots(iv)$$

where $\quad V_{ij}=\left[\frac{\partial^2 V}{\partial q_i\,\partial q_j}\right]_0=\left[\frac{\partial^2 V}{\partial u_i\,\partial u_j}\right]=0$

= constant which is to be evaluated at $q_i=q_i^0$ and $q_j=q_j^0$.

The constant $V_{ij}=V_{ji}$ form a symmetric matrix $V$. In Eq. (iv), we retain the terms quadratic in the coordinates.

The kinetic energy of the system is given by

$$T=\sum_i\sum_j\frac{1}{2}m_{ij}\,\dot{q}_i\dot{q}_j=\sum_i\sum_j\frac{1}{2}m_{ij}\,\dot{u}_i\dot{u}_j \qquad \ldots(v)$$

because the generalized coordinates do not involve time explicitly and therefore the kinetic energy is a homogeneous quadratic function of generalized velocities.

The coefficients are, in general, functions of generalized coordinates and therefore expanding $m_{ij}$ in Taylor's series, we get

$$m_{ij}(q_1,\ldots,q_n)=m_{ij}(q_0^1,\ldots,q_0^n)+\sum_{k=1}^{n}\left[\frac{\partial m_{ij}}{\partial q_k}\right]_0 u_k+\ldots \qquad \ldots(vi)$$

In Eq. (v), the term is already quadratic in the $u_i$'s, we obtain the lowest non-vanishing approximation to $T$ in quadratic form only by retaining the first term in the expansion. If the constant values of the function $m_{ij}$ are denoted by $T_{ij}$, then the kinetic energy is

$$T=\frac{1}{2}\sum_i\sum_j T_{ij}\,\dot{u}_i\dot{u}_j \qquad \ldots(vii)$$

Obviously, the constants $T_{ij}$ are elements of symmetric matrix $T$. Now, the Lagrangian $L\,(=T-V)$ can be written as

$$T=\frac{1}{2}\sum_i\sum_j [T_{ij}\,\dot{u}_i\dot{u}_j - V_{ij}\,u_i u_j] \qquad \ldots(viii)$$

Using $u_i$'s as generalized coordinates, the Lagrange's equations

$$\frac{d}{dt}\left[\frac{\partial L}{\partial \dot{q}_j}\right]-\frac{\partial L}{\partial q_i}=0$$

take the form

$$\sum_{j=1}^{n}\left[T_{ij}\,\ddot{u}_j+V_{ij}\,u_j\right]=0 \qquad \ldots(ix)$$

For $i=1, 2, \ldots, n$, Eq. (ix) represents $n$ equations which are to be solved to obtain the motion near the position of equilibrium.

# Eigen Value Equation

Taking an oscillatory solution of Eq. (ix) in the form

$$u_i = Ca_i e^{i\omega t} \qquad \ldots(x)$$

where, $Ca_i$ is the complex amplitude of the oscillation for each coordinate $u_i$, the factor $C$ being used for convenience as a scale factor, the same for all the coordinates.

Substituting for $u_j$ from Eq. (x) into Eq. (ix), we obtain

$$\sum_{j=1}^{n}[V_{ij}\,a_j\,e^{i\omega t}-\omega^2 T_{ij}a_j e^{i\omega t}]=0$$

$$\Rightarrow \qquad e^{i\omega t}\sum_{j=1}^{n}[V_{ij}a_j-\omega^2 T_{ij}a_j]=0$$

$$\Rightarrow \qquad \sum_{j=1}^{n}[V_{ij}a_j-\omega^2 T_{ij}a_j]=0 \quad (\because e^{i\omega t}\neq 0) \qquad \ldots(xi)$$

In matrix form

$$\mathbf{Va}-\omega^2\mathbf{Ta}=0 \qquad \ldots(xii)$$

where, the matrix **V**, **T** and **a** are

$$\mathbf{V}=\begin{pmatrix} V_{11} & V_{12} & \ldots & V_{1n}\\ V_{21} & V_{22} & \ldots & V_{2n}\\ \ldots & \ldots & \ldots & \ldots\\ V_{n1} & V_{n2} & \ldots & V_{nn}\end{pmatrix},\ \mathbf{T}=\begin{pmatrix} T_{11} & T_{12} & \ldots & T_{1n}\\ T_{21} & T_{22} & \ldots & T_{2n}\\ \ldots & \ldots & \ldots & \ldots\\ T_{n1} & T_{n2} & \ldots & T_{nn}\end{pmatrix}$$

and $\quad \mathbf{a} = \begin{pmatrix} a_1 \\ a_2 \\ \dots \\ a_n \end{pmatrix}$

Eqs. (xi) or (xii) represent $n$ linear, homogeneous, algebraic equations in $a_j$ and $\omega$, *i.e.*,

$$[V_{11} - \omega^2 T_{11}]a_1 + [V_{12} - \omega^2 T_{12}]a_2 + \dots + [V_{1n} - \omega^2 T_{1n}]a_n = 0 \quad \dots\text{(xiii)}$$

$$\dots \quad \dots \quad \dots \quad \dots \quad \dots$$

$$[V_{n1} - \omega^2 T_{n1}]a_1 + [V_{n2} - \omega^2 T_{n2}]a_2 + \dots + [V_{nn} - \omega^2 T_{nn}]a_n = 0$$

Let us assume that inverse of $\mathbf{T}$ matrix exists. Multiplying Eq. (xii) by $\mathbf{T}^{-1}$, we get

$$\mathbf{T}^{-1}\mathbf{V}\mathbf{a} - \omega^2 \mathbf{T}^{-1}\mathbf{T}\mathbf{a} = 0$$

Since, $\mathbf{T}^{-1}\mathbf{T} = \mathbf{I}$, unit matrix and $\mathbf{T}^{-1}\mathbf{V} = \mathbf{P}$ (say), then

$$\mathbf{P}\mathbf{a} - \omega^2 \mathbf{I}\mathbf{a} = 0 \quad \text{or} \quad (\mathbf{P} - \omega^2 \mathbf{I})\mathbf{a} = 0 \quad \dots\text{(xiv)}$$

Eq. (xiv) is the eigen value equation. Here, $\omega^2$ are the eigen values of $\mathbf{P}$ and $\mathbf{a}$ is the eigen vector with $n$ components.

## Solution of the Eigen Value Equation

The eigen values are obtained by solving the determinant

$$\Rightarrow \quad |\mathbf{P} - \omega^2 \mathbf{I}| = 0 \quad \dots\text{(xv)}$$

$$\Rightarrow \quad |\mathbf{V} - \omega^2 \mathbf{T}| = 0$$

$$\Rightarrow \quad \begin{vmatrix} V_{11} - \omega^2 T_{11} & V_{12} - \omega^2 T_{12} & \dots & V_{1n} - \omega^2 T_{1n} \\ V_{21} - \omega^2 T_{21} & V_{22} - \omega^2 T_{22} & \dots & V_{2n} - \omega^2 T_{2n} \\ \dots & \dots & \dots & \dots \\ V_{n1} - \omega^2 T_{n1} & V_{n2} - \omega^2 T_{n2} & \dots & V_{nn} - \omega^2 T_{nn} \end{vmatrix} \quad \dots\text{(xvi)}$$

Eqs. (xv) or (xvi) is called secular equation. This determinantal condition is in effect an algebraic equation of $n$th degree for $\omega^2$ and the roots of the determinant provide $n$ frequencies $(\omega_1^2, \omega_2^2, \dots, \omega_n^2)$. These values are the normal mode frequencies.

For each of the value of $\omega^2$, say $\omega_k^2 (k = 1, 2, .., n)$ in the $k$th mode of vibration, Eq. (xiii) may be solved for amplitudes $a_i$. Corresponding to this $\omega_k^2$, we denote the amplitudes by $a_{ik} (i = 1, 2, \dots, n)$. Thus, $a_{ik}$ is the amplitude in the $k$th mode of the $i$th coordinate. Only for $\omega_k^2 > 0$, the motion is oscillatory about the position of stable equilibrium.

The solutions of the secular Eq. (xvi) are often called as the frequencies of free vibrations or as the resonant frequencies of the system.

The general solution of Eq. (xvi) may be written as

$$u_i = \sum_{k=1}^{n} C_k a_{ik} e^{i\omega_k t} \quad \dots\text{(xvii)}$$

Corresponding to the normal frequency $\omega_k$ the eigen vector is $\mathbf{a}_k$ with $n$ components given by the matrix.

$$\mathbf{a}_k = \begin{pmatrix} a_{1k} \\ a_{2k} \\ \vdots \\ a_{nk} \end{pmatrix}$$

Thus, in all there are $n \times n$ eigen vectors components for the system.

Clearly, for each solution $\omega_k^2$ of the Eq. (xvi), there are two frequencies of vibrations $+\omega_k$ and $-\omega_k$ corresponding to which two different scaling factors $C_k^+$ and $C_k^-$ but the eigen vector $\mathbf{a}_k$ is the same for the two frequencies. Now, Eq. (xvii) is

$$u_i = \sum_{k=1}^{n} a_{ik} [C_k^+ e^{+i\omega_k t} + C_k^- e^{-i\omega_k t}] \quad \dots\text{(xviii)}$$

where real part can be expressed as

$$u_i = \sum_{k=1}^{n} f_k a_{ik} \cos(\omega_k t + \phi_k) \quad \dots\text{(xix)}$$

and which represents the actual solution (*i.e.*, motion) for the system.

Here, $f_k$ and $\phi_k$ are determined from initial conditions.

# SOLVED EXAMPLES

### Type I (*Only one correct option*)

***Example 1.*** *A bead slides on a smooth rod which is rotating about one end in a vertical plane with uniform angular velocity $\omega$. If g denotes the acceleration due to gravity, then the lagrange equation of motion is*

(a) $\ddot{r} = r\omega^2 - g \sin \omega t$

(b) $\ddot{r} = r\omega^2 - g \cos \omega t$

(c) $\ddot{r} = -g \sin \omega t$

(d) $\ddot{r} = -g \cos \omega t$

**Solution.** (a) Let $\dot{p}(r, \theta)$ be the position of the particle at any time. Where, $\theta = \omega =$ angular velocity y.

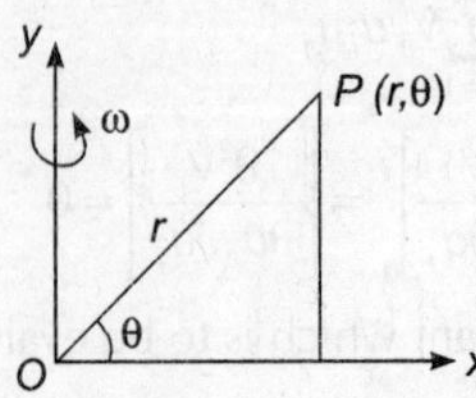


Then, the kinetic energy of the bead is

$$T = \frac{1}{2} m (\dot{r}^2 + r^2 \dot{\theta}^2) = \frac{1}{2} m (\dot{r}^2 + r^2 \omega^2)$$

and the potential energy is

$$V = mgr \sin\theta = mgr \sin wt \quad (\because \theta = wt)$$

Hence, Lagrangian of the motion is

$$L = T - V = \frac{1}{2} m(\dot{r}^2 + r^2\omega^2) - mgr \sin wt$$

Hence, the Lagrange's equation of motion is

$$\frac{d}{dt}\left(\frac{\partial L}{\partial \dot{r}}\right) - \left(\frac{\partial L}{\partial r}\right) = 0$$

$$\Rightarrow \quad m\ddot{r} - m r\omega^2 + mg \sin \omega t = 0$$

$$\Rightarrow \quad \ddot{r} = r\omega^2 - g \sin \omega t$$

***Example 2.*** *Consider a planet of mass m orbiting around the sun under the inverse square law of attraction $\frac{\mu m}{r^2}$, $l > 0$. If the position of the planet at time t given by the polar coordinates $(r, \theta)$, then the Lagrangion L of the system is given by*

(a) $\frac{1}{2} m(\dot{r}^2 + r^2\dot{\theta}^2) - \frac{\mu m}{r}$ (b) $\frac{1}{2} m(\dot{r}^2 + r^2\dot{\theta}^2) + \frac{\mu m}{r}$

(c) $\frac{1}{2} m(\dot{r}^2 + \dot{\theta}^2) + \frac{\mu m}{r}$ (d) $\frac{1}{2} m(\dot{r}^2 + \dot{\theta}^2) - \frac{\mu m}{r}$

**Solution.** (a) Let $(r, \theta)$ be the position of the particle at any instant. Then, kinetic energy of the particle is

$$T = \frac{1}{2}(\dot{r}^2 + r^2\dot{\theta}^2)$$

Since, the particle moves under the force

$$F = \frac{\mu m}{r^2}$$

Hence, potential energy of the particle is

$$V = -\int_\infty^r F\,dr = -\int_\infty^r \frac{\mu m}{r^2}\,dr = -\left[-\frac{\mu m}{r}\right]_\infty^r = \frac{\mu m}{r}$$

Hence, Lagrangian of the motion is

$$L = T - V = \frac{1}{2} m(\dot{r}^2 + r^2\dot{\theta}^2) - \frac{\mu m}{r}$$

***Example 3.*** *A particle of mass m slides down without friction along a curve $z = 1 + \frac{x^2}{2}$ in the xz-plane under the action of constant gravity. Suppose, the z-axis points vertically upwards. Let $\dot{x}$ and $\ddot{x}$ denote $\frac{dx}{dt}$ and $\frac{d^2x}{dt^2}$, respectively.*

*The Lagrangian of the motion is*

(a) $\frac{1}{2} m\dot{x}^2(1 + x^2) - mg\left(1 + \frac{x^2}{2}\right)$

(b) $\frac{1}{2} m\dot{x}^2(1 + x^2) + mg\left(1 + \frac{x^2}{2}\right)$

(c) $\frac{1}{2} m\dot{x}^2 x^2 - mg\left(1 + \frac{x^2}{2}\right)$

(d) $\frac{1}{2} m\dot{x}^2(1 - x^2) - mg\left(1 + \frac{x^2}{2}\right)$

**Solution.** (a) Given that the particle of mass $m$ slides down without friction along a curve

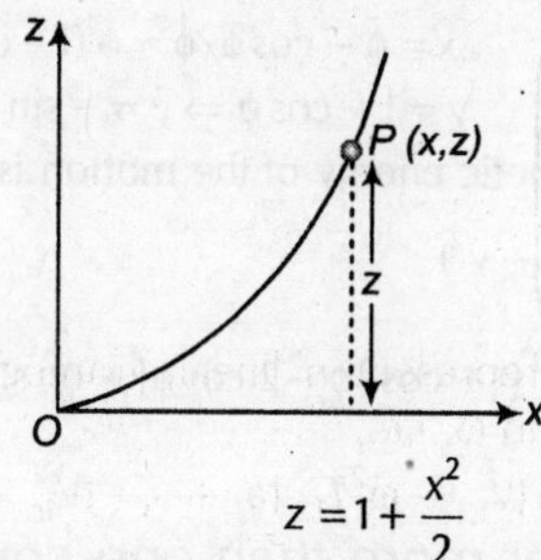


$$z = 1 + \frac{x^2}{2}$$

Let $p(x, y)$ be the position of the particle at any instant, then kinetic energy of the particle is

$$T = \frac{1}{2} m(\dot{x}^2 + \dot{z}^2) = \frac{1}{2} m(\dot{x}^2 + x^2\dot{x}^2) \qquad (\because \dot{z} = x\dot{x})$$

$$= \frac{1}{2} m\dot{x}^2(1 + x^2)$$

and the potential energy of the particle is

$$V = mgz = mg\left(1 + \frac{x^2}{2}\right)$$

Hence, the Lagrangian of the motion is

$$L = T - V = \frac{1}{2} m\dot{x}^2(1 + x^2) - mg\left(1 + \frac{x^2}{2}\right)$$

***Example 4.*** *A particle of unit mass moves in the xy-plane under the influence of a central force depending only on its distance from the origin. If $(r, \theta)$ be the polar coordinates of the particle at a given instant and $V(r)$ the potential due to the given force, then the Lagrangian for such a system is*

(a) $\frac{1}{2}\dot{r}^2 - V(r)$ (b) $\frac{1}{2} m(\dot{r}^2 + \dot{\theta}^2) + V(r)$

(c) $\frac{1}{2} m(\dot{r}^2 + r\dot{\theta}) + V(r)$ (d) $\frac{1}{2} m(\dot{r}^2 + r^2\dot{\theta}^2) - V(r)$

**Solution.** (d) Let $(r, \theta)$ be the polar coordinates of the particle at a given instant. Hence, kinetic energy of the particle is

$$T = \frac{1}{2} m(\dot{r}^2 + r^2\dot{\theta}^2)$$

Now, the force

$$F = F(r)$$

Hence, potential energy of the particle is

$$V = -\int_\infty^r F\,dr = -\int_\infty^r F(r)\,dr = V(r)$$

Hence, Lagrangian of the motion is

$$L = T - V = \frac{1}{2} m(\dot{r}^2 + r^2\dot{\theta}^2) - V(r)$$

***Example 5.*** *A particle of unit mass is moving under gravitational field, along the cycloid $x = \phi - \sin\phi$, $y = 1 + \cos\phi$. Then, the Lagrangian for the motion is*

(a) $\dot{\phi}^2(1 + \cos\phi) - g(1 - \cos\phi)$

(b) $\dot{\phi}^2(1 - \cos\phi) + g(1 + \cos\phi)$

(c) $\dot{\phi}^2(1 - \cos\phi) - g(1 + \cos\phi)$

(d) $2\dot{\phi}^2(1 - \cos\phi) - g(1 + \cos\phi)$

**Solution.** (c) We have,

$$x = \phi - \sin\phi$$

$$\Rightarrow \qquad \dot{x} = \dot{\phi} - \cos\phi \cdot \dot{\phi} = \dot{\phi}(1 - \cos\phi)$$

and $\qquad y = 1 + \cos\phi \Rightarrow \dot{y} = -\sin\phi \cdot \dot{\phi}$

Hence, the kinetic energy of the motion is

$$T = \frac{1}{2}(\dot{x}^2 + \dot{y}^2)$$

$$= \frac{1}{2}[\dot{\phi}^2[1 + \cos^2\phi - 2\cos\phi] + \dot{\phi}^2 \sin^2\phi]$$

$$= \dot{\phi}^2 - \dot{\phi}^2 \cos\phi = \dot{\phi}^2(1 - \cos\phi)$$

and the potential energy is

$$V = gh = gy = g(1 + \cos\phi)$$

Hence, Lagrangian of the motion is

$$L = T - V = \dot{\phi}^2(1 - \cos\phi) - g(1 + \cos\phi)$$

## Type II (*One or more than one correct option*)

***Example 6.*** *In polar coordinate system the Hamiltonian equation of motion are*

(a) $\dot{r} = \frac{p_r}{m}$ (b) $\dot{\theta} = \frac{P\theta}{mr^2}$

(c) $p_r = mr$ (d) $p_\theta = mr^2\dot{\theta}$

**Solution.** (a), (b), (c), (d)

If $r, \theta$ are the polar coordinates of a particle of mass $m$, then

$$x = r\cos\theta \text{ and } y = r\sin\theta$$

$$\Rightarrow \qquad \dot{x} = \dot{r}\cos\theta - r\dot{\theta}\sin\theta$$

and $\qquad \dot{y} = \dot{r}\sin\theta + r\dot{\theta}\cos\theta$

Now, the kinetic energy is

$$T = \frac{1}{2}m(\dot{x}^2 + \dot{y}^2) = \frac{1}{2}m(\dot{r}^2 + r^2\dot{\theta}^2)$$

The potential energy is

$$V = V(r, \theta)$$

and the Lagrangian is

$$L = T - V = \frac{1}{2}m(\dot{r}^2 + r^2\dot{\theta}^2) - V(r, \theta)$$

$\therefore$ Generalized momenta are

$$p_r = \frac{\partial L}{\partial \dot{r}} = m\dot{r}$$

and $\qquad p_\theta = \frac{\partial L}{\partial \dot{\theta}} = mr^2\dot{\theta}$

$$\Rightarrow \qquad \dot{r} = \frac{p_r}{m} \text{ and } \dot{\theta} = \frac{p_\theta}{mr^2}$$

$\therefore$ The Hamiltonian is

$$H = \sum_k p_k\dot{q}_k - L$$

$$= p_r\dot{r} + p_\theta\dot{\theta} - \frac{1}{2}m(\dot{r}^2 + r^2\dot{\theta}^2) + V(r, \theta)$$

$$\Rightarrow \qquad H = \frac{1}{2m}\left(p_r^2 + \frac{p_\theta^2}{r^2}\right) + V(r, \theta) \qquad \text{...(i)}$$

Hence, Hamilton's equations of motion in polar coordinate system are

$$\dot{r} = \frac{\partial H}{\partial p_r} \text{ or } \dot{r} = \frac{p_r}{m}$$

and $\qquad \dot{p}_r = -\frac{\partial H}{\partial r} \text{ or } \dot{p}_r = \frac{p_\theta^2}{mr^3} - \frac{\partial V}{\partial r} \qquad \text{...(ii)}$

and $\qquad \dot{\theta} = \frac{\partial H}{\partial p_\theta} \text{ or } \dot{\theta} = \frac{p_\theta}{mr^2}$

and $\qquad \dot{p}_\theta = -\frac{\partial H}{\partial \theta} \text{ or } \dot{p}_\theta = -\frac{\partial V}{\partial \theta} \qquad \text{...(iii)}$

***Example 7.*** *Given, the transformation,*

$$Q = \sqrt{(2q)}\, e^a \cos p$$

$$P = \sqrt{(2q)}\, e^{-a} \sin p, \textit{ then}$$

(a) it is a canonical transformation

(b) it is not a canonical transformation

(c) $PdQ - pdq \neq dF$ where, $F = \left(\frac{1}{2}q\sin 2p - pq\right)$

(d) $PdQ - pdq \neq dF$ where, $\left(F = \frac{1}{2}q\sin 2p - pq\right)$

**Solution.** (a), (c)

We have,

$$dQ = (2q)^{-1/2} e^a \cos p\, dq - (2q)^{1/2} e^a \sin p\, dp$$

So, $\qquad P\,dQ - p\,dq$

$$= \sin p[\cos p\, dq - 2q\sin p\, dp] - p\,dq$$

$$= (\sin p\cos p - p)\,dq - 2q\sin^2 p\, dp$$

$$= \left(\frac{1}{2}\sin 2p - p\right)dq - 2q\sin^2 p\, dp$$

$$= \frac{\partial}{\partial q}\left(\frac{1}{2}q\sin 2p - pq\right)dq + \frac{\partial}{\partial q}\left(\frac{1}{2}q\sin 2p - pq\right)dp$$

$$= \frac{\partial F}{\partial q}dq + \frac{\partial F}{\partial p}dp = dF$$

which shows that right hand side is an exact differential of the function

$$F = \left(\frac{1}{2}q\sin 2p - pq\right)$$

and hence the transformation is canonical.

***Example 8.*** *A particle of mass m is moving in a plane. In cartesion coordinate*

(a) the kinetic energy is $\frac{1}{2}m(\dot{x}^2 + \dot{y}^2)$

(b) $F_x = \frac{d}{dt}\left(\frac{\partial T}{\partial \dot{x}}\right) - \frac{\partial T}{\partial x}$ where, $T$ is kinetic energy

(c) $F_y = \frac{d}{dt}\left(\frac{\partial T}{\partial \dot{y}}\right) - \frac{\partial T}{\partial y}$ where, $T$ is kinetic energy

(d) $F_x = F_y$

**Solution.** (a), (b), (c)

Let the position of a particle in cartesian coordinate system at time $t$ is $(x, y)$ and $C_x, F_y$ be the force components acting on a particle in $x$ and $y$ directions, respectively.

Hence, the work done by constraints forces in a rigid body is zero and consequently the constraint is conservative in nature.

***Example 13.*** *For the system of four point masses 1 g, 2 g, 3 g and 4 g, located at the points (1, 0, 0), (1, 1, 0), (1,1,1) and (1, 1, – 1) cm.*

(a) $I_{xz} = I_{zx}$

(b) $I_{yz} = I_{zy}$

(c) $I_{xy} = I_{yx}$

(d) The inertia tensor $I$ is $\begin{bmatrix} 16 & -9 & 1 \\ -9 & 17 & 1 \\ 1 & 1 & 19 \end{bmatrix}$

**Solution.** (a), (b), (c), (d)

We have,

$$I_{xx} = \sum_{i=1}^{4} m_i(y_i^2 + z_i^2)$$

$$= 1\times 0 + 2\times 1 + 3\times 2 + 4\times 2 = 16 \text{ g cm}^2$$

$$I_{yy} = \sum_i^4 m_i(x_i^2 + z_i^2) = 17 \text{ g cm}^2$$

and $\quad I_{zz} = \sum_i m_i(x_i^2 + y_i^2) = 19 \text{ g cm}^2$

Also, $\quad I_{xy} = I_{yx} = -\sum_{i=1}^{4} m_i x_i y_i$

$$= -[0 + 2\times 1\times 1 + 3\times 1\times 1 + 4\times 1\times 1]$$

$$= -9 \text{ g cm}^2$$

Similarly, $I_{xz} = I_{zx} = -\sum_i m_i x_i z_i = 1 \text{ g cm}^2$

and $\quad I_{yz} = I_{yz} = -\sum_i m_i y_i z_i = 1 \text{g cm}^2$

Thus, the inertia tensor $I$ is

$$I = \begin{bmatrix} I_{xx} & I_{xy} & I_{xz} \\ I_{yx} & I_{yy} & I_{yz} \\ I_{zx} & I_{zy} & I_{zz} \end{bmatrix} = \begin{bmatrix} 16 & -9 & 1 \\ -9 & 17 & 1 \\ 1 & 1 & 19 \end{bmatrix}$$

***Example 14.*** *For cylindrical coordinates (ρ, φ z), for a particle of mass m moving in a force field of potential V (ρ, φ, z)*

(a) $\dot{\rho} = \dfrac{p_\rho}{m}$ (b) $\dot{\phi} = \dfrac{p_\phi}{m\rho^2}$

(c) $\dot{z} = \dfrac{p_z}{m}$ (d) $\dot{p}_z = -\dfrac{\partial V}{\partial z}$

**Solution.** (a), (b), (c), (d)

In cylindrical coordinates for any point $(x, y, z)$, we have

$$x = \rho\cos\phi,\ y = \rho\sin\phi,\ z = z$$

Hence, the kinetic energy is

$$T = \frac{1}{2}m(\dot{x}^2 + \dot{y}^2 + \dot{z}^2)$$

$$= \frac{1}{2}m(\dot{\rho}^2 + \rho^2\dot{\phi}^2 + \dot{z}^2)$$

Hence, the Lagrangian is

$$I = T - V = \frac{1}{2}m(\dot{\rho}^2 + p^2\dot{\phi}^2 + \dot{z}^2) - V(\rho, \phi, z)$$

So, $\quad p_\rho = \dfrac{\partial L}{\partial \dot{\rho}} = m\dot{\rho}$

$$p_\phi = \frac{\partial L}{\partial \dot{\phi}} = mp^2\dot{\phi}$$

$$p_z = \frac{\partial L}{\partial \dot{z}} = m\dot{z}$$

Evidently, $L$ does not involve $t$ explicitly, thus

The Hamiltonian, is

$$H = T + V = \frac{1}{2}m(\dot{\rho}^2 + \rho^2\dot{\phi}^2 + \dot{z}^2) + V$$

$$= \frac{1}{2}m\left(\frac{p_\rho^{\,2}}{m^2} + \frac{p_\phi^{\,2}}{m^2\rho^2} + \frac{p_z^{\,2}}{m^2}\right) + V$$

$$= \frac{1}{2m}\left(p_\rho^{\,2} + \frac{p_\phi^{\,2}}{\rho} + p_z^{\,2}\right) + V$$

Hence, Hamilton's equations of motion are

$$\dot{p}_\rho = -\frac{\partial H}{\partial \rho} = \frac{p_\phi^{\,2}}{m\rho^3} - \frac{\partial V}{\partial \rho},\ \dot{\rho} = \frac{\partial H}{\partial p_\rho} = \frac{p_\rho}{m}$$

$$\dot{p}_\phi = -\frac{\partial H}{\partial \phi} = -\frac{\partial V}{\partial \phi},$$

$$\dot{\phi} = -\frac{\partial H}{\partial p_\phi} = \frac{p_\phi}{m\rho^2},\ \dot{p}_z = -\frac{\partial H}{\partial z} = -\frac{\partial V}{\partial z},$$

$$\dot{z} = \frac{\partial H}{\partial p_z} = \frac{p_z}{m}$$

***Example 15.*** *Which of the following(s) is/are correct?*

(a) $[u, u] = 0$

(b) $[u, c] = 0$, where $c$ is a constant, independent of $q$ and $p$ explicitly.

(c) $[u + v, w] = [u, w] + [v, w]$

(d) $[u, u] = 1$

**Solution.** (a), (b), (c)

(a) $[u, u] = \sum_i \left(\dfrac{\partial u}{\partial q_i}\dfrac{\partial u}{\partial p_i} - \dfrac{\partial u}{\partial p_i}\dfrac{\partial u}{\partial q_i}\right) = 0$

(b) $[u, c] = \sum_i \left(\dfrac{\partial u}{\partial q_i}\dfrac{\partial c}{\partial p_i} - \dfrac{\partial u}{\partial p_i}\dfrac{\partial c}{\partial q_i}\right) = 0$

where $\dfrac{\partial c}{\partial p_i} = 0 = \dfrac{\partial c}{\partial q_i}$

(c) $\quad [u + v, w]_{q,p} = \sum_i \left(\dfrac{\partial(u+v)}{\partial q_i}\dfrac{\partial w}{\partial p_i} - \dfrac{\partial(u+v)}{\partial p_i}\dfrac{\partial w}{\partial q_i}\right)$

$$= \sum_i \left(\frac{\partial u}{\partial q_i}\frac{\partial w}{\partial p_i} - \frac{\partial u}{\partial p_i}\frac{\partial w}{\partial q_i}\right)$$

$$+ \sum_i \left(\frac{\partial v}{\partial q_i}\frac{\partial w}{\partial p_i} - \frac{\partial v}{\partial p_i}\frac{\partial w}{\partial q_i}\right)$$

$$= [u, w] + [v, w]$$

# Exercise 1 (For Part 'B')

**Directions** (Q. Nos. 1-176) *All questions have only one correct option.*

**1.** For the Lagrangian $L = \frac{1}{2}\dot{q}^2 - q\dot{q} + q^2$, then conjugate momentum $p$ is

(a) $\dot{q} + q$ (b) $q\,\dot{q}$ (c) $\dot{q} - q$ (d) $q - \dot{q}$

**2.** Given, $KE = T = \frac{1}{2}m\dot{r}^2$

and $PE = V = \frac{1}{r}\left(1 + \frac{\dot{r}^2}{c^2}\right)$

What is Hamiltonian $H$ ?

(a) $T + V$ (b) $T + V + \frac{2\dot{r}^2}{rc^2}$

(c) $T + V - \frac{2\dot{r}^2}{rc^2}$ (d) None of these

**3.** For the system described by the Lagrangian $L = \dot{q}_1^2 + \dot{q}_2^2 + \dot{q}_1\dot{q}_2 - q_1^2 - q_2^2$ which one of the following statements is not true?

(a) $p_1 + p_2 = 3(\dot{q}_1 + \dot{q}_2)$

(b) $\dot{p}_1 + \dot{p}_2 = -2(q_1 + q_2)$

(c) $\frac{\dot{p}_1}{\dot{p}_2} = \frac{q_2}{q_1}$

(d) $(q_1 + q_2)$ executes simple harmonic motion

**4.** For the system with Hamiltonian

$$H = q_1 p_1 - q_2 p_2 - aq_1^2 + bq_2^2$$

which one of the following statements is not true?

(a) $q_1 = Ae^t$ (b) $q_2 = Be^t$

(c) $\dot{p}_1 = -p_1 + 2aq_1$ (d) $\dot{p}_2 = p_2 - 2bq_2$

**5.** For the system with Lagrangian $L = \sum_i f_i(q_i)\,\dot{q}_i^2 - \sum_i V_i(q_i)$ which one of the following statements is not correct?

(a) $H = \sum_i \frac{p_i^2}{2f(q_i)} + \sum V_i(q_i)$

(b) $\dot{q}_i = \frac{p_i}{2f_i}$

(c) $\dot{p}_i = \dot{q}_i^2 \frac{\partial f_i}{\partial q_i} - \frac{\partial V_i(q_i)}{\partial q_i}$

(d) $p_i = 2f_i\dot{q}_i$

**6.** For a system with Lagrangian $L = \frac{1}{2Z}\dot{q}^2 - \frac{1}{2}\left(X - \frac{Y^2}{Z}\right) - \frac{Y}{Z}q\dot{q}$, where $X, Y$ and $Z$ are time dependent, which one of the following relation is wrong ?

(a) $H = T + V$ (b) $\dot{q} = Zp + Yq$

(c) $p = \frac{1}{Z}(\dot{q} - Yq)$ (d) $\dot{p} = -(Yp + Xq)$

**7.** For a particle of mass $m$ moving under a potential $V = \frac{K}{q}$, which one of the following relations is correct?

(a) $\dot{p} = -\frac{K}{q^2}$ (b) $\ddot{q} = \frac{K}{mq^2}$

(c) $m\dot{q}^2 + \frac{2K}{q} =$ Constant (d) $p^2 + \frac{2mK}{q} =$ Constant

**8.** For the Hamiltonian $H = \frac{1}{2}(Zp^2 + 2Ypq + Xq^2)$, what is $\dot{q}$?

(a) $\frac{Zp}{2}$ (b) $Zp + Yq$

(c) $-(Yp + qX)$ (d) None of these

**9.** A rigid body moving in space with one point fixed has degree of freedom

(a) 1 (b) 3

(c) 6 (d) 9

**10.** A particle is constrained to move along the inner surface of a fixed hemispherical bowl. The number of degrees of freedom of the particle is

(a) one (b) two

(c) three (d) four

**11.** A rigid body moving freely in space has degrees of freedom

(a) 3 (b) 6

(c) 9 (d) 4

**12.** If the Lagrangian does not depend on time explicitly,

(a) the Hamiltonian is constant

(b) the Hamiltonian cannot be constant

(c) the kinetic energy is constant

(d) the potential energy is constant

**13.** The product of generalized coordinate and its conjugate momentum has the dimensions of

(a) force (b) energy

(c) linear momentum (d) angular momentum

**14.** The Lagrangian of a particle of mass $m$ moving in a plane is given by

$$L = \frac{1}{2}m(v_x'^2 + v_y^2) + a(xv_y - yv_x)$$

where, $v_x$ and $v_y$ are velocity components and a is a constant. The canonical momenta are given by

(a) $p_x = mv_x$ and $p_y = mv_y$

(b) $p_x = mv_x + ay$ and $p_y = mv_y + ax$

(c) $p_x = mv_x - ay$ and $p_y = mv_y + ax$

(d) $p_x = mv_x - ay$ and $p_y = mv_y - ax$

**15.** Hamilton canonical equations of motion for a conservative system are

(a) $-\frac{dq_i}{dt}=\frac{\partial H}{\partial p_i}$ and $-\frac{dp_i}{dt}=\frac{\partial H}{\partial q_i}$

(b) $\frac{dp_i}{dt}=\frac{\partial H}{\partial p_i}$ and $\frac{dp_i}{dt}=\frac{\partial H}{\partial q_i}$

(c) $-\frac{dq_i}{dt}=\frac{\partial H}{\partial p_i}$ and $\frac{dp_i}{dt}=\frac{\partial H}{\partial q_i}$

(d) $\frac{dq_i}{dt}=\frac{\partial H}{\partial p_i}$ and $-\frac{dp_i}{dt}=\frac{\partial H}{\partial q_i}$

**16.** The Lagrangian of a particle moving in a plane under the influence of a central potential is given by $L=\frac{1}{2}m(\dot{r}^2+r^2\dot{\theta}^2)-V(r)$. The generalized momenta corresponding to $r$ and $\theta$ are given by

(a) $m\dot{r}$ and $mr^2\dot{\theta}$ (b) $m\dot{r}$ and $mr\dot{\theta}$

(c) $m\dot{r}^2$ and $mr^2\dot{\theta}$ (d) $m\dot{r}^2$ and $mr^2\dot{\theta}^2$

**17.** The Hamiltonian corresponding to the Lagrangian $L=ax^2+by^2-kxy$ is

(a) $\frac{p_x^2}{2a}+\frac{p_y^2}{2b}+kxy$ (b) $\frac{p_x^2}{4a}+\frac{p_y^2}{4b}-kxy$

(c) $\frac{p_x^2}{4a}+\frac{p_y^2}{4b}+kxy$ (d) $\frac{p_x^2+p_y^2}{4ab}+kxy$

**18.** In case of a rigid body, having $N$ particles, the number of degrees of freedom is

(a) $N$ (b) $3N$

(c) 3 (d) $\infty$

**19.** The generalized momentum $p_x$ of a particle of mass $m$ with velocity $v_x$ in an electromagnetic field is given by

(a) $p_x=mv_x$ (b) $p_x=mv_x+qA_x$

(c) $p_x=mv_x-qA_x$ (d) $p_x=qv_xA_x$

**20.** The frequency of small oscillation of the axis of rotation if the axes is the longest side

(a) 4 rps (b) 8 rps

(c) 3 rps (d) 6 rps

**21.** A flywheel whose moment of inertia about its axis is 200 lb-ft$^2$ makes 10 revolutions per second. What is the kinetic energy (in ft-lb)?

(a) 20000 (b) 25000

(c) 12500 (d) 10000

**22.** For a system with Lagrangian

$$=\frac{1}{2}(\dot{x}^2+\dot{y}^2)-\frac{1}{2}\omega_0^2(x^2+y^2)+\alpha xy\,;\ \alpha>0$$

what should be the value of $\omega_0$ to have two normal modes of vibrations?

(a) $\omega_0=\sqrt{\alpha}$ (b) $\omega_0<\sqrt{\alpha}$

(c) $\omega_0>\sqrt{\alpha}$ (d) None of these

**23.** A particle is placed inside a hollow-sphere and is under the influence of gravity. The sphere is rotating around its vertical axis with constant angular velocity $\omega$. Find the period of small oscillation of the particle around its steady motion ($\theta=\alpha$) ;

(a) $2\pi\sqrt{\frac{a}{g}}$ (b) $2\pi\sqrt{\frac{a}{g}\tan\alpha}$

(c) $2\pi\sqrt{\frac{a}{g}\cot\alpha\,\mathrm{cosec}\,\alpha}$ (d) None of these

**24.** For a system characterised by the Lagrangian

$$L=\frac{1}{2}(\dot{x}^2+\dot{y}^2)-\frac{1}{2}\omega_0^2(x^2+y^2)+\alpha\dot{x}\dot{y}$$

what restriction should be imposed on $\alpha$ for the normal modes of vibrations?

(a) $\alpha>0$ (b) $\alpha<0$

(c) $\alpha>1$ (d) $\alpha\neq1$

**25.** In the preceding problem what are the frequencies of the normal modes of vibration?

(a) $\frac{\omega_0}{\sqrt{1\pm\alpha}}$ (b) $(1\pm\alpha)\omega_0$

(c) $\frac{\omega_0}{1\pm\alpha}$ (d) $\frac{\omega_0}{\sqrt{\alpha}}$

**26.** What are the normal frequencies of normal modes of vibration of the system characterised by the Lagrangian

$$L=(\dot{q}_1^2+\dot{q}_2^2)+\dot{q}_1\dot{q}_2-(q_1^2+q_2^2)$$

(a) $1\,;\ \frac{1}{\sqrt{3}}$ (b) $2\,;\ \sqrt{\frac{2}{3}}$

(c) $\sqrt{2}\,;\ \sqrt{\frac{2}{3}}$ (d) $1;\ \sqrt{\frac{2}{3}}$

**27.** A small mass $m_1$ hangs from a fixed point at the end of very long string of length $l_1$. To $m_1$ is suspended a mass $m_2$ by a string whose length is $l_2$ and is very small compared to $l_1$. What is the period of small oscillation of $m_2$?

(a) $2\pi\sqrt{\frac{m_1(l_1+l_2)}{(m_1+m_2)g}}$ (b) $2\pi\sqrt{\frac{(l_1+l_2)}{(m_1+m_2)g}}$

(c) $2\pi\sqrt{\frac{(l_1+l_2)}{g}}$ (d) $2\pi\sqrt{\frac{m_1l_2}{(m_1+m_2)g}}$

**28.** The Lagrangian of a system is given by

$$L=\frac{1}{2}(\dot{x}_1^2+\dot{x}_2^2+\dot{x}_3^2)-\frac{1}{2}[x_1^2+(x_2-x_1)^2+(x_3-x_2)^2+x_3^2]$$

Find the ratio of eigen frequencies of the normal modes of vibration.

(a) $1:\sqrt{2}:1$ (b) $\sqrt{2}:1:\sqrt{2}$

(c) $1:\sqrt{2}+1:\sqrt{2}-1$ (d) $1:\sqrt{2}+1:\sqrt{3}+1$

**29.** A mass $m$ is connected on either side with a spring each of spring constants $k_1$ and $k_2$. The free ends of springs are tied to rigid supports. The displacement of the mass is $x$ from equilibrium position. Which one of the following is true?

(a) The force acting on the mass is $-(k_1 k_2)^{1/2} x$.
(b) The angular momentum of the mass is zero about the equilibrium point and its Lagrangian is $\frac{1}{2} m\dot{x}^2 - \frac{1}{2}(k_1 + k_2)x^2$.
(c) The total energy of the system is $\frac{1}{2} m\dot{x}^2$.
(d) The angular momentum of the mass is $m x \dot{x}$ and the Lagrangian of the system is $\frac{m}{2}\dot{x}^2 + \frac{1}{2}(k_1 + k_2)x^2$.

**30.** The homogeneity of time leads to the law of conservation of
(a) linear momentum (b) angular momentum
(c) energy (d) parity

**31.** In the double pendulum if mass $m_1$ (of first pendulum) >> $m_2$ (mass of second pendulum), then what is the ratio of eigen frequencies of the normal modes of vibration of the double pendulum?
(a) $l_1 : l_2$ (b) $\sqrt{l_1} : \sqrt{l_2}$
(c) $\sqrt{l_1} : \sqrt{l_1 + l_2}$ (d) $\sqrt{l_1} : \sqrt{l_1 - l_2}$

**32.** In the preceding problem if $m_1 = m_2$ and $l_1 = l_2$, then the ratio of normal frequencies is
(a) $\sqrt{2}+1 : \sqrt{2}-1$ (b) $\sqrt{2}+1 : 1$
(c) $\sqrt{2}-1 : 1$ (d) $\sqrt{\sqrt{2}+1} : \sqrt{\sqrt{2}-1}$

**33.** A particle is constrained to move on a circle under the action of gravity. The circle is placed in a vertical plane and placed on the ground. If the radius vector of the particle makes the angle $\theta$ with the vertical, Lagrange's equation of motion is

$$\dot{\theta}^2 + \frac{2g}{a} f(\theta) = \text{constant}$$

(a) $\sin\theta$ (b) $\cos\theta$ (c) $\frac{1}{\cos\theta}$ (d) $\frac{1}{\sin\theta}$

**34.** If the point of support of simple pendulum oscillates horizontally according to the law $x = a\cos vt$, then the value of the function $F(\theta, t)$ will be where, $\ddot{\theta} + \frac{2}{l}\sin\theta = R(\theta, t)$
(a) $-\frac{av^2}{l}\cos(\theta - vt)$ (b) $-\frac{av^2}{l}\cos vt \cos\theta$
(c) $\frac{av^2}{l}\cos vt \sin\theta$ (d) $\frac{av^2}{l}\sin vt \cos\theta$

**35.** If the point of support of simple pendulum oscillates vertically in the plane of pendulum according to the law $y = a\cos vt$, then the value of the function $F(\theta, t)$ of the equation of motion $\ddot{\theta} + \frac{2}{l}\sin\theta = R(\theta, t)$ will be
(a) $-\frac{av^2}{l}\cos vt \sin\theta$ (b) $-\frac{av^2}{l}\cos vt \cos\theta$
(c) $\frac{av^2}{l}\cos vt \cos\theta$ (d) $\frac{av^2}{l}\cos vt \sin\theta$

**36.** A particle is constrained to move on the arc of a parabola $z = 4ay^2$, (z-axis vertical) under gravity. The parabola is rotating around the Z-axis with constant angular velocity $\omega$. For which value of $\omega$ is the particle at rest on the parabola?
(a) $2\sqrt{2ga}$ (b) $\sqrt{2ga}$
(c) $\sqrt{ga}$ (d) None of these

**37.** The point of support of a simple pendulum moves on an ellipse fixed in the same plane with the parametric equation $x = a\cos\omega t$, $y = b\sin\omega t$, $\omega$ = constant. The Lagrange equation of the motion of the bob for small oscillations is obtained as

$$\ddot{\theta} + \frac{g\theta}{l} F(t) = \frac{a\omega^2}{l}\cos\omega t$$

the value of the function $F(t)$, is
(a) 1 (b) $1 + \frac{b\omega^2}{g}\sin\omega t$
(c) $\frac{b\omega^2}{g}\sin\omega t$ (d) None of these

**38.** A pendulum bob is suspended by a spring and allowed to swing in a vertical plane. What is the additional term in the equation of motion which makes it distinct from that of a simple pendulum of length $l = r$ (*i.e.*, from $\ddot{\theta} + (g/r)\theta = 0$)
(a) $2\dot{r}\dot{\theta}$ (b) $\frac{2\dot{r}\dot{\theta}}{r}$
(c) zero (d) $r^2\dot{\theta}$

**39.** A particle is constrained to move on the surface of an inverted cone with semi-vertical angle $\theta$ under the force $V = V(r, \phi)$ and the Lagrange equations in generalized coordinates $r$ and $\phi$ have been obtained as

$$m\ddot{r} = mf(r, \theta)\dot{\phi}^2 - \frac{\partial V}{\partial r}$$

and

$$mrf(r, \theta)\ddot{\phi} = -\frac{\partial V}{\partial r}$$

the value of function $f(r, \theta)$ is
(a) $r\sin^2\theta$ (b) $r\sin\theta$
(c) $\frac{r}{\sin^2\theta}$ (d) $r^2\sin^2\theta$

**40.** A bead, while thrown upward (along z-axis) follows the path of an inverted conical spiral around the z-axis such that $r = az$ and $\phi = -bz$, $\theta$ = constant where $a$ and $b$ are constants.

The Hamiltonian has been calculated as

$$H = \frac{p_z^2}{2mf(z)} + mgz$$

what is the value of $f(z)$?
(a) 1 (b) $1 + a^2z^2$
(c) $1 + a^2b^2z^2$ (d) $1 + a^2(1 + b^2z^2)$

**41.** The earth is nearly symmetric about the polar axis and slightly bulged at the equator so that $I_3 > I_1$ and $\frac{I_3 - I_1}{I_1} = \frac{1}{300}$. What is the period of precession of the axis of rotation about the symmetry axis?

(a) 360 days (b) 365 days
(c) 300 days (d) 420 days

**42.** If $A, B, C; F, G, H$ are the moments and products of inertia of a rigid body about three mutually perpendicular and concurrent axes, then the moment of inertia of the rigid body about an axis making angles $\alpha = \beta = \gamma = 45°$ with the original axis is

(a) $(A + B + C) - (F + G + H^+)$
(b) $\frac{1}{2}[(A + B + C) - (F + G + H^+)]$
(c) $(A + B + C) - \frac{1}{2}(F + G + H)$
(d) $\frac{A + B + C}{2} - (F + G + H)$

**43.** A particle is contained to move on the surface of a cylinder, with its axis along the z-axis, under the influence of a force directed towards the origin and proportional to its distance from the origin. Which of the following statements is not true?

(a) Motion in the z-direction is simple harmonic.
(b) Angular momentum about z-axis is conserved.
(c) $\dot{p}_z \propto z$
(d) z is cyclic coordinate.

**44.** A particle of mass $m$ is constrained to move on the inclined rod in a vertical plane under the influence of a central potential $V(r) = br^2$. The rod makes an angle $\theta$ with the z-axis and is rotating around the z-axis with a constant angular velocity $\omega$. Ignoring the gravitational effect, find the value of $b$ to keep the particle stationary on the rod

(a) $\omega^2 \sin^2 \theta$ (b) $m\omega^2 \sin^2 \theta$
(c) $\frac{m\omega^2 \sin^2 \theta}{2}$ (d) None of these

**45.** Consider the motion of a particle in the potential $V(x)$ shown in figure.

Suppose, the particle has a total energy $E = V_1$ in the figure. Then, the speed of the particle is zero when it is at

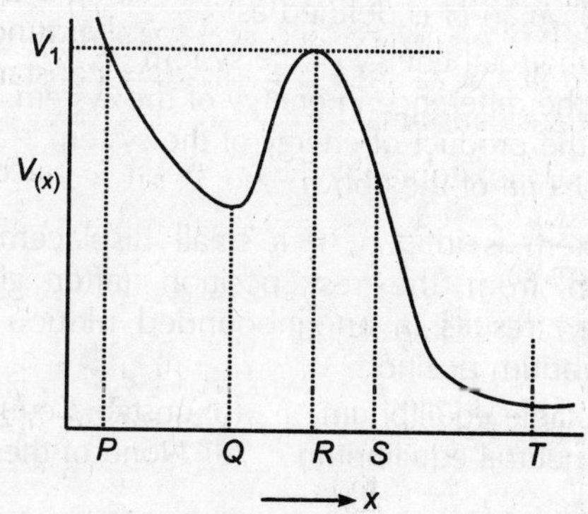


(a) point $P$ (b) point $Q$
(c) point $S$ (d) point $T$

**46.** In the preceding problem which one of the following statement is not correct about the particle?

(a) It experiences no force when its position corresponds to the point $Q$ on the curve.
(b) It experiences no force when its position corresponds to the point $R$ on the curve.
(c) Its speed is the largest when it is at $S$.
(d) It will be in a closed orbit between $P$ and $R$, if $E < V_1$.

**47.** For the Lagrangian $L = q^2 \cdot \dot{q}^2$ in the solution of Lagrange equation, the coordinate will depend on $t$ as (when initially $q = 0$)

(a) $q \propto t$ (b) $q \propto t^{1/2}$ (c) $q \propto t^2$ (d) $q \propto t^{3/2}$

**48.** A particle is constrained to move on the plane curve $xy = c$ (where $c$ is constant) under gravity. Taking y-axis vertical the Lagrange equation is derived as

$$x^2\ddot{x} + c^2 \frac{d}{dt}F(x, \dot{x}) - gc = 0$$

Find the value of the function $F$.

(a) $\dot{x} / x^2$ (b) $\dot{x}\, x^2$
(c) $x\dot{x}$ (d) $\dot{x}^2 x$

**49.** Lagrange's equation of motion of a simple pendulum, whose point of support moves uniformly on a vertical circle of radius $a$ with constant frequency $\nu$, is obtained as

$$\ddot{\theta} + \frac{g}{l}\sin\theta = F(\theta, t)$$

Find the value of the function $F$.

(a) $\frac{a\nu}{l}\cos(\theta - \nu t)$ (b) $\frac{a\nu^2}{l}\cos(\theta - \nu t)$
(c) $\frac{a\nu^2}{l}\sin(\theta - \nu t)$ (d) $\frac{a\nu}{l}\sin(\theta - \nu t)$

**50.** A Lagrangian for a system with two degrees of freedom,

$$L = \dot{q}_1^2 + \dot{q}_2^2 + \dot{q}_1\dot{q}_2 - q_1^2 - q_2^2,$$

yields the Lagrange equation

$$\ddot{X} + 2X = 0 \quad \text{and} \quad \ddot{Y} + KY = 0$$

where, $X = q_1 + q_2$ and $Y = q_1 - q_2$. Find the value of $K$.

(a) 2 (b) 3
(c) 2/3 (d) None of these

**51.** A particle moves on a cycloid $s = 4a\sin\theta$ under the action of gravity. What is the time period of the small oscillation?

(a) $2\pi\sqrt{\frac{a}{g}}$ (b) $2\pi\sqrt{\frac{2a}{g}}$
(c) $2\pi\sqrt{\frac{a}{2g}}$ (d) None of these

**52.** For the Lagrangian $L = \frac{1}{2}q^2\dot{q}^2 - q^3$ with one degree of freedom, the Lagrange equation is obtained as

$$L = nq^3 = \text{constant}$$

Find the value of integer $n$.

(a) 1 (b) 2
(c) −1 (d) −2

**53.** A particle moves in a central field of force (*i.e.*, the potential energy is $V(r)$) and is equation is written as

$$m\ddot{r} = \frac{k}{r^n} - \frac{\partial V}{\partial r}, \text{ where } k \text{ is constant.}$$

Find the value of $n$.

(a) zero (b) one
(c) two (d) three

**54.** A particle moves under the influence of gravity on an frictionless inner surface of a paraboloid of revolution $x^2 + y^2 = az$ with $z$-axis vertical. Which of the following is conserved?

(a) Momentum conjugate to $r$
(b) Momentum conjugate to $\theta$
(c) Momentum conjugate to $z$
(d) None of the above

**55.** The constraints on a bead on a uniformly rotating wire in a force free space is

(a) rheonomous (b) scleronomous
(c) Both (a) and (b) (d) None of these

**56.** If the generalized coordinate is angle $\theta$, the corresponding generalized force has the dimensions of

(a) force (b) momentum
(c) torque (d) energy

**57.** If a generalized coordinate has the dimensions of velocity, generalized velocity has the dimensions of

(a) displacement (b) velocity
(c) acceleration (d) force

**58.** The Lagrangian for a charged particle in an electromagnetic field is

(a) $L = T + q\phi + q(\mathbf{v}.\ \mathbf{A})$ (b) $L = T - q\phi - q(\mathbf{v}.\ \mathbf{A})$
(c) $L = T - q\phi + q(\mathbf{v}.\ \mathbf{A})$ (d) $L = T + q\phi - q(\mathbf{v}.\ \mathbf{A})$

where, $T$ is the kinetic energy and $\phi$ and $A$ are magnetic scalar and vector potentials.

**59.** Identify the points of unstable equilibrium for the potential shown in figure.

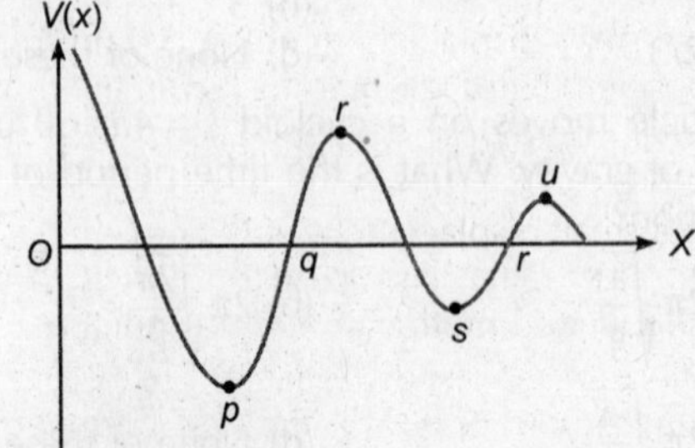


(a) $p$ and $s$ (b) $q$ and $t$ (c) $r$ and $t$ (d) $r$ and $s$

**60.** The curve made by a cable of fixed length suspended from two fixed points for minimum gravitational potential is

(a) circular (b) parabolic
(c) hyperbolic (d) catenary

**61.** Let there exists a generating function $F$, such that $dF/dt = L - K$, where $L, K$ being the Lagrangian in old and new set of coordinates

(a) The transformation is canonical
(b) The transformation is not canonical
(c) Both (a) and (b)
(d) None of the above

**62.** Which of the following statements are true?

(a) The shortest distance between two points in a plane is a straight line.
(b) The shortest distance between two points is a curve.
(c) The shortest distance between two points is a semi-circle.
(d) The shortest distance between two points not a straight line.

**63.** In a simple dynamical conservative system sum of kinetic energy and potential energy

(a) constant (b) not constant
(c) is zero (d) varying

**64.** Hamiltonian function is

(a) $H = L\sum_k p_k q_k$ (b) $H = \sum_k p_k q_k - L$
(c) $H = \sum_k p_k q_k + L$ (d) None of these

**65.** Chasle's theorem states

(a) The general displacement of a rigid body with one point fixed is a rotation about some axis
(b) The general displacement of a rigid body is a translation with rotation
(c) Lagrange's bracket is canonical invariant
(d) Poisson's bracket is invariant under canonical transformation

**66.** Moment of inertia about $X$-axis is

(a) $I_{xx} = \sum_{i=1}^{n} m_i(y_i^2 + z_i^2)$ (b) $I_{yy} = \sum_{i=1}^{n} m_i(z_i^2 + y_i^2)$
(c) $I_{zz} = \sum_{i=1}^{n} m_i(x_i^2 + y_i^2)$ (d) None of these

**67.** Hamiltonian $H$ is defined as

(a) the total energy of the system
(b) the difference in energy of the system
(c) the product of energy of the system
(d) None of the above

**68.** A system is in ......, if a small displacement of the system from the rest position (after giving small energy) results in an unbounded motion about the equilibrium position

(a) stable equilibrium (b) unstable equilibrium
(c) neutral equilibrium (d) None of these

**69.** Rheonomous constraints are
(a) the constraints that can be expressed as equation form
(b) the constraints that cannot be expressed as equation form
(c) equation of constraints that contain time as explicit variable
(d) equation of constraints that does not contains time as explicit variable

**70.** The constraints that cannot be expressed as equation form
(a) holonomic constraints
(b) non-holonomic constraints
(c) rheonomous constraints
(d) scleronomous constraints

**71.** If $f(y, y', x)$ defines a curve $y = y(x)$, then Euler-Lagrange's equation is
(a) $\frac{\partial f}{\partial y}\frac{d}{dx}\left(\frac{\partial f}{\partial y'_k}\right)=0$ (b) $\frac{\partial f}{\partial y}+\frac{d}{dx}\left(\frac{\partial f}{\partial y'_k}\right)=0$
(c) $\frac{\partial f}{\partial y}-\frac{d}{dx}\left(\frac{\partial f}{\partial y'_k}\right)=0$ (d) None of these

**72.** For every action there is always equal and opposite reaction is known as
(a) Law of inertia
(b) Law of force
(c) Law of action and reaction
(d) None of the above

**73.** Moment of inertia about Y-axis is
(a) $I_{xx}=\sum_{i=1}^{n} m_i(y_i^2+z_i^2)$ (b) $I_{yy}=\sum_{i=1}^{n} m_i(z_i^2+y_i^2)$
(c) $I_{zz}=\sum_{i=1}^{n} m_i(x_i^2+y_i^2)$ (d) None of these

**74.** Lagrange's equation of holonomic system are
(a) $\frac{d}{dt}\left(\frac{\partial T}{\partial \dot{q}_k}\right)\frac{\partial T}{\partial q_k}=Q_k \quad (k=1,\ldots,n)$
(b) $\frac{d}{dt}\left(\frac{\partial T}{\partial \dot{q}_k}\right)\Big/\frac{\partial T}{\partial q_k}=Q_k \quad (k=1,\ldots,n)$
(c) $\frac{d}{dt}\left(\frac{\partial T}{\partial \dot{q}_k}\right)-\frac{\partial T}{\partial q_k}=Q_k \quad (k=1,\ldots,n)$
(d) None of the above

**75.** An inertial frame is
(a) non-accelerated frame of reference
(b) accelerated frame of reference
(c) Both (a) and (b)
(d) None of the above

**76.** Newton's First law of motion states
(a) A body continues in its state of rest or uniform motion, unless no external force is applied to it
(b) The time rate of change of momentum is proportional to impressed force
(c) For every action there is always equal and opposite reaction
(d) None of the above

**77.** Generalized coordinates
(a) depend on each other
(b) are independent of each other
(c) are spherical coordinates
(d) None of the above

**78.** The Hamilton's principal states for a conservative holonomic system, the motion of a particle from time $t_1$ to time $t_2$ is such that line integral $S=\int_1^2 L\,dt$ has ...... for the correct path of motion. Here, $S$ is called Hamilton's principal function
(a) stationary (extremum) value
(b) mean value
(c) non-stationary value
(d) None of the above

**79.** Euler's theorem states
(a) The general displacement of a rigid body with one point fixed is a rotation about some axis
(b) The general displacement of a rigid body is translation with a rotation
(c) Lagrange's bracket is canonical invariant
(d) Poisson's bracket is invariant under canonical transformation

**80.** Hamilton's theorem states
(a) $\dot{q}_k=\frac{\partial H}{\partial p_k}$ (b) $-\dot{p}_k=\frac{\partial H}{\partial q_k}$
(c) Bothe (a) and (b) (d) None of these

**81.** Degree of freedom is
(a) the minimum number of independent coordinates (or variables) required to specify the system
(b) the maximum number of independent coordinates (or variables) required to specify the system
(c) the minimum number of dependent coordinates (or variables) required to specify the system
(d) the minimum number of dependent coordinates (or variables) required to specify the system

**82.** If any coordinate $q_k$ is cyclic, *i.e.*, not contained in $H$, then
(a) $\frac{\partial H}{\partial q_k}=0$ (b) $\dot{p}_k=0$
(c) Both (a) and (b) true (d) (a) or (b) are true

**83.** Stable equilibrium
(a) If a small displacement of the system from the rest position (after giving small energy) results in a small bounded motion about the equilibrium position
(b) If a small displacement of the system from the rest position (after giving small energy) results in an unbounded motion about the equilibrium position
(c) If the system on displacement has no tendency to move about or above the equilibrium position
(d) None of the above

**84.** Equation of constraints that does not contain time as explicit variable are referred as
(a) holonomic constraints
(b) rheonomous constraints
(c) non-holonomic constraints
(d) scleronomous constraints

**85.** A particle is constrained to move along the inner surface of a fixed hemi-spherical bowl. The number of degrees of freedom of the particle is
(a) one (b) two (c) three (d) four

**86.** For a one-dimensional harmonic oscillator, the representative point in two-dimensional phase space traces
(a) an ellipse (b) a parabola
(c) a hyperbola (d) always a straight line

**87.** For two coupled oscillators, the equation of motion are
(a) $m\ddot{x}_1 + kx_1 + k'(x_1 + x_2) = 0$
$m\ddot{x}_2 + kx_2 + k'(x_1 + x_2) = 0$
(b) $m\ddot{x}_2 + kx_2 + k'(x_1 + x_2) = 0$ only
(c) $m\ddot{x}_1 + kx_1 + k'(x_1 + x_2) = 0$ only
(d) None of the above

**88.** Limitations imposed on the motion of a system are referred as
(a) constraints (b) frame of reference
(c) degree of freedom (d) None of these

**89.** Which of the following represents the cartesian coordinate
(a) $(x, y, z)$ (b) $(r, \theta, \phi)$
(c) $(r, \theta, z)$ (d) None of these

**90.** The dimensions of generalized momentum
(a) are always those of linear momentum
(b) are always those of angular momentum
(c) may be those of linear momentum
(d) None of the abvoe

**91.** In centre of mass frame of reference
(a) total linear momentum is zero
(b) total linear momentum is less than zero
(c) total linear momentum is greater than zero
(d) None of the above

**92.** Which of the following represents the cylindrical coordinate?
(a) $(x, y, z)$ (b) $(r, \theta, \phi)$
(c) $(r, \theta, z)$ (d) None of these

**93.** An example of stable equilibrium is
(a) a pendulum in the rest position
(b) an egg standing on one end
(c) book placed flat any where on table
(d) None of the above

**94.** Relation between Cartesian and Spherical coordinate system
(a) $\begin{cases} x = r\sin\theta\cos\phi \\ y = r\sin\theta\sin\phi \\ z = r\cos\theta \end{cases}$ (b) $\begin{cases} x = r\sin\theta\sin\phi \\ y = r\sin\theta\sin\phi \\ z = r\sin\theta \end{cases}$
(c) $\begin{cases} x = r\sin\theta\cos\phi \\ y = r\sin\theta\sin\phi \\ z = r \end{cases}$ (d) None of these

**95.** A system is in ......, if the system on displacement has no tendency to move about or above the equilibrium position
(a) stable equilibrium (b) unstable equilibrium
(c) neutral equilibrium (d) None of these

**96.** Non-inertial frame is
(a) non-accelerated frame of reference
(b) accelerated frame of reference
(c) Both (a) and (b)
(d) None of the above

**97.** Relation between cartesian and cylindrical coordinate system
(a) $\begin{cases} r = \sqrt{x^2 y^2 z^2} \\ \theta = \tan^{-1}\frac{y}{x} \\ z = z \end{cases}$ (b) $\begin{cases} r = \sqrt{x^2 + y^2 + z^2} \\ \theta = \tan^{-1}\frac{y}{x} \\ z = z \end{cases}$
(c) $\begin{cases} r = \sqrt{x^2 + y^2 + z^2} \\ \theta = \tan\frac{y}{x} \\ z = z \end{cases}$ (d) None of these

**98.** Which of the following represents the spherical coordinates?
(a) $(x, y, z)$ (b) $(r, \theta, \phi)$
(c) $(r, \theta, z)$ (d) None of these

**99.** The general displacement of a rigid body is a translation with a rotation
(a) Euler's theorem (b) Chasle's theorem
(c) Law of inertia (d) Law of force

**100.** If the work done by forces on the particle around a closed path in the force field is zero
(a) the forces are conservative
(b) the forces are non-conservative
(c) Both (a) and (b) are true
(d) None of the above

**101.** Unstable equilibrium
(a) if a small displacement of the system from the rest position (after giving small energy) results in a small bounded motion about the equilibrium position
(b) if a small displacement of the system from the rest position (after giving small energy) results in an unbounded motion about the equilibrium position
(c) if the system on displacement has no tendency to move about or above the equilibrium position
(d) None of the above

**102.** A frame of reference in which law of inertia holds
(a) galilean frames of reference
(b) non-newtonian frame of reference
(c) accelerated frames
(d) None of the above

**103.** The following $I_{yy} = \sum_{i=1}^{n} m_i (z_i^2 + y_i^2)$ represents
(a) moment of inertia about $X$-axis
(b) moment of inertia about $Y$-axis
(c) moment of inertia about $Z$-axis
(d) None of the above

**104.** The dimensions of generalized momentum
(a) are always those of linear momentum
(b) are always those of angular momentum
(c) may be those of angular momentum
(d) None of the above

**105.** Conservation of total angular momentum
(a) If the total external force on the system is zero, the total linear momentum is constant of motion
(b) In centre of mass frame of reference, total linear momentum is zero
(c) The total angular momentum of a system of particles is conserved
(d) None of the abvoe

**106.** In case of two coupled identical pendulums, oscillating in a plane
(a) each pendulum always execute simple harmonic motion
(b) two pendulum always execute simple harmonic motion
(c) the general motion can be expressed as a superposition of two simple harmonic motions of the same frequency
(d) None of the above

**107.** Principle of virtual work states
(a) The work done is zero in the case of an arbitrary displacement of a system from a position of equilibrium
(b) The work done is non-zero in the case of an arbitrary displacement of a system from a position of equilibrium
(c) The work done is infinite in the case of an arbitrary displacement of a system from a position of equilibrium
(d) None of the above

**108.** The general displacement of a rigid body with one point fixed is a rotation about some axis
(a) Euler's theorem
(b) Chasle's theorem
(c) Law of inertia
(d) Law of force

**109.** Relation between cartesian and spherical coordinate systems

(a) $\left\{\begin{array}{l} r = \sqrt{x^2+y^2+z^2} \\ \theta = \tan^{-1}\sqrt{\dfrac{x^2+y^2}{z}} \\ \phi = \tan^{-1}\dfrac{y}{x} \end{array}\right.$ (b) $\left\{\begin{array}{l} r = \sqrt{x^2y^2z^2} \\ \theta = \tan^{-1}\sqrt{\dfrac{x^2y^2}{z}} \\ \phi = \tan\dfrac{y}{x} \end{array}\right.$

(c) $\left\{\begin{array}{l} r = \sqrt{x^2+y^2/z^2} \\ \theta = \tan\dfrac{yz}{x} \\ \phi = \tan^{-1}\dfrac{y}{x} \end{array}\right.$ (d) None of these

**110.** A body continues in its state of rest or uniform motion, unless no external force is applied to it
(a) law of inertia
(b) law of force
(c) law of action and reaction
(d) None of the above

**111.** Moment of inertia about $Z$-axis is
(a) $I_{xx} = \sum_{i=1}^{n} m_i (y_i^2 + z_i^2)$ (b) $I_{yy} = \sum_{i=1}^{n} m_i (z_i^2 + y_i^2)$
(c) $I_{zz} = \sum_{i=1}^{n} m_i (x_i^2 + y_i^2)$ (d) None of these

**112.** The mechanics based on Newton's law of motion and alternatively developed by Lagrange, Hamilton and others is
(a) classical mechanics (b) relative mechanics
(c) quantum mechanics (d) None of these

**113.** If a coordinate system is attached to a rigid body and one describe the position of any particle relative to it, then such coordinate system is called
(a) frame of reference
(b) space time reference system
(c) coordinate system
(d) None of the above

**114.** Let $f(y_1, y_2, \ldots, y_k, \ldots, y_n, y_1', y_2', \ldots, y_k', \ldots, y_n', x)$ and $y_i(x) = y_i$. Then, Euler Lagrange's equations are
(a) $\dfrac{\partial f}{\partial y_k} + \dfrac{d}{dx}\left(\dfrac{\partial f}{\partial y_k'}\right) = 0, k = 1, 2, \ldots, n$
(b) $\dfrac{\partial f}{\partial y_k} \cdot \dfrac{d}{dx}\left(\dfrac{\partial f}{\partial y_k'}\right) = 0, k = 1, 2, \ldots, n$
(c) $\dfrac{\partial f}{\partial y_k} - \dfrac{d}{dx}\left(\dfrac{\partial f}{\partial y_k'}\right) = 0, k = 1, 2, \ldots, n$
(d) None of the abvoe

**115.** The time rate of change of momentum is proportional to impressed force
(a) law of inertia
(b) law of force
(c) law of action and reaction
(d) None of the above

**116.** Choose the correct statements.

(a) The angular momentum is conserved for systems possessing rotational symmetry.

(b) If the Lagrangian of a system is invariant under translation along a direction, the corresponding linear momentum is not conserved.

(c) If the Lagrangian of a system is not invariant under translation along a direction, one cannot say anything about the corresponding linear momentum.

(d) For a conservative system, the Hamiltonian is not equal to the sum of kinetic and potential energies.

**117.** If $W_{12}$ is the work done by an external force $F$ upon a particle in displacing from point 1 to 2 and the change in potential energy from point 1 to 2 is $V_1$ and $V_2$, respectively. Then,

(a) $W_{12} = \int_1^2 F \cdot dr = V_1 + V_2$

(b) $W_{12} = \int_1^2 F \cdot dr = V_1 - V_2$

(c) $W_{12} = \int_1^2 F \cdot dr = V_1 V_2$

(d) None of the above

**118.** Neutral equilibrium

(a) If a small displacement of the system from the rest position (after giving small energy) results in a small bounded motion about the equilibrium position

(b) If a small displacement of the system from the rest position (after giving small energy) results in an unbounded motion about the equilibrium position

(c) If the system on displacement has no tendency to move about or above the equilibrium position

(d) None of the above

**119.** Newton's second law of motion states

(a) A body continues in its state of rest or uniform motion, unless no external force is applied to it

(b) The time rate of change of momentum is proportional to impressed force

(c) For every action there is always equal and opposite reaction

(d) None of the abvoe

**120.** A rigid body moving freely in space has degrees of freedom

(a) three (b) six

(c) nine (d) twelve

**121.** If the physical phenomena occur in a space, its position is known as .......the time of occurrence and the point taken together are called ...

(a) point event (b) event, point

(c) space, event (d) None of these

**122.** If $W_{12}$ is the work done by an external force $F$ upon a particle in displacing from point 1 to 2 and the change in kinetic energy from point 1 to 2 is $T_1$ and $T_2$, respectively. Then,

(a) $W_{12} = \int_1^2 F \cdot dr = T_2 T_1$

(b) $W_{12} = \int_1^2 F \cdot dr = T_2 + T_1$

(c) $W_{12} = \int_1^2 F \cdot dr = T_2 - T_1$

(d) None of the above

**123.** Poisson's bracket is

(a) invariant under canonical transformation

(b) variant under canonical transformation

(c) Both (a) and (b)

(d) None of the above

**124.** Newton's third law of motion states

(a) A body continues in its state of rest or uniform motion, unless no external force is applied to it

(b) The time rate of change of momentum is proportional to impressed force

(c) For every action there is always equal and opposite reaction

(d) None of the abvoe

**125.** If the Lagrangian does not depend on time explicitly

(a) the Hamiltonian is constant

(b) Hamiltonian not constant

(c) the kinetic energy is constant

(d) the potential energy is constant

**126.** Energy conservation law states

(a) The sum of kinetic energy and potential energy (*i.e.*, total mechanical energy) of a particle remains constant in a conservative force field

(b) The sum of kinetic energy and potential energy (*i.e.*, total mechanical energy) of a particle remains not constant in a conservative force field

(c) The sum of kinetic energy and potential energy (*i.e.*, total mechanical energy ) of a particle remains constant in non-conservative force field

(d) None of the above

**127.** Choose the correct statements

(a) The angular momentum is not conserved for systems possessing rotational symmetry

(b) If the Lagrangian of a system is invariant under translation along a direction, the corresponding linear momentum is not conserved

(c) If the Lagrangian of a system is invariant under translation along a direction, we cannot say anything about the corresponding linear momentum

(d) For a non-conservative system, the Hamiltonian is equal to the sum of kinetic and potential energies

**128.** Classical mechanics that deals with the Newton's laws and their consequences. Here, vector quantities such as force, acceleration, momentum etc are used is referred as

(a) newtonian (Vectorial) mechanics

(b) quantum mechanics

(c) analytical mechanics

(d) None of the above

**129.** Following is true for mechanics?

(a) It deals with physical objects in motion under the influence of external and internal interaction.
(b) It deals with physical objects at rest under the influence of external and internal interaction
(c) Both (a) and (b)
(d) None of the above

**130.** In the case of symmetric mode for two coupled identical spring mass system

(a) Both masses have equal and opposite displacements in phase
(b) Both masses vibrate with the frequency of single spring mass system
(c) Both masses vibrate with a frequency different to the frequency of single spring mass system
(d) None of the above

**131.** Choose the correct statements

(a) The angular momentum is not conserved for systems possessing rotational symmetry
(b) If the Lagrangian of a system is not invariant under translation along a direction, the corresponding linear momentum is conserved
(c) If the Lagrangian of a system is not invariant under translation along a direction, we cannot say anything about the corresponding linear momentum
(d) For a conservative system, the Hamiltonian is equal to the sum of kinetic and potential energies

**132.** Relation between cartesian and polar coordinate system

(a) $\begin{cases} x = r\cos\theta \\ y = r\sin\theta \end{cases}$ (b) $\begin{cases} x = r\sin\theta \\ y = r\cos\theta \end{cases}$

(c) $\begin{cases} x = r\tan\theta \\ y = r\sin\theta \end{cases}$ (d) None of these

**133.** In case of two coupled identical pendulums, in general

(a) the potential energy is a homogeneous quadratic functions, when expressed in terms of actual displacements
(b) the potential energy is not a homogeneous quadratic functions, when expressed in terms of actual displacements
(c) the potential energy is not a homogeneous quadratic functions, when expressed in terms of normal coordinates
(d) None of the above

**134.** Relation between Cartesian and Polar coordinate system

(a) $r = \sqrt{x^2 y^2}$ and $\theta = \tan\dfrac{y}{x}$

(b) $r = \sqrt{x^2 + y^2}$ and $\theta = \tan^{-1}\dfrac{y}{x}$

(c) $r = \sqrt{x^2 / y^2}$ and $\theta = \tan^{-1}\dfrac{y}{x}$

(d) None of the above

**135.** The holonomic constraints are

(a) the constraints that can be expressed as equation form
(b) the constraints that cannot be expressed as equation from
(c) equation of constraints that contain time as explicit variable
(d) Equation of constraints that does not contains time as explicit variable

**136.** Whenever the Lagrangian for a system does not contain a coordinate explicitly

(a) $q_k$ is cyclic coordinate
(b) $p_k$ is cyclic coordinate
(c) $p_k$ is a constant of motion
(d) None of the abvoe

**137.** The following $I_{zz} = \sum_{i=1}^{n} m_i (x_i^2 + y_i^2)$ represents

(a) moment of inertia about $X$-axis
(b) moment of inertia about $Y$-axis
(c) moment of inertia about $Z$-axis
(d) None of the above

**138.** The system is said to be in equilibrium, if the generalized forces acting on the system

(a) are equal to zero (b) are non-zero
(c) are infinite (d) None of these

**139.** Rutherford differential scattering cross section

(a) has the dimensions of area
(b) has the dimensions of solid angle
(c) is proportional to the square of the kinetic energy of the incident particle
(d) None of the above

**140.** The following $(r, \theta, z)$ are the coordinate of

(a) cartesian coordinate system
(b) cylindrical coordinate system
(c) spherical coordinate system
(d) None of the above

**141.** Equation of constraints that contain time as explicit variable are referred as

(a) holonomic constraints
(b) non-holonomic constraints
(c) rheonomous constraints
(d) scleronomous constraints

**142.** In case of two coupled identical pendulums, oscillating in a plane

(a) each pendulums, always execute simple harmonic motion
(b) the general motion can be expressed as a superposition of two simple harmonic motions of the same frequency
(c) the general motion can be expressed as a superposition of two simple harmonic motions of the same frequency
(d) None of the above

**143.** Whenever the Lagrangian for a system does not contain a coordinate explicitly
(a) $p_k$ is cyclic coordinate
(b) $p_k$ the generalized momentum, is a constant of motion
(c) $q_k$ is always zero
(d) None of the abvoe

**144.** In case of two coupled identical pendulums, in general
(a) The potential energy is a homogeneous quadratic functions, when expressed in terms of actual displacements
(b) Two potential energy is not a homogeneous quadratic functions, when expressed in terms of normal coordinates
(c) The potential energy is a homogeneous quadratic functions, when expressed in terms of normal coordinates
(d) None of the above

**145.** Choose the correct statements
(a) The angular momentum is not conserved for systems possessing rotational symmetry
(b) If the Lagrangian of a system is invariant under translation along a direction, the corresponding linear momentum is conserused
(c) If the Lagrangian of a system is not invariant under translation along a direction, we can not say any thing about the corresponding linear momentum
(d) For a conservative system,the Hamiltonian is not equal to the sum of kinetic and potential energies

**146.** A particle is moving under central force about a fixed centre of force. Choose the correct statement
(a) The motion of the particle is always on a circular path
(b) Its kinetic energy remains constant
(c) Motion of the particle takes place in a plane
(d) None of the above

**147.** If the Poisson bracket of a function with the Hamiltonian venusians
(a) the function depends upon time
(b) the function does not depend on time explicitly
(c) the function is not the constant of motion
(d) None of the above

**148.** At the centre of mass-frame of reference. If the total external force on the system is zero
(a) the total linear momentum is constant of motion
(b) total linear momentum is zero
(c) the total angular momentum of a system of particles is conserved
(d) None of the above

**149.** A particle is moving under central force about a fixed centre of force. Choose the correct statement.
(a) The motion of the particle is always on a circular path
(b) Its angular momentum is conserved
(c) Its kinetic evergy remains constant
(d) None of the abvoe

**150.** The constraints that can be expressed as equation form
(a) holonomic constraints
(b) non-holonomic constraints
(c) rheonomous constraints
(d) scleronomous constraints

**151.** The following $(x, y, z)$ are the coordinate of
(a) cartesian coordinate system
(b) cylindrical coordinate system
(c) spherical coordinate system
(d) None of the above

**152.** Generalized coordinates are
(a) A set of dependent coordinates sufficient in number to describe completely the state of configuration of a dynamical system
(b) A set of independent coordinates sufficient in number to describe completely the state of configuration of a dynamical system
(c) A set of dependent coordinates excesses in number to describe completely the state of configuration of a dynamical system
(d) None of the above

**153.** In the force is conservative, the work done on the particle
(a) around a closed path in the force field is zero
(b) around a open path in the force field is zero
(c) around a closed path in the force field is non-zero
(d) None of the above

**154.** An alternative and superior schemes in classical mechanics developed by d'Alembert, Lagrange, Hamilton and others. Here, scalar quantities such s energy rather than vector quantities are used and dynamical relations are obtained by systematic process of differentiation
(a) newtonian (vectorial) mechanics
(b) analytical mechanics
(c) quantum mechanics
(d) None of the above

**155.** Lagrangian is defined as
(a) $L = T - V$, where $T$ is kinetic energy and $V$ potential energy
(b) $L = T\,V$, where $T$ is kinetic energy and $V$ potential energy
(c) $L = T \pm V$, where $T$ is kinetic energy and $V$ potential energy
(d) $L = T/V$, where $T$ is kinetic energy and $V$ potential energy

**156.** The scleronomous constraints are
(a) the constraints that can be expressed as equation form
(b) the constraints that cannot be expressed as equation form
(c) equation of constraints that contain time as explicit variable
(d) equation of constraints that does not contains time as explicit variable

**157.** If we make a canonical transformation from the set of variables $(p_k, q_k)$ to new set of variables $(P_k, Q_k)$ and the transformed Hamiltonian is identically zero, then
(a) the new variables are constant in time
(b) the new variables are not constant in time
(c) the new variables are not cyclic
(d) None of the above

**158.** For a conservative system, generalized force
(a) has necessarily the dimensions of force
(b) is a dimensionless quantity
(c) cannot have dimensions of force
(d) may have the dimensions of torque

**159.** In the case of symmetric mode for two coupled identical spring mass system
(a) both masses have equal displacements in phase
(b) both masses have equal and opposite displacements in phase
(c) both masses vibrate with a frequency different to the frequency of single spring mass system
(d) None of the above

**160.** The following $(r, \theta, \phi)$ are the coordinate of
(a) cartesian coordinate system
(b) cylindrical coordinate system
(c) spherical coordinate system
(d) None of the above

**161.** If we make a canonical transformation from the set of variables $(p_k, q_k)$ to new set of variables $(P_k, Q_k)$ and the transformed Hamiltonian is identically zero, then
(a) the new variables are cyclic
(b) the new variables are not constant in time
(c) the new variables are not cyclic
(d) None of the above

**162.** Lagrange's equations for conservative, non-holonomic system are
(a) $\left(\frac{\partial T}{\partial q_k}\right) - \frac{\partial L}{\partial \dot{q}_k} = \sum_{i=1}^{m} \lambda_i a_{ik}, (k = 1, \ldots, n)$ where $a_{ik}$ are functions of $q_k'$s and $t$ and $\lambda_i$ are constants $(i = 1, \ldots, m)$
(b) $\frac{d}{dt}\left(\frac{\partial T}{\partial \dot{q}_k}\right) = \sum_{i=1}^{m} \lambda_i a_{ik}, (k = 1, \ldots, n)$ where $a_{ik}$ are functions of $q_k$'s and $t$ and $\lambda_t$ are constants $(i = 1, \ldots, m)$
(c) $\frac{d}{dt}\left(\frac{\partial T}{\partial \dot{q}_k}\right) - \frac{\partial L}{\partial q_k} = \sum_{i=1}^{m} \lambda_i a_{ik}, (k = 1, \ldots, n)$ where $a_{ik}$ are functions of $q_k$'s and $t$ and $\lambda_t$ are constants $(i = 1, \ldots, m)$
(d) None of the abvoe

**163.** An example of stable equilibrium is
(a) a hanging spring mass system in the stationary position
(b) an egg standing on one end
(c) a book placed flat anywhere on a table
(d) None of the above

**164.** Hamilton principal function $S$ and Hamilton characteristic function $W$ for conservative system are related as, where $E$ is the total energy and $t$ is the time
(a) $S = W$
(b) $S + W - Et$
(c) $S = W + Et$
(d) None of these

**165.** The centre of mass is defined as
(a) $R = \frac{\sum_i m_i r_i}{\sum_i m_i} = \frac{\sum_i m_i r_i}{M}$, where $\sum_i m_i = M$ (total mass of system)
(b) $R = \frac{\sum_i m_i r_i}{(\sum_i m_i)^2} = \frac{\sum_i m_i r_i}{M^2}$, where $\sum_i m_i = M$ (total mass of system)
(c) $R = \sum_i m_i r_i \sum_i m_i = M \sum_i m_i r_i$, where $\sum_i m_i = M$ (total mass of system)
(d) None of the above

**166.** If $p_k$ and $q_k$ $(k = 1, 2, 3)$ represent the momentum and position coordinates respectively, for a particle
(a) the phase space is six dimensional
(b) the configuration space is six dimensional
(c) the configuration space is three dimensional
(d) None of the above

**167.** Non-holonomic constraints are
(a) the constraints that can be expressed as equation form
(b) the constraints that cannot be expressed as equation form
(c) equation of constraints that contain time as explicit variable
(d) equation of constraints that does not contains time as explicit variable

**168.** d'Alembert's principle is
(a) $\sum_{i=1}^{N} (F_i - p_i) \cdot \delta r_i \neq 0$, where $p_i = \frac{\partial F_i}{\partial t}$ is the reversed effective force
(b) $\sum_{i=1}^{N} (F_i - p_i) \cdot \delta r_i = 0$, where $p_i = \frac{\partial F_i}{\partial t}$ is the reversed effective force
(c) $\sum_{i=1}^{N} (F_i - p_i) \cdot \delta r_i \geq 0$, where $p_i = \frac{\partial F_i}{\partial t}$ is the reversed effective force
(d) $\sum_{i=1}^{N} (F_i - p_i) \cdot \delta r_i \leq 0$, where $p_i = \frac{\partial F_i}{\partial t}$ is the reversed effective force

**169.** Lagrange's equations for a conservative holonomic dynamical system are
(a) $\left(\frac{\partial T}{\partial \dot{q}_k}\right) = \left(\frac{\partial L}{\partial \dot{q}_k}\right) (k = 1, \ldots, n)$
(b) $\left(\frac{\partial T}{\partial \dot{q}_k}\right)^2 = \frac{\partial L}{\partial \dot{q}_k} (k = 1, \ldots, n)$
(c) $\frac{d}{dt}\left(\frac{\partial T}{\partial \dot{q}_k}\right) = \frac{\partial L}{\partial q_k} (k = 1, \ldots, n)$
(d) None of the above

**170.** Relation between cartesian and cylindrical coordinate system

(a) $\begin{cases} x = r\cos\theta \\ y = r\sin\theta \\ z = z \end{cases}$ (b) $\begin{cases} x = r\sin\theta \\ y = r\cos\theta \\ z = z \end{cases}$

(c) $\begin{cases} x = r\cos\theta \\ y = r\sin\theta \\ z = \sin\theta_z \end{cases}$ (d) None of these

**171.** The total angular momentum of a system of particles about a point

(a) is the sum of angular momentum of the system about the centre of mass and the angular momentum about the reference point of the system mass, concentrated at the centre of the mass

(b) is the difference of angular momentum of the system about the centre of mass and the angular momentum about the reference point of the system mass, concentrated at the centre of the mass

(c) is the product of angular momentum of the system about the centre of mass and the angular momentum about the reference point of the system mass, concentrated at the centre of the mass

(d) None of the above

**172.** If a small displacement of the system from the rest position (after giving small energy) results in a small bounded motion about the equilibrium position. Then, system is in

(a) stable equilibrium (b) unstable equilibrium
(c) neutral equilibrium (d) None of these

**173.** Lagrange's bracket is

(a) canonical invariant (b) canonical variant
(c) non-invariant (d) None of these

**174.** If $p_k$ and $q_k$ $(k = 1, 2, 3)$ represent the momentum and position coordinates respectively, for a particle

(a) the phase space is six dimensional
(b) the configuration space is six dimensional
(c) the phase space is three dimensional
(d) None of the above

**175.** Conservation of linear momentum

(a) if the total external force on the system is zero, the total linear momentum is constant of motion
(b) total linear momentum is zero
(c) the total angular momentum of a system of particles is conserved
(d) None of the above

**176.** If the poisson bracket of a function with the Hamiltonian vanishes

(a) the function depends upon time
(b) the function is a constant of motion
(c) the function is not the constant of motion
(d) None of the above

# Exercise 2 (For Part 'C')

**Directions** (Q. Nos. 1-63) *Questions may have one or more than one correct option.*

**1.** If a rigid body is rotating with an angular velocity $\omega$ about an instantaneous axis through a fixed point in the body, even the angular momentum vector **J** about the same point

(a) will be always in the direction of $\omega$.
(b) may be in the direction of $\omega$.
(c) may have different direction to that of $\omega$.
(d) will be always perpendicular to $\omega$.

**2.** According to the principal of least action

(a) $\Delta\int(\sum_k p_k\dot{q}_k - H)dt = 0$

(b) $\Delta\int\sum_k p_k\dot{q}_k\,dt = 0$

(c) $\Delta\int(H + L) = 0$

(d) $\int\sum_k p_k\dot{q}_k\,dt = 0$

**3.** If $I_1, I_2$ and $I_3$ represent the principal moments of inertia of a rigid body and $\omega = (\omega_1, \omega_2, \omega_3)$ is the angular velocity with components along the three principal axes,

(a) the z-component of the torque acting on the body in general is
$$T_3 = I_3\dot{\omega}_3$$

(b) the z-component of the torque acting on the body in general is
$$T_3 = I_3\dot{\omega}_3 + (I_2 - I_1)\omega_1\omega_2$$

(c) for torque free motion of the rigid body, always we have
$$I_3\omega_3 = \text{constant}$$

(d) for torque free motion of the rigid body, in general we have
$$I_3\dot{\omega}_3 = (I_1 - I_2)\omega_1\omega_2$$

**4.** A heavy symmetrical top is rotating under the action of a gravitational angular momentum along the figure axis.

(a) The torque is perpendicular to $L_3$
(b) The angular momentum $L_3$ will change in magnitude.

(c) The angular momentum $L_3$ will remain constant in magnitude.
(d) The angular momentum $L_3$ will remain constant in magnitude as well as in direction.

**5.** Constraint in a rigid body is
(a) holonomic (b) non-holonomic
(c) scleronomic (d) rheonomic

**6.** Generalized coordinates
(a) depend on each other
(b) are independent of each other
(c) are necessarily spherical coordinates
(d) may be cartesian coordinates

**7.** An example of stable equilibrium is/are
(a) a hanging spring mass system in the stationary position
(b) a pendulum in the rest position
(c) an egg standing on one end
(d) a book placed flat anywhere on a table

**8.** Whenever the Lagrangian for a system does not contain a coordinate explicitly,
(a) $q_k$ is cyclic coordinate
(b) $p_k$ is cyclic coordinate
(c) $p_k$, the generalized momentum, is a constant of motion
(d) $q_k$ is always zero

**9.** The dimensions of generalized momentum
(a) are always those of linear momentum
(b) are always those of angular momentum
(c) may be those of linear momentum
(d) may be those of angular momentum

**10.** Choose the correct statements.
(a) The angular momentum is conserved for systems possessing rotational symmetry.
(b) If the Lagrangian of a system is invariant under translation along a direction, the corresponding linear momentum is conserved.
(c) If the Lagrangian of a system is invariant under translation along a direction, we cannot say anything about the corresponding linear momentum.
(d) For a conservative system, the Hamiltonian is equal to the sum of kinetic and potential energies.

**11.** In case of two coupled identical pendulums, oscillating in a plane,
(a) each pendulum always execute simple harmonic motion
(b) two pendulums may execute simple harmonic motions
(c) the general motion can be expressed as a super position of two simple harmonic motions of the same frequency
(d) the general motion can be expressed as a super position of two simple harmonic motions of different frequencies

**12.** In case of a symmetric mode for two coupled identical spring mass systems,
(a) both masses have equal displacements in phase
(b) both masses have equal and opposite displacements
(c) both masses vibrate with the frequency of single spring mass system
(d) both masses vibrate with a frequency different to the frequency of single spring mass system

**13.** In case of two coupled identical pendulums, in general,
(a) the potential energy is a homogeneous quadratic function, when expressed in terms of actual displacements
(b) the potential energy is not a homogeneous quadratic function, when expressed in terms of actual displacements
(c) the potential energy is a homogeneous quadratic function, when expressed in terms of normal coordinates
(d) the potential energy is not a homogeneous quadratic function, when expressed in terms of normal coordinates

**14.** In case of double pendulum, if the masses as well as thread lengths are equal ($m_1 = m_2 = m$, $l_1 = l_2 = l$),
(a) two normal mode frequencies are equal to that of or pendulum of length $2l$ and mass $m$
(b) two normal mode frequencies are equal to that of single pendulum of length $l$ and mass $m$
(c) two normal mode frequencies are different
(d) the sum of squared frequencies of normal modes is equal to four times the squared frequency of a single pendulum of length $l$ and mass $m$

**15.** In case of a linear triatomic of molecule $XY_2$ type, the eigen frequencies $\omega_1, \omega_2$ and $\omega_3$ can be represented as
(a) $\omega_1 = \omega_2 = \omega_3$ (b) $\omega_1 = 0,\ \omega_2 = \omega_3$
(c) $\omega_1 = 0,\ \omega_2 \neq \omega_3$ (d) $\omega_1 \neq \omega_2 \neq \omega_3$

**16.** Consider a particle falling freely under gravity near the surface of earth, then Lagrange's equations of motion are
(a) $\ddot{x} = 0$ (b) $\ddot{y} = 0$
(c) $\ddot{z} = g$ (d) $\ddot{z} + g = 0$

**17.** Given simply supported beam under a uniformly distributed load $w$.
(a) the differential equation governing the deflection $y(x)$ of the beam is $EI\dfrac{d^4y}{dx^4} - w = 0,\ 0 < x < l$
(b) the differential equation governing the deflection $y(x)$ of the beam is $EI\dfrac{d^3y}{dx^3} + w = 0,\ 0 < x < l$
(c) the deflection of the beam is given by
$$\bar{y}(x) = \frac{4wl^4}{\pi^5 EI}\left\{\sin\left(\frac{\pi x}{l}\right) + \frac{1}{243}\sin\left(\frac{3\pi x}{l}\right)\right\}$$

(d) the deflection of the beam is given by

$$\bar{y}(x) = \frac{4wl^3}{\pi EI}\left\{\cos\left(\frac{\pi x}{l}\right) + \frac{1}{46}\sin\left(\frac{3\pi x}{l}\right)\right\}$$

**18.** The path on which a particle in the absence of friction, will slide from one point to another in the shortest time under the action of gravity is

(a) the equation of the path is $x = b(\phi - \sin\phi)$, $y = b(1 - \cos\phi)$

(b) a cycloid

(c) a rectangle

(d) a square

**19.** A particle of mass $m$ falls a given distance $z_0$ in time $t_0 = \sqrt{2z_0/g}$ and the distance travelled in time $t$ is given by $z = at + bt^2$, where constants $a$ and $b$ are such that the time $t_0$ is always the same

(a) the integration $\int_0^{t_0} L\,dt$ is an extremum for real values of the coefficients, when $a = 0$ and $b = g/2$

(b) the kinetic energy of the particle is $\frac{1}{2}m\dot{z}^2$

(c) the Lagrangion is $\frac{1}{2}m\dot{z}^2 + mgz$

(d) the potential energy of the particle is $mgz$

**20.** A particle of mass $m$ falls a given distance $z_0$ in time $t_0 = \sqrt{2z_0/g}$ and the distance travelled in time $t$ is given by $z = at + bt^2$, where constants $a$ and $b$ are such that the time $t_0$ is always the same

(a) the integration $\int_0^{t_0} L\,dt$ is an extremum for real values of the coefficients only when $a = 0$ and $b = g/2$

(b) the integration $\int_0^{t_0} L\,dt$ is an extremum for real values of the coefficients only when $a = 0$ or $b = g/2$

(c) the integral $\int_0^{t_0} L\,dt$ is an extremum if $\frac{d}{dt}\left[\frac{\partial L}{\partial \dot{z}}\right] - \frac{\partial L}{\partial z} = 0$

(d) The integral $\int_0^{t_0} L\,dt$ is an extremum if $\frac{d}{dt}\left[\frac{\partial L}{\partial \dot{z}}\right] = \frac{\partial L}{\partial z}$

**21.** The Lagrangian equation of motion in polar coordinates for a particle of mass $m$ is moving in a plane under an inverse square law attractive force are

(a) $m\ddot{r} - mr\dot{\theta}^2 + \frac{k}{r^2} = 0$ (b) $mr^2\ddot{\theta} + 2mr^2\dot{\theta} = 0$

(c) $mr + mr\dot{\theta}^2 = 0$ (d) $mr^2\dot{\theta}^2 + m\dot{\theta}^2 = 0$

**22.** For two dimensional isotropic harmonic oscillator,

(a) hamiltonian function is

$$H = \frac{1}{2m}(p_x^2 + p_y^2) + \frac{1}{2}k(x^2 + y^2)$$

(b) Hamiltonian equation of motion is $\dot{x} = \frac{p_x}{m}$, $\dot{y} = \frac{p_y}{m}$

(c) equation of motion is $p_x = m\ddot{x}$, $p_y = m\ddot{y}$

$$m\ddot{x} + kx = 0$$
$$m\ddot{y} + kx = 0$$

(d) The equation of motion are $m\ddot{x} + m\ddot{y} = 0$

**23.** An object moves under the influence of gravity on the frictionless inner surface of the elliptic paraboloid given by

$$bx^2 + cy = az$$

where a, b, c are positive constants. The required Lagrangian equations of motion are

(a) $m\ddot{x} = 2bx\lambda$ (b) $m\ddot{y} = 2cy\lambda$

(c) $m\ddot{z} = -mg - a\lambda$ (d) $m\ddot{x} + m\ddot{y} + m\ddot{z} = 0$

**24.** Given, transformation equations $Q = q^m \cos np$ and $P = q^m \sin np$

(a) for $m = \frac{1}{2}$ and $p = 2$ the transformation equations become canonical

(b) for $m = \frac{1}{2}$ and $p = 2$ the transformation equations are not canonical

(c) $F_3 = -\frac{1}{2}Q^2 \tan 2p$ is the generating function

(d) $F_3 = \frac{1}{2}Q^2 \sec^2 p$ is the generating function

**25.** In cylindrical coordinates the Hamiltonian equation of motion are

(a) $\dot{r} = \frac{p_r}{m}$ (b) $\dot{\theta} = \frac{p_\theta}{m}$

(c) $\dot{z} = \frac{p_z}{m}$ (d) $p_r = m\dot{r}$

**26.** Let a bead slides on a wire in the shape of a cycloid described by equations $x = a(\theta - \sin\theta)$

$$y = a(1 + \cos\theta)$$

where $0 \le \theta \le 2\pi$ neglect friction between the bead and the wire, then

(a) the kinetic energy of the bead is $ma^2\dot{\theta}^2(1 - \cos\theta)$

(b) the potential energy of the bead is $mga(1 + \cos\theta)$

(c) the Lagrangian is

$$= ma^2\dot{\theta}^2(1 - \cos\theta) - mga(1 + \cos\theta)$$

(d) the Lagrangian equation of motion is

$$\ddot{\theta}(1 - \cos\theta) + \frac{1}{2}\sin\theta\,\dot{\theta}^2 - \frac{g}{2a}\sin\theta = 0$$

**27.** There is a charged particle of mass $m$ in an electromagnetic field

(a) the kinetic energy of the particle is $\frac{1}{2}mv^2$

(b) the Hamiltonian can be interpreted as the sum of kinetic and electrostatic potential energies of the particle

(c) the Hamiltonian cannot be interpreted as the sum of kinetic and electrostatic potential energies of the particle

(d) the particle have no kinetic energy

**28.** If [ϕ, ψ] be the poisson bracket $\frac{d}{dt}[\phi,\psi]=\left[\frac{d\phi}{dt},\psi\right]+\left[\phi,\frac{d\psi}{dt}\right]$. Then,

(a) $\frac{d}{dt}[\phi,\psi]=\left[\frac{d\phi}{dt},\psi\right]+\left[\phi,\frac{d\psi}{dt}\right]$

(b) $\frac{d}{dt}[\phi,\psi]=\frac{\partial}{\partial t}=\left\{\frac{\partial\phi\partial\psi}{\partial q_i\partial p_i}-\frac{\partial\psi\partial\phi}{\partial q_i\partial i_1}\right\}$

(c) $\frac{d}{dt}[\phi,\psi]=\left[\frac{d\phi}{dt},\psi\right]$

(d) $\frac{d}{dt}[\phi,\psi]=\left[\phi,\frac{d\psi}{dt}\right]$

**29.** A particle of mass $m$ moves in a force field of potential $V$, then in spherical polar coordinates

(a) the kinetic energies $\frac{1}{2}m(\dot{r}^2+r^2\dot{\theta}^2+r^2\,\dot{\phi}^2\sin^2\theta)$

(b) one of the Hamilton equation of motion is $\dot{r}=\frac{Pr}{m}$

(c) one of the Hamilton equation of motion is $\dot{\theta}=\frac{P_\theta}{mr^2}$

(d) one of the Hamilton equation of motion is $\dot{\phi}=\frac{p_\phi}{mr^2\sin^2\theta}$

**30.** If $\{q_l,q_i\}\{p_l,q_j\}$ are the Lagrange brackets and $[q_l,q_j],[p_l,q_j]$. Then,

(a) $\sum_{l=1}^{n}\{q_l,q_i\}[q_l,q_j]+\sum_{l=1}^{n}\{p_l,q_i\}[p_l,q_j]$

(b) $[q_i,q_i]=0$

(c) $\{q_i,q_i\}=0$

(d) $[p_i\,q_i]=-[q_i,p_i]$

**31.** In a spherical pendulum, a small bob (particle) of mass $m$ is constrained to move on a smooth spherical surface, say of radius $R$, $R$ being the length of the pendulum

(a) the Lagrangian is $\frac{1}{2}mk^2(\dot{\theta}^2+\dot{\phi}^2\sin^2\theta)+mg\,R\cos\theta$

(b) $\ddot{\theta}-\frac{1}{2}\sin 2\theta\,\dot{\phi}+\frac{g}{R}\sin\theta=0$, is one of the equation of motion

(c) $mR^2\sin^2\theta\,\dot{\phi}=$ constant, is one of the equation of motion

(d) $mR^2\cos^2\theta\,\dot{\phi}^2=$ constant, is one of the equation of motion

**32.** If the transformation equations between two salts of coordinates are

$$P=2(1+q^{1/2}\cos p)\,q^{1/2}\sin p,$$
$$Q=\log(1+q^{1/2}\cos p),\ \text{then}$$

(a) the transformation is canonical

(b) the generating function of this transformation is $F_3=-(e^Q-1)^2\tan p$

(c) the transformation is not canonical

(d) the generating function of this transformation is $F_3=\tan p$

**33.** For a simple pendulum,

(a) the equation of motion is $l\ddot{\theta}+g\sin\theta=0$

(b) the equation of motion for small θ is $\ddot{\theta}+\frac{g}{l}\theta=0$

(c) the force of constraints is $\partial=-ml\dot{\theta}^2-mg\cos\theta$

(d) the tension is $F=ml\dot{\theta}^2-mg\cos\theta$

**34.** Given, the transformation $Q=\frac{1}{p}$, $P=qp^2$, then

(a) the transformation is canonical

(b) the transformation is not canonical

(c) $\delta PdQ-\delta QdP$ is invariant

(d) $\delta PdQ-\delta QdP$ is not invariant

**35.** If the potential energy in the Lagrangian contains velocity dependent terms. Then, the canonical momentum corresponding to a coordinate of rotation θ of the entire system is not longer the mechanical angular momentum $L_\theta$. Let is given by

$$p_\theta=L_\theta-\sum_i\mathbf{n}\cdot\mathbf{r}_i\times\Delta\mathbf{v}_i\cdot V$$

where $\Delta_v$ is the gradient operator in which the derivatives are with respect to the velocity components and $n$ is the unit vector in the direction of rotation, then

(a) is not longer the mechanical angular momentum $L_\theta$

(b) it is given by $p_\theta=L_\theta-\sum_i\mathbf{n}\cdot\mathbf{r}_i\times\Delta\mathbf{v}_i\cdot V$

(c) is the mechanical angular momentum $L_\theta$

(d) is given by $p_\theta=0$

**36.** A solid homogeneous cylinder of radius $r$, rolls without slipping on the inside of a stationary large cylinder of radius, $R$.

(a) The equation of motion is $\frac{3}{2}(R-r)\ddot{\phi}+g\,\phi=0$

(b) The equation of motion is $\frac{2}{3}R\ddot{\phi}+g\phi=0$

(c) The period of small oscillation is $T=2\pi\sqrt{\frac{3(R-r)}{2g}}$

(d) The period of small oscillation is $T=\pi\sqrt{\frac{3R}{2gr}}$

**37.** A bead slides on a wire in the shape of a cycloid described by equations

$$x=a(\theta-\sin\theta)$$
$$y=a(1+\cos\theta)$$

where $0\le\theta\le 2\pi$

(a) The Lagrangian is $ma^2\dot{\theta}^2(1-\cos\theta)-mga(1+\cos\theta)$

(b) The kinetic energy of the bead is $ma^2\dot{\theta}^2(1-\cos\theta)$

(c) The potential energy of the bead is $mga(1+\cos\theta)$

(d) The equation of motion of the bead is $\ddot{\theta}(1-\cos\theta)+\frac{1}{2}\sin\theta\,\dot{\theta}^2-\frac{g}{2a}\sin\theta=0$

**38.** Let a particle is moving under a central force, then

(a) the kinetic energy of the particle is $\frac{1}{2}m(\dot{r}^2 + r^2\dot{\theta}^2)$

(b) the potential energy of the particle is $-\frac{k}{r}$

(c) the Lagrangion is $\frac{1}{2}m(\dot{r}^2 + r^2\dot{\theta}^2) + \frac{k}{r}$

(d) The equation of motion the particle is

$$\left.\begin{aligned} m\ddot{r} - mr\dot{\theta}^2 + \frac{k}{r^2} &= 0 \\ 2mr\,\dot{r}\dot{\theta} + mr^2\ddot{\theta} &= 0 \end{aligned}\right\}$$

**39.** Which of the following statement is/are true?

(a) The kinetic energy of simple pendulum is $\frac{1}{2}ml^2\dot{\theta}^2$.

(b) The potential energy of simple pendulum is $-mgl\cos\theta$.

(c) The Lagrangion of simple pendulum is $\frac{1}{2}ml^2\dot{\theta}^2 - mgl(1-\cos\theta)$

(d) The equation of motion of simple pendulum $\ddot{\theta} + \frac{g}{l}\sin\theta = 0$.

**40.** Which of the following statement is/are true?

(a) The Lagrange's equation of motion for one dimensional x (say) is given by $\frac{d}{dt}\left(\frac{\partial L}{\partial \dot{x}}\right) - \frac{\partial L}{\partial x} = 0$.

(b) The kinetic energy for linear harmonic oscillator is $\frac{1}{2}m\dot{x}^2$

(c) The potential energy for linear harmonic oscillator is $\frac{1}{2}kx^2 + c$.

where c is constanted, k is spring constant.

(d) $m\ddot{x} + kx = 0$ is equation of linear harmonic oscillator.

**41.** A particle of mass M moves on a plane in the field of force given by

$$F = -\mathbf{r}\,kr\cos\theta$$

where k is constant and **r** is the radial unit vector.

(a) The angular momentum of the particle about the origin be conserved.

(b) The angular momentum of the particle about the origin is not conserved.

(c) The differential equation of the orbit of the particle is $M\ddot{r} - Mr\dot{\theta}^2 + kr\cos\theta = 0$

(d) The kinetic energy of the particle is $\frac{1}{2}M(\dot{r}^2 + r^2\dot{\theta}^2)$

**42.** Which of the following statements is/are true?

(a) The equations of motion of the double pendulum are given by

$$(m_1 + m_2)l_1\ddot{\theta}_1 + m_2 l_2\ddot{\theta}_2 + (m_1 + m_2)g\theta_1 = 0$$

and $l_1\ddot{\theta}_1 + l_2\ddot{\theta}_2 + g\theta_2 = 0$ for small angles $\theta_1, \theta_2$

(b) The kinetic energy of the double pendulum is given by

$$\frac{1}{2}(m_1 + m_2)l_1^2\dot{\theta}_1^2 + \frac{1}{2}m_2 l^2\dot{\theta}_2^2 + m_2 l_1 l_2\,\dot{\theta}_1\dot{\theta}_2\cos(\theta_1 - \theta_2)$$

(c) The potential energy of the double pendulum is given by

$$m_1 g l_1(1-\cos\theta_1) + m_2 g(l_1 + l_2 - l_1\cos\theta_1 - l_2\cos\theta_2)$$

(d) The Lagrangion of the double pendulum is given by

$$\frac{1}{2}(m_1 + m_2)l_1^2\dot{\theta}_1^2 + \frac{l}{2}m_2 l_2\,\dot{\theta}_2^2 + m_2 l_1 l_2\,\dot{\theta}_1\dot{\theta}_2\cos(\theta_1 - \theta_2) - (m_1 - m_2)gl_1(1-\cos\theta_1) - m_2 g l_2(1-\cos\theta_2)$$

**43.** For spherical pendulum. Where spherical bob is constrained to move on a spherer.

(a) The kinetic energy is $\frac{1}{2}mr^2(\dot{\theta}^2 + \sin^2\theta\,\dot{\phi}^2)$

(b) The potential energy is $mgr\cos\theta$

(c) The Lagrangion is

$$\frac{1}{2}mr^2(\dot{\theta}^2 + \sin^2\theta\,\dot{\phi}^2) - mgr\cos\theta$$

(d) The equation of motion are

$$mr^2\ddot{\theta} - mr^2\sin\theta\cos\theta\,\dot{\phi}^2 - mgr\sin\theta = 0$$

$$mr^2\frac{d}{dt}(\sin^2\theta\dot{\phi}) = 0$$

**44.** Given, the Lagrangian L,

$$L = \frac{1}{2}\mu(\dot{r}^2 + r^2\dot{\theta}^2) + \frac{GMm}{r}$$

when $\mu = \frac{mM}{m+M}$. Then,

(a) the general equation of Routhian is $R = \sum_{k=1}^{s} p_k\dot{q}_k - L$

(b) the Routhian of the given Lagrangion is $R = -\frac{1}{2}\mu\dot{r}^2 + \frac{p\theta}{2\mu r^2} - \frac{GMm}{R}$

(c) the general equation of Routhian is $R = \frac{\partial L}{\partial \theta}$

(d) the Routhian of given Lagrangian is $R = \frac{1}{2}\mu r^2 + \theta^2$

**45.** If Hamiltonian function is not an explicit function of t, then

(a) Hamiltonian function is a constant of the motion

(b) Hamiltonian function is variable of the motion

(c) $\frac{dH}{dt} = 0$

(d) $\frac{dH}{dt} \neq 0$

**46.** A particle of mass $m$ moving in a vertical plane along a given curve in gravitational field. The equation of the curve is $x = x(s)$ and $z = z(s)$.

(a) The kinetic energy of the particle $\frac{1}{2}m(x'^2 + z'^2)\dot{s}^2$

(b) The potential energy the particle is $mgz(s)$

(c) The equation of motion of the particle is $\frac{d}{dt}[m(x^2 + z'^2)\dot{s}] - m\dot{s}^2(x'x'' - z'z'') + mgz' = 0$

(d) The Lagrangian in $ms$ of $s$ is $\frac{d}{dt}\left(\frac{\partial L}{\partial \dot{s}}\right) - \frac{\partial L}{\partial s} = 0$

**47.** Given

$$\left.\begin{array}{l} P = q \cot p \\ Q = \log(1/q \sin p) \end{array}\right\}$$

Then,

(a) the generating function is $F = e^{-Q}(1 - q^2e^{2Q})^{1/2} + q\sin^{-1}(qe^Q)$

(b) this transformation is canonical

(c) this transformation is not canonical

(d) the generating functions $F = \sin^{-1}q^2 + \cos^{-1}q^2$

**48.** For $H$ the Hamiltonian function

(a) $\frac{\partial H}{\partial t} = \frac{dH}{dt}$ (b) $\frac{\partial H}{\partial t} \neq \frac{dH}{dt}$

(c) $\frac{\partial H}{\partial t}\frac{dt}{dH} = 1$ (d) $\frac{\partial H}{\partial t} - \frac{dH}{dt} = 0$

**49.** For a simple pendulum of length $l$ and mass of bob $m$ in conservative system

(a) the Lagrangian equation of motion is $\frac{d}{dt}\left(\frac{\partial L}{\partial \dot{\theta}}\right) - \frac{\partial L}{\partial \theta} = 0$

(b) the kinetic energy is $T = \frac{1}{2}ml^2\dot{\theta}^2$

(c) the potential energy is $V = -mgl\cos\theta$

(d) the equation of motion is $\ddot{\theta} + \frac{g}{l}\sin\theta = 0$

**50.** Given a particle of mass $m$, moving in a plane under inverse law of attractive force, in polar coordinates, then

(a) the equation of motion is $m\ddot{r} - mr\dot{\theta}^2 + \frac{k}{r^2} = 0$

(b) the equation of motion is $2m\dot{r}\dot{\theta} + mr^2\ddot{\theta} = 0$

(c) the potential energy is $-\frac{k}{r}$

(d) the kinetic energy is $\frac{1}{2}m(\dot{r}^2 + r^2\dot{\theta}^2)$

**51.** Let particle of mass $m$ moves in a plane. Then, in polar coordinates

(a) the kinetic energy is $\frac{1}{2}(m\dot{r}^2 + (r\dot{\theta})^2$

(b) $\frac{d}{dt}(m\dot{r}) - m\dot{\theta}^2 r = F_r$ is one of the equation of motion

(c) $2m\dot{r}\dot{\theta} + rm\ddot{\theta} = F_\theta$ is one of the equation of motion

(d) the kinetic energy is $\frac{1}{2}mv^2$

**52.** Given the transformation

$$Q = \log\left(\frac{1}{q}\sin p\right), \quad P = q\cot p$$

(a) This transformation is canonical

(b) This transformation is not canonical

(c) $\dot{Q} = \frac{\partial H}{\partial P}$

(d) $\dot{P} = -\frac{\partial H}{\partial Q}$

**53.** The equation of motion of a particle in space in cartesian coordinates are

(a) $m\ddot{x} = F_x$

(b) $m\ddot{y} = F_y$

(c) $m\ddot{z} = F_z$

(d) $m\ddot{x} = m\ddot{y} = m\ddot{z}$

**54.** Given Hamiltonian of a dynamical system

$$H = q_1p_1 - q_2p_2 - aq_1^2 + bq_2^2$$

where $a$, $b$ are constants. What is the solution of the given system?

The solution of the given system are

(a) $q_1 = e^{t + C_1}$

(b) $q_2 = e^{-t + C_2}$

(c) $p_1 = 2ae^{t + C_1} + e^{C_2 - t}$

(d) $p_2 = -2bte^{t + C_2} + e^{t + C_3}$

**55.** If the equations of transformation do not depend explicitly on time and if the potential energy is velocity independent. Then,

(a) Hamiltonian $H$ is the total energy of the system

(b) Hamiltonian $H$ is not the total energy of the system

(c) Hamiltonian $H$ is the sum of kinetic energy and potential energy

(d) Hamiltonian $H$ is not the sum of kinetic energy and potential energy

**56.** Which of the following statement is/are true?

(a) The Lagrange's equation for conservative holonomic dynamical system is

$$\frac{d}{dt}\left(\frac{\partial L}{\partial \dot{q}_k}\right) - \frac{\partial L}{\partial q_k} = 0, \ (k = 1, 2, \ldots, n)$$

(b) The Hamilton's principal is $\delta\int_{t_1}^{t_2} L\,dt = 0$ for conservative, holonomic dynamic system

(c) Both (a) and (b)

(d) Neither (a) nor (a)

**57.** Which of the following statements are true

(a) $\{q_i, q_j\}_{q,p} = 0$ (b) $\{q_i, p_j\} = \begin{cases} 1, \text{ if } i = j \\ 0, \text{ if } i \neq j \end{cases}$

(c) $\{q_i, q_i\}_{q,q} \neq 0$ (d) $\{q_i, p_i\} = \begin{cases} 1, \text{ if } i = i \\ 0, \text{ if } i \neq i \end{cases}$

**58.** Given, the Lagrangian function is given as $L = \dot{q}_k q_k - \sqrt{(1 - \dot{q}_k^2)}$, then

(a) the Lagrangian equation is $\ddot{q}_k = 0$
(b) the Lagrangian equation is $\ddot{q}_k \neq 0$
(c) the Lagrangian equation is given by
$$\frac{d}{dt}\left(\frac{\partial T}{\partial \dot{q}_k}\right) - \frac{\partial L}{\partial q_k} = 0$$
(d) the Lagrangian equation states that generalized acceleration is zero

**59.** Two objects of masses $m_1 = 200$ g and $m_2 = 500$ g possess respectively, velocities $\mathbf{v}_1 = 10\,\hat{\mathbf{i}}$ m/s and $\mathbf{v}_2 = 3\hat{\mathbf{i}} + 5\hat{\mathbf{j}}$ m/s just prior to a collision during which they become permanently attached to each other. Then,

(a) The velocity of the centre of mass is
$$\mathbf{V} = 5\mathbf{i} + \left(\frac{25}{7}\right)\mathbf{j}$$
(b) The final momentum of the combinaton in the laboratory frame is $3.5\mathbf{i} + 2.5\mathbf{j}$
(c) The fraction of the initial total kinetic energy is associated with the motion after collision is
$$\frac{T_f}{T_i} = 0.72$$
(d) $\dfrac{T_f}{T_i} = 1$

**60.** Given, the transformation defined by $q = \sqrt{[2P]}\sin Q$, $p = \sqrt{[2P]}\cos Q$, then

(a) is canonical
(b) is not canonical
(c) it is canonical, if $[Q, P] = 1$
(d) it is canonical, if $[Q, Q] = [P, P] = 0$

**61.** For an ideal spring mass arrangement

(a) the Hamiltonian is $\dot{x} = \dfrac{p_x}{m}$
(b) the Hamiltonian is $\dot{p}_x = -k_x$
(c) the Hamiltonian equation of motion is
$$\ddot{x} + \frac{k}{m}x = 0$$
(d) the Hamiltonian equation of motion is
$$\ddot{x} = kx$$

**62.** Two heavy particles of weights $W_1$ and $W_2$ are connected by a light inextensible string and hang over a fixed smooth circular cylinder of radius $R$, the axis of which is horizontal. The condition of equilibrium of the system by applying the principal of virtual work is

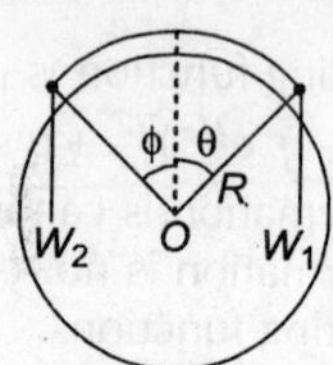


(a) $W_1 \sin\theta + W_2 \sin\phi = 0$
(b) $W_1 \sin\theta - W_2 \sin\phi = 0$
(c) $\dfrac{W_1}{W_2} = \dfrac{\sin\phi}{\sin\theta}$
(d) $\dfrac{W_1}{W_2} = \dfrac{\sin\theta}{\sin\phi}$

**63.** Let function $f$ does not depend on $x$ explicitly *i.e.*, $f = f(y, y', x)$. Then,

(a) $f - y'\dfrac{\partial f}{\partial y'} = \text{Constant}$ (b) $f - y'\dfrac{\partial f}{\partial y} \neq \text{Constant}$

(c) $\dfrac{\partial f}{\partial x} = 0$ (d) $\dfrac{\partial f}{\partial x} \neq 0$

# Answers

## Exercise 1

| | | | | | | | | | |
|---|---|---|---|---|---|---|---|---|---|
| **1.** (c) | **2.** (c) | **3.** (c) | **4.** (d) | **5.** (a) | **6.** (a) | **7.** (c) | **8.** (b) | **9.** (b) | **10.** (b) |
| **11.** (b) | **12.** (a) | **13.** (d) | **14.** (c) | **15.** (d) | **16.** (a) | **17.** (c) | **18.** (b) | **19.** (b) | **20.** (d) |
| **21.** (c) | **22.** (c) | **23.** (c) | **24.** (d) | **25.** (a) | **26.** (c) | **27.** (d) | **28.** (d) | **29.** (b) | **30.** (c) |
| **31.** (b) | **32.** (b) | **33.** (b) | **34.** (b) | **35.** (a) | **36.** (a) | **37.** (b) | **38.** (b) | **39.** (a) | **40.** (d) |
| **41.** (c) | **42.** (d) | **43.** (d) | **44.** (c) | **45.** (b) | **46.** (c) | **47.** (b) | **48.** (a) | **49.** (b) | **50.** (c) |
| **51.** (b) | **52.** (b) | **53.** (d) | **54.** (b) | **55.** (a) | **56.** (c) | **57.** (c) | **58.** (c) | **59.** (c) | **60.** (d) |
| **61.** (a) | **62.** (a) | **63.** (a) | **64.** (b) | **65.** (b) | **66.** (a) | **67.** (a) | **68.** (b) | **69.** (c) | **70.** (b) |
| **71.** (c) | **72.** (c) | **73.** (b) | **74.** (c) | **75.** (a) | **76.** (a) | **77.** (b) | **78.** (a) | **79.** (a) | **80.** (c) |
| **81.** (a) | **82.** (d) | **83.** (a) | **84.** (d) | **85.** (b) | **86.** (a) | **87.** (a) | **88.** (a) | **89.** (a) | **90.** (c) |
| **91.** (a) | **92.** (c) | **93.** (a) | **94.** (a) | **95.** (c) | **96.** (b) | **97.** (b) | **98.** (b) | **99.** (b) | **100.** (a) |
| **101.** (a) | **102.** (a) | **103.** (b) | **104.** (c) | **105.** (c) | **106.** (b) | **107.** (a) | **108.** (a) | **109.** (a) | **110.** (a) |

**111.** (a) **112.** (a) **113.** (a) **114.** (c) **115.** (b) **116.** (a) **117.** (b) **118.** (c) **119.** (b) **120.** (b)
**121.** (a) **122.** (c) **123.** (a) **124.** (c) **125.** (a) **126.** (a) **127.** (c) **128.** (a) **129.** (c) **130.** (b)
**131.** (d) **132.** (a) **133.** (b) **134.** (b) **135.** (a) **136.** (a) **137.** (b) **138.** (a) **139.** (a) **140.** (b)
**141.** (c) **142.** (c) **143.** (b) **144.** (c) **145.** (b) **146.** (c) **147.** (b) **148.** (b) **149.** (b) **150.** (a)
**151.** (a) **152.** (b) **153.** (a) **154.** (b) **155.** (a) **156.** (d) **157.** (a) **158.** (d) **159.** (a) **160.** (c)
**161.** (a) **162.** (c) **163.** (a) **164.** (b) **165.** (a) **166.** (c) **167.** (b) **168.** (b) **169.** (a) **170.** (a)
**171.** (a) **172.** (a) **173.** (a) **174.** (a) **175.** (a) **176.** (b)

## Exercise 2

**1.** (b,c) **2.** (b,c) **3.** (b,d) **4.** (a,c) **5.** (a,c) **6.** (b,d) **7.** (a,b) **8.** (a,c) **9.** (c,d) **10.** (a,b,d)
**11.** (b,d) **12.** (a,c) **13.** (b,c) **14.** (c,d) **15.** (c,d) **16.** (a,b,d) **17.** (a,c) **18.** (a,b) **19.** (a,b,c,d) **20.** (a,c,d)
**21.** (a,b) **22.** (a,b,c) **23.** (a,b,c) **24.** (a,c) **25.** (a,b,c,d) **26.** (a,b,c,d) **27.** (a,b) **28.** (a,b) **29.** (a,b,c,d) **30.** (a,b,c,d)
**31.** (a,b,c) **32.** (a,b) **33.** (a,b,c,d) **34.** (a,c) **35.** (a,b) **36.** (a,c) **37.** (a,b,c,d) **38.** (a,b,c,d) **39.** (a,b,c,d) **40.** (a,b,c,d)
**41.** (a,c,d) **42.** (a,b,c) **43.** (a,b,c,d) **44.** (a, b) **45.** (a,c) **46.** (a,b,c,d) **47.** (a,b) **48.** (a,c,d) **49.** (a,b,c,d) **50.** (a,b,c,d)
**51.** (a,b,c) **52.** (a,c,d) **53.** (a,b,c) **54.** (a,b,c,d) **55.** (a,c) **56.** (c) **57.** (a,b) **58.** (a,c,d) **59.** (a,b,c) **60.** (a,c,d)
**61.** (a,b,c) **62.** (b,c) **63.** (a,c)

# Hints & Solutions

## Exercise 1

**1.** Conjugate momentum is

$$p=\frac{\partial L}{\partial \dot{q}}=\frac{1}{2}(2\dot{q})-q+0=\dot{q}-q$$

**2.** We have, $H=\sum p_k\dot{q}_k-L$ $\quad(k=1\text{ only})$

Here, $\quad q_1=r^k$

$$\Rightarrow\quad p_1=\frac{\partial L}{\partial \dot{q}_1}=\frac{\partial}{\partial \dot{q}_1}(T-V)$$

$$=\frac{\partial T}{\partial \dot{q}_1}-\frac{\partial V}{\partial \dot{q}_1}$$

$$=\frac{\partial T}{\partial \dot{r}}-\frac{\partial V}{\partial \dot{r}}$$

$$=m\dot{r}-\frac{2\dot{r}}{rc^2}$$

Hence, $\quad p_1\dot{q}_1=\left(m\dot{r}-\frac{2\dot{r}}{rc^2}\right)\dot{r}=m\dot{r}^2-\frac{2\dot{r}^2}{rc^2}$

$$\Rightarrow\quad H=p_1\dot{q}_1-L=m\dot{r}^2-\frac{2\dot{r}^2}{rc^2}-(T-V)$$

$$=2T-\frac{2\dot{r}^2}{rc^2}-T+V$$

$$=T+V-\frac{2\dot{r}^2}{rc^2}$$

**3.** We have, $\quad L=\dot{q}_1^2+\dot{q}_2^2+\dot{q}_1\dot{q}_2-q_1^2-q_2^2$

$$p_1=\frac{\partial L}{\partial \dot{q}_1}=2\dot{q}_1+\dot{q}_2$$

$$p_2=\frac{\partial L}{\partial \dot{q}_2}=2\dot{q}_2+\dot{q}_1$$

$$p_1+p_2=3(\dot{q}_1+\dot{q}_2)\qquad\text{...(i)}$$

$$\frac{\partial L}{\partial q_1}-\frac{d}{dt}\left(\frac{\partial L}{\partial \dot{q}_1}\right)=0$$

$$\Rightarrow\quad -2q_1-\dot{p}_1=0$$

$$\Rightarrow\quad \dot{p}_1=-2q_1\qquad\text{...(ii)}$$

Similarly, $\quad \dot{p}_2=-2q_2\qquad\text{...(iii)}$

On adding Eqs. (ii) and (iii), we get

$$\Rightarrow\quad \dot{p}_1+\dot{p}_2=-2(q_1+q_2)\qquad\text{...(iv)}$$

On dividing Eq. (ii) by Eq. (iii), we get

$$\Rightarrow\quad \frac{\dot{p}_1}{\dot{p}_2}=\frac{q_1}{q_2}$$

From Eqs. (i), we get

$$\dot{p}_1+\dot{p}_2=3(\ddot{q}_1+\ddot{q}_2)\qquad\text{...(v)}$$

From Eqs. (iv) and (v), we get

$$\ddot{q}_1+\ddot{q}_2=-\frac{2}{3}(q_1+q_2)$$

Let $\quad q_1+q_2=\theta$

$$\Rightarrow\quad \ddot{Q}+\frac{2}{3}Q=0$$

$$\Rightarrow\quad Q=C_1\cos\sqrt{\frac{2}{3}}t+C_2\sin\sqrt{\frac{2}{3}}t$$

$\Rightarrow$ $Q$ executes simple harmonic motion.

**4.** We have, $\quad H=q_1p_1-q_2p_2-aq_1^2+bq_2^2$

$$\dot{q}_1=\frac{\partial H}{\partial p_1}=q_1,\quad \dot{q}_2=\frac{\partial H}{\partial p_2}=-q_2$$

$$-\dot{p}_1=\frac{\partial H}{\partial q_1}=p_1-2aq_1$$

$$\Rightarrow\quad \dot{p}_1=2aq_1-p_1$$

and $\quad -\dot{p}_2 = \frac{\partial H}{\partial q_2} = -p_2 + 2bq_2$

$\Rightarrow \quad \dot{p}_2 = p_2 - 2bq_2$

**6.** Here, $L$ is time dependent.

$\Rightarrow$ $T - V$ is time dependent.

Hence, $H = T + V$ will not hold.

**7.** We have, $L = T - V = \frac{1}{2} m\dot{q}^2 - \frac{k}{q}$

Using $\frac{\partial L}{\partial q} - \frac{d}{dt}\left(\frac{\partial L}{\partial \dot{q}}\right) = 0$, we get $m\dot{q}^2 + \frac{2k}{q} = \text{Constant}$

**9.** A particle in rigid body needs three coordinates $(x_i, y_i, z_i)$; $i = 1, 2, 3$ to specify its position in space.

Let one point of the rigid body is at origin. Constraint equations for the particle at origin is $x_1 = 0,\ y_1 = 0,\ z_1 = 0$ and constraint equations for the other particles are

$$x_2^2 + y_2^2 + z_2^2 = r_2^2, \quad x_3^2 + y_3^2 + z_3^2 = r_3^2$$

and $\quad (x_2 - x_3)^2 + (y_2 - y_3)^2 + (z_2 - z_3)^2 = r_{23}^2$

Hence, total number of constraints $= 3 + 3 = 6$

$\Rightarrow$ Number of degrees of freedom $= 9 - 6 = 3$

**10.** Coordinate of the particle is $(x_1, y_1)$.

$\Rightarrow$ Number of degrees of freedom $= 2$

**12.** Since, $\quad \frac{dH}{dt} = \frac{\partial H}{\partial t} = -\frac{\partial L}{\partial t}$

when, $L$ is independent of time t.

Then, $\quad \frac{dH}{dt} = 0$

$\Rightarrow$ $H =$ constant

**13.** Let Lagrangian $L$ is

$$L = T - V = \frac{1}{2} m\dot{r}^2 - v(r)$$

Here, generalized coordinate is

$$q_1 = r \Rightarrow \dot{q}_1 = \dot{r}$$

Generalized momenta corresponding to $q_1$ is

$$\frac{\partial L}{\partial \dot{q}_1} = \frac{\partial L}{\partial \dot{r}} = m\dot{r} = m\frac{dr}{dt} = mv$$

Hence, $q_1 \frac{\partial L}{\partial \dot{q}_1} = r(mv) = mvr$ = angular momentum

**14.** $$L = \frac{1}{2} m(\dot{x}^2 + \dot{y}^2) + a(x\dot{y} - y\dot{x})$$

$$\frac{\partial L}{\partial \dot{x}} = m\dot{x} - ay, \quad \frac{\partial L}{\partial \dot{y}} = m\dot{y} + ax$$

$\Rightarrow \quad p_x = mv_x - ay \quad \text{and} \quad p_y = mv_y + ax$

**19.** The Lagrangian $L$ for a charged particle in an electromagnetic field is given by

$$L = T - U = T - [q\phi - q(\mathbf{v} \cdot \mathbf{A})$$

where $U = q\phi - q(\mathbf{v} \cdot \mathbf{A})$ is the generalized potential $\phi$ is the gradient, $\mathbf{A}$ is the magnetic potential.

$\Rightarrow \quad L = \frac{1}{2}\sum_k mv_k^2 + q\sum_k v_k A_k - q\phi$

Now, canonical momenta is

$$\frac{\partial L}{\partial v_k} = mv_k + qA_k$$

$$\frac{\partial V}{\partial v_x} = mv_x + qA_x$$

$\Rightarrow \quad p_x = mv_x + qA_x$

**22.** $L = \frac{1}{2}(\dot{x}^2 + \dot{y}^2) - \frac{1}{2}\omega_0^2(x^2 + y^2) + \alpha xy$

$\Rightarrow \quad \frac{\partial L}{\partial x} - \frac{d}{dx}\left(\frac{\partial L}{\partial \dot{x}}\right) = 0$

$\Rightarrow \quad -\omega_0^2 x + \alpha y - \frac{d}{dx}(\dot{x}) = 0$

$\Rightarrow \quad \ddot{x} = \alpha y - \omega_0^2 x$

Similarly, $\quad \ddot{y} = \alpha x - \omega_0^2 y$

$\Rightarrow \quad \ddot{x} + \ddot{y} = (\alpha - \omega_0^2)(x + y)$

For normal modes of vibration

$$\alpha - \omega_0^2 < 0$$

$\Rightarrow \quad \omega_0^2 > \alpha \quad \Rightarrow \quad \omega_0 > \sqrt{\alpha}$

**24.** $L = \frac{1}{2}(\dot{x}^2 + \dot{y}^2) - \frac{1}{2}\omega_0^2(x^2 + y^2) + \alpha\dot{x}\dot{y}$

$$\frac{\partial L}{\partial x} - \frac{d}{dx}\left(\frac{\partial L}{\partial \dot{x}}\right) = 0$$

$\Rightarrow \quad -\omega_0^2 x - \frac{d}{dx}(\dot{x} - \alpha\dot{y}) = 0$

$\Rightarrow \quad \ddot{x} - \alpha\ddot{y} = -\omega_0^2 x$

Similarly, $\quad \ddot{y} - \alpha\ddot{x} = -\omega_0^2 y$

$\Rightarrow \quad \ddot{x} + \ddot{y} - \alpha(\ddot{x} + \ddot{y}) = -\omega_0^2(x + y)$

$\Rightarrow \quad (\ddot{x} + \ddot{y})(1 - \alpha) = -\omega_0^2(x + y)$

$\Rightarrow \quad \ddot{x} + \ddot{y} = -\frac{\omega_0^2}{1 - \alpha}(x + y)$

Hence, $\alpha \neq 1$ for the normal modes of vibration.

**47.** $$L = q^2\dot{q}^2$$

$$\frac{\partial L}{\partial q} - \frac{d}{dt}\left(\frac{\partial L}{\partial \dot{q}}\right) = 0$$

$\Rightarrow \quad 2q\dot{q}^2 - \frac{d}{dt}(2q^2 \cdot \dot{q}) = 0$

$\Rightarrow \quad q\dot{q}^2 - (q^2\ddot{q} + 2\dot{q}^2 q) = 0$

$\Rightarrow \quad \dot{q}^2 - q\ddot{q} - 2\dot{q}^2 = 0$

$\Rightarrow \quad \ddot{q}q + \dot{q}^2 = 0$

$\Rightarrow \quad d(q\dot{q}) = 0$

$\Rightarrow \quad q\dot{q} = C$

$\Rightarrow \quad q\frac{dq}{dt} = C$

$\Rightarrow \quad q\,dq = C\,dt$

On integration, we get

$$\frac{q^2}{2} = Ct + C'$$

At $t = 0, q = 0 \Rightarrow C' = 0$

Hence, $q^2 = 2Ct \Rightarrow q \propto t^{1/2}$

**61.** By Hamilton's principle the path of a conservative mechanical system between two fixed points time $t_1$ to time $t_2$ is such that the variation of time integral.

$$I = \int_{t_1}^{t_2} L\,dt$$

$$= \int_{t_1}^{t_2} K\,dt \text{ is zero}$$

*i.e.,* $\delta \int_{t_1}^{t_2} dt = 0$ and $\delta \int_{t_1}^{t_2} K\,dt = 0$

Subtracting these, we have

$$\delta \int_{t_1}^{t_2} (L - K)\,dt = 0$$

$$\Rightarrow \quad \delta \int_{t_1}^{t_2} \frac{dF}{dt}\,dt = 0$$

$$\Rightarrow \quad \delta \int_{t_1}^{t_2} \frac{dF}{dt}\,dt = \delta\,[F(t_2) - F(t_1)] = 0$$

By definition of generating function it follows that the transformation is canonical.

**62.** Suppose, $A(x_1, y_1)$ and $B(x_2, y_2)$ are two points in $XY$-plane. An element of length $ds$ of any curve, say $AP'B$, passing through $A$ and $B$ points is given by

$$ds^2 = dx^2 + dy^2$$

or $$ds = \sqrt{1 + y'^2}\,dx = 0 \quad \text{...(i)}$$

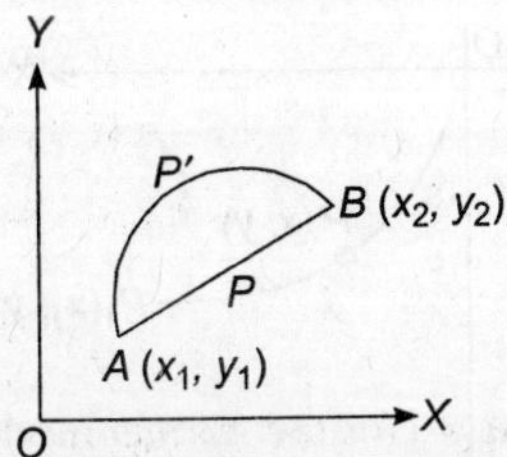


Then, total length of the curve from point $A$ to the point $B$ is given by

$$S = \int_A^B \sqrt{1 + y'^2}\,dx = \int_A^B \alpha\,dx \quad \text{...(ii)}$$

where, $\alpha = \sqrt{1 + y'^2}$. The length of the curve $s$ will be minimum, when $\delta s = 0$. This means that $\alpha$ should satisfy the Euler-Lagrange's equation, *i.e.*,

$$\frac{\partial \alpha}{\partial y} - \frac{d}{dx}\left(\frac{\partial f}{\partial y'}\right) = 0 \quad \text{...(iii)}$$

Here, $\frac{\partial \alpha}{\partial y} = 0$ and $\frac{\partial \alpha}{\partial y'} = \frac{y'}{\sqrt{1 + y'^2}}$

Therefore, Eq. (iii) is

$$\frac{d}{dx}\left(\frac{y'}{\sqrt{1 + y'^2}}\right) = 0$$

or $$\frac{y'}{\sqrt{1 + y'^2}} = C, \text{ a constant}$$

$$\Rightarrow \quad y'^2 = C^2(1 + y'^2)$$

$$\Rightarrow \quad y'^2(1 - C^2) = C^2$$

$$\Rightarrow \quad y' = \frac{C}{\sqrt{1 - C^2}} = a \text{ (Constant)}$$

$$\Rightarrow \quad \frac{dy}{dx} = a \quad \text{...(iv)}$$

Integrating it, we get

$$y = ax + b \quad \text{...(v)}$$

where $b$ is a constant of integration Eq. (iv) represents a straight line. Therefore, the shortest distance between any two points in a plane is a straight line.

**63.** For the conservative system consisting of $N$ particles. Let potential energy $V$, is

$$V = V(q_1, q_2, \dots, q_n)$$

and kinetic energy is

$$T = T(q_1, q_2 \dots, q_n, \dot{q}_1, \dot{q}_2, \dots, \dot{q}_n)$$

The Lagrangian, $L$ is,

$$L = T - V$$

$$= L(q_1, q_2, \dots q_n, \dot{q}_1, \dot{q}_2, \dots, \dot{q}_n)$$

By Lagrange's equations

$$\frac{d}{dt}\left[\sum_{k=1}^{n} \dot{q}_k \frac{\partial L}{\partial \dot{q}_k} - L\right] = \left[\sum_{k=1}^{n} \ddot{q}_k \frac{\partial L}{\partial \dot{q}_k} + \dot{q}_k \frac{\partial}{\partial t}\left(\frac{\partial L}{\partial \dot{q}_k}\right)\right] - \sum_{k=1}^{n}\left(\frac{\partial L}{\partial q_k}\dot{q}_k + \frac{\partial L}{\partial \dot{q}_k}\ddot{q}_k\right)$$

$$= \sum_{k=1}^{n} \dot{q}_k\left[\frac{d}{dt}\left(\frac{\partial L}{\partial \dot{q}_k}\right) - \frac{\partial L}{\partial q_k}\right] = 0$$

Therefore, we have,

$$\sum_{k=1}^{n} \dot{q}_k \frac{\partial L}{\partial \dot{q}_k} = \sum_{k=1}^{n} \dot{q}_k \frac{\partial T}{\partial \dot{q}_k}$$

$$= \frac{1}{2}\sum_{k=1}^{n} \dot{q}_k\left(\frac{\partial}{\partial \dot{q}_k}\sum_{i=1}^{N} m\dot{r}_i\right)$$

$$= \sum_{k=1}^{n} \dot{q}_k\left[\sum_{i=1}^{N} m\dot{\mathbf{r}}_i \cdot \left(\frac{\partial \dot{\mathbf{r}}_i}{\partial \dot{q}_k}\right)\right]$$

$$= \sum_{k=1}^{n} \dot{q}_k\left[\sum_{i=1}^{N} m\dot{\mathbf{r}}_i \cdot \left(\frac{\partial \mathbf{r}_i}{\partial q_k}\right)\right]$$

$$= \sum_{i=1}^{N} m\dot{\mathbf{r}}_i \cdot \left(\sum_{k=1}^{n} \frac{\partial \mathbf{r}_i}{\partial q_k}\dot{\mathbf{q}}_k\right)$$

$$= \sum_{i=1}^{N} m\dot{\mathbf{r}}_i \cdot \dot{\mathbf{r}}_i = 2T \quad \text{...(i)}$$

Since, $\sum_{k=1}^{n} \dot{q}_k \frac{\partial L}{\partial \dot{q}_k} - L = \text{Constant}$ ...(ii)

Hence, by Eqs. (i) and (ii), we have

$$2T - (T - V) = T + V = \text{Constant}$$

## Exercise 2

**2.** According to the principle of least action, we have

$$\Delta \int \sum_k p_k \dot{q}_k \, dt = 0$$

and
$$\sum_k p_k \dot{q}_k = \sum_k \frac{\partial T}{\partial \dot{q}_k} \dot{q}_k = 2T$$
$$= T - V + T + V$$
$$= L + H$$

**8.** For conservative system, the Lagrange's equations are given by

$$\frac{\partial L}{\partial q_k} - \frac{d}{dt}\left(\frac{\partial L}{\partial \dot{q}_k}\right) = 0 \qquad \text{...(i)}$$

Since,
$$p_k = \frac{\partial L}{\partial \dot{q}_k}$$

Hence, from Eq. (i), we have

$$\frac{\partial L}{\partial q_k} - \frac{d}{dt}(p_k) = 0$$

Now, if Lagrangian does not contain a coordinate $q_k$ explicitly,

*i.e.*,
$$\frac{\partial L}{\partial q_k} = 0$$

Then, from Eq. (i), we get

$$-\frac{d}{dt}(p_k) = 0$$

$\Rightarrow$
$$p_k = \text{constant}$$

Hence, the generalized momentum $p_k$ is a constant of motion.

Hence, the coordinate $q_k$ is called cyclic or ignorable.

**16.** Here, $T = \frac{1}{2} m(\dot{x}^2 + \dot{y}^2 + \dot{z}^2)$ and $V = mgz$

$\Rightarrow$
$$L = T - V = \frac{1}{2} m(\dot{x}^2 + \dot{y}^2 + \dot{z}^2) - mgz$$

The Lagrange's equations are

$$\frac{\partial L}{\partial x} - \frac{d}{dt}\left(\frac{\partial L}{\partial \dot{x}}\right) = 0, \qquad \frac{\partial L}{\partial y} - \frac{d}{dt}\left(\frac{\partial L}{\partial \dot{y}}\right) = 0$$

and
$$\frac{\partial L}{\partial z} - \frac{d}{dt}\left(\frac{\partial L}{\partial \dot{z}}\right) = 0$$

$\Rightarrow$
$$\ddot{x} = 0, \quad \ddot{y} = 0, \quad \ddot{z} + g = 0$$

**17.** The differential equation governing the deflection $y(x)$ of the beam is given by

$$EI \frac{d^4 y}{dx^4} - w = 0, \; 0 < x < l \qquad \text{...(i)}$$

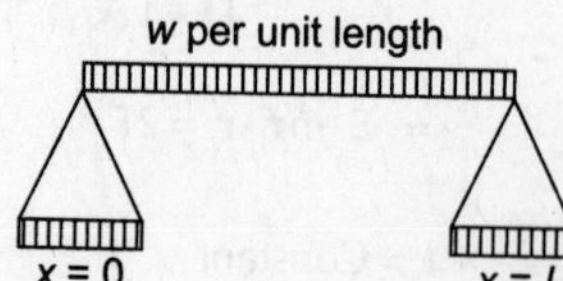


Here, the boundary conditions to be satisfied are

$$y(x = 0) = y(x = l) = 0 \qquad \text{...(ii)}$$

(deflection is zero at ends)

$$\frac{d^2 y}{dx^2}(x = 0) = \frac{d^2 y}{dx^2}(x = l) = 0 \qquad \text{...(iii)}$$

(bending moment zero at ends)

We assume the trial solution $\bar{y}(x) = C_1 \sin(\pi x/l) + C_2 \sin(3\pi x/l)$, which satisfies the boundary conditions (ii) and (iii).

Substituting the trial solution in Eq. (i), we obtain the residual

$$R = EIC_1(\pi/l)^4 \sin(\pi x/l) + EIC_2 (3\pi/l)^4 \sin(3\pi x/l) - w$$

Thus, $\int_0^l R \cdot \sin(\pi x/l) = 0$ and $\int_0^l R \cdot \sin(3\pi x/l) = 0$

Computing these integrals, we get

$$EIC_1(\pi/l)^4 \, l/2 - w \cdot 2l/\pi = 0$$
$$EIC_2(3\pi/l)^4 \, l/2 - w \cdot 2l/3\pi = 0$$

Solving these, we obtain

$$C_1 = \frac{4wl^4}{\pi^5 EI} \text{ and } C_2 = \frac{4wl^4}{243 \, \pi^5 EI}$$

Hence, the deflection of the beam is given by

$$\bar{y}(x) = \frac{4wl^4}{\pi^5 EI}\left\{\sin\left(\frac{\pi x}{l}\right) + \frac{1}{243}\sin\left(\frac{3\pi x}{l}\right)\right\}$$

**18.** Let the particle start sliding on the curve $OP_1$ from $O$ with zero velocity. At time $t$, let the particle be at $P(x, y)$ such that arc $OP = s$

By the principle of work and energy, we have KE at P – KE at $O$ = work done in moving the particle from $O$ to $P$.

$$\frac{1}{2} m\left(\frac{ds}{dt}\right)^2 - 0 = mgy$$

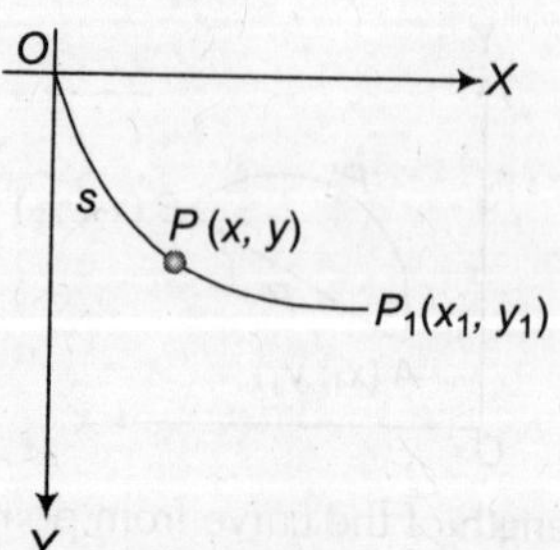


$\Rightarrow$
$$ds/dt = \sqrt{(2gy)} \qquad \text{...(i)}$$

Thus, the time taken by the article to move from $O$ to $P_1$ is

$$T = \int_0^T dt = \int_0^{x_1} \frac{ds}{\sqrt{(2gy)}}$$
$$= \frac{1}{\sqrt{2g}} \int_0^{x_1} \frac{\sqrt{(1 + y'^2)}}{\sqrt{y}} dx$$

Here, $f = \sqrt{[(1 + y'^2)/y]}$ is independent of $x$.

Hence, Euler's equation reduces to $f - y' \frac{\partial f}{\partial y'} =$ constant, C : say

$\Rightarrow$
$$\frac{\sqrt{(1 + y'^2)}}{\sqrt{y}} - y' \frac{\partial}{\partial y'}\left\{\frac{\sqrt{(1 + y'^2)}}{\sqrt{y}}\right\} = C$$

$$\Rightarrow \quad \frac{\sqrt{(1+y'^2)}}{\sqrt{y}} - y'\left\{\frac{y'}{\sqrt{(1+y'^2)}\sqrt{y}}\right\} = C$$

$$\Rightarrow \quad \sqrt{[y(1+y'^2)]} = 1/C = \sqrt{a}, \text{ say}$$

Solving for $y'$, we have $y' = \dfrac{dy}{dx} = \sqrt{\left(\dfrac{a-y}{y}\right)}$

On integration, we get

$$\int_0^x dx = \int_0^y \sqrt{\left(\frac{y}{a-y}\right)}\,dy \qquad [\text{Put } y = a\sin^2\theta]$$

$$\Rightarrow \quad x = \int_0^\theta \sqrt{\left(\frac{a\sin^2\theta}{a - a\sin^2\theta}\right)}\, 2a\sin\theta\cos\theta\, d\theta$$

$$= a\int_0^\theta 2\sin^2\theta\, d\theta$$

$$= a\int_0^\theta (1-\cos 2\theta)\, d\theta$$

$$= \frac{a}{2}(2\theta - \sin\theta) \qquad \ldots\text{(ii)}$$

Put $a/2 = b$ and $2\theta = \phi$, Eqs. (ii) and (i) become $x = b(\phi - \sin\phi)$, $y = b(1-\cos\phi)$ which is a cycloid. The constant $b$ is found the fact that the curve goes through $(x_1, y_1)$.

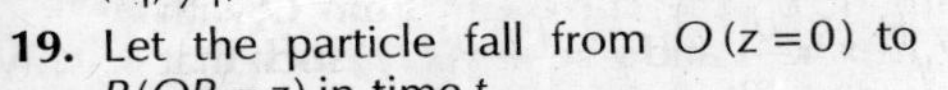

**19.** Let the particle fall from $O(z=0)$ to $P(OP = z)$ in time $t$.

$O$ — $z = 0$; $z$; $z_0$; $P$

Kinetic energy of the particle at $P$,

$$T = \frac{1}{2}m\dot{z}^2$$

Potential energy of the particle at $P$, is given by

$$V = -mgz$$

Hence,

$$L = T - V = \frac{1}{2}m\dot{z}^2 + mgz \qquad \ldots\text{(i)}$$

Hence, by Hamilton's principle,

$$\delta\int_0^{t_0} L\,dt = 0$$

$\Rightarrow \quad \displaystyle\int_0^{t_0} L\,dt$ = extremum, for which

$$\frac{d}{dt}\left[\frac{\partial L}{\partial \dot{z}}\right] - \frac{\partial L}{\partial z} = 0 \qquad \ldots\text{(ii)}$$

is to be satisfied.

Also, by the Hamilton's principle

$$\delta\int_0^{t_0} L\,dt = 0$$

$\Rightarrow \quad \displaystyle\int_0^{t_0} L\,dt$ = Extremum, for which

$$\frac{d}{dt}\left[\frac{\partial L}{\partial \dot{z}}\right] - \frac{\partial L}{\partial z} = 0$$

is to be satisfied.

Here, $\dfrac{\partial L}{\partial \dot{z}} = m\dot{z}$ and $\dfrac{\partial L}{\partial z} = mg$. Hence, Eq. (ii) is

$$\frac{d}{dt}(m\dot{z}) - mg = 0 \text{ or } \ddot{z} = g \qquad \ldots\text{(iii)}$$

But $z = at + bt^2$ and, therefore $\dot{z} = a + 2bt$

and $\qquad \ddot{z} = 2b \qquad \ldots\text{(iv)}$

From Eqs. (iii) and (iv), we have

$$2b = g \text{ or } b = g/2 \qquad \ldots\text{(v)}$$

Also, at $t = t_0$, $z = z_0$, we have

$$z_0 = at_0 + bt_0^2 \qquad \ldots\text{(vi)}$$

But $\qquad t_0 = \sqrt{\dfrac{2z_0}{g}}$

$$\Rightarrow \quad z_0 = \frac{1}{2}gt_0^2 \qquad \ldots\text{(vii)}$$

Hence, by Eqs. (vi) and (vii) and using Eq. (v), we have

$$at_0 + \frac{g}{2}t_0^2 = \frac{1}{2}gt_0^2 \Rightarrow at_0 = 0$$

Since, $\qquad t_0 \neq 0 \quad \Rightarrow \quad a = 0$

Thus, $\displaystyle\int_0^{t_0} L\,dt$ is extremum, when $a = 0$, $b = \dfrac{g}{2}$

**20.** Let the particle fall from $O(z=0)$ to $P(OP = z)$ in time $t$.

Kinetic energy of the particle at $P$,

$$T = \frac{1}{2}m\dot{z}^2$$

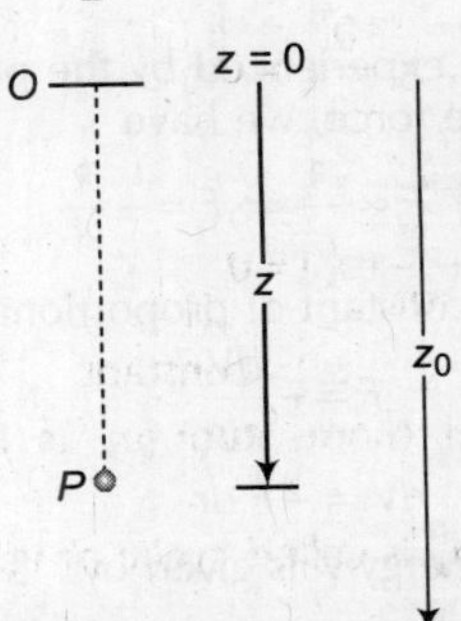


Potential energy of the particle at $P$, is given by

$$V = -mgz$$

Hence, the Lagrangian is

$$L = T - V = \frac{1}{2}m\dot{z}^2 + mgz \qquad \ldots\text{(i)}$$

Hence, by the Hamilton's principle

$$\delta\int_0^{t_0} L\,dt = 0$$

$\Rightarrow \quad \displaystyle\int_0^{t_0} L\,dt$ = Extremum, for which

$$\frac{d}{dt}\left[\frac{\partial L}{\partial \dot{z}}\right] - \frac{\partial L}{\partial z} = 0 \qquad \ldots\text{(ii)}$$

is to be satisfied.

Here, $\dfrac{\partial L}{\partial \dot{z}} = m\dot{z}$ and $\dfrac{\partial L}{\partial z} = mg$. Hence, Eq. (ii) is

$$\frac{d}{dt}(m\dot{z}) - mg = 0$$

$$\Rightarrow \quad \ddot{z} = g \qquad \ldots\text{(iii)}$$

But $z = at + bt^2$ and therefore $\dot{z} = a + 2bt$

and $\qquad \ddot{z} = 2b \qquad \ldots\text{(iv)}$

From Eqs. (iii) and (iv), we have

$$2b = g \Rightarrow b = \frac{g}{2} \quad \text{...(v)}$$

Also, at $t = t_0$, $z = z_0$, we have

$$z_0 = at_0 + bt_0^2 \quad \text{...(vi)}$$

But $$t_0 = \sqrt{\frac{2z_0}{g}}$$

or $$z_0 = \frac{1}{2} gt_0^2 \quad \text{...(vii)}$$

By Eqs. (vi) and (vii) and using Eq. (v), we have

$$at_0 + \frac{g}{2} t_0^2 = \frac{1}{2} gt_0^2$$

$\Rightarrow$ $$at_0 = 0$$

Since, $t_0 \neq 0 \Rightarrow a = 0$

Thus, $\int_0^{t_0} L dt$ is extremum, when aa $= 0$, $b = \frac{g}{2}$.

**21.** Let $(r, \theta)$ be the plane polar coordinates of the particle of mass $m$. Then, the kinetic energy of the particle $T$ is given by

$$T = \frac{1}{2} m (\dot{r}^2 + r^2\dot{\theta}^2)$$

If $F$ is the force experienced by the particle, then by inverse law of attractive force, we have

$$F \propto \frac{1}{r^2} \Rightarrow F = -\frac{k}{r^2}$$

where $k$ is the constant of proportionality.

Since, $$F = -\frac{dV}{dr}$$

$\Rightarrow$ $$dV = -F\, dr$$

and potential energy $V$ is given by

$$V = -\int_\infty^r F\, dr = \int_\infty^r \frac{k}{r^2} dr$$

$$= \left[-\frac{k}{r}\right]_\infty^r$$

$$= -\frac{k}{r}$$

Hence, the Lagrangian $L$ is given by

$$L = T - V$$

$$= \frac{1}{2} m (\dot{r}^2 + r^2\dot{\theta}^2) + \frac{k}{r} \quad \text{...(i)}$$

$$\Rightarrow \left.\begin{aligned} &\frac{\partial L}{\partial \dot{r}} = m\dot{r}, \ \frac{\partial L}{\partial r} = mr\dot{\theta}^2 - \frac{k}{r^2}, \ \frac{\partial L}{\partial \theta} = 0 \\ \text{and} \quad &\frac{\partial L}{\partial \dot{\theta}} = mr^2\dot{\theta} \end{aligned}\right\} \quad \text{...(ii)}$$

The Lagrangian equation or equation of motion in the variable $r$ is

$$\frac{d}{dt}\left(\frac{\partial L}{\partial \dot{r}}\right) - \frac{\partial L}{\partial r} = 0$$

$$\Rightarrow \frac{d}{dt}(m\dot{r}) - \left(mr\dot{\theta}^2 - \frac{k}{r^2}\right) = 0$$

$$\Rightarrow mr - mr\dot{\theta}^2 + \frac{k}{r^2} = 0 \quad \text{...(iii)}$$

The Lagrangian equation in the variable $\theta$ is

$$\frac{d}{dt}\left(\frac{\partial L}{\partial \dot{\theta}}\right) - \frac{\partial L}{\partial \theta} = 0$$

$$\Rightarrow \frac{d}{dt}(mr^2\dot{\theta}) = 0 \quad \text{[from Eq. (ii)]}$$

$$\Rightarrow mr^2\ddot{\theta} + 2mr\dot{r}\dot{\theta} = 0 \quad \text{...(iv)}$$

Eqs. (ii) and (iv) are the Lagrangian equation of motion in polar coordinates.

**22.** (a) **Hamiltonian function**

The kinetic energy is given by

$$T = \frac{1}{2} m (\dot{x}^2 + \dot{y}^2) \quad \text{...(i)}$$

and the potential energy is given by

$$V = \frac{1}{2} kr^2 = \frac{1}{2} k (x^2 + y^2) \quad \text{...(ii)}$$

Hence, the Lagrangian function $L$ is given by

$$L = \frac{1}{2} m (\dot{x}^2 + \dot{y}^2) - \frac{1}{2} k(x^2 + y^2) \quad \text{...(iii)}$$

Since,

$$p_x = \frac{\partial L}{\partial \dot{x}} m\dot{x} \text{ and } p_y + \frac{\partial L}{\partial \dot{y}} = m\dot{y} \quad \text{...(iv)}$$

Hence $$x = \frac{p_x}{m} \text{ and } y = \frac{p_y}{m} \quad \text{...(v)}$$

Substituting these values of $\dot{x}$ and $\dot{y}$ in Eq. (iii), we have

$$L = \frac{1}{2} m \left[\left(\frac{p_x}{m}\right)^2 + \left(\frac{p_y}{m}\right)^2\right]$$

$$= \frac{1}{2} k (x^2 + y^2)$$

$$= \frac{1}{2m} (p_x^2 + p_y^2) - \frac{1}{2} k (x^2 + y^2) \quad \text{...(vi)}$$

Now, the Hamiltonian $H$ is defined as

$$H = \Sigma p_r \dot{q}_r - L = p_x\dot{x} + p_y\dot{y} - L$$

$$= p_x\left(\frac{p_x}{m}\right) + p_y\left(\frac{p_y}{m}\right) - L$$

$$= \frac{p_x^2}{m} + \frac{p_y^2}{m} - \frac{1}{2m}(p_x^2 + p_y^2) + \frac{1}{2} k (x^2 + y^2)$$

$$= \frac{1}{2m}(p_x^2 + p_y^2) + \frac{1}{2} k (x^2 + y^2) \quad \text{...(vii)}$$

(b) **Hamiltonian equation of motion** Here,

$$\left.\begin{aligned} &\frac{\partial H}{\partial p_y} = \frac{p_x}{m}, \ \frac{\partial H}{\partial p_y} = \frac{p_y}{m} \\ &\frac{\partial H}{\partial x} = kx, \ \frac{\partial H}{\partial y} = ky \end{aligned}\right\} \quad \text{...(viii)}$$

Hence, the Hamilton's equations for $\dot{x}$ and $\dot{y}$ are

$$\dot{x} = \frac{\partial H}{\partial p_x}, \ \dot{y} = \frac{\partial H}{\partial p_y}$$

$$\Rightarrow \dot{x} = \frac{p_x}{m}, \ \dot{y} = \frac{p_y}{m} \quad \text{...(ix)}$$

$$\Rightarrow p_x = m\dot{x}, \ p_y = m\dot{y}$$

$$\Rightarrow p_x = m\dot{x}, \ p_y = m\dot{y} \quad \text{...(x)}$$

Eqs. (ix) and (x) are four Hamilton's equation of motion of first order.

(c) **Equation of motion** The Hamilton's equations for $\dot{p}_x$ and $\dot{p}_y$ are

$$\dot{p}_x = -\frac{\partial H}{\partial x}, \dot{p}_y = -\frac{\partial H}{\partial y}$$

or $$\dot{p}_x = -kx, \dot{p}_y = -ky \text{ [from Eq. (viii)]} \quad \text{...(xi)}$$

Substituting the values of $\dot{p}_x$ and $\dot{p}_y$ from Eq. (ix) in Eq. (x), we have

$$-kx = m\ddot{x} \quad \text{and} \quad -kx = m\ddot{y}$$

Therefore, the equation of motion of a two dimensional harmonic oscillator are

$$\left.\begin{aligned} mx + kx &= 0 \\ my + ky &= 0 \end{aligned}\right\}$$

and

**23.** The equation of the paraboloid is $bx^2 + cy^2 = az$,

$$\Rightarrow \quad f \equiv bx^2 + cy^2 - az = 0$$

Hence, the equation of the constraint is given by

$$2bx\, dx + cy\, dy - a\, dz = 0 \quad \text{...(i)}$$

So, the coefficients in the constraint Eq. (i) are

$$A_x = 2bx, A_y = 2\, cy \text{ and } A_z = -a \quad \text{...(ii)}$$

Thus, Lagrangian of the particle is given by

$$L = \frac{1}{2} m(\dot{x}^2 + \dot{y}^2 + \dot{z}^2) - mgz,$$

$$\Rightarrow \left.\begin{aligned} \frac{\partial L}{\partial \dot{x}} &= m\dot{x}, \frac{\partial L}{\partial x} = 0 \\ \frac{\partial L}{\partial \dot{y}} &= m\dot{y}, \frac{\partial L}{\partial y} = 0 \\ \frac{\partial L}{\partial \dot{z}} &= m\dot{z}, \frac{\partial L}{\partial z} = -mg \end{aligned}\right\} \quad \text{...(ii)}$$

Hence, the Lagrange's equations are respectively given by

$$\frac{d}{dt}\left\{\frac{\partial L}{\partial \dot{x}}\right\} - \frac{\partial L}{\partial x} = A_x\lambda$$

$$\frac{d}{dt}\left\{\frac{\partial L}{\partial \dot{y}}\right\} - \frac{\partial L}{\partial y} = A_y\lambda$$

$$\frac{d}{dt}\left\{\frac{\partial L}{\partial \dot{z}}\right\} - \frac{\partial L}{\partial z} = A_z\lambda$$

From Eqs. (ii) and (iii), we have

$$\left.\begin{aligned} m\ddot{x} &= 2bx\,\lambda \\ m\ddot{y} &= 2cy\,\lambda \\ m\ddot{z} + mg &= -a\lambda \end{aligned}\right\} \quad \text{...(iv)}$$

The required Lagrangian equation of motion.

**24.** (a) The transformation is canonical if

$$[Q, P] = 1$$

$$\Rightarrow \left[\frac{\partial Q}{\partial q}\frac{\partial P}{\partial p} - \frac{\partial Q}{\partial p}\frac{\partial P}{\partial q}\right] = 1 \quad \text{...(i)}$$

From transformation equations, we have

$$\left.\begin{aligned} \frac{\partial Q}{\partial q} &= mq^{m-1}\cos np \\ \frac{\partial Q}{\partial p} &= -pq^m \sin np \end{aligned}\right\}$$

and $$\frac{\partial P}{\partial q} = mq^{m-1}\sin np$$

$$\frac{\partial P}{\partial p} = pq^m \cos np$$

Putting in Eq. (i), we get

$$(mq^{m-1}\cos np \cdot pq^m \cos np + pq^m \sin np\, mq^{m-1}\sin np) = 1$$

$$\Rightarrow \quad mpq^{2m-1}(\cos^2 np + \sin^2 np) = 0$$

$$\Rightarrow \quad mpq^{2m-1} = 1$$

Equating the coefficient of $q^0$ on both sides which is possible only f

$$2m - 1 = 0$$

$$\Rightarrow \quad m = \frac{1}{2}$$

and then $$mpq^0 = 1$$

$$\Rightarrow \quad mp = 1$$

$$\Rightarrow \quad \frac{1}{2}p = 1$$

$$\Rightarrow \quad p = 2$$

Thus, $m = \frac{1}{2}$ and $p = 2$ so that equations of transformation now become

$$\left.\begin{aligned} Q &= q^{1/2}\cos 2p \\ P &= q^{1/2}\sin 2p \end{aligned}\right\}$$

(b) The generating function as

$$q = -\frac{\partial F_3}{\partial p}(p, Q)$$

Putting in it $q = Q^2 \sec^2 2p$ from transformation equation, we have

$$Q^2 \sec^2 2p = -\frac{\partial F_3}{\partial p}(p, Q)$$

$$\Rightarrow \quad F_3 = -\int Q^2 \sec^2 2p\, dp$$

$$\Rightarrow \quad F_3 = -\frac{1}{2}Q^2 \tan 2p$$

which is the required generating function.

**25.** Here, $x = r\cos\theta$, $y = r\sin\theta$, $z = z$ and the Lagrangian

$$L = T - V = \frac{1}{2}m(\dot{x}^2 + \dot{y}^2 + \dot{z}^2) - V(x, y, z)$$

$$= \frac{1}{2}m(\dot{r}^2 + r^2\dot{\theta}^2 + \dot{z}^2) - V(r, \theta, z)$$

The generalized momentum is

$$p_r = \frac{\partial L}{\partial \dot{r}} = m\dot{r} \text{ or } \dot{r} = \frac{p_r}{m},$$

and $$\dot{\theta} = \frac{p_\theta}{mr^2}, \dot{z} = \frac{p_z}{m}$$

The Hamiltonian is

$$H = \sum_k p_k\dot{q}_k - L \text{ where } k = r, \theta, z$$

$$\Rightarrow \quad H = p_r\dot{r} + p_\theta\dot{\theta} + p_z\dot{z} - \frac{1}{2}m(\dot{r}^2 + r^2\dot{\theta}^2 + \dot{z}^2) + V(r, \theta, z)$$

$$= \frac{1}{2m}\left(p_r^2 + \frac{p_\theta^2}{r^2} + p_z^2\right) + V(r, \theta, z) \quad \text{...(i)}$$

Hamilton's equations are

$$\dot{q}_k = \frac{\partial H}{\partial p_k} \text{ and } \dot{p}_k = -\frac{\partial H}{\partial q_k}$$

Hence, the required equations are,

$$\dot{r} = \frac{\partial H}{\partial p_r} \text{ or } \dot{r} = \frac{p_r}{m}$$

and $$\dot{p}_r = -\frac{\partial H}{\partial r} \text{ or } \dot{p}_r = \frac{p_\theta^2}{mr^3} - \frac{\partial V}{\partial r} \qquad \ldots(ii)$$

$$\dot{\theta} = \frac{\partial H}{\partial p_\theta} \text{ or } \dot{\theta} = \frac{p_\theta}{m}$$

and $$\dot{p}_\theta = -\frac{\partial H}{\partial \theta} \text{ or } \dot{p}_\theta = -\frac{\partial V}{\partial \theta} \qquad \ldots(iii)$$

$$\dot{z} = \frac{\partial H}{\partial p_z} \text{ or } \dot{z} = \frac{p_z}{m}$$

and $$\dot{p}_z = -\frac{\partial H}{\partial z} \text{ or } \dot{p}_z = -\frac{\partial V}{\partial z} \qquad \ldots(iv)$$

**26.** (a) Let $P(x, y)$ be the position of the bead of the mass $m$ at any instant $t$. The path of bead is a cycloid represented by equations.

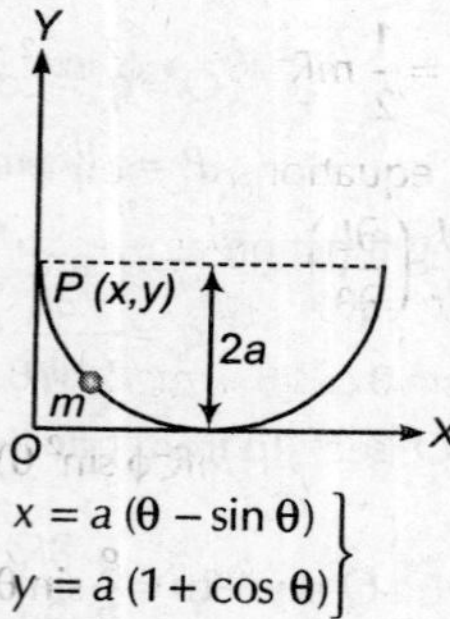


$$\left.\begin{aligned} x &= a(\theta - \sin\theta) \\ y &= a(1 + \cos\theta) \end{aligned}\right\}$$

The kinetic energy of the bead is given by

$$T = \frac{1}{2} m(\dot{x}^2 + \dot{y}^2)$$

$$= \frac{1}{2} m\{a^2(\dot{\theta} - \cos\theta\,\dot{\theta})^2 + a^2(-\sin\theta\,\dot{\theta})^2\}$$

$$= ma^2\dot{\theta}^2(1 - \cos\theta)$$

The potential energy of the bead, (taking $x$-axis as the reference level) is

$$V = mgy = mga(1 + \cos\theta)$$

The Lagrangian is given by

$$L = T - V$$

$$= ma^2\dot{\theta}^2(1 - \cos\theta) - mga(1 + \cos\theta) \qquad \ldots(i)$$

(b) The Lagrange's equation of motion is given by

$$\frac{d}{dt}\left(\frac{\partial L}{\partial \dot{\theta}}\right) - \frac{\partial L}{\partial \theta} = 0 \qquad \ldots(ii)$$

From Eq. (i), we have

$$\frac{\partial L}{\partial \dot{\theta}} = 2ma^2\dot{\theta}(1 - \cos\theta)$$

and $$\frac{\partial L}{\partial \theta} = 2ma^2\dot{\theta}\sin\theta + mga\sin\theta$$

which on substituting in Eq. (ii) gives

$$\frac{d}{dt}[2ma^2\dot{\theta}(1 - \cos\theta)] - [ma^2\dot{\theta}^2\sin\theta + mga\sin\theta] = 0$$

or $$2ma^2\ddot{\theta}(1 - \cos\theta) + 2ma^2\dot{\theta}\sin\theta\,\dot{\theta} - ma^2\dot{\theta}^2\sin\theta - mga\sin\theta = 0$$

or $$\ddot{\theta}(1 - \cos\theta) + \frac{1}{2}\sin\theta\,\dot{\theta}^2 - \frac{g}{2a}\sin\theta = 0 \qquad \ldots(iii)$$

Which is the required equation of motion.

**27.** The kinetic energy of the particle is given by

$$T = \frac{1}{2}mv^2$$

The generalized potential energy $V$ of a charged particle moving in an electromagnetic field is given by

$$V = q\left(\phi - \frac{1}{c}\,\bar{v}\cdot\bar{A}\right)$$

The Lagrangian is given by

$$L = T - q\left(\phi - \frac{1}{c}\,\bar{v}\cdot\bar{A}\right)$$

and $$p_i = \frac{\partial L}{\partial v_i} = mv_i + \frac{q}{c}A_i$$

Hence, the Hamiltonian is given by

$$H = \sum_i p_i v_i - L$$

$$= \sum_i\left(mv_i + \frac{q}{c}A_i\right)v_i - L$$

$$= mv^2 + \frac{q}{c}(\bar{v}\cdot\bar{A}) - L$$

$$= 2T + \frac{q}{c}(\bar{v}\cdot\bar{A}) - \left\{T - q\left(\phi - \frac{1}{c}\,\bar{v}\cdot\bar{A}\right)\right\}$$

$$= T + q\phi$$

$$= \frac{1}{2}mv^2 + q\phi$$

so that $H$ can be interpreted easily as the sum of kinetic and electrostatic potential energies of the particle.

**28.** We have, $$\frac{\partial}{\partial t}[\phi, \psi] = \frac{\partial}{\partial t}\left\{\frac{\partial \phi}{\partial q_i}\frac{\partial \psi}{\partial p_i} - \frac{\partial \psi}{\partial q_i}\frac{\partial \phi}{\partial p_i}\right\}$$

$$= \frac{\partial}{\partial q_i}\left(\frac{\partial \phi}{\partial t}\right)\frac{\partial \psi}{\partial p_i} + \frac{\partial \phi}{\partial q_i}\frac{\partial}{p_i}\left(\frac{\partial \psi}{\partial t}\right) - \frac{\partial}{\partial q_i}\left(\frac{\partial \psi}{\partial t}\right)\frac{\partial \phi}{\partial p_i} - \frac{\partial \psi}{\partial q_i}\frac{\partial}{\partial p_i}\left(\frac{\partial \phi}{\partial t}\right)$$

$$= \left\{\frac{\partial}{\partial q_i}\left(\frac{\partial \phi}{\partial t}\right)\frac{\partial \psi}{\partial p_i} - \frac{\partial \psi}{\partial q_i}\frac{\partial}{\partial p_i}\left(\frac{\partial \phi}{\partial t}\right)\right\} + \left\{\frac{\partial \phi}{\partial q_i}\frac{\partial}{\partial p_i}\left(\frac{\partial \psi}{\partial t}\right) - \frac{\partial}{\partial q_i}\left(\frac{\partial \psi}{\partial t}\right)\frac{\partial \psi}{\partial p_i}\right\}$$

$$= \left[\frac{\partial \phi}{\partial t}, \psi\right] + \left[\phi, \frac{\partial \psi}{\partial t}\right]$$

**29.** The kinetic energy is given by

$$T = \frac{1}{2}m(\dot{r}^2 + r^2\dot{\theta}^2 + r^2\dot{\phi}^2\sin^2\theta) \qquad \ldots(i)$$

Then, the Lagrangian is given by

$$L = T - V = \frac{1}{2} m(\dot{r}^2 + r^2\dot{\theta}^2 + r^2\dot{\phi}^2 \sin^2\theta) - V(r, \theta, \phi) \quad \ldots\text{(ii)}$$

So, $$p_r = \frac{\partial L}{\partial \dot{r}} = m\dot{r}$$

$$p_\theta = \frac{\partial L}{\partial \dot{\theta}} = -mr^2\dot{\theta}$$

$$p_\phi = \frac{\partial L}{\partial \dot{\phi}} = mr^2\dot{\phi}\sin^2\theta$$

Therefore, we get

$$\dot{r} = \frac{p_r}{m}, \dot{\theta} = \frac{p_\theta}{mr^2}, \dot{\phi} = \frac{p_\phi}{mr^2\sin^2\theta} \quad \ldots\text{(iii)}$$

The Hamiltonian is given by

$$H = \sum_{i=1}^{3} p_i\dot{q}_i - L = p_r\dot{r} + p_\theta\dot{\theta} + p_\phi\dot{\phi} - L$$

From Eqs. (ii) and (iii), we get

$$H = \frac{p_r^2}{2m} + \frac{p_\theta^2}{2mr^2} + \frac{p_\phi^2}{2mr^2\sin^2\theta} + V(r, \theta, \phi) \quad \ldots\text{(iv)}$$

The Hamilton's equations of motion are

$$\dot{q}_i = \frac{\partial H}{\partial p_i}, \dot{p}_i = -\frac{\partial H}{\partial q_i}, i = 1, 2, 3$$

Therefore, from Eq. (iv), we have

$$\dot{r} = \frac{\partial H}{\partial p_r} = \frac{p_r}{m} \quad \ldots\text{(v)}$$

$$\dot{\theta} = \frac{\partial H}{\partial p_\theta} = \frac{p_\theta}{mr^2} \quad \ldots\text{(vi)}$$

$$\dot{\phi} = \frac{\partial H}{\partial p_\phi} = \frac{p_\phi}{mr^2\sin^2\theta} \quad \ldots\text{(vii)}$$

and $$\dot{p}_r = -\frac{\partial H}{\partial r} = \frac{p^2\theta}{mr^3} + \frac{p^2\phi}{mr^2\sin^2\theta} - \frac{\partial V}{\partial r} \quad \ldots\text{(viii)}$$

$$\dot{p}_\theta = -\frac{\partial H}{\partial \theta} = \frac{p_\phi^2\cos\theta}{mr^2\sin^3\theta} - \frac{\partial V}{\partial \theta} \quad \ldots\text{(ix)}$$

$$\dot{p}_\phi = -\frac{\partial H}{\partial \phi} = -\frac{\partial V}{\partial \phi} \quad \ldots\text{(x)}$$

Thus, the Hamilton equation of motion are given by Eq. (vi) to Eq. (viii).

**30.** We know that

$$\{q_l, q_i\} = 0$$

and $$[q_l, q_j] = 0$$

Also, $$[p_l, q_i] = -\{q_i, p_l\} = -\delta_{il}$$

and $$[p_l, q_j] = -[q_j, p_l] = -\delta_{jl}$$

Therefore, first factor on the right hand side in the equation to be proved is zero and the second factor gives

$$\sum_{l=1}^{n} \{p_l, q_i\}[p_l, q_j] = -\delta_{il} \times -\delta_{jl} = \delta_{ij}$$

which is the required result.

**31.** The constraint equation is given by

$$x^2 + y^2 + z^2 - R^2 = 0$$

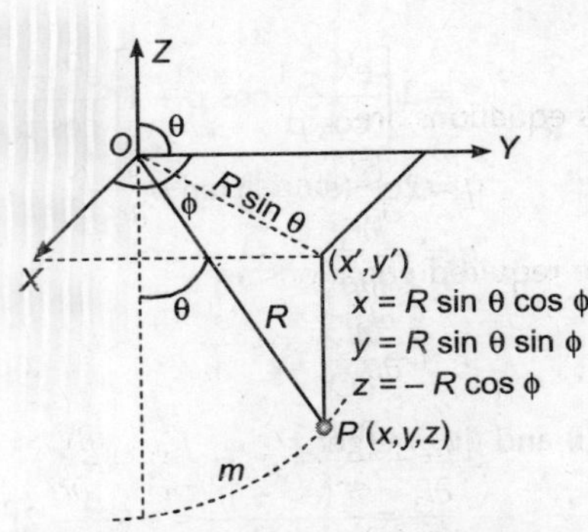


Taking $\theta$ and $\phi$ as the generalized coordinates. The cartesian coordinates of the bob $P$ are

$$x = R\sin\theta'\cos\phi,$$
$$y = R\sin\theta'\sin\phi$$

and $$z = R\cos\theta'$$

$\Rightarrow$ $$x = R\sin\theta\cos\phi$$
$$y = R\sin\theta\sin\phi$$

and $$z = -R\cos\theta \text{ (as } \theta' = \pi - \theta)$$

Now, the Lagrangian is given by

$$L = \frac{1}{2} m(\dot{x}^2 + \dot{y}^2 + \dot{z}^2) - V$$

$$= \frac{1}{2} mR^2(\dot{\theta}^2 + \dot{\phi}^2\sin^2\theta) + mgR\cos\theta$$

Hence, Lagrange's equations of motion are

$$\frac{d}{dt}\left(\frac{\partial L}{\partial \dot{\theta}}\right) - \frac{\partial L}{\partial \theta} = 0 \text{ and } \frac{d}{dt}\left(\frac{\partial L}{\partial \dot{\phi}}\right) - \frac{\partial L}{\partial \phi} = 0$$

$$\Rightarrow mR^2\ddot{\theta} - mR^2\dot{\phi}^2\sin\theta\cos\theta + mgR\sin\theta = 0$$

and $$\frac{d}{dt}(mR^2\dot{\phi}\sin^2\theta) = 0$$

$\Rightarrow$ $$\ddot{\theta} - \frac{1}{2}\sin 2\theta\phi + \frac{g}{R}\sin\theta = 0$$

and $mR^2\sin^2\theta\,\dot{\phi} = \text{Constant}$

Which is the required equation of motion.

**32.** (a) If the given transformation is canonical, then $(p\,dq - P\,dQ)$ must be an exact differential *i.e.*,

$$p\,dq - P\,dQ = p\,dq - 2(1 + q^{1/2}\cos p)q^{1/2}\sin p$$
$$\cos p\,dq - 2q\sin p\,dp\,q^{1/2}(1 + q^{1/2}\cos p)$$
$$= p\,dq - \sin p\cos p\,dq + 2q\sin^2 p\,dp$$
$$= \left(p - \frac{1}{2}\sin 2p\right)dq + q(1 - \cos 2p)\,dp$$
$$= d\left\{q\left(p - \frac{1}{2}\sin 2p\right)\right\}$$

which is an exact differential and hence the transformation is canonical.

(b) We have,

$$Q = \log(1 + q^{1/2}\cos p)$$

$\Rightarrow$ $$e^Q = (1 + q^{1/2}\cos p)$$

$\Rightarrow$ $$q^{1/2} = \frac{e^Q - 1}{\cos p}, \text{ giving } q = \frac{(e^Q - 1)^2}{(\cos p)^2} \quad \ldots\text{(i)}$$

Given, $$P = 2(1 + q^{1/2}\cos p)q^{1/2}\sin p$$

$$= 2\left[\frac{e^Q - 1}{\cos p}\cos p + 1\right]\frac{e^Q - 1}{\cos p}\sin p$$

$$= 2e^Q(e^Q - 1)\tan p \qquad \ldots\text{(ii)}$$

Since, $q = -\dfrac{\partial F_3}{\partial p}$

and $P = -\dfrac{\partial F_3}{\partial Q}$

By Eqs. (i) and (ii), we get

$$\frac{\partial F_3}{\partial p} = -\frac{(e^Q - 1)^2}{\cos^2 p} = -(e^Q - 2)^2\sec^2 p \qquad \ldots\text{(iii)}$$

and $\dfrac{\partial F_3}{\partial Q} = -2e^Q(e^Q - 1)\tan p \qquad \ldots\text{(iv)}$

Integrating Eq. (iii), we get

$$F_3 = -\int (e^Q - 1)^2\sec^2 p\, dp + C_1$$

Taking $C_1 = 0$, we have

$$F_3 = -(e^Q - 1)^2\tan p \qquad \ldots\text{(v)}$$

and integrating Eq. (iv), we get

$$F_3 = -2\int e^Q(e^Q - 1)\tan p\, dQ + C_2$$

Taking $C_2 = 0$, we have,

$$F_3 = -(e^Q - 1)^2\tan p \qquad \ldots\text{(vi)}$$

Since, Eqs. (v) and (vi) are same. Hence, $F_3$ is the generator of the given transformation.

**33.** The Lagrangian $L$ is given by

$$L = \frac{1}{2}mr^2\dot{\theta}^2 + mgr\cos\theta \qquad \ldots\text{(i)}$$

where $V = -mgr\cos\theta$ with respect to position $S$.

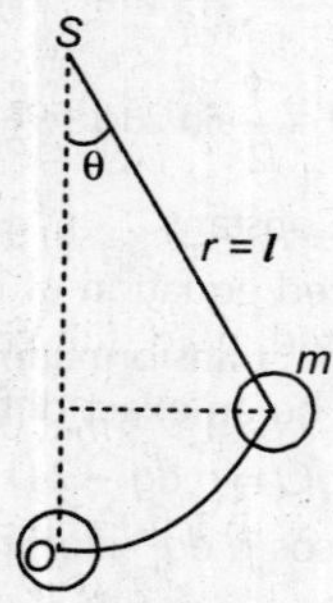


The equation of constraint is given by

$$r = l \text{ or } dr = 0 \qquad \ldots\text{(ii)}$$

Here, there is only one constraint equation, hence only one Lagrange's multiplier $\lambda$ will be needed. There are two coordinates $r$ and $\theta$ and the general constraint equation will be

$$a_r dr + a_\theta d\theta = 0 \qquad \ldots\text{(iii)}$$

Hence, $a_r = 1,\ a_\theta = 0$

Equation of motion are

$$\frac{d}{dt}\left(\frac{\partial L}{\partial \dot{r}}\right) - \frac{\partial L}{\partial r} = \lambda a_r \qquad \ldots\text{(iv)}$$

and $\dfrac{d}{dt}\left(\dfrac{\partial L}{\partial \dot{\theta}}\right) - \dfrac{\partial L}{\partial \theta} = \lambda a_\theta \qquad \ldots\text{(v)}$

Here, $\dfrac{\partial L}{\partial \dot{r}} = 0$

$$\frac{\partial L}{\partial r} = mr\dot{\theta}^2 + mg\cos\theta$$

$$\frac{\partial L}{\partial \dot{\theta}} = mr^2\dot{\theta}$$

$$\frac{\partial L}{\partial \theta} = -mgr\sin\theta$$

Hence, $-mr\dot{\theta}^2 - mg\cos\theta = \lambda \qquad \ldots\text{(vi)}$

$\Rightarrow \quad mr^2\ddot{\theta} + mgr\sin\theta = 0 \qquad \ldots\text{(vii)}$

where $\dot{r} = 0$ from Eq. (ii).

Using $r = l$, (the constraint equation), equation of motion of simple pendulum is given by Eq. (vii),

$$l\ddot{\theta} + g\sin\theta = 0$$

For small $\theta$, $\sin\theta = \theta$ and hence

$$\ddot{\theta} + \frac{g}{l}\theta + 0 \qquad \ldots\text{(viii)}$$

The force of constraint is given by

$$\lambda = -ml\dot{\theta}^2 - mg\cos\theta \qquad \ldots\text{(ix)}$$

which gives the force of constraint *i.e.*, tension $F = ml\dot{\theta}^2 - mg\cos\theta$ in magnitude.

**34.** We have,

$$dQ = \frac{\partial}{\partial p}\left(\frac{1}{p}\right)dp + \frac{\partial}{\partial p}\left(\frac{1}{p}\right)dq = -\frac{1}{p^2}dp + 0$$

and $\delta Q = \dfrac{\partial}{dp}\left(\dfrac{1}{p}\right)\delta p + \dfrac{\partial}{\partial p}\left(\dfrac{1}{p}\right)\delta q$

$$\delta Q = -\frac{1}{p^2}\delta p + 0$$

Similarly, $dP = p^2 dq + 2qp\, dp$ and $\delta P = p^2\delta q + 2qp\,\delta p$

so that $\delta P\, dQ - \delta Q\, dP = (p^2\delta q + 2qp\,\delta p) \times -\dfrac{1}{p^2}dp$

$$-\left(-\frac{1}{p^2}\delta p\right)(p^2\, dq + 2pq\, dp)$$

$$= -\delta q\, dp + \delta p + dq$$

$$= (\delta p\, dq - \delta q\, dp)$$

$\Rightarrow$ The bilinear form is invariant and consequently, the transformaton is canonical.

**35.** We have,

$$p_j = \frac{\partial L}{\partial \dot{q}_j} = \frac{\partial T}{\partial \dot{\mathbf{r}}_i}\cdot\frac{\partial \dot{\mathbf{r}}_i}{\partial \dot{q}_j} - \frac{\partial \mathbf{V}}{\partial \dot{\mathbf{r}}_i}\cdot\frac{\partial \dot{\mathbf{r}}_i}{\partial \dot{q}_j}$$

$$= \sum_i\left(m_i\dot{\mathbf{r}}\cdot\frac{\partial \dot{\mathbf{r}}_i}{\partial \dot{q}_j} - \frac{\partial V}{\partial \dot{\mathbf{r}}_i}\cdot\frac{\partial \dot{\mathbf{r}}_i}{\partial \dot{q}_j}\right)$$

$$= \sum_i m_i\mathbf{v}_i\cdot(\mathbf{n}\times\mathbf{r}_i) - \sum_i\frac{\partial V}{\partial \mathbf{v}_i}\cdot(\mathbf{n}\times\mathbf{r}_i)$$

$$= \sum_i \mathbf{n}\cdot[\mathbf{r}_i\times(m_i\mathbf{v}_i)] - \sum_i \mathbf{n}\cdot\left(\mathbf{r}_i\times\frac{\partial V}{\partial \mathbf{v}_i}\right)$$

$$= \mathbf{n}\cdot\sum_i L_i - \mathbf{n}\cdot\Sigma\mathbf{r}_i\times\frac{\partial V}{\partial \mathbf{v}_i}$$

Therefore, $p_\theta = L_\theta - \sum_i \mathbf{n}(\mathbf{r}_i\times\Delta\mathbf{v}_i\cdot V)$

**36.** Let $\phi$ be the angle which is the radius of larger cylinder makes with the point of contact with the vertical and $\theta$, the angle that a fixed radius of small cylinder makes with the vertical. Distance $00' = (R-r)$.

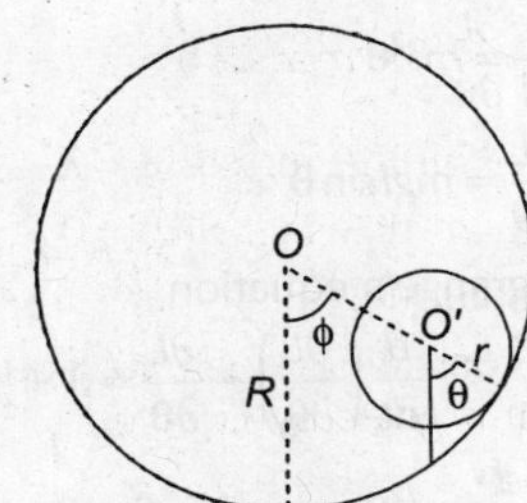


Since, the cylinder rolls without slipping, the equation of constraint is

$$r\theta = (R-r)\phi$$

or $$r\dot{\theta} = (R-r)\dot{\phi} \quad \ldots\text{(i)}$$

Kinetic energy is given by

$T$ = KE of translation of centre of mass + KE of rotation about centre of mass

$$= \frac{1}{2}m[(R-r)\dot{\phi}]^2 + \frac{1}{2}I_2\dot{\theta}^2$$

$$= \frac{1}{2}m[(R-r)\dot{\phi}]^2 + \frac{1}{2}\cdot\frac{1}{2}mr^2\cdot\dot{\theta}^2$$

$$= \frac{3}{4}m(R-r)^2\dot{\phi}^2 \quad \ldots\text{(ii)}$$

Using Eq. (i), we have

Potential energy, $V = -mg(R-r)\cos\phi$

where, $V = 0$ for $\phi = 90°$

The Lagrangian for the system is given by

$$L = T - V$$

$$= \frac{3}{4}m(R-r)^2\dot{\phi}^2 + mg(R-r)\cos\phi \quad \ldots\text{(iii)}$$

(a) The equation of motion is given by

$$\frac{d}{dt}\left(\frac{\partial L}{\partial \dot{\phi}}\right) - \frac{\partial L}{\partial \phi} = 0$$

$$\Rightarrow \quad \frac{3}{2}(R-r)^2\ddot{\phi} + g(R-r)\sin\phi = 0$$

For small oscillations, we have

$$\sin\phi = \phi$$

Hence, $$\frac{3}{2}(R-r)\ddot{\phi} + g\phi = 0 \quad \ldots\text{(iv)}$$

Which is the required equation of motion.

(b) The Eq. (iv) can be rewritten as

$$\ddot{\phi} + \omega^2\phi = 0$$

where $\omega$ the frequency of small oscillations, *i.e.*,

$$\omega = \sqrt{\frac{g}{3/2\,(R-r)}} = \sqrt{\frac{2g}{3(R-r)}}$$

So, the period of small oscillations is given by

$$T = \frac{2\pi}{\omega} = 2\pi\sqrt{\frac{3(R-r)}{2g}}$$

**37.** (a) Let $P(x, y)$ be the position of the bead of the mass $m$ at any instant $t$. The path of bead is a cycloid represented by equations

$$\left.\begin{aligned} x &= a(\theta - \sin\theta) \\ y &= a(1+\cos\theta) \end{aligned}\right\}$$

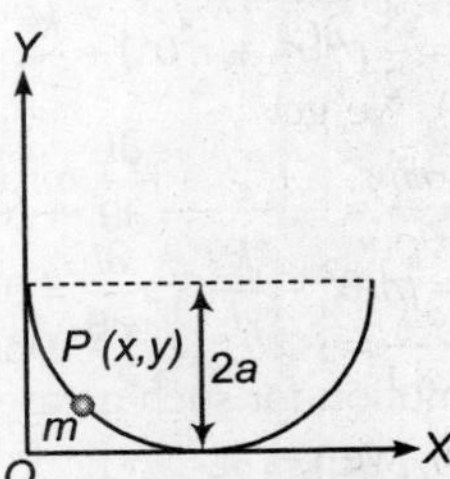


The kinetic energy of the bead is given by

$$T = \frac{1}{2}m(\dot{x}^2 + \dot{y}^2)$$

$$= \frac{1}{2}m\{a^2(\dot{\theta} - \cos\theta\,\dot{\theta})^2 + a^2(-\sin\theta\,\dot{\theta})^2\}$$

$$= ma^2\dot{\theta}^2(1-\cos\theta)$$

The potential energy for the bead, taking $x$-axis as the reference level is given by

$$V = mgy = mga(1+\cos\theta)$$

Hence, the Lagrangian is given by

$$L = T - V = ma^2\dot{\theta}^2(1-\cos\theta) - mga(1+\cos\theta) \quad \ldots\text{(i)}$$

(b) The Lagrange's equation of motion is given by

$$\frac{d}{dt}\left(\frac{\partial L}{\partial \dot{\theta}}\right) - \frac{\partial L}{\partial \theta} = 0 \quad \ldots\text{(ii)}$$

From Eq. (i), we have

$$\frac{\partial L}{\partial \dot{\theta}} = 2ma^2\dot{\theta}(1-\cos\theta)$$

and $$\frac{\partial L}{\partial \theta} = ma^2\dot{\theta}^2\sin\theta + mga\sin\theta$$

which when substituted in Eq. (ii), gives

$$\frac{d}{dt}[2ma^2\dot{\theta}(1-\cos\theta)] - [ma^2\dot{\theta}^2\sin\theta + mga\sin\theta] = 0$$

$$\Rightarrow \quad 2ma^2\ddot{\theta}(1-\cos\theta) + 2ma^2\dot{\theta}\sin\theta\dot{\theta} - ma^2\dot{\theta}^2\sin\theta - mga\sin\theta = 0$$

$$\Rightarrow \quad \ddot{\theta}(1-\cos\theta) + \frac{1}{2}\sin\theta\,\dot{\theta}^2 - \frac{g}{2a}\sin\theta = 0 \quad \ldots\text{(iii)}$$

Which is the required equation of motion.

**38.** Central force is that force which is always directed away or towards a fixed centre and the magnitude of which is a function of the distance from the fixed centre (origin).

Let a particle of mass $m$ moving in a plane and attracted towards the origin of coordinates with a force that is inversely proportional to the square of the distance from it. If $(r, \theta)$ be its plane polar coordinates, the kinetic energy will be

$$T = \frac{1}{2}m(\dot{r}^2 + r^2\dot{\theta}^2),$$

and the potential energy is given by

$$V = -\int_{\infty}^{r} F\,dr = -\int_{\infty}^{r} -\frac{k}{r^2}\,dr = -\frac{k}{r},$$

because force $F$ is attractive in nature and varies inversely as the square of the distance from the origin, *i. e.*, $F = -k/r^2$, where $k$ is a constant of proportionality. The Lagrangian will, thus, become

$$L = T - V$$
$$= \frac{1}{2}m(\dot{r}^2 + r^2\dot{\theta}^2) + \frac{k}{r}, \qquad \text{...(i)}$$

Giving
$$\left.\begin{array}{ll} \dfrac{\partial L}{\partial \dot{r}} = m\dot{r}, & \dfrac{\partial L}{\partial \dot{\theta}} = mr^2\dot{\theta} \\ \dfrac{\partial L}{\partial r} = mr\dot{\theta}^2 - \dfrac{k}{r^2}, & \dfrac{\partial L}{\partial \theta} = 0 \end{array}\right\} \qquad \text{...(ii)}$$

The equations of motion for such a case will be

$$\left.\begin{array}{l} \dfrac{d}{dt}\left(\dfrac{\partial L}{\partial \dot{r}}\right) - \dfrac{\partial L}{\partial r} = 0 \\ \dfrac{d}{dt}\left(\dfrac{\partial L}{\partial \dot{\theta}}\right) - \dfrac{\partial L}{\partial \theta} = 0 \end{array}\right\} \qquad \text{...(iii)}$$

On applying Eq. (ii) to Eq. (iii), we get

$$\frac{d}{dt}(m\dot{r}) - mr\dot{\theta}^2 + \frac{k}{r^2} = 0$$

and
$$\frac{d}{dt'}(mr^2\dot{\theta}) = 0$$

Solving further, we get

$$m\ddot{r} - mr\dot{\theta}^2 + \frac{k}{r^2} = 0$$

and
$$2mr\,\dot{r}\,\dot{\theta} + mr^2\ddot{\theta} = 0 \qquad \text{...(iv)}$$

These are desired equations of motion for the particle moving under the influence of a central force.

**39.** Let $O$ be the point of support and $l$ be the length of pendulum with mass $m$.

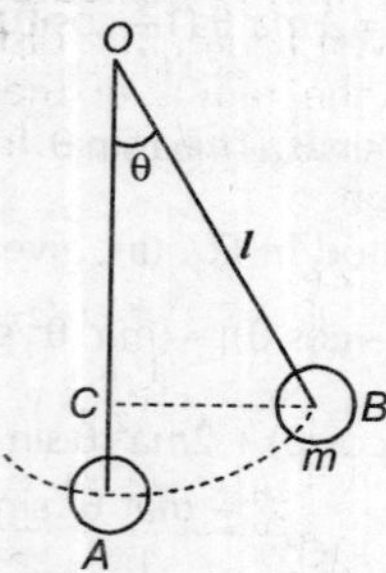


The angle $\theta$ between rest position and deflected position is chosen as generalized coordinate. The kinetic energy is given by

$$T = \frac{1}{2}mv^2 = \frac{1}{2}m(l\dot{\theta})^2 = \frac{1}{2}ml^2\dot{\theta}^2$$

where $m$ is the mass of the bob.

In coming from position $B$ to $A$, the mass has fallen freely through a vertical distance $CA$. Thus, potential energy is

$$V = mg\,(OA - OC)$$
$$= mg\,(l - l\cos\theta)$$
$$= mgl\,(l - \cos\theta)$$

where the reference level or zero level of potential energy has been taken at a distance $l$ below the point of suspension. If reference level is taken through $O$, then

$$V = -mgl\cos\theta$$

Thus, Lagrangian is

$$L = T - V$$
$$= \frac{1}{2}ml^2\dot{\theta}^2 - mgl(1 - \cos\theta).$$

Hence,
$$\frac{\partial L}{\partial \dot{\theta}} = ml^2\dot{\theta}$$

and
$$\frac{\partial L}{\partial \theta} = mgl\sin\theta$$

Substituting in Lagrange's equation

$$\frac{d}{dt}\left(\frac{\partial L}{\partial \dot{\theta}}\right) - \frac{\partial L}{\partial \theta} = 0$$

We get,
$$\frac{d}{dt}(ml^2\dot{\theta}) + mgl\sin\theta = 0$$

$$\Rightarrow \quad ml^2\ddot{\theta} + mgl\sin\theta = 0$$

$$\Rightarrow \quad \ddot{\theta} + \frac{g}{l}\sin\theta = 0$$

If the amplitude of the motion is small enough, *i.e.*, $\sin\theta \simeq \theta$, then

$$\ddot{\theta} + \frac{g}{l}\theta = 0.$$

which is equation for simple harmonic motion.

**40.** Largrnge's equation of motion for one dimension, say $x$, can be written as

$$\frac{d}{dt}\left(\frac{\partial L}{\partial \dot{x}}\right) - \frac{\partial L}{\partial x} = 0 \qquad \text{...(i)}$$

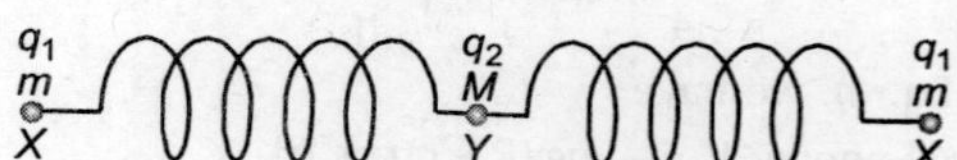


**Linear harmonic oscillator**

The kinetic energy of this system is given by

$$T = \frac{1}{2}m\dot{x}^2$$

and potential energy is given by

$$V = -\int -\mathbf{F}\cdot dx$$
$$= -\int -kx\,dx = \frac{1}{2}kx^2 + C$$

where $C$ is a constant of integration and $k$ is spring constant. If we choose the horizontal plane passing through the position the position of equilibrium as the reference level, then $V = 0$ at $x = 0$ so that $C = 0$. Thus, Lagrangian is

$$L = \frac{1}{2}m\dot{x}^2 - \frac{1}{2}kx^2,$$

Hence,
$$\frac{\partial L}{\partial \dot{x}} = \frac{1}{2}m\dot{x}$$

and
$$\frac{\partial L}{\partial x} = -kx.$$

Eq. (i) takes the form

$$\frac{d}{dt}(m\dot{x}) - (-k\dot{x}) = 0$$

$$\Rightarrow \quad m\ddot{x} + kx = 0$$

which is the required expression for linear harmonic oscillator.

**41.** Suppose, $(r, \theta)$ are the polar coordinates of the particle of mass $M$ in the given plane. The kinetic energy of the particle will be

$$T = \frac{1}{2} M(\dot{r}^2 + r^2\dot{\theta}^2) \quad \ldots\text{(i)}$$

(a) To show it, let us write the Lagranges's equation of motion in terms of $\theta$, *i.e.*,

$$\frac{d}{dt}\left(\frac{\partial T}{\partial \dot{\theta}}\right) - \frac{\partial T}{\partial \theta} = Q_\theta \quad \ldots\text{(ii)}$$

From Eq. (i),

$$\frac{\partial T}{\partial \dot{\theta}} = Mr^2\dot{\theta}$$

$$\frac{\partial T}{\partial \theta} = 0$$

and since the force is only radial, $Q_\theta = 0$. Eq. (ii), therefore, becomes

$$\frac{d}{dt}(Mr^2\dot{\theta}) = 0$$

$$\Rightarrow \quad Mr^2\dot{\theta} = \text{a Constant}$$

The left hand side of above equation is the angular momentum of the particle about the origin and is, therefore, conserved.

(b) The Lagrange's equation is given by

$$\frac{d}{dt}\left(\frac{\partial T}{\partial \dot{r}}\right) - \frac{\partial T}{\partial r} = Q_r \quad \ldots\text{(iii)}$$

From Eq. (i),

$$\frac{\partial T}{\partial \dot{r}} = M\dot{r}$$

$$\frac{\partial T}{\partial r} = Mr\dot{\theta}$$

Also, $Q_r = F_r = kr\cos\theta$. Therefore, Eq. (iii) becomes

$$\frac{d}{dt}(M\dot{r}) - Mr\dot{\theta}^2 = -kr\cos\theta$$

$$\Rightarrow \quad M\ddot{r} - Mr\dot{\theta}^2 + kr\cos\theta = 0$$

The desired differential equation of the orbit of the particle.

**42.** At any time $t$, let the masses $m_1, m_2$ be at $P_1(x_1, y_1)$ and $P_2(x_2, y_2)$, we have

$$\left.\begin{aligned} x_1 &= l_1\sin\theta_1,\ y_1 = l_1\cos\theta_1 \\ x_2 &= l_1\sin\theta_1 + l_2\sin\theta_2,\ y_2 = l_1\cos\theta_1 + l_2\cos\theta_2 \end{aligned}\right\} \quad \ldots\text{(i)}$$

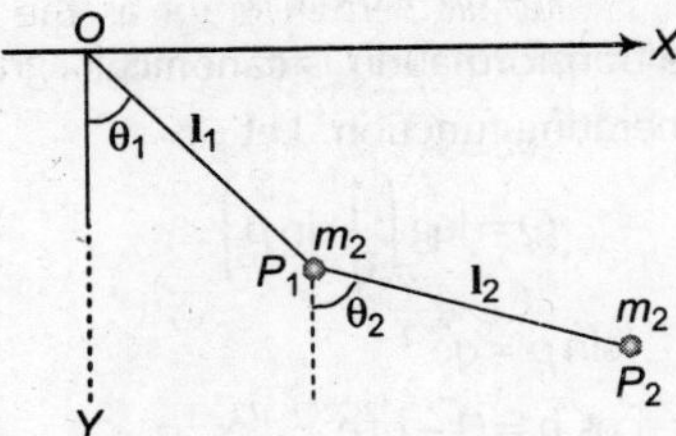


Total kinetic energy is given by

$$T = \frac{1}{2} m_1(\dot{x}_1^2 + \dot{y}_1^2) + \frac{1}{2} m_2(\dot{x}_2^2 + \dot{y}_2^2)$$

$$= \frac{1}{2}(m_1 + m_2) l_1^2\dot{\theta}_1^2 + \frac{1}{2} m_2 l_2^2\dot{\theta}_2^2 + m_2 l_1 l_2\dot{\theta}_1\dot{\theta}_2\cos(\theta_1 - \theta_2)$$

Total potential energy is given by

$$V = m_1 g l_1(1 - \cos\theta_1) + m_2 g(l_1 + l_2 - l_1\cos\theta_1 - l_2\cos\theta_2)$$

Hence, Lagrangian is given by $L = T - V$

$$= \frac{1}{2}(m_1 + m_2) l_1^2\dot{\theta}_1^2 + \frac{1}{2} m_2 l_2^2\dot{\theta}_2^2) + m_2 l_1 l_2\dot{\theta}_1\dot{\theta}_2\cos(\theta_1 - \theta_2) - (m_1 - m_2) g l_1(1 - \cos\theta_1) - m_2 g l_2(1 - \cos\theta_2) \quad \ldots\text{(ii)}$$

The Lagrange's equation corresponding to $\theta_1$, $\frac{\partial L}{\partial \theta_1} - \frac{d}{dt}\left(\frac{\partial L}{\partial \dot{\theta}_1}\right) = 0$, gives

$$-m_2 l_1 l_2\dot{\theta}_1\dot{\theta}_2\sin(\theta_1 - \theta_2) - (m_1 + m_2) g l_1\sin\theta_1 - \frac{d}{dt}[(m_1 + m_2) l_1^2\dot{\theta}_1 + m_2 l_1 l_2\dot{\theta}_2\cos(\theta_1 - \theta_2)] = 0$$

or

$$(m_1 + m_2) l_1\ddot{\theta}_1 + m_2 l_2\ddot{\theta}_2\cos(\theta_1 - \theta_2) + m_2 l_2\dot{\theta}_2^2\sin(\theta_1 - \theta_2) + (m_1 + m_2) g\sin\theta_1 = 0 \quad \ldots\text{(iii)}$$

Lagrange's equation corresponding to $\theta_2$,

$$\frac{\partial L}{\partial \theta_2} - \frac{d}{dt}\left(\frac{\partial L}{\partial \dot{\theta}_2}\right) = 0 \text{ gives}$$

$$m_2 l_1 l_2\dot{\theta}_1\dot{\theta}_2\sin(\theta_1 - \theta_2) - m_2 g l_2\sin\theta_2 - \frac{d}{dt}[m_2 l_2^2\dot{\theta}_2 + m_2 l_1 l_2\dot{\theta}_1\cos(\theta_1 - \theta_2)] = 0$$

or

$$l_2\ddot{\theta}_2 + l_2\ddot{\theta}_1\cos(\theta_1 - \theta_2) - l_1\dot{\theta}_1^2\sin(\theta_1 - \theta_2) + g\sin\theta_2 = 0 \quad \ldots\text{(iv)}$$

Now, since $\dot{\theta}_1$ and $\dot{\theta}_2$ being small, retaining first order terms only, Eqs. (iii) and (iv) reduce to

$$(m_1 + m_2) l_1\ddot{\theta}_1 + m_2 l_2\ddot{\theta}_2 + (m_1 + m_2) g\theta_1 = 0$$

and

$$l_1\ddot{\theta}_1 + l_2\ddot{\theta}_2 g\theta_2 = 0$$

**43.** The position of the bob is located by spherical coordinates $\theta$, $\phi$ as shown in given figure. The distance $r$ of the bob from the origin will be the radius of the sphere on which the particle (or bob) moves. The force in this case is constant in the vertical direction.

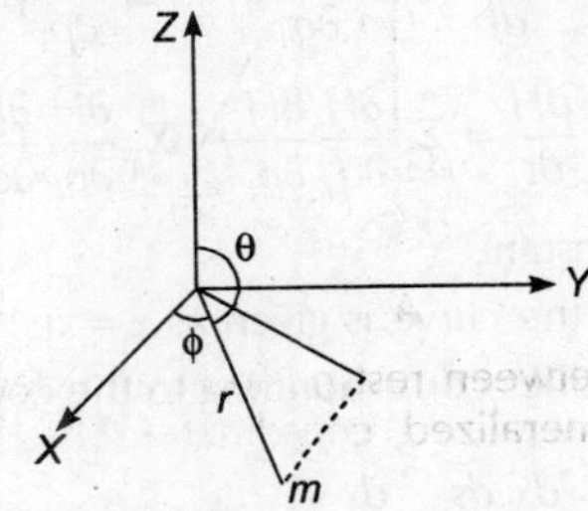


The kinetic energy of the bob is given by $T = \frac{1}{2} mr^2(\dot{\theta}^2 + \sin^2\theta\dot{\phi}^2)$.

The potential energy of the bob due to gravity relative to the horizontal plane

$$V = mgr\cos\theta$$

The Lagrangian for the system is

$$L = T - V$$

$$= \frac{1}{2} mr^2(\dot{\theta}^2 + \sin^2\theta\dot{\phi}^2) - mgr\cos\theta$$

The Lagrange's equations are given by

$$\frac{d}{dt}\left(\frac{\partial L}{\partial \dot\theta}\right)-\frac{\partial L}{\partial \theta}=0,$$

and $$\frac{d}{dt}\left(\frac{\partial L}{\partial \dot\phi}\right)-\frac{\partial L}{\partial \phi}=0 \text{ gives}$$

$$\frac{d}{dt}(mr^2\dot\theta)-mr^2\sin\theta\cos\theta\dot\phi^2-mgr\sin\theta=0$$

and $$\frac{d}{dt}(mr^2\sin^2\theta\,\dot\phi)=0$$

Which solving further, gives

$$m\,r^2\,\ddot\theta-mr^2\sin\theta\cos\theta\,\dot\phi^2-mgr\sin\theta=0$$

and $$mr^2\frac{d}{dt}(\sin^2\theta\dot\phi)=0$$

which are the desired equations of the motion of a spherical pendulum.

**44.** The routhian is

$$R=\sum_{k=1}^{s}p_k\dot q_k-L$$

Since, θ is the cyclic coordinate,

$$R=P_\theta\,\dot\theta-\frac{1}{2}\mu(\dot r^2+r^2\dot\theta^2)-\frac{GMm}{r}$$

Since, $$P_\theta=\frac{\partial L}{\partial\dot\theta}=\mu r^2\,\dot\theta=\text{Constant},$$

Hence, $$\dot\theta=\frac{P_\theta}{\mu r^2}$$

Therefore, $$R=-\frac{1}{2}\mu\dot r^2+\frac{P_\theta}{2\mu r^2}-\frac{GMm}{r}$$

**45.** (i) Since, Hamiltonian $H$ is independent of $t$, we have

$$H=H(q_1,q_2,\ldots,q_n,p_1,p_2,\ldots p_n)$$

$$\Rightarrow\quad 0=\frac{dH}{dt}=\sum_{i=1}^{n}\frac{\partial H}{\partial q_i}\dot q_i+\sum_{i=1}^{n}\frac{\partial H}{\partial p_i}\dot p_i$$

or $$\frac{dH}{dt}=\sum_{i=1}^{n}\frac{\partial H}{\partial q_i}\frac{\partial H}{\partial p_i}-\sum_{i=1}^{n}\frac{\partial H}{\partial p_i}\frac{\partial H}{\partial q_i}=0$$

$$\Rightarrow\quad H=\text{Constant}$$

**46.** The equation of the curve is given as $x = x(s)$ and $z = z(s)$. Hence, the velocities corresponding to the coordinates $x$ and $z$ are

$$\dot x=\frac{dx}{dt}=\frac{dx}{ds}\frac{ds}{dt}=\frac{dx}{ds}\dot s=x'\dot s\qquad\text{where }\frac{dx}{ds}=x'$$

$$\dot z=\frac{dz}{dt}=\frac{dz}{d}\frac{ds}{dt}=z'\dot s$$

where $$z'=\frac{dz}{ds},$$

The kinetic energy of the particle is given by

$$T=\frac{1}{2}m(x'^2+z'^2)\dot s^2$$

The potential energyof the particle is given by

$$V=mgz(s)$$

The Lagrangian is given by

$$L=T-V=\frac{1}{2}m(x'^2+z'^2)\dot s^2-mgz(s)$$

The differentiation with respect ot $\dot s$ and $s$, respectively gives;

$$\frac{\partial L}{\partial\dot s}=m(x'^2+z'^2)\dot s \qquad\ldots\text{(i)}$$

and $$\frac{\partial L}{\partial s}=m\dot s^2(x'x''+z'z'')-mgz' \qquad\ldots\text{(ii)}$$

∴ The Largange's equation in terms of $s$ is

$$\frac{d}{dt}\left(\frac{\partial L}{\partial\dot s}\right)-\frac{\partial L}{\partial s}=0 \qquad\ldots\text{(iii)}$$

Substituting the value of $\frac{\partial L}{\partial\dot s}$ and $\frac{\partial L}{\partial s}$ from Eqs. (i) and (ii) in Eq. (iii), we get

$$\frac{d}{dt}[m(x^2+z'^2)\dot s]-m\dot s^2(x'x''+z'z'')+mgz'=0$$

Which is the required equation motion.

**47.** (a) If $pdq-PdQ=dF$

A transformation is canonical

$$dQ=\frac{\partial Q}{\partial q}dq+\frac{\partial Q}{\partial p}dp$$

$$=\frac{\partial}{\partial q}\left[\log\left(\frac{1}{q}\sin\right)\right]dq+\frac{\partial}{\partial q}\left[\log\left(\frac{1}{q}\sin p\right)\right]dp$$

$$=-\frac{1}{\left(\frac{1}{q}\sin p\right)}\left(\frac{\sin p}{q^2}\right)dq+\frac{1}{\left(\frac{1}{q}\sin p\right)}\left(\frac{\cos p}{q}\right)dp$$

$$=-\frac{dq}{q}+\cot p\,dp$$

Therefore, $$pdq-PdQ=pdq-(q\cot p)\left(-\frac{dq}{q}+\cot p\,dp\right)$$

$$=(p+\cot p)\,dq-q\cot^2 p\,dp$$

$$=\frac{\partial}{\partial q}(qp+q\cot p)\,dq+\frac{\partial}{\partial p}(qp+q\cot p)\,dp$$

$$=\frac{\partial F}{\partial q}dq+\frac{\partial F}{\partial p}dp$$

Here, right hand side is the exact differential of the function

$$F=qp+q\cot p$$

and hence the transformation is canonical.

(b) $F$ is the generating function. Let

$$Q=\log\left(\frac{1}{q}\sin p\right)$$

or $$\sin p=qe^Q$$

Hence, $$\cos p=(1-q^2e^{2Q})^{1/2}$$

and $$\cot p=\frac{(1-q^2e^{2Q})^{1/2}}{qe^Q}$$

On putting these values in the expression for $F$, we get

$$F=q\sin^{-1}(qe^Q)+e^{-Q}(1-q^2e^{2Q})^{1/2}$$

The required generating function.

**48.** Let $q_1, q_2, \ldots, q_n$ be the generalized coordinates, then Hamilton's equations of motion are given by

$$\dot{p}_i = -\frac{\partial H}{\partial q_i} \text{ and } \dot{q}_i = \frac{\partial H}{\partial p_i}, \quad i = 1, 2, \ldots, n \quad \ldots\text{(i)}$$

Since, $\quad H = H(q_1, q_2, \ldots, q_n, p_1, p_2, \ldots, p_n, t) \quad \ldots$(ii)

Therefore, $$\frac{dH}{dt} = \frac{\partial H}{\partial t} + \sum_{i=1}^{n} \frac{\partial H}{\partial q_i}\dot{q}_i + \sum_{i=1}^{n} \frac{\partial H}{\partial p_i}\dot{p} \quad \ldots\text{(iii)}$$

From Eqs. (i) and (ii), we get

$$\frac{dH}{dt} = \frac{\partial H}{\partial t} - \sum_{i=1}^{n} \dot{p}_i \dot{q}_i + \sum_{i=1}^{n} \dot{p}_i \dot{q}_i$$

Hence, $$\frac{dH}{dt} = \frac{\partial H}{\partial t}$$

**49.** Let $\theta$ be the angular displacement from the vertical $Oy$ at any time $t$. And here dynamical system consists of a single particle of mass $m$ and generalised coordinate $\theta$. Since, the system is conservative and hence the Lagrange's equation of motion is

$$\frac{d}{dt}\left(\frac{\partial L}{\partial \dot{\theta}}\right) - \frac{\partial L}{\partial \theta} = 0 \quad \ldots\text{(i)}$$

The kinetic energy is given by $T = \frac{1}{2} ml^2\dot{\theta}^2$

and the potential energy is given by

$$V = -mgl\cos\theta$$

The Lagrangian is given by $L = T - V = \frac{1}{2} l^2\dot{\theta}^2 + mgl\cos\theta$

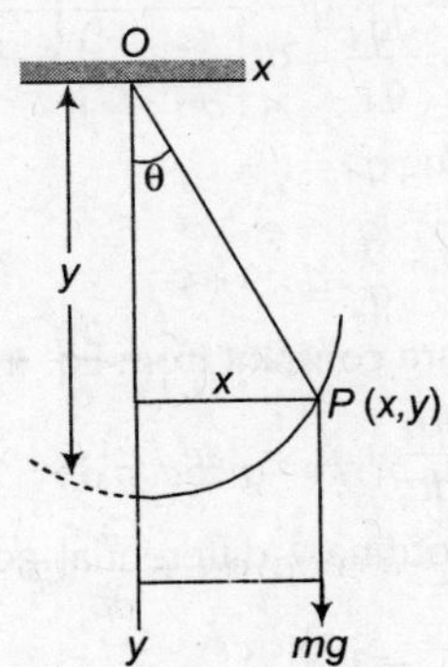


Substituting the value of $L$ in Eq. (i), we have

$$\frac{d}{dt}(ml^2\dot{\theta}) + mgl\sin\theta = 0$$

$$\Rightarrow \quad ml^2\ddot{\theta} + mgl\sin\theta = 0$$

$$\Rightarrow \quad \ddot{\theta} + \frac{g}{l}\sin\theta = 0$$

Which is the required equation of motion.

**50.** Let $(r, \theta)$ be the plane polar coordinates of a particle of mass $m$, Then, the kinetic energy of the particle $T$ is

$$T = \frac{1}{2} m(\dot{r}^2 + r^2\dot{\theta}^2)$$

By inverse law of attractive force, if $F$ is the force experienced by the particle, then $F \propto \frac{1}{r^2}$ or $F = -\frac{k}{r^2}$, where $k$ is the constant of proportionality.

The potential energy is given by

$$V = -\int_{\infty}^{r} F\,dr = -\int_{\infty}^{r} -\frac{k}{r^2}\,dr = -\frac{k}{r}$$

The Lagrangian is given by

$$L = T - V = \frac{1}{2} m(\dot{r}^2 + r^2\dot{\theta}^2) + \frac{k}{r} \quad \ldots\text{(i)}$$

We have
$$\left.\begin{aligned} \frac{\partial L}{\partial \dot{r}} &= m\dot{r}, & \frac{\partial L}{\partial \dot{\theta}} &= mr^2\dot{\theta} \\ \frac{\partial L}{\partial r} &= mr\dot{\theta}^2 - \frac{k}{r^2}, & \frac{\partial L}{\partial \theta} &= 0. \end{aligned}\right\} \quad \ldots\text{(ii)}$$

Hence, the equation of motion are

$$\left.\begin{aligned} \frac{d}{dt}\left(\frac{\partial L}{\partial \dot{r}}\right) - \frac{\partial L}{\partial r} &= 0 \\ \frac{d}{dt}\left(\frac{\partial L}{\partial \dot{\theta}}\right) - \frac{\partial L}{\partial \theta} &= 0 \end{aligned}\right\} \quad \ldots\text{(iii)}$$

On applying Eq. (ii) to Eq. (iii), we have

$$\frac{d}{dt}(m\dot{r}) - mr\dot{\theta}^2 + \frac{k}{r^2} = 0$$

and $$\frac{d}{dt}(mr^2\dot{\theta}) = 0$$

or $$\left.\begin{aligned} m\ddot{r} - mr\dot{\theta}^2 + \frac{k}{r^2} &= 0 \\ \text{and} \quad 2m\dot{r}\dot{\theta} + mr^2\ddot{\theta} &= 0 \end{aligned}\right\} \quad \ldots\text{(iv)}$$

There are the desired equations of motion for the particle moving under the influence of a central force.

**51.** Here, $x = r\cos\theta$, $y = r\sin\theta$. Hence

$$\dot{x} = \dot{r}\cos\theta - r\dot{\theta}\sin\theta,$$
$$\dot{y} = \dot{r}\sin\theta + r\dot{\theta}\cos\theta$$

Then, kinetic energy is given by

$$T = \frac{1}{2} m(\dot{x}^2 + \dot{y}^2)$$
$$= \frac{1}{2} m\dot{r}^2 + (r\dot{\theta})^2$$

Since, $$Q_j = \sum_{i=1}^{N} \mathbf{F}_i \cdot \frac{\partial \mathbf{r}_i}{\partial q_j}$$

Hence, $$Q_r = \mathbf{F} \cdot \frac{\partial \mathbf{r}}{\partial r} = F_r$$

and $$Q_\theta = \mathbf{F} \cdot \frac{\partial \mathbf{r}}{\partial \theta} = \mathbf{F} \cdot r\mathbf{n} = rF_\theta$$

**n** is the unit vector perpendicular to the direction of **r**. We have,

$$\frac{d}{dt}\left(\frac{\partial T}{\partial \dot{r}}\right) - \frac{\partial T}{\partial r} = Q_r$$

$$\Rightarrow \quad \frac{d}{dt}(m\dot{r}) - m\dot{\theta}^2 r = F_r \quad \ldots\text{(i)}$$

Also, $$\frac{d}{dt}\left(\frac{\partial T}{\partial \dot{\theta}}\right) - \frac{\partial T}{\partial \theta} = Q_\theta$$

$$\Rightarrow \quad \frac{d}{dt}(mr^2\dot{\theta}) = rF_\theta$$

Hence, $$2m\dot{r}\dot{\theta} + rm\ddot{\theta} = F_\theta \quad \ldots\text{(ii)}$$

Thus, the required equation of motion are given by Eqs. (i) and (ii).

**52.** The Hamilton's equations are

$$\dot{q} = \frac{\partial H}{\partial p} \text{ and } \dot{p} = -\frac{\partial H}{\partial q}$$

where, $H$ is the Hamiltonian. Now,

$$\dot{Q} = \frac{q}{\sin p} \frac{q\dot{p}\cos p - \dot{q}\sin p}{q^2}$$

$$= \frac{q\dot{p}\cos p - \dot{q}\sin p}{q \sin p}$$

$$= (-\cot p)\frac{\partial H}{\partial q} - \frac{1}{q}\frac{\partial H}{\partial p}$$

$$= (-\cot p)\frac{\partial H}{\partial P}\frac{\partial P}{\partial q} - \frac{1}{q}\frac{\partial H}{\partial P}\frac{\partial P}{\partial p}$$

$$= (-\cot^2 p)\frac{\partial H}{\partial P} + \frac{q\operatorname{cosec}^2 p}{q}\frac{\partial H}{\partial P}$$

$$= (-\cot^2 p)\frac{\partial H}{\partial P} + (\operatorname{cosec}^2 p)\frac{\partial H}{\partial P}$$

$$= (\operatorname{cosec}^2 p - \cot^2 p)\frac{\partial H}{\partial P}$$

$$= \frac{\partial H}{\partial P}$$

and $\dot{P} = \dot{q}\cot p - q\dot{p}\operatorname{cosec}^2 p$

$$= \frac{\partial H}{\partial p}\cot p + q(\operatorname{cosec}^2 p)\frac{\partial H}{\partial q}$$

$$= (\cot p)\frac{\partial H}{\partial Q}\frac{\partial Q}{\partial p} + q(\operatorname{cosec}^2 p)\frac{\partial H}{\partial Q}\frac{\partial Q}{\partial q}$$

$$= (\cot p)\frac{\partial H}{\partial Q}\frac{q}{\sin p}\frac{\cos p}{q} + q(\operatorname{cosec}^2 p)\frac{q}{\sin p}\frac{-\sin p}{q^2}\frac{\partial H}{\partial Q}$$

$$= (\cot^2 p)\frac{\partial H}{\partial Q} - (\operatorname{cosec}^2 p)\frac{\partial H}{\partial Q}$$

$$= -\frac{\partial H}{\partial Q}$$

Since, $\dot{Q} = \dfrac{\partial H}{\partial P}$ and $\dot{P} = -\dfrac{\partial H}{\partial Q}$

Thus, the given transformation is canonical.

**53.** In cartesian coordinate system the generalized force components are $F_x, F_y, F_z$, and kinetic energy

$$T = \frac{1}{2}m(\dot{x}^2 + \dot{y}^2 + \dot{z}^2)$$

$$\Rightarrow \quad \frac{\partial T}{\partial x} = \frac{\partial T}{\partial y} = \frac{\partial T}{\partial z} = 0$$

and $\quad \dfrac{\partial T}{\partial \dot{x}} = m\dot{x}, \dfrac{\partial T}{\partial \dot{y}} = m\dot{y}$

$$\frac{\partial T}{\partial \dot{z}} = m\dot{z}$$

Lagrange's equations of motions are

$$\frac{d}{dt}\left(\frac{\partial T}{\partial \dot{q}_j}\right) - \frac{\partial T}{\partial q_j} = Q_j$$

For $j = 1$, we have

$$\frac{d}{dt}\left(\frac{\partial T}{\partial \dot{x}}\right) - \frac{\partial T}{\partial x} = F_x$$

Therefore, we have

$$\frac{d}{dt}(m\dot{x}) = F_x$$

$$\Rightarrow \quad m\ddot{x} = F_x \quad \ldots\text{(i)}$$

For $j = 2$,

$$\frac{d}{dt}\left(\frac{\partial T}{\partial \dot{y}}\right) = F_y$$

$$\Rightarrow \quad m\ddot{y} = F_y \quad \ldots\text{(ii)}$$

For $j = 3$,

$$m\ddot{z} = F_z \quad \ldots\text{(iii)}$$

So, $m\ddot{x} = F_x$, $m\ddot{y} = F_y$ and $m\ddot{z} = F_z$ are required equation of motion of a particle in space.

**54.** We have the Hamiltonian

$$H = q_1p_1 - q_2p_2 - aq_1^2 + bq_2^2 \quad \ldots\text{(i)}$$

and so the Hamilton canonical equations are

$$\dot{q}_1 = \frac{\partial H}{\partial p_i}, \dot{p}_i = -\frac{\partial H}{\partial q_i}, i = 1, 2$$

From Eq. (i), we have

$$\dot{q}_1 = q_1 \quad \ldots\text{(ii)}$$

$$\dot{q}_2 = q_2 \quad \ldots\text{(iii)}$$

$$\dot{p}_1 = -(p_1 - 2aq_1) \quad \ldots\text{(iv)}$$

$$\dot{p}_2 = p_2 - 2bq_2 \quad \ldots\text{(v)}$$

From Eq. (ii), we have

$$\frac{dq_1}{q_1} = dt$$

$$\Rightarrow \quad \log q_1 = t + C_1$$

$$\Rightarrow \quad q_1 = e^{t + C_1} \quad \ldots\text{(vi)}$$

Similarly, $\quad q_2 = e^{-t + C_2} \quad \ldots\text{(vii)}$

where, $C_1$ and $C_2$ are constant from Eq. (iv) and (vi), we have

$$\frac{dp_1}{dt} + p_1 = 2ae^{t + C_1}$$

which is a linear ordinary differential equation, integration gives

$$p_1 = 2ae^{t + C_1} + e^{C_2 - t} \quad \ldots\text{(viii)}$$

From Eq. (v) and (vii), we have

$$\frac{dp_2}{dt} - p_2 = -2be^{t + C_2}$$

Integrating, we get

$$p_2 = -2bte^{t + C_2} + e^{t + C_3} \quad \ldots\text{(ix)}$$

They the solution of the problem is given by Eq. (vi) to Eq. (ix).

**55.** Consider a dynamical system with $N$ particles. The position vector of the $i$-particle is

$$\mathbf{r}_i = \mathbf{r}_i(q_1, q_2, \ldots, q_n), (i = 1, 2, \ldots, N) \quad \ldots\text{(i)}$$

Potential energy is givne by

$$V = V(q_1, q_2, \ldots, q_n)$$

Kinetic energy is given by

$$T = \frac{1}{2}\sum_{i=1}^{N} m_i \dot{r}_1^2$$

Hence, $\mathbf{r}_i = \sum_{j=1}^{n} \frac{\partial r_i}{\partial q_j} \dot{q}_j,\ i = 1, 2, \ldots, N$

and $T = \frac{1}{2} \sum_{i=1}^{N} m_i \left( \sum_{j=1}^{n} \frac{\partial \mathbf{r}_i}{\partial q_j} \dot{q}_j \right)^2$

Thus, $T$ reduces to a homogeneous quadratic function of $\dot{q}_1, \dot{q}_2, \ldots, \dot{q}_n$.

Therefore, by Euler's theorem we get

$$\sum_{j=1}^{n} \dot{q}_j \frac{\partial i}{\partial \dot{q}_j} = 2T \qquad \ldots\text{(ii)}$$

The Hamiltonian is given by

$$H = \sum_{j=1}^{N} p_j \dot{q}_j - L$$

$$\Rightarrow \quad H = \sum_{j=1}^{N} \dot{q}_j \frac{\partial L}{\partial \dot{q}_j} - L \qquad \left( \because p_j = \frac{\partial L}{\partial \dot{q}_j} \right)$$

$$\Rightarrow \quad H = \sum_{j=1}^{n} \dot{q}_j \frac{\partial T}{\partial \dot{q}_j} - (T - V) \qquad \left( \because \frac{\partial V}{\partial \dot{q}_j} = 0 \right)$$

Therefore, from Eq. (ii), we get $H = 2T - (T - V)$. Thus, $H = T + V$ = Total energy of the mechanical system.

**56.** Lagrange's equations for conservative, holonomic dynamical system, is given by

$$\frac{d}{dt}\left( \frac{\partial L}{\partial \dot{q}_k} \right) - \frac{\partial L}{\partial q_k} = 0 \ (k = 1, 2, \ldots, n)$$

Now, $\delta \int_{t_1}^{t_2} L\,dt = \int_{t_1}^{t_2} L\,dt$

$$= \int_{t_1}^{t_2} \left[ \sum_{k=1}^{n} \left( \frac{\partial L}{\partial q_k} \delta q_k + \frac{\partial L}{\partial \dot{q}_k} \delta \dot{q}_k \right) \right] dt$$

$$= \int_{t_1}^{t_2} \left( \sum_{k=1}^{n} \frac{\partial L}{\partial q_k} \delta q_k \right) dt - \int_{t_1}^{t_2} \left[ \sum_{k=1}^{n} \frac{d}{dt} \left( \frac{\partial L}{\partial \dot{q}_k} \right) \delta q_k \right] dt$$

$$= \int_{t_1}^{t_2} \left[ \sum_{k=1}^{n} \left( \frac{\partial L}{\partial q_k} - \frac{d}{dt} \left( \frac{\partial L}{\partial \dot{q}_k} \right) \delta \dot{q}_k \right) \right] dt = 0$$

$$\Rightarrow \quad \delta \int_{t_1}^{t_2} L dt = 0$$

which is the Hamilton's principle.

**57.** (a) We have,

$$\{q_i, q_j\}_{q,p} = \sum_k \left( \frac{\partial q_k}{\partial q_i} \frac{\partial p_k}{\partial q_j} - \frac{\partial q_k}{\partial q_j} \frac{\partial p_k}{\partial q_i} \right)$$

where $p$ and $q$ are independent.

Hence $\frac{\partial p_k}{\partial q_j} = 0 = \frac{\partial p_k}{\partial q_i}$

Therefore, $\{q_i, q_j\}_{q,p} = 0$.

(b) We have,

$$\{q_i, p_j\}_{q,p} = \sum_k \left( \frac{\partial q_k}{\partial q_i} \frac{\partial p_k}{\partial p_j} - \frac{\partial q_k}{\partial p_j} \frac{\partial p_k}{\partial q_i} \right)$$

Since, $p$, and $q$ are independent.

$$\Rightarrow \quad \frac{\partial q_k}{\partial p_j} = \frac{\partial p_k}{\partial q_i} = 0$$

Therefore, we get

$$\{q_i, p_j\}_{q,p} = \sum_k \frac{\partial q_k}{\partial q_i} \frac{\partial p_k}{\partial p_j} = \sum \delta_{ki}\, \delta_{kj} = \delta_{ij}$$

where $\delta_{ij}$ is Kronecker delta. Hence,

$$\{q_i, p_j\} = \begin{cases} 1, & \text{if } i = j \\ 0, & \text{if } i \neq j \end{cases}$$

**58.** Given,

$$L = \dot{q}_k\, q_k - \sqrt{(1 - \dot{q}_k^2)} \qquad \ldots\text{(i)}$$

$$\Rightarrow \quad \frac{\partial L}{\partial q_k} = \dot{q}_k \qquad \ldots\text{(ii)}$$

and

$$\frac{\partial L}{\partial \dot{q}_k} = q_k - \frac{1}{2}(1 - \dot{q}_k^2)^{-1/2}(-2\dot{q}_k)$$

$$= q_k + \frac{\dot{q}_k}{\sqrt{(1 - \dot{q}_k^2)}} \qquad \ldots\text{(iii)}$$

The Lagrangian equations is given by

$$\frac{d}{dt}\left( \frac{\partial T}{\partial \dot{q}_k} \right) - \frac{\partial L}{\partial q_k} = 0 \qquad \ldots\text{(iv)}$$

By Eqs. (ii), (iii) and (iv), we get

$$\Rightarrow \quad \frac{d}{dt}\left\{ q_k + \frac{\dot{q}_k}{\sqrt{(1 - \dot{q}_k^2)}} \right\} - \dot{q}_k = 0$$

$$\Rightarrow \quad \dot{q}_k + \frac{\ddot{q}_k (1 - \dot{q}_k^2)^{\frac{1}{2}} - \frac{1}{2}(1 - \dot{q}_k^2)^{1/2}(-2\dot{q}_k)\ddot{q}_k \dot{q}_k}{(1 - \dot{q}_k^2)} - \dot{q}_k = 0$$

$$\Rightarrow \quad \ddot{q}_k (1 - \dot{q}_k^2) + \frac{\dot{q}_k^2\, \ddot{q}_k}{\sqrt{(1 - \dot{q}_k^2)}} = 0$$

$$\Rightarrow \quad \frac{\ddot{q}_k (1 - \dot{q}_k^2) + \dot{q}_k^2\, \ddot{q}_k}{\sqrt{(1 - \dot{q}_k^2)}} = 0$$

$$\Rightarrow \quad \ddot{q}_k (1 - \dot{q}_k^2 + \dot{q}_k^2) = 0$$

$$\Rightarrow \quad \ddot{q}_k = 0$$

Which is the requied Lagrange's equation.

Since, $\ddot{q}_k = 0$, the generalised acceleration is zero.

**59.** (a) The velocity of centre of mass is

$$\mathbf{V} = \frac{m_1 \mathbf{v}_1 + m_2 \mathbf{v}_2}{m_1 + m_2} = \frac{0 \cdot 2(10\,\mathbf{i}) + 0 \cdot 5\,(3\mathbf{i} + 5\mathbf{j})}{0 \cdot 2 + 0 \cdot 5}$$

$$= 5\mathbf{i} + \left( \frac{25}{7} \right) \mathbf{j}$$

(b) The final momentum $= (m_1 + m_2)\, \mathbf{V} = 0 \cdot 7$

$$\mathbf{V} = 3.5\,\mathbf{i} + 2.5\,\mathbf{j}$$

(c) Let $\mathbf{T}_i$ be the initial total kinetic energy and $\mathbf{T}_f$ be the final total kinetic energy. Then,

$$\mathbf{T}_i = \frac{1}{2} m_1 v_1^2 + \frac{1}{2} m_2 v_2^2$$

$$= \frac{1}{2}(0.2)(10)^2 + \frac{1}{2}(0.5)(3^2 + 5^2)$$

$$= 10 + 8.5 = 18.5 \text{ joule}$$

By the law of conservation of momentum, we have

$$m_1 \mathbf{v}_1 + m_2 \mathbf{v}_2 = (m_1 + m_2)\mathbf{v}$$

where, **v** is the final velocity of the combined particle in the laboratory system.
Since, **v** is identical to **v**
*i.e.*, **v** = 5**i** + (25/7)**j**

Therefore, we get $\mathbf{T}_f = \frac{1}{2}(m_1 + m_1)\mathbf{v}^2$

$$= \frac{1}{2} \times 0.7\left[5^2 + \left(\frac{25}{7}\right)^2\right] = 13.2 \text{ joule}$$

and $\frac{\mathbf{T}_f}{\mathbf{T}_i} = \frac{13.2}{18.5} = 0.72$

**60.** Rewriting the given transformation, we have

$$\tan Q = \frac{q}{p} \qquad \ldots\text{(i)}$$

$$P = \frac{1}{2}(q^2 + p^2)$$

By Poisson bracket condition, is the transformation is canonical, if

$$[Q, Q] = [P, P] = 0$$

and $$[Q, P] = 1$$

(a) The first condition is already satiafied,
(b) Now, we have to show that

$$[Q, P] = 1$$

From Eq. (i), we have

$$\sec^2 Q \frac{\partial Q}{\partial q} = \frac{1}{p}, \frac{\partial P}{\partial q} = q$$

$$\sec^2 Q \frac{\partial Q}{\partial p} = -\frac{q}{p^2}, \frac{\partial P}{\partial p} = p$$

Then, $[Q, P] = \left[\frac{\partial Q}{\partial q}\frac{\partial P}{\partial p} - \frac{\partial Q}{\partial p}\frac{\partial P}{\partial q}\right]$

$$= \left[\left(\frac{1}{p}\cos^2 Q\right)p + \left(\frac{q}{p^2}\cos^2 Q\right)q\right]$$

$$= \cos^2 Q\left(1 + \frac{q^2}{p^2}\right)$$

$$= \cos^2 Q(1 + \tan^2 Q) = 1$$

Hence, the transformation is canonical.

**61.** Here, the Lagrangian is given by

$$L = \frac{1}{2}m\dot{x}^2 - \frac{1}{2}kx^2$$

where, $k$ is the force constant of the spring.

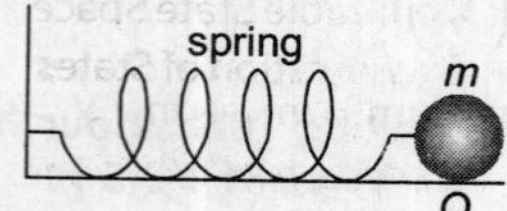


$$p_x = \frac{\partial L}{\partial \dot{x}} = m\dot{x} \quad \text{or} \quad \dot{x} = \frac{p_x}{m}$$

The Hamiltonian, is given by

$$H = \sum_k p_k \dot{q}_k - L = p_x\dot{x} - \left[\frac{1}{2}m\dot{x}^2 + \frac{1}{2}kx^2\right]$$

$$= \frac{1}{2}m\dot{x}^2 - \frac{1}{2}kx^2 = \frac{p_x^2}{2m} + \frac{1}{2}kx^2$$

Hamilton's equations are given by

$$\dot{x} = \frac{\partial H}{\partial p_k} = \frac{p_x}{m} \quad \text{and} \quad \dot{p}_x = -\frac{\partial H}{\partial x} = -kx$$

Thus, the equation of motion of spring-mass system is given by

$$m\ddot{x} = -kx \quad \text{or} \quad \ddot{x} + \frac{k}{m}x = 0$$

**62.** By the principle of virtual work, we have

$$\sum_{i=1}^{N} \mathbf{F}_i \cdot \delta\mathbf{r}_i = 0$$

Here, $i = 1, 2$ and, therefore,

$$W_1 \sin\theta\, \delta r_1 + W_2 \sin\phi\, \delta r_2 = 0$$

But $\delta r_1 = R\, d\theta, \delta r_2 = R d\phi$

Hence, $W_1 \sin\theta\, \delta\theta + W_2 \sin\phi\, \delta\phi = 0$

But $\theta + \phi =$ Constant

Therefore, $\delta\theta + \delta\phi = 0$ or $\phi = \delta\theta$

Thus, $(W_1 \sin\theta - W_2 \sin\phi)\,\delta\theta = 0$

Since, $\delta\theta \neq 0$, the condition of equilibrium of the system is

$$W_1 \sin\theta - W_2 \sin\phi = 0 \text{ or } \frac{W_1}{W_2} = \frac{\sin\phi}{\sin\theta}$$

**63.** The Euler-Lagrange differential equation is given by

$$\frac{d}{dx}\left(\frac{\partial f}{\partial y'}\right) - \frac{\partial f}{\partial y} = 0$$

Multiplying above equation by $y'$ and adding and subtracting the expression $y''\frac{\partial f}{\partial y''}$

$\left(\text{where, } y'' = \frac{\partial y'}{\partial x} \text{ and } y' = \frac{\partial y}{\partial x}\right)$, we get

$$y'\frac{d}{dx}\left(\frac{\partial y}{\partial y'}\right) - y'\frac{\partial f}{\partial y} + y''\frac{\partial f}{\partial y'} - y''\frac{\partial f}{\partial y'} = 0$$

$$\Rightarrow \quad y'\frac{d}{dx}\left(\frac{\partial f}{\partial y'}\right) + y''\frac{\partial f}{\partial y'} - y''\frac{\partial f}{\partial y'} - y'\frac{\partial f}{\partial y} = 0$$

$$\Rightarrow \quad \frac{d}{dx}\left(y'\frac{\partial f}{\partial y'}\right) - y''\frac{\partial f}{\partial y'} - y'\frac{\partial f}{\partial y} - y\frac{\partial f}{\partial x} + \frac{\partial f}{\partial x} = 0$$

$\left(\text{by adding and subtracting } \frac{\partial f}{\partial x}\right)$

$$\Rightarrow \quad \frac{d}{dx}\left(y''\frac{\partial f}{\partial y'}\right) - \left[y'\frac{\partial f}{\partial y} - y'\frac{\partial f}{\partial y} + \frac{\partial f}{\partial x}\right] + \frac{\partial f}{\partial x} = 0$$

$$\Rightarrow \quad \frac{d}{dx}\left(y'\frac{\partial f}{\partial y'}\right) - \frac{\partial f}{\partial y'} + \frac{\partial f}{\partial x} = 0 \quad [\because f = f(y, y', x)]$$

$$\Rightarrow \quad \frac{d}{dx}\left[y'\frac{\partial f}{\partial y'} - f\right] + \frac{\partial f}{\partial x} = 0 \qquad \ldots\text{(i)}$$

If $f$ does not depend upon $x$ explicitly, then $\frac{\partial f}{\partial x} = 0$ and hence, we must have

$$\frac{d}{dx}\left[y'\frac{\partial f}{\partial y'} - f\right] = 0 \Rightarrow y'\frac{\partial f}{\partial y'} - f = \text{Constant}$$

$$\Rightarrow \quad f - y'\frac{\partial f}{\partial y'} = \text{Constant} \qquad \ldots\text{(ii)}$$

# 22 Descriptive Statistics Theory of Probability

## Syllabus

- Sample Space
- Discrete Probability
- Independent Events
- Baye's Theorem
- Random Variables and Distribution Functions (Univariate and Multivariate
- Expectation and Moments
- Independent Random Variables
- Marginal and Conditional Distributions
- Characteristic Functions
- Probability Inequalities
- Tchebyshef, Markov, Jensen
- Modes of Convergence
- Weak and Strong Laws of Large Numbers
- Central Limit Theorems (i.i.d. case)
- Markov Chains with Finite and Countable State Space
- Classification of States
- Limiting Behaviour of n-step Transition Probabilities
- Stationary Distribution
- Poisson and Birth-and-death Processes
- Standard Discrete and Continuous Univariate Distributions
- Sampling Distributions
- Standard Errors and Asymptotic Distributions
- Distribution of Order Statistics and Range

## Statistics

Single observation does not form statistics. Statistics are a sum total of observations.
Statistics are expressed quantitatively and not quantitatively.
Statistics are collected with a definite purpose.
Statistics in an experiment are comparable and can be classified into various groups.

## Data

It means information (given facts). It is of two types, primary and secondary.

**Primary data** When data is collected with a, definite plan or design it is called primary data.

**Secondary data** Data which are not primarily collected but obtained from pub ished or unpublished scenes are known as secondary data.

## Presentation of Data

The collected data is put in some suitable tabular form in order to study its silent features. This is called presentation of data in tabular form. The data can be arranged in the following ways

**(i)** In serial order or alphabetic order
**(ii)** Ascending order
**(iii)** Descending order

The raw data put in ascending or descending order of magnitude is called an array or array data.

For large data to put, it in serial order is tedins work. For simplicity, we put it in tabular form. In the first column of the table data is put in from lowest to greatest value.

For first value, we put 1 bar (a verticle line segment) in second column oppos te to it if, for second repeated value 2nd bar is put and so on. This process is repeated for each value of data. For same value of data number of times. It is repeated the same number of bars are put in the 2nd column opposite to it. And for different value of data same process is repeated.

The bars drawn in the 2nd column are known as tally marks. And to facilitate it we record tally marks in the bunches of five bars.

In the third column of the table corresponding to each data, the counting of tally marks is put opposite to it. This is called frequency of the data value (observation).

This way of presentation of data in tabular form is known as frequency distribution values of data (obseration) are called variates, the number of times observation occurs is called frequency of the observation.

When collection of data is very large, we divide the whole range (highest value-lowest value) into a number of classes.

Then, for values of variates in the same class are tallied and then counted.

This gives grouped frequency distribution.

There are two methods of classifying data according to the class intervals.

**(i)** Exclusive method (in it upper limit of one class is the lower limit of another class).

**(ii)** Inclusive method (In it upper limit of the class is included in the same class).

# Cumulative Frequency Distribution

## Cumulative Frequency

In a discrete frequency distribution the cumulative frequency of a particular value of the variable is the total of all the frequencies of the values of the variable which are less than or equal to the particular value.

Two types of cumulative frequencies

**(i)** Less than (we add up the frequencies from above)

**(ii)** Greater than (we add up frequencies from below)

The values of the variable and the corresponding frequencies together form cumulative frequencies distribution.

# Graphical Representation of Statistical Data

## Bar Graph

A bar graph is a pictorial representation of the numerical data by a number of bars (rectangles) of uniform width erected horizontally or vertically with equal spacing between them.

## Histogram

A histogram or frequency histogram is a graphical representation of a frequency distribution in the form of rectangles with class intervals as bases and heights proportional to corresponding frequencies such that there is no gap between any two successive rectangles.

It is a two dimensional diagram.

## Frequency Polygon

It is another method of representing frequency distribution graphically. It can be drawn in two ways

**(i)** Using histogram

**(ii)** Without using histogram

# Measure of Central Tendency

**(i)** Arithmetic mean for $x_i, i = 1, 2, \ldots, n$

(a) $\bar{x} = \frac{1}{n}(x_1 + x_2 + \ldots + x_n) = \frac{1}{n}\sum_{i=1}^{n} x_i$

(b) $\bar{x} = \frac{\left(\sum_{i=1}^{n} f_i x_i\right)}{\sum_{i=1}^{n} f_i} = \frac{1}{N}\sum_{i=1}^{n} f_i x_i$

where $N = f_1 + f_2 + \ldots + f_n$, for data : $x_i/f_i$

(c) $\bar{x} = A + \frac{1}{N}\sum f_i d_i$

where, $A$ is assumed mean

$d_i = x_i - A$

(d) $\bar{x} = A + \frac{h}{N}\sum_{i=1}^{n} f_i d_i$

where, $A$ is assumed mean

$d_i = \frac{x_i - A}{n}$, h being common value of interval (class)

**Properties of mean**

**(i)** $\sum_{i=1}^{n} f_i(x_i - \bar{x}) = 0$

**(ii)** $Z = \sum_{i=1}^{n} f_i(x_i - A)^2$

is minimum at the point $A = \bar{x}$

$$\bar{x} = \sum_{i=1}^{n} \frac{n_i \bar{x}_i}{\sum_{i=1}^{n} n_i}$$

**(ii)** Median $= l + \frac{h}{f}\left(\frac{N}{2} - c\right)$ for continuous frequency distribution

For discrete distribution

(a) find $N/2$ , $N = \sum_{i=1}^{n} f_i$

(b) Cumulative frequency $> N/2$

(c) $x$ corresponding to the cumulative frequency is median.

**(iii)** Mode $= l + \frac{h(f_1 - f_0)}{(f_1 - f_0) - (f_2 - f_1)}$

For a symmetrical distribution

Mean = Median = Mode

For moderately asymmetrical distribution Mean – Median $= \frac{1}{3}$ (Mean – mode)

**(iv)** Geometric mean

$$G = (x_1 \cdot x_2 \ldots . x_n)^{1/n}$$

**(v)** Harmonic mean

(a) $H = \dfrac{1}{\frac{1}{n}\sum_{i=1}^{n}\frac{1}{x_i}}$

(b) $H = \dfrac{1}{\frac{1}{N}\sum_{i=1}^{n} f_i/x_i}$ for data $x_i/f_i$

# Measure of Dispersion

Average or the measure of central tendency gives us an idea of the cementration of the observations about the central part of the distribution. It does not give complete idea of the distribution. For it we need to measure the dispersion of the data. Dispersion (or scatteredness) may be homogeneous (less dispersed) or heterogeneous (mere scattered).

## Characteristic of Data for an Ideal Measure of Dispersion

**(i)** It should be rigidly defined.
**(ii)** It should be easy to calculate and easy to understand.
**(iii)** If should be based on all observations.
**(iv)** It should be amendable to further treatment (mathematical).
**(v)** Fluctuations of sampling should have little effect on it.

There are four measure of dispersion.

**(i)** Range
**(ii)** Quartile deviation or semi-interquartile range
**(iii)** Mean deviation
**(iv)** Standard deviation

### (i) Range

Range = Greatest observation – Smallest observation

### (ii) Quartile Deviation or Semi-interquartile Range $Q$

$$Q = \frac{1}{2}(Q_3 - Q_1)$$

$Q_1$ = First quartile,
$Q_3$ = Third quartile of the distribution

### (iii) Mean deviation

Given, $X_i | f_i, i = 1, 2, \ldots, n$ (frequency distribution)

Mean deviation $= \frac{1}{N}\Sigma f_i | x_i - A|$

where, $\Sigma f_i = N$

$|x_i - A|$ = Absolute value of the deviation $x_i - A$

### (iv) Standard deviation (Root Mean Square Deviation)

Given, frequency distribution $x_i | f_i, i = 1, 2, \ldots$

$\sigma$ = (Standard deviation)

$$= \sqrt{\frac{1}{N}\sum_i f_i(x_i - \bar{x})^2}$$

$$N = \sum_{i=1}^{n} f_i$$

$\sigma^2 = \frac{1}{N}\sum_i f_i(x_i - \bar{x})^2$ is called variance.

If $A$ is any arbitrary number, then

Root mean square deviation $S = \sqrt{\frac{1}{N}\sum_i f_i(x_i - A)^2}$

Relation between $\sigma$ and $S$

$$S^2 = \sigma^2 + d^2$$

where, $d = \bar{x} - A$

# Coefficient of Dispersion

**(i)** CD based on range $= \dfrac{A - B}{A + B}$

$A$ — greatest value, $B$ — smallest value in the data

**(ii)** CD based on quartile deviation $= \dfrac{(Q_3 - Q_1)/2}{(Q_3 + Q_1)/2}$

**(iii)** CD based on mean deviation

$$= \frac{\text{Mean deviation}}{\text{Average from which it is calculated}}$$

**(iv)** CD based on standad deviation $= \dfrac{\text{SD}}{\text{Mean}} = \dfrac{\sigma}{x}$

# Coefficient of Variation

100 times the coefficient of dispersion based upon standard deviation is called coefficient of variation (CV)

$$CV = 100 \times \frac{\sigma}{\sqrt{x}}$$

Moments $\mu'_r = \frac{1}{N}\sum_i f_i(x_i - A)^r$

where, $\sum_i f_i = N$

$$\mu_r = \frac{1}{N}\Sigma f_i(x_i - \bar{x})^r$$

- Relation between moments about mean and moments about a point.

$$\mu_2 = \mu'_2 - \mu'^2_1$$

$$\mu_3 = \mu'_3 - 3\mu'_2\mu'_1 + 2\mu'^3_1$$

$$\mu_4 = \mu'_4 - 4\mu'_3\mu'_1 + 6\mu'_2\mu'^2_1 - 3\mu'^4_1$$

$$\mu_2' = \mu_2 + \mu_1'^2$$
$$\mu_3' = \mu_3 - 3\mu_2\mu_1' + \mu_1'^3$$
$$\mu_4' = \mu_4 - 4\mu_3\mu_1' + 6\mu_2\mu_1'^2 + \mu_1'^4$$

- Sheppard's correction for moments.

$$\mu_2(\text{corrected}) = \mu_2 - \frac{h^2}{12}$$
$$\mu_3(\text{corrected}) = \mu_3$$
$$\mu_4(\text{corrected}) = \mu_4 - \frac{1}{2}h^2\mu_2 + \frac{7}{240}h^4$$

- Pearson's $\beta$ and $\gamma$ coefficients.

$$\beta_1 = \frac{\mu_3^2}{\mu_2^3}, \ \gamma_1 = +\sqrt{\beta_1}$$
$$\beta_2 = \frac{\mu_4}{\mu_2^2}, \ \gamma_2 = \beta_2 - 3$$

- $r$th absolute moments about origin

For $\frac{x_i}{f_i}$, $i = 1, 2, \ldots$

$$= \frac{1}{N}\sum_{i=1}^{n} f_i\,|x_i^r|, \quad N = \Sigma f_i$$

- $r$th absolute moment about mean

For $x_i/f_i$, $i = 1, 2, 3, \ldots$

$$= \frac{1}{N}\sum_{i=1}^{n} f_i\,|x_i - \bar{x}|^r$$

- Based upon moments, coefficient of skewness.

$$S_K = \frac{\sqrt{\beta_1}\,(\beta_2 + 3)}{2(5\beta_2 - 6\beta_1 - 9)}$$

- For symmetric distribution

$S_K = 0 \Rightarrow$ Either $\beta_1 = 0$ or $\beta_2 = -3$.

As $\beta_2 = \frac{\mu_4}{\mu_2^2} \Rightarrow \beta_2 \not< 0$

So, $S_K = 0 \Leftrightarrow \beta_1 = 0$

$\Rightarrow \beta_1$ is the measure of skewness.

- For symmetric distribution

$$\beta_1 = 0$$

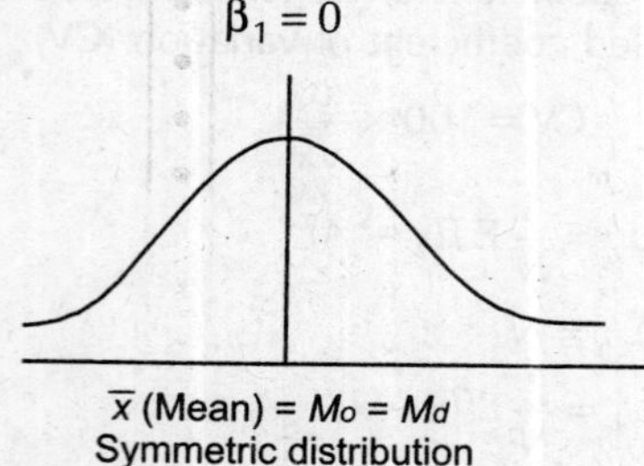

$\bar{x}$ (Mean) = $M_o$ = $M_d$
Symmetric distribution

The skewness is positive, if the larger tail of the distribution lies towards the higher values of the variate, *i.e.*, the curve drawn with the help of the given data is stretched more to the right than to the left and is negative in the centrary case.

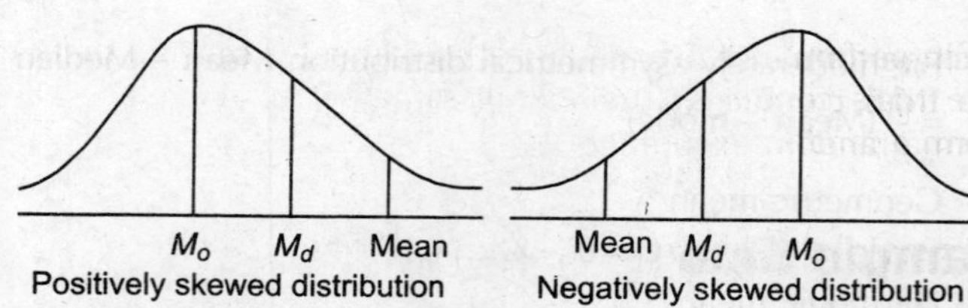


Positively skewed distribution    Negatively skewed distribution

A distribution is said to be skewed if

**(i)** Mean, Median and Mode fall at different points,

Mean ≠ Median ≠ Mode

**(ii)** Quartiles are not equidistant from median.

**(iii)** The curve drawn with the help of given data is not symmetrical but stretched more to one side than the other.

# Kurtosis

If we know

**(i)** the measure of central tendency
**(ii)** dispersion
**(iii)** skewness

We do not get the idea of flatness or peakedness from there. Karl Pearson used the concept of 'convexity of curve' or Kurtosis to measure the flatness or peakedness of the curve. It is measured by the coefficient

$$\beta_2 = \frac{\mu_4}{\mu_2^2}, \ \gamma_2 = \beta_2 - 3$$

Curve of the type '*A*' which is neither flat nor peaked is called normal curve or mesokurtic curve, for such curve $\beta_2 = 3$, *i.e.*, $\gamma_2 = 0$

Curve of type '*B*' is flatter than the normal curve. It is known as platykurtic. For it $\beta_2 < 3$, *i.e.*, $\gamma_2 < 0$.

Curve of type '*C*' is more peaked than the normal curve is called leptokurtic. For it $\beta_2 > 3$ *i.e.*, $\gamma_2 > 0$.

# Theory of Probability

## Random Experiment

The theory of probability provides mathematical models for 'real world phenomena' involving games and chance such as tossing of a coin or a dice etc.

Probability has additive property and frequency interpretation. To deal with these properties of probabilistic situations we need a mathematical description or model.

Any such probabilistic situation is referred to as 'random experiment', and is denoted by *E* (say), *E* may be tossing of a coin or a dice or taking a card from a pack of 52 cards (playing), etc.

Each performance in a random experiment is called a trial. All the trials conducted under the same set of conditions also form a random experiment.

## Sample Space

The result of a trial in a random experiment is called an outcome (or an elementary event or a sample point).

The totality of all possible outcomes constitutes sample space $S$ (say).

We suppose total outcomes is finite say $n: e_1, e_2, \ldots, e_n$, such that no two or more outcomes occur simultaneously and exactly one of the outcomes must occur. Then, $S = \{e_1, e_2, \ldots, e_n\}$ and $\{e_1\}, \{e_2\}, \ldots, \{e_n\}$ are called elementary events of $S$.

Here, $\{e_i\} = S, \forall\, i = 1, 2, \ldots, n.$

A sample space $S$ may be finite or countably infinite (countable or discrete) or uncountable (non-discrete).

**Examples of discrete $S$.**

$S$ is finite

Tossing of a coin one time gives

$$S = \{H, T\}$$

Its tossing two times gives

$$S = \{HH, HT, TH, TT\}$$

- Tree diagram of outcomes is

| Tossing 1st | 2nd | Outcomes |
|---|---|---|
| H | H | HH |
| | T | HT |
| T | H | TH |
| | T | TT |

- Its tossing three times gives tossing

| Tossing 1st | 2nd | 3rd | Outcomes |
|---|---|---|---|
| H | H | H | HHH |
| | | T | HHT |
| | T | H | HTH |
| | | T | HTT |
| T | H | H | THH |
| | | T | THT |
| | T | H | TTH |
| | | T | TTT |

$$S = \{HHH, HHT, HTH, HTT, THH, THT, TTH, TTT\}$$

Tossing of a dice gives $S = \{1, 2, 3, 4, 5, 6\}$

Tossing of a pair of dice gives

| Dot on Top face↓ | 1 | 2 | 3 | 4 | 5 | 6 |
|---|---|---|---|---|---|---|
| 1 | (1, 1) | (1, 2) | (1, 3) | (1, 4) | (1, 5) | (1, 6) |
| 2 | (2, 1) | (2, 2) | (2, 3) | (2, 4) | (2, 5) | (2, 6) |
| 3 | (3, 1) | (3, 2) | (3, 3) | (3, 4) | (3, 5) | (3, 6) |
| 4 | (4, 1) | (4, 2) | (4, 3) | (4, 4) | (4, 5) | (4, 6) |
| 5 | (5, 1) | (5, 2) | (5, 3) | (5, 4) | (5, 5) | (5, 6) |
| 6 | (6, 2) | (6, 2) | (6, 3) | (6, 4) | (6, 5) | (6, 6) |

$6^2 = 36$ outcomes in the form of pairs representing $S$.

$S$ is infinite.

Tossing of a coin until a head appears

$$S = \{1, 2, 3, \ldots, n, \ldots, \infty\}$$

$n$ = number of times coin is tossed $\infty$ refers to the case when head never appears.

It shows every positive integer is an element of $S$.

$S$ is infinite.

As $N = \{1, 2, 3, \ldots, n, \ldots, \infty\}$ and $S$ has one-to-one correspondence $N$ is countably infinite, so $S$ is countably infinite.

Here, $N$ is the set of all natural numbers.

*e.g.*, A card is drawn from an ordinary deck of 52 cards. The sample space $S$ consists of the four suits, clubs ($C$), diamonds $D$ and spades ($S$), where each suit has 13 cards, numbered from 2 to 1C, end jack ($J$), queen ($Q$), king ($K$) and ace ($A$). The hearts ($H$) and diamonds ($D$) are red cards and spades ($S$) and clubs ($C$) are black cards.

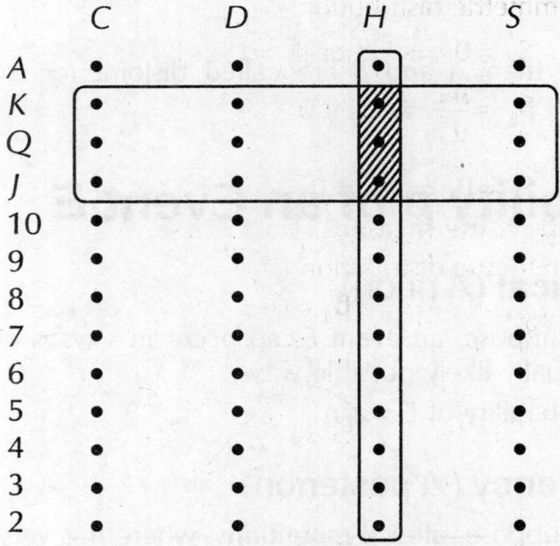


Let $E$ be the event of a picture card, *i.e.*, jack ($J$), queen ($Q$) or king ($K$) and let $F$ be the event of a heart. Then,

$$E \cap F = \{JH, QH, KH\}$$

is the event of a heart and a picture card, as shaded in the figure.

## Continuous Sample Space

A sample space is continuous, if it is an interval or a product of intervals. In such case, only its measurable subsets are events.

*e.g.*, Let a pencil drop, head first, into a rectangular box and note the point at the bottom of the box that the pencil first touches.

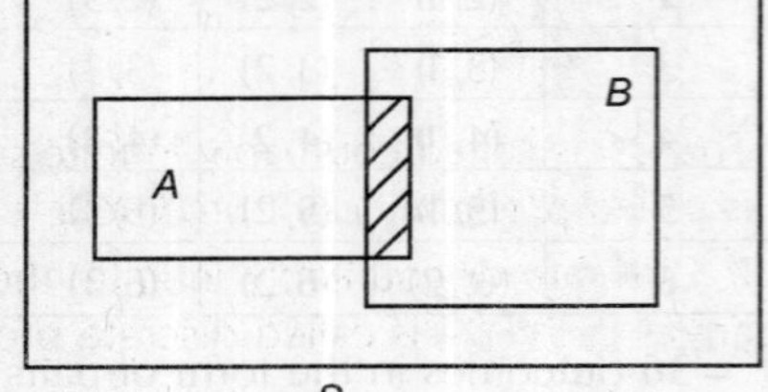


Here, $S$ consists of all the points on the bottom of the box. Let in the figure rectangular area represent these points.

Let $A$ and $B$ be the events that the pencil drops into the corresponding areas.

Then, $A \cap B$ is the event that pencil drops in the shaded region ("As shown in the figure.)

## Events and Operations on Events

For $A \subseteq S$, $A$ is called event of $S$.

$\phi \subseteq S$, $\phi$ = null set. It is called impossible event.

$S \subseteq S$. $S$ is universal set. It is called sure event.

Two or more events can be combined using $\cup$ (union), $\cap$ (intersection) and C (complement).

For $A, B \subseteq S$,

$A \cup B$ denotes events $A$ or $B$ or both.

$A \cap B$ denotes events $A$ and $B$ both.

$A^c$ denotes complement of $A$.

$$A^c = S - A.$$

If $A \cap B = \phi$ then $A$ and $B$ are called disjoint (or mutually exclusive).

## Probability *p* of an Event *E*

### (a) Classical (*A* priori)

**Definition** Suppose, an event $E$ can occur in $s$ ways out of a total of $n$ equally likely possible ways.

Then, $p$ (probability of $E$) = $s/n$.

### (b) Frequency (*A* posterion)

**Definition** Suppose, after $n$ repetitions, where $n$ is very large, an event $E$ occurs $s$ times.

Then, (probability of $E$) = $s/n$.

(It is a relative measurement of frequency of $E$ to the frequency of $S$).

Concept of probability is from time unknown in human civilization. Laplace, Pascal etc., give them mathematical interpretation, which is growing very fast.

## Axiomatic Definition of Probability

Let $S$ be a sample space.

Let $\varepsilon$ be a collection of subsets (events) of $S$ s.t.

**(i)** For $A, B \in \varepsilon$, $A - B \in \varepsilon$

**(ii)** For $A_i \in \varepsilon$, $i = 1, 2, \ldots, \infty$ $\bigcup_{i=1}^{\infty} A_i \in \varepsilon$

Let $P : \varepsilon \longrightarrow [0, 1]$ s.t.,

A-I. $P(A_i) \geq 0, \forall A_i \in \varepsilon$

A-II. $P(S) = 1$

A-III. $\forall A, B \in \varepsilon$, $A \cap B = \phi$, $P(A \cup B) = P(A) + P(B)$

Then, $P$ is called probability function, $P(A)$ is called probability of event $A$, and the triplet $(S, \varepsilon, P)$ is called probability space. When understood $(S, \varepsilon, P)$ is simply represented by $S$, and then $S$ is treated as probability space. A-I, A-II, A-III are called axioms of probability

Generalization of A-III to any finite number of mutually disjoint events $A_1, A_2, \ldots, A_n$;

$P(A_1 \cup A_2 \cup \ldots \cup A_n) = P(A_1) + P(A_2) + \ldots + P(A_n)$

(By principle of mathematical induction)

## Important Theorems on Probability

***Theorem 1.*** $P(\phi) = 0$

***Proof.*** For any event $A$, $A \cup \phi = A$, $A \cap \phi = \phi$.

So, $P(A \cup \phi) = P(A) + P(\phi)$

or $P(A) = P(A) + P(\phi)$

$\Rightarrow$ $P(\phi) = 0$

***Theorem 2.*** For any event $A$,

$$P(A^c) = 1 - P(A)$$

***Proof.*** We know $A^c = S - A$ = Complement of $A$.

$A \cap A^c = \phi$ and $A \cup A^c = S$

$\Rightarrow$ $P(S) = P(A \cup A^c) = P(A) + P(A^c)$

or $1 = P(A) + P(A^c)$

$\Rightarrow$ $P(A^c) = 1 - P(A)$

***Theorem 3.*** For any event $A$,

$$0 \leq P(A) \leq 1.$$

***Proof.*** We know $P(A) \geq 0$.

We know $S = A \cup A^c$

$\Rightarrow$ $P(S) = P(A \cup A^c) = P(A) + P(A^c)$

$\Rightarrow$ $1 = P(A) + P(A^c) \Rightarrow 1 \geq P(A)$

As, $P(A^c) \geq 0$

Thus, $0 \leq P(A) \leq 1$

***Theorem 4.*** If $A \subseteq B$, then $P(A) \leq P(B)$

***Proof.*** If $A \subseteq B$, then $B = A \cup (B - A)$

where $A \cap (B \setminus A) = \phi$.

So, $P(B) = P(A \cup (B \setminus A)) = P(A) + P(B \setminus A)$

$\Rightarrow$ $P(B) \geq P(A)$ (As $P(B \setminus A) \geq 0$)

***Theorem 5.*** For any two events $A$ and $B$

$$P(A \setminus B) = P(A \cap B^c) = P(A) - P(A \cap B)$$

***Proof.*** As $A = (A \setminus B) \cup (A \cap B)$,

and $(A - B) \cap (A \cap B) = \phi$

$\Rightarrow$ $P(A) = P[(A \setminus B) \cup (A \cap B)]$

$= P(A \setminus B) + P(A \cap B)$

$P(A) = P(A \cap B^c) + P(A \cap B)$

$\Rightarrow$ $P(A \cap B^c) = P(A) - P(A \cap B)$

***Theorem 6.*** Addition rule

***Proof.*** For any two events $A$ and $B$,

$$P(A \cup B) = P(A) + P(B) - P(A \cap B)$$

$$A \cup B = (A \mid B) \cup B$$

where $(A \mid B) \cap B = \phi$

So, $P(A \cup B) = P(A \mid B) + P(B)$

$= P(A) - P(A \cap B) + P(B)$

or $P(A \cup B) = P(A) + P(B) - P(A \cap B)$

Similarly, for any three events $A$, $B$ and $C$.

$P(A \cup B \cup C) = P(A) + P(B) + P(C) - P(A \cap B)$

$-P(A \cap C) - P(B \cap C) + P(A \cap B \cap C)$

## Finite Probability Space

Let sample space $S$ be finite

$$S = \{a_1, a_2, \ldots, a_n\}$$

Let $p(a_i) = p_i \in [0, 1]$, $i = 1, 2, \ldots, n$ s.t.,

**(i)** $p_i \geq 0$

**(ii)** $- p_1 + p_2 + \ldots + p_n = 1$

Then, $p_i$ is called probability of $a_i$.

For $A \subseteq S$, $P(A) = \sum_{a_i \in A} p(a_i) = \sum_{a_i \in A} p_i$

Thus, we have distribution of probability with respect to outcomes of $S$ as follows

| **Outcome** | $a_1$ | $a_2 \ldots\ldots a_n$ |
|---|---|---|
| **Probability** | $p_1$ | $p_2$ $p_n$ |

This is called probability distribution.

## Finite Equiprobable Space

A probability space $(S, \varepsilon, P)$, $S$ being finite, s.t., each outcome has equal probability, is called a finite equiprobable space.

In other words, if S has $n$ elements, then each point in $S$ is assigned the probability $1/n$ and each event $A$ containing $r$ points is assigned the probability $r/n$.

Thus, $P(A) = \dfrac{\text{Number of elements of } A}{\text{Number of elements of } S} = \dfrac{n(A)}{n(S)}$

## Discrete Space, Countably Infinite Sample Space

Let $S = \{a_1, a_2, \ldots\ldots\}$

for $a_i \in S$, $p(a_i) = p_i \in [0, 1]$

s.t., **(i)** $p_i \geq 0$, $\forall_i$

**(ii)** $\sum_{i=1}^{\infty} p_i = 1$

Then, $S$ is called countably infinite sample space and $p(a_i) = p_i$ is called probability of outcome $a_i$.

If $S$ is finite or countably infinite, then it is called discrete; for any $A \subseteq S$, $P(A)$ is called discrete probability of $A_1$.

## Uncountable Space

Here, we shall consider the uncountable sample spaces as having points with some finite geometrical measurement $m(S)$, such as length, area, or volume, and where a points in $S$ is selected at random.

The probability of an event $A$, *i.e.*, that the selected point belongs to A, is then the ratio of $m(A)$ to $m(S)$.

Thus, $P(A) = \dfrac{\text{Lenght of } A}{\text{Length of } S}$

or $P(A) = \dfrac{\text{Area of } A}{\text{Area of } S}$

or $P(A) = \dfrac{\text{Volume of } A}{\text{Volume of } S}$

Such a probability space $S$ is said to be uniform.

$P(A)$ is called non-discrete probability or continuous probability.

# Conditional Events and Conditional Probabilities

Let $A$ anc $B$ be events of $A$ sample space $S$ s.t., happening of $A$ depends upon happening of $B$. Then, it is said that 'event $A$ is conditior ed by $B$'. It is also expressed as '$A$ is conditional event with respect to $B$' and is denoted by $A/B$.

The conditional probability of $A$ given $B$ is defined as

$$P(A / B) = \frac{n(A \cap B)}{n(B)}, \quad n(B) \neq 0.$$

Here, $n(B)$ denotes number of points in $B$, etc.

## Multiplication Theorem for Conditional Probability

Let $A$ and $B$ be events of $S$. Then,

**(i)** $P(B / A) = \dfrac{P(A \cap B)}{P(A)}$, provided $P(A) > 0$.

**(ii)** $P(A / B) = \dfrac{P(A \cap B)}{P(B)}$, provided $P(B) > 0$.

These imply

$$P(A \cap B) = P(A)P(B/A), \text{ if } P(A) > 0$$
$$= P(B)P(A/B), \text{ if } P(B) > 0.$$

For three independent events $A, B, C$, the multiplication law is

$$P(A \cap B \cap C) = P(A)P(B/A)P(C/A \cap B).$$

Here, $P(A)$ = Probability that $A$ occurs.

$P(B/A)$ = Probability that $B$ occurs assuming that $A$ occurred.

$P(C/A \cap B)$ = Probability that $C$ occurs assuming that $A$ and $B$ have occurred.

### Finite Stochastic Process and Tree Diagrams

A finite stochastic process is a finite sequence of experiments where each experiment has a finite number of outcomes with given probabilities.

A convenient way of describing such a process is by means of a labelled tree diagram.

## Independent Events

Events $A$ and $B$ in probability space $S$ are said to be independent, if the occurrence one of them does not influence the occurrence of other.

In terms of probability, $B$ is independent of $A$, if

$$P(B) = P(B/A) \text{ and } \quad P(A) = P(A/B).$$

**Property of independent events** If $A$ and $B$ are independent events, then

$$P(A \cap B) = P(A) \cdot P(B)$$

We know $\quad P(A \cap B) = P(A)P(B/A)$, if $P(A) > 0$.

$$= P(A) \cdot P(B)$$

Also, $\quad P(A \cap B) = P(B)(A/B)$, if $P(B) > 0$

$$= P(B)P(A)$$

**Generalization** For $n$ independent events $A_1, A_2 \dots A_n$

$$P(A_1 \cap A_2 \cap \dots \cap A_n) = P(A_1) \cdot P(A_2) \dots P(A_n)$$

***Theorem*** If $A$ and $B$ are mutually exclusive (*i.e.*, $A \cap B = \varphi$), and independent then either $P(A) = 0$ or $P(B) = 0$.

***Proof*** Here, $\quad P(A)P(B) = P(A \cap B) = P(\phi) = 0$

$\Rightarrow$ Either $P(A) = 0$ or $P(B) = 0$,

Hence proved.

## Partitions, Total Probability and Baye's Formula

Suppose, a set $S$ is the union of mutually disjoint subsets $A_1, A_2 \dots, A_n$. Then, it is said that $\{A_1, A_2, \dots, A_n\}$ is a partition of S.

Here, $A_i \cap A_j = \phi$ for $i \neq j$, $i, j = 1, 2, \dots n$, and

$$S = A_1 \cup A_2 \cup \dots \cup A_n.$$

Let for $n = 3$, $\{A_1, A_2, A_3\}$ is a partition of $S$.

Let $E \subseteq S$.

The Venn diagram representation is

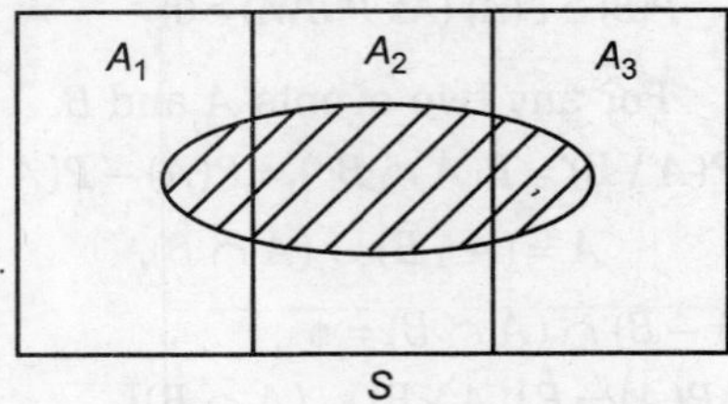


Then, $\quad E = E \cap S$

$$= E \cap (A_1 \cup A_2 \cup A_3)$$
$$= (E \cap A_1) \cup (E \cap A_2) \cup (E \cap A_3)$$

This shows $\{E \cap A_1, E \cap A_2, E \cap A_3\}$ is a partition of $E$.

**Generalization** Let $\{A_1, A_2, \dots, A_n\}$ be a partition of $S$, and $E \subseteq S$.

Then, $\quad E = E \cap S = E \cap (A_1 \cup A_2 \cup \dots \cup A_n)$

$$= (E \cap A_1) \cup (E \cap A_2) \cup \dots \cup (E \cap A_n)$$

$\Rightarrow \quad \{E \cap A_1, E \cap A_2, \dots, E \cap A_n\}$ is a partition of $E$.

## Total Probability of *E*

$$P(E) = P[(E \cap A_1) \cup (E \cap A_2) \cup \dots \cup (E \cap A_n)]$$
$$= P(E \cap A_1) + P(E \cap A_2) + \dots + P(E \cap A_n)$$
$$= P(A_1)P(E/A_1) + P(A_2)P(E/A_2) + \dots + P(A_n)P(E/A_n)$$
$$= \sum_{k=1}^{n} P(A_k)P(E/A_k)$$

## Baye's Formula

$$P(A_k/E) = \frac{P(E \cap A_k)}{P(E)} = \frac{P(A_k)P(E/A_k)}{P(E)}$$
$$= \frac{P(A_k)P(E/A_k)}{\sum_{k=1}^{n} P(A_k)P(E/A_k)}$$

This is baye's formula, after English, Mathematician Thomas Baye's (s(1702 – 1761).

## Bayes' Formula for Future Event

Given **(i)** $F \subseteq S$

**(ii)** $P(F/E \cap A_k)$, $k = 1, 2, \dots, n$.

Then, $\quad P(F/E) = \dfrac{\sum_{k=1}^{n} P(A_k)P(E/A_k)P(F/E \cap A_k)}{\sum_{k=1}^{n} P(A_k)P(E/A_k)}$

## Stochastic Interpretation of Total Probability and Baye's Formula

For the sake of simplicity, we consider three mutually exclusive events which partition $S$.

Let $E$ be any even of S.

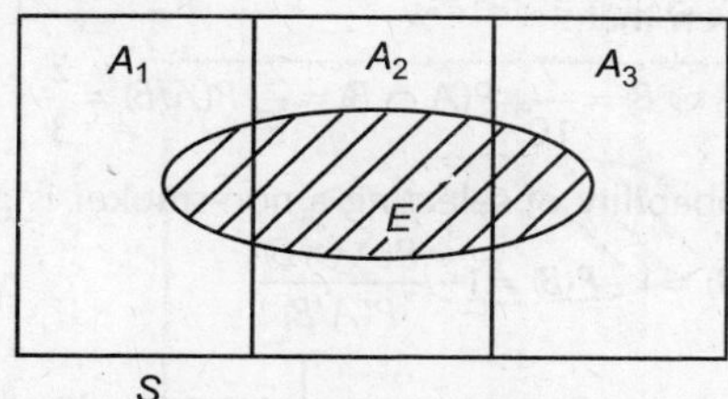


Venn diagram representation of $S$ and $A_1, A_2$ and $A_3$, $E$. Corresponding to it stochastic tree diagram is

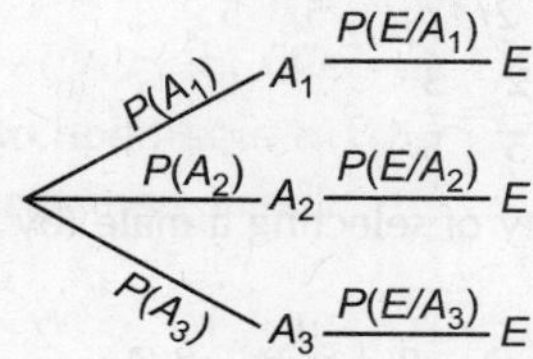


We want $P(E)$. Using tree diagram is

$$P(E) = P(A_1)P(E/A_1) + P(A_2)P(E/A_2) + P(A_3)P(E/A_3)$$

For $k = 1, 2, 3$,

$$P(E)P(A_k/E) = P(E \cap A_k)$$

$$= P(A_k \cap E) = P(A_k)P(E/A_k)$$

$$\Rightarrow \quad P(A_k/E) = \frac{P(A_k)P(E/A_k)}{P(E)}$$

$$= \frac{P(A_k)P(E/A_k)}{P(A_1)P(E/A_1) + P(A_2)P(E/A_2) + P(A_3)P(E/A_3)}$$

This stochastic process applies to any positive integer $n$.

# Repeated Trials as a Stochastic Process

The probability space of a repeated trial process may be viewed as a stochastic process whose tree diagram has the following properties

**(i)** each branch point has the same outcomes

**(ii)** All branches leading to the same outcome have the same probability.

***Example 1.*** *Twenty five books are placed at random in a shelf. Find the probability that a particular pair of books shall be (i) always together, and (ii) never together.*

**Solution.** Since, 25 books can be arranged among themselves in 25! ways, the exhaustive number of cases is 25!.

(i) Let us now regard that the two particular books are tagged together, so that we shall regard them as single book. Now, we have (25 – 1) = 24 books which can be arranged among themselves in 24! ways. But the two books which are fastened together can be arranged among themselves is 2! ways. Therefore, associating these two operations, the number of favourable cases for getting a particular pair of books always together is $24! \times 2!$.

Hence, required probability $= \dfrac{24! \times 2!}{25!} = \dfrac{2}{25}$

(ii) Total number of arrangements of 25 books among themselves is 25! and the total number of arrangements that a particular pair of books will always be together is $24! \times 2$. Hence, the number of arrangements in which a particular pair of books is never together is

$25! - 2 \times 24! = (25 - 2) \times 24! = 23 \times 24!$.

Hence, required probability $= \dfrac{23 \times 24!}{25!} = \dfrac{23}{25}$

**Alternate Method** $P$ [A particular pair of books shall never be together]

$= 1 - P$ [A particular pair of books is always together]

$$= 1 - \frac{2}{25} = \frac{23}{25}$$

***Example 2.*** *If 6n tickets numbered 0, 1, 2,..., 6n – 1 are placed in a bag and three are drawn out, show that the chance that the sum of the numbers on them is equal to 6n is 3n/(6n – 1) (6n – 2).*

**Solution.** The total number of ways of drawing 3 tickets out of $6n$ is given by

$$^{6n}C_3 = n(6n-1)(6n-2)$$

Favourable cases for obtaining a sum of $6n$ on the three drawn tickets are given below

$(0, 1, 6n-1)$; $(0, 2, 6n-2)$;...; $(0, 3n-1, 3n+1)$, *i.e.*, $(3n-1)$ cases

$(1, 2, 6n-3)$ $(1, 3, 6n-4)$;...; $(1, 3n-1, 3n)$, *i.e.*, $(3n-2)$ cases

$(2, 3, 6n-5)$; $(2, 4, 6n-6)$; ...; $(2, 3n-2, 3n)$, *i.e.*, $(3n-4)$ cases

$(3, 4, 6n-7)$; $(3, 5, 6n-8)$; ...; $(3, 3n-2, 3n-1)$, *i.e.*, $(3n-5)$ cases

⋮ ⋮ ⋮

$(2n-2, 2n-1, 2n+3)$; $(2n-2; 2n, 2n+2)$ *i.e.*, 2 cases

$(2n-1, 2n, 2n+1)$ *i.e.*, 1 case

Hence, total number of favourable cases

$$= \{(3n-1) + (3n-4) + \ldots + 5 + 2\} + \{(3n-2) + (3n-5) + \ldots + 4 + 1\} \quad \ldots\text{(i)}$$

The expression in each bracket of eq. (i) is the sum of $n$ terms of an arithmetic progression (AP) series.

Hence, Total number of favorable cases

$$= \{2 + 5 + \ldots + (3n-4) + (3n-1)\} + \{1 + 4 + \ldots + (3n-5) + (3n-2)\}$$

$$= \frac{n}{2}\{2 \times 2 + (n-1)3\} + \frac{n}{2}\{2 \times 1 + (n-1) \times 3\}$$

$$= \frac{n}{2}(4 + 3n - 3 + 2 + 3n - 3) = 3n^2$$

Hence, the required probability

$$= \frac{3n^2}{n(6n-1)(6n-2)}$$

$$= \frac{3n}{(6n-1)(6n-2)}$$

***Example 3.*** *There are $(N+1)$ identical urns marked 0, 1, 2,..., N each of which contains N white and red balls. The kth urn contains k red and $N-k$ white balls, $(k = 0, 1, 2, \ldots, N)$. An urn is chosen at random and n random drawing of a ball are made from its the ball drawn being replaced after each draw. If the balls drawn are all red, shown that the probability that the next drawing will also yield a red ball is approximately $(n+1)/(n+2)$ when N is large.*

**Solution.** Let $E_k$ denote the event that the kth urn is chosen, $(k = 0, 1, 2, \ldots, N)$, Then, the event, $E_0, E_1, E_2, \ldots, E_n$ are pairwise mutually exclusive, one of which certainly occurs.

Then, $P(E_1) = P(E_2) = \ldots = P(E_n) = \dfrac{1}{N+1}$ (from symmetry) ...(i)

Let $A$ denote the event of getting $n$ red balls successively in $n$ draws (with replacement from an urn chosen at random).

Then, $$P(A/E_k) = \frac{k}{N}\cdot\frac{k}{N}\cdots\frac{k}{N} = \left(\frac{k}{N}\right)^n \quad \text{...(ii)}$$

and $$P(A) = \sum_{k=0}^{N} P(E_k)\, P(A/E_k) = \frac{1}{N+1}\sum_{k=0}^{N}\left(\frac{k}{N}\right)^n$$

Now, using Baye's theorem, we have

$$P(E_k/A) = \frac{P(E_k)\,P(A/E_k)}{\sum\limits_{k=0}^{N} P(E_k)\,P(A/E_k)} = \frac{\dfrac{1}{N+1}\cdot\left(\dfrac{k}{N}\right)^n}{\dfrac{1}{N+1}\sum\limits_{k=0}^{N}\left(\dfrac{k}{N}\right)^n}$$

Let $C$ be the future event that $(n+1)$th draw also yields a red ball. Then, on the same lines, it can be shown that

$$P(A \cap C) = \frac{1}{N+1}\sum_{k=0}^{N}\left(\frac{k}{N}\right)^{n+1}$$

Hence, the required probability is, given by

$$P(C/A) = \frac{P(A \cap C)}{P(A)} = \frac{\dfrac{1}{N+1}\sum\limits_{k=0}^{N}\left(\dfrac{k}{N}\right)^{n+1}}{\dfrac{1}{N+1}\sum\limits_{k=0}^{N}\left(\dfrac{k}{N}\right)^n}$$

If $N$ is very large, then we have

$$P(A) = \frac{1}{N}\sum_{k=0}^{N}\left(\frac{k}{N}\right)^n = \int_0^1 x^n dx = \frac{1}{n+1}$$

and $$P(A \cap C) \simeq \frac{1}{N}\sum_{k=0}^{N}\left(\frac{k}{N}\right)^{n+1} = \int_0^1 x^{n+1} dx = \frac{1}{n+2}$$

Hence, $$P(C/A) = \frac{n+1}{n+2}$$

This is known is law of Succession due to Laplace.

***Example 4.*** *From a city population, the probability of selecting (i) a male or a smoker is 7/10 (ii) a male smoker is 2/5 and (iii) a male, if a smoker is already selected is 2/3. Find the probability of selecting (a) a non-smoker (b) a male and (c) a smoker, if a male is first selected.*

**Solution.** Define the following events

$A$ : a male is selected, $B$ : a smoker is selected

We are given that,

$$P(A \cup B) = \frac{7}{10},\ P(A \cap B) = \frac{2}{5},\ P(A/B) = \frac{2}{3}$$

(a) The probability of selecting a non-smoker is given by.

$$P(\bar{B}) = 1 - P(B) = 1 - \frac{P(A \cap B)}{P(A/B)}$$

$$\left[\text{since, } P(A/B) = \frac{P(A \cap B)}{P(B)}\right]$$

$$= 1 - \frac{2/5}{2/3} = 1 - \frac{3}{5} = \frac{2}{5}$$

$$\Rightarrow \quad P(B) = 1 - \frac{2}{5} = \frac{3}{5}$$

(b) The probability of selecting a male (by addition theorem) is given by

$$P(A) = P(A \cup B) + P(A \cap B) - P(B) = \frac{7}{10} + \frac{2}{5} - \frac{3}{5} = \frac{1}{2}$$

(c) The probability of selecting a smoker, if a male is first selected is given by

$$P(B/A) = \frac{P(A \cap B)}{P(A)} = \frac{2/5}{1/2} = \frac{4}{5}$$

***Example 5.*** *An urn contains 5 white and 5 black balls, 4 balls are drawn from this urn and put into another urn. From this second urn a ball is drawn and is found to be white. What is the probability of drawing a white ball again at the next draw. (The first white ball drawn is not replaced.)*

**Solution.** The event of drawing 4 balls from the urn is associated with five mutually exclusive events as follows

$E_0$ = the event of drawing 0 white and 4 black balls

$E_1$ = the event of drawing 1 white and 3 black balls

$E_2$ = the event of drawing 2 white and 2 black balls

$E_3$ = the event of drawing 3 white and 1 black balls

$E_4$ = the event of drawing 4 white and 0 black balls

Then, we have

$$P(E_0) = \frac{^5C_4}{^{10}C_4} = \frac{1}{42},\ P(E_1) = \frac{^5C_1 \times {^5C_3}}{^{10}C_4} = \frac{5}{21},$$

$$P(E_2) = \frac{^5C_2 \times {^5C_2}}{^{10}C_4} = \frac{10}{21},\ P(E_3) = \frac{^5C_3 \times {^5C_1}}{^{10}C_4} = \frac{5}{21}$$

and $$P(E_4) = \frac{^5C_4}{^{10}C_4} = \frac{1}{42}$$

Let $A$ denote the event of drawing a white ball from the second urn in the first draw. Then, we have

$$P(A/E_0) = 0,\ P(A/E_1) = \frac{1}{4},\ P(A/E_2) = \frac{2}{4},$$

$$P(A/E_3) = \frac{3}{4} \text{ and } P(A/E_4) = \frac{4}{4} = 1$$

Let $C$ denote the future event, *i.e.*, the next ball drawn from the remaining 3 balls in the second urn is white.

Hence, $P(C/A \cap E_0) = 0,\ P(C/A \cap E_1) = 0,\ P(C/A \cap E_2) = \dfrac{1}{3},$

$$P(C/A \cap E_3) = \frac{2}{3} \text{ and } P(C/A \cap E_4) = \frac{3}{3} = 1$$

Hence. $P(C/A) = \frac{\sum_{i=0}^{4} P(E_i)\, P(A/E_i)\, P(C/A \cap E_i)}{\sum_{i=0}^{4} P(E_i)\, P(A/E_i)}$

$$= \frac{\frac{1}{42} \times 0 \times 0 + \frac{5}{21} \times \frac{1}{4} \times 0 + \frac{10}{21} \times \frac{2}{4} \times \frac{1}{3} + \frac{5}{21} \times \frac{3}{4} \times \frac{2}{3} + \frac{1}{42} \times 1 \times 1}{\frac{1}{42} \times 0 + \frac{5}{21} \times \frac{1}{4} + \frac{10}{21} \times \frac{2}{4} + \frac{5}{21} \times \frac{3}{4} + \frac{1}{42} \times 1}$$

$= 49$

# Random Variable (or Random Vector)

Let $(S, \varepsilon, P)$ be a probability space.

Let $X : S \longrightarrow R, R = ]-\infty, \infty[$, such that for every $a \in R$, $\{x \in S \mid f(x) \leq a\} \in \varepsilon$.

Then, $X$ is called one dimensional random variable.

If $X : S \longrightarrow R^2$, then $X$ is having value which has two components. Its elements are in the form of pairs.

In this case, $X$ is 2-dimensional random variable.

Similarly, if $X : S \rightarrow R^n$, then $X$ is having values as $n$-tuples $(x_1, x_2, \ldots, x_n)$ and $X$ is called $n$-dimensional random variable

> **Note** If dimension of a random variable is not specified, then it would be considered as one dimensional random variable.

# Important Theorems on Random Variables (Measurable Functions)

***Theorems 1.*** Let $X : S \longrightarrow R(]-\infty, \infty[)$.

Then, $X$ is a random variable if and only if

$$\{x \in S \mid X(x) < a\} \in \varepsilon$$

where, $a$ is any real $\in R$.

***Theorem 2.*** If $X_1 : S \longrightarrow R, X_2 : S \longrightarrow R$

be two random variables and $C$ be a constant (real or complex), then $CX_1$, $X_1 + X_2$, and $X_1X_2$ are also random variables.

***Theorem 3.*** For any constants $C_1$ and $C_2$ and $X_1 : S \longrightarrow R, X_2 : S \longrightarrow R$, two random variables.

$C_1X_1 + C_2X_2$ is also a random variable.

***Theorem 4.*** If $\{X_n \mid n \geq 1\}$ is a collection of random variables defined on $S$, then $\sup_n X_n, \inf_n X_n, \lim_{n\to\infty} \sup X_n, \lim_{n\to\infty} \inf X_n$ are all random variables whenever they are finite for all $x \in S$.

***Theorem 5.*** If $X$ is a random variable, then

**(i)** $\frac{1}{X}$, where $\frac{1}{X}(x) = \infty$, if $X(x) = 0$

**(ii)** $X_+(x) = \max[0, X(x)]$

**(iii)** $X_-(x) = -\min[0, X(x)]$

**(iv)** $|X|$

are random variables.

***Theorem 6.*** If $X_1$ and $X_2$ are random variables, then

**(i)** $\max(X_1, X_2)$

**(ii)** $\min(X_1, X_2)$

are also random variables.

***Theorem 7.*** If $X$ is a random variable and $f$ is a continuous function, then $f(x)$ is also a random variable.

***Theorem 8.*** If $X$ is a random variable and $f$ is increasing function, then $f(x)$ is a random variable.

***Theorem 9.*** If $X$ is a random variable and $f$ is of bounded variation, then $f(x)$ is a random variable.

# Characteristic Random Variable

Let $(S, \varepsilon, P)$ be a probability space. Let $A \subseteq S$.

Let $\Psi_A : S \longrightarrow \{0, 1\}$ be defined as follows

$$\Psi_A(x) = \begin{cases} 1, & \text{if } x \in A \\ 0, & \text{if } x \notin A \end{cases}$$

It satisfies following properties

**(i)** $\Psi_\phi(x) = 0$

Here, $\phi$ is null set.

**(ii)** $\Psi_S(x) = 1$, $S$ being sample sapce.

**(iii)** $A = B \Rightarrow \Psi_A(x) = \Psi_B(x)$, $A, B \subseteq S$.

**(iv)** If $A \subseteq B$, then $\Psi_A(x) \leq \Psi_B(x)$, $A, B \subseteq S$.

**(v)** $\Psi_A(x) + \Psi_{\bar{A}}(x) = 1$, $A \subseteq S$, $\bar{A} = S - A$.

**(vi)** $\Psi_{A \cap B}(x) = \Psi_A(x)\Psi_B(x)$

**(vii)** $\Psi_{A \cup B}(x) = \Psi_A(x) + \Psi_B(x) - \Psi_A(x)\Psi_B(x)$

# Discrete and Continuous Random Variable

If it takes countable number of values, then it is called discrete random variable.

If it takes non-discrete random values (uncountable number of values), then, it is called continuous random variable.

or

If its values cannot be put in one-to-one correspondence with a set of positive integers, then it is called continuous random variable.

The set of values which random variable $X$ takes is called spectrum of $X$.

e.g., (a random variable $X$ having countably infinite values)

A coin is tossed until a head appears. Its sample space is

$$S = \{H, TH, TTH, TTTH, \ldots, T^nH, \ldots, T^\infty\}$$

Let $X$ denote the number of times the coin is tossed. Then, $X$ is a random variable

$$X = \{1, 2, 3, \ldots, \infty\}$$

In it '$\infty$' is for the case that only tails occur.

Here, $X$ is infinite (countably) discrete random variable.

e.g., (continuous random variable)

A point is chosen in a circle $C$ of radius $r$.

Let $X$ denote the distance of the point from the centre.

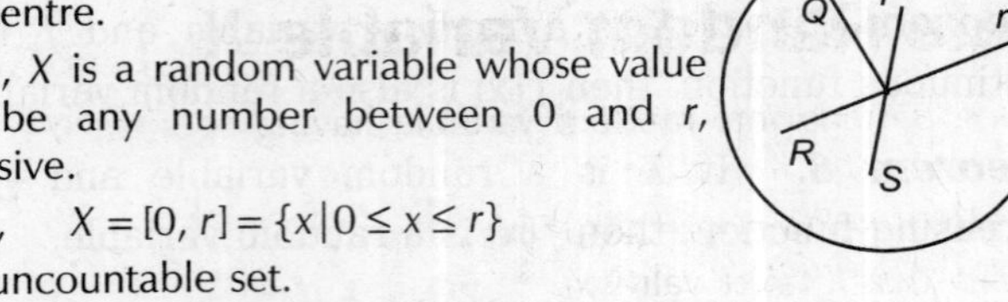


Then, $X$ is a random variable whose value can be any number between 0 and $r$, inclusive.

Thus, $\quad X = [0, r] = \{x \mid 0 \le x \le r\}$

$X$ is uncountable set.

It is as continuous random variable.

e.g., a linear array EMPLOYEE has $n$ elements. Suppose, NAME appears randomly in the array and there is a linear search to find the location $K$ of NAME, *i.e.*, to find $K$ such that EMPLOYEE [$K$] = NAME. Let $f(n)$ denote the number of comparisons in the linear search.

(a) Let $X = f(n) =$ The number of comparisons in the linear search.

Since, NAME can appear in any position in the array with the same probability of $\frac{1}{n}$, so $X = 1, 2, \ldots, n$.

Its probability distribution is

| $X$ | 1 | 2 | ... | $n$ |
|---|---|---|---|---|
| $P(X)$ | $1/n$ | $1/n$ | ... | $1/n$ |

$$E(X) = 1\cdot\frac{1}{n} + 2\cdot\frac{1}{n} + \ldots + n\cdot\frac{1}{n}$$

$$= (1 + 2 + \ldots + n)\frac{1}{n} = \frac{1}{2}\frac{n(n+1)}{n}$$

$$= \frac{(n+1)}{2}$$

If the NAME appears at the end of the array, then $f(x) = n$, It is worst possible case.

***Example 6.*** *Let $X$ be a continuous random variable with pdf*

$$f(x) = \begin{cases} ax, & 0 \le x \le 1 \\ a, & 1 \le x \le 2 \\ -ax + 3a, & 2 \le x \le 3 \\ 0, & \text{elsewhere} \end{cases}$$

*(i) Determine the constant a (ii) compute $P(X \le 1.5)$.*

**Solution.** (i) Constant '$a$' is determined from the consideration that total probability is unity, *i.e.*, $\int_0^\infty f(x)\,dx = 1$

$$\Rightarrow \int_{-\infty}^0 f(x)\,dx + \int_0^1 f(x)\,dx + \int_1^2 f(x)\,dx + \int_2^3 f(x)\,dx + \int_3^\infty f(x)\,dx = 1$$

$$\Rightarrow \int_0^1 ax\,dx + \int_0^2 a\cdot dx + \int_2^3 (-ax + 3a)\,dx = 1$$

$$\Rightarrow \quad a\left|\frac{x^2}{2}\right|_0^1 + a\,|x|_1^2 + a\left|-\frac{x^2}{2} + 3x\right|_2^3 = 1$$

$$\Rightarrow \quad \frac{a}{2} + a + a\left\{\left(-\frac{9}{2} + 9\right) - (-2 + 6)\right\} = 1$$

$$\Rightarrow 2a = 1 \Rightarrow a = \frac{1}{2} \qquad \ldots(i)$$

(ii) We have,

$$P(X \le 1.5) = \int_{-\infty}^{1.5} f(x)\,dx = \int_{-\infty}^0 f(x)\,dx + \int_0^1 f(x)\,dx + \int_1^{1.5} f(x)\,dx$$

$$= a\int_0^1 x\,dx + \int_1^{1.5} a\,dx$$

$$= a\left|\frac{x^2}{2}\right|_0^1 + a\,|x|_1^{1.5} = \frac{a}{2} + 0.5\,a = a = \frac{1}{2}$$

[from Eq. (i) in Part (i)]

***Example 7.*** *A random variable $X$ has the following probability function*

| **Values of X, x** | 0 | 1 | 2 | 3 | 4 | 5 | 6 | 7 |
|---|---|---|---|---|---|---|---|---|
| **P (x)** | 0 | $k$ | $2k$ | $2k$ | $3k$ | $k^2$ | $2k^2$ | $7k^2 + k$ |

*(i) Find k*

*(ii) Evaluate $P(X < 6)\,P(X \ge 6)$ and $P(0 < X < 5)$*

*(iii) If $P(X \le a) > \frac{1}{2}$, find the minimum value of a and*

*(iv) Determine the distribution function of X.*

**Solution.** (i) $\because \quad \sum_{x=0}^{7} p(x) = 1, \; k + 2k + 2k + 3k + k^2 + 2k^2 + 7k^2 + k = 1$

$$\Rightarrow \quad 10k^2 + 9k - 1 = 0$$

$$\Rightarrow \quad (10k - 1)(k + 1) = 0$$

$$\Rightarrow \quad k = \frac{1}{10} \text{ or } k = -1$$

But since $p(x)$ cannot be negative, $k = -1$ is rejected.

Hence, $k = \frac{1}{10}$.

(ii) We have, $P(X < 6) = P(X = 0) + P(X + 1) + \ldots + P(X = 5)$

$$= \frac{1}{10} + \frac{2}{10} + \frac{2}{10} + \frac{3}{10} + \frac{1}{100} = \frac{81}{100}$$

Now, $\quad P(X \ge 6) = 1 - P(X < 6) = 1 - \frac{81}{100} = \frac{19}{100}$

$$P(0 < X < 5) = P(X = 1) + P(X = 2) + P(X = 3) + P(X = 4) = 8k = \frac{4}{5}$$

(iii) We have, $P(X \le a) > \frac{1}{2}$. By trial, we get $a = 4$.

(iv) The distribution function $F_X(x)$ of $X$ is given in the adjoining table.

| $X$ | $F_X(x) = P(X \le x)$ |
|---|---|
| 0 | 0 |
| 1 | $k = \frac{1}{10}$ |
| 2 | $3k = \frac{3}{10}$ |
| 3 | $5k = \frac{5}{10}$ |
| 4 | $8k = \frac{4}{5}$ |
| 5 | $8k + k^2 = \frac{81}{100}$ |
| 6 | $8k + 3k^2 = \frac{83}{100}$ |
| 7 | $9k + 10K^2 = 1$ |

***Example 8.*** *Let $X$ be a random variable whose density function $f$. Forms an isosceles triangle above the unit interval $I = [0, 1]$ and 0 elsewhere. Then, prove that*

(a) *Height of the triangle is 2.*

(b) *Formula for pdf is*

$$f(x) = \begin{cases} 4x, & \text{if } 0 \le x \le 1/2 \\ -4x + 4, & \text{if } 1/2 \le x \le 1 \\ 0, & \text{elsewhere} \end{cases}$$

(c) *The mean $\mu = E(X)$ of $X$ is $1/2$.*

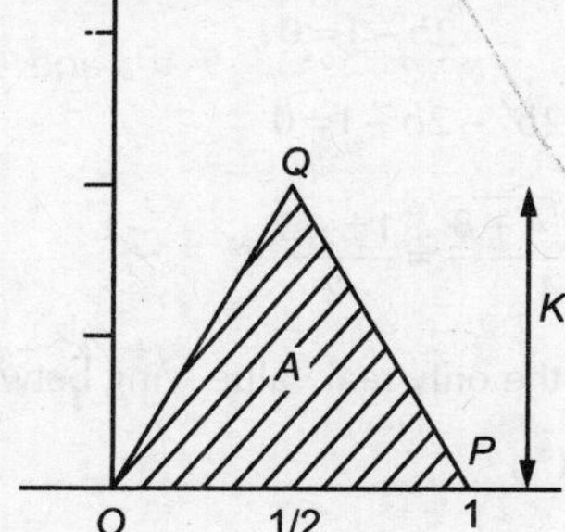


**Solution.** Let $OPQ$ be isosceles triangle of height say $K$, base being $OP = [0, 1]$. As pdf : $f$ forms $OPQ$, so area of $OPQ = 1$.

$$\Rightarrow \quad \frac{1}{2} \cdot OP \cdot K = 1 \quad \Rightarrow \quad \frac{1}{2} \cdot 1 \cdot K = 1$$

$$\Rightarrow \quad K = 2$$

As $f$ is linear between $X = 0$ and $x = 1/2$, represented by $OQ$,

Its slope $\quad m = \frac{K}{1/2} = \frac{2}{1/L} = 4.$

Again, $f$ is linear between $x = 1/2$ and $x = 1$, represented by $QP$, its slope $m = \frac{-K}{1-(1/2)} = -4.$

Hence, $\quad f(x) = \begin{cases} 4x, & \text{if } 0 \le x \le 1/2 \\ -4x + 4, & \text{if } 1/2 \le x \le 1 \\ 0, & \text{elsewhere} \end{cases}$

We may view probability as weight or mass and the mean as the centre of gravity.

Since, triangle is symmetric,

$$\mu = E(X) = 1/2$$

The mid-point of the base of triangle between 0 to 1.

$$\mu = E(X) = \int_{-\infty}^{\infty} xf(x)dx = \int_0^{1/2} x(4x)dx + \int_{1/2}^{1} x(-4x + x)dx$$

$$= 1/2$$

## Probability Mass Function and Probability Distribution for a Discrete Random Variable $X$

Let $X$ be one dimensional random variable having countably infinite values $x_1, x_2, \dots, x_n, \dots$.

For each $x_i$, let $p_i = P(X = x_i) = p(x_i)$ be probability that $X$ takes value $x_i$.

It satisfies

(i) $p(x_i) \ge 0, \forall i$

(ii) $\sum_{i=1}^{\infty} p(x_i) = 1$

Here, $p : \{x_1, x_2, \dots, x_n, \dots\} \longrightarrow [0, 1]$

It is called probability mass function of $X$.

The set $\{(x_i, p(x_i)) \mid x_i \in X, p_i \ge 0, \sum_{i=1}^{\infty} p_i = 1\}$

is called probability distribution of $X$.

In tabular form probability distribution of $X$

| **X** | $x_1,$ | $x_2,$ | ...., | $x_n$ | ...., |
|---|---|---|---|---|---|
| **P(X)** | $P(x_1),$ | $P(x_2),$ | ...., | $P(x_n)$ | ...., |

## Distribution Function

Let $X$ be a random variable an $(S, \varepsilon, P)$. Let

$$F_X : X \longrightarrow [0, 1]$$

be such that $F_x(a) = P(X \le a)$

$$= P\{x \mid X(x) \le a\}.$$

where, $-\infty < a < \infty$ is called the distribution function of $X$.

## Properties of Distribution Function

**1.** If $F$ is a distribution function of the random variable $X$ and if $a < b$, then

$$P(a < x \le b) = F(b) - F(a)$$

**2.** If $F$ is the distribution function of one-dimensional random variable $X$, then

(i) $0 \le F(x) \le 1$

(ii) $F(x) \le F(y)$, if $x < y$

*i.e.*, all distribution functions are monotonically non-decreasing and lie between 0 and 1.

3. If $F$ is a distribution function of one-dimensional random variable $X$, then

$$F(-\infty) = \lim_{x \to -\infty} F(x) = 0$$

and $$F(\infty) = \lim_{x \to \infty} F(x) = 1$$

**Cumulative Distribution Function**

(or simply distribution function)

Let $X$ be a random variable.

Let $F : R \longrightarrow [0, 1]$ such that

$$\forall\ x \in R,\ F(x) = P(X \le x).$$

Then, $F$ is called cumulative distribution function.

If $X$ is discrete having probability distribution say $\{(x_i, p(x_i)) \mid i = 1, 2, \ldots\}$

Then, $$F(x) = \sum_{i|x_i \le x} p(x_i)$$

It is called cumulative discrete distribution function.

It is a 'step function' having jump $p_i$ at $i$ and is constant between each pair of integers.

# Probability Density Function

Let $X$ be a continuous random variable.

Let $x \in X$. Let $dx$ be very small increment in the value of $x$.

We consider interval $]x, x + dx[$.

Let $f : X \to [0, 1]$ such that

$\forall\ x \in ]x, x + dx[$,

$$f(x)dx = P(x \le X \le x + dx).$$

Then, $f$ is called probability density function of $X$.

$$dF = f(x)dx$$

is called probability differential, $y = f(x)$ is called probability curve, it satisfies

(i) $f(x) \ge 0,\ -\infty < x < \infty$

(ii) $\int_{-\infty}^{\infty} f(x)dx = 1$

(iii) $P(X \le x) = \int_{-\infty}^{x} f(x)dx$

# Continuous Distribution Function

Let $X$ be a continuous random variable with probability density function $f(x)$.

Then, $$f_x : R \longrightarrow [0, 1]$$

defined by $$F_x(x) = P(X \le x)$$

$$= \int_{-\infty}^{x} f(t)dt,\ -\infty \le x \le \infty,$$

is called cumutative distribution function for $X$.

***Example* 9.** *The diameter of an electric cable, say $X$ is assumed to be a continuous random variable with pdf*

$$f(x) = 6x(1 - x),\ 0 \le x \le 1$$

*(i) Check that $f(x)$ is pdf and*

*(ii) Determine a number $b$ such that $P(X < b) = P(X > b)$.*

**Solution.** Obviously, for $0 \le x \le 1$, $f(x) \ge 0$.

Now, $$\int_0^1 f(x)\,dx = 6\int_0^1 x(1 - x)\,dx = 6\int_0^1 (x - x^2)\,dx = 6\left|\frac{x^2}{2} - \frac{x^3}{3}\right|_0^1 = 1$$

Hence, $f(x)$ is the pdf of real value $X$.

(ii) We have, $$P(X < b) = P(X > b)$$

$$\Rightarrow \int_0^b f(x)\,dx = \int_b^1 f(x)\,dx$$

$$\Rightarrow 6\int_0^b x(1 - x)\,dx = 6\int_b^1 x(1 - x)\,dx$$

$$\Rightarrow \left|\frac{x^2}{2} - \frac{x^3}{3}\right|_0^b = \left|\frac{x^2}{2} - \frac{x^3}{3}\right|_b^1$$

$$\Rightarrow \left(\frac{b^2}{2} - \frac{b^3}{3}\right) = \left[\left(\frac{1}{2} - \frac{1}{3}\right) - \left(\frac{b^2}{2} - \frac{b^3}{3}\right)\right]$$

$$\Rightarrow 3b^2 - 2b^3 = (1 - 3b^2 + 2b^3)$$

$$\Rightarrow 4b^3 - 6b^2 + 1 = 0$$

$$\Rightarrow (2b - 1)(2b^2 - 2b - 1) = 0$$

$$\therefore 2b - 1 = 0$$

$$\Rightarrow b = \frac{1}{2} \text{ or } 2b^2 - 2b - 1 = 0$$

$$\Rightarrow b = \frac{2 \pm \sqrt{4 + 8}}{4} = \frac{1 \pm \sqrt{3}}{2}$$

Hence, $b = \frac{1}{2}$ is the only real value lying between 0 and 1 and satisfying (*).

# Joint Probability Law

Let $(s, \varepsilon, P)$ be a probability space.

Let $X : S \to R$ and $Y : S \to R$ be two random variables, so that for any $a \in R$

$$\{x \in S \mid X(x) \le a\} \in \varepsilon, \quad \{x \in S \mid Y(x) \le a\} \in \varepsilon$$

*i.e.*, $\{x \in S \mid Y(x) \le a\}$

and $\{x \in S \mid Y(x) \le a\}$ are events of $S$.

Here, $X$ and $Y$ have same probability space.

We conside, $X \times Y = \{(x, y) \mid x \in Y, y \in Y\}$

If $$p_{xy}(x, y) = P[(x, y) \in E]$$

Then, it represents probability of the event $E$.

**Joint probability function of *X* and *Y*.**

Let $S$ be a sample space; $X : S \to R$ and $Y : S \to R$ be two random variables defined on it.

We take

$$X \times Y = \{(x, y) \mid x \in X(s), y \in Y(s)\}.$$

It is a two dimensional random variable on $S$.

It is also called two dimensional random vector on $S$.

Where $X$ and $Y$ are discrete random variable.

Let $X(S) = \{x_1, x_2, \ldots, x_n\}$

$Y(X) = \{y_i, y_2, \ldots, y_n\}$

Then, $X \times Y = \{(x_i, y_i) \mid x_i \in X(s), y_i \in Y(s)\}$

and joint probability function of $X$ and $Y$ is

$$p_{ij} = P(X = x_i \cap Y = y_i) = p(x_i, y_i)$$

In tabular form it is given as follows

| X \ Y | $y_1$ | $y_2$ | ... | $y_j$ | $y_m$ | Total |
|---|---|---|---|---|---|---|
| $x_1$ | $p_{11}$ | $p_{12}$ | ... | $p_{1j}$ | $p_{1m}$ | $p_1$ |
| $x_2$ | $p_{21}$ | $p_{22}$ | ... | $p_{2j}$ | $p_{2m}$ | $p_2$ |
| $x_i$ | $p_{i1}$ | $p_{i2}$ | ... | $p_{ij}$ | $p_{im}$ | $p_i$ |
| $x_n$ | $p_{n1}$ | $p_{n2}$ | ... | $p_{nj}$ | $p_{nm}$ | $p_n$ |
| **Total** | $p_1$ | $p_2$ | ... | $p_j$ | $p_m$ | 1 |

It satisfies following

$$\sum_{i=1}^{n} \sum_{j=1}^{m} p_{ij} = 1$$

## The Probability Distribution of $X$

$$p_x(x_i) = P(X = x_i) = \sum_{j=i}^{m} P(X = x_i \cap Y = y_j)$$

$$= \sum_{j=1}^{m} p_{ij} = \sum_{i=1}^{m} p(x_i, y_j) = p_i$$

It is known as marginal probability function of $X$.

It satisfies $\sum_{i=1}^{n} p_i = 1.$

## The Probability Distribution of $y$

$$p_y(y_i) = \sum_{i=1}^{n} P(X = x_i \cap Y = y_j) = \sum_{i=1}^{n} p_{ij}$$

$$= \sum_{i=1}^{n} p(x_i, y_j) = p_j$$

It is called marginal probability function of $Y$.

It satisfies $\sum_{j=1}^{m} p_j = 1.$

## For Joint Distribution, Conditional Probabilities

$$P(X = x_i \mid Y = y_j) = \frac{P(X = x_i \cap Y = y_j)}{P(Y = y_j)} = \frac{p(x_i, y_j)}{p_y(y_j)} = \frac{p_{ii}}{p_j}$$

is called conditional probability function of $X$, given $Y = y_j$.

$$P(Y = y_j \mid X = x_i) = \frac{p(x_i, y_j)}{p_X(x_i)} = \frac{p_{ij}}{p_i}.$$

is called conditional probability function of $Y$, given $X = x_i$.

Here, $$\sum_{i=1}^{n} \frac{pij}{pj} = \frac{p_j}{p_j} = 1$$

and $$\sum_{j=1}^{m} \frac{p_{ij}}{p_i} = \frac{p_i}{p_i} = 1$$

For Joint Distribution $X$ and $Y$ $(r \cdot v_s)$ are Independent, if

$P(X = x_i, Y = y_j) = P(X = x_i) \cdot P(Y = y_j)$.

If it is not so, then $X$ and $Y$ are called dependent.

## Independent Random Variables in Terms of pdf's

Let $X$ and $Y$ have joint pdf as $f_{xy}(x, y)$ and marginal pdf's $f_x(x)$ and $f_y(y)$, respectively. They are said to be stochastically independent, if

$$f_{xy}(x, y) = f_x(x) \cdot f_y(y)$$

## In Terms of Distribution Function

$X$ and $Y$ are stochastically independent if and only if there joint distribution function.

$F_{xy}(x, y)$ is the product of their marginal distribution functions $F_x(x), F_y(y)$.

Two variables which are not stochastically independent are said to be stochastically dependent.

## Joint Probability Distribution Function for Continuous Random Variables

Let $X$ and $Y$ be two random variables. Then, $(X, Y)$ is two dimensional random variable.

Its corresponding point distribution function is denoted by $F_{xy}(x, y)$.

It is defined as the probability that simultaneously the observation $(X, Y)$ will have the property $(X \le x$ and $Y \le y)$ *i.e.*,

$$F_{xy}(xy) = P(-\infty < X \le x, -\infty \le Y \le y)$$

$$= \int_{-\infty}^{x} \int_{-\infty}^{y} f_{xy}(x, y) dxdy$$

where, $f_{xy}(x, y) \ge 0$

and $\int_{-\infty}^{\infty} \int_{-\infty}^{\infty} f_{xy}(x, y)\, dxdy = 1$

### Properties of Joint Distribution Functions

**(i)** Distribution function $F(x, y)$ is monotonically non-decreasing and continuous from the right with respect to each coordinate.

**(ii)** $F(-\infty, y) = 0$

$F(x, \infty) = 0$

$F(-\infty, \infty) = 1$

**(iii)** For, $\forall\, a_1, b_1, a_2, b_2 \in R$

$a_1 \le b_1,\ a_2 \le b_2$

$$P(a_1 < x < b_1, a_2 < y < b_4 < b_2) = F_{xy}(b_1, b_2) + F_{xy}(a_1, a_2) - F_{xy}(a_1, b_2) - F_{xy}(b_1, a_2)$$

# Marginal Distribution Function

Marginal distribution functions of $X$ and $Y$ means individual distribution functions $F_x(x)$ and $F_y(y)$ of $X$ and $Y$, respectively.

Given, joint distribution function of $X$ and $Y$ : $F_{xy}(x, y)$.

Then,
$$\begin{aligned} F_x(x) &= P(X \le x) \\ &= P(X \le x, Y < \infty) \\ &= \lim_{y \to \infty} F_{xy}(x, y) \\ &= F_{xy}(x, \infty) \end{aligned}$$

Similarly,
$$\begin{aligned} F_y(y) &= P(Y \le y) \\ &= P(-\infty < X < \infty, Y \le y) \\ &= \lim_{x \to \infty} F_{xy}(x, y) = F_{xy}(\infty, y) \end{aligned}$$

From joint distribution function $F_{xy}(x, y)$, we can find individual distribution functions $F_x(x), F_y(y)$. These are called marginal distribution functions of $X$ and $Y$, respectively.

In case of joint discrete random variable, marginal distribution functions are given as follows

$$F_x(x) = \sum_y P(X \le x, Y = y)$$

$$F_y(y) = \sum_x P(X = x, Y \le y)$$

Similarly, for joint continuous random variable, marginal distribution functions are as follows

$$F_x(x) = \int_{-\infty}^{x} \left\{ \int_{-\infty}^{\infty} f_{xy}(x, y)dy \right\} dx$$

$$F_x(y) = \int_{-\infty}^{y} \left\{ \int_{-\infty}^{\infty} f_{xy}(x, y)dx \right\} dy$$

Let $F_{xy}(x, y)$ be two dimensional continuous joint distribution function.

Then, corresponding to it, joint probability density function is

$$\begin{aligned} f_{xy}(x, y) &= \frac{\partial^2 F_{xy}(x, y)}{\partial x \partial y} \\ &= \lim_{\substack{\delta x \to 0 \\ \delta y \to 0}} \frac{P(x \le X \le x + \delta x, y \le Y \le y + \delta y)}{\delta x\, \delta y} \end{aligned}$$

The probability that the point $(x, y)$ will lie in the infinite small rectangular region of area $dx\, dy$ is given by

$$\begin{aligned} &P\left(x - \frac{1}{2}dx \le X \le x + \frac{1}{2}dx, y - \frac{1}{2}dy \le Y \le y + \frac{1}{2}dy\right) \\ &= d\, F_{xy}(x, y) \end{aligned}$$

It is denoted by $f_{xy}(x, y)dx\, dy$.

Where, $f_{xy}$ is called joint probability density function of $X$ and $Y$.

## The Marginal Probability

Density function of $Y$ and $X$ are given, respectively as follows

$$f_y(y) = \int_{-\infty}^{\infty} f_{xy}(x, y)dx \quad \text{(for continuous variables)}$$
$$= \sum_x p_{xy}(x, y) \quad \text{(for discrete variables)}$$
$$f_x(x) = \int_{-\infty}^{\infty} f_{xy}(x, y)dx \quad \text{(for continuous variables)}$$
$$= \sum_y p_{xy}(x, y) \quad \text{(for discrete variables)}$$

From joint distribution function, we have

$$f_x(x) = \frac{dF_X(x)}{dx} = \int_{-\infty}^{\infty} f_{xy}(x, y)dy$$
$$f_y(y) = \frac{dF_Y(y)}{dy} = \int_{-\infty}^{\infty} f_{xy}(x, y)dx$$

from the joint pdfs (pmfs) $f_{xy}(x, y)$ of two random variables $X$ and $Y$, we can obtain the individual distributions of $X$ and $Y$ in the form of their marginal pdfs (pmfs) $f_x(x)$ and $f_y(y)$, using

$$f_x(x) = \frac{dF_x(x)}{d_x} = \int_{-\infty}^{\infty} f_{xy}(x, y)dy$$

and
$$f_y(y) = \frac{dF_y(y)}{dy} = \int_{-\infty}^{\infty} f_{xy}(x, y)dx$$

Its converse is not true; from the marginal distribution functions of two jointly distributed random variables, we cannot determine the joint distributions of these two random variables.

## Conditional Distribution Functions

Let $(X, Y)$ be two dimensional random variable having joint distribution function

$$F_{xy}(x, y) = P(X \le x, Y \le y)$$

Let $A$ be the event $(Y \le y)$ that is event $A$ is said to occur when $Y$ assumes values upto $y$ (including it).

Then,
$$\begin{aligned} F_{y/x}(y|x) &= P(A|X = x) \\ &= P(Y \le y|X = x) \end{aligned}$$

represents conditional distribution function of $Y$ when $X$ has already taken particular value $x$

In terms of $F_{y|x}(y|x)$, joint distribution function $F_{xy}(x, y)$ is given as

$$F_{xy}(x, y) = \int_{-\infty}^{x} F_{y|x}(y|x)\, dF_x(x)$$

Similarly,
$$\begin{aligned} F_{x|y}(x|y) &= P(A|Y = y) \\ &= P(X \le x|Y = y) \end{aligned}$$

and
$$F_{xy}(x, y) = \int_{-\infty}^{y} F_{x|y}(x|y)\, dF_y(y)$$

The conditional probability density function of $Y$ given $X$, for two random variables $X$ and $Y$ which are continuous and jointly distributed

$$f_{y|x}(y|x) = \frac{\partial}{\partial y} F_{y|x}(y|x)$$

**Properties**

**(i)** If $f_x(x) > 0$, then

$$f_{y|x}(y|x) = \frac{f_{xy}(x,y)}{f_x(x)}$$

**(ii)** If $f_y(y) > 0$, then

$$f_{x|y}(x|y) = \frac{f_{xy}(x,y)}{f_y(y)}$$

**(iii)** In terms of differentials,

$$P(x < X \le x + dx / y < Y \le y + dy)$$
$$= \frac{P(x < X \le x + dx, y < Y \le y + dy)}{P(y < Y \le y + dy)}$$
$$= \frac{f_{xy}(x,y)dxdy}{f_y(y)dy}$$
$$= \frac{f_{xy}(x,y)dx}{f_y(y)} = f_{x|y}(x|y)dx$$

$f_{x|y}(x|y) =$ Conditional density function of $X$ when $Y = y$

# Mathematical Expectation

Let $X$ be a random variable (*rv*) with pdf (pmf) $f(x)$. Then, its mathematical expectation denoted by $E(x)$ is

$$E(x) = \int_{-\infty}^{\infty} x f(x) dx \text{ (for continuous } rv)$$
$$= \sum_{x=-\infty}^{\infty} x f(x) \quad \text{(for discrete } rv)$$

povided the right hand integral (or series) is absolutely convergent *i.e.*,

$$\int_{-\infty}^{\infty} |xf(x)|\, dx < \infty \quad \text{or} \quad \sum_x |xf(x)| < \infty$$

## Properties of Mathematical Expectations

1. Let $X$ be a random variable and $K$ be a real number. Then,
   (i) $E(kx) = kE(x)$
   (ii) $E(x + k) = E(x) + k$
   (iii) $E(ax + b) = aE(x) + b$
2. (i) Let $X$ and $Y$ be random variables on the same sample space $S$.
   Then, $E(x + y) = E(x) + E(y)$
   (ii) Let $X_1, X_2, \ldots, X_n$ be random variables on same sample space $S$.
   Then, $E(X_1 + X_2 + \ldots + X_n) = E(x_1) + E(x_2) + \ldots + E(x_n)$.

## Expectation of a Function of a Random Variable

Let $X$ be a random variable with pdf (pmf) $f(x)$ and distribution function $F(x)$. If $g(\cdot)$ is a function such that $g(x)$ is a random variable and $E(g(x))$ exists, then

$$E(g(x) = \int_{-\infty}^{\infty} g(x) dF(x)$$
$$= \int_{-\infty}^{\infty} g(x) \cdot f(x) dx \text{ (for continuous } rv)$$
$$= \sum_x g(x) \cdot f(x) \quad \text{(for discrete } rv)$$

# Moments

We know that, $E(g(x)) = \int_{-\infty}^{\infty} g(x) f(x) dx$

1. If $g(x) = x^r$, $r$ being a positive integer, then
   $$E(X^r) = \int_{-\infty}^{\infty} x^r f(x) dx$$
   It is denoted by $\mu_r'$, the $r$th moment (about origin) of the probability distribution.
   Thus, $\mu_r'$ (about origin) $= E(X^r)$
   $\mu_1'$ (about origin) $= E(X)$
   $\mu_2'$ (about origin) $= E(x^2)$
   Mean $= \bar{x} = \mu_1'$ (about origin) $= E(x)$
2. If $g(x) = [X - E(x)]^r = (X - \bar{x})^r$,
   then $E[g(x)] = E[(X - E(x))^r]$
   $$= \int_{-\infty}^{\infty} (x - \bar{x})^r f(x) dx$$
   It is denoted by $\mu_r$ and is called $r$th moment about mean.
   If $r = 2$,
   $$\mu_2 = E[X - E(x)]^2 = \int_{-\infty}^{\infty} (x - \bar{x})^2 f(x) dx$$
   $\mu_2$ is called variance of the probability distribution of a *rv* $X$ in terms of expectation.
   $\mu_2$ is also denoted by $\sigma_x^2$.
   The positive square root of $\sigma_x^2 = +\sigma_x$. It is called standard deviation of $X$.

# Covariance

Let $X$ and $Y$ be two random variables. Then, covariance between them is denoted by cov $(x, y)$ and is defined as follows

$$\text{Cov}(X, Y) = E[(X - E(x))(Y - E(y))] = E(XY) - E(x)E(y)$$

If $X$ and $Y$ are independent, then $E(xy) = E(x)E(y)$ and so cov $(x, y) = E(x)E(y) - E(x)E(y) = 0$.

# Correlation Coefficient

Let $X$ and $Y$ be two random variables. The correlation coefficient between them is denoted by $P_{xy}$ or $r_{xy}$ and is defined as follows

$$r_{xy} = \frac{\text{cov}(x, y)}{\sigma_x \sigma_y}$$

cov $(x, y)$ is covariance between $X$ and $Y$ and $\sigma_x$ and $\sigma_y$ are standard deviations of $X$ and $Y$, respectively.

## Properties of $r_{xy}$

**(i)** correlation $r_{xy}$ is dimensionless.

**(ii)** $r(x, y) = r(y, x)$

**(iii)** $-1 \le r_{xy} \le 1$

**(iv)** $r_{xx} = 1$

**(v)** $r_{(x,-x)} = -1$

**(vi)** $r(ax + b, cy + d) = r(x, y)$, if $a, c \ne 0$.

A pair of random variables with identical individual distributions can have distinct covariances and correlations.

cov $(x, y)$ and $r_{xy}$ are measurements of the way that $X$ and $Y$ are interrelated.

# Expectation and Games of Chance

Let a game consists of $n$ outcomes $S = \{a_1, a_2, \ldots, a_n\}$ such that probability of $a_i$ is $p_i$ $(i = 1, 2, \ldots, n)$. Let the payoff to a player be $w_i$ for the outcome $a_i$, if $w_i > 0$, then player wins, if $w_i < 0$ player losses, $i = 1, 2, \ldots, n$.

Then, $E(w) = w_1 p_1 + w_2 p_2 + \ldots + w_n p_n$.

where, $w = \{w_1, w_2, \ldots, w_n\}$ = Random variable on $S$.

The game is fair, if $E = 0$, favourable of the player, if $E > 0$ and unfavourable to him, if $E < 0$.

## Properties of Variance

Let $X$ be a random variable and let $a$ and $b$ be constants. Then,

$$\text{var}(ax + b) = a^2 \text{ var}(x)$$

$$\sigma_{ax+b} = |a| \sigma_x$$

# Moment Generating Function

Let $X$ be a random variable. Let $h > 0$ such that $-h < t < h$ and $E(e^{tx})$ exist.

Then, $M_x(t) = E(e^{tx})$ is called moment generating function of $X$.

If $X$ is discrete random variable with probability distribution

$p(x_i) = P(X = x_i)$, $i = 1, 2, \ldots$, then $M_x(t) = \sum_{i=1}^{\infty} e^{tx_i} p(x_i)$

provided the sum is finite.

If $X$ is continuous random variable with probability density function $f(x)$, then

$$M_x(t) = \int_{-\infty}^{\infty} x f(x)\, dx$$

provided integral exists.

# Probability Generating Function (PGF)

Probability generating function of a random variable $X$ is defined as

$P(S) = E(s^x)$

provided it exist.

We know that mgf of $X$ is given by $M_x(t) = E(e^{tx})$, where $-h < t < X$.

Putting $e^t = S$ in it, *i.e.*, $E = \log_e S$

we get, $M_x(\log_e S) = E[(e^t)^x] = E(S^x) = P(S)$

Thus, $P(S) = M_x(\log_e S) = E(S^x)$

$= \sum S^{xi} p_i$ provided $|S| \le 1$.

Since, coefficient of $S^{x_i}$ in it is $p_i$ so it generates probabilities.

For continuous random variable $X$ with probability density function $f(x)$,

$$P(S) = \int_{-\infty}^{\infty} s^x f(x) dx,$$

provided integral exists.

# Characteristic Function

For all real numbers $t$, the characteristic function $\psi_x(t)$ of a random variable $X$ is defined as follows

$$\psi_x(t) = E(e^{itX}), \quad i = \sqrt{-1}.$$

Thus, $\psi_x : R \longrightarrow [0, 1]$

## Properties of Characteristic Function

**(i)** The characteristic function of a random variable $X$ always exists.

**(ii)** $|\psi_x(t)| \le 1$ for all real numbers $t$,

**(iii)** $\psi_x(0) = 1$ and $\psi_x(t) = \overline{\psi_x(-t)}$

**(iv)** $\psi_x(t)$ is continuous function of $t$, $(-\infty < t < \infty)$.

**(v)** For constants $a$ and $b$, $\psi_{ax+b}(t) = e^{ibt} \psi_x(at)$

## Multivariate Characteristic Function

Let $X = \begin{bmatrix} X_1 \\ X_2 \\ \vdots \\ X_n \end{bmatrix}_{n \times 1}$ be $n$ tuple

random variable *i.e.*, $n$-dimensional random variable.

Let $t = \begin{bmatrix} t_i \\ t_2 \\ \vdots \\ t_n \end{bmatrix}_{n \times 1} \in R^n$, $t$ being real.

Then, characteristic function of $X$ is defined as

$$\phi_x(t) = E(e^{itx}) = E[e^{it(x_1 + x_2 + \ldots + x_n)}]$$

$$= E(e^{i(t_1 x_1 + t_2 x_2 + \ldots + t_n x_n)})$$

It is also denoted by

$$\phi_{X_1, X_2, \ldots, X_n}(t_1, t_2, \ldots, t_n) \text{ or } \phi_X(t_1, t_2, \ldots, t_n).$$

## Jenson's Inequality

For a random variable $X$ and a convex function $f(x)$ $E(f(x) \geq f(E(x)))$.

## Markov's Inequality

Let $X$ be a random variable such that $P(y \geq 0) = 1$, then for $t > 0$,

$$P(y \geq t) \leq \frac{E(Y^a)}{t^a}, \text{ for fixed } a \geq 0.$$

## Chebyshev's Inequality

Let $X$ be a random variable with probability density function $f(x)$, mean $\mu$ and variance $\sigma^2$.

Then, $\quad P[|x - \mu| \geq \delta] \leq \dfrac{\sigma^2}{\delta^2}$ for fixed $\delta > 0$.

This leads to

$$P[|x - \mu| < \delta] \geq 1 - \frac{\sigma^2}{\delta^2} \text{ for fixed } \delta > 0.$$

or $\quad P(\mu - \delta \leq X \leq \mu + \delta) \geq 1 - \dfrac{\sigma^2}{S^2}$ for fixed $\delta > 0$.

## Convergence in Probability

Let $X_n$ be a sequence of random variables. Then, $\{X_n\}$ converges in probability to a random variable $X$ *i.e.*, $X_n \xrightarrow{p} X$, if for every $\in > 0$,

$$P\{|X_n - x| > \in\} \longrightarrow 0 \text{ as } n \longrightarrow \infty$$

convergence in probability is also called stochastic convergence or weak convergence.

***Theorem*** Let $\quad X_n \xrightarrow{p} X$

and $\quad Y_n \xrightarrow{p} Y$,

Then,

(a) $cX_n \xrightarrow{p} cX$ for c real.

(b) $X_n + Y_n \xrightarrow{p} X + Y$

(c) $X_n Y_n \xrightarrow{p} XY$;

(d) $\dfrac{X_n}{Y_n} \xrightarrow{p} \dfrac{X}{Y}$;

If $P(Y_n = 0)_{=0}$ for every $n$ and $P(y = 0) = 0$;

(e) for a continuous and real valued function $f(x)$, $f(X_n) \xrightarrow{p} f(x)$.

## Convergence in Distribution

A sequence of random variables $\{X_n\}$ converges to a random variable $X$ in distribution or in law *i.e.*,

$$X_n \xrightarrow{d} X \text{ or } X_n \xrightarrow{L} X$$

If $\lim_{n \to \infty} F_{X_n}(t) = F_x(t)$ at each point $t$, where $F_x(\cdot)$ is continuous.

***Theorem*** Let $X_n \xrightarrow{d} X$ and $Y_n \xrightarrow{d} C$ for $C$ constant. Then,

**(i)** $X_n + Y_r \xrightarrow{d} X + C$;

**(ii)** $X_n Y_n \xrightarrow{d} CX$;

**(iii)** $\dfrac{X_n}{Y_n} \xrightarrow{c} \dfrac{X}{C}$, if $C \neq 0$

## Almost Sure Convergence or Convergence Almost Everywhere

A sequence of random variables $\{X_n\}$ converges to $X$ almost surely or almost everywhere (*i.e.* $X_n \xrightarrow{a.s} X$) (or $X_n \xrightarrow{a.e.} X$), if $P[\lim_{n \to \infty} X_n = X] = 1$

Convergence almost sure is also called strong convergence.

## Convergence in Mean Square

A sequence of random variables $\{X_n\}$ converges to $X$ in mean squares (*i.e.*, $X_n \xrightarrow{L_2} X$), if $\lim_{n \to \infty} E(X_n \longrightarrow X)^2 = 0$

***Theorems***

**(i)** $X_n \xrightarrow{as} X \Rightarrow X_n \xrightarrow{p} X$

$\Rightarrow X_{n_k} \xrightarrow{as} X$ (where, $n_k$ is a subsequence);

**(ii)** $X_n \xrightarrow{L_2} X \Rightarrow X_n \xrightarrow{p} X$;

**(iii)** $X_n \xrightarrow{p} X \Rightarrow X_n \xrightarrow{d} X$

**(iv)** for constant $k$,

$X_n \xrightarrow{d} k \Rightarrow X_n \xrightarrow{p} k$

## Law of Large Numbers

For any positive integer $\alpha$, no matter how small, $P(\mu - \alpha \leq \overline{X_n} \leq \mu + \alpha) \longrightarrow) 1$ as $n \to \infty$ that is, the probability that the sample mean $\overline{X_n}$ has a value in the interval $[\mu - \alpha, \mu + \alpha]$ approaches 1 as $n$ approaches $\infty$.

## Weak Law of Large Numbers

Let $X_1, X_2, \ldots, X_n$ be random variables such that $E(X_i) = a$, $V(X_i) = b^2$ and are finite for $i = 1, 2, \ldots, n$.

Then, weak law of large number holds, if

$$\bar{x} = \frac{x_1 + x_2 + \ldots + x_n}{n} = \frac{S_n}{n} \longrightarrow a \text{ in probability}$$

In WLLN, the random variables need not be identically distributed. They need only to have same mean and same finite variance.

## Strong Law of Large Numbers (SLLN)

Let $X_1, X_2, \ldots, X_n$ be independent random variables such that $E(X_n) = a$ for $n \geq 1$.

Then, strong law of large numbers holds, if $\bar{x} = \frac{x_1 + x_2 + \ldots + x_n}{n} \longrightarrow a$ almost surely.

Strong law of large numbers holds, if either $V(X_n) \le A$ for every $n \ge 1$ and positive $A$ or $\sum_n \frac{V(X_n)}{n^2} < \infty$.

Strong law of large numbers implies weak law of large numbers.

## Central Limit Theorem

Let $X_1, X_2, \ldots, X_n$ be a sequence of independent random variables with the same distribution and with mean $\mu$ and variance $\sigma^2$.

Let $$Z_n = \frac{\overline{X_n} - \mu}{\sigma / \sqrt{n}}$$

where $\overline{X_n} = (X_1 + X_2 + \ldots + X_n) / n$.

Then, for large $n$ and any interval $[a, b]$, $a \le x \le b$,

$$P(a \le Z_n \le b) \cong P(a \le \phi \le \beta)$$

where $\phi$ is the standard normal distribution.

Here, $\overline{X_n}$ = sample mean of random variables $X_1, X_2, \ldots, X_n$

$Z_n$ = standardized sample mean.

CLT says that in any sequence of repeated trials, the standardized sample mean approaches the standard normal variable as the number of trials increases.

***Example 10.*** *A box contains $2^n$ tickets among which ${}^nC_i$ tickets bear the number $i$, $i = 0, 1, 2, \ldots, n$. A group of $m$ tickets is drawn. What is the expectation of the sum of their numbers?*

**Solution.** Let $X_i$; $i = 1, 2, \ldots, m$ be the variable representing the number on the $i$th ticket drawn. Then, the sum '$S$' of the numbers on the tickets drawn is given by

$$S = X_1 \times X_2 + \ldots + X_m = \sum_{i=1}^{m} X_i, \text{ so that } E(S) = \sum_{i=1}^{m} E(X_i)$$

$X_i$ is a random variable which can take any one of the possible values 0, 1, 2,..., $n$ with respective probabilities ${}^nC_0/2^n, {}^nC_1/2^n, {}^nC_2/2^n, \ldots, {}^nC_n/2^n$.

Hence, $$E(X_i) = \frac{1}{2^n}(1 \cdot {}^nC_1 + 2 \cdot {}^nC_2 + 3 \cdot {}^nC_3 + \ldots + n \cdot {}^nC_n)$$

$$= \frac{1}{2^n}\left(1 \cdot n + 2 \cdot \frac{n(n-1)}{2!} + 3\,\frac{n(n-1)(n-2)}{3!} + \ldots + n \cdot 1\right)$$

$$= \frac{n}{2^n}\left\{1 + (n-1) + \frac{(n-1)(n-2)}{2!} + \ldots + 1\right\}$$

$$= \frac{n}{2^n}({}^{n-1}C_0 + {}^{n-1}C_1 + {}^{n-1}C_2 + \ldots + {}^{n-1}C_{n-1}) = \frac{n}{2^n} \cdot (1+1)^{n-1} = \frac{n}{2}$$

***Example 11.*** *What is the expectation of the number of failures preceding the first success in an infinite series of independent trials with constant probability $p$ of success in each trial?*

**Solution.** Let the random variable $X$ denote the number of failures preceding the first success. Then $X$ can take the values 0, 1, 2,..., $\infty$. We have,

$P(x = n) = p(x)$ ($x$ failures precede the first success) $= q^x p$, where $q = 1 - p$ is the probability of failure in a trail.

Then, by definition,

$$E(X) = \sum_{x=0}^{\infty} xp(x) = \sum_{x=0}^{\infty} x q^x p = pq \sum_{x=1}^{\infty} x q^{x-1}$$

$$= pq\,(1 + 2q + 3q^2 + 4q^3 + \ldots) \qquad \ldots(*)$$

Now, $1 + 2q + 3q^2 + 4q^3 + \ldots$ is an infinite arithmetic geometric series.

Let $$S = 1 + 2q + 3q^2 + 4q^3 + \ldots$$

$$qS = q + 2q^2 + 3q^3 + \ldots$$

Hence $$(1-q)S = 1 + q + q^2 + q^3 + \ldots = \frac{1}{1-q}$$

$$\Rightarrow \quad S = \frac{1}{(1-q)^2}$$

Hence, $$1 + 2q + 3q^2 + 4q^3 + \ldots = \frac{1}{(1-q)^2}$$

Hence, $$E(X) = \frac{pq}{(1-q)^2} = \frac{pq}{p^2} = \frac{q}{p} \qquad \text{[from (*)]}$$

***Example 12.*** *Let the rv $x$ assume that value 'r' with the probability law $P(X = r) = q^{r-1}p$; $r = 1, 2, 3, \ldots$. Find the mgf of $X$ and hence, its mean and variance.*

**Solution.** $$M_X(t) = E(e^{tX}) = \sum_{r=1}^{\infty} e^{tr} q^{r-1} p = \frac{p}{q} \sum_{r=1}^{\infty} (qe^t)^r$$

$$= \frac{p}{q} qe^t \sum_{r=1}^{\infty} (qe^t)^{r-1} = pe^t\{1 + qe^t + (qe^t)^2 + \ldots\} = \left(\frac{pe^t}{1 - qe^t}\right)$$

If dash (′) denotes the differentiation *wrt* to $t$, then we have

$$M_x'(t) = \frac{pe^t}{(1 - qe^t)^2}, \quad M_x''(t) = pe^t \frac{(1 + qe^t)}{(1 - qe^t)^3}$$

Hence, $$\mu_1' \text{ (about origin)} = M_x'(0) = \frac{p}{(1-q)^2} = \frac{1}{p}$$

$$\mu_2' \text{ (about origin)} = M_x''(0) = \frac{p(1+q)}{(1-q)^3} = \frac{1+q}{p^2}$$

Hence, $$\text{mean} = \mu_1' \text{ (about origin)} = \frac{1}{p}$$

and $$\text{variance} = \mu_2 = \mu_2' - \mu_1'^2 = \frac{1+q}{p^2} - \frac{1}{p^2} = \frac{q}{p^2}$$

## Stochastic Process (or Chance or Random Process)

It is a family of random variables $\{X(t) | t \in T\}$ defined on a common sample space $S$ and indexed by the parameter $t$, $t \in T$ (index set).

The values of $X(t)$ are called states.

The set of all possible values of $X(t)$ form the state space of the process and is denoted by I

If the state space is discrete, the stochastic process is known as a chain. In this case, state space is assumed to be {0, 1, 2, 3, .....}.

A finite stochastic process consists of a sequence of experiments in which each experiment has a finite number of outcomes with given probabilities.

# Markov Process (Memoryless Process)

A Markov (memoryless) process is a stochastic process whose entire past history is summarized in its current (present) state *i.e.*, the "future" is independent of its "past."

## Markov Chain

It is a markov process in which the state space I is discrete (finite or countably infinite). Thus, a finite markov chain is a finite stochastic process consisting of a sequence of trials whose outcomes say $x_1, x_2, \ldots$ satisfy the following two conditions.

(a) Each outcome belongs to the state space $I = \{a_1, a_2, \ldots \pi_m\}$ Which is the finite set of outcomes.

(b) The outcomes of any trial depends atmost upon the outcome of the immediate preceeding trials and not upon any other previous outcomes *i.e.*,

$$P(X_n = i_n \mid x_0 = i_0, X_1 = i_1, \ldots, X_{n-1} = i_{n-1})$$
$$= P(X_n = i_n \mid X_{n-1} = i_{n-1})$$

# System is in a State '$a_1$' at time '$n$'

The system is said to be in a state '$a_i$' at time '$n$' or at the $n$th step, if $a_i$ is the outcome on the $n$th trial.

Associated with each ordered pair of states $(a_i, a_j)$, the number $P_{ij}$ is the probability that the system changes from the $i$th state to the $j$th state, *i.e.*, $p_{ij}$ is the probability that $a_j$ occurs immediately after $a_i$ occurs. The numbers $P_{ij}$ are known as transition probabilities.

**Transition matrix *P***

It is a square matrix of transition probabilities.

$$P = \begin{matrix} & a_1 & a_2 & \cdots & a_m \\ a_1 \\ a_2 \\ \vdots \\ a_m \end{matrix} \begin{pmatrix} p_{11} & p_{12} & \cdots & p_{1m} \\ p_{21} & p_{22} & \cdots & p_{2m} \\ \vdots & \vdots & & \\ p_{m1} & p_{m2} & \cdots & p_{mn} \end{pmatrix}$$

The $i$th row of $P$ namely $(p_{i1}, p_{i2}, \ldots p_{im})$ represents the probabilities of that system will change from $a_i$ to $a_1, a_2, \ldots a_m$.

# Probability Vector

It is a vector $v = (v_1, v_2, \ldots, v_n)$, if $v_i \geq 0$ for every $i$, and $\sum_{i=1}^{n} v_i = 1$.

A vector whose components are non-negative, but their sum is not one, can be converted into a probability vector by dividing each component by the sum of the components.

# Stochastic Matrix

$P$ is a square matrix with each row being a probability vector. In other words, all the entries of $P$ are non-negative and the sum of the entries of any row is one.

A vector $v$ is said to be a fixed vector or a fixed point of a matrix $A$, if $vA = v$ and $v \neq 0$.

If $v$ is a fixed vector or a fixed point of a matrix $A$, if $vA = v$ and $v \neq 0$.

If $v$ is a fixed vector of $A$, so is $Kv$ same $(Kv)A = K(vA) = K(v) = Kv$.

***Theorem 1*** If $v = (v_1, v_2, \ldots, v_n)$ is a probability vector of a $n$-square stochastic matrix $P$, then $vP$ is also a probability vector.

***Theorem 2*** Let $P$ be a regular stochastic matrix, then

**(i)** $P$ has a unique fixed probability vector $t$ and the components of $t$ are all positive.

**(ii)** The sequence $P, P^2, P^3, \ldots$ of powers of $P$ approaches the matrix $T$ whose rows are each the fixed point $t$.

**(iii)** If $P$ is any probability vector, then the sequence vectors $pP, pP^2, \ldots$ approaches the fixed point '$t$'.

# Definition

A matrix $A$ approaches matrix $B$, means every entry of $A$ approaches the corresponding entry of $B$.

The entry $p_{ij}$ in the transition probability matrix $P$ is the probability that the system moves from the state $a_i$ to the state $a_j$ in one step *i.e.*, $a_i \to a_j$.

One step transition probabilities in $P$ can also be described by a directed graph function as state transition diagram or simply transition diagram of the markov chain.

A node labelled $i$ of the transition diagram represents state $i$ of the markov chain.

A branch labelled $p_{ij}$ from node $i$ to node $j$ represents the conditional probability (or the one step transition probability) defined by

$$P_{ij} = P(X_n = j \mid X_{n-1} = i)$$

## $n$th Step Transition Probabilities

The probability that a markov chain will move from state $i$ to state $j$ in exactly $n$ steps, is denoted by $p_{ij}(n)$ or $p_{ij}^{(n)}$ and is given by

$$p_{ij}^{(n)} = p_{ij}(n) = P(X_{m+n} = j \mid X_m = i)$$

i.e., $a_i \longrightarrow a_{k_1} \longrightarrow a_{k_2} \longrightarrow \ldots\ldots \longrightarrow a_{k_{n-1}} \longrightarrow a_j$

***Example 13.*** *The figure shows four*

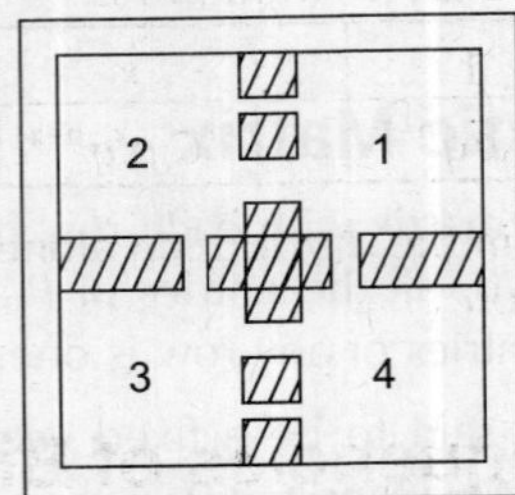


*compartments with door leading from one to another. A mouse in any compartment is equally likely to pass through each of the doors of the compartment. Then, transition matrix of the markov chain. Draw the transition diagram.*

**Solution.** The 4 rooms are considered as four states say 1, 2, 3 and 4. Since, mouse is moving, it does not stay in the same room. From room 1 it can move to 1 with probability 0 to 2 with probability 2/3 to 4 with probability 1/3.

The first row consists of 0, 2/3, 0, 1/3 and so transition matrix is

|   | 1 | 2 | 3 | 4 |
|---|---|---|---|---|
| 1 | 0 | 2/3 | 0 | 1/3 |
| 2 | 2/3 | 0 | 1/3 | 0 |
| 3 | 0 | 1/2 | 0 | 1/2 |
| 4 | 1/2 | 0 | 1/2 | 0 |

The transition diagram is

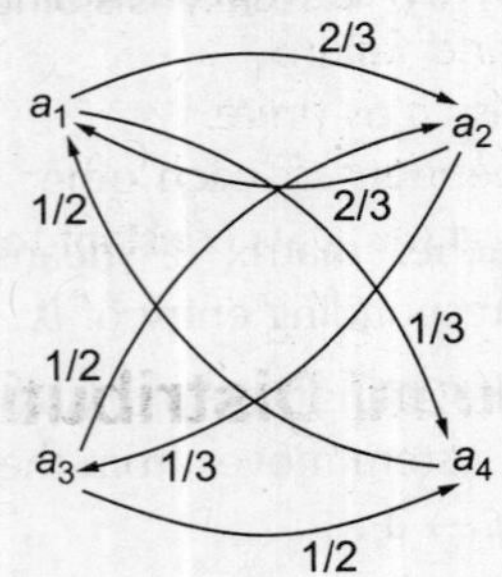


## Chapman-Kolmogorov Equation

$$p_{ij}(m+n) = \sum_K p_{iK}(m) p_{Kj}(n)$$

$$p^{(n)} = p^n$$

The matrix of $n$-step transition probabilities $p^{(n)}$ is obtained by multiplying the matrix of one step transition probabilities $P$ by itself $(n-1)$ times.

***Theorem 1*** If $P$ is the transition matrix of a markov chain, then the $n$-step transition matrix $P^{(n)}$ is equal to the nth power of $P$, i.e., $P^{(n)} = P^n$.

In other words, the problem of finding the $n$-step transition probabilities is reduced to one of the forming powers of a given matrix.

Probability distribution of the system at some arbitrary time is denoted by the probability vector

$$P = (p_1, p_2, \ldots\ldots, p_m)$$

where $p_i$ denotes the probability that the system is in the '$i$th' state.

At the time $t = 0$, when the process begins, the corresponding probability vector

$$p^0 = (p_1^0, p_2^0, \ldots\ldots, p_i^0, \ldots, p_m^0)$$

denotes the initial probability distribution.

Similarly, the $n$th step probability distribution, i.e., the distribution after the 1st $n$-steps is denoted by

$$p^n = (p_1^{(n)}, p_2^{(n)}, \ldots, p_m^{(n)})$$

The (marginal) pmf of the random variable $X_n$ can be obtained from the $n$th step transition probabilities and the initial distribution as follows

$$p^{(n)} = p^{(0)} p^{(n)} = p^{(0)} p^n$$

Thus, the probability distributions of a homogeneous Markov chain are completely determined from the one step transition probability matrix $P$ and the initial probability distribution $p^{(0)}$.

***Theorem 2*** The probability distribution of the system n-steps later is given by $p^{(n)} = p^{(0)} p^n$

## Stationary Distribution of Regular Markov Chain

***Theorem*** Let $P$ be a regular transition matrix of a Markov chain. Then, in the long run, the probability that any state $a_i$ occurs is approximately equal to the component $t_j$ of the unique fixed probability vector $t$ of $P$.

**Stationary Distribution** Stationary distribution of a Markov chain is the unique fixed probability vector $t$ of the regular transition matrix $P$ of the Markov chain because every sequence of probability distribution approaches $t$.

## Absorbing States

A state $a_i$ of a Markov chain is said to be an absorbing state, if the system remains in the state $a_i$ once it enters there i.e., a state is absorbing, if $p_{ii} = 1$.

### Important Theorems

***Theorem 1*** A stochastic matrix $P$ is not regular, if a '1' occurs in the principal main diagonal.

***Theorem 2*** If $P$ and $Q$ are stochastic matrices, then their product $PQ$ is also stochastic matrix. Thus, $p^n$ is stochastic matrix for all positive integer values of $n$.

***Theorem 3*** Let $t = (t_1, t_2, \ldots, t_m)$ be a vector and $T$ be a square matrix whose rows are each the same vector $t$. Then, $p^T = t$, where $P = (p_1, p_2 \ldots, p_m)$ is a probability vector.

***Theorem 4*** The transition matrix $P$ of a Markov chain is a stochastic matrix.
A stochastic matrix $P$ is said to be regular, if all the entries of some power $p^m$ are positive.

## Bernoulli's Distribution

A random variable $X$ which takes two values 0 and 1 with probabilities $q$ and $p$, respectively *i.e.*, $p(x=0)=q$, $p(x=1)=p=1-q$, is called Bernoulli's variate and is said to have Bernoulli's distribution. Sometimes, the two values are +1 and −1 instead of 1 and 0.

## Binomial Distribution

A random variable $X$ is said to follow binomial distribution, if it assumes only non-negative values and its probability mass function is given by,

$$P(X=x)=p(x)=\begin{cases} {}^nC_x p^x q^{n-x}, x=0,1,\ldots,n, \\ \text{and} \quad q=1-p \\ 0, \quad \text{otherwise} \end{cases}$$

$n$ and $p$ are known as parameters of the binomial distribution.

$n$ is sometimes called degree of the binomial distribution.

Binomial distribution is a discrete distribution as $X$ can take only discrete values *viz* $0, 1, 2, \ldots, n$.

Let a random experiment be a set of $n$ independent bernoullian trials, $n$ being finite.

The probability of succes in each trial is a constant $p$, and that of failure be $q = 1-p$.

Then, the probability of $x$ successes and $n-x$ failures in $n$ independent trials, say in the order

$$\underbrace{SS.....S}_{x\text{ times}}\ \underbrace{FF.....F}_{(n-x)\text{ times}} \text{ is}$$

$$p(\underbrace{SS\ldots S}_{x\text{ times}}\ \underbrace{FF\ldots F}_{(n-x)\text{ times}}) = \underbrace{p(S)p(S)\ldots p(S)}_{x\text{ times}}\underbrace{p(F)\ldots p(F)}_{(n-x)\text{ times}}$$

$$= \underbrace{pp\ldots p}_{x\text{ times}}\ \underbrace{qq\ldots q}_{(n-x)\text{ times}}$$

$$= p^x q^{n-x}$$

Any variable which follows binomial distribution is known as binomial variate,

Probability $p(x)$ is sometimes denoted by $b(x, n, p)$.

## Derivation

In $n$ trials $x$ successes can occur in ${}^nc_x$ ways, each with probability $p^x q^{n-x}$.

Hence, probability of $x$ successes in $n$ trials in any of these ways is given by

$${}^nc_x p^x q^{n-x},$$

Where $x = 0, 1, 2, \ldots, n$.

Thus, binomial probability distribution is

| $x$ | 0 | 1 | ... | $x$ | ... | $n$ |
|---|---|---|---|---|---|---|
| $p(x)$ | ${}^nC_0 p^0 q^n$ | ${}^nC_1 pq^{n-1}$ | | ${}^nC_x p^x q^{n-x}$ | ... | ${}^nC_n p^n q^0$ |

The successive terms in the distribution alone can be obtained from $(q+p)^n$ expansion.

## Expected Frequencies of Binomial Distribution

Let us suppose that $n$ trials constitute an experiment. If this experiment is repeated $n$ times, the frequency function of binomial distribution is given by

$$f(x) = Np(x)$$
$$= N\,{}^nC_x p^x q^{n-x}, \quad n = 0, 1, 2, \ldots, n$$

and the expected frequencies of $0, 1, 2, \ldots, n$ successes are successive terms of the binomial expansion $N(q+p)^n$, where $q + p = 1$

$$\sum_{x=0}^{n} p(x) = \sum_{x=0}^{n} {}^nC_x p^x q^{n-x} = (q+p)^n = 1^n = 1$$

## Physical Conditions for Binomial Distribution

**(i)** Each trial results in two mutually disjoint outcomes, termed as success and failure.

**(ii)** The number of trials '$n$' is finite.

**(iii)** The trials are independent of each other.

**(iv)** The probability fo success '$p$' is constant for each trial.

## Moments of Binomial Distribution

$$\mu_1' = np$$
$$\mu_2' = n(n-1)p^2 + np$$
$$\mu_3' = n(n-1)(n-2)p^3 + 3n(n-1)p^2 + np$$
$$\mu_4' = n(n-1)(n-2)(n-3)p^4 + 6n(n-1)(n-2)p^3 + 7n(n-1)p^2 + np$$

## First Four Central Moments of Binomial Distributions

$$\mu_1 = 0$$
$$\mu_2 = \mu_2' - \mu_1'^2 = npq$$

$$\mu_3 = \mu_3' - 3\mu_2'\mu_1' + 2\mu_1'^3 = npq(q-p)$$
$$\mu_4 = \mu_4' - 4\mu_3'\mu_1' + 6\mu_2'\mu_1'^2 - 3\mu_1'^4$$
$$= npq(1+3(n-2)pq)$$

Pearson's $\beta$ coefficients and $\gamma$ coefficients

$$\beta_1 = \frac{\mu_3^2}{\mu_2^3} = \frac{(1-2p)^2}{npq}$$
$$\beta_2 = \frac{\mu_4}{\mu_2^2} = \frac{1-6pq}{npq}$$
$$\gamma_1 = \sqrt{\beta_1} = \frac{1-2p}{\sqrt{npq}}$$
$$\gamma_2 = \beta_2 - 3 = \frac{1-6pq}{npq}$$

***Example 14.*** *In a binomial distribution consisting of 5 independent trials, probabilities of 1 and 2 successes are 0.4096 and 0.2048, respectively. Find the parameter 'p' of the distribution.*

**Solution.** Let $X \sim B(n, p)$. In usual notations, we are given

$$n = 5,\ p(1) = 0.4096 \text{ and } P(2) = 0.2048$$

According to Binomial probability law,

$$P(X = x) = p(x) = \binom{5}{x} p^x (1-p)^{5-x},\ x = 0, 1, 2, \ldots, 5$$

Now, $$p(1) = \binom{5}{1} p(1-p)^4 = 0.4096 \quad \ldots\text{(i)}$$

and $$p(2) = \binom{5}{2} p^2 (1-p)^3 = 0.2048 \quad \ldots\text{(ii)}$$

Dividing Eq. (i) by Eq. (ii), we have

$$\frac{\binom{5}{1} p(1-p)^4}{\binom{5}{2} p^2 (1-p)^3} = \frac{0.4096}{0.2048}$$

$$\Rightarrow \frac{5(1-p)}{10p} = 2 \Rightarrow p = \frac{1}{5} = 0.2$$

# Poisson Distribution

(As an approximation of binomial distribution)
It is a limiting case of binomial distribution.
In binomial distribution, if

**(i)** $n$ (the number of trials) $\to \infty$,

**(ii)** $p$ (the constant probability of success for each trial is indefinitely small, *i.e.*, $p \to o$,

**(iii)** $np = \lambda$ (say) is finite, then

$$b(n, p) \to p(x) = \frac{e^{-x}\lambda^x}{x!}$$

It is poisson distribution.
A random variable $X$ is said to follow a poisson distribution, if it assumes only non-negative values and its probability mass function is

$$p(x, \lambda) = P(X = x) = \frac{e^{\lambda}\lambda^x}{x!}, x = 0, 1, 2, \ldots$$
$$= 0, \text{ otherwise}$$

Here, $\lambda > 0$ is called parameter of the distribution.
Poisson distribution satisfies following properties

$$\sum_{K=0}^{\infty} P(X = x) = e^{-\lambda} \sum_{x=0}^{\infty} \frac{\lambda^x}{x!}$$
$$= e^{-\lambda} e^{\lambda} = 1$$

The corresponding distribution function is

$$F(x) = P(X \le x) = \sum_{r=0}^{x} p(r) = e^{-\lambda} \sum_{r=0}^{x} \frac{\lambda^r}{r!};\ x = 0, 1, \ldots$$

## Occurrences of Poisson Distribution

Poisson distribution occurs when there are events which do not occur as outcomes of a definite number of trials (unlike that in binomial) of an experiment but which occurs at random points of time and space where in our interest lies only in the number of occurrences of the event, not in the non-occurrences.

## Moments of the Poisson Distribution

$$\mu_1' = \lambda$$
$$\mu_2' = \lambda^2 + \lambda$$
$$\mu_3' = \lambda^3 + 3\lambda^2 + \lambda$$
$$\mu_4' = \lambda^4 + 6\lambda^3 + 7\lambda^2 + \lambda$$

Also, moments about mean

$$\mu_2 = \lambda$$
$$\mu_3 = \lambda$$
$$\mu_4 = 3\lambda^2 + \lambda$$

## Poisson Approximation to Binomial Distribution

For large $n$, the calculation of binomial probabilities is very cumbersome. In such cases, they are computed by approximation procedures.
For (1) $n \to \infty$,
(2) $p \to 0$,
Binomial distribution can be approximated by poisson distribution with $\lambda = np$.

## Negative Binomial Distribution

**Definition** A random variable $X$ is said to follow a negative binomial distribution, if its probability mass function is given by

$$p(x) = P(X = x) = \begin{cases} {}^{x+r-1}C_{r-1} p^r q^x, & \text{if } x = 0, 1, 2, \ldots \\ 0, & \text{otherwise} \end{cases}$$

***Example 15.*** *A car hire firm has two cars, which it hires out day by day. The number of demands for a car on each day is distributed as a Poisson distribution with mean 1.5. Calculate the proportion of days on which (i) neither car is used and (ii) the proportion of days on which some demand is refused.*

**Solution.** Here, the random variable $X$, which denotes the number of demands for a car on any day follows Poisson distribution with mean $\lambda = 1.5$. The proportion of days on which there are $x$ demands for a car is given by

$$P(X = x) = \frac{e^{-1.5}(1.5)^x}{x!};\ x = 0, 1, 2, \ldots$$

(i) Proportion of days on which neither car is used is given by

$$P(x = 0) = e^{-1.5} = \left\{-1 - 1.5 + \frac{(1.5)^2}{2!} - \frac{(1.5)^3}{3!} + \frac{(1.5)^4}{4!} - \ldots\right\}$$

$$= 0.2231$$

(ii) Proportion of days on which some demand is refused is

$$P(X > 2) = 1 - P(X \le 2) = 1 - \{P(X = 0) + P(X = 1) + P(X = 2)\}$$

$$= 1 - e^{-1.5}\left\{1 + 1.5 + \frac{(1.5)^2}{2!}\right\} = 1 - 0.2231 \times 3.625 = 0.19126$$

***Example 16.*** *A manufacturer, who produces medicine bottles, finds that 0.1% of the bottles are defective. The bottles are packed in boxes containing 500 bottles. A drug manufacturer buys 100 boxes from the producer of bottles. Using Poisson distribution, find how many boxes will contain* (i) no defective and (ii) atleast two defective.

[given, $e^{-0.5} = 0.6065$]

**Solution.** In the usual notations, we are given $N = 100, n = 500, p =$ Probability of a defective bottle $= 0.001$ and $\lambda = np = 500 \times 0.001 = 0.5$

Let the random variable $X$ denote the number of defective bottles in a box of 500. Then, by Poisson probability law, the probability of $x$ defective bottles in a box is

$$P(X = x) = \frac{e^{-0.5}(0.5)^x}{x!} = \frac{0.6065 \times (0.5)^x}{x!};\ x = 0, 1, 2, \ldots$$

Hence, in a consignment of 100 boxes, the frequency (number) of boxes containing $x$ defective bottles is

$$f(x) = N \cdot P(X = x) = \frac{100 \times 0.6065 \times (0.5)^x}{x!}$$

(i) Number of boxes containing no defective bottle

$$= 100 \times P(X = 0) = 100 \times 0.6065 \simeq 61$$

(ii) Number of boxes containing atleast two defective bottles

$$= 100\,[P(X \ge 2)] = 100\,\{1 - (X = 0) - P(X = 1)\}$$

$$= 100\,(1 - 0.6065 - 0.6065 \times 0.5) = 100 \times 0.09025 \simeq 9$$

## Geometric Distribution

If $p(x) = q^x p,\ x = 0, 1, 2, \ldots$, then it is called probability function of geometric distribution.

Negative binomial distribution may be regarded as the generalization of geometric distribution.

## Discrete Uniform Distribution

A random variable $X$ is said to have uniform distribution on $n$ points $\{x_1, x_2, \ldots, x_n\}$, if its pmf is given by

$$P(X = x_i) = \frac{1}{n},\ i = 1, 2, \ldots, n$$

## Hypergeometric Distribution

### Conditions

(i) Population is finite,

(ii) Sampling is done without replacement.

(iii) Events are random and stochastically dependent. Under these conditions, probability distribution is called hypergeometric distribution.

### Definition

A discrete random variable $X$ is said to follow the hypergeometric distribution, if it assumes only non-negative values and its probability mass function is given by

$$P(X = k) = h(k, N, M, n)$$

$$= \frac{\binom{M}{k}\binom{N-M}{n-k}}{\binom{N}{n}} = \frac{{}^{M}C_k\ {}^{N-M}C_{n-k}}{{}^{N}C_n}$$

$$k = 0, 1, 2, \ldots, \min(n, M)$$
$$= 0, \text{ otherwise}$$

$N$, $M$ and $n$ are known as the three parameters of hypergeometric distribution.

$$\text{Mean } E(X) = \frac{nM}{N}$$

$$V(X) = \frac{NM(N - M)(N - n)}{N^2(N - 1)}$$

## Approximation to Binomial Distribution

Hypergeometric distribution tends to binomial distribution as $N \to \infty$ and $\frac{M}{N} \to P$.

## Multinomial Distribution

It is generalization of binomial distribution.

**Condition** There are more than two mutually exclusive outcomes of a trial.

Then, the probability distribution is called multinomial distribution.

Let $E_1, E_2, \ldots, E_k$ be $k$ mutually exclusive and exhaustive outcomes of a trial with their respective probabilities $p_1, p_2, \ldots, p_k$.

Let $E_1$ occurs $x_1$ times,

$E_2$ occurs $x_2$ times,

$\vdots$

$E_k$ occurs $x_k$ times,

in $n$ independent trials.

Then, $p(E_1^{x_1}, E_2^{x_2}, \ldots, E_k^{x_k}) = C \cdot p_1^{x_1}, p_2^{x_2}, \ldots, p_k^{x_k}$,

where $C$ is the number of permutations of $n$ objects of which $x_1$ are of one kind, $x_2$ are of another kind, .... $x_k$ are of $k$th kind, and

$$C = \frac{n!}{x_1!x_2!\ldots x_k!}, 0 \le x_i \le n, i = 1, 2, \ldots, n$$

# Theoritical Continuous Distribution

Rectangular (or uniform) distribution probability density function

$$f(x) = \begin{cases} K, & a < x < b \\ 0, & \text{otherwise} \end{cases}$$

Total probability = 1

$$\Rightarrow \quad \int_a^b f(x)\,dx = 1 \quad \Rightarrow \int_a^b K\,dx = 1$$

$$\Rightarrow \quad K(b-a) = 1 \quad \Rightarrow K = \frac{1}{b-a}$$

Thus, $$f(x) = \begin{cases} \dfrac{1}{b-a}, & a < x < b \\ 0, & \text{otherwise} \end{cases}$$

> ***Note*** **(a)** $a$ and $b$ are two parameters of the uniform distribution on $[a, b]$.
>
> **(b)** Uniform distribution is also known as rectangular distribution. Its distribution function is
>
> 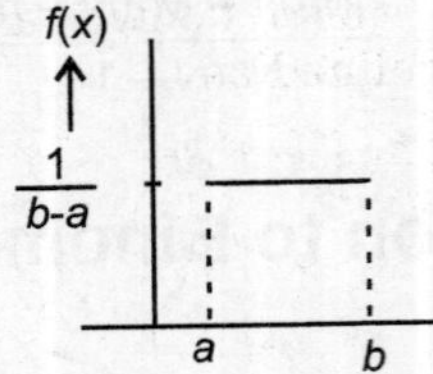
> 
>
> $$F(x) = \begin{cases} 0, & \text{if } -\infty < x < a \\ \dfrac{x-a}{b-a}, & \text{if } a \le x \le b \\ 1, & \text{if } b < x < \infty \end{cases}$$
>
> Probability density function 'curve' for uniform distribution.
>
> 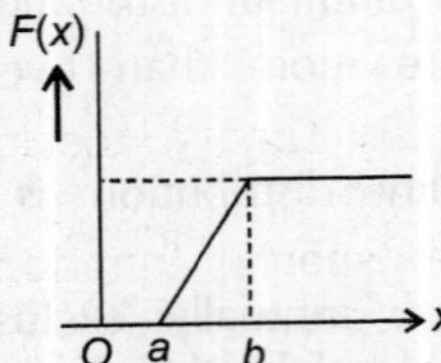
> 
>
> Cumulative distribution function 'curve' for uniform distribution.

**Properties**

**(i)** Mean $= E(x) = \dfrac{b+a}{2}$

**(ii)** $\mu_2 = \sigma^2 = \dfrac{1}{12}(b-a)^2$

**(iii)** $E(X - \bar{x}) =$ Mean deviation from mean $= \dfrac{b-a}{4}$

# Triangular Distribution

Probability density function for triangular distribution

$$f(x) = \begin{cases} \dfrac{2(x-a)}{(b-a)(c-a)}, & a \le x \le c \\ \dfrac{2(b-x)}{(b-a)(b-c)}, & c < x < b \end{cases}$$

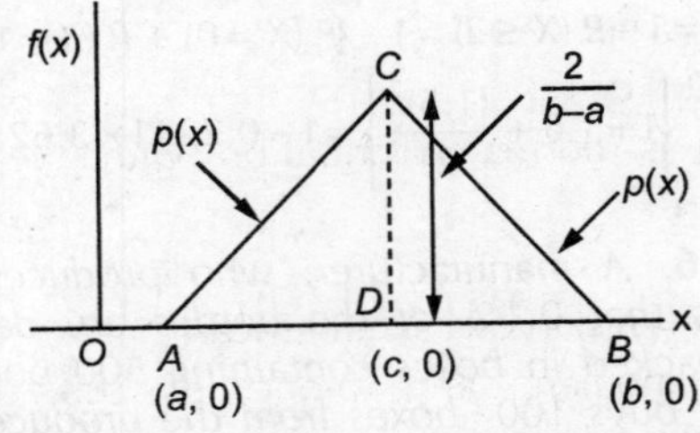


Probability density curve for a triangular distribution.

# Normal Distribution

A random variable $X$ is said to have a normal distribution with parameters $\mu$(called "mean") and $\sigma^2$ (called "variance"), if its density function is given by the probability law

$$f(x, \mu, \sigma) = \frac{1}{\sigma\sqrt{2\pi}} e^{-\frac{1}{2}\left(\frac{x-\mu}{\sigma}\right)^2},$$

$$-\infty < x < \infty, \quad -\infty < \mu < \infty, \sigma > 0$$

Random variable $X$ with mean $\mu$ and variance $\sigma^2$ is represented by $X \sim N(\mu, \sigma^2)$.

If $X \sim N(\mu, \sigma^2)$, then $Z = \dfrac{X-\mu}{\sigma}$ is called standard normal variate with $E(z) = 0$, and $\text{var}(z) = 1$, and then $z \sim N(0, 1)$.

The probability density function,

$$\phi(z) = \frac{1}{\sqrt{2\pi}} e^{-z^2/2}, \quad \infty < z < \infty$$

(of standard normal variate $z$).

# Probability Distribution Function

$$\phi(Z) = P(Z \le z) = \int_{-\infty}^{z} \phi(u)\,du$$

**Properties**

**(i)** $\phi(-z) = 1 - \phi(z)$

**(ii)** $P(a \le X \le b) = \phi\left(\dfrac{b-\mu}{\sigma}\right) - \phi\left(\dfrac{a-\mu}{\sigma}\right)$

The graph of probability density function $\phi(z)$ is bell shaped curve.

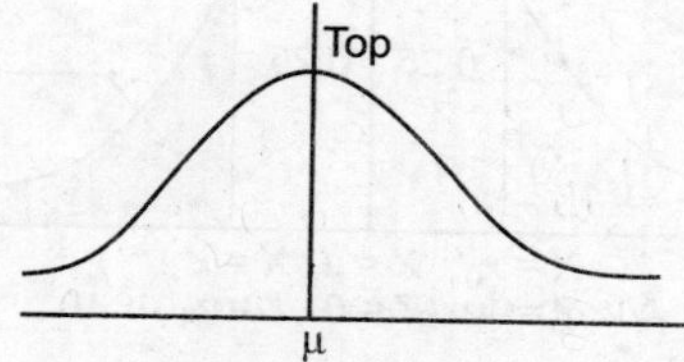


For large σ, curve tends to flatten out.

For smaller σ, curve tends to have sharp peak.

## Normal Distribution as a Limiting Form (or an approximation) of a Binomial Distribution

In $B(n, p)$, if

**(i)** $n \to \infty$

**(ii)** neither $p$ nor $q \to 0$,

then $B(n, p) \sim N(\mu, \sigma^2)$

Here, $N(\mu, \sigma^2)$ is normal distribution with mean μ and variance $\sigma^2$.

**Properties**

**(i)** About $x = h$ curve is symmetrical.

**(ii)** Mean, median, and mode of the distribution coincide.

**(iii)** As $x$ increases, $f(x)$ decreases.

$$[p(x)]_{max} = \frac{1}{\sigma\sqrt{2\pi}}$$

**(iv)** $\beta_1 = 0, \beta_2 = 3$

**(v)** $\mu_{2r+1} = 0,\ r = 0, 1, 2, \ldots$

$\mu_{2r} = 1\cdot 3\cdot 5\ldots(2r-1)\sigma^{2r},\ r = 0, 1, 2, \ldots$

**(vi)** $f(x) \geq 0$

**(vii)** $x$-axis is asymptote.

**(viii)** Point of inflexion is $x = \mu \pm \sigma$, $f(x) = \frac{1}{\sigma\sqrt{2\pi}} e^{-\frac{1}{2}x}$

**(ix)** Mean deviation about mean is

$$\sqrt{\frac{2}{\pi}}\sigma \cong \frac{4}{5}\sigma \text{ (approximately)}$$

$$QD = \frac{Q_3 - Q_1}{2} = \frac{2}{3}\sigma$$

$$QD : MD : SD = \frac{2}{3}\sigma : \frac{4}{5}\sigma : \sigma$$

$$= \frac{2}{3} : \frac{4}{5} : 1$$

$$= 10 : 12 : 15$$

**(x)** Area property

$P(\mu - \sigma < x < \mu + \sigma) = 0.6826$

$P(\mu - 2\sigma < x < \mu + 2\sigma) = 0.9544$

$P(\mu - 3\sigma < x < \mu + 3\sigma) = 0.9973$

## Fitting of Normal Distribution

In order to fit normal distribution to the given data, we first calculate the mean μ (say) and standard deviation σ (say) from the given data, then the normal curve fitted to the given data is given by,

$$f(x) = \frac{1}{\sigma\sqrt{2\pi}} e^{\frac{-(x-\mu)^2}{2\sigma^2}}, -\infty < x < \infty$$

To calculate the expected normal frequencies we first find the standard normal variates corresponding to the lower limits of each of the class intervals, *i.e.*, compute $Z_i = \frac{x_i' - \mu}{\sigma}$, where $x_i'$ is the lower limit of the *i*th class intervals. Then, the areas under the normal curve to the left of the ordinate at $z = z_i$, say, $\phi(z_i)$ are computed from the table. Finally the areas for the successive class intervals are obtained by subtraction, *viz.*, $\phi(z_{i+1}) - \phi(z_i)$, $(i = 1, 2, \ldots, n)$ and on multiplying these areas by $N$, we get expected normal frequencies.

Normal approximation to Binomial distribution.

For **(i)** $n \to \infty$

**(ii)** $p \not\to 0$

Binomial distribution tends to normal distribution.

***Theorem*** Let $X$ be a binomial random variate with mean $\bar{X} = np$ and SD $= \sqrt{npq}$, then the limiting form of the distribution of

$$Z = \frac{X - np}{\sqrt{npq}}$$

as $n \to \infty$ is standard normal distribution $N(z, 0, 1)$.

Normal distribution is fairly good even when

**(i)** $n$ is small and $p$ is near to 1/2.

**(ii)** both $np$ and $nq$ are $\geq 5$.

Error function of $x$ (also known as error integral), denoted by erf $x$, is defined as

$$\text{erf}(x) = \frac{2}{\sqrt{\pi}} \int_0^x e^{-t^2} dt \qquad \ldots(i)$$

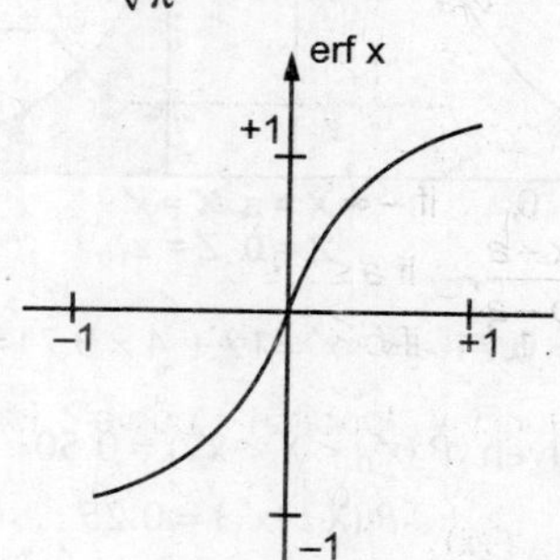


It is used in probability theory, thermodynamics, heat conduction problems, etc.

Erf $x$ is known as a 'special function'. Since, Eq. (i) cannot be evaluated in terms of 'elementary functions' by the usual method of calculus.

***Example 17.*** *X is normally distributed and the mean of X is 12 and SD is 4. Find out the probability of the following*

(a) (i) $X \geq 20$, (ii) $X \leq 20$ and (iii) $0 \leq X \leq 12$

(b) *Find x′, when* $P(X > x') = 0.24$

(c) *Find* $x'_0$ *and* $x'_1$, *when* $P(x'_0 < X < x'_1) = 0.50$ *and* $P(X > x'_1) = 0.25$.

**Solution.** (a) We have $\mu = 12, \sigma = 4$, *i.e.*, $X \sim N(12, 16)$

(i) $P(X \geq 20) = ?$

when $X = 20$, $Z = \dfrac{20-12}{4} = 2$

$\therefore \quad P(X \geq 20) = P(Z \geq 2) = 0.5 - P(0 \leq Z \leq 2)$

$= 0.5 - 0.4772 = 0.0228$

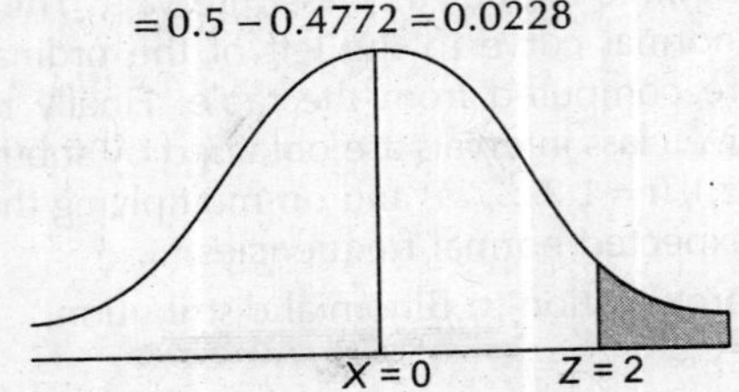


(ii) $P(X \leq 20) = 1 - P(X \geq 20) = 1 - 0.0228 = 0.9722$ [from part (i)]

(iii) $P(0 \leq X \leq 12) = P(-3 \leq Z \leq 0), \left(Z = \dfrac{X-12}{4}\right)$

$= P(0 \leq Z \leq 3) = 0.49865$, (from symmetry)

(b) when $X = x'$, $Z = \dfrac{x'-12}{4} = z_1$, (say)

Then, we are given

$P(X > x') = 0.24 \Rightarrow P(Z > z_1) = 0.24$

$\Rightarrow \quad P(0 < Z < z_1) = 0.26$

Hence, from normal tables, $z_1 = 0.71$ (approx)

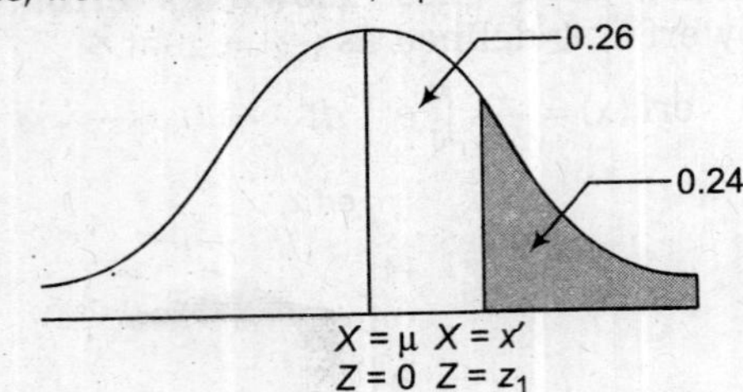


$\therefore \quad \dfrac{x'-12}{4} = 0.71 \Rightarrow x' = 12 + 4 \times 0.71 = 14.84$

(c) We are given $P(x'_0 < X < x'_1) = 0.50$

and $\qquad P(X > x'_1) = 0.25 \qquad$ ...(i)

From Eq. (i), obviously, the points $x'_0$ and $x'_1$ are located as shown in following adjoining.

when $\qquad X = x'_1, Z = \dfrac{x'_1 - 12}{4} = z_1$ (say)

and when $\qquad X = x'_0, Z = \dfrac{x'_0 - 12}{4} = -z_1$

(It is obvious from the figure)

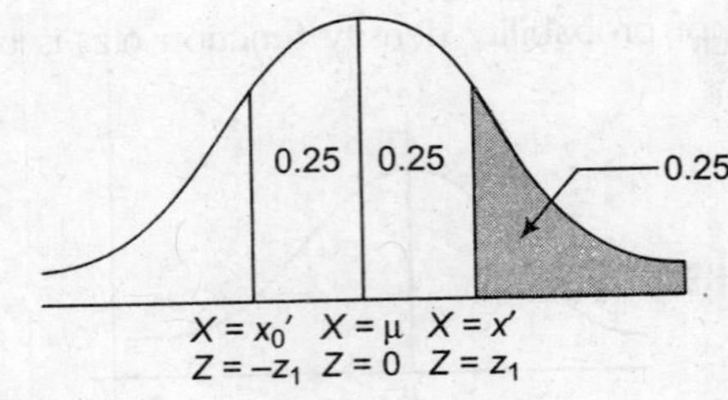


$\Rightarrow \quad P(Z > z_1) = 0.25$

$\Rightarrow \quad P(0 < Z < z_1) = 0.25$

$z_1 = 0.67$ (from table)

$\therefore \quad \dfrac{x'_1 - 12}{4} = 0.67 \Rightarrow x'_1 = 12 + 4 \times 0.67 = 14.68$

and $\quad \dfrac{x_0' - 12}{4} = -0.67$

$\Rightarrow \quad x'_0 = 12 - 4 \times 0.67 = 9.32$

***Example 18.*** *The marks obtained by a number of students for a certain subject are assumed to be approximately normally distributed with mean value 65 and with a standard deviation of 5. If 3 students are taken at random from this set, what is the probability that exactly 2 of them will have marks over 70?*

**Solution.** Let the real value X denote the marks obtained by the given set of students in the given subject. Then, we are given that $X \sim N(\mu, \sigma^2)$, where $\mu = 65$ and $\sigma = 5$. The probability '$p$' that a randomly selected student from the given set gets marks over 70 is given by $p = P(X > 70)$.

When $\qquad X = 70, Z = \dfrac{X-\mu}{\sigma} = \dfrac{70-65}{5} = 1$

Hence, $\qquad p = P(X > 70) = P(Z > 1) = 0.5 - P(0 \leq Z \leq 1)$

$= 0.5 - 0.3413 = 0.1587$ [from normal probability tables]

Since, this probability is same for each student of the set, the required probability that out of 3 students selected at random from the set, exactly 2 will have marks over 70, is given by the binomial probability law

$${}^3C_2\, p^2 (1-p) = 3 \times (0.1587)^2 \times (0.8413) = 0.06357$$

## Gamma Distribution

$$f(x) = \begin{cases} \dfrac{e^{-x} x^{\lambda}}{\lambda}, & \lambda > 0, 0 < x < \infty \\ 0, & \text{otherwise} \end{cases}$$

$\lambda$ being parameter.

Cumulative distribution function.

$$F_X(x) = \begin{cases} \int_0^x f(u)\,du \\ 0 \end{cases}$$

Mean $\left.\begin{aligned} \bar{x} &= \lambda \\ \mu_2 &= \lambda \end{aligned}\right\}$

$$\beta_1 = \frac{u}{\lambda}, \beta_2 = 3 + \frac{6}{\lambda}$$

Standard gamma variate tends to standard normal variate as $\lambda \to \infty$.

Here, $\bar{x} = \mu_2$ (like in Poisson distribution).

## Beta Distribution Function of First Kind

$$f(x) = \begin{cases} \frac{1}{B(\mu, \nu)} x^{\mu-1}(1-x)^{\nu-1}, \text{ for } \mu, \nu > 0 \\ \qquad\qquad 0 < x < 1 \\ 0, \quad \text{otherwise} \end{cases}$$

where $\beta(\mu, \nu)$ is called Beta function, $\mu$ and $\nu$ being its parameters. It is denoted by $\beta$, $(\mu\ u)$.

Its coumulative distribution function is denoted by

$$f(x) = \begin{cases} 0 & , \text{if } x < 0 \\ \int_0^x \frac{1}{B(\mu, \nu)} u^{\mu-1}(1-u)^{\nu-1} du, & \text{if } 0 < x < 1, (\mu, \nu) > 0 \\ 1 & , \text{if } x > 1 \end{cases}$$

## Beta Distribution Function of Second Kind

For it pdf is given by,

$$f(x) = \begin{cases} \frac{1}{\beta(\mu, \nu)} \frac{x^{\mu-1}}{(1+x)^{\mu+\nu}}, \text{ if } \mu, \nu > 0 \text{ and } 0 < x < 1 \\ 0 \qquad\qquad, \text{otherwise} \end{cases}$$

Here, $\beta(\mu, \nu)$ is beta function $\mu$, $\nu$ being its parameters. Beta distribution function of 2nd kind is denoted by $\beta_2(\mu, \nu)$.

## Exponential Distribution

Its pdf is

$$f(x) = \begin{cases} \theta e^{-\theta x}, \text{ if } x \geq 0 \\ 0 \qquad, \text{otherwise} \end{cases}$$

Its cumulative probability distribution function is given by,

$$f(x) = \begin{cases} 1 - e^{-\theta x}, \text{ if } x \geq 0 \\ 0 \qquad, \text{otherwise} \end{cases}$$

## Laplace (Double Exponential Distribution)

$$f(x) = \frac{1}{2} e^{-|x|}, \quad -\infty < x < \infty.$$

## Weibul Distribution

Its pdf is given by,

$$f(x) = ce^{c-1}e^{-x^c}, \quad x > 0, c > 0$$

c being parameter.

## Logistic Distribution

Its pdf is

$$f(x) = \frac{1}{2}\left[1 + \tanh\left\{\frac{1}{2}\frac{(x-\alpha)}{\beta}\right\}\right], \beta > 0$$

## Cauchy's Distribution

Its pdf is

$$f(x) = \frac{1}{\pi(1+x^2)}, \quad -\infty < x < \infty$$

$$d\,p(\theta) = \begin{cases} \frac{1}{\pi} d\theta, -\frac{\pi}{2} \leq \theta \leq \frac{\pi}{2} \\ 0, \qquad \text{otherwise} \end{cases}$$

## Order Statistics

Let $X_1, X_2, \ldots, X_n$ be $n$ independent and identically distributed variates, each with cumulative distribution function $F(x)$. If these variables are arranged in ascending order of magnitude

$$X_{(1)} \leq X_{(2)} \leq \ldots \leq X_{(n)},$$

we call $X_{(r)}$ as the $r$th order statistic, $r = 1, 2, \ldots, n$.

$$\begin{aligned} F_n(x) &= P(X_n \leq x), \quad i = 1, 2, \ldots, n \\ &= P[(X_1 \leq x) \cap (X_2 \leq x) \cap \ldots \cap (X_n \leq x)] \\ &= P(X_1 \leq x)P(X_2 \leq x) \ldots P(X_n \leq x) \\ &= \underbrace{F(x) \cdot F(x) \cdot \ldots \cdot F(x)}_{n \text{ times}} \end{aligned}$$

$$F_n(x) = [F(x)]^n$$

## Distribution of Range

$W = X_n - X_1$. Its pdf is

$$g(w) = n(n-1)\int_{-\infty}^{\infty} f(x)[f(x+w) - f(x)]^{n-2} f(x+w)\,dx, w \geq 0$$

Its cumulative distribution function is

$$G(w) = n\int_{-\infty}^{\infty} f(x)[f(x+w) - f(x)]^{n-1} dx.$$

## Random Sample

It is the collection of members of a population in which each member has equal chance (or probability) of being included in the sample.

## Degrees of Freedom (dof or df)

Degrees of freedom of a statistic is a positive integer, (denoted by $\nu$), $\nu = n - k$, where $n$ is the number of independent observations of the random sample and $k$ is the number of population parameters which are calculated with the sample data.

Thus, the dof $\nu = n - k$ is the difference between $n$ the sample size and $k$ the number of independent constraints imposed on the observations in the sample.

## Sampling Distribution

Let population be finite of size $N$ and each sample drawn from it be of size $n$.

Then, total number of samples is given by,

$$N_{C_n} = \frac{N!}{n!N-n!} = k \text{ say}$$

Let $S$ be a statistic (such as mean, standard deviation, median, mode etc.). Its value is found for each sample.

If given sample is $\{x_1, x_2, \ldots, x_n\}$, then $S = S(x_1, x_2, \ldots, x_n)$

Since, there are $k$ samples, so statistic $S$ has $k$ values

| Sample number | 1 | 2 | ... | $k$. |
|---|---|---|---|---|
| Statistic $S$ | $S_1$ | $S_2$ | ... | $S_k$. |

Sampling distribution (SD) of the statistic is the set of values $\{S_1, S_2, \ldots, S_k\}$ of the statistic, $S$ obtained one for each sample.

## Standard Error (SE)

It is the standard deviation of the sampling distribution of a statistic $S$. It gives an index of the precision of the estimate of the parameters. As the sample size increases, standard error (SE) decreases.

## Sampling Distribution of Mean ($\sigma$ unknown) *t*-Distribution

For small sample of size $n$ (< 30), the unknown $\sigma$ can be substituted by $s$, where

$$s^2 = \sum_{n=1}^{n} \frac{(x_i - \bar{x})^2}{n-1}$$

provided. We make assumption that the sample is drawn from a normal population.

In this case, statistic for inference on population mean $\mu$ is

$$t = \frac{\bar{x} - \mu}{s/\sqrt{n}}$$

The graph of $t$-distribution is

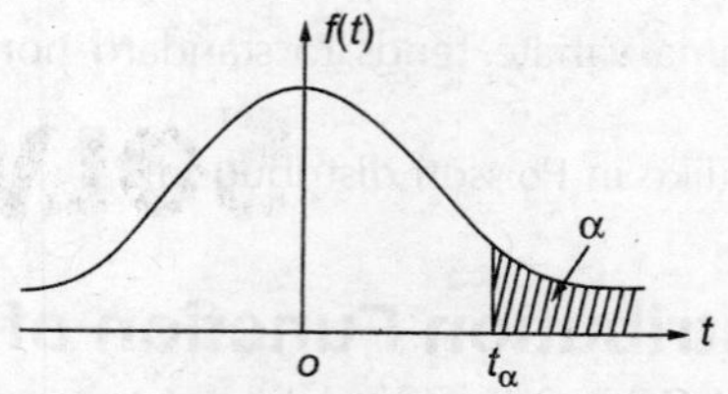


The $t$-distribution curve is symmetric about the mean $O$, unimodal, bell shaped and asymptotic on both sides of $t$-axis. It is similar to normal curve.

Variance for it is more than 1. (Variance for normal distribution is 1) $t$-distribution is more variable.

As $n \to \infty$, variance of $t$-distribution approaches 1, and $t$-distribution itself approaches the standard normal distribution.

(For $n \geq 30$, standard normal distribution provides a good approximation to the $t$-distribution.)

## Chi-square Variate ($\chi^2$-Variate)

Chi-square variate the square of a standard normal variate is known as a chi-square variate with 1 degree of freedom.

If $X \sim N(\mu, \sigma^2)$, then

$$Z = \frac{X - \mu}{\sigma} \sim N(0, 1)$$

and $Z^2 = \left(\frac{X-\mu}{\sigma}\right)^2$ is a chi-square variate with 1 df (degree of freedom).

## *F*-statistic

If $X$ and $Y$ are two independent chi-square variates with $\nu_1$ and $\nu_2$ df, respectively. Then, $F$-statistic is defined by

$$F = \frac{X/\nu_1}{Y/\nu_2}$$

## Fisher's *z*-Distribution

If $F$-distribution with $(\nu_1, \nu_2)$ df is put in the form

$$F = \exp(2z),$$

then $$Z = \frac{1}{2}\log_e F$$

This $Z$ is called fisher's $z$-variate with $(\nu_1, \nu_2)$ degrees of freedom.

# SOLVED EXAMPLES

## Type I (*Only one correct option*)

***Example 1.*** *If $X_1$ and $X_2$ are independent Cauchy variates with parameters $(\lambda_1, \mu_1)$ and $(\lambda_2, \mu_2)$ respectively, then $X_1 + X_2$ is*

(a) a normal variate $N(\lambda_1+\lambda_2, \mu_1+\mu_2)$.

(b) a normal variate $N(\lambda_1+\lambda_2, \mu_1^2+\mu_2^2)$.

(c) a cauchy variate with parameters $(\lambda_1+\lambda_2, \mu_1+\mu_2)$.

(d) a cauchy variate with parameters $(\lambda_1-\lambda_2, \mu_1-\mu_2)$.

**Solution.** (c) Using characteristic function $\phi_{X_j}(t) = e^{i(\mu_j t - \lambda_j |t|)}$, $j = 1, 2, ..$

$$\text{Now, } \phi_{X_1+X_2}(t) = e^{i[(\mu_1+\mu_2)t-(\lambda_1+\lambda_2|t|)]}$$

$$= e^{i(\mu_1 t-\lambda_1|t|)+i(\mu_2 t-\lambda_2|t|)}$$

$$= e^{i(\mu_1 t-\lambda_1|t|)}e^{i(\mu_2 t-\lambda_2|t|)} = \phi_{X_1}(t)\,\phi_{X_2}(t)$$

The characteristic function being unique, so $X_1 + X_2$ is a cauchy variate with parameters $(\lambda_1+\lambda_2, \mu_1+\mu_2)$.

***Example 2.*** *For Gamma distribution of a random variable X, which is true?*

(a) $E(X) = \text{var}(X)$  (b) $[E(X)]^2 = \text{var}(X)$

(c) $E(X) = [\text{var}(X)]^2$  (d) None of these

**Solution.** (a) We know cumulant generating function of Gamma distribution is $K_X(t) = \log M_X(t)$

$$= \log(1-t)^{-\lambda} \qquad |t| < 1$$

$$= -\lambda \log(1-t)$$

$$= -\lambda\left[-t - \frac{t^2}{2} - \frac{t^3}{3} - \dots\right]$$

$$= \lambda\left[t + \frac{t^2}{2} + \frac{t^3}{3} + \dots\right]$$

Mean $= K_1 =$ coefficient of $t$ in $K_X(t) = \lambda$

$\mu_2 = K_2 =$ coefficient of $\dfrac{t^2}{2!}$ in $K_X(t) = \lambda$

Thus, mean $E(X) = \text{var}(X) = \mu_2$.

***Example 3.*** *Moment generating function of Gamma distribution about origin, $M_X(t)$ is*

(a) $(1+t)^{\lambda}, |t| < 1$  (b) $(1-t)^{\lambda}, |t| < 1$

(c) $(1+t)^{-\lambda}, |t| < 1$  (d) $(1-t)^{-\lambda}, |t| < 1$

**Solution.** (d) $M_X(t) = E(e^{tx}) = \int_0^\infty e^{tx} f(x)\, dx$

$$= \int_0^\infty e^{tx} \frac{1}{\Gamma\lambda} e^{-x} x^{\lambda-1} dx$$

$$= \frac{1}{\Gamma\lambda}\int_0^\infty e^{-(1-t)x} x^{\lambda-1} dx$$

$$= \frac{1}{\Gamma\lambda}\cdot\frac{\Gamma\lambda}{(1-t)^\lambda}, |t| < 1$$

$$M_x(t) = (1-t)^{-\lambda}, |t| < 1$$

***Example 4.*** *Let $X \sim N(\mu, \sigma^2)$. If $\sigma^2 = \mu^2$, $(\mu > 0)$, then the value of $p(X < -\mu \mid X < \mu)$ in terms of cumulative function of N(0, 1) is*

(a) $2[1 - p(z \le 1)]$  (b) $2[1 - p(z \le 2)]$

(c) $[1 - p(z \le 1)]$  (d) $[1 - p(z \le 2)]$

**Solution.** (b) $P(X < -\mu \mid X < \mu)$

$$= P\frac{(X < -\mu \cap X < \mu)}{P(X < \mu)} = \frac{P(X < -\mu)}{P(X < \mu)} \qquad (\text{here, } \mu > 0)$$

$$= \frac{P\left(\dfrac{X-\mu}{\sigma} < -\dfrac{2\mu}{\sigma}\right)}{P\left(\dfrac{X-\mu}{\sigma} < \dfrac{\mu-\mu}{\sigma}\right)}$$

$$= \frac{P\left(\dfrac{X-\mu}{\sigma} < -2\right)}{P\left(\dfrac{X-\mu}{\sigma} < 0\right)} \qquad (\text{as } \mu^2 = \sigma^2)$$

$$= \frac{P(Z < -2)}{P(Z < 0)} = \frac{P(Z > 2)}{P(Z < 0)} \qquad (\text{by symmetry})$$

$$= \frac{P(Z > 2)}{1/2} = 2P(Z > 2)$$

$$= 2[1 - P(Z \le 2)]$$

***Example 5.*** *A fair dice is tossed 7 times. The probability that a 5 or a 6 occurs atleast once is*

(a) $1-(1/3)^7$  (b) $1-(2/3)^7$

(c) $(2/3)^7$  (d) $(1/3)^7$

**Solution.** (b) $p = \dfrac{1}{3}, q = \dfrac{2}{3}$

$q =$ probability that 1, 2, 3 or 4 occurs in one toss.

***Example 6.*** *A distributor of bean seeds determine from extensive tests that 5% of large batch of seeds will not germinate. He sells the seeds in packets of 200 and guarantees 90% germination. The probability that a particular packet will violate the guarantee is*

(a) $1 - \sum_{x=0}^{20} \dfrac{e^{-10}\cdot 10^x}{x!}$  (b) $1 - \sum_{x=0}^{20} \dfrac{e^{-10}\cdot x^{10}}{10!}$

(c) $\sum_{x=0}^{20} \dfrac{e^{-10}\cdot 10^x}{x!}$  (d) $\sum_{x=0}^{20} \dfrac{e^{-x}\cdot x^{10}}{x!}$

**Solution.** (a) $p =$ probability of not germinating $= \dfrac{5}{100}$

$\lambda =$ mean number of seeds in a sample of 200 which do not germinate $= np = 10$

$X =$ number of seeds that do not germinate

(= random variable)

$$P(X > 20) = 1 - P(x \le 20) = 1 - \sum_{x=0}^{20} \frac{e^{-10}10^x}{x!}$$

$P(X > 20)$ = Probability that the guarantee is violated.

***Example 7.*** *The mean and standard deviation of an examination in which grades 70 and 88 corresponds to scores of –0.6 and 1.4, respectively are*

(a) $\bar{x} = 75.4, \sigma = 9$ (b) $\bar{x} = 9, \sigma = 75.4$
(c) $\bar{x} = 75, \sigma = 9.4$ (d) $\bar{x} = 9.4, \sigma = 75$

**Solution.** (a) $z = \dfrac{X - \bar{X}}{\sigma}$

For $z = -0.6, X = 70, \quad -0.6 = \dfrac{70 - \bar{X}}{\sigma}$

For $z = 1.4, X = 88, \quad 1.4 = \dfrac{88 - \bar{X}}{\sigma}$

$\Rightarrow \sigma = 9, \bar{x} = 75.4$

**Directions** (Q. Nos. 8-10) *Two independent random variates X and Y are both normally distributed with means 1 and 2 and standard deviations 3 and 4, respectively.*
*If* $Z = X - Y$

***Example 8.*** *The probability density function of Z is*

(a) $p(z) = \dfrac{1}{5\sqrt{2\pi}} \exp\left[-\dfrac{1}{2}\left(\dfrac{z+1}{5}\right)^2\right], -\infty < z < \infty$

(b) $p(z) = \dfrac{1}{5\sqrt{2\pi}} \exp\left[-\dfrac{1}{2}\left(\dfrac{z-1}{5}\right)^2\right], -\infty < z < \infty$

(c) $p(z) = \dfrac{1}{3\sqrt{2\pi}} \exp\left[-\dfrac{1}{2}\left(\dfrac{z+1}{3}\right)^2\right], -\infty < z < \infty$

(d) $p(z) = \dfrac{1}{3\sqrt{2\pi}} \exp\left[-\dfrac{1}{2}\left(\dfrac{z-1}{3}\right)^2\right], -\infty < z < \infty$

**Solution.** (a) Since, $X \sim N(1, 9)$,

$Y \sim N(2, 16)$.

So, $Z = X - Y \sim N(1-2, 9+16) = N(-1, 25)$

Thus, $\mu = -1, \sigma^2 = 25$

$$f(z) = \frac{1}{\sigma\sqrt{2\pi}} \exp\left[-\frac{1}{2}\left(\frac{x-\mu}{\sigma}\right)^2\right]$$

gives required answer.

***Example 9.*** *The mean, median and standard deviations are*

(a) Mean = Median = –1, Standard Deviation (SD) = 5
(b) Mean = Median = 1, (SD) = 5
(c) Mean = 1, Median = –1, (SD) = 25
(d) Mean = –1, Median = 1, (SD) = 25

**Solution.** (a) For normal distribution

Mean = Median = Mode = –1

$SD = \sigma = \sqrt{\sigma^2} = \sqrt{25} = 5$

***Example 10.*** $P(Z + 1 \le 0)$ *is*

(a) 0.4 (b) 0.5
(c) 0.6 (d) 0.7

**Solution.** (b) $P(Z + 1 \le 0) = P\left(\dfrac{Z+1}{5} \le \dfrac{0}{5}\right)$

$= P\left(\dfrac{Z+1}{5} \le 0\right)$

$= P(U \le 0)$ where $\dfrac{Z+1}{5} = U$

$= 0.5$

Thus, $P(Z + 1 \le 0) = 0.5$

***Example 11.*** *If X is normal with mean 2 and standard deviation 3, then the distribution of* $Y = \dfrac{1}{2}X - 1$ *is*

(a) $N(0, 9/4)$ (b) $N(1, 9/4)$
(c) $N(0, 3/4)$ (d) $N(1, 3/4)$

**Solution.** (a) $X \sim N(\mu, \sigma^2) = N(2, 3^2) = N(2, 9)$

$E(Y) = E(aX + b) = aE(X) + b$

$= a\mu + b$

$\text{var}\, Y = a^2\, \text{var}(X) = a^2\sigma^2$

Here, $\mu = 2, \sigma^2 = 9, a = \dfrac{1}{2}, b = 1$

So, $Y = \dfrac{1}{2}X - 1 \sim N\left(\dfrac{1}{2}\cdot 2 - 1, \dfrac{1}{4}\cdot 9\right) = N\left(0, \dfrac{9}{4}\right)$

***Example 12.*** *Which vector is a probability vector?*

(a) $\left(\dfrac{1}{4}, \dfrac{3}{2}, -\dfrac{1}{4}, \dfrac{1}{2}\right)$ (b) $\left(\dfrac{5}{2}, 0, \dfrac{8}{3}, \dfrac{1}{6}, \dfrac{1}{6}\right)$

(c) $\left(\dfrac{1}{12}, \dfrac{1}{2}, \dfrac{1}{6}, 0, \dfrac{1}{4}\right)$ (d) $(3, 0, 2, 5, 3)$

**Solution.** (c) Each component is non-negative and sum of the components is 1.

***Example 13.*** *Which matrix is stochastic matrix?*

(a) $\begin{pmatrix} 0 & 1 & 0 \\ 1/2 & 1/4 & 1/4 \end{pmatrix}$ (b) $\begin{pmatrix} 1/2 & 1/2 \\ 1/2 & 1/2 \end{pmatrix}$

(c) $\begin{pmatrix} 0 & 1 \\ 1/2 & 1/4 \end{pmatrix}$ (d) $\begin{pmatrix} 0 & 1 \\ -1/2 & 3/2 \end{pmatrix}$

**Solution.** (b) It is square, its each entry is non-negative and sum of each row is one.

***Example 14.*** *The transition diagram is as follows*

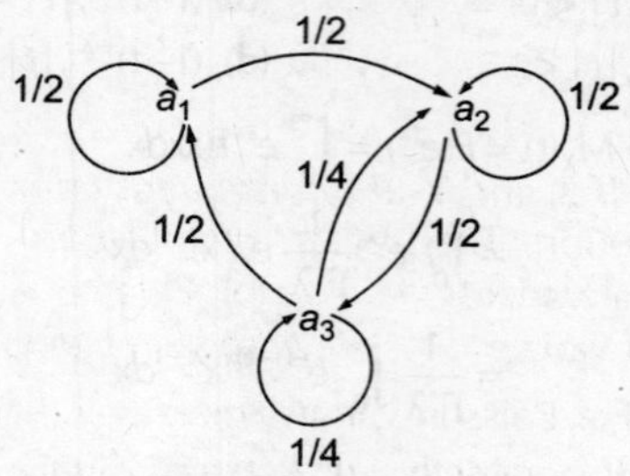


*Its transition matrix is*

(a) $\begin{matrix} & a_1 & a_2 & a_3 \\ a_1 & 1/2 & 1/2 & 0 \\ a_2 & 0 & 1/2 & 1/2 \\ a_3 & 1/2 & 1/4 & 1/4 \end{matrix}$ (b) $\begin{pmatrix} 1/2 & 1/3 & 0 \\ 0 & 1/2 & 1/2 \\ 0 & 1/4 & 3/4 \end{pmatrix}$

(c) $\begin{pmatrix} 2/3 & 0 & 1/3 \\ 1/2 & -1/2 & 1 \\ 1 & 0 & 1 \end{pmatrix}$ (d) $\begin{pmatrix} 1 & 0 & 0 \\ 0 & 1/2 & 1/3 \\ 2/3 & 1/3 & 1/2 \end{pmatrix}$

**Solution.** (a) It is square matrix which satisfies given transition diagram.

***Example 15.*** *The unique fixed probability vector of matrix*

$$A = \begin{pmatrix} 2/3 & 1/3 \\ 2/5 & 3/5 \end{pmatrix} \text{ is}$$

(a) $\left(\frac{6}{11}, \frac{5}{11}\right)$ (b) $\left(\frac{3}{11}, \frac{8}{11}\right)$

(c) $\left(\frac{4}{11}, \frac{7}{11}\right)$ (d) $\left(\frac{5}{11}, \frac{6}{11}\right)$

**Solution.** (a) $(x_1, x_2)A = (x_1, x_2)$

On solving this for $x_1, x_2$, we get required answer.

***Example 16.*** *The unique fixed probability vector t of*

$$P = \begin{pmatrix} 0 & 3/4 & 1/4 \\ 1/2 & 1/2 & 0 \\ 0 & 1 & 0 \end{pmatrix} \text{ is}$$

(a) $\left(\frac{4}{13}, \frac{8}{13}, \frac{1}{13}\right)$ (b) $\left(\frac{4}{13}, \frac{6}{13}, \frac{1}{13}\right)$

(c) $\left(\frac{6}{13}, \frac{2}{13}, \frac{4}{13}\right)$ (d) $\left(\frac{1}{13}, \frac{5}{13}, \frac{6}{13}\right)$

**Solution.** (a) Let $t = (x, y, z)$ be fixed project.

Then, $x + y + z = 1$. So, $t = (x, y, 1 - x - y)$.

Using $t, p = t$, we get

$$\frac{1}{2}y = x$$

$$\frac{3}{4}x + \frac{1}{2}y + 1 - x - y = y$$

$$\frac{1}{4}x = 1 - x - y$$

On solving above equations, we get

$$x = \frac{4}{13}, y = \frac{8}{13}, z = \frac{1}{13}$$

So, $t = (x, y, z)$

***Example 17.*** *If X and Y are correlated variates each having poisson distribution. Then, X + Y cannot be*

(a) Binomial variate (b) Poisson variate

(c) Normal variate (d) Hypergeometric variate

**Solution.** (b) For Poisson variate, mean = variance.

Let $\lambda$ and $\mu$ parameters of Poisson variate $X$ and $Y$. Then, $X \sim P(\lambda), Y \sim P/(\mu)$

$(X, Y)$ are correlated

$$E(X + Y) = E(X) + E(Y) = \lambda + \mu$$

$$\begin{aligned} \text{var}(X + Y) &= \text{var}(X) + \text{var}(Y) + 2\,\text{cov}(X, Y) \\ &= \lambda + \mu + 2\rho\sqrt{\lambda - \mu} \quad (\rho \neq 0) \\ &= E(X + Y) + 2\rho\sqrt{\lambda - \mu} \end{aligned}$$

As $E(X + Y) \neq \text{var}(X + Y)$

So, $X + Y$ is not a poisson variate.

***Example 18.*** *Let X be a random variable taking values in a set E. Let $p(x > a + b \mid X > a) = p(X > b)$ for all $a, b \in E$ Then, which of the following is a possible distribution of X?*

(a) Poisson (b) Geometric

(c) Long-normal (d) Exponential

**Solution.** (d) First, we consider $a < b$

0 a a+b

Then, $\{x \in R \mid x > a + b\} \cap \{x \in R \mid x > a\} = \{x \in R \mid x > a + b\}$

Thus, $]a + b, \infty[ \cap ]a, \infty[ = ]a + b, \infty[$

Now, $P(x > a + b \mid X > a)$

$$= \frac{P[(x > a + b) \cap (x > a)]}{P(x > a)}$$

$$= \frac{P(x > a + b)}{P(x > a)}$$

$$\text{or } P(x > a + b \mid X > a) = \frac{\int_{a+b}^{\infty} f(x)\,dx}{\int_a^{\infty} f(x)\,dx} \quad \text{...(i)}$$

For $f(x) = \theta e^{-\theta x}, \theta > 0, -\infty < x < \infty$

Eq. (i) gives,

$$P(x > a + b \mid X > a) = \frac{\int_{a+b}^{\infty} \theta e^{-\theta x} dx}{\int_a^{\infty} \theta e^{-\theta x} dx}$$

$$= \theta\left[\frac{e^{-\theta x}}{-\theta}\right]_{a+b}^{\infty} \Big/ \theta\left[\frac{e^{-\theta x}}{-\theta}\right]_a^{\infty}$$

$$= e^{-\theta b} = P(X > b)$$

$\Rightarrow$ The possible distribution of $X$ is exponential.

***Example 19.*** *Which of the following is/are cumulative distribution function(s) (cdf) of random variable(s)?*

(a) $F_1(x) = \begin{cases} 0, & x \le 0 \\ e^{-x}, & x > 0 \end{cases}$ (b) $F_2(x) = \begin{cases} 0, & x \le 0 \\ 1 - e^{-x}, & x > 0 \end{cases}$

(c) $F_3(x) = \begin{cases} 0 & x \le 0 \\ 1 & x > 0 \end{cases}$ (d) $F_4(x) = \begin{cases} 0, & x < 0 \\ 1/2, & 0 \le x < 1 \\ 1, & x \ge 0 \end{cases}$

**Solution.** (b) $f(x) = \dfrac{d}{dx} F_2(x) = \begin{cases} 0 & \text{, if } x \le 0 \\ \dfrac{d}{dx}(1 - e^{-x}), & \text{if } x > 0 \end{cases}$

$$= \begin{cases} 0, & \text{if } x \le 0 \\ e^{-x}, & \text{if } x > 0 \end{cases}$$

$$\int_{-\infty}^{\infty} f(x)\,dx = \int_{-\infty}^{0} f(x)\,dx + \int_0^{\infty} f(x)\,dx$$

$$= 0 + \int_0^{\infty} e^{-x} dx$$

$$= -[e^{-x}]_0^{\infty} = -\left[\frac{1}{\infty} - \frac{1}{1}\right] = 1$$

$\Rightarrow F_2(x)$ is a cumulative distribution function.

***Example 20.*** *Suppose X and Y are independent N(0, 1) random variables. Let* $U = \frac{X}{Y}$ *and* $V = \frac{X}{|Y|}$. *Then,*

(a) $U$ and $V$ are independent
(b) $U$ and $V$ have the same distribution
(c) $P(U = V) = \frac{1}{2}$
(d) $P(U < V) = \frac{1}{2}$

**Solution.** (b) Given,

(i) $X \sim N(0,1], Y \sim N(0,1]$,
(ii) $X$ and $Y$ are independent.

So, joint probability distribution of $X$ and $Y$ is

$$f_{XY}(x, y) = f_X(x) \cdot f_y(y)$$

$$= \frac{1}{\sqrt{2\pi}} e^{-x^2/2} \cdot \frac{1}{\sqrt{2\pi}} e^{-y^2/2}$$

$$= \frac{1}{2\pi} e^{-(x^2+y^2)/2}$$

Now, we take $U = X/Y$.

Let $W = Y$

Then, $X = YU = WU$

$Y = W$

$$\text{Jacobian, } J = \frac{\partial(X, Y)}{\partial(V, W)} = \begin{vmatrix} W & U \\ 0 & 1 \end{vmatrix} = W$$

$|J|$ = absolute value of $J = |W| = |Y|$

Hence, joint probability density function of $U$ and $W$ becomes

$$g_{UW}(u, w) = f_{XY}(x, y)|J|$$

$$= \frac{1}{2\pi} e^{-(x^2+y^2)/2} |Y|$$

$$= \frac{1}{2\pi} e^{-(W^2u^2+w^2)/2} |W|$$

$$= \frac{1}{2\pi} e^{-(1+u^2)w^2/2} |w|, \; -\infty < (u, w) < \infty$$

Marginal probability density function of $U$ is

$$g_U(u) = \frac{1}{2\pi} \int_{-\infty}^{\infty} e^{-(1+u^2)w^2/2} |w| \, dw$$

$$= \frac{1}{\pi} \int_0^{\infty} e^{-(1+u^2)w^2/2} |w| \, dw \qquad \left(\text{putting } (1+u^2)\frac{w^2}{2} = t\right)$$

$$= \frac{1}{\pi} \int_0^{\infty} e^{-t} \frac{dt}{1+a^2}$$

$$g_U(u) = \frac{1}{\pi} \frac{1}{(1+u^2)}, \; -\infty < u < \infty$$

pdf of standard cauchy distribution.

Similarly, on considering

$$\left.\begin{matrix} V = \dfrac{X}{|Y|} = \dfrac{X}{Z} \end{matrix}\right\}, \text{ we get } X = VW$$

$$W = |Y| \qquad Z = |Y| = W$$

$$\text{Then, Jacobian } J_1 = \frac{\partial(X, Z)}{\partial(V, W)} = W$$

And repeating the same procedure, we get

$$g_V(v) = \frac{1}{\pi(1+v^2)}, \; -\infty < v < \infty$$

It is pdf of Cauchy's distribution.

These show that $U$ and $Y$ have same distribution.

***Example 21.*** *If X and Y be two independent random variables, each representing the number of failures preceding the first success in a sequence of Bernoulli trials with p as probability of success in a single trial and q as probability of failure, then p(X = Y) is*

(a) $\frac{p}{1+q}$ (b) $\frac{q}{1+p}$ (c) $\frac{p}{1+p}$ (d) $\frac{q}{1+q}$

**Solution.** (a) $P(X = r) = P(Y = r) = q^r p, \quad r = 0, 1, 2, \ldots$

$$P(X = Y) = \sum_{r=0}^{\infty} P(X = r \cap Y = r)$$

$$= \sum_{r=0}^{\infty} P(X = r) \cdot P(Y = r)$$

(as $X$ and $Y$ being independent)

$$= \sum_{r=0}^{\infty} q^r \cdot p \cdot q^r \cdot p = p^2 \sum_{r=0}^{\infty} q^{2r}$$

$$= \frac{p^2}{1-q^2} = \frac{p}{1+q}$$

***Example 22.*** *Let X have a standard cauchy distribution. Then, probability density function of* $X^2$ *is of*

(a) Cauchy distribution (b) Exponential distribution
(c) Normal distribution (d) Beta distribution

**Solution.** (d) pdf of Cauchy distribution

$$f(x) = \frac{1}{\pi} \frac{1}{1+x^2}, \; -\infty < x < \infty$$

The distribution function of $Y = X^2$

$$G_Y(y) = P(Y \le y) = P(X^2 \le y) = P(-\sqrt{y} \le X \le \sqrt{y})$$

$$= \int_{-\sqrt{y}}^{y} f(x)\, dx = \frac{2}{\pi} \tan^{-1} \sqrt{y}, \; 0 < y < \infty$$

$$\text{Its pdf, } g_Y(y) = \frac{d}{dy} G_Y(y)$$

$$= \frac{2}{\pi} \frac{1}{(1+y)2\sqrt{y}}$$

$$= \frac{1}{B(1/2, 1/2)} \frac{y^{1/2-1}}{(1+y)^{1/2+1/2}}, \; y > 0$$

Thus, $X^2 \sim B_2(1/2, 1/2)$ = Beta variate of 2nd kind with parameters $(1/2, 1/2)$.

***Example 23.*** *Let* $X_1, X_2, \ldots, X_n$ *be independent random variables,* $X_i$ *having exponential distribution with parameter* $\theta_i, i = 1, 2, \ldots, n$.

*Then,* $Z = \min(X_1, X_2, \ldots, X_n)$ *has*

(a) Normal distribution $N(\mu, \sigma^2)$

(b) Exponential distribution with parameter $\sum_{i=1}^{n} \theta_i$

(c) Geometric distribution

(d) Cauchy distribution

**Solution.** (b) $G_Z(x) = p(Z \le z) = 1 - P(Z > z)$

$$= 1 - P(\min(X_1, X_2, \dots, X_n) < z)$$

$$= 1 - P(X_i > z \mid i = 1, 2, \dots, n)$$

$$= 1 - \prod_{i=1}^{n} P(X_i > z) = 1 - \prod_{i=1}^{n} (1 - P(X_i < z))$$

$$= 1 - \prod_{i=1}^{n} [1 - F_{X_i}(z)]$$

$$= 1 - \prod_{i=1}^{n} [1 - (1 - e^{-\theta iz})]$$

$$= \begin{cases} 1 - \prod_{i=1}^{n} e^{-\theta iz} = 1 - e^{-\left(\sum_{i=1}^{n} \theta_i\right) z}, & z > 0 \\ 0, & \text{otherwise} \end{cases}$$

$$\text{pdf } g_Z(z) = \frac{d}{dz} G_Z(z) = \begin{cases} \sum_{i=1}^{n} \theta_i \, e^{-\left(\sum_{i=1}^{n} \theta_i\right) z_i}, & z_i > 0 \\ 0, & \text{otherwise} \end{cases}$$

$\Rightarrow$ Z has Exponential distribution.

***Example 24.*** *Let A and B be events with $P(A) = \frac{3}{8}$, $P(B) = \frac{5}{8}$ and $P(A \cup B) = \frac{3}{4}$. Then,*

**(i)** *$P(A^c)$ is*

(a) $\frac{5}{8}$ (b) $\frac{3}{8}$ (c) $\frac{1}{4}$ (d) $\frac{2}{5}$

**(ii)** *$P(B^c)$ is*

(a) $\frac{5}{8}$ (b) $\frac{3}{8}$ (c) $\frac{1}{4}$ (d) $\frac{2}{5}$

**(iii)** *$P(A \cap B)$ is*

(a) $\frac{5}{8}$ (b) $\frac{3}{8}$ (c) $\frac{1}{4}$ (d) $\frac{2}{3}$

**(iv)** *$P(A / B)$ is*

(a) $\frac{3}{8}$ (b) $\frac{1}{4}$ (c) $\frac{2}{5}$ (d) $\frac{2}{3}$

**(v)** *$P(B / A)$ is*

(a) $\frac{3}{8}$ (b) $\frac{1}{4}$ (c) $\frac{2}{5}$ (d) $\frac{2}{3}$

**Answer** (i)—(a); (ii) — (b); (iii) —(c); (iv) —(c); (v)—(d).

**Solution.**

(i) $P(A^c) = 1 - P(A) = 1 - \frac{3}{8} = \frac{5}{8}$

(ii) $P(B^c) = 1 - P(B) = 1 - \frac{5}{8} = \frac{3}{8}$

(iii) $P(A \cap B) = P(A) + P(B) - P(A \cup B)$

$$= \frac{3}{8} + \frac{5}{8} - \frac{3}{4} = \frac{1}{4}$$

(iv) $P(A / B) = \frac{P(A \cap B)}{P(B)} = \frac{1/4}{5/8} = \frac{2}{5}$

(v) $P(B / A) = \frac{P(A \cap B)}{P(A)} = \frac{1/4}{3/8} = \frac{2}{3}$

***Example 25.*** *Three horses A, B, C are in a race, A is twice as likely to win as B, and B is twice as likely to win as C. Then,*

**(i)** *Probability that A wins, P(A) =*

(a) $\frac{1}{7}$ (b) $\frac{2}{7}$ (c) $\frac{3}{7}$ (d) $\frac{4}{7}$

**(ii)** *Probability that B wins, P(B) =*

(a) $\frac{1}{7}$ (b) $\frac{2}{7}$ (c) $\frac{3}{4}$ (d) $\frac{4}{7}$

**(iii)** *Probability that C wins P(c) =*

(a) $\frac{1}{7}$ (b) $\frac{2}{7}$ (c) $\frac{3}{7}$ (d) $\frac{4}{7}$

**(iv)** *Probability that B or C wins, $P(B \cup C) =$*

(a) $\frac{2}{7}$ (b) $\frac{3}{4}$ (c) $\frac{3}{7}$ (d) $\frac{4}{7}$

**(v)** *Probability that A, B or C wins, $P(A \cup B \cup C) =$*

(a) 0 (b) 1 (c) $\frac{1}{7}$ (d) $\frac{5}{7}$

**Answer**

(i) —(d); (ii) — (b); (iii) —(a); (iv) —(c); (v)—(b).

**Solution.**

Let P(c) = p

Then, $P(B) = 2P(C) = 2p$

$$P(A) = 2\,P(B) = 2(2p) = 4p.$$

As one of the horses has to win the race, so the sum of the probabilities must be 1.

$$\Rightarrow \quad p + 2p + 4p = 1 \Rightarrow 7p = 1 \text{ or } p = \frac{1}{7}.$$

Thus, $P(A) = \frac{4}{7}, P(B) = \frac{2}{7}, P(C) = \frac{1}{7}$

$$P(B \cup C) = P(B) + P(C) = \frac{2}{7} + \frac{1}{7} = \frac{3}{7}$$

$$P(A \cup B \cup C) = \frac{4}{7} + \frac{2}{7} + \frac{1}{7} = \frac{7}{7} = 1$$

***Example 26.*** *A card is selected at random from a deck of 52 cards. Picture cards : Jack (J), Queen (Q) King (K), Heart (H), Diamond (D), are red Spade (S), Club (C) are black ace (A) Then,*

**(i)** *Probability that it is heart, P(F) is [F = event of heart]*

(a) $\frac{1}{4}$ (b) $\frac{3}{13}$ (c) $\frac{4}{13}$ (d) $\frac{11}{26}$

**(ii)** *Probability that it is a face card, P(E) is [E event of face card]*

(a) $\frac{3}{13}$ (b) $\frac{1}{4}$ (c) $\frac{1}{26}$ (d) $\frac{11}{26}$

**(iii)** *Probability that it is heart of face card, $P(E \cap F)$ is*

(a) $\frac{3}{13}$ (b) $\frac{3}{52}$ (c) $\frac{11}{26}$ (d) $\frac{1}{4}$

**(iv)** *Probability that it is either a heart or a face card, $P(E \cup F)$ is*

(a) $\frac{11}{26}$ (b) $\frac{1}{4}$ (c) $\frac{3}{13}$ (d) $\frac{3}{52}$

**Answer**

(i) —(a); (ii) — (a); (iii) —(b); (iv) —(a)

**Solution.**

(i) There are 13 cards of heart out of 52 cards.

So, $P(F) = \frac{13}{52} = \frac{1}{4}$

(ii) There are 12 face cards out of 52 cards.

So, $P(E) = \frac{12}{52} = \frac{3}{13}$

(iii) Here, $E \cap F = \{JH, QH, KH\}$

So, $P(E \cap F) = \frac{3}{52}$

(iv) $P(E \cup F) = P(E) + P(F) - P(E \cap F)$

$$= \frac{3}{13} + \frac{1}{4} - \frac{3}{52} = \frac{12+13-3}{52} = \frac{11}{26}$$

***Example 27.*** *Let A and B be two events of a sample space S, probability of A, $P(A) > 0$.*

**(i)** *If A is a subset of B, then $P(B / A)$ is*

(a) 0 (b) 1

(c) 1/2 (d) None of these

**(ii)** *If A and B are mutually exclusive, then $P(B / A)$ is*

(a) 0 (b) 1

(c) $\frac{1}{2}$ (d) None of these

**Answer** (i) →(b); (ii) → (a)

***Example 28.*** *Let E be an event for which $P(E) > 0$. Then,*

**(i)** For any event A

(a) $P(A/E) \geq 0$ (b) $P(A/E) = 0$

(c) $P(A/E) = 1$ (d) None of these

**(ii)** For any certain event S, $P(S / E)$ is

(a) 0

(b) 1

(c) $0 < P(S/E) < 1$

(d) None of the above

**(iii)** For any two disjoint events A and B, $P(A \cup B / E)$ is equal to

(a) 0

(b) 1

(c) $P(A \cap B)$

(d) $P(A/E) + P(B/E)$

**(iv)** *For any infinite sequence of mutually exclusive events $A_1, A_2, \ldots$, $P(A_1 \cup A_2 \cup \ldots /E)$ is equal to*

(a) 0

(b) 1

(c) $P(A_1 \cap A_2 \cap \ldots)$

(d) $P(A_1 / E) + P(A_2 / E) + \ldots$

**Answer** (i) →(a); (ii) → (b); (iii) →(d); (iv) →(d)

***Example 29.*** *Suppose a coin, weighted so that $P(H) = \frac{2}{3}$ and $P(T) = \frac{1}{3}$, is tossed. If head appears, then a number is selected at random from numbers 1 through 9, i.e, from $\{1, 2, 3, 4, 5, 6, 7, 8, 9\}$; if tail appears, then a number is selected from the numbers 1 through 5. Then,*

**(i)** *The probability that an even number '$E_v$' appears, i.e., $P(E_v)$ is*

(a) $\frac{58}{135}$ (b) $\frac{68}{135}$

(c) $\frac{77}{135}$ (d) $\frac{87}{135}$.

**(ii)** *The probability that an odd number '$O_d$' appears, i.e, $P(Od)$ is*

(a) $\frac{58}{135}$ (b) $\frac{68}{135}$

(c) $\frac{77}{135}$ (d) $\frac{87}{135}$

**Answer** (i) →(a); (ii) →(c)

**Solution.**

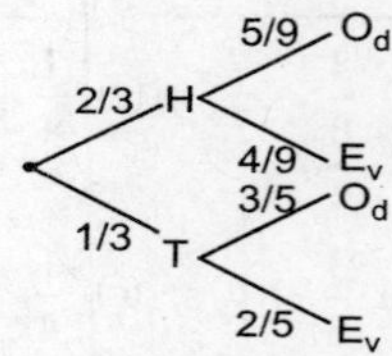


(i) $P(E_v) = P(H) \cdot P(E_v / H) + P(T) \cdot P(E_v / T)$

$$= \frac{2}{3} \cdot \frac{4}{9} + \frac{1}{3} \cdot \frac{2}{3} = \frac{58}{135}$$

(ii) $(O_d) = P(H) \cdot P(O_d / H) + P(T) \cdot P(O_d / T)$

$$= \frac{2}{3} \cdot \frac{5}{9} + \frac{1}{3} \cdot \frac{3}{5} = \frac{77}{135}$$

***Example 30.*** Three horses $a, b, c$ race together their respective probabilities of winning are $\frac{1}{2}, \frac{1}{3}, \frac{1}{6}$.

*The probability that c wins the first race and a wins the second race P(ca) is*

(a) $\frac{1}{12}$ (b) $\frac{1}{18}$

(c) $\frac{1}{36}$ (d) $\frac{1}{42}$

**Solution.** (a) Sample space for first race

$$S_1 = \{a, b, c\}$$

Given, probability that horse 'a' win the race, $P(a) = \frac{1}{2}$

Similarly, $P(b) = \frac{1}{3}$

$P(c) = \frac{1}{6}$

After second race, sample space for two races ( two repeated trials),

$$S_2 = \{aa, ab, ac, ba, bb, bc, ca, cb, cc\}$$

Here, $aa$ represents $(a, a)$

$ab$ represents $(a, b)$ etc.

Probability of each point in $S_2$

$P(a \cdot a) = P(a) \cdot p(a) = \frac{1}{2} \cdot \frac{1}{2} = \frac{1}{4}$, $P(ba) = \frac{1}{6}$, $p(ca) = \frac{1}{12}$

$P(a \cdot b) = p(a) \cdot p(b) = \frac{1}{2} \cdot \frac{1}{3} = \frac{1}{6}$, $p(bb) = \frac{1}{9}$, $p(cb) = \frac{1}{18}$

$P(a \cdot c) = p(a) \cdot p(c) = \frac{1}{2} \cdot \frac{1}{6} = \frac{1}{12}$, $p(bc) = \frac{1}{18}$, $P(cc) = \frac{1}{36}$

Probability that C wins first and a wins second is $P(ca) = \frac{1}{12}$

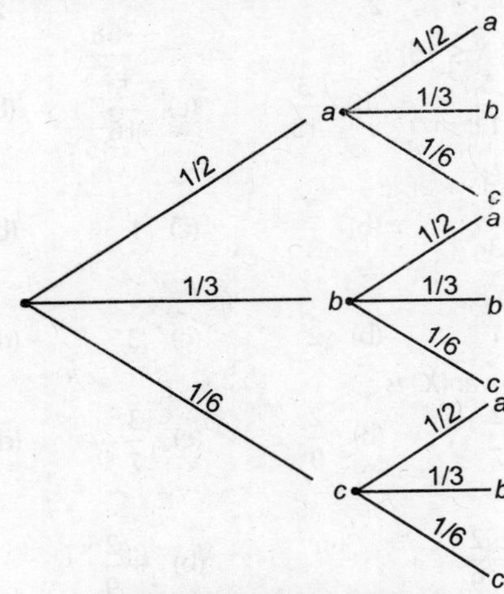


Tree diagram for the repeated trial (Stochastic process).

***Example 31.*** *A factory uses three machines X, Y, Z to produce certain items*

*X produces 50% of the items of which three per cent are defective.*

*Y produces 30% of the items of which 4% are defective.*

*Z produces 20% of the items of which 5% are defective. Let D be defective and $\overline{D}$ be non-defective item.*

*Then,*

**(i)** *Probability that randomly selected item is defective, P(D) is*

(a) $\frac{37}{100}$ (b) $\frac{41}{1000}$

(c) $\frac{47}{100}$ (d) $\frac{49}{1000}$

**(ii)** *The probability that defective item is from machine Z, P(Z/D) is*

(a) $\frac{10}{37}$ (b) $\frac{29}{100}$

(c) $\frac{31}{100}$ (d) $\frac{33}{100}$

**Answer** (i) → (a); (ii) → (a)

**Solution** (i) $P(D) = P(X) \cdot P(D/X) + P(Y) \cdot P(D/Y) + P(Z) \cdot P(D/Z)$

$$= \frac{50}{100} \cdot \frac{3}{100} + \frac{30}{100} \cdot \frac{4}{100} + \frac{20}{100} \cdot \frac{5}{100} = \frac{37}{100}$$

(ii) $P(X/D) = \frac{P(X) \cdot P(D/X)}{P(D)} = \frac{\frac{50}{100} \cdot \frac{3}{100}}{\frac{37}{1000}} = \frac{15}{37}$

$P(Y/D) = \frac{P(Y) \cdot P(D/Y)}{P(D)} = \frac{\frac{30}{100} \cdot \frac{4}{100}}{\frac{37}{1000}} = \frac{12}{37}$

$P(Z/D) = \frac{P(Z)\, P(D/Z)}{P(D)} = \frac{\frac{20}{100} \cdot \frac{5}{100}}{\frac{37}{1000}} = \frac{10}{37}$.

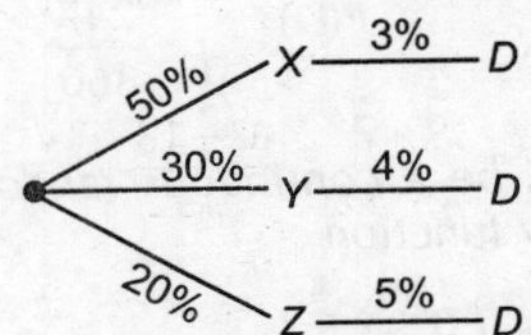


Tree Diagram for stochastic process (Stochastic tree)

***Example 32.*** *Given, three boxes X, Y, Z*

*X has 10 lightbulbs of which 4 are defective.*

*Y has 6 lightbulbs of which 1 is defective.*

*Z has 8 lightbulbs of which 3 are defective.*

*A box is chosen at random and then a bulb is randomly selected from the chosen box.*

*Let D denote defective bulb and $\overline{D}$ denote non-defective bulb.*

*Then,*

**(i)** *Probability that the bulb is non-defective $P(\overline{D})$ is*

(a) $\frac{247}{360}$ (b) $\frac{248}{360}$ (c) $\frac{249}{360}$ (d) $\frac{250}{360}$

**(ii)** *If the bulb is non-defective probability that it came from Z, $P(Z/\overline{D})$ is*

(a) $\frac{72}{247}$ (b) $\frac{73}{247}$ (c) $\frac{74}{247}$ (d) $\frac{75}{247}$

**Answer** (i) → (a) ; (ii) → (d)

**Solution.** Let $D$ be the event of defective bulb.

Then, $\overline{D}$ is the event of non-defective bulb.

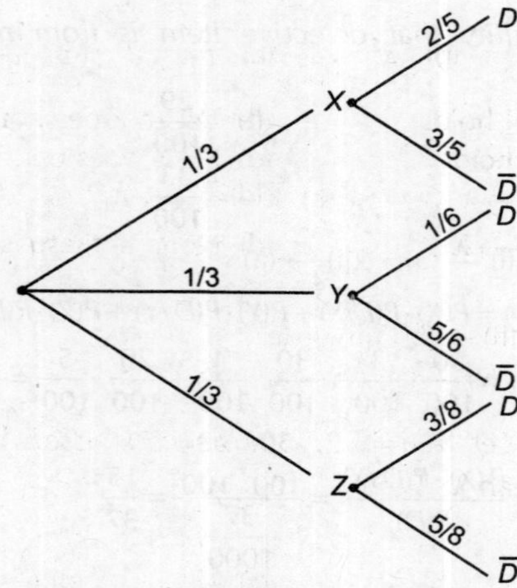


Tree diagram for stochastic process (stochastic tree)

$$P(\overline{D}) = P(X)\cdot P(\overline{D}/X) + P(Y)\cdot P(\overline{D}/Y) + P(Z)\cdot P(\overline{D}/Z)$$

$$= \frac{1}{3}\cdot\frac{3}{5} + \frac{1}{3}\cdot\frac{5}{6} + \frac{1}{3}\cdot\frac{5}{8} = \frac{247}{360}$$

$$P(Z/\overline{D}) = \frac{P(Z)\cdot P(\overline{D}/Z)}{P(\overline{D})} = \frac{\frac{1}{3}\cdot\frac{5}{8}}{\frac{247}{360}} = \frac{75}{247}$$

***Example 33.*** *Let X be a continuous random variable with the following density function*

$$f(x) = \begin{cases} \frac{1}{2}x^2, & \text{if } 0 \le x \le 2 \\ 0, & \text{elsewhere} \end{cases}$$

*Then,*

(*i*) *Cumulative distribution function F of X is*

(a) $F(x) = \begin{cases} \frac{1}{4}x^2, & \text{if } 0 \le x \le 2 \\ 0, & \text{elsewhere} \end{cases}$

(b) $F(x) = \begin{cases} 0, & \text{if } x < 0 \\ \frac{1}{4}x^2, & \text{if } 0 \le x \le 1 \\ 1, & \text{if } x > 1 \end{cases}$

(c) $F(x) = \begin{cases} 0 & \text{if } x < 0 \\ \frac{1}{4}x^2 & \text{if } 0 \le x \le 2 \\ 1 & \text{if } x > 2 \end{cases}$

(d) None of the above

(*ii*) *Graph of f (pdf)*

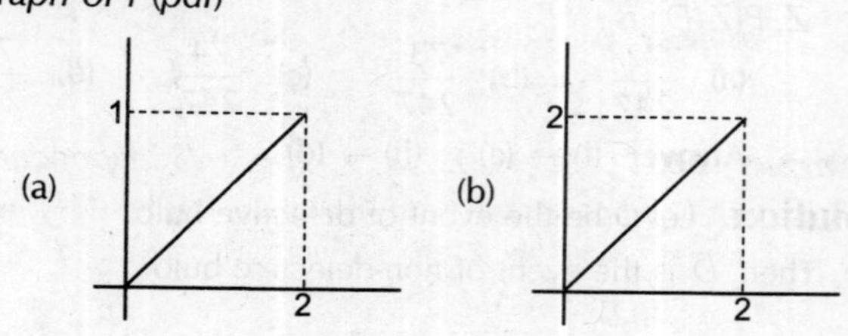


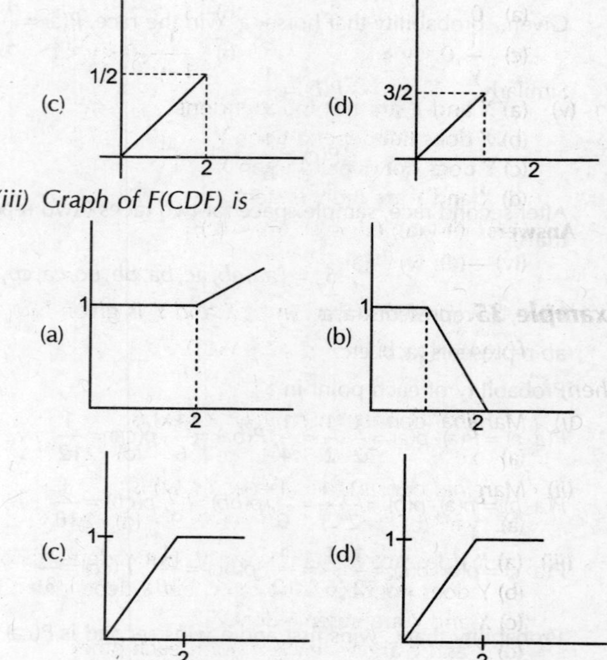


(*iii*) *Graph of F(CDF) is*

(*iv*) $P(1 \le X \le 1.5)$ *is*

(a) $\frac{5}{11}$ (b) $\frac{5}{13}$ (c) $\frac{5}{16}$ (b) $\frac{5}{18}$

(*v*) $E(X)$ *is*

(a) $\frac{1}{3}$ (b) $\frac{2}{3}$ (c) 1 (b) $\frac{4}{3}$

(*vi*) $E(X^2)$ *is*

(a) 1 (b) 2 (c) 3 (d) 4

(*vii*) $\sigma_x^2 = \text{var}(X)$ *is*

(a) $\frac{2}{7}$ (b) $\frac{2}{9}$ (c) $\frac{3}{7}$ (d) $\frac{3}{10}$

(*viii*) $\sigma_x$ *is*

(a) $-\frac{2}{9}$ (b) $+\frac{2}{9}$

(c) $-\frac{\sqrt{2}}{9}$ (d) $+\frac{\sqrt{2}}{9}$

***Example 34.*** *The joint probability density function of a two dimensional random variable (X, Y) is given by*

$$f(x, y) = 2, \quad 0 < x < 1, 0 < y < x = 0 \text{ elsewhere}$$

*Then,*

(*i*) *Marginal density function of X,* $f_X(x)$

(a) 0 (b) 1 (c) 2 (d) 3

(*ii*) *Marginal density function of Y,* $f_Y(x)$

(a) 0 (b) 1 (c) 2 (d) 3

(*iii*) *Conditional density function of Y given,* $X = x, f_{y/x}(y/x)$

(a) 0 (b) 1

(c) $\frac{1}{x}, 0 < x < 1$ (d) $\frac{1}{x^2}, 0 < x < 1$

(iv) *Conditional density function of X given Y,* $f_{X/Y}(x/y)$

(a) 0 (b) 1

(c) $\frac{1}{y}, 0<y<1$ (d) $\frac{1}{1-y}, 0<y<1$

(v) (a) *X* and *Y* are not independent

(b) *X* does not depend upon *Y*

(c) *Y* does not depend upon *X*

(d) *X* and *Y* are independent

**Answers** (i)—(a); (ii) —(a); (iii) —(c);

(iv) —(d); (v) —(a)

***Example 35.*** *Joint distribution of X and Y is given by* $f(x, y) = 4xy\, e^{-(x^2+y^2)}, x \geq 0\ y \geq 0.$

*Then,*

(i) *Marginal density function of X* $f_X(x)$ *is*

(a) $xe^{-x}$ (b) $xe^{-2x}$ (c) $xe^{-x^2}$ (d) $2xe^{-x^2}$

(ii) *Marginal density function of Y* $f_Y(y)$ *is*

(a) $y\,e^{-x}$ (b) $ye^{-2y}$ (c) $ye^{-y^2}$ (d) $2ye^{-y^2}$

(iii) (a) *X* does not depend upon *Y*, but *Y* depends on *X*.

(b) *Y* does not depend upon *X*, but *X* depends on *Y*.

(c) *X* and *Y* are independent.

(d) *X* and *Y* are dependent upon each other.

(iv) *Conditional distribution of X for given Y is*

$$f(X = x / Y = y) = \frac{f(x, y)}{f_Y(y)}$$

(a) $xe^{-x}$ (b) $2xe^{-x}$ (c) $2xe^{-x^2}$ (d) $xe^{-2x^2}$

**Answer** (i) — (d); (ii) —(d); (iii)—(c); (iv)—(c);

***Example 36.*** *Let $X_i$ be independent and identically distributed (iid) random variable following binomial distribution B(n, p), with $E(x_i) = p$,*

$$V(x_i) = E(X_i^2) - [E(X_i)]^2 = p(1-p)$$

$$i = 1, 2, 3, \ldots, n \text{ and } 0 < p < 1.$$

Then,

(a) WLLN holds (b) WLLN does not holds

(c) SLLN holds (d) SLLN does not holds

**Answers** (a)

***Example 37.*** *Let $X_i$ be independent and identically distributed (iid) random variable such that each $X_i$ has probability density function*

$$f(x) = \frac{1}{\lambda} e^{-x/\lambda}, x > 0$$

*Then,*

(i) $E(X_i)$ *is*

(a) $\lambda$ (b) $\lambda^2$ (c) $n\lambda$ (d) $\frac{\lambda}{n}$

(ii) $V(X_i)$ *is*

(a) $\lambda$ (b) $\lambda^2$ (c) $n\lambda^2$ (d) $\frac{\lambda^2}{n}$

(iii) $E(\overline{X})$ *is*

(a) $\lambda$ (b) $\lambda^2$ (c) $n\lambda^2$ (d) $\frac{\lambda^2}{n}$

(iv) $V(\overline{X})$ *is*

(a) $\lambda$ (b) $\lambda^2$ (c) $n\lambda$ (d) $\frac{\lambda^2}{n}$

(v) (a) WLLN holds (b) WLLN does not hold

(c) SLLN holds (d) SLLN does not hold

(vi) (a) $\overline{X} \xrightarrow{p} \lambda$ (b) $\overline{X} \xrightarrow{qe} \lambda$

(c) $\overline{X} \xrightarrow{L_2} \lambda$ (d) None of these is true

**Answer**

(i) — (a); (ii) — (b); (iii) — (a)

(iv) — (d); (v) — (a); (vi)—(a)

***Example 38.*** *Let $X_i$ $(i = 1, 2, \ldots, n)$ be iid poisson random variables with mean $\lambda$. Then,*

(i) $E(X_i)$ *is*

(a) $\lambda$ (b) $\lambda^2$ (c) $n\lambda$ (d) $\frac{\lambda}{n}$

(ii) $V(X_i)$ *is*

(a) $\lambda$ (b) $\lambda^2$ (c) $n\lambda$ (d) $\frac{\lambda}{n}$

(iii) $E(\overline{X})$ *is*

(a) $\lambda$ (b) $\lambda^2$ (c) $n\lambda$ (d) $\frac{\lambda}{n}$

(iv) $V(\overline{X})$ *is*

(a) $\lambda$ (b) $\lambda^2$ (c) $n\lambda$ (d) $\frac{\lambda}{n}$

**Answers** (i) — (a); (ii) —(a); (iii) — (a); (iv) — (d)

***Example 39.*** Let $P = \{X_n = \pm 2^n\} = \frac{1}{2^{2n+1}}$ *and* $P\{X_n = 0\} = 1 - \frac{1}{2^{2n}}$ *for* $n = 1, 2, \ldots$

Then,

(i) $E(X_n)$ *is*

(a) 0 (b) 1 (c) $n^{1/2}$ (d) $n^{3/2}$

(ii) $V(X_n)$ *is*

(a) 0 (b) 1 (c) $n^{1/2}$ (d) $n^{3/2}$

(iii) $E(\overline{X})$ *is*

(a) 0 (b) 1 (c) $n^{1/2}$ (d) $n^{3/2}$

(iv) $V(\overline{X})$ *is*

(a) 0 (b) 1 (c) $\frac{1}{n}$ (d) $\frac{1}{n^2}$

(v) (a) WLLN holds

(b) WLLN does not hold

(c) SLLN holds

(d) WLLN and SLLN both hold

**Answer** (i) — (a); (ii) —(b); (iii) —(a);

(iv) —(c); (v) —(c);

***Example 40.*** *Let $X_1, X_2, \ldots, X_n$ be n independent and identically distributed random variables each with mean $\mu$ and variance $\sigma^2$, and let $\overline{X}_n$ be the sample mean, i.e.,*

$$\overline{X}_n = \frac{X_1 + X_2 + \ldots + X_n}{n}$$

*Then,*

*(i) Mean of $\bar{X}_n$ is*

(a) 0 (b) $\mu$ (c) $2\mu$ (d) $n\mu$

**Solution.** (b) $\mu_{\bar{X}_n} = E(\bar{X}_n) = \dfrac{E(X_1 + X_2 + \ldots + X_n)}{n}$

$$= \frac{1}{n} E(X_1 + X_2 + \ldots + X_n)$$

$$= \frac{1}{n}[E(X_1) + E(X_2) + \ldots + E(X_n)]$$

$$= \frac{1}{n}(\mu + \mu + \ldots + \mu)$$

$$= \frac{n\mu}{n} = \mu$$

or $\mu_{\bar{X}_n} = \mu$

*(ii) Variance of $\bar{X}_n$ is*

(a) 0 (b) $\sigma$ (c) $n\sigma^2$ (d) $\dfrac{\sigma^2}{n}$

**Solution.** (d) $\text{Var}(\bar{X}_n) = \text{Var}\dfrac{(X_1 + X_2 + \ldots + X_n)}{n}$

$$= \frac{1}{n^2}[\text{Var}(X_1) + \text{Var}(X_2) + \ldots + \text{Var}(X_n)]$$

$$= \frac{1}{n^2}(\sigma^2 + \sigma^2 + \ldots + \sigma^2) = \frac{n\sigma^2}{n^2} = \frac{\sigma^2}{n}$$

*(iii) For any $\alpha > 0$, as $n \to \infty$*

$P(\mu - \alpha \le \bar{X}_n \le \mu + \alpha) \to$

(a) 0 (b) 1 (c) $\mu$ (d) $\sigma$

**Solution.** (b) We know from Chebyshev's inequality for any random variable $X$, with mean $\mu$ and variance $\sigma^2$.

$$P(\mu - \delta \le X_n \le \mu + \delta) \ge 1 - \frac{\sigma^2}{\delta^2}$$

On putting $\sigma = \dfrac{\delta}{n}$, $X = X_n$, we get

$$P(\mu - \delta \le X_n \le \mu + \delta) \ge 1 - \frac{\delta^2}{n^2\delta^2} = 1 - \frac{1}{n^2}$$

On taking limit as $n \to \infty$

$$\lim_{n \to \infty} P(\mu - \delta \le X_n \le \mu + \delta) \ge \lim_{n \to \infty}\left(1 - \frac{1}{n^2}\right)$$

$$\Rightarrow \lim_{n \to \infty} P(\mu - \delta \le X_n \le \mu + \delta) = 1$$

***Example 41.*** *A bag contains $n + 1$ coins. It is known that one of these coins shows heads on both sides, whereas the other coins are fair. Once coin is selected at random and tossed. If the probability that toss results in heads is $\dfrac{7}{12}$. Then, the value of n is*

(a) 3 (b) 4 (c) 5 (d) None of these

**Solution.** (c) Let $E_1$ denote the event 'a coin with two heads' is selected and $E_2$ denote the event 'a fair coin is selected'. Let $A$ be the event 'the toss results in heads'

Then, $P(E_1) = \dfrac{1}{n+1}$, $P(E_2) = \dfrac{n}{n+1}$, $P\left(\dfrac{A}{E_1}\right) = 1$

and $P\left(\dfrac{A}{E_2}\right) = \dfrac{1}{2}$

$$\therefore \quad P(A) = P(E_1)\, P\left(\frac{A}{E_1}\right) + P(E_2)\, P\left(\frac{A}{E_2}\right)$$

$$\Rightarrow \quad \frac{7}{12} = \frac{1}{n+1} \times 1 + \frac{n}{n+1} \times \frac{1}{2}\left[\because P(A) = \frac{7}{12}\right]$$

$$\Rightarrow \quad 12 + 6n = 7n + 7 \Rightarrow n = 5$$

***Example 42.*** *Two numbers b and c are chosen at random with replacement from the numbers 1, 2, 3, 4, 5, 6, 7, 8 and 9. The probability that $x^2 + bx + c > 0$ for all $x \in R$ is*

(a) $\dfrac{10}{27}$ (b) $\dfrac{31}{81}$ (c) $\dfrac{32}{81}$ (d) $\dfrac{11}{27}$

**Solution.** (c) Since, $b$ and $c$ both can assume values from 1 to 9. So, total number of ways of choosing $b$ and $c$ is

$$9 \times 9 = 81$$

Now, $x^2 + bx + c > 0$ for all $x \in R \Rightarrow D < 0$ *i.e.*,

$$b^2 - 4c < 0$$

The following table shows the possible values of $b$ and $c$ for which $b^2 - 4c < 0$

| c | b | Total |
|---|---|---|
| 1 | 1 | 1 |
| 2 | 1, 2 | 2 |
| 3 | 1, 2, 3 | 3 |
| 4 | 1, 2, 3 | 3 |
| 5 | 1, 2, 3, 4 | 4 |
| 6 | 1, 2, 3, 4 | 4 |
| 7 | 1, 2, 3, 4, 5 | 5 |
| 8 | 1, 2, 3, 4, 5 | 5 |
| 9 | 1, 2, 3, 4, 5 | 5 |

So, favourable number of ways = 32

Hence, required probability $= \dfrac{32}{81}$

***Example 43.*** *The PDF of x is*

$$f(x) = \begin{cases} 3e^{-3x}, & x > 0 \\ 0, & \text{elsewhere} \end{cases}$$

*The cumulative distribution function of x is*

(a) $F(x) = \begin{cases} 0, & x \ge 0 \\ 1 - e^{-3x}, & x < 0 \end{cases}$

(b) $F(x) = \begin{cases} 0, & x \le 0 \\ 1 + e^{-3x}, & x > 0 \end{cases}$

(c) $F(x) = \begin{cases} 0, & x \le 0 \\ 1 - e^{-3x}, & x > 0 \end{cases}$

(d) None of the above

**Solution.** (c) The PDF of $f(x)$ is defined as

$$F(x) = \int_{-\infty}^{x} f(x)\,dx = \int_{-\infty}^{0} 0\,dx + \int_{0}^{x} 3e^{-3x}\,dx$$

$$= -(e^{-3x} - 1)$$

$$\therefore \quad F(x) = \begin{cases} 0, & x \le 0 \\ 1 - e^{-3x}, & x > 0 \end{cases}$$

***Example 44.*** *The PDF of a continuous random variate is*

$$f(x) = \begin{cases} 0, & x < 2 \\ \dfrac{(3+2x)}{18}, & 2 \le x \le 4 \\ 0, & x > 4 \end{cases}$$

*Then, probability that x will lie between $2 \le x \le 3$ is*

(a) 4/9 (b) 2/9 (c) 5/9 (d) – 2/9

**Solution.** (a) $P(2 \le x \le 3) = \int_2^3 f(x)\,dx = \int_2^3 \dfrac{3+2x}{18}\,dx = \dfrac{4}{9}$

***Example 45.*** *The value of c for which function*

$$f(x) = \begin{cases} \dfrac{c}{\sqrt{x}}, & 0 < x < 4 \\ 0, & \text{elsewhere} \end{cases}$$

*is a PDF, $P(x > 1)$ is*

(a) 1/4, 0 (b) – 1/4, 1/2

(c) 1/4, 1/2 (d) 1/2, 1

**Solution.** (c) $\int_{-\infty}^{\infty} f(x)\,dx = \int_{-\infty}^{0} 0\,dx + \int_0^4 \dfrac{c}{\sqrt{x}}\,dx + \int_4^{\infty} 0\,dx = 1$

or $\quad [2cx^{1/2}]_0^4 = 1$ or $c = \dfrac{1}{4}$

$$\therefore \quad P(x > 1) = \frac{1}{4}\int_1^4 x^{-1/2}\,dx = \frac{1}{2}$$

***Example 46.*** *The value of k, for which function*

$$f(x) = \begin{cases} k\,e^{-3x}, & x > 0 \\ 0, & \text{elsewhere} \end{cases} \quad \textit{is a PDF.}$$

(a) 3 (b) 1/3 (c) 2 (d) – 3

**Solution.** (a) We know that, $f(x)$ is a PDF, if

$$\int_{-\infty}^{\infty} f(x)\,dx = 1 \text{ or } \int_{-\infty}^{0} 0\,dx + k\int_0^{\infty} e^{-3x}\,dx = 1$$

or $\quad \dfrac{k}{-3}[e^{-3x}]_0^{\infty} = \dfrac{k}{3} = 1$

$\therefore \quad k = 3$

***Example 47.*** *The value of mode for the frequency curve*

$$y = \left(\frac{1}{2}\right)\sin x,\ 0 \le x < \pi \text{ is}$$

(a) $\pi$ (b) $\pi/3$

(c) $\pi/4$ (d) $\pi/2$

**Solution.** (d) As, mode is the highest frequency element

$\therefore \quad y = \dfrac{1}{2}\sin x,\ 0 \le x \le \pi$ has maximum frequency

when $\quad x = \dfrac{\pi}{2}$

$\therefore \quad y = \dfrac{1}{2}$ at $x = \dfrac{\pi}{2}$

## Type II (*One or more than one correct option*)

***Example 48.*** *If A, B and C are three events, then which of the following is/are correct?*

(a) $p$ (exactly of $A, B, C$ occur)

$\le P(A \cap B) + P(B \cap C) + P(C \cap A)$

(b) $P(A \cup B \cup C) \le P(A) + P(B) + P(C)$

(c) $P$ (exactly one of $A, B, C$ occur)

$\le P(A) + P(B) + P(C) - P(B \cap C) - P(C \cap A) - P(A \cap B)$

(d) $P$ ($A$ and atleast one of $B, C$ occurs)

$\le P(A \cap B) + P(A \cap C)$

**Solution.** (a), (b), (c), (d) We have,

$P$(exactly two of $A, B, C$ occur)

$$= P(A \cap B \cap \bar{C}) + P(A \cap \bar{B} \cap C) + P(\bar{A} \cap B \cap C)$$

$$= P(A \cap B) - P(A \cap B \cap C) + P(A \cap C) - P(A \cap B \cap C) + P(B \cap C) - P(A \cap B \cap C)$$

$$= P(A \cap B) + P(B \cap C) + P(A \cap C) - 3P(A \cap B \cap C) \le P(A \cap B) + P(B \cap C) + P(A \cap C)$$

Also, $P(A \cup B \cup C)$

$$= P(A \cup B) + P(C) - P\{(A \cup B) \cap C\}$$

$$\le P(A \cup B) + P(C)$$

$$\le P(A) + P(B) + P(C) \quad [\because P(A \cup B) \le P(A) + P(B)]$$

Now, $P$ (exactly one of $A, B, C$ occur)

$$= P(A \cap \bar{B} \cap \bar{C}) + P(\bar{A} \cap B \cap \bar{C}) + P(\bar{A} \cap \bar{B} \cap C)$$

$$= P(A \cap \overline{B \cup C}) + P(\overline{A \cup B} \cap C) + P(B \cap \overline{A \cup C})$$

$$= P(A) - P\{A \cap (B \cup C) \cup (A \cap C)\} + P(C) - P\{(C \cap A) \cup (C \cap B)\} + P(B) - P\{(B \cap A) \cup (B \cap C)\}$$

$$= P(A) + P(B) + P(C) - 2P(A \cap B) - 2P(B \cap C) - 2P(A \cap C) + 3P(A \cap B \cap C)$$

$$= [P(A) + P(B) + P(C) - P(A \cap B) - P(B \cap C) - P(A \cap C)] - [P(A \cap B) + P(B \cap C) + P(A \cap C) - 3P(A \cap B \cap C)]$$

$$= P(A) + P(B) + P(C) - P(A \cap B) - P(B \cap C) - P(A \cap C) - P(\text{exactly two of } A, B, C \text{ occur})$$

$$\le P(A) + P(B) + P(C) - P(A \cap B) - P(B \cap C) - P(A \cap C)$$

Finally, P ($A$ and atleast one of $B, C$ occurs)

$$= P[A \cap (B \cup C)]$$

$$= P[(A \cap B) \cup (A \cap C)]$$

$$= P(A \cap B) + P(A \cap C) - P[(A \cap B) \cap (A \cap C)]$$

$$= P(A \cap B) + P(A \cap C) - P(A \cap B \cap C)$$
$$\le P(A \cap B) + P(A \cap C)$$

***Example 49.*** *A Poisson distribution has a double mode at $x = 3$ and $x = 4$.*

(a) The probability that $x = 4$ is $\frac{32\,e^{-4}}{3}$.

(b) The probability that $x = 3$ or is $\frac{32\,e^{-4}}{3}$.

(c) The probability that $x = 3$ or $x = 4$ is $\frac{64}{3}\,e^{-4}$.

(d) The probability that $x = 3$ or $x = 4$ is 1.

**Solution.** (a), (b), (c)

The two modes in Poisson distribution

$$P(x:\lambda) = \frac{e^{-\lambda}\,\lambda^{x-}}{x!} \text{ are } \lambda \text{ and } \lambda - 1$$

$$\therefore \quad \lambda = 4$$

$$\therefore \quad P(x = 4) = \frac{e^{-4}\,\lambda^4}{4!} = \frac{32\,e^{-4}}{3}$$

$$P(x = 3) = \frac{e^{-4}\,(4)^3}{3!} = \frac{32\,e^{-4}}{3}$$

$$\therefore \quad P[(x = 3) \cup (x = 4)]$$
$$= P(x = 3) + P(x = 4) = \frac{64}{3}\,e^{-4}$$

***Example 50.*** *A biased coin with probability $p$, $0 < p < 1$ of heads is tossed until a head appears for the first time. If the probability that the number of tosses required is even $\frac{2}{5}$, then $p$ equals*

(a) $\frac{1}{3}$ (b) $\frac{2}{3}$ (c) $\frac{2}{5}$ (d) $\frac{3}{5}$

**Solution.** (a) Let $q = 1 - p$. Since, head appears first time is an even throw *i.e.*, 2 or 4 or 6 etc.

$$\therefore \quad \frac{2}{5} = qp + q^3p + q^5p + \ldots$$

$$\Rightarrow \quad \frac{2}{5} = \frac{qp}{1 - q^2}$$

$$\Rightarrow \quad \frac{2}{5} = \frac{(1-p)}{1-(1-p)^2} = \frac{1-p}{2-p}$$

$$\Rightarrow \quad 2(2 - p) = 5(1 - p) \Rightarrow p = \frac{1}{3}$$

***Example 51.*** *An ordinary six faced die is thrown four times. The probability of getting*

(a) 0 aces is $(5/6)^4$ (b) 2 aces ${}^4C_3\left(\frac{5}{6}\right)\cdot\left(\frac{1}{6}\right)^3$

(c) 3 aces ${}^4C_2\left(\frac{5}{6}\right)^2\left(\frac{1}{6}\right)^2$ (d) 4 aces is $\left(\frac{1}{6}\right)^3$

**Solution.** (a), (d)

$$P(\text{an ace}) = p = \frac{1}{6}$$

$$q = 1 - p = \frac{5}{6}\; n = 4$$

By Bernoulli's trials, the probability of

$$0 \text{ ace} = \text{1st term of } \left(\frac{5}{6} + \frac{1}{6}\right)^4 = \left(\frac{5}{6}\right)^4$$

$$1 \text{ ace} = \text{2nd term of } \left(\frac{5}{6} + \frac{1}{6}\right)^4$$
$$= {}^4C_1\left(\frac{5}{6}\right)^3\cdot\left(\frac{1}{6}\right)$$

$$2 \text{ aces} = \text{3rd term of } \left(\frac{5}{6} + \frac{1}{6}\right)^4$$
$$= {}^4C_2\left(\frac{5}{6}\right)^2\cdot\left(\frac{1}{6}\right)^2$$

$$3 \text{ aces} = \text{4th term of } \left(\frac{5}{6} + \frac{1}{6}\right)^4$$
$$= {}^4C_3\left(\frac{5}{6}\right)\cdot\left(\frac{1}{6}\right)^3$$

$$4 \text{ aces} = \text{5th or last term of } \left(\frac{1}{6}\right)^4$$

$$(p + q)^n = \left(\frac{5}{6} + \frac{1}{6}\right)^4$$

***Example 52.*** *The probability of the simultaneous occurrence of two events A and B is p. If the probability that exactly one of A and B occurs is q. Then, which of the following option(s) is/are correct?*

(a) $P(\bar{A}) + P(\bar{B}) = 2 + 2q - p$

(b) $P(\bar{A}) + P(\bar{B}) = 2 - 2p - q$

(c) $P(A \cap B / A \cup B) = \frac{p}{p + q}$

(d) $P(\bar{A} \cap \bar{B}) = 1 - p - q$

**Solution.** (b), (c), (d)

We have,

$$P(A \cap B) = p \text{ and } P(A) + P(B) - 2P(A \cap B) = q$$

$$\Rightarrow \quad P(A) + P(B) - 2p = q$$

$$\Rightarrow \quad P(A) + P(B) = 2p + q$$

$$\Rightarrow \quad 1 - P(\bar{A}) + 1 - P(\bar{B}) = 2p + q$$

$$\Rightarrow \quad P(\bar{A}) + P(\bar{B}) = 2 - 2p - q$$

Now, $P\{(A \cap B)/(A \cup B)\}$

$$= P\,\frac{[(A \cap B) \cap (A \cup B)]}{P(A \cup B)}$$

$$= \frac{P(A \cap B)}{P(A \cup B)}$$

$$= \frac{P(A \cap B)}{P(A) + p(B) - P(A \cap B)}$$

$$= \frac{p}{2p + q - p} = \frac{p}{p + q}$$

Finally, $P(\bar{A} \cap \bar{B}) = P(\overline{A \cup B}) = 1 - P(A \cup B)$

$$= 1 - [P(A) + P(B) - P(A \cap B)]$$
$$= 1 - [2p + q - p] = 1 - p - q$$

# Exercise 1 (For Part 'B')

**Directions** (Q. Nos. 1-382) *All questions have only one correct option.*

**1.** A cricket club has 15 members of which only 5 can bowl. If the names of 15 members are put into a box and 11 names are drawn at random, then the probability of obtaining 11 members team containing exactly three bowlers is

(a) $\frac{18}{91}$ (b) $\frac{30}{91}$

(c) $\frac{15}{91}$ (d) None of these

**2.** These houses are available in a locality, 3 persons apply for the houses. Each applies for one house without consulting others. The probability that all the three apply for the same house is

(a) $\frac{2}{9}$ (b) $\frac{1}{9}$ (c) $\frac{8}{9}$ (d) $\frac{7}{9}$

**3.** Let $A$ and $B$ be two events such that $P(\overline{A \cup B}) = 1/6$, $P(A \cap B) = 1/4$ and $P(\overline{A}) = 1/4$, where $\overline{A}$ stands for complement of event $A$. Then, events $A$ and $B$ are

(a) equally likely and mutually exclusive
(b) equally likely but not independent
(c) independent but not equally likely
(d) mutually exclusive and independent

**4.** If the probability that $A$ and $B$ will die within a year are $p$ and $q$ respectively, then the probability that only one of them will be alive at the end of the year is

(a) $p+q$ (b) $p+q-2pq$

(c) $p+q-pq$ (d) $p+q+pq$

**5.** An unbiased coin is tossed to get 2 points for turning up a head and one point for the tail. If three unbiased coins are tossed simultaneously, then the probability of getting a total of odd number of points is

(a) $\frac{1}{2}$ (b) $\frac{1}{4}$ (c) $\frac{1}{8}$ (d) $\frac{3}{8}$

**6.** A six faced dice is a biased one. It is thrice more likely to show an odd number than to show an even number. It is thrown twice. The probability that the sum of the numbers in the two throws is even is

(a) $\frac{1}{2}$ (b) $\frac{5}{9}$

(c) $\frac{5}{8}$ (d) None of these

**7.** Let $A$ and $B$ be two independent events. The probability that both $A$ and $B$ occur is 1/2 and the probability that neither $A$ nor $B$ occurs is 1/2. The respective probabilities of $A$ and $B$ are

(a) $\frac{1}{6}$ and $\frac{1}{2}$ (b) $\frac{1}{2}$ and $\frac{1}{6}$

(c) $\frac{1}{3}$ and $\frac{1}{4}$ or $\frac{1}{4}$ and $\frac{1}{3}$ (d) None of these

**8.** The probability that a teacher will give an unannounced test during any class is 1/5. If a student is absent twice, then the probability that he misses atleast one test is

(a) $\frac{2}{5}$ (b) $\frac{4}{5}$ (c) $\frac{7}{25}$ (d) $\frac{9}{25}$

**9.** From 4 children, 2 women and 4 men, 4 women selected. The probability that there are exactly 2 children among the selected is

(a) 11/21 (b) 9/21

(c) 10/21 (d) None of these

**10.** Suppose $E$ and $F$ are two events of a random experiment. If the probability of occurrence of $E$ is 1/5 and the probability of occurrence of $F$ given $E$ is 1/10, then the probability of non-occurrence of atleast one of the events $E$ and $F$ is

(a) $\frac{1}{18}$ (b) $\frac{1}{2}$ (c) $\frac{49}{50}$ (d) $\frac{1}{50}$

**11.** If three unbiased coins are tossed, find the probability of getting atleast two tails and atmost two tails.

(a) $\frac{1}{2}, \frac{3}{8}$ (b) $\frac{1}{2}, \frac{5}{8}$

(c) $\frac{1}{2}, \frac{7}{8}$ (d) None of these

**12.** In a competition $A$, $B$ and $C$ are participating. The probability that $A$ wins is twice that of $B$; the probability that $B$ wins is twice that of $C$. The probability that $A$ loses is

(a) $\frac{1}{7}$ (b) $\frac{2}{7}$ (c) $\frac{4}{7}$ (d) $\frac{3}{7}$

**13.** A number $n$ is chosen at random from $S = \{1, 2, 3, \ldots, 50\}$. Let $A = \left\{n \in S : n + \frac{50}{n} > 27\right\}$, $B = \{n \in S : n \text{ is a prime}\}$ and $C = \{n \in S : n \text{ is a square}\}$. The correct order of their probabilities is

(a) $P(A) < P(B) < P(C)$ (b) $P(A) > P(B) > P(C)$

(c) $P(B) < P(A) < P(C)$ (d) $P(A) > P(C) > P(B)$

**14.** From a well shuffled pack of 52 cards, 3 cards are drawn at random. Find the probability that three cards drawn contain two kings and one ace.

(a) $\frac{4}{5525}$ (b) $\frac{5}{5525}$ (c) $\frac{6}{5525}$ (d) $\frac{7}{5525}$

**15.** A rifleman is firing at a distant target and has only 10% chance of hitting it. The number of rounds, he must fire in order to have 50% chance of hitting it atleast once is

(a) 11 (b) 9 (c) 7 (d) 5

**16.** A fair coin is tossed three times. Find the probability of getting atmost one head and two consecutive heads.

(a) $\frac{1}{2}, \frac{1}{3}$ (b) $\frac{1}{3}, \frac{1}{4}$ (c) $\frac{1}{2}, \frac{1}{4}$ (d) $-\frac{1}{2}, -\frac{3}{4}$

**17.** The probability of India winning a test match against West Indies is 1/2. Assuming independence from match-to-match the probability that in a three match series India's second win occurs at the third test is

(a) $\frac{2}{3}$ (b) $\frac{1}{2}$ (c) $\frac{1}{4}$ (d) $\frac{1}{8}$

**18.** If the probability that a man aged $x$ years will die within a year be $p$, then the chance that out of 5 men $A, B, C, D$ and $E$, each aged $x$ years. $A$ will die during the year and be the first to die is

(a) $\frac{1}{5} p(1-p)^4$ (b) $\frac{1}{5}(1-(1-p)^5)$

(c) $5(1-(1-p)^5)$ (d) None of these

**19.** A pair of dice is rolled again-and-again till a total of 5 or 7 is obtained. The chance that a total of 5 comes before a total of 7 is

(a) $\frac{2}{5}$ (b) $\frac{3}{7}$

(c) $\frac{3}{13}$ (d) None of these

**20.** A bag $X$ contains 2 white and 3 black balls and another bag $Y$ contains 4 white and 2 black balls. One bag is selected at random and a ball is drawn from it. Then, the probability for the ball chosen be white is to

(a) $\frac{2}{15}$ (b) $\frac{7}{15}$ (c) $\frac{8}{15}$ (d) $\frac{14}{15}$

**21.** The probability that a man can hit a target is 3/4. He tries 5 times. The probability that he will hit the target atleast three times is

(a) $\frac{291}{364}$ (b) $\frac{371}{464}$ (c) $\frac{471}{502}$ (d) $\frac{459}{512}$

**22.** The probability of getting qualified in IIT-JEE and AIEEE by a student are respectively $\frac{1}{5}$ and $\frac{3}{5}$. The probability that the student gets qualified for one of these tests is

(a) $\frac{3}{25}$ (b) $\frac{17}{25}$ (c) $\frac{22}{25}$ (d) $\frac{8}{25}$

**23.** Four persons are chosen at random from a group of 3 men, 2 women and 4 children. The chance that exactly 2 of them are children, is

(a) $\frac{10}{21}$ (b) $\frac{11}{13}$ (c) $\frac{13}{25}$ (d) $\frac{21}{32}$

**24.** A biased coin with probability $p$; $(0 < p < 1)$ of getting a head is tossed until a head appears for the first time. If 2/5 is the probability that the number of tosses required is even, then $p$ is equal to

(a) $\frac{2}{5}$ (b) $\frac{3}{5}$ (c) $\frac{1}{3}$ (d) $\frac{2}{3}$

**25.** Events $A$, $B$ and $C$ are mutually exclusive events such that $P(A) = \frac{3x+1}{3}$, $P(B) = \frac{1-x}{4}$ and $P(C) = \frac{1-2x}{4}$. The set of possible values of $x$ are in the interval

(a) $\left[\frac{1}{3}, \frac{1}{2}\right]$ (b) $\left[\frac{1}{3}, \frac{2}{3}\right]$ (c) $\left[\frac{1}{3}, \frac{13}{3}\right]$ (d) $[0, 1]$

**26.** Two events $A$ and $B$ have probabilities 0.25 and 0.50, respectively. The probability that both $A$ and $B$ occur simultaneously is 0.14. Then, the probability that neither $A$ nor $B$ occurs is

(a) 0.39 (b) 0.375 (c) 0.89 (d) 0.86

**27.** A box contain 10 mangoes out of which 4 are rotten. 2 mangoes are taken out together. If one of them is found to be good, then probability that the other is also good is

(a) $\frac{1}{3}$ (b) $\frac{8}{15}$ (c) $\frac{5}{13}$ (d) $\frac{2}{3}$

**28.** A card is drawn at random from a well shuffled pack of 52 cards. The probability of getting a heart or a diamond is

(a) $\frac{1}{26}$ (b) $\frac{1}{2}$

(c) $\frac{3}{13}$ (d) 1

**29.** A man has the choice of running either a hot snack stall or an ice cream stall at a sea side resort during the summer season. If it is a fairly cool summer he should make ₹ 5000 by running the hot snack stall but if the summer is quite hot he can only expect to make ₹ 1000. On the other hand, if he operates the ice cream stall, his profit is estimated at ₹ 6500, if the summer is hot, but only ₹ 1000 if it is cool. There is a 40 per cent chance of the summer being hot. Should he opt for running the hot snack stall or the ice-cream stall? Give mathematical arguments?

(a) Ice cream stall (b) Hot snack

(c) Both (a) and (b) (d) Data is incomplete

**30.** $A$ throws a coin 3 times. If he gets a head all the three times he is to get a prize of ₹ 160. The entry fee for the game is ₹ 16. The mathematical expectation of $A$ is

(a) ₹ 7 (b) ₹ 6 (c) ₹ 9 (d) ₹ 5

**31.** The probability that there is atleast one error is an account statement prepared by $A$ is 0.3 and for $B$ and $C$, they are 0.4 and 0.45, respectively. $A$, $B$ and $C$ prepared 20, 10 and 40 statements, respectively. The expected number of correct statements in all is

(a) 42 (b) 32 (c) 47 (d) 27

**32.** The probability that tthere is atleast one error in an account statement prepared by $A$ is 0.2 and for $B$ and $C$, they are 0.25 and 0.4, respectively. $A$, $B$ and $C$ prepared 10, 16 and 20 statements, respectively. Find the expected number of correct statements in all.

(a) 20 (b) 25 (c) 30 (d) 32

**33.** A firm plans to bid ₹ 300 per tonne for a contract to supply 1000 tonnes of a metal. It has two competitors *A* and *B* and it assumes that the probability that *A* will bid less than ₹ 300 per tonne is 0.3 and that *B* will bid less than ₹ 300 per tonne is 0.7. If the lowest bidder gets all the business and the firms bid independently, what is the expected value of the contract to the firm?

(a) ₹63000 (b) ₹27000 (c) ₹147000 (d) ₹237000

**34.** A player tosses three fair coins. He wins ₹ 8, if 3 heads occur; ₹ 3, if 2 heads occur and ₹ 1, if only 1 head occur. If the game is fair, how much would he lose, if no head occur?

(a) ₹ 20 (b) ₹ 30
(c) ₹ 15 (d) ₹ 35

**35.** An urn contains 7 white and 3 red balls. Two balls are drawn together at random, from this urn. Compute the probability that neither of them is white. Find also the probability of getting one white and one red ball. Hence, compute the expected number of white balls.

(a) 1 (b) 2 (c) 3 (d) 1.4

**36.** A man draws 2 balls from a bag containing 3 white and 5 black balls. If he is to receive ₹ 14 for every white ball which he draws and ₹ 7 for every black ball, what is his expectation?

(a) ₹ 20.25 (b) ₹ 19.25
(c) ₹ 18.25 (d) None of these

**37.** A bag contain 5 white and 7 black balls. Find the expectations of a man who is allowed to draw two balls from the bag and who is to receive one rupee for each black ball and two rupees for each white ball drawn.

(a) ₹ 2.83 (b) ₹ 3.83
(c) ₹ 4.83 (d) ₹ 5.83

**38.** Two cards are taken out one-by-one from the 52 normal playing cards. What is the chance that the first card is an ace and second card is an honours card, the first card is not taken back into the pack before the second is drawn?

(a) $\frac{5}{221}$ (b) $\frac{3}{221}$
(c) $\frac{7}{221}$ (d) $\frac{9}{221}$

**39.** If *A* and *B* are two events such that $P(A) > 0$ and $P(B) \neq 1$, then $P(\bar{A}/\bar{B})$ is equal to

(a) $1 - P(A/B)$ (b) $1 - \frac{P(A)}{P(B)}$
(c) $\frac{1 - P(A \cup B)}{P(\bar{B})}$ (d) $\frac{P(\bar{A})}{P(\bar{B})}$

**40.** The odds against an event *A* are 5 : 2 and odds in favour of another independent event *B* are 6 : 5. The chances that neither *A* nor *B* occurs is

(a) $\frac{52}{77}$ (b) $\frac{25}{77}$ (c) $\frac{10}{77}$ (d) $\frac{12}{77}$

**41.** Three letters are written to different persons and addresses on the envelops are also written. Without looking at the addresses, the letters are put into the envelops; the probability that letters go into right envelops is

(a) $\frac{1}{27}$ (b) $\frac{1}{6}$ (c) $\frac{1}{9}$ (d) $\frac{1}{8}$

**42.** In a non-leap year, the probability of getting 53 Sundays or 53 Tuesdays or 53 Thursdays is

(a) $\frac{1}{7}$ (b) $\frac{2}{7}$ (c) $\frac{3}{7}$ (d) $\frac{4}{7}$

**43.** Mr *A* gave his telephone number of Mr *B*. Mr *B* remembers that the first two digits were 40 and the remaining four digits were two 3s, one 6 and one 8. He is not certain about the order of the digits. Mr *B* dials 403638. The probability that he will get *A*'s house is

(a) $\frac{1}{2}$ (b) $\frac{1}{4}$ (c) $\frac{1}{8}$ (d) $\frac{1}{12}$

**44.** A number of five digits is formed by using the digits 0, 1, 2, 3, 4, no digit being repeated in any number. The probability that it is a number divisible by 4 is

(a) $\frac{1}{3}$ (b) $\frac{5}{16}$ (c) $\frac{1}{4}$ (d) $\frac{4}{15}$

**45.** Box *A* contains 2 black and 3 red balls while box *B* contains 3 black and 4 red balls. Out of these two boxes one is selected at random and the probability of choosing box *A* is double that of box *B*. If a red ball is drawn from the selected box, then the probability that it has come from box *B* is

(a) $\frac{21}{41}$ (b) $\frac{10}{31}$ (c) $\frac{12}{31}$ (d) $\frac{13}{41}$

**46.** If a balanced coin is flipped twice, what is the probability of getting atleast one head?

(a) $\frac{3}{4}$ (b) $\frac{1}{2}$ (c) $\frac{1}{4}$ (d) $\frac{2}{3}$

**47.** A shopkeeper purchases magazine for ₹ 10 each and sells them for ₹ 15 each. He cannot return unsold magazines. The probability distribution of the sale of magazines is

| **Number of customers** | 28 | 29 | 30 | 31 | 32 |
|---|---|---|---|---|---|
| **Probability** | 3.0 | 0.2 | 0.2 | 0.2 | 0.1 |

The number of magazines the shopkeeper should stock is

(a) 29 (b) 28 (c) 30 (d) 31

**48.** Experience has shown that a certain lie detector will show a positive reading (indicates a lie) 10% of the time when a person is telling the truth and 95% of the time when a person is lying. Suppose that, a random sample of 5 suspects is subjected to a lie detector test regarding a recent one person crime. Then, the probability of observing no positive reading, if all suspects plead innocent and are telling the truth is

(a) 0.409 (b) 0.735
(c) 0.00001 (d) 0.591

**49.** We have a biased die such that, each even number is twice likely to occur for odd number. What is the probability of getting a numbers greater than 3, in a single roll of die?

(a) $\frac{4}{9}$ (b) $\frac{5}{9}$ (c) $\frac{3}{9}$ (d) $\frac{1}{9}$

**50.** The standard deviation for the set of numbers 1, 4, 5, 7, 8 is 2.45 nearly. If 10 is added to each number, then new standard deviation is

(a) 24.45 (b) 12.45 (c) 2.45 (d) 0.245

**51.** A car has four traffic lights on its route. Each of them allows it to move ahead or stop with probability 0.5. If $X$ represents the number of lights passed before the car stops for the time, then

(a) $P(X=3) > P(X=4)$ (b) $P(X=3) = P(X=4) > 0$
(c) $P(X=3) < P(X=4)$ (d) $P(X=3) = P(X=4) = 0$

**52.** Let $X$ has the probability density function

$$f(x) = \begin{cases} 0.75\,(1-x^2),\ x \in [-1, 1] \\ 0, \quad \text{otherwise} \end{cases}$$

What is probability $P\left(-\frac{1}{2} \le X \le \frac{1}{2}\right)$?

(a) 0.68 (b) 0.60
(c) 0.65 (d) None of these

**53.** For a given probability distribution

$$f(x) = \frac{1}{8}\binom{3}{x},\ x = 0, 1, 2, 3$$

for a random variable $X$, the moment generating function of this is

(a) $\frac{1}{8}(1+e^t)^3$ (b) $\frac{1}{4}e^t$ (c) $(1+e^t)^2$ (d) $e^t$

**54.** The number of arrivals per hour at an automatic teller machine is Poisson distributed with a mean of 3.5 arrivals/h. What is the probability that more than three arrivals occur in an hour?

(a) 0.3209 (b) 0.4633 (c) 0.5367 (d) 0.6791

**55.** Marks on a Chemistry test follow a normal distribution with a mean of 65 and a standard deviation of 12. Approximately what percentage of the students have scores below 50?

(a) 11% (b) 89% (c) 15% (d) 18%

**56.** The standard deviation of the wages of 85 employees is ₹ 15.40. After one year each of

(a) 15.40 (b) 40.40 (c) 20.40 (d) 10.40

**57.** $X_i$, $i = 1, 2, \ldots, n$ are i id random variables with cdf $F(x)$ and pdf $f(x)$. Then, the pdf $g_z(x)$, where $Z = \max[X_1, X_2, \ldots, X_n]$ is

(a) $n[F(x)]^{n-1}f(x)$ (b) $n[1-F(x)]^{n-1}f(x)$
(c) $[F(x)]^{n-1}f(x)$ (d) $[1-F(x)]^{n-1}f(x)$

**58.** Let $X$ have the probability density function

$$f(x) = \begin{cases} 0.75\,(1-x^2),\ x \in [-1, 1] \\ 0, \quad \text{otherwise} \end{cases}$$

The probability distribution function $F(x)$ is given by

(a) $F(x) = 0.5 + 0.75x - 0.25x^3$, $x \in (-1, 1]$
(b) $F(x) = 0.75x - 0.25x^3$, $x \in (1, 1)$
(c) $F(x) = 0.5 - 0.25x^2$, $x \in (-1, 1]$
(d) $F(x) = 0.5x^2 - 0.2x^2$, $x \in (-1, 1]$

**59.** What is the second mean about the origin for a random variable $X$ with probability density

$$f(x) = \begin{cases} \frac{x}{2},\ 0 < x < 2 \\ 0, \text{ otherwise} \end{cases}$$

(a) 2 (b) 3
(c) 4 (d) None of these

**60.** A can company reports that the number of breakdowns per 8 h shift on its machine operated assembly line follows a Poisson distribution with a mean of 1.5. Assuming that the machine operates independently across shifts, what is the probability of no breakdowns during three consecutive 8 h shifts?

(a) 0.0744 (b) 0.0498
(c) 0.6065 (d) 0.0111

**61.** One of the side effects of flooding a lake in northern boreal forest areas (e.g., for a hydroelectric project) is that mercury is leached from the soil, enters the food chain and eventually contaminates the fish. The concentration in fish will vary among individual fish because of differences in eating patterns, movements around the lake, etc. Suppose that the concentrations of mercury is individual fish follows an approximate normal distribution with a mean of 0.25 ppm and a standard deviation of 0.08 ppm. Fish are safe to eat if the mercury level is below 0.30 ppm. What proportion of fish are safe to eat?

(a) 63% (b) 23%
(c) 73% (d) 27%

**62.** If the standard deviation of the observation $-5, -4, -3, -2, -1, 0, 1, 2, 3, 4, 5$ is $\sqrt{10}$. The standard deviation of observations 15, 16, 17, 18, 19, 20, 21, 22, 23, 24, 25 will be

(a) $\sqrt{10}+20$ (b) $\sqrt{10}+10$
(c) $\sqrt{10}$ (d) None of these

**63.** $X_1, X_2$ are two independent random variables each having the same distribution $P(X_i = k) = \frac{1}{2^{k+1}}$, $k = 0, 1, 2, \ldots$; then the probability that $X_1 + X_2 = 5$ is

(a) $\frac{6}{2^7}$ (b) $\frac{5}{2^6}$
(c) $\frac{3}{2^6}$ (d) $\frac{4}{2^7}$

**64.** Which of the following can serves as probability distribution?

(a) $f(x) = \frac{x-2}{2}$, x = 1, 2, 3, 4

(b) $h(x) = \frac{x^2}{25}$, x = 1, 2, 3, 4

(c) $f(x) = \frac{x-2}{5}$, x = 1, 2, 3, 4

(d) $g(x) = \frac{1}{4}$, x = 1, 2, 3, 4

**65.** Given, probability density function of random variable $X$

$$f(x) = \begin{cases} \frac{4}{\pi(1+x^2)}, & 0 < x < 1 \\ 0, & \text{otherwise} \end{cases}$$

The second moment about the origin of a random variable $X$ is

(a) $\frac{4}{\pi}$ (b) $\frac{4}{\pi} - 1$ (c) $4\pi$ (d) $\frac{\pi}{4} - 1$

**66.** The distribution of phone calls arriving in one minute periods at a switchboard is assumed to be Poisson with the parameter $\lambda$. During 100 periods, the following distribution was obtained

| **# (calls)** | 0 | 1 | 2 | 3 | 4 or more |
|---|---|---|---|---|---|
| **Frequency** | 30 | 43 | 21 | 6 | 0 |

An estimate for $\lambda$ based on this data set is

(a) 1.00 (b) 1.03 (c) 1.04 (d) 1.33

**67.** It has been estimated that about 20% of people between the ages of 18 and 25 have used marijuana in the last year. Which of the following is correct about this statement?

(a) Five people of this age group were randomly selected. This means that exactly one of them must have used marijuana in the last year.

(b) Twenty people were randomly selected from this age group. Eighteen of them use marijuana in the last year. The next person selected at random will have a lower probability of using marijuana.

(c) Ten people were randomly selected from this age group. None of them have used marijuana in the last year. The next person selected must have a higher probability of using marijuana in the last year.

(d) A thousand people from this age group were randomly selected. It is not unusual to find that 217 of them have used marijuana in the last year.

**68.** The standard deviations of two sets containing 10 and 20 members are 2 and 3, respectively measured from their common mean 5. The SD for the whole set of 30 members is

(a) $\frac{2}{\sqrt{3}}$ (b) $\sqrt{6}$ (c) $\sqrt{\left(\frac{22}{3}\right)}$ (d) $\sqrt{3}$

**69.** The folded normal distribution has density function $f(x) = c - \frac{1}{\sqrt{2\pi}} e^{-x^2/2}$; $x > 0$, then the mean of the distribution is

(a) $\sqrt{\frac{2}{\pi}}$ (b) $\frac{2}{\pi}$ (c) $\frac{\pi}{2}$ (d) $0.7\pi$

**70.** Which of the following cannot serves as the probability distribution?

(a) $f(x) = \frac{1}{6}$ for x = 1, 2, 3, 4, 5, 6

(b) $f(x) = \frac{1}{2}$ for x = 1, 2

(c) $f(x) = \frac{1}{3}$ for x = 1, 2, 3

(d) $f(x) = \frac{1}{4}$ for x = 1, 2

**71.** The relationship between mean, $\mu$ variance, $\sigma^2$ and second moment about the origin $\mu_2'$ is

(a) $\sigma^2 = \mu_2' - \mu^2$ (b) $\sigma^2 = \mu\,\mu_2'$

(c) $\sigma^2 = \mu_2' + \mu$ (d) None of these

**72.** Suppose that the allele for tallness ($T$) is dominant over shortness ($t$); that for Yellow ($Y$) is dominant over green ($y$); and that for roundness ($W$) is dominant over wrinkled ($w$). Suppose we cross two plants with genotypes TTYyWw and TtYyWw. The probability of a Tall, Yellow, Round plant is

(a) 9/16 (b) 2/32

(c) 1/16 (d) 3/32

**73.** If $A_1$, $A_2$ and $A_3$ are three event, then $P(A_1 \cup A_2 \cup A_3)$ is

(a) $\sum_1^3 P(A_i) - \sum_{i=1}^3 \sum_{j=1}^3 P(A_i \cap A_j)$

(b) $\sum_1^3 P(A_i)$

(c) $\sum_1^3 P(A_i) - \sum_{i<j=1}^3 \sum P(A_i \cap A_j) + P(A_1 \cap A_2 \cap A_3)$

(d) $\sum_i^3 P(A_i) - P(A_1 \cap A_2 \cap A_3)$

**74.** If $X$ is a Poisson variate such that $P(X = 2) = [9 \cdot P(X = 4) + 90 \cdot P(X = 6)]$, the mean of the distribution is

(a) 1 (b) 2 (c) 3 (d) 4

**75.** If $f(x)$ is a probability density function of a continuous random variable, then

(a) $\int_{-\infty}^{\infty} f(x)dx = 0$ (b) $\int_{-\infty}^{\infty} f(x)dx = 1$

(c) $\int_{-\infty}^{\infty} f(x)dx > 1$ (d) $\int_{-\infty}^{\infty} f(x)dx < 0$

**76.** The third moment about the mean is referred as ...... of a distribution.

(a) Symmetry or skewness

(b) Expatiation

(c) Kurtosis

(d) None of the above

**77.** The number of telephone calls that pass through a switchboard has a Poisson distribution with mean equal to 2 per minute. The probability that no telephone calls pass through the switchboard in two consecutive minutes is

(a) 0.2707 (b) 0.0517 (c) 0.0183 (d) 0.0366

**78.** A random variable $X$ has a probability distribution as follows

| $r$ | 0 | 1 | 2 | 3 |
|---|---|---|---|---|
| $P(R=r)$ | $2k$ | $3k$ | $13k$ | $2k$ |

Then, the probability that $pr\ (x > 2.0)$ is equal to

(a) 0.90 (b) 0.25 (c) 0.65 (d) 0.15

**79.** Consider two independent Poisson processes $\{X_1(t)\}$ and $\{X_2(t)\}$ with rates 1 and 2 per unit time, respectively. Then, the conditional mean of $X_1(t)$ given $X_1(t) + X_2(t) = 9$ is

(a) 9 (b) 3 (c) 6 (d) 1

**80.** Let $X$ be a random variable with probability density function

$$f(x) = \frac{1}{2} e^{\left[\frac{-(x-3)}{3}\right]}, \quad x \geq 3 = 0,$$

otherwise, then $E(X)$ is

(a) 4 (b) 5 (c) 7 (d) 12

**81.** For any real numbers $a$ and $b$, $a \leq b$, the probability density function of a continuous random variable $X$ is given by

(a) $P(a \leq X \leq b) = \int_a^b f(x)\,dx$

(b) $P(a \leq X \leq b) = \int_a^b f(x)\,dx$

(c) $P(a \leq X \leq b) = 1 - \int_a^b f(x)\,dx$

(d) $P(a \leq X \leq b) = \int_a^b f(x)\,dx - 1$

**82.** For any random variable $X$ for which $E(X)$ exist. The zeroth moment about the mean, $\mu_0$ is

(a) zero (b) one
(c) mean itself (d) None of these

**83.** In a biological cell the average member of genes that will change into mutant genes, when treated radioactively, is 2.4. Assuming Poisson probability distribution find the probability that there are atmost 3 mutant genes in a biological cell after the radioactive treatment

(a) 0.2090 (b) 0.7576
(c) 0.5697 (d) 0.7787

**84.** A random variable $Y$ has the following distribution

| $Y$ | $-1$ | 0 | 1 | 2 |
|---|---|---|---|---|
| $P(Y)$ | $3C$ | $2C$ | 0.4 | 0.1 |

The value of the constant $C$ is

(a) 0.10 (b) 0.15
(c) 0.20 (d) 0.25

**85.** Let $X$ and $Y$ be independent Poisson variable with mean 5. Then, given $X + Y = 10$, the distribution of $X$ is

(a) Binomial $\left(10, \frac{1}{2}\right)$ (b) Poisson (5)

(c) Binomial $\left(5, \frac{1}{2}\right)$ (d) Poisson (10)

**86.** Suppose $\{X_n\}$ is a sequence of independent random variable, having uniform distribution over the interval $\left(-1-\frac{1}{n}, 1+\frac{1}{n}\right)$ and $\bar{X}_n = (X_1 + X_2 + \ldots\ldots + X_n)/n$, then, as $n \to \infty$

(a) $\bar{X}_n \to 1$ is probability
(b) $\bar{X}_n \to 0$ in distribution
(c) $\bar{X}_n \to X$, where $X$ has uniform distribution over $(-1, 1)$
(d) $\bar{X}_n$ does not converge to any random variable in probability

**87.** The probability distribution function always satisfies the probability postulates

(a) always true (b) partially true
(c) always false (d) partially false

**88.** For any random variable, for which mean $\mu$ exist, the first moment about the mean is equal to

(a) zero (b) one
(c) mean itself (d) None of these

**89.** Which of the following is not applicable to a Poisson Distribution?

(a) It is used to compute the probability of rare events.
(b) Every event is independent of every other event.
(c) It is parameterized by the sample size and the probability that an event will occur.
(d) The theoritical range for the number of events that could occur is 0, 1, 2, 3,...

**90.** The chance that a person will contract AIDS after a sexual contact with an infected partner has been estimated to be 1/4. This means

(a) a person will be infected after exactly 4 sexual contacts with infected partners
(b) of 1000 people having sexual contacts with infected partners, exactly 250 will become infected
(c) of 200 people having sexual contacts with infected partners, about 50 will become infected
(d) in exactly 25% of all sexual contacts with infected partners, the infection will spread

**91.** Let $X$ and $Y$ be iid random variables having any probability distribution with finite mean. Then, $E(X \mid X + Y = k)$

(a) cannot be determined
(b) need not exist
(c) is $E(X)$
(d) is $k/5$

**92.** The pdf of a random variable $X$ is $f(x)=\frac{2}{x^3}$, $1< x < \infty$, then

(a) both mean and variance are finite
(b) both mean and variance are in finite
(c) mean is finite and variance is infinite
(d) mean is infinite and variance is finite

**93.** Which of the following function can be represented as the probability distribution of a random variable with the given range for x = 1, 2, 3, 4?

(a) $f(x)=\frac{x-2}{5}$ (b) $f(x)=\frac{x^2}{50}$
(c) $f(x)=\frac{1}{5}$ (d) None of these

**94.** The moment of 'inertia of a rod' is equivalent to

(a) first moment about the origin
(b) second moment about the origin
(c) third moment about the origin
(d) None of the above

**95.** The number of bacteria in a drop of water from a lake has a Poisson distribution with an average of 0.5 bacteria/drop. A small dish containing four drops of water from the lake is placed under a microscope. The probability of observing atmost one bacteria in the sample is

(a) 0.910 (b) 0.406 (c) 0.271 (d) 0.135

**96.** The chances that you will ticketed for illegal parking on campus are about 1/3. During the last nine days, you have illegally parked everyday and have not been ticketed (you lucky person)! Today, on the 10th day, you again decide to park illegally. The chances that you will be caught are

(a) greater than 1/3 because you were not caught in the last nine days
(b) less than 1/3 because you were not caught in the last nine days
(c) still equal to 1/3 because the last nine days do not affect the probability
(d) equal to 1/10 because you were not caught in the last nine days.

**97.** Let $X$ and $Y$ be iid $N(\mu, \sigma^2)$. Define $U = X + Y$ and $V = X - Y$. Then, the conditional distribution of $V$ given $U = s$ is

(a) a point mass at 0 (b) $U\left(\mu-\frac{s}{2}, \mu+\frac{s}{2}\right)$
(c) $N(0, 2\sigma^2)$ (d) $N(0, s^2)$

**98.** Let $\{x_n\}$ be a sequence of random variables and $\{u_n\}$ be their expectations. Let $V_n = \text{Var}\{X_1 + X_2 + \ldots\ldots + X_n\}$. The condition $\frac{V_n}{n^2} \to 0$ as $n \to \infty$ for existence of weak law of large numbers is

(a) necessary but not sufficient
(b) sufficient but not necessary
(c) necessary as well as sufficient
(d) neither necessary nor sufficient

**99.** If $F(x)$ is a distribution function of a random variable $X$ and given statements

I. $F(-\infty) = 0$ and $F(+\infty) = 1$
II. $F(-\infty) = 1$ and $F(+\infty) = 0$
III. $a < b \Rightarrow F(a) \le F(b)$ for real $a$ and $b$
IV. $a < b \Rightarrow F(a) \ge F(b)$ for real $a$ and $b$

(a) I and IV are true
(b) II and IV are true
(c) I and III are true
(d) II and III are true

**100.** In Physics 'mean' represents

(a) centre of gravity (b) moment of inertia
(c) gravitational forces (d) None of these

**101.** Bacteria in hamburger are distributed through out the meat. Suppose that a large batch of hamburger has an average contamination of 0.3 bacteria/gram. Then, the probability that a 10 gram sample will contain one or fewer bacteria is

(a) 0.2222 (b) 0.7408 (c) 0.9603 (d) 0.1992

**102.** The probability that the Red River will flood in any given year has been estimated from 200 yr of historical data to be one in four. This means

(a) the red river will flood every four year
(b) in the next 100 yr, the red river will flood exactly 25 times
(c) in the last 100 yr, the red river flooded exactly 25 times
(d) in the next 100 yr, the red river will flood about 25 times

**103.** Let $X \sim N(2, 1)$ and define

$$Y = \begin{cases} -1, & \text{if } X \le 0 \\ +1, & \text{if } X > 0 \end{cases}$$

Then, $E(Y)$ is

(a) equal to 0 (b) less than 0
(c) greater than 0 (d) equal to 2

**104.** Let $X_1, X_2, \ldots, X_9$ be a random sample from a continuous population with mean $\mu$ and variance $\sigma^2$. According to Chebyshev's inequality

$$p\left[\left|\frac{X_1 + X_2 + \ldots\ldots + X_9}{9} - \mu\right| \le \sigma\right]$$

is greater than or equal to

(a) 0.9973 (b) $\frac{1}{9}$ (c) $\frac{8}{9}$ (d) $\frac{8}{9^2}$

**105.** The function $f(x)=\frac{x+2}{25}$ for x = 1, 2, 3, 4, 5 can be represented as probability distributions function

(a) always true (b) always false
(c) partially true (d) can't say

**106.** The first moment about the origin is

(a) variance (b) mean
(c) standard deviation (d) None of these

**107.** In a certain communications system, there is an average of 1 transmission error per 10s Let the distribution of transmission errors be Poisson. What is the probability of more than 1 error in a communication one-half minute in duration?
(a) 0.950 (b) 0.262 (c) 0.738 (d) 0.801

**108.** An insurance company issues a policy on a small boat under the following conditions

The replacement cost (₹ 5000) will be paid for a total loss. If it is not a total loss, but the damage is more than ₹ 2000, then ₹1500 will be paid. Nothing will be paid for damage costing ₹ 2000 or less and of course nothing is paid out if there is no damage. The company estimates the probability of the first three events as 0.02, 0.10 and 0.30, respectively. The amount the company should charge if it wishes to make a profit of ₹ 50 above the expected amount paid out in a year is
(a) ₹ 250 (b) ₹ 201 (c) ₹ 300 (d) ₹ 1200

**109.** In two independent tosses of a fair die the probability that the sum of the outcomes is 7, is
(a) 1/6 (b) 3/5 (c) 1/12 (d) 1/3

**110.** The ratio frequency to the width of the class interval is known as
(a) frequency density (b) relative frequency
(c) class density (d) relative density

**111.** If $A$ and $B$ are mutually exclusive events, then
(a) $P(A \cap B) = 1$ (b) $P(A \cap B) = 0$
(c) $P(A) = P(B)$ (d) $P(A \cap B) = P(A)P(B)$

**112.** The second moment about the mean is
(a) variance (b) mean
(c) standard deviation (d) None of these

**113.** The rate at which a particular defect occurs in lengths of plastic film being produced by a stable manufacturing process is 4.2 defects per 75 m length. A random sample of the film is selected and it was found that the length of the film in the sample was 25 m. What is the probability that there will be atmost 2 defects found in the sample?
(a) 0.2102 (b) 0.2417
(c) 0.8335 (d) 0.1323

**114.** The average length of stay in a hospital is useful for planning purposes. Suppose that the following is the distribution of the length of stay in a hospital after a minor operation

| **Days** | 2 | 3 | 4 | 5 | 6 |
|---|---|---|---|---|---|
| **Prob.** | 0.05 | 0.20 | 0.40 | 0.20 | ? |

The average length of stay is
(a) 0.15 (b) 0.17 (c) 3.3 (d) 4.0

**115.** If $X$ is a Poisson random variable with $P(X = 1) = 2P(X = 3)$, what is the expected value of $X$?
(a) 3 (b) $\sqrt{3}$ (c) $\sqrt{6}$ (d) 2

**116.** With the increase in the number of observations and classes, the shape of the frequency polygon
(a) tends to become increasingly smooth
(b) tends to become jagged
(c) remains the same
(d) varies only if data becomes

**117.** In rolling a fair die, what is the probability of obtaining even number?
(a) $\frac{1}{2}$ (b) $\frac{1}{6}$
(c) $\frac{1}{3}$ (d) None of these

**118.** The random variable $X$ takes the value 0,1, 2 and 3 with probabilities $\frac{1}{125}, \frac{123}{125}, \frac{48}{125}$ and $\frac{64}{125}$ the value of $E(X)$ is
(a) $\frac{12}{4}$ (b) $\frac{12}{7}$
(c) $\frac{12}{5}$ (d) None of these

**119.** Suppose flaws (cracks, chips, specks, etc.) occur on the surface of glass with density of 3 per sq m. What is the probability of there being exactly 4 flaws on a sheet of glass of area 0.5 sq m?
(a) 0.047 (b) 0.168 (c) 0.981 (d) 0.815

**120.** A business evaluates a proposed venture as follows. It stands to make a profit of ₹ 10000 with probability 3/20, to make a profit of ₹ 5000 with probability 9/20, to break even with probability 1/4 and to lose ₹ 5000 with probability 3/20. The expected profit in dollars is
(a) 1500 (b) 0 (c) 3000 (d) 3250

**121.** If $A$ and $B$ are events and $A^c$ denotes the complement of $A$, then which of the following is always an upper bound of $P(A) - P(B)$?
(a) $P(AB^c)$ (b) $P(A^cB)$ (c) $P(AB)$ (d) $P(A^cB^c)$

**122.** If the probability of getting 10-20, 21-30, 31-40 over 40 cars for service at a day is 0.20, 0.35, 0.25, 0.12, respectively. What is the probability of getting atleast 21 cars at that day?
(a) 0.72 (b) 0.62
(c) 0.35 (d) 0.12

**123.** It is sometimes possible to obtain approximate probabilities associated with values of a random variable by using the probability distribution of a different random variable. For example, binomial probabilities using the Poisson probability function, binomial probabilities using the normal etc. In order for the Poisson to give 'good' approximate values for binomial probabilities we must have the condition(s) that
(a) the population size is large relative to the sample size
(b) the sample size is large

(c) the probability, $p$,is small and the sample size is large

(d) the probability, $p$ is close to 0.5 and the sample size is large

**124.** Before planting a crop for the next year, a producer does a risk assesment. According to her assessment, she concludes that there are three possible net outcomes : a ₹ 7000 gain, a ₹ 4000 gain, or a ₹ 10000 loss with probabilities 0.55, 0.20 and 0.25, respectively. The expected profit is

(a) ₹ 3850 (b) ₹ 0
(c) ₹ 2150 (d) ₹ 2500

**125.** Let $X$ and $Y$ be jointly distributed random variables such that the conditional distribution of $Y$, given $X = x$, is uniform on the interval $(x - 1, x + 1)$. Suppose $E(X) = 1$ and $\text{Var}(X) = \frac{5}{3}$. The variance of the random variable $Y$ is

(a) $\frac{1}{2}$ (b) $\frac{2}{3}$
(c) 1 (d) 2

**126.** If $A$ and $B$ are independent events, then

(a) $P(A/B) = P(A) \cdot P(B)$ (b) $P(A/B) = P(B)$
(c) $P(A/B) = P(A)$ (d) None of these

**127.** Lice are a pesky problem for school aged children and is unrelated to cleanliness. The lifetimes of lice that have fallen off the scalp onto bedding is approximately normally distributed with a mean of 2.2 days and a standard deviation of 0.4 days. We would expect that approximately 90% of the lice would die within

(a) about 2.6 days (b) about 3.9 days
(c) about 2.5 days (d) about 2.7 days

**128.** An insurance company has estimated the following cost probabilities for the next year on a particular model of car

| Cost | ₹ 0 | ₹ 500 | ₹ 1000 | ₹ 2000 |
|---|---|---|---|---|
| Prob | 0.60 | 0.05 | 0.13 | ? |

The expected cost to the insurance company is (approximately)

(a) ₹ 155 (b) ₹ 595 (c) ₹ 875 (d) ₹ 645

**129.** Let $X$ and $Y$ be jointly distributed random variables such that the conditional distribution of $Y$, given $X = x$, is uniform on the interval $(x - 1, x + 1)$. Suppose, $E(X) = 1$ and $\text{Var}(X) = \frac{5}{3}$. The mean of random variable $Y$ is

(a) $\frac{1}{2}$ (b) 1 (c) $\frac{3}{2}$ (d) 2

**130.** If $P(B/A) = P(B)$ and $P(A) \neq 0$, $P(B) \neq 0$, then

(a) $P(A/B) = P(A)$ (b) $P(A/B) = P(A) \cdot P(B)$
(c) $P(A/B) = P(A)/P(B)$ (d) $P(A/B) = P(B)$

**131.** The measurement of the width of the index finger of a human right hand is a normally distributed variable with a mean of 6 cm and a standard deviation of 0.5 cm. What is the probability that the finger width of a randomly selected person will be between 5 cm and 7.5 cm?

(a) 0.9759 (b) 0.0241 (c) 0.9500 (d) 1.000

**132.** A restaurant manager is considering a new location for her restaurant. The projected annual cash flow for the new location is

| Annual Cash Flow | ₹ 10000 | ₹ 30000 | ₹ 70000 | ₹ 90000 | ₹ 100000 |
|---|---|---|---|---|---|
| Probability | 0.10 | 0.15 | 0.50 | 0.15 | ? |

The expected cash flow for the new location is

(a) ₹ 12800 (b) ₹ 64000
(c) ₹ 70000 (d) ₹ 60000

**133.** Consider two identical boxes $B_1$ and $B_2$, where the box $B_i (i = 1, 2)$ contains $i + 1$ red and $5 - i - 1$ white balls. A fair die is cast. Let the number of dots shown on the top face of the die be $N$. If $N$ is even or 5, then two balls are drawn with replacement from the box $B_1$, otherwise, two balls are drawn with replacement from the box $B_2$. The probability that the two drawn balls are of different colors is

(a) $\frac{7}{25}$ (b) $\frac{9}{25}$
(c) $\frac{12}{25}$ (d) $\frac{16}{25}$

**134.** If $A$ is an event of a sample space $S$, then choose the correct statement?

(a) $P(A) \leq P(S)$ (b) $P(A) > P(S)$
(c) $P(A) > 1$ (d) $P(A) < 0$

**135.** Which of the following is not correct about a standard normal distribution?

(a) $P(0 \leq Z \leq 1.50) = 0.4332$
(b) $P(Z \leq -1.0) = 0.1587$
(c) $P(Z \geq 2.0) = 0.0228$
(d) $P(Z \geq -2.5) = 0.4938$

**136.** A rock concert producer has scheduled an outdoor concert. If it is warm that day, she expects to make a ₹ 20000 profit. If it cool that day, she expects to make a ₹ 5000 profit. If it is very cold that day, she expects to suffer a ₹ 12000 loss. Based upon historical records, the weather office has estimated the chances of a warm day to be 0.60; the chances of a cool day to be 0.25. What is the producer's expected profit?

(a) ₹ 5000 (b) ₹ 13000
(c) ₹ 15050 (d) ₹ 11450

**137.** If $A$ and $A'$ are complementary events in a sample space $S$, then

(a) $P(A) + P(A') = 0$ (b) $P(A) - P(A') = 0$
(c) $P(A) + P(A') = 1$ (d) $P(A) - P(A') = 1$

**138.** Let $A$, $B$ and $C$ be three events such that $P(A) = 0.4$, $P(B) = 0.5$, $(A \cup B) = 0.6$, $P(C) = 0.6$ and $P(A \cap B \cap C^c) = 0.1$. Then, $P(A \cap B | C)$ is equal to

(a) $\frac{1}{2}$ (b) $\frac{1}{3}$ (c) $\frac{1}{4}$ (d) $\frac{1}{5}$

**139.** The daily milk production of Guernsey cows is approximately normally distributed with a mean of 35 kg/day and a standard deviation of 6 kg/day. The probability that a days production for a single animal will be less than 28 kg is approximately

(a) 0.41 (b) 0.09
(c) 0.38 (d) 0.12

**140.** A crop insurance company establishes the following loss table based upon previous claims

| Per cent loss | 0 | 25 | 50 | 100 |
|---|---|---|---|---|
| Probability | 0.90 | 0.05 | 0.02 | ? |

If they write policy that pays a maximum of ₹ 150/hectare, their expected loss in ₹/hectare is approximately

(a) 5.2 (b) 7.9
(c) 4.5 (d) 37.5

**141.** Let $X$ and $Y$ be jointly distributed random variables having the joint probability density function

$$f(x, y) = \begin{cases} \frac{1}{\pi}, & \text{if } x^2 + y^2 \le 1 \\ 0, & \text{otherwise} \end{cases}$$

Then, $P(Y > \max(X, -X))$ is equal to

(a) $\frac{1}{2}$ (b) $\frac{1}{3}$ (c) $\frac{1}{4}$ (d) $\frac{1}{6}$

**142.** Which of the Following statement is false?
If $P(A) \ne 0$

(a) $P(B/A) \ge 0$ (b) $P(A/A) = 1$
(c) $P(B/A) \ge P(B)$ (d) $P(B/A) = P(B)/P(A \cup B)$

**143.** The distribution of weights of a large group of high school students is normally distributed with $\mu = 55$ kg and $\sigma = 5$ kg. Which of the following is true?

(a) About 16 per cent of the students will be over 60 kg
(b) About 2.5 per cent will be below 45 kg
(c) Half of them can be expected to weigh less than 55 kg
(d) All of the above are true

**144.** Cans of soft drinks cost ₹ 0.30 in a certain vending machine. What is the expected value and variance of daily revenue ($Y$) from the machine, if $X$, the number of cans sold per day has $E(X) = 125$, and Var $(X) = 50$?

(a) $E(Y) = 37.5$, $\text{Var}(Y) = 50$
(b) $E(Y) = 37.5$, $\text{Var}(Y) = 4.5$
(c) $E(Y) = 37.5$, $\text{Var}(Y) = 15$
(d) $E(Y) = 37.5$, $\text{Var}(Y) = 15$

**145.** Let $X$ and $Y$ be independent Poisson random variables with parameters 1 and 2, respectively.
Then, $P$ is $\left(X = 1 | \frac{X+Y}{2} = 2\right)$

(a) 0.426 (b) 0.293
(c) 0.395 (d) 0.512

**146.** For any event $A$, events $A$ and $\phi$ are

(a) independent events (b) dependent event
(c) (a) and (b) are false (d) (a) is false, (b) is true

**147.** The distribution of weights in a large group is approximately normally distributed. The mean is 80 kg and approximately 68% of the weights are between 70 and 90 kg. The standard deviaton of the distribution of weights is equal to

(a) 20 (b) 5
(c) 40 (d) 10

**148.** Consider 100 blood donors chosen randomly from a population where the probability of type $A$ is 0.40? What is the approximate probability that atleast 43 donors will have type blood?

(a) About 0.43 (b) About 0.62
(c) About 0.73 (d) About 0.27

**149.** Let $|X_n|$ be a sequence of independent random variables with

$$p(X_n = n^\alpha) = p(X_n = -n^\alpha) = \frac{1}{2}$$

The sequence $|X_n|$ obeys the weak law of large numbers if

(a) $\alpha < \frac{1}{2}$ (b) $\alpha = \frac{1}{2}$ (c) $\frac{1}{2} < \alpha \le 1$ (d) $\alpha > 1$

**150.** Three events $A$, $B$ and $C$ are independent events iff

(a) $P(A \cap B \cap C) = P(A) + P(B) + P(C)$
(b) $P(A \cap B \cap C) = P(A)\,P(B)\,P(C)$
(c) $P(A \cap B \cap C) = P(A) + P(B) + P(C) - P(A \cup B \cup C)$
(d) $P(A \cap B \cap C) = P(A) + P(B) + P(C) + P(A \cap B \cap C)$

**151.** The height of an adult male is known to be normally distributed with a mean of 69 inches and a standard deviation of 2.5 inches. The height of the doorway such that 96 per cent of the adult males can pass through it without having to bend is

(a) 1.8 (b) about 65
(c) about 74 (d) about 80

**152.** Consider 8 blood donors chosen randomly from a population. The probability that the donor has type $A$ blood is 0.40. Which of the following is correct?

(a) The probability of 1 or fewer donors having type $A$ blood is about 0.11.
(b) The probability of 7 or more donors not having type $A$ blood is about 0.0087.
(c) The probability of exactly 5 donors having type $A$ blood is about 0.28.
(d) The probability of exactly 5 donors not having type $A$ blood is about 0.12.

**153.** Let $X_1$ and $X_2$ be independent binomial random variables with $E(X_i) = n_i P$ and Var $(X_i) = n_i\, p(1-p)$, $0 < p < 1$, $i = 1, 2$. Then, the distribution of the random variable $Z = n_1 + n_2 - X_1 - X_2$ is

(a) binomial with mean $(n_1 + n_2)p$
(b) binomial with mean $(n_1 + n_2)(1-p)$
(c) poisson with mean $(n_1 + n_2)p$
(d) poisson with mean $(n_1 + n_2)(1-p)$

**154.** If *A*, *B* and *C* are three events in a sample space *S* such that $(A \cap B) \neq 0$, then

(a) $P(A \cap B \cap C) = P(A) \cdot P\left(\frac{B}{A}\right) \cdot P\left(\frac{C}{A} \cap B\right)$
(b) $P(A \cap B \cap C) = P(A) \cdot P\left(\frac{A}{B}\right) \cdot P\left(\frac{A}{B} \cap C\right)$
(c) $P(A \cap B \cap C) = P(A) \cdot P\left(\frac{B}{C}\right)$
(d) $P(A \cap B \cap C) = P(A) \cdot P\left(\frac{C}{B}\right)$

**155.** The heights of students at a college are normally distributed with a mean of 175 cm and a standard deviation of 6 cm. One might expect in a sample of 1000 students that the number with heights less than 163 cm is

(a) 997 (b) 23 (c) 477 (d) 228

**156.** Newsweek in 1989 reported that 60% of young children have blood lead levels that could impair their neurological development. Assuming that a class in a school is a random sample from the population of all children at risk, the probability that atleast 5 children out of 10 in a sample taken from a school may have a blood level that may impair development is

(a) about 0.25 (b) about 0.20
(c) about 0.84 (d) about 0.16

**157.** Suppose that $X_1, \ldots, X_n$ are random variables such that the variance of each variable is 1 and the correlation between each pair of different variables is $\frac{1}{4}$. Then,

Var $(X_1 + X_2 + \ldots + X_n)$ is

(a) $\frac{n(n+1)}{2}$ (b) $\frac{n(n+2)}{4}$
(c) $\frac{n(n+3)}{4}$ (d) $\frac{n(n+3)}{2}$

**158.** What is the probability to get two aces in succession (with replacement) from a deck of 52 cards?

(a) $\frac{1}{52}$ (b) $\frac{2}{169}$ (c) $\frac{2}{159}$ (d) $\frac{1}{169}$

**159.** The height of an adult male is known to be normally distributed with mean of 175 cm and standard deviation 6 cm. The 20th percentile of the distribution of heights is

(a) 175 (b) 179 (c) 170 (d) 172

**160.** There are 10 patients of the Neo-Natal Ward of a local hospital who are monitored by 2 staff members. If the probability (at any one time) of a patient requiring emergency attention by a staff member is 0.3, assuming the patients to be behave independently, what is the probability at any one time that there will not be sufficient staff to attend all emergencies?

(a) 0.3828 (b) 0.3000 (c) 0.0900 (d) 0.6172

**161.** The probability that exactly one of the events *E* or *F* occurs is equal to

(a) $P(E) + P(F) - P(EF)$ (b) $P(E) + P(F) - 2P(EF)$
(c) $P(E^C) + P(F) - 2P(E^C F)$ (d) $P(E) + P(F)$

**162.** What is the probability to get two aces in succession from an ordinary deck of 52 cards without replacement?

(a) $\frac{2}{221}$ (b) $\frac{1}{221}$ (c) $\frac{3}{221}$ (d) $\frac{4}{221}$

**163.** Heights of males are approximately normally distributed with a mean of 170 cm and a standard deviation of 8 cm. What fraction of males are taller than 176 cm?

(a) 0.7500 (b) 0.6000 (c) 0.2734 (d) 0.2266

**164.** The probability that a certain machine will produce a defective item is 0.20. If a random sample of 6 items is taken from the output of this machine, what is the probability that there will be 5 or more defectives in the sample?

(a) 0.0001 (b) 0.0154 (c) 0.0015 (d) 0.0016

**165.** The joint probability density function of the random variables *X*, *Y* and *Z* is

$f(x, y, z) = 8xyz,\ 0 < x, y, z < 1$
$= 0$, otherwise

The $P(X < Y < Z)$ is

(a) $\frac{1}{8}$ (b) $\frac{1}{3}$ (c) $\frac{1}{6}$ (d) $\frac{3}{8}$

**166.** The time required to assemble an electronic component is normally distributed with a mean of 12 min and a standard deviation of 1.5 min. Find the probability that a particular assembly takes more than 14.25 min

(a) 0.9332 (b) 0.0668 (c) 0.3413 (d) 0.4332

**167.** If you buy one ticket in the Provincial Lottery, then the probability that you will win a prize is 0.11. If you buy one ticket each month for five months, what is the probability that you will win atleast one prize

(a) 0.55 (b) 0.50 (c) 0.44 (d) 0.45

**168.** What is the probability of getting, four sixes and another number in five random rolls of a balanced die?

(a) $\frac{4}{7776}$ (b) $\frac{3}{7776}$ (c) $\frac{5}{7776}$ (d) $\frac{2}{7776}$

**169.** A random variable $X$ has Poisson distribution.

If $2P(X=2) = P(x=1) + 2P(X=0)$

Then, the variance of $X$ is

(a) $\frac{3}{2}$ (b) 2 (c) 1 (d) $\frac{1}{2}$

**170.** It is known that the resistance of carbon resistors is normally distributed with $\mu = 1200$ ohms and $\sigma = 120$ ohms. What proportion of the resistors have resistances that differ from the mean resistance by more than 120 ohms?

(a) 0.9544 (b) 0.3413 (c) 0.1587 (d) 0.3174

**171.** Suppose 60% of a herd of cattle is infected with a particular disease. Let $Y$ = the number of non-diseased cattle in a sample of size 5. The distribution of $Y$ is

(a) binomial with $n=5$ and $p=0.6$
(b) binomial with $n=5$ and $p=0.4$
(c) binomial with $n=5$ and $p=0.5$
(d) the same as the distribution of $X$, the number of infected cattle

**172.** A box contains two coins, one of which is fair and the other two headed. One coin is chosen at random and tossed twice. If two heads appear, then the probability that the chosen coin was two headed is

(a) $\frac{1}{2}$ (b) $\frac{1}{4}$ (c) $\frac{1}{3}$ (d) $\frac{4}{5}$

**173.** What is the probability of getting, three heads, in three random tosses of a balance coin?

(a) $\frac{1}{18}$ (b) $\frac{1}{8}$ (c) $\frac{1}{4}$ (d) $\frac{1}{3}$

**174.** The time that a skier takes on a downhill course has a normal distribution with a mean of 12.3 min and standard deviation of 0.4 min. The probability that on a random run the skier takes between 12.1 and 12.5 min is

(a) 0.1915 (b) 0.3830 (c) 0.3085 (d) 0.6170

**175.** The probability that a certain machine will produce a defective item is 1/4. If a random sample of 6 items is taken from the output of this machine, what is the probability that there will be 5 or more defectives in the sample?

(a) 1/4096 (b) 3/4096 (c) 4/4096 (d) 19/4096

**176.** Two independent events $E$ and $F$ are such that

$$P(E \cap F) = \frac{1}{6},\ P(E^C \cap F^C) = \frac{1}{3}$$

and $P(E) > P(F)$. Then, $P(E)$ is

(a) $\frac{1}{2}$ (b) $\frac{2}{3}$ (c) $\frac{1}{3}$ (d) $\frac{1}{4}$

**177.** Which of the following inequality is correct?

(a) $P(A \cap B) \le P(A) + P(B)$
(b) $P(A \cap B) \ge P(A) + P(B)$
(c) $P(A \cap B) \ge 0$
(d) $P(A \cap B) = P(A) + P(B) + P(A \cup B)$

**178.** The cost of treatment per patient for a certain medical problem was modeled by one insurance company as a normal random variable with mean \$775 and standard deviation \$150. What is the probability that the treatment cost of a patient is less than \$1000, based on this model?

(a) 0.5000 (b) 0.6826 (c) 0.8531 (d) 0.9332

**179.** Fifteen per cent of new residential central air conditioning units installed by a supplier need additional adjustments requiring a service call. Assume that a recent sample of seven such units constitutes a Bernoulli process. Interest centres on $X$, the number of units among these seven that need additional adjustments. The mean and variance of $X$ are respectively

(a) 0.15 ; 0.85 (b) 0.15 ; 1.05
(c) 0.15 ; 0.8925 (d) 1.05 ; 0.8915

**180.** If $X$ and $Y$ are independent $N(0, 1)$ variables, then the characteristic function of $XY$ is

(a) $e^{-t^2}$ (b) $(1+t^2)^{-1/2}$
(c) $(1+t)^{1/2}$ (d) $(1+t^2)^{-1}$

**181.** In a sample survey, the chances of young professionals courses MBA degree, MCA degree or both are 0.86, 0.35 and 0.29, respectively. What is the probability of owning either or both degrees?

(a) 0.82 (b) 0.92 (c) 0.08 (d) 0.18

**182.** Bolts that are used in the construction of an electric transformer are supposed to be 0.060 inches in diameter, and any bolt with diameter less than 0.058 inches or greater than 0.062 inches must be scrapped. The machine that makes these bolts is set to produce bolts of 0.060 inches in diameter, but it actually produces bolts with diameters following a normal distribution with $\mu = 0.060$ inches and $\sigma = 0.060$ inches and $\sigma = 0.001$ inches. The proportion of bolts that must be scrapped is equal to

(a) 0.0456 (b) 0.0228 (c) 0.9772 (d) 0.3333

**183.** It has been estimated that as many as 70% of the fish caught in certain areas of the Great Lakes have liver cancer due to the pollutants present. Find an approximate 95% range for the number of fish with liver cancer present in a sample of 130 fish

(a) (80, 102) (b) (86, 97)
(c) (63, 119) (d) (36, 146)

**184.** Let $X_n$ denote the sum of points obtained when $n$ fair dice are rolled together. The expectation and variance of $X_n$ are

(a) $\frac{7}{2}n$ and $\frac{35}{12}n^2$, respectively
(b) $\frac{7}{2}n$ and $\frac{35}{12}n$, respectively
(c) $\left(\frac{7}{2}\right)^n$ and $\left(\frac{35}{12}\right)^n$, respectively
(d) None of the above

**185.** Suppose the test scores of 600 students are normally distributed with a mean of 76 and standard deviation of 8. The number of students scoring between 70 and 82 is

(a) 272 (b) 164 (c) 260 (d) 328

**186.** In a triangle test a tester is presented with three food samples, two of which are alike, and is asked to pick out the odd one by testing. If a tester has no well developed sense and can pick the odd one only, by chance, what is the probability that in five trials he will make four or more correct decisions?

(a) 11/243 (b) 1/243 (c) 10/243 (d) 233/243

**187.** If $A$ and $B$ are two events in a sample space $S$, then $P(A \cup B)$

(a) $P(A)+P(B)$ (b) $P(A)+P(B)+P(A \cap B)$

(c) $P(A)+P(B)-P(A \cap B)$ (d) None of these

**188.** If $x$ and $y$ are deviations from arithmetic mean, $r = 0.8$, $\Sigma xy = 60$, $\sigma_y = 25$ and $\Sigma x^2 = 90$, then number of items in the series, is

(a) 10 (b) 15

(c) 18 (d) None of these

**189.** The diameters of steel disks produced in a plant are normally distributed with a mean of 2.5 cm and standard deviation of 0.02 cm. The probability that a disk picked at random has a diameter greater than 2.54 cm is about

(a) 0.5080 (b) 0.2000 (c) 0.1587 (d) 0.0228

**190.** Which of the following is not an assumption of the binomial distribution?

(a) All trials must be identical.

(b) All trials must be independent.

(c) Each trial must be classified as a success or a failure.

(d) The probability of success is equal to 0.5 in all trials.

**191.** Suppose $P$ and $Q$ are independent events of an experiment $E$. Then, it follows that

(a) $P^C$ and $Q^C$ are dependent

(b) $P$ and $Q$ are mutually exclusive

(c) $P$ and $Q^C$ are dependent

(d) $P^C$ and $Q$ are independent

**192.** Given, $P(A_i) = \left(\frac{1}{2}\right)^1$ and $\bigcup_{i=1}^{\infty} A_i = S$, the sample space where $A_i$ are mutually exclusive events, then $P(S)$ is

(a) 0 (b) 1

(c) $\infty$ (d) None of these

**193.** A random sample of 15 people is taken from a population in which 40% favour a particular political stand. What is the probability that exactly 6 individuals in the sample favour this political stand?

(a) 0.4000 (b) 0.5000

(c) 0.4000 (d) 0.2066

**194.** If $A$ and $B$ are two events and the probability $P(B) \neq 1$, then

$\dfrac{P(A) - P(A \cap B)}{1 - P(B)}$ equals

(a) $P\left(\frac{A}{B}\right)$ (b) $P\left(\frac{A}{\overline{B}}\right)$

(c) $P\left(\frac{\overline{A}}{B}\right)$ (d) $P\left(\frac{\overline{A}}{\overline{B}}\right)$

**195.** For Bernoulli's distribution the mean and variation is related by

(a) $\sigma^2 = p\mu$ (b) $\sigma^2 = \dfrac{p}{\mu}$

(c) $\sigma = p\mu$ (d) None of these

**196.** When a card is drawn from the pack of cards. The probability of getting red cards is

(a) 3 (b) 1 (c) $\frac{1}{4}$ (d) $\frac{1}{2}$

**197.** If the joint probability function of $X_1, X_2, X_3$ is $P(X_1 = x_1, X_2 = x_2, X_3 = x_3)$

$$= \begin{cases} \dfrac{x_1 x_2 x_3}{72}, & \text{if } x_1 = 1, 2;\ x_2 = 1, 2, 3;\ x_3 = 1, 3 \\ 0 & \text{otherwise} \end{cases}$$

then the marginal probability function, $P(X_1 = x_1)$ of $X_1$ is

(a) $\frac{x_1}{3}$, if $x_1 = 1, 2$ and 0 otherwise

(b) $\frac{1}{2}$, if $x_1 = 1, 2$ and 0 otherwise

(c) $\frac{x_3}{3}$, if $x_1 = 1, 2$ and 0 otherwise

(d) None of the above

**198.** The second moment about the origin is $\mu'_2$ and the mean is $\mu$, then the variance is given by

(a) $\sigma^2 = \mu'_2 + \mu^2$ (b) $\sigma^2 = \mu'_2 - \mu^2$

(c) $\sigma^2 = \dfrac{\mu'_2}{\mu^2}$ (d) None of these

**199.** For two events $A$ and $B$. Let $P(A) = \frac{1}{3}$, $P(B) = \frac{1}{4}$ and $P(A \cup B) = \frac{1}{2}$, then $P\left(\frac{A}{B}\right)$ is

(a) $\frac{1}{3}$ (b) $\frac{1}{2}$

(c) $\frac{1}{4}$ (d) 1

**200.** If for a binomial distribution mean = 7 and variance = 6, then the probability of success $p$ is equal to

(a) $\frac{1}{49}$ (b) $\frac{1}{42}$

(c) $\frac{1}{7}$ (d) $\frac{6}{7}$

**201.** In binomial distribution the variance $\sigma^2$ and mean $\mu$ are related by

(a) $\sigma^2 = q\mu$ (b) $\sigma^2 = \frac{\mu}{q}$

(c) $q^2 \sigma^2 = \mu$ (d) None of these

**202.** What is the probability of getting 4 cards, belongs to different suits, when they are drawn without replacement from the pack of 52 cards?

(a) $\frac{2197}{20825}$ (b) $\frac{219}{202}$

(c) $\frac{200}{326}$ (d) None of these

**203.** Which one of the following is least affected by extreme values?

(a) Range
(b) Mean deviation
(c) Standard deviation
(d) Quartile deviation

**204.** Which one of the following statements is correct for a pair of random variables $(X, Y)$?

(a) If the marginal distribution are normal, then their joint distribution is necessarily bivariate normal.
(b) If the joint distribution is bivariate normal, then the marginal distributions are necessarily normal.
(c) If the correlation coefficient between the variables is zero, then the variables must be independent.
(d) The conditional mean of $X$ given $Y = y$ is a linear function of $y$.

**205.** 6 coins are tossed 6400 times. What is the probability of getting 6 holds, $x$ times.

(a) $e^{-100x}$ (b) $\frac{1}{x} e^{-100x}$

(c) $e^{-100} \frac{100^x}{x!}$ (d) None of these

**206.** What is the probability of getting the sum of two dice 7, when they are thrown simultaneously?

(a) $\frac{1}{3}$ (b) $\frac{1}{4}$

(c) $\frac{1}{6}$ (d) $\frac{1}{2}$

**207.** The harmonic mean of a $n$ observations can be computed as square of geometric mean divided by arithmetic mean, if $n$ is equal to

(a) 2 (b) 3
(c) 4 (d) 5

**208.** If $X$ and $Y$ are iid geometric random variables *i.e*, $P[X = n] = qp^n$ for $n = 0, 1, 2, \ldots$ where $0 < p < 1$, $q = 1 - p$, then $P\{Y = y \mid X + Y = k\}$ is equal to

(a) $\frac{1}{k+1}$ (b) $pq^{y-1}$

(c) $pq^{k-1}$ (d) $\binom{k}{y} p^y q^{k-y}$

**209.** The moment generating function of the random variable $X$. Whose moments are $\mu'_r = (r+1) \cdot 2^r$ is

(a) $(1-2t)^{-1}$ (b) $(1-2t)$ (c) $2t$ (d) $\frac{1}{2t}$

**210.** A card is drawn at random from the pack of playing cards. The probability of getting a face card is

(a) $\frac{4}{13}$ (b) 13

(c) $\frac{3}{13}$ (d) None of these

**211.** The weighted arithmetic mean of the first $n$ natural numbers, the weights being the numbers themselves, is

(a) $\frac{(n+1)}{2}$ (b) $\frac{(2n+1)}{3}$

(c) $\frac{(2n+1)}{6}$ (d) $\frac{(n+1)^2}{2}$

**212.** If $X$ and $Y$ are independent random variables with binomial distributions with the same parameter $p$, then the conditional distribution of $X$ given $X + Y$ is

(a) binomial (b) discrete uniform
(c) poisson (d) hypergeometric

**213.** The average incoming call rate is 4 per min. The probability that there are not more than 3 calls is

(a) $\frac{71}{3} e^{-4}$ (b) $e^{-6}$

(c) $-\frac{71}{3}$ (d) $-e^4$

**214.** What is the probability that 3 out of 10 student will pass the exam, given that anyone of that can pass it with probability 0.80?

(a) 0.30 (b) 0.10
(c) 0.20 (d) None of these

**215.** The standard deviation of the observations : $-\sqrt{7}, -\sqrt{6}, -\sqrt{5}, -\sqrt{4}, -\sqrt{3}, -\sqrt{2}, -1, 1, \sqrt{2}, \sqrt{3}, \sqrt{4}, \sqrt{5}, \sqrt{6}, \sqrt{7}$ is

(a) $\sqrt{2}$ (b) 2 (c) $2\sqrt{2}$ (d) 4

**216.** In a binomial distribution with parameters $n$ and $p$, the covariance between the number of successes and the number of failures is

(a) 0 (b) 1
(c) $np(1-p)$ (d) $-np(1-p)$

**217.** A manufacture of steel blades found 5% of its blade deffective. He sells blades in packets each containing 5 blades. The probability that a packet contains one defective blade is

(a) $0.25e^{-0.25}$ (b) 0.5
(c) $e^{-0.25}$ (d) 0.25

**218.** What is the probability of getting seven heads in 12 flips of a balanced coin?

(a) 0.90 (b) 0.19
(c) 0.39 (d) 0.49

**219.** Match List-I with List-II and select the correct answer using the codes given below the lists

| | List I (Statements) | | List-II (Measures of location or dispersion) |
|---|---|---|---|
| A. | It is heavily influenced by extreme values | 1. | Mean |
| B. | It is affected by a change of origin but not by a change of scale | 2. | Mode |
| C. | It is not unduly affected by extreme values | 3. | Coefficient of variation |
| D. | It is affected by changes of scale of origin | 4. | Range |

**Codes**

| | A | B | C | D |
|---|---|---|---|---|
| (a) | 4 | 3 | 2 | 1 |
| (b) | 4 | 3 | 1 | 2 |
| (c) | 3 | 4 | 2 | 1 |
| (d) | 3 | 4 | 1 | 2 |

**220.** The data plotted on a semi-logarithmic scale will give a straight line graph if

(a) $y = a + b^x$ (b) $y = a + b \log x$

(c) $y = ab^x$ (d) $y = \dfrac{a}{1+e^{bx}}$

**221.** $X$ is a non-negative integer valued random variable with $P[X = x]$

$$= \begin{cases} \dfrac{(x+1)}{2^{x+2}}, & x = 0, 1, 2.. \\ 0, & \text{otherwise} \end{cases}$$

Then, mean and variance of $X$ are respectively

(a) (2 and 4) (b) (4 and 2)

(c) (2 and 3) (d) (2 and 2)

**222.** If a random variable $X$ takes the value 1, 2,... with probability function

$\dfrac{\lambda^r}{r!}$, $r = 1, 2, 3,..., \infty$. The value of $\lambda$ is

(a) $\log_e 2$ (b) $\log_e 1$

(c) $\log_e 5$ (d) None of these

**223.** The number of parameters is Bernoulli distribution are

(a) 1 (b) 2

(c) 3 (d) None of these

**224.** The minimum value of Var $(Y - aX)$, over all the values of $a$, is given by

(a) $\rho^2$ Var $(Y)$ (b) $(1-\rho^2)$ Var $(Y)$

(c) $\dfrac{\text{Var}(Y)}{\text{Var}(X)}\rho^2$ (d) $\dfrac{\text{Var}(X)}{\text{Var}(Y)}\rho^2$

**225.** Two dice are thrown. The probability that the sum of the numbers coming up on them is 9, if it is known that the number 5 always occurs on the first die, is

(a) $\dfrac{1}{6}$ (b) $\dfrac{1}{3}$

(c) $\dfrac{2}{3}$ (d) None of these

**226.** If $X_1$, $X_2$ are iid Poisson random variables, then the conditional distribution of $X_1$ given $X_1 + X_2$ is

(a) Binomial (b) Hypergeometric

(c) Geometric (d) Discrete uniform

**227.** Let $X_1$ and $X_2$ be two independent random variables, then moment generating function of $M_{(X_1+X_2)}(t)$ is

(a) $M_{X_1}(t)$ (b) $M_{X_2}(t)$

(c) $M_{X_1}(t)M_{X_2}(t)$ (d) $\dfrac{M_{X_1}(t)}{M_{X_2}(t)}$

**228.** Repeated trials are normally referred to

(a) uniform distribution

(b) bernoulli distribution

(c) gamma distribution

(d) None of the above

**229.** If the first of two samples has 100 items with mean 15 and the whole group has 250 items with mean 15.6, then the mean of the second group is

(a) 15 (b) 16

(c) 14 (d) None of these

**230.** There are four machines and it is known that exactly two of them are faulty. They are tested, one by one, in a random order till both the faulty machines are idenified. Then, the probability that only two tests are needed is

(a) 1/3 (b) 1/6

(c) 1/2 (d) 1/4

**231.** If the random variable $X$ has a Poisson distribution with parameter $\lambda$ and the random variable $y$ has a binomial distribution with parameters $n$ and $p$ as its conditional distribution given $X = n$, then which one of the following is the distribution of $Y$?

(a) A Poisson distribution with parameter $\lambda_p$.

(b) A Poisson distribution with parameter $\lambda_q$ $(q = 1 - p)$.

(c) A Poisson distribution with parameter.

(d) A Geometric distribution.

**232.** Given the probability density function $f(x) = \begin{cases} e^{-x}, & x \geq 0 \\ 0, & x < 0 \end{cases}$, then cumulative probability function $F(2)$ is

(a) $1 + e^{-2}$ (b) $e^{-2}$

(c) $e^{-1}$ (d) $1 - e^{-2}$

**233.** The Bernoulli distribution has a mean

(a) $p^2$ (b) $\dfrac{p}{q}$

(c) $p$ (d) $pq$

**234.** Let $A$, $B$, $C$ be three events such that $P(A) = 0.3$, $P(B) = 0.4$, $P(C) = 0.8$, $(A \cap B) = 0.08$, $P(A \cap C) = 0.28$, $P(A \cap B \cap C) = 0.09$. If $P(A \cup B \cup C) \geq 0.75$, then

(a) $0.23 \leq P(B \cap C) \leq 0.48$ (b) $0.23 \leq P(B \cap C) \leq 0.75$
(c) $0.48 \leq P(B \cap C) \leq 0.75$ (d) None of these

**235.** If $X_1, X_2, \ldots, X_n$ are iid standard Cauchy random variables, then the distribution of $\overline{X}_n = \frac{1}{n}\sum_{i=1}^{n} x_i$ is

(a) normal
(b) nearly normal for all large $n$
(c) laplace
(d) standard cauchy

**236.** Given, a probability density function

$$f(x) = \begin{cases} e^{-x} & x \geq 0 \\ 0 & x < 0 \end{cases}$$

Find the probability $P(1 \leq x \leq 2)$

(a) $e^{-1} + e^{-2}$ (b) $e^{-2}$ (c) $e^{-1}$ (d) $e^{-1} - e^{-2}$

**237.** The range of the Bernoulli random variable is the set

(a) $\{0, 1\}$ (b) set of real numbers
(c) set of integers (d) None of these

**238.** If an odd numbers $X_1, \ldots, X_{2n+1}$ of random variables following the uriform distribution over (0, 1) are taken, then expected value of their median will be

(a) $\frac{(n+1)}{(2n+1)}$ (b) $\frac{1}{2}$
(c) $\frac{n+1}{2n}$ (d) $\frac{n}{(2n+1)}$

**239.** If $A$ and $B$ are two events such that $P(A) > 0$ and $P(B) \neq 1$, then $P\left(\frac{\overline{A}}{\overline{B}}\right)$ is equal to

(a) $1 - P\left(\frac{A}{\overline{B}}\right)$ (b) $1 - P\left(\frac{\overline{A}}{B}\right)$
(c) $\frac{1 - P(A \cap B)}{P(\overline{B})}$ (d) $\frac{P(\overline{A})}{P(\overline{B})}$

**240.** Let the random variable $T$ have a exponential distribution. If $[T]$ denotes the greatest integer less than or equal to $T$, then the distribution of $[T]$ is

(a) poisson
(b) negative binomial other than geometric
(c) geometric
(d) None of the above

**241.** $E[(aX + b)^n]$ is equal to

(a) $\sum_{i=0}^{n} \binom{n}{i} a^{n-i} b^i E(X^{n-i})$
(b) $aE(X) + b^n$
(c) $E(a^n X) + b^n$
(d) $\sum_{i=1}^{n} \binom{n}{i} a^{n-i} b^{n-i} E(X^{n-i})$

**242.** For the given exponential distribution $f(x) = \frac{1}{c} e^{-x/c}$, $c > 0$. The first mean about the origin is

(a) $c^4$ (b) $c^3$ (c) $c^2$ (d) $c$

**243.** The variance of the Bernoulli distribution is

(a) $p^2$ (b) $pq$
(c) $q^2$ (d) $\frac{p}{q}$

**244.** A simple random sample of size 3 is drawn from a population consisting of $N$ distinct elements. Now, consider the following statements :

The probability that the sample consists of three distinct units is

I. $\frac{(N-1)(N-2)}{N^2}$, when sample is drawn without replacement.

II. $\frac{1}{N^3}$, when the sample is drawn without replacement.

Select the correct answer from the following alternatives :

(a) Only I is correct
(b) Only II is correct
(c) Both I and II are correct
(d) Neither I nor II is correct

**245.** A fair coin is tossed repeatedly. If tail appears on first four tosses, then the probability of head appearing on fifth toss equals

(a) 1/2 (b) 1/32
(c) 31/32 (d) 1/5

**246.** If $P(s)$ is the probability generating function of a non-negative integer valued random variable $X$, then $\int_0^1 P(s^2)\, dx$ equals

(a) $E(X^2)$ (b) $E(\sqrt{X})$
(c) $E\left(\frac{1}{X+1}\right)$ (d) $E\left(\frac{1}{2X+1}\right)$

**247.** If $c_1$ and $c_2$ are two constants, then following statement is false

(a) $E[c_1 X + c_2] = c_1 E(X) + c_2$
(b) $E[c_1 X + c_2 X] = c_1 E(X) + c_2 E(X)$
(c) $E[(c_1 + c_2) X] = (c_1 + c_2) E(X)$
(d) $E[c_1 X + c_2] = c_1 + c_2$

**248.** If random variable $X$ has a probability generating function $P_x(t)$. The probability generating function of 2x is

(a) $P_X(t^2)$ (b) $P_X(t)$ (c) $P_X(1-t)$ (d) $P_X(t^3)$

**249.** When $n \to \infty$, the Binomial distribution can be approximated by

(a) Bernoulli distribution (b) Uniform distribution
(c) Poisson distribution (d) None of these

**250.** A fair coin is tosssed till two heads occur in succession. The probability that the number of tosses required is less than 6 is

(a) $\frac{15}{32}$ (b) $\frac{5}{64}$ (c) $\frac{19}{32}$ (d) $\frac{31}{64}$

**251.** The probability that in a group of $N$ people atleast two will have the same birthday is

(a) $1-\frac{(365)^N (365)!}{(365-N)!}$ (b) $1+\frac{(365)^N (365)!}{(365-N)!}$

(c) $1-\frac{(365)^N (365)!}{(365+N)!}$ (d) None of these

**252.** If the joint p d f of X and Y is

$$f(x, y)=\frac{1}{\pi\sqrt{2}} e^{(x^2+y^2-\sqrt{2}xy)}, \quad -\infty < x, y < \infty,$$

then the coefficients of linear correlation between $X$ and $Y$ is

(a) $\frac{1}{\sqrt{2}}$ (b) $-\frac{1}{\sqrt{2}}$ (c) $\frac{1}{2}$ (d) $-\frac{1}{2}$

**253.** For constants $a$ and $b$, the expected value of $aX + b$ is

(a) $E(aX + b) = aX$ (b) $E(aX + b) = b$

(c) $E(aX + b) = a\,E(X) + b$ (d) $E(aX + b) = aX + E(b)$

**254.** Let $X_1,\ldots, X_n$ are independent variables, then $F(x_1, x_2, \ldots, x_n)$ is equal to

(a) $F_1(x_1)\cdot F_2(x_2)\ldots F_n(x_n)$

(b) $F_1(x) F_2(x_2)\ldots F_n(x)$

(c) $F(x_1) F(x_2) F(x_3)\ldots F(x_n)$

(d) None of the above

**255.** The Binomial distribution have the mean

(a) $n^2p$ (b) $np$

(c) $npq$ (d) None of these

**256.** Let $X_1,\ldots, X_n$ be iid random variables with the uniform distribution over (0, 1) as their common distribution. If $R = (\max X_i - \min X_i)$ is the range of the $X_i$' s, then the expected value of $R$ will be

(a) $\frac{n-1}{n}$ (b) $\frac{n-1}{n+1}$ (c) $\frac{n}{n+1}$ (d) $\frac{n-2}{n}$

**257.** A bag contains $n$ tickets marked 1, 2, 3..., $n$. If two tickets are drawn, then the chance that the difference of the numbers on the tickets exceed $m < (n - 1)$ is

(a) $\frac{(n-m)(n-m+1)}{n(n-1)}$ (b) $\frac{(n-m)(m-n+1)}{n(n-1)}$

(c) $\frac{(n-m)(n-m-1)}{n(n-1)}$ (d) None of these

**258.** Let $X$ and $Y$ be two arbitrary random variables with $E(X) = E(Y)$ and var $(X) =$ Var $(Y)$. If $U = X + Y$ and $V = X - Y$, then $U$ and $V$ are

(a) independent

(b) correlated

(c) uncorrelated and thus independent

(d) uncorrelated but not independent

**259.** The expected value of the constant $b$ is

(a) 0 (b) 1 (c) $\frac{1}{b}$ (d) $b$

**260.** The mean and variance of a standardized random variable are

(a) $u = 1, \sigma^2 = 0$ (b) $\mu = 0, \sigma^2 = 1$

(c) $\mu = 0 = \sigma^2$ (d) $\mu = \sigma^2 = 1$

**261.** What is the probability of getting 6 when balanced die is rolled once?

(a) $\frac{1}{2}$ (b) $\frac{1}{6}$ (c) $\frac{2}{3}$ (d) $\frac{1}{3}$

**262.** If $\eta$ denotes the correlation ratio, then

(a) $-1 \le \eta \le 1$ (b) $-1 \le \eta \le 0$

(c) $0 \le \eta \le 1$ (d) $-1 < \eta < 1$

**263.** 3 mangoes and 3 apples are in a box. If fruits are chosen at random, the probability that one is a mango and the other is an apple, is

(a) 3/5 (b) 5/6

(c) 1/36 (d) None of these

**264.** Let $X$ be a discrete random variable with probability mass function

$$P(X = 0) = 1 - \frac{1}{C^2}, \quad P(X = -1) = P(X = +1) = \frac{1}{2C^2}$$

where $C > 1$ is a constant. If $\sigma^2$ denotes the variance of $X$, then $[(|X| > C\sigma)]$ is

(a) less than $1-\frac{1}{C^2}$ (b) less than $\frac{1}{C^2}$

(c) greater than $\frac{1}{C^2}$ (d) equal to $\frac{1}{C^2}$

**265.** If $X$ has the probability density

$$f(x) = \begin{cases} e^{-x}, & x > 0, \\ 0, & \text{otherwise} \end{cases} \quad \text{and } g(X) = e^{3X/4}$$

What is the expected value of $g(X)$?

(a) 4 (b) 3 (c) 2 (d) 1

**266.** Let $X_1$ and $X_2$ are two independent variables and $Y = a_1X_1 + a_2X_2$, then var $(Y)$ is

(a) $a_1$ var $(X_1) + a_2$ var $(X_2)$ (b) $a_1X_1 + a_2X_2$

(c) $a_1^2$ var $(X_1) + a_2^2$ var $(X_2)$ (d) None of these

**267.** What is the probability of getting head when we toss a coin once?

(a) $\frac{1}{2}$ (b) $\frac{1}{4}$ (c) 1 (d) 0

**268.** A radar unit tracking a target detects it with probability $p$ during a surveillance cycle. The detection of the target in each cycle is independent of other cycles. The probability that the target will be detected within the first $n$ cycles is

(a) $p^n$ (b) $1-(1-p)^n$

(c) $\sum_{k=1}^{n} p^k$ (d) $(1-p)^n$

**269.** The following table represents a probability distribution for a random variable $X$

| $X$ | 1 | 2 | 3 | 4 | 5 | 6 |
|---|---|---|---|---|---|---|
| $P\ (X = X)$ | 0.1 | 2k | k | 0.2 | 3k | 0.1 |

Then, the value of $k$ is

(a) 0.1 (b) 0.2 (c) 0.3 (d) 0.4

**270.** A table of rates of daily wages and number of employees is given below

| Daily wage in ₹ | Number of employees |
|---|---|
| 80 and less than 90 | 2 |
| 90 and less than 100 | 6 |
| 100 and less than 110 | 10 |
| 110 and less than 120 | 14 |
| 120 and less than 130 | 9 |
| 130 and less than 140 | 7 |
| 140 and less than 150 | 2 |

Consider the following interferences drawn from the data in the table given above.

I. Wages of about two third of the employees ranged from ₹ 100 to ₹ 129.

II. Exact range of wages is ₹ 70.

III. Ninety per cent of the employees earn, atleast ₹ 100 per day.

Which of the above inferences valid?

(a) I and III (b) I and II
(c) II and III (d) I, II and III

**271.** The expected value of the random variable $X$ whose probability density is given by

$$f(x) = \begin{cases} \dfrac{x+1}{8}, & 2 < x < 4 \\ 0, & \text{otherwise} \end{cases}$$

(a) $\dfrac{37}{6}$ (b) $\dfrac{37}{12}$ (c) $\dfrac{37}{18}$ (d) $\dfrac{37}{24}$

**272.** Let $X_1$ and $X_2$ are two independent variables and $Y = a_1X_1 + a_2X_2$, then $E(Y)$ is

(a) $a_1E(X_1) + a_2E(X_2)$ (b) $a_1X_1 + a_2X_2$
(c) $X_1 + X_2$ (d) None of these

**273.** The variance of the uniform (discrete) probability distribution is given by

(a) $\Sigma \dfrac{(x_i - \mu)^2}{k^2}$ (b) $\Sigma x_i / k$
(c) $\Sigma x_i$ (d) $k$

**274.** Let $(X, Y)$ be jointly distributed with density function $f(x, y) = e^{-y}$, $0 < x < y < \infty$
$= 0$, otherwise

Now, consider the following statements

I. $E[X|y]$ is $\dfrac{y}{2}$

II. $E[y|x]$ is $x + 1$

Select the correct answer from the following alternatives

(a) Only I is correct
(b) Only II is correct
(c) Both I and II are correct
(d) Neither I nor II is correct

**275.** Suppose $X$ follows a binomial distribution with parameters $n$ and $p$, where $0 < p < 1$, if $\dfrac{P(X-r)}{P(X = n-r)}$ is independent of $n$ and $r$, then

(a) $p = \dfrac{1}{2}$ (b) $p = \dfrac{1}{3}$
(c) $p = \dfrac{1}{4}$ (d) None of these

**276.** Let $X_1, X_2, \ldots,$ be independent random variables each distributed uniformly over the interval (0, 2). The number to which $\dfrac{1}{n}(X_1^2 + \ldots + X_n^2)$ converges in probability as $n \to \infty$ is

(a) 0 (b) $\dfrac{4}{3}$ (c) 1 (d) $\dfrac{1}{3}$

**277.** Let $X$ be a random variable, denotes the number of points rolled with a balanced die. The expected value of $g(X) = 2X^2 + 1$ is

(a) $\dfrac{94}{4}$ (b) $\dfrac{94}{3}$
(c) $\dfrac{94}{2}$ (d) 94

**278.** For given constants $a$ and $b$, $E(aX + b)$ is equal to

(a) $aE(X) + b$ (b) $aE(X) + E(b)$
(c) $aE(X)$ (d) $a + b$

**279.** Let $\phi(x)$ be a standard normal distribution function. Then, following relation holds

(a) $\phi(-x) = 1 - \phi(x)$ (b) $\phi(-x) = \phi(x)$
(c) $\phi(-x) = \phi(x) - 1$ (d) None of these

**280.** Two digits are chosen without replacement form the ten digits between 0 and 9. The probability that the sum of the two digits is even and their product is odd, is

(a) $\dfrac{1}{4}$ (b) $\dfrac{1}{2}$
(c) $\dfrac{2}{9}$ (d) $\dfrac{7}{9}$

**281.** One card is drawn from a pack of 52 cards. The probability that it is the card of a king or spade is

(a) 1/26 (b) 3/26 (c) 4/13 (d) 3/13

**282.** If $M(t)$, the moment generating function of a random variable $X$, exists for $-h < t < h$ (for some $h > 0$), then for any real $a$, which one of the following statements is always correct (for $-h < t < h$)?

(a) $\Pr[X \geq a] \leq e^{-at} M(t)$ (b) $\Pr[X \geq a] \geq e^{-at} M(t)$
(c) $\Pr[X \leq a] \leq e^{-at} M(t)$ (d) $\Pr[X \leq a] \geq e^{-at} M(t)$

**283.** The random variable $X$ have the probability density function $f(x) = \begin{cases} \dfrac{4}{\pi(1+x^2)}, & 0 < x < 1 \\ 0 & \text{otherwise} \end{cases}$

What is the expected value?

(a) $\log 4$ (b) $\log \pi$

(c) $\dfrac{\log 4}{\pi}$ (d) $\dfrac{\pi}{\log 4}$

**284.** If $X$ and $Y$ are independent, then their covariance $E[(X_1 - \mu_X)(Y - \mu_Y)]$ is equal to

(a) zero (b) one (c) two (d) three

**285.** Let $F(x)$ be a distribution function of normal distribution and $\phi(x)$ be a standard distribution function. Then, following relation holds

(a) $F(x) = \phi\left(\dfrac{x-\mu}{\sigma}\right)$ (b) $F(x) = \phi\left(\dfrac{x}{\sigma}\right)$

(c) $F(x) = \phi(x)$ (d) None of these

**286.** Consider the following statements regarding the two independent events $A_1$ and $A_2$

I. $\overline{A}_1$ and $\overline{A}_2$ are independent

II. $\overline{A}_1$ and $A_2$ are independent

III. $A_1$ and $\overline{A}_2$ are independent

Which of these is/are correct?

(a) Only I (b) I and II

(c) II and III (d) I, II and III

**287.** $X$ follows a binomial distribution with parameters $n$ and $p$ and $Y$ follows a binomial distribution with parameters $m$ and $p$. Then, if $X$ and $Y$ are independent $P(X = r | X + Y = r + s) =$

(a) $\dfrac{({}^mC_r)({}^nC_s)}{{}^{m+1}C_{rs}}$ (b) $\dfrac{{}^mC_s\,{}^nC_r}{{}^{m+n}C_{r+s}}$

(c) $\dfrac{{}^mC_s}{{}^{m+n}C_r}$ (d) None of these

**288.** A company engaged in the manufacture of talcum powder of various varieties has found a new perfume for the talcum powder. It wants to bring out new perfumed powder to the market in only one size. It has data on sales of various sizes of its existing product. Based on which measure of central tendency would be company decide on the size of the new product to be marketed?

(a) Mean

(b) Median

(c) Mode

(d) Weighted arithmetic mean

**289.** For any real constants $a$ and $b$ with $a \le b$ and $F(x)$ the probability distribution function of random variable $X$, the following is true

(a) $P(a \le X \le b) = F(b) - F(a)$

(b) $P(a \le X \le b) = F(a) - F(b)$

(c) $P(a \le X \le b) = F(b)$

(d) $P(a \le X \le b) = F(a)$

**290.** If $X$ and $Y$ are independent variables with variance $\sigma_X^2$ and $\sigma_Y^2$ respectively, then the variance of $X + Y$ is

(a) $\sigma_{x^2}\,\sigma_{y^2}$ (b) $\sigma_{x^2} + \sigma_{y^2}$

(c) $\dfrac{\sigma_{x^2}}{\sigma_{y^2}}$ (d) None of these

**291.** In normal distribution, the curve of $f(x)$ is symmetric with respect to

(a) $x = \sigma$ (b) $x = \mu$

(c) $x = \dfrac{1}{\sigma}$ (d) None of these

**292.** A family has three children and it is known that it has atleast one boy. Assuming that all sex distributions are equally likely, the probability that there are exactly two boys in the family is

(a) $\dfrac{3}{8}$ (b) $\dfrac{3}{7}$ (c) $\dfrac{4}{7}$ (d) $\dfrac{1}{2}$

**293.** A coin is tossed $m + n$ times, with $m > n$. The probability of getting $m$ consecutive heads is

(a) $\dfrac{(n+2)}{2^{m+1}}$ (b) $\dfrac{n}{2^{m+1}}$

(c) $\dfrac{1+n}{2^{m+1}}$ (d) None of these

**294.** Which one of the following is not a graphical presentation of frequency distribution?

(a) Histogram (b) Frequency polygon

(c) Ogive (d) Scatter diagram

**295.** The probability density function for the random variable whose probability distribution is given by $F(x) = \begin{cases} x, & 0 \le x \le 1 \\ 0, & \text{otherwise} \end{cases}$ ?

(a) $f(x) = \begin{cases} 1, & 0 \le x \le 1 \\ 0, & \text{otherwise} \end{cases}$ (b) $f(x) = \begin{cases} x, & 0 \le x \le 1 \\ 0, & \text{otherwise} \end{cases}$

(c) $f(x) = \begin{cases} 0, & 0 \le x \le 1 \\ 1, & \text{otherwise} \end{cases}$ (d) $f(x) = \begin{cases} 0, & x \le x \le 1 \\ x, & \text{otherwise} \end{cases}$

**296.** If $X$ and $Y$ are independent variables with mean $\mu_X$ and $\mu_Y$, then $(X + Y)$ have the mean equal to

(a) $\mu_X + \mu_Y$ (b) $\mu_X\,\mu_Y$

(c) $\mu_X - \mu_Y$ (d) None of these

**297.** We get standard normal distribution from normal distribution if

(a) $\mu = 0, \sigma = 1$ (b) $\mu = 1, \sigma = 0$

(c) $\mu = \sigma = 0$ (d) $\mu = \sigma = 1$

**298.** If for the events $A$ and $B$, $P(A|B) = \dfrac{1}{4}$, and $P(B|A) = \dfrac{1}{2}$, then which one of the following is not correct?

(a) $A$ and $B$ are mutually exclusive

(b) $A$ and $B$ are independent

(c) $(A^c|B) = \dfrac{3}{4}$

(d) $P(B^c|A) = \dfrac{1}{2}$

**299.** Two players $A$ and $B$ toss a coin alternately. A begins the game and the player who first throws heads is the winner. $B$'s coin is fair but $A$'s is biased and has probability $p$ of showing heads. The value of $p$ so that the game is equiprobable to both players

(a) 2/3 (b) 1/3
(c) 2/5 (d) None of these

**300.** If $x_1$ and $y_1$ $(i = 1, 2, ..., n)$ are the observations on two variables $x$ and $y$ with geometric means $G_1$ and $G_2$ respectively, then the geometric mean of the ratio $\frac{x}{y}$ is

(a) antilog $\left(\frac{G_1}{G_2}\right)$ (b) $\frac{G_1}{G_2}$
(c) $\log G_1 - \log G_2$ (d) None of these

**301.** The random variable $X$ has the probability density function $f(x) = \begin{cases} ke^{-3x}, & x > 0 \\ 0, & \text{otherwise} \end{cases}$.

The value of $k$ is

(a) 1 (b) 2 (c) 3 (d) 4

**302.** If $X_1$ has the mean 3 and $X_2$ has the mean 7 and $X$, $X_2$ are independent random variables, then mean of $X_1 + X_2$ is

(a) 10 (b) 3 (c) 7 (d) 4

**303.** What is the probability of getting two 'six' in rolling a die 4 times?

(a) $\frac{179}{1296}$ (b) $\frac{170}{1296}$ (c) $\frac{2}{1296}$ (d) $\frac{171}{1296}$

**304.** For any two events $A$ and $B$ in a sample space; $P(A \cap B) \geq P(A) + P(B) + \delta$, then $\delta$ is equal to

(a) $-1$ (b) 1 (c) 0 (d) 2

**305.** Three dice are thrown. The probability of getting a sun which is a perfect square is

(a) 2/5 (b) 9/20
(c) 1/4 (d) None of these

**306.** The mean squared deviation from a point a for a given set $x_1, ..., x_n$ of observations on a random variable $X$ is defined by $\frac{1}{n}\Sigma(x_i - a)^2$. The above quantity will attain its minimum value

(a) for none of the values of $a$
(b) when $a$ = the arithmetic mean of $x_i$
(c) when $a$ = the median of $x_i$
(d) when $a$ = the mode of $x_i$

**307.** Let $f(x) = \frac{1}{\pi l}$, $0 \leq x \leq \pi l$ be a probability density function. The probability distribution function $F(x)$ is given by

(a) $\frac{x}{\pi l}$ (b) $\frac{1}{\pi l}$
(c) $x\pi l$ (d) $\frac{\pi l}{x}$

**308.** If $X_1$ has the mean 4 and $X_2$ has the mean 2 and $X_1$ and $X_2$ are independent random variables, then $E(2X_1 + X_2 - 5)$ is

(a) 1 (b) 2 (c) 3 (d) 4

**309.** When $n \to \infty$, the binomial distribution can be approximated by

(a) bernoulli distribution (b) uniform distribution
(c) poisson distribution (d) None of these

**310.** The first of three urns contains 5 white and 8 black balls, the second contains 6 white and 7 black balls and the third contains 11 white balls. An urn is chosen at random and a ball is drawn from it. It turns out to be white. The probability that the ball came from the third urn, is

(a) 1 (b) $\frac{8}{13}$ (c) $\frac{1}{11}$ (d) $\frac{13}{24}$

**311.** A fair coin is tossed $2n$ times. The probability of getting as many heads in the first $n$ tosses as in the last $n$ is

(a) $\frac{^{2n}C_n}{2^{2n}}$ (b) $\frac{^nC_{n-1}}{2^n}$
(c) $\frac{n}{2^{2n}}$ (d) None of these

**312.** Which one of the following measures of central tendency is not affected by extreme values?

(a) Arithmetic mean (b) Median
(c) Geometric mean (d) Harmonic mean

**313.** Cataracts are a very rare birth defect. In Canada, they occur at a rate of approximately 3 babies in every 100000 births. In 1989, there were approximately 57000 births in BC. The probability that more than 5 babies will be born with cataracts is approximately

(a) about 0.1080 (b) about 0.0295
(c) about 0.0216 (d) about 0.0080

**314.** Let $X_1, X_2, ..., X_n$ be independent random variables with pdf of $X_i$ $(i = 1, 2, ..., n)$ as

$$f(x_i, \theta) = \begin{cases} (x_i, 0 = \ 0.e^{-\theta x_i};\ \theta > 0, x_i > 0 \\ 0 \quad ;\text{otherwise} \end{cases}$$

Then, the pdf of $u = X_1 + X_2 + ... + X_n$ is

(a) $\frac{\theta^n}{(n-1)!}u^{n-1}e^{-\theta u}$; $\theta > 0, u > 0$

(b) $\frac{\theta^n}{n!}u^n e^{-\theta u}$; $\theta > 0, u > 0$

(c) $\frac{\theta^n}{n!}u^{n-1}e^{-\theta u}$; $\theta > 0, u > 0$

(d) $\frac{\theta^n}{(1-n)!}u^n e^{-\theta u}$; $\theta > 0, u > 0$

**315.** In order to get atleast once a head with probability $\geq 0.9$, the number of times a coin needs to be tossed is

(a) 6 (b) 4
(c) 5 (d) None of these

**316.** The point of intersection of the 'less than' and the 'greater than' ogives is the

(a) mean (b) median
(c) geometric mean (d) harmonic mean

**317.** Let the probability density function $f(x) = \begin{cases} kx^2, & 0 \le x \le 2 \\ 0, & \text{otherwise} \end{cases}$

the value of $k$ is given by

(a) $\frac{1}{8}$ (b) $\frac{3}{8}$
(c) $\frac{2}{5}$ (d) None of these

**318.** The variance of Poisson distribution is given by

(a) $\sigma^2 = \lambda$ (b) $\sigma^2 = \frac{1}{\lambda}$
(c) $\sigma^2 = \frac{1}{\lambda^2}$ (d) None of these

**319.** A fisherman arrives at his favourite fishing spot. From past experience he knows that the number of fish he catches per hour follows a Poisson distribution at 0.5 fish/h. The probability that he catches atleast 3 fish in four hours is

(a) 0.0126 (b) 0.0144
(c) 0.1804 (d) 0.3233

**320.** The Geometric mean, if the series 1, 2, 4,..., $2^n$, is

(a) $2^{n+(1/2)}$ (b) $2^{(n+1)/2}$
(c) $2^{n-(1/2)}$ (d) $2^{n/2}$

**321.** The joint density function of $X$ and $Y$ is $f(x, y) = \frac{2}{(1+x+y)^3}$; $x>0$, $y>0$, then the marginal density function of $X$ is

(a) $\frac{1}{(1+x)^3}$; $x>0$ (b) $\frac{1}{(1+x)^2}$; $x>0$
(c) $\frac{1}{1+x}$; $x>0$ (d) $\frac{1}{1+x+y}$; $x>0, y>0$

**322.** Let the probability distribution function be $F(x) = \begin{cases} 0, & x<0 \\ 1-e^{-x}, & x>0 \end{cases}$ find the probability density function

(a) $f(x) = \begin{cases} 0, & x<0 \\ e^{-x}, & x>0 \end{cases}$ (b) $f(x) = 1 - e^{-x}$
(c) $f(x) = \begin{cases} 0, & x<0 \\ e^{x}, & x>0 \end{cases}$ (d) None of these

**323.** The moment generating function of a Poisson distribution is given by

(a) $M_X(t) = e^{\lambda(e^t-1)} - 1$
(b) $M_X(t) = e^{\lambda}$
(c) $M_X(t) = e^{\lambda(e^t-1)}$
(d) None of the above

**324.** The number of babies born with a particular severe eye defect each year varies randomly, but at a rate of about 30/10000 live births. Last year there were about 15000 live births. The approximate probability that there will be more than 58 babies born with this eye defect is

(a) about 16% (b) about 5%
(c) about 1% (d) about 2.5%

**325.** In some courses, students are graded on a 'normal curve'. For example, students within's 0.5 standard deviations of the mean receive a C; between 0.5 and 1.0 standard deviations above the mean receive a C+; between 1.0 and 1.5 standard deviations above the mean receive a B; between 1.5 and 2.0 standard deviations above the mean receive a B+, etc. The class average in an exam was 60 with a standard deviation of 10. The bounds for a B grade and the percentage of students who will receive a B grade if the marks are actually normal distributed are

(a) (65, 75), 24.17% (b) (70, 75), 18.38%
(c) (70, 75), 9.19% (d) (65, 75), 12.08%

**326.** The variance of 6, 8, 10, 12, 14 is

(a) 1 (b) 8 (c) 12 (d) 16

**327.** If $f(x, y) = 1$; $0 \le x \le 1$, $0 \le y \le 1 = 0$; otherwise

then $P\left\{x^2 + y^2 < \frac{1}{4}\right\}$, is

(a) $\frac{\pi}{2}$ (b) $\frac{\pi}{4}$ (c) $\frac{\pi}{8}$ (d) $\frac{\pi}{16}$

**328.** For the random variable $X$, which has the probability function $f(x) = \frac{k}{x!}$ $(x = 0, 1, 2, \ldots)$ the distribution function is

(a) $ke$ (b) $\frac{k}{e}$
(c) $e$ (d) None of these

**329.** The Binomial distribution have mean equals to

(a) $\mu = np$ (b) $\mu = p$
(c) $\mu = npq$ (d) None of these

**330.** The number of deaths due to stroke in the Vancouver region each year varies randomly with a mean of about 555 deaths per year. Assuming that the number of deaths has an approximate Poisson distribution, then the probability that there will be atleast 600 deaths due to stroke in anyone year is

(a) about 1% (b) about 32%
(c) about 16% (d) about 2.5%

**331.** The grade point averages of students at the University of Manitoba are approximately normally distributed with mean equal to 2.4 and standard deviation equal to 0.8. What fraction of the students will possess a grade point average in excess of 3.0?

(a) 0.7500 (b) 0.6000
(c) 0.2734 (d) 0.2266

**332.** The geometric mean of observations 2, 4, 16 and 32 is

(a) 6 (b) 7 (c) 8 (d) 9

**333.** Random variable $X$ follows a normal distribution with mean 50 and standard deviation 10. Let $\Phi$ (*) be the cumulative distribution function of $N(0, 1)$. If $P\{|X - 75| \le 10\} = \Phi(z_1) - \Phi(z_2)$, then

(a) $z_1 = 2.5, z_2 = 1.5$ (b) $z_1 = 3.5, z_2 = 2.5$
(c) $z_1 = 3.5, z_2 = 1.5$ (d) $z_1 = 2.5, z_2 = 0.5$

**334** If random variable X has the probability function $f(x) = \frac{k}{x!}$ $(x = 0, 1, 2, \ldots)$, the value of $k$ is

(a) $\frac{1}{e}$ (b) e
(c) $1 - \frac{1}{e}$ (d) None of these

**335.** The Binomial distribution have number of parameters

(a) one (b) two (c) three (d) four

**336.** The marketing manager of a company has noted that she usually receives 10 complaint calls during a week (consisting of five working days), and that the calls occur at random. Let us suppose that the number of calls during a week follows the Poisson distribution. The probability that she gets five such calls in one day is

(a) 0.0361 (b) 0.0378
(c) 0.9834 (d) 0.2000

**337.** The marks on a statistics test are normally distributed with a mean of 62 and a variance of 225. If the instructor wishes to assign *B*'s or higher to the top 30% of the students in the class, what marks is required to get a *B* or higher?

(a) 68.7 (b) 71.5 (c) 73.2 (d) 69.9

**338.** The standard deviation of a set of variables is 2.5. Now, 16 is added to each observation, the standard deviation of the new set is

(a) 2.5 (b) 6.5
(c) 18.5 (d) None of these

**339.** The mean and variance of Poisson distribution are same

(a) always true (b) always false
(c) partially true (d) partially false

Directions (Q. Nos. 340 and 341) Significant birth defects occur at a rate of about 4 per 1000 births in human populations. After a nuclear accident, there were 10 defects observed in the next 1500 births.

**340.** An approximate 95% interval for the number of defects that would occur in 1500 births (assuming that the rate has not changed) is

(a) (4,8) (b) (2,10) (c) (2,6) (d) (0,8)

**341.** Find the probability of observing atleast 10 defects in this sample, if the rate had not changed after the accident

(a) 0.008 (b) 0.003 (c) 0.041 (d) 0.084

**Directions** (Q. Nos. 342 and 343) A newborn baby whose Apgar score is over 6 is classified as normal and this happens in 80% of births. As a quality control check, an auditor examined the records of 100 births. He would be suspicious if the number of normal births in the sample of 100 births fell above the upper limit of a "95% normal-range"

**342.** Babies that have Apgar scores of 6 or lower require more expensive medical care. What is the probability that in the next 10 births 3 or more babies will have Apgar scores of 6 or lower?

(a) 0.2013 (b) 0.3222
(c) 0.9999 (d) 0.0001

**343.** What is this upper limit?

(a) 112 (b) 72
(c) 88 (d) 8

**Directions** (Q. Nos. 344 and 345) The following two questions refer to the following situation.

All human blood can be 'ABO' typed as belonging to one of A, B, O or AB type. The actual distribution varies slightly among different groups of people, but for a randomly chosen person from North America, the following are the approximate probabilities

| **Blood type** | O | A | B | AB |
|---|---|---|---|---|
| **Probability** | 0.45 | 0.40 | 0.11 | 0.04 |

**344.** What is the probability that both people in a couple will have the same blood type if matings are random with respect to blood type, *i.e.*, one partner's blood type does not influence the blood type of the other partner

(a) about 0.21 (b) about 0.16
(c) about 0.002 (d) about 0.38

**345.** Consider an accident victim with type B blood. She can only receive a transfusion from a person with type B or type O blood. What is the probability that a randomly chosen person will be suitable donor?

(a) About 0.11 (b) About 0.04
(c) About 0.15 (d) About 0.56

**Directions** (Q.Nos. 346 and 347) Seventeen people have been exposed to a particular disease. Each one independently has a 40% chance of contracting the disease. A hospital has the capacity to handle 10 cases of the disease.

**346.** Planners need to have enough beds available to handle a proportion of all outbreaks. Suppose a typical outbreak has 100 people exposed, each with a 40% chance of coming down with the disease. Which is not correct?

(a) This experiment satisfies the assumptions of a binomial distribution.

(b) About 95% of the time between 30 and 50 people will contract the disease.

(c) Almost all of the time, between 25 and 55 people will contract the disease.

(d) Almost all of time, less than 40 people will be infected.

**347.** What is the probability that the hospital's capacity will be exceeded?

(a) 0.965 (b) 0.035
(c) 0.989 (d) 0.011

**Directions** (Q. Nos. 348 and 349) It has been estimated that about 30% of frozen chicken contain enough salmonella bacteria to cause illness if improperly cooked. A consumer purchases 12 frozen chickens.

**348.** Suppose that a supermarket buys 1000 frozen chickens from a supplier. Find an approximate 95% interval for the number of frozen chickens that may be contaminated

(a) (90, 510) (b) (285,315)
(c) (0,730) (d) (270,330)

**349.** What is the probability that the consumer will have more than 6 contaminated chickens?

(a) 0.961 (b) 0.118
(c) 0.882 (d) 0.039

**Directions** (Q. Nos. 350 and 351) Suppose that the probability that a cross between two varieties will express a particular gene is 0.20.

**350.** Suppose that 120 crosses are bred. Find a likely 95% range for the number of progeny that will express the gene

(a) 24s'19.2 (b) 24s'4.4
(c) 24s'8.8 (d) 24s'4.9

**351.** What is the probability that in 8 progeny plants, two or fewer plants will express the gene?

(a) 0.2936 (b) 0.3355 (c) 0.1678 (d) 0.7969

**352.** The number of traffic accidents per week in a small city has a Poisson distribution with mean equal to 1.3. What is the probability of atleast two accidents in 2 weeks?

(a) 0.2510 (b) 0.3732
(c) 0.5184 (d) 0.7326

**353.** The number of traffic accidents per week in a small city has Poisson distribution with mean equal to 3. What is the probability of atleast one accident in 2 weeks?

(a) 0.0174 (b) 0.9502
(c) 0.9975 (d) 0.1991

**354.** Suppose 50 men out of 10000 and 25 women out of 10000 are colour blind. A colour blind person is chosen at random. Assuming that males and females are equally likely, the probability of the person being male is

(a) 1/2 (b) 1/3 (c) 2/3 (d) 0.005

**355.** Events $A_1, A_2, A_3$, are pairwise independent which of the following statements is not true in general?

(a) $P(A_1^c A_2) = P(A_1^c)P(A_2)$
(b) $P(A_1 \cup A_2) = 1 - [1 - P(A_1)][1 - P(A_2)]$
(c) $P(A_1^c A_2 A_3) = P(A_1^c)P(A_2) \cdot P(A_3)$
(d) $P(A_1^c A_3^c) = P(A_1^c)P(A_3^c)$

**356.** Which of the following is not a characteristic function?

(a) $(q + pe^{it})^n$ (b) cost
(c) $\exp(e^{t^2/2})$ (d) $(\cos t)^2$

**357.** A biased coin is tested 4 times or until a head turns up whichever occurs earlier. The distribution of the number of fails turning up is

(a) Binomial (b) Geometric
(c) Both (a) and (b) (d) Negative binomial

**358.** The expectation of the total number of points obtained when three fair dice are rolled together once is

(a) 6.0 (b) 10.5 (c) 12.5 (d) 11.0

**359.** If $A$ and $B$ are independent events, $P(A) = 0.5$ and $P(A \cup B) = 0.6$, then $P(B)$ is

(a) 0.1 (b) 0.2 (c) 0.3 (d) 0.5

**360.** The sequence $\{X_n\}$ of random variables is said to converge to $x$ in probability, if as $n \to \infty$.

(a) $P\{|X_n - X| > \epsilon\} \to 0$ for some $\epsilon > 0$
(b) $P\{|X_n - X| < \epsilon\} \to 0$ for some $\epsilon < 0$
(c) $P\{|X_n - X| > \epsilon\} \to 0$, for all $\epsilon > 0$
(d) $P\{|X_n - X| < \epsilon\} \to 0$ for all $\epsilon > 0$

**361.** If $X$ has the geometric distribution $P[P = x], = pq^x, X = 0, 1, 2, \ldots$ with $P = \frac{2}{5}$, then the second raw moment is

(a) 12 (b) 6 (c) 4 (d) 8

**362.** If random variables $X$ and $Y$ are independent, then $E(XY)$ is equal to

(a) $E(X) + E(Y)$ (b) $E(X) - E(Y)$
(c) $E(X)E(Y)$ (d) $E(X)E(Y) + \sigma_{XY}$

**363.** If $x$ is a Poisson random variate with mean 3, then $P(|X - 3| < 1)$ will be

(a) $\frac{1}{2}e^{-3}$ (b) $3e^{-3}$
(c) $\frac{9}{2}e^{-3}$ (d) $\left(\frac{99}{8}\right)e^{-3}$

**364.** Let $X$ be a normal random variable with mean zero and variance 9. If $a = P(X \geq 3)$, then $P(|X| \leq 3)$ equals

(a) $a$ (b) $1 - a$
(c) $2a$ (d) $1 - 2a$

**365.** A coin is tossed 5 times, probability of head is $\frac{1}{2}$. The probability exactly 2 heads is

(a) $\frac{5}{16}$ (b) $\frac{1}{16}$
(c) $\frac{2}{3}$ (d) $\frac{1}{3}$

**366.** If $X$ and $Y$ are independent random variables, then $\sigma_{XY}$ is equal to

(a) zero (b) one
(c) two (d) $E(XY) - E(X)E(Y)$

**367.** An urn contains 2 white and 3 blacks. A ball is drawn at random and its colour is noted. The ball drawn is replaced and 2 more balls of the same colour are added to the urn. If now a ball is chosen at random from the urn, then the probability that it is white, is

(a) $\frac{4}{5}$ (b) $\frac{3}{5}$ (c) $\frac{2}{5}$ (d) $\frac{1}{5}$

**368.** For the constants $a$ and $b$, $E(aX+b)$ is

(a) $aE(X)+b$ (b) $E(X)$
(c) $aE(X)$ (d) None of the above

**369.** If $X_1, X_2, \dots, X_n$ are $n$-independent random variables each have the same distribution with variance $\sigma^2$. Then, mean $\bar{X}$ have variance $\sigma_{\bar{X}}^2$ is

(a) $\sigma^2$ (b) $\frac{\sigma^2}{n}$
(c) $\frac{\sigma^2}{n^2}$ (d) None of these

**370.** For the three arbitrary events, $A$, $B$ and $C$ assuming all the conditional probabilities to be defined, $P(A|B\cap C)$ equals

(a) $P(A|B)\cdot P(A|C)$ (b) $\frac{P(A\cap B|C)}{P(B|C)}$
(c) $\frac{P(A\cap B|C)}{P(C|B)}$ (d) $\frac{P(B\cap C|A)}{P(A|B\cup C)}$

**371.** $P(A/A\cup B)$ is equal to when $P(A\cap B)=0$

(a) $\frac{P(A)}{P(B)}$ (b) $\frac{P(A)}{P(B)+P(A\cup B)}$
(c) $\frac{P(A)}{P(A)+P(B)}$ (d) $\frac{P(B)}{P(A)+P(B)}$

**372.** For any two events $A$ and $B$

(a) $P(A\cup B)\le P(A)+P(B)$ (b) $P(A\cup B)=P(A)+P(B)$
(c) $P(A\cup B)\ge P(A)+P(B)$ (d) None of these

**373.** If $A$ and $B$ are two events on some probability space such that

$P(A\cup B)=\frac{5}{6}, P(A\cap B)=\frac{1}{3}, P(B^c)=\frac{1}{2}$, then

(a) such $A$ and $B$ cannot exist
(b) $A$ and $B$ are mutually exclusive
(c) $A$ and $B$ are independent
(d) $A$ and $B$ have the same probability of occurrence

**374.** Let $p_1=P(A)$, $p_2=P(B)$, $p_3=P(A\cap B)$, then $P(A/B)$ is

(a) $\frac{p_3}{p_2}$ (b) $\frac{p_2}{p_3}$
(c) $p_3p_2$ (d) $p_1p_2$

**375.** What is the probability of getting doublets when two dice are thrown simultaneously?

(a) $\frac{1}{2}$ (b) $\frac{1}{3}$
(c) $\frac{1}{6}$ (d) $\frac{2}{3}$

**376.** A fair die is rolled repeatedly. If $A$ denotes the event that the number of 3 will show up before the number 6, then $P(A)$ is

(a) $\frac{1}{9}$ (b) $\frac{1}{3}$
(c) $\frac{1}{2}$ (d) $\frac{2}{3}$

**377.** The mean and variance of Binomial distribution $b(x:n,p)$ are 4 and $\frac{4}{3}$, respectively. What is the probability of getting 2 successes?

(a) 20 (b) $\frac{20}{423}$
(c) $\frac{20}{243}$ (d) $\frac{1}{243}$

**378.** A card is drawn at random from a pack of cards. What is the probability of getting an ace of spade or knave of club?

(a) $\frac{2}{3}$ (b) $\frac{2}{13}$
(c) $\frac{1}{26}$ (d) $\frac{1}{3}$

**379.** The pdf of a random variable $X$ is given by

$$f(x)=\begin{cases} kx(1-x), & 0<x<1 \\ 0, & \text{otherwise}\end{cases}$$

where $k$ is an appropriate positive constant. The value of $P\left(X<\frac{1}{k}\right)$ is

(a) $\frac{1}{81}$ (b) $\frac{1}{9}$
(c) $\frac{2}{27}$ (d) $\frac{1}{3}$

**380.** For Binomial distribution, $n=10$ and $p=0.6$, $E(X^2)$ is

(a) 30 (b) 38
(c) 8 (d) 38.4

**381.** What is the probability that non-leap year have 53 Sundays?

(a) $\frac{1}{6}$ (b) $\frac{1}{5}$
(c) $\frac{1}{4}$ (d) $\frac{1}{7}$

**382.** A random variable $X$ has the cumulative distribution function

$$F(x)=\begin{cases} 1-\exp\left(-\frac{x^2}{2\sigma^2}\right) & \text{for } x\ge 0 \\ 0, & \text{otherwise}\end{cases}$$

(a) $\frac{\sigma}{2}$ (b) 0
(c) $\sigma$ (d) $2\sigma$

# Exercise 2 (For Part 'C')

**Directions** (Q. Nos. 1-22) *Questions may have one or more than one correct option.*

**1.** Out of 40 students, 25 are boys, 16 are married students, 10 are married boys.

(a) Number of unmarried girls is 9.

(b) Number of unmarried girls is null.

(c) The probability that chosen student is unmarried girl is $\frac{9}{40}$.

(d) The probability that chosen student is unmarried girl is 0.

**2.** If $A$ and $B$ are two events, the probability that exactly one of them occurs is given by

(a) $P(A)+P(B)-2P(A\cap B)$

(b) $P(A\cap\overline{B})+P(\overline{A}\cap B)$

(c) $P(A\cup B)-P(A\cap B)$

(d) $P(\overline{A})+P(\overline{B})-2P(\overline{A}\cap\overline{B})$

**3.** In a book of 520 pages, 390 typographical errors occurs.

(a) The probability that random sample of 1 page will not contain error is $e^{-3/4}$

(b) The probability that random sample of 4 pages will not contain error is $e^{-3}$.

(c) $\lambda = 3/4$

(d) The probability that random sample of 4 pages will have no error is 0.

**4.** The probabilities that a student passes in Mathematics. Physics and Chemistry are $m$, $p$ and $c$, respectively. Of these subjects, the student has 75% chance of passing in atleast one, a 50% chance of passing in atleast two and a 40% chance of passing in exactly two Which of the following relations are true?

(a) $p+m+c=\frac{19}{20}$ (b) $p+m+c=\frac{27}{20}$

(c) $pmc=\frac{1}{10}$ (d) $pmc=\frac{1}{4}$

**5.** If $A$ and $B$ are two independent events such that $P(\overline{A}\cap B)=2/15$ and $P(A\cap\overline{B})=1/6$, then $P(B)$ is

(a) $\frac{4}{5}$ (b) $\frac{1}{6}$ (c) $\frac{1}{5}$ (d) $\frac{5}{6}$

**6.** When one dice is thrown, then

(a) the associated sample space is {1, 2, 3, 4, 5, 6}.

(b) the number of sample points are 6.

(c) the probability of getting 5 is 6.

(d) the probability of getting 5 is 1/6.

**7.** If $P(A)=3/5$ and $P(B)=2/3$, then which of the following option (s) is/are correct?

(a) $P(A\cup B)\geq 2/3$

(b) $4/15\leq P(A\cap B)\leq 3/5$

(c) $2/5\leq P(A/B)\leq 9/10$

(d) $P(A\cap\overline{B})\leq 1/3$

**8.** Out cf 52 cards 4 are drawn at random without replacement.

(a) Number of ways of selecting 4 cards from a pack cf 52 cards is ${}^{52}C_4$

(b) Number of ways 2 red cards are drawn from 26 red cards is ${}^{26}C_2$

(c) Probability that two are black and two are red is 325/833.

(d) Probability that two are black and two are red is 1.

**9.** If $A$ and $B$ are two events such that $P(A)=\frac{1}{2}$ and $P(B)=\frac{2}{3}$, then which of the following is correct?

(a) $P(A\cup B)\geq\frac{2}{3}$ (b) $P(A\cap\overline{B})\leq\frac{1}{3}$

(c) $\frac{1}{6}\leq P(A\cap B)\leq\frac{1}{2}$ (d) $\frac{1}{6}\leq P(\overline{A}\cap B)\leq\frac{1}{2}$

**10.** A dice is thrown, the probability of getting

(a) less than 4 is 1 (b) odd number is 0

(c) less than 4 is $\frac{1}{2}$ (d) odd number is $\frac{1}{2}$

**11.** An urn contains 5 black and 11 white balls probability of getting

(a) black ball when it is drawn at random is 0

(b) white ball when drawn ball is replaced is 1

(c) white ball when drawn ball is replaced is $\frac{11}{16}$

(d) black ball when it is drawn at random is $\frac{5}{16}$

**12.** Given, the exponential distribution

$$f(x)=\frac{1}{c}e^{-x/c},$$

$$0\leq x\leq\infty,\ c>0.$$

(a) The moment generating function is $1+ct+c^2t^2+\dots$

(b) The moment generating function is $1+t+t^2+\dots$

(c) The second moment about the origin is $2c^2$.

(d) The second moment about the origin is $c^3$.

**13.** Let $P(A)=\frac{2}{3}$, $P(B)=\frac{1}{4}$, $P(C)=\frac{1}{6}$ for disjoints sets.

(a) $P(A\cup B\cup C)=1$

(b) $P(A\cup B\cup C)=0$

(c) $P(A\cup B\cup C)=P(A)+P(B)+P(C)$

(d) $P(A\cup B\cup C)=P(A)P(B)P(C)$

**14.** Two dice are thrown simultaneously. Find the probability of getting

(a) an odd number on the first die is $\frac{1}{2}$

(b) an ace on atleast one of the dice is $\frac{11}{36}$

(c) an odd number on the first die is $\frac{1}{2}$

(d) an ace on atleast one of the dice is 1/3

**15.** If the independent event $A$ and $B$ are such that $0 < P(A) < 1$ and $0 < P(B) < 1$, then which of the following option (s) is/are correct?

(a) $A$ and $B$ are mutually exclusive.
(b) $A$ and $\bar{B}$ are independent.
(c) $\bar{A}$ and $\bar{B}$ are independent.
(d) $P(A/B) = P(\bar{A}/B) = 1$.

**16.** Given, the function $f(x) = \begin{cases} e^{-x}, & x \geq 0 \\ 0, & x < 0 \end{cases}$

(a) $\int_{-\infty}^{\infty} f(x)\,dx = 1$
(b) $f(x) \geq 0, \forall x$
(c) $f(x)$ is defined as density function
(d) $f(x)$ is not defined as density function

**17.** For any two events $A$ and $B$ defined on a sample space.

(a) $P(A/B) \geq \frac{P(A) + P(B) - 1}{P(B)}, P(B) \neq 0$ is always true
(b) $P(A \cap \bar{B}) = P(A) - P(A \cap B)$
(c) $P(A \cup B) = 1 - P(A^c) \cdot P(B^c)$, if $A$ and $B$ are independent
(d) $P(A \cup B) = 1 - P(A^c) \cdot P(B^c)$, if $A$ and $B$ are disjoint

**18.** If $A$ and $B$ are two events. The probability that atmost one of $A$, $B$ occurs is

(a) $1 - P(A \cap B)$
(b) $P(\bar{A}) + P(\bar{B}) - P(\bar{A} \cap \bar{B})$
(c) $P(\bar{A}) + P(\bar{B}) + P(A \cup B) - 1$
(d) $P(A \cap \bar{B}) + P(\bar{A} \cap B) + P(\bar{A} \cap \bar{B})$

**19.** If $A$ and $B$ are two independent events such that $P(A) = \frac{1}{2}$ and $P(B) = \frac{1}{5}$, then which of the following is/are correct?

(a) $P(A \cup B) = \frac{3}{5}$ (b) $P\left(\frac{A}{B}\right) = \frac{1}{2}$

(c) $P\left(\frac{A}{A \cup B}\right) = \frac{5}{6}$ (d) $P(A \cap B/\bar{A} \cup \bar{B}) = \frac{1}{2}$

**20.** If $E_1$ and $E_2$ are two events such that $P(E_1) = 1/4$, $P(E_2/E_1) = 1/2$ and $P(E_1/E_2) = 1/4$,

(a) then $E_1$ and $E_2$ are independent
(b) $E_1$ and $E_2$ are exhaustive
(c) $E_2$ is twice as likely to occur as $E_1$
(d) probabilities of the events $E_1 \cap E_2$, $E_1$ and $E_2$ are in GP

**21.** If $A$ and $B$ are two events such that $P(B) \neq 1$, $B^c$ denotes the event complementary to $B$, then

(a) $P(A/B^c) = \frac{P(A) - P(A \cap B)}{1 - P(B)}$
(b) $P(A \cap B) \geq P(A) + P(B) - 1$
(c) $P(A) >< P(A/B)$ according as $P(A/B^c) >< P(A)$
(d) $P(A/B^c) + P(A^c/B^c) =$

**22.** There are 100 tickets numbered from 1 to 100. They are all well shuffled and a ticket is drawn at random. The probability that the number on the ticket drawn is

(a) an even number is 0.5
(b) 5 or multiple of 5 is 0.2
(c) greater than 75 is 0.25
(d) is a square of integers is 0.1

# Answers

## Exercise 1

| | | | | | | | | | |
|---|---|---|---|---|---|---|---|---|---|
| **1.** (b) | **2.** (b) | **3.** (c) | **4.** (b) | **5.** (a) | **6.** (c) | **7.** (c) | **8.** (d) | **9.** (b) | **10.** (c) |
| **11.** (c) | **12.** (d) | **13.** (b) | **14.** (c) | **15.** (c) | **16.** (c) | **17.** (c) | **18.** (b) | **19.** (a) | **20.** (c) |
| **21.** (d) | **22.** (b) | **23.** (a) | **24.** (c) | **25.** (a) | **26.** (a) | **27.** (c) | **28.** (b) | **29.** (b) | **30.** (b) |
| **31.** (a) | **32.** (d) | **33.** (d) | **34.** (a) | **35.** (d) | **36.** (b) | **37.** (a) | **38.** (a) | **39.** (c) | **40.** (b) |
| **41.** (b) | **42.** (c) | **43.** (d) | **44.** (b) | **45.** (b) | **46.** (a) | **47.** (c) | **48.** (d) | **49.** (b) | **50.** (c) |
| **51.** (a) | **52.** (a) | **53.** (a) | **54.** (b) | **55.** (a) | **56.** (a) | **57.** (a) | **58.** (a) | **59.** (a) | **60.** (d) |
| **61.** (c) | **62.** (c) | **63.** (a) | **64.** (d) | **65.** (b) | **66.** (b) | **67.** (d) | **68.** (c) | **69.** (a) | **70.** (c) |
| **71.** (a) | **72.** (a) | **73.** (c) | **74.** (a) | **75.** (b) | **76.** (a) | **77.** (c) | **78.** (b) | **79.** (b) | **80.** (b) |
| **81.** (a) | **82.** (b) | **83.** (d) | **84.** (a) | **85.** (a) | **86.** (a) | **87.** (a) | **88.** (a) | **89.** (c) | **90.** (c) |
| **91.** (d) | **92.** (c) | **93.** (b) | **94.** (b) | **95.** (b) | **96.** (c) | **97.** (c) | **98.** (b) | **99.** (c) | **100.** (a) |
| **101.** (d) | **102.** (d) | **103.** (c) | **104.** (c) | **105.** (a) | **106.** (b) | **107.** (d) | **108.** (c) | **109.** (a) | **110.** (a) |
| **111.** (b) | **112.** (a) | **113.** (c) | **114.** (c) | **115.** (b) | **116.** (a) | **117.** (a) | **118.** (c) | **119.** (a) | **120.** (c) |
| **121.** (a) | **122.** (a) | **123.** (c) | **124.** (c) | **125.** (d) | **126.** (c) | **127.** (d) | **128.** (b) | **129.** (b) | **130.** (a) |
| **131.** (a) | **132.** (b) | **133.** (c) | **134.** (a) | **135.** (d) | **136.** (d) | **137.** (c) | **138.** (b) | **139.** (d) | **140.** (b) |
| **141.** (c) | **142.** (d) | **143.** (d) | **144.** (b) | **145.** (c) | **146.** (a) | **147.** (d) | **148.** (d) | **149.** (c) | **150.** (a) |
| **151.** (c) | **152.** (a) | **153.** (b) | **154.** (a) | **155.** (b) | **156.** (c) | **157.** (c) | **158.** (d) | **159.** (c) | **160.** (d) |

**161.** (b) **162.** (b) **163.** (d) **164.** (d) **165.** (c) **166.** (b) **167.** (c) **168.** (c) **169.** (b) **170.** (d)
**171.** (b) **172.** (d) **173.** (b) **174.** (b) **175.** (d) **176.** (c) **177.** (a) **178.** (d) **179.** (d) **180.** (b)
**181.** (b) **182.** (a) **183.** (a) **184.** (b) **185.** (d) **186.** (a) **187.** (c) **188.** (a) **189.** (d) **190.** (d)
**191.** (d) **192.** (b) **193.** (d) **194.** (a) **195.** (a) **196.** (d) **197.** (c) **198.** (b) **199.** (a) **200.** (c)
**201.** (a) **202.** (a) **203.** (c) **204.** (b) **205.** (c) **206.** (c) **207.** (a) **208.** (a) **209.** (a) **210.** (c)
**211.** (b) **212.** (b) **213.** (a) **214.** (c) **215.** (b) **216.** (b) **217.** (a) **218.** (b) **219.** (a) **220.** (c)
**221.** (a) **222.** (a) **223.** (a) **224.** (a) **225.** (c) **226.** (a) **227.** (c) **228.** (b) **229.** (d) **230.** (a)
**231.** (a) **232.** (d) **233.** (c) **234.** (a) **235.** (b) **236.** (d) **237.** (a) **238.** (c) **239.** (a) **240.** (b)
**241.** (a) **242.** (d) **243.** (b) **244.** (a) **245.** (a) **246.** (b) **247.** (d) **248.** (a) **249.** (c) **250.** (a)
**251.** (a) **252.** (c) **253.** (c) **254.** (a) **255.** (b) **256.** (c) **257.** (c) **258.** (c) **259.** (d) **260.** (b)
**261.** (b) **262.** (c) **263.** (a) **264.** (a) **265.** (a) **266.** (c) **267.** (a) **268.** (b) **269.** (a) **270.** (a)
**271.** (b) **272.** (a) **273.** (a) **274.** (c) **275.** (a) **276.** (d) **277.** (b) **278.** (a) **279.** (a) **280.** (c)
**281.** (c) **282.** (b) **283.** (c) **284.** (a) **285.** (a) **286.** (d) **287.** (a) **288.** (c) **289.** (b) **290.** (b)
**291.** (b) **292.** (b) **293.** (a) **294.** (d) **295.** (a) **296.** (d) **297.** (a) **298.** (a) **299.** (b) **300.** (b)
**301.** (c) **302.** (a) **303.** (d) **304.** (a) **305.** (d) **306.** (b) **307.** (a) **308.** (a) **309.** (c) **310.** (d)
**311.** (a) **312.** (c) **313.** (d) **314.** (a) **315.** (b) **316.** (b) **317.** (b) **318.** (a) **319.** (d) **320.** (b)
**321.** (b) **322.** (a) **323.** (c) **324.** (d) **325.** (c) **326.** (b) **327.** (d) **328.** (a) **329.** (a) **330.** (d)
**331.** (d) **332.** (c) **333.** (c) **334.** (a) **335.** (b) **336.** (a) **337.** (d) **338.** (a) **339.** (a) **340.** (b)
**341.** (d) **342.** (b) **343.** (c) **344.** (d) **345.** (d) **346.** (d) **347.** (b) **348.** (d) **349.** (d) **350.** (d)
**351.** (c) **352.** (d) **353.** (c) **354.** (c) **355.** (c) **356.** (c) **357.** (b) **358.** (b) **359.** (b) **360.** (c)
**361.** (c) **362.** (b) **363.** (c) **364.** (d) **365.** (a) **366.** (a) **367.** (c) **368.** (a) **369.** (b) **370.** (b)
**371.** (c) **372.** (a) **373.** (c) **374.** (a) **375.** (c) **376.** (c) **377.** (c) **378.** (c) **379.** (c) **380.** (d)
**381.** (d) **382.** (b)

## Exercise 2

**1.** (a,c) **2.** (d) **3.** (a,b,c) **4.** (b,c) **5.** (a,b) **6.** (a,b,d) **7.** (a,b,c,d) **8.** (a,b,c) **9.** (a,b,c,d) **10.** (c,d)
**11.** (c,d) **12.** (a,c) **13.** (c) **14.** (a,b) **15.** (b,c,d) **16.** (a,b,c) **17.** (a,b,c) **18.** (a,b,c,d) **19.** (a,b,c) **20.** (a,d)
**21.** (a,b,c,d) **22.** (a,b,c,d)

# Hints & Solutions

## Exercise 1

**1.** Required probability is

$$= \frac{{}^5C_3 \times {}^{10}C_8}{{}^{15}C_{11}} = \frac{{}^5C_2 \times {}^{10}C_2}{{}^{15}C_4}$$

$$= \left(\frac{5 \times 4}{2!}\right)\left(\frac{10 \times 9}{2!}\right)\left(\frac{4!}{15 \times 14 \times 13 \times 12}\right)$$

**2.** Number of ways of applying for houses 3 persons $= 3 \times 3 \times 3$

(Note that the expt. is a random expt.)

Number of ways in which all the 3 apply for the same house = 3

$\therefore$ Required probability $= \frac{3}{27} = \frac{1}{9}$

(If the houses are *a*, *b*, *c* possible sample points are (*a*, *a*, *a*), (*a*, *a*, *b*), (*a*, *a*, *c*),…, (*c*, *c*, *a*), (*c*, *c*, *b*), (*c*, *c*, *c*), favourable sample points are (*a*, *a*, *a*), (*b*, *b*, *b*), (*c*, *c*, *c*)).

**3.** We have $P(\overline{A \cup B}) = \frac{1}{6}$

$$\Rightarrow \quad P(\overline{A \cup B}) = 1 - P(A \cup B)$$

$$\Rightarrow \quad P(A \cup B) = 1 - \frac{1}{6} = \frac{5}{6}$$

Also, $\quad P(A \cap B) = \frac{1}{4}$

and $\quad P(A) = 1 - P(\overline{A}) = 1 - \frac{1}{4} = \frac{3}{4}$

By the addition theorem,

$$P(A \cup B) = P(A) + P(B) - P(A \cap B)$$

$$\Rightarrow \quad \frac{5}{6} = \frac{3}{4} + P(B) - \frac{1}{4}$$

$$\Rightarrow \quad P(B) = \frac{5}{6} - \frac{1}{2} = \frac{2}{6} = \frac{1}{3}$$

Since. $\quad P(A) \times P(B) = \frac{3}{4} \times \frac{1}{3} = \frac{1}{4}$

$= P(A \cap B)$ and $P(A) \neq P(B)$, we have *A*, *B* as independent but not equally likely.

**4.** Let $E_1$ : '*A* is alive after a year,' and $E_2$ :' *B* is alive after a year,' then $P(E_1) = 1 - p$ and $P(E_2) = 1 - q$.

Required probability

$$= P(E_1 \cap E_2') + P(E_2 \cap E_1')$$

$$= P(E_1)(1-P(E_2)) + P(E_2)(1-P(E_1))$$
$$= (1-p)q + (1-q)p = p + q - 2pq$$

**5.** To get odd number of points on 3 coins, we should have $T(1), T(1), T(1)$ or $H(2), H(2), T(1)$ and number of ways $= 1 + {}^3C_2 \cdot {}^1C_1 = 4$

Total number of ways $= 2 \times 2 \times 2 = 8$

$$\text{Probability} = \frac{4}{8} = \frac{1}{2}$$

**6.** Let $p$ be the probability that the dice shows an odd number and $q$, that of the dice showing an even number, then $p + q = 1$

But $p = 3q$, therefore, $p = \frac{3}{4}$ and $q = \frac{1}{4}$

$P$ (sum of two throws is even)

$= P$ (both throws show an odd number)

$+ P$ (both throws show an even number)

$$= p \times p + q \times q = p^2 + q^2$$
$$= \left(\frac{3}{4}\right)^2 + \left(\frac{1}{4}\right)^2 = \frac{10}{16} = \frac{5}{8}$$

**7.** If $P(A) = x$ and $P(B) = y$, then

$$P(A \cap B) = \frac{1}{12} \Rightarrow P(A)P(B) = \frac{1}{12}$$

or $\quad xy = \frac{1}{12}$

and $P$ (neither $A$ nor $B$ occurs) $= P(A')P(B') = \frac{1}{2}$

$$\Rightarrow \quad P(A')P(B') = \frac{1}{2} \quad \text{or} \quad (1-x)(1-y) = \frac{1}{2}$$

**8.** Required probability

$= 1 - P$ (student does not miss any test)

$= 1 - P$ (the teacher does not give test on both days)

$$= 1 - \left(1 - \frac{1}{5}\right)\left(1 - \frac{1}{5}\right) = 1 - \frac{26}{25} = \frac{9}{25}$$

**9.** 4 can be selected out of 10 in ${}^{10}C_4 = 210$ ways. 2 children can be selected in three combinations

(i) 2 children and 2 women $= {}^4C_2 \times {}^2C_2 = 6$

(ii) 2 children and 2 men $= {}^4C_2 \times {}^4C_2 = 36$

(iii) 2 children, 1 man, 1 women

$$= {}^4C_2 \times {}^4C_1 \times {}^2C_1 = 48$$

Hence, Total number of favourable cases

$$= 48 + 36 + 6 = 90$$

Hence, Required probability $= \frac{90}{210} = \frac{9}{21}$

**10.** Given, $P(E) = \frac{1}{5}$, $P(F/E) = \frac{1}{10}$

Hence $\quad P(E \cap F) = P(E) \cdot P(F/E)$

$$= \frac{1}{5} \cdot \frac{1}{10} = \frac{1}{50}$$

Hence, probability of non-occurence of atleast one of the events $E$ and $F$

$$= 1 - P(E \cap F) = 1 - \frac{1}{50} = \frac{49}{50}$$

**11.** The sample space $S$ is given by,

$S = \{HHH, HHT, HTH, HTT, THH, THT, TTH, TTT\}$

The number of sample points $= n(S) = 8$

Let $A$ be the event that of getting atleast two tails. Atleast two tails means two tails or three tails.

$$A = \{HTT, THT, TTH, TTT\}$$

$$\therefore \quad n(A) = 4, \quad P(B) = \frac{n(A)}{n(S)} = \frac{4}{8} = \frac{1}{2}$$

Let $B$ be the event that of getting atmost two tails. Atmost two tails means two tails or one tail or no tail (all heads).

$B = \{HHH, HHT, HTH, HTT, THH, THT, TTH\}$

$$n(B) = 7, \quad P(B) = \frac{n(B)}{n(S)} = \frac{7}{8}$$

**12.** We have $P(C) = x$, $P(B) = 2x$, $P(A) = 2P(B) = 4x$

$$P(A) + P(B) + P(C) = 7x = 1 \qquad (\because A \cup B \cap C = 5)$$

$$\Rightarrow \quad x = P(C) = \frac{1}{7}$$

$$\therefore \quad P(A) = 4x = \frac{4}{7}$$

$$P(\bar{A}) = 1 - \frac{4}{7} = \frac{3}{7}$$

**13.** We have $n \in S$, $n + \frac{50}{n} > 27$

$$\Rightarrow \quad n^2 - 27n + 50 > 0$$
$$\Rightarrow \quad (n-2)(n-25) > 0$$
$$\Rightarrow \quad n = 1, 26, 27, 28, \ldots, 50$$
$$\Rightarrow \quad P(A) = \frac{25}{50}$$

$n$ is prime, $n = 2, 3, 5, 7, 11, 13, 17, 19, 23, 29, 31, 37, 41, 43, 47$

$$\Rightarrow \quad P(B) = \frac{15}{50}$$

$n$ is square, $n = 1, 4, 9, 16, 25, 36, 49$

$$\Rightarrow \quad P(C) = \frac{7}{50}$$

Hence $\quad P(A) > P(B) > P(C)$

**14.** 3 cards out of 52 cards can be drawn in ${}^{52}C_3$ ways.

The number of sample points

$$= n(S) = {}^{52}C_3 = \frac{52 \times 51 \times 50}{1 \times 2 \times 3}$$
$$= 52 \times 17 \times 25 = 22100$$

Let $A$ be the event that 3 cards drawn contains two kings and one ace card

$$n(A) = {}^4C_2 \cdot {}^4C_1 = \frac{4 \times 3}{1 \times 2} \times 4 = 24$$

Hence $P(A) = \frac{n(A)}{n(S)} = \frac{24}{22100} = \frac{6}{5525}$

**15.** Suppose that the man fires $n$ shots.

$P$ (target being hit atleast once)

$= 1 - P$ (target is not hit any time

$$= 1 - \left(1 - \frac{10}{100}\right)^n = 1 - \left(\frac{9}{10}\right)^n$$

So, we must have $1-\left(\frac{9}{10}\right)^n \geq \frac{50}{100}$

$\Rightarrow \left(\frac{9}{10}\right)^n \leq \frac{1}{2} \Rightarrow \left(\frac{10}{9}\right)^n \geq 2$

$\Rightarrow \quad n\log\frac{10}{9} \geq \log 2$

$\Rightarrow \quad n \geq \frac{\log 2}{\log 10 - \log 9} = \frac{0.3010}{1-0.9542}$

$\Rightarrow \quad n \geq \frac{0.3010}{0.0458} = 6.6 \simeq 7$

Hence, minimum value of $n$ is 7.

**16.** The sample space $S$ is given by,
$S = \{HHT, HHT, HTH, HTT, THH, THT, TTH, TTT\}$
The number of sample points $= n(S) = 8$
Let $A$ be the event that of getting atmost one head, *i.e.*, one head or no head (all tails.)

$$A = \{HTT, THT, TTH, TTT\}$$

$\therefore \quad n(A) = 4, \quad P(A) = \frac{n(A)}{n(S)} = \frac{4}{8} = \frac{1}{2}$

Let $B$ be the event that of getting two consecutive heads $B = \{THH, HHT\}$

$$P(B) = \frac{n(A)}{n(S)} = \frac{2}{8} = \frac{1}{4}$$

**17.** Probability for India to win the match $= \frac{1}{2}$

Probability for India to loose the match $= 1-\frac{1}{2} = \frac{1}{2}$

Hence, required probability $= \frac{1}{2}\cdot\frac{1}{2}\cdot\frac{1}{2} + \frac{1}{2}\cdot\frac{1}{2}\cdot\frac{1}{2}$

(1st won, 2nd lost, 3rd won)

or (1st lost, 2nd won, 3rd won) $= \frac{1}{4}$

**18.** The probability that a man aged $x$ years will not die within a year is $1-p$, therefore, the chance that neither of the five persons die within a year is $(1-p)^5$.
Hence, $P$ (atleast one man dies within a year)

$$= 1-(1-p)^5$$

Since, there are five persons and anyone has the same chance of being dead first, therefore, the required probability that $A$ will die and be the first to die within a year

$$= \frac{1}{5}\{1-(1-p)^5\}$$

**19.** $P$ (a total of 5 comes up)

$$= \frac{4}{36} = \frac{1}{9} = p \text{ (say)}$$

$P$ (neither a total of 5 nor a total of 7 comes up)

$$= 1-\left(\frac{1}{9}+\frac{1}{6}\right) = \frac{13}{18} = q \text{ (say)}$$

Hence, required probability

$$= p + qp + q^2p + \ldots \text{upto } \infty$$

$$= \frac{p}{1-q} = \frac{1/9}{1-\frac{13}{18}} = \frac{2}{5}$$

**20.** Probability of choosing a bag and a white ball from it are independent.
Probability of choosing a white ball from

$$X = \frac{1}{2}\times\frac{2}{5} = \frac{1}{5} \quad \ldots\text{(i)}$$

and probability of choosing a white ball from

$$Y = \frac{1}{2}\times\frac{4}{6} = \frac{1}{3} \quad \ldots\text{(ii)}$$

The events in Eqs. (i) and (ii) are mutually exclusive.

$\therefore$ Required probability $= \frac{1}{5}+\frac{1}{3} = \frac{8}{15}$

**21.** It is a case of Bernoullian trials with

$$n = 5, p = \frac{3}{4}, q = \frac{1}{4}$$

Hence, required probability

$$= P(3) + P(4) + P(5)$$

$$= {}^5C_3p^3q^2 + {}^5C_4p^4q + {}^5C_5p^5$$

$$= \frac{459}{512}$$

**22.** The probability that the student is selected for IIT–JEE

$$= P(E_1) = \frac{1}{5} \Rightarrow P(\bar{E}_1) = \frac{4}{5}$$

The probability that the student is selected for AIEEE

$$= P(E_2) = \frac{3}{5} \Rightarrow P(\bar{E}_2) = \frac{2}{5}$$

The probability that he is selected for one of the examinations

$$= 1-P(\bar{E}_1)P(\bar{E}_2) = 1-\frac{4}{5}\times\frac{2}{5} = \frac{17}{25}$$

**23.** Let $S$ be the sample space and $E$ be the event of choosing four persons, such that 2 of them are children. Then,
$n(S)$ = Number of ways of choosing 4 persons out of 9

$$= {}^9C_4 = \frac{9\times8\times7\times6}{4\times3\times2\times1} = 126$$

$n(E)$ = Number of ways of choosing 2 children out of 4 and 2 persons out of $(3+2)$ persons

$$= ({}^4C_2 \times {}^5C_2) = \frac{4\times3}{2\times1}\times\frac{5\times4}{2\times1} = 60$$

Hence, $\quad P(E) = \frac{n(E)}{n(S)} = \frac{60}{126} = \frac{10}{21}$

**24.** Probability of getting a head $= p$ and probability of not getting a head (getting a tail) $= q$, such that $p+q=1$.
Head may be got in 2nd or 4th or 6th or...throws.
The events of getting a head or a tail or independent.
Hence, required probability

$$= q\cdot p + q\cdot q\cdot q\cdot p + q\cdot q\cdot q\cdot q\cdot q\cdot p + \ldots = \frac{2}{5} \text{ (given)}$$

$\Rightarrow \quad qp + q^3p + q^5p + \ldots = \frac{2}{5}$ (Infinite GP)

$\Rightarrow \quad \frac{qp}{1-q^2} = \frac{2}{5} \Rightarrow \frac{(1-p)p}{1-(1-p)^2} = \frac{2}{5}$

$\Rightarrow \quad 5p - 5p^2 = 4p - 2p^2$

$\Rightarrow \quad 3p^2 = 1p \Rightarrow p = \frac{1}{3} \quad (\because p \neq 0)$

**25.** We have $P(A)=\frac{3x+1}{3}, P(B)=\frac{1-x}{4}, P(C)=\frac{1-2x}{2}$

Hence, these are mutually exclusive.

$$0\le\frac{3x+1}{3}\le 1, 0\le\frac{1-x}{4}\le 1, \text{ and } 0\le\frac{1-2x}{2}\le 1$$

$$\Rightarrow \quad -1\le 3x\le 2, -3\le x\le 1 \text{ and } -1\le 2x\le 1$$

$$\Rightarrow \quad -\frac{1}{3}\le x\le\frac{2}{3}, -3\le x\le 1 \text{ and } -\frac{1}{2}\le x\le\frac{1}{2}$$

Also, $0\le\frac{1+3x}{3}+\frac{1-x}{4}+\frac{1-2x}{2}\le 1$

$$\Rightarrow \quad 0\le 13-3x\le 12 \quad\Rightarrow\quad 1\le 3x\le 13$$

$$\Rightarrow \quad \frac{1}{3}\le x\le\frac{13}{3}$$

$$\max\left\{-\frac{1}{3},-3,-\frac{1}{2},\frac{1}{3}\right\}\le x$$

$$\le\min\left\{\frac{2}{3},1,\frac{1}{2},\frac{13}{3}\right\}$$

$$\Rightarrow \quad \frac{1}{3}\le x\le\frac{1}{2} \quad\Rightarrow\quad x\in\left[\frac{1}{3},\frac{1}{2}\right]$$

**26.** $P$ (neither $A$ nor $B$)

$$=1-P(\text{either } A \text{ or } B)=1-P(A\cup B)$$

$$=1-\{P(A)+P(B)-P(A\cap B)\}$$

$$=1-\{0.25+0.50-0.14\}=0.39$$

**27.** Let $E_1$ : "one mango is good" and $E_2$ : "both the mangoes are good", then

$P(E_1)=P$ (one mango is good)

$=P$ (atleast one mango is good)

$=1-P$ (no mango is good)

$$=1-\frac{^4C_2}{^{10}C_2}=1-\frac{4\times 3}{10\times 9}$$

$$=1-\frac{2}{15}=\frac{13}{15}$$

and $P(E_2)=P$ (both the mangoes are good)

$$=\frac{^6C_2}{^{10}C_2}=\frac{6\times 5}{10\times 9}=\frac{1}{3}$$

Hence, required probability

$$=P(E_2/E_1)=\frac{P(E_2\cap E_1)}{P(E_1)}$$

$$=\frac{P(E_2)}{P(E_1)}=\frac{(1/3)}{(13/15)}=\frac{5}{13} \quad (\text{note that } E_2\subset E_1)$$

**28.** A card can be drawn out of 52 in 52 ways. It can be a heart or a diamond in 26 ways.

(∵ there are 13 hearts and 13 diamonds)

Hence, required probability $=\frac{26}{52}=\frac{1}{2}$

**29.** Probability of hot summer

$$=p_1=40\%=\frac{40}{100}=0.4$$

Probability of cool summer

$$=p_2=1-0.4=0.6$$

| Weather | Probability $p$ | Income from hot snack stall $x$ | Income from ice-cream stall $y$ |
|---|---|---|---|
| Summer Hot | 0.4 | ₹1000 | ₹6500 |
| Summer cool | 0.6 | ₹5000 | ₹1000 |

Expected income from hot snack stall

$$E(x)=x_1\cdot p_1+x_2\cdot p_2$$

$$=1000\times 0.4+5000\times 0.6$$

$$=400+3000=₹3400$$

Expected income from ice-cream stall

$$E(y)=y_1\cdot p_1+y_2\cdot p_2$$

$$=6500\times 0.4+1000\times 0.6$$

$$=2600+600=₹3200$$

Expected income from the hot snack stall is greater than that of the ice-cream stall. Hence, he should opt for running the hot snack stall.

**30.** Probability of getting a head from a single coin $=\frac{1}{2}$

Hence, $A$'s probability of winning is

$$p=\frac{1}{2}\times\frac{1}{2}\times\frac{1}{2}=\frac{1}{8}$$

$A$'s probability of losing is

$$q=1-\frac{1}{8}=\frac{7}{8}$$

Mathematical Expectation of $A=a\times p+(-b\times q)$, where '$a$' represents the prize money, '$b$' represents the entry fee and $p$ and $q$ refer to probabilities of winning and losing.

Hence, $E(A)=ap-bq$

$$=160\times\frac{1}{8}+\left(-16\times\frac{7}{8}\right)$$

$$=20-14=₹6$$

Thus, $A$'s expectation is ₹6.

**31.** Let $p_1, p_2, p_3$, respectively denote the probability of the events that there is no error in the accounts prepared by $A$, $B$ and $C$. Then,

$p_2=1-$ (probability of atleast one error occurring in the account statement prepared by $A$) $=1-0.3=0.7$

Similarly, $p_2=1-0.4=0.6$, and $p_3=1-0.45=0.55$

Now, $E(X)=\Sigma p_ix_i=(0.7)\times 20+(0.6)\times 10+(0.55)\times 40$

$$=14+6+22=42$$

**32.** Let $p_1, p_2, p_3$, respectively denote the probability of the events that there is no error in the account prepared by $A$, $B$ and $C$. Then,

$p_1=1-$ (probability of atleast one error in the account statement prepared by $A$) $=1-0.2=0.8$

Similarly, $p_2=1-0.25=0.75$, and $p_3=1-0.4=0.6$

Also, $x_1=10, x_2=16, x_3=20$

$$E(X)=p_1x_1+p_2x_2+p_3x_3+\ldots+p_nx_n$$

$$E(X)=(0.8\times 10)+(0.75\times 16)+(0.6\times 20)$$

$$=8+12+12=32$$

Hence, the expected number of all correct statements would be 32.

**33.** There are two competitors $A$ and $B$ and the lowest bidder gets the contract.

Value of Plan $= 300 \times 1000 =$ ₹ 300000

I. If both bid less than ₹ 300;

Probability $0.3 \times 0.7 = 0.21$

Hence, Plan value $= 300000 \times 0.21 =$ ₹ 63000

II. If only $A$ bids less than ₹ 300 and $B$ bids more than ₹ 300

Probability $0.3 \times 0.3 = 0.09$

Hence, Plan value $= 300000 \times 0.09 =$ ₹ 270000

III. If only $B$ bids less than ₹ 300 and $A$ bids more than ₹ 300;

Probability $0.7 \times 0.7 = 0.49$

Hence, Plan value $= 300000 \times 0.49 =$ ₹ 147000

Thus, the value of plan is ₹ 63000 + 2700 + 147000

= ₹ 237000

**34.** Let $x_1, x_2, x_3, x_4$ denotes the value of 0, 1, 2, 3 heads, respectively with probabilities $p_1, p_2, p_3, p_4$. Then,

$$p_1 = \frac{1}{2} \times \frac{1}{2} \times \frac{1}{2} = \frac{1}{8}$$

$$p_2 = 3\left(\frac{1}{2} \times \frac{1}{2} \times \frac{1}{2}\right) = \frac{3}{8}$$

$$p_3 = 3\left(\frac{1}{2} \times \frac{1}{2} \times \frac{1}{2}\right) = \frac{3}{8}$$

$$p_4 = \frac{1}{2} \times \frac{1}{2} \times \frac{1}{2} = \frac{1}{8}$$

We want to find the value of $x_1$ such that $E(X) = 0$.

Hence, $E(X) = p_1x_1 + p_2x_2 + p_3x_3 + p_4x_4 = 0$

$$\Rightarrow \quad x_1 \times \frac{1}{8} + 1 \times \frac{3}{8} + 3 \times \frac{3}{8} + 8 \times \frac{1}{8} = 0$$

$$\Rightarrow \quad \frac{x_1 + 3 + 9 + 8}{8} = 0 \quad \Rightarrow \quad x_1 = -20$$

He will lose ₹ 20, if no head occurs.

**35.** (a) Computation of probability :

2 balls drawn may be (i) either both are white or (ii) both are red or (iii) one is white and one is red. Then,

1. Probability of drawing 2 red balls

$$= p_1 = \frac{{}^9C_2}{{}^{10}C_2} = \frac{3}{45} = \frac{1}{15}$$

When 2 balls drawn are red, then neither of them is white.

Hence, probability that neither of the 2 balls drawn is white

$$= \frac{1}{15}$$

2. Probability of drawing 1 white ball and 1 red ball.

$$= p_2 = \frac{{}^7C_1 \times {}^3C_1}{{}^{10}C_2} = \frac{21}{45} = \frac{7}{15}$$

(b) Computation of expected number of white balls

Out of 2 balls drawn, the number of white balls may be 0, 1, 2.

Hence, probability of 0 white ball

$$= p_1 = \frac{{}^7C_0 \cdot {}^3C_2}{{}^{10}C_2} = \frac{1 \times 3}{45} = \frac{3}{15}$$

Hence, probability of 1 white ball

$$= p_2 = \frac{{}^7C_1 \cdot {}^3C_1}{{}^{10}C_2} = \frac{7 \times 3}{45} = \frac{7}{15}$$

Hence, probability of 2 white balls

$$= p_3 = \frac{{}^7C_2 \cdot {}^3C_0}{{}^{10}C_2} = \frac{21 \times 1}{45} = \frac{7}{15}$$

Hence, expected number of white balls

$$= x_1 \cdot p_1 + x_2 \cdot p_2 + x_3 \cdot p_3$$

$$= 0 \times \frac{3}{15} + 1 \times \frac{7}{15} + 2 \times \frac{7}{15}$$

$$= 0 + \frac{7}{15} + \frac{14}{15} = \frac{21}{15} = 1.4$$

**36.** 2 balls drawn may be either (i) both are white, or (ii) both are black, or (iii) one is white and one is black. Then,

(i) Probability of drawing 2 white balls

$$= p_1 = \frac{{}^3C_2}{{}^8C_2} = \frac{3}{28}$$

(ii) Probability of drawing 2 black balls

$$= p_2 = \frac{{}^5C_2}{{}^8C_2} = \frac{10}{28}$$

(iii) Probability of drawing 1 white ball and 1 black ball

$$= p_3 = \frac{{}^3C_1 \times {}^5C_1}{{}^8C_2} = \frac{15}{28}$$

(a) Amount to be received for 2 white balls $= x_1 =$ ₹ $14 \times 2$ = ₹ 28

(b) Amount to be received for 2 black balls $= x_2 =$ ₹ $7 \times 2$ = ₹ 14

(c) Amount to be received for 1 white ball and 1 black ball $= x_3 =$ ₹ 14 + ₹ 7 = ₹ 21

∴ His expectation

$$= E(x) = x_1 \cdot p_1 + x_2 \cdot p_2 + x_3 \cdot p_3$$

$$= 28 \times \frac{3}{28} + 14 \times \frac{10}{28} + 21 \times \frac{15}{28}$$

$= 3 + 5 + 11.25 =$ ₹ 19.25

**37.** 2 balls drawn may be either (i) both are white or (ii) both are black or (iii) 1 is white and 1 is black. Then,

(i) Probability of drawing 2 white balls

$$= p_1 = \frac{{}^5C_2}{{}^{12}C_2} = \frac{10}{66}$$

(ii) Probability of drawing 2 black balls

$$= p_2 = \frac{{}^7C_2}{{}^{12}C_2} = \frac{21}{66}$$

(iii) Probability of drawing 1 white ball and 1 black ball

$$= p_3 = \frac{{}^5C_1 \times {}^7C_1}{{}^{12}C_2} = \frac{35}{66}$$

(a) Amount to be received for 2 white balls

$= x_1 =$ ₹ $2 \times 2 =$ ₹ 4

(b) Amount to be received for 2 black balls $x_2 =$ ₹ $1 \times 2 =$ ₹ 1

(c) Amount to be received for 1 white ball and 1 black ball
$$= x_3 = ₹ 2 + ₹ 1 = ₹ 3$$

Hence, expectation of the mean
$$= E(x) = x_1 \cdot p_1 + x_2 \cdot p_2 + x_3 \cdot p_3$$
$$= 4 \times \frac{10}{66} + 2 \times \frac{21}{66} + 3 \times \frac{35}{66}$$
$$= ₹ 2.83$$
$$= \frac{40}{66} + \frac{42}{66} + \frac{105}{66} = \frac{187}{66} = ₹ 2.83$$

**38.** Required probability $= \frac{4}{52} \times \frac{15}{51} = \frac{5}{221}$

(When one ace has been drawn at first draw, only 15 honours will be felt in the pack)

**39.** $P(\overline{A}/\overline{B}) = \frac{P(\overline{A} \cap \overline{B})}{P(\overline{B})} = \frac{P(\overline{A \cup B})}{P(\overline{B})} = \frac{1 - P(A \cup B)}{P(\overline{B})}$

**40.** Given, $P(A) = \frac{2}{7}$ and $P(B) = \frac{6}{11}$

Required probability
$$= P(A' \cap B') = (1 - P(A))(1 - P(B))$$
$$= \frac{5}{7} \times \frac{5}{11} = \frac{25}{77}$$

**41.** There are three letters and three directed envelopes, therefore, they can be put into the envelopes in ${}^3P_3 = 3! = 6$ ways out of which only one is correct.

Required probability $= \frac{1}{6}$

**42.** A non-leap year contains 365 days, *i.e.*, 52 complete weeks and an additional day which may be Sunday, Monday, Tuesday, Wednesday, Thursday, Friday or Saturday. Out of these 7 possible days, the favourable are Sunday, Tuesday, Thursday.

$\therefore$ Required probability $= \frac{3}{7}$

**43.** Two 3s, one 6 and one 8 can be dialled in $\frac{4!}{2!} = 12$ ways of which only one is the correct way of dialling.

$\therefore$ Required probability $= \frac{1}{12}$

**44.** Number of all possible five digit numbers is $4P(4, 4) = 4 \times 24 = 96$ and the numbers which are divisible by 4 must end in 04, 20, 40 or in 12, 24, 32. Number of numbers of the first kind in $3P(3, 3) = 3 \times 6 = 18$ and that of second kind is $3 \times 2P(2, 2) = 12$

Required probability $= \frac{(18 + 12)}{96} = \frac{5}{16}$

**45.** Required probability $= \dfrac{\frac{1}{3} \times \frac{4}{7}}{\frac{2}{3} \times \frac{3}{5} + \frac{1}{3} \times \frac{4}{7}} = \frac{4}{21} \times \frac{21 \times 5}{62} = \frac{10}{31}$

**46.** Sample space $S = \{HH, HT, TH, TT\}$

Since, the coin is balanced, each outcome has probability $\frac{1}{4}$

Since, $A = \{HH, HT, TH\}$

Hence, $P(A) = P(HH) + P(HT) + P(TH)$
$$= \frac{1}{4} + \frac{1}{4} + \frac{1}{4} = \frac{3}{4}$$

**49.** We have $S = \{1, 2, 3, 4, 5, 6\}$

If $w$ is the probability of occurrence of odd number, then $2w$ is of even number and
$$w + 2w + w + 2w + w + 2w = 1$$
$$\Rightarrow \quad w = \frac{1}{9}$$
$$P\{\text{a number greater than } 3\} = \frac{2}{9} + \frac{1}{9} + \frac{2}{9} = \frac{5}{9}$$

**52.** We have $P(a \le X \le b) = F(b) - F(a) = \int_a^b f(t)\,dt$
$$\Rightarrow \quad P\left(-\frac{1}{2} \le X \le \frac{1}{2}\right) = F\left(\frac{1}{2}\right) - F\left(-\frac{1}{2}\right)$$
$$= 0.75 \int_{-\frac{1}{2}}^{\frac{1}{2}} (1 - t^2)\,dt = 0.68$$

**53.** We have $M_X(t) = E(e^{tX}) = \frac{1}{8} \sum_{x=0}^{3} e^{tx} \binom{3}{x} = \frac{1}{8}(1 + e^t)^3$

**58.** We have $F(x) = \int_{-\infty}^{x} f(t)\,dt$
$$= 0.75 \int_{-1}^{x} (1 - t^2)\,dt$$
$$= 0.5 + 0.75x - 0.25x^3$$

For $x \in (-1, 1]$

and $F(x) = 0$, if $x \le 1$

$F(x) = 1$, if $x > 1$

**59.** We have $\mu_2' = \int_0^2 \frac{x^3}{2} = \frac{1}{2} \frac{x^4}{4} \Big|_0^2 = \frac{1}{2} \cdot \frac{16}{4} = 2$

**64.** (a) $f(1) = -\frac{1}{2}$ negative

(b) $\sum_x f(x) = \frac{6}{5} \ne 1$

(c) $f(1) = \frac{-1}{5}$ negative

(d) $\sum_x g(x) = 1$

**65.** We have $\mu_r' = E(X^r) = \int_{-\infty}^{\infty} x^r f(x)\,dx$
$$\Rightarrow \quad \mu_2' = \frac{4}{\pi} \int_0^1 \frac{x^2}{1 + x^2}\,dx = \frac{4}{\pi} - 1$$

**70.** For $f(x) = \frac{1}{4}$
$$\sum_x f(x) \ne 1$$
So, it cannot serve as probability distribution.

**71.** We have $\sigma^2 = E[(X - \mu)^2]$
$$= E[X^2 - 2\mu X + \mu^2)]$$
$$= E(X^2) - 2\mu E(X) + E(\mu^2)$$
$$= \mu_2' \quad 2\mu \cdot \mu + \mu^2$$
$$= \mu_2' - \mu^2$$

**82.** We have $\mu_r = E[(X - \mu)^r] = \sum_x (x - \mu)^r f(x)$
$$\Rightarrow \quad \mu_0 = \sum_x (x - \mu)^0 f(x) = \sum_x f(x) = 1$$

**87.** Probability distribution function always satisfies probability postulate.

**88.** We have $\mu_r = E[(X-\mu)^r] = \sum_x (x-\mu)^r f(x)$

$\Rightarrow$ $\mu_1 = \sum_x x\, f(x) - \mu \sum_x f(x)$

$= \mu - \mu \cdot 1$ $\quad [\because \sum_x f(x) = 1]$

$= 0$

**93.** For $f(x) = \dfrac{x^2}{50}$

$\sum_x f(x) = 1$

**105 .** For the function to serve as probability distribution $\sum_x f(x) = 1$

$f(1) + f(2) + f(3) + f(4) + f(5) = \dfrac{3}{25} + \dfrac{4}{25} + \dfrac{5}{25} + \dfrac{6}{25} + \dfrac{7}{25} = 1$

and $f(x) \geq 0$

For all $x = 1, 2, 3, 4, 5$

**117.** We have $S = \{1, 2, 3, 4, 5, 6\},\ n(S) = 6$

$A = \{2, 4, 6\},\ n(A) = 3$

$P(A) = \dfrac{n(A)}{n(S)} = \dfrac{3}{6} = \dfrac{1}{2}$

**118.** We have $E(X) = \sum_x x f(x)$

$= 0 \cdot \dfrac{1}{125} + 1 \cdot \dfrac{12}{125} + 2 \cdot \dfrac{48}{125} + 3 \cdot \dfrac{64}{125} = \dfrac{12}{5}$

**122.** Since, the events are mutually exclusive

$P(\text{Atleast 3 cars}) = 0.35 + 0.25 + 0.12 = 0.72$

**126.** We have $P(A/B) = \dfrac{P(A \cap B)}{P(B)} = \dfrac{P(A) \cdot P(B)}{P(B)}$

$= P(A)$

**130.** We have $P(A/B) = \dfrac{P(A \cap B)}{P(B)} = \dfrac{P(A) \cdot P(B/A)}{P(B)} = \dfrac{P(A) \cdot P(B)}{P(B)}$

$= P(A)$

**134.** $A \subset S \Rightarrow P(A) \leq P(S)$

**137.** $A \cup A' = S$

$P(S) = P(A \cup A')$

$= P(A) + P(A') = 1$

**142.** We have (a) $P(B/A) = \dfrac{P(A \cap B)}{P(A)} \geq 0$

(b) $P(A/A) = \dfrac{P(A \cap A)}{P(A)} = \dfrac{P(A)}{P(A)} = 1$

(c) By definition

(d) Is false

**146.** By the definition of independent event

$P(A \cap \phi) = P(A) \cdot P(\phi) = P(A) \cdot 0 = 0$

**154.** $A \cap B \cap C = (A \cap B) \cap C$

Use $P(A \cap B) = P(A) \cdot P(B/A)$

We have

$P((A \cap B) \cap C) = P(A \cap B) \cdot P(C/A \cap B)$

$= P(A) P(B/A) \cdot P(C/A \cap B)$

**158.** When first is replaced before the second card is drawn, we have

$\dfrac{4}{52} \cdot \dfrac{4}{52} = \dfrac{1}{169}$

**162.** When first card is not replaced before the second card is drawn, we have

$\dfrac{4}{52} \cdot \dfrac{3}{51} = \dfrac{1}{221}$

**168.** Multiplying the respective probabilities

$\dfrac{1}{6} \cdot \dfrac{1}{6} \cdot \dfrac{1}{6} \cdot \dfrac{1}{6} \cdot \dfrac{5}{6} = \dfrac{5}{7776}$

**173.** Multiplying the respective probabilities,

$\dfrac{1}{2} \cdot \dfrac{1}{2} \cdot \dfrac{1}{2} = \dfrac{1}{8}$

**177.** By additional law of probability

$P(A \cup B) = P(A) + P(B) - P(A \cap B)$

$P(A \cup B) + P(A \cap B) = P(A) + P(B)$

$\because$ $P(A \cup B) \geq 0$

Hence $P(A \cap B) \leq P(A) + P(B)$

**181.** We have $P(A) = 0.86,\ P(B) = 0.35,\ P(A \cap B) = 0.29$

Hence, $P(A \cup B) = P(A) + P(B) - P(A \cap B) = 0.92$

**192.** We have $P(S) = P(\cup A_i) = P(A_1) + P(A_2) + \ldots$

$= \dfrac{1}{2} + \left(\dfrac{1}{2}\right)^2 + \left(\dfrac{1}{2}\right)^3 + \ldots = \dfrac{1/2}{1 - 1/2} = 1$

**196.** We have $N(S) = 52$

$R =$ Event 'Red cards'

$N(R) = 26$

Hence, $P(R) = \dfrac{N(R)}{N(S)} = \dfrac{26}{52} = \dfrac{1}{2}$

**199.** We have $P(A \cap B) = P(A) + P(B) - P(A \cup B)$

$= \dfrac{1}{3} + \dfrac{1}{4} + \dfrac{1}{2} = \dfrac{1}{12}$

Hence, $P(A/B) = \dfrac{P(A \cap B)}{P(B)} = \dfrac{1/12}{1/4} = \dfrac{1}{3}$

**201.** For binomial distribution

Mean $\mu = np$

Variance $\sigma^2 = npq = \mu q$

**202.** Number of ways of selecting 4 cards from a pack of 52 cards

$^{52}C_4 = \dfrac{52 \times 51 \times 50 \times 49}{1 \times 2 \times 3 \times 4} = 270725$

$A =$ Event four cards belongs to different suits

$N(A) = {}^{13}C_1 \times {}^{13}C_1 \times {}^{13}C_1 \times {}^{13}C_1$

$= 13 \times 13 \times 13 \times 13$

Hence, $P(A) = \dfrac{13 \times 13 \times 13 \times 13}{270725} = \dfrac{2197}{20825}$

**205.** Here, $\lambda = np = 6400 \times \left(\dfrac{1}{2}\right)^6 = 100$

$P(X = x) = e^{-\lambda} \dfrac{\lambda^x}{x!} = e^{-100} \dfrac{100^x}{x!}$

**206.** We have $N(S) = 36$

$E =$ Sum is 7

$= \{(6, 1), (5, 2), (4, 3), (3, 4), (2, 5), (1, 6)\}$

$N(E) = 6$

Hence, $P(E) = \dfrac{6}{36} = \dfrac{1}{6}$

**209.** Here, $M_x(t) = 1 + \mu_1^1 t + \mu_2^1 \frac{t^2}{2!} + \ldots$

$$= 1 + 2t + 2!2^2 \frac{t^2}{2!} + 3!2^3 \frac{t^3}{3!} + \ldots$$

$$= 1 + 2t + (2t)^2 + (2t)^3 + \ldots = (1-2t)^{-1}$$

**210.** We have $N(S) = 52$

$E$ = Event getting face card

$N(E) = 12$

Hence $P(E) = \frac{12}{52} = \frac{3}{13}$

**213.** $X$ = Number of calls per minute

$$P(X = x) = e^{-\lambda} \frac{\lambda^x}{x!}$$

$$P(X \not> 3) = P(X \le 3)$$

$$= \sum_{x=0}^{3} e^{-\lambda} \frac{\lambda^x}{x!}\bigg|_{\lambda=4}$$

$$= e^{-4}\left[1 + \frac{4}{1} + \frac{4^2}{2!} + \frac{4^3}{3!}\right] = \frac{71}{3} e^{-4}$$

**214.** We have $x = 3$, $n = 10$, $p = 0.80$

$$b(x; n, p) = \binom{10}{3} (0.80)^3 (1 - 0.80)^{10-7} = 0.20$$

**217.** Here, $p = 5\% = 0.05$

$n = 5$

$\lambda = np = 0.05 \times 5 = 0.25$

Let $X$ = Number of defective blades

Poisson law $P(X = x) = e^{-\lambda} \frac{\lambda^x}{x!}$

$P(X = 1) = 0.25 e^{-0.25}$

**218.** We have $x = 7$, $n = 12$, $p = \frac{1}{2}$

By binomial distribution, the probability of getting 7 heads in 12 flips is

$$b(x; n, p) = \binom{12}{7}\left(\frac{1}{2}\right)^7 \left(1 - \frac{1}{2}\right)^5 = 0.19$$

**222.** We have $\Sigma f(x) = 1$

$$\Rightarrow \quad \sum_{r=0}^{\infty} \frac{\lambda^r}{r!} = \frac{\lambda}{1!} + \frac{\lambda^2}{2!} + \frac{\lambda^3}{3!} + \ldots = 1$$

$$\Rightarrow \quad e^{\lambda} - 1 = 1 \quad \left(\because e^{\lambda} = 1 + \lambda + \frac{\lambda^2}{2!} + \frac{\lambda^3}{3!} + \ldots\right)$$

$$\Rightarrow \quad e^{\lambda} = 2$$

$$\Rightarrow \quad \lambda \log_e e = \log_e 2$$

$$\Rightarrow \quad \lambda = \log_e 2$$

**227.** We have $M_{(X_1 + X_2)}(t) = [e^{t(X_1 + X_2)}] = E(e^{tX_1} \cdot e^{tX_2}) = E(e^{tX_1}) E(e^{tX_2})$

($\because X_1$ and $X_2$ are independent)

$$= M_{X_1}(t) M_{X_2}(t)$$

**232.** We have $F(2) = \int_{-\infty}^{2} f(x)dx = \int_{-\infty}^{0} 0 \cdot dx + \int_0^2 e^{-x} dx = 1 - e^{-2}$

**236.** We have $P(1 \le x \le 2) = \int_1^2 f(x)dx = \int_1^2 e^{-x}dx = e^{-1} - e^{-2}$

**241.** By Binomial theorem

$$(ax + b)^n = \sum_{i=0}^{n} \binom{n}{i} (ax)^{n-1} b^i$$

$$\Rightarrow \quad E[(aX + b)] = E\left[\sum_{i=0}^{n} \binom{n}{i} a^{n-i} b^i X^{n-i}\right]$$

$$= \sum_{i=0}^{n} \binom{n}{i} a^{n-i} b^i E(X^{n-i})$$

**242.** We have $M_0(t) = \int_0^{\infty} e^{tx} \cdot f(x)dx = \int_0^{\infty} e^{tx} \cdot \frac{1}{c} e^{-x/c} dx$

$$= \frac{1}{c} \int_0^{\alpha} e^{\left(t - \frac{1}{c}\right)x} dx$$

$$= \frac{1}{c} \frac{1}{\left(t - \frac{1}{c}\right)} \cdot e^{\left(t - \frac{1}{c}\right)x} \Big|_0^{\infty}$$

$$= (1 - ct)^{-1} = 1 + ct + c^2t^2 + \ldots,$$

Then $\mu_1' = \frac{d}{dt} M_0(t)\Big|_{t=0}$

$$= (c + 2c^2 t + 3c^3 t^2 + \ldots)_{t=0} = c$$

**265.** We have $E[g(X)] = \int_{-\infty}^{\infty} g(x) f(x)dx$

$$= \int_0^{\infty} e^{3x/4} \cdot e^{-x} dx$$

$$= \int_0^{\infty} e^{-x/4} dx = 4$$

**271.** We have $E(X) = \int_{-\infty}^{\infty} x \cdot f(x)dx = \int_2^4 x \cdot \frac{x+1}{8} dx = \frac{37}{12}$

**277.** For balanced die $f(x) = \frac{1}{6}$, $x = 1, 2, \ldots, 6$

$$E[g(X)] = \sum_x g(x) f(x) = \sum_{x=1}^{6} (2x^2 + 1) \cdot \frac{1}{6} = \frac{94}{3}$$

**283.** We have $E(X) = \int_{-\infty}^{\infty} x \cdot f(x)dx = \int_0^1 \frac{4}{\pi(1 + x^2)} dx = \frac{\log 4}{\pi}$

**285.** Substitute $x = \frac{x - \mu}{\sigma}$ in standard normal distribution, we get normal distribution function.

**295.** We have $f(x) = \frac{dF(x)}{dx} = \begin{cases} 1, & 0 \le x \le 1 \\ 0, & \text{otherwise} \end{cases}$

**301.** We have $\int_{-\infty}^{\infty} f(x)\, dx = 1$

$$\Rightarrow \quad \int_0^{\infty} ke^{-3x} dx = k \int_0^{\infty} e^{-3x} dx = \frac{k}{3} = 1 \quad \Rightarrow k = 3$$

**303.** We have $p = \frac{1}{6}$, $q = 1 - \frac{1}{6} = \frac{5}{6}$, $n = 4$

Hence, $P(X \ge 2) = f(2) + f(3) + f(4) = \binom{4}{2}\left(\frac{1}{6}\right)^2 \left(\frac{5}{6}\right)^2$

$$+ \binom{4}{3}\left(\frac{1}{6}\right)^3 \left(\frac{5}{6}\right) + \binom{4}{4}\left(\frac{1}{6}\right)^4$$

$$= \frac{171}{1296}$$

**307.** We have $F(x) = \int_0^x f(t)\, dt = \int_0^x \frac{1}{\pi l}\, dx = \frac{x}{\pi l}, 0 \le x \le \pi l$

**308.** We have $E(2X_1 + X_2 - 5) = E(2X_1 + X_2) - 5$

$$= 2E(X_1) + E(X_2) - 5$$
$$= 2\mu_1 + \mu_2 - 5$$
$$= 2 \times 4 + (-2) - 5 = 1$$

**317.** We have $\int_{-\infty}^{\infty} f(x)\, dx = 1$

$$\Rightarrow \quad \int_0^2 f(x)\, dx = \int_0^2 kx^2\, dx = k\int_0^2 x^2\, dx = k\left(\frac{x^3}{3}\right)_0^2 = 1$$

$$\Rightarrow \quad k\left(\frac{8}{3} - 0\right) = 1 \Rightarrow k = \frac{3}{8}$$

**322.** We have $f(x) = \frac{dF(x)}{dx} = \begin{cases} 0, & x < 0 \\ e^{-x}, & x > 0 \end{cases}$

**328.** We have $F(x) = P(X \le x) = \sum_x \left(\frac{k}{x!}\right) = ke$

**334.** We have $\sum_x f(x) = 1$

$$\Rightarrow \quad k\sum_x \frac{1}{x!} = 1 \Rightarrow ke = 1 \Rightarrow k = \frac{1}{e}$$

**365.** We have $P(\text{a head}) = P = \frac{1}{2}, q = 1 - p = \frac{1}{2}, n = 5$

The probability no head, one head, two head...are the successive terms of binomial expression $(p + q) S$

$$\therefore \quad P(\text{2 heads}) = {}^5C_2\left(\frac{1}{2}\right)^2\left(\frac{1}{2}\right)^3 = \frac{5}{2}\left(\frac{1}{2}\right)^5 = \frac{5}{16}$$

**368.** We have $E(aX + b) = E(aX) + E(b) = aE(X) + b$

**369.** We have $\bar{X} = \frac{X_1 + X_2 + \ldots + X_n}{n} = \frac{1}{n}X_1 + \frac{1}{n}X_2 + \ldots + \frac{1}{n}X_n$

$$\sigma_{\bar{x}}^2 = \text{var}(\bar{X})$$
$$= \frac{1}{n^2}\text{var}(X_1) + \frac{1}{n^2}\text{var}(X_2) + \ldots + \frac{1}{n^2}\text{var}(X_n)$$
$$= \sum_{i=1}^{n}\left(\frac{1}{n}\right)^2 \sigma^2 = \frac{1}{n^2}n\sigma^2 = \frac{\sigma^2}{n}$$

**371.** We have $P(A/A \cup B) = \frac{P[A \cap (A \cup B)]}{P(A \cup B)} = \frac{P(A)}{P(A) + P(B)}$

$(\because P(A \cup B) = P(A) + P(B)$

and $\quad A \cap (A \cup B) = A$

**372.** We have $P(A \cup B) = P(A) + P(B) - P(A \cap B)$

$\Rightarrow \quad P(A \cap B) = P(A) + P(B) - P(A \cup B)$

$\because \quad P(A \cap B) \ge 0$

$\Rightarrow \quad P(A) + P(B) - P(A \cup B) \ge 0$

$\Rightarrow \quad P(A) + P(B) \ge P(A \cup B)$

**375.** We have $N(S) = 6 \times 6 = 36$

$$E = \text{Doublets} = \{(x, x) : x = 1..6\}$$
$$N(E) = 6$$
$$P(E) = \frac{6}{36} = \frac{1}{6}.$$

**377.** We have $p(x) = {}^nC_x\, p^x q^{n-x}$

and mean $= np = 4$

and variance $= npq = \frac{4}{3}$

$\therefore \quad \frac{npq}{np} = q = \frac{4}{3} \div 4\frac{1}{3}$

$\therefore \quad p = 1 - q - \frac{1}{3} = \frac{2}{3}$

and $n = \frac{4}{p} = 4 \times \frac{3}{2} = 6$

$\therefore p(X = 2) = \frac{20}{243}$

**378.** We have $N(S) = 52$

$A =$ Card is ace of Spade, $N(A) = 1$

$B =$ Card is knave of club, $N(B) = 1$

and $A \cap B = \phi$, independent events

By addition law,

$$P(A \cup B) = P(A) + P(B)$$
$$= \frac{1}{52} + \frac{1}{52} = \frac{1}{26}$$

**380.** We have $E(X^2) = n(n-1)p^2 + np$

$$= 10 \times 9 \times (0.6)^2 + (0.6)10 = 38.4$$

**381.** Non-leap year have 53 week + 1 day

This 1 day will be any of the day from Sunday to Saturday

$\therefore \quad N(S) = 7$

$A \equiv 1$ day is Sunday, $N(A) = 1$

Hence, $\quad P(A) = \frac{1}{7}$

## Exercise 2

**1.** We have $N(S) = 40$

$N(A) =$ Number of boys $= 25$

$N(B) =$ Number of married students $= 16$

$N(A^C) =$ Number of girls

$N(B^C) =$ Number of unmarried students

$N(A \cup B) = 10$

Hence, number of unmarried girl is

$$= N(A^C \cap B^C)$$
$$= N(S) - N(A \cup B)$$
$$= N(S) - N(A) - N(B) + N(A \cap B)$$
$$= 40 - 25 - 16 + 10 = 9$$

Hence, $\quad P(A^C \cap B^C) = \frac{9}{40}$

**2.** We have,

$P$ (Exactly one of $A$, $B$ occurs)

$$= P[(A \cap \bar{B}) \cup (\bar{A} \cap B)]$$
$$= P(A \cap \bar{B}) + P(\bar{A} \cap B)$$
$$= P(A) - P(A \cap B) + P(B) - P(A \cap B)$$

$= P(A) + P(B) - 2P(A \cap B)$
$= P(A \cup B) - P(A \cap B)$

Also, $P$ (Exactly one of $A$, $B$ occurs)

$= P(A \cup B) - P(A \cap B)$
$= \{1 - P(\overline{A \cup B})\} - \{1 - P(\overline{A \cap B})\}$
$= \{1 - P(\bar{A} \cap \bar{B})\} - [1 - P(\bar{A} \cup \bar{B})]$
$= P(\bar{A} \cup \bar{B}) - P(\bar{A} \cap \bar{B})$
$= P(\bar{A}) + P(\bar{B}) - 2P(\bar{A} \cap \bar{B})$

Hence, option (d) is incorrect.

**3.** We have $\lambda = \frac{390}{520} = \frac{3}{4}$

and let $X$ = Number of error per page

Hence $P(X = x) = e^{-\lambda} \frac{\lambda^x}{x!} = e^{-3/4} \frac{(3/4)^x}{x!}$

$\Rightarrow \quad P(X = 0) = e^{-3/4} \frac{(3/4)^0}{0!} = e^{-3/4}$

Hence, probability that random sample of 4 pages will contain no error is

$$[P(X = 0)]^4 = e^{-(3/4) \times 4} = e^{-3}$$

**4.** We have, $P(A \cup B \cup C) = \frac{3}{4}$

*i.e.*, $P(A) + P(B) + P(C) - P(A \cap B) - P(B \cap C) - P(A \cap C)$

$$+ P(A \cup B \cup C) - \frac{3}{4} \quad \text{...(i)}$$

$$P(A \cap B) + P(B \cap C) + P(A \cap C) - 2P(A \cap B \cap C) = \frac{1}{2} \quad \text{...(ii)}$$

and $\quad P(A \cap B) + P(B \cap C) + P(A \cap C) - 3P(A \cap B \cap C) = \frac{2}{5} \quad \text{...(iii)}$

Form Eqs. (ii) and (iii), we get

$$P(A \cap B \cap C) = \frac{1}{2} - \frac{2}{5} = \frac{1}{10} \quad \text{...(iv)}$$

$\Rightarrow \quad P(A)\,P(B)\,P(C) = \frac{1}{10}$

$$pmc = \frac{1}{10}$$

From Eqs. (i), (ii) and (iii) we have

$$P(A) + P(B) + P(c) - \left(\frac{1}{2} + \frac{2}{10}\right) + \frac{1}{10} = \frac{3}{4}$$

$\Rightarrow \quad p - m + c = \frac{27}{20}$

**5.** Let $P(A) = x$ and $P(B) = y$. Since, $A$ and $B$ are independent events. Therefore,

$P(\bar{A} \cap B) = 2/15$
$\Rightarrow \quad P(\bar{A})\,P(B) = 2/15$
$\Rightarrow \quad \{1 - P(A)\}\,P(B) = 2/15$
$\Rightarrow \quad (1 - x)y = 2/15$
$\Rightarrow \quad y - xy = 2/15 \quad \text{...(i)}$

and $\quad P(A \cap \bar{B}) = \frac{1}{6}$

$\Rightarrow \quad P(A)\,P(\bar{B}) = \frac{1}{6} \Rightarrow x(1 - y) = \frac{1}{6}$

$\Rightarrow \quad x - xy = \frac{1}{6} \quad \text{...(ii)}$

Subtracting Eq. (i) From Eq. (ii), we get

$$x - y = \frac{1}{30} \Rightarrow x = \frac{1}{30} + y$$

Putting this value of $x$ in Eq. (i), we get

$$y - y\left(\frac{1}{30} + y\right) = \frac{2}{15}$$

$\Rightarrow \quad 30y - y - 30y^2 = 4$
$\Rightarrow \quad 30y^2 - 29y + 4 = 0$
$\Rightarrow \quad (6y - 1)(5y - 4) = 0$
$\Rightarrow \quad y = 1/6 \text{ or } y = 4/5$
$\Rightarrow \quad P(B) = 1/6 \text{ or } P(B) = 4/5$

**6.** The associated sample space is

$$S = \{1, 2, 3, 4, 5, 6\}$$

Hence, number of sample points in

$$N(S) = 6$$

Let $A$ be the event of getting 5, then

$$A = \{5\} \text{ and } N(A) = 1$$

Hence, probability of getting 5 is

$$P(5) = \frac{N(A)}{A(S)} = \frac{1}{6}$$

**7.** Since, $B \subseteq A \cup B$. Therefore,

$$P(B) \le P(A \cup B) \Rightarrow P(A \cup B) \ge 2/3$$

So, option (a) is correct.

Now, $\quad P(A \cap B) = P(A) + P(B) - P(A \cup B)$
$\Rightarrow \quad P(A \cap B) \ge P(A) + P(B) - 1$
$\Rightarrow \quad P(A \cap B) \ge \frac{3}{5} + \frac{2}{3} - 1 = \frac{4}{15}$

Also, $\quad A \cap B \subseteq A$
$\Rightarrow \quad P(A \cap B) \le P(A)$
$\Rightarrow \quad P(A \cap B) \le 3/5$

Hence, $\quad \frac{4}{15} \le P(A \cap B) \le \frac{3}{5}$

So, option (b) is correct.

Now, $\quad \frac{4}{15} \le P(A \cap B) \le \frac{3}{5}$
$\Rightarrow \quad \frac{4}{15} \le P(A/B)\,P(B) \le \frac{3}{5}$
$\Rightarrow \quad \frac{4}{15} \le \frac{2}{3} P(A/B) \le \frac{3}{5}$
$\Rightarrow \quad \frac{2}{5} \le P(A/B) \le \frac{9}{10}$

So, option (c) is correct.

Finally, $P(A \cap \bar{B}) = P(A) - P(A \cap B) \le \frac{3}{5} - \frac{4}{15} = \frac{1}{3}$

So, option (d) is also correct.

**8.** Number of ways of selecting 4 cards from a pack of 52 cards is

$${}^{52}C_4 = \frac{52!}{(52-4)!\,4!} = \frac{52 \times 51 \times 50 \times 49}{1 \times 2 \times 3 \times 4} = 270725$$

$A \equiv$ Event two cards are black and two cards are red

$N(A) =$ (Number of ways 2 red cards are drawn from 26 red cards) $\times$ (Number of ways 2 black cards drawn from 26 black cards)

$$= {}^{26}C_2 \times {}^{26}C_2 = 325 \times 325$$

Hence, $$P(A) = \frac{325 \times 325}{270725} = \frac{325}{833}$$

**9.** We have, $P(A \cup B) \geq \max\{P(A), P(B)\} = \frac{2}{3}$

and $$P(A \cap B) \leq \min\{P(A), P(B)\} = \frac{2}{3}$$

Now, $$P(A \cap B) = P(A) + P(B) - P(A \cup B)$$

$$\Rightarrow \quad P(A \cap B) = P(A) + P(B) - 1 = \frac{1}{6}$$

Hence, $$\frac{1}{6} \leq P(A \cap B) \leq \frac{1}{2}$$

Also, $P(A \cap \overline{B}) = P(A) - P(A \cap B) \leq \frac{1}{2} - \frac{1}{6} = \frac{1}{3}$

and $P(\overline{A} \cap B) = P(B) - P(A \cap B) \leq \frac{2}{3} - \frac{1}{6} = \frac{1}{2}$

Hence, $\frac{2}{3} - \frac{1}{2} \leq P(\overline{A} \cap B) \leq \frac{2}{3} - \frac{1}{6}$

$$\Rightarrow \quad \frac{1}{6} \leq P(\overline{A} \cap B) \leq \frac{1}{2}$$

**10.** Sample space

$$S = \{1, 2, 3, 4, 5, 6\},$$
$$N(S) = 6$$

(a) $E \equiv$ Event of getting less than 4,

then $E = \{1, 2, 3\}$, $N(E) = 3$

Hence, $P(E) = \frac{N(E)}{N} = \frac{3}{6} = \frac{1}{2}$

(b) $E \equiv$ The event of getting odd number,

then $E = \{1, 3, 5\}$, $N(E) = 3$

Hence, $$P(E) = \frac{3}{6} = \frac{1}{2}$$

**11.** Total number of possible outcomes is

$$N(S) = 11 + 5 = 16$$

(a) $E \equiv$ Event of black ball is drawn,

$N(E) = 5$

Hence, $$P(E) = \frac{N(E)}{N(S)} = \frac{5}{16}$$

(b) $F \equiv$ Event of white ball is drawn

Hence, $$P(F) = 1 - P(E) = 1 - \frac{5}{16} = \frac{11}{16}$$

**12.** The moment generating function about the origin is

$$M_0(t) = \int_0^\infty e^{tx} f(x)\,dx = \int_0^\infty e^{tx}\left(\frac{1}{c}e^{-x/c}\right)dx$$

$$= \frac{1}{c}\int_0^\infty e^{(t-1/c)x}\,dx$$

$$= \frac{1}{c}\,\frac{e^{(t-1/c)x}\big|_0^\infty}{t - \frac{1}{c}}$$

$$= (1 - ct)^{-1} = 1 + ct + c^2t^2 + \ldots$$

$$\mu_2' = \frac{d^2}{dt^2} M_0(t)\bigg|_{t=0} = 2c^2$$

**13.** We have $P(A) = \frac{1}{6}$, $\frac{2}{3}P(B) = \frac{1}{6}$

$$\Rightarrow \quad P(B) = \frac{1}{6} \times \frac{3}{2} = \frac{1}{4}$$

$$\frac{1}{4}P(C) = \frac{1}{6} \quad \Rightarrow \quad P(C) = \frac{1}{6} \times \frac{4}{3} = \frac{2}{3}$$

Hence, $P(A \cup B \cup C) = P(A) + P(B) + P(C)$, ($A, B, C$ are disjoint sets)

$$= \frac{1}{6} + \frac{1}{4} + \frac{2}{3} = \frac{13}{12} > 1$$

$\therefore$ Probability law does not holds.

**14.** Number of possible outcomes is

$$N = 6 \times 6 = 36$$

(a) $A =$ Odd number on first die

$$= \{(x, y) : x = 1, 3, 5,\ y = 1, 2, 3, 4, 5, 6\}$$

$N(A) = 3 \times 6 = 18$

Hence, $P(A) = \frac{18}{36} = \frac{1}{2}$

(b) $A =$ Ace on atleast one die $= \{(1, x) : x = 1, 2, \ldots, 6\}$
$\cup \{(x, 1) : x = 1, 2, \ldots, 6\} \cap \{(1, 1)\}$

$N(A) = 6 + 6 - 1 = 11$

Hence, $$P(A) = \frac{11}{36}$$

**15.** Since, $A$ and $B$ are independent events.

$$P(A \cap B) = P(A)\,P(B) \neq 0$$

So, $A$ and $B$ cannot be mutually exclusive events.

Now, $P(A \cap \overline{B}) = P(A) - P(A \cap B)$

$$= P(A) - P(A)\,P(B)$$
$$= P(A)(1 - P(B))$$
$$= P(A)\,P(\overline{B})$$

and $$P(\overline{A} \cap \overline{B}) = P(\overline{A \cup B})$$
$$= P(\overline{A \cup B})$$
$$= 1 - P(A \cup B)$$
$$= 1 - \{1 - P(\overline{A})\,P(\overline{B})\}$$

[$\because$ $A$ and $B$ are independent]

$$= P(\overline{A})\,P(\overline{B})$$

So, $A$ and $\overline{B}$ as well as $\overline{A}$ and $\overline{B}$ are independent events.

Finally, $P(A/B) + P(\overline{A}/B)$

$$= \frac{P(A \cap B)}{P(B)} + \frac{P(\overline{A} \cap B)}{P(B)}$$

$$= \frac{P(A \cap B) + P(\overline{A} \cap B)}{P(B)} = \frac{P(B)}{P(B)} = 1$$

Hence, option (a) is incorrect.

**16.** $f(x)$ is defined as density function

(i) $f(x) \geq 0,\ -\infty < x < \infty$

(ii) $\int_{-\infty}^{\infty} f(x)\,dx = 1$

Here, $f(x) \geq 0, \forall x$

and $\int_{-\infty}^{\infty} f(x)\,dx = \int_{-\infty}^{\infty} 0 \cdot dx + \int_0^{\infty} e^{-x} dx = 1$

**17.** For $A$ $P(A/B) = \dfrac{P(A \cap B)}{P(B)}$

$\Rightarrow$ TPT $P(A \cap B) \geq P(A) + P(B) - 1$

or TPT, $1 \geq P(A) + P(B) - P(A \cap B)$

or TPT, $1 \geq P(A \cup B)$

which is true $\Rightarrow$ (a) is correct

(b) and (c) are obvious.

Hence, (a), (b) and (c) are the correct answers.

**18.** We have, required probability

$= P(\overline{A} \cup \overline{B}) = P(\overline{A \cap B}) = 1 - P(A \cap B)$

So, option (a) is correct.

Again, $P(\overline{A} \cup \overline{B}) = P(\overline{A}) + P(\overline{B}) - P(\overline{A} \cap \overline{B})$

[By add. theorem]

So, option (b) is correct.

Again, $P(\overline{A} \cup \overline{B})$

$$= P(\overline{A}) + P(\overline{B}) - P(\overline{A} \cap \overline{B})$$
$$= P(\overline{A}) + P(\overline{B}) - P(\overline{A \cup B})$$
$$= P(\overline{A}) + P(\overline{B}) = -\{1 - P(A \cup B)\}$$
$$= P(\overline{A}) + P(\overline{B}) + P(A \cup B) - 1$$

So, option (c) is correct.

Finally,

$P(\overline{A} \cup \overline{B}) = P[(A \cap \overline{B}) \cup (\overline{A} \cap B) \cup (\overline{A} \cap \overline{B})]$

$\Rightarrow P(\overline{A} \cup \overline{B}) = P(A \cap \overline{B}) + P(\overline{A} \cap B) + P(\overline{A} \cap \overline{B})$

Since, $A \cap \overline{B}$, $\overline{A} \cap B$ and $\overline{A} \cap \overline{B}$ are mutually exclusive events such that

$\overline{A} \cup \overline{B} = (A \cap \overline{B}) \cup (\overline{A} \cap B) \cup (\overline{A} \cap \overline{B})$

Hence, $P(\overline{A} \cup \overline{B}) = P[(\overline{A} \cap B) \cup (\overline{A} \cap B) \cup (\overline{A} \cap \overline{B})]$

$\Rightarrow P(\overline{A} \cup \overline{B}) = P(A \cap \overline{B}) + P(\overline{A} \cap B) + P(\overline{A} \cap \overline{B})$

So, option (d) is correct.

**19.** Since, $A$ and $B$ are independent events. Therefore,

$P(A \cap B) = P(A)\,P(B) = \dfrac{1}{2} \times \dfrac{1}{5} = \dfrac{1}{10}$

and $\quad P(A/B) = P(A) = \dfrac{1}{2}$

So, option (b) is correct.

Now, $P(A \cup B) = P(A) + P(B) - P(A \cap B)$

$$= \frac{1}{2} + \frac{1}{5} - \frac{1}{10} = \frac{3}{5}$$

So, option (a) is correct.

Now, $P(A/A \cup B) = \dfrac{P[A \cap (A \cup B)]}{P(A \cup B)} = \dfrac{P(A)}{P(A \cup B)}$

$$= \frac{1/2}{3/5} = \frac{5}{6}$$

So, option (c) is correct.

And $P(A \cap B / \overline{A} \cup \overline{B}) = P(A \cap B / (\overline{A \cap B})) = 0$

So, option (d) is not correct.

**20.** We have $P(E_2/E_1) = \dfrac{P(E_1 \cap E_2)}{P(E_1)}$

$$\frac{1}{2} = \frac{P(E_1 \cap E_2)}{1/4}$$

$\Rightarrow P(E_1 \cap E_2) = \dfrac{1}{8} = P(E_2) \cdot P(E_1/E_2)$

$= P(E_1) = \dfrac{1}{4} \quad \Rightarrow \quad P(E_2) = \dfrac{1}{2}$

Since, $P(E_1 \cap E_2) = \dfrac{1}{8} = P(E_1) \cdot P(E_2)$

$\Rightarrow$ Events are independent.

Also, $P(E_1 \cup E_2) = \dfrac{1}{2} + \dfrac{1}{4} - \dfrac{1}{8} = \dfrac{5}{8}$

$\Rightarrow E_1$ and $E_2$ are non-exhaustive.

$\Rightarrow$ Hence, (a), (c) and (d) are the correct answers.

**21.** (b) $1 \geq P(A) + P(B) - P(A \cap B)$

or $\quad P(A \cap B) \geq P(A) + P(B) - 1$

(c) Let $\quad P(A) > P(A/B)$

or $\quad P(A) > \dfrac{P(A \cap B)}{P(B)}$

$$P(A) \cdot P(B) > P(A \cap B) \quad \text{...(i)}$$

TPT $\quad P(A/B^c) > P(A)$

$$\frac{P(A \cap B^c)}{P(B^c)} > P(A)$$

$$P(A) - P(A \cap B) > P(A)[1 - P(B)]$$

$$-P(A \cap B) > -P(A) \cdot P(B)$$

or $\quad P(A) \cdot P(B) > P(A \cap B) \quad$ ...(ii)

From Eqs. (i) and (ii), $P(A) > P(A/B)$

$\Rightarrow \quad P(A/B^c) > P(A)$

Hence, (a), (b), (c) and (d) are the correct answers.

**22.** $N(S) = 100$

(a) $A \equiv$ Even number $= \{2, 4, 6, \ldots, 100\}$

$N(A) = 50$

Hence, $\quad P(A) = \dfrac{N(A)}{N(S)} = \dfrac{50}{100} = \dfrac{1}{2}$

(b) $A \equiv$ Event of getting 5 or multiple of 5

$= \{5, 10, 15, \ldots, 100\}$,

$N(A) = 20$

$P(A) = \dfrac{N(A)}{N(S)} = \dfrac{20}{100} = \dfrac{1}{5}$

(c) $A \equiv$ Event of getting more than 75

$= \{76, 77, \ldots, 100\}$

$N(A) = 25$

$P(A) = \dfrac{N(A)}{N(S)} = \dfrac{25}{100} = \dfrac{1}{4}$

(d) $E \equiv$ Square of an integer

$= \{1, 4, 9, 25, 36, 49, 64, 81, 100\}$

$N(E) = 10$

$P(E) = \dfrac{N(E)}{N(S)} = \dfrac{10}{100} = \dfrac{1}{10}$

# 23 Statistical Inferences & Gauss Markov Model

## Syllabus

- Methods of Estimation
- Properties of Estimators
- Confidence Intervals
- Tests of Hypothesis
- Most powerful and Uniformly most Powerful Tests
- Likelihood Ratio Tests
- Analysis of Discrete Data and chi-square Test of goodness of Fit
- Large Sample Tests
- Simple Non-parametric Tests for One and Two Sample Problems
- Rank Correlation and Test for Independence
- Elementary Bayesian Inference
- Gauss-Markov Models
- Estimability of Parameters
- Best Linear Unbiased Estimators
- Tests for Linear Hypothesis and Confidence Intervals
- Analysis of Variance and Covariance
- Fixed, Random and Mixed Effects Models
- Simple and Multiple Linear Regression
- Elementary Regression Diagnostics
- Logistic Regression
- Multivariate Normal Distribution
- Wishart distribution and their Properties
- Distribution of Quadratic Forms
- Inference for Parameters
- Partial and Multiple Correlation Coefficients and Related Tests
- Data Reduction Techniques
- Principle Component Analysis,.
- Discriminant Analysis
- Cluster Analysis
- Canonical Correlation.
- Simple RandomSampling
- Stratified Sampling and Systematic Sampling
- Probability Proportional to Size Sampling
- Ratio and Regression Methods
- Completely Randomized
- Randomized Blocks and Latin-square Designs
- Connectedness and Orthogonality of Block Designs
- BIBD. 2k Factorial Experiments
- Confounding and Construction
- Series and Parallel Systems
- Hazard Function and Failure Rates
- Censoring and Life Testing

## Methods of Estimation

'To estimate' means 'to judge'.

If estimating parameter has a particular value (quantitative in the form of real number), then for it method of estimation is called point estimation.

If estimating parameter has a value (quantity in the form of real number) lying in an interval, then for it method of estimation is called interval estimation.

## Characteristics of Estimators

- Consistency
- Unbiasedness
- Efficiency
- Sufficiency

Let $X$ be a random variable with pdf $f(x, \theta)$, $\theta$ being a parameter.

Problem is to find the value of $\theta$.

The collection of all possible values that $\theta$ can take is denoted by $\Theta$ and is called parameter space.

In set theory notation above information can be expressed as $\{f(x,\theta)\,|\,\theta\in\Theta\}$,

we consider a random sample $x_1, x_2, \ldots, x_n$ of size $n$ from a population with probability density function.

$$f(x;\ \theta_1, \theta_2, \ldots, \theta_k)$$

Where $\theta_1, \theta_2, \ldots, \theta_k$ are unknown population parameters.

A function of sample values used to estimate one or more parameters is called a statistic.

An infinite number of statistics can be created to estimate population parameters.

Among these statistics, a statistic which has value nearest to the parameter value (under study) is called best estimate of the parameter.

Symbolically, if $x_1, x_2, \ldots, x_n$ is a sample of size $n$.

$T_1 = \hat{\theta}_1(x_1, x_2, \ldots, x_n)$, $T_2 = \hat{\theta}_2(x_1, x_2, \ldots, x_n) \ldots T_k = \hat{\theta}_k(x_1, x_2, \ldots, x_n)$ be functions of sample values (*i.e.*, statistics), which have values near to population parameters, then problem is to find the statistic which is best estimate of the population parameter (*s*).

These statistics are called estimators.

## Consistency

Let $\{x_1, x_2, \ldots, x_n\}$ be a random sample of size $n$.

Let $T_n = T(x_1, x_2, \ldots, x_n)$, $n = 1, 2, \ldots$ be a sequence of estimators of $\gamma(\theta)$, $\theta \in \Theta$.

$r(\theta)$ is a function of $\theta$.

This $T_n$ is said to be consistent if

$$\lim_{n\to\infty} T_n \xrightarrow{p} \gamma(\theta)$$

This can also be expressed as $T_n$ is said to be consistent to $r(\theta)$, if for any arbitrarily chosen $\in > 0$ and $n > 0$ there exists a positive integer $m$. (depending upon $\in$ and $\eta$) such that

$$P[|T_n - \gamma(\theta)| > \in] \to 1 \text{ as } n \to \infty$$

*i.e.*, $$P[|T_n - \gamma(\theta)| < \in] > 1 - \eta, \quad \forall\, n \ge m$$

Here, $T_n = T(x_1, x_2, \ldots, x_n)$ is an estimator of $r(\theta)$. Its value depends upon the sample size $n$. As $n$ increases, $T_n$ may change on making $n$ very large, we study how does $T_n$ behave.

***Theorem*** Invariance Property of Consistent Estimators. If $T_n$ is a consistent estimator of $r(\theta)$ and $\psi(\gamma(\theta))$ is a continuous function of $\gamma(\theta)$, then $\psi(T_n)$ is a consistent estimator of $\psi(\gamma(\theta))$.

***Theorem*** Sufficient Condition for Consistency. Let $\{T_n\}$ be a sequence of estimators such that for all $\theta \in \Theta$

(i) $E_\theta(T_n) \to \gamma(\theta), n \to \infty$

and (ii) $\text{Var}_\theta(T_n) \to 0$ as $n \to \infty$

Then, $T_n$ is a consistent estimator of $\gamma(\theta)$.

## Unbiasedness

Unbiasedness is associated with sample size $n$.

A statistic $T_n = T(x_1, x_2, \ldots, x_n)$, is said to be an unbiased estimator of $\gamma(\theta)$, if

$$E(T_n) = \gamma(\theta), \forall \theta \in \Theta$$

If $E(T_n) > \gamma(\theta)$, then $T_n$ is said to be positively biased and if $E(T_n) < \gamma(\theta)$, it is said to be negatively biased.

The amount of bias $b(\theta)$ is given by

$$b(\theta) = E(T_n) - \gamma(\theta), \theta \in \Theta$$

## Unbiased Estimate for Population Mean ($\mu$) and Variance ($\sigma^2$)

Let a large population be $\{X_1, X_2, \ldots, X_N\}$ (of size $N$) with mean $\mu$ and variance $\sigma^2$.

Let $\{x_1, x_2, \ldots, x_n\}$ be a random sample of size $n$ taken from it. Then, sample mean $\bar{x}$ is given by

$$\bar{x} = \frac{1}{n}(x_1 + x_2 + \ldots + x_n)$$

$$= \frac{1}{n}\sum_{i=1}^{n} x_i$$

and sample variance,

$$s^2 = \frac{1}{n}\sum_{i=1}^{n}(x_i - \bar{x})^2$$

Now, $E(\bar{X}) = E\left(\frac{1}{n}\sum_{i=1}^{n} x_i\right) = \frac{1}{n}\sum_{i=1}^{n} E(x_i)$

In the sample, each $x_i$ is from the population $\{X_1, X_2, \ldots, X_N\}$ and so $x_i$ can take anyone of the values $X_1, X_2, \ldots, X_n$ each with equal probability $1/N$.

Thus, probability distribution for $x_i$

| $x_i$ | $X_1$ | $X_2$ | ....... | $X_N$ |
|---|---|---|---|---|
| $P_i$ | $1/N$ | $1/N$ | ...... | $1/N$ |

Therefore, $$E(x_i) = \frac{1}{N}X_1 + \frac{1}{N}X_2 + \ldots + \frac{1}{N}X_N$$

$$= \frac{1}{N}(X_1 + X_2 + \ldots + X_N) = \mu$$

Now, $$E(\bar{x}) = \frac{1}{n}\cdot\sum_{i=1}^{n} E(x_i) = \frac{1}{n} n\mu = \mu$$

$\Rightarrow$ Sample mean $\bar{x}$ is unbiased estimate of the population mean ($\mu$).

Now, $$E(s^2) = E\left[\frac{1}{n}\sum_{i=1}^{n}(x_i - \bar{x})^2\right]$$

$$= E\left[\frac{1}{n}\sum_{i=1}^{n}(x_i^2 + \bar{x}^2 - 2x_i\bar{x})\right]$$

$$= E\left[\frac{1}{n}\sum_{i=1}^{n} x_i^2 + n\bar{x}^2 - 2n\bar{x}^2\right]$$

$$= E\left[\frac{1}{n}\sum_{i=1}^{n} x_i^2 - \bar{x}^2\right]$$

$$E(s^2) = \frac{1}{n}\sum_{i=1}^{n} E(x_i^2) - E(\bar{x}^2)$$

We know,

$$V(x_i) = \text{variance of } x_i$$

$$= E[x_i - E(x_i)]^2$$

$$= E[x_i - \mu]^2$$

$$= \frac{1}{N}(x_1 - \mu)^2 + \frac{1}{N}(x_2 - \mu)^2 + \ldots + \frac{1}{N}(X_N - \mu)^2$$

or $$V(x_i) = \frac{1}{N}\sum_{i=1}^{N}(x_i - \mu)^2 = \sigma^2$$

Also, we know

$$V(x) = E(x^2) - [E(x)]^2 \quad \ldots\text{(i)}$$

For $x = x_i$, this gives

$$V(x_i) = E(x_i^2) - [E(x_i)]^2$$

$\Rightarrow$ $$E(x_i^2) = V(x_i) + [E(x_i)]^2 = \sigma^2 + \mu^2 \quad \ldots\text{(ii)}$$

for $x = \bar{x}$, Eq. (i) gives

$$V(\bar{x}) = E(\bar{x}^2) - [E(\bar{x})]^2 \quad \ldots\text{(iii)}$$

Also, $$V(\bar{x}) = V\left(\frac{1}{n}\sum_{i=1}^{n} x_i\right) = \frac{1}{n^2}\sum_{i=1}^{n} V(x_i)$$

$$= \frac{1}{n^2}[V(x_1) + V(x_2) + \ldots + V(x_n)]$$

$$= \frac{1}{n^2}(\underbrace{\sigma^2 + \sigma^2 + \ldots + \sigma^2}_{n\text{-times}})$$

$$= \frac{1}{n^2}\cdot n\sigma^2 = \frac{\sigma^2}{n}$$

or $$V(\bar{x}) = \frac{\sigma^2}{n} \quad (\sigma^2 \text{ being population variance}) \quad \ldots\text{(iv)}$$

from Eqs. (iii) and (iv), we get

$$E(\bar{x}^2) - [E(\bar{x})]^2 = \frac{\sigma^2}{n}$$

or $$E(\bar{x}^2) = \frac{\sigma^2}{n} + \mu^2, \qquad [\text{As } E(\bar{x}) = \mu] \quad ...(v)$$

Now, $$E(s^2) = \frac{1}{n}\sum_{i=1}^{n} E(x_i^2) - E(\bar{x}^2)$$

$$= \frac{1}{n}\sum_{i=1}^{n}(\sigma^2 + \mu^2) - \left(\frac{\sigma^2}{n} + \mu^2\right)$$

Using Eqs. (ii) and (v), we get

$$= \frac{1}{n}(n(\sigma^2 + \mu^2)) - \left(\frac{\sigma^2}{n} + \mu^2\right)$$

$$= \sigma^2 + \mu^2 - \frac{\sigma^2}{n} + \mu^2$$

$$= \left(1 - \frac{1}{n}\right)\sigma^2 = \left(\frac{n-1}{n}\right)\sigma^2$$

$$\Rightarrow \quad E(s^2) = \frac{(n-1)}{n}\sigma^2 \neq \sigma^2$$

$\Rightarrow$ Sample variance is not an unbiased estimate of population variance.

We know $$E(s^2) = \frac{n-1}{n}\sigma^2$$

$$\Rightarrow \quad \frac{n}{n-1}E(s^2) = \sigma^2$$

$$\Rightarrow \quad E\left(\frac{n}{n-1}s^2\right) = \sigma^2$$

$$\Rightarrow \quad E\left[\frac{n}{(n-1)}\frac{1}{n}\sum_{i=1}^{n}(x_i - \bar{x})^2\right] = \sigma^2$$

$$\Rightarrow \quad E\left[\frac{1}{(n-1)}\sum_{i=1}^{n}(x_i - \bar{x})^2\right] = \sigma^2$$

Putting $S^2 = \frac{1}{n-1}\sum_{i=1}^{n}(x_i - \bar{x})^2$,

We get $E(S^2) = \sigma^2$

$\Rightarrow$ $S^2$ is unbiased estimate of the population variance, $\sigma^2$.

We know $$s^2 = \frac{1}{n}\sum_{i=1}^{n}(x_i - \bar{x})^2$$

$$S^2 = \frac{1}{n-1}\sum_{i=1}^{n}(x_i - \bar{x})^2$$

$$\Rightarrow \quad ns^2 = (n-1)S^2$$

$$\Rightarrow \quad s^2 = \left(1 - \frac{1}{n}\right)S^2$$

for very large sample, $n \to \infty$ and so $s^2 = S^2$

$\Rightarrow s^2$ becomes unbiased estimate of population variance.

# Test of Significance for Sample Mean

For large samples, the standard normal variate corresponding to $\bar{x}$ is

$$Z = \frac{\bar{x} - \mu}{\sigma / \sqrt{n}}$$

Null Hypothesis, $H_0$ = The sample has been drawn from a population with mean $\mu$ and variance $\sigma^2$, *i.e.*, there is no significant difference between the sample mean ($\bar{x}$) and population mean ($\mu$), the test statistic (for large samples) is

$$Z = \frac{\bar{x} - \mu}{\sigma / \sqrt{n}}$$

If $\sigma$ is unknown, its estimate is $\hat{\sigma}^2 = s^2$ or $\sigma = s$ for large sample.

Confidence limits for $\mu$ 95% confidence interval for $\mu$ is given by

$$|Z| \leq 1.96, \quad i.e., \left|\frac{\bar{x} - \mu}{\sigma / \sqrt{n}}\right| \leq 1.96$$

$\Rightarrow \bar{x} \pm 1.96\frac{\sigma}{\sqrt{n}}$ are known as 95% confidence limits for $\mu$ as

$$\bar{x} - 1.96\frac{\sigma}{\sqrt{n}} \leq \mu \leq \bar{x} + 1.96\frac{\sigma}{\sqrt{n}}$$

Similarly, 99% confidence limits for $\mu$ are $\bar{x} \pm 2.58\frac{\sigma}{\sqrt{n}}$

and 98% confidence limits for $\mu$ are $\bar{x} \pm 2.33\frac{\sigma}{\sqrt{n}}$.

In sampling from a finite population of size $N$, 95% confidence limits for $\mu$ are $\bar{x} \pm 1.96\frac{\sigma}{\sqrt{n}}\sqrt{\frac{N-n}{N-1}}$

and 99% confidence limits for $\mu$ are $\bar{x} \pm 2.58\frac{\sigma}{\sqrt{n}}\sqrt{\frac{N-n}{N-1}}$

Confidence limits for any parameter are also known as its fiducial limits.

## Efficiency

Let $T_1$ and $T_2$ be two consistent estimator of certain parameter $\theta$ such that $\text{var}(T_1) < \text{var}(T_2), \forall n$

(In short $V(T_1) < V(T_2), \forall n$),

Then, $T_1$ is said to be more efficient than $T_2$ for all sample sizes.

Let $\mathfrak{I}$ be a collection of all consistent estimators of a parameter.

Let $T \in \mathfrak{I}$ be such that $\forall t \in \mathfrak{I}$

$$\text{var}(T) < \text{var}(t)$$

Then, $T$ is said to be most efficient estimator.

If $T, T_1, T_2, \ldots, T_n$ be estimators of $\gamma(\theta)$ and $\text{var}(T)$ is minimum, then efficiency $E_i$ of $T_1$ $(i = 1, 2, \ldots, n)$ is defined as

$$E_i = \frac{\text{var}(T)}{\text{var}(T_i)}, i = 1, 2, \ldots, n$$

Here, $$E_i \leq 1, \; i = 1, 2, \ldots, n$$

# Minimum Variance Unbiased (MVU) Estimators

If a statistic $T = T(x_1, x_2, \ldots, x_n)$ based on sample of size $n$ is such that

**(i)** $T$ is unbiased for $\gamma(\theta)$, for all $\theta \in \Theta$ and

**(ii)** It has the smallest variance among the class of all unbiased estimators of $\gamma(\theta)$,

then $T$ is called the minimum variance unbiased estimator (MVUE) of $\gamma(\theta)$.

*i.e.*, $T$ is MVUE of $\gamma(\theta)$

if $\quad E_\theta(T) = \gamma(\theta), \forall \theta \in \Theta$

and $\quad \text{var}_\theta(T) = \text{var}(T'), \forall \theta \in \Theta$

Where $T'$ is another unbiased estimator of $\theta$.

***Theorem 1*** An MVUE is unique in the sense that, if $T_1$ and $T_2$ are MVU estimators of $\gamma(\theta)$, then $T_1 = T_2$ almost surely.

***Theorem 2*** Let $T_1$ and $T_2$ be unbiased estimators of $\gamma(\theta)$ with efficiencies $e_1$ and $e_2$ respectively, and $\rho = \rho_\theta$ be the correlation coefficient between them. Then,

$$\sqrt{e_1 e_2} - \sqrt{(1-e_1)(1-e_2)} \le \rho \le \sqrt{e_1 e_2} + \sqrt{(1-e_1)(1-e_2)} \quad \ldots \text{(i)}$$

In particular $\quad$ If $e_1 = 1, e_\alpha = e$, then Eq. (i) gives

$$\sqrt{e} \le \rho \le \sqrt{e} \Rightarrow \rho = \sqrt{e}$$

***Theorem 3*** If $T_1$ is an *MVU* estimator of $\gamma(\theta)$, $\theta \in \Theta$ and $T_2$ is any other unbiased estimator of $\gamma(\theta)$ with efficiency $e = e_\theta$, then the correlation coefficient between $T_1$ and $T_2$ is given by $= \sqrt{e}$, *i.e.*, $\rho'_\theta = \sqrt{e_\theta}, \forall \theta \in \Theta$

***Theorem 4*** If $T_1$ is an MVUE of $\gamma(\theta)$ and $T_2$ is any other unbiased estimator of $\gamma(\theta)$ with efficiency $e < 1$, then no unbiased linear combination of $T_1$ and $T_2$ can be an MVUE of $\gamma(\theta)$.

# Sufficiency

An estimator is said to be sufficient for a parameter, if it contains all the informations in the sample regarding the parameter.

## Factorization Theorem (Neymon)

$T = t(x)$ be sufficient estimator for $\theta$ if and only if the joint density function $L$(say), of the sample values can be expressed in the form.

$$L = g_\theta[t(x)].\, h(x)$$

Where, $g_\theta[t(x)]$ depends on $\theta$ and $x$ only through the value of $t(x)$ and $h(x)$ is independent of $\theta$.

## Invariant Property of Sufficient Estimator

If $T$ is sufficient estimator for the parameter $\theta$ and if $\psi(T)$ is a one-to-one function of $T$, then $\psi(T)$ is sufficient for $\psi(\theta)$.

## Fisher Neyman Criterion

A statistic $t_1 = t_1(x_1, x_2, \ldots, x_n)$ is sufficient estimator of parameter $\theta$ if and only if the likelihood function (joint pdf the sample) can be expressed as

$$L = \prod_{i=1}^{n} f(x_i, \theta)$$

$$= g_1, 1(t_1, \theta) \cdot K(x_1, x_2, \ldots, x_n)$$

The most general form of the distributions admitting sufficient statistic is Koopman's form and is given by $L = L(x, \theta) = g(x) \cdot h(\theta) \exp\, [a(\theta)\psi(x)]$, where $h(\theta)$ and $a(\theta)$ are functions of parameter $\theta$ only and $g(x)$ and $\psi(x)$ are the functions of sample observations only.

# Methods of Estimation

**(i)** Method of Maximum Likelihood Estimation

**(ii)** Method of Minimum Variance

**(iii)** Method of Moments

**(iv)** Method of Least Squares

**(v)** Method of Minimum Chi-square

**(vi)** Method of Inverse Probability

## Properties of Maximum Likelihood Estimators

**(i)** The first and second derivatives *viz.*, $\frac{\partial}{\partial \theta} \log L$ and $\frac{\partial^2}{\partial \theta^2} \log L$ exist and are continuous functions of $\theta$ in a range $R$ (including the true Value $\theta_0$ of the parameter) for almost all $x$.

**(ii)** The third derivative exists *i.e.*, $\frac{\partial^3}{\partial \theta^3} \log L$ exists such that $\left| \frac{\partial^3}{\partial \theta^3} \log L \right| < M(x)$.

Where, $E[M(x)] < K$, $K$ being positive real number.

**(iii)** For every $\theta$ in $R$,

$$E\left(-\frac{\partial^2}{\partial \theta^2} \log L\right) = \int_{-\infty}^{\infty} \left(-\frac{\partial^2}{\partial \theta^2} \log L\right) \cdot L dx$$

$$= I(\theta)$$

is finite and non-zero.

**(iv)** The range of integration is independent of $\theta$.

***Theorem 1*** (Cramer-Rao Theorem) "With probability approaching unity as $n \to \infty$, the likelihood equation $\frac{\partial}{\partial \theta} \log L = 0$, has a solution which converges in probability to the true value $\theta_0$." In other words MLE's are consistent.

MLE's are always consistent but need not be unbiased.

***Theorem 2*** (Hazoor Bazar's Theorem) Any consistent solution of the likelihood equation is asymptotically normally distributed about the true value $\theta_0$. Thus,

$\hat{\theta} \sim N\left(\theta_0, \frac{1}{I(\theta_0)}\right)$ as $n \to \infty$.

The variance of MLE is given by

$$V(\hat{\theta}) = \frac{1}{I(\theta)} = \frac{1}{E\left[-\frac{\partial}{\partial\theta^2}\log L\right]}$$

***Theorem 3*** If MLE exists, it is the most efficient in the class of such estimators.

***Theorem 4*** If a sufficient estimator exists, it is a function of maximum likelihood estimator.

(This theorem is useful in finding, if a sufficient estimator exists or not).

***Theorem 5*** If for a given population with pdf $f(x,\theta)$, MVB (Minimum variance bound) estimator $T$ exists for $\theta$, then the likelihood equation will have a solution equal to the estimator $T$.

***Theorem 6*** (Invariance property of MLE) If $T$ is the MLE of $\theta$ and $\psi(\theta)$ is one-to-one function of $\theta$, then $\psi(T)$ is the MLE of $\psi$ ($\theta$).

***Theorem 7*** Cramer-Rao Inequality. If $t$ is an unbiased estimator for $\gamma(\theta)$, a function of parameter $\theta$, then

$$\text{var}(t) \geq \frac{\left[\frac{d}{dt}\gamma(\theta)\right]^2}{E\left[\frac{\partial}{\partial\theta}\log L\right]^2} = \frac{[\gamma'(\theta)]^2}{I(\theta)}$$

Where, $I(\theta)$ is the information on $\theta$ supplied by the sample.

## Regularity Conditions for Cramer-Rao Inequality

**(i)** The parameter space $\Theta$ is a non-degenerate open interval on the real line $R' = ]-\infty, \infty[$.

**(ii)** For almost all $x = (x_1, x_2, \ldots, x_n)$, and for all $\theta \in \Theta$, $\frac{\partial}{\partial x} L(x,\theta)$ exists the exceptional set, if any is independent of $\theta$.

**(iii)** The range of integration is independent of the parameter $\theta$, so that $f(x,\theta)$ is differentiable under integral sign.

**(iv)** The conditions of uniform convergence of integrals are satisfied so that differentiation under the integral sign is valid.

**(v)** $I(\theta) = E\left[\left\{\frac{\partial}{\partial\theta}\log L(x,\theta)\right\}^2\right]$ exists and is positive for all $\theta \in \Theta$ corollary.

**(vi)** If $t$ is an unbiased estimator of $\theta$ *i.e.*, $E(t) = \theta$

$\Rightarrow$ $\gamma(\theta) = \theta \Rightarrow \gamma'(\theta) = 1$

So $$\frac{[\gamma'(\theta)]^2}{E\left[\left(\frac{\partial}{\partial\theta}\log L\right)^2\right]} \leq \text{var}(t)$$

$$\Rightarrow \quad \frac{1}{I(\theta)} = \frac{1}{E\left[\left(\frac{\partial}{\partial\theta}\log L\right)^2\right]} \leq \text{var}(t)$$

where, $I[\theta] = E\left[\left(\frac{\partial}{\partial\theta}\log L\right)^2\right]$ is called the amount of information on $\theta$ supplied by the sample $\{x_1, x_2, \ldots, x_n\}$ and its reciprocal $\frac{1}{I(\theta)}$ as the information limit to the variance of estimator $t = t(x_1, x_2, \ldots, x_n)$

(It is by RA Fisher)

## MVBE

An unbiased estimator $t$ of $\gamma(\theta)$ for which Cramer-Rao lower bound in

$$\text{var}(t) \Rightarrow \frac{\left(\frac{d}{d\theta}\gamma(\theta)\right)^2}{E\left[\frac{\partial}{\partial\theta}\log L\right]^2} = \frac{[\gamma'(\theta)]^2}{I(\theta)}$$

is attained is called a minimum variance bound estimator (MVBE).

## Condition for the Equality Sign in Crammer-Rao (C-R) inequality

C-R inequality is

$$\frac{[\gamma'/(\theta)]^2}{E\left[\left(\frac{\partial}{\partial\theta}\log L\right)^2\right]} \leq \text{var}(t) = E[t-\gamma(\theta)]^2$$

The necessary and sufficient condition for an unbiased estimator $t$ to attain the lower bound of its variance is given by

$$\frac{\partial}{\partial\theta}\log L = \frac{t-\gamma(\theta)}{\lambda(\theta)} = [t-\gamma(\theta)]A(\theta)$$

where, $$A = A(\theta) = \frac{1}{\lambda(\theta)} \text{ say}$$

***Theorem 1*** If the likelihood function $L$ is expressible as

$$\frac{\partial}{\partial\theta}\log L = \frac{t-\gamma(\theta)}{\lambda(\theta)} = [t-\gamma(\theta)]A(\theta),$$

then

(i) $t$ is an unbiased estimator of $\gamma(\theta)$.

(ii) Minimum Variance Bound (MVB) estimator $t$ for $\gamma(\theta)$ exists and

(iii) $\text{var}(t) = \frac{\gamma'(\theta)}{A(\theta)} = [\gamma'(\theta)\lambda(\theta)]$

***Theorem 2*** A MVB estimator for $\gamma(\theta)$ exists if and only if there exists a sufficient estimator for $\gamma(\theta)$.

# Complete Family of Distributions

Let a statistic $T = T(x_1, x_2, x_3, \ldots, x_n)$ be based on a random sample of size $n$ from the population $f(x, \theta), \theta \in \Theta$.

The distribution of the statistic $T$ will, in general depend on $\theta$. So, corresponding to $T$, we again have a family of distributions, say $\{g(t, \theta), \theta \in \Theta\}$.

**Definition** The statistic $T = t(x_1, x_2, \ldots, x_n)$ or more precisely, the family of distributions $\{g(t, \theta) | (\theta \in \Theta)\}$ is said to be complete for $\theta$ if

$$E_\theta[h(T)] = 0 \text{ for all } \theta$$

$$\Rightarrow \quad P_\theta[h(T) = 0] = 1$$

i.e., $\int h(t) \cdot g(t, \theta) dt = 0, \forall \theta \in \Theta$

or $\Sigma\, h(t) \cdot g(t, \theta) = 0, \forall \theta \in \Theta$

$\Rightarrow \quad h(T) = 0\ \forall \theta \in N$ almost surely (a.s)

# MVUE (Minimum Variance Unbiased Estimator) and Blackmellisation

***Theorem*** (Rao-Blackwell Theorem) Let $X$ and $Y$ be random variables such that

$$E(Y) = \mu \text{ and } \text{var}(Y) = \sigma^2 y > 0$$

Let $E(Y | X = x) = \phi(x)$

Then, (i) $E(\phi(x)) = \mu$

(ii) $\text{var}[\phi(x)] \le \text{var}(y)$

# The Principle of Maximum Likelihood Estimation

It consists of finding an estimator $\hat{\theta}$ for the unknown parameter $\theta = (\theta_1, \theta_2, \ldots, \theta_k)$ say, which maximises the likelihood function $L(\theta)$ for variations in parameter, i.e.,

To find $\hat{\theta} = (\hat{\theta}_1, \hat{\theta}_1, \ldots, \hat{\theta}_k)$

such that $L(\hat{\theta}) > L(\theta), \forall \theta \in \Theta$

or $L(\hat{\theta}) = \sup L(\theta), \forall \theta \in \Theta$

$\hat{\theta}$ is called Maximum Likelihood Estimator (MLE)

$\hat{\theta}$ is the solution of

$$\frac{\partial L}{\partial \theta} = 0 \text{ and } \frac{\partial^2 L}{\partial \theta^2} < 0 \quad \ldots(i)$$

Eq. (i) can also be written as

$$\frac{1}{L} \frac{\partial L}{\partial \theta} = 0 \text{ or } \frac{\partial}{\partial \theta} \log L = 0 \quad \ldots(ii)$$

If $\theta$ is a vector valued parameter, then

$$\hat{\theta} = (\hat{\theta}_1, \hat{\theta}_2, \ldots, \hat{\theta}_k)$$

is given by the solution of simultaneous equations

$$\frac{\partial}{\gamma \theta i} \log L = \frac{\partial}{\partial \theta i} \log L(\theta_1, \theta_2, \ldots, \theta_k)$$

$$= 0; i = 1, 2, \ldots, K \quad \ldots(iii)$$

Eqs. (ii) and (iii) are referred as the likelihood equations for estimating the parameters.

# Confidence Interval and Confidence Limit

We fix$\alpha$ (say 5% or 1%) and determine two constants $C_1$ and $C_2$ such that $P(C_1 < \theta < C_2 | t) = 1 - \alpha$

The $C_1$ and $C_2$ so determined are known as confidence limits or fidenicial limits, and the interval $[c_1, c_2]$ within which the unknown value of the population parameter is expected to lie, is called the confidence interval and $1 - \alpha$ is called the confidence coefficient.

For $\alpha = 0.05$ (or 0.01), we get 95% (or 99%) confidence limit.

To find $C_1$ and $C_2$: Let $T_1$ and $T_2$ be two statistics such that

$$P(T_1 > \theta) = \alpha_1 \quad \ldots(i)$$

and

$$P(T_2 < \theta) = \alpha_2 \quad \ldots(ii)$$

$\alpha_1$ and $\alpha_2$ are constants independent of $\theta$. In Eqs. (i) and (ii) $T_1$ and $T_2$ may be taken as $C_1$ and $C_2$.

On combining Eqs. (i) and (ii), we get

$$P(T_1 < \theta < T_2) = 1 - \alpha,$$

Where, $\alpha = \alpha_1 + \alpha_2$

# Test of Significance

It enables us to decide on the basis of the sample results, if

(i) The deviation between the observed sample static and the hypothetical parameter value, or

(ii) The deviation between two independent sample statistics is significant or might be attributed to chame or the fluctuations of the sampling.

Since, for large $n$, almost all the distributions (binomial, poisson, hypergeometric, $t, F, \chi^2$ etc.,) can be approximated very closely by a normal probability curve, so we use the normal test of significance for large samples.

The $t$-test, $F$-test and $\chi^2$-tests and Fisher's $z$-transformations are used for small samples to study such differences.

# Null Hypothesis

To apply test of significance on samples, the hypothesis is set up first; it is a statement about the population parameter. It is usually a hypothesis of no difference. It is called null hypothesis, and is denoted by $H_0$.

Thus, $H_0$ (Null Hypothesis) The sample statistic does not differ significantly from the hypothetical parameter value

In case of two statistics,

$H_o$: The sample statistics do not differ significantly.

In the next step, we calculate probability that the deviation between the observed sample statistic and the population parameter value is due to fluctuations of sampling.
If the deviation is significant (test of significance), then the null hypothesis is rejected.
If the deviation is not significant the null hypothesis is retained.

## Alternative Hypothesis

Any hypothesis which is complementary to the null hypothesis is called an alternative hypothesis. It is usually denoted by $H_1$.
e.g., If $H_0 : \mu = \mu_0$ (the population has specified mean $\mu_0$), then alternative hypothesis could be

**(i)** $H_1$: $\mu \neq \mu_0$ (*i.e.*, $H_1 : \mu > \mu_0$ or $H_1$: $\mu < \mu_0$)
**(ii)** $H_1$: $\mu > \mu_0$
**(iii)** $H_1$: $\mu < \mu_0$

The alternative hypothesis in

**(i)** is known as a two tailed alternative hypothesis.
**(ii)** is right tailed alternative hypothesis.
**(iii)** is left tailed alternative hypothesis.

## Critical Value or Significant Value

The value of text statistic which separates the critical (or rejection) region and the acceptance region is called the critical value or significant value.
It depends upon

**(i)** the level of significance used.
**(ii)** the alternative hypothesis, whether it is two tailed or single tailed.

For large samples, corresponding to statistic $t$,

$$Z = \frac{t - E(t)}{S.E(t)} \sim N(0, 1) \quad \dots \text{(i)}$$

asymptotically as $n \to \infty$
The value of $Z$ given by Eq. (i) is known as test statistict,
For two tailed test, at '$\alpha$' level of significance, $Z$ is denoted by $Z_\alpha$. Thus, $P(|Z| > Z_\alpha) = \alpha$.
The level of significance is the size of the type I error (or the maximum producer's risk). It is generally 5% or 1%. It is fixed in advance before collecting the sample information.

## Errors in Sampling

The main objective of sampling theory is to draw conclusion about the population parameters on the basis of sample results.
It is generally in the form : To accept or reject the population after examining a sample from it. In this working there may be possibility of error. It is of two types

Type I Error: Reject $H_0$, when it is true.
Type II Error: Accept $H_0$, when it is wrong, *i.e.*, accept Ho when $H_1$ is true.

Let $P\{$ Reject $H_0$ when it is true$\}$

$= P\{$ Reject $H_0 \mid H_0\} = \alpha$

and $P\{$ Accept $H_0$ when it is wrong$\}$

$= P\{$ Accept $H_0 \mid H_1\} = \beta$

Then, $\alpha$ is called size of type I error, $\beta$ is called size of type II error.
$\alpha$ is also called Producer's risk and $\beta$ is called consumer's risk.
In two dimensional space test statistics $t = t(x_1, x_2, \dots, x_n)$ each element is in the form of ordered pairs.

Thus, $x_i = (y_i', y_i'')$

The values can be plotted in 2-dimensional plane.

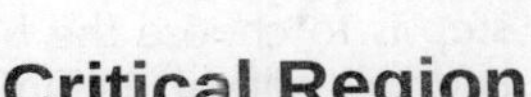

## Critical Region

A region (corresponding to a statistic $t$) in the sample space $S$ which amounts to rejection of $H_o$ is termed as critical region or region of rejection.
If $W$ is the critical region and if $t = t(x_1, x_2, \dots, x_n)$ is the value of the statistic based on a random sample of size $n$, then

$$P(t \in W / H_0) = \alpha$$
$$P(t \in \overline{W} / H_1) = \beta$$

$\overline{W}$ (complement of $W$) is called acceptance region.
Here, $W \cup \overline{W} = S, W \cap \overline{W} = \phi$
Probability '$\alpha$' that a random value of the statistic $t$ belongs to the critical region is known as the level of significance.
Power of the test
We know

$\alpha =$ Probability of type I error
$= P$ (Reject $H_0 | H_0$ is true)
$\beta =$ Probability of type II error
$= P$(Accept $H_0 | H_0$ is false)

Power of the test is defined as $1 - \beta$. It is also called power function of the test hypothesis $H_0$ against the alternative hypothesis $H_1$.
The value of the power function at a parameter point is called the power of the test at that point.

## Steps in Solving Testing of Hypothesis Problem

**(i)** From the problem, to know the form of the population distribution, and the parameter(s) about which the hypothesis are set up.
**(ii)** Setting up of the null hypothesis $H_0$ and the alternative hypothesis $H_1$ in terms of the range of the parameter values.
**(iii)** Choosing of statistic $t = t(x_1, x_2, \dots, x_n)$ called test statistic which controls to $\alpha$ and $\beta$ to minimum level.
**(iv)** Partition the set of all possible values of statistic $t$ into two disjoint sets $W$ (rejection region or critical region) and $\overline{W}$ (acceptance region) such that

(a) Reject $H_0$ (*i.e.*, accept $H_1$), if the value of $t$ falls in $W$.

(b) Accept $H_0$, if the value of $t$ fall in $\overline{W}$.

**(v)** Take observation (Experimentally sample observations) calculate test statistic and further follow the steps and take decision.

## Optimum Test under Different Situations

In any testing problem the first two steps, *viz.*,

**(i)** the form of population distribution

**(ii)** the parameter(s) of interest are considered from the problem. The most important step is to choose the best test, *i.e.*, the best statistic '$t$' and the critical region $W$ where by the best test we mean one which in addition to controlling $\alpha$ at any desired low level has the minimum type II error $\beta$ or maximum power $1-\beta$, compared to $\beta$ of all other tests having this $\alpha$.

# Most Powerful Test (MP test)

Let test hypothesis be

$$H_0: \theta = \theta_0$$
$$H_1: \theta \neq \theta_0$$

The critical region $W$ is the most powerful (MP) critical region of size $\alpha$ (and corresponding test a most powerful test of level $\alpha$) for testing $H_0: \theta = \theta_0$ against $H_1: \theta = \theta_1$, if

$$P(x \in W | H_0) = \int_W L_0 \, dx = \alpha \qquad \text{... (i)}$$

and $$P(x \in W / H_1) \geq P(x \in W_1 | H_1) \qquad \text{... (ii)}$$

for every other critical region $W_1$ satisfying Eq. (i).

## Uniformly Most Powerful Text (UMP Test)

Let $$H_0: \theta = \theta_0$$
$$H_1: \theta \neq \theta_0$$

Then, for a predetermined $\alpha$, the best test for $H_0$ is called the uniformly most powerful test of level $\alpha$.

**Definition** The region $W$ is called uniformly most powerful (UMP) critical region of size $\alpha$ (and corresponding test as uniformly most powerful (UMP) test of level $\alpha$) for testing $H_0: \theta = \theta_0$ against $H_1: \theta \neq \theta_0$ *i.e.*,

$$H_1: \theta = \theta_1 \neq \theta_0 \text{ if}$$

$$P(x \in W | H_0) = \int_W L_0 \, dx = \alpha \qquad \text{...(i)}$$

and $$P(x \in W | H_1) \geq P(x \in W_1 | H_1) \qquad \text{...(ii)}$$

for all $\theta \neq \theta_0$

Whatever the region $W_1$ satisfying Eq. (i) may be.

## Neyman-Pearson Lemma

Let $\{x_1, x_2, \ldots, x_n\}$ be a random sample of size $n$ from the population whose density function is $f(x, \theta)$.

Let null hypothesis be $H_0: \theta = \theta_0$ and alternative hypothesis be $H_1: \theta = \theta_1$

Let $K > 0$, be a constant and $W$ be a critical region of size $\alpha$ such that

$$W = \left\{x \in S : \frac{f(x, \theta_1)}{f(x, \theta_0)} > K\right\}$$

$$\Rightarrow \qquad W = \left\{x \in S : \frac{L_1}{L_0} > K\right\}$$

and $$\overline{W} = \left\{x \in S : \frac{L_1}{L_0} \leq K\right\}$$

Where, $L_0$ and $L_1$ are the likelihood functions of the sample observations $x = (x_1, x_2, \ldots, x_n)$ under $H_0$ and $H_1$ respectively. Then, $W$ is the most powerful critical region of the test hypothesis $H_0: \theta = \theta_0$ against the alternative $H_1: \theta = \theta_1$

Let $$W = \left\{x \in S \middle| \frac{L_1}{L_0} > K\right\}$$

be the most powerful $H_1: \theta = \theta\hat{1}$ critical region of size $\alpha$ for testing $H_0: \theta = \theta_0$ against and let it be independent of $\theta_1 \in \Theta_1 = \Theta - \Theta_0$, where $\Theta_0$ is the parameter space under $H_0$. Then, we say that critical region $W$ is the uniformly most powerful critical region (UMP CR) of size $\alpha$ for testing $H_0: \theta = \theta_0$ against $H_1: \theta \in \Theta_1$.

## Unbiased Test and Unbiased Critical Region

Let testing be of

$$H_0: \theta = \theta_0 \text{ against}$$
$$H_1: \theta = \theta_1$$

The critical region $W$ and consequently the test based on it is said to be unbiased, if the power of the test exceeds the size of the critical region, *i.e.*, if

power of the test $\geq$ size of the C.R.

$$\Rightarrow \qquad 1 \beta \geq \alpha$$

$$\Rightarrow \qquad P_{\theta_1}(W) \geq P_{\theta_0}(W)$$

$$\Rightarrow \qquad P[x | x \in W | H_1] \geq P[x | x \in W | H_0]$$

In other words, the critical region $W$ is said to be unbiased, if $P_\theta(W) \geq P_{\theta_0}(W), \forall \theta (\neq \theta_0) \in \Theta$

***Theorem*** Every most powerful (MP) or uniformly most powerful (UMP) (CR) is necessarily unbiased.

(i) If $W$ be MPCR of size $\alpha$ for testing $H_0: \theta = \theta_0$ against $H_1: \theta = \theta_1$, then it is necessarily unbiased.

(ii) Similarly, if $W$ be UMPCR of size $\alpha$ for testing $H_0: \theta = \theta_0$ against $H_1: \theta \in \Theta_1$, then it is also unbiased.

# Optimum Regions and Sufficient Statistics

Let $X_1, X_2, \ldots, X_n$ be a random sample of size $n$ from a population with pdf (or pmf) $f(x, \theta)$ where parameter $\theta$ may be a vector, Let $T$ be a sufficient statistic for $\theta$. Then, by factorization theorem.

$$L(x,\theta)=\prod_{i=1}^{n} f(x_i,\theta)=g_\theta[t(x)]h(x) \quad \text{...(i)}$$

Where, $g_\theta(t(x))$ is the marginal distribution of the statistic $T=t(x)$. By NP–Lemma, the MPCR for testing $H_0:\theta=\theta_0$ against $H_1:\theta=\theta_1$ is given by

$$W=\{x|\,L(x,\theta_1)\geq KL(x,\theta_0)\},\forall K>0 \quad \text{...(ii)}$$

from Eqs. (i) and (ii), we get

$$W=\{x|\,g_{\theta_1}(t(x))\cdot h(x)\geq K.g_{\theta_0}(t(x)).h(x)\},\forall K>0$$
$$=\{x|\,g_{\theta_1}(t(x))\geq K\cdot g_{\theta_0}(t(x))\},\ \forall K>0$$

Hence, if $T=t(x)$ is sufficient statistic for $\theta$ then MPCR for the test is given in terms of marginal distribution of $T=t(x)$ rather than the joint distribution of $X_1,X_2,\ldots,X_n$.

## Likelihood Function

Let $x_1,x_2,\ldots,x_n$ be a random sample of size $n$ from a population with density function $f(x,\theta)$. Then, the likelihood function of the sample values $x_1,x_2,\ldots,x_n$ is denoted by $L=L(\theta)$, and is defined as their joint density function given by

$$L=f(x,\theta)\cdot f(x_2,\theta),\ldots,f(x_n,\theta)=\prod_{i=1}^{n} f(x_i,\theta)$$

$L$ gives the relative likelihood that the random variables assume a particular set of values $x_1,x_2,\ldots,x_n$.

For a given sample $x_1,x_2,\ldots,x_n$ $L$ becomes a function of the variable $\theta$, the parameter.

## Likelihood Ratio Test

Let $x_1,x_2,\ldots,x_n$ be a random sample of size $n>1$ from a population with pdf $f(x,\theta_1,\theta_2,\ldots,\theta_k)$, where, $\Theta$ the parameter space is the totality of all points that $(\theta_1,\theta_2,\ldots,\theta_k)$ can assume.

We want to test the null hypothesis $H_0:(\theta_1,\theta_2,\ldots,\theta_k)\in N_0$ against the alternative hypothesis of the type $H_1:(\theta_1,\theta_2,\ldots,\theta_k)\in\Theta-\Theta_0$. The likelihood function of the sample observations is given by

$$L=\prod_{i=1}^{n} f(x_i,\theta_1,\theta_2,\ldots,\theta_k) \quad \text{...(i)}$$

By the principle of maximum likelihood,

The likelihood equation for estimating any parameter $\theta_i$ is given by

$$\frac{\partial L}{\partial\theta_i}=0,\ (i=1,2,\ldots,\ k) \quad \text{...(ii)}$$

Using $\dfrac{\partial L}{\partial\theta_i}=0,\ (i=1,2,\ldots,\ k)$

We can obtain the maximum likelihood estimates for the parameters $(\theta_1,\theta_2,\ldots,\theta_k)$ these parameters vary over the parameter space $\Theta$ and subspace $\Theta_0$.

Using the maximum likelihood estimates so obtained, in

$$L=\prod_{i=1}^{n} f(x_i,\theta_1,\ \theta_2,\ldots,\theta_k) \quad \text{...(i}$$

We obtain maximum values of the likelihood function for variation of the parameters in $\Theta$ and $\Theta_0$, respectively.

The likelihood ratio test is defined as the quotient of these two maximas, given by

$$\lambda=\lambda(x_1,x_2,\ldots,x_n)=\frac{L(\hat{\Theta}_0)}{L(\hat{\Theta})}=\frac{\sup_{\theta\in\Theta_0} L(x,\theta)}{\sup_{\theta\in\Theta} L(x,\theta)}$$

Where, $L(\Theta_C)$ and $L(\Theta)$ are the maxima of the likelihood function (i) with respect to the parameters in the regions $\Theta_0$ and $\Theta$, respectively.

***Theorem 1*** If $\lambda$ is the likelihood ratio test for testing a null hypothesis $H_0$ and if $\cup=\phi(\lambda)$ is a monotonic increasing (decreasing) function of $\lambda$, then the test based on $\cup$ is equivalent to the likelihood ratio test. The critical region of the test based on $\cup$ is

$$\phi(0)<\cup<\phi(\lambda_0)$$
$$[\phi(\lambda_0)<\cup<\phi(0)]$$

***Theorem 2*** Let $x_1,x_2,\ldots,x_n$ be a random sample from a population with Pdf $f(x;\theta_1,\theta_2,\ldots,\theta_k)$ where the parameter space $N$ is $k$-dimensional. Suppose, we want to test the composite hypothesis.

$$H_0:\ \theta_1=\theta_1',\ \theta_2=\theta_2',\ldots,\ \theta_r=\theta_r',\ r<k$$

Where $\theta_1',\theta_2',\ldots\theta_r'$ are specified numbers. When, $H_0$ is true, $-2\log_e\lambda$ is asymptotically distributed as chi-square with $r$ degrees of freedom *i.e.*, under $H_0$, $-2\log\lambda\sim\chi_r^2$, if $n$ is large.

Test for the mean of a normal population $N(\mu,\sigma^2)$.

Let $\{x_1,x_2,\ldots,x_n\}$ be a random sample of size $n$ from it

Let $H_0:\mu=\mu_0$ (specified) $0<\sigma^2<\infty$

$$H_1:\ \mu\neq\mu_0,0<\sigma^2<\infty$$

$\Theta$ (Parameter space)

$$=\{(\mu,\sigma^2)|-\infty<\mu<\infty,0<\sigma^2<\infty\}$$
$$\Theta_0=\{(\mu,\sigma^2)|\,\mu=\mu_0,0<\sigma^2<\infty\}$$

$\Theta_0$ being subspace of $\Theta$ determined by the null hypothesis $H_0$.

## Test for the Equality of Means of Two Normal Populations

$N(\mu_1,\sigma_1^2),N(\mu_2,\sigma_2^2)$

$\mu_1,\mu_2,\sigma_1^2.\sigma_2^2$ are unspecified. Then,

$$H_0:\mu_1=\mu_2=\mu$$
$$H_1:\mu_1\neq\mu_2$$
$$\Theta=\{(\mu_1,\ \mu_2,\ \sigma_1^2,\ \sigma_2^2)|-\infty<\mu_i<\infty,\ \sigma_i^2>0,\ i=1,2\}$$
$$\Theta=\{(\mu,\ \sigma_1^2,\ \sigma_2^2)|-\infty<\mu<\infty,\ \sigma_i^2>0,\ i=1,2\}$$

In case cf population variances are unequal, $\sigma_1^2\neq\sigma_2^2$

In case cf population variances are equal, $\sigma_1^2=\sigma_2^2=\sigma^2$.

### Test for the Equality of Means of Several Normal Populations having Unknown Common Variance $\sigma^2$

Let $H_0 = \mu_1 = \mu_2 = \ldots = \mu_k = \mu$

$\sigma_1^2 = \sigma_2^2 = \ldots = \sigma_k^2 = \sigma^2$

$H_1 = \mu_i$ are not all equal

$\sigma_1^2 = \sigma_2^2 = \ldots = \sigma_k^2 = \sigma^2$

### Test for the Variance of a Normal Population

$N(\mu, \sigma^2)$

Let $H_0 : \sigma^2 = \sigma_0^2$ (specified)

$H_1 : \sigma^2 \neq \sigma_0^2$

### Test for Equality of Variance of Two Normal Populations

$N(\mu_1, \sigma_1^2)$ and $N(\mu_2, \sigma_2^2)$

$H_0 : \sigma_1^2 = \sigma_2^2 = \sigma^2$ (unspecified)

$\mu_1$ and $\mu_2$ are unspecified.

$H_1 : \sigma_1^2 \neq \sigma_2^2, \mu_1, \mu_2$ (unspecified)

### Test for the Equality of Variances of Several Normal Populations

$N(\mu_i, \sigma_i^2)$ $\quad i = 1, 2, \ldots k.$

$H_0 : \sigma_1^2 = \sigma_2^2 = \ldots = \sigma_k^2 = \sigma^2$ (unspecified)

With $\mu_1, \mu_2, \ldots, \mu_k$ (unspecified)

$H_1 = \sigma_1^2 (i = 1, 2, \ldots, k)$ are not all equal ;

$\mu_1, \mu_2, \ldots, \mu_k$. (unspecified)

### IIDR Variables

A collection of random variables is independent and identically distributed (IID) if each random variable has the same probability distribution as the others and all are mutually independent.

**Central Limit Theorem** The probability distribution of the sum (or average) of IID variables with finite variance approaches a normal distribution.

Example of IID

(i) A sequence of fair due rolls is IID

(ii) A sequence of fair coin flips is IID

## Chi-square Test of Goodness of Fit

It tests if the deviation of the experiment from theory is just by chance or is it really due to the inadequacy of theory to fit the observed data.

If $O_i$ and $E_i$, $(i = 1, 2, \ldots, k)$, be a set of observed and expected frequencies, then

$$\chi^2 = \sum_{i=1}^{k} \frac{(O_i - E_i)^2}{E_i}, \qquad \sum_{i=1}^{k} O_i = \sum_{i=1}^{k} E_i$$

follows chi-square distribution with $(k - 1)$ df

**Conditions**

**(i)** Sample observations should be independent

**(ii)** Constraints on the cell frequencies if any should be linear,

e.g., $\Sigma n_i = \Sigma \lambda_i$, or $\Sigma o_i = \Sigma E_i$

**(iii)** $N$, the total frequency should be reasonably large, say greater than 50.

**(iv)** No theoritical cell frequency should be less than the chi-square is a continuous distribution, but it cannot maintain its character of continuity if cell frequency is less than 5. It is a non-parametric test (or distribution free test).

## Degrees of Freedom (DF)

The number of independent variates which make up the statistic (e.g., $\chi^2$) is known as the degrees of freedom (df) and is usually denoted by $\nu$.

The number of degrees of freedom is the total number of observations less the number of independent constraints imposed on the observations.

If $k$ is the number of independent constraints in the set of data of $n$ observations, then $\nu = n - k$.

If a random variable $X$ has a chi-square distribution with $n$-degrees of freedom, then we write it as $X \sim \chi^2_{(n)}$.

Its probability density function is given by

$$f(x) = \frac{1}{2^{n/2} \Gamma n/2} e^{-x/2} x^{(n/2)-1}, 0 \leq x < \infty$$

### Properties of Degree of Freedom

**(i)** If $X_i, i = 1, 2, \ldots, n$ are $n$ independent normal variates with mean $\mu_i$ and standard deviation $\sigma_i$, then $\sum_{i=1}^{n} \left( \frac{X_i - \mu}{\sigma_i} \right)^2$ is a $\chi^2$-variate with $n$ degrees of freedom.

**Normal distribution is a particular case of $\chi^2$-distribution** when $n = 1$

We know pdf for $\chi^2$ distribution is

$$f(x) = \frac{1}{2^{n/2} \Gamma(n/2)} e^{-x/2} x^{\frac{n}{2}-1}; \ 0 \leq x < \infty$$

Putting $x = \chi^2$, probability differential is given by

$$dP(\chi^2) = f(\chi^2) d\chi^2$$

$$= \frac{1}{2^{n/2} \Gamma(n/2)} e^{-\chi^2/2} (\chi^2)^{(n/2-1)} d\chi^2, 0 \leq \chi^2 < \infty$$

for $n = 1$,

$$dP(\chi^2) = f(\chi^2) d\chi^2 = \frac{1}{2^{1/2} \Gamma(1/2)} e^{-\chi^2/2} (\chi^2)^{(1/2-1)} d\chi^2$$

$$= \frac{1}{\sqrt{2\pi}} e^{-\chi^2/2} d\chi, -\infty < \chi < \infty$$

$\Rightarrow \chi^2$ is a standard normal variate.

**(ii)** In random sampling from a normal population with mean $\mu$ and standard deviation $\sigma$, $\bar{X}$ is distributed normally about mean $\mu$ with standard deviation $\sigma/\sqrt{n}$.

So, $$\frac{\bar{X}-\mu}{\sigma/\sqrt{n}} \sim N(0,1)$$

$\Rightarrow$ $$\left[\frac{\bar{x}-\mu}{\sigma/\sqrt{n}}\right]^2 \text{ is a } \chi^2\text{-variate}$$

with (i) degree of freedom.

**(iii)** Standard $\chi^2$ variate tends to standard normal variate as $n \to \infty$. So, $\chi^2$-distribution tends to normal distribution for large degrees of freedom. In practice for $n \geq 30$, the $\chi^2$-approximation to normal distribution is fairly good.

## Mode of Chi-square Distribution with *n* Degrees of Freedom is $(n-2)$

Mean $= \mu_1' = n$

Variance $= \mu_2 = 2n$

$$\mu_3 = 8n,$$
$$\mu_4 = 48n + 12n^2$$
$$\beta_1 = \frac{8}{n}$$
$$\beta_2 = \frac{12}{n} + 3$$

Karl Pearson's coefficient of skewness is given by

$$\text{Skewness} = \frac{\text{Mean} - \text{Mode}}{\text{SD}} = \frac{n-(n-2)}{\sqrt{2n}} = \sqrt{\frac{2}{n}}$$

Skewness > 0 for $n \geq 1$. So, $\chi^2$- distribution is positively skewed.

As skewness $\propto \frac{1}{\sqrt{n}} = \frac{1}{\sqrt{d.f}}$, So chi-square distribution rapidly tends to symmetry as $n \to \infty$ and so $n \to \infty$ implies $\chi^2$-distribution tends to normal distribution.

for $n \geq 1$, as $x$ increases

$$f(x) = \frac{1}{2^{n/2}\Gamma(n/2)} e^{-x/2} x^{n/2-1}, \; 0 \leq x < \infty$$

decreases rapidly and finally tends to zero as $x \to \infty$.

For $n > 1$, the $\chi^2$-probability curve is positively skewed towards higher values of $x$. $x$-axis is an asymptote to the curve.

The shape of the curve for $n = 1, 2, 3, 4, 5, 6$.

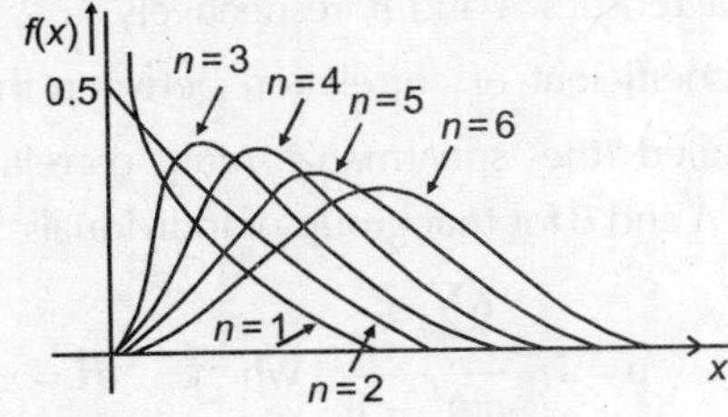


Probability curve of chi-square distribution.

## Critical Values of $\chi^2$-Distribution

Let $\chi_n^2(\alpha)$ be the value of chi-square variate for $n$ degrees of freedom such that

$$P[\chi^2 > \chi_n^2(\alpha)] = \alpha \quad \text{...(i)}$$

The value $\chi_n^2(\alpha)$ given by Eq. (i) is known as the upper (right tailed) $\alpha$-point or critical value or significant value of chi-square for $n$ degrees of freedom.

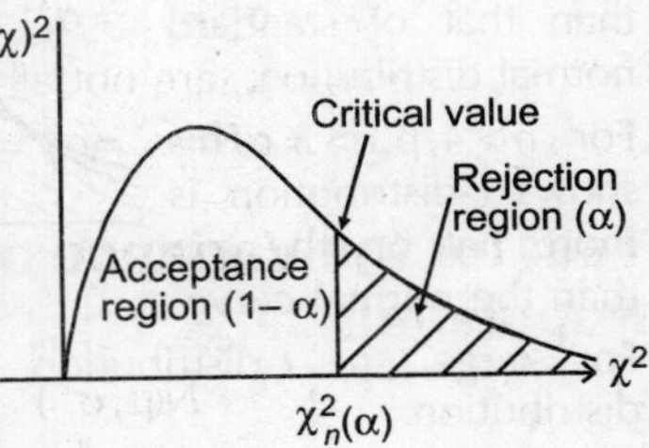


The critical values of $\chi^2$ increases as df $n$ increases and level of significance ($\alpha$) decreases.

## Student's *t*-Statistic

Assumptions for student's t-test

**(i)** The parent population is normal.

**(ii)** Sample observations are independent (sample is randomly chosen).

**(iii)** The population standard deviation $\sigma$ is unknown.

**Definition** Let $\{x_1, x_2, \ldots, x_n\}$ be a random sample of size $n$ from a normal population with mean $\mu$ and variance $\sigma^2$. Then, student's $t$ is defined by the statistic

$$t = \frac{\bar{x}-\mu}{S/\sqrt{n}}$$

where, $$\bar{x} = \frac{1}{n}\sum_{i=1}^{n} x_i$$

$$S^2 = \frac{1}{n-1}\sum_{i=1}^{n}(x_i - \bar{x})^2$$

Its degree of freedom is $\nu = n - 1$.

Student's $t$-distribution with degree of freedom 1 is a Cauchy's distribution

$$f(t) = \frac{1}{\pi}\frac{1}{(1+t^2)}, \; -\infty < t < \infty$$

The probability density function of $t$-distribution with $n$ degrees of freedom is

$$f(t) = c\left[1 + \frac{t^2}{n}\right]^{-(n+1)/2}, \; -\infty < t < \infty$$

It shows $f(-t) = f(t)$

So, the probability curve is symmetrical about the line $t = 0$.

As $t$ increases, $f(t)$ decreases rapidly and tends to 0 as $t \to \infty$, So, $t$-axis is asymptote to the curve.

Mean of $t$-distribution $\mu_1' = 0$

$\mu_{2r+1}$ (about origin) $= 0, r = 1, 2, \ldots$

$$\mu_{2r} = \mu'_{2r} = \frac{n^r(2r-1)(2r-3)\ldots 3.1}{(n-2)(n-4)\ldots(n-2r)}$$

where, $\frac{n}{2} > r$

$$\mu_2 = \frac{n}{n-2}, n > 2; \beta_\alpha = \frac{3(n-2)}{(n-4)}, n > 4$$

These show, for $n > 2$, $\mu_2 > 1$. This implies variance of $t$-distribution is greater than that of standard normal distribution.

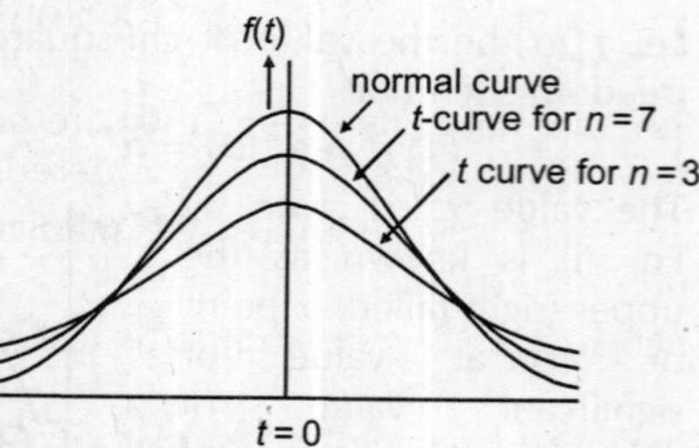


For $n > 4, \beta_\alpha > 3$. This shows $t$-distribution is more flat on the top than the normal curve.

For large. $n$, $t$-distribution tends to standard normal distribution.

## Critical Values of *t*

The critical values (or significant values) of $t$ at level of significance $\alpha$ and df $\nu$ for two tailed test are given by

$$P[|t| > t_\nu(\alpha)] = \alpha \quad \Rightarrow \quad P[|t| \le t_\nu(\alpha)] = 1 - \alpha$$

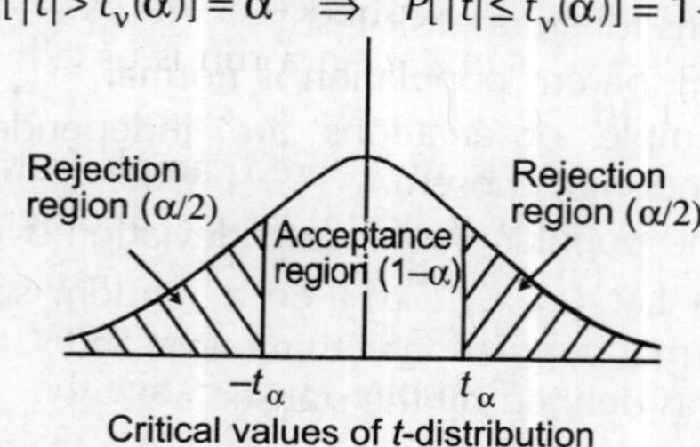


Critical values of *t*-distribution

## Snedecor's *F*-Distribution

The sampling distribution of $F$-statistic does not involve any population parameter and depends only on the degrees of freedoms $\nu_1$ and $\nu_2$.

A statistic $F$ with $(\nu_1, \nu_2)$ degrees of freedom (df) is denoted by $F \sim F(\nu_1 \nu_2)$.

It is defined as follows

$$F = \frac{X / \nu_1}{Y / \nu_2}$$

Where $X$ and $Y$ are two independent chi-square variates with $\nu_1$ and $\nu_2$ df, respectively.

For $F$-distribution with $(\nu_1, \nu_2)$ degrees of freedom the probability function is given by

$$f(F) = \frac{\left(\frac{\nu_1}{\nu_2}\right)^{\nu_1/2}}{B\left(\frac{\nu_1}{2}, \frac{\nu_2}{2}\right)} \cdot \frac{F^{\frac{\nu_1}{2}-1}}{\left[1 + \frac{\nu_1}{\nu_2} F\right]^{\frac{(\nu_1+\nu_2)}{2}}}, 0 \le F < \infty$$

### Properties of *F*-statistics

**(i)** Mean $\mu_1' = \frac{\nu_2}{\nu_2 - 2}, \nu_2 > 2$

**(ii)** Variance $\mu_2 = \frac{2\nu_2^2(\nu_2 + \nu_1 - 2)}{\nu_1(\nu_2 - 2)^2(\nu_2 - 4)}, \nu_2 > 4$

**(iii)** For large $\nu_1$ and $\nu_2$, $F$-statistic tends to $N\left[1, 2\left(\frac{1}{\nu_1} + \frac{1}{\nu_2}\right)\right]$ variate.

**(iv)** Mode of $F$-distribution exists if any only if $\nu_1 > 2$.

If mode exists, then mode $= \frac{\nu_2}{(\nu_2 + 2)} \frac{(\nu_1 - 2)}{\nu_1}$ and (Mode) < 1.

**(v)** Points of inflexion of $F$-distribution exist for $\nu_1 > 4$ and are equidistant from mode.

**(vi)** Karl Pearson's coefficient of skewness is

$$S_k = \frac{\text{Mean}-\text{Mode}}{\sigma} > 0,$$

as mean > 1 and mode < 1. So, $F$-distribution is highly positively skewed.

**(vii)** The probability $P(F)$ increases steadily at first until if reaches its peak (corresponding to the modal value which is less than 1) and then decreases slowly so as to became tangential at $F = \infty$, *i.e.*, $F$-axis is an asymptote to the right tail.

## Critical Values of *F*-Distribution

The significant value $F_\alpha(n_1, n_2)$ at level of significance $\alpha$ and $(n_1, n_2)$ *d.f.* is determined by

$$P[F > F_\alpha(n_1, n_2)] = \alpha$$

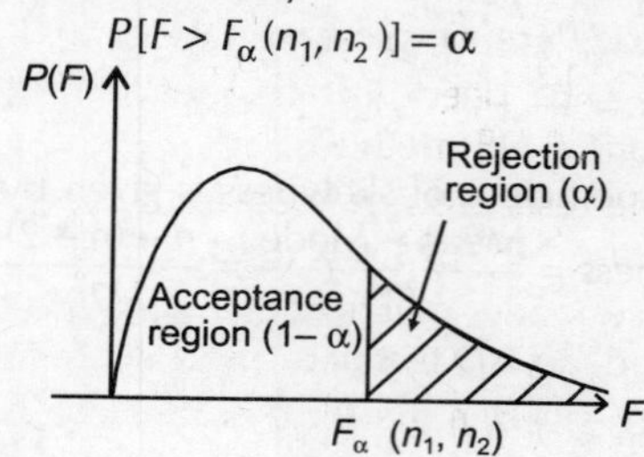


## Fisher's *Z*-Distribution

Given, Snedecor's F-distribution with $(\nu_1, \nu_2)$ degrees of freedom. We take, $Z = \frac{1}{2} \log_e F$.

Then, $Z$ is having fisher's $Z$-distribution with $(\nu_1, \nu_2)$ degrees of freedom.

## Rank Correlation

Let $\{(x_i, y_i) | i = 1, 2, \ldots, n\}$ be the ranks of the $i$th individual in two characteristics $A$ and $B$, respectively,

Pearson coefficient of correlation between the ranks $x_i's$ and $y_i's$ is called the spearman's rank correlation coefficient between $A$ and $B$ for that group of individuals, and is given by

$$\rho = 1 - \frac{6\sum_{i=1}^{n} d_i^2}{n(n^2 - 1)} \quad \text{where,} \quad d\hat{i} = x_i - y_i$$

# Non-parametric Test

Almost all exact (small) sample tests of significance are based on the fundamental assumption that the parent population is normal and are concerned with testing or estimating the means and variances of these populations such tests, which deal with the parameters of the population are known as parametric tests. Thus, a parametric test is a test whose model specifies certain conditions about the parameters of the population from which samples are drawn.

Non-parametric (NP) test does not depend on the particular form of the basic frequency function from which the samples are drawn. In other words, non-parametric test does not make any assumption regarding the form of the population, *i.e.*, does not make any assumption about the parameters of the population.

Since, NP tests do not depend upon the frequency distribution of population so they are also called distribution freetests.

*e.g.*, ρ (rank correlation coefficient is a distribution free test, (NP test).

## Advantages of NP Tests

- **(i)** NP methods are simple and easy to apply.
- **(ii)** There is no need of frequency distribution of population in NP methods.
- **(iii)** Parametric tests are not used for 'Classification data'. In such case NP tests are used.
- **(iv)** Social, economic, psychological data are not normally distributed, so NP tests are used in them.
- **(v)** The datas' given in the form of rank are dealt with NP tests.

## Assumptions Associated with Non-parametric Tests (NP Tests)

- **(i)** Sample observations are independent
- **(ii)** The variable under study is continuous.
- **(iii)** Probability density function is continuous.
- **(iv)** Lower order moments exist.

## Disadvantages of NP (Non-parametric Tests)

- **(i)** NP Tests can be used only if the measurements are nominal or ordinal.
- **(ii)** There is no NP methods for testing interactions in 'Analysis of variance' model unless special assumptions about the additivity of the model are made.
- **(iii)** NP tests are designed to test statistical hypothesis only and not for estimating the parameters.

# Ordered Sample

By saying that $x_1, x_2, \ldots, x_n$ is an ordered sample we mean $x_1 \le x_2 \le \ldots \le x_n$.

Non-parametric methods (tests) are based on ordered statistic theory (in which samples are ordered).

Non-Parametric methods use median, range, quartile, inter quartile range etc.

The structure of non-parametric test is based on the following

## Fundamental Property of Ordered Statistics

The distribution of the area under the density function between any two ordered observations is independent of the form of the density function.

# World-Wolfowitz Run Test

Run (Definition). A run is defined as a sequence of letters of one kind surrounded by sequence of letters of the other kind, and the number of elements in a run is usually referred to as the length ($l$) of the run.

Suppose, $x_1, x_2, \ldots, x_n$, is an ordered sample from a population with density $f_1(\cdot)$ and $y_1, y_2, \ldots, y_{n_2}$ is another independent ordered sample from another population with density $f_2(\cdot)$.

$$H_0: f_1(\cdot) = f_2(\cdot)$$

We combine the two samples and arrange the observations in order of magnitude to give the combined ordered sample as (say).

$$x_1 x_2 y_1 y_2 y_3 x_3 y_4 x_4 x_5 y_5 \quad \ldots \text{(i)}$$

In Eq. (i) in order a run of $x$, $l = 2$ a run of $y$, $l = 3$; a run of $x$, $l = 1$; a run of $y$, $l = 1$, etc.

If both the samples come from the same population, then the number of runs in the combined sample would be large.

If the samples come from two different populations, their range do not overlap, there would be only two runs: $x_1, x_2, \ldots, x_{n1}$ and $y_1, y_2, \ldots, y_{n_2}$ mean and variance would tend to reduce the number of runs. And alternative hypothesis is $H_1$:only few runs.

# Test for Randomness

Let $x_1, x_2, \ldots, x_n$ be the set of observations arranged in the order in which they occur, *i.e.*, $x_i$ is the $i$th observation in the outcome of an experiment.

We calculate the median of the observation.

If $x_i$ is alone median we write $A$ at $i$th position if $x_i$ is below median we write $B$ at then position. Here, $i = 1, 2, \ldots, n$, $j = 1, 2, \ldots, n$. Thus, we get a sequence of $A$'s and $B$'s of the type

$$ABBAAABABB \quad \ldots \text{(i)}$$

$H_0$: The set of observations is random, the number of runs $U$ Eq. (i) is a random variable with

$$E(U) = \frac{n+2}{2} \text{ and } \operatorname{var}(U) = \frac{n(n-2)}{4(n-1)}$$

for large $n$ (say> 25), $U$ may be regarded as asymptotically normal and so normal test may be used.

## Median Test

It is used to test if two independent ordered samples differ in their central tendencies.

Let $x_1, x_2, \ldots, x_{n_1}$ and $y_1, y_2, \ldots, y_{n_2}$ be two independent ordered samples from the populations with pdf's $f_1(\cdot)$ and $f_2(\cdot)$, respectively. The measurements must be atleast ordinal. Let $z_1, z_2, \ldots, z_{n_1+n_2}$ be the combined ordered sample. Let $m_1$ be the number of $x'$s and $m_2$ be the number of $y'$s exceeding the median value $M$(say), of the combined sample.

$H_0$: The samples come from same population

Or

$H_0$: The samples come from different populations with the same median.

Thus, $\quad H_0: f_1(\cdot) = f_2(\cdot)$

Joint distribution of $m_1, m_2$ is hypergeometric distribution with probability function

$$P(m_1, m_2) = \frac{\binom{n_1}{m_1}\binom{n_2}{m_2}}{\binom{n_1+n_2}{m_1+m_2}}$$

If $m_1 < n/2$, then the critical region corresponding to the size of type I error $\alpha$ is given by $m_1 < m_1'$ where $m_1'$ is found from

$$\sum_{m_1=1}^{m_1'} P(m_1, m_2) = \alpha$$

The distribution of $m_1$ under $H_0$ is also hypergeometric with

$$E(m_1) = \frac{n_1}{2}, \text{ if } N = n_1 + n_2 \text{ is even.}$$

$$= \frac{n_1}{2} \cdot \frac{(N-1)}{N}, \text{ if } N \text{ is odd.}$$

and $\quad \text{var}(m_1) = \dfrac{n_1 n_2}{4(N-1)}$, if $N$ is even.

$$= \frac{n_1 n_2 (N+1)}{4N^2}, \text{ if } N \text{ is odd.}$$

for large samples, $m_1$ is asymptotically normal. Thus,

$$Z = \frac{m_1 - E(m_1)}{\sqrt{\text{var}(m_1)}} \sim N(0, 1) \text{ asymptotically.}$$

## Sign Test

It is used in following conditions

**(i)** When there are pairs of observations on two things being compared.

**(ii)** For any given pair, each of the two observations is made under similar extraneous conditions.

**(iii)** Different pairs are observed under different conditions.

## Assumptions of Sign Test

**(i)** Measurements are such that the deviations $d_1 = x_i - y_i$ can be expressed in terms of positive or negative signs.

**(ii)** Variables have continuous distribution.

**(iii)** di's are independent.

Let $(x_i, y_i), i = 1, 2, \ldots, n$ be $n$ paired sample observations drawn from the two populations with pdf's

$$f_1(\cdot) \text{ and } f_2(\cdot)$$

$$H_0: f_1(\cdot) = f_2(\cdot)$$

To test $H_0$, we consider

$$d\hat{i} = x_i - y_i, (i = 1, 2, \ldots, n)$$

Let $\quad u_i = \begin{cases} 1, & \text{if } x_i - y_i > 0 \\ 0, & \text{if } x_i - y_i < 0 \end{cases}$

## Mann-Whitney-Wilcoxon U-Test

When, we do not make the $t$-test assumptions about the parent population, $U$-test is used.

Let $x_i (i = 1, 2, \ldots, n_1)$ and $y_j (j = 1, 2, \ldots, n_2)$ be two independent ordered samples of size $n_1$ and $n_2$ from populations with pdf $f_1(\cdot)$ and $f_2(\cdot)$, respectively.

$$H_0: f_1(\cdot) = f_2(\cdot)$$

Let $T$ denote the sum of ranks of the $y'$s in the combined ordered sample.

The test statistic $U$ is then defined in terms of $T$ as follows

$$U = n_1 n_2 + \frac{n_2(n_2+1)}{2} - T$$

If $T$ is significantly large or small, then

$$H_0: f_1(\cdot) = f_2(\cdot) \text{ is rejected.}$$

The problem is to find the distribution of $T$ under $H_0$.

***Example 1.*** *Let $X_1, X_2, \ldots, X_n$ be a random sample from $N(0, 1)$.*

*Define* $\quad \overline{X}_K = \dfrac{1}{K}\displaystyle\sum_{i=1}^{K} X_i$

*and* $\quad \overline{X}_{n-K} = \dfrac{1}{n-K}\displaystyle\sum_{K+1}^{n} X_i$

*Then,*

*(i) Find statistic of* $\frac{1}{2}(\overline{X}_K + \overline{X}_{n-K})$

*(ii) Find statistic of* $K \cdot \overline{X}_k^2 + (n-k)\,\overline{X}_{n-K}^2$

*(iii) Find* $\dfrac{X_1^2}{X_2^2}$

*(iv) Find* $\dfrac{X_1}{X_2}$

**Solution.**

(i) Given, $X_1, X_2, \ldots, X_n$ is a random sample from $N(0, 1)$.

$$\overline{X}_K = \frac{1}{K}(X_1 + X_2 + \ldots + X_K)$$

So, $\overline{X}_K \sim N\left(0, \frac{1}{K}\right)$

$$\text{var}(\overline{X}_K) = \frac{1}{K^2}(\text{var } X_1 + \text{var } X_2 + \ldots + \text{var } X_K)$$

$$= \frac{1}{K^2}\underbrace{(1+1+\ldots+1)}_{K \text{ times}} = \frac{1}{K^2} \times K = \frac{1}{K}$$

$$E(\overline{X}_K) = \frac{1}{K}E(X_1 + X_2 + \ldots + X_K)$$

$$= \frac{1}{K}(E(X_1) + E(X_2) + \ldots + E(X_K))$$

$$= \frac{1}{K}(0 + 0 + \ldots + 0) = 0$$

So, $\overline{X}_k \sim N\left(0, \frac{1}{K}\right)$

Similarly, we can show that

$$\overline{X}_{n-K} \sim N\left(0, \frac{1}{n-K}\right)$$

Again, since $(X_1, X_2, \ldots, X_K)$ and $(X_{K+1}, Y_{K+2}, \ldots, X_n)$ are independent, $\overline{X}_k$ and $\overline{X}_{n-K}$ are independent.

Hence, $\frac{1}{2}(\overline{X}_K + \overline{X}_{n-K}) = \frac{1}{2}\overline{X}_K + \frac{1}{2}\overline{X}_{n-K}$

$$\sim N\left(0, \frac{1}{4K} + \frac{1}{4(n-K)}\right)$$

$$\Rightarrow \frac{1}{2}(\overline{X}_K + \overline{X}_{n-K}) \sim N\left(0, \frac{n}{4K(n-K)}\right)$$

$\Rightarrow \frac{1}{2}(\overline{X}_K + \overline{X}_{n-1})$ has normal distribution with mean 0 and variance $\frac{n}{4K(n-K)}$.

(ii) We know

$$\overline{X}_K = \frac{1}{K}(X_1 + X_2 + \ldots + X_K)$$

$$\Rightarrow \text{var}(\overline{X}_K) = \frac{1}{K^2}(\text{var}(X_1) + \text{var}(X_2) + \ldots + \text{var}(X_K))$$

$$= \frac{1}{K^2}\underbrace{(1+1+\ldots+1)}_{K \text{ times}} = \frac{K}{K^2} = \frac{1}{K}$$

or $K\,\text{var}(\overline{X}_K) = 1$ or $\text{var}(\sqrt{K}\overline{X}_K) = 1$

or $\text{var}\left(\frac{\overline{X}_K}{\sqrt{1/K}}\right) = 1$

$$\frac{\overline{X}_K}{\sqrt{1/K}} \sim N(0,1)$$

Similarly, we can show that $\frac{\overline{X}_{n-K}}{\sqrt{\frac{1}{n-K}}} \sim N(0,1)$

$\Rightarrow \left(\frac{\overline{X}_K}{\sqrt{\frac{1}{K}}}\right)^2 \sim$ is a chi-square variate with one degree of freedom *i.e.*, $K\overline{X}_K^2 \sim \chi^2_{(1)}$.

Similarly, $(n-K)\overline{X}_{n-K}^2 \sim \chi^2_{(1)}$

Since, $\overline{X}_K$ and $\overline{X}_{n-K}$ are independent, by addition property of chi-square distribution,

$$K\overline{\chi}_K^2 + (n-K)\overline{\chi}_{n-K}^2 \sim \chi^2_{(1+1)} = \chi^2_{(2)}$$

Thus, $K \cdot \overline{\chi}_K^2 + (n-K)\overline{\chi}_{n-K}^2$ is a Chi-square variate with 2 degrees of freedom.

(iii) $X_1^2 / X_2^2$

Since, $X_1 \sim N(0,1)$ and $X_1 \sim N(0,1)$ are independent,

$X_1^2 \sim \chi^2$ and $X_2^2 \sim \chi^2_{(1)}$ are also independent.

So, by the definition of

F-statistic, $\frac{(X_1^2/1)}{(X_2^2/1)} \sim F_{(1,1)}$

$$\Rightarrow \frac{X_1^2}{X_2^2} \sim F_{(1,1)}$$

$\Rightarrow \frac{X_1^2}{X_2^2}$ is *F*-statistic with (1,1) degrees of freedom, and so its distribution is *F*-distribution.

(iv) $X_1 / X_2$

Given, $X_1 \sim N(0,1)$, $X_2 \sim N(0,1)$. $X_1$ and $X_2$ being independent.

We know the ratio of two independent standard normal variates is a Cauchy variate. So, $\frac{X_1}{X_2}$ is a Cauchy's variate and hence its distribution is Cauchy's distribution.

# Gauss-Markov Model

A Gauss-Markov linear model is a linear statistical model that satisfies all the conditions of a general linear model except. The normality of the error terms.

Simple linear regression model is

$$Y = \alpha + \beta x + \varepsilon \qquad \ldots\text{(i)}$$

where, α and β are unknown intercept and slope parameters, respectively. Here ε known as random error or random disturbance is assumed to be normally distributed with mean $E(\varepsilon) = 0$ and variance var $(\varepsilon) = \sigma^2$. The quantity $\sigma^2$ is known as residual variance or error variance. $T_o$ estimate of regression coefficients α and β a regression line is fitted $\mathbf{Y} = a_0 + a_1 x$ is fitted according to the principle of least squares. Here, **Y** is the predicted or fitted or estimated value.

The least square estimates of α and β are $a_0$ and $a_1$ given by

$$\Sigma y_i = Na_0 + a_1 \Sigma x_i \qquad \ldots\text{(ii)}$$

$$\Sigma y_i x_i = a_0 \Sigma x_i + a_i \Sigma x_i^2 \qquad \ldots\text{(iii)}$$

The slope of regression line β is the change in mean of *y*'s corresponding to a unit increase in $x_i$.

# Gauss-Markov Theorem

The least square estimates $a_0$ and $a_1$ for the actual regression coefficients α and β have the smallest variance and hence most reliable among all unbiased estimators.

## Confidence Intervals

A $(1-\alpha)$ 100% confidence interval for the parameter $\beta$ is

$$a_1 - \frac{t_{\alpha/2} S_\varepsilon \sqrt{n}}{\sqrt{S_{xx}}} < \beta < a_1 + \frac{t_{\alpha/2} S_\varepsilon \sqrt{n}}{\sqrt{S_{xx}}}$$

Where, $t_{\alpha/2}$ is the value of the $t$-distribution with $n$ 2 degrees of freedom.

A $(1-\alpha)$100% confidence interval for $\alpha$ is

$$a_0 - t_{\alpha/2} S_\varepsilon \sqrt{\frac{S_{xx} + (n\bar{x})^2}{nS_{xx}}} < \alpha < a_0 + t_{\alpha/2} S_\varepsilon \sqrt{\frac{S_{xx} + (n\bar{x})^2}{nS_{xx}}}$$

Here, $S_\varepsilon^2$ = (unbiased) estimate of $\sigma^2$

$$= \frac{S_{xx} S_{yy} - (S_{xy})^2}{n(n-2) S_{xx}}$$

## Testing of Hypothesis

Statistics for inferences about $\alpha$ and $\beta$

For slope $\beta$

$$t = \frac{a_1 - \beta}{S_\varepsilon} \sqrt{\frac{S_{xx}}{n}}$$

For intercept $\alpha$

$$t = \frac{a_0 - \alpha}{S_\varepsilon} \sqrt{\frac{nS_{xx}}{S_{xx} + (n\bar{x})^2}}$$

Here, $t$-distribution is of $(n-2)$ degrees of freedom.

## G-M *m*-Dimensional Model

If $Y$ is an $m$-dimensional response variable vector and

$$Z_i = Z_i(X), \quad i = 1, 2, \ldots, k$$

are $m$-dimensional functions of the explanatory variable vector $X$, the Gauss-Markov linear model has the form

$$Y = \beta_0 Z_0 + \beta_1 Z_1 + \ldots + \beta_K Z_K + \varepsilon$$

with (i) $E(\varepsilon) = 0$

(ii) $\text{Var}(\varepsilon) = \sigma^2$

$\sigma^2$ is known as residual variance or error variance. In other words, the observed responses $Y_i$, $i = 1, 2, \ldots, m$ are not assumed to be normally distributed and are not correlated with one another and have a common variance $\text{Var}(Y_i) = \sigma^2$.

## Gauss-Markov Mc Theorem (*M* for *m*-dimension)

Suppose, the response variable $Y (= Y_1, Y_2, \ldots, Y_m)$ and the explanatory variables $X$ satisfy a Gauss-Markov linear model. We consider

$$Y = \sum_{i=1}^{m} C_i Y_i, \quad C_i \in R \qquad \ldots(i)$$

If $\mu_i$ is estimator of $Y_i$ and parameter

$$\theta = \sum_{i=1}^{m} C_i \mu_i \qquad \ldots(ii)$$

is estimator for $Y$, then among all unbiased estimators for $Y$, in the form of Eq. (ii), the ordinary least square estimator (OLS)

$$\hat{\theta} = \sum_{i=1}^{m} C_i \hat{\mu}_i \qquad \ldots(iii)$$

gives the smallest variance. In other words, OLS estimator is the uniformly minimum unbiased estimator.

The $\hat{\theta}$ in Eq. (iii) is known as the best linear unbiased estimator (BLUE) for a linear combination of the responses in a Gauss-Markov linear model.

# Analysis of Variance

It is a statistical tool for test of significance, and is used to test the hemogeneity of several means.

It was introduced by Prof. R A Fisher in 1920, in agronomical data variation is inherent in nature. The total variation in any set of numerical data is due to a number of causes which may be classified as

(i) assignable causes and (ii) chame causes.

## Definition

Analysis of variance (ANOVA) is the "separation of variance ascribable to one group of causes from the variance ascribable to other group".

ANOVA test is based on test statistic $F$ (or variance ratio test). By the technique of the analysis of variance (ANOVA). The total variation in the sample data is expressed as the sum of its non-negative components where each of these components is a measure of the variation due to some specific independent source or factor or cause.

The ANOVA consists in the estimation of the amount of variation due to each of the independent factors (causes) separately and then comparing these estimates due to assignable factors (causes) with the estimate due to chame factors (causes), the later being known as experimental error or simply error.

## Assumptions for ANOVA Test

**(i)** The observations are independent.

**(ii)** Parent population is normal.

**(iii)** Various treatments and environmental effects are additive in nature.

## Cochran's Theorem

Let $X_1, X_2, \ldots, X_n$ denote a random sample from normal population $N(0, \sigma^2)$. Let the sum of the squares of these values be written in the form

$$\sum_{i=1}^{n} X_i^2 = Q_1 + Q_2 + \ldots + Q_K$$

Where, $Q_j$ is a quadratic form in $X_1, X_2, \ldots, X_n$, with rank (degrees of freedom) $r_j$, $j = 1, 2, \ldots, k$. Then, the random variables $Q_1, Q_2, \ldots, Q_K$ are mutually independent and $\dfrac{Q_j}{\sigma^2}$ is $\chi^2$-variate with $r_j$ degrees of freedom if and only if $\sum_{j=1}^{k} r_j = n$.

## One Way Classification

Let $Y$ be a random variable having $N$ observations $y_{ij}$ $(i = 1, 2, \ldots, k, j = 1, 2, \ldots n_i)$ grouped on some basis into $K$ classes of sizes $n_1, n_2, \ldots, n_K$ respectively, $N = \sum_{j=1}^{k} n_i$ as shown in the table.

| Class | Sample Observation | | | | Total | Mean |
|---|---|---|---|---|---|---|
| 1 | $y_{11}$ | $y_{12}$ | ...... | $y_{1n_1}$ | $T_1$ | $\bar{y}_1$ |
| 2 | $y_{21}$ | $y_{22}$ | ...... | $y_{2n_2}$ | $T_2$ | $\bar{y}_2$ |
| ⋮ | ⋮ | ⋮ | | ⋮ | ⋮ | ⋮ |
| $i$ | $y_{i1}$ | $y_{i2}$ | ...... | $y_{in_i}$ | $T_i$ | $\bar{y}_i$ |
| ⋮ | ⋮ | ⋮ | | ⋮ | ⋮ | ⋮ |
| $k$ | $y_{k1}$ | $y_{k2}$ | ...... | $y_{kn_k}$ | $T_k$ | $\bar{y}_k$ |

The total variation in the observation $y_{ij}$ can be split into the following two components.

**(i)** The variation between the classes or variation due to different bases of classification, commonly known as treatments.

**(ii)** The variation within the classes, *i.e.*, inherent variation of the random variable within the observations of a class.

# Example of Mathematical Model

Consider the effect of $K$-different rations on the yield in milk of $N$ cows (of the same breed and stock) divided into $K$ classes of sizes $n_1, n_2, \ldots, n_K$ respectively, $N = \sum_{i=1}^{K} n_i$

$$\begin{aligned} y_{ij} &= \mu_i + \varepsilon_{ij} = \mu + (\mu_i - \mu) + \varepsilon_{ij} \\ &= \mu + \alpha_i + \varepsilon_{ij} (i = 1, 2, \ldots, k, j = 1, 2, \ldots, n_i) \quad \ldots\text{(i)} \end{aligned}$$

Here,

**(i)** $y_{ij}$ is the yield from the $j$th cow, $(j = 1, 2, \ldots, n_i)$ fed on the $i$th ration $(i = 1, 2, \ldots, k)$ ...(ii)

**(ii)** $\mu$ is the general mean effect

$$\mu = \sum_{i=1}^{k} n_i \mu_i / N \quad \ldots\text{(iii)}$$

where $\mu_i$ is the fixed effect due to the $i$th ration, *i.e.*, if there were no treatment differences and no chance causes, then the yield of each cow will be $\mu$.

**(iii)** $\alpha_i$ is the effect of the $i$th ration

$$\alpha_i = \mu_i - \mu \ (i = 1, 2, \ldots, k)$$

*i.e.*, the $i$th ration increases (or decreases) the yield by an amount $\alpha_i$.

On using Eqs. (ii) and (iii), we get

$$\begin{aligned} \sum_{i=1}^{k} n\alpha_i &= \sum_{i=1}^{k} n_i(\mu_i - \mu) \\ &= \Sigma n_i \mu_i - \mu \Sigma n_i \\ &= N\mu - \mu N = 0 \end{aligned}$$

**(iv)** $\varepsilon_{ij}$ is the error factor due to chame.

## Fixed Effect Model

Suppose, the $K$ levels of the factor (treatment) under consideration are the only levels of interest and all these are included in the experiment by the investigator or

Out of a large number of classes, the $k$ classes (treatments) in the model (i) are specifically chosen by the experimenter.

In such a case, $\alpha_i$, representing $i$th class or $i$th level of the factor (treatment) $i = 1, 2, \ldots, k$, are fixed constant (unknown) and model (i) is known as the fixed effect model.

In this model problem is to estimate $\alpha_i$'s and to test same hypothesis about $\alpha_i$'s.

# Random Effect Model

Suppose, we have a large number of classes (levels of factor under consideration) and we want to test, through an experiment, if all the classes effects are equal or not. Due to consideration of time, money or administrative convenience, it may be possible to include all the factor levels in the experiment. In such a situation, we take only a random sample of classes (factor levels) in the experiment and after studying and analysing the sample data, we want to draw conclusions which would be valid for all the classes (factor levels), whether included in the experiment or not. In such a situation the parameters $\alpha_i$'s in the model (i) will not be fixed constants but will be random samples and model (i) is termed as random effect model.

## ANOVA for Fixed Effect Model

If the factor levels under consideration are the only levels of interest, then the fixed effect or parametric model is used. Parametric or fixed effect model.

$$\begin{aligned} y_{ij} &= \mu_i + \varepsilon_{ij} \\ &= \mu_i + \alpha_i + \varepsilon_{ij} (i = 1, 2, \ldots, k;\ j = 1, 2, \ldots n_i) \end{aligned}$$

Where, $\alpha_i$'s are fixed (unknown) constants and all the symbols have their usual meaning.

### Assumptions in the Fixed Effect Model

**(i)** All the observations ($y_{ij}$'s) are independent and

$$y_{ij} \sim N(\mu_i, \sigma_e^2).$$

**(ii)** Different effects are additive in nature.

**(iii)** $\varepsilon_{ij}$ are *i.i.d.* $N(0, \sigma_0^2)$, *i.e.*, $E(\varepsilon_{ij}) = 0$ and $V(\varepsilon_{ij}) = 0$, $\forall$ $i$ and $j$.

Under the third assumption, the model becomes

$$E(y_{ij}) = \mu_i + \mu + \alpha_{ij} \quad (i = 1, 2, \ldots, k, j = 1, 2, \ldots, n)$$

## Statistical Analysis of the Fixed Effect Model

### Null Hypothesis

We want to test the equality of the population means, *i.e.*, the homogeneity of different rations.

This can also be expressed as

$$H_0 : \mu_1 = \mu_2 = \ldots = \mu_k = \mu$$

In terms of $\alpha_i$'s

$$H_0 : \alpha_1 = \alpha_2 = \ldots = \alpha_k = 0$$

$H_1$ = Alternative hypothesis : Atleast two of the means are different.

Let $\bar{y}_i$ = Mean of the $i$th class

$$= \sum_{j=1}^{n_i} \frac{y_{ij}}{n_i}, \quad i = 1, 2, \ldots, k$$

and $\bar{y}_{i,j}$ = Grand mean or (Overall mean)

$$= \frac{1}{N} \sum_{i=1}^{k} \sum_{j=1}^{n_i} y_{ij} = \frac{1}{N} \sum_{i=1}^{k} n_i \bar{y}_i$$

## Least Square Estimates of Parameters

The parameters $\mu$ and $\alpha_i$ in the fixed effect model are estimated by the principle of least squares on minising the error (residual) sum of the squares given by

$$E = \sum_i \sum_j \varepsilon_{ij}^2 = \sum_i \sum_j (y_{ij} - \mu - \alpha_i)^2$$

Now, the model becomes

| $y_{i,j}$ | $=$ | $\bar{y}_{ii}$ | $+$ | $(\bar{y}_i - \bar{y}_{ij})$ | $+$ | $(y_{ij} - \bar{y}_j)$ |
|---|---|---|---|---|---|---|
| observation | | Grand Mean | | Deviation due to $i$th treatment | | Residual or error component |

**ANOVA Table for One Way classified Data**

| Source of variation | Sum of squares | $d_1 f$ | Mean sum of squares | Variance ratio |
|---|---|---|---|---|
| Treatment (Ratio) | $S_t^2$ | $K-1$ | $s_t = \frac{S_t^2}{K-1}$ | $F = \frac{s_t^2}{s_E^2}$ |
| Error | $S_E^2$ | $N-K$ | $s_E^2 = \frac{S_E^2}{N-K}$ | $= F_{K-1, N-K}$ |
| Total | $S_T^2$ | $N-1$ | | |

## ANOVA for Random Effect Model for One Way Classified Data

In the fixed effect model $\alpha_i$'s are supposed to be constants.

In the random effect model, we suppose that there is only one source of variation, say, factor $A$, whose $k$ levels, say $A_1, A_2, \ldots, A_k$ have been selected at random from a large population of levels. The linear model (for random effects) is given by

$$y_{ij} = \mu + a_i + \varepsilon_{ij}, \quad \ldots(i)$$

$$i = 1, 2, \ldots, k$$

$$j = 1, 2, \ldots, n.$$

Here, it is supposed that all the classes are of equal size, say $n$, *i.e.*, each factor of $A$ is repeated an equal number of $n$ times.

In Eq. (i), $\mu$ = General mean effect $= \frac{1}{k} \sum_{i=1}^{k} \mu_i$

$a_i$ = Additional effect due to the $i$th level of $A$, $i = 1, 2, \ldots, k$.

(which is not constant; it is a random variable)

$\varepsilon_{ij}$ = The error effect due to chance.

Again, we assume that

$a_i$ *i.i.d.* $N(0, \sigma_a^2)$, $i = 1, 2, \ldots, k$

$\varepsilon_{ij}$ *i.i.d.* $N(0, \sigma_e^2)$, $i = 1, 2, \ldots, k$; $j = 1, 2, \ldots, n$

and $a_i$'s and $\varepsilon_{ij}$'s are mutually independent.

$$\text{var } (y_{ij}) = \text{var}(\mu + a_i + \varepsilon_{ij})$$

$$= \text{var}(a_i + \varepsilon_{ij})$$

[Variance is independent of change of origin]

$$= \text{var}(a_i) + \text{var}(\varepsilon_{ij})$$

$$= \sigma_a^2 + \sigma_e^2 \quad (a_i \text{ and } \varepsilon_{ij} \text{ are independent})$$

$\sigma_a^2$ and $\sigma_e^2$ are known as the components of the variance of $Y$ and the model (i) is known as variance component model.

**ANOVA Table For One Way Classified Data Random Effect Model.**

| Source of variation | Sum of squares | Degree of freedom | Mean S.S. | Variance ratio |
|---|---|---|---|---|
| Factor $A$ | $S_A^2$ | $K-1$ | $s_A^2 = \frac{S_A^2}{K-1}$ | $F = \frac{s_A^2}{s_E^2}$ |
| Error | $S_E^2$ | $N-K$ | $s_E^2 = \frac{S_E^2}{N-K}$ | |
| Total | $S_T^2$ | $N-1$ | | |

## Analysis of Covariance (ANOCOVA)

Analysis of covariance (ANOCOVA) is a technique in which it is possible to control certain sources of variation by taking additional observations on each of the experimental units.

Let in an experiment, $y$ be the response variable and $x$ be another variable, linearly related to $y$. Moreover, $x$ cannot be controlled experimentally; it can be observed along with the $y$'s. The variable $x$ is called the covariate/ concomitant/independent/auxiliary variable.

In analysis of covariance (ANOCOVA), we adjust the variation in the response variable ($y$) for the linear regression (effect) of the independent variable ($x$). If this is not done, then the error mean square will be inflated due to the linear effect of $x$, and makes it difficult to detect the true differences in the response variable.

ANOCOVA procedure is a combination of the analysis of variance (ANOVA) and regression analysis.

In a experimental data, whenever it is possible to take additional observations on one or more of the variables along with the response variable under study, the ANOCOVA technique is useful.

*e.g.*,

(i) Suppose, we want to compare the effect of some rations (diets) on the weight of animals, for it we use ANOCOVA. We consider

$y$ : The final weight of the animals taking ration (diet) after a specified period (days/weeks/months) as the response variable.

$x$ : The initial weight of the animals at the time of starting the experiment as the concomitant variable.

To ensure that the real difference in the final weights $y$ are due to the rations we must adjust for the linear effect of the initial weight ($x$) on $y$.

(ii) Suppose, we want to compare the differences in strength of the filament fibre ($y$) produced by different machines. Obviously, $y$ depends on the thickness ($x$) of the fibre—thicker the fibre, stronger it is. The effect of thickness ($x$) on the strength ($y$) can be eliminated by performing ANOCOVA between the response variable ($y$) and the concomitant variable ($x$), for testing the difference in the strength of the fibre produced by different machines.

## Analysis of Covariance (ANOCOVA) for One Way Classification with Single Concomitant Variable in CRD Layout

Let the problem to be compare $\nu$ treatments $t_1, t_2, \ldots, t_\nu$, $i$th treatment replicated $r_i$ times $i = 1, 2, \ldots, \nu$.

and $n = \sum_{i=1}^{\nu} r_i$ = The total number of experimental units.

We suppose that the experiment is conducted with a Completely Randomised Design (CRD) layout.

Let response variable by $y$ (dependent) and corresponding to it a single concomitant variable $x$. Then, the linear ANOCOVA model consists of the sum of two components one is the same component as in ANOVA and second is due to the regression of $y$ on the concomitant variable $x$.

Assuming a linear relationship between the response variable ($y$) and the concomitant variable ($x$), the appropriate statistical model (for fixed effects) for ANOCOVA for Completely Randomised Design (CRD) with one concomitant variable is given by

$$y_{ij} = \mu + \alpha_i + \beta(x_{ij} - \bar{x}\ldots) + \varepsilon_{ij}$$
$$(i = 1, 2, \ldots, r;\ j = 1, 2, \ldots, r_i)$$

where, in the usual notation of ANOVA.

**(i)** $\mu$ is the general mean effect.

**(ii)** $\alpha_i$ is the (fixed) additional effect due to the $i$th treatment ($i = 1, 2, \ldots, \nu$).

**(iii)** $\varepsilon_{ij}$ is the random error effect.

**(iv)** $\beta$ is the coefficient of regression of $y$ on $x$ and

**(v)** $x_{ij}$ is the value of concomitant variable corresponding to the response variable $y_{ij}$, so that

(a) $\sum_{i=1}^{k} \alpha_i = 0$

(b) $\varepsilon_{ij}\ \underbrace{i.i.d}\ N(o, \sigma_e^2)$

**Table : ANOVA Table (CRD)**

| Source of variation | Sum of squares and products | | | | Estimate of $\beta$ | Adjusted $SS_{xy}$ | Adjusted d.f. |
|---|---|---|---|---|---|---|---|
| | d.f. | $SS_{xx}$ | $SS_{xy}$ | $SS_{yy}$ | | | |
| Classes (Treatments) | $\nu-1$ | $T_{xx}$ | $T_{xy}$ | $T_{yy}$ | $\frac{E_{xy}}{E_{xx}}$ | $SSE$ | $n-\nu-1$ |
| Error | $n-\nu$ | $E_{xx}$ | $E_{xy}$ | $E_{yy}$ | $\frac{E'_{xy}}{E'_{xx}}$ | $(SSE^*)$ | $n-2$ |
| Total difference total error | $n-1$ | $E'_{xx}$ | $E'_{xy}$ | $E'_{yy}$ | | $(SSE^*) - (SSE)$ | $\nu-1$ |

Here, $E'_{xx} = \sum_i \sum_j (x_{ij} - \bar{x})^2 = SS_{xx} = T_{xx} + E_{xx}$

$$E'_{yy} = \sum_i \sum_j (y_{ij} - \bar{y})^2 = SS_{yy} = T_{yy} + E_{yy}$$

$$E'_{xy} = \sum_i \sum_j (x_{ij} - \bar{x})(y_{ij} - \bar{y})$$
$$= SS_{xy} = T_{xy} + E_{xy}$$

**Table : ANOVA Table (RBD)**

| Source of variation | d.f. | Sum of squares and products | | | Estimate of $\beta$ | Adusted $SS_{xy}$ | Adjusted d.f. |
|---|---|---|---|---|---|---|---|
| | | $SS_{xx}$ | $SS_{xy}$ | $SS_{yy}$ | | | |
| Blocks | $r-1$ | $B_{xx}$ | $B_{yy}$ | $B_{xy}$ | $\hat{\beta} = \frac{E_{xy}}{E_{xx}}$ | $SSE$ | $(r-1)(\nu-1)-1$ |
| Treatments | $\nu-1$ | $T_{xx}$ | $T_{yy}$ | $T_{xy}$ | $\hat{\beta}' = \frac{E'_{xy}}{E'_{xx}}$ | $SSE^*$ | $r(\nu-1)-1$ |
| Error | $(r-1)(\nu-1)-1$ | $E_{xx}$ | $E_{yy}$ | $E_{xy}$ | | $(SSE)^* -(SSE)$ | $\nu-1$ |
| Treatment + error difference | $r(\nu-1)$ | $E'_{xx}$ | $E'_{yy}$ | $E'_{xy}$ | | | |

$$E'_{xx} = T_{xx} + E_{xy}$$
$$E'_{yy} = T_{yy} + E_{yy}$$
$$E'_{xy} = T_{xy} + E_{xy}$$

## Mixed Effect Model

Consider two sources (factors) of variation, say $A$ and $B$, $A$ being at $p$ levels $A_i$, $i = 1, 2, \ldots, p$, and $B$ being at $q$ levels $B_j$, $j = 1, 2, \ldots, q$.

Let data observation be selected at random from a large population at levels $A$ and $B$, respectively.

Let $y_{ij}$ denote the observation under the $i$th level of $A$ and $j$th level of $B$. Then, the linear mathematical model (for random effect) will be

$$y_{ij} = \mu + a_i + b_j + c_{ij} + \varepsilon_{ij} \quad \ldots(i)$$
$$(i = 1, 2, \ldots, p;\ j = 1, 2, \ldots, q)$$

where, $a_i\ \underbrace{i.i.d.}\ N(0, \sigma_a^2)$

$b_j \ \underline{i.i.d.}\ N(0, \sigma_b^2)$
$c_{ij} \ \underline{i.i.d.}\ N(0, \sigma_{ab}^2)$
$\varepsilon_{ij} \ \underline{i.i.d.}\ N(0, \sigma_e^2)$

and $a_i$'s, $b_j$'s, $c_{ij}$'s and $\varepsilon_{ij}$'s are mutually uncorrelated, and $\mu$ is the general mean effect $a_i$ is the additional effect due to $i$th level of $A$, $b_j$ is the additional effect due to the $j$th level of $B$, $\varepsilon_{ij}$ is the random error effect and $c_{ij}$ is the interaction effect.

If all the levels of one of the factors, say $A$ are included in the experiment, *i.e.*, if $\alpha_i$'s are fixed constants and all the levels of the other factor, say $B$ are not included in the experiment, *i.e.*, if $B_j$'s are random variables then the model (1) is known as mixed effect model.

## Regression Analysis

Sir Francis Galton (1822-1911) used regression analysis to study whether the offspring having either short or tall parents, revert (regress) back to average height of the general population.

It is the study of actual relationship, if it exists between two (or more variables) by determining mathematical equations between them.

It predicts or estimates one (dependent) variable (response) in terms of other (independent) variable(s); (regression(s)).

It is used in optimization, to determine the values of independent variable (s) for which dependent variable attains maximum or minimum value.

## Simple Regression and Multiple Linear Regression

Simple regression is the relationship between two variables (one dependent variable and one independent variable).

In multiple regression the number of variables is more than two (with one dependent variable and two or more independent variables).

If the relationship between variables, then the regression is called linear.

## Regression Line of Y on X

If $Y$ is dependent on $X$, then the simple linear relation

$$Y = a_0 + a_1 X \qquad \text{...(i)}$$

is known as regression line of $Y$ on $X$.

Similarly, if $X$ depends on $Y$, then

$$X = b_0 + b_1 Y \qquad \text{...(ii)}$$

is known as regression line of $X$ on $Y$.

Multiple regression equation is given by

$$Y = f(X_1, X_2, \ldots\ldots, X_n) \qquad \text{...(iii)}$$

If Eq. (iii) is in the form

$$Y = b_0 + b_1 X_1 + b_2 X_2 + \ldots + b_n X_n,$$

then it represents multiple linear regression.

If Eq. (iii) is the form say,

$$Y = b_0 + b_1 X + b_2 X_2 + b_3 X_1 X_2 + \ldots + b_k X_k^k$$

Then, it represents multiple non-linear regression.

## Logistic Regression

In statistic, logistic regression (logistic model or logit model) is used for prediction of the probability of occurrence of an event by fitting data to a logit function (or logistic curve).

It is a generalized linear model used for binomial regression. It makes use of several predictor variables that may be either numerical or categorical.

Logistic curve always takes values between 0 and 1.

$$f(z) = \frac{e^z}{e^z + 1} = \frac{1}{1 + e^{-z}}, -\infty < z < \infty,$$

and $0 < f(z) < 1$

The variable $z$ is the measure of the total contribution of all the independent variables used in the model and is known as logit.

$z$ is defined as

$$z = \beta_0 + \beta_1 x + \beta_2 x^2 + \ldots + \beta_k x^k$$

where, $\beta_0$ is called intercept $\beta_1, \beta_2, \ldots, \beta_k$ are called regression coefficients of $x_1, x_2, \ldots, x_k$, respectively.

Logistic regression analysis binomially distributed data of the form

$$y_i \sim B(n_i, p_i) \text{ for } n = 1, 2, \ldots, m.$$

Where, the numbers of Bernoullian trials $n_i$ are known and probabilities of success $p_i$ are unknown.

The model proposes for each trial $i$, there is a set of explanatory variables that might infirm the final probability. These explanatory variables can be though of as being in a $k$-dimensional vector $X_i$, and model, then takes the form.

$$p_i = E\left(\frac{Y_i}{n_i} \middle| X_i\right)$$

The logit, natural log $s$ of the odds of the unknown binomial probabilities are modelled as the linear function of $X_i$,

$$\text{logit}(p_i) = \ln\left(\frac{p_i}{1 - p_i}\right)$$

$$= \beta_0 + \beta_1 x_{1,i} + \beta_2 x_{2,i} + \ldots + \beta_k x_{k,i}$$

## Multivariate Normal Distribution

The multivariate normal distribution of a $k$-dimensional random vector $X = [X_1, X_2, \ldots, X_k]$ is represented by $X \sim N(h, \Sigma)$ or $X \sim N_k(h, \Sigma)$ with $k$-dimensional mean vector

$$\mu = [E(X_1), E(X_2), \ldots, E(X_k)]$$

and $k \times k$ covariance matrix

$$\Sigma = [\text{Cov}(X_i, X_j)] = [\sigma_{ij}]_{k \times k}$$

$$i = 1, 2, \ldots, k; \ j = 1, 2, \ldots, k$$

$$= [\sigma_{ij}]_{k \times k}$$

where, $\sigma_{ij} = \sigma_{ji}$

The random $k$ vector $X$ is said to be multivariate normal if and only if the linear function $a'X = a_1X_1 + a_2X_2 + \ldots + a_kX_k$ where, $a' = (a_1, a_2, \ldots, a_k)$ is normal for all '$a$'.

***Theorem*** If $X$ is $k$ variate normal with mean $\mu$ and covariance matrix $\Sigma = [\sigma_{ij}]$ which is non-singular, then $X$ has a probability density function given by

$$f_X(x) = \frac{1}{(2\pi)^{k/2}|\Sigma|^{1/2}} e^{-\frac{1}{2}(x-\mu)\Sigma^{-1}(x-\mu)}$$

## The Wishart Distribution

If the mean of $X \sim N_p(\mu, \Sigma)$ is known to be $\mu = 0$, then for a data matrix $X(n \times p)$ the estimated covariance matrix is proportional to $X^TX$.

The distribution of $X^T$ is called Wishart distribution and is denoted by $W_p(\Sigma, n)$.

$$X = (x_1, x_2, \ldots, x_n)$$

It is used in the analysis of estimated covariance matrices.

For $p = 1$, $X \sim N_1(0, \sigma^2)$, for if the data matrix of the observations $X = (x_1, x_2, \ldots, x_n)^T$ with $M = X^TX = \Sigma x_i x_i^T$ leads to the Wishart distribution $W_1(\sigma^2, n) = \sigma^2 X_n^2$. This shows that one dimensional Wishart distribution is a $\chi^2_{(1)}$ (Chi-square) distribution.

***Theorem 1*** If $M \sim W_p(\Sigma, n)$ and $B(p \times q)$, then the distribution of $B^TMB$ is Wishart $W_q(B^T\Sigma B, n)$.

***Theorem 2*** If $M \sim W_p(\Sigma, m)$ and $a \in R^p$ with $a^T\Sigma a \neq 0$, then the distribution of $\dfrac{a^TMa}{a^T\Sigma a}$ is $\chi^2_m$ (Chi-square) distribution with $m$ degrees of freedom.

***Theorem 3*** (Co.chran) Let $\chi(n \times p)$ be a data matrix from a $N_p(0, \Sigma)$ distribution and let $C(n \times n)$ be a symmetric matrix. Then,

**(i)** $X^TCX$ has the distribution of weighted Wishart random variables, *i.e.*,

$$\chi^TCX = \sum_{i=1}^{n} \lambda_i W_p(\Sigma, 1)$$

where, $\lambda_i, i = 1, 2, \ldots, n$ are the eigen values of $C$.

**(ii)** $X^TCX$ has Wishart distribution if and only if $C^2 = C$. In this case, $X^TCX \sim W_p(\Sigma, r)$, and $r = \text{rank}(C) = \text{tr}(C)$.

**(iii)** $nS = \chi^TH\chi$ is distributed as $W_p(\Sigma, n-1)$, $S$ being sample covariance matrix.

**(iv)** $\bar{x}$ and $S$ are independent.

## The Properties of Wishart Distribution

**(i)** If $M \sim W_p(\Sigma, n)$, then $E(M) = n\Sigma$.

**(ii)** If $M_i$ are independent Wishart $W_p(\Sigma, n_i)$, $i = 1, \ldots, k$, then

$$M = \sum_{i=1}^{k} M_i \sim W_p(\Sigma, n) \text{ where } n = \sum_{i=1}^{k} n_i$$

**(iii)** The density function of $W_p(\Sigma, n-1)$ for a positive definite $M$ is given by

$$f_{\Sigma, n-1}(M) = \frac{|M|^{\frac{1}{2}(n-p-2)} e^{-\frac{1}{2}\text{tr}(M\Sigma^{-1})}}{2^{\frac{1}{2}p(n-1)} \Pi^{\frac{1}{4}p(p-1)} |\Sigma|^{\frac{1}{2}(n-1)} \prod_{i=1}^{p} \left|\frac{n-i}{2}\right.}$$

Where, $\Gamma$ is the gamma function.

## Partial Correlation and Partial Regression

When the values of one variable are associated with or influenced by other variable, Karl Pearson's coefficient of correlation is used as a measure of linear relationship between them.

When the values of one variable are influenced by a group of variables, then the study of the joint effect of the group of variables upon a variable (not included in the group) is called multiple correlation and multiple regression.

When in multivariate distribution we are interested in the relationship between two variables only then there arise two alternatives

**(i)** We consider only those two members of the observed data in which the other members have specified values.

**(ii)** We may eliminate mathematically the effect of other variates on two variates.

The first method has disadvantage that it limits the size of the data and also it will be applicable to only the data in which other variates has assigned values.

In the second method it may not be possible to eliminate the entire influence of the variates but the linear effect can be easily eliminated.

The correlation and regression between only two variates eliminating the linear effect of other variates in them is called the partial correlation and partial regression.

# Data Reduction Techniques

When there is a very large amount of data, it becomes difficult to manage and analyse in a limited given time.

In order to make a given data to a manageable size a data reduction technique is used.

Subsampling is a data reduction technique which reduces a very large amount of data to a manageable size which can be easily analysed in a given time. In subsampling, observation values (training points) are randomly removed.

Feature selection is another data reduction technique, which tries to retain only the best features of a data set.

Let $x = (x_1, x_2, \ldots, x_n) \in R^n$ be a set of data.

Let $S : R^n \to \mathcal{R}$ be a statistic.

Its example mean statistic is simply the average value of the data points.

Subsampling does not preserve the entire set of data; it preserves all statistics on a random subset of the data.

## Principal Component Analysis (PCA)

It is a mathematical procedure that uses an orthogonal transformation to convert a set of observations of possibly correlated variables into a set of values of uncorrelated variables called principal components.

The number of principal components is less than or equal to the number of original variables.

## Discriminant Analysis

It is a technique for classifying a set of observations into predefined classes.

The set of observations is referred to as training set. Based on training set, the technique constructs a set of linear functions of the predictors, known as discriminant functions such that

$$L = b_1x_1 + b_2x_2 + \dots + b_nx_n + c,$$

where, the $b$'s are discriminant coefficients, the $x$'s are the input variables or predictors and $c$ is a constant.

These discriminant functions are used to predict the class of a new observation with unknown class. For a $k$-class problem, $k$ discriminant functions are constructed. Given a new observation, all the $k$ discriminant functions are evaluated and the observation is assigned to class $i$, if the $i$th discriminant function has the highest value.

## Cluster Analysis

Cluster analysis or clustering is the task of assigning a set of objects into groups (called clusters) so that the objects in the same cluster are more similar (in same sense or another) to each other than to those in other clusters.

## Canonical Analysis (Correlation)

Canonical correlation is a procedure for assessing the relationship between two sets of variables.

## Computation of Eigen Values

Eigen values are proportion of variance amounted for by the correlation between the respective canonical variates. These are weighted sum scores of two sets of variables.

## Successive Eigen Values

Canonical correlations are the correlations between successively extracted canonical variates.

## Significance of Roots

Different canonical correlations are tested, one by one, beginning with the largest one, only those roots that are statistically significant are then retained for subsequent interpretation.

## Canonical Weights

Each significated canonical root represents two weighted sums, one for each set of variables. These weights are called canonical weights.

***Example 2.*** *If $ax + by + c = 0$ is line of regression of $y$ on $x$ and $a_1x + b_1y + c_1 = 0$ is line of regression of $x$ on $y$, then show that $|ab_1| \le |a_1 b|$.*

**Solution.** Line of regression of $y$ on $x$ is

$$ax + by + c = 0$$

or
$$y = -\frac{a}{b}x - \frac{c}{b}$$

$\therefore$
$$r_1 = -\frac{a}{b}$$

Line of regression of $x$ on $y$ is

$$x = -\frac{b_1}{a_1}y - \frac{c_1}{a_1}$$

$\therefore$
$$r_2 = -\frac{b_1}{a_1}$$

Then, $|r_1 r_2| \le 1$ or $|ab_1| \le |a_1 b|$.

***Example 3.*** *If $a, b, c, d$ are constants such that $a$ and $c$ are of opposite signs and $r$ is coefficient of correlation between $X$ and $Y$, then find correlation coefficient between $ax + b$ and $cy + d$.*

**Solution.** Let $U = aX + b, V = cY + d$, we can write

$$X = aU + b,\ y = cV + d, \text{ and}$$

$\therefore$
$$x_i - X = a(u_i - U), y_i - Y = c(v_i - V)$$

$\therefore$
$$r = \frac{\Sigma\, ac\,(u_i - U)\,(v_i - V)}{\sqrt{\{\Sigma a^2(u_i - U)^2\}}\sqrt{\{\Sigma\, c^2\,(v_i - V)^2\}}}$$

$$= \frac{ac\,\Sigma\,(u_i - U)\,(v_i - V)}{\pm\, ac\sqrt{\Sigma\,(u_i - U)^2}\sqrt{\Sigma\,(v_i - V)^2}}$$

or $r(X, Y) = \pm\, r(U, V)$

$r(X, Y) = r(U, V)$, if $a$ and $c$ have same sign and $r(X, Y) = -r(U, V)$, if $a$ and $c$ have opposite sign.

***Example 4.*** *If a linnear relation $aX + bY + c = 0$ exists between the variables $X$ and $Y$ and $ab < 0$, then find coefficient of correlation between $X$ and $Y$.*

**Solution.** Given $aX + bY + c = 0$ ...(i)

$\therefore$ $a\overline{X} + b\overline{Y} + c = 0$ ...(ii)

From Eqs. (i) and (ii), we get

$$a(X - \overline{X}) + b(Y - \overline{Y}) = 0$$

$\Rightarrow$
$$X - \overline{X} = -\frac{b}{a}(Y - \overline{Y}) \quad \text{...(iii)}$$

$$\text{cov}(X, Y) = \frac{1}{n}\Sigma(x_i - \overline{X})(y_i - \overline{Y}) = -\frac{b}{a}\left[\frac{1}{n}\Sigma(y_i - \overline{Y})^2\right]$$

$$= -\frac{b}{a}\text{var}(Y) \qquad \text{...(iv)}$$

Also, $\text{var}(X) = \frac{1}{n}\Sigma(x_i - X)^2 = \frac{b^2}{a^2}\left[\frac{1}{n}\Sigma(y_i - \overline{Y})^2\right]$

$$= \frac{b^2}{a^2}\text{var}(Y) \qquad \text{...(v)}$$

$$\therefore \text{cov}(X, Y) = \frac{-\frac{b}{a}\text{var}(Y)}{\sqrt{\left\{\frac{b^2}{a^2}\text{var}(Y)\right\}}\sqrt{\{\text{var}(Y)\}}} = \frac{-\frac{b}{a}}{\left|\frac{b}{a}\right|}$$

($\because ab < 0 \Rightarrow a$ and $b$ are of opposite sign)

$$= \frac{-b/a}{-b/a} = 1$$

***Example 5.*** *If variance of X, Y, X – Y are respectively,* $\sigma_x^2, \sigma_y^2, \sigma_{x-y}^2$, *then find coefficient of correlation r between two variables X and Y.*

**Solution.** Let $Z = X - Y \quad \therefore \overline{Z} = \overline{X} - \overline{Y}$

$$Z - \overline{Z} = X - \overline{X} - (Y - \overline{Y})$$

$$(Z - \overline{Z})^2 = (X - \overline{X})^2 + (Y - \overline{Y})^2 - 2(X - \overline{X})(Y - \overline{Y})$$

$$\frac{1}{n}\Sigma(Z - \overline{Z})^2 = \frac{1}{n}\Sigma(X - \overline{X})^2 + \frac{1}{n}\Sigma(Y - \overline{Y})^2 - \frac{2}{n}\Sigma(X - \overline{X})(Y - \overline{Y})$$

$$\Rightarrow \quad \sigma_z^2 = \sigma_x^2 + \sigma_y^2 - 2\,\text{cov}(X\,Y)$$

$$\Rightarrow \quad \sigma_{x-y}^2 = \sigma_x^2 + \sigma_y^2 - 2r\,\sigma_x\,\sigma_y$$

$$\therefore \quad r = \frac{\sigma_x^2 + \sigma_y^2 - \sigma_{x-y}^2}{2\sigma_x\,\sigma_y}$$

# Design of Experiments (Theory of Sampling)

## 1. Sampling

It is the selection of same part of an aggregate or totality on the basis of which a judgement or inference about the aggregate or totality is made.

## 2. Elements of Sampling

It has three elements

**(i)** Selection of the sample.
**(ii)** Collection of information about the population.
**(iii)** Making an inference about the population.

## 3. Sample

A sample is a part of the universe which we select for the purpose of investigation.

## 4. Universe

Universe is the total of the items or units in any field of enquiry.

## 5. Types of Universe

(a) **Finite and Infinite Universe** If the number of units or items or members in a universe is definite and fixed it is a finite universe, otherwise it is infinite.

(b) **Existent and Hypothetical Universe** An existent universe is one which comprises concrete items or units *e.g.*, the number of units in a jungle.
A hypothetical universe is one which is non-existent; it is imaginary.
*e.g.*, Throw of coins or dice.

## 6. Population

It is the total of the items about which information is needed.

## 7. Characteristics

The attributes which are the objects of study, are the characteristics of the elementary units.

## 8. Elementary Units

The units which possess the characteristics of the population are called elementary units.

## 9. Difference between Sample and Population

| | Population | Sample |
|---|---|---|
| 1. | Collection of items in totality being considered for study. | Part or portion of the population, is chosen for study. |
| 2. | Characteristics of the population are known as parameters. | The corresponding characteristics of the known as statistics. |
| 3. | Population size = $N$ | Sample size = $n$ |
| 4. | Population mean = $\mu$ | Sample mean = $\overline{x}$ |
| 5. | Population standard deviation = SD | Sample standard deviation = $S_i$ |

# Sampling Design

It is a definite plan for obtaining a sample from the population. It refers to the technique or procedure of selecting some sampling units from which inferences about the population are drawn.

# Sampling Frame

It refers to the (population frame) listing of all items in the population under study.

## Sampling Error

In a sample survey, only a small part of the universe or population is studied. In such study there is every possibility that its results would differ to some extent from that of the universe. Even if two or three samples of the universe are taken, the result would differ from each other. These differences among sample constitute the sampling error.

## Statistics and Parameters

A statistics is a characteristic of a sample and parameter is the characteristic of the universe or the population.

## Simple Random Sampling (SRS)

It is the technique of drawing a sample in such a way that each unit of the population has an equal and independent chance of being included in the sample.

## Stratified Random Sampling

Stratification means division into layers. Auxiliary information (past data or some other information) related to the character under study may be used to divide the population into various groups such that

(i) units within each group are as homogeneous as possible.

(ii) the group means are as widely different as possible.

Thus, a population consisting of $N$ sampling units is divided, into $K$ relatively homogeneous mutually disjoint (non-overlapping) subgroups, termed as strata, of sizes $N_1, N_2, \ldots, N_k$, such that $N = \sum_{i=1}^{K} N_i$.

If a simple random sample (generally without replacement) of size $n_i$, $(i = 1, 2, \ldots, K)$ is drawn. From each of the stratum, respectively such that $n = \sum_{i=1}^{K} n_i$, the sample is termed as Stratified Random Sample of size $n$, and the technique of drawing such a sample is called stratified Random Sampling.

## Systematic Sampling

Systematic sampling is a commonly employed technique if the complete and up-to-date list of sampling units is available. This consists in selecting only the first unit at random, the rest being automatically selected according to some predetermined pattern involving regular spacing of units.

Let us suppose that $N$ sampling units are serially numbered from 1 to $N$ in some order and a sample of size $n$ is to be drawn such that

$$N = nK \Rightarrow K = \frac{N}{n}$$

Where $K$, usually called sampling interval, is an integer.

Systematic sampling consists in drawing a random number, say $i \leq K$ and selecting the unit corresponding to this number and every $k$th unit subsequently.

Thus, the systematic sample of size $n$ will consists of the units $i$, $i + K, i + 2K, \ldots, i + (n - 1)K$.

The random number '$i$' is called the random start, and its value determines, as a matter of fact, the whole sample.

## Experimental Design

Experimental design is the plan, structure and strategy of investigation conceived as to obtain answers to research questions and to control variance.

### Plan

The plan is the overall scheme or paradigm of research. It includes an outline of what the investigation will do from writing the hypothesis and their operational implications to the final analysis of data.

### Structure

The structure of research is the outline, the scheme, the paradigm of the operation of the variables.

### Strategy

Strategy implies how the research objective will be reached and how the problems encountered will be treated. Strategy includes the methods to be used to gather and analyze the data.

### Purpose

**(a)** Experimental design helps the investigation obtain answers to the questions of experiment and also helps to control the extraneous and error variance of the particular experimental problems under study.

**(b)** Experimental design has two basic purposes.

(i) To provide answers to research questions.

(ii) To control variance.

### Construction

**1.** To maximize the variance of the variable or variables of the substantive research hypothesis.

**2.** To control the variance of extraneous or unwated variables.

**3.** To minimize the error or random variance.

## Maximization of Experimental Variances

Experimental variance simply refers to variance in the dependent variables influenced by the independent variable or variables of the substantive hypothesis. If the independent variable does not vary substantially there is little chance of separating its effect from the total variance of the dependent variables. For this purpose it is needed to design, plan and conduct the research so that the experimental conditions would be as different as possible.

### Control of Extraneous Variables

The influences of independent variables extraneous to the purpose of the study are minimized, nullified or isolated.

The ways to control the extraneous variables

**(i)** Subjects are as homogeneous as possible.

**(ii)** Through randomization.

**(iii)** Build it right into the design as an independent variable.

**(iv)** To match subjects.

## Sampling Distribution

If we take certain number of samples and compute statistical measures respectively, then the values of a particular statistic, (say mean) obtained from each sample, together with their relative frequencies will constitute the sampling distribution of the statistics (here mean).

### Precision

It is the range within which the population average or other parameters will lie in accordance with the reliability specified in the confidence level as a percentage of the estimate ± or as a numerical quantity.

### Confidence Level and Significance Level

The confidence level or reliability is the expected percentage of times that the actual value will fall within the stated precision limits. While the significance level indicates the likelihood that the answer will fall outside the range. If the confidence level is $x\%$, then the significance level will be $(100 - x)\%$.

### Replication

Replication means the repetition of the treatments under investigation. An experimenter resorts to replication in order to average out the influence of the chance factors on different experimental units. Thus, the repetition of treatments results in more reliable estimate than is possible with a single observation.

### Randomisation

In the absence of the prior knowledge of the variability of the experimental material, a process of assigning the treatments to various experimental units in a purely chance manner is called randomisation.

### Local Control

The process of reducing the experimental error by dividing the relatively heterogeneous experimental area (field) into homogeneous blocks (due to physical contiguity as fas as field experiments are concerned) is known as local control.

### Shape of Blocks and Plots

The shape and size of the blocks will usually depend upon the shape and size of the plots.

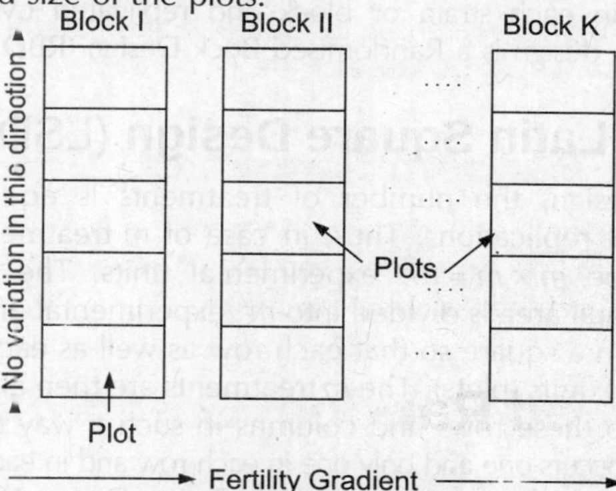


In order to control the experimental error it is desirable to divide the whole experimental area into different subgroups (blocks) such that within each block there is as much homogeneity as possible but between blocks there is maximum variation. Further, each block is divided into as many plots as the number of treatments.

For maximum precision the plots should be rectangular in shape with their long sides parallel to the direction of the fertility gradient and the blocks should be arranged one after the other along the fertility gradient as shown in the figure.

### Completely Randomised Design (CRD)

It is based an principles of randomisation and replication.

In this design treatments are allocated at random to the experimental units over the entire experimental material.

Let there be v treatments, the $i$th treatment being replicated $r_i$ times, $i = 1, 2, \dots, v$. Then, the whole experimental material is divided into $n = \Sigma r_i$ experimental units and the treatments are distributed completely at random over the units subject to the condition that the $i$th treatment occurs $r_i$ times. Randomisation assures that extraneous factors do not continually influence are treatment. In particular case, if

$$r_i = r, \forall\ i = 1, 2, \dots v$$

*i.e.*, if each treatment is repeated an equal number of times $r$, then $n = rv$ and randomisation gives every group of $r$ units an equal chance of receiving the treatments.

In general, equal number of replications for each treatment should be made except in particular cases when some treatments are of greater interest than others or when practical limitations dictate otherwise.

## Randomised Block Design (RBD)

In field experimentations, if the whole of the experimental area is not homogeneous and the fertility gradient is only in one direction, then a simple method of controlling the variability of the experimental material consists in stratifying or grouping the whole area into relatively homogeneous strata or subgroups (or blocks or replicates, as they are called), perpendicular to the direction of the fertility gradient. Now, if the treatments are applied at random to relatively homogeneous units within each strata or block and replicated over all the blocks, the design is a Randomised Bock Design (RBD).

## $m \times m$ Latin Square Design (LSD)

In this design, the number of treatments is equal to the number of replications. Thus, in case of $m$ treatments, there have to be $m \times m = m^2$ experimental units. The whole of experimental area is divided into $m^2$ experimental units (plots) arranged in a square so that each row as well as each column contains $m$ units (plots). The $m$ treatments are then allocated at random to these rows and columns in such a way that every treatment occurs one and only one in each row and in each column. Such a layout is known as $m \times m$ Latin Square Design (LSD).

## Balanced Incomplete Block Design (BIBD)

An arrangement of $v$ treatments in $b$ blocks of $k$ plots each $(k < v)$ is known as Balanced Incomplete Block Design, if

**(i)** each treatment occurs once and only once in $r$ blocks and

**(ii)** each pair of treatments occurs together in $\lambda$ blocks.

The variance of the estimate of any treatment (varity) mean which has been replicated $r$ times (*i.e.*, it occurs in $r$ blocks of the design) is $\frac{\sigma^2}{r}$ where $\sigma^2$ is error variance. Thus, in balanced Incomplete Block Design all the treatments are estimated with equal precision.

In CRD or RBD or LSD, primary concern is with the comparison and estimation of the effects of a single set of treatments like varieties of wheat, manure or different methods of cultivation etc. Such experiments which deal with one factor only may be called simple experiments.

In factorial experiment, the effects of several factors of variation are studied and investigated simultaneously, the treatments being all the combinations of different factors under study. In these experiments an attempt is made to estimate the effects of each of the factors and also the interaction effects, *i.e.*, the variation in the effect of one factor as a result to different levels of other factors.

## Basic Ideas and Notations in the $2^n$-Factorial Experiment

In the design of the $2^n$-factorial experiment there are $n$ factors, each factor having two levels.

Levels may be two quantitative levels or concentration of say, a fertilizer or it may mean two qualitative alternatives, like two species of a plant. In some cases one level is simply the control group, *i.e.*, the absence of the factor and the other is its presence.

## Confounding

The process by which unimportant comparisons are deliberately confused or mixed up or entangled with the block comparisons, for the purpose of assessing more important comparisons with greater precision is called confounding.

Confounding is also defined as the technique of reducing the size of a replication over a number of blocks at the cost of losing some information on some effect which is not of much practical importance.

The device of confounding consists of subdividing the replicate into two or more equal subgroups (blocks) and the various treatment combinations into two or more groups of equal size following certain rules by which we sacrifice some information on certain higher order interactions and allocating the treatment combinations of any group to any block at random.

## $2^2$-Design

Here, we have two factors each at two levels (0, 1), say so that there are $2 \times 2 = 4$ treatment combinations in all, using Yates' notation, let capital letters $A$ and $B$ indicate the name of the two factors under study and let the small letters $a$ and $b$ denote one of the two levels of each of the corresponding factors and this will be called second level. The first level of $A$ and $B$ is generally expressed by the absence of the corresponding letters in the treatment combinations. The four treatment combinations can be enumerated as follows

$a_0b_0$ or 1 : Factor $A$ and $B$, both at first level
$a_1b_0$ or $a$ : $A$ at second level, $B$ at first level
$a_0b_1$ or $b$ : $A$ at first level, $B$ at second level
$a_1b_1$ or $ab$ : $A$ and $B$ both at second level

These four treatment combinations can be compared by laying out the experiment in

**(i)** RBD with $r$ replicates (say), each replicate containing 4 units, or

**(ii)** $4 \times 4$ LSD and ANOVA can be carried out accordingly.

In the above cases there are 3 df associated with the treatment effects.

In factorial experiment our main objective is to carry out separate tests for the main effects $A$, $B$ and the interaction $AB$, splitting the treatment S. S with 3 df into three orthogonal components each with 1 df and each associated either with the main effect $A$ and $B$ or the intersection $AB$.

## $2^n$-Factorial Experiment

In $2^n$ factorial experiment we consider $n$ factors each at 2 levels. Suppose, $A, B, C, \ldots, K$ are the factors each at two levels (0, 1). Corresponding small letters $a, b, c, \ldots, k$ denote the corresponding factors at the second level, the first level of any factor being signified by the absence of the corresponding small letters. The treatment combinations, in standard order, can be written as

1, a, b, ab, c, ac, bc, abc, d, ad, bd, abd, cd, acd, bcd, abcd, e, ae, be, abe, ce, ace, bce, abce, de, ade, bde, abde, cde,

acde, bcde, abcde, etc.

For $2^n$ experiment, the various factorial effects are enumerated as follows

Main effects : $\binom{n}{1}$ in number

Two factor interactions : $\binom{n}{2}$ in number

Three factor interactions : $\binom{n}{3}$ in number

... ... ...

... ... ...

$n$ factor interaction : $\binom{n}{n}$ in number.

Hence, the total number of factorial effects in $2^n$ experiment are

$$\binom{n}{1}+\binom{n}{2}+\ldots+\binom{n}{n}=\binom{n}{0}+\binom{n}{1}+\binom{n}{2}+\ldots+\binom{n}{n}-\binom{n}{0}$$

$$=(1+1)^n-1=2^n-1$$

## Hazard Function (or Failure Rate or Hazard Rate or Fare of Mortality)

$h(x)$ is the ratio of the probability function $P(x)$ to the survival function $S(x)$.

Thus, $$h(x)=\frac{P(x)}{S(x)}=\frac{P(x)}{1-D(x)}$$

where, $D(x)=1-S(x)$

$D(x)$ is called distribution function.

Let $f(t)$ be probability density function of failure per unit of time.

Cumulative distribution function of failure, $F(t)$ is given by

$$F(t)=\int_0^t f(t)\,dt$$

$F(t)$ is also called unreliability.

Survival function (or reliability function) $R(t)=1-F(t)$

Hazard rate $h(t)=\dfrac{f(t)}{R(t)}$.

The conditional probability of failure

$$=\frac{R(t)-R(t+L)}{R(t)}$$

= Probability that the item fails in the interval $[t, t+L]$, given that it has not failed up to time $t$.

Its graph resembles the shape of the hazard rate curve, when the interval length is small enough, the conditional probability of failure is approximately $h(t)\cdot L$

$H(t)=$ cumulative hazard function

$$=\int_{-0}^{t} h(t)\,dt$$

## Censoring

When we have a problem to investigate a population to determine reliability of its units with respect to their functioning during a fixed time say $T$, then the data obtained is called censored type I data.

During the $T$ hours of test we observe $r$ failures (where $r$ can be any number from 0 to $n$). Let the exact failure times be $t_1, t_2, \ldots, t_r$ and there be $(n-r)$ units which survived the entire $T$ hour test without failing. This type of 'censoring is censored type I data' or 'right censored data'.

When we observe $t_1, t_2, \ldots, t_r$, exactly $r$ failure times in advance and test units until they occur, then test ends at time $T=t_r$ and $(n-r)$ units survive. Then, data obtained is called censored type II data.

## Readout or Interval Data

Sometimes exact times of failure are not know, only an interval of time in which the failure occurred is recorded. This kind of data is called readout or interval data and the situation is as follows

n units → start test; 0, $T_1$ ($r_1$ fail), $T_2$ ($r_2$ fail), $T_3$ ($r_3$ fail), $T_k=T$ ($n-\Sigma r_i$ left)

## Rate of a Vital Event

It is defined as the ratio of the total number of occurrences of the event to the total number of persons exposed to the risk of occurrence of that event.

## Sex Ratio

It is defined as the total number of females per thousand males.

$$\text{Sex ratio}=\frac{\text{Female population}}{\text{Male population}}\times 1000$$

$$=\frac{f_p}{m_p}\times 1000$$

Usually, the population $P_t$ is not constant and keeps changing from time to time. An estimate of the population in the middle of the period $[t_1, t_2]$ is given by the mean of the population at the extremities, *i.e.*,

$$P_{\left(\frac{t_1+t_2}{2}\right)}=\frac{1}{2}[P_{t_1}+P_{t_2}]$$

## Crude Death Rate (CDR)

It is defined as the number of deaths (from all causes) per $k$ persons in the population of any given region or community during a given period.

In particular, annual crude death rate (CDR) denoted by $m$, for any given region or community is given by

$$m = \frac{\text{Annual deaths}}{\text{Annual mean population}} \times k$$

where, $k = 1000$ (usually)

The crude death rate for any period gives the rate at which the population is depleted through deaths over the course of the period.

***Example 6.*** *The minimum number of replications so that an observed difference of 10% of the mean will be taken as significant at 5% level, find the CV of the plot values being 12%.*

**Solution.** Let $r$ be the required number of replications and $\mu$ be the common mean.

Then, coefficient of variation CV = 12

We know $\quad CV = 100\frac{\sigma}{\mu}$

$$\Rightarrow \quad \sigma = \frac{\mu \cdot (CV)}{100} = \frac{\mu \times 12}{100} = 0.12\mu$$

Given, $\bar{x}_1 - \bar{x}_2 = 10\%$ of $\mu = \frac{10}{100}\mu = 0.10\mu$

So, $$t = \frac{\bar{x}_1 - \bar{x}_2}{\sigma\sqrt{2/r}} = \frac{0.10\mu}{0.12\mu\sqrt{(2/r)}}$$

for $t$ to be significant at 5% level of significance,

$$|t| > 1.96 \Rightarrow \frac{10}{12}\sqrt{\frac{r}{2}} > 1.96$$

$$\Rightarrow \quad r > 2(1.96 \times 1.2)^2 = 11.1$$

Hence, the required (minimum) number of replication is 12 (the next integer greater than 11.1)

***Example 7.*** *Consider a population of 6 units with values 1, 2, 3, 4, 5, 6. Draw all possible samples of size 2 without replacement from the population. Then, Show that*

1. sample mean is unbiased estimate of the population mean
2. sampling variance is same as the variance of the sample mean
3. variance (srswor) < variance (srswr)

**Solution.**

| Y | $Y^2$ |
|---|---|
| 1 | 1 |
| 2 | 4 |
| 3 | 9 |
| 4 | 16 |
| 5 | 25 |
| 6 | 36 |
| **Total** 21 | 91 |

Mean of the population

$$\bar{y} = \frac{1}{N}\Sigma Y = \frac{21}{6} = 3.5$$

Mean square for the population

$$S^2 = \frac{1}{N-1}\Sigma(Y-\bar{Y})^2$$
$$= \frac{1}{N-1}\Sigma(Y^2 + \bar{Y}^2 - 2Y\bar{Y})$$
$$= \frac{1}{N-1}\Sigma(Y^2 + N\bar{Y}^2 - 2N\bar{Y}\bar{Y})$$
$$= \frac{1}{N-1}\Sigma(Y^2 - N\bar{Y}^2)$$
$$= \frac{1}{6-1}(91 - 6\times(3.5)^2)$$
$$= \frac{1}{5}(91 - 6\times 12.25) = 3.5$$

$$\text{Population variance } \sigma^2 = \frac{1}{N}\Sigma(Y-\bar{Y}^2)$$
$$= \frac{(N-1)}{N}S^2 = \frac{5}{6}\times 3.5 = 2.917$$

1. The total number of samples of size $n = 2$ from a population of $N = 6$ units is ${}^6C_2 = 15$.

| Sample Number | Sample Values $y$ | Sample Mean $\bar{y}$ | $(\bar{y} - \bar{Y})$ | $(\bar{y} - \bar{Y})^2$ |
|---|---|---|---|---|
| 1 | (1, 2) | 1+2/2 = 1.5 | −2.0 | 4.00 |
| 2 | (1, 3) | 1+3/2 = 2.0 | −1.5 | 2.25 |
| 3 | (1, 4) | 2.5 | −1.0 | 1.00 |
| 4 | (1, 5) | 3.0 | −0.5 | 0.25 |
| 5 | (1, 6) | 3.5 | 0 | 0.00 |
| 6 | (2, 3) | 2.5 | −1.0 | 1.00 |
| 7 | (2, 4) | 3.0 | −0.5 | 0.25 |
| 8 | (2, 5) | 3.5 | 0 | 0.00 |
| 9 | (2, 6) | 4.0 | 0.5 | 0.25 |
| 10 | (3, 4) | 3.5 | 0 | 0.00 |
| 11 | (3, 5) | 4.0 | 0.5 | 0.25 |
| 12 | (3, 6) | 4.5 | 1.0 | 1.00 |
| 13 | (4, 5) | 4.5 | 1.0 | 1.00 |
| 14 | (4, 6) | 5.0 | 1.5 | 2.25 |
| 15 | (5, 6) | 5.5 | 2.0 | 4.00 |
| **Total** | | 52.5 | 0 | 17.50 |

$$E(\bar{y}) = \frac{\sum_{i=1}^{6}\bar{y}_i}{\binom{N}{n}} = \frac{52.5}{15} = 3.5 = \bar{Y}$$

Thus, $E(\bar{y}) = \bar{Y}$

$\Rightarrow$ Sample mean $\bar{y}$ is an unbiased estimate of population mean $\bar{Y}$.

2. $$\text{var}(\bar{y}) = \frac{1}{\binom{N}{n}}\sum_{i=1}^{15}(\bar{y}_i - \bar{Y})^2 = \frac{1}{15}\sum_{i=1}^{15}(\bar{y}_i - \bar{Y})^2$$
$$= \frac{17.50}{15} = 1.167$$

In simple random sampling without replacement (srswor), variance of sample mean

$$= \frac{N-n}{Nn} S^2 = \frac{(6-2)}{(6\times 2)} \cdot (3.5)$$

$$= \frac{3.5}{3} = 1.167$$

This, shows that sampling variance is same as the variance of the sample mean.

3. $\text{var}(\bar{y})$ in (srswor) $= 1.167$

$$\text{var}(\bar{y}) \text{ in (srswr)} = \frac{\sigma^2}{n} = \frac{2.917}{2} = 1.458$$

$\Rightarrow$ $\text{var}(\bar{y})$ in (srswr) > $\text{var}(\bar{y})$ in (srswor)

***Example 8.*** *A sample of 30 students is to be drawn from a population consisting of 300 students belonging to two colleges A and B. The means and standard deviations of their marks are given below*

| | Total Number of Students ($N_i$) | Mean ($\bar{Y}_{N_i}$) | Standard Deviation ($\sigma_i$) |
|---|---|---|---|
| College $A$ | 200 | 30 | 10 |
| College $B$ | 100 | 60 | 40 |

*Using proportional allocation technique determine the sample sizes for colleges A and B.*

**Solution.** 1. We consider the colleges $A$ and $B$ as representing two strata. Then, the problem is to draw a stratified random sample of size 30 using technique of proportional allocation. In proportional allocation, we have

$$n_i = \frac{n}{N} \cdot N_i = \frac{30}{300} N_i$$

$\Rightarrow$ For college $A$, $n_1 = \frac{1}{10} \times 200 = 20$

For college $B$, $n_2 = \frac{1}{10} \times 100 = 10$

Thus, the required sample sizes for the colleges $A$ and $B$ are 20 and 10, respectively.

2. Determine the variance of the estimate of population mean in stratified random sampling with proportional allocation and variance of the estimate of population mean in unstratified simple random sampling.

To calculate $\text{var}(\bar{Y}_{st})_P$ and $\text{var}(\bar{Y}_n)_R$

| College | $N_i$ | $\bar{Y}_{N_i}$ | $\sigma_i$ | $\sigma_i^2$ | $S_i^2 = \frac{N}{N-1}\sigma_i^2$ |
|---|---|---|---|---|---|
| **A** | 200 | 30 | 10 | 100 | 100.3344 |
| **B** | 100 | 60 | 40 | 1600 | 1605.3511 |
| Total | | 90 | | 1700 | 1705.6855 |

| $N_i\bar{Y}_{N_i}$ | $N_i\bar{Y}_{N_i}^2$ | $N_iS_i^2$ | $N_i\sigma_i^2$ |
|---|---|---|---|
| 6000 | 180000 | 20066.88 | 20000 |
| 6000 | 360000 | 160535.11 | 16000 |
| 12000 | 540000 | 180601.99 | 180000 |

Here, $N = 300, n = 30$

$$\bar{Y}_N = \frac{1}{N}\sum_{i=1}^{2} N_i\bar{Y}_{N_i} = \frac{1}{300} \times 12000 = 40$$

$$\bar{Y}_N = 40$$

$$S^2 = \frac{1}{N-1}\Sigma\Sigma(Y_{ij} - \bar{Y}_N)^2$$

$$= \frac{1}{N-1}\Sigma\Sigma(Y_{ij} - \bar{Y}_{N_i} + \bar{Y}_{N_i} - \bar{Y}_N)^2$$

$$= \frac{1}{N-1}\left[\sum_{i=1}^{2} N_i\sigma_i^2 + \sum_{i=1}^{2} N_i(\bar{Y}_{N_i} - \bar{Y}_N)^2\right]$$

$$= \frac{1}{299}[180000 + 540000 - 480000]$$

$$= \frac{240000}{299}$$

In srswor, $\text{var}(\bar{Y}_n)_R = \frac{N-n}{Nn} \cdot S^2$

$$= \frac{(300-30)}{300\times 30} \cdot \frac{240000}{299}$$

$$= \frac{7200}{299} = 24.08$$

$$\text{var}(\bar{Y}_{st})_P = \frac{N-n}{nN^2}\sum_{i=1}^{2} N_iS_i^2$$

$$= \frac{(300-30)}{30\times(300)^2} \times 180601.99$$

$$= \frac{270 \times 180601.99}{2700000} = 18.0602$$

3. What is the gain in efficiency due to stratified random sampling (proportional allocation) over srswor.

Required gain in efficiency

$$= \frac{\text{var}(\bar{y}_n)_R - \text{var}(\bar{y}_{st})_P}{\text{var}(\bar{Y}_{st})_P}$$

$$= \frac{24.08 - 18.06}{18.06} = 0.333$$

So, gain in efficiency = 33.3%

***Example 9.*** *In simple random sampling without replacement (srswor), the sample mean is an unbiased estimate of the population mean.*

**Solution.** $E(\bar{Y}_n) = E\left[\frac{1}{n}\sum_{i=1}^{N} a_iY_i\right] = \frac{1}{n}\sum_{i=1}^{N} E(a_i)Y_i$

Since, $a_i$ takes only two values 1 and 0,

$$E(a_i) = 1 \cdot P(a_i = 1) + 0 \cdot P(a_i = 0)$$

$= 1 \cdot P$ ($i$th unit is included in a sample of size $n$) + $0 \cdot P$ ($i$th unit is not included in a sample of size $n$)

$$= 1 \cdot \frac{n}{N} + 0 \cdot \left(1 - \frac{n}{N}\right) = \frac{n}{N}$$

Hence, $E(\bar{y}_n) = \frac{1}{n}\sum_{i=1}^{N}\frac{n}{N}Y_i = \sum_{i=1}^{N}\frac{Y_i}{N} = \frac{1}{N}\sum_{i=1}^{N} Y_i$

or $E(\bar{y}_n) = \bar{Y}_N$

$\Rightarrow$ Sample mean is an unbiased estimate of the population mean.

# SOLVED EXAMPLES

## Type I (Only one correct option)

***Example 1.*** *If $x = 4$ of $n = 20$ patients suffered serious side effects from a new medication, testing the null hypothesis $\theta = 0.50$ against the alternative hypothesis $\theta \neq 0.50$ at the 0.05 level of significance, Here, $\theta$ is the true proportion of patients suffering serious side effects from the new medication. Then,*

(a) the null hypothesis must be rejected
(b) the null hypothesis is accepted
(c) the *p*-value is zero
(d) the *p*-value is one

**Solution.** (a) 1. $H_0 : \theta = 0.50$

$H_1 : \theta \neq 0.50, \alpha = 0.05$

2. Use the test statistic $X$, the observed number of successes.
3. $x = 4$, and since $P(X \le 4) = 0.0059$, the *P*-value is $2\,(0.0059) = 0.0118$.
4. Since, the *P*-value, 0.0118 is less than 0.05, the null hypothesis must be rejected; we conclude that $\theta \neq 0.50$.

***Example 2.*** *If the joint density of $X_1$, $X_2$ and $X_3$ is given by*

$$f(x_1, x_2, x_3) = \begin{cases} (x_1 + x_2)\, e^{-x_3} & \text{for } 0 < x_1 < 1, 0 < x_2 < 1, x_3 > 0 \\ 0, & \text{elsewhere} \end{cases}$$

*Then, the regression equation of $X_2$ on $X_1$ and $X_3$ is*

(a) $\dfrac{x_1 + \frac{2}{3}}{2x_1 + 1}$ (b) $\dfrac{x_1}{x_1 + 1}$

(c) $x_1 + x_2$ (d) $\dfrac{x_1 + x_2}{x_3}$

**Solution.** (a) The joint marginal density of $X_1$ and $X_3$ is given by

$$m(x_1, x_3) = \begin{cases} \left(x_1 + \dfrac{1}{2}\right) e^{-x_3} & \text{for } 0 < x_1 < 1, x_3 > 0 \\ 0 & \text{elsewhere} \end{cases}$$

Therefore,

$$\mu_{x_2 | x_1, x_3} = \int_{-\infty}^{\infty} x_2 \cdot \frac{f(x_1, x_2, x_3)}{m(x_1, x_3)}\, dx_2$$

$$= \int_0^1 \frac{x_2 (x_1 + x_2)}{\left(x_1 + \dfrac{1}{2}\right)}\, dx_2 = \frac{x_1 + \frac{2}{3}}{2x_1 + 1}$$

***Example 3.*** *A study is made to determine the proportion of voters in a sizeable community who favour the construction of a nuclear power plant. If 140 of 400 voters selected at random favour the project and we use $\hat{\theta} = \dfrac{140}{400} = 0.35$ as an estimate of the actual proportion of all voters in the community who favour the project.*

(a) With 99% confidence the error is less than 0.06
(b) With 99% confidence the error is greater than 0.06
(c) With 90% confidence the error is less than 0.05
(d) With 90% confidence the error is greater than 0.05

**Solution.** (a) Substituting $n = 400$, $\hat{\theta} = 0.35$, and $z_{0.005} = 2.575$ into the formula of

$$z_{\alpha/2} \cdot \sqrt{\frac{\hat{\theta}(1 - \hat{\theta})}{n}}$$

We get $2.575 \cdot \sqrt{\dfrac{(0.35)(0.65)}{400}} = 0.061$

or 0.06 rounded to two decimals. Thus, if we use $\hat{\theta} = 0.35$ as an estimate of the actual proportion of voters in the community who favour the project, we can assert with 99% confidence that the error is less than 0.06

***Example 4.*** *In a random sample, 136 of 400 persons given a flu vaccine experienced some discomfort. Construct a 95% confidence interval for the true proportion of persons who will experience some discomfort from the vaccine,*

(a) (0.204, 0.306) (b) (0.29, 0.39)
(c) [1, 2] (d) [0.6, 0.9]

**Solution.** (b) Substituting $n = 400$, $\hat{\theta} = \dfrac{136}{400} = 0.34$ and $z_{0.025} = 1.96$ into the confidence interval

formula of $\hat{\theta} - z_{\alpha/2} \cdot \sqrt{\dfrac{\hat{\theta}(1 - \hat{\theta})}{n}} < \theta < \hat{\theta}0 + z_{\alpha/2} \cdot \sqrt{\dfrac{\hat{\theta}(1 - \hat{\theta})}{n}}$,

We get $0.34 - 1.96 \sqrt{\dfrac{(0.34)(0.66)}{400}} < \theta < 0.34 + 1.96 \sqrt{\dfrac{(0.34)(0.66)}{400}}$

$$0.29 < \theta < 0.386$$

or rounding to two decimals, $0.29 < \theta < 0.39$

***Example 5.*** *A company manufactures impellers for use in jet-turbine engines. One of the operations involves grinding a particular surface finish on a titanium alloy component. Two different grinding processes can be used, and both processes can produce parts at identical mean surface roughness. The manufacturing engineer would like to select the process having the least variability in surface roughness. A random sample of $n_1 = 11$ parts from the first process results in a sample standard deviation $s_1 = 5.1$ microinches, and a random sample of $n_2 = 16$ parts from the second process results in a sample standard deviation of $s_2 = 4.7$ microinches. Find a 90% confidence interval on the ratio of the two standard deviations, $\sigma_1/\sigma_2$.*

(a) The standard deviations of surface roughness for the two processes are different at the 90% level of confidence.

(b) The standard deviations of surface roughness for the two processes are same at the 90% level of confidence
(c) Both (a) and (b)
(d) Neither (a) nor (b)

**Solution.** (a) Assuming that the two processes are independent and that surface roughness is normally distributed, we get

$$\frac{s_1^2}{s_2^2} f_{0.95,15,10} \le \frac{\sigma_1^2}{\sigma_2^2} \le \frac{s_1^2}{s_2^2} f_{0.95,15,10}$$

$$\frac{(5.1)^2}{(4.7)^2} 0.39 \le \frac{\sigma_1^2}{\sigma_2^2} \le \frac{(5.1)^2}{(4.7)^2} 2.85$$

or upon completing the implied calculations and taking square roots,

$$0.678 \le \frac{\sigma_1}{\sigma_2} \le 1.887$$

Here, $f_{0.95,15,10} = 1/f_{0.05,10,15} = 1/2.54 = 0.39$ Since this confidence interval includes unity, we cannot claim that the standard deviations of surface roughness for the two processes are different at the 90% level of confidence.

***Example 6.*** *If the two lines of regression are perpendicular to each other, then the relation between the regression coefficients is*

(a) $\beta_{xy} = \beta_{yx}$ (b) $\beta_{xy} \cdot \beta_{yx} = 1$
(c) $\beta_{xy} + \beta_{yx} = 1$ (d) $\beta_{yx} + \beta_{xy} = 0$

**Solution.** (d) We have, $\tan\phi_1 = r\frac{\sigma_y}{\sigma_x} = b_{xy}$

and $$\tan\phi_2 = \frac{\sigma_y}{r\sigma_x} = \frac{1}{b_{yx}}$$

$\therefore$ $$\tan(\phi_1 - \phi_2) = \frac{\tan\phi_1 - \tan\phi_2}{1 + \tan\phi_1 \tan\phi_2}$$

$\Rightarrow$ $$\tan\phi_1 \tan\phi_2 + 1 = 0$$

$$r\frac{\sigma_y}{\sigma_x} \cdot \frac{\sigma_y}{r\sigma_x} + 1 = 0$$

$$b_{xy}\frac{1}{b_{yx}} + 1 = 0$$

$$b_{xy} + b_{yx} = 0$$

***Example 7.*** *Let $b_{yx}$ and $b_{xy}$ denote the regression coefficient of y on x and of x on y, respectively. Then, $b_{yx} = b_{xy}$ implies that*

(a) $\sigma_y = \sigma_x$ (b) $\rho = 1$
(c) $\rho = 0$ (d) None of these

**Solution.** (a) We have, $b_{yx} = \sigma_{xy} \Rightarrow r\frac{\sigma_y}{\sigma_x} = r\frac{\sigma_x}{\sigma_y}$

$\Rightarrow \sigma_y^2 = \sigma_x^2 \Rightarrow \sigma_y = \sigma_x$

***Example 8.*** *95% confidence limits and the confidence intervals for a correlation coefficient which is computed to be 0.60 from a sample of size 28 is*

(a) 0.29236, 0.7951 and [0.29236, 0.7951]
(b) 0.19236, 0.9951 and [0.19236, 0.951]
(c) 0.09236, 0.4951 and [0.09236, 0.4951]
(d) None of the above

**Solution.** (a) We have, $r = 0.60$, $n = 28$, and $\alpha = 0.05$

Confidence limits (CL) for $\mu_2$ are $z \pm 1.96\sigma_z$.

Where, for $r = 0.60$, $z = 0.693$

and $$\sigma_2 = \frac{1}{\sqrt{n-3}} = \frac{1}{\sqrt{28-3}} = \frac{1}{5} = 0.2$$

So, $\mu_2$ has limits as

$$0.693 \pm 1.96(0.2)$$
$$= 0.3011516,\ 1.0851516$$

So, confidence interval for $\mu_2$ is

$$(0.3011516,\ 1.0851516)$$

Using $$\mu_2 = \frac{1}{2}\log_e\frac{(1+\rho)}{(1-\rho)}$$
$$= 1.1513\log_{10}\frac{(1+\rho)}{(1-\rho)}$$

We have, for $0.30115 = \mu_z = 1.1513\log_{10}\frac{(1+\rho)}{(1-\rho)}$

$\Rightarrow$ $$\rho = \frac{0.826}{2.826} = 0.29236$$

for $$1.0851 = \mu_z = 1.1513\log_{10}\frac{(1+\rho)}{(1-\rho)}$$

$\Rightarrow$ $$\rho = \frac{7.7608}{9.7608} = 0.7951$$

So, confidence limits are 0.29236, and 0.7951 and confidence interval is [0.29236, 0.7951].

***Example 9.*** *Given two variables x and y, x being our velocity in cm/s, and y, evaporation coefficient in mm²/s of burning fuel droplets in an impulse engine, with $n = 10$ and $r = 0.9515$.*
*Null hypothesis $H_0 : \rho = 0$*
*Alternative hypothesis $H_1 : \rho \ne 0$.*
*Then,*

(a) $H_0$ is rejected (b) $H_0$ is accepted
(c) It is one tailed test (d) None of these

**Solution.** (a) We have, $H_0 : \rho = 0$
$H_1 : \rho \ne 0$

As, $r = 0.9515 = 0.95 = 95\%$
So, $\alpha = 5\% = 0.05$

$\alpha$ is level of significance.

Critical region : (two tailed test)

$H_0$ is rejected, if $z > z_{\alpha/2} = 1.96$
or $z < -z_{\alpha/2} = -1.96$

For $r = 0.95$ from the table, we get

$$z^* = \frac{1}{2}\log_e\frac{1+r}{1-r} = 1.832$$

So, $$z = \sqrt{n-3}\ z^* = (\sqrt{10-3})(1.832)$$
$$= 4.847$$

As, $$z = 4.847 > 1.96 = z_{\alpha/2}$$

$\Rightarrow H_0$ is rejected and there is linear relation between x and y.

**Example 10.** *In a certain paired data $n = 18$ and $r = 0.44$*
*Null hypothesis $H_0$* : $\rho = 0.30$
*Alternative hypothesis $H_1$* : $\rho > 0.30$
*Level of significance $\alpha = 0.01$*
*Then,*

(a) $H_0$ is accepted
(b) $H_0$ is rejected
(c) It is two tailed test
(d) None of these

**Solution.** (a) Here, null hypothesis $H_0 : \rho = 0.30$

Alternative hypothesis $H_1 : \rho > 0.30$

Level of significance $\alpha = 0.01$

Critical region : Right one tailed test

Reject null hypothesis test of $z > 2.33 = z_\alpha$

For $r = 0.44$ from table, we get

$$z^* = \frac{1}{2}\log_e\left(\frac{r+1}{r-1}\right) = 0.472$$

So, $z = \sqrt{n-3}\, z^* = \sqrt{18-3}\ (0.472)$

$= 1.828$ .

As $z = 1.828 < z_\alpha = 2.33,$

So, null hypothesis $H_0 : \rho = 0.30$ is accepted.

**Example 11.** *Let $z = ax + by$ and $r$ be the correlation coefficient between x and y.*

(i) *Then,*

(a) $\sigma_z^2 = a^2\sigma_x^2 + b^2\sigma_y^2 - 2abr\,\sigma_x\sigma_y$

(b) $\sigma_z^2 = a^2\sigma_x^2 + b^2\sigma_y^2 + 2abr\,\sigma_x\sigma_y$

(c) $\sigma_z^2 = r(a^2\sigma_x^2 + b^2\sigma_y^2)$

(d) None of the above

(ii) *Then,*

(a) $r = \dfrac{\sigma_x^2 + \sigma_y^2 - \sigma_{x+y}^2}{2\sigma_x\sigma_y}$
(b) $r = \dfrac{\sigma_x^2 + \sigma_y^2 - \sigma_{x-y}^2}{2\sigma_x\sigma_y}$

(c) $r = \dfrac{\sigma_x^2 + \sigma_y^2}{2\sigma_x\sigma_y}$
(d) None of these

**Solution.**

(i) (b) We have, $z = ax + by$

$\Rightarrow$ $E(z) = aE(x) + bE(y)$

$z - E(z) = (ax + by) - [aE(x) + bE(y)]$

or $z - E(z) = a(x - E(x)) + b(y - E(y))$

On squaring both sides, we get

$$[z - E(z)]^2 = a^2[x - E(x)]^2 + b^2[y - E(y)]^2 + 2ab[x - E(x)][y - E(y)]$$

On taking expectation of both sides, we get

$$E[z - E(z)]^2 = a^2E[x - E(x)]^2 + b^2E[y - E(y)]^2 + 2abE[x - E(x)][y - E(y)]$$

or $\sigma_z^2 = a^2\sigma_x^2 + b^2\sigma_y^2 + 2abr\sigma_x\sigma_y$

$\left[\text{As, } r = \dfrac{\text{cov}(x,y)}{\sigma_x\sigma_y} = \dfrac{E[(x - E(x))(y - E(y))]}{\sigma_x\sigma_y}\right]$

(ii) (b) We know that, if $z = ax + by$, then

$$\sigma_z^2 = a^2\sigma_x^2 + b^2\sigma_y^2 + 2abr\,\sigma_x\sigma_y$$

Putting $a = 1$, $b = -1$, we get $z = x - y$

Then, $\sigma_{x-y}^2 = \sigma_x^2 + \sigma_y^2 - 2r\,\sigma_x\sigma_y$

$\Rightarrow$ $r = \dfrac{\sigma_x^2 + \sigma_y^2 - \sigma_{x-y}^2}{2\sigma_x\sigma_y}$.

**Example 12.** *In the case of perfect correlation both the lines of regression.*

(a) are perpendicular to each other

(b) are coincident

(c) make angle of $\pi/4$ with each other

(d) make angle of $\pi/6$ with each other

**Solution.** (b) In the case of perfect correlation, positive or negative,

$r =$ coefficient of correlation $= \pm 1$.

The equation of line of regression of y on x becomes

$$Y - \bar{y} = \pm\frac{\sigma_y}{\sigma_x}(x - \bar{x})$$

$$\Rightarrow \quad \frac{Y - \bar{y}}{\sigma_y} = \pm\frac{(x - \bar{x})}{\sigma_x} \quad \text{...(i)}$$

Similarly, the equation of the line of regression of x and y becomes

$$X - \bar{x} = \pm\frac{\sigma_x}{\sigma_y}(y - \bar{y})$$

$$\Rightarrow \quad \frac{Y - \bar{y}}{\sigma_y} = \pm\frac{(x - \bar{x})}{\sigma_x} \quad \text{...(ii)}$$

From Eqs. (i) and (ii), we see in the case of perfect correlation ($r = \pm 1$) both the lines of regression coincide.

**Example 13.** *The variables x and y are connected by the equation $ax + by + c = 0$. Then, the correlation between them is*

(a) $+1, \ \forall\ a, b$

(b) $-1, \ \forall\ a, b$

(c) $\pm 1$ if a and b are of opposite sign or of same sign

(d) $\pm 1$ if a and b are of same sign or of opposite sign

**Solution.** (d) We have, $ax + by + c = 0$

$\Rightarrow$ $aE(X) + bE(Y) + c = 0$

From these we have

$a(X - E(X)) + b(Y - E(Y)) = 0$

or $(X - E(X)) = -\dfrac{b}{a}(Y - E(Y))$

Now, $\text{cov}(X,Y) = E(X - E(X))(Y - E(Y))$

$$= E\left[-\frac{b}{a}(Y - E(Y))(Y - E(Y))\right]$$

$$= -\frac{b}{a}E(Y - E(Y))^2$$

$$= -\frac{b}{a}\sigma_Y^2$$

Also, $E[X - E(X)]^2 = \dfrac{b^2}{a^2}E(Y - E(Y))^2$

$$= \frac{b^2}{a^2}\sigma_Y^2$$

Now, $$r = \frac{\text{cov}(X,Y)}{\sigma_x\sigma_y} = \frac{-\frac{b}{a}\sigma_Y^2}{\sqrt{\sigma_X^2}\sqrt{\sigma_Y^2}}$$

$$= \frac{-\frac{b}{a}\sigma_Y^2}{\left|\frac{b}{a}\right|\sigma_Y \cdot \sigma_Y} = -\frac{\left(\frac{b}{a}\right)}{\left|\frac{b}{a}\right|}$$

$= +1$, if $b$ and $a$ are of opposite sign

$= -1$, if $b$ and $a$ are of same sign

***Example 14.*** *A computer while calculating correlation coefficient between two variables X and Y from 25 pairs of observations observed from the following results*

$$n = 25,\ \Sigma X = 125,\ \Sigma X^2 = 650$$

$$\Sigma Y = 100,\ \Sigma Y^2 = 460,\ \Sigma XY = 508$$

*It was, however, later discovered at the time of checking that he has copied down two pairs as*

| X | Y |
|---|---|
| 6 | 14 |
| 8 | 6 |

*while the correct values were.*

| X | Y |
|---|---|
| 8 | 12 |
| 6 | 8 |

*Then, the correct value of correlation coefficient is*

(a) 0.17 (b) 0.37
(c) 0.67 (d) 0.97

**Solution.** (c) Corrected $\Sigma X = 125 - 6 - 8 + 8 + 6 = 125$

Corrected $\Sigma Y = 100 - 14 - 6 + 12 + 8 = 100$

Corrected $\Sigma X^2 = 650 - 6^2 - 8^2 + 8^2 + 6^2 = 650$

Corrected $\Sigma Y^2 = 460 - 14^2 - 6^2 + 12^2 + 8^2 = 436$

Corrected $\Sigma XY = 508 - 6\times14 - 8\times6 + 8\times12 + 6\times8 = 520$

$$\overline{X} = \frac{1}{n}\Sigma X = \frac{1}{25}\times125 = 5$$

$$\overline{Y} = \frac{1}{n}\Sigma Y = \frac{1}{25}\times100 = 4$$

$$\text{cov}(X,Y) = \frac{1}{n}\Sigma XY - \overline{X}\overline{Y} = \frac{1}{25}\times520 - 5\times4 = \frac{4}{5}$$

$$\sigma_x^2 = \frac{1}{n}\Sigma X^2 - \overline{X}^2 = \frac{1}{25}\times650 - 5^2 = 1$$

$$\sigma_y^2 = \frac{1}{n}\Sigma Y^2 - \overline{Y}^2 = \frac{1}{25}\times436 - 16 = \frac{36}{25}$$

$$\text{Corrected } r(X,Y) = \frac{\text{cov}(X,Y)}{\sigma_x\sigma_y} = \frac{\frac{4}{5}}{1\times\frac{6}{5}} = \frac{2}{3} = 0.67$$

***Example 15.*** *For two cities Calcutta and Bombay prices of commodities are given in the following data*

| | Calcutta | Bombay |
|---|---|---|
| Average price | 65 | 67 |
| Standard deviation | 2.5 | 3.5 |

*Correlation coefficient between the prices of commodities in the two cities is 0.8.*

*Then, the most likely price in Bombay corresponding to the price of ₹ 70 at Calcutta is*

(a) 56.5 (b) 22.6
(c) 72.6 (d) 90.5

**Solution.** (c) Let the prices, (in Rupees), in Bombay and Calcutta be denoted by $Y$ and $X$, respectively. Then, we are given

$$\overline{X} = 65,\quad \overline{Y} = 67$$

$$\sigma_x = 2.5,\quad \sigma_y = 3.5$$

$$r = r(X,Y) = 0.8$$

We want $Y$ for $X = 70$

The line of regression of $y$ on $x$ is

$$Y - \overline{Y} = r\frac{\sigma_y}{\sigma_x}(X - \overline{X})$$

$$\Rightarrow \quad Y = \overline{Y} + r\frac{\sigma_y}{\sigma_x}(X - \overline{X})$$

$$= 67 + 0.8\times\frac{3.5}{2.5}(X - 65)$$

When, $X = 70$

$$Y = 67 + 0.8\times\frac{3.5}{2.5}(70 - 65)$$

$$= 67 + 0.8\times\frac{3.5}{2.5}\times5$$

$$= 67 + 5.6$$

$$\hat{Y} = 72.6$$

Thus, corresponding to the price of ₹ 70 at Calcutta, the most likely price in Bombay is ₹ 72.6.

***Example 16.*** *In a partially destroyed laboratory record of an analysis of correlation data, the following results are only legible.*

*Variance of X = 9*

*Regression equations are*

$$8X - 10Y + 66 = 0$$

$$40X - 18Y = 214$$

*Then,*

(i) *the mean values of X and Y*

(a) $\overline{X} = 13,\ \overline{Y} = 17$ (b) $\overline{X} = 17,\ \overline{Y} = 13$
(c) $\overline{X} = 15,\ \overline{Y} = 18$ (d) $\overline{X} = 14,\ \overline{Y} = 18$

(ii) *The correlation coefficient between x and y is*

(a) +0.1 (b) −0.1 (c) +0.6 (d) −0.5

(iii) *The standard deviation of Y, $\sigma_y$ is*

(a) 1 (b) 2 (c) 3 (d) 4

**Solution.**

(i) (a) Given, regression lines are

$$8X - 10Y + 66 = 0$$
$$40X - 18Y = 214$$

Since, both the lines pass through $(\overline{X}, \overline{Y})$, we have

$$8\overline{X} - 10\overline{Y} + 66 = 0$$
$$40\overline{X} - 18\overline{Y} = 214$$

On solving these equations, we get

$$\overline{X} = 13, \overline{Y} = 17$$

(ii) (c) Let regression line of $Y$ on $X$ be

$$8X - 10Y + 66 = 0$$

and regression line of $X$ on $Y$ be

$$40X - 18Y = 214$$

These can be put as

$$Y = \frac{8}{10}X + \frac{66}{10} \text{ and } X = \frac{18}{40}Y + \frac{214}{40}$$

Therefore, $b_{yx}$ = Regression coefficient of $Y$ on $X$

$$= \frac{8}{10} = \frac{4}{5}$$

and $b_{xy}$ = Regression coefficient of $X$ on $Y$

$$= \frac{18}{40} = \frac{9}{20}$$

Here, $r^2 = b_{yx} \cdot b_{xy} = \frac{4}{5} \times \frac{9}{20} = \left(\frac{3}{5}\right)^2$

$$\Rightarrow \quad r = \pm\frac{3}{5} = \pm 0.6$$

Since, both the regression coefficients are positive. So, $r = +\text{ve}$. Thus, $r = +0.6$.

(iii) (d) We know, $b_{yx} = r\frac{\sigma_y}{\sigma_x}$

$$\Rightarrow \quad \frac{4}{5} = \frac{3}{5}\frac{\sigma_y}{3} \Rightarrow \sigma_y = 4$$

## Type II (*One or more than one correct option*)

***Example 17.*** *Under the assumptions required by the signed-rank test. $T^+$ is a value of a random variable*

(a) with the mean $\mu = \frac{n(n+1)}{4}$

(b) with the variance $\sigma^2 = \frac{n(n+1)(2n+1)}{24}$

(c) with the mean $\mu = \frac{n}{2}$

(d) with the variance $\sigma^2 = \frac{n(n+1)}{6}$

**Solution.** (a), (b)

Expressed in terms of ranks and signed differences, the null hypothesis for the one-sample and paired-sample signed-rank tests may be stated as follows : For each rank, the probabilities that it will be assigned to a positive difference or to a negative difference are both $\frac{1}{2}$.

Thus, we have

$$T^+ = 1 \cdot x_1 + 2 \cdot x_2 + \ldots + n \cdot x_n$$

where $x_1, x_2 \ldots, x_n$ are values of independent random variables having the Bernoulli distribution with $\theta = \frac{1}{2}$. Since $E(X_i) = \theta = \frac{1}{2}$ and $\text{var}(X_i) = \theta(1-\theta) = \frac{1}{4}$ for $i = 1, 2 \ldots, n$ with $n = 1$, it follows

$$\mu = 1 \cdot \frac{1}{4} + 2 \cdot \frac{1}{2} + \ldots + n \cdot \frac{1}{2}$$
$$= \frac{1 + 2 + \ldots + n}{2} = \frac{n(n+1)}{4}$$

and $\sigma^2 = 1^2 \cdot \frac{1}{4} + 2^2 \cdot \frac{1}{4} + \ldots + n^2 \cdot \frac{1}{4}$

$$= \frac{1^2 + 2^2 + \ldots + n^2}{4} = \frac{n(n+1)(2n+1)}{24}$$

***Example 18.*** *Checking on elm trees that were planted many years ago along a country road, a county official obtained the following arrangement of healthy, H and diseased, D, trees*

*HHHHDDDHHHHHHHDDHHDDDD*

*Test at the 0.5 level of significance whether this arrangement may be regarded as random.*

(a) Null hypothesis must be rejected

(b) Null hypotheis must not be rejected

(c) The diseased trees come in clusters

(d) The arrangement of healthy and diseased elm trees is not random

**Solution.** (a), (c), (d)

1. $H_0$ : Arrangement is random
   $H_1$ : Arrangement is not random.
   and $\alpha = 0.05$
2. Since, $n_1 = 13$ and $n_2 = 9$, reject the null hypothesis if $u \leq 6$ or $u \geq 17$, where 6 and 17 are the corresponding values of $u'_{0.025}$ and $u_{0.025}$.
3. $u = 6$ by inspection of the data.
4. Since, $u = 6$ is equal to $u_{0.025} = 6$, the null hypothesis must be rejected; the arrangement of healthy and diseased elm trees is not random. It appears that the diseased trees come in clusters

***Example 19.*** *If $x_1, x_2, \ldots, x_n$ are the values of a random sample of size n from a uniform population with $\alpha = 0$*

(a) the likelihood function is $L(\beta) = \left(\frac{1}{\beta}\right)^n$

(b) the likelihood function is $L(\beta) = (\beta)^n$

(c) the maximum likelihood estimator of $\beta$ is the $n$th order statistic

(d) no maximum likelihood estimator of $\beta$ is exist

**Solution.** (a), (c)

The likelihood function is given by

$$L(\beta) = \prod_{i=1}^{n} f(x_i ; \beta) = \left(\frac{1}{\beta}\right)^n$$

for β greater than or equal to the largest of the *x*s and 0 otherwise. Since, the value of this likelihood function increases as β decreases, we must make β as small as possible, and it follows that the maximum likelihood estimator of β is $Y_n$, the *n*th order statistic.

***Example 20.*** *An automatic filling machine is used to fill bottles with liquid detergent. A random sample of 20 bottles results in a sample variance of fill volume of* $s^2 = 0.0153$ *(fluid ounces)*$^2$. *If the variance of fill volume is too large, an unacceptable proportion of bottles will be under or overfilled. We will assume that the fill volume is approximately normally distributed.*

(a) At the 95% level of confidence, the data indicate that the process standard deviation could be as large as 0.17 fluid ounce

(b) At the 95% level of confidence, the data indicate that the process standard deviation cannot be as large as 0.17 fluid ounce

(c) $\sigma^2 \le 0.0287$ (fluid ounce)$^2$

(d) $\sigma^2 \ge 0.0277$ (fluid ounce)$^2$

**Solution.** (a), (c)

A 95% upper confidence interval is found from as follows

$$\sigma^2 \le \frac{(n-1)S^2}{\chi^2_{0.95,\,19}}$$

$$\Rightarrow \quad \sigma^2 \le \frac{(19)\,0.0153}{10.117} = 0.0287 \text{ (fluid ounce)}^2$$

This last expression may be converted into a confidence interval on the standard deviation σ by taking the square root of both sides, resulting in

$$\sigma \le 0.17$$

Therefore, at the 95% level of confidence, the data indicate that the process standard deviation could be as large as 0.17 fluid ounce.

***Example 21.*** *Suppose that 100 tires made by a certain manufacturer lasted on the average 21819 miles with a standard deviation of 1295 miles, Testing the null hypothesis* $\mu = 22000$ *miles against the alternative hypothesis* $\mu < 22000$ *miles at the 0.05 level of significance.*

(a) Null hypothesis can be rejected

(b) Null hypothesis cannot be rejected

(c) $z = 1.40$

(d) $z = -1.40$

**Solution.** (b), (d)

1. $H_0 : \mu = 22000$
   $H_1 : \mu < 22000$
   $\alpha = 0.05$
2. Reject the null hypothesis, if $z \le -1.645$, where
   $$z = \frac{\bar{x} - \mu_0}{\sigma/\sqrt{n}}$$
3. Substituting $\bar{x} = 21819$, $\mu_0 = 22000$, $s = 1295$ and σ for $n = 100$, we get
   $$z = \frac{21819 - 22000}{1295/\sqrt{100}} = -1.40$$
4. Since $z = -1.40$ is greater than $-1.645$, the null hypothesis cannot be rejected; there is no real evidence that the tires are not as good as assumed under the null hypothesis.

***Example 22.*** *Which of the following(s) is/are correct?*

(a) $\bar{X}$ is a sufficient estimator of the mean μ of a normal population with the known variance $\sigma^2$

(b) $\bar{X}$ is not a sufficient estimator of the mean μ of a normal population with the known variance $\sigma^2$

(c) $\sum_{i=1}^{n} (x_i - \mu)^2 = \sum_{i=1}^{n} [(x_i - \bar{x}) - (\mu - \bar{x})]^2$

(d) $f(x_1, x_2, \ldots, n_n; \mu) = \left(\frac{1}{\sigma\sqrt{2\pi}}\right)^n \cdot e^{-\frac{1}{2}\sum_{i=1}^{n}\left(\frac{x_i - \mu}{\sigma}\right)^2}$

**Solution.** (a), (c), (d)

Making use of the fact that

$$f(x_1, x_2, \ldots, n_n; \mu) = \left(\frac{1}{\sigma\sqrt{2\pi}}\right)^n \cdot e^{-\frac{1}{2}\sum_{i=1}^{n}\left(\frac{x_i - \mu}{\sigma}\right)^2}$$

and that

$$\sum_{i=1}^{r} (x_i - \mu)^2 = \sum_{i=1}^{n} [(x_i - \bar{x}) - (\mu - \bar{x})]^2$$

$$= \sum_{i=1}^{n} (x_i - \bar{x})^2 + \sum_{i=1}^{n} (\bar{x} - \mu)^2 = \sum_{i=1}^{n} (x_i - \bar{x})^2 + n(\bar{x} - \mu)^2$$

Thus, we get,

$$f(x_1, x_2, \ldots, x_n; \mu) = \left\{\frac{\sqrt{n}}{\sigma\sqrt{2\pi}} \cdot e^{-\frac{1}{2}\left(\frac{\bar{x} - \mu}{\sigma/\sqrt{n}}\right)^2}\right\} \times \left[\frac{1}{\sqrt{n}}\left(\frac{1}{\sigma\sqrt{2\pi}}\right)^{n-1} \cdot e^{-\frac{1}{2}\sum_{i=1}^{n}\left(\frac{x_i - \bar{x}}{\sigma}\right)^2}\right]$$

where the first factor on the right hand side depends only on the estimate $\bar{x}$ and the population mean μ, and the second factor does not involve μ.

Thus, it follows that $\bar{X}$ is a sufficient estimator of the mean μ of a normal population with the known variance $\sigma^2$.

# Exercise 1 (For Part 'B')

**Directions** (Q. Nos. 1-402) *All questions have only one correct option.*

**1.** If it is known that the 95% LCL and UCL to population mean are 48.04 and 51.96, respectively. What is the value of the population variance, when the sample size is 100?

(a) 8 (b) 10
(c) 12 (d) 12.50

**2.** If $T_1$ and $T_2$ are unbiased estimate of $\theta$ and $\theta^2$ $(0 < \theta < 1)$ and $T$ is a sufficient statistic, then $E\left(\frac{T_1}{T}\right) - E\left(\frac{T_2}{T}\right)$ is

(a) minimum variance unbiased estimator $\theta$
(b) always the minimum variance unbiased estimator of $\theta(1-\theta)$
(c) always an unbiased estimator of $\theta(1-\theta)$, which has variance not exceeding that of $T_1 - T_2$
(d) not an unbiased estimator of $\theta(1-\theta)$

**3.** Consider the following graph of the mean yield of barley in 1980, 1984 and 1988 along with a 95% confidence interval.

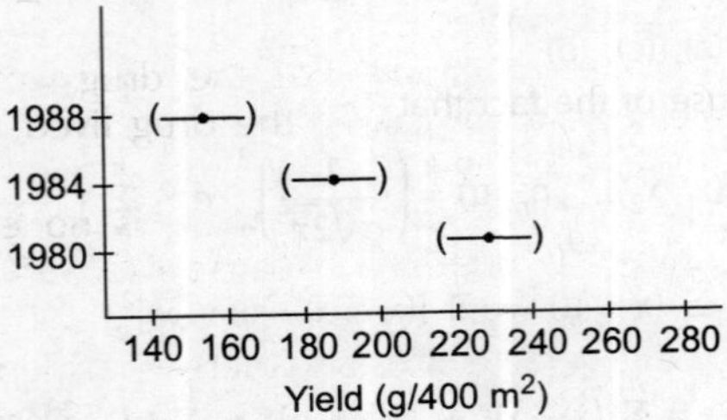


Which of the following is incorrect?

(a) Since, the confidence intervals for 1984 and 1980 have considerable overlap, there is little evidence that the sample means differ.
(b) Since, the confidence intervals for 1988 and 1980 do not overlap, there is good evidence that their respective population means differ.
(c) The sample mean for 1984 is about 195 g /400 $m^2$.
(d) The sample mean for 1988 is less than the sample mean for 1984.

**4.** The above confidence intervals are of the orders 6 percentage points. What sample size for each poll would be needed, so that we are 95% confident of being within 2 percentage points of the true difference assuming that the above proportions are reasonable estimates of the proportions in the population?

(a) 6000 (b) 1000
(c) 15000 (d) 4000

**5.** Two vaccines against measles are being tested. It is important to know the difference in success rate very accurately, *i.e.*, to be 95% sure that the estimated difference is within 0.01 of the true difference. If both vaccines are expected to have an approximate success rate of 80%, then the required sample size is

(a) about 750 in each group for a total of 1500 people
(b) about 1500 in each group for a total of 3000 people
(c) about 3000 in each group for a total of 6000 people
(d) about 12000 in each group for a total of 24000 people

**6.** Samples of hamburger were selected from two different outlets of a large supermarket to measure the percentage of fat present in the meat, with the following summary data.

| | Outlet 1 | Outlet 2 | |
|---|---|---|---|
| $n$ | 5 | 10 | |
| Mean | 10.3 | 10.7 | per cent |
| std. dev | 1.6 | 2.3 | per cent |

It is reasonable to believe that both outlets have the same variability. Hence, the pooled standard deviation is

(a) 1.95 (b) 2.08 (c) 4.38 (d) 2.11

**7.** The degrees of freedom of the pooled estimate in the previous question is

(a) 15 (b) 13 (c) 7.5 (d) 5

**8.** The government claims that students earn an average of \$ 4500 during their summer break from studies. A random sample of students gave a sample average of \$ 3975 and a 95% confidence interval was found to be (\$ 3525 < $\mu$ < \$ 4425). This interval is interpreted to mean that

(a) if the study were to be repeated many times, there is a 95% probability that the true average summer earnings is not \$ 4500 as the government claims
(b) because our specific confidence interval does not contain the value \$4500 there is a 95% probability that the true average summer earnings is not \$ 4500
(c) if we were to repeat our survey many times, then about 95% of all the confidence intervals will contain the value \$4500
(d) if we repeat our survey many times, then about 95% of our confidence intervals will contain the true value of the average earnings or students

**9.** A random sample of the heights of 100 students from a large population of students from standard deviation as 0.35 m show an average height of 1.75 m. What are the 95% confidence limits for the average height of all the students forming the population?

(a) [1.68 m, 1.82 m] (b) [1.58 m, 1.90 m]
(c) [1.58 m, 1.92 m] (d) [1.5 m, 2.0 m]

**10.** Which one of the following statement is correct?

(a) If a test is significant at 5% level, then the probability of the null hypothesis being true is atleast 0.05.
(b) If a test is significant at 1% level, then the value of the test statistic must be quite large.
(c) If the *p*-value of a test statistics is 0.16, then the test is in significant at 10% level.
(d) If the sample mean based on a random sample of size 1000 from a population turns out to be 0.003, then the hypothesis that the population mean is 0 should be rejected.

**11.** One class decided 10 estimate the proportion of cars that are red in a parking lot. They took a random sample of the cars in the closest parking lot to the calls.

Which of the following is not correct?

(a) Even though the sample was random sample of cars in the parking lot, the sample may not be representative of the population of cars driven by SFU students because the decision to park in *B*-lot is a self-selected sample.
(b) If another sample of cars was taken, it is likely that a different proportion for Japanese made cars would be found. The set of all possible values for the proportion is known as the sampling distribution.
(c) The confidence interval computed refers to the proportion of cars in the sample that were red.
(d) The sample was a simple random sample from cars parked. This means that every car in the lot had an equal chance of being selected.

**12.** A statistics professor would like to determine, whether students in his class showed improved performance on the final examination as compared to the mid-term examination. A random sample of 4 students selected from a large class revealed the following mid-term and final scores

| **Student** | #1 | #2 | #3 | #4 |
|---|---|---|---|---|
| **Mid-term** | 70 | 62 | 57 | 68 |
| **Final** | 80 | 79 | 87 | 88 |

Making the appropriate assumptions, the value of the test statistic is

(a) 19.25/8.30
(b) 19.25/(8.30/2)
(c) $19.25/\sqrt{28.295/4 + 28.295/4}$
(d) $19.25 \cdot \sqrt{34.92/4 + 21.67/4}$

**13.** Two vaccines against measles are being tested. It is important to know the difference in success rate very accurately, *i.e.*, to be 95% sure that the estimated difference is within 0·01 of the true difference. If both vaccines are expected to have an approximate success rate of 80%, then the required sample size for each group is obtained by solving

(a) $0.01 = 1.96\sqrt{\dfrac{0.8(0.2)}{n} + \dfrac{0.8\,(0.2)}{n}}$
(b) $0.02 = 1.96\sqrt{\dfrac{0.8(0.2)}{n} + \dfrac{0.8\,(0.2)}{n}}$
(c) $0.01 = 1.96\sqrt{\dfrac{0.5(0.5)}{n} + \dfrac{0.5\,(0.5)}{n}}$
(d) $0.02 = 1.96\sqrt{\dfrac{0.5(0.5)}{n} + \dfrac{0.5\,(0.5)}{n}}$

**14.** A study was conducted to investigate the effectiveness of a new drug for treating State 4 AIDS patients. A group of AIDS patients was randomly divided into two groups One group received the new drug; the other group received a placebo. The difference in mean subsequent survival (those with drugs, those without drugs) was found to be 1.04 yr and a 95% confidence interval was found to be 1.04 ± 2.37 yr. Based upon this information

(a) we can conclude that the drug was effective because those taking the drug lived, on average, 1.04 yr longer
(b) we can conclude that the drug was ineffective because those taking the drug lived, on average, 1.04 yr less
(c) we can conclude that there is no evidence the drug was effective because the 95% confidence interval covers zero
(d) we can conclude that there is evidence the drug was effective because the 95% confidence interval does not cover zero

**15.** Which of the following statements about confidence intervals is incorrect?

(a) If we keep the sample size fixed, the confidence interval gets wider as we increase the confidence coefficient.
(b) A confidence interval for a mean always contains the sample mean.
(c) If we keep the confidence coefficient fixed, the confidence interval gets narrower as we increase the sample size.
(d) If the population standard deviation increases, the confidence interval decreases in width.

**16.** In a marketing survey for the introduction of a new product in a town a sample of 400 persons was drawn: When they were aproached for sale, 80 of them purchased the product. Find 95% confidence limits for the percentage of persons who would buy the product in the town.

(a) [16.08, 23.92] (b) [16.28, 24.92]
(c) [17.08, 23.95] (d) None of these

**17.** To test the equality of the population means of two normal populations $(\mu_1, \sigma_1^2)$ and $N(\mu_2, \sigma_2^2)$ consider test statistic $t = \dfrac{\bar{x}_1 - \bar{x}_2}{S\sqrt{\dfrac{1}{n_1} + \dfrac{1}{n_2}}}$, where $S^2$ is the pooled sample variance based on samples of sizes $n_1$ and $n_2$ from the populations, then

(a) the distribution of $t$ is students $t$ is $\sigma_1^2 \neq 0$ but unknown
(b) the distribution of $t$ is $N(0, 1)$, if $\sigma_1^2 = \sigma_2^2$ known
(c) the distribution of $t$ is students $t$, if $\sigma_1^2 = \sigma_2^2 = \sigma^2$ but unknown
(d) the distribution of $t$ is students $t$, if $\sigma_1^2$ and $\sigma_2^2$ are known and distinct

**18.** A study conducted by an airline showed that a random sample of nine of its passengers disembarking at the winnipeg airport, took an average of 24.1 min to claim their luggage. From a previous survey it was willing to assume that time to claim luggage is normally distributed with a variance of 18 (min$^2$). A 95% confidence interval for the mean time to claim one's luggage has end-points

(a) $24.1 \pm 8.32$
(b) $24.1 \pm 3.92$
(c) $24.1 \pm 2.77$
(d) $24.1 \pm 3.26$

**19.** Two surgical procedures are widely used to treat a certain type of cancer. To compare the success rates of the two procedures, a random sample from each type of procedure is obtained and the number of patients with no reoccurrence of the disease after 1 yr was recorded. Here, is the data

| | $n$ | No Occurrence |
|---|---|---|
| Procedure *A* | 100 | 78 |
| Procedure *B* | 120 | 102 |

A 95% confidence interval for the difference in success rates is

(a) $0.07 \pm 0.053$ (b) $0.07 \pm 0.0054$
(c) $0.07 \pm 0.103$ (d) $0.07 \pm 0.115$

**20.** A new insect spray, type *A*, is to be compared with a spray, type *B*, that is currently in use. Two rooms of equal size are sprayed with the same amount of spray, one room with type *A* and the other with type *B*. Two hundred insects are released into each room and after one hour the numbers of dead insects are counted. The results are given in the following table.

| | Spray *A* | Spray *B* |
|---|---|---|
| Total number of insects | 200 | 200 |
| Total number of dead insects | 140 | 100 |

A 90% confidence interval for the difference in the rates of kill for the two sprays, is

(a) $0.2 \pm 1.645\sqrt{\dfrac{0.46}{200}}$ (b) $0.2 \pm 1.645\sqrt{\dfrac{0.48}{200}}$
(c) $0.2 \pm 1.96\sqrt{\dfrac{0.46}{200}}$ (d) $0.2 \pm 1.96\sqrt{\dfrac{0.48}{200}}$

**21.** In a study of iron deficiency among infants, random samples of infants following different feeding programs were compared. One group contained breast-fed infants, while the children in another group were fed by a standard baby formula without any iron supplements. Here, are summary results of blood hemoglobin levels at 12 months of age.

| Group | Sample Size | Sample Mean | Sample Std Deviation |
|---|---|---|---|
| Breast-fed | 8 | 13.3 | 1.7 |
| Formula-fed | 10 | 12.4 | 1.8 |

A 98% confidence interval for the mean difference in hemoglobin level between the two populations of infants is

(a) $0.9 \pm 1.94$ (b) $0.9 \pm 2.08$
(c) $0.9 \pm 2.13$ (d) $0.9 \pm 2.15$

**22.** What is a statistical inference?

(a) A decision, estimate, prediction, or generalization about the population based on information contained in a sample.
(b) A statement made about a sample based on the measurements in that sample.
(c) A set of data selected from a larger set of data.
(d) A decision, estimate, prediction or generalization about sample based on information contained in a polulation.

**23.** For a given sample of 200 items drawn from a large population, the mean is 65 and the standard deviation is 8. Find the 95% confidence limits for the population mean.

(a) [65.11, 63.89] (b) [66.11, 63.89]
(c) [67.11, 64.89] (d) None of these

**24.** 500 apples are taken at random from a large basket and 50 are found to be bad. Estimate the proportion of bad apples in the basket and assign limits within which the percentage most probably lie. A random sample of 700 units from a large consignment showed that 200 were damaged. Find (i) 95% confidence limits for the proportion of damgaed units in the consignment.

(a) [0.26, 0.32] (b) [0.253, 0.319]
(c) [0.273, 0.419] (d) None of these

**25.** An electrical firm which manufactures a certain type of bulb wants to estimate its mean life. Assuming that the life of the light bulb is normally distributed and that the standard deviation is known to be 40 h, how many bulbs should be tested so that we can be 90 per cent confident that the estimate of the mean will not differ from the true mean life by more than 10 h?

(a) 7 (b) 44 (c) 8 (d) 62

**26.** Two vaccines against measles are being tested,. It is important to know the difference in success rate very accurately, *i.e.*, to be 95% sure that the estimated difference is within 0.01 of the true difference. If both vaccines are expected to have an approximate success rate of 80%, then the required sample size for each group is obtained by solving

(a) $0.01 = 1.96\sqrt{\frac{0.8\,(0.2)}{n}+\frac{0.8\,(0.2)}{n}}$

(b) $0.02 = 1.96\sqrt{\frac{0.8\,(0.2)}{n}+\frac{0.8\,(0.2)}{n}}$

(c) $0.01 = 1.96\sqrt{\frac{0.5\,(0.5)}{n}+\frac{0.5\,(0.5)}{n}}$

(d) $0.02 = 1.96\sqrt{\frac{0.5\,(0.5)}{n}+\frac{0.5\,(0.5)}{n}}$

**27.** There may be a cure for male pattern baldness (at least millions of males hope there will be) using the blood pressure drug Minoxidil. A group of males was randomly assigned to two groups one group received topical applications of the drug; the other group recevied applicatiobns of an identical looking placebo. The summary data

| | **Number with Sample Size** | **New $H-A$ir Growth** |
|---|---|---|
| Minoxidil group | 310 | 100 |
| Placebo group | 100 | 25 |

A 95% confidence interval for the difference in the proportion of males showing new hair growth is

(a) $0.073 \pm 0.152$ (b) $0.073 \pm 0.048$
(c) $0.073 \pm 0.024$ (d) $0.073 \pm 0.099$

**28.** A seed company claims that 80% of the seeds of a certain variety of tomato will germinate if sown under normal growing conditions. A government inspector is intersested in whether or not the proportion of seeds germinating is living upto the company's claim. He randomly selects a sample of 200 seeds from a large shipment and tests the sample for percentage germination. If 155 of the 200 seeds germinate, then the calculated value of the test statistic used to test the hypothesis of interest is

(a) $-847$ (b) $-884$
(c) $-897$ (d) $-825$

**29.** You have measured the systolic blood pressure of a random sample of 25 employees of a company. A 95% confidence interval for the mean systolic blood pressure for the employees is computed to be (122,138). Which of the following statements gives a valid interpretation of this interval?

(a) About 95% of the sample of employees have a systolic blood pressure between 122 and 138.
(b) About 95% of the employees in the company have a systolic blood pressure between 122 and 138.
(c) If the sampling procedure were repeated many times, then approximately 95% of the resulting confidence intervals would contain the mean systolic blood pressure for employees in the company.
(d) If the sampilmg procedure were repeatyed many times, then approximately 95% of the sample means would be between 122 and 138.

**30.** A dice is thrown 9000 times and a throw of 3 or 4 is observed 3240 times. Find the limits between which the probability of a throw of 3 or 4 lies.

(a) [0.345, 0.375] (b) [0.365, 0.395]
(c) [0.360, 0.391] (d) None of these

**31.** A random of 100 ball bearings selected from a shipment of 2000 ball bearing has an average diameter of 0.354 cm with a SD = 0.048 cm. Find 95% confidence interval for the average diameter of these 2000 ball bearings.

(a) [0.345, 0.363] (b) [0.445, 0.463]
(c) [0.245, 0.263] (d) None of these

**32.** In an investigation on toxins produced by molds that infect corn crops, a biochemist prepares extracts of the mold culture and then measures the amount of the toxic substance per gram of solution. From six preparations of the mold culture the following observations on toxic substances (mg) are obtained 1.2, 0.8, 0.6, 1.1, 1.2, 0.8

A 95% confidence interval for the mean amount of toxic substances is

(a) 0.95 $ 2.57 (0.10) (b) 0.95 $ 1.96 (0.10)
(c) 0.95 $ 2.57 (0.25) (d) 0.95 $ 1.96 (0.25)

**33.** The average time between infection with the AIDS virus and developing AIDS has been estimated to be 8 yr with a standard deviation of about 2 yr. Approximately, what fraction of people develop AIDS with in 4 yr of infection?

(a) 5% (b) 2.5%
(c) 32% (d) 16%

**34.** Two surgical procedures are widely used to treat a certain type of cancer. To compare the success rates of the two procedures, a random sample from each type of procedure is obtained and the number of patients with no reoccurrence of the disease after 1 yr was recorded. Here, is the data.

| | ***n*** | **No Occurrence** |
|---|---|---|
| Procedure *A* | 100 | 78 |
| Procedure *B* | 120 | 102 |

A 95% confidence interval for the difference in success rates is

(a) $0.07 \pm 0.053$ (b) $0.07 \pm 0.0054$
(c) $0.07 \pm 0.103$ (d) $0.07 \pm 0.115$

**35.** Consider a binomial parameter $p$ and the test of $H_0 : p = 0.7$. If $X$ represents the number of successes in 15 trials and if the null hypothesis is rejected, if $X \geq 13$. What is the probability of type I error for this test?

(a) 0.004 (b) 0.035
(c) 0.050 (d) 0.127

**36.** We want to test $H_0 : \mu = 1.5$ vs, $H_1 : \mu \neq 1.5$ at $\alpha = 0.05$. A 95% confidence interval for $\mu$ calculated from a given random sample is (1.4, 3.6). Based on this finding we

(a) fail to reject $H_0$
(b) reject $H_0$
(c) cannot make any decision at all because the value of the test statistic is not available
(d) cannot make any decision at all because the distribution of the population is unknown

**37.** Out of a consignment of 100000 tennis balls, 400 were selected at random and examined. It was found that 200 of these were defective . How many defective balls can you reasonably expect to have in the whole consignment at 95% confidence level?

(a) [4865, 5135] (b) [4765, 5035]
(c) [4875, 5235] (d) None of these

**38.** The mean height obtained from a sample of size 100 taken radomly from a population is 164 cm. If the standard deviation of the height distribution of the population is 3 cm, setup 95% confidence limits for the mean height of the population.

(a) [163.41, 164.59] (b) [153.41, 154.59]
(c) [173.41, 174.59] (d) None of these

**39.** An analyst, using a random sample of $n = 500$ familes, obtained a 90 per cent confidence interval for mean monthly family income for a large population; ($600, $800). If the analyst had used a 99 per cent confidence coefficient instead, the confidence interval would be

(a) narrower and would involve a larger risk of being incorrect
(b) wider and would involve a smaller risk of being incorrect
(c) narrower and would involve a smaller risk of being incorrect
(d) wider and would involve a larger risk of being incorrect

**40.** The output from a sewage treatment plant is constantly monitored to assess treatement efficacy. Suppose that the mean coliform content is 20 becteria/mL with a standard deviation of 4 bacteria/mL. An automatic measuring device is being used to monitor the bacterial levels. An alarm should ring, whenever the bacterial level exceeds the 97.5th percentile. The upper bound should be

(a) 20 per mL (b) 24 per mL
(c) 28 per mL (d) 32 per mL

**41.** A company operates a production line producing a large number of manufactured parts in three shifts of 8 h each. The following table provides data obtained from a sample of 162 manufactured parts not conforming to specifications.

| | Shift 1 | Shift 2 | Shift 3 | Shift 4 |
|---|---|---|---|---|
| Non-conforming | 50 | 44 | 68 | 162 |

A test of the hypothesis that the non-conforming parts are uniformly distributed among the three shifts can be based upon which of the following values of the test statistic?

(a) 5.78 with 3 degrees of freedom
(b) 5.78 with 2 degrees of freedom
(c) 5.48 with 2 degrees of freedom
(d) 5.48 with 3 degrees of freedom

**42.** A large supermarket chain will increase its stock of bakery products if more than 20% of its customers are purchasers of bakery products. A random sample of 100 customers found 28% purchased bakery items. A 5% significance test is conducted to determine if the chain should increase its bakery stock. The $p$-value for this situation is

(a) 0.0500 (b) 0.0750 (c) 0.0375 (d) 0.0228

**43.** A 95% confidence interval for $\mu$ is calculated to be (1·7, 3·5). It is now decided to test the hypothesis $H_0 : \mu = 0$ vs $H_A : \mu \neq 0$ at the $\alpha = 0.05$ level, using the same data as was used to construct the

(a) we cannot test the hypothesis without the original data
(b) we cannot test the hypothesis at the $\alpha = 0.50$ level becuse the $\alpha = 0.50$ test is connected to the 97.5% confidence interval
(c) we can only make the connection between hypothesis tests and *ci*, if the sample sizes are large
(d) we would reject $H_0$ at level $\alpha = 0.05$

**44.** In a sample of 1000 TV viewers, 340 watched a particular programme. Find 99% confidence limits for the percentage of all viewers who watch this programme.

(a) [30.13, 35.89] (b) [30.13, 37.87]
(c) [31.13, 38.87] (d) None of these

**45.** A horticulturist wishes to estimate the mean growth of seedlings in a large timber plot last year. A random sample of $n = 100$ seedlings is selected and the one year growth for each is measured. The sample results are : $X = 5.62$ cm and $s = 2.50$ cm. The 95 per cent confidence interval for the mean growth is

(a) (3.12, 8.12) (b) (4.98, 6.26)
(c) (5.13, 6.11) (d) (5.37, 5.87)

**46.** A simple random sample of size 66 was drawn in the process of estimating the mean annual income of 950 families of a certain township. The mean and standard deviation of the samples were found to be ₹ 4730 and ₹ 7.65, respectively. Find a 95%

confidence interval for the population mean (Table value of $Z$ for confidence level at 95% is 1.96).

(a) [4728.15, 4731.85] (b) [4278.15, 4308.85]
(c) [4782.15, 4796.85] (d) None of these

**47.** A research biologist has carried out an experiment on a random sample of 15 experimental plots in a field. Following the collection of data, a test of significance was conducted under appropriate null and alternative hypothesis and the $P$ value was determined to be approximately 0·03. This indicates that

(a) this result is statistically significant at the 0.01 level
(b) the probability of being wrong in this situation is only 0.03.
(c) there is some reason to believe that the null hypothesis is incorrect
(d) if this experiment were repeated 3 per cent of the time we would get this same result

**48.** The following table gives the number of wins for each of the first four post positions at assiniboine downs for 80 races during the 1978 horse racing season

| **Post position** | 1 | 2 | 3 | 4 |
|---|---|---|---|---|
| **Number of wins** | 24 | 17 | 19 | 20 |

For testing the hypothesis that the probability of winning is the same for all four post positions, the calculated value of the test statistic is

(a) 26.00 (b) 1.25
(c) 1.30 (d) 0.40

**49.** It is believed that atleast 60% of voters from a certain region in Canada favour the free trade agreement (FTA). A recent poll indicated that out of 400 randomly selected individuals, 250 favoured the FTA. At the 5% level of significance, we would

(a) fail to reject $H_0$ because the calculated value of the test statistic is 1.033 which is less than 1.645
(b) fail to reject $H_0$ because the calculated value of the test statistic is 1.033 which is less than 1.96
(c) fail to reject $H_0$ because the calculated value of the test statistic is 1.0204 which is less than 1.96
(d) fail to reject $H_0$ because the calculated value of the test statistic is 1.0204 which is less than 1.645

**50.** In testing $H : \mu = 100$ against, $A : \mu \neq 100$ at the 10% level of significance, $H$ is rejected, if

(a) 100 is contained in the 90% confidence interval
(b) the value of the test statistic is in the acceptance region
(c) the $p$-value is less than 0.10
(d) the $p$-value is greater than 0.10

**51.** A random sample of 100 items taken from a large batch of articles contains 5 defective items.
Setup 96 per cent confidence limits for the proportion of defective items in the batch.

(a) [0.005, 0.095] (b) [0.006, 0.095]
(c) [0.015, 0.095] (d) None of these

**52.** The incidence of a particular disease in an area is such that 20 per cent people of that area suffers from it. What size of sample should be taken so as to ensure that the error of estimation of the proportion should not be more than 5 per cent with 95 per cent confidence?

(a) 246 (b) 236
(c) 226 (d) 286

**53.** The average yield of gain on 9 randomly picked experimental plots of farm was found to be 150 bushels. If the yield in bushels per plot in previous studies was found to be approximately normally distributed with a variance of 400 bushels$^2$ a 98% confidence Interval for the mean yield is

(a) (13.9, 163.1) (b) (144.8, 155.2)
(c) (132.8, 167.2) (d) (134.5, 165.5)

**54.** A proponent of innovative teaching methods wishes to compare the effectiveness of teaching English by the traditional class room lecture system ($T$) and by the extensive use of audio visual aids. To do so a class of 250 is randomly divided into two groups
100 are taught by method $T$; of these 63 pass a test
150 are taught by method A; of these 105 pass a test
The appropriate test statistic for testing whether the traditional method has a lower passing rate than the audio visual methods

(a) $\dfrac{0.63-0.70}{\sqrt{\dfrac{0.672\times 0.328}{100}+\dfrac{0.672\times 0.328}{150}}}$

(b) $\dfrac{0.63-0.70}{\sqrt{\dfrac{0.630\times 0.370}{100}+\dfrac{0.700\times 0.300}{150}}}$

(c) $\dfrac{0.63-0.70}{\sqrt{\dfrac{0.667\times 0.333}{100}+\dfrac{0.667\times 0.333}{150}}}$

(d) $\dfrac{(63-67.2)^2}{67.2}+\dfrac{(37-32.8)^2}{32.8}+\dfrac{(105-100.8)^2}{100.8}+\dfrac{(45-49.2)^2}{49.2}$

**55.** On a particularly difficult multiple choice question having five choices, the instructor suspected that all 300 students who answered the question simply picked an answer at random. The distribution of students answers to the question is as follows

| **Answer** | **Frequency** |
|---|---|
| $A$ | 68 |
| $B$ | 53 |
| $C$ | 61 |
| $D$ | 75 |
| $E$ | 43 |

It is desired to conduct a test involving the hypothesis $H_0 : p_1 = p_2 = p_3 = p_4 = p_5 = 0.2$ and $H_1$ : not all $p_i = 0.2$, where $p_i$ denotes the probability of choosing answer *i*. Then, the value of the test statistic is

(a) 11.60 (b) 10.47
(c) 190.76 (d) 310.47

**56.** A random sample of 100 voters in a community produced 59 voters in favour of candidate A. The observed value of the test statistic for testing the null hypothesis $H : p = 0.5$ versus the alternative hypothesis $A : p \neq 0.5$ is

(a) 1.80 (b) 1.90
(c) 1.83 (d) 1.28

**57.** A Canadian railway company claims that its trains block crossings no more that 5 min per train on the average. The actual times (minutes) that 10 randomly selected trains block crossings were

10.4 9.7 6.5 9.5 8.8 11.2 7.2 10.5 8.2 9.3

Giving, $X = 9.130$ and $s^2 = 2.209$. In testing this claim, at the significance level of 0·05 and assuming that the crossing times are normally distributed, the value of the test statistic and the critical value are, respectively

(a) 5.91 and 2.2622 (b) 8.79 and 1.8331
(c) 5.91 and 1.8331 (d) 8.79 and 2.2622

**58.** In a sample of 900 shareholders of companies, 400 stated that their major aim in holding stocks is capital application. What is the 90% confidence range within, which lies the population of stock holders, who hold stocks for appreciation?

(a) [0.317, 0.372] (b) [0.417, 0.472]
(c) [0.517, 0.572] (d) None of these

**59.** A random sample of 100 days shows an average daily sale of ₹ 1000 with a standard deviation of ₹ 250 in a particular shop. Assuming a normal distribution, find the limits which have a 95% chance of including the expected sales per day.

(a) [₹ 950.75, ₹ 949.25]
(b) [₹ 950.75, ₹ 1049.25]
(c) [₹ 950.75, ₹ 1149.25]
(d) None of the above

**60.** Referring to the previous question, about how many animals should be sampled (in total) in order to be 95% confident of determining the true mean weight within 2 kg?

(a) 140 (b) 170
(c) 550 (d) 100

**61.** A new insect spray, type A is to be compared with a spray, type *B*, that is currently in use. Two rooms of equal size are sprayed with the same amount of spray, one room with type *A* and the other with type *B*. Two hundred insects are released into each room, and after one hour the numbers of dead insects are counted. The results are given in the following table

| | **Spray *A*** | **Spray *B*** |
|---|---|---|
| Total number of insects | 200 | 200 |
| Total number of dead insects | 140 | 100 |

A 90% confidence interval for the difference in the rates of kill for the two sprays, is

(a) $0.2 \pm 1.645\sqrt{\dfrac{0.46}{200}}$ (b) $0.2 \pm 1.645\sqrt{\dfrac{0.48}{200}}$

(c) $0.2 \pm 1.96\sqrt{\dfrac{0.46}{200}}$ (d) $0.2 \pm 1.96\sqrt{\dfrac{0.48}{200}}$

**62.** A die was rolled 30 times with the results shown below

| **Number of spots** | 1 | 2 | 3 | 4 | 5 | 6 |
|---|---|---|---|---|---|---|
| **Frequency** | 1 | 4 | 9 | 9 | 2 | 5 |

If a chi-square goodness of fit test is used to test the hypothesis that the die is fair at a significance level of $\alpha = 0.05$, then the value of the chi-square statistic and the decision reached are

(a) 11.6; reject hypothesis
(b) 11.6; accept hypothesis
(c) 22.1; reject hypothesis
(d) 22.1; accept hypothesis

**63.** Let *p* represent the proportion of defectives in a manufacturing process. To test $H : p = 0.25$ vs $A : p > 0.25$, a random sample of size 5 is taken from the process. If the number of defectives is 4 or more, the null hypothesis is rejected. What is the probability of rejecting *H*, if $p = 0.20$?

(a) 0.00192 (b) 0.9933
(c) 0.0096 (d) 0.0067

**64.** A telephone company's records indicate that private customers pay on average ₹ 17.10 per month for long-distance telephone calls. A random sample of 10 customers' bills during a given month produced a sample mean of ₹ 22.10 expended for long distance calls and a sample variance of 45. A 5% significance test is to be performed to determine if the mean level of billing for long distance calls per month is in excess of ₹ 17.10. The calculated value of the test statistic and the critical value respectively are

(a) (2.36, 1.8331) (b) (1.17, 2.2622)
(c) (2.36, 2.2622) (d) (1.17, 1.8331)

**65.** A statistic $T_n$ such that var $(T_n)$ for all θ, is consistent as an estimator of θ as $n \to \infty$

(a) if an only if $E_q(T_n) \to \theta$ for all θ
(b) if but not only if $E_q(T_n) \to \theta$ for all θ
(c) if and only if $E_q(T_n) = \theta$ for all θ for every *n*
(d) if and only if $E_q(T_n) - \theta/\text{var}(T_n) \to 0$ for all θ

**66.** A factory produces 60000 pairs of shoes on a daily basis. from a sample of 600 pairs, 3 per cent were found to be of inferior quality. Estimate the number of pairs that can be reasonably expected to be spoiled in the daily production process at 95% level of confidence.

(a) [989, 2612] (b) [782, 2618]
(c) [882, 2618] (d) None of these

**67.** A random sample of 4 herefords, each with a frame size of three (on a one-to-seven scale), gave a sample mean weight of 452 kg and a sample standard deviation of 12 kg. A 95% confidence interval for the average weight of all herefords of this frame size is (using an 'exact' confidence interval)

(a) (435.3, 468.7) (b) (432.9, 471.1)
(c) (440.2, 463.8) (d) (428.5, 475.5)

**68.** A regression of the amount of calories In a serving of breakfast cereal vs the amount of fat gave the following results : calories 97.1053 + 9.6525 fat. Which of the following is false?

(a) It is estimated that for every additional gram of fat in the cereal, the number of calories increases by about 9.
(b) It is estimated that in cereals with no fat, the total amount of calories is about 97.
(c) If a cereal has 2 g of fat, then it is estimated that the total number of calories is about 115.
(d) One cereal has 140 calories and 5 g of fat. Its residual is about 5 calories.

**69.** A researcher wants to see, if birds that build larger nests lay larger eggs. She selects two random samples of nests : one of small nests and the other of large nests. She weights one egg from each nest. The data are summarized below

| | Small nests | Large nests |
|---|---|---|
| Sample size | 60 | 159 |
| Sample mean (g) | 37.2 | 35.6 |
| Sample variance | 24.7 | 39.0 |

A 95% confidence interval for the difference between the average mass of eggs in small and large nests

(a) $1.6 \pm 1.33 = (0.27, 2.93)$
(b) $1.6 \pm 1.48 = (0.12, 3.08)$
(c) $1.6 \pm 1.59 = (0.01, 3.19)$
(d) $1.6 \pm 1.76 = (-0.16, 3.36)$

**70.** The power takeoff driveline on tractors used in agriculture is a potentially serious hazard to operators of farm equipment. The driveline is covered by a shield in new tractors but for a variety of reasons, the shield is often missing on older tractors. Two type of shields are the bolt-on and the flip-up. It was believed that the bolt-on shield was perceived as a nuisance by the operators and deliberately removed but the flip-up shield is easily lifted for inspection and maintenance and may be left in place. In a study initiated by the National Safety Council of the US, a sample of older tractors with both types of shields was taken to see what proportion were removed of 183 tractors designed to have bolt on shields, 35 had been removed of the 136 tractors with flip-up shields, 15 were removed. We wish to test the hypothesis $H: p_b = p_f$ vs $A: p_b \neq p_f$, where $p_b$ and $p_f$ are the proportion of tractors with the bolt-on and flip-up shields removed, respectively. The test-statistic is computed to be 1.97. The $p$-value is

(a) 0.025 (b) 0.049
(c) 0.012 (d) 0.975

**71.** In order to study the amounts owed to the city a city clerk takes a random sample of 16 files from a cabinet containing a large number of delinquent accounts and finds the average amount $X$ owed to the city to be ₹ 230 with a sample standard deviation of ₹ 36. It has been claimed that the true mean amount owed on accounts of this type is greater than ₹ 250. If it is appropriate to assume that the amount owed is a normally distributed random variable, the value of the test statistic appropriate for testing the claim is

(a) $-3.33$ (b) $-1.96$ (c) $-2.22$ (d) $-0.55$

**72.** Let $y_1$, $y_2$ and $y_3$ be independent and identically distributed normal variables with mean 3 and variance 1. Let $\bar{y} = \dfrac{y_1 + y_2 + y_3}{3}$

Then, $\sum_{i=1}^{3} (y_i - \bar{y})$ has a

(a) chi-square distribution with 3 degrees of freedom
(b) chi-square distribution with 2 degrees of freedom
(c) chi-square distribution with 1 degrees of freedom
(d) non-central chi-square distribution

**73.** If $X_1$ and $X_2$ are independent standard normal variates, then the distribution of $\dfrac{X_1^2}{X_2^2}$ is

(a) standard normal
(b) student'st
(c) Cauchy
(d) $F$-distribution with (1, 1) degrees of freedom

**74.** The diameter of ball bearings are known to be normally distributed with unknown mean and variance. A random sample of size 25 gave a mean 2.5 cm. The 95% confidence interval had length 4 cm. Then,

(a) the sample variance is 4.86
(b) the sample variance is 26.03
(c) the population variance is 4.84
(d) the sample variance is 23.47

**75.** The following data give uric acid levels (in milligrams per 100 mL) for 5 subjects before and after a special diet

| Subject | Before | After |
|---|---|---|
| 1 | 5.2 | 5.2 |
| 2 | 6.3 | 6.2 |
| 3 | 6.4 | 6.3 |
| 4 | 5.5 | 5.6 |
| 5 | 5.9 | 5.6 |

…st the hypothesis that the diet reduces the uric acid eve!, we might use

(a) a two sample $t$-test because the uric acid levels before and after the diet can be assumed independent
(b) a sign test
(c) a paired $t$-test
(d) Both (b) and (c)

**76.** An experiment was conducted to compare the efficacies of two drugs in the prevention of tapeworms in the stomachs of a new breed of sheep. Samples of size 5 and 8 from each breed were given the drug and the two sample means were 28.6 and 40.0 worms per sheep. From previous studies, it is known that the variances in the two groups are 198 and 232, respectively and that the number of worms in the stomachs has an approximate normal distribution. A 95% confidence interval for the difference in the mean number of worms per sheep is

(a) $-11.4 \pm 18.6$ (b) $11.4 \pm 18.2$
(c) $-11.4 \pm 17.9$ (d) $11.4 \pm 16.2$

**77.** In a test of $H_0$ : $p = 0.4$ against $H_a$ : $p \neq 0.4$, a sample of size 100 produces $Z = 1.28$ for the value of the test statistic. Thus, the $p$-value (or observed level of significance) of the test is approximately equal to

(a) 0.90 (b) 0.40
(c) 0.05 (d) 0.20

**78.** We wish to test $H_0$ that the average family income of Manitoba families is atleast \$15000 at level of significance $\alpha = 0.05$. In order to test the null hypothesis a sample of size 1000 is selected from the population and the $p$-value of the test is determined to be 0.02. Then, we

(a) reject $H_0$ because the data are sufficiently unuusual if the null hypothesis were false
(b) reject $H_0$ because the data are sufficiently nusual if the null hypothesis were true
(c) fail to reject $H_0$ because the data are not sufficiently unusual if the null hypothesis were true
(d) fail to reject $H_0$ because the data are not sufficiently unusual if the null hypothesis were false

**79.** $X$ has a normal distribution with mean 1 and variance 4. Then, $\frac{1}{4}(X^2 - 2X + 1)$ has

(a) normal distribution with mean 0 and variance 4
(b) standard normal distribution
(c) normal distribution with mean 1 and variance 16
(d) chi-square distribution with one degree of freedom

**80.** A turkey producer knows from previous experience that profits are maximized by selling turkeys when their average weight is 12 kg. Before determining whether to put all their full grown turkeys on the market this month, the producer wishes to estimate their mean weight. Prior know ledge indicates that turkey weights have a standard deviation of around 1.5 kg. The number of turkeys that must be sampled in order to estimate their true mean weight to within 0.5 kg with 95% confidence is

(a) 35 (b) 5 (c) 65 (d) 10

**81.** Two vaccines against measles are being tested. It is important to know the difference in success rate very accurately, *i.e.*, to be 95% sure that the estimated difference is within 0.01 of the true difference. If both vaccines are expected to have an approximate success rate of 80%, then the required sample size is

(a) about 750 in each group for a total of 1500 people
(b) about 1500 in each group for a total of 3000 people
(c) about 3000 in each group for a total of 6000 people
(d) about 12000 in each group for a total of 24000 people

**82.** Popular wisdom is that eating pre-sweetened cereal tends to increase the number of dental caries (cavities) in children. A sample of children was (with parental consent) entered into a study and followed for several years. Each child was classified as a sweetened-cereal lover or a non-sweetened cereal lover. At the end of the study, the amount of tooth damage was measured. Here is the summary data

| Group | $n$ | mean | SD |
|---|---|---|---|
| **Sugar Bombed** | 10 | 6.41 | 5.0 |
| **No sugar** | 15 | 5.20 | 15.0 |

An approximate 95% confidence interval for the difference in the mean tooth damage is

(a) $(6.41 - 5.20) \pm 2.26\sqrt{\frac{5}{10} + \frac{15}{15}}$

(b) $(6.41 - 5.20) \pm 2.26\sqrt{\frac{25}{10} + \frac{225}{15}}$

(c) $(6.41 - 5.20) \pm 1.96\sqrt{\frac{25}{10} + \frac{225}{15}}$

(d) $(6.41 - 5.20) \pm 2.07\sqrt{\frac{146}{10} + \frac{146}{15}}$

**83.** A statistical procedure to estimate the mean shell thickness of eggs from chikens contaminated with PCBs obtains a point estimate of 0.70 mm and an estimated standard error of 0.05 mm. This means

(a) the standard deviation of actual shell thickness in the sample was 0.05 mm
(b) we are 95% confident that the sample mean shell thickness is accurate to with 0.05 mm
(c) an estimate of the standard deviation of the sample mean shell thickness over repeated samples is 0.05 mm
(d) the standard deviation of the population mean over all eggs is about 0.05 mm

**84.** The average time it takes for a person to experience pain relief from aspirin is 25 min. A new ingredient is added to help speed up relief. Let μ denote the average time to obtain pain relief with the new product. An experiment is conducted to verify if the new product is better. What are the null and alternative hypothesis?

(a) $H_0 : \mu = 25$ vs $H_A : \mu \neq 25$
(b) $H_0 : \mu = 25$ vs $H_A : \mu < 25$
(c) $H_0 : \mu < 25$ vs $H_A : \mu = 25$
(d) $H_0 : \mu < 25$ vs $H_A : \mu > 25$

**85.** To test the hypothesis $H_0$ : that a coin is unbaised against that it has a positive bias for heads the following procedure is suggested. Throw the coin thrice. If there are 3 heads reject $H_0$ anmd if there is no more than 1 head accept it. If there are jsut 2 heads, throw the coin another three times and reject $H_0$ if and only all, three additional throws shows heads. The size of the test is

(a) $\frac{1}{8}$ (b) $\frac{11}{64}$
(c) $\frac{1}{4}$ (d) $\frac{1}{64}$

**86.** A 95 per cent confidence interval for the mean time taken to process new insurance policies is (11, 12) days. This interval can be interpreted to mean that

(a) only 5 per cent of all policies take less than 11 or more than 12 days to process
(b) only 5 per cent of all policies take between 11 and 12 days to process
(c) about 95% out of every 100 such intervals construted from random samples of the same size will contain the population mean processing time
(d) the probability is 0.95 that all policies take between 11 and 12 days to process

**87.** A sample of 8 patients had their lung capactiy measured before and after a certain treatment with the following results

| Patient | Before | After |
|---|---|---|
| 1 | 750 | 850 |
| 2 | 860 | 880 |
| 3 | 950 | 930 |
| 4 | 830 | 860 |
| 5 | 750 | 800 |
| 6 | 680 | 740 |
| 7 | 720 | 760 |
| 8 | 810 | 800 |

The sign test is used to test the hypothesis that the treatment provides no increase in lung capacity. The probability under $H_0$ of obtaining the observed result or a more extreme one (*i.e.*, the *p*-value or observec level of significance) is

(a) 0.0352 (b) 0.1094 (c) 0.0498 (d) 0.1445

**88.** A study was conducted to estimate the effectiveness of doing assignments in an introductory satistics course. Students in one section taught by instructor. *A* received no assignments. Students in another section taught by instructor *B*, received assignments. The final grade of each student was recorded. A 95% confidence interval for the difference in the mean grades (section *A*-section *B*) was computed to be $-3.5 \pm 1.8$. This means

(a) there is evidence that doing assignments improves the average grade because the difference in the population means is less than zero
(b) there is little evidence that doing assignments improves the average grade becuase the 95% confidence interval does not cover zero.
(c) there is evidence that doing assignments improves the average grade because the 95% confidence interval does not cover zero.
(d) there is evidence that doing assignments does not improve the average grade becuase the 95% confidence interval does not cover zero.

**89.** Auditor *A* is faced with a population of 1000 accounts (population *A*). He is going to select a random sample of 30 accounts from population *A* and he is going to use the average amount owing in these sampled accounts as an estimate of the average amount owing in population *A*. Auditor *B* is faced with a population of 10000 accounts (population *B*). He is going to select a random sample of 30 accounts from population *B* and he is going to use the average amount owing in these sample accounts as an estimate of the average amount owing in population *B*. Other things being equal to

(a) auditor *A*'s estimate will be about 10 times more accurate than Auditor *B*'s estimate
(b) auditor *B*'s estimate will be about 10 times more accurate than Auditor *A*'s estimate
(c) auditor *A*'s estimate will be about 3.16 times more accurate than Auditor *B*'s estimate
(d) the accuracy of the two estimate will be about the same

**90.** The profit per new car sold by a small automobile dealer varies from car to car. The average profit per sale tabulated for the past 6 days was ₹ 368 with a standard deviation of ₹ 190. To test if there is sufficient evidence to indicate that average profit per sale is less than ₹ 480, the appropriate null and alternative hypothesis for the test are :

(a) $H : \mu =$ ₹ 368 vs $A : \mu <$ ₹ 480
(b) $H : \mu =$ ₹ 480 vs $A : \mu >$ ₹ 480
(c) $H : \mu =$ ₹ 480 vs $A : \mu >$ ₹ 480
(d) $H : \mu =$ ₹ 480 vs $A : \mu \neq$ ₹ 480

**91.** $X_1, X_2, \ldots, X_n$ are iid Bernoulli random variables with $E(X_i) = 0$ and $S_n = \sum_i^n X_i$. Then, for a sequence of non-negative number $\{K_n\}$, $T_n = \frac{S_n + K_n}{n + K_n}$ is a consistent estimator of θ

(a) if $\frac{k_n}{n} \to 0$ as $n \to \infty$
(b) if and only if $k_n = 0, \forall n$
(c) if and only if $k_n$ is bounded as $n \to \infty$
(d) whatever $\{k_n\}$ is

**92.** An experiment was conducted to estimate the mean yield of a new variety of oats. A sample of 20 plots gave a mean yield of 2.9 t/hectare and a 95% confidence interval of (2.48, 3.32) t/hectare. This means
(a) we are sure the true mean yield of this new variety is between 2.48 and 3.32 t/hectare
(b) we are 95% confident that the true mean yield of this variety is 2.9 t/hectare
(c) about 95% of the yields of the new variety will be between 2.48 and 3.32 t/hectare
(d) we are 95% confident that the true mean yield of this variety is between 2.48 and 3.32 t/hactare

**93.** You wish to estimate μ, the average lifetime of a particular type of battery. You are planning to select *n* batteries of this type and to operate them continuously until they fail. You have some feeling that he standard deviation of the lifetimes should be around 20 h and you wish your estimate of μ to be within 1 h of μ with probability 0.95. How many batteries should you select?
(a) 1537 (b) 784 (c) 40 (d) 77

**94.** Two surveys were conducted before and after the recent autopac rate increases to find the proportion of voters who state they would vote for the current government. The results were as follows

| | Weak 1 | Weak 2 | Total over both weeks |
|---|---|---|---|
| Noumber surveyed | 400 | 600 | 1000 |
| Noumber in favour of current government | 150 | 150 | 300 |

An approximate 95% confidence interval for the change in support is
(a) $(0.375 - 0.250) \pm 1.96\sqrt{\frac{(0.375)(0.625)}{400} + \frac{(0.250)(0.750)}{600}}$
(b) $(0.375 - 0.250) \pm 1.96\sqrt{\frac{(0.375)(0.625)}{1000} + \frac{(0.250)(0.750)}{1000}}$
(c) $(0.375 - 0.250) \pm 1.96\sqrt{\frac{(0.300)(0.700)}{400} + \frac{(0.300)(0.700)}{600}}$
(d) $(0.375 - 0.250) \pm 1.96\sqrt{\frac{(0.300)(0.700)}{1000} + \frac{(0.300)(0.700)}{1000}}$

**95.** In a test of $H_0 : \mu = 100$ against $H_A : \mu \neq 100$, a sample of size 10 produces a sample mean of 103 and a *p*-value of 0.08. Thus, at the 0.05 level of significance
(a) there is sufficient evidence to conclude that $\mu \neq 100$,
(b) there is sufficient evidence to conclude that $\mu = 100$
(c) there is insufficient evidence to conclude that $\mu = 100$
(d) there is insufficient evidence to conclude that $\mu \neq 100$

**96.** The chi-square goodness of fit is based on
(a) multinomial distribution
(b) hypergeometric distribution
(c) the assumption that the character under study is normal
(d) None of the above

**97.** Does playing music to dairy cattle increase their milk production? An experiment was conducted where a group of dairy cattle was divided into two groups. Music was played to one group; the control group did not have music played. The average increase in production was 2.5 L/cow over the time period in question. A 95% confidence interval for the difference (treatment-control) in the mean production was computed to be (1.5, 3.5) L/cow. This means
(a) 95% of the cows increased their production by between 1.5 and 3.5 L
(b) we are 95% confident that the average increase in production in the sample is 2.5L/cow
(c) becuase the confidence interval does not contain zero, we are 95% confident that there was no effect of playing music
(d) we don't know the true increase in production, but we are 95% confident that the increase in the mean production is in this interval

**98.** For the problem outlined above, the critical value (table value) of the test statstic when the level of significance is $\alpha = 0.05$, is
(a) 0.1026 (b) 7.3778
(c) 5.9915 (d) 12.5916
(e) 7.8147

**99.** A very simple interval estimator for μ is $(\bar{Y} - 2se \to \bar{Y} + 2se)$. Which of the following statement is/are true if the sample size, *n* is 'large'?
(a) This interval will contain the true value of μ approximately 95 times out of one hundred.
(b) This interval is an approximate 95% confidence interval for μ.
(c) This interval is too narrow to be a useful interval estimator for μ.
(d) Both (a) and (b) are true.

**100.** In a test of $H_0 : \mu = 100$ against $H_A : \mu \neq 100$ a sample of size 80 produces $Z = 0.8$ for the value of the test statistic. The *p*-value of the test is thus equal to
(a) 0.20 (b) 0.40
(c) 0.29 (d) 0.42

**101.** The curve, which is especially useful in graphically estimating percentiles is

(a) ogive (b) frequency curve
(c) normal curve (d) frequency polygon

**102.** Trace metals in drinking water wells affect the flavour of the water and unusually high concentrations can pose a health hazard. Furthermore, the water in well may vary in the concentration of the trace metals depending upon from where it is drawn. In the paper, 'Trace Metals of South Indian River Region' (Environmental Studies, 1982, 62-6), trace metal concentrations (mg/L) on zinc were found from water drawn from the bottom and the top of each of 6 wells. The data follows

| Location | Bottom | Top |
|---|---|---|
| 1 | 0.430 | 0.415 |
| 2 | 0.266 | 0.238 |
| 3 | 0.567 | 0.390 |
| 4 | 0.531 | 0.410 |
| 5 | 0.707 | 0.605 |
| 6 | 0.716 | 0.609 |

A 95% confidence interval for the mean difference in the zinc concentrations in this area between water drawn from the top and bottom of wells is

(a) $0.0917 \pm 2.57(0.061)$ (b) $0.0917 \pm 2.45(0.061)$
(c) $0.0917 \pm 2.57(0.025)$ (d) $0.0917 \pm 2.45(0.025)$

**103.** A student is interested in estimating the average number of showers per week taken by college sudents. Based on a preliminary sample he believes that $\sigma^2$ is close to 2.1. How large a sample is needed if his estimate is to be within 0.3 with probability 0.95?

(a) 183 (b) 253 (c) 64 (d) 90

**104.** We wish to test if a new feed increases the mean weight gain compared to an old feed. At the conclusion of the experiment it was found that the new feed gave a 10 kg bigger gain than the old feed. A two-sample *t*-test with the proper one-sided alternative was done and the resulting *p*-value was 0.082. This means

(a) there is an 8·2% chance the null hypothesis is true
(b) there was only a 8.2% chance of observing an increase greater than 10 kg (assuming the null hypothesis was true)
(c) there was only an 8·2% chance of observing an increase greater than 10 kg (assuming the null hypothesis was false)
(d) there is an 8·2% chance the alternate hypothesis is true

**105.** Let $(X_1, X_2)$ be a random sample from $N(0, 1)$. Then, the distribution of $\frac{(X_2 - X_1)^2}{2}$ is

(a) chi-square with one degree of freedom
(b) standard normal
(c) Cauchy
(d) *F*-distribution with (2, 2) degree of freedom

**106.** The following are percentages of fat found in 5 samples of each of two brands of ice cream :

| *A* | 5.7 | 4.5 | 6.2 | 6.3 | 7.3 |
|---|---|---|---|---|---|
| *B* | 6.3 | 5.7 | 5.9 | 6.4 | 5.1 |

Which of the following procedures is appropriate to test the hypothesis of equal average fat content in the two types of ice cream?

(a) Paired *t*-test with 5 df
(b) Two sample *t*-test with 8 df
(c) Paired *t*-test with 4 df
(d) Two sample *t*-test with 9 df

**107.** The United States Golf Association (USGA) tests new brands of golf balls to assure that they meet USGA specifications. One test involves measuring the average distance traveled when the ball is hit by a machine called 'Iron Byron''. Past tests have indicated that the standard deviation of the distances 'Iron Byron' hits golf balls is 10 m How many golf balls should be hit by 'Iron Byron' in order to estimate the mean distance for a new brand with a 90% conf dence inteval of width 2 m?

(a) 17 (b) 9
(c) 384 (d) 271

**108.** The excellent drug company claims its aspirin tablets will relieve headaches faster than any other aspirin on the market, To determine whether excellent's claim is valid, random samples of size 15 are chosen from aspirins made by excellent and the simple drug company. An aspirin is given to each of the 30 randomly selected persons suffering from headaches and the number of minutes required for each to recover from the headache is recorded. The sample results are

| | ₹/overline {X} ₹ | ₹ S~₹ 2 |
|---|---|---|
| Excellent (E) | 8.4 | 4.2 |
| Simple (S) | 8.9 | 4.6 |

A 5% significance level test is performed to determine whether Excellent's aspirin cures headaches significantly faste than Simple's aspirin. The appropriate hypothesis to be tested is

(a) $H : \mu E - \mu S = 0$ $A : \mu E - \mu S > 0$
(b) $H : \mu E - \mu S = 0$ $A : \mu E - \mu S \neq 0$
(c) $H : \mu E - \mu S = 0$ $A : \mu E - \mu S < 0$
(d) $H : \mu E - \mu S < 0$ $A : \mu E - \mu S = 0$

**109.** The life, in months of service, before a failure of the colour television picture tube in a random sample of 6 television sets manufactured by company *A* and 8 television sets manufactured by company *B* are as follows

| Company | Life of picture tube (Months) | | | | | | | |
|---|---|---|---|---|---|---|---|---|
| *A* | 32 | 25 | 40 | 31 | 35 | 29 | | |
| *B* | 45 | 32 | 47 | 34 | 37 | 27 | 35 | 44 |

The calculated value of the Rank sum test statistic for testing the null hypothesis that the life, in months of service, before failure of picture tube is the same both companies is

(a) 75 (b) 71 (c) 32 (d) 33

**110.** A study was carried out to investigate the effectiveness of a treatment. 1000 subjects participated in the study with 500 being randomly assigned to the 'treatment group' and the other 500 to the 'control (or placebo) group'. A statistically significant difference was reported between the responses of the two groups ($P < 0.005$). Thus,

(a) there is a large difference between the effects of the treatment and the placebo
(b) there is strong evidence that the treatment is very effective
(c) there is strong evidence that there is some difference in effect between the treatment and the placebo
(d) there is little evidence that the treatment has any effect

**111.** A research group was interested in predicting the number of bus riders per capita in census districts. They felt that the rider-ship per capita, $Y$ could be predicted using the average income $X$ for the census district. A sample of 29 census districts were taken and the observations on the samples were used to obtain $n = 29$, $Y = 62.1429$, $X = 3452.178$; $\Sigma(X - X)(Y - Y) = 189$ 312.0; $\Sigma(X - X)^2 = 19910691.0$; $\Sigma(Y - Y)^2 = 13369.381$; MSE $= 428.5$ based on this data, a 98% confidence interval for $\beta_1$ is

(a) $0.0095 \pm (2.473)(20.7894)$
(b) $0.0095 \pm (2.33)(0.0046)$
(c) $0.0095 \pm (2.33)(20.7894)$
(d) $0.0095 \pm (2.473)(0.0046)$

**112.** A researcher in biochemistry is attempting to summarize the results of an experiment. The experiment involved measuring enzyme active under a variety of conditions. The analysis has yielded the following statistics :

| $n$ | 10 |
|---|---|
| Median | 157.00 |
| Mean | 163.50 |
| Variance | 45.29 |
| SD | 6.73 |
| Range | 38.00 |

A 95% confidence interval for the mean enzyme activity is

(a) (161.4, 165.6) (b) (154.9, 159.1)
(c) (158.8, 168.2) (d) (158.7, 168.3)

**113.** If $X_1, \ldots, X_n$ is a random sample from the poisson distribution with mean $\lambda$. The Cramer-Rao lower bound to the variance of any unbiased estimator of $\lambda$ is given by

(a) $\dfrac{\lambda^2}{n}$ (b) $\dfrac{\lambda}{n}$ (c) $\dfrac{\sqrt{\lambda}}{n}$ (d) $\dfrac{e^{-\lambda}}{n}$

**114.** Following the analysis of some data on two samples drawn from populations in which the variable of interest is normally distributed, the $p$-value for the comparison of the two sample means under the null hypothesis that the two population means are equal ($H_0 \mu_1 = \mu_2$) against $H_A : \mu_1 \neq \mu_2$ was found to be 0·0063. This $ps$ value indicates that

(a) there is very little evidence in the data for a conclusion to be reached
(b) there is rather strong evidence against the null hypothesis
(c) the evidence against the null hypothesis is not strong
(d) the null hypothesis should be accepted

**115.** Let $\{x_1, x_2, \ldots, x_n\}$ be a random sample from a normal population $N(\mu, 1)$. Then, an unbiased estimator of $\mu^2 + 1$ is

(a) $\dfrac{1}{n}\sum_{i=1}^{n} x_i$ (b) $\dfrac{1}{n}\sum_{i=1}^{n} x_i^2$
(c) $\sum_{i=1}^{n} x_i$ (d) $\sum_{i=1}^{n} x_i^2$

**116.** Let $T$ be an unbiased estimator for $\theta$ $V(T) > 0$. Then,

(a) $T$ is unbiased estimator of $\theta^2$
(b) $T^2$ is unbiased estimator of $\theta^2$
(c) $T^2$ is also unbiased estimator of $\theta^3$
(d) $T^2$ is biased estimator of $\theta^2$

**117.** From a normal population $N(\mu, \sigma^2)$,

(a) the sample mean is not consistent estimator of $\mu$
(b) sample mean is not consistent estimator of $\sigma^2$
(c) sample mean is consistent estimator of $\mu$
(d) sample mean is consistent estimator of $\sigma^2$

**Directions** (Q. Nos. 118-120) In random sampling from normal population $N(\mu, \sigma^2)$, the maximum likelihood estimator for

**118.** $\mu$, when $\sigma^2$ is known as

(a) $n\mu$ (b) $\sqrt{n}\,\mu$
(c) $\bar{x}$ (d) $n\bar{x}$

**119.** $\sigma^2$, when $\mu$ is known as

(a) $\hat{\sigma}^2 = \dfrac{1}{n}\sum_{i=1}^{n}(x_i - \mu)^2$ (b) $\hat{\sigma}^2 = \dfrac{1}{n-1}\sum_{i=1}^{n}(x_i - \mu)^2$
(c) $\hat{\sigma}^2 = \dfrac{n}{n-1}\sum_{i=1}^{n}(x_i - \mu)^2$ (d) $\hat{\sigma}^2 = \sum_{i=1}^{n}(x_i - \mu)^2$

**120.** Simultaneous estimation of $\mu$ and $\sigma^2$ is

(a) $\hat{\mu} = \bar{x}, \hat{\sigma}^2 = \dfrac{1}{n}\sum_{i=1}^{n}(x_i - \bar{x})^2 = s^2$
(b) $\hat{\mu} = \bar{x}, \hat{\sigma}^2 = \dfrac{n}{n-1}s^2$
(c) $\hat{\mu} = \bar{x}, \hat{\sigma}^2 = \sigma^2$
(d) None of the above

**121.** The minimum variance bound (MVB) estimator for $\mu$ in the normal population $N(\mu, \sigma^2)$, where $\sigma^2$ is known as

(a) $\bar{x}$ (b) $n\bar{x}$
(c) $\sigma^2$ (d) $n\sigma^2$

**122.** The minimum variance bound (MVB) estimator for $\theta$ in the Cauchy's population is

(a) $\bar{x}$ (b) $n\bar{x}$

(c) $\sigma^2$ (d) not in existence

**123.** A random sample $\{x_1, x_2, \ldots, x_n\}$ is taken from a normal population with mean zero and variance $\sigma^2$. Then, MVB estimator for $\sigma^2$ is

(a) $\frac{\Sigma x_i}{n}$ (b) $\sum_{i=1}^{n} \frac{x_i^2}{n}$

(c) $\Sigma x_i$ (d) $\Sigma x_i^2$

**Directions** (Q. Nos. 124-126) If $x \geq 1$, is the critical region for testing $H_0 : \theta = 2$ against the alternative $\theta = 1$, on the basis of the single observation from the population,

$$f(x, \theta) = \theta \exp(-\theta x),\ 0 \leq x < \infty.\ \text{Then,}$$

**124.** Size of type I error is

(a) $e$ (b) $\frac{1}{e}$

(c) $e^2$ (d) $\frac{1}{e^2}$

**125.** Size of type II error is

(a) $\frac{1}{e}$ (b) $1 - \frac{1}{e}$

(c) $e$ (d) $1 - e$

**126.** Power of the test is

(a) $e$ (b) $\frac{1}{e}$

(c) $1 - e$ (d) $1 - \frac{1}{e}$

**127.** If $X_1, X_2, \ldots, X_n$ are random observations on a Bernoulli variable $X$ taking value 1 with probability $p$ and the value 0 with probability $1-p$, then the consistent estimator of $p(1-p)$ is

(a) $\bar{X}(1-\bar{X})$ (b) $\frac{1}{n}\bar{X}(1-\bar{X})$

(c) $\frac{\bar{X}^2}{n}$ (d) $\frac{n}{1-n}(1-\bar{X})$

**128.** For Cauchy's distribution, which one is true?

(a) Sample mean and sample median are consistent estimators of population mean and population median.

(b) Sample mean is consistent but sample median is not consistent estimator of the population mean.

(c) Sample mean is non-consistent estimator but sample median is consistent estimator of the population mean.

(d) Sample mean and sample median both are not consistent estimators of population mean.

**129.** Let $X_1, X_2, \ldots, X_n$ be a random sample from a population with pdf

$$f(x, \theta) = \theta x^{\theta-1},\ 0 < x < 1,\ \theta > 0.$$

Then, $t = \prod_{i=1}^{n} X_i$ is

(a) sufficient estimate for $\theta$

(b) not sufficient estimate for $\theta$

(c) sufficient estimate for $n\theta$

(d) not sufficient estimate for $n\theta$

**Directions** (Q. Nos. 130-131) The maximum likelihood estimate of the parameter $\alpha$ of a population having density function

$$\frac{2}{\alpha^2}(\alpha - x),\ 0 < x < \alpha$$

**130.** For a sample of unit size is

(a) $x$ (b) $2x$

(c) $3x$ (d) $\frac{x}{2}$

**131.** The maximum likelihood estimate of the parameter $\alpha$ of a population $\frac{2}{\alpha^2}(\alpha - x),\ 0 < x < \alpha$ for a sample of unit size is

(a) biased (b) unbiased

(c) $x$ (d) $\sqrt{x}$

**132.** Maximum likelihood estimate for the parameter $\lambda$ of a Poisson distribution on the basis of a sample of size $n$ is

(a) $\bar{x}$ (b) $n\bar{x}$

(c) $\frac{\bar{x}}{n}$ (d) $\frac{\bar{x}}{\sqrt{n}}$

**133.** The variance of maximum likelihood estimate for the parameter $\lambda$ of a Poisson distribution on the basis of a sample of size $n$ is

(a) $\lambda$ (b) $\frac{n}{\lambda}$

(c) $\frac{\lambda}{n}$ (d) $\frac{\lambda}{n^2}$

**134.** The sufficient estimator for estimating the parameter $\lambda$ of the Poisson distribution is

(a) $\bar{X}$ (b) $n\bar{X}$

(c) $\frac{\bar{X}}{n}$ (d) $\frac{\bar{X}}{n^2}$

**135.** A study was conducted to examine the quality of fish after seven days in ice storage. For this study

$Y$ = measurement of fish quality (on a 10 point scale with 10 = BEST.)

X = # of hours after being caught that the fish were packed in ice.

The sample linear regression line is $\hat{Y} = 8.5 - 0.5X$. From this we can say that

(a) a one hour delay in packing the fish in ice decreases the estimated quality by 0.5

(b) a one hour delay in packing the fish in ice increases the estimated quality by 0.5

(c) if the estimated quality increases by 1, then the fish have been packed in ice one hour sooner

(d) if the estimated quality increases by 1 the fish have been packed in ice two hours later

**136.** Refer to the previous question. If the number of weeks after planting ranged from 2 to 8. What is the predicted height for a seedling afler 12 weeks?

(a) Should not be determined because the relationship between $Y$ and $X$ may not be linear beyond 8 weeks.

(b) 9·467

(c) 24·804

(d) 28·584

**137.** There is an approximate linear relationship between the height of females and their age (from 5 to 18 yr) described by

height = 50.3 + 6.01 (age)

where, height is measured in cm and age in years. Which of the following is not correct?

(a) The estimated slope is 6·01 which implies that children increase by about 6 cm for each year they grow older.

(b) The estimated height of a child who is 10 yr old is about 110 cm.

(c) The estimated- intercept is 50.3 cm which implies that children reach this height when they are $\frac{50.3}{6.01} = 8.4$ yr old.

(d) The average height of children when they are 5 yr old is about 50% of the average height when they are 18 yr old

**138.** A botanist investigates the relationship between $Y$ the heights of seedlings (in inches) and $X$, the number of weeks after planting. The summary data are $n = 6$, $\overline{X} = 4.67$, $\overline{Y} = 9.467$, $\Sigma X^2 = 154$, $\Sigma Y^2 = 696.54$ $\Sigma XY = 325.9$. The fitted regression line for seedling height on the number of weeks after planting is

(a) $\hat{\mathbf{Y}} = 2.8 + 2.62\,X$ (b) $\hat{\mathbf{Y}} = -2.8 + 2.62\,X$

(c) $\hat{\mathbf{Y}} = 2.62 + 2.8\,X$ (d) $\hat{\mathbf{Y}} = 9.5 + 2.62\,X$

**139.** The least squares regression line is the line

(a) which is determined by use of a function of the distance between the observed $Y$'s and the predicted $Y$'s

(b) which has the smallest sum of the squared residuals of any line through the data values

(c) for which the sum of the residuals about the line is zero

(d) which has all of the above properties

**140.** A selection of cereals was sampled and the number of calories was plotted against the number of grams of protein with the following results

**Parameter Estimates**

| Term | Estimate | Std Error | Lower 95% | Upper 95% |
|---|---|---|---|---|
| Intercept | 106.01939 | 5.687496 | 4.689284 | 117.3495 |
| Protein | 0.3393214 | 2.054662 | −3.753788 | 4.4324306 |

Which of the following is not correct?

(a) The 95% confidence interval for the number of calories per gram of protein indicates that the known true value of 4 calories/g may be consistent with the data.

(b) It is estimated that cereals with no protein would have just over 100 calories/serving.

(c) The observed regression line is $Y = 106.0 + 0.339$ (Protein).

(d) The standard error for the slope indicates how much the calories may vary among different cereals in the sample

**141.** A survey was conducted to investigate, whether alcohol consumption and smoking are related. The following information was compiled for 600 individuals.

| | Smoker | Non-smoker |
|---|---|---|
| Drinker | 193 | 165 |
| Non-drinker | 89 | 153 |

Which of the following statements is true?

(a) The appropriate alternative hypothesis is $A$ : Smoking and alcohol consumption are independent

(b) The appropriate null hypothesis is $H$ : Smoking and alcohol consumption are not independent.

(c) The culculated value of the text stastistic is 3.84.

(d) At level 0.01 We conclude that smoking and alcohol consumption are related.

**142.** The average height of children is believed to have increased in the last 50 yr due to better nutrition and better health services. To examine this hypothesis, measurement of the heights (in cm) of 10 pairs of mothers and their eldest adult daughters yielded the following results

| Pair | Mother | Daughter | Pair | Mother | Daughter |
|---|---|---|---|---|---|
| 1 | 178.2 | 178.2 | 6 | 166.6 | 172.8 |
| 2 | 173.4 | 168.6 | 7 | 157.4 | 152.0 |
| 3 | 163.0 | 164.2 | 8 | 176.4 | 176.4 |
| 4 | 152.2 | 157.4 | 9 | 162.0 | 159.4 |
| 5 | 155·8 | 165·2 | 10 | 165.1 | 159·0 |

Consider the differences computed by taking the mother's height, the daughter's height. The value of the Signed Rank test statistic is

(a) 36 (b) 19

(c) 16 (d) 6

**143.** A manufacturer wished to compare the wearing qualities of two different types of automobile tires $A$ and $B$. To make the comparison, a tire of type $A$ and one of type $B$ were randomly assigned and mounted on the rear wheels of each of five automobiles. The automobiles were then operated for a specified number of miles and the. amount of wear was recorded for each tire. These measurements appear below

| Automobile | Tire A | Tire B |
|---|---|---|
| 1 | 10·6 | 10.2 |
| 2 | 9·8 | 9.4 |
| 3 | 12·3 | 11.8 |
| 4 | 9·7 | 9.1 |
| 5 | 8.8 | 8.3 |

The absolute value of the test statistic calculated from the data for testing the null hypothesis that there is no difference in the average wear for the two types of tires is

(a) 12.83 (b) 5.7 (c) 8·35 (d) 10.72

**144.** Coefficient of correlation is unaffected by change of

(a) origin but not scale
(b) scale but not origin
(c) origin as well as scale in only one of the variables
(d) origin as well as scale in either or both the variables

**145.** To determine the reliability of experts used in interpreting the results of polygraph examinection in criminal investigations, 280 cases were studied. The results were

| | | True Status | |
|---|---|---|---|
| | | **Innocent** | **Guilty** |
| Examiner's | Innocent | 131 | 15 |
| Decision | Guilty | 9 | 225 |

If the hypotheses were $H$ : Suspect is Innocent vs A : suspect is guilty, then we could estimate the probability of making a type II error as

(a) 15/280 (b) 9/280 (c) 15/140 (d) 9/140

**146.** During the pre-flight check, Pilot Jones discovers a minor problem a warning light indicates that the fuel gauge may be broken. If Jones decides to check the fuel level by hand, it will delay the flight by 45 min. If Jones decides to ignore the warning, the aircraft may run out of fuel before it gets to Gimli. In this situation, what would be

(i) the appropriate null hypothesis? and;
(ii) a type I error?

(a) Null Hypothesis: assume that the warning can be ignored.
Type I error : decide to check the fuel by hand when there is in fact enough fuel.
(b) Null Hypothesis: assume that the warning can be ignored.
Type I error : decide to ignore the warning when there is in fact not enough fuel
(c) Null Hypothesis: assume that the fuel should be checked by hand.
Type I error : decide to ignore the warning when there is in fact not enough fuel.
(d) Null Hypothesis : assume that the fuel should be checked by hand.
Type 1 error : decide to check the fueled by hand when there is in fact enough fuel.

**147.** The correlation coefficient provides

(a) a measure of the extent to which changes in one variable cause changes in another variable
(b) a measure of the strength of the linear association between two categorical variables
(c) a measure of the strength of the association (not necessarily linear) between two categorical variables
(d) a measure of the strength of the linear association between two quantitative variables

**148.** If $X_1, \ldots, X_n$ are pair wise uncorrelated random variables with the same variance, then the correlation coefficient between $X_1$ and $\bar{X}$ (the mean of the random variables) is

(a) 0 (b) 1
(c) $1/\sqrt{n}$ (d) $1/n$

**149.** In hypothesis testing, $\beta$ is the probability of committing an error of type II. The power of the test, $1-\beta$ is, then

(a) the probability of rejecting $H_0$ when $H_A$ is true
(b) the probability of failing to reject $H_0$ when $H_A$ is true
(c) the probability of failing to reject $H_0$ when $H_0$ is true
(d) the probability of rejecting $H_0$ when $H_0$ is true

**150.** For children, there is approximately a linear relationship between 'height' and 'age'. One child was measured monthly. Her height was 75 cm at 3 yr of age and 85 cm when she was measured 18 months later. A least squares line was fit to her data. The slope of this line is approximately

(a) 0.55 cm/m (b) 10 cm/m
(c) 25 cm/m (d) 1.57 cm/m

**151.** For children between the ages of 18 months and 29 months, there is approximately a linear relationship, between 'height and 'age'. The relationship can be represented by : $\hat{Y} = 64.93 + 0.63(x)$, where $Y$ represents height (in cm) and $X$ represents age (in month). Joseph is 22.5 monthrs old and is 80 cm tall. What is Joseph's residual?

(a) 79.1 (b) – 0.9
(c) + 0.9 (d) 56.6

**152.** If $x$ and $y$ are independent variables, then cov $(x, y)$ is

(a) $\sigma_x\sigma_y$ (b) $\frac{\sigma_x}{\sigma_y}$
(c) $\frac{\sigma_y}{\sigma_x}$ (d) 0

**153.** Since, $\alpha$ = probability of type I error, then $1-\alpha$

(a) probability of rejecting $H_0$ when $H_0$ is true
(b) probability of not rejecting $H_0$ when $H_0$ is true
(c) probability of not rejecting $H_0$ when $H_A$ is true
(d) probability of rejecting $H_0$ when $H_A$ is true

**154.** On May 11th, 50 randomly selected subjects had their systolic blood pressure (SBP) recorded twice, the first time at about 9:00 am and the second time at about 2:00 pm If one were to examine the relationship between the morning and afternoon readings, then one might expect

(a) the correlation to be near zero, as the morning and afternoon readings should be independent of one another

(b) the correlation to be high and positive, as those with relatively high readings in the morning will tend to have relatively high readings in the afternoon

(c) the correlation to be high and negative, as those with relatively high readings in the morning will tend to have relatively low readings in the afternoon

(d) the correlation to be near zero, as correlation measures the strength of the linear association

**155.** Angle between two lines of regression is

(a) $\tan^{-1}\left(\frac{r_1 - 1/r_2}{1 + r_2/r_1}\right)$ (b) $\tan^{-1}\left(\frac{r_1 r_2 - 1}{r_1 + r_2}\right)$

(c) $\tan^{-1}\left(\frac{r_2 - 1/r_1}{1 + r_2/r_1}\right)$ (d) $\tan^{-1}\left(\frac{r_1 - r_2}{1 + r_1 r_2}\right)$

where, $r_1$ is coefficient of line of regression of $y$ on $x$ and $r_2$ of $x$ on $y$.

**156.** In a statistical test of hypothesis, what happens to the rejection region when $\alpha$ the level of significance, is reduced?

(a) The answer depends on the value of $\beta$.

(b) The rejection region is reduced in size.

(c) The rejection region is increased in size.

(d) The rejection region is unaltered.

**157.** Are all employees equally prone to having accidents? To investigate this hypothesis, Parry (1985) looked at a light manufacturing plant and classified the accidents by type and by age of the employee.

| | Accident Type | | |
|---|---|---|---|
| **Age** | **Sprain** | **Burn** | **Cut** |
| Under 25 | 9 | 17 | 5 |
| 25 or over | 61 | 13 | 12 |

A chi-square test gave a test-statistic of 20.78. If we test at $\alpha = 0.05$

(a) there appears to be no association between accident type and age

(b) age seems to be independent of accident type

(c) accident type does not seem to be independent of age

(d) there appears to be a 20.78% correlation between accident type and age

**158.** If $x = X - M_x$, $y = Y - M_y$ and $\Sigma xy = 40$, $\Sigma x^2 = 80$ and $\Sigma y^2 = 20$. Then, coefficient of correlation between $X$ and $Y$ is

(a) 0 (b) 0.5 (c) $-1$ (d) 1

**159.** If the correlation coefficient between two variables $x$ and $y$ is 0.4 and regression coefficient $x$ on $y$ is 0.2, then regression coefficient of $y$ on $x$, is

(a) 0.4 (b) $\pm 0.8$
(c) 0.8 (d) 0.6

**160.** Seven sets of identical twins are given psychological tests to determine whether the firstborn of the twins tends to be more aggressive than the second born. The results are shown in the following table, where the higher score represents greater aggressiveness.

| Set | First born | Second born | Difference |
|---|---|---|---|
| 1 | 86 | 88 | $-2$ |
| 2 | 77 | 65 | 12 |
| 3 | 91 | 90 | 1 |
| 4 | 70 | 65 | 5 |
| 5 | 75 | 80 | $-5$ |
| 6 | 88 | 81 | 7 |
| 7 | 87 | 72 | 15 |

If we are willing to assume that the distribution of differences is symmetric about the median but not necessarily normal, then the value of the appropriate test statistic is

(a) 22·5 and we would reject $H_0$ at $\alpha = 0.05$

(b) 40 and we would reject $H_0$ at $\alpha = 0.05$

(c) 1·71 and we would not reject $H_0$ at $\alpha = 0.05$

(d) 22.5 and we would not reject $H_0$ at $\alpha = 0.05$

**161.** If two regression lines are coincident, then which is correct?

(a) $r = 0$ (b) $r = -1/2$
(c) $r = 1/2$ (d) $r = \pm 1$

**162.** If $\Sigma x = 30, \Sigma y = 42$, $\Sigma xy = 199, \Sigma x^2 = 184$, $\Sigma y^2 = 318$ and $n = 6$, then regression coefficient $b_{xy}$ is

(a) $-0.36$ (b) 0.46
(c) 0.26 (d) 0.38

**163.** In a statistical test for the equality of a mean, such as $H_0: \mu = 10$, if $\alpha = 0.05$

(a) 95% of the time we will make an incorrect inference

(b) 5% of the time we will say that there is a real difference when there is no difference

(c) 5% of the time we will say that there is no real difference when there is a difference

(d) 95% of the time the null hypothesis will be correct

**164.** Men tend to marry women who are slightly younger than themselves. Suppose that every man married a woman who was exactly 0.5 of a year younger than themselves. Which of the following is correct?

(a) The correlation is $-0.5$.

(B) The correlation is 0.5.

(c) The correlation is 1.

(d) The correlation is $-1$.

**165.** The two lines of regression are $x + 2y - 5 = 0$ and $x + 3y - 8 = 0$. The coefficient of correlation between x and y is

(a) – 0.82 (b) 0.82
(c) 0.72 (d) 0.73

**166.** If $b_{xy} = 1.6$ and $b_{xy} = 0.4$ and the angle between two regression lines is θ, then tan θ is

(a) 0.18 (b) 0.16
(c) 0.3 (d) 0.24

**167.** The usual statistic to test atis whether bivariate normal population correlation coefficient ρ is zero, is

(a) $\left(\frac{r}{\sqrt{1-r^2}}\right)\sqrt{n-2}$ (b) $\left(\frac{r}{\sqrt{1-r^2}}\right)\sqrt{n-1}$

(c) $\frac{1}{2\log\frac{1+r}{1-r}}$ (d) $\frac{r}{\sqrt{n}}$

**168.** Which of the following statements is correct?

(a) An extremely small *p*-value indicates that the actual data differs markedly from that expected, if the null hypothesis were true.
(b) The *p*-value measures the probability that the hypothesis is true.
(c) The *p*-value measures the probability of making a type II error.
(d) The larger the p-value, the stronger the evidence against the null hypothesis.

**169.** Which of the following is not correct?

(a) The probability of a type I error is controlled by the selection of the α level.
(b) The probability of a type II error is controlled by the sample size.
(c) The power of a test depends upon the sample size and the distance between the null and alternate hypothesis.
(d) The *p*-value measures the probability that the null hypothesis is true.

**170.** The coefficient of correlation between x and y is

| *x* | 1 | 2 | 3 | 4 | 5 |
|---|---|---|---|---|---|
| *y* | 3 | 7 | 12 | 19 | 28 |

(a) – 1 (b) – 0.82
(c) 0.82 (d) 0.988

**171.** If cov $(x, y) = 40$, var $(x) = 120$ and var $(y) = 30$, then coefficient of correlation between x and y is

(a) 0.62 (b) 0.66
(c) 1.20 (d) – 0.360

**172.** If $X_i$, $i = 1, 2, \ldots, n$ are the ranks on variables X and Y for n individuals, then the value of $\sum_{i=1}^{n}(X_i - Y_i)^2$ is always less than

(a) $n(n^2-1)$ (b) $\frac{(n^2-1)}{3}$ (c) $n^2 - 1$ (d) $\frac{n(n^2-1)}{3}$

**173.** A student wishes to examine the effect of wing width and wing length on the length of flight of a paper airplane. There are 4 different models of airplanes. Which of the following is not correct?

(a) A factor (such as wing width) is an experimental variable under control of the experimenter.
(b) The order of flights was randomized to remove the influence of any other variables upon the light distance of each flight.
(c) It would be better to make four copies of each model of plane to give some feel for the plne-to-plane variations. Flying a single copy four times gives information about the internal variation.
(d) Interaction between two factors means that the effect of a factor at one level depends on the level of the second factor.

**174.** The power takeoff driveline on tractors used in agriculture is a potentially serious hazard to operators of farm equipment. The driveline is covered by a shield in new tractors, but for a variety of reasons, the shield is often missing on older tractors. Two type of shields are the bolt-on and the flip-up. It was believed that the bolt-on shield was perceived as a nuisance by the operators and deliberately removed, but the flip-up shield is easily lifted for inspection and maintenance and may be left in place. In a easily lifted for inspection and maintenance and may be left in place. In a study initiated by the National Safety Council of the US, a sample of older tractors with both types of shields was taken to see what proportion were removed of 183 tractors designed to have bolt-on shields, 35 had been removed of the 136 tractors with flip-up shields, 15 were removed. We wish to test the hypothesis $H: p_b = p_f$ vs $A: p_b \neq f_f$, where $p_b$ and $p_f$ are the proportion or tractors with the bolt-on and flip-up shields removed, respectively. The test-statistic is computed to be 1.97. The *p*-value is

(a) 0.025 (b) 0.049
(c) 0.012 (d) 0.975

**175.** The two lines of regression are $13x - 10y + 11 = 0$ and $2x - y - 1 = 0$, then mean of x and y series are

(a) 3, – 5 (b) 3, 5 (c) – 3, 10 (d) – 3, – 5

**176.** The point that lies on both the lines of regression for a bivariate distribution, is

(a) (0, 0) (b) $(\bar{x}, \bar{y})$ (c) $(\sigma_x, \sigma_y)$ (d) $(r_1, r_2)$

**177.** Let $X_1, X_2, \ldots, X_p$ be random variables with finite moments of second order. Let $\hat{\mathbf{X}}_1$ be the multiple linear regression of $(X_2, X_3, \ldots, X_p)$ on $X_1$. Now, consider the following statements

1. $X_1$ and $\hat{\mathbf{X}}_1$ are positively correlated
2. $X_1$ and $X_1 - \hat{\mathbf{X}}_1$, are uncorrelated

Select the correct answer from the following alternatives

(a) both I and II are correct
(b) neither I nor II is correct
(c) only II is correct
(d) only I is correct

**178.** An experiment was designed an experiment to investigate the effect of the amount of water and seed variety upon subsequent growth of plants. Each plant was potted in a clay plot and a measured amount of water was given weekly. The height of the plant at the end of the experiment was measured.
Which of the following is not correct?

(a) The response variable is the plant height.
(b) The explanatory variables are the amount of water and seed variety.
(c) Randomization was used to eliminate the effect of other possible factors upon the growth of the plants.
(d) A possible uncontrollable factor in this experiment is any nutrients that might be present in the clay pots.

**179.** Two different medical procedures are widely used to treat a disease. One hundred patients were randomly selected for each procedure in a recent clinical trial, with the following results

| | $n$ | Number of successes (no recurrence of disease) |
|---|---|---|
| Procedure 1 | 100 | 78 |
| Procedure 2 | 100 | 87 |

What is the absolute value of the test statistic calculated from the data for testing the null hypothesis that there is no difference between the success rates between procedure 1 and procedure 2?

(a) + 0.658 (b) +1.675 (c) +2.385 (d) +2.575

**180.** The two lines of regression are $8x - 10y = 66$ and $40x - 18y = 214$ and variance of $x$ is 9. The standard deviation of $y$ series is

(a) 8 (b) 6 (c) 4 (d) 3

**181.** If $r_1$ and $r_2$ are regression coefficients of $Y$ on $X$ and $X$ on $Y$ respectively, then

(a) $r_1 + r_2 = 2r$ (b) $r_1 + r_2 < 2r$
(c) $r_1 + r_2 \geq 2r$ (d) None of these

**182.** Partial correlation coefficient $r_{23.1}$ is strictly positive, if

(a) $r_{23}^2 > r_{12}r_{13}$ (b) $r_{32}^2 < r_{12}r_{13}$
(c) $r_{23} < r_{12}r_{13}$ (d) $r_{32} > r_{12}r_{13}$

**183.** A study found a correlation of $r = -0.61$ between the sex of a worker and his or her income. You conclude that

(a) women earn more than men on average
(b) women earn less than men on average
(c) an arithmetic mistake was made; this is not a possible value of $r$
(d) this is non-sense because $r$ makes no sense here

**184.** Suppose the $p$-value was found to be 0.053. This means

(a) the probability that the proportion of smokers has not changed is 0.053
(b) the proportion of smokers has definitely decreased
(c) there is some but not overwhelming evidence, that the proportion of smokers has decreased
(d) there is no evidence that the proportion of smokers is the same in both years

**185.** Two variables have least square regression lines $3x + 2y = 26$ and $6x + y = 31$, then correlation between $x$ and $y$ is

(a) 0.5 (b) 0.7 (c) – 0.7 (d) – 0.5

**186.** The coefficieint of correlation between $x$ and $y$ is 0.5 and their covariance is 16 and SD of $x$ is 4, then SD of $y$ is

(a) 4 (b) 8 (c) 16 (d) 64

**187.** Let $X$ and $Y$ be the number of heads and number of tails in tossing a coin $n$ times. Then, the coefficient of $Y$ on $X$ is

(a) 0 (b) – 1 (c) 1 (d) $\frac{1}{2}$

**188.** A random sample of 100 members of a union are asked to respond to two questions :

Question 1. Are you happy with your financial situation? Question 2. Do you approve of the Federal government's economic policies? The responses are

| | | Question 1 | | |
|---|---|---|---|---|
| | | Yes | No | Total |
| Question 2 | Yes | 22 | 48 | 70 |
| | No | 12 | 18 | 30 |
| | Total | 34 | 66 | 100 |

To test null hypothesis that response to Question 1 is independent of response to Question 2 at 5% level, the expected frequency for the cell (Yes, Yes) and the critical value of the associated test statistic are

(a) 23.8 and 1.96, respectively
(b) 10.2 and 3.84, respectively
(c) 23.8 and 3.84, respectively
(d) 23.8 and 7.81, respectively

**189.** In a similar study of adult makes, the p-value was found to be 0.053. This means

(a) the probability that the proportion of male smokes has not changed is 0.053
(b) the proportion of male smokers has definitely decreased
(c) if the proportion of male smokers has not changed, than there is only a 0.053 chance of seeing the observed drop in the smoking rate in the survey
(d) if the proportion of male smokers has changed, then there is only a 0.053 chance of detecting a difference

**190.** If cov $(x, y) = -16.5$, var $(x) = 2.89$, var $(y) = 100$, the coefficient of correlation is

(a) $-0.97$ (b) $-0.87$
(c) $-0.97$ (d) None of these

**191.** For 12 pair of observation on $x$ and $y$ the $r$ calculated is 0.674. The standard error is

(a) 0.2563 (b) 0.1573
(c) 0.4384 (d) None of these

**192.** The table given below the shows the ranks assigned to candidates $A$, $B$, $C$ and $D$ by two judges :

| Candidate | $A$ | $B$ | $C$ | $D$ |
|---|---|---|---|---|
| Judge 1 | 2 | 1 | 3 | 4 |
| Judge 2 | 1 | 2 | 4 | 3 |

Based on this data, spearman's rank correlation coefficient will be

(a) $\frac{1}{2}$ (b) $\frac{2}{5}$
(c) $\frac{3}{5}$ (d) $\frac{4}{5}$

**193.** If the correlation between body weight and annual income where high and positive, we could conclude that

(a) high incomes cause people to eat more food
(b) low incomes cause people to eat less food
(c) high income people tend to spend a greater proportion of their income on food than low income people, on average
(d) high income people tend to be heavier than low income people people, on average

**194.** In testing statistical hypothesis, which of the following statements is false?

(a) The critical regions is the values of the test statistic for which we reject the null hypothesis.
(b) The level of significance is the probability of type I error.
(c) For testing $H_0 \mu = \mu_0$ $H_A : \mu > \mu_0$, we reject $H_0$ for high values of the sample mean $X$.
(d) The p-value measures the probability that the null hypothesis is true.

**195.** If $x$ and $y$ are independent variables, then two lines of regression are

(a) $x = 0, y = 0$
(b) $x = 0, y =$ constant
(c) $x =$ constant, $y = 0$
(d) $x =$ constant, $y =$ constant

**196.** The correlation coefficient 0.5 between $x$ and $y$ means

(a) 50% of data are explained
(b) 25% of variations are explained
(c) out of total variations of $y$ only 25% is due to $x$ and rest due to other factors
(d) out to total variation of $y$ only 50% is due to to $x$ and rest due to other factors

**197.** Let the random variable $X$ have uniform distribution over (0,1) Then, the correlation coefficient between $X$ and its distribution function is

(a) 0 (b) 0.5 (c) 1 (d) $-1$

**198.** A research study has reported that there is a correlation of $r = -0.59$ between the eye colour (brown, green and blue) of an experimental animal and the amount of nicotine that is fatal to the animal when consumed. This indicates

(a) nicotine is less harmful to one eye colour than the others
(b) the lethal of nicotine goes down as the eye colour of the animal changes
(c) one must always consider the eye colour of animals in making statements about the effect of nicotine consumption
(d) the researchers need to take a course in statistics because correlation is not an appropriate measure of association in this situation

**199.** In a hypothesis testing problem

(a) the null hypothesis will not be rejected unless the data are not unusual (given that the hypothesis is true)
(b) the null hypothesis will not be rejected unless the p-value indicates the data are very unusual (given that the hypothesis is true)
(c) the null hypothesis will not be rejected only if the probability of observing the data provide convincing evidence that it is true
(d) The null hypothesis is also called the research hypothesis; the alternative hypothesis often represents the status quo

**200.** Last year a small statistical consulting company paid each of its five statistical clerks \$22000 two statistical analysts \$50000 each and the senior statistician/owner \$270000 The number of employees earning less than the mean salary is

(a) 0 (b) 4 (c) 5 (d) 7

**201.** A sample of underweight babies was fed a special diet and the following weight gains (lbs) were observed at the end of three montns.

6.7 2.7 2.5 3.6 3.4 4.1 4.8 5.9 8.3

The mean and standard deviation are

(a) 4.67,3.82 (b) 3.82,4.67
(c) 4.67,1.95 (d) 1.95,4.67

**202.** The Central Limit Theorem states that

(a) if $n$ is large, then the distribution of the sample can be approximated closely by a normal curve
(b) if $n$ is large and if the population is normal, then the variance of the sample mean must be small
(c) if $n$ is large, then the sampling distribution of the sample mean can be approximated closely by a normal curve
(c) if $n$ is large and if the population is normal, then the sampling distribution of the sample mean can be approximated closely by a normal curve

**203.** The term test scores of 15 students enrolled in a business statistics class were recorded in ascending order as follows

4, 7, 7, 9, 10, 11, 13, 15, 15, 15, 17, 17, 19, 19, 20

After calculating the mean, median, and mode an error is discovered : one of the 15' s is really a 17. The measures of central tendency which will change are

(a) the mean only (b) the mode only
(c) the median only (d) the mean and mode

**204.** The central limit theorem tells us that the sampling distribution approximately normal. Which of the following conditions are necessary for the theorem to be valid?

(a) The sample size has to be large.
(b) We have to be sampling from a normal population.
(c) The population has to be symmetric.
(d) population variance has to be small.

**205.** Suppose a frequency distribution is skewed with a median of $75 and a mode of $80. Which of the following is a possible value for the mean of distribution?

(a) $86 (b) $91
(c) $64 (d) $75

**206.** Which of the following statement is not true?

(a) In a symmetric distribution, the means and the median are equal.
(b) The first quartile is equal to the twenty-fifth percentile.
(c) In a symmetric distribution, the median is halfway between the first and the third quartiles.
(d) The median is always greater than the mean.

**207.** A scientist is weighing each of 30 fish. She obtains a mean of 30 g and a standard deviation of 2 g. After completing the weighing, she finds that the scale was misaligned and always under reported every weight 2 g,*i.e..*, a fish that really weighed 26 g was reported to weigh 24 g. What is mean and standard deviation after correcting for the error in the scale ?

(a) 28 g, 2g (b) 30 g, 4 g,
(c) 32 g, 2g (d) 32 g, 4 g

**208.** The Central Limit Theorem is important in statistics because it allows us to use the normal distribution to make inferences concerning the population mean

(a) provided that the population is normally distributed and the sample size is reasonably large
(b) provided that the population is normally distributed (for any sample size)
(c) provided that the sample size is reasonably large (for any population)
(d) provided that the population is normally distributed and the population variance is known (for any sample size)

**209.** Rainwater was collected in water collectors at thirty different sites near an industrial basin and the amount of acidity (pH level) was measured. The mean and standard deviation of the values are 4.60 and 1.10, respectively. When the pH metre was recaliprated back at the laboratory, it was found to be in error. The error can be corrected by adding 0.1 pH units to all of the values and then multiply the result by 1.2. The mean and standard deviation of the corrected pH measurements are

(a) 5.64,1.44 (b) 5.64, 1.32
(c) 5.40, 1.44 (d) 5.40, 1.32

**210.** An experiment was conducted by the Schwarz family to took at the yield of popcorn (total grams that popped when 15 g of popcorn were heated) when two variables (the type of popcorn : gourmet or plain) and the amount of oil (little or lots) was used.A profile plot of the results in below

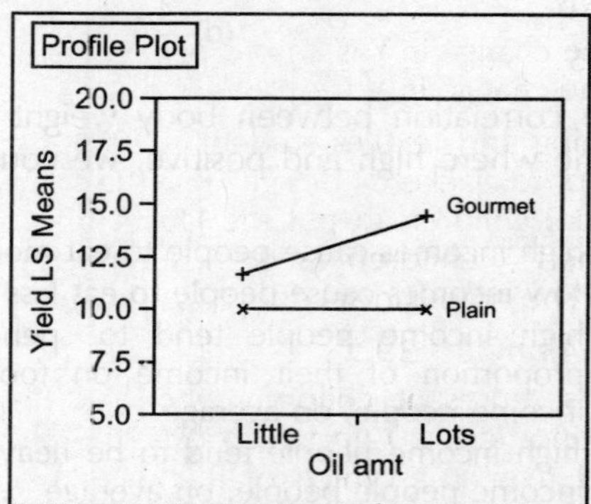


Which of the following is not correct?

(a) Because the lines are not parallel, there appears to be evidence of interaction between the two variables.
(b) The two explanatory factors are the amount of oil and the type of popcorn. The response variable is the yield of popcorn.
(c) The difference in yield between gourmet and plain popcorn is estimated to increase about 6 g when lots oil were used.
(d) An interaction would exist if the increase in yield from going from little to lots of oil were the same for both types of popcorn.

**211.** 'Normal' body temperature varies by times of day. A series of readings was taken of the body temperature of a subject. The mean reading was found to be 36.5 r̂ C with a standard deviation of 0.3 r̂ C with a standard deviation of 0.3 *r* C. When converted to r̂ F, the mean and standard deviation are

(r̂ F = r̂ C (1.8) + 32)

(a) 97.7, 32 (b) 97.7, 0.30
(c) 97.7, 0.54 (d) 97.7, 0.97

**212.** The Central Limit Theorem is important in statistics because

(a) it tells us that large samples do not need to be selected

(b) it guarantees that when it applies, the samples that are drawn are always randomly selected

(c) it enables reasonably accurate probabilities to be determined for events involving the sample average when the sample size is large regardless of the distribution of the variable

(d) it tells us that, if several samples have produced sample averages which seem to be different than expected, the next sample average will likely be close to its expected value

**213.** Given that, we have collected pairs of observations on two variables *X* and *Y*, we would consider fitting a straight line with *X* as an explanatory variable, if

(a) the change in *Y* is an additive constant

(b) the change in *Y* is a constant for each unit change in *X*

(c) the change in *Y* is a fixed per cent of *Y*

(d) the change in *Y* is exponential

**214.** A clothing and textiles student is trying to assess the effect of a jacket's design on the times it takes preschool children to put the jacket on. In a pretest, she timed 7 children as they put on her prototype jacket. The times (in seconds) are provided below

*n n* 65 43 *n* 119 39

The n s represent children who had not put the jacket on after 120 (in which case the children were allowed to stop). Which of following would be the best value to use as the typical time required to put on the jacket?

(a) The median time, which was 43

(b) The mean time which was 66

(c) The median time, which was 52

(d) The median time, which was 119

**215.** The following table represents the relative frequency of accidents per day in a city

| Accidents | 0 | 1 | 2 | 3 | 4 or more |
|---|---|---|---|---|---|
| Relative Frequency | 0.55 | 0.20 | 0.10 | 0.15 | 0 |

Which of the following statements are true?

I. The mean and modal number of accidents are equal.

II. The mean and median number of accidents are equal.

III. The median and modal number of accidents are equal.

(a) I (b) Only II (c) Only III (d) I, II and III

**216.** A student discovers that his grade on a recent test was the 72nd percentile. If 90 students wrote the test, then approximately how many students received a higher grade than he did?

(a) 65 (b) 25 (c) 72 (d) 71

**217.** Consicer the following output from data desk when analyz ng the pH values of the 1986 collected on precip tation events.

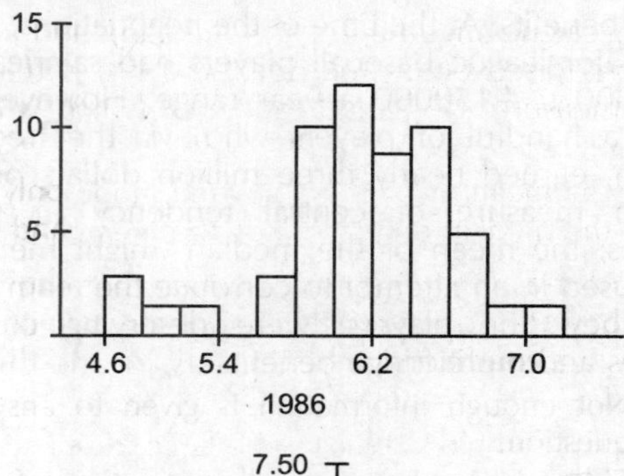


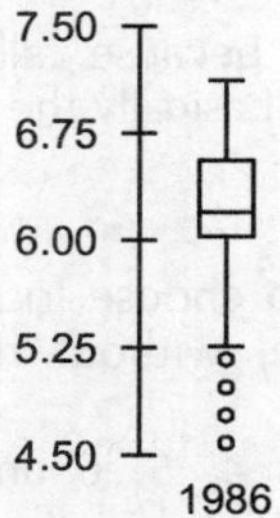


Summary stats for 1986

NumNumeric = 55

NumNonNumeric = 0

NumCases = 55

Mean = 6.0673

Median = 6.1000

Std deviation = 0.47339

Range = 2.4000

Minimum = 4.6000

Maximum = 7

75th percentile = 6.4000

Which of the following is not correct?

(a) The 25th percentile is about 5.9.

(b) Some outliers appear to be present below a pH of 5.4.

(c) About 95% of the observations have pH values in the approximate range $6 \pm 1$.

(d) About 10% of the values are in the range 5.8 to 5.0.

**218.** The frequency distribution of the amount of rainfall in December in a certain region for a period of 30 yr is given below

| Rainfall (in inches) | Number of Years |
|---|---|
| 2.0 - 4.0 | 3 |
| 4.0 - 6.0 | 6 |
| 6.0 - 8.0 | 8 |
| 8.0 - 10.0 | 8 |
| 10.9 - 12.0 | 5 |

The mean amount of rainfall (in inches) is

(a) 7.30 (b) 7.25 (c) 7.40 (d) 8.40

**219.** During the past few months, major league baseball players were in the process of negotiating with the team owners for higher minimum salaries and more fringe benefits. At the time of the negotiations, most of the major league baseball players had salaries in the \$100000 *u* #150000 a year range. However, there were a handful of players who, *via* the free agent system, earned nearly three million dollars per year. Which measure of central tendency of player's salaries, the mean or the median ,might the players have used in an attempt to convince the team owners that they (the players) were deserving of higher salaries and more fringe benefits?

(a) Not enough information is given to answer the question.
(b) Either one, because all measures of central tendency are basically the same.
(c) Mean
(d) Median

**220.** You are allowed to choose four whole numbers from 1 to 10 (inclusive, without repeats). Which of the following is false?

(a) The numbers 4, 5, 6 and 7 have the smallest possible standard deviation.
(b) The numbers 1, 2, 3 and 4 have the smallest possible standard deviation.
(c) The numbers 1, 5, 6 and 10 have the largest possible standard deviation.
(d) The numbers 1, 2, 9 and 10 have the largest possible standard deviation.

**221.** Which of the following is incorrect about the use of a paired experiment?

(a) The object of pairing (or blocking) is to account for the ring effect of possible other factors (such as fertility of soils).
(b) The analysis of paired data starts by finding the difference between the values of the pair. The order of the difference (as long as it is consistent) is unimportant.
(c) It is crucial to recognize pairing. If pairing is not recognized, the results will not be as accurate and precise as possible.
(d) Because pairing is beneficial, we can pair all data by matching the smallest value of each sample, the second smallest value of each sample, the third smallest value of each sample etc.

**222.** Which of the following is false?

(a) The numbers 3, 3 and 3 have a standard deviation of 0.
(b) The number 3, 4 and 5, have the same standard deviation as 1003, 1004, 1005.
(c) The standard deviation is a measure of spread around the centre of the data.
(d) The numbers 1, 5 and 9 have a smaller standard deviation than 101, 105, 109.

**223.** Recently, the City of Winnipeg has been criticized for its excessive discharges of untreated sewage into the Red River. A microbiologist take 45 samples of water downstream from the treated sewage outlet and measures the number of caliform bacteria present. A summary table is as follows :

| Number of Bacteria | Number of Samples |
|---|---|
| 20 - 30 | 5 |
| 30 - 40 | 20 |
| 40 - 50 | 15 |
| 50 - 60 | 5 |

The 80th percentile is approximately

(a) 45 (b) 47
(c) 80 (d) 48

**224.** From tax records, it is relative easy to determine the amount of liquor consumed per capita and the number of cigarettes consumed per capita for each of the 10 provinces of Canada. These are plotted on a scatter plot and a high positive correlation is found. Which of the following is correct?

(a) This implies that heavy smoking causes people to drink more.
(b) This implies that heavy drinking causes people to smoke more.
(c) We cannot conclude cause and effect but this also implies that there is a high positive correlation between cigarette smoking and alcohol consumption for individuals.
(d) This could be an example of a correlation caused by common cause because both activities are highly correlated with average family income and average income varies widely among the provinces.

**225.** A weed killer is to be applied at rate of two ounces per 1000 gallons of water, *i.e.*, 2 oz/1000 gallons. What is the application rate in mL/1000L, if there are 28.375 mL/oz and 4.5 L/gallon?

(a) 255.4 (b) 12.6
(c) 0.32 (d) 0.014

**226.** You are allowed to choose any four integers, without limits but without repeats. Which of the following is false?

(a) The numbers 4, 5, 6 and 7 has the same standard deviation as the numbers 1231, 1232, 1233, 1234.
(b) The numbers 1, 5, 7 and 9 has a smaller standard deviation than the numbers 1231, 1235, 1237, 1239.
(c) The numbers 1, 5, 6 and 10 has a larger standard deviation than the numbers 1231, 1232, 1233, 1234.
(d) The numbers 1, 2, 9 and 10 has the same standard deviation as the numbers 1231, 1232, 1239, 1240.

**227.** Consider the following box-plot of the yield of barley drawn using the convention that the wiskers reach the 10 and 90th percentiles.

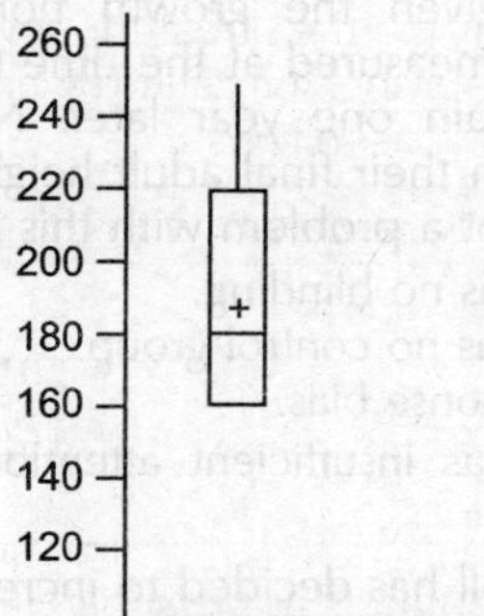


Which of the following is not correct?

(a) The mean is about 200g /400 m$^2$.

(b) The median is about 180g /400 m$^2$.

(c) About 50% of the yields are between 160 and 220g /400 m$^2$.

(d) About 25% of the yields are below 220g/400 m$^2$.

**228.** Recall in one assignment, you conducted a two factor experiment to compare the flying distances of paper airplanes. One factor was wing length with two levels; the second factor was wing depth also with two factors.

Which of the following is correct?

(a) A good experiment would fly all four copies of the different airplanes in sequential order.

(b) A good experiment would control for the person launching the planes by having the same person do all the launches.

(c) A good experiment would make a single copy of each treatment combination and test each copy 10 times.

(d) A good experiment would examine the effect of paper weight on flying by making all planes of the same weight of paper.

**229.** An experiment was performed where students examined a set of circles. For each circle they guessed the actual area and then measured the actual area. The scatter plot had the guessed areas on the vertical axis and the actual areas on the horizontal axes. A fitted line was fit to these data points. One student's fitted line was Guessed area = 5 + 0.65 Actual area. Which of the following is not correct?

(a) The student guessed that a circle has an area of 125 mm$^2$. A better guess would be 86 mm$^2$.

(b) The slope in the above equation indicates that, on average, a student increases her guess by only 0.65 mm$^2$ for every 1 mm$^2$ increase in actual area.

(c) 'Calibration' refers to the process where the relationship between the guessed and real areas is used to correct future guesses.

(d) If the fitted regression line tends to fall below the '45 f line', then this student tends to underestimate real areas.

**230.** Herbicide *A* has been used for years in order to kill a particular type of weed, but an experiment is to be conducted in order to see whether a new herbicide, Herbicide *B*, is more effective than Herbicide *A*. Herbicide *A* will continue to be used unless there is sufficient evidence that Herbicide *B* is more effective. The alternative hypothesis in this problem is that

(a) Herbicide A is more effective than Herbicide *B*

(b) Herbicide *B* is more effective than Herbicide *A*

(c) Herbicide *A* is not more effective than Herbicide *B*

(d) Herbicide *B* is not more effective than Herbicide *A*

**231.** Which of the following is not a necessary assumption underlying the use of the analysis of variance technique?

(a) The samples are independent and randomly selected.

(b) The populations are normally distributed.

(c) The variances of the populations are the same

(d) The means of the populations are equal.

**232.** The sample mean is an unbiased estimator for the population mean. This means

(a) the sample mean always equals the population mean

(b) the average sample mean, overall possible samples, equals the population mean

(c) the sample mean is always very close to the population mean

(d) the sample mean will only very a little from the population mean

**233.** A researcher wishes to calculate the average height of patients suffering from a particular disease. From patient records, the mean was computed as 156 cm, and standard deviation as 5 cm. Further, investigation reveals that the scale was misaligned and that all reading are 2 cm too large. e.g., a patient whose height is really 180 cm was measured as 182 cm. Furthermore, the researcher would like to work with statistics based on metres. The correct mean and standard deviation are

(a) 1·56 m, 0·05 m (b) 1·54 m, 0·05 m

(c) 1.56 m, 0.03 m (d) 1.58 m, 0.05 m

**234.** A wholesale distributor has found that the amount of a customer's order is a normal random variable with a mean of \$ 200 and a standard deviation of \$ 50. What is the probability that the total amount in a random smaple of 20 orders is greater than \$ 4500?

(a) 0.1915 (b) 0.0125

(c) 0.3085 (d) 0.0228

**235.** Which of the following statements is incorrect about the sampling distribution of the sample mean?

(a) The standard error of the sample mean will decrease as the sample size increases.

(b) The standard error of the sample mean is a measure of the variability of the sample mean among repeated samples.

(c) The sample mean is unbiased for the true (unknown) population mean.
(d) The sampling distribution shows how the sample was distributed around the sample mean.

**236.** Can of salmon have a nominal net weight of 250 g; However, due to variation in the canning process, the actual net weight has an approximate normal distribution with a mean of 255 g and a standard deviation of 10 g. According to consumer affairs, a sample of 16 tins should have less than a 5% chance that the mean weight is less than 250 g. What is the actual probability that a sample of 16 tins will have a mean weight less than 250 g?

(a) 0.1915 (b) 0.3085
(c) 0.0228 (d) 0.4772

**237.** A random sample Of 500 households in Vancouver was selected and several variables are recorded for each household. Which of the following is not correct?

(a) Household total income is a ratio scaled variable.
(b) Household income (which averages about \$ 35000) and was rounded to the nearest \$100 can be treated as a continuous variable even though it is 'discrete'.
(c) Socio-economic status was coded as 1= low income, 2 = middle income, 3 = high income and is an interval scaled variable.
(d) The primary language used at home is a nominal scaled variable.

**238.** A random sample of size $n = 30$ is taken from a population or size $N = 300$. Which statement is generally correct?

(a) $\mu$ is an estimate of $\overline{X}$ ; $s$ is an estimate of $s$.
(b) $\overline{X}$ is an estimate of $\mu$; $\sigma$ is an estimate of $\sigma$.
(c) $\mu$ is an estimate of $\overline{X}$ ; $s$ is an estimate of the standard deviation of the sample mean.
(d) $X$ is an estimate of $\mu$; $s$ is an estimate of the standard deviation of the sample mean.

**239.** Which of the following statements is not correct?

(a) In a proper random sampling, every element of the population has a known (and often equal) chance of being selected.
(b) The precision of a sample mean or sample proportion depends only upon the sample size (and not the population size) in a proper random sample.
(c) Convenience sampling often leads to biases in estimates because the sample is often not representative of the population.
(d) If a sample of 1000000 families is randomly selected from all or Canada (with about 8000000 families) and the average family income is computed, then the true value of the family income for all families in Canada is known.

**240.** An experiment to measure the effect of giving growth hormones to girls affected by Turner's Syndrome was carried out recently in Vancouver. All 34 girls in the study were given the growth hormone and their heights were measured at the time the hormone was given and again one year later. No measurements were made on their final adult heights. Which of the following is not a problem with this experiment?

(a) There was no blinding.
(b) There was no control group.
(c) Non-response bias.
(d) There was insufficient attention to the placebo effect.

**241.** The Gallup Poll has decided to increase the size of its random sample of Canadian voters from about 1500 people to about 4000 people. The effect of this increase is to

(a) reduce the bias of the estimate
(b) increase the standard error of the estimate
(c) reduce the variability of the estimate
(d) increase the confidence interval width for the parameter

**242.** A survey was conducted by visiting a student parking lot to estimate the proportion of cars that were red. Which of the following is not correct?

(a) If the sampled stall was empty, we can simply choose another stall at random, to take its place because it is not likely that the stall being vacant is related to a car being red.
(b) The sample would be representative of the population if 100 cars were chosen regardless if randomization was used or not.
(c) Even though a random sample was taken from ears in the parking lot, the sample may not be representative or the cars driven by SFU students because the decision to park in *B*-lot is self-selected.
(d) If a another sample of cars was chosen, it is likely that a different proportion of cars' that are red would be obtained.

**243.** If a random sample of 500 organges produces 25 rotten organes, then the estimate of SE of the proportion of rotten organges in the sample is

(a) 0.01 (b) 0.05
(c) 0.028 (d) 0.0593

**244.** Recall in one assignment you surveyed cars in a parking lot to estimate the proportion that were red or the proportion that were from a Japanese manufacturer. Which of the following is not correct?

(a) A convenience sample of the cars closest to the applied science building may give a biased estimate of the proportion of cars which are from a Japanese manufacturer.
(b) Different students may get different answers for the proportion of cars that are red.

(c) The sample proportion of cars that are red is an unbiased estimate of the population proportion, if the sampling is a simple random sample.

(d) A sample of 100 ears in a convenience sample is always better than a sample of 20 cars from a proper random sample.

**245.** The following numbers are extracted from a table of random digits: 38683 50279 38224 09844 13578 28251 12708 24684

A scientist will be measuring the total amount of woody debris in a random sample of sites selected without replacement from a population of 45 sites. The sites are labelled 01, 02, ... , 45 and she starts at the beginning of the line of random digits and takes consecutive pairs of digits. Which of the following is correct?

(a) Her sample is 38, 25, 02, 38 and 22.
(b) Her sample is 38, 68, 35, 02 and 22.
(c) Her sample is 38, 35, 27, 28 and 08.
(d) Her sample is 38, 35, 02, 22 and 40.

**246.** If the population SD is known to be 5 for a population containing 80 units, then the standard error of sample mean for a sample of size 25 without replacement is

(a) 5 (b) 0.20 (c) 1 (d) 0.85

**247.** Which of the following statement is not correct?

(a) The sample standard deviation measures variability of our sample values.

(b) A larger sample will give answers that very less from the true value than smaller samples (assuming both are properly chosen).

(c) The sampling distribution describes how our estimate (answer) will very, if a new sample is taken.

(d) A large sample size always gives unbiased estimators biased regardless of how the sample is chosen.

**248.** A survey was done to estimate the proportion of cars that are red and are Japanese made in the city of Vancouver by taking a random sample of size 25 from a student parking lot at Simon Fraser University. Which of the following is not correct?

(a) This sample may not be representative of the cars in Vancouver because mainly students park at SFU.

(b) If the particular stall is vacant, we can simply select another stall at random because it is unlikely that a stall is vacant is related to the colour or manufacturer of the car

(c) It would be dangerous to simply select the first 25 stalls in the lot closest to the applied science building because there are a number of stall reserved for service vehicles whose primary colour is white.

(d) Different students obtained different answers for their sample proportions. This is an example of a sampling distribution for an estimator

**249.** A properly conducted random survey selected 1000 Canadians (from a total population of about 30 million) and 1000 Americans (from a total population of about 300 million). Which of the following is false?

(a) Randomization ensures that both samples are representative or their respective populations.

(b) The precision is determined by the ratio of the sample size to the total population size.

(c) A smaller proportion of the American population has been chosen. Therefore, a particular person has a smaller chance of being selected in America than in Canada.

(d) A potential stratification variable for both countries could be location eastern, middle, or western continental.

**250.** A sample of size 3 is taken from a population of 10 members with replacement. If the sample observations are 1, 3 and 5, what is the estimate of the standard error of sample mean?

(a) 1.96 (b) 1.02
(c) 2.25 (d) 2.28

**251.** Random samples of 1000 bolts manufactured by machine *A* and 1000 bolts manufactured by machine *B* showed 52 and 23 defective bolts, respectively. The observed value of the test statistic for testing the null hypothesis that there is no difference in the performance of the machines is

(a) 3.29 (b) 2.47
(c) 8.56 (d) 3.41

**252.** The heights in centimetres of 5 students are 165, 175, 176, 159 and 170.

The sample median and sample mean respectively

(a) 170, 169 (b) 170, 170
(c) 169, 170 (d) 176, 169

**253.** A recent survey by a large circulation Canadian magazine on the contribution of universities to the economy was circulated to 394 people who the magazine decided 'are the most likely to know how important are universities to the Canadian economy' The main problem with using these results to draw conclusions about the general public's perception is

(a) selection bias
(b) insufficient attention to the placebo effect
(c) no control group
(d) non-response bias

**254.** A simple random sample of size 10 is drawn without replacement from a universe containing 85 units. If the mean and SD as obtained from the sample, 90 are 90 and 4 respectively, what is the estimate of the standared error of sample mean?

(a) 0.58 (b) 1.26
(c) 0.67 (d) 0.72

**255.** A new headache remedy was given to a group of 25 subjects who had headaches. Four hours after talking the new remedy, 20 of the subjects reported that their headaches had disappeared. From this information you conclude

(a) that the remedy is effective for the treatment of headaches
(b) nothing because the sample size is too small
(c) nothing because there is no control group for comparison
(d) that the new treatment is better than aspirin

**256.** The following statistics were collected on two groups of cattle.

| | Group *A* | Group *B* |
|---|---|---|
| Sample size | 45 | 30 |
| Sample mean | 1000 lbs | 800 lbs |
| Sample std dev | 80 lbs | 70 lbs |

Which of the following statements is correct?

(a) Group *A* is less variable than Group *B* because Group *A*'s standard deviation is larger.
(b) Group *A* is relatively less variable than Group *B* because Group *A*'s coefficient of variation (the ratio or the standard deviation to the mean) is smaller.
(c) Group *A* is less variable than Group *B* because the standard deviation per animal is smaller.
(d) Group *A* is relatively more variable than Group *B* because the sample mean is larger.

**257.** In class, we performed a randomized, response survey to estimate the proportion of class who used marijuana in the last year. Each student obtained a random digit between 0 and 9 (inclusive). Of those who received the digits 0, l, 2, 3, or 4, these students answered the question on marijuana usage. Of those who received the digits 5, 6, 7, 8 and 9 these students answered the question, if their favourite person's birthday was in January to June (inclusive). We obtained a total of 150 yes and 250 no responses. Which of the following is false?

(a) We estimate that about 25% of students have used marijuana in the last year.
(b) About 50% of people have birthdays in January-June (inclusive).
(c) Of the 150 yeses, about 66% = 100/150 of these had favourite people with birthdays in January-June (inclusive).
(d) About 37% = 150/400 said yes to having used marijuana in the last year.

**258.** We wish to draw a sample of size 5 without replacement from a population 50 households. Suppose, the households are numbered 01, 02,...,50 and suppose that the relevant line of the random number table is digits 11362 35692 96237 90842 46843 62719 64049 17823

Then, the households selected are

(a) households 11 13 36 62 73
(b) households 11 36 23 08 42
(c) households 11 36 23 23 08
(d) households 11 36 23 56 92

**259.** There is a positive association between the number of drownings and ice cream sales. This is an example of an association likely caused by

(a) coincidence
(b) cause and effect relationship
(c) confounding factor
(d) common cause

**260.** A sample of 99 distances has a mean of 24 feet and a median of 24·5 feet. Unfortunately, it has just been discovered that an observation which was erroneously recorded as '30' actually had a value of '35'. If we make this correction to the data, then

(a) the mean remains the same, but the median is increased
(b) the mean and median remain the same
(c) the median remains the same but the mean is increased
(d) the mean and median are both increased

**261.** Each person in a random sample of males and females was asked to state his/her sex and preferred colour. The resulting frequencies are shown below

| | | Colour | | |
|---|---|---|---|---|
| | | Red | Blue | Green |
| Sex | Male | 3 | 11 | 6 |
| | Female | 17 | 11 | 2 |

Which of the following is false?

(a) 55% of males prefer the colour blue.
(b) Of those who prefer the colour green, 75% are males.
(c) 44% of people surveyed prefer the colour blue.
(d) 45% of people are males who prefer the colour red.

**262.** A researcher wishes to estimate the mean of a population by using sufficiently large sample. The probability is 0.95 that the sample mean will not differ from the true mean by more than 25% of the standard deviation. How large sample should be taken?

(a) 52 (b) 42 (c) 62 (d) 72

**263.** A nutritionist wants to study the effect of storage time (6, 12 and 18 months) on the amount of vitamin C present in freeze dried fruit when stored for these lengths of time. Vitamin C is measured in milligrams per 100 milligrams of fruit. Six fruit packs were randomly assigned to each of the three storage times. The treatment, experimental unit, and response are respectively

(a) a specific storage time, amount of vitamin C, a fruit pack

(b) a fruit pack, amount of vitamin C, a specific storage time

(c) random assignment, a fruit pack, amount of vitamin C

(d) a specific storage time, a fruit pack, amount of vitamin C

**264.** A simple random sample of size 16 is drawn from a population with 50 members. What is the SE of sample mean if the population variance is known to be 25 given that the sampling is done with replacement?

(a) 1.25 (b) 6.25
(c) 1.04 (d) 1.56

**265.** An experiment was conducted where a person's heart rate was measured 4 times in the space of 10 min. This was repeated on a sample of 20 people. Which of the following is not correct?

(a) The standard deviation within subjects refers to the repeated measurements of a single person's heart rate.

(b) The standard deviation among subjects refers to the variation in heart rates among different people

(c) The variation among subject was larger than the variation within subjects.

(d) The variation in heart rates base on measurements taken for 30 s was larger than the variation of heart rates based on measurements taken for 15 s.

**266.** A firm wishes to estimate with an error of not more than 0.03 and a level or confidence of 98%, the proportion of consumers that prefers its brand of household detergent. Sales reports indicate that about 0.20 of all consumers prefer the firm's brand. What is the requisite sample size?

(a) 965 (b) 975
(c) 985 (d) 995

**267.** A survey is to be undertaken of recent nursing graduates in order to compare the starting salaries of women and men. For each graduate, three variables are to be recorded (among others) ů sex, starting salary and area of specialization

(a) sex and starting salary are explanatory variables; area of specialization is a resoponse variable

(b) sex is an explanatory variable; starting salary and area of specialization are response variables

(c) sex is an explanatory variable; starting salary is a response variable, area of specialization is a possible confounding variable

(d) sex is a response variable, starting salary is an explanatory variable, area of specialization is a possible confounding variable

**268.** In general, which of the following statements is false?

(a) The sample mean is more sensitive to extreme values than the median.

(b) The sample range is more sensitive to extreme values than the standard deviation.

(c) The sample standard deviation is a measure of spread around the sample mean.

(d) The sample standard deviation is a measure of central tendency around the median.

**269.** The sampling distribution of refers to

(a) the distribution of the various sample sizes which might be used in a given study

(b) the distribution of the different possible values of the sample mean together with their respective probabilities of occurence

(c) the distribution of the values of the items in the population

(d) the distribution of the values of the items actually selected in a given sample

**270.** It is known that population standard deviation in waiting time for new gas connection in a particular town is 20 days. How large sample should be chosen to the 95% confident that the average waiting time is within 3 days of true average?

(a) 58 (b) 59 (c) 61 (d) 62

**271.** Consider an experiment to investigate the efficacy of different insecticides in controlling pests and their effects on subsequent yield. What is the best reason for randomly assigning treatment levles (spraying or not sparying) to the experimental units (farms)?

(a) Randomization make the experiment easier to conduct because we can apply the insecticide in any pattern rather than in a systematic fashion.

(b) Randomization makes the analysis easier because the data can be collected and entered into the computer in any order.

(c) Randomization is required by statistical consultants before they will help you analyze the experiment.

(d) Randomization will tend to average out all other uncontrolled factors such as soil fertility so that they are not confounded with the treatment effects.

**272.** Many professional schools require applicants to take a standardized test. Suppose that, 1000 students write the test and you find that your mark of 63 (out of 100) was the 73rd percentile. This means

(a) atleast 73% of the people got 63 or better

(b) atleast 270 people got 73 or better

(c) atleast 270 people got 63 or better

(d) atleast 27% of the people got 73 or worse

**273.** A random sample of 100 observations is to be drawn from a population with a mean of 40 and a standard deviation of 25. The probability that the mean of the sample will exceed 45 is

(a) 0.4772 (b) 0.4207
(c) 0.0793 (d) 0.0228

**274.** Which of the following statements is false?

(a) Non-response can cause bias in surveys becuase non-respondents often tend to behave differently from people who respond.

(b) Non-sampling errors are often bigger than the random sampling errors in surveys.

(c) Slight changes in the wording of questions can make a measurable difference to survey results.

(d) Sophisticated statistical methods can always correct the result, if the population you are sampling from is different from the population of interest, *e.g.*, due to under-coverage.

**275.** The average monthly mortgage payment for recent home buyers in winnipeg is $\mu = \$732$, with standard deviation of $\sigma = \$421$ a random sample of 125 recent home buyers is selected. The approximate probability that their average monthly mortgage payment will be more than \$782 is

(a) 0.9082 (b) 0.4522
(c) 0.4082 (d) 0.0918

**276.** A manufacturing concern wants to estimate the average amount of purchase of its product in a month by the customers. If the standard deviation is ₹ 10, find the sample size if the maximum error is not to exceed ₹ 3 with a probability of 0.99.

(a) 72 (b) 73 (c) 74 (d) 75

**277.** Which of the following is correct?

(a) We do not need to randomize if our sample size is sufficiently large.

(b) A large sample size always ensures that our sample is representative of the population.

(c) If all other things are equal, we need a larger sample size for a larger population.

(d) In a properly chosen sample, an estimate will be less variable with a large sample size and hence more precise.

**278.** A simple random sample of size three units is drawn with replacement from a population of size *N*. The probability that the sample consists of three distinct units is

(a) $\dfrac{1}{N^2}$ (b) $\dfrac{1}{N^3}$

(c) $\dfrac{(N-1)(N-2)}{N^2}$ (d) $\dfrac{(N-1)^2}{N^3}$

**279.** An experimenter wishes to test whether or not two types of fish food (a standard fish food and a new product) work equally well at producing fish of equal weight after a 2 months feeding program. The experimenter has 2 indentical fish tanks (1 and 2) to put fish in and is considering how to assign the 40 tagged fish to the tanks. To properly assign the fish, one step would be to

(a) put all the odd tagged numbered fish in one tank, the even in the other and give the standard food type to the odd numbered ones

(b) obtain pairs of fish whose weights are virtually equal at the start of the experiment and randomly assign one of the group tank 1, the other to tank 2 with the feed assigned at random to the tanks

(c) proceed as in (b) but put the heavier of the pair into tank 2

(d) assign the fish at random to the two tanks and give the standard feed to tank 1

**280.** A consumer affairs agency wants to check the average weight of a new product on the market. A random sample of 25 items of the product was taken and the weights (in grams) of these items were classified as follows

| Class Limits | Frequency |
|---|---|
| 74 - 77 | 3 |
| 77 - 80 | 6 |
| 80 - 83 | 9 |
| 83 - 86 | 3 |
| 86 - 89 | 4 |

The 3rd quartile of the weight in this sample is qual to

(a) 83.00 (b) 75.00 (c) 83.75 (d) 18.75

**281.** Recall in one assignment you surveyed cars in a parking lot to estimate the proportion that were red or the proportion that were from a Japanese manufacturer. Which of the following is not correct?

(a) A convenience sample of the cars closest to the applied science building may give a biased estimate of the proportion of cars which are from a Japanese manufacturer.

(b) Different students may get different answers for the proportion of cars that are red.

(c) The sample proportion of cars that are red is an unbiased estimate of the population proportion, if the sampling is a simple random sample.

(d) A sample of 100 cars in a convenience sample is always better than a sample of 20 cars from a proper random sample.

**282.** The variance of the population total in systematic sampling is smaller than the variance of the population total in without replacement simple random sampling if and only if the correlation coefficient(s) between pairs of units in the sample systematic sample is

(a) equal to $\dfrac{-1}{(N-1)}$ (b) greater than $\dfrac{-1}{(N-1)}$

(c) less than $\dfrac{-1}{(N-1)}$ (d) Less than zero

where, *N* is the number of units in the population.

**283.** A researcher wishes to compare the effects of 2 fertilizers on the yield of a soyabean crop. She has 20 plots of land available and she decides to use a paired experiment using 10 pairs of plots. Thus, she will

(a) use a table of random numbers to divide the 20 plots into 10 pairs and then for each pair, flip a coin to assign the fertilizers to the 2 plots

(b) subjectively divide the 20 plots into 10 pairs (making the plots within a block as similar as possible) and then, for each pair, flip a coin to assign the fertilizers to the 2 plots

(c) use a table of random numbers to divide the 20 plots into 10 pairs and then use the table of random numbers a second time to decide upon the fertilizer to be applied to each pair

(d) flip a coin to divide the 20 plots into 10 pairs and then, for each pair, use a table of random numbers to assign the fertilizers to the 2 plots

**284.** The Federal government periodically tests packaged products to check that the manufacturer is not short-weighting the product (*i.e.*, underfilling products). To allow for variation in the filling process, the federal government takes a sample of bottles of 16 beer with nominal capacity of 344 mL and if the mean volume in the bottles is less than 340 mL, the manufacturer is fined. Suppose an unscrupulous brewer sets the machine to fill, on average, 342 mL. The machine has a standard deviation of 4 mL. The probability that a type II error will be made is

(a) 0.4772 (b) 0.0228 (c) 0.9772 (d) 0.1915

**285.** Fill in the missing words to the quote : 'Statistical methods may be described as methods for drawing conclusions about......based on..............computed from the.....................

(a) statistics, samples, populations
(b) populations, parameters, samples
(c) statistics, parameters, samples
(d) populations, statistics, samples

**286.** A random sample of a group of people is taken and 120 were found to be in favour of liberalizing licensing regulations. If the proportion of people in the population found in favour of liberlization with 95% confidence lies between 0.683 and 0.817, then the number of people in the group is

(a) 140 (b) 150
(c) 160 (d) 175

**287.** The yield of a variety of wheat was measured on a series of small plots. The 2nd and 98th percentile were found to be 29 bushels/acre and 41 bushels/acre, respectively. The standard deviation (bushels/acre) is approximately

(a) 12 (b) 6 (c) 3 (d) 4

**288.** Consider the following 0 give of the scores of students in an introductory statistics course

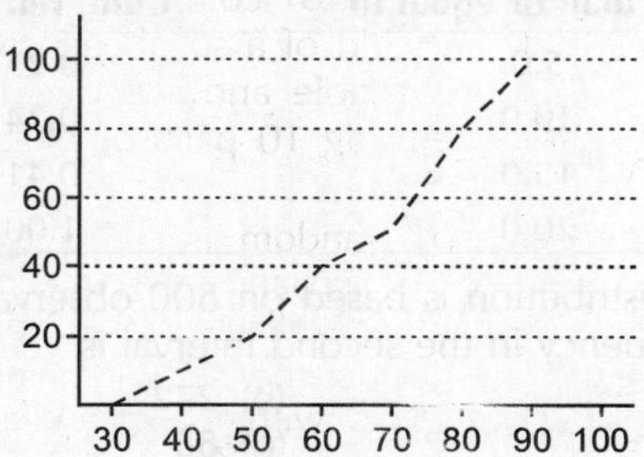


A grade of C or C+ is assigned to a student who scores between 55 and 70. The percentage of students that obtained a grade of C of C+ is

(a) 25% (b) 30%
(c) 20% (d) 50%

**289.** Recently, the city of winnipeg has been criticized for its excessive discharges of untreated sewage into the red river. A microbiologist take 50 samples of water downstream from the treated sewage outlet and measures the number of coliform bacteria present. A summary table is as follows

| Number of Bacteria | Number of Samples |
|---|---|
| 50 - 60 | 5 |
| 60 - 70 | 20 |
| 70 - 80 | 10 |
| 80 - 90 | 15 |

The mean number of bacteria per sample is

(a) 70 (b) 71
(c) 72 (d) 76

**290.** The yield of a grain $Y$ (t/ha), appears to be linearly related to the amount of fertilizer applied $X$ (kg/ha). An experiment was conducted by applying different amounts of fertilizer (0 to 10 kg/ha) to plots of land and measuring the resulting yields. The following estimated regression line was obtained

yield = 4.85 + 0.05 (fertilizer)

Which of the following is not correct?

(a) If no fertilizer was used, the yield is estimated to be 4.85 t/ha.
(b) If fertilizer is applied at 10 kg/ha, the estimated yield is 5.35 t/ha.
(c) For every additional kg/ha of fertilizer applied, the yield is estimated to increase 0.05 t/ha.
(d) If the current level of fertilizer is changed from 7.0 to 9.0 kg/ha, the yield is estimated to increase by 0.20 t/ha.

**291.** Consider the following table in reference to the testing of a null hypothesis

| | $H-0$ True | $H-0$ False |
|---|---|---|
| Accept $H-0$ | 1 | 2 |
| Reject $H-0$ | 3 | 4 |

Which of the following is incorrect?

(a) Entires (1) and (4) are correct decisions.
(b) The $P$ (making entry (2)) is controlled by the sample size for a given $\alpha$-level.
(c) A type I error occurs, if entry (3) occurs.
(d) A type II error occurs when entry (1) is made.

**292.** Which of the following is not correct about the principles of causal inference?

(a) Lack of Temporal Ambiguity means that the cause should precede the effect.

(b) A Dose-response Relationship means that the size of an effect shout vary with the size of the cause.

(c) Coherence means that there is biological or theoretical basis for the hypothesized cause and effect.

(d) Specificity means that the effects are associated primarily with one cause.

**293.** Refer to the previous question. We wish to be 95% confident of being within 1.0 g of the true value. What is the approximate sample size is needed for each group?

(a) 240 (b) 60 (c) 8000 (d) 2000

**294.** Consider the following statement concerned with the collection of data and determine the best selection of terms to complete the statement. "The entire group of objects or people about which information is wanted, is called the...........Individual members are called. The..................is the part that is actually examined in order to gather information".

(a) population, explanatory variables, sub-group
(b) whole, items of interest, stratum
(c) response group, respondents, non-response group
(d) population, units, sample

**295.** When testing water for chemical impurities results are often reported as bdl, *i.e.*, below detection limit. The following are the measurements of the amount of lead in a series of water samples taken from inner city households (ppm).

5, 7, 12, bdl, 10, 8, bdl, 20, 6

Which of the following is correct?

(a) The mean lead level in the water is about 10 ppm.
(b) The mean lead level in the water is about 8 ppm.
(c) The median lead level in the water is 7 ppm.
(d) The median lead level in the water is 8 ppm.

**296.** If a store runs out of advertised material during a sale, customers become upset and the firm loses not only the sale but also goodwill. From past experience, a record store finds that the mean number of albums sold in a sale is 845, the variance is 225 and that a histogram of the demand appears mound shaped. The manager is willing to accept a 2.5% chance that an album will be sold out. About how many albums should the manager order for an upcoming sale?

(a) 1295 (b) 875
(c) 1070 (d) 935

**297.** We wish to investigate, if a new medicine is effective in reducing the length and severity of the flu. We take the next 20 patients that come to the walk-in clinic complaining of flu and after a medical exam to verify that the patients do have the flu, we give them the new medicine and tell them about the new drug we are giving them. One week later, the patients are contacted and 15 patients state the new remedy was helpful in reducing the severity and length of the illness. Which of the following is not correct?

(a) This is a poor experiment because there is no control group. We do not know how many would feel better in a week without treatment.

(b) This is a poor experiment because it is not double-blinded. The patients may feel relief because they thought the drug should work.

(c) This is a poor experiment because a convenience sample was selected. Patients who come to the a walk-in clinic may have more severe flu than people who do not.

(d) This is a poor experiment because we didn't give the remedy to people without the flu to assess its effect in a control group.

**298.** Which fo the following is not correct about constructing histograms?

(a) The approximate numbers of classes is $1+ 3.3 \log (n)$.
(b) All class intervals should be of equal width.
(c) The bars of the histogram are centred over the class mark (mid-point).
(d) The first and last classes should be open-ended to account for extreme points.

**299.** In an experiment to determine, if antibiotics increase the final dressed weight of cattle, the following were measured on each animal in the study.

Sex, initial weight, weight gain, grade of meat.

where, grade is recorded as (*A*, *B* or *C*). The scale of measurement of these variable are

(a) nominal, ratio, interval, nominal
(b) nominal, ratio, ratio, nominal
(c) nominal, ratio, ratio, ordinal
(d) ordinal, ratio, ratio, ordinal

**300.** The best way to recognize whether or not a variable is growing exponentially over time is by

(a) plotting the variable against time and looking for a straight-line pattern
(b) calculating the least squares regression line of the variable against time and examining the residuals
(c) plotting the logarithm of the variable against time and looking for a straight line pattern
(d) smoothing the time series by running medians of three or five

**301.** Consider the following cumulative relative frequency distribution

| Less than or equal to | Cum. rel. freq. |
|---|---|
| 5.0 | 0.23 |
| 10.0 | 0.34 |
| 15.0 | 0.41 |
| 20.0 | 1.00 |

If this distribution is based on 800 observations, then the frequency in the second interval is

(a) 34 (b) 272
(c) 80 (d) 88

**302.** Forest companies routinely take samples from tracts that have been replanted to monitor the growth of the trees. Suppose that in a recent sample of two tracts, the diameter of the trees was measured with the following results

| Tracts | A | B |
|---|---|---|
| Trees | 75 | 210 |
| Range | 232-315 | 215-250 (mm) |

Histograms to compare the two groups are to be constructed. Which of the following is not recommended?

(a) The number of classes in Group *A* and Group *B* should be around 7 or 8.
(b) The class width of both groups will be 10 mm
(c) The class bounds will be 232-242 mm 242-252 mm, etc., for Group *A* and 215-225 mm, 225-235 mm, etc., for Group *B*.
(d) The verticle scale for both groups should be relative frequency (%).

**303.** In an aquaculture study, the following variables were measured on each fish

Sex, initial weight(g), body temperature (C) weight gain (g).

The scale of these four variables (in order) are

(a) nominal, ratio, ratio, ratio
(b) nominal, ratio, interval, interval
(c) ordinal, ratio, inverval, ratio
(d) nominal, ratio, interval, ratio

**304.** There may be a cure for male pattern baldness (at least millions of males hope there will be) using the blood pressure durg Minoxidil. A group of males was randomly assigned to two groups. One group received topical applications of the drug; the other group received applications of an identical looking placebo, the summary data

| Number with Sample Size | | New $H-A$ir Growth |
|---|---|---|
| Minoxidil group | 310 | 100 |
| Placebo group | 100 | 25 |

A 95% confidence interval for the difference in the proportion of males showing new hair growth is

(a) $0.073 \pm 0.152$ (b) $0.073 \pm 0.048$
(c) $0.073 \pm 0.024$ (d) $0.073 \pm 0.099$

**305.** Discriminant analysis is a statistical technique, which attempt to find a set of variables to allow you distinguish among groups, *e.g.,* in one of the assignments, you tried to distinguish among authors based on sentence length and other statistic. Which of the following is not correct?

(a) We need to adjust some variables to a 'per 100 word basis' or to a 'per sentence basis' to adjust for the different number of words in the texts, where authorship is known.
(b) Potentially useful variables are selected by finding variables whose distribution are as similar as possible for all the authors.
(c) Another example of this method might be a bank making a decision on granting a student a loan based on characteristics such as grade point average, past credit history, etc.
(d) We looked at many pairs of plots to find the pair of variables that gave the best separation between the two authors.

**306.** A single stem and leaf plot is a useful tool because

(a) it includes the average and the standard deviation
(b) it shows the percentage distribution of the data values
(c) it enables us to examine the data values for the presence of trends, cycles and seasonal variation
(d) it enables us to locate the centre of the data, see the overall shape of the distribution, and look to marked deviations from the overall shape

**307.** A study was conducted to investigate the effect of a coal-fire generating plant upon the water quality of a river. As part of an environmental impact study, fish were captured, tagged and released. The following information was recorded for each fish

Sex (0 = female, 1 = male),
Length (cm)
Maturation (0 = young, 1 = adult),
Weight (g).

The scale of these variables is

(a) nominal, ratio, nominal, ratio
(b) nominal, interval, ordinal, ratio
(c) nominal, ratio, ordinal, ratio
(d) ordinal, ratio, nominal, ratio

**308.** Doctors' practices have been categorized as to being Urban, Rural, or Intermediate. The number of doctors who prescribed tetracycline to atleast one patient under the age of 8 were recorded for each of these practice areas. The results are

| | Urban | Intermediate | Rural |
|---|---|---|---|
| Tetracycline | 95 | 74 | 31 |
| No tetracycline | 126 | 84 | 30 |

If the country type of practice and the use of tetracycline are independent, then the expected number of rural doctros who prescribe tetracycline is

(a) 31.0 (b) 27.7
(c) 1.37 (d) 51%

**309.** An experiment was conducted, where you flew paper airplanes after modifying wing depth and wing length. There were four different models of airplane. One design consideration was the choice between flying each plane four times or making four copies of each model, each of which is folwn once.

Which of the following is not correct?

(a) Flying multiple copies of each model (*i.e.*, separate planes of each model) could give information on variability in flight due to fabrication effects (*i.e.*, how you made the plane).
(b) Flying a single copy of each model four times could give information on variability in flight due to changes in initial launch conditions.
(c) The differences in flight length among the different models gives information on the 'effects' of the design factors wing depth and wing length.
(d) Interaction between the effects of wing depth and wing width implies that the effects of wing depth are the same for all wing widths.

**310.** Forty students wrote a Statistics examination having a maximum of 50 marks. The mark distribution is given in the following steam and leaf plot

0 | 28
1 | 2245
2 | 01333358889
3 | 001356679
4 | 22444466788
5 | 000

The third quartile of the mark distribution is equal to

(a) 75 (b) 44 (c) 32 (d) 37.5

**311.** As part of a study to investigate the effects of stubble burning, the following variables were measured at several sites around Winnipeg

pH of soil (to one decimal place, *e.g.*, 6.3) ; crop grown (0 = wheat, 1 = barley, 2 = oats, 3 = other); amount of stubble (0 = light, 1 = medium, 2 = heavy); data of final harvesting (*e.g.*, 10 Oct, 92)

The scales of these variables are

(a) interval, ordinal, ratio, ratio
(b) interval, nominal, nominal, interval
(c) interval, nominal, ordinal, interval
(d) ratio, ordinal, ordinal, ratio

**312.** A marine biologist wants to test the effect of water temperature on the average dive duration for sea otters. Five otters are available for an experiment and each otter is observed diving in both warm and cold water (with the order being random). The biologist collects the following data

| Dive Duration (Sec) | | |
|---|---|---|
| **Otter** | **Warm Water** | **Cold Water** |
| *J2* | 97 | 92 |
| *B7* | 65 | 60 |
| *M3* | 75 | 77 |
| *D4* | 103 | 43 |
| *B8* | 90 | 81 |

Test for any difference in the length of dives using a non-parametric procedure

(a) rank sum procedure, $W_{cold} = 25$; $p$-value $> 0.111$
(b) rank sum procedure, $W_{cold} = 25$, $p$-value $> 0.222$
(c) signed rank procedure, $W^- = 1$; $p$-value $= 0.062$
(d) signed rank procedure, $W^- = 1$; $p$-value $= 0.124$

**313.** An experiment was conducted where 0 you tried to distinguish among authors based on sentence length and other satistics. Which of the following is not correct?

(a) We needed to adjust some variables to a 'per 100 word basis' to adjust for the different number of words on a page.
(b) This was a simplified form of discriminant analysis where, in general, one wishes to distinguish among groups of objects based on characteristics observed.
(c) Another example of his method might be a bank making a decision on granting a student a loan based on characteristics such as grade point average, past credit history, etc.
(d) Potentially useful variable are selected by finding variables whose distribution are as similar as possible for all the authors.

**314.** Thirty students wrote a statistics examination having a maximum of 50 marks. The mark distribution is given in the following stem and leaf plot

0 | 9
1 | 225
2 | 013335889
3 | 00136679
4 | 02244478
5 | 0

The median mark is equal to

(a) 30.5 (b) 30.0 (c) 25.0 (d) 28.5

**315.** A study was conducted to measure the effect of smoking upon the birth weight of a baby. The following variables were measured for each women in the study

Smoking status (yes, no), baby birth weight (g), APGAR score, birth date.

The scales of these variables are

(a) Nominal, ratio, ratio, ratio
(b) Ordinal, ratio, interval, interval
(c) Nominal, ratio, ordinal, ratio
(d) Nominal, ratio, ordinal, interval

**316.** Earthquake intensities are measured using a device called a seismograph which is designed to be most sensitive for earthquakes with intensities between 4.0 and 9.0 on the open-ended Richter scale. Measurements of nine earthquakes gave the following readings

4.5 L 5.5 H 8.7 8.9 6.0 H 5.2 where L indicates that the earthquake had an intensity below 4.0 and a H indicates that the earthquake has an intensity above 9.0. The median earthquake intensity of the sample is

(a) cannot be computed because all of the values are not known
(b) 8.70
(c) 5.75
(d) 6.00

**317.** An experiment was conducted where you analyzed the results of the plant growth experiment after you manipulated the amount of water and seed variety, Which of the following is correct?

(a) We randomized the plants to plots to eliminate any effect of hidden variables.
(b) We could determine the best combination of water and seed variety by examining the difference in the plant height in the final week of the experiment.
(c) The variability in growth among plants of the same variety who received the same amount of water was constant over time.
(d) The growth of a particular plant in week 3 is likely to be independent (unrelated) of the growth of the same plant in week 2.

**318.** Which one of the following statements is false?

(a) Pie charts are better than bar graphs for comparing relative sizes.
(b) Data that are nominal scale are presented using frequency tables.
(c) Means and standard deviation of ordinal data are meaningless.
(d) The scatter plot is the basic graphic tool for investigating relationships between two intervals or ratio scaled variables.

**319.** An experiment was performed upon rats to investigate the effect of ingesting Alar (a chemical sprayed on apple trees to keep fruit from dropping before ripe) upon subsequent cancer rates. The following variables were measured

Gender (0 = female, 1 = male);
Weight (g);
dose of Alar (nil, low, high);
number of tumors

The typical weight of a rat is about 800 g and the weights were rounded to the nearest gram. The number of tumors is around 10.

Which of the following is false?

(a) Gender is nominal scale; dose is ordinal scale.
(b) Gender is discrete; weight is continuous.
(c) Number of tumors is discrete and is interval scale.
(d) Dose is ordinal scale and discrete.

**320.** Earthquake intensities are measured using a device called a seismograph which is designed to be most sensitive for earthquakes with intensities between 4.0 and 9.0 on the open-ended Richter scale. Measurements of ten earthquakes gave the following readings

4.5 L 5.5 H 8.7 8.9 6.0 H 5.2 7.2

Where L indicates that the earthquake had an intensity below 4.0, and a H indicates that the earthquake had an intensity above 9.0. One measure of central tendency is the x% trimmed mean computed after trimming x% of the upper values and x% of the bottom values. The value of the 20% trimmed mean is

(a) cannot be computed because all of the values are not known
(b) 6.00
(c) 6.60
(d) 6.92

**321.** A researcher is studying the hatching Yellow Bellied Sapsuckers. She has a study group of 40 eggs. A similar study has shown that the eggs hatching times shoulc have a mean of 42 days and a variance of 9 days (note that variance is (std dev)$^2$). Her thesis advisor has suggested that the distribution of hatching times will have the same shape as that of the Purple Throated Tree-tappers; which is 'mound shaped', If the researcher is willing to assume that her advisor is correct, how may eggs will have hatching times between 36 and 48 days?

(a) Approximately 55%, or around 22 eggs
(b) Approximately 68%, or around 27 eggs
(c) Approximately 75%, or around 30 eggs
(d) Approximately 95%, or around 38 eggs

**322.** Which of the following is not correct?

(a) The scatterplot is the basic graphical tool for nvestigating relationships between two continuous nterval or ratio scaled variables.
(b) The frequency table is useful for summarizing data from a nominal scaled variable.
(c) Means and standard deviations of nominal or ordinal scaled, variables are useful summary measures.
(d) Pie charts don't perform well because people have difficulty in accurately quantifying angles.

**323.** The following is a histogram showing the actual frequency of the closing prices on the New York exchange of a particular stock.

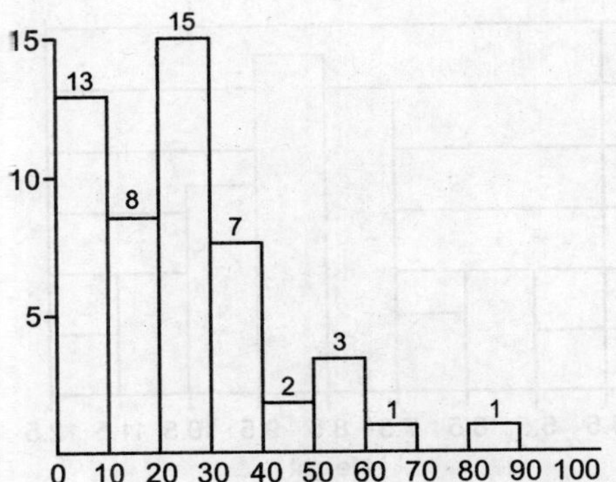

Based on the above frequency histogram for New York Stock exchange. the class that contains the 80th percentile is

(a) 20–30 (b) 10–20 (c) 40–50 (d) 30–40

**324.** An airplane is only allowed a gross passenger weight of 8000 kg. If the weights of passengers travelling by air between Toronto and Vancouver have a mean of 78 kg and a standard deviation of 7 kg, the approximate probability that the combined weight of 100 passengers will exceed 8000 kg is

(a) 0.4978 (b) 0.3987 (c) 0.1103 (d) 0.0022

**325.** The distribution of the heights of students in a large class is roughly bell-shaped. Moreover, the average height is 68 inches, and approximately 95% of the heights are between 62 and 74 inches. Thus, the standard deviation of the height distribution is approximately equal to

(a) 2 (b) 3 (c) 6 (d) 9

**326.** The following is a display comparing the favourite TV shows selected from a specified set by gender. Each person had to select one preferred show from the three shows given below

<-------Per cent-------> Sample

10 20 30 40 50 60 70 80 90 100 Size

|--|--|--|--|--|--|--|--|--|--|

Male: sssssssssssssssffffffffffffbbbbbbbb 100

Female: sssssssffffffffffffffffffffffbbbbbbb 300

Star Trek; ffff = Friends; bbbb = Baywatch;

Which of the following is false?

(a) A greater percentage of males have Star Trek as their favourite show than females.

(b) More females (in absolute number) selected Baywatch as their favourite show than males.

(c) About 1/5 of females surveyed selected Star Trek as their favourite show from the three given.

(d) About twice as many females (in relative numbers) enjoy Star Trek than males.

**327.** A histogram of the heights of 39 plants is as follows The 75th percentile of the height distribution is approximately

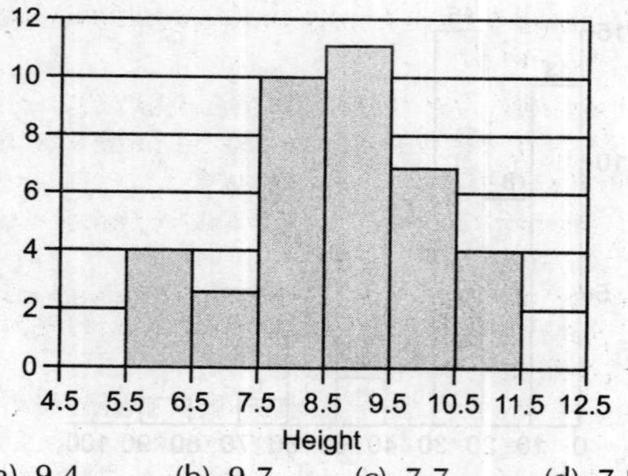


(a) 9.4 (b) 9.7 (c) 7.7 (d) 7.5

**328.** Government regulations indicate that the total weight of cargo in a certain kind of airplane cannot exceed 330 kg. On a particular day a plane is loaded with 100 boxes of goods. If the weight distribution for individual boxes is normal with mean 3.2 kg and standard deviation 7 kg, what is the probability that the regulations will not be met

(a) 1.5% (b) 92%

(c) 8% (d) 15%

**329.** For the following histogram, what is the proper ordering of the mean, median, and mode? Note that the graph is not numerically precise only the relative positions are important.

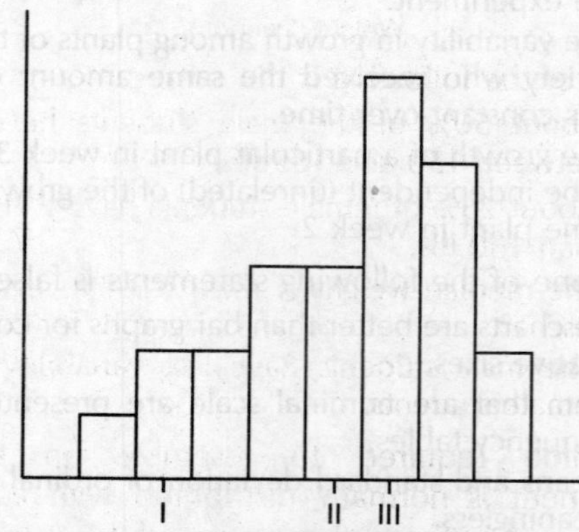


(a) I = mean II = median III = mode

(b) I = mode II = median III = mean

(c) I = median II = mean III = mode

(d) I = mode II = mean III = median

**330.** An experiment was conducted to investigate the effect of a new weed killer to suppress weed germination in onion crops. Two chemicals were used, the standard week killer (C) and the new chemical (W). Both chemicals were tested at high and low concentrations. Measurements are made on each of 50 plots for each treatment combinations of the % weed germination, Here are some box-plots of the results where the whiskers extend to the min and max of the data.

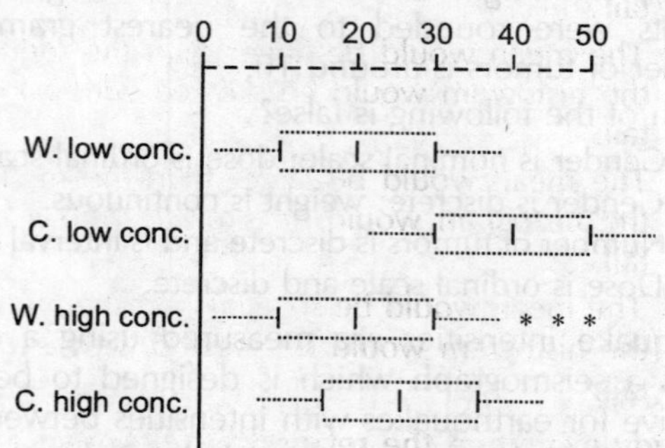


Which of the following is not a feature of this data?

(a) At either high or low concentrations, the new chemical (W) gives better control of weed germination than the control (C).

(b) Fewer weeds germinate at higher concentrations of both chemicals.

(c) The results from the control chemical are less variable than the new chemical.

(d) High or low concentrations of either chemical have approximately the same effects on weed germination.

**331.** The weights of the male and female students in a class are summarized in the following box plots

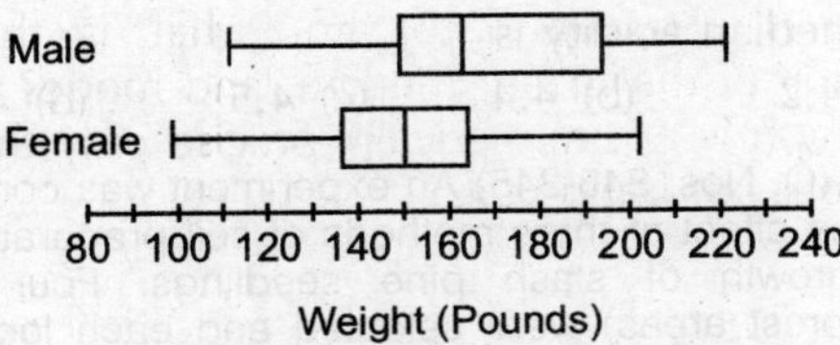


Which of the following is not correct?

(a) About 50% of the male students have weights between 150 and 185 lbs.

(b) About 25% of female students have weights more than 130 lbs.

(c) The median weight of male students is about 162 lbs.

(d) The male students have less variability than the female students.

**332.** The time required to assemble an electronic component is normally distributed with a mean of 12 min and a standard deviation of 1.5 min. Find the probability that the time 'required to assemble all nine components (*i.e.*, the total assembly time) is greater than 117 min

(a) 0.2514 (b) 0.2486
(c) 0.4772 (d) 0.0228

**333.** If most of the measurements in a large data set are of approximately the same magnitude except for a few measurements that are quite a bit larger, how would the mean and median of the data set compare and what shape would a histogram of the data set have?

(a) The mean would be smaller than the median and the histogram would be skewed with a long left tail.

(b) The mean would be larger than the median and the histogram would be skewed with a long right tail.

(c) The mean would be larger than the median and the histogram would be skewed with a long left tail.

(d) The mean would be smaller than the median and the histogram would be skewed with a long right tail.

**334.** A study examined the relationship between the sepal length and sepal width for two varieties of an exotic tropical plant. Varieties *A* and *B* are represented by x's and o's, respectively, in the following plot

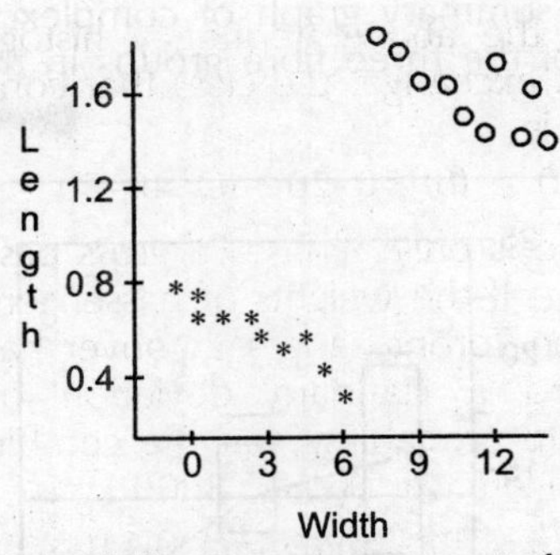


Which of the following statements is false?

(a) Considering variety *A* alone, there is a negative correlation between sepal length and sepal width.

(b) Considering variety *B* alone, the least squares regression line for predicting sepal length from sepal width has a negative slope.

(c) Considering both varieties together, there is a positive correlation between sepal length and sepal width.

(d) Considering each variety separately, there is a positive correlation between sepal length and sepal width.

**335.** Consider the following box plots of the grades in a course in statistics for each sex drawn according to the convention that the whiskers reach the 10th and 90th percentiles.

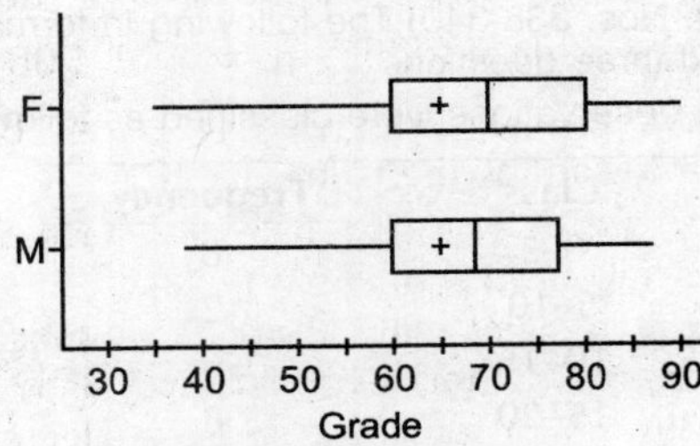


Which of the following is correct?

(a) The mean grade of the female students is about 72.

(b) The median grade for the male students is about 68.

(c) About 25% of female students get grades above 72.

(d) About 50% of female students get grades between 62 and 82.

**336.** In measuring the centre of the data from a skewed distribution, the median would be preferred over the mean for most purposes because

(a) the median is the most frequent number while the mean is most likely

(b) the mean may be too heavily influenced by the larger observations and this gives too high an indication of the centre

(c) the median is less than the mean and smaller numbers are always appropriate for the centre

(d) the mean measures the spread in the data

**337.** Here is a summary graph of complex carbohydrates for each of the three fibre groups in the cereal data set.

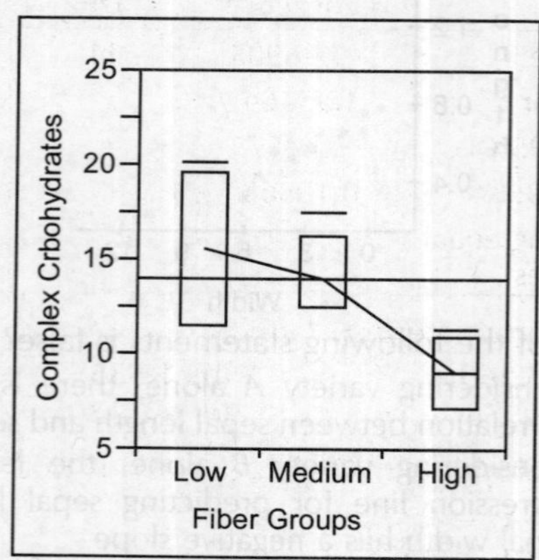


Which of the following is not correct?

(a) The low fibre group is more variable than the medium fibre group because the central box is larger.

(b) About 25% of low fibre cereals have less than 12 g of complex carbohydrates per serving.

(c) About 50% of medium fibre cereals have more than 15 g of complex carbohydrates per serving.

(d) About 25% of the medium fibre cereals have less than 10 g of complex carbohydrates.

**Directions** (Q. Nos. 338-340) The following in formation will be used in the next three questions.

A sample of 35 observations were classified as follows

| Class | Frequency |
|---|---|
| 0–5 | 8 |
| 5–10 | 2 |
| 10–15 | 6 |
| 15–20 | 8 |
| 20–25 | 5 |
| 25–30 | 5 |
| 30–35 | 0 |
| 35–40 | 1 |

**338.** The sample mean of the above grouped data is

(a) 14.89 (b) 14.23

(c) 15.35 (d) 15.11

**339.** The class mark of the third class is

(a) 10.0 (b) 12.5

(c) 15.0 (d) 7.5

**340.** The 80th percentile of the above grouped data is

(a) 27 (b) 22

(c) 19 (d) 24

**Directions** (Q. Nos. 341-342) Rainwater was collected in water collectors at thirty different sites near an industrial basin and the amount of acidity (pH level) was measured. The following stem-and-leaf diagram shows the pH values that ranged from 2.6 to 6.3.

| Stems | Leaves |
|---|---|
| 2 | 679 |
| 3 | 237789 |
| 4 | 1222446899 |
| 5 | 0556788 |
| 6 | 0233 |

**341.** The inter quartile range is

(a) 7.75 (b) 23.25 (c) 56.25 (d) 1.855

**342.** The median acidity is

(a) 4.2 (b) 4.4 (c) 4.5 (d) 4.6

**Directions** (Q. Nos. 343-345) An experiment was conducted to determine the effect of three methods of soil preparation on the first year growth of slash pine seedlings. Four locations (provincial forest areas) were selected and each location was divided into three plots. Three methods of soil preparation were used. No preparation, light fertilization and burning. One treatment was randomly assigned to the plots within each location and all three treatments were applied at each locations. On each plot, the same number of seedlings was planted, and the average first year growth for the seedlings on the plot was recorded. Two outputs appear below-only one of which is a 'correct' way of analyzing this data–

| Source | df | SS | Prob |
|---|---|---|---|
| prep | * | 38 | 0.1517 |
| Error | * | 73 | |
| Total | * | 111 | |
| prep | Mean | | |
| burn | 12.0 | | |
| fertilize | 16.0 | | |
| none | 12.5 | | |
| Source | df | SS | Prob |
| prep | * | 38.0 | 0.0121 |
| locn | * | 61.7 | 0.0077 |
| Error | * | 11.3 | |
| Total | * | 11 | |
| prep | Mean | | |
| burn | 12.0 | | |
| fertilize | 16.0 | | |
| none | 12.5 | | |

**343.** The LSD for comparing two means is

(a) 2.1 (b) 4.3

(c) 2.7 (d) 2.4

**344.** The value of the test statistic for testing the appropriate hypothesis is

(a) 2.3 (b) 10.1

(c) 10.9 (d) 2.6

**345.** Based upon the results of this study, we wish to be 80% confident of detecting a difference between the 'burn' and the 'none' treatments in the mean growth when testing at $\alpha = 0.05$. The required sample size for each treatment is

(a) > 17 (b) 4 (c) >21 (d) 12

**Directions** (Q. Nos. 346-347) A new drug has been developed for treating stage four (near terminal) AIDS patients. Patients were randomized to the old and new drug and the time to death (months) was recorded

OLD 32 <25 40 31 35 29

NEW 45 32 >48 34 37 27 35 >48

One patient died before twenty five months, but it was not known when. Two patients were still alive after four years when the study was terminated.

**346.** Which of the following is not correct?

(a) Non-parametric procedures require fewer assumptions than parametric procedures.

(b) The SIGNED-RANK test should be used for paired data.

(c) Non-parametric procedures can be used with ordinal data because all that is needed are the relative sizes of the values.

(d) The assumption of independence is not important for non-parametric procedures.

**347.** The value of the test statistic (computed on the OLD drug) for testing if the new drug gave an increased life span is

(a) 75 (b) 71
(c) 32 (d) 33

**Directions** (Q. Nos. 348-349) Different varieties of fruits and vegetables have different amount of nutrients. These differences are important when these products are used to make baby food. We wish to compare the carbohydrate content of two varieties of peaches. The data was analyzed with JMP and the following output was obtained

***t*-Test**

| | Difference | DF | Prob > \|t\| |
|---|---|---|---|
| Estimate | 4.2636 | 10 | 0.2039 |
| Std Error | 3.1366 | | |
| Lower 95% | – 2.7251 | | |
| Upper 95% | 11.2524 | | |
| Assuming equal variances | | | |

**348.** The test statistic, and *p*-value are

(a) 1.359.2039 (b) 4.264.1020
(c) 3.137.2039 (d) 10.2039

**349.** We wish to test if the two varieties are significantly different in their mean carbohydrate content. The null and alternative hypothesis are

(a) $H:\mu_1=\mu_2;\ A:\mu_1<\mu_2$

(b) $H:\mu_1=\mu_2;\ A:\mu_1>\mu_2$

(c) $H:\mu_1=\mu_2;\ A:\mu_1\neq\mu_2$

(d) $H:X_1=X_2;\ A:X_1<X_2$

**Directions** (Q. Nos. 350-352) In order to compare two kinds of feed, thirteen pigs are split into two groups, and each group received one feed. The following are the gains in weight (kilograms) after a fixed period of time.

| Feed A | 8.0 | 7.4 | 5.8 | 6.2 | 8.8 | 9.5 | |
|---|---|---|---|---|---|---|---|
| Feed B | 12.0 | 18.2 | 8.0 | 9.6 | 8.2 | 9.9 | 10.3 |

We wish to test the hypothesis that Feed B gives rise to larger weight gains. The output form JMP is as follows

*t*-test

| | Difference | DF | Prob>\|t\| |
|---|---|---|---|
| Estimate | – 3.26905 | 11 | 0.0566 |
| Std Error | 1.53464 | | |
| Lower 95% | – 6.64677 | | |
| Upper 95% | 0.10868 | | |
| Assuming equal variances | | | |

**350.** The appropriate test statistic is

(a) – 3.269 (b) 1.535
(c) 0.0566 (d) – 2.130

**351.** The appropriate null and alternate hypothesis are

(a) $H:X_A=X_B;\ A:X_A\neq X_B$

(b) $H:\mu_A=\mu_B;\ A:\mu_A\neq\mu_B$

(c) $H:\bar{X}_A=\bar{X}_B;\ A:\bar{X}_A<\bar{X}_B$

(d) $H:\mu_A=\mu_B;\ A:\mu_A<\mu_B$

(e) $H:\bar{X}_A=\bar{X}_B;\ A:\bar{X}_A>\bar{X}_B$

**352.** The p-value for the test is

(a) 0.0566 (b) 0.0283 (c) 0.1132 (d) 0.1087

**Directions** (Q. Nos. 353-354) A Canadian railway company claims that its trains block crossings no more that 8 min per train on the average. The actual times (minutes) that 10 randomly selected trains block crossings were recorded.

10.1 9.5 6.5 8.0 8.8 >12 7.2 10.5 8.2 9.3

**353.** The *p*-value is

(a) 0.101 (b) 0.053 (c) 0.248 (d) 0.049

**354.** The value of an appropriate test-statistics for testing the claim is

(a) 37 (b) 33 (c) 44 (d) 29

**Directions** (Q. Nos. 355-358) DDT is an insecticide that accumulates up the food chain. Predator birds can be contaminated with quite high levels of the chemical by eating many lightly contaminated prey. One effect of DDT upon birds is to inhibit the production of the enzyme carbonic anhydrase which controls calcium metabolism. It is believed that this causes egg shells to be thinner and weaker than normal and makes the eggs more prone to breakage. (this in one of reasons why the condor in California is near extinction.) An experiment was conducted where 16 sparrow hawks were fed a mixture of 3 ppm dieldrin and 15 ppm DDT (A combination often found in contaminated prey). The first egg laid by each bird was measured and the mean shell thickness was found to be 0.19 mm with a standard deviation of 0.01 mm. A normal egg shell has a mean thickness of 0.2 mm.

**355.** The value of the statistic is

(a) – 1.00 (b) – 4.00
(c) 0.01 (d) 1.96

**356.** The null and alternate hypothesis are

(a) $H:\mu=0.2,\ A:\mu<0.2$

(b) $H:\mu<0.2,\ A:\mu=0.2$

(c) $H:\bar{X}=0.2,\ A:\bar{X}<0.2$

(d) $H=\bar{X}=0.19,\ A:\bar{X}=0$

**357.** It is important to detect a decrease in the average thickness to 0.18 mm because then the eggs are so fragile that few survive. What sample size would be needed to be 80% sure of detecting this decrease at $\alpha = 0.05$?

(a) 8 (b) > 128
(c) 34 (d) 27

**358.** The null hypothesis will be rejected ($\alpha = 0.05$) if the test statistic is less than : (note that if the rejection region is two sided, only one side has been shown).

(a) – 2.1314 (b) – 1.7530
(c) – 1.9600 (d) – 1.6450

**Directions** (Q. Nos. 359-360) Winnipeg Tribune claims that the time of travel from downtown to the University *via* the pembina bus has an average of $\mu = 27$ min. A student who normally takes this bus believes that $\mu$ is greater than 27 min. A sample of six ride-times taken to test the hypothesis of interest gave $\overline{X} = 27.5$ min and standard deviation $s = 2.43$ min.

**359.** The value of the test statistic for testing this hypothesis is :

(a) – 0.532 (b) – 0.460
(c) – 0.504 (d) 0.504

**360.** In the previous question, the appropriate critical region and conclusion when testing at a = 0.05 are

(a) $T^* > 2.015$; and we fail to reject $H_0$
(b) $T^* > 2.571$; and we fail to reject $H_0$
(c) $T^* < 2.015$; and we fail to reject $H_0$
(d) $T^* < 2.571$; and we fail to reject $H_0$

**Directions** (Q. Nos. 361-362) In some mining operations, a by product of the processing is mildly radioactive. Of prime concern is the possibility that release of these byproducts into the environment may contaminate the fresh water supply. There are strict regulations for the maximum allowable radioactivity in supplies of drinking water, namely an average of 5 picocuries per litre (pCi/L) or less. However, it is will known that even safe water has occasional hot spots that eventually get diluted, so samples of water are assumed safe unless there is evidence to the contrary. A random sample of 25 specimens of water from a city's water supply gave a mean of 5.39 pCi/L and a standard deviation of 0.87 pCi/L.

**361.** The value of the test statistic, the rejection region ($\alpha = 0.05$) and the *p*-value (computed by a computer) are

(a) $Z^* = 2.24$ reject if $Z^* > 1.960$; *p*-value = 0.0125
(b) $Z^* = 2.24$ reject if $Z^* > 1.645$; *p*-value = 0.0125
(c) $T^* = 2.24$ with 25 df; reject if $T^* > 1.708$; *p*-value = 0.0171
(d) $T^* = 2.24$ with 24 df; reject if $T^* > 1.711$; *p*-value = 0.0173

**362.** The appropriate null and alternative hypothesis are

(a) $H_0 : \mu = 5.39$ vs $H_A : \mu \neq 5.39$
(b) $H_0 : \mu = 5.39$ vs $H_A : \mu < 5.00$
(c) $H_0 : \mu = 5$ vs $H_A : \mu = 5.39$
(d) $H_0 : \mu = 5$ vs $H_A : \mu > 5$

**Directions** (Q. Nos. 363-367) Resting pulse rate is an important measure of the fitness of a person's cardiovascular system with a lower rate indicative of greater fitness. The mean pulse rate for all adult males is approximately 72 beats per min. A random sample of 25 male students currently enrolled the faculty of Agriculture and now taking 5.211 was selected and the mean pulse resting pulse rate was found to be 80 beats per min with a standard deviation of 20 beats per minute. The experimenter wishes to test if the students are less fit, on average, than the general population.

**363.** The value of the test statistic is

(a) 0.32 (b) 2.00
(c) – D.32 (d) 1.64

**364.** The null and alternate hypothesis are

(a) $H : \mu = 72; A : \mu < 72$ (b) $H : X = 72; A : X < 72$
(c) $H : \mu = 80; A : \mu = 72$ (d) $H : \mu = 72; A : \mu > 72$

**365.** The null hypothesis will be rejected at $\alpha = 0.05$ if the test statistic exceeds

(a) 1.9600 (b) 1.6450
(c) 1.7109 (d) 2.0639

**366.** The *p*-value is estimated to be

(a) between 0.025 and 0.05
(b) between 0.020 and 0.025
(c) between 0.05 and 0.10
(d) 7.25

**367.** A possible Type II error would be to

(a) conclude that the students are less fit (on average) than the general population when in fact they have equal fitness on average
(b) conclude that the students have the same fitness (on average) as the general population when in fact they are less fit on average
(c) conclude that the students have the same fitness (on average) as the general population when in fact they are the same fitness level on average
(d) Conclude that the students are less fit (on average) than the general population when, in fact, they are less fit on average

**Directions** (Q. Nos. 368-370) The average growth of a certain variety of pine tree is 10.1 inches in three years. A biologist claims that a new variety will have a greater three-year growth. A random sample of 25 of the new variety has an average three year growth of 10.8 inches and a standard deviation of 2.1 inches.

**368.** At the 5% level of significance, the null hypothesis is

(a) rejected because the calculated value of the test statistic is less than the appropriate critical value 1.711
(b) rejected because the calculated value of the test statistic is greater than the appropriate critical value 1.645
(c) accepted because the calculated value of the test statistic is less than the appropriate critical value 1.711
(d) Accepted because the calculated value of the test statistic is less than the appropriate critical value 1.708

**369.** The appropriate null and alternate hypothesis to test the biologist's claim are
(a) $H:\mu = 10.8$ against $A:\mu > 10.8$
(b) $H:\mu = 10.8$ against $A:\mu \neq 10.8$
(c) $H:\mu = 10.1$ against $A:\mu > 10.1$
(d) $H:\mu = 10.1$ against $A:\mu < 10.1$

**370.** The *p*-value for the previous test is computed to be
(a) between 0.005 and 0.010
(b) between 0.010 and 0.015
(c) between 0.015 and 0.025
(d) between 0.050 and 0.100

**Directions** (Q. Nos. 371-372) A recent estimate by a large distributor of gasoline claims that 60% of all cars stopping at their service stations chose unleaded gas and that super unleaded and regular were each selected 20% of the time. In order to check the validity of these proportions, a study was conducted of cars stopping at the distributor's service stations in a large city. The results were as follows

| Gasoline selected | | |
|---|---|---|
| Regular | Unleaded | Super Unleaded |
| 51 | 261 | 88 |

**371.** If $\alpha = 0.05$, then the value of the appropriate test statistic and the critical value respectively, are
(a) 21.75, 5.99 (b) 13.15, 5.99
(c) 21.75, 7.81 (d) 13.15, 7.81

**372.** The expected cell counts assuming the distributor's claim is correct, are
(a) 100, 200, 100 (b) 51, 261, 88
(c) 80, 240, 80 (d) 133, 133, 133

**Directions** (Q. Nos. 373-374) The paper 'Linkage Studies of the Tomato' (Trans. Royal Canad. Inst. (1931)) reported the accompanying data on phenotypes resulting from crossing tall cut-leaf tomatoes with dwarf Potato-leaf tomatoes. We wish to investigate if the frequencies below are consistent with the Mandellian laws which state the phenotype should occur in the ratio 9 : 3 : 3 : 1.

| | Phenotype | | | |
|---|---|---|---|---|
| | **Tall** | **Tall** | **Dwarf** | **Dwarf** |
| | Cut leaf | Pot leaf | Cut leaf | Pot leaf |
| Frequency | 926 | 288 | 293 | 104 |

**373.** The hypothesis would be rejected at $\alpha = 0.05$ if the test statistic exceeds
(a) 7.81 (b) 5.99
(c) 3.84 (d) 9.49

**374.** The computed test statistic is
(a) 7.81 (b) 5.99
(c) 1.18 (d) 1.47

**Directions** (Q. Nos. 375-378) There are extensive breeding programs for salmon on the West Coast of Canada to enhance the salmon fishery. One question of interest is whether inbreeding affects subsequent fitness of the fish. An experiment was conducted where released salmon were classified as unrelated if the parents were unrelated, half-sibs if the one of the parents was in common and full sibs if both parents were in common. In one release, 25% of the fish were half-sibs, 40% were unrelated and 35% were full sibs. Of 237 returning adult salmon, 45% were unrelated, 25% were full-sibs, and 30% were half-sibs.

Here is some output form JMP

| Test probabilities | | | |
|---|---|---|---|
| **Test** | **chi-square** | **DF** | **Prob>chisq** |
| Likelihood ratio | 11.3939 | 2 | 0.0034 |
| Pearson | 10.8153 | 2 | 0.0045 |

**375.** The null hypothesis is
(a) the return rate is independent of the relatedness of the fish
(b) the return rate is dependent upon the relatedness of the fish
(c) the return rates are 45%, 25% and 30% for unrelated, full-sibs, and half-sibs, respectively
(d) the return rates are 40%, 35% and 25% for unrelated, full-sibs, and half-sibs, respectively

**376.** The *p*-value is
(a) $< 0.005$
(b) between 0.005 and 0.01
(c) between 0.01 and 0.02
(c) between 0.02 and 0.05

**377.** The expected number of half-sibs is
(a) 0.29958 (b) 71
(c) 10.81 (d) 59.25

**378.** The *p*-value is
(a) 0.0034 (b) 0.0068
(c) 0.0090 (d) 0.0045

**Directions** (Q. Nos. 379-380) One criticism of reforestation efforts after timber harvesting is that too few of the seedling survive. An experiment was conducted to assess if mulching the slash (limbs, roots, small branches, etc.) and leaving the mulch on the ground improves the survival rate campared to just leaving the slash on the ground. It is believed that mulching will cause the material to break down sooner and release the nutrients to the seedlings. A total of 500 seedlings were randomly assigned to the two treatments and the two year survival rate was measured. Of the 250 seedling receiving the 'mulching' treatment, 75 survived; of the 250 seedling receiving the 'control' treatment, 55 survived.

**379.** The value of the test statistic and the *p*-value are
(a) 2.76, 0.003
(b) 2.05, 0.042
(c) 2.76, 0.006
(d) 2.05, 0.021

**380.** The null and alternate hypothesis are
($m$ = mulch, $c$ = control)
(a) $H:p_m = 0.22\ A:p_m > 0.22$
(b) $H:\mu_m = 0.22\ A:\mu_m > 0.22$
(c) $H:p_m - p_c = 0\ A:p_m - p_c > 0$
(d) $H:\mu_m - \mu_c = 0\ A:\mu_m - \mu_c > 0$

**Directions** (Q. Nos. 381-382) Two surveys were conducted before and after the recent Autopac rate increases to find the proportion of voters who state they would vote for the current government. The results were as follows

| | Week 1 | Week 2 | Total over both weeks |
|---|---|---|---|
| No. surveyed | 400 | 600 | 1000 |
| No. in favor of current gov't | 150 | 150 | 300 |

**381.** The above confidence intervals are of the order's percentage points. What sample size for each poll would be needed so that we are 95% confident of being within 2 percentage points of the true difference assuming that the above proportions are reasonable estimates of the proportions in the population?

(a) 6000 (b) 1000
(c) 15000 (d) 4000

**382.** An approximate 95% confidence interval for the change in support, is

(a) $(0.375-0.250)\pm 1.96\sqrt{\frac{(0.375)(0.625)}{400}+\frac{(0.250)(0.750)}{600}}$

(b) $(0.375-0.250)\pm 1.96\sqrt{\frac{(0.375)(0.625)}{1000}+\frac{(0.250)(0.750)}{1000}}$

(c) $(0.375-0.250)\pm 1.96\sqrt{\frac{(0.300)(0.700)}{400}+\frac{(0.300)(0.700)}{600}}$

(d) $(0.375-0.250)\pm 1.96\sqrt{\frac{(0.300)(0.700)}{1000}+\frac{(0.300)(0.700)}{1000}}$

**Direictions** (Q. Nos. 383-385) In the past decade there have been extensive anti-smoking campaigns to try and reduce the proportion of smokers in the population. In 1982, a survey of 350 adult females revealed that 148 smoked. In 1989, 488 adult females were surveyed and 163 smoked. Let *p* represent the proportion of adult female smokers.

**383.** The null and alternate hypothesis are

(a) $H: p_{1982}=p_{1989}\ A: p_{1982}>p_{1989}$
(b) $H: p_{1982}\neq p_{1989}\ A: p_{1982}=p_{1989}$
(c) $H: p_{1982}=0.423\ A: p_{1889}<0.423$
(d) $H: p_{1982}=0.334\ A: p_{1982}>0.334$

**384.** The *p*-value is found to be

(a) 2.63 (b) 0.004
(c) 0.009 (d) 0.496

**385.** The test statistic would be computed as

(a) $0.09/\sqrt{\frac{0.423(1-0.423)}{350}+\frac{0.334(1-0.334)}{488}}$

(b) $0.09/\sqrt{\frac{0.423(1-0.423)}{838}+\frac{0.334(1-0.334)}{838}}$

(c) $0.09/\sqrt{\frac{0.371(1-0.371)}{838}}$

(d) $0.9/\sqrt{\frac{0.371(1-0.371)}{350}+\frac{0.371(1-0.371)}{488}}$

**Directions** (Q. Nos. 386-388) Growth hormones are often used to increase the weight gain of chickens. In an experiment using 15 chickens, five different doses of growth hormone (0, 0.2, 0.4, 0.8, and 1.0 mg/kg) were injected into chickens (three for each dose) and the subsequent weight gain was recorded. An experimenter plots the data and finds that a linear relationship appears to hold. The output from JMP follows

**Parameter Estimates**

| Term | Estimate | Std Error | *t*-Ratio | Prob > \|*t*\| | Lower 95% | Upper 95% |
|---|---|---|---|---|---|---|
| Intercept | 4.545853 3 | 0.616581 | + 737 | <0.0001 | 3.2138128 | 5.8778937 |
| dose | 4.832342 6 | 1.016403 | 4.75 | 0.0004 | | |

**386.** It is suspected that the weight gain should increase with dose. An appropriate null and alternate hypothesis to test the slope, the test statistic, and the *p*-value are

(a) $H:\beta_1=0; A:\beta_1\neq 0; T^*=7.37$; *p*-value $<0.0001$
(b) $H:\beta_0=0; A:\beta_0\neq 0; T^*=4.75$; *p*-value $=0.0004$
(c) $H:b_1=0; A:b_1>0; T^*=7.37$; *p*-value $=0.0002$
(d) $H:\beta_1=0; A:\beta_1>0; T^*=4.75$; *p*-value $=0.0002$

**387.** The fitted regression line is

(a) $\hat{Y}=4.55+0.617X$ (b) $\hat{Y}=4.83+4.55X$
(c) $\hat{Y}=4.83+1.02X$ (d) $\hat{Y}=4.55+4.83X$

**388.** An approximate 95% confidence interval for the slope is

(a) $4.55\pm 0.617$ (b) $4.83\pm 2.03$
(c) $4.83\pm 1.02$ (d) $4.83\pm 4.75$

**Directions** (Q. Nos.389-391) Growth harmones are often used to increase the weight gain of chickens. In an experiment using 15 chickens, five different doses of growth hormone (0, 0.2, 0.4, 0.8, and 1.0 mg/k) were injected into chickens (three for each dose) and the subsequent weight gain was recorded. An experimenter plots the data and finds that a liner relationship appears to hold. The output form SAS follows

| Source | dF | Sum of Squares | Mean Square | F Value | Pr > F |
|---|---|---|---|---|---|
| Model | 1 | 78.4083 | 78.4083 | 8.11 | .0137 |
| Error | 13 | 125.7410 | 9.6723 | | |
| Corrected Total | 14 | 204.1493 | | | |
| T For HO : PR > | \|T\| | STD ERROR OF | | | |
| Parameter Estimate | | Parameter = 0 | | | Estimate |
| Intercept | 3.7816 | 3.23 | 0.0066 | | 1.1705 |
| Dose | 4.0416 | 2.85 | 0.0137 | | 1.4195 |

**389.** It is suspected that weight gain should increase with dose. An appropriate null and alternate hypothesis to test the slope, the test statistic, and the $p$-value are

(a) $H:\beta_1 = 0; A:\beta_1 \neq 0; T^* = 2.85; p\text{-value} = 0.0069$
(b) $H:\beta_1 = 0; A:\beta_0 \neq 0; T^* = 3.23; p\text{-value} = 0.0066$
(c) $H:\beta_1 = 0; A:\beta_1 > 0; T^* = 2.85; p\text{-value} = 0.0137$
(d) $H:\beta_1 = 0; A:\beta_1 > 0; T^* = 2.85; p\text{-value} = 0.0069$

**390.** The fitted regression line is

(a) $\hat{Y} = 4.04 + 3.78X$ (b) $\hat{Y} = 3.23 + 2.85X$
(c) $\hat{Y} = 2.85 + 3.23X$ (d) $\hat{Y} = 3.78 + 4.04X$

**391.** A 95% confidence interval for the slope is

(a) $4.04 \pm 1.96(1.42)$ (b) $4.04 \pm 1.77(1.42)$
(c) $4.04 \pm 2.16(1.42)$ (d) $3.78 \pm 1.77(1.17)$

**Directions** (Q. Nos. 392-395) A study was conducted to determine if the fatality rate depends on the size of the automobile. The analysis of accidents is as follows (with some values hidden)

| Death Frequency | m | Size s | L | Total |
|---|---|---|---|---|
| No | 63 | 128 | 46 | 237 |
| Yes | 26 | 95 | 16 | 137 |
| Total | 89 | 223 | 62 | 374 |

**Statistics for Table of Death by size**

| Statistic | DF | Value | Prob |
|---|---|---|---|
| Chi-square | * | 8.663 | ***** |
| Likelihood Ration Chi-Square | * | 8.838 | ***** |

**392.** Which of the following is not correct?

(a) The accidents were cross-classified by size of automobile and fatality.
(b) The null hypothesis is that the fatality status is independent of the size the automobile.
(c) The null hypothesis is that the proportion of fatality status is the same for all three size of automobiles.
(d) If we reject the null hypothesis than we have proven that the size of the automobile affects the chances of a fatality.

**393.** Under a suitable null hypothesis, the expected frequency for the cell corresponding to fatal type of accident and small some automobile is

(a) 81.86 (b) 67.00
(c) 61.43 (d) 63.41

**394.** The null hypothesis will be rejected at $\alpha = 0.05$ if the test statistic exceeds

(a) 12.59 (b) 7.81
(c) 5.99 (d) 3.84

**395.** The approximate $p$-value is

(a) less than 0.005
(b) between 0.005 and 0.010
(c) between 0.010 and 0.025
(d) between 0.050 and 0.100

**Directions** (Q. Nos. 396-400) The effects of a toxic pollutant upon fish was examined by placing fish in a two litre solution of water with various concentrations of the pollutant. The time (in minutes) until the fish showed distress was recorded at which time the fish were removed from the container. A total of 18 different experiments were performed. Note that the pollutant is measured on a logarithmic scale where a change of one unit represents an increase of 10 fold in the pollution concentration. A preliminary plot of the data showed that the relationship of time vs. log(pollution) was approximately linear. The output appears below

| Source | DF | Sum of Squares | Mean Square | F Value | PR > F |
|---|---|---|---|---|---|
| Model | 1 | 2.21459712 | 2.21459712 | 5.49 | 0.0324 |
| Error | 16 | 6.45556062 | 0.40347254 | | |
| Corr. Total | 17 | 8.67015774 | | | |
| T For HO : | PR | \|T\| | STD ERROR OF | | |
| Parameter | Estimate | | Parameter = 0 | | Estimate |
| Intercept | 7.5641 | | 3.82 | 0.0015 | 1.978 |
| Logpollut | – 1.0269 | | – 2.34 | 0.0324 | 0.438 |

**396.** An appropriate null and alternate hypothesis to test the slope, the test statistic and the $p$-value are

(a) $H:\beta_1 = 0; A:\beta_1 \neq 0; T^* = -2.34; p\text{-value} = 0.0324$
(b) $H:\beta_0 = 0; A:\beta_0 \neq 0; T^* = 3.82; p\text{-value} = 0.0007$
(c) $H:\beta_1 = 0; A:\beta_1 < 0; T^* = -2.34; p\text{-value} = 0.0324$
(d) $H:\beta_1 = 0; A:\beta_1 < 0; T^* = -2.34; p\text{-value} = 0.0162$

**397.** The fitted regression line is

(a) $\hat{Y} = -1.03 + 7.56X$ (b) $\hat{Y} = 7.56 - 1.03X$
(c) $\hat{Y} = 3.28 - 2.34X$ (d) $\hat{Y} = 7.56 + 10.27X$

**398.** A 95% confidence interval for the slope is

(a) $7.56 \pm 1.96(1.978)$ (b) $-1.03 \pm 1.96(0.438)$
(c) $7.56 \pm 2.1098(1.978)$ (d) $-1.03 \pm 2.1199(0.438)$

**399.** A similar experiment was performed using a third pollutant. A scatter-plot and the fitted regression line are shown below

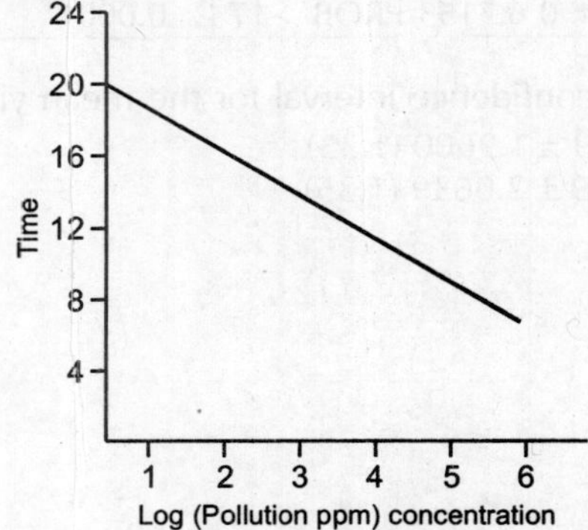

Which of the following is the best description of this plot?

(a) $\hat{Y} = 20 - 2X; r = -0.6$

(b) $\hat{Y} = 20 - 4X; r = -0.6$

(c) $\hat{Y} = 20 - 2X; r = -0.9$

(d) $\hat{Y} = 20 - 4X; r = -0.9$

**400.** A similar experiment was performed using a second pollutant. The estimated regression line is found to be $\hat{Y} = 27.63 - 2.03X$.

Which of the following is not correct?

(a) If the concentration of the pollutant is increased 100 times (represented by an increase of 2 on the logarithmic scale), the average time to distress decreases by 4.06 min.

(b) In order to obtain an estimate time to distress of 25 min, the log (concentration) of the pollutant should be 1.30.

(c) A ten-fold increase in pollution (represented by an increase of one unit on the log scale) decreases the fime to distress by 20.3 min.

(d) It would be inadvisable to extrapolating the line outside of the observed values of the pollutant concentration.

**401.** The effect of acid rain upon the yield of crops is of concern in many places. In order to determine baseline yields, a sample of 13 fields was selected, and the yield of barley (g/400m$^2$) was determined. The output from SAS appears below

| | | | | | Quantiles (DEF = 4) | | | | Extremes | |
|---|---|---|---|---|---|---|---|---|---|---|
| N | 13 | SUM WGTS | 13 | 100% | MAX | 392 | 99% | 392 | LOW | HIGH |
| MEAN | 220.231 | SUM | 2863 | 75% | Q3 | 234 | 95% | 392 | 161 | 225 |
| SD | 58.5721 | VAR | 3430.69 | 50% | MED | 221 | 90% | 330 | 168 | 232 |
| SKEW | 2.21591 | KURT | 6.61979 | 25% | Q1 | 174 | 10% | 163 | 169 | 236 |
| USS | 671689 | CSS | 41168.3 | 0% | MIN | 161 | 5% | 161 | 179 | 239 |
| CV | 26.5958 | STD MEAN | 16.245 | | | | 1% | 161 | 205 | 392 |

The mean, standard deviation, median and the highest value are

(a) 220.231 3430.60 50% 225

(b) 220.231 58.5721 50% 392

(c) 220.231 16.245 221 225

(d) 220.231 58.5721 221 392

**402.** The effect of salinity upon the growth of grasses is of concern in many places where excess irrigation is causing salt to rise to the surface. In order to determine baseline yields, a sample of 24 fields was selected, and the biomass of grasses in a standard sized plot was measured (kg). The output from SAS appears below

| | | | | | Quantiles (DEF = 40) | | | | Extremes | |
|---|---|---|---|---|---|---|---|---|---|---|
| N | 24 | SUM WGTS | 24 | 100% | Max | 22.6 | 99% | 22.6 | Low | High |
| MEAN | 9.09 | SUM | 218.3 | 75% | Q3 | 11.45 | 95% | 22.52 | 0.7 | 15.1 |
| SD | 6.64 | VARIANCE | 44.0 | 50% | MED | 8.15 | 90% | 21.8 | 1 | 19.8 |
| SKEWNE | 0.924 | KURTO | – 0.0209 | 25% | Q1 | 3.775 | 10% | 1.6 | 2.2 | 21.3 |
| USS | 2998 | CSS | 1012.73 | 0% | MIN | 0.7 | 5% | 0.77 | 2.2 | 22.3 |
| CV | 72 | STD MEAN | 1.35 | | | | 1% | 0.7 | 2.8 | 22.6 |
| T : MEAN = 0 6.7153 PROB > \|T\| | | | 0.0001 | | RANGE 21.9 | | | | | |

A 95% confidence interval for the mean yield is

(a) $9.09 \pm 1.9600\ (1.35)$

(b) $9.09 \pm 2.0639\ (1.35)$

(c) $9.09 \pm 2.0639\ (6.64)$

(d) $9.09 \pm 2.0687 (1.35)$

# Exercise 2 (For Part 'C')

**Directions** (Q. Nos. 1-41) *Questions may have one or more than one correct option.*

**1.** The chi-square goodness of fit is based on
(a) multinational distribution
(b) hypergeometric distribution
(c) the assumption that the character under study is normal
(d) None of the above

**2.** To test the equality of the population mean of two normal populations $N(\mu_1, \sigma_1^2)$ and $N(\mu_2, \sigma_2^2)$ consider test statistic

$$t = \frac{\bar{x}_1 - \bar{x}_2}{S\sqrt{\frac{1}{n_1} + \frac{1}{n_2}}}$$

where, $S^2$ is the pooled sample variance based on samples of sizes $n_1$ and $n_2$ from the population. Then,
(a) the distribution of '$t$' is students $t$ with $\sigma_1^2 \neq 0$ but unknown
(b) the distribution of $t$ is $N(0, 1)$, if $\sigma_1^2 = \sigma_2^2$ known
(c) the distribution of $t$ is students $t$, if $\sigma_1^2 = \sigma_2^2 = \sigma^2$ but unknown
(d) the distribution of $t$ is students $t$, if $\sigma_1^2$ and $\sigma_2^2$ are known and distinct

**3.** The following described a new method of measuring the thermal conductivity of Armco iron. Using a temperature of 100°F and a power input of 550 watts, the following 10 measurements of thermal conductivity (in Btu/hr-ft-°F) were obtained

41.60,41.48,42.34, 41.95,41.86,
42.18,41.72,42.26,41.81,42.04

(a) A point estimate of the mean thermal is 41.924 Btu/hr-ft-°F
(b) The point estimate of the mean thermal is 2.65 Btu/hr-ft-°F
(c) Highly confident that the true mean thermal conductivity is with the interval $41.924 \pm 0.1756$
(d) The standard error is about 0.2 per cent of the sample mean

**4.** The increased availability of light materials with high strength has revolutionized the design and manufacture of golf clubs, particularly drivers. Clubs with hollow heads and very thin faces can result in much longer the shots, especially for players of modest skills. This is due partly to the "spring-like effect" that the thin face imparts to the ball. Firing a golf ball at the head of the club and measuring the ratio of the outgoing velocity of the ball to the incoming velocity can quantify this spring-like effect. The ratio of velocities is called the coefficient of restitution of the club. An experiment was performed in which 15 drivers produced by a particular club maker were selected at random and their coefficients of restitution measured. In the experiment the golf balls were fired from an air cannon so that the incoming velocity and spin rate of the ball could be precisely controlled. It is of interest to determine if there is evidence (with $\alpha = 0.05$) to support a claim that the mean coefficient of restitution exceeds 0.82. The observations follow

0.8411 0.8191 0.8182 0.8125 0.8750
0.8580 0.8532 0.8483 0.8276 0.7983
0.8042 0.8730 0.8282 0.8359 0.8660

The sample mean and sample standard deviation are $\bar{x} = 0.83725$ and $s = 0.02456$. The normal probability plot of the data in given figure supports the assumption that the coefficient of restitution is normally distributed. Since, the objective of the experimenter is to demonstrate that the mean coefficient of restitution exceeds 0.82 a one sided alternative hypothesis is appropriate.
(a) The parameter of interest is the mean coefficient of restriction
(b) At 0.05 level of significance the mean coefficient of restitution exceeds 0.82
(c) At 0.05 level of significance the mean coefficient of restitution does not exceeds 0.82
(d) The test statistic $t_0$ is 2.72

**5.** The following are 15 measurements of the octane rating of a certain kind of gasoline 97.5, 95.2, 97.3, 96.0, 96.8, 100.3, 97.4, 95.3, 93.2, 99.1, 96.1, 97.6, 98.2, 98.5, and 94.9. Use the signed-rank test at the 0.05 level of significance to test whether or not the mean octane rating of the given kind of gasoline is 98.5.
(a) The mean octane rating of the given kind of gasoline is not 98.5
(b) The mean octane rating of the given kind of gasoline is 98.5
(c) $T_{0.05} = 21$ for $n = 14$
(d) $T_{0.05} = 61$ for $n = 14$

**6.** If $X_1, X_2, \ldots, X_n$ constitute a random sample of size $n$ from a Bernoulli population,
(a) $\hat{\theta} = \frac{X}{n}$ is a sufficient estimator of $\theta$
(b) $\hat{\theta} = X$ is a sufficient estimator of $\theta$
(c) $\hat{\theta} = \frac{n}{X}$ is a sufficient estimator of $\theta$
(d) there is no sufficient estimator of $\theta$

**7.** The one of the survey compares several methods for predicting the shear strength for steel plate girders. Data for two of these methods, the Karlsruhe and Lehigh procedures, when applied to nine specific girders, are shown in Table (a). We wish to determine whether there is any difference (on the average) between the two methods.

(a) Strength prediction methods yields different results
(b) Strength prediction methods yields same results
(c) The data indicate that the Karlsruhe method produces, on the average, higher strength predictions than does the Lehigh method
(d) The *P*-value for $t_0 = 6.05$ is $P = 0.0002$

**8.** If $x_1, x_2, \ldots\ldots, x_n$ are the values of a random sample from an exponential population,

(a) likelihood function $L(\theta) = \left(\frac{1}{\theta}\right)^n \cdot e^{-\frac{1}{\theta}\left(\sum_{i=1}^{n} x_i\right)}$
(b) likelihood function $L(\theta) = \frac{1}{\theta^2}$
(c) the maximum likelihood estimator is $\hat{\theta} = \overline{X}$
(d) the maximum likelihood estimator is $\hat{\theta} = \frac{1}{\overline{X}}$

**9.** Suppose that *X* is a random variable with mean $\mu$ and variance $\sigma^2$. Let $X_1, X_2, \ldots, X_n$ be a random sample of size *n* from the population represented by *X*.

(a) Sample mean $\overline{X}$ is equal to $\sigma^2$
(b) Sample mean $\overline{X}$ is equal to $\mu$
(c) Sample variance $S^2$ is equal to $\sigma^2$
(d) Sample variance $S^2$ is equal to $\mu$

**10.** A product developer is interested in reducing the drying time of a primer paint. Two formulations of the paint are tested; formulation 1 is the standard chemistry, and formulation 2 has a new drying ingredient that should reduce the drying time. From experience, it is known that the standard deviation of drying time is 8 min and this inherent variability should be unaffected by the addition of the new ingredient. Ten specimens are painted with formulation 1, and another 10 specimens are painted with formulation 2; the 20 specimens are painted in random order. The two sample average drying ti mes are $\bar{x}_1 = 121$ min and $\bar{x}_2 = 112$ min, respectively. What conclusions can the product developer draw about the effectiveness of the new ingredient, using $\alpha = 0.05$?

(a) Adding the new ingredient to the point significantly reduces the drying time
(b) Adding the new ingredient to the point significantly increase the drying time
(c) The *p*-value for the test is 0.0059
(d) The *p*-value for the test is 6

**11.** If $X_1, X_2, \ldots, X_n$ constitute a random sample from a uniform population with $\alpha = 0$, then the largest sample value (*i.e.*, the *n*th order statistic, $Y_n$) is a biased estimator of the parameter $\beta$ to make it unbiased.

(a) The largest sample value (*n*th order statistic) is a biased estimator of parameter $\beta$
(b) The largest sample value $\beta$ (*n*th order statistic) is not a biased estimator of parameter $\beta$
(c) $\frac{n+1}{n}$ times the largest sample value is an unbiased estimator of the parameter $\beta$
(d) $\frac{n+1}{n}$ times the largest sample value is not an unbiased estimator of the parameter $\beta$

**12.** On the basis of a single observation, we want to test the simple null hypothesis that the probability distribution *X* is

| *x* | 1 | 2 | 3 | 4 | 5 | 6 | 7 |
|---|---|---|---|---|---|---|---|
| *f*(*x*) | $\frac{1}{12}$ | $\frac{1}{12}$ | $\frac{1}{12}$ | $\frac{1}{4}$ | $\frac{1}{6}$ | $\frac{1}{6}$ | $\frac{1}{6}$ |

against the composite alternative that the probability distribution is

| *x* | 1 | 2 | 3 | 4 | 5 | 6 | 7 |
|---|---|---|---|---|---|---|---|
| *g*(*x*) | $\frac{a}{3}$ | $\frac{b}{3}$ | $\frac{c}{3}$ | $\frac{2}{3}$ | 0 | 0 | 0 |

where $a + b + c = 1$

(a) The critical region obtained by means of the likelihood ratio technique is inadmissible
(b) The critical region obtained by means of the likelihood ratio technique is not inadmissible
(c) Neither (a) nor (b)
(d) None of the above

**13.** The following are the speeds (in miles per hour) at which every fifth passenger car was timed at a certain check point

46, 58, 60, 56, 70, 66, 48, 54, 62, 41, 39, 52, 45, 62, 53, 69, 65, 65, 67, 76, 52, 52, 59, 59, 67, 51, 46, 61, 40, 43, 42, 77, 67, 63, 59, 63, 63, 72, 57, 59, 42, 56, 47, 62, 67, 70, 63, 66, 69 and 73.

Testing the null hypothesis of randomness at the 0.05 level of significance.

(a) Null hypothesis cannot be rejected
(b) Null hypothesis can be rejected
(c) There is no real evidence that the sample should not be regarded as random
(d) There is a real evidence that the sample should not be regarded as random

**14.** Let *X* be exponentially distributed with parameter $\lambda$.

(a) Maximum likelihood estimator of $\lambda$ is the reciprocal of sample mean
(b) Maximum likelihood estimator of $\lambda$ is the proportional of sample mean
(c) $\hat{\lambda} = \frac{1}{\overline{X}}$
(d) $\hat{\lambda} = \overline{X}$

**15.** A company has to choose among three pension plans. Management wishes to know whether the preference for plans is independent of job classification and wants to use $\alpha = 0.05$. The opinions of a random sample of 500 employees are shown in table (a).

**Table (a) Observed Data**

| | **Pension Plan** | | | |
|---|---|---|---|---|
| Job Classification | 1 | 2 | 3 | Total |
| Salaried workers | 160 | 140 | 40 | 340 |
| Hourly workers | 40 | 60 | 60 | 160 |
| Total | 200 | 200 | 100 | 500 |

**Table (b) Expected Frequencies**

| | **Pension Plan** | | | |
|---|---|---|---|---|
| Job Classification | 1 | 2 | 3 | Total |
| Salaried workers | 136 | 136 | 68 | 340 |
| Hourly workers | 64 | 64 | 32 | 160 |
| **Total** | 200 | 200 | 100 | 500 |

(a) The preference for pension plans is independent for job classification
(b) The preference for pension plans is dependent for job classification
(c) The *P*-value for $\chi_0^2 = 49.63$ is $1.671 \times 10^{-11}$
(d) The *P*-value for $\chi_0^2 = 49.63$ is zero

**16.** The following are the weight gains (in pounds) of two random samples of young turkeys fed two different diets but otherwise kept under identical conditions

**Diet I** 16.3, 10.1, 10.7, 13.5, 14.9, 11.8, 14.3, 10.2, 12.0, 14.7, 23.6, 15.1, 14.5, 18.4, 13.2, 14.0

**Diet II** 21.3, 23.8, 15.4, 19.6, 12.0, 13.9, 18.8, 19.2, 15.3, 20.1, 14.8, 18.9, 20.7, 21.1, 15.8, 16.2

Using the *U*-test at the 0.01 level of significance to test the null hypothesis that the two populations sampled are identical against the alternative hypothesis that on the average the second diet produces a greater gain in weight.
(a) The null hypothesis must be rejected
(b) The null hypothesis must not be rejected
(c) On the average the second diet produces a greater gain in weight
(d) On the average the second diet does not produce greater gain in weight

**17.** Which of the following is/are correct?
(a) $\bar{X}$ is a minimum variance unbiased estimator of the mean $\mu$ of a normal population
(b) $\bar{X}$ is not a minimum variance unbiased estimator of the mean $\mu$ of a normal population
(c) Neither (a) nor (b)
(d) None of the above

**18.** In a random sample of 85 automobile engine crankshaft bearings, 10 have a surface finish that is rougher than the specifications allow. Therefore, a point estimate of the proportion of bearings in the population that exceeds the roughness specification is $\hat{p} = x/n = 10/85 = 0.12$. The 95% two sided confidence interval for *p*.
(a) The upper bound for 95% confidence for *p* is 0.19
(b) The lower bound for 95% confidence for *p* is 0.05
(c) The 95% two sided confidence interval for *p* is $0.05 \le p \le 0.19$
(d) No 95% two sided confidence interval for *p* exist

**19.** ASTM standard E 23 defines standard test methods for notched bar impact testing of metallic materials. The Charpy V-notch (CVN) technique measures impact energy and is often used to determine whether or not a material experiences a ductile-to-brittle transition with decreasing temperature. Ten measurements of impact energy (J) on specimens of A 238 steel cut at 60°C are as follows : 64.1, 64.7, 64.5, 64.6, 64.5, 64.3, 64.6, 64.8, 64.2, and 64.3. Assume that impact energy is normally distributed with $\sigma = 1$ J
(a) A range of highly plausible values lor mean impact energy for A 238 steel at 60°C is 63.84 J $\le \mu \le$ 65.08 J.
(b) Sample mean $\bar{x} = 64.46$
(c) Sample mean $\bar{x} = 42.5$
(d) A range of highly plausible value for mean impact energy for A 288 steel at 60°C is 14 J $\le \mu \le$ 14.5 J

**20.** Let X be normally distributed with unknown $\mu$ and known variance $\sigma^2$.
(a) Simple mean is the maximum likelihood estimator of $\mu$
(b) Simple mean is not the maximum likelihood estimator of $\mu$
(c) $\hat{\mu} = \bar{X}$
(d) $\hat{\mu} \neq \bar{X}$

**21.** Two catalysts are being analyzed to determine how they affect the mean yield of a chemical process. Specifically, catalyst 1 is currently in use, but catalyst 2 is acceptable. Since, catalyst 2 is cheaper, it should be adopted, providing it does not change the process yield. A test is run in the pilot plant and results in the data shown in table. Using $\alpha = 0.05$, and assume equal variances.

**Table Catalyst Yield Data**

| Observation Number | Catalyst 1 | Catalyst 2 |
|---|---|---|
| 1 | 91.50 | 89.19 |
| 2 | 94.18 | 90.95 |
| 3 | 92.18 | 90.46 |
| 4 | 95.39 | 93.21 |
| 5 | 91.79 | 97.19 |
| 6 | 89.07 | 97.04 |
| 7 | 94.72 | 91.07 |
| 8 | 89.21 | 92.75 |
| | $\bar{x}_1 = 92.255$ | $\bar{x}_2 = 92.733$ |
| | $s_1 = 2.39$ | $s_2 = 2.98$ |

(a) There is no difference between the mean yield
(b) There is a difference between the mean yield
(c) $s_p = 2.70$
(d) $t_0 = -0.35$

**22.** The following are the final examination grades of samples from three groups of students who were taught German by three different methods (classroom instruction and language laboratory, only classroom instruction and only self study in language laboratory)

First method 94, 88, 91, 74, 87, 97
Second method 85, 82, 79, 84, 61, 72, 80
Third method 89, 67, 72, 76, 69

Using the *H*-test at the 0.05 level of significance to test the null hypothesis that the three methods are equally effective.

(a) The null hypothesis must be rejected
(b) The null hypothesis must not be rejected
(c) The three methods are not equally effective
(d) The three methods are equally effective

**23.** Which of the following is/are correct?

(a) $Y = \frac{1}{6}(X_1 + 2X_2 + 3X_3)$ is not a sufficient estimator of the Bernoulli parameter $\theta$
(b) $Y = \frac{1}{6}(X_1 + 2X_2 + 3X_3)$ is a sufficient estimator of the Bernoulli parameter $\theta$
(c) Neither (a) nor (b)
(d) None of the above

**24.** The specifications for a certain kind of ribbon call for a mean breaking strength of 185 pounds. If five pieces randomly selected from different rolls have breaking strengths of 171.6, 191.8, 178.3, 184.9 and 189.1 pounds, testing the null hypothesis $\mu = 185$ pounds against the alternative hypothesis $\mu < 185$ pounds at the 0.05 level of significance.

(a) A null hypothesis can be rejected
(b) Null hypothesis cannot be rejected
(c) $t = 0.49$
(d) $t = -0.49$

**25.** An automotive engineer is investigating two different types of metering devices for an electronic fuel injection system to determine whether they differ in their fuel mileage performance. The system is installed on 12 different cars and a test is run with each metering device on each car. The observed fuel mileage performance data, corresponding differences and their signs are shown in table. Use the sign test to determine whether the median fuel mileage performance is the same for both devices using $\alpha = 0.05$.

**Table : Performance of Flow Metering Devices**

| | Metering Device | | | |
|---|---|---|---|---|
| Car | 1 | 2 | Difference, $d_j$ | Sign |
| 1 | 17.6 | 16.8 | 0.8 | + |
| 2 | 19.4 | 20.0 | −0.6 | − |
| 3 | 19.5 | 18.2 | 1.3 | + |
| 4 | 17.1 | 16.4 | 0.7 | + |
| 5 | 15.3 | 16.0 | −0.7 | − |
| 6 | 15.9 | 15.4 | 0.5 | + |
| 7 | 16.3 | 16.5 | −0.2 | − |
| 8 | 18.4 | 18.0 | 0.4 | + |
| 9 | 17.3 | 16.4 | 0.9 | + |
| 10 | 19.1 | 20.1 | −1.0 | − |
| 11 | 17.8 | 16.7 | 1.1 | + |
| 12 | 18.2 | 17.9 | 0.3 | + |

(a) The two devices provide the same median fuel mileage performance
(b) The two devices provide the different median fuel mileage performance
(c) The test statistic is $r = \min(r^+, r^-)$
(d) The test statistic is $r = \max(r^+, r^-)$

**26.** Let $X$ be normally distributed with mean $\mu$ and variance $\sigma^2$, where both $\mu$ and $\sigma^2$ are unknown

(a) $\hat{\mu} = \bar{X}$
(b) $\hat{\sigma}^2 = \frac{1}{n}\sum_{i=1}^{n}(X_i - \bar{X})^2$
(c) $X = \hat{\mu}$
(d) $\hat{\sigma}^2 = \hat{\mu}X$

**27.** Aircrew escape systems are powered by a solid propellant. The burning rate of this propellant is an important product characteristic. Specifications require that the mean burning rate must be 50 cm/s. We know that the standard deviation of burning rate is $\sigma = 2$ cm/s. The experimenter decides to specify a type I error probability or significance level of $\alpha = 0.05$ and selects a random sample of $n = 25$ and obtains a sample average burning rate of $\bar{x} = 51.3$ cm/s.

(a) Mean burning rate $\mu = 50$ cm/s can be rejected
(b) Mean burning rate $\mu = 50$ cm/s cannot be rejected
(c) There is a strong evidence that mean burning rate exceeds 50 cm/s
(d) There is a strong evidence that mean burning rate does not exceeds 50 cm/s

**28.** The following is an arrangement of men, M and women W, lined upto purchase tickets for a rock concert

M W M W W M M M W M W M M M W W M M M M W W M W M

M M W M M M W W W W M M M M W M W W M M M M W W M

Testing for randomness at the 0.05 level of significance.

(a) Null hypothesis cannot be rejected
(b) Null hypothesis can be rejected

(c) There is no real evidence to indicate that the arrangement is not random

(d) There is an real evidence to indicate that the arrangement is random

**29.** Suppose that it is known from experience that the standard deviation of the weight of 8-ounce packages of cookies made by a certain bakery is 0.16 ounce. To check whether its production is under control on a given day, namely, to check whether the true average weight of the packages is 8 ounces, employees select a random sample of 25 packages and find that their mean weight is $\bar{x} = 8.091$ ounces. Since, the bakery stands to lose money when $\mu > 8$ and the customer loses out when $\mu < 8$, testing the null hypothesis $\mu = 8$ against the alternative hypothesis $\mu \neq 8$ at the 0.01 level of significance.

(a) Null hypothesis must be rejected

(b) Null hypothesis must not be rejected

(c) $z = 2.84$

(d) $z = 6.95$

**30.** Montgomery, Peck, and Vining (2001) report on a study in which a rocket motor is formed by binding an igniter propellant and a sustainer propellant together inside a metal housing. The shear strength of the bond between the two propellant types in an important characteristic. The results of testing 20 randomly selected motors are shown in table. Test the hypothesis that the median shear strength is 2000 psi, using $\alpha = 0.05$.

**Table : Propellant Shear Strength Data**

| Observation $i$ | Shear Strength $x_i$ | Differences $x_i - 2000$ | Sign |
|---|---|---|---|
| 1 | 2158.70 | + 158.70 | + |
| 2 | 1678.15 | − 321.85 | − |
| 3 | 2316.00 | + 316.00 | + |
| 4 | 2061.30 | + 61.30 | + |
| 5 | 2207.50 | + 207.50 | + |
| 6 | 1708.30 | − 291.70 | − |
| 7 | 1784.70 | − 215.30 | − |
| 8 | 2575.10 | + 575.10 | + |
| 9 | 2357.90 | + 357.90 | + |
| 10 | 2256.70 | + 256.70 | + |
| 11 | 2165.20 | + 165.20 | + |
| 12 | 2399.55 | + 399.55 | + |
| 13 | 1779.80 | − 220.20 | − |
| 14 | 2336.75 | + 336.75 | + |
| 15 | 1765.30 | − 234.70 | − |
| 16 | 2053.50 | + 53.50 | + |
| 17 | 2414.40 | + 414.40 | + |
| 18 | 2200.50 | + 200.50 | + |
| 19 | 2654.20 | + 654.20 | + |
| 20 | 1753.70 | − 246.30 | − |

(a) The median shear strength is 2000 psi

(b) The median shear strength is not 2000 psi

(c) The test statistic is the observed number of plus differences in given table or $r^+ = 14$

(d) $p$-value is 0.1153

**31.** To cetermine the effectiveness of a new traffic control system, the number of accidents that occurred at 12 dangerous intersections during four weeks before and four weeks after the installation of the new system was observed, and the following data were obtained 3 and 1, 5 and 2, 2 and 0, 3 and 2, 3 and 2, 3 and 0 0 and 2, 4 and 3, 1 and 3, 6 and 4, 4 and 1, 1 and 0 Using the paired sample sign test at the 0.05 level of sign ficance to test the null hypothesis that the new traffic control system is only as effective as the old system.

(a) The new traffic control system is not effective in reducing the number of accidents at dangerous intersections

(b) The new traffic control system is effective in reducing the number of accidents at dangerous intersections

(c) The $p$-value is 0.0192

(d) The $p$-value is 1.006

**32.** The following article describes the results of tensile adhesion tests on 22 U-700 alloy specimens. The load at specimen failure is as follows (in megapascals)

19.8 10.1 14.9 7.5 15.4 15.4
15.4 18.5 7.9 12.7 11.9 11.4
11.4 14.1 17.6 16.7 15.8
19.5 8.8 13.6 11.9 11.4

The sample mean is $\bar{x} = 13.71$ and the sample standard deviation is $s = 3.55$. Figures (a) and (b) show a box plot and a normal probability plot of the tensile adhesion test data, respectively.

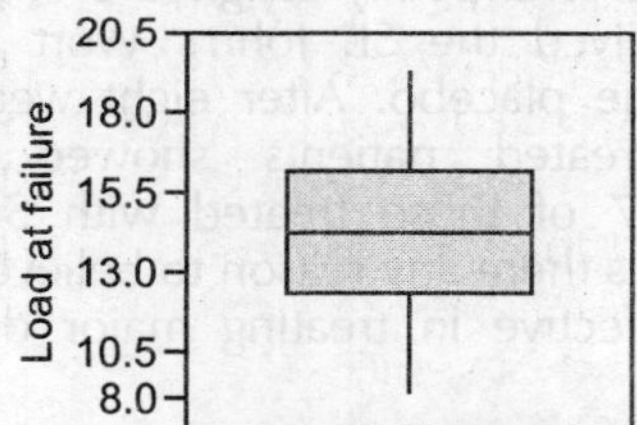


Fig. (a) Box and whisker plot for the laod at failure data

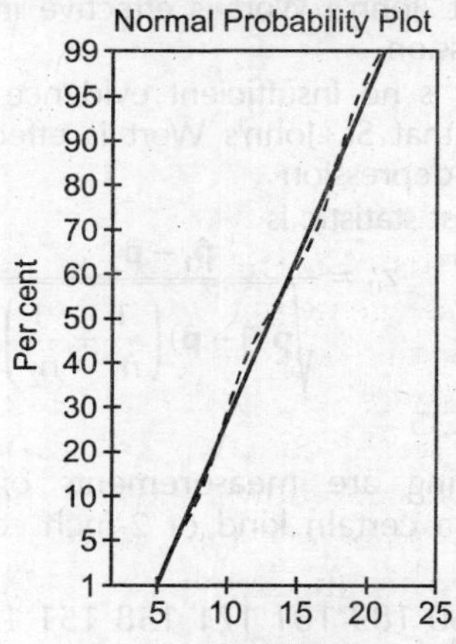


(b) Normal probability plot of the load at failure data

(a) Population is normally distributed
(b) Population is not normally distributed
(c) The CI is fairly wide because there is a lot of variability in the tensile adhesion test measurements
(d) The CI is not fairly wide because there is a lot of variability in the tensile adhesion test measurements

**33.** Determine, on the basis of the sample data shown in the following table, whether the true proportion of shoppers favouring detergent *A* over detergent *B* is the same in all three cities

| | Number Favouring Detergent *A* | Number Favouring Detergent *B* | |
|---|---|---|---|
| Los Angeles | 232 | 168 | 400 |
| San Diego | 260 | 240 | 500 |
| Fresno | 197 | 203 | 400 |

Use the 0.05 level of significance.
(a) The true proportions of shoppers favouring detergent *A* over detergent *B* in the three cities are not the same
(b) $\chi^2 = 6.48$
(c) $\chi^2 = 1$
(d) The true proporitions of shoppers favouring detergent *A* over detergent *B* in the three cities is same

**34.** Extracts of St. John's Wort are widely used to treat depression. An article compared the efficacy of a standard extract of St. John's Wort with a placebo in 200 outpatients diagnosed with major depression. Patients were randomly assigned to two groups; one group received the St. John's Wort and the other received the placebo. After eight weeks, 19 of the placebo treated patients showed improvement, whereas 27 of those treated with St. John's Wort improved. Is there any reason to believe that St. John's Wort is effective in treating major depression? use $\alpha = 0.05$.
(a) There is insufficient evidence to support the claim that St. John's Wort is effective in treating major depression
(b) There is no insufficient evidence to support the claim that St. John's Wort is effective in treating major depression
(c) The test statistic is

$$z_0 = \frac{\hat{p}_1 - \hat{p}_2}{\sqrt{\hat{p}(1-\hat{p})\left(\frac{1}{n_1}+\frac{1}{n_2}\right)}}$$

(d) $z_0 = 1.35$

**35.** The following are measurements of the breaking strength of a certain kind of 2-inch cotton ribbon in pounds
163 165 160 189 161 171 158 151 169 162
163 139 172 165 148 166 172 163 187 173

Using the sign test to test the null hypothesis $\mu = 160$ against the alternative hypothesis $\mu > 160$ at the 0.05 level of significance.
(a) The mean breaking strength of the given kind of ribbon exceeds 160 ponds
(b) The mean breaking strength of given kind of ribbon does not exceeds 160 ponds
(c) The *p*-value 0.0095 is less than 0.05
(d) The *p*-value 0.0095 is greater than 0.05

**36.** In comparing the variability of the tensile strength of two kinds of structural steel an experiment yielded the following results $n_1 = 13$, $s_1^2 = 19.2$, $n_2 = 16$, and $s_2^2 = 3.5$, where the units of measurement are 1,000 pounds per square inch.
Assuming that the measurements constitute independent random samples from two normal populations, testing the null hypothesis $\sigma_1^2 = \sigma_2^2$ against the alternative $\sigma_1^2 \neq \sigma_2^2$ at the 0.02 level of significance.
(a) The variability of the tensile strength of the two kinds of steel is same
(b) The variability of the tensile strength of the two kinds of steel is different
(c) $\frac{s_1^2}{s_2^2} = 5.49$
(d) $\frac{s_1^2}{s_2^2} \leq 0$

**37.** Oxide layers on semi-conductor wafers, are etched in a mixture or gases to achieve the proper thickness. The variability in the thickness of these oxide layers is a critical characteristic of the wafer, and low variability is desirable for subsequent processing steps. Two different mixtures of gases are being studied to determine whether one is superior in reducing the variability of the oxide thickness. Twenty wafers are etched in each gas. The sample standard deviations of oxide thickness are $s_1 = 1.96$ angstroms and $s_2 = 2.13$ angstroms, respectively. Is there any evidence to indicate that either gas is preferable? Use $\alpha = 0.05$
(a) There a strong evidence that indicate that either gas results in a smaller variance of oxide thickness
(b) There is no strong evidence to indicate that either gas results in a smaller variance of oxide thickness
(c) The test statistic is given by $f_0 = \frac{s_1^2}{s_2^2}$
(d) $f_0 = 0.85$

**38.** A semi-conductor manufacturer produces controllers used in automobile engine applications. The customer requires that the process fallout or fraction defective at a critical manufacturing step not exceed 0.05 and that the manufacturer demonstrate process capability at this level of quality using $\alpha = 0.05$. The semi-conductor manufacturer takes a random sample of 200 devices and finds that four of them are defective.

(a) The manufacturer demonstrate process capability for the customer
(b) The manufacturer does not demonstrate process capability for the customer
(c) The test statistic $z_0$ is – 1.95
(d) The test statistic $z_0$ is 1.06

**39.** Suppose that the thickness of a part used in a semi-conductor is its critical dimension and that measurements of the thickness of a random sample of 18 such parts have the variance $s^2 = 0.68$, where the measurements are in thousandths of an inch. The process is considered to be under control, if the variation of the thicknesses is given by a variance not greater than 0.36. Assuming that the measurements constitute a random sample from a normal population, testing the null hypothesis $\sigma^2 = 0.36$ against the alternative hypothesis $\sigma^2 > 0.36$ at the 0.05 level of significance.
(a) Null hypothesis must be rejected
(b) Null hypothesis must be accepted
(c) $\chi^2 = 32.11$
(d) The process used in the manufacturing of the parts must be adjusted

**40.** An automatic filling machine is used to fill bottles with liquid detergent. A random sample of 20 bottles results in a sample variance of fill volume of $s^2 = 0.0153$ (fluid ounces)$^2$. If the variance of fill volume exceeds 0.01 (fluid ounces)$^2$, an unacceptable proportion of bottles will be underfilled or overfilled. Use $\alpha = 0.05$, and assume that fill volume has a normal distribution.
(a) There is no strong evidence that the variance of fill volume exceeds 0.01 (fluid ounces)$^2$
(b) There is a strong evidence that the variance of fill volume exceeds 0.01 (fluid ounces)$^2$
(c) The test statistic $\chi_0^2 = 29.07$
(d) The test statistic $\chi_0^2 = 0.01$

**41.** Let $X_1, X_2, \ldots, X_n$ constitute a random sample of size $n$ from a normal population with the mean $\mu$ and the variance $\sigma^2$,
(a) $\hat{\mu} = \bar{x}$ (b) $\hat{\sigma}^2 = \frac{1}{n}\sum_{i=1}^{n} (x_i = \bar{x})^2$
(c) $\hat{\mu} = \hat{\sigma}^2$ (d) $\mu = \bar{x}$

# Answers

## Exercise 1

| | | | | | | | | | |
|---|---|---|---|---|---|---|---|---|---|
| **1.** (b) | **2.** (a) | **3.** (a) | **4.** (d) | **5.** (d) | **6.** (d) | **7.** (b) | **8.** (d) | **9.** (c) | **10.** (a) |
| **11.** (c) | **12.** (b) | **13.** (a) | **14.** (c) | **15.** (d) | **16.** (a) | **17.** (d) | **18.** (c) | **19.** (c) | **20.** (a) |
| **21.** (d) | **22.** (a) | **23.** (b) | **24.** (b) | **25.** (b) | **26.** (a) | **27.** (d) | **28.** (b) | **29.** (c) | **30.** (a) |
| **31.** (a) | **32.** (a) | **33.** (b) | **34.** (c) | **35.** (d) | **36.** (a) | **37.** (a) | **38.** (a) | **39.** (b) | **40.** (c) |
| **41.** (b) | **42.** (b) | **43.** (b) | **44.** (b) | **45.** (c) | **46.** (a) | **47.** (c) | **48.** (c) | **49.** (d) | **50.** (c) |
| **51.** (a) | **52.** (a) | **53.** (d) | **54.** (a) | **55.** (b) | **56.** (a) | **57.** (b) | **58.** (b) | **59.** (b) | **60.** (a) |
| **61.** (a) | **62.** (a) | **63.** (d) | **64.** (a) | **65.** (c) | **66.** (a) | **67.** (b) | **68.** (d) | **69.** (c) | **70.** (b) |
| **71.** (c) | **72.** (b) | **73.** (d) | **74.** (d) | **75.** (d) | **76.** (d) | **77.** (d) | **78.** (b) | **79.** (d) | **80.** (a) |
| **81.** (d) | **82.** (b) | **83.** (c) | **84.** (b) | **85.** (a) | **86.** (c) | **87.** (d) | **88.** (c) | **89.** (d) | **90.** (b) |
| **91.** (b) | **92.** (d) | **93.** (a) | **94.** (a) | **95.** (d) | **96.** (a) | **97.** (d) | **98.** (c) | **99.** (d) | **100.** (d) |
| **101.** (a) | **102.** (c) | **103.** (d) | **104.** (b) | **105.** (a) | **106.** (b) | **107.** (d) | **108.** (c) | **109.** (d) | **110.** (c) |
| **111.** (d) | **112.** (d) | **113.** (b) | **114.** (b) | **115.** (d) | **116.** (d) | **117.** (c) | **118.** (c) | **119.** (a) | **120.** (a) |
| **121.** (b) | **122.** (a) | **123.** (b) | **124.** (d) | **125.** (b) | **126.** (b) | **127.** (a) | **128.** (a) | **129.** (a) | **130.** (b) |
| **131.** (b) | **132.** (a) | **133.** (b) | **134.** (a) | **135.** (a) | **136.** (a) | **137.** (c) | **138.** (b) | **139.** (b) | **140.** (d) |
| **141.** (d) | **142.** (c) | **143.** (b) | **144.** (d) | **145.** (c) | **146.** (a) | **147.** (d) | **148.** (c) | **149.** (a) | **150.** (a) |
| **151.** (c) | **152.** (d) | **153.** (b) | **154.** (b) | **155.** (b) | **156.** (b) | **157.** (c) | **158.** (d) | **159.** (c) | **160.** (d) |
| **161.** (d) | **162.** (b) | **163.** (b) | **164.** (c) | **165.** (a) | **166.** (b) | **167.** (a) | **168.** (a) | **169.** (d) | **170.** (d) |
| **171.** (b) | **172.** (d) | **173.** (b) | **174.** (b) | **175.** (b) | **176.** (b) | **177.** (b) | **178.** (c) | **179.** (b) | **180.** (c) |
| **181.** (c) | **182.** (d) | **183.** (d) | **184.** (c) | **185.** (d) | **186.** (b) | **187.** (a) | **188.** (c) | **189.** (c) | **190.** (a) |
| **191.** (b) | **192.** (c) | **193.** (d) | **194.** (d) | **195.** (d) | **196.** (b) | **197.** (c) | **198.** (d) | **199.** (b) | **200.** (d) |
| **201.** (c) | **202.** (c) | **203.** (d) | **204.** (a) | **205.** (c) | **206.** (d) | **207.** (c) | **208.** (c) | **209.** (b) | **210.** (d) |
| **211.** (c) | **212.** (c) | **213.** (b) | **214.** (d) | **215.** (c) | **216.** (b) | **217.** (d) | **218.** (c) | **219.** (d) | **220.** (c) |
| **221.** (d) | **222.** (d) | **223.** (b) | **224.** (d) | **225.** (b) | **226.** (b) | **227.** (d) | **228.** (b) | **229.** (a) | **230.** (b) |
| **231.** (d) | **232.** (b) | **233.** (b) | **234.** (b) | **235.** (d) | **236.** (c) | **237.** (c) | **238.** (b) | **239.** (d) | **240.** (c) |
| **241.** (c) | **242.** (b) | **243.** (a) | **244.** (d) | **245.** (d) | **246.** (d) | **247.** (d) | **248.** (c) | **249.** (b) | **250.** (b) |
| **251.** (d) | **252.** (a) | **253.** (a) | **254.** (b) | **255.** (c) | **256.** (b) | **257.** (d) | **258.** (b) | **259.** (d) | **260.** (c) |
| **261.** (d) | **262.** (c) | **263.** (d) | **264.** (a) | **265.** (d) | **266.** (a) | **267.** (c) | **268.** (d) | **269.** (b) | **270.** (d) |
| **271.** (d) | **272.** (c) | **273.** (d) | **274.** (d) | **275.** (d) | **276.** (c) | **277.** (d) | **278.** (c) | **279.** (d) | **280.** (c) |
| **281.** (d) | **282.** (a) | **283.** (b) | **284.** (a) | **285.** (d) | **286.** (c) | **287.** (c) | **288.** (c) | **289.** (c) | **290.** (d) |

| | | | | | | | | | |
|---|---|---|---|---|---|---|---|---|---|
| **291.** (d) | **292.** (c) | **293.** (a) | **294.** (d) | **295.** (c) | **296.** (b) | **297.** (d) | **298.** (d) | **299.** (c) | **300.** (c) |
| **301.** (d) | **302.** (c) | **303.** (d) | **304.** (d) | **305.** (b) | **306.** (d) | **307.** (c) | **308.** (b) | **309.** (d) | **310.** (b) |
| **311.** (c) | **312.** (d) | **313.** (d) | **314.** (a) | **315.** (d) | **316.** (d) | **317.** (b) | **318.** (a) | **319.** (c) | **320.** (d) |
| **321.** (d) | **322.** (c) | **323.** (d) | **324.** (d) | **325.** (b) | **326.** (d) | **327.** (b) | **328.** (c) | **329.** (a) | **330.** (d) |
| **331.** (d) | **332.** (d) | **333.** (b) | **334.** (d) | **335.** (d) | **336.** (b) | **337.** (d) | **338.** (c) | **339.** (b) | **340.** (b) |
| **341.** (d) | **342.** (c) | **343.** (d) | **344.** (b) | **345.** (a) | **346.** (d) | **347.** (d) | **348.** (a) | **349.** (c) | **350.** (d) |
| **351.** (d) | **352.** (b) | **353.** (d) | **354.** (a) | **355.** (b) | **356.** (a) | **357.** (d) | **358.** (b) | **359.** (c) | **360.** (a) |
| **361.** (d) | **362.** (d) | **363.** (b) | **364.** (d) | **365.** (c) | **366.** (a) | **367.** (b) | **368.** (c) | **369.** (c) | **370.** (d) |
| **371.** (b) | **372.** (c) | **373.** (a) | **374.** (d) | **375.** (d) | **376.** (b) | **377.** (d) | **378.** (d) | **379.** (d) | **380.** (c) |
| **381.** (b) | **382.** (a) | **383.** (a) | **384.** (b) | **385.** (d) | **386.** (d) | **387.** (d) | **388.** (b) | **389.** (d) | **390.** (d) |
| **391.** (c) | **392.** (d) | **393.** (a) | **394.** (c) | **395.** (c) | **396.** (d) | **397.** (b) | **398.** (d) | **399.** (a) | **400.** (c) |
| **401.** (d) | **402.** (d) | | | | | | | | |

## Exercise 2

| | | | | | | | | | |
|---|---|---|---|---|---|---|---|---|---|
| **1.** (c) | **2.** (c) | **3.** (c,d) | **4.** (a,b,d) | **5.** (a,c) | **6.** (a) | **7.** (a,c,d) | **8.** (a,c) | **9.** (b,c) | **10.** (a,c) |
| **11.** (a,c) | **12.** (a) | **13.** (a,c) | **14.** (a,c) | **15.** (a,c) | **16.** (a,c) | **17.** (a,c) | **18.** (a,b,c) | **19.** (a,b) | **20.** (a,c) |
| **21.** (a,c,d) | **22.** (a,c) | **23.** (a) | **24.** (b,d) | **25.** (a,c) | **26.** (a,b) | **27.** (a,c) | **28.** (a,c) | **29.** (a,c) | **30.** (a,c,d) |
| **31.** (b,c) | **32.** (a,c) | **33.** (a,b) | **34.** (a,c,d) | **35.** (a,c) | **36.** (a,c) | **37.** (b,c,d) | **38.** (a,c) | **39.** (a,c,d) | **40.** (a,c) |
| **41.** (a,b,d) | | | | | | | | | |

# Hints & Solutions

## Exercise 1

**1.** We have, $\mu - SE(\bar{x})Z_\alpha = 48.04$

$\Rightarrow \quad \mu - SE(\bar{x}) \times 1.96 = 48.04$

$\mu + SE(\bar{x})Z_\alpha = 51.96$

$\Rightarrow \quad \mu + SE(\bar{x}) \times 1.96 = 51.96$

Subtracting, we get

$2\,SE(\bar{x}) \times 1.96 = 3.92$

$\Rightarrow \quad SE(\bar{x}) = 3.92/(2 \times 1.96) = 1$

But $SE(\bar{x}) = \dfrac{\sigma}{\sqrt{n}} = 1$ or $\dfrac{\sigma}{\sqrt{100}} = 1$

$\Rightarrow \quad \sigma = 10$

**9.** We have, $\sigma = 0.35$, $\bar{x} = 1.75$

$Z_\alpha = 1.96$

$$SE(\bar{x}) = \frac{\sigma}{\sqrt{n}} = \frac{0.35}{\sqrt{100}} = 0.035$$

Confidence Limits $= [\bar{x} \mp Z_\alpha \times SE\,\bar{x}]$

$= [175 \mp 0.35 \times 1.96]$

$= [175 \mp 0.0686] = [1.68\text{ m}; 1.82\text{ m}]$

**16.** We have, $p = 80/400 = 0.2$;

$q = 1 - p = 1 - 0.2 = 0.8$

$\therefore$ 95% confidence limits are

$p \pm 1.96 \times \sqrt{(pq)/n}$

$= 0.2 \pm 1.96 \times \sqrt{(0.2 \times 0.8)/400}$

$= 0.1608, 0.2392$

Hence, 95% limits for the percentage of persons who would buy the product are 16.08 to 23.92.

**23.** We have, 95% confidence limits for population

$$\text{mean} = \bar{x} \pm \frac{s}{\sqrt{n}} Z_\alpha = 65 \pm \frac{1.96 \times 8}{\sqrt{200}}$$

$= 65 \pm 1.11 = (66.11, 63.89)$

**24.** Here, $p = \dfrac{200}{700} = 0.286$

$q = 1 - 0.286 = 0.714$

Hence, $SE(p) = \sqrt{\dfrac{pq}{n}} = \sqrt{\dfrac{0.286 \times 0.714}{700}} = 0.017$

95% confidence limits

$= 0.286 \pm 1.96 \times 0.017 = 0.286 \pm 0.033$

$= (0.253, 0.319)$

**30.** Here, $n = 9000$, $p = 3240/9000 = 0.36$, $q = 0.64$

$SE(p) = \sqrt{pq/n} = \sqrt{(0.36 \times 0.64)/9000} = 0.005$

The most probable limits (99.73% confidence limits) for the population proportion of getting a throw of 3 or 4 are $p \pm 2$ SE $(p) = 0.36 \pm 3 \pm 3 \times 0.005 = 0.360 \pm 0.015$

$= [0.365, 0.345]$

**31.** We have, $SE(\bar{x}) = \dfrac{s}{\sqrt{n}} \times \sqrt{\dfrac{N-n}{N-1}} = \dfrac{0.048}{\sqrt{100}} \times \sqrt{\dfrac{2000-100}{2000-1}}$

$= 0.00468$

95% confidence limits

$= \bar{x} \pm 1.96\,SE(\bar{x})$

$= 0.354 \pm (1.96 \times 0.0046)$

$= 0.354 \pm 0.0092 = 0.345$ and $0.363$

**37.** Here, $p = 20/400 = 0.05,\ q = 0.95;$

$\bar{x} = np = 100000 \times 0.05 = 5000$

$\text{SE} = \sqrt{npq}$

$= \sqrt{100000 \times 0.05 \times 0.95} = 68.9$

95% of confidence limits are

$\bar{x} \pm 1.96 \times \text{SE} = 5000 \pm 1.96 \times 68.9$

$= 5135 \text{ and } 4865$

**38.** Here, $n = 100,\ \bar{x} = 164,\ \sigma = 3,$

$Z_\alpha = 1.96;\ \text{SE} = \dfrac{\sigma}{\sqrt{n}} = \dfrac{3}{100} = 0.3 \text{ cm}$

Confidence limits

$= 164 \pm 1.96 \times (0.3) = 164 \pm 0.588$

*i.e.,* 163.412 to 164.59

**44.** Confidence limits

$0.34 \pm 2.58 \times \sqrt{0.34 \times 0.66/1000}$

$= 0.34 \pm 2.58 \times 0.015 = 0.34 \pm 0.0387$

$= [0.3013,\ 0.3787]$

Here, 99% confidence limits for the percentage of all viewers who watch this programme are 30.13 and 37.87.

**46.** We have, $\text{SE}(\bar{x}) = \dfrac{\sigma}{\sqrt{n}} = \dfrac{7.65}{\sqrt{66}} = 0.942$

Confidence limits of population mean

$= \bar{x} \pm 1.96 \times \text{SE}(\bar{x})$

$= 4730 \pm 1.96(0.942)$

$= 4730 \pm 1.846,$ [*i.e.,* 4728.15 to 4731.85]

**51.** We have, $n = 100$; $p$ = sample proportion of defectives $= 5/100 = 0.05$

$\text{SE}\ (p) = \sqrt{pq/n}$

$= \sqrt{0.05 \times 0.95/100}$

$= 0.02179 = 0.022$

From the tables of normal probability curve, we find that

$P(-2.05 \le Z \le 2.05) = 0.96$

$\Rightarrow \quad P(|Z| \le 2.05) = 0.96$

Hence, the significant value of $Z$ at confidence level 96% is 2.05. Hence, 96% confidence limits for the population proportion of defectives are

$p \pm 2.05\ \text{SE}\ (p) = 0.05 \pm 2.05 \times 0.022 = 0.005 \text{ and } 0.095.$

**52.** Here, $P = 0.2,\ Q = 1 - P = 0.8$

$Z_\alpha = 1.96$ and $E = 0.05,\ n = ?$

$n = \dfrac{PQZ_\alpha}{E^2} = \dfrac{0.2 \times 0.8 \times (1.96)^2}{(0.05)^2}$

$= 246$

**58.** We have, $p = \dfrac{400}{900} = \dfrac{4}{9} = 0.4444;\ q = 1 - \dfrac{4}{9} = \dfrac{5}{9}$

$\therefore\ \text{SE}\ (p) = \sqrt{\dfrac{pq}{n}} = \sqrt{\dfrac{4}{9} \times \dfrac{5}{9} \times \dfrac{1}{100}} = 0.0166$

95% confidence limits $= p = \pm 1.645 \sqrt{\dfrac{pq}{n}}$

$= 0.444 \pm 1.645 \times 0.0166$

$= [0.417,\ 0.472]$

**59.** Confidence Interval

$= \left[\bar{x} \mp 1.96 \times \dfrac{s}{\sqrt{n-1}}\right]$

$= ₹\left[1000 \mp 1.96 \times \dfrac{250}{\sqrt{99}}\right]$

$[\because s = 250, n = 100]$

$= ₹[1000 \mp 49.25]$

$= [₹950.75,\ ₹1049.25]$

**66.** Here, we are given $p = 0.03$, $n = 600$ and $N = 60000$

Hence, $\text{SE}\ (p) = \sqrt{\dfrac{pq}{n}} \sqrt{\dfrac{N-n}{N-1}}$ (including fpe)

$= \sqrt{\dfrac{0.03\ (1 - 0.03)}{600}} \times \sqrt{\dfrac{60000 - 600}{60000 - 1}}$

$= 0.0069$

or 95% confidence limit to $p$

$= [p - 1.96 \times \text{SE}\ (p),\ p + 1.96\ \text{SE}\ (p)]$

$= 0.03 - 1.96 \times 0.0069,\ 0.03 + 1.96 \times 0.0069]$

$= [0.01648,\ 0.04353]$

Thus, the number of pairs, then can be reasonably expected to be spoiled in the entire production process on a daily basis at 95% level of confidence lies in

$= [0.01648 \times 60000,\ 0.04353 \times 60000]$

$= [989,\ 2612]$

**115.** We are given

$E(x_i) = \mu,\ V(x_i) = 1,\ \forall\ i = 1, 2, \ldots, n$

Now, $E(x_i^2) = V(x_i) + [E(x_i)]^2$

$= 1 + \mu^2$

$E(t) = E\left[\dfrac{1}{n}\sum_{i=1}^{n} x_i^2\right] = \dfrac{1}{n}\sum_{i=1}^{n} E(x_i^2)$

$= \dfrac{1}{n}\sum_{i=1}^{n}(1 + \mu^2) = \dfrac{1}{n} n(1 + \mu^2)$

$= 1 + \mu^2$

Thus, $E(t) = 1 + \mu^2$

$\Rightarrow$ $t$ is an unbiased estimator of $1 + \mu^2$.

**116.** $T$ is unbiased estimator for $\theta$.

$\Rightarrow \quad E(T) = \theta$

Also, $V(T) = E(T^2) - [E(T)]^2 = E(T^2) - \theta^2$

$\Rightarrow \quad E(T^2) = \theta^2 + V(T) \neq \theta^2$ (as $V(T) > 0$)

Thus, $E(T^2) \neq \theta^2$

$\Rightarrow$ $T^2$ is a biased estimator for $\theta^2$.

**117.** In sampling from a normal population $N(\mu, \sigma^2)$, the sample mean $\bar{x}$ is also normally distributed as $N\left(\mu, \dfrac{\sigma^2}{n}\right)$.

$\Rightarrow \quad E(\bar{x}) = \mu$ and $V(\bar{x}) = \dfrac{\sigma^2}{n}$

And as $n \to \infty$ $\lim_{n \to \infty} V(\bar{x}) = 0$

So, by inversion theorem, $\bar{x}$ is a consistent estimator for $\mu$.

**Solutions** (Q. Nos. 118-120)

As $X \sim N(\mu, \sigma^2)$

sample of size $n$ is $\{x_1, x_2, \dots, x_n\}$.

So,
$$L = \prod_{i=1}^{n}\left[\frac{1}{\sigma\sqrt{2\pi}}\exp\left\{-\frac{1}{2\sigma^2}(x_i-\mu)^2\right\}\right]$$
$$= \left(\frac{1}{\sigma\sqrt{2\pi}}\right)^n \exp\left\{-\sum_{i=1}^{n}\frac{(x_i-\mu)^2}{2\sigma^2}\right\}$$
$$\Rightarrow \log L = -\frac{n}{2}\log 2\pi - \frac{n}{2}\log\sigma^2 - \frac{1}{2\sigma^2}\sum_{i=1}^{n}(x_i-\mu)^2$$

**118.** When $\sigma^2$ is known, the likelihood equation for estimating $\mu$ is
$$\frac{\partial}{\partial\mu}\log L = -\frac{1}{2\sigma^2}\sum_{i=1}^{n}2(x_i-\mu)\cdot(-1) = 0$$
$$\Rightarrow \sum_{i=1}^{n}(x_i-\mu) = 0 \Rightarrow \sum_{i=1}^{n}x_i - n\mu = 0$$
$$\Rightarrow \hat{\mu} = \frac{1}{n}\sum_{i=1}^{n}x_i = \bar{x}$$

Hence, maximum likelihood estimator for $\mu$ is the sample mean $\bar{x}$.

**119.** When $\mu$ is known, the likelihood equation for estimating $\sigma^2$ is
$$\frac{\partial}{\partial\sigma^2}\log L = 0 \Rightarrow -\frac{n}{2}\frac{1}{\sigma^2} - \frac{1}{2}\frac{(-2)}{\sigma^4}\sum_{i=1}^{n}(x_i-\mu)^2 = 0$$
$$\Rightarrow n - \frac{1}{\sigma^2}\sum_{i=1}^{n}(x_i-\mu)^2 = 0$$
$$\Rightarrow \hat{\sigma}^2 = \frac{1}{n}\sum_{i=1}^{n}(x_i-\mu)^2$$

**120.** The likelihood equations for simultaneous estimation of $\mu$ and $\sigma^2$ are
$$\frac{\partial}{\partial\mu}\log L = 0 \text{ and } \frac{\partial}{\partial\sigma^2}\log L = 0$$
$$\Rightarrow \hat{\mu} = \bar{x}$$
and
$$\hat{\sigma}^2 = \frac{1}{n}\sum_{i=1}^{n}(x_i-\bar{x})^2 \quad (\text{as } \bar{x} = \mu)$$
$$= s^2, \text{ the sample variance}$$

**121.** Let $\{x_1, x_2, \dots, x_n\}$ be a sample of size $n$ from a normal population. Then,
$$L = \prod_{i=1}^{n}f(x_i, \mu) = \prod_{i=1}^{n}\left[\frac{1}{\sigma\sqrt{2\pi}}\cdot e^{\frac{-(x_i-\mu)^2}{2\sigma^2}}\right]$$
$$= \left(\frac{1}{\sigma\sqrt{2\pi}}\right)^n \cdot e^{-\sum_{i=1}^{n}\frac{(x_i-\mu)^2}{2\sigma^2}}$$
$$\log L = -n\log(\sqrt{2\pi}\cdot\sigma) - \frac{1}{2\sigma^2}\sum_{i=1}^{n}(x_i-\mu)^2$$
$$= k - \frac{1}{2\sigma^2}\sum_{i=1}^{n}(x_i-\mu)^2$$

where, $k$ is constant independent of $\mu$, ($\sigma$ being known)
$$\frac{\partial}{\partial\mu}\log L = -\frac{1}{2\sigma^2}\sum_{i=1}^{n}2(x_i-\mu)(-1)$$
$$= \sum_{i=1}^{n}\frac{(x_i-\mu)}{\sigma^2} = \frac{n\bar{x}-n\mu}{\sigma^2}$$
$$= \frac{\bar{x}-\mu}{\sigma^2/n}$$

It is in the form
$$\frac{\partial}{\partial\theta}\log L = [t-\gamma(\theta)]A(\theta)$$

Hence, $\bar{x}$ is an *MVB* unbiased estimator for $\mu$ and
$$V(\hat{\mu}) = V(\bar{x}) = \frac{\sigma^2}{n}$$

**122.** Here,
$$L = \prod_{i=1}^{n}f(x_i, \theta)$$
$$= \left(\frac{1}{\pi}\right)^n\prod_{i=1}^{n}\left(\frac{1}{1+(x_i-\theta)^2}\right)$$
$$\Rightarrow \log L = -n\log\pi - \sum_{i=1}^{n}\log[1+(x_i-\theta)^2]$$
$$\Rightarrow \frac{\partial}{\partial\theta}\log L = -\sum_{i=1}^{n}\frac{1\cdot 2(x_i-\theta)\cdot(-1)}{1+(x_i-\theta)^2}$$
$$= 2\sum_{i=1}^{n}\left(\frac{(x_i-\theta)}{1+(x_i-\theta)^2}\right)$$

This cannot be expressed in the form
$$\frac{\partial}{\partial\theta}\log L = [t-\gamma(\theta)]A(\theta)$$

So, *MVB* estimator does not exist for $\theta$, in the Cauchy's population.

And also Cramer Rao lower bound is not attainable by the variance of any unbiased estimator $\theta$.

**123.** Given, $X \sim N(0, \sigma^2)$.
$$f(x, \sigma^2) = \frac{1}{\sigma\sqrt{2\pi}}\exp\left(-\frac{x^2}{2\sigma^2}\right), -\infty < x < \infty$$
$$L = \prod_{i=1}^{n}f(x_i, \sigma^2) = \left(\frac{1}{\sigma\sqrt{2\pi}}\right)^n \exp\left(-\sum_{i=1}^{n}\frac{x_1^2}{2\sigma^2}\right)$$
$$\Rightarrow \text{Log } L = \frac{-n}{2}\log 2\pi - \frac{n}{2}\log\sigma^2 - \frac{1}{2\sigma^2}\sum_{i=1}^{n}x_i^2$$
$$\frac{\partial}{\partial\sigma^2}\log L = \frac{-n}{2\sigma^2} + \frac{1}{2\sigma^4}\sum_{i=1}^{n}x_i^2$$
$$= \frac{\sum_{i=1}^{n}x_i^2 - n\sigma^2}{2\sigma^4} = \frac{\sum_{i=1}^{n}\frac{x_i^2}{n} - \sigma^2}{2\sigma4/n}$$

It is in the form
$$\frac{\partial}{\partial\theta}\log L = \frac{(t-r(t)}{-1(\theta)} = [(t-r\gamma\theta)]A(\theta)$$

So, $\hat{\sigma}^2 = \sum_{i=1}^{n}\frac{x_1^2}{n}$ is an MVB estimator of $\sigma^2$ and $V(\hat{\sigma}^2) = \frac{2\sigma^4}{n}$

**Solutions** (Q. Nos. 124-126)

Here, $W = \{x \mid x \geq 1\}$

$\overline{W} = \{x \mid x < 1\}$

$H_0 : \theta = 2,$

$H_1 : \theta = 1,$

**124.** We have, $\alpha$ = size of type Ist error

$$= p\{x \in W \mid H_0\} = p\{x \geq 1 \mid \theta = 2\}$$

$$= \int_1^\infty f(x, \theta)_{\theta=2}\, dx = \int_1^\infty (\theta e^{-\theta x})_{\theta=2}\, dx$$

$$= \int_1^\infty 2e^{-2x} dx = 2\left[\frac{e^{-2x}}{-2}\right]_1^\infty$$

$$= -\left[\frac{1}{e^\infty} - \frac{1}{e^{+2}}\right] = \frac{1}{e^2}$$

**125.** We have, $\beta$ = Size of type II error

$$= p[x \in \overline{W} \mid H_1] = p\{x < 1 \mid \theta = 1\}$$

$$= \int_0^1 e^{-x} dx = \left[\frac{e^{-x}}{-1}\right]_0^1 = 1 - e^{-1}$$

**126.** Power of the test $= 1 - \beta = 1 - \left(1 - \frac{1}{e}\right) = \frac{1}{e}$

**127.** Here, $X_1, X_2, \ldots, X_n$ are iid Bernoulli variates with the parameter '$p$'.

We know that, $T = (x_1 + x_2 + \ldots + x_n) \sim B(n, p)$

$$\Rightarrow \quad E(T) = E(x_1 + x_2 + \ldots + x_n)$$

$$= E(x_1) + E(x_2) + \ldots + E(x_n)$$

$$= \underbrace{p + p + \ldots + p}_{n-\text{ times}} = np$$

As

| $x_1$ | 0 | 1 |
|---|---|---|
| $p$ | $1-p$ | $p$ |

Hence, $E(x_1) = p$

Similarly, $E(x_2) = E(x_3) = \ldots = E(x_n) = p$

$$\text{Var}(T) = npq$$

$$E(\overline{X}) = \frac{1}{n}E(T) = \frac{1}{n}np = p$$

$$\text{Var}(\overline{X}) = \text{Var}\left(\frac{T}{n}\right) = \frac{1}{n^2}\text{Var}(T) = \frac{npq}{n^2} = \frac{pq}{n}$$

and as $n \to \infty$ var$(\overline{X}) \to 0$

As $\left.\begin{matrix} E(\overline{X}) \to p \\ Var(\overline{X}) \to 0 \text{ as } n \to \infty \end{matrix}\right\}$

$\Rightarrow$ $\overline{X}$ is a consistent estimator of $p$.

Also, $\frac{\Sigma X_i}{n}\left(1 - \frac{\Sigma x_i}{n}\right) = \overline{x}(1 - \overline{X})$ is a polynomial in $\overline{X}$. So, $\overline{X}(1 - \overline{X})$ is a continuous function of $\overline{X}$.

As $\overline{X}$ is consistent estimator of $p$ and continuous function of a consistent estimator is consistent (invariance property of consistent estimator), so $\overline{X}(1 - \overline{X})$ is a consistent estimator of $p(1-p)$.

**128.** For Cauchy's population the probability function is

$$dF(x) = \frac{1}{\Pi}\frac{dx}{1 + (x - \mu)^2}, \; -\infty < x < \infty$$

We assume that the mean of the distribution is at $x = \mu$.

Let $\overline{x}$ be sample mean estimating $\mu$.

Then, sampling distribution of $\overline{x}$ is

$$dF(\overline{x}) = \frac{1}{\Pi} \cdot \frac{d\overline{x}}{1 + (\overline{x} - \mu)^2}, \; -\infty < \overline{x} < \infty$$

(as in Cauchy's distribution, the distribution of $\overline{x}$ is same as the distribution of x).

Since, distribution of $\overline{x}$ is same as the distribution of any single observation, so it does not change with increasing $n$.

$\Rightarrow$ $E(\overline{X}) = \mu$ and Var $(\overline{X}) = V(|\gamma| X) \neq 0$ as $n \to \infty$

We know that, if $\{T_n\}$ is a sequence of estimators such that for all $\theta \in \Theta$ (i) $E_\theta(T_n) \to \gamma(\theta)$, $n \to \infty$

(ii) $\text{Var}_\theta(T_n) \to 0$, as $n \to \infty$

Then, $T_n$ is a consistent estimator of $\gamma(\theta)$.

Using this result we see that sample mean is not consistent estimator of population mean.

The Cauchy's distribution is given by

$$d\,F(x) = \frac{1}{\Pi}\frac{dx}{1 + (x - \mu)^2}, \; -\infty < x < \infty \qquad \ldots(i)$$

Let sample median be $Md$.

Eq. (i) shows that

$$E(Md) = \mu \qquad \ldots(ii)$$

where, $\mu$ = Population mean

For large $n$, the sampling distribution of median is asymptotically normal, so

$$d\,F \propto \exp[-2nf_1^2(x - \mu)^2]\,dx$$

where, $f_1$ is the median ordinate of the parent population.

$$i.e., \quad d\,F \propto \exp\left\{-\frac{(x - \mu)^2}{1/2nf_1^2}\right\} \qquad \ldots(iii)$$

But $\quad f_1$ = Median ordinate of Eq. (i)

= Mode ordinate of Eq. (i)

$$= [f(x)]_{x=\mu} = \frac{1}{\Pi}$$

From Eq. (iii), the variance of the sampling distribution is

$$V(Md) = \frac{1}{4nf_1^2} = \frac{1}{4n(1/\pi)^2} = \frac{\pi^2}{4n} \to 0 \text{ as } n \to \infty \qquad \ldots(iv)$$

So, for Cauchy's distribution, median is a consistent estimator for $\mu$.

**129.** We take likelihood function

$$L(x, \theta) = \prod_{i=1}^n f(x_i, \theta) = \theta^n \prod_{i=1}^n x_i^{\theta - 1}$$

$$= \theta^n \left(\prod_{i=1}^n x_i\right)^\theta \cdot \frac{1}{\left(\prod_{i=1}^n x_i\right)}$$

$$= g(t_1, \theta)\, h(x_1, x_2, \ldots, x_n) \text{ say}$$

$$g(t_1, \theta) = \theta^n \left(\prod_{i=1}^{n} x_i\right)^\theta$$

$$h(x_1, x_2, \ldots, x_n) = \frac{1}{\left(\prod_{i=1}^{n} x_i\right)}$$

Hence, $t_1 = \prod_{i=1}^{n} X_i$ is sufficient estimator for $\theta$.

**Solutions** (Q. Nos. 130-131)

**130.** For a random sample of unit size ($n = 1$), the likelihood function is

$$L(\alpha) = f(x, \alpha) = \frac{2}{\alpha^2}(\alpha - x),\ 0 < x < \alpha$$

The likelihood equation is

$$\frac{\partial}{\partial \alpha} \log L = 0 \Rightarrow \frac{\partial}{\partial \alpha}[\log 2 - 2\log \alpha + \log(\alpha - x)] = 0$$

$$\Rightarrow \quad \frac{-2}{\alpha} + \frac{1}{\alpha - x} = 0 \Rightarrow -2(\alpha - x) + \alpha = 0$$

$$\Rightarrow \quad -\alpha + 2x = 0 \Rightarrow \alpha = 2x$$

Thus, maximum likelihood estimate of $\alpha$ is given by $\hat{\alpha} = 2x$.

**131.** We take $\quad E(\hat{\alpha}) = E(2x)$

$$= \int_0^\alpha 2x f(x, \alpha)\, dx$$

$$= \int_0^\alpha 2x \cdot \frac{2}{\alpha^2}(\alpha - x)\, dx = \frac{4}{\alpha^2}\left[\frac{\alpha x^2}{2} - \frac{x^3}{3}\right]_0^\alpha$$

$$= \frac{2}{3}\alpha$$

As, $E(\hat{\alpha}) \neq \alpha$, $\hat{\alpha} = 2x$ is not an unbiased estimate of $\alpha$, *i.e.*, $\hat{\alpha} = 2x$ is biased.

**132.** The probability function of the Poisson distribution with parameter $\lambda$ is given by

$$P(X = x) = f(x, \lambda) = \frac{e^{-\lambda}\lambda^x}{x!},\ x = 0, 1, 2, \ldots$$

likelihood function of random sample $x_1, x_2, \ldots, x_n$ of $n$ observations from the population is

$$L = \prod_{i=1}^{n} f(x_i, \lambda) = \prod_{i=1}^{n} \frac{e^{-\lambda}\lambda^{x_i}}{x_i!}$$

$$= \frac{e^{-\lambda}\lambda^{x_1}}{x_1!} \cdot \frac{e^{-\lambda}\lambda^{x_2}}{x_2!} \cdots \frac{e^{-\lambda}\lambda^{x_n}}{x_n!}$$

$$L = \frac{e^{-n\lambda}\lambda^{x_1 + x_2 + \ldots + x_n}}{x_1!\, x_2! \ldots x_n!} = \frac{e^{-n\lambda}\lambda^{\sum_{i=1}^{n} x_i}}{x_1!\, x_2! \ldots x_n!}$$

$$\log L = -n\lambda + \left(\sum_{i=1}^{n} x_i\right)\log \lambda - \sum_{i=1}^{n} \log(x_i!)$$

$$= -n\lambda + n\bar{x}\log \lambda - \sum_{i=1}^{n} \log x_i!$$

The likelihood equation for estimating $\lambda$ is

$$\frac{\partial}{\partial \lambda} \log L = 0 \Rightarrow -n + \frac{n\bar{x}}{\lambda} = 0$$

$$\Rightarrow \quad \lambda = \bar{x}$$

Thus, maximum likelihood estimator for $\lambda$ is sample mean $\bar{x}$.

**133.** Let variance of the estimate be $V(\hat{\lambda})$.

Then, $\quad V(\hat{\lambda}) = \dfrac{1}{E\left[-\dfrac{\partial^2}{\partial \lambda^2}\log L\right]}$

$$= \frac{1}{E\left[-\dfrac{\partial}{\partial \lambda}\left(-n + n\dfrac{\bar{x}}{\lambda}\right)\right]} = \frac{1}{E\left[-\left(\dfrac{-n\bar{x}}{\lambda^2}\right)\right]}$$

$$= \frac{n}{\lambda^2}E(\bar{X}) = \frac{n\lambda}{\lambda^2} \qquad [\text{as } E(\bar{X}) = \lambda]$$

$$= \frac{n}{\lambda}$$

Thus, $\quad V(\hat{\lambda}) = \dfrac{n}{\lambda}$

**134.** For Poisson distribution with parameter $\lambda$,

$$\frac{\partial}{\partial \lambda}\log L = -n + \frac{n\bar{x}}{\lambda} = -n\left(1 - \frac{\bar{x}}{\lambda}\right) = \psi(\bar{X}, \lambda)$$

= a function of $\bar{x}$ and $\lambda$ only.

So, $\bar{x}$ is sufficient estimator for estimating parameter $\lambda$.

**243.** We have, $p = \dfrac{25}{500} = \dfrac{1}{20} = 0.05$, so

$$q = 1 - p = 0.95,\ n = 25$$

Hence, $\quad SE(p) = \sqrt{\dfrac{pq}{n}} = \sqrt{\dfrac{0.05 \times 0.95}{500}}$

$$= 0.0097 = 0.001$$

**246.** We have, $\sigma = 5$, $N = 80$, $n = 25$,

Here, $\dfrac{n}{N} = \dfrac{25}{80} = 0.3125 > 0.05$, so the finite population correction factor is required

Hence, $SE(\bar{x}) = \dfrac{\sigma}{\sqrt{n-1}}\sqrt{\dfrac{N-n}{N-1}} = \dfrac{5}{\sqrt{24}} \times \sqrt{\dfrac{80-25}{80-1}}$

$$= \frac{5}{4.899} \times \sqrt{0.696} = \frac{5}{4.899} \times 0.834$$

$$= 0.85$$

**250.** Here, $\Sigma x = 9$, $\Sigma x^2 = 1 + 9 + 25 = 35$

$$SD = \sqrt{\frac{\Sigma x^2}{n} - \left(\frac{\Sigma x}{n}\right)^2};$$

Hence, $\sqrt{\dfrac{35}{3} - \left(\dfrac{9}{3}\right)^2} = \sqrt{2.666} = 1.633$

Also, $\dfrac{n}{N} = \dfrac{3}{10} = 0.3 > 0.05$, so *fpc* is required

Hence, $SE(\bar{x}) = \dfrac{s}{\sqrt{n-1}} \times \sqrt{\dfrac{N-n}{N-1}} = \dfrac{1.633}{\sqrt{2}} \times \sqrt{\dfrac{10-3}{10-1}}$

$$= \frac{1.633}{1.4142} \times 0.882 = 1.02$$

**254.** Here, $n = 10$, $N = 85$, $\dfrac{n}{N} = \dfrac{16}{85}$

$= 0.1176 > 0.05$, so $\in$ *fpc* is required.

Hence, $SE(\bar{x}) = \frac{\sigma}{\sqrt{n-1}} \times \sqrt{\frac{N-n}{N-1}} = \frac{4}{\sqrt{10-1}} \times \sqrt{\frac{85-10}{85-1}}$

$= \frac{4}{\sqrt{9}} \times \sqrt{\frac{75}{84}} = \frac{4}{3} \times \sqrt{0.893}$

$= \frac{4}{3} \times 0.945$

$= 1.26$

**262.** We have, $P[|\bar{x} - \mu| \le 25\% \text{ of SD}] = 0.95$

$\Rightarrow \quad P\left[|\bar{x} - \mu| \le \frac{\sigma}{4}\right] = 0.95 \quad \ldots\text{(i)}$

Also, $\quad P\left[|\bar{x} - \mu| \le 1.96 \frac{\sigma}{\sqrt{n}}\right] = 0.95 \quad \ldots\text{(ii)}$

From Eqs. (i) and (ii), we get

$\Rightarrow \quad 1.95 \frac{\sigma}{\sqrt{n}} = \frac{\sigma}{4}$

$\Rightarrow \quad n \simeq 62$

**264.** We have, $n = 16$, $\sigma = 5$,

$$SE(\bar{x}) = \frac{\sigma}{\sqrt{n}} = \frac{5}{\sqrt{46}} = 1.25$$

**266.** We have, $n = \frac{Z^2 PQ}{E^2} = \frac{(2.33)^2 \times 0.2 \times 0.8}{(0.03)^2}$

$= 965.14$

Hence, sample size should be $n = 965$.

**270.** We have, $n = \left(\frac{\sigma Z}{E}\right)^2 = \left(\frac{1.96 \times 20}{5}\right)^2 = 61.46 \simeq 62$

**276.** We have, $n = \left(\frac{\sigma Z_a}{E}\right)^2 = \left(\frac{10 \times 2.58}{3}\right)^2 = (8.6)^2 \simeq 74$

**286.** We have, $\mu + SE(\bar{x})Z_\alpha = 0.817$

$\mu - SE(x)Z_\alpha = 0.683$

$2\mu = 1.5 \Rightarrow \mu = 0.75$

$\frac{120}{N} = 0.75 \Rightarrow N = \frac{120}{0.75} = 160$

## Exercise 2

**1.** The Chi-square goodness of fit is based on the assumption that the character under study is normal.

**2.** Given, two normal populations $N(\mu_1, \sigma_1^2)$, and $N(\mu_2, \sigma_2^2)$.

Test statistic $t = \frac{\bar{x}_1 - \bar{x}_2}{S\sqrt{\frac{1}{n_1} + \frac{1}{n_2}}}$

where, $S^2$ is the pooled sample variance based on samples of sizes $n_1$ and $n_2$.

In this case '$t$' is student's $t$ statistic and $\sigma_1^2 = \sigma_2^2 = \sigma^2$(unknown).

**3.** A point estimate of the mean thermal conductivity at 100°F and 550 watts is the sample mean or

$$\bar{x} = 41.924 \text{ Btu/hr-ft-°F}$$

The standard error of the sample mean is $\sigma\bar{x} = \sigma / \sqrt{n}$, now since $\sigma$ is unknown, we may replace it by the sample standard deviation $s = 0.284$ to obtain the estimated standard error of $\bar{X}$ as

$$\hat{\sigma}\bar{x} = \frac{s}{\sqrt{n}}$$

$$= \frac{0.284}{\sqrt{10}} = 0.0898$$

Here, the standard error is about 0.2 per cent of the sample mean, implying that we have obtained a relatively precise point estimate of thermal conductivity. If we can assume that thermal conductivity is normally distributed, 2 times the standard error is $2\hat{\sigma}\bar{x} = 2\,(0.0898) = 0.1796$, and we are highly confident that the true mean thermal conductivity is with the interval $41.924 \pm 0.1756$ or between 41.744 and 42.104.

**4.** 1. The parameter of interest is the mean coefficient of restitution $\mu$

2. $H_0 : \mu = 0.82$

3. $H_1 : \mu > 0.82$. We want to reject $H_0$, if the mean coefficient of restitution exceeds 0.82.

4. $\alpha = 0.05$

5. The test statistic is

$$t_0 = \frac{\bar{x} - \mu_0}{s/\sqrt{n}}$$

6. Reject $H_0$, if $t_0 > t_{0.05,\,14} = 1.761$

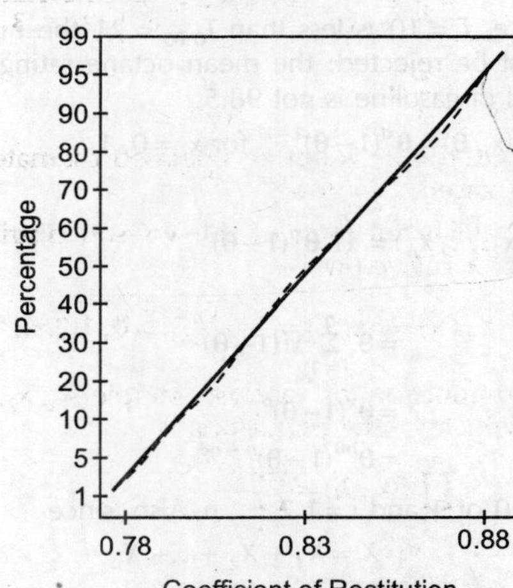


Normal probability plot of the coefficient of restitution data.

7. Computations : Since, $\bar{x} = 0.83725$, $s = 0.02456$, $\mu_{,C} = 0.82$ and $n = 15$, we have

$$t_0 = \frac{0.83725 - 0.82}{0.02456/\sqrt{15}}$$

$$= 2.72$$

8. Conclusions : Since, $t_0 = 2.72 > 1.761$, we reject $H_0$ and conclude at the 0.05 level of significance that the mean coefficient of restitution exceeds 0.82.

**5.** 1. $H_0 : \mu = 98.5$

$H_1 : \mu \ne 98.5$

$\alpha = 0.05$

2. Reject the null hypothesis, if $T \le T_{0.05}$, where $T_{0.05}$ must be read from table the appropriate value of $n$.
3. Subtracting 98.5 from each value and ranking the differences without regard to their sign, we get

| Measurement | Difference | Rank |
|---|---|---|
| 97.5 | −1.0 | 4 |
| 95.2 | −3.3 | 12 |
| 97.3 | −1.2 | 6 |
| 96.0 | −2.5 | 10 |
| 96.8 | −1.7 | 7 |
| 100.3 | 1.8 | 8 |
| 97.4 | −1.1 | 5 |
| 95.4 | −3.2 | 11 |
| 93.2 | −5.3 | 14 |
| 99.1 | 0.6 | 2 |
| 96.1 | −2.4 | 9 |
| 97.6 | −0.9 | 3 |
| 98.2 | −0.3 | 1 |
| 98.5 | 0.0 | |
| 94.9 | −3.6 | 13 |

so that, $T = 4+12+6+10+7+5+11+14+9+3+1+13 = 95$, $T^+ = 8+2 = 10$, $T = 10$. We have, $T_{0.5} = 21$ for $n = 14$.

4. Since, $T = 10$ is less than $T_{0.05} = 21$, the null hypothesis must be rejected; the mean octane rating of the given kind of gasoline is not 98.5.

**6.** Here, $f(x_i, \theta) = \theta^{xi}(1-\theta)^{1-xi}$ for $x_i = 0, 1$

Hence,

$$f(x_1, x_2, \ldots, x_n) = \prod_{i=1}^{n} \theta^{xi}(1-\theta)^{1-xi}$$

$$= \theta^{\sum_{i=1}^{n} xi}(1-\theta)^{n-\sum_{i=1}^{n} xi}$$

$$= \theta^{x}(1-\theta)^{n-x}$$

$$= \theta^{n\hat{\theta}}(1-\theta)^{n-n\hat{\theta}}$$

for $x_i = 0$ or 1 and $i = 1, 2, \ldots, n$. Also, since

$$X = X_1 + X_2 + \ldots + X_n$$

is a binomial random variable with the parameters $\theta$ and $n$, its distribution is given by

$$b(x; n, \theta) = \binom{n}{x}\theta^{x}(1-\theta)^{n-x}$$

and the transformation of variable technique yields

$$g(\hat{\theta}) = \binom{n}{n\hat{\theta}}\theta^{n\hat{\theta}}(1-\theta)^{n-n\hat{\theta}}$$

for $\hat{\theta} = 0, \frac{1}{n}, \ldots, 1$

which one substituting into the formula for $f(x_1, x_2, \ldots, x_n|\hat{\theta})$ gives,

$$\frac{f(x_1, x_2, \ldots, x_n, \hat{\theta})}{g(\hat{\theta})} = \frac{f(x_1, x_2, \ldots, x_n)}{g(\hat{\theta})}$$

$$= \frac{\theta^{n\hat{\theta}}(1-\theta)^{n-n\hat{\theta}}}{\binom{n}{n\hat{\theta}}\theta^{n\hat{\theta}}(1-\theta)^{n-n\hat{\theta}}}$$

$$= \frac{1}{\binom{n}{n\hat{\theta}}} = \frac{1}{\binom{n}{x}}$$

$$= \frac{1}{\binom{n}{x_1 + x_2 + \ldots + x_n}}$$

for $x_i = 0$ or 1 and $i = 1, 2, \ldots, n$. Evidently, this does not depend on $\theta$ and we have shown,

Hence, that $\hat{\theta} = \frac{X}{n}$ is a sufficient estimator of $\theta$.

**7. Table (a) Strength Predictions for Nine Steel Plate Girders (Predicted Load/Observed Load)**

| Girder | Karlsruhe Method | Lehigh Method | Difference $d_j$ |
|---|---|---|---|
| S1/1 | 1.186 | 1.061 | 0.119 |
| S2/1 | 1.151 | 0.992 | 0.159 |
| S3/1 | 1.322 | 1.063 | 0.259 |
| S4/1 | 1.339 | 1.062 | 0.277 |
| S5/1 | 1.200 | 1.065 | 0.138 |
| S2/1 | 1.402 | 1.178 | 0.224 |
| S2/2 | 1.365 | 1.037 | 0.328 |
| S2/3 | 1.537 | 1.086 | 0.451 |
| S2/4 | 1.559 | 1.052 | 0.507 |

The eight-step procedure is applied as follows

1. The parameter of interest is the difference in mean shear strength between the two methods, say $\mu_D = \mu_1 - \mu_2 = 0$
2. $H_0 : \mu_D = 0$
3. $H_1 : \mu_D \ne 0$
4. $\alpha = 0.05$
5. The test statistic is
$$t_0 = \frac{\bar{d}}{s_D/\sqrt{n}}$$
6. Reject $H_0$, if $t_0 > t_{0.025,8} = 2.306$ or if $t_0 < -t_{0.025,8} = -2.306$.
7. Computations : The sample average and standard deviation of the differences $d_j$ and $\bar{d} = 0.2736$ and $s_D = 0.1356$, so the test statistic is
$$t_0 = \frac{\bar{d}}{s_D/\sqrt{n}}$$
$$= \frac{0.2736}{0.1356/\sqrt{9}} = 6.05$$
8. Conclusions : Since, $t_0 = 6.05 > 2.306$, we conclude that the strength prediction methods yield different results. Specifically, the data indicate that the Karlsruhe method produces, on the average, higher strength predictions than does the Lehigh method. The p-value for

$t_0 = 6.05$ is $P = 0.0002$, so the test statistic is well into the critical region.

**8.** Since, the likelihood function is

$$L(\theta) = f(x_1, x_2, \ldots, x_n; \theta) = \prod_{i=1}^{n} f(x_i, \theta) = \left(\frac{1}{\theta}\right)^n \cdot e^{-\frac{1}{\theta}\left(\sum_{i=1}^{n} x_i\right)}$$

On differentiation of ln $L(\theta)$ *wrt*, we get

$$\frac{d[\ln L(\theta)]}{d\theta} = -\frac{n}{\theta} + \frac{1}{\theta^2} \cdot \sum_{i=1}^{n} x_i$$

Equating this derivative to zero and solving for $\theta$, we get the maximum likelihood estimate

$$\hat{\theta} = \frac{1}{n} \sum_{i=1}^{n} x_i = \bar{x}$$

Hence, the maximum likelihood estimator is $\hat{\theta} = \bar{x}$.

**9.** First consider the sample mean. We know that $E(\bar{X}) = \mu$. Therefore, the sample mean $\bar{X}$ is an unbiased estimator of the population mean $\mu$.

Now consider the sample variance,

$$E(S^2) = E\left[\frac{\sum_{i=1}^{n}(X_i - \bar{X})^2}{n-1}\right]$$

$$= \frac{1}{n-1} E \sum_{i=1}^{n}(X_i - \bar{X})^2$$

$$= \frac{1}{n-1} E \sum_{i=1}^{n}(X_i^2 + \bar{X}^2 - 2\bar{X}X_i)$$

$$= \frac{1}{n-1} E\left(\sum_{i=1}^{n} X_i^2 - n\bar{X}^2\right)$$

$$= \frac{1}{n-1}\left[\sum_{i=1}^{n} E(X_i^2) - nE(\bar{X})^2\right]$$

Since, $E(X_i^2) = \mu^2 + \sigma^2$ and $E(\bar{X})^2 = \mu^2 + \sigma^2/n$,

Hence, $$E(S^2) = \frac{1}{n-1}\left[\sum_{i=1}^{n}(\mu^2 + \sigma^2) - n(\mu^2 + \sigma^2/n)\right]$$

$$= \frac{1}{n-1}(n\mu^2 + n\sigma^2 - n\mu^2 - \sigma^2) = \sigma^2$$

Therefore, the sample variance $S^2$ is an unbiased estimator of the population variance $\sigma^2$.

**10.** 1. The quantity of interest is the difference is mean drying times, $\mu_1 - \mu_2$ and $\Delta_0 = 0$.

2. $H_0 : \mu_1 - \mu_2 = 0$ or $H_0 : \mu_1 = \mu_2$

3. $H_1 : \mu_1 > \mu_2$. We want to reject $H_0$, if the new ingredient reduces mean drying time.

4. $\alpha = 0.05$

5. The test statistic is

$$z_0 = \frac{\bar{x}_1 - \bar{x}_2 - 0}{\sqrt{\frac{\sigma_1^2}{n_1} + \frac{\sigma_2^2}{n_2}}}$$

where, $\sigma_1^2 = \sigma_2^2 = (8)^2 = 64$ and $n_1 = n_2 = 10$.

6. Reject $H_0 : \mu_1 = \mu_2$, if $z_0 > 1.645 = z_{0.05}$

7. Computations : Since, $\bar{x}_1 = 121$ min and $\bar{x}_2 = 112$ min, the test statistic is

$$z_0 = \frac{121 - 112}{\sqrt{\frac{(8)^2}{10} + \frac{(8)^2}{10}}} = 2.52$$

8. Conclusion : Since, $z_0 = 2.52 > 1.645$, we reject $H_0 : \mu_1 = \mu_2$ at the $\alpha = 0.05$ level and conclude that adding the new ingredient to the paint significantly reduces the drying time. Alternatively, we can find the *P*-value for this test as

$$P\text{-value} = 1 - \Phi(2.52) = 0.0059$$

Therefore, $H_0 : \mu_1 = \mu_2$ would be rejected at any significance level $\alpha \geq 0.0059$

**11.** The sampling distribution of $Y_n$ is

$$g_n(y_n) = n \cdot \frac{1}{\beta} \cdot \left(\int_0^{y_n} \frac{1}{\beta} dx\right)^{n-1} = \frac{n}{\beta^n} \cdot y_n^{n-1}$$

For $0 < y_n < \beta$ and $g_n(y_n) = 0$ elsewhere,

Hence, $$E(Y_n) = \frac{n}{\beta_n} \int_0^{\beta} y_n^n dy_n = \frac{n}{n+1} \cdot \beta$$

Thus, $E(Y_n) \neq \beta$ and the *n*th order statistic is a biased estimator of the parameter $\beta$. However, since

$$E\left(\frac{n+1}{n} \cdot Y_n\right) = \frac{n+1}{n} \cdot \frac{n}{n+1} \cdot \beta = \beta$$

it follows that $\frac{n+1}{n}$ times the largest sample value is an unbiased estimator of the parameter $\beta$.

**12.** The composite alternative hypothesis includes all the probability distributions that we get by assigning different values from 0 to 1 to *a*, *b* and *c*, subject only to the restriction that $a + b + c = 1$. To determine $\lambda$ for each value of *x*, we first let $x = 1$. For this value we get max $L_0 = \frac{1}{12}$, max $L = \frac{1}{3}$ (corresponding to $a = 1$), and hence, $\lambda = \frac{1}{4}$. Determining $\lambda$ for the other values of *x* in the same way, we get the results shown in the following table

| $x$ | 1 | 2 | 3 | 4 | 5 | 6 | 7 |
|---|---|---|---|---|---|---|---|
| $\lambda$ | $\frac{1}{4}$ | $\frac{1}{4}$ | $\frac{1}{4}$ | $\frac{3}{8}$ | 1 | 1 | 1 |

If the size of the critical region is to be $\alpha = 0.25$, we find that the likelihood ratio technique yields the critical region for which the null hypothesis is rejected when $\lambda = \frac{1}{4}$, namely, when $x = 1$, $x = 2$ or $x = 3$; clearly, $f(1) + f(2) + f(3) = \frac{1}{12} + \frac{1}{12} + \frac{1}{12} = 0.25$. The corresponding probability of a type II error is given by $g(4) + g(5) + g(6) + g(7)$, and hence, it equals $\frac{2}{3}$. $t_0 = 6.05$

Now, let us consider the critical region for which the null hypothesis is rejected only when $x = 4$. Its size is also $\alpha = 0.25$, since $f(4) = \frac{1}{4}$ but the corresponding probability of a type II error is

$$g(1) + g(2) + g(3) + g(5) + g(6) + g(7)$$
$$= \frac{a}{3} + \frac{b}{3} + \frac{c}{3} + 0 + 0 + 0$$
$$= \frac{1}{3}$$

Since, this is less than $\frac{2}{3}$, the critical region obtained by means of the likelihood ratio technique is inadmissible.

**13.** 1. $H_0$ : The sample is random

$H_1$ : The sample is not random

$$\alpha = 0.05$$

2. Reject the null hypothesis, if $z \le -1.96$ or $z \ge 1.96$, where

$$z = \frac{u - \mu}{\sigma}$$

$u$ is the number of runs above and below the median.

3. Since, the median of the speeds is 59.5, we get the following arrangement of $a$'s and $b$'s.

*b b a b a a b b a b b b b a b a a a a a b b b b a b b a b b b a a a b a a a b b b b b a a a a a a a*

Then, since $n_1 = 25$, $n_2 = 25$ and $u = 20$, we get

$$\mu = \frac{2 \cdot 25 \cdot 25}{25 + 25} + 1 = 6$$

$$\sigma^2 = \frac{2 \cdot 25 \cdot 25 (2 \cdot 25 \cdot 25 - 25 - 25)}{(25 + 25)^2 (25 + 25 - 1)}$$
$$= 12.2$$

and

$$z = \frac{20 - 26}{\sqrt{12.2}}$$
$$= -1.72$$

4. Since, $z = -1.72$ falls between $-1.96$ and $1.96$ the null hypothesis cannot be rejected; there is no real evidence that the sample should not be regarded as random.

**14.** The likelihood function of a random sample of size $n$, say $X_1, X_2, \ldots, X_n$, is given by

$$L(\lambda) = \prod_{i=1}^{n} \lambda e^{-\lambda x_i} = \lambda^n e^{-\lambda} \sum_{i=1} x_i$$

The log likelihood is given by

$$\ln \quad L(\lambda) = n \ln \lambda - \lambda \sum_{i=1}^{n} x_i$$

Now,
$$\frac{d \ln L(\lambda)}{d\lambda} = \frac{n}{\lambda} - \sum_{i=1}^{n} x_i$$

and upon equating this last result to zero, we obtain

$$\hat{\lambda} = \frac{n}{\sum_{i=1}^{n} X_i} = \frac{1}{\overline{X}}$$

Thus, the maximum likelihood estimator of $\lambda$ is the reciprocal of the sample mean.

**15.** The eight step hypothesis testing procedure may now be applied to this problem.

1. The variable of intrest is employee preference among pension plans.
2. $H_0$ : Preference is independent of salaried versus hourly job classification.
3. $H_1$ : Preference is not independent of salaried versus hourly job classification.
4. $\alpha = 0.05$
5. The test statistic is

$$\chi_0^2 = \sum_{i=1}^{r} \sum_{j=1}^{c} \frac{(o_{ij} - E_{ij})^2}{E_{ij}}$$

6. Since, $r = 2$ and $c = 3$, the degrees of freedom for chi-square are $(r - 1)(c - 1) = (1)(2) = 2$ and we would reject $H_0$, if $\chi_0^2 > \chi^2_{0.05,2} = 5.99$
7. Computations

$$\chi_0^2 = \sum_{i=1}^{2} \sum_{j=1}^{3} \frac{(o_{ij} - E_{ij})^2}{E_{ij}}$$
$$= \frac{(160 - 136)^2}{136} + \frac{(140 - 136)^2}{136} + \frac{(40 - 68)^2}{68}$$
$$+ \frac{(40 - 64)^2}{64} + \frac{(60 - 64)^2}{64} + \frac{(60 - 32)^2}{32}$$
$$= 49.63$$

8. Conclusions : Since $\chi_0^2 = 49.63 > \chi^2_{0.05,2} = 5.99$, we reject the hypothesis of independence and conclude that the preference for pension plans is not independent of job classification. The $P$-value for $\chi_0^2 = 49.63$ is $P = 1.671 \times 10^{-11}$.

**16.** 1. $H_0 : \mu_1 = \mu_2$

$H_1 : \mu_1 < \mu_2$

$$\alpha = 0.01$$

2. Reject the null hypothesis, if $z \le -2.33$, where

$$z = \frac{U_1 - \mu}{\sigma}$$

3. Ranking the data jointly according to size, we find that the values of the first sample occupy ranks 21, 1, 3, 8, 15, 4, 11, 2, 5.5, 13, 31, 16, 12, 22, 7 and 10. (The fifth and sixth values are both 12.0, so we assigned each the rank 5.5). Thus,

$$W_1 = 1 + 2 + 3 + 4 + 5.5 + 7 + 8 + 10 + 11 + 12 + 13 + 15 + 16 + 21 + 22 + 31$$
$$= 181.5$$

and

$$U_1 = 181.5 - \frac{16.17}{2} = 45.5$$

Since,
$$\mu = \frac{16 \cdot 16}{2} = 128$$

and
$$\sigma^2 = \frac{16 \cdot 16 \cdot 33}{12} = 704, \text{ we get}$$

$$z = \frac{45.5 - 128}{\sqrt{704}}$$
$$= -3.11$$

4. Since, $z = -3.11$ is less than $-2.33$, the null hypothesis must be rejected; we conclude that on the average the second diet produces a greater gain in weight.

**17.** Since,

$$f(x) = \frac{1}{\sigma\sqrt{2\pi}} \cdot e^{-\frac{1}{2}\left(\frac{x-\mu}{\sigma}\right)^2} \quad \text{for } -\infty < x < \infty$$

$$\Rightarrow \quad \ln f(x) = -\ln \sigma\sqrt{2\pi} - \frac{1}{2}\left(\frac{x-\mu}{\sigma}\right)^2$$

Hence, $\dfrac{\partial \ln f(x)}{\partial \mu} = \dfrac{1}{\sigma}\left(\dfrac{x-\mu}{\sigma}\right)$

Hence, $E\left[\left(\dfrac{\partial \ln f(X)}{\partial \mu}\right)^2\right] = \dfrac{1}{\sigma^2} \cdot E\left[\left(\dfrac{X-\mu}{\sigma}\right)^2\right]$

$$= \frac{1}{\sigma^2} \cdot 1 = \frac{1}{\sigma^2}$$

Thus,

$$\frac{1}{n \cdot E\left[\left(\dfrac{\partial \ln f(X)}{\partial \mu}\right)^2\right]} = \frac{1}{n \cdot \dfrac{1}{\sigma^2}} = \frac{\sigma^2}{n}$$

and since $\bar{X}$ is unbiased and $\text{var}(\bar{X}) = \dfrac{\sigma^2}{n}$ it follows that $\bar{X}$ is a minimum variance unbiased estimator of $\mu$.

**18.** A 95% two sided confidence interval for $p$.

$$\hat{P} - z_{0.025}\sqrt{\frac{\hat{P}(1-\hat{P})}{n}} \le p \le \hat{P} + z_{0.025}\sqrt{\frac{\hat{P}(1-\hat{P})}{n}}$$

or $\quad 0.12 - 1.96\sqrt{\dfrac{0.12\,(0.88)}{85}} \le p \le 0.12$

$$+ 1.96\sqrt{\frac{0.12\,(0.88)}{85}}$$

which simplifies to

$$0.05 \le p \le 0.19$$

**19.** The required quantities are $z_{\alpha/2} = z_{0.025} = 1.96$, $n = 10$, $\sigma = 1$ and $\bar{x} = 64.46$.

The resulting 95% CI is as follows

$$\bar{x} - z_{\alpha/2}\frac{\sigma}{\sqrt{n}} \le \mu \le \bar{x} + z_{\alpha/2}\frac{\sigma}{\sqrt{n}}$$

$$64.46 - 1.96\frac{1}{\sqrt{10}} \le \mu \le 64.46 + 1.96\frac{1}{\sqrt{10}}$$

$$63.84 \le \mu \le 65.08$$

This is based on the sample data, a range of highly plausible values for mean impact energy for $A$ 238 steel at 60°C is $63.84\text{ J} \le \mu \le 65.08\text{ J}$.

**20.** The likelihood function of a random sample of size $n$, say $X_1, X_2, \ldots, X_n$ is

$$L(\mu) = \prod_{i=1}^{n} \frac{1}{\sigma\sqrt{2\pi}}\, e^{-(x_i-\mu)^2/(2\sigma^2)}$$

$$= \frac{1}{(2\pi\sigma^2)^{n/2}}\, e^{-(1/2\sigma^2)\sum\limits_{i=1}^{n}(x_i-\mu)^2}$$

Now, $\quad \ln L(\mu) = -(n/2)\ln(2\pi\sigma^2) - (2\sigma^2)^{-1}\sum\limits_{i=1}^{n}(x_i-\mu)^2$

$$\Rightarrow \quad \frac{d\ln L(\mu)}{d\mu} = (\sigma^2)^{-1}\sum_{i=1}^{n}(x_i-\mu)$$

Equating this last result to zero and solving for $\mu$ yields.

$$\hat{\mu} = \frac{\sum\limits_{i=1}^{n} X_i}{n} = \bar{X}$$

Thus, the sample mean is the maximum likelihood estimator of $\mu$.

**21.** The solution using the eight step hypothesis testing procedure is as follows

1. The parameters of interest are $\mu_1$ and $\mu_2$, the mean process yield using catalysts 1 and 2, respectively and we want to know, if $\mu_1 - \mu_2 = 0$.
2. $H_0 : \mu_1 - \mu_2 = 0$ or $H_0 : \mu_1 = \mu_2$
3. $H_1 : \mu_1 \ne \mu_2$
4. $\alpha = 0.05$
5. The test statistic is
$$t_0 = \frac{\bar{x}_1 - \bar{x}_2 - 0}{s_p\sqrt{\dfrac{1}{n_1} + \dfrac{1}{n_2}}}$$
6. Reject $H_0$; if $t_0 > t_{0.025,\,14} = 2.145$ or if $t_0 < -t_{0.025,\,14} = -2.145$.
7. Computations : From given table, we have $\bar{x}_1 = 92.255$, $s_1 = 2.39$, $n_1 = 8$, $\bar{x}_2 = 92.733$, $s_2 = 2.98$ and $n_2 = 8$. Therefore,
$$s_p^2 = \frac{(n_1-1)\,s_1^2 + (n_2-1)\,s_2^2}{n_1+n_2-2}$$
$$= \frac{(7)(2.39)^2 + 7(2.98)^2}{8+8-2} = 7.30$$
$$s_p = \sqrt{7.30} = 2.70$$
and
$$t_0 = \frac{\bar{x}_1 - \bar{x}_2}{2.70\sqrt{\dfrac{1}{n_1}+\dfrac{1}{n_2}}} = \frac{92.255 - 92.733}{2.70\sqrt{\dfrac{1}{8}+\dfrac{1}{8}}} = -0.35$$
8. Conclusions : Since $-2.145 < t_0 = 0.35 < 2.145$, the null hypothesis cannot be rejected. *i.e.*, At the 0.05 level of significance, we do not have strong evidence to conclude that catalyst 2 results in a mean yield that differs from the mean yield when catalyst 1 is used.

**22.** 1. $H_0 : \mu_1 = \mu_2 = \mu_3$

$H_1 : \mu_1, \mu_2$ and $\mu_3$ are not all equal

$\alpha = 0.05$

2. Reject the null hypothesis, if $H \ge 5.991$, where 5.991 is the value of $\chi^2_{0.05,2}$
3. Ranking the grades from 1 to 18, we find that $R_1 = 6 + 13 + 14 + 16 + 17 + 18 = 84$, $R_2 = 1 + 4.5 + 8 + 9 + 10 + 11 + 12 = 55.5$ and $R_3 = 2 + 3 + 4.5 + 7 + 15 = 31.5$ where there is one tie and the tied grades are each assigned the rank 4.5. Substituting the value of $R_1$, $R_2$ and $R_3$ together with $n_1 = 6$, $n_2 = 7$, $n_3 = 5$ and $n = 18$ into the formula for $H$, we get

$$H = \frac{12}{18 \cdot 19}\left(\frac{84^2}{6} + \frac{55.5^2}{7} + \frac{31.5^2}{5}\right) - 3 \cdot 19$$
$$= 6.67$$

4. Since, $H = 6.67$ exceeds $\chi^2_{0.05,2} = 5.991$, the null hypothesis must be rejected; we conclude that the three methods are not all equally effective.

**23.** We must shown that

$$f(x_1, x_2, x_3 | y) = \frac{f(x_1, x_2, x_3, y)}{g(y)}$$

is not independent of $\theta$ for some values of $X_1$, $X_2$ and $X_3$, let us consider the case where $x_1 = 1$, $x_2 = 1$ and $x_3 = 0$. Thus,

$$y = \frac{1}{6}(1 + 2 \cdot 1 + 3.0) = \frac{1}{2} \text{ and}$$

$$f\left(1, 1, 0 | Y = \frac{1}{2}\right)$$

$$= \frac{P\left(X_1 = 1, X_2 = 1, X_3 = 0, Y = \frac{1}{2}\right)}{P\left(Y = \frac{1}{2}\right)}$$

$$= \frac{f(1, 1, 0)}{f(1, 1, 0) + f(0, 0, 1)}$$

where, $f(x_1, x_2, x_3) = \theta^{x_1 + x_2 + x_3}(1-\theta)^{3-(x_1 + x_2 + x_3)}$ for $x_1 = 0$ or 1 and $i = 1, 2, 3$. Since, $f(1, 1, 0) = \theta^2(1-\theta)$ and $(0, 0, 1) = \theta(1-\theta)^2$, it follows that

$$f\left(1, 1, 0 | Y = \frac{1}{2}\right) = \frac{\theta^2(1-\theta)}{\theta^2(1-\theta) + \theta(1-\theta)^2} = \theta$$

and it can be seen that this conditional probability depends on $\theta$. We have thus shown that $Y = \frac{1}{6}(X_1 + 2X_2 + 3X_3)$ is not a sufficient estimator of the parameter $\theta$ of a Bernoulli population.

**24.** 1. $H_0 : \mu = 185$
$H_1 : \mu < 185$
$\alpha = 0.05$

2. Reject the null hypothesis, if $t \le 2.132$, where $t$ is determined by means of the formula given above and 2.132 is the value of $t_{0.05,4}$.
3. First we calculate the mean and the standard deviation, getting $\bar{x} = 183.1$ and $s$ 8.2. Then, substituting these values together with $\mu_0 = 185$ and $n = 5$ into the formula for $t$, we get

$$t = \frac{183.1 - 185}{8.2/\sqrt{5}} = -0.49$$

4. Since, $t = -0.49$ is greater than $-2.132$, the null hypothesis cannot be rejected. If we went beyond this and concluded that the rolls of ribbon from which the sample was selected meet specifications, we would, of course, be exposed to the unknown risk of committing a type II error.

**25.** The eight step procedure follows

1. The parameters of interest are the median fuel mileage performance for the two metering devices
2. $H_0 : \tilde{\mu}_1 = \tilde{\mu}_2$ or equivalently, $H_0 : \tilde{\mu}_D = 0$
3. $H_1 : \tilde{\mu}_1 \ne \tilde{\mu}_2$ or equivalently, $H_1 : \tilde{\mu}_D \ne 0$
4. $\alpha = 0.05$
5. We will use Appendix Table VII to conduct the test, so the test statistic is $r = \min(r^+, r^-)$.
6. Since, $\alpha = 0.05$ and $n = 12$, Appendix table VII gives the cri.ical values as $r^*_{0.05} = 2$. We will reject $H_0$ in favour of $H_1$, if $r \le 2$.
7. Computations : Given table shows the differences and their signs and we note that $r^+ = 8$, $r^- = 4$ and so $r = \min(8, 4) = 4$
8. Conclusions : Since, $r = 4$ is not less than or equal to the critical value $r^*_{0.05} = 2$, we cannot reject the null hypothesis that the two devices provide the same median fuel mileage performance.

**26.** The likelihood function for a random sample of size $n$ is

$$L(\mu, \sigma^2) = \prod_{i=1}^{n} \frac{1}{\sigma\sqrt{2\pi}} e^{-(x_i - \mu)^2/(2\sigma^2)}$$

$$= \frac{1}{(2\pi\sigma^2)^{n/2}} e^{-(1/2\sigma^2)} \sum_{i=1}^{n}(x_i - \mu)^2$$

and

$$\ln L(\mu, \sigma^2) = -\frac{n}{2}\ln(2\pi\sigma^2) - \frac{1}{2\sigma^2}\sum_{i=1}^{n}(x_i - \mu)^2$$

$$\Rightarrow \quad \frac{\partial \ln L(\mu, \sigma^2)}{\partial \mu} = \frac{1}{\sigma^2}\sum_{i=1}^{n}(x_i - \mu) = 0$$

$$\frac{\partial \ln L(\mu, \sigma^2)}{\partial (\sigma)^2} = -\frac{n}{2\sigma^2} + \frac{1}{2\sigma^4}\sum_{i=1}^{n}(x_i - \mu)^2 = 0$$

The solutions to the above equation yield the maximum likelihood estimators

$$\hat{\mu} = \bar{X}$$
$$\hat{\sigma}^2 = \frac{1}{n}\sum_{i=1}^{n}(X_i - \bar{X})^2$$

**27.** 1. The parameter of interest is $\mu$, the mean burning rate.

2. $H_0 : \mu = 50$ cm/s
3. $H_1 : \mu \ne 50$ cm/s
4. $\alpha = 0.05$
5. The test statistic is $z_0 = \dfrac{\bar{x} - \mu_0}{\sigma/\sqrt{n}}$
6. Reject $H_0$, if $z_0 > 1.96$ or if $z_0 < -1.96$. Note that this results from step 4, where we specified $\alpha = 0.05$ and so the boundaries of the critical region are at $z_{0.025} = 1.96$ and $-z_{0.025} = -1.96$
7. Computations : Since, $\bar{x} = 51.3$ and $\sigma = 2$

$$z_0 = \frac{51.3 - 50}{2/\sqrt{25}} = 3.25$$

8. Conclusion : Since, $z_0 = 3.25 > 1.96$, we reject $H_0 : \mu = 50$ at the 0.05 level of significance. Stated more completely, we conclude that the mean burning rate differs from 50 cm/s based on a sample of 25 measurements. In fact, there is strong evidence that the mean burning rate exceeds 50 cm/s.

**28.** 1. $H_0$ : Arrangement is random
$H_1$ : Arrangement is not random
$\alpha = 0.05$

2. Reject the null hypothesis, if $z \le -1.96$ or $z \ge 1.96$, where

$$z = \frac{u - \mu}{\sigma}$$

and $\mu$ and $\sigma^2$ are given.

3. Since, $n_1 = 30$, $n_2 = 18$ and $u = 27$, we get

$$u = \frac{2 \cdot 30 \cdot 18}{30 + 18} + 1 = 23.5$$

$$\sigma = \sqrt{\frac{2 \cdot 30 \cdot 18\,(2 \cdot 30 \cdot 18 - 30 - 18)}{(30 + 18)^2\,(30 + 18 - 1)}} = 3.21$$

and hence

$$z = \frac{27 - 23.5}{3.21} = 1.09$$

4. Since, $z = 1.09$ falls between $-1.96$ and $1.96$, the null hypothesis cannot be rejected; in other words, there is no real evidence to indicate that the arrangement is not random.

**29.** 1. $H_0 : \mu = 8$

$H_1 : \mu \ne 8$

$\alpha = 0.01$

2. Reject the null hypothesis, if $z \le -2.575$ or $z \ge 2.575$, where

$$z = \frac{\bar{x} - \mu_0}{\sigma/\sqrt{n}}$$

3. Substituting $\bar{x} = 8.091$, $\mu_0 = 8$, $\sigma = 0.16$ and $n = 25$, we get

$$z = \frac{8.091 - 8}{0.16/\sqrt{25}} = 2.84$$

4. Since, $z = 2.84$ exceeds 2.575, the null hypothesis must be rejected and suitable adjustments should be made in the production process.

**30.** 1. The parameter of interest is the median of the distribution of propellant shear strength.

2. $H_0 : \tilde{\mu} = 2000$ psi

3. $H_1 : \tilde{\mu} \ne 2000$ psi

4. $\alpha = 0.05$

5. The test statistic is the observed number of plus differences in given table or $r^+ = 14$.

6. We will reject $H_0$, if the $P$-value corresponding to $r^+ = 14$ is less than or equal to $\alpha = 0.05$.

7. Computations : Since, $r^+ = 14$ is greater than $n/2 - 20/2 - 10$. we calculate the $P$-value from

$$P = 2P\left(R^+ \ge 14 \text{ when } P = \frac{1}{2}\right)$$

$$= 2\sum_{r=14}^{20} \binom{20}{r} (0.5)^r\,(0.5)^{20-r} = 0.1153$$

8. Conclusion : Since, $P = 0.1153$ is not less than $\alpha = 0.05$, we cannot reject the null hypothesis that the median shear strength is 2000 psi. Another way to say this is that the observed number of plus signs $r^+ = 14$ was not large or small enough to indicate that median shear strength is different from 2000 psi at the $\alpha = 0.05$ level of significance.

**31.** 1. $H_0 : \mu_1 = \mu_2$

$H_1 : \mu_1 > \mu_2$

$\alpha = 0.05$

$2^1$. Use the test statistic $X$, the observed number of plus signs.

$3^1$. Replacing each positive difference by a plus sign and each negative difference by a minus sign, we get

+ + + + + + − + − + + +

So that $n = 12$ and $x = 10$ we find that $P(X \ge 10) = 0.0192$ for $\theta = \frac{1}{2}$.

$4^1$. Since, the $P$-value, 0.0192 is less than 0.05, the null hypothesis must be rejected and we conclude that the new traffic control system is effective in reducing the number of accidents at dangerous intersections.

**32.** These displays provide good support for the assumption that the population is normally distributed. We want to find a 95 % CI on $\mu$. Since, $n = 22$, we have $n - 1 = 21$ degrees of freedom for $t$, so $t_{0.025,21} = 2.080$ The resulting CI is

$$\bar{x} - t_{\alpha\backslash 2, n-1}\, s/\sqrt{n} \le \mu \le \bar{x} + t_{\alpha\backslash 2, n-1}\, s/\sqrt{n}$$

$$13.71 - 2.080\,(3.55)/\sqrt{22} \le \mu \le 13.71 + 2.080\,(3.55)/\sqrt{22}$$

$$13.71 - 1.57 \le \mu \le 13.71 + 1.57$$

$$12.14 \le \mu \le 15.28$$

The CI is fairly wide because there is a lot of variability in the tensile adhesion test measurements.

**33.** 1. $H_0 : \theta_1 = \theta_2 = \theta_3$

$H_1 : \theta_1, \theta_2$ and $\theta_3$ are not all equal.

$\alpha = 0.05$

2. Reject the null hypothesis, if $\chi^2 \ge 5.991$, where

$$\chi^2 = \sum_{i=1}^{3} \sum_{j=1}^{2} \frac{(f_{ij} - e_{ij})^2}{e_{ij}}$$

and 5.991 is the value $\chi^2_{0.05,2}$

$$\hat{\theta} = \frac{232 + 260 + 197}{400 + 500 + 400}$$

$$= \frac{689}{1300} = 0.53$$

3. The expected cell frequencies are

$e_{11} = 400\,(0.53) = 212$

and $e_{12} = 400\,(0.47) = 188$

$e_{21} = 500\,(0.53) = 265$

and $e_{22} = 500\,(0.47) = 235$

$e_{31} = 400\,(0.53) = 212$

and $e_{32} = 400\,(0.47) = 188$

and substitution into the formula for $\chi^2$ given above yields

$$\chi^2 = \frac{(232 - 212)^2}{212} + \frac{(260 - 265)^2}{265} + \frac{(197 - 212)^2}{212} + \frac{(168 - 188)^2}{188} + \frac{(240 - 235)^2}{235} + \frac{(203 - 188)^2}{188}$$

$$= 6.48$$

4. Since, $\chi^2 = 6.48$ exceeds 5.991, the null hypothesis must be rejected; in other words, the true proportions of shoppers favouring detergent *A* over detergent *B* in the three cities are not the same.

**34.** The eight step hypothesis testing procedure leads to the following results

1. The parameters of interest are $p_1$ and $p_2$, the proportion of patients who improve following treatment with St. John's Wort ($p_1$) or the placebo ($p_2$).
2. $H_0 : p_1 = p_2$
3. $H_1 : p_1 \neq p_2$
4. $\alpha = 0.05$
5. The test statistic is

$$z_o = \frac{\hat{p}_1 - \hat{p}_2}{\sqrt{\hat{p}(1-\hat{p})\left(\frac{1}{n_1} + \frac{1}{n_2}\right)}}$$

where $\hat{p}_1 = 27/100 = 0.27$, $\hat{p}_2 = 19/100 = 0.19$ $n_1 = n_2 = 100$ and

$$\hat{p} = \frac{x_1 + x_2}{n_1 + n_2} = \frac{19 + 27}{100 + 100} = 0.23$$

6. Regect $H_0 : p_1 = p_2$; if $z_0 > z_{0.025} = 1.96$ or if $z_0 <= z_{0.025} = 1.96$
7. Computations : The value of the test statistic is

$$z_0 = \frac{0.27 - 0.19}{\sqrt{0.23\,(0.77)\left(\frac{1}{100} + \frac{1}{100}\right)}} = 1.35$$

8. Conclusions : Since,' $z_o = 1.35$ does not exceed $z_{0.025}$ we cannot reject the null hypothesis. Note that the *p*-value is $P \simeq 0.177$. There is insufficient evidence to support the claim that St. John's Wort is effective in treating major depression.

**35.** 1. $H_1 : \mu = 160$

$H_1 : \mu > 160$

$\alpha = 0.05$

2[1]. Use the test statistic *X*, the observed number of plus signs.

3[1]. Replacing each value exceeding 160 with a plus sign, each value less than 160 with a minus sign, and discarding the one value which equals 160, we get

$$+ + + + + - - + + + - + + - + + + + +$$

So that $n = 19$ and $x = 15$ .Thus $P(X \geq 15) = 0.0095$ for $\theta = \frac{1}{2}$ 4[1]. Since, the *p*-value,0.0095 is less than 0.05 the null hypothesis must be rejected and we conclude that the mean breaking strength of the given kind of ribbon exceeds 160 pounds.

**36.** $H_0 : \sigma_1^2 = \sigma_2^2$

$H_1 : \sigma_1^2 \neq \sigma_2^2$

2. Since, $s_1^2 \geq s_2^2$, reject the null hypothesis, if $\frac{s_1^2}{s_2^2} \geq 3.67$, where 3.67 is the value of $f_{0.01,\, 12,\, 15}$
3. Substituting $s_1^2 = 19.2$ and $s_2^2 = 3.5$ we get

$$\frac{s_1^2}{s_2^2} = \frac{19.2}{3.5} = 5.49$$

4. Since, $f = 5.49$ exceeds 3.67, the null hypothesis must be rejected; we conclude that the variability of the tensile strength of the two kinds of steel is not the same.

**37.** The eight step hypothesis testing procedure may be applied to this problem as follows

1. The parameters of interest are the variances of oxide thickness $\sigma_1^2$ and $\sigma_2^2$. We will assume that oxide thickness is a normal random variable for both gas mixture.
2. $H_0 : \sigma_1^2 = \sigma_2^2$
3. $H_1 : \sigma_1^2 \neq \sigma_2^2$
4. $\alpha = 0.05$
5. The test statistic is given by

$$f_0 = \frac{s_1^2}{s_2^2}$$

6. Since, $n_1 = n_2 = 20$, we will reject $H_0 : \sigma_1^2 = \sigma_2^2$, if $f_0 > f_{0.025,\,19,\,19} = 2.53$ or if $f_0 < f_{0.975,19,19} = 1 \backslash f_{0.025,\,19,\,19} = 1 \backslash 2.53 = 0.40$
7. Computations : Since, $s_1^2 = (1.96)^2 = 3.84$ and $s_2^2 = (2.13)^2 = 4.54$, the test statistic is

$$f_0 = \frac{s_1^2}{s_2^2} = \frac{3.84}{4.54} = 0.85$$

8. Conclusions : Since,

$$f_{0.975,\,19,\,19,} = 0.40 < f_0 = 0.85 < f_{0.025,\,19,\,19,} = 2.53,$$

we cannot reject the null hypothesis $H_0 : \sigma_1^2 = \sigma_2^2$ at the 0.05 level of significance.Therefore, there is no strong evidence to indicate that either gas results in a smaller variance of oxide thickness.

**38.** 1. The parameter of interest is the process fraction defective *p*.

2. $H_0 : p = 0.05$
3. $H_1 : p < 0.05$

This formulation of the problem will allow the manufacturer to make a strong claim about process capability, if the null hypothesis $H_0 : p = 0.05$ is rejected.

4. $\alpha = 0.05$.
5. The test statistic is $z_o = \frac{x - np_0}{\sqrt{np_0\,(1 - p_0)}}$

where, $x = 4$, $n = 200$ and $p_0 = 0.05$

6. Reject $H_0 : p = 0.05$, if $z_o < {}^{-}z_{0.05} = -1.645$
7. Computation : The test statistic is

$$z_0 = \frac{4 - 200\,(0.05)}{\sqrt{200\,(0.05)(0.95)}} = -1.95$$

8. Conclusions : Since, $z_o = -1.95 < {}^{-}z_{0.05} = -1.645$, we reject $H_0$ and conclude that the process fraction defective *p* is less than 0.05 The *P*-value for this value of the test statistic $z_0$ is $P = 0.0256$, which is less than $\alpha = 0.05$. We conclude that the process is capable.

**39.** 1. $H_0 : \sigma^2 = 0.36$

$H_1 : \sigma^2 > 0.36$

$\alpha = 0.05$

2. Reject the null hypothesis, if $\chi^2 \geq 27.587$

where,

$$\chi^2 = \frac{(n-1)\, s^2}{\sigma_0^2}$$

and 27.587 is the value of $\chi^2_{0.05,\, 17}$

3. Substituting $s^2 = 0.68$, $\sigma_0^2 = 0.36$ and $n = 18$, we get

$$\chi^2 = \frac{17\,(0.68)}{0.36} = 32.11$$

4. Since, $\chi^2 = 32.11$ exceeds 27.587, the null hypothesis must be rejected and the process used in the manufacture of the parts must be adjusted.

**40.** Using the eight step procedure results in the following

1. The parameter of interest is the population variance $\sigma^2$.
2. $H_0 : \sigma^2 = 0.01$
3. $H_1 : \sigma^2 > 0.01$
4. $\alpha = 0.05$
5. The test statistic is $\chi_0^2 = \dfrac{(n-1)s^2}{\sigma_0^2}$
6. Reject $H_0$, if $\chi_0^2 > \chi^2_{0.05,\, 19} = 30.14$
7. Computations : $\chi_0^2 = \dfrac{19(0.0153)}{0.01} = 29.07$
8. Conclusions : Since, $\chi_0^2 = 29.07 < \chi^2_{0.05,\, 19} = 30.14$ we conclude that there is no strong evidence that the variance of fill volume exceeds 0.01 (fluid ounces)$^2$.

**41.** Since, the likelihood function is given by

$$L(\mu, \sigma^2) = \prod_{i=1}^{n} n\,(x_i; \mu, \sigma)$$

$$= \left(\frac{1}{\sigma\sqrt{2\pi}}\right)^n \cdot e^{-\frac{1}{2\sigma^2}\sum_{i=1}^{n}(x_i-\mu)^2}$$

Partial differentiation of $\ln L(\mu, \sigma^2)$ *wrt* $\mu$ and $\sigma^2$ yields

$$\frac{\partial\,[\ln L(\mu, \sigma^2)]}{\partial \mu} = \frac{1}{\sigma^2} \cdot \sum_{i=1}^{n} (x_i - \mu)$$

$$\Rightarrow \quad \frac{\partial\,[\ln L(\mu, \sigma^2)]}{\partial \sigma^2} = -\frac{n}{2\sigma^2} + \frac{1}{2\sigma^4} \cdot \sum_{i=1}^{n} (x_1 - \mu)^2$$

Equating the first of these two partial derivatives to zero and solving for $\mu$, we get.

$$\hat{\mu} = \frac{1}{n} \cdot \sum_{i=1}^{n} (x_i = \bar{x})$$

and equating the second of these partial derivatives to zero and solving for $\sigma^2$ after substituting $\mu = \bar{x}$, we get

$$\hat{\sigma}^2 = \frac{1}{n} \sum_{i=1}^{n} (x_i - \bar{x})^2$$

# 24 Linear Programming and Queuing Theory

## Syllabus

- Linear Programming Problem
- Simplex Methods, Quality
- Elementary Queuing and Inventory Models
- Steady State Solution of Markovian Queuing
- Models : $M/M/1$, $M/M/1$ with limited waiting space, $M/M/C$, $M/M/C$ with limited waiting space, $M/G/1$

## Linear Programming Problem

A problem which requires defining the variable involved, establishing relationship between them and formulating the objective function and the constraints, is called a programming problem.

If objective function and constraints are all linear, then the problem is called linear programming problem.

The variables that enter into the problem are called decision variables.

Objective function is expressed in terms of decision variables. Constraints are equalities (=) or inequalities. Which are relations in terms of decision variables.

If objective function is quadratic expression in terms of decision variables, then the problem is called quadratic programming problem.

Any linear programming problem involving more than two variables may be expressed as follows.

Find the values of the variables $x_1, x_2, \ldots, x_n$ which maximize (or minimize) the objective function

$$Z = c_1x_1 + c_2x_2 + \ldots + c_nx_n \qquad \ldots(i)$$

Subject to the constraints

$$\left.\begin{array}{l} a_{11}x_1 + a_{12}x_2 + \ldots + a_{1n}x_n \le b_1 \\ a_{21}x_1 + a_{22}x_2 + \ldots + a_{2n}x_n \le b_2 \\ \vdots \\ a_{m1}x_1 + a_{m2}x_2 + \ldots + a_{mn}x_n \le b_m \end{array}\right\} \qquad \ldots(ii)$$

and meet the non-negative restrictions

$$x_1, x_2, \ldots, x_n \ge 0.$$

A set of values $x_1, x_2, \ldots, x_n$ which satisfies the constraints of the LPP is called its solution.

Any solution to a LPP which satisfies the non-negative restrictions of the problem is called its feasible solution.

Any feasible solution which maximizes (or minimizes) the objective function of the LPP is called its optimal solution.

Some constraints in LPP may be equalities (=) others may be inequalities [(≤) and or (≥)].

The inequality constraints are changed to equalities by adding and or subtracting non-negative variables to (and or from) the left hand side of such constraints.

**Definition** If the constraints of a general LPP be

$$\sum_{j=1}^{n} a_{ij}\, x_i \le b_i \qquad (i = 1, 2, \ldots, k)$$

Then, the non-negative variables $s_i$ which satisfy

$$\sum_{j=1}^{n} a_{ij}\, x_i + s_i = b_i \qquad (i = 1, 2, \ldots, k)$$

are called slack variables.

**Definition** If the constraints of a general linear programming problem be

$$\sum_{j=1}^{n} a_{ij}\, x_i \ge b_i \qquad (i = k, k+1, \ldots)$$

Then, the non-negative variables $s_i$ which satisfy

$$\sum_{j=1}^{n} a_{ij}\, x_i - s_i = b_i, \qquad (i = k, k+1, \ldots)$$

are called surplus variables.

## Canonical Form of LPP

The general linear programming problem can always be expressed in the following form

Maximize $Z = c_1x_1 + c_2x_2 + \ldots + c_nx_n$

subject to the constraints

$$a_{i1}x_1 + a_{i2}x_2 + \ldots + a_{in}x_n \le b_i,$$

$i = 1, 2, \ldots, m$

$$x_1, x_2, \ldots, x_n \ge 0,$$

By making some elementary transformations. This form of the LPP is called its canonical form.

This form is used in duality theory. It has following characteristics

**(i)** Objective function is of maximization type

**(ii)** All constraints are of ($\le$) type.

**(iii)** All variables $x_i$ are non-negative.

## Standard Form of LPP

The general linear programming problem can also be put in the following form

Maximize $Z = c_1x_1 + c_2x_2 + \ldots + c_nx_n$

Subject to the constraints

$$a_{i1}x_1 + a_{i2}x_2 + \ldots + a_{in}x_n = b_i; \qquad (i = 1, 2, \ldots, m)$$

$$x_1, x_2, \ldots, x_n \ge 0.$$

This form of the LPP is called standard form.

It has following characteristics

**(i)** Objective function is of maximization type.

**(ii)** All constraints are expressed as equations.

**(iii)** Right hand side of each constraint is non-negative.

**(iv)** All variables are non-negative.

***Example 1.*** *Express the following problem in the standard form*

*Minimize* $Z = 3x_1 + 4x_2$

*subject to* $2x_1 - x_2 - 3x_3 = -4,\ 3x_1 + 5x_2 + x_4 = 10,$

$x_1 - 4x_2 = 12,\ x_1, x_2, x_3, x_4 \ge 0.$

**Solution.** Here, $x_3, x_4$ are the slack/surplus variables and $x_1, x_2$ are the decision variables. As $x_2$ is unrestricted, let $x_2 = x_2' - x_2''$, where $x_2', x_2'' \ge 0$.

Hence, the problem in standard form is

Maximize $Z' (= -Z) = -3x_1 - 4x_2' + 4x_2''$

subject to

$$-2x_1 + x_2' - x_2'' + 3x_3 = 4$$

$$3x_1 + 5x_2' - 5x_2'' + x_4 = 10$$

$$x_1 - 4x_2' + 4x_2'' = 12$$

$$x_1, x_2', x_2'', x_3, x_4 \ge 0$$

***Example 2.*** *Convert the following LPP to the standard form*

*Maximize* $Z = 3x_1 + 5x_2 + 7x_3$

*Subject to the constraints*

$$6x_1 - 4x_2 \le 5,\ 3x_1 + 2x_2 + 5x_3 \ge 11,$$

$$4x_1 + 3x_3 \le 2,\ x_1, x_2 \ge 0.$$

**Solution.** As $x_3$ is unrestricted, let $x_3 = x_3' - x_3''$ where $x_3', x_3'' \ge 0$.

Now, the given constraints can be expressed as

$$6x_1\ 4x_2 \le 5,$$

$$3x_1 + 2x_2 + 5x_3' - 5x_3'' \ge 11$$

$$4x_1 + 3x_3' - 3x_3'' \le 2$$

$$x_1, x_2\ x_3', x_3'' \ge 0$$

Introducing the slack/surplus variables, the problem in standard form becomes

Maximize $Z = 3x_1 + 5x_2 + 7x_3' - 7x_3''$

Subject to the constraints

$$6x_1 - 4x_2 + s_1 = 5$$

$$3x_1 + 2x_2 + 5x_3' - 5x_3'' - s_2 = 11$$

$$4x_1 + 3x_3' - 3x_3'' + s_3 = 2$$

$$x_1, x_2, x_3', x_3'', s_1, s_2, s_3 \ge 0$$

# Solution of LPP

## Graphical Method to Solve LPP

Linear programming problems involving only two variables can be efectively solved by a graphical technique.

It provides a pictorial representation of the solution.

### Working Procedure

**Step 1** Formulate the given problem as a linear programming problem.

**Step 2** Plot the given constraints as inequalities on $x_1 - x_2$ coordinate plane and determine the convex region formed by them.

**Step 3** Determine the vertices of the convex region and find the value of the objective function at each vertex. The vertex which gives the optimal (maximum or minimum) value of the objective function gives the desired optimal solution of the problem.

Otherwise, draw the dotted line through the origin representing the objective function with $Z = 0$. As $Z$ is increased from zero, this line moves to the right remaining parallel to itself. We go on sliding this line (parallel to itself), till it is farthest away from the origin and passes through only one vertex of the convex region. This is the vertex, where maximum value of $Z$ is attained.

When it is required to minimize $Z$, value of $Z$ is increased till the dotted line passes through the nearest vertex of the convex region.

While solving an LPP graphically, the region of feasible solution is found to be convex, bounded by vertices and edges joining them.

The optimal solution occurs at same vertex. If the optimal solution is not unique, the optimal points are on an edge.

***Example 3.*** *Maximize* $z = 3x + 4y$

*Subject to the constraints*

$$2x + 2y \le 80$$
$$2x + 4y \le 120$$
$$x, y \ge 0$$

**Solution.** First, we find the feasible region which consists of the set of all points whose coordinates simultaneously satisfy all constraints including non-negative restrictions. The above system of inequalities leads to the feasible region shown in figure.

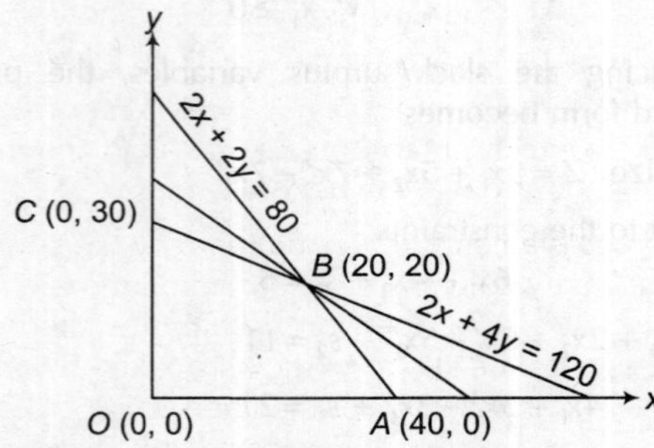


The corner points of the feasible region are $O$ (0, 0), $A$ (40, 0), $B$ (20, 20) and $C$ (0, 30). Note that, the coordinates of the points $B$ have been obtained by solving $2x + 2y = 80$ and $2x + 4y = 120$, simultaneously for $x$ and $y$. The value of the objective function at these corner points is given the following table

| Corner point $(x, y)$ | Value of the objective function $z = 3x + 4y$ |
|---|---|
| $O$ (0, 0) | $3(0) + 4(0) = 0$ |
| $A$ (40, 0) | $3(40) + 4(0) = 120$ |
| $B$ (20, 20) | $3(20) + 4(20) = 140$ |
| $C$ (0, 30) | $3(0) + 4(30) = 120$ |

The maximum value of $z$ is found at the corner point $B$.

Hence, optimum occurs at $x = 20$ and $y = 20$, resulting maximum value of $z$ is 140.

***Example 4.*** *By graphical method, find the solution of linear programming problem*

*Maximize* $z = 3x_1 + 5x_2$

*subject to the constraints*

$$3x_1 + 2x_2 \le 18$$
$$x_1 \le 4,\ x_2 \le 6$$
$$x_1 \ge 0,\ x_2 > 0$$

**Solution.** We draw the graph of $x_1 \le 4$, $x_2 \le 6$, $\frac{x_1}{6} + \frac{x_2}{9} \le 1$

Different point of covex polygon are

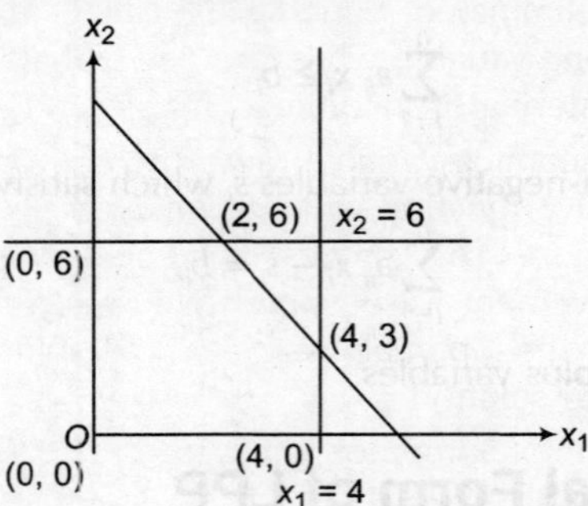


$$(0, 0), (4, 0), (4, 3), (2, 6) \text{ and } (0, 6)$$

Maximum value of $z = 3x_1 + 5x_2$ is at (2, 6)

Hence, $x_1 = 2$, $x_2 = 6$, $z = 36$ is the required solution.

## Simplex Method to Solve LPP

It consists of moving step by step from one vertex to the adjacent one of all the adjacent vertices, the one giving better value of the objective function over that of the preceding vertex, is chosen. This method of jumping from one vertex to the other is then repeated. Since, the number of vertices is finite, the simplex method leads to an optimal vertex in a finite number of steps.

In simplex method, an infinite number of solutions is reduced to a finite number of promising solutions by using the following facts

**(i)** When there are $m$ constraints and $m + n$ (decision and slack) variables ($m \le n$), the starting solution is found by setting $n$ variables equal to zero and then solving the remaining $m$ equations provided the solution exists and is unique.

The '$n$' zero variables are known as non-basic variables while the remaining '$m$' variables are called basic variables and they form a basic solution. This reduces the number of alternatives (basic solutions) for obtaining the optimal solution to ${}^{m+n}C_m$ only.

**(ii)** In an LPP, the variables must always be non-negative. Some of the basic solutions may contain negative variables. Such solutions are called basic infeasible solutions and should not be considered. To achieve this. We start with a basic solution, which is non-negative. The next basic solution must always be non-negative. This is ensured by the feasibility condition. Such a solution is known as basic feasible solution.

If all the variables in the basic feasible solution are non-zero, then it is called non-degenerate solution and if some of the variables are zero, it is called degenerate solution.

**(iii)** A new basic feasible solution may be obtained from the previous one by equating one of the basic variables to zero and replacing it by a new non-basic variables.

The eliminated variable is called the leaving or outgoing variable while the new variable is known as the entering or incoming variable.

The incoming variable must improve the value of the objective function which is ensured by the optimality condition. This process is repeated till no further improvement is possible. The resulting solution is called the optimal basic feasible solution or simply optimal solution.

The simplex method is based on two conditions.

(i) **Feasibility condition** It ensures that, if the starting solution is basic feasible. The subsequent solutions will also be basic feasible.

(ii) **Optimality condition** It ensures that only improved solutions will be obtained.

***Example 5.*** *Using simplex method solve*

*Maximize* $Z = 5x_1 + 3x_2$

*Subject to the constraints*

$$x_1 + x_2 \le 2$$
$$5x_1 + 2x_2 \le 10,$$
$$3x_1 + 8x_2 \le 12,$$
$$x_1, x_2 \ge 0$$

**Solution.** Simplex method consists of the following steps

**Step 1** Check whether the objective function is to be maximized and all *b*'s are positive.

Here, the problem being of maximization type and all *b*'s being $\ge 0$, here this step is not necessary.

**Step 2** Express the problem in the standard form.

Here, by introducing the slack variables $s_1$, $s_2$ and $s_3$, then the problem in standard form becomes

Maximize $Z = 5x_1 + 3x_2 + 0s_1 + 0s_2 + 0s_3$

Subject to the constraints

$$x_1 + x_2 + s_1 + 0s_2 + 0s_3 = 2 \quad \text{...(i)}$$
$$5x_1 + 2x_2 + 0s_1 + s_2 + 0s_3 = 10 \quad \text{...(ii)}$$
$$3x_1 + 8x_2 + 0s_1 + 0s_2 + s_3 = 12 \quad \text{...(iii)}$$
$$x_1, x_2, s_1, s_2, s_3 \ge 0$$

**Step 3** Find an initial basic feasible solution.

Since, there are three equations involving five unknowns and for obtaining a solution, we assign zero values to any two of the variables. We start with a basic solution for which we set $x_1 = 0$ and $x_2 = 0$. (This basic solution corresponds to the origin in the graphical method). Substituting $x_1 = x_2 = 0$ in Eqs. (i), (ii) and (iii), we get the basic solution as

$$s_1 = 2,\ s_2 = 10,\ s_3 = 12$$

Since, all $s_1$, $s_2$ and $s_3$ are positive, then the basic solution is also feasible and non- degenerate.

Therefore, the basic feasible solution is

$x_1 = x_2 = 0$ (non-basic) and $s_1 = 2, s_2 = 10, s_3 = 12$ (basic)

Hence, initial basic feasible solution is given by the following table

| | $c_j$ | ⑤ | 3 | 0 | 0 | 0 | | |
|---|---|---|---|---|---|---|---|---|
| $C_B$ | Basis | $x_1$ | $x_2$ | $s_1$ | $s_2$ | $s_3$ | $b$ | θ |
| 0 | $s_1$ | 1 | 1 | 1 | 0 | 0 | 2 | 2=2/1← |
| 0 | $s_2$ | 5 | 2 | 0 | 1 | 0 | 10 | 2=10/5 |
| 0 | $s_3$ | 3 | 8 | 0 | 0 | 1 | 12 | 4=12/3 |
| | $Z_j = \Sigma\, c_B\, a_{ij}$ | 0 | 0 | 0 | 0 | 0 | 0 | |
| | $C_j = c_j - Z_j$ | 5 ↑ | 3 | 0 | 0 | 0 | | |

[For $x_1$ column $(j = 1)$, $Z_j = \Sigma c_B a_{i1} = 0\,(1) + 0\,(5) + 0\,(3) = 0$ and for $x_2$ column $(j = 2)$, $Z_j = \Sigma c_B a_{i2} = 0\,(1) + 0(2) + 0(8) = 0$

Similarly, for $x_3$ column $1j = 3$

$$Z_j = 0\,(2) + 0\,(10) + 0\,(12) = 0]$$

**Step 4** Apply optimality test.

As $C_j$ is positive under some columns. Hence, the initial basic feasible solution is not optimal (*i.e.*, can be improved) and we proceed to the next step.

**Step 5** (i) Identify the incoming and outgoing variables.

Since, the above table shows that $x_1$ is the incoming variable as its incremental contribution $C_j$ (= 5) is maximum and the column in which it appears is the key column (shown marked by an arrow at the bottom).

Dividing the elements under column *b* by the corresponding elements of key column, we find minimum positive ratio θ is 2 in two rows. We, therefore, arbitrarily choose the row containing $s_1$ as the key row (shown marked by an arrow on its right end). The element at the intersection of key row and the key column *i.e.*, ① is the key element. Therefore, $s_1$ is the outgoing basic variable which will now become non-basic.

Having decided that $x_1$ is to enter the solution, we have tried to find as to what maximum value $x_1$ could have without violating the constraints. So, removing $s_1$, the new basis will contain $x_1$, $s_2$ and $s_3$ as the basic variables.

(ii) Iterate towards the optimal solution,

To transform the initial set of equations with a basic feasible solution into an equivalent set of equations with a different basic feasible solution, we make the key element unity. Now here, the key element being unity, we retain the key row as it is. Then, to make all other elements in key column zero, we subtract proper multiples of key row from the other rows. Now, we subtract, 5 times the elements of key row from the second row and 3 times the elements of key row from the third row. These become the second and the third rows of the next table. We also change, the corresponding value under $c_B$ column from 0 to 5, while replacing $s_1$ by $x_1$ under the basis. Thus, the second basic feasible solution is given by the following table

| | $c_j$ | 5 | 3 | 0 | 0 | 0 | | |
|---|---|---|---|---|---|---|---|---|
| $c_B$ | Basis | $x_1$ | $x_2$ | $s_1$ | $s_2$ | $s_3$ | $b$ | $\theta$ |
| 5 | $x_1$ | 1 | 1 | 1 | 0 | 0 | 2 | |
| 0 | $s_2$ | 0 | $-3$ | $-5$ | 1 | 0 | 0 | |
| 0 | $s_3$ | 0 | 5 | $-3$ | 0 | 1 | 6 | |
| | $Z_j = \Sigma c_B a_{ij}$ | 5 | 5 | 5 | 0 | 0 | 10 | |
| | $C_j = c_j - Z_j$ | 0 | $-2$ | $-5$ | 0 | 0 | | |

As $C_j$ is either zero or negative under all columns, the above table gives the optimal basic feasible solution. This optimal solution is given by $x_1 = 2$, $x_2 = 0$ and maximum $Z = 10$.

## Definition of Primal Dual Problem

**Primal problem** Find $x_1, x_2, \ldots, x_n$, which maximize $z_x = c_1x_1 + c_2x_2 + \ldots + c_nx_n$

Subject to the constraints,

$$\left.\begin{aligned} a_{11}x_1 + a_{12}x_2 + \ldots + a_{1n}x_n &\le b_1 \\ a_{21}x_1 + a_{22}x_2 + \ldots + a_{2n}x_n &\le b_2 \\ &\vdots \\ a_{m1}x_1 + a_{m2}x_2 + \ldots + a_{mn}x_n &\le b_m \\ x_1, x_2, \ldots, x_n &\ge 0 \end{aligned}\right\} \quad \ldots(i)$$

The signs of all parameters ($a$, $b$, $c'$ s) are arbitrary.

The dual of the above problem is obtained by

**(i)** Transposing the coefficient matrix.

**(ii)** Interchanging the role of constant terms and the coefficients of the objective function.

**(iii)** Reverting the inequalities.

**(iv)** Minimizing the objective function instead of maximizing it.

## Dual Problem

Find $w_1, w_2, \ldots, w_m$ which

Minimize $\quad z_w = b_1w_1 + b_2w_2 + \ldots + b_mw_m$

Subject to the constraints,

$$\left.\begin{aligned} a_{11}w_1 + a_{21}w_2 + \ldots + a_{m1}w_m &\ge c_1 \\ a_{12}w_1 + a_{22}w_2 + \ldots + a_{m2}w_m &\ge c_2 \\ &\vdots \\ a_{1n}w_1 + a_{2n}w_2 + \ldots + a_{mn}w_m &\ge c_n \end{aligned}\right\} \quad \ldots(ii)$$

and $\quad w_1, w_2, \ldots, w_m \ge 0$

The problem (ii) is called dual of problem (i). Problem (i) is called primal problem.

In Eq. (ii) $w_1, w_2, \ldots, w_m$ are called dual variables.

## Matrix Form of Symmetric Primal and Its Dual

**Primal problem** Find a column vector $x \in R^n$, which maximizes $Z_x = cX$, $c \in R^n$ (primal objective function) subject to the constraints

$$AX \le b, b \in R^m, x \ge 0$$

where, $A$ is $m \times n$ real matrix.

**Dual problem** Find a column vector $w \in R^m$, which minimizes $Z_w = b^T w$, $b \in R^m$ (dual objective function) Subject to the constraints,

$$A^T w \ge c^T, c \in R^n, w \ge 0,$$

Where, $w = (w_1, w_2, \ldots, w_m)$ and $A^T, b^T, c^T$ are the transpose of $A$, $b$ and $c$ (given in the primal), respectively.

***Example 6.*** *Construct the dual of the LPP*

*Maximize* $\quad Z = 4x_1 + 9x_2 + 2x_3$

*Subject to the constraints*

$$2x_1 + 3x_2 + 2x_3 \le 7$$
$$3x_1 - 2x_2 + 4x_3 = 5$$
$$x_1, x_2, x_3 \ge 0$$

**Solution.** Let $y_1$ and $y_2$ by the dual variables associated with the first and second constraints. Then, the dual problem is

Minimize $\quad W = 7y_1 + 5y_2$

Subject to the constraints

$$2y_1 + 3y_2 \le 4, \; 3y_1 - 2y_2 \le 9,$$
$$2y_1 + 4y_2 \le 2, \; y_1 \ge 0 \text{ and } y_2 \text{ is unrestricted in sign.}$$

***Example 7.*** *Write the dual of the LPP*

*Minimize* $\quad Z = 3x_1 - 2x_2 + 4x_3$

*Subject to the constraints*

$$3x_1 + 5x_2 + 4x_3 \ge 7$$
$$6x_1 + x_2 + 3x_3 \ge 4$$
$$7x_1 - 2x_2 - x_3 \le 10$$
$$x_1 - 2x_2 + 5x_3 \ge 3$$
$$4x_1 + 7x_2 - 2x_3 \ge 2$$
$$x_1, x_2, x_3 \ge 0$$

**Solution.** Since, the problem is of minimization, all constraints should be of $\ge$ type. We multiply the third constraint throughout by $-1$, so that $-7x_1 + 2x_2 + x_3 \ge -10$.

Let $y_1, y_2, y_3, y_4$ and $y_5$ be the dual variables associated with the above five constraints, Then, the dual problem is given by

Maximize $\; W = 7y_1 + 4y_2 - 10y_3 + 3y_4 + 2y_5$

Subject to the constraints

$$3y_1 + 6y_2 - 7y_3 + y_4 + 4y_5 \le 3$$
$$5y_1 + y_2 + 2y_3 - 2y_4 + 7y_5 \le -2$$
$$4y_1 + 3y_2 + y_3 + 5y_4 - 2y_5 \le 4$$
$$y_1, y_2, y_3, y_4, y_5 \ge 0.$$

## Symmetrical Nature of Dual and Primal

(i) The casts associated with the objective function of one problem are just the requirements in the other's set of constraints.

(ii) The constraint coefficient matrix associated with one problem just the requirements is simply the transpose of the constraint coefficient matrix associated with the other.

> ***Note*** Primal is a maximization problem while dual is a minimization problem.

# Queuing Theory

1. Queuing system is a system that functions in following manners

   Input ⟶Service ⟶ Output

   The input is referred as arrival output as departure.
2. The principal anchors in the queuing (theory) system are the customers and the server. If customer arrives, he can get service immediately or have to wait in a queue.
3. The arrival of the customer is referred in terms of inter arrival time and the service is described by service time.
4. Queue size is the number of customers in the queue.
5. Queue discipline is the order in which customers are served.
6. System capacity is the maximum number of customers allowed in the system.
7. The queuing description $a/b/c/d/e/f$

   $a \equiv$ Arrival distribution

   $b \equiv$ Departure (service time) distribution

   $c \equiv$ Number of parallel servers $(1, 2, 3, \ldots, \infty)$

   $d \equiv$ Queue discipline

   $e \equiv$ Maximum number of customers in system

   $f \equiv$ calling source

for (d)

*FCFS* ≡ first come, first served

*LCLS* ≡ last come, last served

*LCFS* ≡ last come, first served

*SIRO* ≡ service in random order

*GD* ≡ general discipline.

For (a and b).

$M \equiv$ Markovian (poisson) arrival or departures distribution (exponential inter arrival or service distribution)

$D \equiv$ Deterministic (constant) time

$E_k \equiv$ Erlang or gamma distribution

$GI \equiv$ General distribution of inter arrival time

$G \equiv$ General distribution of service time

## Performance Measures

Let $C$ be the number of identical servers and arriving unit requires service from any of the server.

Define $p_n(t) = P_r$ {exactly $n$ units in the system at time $t$}. Then,

1. $L_s(t)$ = Expected number of units in the system at time $t$

$$= \sum_{n=1}^{\infty} np_n(t)$$

2. $L_q(t)$ = Expected number of units in a queue at time $t$

$$= \sum_{n=c+1}^{\infty} (n-c)p_n(t)$$

3. $C(t)$ = Expected number of busy servers at time $t$

$$= c\sum_{n=c}^{\infty} p_n(t) + \sum_{n=1}^{c-1} np_n(t)$$

4. $\bar{C}(t)$ = Expected number of servers not busy at time $t$

$$= c - c(t) = \sum_{n=0}^{\infty} (c-n)p_n(t)$$

5. $\sum_{n=0}^{C} p_n(t) = p_r$ {no arrival is waiting for service at time $t$, *i.e.*, no queue}

$$L_s = L_q(t) + C(t)$$

6. For steady state,

$$p_n = \lim_{t\to\infty} p_n(t)$$

7. For steady state,

$W_s$ = Expected waiting time in system

$W_q$ = Expected waiting time in queue

**Little's formulas**

**(i)** $L_s = \lambda W_s$

and $L_q = LW_q$

where, $\lambda$ is an arrival rate at the system.

**(ii)** $W_s = W_q + \dfrac{1}{\mu}$

where, $\mu$ is service rate of the system.

**(iii)** $c = \dfrac{\lambda}{\mu}$

## The Exponential Distribution and its Axioms (Markovian Assumptions)

**Axiom 1** (Memory less property) Let $p_n(t)$ be the probability that $n$ arrivals occurs in interval $(0, t)$. Then, the probability of next arrival in $(0, t+\Delta t)$, $p_{n+1}(t+\Delta t)$ is independent of previous arrival in $(0, t)$ and it depends only on the time interval $(t, t+\Delta t)$.

**Axiom 2** The probability of an arrival in $\Delta t$ is always less than one but greater than zero (*i.e.*, arrival occurs).

**Axiom 3** No more than one arrival occurs in an interval $\Delta t$.

Using axioms 1, 2 and 3, we have

$$p_0(t) = e^{-\lambda t}, \quad t > 0$$

Based on the above axioms, the inter arrival time is exponential with mean $1/\lambda$, where $\lambda$ is the arrival rate given by exponential distribution $f(t) = \lambda e^{-\lambda t}$, $t > 0$.

The pure birth and pure death models. Relation between exponential and poisson distribution.

Pure birth model (Markovian Arrival)

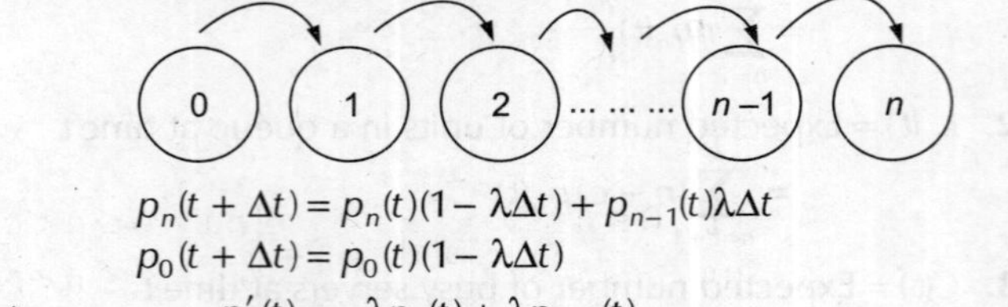

$$p_n(t+\Delta t) = p_n(t)(1-\lambda\Delta t) + p_{n-1}(t)\lambda\Delta t$$

$$p_0(t+\Delta t) = p_0(t)(1-\lambda\Delta t)$$

$$\Rightarrow \quad p_n'(t) = -\lambda p_n(t) + \lambda p_{n-1}(t)$$

$$p_0'(t) = -\lambda p_0(t) = -\lambda e^{-\lambda t}, \quad [\text{As, } p_0(t) = e^{-\lambda t}]$$

And also by recurrence relation

$$p_n(t) = \frac{(\lambda t)^n e^{-\lambda t}}{n!}, \; n = 0, 1, 2, \ldots$$

It is a poisson distribution with mean = $\lambda t$ = variance.

Thus, we have 'if the inter arrival time is exponential with mean $\frac{1}{\lambda}$, then the number of arrivals in time $(0, t)$ is poisson with mean $\lambda t$.'

## Pure Death Model (Markovian Departure)

Let there be $N$ customers at time $t$ and $\mu$ be the departure rate (service rate) with exponential distribution.

Then, $\quad p_N'(t) = -\mu p_N(t)$

$$p_n'(t) = -\mu p_n(t) + \mu p_{n+1}(t), \; 0 < n < N$$

$$p_0'(t) = -\mu p_0(t)$$

These imply, $p_n(t) = \dfrac{(\mu t)^{N-n} e^{\mu t}}{(N-n)!}, \; n = 1, 2, 3, \ldots, N$

(truncated poisson distribution)

$$p_0(t) = 1 - \sum_{n=1}^{N} p_n(t)$$

## Steady State Solution for *M*/*M*/1 Queuing Model

In $M/M/1$ queuing model arrival and service time distributions are Markovian (poisson) distributed (*i.e.*, arrival and service time distribution are exponential), number of server is one, the system size is infinite.

Let $\lambda$ be the arrival rate, $\mu$ be the service rate and $p_n$ probability of $n$ customers in the system.

For steady state

**1.** $p_{n+1} = \dfrac{\lambda+\mu}{\mu} p_n - \dfrac{1}{\mu} p_{n-1}, \; n = 1, 2, 3, \ldots$

$$p_1 = \frac{1}{\mu} p_0$$

It gives, $\quad p_n = \left(\dfrac{\lambda}{\mu}\right)^n p_0 = \rho^n p_0$

where, $\quad \rho = \dfrac{\lambda}{\mu}$ is known as traffic intensity.

Here, $\displaystyle\sum_{n=0}^{\infty} p_n = 1 \Rightarrow p_0 = \frac{1}{\sum_{n=0}^{\infty} \rho^n}$

**2.** As, $\displaystyle\sum_{n=0}^{\infty} \rho^n = \frac{1}{1-\rho}, \; (\rho < 1)$ (being geometric series)

So, $p_0 = 1 - \rho$

**3.** The steady state solution for $M/M/1$ is

$$p_n = \rho^n(1-\rho), \; \rho = \frac{\lambda}{\mu} < 1$$

**4.** The performance measures for $M/M/1$ model are

$$L_s = \sum_{n=0}^{\infty} n p_n = \frac{\rho}{1-\rho}$$

$$W_s = \frac{L_s}{\lambda} = \frac{1}{\mu(1-\rho)}$$

$$W_q = W_s - \frac{1}{\mu} = \frac{\rho}{\mu(1-\rho)}$$

$$L_q = \lambda W_q = \frac{\rho^2}{1-\rho}$$

$$C = L_s - L_q = r$$

## Steady State Solution for *M*/*M*/1/*N* Queuing Model

In $M/M/1/N$ queuing model arrival and service time distribution are Markovian, the number of service channels is one and system capacity in $N$ (finite).

Let $\lambda$ be an (expected) arrival rate, $\mu$ the service rate and $p_n$ = probability (there are $n$ customers in the system).

For steady state

**1.** Probability that there is no customer in the system

$$p_0 = \begin{cases} \dfrac{1-(\lambda/\mu)}{1-(\lambda/\mu)^{N+1}}, & \dfrac{\lambda}{\mu} \neq 1 \\[2ex] \dfrac{1}{1+N}, & \lambda = \mu \end{cases}$$

**2.** Probability that there are $n$ customers in the system

$$p_n = \begin{cases} \left(\dfrac{\lambda}{\mu}\right)^n p_0, & \text{if } n \le N \\ 0 & \text{if } n > N \end{cases}.$$

**3.** Expected number of customers in the queue

$$L_s = \sum_{n=0}^{N} n p_n$$

$$= \begin{cases} \dfrac{\left(\dfrac{\lambda}{\mu}\right)\left[1-(N+1)\left(\dfrac{\lambda}{\mu}\right)^N + N\left(\dfrac{\lambda}{\mu}\right)^{N+1}\right]}{\left(1-\dfrac{\lambda}{\mu}\right)\left(1-\left(\dfrac{\lambda}{\mu}\right)^{N+1}\right)}, & \text{if } \lambda \neq \mu \\[3ex] \dfrac{N}{2} & \text{if } \lambda = \mu \end{cases}$$

**4.** $W_s = \frac{L_s}{\lambda}$

**5.** $L_q = \lambda W_q$

**6.** $W_q = W_s - \frac{1}{\mu}$

**7.** $C = L_s - L_q$

# Steady State Solutions for *M*/*M*/*C* Queuing Models

In *M*/*M*/*C* queuing model arrival and service time are Markovianly (exponentially) distributed, the number of service channels are *c* and the system capacity is infinite. Let $\lambda$ be the arrival rate, $\mu$ be the service rate per channel, and $p_n$ = probability that there are *n* customers in the system

$p = \frac{\lambda}{\mu}$, is the utilization factor.

For steady state

**1.** $$p_{n+1} = \frac{\lambda_n + \mu_n}{\mu_n} p_n - \frac{\lambda_n}{\mu_n} p_{n-1}, \; n \ge 1$$

$$p_1 = \frac{\lambda_n}{\mu_n} p_0$$

where, $$\mu_n = \begin{cases} n\mu, & \text{if } 1 \le n < c \\ c\mu, & \text{if } n \ge c \end{cases}$$

and $\lambda_n = \lambda$

**2.** Probability that there are *n* customers in the system, $p_n$ is given by

$$p_n = \begin{cases} \left(\frac{\lambda}{\mu}\right)^n \cdot p_0, & \text{if } 1 \le n \le c \\ \left(\frac{\lambda}{\mu}\right)^n \cdot \frac{p_0}{(Lc)(c)^{n-c}}, & \text{if } n > c \end{cases}$$

**3.** Probability that there is no customer in the system

$$p_0 = \left[\sum_{n=0}^{c-1} \frac{(\lambda/\mu)^n}{n!} + \frac{(\lambda/\mu)^c}{c!} \cdot \frac{1}{\left(1 - \frac{1}{c} \cdot \frac{\lambda}{\mu}\right)}\right]^{-1}$$

**4.** Expected number of customers in the queue

$$L_q = \sum_{n=0}^{\infty} (n-c) p_n = \frac{\rho^{c+1}}{c-1!(c-\rho)^2} p_0$$

**5.** Expected number of customers in the system

$$L_s = L_q + \frac{\rho}{c}, \; \rho < 1$$

# Steady State Solution for *M*/*M*/*c*/*N* Queuing Model

In *M*/*M*/*c*/*N* queuing model arrival and service time are Markovian, the number of service channels are *c* and system capacity is finite.

Let $\lambda_n$ be the arrival rate, $\mu$ be the service rate per channel and $p_n$ = Probability that there are *n* customers in the system. For steady state

**1.** $$p_{n+1} = \frac{\lambda_n + \mu_n}{\mu_n} p_n - \frac{\lambda_n}{\mu_n} p_{n-1}, \; n \ge 1$$

$$p_1 = \frac{\lambda}{\mu} p_0$$

where, $$\lambda_n = \begin{cases} 1, & 0 \le n \le N \\ 0, & n > N \end{cases} \quad \text{and} \quad \mu_n = \begin{cases} n\mu, & 0 \le n < c \\ c\mu, & c \le n < N \end{cases}$$

**2.** Probability that there are *n* customers in the system is

$$p_n = \begin{cases} \frac{(\lambda/\mu)^n}{n!} p_0, & 0 \le n < c \\ \frac{1}{c!\, c^{n-c}}, & c \le n \le N \end{cases}$$

**3.** Probability that there are no customers in the system,

$$p_0 = \begin{cases} \left[\sum_{n=0}^{c-1} \frac{(\lambda/\mu)^n}{n!} + \frac{\left(\frac{\lambda}{\mu}\right)^c \left(1 - \left(\frac{\lambda}{c\mu}\right)^{N-c+1}\right)}{c!\left(1 - \frac{\lambda}{c\mu}\right)}\right]^{-1}, & \frac{\lambda}{c\mu} \ne 1 \\ \left[\sum_{n=0}^{c-1} \frac{(\lambda/\mu)^n}{n!} + \frac{(\lambda/\mu)^c}{c!}(N - c + 1)\right]^{-1}, & \frac{\lambda}{c\mu} = 1 \end{cases}$$

**4.** Expected number of customers in the queue

$$L_q = \sum_{n=0}^{N} (n-c) p_n$$

$$= \frac{(\lambda/\mu)^{c+1}}{c-1!\left(c - \frac{\lambda}{\mu}\right)^2} \left[1 - \left(\frac{\lambda}{c\mu}\right)^{N-c+1} - (N-c+1)\left(1 - \frac{\lambda}{c\mu}\right)\left(\frac{\lambda}{c\mu}\right)^{N-c}\right] p_0$$

when $\frac{\lambda}{c\mu} = 1$, then

$$L_q = \left(\frac{\lambda}{\mu}\right)^c \frac{(N-c)(N-c+1)}{2c!} p_0$$

# Model (*M*/*G*/*I*) : ($\infty$/*GD*)

In this model, *M* $\rightarrow$ Poisson arrivals,

*G* $\rightarrow$ general output distribution,

$\infty \rightarrow$ waiting room capacity is infinite

*GD* $\rightarrow$ general service discipline such as *FCFS*, *LCFS*, *SIRO*, etc.

To determine the mean queue length and mean waiting time for this system.

Let $f(t) \rightarrow$ pdf (Probability density function) of service time distribution with mean $E(t)$ and var $(t)$.

$n \rightarrow$ number of customers in the system just after a customer departs

$t \rightarrow$ time to serve the customer following the one already departed.

$k \rightarrow$ number of new arrivals during time $t$

$n' \rightarrow$ number of customers left behind the next departing customer.

| | Queue | Service | Departure |
|---|---|---|---|
| $T$ | $n-1$ | $(j+1\text{st})$ | $j+h$ |
| $T+t$ | $n-2$ | $(j+2\text{nd})$ | $(j+1\text{st})$ |

$$n' = \begin{cases} k & , \text{ if } n = 0 \\ (n-1)+k, & \text{if } n > 0 \end{cases} \quad (k = 0, 1, 2, \ldots)$$

Using $\delta = \begin{cases} 1, & \text{if } n = 0 \\ 0, & \text{if } n > 0 \end{cases}$

$$n' = n - 1 + \delta + k$$

$$\Rightarrow \quad E(n') = E(n) + E(\delta) + E(k) - 1$$

In steady state, $E(n') = E(n)$

So, $0 = E(\delta) + E(k) - 1$

$$\Rightarrow \quad E(\delta) = E(k) - 1$$

$$E(n) = \frac{E(k^2) + E(k) - 2E^2(k)}{2[1 - E(k)]}$$

Since, the arrivals in time $t$ follow the poisson distribution,

$$E\left(\frac{k}{t}\right) = \lambda t, \quad E\left(\frac{k^2}{t}\right) = (\lambda t)^2 + \lambda t$$

$$V\left(\frac{k}{t}\right) = E\left(\frac{k^2}{t}\right) - E^2\left(\frac{k}{t}\right)$$

So,
$$E(k) = \lambda\, E(t)$$
$$E(k^2) = \lambda^2 V(t) + \lambda^2 E^2(t) + \lambda E(t)$$

And
$$L_S = E(n) = \lambda E(t) + \frac{\lambda^2[E^2(t) + V(t)]}{2[1 - \lambda E(t)]}$$

This is called the Pollaczek khintchive $(R-K)$ formula.

$$\lambda E(t) < 1$$

Let $a = M$, then

$$\text{var}(t) = \frac{1}{\mu^2}, \; E(t) = \frac{1}{\mu},$$

$$L_S = \frac{\lambda}{\mu} + \frac{\lambda^2[(1/\mu^2) + (1/\mu^2)]}{2\left(1 - \frac{\lambda}{\mu}\right)}$$

$$L_S = \rho + \frac{2\rho^2}{2(1-\rho)} = \frac{\rho}{(1-\rho)}$$

It is same as for $(M/M/I)$ model.

Efficiency of a queuing system

$$= \frac{W_q}{E(t)} = \frac{\text{Average waiting time in queue}}{\text{Average service time}}$$

$$= \frac{\text{Useless time}}{\text{Useful time}}$$

Thus, smaller the ratio, better will be the system.

## Inventory Problems

**(i) Inventory control** It is the function of directing the movement of goods through the entire manufacturing cycle from the requisitioning of raw materials to the inventory of finished goods in an orderly manner to meet the objectives of maximum customer service with minimum investment and efficient (low cost) plant operation.

**(ii)** Raw material inventory, *i.e.*, raw materials which are kept in stock for use in the product of goods.

**(iii)** Work in process inventory, *i.e.*, semi-finished goods or goods in process which are stored during the production process.

**(iv)** Finished goods inventory, *i.e.*, finished goods a waiting shipment from the factory.

**(v)** Inventory also include: furniture, machinery, fixtures etc.

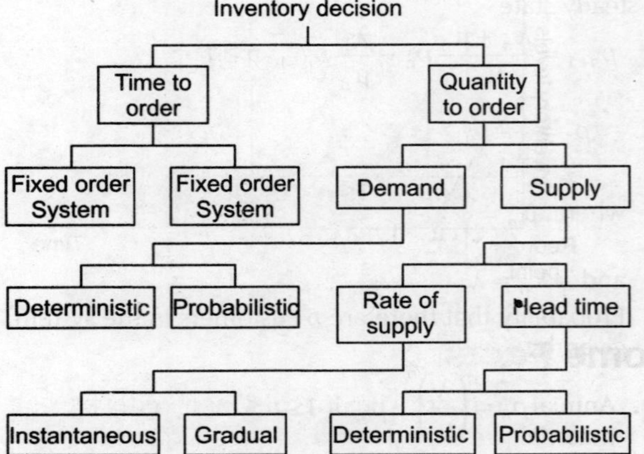


## Basic Characteristic

1. **Inventory costs**
   - **(i)** Purchasing cost — It depends upon price per unit.
   - **(ii)** Setup cost — Fixed prices associated with order.
   - **(iii)** Holding cost — Depends on the maintenance, storage and handling units.
   - **(iv)** Storage cost — Penalty incurred with shortage of items.
   - **(v)** Total inventory cost — Purchasing cost + setup cost + holding cost + shortage cost.
2. **Order cycle** The time interval between the placement of two successive orders. It may be fixed or based on review.
3. **Lead time** The time between ordering a replenishment of an item and actually receiving of the item. When lead time is zero, it is referred to as instantaneous delivery.
4. **Stock replenishment** Instant or uniform.
5. **Time horizon** Period over which inventory level is controlled. It may be finite or infinite.
6. **Maximum stock** Allowable stock inventory.

7. **Buffer stock** Minimal stock inventory maintained.
8. **Reordering level** A point fixed between maximum and minimum stock level to place an order.
9. **Reorder quantity** The quantity of replacement of order.
10. **Economic order** quantity (EOQ) The order quantity which minimizes the cost of inventory.

# Model I

## Classic EOQ Model (With no Shortage and Instant Replenishment)

An inventory model with constant rate demand, with instantaneous order replenishment and no shortage.

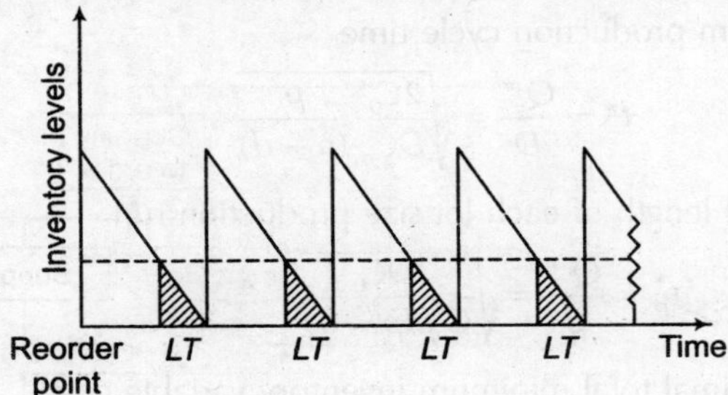


## Some Facts

1. Annual demand, carrying cost and ordering cost for a material are known with certainty and is constant with time.
2. Average inventory level for a material is order quantity divided by two.
3. Inventory is replenished immediately as the stock level is almost zero.
4. Lead time is known as well as fixed and is equal to or greater than zero.

Here,
$D$ = Annual demand for a material (units per year)
$Q$ = Quantity of material ordered at each order point (units per order)
$C_n$ = Cost of carrying (or holding) one unit in inventory for one year (₹ per unit per year)
$C_0$ = Average cost of completing an order for material
TSC = Total annual stocking costs for a material.

## Cost Formulas

1. Annual carrying (or holding) cost
= Average inventory level × Carrying cost per unit per year

$$= \frac{Q}{2} C_n$$

2. Annual ordering cost = Number of orders placed per year × ordering cost per order

$$= \frac{\text{(Annual demand) (ordering cost per order)}}{\text{(Number of units in each order)}} = \frac{D}{Q} \cdot C_0$$

3. Total annual cost = Annual carrying cost + Annual ordering cost

$$= \left(\frac{Q}{2}\right) C_n + \left(\frac{D}{Q}\right) C_0$$

## Economic Order Quantity Formulas

The optimal order quantity occurs, when the annual ordering costs for a material are exactly equal to the annual carrying cost. So,

$$\frac{Q}{2} C_n = \frac{D}{Q} C_0$$

$$\Rightarrow \quad Q^2 = \frac{2DC_0}{C_n} \Rightarrow Q = \sqrt{\frac{2DC_0}{C_n}}$$

So, EOQ is $Q^k = \sqrt{\frac{2DC_0}{C_n}}$

This formula is due to RM Willson.
Average inventory level = $Q/2$
The optimal number of orders or manufacturing runs per year ($N^*$) is given by $N^* = \frac{D}{Q^*} = \sqrt{\frac{DC_n}{2C_0}}$

The optimal time between two successive orders (inventory cycle time)

$$T^* = \frac{\text{Number of working days in a year}}{N^*}$$

Minimum total yearly inventory variable cost

$$TC(Q^*) = \sqrt{2DC_0C_n}$$

# Model II

## Classic EOQ Model (With no Shortage and Gradual Deliveries)

Inventory model with constant rate of demand, with gradual deliveries and no shortage.

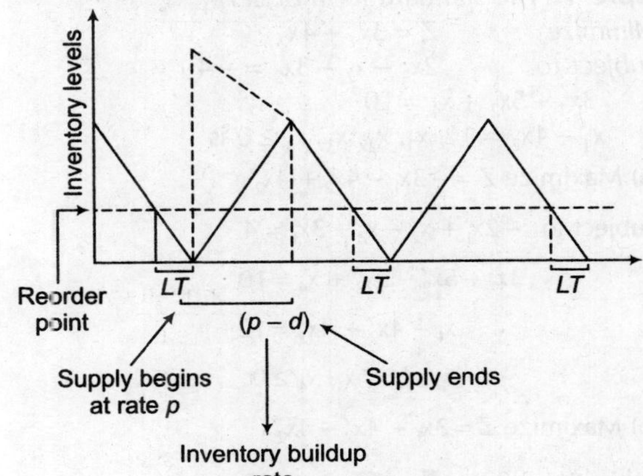

## Assumptions

1. Annual demand, carrying cost and ordering cost for a material can be estimated with certainty.
2. No safety stock is utilized, materials are supplied at a uniform rate ($p$) and used at a uniform rate ($d$) and materials are entirely used up, where the next order begins to arrive.
3. Volume discounts do not exist.
4. Supply or production rate $p$, is greater than usage (or demand) rate ($d$).

All of the definitions of Model I apply also to model II. Additionally,

$d$ = Rate at which units are used out of inventory (units per time period)

$p$ = Rate at which units are supplied to inventory (same as $d$)

Maximum inventory level $= (p-d) \times \dfrac{Q}{p}$

= (Inventory accumulation rate) × (period of delivery)

Minimum inventory level = 0

Average inventory level

$$= \frac{1}{2}\left(\frac{Q}{p}\cdot(p-d)+0\right) = \frac{Q}{2}\frac{(p-d)}{p}$$

Annual inventory carrying (or holding) cost

$$= \frac{Q}{2}\frac{(p-d)}{p}C_n$$

Annual ordering (or setup) cost $= \dfrac{D}{Q}C_0$

Total annual stocking (or variable) cost

$$= TSC = \frac{Q}{2}\frac{(p-d)}{p}C_n + \frac{D}{Q}C_0$$

## Economic Order Quantity Formula

The optimal order quantity occurs when the annual ordering costs are exactly equal to annual carrying costs.

$$\Rightarrow \quad \frac{Q}{2}\frac{(p-d)}{p}C_n = \frac{D}{Q}C_0$$

$$\Rightarrow \quad Q^2 = \frac{2DC_0}{C_n}\frac{p}{(p-d)}$$

$$\Rightarrow \quad Q^* = \sqrt{\frac{2DC_0}{C_n}\cdot\frac{p}{(p-d)}}$$

where, $EOQ = Q^*$

The optimal number of production run per year

$$N^* = \frac{D}{Q^*} = \sqrt{\frac{DC_n(p-d)}{2C_0 p}}$$

Optimum production cycle time

$$t^* = \frac{Q^*}{D} = \sqrt{\frac{2C_0}{DC_n}\frac{p}{(p-d)}}$$

Optimal length of each lot size production run

$$t_p^* = \frac{Q^*}{p} = \sqrt{\frac{2DC_0}{C_n p(p-d)}}$$

The optimal total minimum inventory variable cost

$$TC(Q^*) = \sqrt{2DC_0C_n\frac{(p-d)}{p}}$$

# SOLVED EXAMPLES

## Type I (*Only one correct option*)

***Example 1.*** *The standard form of LPP*

*Minimize* $Z = 3x_1 + 4x_2$

*Subject to* $2x_1 - x_2 - 3x_3 = -4$

$3x_1 + 5x_2 + x_4 = 10$

$x_1 - 4x_2 = 12,\ x_1, x_2, x_3, x_4 \geq 0$ is

(a) Maximize $Z = -3x_1 - 4x_2' + 4x_2''$

Subject to $-2x_1 + x_2' - x_2'' + 3x_3 = 4$

$3x_1 + 5x_2' - 5x_2'' + x_4 = 10$

$x_1 - 4x_2' + 4x_2'' = 12$

$x_1, x_2', x_2'' x_3, x_4 \geq 0$

(b) Maximize $Z = 3x_1 + 4x_2' - 4x_2''$

Subject to $2x_1 + x_2' - x_2'' + 3x_3 = 10$

$3x_1 + 5x_2' + 5x_2'' + x_4 = 4$

$x_1 + 4x_2' - 4x_2'' = 12$

$x_1, x_2', x_2'', x_3, x_4 \geq 0$

(c) Maximize $Z = 3x_1 - 4x_2' + 4x_2''$

Subject to $2x_1 + x_2' - x_2'' - 3x_3 = 4$

$3x_1 + 5x_2' - 5x_2'' + x_4 = 10$

$x_1 - 4x_2' + 4x_2'' = 12$

$x_1, x_2', x_2'', x_3, x_4 \geq 0$

(d) None of the above

**Solution.** (a) Here, $x_3$, $x_4$ are the slack/surplus variables and $x_1, x_2$ are the decision variables. As $x_2$ is unrestricted, let $x_2 = x_2' - x_2''$, where $x_2', x_2'' \geq 0$.

Hence, the problem in standard form is

Maximize $\quad Z'(= -Z) = -3x_1 - 4x_2' + 4x_2''$

Subject to $\quad -2x + x_2' - x_2'' + 3x_3 = 4$

$$3x_1 + 5x_2' - 5x_2'' + x_4 = 10$$

$$x_1 - 4x_2' + 4x_2'' = 12$$

$$x_1, x_2', x_2'', x_3, x_4 \geq 0$$

***Example 2.*** *The maximum value of $Z = 2x + 3y$ subject to the constraints $x + y \leq 30$, $y \geq 3$, $0 \leq y \leq 12$, $x - y \geq 0$, and $0 \leq x \leq 20$ is*

(a) 11 (b) 72 (c) 33 (d) 36

**Solution.** (b) Any point $(x, y)$ satisfying the conditions $x \geq 0, y \geq 0$ lies in the first quadrant only. Also, since $x + y \leq 30$, $y \geq 3$, $y \leq 12$, $x \geq y$ and $x \leq 20$, the desired point $(x, y)$ lies within the convex region *ABCDE* (shown shaded in figure, Its vertices are $A(3, 3), B(20, 3), C(20, 10), D(18, 12)$ and $E(12, 12)$.

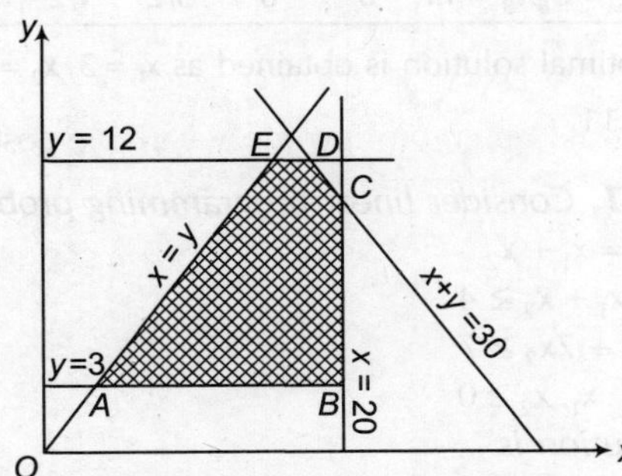


The values of $Z$ at these five vertices are

$Z(A) = 15$, $Z(B) = 49$, $Z(C) = 70$, $Z(D) = 72$ and $Z(E) = 60$.

Since, the maximum value of $Z$ is 72 which occurs at the vertex $D$, the solution to the LPP is $x = 18$, $y = 12$ and maximum $Z = 72$.

**Directions** (Q. Nos. 3-8) *Given,*

*Minimize* $\quad -3x_1 - 2x_2,$

*Subject to* $\quad x_1 - x_2 \geq 1, y_1$

$$-3x_1 + 2x_2 \geq -2, y_2$$

$x_1 \geq 0$, $x_2$ *is unrestricted in sign.*

***Example 3.*** *In the dual, we have*

(a) Min $y_0 = y_1 - 2y_2$ (b) Max $y_0 = y_1 - 2y_2$

(c) Min $-3x_1 - 2x_2$ (d) None of these

***Example 4.*** *The optimal solution is*

(a) $x_1 = 10, x_2 = -11$ (b) $x_1 = 1, x_2 = 2$

(c) $x_1 = 0, x_2 = -1$ (d) $x_1 = x_2 = -1$

***Example 5.*** *The min $-3x_1 - 2x_2$ is*

(a) 12 (b) 20 (c) 2 (d) 5

***Example 6.*** *The dual variables are*

(a) positive (b) negative

(c) non-negative (d) non-positive

***Example 7.*** *In the dual of the given primal*

(a) $y_1 - 3y_2 \leq -3x_1$ (b) $y_1 - 3y_2 \geq -3x_1$

(c) $y_1 - 3y_2 = 0$ (d) None of these

***Example 8.*** *In the dual of above primal is*

(a) $-y_1 + 2y_2 = -2x_2$ (b) $-y_1 + 2y_2 > -2x_2$

(c) $-y_1 + 2y_2 < -2x_2$ (d) None of these

**Solutions.** (Q. Nos. 3-8) **3.** (b), **4.** (c), **5.** (c), **6.** (c), **7.** (a)

**8.** (a) The dual is

Max $\quad y_0 = y_1 - 2y_2$

Subject to $\quad y_1 - 3y_2 \leq -3, x_1$

$$-y_1 + 2y_2 = -2, x_2,$$

$$y_1, y_2 \geq 0$$

For solving the above by simplex method, we must make the right hand sides of constraints non-negative. Thus, the above becomes

Max $\quad y_0 = y_1 - 2y_2$

Subject to the constraints $-y_1 + 3y_2 - s_1 + R_1 = 3, -x_1$

$$y_1 - 2y_2 + R_2 = 2, -x_2$$

$$y_1, y_2 \geq 0$$

Observe that both $x_1$ and $x_2$ become $-x_1$ and $-x_2$. Finally, $C_B^T B^{-1}$ of optimal primal table will give $-x_1$ and $-x_2$. We solve above by two phase method. We have

| Basis | $y_1$ | $y_2$ | $s_1$ | $R_1$ | $R_2$ | Sol |
|---|---|---|---|---|---|---|
| $r_0$ | 0 | 1 | $-1$ | 0 | 0 | 5 |
| $R_1$ | $-1$ | 3 | $-1$ | 1 | 0 | 3 |
| $R_2$ | 1 | 2 | 0 | 0 | 1 | 2 |
| $r_0$ | $\frac{1}{3}$ | 0 | $-\frac{2}{3}$ | $-\frac{1}{3}$ | 0 | 4 |
| $y_2$ | $-\frac{1}{3}$ | 1 | $-\frac{1}{3}$ | $\frac{1}{3}$ | 0 | 1 |
| $R_2$ | $\frac{1}{3}$ | 0 | $-\frac{2}{3}$ | $\frac{2}{3}$ | 1 | 4 |
| $y_0$ | 0 | 0 | 0 | 0 | 1 | 2 |
| $y_2$ | 0 | 1 | $-1$ | 1 | 1 | 5 |
| $y_1$ | 1 | 0 | $-2$ | 2 | 3 | 12 |

The optimal solution of dual (that is of given problem)

$$= C_B^T B^{-1} \text{ of optimal primal problem}$$

$$= (-2, 1)\begin{bmatrix} 1 & 1 \\ 2 & 3 \end{bmatrix} = (0, 1)$$

Thus, $\quad (0, 1) = (-x_1, -x_2)$

Hence, the optimal solution of given problem is $x_1 = 0$, $x_2 = -1$ and min $x_0 = 2$.

***Example 9.*** *Consider the LP problem*

*Maximize* $x_1 + x_2$

*subject to* $x_1 - 2x_2 \le 10$

$x_2 - 2x_1 \le 10$

$x_1, x_2 \ge 0$

*Then,*

(a) the LP problem admits an optimal solution
(b) the LP problem is unbounded
(c) the LP problem admits no feasible solution
(d) the LP problem admits a unique feasible solution

**Solution.** (b) Objective function Max $x_1 + x_2$

constraints $x_1 - 2x_2 \le 10$

$x_2 - 2x_1 \le 10$

$x_1, x_2 \ge 0$

Graphically drawing

$$x_1 - 2x_2 = 10$$

$$x_2 - 2x_1 = 10$$

We get

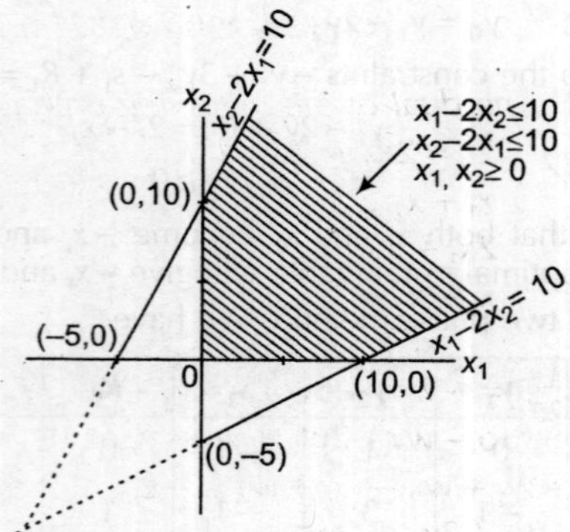


The shaded region is the feasible region which is unbounded. Thus, the LP problem is unbounded.

***Example 10.*** *Consider the linear programming problem*

*Maximize* $z = 3x_1 + 2x_2$

*Subject to* $x_1 + x_2 \le 4$

$x_1 - x_2 \le 2$

$x_1, x_2 \ge 0$

*Then, its solution is*

(a) $x_1 = 3, \quad x_2 = 1$, Max $z = 11$
(b) $x_1 = 1, \quad x_2 = 3$, Max $z = 10$
(c) $x_1 = 2, \quad x_2 = 1$, Max $z = 11$
(d) $x_1 = 1, \quad x_2 = 2$, Max $z = 10$

**Solution.** (a) Introducing the slack (or surplus) variables $S_1, S_2$ the problem takes the form

Maximize $z = 3x_1 + 2x_2 + 0S_1 + 0S_2$

subject to $x_1 + x_2 + S_1 + 0S_2 = 4$

$x_1 - x_2 + 0S_1 + S_2 = 2$

$x_1, x_2, S_1, S_2 \ge 0$

Putting $x_1 = 0, x_2 = 0$ in the above equations, we get

$$S_1 = 4, \quad S_2 = 2$$

Thus, initial basic feasible solution is

$$x_1 = 0, x_2 = 0, S_1 = 4, S_2 = 2$$

**Simplex Computation**

| | | $C_j$ | 3 | 2 | 0 | 0 | |
|---|---|---|---|---|---|---|---|
| Basic variable | $C_B$ | $X_B$ | $x_1$ | $x_2$ | $S_1$ | $S_2$ | Min Ratio $(X_B/X_K)$ |
| $S_1$ | 0 | 4 | 1 | 1 | 1 | 0 | 4/1 |
| $S_2$ | 0 | 2 | 1 | $-1$ | 0 | 1 | 2/1 ← min |
| $x_1 = x_2 = 0$ | $z = C_BX_B = 0$ | | $-3^*$↑ | $-2$ | 0 | 0 ↓ | $\Delta_j = z_j - C_j$ |
| $S_1$ | 0 | 2 | 0 | 2 | 1 | $-1$ | 2/2 min ← |
| $x_1$ | 3 | 2 | 1 | $-1$ | 0 | 1 | — |
| $x_2 = S_2 = 0$ | $Z = C_BX_B = 6$ | | 0 | $-5^*$ ↑ | 0 ↓ | 3 | ← $\Delta_j$ |
| $x_2$ | 2 | 1 | 0 | 1 | 1/2 | $-1/2$ | |
| $x_1$ | 3 | 3 | 1 | 0 | 1/2 | 1/2 | |
| $S_1 = S_2 = 0$ | $z = C_BX_B = 11$ | | 0 | 0 | 5/2 | 1/2 | $\Delta_j \ge 0$ |

Thus, optimal solution is obtained as $x_1 = 3, x_2 = 1$

Max $z = 11$

***Example 11.*** *Consider linear programming problem*

*Minimize* $z = x_1 + x_2$

*Subject to* $2x_1 + x_2 \ge 4$

$x_1 + 7x_2 \ge 7$

$x_1, x_2 \ge 0$

*Then, its solution is*

(a) $x_1 = \frac{21}{13}, x_2 = \frac{10}{13}$, Max $z = \frac{31}{13}$

(b) $x_1 = \frac{10}{13}, x_2 = \frac{21}{13}$, Max $z = \frac{13}{31}$

(c) $x_1 = \frac{20}{13}, x_2 = \frac{5}{13}$, Max $z = \frac{31}{13}$

(d) None of the above

**Solution.** (a) Transforming the problem into maximization problem, we get

Max $z' = $ Max $(-z) = -x_1 - x_2$, $z' = -z$

such that $2x_1 + x_2 \ge 4$

$x_1 + 7x_2 \ge 7$

On introducing surplus variables $x_3$ and $x_4$, $(x_3 \ge 0, x_4 \ge 0)$ and artificial variables $a_1, a_2$, it becomes

$$2x_1 + x_2 - x_3 + a_1 = y$$

$$x_1 + 7x_2 - x_4 + a_2 = 7$$

**Phase 1** Put $x_1 = 0, x_2 = 0, x_3 = 0, x_4 = 0$

We get, $a_1 = 4, a_2 = 7$

**Phase 1 Simplex table**

| | | 0 | 0 | 0 | 0 | – 1 | – 1 |
|---|---|---|---|---|---|---|---|
| Basic variable | $X_B$ | $X_1$ | $X_2$ | $X_3$ | $X_4$ | $A_1$ | $A_2$ |
| $a_1$ | 4 | 2 | 1 | – 1 | 0 | 1 | 0 |
| $\leftarrow a_2$ | 7 | 1 | 7 | 0 | – 1 | 0 | 1↓ |
| $a_1$ | 3 | 13/7 | 0 | – 1 | 1/7 | 1 | – 1/7 |
| $x_2$ | 1 | 1/7 | 1 | 0 | – 1/7 ↑ | 0 ↓ | 1/7 |
| $x_4$ | 21 | 13 | 0 | – 7 | 1 | 7 | × |
| $x_2$ | 4 | 2 | 1 | – 1 | 0 | 1 | × |

Thus, initial basic feasible solution is

$$x_1 = 0, x_2 = 4, x_3 = 0, x_4 = 21$$

Phase 2 Simplex table

| | | $C_j$ | – 1 | – 1 | 0 | 0 | |
|---|---|---|---|---|---|---|---|
| Basic Variable | $C_B$ | $X_B$ | $X_1$ | $X_2$ | $X_3$ | $X_4$ | Min Ratio |
| $x_4$ | 0 | 21 | 13 | 0 | – 7 | 1 | 21/13 |
| $x_2$ | – 1 | 4 | 2 | 1 | – 1 | 0 | 4/2 |
| | $z' = -4$ | | – 1 | 0 | 1 | 0 | $\leftarrow \Delta_j$ |
| $x_1$ | – 1 | 21/13 | 1 | 0 | – 7/13 | 1/13 | |
| $x_2$ | – 1 | 10/13 | 0 | 1 | 1/110 | 2/13 | |
| | $z' = -31/13$ | | 0 | 0 | 6/13 | 1/13 | $\leftarrow \Delta_j \geq 0$ |

Thus, desired solution

$$x_1 = \frac{21}{13}, x_2 = \frac{10}{13}, \text{Max } z = \frac{31}{13}$$

**Directions** (Q. Nos. 12-13) *An aircraft uses rivets at an approximately constant rate of* 5000 kg *per year. The rivets cost ₹ 20 per kg and the company personnel estimate that it costs ₹ 20 to replace an order, and the carrying cost of inventary is* 10% *per year.*

***Example 12.*** *How frequently should orders for rivets be placed and what quantities should be ordered for?*

(a) 5 orders, 1000 units
(b) 10 orders 2000 units
(c) 15 orders 1500 units
(d) 10 orders 1000 units

***Example 13.*** *If the actual costs are ₹ 500 to plane an order and 15% for carrying cost, the optimum policy would change. How much is the company losing per year because of imperfect cost information.*

(a) 873 units
(b) 1873 units
(c) 1000 units
(d) 1500 units

**Solution.** (Q. Nos. 12-13)

Here, we are given

Demand rate ($D$) = 5000 kg per year

Cost ($C$) = ₹ 20 per kg

Inventory carrying rate $I$ = 10% per year

Inventory carrying cost ($C_h$)

$= I \times C = 20 \times 0.1 =$ ₹ 2 per year

Ordering cost $C_0$ = ₹ 200 per order.

**12.** (a) $Q^*(EOQ) = \sqrt{\frac{2DC_0}{C_h}} = \sqrt{\frac{2 \times 5000 \times 200}{2}}$

$= 1000$ units

Optimum number of orders per year

$$N^* = \frac{D}{Q^*} = \frac{5000}{1000} = 5 \text{ orders}$$

**13.** (b) Total minimum variable inventory cost corresponding to $Q^*$ (= 1000 units)

$= TVC^* = \sqrt{2DC_0C_h} = \sqrt{2 \times 5000 \times 200 \times 2}$

$= 2 \times 1000 = 2000$

If $C_0$ = ₹ 500 per order and $I = 0.15$

Then, $Q^* = \sqrt{\frac{2 \times 5000 \times 500}{20 \times 0.15}} = 1291$ units

and $TVC^* = \sqrt{2DC_0 \cdot C_h}$

(Here $C_h = I \times C = 0.15 \times 20 = 3.0$)

So, $TVC^* = \sqrt{2 \times 5000 \times 500 \times 3} = 3873$

So the loss per year due to imperfect information

$= 3873 - 2000 = 1873$ units

***Example 14.*** *The dual of the following primal problem*

*Min* $z_x = 2x_2 + 5x_3$

*Subject to* $x_1 + x_2 \geq 2,$

$2x_1 + x_2 + 6x_3 \leq 6$

$x_1 - x_2 + 3x_3 = 4$

*and* $x_1, x_2, x_3 \geq 0$ *is*

(a) Min $Z'_w = -2w_1 + 6w_2 + 4w_3 - 4w_4$

subject to $-w_1 + 2w_2 + w_3 - w_4 \geq 0$

$-w_1 + w_2 - w_3 + w_4 \geq -2$

$6w_2 + 3w_3 - 3w_4 \geq -5$

$w_1, w_2, w_3, w_4 \geq 0$

(b) Min $Z'_w = -2w_1 - 6w_2 - 4w_3 + 4w_4$

Subject to $-w_1 + 2w_2 + w_3 - w_4 \geq 0$

$-w_1 + w_2 - w_3 + w_4 \geq 2$

$6w_2 + 3w_3 - 3w_4 \geq 5$

$w_1, w_2, w_3, w_4 \geq 0$

(c) Min $z'_w = 2w_1 + 6w_2 - 4w_3 - 4w_4$

Subject to $w_1 - 2w_2 + w_3 - w_4 \geq 0$

$w_1 + w_2 + w_3 - w_4 \geq 2$

$6w_2 + 3w_3 - 3w_4 \geq -5$

$w_1, w_2, w_3, w_4 \geq 0$

(d) None of the above

**Solution.** (a) the standard primal form of the given problem is

Max $z'_x = -2x_2 - 5x_3$, where $z'_x = -z_x$

Subject to $-x_1 - x_2 \leq -2$

$2x_1 + x_2 + 6x_3 \leq 6$

$x_1 - x_2 + 3x_3 \leq 4$

$-x_1 + x_2 - 3x_3 \leq -4$

$x_1, x_2, x_3 \geq 0$

The dual of the above problem is obtained by

(a) transposing the coefficient matrix

(b) interchanging the role of constant terms and the coefficients of the objective function

(c) reverting the inequalities

(d) minimizing the objective function instead of maximizing it

So, the dual problem is to find $w_1, w_2, w_3$ and $w_4$ which minimize

Min $Z'_w = -2w_1 + 6w_2 + 4w_3 - 4w_4$

Subject to

$$-w_1 + 2w_2 + w_3 - w_4 \geq 0$$
$$-w_1 + w_2 - w_3 + w_4 \geq -2$$
$$6w_2 + 3w_3 - 3w_4 \geq -5$$
$$w_1, w_2, w_3, w_4 \geq 0$$

***Example 15.*** *The dual of the problem*

*Min* $z = 2x_1 + 3x_2 + 4x_3$

*Subject to the constraints*

$$2x_1 + 3x_2 + 5x_3 \geq 2$$
$$3x_1 + x_2 + 7x_3 = 3$$
$$x_1 + 4x_2 + 6x_3 \leq 5$$

$x_1, x_2 \geq 0$ *and* $x_3$ *is unrestricted is*

(a) Min $Z'_w = 2w_1 - 3w_2 + 5w_3$

Subject to $-2w_1 + 3w_2 + w_3 \geq -2$

$-3w_1 + w_2 + 4w_3 \geq -3$

$5w_1 - 7w_2 - 6w_3 = 4$

$w_1, w_3 \geq 0$ and $w_2$ is unrestricted.

(b) Min $z'_w = -2w_1 + 3w_2 + 5w_3$

Subject to, $-2w_1 + 3w_2 + w_3 \geq -2$

$-3w_1 + w_2 + 4w_3 \geq -3$

$5w_1 - 7w_2 - 6w_3 = 4$

$w_1, w_3 \geq 0$ and $w_2$ is unrestricted.

(c) Min $z'_w = 2w_1 - 3w_2 + 5w_3$

Subject to $2w_1 + 3w_2 - w_3 \geq 2$

$3w_1 - w_2 - 4w_3 \geq 3$

$5w_1 - 7w_2 + 6w_3 = 4$

$w_1, w_3 \geq 0$ and $w_2$ is unrestricted.

(d) None of the above

**Solution.** (b) In the given problem $x_3$ is unrestricted, we consider

$x_3 = x_3' - x_3''$ where $x_3', x_3'' \geq 0$

Therefore standard primal problem of the above problem in terms of restricted variables is

Max $z'_x = -2x_1 - 3x_2 - 4(x_3' - x_3'')$

Subject to $-2x_1 - 3x_2 - 5(x_3' - x_3'') \leq -2$

$$3x_1 + x_2 + 7(x_3' - x_3'') \leq 3$$
$$-3x_1 - x_2 - 7(x_3' - x_3'') \leq -3$$
$$x_1 + 4x_2 + 6(x_3' - x_3'') \leq 5$$
$$x_1, x_2, x_3', x_3'' \geq 0$$

The dual of the given standard primal is

Min $z'_w = -2w_1 + 3(w_2' - w_2'') + 5w_3$

Subject to the constraints

$$-2w_1 + 3(w_2'' - w_2'') + w_3 \geq -2$$
$$-3w_1 + (w_2' - w_2'') + 4w_3 \geq -3$$
$$-5w_1 + 7(w_2' - w_2'') + 6w_3 \geq -4$$
$$5w_1 - 7(w_2' - w_2'') - 6w_3 \geq 4$$
$$w_1, w_2', w_2'', w_3 \geq 0$$

This problem can be written as

Min $z'_w = -2w_1 + 3w_2 + 5w_3$

Subject to the constraints

$$-2w_1 + 3w_2 + w_3 \geq -2$$
$$-3w_1 + w_2 + 4w_3 \geq -3$$
$$5w_1 - 7w_2 - 6w_3 = 4$$

$w_1, w_3 \geq 0$ and $w_2$ is unrestricted.

**Directions** (Q. Nos. 16-17) *A TV repairman finds that the time spent on his job has an exponential distribution with mean 30 min. He repairs sets in the order in which they came in and the arrival of sets is approximately poisson with an average rate of 10 per 8 h day.*

***Example 16.*** *What is repairman's expected idle time each day?*

(a) 2 h (b) 3 h

(c) 4 h (d) 5 h

***Example 17.*** *How many jobs are ahead of the average set just brought in?*

(a) 1 (b) 2

(c) $1\frac{1}{2}$ (d) $1\frac{2}{3}$

**Solution.** (Q. Nos. 16-17)

Here, service rate (average) $\mu = \frac{1}{30}$

Average arrival rate $\lambda = \frac{10}{8 \times 60} = \frac{1}{48}$

We know the fraction of the time the repairman is busy (*i.e.*, traffic intensity $1 = \frac{\lambda}{\mu}$

**16.** (b) So, the number of hours per which the repairman remains busy in a 8 h day is

$$= 8\left(\frac{\lambda}{\mu}\right) = 8 \times \frac{30}{48} = 5 \text{ h}$$

And the time for which the repairman remains idle in 8 h day

$$= (8 - 5) \text{ h} = 3 \text{ h}$$

**17.** (d) The expected number of jobs are

$$L_s = \frac{\lambda/\mu}{1-\frac{\lambda}{\mu}} = \frac{\lambda}{\mu-\lambda} = \frac{\frac{1}{48}}{\frac{1}{30}-\frac{1}{48}}$$

$$= \frac{30 \times 48}{48 \times 18} = \frac{5}{3} = 1\frac{2}{3} \text{ jobs}$$

**Directions** (Q. Nos. 18-22) *In a railway marshalling yard, goods trains arrive at a rate of 30 trains per day. Assume that the inter arrival time follows an exponential distribution and the service time (the time taken to hump a train) distribution is also exponential with an average 36 min. Then,*

***Example 18.*** *The average number of trains in the queue is*

(a) 2 (b) 3
(c) 4 (d) 5

***Example 19.*** *The probability that the queue size exceeds 10 is*

(a) $\left(\frac{1}{2}\right)$ (b) $\left(\frac{2}{3}\right)^{10}$
(c) $\left(\frac{3}{4}\right)^{10}$ (d) $\left(\frac{4}{5}\right)^{10}$

***Example 20.*** *Expected waiting time in the queue is*

(a) 12 min (b) 48 min
(c) 84 min (d) 108 min

***Example 21.*** *The probability that the number of trains in the system exceeds 10 is*

(a) $\left(\frac{1}{2}\right)^{10}$ (b) $\left(\frac{2}{3}\right)^{10}$
(c) $\left(\frac{3}{4}\right)^{10}$ (d) $\left(\frac{4}{5}\right)^{10}$

***Example 22.*** *The average number of trains in the queue is*

(a) 2 (b) 5 (c) 7 (d) 10

**Solutions** (Q. Nos. 18-22)

Here, average arrival rate $\lambda = \frac{30}{60 \times 24}$ trains/min

$= \frac{1}{48}$ trains/min

Average service time $= \frac{1}{36}$ trains/min

So, $\rho$ = traffic intensity $= \frac{\text{mean arrival rate}}{\text{mean service rate}}$

$$= \frac{\lambda}{\mu} = \frac{\frac{1}{48}}{\frac{1}{36}} = \frac{36}{48} = \frac{3}{4}$$

**18.** (b) The average number of trains in the queue, $L_s = \frac{\rho}{1-\rho}$

$$= \frac{\frac{3}{4}}{1-\frac{3}{4}} = \frac{\frac{3}{4}}{\frac{1}{4}} = 3 \text{ trains}$$

**19.** (c) The probability that queue size exceeds 10

$$= \text{Probability (queue size} \geq 10) = \rho^{10} = \left(\frac{3}{4}\right)^{10}$$

**20.** (d) Expected waiting time in the queue

$$W_q = \frac{\lambda}{\mu(\mu-\lambda)} = \frac{\frac{1}{48}}{\frac{1}{36}\left(\frac{1}{36}-\frac{1}{48}\right)} = 108 \text{ min}$$

**21.** (c) The probability that the number of trains in the system exceeds 10 = $P$ (number of trains $\geq 10$) $= (\rho)^{10} = \left(\frac{3}{4}\right)^{10}$

**22.** (a) Average number of trains in the queue

$$L_q = \frac{\lambda^2}{\mu(\mu-\lambda)} = \frac{\left(\frac{1}{48}\right)^2}{\frac{1}{36}\left(\frac{1}{36}-\frac{1}{48}\right)} = \frac{108}{48} = 2.25 \cong 2 \text{ trains}$$

## Type II (*One or more than one correct option*)

***Example 23.*** *Maximize* $z = 107x_1 + x_2 + 2x_3$
*Subject to the constraints*

$$14x_1 + x_2 - 6x_3 + 3x_4 = 7$$
$$16x_1 + \frac{1}{2}x_2 - 6x_3 \leq 5$$
$$3x_1 - x_2 - x_3 \leq 0$$
$$x_1, x_2, x_3, x_4 \geq 0$$

*In standard linear programming problem*

(a) The number of constraints are three
(b) The number of decision variables are six
(c) The number of constraints are six
(d) The number of decision variables are three

**Solution.** (a), (b)

By introducing slack variables, $x_5 \geq 0$ and $x_6 \geq 0$ respectively, the set of constraints of the given LPP are converted into the system of equations,

$$\begin{pmatrix} 14/3 & 1/3 & -2 & 1 & 0 & 0 \\ 16 & 1/2 & -6 & 0 & 1 & 0 \\ 3 & -1 & -1 & 0 & 0 & 1 \end{pmatrix} \begin{bmatrix} x_1 \\ x_2 \\ x_3 \\ x_4 \\ x_5 \\ x_6 \end{bmatrix} = \begin{bmatrix} 7/3 \\ 5 \\ 0 \end{bmatrix}$$

which has three constraints in six variable.

***Example 24.*** *Given,*

*Maximize* $f(x) = 2x_1 + 5x_2 + 6x_3$

*subject to the constraints*

$$5x_1 + 6x_2 - x_3 \le 3$$
$$-2x_1 + x_2 + 4x_3 \le 4$$
$$x_1 - 5x_2 + 3x_3 \le 1$$
$$-3x_1 - 3x_2 + 7x_3 \le 6$$
$$x_1, x_2, x_3 \ge 0$$

*Let $w_1$, $w_2$, $w_3$ and $w_4$ are the associated dual variables to primal problem, then in the dual of the given problem*

(a) Minimize $g(w) = 3w_1 + 4w_2 + w_3 + 6w_4$

(b) $5w_1 - 2w_2 + w_3 - 3w_4 \ge 2$

$6w_1 + w_2 - 5w_3 - 3w_4 \ge 5$

$-w_1 + 4w_2 + 3w_3 + 7w_4 \ge 6$

$w_1, w_2, w_3, w_4 \ge 0$

(c) Minimize $g(w) = (3, 4, 1, 6)\,[w_1, w_2, w_3, w_4]$

(d) $\begin{bmatrix} 5 & -2 & 1 & -3 \\ 6 & 1 & -5 & -3 \\ -1 & 4 & 3 & 7 \end{bmatrix}\begin{bmatrix} w_1 \\ w_2 \\ w_3 \\ w_4 \end{bmatrix} \ge \begin{bmatrix} 2 \\ 5 \\ 6 \end{bmatrix}$

$w_1, w_2, w_3, w_4 \ge 0$

**Solution.** (a), (b), (c), (d)

Maximize $f(x) = cx$

subject to the constraints

$$Ax \le b, \; x \ge 0$$

where, $A = \begin{bmatrix} 5 & 6 & -1 \\ -2 & 1 & 4 \\ 1 & -5 & 3 \\ -3 & -3 & 7 \end{bmatrix}$, $b = \begin{bmatrix} 3 \\ 4 \\ 1 \\ 6 \end{bmatrix}$ and $c = (2\;5\;6)$

**Dual problem** Let $w = [w_1, w_2, w_3, w_4]$ be the dual variables, minimize $g(w) = (3, 4, 1, 6)\,[w_1, w_2, w_3, w_4]$

subject to the constraints

$$\begin{bmatrix} 5 & -2 & 1 & -3 \\ 6 & 1 & -5 & -3 \\ -1 & 4 & 3 & 7 \end{bmatrix}\begin{bmatrix} w_1 \\ w_2 \\ w_3 \\ w_4 \end{bmatrix} \ge \begin{bmatrix} 2 \\ 5 \\ 6 \end{bmatrix}$$
$$w_1, w_2, w_3, w_4 \ge 0$$

Hence, minimize $g(w) = 3w_1 + 4w_2 + w_3 + 6w_4$

Subject to the constraints

$$5w_1 - 2w_2 + w_3 - 3w_4 \ge 2$$
$$6w_1 + w_2 - 5w_3 - 3w_4 \ge 5$$
$$-w_1 + 4w_2 + 3w_3 + 7w_4 \ge 6$$
$$w_1, w_2, w_3, w_4 \ge 0$$

***Example 25.*** *In the dual of the given problem,*

*Given, Min* $z = 5x_1 - 7x_2$

*subject to*

$$x_1 - 9x_2 \le 9$$
$$-2x_1 + 3x_2 \le 6$$
$$x_1 + x_2 \le 12, \; x_1 \ge 2, \; x_1, x_2 \ge 0$$

(a) Max $w = -9y_1 - 6y_2 - 12y_3 + 2y_4$

(b) Min $w = -9y_1 + 6y_2 + 4y_3$

(c) $-y_1 + 2y_2 - y_3 + y_4 \le -5$

$9y_1 \;\; 3y_2 \;\; y_3 \le 7$

$y_1, y_2 \ge 0$

(d) $-x_1 + 9x_2 \ge -9$

$2x_1 - 3x_2 \ge -6$

$-x_1 - x_2 \ge -12$

$x_1 \ge 2, \; x_1, x_2 \ge 0$

**Solution.** (a), (c)

Convert the given problem into canonical form. The canonical form is

Min $z = -5x_1 + 7x_2$

Subject to constraints

$$-x_1 + 9x_2 \ge -9 \qquad y_1$$
$$2x_1 - 3x_2 \ge -6 \qquad y_2$$
$$-x_1 - x_2 \ge -12 \qquad y_3$$
$$x_1 \ge 2 \qquad y_4$$
$$x_1, x_2 \ge 0$$

where, $y_1$, $y_2$, $y_3$ and $y_4$ are the associated dual variables to primal constraints. The dual problem is

Max $w = -9y_1 - 6y_2 - 12y_3 + 2y_4$

Subject to constraints

$$-y_1 + 2y_2 - y_3 + y_4 \le -5$$
$$9y_1 - 3y_2 - y_3 \le 7, \; y_1, y_2 \ge 0$$

***Example 26.*** *Customers arrive at a one window drive in bank according to a poisson distribution with mean 10 per hour. Service time per customer is exponential with mean 5 min. The space infront of the window, including that for the serviced car can accommodate a maximum of 3 cars. Other cars can wait outside this space.*

(a) The probability that an arriving customer can drive directly to the space infront of the window is 0.42

(b) The probability that an arriving customer will have to wait outside the indicated space is 0.48

(c) Expected waiting time of a customer in queue is 5/12

(d) Probability that there will be no or one car in the space is 30

**Solution.** (a), (b), (c), (d)

Here, mean arrival rate, is

$$\lambda = 10 \text{ customer/h}$$

Mean service rate is $\mu = \frac{1}{5} \times 60 = 12$ customer/h

Utilization factor is

$$\rho = \frac{\lambda}{\mu} = \frac{10}{12} \text{ or } \frac{5}{6}$$

(a) The probability that an arriving customer can drive directly to the space infront of the window is

$$= P_0 + P_1 + P_2 = (1-\rho) + \rho(1-\rho) + \rho^2(1-\rho)$$

$$= (1-\rho)(1+\rho+\rho^2) = \frac{1}{6}\left(1+\frac{5}{6}+\frac{25}{36}\right) = 0.42$$

(b) The probability that an arriving customer has to wait outside the indicated space is

= Probability that there are atleast 3 customers in front of the window is

$$= 1-(P_0+P_1+P_2+P_3) = 1-0.42-P_3$$

$$= 0.58 - \{\rho^3(1-\rho)\}$$

$$= 0.58 - \left\{\left(\frac{5}{6}\right)^3 \frac{1}{6}\right\} = 0.58 - 0.10 = 0.48$$

(c) Expected waiting time of a customer in queue is

$$W_q = \frac{\lambda}{\mu(\mu-\lambda)} = \frac{10}{12(12-10)} = \frac{5}{12} \text{ or } 0.417 \text{ h}$$

(d) We have, $P_0 = 1-\frac{\lambda}{\mu} = 1-\frac{5}{6} = 0.16;$

$$P_1 = \frac{\lambda}{\mu}P_0 = \frac{5}{6}\left(\frac{1}{6}\right) = 0.14$$

$P_0 + P_1$ = Probability that there will be no or one car in the space = 0.30.

***Example 27.*** *Given system of linear equations,*

$$2x_1 + x_2 - x_3 = 2, \quad 3x_1 + 2x_2 + x_3 = 3$$

*For the given system,*

(a) $x_3 = 0$ (non-basic), $x_1 = 1$, $x_2 = 0$ (basic)

(b) $x_2 = 5/3$, $x_3 = -1/3$ (basic), $x_1 = 0$ (non-basic)

(c) $x_1 = 1$, $x_3 = 0$ (basic), $x_2 = 0$ (non-basic)

(d) Here, two of the basic solutions are degenerate solutions

**Solution.** (a), (b), (c), (d)

The given system of equations is $Ax = b$

where $A = \begin{pmatrix} 2 & 1 & -1 \\ 3 & 2 & 1 \end{pmatrix}, b = \begin{bmatrix} 2 \\ 3 \end{bmatrix}$ and $x = \begin{bmatrix} x_1 \\ x_2 \\ x_3 \end{bmatrix}$

Since, rank $(A) = 2$

The maximum number of linearly independent columns of $A$ is 2. Thus, we can take any of the following $2 \times 2$ submatrices of $A$, as basis matrix $B$.

$$\begin{pmatrix} 2 & 1 \\ 3 & 2 \end{pmatrix} \begin{pmatrix} 1 & -1 \\ 1 & 1 \end{pmatrix} \text{ and } \begin{pmatrix} 2 & -1 \\ 3 & 2 \end{pmatrix}$$

The variables not associated with the columns of these submatrices are, respectively $x_3$, $x_1$ and $x_2$.

Considering $B = \begin{pmatrix} 2 & 1 \\ 3 & 2 \end{pmatrix}$

A basic solution to the given system is obtained by setting $x_3 = 0$ and solving the system

$$\begin{pmatrix} 2 & 1 \\ 3 & 2 \end{pmatrix} \begin{bmatrix} x_1 \\ x_2 \end{bmatrix} = \begin{bmatrix} 2 \\ 3 \end{bmatrix}$$

Thus, basic solution to the given system is

$$x_1 = 1,\ x_2 = 0;\ \text{(non-basic)},\ x_3 = 0$$

Similarly, the other two basic solutions are

$$x_2 = 5/3,\ x_3 = -1/3;\ \text{(non-basic)},\ x_1 = 0$$

and $\quad x_1 = 1,\ x_3 = 0$ (non-basic), $x_2 = 0$

In each of the two basic solutions, atleast one of the basic variables is zero. Hence, two of the basic solutions are degenerate solutions.

***Example 28.*** *An animal feed company must produce 200 kg of a mixture consisting of ingredients $X_1$ and $X_2$. The ingredient $X_1$ costs ₹ 3 per kg and $X_2$ costs ₹ 5 per kg. Not more than 80 kg of $X_1$ can be used and atleast 60 kg of $X_2$ must be used.*

(a) The number of constraints are three

(b) The number of decision variables are two

(c) The problem has only are feasible point

(d) The optimal solution is to mix 80 kg of ingredients $X_1$ and 120 kg of ingredients $X_2$ to have a minimum cost of ₹ 840

**Solution.** (a), (b), (c), (d)

The appropriate mathematical formulation of the given problem as LP model is

Minimize (total cost) $= 3x_1 + 5x_2$

Subject to the constraints

$$x_1 + x_2 = 200, \quad x_1 \le 80, x_2 \ge 60, \quad x_1 \ge 0 \text{ and } x_2 \ge 0$$

Drawing the lines $x_1 + x_2 = 200$, $x_1 = 80$ and $x_2 = 60$ on a graph sheet, we get the following figure

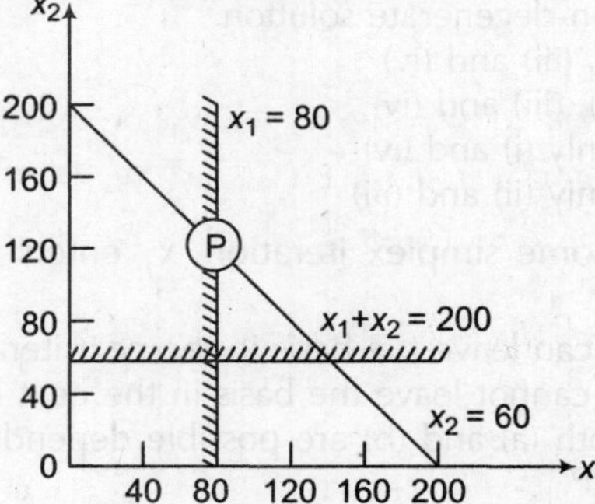


From figure it may be observed from the adjoining figure that the given problem has no feasible solution space (shaded area) but has only one feasible point with its coordinates $x_1 = 80$ and $x_2 = 120$.

Therefore, the optimal solution is to mix 80 kg of ingredients $X_1$ and 120 kg of ingredients $X_2$ to have a minimum cost of ₹ 840.

# Exercise 1 (For Part 'B')

**Directions** (Q. Nos. 1-396) *All questions have only one correct option.*

**1.** Let $f(x)$ denote the objective function of an LPP, then
(a) Max $f(x) = -$ min $[-f(x)]$
(b) Max $f(x) = -$ min $[f(-x)]$
(c) Max $f(x) = -$ min $[f(x)]$
(d) Max $f(x) =$ min $[-f(-x)]$

**2.** The maximum value of $z = 4x + 2y$ subject to $2x + 3y \le 18$, $x + y \ge 10$, $x, y \ge 0$ is
(a) 36 (b) 40
(c) 20 (d) None of these

**3. A.** Every solution of linear programming problem is optimal solution.
**B.** Every optimal solution of linear programming problem is solution.
(a) A and B both true
(b) A is true only
(c) B is true only
(d) Both A and B false

**4.** Which of the following is/are correct?
(i) The artificial variable are only a computational device for getting a starting solution.
(ii) With the help of artificial variable it is not necessary that we get a starting solution.
(iii) The choose the variable as entering variable corresponding which we get $z_j - c_j$ most negative, is always the best strategy (for maximizing objective function).
(iv) If all the basic variables in the basic feasible solution are positive, then it is called non-degenerate solution.
(a) (i), (iii) and (iv)
(b) (ii), (iii) and (iv)
(c) Only (i) and (iv)
(d) Only (ii) and (iii)

**5.** Let in some simplex iteration, $x_j$ enters in the basis. Then,
(a) $x_j$ can leave the basis in the next iteration
(b) $x_j$ cannot leave the basis in the next iteration
(c) Both (a) and (b), are possible depending upon the LPP
(d) None of the above

**6.** Which of the following is not associated with an LPP
(a) Proportionality (b) Uncertainty
(c) Divisibility (d) Additively

**7.** In linear programming problem
(a) objective function, constraints and variables are all linear
(b) only objective function to be linear
(c) only constraints are to be linear
(d) only variables are to be linear

**8.** Let $Ax = b$ be a system of $m$ equation and $n$ unknowns $(m \le n)$. Suppose, column vector $b$ is not a linear combination of column of $A$ and rank of $A$ is $r < m$. Then, the number of basic solutions for this system is
(a) ${}^nC_m$ (b) $\le {}^nC_m$ (c) $\le {}^nC_r$ (d) 0

**9.** Let $\hat{X}$ be a possible solution to primal LPP Min $\phi(X) = C^T X$, subject to $AX \ge b$, $X \ge 0$ and $\hat{Y}$ be a feasible solution to dual LPP
Max $\psi(Y) = b^T Y$ subject to $A^T Y \le C$, $Y \ge a$. Then,
(a) $\phi(\hat{X}) = \psi(\hat{Y})$ (b) $\phi(\hat{X}) \ge \psi(\hat{Y})$
(c) $\phi(\hat{X}) \le \psi(\hat{Y})$ (d) Can't say

**10.** If, in cost matrix of an assignment problem, we multiply each entry of one row by a non-zero constant $k > 0$, then for the changed problem
(a) the optimal solution remains same but the optimal value of objective function may be changed
(b) the optimal solution may change but the optimal value of the objective function remains same
(c) both, the optimal solution and optimal value of objective function, remains same
(d) both, the optimal solution and optimal value of objective function, may be changed

**11.** If in linear programming problems, we get the solution with some variables are of the form $\log x_j$. Then, given problem is
(a) linear programming problem always
(b) it can't be a linear programming problem
(c) it can be a linear programming problem
(d) None of the above

**12.** In the last simplex table of a maximization LPP, the column corresponding to a variable $x_j$ is $(-6, -2, -1, 0)^T$ and $z_j - c_j = -3$. Then, this shows that
(a) feasible region of the LPP is bounded
(b) feasible region of the LPP is unbounded in $x_j$ direction
(c) solution is unbounded
(d) None of the above

**13.** Simplex table for phase I of the simplex algorithm for an LPP is given below ($x_3$, $x_4$ and $x_5$ are artificial variables)

| Basic | $x_1$ | $x_2$ | $x_3$ | $x_4$ | $x_5$ | RHS |
|---|---|---|---|---|---|---|
| $z_j - c_j$ | 0 | 0 | 0 | 0 | 0 | 0 |
| $x_1$ | 1 | 0 | 3/5 | 1/5 | 0 | 2 |
| $x_2$ | 0 | 0 | $-2/5$ | 1/5 | 0 | 0 |
| $x_3$ | 0 | 0 | $-1$ | $-1$ | 1 | 0 |

Consider the following statements

(i) The table does not show the end of phase I, since the artificial variable $x_5$ is in the basis.

(ii) The table does show the end of phase I, since the value of the phase I objective function is zero.

(iii) The constraints for the original LPP are redundant.

(iv) The original LPP does not have a feasible solution

Then,

(a) (ii) and (iii) are true (b) (ii) and (iv) are true
(c) (i) and (iv) are true (d) Only (ii) is true

**14.** Which of the following is correct?

(a) If primal has a feasible solution, then its dual will also have a feasible solution.
(b) If primal has no feasible solution, then its dual will also have no feasible solution.
(c) If both, primal and dual, have feasible solution, then both will have bounded optimal solution.
(d) If primal has no feasible solution, then its dual will have an unbounded solution.

**15.** The variables to be determined in LPP are always

(a) positive only (b) negative only
(c) non-negative (d) non-positive

**16.** In applications of dual simplex method the availability vector (RHS vector) must be

(a) $\geq 0$
(b) $\leq 0$
(c) no restriction of type (a) or (b) is required
(d) None of the above

**17.** The function $f(x) = C^T x + d$ is linear

(a) convex
(b) concave
(c) both convex and concave
(d) either convex and concave

**18.** If $L_s$ and $W_s$ the expected length of customers in the system and $W_s$ be the expected waiting time in the system, by Little's formula, for arrival rate $\lambda$ in the system

(a) $L_s = \lambda W_s$ (b) $L_s W_s = \lambda$
(c) $W_s = \lambda L_s$ (d) None of these

**19.** If $x_j$ is a basic variable in a simplex table. Then, the relative cost is

(a) $z_j - c_j < 0$
(b) $z_j - c_j > 0$
(c) $z_j - c_j = 0$
(d) either $z_j - c_j = 0$ or $z_j - c_j > 0$

**20.** In dual simplex method, leaving variable position is positive after the iteration, then in next iteration or in some later iterations the variable occupying the place of this variable in the table

(a) can become negative
(b) cannot become negative
(c) will always become negative
(d) None of the above

**21.** A set $C$ in $n$ dimensional space is said to be convex, if every point on the line segment joining any two distinct points of $C$ lie in

(a) $R$
(b) $C$
(c) Neither (a) nor (b)
(d) Both (a) and (b)

**22.** In linear programming problem, if

**A.** Every optimal solution is solution.

**B.** Every optimal solution is feasible solution

(a) A and B both false (b) A is true only
(c) B is true only (d) A and B both true

**23.** If in a simplex table the relative cost $z_j - c_j$ for a non-basic variables is zero, then there exists an alternate optimal solution, provided

(a) it is starting simplex table
(b) it is optimal simplex table
(c) it can be any simplex table
(d) None of the above

**24.** In dual simplex method,

(a) the iterations move towards feasibility maintaining optimality
(b) the iterations move towards optimality maintaining feasibility
(c) the iteration maintain both feasibility and optimality
(d) None of the above

**25.** Any point $P$ in a convex set $S$ is called an extreme point, if $P$ cannot be expressed as a convex combination of any other

(a) two points
(b) three points in $S$
(c) two distinct points in $S$
(d) None of the above

**26.** Let $\bar{c} \neq 0$ be a $n$ component vector and $z$ a given scalar, then the equation of a hyper plane in $E^n$ is a set of points

(a) $\{\bar{x} \mid \bar{c}\,\bar{x} > z\}$ (b) $\{\bar{x} \mid \overline{cx} \geq z\}$
(c) $\{\bar{x} \mid \bar{c}\,\bar{x} = z\}$ (d) None of these

**27.** If in the primal the number of constraints are $m$ and in dual the number of variables are $n$. Then,

(a) $m \geq n$ (b) $m \leq n$
(c) $m = n$ (d) None of these

**28.** Let $S$ be a closed convex set and $x$ is an extreme point of $S$, then $S - \{x\}$ is

(a) convex
(b) non-convex
(c) may or may not be convex
(d) None of the above

**29.** The equation for hyperplane in $E^n$ is given by

(a) $c_1x_1 + c_2x_2 + \ldots + c_nx_n = z$
(b) $c_1x_1 + c_2x_2 + \ldots + c_nx_n > z$
(c) $c_1x_1 + c_2x_2 + \ldots + c_nx_n \leq z$
(d) $c_1x_1 + c_2x_2 + \ldots + c_nx_n \geq z$

**30.** If the primal has no feasible solution. Then, its dual has
(a) unbounded solution
(b) either unbounded or no feasible solution
(c) no feasible solution
(d) feasible solution but not optimal solution

**31.** Which of the following sets is convex sets?
(a) $\{(x, y): x^2 + y^2 \geq 1\}$
(b) $\{(x, y): y^2 \leq x\}$
(c) $\{(x, y): 3x^2 + 3y^2 \geq 5\}$
(d) $\{(x, y): y \geq 2, y \leq 4\}$

**32.** The hyperplane in $E^n$ passing through the origin for given $z$, is
(a) $\{x \mid cx = z\}$ (b) $\{x \mid cx = 0\}$
(c) $\{x \mid cx > z\}$ (d) None of these

**33.** Consider the following
LPP Max $z = x_1$ subject to $x_1 + x_2 \geq 1$, $x_1 - x_2 \geq 1$ $x_1 \geq 0$, $x_2 \geq 0$. Then, the solution to its dual is
(a) unbounded (b) infeasible
(c) degenerate (d) bounded

**34.** Consider the set $S = \{x \in R^2 : |x| < 1\}$, then
(a) $S$ has no vertex as it is not convex
(b) $S$ has no vertex as it is not closed
(c) $S$ has no vertex as it is bounded
(d) $S$ has infinitely many vertices

**35.** The set $S = \{(x_1, x_2): x_1 + x_2 = 1\}$ has
(a) no vertex
(b) exactly two vertices
(c) more than two vertices
(d) None of the above

**36.** Which of the following is not convex?
(a) $\{(x, y): 3 \leq x^2 + y^2 \leq 5\}$
(b) $\{(x, y): 3x^2 + 3y^2 \leq 6\}$
(c) $\{(x, y): y^2 \leq x\}$
(d) $\{(x, y): x \geq 2, x \leq 3\}$

**37.** The hyperplanes $\bar{c}_1\bar{x} = z_1$ and $\bar{c}_2\bar{x} = z_2$ are parallel, if
(a) $c_1 = \lambda c_2, \lambda \neq 0$ (b) $z_1 = \lambda c_2, \lambda \neq 0$
(c) $\lambda c_1 = z_1$ (d) $\lambda c_2 = z_2$

**38.** Let $x$ be a non-optimal feasible solution of a linear programming maximization problem and $y$ a dual feasible solution. Then,
(a) the primal objective value at $x$ is greater than the dual objective value at $y$
(b) the primal objective value at x can be equal to the dual objective value at $y$
(c) the primal objective value at $x$ is less than the dual objective value at $y$
(d) the dual can be unbounded

**39.** Locus of points obtained by all convex combinations of two points represent
(a) straight line
(b) a line segment
(c) a hyperplane
(d) a hypersphere

**40.** Given the hyperplane $\bar{c}x = z$ in $E^n$ $(\bar{c}_2 \neq 0)$, then
(a) vector $\bar{c}$ is normal to the hyperplane
(b) vector $\bar{c}$ is not normal to the hyperplane
(c) vector $\bar{c}$ is unit vector
(d) None of the above

**41.** Consider the primal problem (LP)
max $4x_1 + 3x_2$ subject to $x_1 + x_2 \leq 8$, $2x_1 + x_2 \leq 10$, $x_1 \geq 0$, $x_2 \geq 0$ together with its dual (LD). Then,
(a) (LP) and (LD) both are infeasible
(b) (LP) and (LD) both are feasible
(c) (LP) is feasible but (LD) is infeasible
(d) (LP) is infeasible but (LD) is feasible

**42.** A simplex in $n$ dimension is a convex polyhedron having exactly
(a) $(n - 1)$ vertices
(b) $n$ vertices
(c) $(n + 1)$ vertices
(d) $(n + 2)$ vertices

**43.** Consider the following LPP Max $z = x_1$ subject to $x_1 + x_2 \leq 1$, $x_1 - x_2 \geq 1$, $x_1 \geq 0$, $x_2 \geq 0$. Then, the solution to its dual is
(a) unbounded (b) infeasible
(c) degenerate (d) bounded

**44.** Polytope is intersection of
(a) finite number of open half spaces
(b) arbitrary number of open half spaces
(c) finite number of closed half spaces
(d) arbitrary number of closed half spaces

**45.** Given, hyperplane $\bar{c}\,\bar{x} = z$ in $E^n$, $\bar{c}$ is normal to hyperplane, then
(a) $\lambda\bar{c}$ is also normal to hyperplane, $\lambda \neq 0$
(b) $\lambda\bar{c}$ is not normal to hyperplane, $\lambda \neq 0$
(c) $\lambda\bar{c}$ is parallel to hyperplane, $\lambda \neq 0$
(d) None of the above

**46.** If a slack or surplus variable $s_1$ is in optimal primal basis, then in the optimal dual solution
(a) the dual variable corresponding to $i$th primal constraint is zero
(b) the slack or surplus variable attached to $i$th dual constraint is zero
(c) the dual variable corresponding to $i$th primal constraint is unrestricted in sign
(d) None of the above

**47.** Phase I of simplex method
(a) optimize the objective function of the given problem
(b) given a starting BFS
(c) is required, if a variable is unrestricted in sign
(d) None of the above

**48.** **A.** Every feasible solution is solution to LPP
**B.** Every solution is feasible solution to LPP
(a) A and B both true (b) A is true only
(c) B is true only (d) Both A and B false

**49.** Let (D) be the dual of the (P) primal LPP
Minimize $(x_1 + 2x_2)$
subject to $x_1 + x_2 \leq 1$ and $x_1 + x_2 \geq 2$. Then,
(a) both (P) and (D) are feasible problems
(b) both (P) and (D) are infeasible problems
(c) (P) is feasible but (D) is infeasible
(d) (P) is infeasible but (D) is feasible

**50.** The set $S = \{(x_1, x_2) : -x_1 + 2x_2 \leq 3, -x_1 + 4x_2 \leq 9\}$ is
(a) convex
(b) convex iff $x_1 \geq 0$ and $x_2 \geq 0$
(c) not convex
(d) None of the above

**51.** A set $A \subset E^n$ is open set, then
(a) it contains all its boundary points
(b) it contains all its interior points
(c) (A) and (B) both true
(d) (A) and (B) both false

**52. A.** Every solution satisfies non-negativity restriction in LPP
**B.** Every feasible solution satisfies non-negativity restriction.
(a) A and B both true (b) A is true
(c) B is true (d) Both A and B false

**53.** Consider an LPP in three variables with objective function minimize $(2x_1 - 3x_2 + 4x_3)$. Suppose, $x_1 = 1$, $x_2 = 0$, $x_3 = 5$ is a feasible solution to this problem. Then, the optimal value of the dual objective function is
(a) equal to 22
(b) less than 22
(c) greater than or equal to 22
(d) less than or equal to 22

**54.** If $f(x)$ is convex function, then $-f(x)$ is
(a) convex function
(b) concave function
(c) strictly convex function
(d) strictly concave function

**55.** The set $\{(x_1, x_2) \mid x_1^2 + x_2^2 \leq 1\}$ is
(a) open set
(b) closed set
(c) neither open nor closed
(d) open and closed both

**56. A.** Every optimal solution is feasible solution in LPP
**B.** Every feasible solution is optimal solution in LPP
(a) A and B both true
(b) A is true
(c) B is true
(d) Both A and B false

**57.** Which of the following is not correct?
(a) If any of the constraints in the primal is a perfect equality, then the corresponding dual variable is unrestricted in sign.
(b) If any of the primal variables is unrestricted in sign, then the corresponding dual constraint is a perfect equality.
(c) If primal has a feasible solution and its dual has no feasible solution, then the optimal value of primal may or may not be finite.
(d) Both the primal and the dual, can have infeasible solutions.

**58.** Let $H$ and $K$ be two subsets of $R^n$ and let $<H>$ and $<K>$ denotes the convex hulls of $H$ and $K$, respectively. Then,
(a) $H \subset <H>$ and $K \subset <K> \Rightarrow H$ and $K$ both are convex sets
(b) $H = <H>$ and $K \subset <K> \Rightarrow H$ is convex but $K$ is not convex
(c) $H = <H>$ and $K \subset <K> \Rightarrow H$ is non-convex but $K$ is convex
(d) $H \subset <H>$ and $K \subset <K> \Rightarrow H$ and $K$ may or may not be convex sets

**59.** A set $A \subset E^n$ is closed set, then
(a) it contains all its boundary points
(b) it contains all its interior points
(c) A and B both true
(d) A and B both false

**60.** All $x_i$'s equal to zero, in LPP are
(a) solution to LPP
(b) feasible solution to LPP
(c) optimal solution to LPP
(d) no solution to LPP

**61.** Whch of the following statement is correct?
(a) Dual simplex method is always applicable
(b) Dual simplex method cannot give an unbounded solution to the primal
(c) Dual simplex method is applicable only when all all $b_i \leq 0$
(d) All of the above statements are correct

**62.** The feasible region of LPP is always a
(a) convex polyhedron (b) polytope
(c) hyperplane (d) None of these

**63.** The set $\{(x_1, x_2) \mid x_1^2 + x_2^2 < 1\}$ is a
(a) open set
(b) closed set
(c) neither open nor closed
(d) open and closed both

**64.** Every solution to linear programming problem is
(a) linear only
(b) non-linear only
(c) linear and non-linear both
(d) None of the above

**65.** For the problem
Max $z = 2x_1 + x_2 + 5x_3 + 6x_4$
subject to $2x_1 + x_3 + x_4 \leq 8$,
$2x_1 + 2x_2 + x_3 + 2x_4 \leq 12, \forall x_1 \geq 0$,

It is known that $x_1 = 0$, $x_2 = 0$, $x_3 = 4$ and $x_4 = 4$ is the optimal solution. Then, optimal solution of its dual is

(a) $w_1 = 1, w_2 = 4$ (b) $w_1 = 1, w_2 = 3$
(c) $w_1 = 4, w_2 = 1$ (d) $w_1 = 0, w_2 = 0$

**66.** The inside of the sphere in $E^3$, with centre $\bar{a}$ and radius $\varepsilon > 0$, is the set of points

(a) $\{x \mid |\bar{x} - \bar{a}| < \varepsilon\}$ (b) $\{x \mid |\bar{x} - \bar{a}| > \varepsilon\}$
(c) $\{x \mid |\bar{x} - \bar{a}| = \varepsilon\}$ (d) None of the above

**67.** For given $2x_1 + x_2 - x_3 = 2$ and $3x_1 + 2x_2 + x_3 = 3$ one of the basic solution is

(a) (1, 2) (b) (1, 0)
(c) (0, 0) (d) None of these

**68.** Let $E^3$ is an Euclidean space, an equation of sphere with centre $\bar{a}$ and radius $\varepsilon$ is

(a) $|\bar{x} - \bar{a}| < \varepsilon$ (b) $|\bar{x} - \bar{a}| > \varepsilon$
(c) $|\bar{x} - \bar{a}| = \varepsilon$ (d) None of these

**69.** Given, $\begin{pmatrix} 1 & 2 & 1 \\ 2 & 1 & 5 \end{pmatrix}\begin{pmatrix} x_1 \\ x_2 \\ x_3 \end{pmatrix} = \begin{pmatrix} 4 \\ 5 \end{pmatrix}$ the maximum possible basic solution is

(a) 3 (b) 4
(c) 2 (d) 6

**70.** Any convex combination of *k*-different optimal solutions to a linear programming problem is

(a) an optimal solution
(b) non-optimal solution
(c) no solution exist
(d) None of the above

**71.** A linear programming problem have

(a) never more that optimal solution
(b) only one optimal solution
(c) one or more optimal solution
(d) None of the above

**72.** If linear programming problem have basic feasible solution, if we drop one basis vector and introduce a non-basis vector in basis, then new solution obtained is

(a) a basic feasible solution
(b) a non-basic feasible solution
(c) no solution exist
(d) None of the above

**73.** The non-negative condition means, decision variables in linear programming problems are

(a) negative (b) positive
(c) non-negative (d) None of these

**74.** For given linear programming problem, if z is an objective function

(a) max $z = -$ min $z$
(b) max $z =$ min $(-z)$
(c) max $(-z) =$ max $z$
(d) None of the above

**75.** Any solution which satisfies atleast one constraints in linear programming problem, is included in

(a) feasible region
(b) non-feasible region
(c) boundary
(d) None of the above

**76.** Given a system of linear equations $\bar{A}\bar{x} = \bar{b}$, if $\bar{x}_B$ is one of the basic solution for given basic $B$, then

(a) $\bar{x}_B = \bar{B}^{-1}\bar{b}^{-1}$ (b) $\bar{x}_B\bar{b} = \bar{B}^{-1}$
(c) $\bar{x}_B = \bar{B}^{-1}b$ (d) None of these

**77.** For given $x_1 + 2x_2 + x_3 = 4$ and $2x_1 + x_2 + 5x_3 = 5$ one basic solution is

(a) (2, 1) (b) (5, 6)
(c) (2, 2) (d) None of these

**78.** Linear programming problem tackles only constrains and objective functions that are

(a) linear only (b) non-linear only
(c) integer only (d) None of these

**79. A.** If linear programming problem have feasible solution, then it also has a basic feasible solution.

**B.** There exist only finite number of feasible solutions.

(a) A and B both false (b) A is true only
(c) B is true only (d) A and B both true

**80.** Let $X$ be a set in $E^n$ and $\bar{x}_1, \bar{x}_2 \in X$. The set $X$ is connected, if

(a) line segment joining $\bar{x}_1$ and $\bar{x}_2$ belongs to $X$
(b) line segment joining $\bar{x}_1$ and $\bar{x}_2$ does not belongs to $X$
(c) polygonal path joining $\bar{x}_1$ and $\bar{x}_2$ belongs to $X$
(d) polygonal path joining $\bar{x}_1$ and $\bar{x}_2$ does not belongs to $X$

**81.** A square is a convex set, its exterior points are

(a) vertices of square (b) sides of square
(c) inside of square (d) None of these

**82.** Set $A \subset E^n$ is bounded above, then there exist

(a) upper limit (b) lower limit
(c) upper and lower both (d) None of these

**83.** Let $X$ be a set in $E^n$ and any $\bar{x}_1, \bar{x}_2 \in X$. Then, set $X$ is convex, if

(a) line segment joining $\bar{x}_1$ and $\bar{x}_2$ belongs to $X$
(b) line segment joining $\bar{x}_1$ and $\bar{x}_2$ does not belongs to $X$
(c) polygonal path joining $\bar{x}_1$ and $\bar{x}_2$ belongs to $X$
(d) polygonal path joining $\bar{x}_1$ and $\bar{x}_2$ does not belongs to $X$

**84.** Linear programming deals with problems involving

(a) single objective function
(b) double objective function
(c) no objective function
(d) None of the above

**85.** Set $A \subset E^n$ is bounded below for $\bar{r} < \infty$, every $\bar{a} \in A$, is

(a) $\bar{r} \le \bar{a}$ (b) $\bar{r} \ge \bar{a}$
(c) $\bar{r} = \bar{a}$ (d) $\bar{r} > \bar{a}$

**86.** The dimension of a cone C is
(a) minimum number of linearly independent vectors in C
(b) maximum number of linearly independent vectors in C
(c) maximum number of linearly dependent vectors in C
(d) minimum number of linearly dependent vectors in C

**87.** Given, $\Sigma a_{ij} x_j \ge b_i$, to convert it into equality we introduce
(a) slack variable (b) surplus variable
(c) unrestricted variable (d) None of the above

**88.** Set $A \subset E^n$ is bounded above, if for $\bar{r} < \infty$, every o $\bar{a}$ A, is
(a) $\bar{r} \le \bar{a}$ (b) $\bar{r} \ge \bar{a}$
(c) $\bar{r} = \bar{a}$ (d) None of these

**89.** The circumference of the circle is
(a) both boundary and extreme point
(b) boundary point only
(c) extreme point only
(d) interior point

**90.** Every basic feasible solution in convex set of solution is
(a) extreme point (b) boundary point
(c) non-extreme point (d) non-boundary point

**91.** Set $A \subset E^n$ is strictly bounded, if for $r > 0$, every $\bar{a} \in A$
(a) $|\bar{a}| \le r$ (b) $|\bar{a}| \ge r$
(c) $|\bar{a}| = r$ (d) $|\bar{a}| < r$

**92.** A convex combination of a finite number of points $\bar{x}_1, \dots, \bar{x}_m$ is $\bar{x} = \sum_{i=1}^{m} \mu_i \bar{x}_i$ subject to the condition
(a) $\mu_i \le 0, \forall i, \Sigma\mu_i = 1$ (b) $\mu_i \ge 0, \forall i, \Sigma\mu_i = 1$
(c) $\mu_i \ge 0, \forall i, \Sigma\mu_i \ge 0$ (d) $\mu_i \ge 0, \forall i, \Sigma\mu_i \le 0$

**93.** Set of feasible solutions to $\bar{A}\bar{x} = \bar{b}$ is
(a) convex set (b) non-convex set
(c) disconnected set (d) None of these

**94.** The complement of a set $\{x \mid x_1^2 + x_2^2 = 1\}$, where $x = (x_1, x_2)$ is
(a) $\{x \mid x_1^2 + x_2^2 = 1\}$
(b) $\{x \mid x_1^2 + x_2^2 \le 1\}$
(c) $\{x \mid x_1^2 + x_2^2 < 1\}$ and $\{x \mid x_1^2 + x_2^2 > 1\}$
(d) None of the above

**95.** The set $\{(x_1, x_2) \mid x_1^2 + x_2^2 \le 1\}$ is a
(a) convex set (b) concave set
(c) open set (d) None of these

**96.** If $\bar{x}_B$ and $\overset{\Delta}{x}_B$ are two basic feasible solution to linear programming problem max $z = \bar{c}\bar{x}$, subject to $\bar{A}\bar{x} = \bar{b}$, $\bar{x} \ge 0$ and $\bar{c}_B$ and $\overset{\Delta}{c}_B$ are respected cost associated vector to $\bar{x}_B$ and $\overset{\Delta}{x}_B$. Then, $\overset{\Delta}{x}_B$ is improved basic feasible solution, then $\bar{x}_B$, if
(a) $\overset{\Delta}{c}_B \overset{\Delta}{x}_B \le \bar{c}_B \bar{x}_B$ (b) $\overset{\Delta}{c}_B \overset{\Delta}{x}_B \ge \bar{c}_B \bar{x}_B$
(c) $\bar{c}_B \bar{x}_B < \overset{\Delta}{c}_B \overset{\Delta}{x}_B$ (d) $\bar{c}_B \bar{x}_B < \overset{\Delta}{c}_B \overset{\Delta}{x}_B$

**97.** Two hyperplanes $\bar{c}_1\bar{x} = z_1$ and $\bar{c}_2\bar{x} = z_2$ are parallel, if
(a) $\bar{c}_1 = \lambda \bar{c}_2$ for same $\lambda \ne 0$
(b) $z_1 = \lambda z_2$ for same $\lambda \ne 0$
(c) $\bar{c}_1 \ne \lambda \bar{c}_2$ for same $\lambda \ne 0$
(d) None of the above

**98.** Given, an Euclidean space $E^n$ and $\bar{c}\bar{x} = z$ is represents an hyperplane in $E^n$. Then, this hyperplane passes through the origin, if
(a) $\bar{c}\bar{z} = 0$ (b) $\bar{c}\bar{z} \ge 0$
(c) $\bar{c}\bar{x} = 0$ (d) None of these

**99.** A triangle and its interior form a
(a) convex set (b) concave set
(c) disconnected set (d) None of these

**100.** Given, $\Sigma a_{ij} x_j \le b_i$ to convert it into equality, we introduce
(a) slack variable (b) surplus variable
(c) Unrestricted variable (d) None of these

**101.** The complement of a set $\{x \mid x_1^2 + x_2^2 < 1\}$, where $x = (x_1, x_2)$ is
(a) $\{x \mid x_1^2 + x_2^2 > 1\}$ (b) $\{x \mid x_1^2 + x_2^2 < 1\}$
(c) $\{x \mid x_1^2 + x_2^2 = 1\}$ (d) $\{x \mid x_1^2 + x_2^2 \ge 1\}$

**102.** A basic solution to the system $\bar{A}\bar{x} = \bar{b}$ is non-degenerated, if
(a) no basic variable is equal to zero
(b) no basic variable is negative
(c) no basic variable is positive
(d) None of the above

**103.** The complement of a closed set is
(a) open set (b) closed set
(c) both open and closed (d) None of these

**104.** A boundary point of a convex set are always
(a) extreme point (b) not extreme points
(c) interior points (d) None of these

**105.** Two hyperplanes are parallel
(a) they have same unit normals
(b) they have distinct unit normals
(c) the product of unit normal is unity
(d) None of the above

**106.** A set of feasible solution in linear programming problem is
(a) non-convex set (b) convex set
(c) disconnected set (d) None of these

**107.** The complement of a open set is
(a) open set
(b) closed set
(c) neither open nor closed
(d) None of the above

**108.** An extreme point of a convex set is
(a) boundary point (b) interior point
(c) convex point (d) None of these

**109.** If $\bar{c}\bar{x} = z\ (z \neq 0)$ is a hyperplane and $\bar{x}_1$ and $\bar{x}_2$ are two points on this hyperplane, then
(a) $\bar{c}\,\bar{x}_1 \neq \bar{c}\,\bar{x}_2$ (b) $\bar{c}\,\bar{x}_1 > \bar{c}\,\bar{x}_2$
(c) $\bar{c}\,\bar{x}_1 = \bar{c}\,\bar{x}_2$ (d) None of these

**110.** A hyperplane is
(a) convex set (b) not a convex set
(c) disk with hole (d) None of these

**111.** The Euclidean space $E^n$ have
(a) no boundary point (b) one boundary point
(c) two boundary point (d) $n$ boundary point

**112.** A point $\bar{x} \in X$ is an extreme point of convex set $X$ iff there do not exist points $\bar{x}_1, \bar{x}_2\ (\bar{x}_1 \neq \bar{x}_2)$ in $X$ such that
(a) $\bar{x} = (1-\lambda)\bar{x}_1 + \lambda\bar{x}_2,\ 0 < \lambda < 1$
(b) $\bar{x} = (1-\lambda)\bar{x}_1 + \lambda\bar{x}_2,\ 0 \leq \lambda \leq 1$
(c) $\bar{x} = (1-\lambda)\bar{x}_1 + \lambda\bar{x}_2$, $\lambda$ real
(d) None of the above

**113.** The set $\{x_1, x_2 \mid x_1 \geq 1,\ x_1 \geq x_2\}$ is
(a) convex set (b) not convex set
(c) closed set (d) None of these

**114.** For given $\bar{c} = (2, 6, 7)$ and $z = 4$, the equation of hyperplane is given by
(a) $2x_1 + 6x_2 + 7x_3 \neq 4$ (b) $2x_1 + 6x_2 + 7x_3 > 4$
(c) $2x_1 + 6x_2 + 7x_3 = 4$ (d) None of these

**115.** The Euclidean space $E^n$ is
(a) open set
(b) closed set
(c) both open and closed set
(d) Neither open nor closed

**116.** The convex combination of two points $\bar{x}_1, \bar{x}_2 \in X$ is referred as
(a) $(1-\lambda)\bar{x}_1 + \lambda\bar{x}_2,\ 0 \leq \lambda \leq 1$
(b) $(1-\lambda)\bar{x}_1 + \lambda\bar{x}_2$, $\lambda$ any real number
(c) $\lambda\bar{x}_1 + \lambda\bar{x}_2,\ 0 \leq \lambda \leq 1$
(d) $\lambda\bar{x}_1 + \lambda\bar{x}_2$, $\lambda$ any real number

**117.** The vector $\bar{a}$ is orthogonal to vector $\bar{b}$, if
(a) $\bar{a}\bar{b} = 0$ (b) $\bar{a}\bar{b} \geq 0$
(c) $\bar{a}\bar{b} \leq 0$ (d) None of these

**118.** For a given $\bar{c} = (2, 3)$ and $z = 7$, the positive closed space is a set
(a) $\{2x_1 + 3x_2 \geq 7\}$ (b) $\{2x_1 + 3x_2 \leq 7\}$
(c) $\{2x_1 + 3x_2 > 7\}$ (d) $\{2x_1 + 3x_2 < 7\}$

**119.** The inside of a circle with radius $\varepsilon > 0$ and centre $\bar{a}$ is the set of points
(a) $\{x / |\bar{x} - \bar{a}| < \varepsilon\}$ (b) $\{x / |\bar{x} - \bar{a}| > \varepsilon\}$
(c) $\{x / |\bar{x} - \bar{a}| = \varepsilon\}$ (d) None of these

**120.** Two vertices of the feasible region $P$ of an LPP are $x_1 = (0, 1, 1, 2,)$ and $x_2 = (3, 0, 0, 1)$. Then, a point which cannot be vertex of $P$ is
(a) (1, 2/3, 2/3, 5/3) (b) (6, –1, –1, 0)
(c) (1/2, 5/6, 5/6, 11/6) (d) All of these

**121.** Match the following primal with their dual Primal
(i) Max $Z_x = CX$ subject to $AX \leq b$; $X \geq 0$
(ii) Min $Z_x = CX$ subject to $AX \leq b$; $X \geq 0$
(iii) Max $Z_x = CX$ subject to $AX = b$; $X$ are unrestricted in sign
Dual
(A) Min $Z_w = b^T W$ subject to $A^T W = C^T$, $W$ is unrestricted in sign
(B) Min $Z_w = b^T W$ subject to $A^T W \geq C^T; W \geq 0$
(C) Max $Z_w = b^T W$ subject to $A^T W \leq C^T; W \leq 0$
(D) Max $Z_w = b^T W$ subject to $A^T W \geq C^T;\ W \geq 0$,
Then,

| | (i) | (ii) | (iii) |
|---|---|---|---|
| (a) | B | C | A |
| (b) | A | C | D |
| (c) | B | D | A |
| (d) | D | B | C |

**122.** Simplex method is the
(a) algebraic procedure for solving LPP
(b) geometric procedure for solving LPP
(c) both (a) and (b)
(d) None of the above

**123.** Let $E^2$ is Euclidean plane, a equation of circle with centre (0, 0) and radius $\varepsilon$ is
(a) $|\bar{x}| < \varepsilon$ (b) $|\bar{x}| > \varepsilon$
(c) $|\bar{x}| = \varepsilon$ (d) None of these

**124.** Let $S$ be a convex set and $w$ be its a boundary point, then a hyperplane $H$ is said to be a supporting hyperplane of $S$ at $w$, if
(a) $S$ lies in one of its closed half spaces
(b) $w$ lies on $H$
(c) either (a) or (b)
(d) Both (a) and (b)

**125.** If there exist feasible solutions to both the primal and its dual. Then,
(a) the primal may have an unbounded solution while the dual a bounded solution
(b) the primal may have a bounded solution while the dual an unbounded solution
(c) both, the primal and the dual, may have unbounded solutions
(d) both, the primal and the dual, must have bounded optimal solutions

**126.** In linear programming problem, the solution exists in convex set and the convex set have optimal solution at
(a) extreme points (b) boundary point
(c) inside point (d) None of these

**127.** The intersection of finite number of convex sets is
(a) convex set (b) open set
(c) closed set (d) None of these

**128.** The set $S = \{(x_1, x_2) : x_1^2 + x_2^2 \leq 1,\ x_1^2 - x_2 \geq 0\}$ is
(a) non-empty and convex set
(b) non-empty and non-convex set
(c) empty and convex set
(d) empty and non-convex set

**129.** The optimal basis of primal consists of variables $x_1$ and $x_2$. The cost of these are 3 and 0 respectively and the corresponding columns are $(3, 2)^T$ and $(0, -1)^T$, respectively. Then, the optimal solution $(w_1, w_2)$ of its dual is

(a) (3, 0) (b) (1, 0)
(c) (1, 2) (d) None of these

**130.** If there is an optimal solution to linear programming problem, then optimal solution exists at

(a) extreme point (b) inside point
(c) boundary point (d) None of these

**131.** The intersection of two convex sets is a

(a) convex set (b) concave set
(c) open set (d) None of these

**132.** If $S = \{(2, 3), (4, 5)\} \subset R^2$, then convex Hull $< S >$ of $S$ is

(a) $\{(x, y): y = x + 1, 2 \le x \le 4, 3 \le y \le 5\}$
(b) $\{(x, y): y = x + 1, 2 \le x \le 3, 4 \le y \le 5\}$
(c) $\{(x, y): y = x - 1, 2 \le x \le 4, 3 \le y \le 5\}$
(d) $\{(x, y): y = x - 1, 2 \le x \le 3, 4 \le y \le 5\}$

**133.** The shadow prices (or opportunity cost) of the LPP Max $z = 3x_1 + 2x_2$ subject to $x_1 + x_2 \le 4$, $x_1 - x_2 \le 2$ and $x_1, x_2 \ge 0$; (given that optimal solution of this LPP is $x_1 = 3$, $x_2 = 1$ and $z = 11$); are

(a) $\frac{5}{2}, \frac{1}{2}$ (b) $2, \frac{3}{2}$
(c) $\frac{1}{2}, \frac{3}{2}$ (d) $\frac{3}{2}, \frac{1}{2}$

**134.** If a feasible solution of linear programming problem exist, the region of feasible solution is

(a) convex set (b) connected set
(c) non-convex set (d) None of these

**135.** A hyperplane is

(a) concave set (b) convex set
(c) disconnected set (d) None of these

**136.** If $S_1 = \{x : |x| = 5\}$ and $S_2 = \{x : |x| > 5\}$, then convex hulls of $S_1$ and $S_2$ are, respectively.

(a) $\{x : |x| \ge 5\}$ and $\{x : |x| \ge 5\}$
(b) $\{x : |x| \le 5\}$ and $\{x : |x| \ge 5\}$
(c) $\{x : |x| \le 5\}$ and $R$
(d) $R$ and $\{x : |x| \ge 5\}$

**137.** Non-negativity restriction states, if $x_j$ are some variables, then

(a) $x_j \ge 0$ (b) $x_j = 0$ (c) $x_j \le 0$ (d) $x_j > 0$

**138.** A holed disk is

(a) convex set (b) connected set
(c) disconnected set (d) None of these

**139.** The set $S = \{(x, y) : x^2 + y^2 = 1\}$ *i.e.*, a circle of unit radius is a

(a) convex set
(b) non-convex set
(c) convex hull of finite number of points
(d) None of the above

**140.** If primal : max $z_x = x_1 + x_2 + x_3$, $x_1 \ge 0$, $x_2 \ge 0$, $x_3 \ge 0$, then the solutions of primal and its dual are respectively,

(a) infeasible, infeasible (b) feasible, feasible
(c) feasible, infeasible (d) infeasible, feasible

**141.** If $x_j's$ are feasible solution to LPP, then

(a) $x_j \ge 0$ (b) $x_j \le 0$
(c) $x_j = 0$ (d) None of these

**142.** A square is a convex set, its boundary points are

(a) vertices and sides (b) vertices only
(c) sides only (d) inside

**143.** A subset $S \subset R^n$, is said to be convex iff for any $x_1$, $x_2 \in S$ imply

(a) $\lambda_1 x_1 + \lambda_2 x_2 \in S, \lambda_1 + \lambda_2 = 1$
(b) $\lambda_1 x_1 + \lambda_2 x_2 \in S, \lambda_1 \ge 0, \lambda_2 \ge 0$
(c) $\lambda_1 x_1 + \lambda_2 x_2, \lambda_1 > 0, \lambda_2 > 0, \lambda_1 + \lambda_2 = 1$
(d) $\lambda_1 x_1 + \lambda_2 x_2 \in S, \lambda_1 \ge 0, \lambda_2 \ge 0, \lambda_1 + \lambda_2 = 1$

**Direction** (Q. Nos. 144-148) The dual is

$$\text{Max } y_1 - 3y_2 - 7y_3 + 5y_4$$
$$\text{Subject to } 5y_1 - y_2 + y_3 - 4y_4 \le 10$$
$$-5y_1 + y_2 + 4y_4 \le 5$$
$$-3y_1 - y_3 + y_4 \le 5,$$
$$y_i = 0 \ (i = 1, 2, 3, 4)$$

The iterations are given as follow. The solution is unbounded, Hence, there is no feasible solution of the given LP.

**Table**

| Basic | $y_1$ | $y_2$ | $y_3$ | $y_4$ | $s_1$ | $s_2$ | $s_3$ | sol |
|---|---|---|---|---|---|---|---|---|
| $y_0$ | $-1$ | 3 | 7 | $-5$ | 0 | 0 | 0 | 0 |
| $s_1$ | 5 | $-1$ | 1 | $-4$ | 1 | 0 | 0 | 10 |
| $s_2$ | $-5$ | 1 | 0 | 4 | 0 | 1 | 0 | 5 |
| $s_3$ | $-3$ | 0 | $-1$ | 1 | 0 | 0 | 1 | 5 |
| | $-\frac{29}{4}$ | $\frac{17}{4}$ | 7 | 0 | 0 | $\frac{5}{4}$ | 0 | $\frac{25}{4}$ |
| $s_1$ | 0 | 0 | 1 | 0 | 1 | 1 | 0 | 15 |
| $y_4$ | $-\frac{5}{4}$ | $\frac{1}{4}$ | 0 | 1 | 0 | $\frac{1}{4}$ | 0 | $\frac{5}{4}$ |
| $s_3$ | $-\frac{7}{4}$ | $-\frac{1}{4}$ | $-1$ | 0 | 0 | $-\frac{1}{4}$ | 1 | $\frac{15}{4}$ |

**144.** The problem have

(a) possible solution (b) no feasible solution
(c) bounded solution (d) None of these

**145.** In the dual, we have

(a) Max $y_1 - 3y_2 - 7y_3 + 5y_4$ and $y_i \ge 0, i = 1, 2, 3, 4$
(b) Min $y_1 - 3y_2 - 7y_3 + 5y_4$ and $y_i \le 0, i = 1, 2, 3, 4$
(c) (a) and (b) both true
(d) None is true

**146.** In the dual of this problem we have

(a) Max $y_1 - 3y_2 - 7y_3 + 5y_4$
(b) Max $10x_1 + 5x_2 + 5x_3$
(c) Max $5x_1 - 5x_2 - 3x_3 \ge 1$
(d) None of the above

**147.** The dual of the problem have
(a) non-negative variables (b) negative variables
(c) unrestricted variables (d) None of these

**148.** The problem have
(a) bounded solution (b) unbounded solution
(c) feasible solution (d) None of these

**Directions** (Q. Nos. 149-151) M/s Upkar Prakashan uses 10000 envelopes per year. Each envelope costs ₹ 32. The production department estimates setup cost as ₹ 55 and accounting department estimates the holding cost as 12.5% of the value of inventory. Replenishment rate is uniform 120 envelops per day. Assuming 250 working days.

**149.** What is the total inventory cost on the basis of optimal policy?
(a) ₹ 2644 (b) ₹ 1564 (c) ₹ 1714 (d) ₹ 1800

**150.** What is the optimal order quantity?
(a) ₹ 703 (b) ₹ 600 (c) ₹ 643 (d) ₹ 896

**151.** What are the optimal number of setups?
(a) 5 setups (b) 8 setups
(c) 10 setups (d) 16 setups

**Directions** (Q. Nos. 152-153) Suppose that *XYZ* has a product for which the assumption of the inventory model with planned shortages are valid. The following data is given for the company

Annual demand = 2000 units per year
Cost of an item = ₹ 50 per unit
Ordering cost = ₹ 25 per order
Inventory carrying cost = 20%
Back order cost = ₹ 30 units per year

**152.** What are the maximum number of back order units
(a) 29 units (b) 50 units (c) 46 units (d) 55 units

**153.** What is the minimum cost order quantity?
(a) 100 units (b) 115 units
(c) 130 units (d) 60 units

**154.** From the given table

| Basic | $C_j =$ | 0 | 5 | 0 | 0 | 0 | 0 |
|---|---|---|---|---|---|---|---|
| Var | $C_B$ | $X_B$ | $X_1$ | $X_2$ | $X_3$ | $X_4$ | $X_5$ |
| $X_2$ | 5 | 2 | 0 | 1 | 0 | 0 | 2 |
| $X_3$ | 0 | 4 | 0 | 0 | 1 | −1 | −1 |
| $X_1$ | 0 | 3 | 1 | 0 | 0 | −3 | 1 |

(where, $x_4$ and $x_5$ are slack variables)
we get,
(a) alternatives basic feasible solution, with unbounded region
(b) alternative basic feasible solution with bounded region
(c) alternative non-basic feasible solution with bounded region
(d) alternative non-basic feasible solution with unbounded region

**155.** The variables to be determined in LPP are
(a) linear only
(b) non-linear only
(c) linear and non-linear both
(d) None of the above

**156.** In the dual simplex method, let $x_j$ be a basic variable having negative value. Let all other entries in $x_j$ row of this dual simplex table be greater than or equal to zero. Then,
(a) the set of all feasible solutions is empty
(b) the LPP has an unbounded solution
(c) the LPP has the optimal solution
(d) None of the above

**157.** Which of the following is/are correct?
(a) In simplex method, we seek to eliminate primal infeasibility and seek to maintain dual feasibility
(b) In simplex method, we seek to eliminate dual infeasibility and seek to maintain primal feasibility
(c) In dual simplex method we seek to eliminate dual infeasibility and seek to maintain primal feasibility
(d) None of the above

**158.** The case of degeneracy can be arise
(a) at initial table
(b) at any stage of iteration
(c) at final table
(d) at any stage of iteration except initial stage

**159.** An objective function in general LPP contains
(a) constant term
(b) only term with variables
(c) terms other than variables
(d) None of the above

**160.** Suppose, there are 5 teachers and 5 courses one course to be given to one teacher. Suppose, we also have from the past records of evaluations by students, an average rating for each teacher's ability to teach each of the five courses. The problem of optimally assigning courses to teachers can be modeled as
(a) a network model in which a shortest path is required
(b) a sequencing model is which an optimal sequencing of courses is required
(c) an assignment model in which a linear function is to be maximized
(d) None of the above

**161.** In solving an LPP (having a finite optimal solution) by simplex method, the termination of iterations of the method indicates that
(a) the feasible solution of the primal problem has been attained.
(b) the feasible solution of the dual problem has been attained
(c) both (a) and (b) simultaneously
(d) None of the above

**162.** About an LPP, consider the following two statements

**A.** LPP has an infinite number of optimal solutions.

**B.** LPP has atleast two basic optimal solutions.

Which of the following statements is true?

(a) If A is true, then B is true
(b) If B is true, then B is false
(c) If B is false, then A is false
(d) None of the above

**163.** The constraints in the general LPP are

(a) linear function
(b) non-linear function
(c) constant function
(d) None of the above

**164.** If in cost matrix of an assignment problem, we multiply each $c_{ij}$ by a non-zero constant $k > 0$, then for the changed problem

(a) the optimal solution remains same but the optimal value of objective function may be changed
(b) the optimal solution may change but the optimal value of the objective function remains same
(c) both the optimal solution and optimal value of objective function, remains same
(d) both the optimal solution and optimal value of objective function, may be changed

**165.** In maximization LPP, if a variable corresponding to positive $z_j - c_j$ is entered and leaving variable rule is properly followed (solution space is not unbounded), then

(a) the next basic solution will be not BFS
(b) the solution may be bounded or unbounded
(c) the value of the objective function will decrease
(d) the value of objective function will increase

**166.** In context of LPP, which of the following statement is/are true?

(a) The number of extreme points of the convex set of feasible solutions may be lesser than the number of basic feasible solutions.
(b) In an extreme point, vectors associated to the positive $x_i$'s may be LI or LD.
(c) There is always a one-to-one correspondence between the extreme points and basic feasible solutions
(d) None of the above

**167.** An objective function in general LPP is

(a) linear function
(b) non-linear function
(c) constant function
(d) None of the above

**168.** Consider the primal problem (LP)

Max $\quad z_x = 4x_1 + 3x_2$

Subject to

$$x_1 + x_2 \le 8$$
$$2x_1 + x_2 \le 10$$
$$x_1 \ge 0,\ x_2 \ge 10$$

Together with its dual (LD). Then,

(a) (LP) and (LD) both are infeasible
(b) (LP) and (LD) both are feasible
(c) (LP) is feasible but (LD) is infeasible
(d) (LP) is infeasible but (LD) is feasible

**169.** The final simplex table for a LPP is given below, where $x_3$ and $x_4$ are slack variables.

| Basic | $x_1$ | $x_2$ | $x_3$ | $x_4$ | RHS |
|---|---|---|---|---|---|
| $x_1$ | 1 | 0 | 0 | 1 | 4 |
| $x_2$ | 0 | 0 | −1 | 2 | 6 |
| $z_j - c_j$ | 0 | 0 | 2 | 2 | $z = 12$ |

Then,

(a) the feasible region is unbounded but the optimal value is bounded
(b) both the feasible region and the optimal value are unbounded
(c) both the feasible region and the optimal value are bounded
(d) None of the above

**170.** If the dual of the problem has infeasible solution, then the value of objective function is

(a) unbounded
(b) bounded
(c) no solution
(d) None of the above

**171.** For an LPP having $n$ decision variables and $m$ constraints, then any extreme point (let us say $x = [x_1, x_2, \ldots, x_n]^T$ be an extreme point) can have atmost

(a) $n$ positive $x_i$'s
(b) $m$ positive $x_i$'s
(c) $k$ positive $x_i$'s, where $m \le k < n$
(d) None of the above

**172.** If for basic feasible solution $\bar{x}_B$, the problem min $z = \bar{c}\,\bar{x}$, subject to $A\bar{x} = \bar{b}$, $\bar{x} \ge \bar{0}$, $z_j - c_j \le 0$ for all $j$, then $\bar{x}_B$ is a

(a) optimal solution
(b) non-optimal solution
(c) only basic feasible solution
(d) None of the above

**173.** In context of an LPP, which of the following is incorrect?

(a) Key column in simplex table indicates the incoming basic currently non-basic variable and the key row represents the basic variable that will become non-basic.
(b) If all the entries in the key column are negative or zero and the corresponding $(z_i - c_j) < 0$, (for a maximization problem), then there is an unbounded solution to the LPP.
(c) In improving a non-optimum solution the key element may be positive, negative or zero.
(d) For a minimization problem, the feasible solution can be unbounded.

**174.** The assignment problem is a
(a) non-linear programming problem
(b) dynamic programming problem
(c) integer linear programming problem
(d) integer non-linear programming problem

**175.** Which of the following statements is true?
(a) An LPP has a basic feasible solution, if it has feasible solution.
(b) An LPP always has a feasible solution.
(c) An LPP has a unique optimal solution, if it has a feasible solution.
(d) None of the above

**176.** If there is an optimal basic feasible solution to a linear programming problem and for same $\bar{a}_j$ not in the basis, $z_j - c_j = 0$ , $y_{ij} \leq 0$ for all *i*, then
(a) non-basic optima will exist
(b) non-basic optima will not exist
(c) Sometimes optima will exist
(d) None is true

**177.** In regular simplex method,
(a) the iterations move towards feasibility maintaining optimality
(b) the iterations move towards optimality maintaining feasibility
(c) the iterations maintain both feasibility and optimality
(d) None of the above

**178.** If in linear programming problem the number of variable in primal are *n* and number of constraints in its dual are *m*, then
(a) $m \geq n$ (b) $m \leq n$
(c) $m = n$ (d) None of these

**179.** The set of basic optimal solutions to an LPP is
(a) finite
(b) convex
(c) either singleton or infinite
(d) None of the above

**180.** if $\bar{x}_1, \bar{x}_2, \ldots, \bar{x}_k$ are different optimal solution to linear programming problem, then any convex combination of $\bar{x}_1, \bar{x}_2, \ldots, \bar{x}_k$ is
(a) not an optimal solution (b) an optimal solution
(c) non-feasible solution (d) None of these

**181.** At any iteration of the usual simplex method (maximization problem), if there is atleast one basic variable in the basis at zero level and all $(z_i - c_j) \geq 0$, then the current solution is
(a) infeasible (b) unbounded
(c) non-degenerate (d) degenerate

**182.** Consider the LPP

$$Z_{max} = 7x_1 + 4x_2 + 3x_3 + 5x_4$$

subject to $2x_1 + x_2 + 5x_3 - x_4 = 5$
$x_1 + 7x_2 - x_3 + 3x_4 = 9$
$x_1, x_2, x_3, x_4 \geq 0$. Then, the solution
$x_1 = 2, x_2 = 1, x_3 = 0, x_4 = 0$ is a
(a) feasible solution but not a basic feasible solution
(b) feasible solution and a degenerate basic feasible solution
(c) feasible solution and a non-degenerate basic feasible solution
(d) basic solution but not a feasible solution

**183.** Two hyperplanes are parallel, if they have
(a) same unit normal (b) distinct unit normal
(c) same normal (d) None of these

**184.** If in phase I of the simplex method, an artificial variable remains at positive level in the optimal table of phase I, then
(a) the solution is unbounded
(b) there exists an optimal solution
(c) there exists no solution
(d) None of the above

**185.** Let $X_1$ be a feasible solution to Min $\phi(X) = c^T X$ subject to $AX \geq b$, $X \geq 0$ and $Y_1$ be a feasible solution to Max $\psi(Y) = b^T Y$, subject to $A^T Y \leq c$, $Y \geq 0$, then
(a) $\phi(X_1) \geq \psi(Y_1)$ (b) $\phi(X_1) \leq \psi(Y_1)$
(c) $\phi(X_1) = \psi(Y_1)$ (d) None of these

**186.** Let *f* be a function defined on a convex set $S \subset R^n$, then *f* is said to be convex function over *S*, if for any two points $x_1$ and $x_2$ in *S* and for all $\lambda \in [0, 1]$, we have
(a) $f[(1-\lambda)x_1 + \lambda x_2] \geq (1-\lambda)f(x_1) + \lambda f(x_2)$
(b) $f[(1-\lambda)x_1 + \lambda x_2] \leq (1-\lambda)f(x_1) + \lambda f(x_2)$
(c) $f[(1-\lambda)x_1 + \lambda x_2] < (1-\lambda)f(x_1) + \lambda f(x_2)$
(d) $f[(1-\lambda)x_1 + \lambda x_2] > (1-\lambda)f(x_1) + \lambda f(x_2)$

**187.** For given $\bar{c} = (6, 7, 8)$, $z = 9$, the negative closed half plane is the set
(a) $6x_1 + 7x_2 + 8x_3 \geq 9$ (b) $6x_1 + 7x_2 + 8x_3 \leq 9$
(c) $6x_1 + 7x_2 + 8x_3 = 9$ (d) None of these

**188.** Which of the following statements is not correct?
(a) It is possible for the initial solution to an LPP be degenerate.
(b) As and when a degenerate variable is outgoing no change will take place in the value of objective function.
(c) In a simplex table, the key column element are 2, 7, 5 and corresponding $X_{Bi}$ values are 4, 18 and 10. This indicate the degenerate solution in the next simplex table.
(d) None of the above

**189.** In simplex iteration, $x_j$ enters the basis. Then,
(a) $x_j$ can leave the basis in the next iteration
(b) $x_j$ cannot leave the basis in next iteration
(c) Both (A) and (B) are true
(d) None of the above

**190.** Let the optimal of an LPP occur at two vertices $x_1$ and $x_2$, then it also occurs at $x = (1-\lambda)x_1 + \lambda x_2$, $0 < \lambda < 1$ and
(a) *x* is a basic solution
(b) *x* is a basic feasible solution
(c) *x* is a non-basic soluton
(d) None of the above

**191.** Given, $\bar{c} = (2, 3)$ and $z = 7$, the hyperplane in $E^2$ is defined by

(a) $2x_1 + 3x_2 = 7$ (b) $2x_1 + 3x_2 \geq 7$
(c) $2x_1 + 3x_2 \leq 7$ (d) None of these

**192.** The minimum ratio criterion in the simplex method ensures that

(a) there is a maximum possible improvement in the objective function
(b) the next iterative solution obtained is basic
(c) the next iterative solution obtained is feasible
(d) the column indroduced is independent of the columns constituting the present basic

**193.** In a two phase simplex method, if in phase I an artificial variable remains at positive level in the optimal table of phase I, then

(a) the solution is unbounded
(b) there exist no solution
(c) there exist an optimal solution
(d) None of the above

**194.** The solution of LPP

$$Z_{max} = -x_1 + 5x_2 - 8x_3$$

subject to $2x_1 - x_2 + 2x_3 \leq 2$

$$x_1, x_2, x_3 \geq 0$$

(a) –8 (b) –10
(c) 2 (d) None of these

**195.** The line segment between $\bar{x}_1$ and $\bar{x}$ is the set of points such that

(a) $\{\bar{x} \mid \bar{x} = \lambda\bar{x}_2 + (1-\lambda)\bar{x}_1, 0 \leq \lambda \leq 1\}$
(b) $\{\bar{x} \mid \bar{x} = \lambda\bar{x}_2 + (1-\lambda)\bar{x}_1, \lambda = 1\}$
(c) $\{\bar{x} \mid \bar{x} = \lambda\bar{x}_2 + (1-\lambda)\bar{x}_1, \lambda$ any number$\}$
(d) None of the above

**196.** The variable which is unrestricted in sign is equivalent to the difference of two

(a) negative variables (b) non-negative variables
(c) neither (a) nor (b) (d) Both (a) and (b)

**197.** If the primal has alternate optimal solution, then dual has

(a) alternate optimal solution
(b) degenerate optimal solution
(c) unbounded solution
(d) non-feasible solution

**198.** A basic solution to the system $Ax = b$ is called degenerate, if

(a) atmost one of the basic variables vanishes
(b) exactly one of the basic variables vanishes
(c) atleast one of the basic variables vanishes
(d) more than one of the basic variables vanishes

**199.** The availability vector is in dual simplex method must be of type

(a) $\geq 0$
(b) $\leq 0$
(c) Both a) and (b) are ture
(d) None of the above

**200.** The equation of line passing through points $\bar{x}_1$ and $\bar{x}_2$ $(\bar{x}_1 \neq \bar{x}_2)$ in $E^n$ is

(a) $\lambda\bar{x}_2 + (1-\lambda)\bar{x}_1 = \bar{x} \in E^n$, $\lambda$ any real number
(b) $\lambda\bar{x}_2 + (1-\lambda)\bar{x}_1 = \bar{x} \in E^n, \lambda < 0$
(c) $\lambda\bar{x}_2 + (1-\lambda)\bar{x}_1 = \bar{x} \in E^n, 1 < x < 0$
(d) None of the above

**201.** Consider the following LPP

$$\text{Min } z = 10x_1 + x_2 + 5x_3$$

subject to $5x_1 - 7x_2 + 3x_3 \geq 50$, $x_1, x_2, x_3 \geq 0$, then its optimal value is

(a) $\frac{50}{3}$ (b) $\frac{10}{3}$
(c) $\frac{250}{3}$ (d) $\frac{100}{3}$

**202.** Given, $2x_1 + x_2 - x_3 = 2$ and $3x_1 + 2x_2 + x_3 = 3$, then one of the basis is

(a) $\begin{pmatrix} 2 & 1 \\ 3 & 2 \end{pmatrix}$ (b) $\begin{pmatrix} 1 & 0 \\ 0 & 1 \end{pmatrix}$
(c) $\begin{pmatrix} 2 & 1 & -1 \\ 3 & 2 & 1 \end{pmatrix}$ (d) None of these

**203.** The LPP

$$\text{Max } z = x_1 + 2x_2 + 3x_3 + 4x_4$$

subject to $\frac{x_1}{2} + x_2 + \frac{3x_3}{2} + 2x_4 \geq 8$

$x_1, x_2, x_3, x_4 \geq 0$ has

(a) no feasible solution
(b) unique optimal solution
(c) an unbounded solution
(d) None of the above

**204.** In simplex method, the variable $x_j$ leave the basis in some iteration. Then,

(a) $s_j$ can enter the basis in the next iteration
(b) $x_j$ does not enter the basis in next iteration
(c) (a) and (b) both true
(d) None of the above

**205.** The set $\{\bar{x} \mid x_1^2 + x_2^2 \leq 6\}$ is

(a) connected set (b) disconnected set
(c) open set (d) None of these

**206.** Which of the following statement is true?

(a) For every instance of an LP the set of optimal solutions is finite.
(b) For every instance of an LP the set of feasible points is unbounded.
(c) For every instance of an LP the set of basic feasible solution is finite.
(d) None of the above

**207.** In a linear programming problem in standard form, there are six variables and four constraints. Then, the number of basic feasible solution are

(a) 15 (b) less than 15
(c) more than 15 (d) None of these

**208.** For given hyperplane $\bar{c}\,\bar{x} = z$ in $R^n$. Then, the following sets define closed half spaces
(a) $\{\bar{x} \mid \bar{c}\,\bar{x} \le z\}$ and $\{\bar{x} \mid \bar{c}\,\bar{x} \ge z\}$
(b) $\{\bar{x} \mid \bar{c}\,\bar{x} < z\}$ and $\{\bar{x} \mid \bar{c}\,\bar{x} > z\}$
(c) $\{\bar{x} \mid \bar{x} < \bar{c}\}$ and $\{\bar{x} \mid \bar{x} > \bar{c}\}$
(d) None of the above

**209.** The line passing through two points $x_1$ and $x_2$ is the set
(a) $\{x : x = (1-\lambda)x_1 + \lambda x_2, \lambda \in R\}$
(b) $\{x : x = (1-\lambda)x_1 + \lambda x_2, 0 \le \lambda \le 1\}$
(c) $\{x : x = (1-\lambda)x_1 + \lambda x_2, 0 \ge \lambda \ge 1\}$
(d) $\{x : x = (1-\lambda)x_1 + \lambda x_2, 0 < \lambda < 1\}$

**210.** Dual simplex method is applicable, if
(a) optimality condition is satisfied in the initial table
(b) optimality condition is satisfied in the starting table
(c) optimal condition does not satisfy
(d) None of the above

**211.** Given, $\bar{c}\,\bar{x} = z$ an hyperplane in $R^n$, then the following sets define open half space
(a) $\{\bar{x} \mid \bar{c}\,\bar{x} \le z\}$ and $\{\bar{x} \mid \bar{c}\,\bar{x} \ge z\}$
(b) $\{\bar{x} \mid \bar{c}\,\bar{x} < z\}$ and $\{\bar{x} \mid \bar{c}\,\bar{x} > z\}$
(c) $\{\bar{c} \mid \bar{x} \ge z\}$ and $\{\bar{c} \mid \bar{x} \le z\}$
(d) None of the above

**212.** For the system

$$x_1 + 2x_2 + x_3 + x_4 = 2,$$
$$x_1 + 2x_2 + \frac{x_3}{2} + x_5 = 2$$

which of the following is a basic feasible solution?
(a) $x_1 = -1, x_2 = 1/2, x_3 = x_4 = x_5 = 0$
(b) $x_1 = 1, x_1 = 1/2, x_3 = x_4 = x_5 = 0$
(c) $x_1 = 1, x_3 = 1/2, x_2 = x_4 = x_5 = 0$
(d) None of the above

**213.** A linear programming problem in which all or some of the variables, are constrained to assume non-negative integer values is referred as
(a) integer programming problem
(b) dynamic programming problem
(c) non-linear programming problem
(d) None of the above

**214.** The set $\{\bar{x} \mid \bar{x}_1^2 + \bar{x}_2^2 < 1 \text{ or } (x_1 - 5)^2 + (x_2 - 6)^2 < 1\}$
(a) connected set
(b) disconnected set
(c) closed set
(d) None of the above

**215.** The given system
$2x_1 + 3x_2 + 4x_3 + 2x_4 = 2$
$3x_1 + 4x_2 + 6x_3 = 3$ has
(a) 5 degenerate basic solution
(b) 6 basic solution and all are non-degenerate solution
(c) 5 basic solution but 6 degenerate solution
(d) 5 basic solution in which 4 solution are degenerate

**216.** Let $B = (A_1, A_4, A_6)$ constitute a basis for linear programming problem. Let $A_2 = aA_1 + bA_4 + cA_6$. Let in $B$ the column $A_4$ be replaced by $A_2$. Then, new $B$ will be again be a basis provided
(a) $a$, $b$ and $c$ all are positive
(b) $b = 0$
(c) $b \ne 0$
(d) None of the above

**217.** The set $\{(x_1, x_2) \mid (x_1 - 1)^2 + (x_2 - 3) \le 2\}$ is
(a) strictly bounded
(b) bounded above
(c) bounded below
(d) None of the above

**218.** The number of basic solution to the system

$$x_1 + 2x_2 + 10x_3 + 4x_4 = 5$$
$$x_1 + x_2 + 5x_3 + 4x_4 = -8 \text{ is}$$

(a) 0 (b) 4
(c) 6 (d) Infinite

**219.** For the given problem

$$x_1 + x_2 - x_3 - 2x_4 - 5x_5 = 2$$
$$x_2 + x_3 + 5x_4 - 5x_5 = 2$$

The solution $x_1 = x_3 = x_4 = 0, x_2 = 7, x_5 = 1$ is
(a) not a basic solution
(b) a basic feasible solution
(c) a basic solution
(d) None of the above

**220.** If in the primal the number of constraints are $m$ and in dual the number of variables are $n$, then
(a) $m \ge n$ (b) $m \le n$
(c) $m = n$ (d) None of these

**221.** The set $A \subset E^n$ is bounded below, if there exist
(a) upper limit
(b) lower limit
(c) upper and lower both limits
(d) None of the above

**222.** The number of the degenerate basic solutions of the system $x_1 + 2x_2 + x_3 = 4$, $2x_1 + x_2 + 5x_3 = 5$ is
(a) 0 (b) 1
(c) 2 (d) 3

**223.** The simplex multiplier
(a) is a feasible solution of the dual
(b) is a basic feasible solution of the dual
(c) corresponding to optimal primal table, is the optimal solution of dual
(d) None of the above

**224.** In linear programming problem, if in primal objective function is of maximization, then for its dual the objective function is of
(a) maximization
(b) minimization
(c) optimization
(d) None of the above

**225.** Given, $\begin{pmatrix} 2 & 1 & -1 \\ 3 & 2 & 1 \end{pmatrix}\begin{pmatrix} x_1 \\ x_2 \\ x_3 \end{pmatrix} = \begin{pmatrix} 2 \\ 3 \end{pmatrix}$, then the one of the basis is

(a) $\begin{pmatrix} 2 & 1 \\ 3 & 2 \end{pmatrix}$ (b) $\begin{pmatrix} 2 & 1 & -1 \\ 3 & 2 & 1 \end{pmatrix}$

(c) $\begin{pmatrix} 2 & 3 \\ 2 & 3 \end{pmatrix}$ (d) $\begin{pmatrix} 1 & 6 \\ 3 & 4 \end{pmatrix}$

**226.** Which of the following statements is correct?

(a) Every LPP admits an optimal solution.
(b) Every LPP admits unique optimal solution.
(c) If an LPP admits two optimal solution it has an infinite no of optimal solutions.
(d) The set of all feasible solutions to an LPP is not a convex set.

**227.** If the primal of LPP has unbounded solution, then dual of the problem

(a) has an optimal solution
(b) has no solution
(c) has an unbounded solution
(d) None of the above

**228.** If a slack or surplus variable $s_j$ is in optimal primal basis, then the optimal dual solution

(a) the dual variable corresponding to $j$th primal constraint is zero
(b) the slack or surplus variable attached to $j$th dual constraint is zero
(c) (a) and (b) both true
(d) None is true

**229.** The basis of $\begin{pmatrix} 1 & 2 & 3 \\ 2 & 1 & 5 \end{pmatrix}\begin{pmatrix} x_1 \\ x_2 \\ x_3 \end{pmatrix} = \begin{pmatrix} 4 \\ 5 \end{pmatrix}$ is

(a) $\begin{pmatrix} 1 & 2 \\ 2 & 1 \end{pmatrix}$ (b) $\begin{pmatrix} 1 & 2 \\ 1 & 2 \end{pmatrix}$

(c) $\begin{pmatrix} 1 & 3 & 1 \\ 5 & 6 & 2 \end{pmatrix}$ (d) $\begin{pmatrix} 1 & 2 & 3 \\ 2 & 1 & 5 \end{pmatrix}$

**230.** The constraints of linear programming problem including non-negativity restrictions are

(a) closed half space only
(b) hyperplane only
(c) either closed half spaces or hyperplanes
(d) None of the above

**231.** In a maximization linear programming problem the variables corresponding to minimum ratio on with solution column leaves the basis. This ensures

(a) that next solution will be basic feasible solution
(b) the next solution will not be a basic feasible solution
(c) this solution is feasible
(d) None of the above

**232.** If the primal of LPP has no solution, then dual of the problem

(a) has either no solution or is unbounded
(b) has unbounded solution
(c) has an optimal solution
(d) None of the above

**233.** A basic solution to the system is degenerated, if

(a) some basic variables are non-zero
(b) some basic variables are equal to zero
(c) some basic variables are positive
(d) Some basic variables are negative

**234.** The number of feasible solutions to an LPP cannot be

(a) exactly one (b) exactly two
(c) infinite (d) finite

**235.** In two phase simplex metod, phase I

(a) gives a starting basic feasible solution
(b) optimize the objective function
(c) provides optimal solution
(d) None of the above

**236.** The constraints of a linear programming problem including non-negativity restrictions are

(a) closed half spaces only
(b) hyperplanes only
(c) either closed half spaces or hyperplanes
(d) None of the above

**237.** Let $\bar{a} \in E^n$ is an interior point of set $A \subset E^n$ and $N_\epsilon$ is the ε-neighbourhood of $\bar{a}$, then

(a) $N_\varepsilon = \{x \mid x \in A\}$
(b) $N_\varepsilon = \{x \mid x \in A^c\}$
(c) $N_\varepsilon = \{x \mid x \notin A\}$
(d) None of the above

**238.** Which of the following statements is false?

(a) The set of feasible solutions of a linear programming problem is convex.
(b) All functions in an LPP are linear.
(c) Every point lying on the line segment joining two optimal solution to a linear programming problem is also optimal solution.
(d) The set of all optimal solutions to an LPP need not be convex.

**239.** Let the optimal of a linear programming problem occur at two vertices $X_1$ and $X_2$. Then, we know that it also occurs at every $X = (1 - \lambda)X_1 + \lambda X_2$, $0 < \lambda < 1$

(a) $X$ is a basic solution
(b) $X$ is a basic feasible solution
(c) $X$ is not a basic solution
(d) None of the above

**240.** If ir a simplex table, there is a tie in the leaving variable, then

(a) the next basic feasible solution (BFS) will be a non-degenerate BFS
(b) the next BFS will be degenerate BFS
(c) the next BFS will be optimal
(d) None of the above

**241. Assertion (A)** Every solution satisfies non-negative restriction in LPP.

**Reason (R)** Every solution is feasible solution to LPP. Then,

(a) A is true because R is true
(b) A is true but R is not true
(c) R is true but A is not true
(d) Neither A nor R is true

**242.** If in a simplex table, the relative cost $Z_j - C_j$ is zero for a non-basic variable, then there exists an alternate optimal solution, provided

(a) it is starting simplex table
(b) it can be any simplex table
(c) it is optimal simplex table
(d) None of the above

**243.** If $x_j$ is a basic variable in a simplex table, then the relative cost

(a) $Z_j - C_j < 0$ (b) $Z_j - C_j > 0$
(c) $Z_j - C_j = 0$ d) None of these

**244.** Let $\bar{a} \in E^n$ is a boundary point of set $A \subset E^n$ and $N_\varepsilon$ is the ε-neighbourhood of $\bar{a}$, then

(a) $N_\varepsilon = \{x \mid x \in A \text{ or } x \in A^c\}$
(b) $N_\varepsilon = \{x \mid x \in A, x \notin A^c\}$
(c) $N_\varepsilon = \{x \mid x \notin A, x \in A^c\}$
(d) None of the above

**245.** The LPP

$$\text{Max } z = \frac{3}{2}x_1 - x_2$$

subject to

$$3x_1 - 2x_2 \le 12$$
$$x_1 \le 6$$
$$x_1, x_2 \ge 0 \text{ has}$$

(a) unique optimal solution
(b) alternative optimal solution
(c) unbounded solution
(d) no feasible solution

**246.** In simplex table of a maximization LPP the column corresponding to a variable $x_j$ is $(2; -1, 0, -3)^T$. The $Z_j - C_j = 2$ is not most negative. Then,

(a) the solution is unbounded
(b) the solution is bounded
(c) the solution may be bounded or unbounded
(d) None of the above

**247.** To find dual of linear programming problem, the primal must be in

(a) standard form (b) canonical form
(c) with ≤, =, ≥ signs (d) None of these

**248.** The ε-neighbourhood about a point $\bar{a}$ is the set of points

(a) $\{x \mid \bar{x} - \bar{a}| > \varepsilon\}$ (b) $\{x \mid \bar{x} - \bar{a}| < \varepsilon\}$
(c) $\{x \mid \bar{x} - \bar{a}| = \varepsilon\}$ (d) None of these

**249.** The LPP max $z = 3x_1 + 4x_2$ subject to $x_1 + x_2 \le -2$, $x_1, x_2 \ge 0$ has

(a) no feasible solution
(b) unbounded solution
(c) unique optimal solution
(d) multiple optimal solution

**250.** In a maximization LPP, if a variable corresponding to positive $Z_j - C_j$ is entered, the leaving variable rule is followed (and solution space is not unbounded), then

(a) the next basic solution will not be basic feasible solution
(b) the value of the objective function will decrease
(c) the value of the objective function will increase
(d) the value of the objective function remains constant

**251.** In a linear programming problem,

(a) number of basic feasible solutions ≤ number of vertices
(b) number of basic feasible solutions ≥ number of vertices
(c) number of basic feasible solutions = number of vertices
(d) None of the above

**252.** The inside of a hypersphere with centre at $\bar{a}$ and radius $\varepsilon > 0$, is the set of points

(a) $\{\bar{x} \mid |\bar{x} - \bar{a}| < \varepsilon\}$ (b) $\{\bar{x} \mid |\bar{x} - \bar{a}| > \varepsilon\}$
(c) $\{\bar{x} \mid |\bar{x} - \bar{a}| = \varepsilon\}$ (d) None of these

**253.** About an LPP (with two decision variables) Consider the following two statements

**A.** A constraint of the LPP is parallel to its objective function.

**B.** There exist and infinite number of optimal solutions to the problem.

Which of the following statements is true?

(a) If A is true, then B is true
(b) If B is true, then A is true
(c) A is true if and only if B is true
(d) None of the above

**254.** The linear programming relaxation of an integer linear programming

(a) permits a non-linear objective function
(b) ignores the integrality restrictions on the decision variables
(c) relaxes non-negativity restriction
(d) None of the above

**255.** In some simplex table of minimization LPP, the column corresponding to a variable $x_j$ is $(2; -1, 0, -3)^T$. The $Z_j - C_j$ is not most positive. Then,

(a) the solution is unbounded
(b) the solution is bounded
(c) the solution may be bounded or unbounded
(d) None of the above

**256.** Let $E^n$ be an Euclidean space, a hypersphere in $E^n$ with centre at $\bar{a}$ and radius $\varepsilon > 0$ is a set of points

(a) $\{\bar{x} \mid |\bar{x} - \bar{a}| > \varepsilon\}$ (b) $\{\bar{x} \mid |\bar{x} - \bar{a}| < \varepsilon\}$
(c) $\{\bar{x} \mid |\bar{x} - \bar{a}| = \varepsilon\}$ (d) None of these

**257.** Let $P = \{x \in R^n : Ax \le b\}$ be the feasible region of the LPP : $\max_{\lambda \in P} c^T x$ consider the following statements

**A.** $P$ is unbounded.

**B.** The optima of the LPP is unbounded

Which of the following statements is true?

(a) If A is true, then B is true
(b) If B is false, then A is false
(c) If A is false, then B is false
(d) None of the above

**258.** In an integer linear programming problem

(a) all decision variables are integers
(b) all decision variables are real numbers
(c) all decision variables are complex numbers
(d) all decision variables are non-negative

**259.** Let primal LPP be max $f(X) = C^T X$, $AX \le b$, $X \ge 0$ and dual be min $g(Y) = b^T Y$, $A^T Y \ge C$, $Y \ge 0$. Let $X^*$ and $Y^*$ be feasible solution of primal and dual. Then,

(a) $f(X^*) \le g(Y^*)$ (b) $f(X^*) \ge g(Y^*)$
(c) $f(X^*) = g(Y^*)$ (d) None of these

**260.** Consider the LPP max $z = x_1$

subject to
$$3x_1 + 4x_2 \le 10;$$
$$5x_1 - x_2 \le 9$$
$$3x_1 - 2x_2 \ge -2$$
$$x_1 - 3x_2 \le 3$$
$$x_1, x_2 \ge 0$$

Then, the value of the LPP is

(a) 9/5 (b) 2 (c) 3 (d) 10/3

**261.** If all the decision variables of an integer programming problem assumes 0 or 1 value, then the problem is called

(a) pure integer programming problem
(b) mixed integer programming problem
(c) zero one programming problem
(d) None of the above

**262.** Let $X_1$ be a possible solution to linear programming problem

max $\phi(X) = C^T X$, subject to $AX \le b$, $X \ge 0$ and $Y$ be a feasible solution to LPP

min $\psi(Y) = b^T Y$, subject to $A^T Y \ge C$, $Y \ge 0$, then

(a) $\phi(X_1) \le \psi(Y_1)$
(b) $\phi(X_1) \ge \psi(Y_1)$
(c) $\phi(X_1) = \psi(Y_1)$
(d) None of the above

**263.** Consider the statements about linear programming

(i) The number of feasible solutions is infinite and hence the number of optimal solutions is also infinite.
(ii) An LPP may have no feasible solution.
(iii) The number of optimal solutions, if exist is finite.
(iv) If one can get two optimal solutions, then one can obtain an infinite number of optimal solutions.

out of the above statements

(a) Only (i) and (iii) are true
(b) Only (ii) and (iv) are true
(c) Only (ii) is false
(d) Only (iii) is true

**264.** Consider the following LPP

min $z = -x_1 - 2x_2$

subject to $x_1 - 2x_2 \le 2$, $x_1 + x_2 \le 4$
$x_1 \ge 0$, $x_2 \ge 0$. Then,

(a) the feasible region is unbounded but the optimal value is bounded
(b) both the feasible region and the optimal value are unbounded
(c) the optimal value is unbounded but the feasible region is bounded
(d) None of the above

**265.** The primal LPP is

max $Z = y_1 - 2y_2$

Subject to
$$y_1 - 3y_2 \le -3$$
$$-y_1 + 2y_2 = -2$$
$$y_1, y_2 \ge 0$$

Then, $C_B^T B^{-1}$ of optimal table of above is (0, 1). Then, the optimal solution $(x_1, x_2)$ of dual is

(a) (0, 1)
(b) (0, −1)
(c) (0, 0)
(d) None of the above

**266.** If a variable $x_j$ is unrestricted in sign in the primal linear programming problem, then the corresponding (*i.e.*, the *j*th) dual constraint is

(a) with $\le$ sign, if the primal is a minimization problem
(b) with $\ge$ sign, if the primal in a maximization problem
(c) with equality sign
(d) None of the above

**267.** The LPP

Max $z = -3x_1 + x_2$

subject to
$$2x_1 + x_2 \le 4,$$
$$-x_1 + x_2 \le 1,$$
$$x_1 + x_2 \ge 1,$$
$$-3x_1 + x_2 \ge -3,$$
$$x_1, x_2 \ge 0 \text{ has}$$

(a) unique optimal solution
(b) alternative optimal solution
(c) constraints leading to an infeasible region
(d) constraints leading to an unbounded solution

**268.** If the value of the objective function is unbounded in primal, then the dual of the problem have

(a) infeasible solution (b) feasible solution
(c) bounded solution (d) unbounded solution

**269.** The dual of Max $Z = 5x_1 + 12x_2 + 4x_3$

subject to $x_1 + 2x_2 + x_3 \le 5$
$2x_1 - x_2 + 3x_3 = 2$
$x_1, x_2, x_3 \ge 0$

is

(a) Min $W = 5y_1 + 2y_2$
Subject to
$y_1 + 2y_2 \ge 5$
$2y_1 - y_2 \ge 12$
$y_1 + 3y_2 \ge 4$
$y_1 \ge 0$ and $y_2$
unrestricted in sign

(b) Min $W = 5x_1 + 12x_2 + 4x_3$
Subject to
$x_1 + 2x_2 + x_3 \le 5$
$2x_1 - x_2 + 3x_3 = 2$
$x_1, x_2, x_3 \ge 0$

(c) Max $W = 5x_1 + 12x_2 + 3x_3$
Subject to
$x_1 + x_2 + x_3 = 5$
$x_1 + x_2 \ge 5$
$x_1 + x_2 \le 2$

(d) None of the above

**270.** The LPP

max $z = 2x_1 + 3x_2$
subject to $x_1 + x_2 \le 2$
$2x_1 + x_2 \le -2$
$x_1, x_2 \ge 0$ has

(a) no feasible solution
(b) a unique optimal solution
(c) unbounded solution
(d) multiple optimal solution

**271.** The optimal basis of primal consists of variables $x_1$ and $x_2$. The cost of these are 3 and 0 and the corresponding columns all $(3, 2)^T$ and $(0, -1)^T$. Then, the optimal solution $(y_1, y_2)$ of dual is

(a) (3, 0) (b) (1, 0)
(c) (1, 2) (d) (0, 0)

**272.** The dual of PP

Min $Z = 4x_1 + 6x_2 + 18x_3$
Subject to $x_1 + 3x_2 \ge 3$
$x_2 + 2x_3 \ge 5$
$x_j \ge 0 \ (j = 1, 2, 3)$ is

(a) Max $Z^* = 3w_1 + 5w_2$
Subject to $w_1 \le 4$
$3w_1 + w_2 \le 6$
$2w_2 \le 18$
$w_1, w_2 \ge 0$

(b) Min $Z^* = 3w_1 + 5w_2$
Subject to
$x_1 + 3x_2 \le 3$
$x_1 + 2x_2 \ge 5$
$x_j \le 0$

(c) Min $Z = 4x_1 + 6x_2 + 18x_3$
Subject to
$x_1 + 3x_2 \le 3$
$x_2 + 2x_3 \le 5$
$x_j \le 0$

(d) None of the above

**273.** If *i*th constraint in the primal linear programming problem is an equality, then the corresponding (*i.e.*, *i*th) dual variable is

(a) unrestricted in sign
(b) restricted to greater than zero
(c) restricted to less than zero
(d) None of the above

**274.** The dual of LPP Max $Z = 5x_1 + 6x_2$

Subject to $x_1 + 9x_2 \le 60$
$2x_1 + 3x_2 \le 45$
$5x_1 - 2x_2 \le 20$
$x_2 \le 30$
and $x_1, x_2 \ge 0$

is

(a) Min $W = 60y_1 + 45y_2 + 20y_3 + 30y_4$
$y_1 + 2y_2 + 5y_3 \ge 5$
$9y_1 + 3y_2 - 2y_3 + y_4 \ge 6$
$y_1, y_2, y_3, y_4 \ge 0$

(b) Min $Z = 5x_1 + 6x_2$
Subject to
$x_1 + 9x_2 \le 60$
$2x_1 + 3x_2 \le 45$
$5x_1 - 2x_2 \le 20$
$x_2 \le 30$
$x_1, x_2 \ge 0$

(c) Max $W = 5x_1 + 6x_2$
Subject to
$x_1 + x_2 + x_3 = 0$
$x_1 + x_2 = 6$

(d) None of the above

**275.** In an LPP, if the objective function is parallel to a constraint and the feasible region is non-empty, then the objective function may assume

(a) an unbounded solution
(b) unique optimal solution
(c) multiple optimal solution
(d) any one of the above

**276.** The dual of a dual linear programming problem is

(a) primal
(b) dual
(c) dual of a dual
(d) None of the above

**277.** The dual of LPP

Max $Z = 3x_1 + 4x_2$

Subject to

$2x_1 + 3x_2 \leq 16$

$5x_1 + 2x_2 \geq 20$

$x_1, x_2 \geq 0$ is

(a) Min $Z = 3x_1 + 4x_2$
Subject to
$$2x_1 + 3x_2 \geq 16$$
$$5x_1 + 2x_2 \leq 20$$
$$x_1, x_2 \leq 0$$

(b) Min $Z^* = 16y_1 + 20y_2$
Subject to
$$2y_1 - 5y_2 \geq 3$$
$$3y_1 - 2y_2 \geq 4$$
$$y_1, y_2 \geq 0$$

(c) Min $Z = 16x_1 + 20x_2$
Subject to
$$x_1 + x_2 = 3$$
$$x_1 + x_3 = 4$$
$x_1, x_2$ unrestricted is sign

(d) None of the above

**278.** Consider an LPP min $z = 6x + 10y$ subject to $x \geq 6$, $y \geq 2$, $2x + y \geq 10$, $x, y \geq 0$. Redundant constraint in this LPP is

(a) $x \geq 6$ (b) $2x + y \geq 10$
(c) both (a) and (b) (d) None of these

**279.** The maximum value of $P = 4x + 2y$ subject to $4x + 2y \leq 46$, $x + 3y \leq 24$, $x \geq 0$ and $y \geq 0$ occurs at

(a) one point
(b) two point
(c) four points
(d) infinite number of points

**280.** If the dual of the linear programming problem have a finite optimal solution, then primal process

(a) finite optimal solution
(b) unbounded solution
(c) no solution
(d) infinite solution

**281.** If the optimum of an LPP with a non-constant objective function $f(x)$ occurs at vertices $A$ and $B$ of the feasible region $S$, then

(a) $A$ and $B$ may be any two vertices
(b) $A$ and $B$ must be adjacent vertices
(c) there exists a third vertex $C$ of $S$ at which also optimum occurs
(d) None of the above

**282.** The dual of LPP maximize $3x_1 + 5x_2$

Subject to

$2x_1 - 3x_2 = 8$

$4x_1 + x_2 \geq 3$

$x_2 \leq 1$

and

$x_1, x_2 \geq 0$ is

(a) Min $8u_1 - 3u_2 + u_3$
Subject to
$$2u_1 - 4u_2 \geq -3$$
$$-3u_1 - u_2 + u_3 \geq -5$$
$u_1$ unrestricted and
$$u_2, u_3 \geq 0$$

(b) Min $3x_1 + 5x_3$
Subject to
$$2x_1 - 3x_2 \leq 8$$
$$4x_1 + x_2 \leq 3$$
$$x_2 \geq 1$$
$$x_1, x_2 \leq 0$$

(c) (a) and (b) both true
(d) None of the above

**283.** The car and parking in queueing system identifies

(a) customer and server (b) server and customer
(c) both customers (d) None of these

**284.** The set $\{(x, y) : y < x^2 + 2x + 1\}$ is

(a) convex set
(b) non-convex set
(c) convex polyhedron
(d) None of the above

**285.** For M/M/1 queueing system, the expected number of customers in system are

(a) $L_s = \dfrac{\lambda}{\mu - \lambda}$ (b) $L_s = \dfrac{\lambda - \mu}{\lambda}$

(c) $L_s = \dfrac{\mu}{\mu - \lambda}$ (d) None of these

**286.** The set $S = \{(x, y) : xy \leq 0\}$ is

(a) convex and unbounded
(b) convex and bounded
(c) non-convex and unbounded
(d) non-convex and bounded

**287.** The passenger and the train in queueing system describers

(a) customer and server (b) server and customer
(c) both server (d) None of these

**288.** For M/M/1 queueing system, the expected number of customers in the system are

(a) $L_s = \dfrac{\rho}{1 - \rho}$ (b) $L_s = \dfrac{1 - \rho}{\rho}$

(c) $L_s = 1 - \rho$ (d) None of these

**289.** If the injured goes to doctor for treatment, then in queueing system, the doctor and injured are respectively

(a) server and customer (b) customer and server
(c) both customer (d) None of these

**290.** The traffic intensity for M/M/1 system is given by

(a) $\rho = \lambda / \mu$
(b) $\rho = \mu / \lambda$
(c) $\rho = \lambda\mu$
(d) None of the above

**291.** The mean and variance of the poisson distribution are
(a) equal (b) mean > variance
(c) mean < variance (d) None of these

**292.** For $M/M/1/N$ queue model, the probability $p_0$, that there are no customers in the system is

(a) $p_n = \begin{cases} \dfrac{1-\rho}{1-\rho^{N+1}}\rho^n, & \rho \neq 1 \\ \dfrac{1}{N+1}, & \rho = 1 \end{cases}$

(b) $p_n = \begin{cases} \dfrac{1-\rho}{\rho^{N+1}}\rho^n, & \rho \neq 1 \\ 1, & \rho = 1 \end{cases}$

(c) $p_n = \begin{cases} \dfrac{1+\rho^{N+1}}{\rho}, & \rho \neq 1 \\ N+1, & \rho = 1 \end{cases}$

(d) None of the above

**Directions** (Q. Nos. 293-296) An annual demand for safety suits in 3200 units. The unit cost is ₹ 6 and carrying charges 25% per annum. If the cost of procurement is ₹ 150.

**293.** Number of orders per year
(a) 4 (b) 2
(c) 3 (d) 1

**294.** What is the economic order quantity?
(a) 200 units (b) 600 units
(c) 800 units (d) 100 units

**295.** What is the time between two consecutive order?
(a) 13 months (b) 3 months
(c) 6 months (d) 2 months

**296.** What is the optimal cost?
(a) ₹ 20 (b) ₹ 20400
(c) ₹ 10000 (d) ₹ 5000

**297.** If rate of birth is 12 per min. Then, the average number of birth per year is
(a) 43800 (b) 45000
(c) 40000 (d) None of these

**298.** The arrival of customers (with no departure) in system, in queueing theory can be stated as
(a) the pure birth process
(b) the pure death process
(c) the birth death process
(d) None of the above

**299.** When $\rho = 1$, for $M/M/1/N$ queueing system, expected number of customers in the system are
(a) $N/2$ (b) $N/6$
(c) $N$ (d) None of these

**300.** A certain items setup cost and scrap value is constant with respect to time but its maintenance cost starts increasing with respect to time. If $f(n)$ is the maintenance cost function and $A(n)$ is the average total annual cost, then it is better to replace that item, when
(a) $f(n) = A(n)$ (b) $f(n) < A(n)$
(c) $f(n) =$ constant (d) $A(n) =$ constant

**301.** If the inter-arrival time is exponential with mean $1/\lambda$, then the number of arrivals is $(0, t)$ is
(a) poisson distributed
(b) binomial distributed
(c) exponential distributed
(d) None of the above

**302.** The withdrawal of items from certain inventory without refilling in queueing systems can be stated as
(a) the pure birth process
(b) the pure death process
(c) the birth-death process
(d) None of the above

**303.** For $M/M/1/N$ system, the expected waiting time in the system for $\rho = 1$ is
(a) $W_s = \dfrac{N}{2\lambda}$ (b) $W_s = \dfrac{N}{2}$
(c) $W_s = \dfrac{1}{\lambda}$ (d) None of these

**304.** When the equipment starts deteriorating with respect to time, its maintenance cost gradually starts
(a) increasing
(b) decreasing
(c) constant
(d) None of the above

**305.** If the number of arrivals are Poisson distributed, then the inter-arrival time is
(a) poisson distributed
(b) exponential distributed
(c) binomial distributed
(d) None of the above

**306.** The arrival and departure of quests in a hotel in queueing systems can be stated as
(a) the pure death process
(b) the pure birth process
(c) the birth-death process
(d) None of the above

**307.** The expected waiting time in the queue for $\rho = 1$ in $M/M/1/N$ system is
(a) $W_q = \dfrac{N}{2\lambda} - \dfrac{1}{\mu}$ (b) $W_q = \dfrac{1}{\mu}$
(c) $W_q = \dfrac{N}{2\lambda}$ (d) None of these

**308.** Replacement problems are associated with
(a) setup cost
(b) maintenance cost
(c) value of the equipments
(d) None of the above

**309.** In a pure birth model, if $\lambda$ is an arrival rate, $p_0(t)$ the probability of 0 arrivals, then
(a) $p_0'(t) = -\lambda/p_0$ (b) $p_0'(t) = \lambda p_0(t)$
(c) $p_0'(t) = p_0(t)$ (d) None of these

**310.** The certain situation the customer arrives from one gate and departure takes from another gate. This situation of incoming and outgoing can be started as
(a) the pure birth process
(b) the pure death process
(c) the birth-death process
(d) None of the above

**311.** The expected number of customers in the queue for $M/M/1/N$ system are
(a) $L_q = L_s - \rho$ (b) $L_q = L_s$
(c) $L_q = L_s + 1$ (d) None of these

**312.** In certain replacement model, the average maintenance cost of the system remains constant. Is it better to replace the item on the decision made on maintenance cost
(a) yes (b) no
(c) can't say (d) None of these

**313.** The inter-departure time, corresponding to truncated Poisson distribution in a pure death model is
(a) exponential distributed
(b) poisson distributed
(c) binomial distributed
(d) None of the above

**314.** There are $N$ inventories in the system, one-by-one all the inventories are consumed with replacing the inventories. This process is stated as
(a) the pure death process
(b) the pure birth process
(c) the birth-death process
(d) None of the above

**315.** Let $N = 10$, arrival rate $\lambda = 2$, then for $M/M/1/N$ system the expected waiting time in the system for $\rho = 1$ is
(a) $W_s = \frac{10}{3}$ (b) $W_s = \frac{5}{2}$
(c) 3 (d) None of these

**316.** Replacement models discuss the problem where we wish to
(a) maximize operational (maintenance) cost
(b) minimize operational cost
(c) maximize setup cost
(d) minimize setup cost

**317.** Let $p_n$ be the probability that $n$ service occured out of $N$ in (Pure death model) time $t$ with inter-departure time exponential distributed with mean $\mu$
(a) $p_n = \frac{(\mu t)^{N-n} e^{-\mu t}}{N-n!}, 0 < n < N$
(b) $p_n = \frac{(\mu t)^N e^{-\mu t}}{N!}$
(c) $p_n = \frac{(\mu t)^n - e^{-\mu t}}{n!}$
(d) None of the above

**318.** Under the exponential assumptions. Let $\lambda$ be the arrival rate, then $P_r$ {an arrival occur in infinitesimal interval $\Delta t = 0$} is
(a) $\lambda \Delta t + 0(t)$ (b) $\lambda \Delta t$
(c) $0(\Delta t)$ (d) None of these

**319.** Let $N = 15$, then for $\rho = 1$, $p_n$, then the probability of $n$ customer in the system for $M/M/1/N$ queueing system is
(a) $p_n = \frac{1}{10}$ (b) $p_n = \frac{1}{16}$
(c) $p_n = \frac{1}{3}$ (d) None of these

**Directions** (Q. Nos. 320-323) The cost of parameters and other factors for a production inventory system of automobile pistons are given below

Demand per year = 6000 units
Unit cost = ₹ 40
Setup cost = ₹ 500
Production rate per year = 36000 units
Holding cost per year = ₹ 8
Shortage cost per unit per year = ₹ 20

**320.** The number of shortage is
(a) 567 units (b) 157 units
(c) 267 units (d) None of these

**321.** The optimal lot size is
(a) No unit (b) 2000 units
(c) 500 units (d) 1123 units

**322.** The setup time is
(a) $2\frac{1}{4}$ months (b) 5 months
(c) 8 months (d) None of these

**323.** The manufacturing time is
(a) 2 days (b) approx 12 days
(c) approx 20 days (d) approx 50 days

**324.** Under the axioms of exponential distribution, the number of arrivals of during a sufficient small time interval is
(a) more than one (b) less than one
(c) atmost one (d) None of the above

**325.** Under exponential assumptions, let $\mu$ be the service rate, then $P_r$ {Service completion in $\Delta t = 0$/system no empty} is
(a) $\mu \Delta t + 0(t)$ (b) $\mu \Delta t$
(c) $0(t)$ (d) None of these

**Directions** (Q. Nos. 326-329) M/s Bakar and Co. supplies 600 units of its products per year. Shortage is not allowed and inventory carrying cost amount to 60 pais e, per unit year. The setup cost run is ₹ 80.

**326.** What are the optimal numbers of order per year?
(a) 2/6 (b) 1/3 (c) 2/3 (d) 3/2

**327.** What is the minimal average yearly cost?
(a) ₹ 500 (b) ₹ 240
(c) ₹ 300 (d) ₹ 640

**328.** What is the optimal period of supply per optimal order?
(a) 3/2 (b) 2/3 (c) 1/3 (d) 6/2

**329.** What is the increase in total cost associated with ordering 20 per cent more?

(a) ₹ 45 (b) ₹ 4 (c) ₹ 50 (d) ₹ 30

**330.** In the *EOQ* model with backlogging the optimal number of orders to backlog is

(a) directly proportional to
(b) directly proportional to the square root of
(c) not dependent on
(d) directly proportional to the reciprocal of

**331.** Under the axioms of exponential distribution, then the probability of arrival

(a) depends on previous arrival
(b) independent of previous arrival
(c) dependent as well as independent
(d) None of the above

**332.** Under exponential assumptions, $P_r$ {more than one arrivals occurs in $\Delta t = 0$} is

(a) zero (b) positive
(c) negative (d) None of these

**333.** The optimal number of orders per year increases, when

(a) price increases
(b) carry cost decreases
(c) total annual rupee value decreases
(d) None of the above

**334.** The statement 'The next arrival of a customer is independent of previous arrival of customer' is stated as

(a) memoryless property (b) memorable property
(c) shortage property (d) None of these

**335.** Under exponential assumptions, $P_r$ {more than one service is completion in $\Delta t \approx 0$ per more than one unit in system}

(a) zero (b) positive
(c) negative (d) None of these

**336.** In the *EOQ* model,

(a) orders arrival in abatch
(b) demand is known and occurs at a constant rate
(c) all demand must be satisfied
(d) All of the above

**337.** The departure and arrivals in queueing system are normally considered respectively as

(a) births and deaths (b) deaths and births
(c) births (d) deaths

**338.** Under the exponential assumptions, the probability that an event will occur in sufficient small interval is

(a) always positive (b) always negative
(c) always zero (d) None of these

**339.** In the production lot sizer model, increasing the rate of production

(a) increase the optimal number of orders to place each year
(b) does not influence the optimal number of order
(c) decreases the optimal number of orders to place each year
(d) None of the above

**340.** A barber shop has two barbers and three chairs for customers. Assume that customers arrive in a poission fashion at a rate 5 rate h and that each barber services customers according to an exponential distribution with mean of 15 min. Further, if a customer arrive and there are no empty chair in the shop he will leave. Then, the probability of the shop to be empty is

(a) $\frac{256}{901}$ (b) $\frac{153}{724}$
(c) $\frac{89}{301}$ (d) None of these

**341.** Under the exponential assumptions, the probability that an event occur in sufficient small interval is

(a) greater than one (b) less than one
(c) equals to one (d) None of these

**342.** For *M*/*M*/1/*N* queue models, the probability $p_n$ that there are *n* customers in the system is

(a) $\rho^n p_0$ (b) $\rho p_0$
(c) $p_0^n$ (d) None of these

**343.** A company has a steady demand of a product of 40 items per month the purchase cost is ₹ 6 per item and the cost of ordering and procuring the material is ₹ 15 per occasion. If stock holding cost is 20% per annum, how frequently should the company replenish the stock?

(a) 4.36 (b) 4.8
(c) 3.2 (d) None of these

**344.** The *EOQ* model is based on all the following assumptions except

(a) annual demand is known and constant
(b) estimates of carrying and ordering costs are accurate
(c) the ratio of ordering cost per order placed to carrying cost as a percentage of average inventory is always constant
(d) instantaneous receipt of orders occurs exactly, when previous invetory is just used up

**345.** In queue description *M*/*M*/1, the number of servers are

(a) 1 (b) *M*
(c) 2 (b) None of these

**346.** The interarrival time is 10 min, the arrival rate is

(a) 8 (b) 1/10
(c) 3 (d) 2

**347.** For *M*/*M*/1/*N*, the identity holds

(a) $\sum_{n=0}^{N} p_n = 1$ (b) $\sum_{n=0}^{N} p_n > 1$
(c) $\sum_{n=0}^{N} p_n < 1$ (d) None of these

**348.** Which of the following relationship is not true?
(a) $W_s = W_q + 1/\mu$ (b) $L_s = \lambda W^q$
(c) $L_s = L_q + 1^s/\lambda$ (d) $L_q = \lambda W_q$

**349.** All of the following may be used to find the *EOQ* except
(a) optimal number of days supply to order
(b) number of orders which minimize ordering costs
(c) optimal number of rupees per order
(d) optimal number of orders per year

**350.** The mean and standard deviation of exponential distribution are
(a) equal (b) mean > SD
(c) mean < SD (d) None of these

**351.** In queueing description *M/M/*1, the arrival and departure distribution
(a) both Markovian (b) binomial
(c) general (d) None of these

**352.** For *M/M/*1*/N* queue models, if $p_n$ is the number of customers in the system, then
(a) $p_n = 0$ for $n > N$ (b) $p_n \neq 0$ for $n > N$
(c) $p_n = 1$ for $n > N$ (d) None of these

**353.** For the queueing modes (*M/M/*1) : (∞*/FCFS*), the average waiting time of customer in the queue is
(a) $\dfrac{\lambda}{\mu(\mu-\lambda)}$ (b) $\dfrac{\lambda^2}{\mu(\mu-\lambda)}$
(c) $\dfrac{1}{\mu-\lambda}$ (d) $\dfrac{\mu}{\lambda(\mu-\lambda)}$

**354.** The *EOQ* model is of particular importance because
(a) it is fairly simple and easy to understand
(b) it is the most realistic model which can be formulated
(c) there are only a few assumptions to satisfy and the needed information is always easy to obtain
(d) no other model can be applied, if it cannot be used

**355.** Let *p* be the probability that an arrival occurs in $\Delta t \approx 0$ under exponential assumptions
(a) $0 \le p \le 1$ (b) $0 < p \le 1$
(c) $0 < p < 1$ (d) $0 \le 1 < 1$

**356.** *M/G/*2 queue description, the departure arrival distribution respectively are
(a) general and markovian
(b) markovian and general
(c) markovian
(d) None of the above

**357.** If arrival rate is 3 customers per day and service rate is 5 customer per day for *M/M/*1 queueing system the expected number of customer in the system at certain day is
(a) 1.5 (b) 2
(c) 3 (d) 5

**358.** A typist in an office receives on the average 22 latter per day for typing in poisson fashion. The typist works 8 h a day and it takes of the average 20 min to type a letter and the time distributed exponentially, then the average waiting time needed to have a letter typed
(a) 11/12 day (b) 2/3 day
(c) 1/2 day (d) None of these

**359.** Let *q* be the probability that no arrival occur in $\Delta t \approx 0$ under exponential assumptions is
(a) $0 \le q \le 1$ (b) $0 < q < 1$
(c) $0 \le q < 1$ (d) $0 < 1 \le 1$

**360.** What is the total annual cost?
(a) ₹ 560 (b) ₹ 986 (c) ₹ 867 (d) ₹ 800

**361.** For *M/M/*1 model, the expected number of busy servers are equal to
(a) traffic intensity ρ (b) arrival rate λ
(c) service rate μ (d) None of these

**362.** A super market has two girls ringing up shales at the counters. If the service time for each customer is exponential with mean 4 min and if people arrive in poisson fashion at the counter at the rate of 10 per h. Then the expected percentage of idle time for each girl is
(a) 67% (b) 50% (c) 13% (d) 4%

**363.** What is the time between orders?
(a) 30 day (b) 21 day
(c) 60 day (d) 5 day

**364.** What is the maximum inventory level?
(a) 86 units (b) 50 units
(c) 36 units (d) 46 units

**365.** If $p_0(t)$ states the probability that no event occurs in (0, *t*). Then, under exponential assumptions
(a) $p_0(t) = e^{-\lambda t}, t > 0$ (b) $p_0(t) = 1$
(c) $p_0(t)\dfrac{e^{-\lambda t}}{t}, t < 0$ (d) None of these

**366.** Under memoryless assumption, the arrival of the customer is independent of
(a) previous arrival (b) future arrival
(c) state of the system (d) None of these

**367.** *M/M/*3*/N*, queue description states, the number of servers and buffer capacity as
(a) 3 and *M* (b) *M* and 3
(c) 3 and *N* (d) None of these

**368.** For *M/M/*1 model, the probability that there is no customer in the system is
(a) $1-\rho$ (b) ρ
(c) $1/\rho$ (d) None of these

**369.** A company uses rivets at a rate of 5000 kg per year, rivets costing ₹ 2.00 per kg. It costs ₹ 20 to place order and carrying cost of inventory is 10% per year. Order for rivets should be placed for
(a) 4.8 months (b) 3 months
(c) 2 months (d) 6 months

**370.** Let

A : The number of units in the system.

B : The number of units waiting for service.

C : The number of servers.

The following relation holds

(a) $C = A - B$ (b) $C = A + B$

(c) $C = A/B$ (d) None of these

**371.** For *M*/*M*/1 system, the expected waiting time in the queue is

(a) $\frac{\lambda}{\mu}$ (b) $\frac{\lambda}{\mu(\mu - \lambda)}$

(c) $\frac{\lambda}{\mu - \lambda}$ (d) None of these

**372.** Arrivals at a telephone booth are considered to be poisson, with an average time of 10 min between one arrival and the next. The length of a phone call assumed to be distributed exponentially with mean 3 min. Then, the probability that a person arriving at the path will have to wait is given by

(a) 1/3 (b) 2/3

(c) 3/10 (d) 1/4

**373.** Let $L_s$ be the expected number of customers in system and C expected number of busy servers providing services and $L_q$ the number of customers is a queue. When $L_q \equiv 0$, then the following relation holds

(a) $L_s < C$

(b) $L_s > C$

(c) $L_s = C$

(d) None of the above

**374.** For *M*/*M*/1 system, the expected queueing length is

(a) $\frac{\lambda^2}{\mu}$ (b) $\frac{\lambda^2}{\mu(\mu - \lambda)}$

(c) $\frac{\lambda}{\mu - \lambda}$ (d) None of these

**375.** A bank has 5 computers in its main branch and one hardware specialist, who attends to any computer that malfunctions. A computer may work for a length of time that is distributed exponentially before a break down occurs. The time that the specialist takes to repair a broken down machine is also distributed exponentially. In the associated queueing model, which one of the following statements is true?

(a) The arrival rate $\lambda$ and the service rate $\mu$ are constant and for the steady state to be achieved, we require $\frac{\lambda}{\mu} < 1$

(b) The arrival rate $\lambda$ and service rate $\mu$ depend on the number of computers that are not yet down and for steady state to be achieved we require $\frac{\lambda_1\lambda_2\lambda_3\lambda_4\lambda_5}{\mu_1\mu_2\mu_3\mu_4\mu_5} < 1$

(c) The arrival rate depends on the number of computers that are not down and service rate is constant

(d) The arrival rate is constant but the service rate depends on the computers broken down

**376.** Consider the situation, when no server is working, then the number of customers in the system are

(a) equal to number of customers in queue

(b) more than number of customers in queue

(c) less than number of customers in queue

(d) None of the above

**377.** For *M*/*M*/1 queueing system arrival rate $\lambda = 4$ cars per day, $\mu = 6$ cars per day, then $p_5$ is equal to

(a) 0.4390 (b) 0.14815

(c) 0.2222 (d) None of these

**378.** Find the optimal *EOQ* for the following Annual Usage = 1000 pieces, cost per piece = ₹ 250, ordering cost = ₹ 6 per order, expending cost = ₹ 4 per order, inventory holding cost = 20% average inventory, Material holding cost = ₹ 1 per piece, is

(a) 20

(b) 10

(c) 25

(d) The above informations are insufficient

**379.** On a certain day, number of customers in a system are 20 and number of customers in service are 12, then the number of customers waiting are

(a) 10 (b) 8

(c) 20 (d) None of these

**380.** *M*/*M*/3/*FCFS*/*N*, queue description, *FCFS* and *N* are

(a) queue discipline and arrival pattern

(b) queue discipline and buffer capacity

(c) arrival and departure distribution

(d) None of the above

**381.** If arrival rate is 20 customers per week and service rate is 50 customers per week, then the expected number of busy servers for *M*/*M*/1 queueing system are

(a) 2/5 (b) 5/2

(c) 5 (d) None of the abive

**382.** Let C be the expected number of servers in the system, $\bar{C}$ the expected number of servers not busy and C the expected number of servers busy, then

(a) $\bar{C} = C - C$ (b) $\bar{C} = C - C$

(c) $C = \bar{C}/C$ (d) $C = C/\bar{C}$

**383.** Selected the correct statement

(a) *EOQ* is that quantity at which price paid by the buyer is minimum

(b) If annual demand doubled with all other parameters remaining constant, the *EOQ* is doubled

(c) Total ordering cost equals total holding cost

(d) Stock out cost are never permitted

**384.** If arrival rate is 15 customers per min and service rate is 30 customers per min, then for $M/M/1$ queueing system, its traffic intensity is given by

(a) 1/2 (b) 2
(c) 4 (d) None of these

**385.** Let $p_n$ be the brobability of $n$ units in the system then expected number of units $L_s$ in the system are

(a) $L_s = \sum_{n=0}^{\infty} np_n$ (b) $L_n = np_n$
(c) $L_s = n \sum_{n=0}^{\infty} p_n$ (d) None of these

**386.** For $M/M/1$ queueing system, if arrival rate is 10 customers per day and service rate is 30 customers per day, then expected number of customers in the queue on a certain day is

(a) $\frac{1}{3}$ (b) $\frac{1}{6}$
(c) 6 (d) None of these

**387.** Let $C$ be the number of servers, $p_n$ be the probability of $n$ units in the system and then expected queue size $L_q$ is

(a) $\sum_{n=1}^{\infty} C_n p_n$
(b) $\sum_{n=C+1}^{\infty} (n-C)p_n$
(c) $\sum_{n=C+1}^{\infty} (n+C)p_n$
(d) None of the above

**388.** If $L_s$ be the number of customers in the system, $L_q$ be the number of customers in the queue, in the system, then

(a) $L_s \le L_q$ always
(b) $L_s < L_q$ always
(c) $L_s \ne L_q$ always
(d) $L_q < L_s$ never

**389.** Let $\lambda$ be the arrival rate in the system, $\mu$ be an service rate of the system, $L_s$ and $L_q$ be the number of eustomers in the systemand queue, then

(a) $\mu\lambda = L_s - L_q$
(b) $\frac{\lambda}{\mu} = L_s + L_q$
(c) $L_s = L_q + \frac{\lambda}{\mu}$
(d) None of the above

**390.** Let $\lambda$ be an arrival rate of customer in a system, $\mu$ be an service rate of the system, then the expected number of busy servers are

(a) $\lambda/\mu$ (b) $\lambda + \mu$
(c) $\lambda\mu$ (d) None of these

**391.** The relationship between expected number of customer in the system, $L_s$ expected number of customers in queue $L_q$, arrival rate of customers at system $\lambda$ and service rate of customers in system $\mu$ is

(a) $L_s - L_q = \lambda/\mu$
(b) $L_s + L_q = \lambda/\mu$
(c) $L_s/L_q = \lambda/\mu$
(d) None of the above

**392.** The expected waiting time in the system is 10 min and expected waiting time in the queue is 5 min, then the service rate is

(a) 1/10 (b) 1/5
(c) 5 (d) 10

**393.** Let $W_s$ and $W_q$ be the expected waiting time in system and queue and $L_s$ and $L_q$ be the expected number of customers in system and queue, then

(a) $\frac{L_s}{W_s} < \frac{L_q}{W_q}$ (b) $\frac{L_s}{W_s} > \frac{L_q}{W_q}$
(c) $\frac{L_s}{W_s} = \frac{L_q}{W_q}$ (d) None of these

**394.** For $M/M/1$ queueing model, the steady state solution is

(a) $p_n = \rho^n(1-\rho)$
(b) $p_n = \rho^n$
(c) $p_n = 1-\rho$
(d) None of the above

**395.** Little formula state the relationship between

(a) $W_s, W_q$ and $\lambda$
(b) $L_s, L_q$ and $\lambda$
(c) $W_s, L_s$ and $\lambda$
(d) None of the above

**396.** For $M/M/1$ queueing model, following identity holds

(a) $\sum_{n=0}^{\infty} p_n = 1$
(b) $\sum_{n=0}^{\infty} p_n > 0$
(c) $\sum_{n=0}^{\infty} p_n \ne 1$
(d) None of the above

# Exercise 2 (For Part 'C')

**Directions** (Q. Nos. 1-49) *Questions may have one or more than one correct option.*

**1.** *XYZ* farm is engaged in breeding pigs. The pigs are fed an various products grown on the farm because of the need to ensure certain nutrient constitutents. It is necessary to buy additional one or two products, which we shall call *A* and *B*. The nutrient constituents (vitamins and proteins) in each unit of the product are given below

| Nutrient constituents | Nutrient constituent in the product | | Minimum requirement of nutrient constituents |
|---|---|---|---|
| | *A* | *B* | |
| 1 | 36 | 6 | 108 |
| 2 | 3 | 12 | 36 |
| 3 | 20 | 10 | 100 |

Product *A* costs ₹ 20 per unit and product *B* costs ₹ 40 per unit. Determine how much of products *A* and *B* must be purchased, so as to provide the pigs nutrients not less than the minimum required, at the lowest possible cost. Then,

(a) the minium cost is ₹ 160

(b) a firm purchase null unit of *A* and units 10 units of *B* for minimum cost

(c) a firm purchase null unit of *B* and 10 units of *A* for minimum cost

(d) a firm purchase 4 units of *A* and 2 units of products *B* for miniumum cost

**2.** In a single server model, the arrival rate is 12 customer per h and service rate is 30 customer per h.

(a) probability of *n* customers in the system is $\left(1-\frac{\lambda}{\mu}\right)\left(\frac{\lambda}{\mu}\right)^n$

(b) probability of no customer in the system is $\left(1-\frac{\lambda}{\mu}\right)$

(c) the probability that there is no customer in the system is 0.6

(d) the probability that there is no customer in the system is 1

**3.** In a paints manufacturing unit, each type of paint is to be ground to a specified degree of fineness. The manufacturer uses the same ball mill for a variety of paints and after completion of each batch, the mill has to be cleaned and the ball charge properly made up. The change-over from one type of paint to another, is estimated to cost ₹ 90 per batch. The annual sales of a particular grade of paint are 30000 L and the inventory carrying cost is ₹ 1 per L. Given that, the rate of production is 3 times the sales rate, determine the optimal production lot size and the number of production runs.

(a) the optimal production lot size is 2683.28 L

(b) the number of production runs are nil

(c) the optimal prodction lot size is nil

(d) the number of production runs are 11.18 runs

**4.** The LPP

$$\text{Max } (z) = \frac{3}{z}x_1 - x_2$$

$$\text{Subject to } \quad 3x_1 - 2x_2 \le 12$$

$$x_1 \le 6$$

$$x_1, x_2 \ge 0 \text{ has}$$

(a) no feasible solution

(b) unique optimal solution

(c) alternating optimal solution

(d) unbounded solution

**5.** The maximum value of

$$P = 4x + 2y$$

$$\text{Subject to } 4x + 2y \le 46$$

$$x + 3y \le 24$$

$$x \ge 0,\ y \ge 0 \text{ occurs at}$$

(a) one point (b) two points

(c) four points (d) infinite number of points

**6.** An advertising firm desires to reach two types of audiences—customers with annual income of more than ₹ 40000 (target audience *A*) and customers with annual income of less than ₹ 40000 (target audience *B*). The total advertising budget is ₹ 200000. One programme of TV advertising costs ₹ 50000. One programme of radio advertising costs ₹ 20000. Contract conditions ordinarily require that there should be atleast 3 programmes on TV and the number of programmes on radio must not exceed 5. Survey indicates that a single TV programme reaches 750000 customers in target audience *A* and 150000 in target audience *B*. One radio programme reaches 40000 customers in target audience *A* and 260000 in target audience *B*.

Let $x_1$ is the number of programmes on TV and $x_2$ number of programmes on radio, then

(a) the objective function can be expressed as Maximize (total audience)

$$Z = (750000 + 150000)\,x_1 + (40000 + 260000)\,x_2$$

(b) the constraints of the given problem can be expressed as $50000\ x_1 + 20000\ x_2 \le 200000$ or $5x_1 + 2x_2 \le 20$

$$x_1 \ge 3$$

$$x_2 \le 5$$

$$\text{and} \quad x_1 \ge 0,\ x_2 \ge 0$$

(c) the optimal solution is to given 4 programmes on TV and no programme on radios in order to achieve a maximum audience reach of 3600000 audiences

(d) no optimal solutions exist

**7.** It has been determined from an analysis of accounting and production data for part number 625, that its cost to purchase is ₹ 36 per order and ₹ 2 per part. Its inventory carrying charge is 9 per cent of the average inventory. The demand of his part is 10000 units per annum.

(a) the economic order quantity it is 2000 units
(b) the economic order quantity is 6000 units
(c) the optimal number of orders are 5 orders
(d) the optimal number of orders are 65 orders

**8.** The LPP

Max $z = x_1 + x_2$

Subject to $x_1 + x_2 \geq 1$

$x_1, x_2 \geq 0$ has

(a) feasible region closed
(b) feasible region unbounded
(c) alternating solution or multiple optimal solution
(d) unbounded optimal solution

**9.** The LPP

Max $z = x_1 + x_2$

Subject to $x_1 + x_2 \leq 1$

$x_1 + x_2 \geq 2$

$x_1 + x_2 \geq 0$

$x_1, x_2 \geq 0$ has

(a) no feasible solution (b) no solution
(c) no optimal solution (d) None of these

**10.** The LPP

Max $(z) = -x_1 + 2x_2$

Subject to $-x_1 + x_2 \leq 1$

$-x_1 + 2x_2 \leq 4$

$0 \leq x_1 \leq 5$

$x_2 \geq 0$ has

(a) closed feasible region
(b) alternating optimal solution
(c) bounded optimal solution
(d) uncountable number of optimal solution

**11.** Which of the following is/are LPP?

(a) Max $(z) = -x_1 + 2x_2$
Subject to $x_1 + 2x_2 \geq 1$
$x_2 \geq 0$

(b) Min $(z) = x_1 + 3x_2$
Subject to $x_1 + x_2 \geq 1, x_1 + x_2 \leq 2$
$x_1 x_2 \geq 0$

(c) Max $(z) = x_1 - x_2$
Subject to $x_1 + x_2 > 0$
$x_1 + 2x_2 \leq 0$
$x_1 x_2 \geq 0$

(d) Min $(z) = 3x_1 - 2x_2$
Subject to $x_1 + x_2 \leq 1$
$x_1, x_2 \geq 0$

**12.** A bank has one drive-in counter. It is estimated that cars arrive according to poisson distribution at the rate of 2 every 5 min and that there is enough space to accommodate a line of 10 cars. Other arriving cars can wait outside this space, if necessary. It takes 1.5 min on an average to serve a customer but the serv ce time actually varies according to an exponential distribution. Then,

(a) the probability of time, that the facility remains idle is 0.4
(b) the expected number of customer waiting but currently not being served at a particular point of time is 0.9
(c) the expected time a customer spends in the system is 3.75 min
(d) mean arrival rate is 40 per h

**13.** Which of the following is/are correct?

(a) A is a convex set
(b) C is a convex set
(c) B is a non-convex set
(d) D is a non-convex set

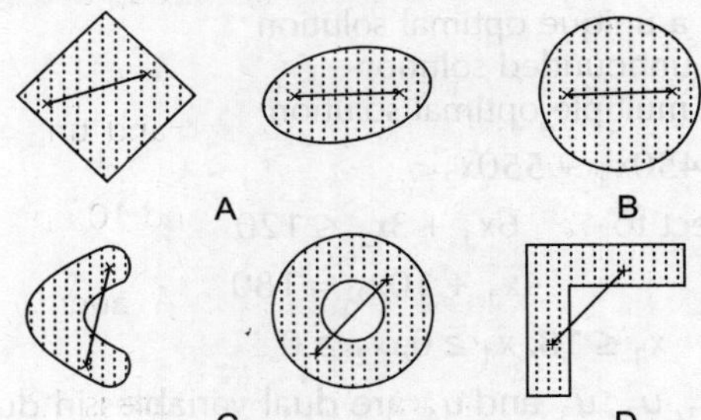


**14.** Let the value of money be assumed to be 10% year and suppose that, machine A is replaced after every 3 yr, whereas machine B replaced after every 6 yr. The yearly cost of both the machines are given as under

| Year | 1 | 2 | 3 | 4 | 5 | 6 |
|---|---|---|---|---|---|---|
| Machine A | 1000 | 200 | 400 | 1000 | 200 | 400 |
| Machine B | 1700 | 100 | 200 | 300 | 400 | 500 |

Determine which machine should be purchased.

(a) average cost per year of machine A is ₹ 552.87
(b) average cost per year of machine B is ₹ 577.19
(c) machine A should be replaced by machine B
(d) machine A should not be repalced by machine B

**15.** Max value of LPP

Max $(z) = 2x + 3y$

Subject to $2x + y \leq 10$

$x + 2y \leq 10, x, y \geq 0$

(a) $\frac{25}{3}$ (b) $\frac{26}{3}$

(c) $\frac{50}{3}$ (d) $\frac{52}{3}$

**16.** Which of the followings is/are true for an LPP?
(a) Feasible region is always closed
(b) Optimal value of LPP always exists at vertex or extreme point
(c) Decision variables are linear and continuous
(d) Decision variables linear but not continuous

**17.** The LPP

Max $(z) = 6x_1 - 2x_2$

Subject to $2x_1 - x_2 \le 2$

$x_1 \le 4$

$x_1, x_2 \ge 0$ has

(a) optimal solution is bounded
(b) uncountable optimal solution
(c) feasible region is unbounded
(d) no solution

**18.** The LPP

Max $(z) = 2x_1 + 3x_2$

Subject to $x_1 + x_2 \le 2$

$2x_1 + x_2 \le -2$

$x_1, x_2 \ge 0$ has

(a) no feasible solution
(b) a unique optimal solution
(c) unbounded solution
(d) multiple optimal solution

**19.** Max $450x_1 + 550x_2$

Subject to $6x_1 + 3x_2 \le 120$

$4x_1 + 10x_2 = 180$

$x_1 \le 18,\ x_1 \ge 0,\ x_2 \ge 0$

Let $u_1, u_2, u_3$ and $u_4$ are dual variables in dual of the given problem, then

(a) Minimize $120u_1 + 180u_2 + 180u_3 + 18u_4$
(b) $6u_1 + 4u_2 - 4u_3 + u_4 \ge 450$
$3u_1 + 10u_2 - 10u_3 \ge 550$
(c) $u_2 - u_3$ is unrestricted in sign
(d) all dual variables are unrestricted

**20.** Minimize $Z = 5x_1 - 6x_2 + 4x_3$

Subject to constraints

$3x_1 + 4x_2 + 6x_3 \ge 9$

$x_1 + 3x_2 + 2x_3 \ge 5$

$7x_1 \quad 2x_2 \quad x_3 \le 10$

$x_1 - 2x_2 + 4x_3 \ge 4$

$2x_1 + 5x_2 - 3x_3 \ge 3$

$x_1 \ge 0,\ x_2 \ge 0,\ x_3 \ge 0$

If $y_1, y_2, y_3, y_4$ and $y_5$ are dual variables, then in the dual of following problem

(a) Maximize $Z^* = 9y_1 + 5y_2 - 10y_3 + 4y_4 + 3y_5$
(b) $3y_1 + y_2 - 7y_3 + y_4 + 2y_5 \le 5$
$4y_1 + 3y_2 + 2y_3 - 2y_4 + 5y_5 \le -6$
$6y_1 + 2y_2 + y_3 + 4y_4 - 3y_5 \le 4$
(c) $y_1, y_2, y_3, y_4, y_5 \ge 0$
(d) All variables $y_i$ is are unrestricted

**21.** Maximize $Z = 0.1x_1 + 0.2x_2$.

Subject to the constraints

$x_1 + x_2 \le 100000$

$x_1 \le 75000,\ x_2 \le 75000$

$0.1x_1 + 0.2x_2 \ge 0.12\,(x_1 + x_2)$

(a) max $Z =$ ₹ 14000
(b) for maximum value of $Z$, $x_1 = 60000$
(c) for maximum value of $Z$, $x_2 = 40000$
(d) for maximum value of $Z$, $x_1 = x_2$

**22.** In an LPP, if the objective function is parallel to a constraints and the feasible region is non-empty. Then, the objective function may assume
(a) unique optimal solution
(b) an unbounded solution
(c) multiple optimal solution
(d) any one of the above

**23.** Consider the following LPP

Min $z = -x_1 - 2x_2$

Subject to $x_1 - 2x_2 \le 2$

$-x_1 + x_2 \le 4$

$x_1 \ge 0,\ x_2 \ge 0$, then

(a) the feasible region is unbounded but the optimum value is bounded
(b) both the feasible region and the optimal value are unbounded
(c) the optimum value is unbounded but the feasible region is bounded
(d) None of the above

**24.** Given, system of linear equation

$x_1 + 2x_2 + x_3 = 4$

$3x_1 + x_2 + 5x_3 = 5$

(a) (basic) $x_2 = 5/8,\ x_3 = -2/8;\ x_1 = 0$ (non-basic)
(b) (basic) $x_1 = 5,\ x_3 = -1;\ x_2 = 0$ (non-basic)
(c) (basic) $x_1 = 2,\ x_2 = 1;\ x_3 = 0$ (non-basic)
(d) all the basic solutions are non-degenerate solutions

**25.** Given, LPP

Max $(Z) = 4x_1 + 5x_2 + 3x_3$

Subject to the constraints

$x_1 + x_2 + x_3 = 10$

$x_1 + x_2 \ge 1$

$2x_1 + 3x_2 + x_3 \le 30$

(a) standard form is Maximize
$Z = 4x_1 + 5x_2 - 3x_3 + 0s_1 + 0s_2 - MA_1 - MA_2$
(b) $x_1 + x_2 + x_3 + A_1 = 10,\ x_1 - x_2 - s_1 + A_2 = 1$
$2x_1 + 3x_2 + x_3 + s_2 = 30$
where, $x_1 \ge 0,\ x_2 \ge 0,\ s_1 \ge 0,\ s_2 \ge 0$
$A_1 \ge 0,\ A_2 \ge 0$

(c) the optimal solution is

$$x_1 = \frac{11}{2}, x_2 = \frac{9}{2}, x_3 = 0$$

(d) the optimal value is $z = \frac{89}{2}$

**26.** If the customer arrival rate is 20 per hour and service rate is 40 per h, then for single server model

(a) probability no customer in the system is 0.4

(b) expected number of customers in waiting line is 0.9

(c) expected time a customer spend in system is $\frac{1}{16}$ h

(d) expected number of customers in waiting line is 26

**27.** Consider the statement about linear programming problem

(i) An LPP may have no feasible solution.

(ii) The number of optimal solutions, if exists is finite.

(iii) The number of feasible solution is infinite and hence the number of optimal solutions is also infinite.

(iv) If one can get two optimal solutions, then one can obtain an infinite number of optimal solutions.

Out of the above statements

(a) Only (i) and (iv) are true

(b) Only (ii) and (iv) are true

(c) Only (i) is true

(d) Only (iv) is true

**28.** Given,

Minimize $z = x_1 - 3x_2 - 2x_3$

Subject to the constraints

$$3x_1 - x_2 + 2x_3 \le 7$$
$$2x_1 - 4x_2 \ge 12$$
$$-4x_1 + 3x_2 + 8x_3 = 10$$

$x_1, x_2 > 0$ and $x_3$ is unrestricted. If $w_1, w_2, w_3$ are the dual variables, then in the dual of the given problem

(a) Maximize $z^* = 7w_1 + 12w_2 + 10w_3$

(b)
$$3w_1 + 2w_2 - 4w_3 \le 1$$
$$w_1 + 4w_2 - 3w_3 \ge 3$$
$$-2w_1 - 8w_3 = 2$$

(c) $w_1 \le 0$ and $w_2 \ge 0$, also $w_3$ is unrestricted

(d) there is no unrestricted variable

**29.** Given,

Minimize $Z = 40x_1 + 120x_2$

Subject to the constraints

$$x_1 - 2x_2 \le 8$$
$$3x_1 + 5x_2 = 90$$
$$15x_1 + 44x_2 \le 660$$
$$x_1 \ge 0, x_2 \ge 0$$

Let $y_1, y_2, y_3$ and $y_4$ are dual variables, then in the dual of given problem

(a) Maximize $Z_y = 8y_1 + 90y - 660y_4$

(b)
$$-y_1 + 3y - 15y_4 \le 40$$
$$2y_1 + 5y - 44y_4 \le 120$$
$$y_1 \ge 0, y_4 \ge 0$$

(c) $y_2$ is unrestricted in sign

(d) no unrestricted variable

**30.** Given, the set $S = [(x_1, x_2) : 3x_1^2 + 2x_2^2 \le 6]$

(a) the set is convex

(b) the set is concave

(c) both (a) and (b)

(d) neither (a) nor (b)

**31.** A typist at an office receives on the average 22 letters per day for typing. The typist works 8 h a day and it takes on the average 20 min to type a letter.

(a) the typist's utilization rate is 0.917

(b) the average number of letters waiting to be typed is 10.8083 letters per day

(c) the average waiting time needed to have a letter typed is 4 h

(d) the typist utilization rate is 0.6213

**32.** The LPP

Min $Z = x_1 + x_2$

Subject to $x_1 + x_2 \le 1$

$x_1, x_2 \ge 0$

has

(a) unique optimal solution

(b) feasible region is bounded

(c) uncountable optimal solution

(d) bounded optimal solution

**33.** The LPP

Max $z = -x_1 + 2x_2$

Subject to $-x_1 + x_2 \le 1$

$-x_1 + 2x_2 \le 4$

$x_1, x_2 \ge 0$

has

(a) feasible region is unbounded

(b) alternating optimal solution

(c) bounded optimal solution but decision variable has no bounds

(d) infinite optimal solution but the solution exists at only one vertex

**34.** The charitable hospital provides free clinical service to the patients on every morning. There are three doctors on duty, who are equally qualified and experienced. It takes, on an average 20 min for a patient to get treatment and the actual time taken is known to vary approximately exponentially around this average. The patients arrive according to the Poisson distribution with an average of 6 per hour. The medical superintendent of the hospital wants to investigate the following.

(a) The expected number of patients waiting in the queue is 0.889.
(b) The average time that a patient spends at the clinic is 28.9 min.
(c) The probability that a patient has to wait before he gets service is 0.444.
(d) The average percentage idle time for each of the dentists is 1/3.

**35.** In a university cafeteria, the customers (students) have to pass through three counters. The customers buy coupons at the first counter select and collect the snacks at the second counter and collect coffee or tea at the third. The server at each counter takes on an average 2 min although the distribution of the time of service is approximately exponential. If the arrivals of customers to the cafeteria are approximate by poisson at an average rate of eight per hour.
(a) The average time a customer spends waiting in the cafeteria is 16 min.
(b) The average time of getting the service is 16 min.
(c) The most probable time in getting the service is 4 min.
(d) Arrial rate is 2 min.

**36.** Min $Z = x_1 + 2x_2$

Subject to $2x_1 + x_2 \geq 2$

$3x_1 + 4x_2 \leq 12$

$x_1, x_2 \geq 0$

has
(a) no feasible solution
(b) solution exists
(c) no optimal solution
(d) feasible region is unbounded

**37.** The LPP

Max $Z = x_1 + 4x_2$

Subject to $x_1 + x_2 \geq 1$

$x_1 \leq 2$

$x_1, x_2 \geq 0$

has
(a) unbounded optimal solution
(b) feasible region is unbounded
(c) no optimal value
(d) feasible region is closed

**38.** *ABC* plumbing supply company stocks thousands of plumbing items sold to regional plumbers, contractors and retailers. Mr Ramesh the firm's general manage:, wonders how much money could be saved annually, if *EOQ* were used instead of the firm's present rules of thumb. He instructs Mr Ram to conduct an analysis of one material only to examine, if significant savings might result from using the *EOQ* Mr Ram develops the following estimates from accounting information

$D = 10000$

$Q = 400$ valves per order (present order quantity)

$C_h$ = ₹ 4 per unit per year

$C_0$ = ₹ 55 per order
(a) the present total annual stocking cost is ₹ 2175
(b) the economic order quantity is 524.4 units
(c) the total annual stocking cost, if *EOQ* is applied is 2097.6 units
(d) if the annual savings on this one material were applied to the thousands of items in inventory, the savings from *EOQ* would be significant.

**39.** A manufacturer of leather belts makes three types of belts. *A*, *B* and *C*, which are processed on three machines $M_1$, $M_2$ and $M_3$. Belt *A* requires 2 h on machine $M_1$ and 3 h on machine $M_3$. Belt *B* requires 3 h on machine $M_1$, 2 h on machine $M_2$ and 2 h on machines $M_3$ and Belt *C* requires 5 h on machine $M_2$ and 4 h on machine $M_3$. There are 8 h of time per day available on machine $M_1$, 10 h of time per day available on machine $M_2$ and 15 h of time per day available or machine $M_3$. The profit gained from belt *A* is ₹ 3.00 per unit, from Belt *B* is ₹ 5.00 per unit, from belt *C* is ₹ 4.00 per unit.
(a) The number of constraints are three
(b) The number of decision variables are three
(c) The number of constraints are two
(d) The number of constraints are six

**40.** The LPP

Max $Z = -3x_1 + x_2$

Subject to $2x_1 + x_2 \leq 4$

$-x_1 + x_2 \leq 1$

$x_1 + x_2 \geq 1$

$-3x_1 + x_2 \geq -3$

$x_1, x_2 \geq 0$

has
(a) unique optimal solution
(b) alternating optimal solution
(c) constraints leading to an infeasible region
(d) constraints leading to an unbounded solution

**41.** Consider an LPP

Min $z = 6x + 10y$

Subject to $x \geq 6$

$y \geq 2$

$2x + y \geq 10$

$x \geq 0, y \geq 0$

The redundant constraints in this LPP is
(a) $x \geq 6$
(b) $2x + y \geq 10$
(c) Both (a) and (b)
(d) None of the above

**42.** A manager has decided to place order for a minimum quantity of 500 units of a particular item in order to get a discount of 10%. From the records, it was found out that in the last year, 8 orders each of size 200 units have been placed. Given, ordering cost = ₹ 500 per order. Inventory carrying cost = 40% of the inventory value and the cost per unit = ₹ 400.

(a) The manager's decision is justified
(b) The manager's decision cannot be justified
(c) The savings are of ₹ 46400
(d) The manager is loss of ₹ 49000

**43.** The terminal operates with four unloading bays. Each bay requires a crew of two employer. The truck arrive at an average rate of three per hour, according to Poisson distribution. A crew unload a semitrailer rig with average of one hour, having exponential service time distribution.

(a) Probability that there are no trucks in the system is 0.0377.
(b) Average waiting time in queue for trucks is 0.51 h.
(c) Average waiting time spend in the system is 1.51 h.
(d) Average number of trucks in the system is 4.53 trucks.

**44.** In a single server model, the arrival rate is 5 customer per hour and service rate is 8 customers per hour.

(a) Expected time of customer in a queue is 5/24 h.
(b) Probability of atleast two customers in the system is $(5/8)^3$.
(c) Probability that server is ideal is 15/64.
(d) Probability that server is ideal is 1.

**45.** The maximum value of

$$z = 4x + 2y$$

Subject to $2x + 3y \le 18$

$$x + y \ge 10$$

$$x, y \ge 0$$

is

(a) 36 (b) 40
(c) 20 (d) None of these

**46.** About an LPP (with two decision variables) Consider the following two statements

**A.** A constraints of LPP is parallel to its objective function.

**B.** There exists an infinite number of optimal solutions to the problem.

Which of the following is true?

(a) If B *is true, then* A *is true*
(b) If B is true, then B is true
(c) A is true iff B is true
(d) None of the above

**47.** A firm makes two products *X* and *Y* and has a total production capacity of 9 tonnes per day, *X* and *Y* requiring the same production capacity. The firm has a permanent contract to supply atleast 2 tonnes of *X* and atleast 3 tonnes of *Y* per day to another company. Each tonne of *X* required 20 machine hours production time and each tonne of *Y* requires 50 machine hour production time, the daily maximum possible number of machine hour is 360. All the firm's output can be sold and the profit made is ₹ 80 per tonne of *X* and ₹ 120 per tonne of *Y*.

(a) The objective function is Maximize
$$Z = 10000x + 8500y$$
(b) The constraints are
$$6x + 5y \le 60$$
$$x + y = 11$$
with $x, y \ge 0$
(c) Optimal solution to the gevin LP problem is $x = 5, y = 6$, Max $Z = 101000$
(c) No optimal solution exist

**48.** The LPP

Max $Z = 3x_1 + 4x_2$

Subject to $x_1 + x_2 \le -2$

$$x_1, x_2 \ge 0$$

has

(a) no feasible solution
(b) unbounded solution
(c) unique optimal solution
(d) multiple optimal solution

**49.** Which of the following statement(s) is/are true?

(a) The set of feasible solutions of a linear programming problem is convex.
(b) All functions in an LPP are linear.
(c) The set of all optimal solutions to an LPP need not be convex.
(d) Every point lying on the line segment joining two optimal solution to a linear programming problem is also optimal solution.

# Answers

## Exercise 1

1. (a) 2. (d) 3. (b) 4. (c) 5. (c) 6. (b) 7. (a) 8. (d) 9. (b) 10. (d)
11. (b) 12. (b) 13. (a) 14. (c) 15. (c) 16. (c) 17. (c) 18. (a) 19. (c) 20. (a)
21. (c) 22. (d) 23. (b) 24. (a) 25. (c) 26. (c) 27. (c) 28. (c) 29. (a) 30. (b)
31. (d) 32. (b) 33. (b) 34. (b) 35. (a) 36. (a) 37. (a) 38. (c) 39. (b) 40. (a)
41. (b) 42. (c) 43. (d) 44. (c) 45. (a) 46. (a) 47. (b) 48. (b) 49. (d) 50. (a)
51. (b) 52. (c) 53. (d) 54. (b) 55. (b) 56. (b) 57. (c) 58. (b) 59. (c) 60. (b)
61. (b) 62. (b) 63. (a) 64. (a) 65. (c) 66. (a) 67. (b) 68. (c) 69. (a) 70. (b)
71. (c) 72. (a) 73. (c) 74. (b) 75. (b) 76. (d) 77. (a) 78. (a) 79. (d) 80. (c)
81. (a) 82. (a) 83. (a) 84. (a) 85. (a) 86. (b) 87. (b) 88. (b) 89. (a) 90. (a)
91. (d) 92. (b) 93. (a) 94. (c) 95. (a) 96. (c) 97. (a) 98. (c) 99. (a) 100. (a)
101. (d) 102. (a) 103. (a) 104. (b) 105. (a) 106. (b) 107. (b) 108. (a) 109. (a) 110. (a)
111. (a) 112. (a) 113. (b) 114. (c) 115. (c) 116. (a) 117. (a) 118. (a) 119. (a) 120. (d)
121. (a) 122. (a) 123. (a) 124. (d) 125. (b) 126. (a) 127. (a) 128. (b) 129. (b) 130. (a)
131. (a) 132. (a) 133. (a) 134. (a) 135. (b) 136. (c) 137. (b) 138. (b) 139. (b) 140. (c)
141. (a) 142. (a) 143. (d) 144. (b) 145. (a) 146. (a) 147. (a) 148. (b) 149. (c) 150. (c)
151. (d) 152. (a) 153. (b) 154. (d) 155. (a) 156. (a) 157. (b) 158. (b) 159. (b) 160. (c)
161. (c) 162. (d) 163. (a) 164. (a) 165. (c) 166. (a) 167. (a) 168. (d) 169. (a) 170. (a)
171. (b) 172. (a) 173. (c) 174. (c) 175. (a) 176. (a) 177. (b) 178. (c) 179. (a) 180. (b)
181. (d) 182. (c) 183. (a) 184. (c) 185. (a) 186. (b) 187. (b) 188. (d) 189. (b) 190. (c)
191. (a) 192. (c) 193. (b) 194. (d) 195. (a) 196. (b) 197. (a) 198. (c) 199. (c) 200. (a)
201. (c) 202. (a) 203. (c) 204. (b) 205. (a) 206. (c) 207. (b) 208. (a) 209. (a) 210. (b)
211. (b) 212. (d) 213. (a) 214. (a) 215. (d) 216. (c) 217. (a) 218. (b) 219. (a) 220. (c)
221. (b) 222. (a) 223. (c) 224. (b) 225. (a) 226. (c) 227. (b) 228. (a) 229. (a) 230. (c)
231. (a) 232. (a) 233. (b) 234. (b) 235. (a) 236. (c) 237. (a) 238. (d) 239. (c) 240. (b)
241. (d) 242. (c) 243. (c) 244. (a) 245. (b) 246. (a) 247. (b) 248. (b) 249. (a) 250. (b)
251. (b) 252. (a) 253. (b) 254. (b) 255. (a) 256. (c) 257. (c) 258. (a) 259. (a) 260. (b)
261. (c) 262. (a) 263. (b) 264. (b) 265. (b) 266. (c) 267. (a) 268. (a) 269. (a) 270. (b)
271. (b) 272. (a) 273. (a) 274. (a) 275. (d) 276. (a) 277. (b) 278. (d) 279. (d) 280. (a)
281. (b) 282. (a) 283. (a) 284. (b) 285. (a) 286. (c) 287. (a) 288. (a) 289. (a) 290. (a)
291. (a) 292. (a) 293. (a) 294. (c) 295. (b) 296. (b) 297. (a) 298. (a) 299. (a) 300. (a)
301. (a) 302. (b) 303. (a) 304. (a) 305. (b) 306. (c) 307. (a) 308. (b) 309. (a) 310. (c)
311. (a) 312. (b) 313. (a) 314. (a) 315. (b) 316. (b) 317. (a) 318. (a) 319. (b) 320. (c)
321. (d) 322. (a) 323. (b) 324. (c) 325. (a) 326. (d) 327. (b) 328. (b) 329. (b) 330. (d)
331. (b) 332. (a) 333. (d) 334. (a) 335. (a) 336. (d) 337. (b) 338. (a) 339. (a) 340. (a)
341. (b) 342. (a) 343. (a) 344. (c) 345. (a) 346. (b) 347. (a) 348. (c) 349. (d) 350. (a)
351. (a) 352. (a) 353. (a) 354. (c) 355. (c) 356. (a) 357. (a) 358. (c) 359. (b) 360. (c)
361. (a) 362. (a) 363. (b) 364. (a) 365. (a) 366. (a) 367. (c) 368. (a) 369. (a) 370. (a)
371. (b) 372. (c) 373. (c) 374. (b) 375. (b) 376. (a) 377. (a) 378. (a) 379. (b) 380. (b)
381. (a) 382. (a) 383. (c) 384. (a) 385. (a) 386. (a) 387. (b) 388. (a) 389. (c) 390. (a)
391. (a) 392. (b) 393. (c) 394. (a) 395. (c) 396. (a)

## Exercise 2

1. (a,d) 2. (a,b,c) 3. (a,d) 4. (b) 5. (d) 6. (a,b,c) 7. (a,c) 8. (a,b,c,d) 9. (a,b,c) 10. (a,b,c,d)
11. (a,b,d) 12. (a,b,c,d) 13. (a,d) 14. (a,b,d) 15. (c) 16. (a,b,c) 17. (a,c) 18. (b) 19. (a,b,c) 20. (a,b,c)
21. (a,b,c) 22. (d) 23. (b) 24. (a,b,c,d) 25. (a,b,c,d) 26. (a,b,c) 27. (a) 28. (a,b,c) 29. (a,b,c) 30. (a)
31. (a,b,c) 32. (a,b,d) 33. (a,b,c,d) 34. (a,b,c,d) 35. (a,c) 36. (a,b,c,d) 37. (a,b,c,d) 38. (a,b,c,d) 39. (a,b) 40. (a)
41. (a) 42. (a,c) 43. (a,b,c) 44. (a,b,c) 45. (d) 46. (c) 47. (a,b,c) 48. (a) 49. (b,c,d)

# Hints & Solutions

## Exercise 1

**67.** We have,

$$\begin{pmatrix} 2 & 1 & -1 \\ 3 & 2 & 1 \end{pmatrix}\begin{pmatrix} x_1 \\ x_2 \\ x_3 \end{pmatrix} = \begin{pmatrix} 2 \\ 3 \end{pmatrix}$$

One of the basis is $\begin{pmatrix} 2 & 1 \\ 3 & 2 \end{pmatrix}$ which gives

$$\bar{x}_B = \bar{B}^{-1}\bar{b}$$
$$= \begin{pmatrix} 2 & 1 \\ 3 & 2 \end{pmatrix}\begin{pmatrix} 2 \\ 3 \end{pmatrix}$$
$$= \begin{pmatrix} 1 \\ 0 \end{pmatrix}$$

**69.** The maximum number of basic solution are

$$\frac{n!}{m!(n-m)!}$$
$$\therefore \quad = \frac{3!}{2!1!} = 3$$

**77.** We have,

$$\begin{pmatrix} 1 & 2 & 1 \\ 2 & 1 & 5 \end{pmatrix}\begin{pmatrix} x_1 \\ x_2 \\ x_3 \end{pmatrix} = \begin{pmatrix} 4 \\ 5 \end{pmatrix}$$

One of the basis is $\begin{pmatrix} 1 & 2 \\ 2 & 1 \end{pmatrix}$ which gives

$$\bar{x}_B = \bar{B}^{-1}\bar{b}$$
$$= \begin{pmatrix} 1 & 2 \\ 2 & 1 \end{pmatrix}^{-1}\begin{pmatrix} 4 \\ 5 \end{pmatrix} = \begin{pmatrix} 2 \\ 1 \end{pmatrix}$$

**Solutions** (Q. Nos. 149-151)

$D = 10000$ valves per year,
$C =$ ₹ 32 per valve
$C_0 =$ ₹ 55 per setup
$C_h = 12.5\%$ of ₹ 32 = ₹ 4 per year
$p = 120$ valves per day
$d = \frac{10000}{250} = 40$ valves per day

**149.** Optimal total annual stocking cost is

$$TC(Q^*) = \frac{Q}{2}\left(\frac{p-d}{p}\right)C_h + \left(\frac{D}{Q^*}\right)C_0$$
$$= \frac{642.26}{2}\left(\frac{120-40}{120}\right)4 + \left(\frac{10000}{642.26}\right)55$$
$= ₹ 856.8 + 856.35$
$= ₹ 1713.15$ per year
$= ₹ 1714$ (approx)

**150.** We have, $EOQ$, $Q^* = \sqrt{\frac{2DC_0}{C_h}\left(\frac{p}{p-d}\right)}$

$$= \sqrt{\frac{2\times 10000 \times 55}{4}\left(\frac{120}{120-40}\right)}$$
$= 642.26$ valve

**151.** Optimal number of setups,

$$\frac{D}{Q^*} = \frac{10000}{642.26} = 16 \text{ setups}$$

**Solutions** (Q. Nos. 152-153)

From the given data the problem, in usual notations
Annual demand, $D = 2000$ units
Cost of an item, $C =$ ₹ 50
Ordering cost, $C_0 =$ ₹ 25
Inventory carrying cost, $C_h = 20\%$ of ₹ 50 = ₹ 10
Back order cost, $C_b =$ ₹ 10

**152.** Maximum number of back order units is given by

$$S^* = Q^*\left(\frac{C_h}{C_h + C_b}\right)$$
$$= 115\left(\frac{10}{10+30}\right) = 29 \text{ units}$$

**153.** Minimum cost order quantity or $EOQ$ is given by

$$Q^* = \sqrt{\frac{2DC_0}{C_h}\left(\frac{C_h + C_b}{C_b}\right)}$$
$$= \sqrt{\frac{2\times 2000 \times 25}{10}\left(\frac{10+30}{30}\right)}$$
$= 115$ units

**269.** Max $Z = 5x_1 + 12x_2 + 4x_3$,
Subject to the constraints,

$$x_1 + 2x_2 + x_3 \le 5,$$
$$2x_1 - x_2 + 3x_3 = 2,$$
$$x_1, x_2, x_3 \ge 0$$

We change the equality into inequalities and bring the LPP in canonical form.

$$\text{Max } Z = 5x_1 + 12x_2 + 4x_3,$$

Subject to the constraints

$$x_1 + 2x_2 + x_3 \le 5, \quad y_1$$
$$2x_1 - x_2 + 3x_3 \le 2, \quad y_2^+$$
$$-2x_1 + x_2 - 3x_3 \le -2, \quad y_2^-$$
$$x_1, x_2, x_3 \ge 0$$

The dual of above is
Min $W = 5y_1 + 2(y_2^+ - y_2^-)$
Subject to the constraints

$$y_1 + 2(y_2^+ - y_2^-) \ge 5,$$
$$2y_1 - (y_2^+ - y_2^-) \ge 12,$$

$$y_1 + 3(y_2^+ - y_2^-) \geq 4,$$
$$y_1, y_2^+, y_2^- \geq 0$$

The above is same as

Min $\quad W = 5y_1 + 2y_2$

Subject to the constraints,

$$y_1 + 2y_2 \geq 5$$
$$2y_1 - y_2 \geq 12,$$
$$y_1 + 3y_2 \geq 4,$$

$y_1 \geq 0$ and $y_2$ unrestricted in sign.

**272.** Given, Minimize

$$Z = 4x_1 + 6x_2 + 18x_3$$

Subject to the constraints

$$x_1 + 3x_2 \geq 3$$
$$x_2 + 2x_3 \geq 5$$
$$x_j \geq 0 \qquad (j = 1, 2, 3)$$

**Standard Primal** Introducing surplus variables $x_4 \geq 0$ and $x_5 \geq 0$, the standard form of the LPP is

$$\text{Minimize } Z = 4x_1 + 6x_2 + 18x_3 + 0 \cdot x_4 + 0 \cdot x_5$$

Subject to the constraints

$$x_1 + 3x_2 - x_4 = 3,$$
$$0 \cdot x_1 + x_2 + 2x_3 - x_5 = 5$$
$$x_j \geq 0 \qquad (j = 1, 2, 3, 4, 5)$$

**Dual** Let $w_1$ and $w_2$ we the dual variables corresponding to each primal constraint,

Max $\quad Z^* = 3w_1 + 5w_2,$

Subject to the constraints

$$w_1 + 0 \cdot w_2 \geq 4$$
$$3w_1 + w_2 \leq 6,$$
$$0 \cdot w_1 + 2w_2 \leq 18$$
$$-w_1 + 0 \cdot w_2 \leq 0$$
$$0 \cdot w_1 - w_2 \leq 0,$$

$w_1$ and $w_2$ unrestricted (redundant).

Eliminating redundancy, the dual problem is given by

Max $\quad Z^* = 3w_1 + 5w_2,$

Subject to the constraints

$$w_1 \leq 4, 3w_1 + w_2 \leq 6$$
$$2w_2 \leq 18$$
$$w_1 \geq 0$$
$$w_2 \geq 0$$

**274.** The dual of LPP

Max $\quad Z = 5x_1 + 6x_2,$

Subject to the constraints.

$$x_1 + 9x_2 \leq 60, \quad y_1$$
$$2x_1 + 3x_2 \leq 45, \quad y_2$$
$$5x_1 - 2x_2 \leq 20, \quad y_3$$
$$x_2 \leq 30, \quad y_4$$
$$x_1, x_2 \geq 0$$

is Min $W = 60y_1 + 45y_2 + 20y_3 + 30y_4$

Subject to the constraints

$$y_1 + 2y_2 + 5y_3 \geq 5$$
$$9y_1 + 3y_2 - 2y_3 + y_4 \geq 6$$
$$y_1, y_2, y_3, y_4 \geq 0$$

**277.** Given, maximize

$$Z = 3x_1 + 4x_2$$

Subject to the constraints,

$$2x_1 + 3x_2 \leq 16$$
$$5x_1 + 2x_2 \geq 20$$
$$x_1, x_2 \geq 0$$

Since, the objective function of the given LP problem is of maximization, the direction of each inequality of '≥' type has to be changed.

Multiplying the second constraints on both sides by – 1, we have

$$(-1)(5x_1 + 2x_2) \geq (-1)20$$

or $\quad -5x_1 - 2x_2 \leq -20$

The standard primal LP problem is

Maximize $\quad Z_x = 3x_1 + 4x_2$

Subject to the constraints

$$2x_1 + 3x_2 \leq 16$$
$$5x_1 - 2x_2 \leq -20$$
$$x_1 \geq 0, x_2 \geq 0$$

If $y_1$ and $y_2$ are dual problems corresponding to the two primal constraints in given order, then the dual is

Minimize $\quad Z_y = 16y_1 - 20y_2$

Subject to the constraints

$$2y_1 - 5y_2 \geq 3$$
$$3y_1 - 2y_2 \geq 4$$

and $\quad y_1 \geq 0, y_2 \geq 0$

**282.** Given, maximize $3x_1 + 5x_2$

Subject to the constraints,

$$2x_1 - 3x_2 = 8$$
$$4x_1 + x_2 \geq 3$$
$$x_2 \leq 1$$
$$x_1 \geq 0, x_2 \geq 0$$

Writing this in standard form leaving the equation in the constraints as it is, the primal is

Maximize $-3x_1 - 5x_2$

Subject to the constraints,

$$2x_1 - 3x_2 = 8$$
$$4x_1 - x_2 \leq -3$$
$$x_2 \leq 1$$
$$x_1 \geq 0$$
$$x_2 \geq 0$$

Now, the dual is

Minimize $8u_1 - 3u_2 + u_3$

Subject to the constraints

$$2u_1 - 4u_2 \geq -3$$
$$-3u_1 - u_2 + u_3 \geq -5$$
$$u_2 \geq 0, u_3 \geq 0$$

and $u_1$ is unrestricted in sign.

**283.** Car—Customer
Parking—Server

**285.** We have, $L_s = \dfrac{\rho}{1-\rho} = \dfrac{(\lambda/\mu)}{1-(\lambda/\mu)} = \dfrac{\lambda}{\mu-\lambda}$

**287.** Passenger—Customer
Train—Server

**288.** We have, $L_s = \sum_{n=0}^{\infty} np_n = \dfrac{\rho}{1-\rho}$

**289.** Injured—Customer
Doctor—Server

**290.** We have, $\rho = \dfrac{\text{Arrival rate}}{\text{Departure rate}}$

**291.** For Poisson, distribution mean = $\lambda t$ = Variance

**292.** For $M/M/1/N$ queue,

$$p_0 = \begin{cases} \dfrac{1-\rho}{1-\rho^{N+1}}, \rho \neq 1 \\ \dfrac{1}{N+1}, \rho = 1 \end{cases} \quad \text{and} \quad p_n = \rho^n p_0 = \begin{cases} \dfrac{(1-\rho)}{1-\rho^{N+1}}\rho^n, \rho \neq 1 \\ \dfrac{1}{N+1}, \rho = 1 \end{cases}$$

**Solutions** (Q. Nos. 293-296)
$D = 3200$ units per year, ₹1 = 0.25,
$C =$ ₹6, $C_0 =$ ₹150

**293.** Number of orders per year is $= \dfrac{D}{Q^*} = \dfrac{3200}{800} = 4$

**294.** We have, $EOQ, Q^* = \sqrt{\dfrac{2DC_0}{C_h}} = \sqrt{\dfrac{2 \times 150 \times 3200}{6 \times 1.25}}$

$= 800$ units

**295.** Optimal time between two consecutive orders is

$$T^* = \frac{Q}{D} = \frac{800 \times 12}{3200} = 3 \text{ months}$$

**296.** Since, cost of one unit is ₹6, cost of 3200 units are $6 \times 3200 =$ ₹19200

Hence, optimal cost $= 6D + \sqrt{2DC_0C_h}$
$= 6 \times 3200 + \sqrt{2 \times 3200 \times 150 \times 6 \times 0.25}$
$=$ ₹20400

**297.** Birth per day $\lambda = \dfrac{24 \times 60}{12} = 120$ per day

Hence, birth per year $= \lambda t = 120 \times 365$
$= 43800$ per year

**298.** Under pure birth process only arrival occurs.

**299.** We have, $L_s = \sum_{n=0} np_n = \dfrac{1}{N+1}\left(\sum_{n=0}^{N} n\right)$

$$= \frac{1}{N+1} \cdot \frac{(N+1)N}{2} = \frac{N}{2}$$

Since, $\sum_{n=0}^{N} n = \dfrac{(N+1)N}{2}$

and $p_n = \dfrac{1}{N+1}$ for $\rho = 1$

**301.** If the number of arrivals in $(0, t)$ is poisson with mean $\lambda t$, then the inter-arrival time is exponential with mean $1/\lambda$.

**302.** Under pure death process only departure occurs.

**303.** We have, $W_s = \dfrac{L_s}{\lambda} = \dfrac{N}{2} \times \dfrac{1}{\lambda}$ for $\rho = 1$

**306.** The arrival represents birth and departure represents death.

**307.** We have, $W_q = W_s - \dfrac{1}{\mu} = \dfrac{L_s}{\lambda} - \dfrac{1}{\mu} = \dfrac{N}{2\lambda} - \dfrac{1}{\mu}$ for $\rho = 1$

**309.** We have, $p_0(t + \Delta t) = p_0(t)(1 - \lambda\Delta t)$

$$\Rightarrow \quad \lim_{\Delta t \to 0} \frac{p_0(t+\Delta t) - p_0(t)}{\Delta t} = -\lambda p_0(t)$$

$$\Rightarrow \quad p_0'(t) = -\lambda p_0(t)$$

**311.** We have, $L_q = \lambda W_q = \lambda\left(W_s - \dfrac{1}{\mu}\right)$

$$= \lambda\left(\frac{L_s}{\lambda} - \frac{1}{\mu}\right) = L_s - \frac{\lambda}{\mu}$$

$$= L_s - \rho$$

**314.** One-by-one consumption of inventory represents the death.

**315.** We have, $W_s = \dfrac{N}{2\lambda}$ for $\rho = 1$

Hence, $W_s = \dfrac{10}{4} = \dfrac{5}{2}$

$$p_n = \frac{1}{N+1} \text{ for } \rho = 1$$

$$= \frac{1}{15+1} = \frac{1}{16}$$

**Solutions** (Q. Nos. 320-323) From the data of the problem $D = 6000$ units/yr, $C_0 =$ ₹500; $C_h =$ ₹8; $C_b =$ ₹20, $C =$ ₹40, $P = 36000$ units 1 yr.

**320.** We have, $S^* = Q^*\left(\dfrac{C_h}{C_h + C_b}\right)\left(\dfrac{p-d}{p}\right)$

$$= 1123\left(\frac{8}{8+20}\right)\left(\frac{36000-6000}{36000}\right) = 267 \text{ units}$$

**321.** We have, $EOQ, Q^*$

$$= \sqrt{\frac{2DC_0}{C}\left(\frac{p}{p-d}\right)\left(\frac{C_h + C_b}{C_b}\right)}$$

$$= \sqrt{\frac{2 \times 6000 \times 500}{8}\left(\frac{36000}{36000-6000}\right)\left(\frac{8+20}{20}\right)}$$

$$= \sqrt{1260000} = 1123 \text{ units}$$

**322.** We have, $t^* = \dfrac{Q^*}{D} = \dfrac{1123}{6000} = 0.19 \text{ yr} = 2.28$ months

**323.** We have, $t_1^* = \dfrac{Q^*}{p} = \dfrac{1123}{36000} = 0.031 \text{ yr} = 12$ day

**324.** $P_r$ {Arrival occurs more than one in $\Delta T$} $\approx 0$
$= 0$

**Solutions** (Q. Nos. 326-329) $D$, total number of units supplied per unit time period = 600 units

$C_0$, setup cost per run = ₹80

$C_h$, inventory carrying cost per unit per year = ₹0.60

**326.** The optimal number of orders per year,

$$N^* = \frac{D}{Q^*} = \frac{600}{400} = \frac{3}{2}$$

**327.** Minimum average yearly cost is given by

$$TC(Q^*) = \frac{D}{Q^*} C_0 + \frac{Q_2^*}{2} C_h$$

$$= \frac{600 \times 80}{400} + \frac{1}{2} \times 400 \times 0.60 = ₹\,240$$

**328.** The optimal period of supply per optimal order is

$$T^* = \frac{1}{N^*} = \frac{2}{3}$$

**329.** Ordering 20% higher than *EOQ*

$$\text{Ordering quantity} = \frac{120}{100} \times 400 = 480 \text{ units with}$$

$$Q^* = 400 \text{ and } Q = 480$$

$$k = \frac{480}{400} = 1.2$$

Also, $\frac{TC(Q)}{TC(Q^*)} = \frac{1}{2}\left(\frac{1}{k} + k\right) = \frac{1}{2}\left(\frac{1}{1.2} + 1.2\right) = \frac{61}{60}$

Thus, the cost would increase by $\frac{1}{80}$th

or $240 \times \frac{1}{60} = ₹\,4$

**331.** If $p_n(t)$ is the probability of arrival of $n$ customer in $(0, t)$, then the probability of net arrival depends only on $(t, t + \Delta t)$, not on $(0, t)$.

**332.** Under exponential assumptions in $\Delta t \approx 0$, atmost one arrival can occur.

**335.** Under exponential assumption $\Delta t + 0$, atmost one service can occur.

**337.** Departure represents death and arrival represents birth.

**341.** If $p(\Delta t)$ is the probability of arrival in $\Delta t \approx 0$, then $0 < p(\Delta t) < 1$.

**342.** We have, $p_n = \rho^n p_0$

**345.** $a/b/c$, the third position '$c$' represents number of servers, *i.e.*, $c = 1$.

**346.** We have, $\frac{1}{\lambda} = 10 \Rightarrow \lambda = \frac{1}{10}$

**347.** For $M/M/1/N$, for $n \geq N$, $p_n = 0$

Hence, $\sum_{n=0}^{\infty} p_n = 1 \Rightarrow \sum_{n=0}^{N} p_n + \sum_{n=N+1}^{\infty} p_n = 1$

$$\Rightarrow \sum_{n=0}^{N} p_n = 1$$

**350.** For exponential distribution, the mean $= \lambda$ and standard deviation $= \lambda$

**351.** $M$ represents Markovian (exponential/poisson) distribution for arrival (departure).

**352.** We have, $p_n = 0$ for $n > N$ for $M/M/1/N$.

**356.** We have, $a/b/c$

$a \equiv$ Arrival distribution

$b \equiv$ Departure distribution

Here, arrival is Markovian and departure is general.

**357.** We have, $\lambda = 3, \mu = 5 \Rightarrow \rho = \frac{3}{5}$

$$L_s = \frac{\rho}{1-\rho} = \frac{3/5}{1-(3/5)} = \frac{3}{2} = 1.5$$

**359.** $p$ : the probability an arrival occurs in $\Delta t \approx 0$

$$q = 1 - p$$

Since, $0 < p < 1 \Rightarrow 1 < q < 1$

**360.** Total annual inventory cost, $TC(Q^*)$ is given by

$$TC(Q^*) = \frac{D}{Q^*} C_0 + \frac{(Q^* - S^*)^2}{2Q^*} C_h + \frac{S^{*2}}{2Q^*} \times C_b$$

**361.** Expected number of busy servers = traffic intensity

**363.** Time between orders $= \frac{Q^*}{D} = \frac{115}{2000} \times 365 = 21$ day

**364.** Maximum inventory level is

$$I_{max} = Q^* - S^* = 115 - 29 = 86 \text{ units}$$

**367.** We have, $a/b/c/d$

$c \equiv$ Number of servers, here $c = 3$

$d \equiv$ System capacity, here $d = 4$

**368.** We have, $p_0 = (1 - \rho)$

$$= \frac{2000}{115} \times 25 + \frac{(86)^2}{2\,(115)} \times 10 + \frac{(29)^2}{2\,(115)} \times 30$$

$$= 435 + 321.6 + 109.7 = ₹\,866.3$$

**371.** We have, $W_q = \frac{\rho}{\mu(1-\rho)} = \frac{\lambda/\mu}{\mu\left(1 - \frac{\lambda}{\mu}\right)} = \frac{\lambda}{\mu(\mu - \lambda)}$

**373.** We have, $L_s = L_q + C$, when $L_q = 0$, $L_s = C$

**374.** We have, $L_q = \frac{\rho^2}{1-\rho} = \frac{(\lambda/\mu)^2}{1 - \lambda/\mu} = \frac{(\lambda/\mu)^2}{\frac{\mu - \lambda}{\mu}} = \frac{\lambda^2}{\mu(\mu - \lambda)}$

**376.** We have, $L_s = L_q + C$ Here, $L_q = 0$

Hence, $L_s = C$

**377.** We have, $\rho = \frac{\lambda}{\mu} = \frac{4}{6} = \frac{2}{3}$

$$p_n = \rho^n (1 - \rho)$$

$$p_5 = \left(\frac{2}{3}\right)^5 \left(1 - \frac{2}{3}\right) = 0.04390$$

**379.** We have, $L_s = 20$, $C = 12$, $L_q = L_s - C = 20 - 12 = 8$

**380.** We have, $a/b/c/d/e$

$d \equiv$ Queue discipline, here *FCFS* in queue discipline

$e \equiv$ System capacity, *i.e.*, buffer capacity, here it is $N$.

**381.** We have, $\lambda = 20$

$$\mu = 50$$

$$C = \frac{\lambda}{\mu} = \frac{20}{50} = \frac{2}{5}$$

**382.** Expected number of servers busy + Expected number of severs idle = Expected number of servers

**384.** We have, $\lambda = 15$

$$\mu = 30$$

Traffic intensity, $\rho = \frac{\lambda}{\mu} = \frac{15}{30} = \frac{1}{2}$

**385.** We have, $L_s = \sum_{n=0}^{\infty} np_n$

**386.** We have, $\lambda = 10, \mu = 30$

Hence, $\rho = \frac{\lambda}{\mu} = \frac{1}{3}$

$$L_q = \frac{\rho^2}{1-\rho} = \frac{(1/3)^2}{1-(1/3)} = \frac{(1/9)}{\frac{3-1}{3}} = \frac{1}{6}$$

**387.** We have, $L_q = \sum_{n=C+1}^{\infty} (n-C)p_n$

**388.** We have, $L_s = L_q + C \Rightarrow L_s \geq L_q$

**389.** We have, $W_s = W_q + \frac{1}{\mu}$

$$\Rightarrow \frac{L_s}{\lambda} = \frac{L_q}{\lambda} + \frac{1}{\lambda} \text{ or } L_s = L_q + \frac{\lambda}{\mu}$$

**390.** We have, traffic intensity $= \frac{\lambda}{\mu}$

**391.** We have, $L_s - L_q$ = traffic intensity

**392.** We have, $W_s = W_q + \frac{1}{\mu}$

$$\Rightarrow 10 = 5 + \frac{1}{\mu} \text{ or } \mu = \frac{1}{5}$$

**393.** We have, littles formula, $L_s = \lambda W_s$ and $L_q = \lambda W_q$

$$\Rightarrow \frac{L_s}{W_s} = \frac{L_q}{W_q}$$

**394.** We have, $p_n = \rho^n(1-\rho), \rho < 1$

**395.** We have, $L_s = \lambda W_q$

**396.** Sum of all probabilities is equal to one.

i.e., $\sum_{n=0}^{\infty} p_n = 1$

## Exercise 2

**1.**

| Decision variables | Name of product | Type of nutrient constituent | | | Cost of product |
|---|---|---|---|---|---|
| $x_1$ | A | 36 | 3 | 20 | 20 |
| $x_2$ | B | 6 | 12 | 10 | 40 |
| Minimum requirement | | 108 | 36 | 100 | |

Hence, the problem can be formulated as follows

Minimize (total cost) $Z = 20x_1 + 40x_2$

Subject to

$$36x_1 + 6x_2 \geq 108;\ 3x_1 + 12x_2 \geq 36;$$
$$20x_1 + 10x_2 \geq 100;\quad x_1 \geq 0;\ x_2 \geq 0$$

Since, each of them happened to be of 'greater than or equal to type', the points $(x_1, x_2)$ sastisfying them all will lie in the region that falls towards the right of each of these straight lines.

The solution space is the intersection of all these regions in the first, quadrant. This is shown shaded in the following figure.

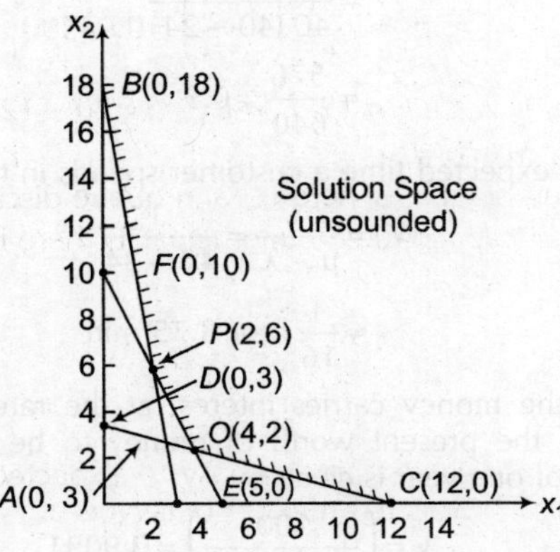


The solution spaces open with B, P, Q and C as extreme points.

| Extreme point | Coordinates | Objective function value $Z = 20x_1 + 40x_2$ |
|---|---|---|
| B | (0, 18) | $Z(B) = 20(0) + 40(18) = 720$ |
| P | (2, 6) | $Z(P) = 20(2) + 40(6) = 280$ |
| Q | (4, 2) | $Z(Q) = 20(4) + 40(2) = 160$ |
| C | (12, 0) | $Z(C) = 20(12) + 40(0) = 240$ |

Since, the minimum cost of ₹ 160 is found at point Q (4, 2) *i.e.*, $x_1 = 4$ and $x_2 = 2$, the optimal solution for the firm is to purchase 4 units of product A and 2 units of product B in order to maintain a minimum cost of ₹ 160.

**2.** We have, arrival rate $\lambda = 12$

and service rate $\mu = 30$

$P_n$ = Probability of $n$ customers in the system

$$= \left(1 - \frac{\lambda}{\mu}\right)\left(\frac{\lambda}{\mu}\right)^n = \left(1 - \frac{12}{30}\right)\left(\frac{12}{30}\right)^n$$

$$\therefore \quad P_0 = \left(1 - \frac{12}{30}\right) = 1 - 0.4 = 0.6$$

**3.** We have,

$$p = 90000;\ D = 30000$$
$$C_0 = ₹\,80;\ C_h = ₹\,1$$
$$Q^* = \sqrt{\frac{2DC_0}{C_h}\left(\frac{p}{p-d}\right)}$$
$$= \sqrt{\frac{2 \times 30000 \times 80}{1}\left(\frac{90000}{90000 - 30000}\right)}$$
$$= 2683.28 \text{ L}$$

and $N^* = \frac{D}{Q^*} = \frac{30000}{2683.28} = 11.18$ runs

**6.** The appropriate mathematical formulation of the given problem as LP model is as follows

Maximize (total audience)

$Z = (750000 + 150000)\,x_1 + (40000 + 260000)\,x_2$

Subject to the constraints

$$50000\ x_1 + 20000\ x_2 \leq 200000 \text{ or } 5x_1 + 2x_2 \leq 20$$
$$x_1 \geq 3,\ x_2 \leq 5 \text{ and } x_1 \geq 0,\ x_2 \geq 0$$

where, $x_1$ = Number of programming on TV

$x_2$ = Number of programmes on Radio

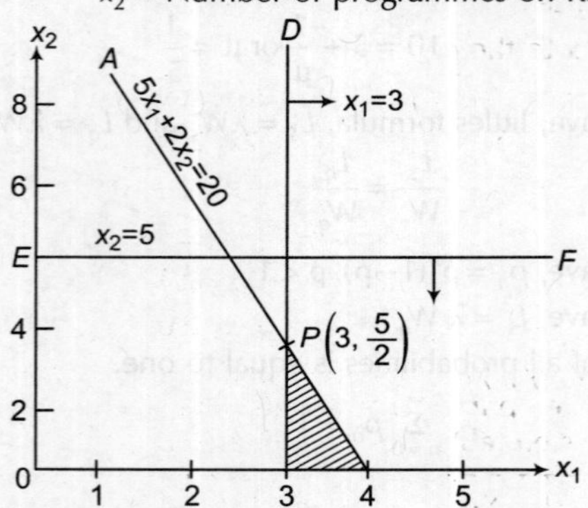


Clearly, each point $(x_1, x_2)$ satisfying the constraints $x_1 \geq 0$, $x_2 \geq 0$ must lie in the first quadrant only. Also, since $5x_1 + 2x_2 \leq 20$, $x_1 \geq 3$ and $x_2 \leq 5$, the desired point $(x_1, x_2)$ lies somewhere on the convex region *BCP*. The coordinates of the extreme points of this feasible region are given by

$$B = (4, 0),\ C = (3, 0) \text{ and } P = \left(3, \frac{5}{2}\right)$$

| Extreme point | Coordinates | Objective function value $Z = 4x_1 + 3x_2$ |
|---|---|---|
| B | (4, 0) | $Z(B) = 900000 \times 4 + 300000 \times 0 = 3600000$ |
| C | (3, 0) | $Z(C) = 900000 \times 3 + 300000 \times 0 = 2700000$ |
| P | (3, 5/2) | $Z(P) = 900000 \times 3 + 300000 \times 5/2 = 3450000$ |

Since, the maximum value of $Z = 3600000$ occurs at the point $B(4, 0)$, the solution to the given problem is $x_1 = 4$, $x_2 = 0$ and max 3600000.

Therefore, the optimal solution is to give 4 programmes on TV and no programme on radios in order to achieve a maximum audience reach of 3600000 audiences.

**7.** Demand of parts per annum $D = 10000$

and purchase or ordering cost per order,

$$C_0 = ₹\,36 \text{ per order}$$

and cost of one part, $C = ₹\,2$

Inventory carrying costs (expressed as a percentage of the value of average inventory), $1 = ₹\,0.09$.

Here, $Q^*$ = Economic order quantity

$TC^*$ = Total inventory cost

Now, cost of inventory = $DC = ₹\,10000 \times 2$

The total inventory carrying cost over a period is given by

(average inventory during the period) × (cost of the unit) × (Inventory carrying cost as percentage)

$$= \left(\frac{1}{2} Q\right) \times (₹\,2) \times (₹\,0.09) = 0.09\,Q$$

The total ordering cost is given by

(number of orders per period) × (ordering cost per order)

$$= \left(\frac{10000}{Q}\right) \times 36$$

Hence, $$TC = 10000 \times 2 + \frac{360000}{Q} + 0.09Q$$

Differentiating *Wrt* $Q$,

$$\frac{d(TC)}{dQ} = \frac{-360000}{Q^2} + 0.09$$

Equating it equal to zero, we get

$$\frac{360000}{Q^2} = 0.09$$

or $$Q = 2000 \text{ units}$$

At $$Q = 2000 \text{ units}$$

$$\frac{d^2(TC)}{dQ^2} = -\frac{720000}{Q^2} > 0$$

Hence, *TC* is minimum, when $Q = 2000$ units.

Thus, *EOQ*, $Q^* = 2000$ units.

(ii) Optimal number of orders $= \frac{\text{Demand}}{EOQ} = \frac{D}{Q^*}$

$$= \frac{10000}{2000} = 5 \text{ orders}$$

**12.** We have,

Mean arrival rate, $\lambda = \frac{2 \times 60}{5}$ or 24 per h

and Mean service rate, $\mu = \frac{60}{1.5}$ or 40 per h

(a) The proportion of time, the facility remains idle is

$$P_0 = 1 - \frac{\lambda}{\mu} = 1 - \frac{24}{40} = 0.4$$

*i.e.*, 40% of the time facility remains idle.

(b) The expected number of customers in the waiting line is

$$L_q = \frac{\lambda^2}{\mu(\mu - \lambda)}$$
$$= \frac{24 \times 24}{40\ (40 - 24)}$$
$$= \frac{576}{640} = 0.9$$

(c) The expected time a customer spends in the system is

$$W_s = \frac{1}{\mu - \lambda} = \frac{1}{40 - 24}$$
$$= \frac{1}{16} \text{ h or } 3.75 \text{ min}$$

**14.** Since, the money carries interest at the rate of 10% per annum, the present worth of money to be spent over a period of one year is given by

$$v = \left(\frac{100}{(100 + 10)}\right) = 0.9091$$

Computation of present worth of machines *A* and *B*

| Year | Discount factor $v^{n-1}$ | Machine A | | Machine B | |
|---|---|---|---|---|---|
| | | Yearly cost $C_n$ | Present value $C_n v^{n-1}$ | Yearly cost $C_n$ | Present value $C_n v^{n-1}$ |
| 1 | 1.0000 | 1000 | 1000.00 | 1700 | 1700 |
| 2 | 0.9091 | 200 | 181.82 | 100 | 90.91 |
| 3 | 0.8265 | 400 | 330.60 | 200 | 165.30 |
| 4 | 0.7514 | 1000 | 751.40 | 300 | 225.42 |
| 5 | 0.6830 | 200 | 136.60 | 400 | 273.20 |
| 6 | 0.6209 | 400 | 248.36 | 500 | 310.45 |

The total discounted cost or present worth for machine *A* over 3 yr

$$= 1000 \times 1 + 200 \times 0.9091 + 400 \times (0.9091)^2$$
$$= 1000 + 181.82 + 330.60 = ₹1512.42$$

Hence, average cost per year of machine *A*

$$= \frac{1512.42}{2.7356} = ₹552.87$$

The total discounted cost or present worth for machine *B* over six year is

$$= 1700 \times 1 + 100 \times 0.9091 + 200 \times (0.9091)^2$$
$$+ 300 \times (0.9091)^3 + 400 \times (0.9091)^4 + 500\,(0.9091)^5$$
$$= 1700 + 90.91 + 165.30 + 225.42 + 273.20 + 310.45$$
$$= ₹2765.25$$

Hence, average cost per year of machine *B*

$$= \frac{2765.25}{4.7909} = ₹577.19$$

Since, the weighted average cost of machine *A* is less than that of *B*, machine *A* should not be replaced by machine *B*.

**19.** Primal of the given problem in standard form is

Max $\quad 450x_1 + 550x_2$

Subject to constraints

$$6x_1 + 3x_2 \le 120$$
$$4x_1 + 10x_2 \le 180$$
$$-4x_1 - 10x_2 \le -180$$
$$x_1 \le 18$$
$$x_1 \ge 0$$
$$x_2 \ge 0$$

The dual linear programming problem is

Minimize $120u_1 + 180u_2 + 180u_3 + 18u_4$

Subject to constraints

$$6u_1 + 4u_2 - 4u_3 + u_4 \ge 450$$
$$3u_1 + 10u_2 - 10u_3 \ge 550$$
$$u_1 \ge 0, u_2 \ge 0, u_3 \ge 0, u_4 \ge 0$$

Writing $u_2^* = u_2 - u_3$, the dual is

Minimize $120u_1 + 180u_2^* + 18u_4$

Subject to constraints

$$6u_1 + 4u_2^* + u_4 \ge 450$$
$$3u_1 + 10u_2^* \ge 550$$

$u_1 \ge 0, u_4 \ge 0, u_2^*$ is unrestricted in sign.

**20.** Since, the objective function of the given LP problem is of minimization, the direction of each inequality of '≤' type has to be changed.

We have,

Minimize $\quad Z = 5x_1 - 6x_2 + 4x_3$

Subject to the constraints

$$3x_1 + 4x_2 + 6x_3 \ge 9$$
$$x_1 + 3x_2 + 2x_3 \ge 5$$
$$-7x_1 + 2x_2 + x_3 \ge -10$$
$$x_1 - 2x_2 + 4x_3 \ge 4$$
$$2x_1 + 5x_2 - 3x_3 \ge 3$$
$$x_1 \ge 0, x_2 \ge 0, x_3 \ge 0$$

If $y_1, y_2, y_3, y_4$ and $y_5$ are dual variables corresponding to the five primal constraints in given order, then the conversion table may be written as

| | $y_1$ | $y_2$ | $y_3$ | $y_4$ | $y_5$ | |
|---|---|---|---|---|---|---|
| $x_1$ | 3 | 1 | −7 | 1 | 2 | ≤5 |
| $x_2$ | 4 | 3 | 2 | −2 | 5 | ≤−6 |
| $x_3$ | 6 | 2 | 1 | 4 | −3 | ≤4 |
| | ≥9 | ≥5 | ≥−10 | ≥4 | ≥3 | |

The dual is given by maximize

$$Z^* = 9y_1 + 5y_2 - 10y_3 + 4y_4 + 3y_5$$

Subject to the constraints

$$3y_1 + y_2 - 7y_3 + y_4 + 2y_5 \le 5$$
$$4y_1 + 3y_2 + 2y_3 - 2y_4 + 5y_5 \le -6$$
$$6y_1 + 2y_2 + y_3 + 4y_4 - 3y_5 \le 4$$
$$y_1, y_2, y_3, y_4, y_5 \ge 0$$

**21.** The extreme points of the feasible region *ABCD* *A*(0, 0), *B*(60000; 40000), *C*(75000; 25000) and *D*(75000; 18750)

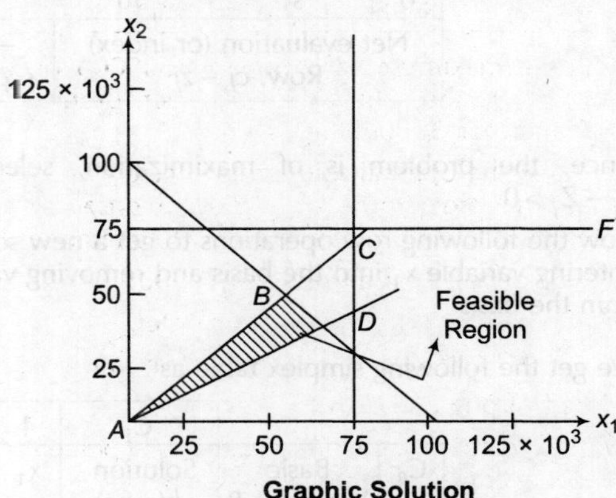

**Graphic Solution**

Hence, the value of objective function at extreme points are

$$Z(C) = 7500 + 5000 = ₹12500$$
$$Z(D) = 7500 + 3750 = ₹11250$$
$$Z(B) = 6000 + 8000 = ₹14000$$

Since, the maximum value of *Z* occurs at extreme point *B*, the optimal solution the problem is $x_1 = 60000$; $x_2 = 40000$ and max $Z = ₹14000$.

**24.** The given system of equations can be written in the matrix form as

$$\bar{A}\bar{x} = \bar{b}$$

where, $\bar{A} = \begin{pmatrix} 1 & 2 & 1 \\ 2 & 1 & 5 \end{pmatrix}$

$$\bar{x} = \begin{bmatrix} x_1 \\ x_2 \\ x_3 \end{bmatrix} \text{ and } \bar{b} = \begin{bmatrix} 4 \\ 5 \end{bmatrix}$$

Here, rank $(A) = 2$

The maximum number of linearly independent columns of $A$ is 2. Therefore, we can take any of the following $2 \times 2$ sub-matrices as basis matrix $B$

$$\begin{pmatrix} 1 & 2 \\ 2 & 1 \end{pmatrix}, \begin{pmatrix} 1 & 1 \\ 2 & 5 \end{pmatrix} \text{ and } \begin{pmatrix} 2 & 1 \\ 1 & 5 \end{pmatrix}$$

The variables not associated with the columns of $B$ are $x_3$, $x_2$ and $x_1$ respectively, in the three different cases.

Let us take $B = \begin{pmatrix} 1 & 2 \\ 2 & 1 \end{pmatrix}$

Hence, a basic solution to the given system is now obtained by setting $x_3 = 0$ and solving the system

$$\begin{pmatrix} 1 & 2 \\ 2 & 1 \end{pmatrix} \begin{bmatrix} x_1 \\ x_2 \end{bmatrix} = \begin{bmatrix} 4 \\ 5 \end{bmatrix}$$

Hence, a basic (non-basic) solution to the given system is (basic) $x_1 = 2$, $x_2 = 1$; $x_3 = 0$ (non-basic)

Similarly, the other two basic and non-basic solutions are (basic) $x_1 + 5$, $x_3 = -1$; $x_2 = 0$ (non-basic)

and (basic) $x_2 = \frac{5}{8}$, $x_3 = \frac{2}{8}$; $x_1 = 0$ (non-basic)

We observe that all the above, three basic solutions are non-degenerate solution.

**25.** By adding slack, surplus and artificial variables in the set of constraints and assigning appropriate costs to these variables in the objective function. The standard form is given by

Maximize $Z = 4x_1 + 5x_2 - 3x_3 + 0s_1 + 0s_2 - MA_1 - MA_2$

Subject to $\quad x_1 + x_2 + x_3 + A_1 = 10$

$$x_1 - x_2 - s_1 + A_2 = 1$$

$$2x_1 + 3x_2 + x_3 + s_2 = 30$$

Where, $x_1 \geq 0$, $x_2 \geq 0$, $s_1 \geq 0$, $s_2 \geq 0$, $A_1 \geq 0$, $A_2 \geq 0$

An initial basic feasible solution is obtained by setting

$$x_1 = x_2 = x_3 = s_1 = 0$$

Hence, $\quad A_1 = 10$

$A_2 = 1$ and $s_2 = 30$

and $\quad Z = -M$

The initial simplex table is

| | | $C_j$ | 4 | 5 | $-3$ | 0 | 0 | $-M$ | $-M$ | Min Ratio |
|---|---|---|---|---|---|---|---|---|---|---|
| $C_B$ | Basic Variables $B$ | Solution $b(=x_B)$ | $x_1$ | $x_2$ | $x_3$ | $s_1$ | $s_2$ | $A_1$ | $A_2$ | $x_B/x_1$ |
| $-M$ | $A_1$ | 10 | 1 | 1 | 1 | 0 | 0 | 1 | 0 | 10 |
| $-M$ | $A_2$ | 1 | 1 | $-1$ | 0 | $-1$ | 0 | 0 | 1 | $1 \rightarrow$ |
| 0 | $s_2$ | 30 | 2 | 3 | 1 | 0 | 1 | 0 | 0 | 15 |
| Net evaluation (or index) | | | $-2M$ | 0 | $-M$ | $M$ | 0 | $-M$ | $-M$ | |
| Row. $cj - zj$ | | | $4 + 2M\uparrow$ | 5 | $-3 + M$ | $-M$ | 0 | 0 | 0 | |

Since, the problem is of maximization, select largest $C_j - Z_j > 0$.

Now the following row operations to get a new solution by entering variable $x_1$ into the basis and removing variable $A_2$ from the basis

(i) $R_2(\text{new}) \rightarrow R_2$ (old)

(ii) $R_1(\text{new}) \rightarrow R_1(\text{old}) - R_2$ (new) and

(iii) $R_3(\text{new}) \rightarrow R_3(\text{old}) - 2R_2$ (new)

We get the following simplex table as

| | | $C_j$ | 4 | 5 | $-3$ | 0 | 0 | $-M$ | $-M$ | Min. Ratio |
|---|---|---|---|---|---|---|---|---|---|---|
| $C_B$ | Basic Variables $B$ | Solution $b(=x_B)$ | $x_1$ | $x_2$ | $x_3$ | $s_1$ | $s_2$ | $A_1$ | $A_2$ | $x_B/x_2$ |
| $-M$ | $A_1$ | 9 | 0 | 2 | 1 | 0 | 0 | | $-1$ | $9/2 \rightarrow$ |
| 4 | $x_1$ | 1 | 1 | $-1$ | 0 | $-1$ | 0 | | 1 | — |
| 0 | $s_2$ | 28 | 0 | 5 | 1 | 2 | 1 | | $-2$ | 28/5 |
| $0Z_j$ | | | 4 | $-2M - 4$ | $-M$ | $-4$ | 0 | | $M+4$ | |
| Net evaluation (or index) Row $C_j - Z_j$ | | | 0 | $1 + 2M\uparrow$ | $-3 + M$ | 4 | 0 | | $-4$ | |

Applying the following row operations to get a new solution by entering variable $x_2$ into the basis and removing variable $A_1$ from the basis,

(i) $R_1(\text{new}) \to \frac{1}{2}R_1$ (old)

(ii) $R_2(\text{new}) \to R_2(\text{old}) + R_1$ (new) and

(iii) $R_3(\text{new}) \to R_3(\text{old}) - 5R_1$ (new)

We have the simplex table as

| | | $C_j$ | 4 | 5 | −3 | 0 | 0 | −M | −M |
|---|---|---|---|---|---|---|---|---|---|
| $C_B$ | Basic Variable s B | Solution Values $b(=x_B)$ | $x_1$ | $x_2$ | $x_3$ | $s_1$ | $s_2$ | $A_1$ | $A_2$ |
| 5 | $x_2$ | $\frac{9}{2}$ | 0 | 1 | $\frac{1}{2}$ | 0 | 0 | | |
| 4 | $x_1$ | $\frac{11}{2}$ | 1 | 0 | $\frac{1}{2}$ | −1 | 0 | | |
| 0 | $s_2$ | $\frac{11}{2}$ | 0 | 0 | $-\frac{3}{2}$ | 2 | 1 | | |
| | $Z_j$ | | 4 | 5 | $\frac{9}{2}$ | −4 | 0 | | |
| $C_j - Z_j$ | | | 0 | 0 | $\frac{15}{2}$ | 4 | 0 | | |

Since, all entries in the net evaluation row are either positive or zero, further improvement in the objective function is not possible. Hence, the optimal solution is being attained and hence, we have

$x_1 = \frac{11}{2}$, $x_2 = \frac{9}{2}$, $x_3 = 0$, $s_1 = 0$ and maximum value of $Z$ is $\frac{89}{2}$.

**26.** (a) We have, $p_0 = 1 - \frac{\lambda}{\mu} = 1 - \frac{24}{40} = 4$

(b) We have, $L_q = \frac{\lambda^2}{\mu(\mu-\lambda)} = \frac{24 \times 24}{40(40-24)}$

$$= \frac{576}{640} = 0.9$$

(c) We have, $W_s = \frac{1}{\mu - \lambda} = \frac{1}{40-24} = \frac{1}{16}$ h

**28.** Introducing a slack variable $x_4 \geq 0$ and a surplus variable $x_5 \geq 0$. Then, the primal is

Minimize $Z = cx$, subject to the constraints

$$Ax = b$$

and $\quad x > 0$

Where, $x = [x_1, x_2, x_3^+, x_3^-, x_4, x_5]$

$$c = [1, -3, -2, 2, 0, 0]$$

$$b = [7, 12, 10]$$

and $A = \begin{pmatrix} 3 & -1 & 2 & -2 & 1 & 0 \\ 2 & -4 & 0 & 0 & 0 & -1 \\ -4 & 3 & 8 & -8 & 0 & 0 \end{pmatrix}$

When, $x_3 = x_3^+ - x_3^-$

If $w = [w_1, w_2, w_3]$ are the dual variables, the dual is

Maximize $\quad Z^* = 7w_1 + 12w_2 + 10w_3$

Subject to the constraints

$$3w_1 + 2w_2 - 4w_3 \leq 1$$
$$-w_1 - 4w_2 + 3w_3 \leq -3$$

$$\Rightarrow \quad w_1 + 4w_2 - 3w_3 \geq 3$$

$$\left.\begin{array}{l} 2w_1 + 8w_3 \leq -2 \\ -2w_1 - 8w_3 \leq 2 \end{array}\right\}$$

$$\Rightarrow \quad 2w_1 + 8w_3 = 2$$

$$\left.\begin{array}{l} w_1 \leq 0 \\ -w_1 \leq 0 \end{array}\right\}$$

$$\Rightarrow \quad w_1 \leq 0$$

and $\quad w_2 \geq 0$

$w_1$, $w_2$ and $w_3$ are unrestricted.

Eliminating redundancy, dual variables are $w_1 \leq 0$, $w_2 \geq 0$ and $w_3$ unrestricted. We have,

Maximize $\quad Z^* = 7w_1 + 12w_2 + 10w_3$

Subject to the constraints

$$3w_1 + 2w_2 - 4w_3 \leq 1$$
$$w_1 + 4w_2 - 3w_3 \geq 3$$
$$-2w_1 - 8w_3 = 2$$
$$w_1 \leq 0$$

and $\quad w_2 \geq 0$, $w_3$ unrestricted

**29.** Transform the '≤' type constraint to a '≥' type constraint by multiplying the constraint by −1. Also, write the '=' type constraint equivalent to two constraints of the type ≥ and ≤. The given primal problem can be written as follows

We have minimize $Z = 40x_1 + 120x_2$

Subject to the constraints

$$-x_1 + 2x_2 \geq -8$$
$$3x_1 + 5x_2 \geq 90$$
$$3x_1 + 5x_2 \leq 90$$

or $\quad -3x_1 - 5x_2 \geq -90$

$$-15x_1 - 44x_2 \geq -660$$
$$x_1 \geq 0,\ x_2 \geq 0$$

Let $y_1$, $y_2$, $y_3$ and $y_4$ be the dual variables corresponding to the four constraints in given order, then the dual of the given primal problem can be formulated as follows

Minimize $\quad Z^* = 8y_1 + 90y_2 - 90y_3 - 660y_4$

Subject to the constraints

$$-y_1 + 3y_2 - 3y_3 - 15y_4 \leq 40$$
$$2y_1 + 5y_2 - 5y_3 - 44y_4 \leq 120$$
$$y_1 \geq 0,\ y_2 \geq 0,\ y_3 \geq 0,\ y_4 \geq 0$$

Let $y = y_2 - y_3$, then the above dual problem reduces to the form.

Hence, maximize $Z_y = 8y_1 + 90y - 660y_4$

Subject to the constraints

$$-y_1 + 3y - 15y_4 \leq 40$$
$$2y_1 + 5y - 44y_4 \leq 120$$
$$y_1 \geq 0,\ y_4 \geq 0;$$

$y$ is unrestricted in sign.

Since, the second constraint in the primal is equality. Therefore, the corresponding second dual variable $y_2$ is unrestricted in sign.

**30.** Let $x, y \in S$, where $x = (x_1, x_2)$ and $y = (y_1, y_2)$

The line segment joining $x$ and $y$ is the set

$$[u : u = \lambda x + (1-\lambda)y,\ 0 \le \lambda \le 1]$$

For some $\lambda$, $0 \le \lambda \le 1$, let $u = (u_1, u_2)$ be a point of this set, so that

$$u_1 = \lambda x_1 + (1-\lambda)y_1 \text{ and } u_2 = \lambda x_2 + (1-\lambda)y_2$$

Now, $3u_1^2 + 2u_2^2$

$$= 3[\lambda x_1 + (1-\lambda)y_1]^2 + 2[\lambda x_2 + (1-\lambda)y_2]^2$$

$$= \lambda^2(3x_1^2 + 2x_2^2) + (1-\lambda)^2[3y_1^2 + 2y_2^2] + 2\lambda(1-\lambda)(3x_1y_1 + 2x_2y_2)$$

$$\le 6\lambda^2 + 6(1-\lambda)^2 + 12\lambda(1-\lambda)$$

Since, $(3x_1y_1 + 2x_2y_2)$

$$\le \sqrt{(x_1\sqrt{3})^2 + (x_2\sqrt{2})^2}\ \sqrt{(y_1\sqrt{3})^2 + (y_2\sqrt{3})^2}$$

Thus, $3u_1^2 + 2u_2^2 \le 6$; and hence $u = (u_1, u_2)$ is also a point of $S$.

Hence, $S$ is a convex set.

**31.** (a) Here, the typist's utilization rate

$$= P = \frac{\lambda}{\mu} = \frac{22}{24} = 0.917$$

(b) Here, the average number of letters waiting to be typed

$$L_q = \frac{\lambda^2}{\mu(\mu-\lambda)} = \frac{22\times 22}{24(24-22)}$$

$$= 10.8083 \text{ letters per day}$$

(c) Here, the average waiting time needed to have a letter typed

$$W_s = \frac{1}{\mu-\lambda} = \frac{1}{24-22}$$

$$= \frac{1}{2} \text{ day or 4 h}$$

**34.** Here,

$\lambda = 6$ patients per hour, $\mu = \frac{1}{20}$ min or 3 patients per hour, $k = 3$.

Probability of no patient in system

$$P_0 = \left[\sum_{n=0}^{k-1} \frac{1}{n!}\left(\frac{\lambda}{\mu}\right)^n + \frac{1}{k!}\left(\frac{\lambda}{\mu}\right)^k \cdot \frac{1}{\{1-(\lambda/k\mu)\}}\right]^{-1}$$

$$= \left[1 + 2 + \frac{2^2}{2!} + \frac{2^3}{3!\{1-6/9\}}\right]^{-1} = \frac{1}{9}$$

(a) Hence, expected number of patients waiting in the queue

$$L_q = \left[\frac{1}{(k-1)!}\left(\frac{\lambda}{\mu}\right)^k \cdot \frac{\lambda\mu}{(k\mu-\lambda)^2}\right]P_0$$

$$= \frac{1}{2!}\times 2^3 \times \frac{6\times 3}{(3\times 3-6)^2}\times\frac{1}{9}$$

$$= \frac{8}{9} \text{ or } 0.889$$

(b) Hence, average time a patient spends in the system

$$W_s = W_q + \frac{1}{\mu}$$

$$= \frac{L_q}{\lambda} + \frac{1}{\mu} = \frac{8}{9}\times\frac{1}{6} + \frac{1}{3}$$

$$= \frac{13}{27} \text{ h or 28.9 min}$$

(c) Hence, probability that a patient has to wait

$$P(n \ge k) = \frac{1}{k!}\left(\frac{\lambda}{\mu}\right)^k \frac{1}{\{1-(\lambda/k\mu)\}} P_0$$

$$= \frac{1}{3!}\times 2^3 \times \frac{1}{[1-(6/9)]}\times\frac{1}{9}$$

$$= \frac{4}{9} \text{ or } 0.444$$

(d) Hence, the fraction of time the doctors are busy,

$$\rho = \frac{\lambda}{k\mu} = \frac{2}{3}$$

Therefore, the expected idle time for each doctor

$$= 1 - \frac{2}{3} = \frac{1}{3}$$

**35.** We have,

$$\text{Arrival rate } \lambda = 8 \text{ customers/h}$$

$$\text{Service time per phase} = 2 \text{ min}$$

$$k = 3$$

Hence, service rate $\mu$

$$= 2\times 3 \text{ customers/min}$$

$$= 10 \text{ customers/h,}$$

(a) Average time a customer spends waiting in the cafeteria

$$W_q = \frac{k+1}{3k}\cdot\frac{\lambda}{\mu(\mu-\lambda)}$$

$$W_q = \frac{3+1}{2(3)}\times\frac{8}{10(10-8)}$$

$$= \frac{32}{120} \text{ h or 16 min}$$

(b) Average time of getting the service is the average of the time when it is following the third phase of service. Thus, average time spent in getting the service is

$$\frac{1}{\mu} = \frac{1}{10} \text{ h or 6 min}$$

(c) The most probable time spent in getting the service is the model value of service time for the third phase of service. Thus, most probable time spent is

$$\frac{k-1}{k\mu} = \frac{3-1}{3\times 10} = \frac{1}{15} \text{ h or 4 min}$$

**38.** The present total annual stocking cost is

$$TSC_1 = \frac{Q}{2}\times C_h + \frac{D}{Q}\times C_0$$

$$= \frac{400}{2}\times 4 + \frac{10000}{400}\times 55$$

$$= 800 + 1375$$

$$= ₹2175$$

$$EOQ, \quad Q^* = \sqrt{\frac{2DC_0}{C_h}} = \sqrt{\frac{2 \times 10000 \times 55}{4}}$$
$$= \sqrt{275000}$$
$$= 524.4 \text{ units}$$

The total annual stocking cost, if *EOQ* were employed is

$$TSC_2 = \frac{Q^*}{2} \times C_h + \frac{D}{Q^*} \times C_0$$
$$= \frac{524.4}{2} \times 4 + \frac{10000}{524.4} \times 55$$
$$= ₹\,2097.6$$

The estimated annual savings in stocking costs

$$= TSC_1 - TSC_2$$
$$= 2175 - 2097.6$$
$$= ₹\,77.4$$

Hence, Mr Ram concluded that, if the annual savings on this one material were applied to the thousands of items in inventory, the savings from *EOQ* would be significant.

**39.** Let the manufacturer decide to produce $x_1$, units of type *A* belt, $x_2$ units of type *B* belt and $x_3$ units of type *C* belt.

Then, the given problem can be put in the following mathematical form

Maximize $\quad Z = 3x_1 + 5x_2 + 4x_3$

Subject to the constraints

$$2x_1 + 3x_2 \le 8$$
$$2x_2 + 5x_3 \le 10$$
$$3x_1 + 2x_2 + 4x_3 \le 15$$
$$x_1, x_2, x_3 \ge 0$$

**42.** In the usual notations, we are given

Annual demand,

$$D = 8 \times 200 = 1600 \text{ units per yr}$$

Ordering cost,

$$C_0 = ₹\,500 \text{ per order}$$

Cost per unit,

$$C = ₹\,400 \text{ per units}$$

Inventory carrying cost,

$$C_h = 40\% \text{ of } ₹\,400$$
$$= ₹\,160$$

(i) If $Q^*$ is the optimal order quantity, we have

$$EOQ, \ Q^* = \sqrt{\frac{2DC_0}{C_h}} + \sqrt{\frac{2 \times 1600 \times 500}{160}}$$
$$= 100 \text{ units}$$

Total inventory cost as per *EOQ* approach

$$TC(Q^*) = DC + \frac{D}{Q^*} \times C_0 + \frac{Q^*}{2} \times CI$$

or $\quad TC(100) = 1600 \times 400 + \frac{1600}{100} \times 500 + \frac{100}{2} \times (400 \times 0.4)$

$$= ₹\,640000 + 8000 + 8000$$
$$= ₹\,656000 \quad \ldots(i)$$

(ii) Total cost as per present policy, *i.e.*, for order size of 200 units

$$TC(100) = 1600 \times 400 + \frac{1600}{200} \times 500 + \frac{200}{2} \times (400 \times 0.4)$$
$$= ₹\,640000 + 4000 + 16000$$
$$= ₹\,660000 \quad \ldots(ii)$$

(iii) Proposed inventory costs. If the manager decides to place an order for a minimum quantity of 500 items to avail a discount of 10%, the cost per item becomes $₹\,400 \times 0.4 = ₹\,360$

$$TC(500) = 1600 \times 360 + \frac{1600}{500} \times 500 + \frac{500}{2} \times (360 \times 0.4)$$
$$= ₹\,576000 + 1600 + 36000$$
$$= ₹\,613600 \quad \ldots(iii)$$

From Eqs. (i), (ii) and (iii) above, it is quite evident that if the manager decides to place an order for a minimum quantity of 500 items, he will save ₹ (660000 − 613600) = ₹ 46400 over the present policy of placing an order of size 200 units. Also, he will save ₹ (656000 − 613600) = ₹ 42400 over the policy of placing order of economic size, *i.e.*, an order of size 100 units.

Hence, the manager's decision is justified and it will save ₹ 45400.

**43.** $P_0 \equiv$ Probability that there are no truck in the system

Here, $\lambda = 3$ per hour, $\mu = 1$ per hour, $C = 4$ bays and $\rho = 3 = \lambda/\mu$

This is the *M/M/C* queueing model with infinite capacity.

(a) $$P_0 = \left[\sum_{n=0}^{C-1} \frac{(\lambda/\mu)^n}{n!} + \frac{(\lambda/\mu)^C}{C}\left(\frac{1}{1-(\lambda/\mu)}\right)\right]^{-1}$$
$$= \left[1 + 3 + \frac{9}{2} + \frac{27}{6} + \frac{81}{24\,(1-0.75)}\right]^{-1}$$
$$= 0.0377$$

(b) Average number of trucks in the queue

$$L_q = \frac{\rho^{C+1}}{C-1!(C-\rho)^2}$$
$$P_0 = \frac{(3)^5}{3!(4-3)^2}(0.0377)$$
$$= 1.53 \text{ h}$$
$$W_q = \frac{L_q}{\lambda} = \frac{1.5}{3} 0.51 \text{ h}$$

(c) $W_s = W_q + \frac{1}{\mu} = 0.51 + 1 = 1.51 \text{ h}$

(d) $L_s = \lambda W_s = 3(1.51) = 4.53$ trucks

**44.** (a) Expected time of customer in queue is

$$W_q = \frac{\lambda}{\mu(\mu - \lambda)}$$
$$= \frac{5}{8(8-5)} = \frac{5}{24} \text{ h}$$

(b) Probability (atleast two customers in the system)

$$= P(n \geq 2)$$

$$\left(\frac{\lambda}{\mu}\right)^{n+1} = \left(\frac{\lambda}{\mu}\right)^{2+1}$$

$$= \left(\frac{5}{8}\right)^{3}$$

(c) Probability (the server is idle)

$$= \rho\,(1-\rho)$$

$$= \frac{5}{8}\left(1-\frac{5}{8}\right)$$

$$= \frac{15}{64}$$

**47.** The appropriate mathematical formulation of the given as LP model is

Maximize $Z = 10000x + 8500y$

Subject to $6x + 5y \leq 60$

$x + y = 11$

with $x, y \geq 0$

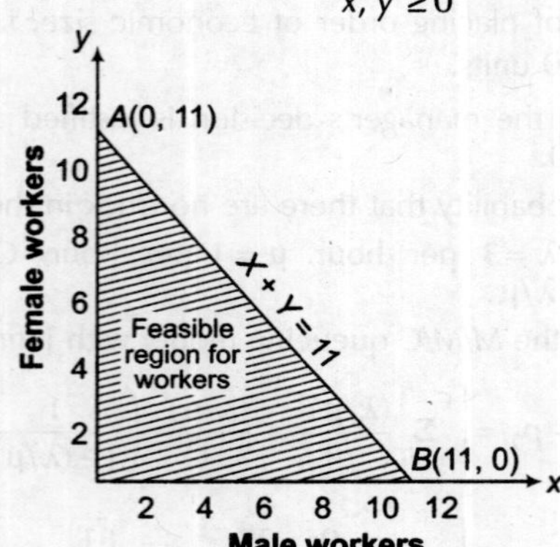


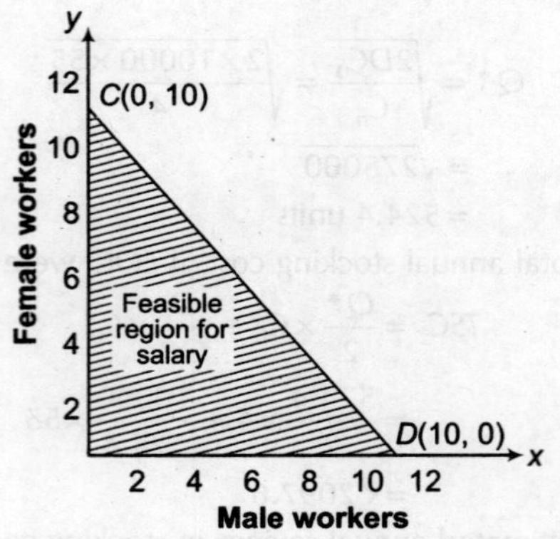


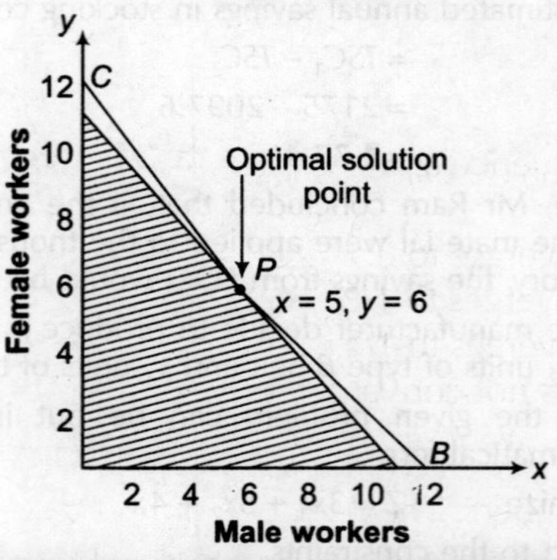


| Extreme Point | Coordinates $(x, y)$ | Objective Function Value $Z = 10000x + 8500y$ |
|---|---|---|
| $O$ | (0, 0) | $10000 + 8500(0) = 0$ |
| $A$ | (0, 11) | $10000(0) + 8500(11) = 93500$ |
| $P$ | (5, 6) | $10000(5) + 8500(6) = 101000$ |
| $D$ | (10, 0) | $10000(10) + 8500(0) = 100000$ |

The maximum value of the objective function $Z = 101000$ occurs at the extreme point $P(5, 6)$. Hence, optimal solution to the given LP problem is $x = 5$ , $y = 6$, Max $Z = 101000$.

# Solutions of Sample Questions Provided on CSIR Website

## Part 'B'

**21.** The sequence $a_n = \frac{1}{n^2} + \frac{1}{(n+1)^2} + \ldots + \frac{1}{(2n)^2}$

(a) converges to 0
(b) converges to 1/2
(c) converges to 1/4
(d) does not converge

**22.** Let $x_n = n^{1/n}$ and $y_n = (n!)^{1/n}$, $n \geq 1$ be two sequences of real numbers. Then,

(a) $(x_n)$ converges, but $(y_n)$ does not converge
(b) $(y_n)$ converges, but $(x_n)$ does not converge
(c) both $(x_n)$ and $(y_n)$ converge
(d) neither $(x_n)$ nor $(y_n)$ converges

**23.** The set $\{x \in \mathbb{R} : x \sin x \leq 1, x \cos x \leq 1\} \subset \mathbb{R}$ is

(a) a bounded closed set
(b) a bounded open set
(c) an unbounded closed set
(d) an unbounded open set

**24.** Let $f : [0, 1] \to \mathbb{R}$ be continuous such that $f(t) \geq 0$, for all $t$ in $[0, 1]$. Define $g(x) = \int_0^x f(t)\, dt$, then

(a) $g$ is monotone and bounded
(b) $g$ is monotone but no bounded
(c) $g$ is bounded but not monotone
(d) $g$ is neither monotone nor bounded

**25.** Let $f$ be a continuous function on [0, 1] with $f(0) = 1$. Let $G(a) = \frac{1}{a}\int_0^a f(x)\, dx$

(a) $\lim_{a \to 0} G(a) = \frac{1}{2}$
(b) $\lim_{a \to 0} G(a) = 1$
(c) $\lim_{a \to 0} G(a) = 0$
(d) the limit $\lim_{a \to 0} G(a)$ does not exist

**26.** Let $\alpha_n = \sin\left(\frac{1}{n^2}\right)$, $n = 1, 2, \ldots$ Then,

(a) $\sum_{n=1}^{\infty} \alpha_n$ converges
(b) $\limsup_{n \to \infty} \alpha_n \neq \liminf_{n \to \infty} \alpha_n$
(c) $\lim_{n \to \infty} \alpha_n = 1$
(d) $\sum_{n=1}^{\infty} \alpha_n$ diverges

**27.** If for $x \in \mathbb{R}$, $\varphi(x)$ denotes the integer closest to $x$ (if there are two such integers take the larger one), then $\int_{10}^{12} \varphi(x)\, dx$ equals

(a) 22
(b) 11
(c) 20
(d) 12

**28.** Let $P$ be a polynomial of degree $k > 0$ with a non-zero constant term. Let $f_n(x) = P\left(\frac{x}{n}\right)$, $\forall x \in (0, \infty)$.

(a) $\lim_{n \to \infty} f_n(x) = \infty$, $\forall x \in (0, \infty)$
(b) $\exists x \in (0, \infty)$, such that $\lim_{n \to \infty} f_n(x) > P(0)$
(c) $\lim_{n \to \infty} f_n(x) = 0$, $\forall x \in (0, \infty)$
(d) $\lim_{n \to \infty} f_n(x) = P(0)$, $\forall x \in (0, \infty)$

**29.** Let $C$ [0, 1] denote the space of all continuous functions with supremum norm.

Then, $K = \left\{f \in C\,[0, 1] : \lim_{n \to \infty} f\left(\frac{1}{n}\right) = 0\right\}$

(a) vector space but not closed in $C$ [0, 1]
(b) closed but does not form a vector space
(c) a closed vector space but not an algebra
(d) a closed algebra

**30.** Let $u, v, w$ be three points in $\mathbb{R}^3$ not lying in any plane containing the origin.

Then,
(a) $\alpha_1 u + \alpha_2 v + \alpha_2 w = 0 \Rightarrow \alpha_1 = \alpha_2 = \alpha_3 = 0$
(b) $u, v, w$ are mutually orthogonal
(c) one of $u, v, w$ has to be zero
(d) $u, v, w$ cannot be pairwise orthogonal

**31.** Let $x, y$ be linearly independent vectors in $\mathbb{R}^2$, suppose $T : \mathbb{R}^2 \to \mathbb{R}^2$ is a linear transformation, such that $Ty = \alpha x$ and $Tx = 0$. Then, with respect to some basis in $\mathbb{R}^2$, $T$ is of the form
(a) $\begin{pmatrix} a & 0 \\ 0 & a \end{pmatrix}, a > 0$ (b) $\begin{pmatrix} a & 0 \\ 0 & b \end{pmatrix}, a, b > 0; a \neq b$
(c) $\begin{pmatrix} 0 & 1 \\ 0 & 0 \end{pmatrix}$ (d) $\begin{pmatrix} 0 & 0 \\ 0 & 0 \end{pmatrix}$

**32.** Suppose $A$ is an $n \times n$ real symmetric matrix with eigen values $\lambda_1, \lambda_2, \ldots, \lambda_n$, then
(a) $\prod_{i=1}^{n} \lambda_i < \det(A)$
(b) $\prod_{i=1}^{n} \lambda_i > \det(A)$
(c) $\prod_{i=1}^{n} \lambda_i = \det(A)$
(d) if $\det(A) = 1$, then $\lambda_j = 1$ for $j = 1, \ldots, n$.

**33.** Let $f$ be analytic on $D = \{z \in \mathbb{C} : |z| < 1\}$ and $f(0) = 0$. Define

$$g(z) = \begin{cases} \dfrac{f(z)}{z}; & z \neq 0 \\ f'(0); & z = 0 \end{cases}$$

Then,
(a) $g$ is discontinuous at $z = 0$ for all $f$
(b) $g$ is continuous, but not analytic at $z = 0$ for all $f$
(c) $g$ is analytic at $z = 0$ for all $f$
(d) $g$ is analytic at $z = 0$ only if $f'(0) = 0$

**34.** Let $\Omega \subseteq \mathbb{C}$ be a domain and let $f(z)$ be an analytic function on $\Omega$ such that $|f(z)| = |\sin z|$ for all $z \in \Omega$, then
(a) $f(z) = \sin z$ for all $z \in \Omega$
(b) $f(z) = \sin(\bar{z})$ for all $z \in \Omega$
(c) there is a constant $c \in \mathbb{C}$ with $|c| = 1$ such that $f(z) = c \sin z$ for all $z \in \Omega$
(d) such a function $f(z)$ does not exist

**35.** The radius of convergence of the power series $\sum_{n=0}^{\infty} (4n^2 - n^3 + 3) z^n$ is
(a) 0 (b) 1 (c) 5 (d) $\infty$

**36.** Let $\mathbb{F}$ be a finite field such that for every $a \in \mathbb{F}$ the equation $x^2 = a$ has a solution in $\mathbb{F}$. Then,
(a) the characteristic of $\mathbb{F}$ must be 2
(b) $\mathbb{F}$ must have a square number of elements
(c) the order of $\mathbb{F}$ is a power of 3
(d) $\mathbb{F}$ must be a field with prime number of elements

**37.** Let $\mathbb{F}$ be a field with $5^{12}$ elements. What is the total number of proper subfields of $\mathbb{F}$?
(a) 3 (b) 6 (c) 8 (d) 5

**38.** Let $K$ be an extension of the field $Q$ of rational numbers
(a) If $K$ is a finite extension, then it is an algebraic extension
(b) If $K$ is an algebraic extension, then it must be a finite extension
(c) If $K$ is an algebraic extension, then it must be an infinite extension
(d) If $K$ is a finite extension, then it need not be an algebraic extension

**39.** Consider the group $S_9$ of all the permutations on a set with 9 elements. What is the largest order of a permutation in $S_9$?
(a) 21 (b) 20
(c) 30 (d) 14

**40.** Suppose $V$ is a real vector space of dimension 3. Then, the number of pairs of linearly independent vectors in $V$ is
(a) one (b) infinity
(c) $e^3$ (d) 3

**41.** Consider the differential equation $\dfrac{dy}{dx} = y^2$, $(x, y) \in \mathbb{R} \times \mathbb{R}$

Then,
(a) all solutions of the differential equation are defined on $(-\infty, \infty)$
(b) no solution of the differential equation is defined on $(-\infty, \infty)$
(c) the solution of the differential equation satisfying the initial condition $y(x_0) = y_0$, $y_0 > 0$ is defined on $\left(-\infty, x_0 + \dfrac{1}{y_0}\right)$
(d) the solution of the differential equation satisfying the initial condition $y(x_0) = y_0$, $y_0 > 0$ is defined on $\left(x_0 - \dfrac{1}{y_0}, \infty\right)$

**42.** The second order partial differential equation

$$(1 - \sqrt{xy})\frac{\partial^2 u}{\partial x^2} + 2\frac{\partial^2 u}{\partial x \partial y}(1 + \sqrt{xy})\frac{\partial^2 u}{\partial y^2} = 0 \text{ is}$$

(a) hyperbolic in the second and the fourth quadrants
(b) elliptic in the first and the third quadrants
(c) hyperbolic in the second and elliptic in the fourth quadrant
(d) hyperbolic in the first and the third quadrants

**43.** A general solution of the equation $\frac{\partial u(x, y)}{\partial x} + u(x, y) = e^{-x}$ is

(a) $u(x, y) = e^{-x} f(y)$
(b) $u(x, y) = e^{-x} f(y) + xe^{x}$
(c) $u(x, y) = e^{+x} f(y) + xe^{+x}$
(d) $u(x, y) = e^{-x} f(y) + xe^{-x}$

**44.** Consider the application of Trapezoidal and Simpson's rules to the following integral

$$\int_0^4 (2x^3 - 3x^2 + 5x + 1)\, dx$$

(a) both Trapezoidal and Simpson's rules will give results with same accuracy.
(b) the Simpson's rule will give more accuracy than the Trapezoidal rule but less accurate than the exact result.
(c) the Simpson's rule will give the exact result.
(d) both Trapezoidal rule and Simpson's rule will give the exact results.

**45.** The integral equation

$$g(x)\, y(x) = f(x) + \lambda \int_\alpha^\beta k(x, t)\, y(t)\, dt$$

with $f(x)$, $g(x)$ and $k(x, t)$ as known functions, $\alpha$ and $\beta$ as known constants and $\lambda$ as a known parameter is a

(a) linear integral equation of Volterra type
(b) linear integral equation of Fredholm type
(c) non-linear integral equation of Volterra type
(d) non-linear integral equation of Fredholm type

**46.** Let $y(x) = f(x) + \lambda \int_a^b k(x, t)\, y(t)\, dt$, where $f(x)$ and $k(x, t)$ are known functions $a$ and $b$ are known constants and $\lambda$ is a known parameter. If $\lambda_i$ be the eigen values of the corresponding homogeneous equation, then the above integral equation has in general,

(a) many solutions for $\lambda \neq \lambda_i$
(b) no solution for $\lambda \neq \lambda_i$
(c) a unique solution for $\lambda = \lambda_i$
(d) either many solutions or no solution at all for $\lambda = \lambda_i$, depending on the form of $f(x)$

**47.** The equation of motion of a particle in the $xz$– plane is given by $\frac{d\mathbf{v}}{dt} = -\mathbf{v} - \hat{\mathbf{k}}$ with $\mathbf{v} = \alpha\hat{\mathbf{k}}$, where $\alpha = \alpha(t)$ and $\hat{\mathbf{k}}$ is the unit vector along the $z$-direction. If initially (*i.e.*, $t = 0$) $\alpha = 1$, then the magnitude of velocity at $t = 1$ is

(a) $2/e$ (b) $2 + e/3$
(c) $\frac{2-e}{e}$ (d) 1

**48.** Consider the functional

$$F(u, v) = \int_0^{\pi/2} \left[ \left(\frac{du}{dx}\right)^2 + \left(\frac{dv}{dx}\right)^2 + 2u(x)v(x) \right] dx$$

with $u(0) = 1, v(0) = -1$ and $u\left(\frac{\pi}{2}\right) = 0, v\left(\frac{\pi}{2}\right) = 0$

Then, the extremals satisfy

(a) $u(\pi) = 1, v(\pi) = -1$
(b) $u(\pi) + v(\pi) = 0, u(\pi) - v(\pi) = 2$
(c) $u(\pi) = -1, v(\pi) = 1$
(d) $u(\pi) + v(\pi) = -2, u(\pi) - v(\pi) = 0$

**49.** The pairs of observations on two random variables $x$ and $y$ are

| $x$ | 2 | 5 | 7 | 11 | 13 | 19 |
|---|---|---|---|---|---|---|
| $y$ | 0 | 15 | 25 | 45 | 55 | 85 |

Then, the correlation coefficient between $x$ and $y$ is

(a) 0 (b) 1/5
(c) 1/2 (d) 1

**50.** Let $X_1, X_2, X_3$ be independent random variables with $P(X_i = +1) = P(X_i = -1) = 1/2$.

Let $Y_1 = X_2X_3$, $Y_2 = X_1X_3$ and $Y_3 = X_1X_2$.

Then, which of the following is not true?

(a) $Y_i$ and $X_i$ have same distribution for $i = 1, 2, 3$
(b) $(Y_1, Y_2, Y_3)$ are mutually independent
(c) $X_1$ and $(Y_2, Y_3)$ are independent
(d) $(X_1, X_2)$ and $(Y_1, Y_2)$ have the same distribution

**51.** Let $X$ be an exponential random variable with parameter $\lambda$. Let $Y = [X]$, where $[x]$ denotes the largest integer smaller than $x$. Then,

(a) $Y$ has a geometric distribution with parameter $\lambda$.
(b) $Y$ has a geometric distribution with parameter $1 - e^{-l}$.
(c) $Y$ has a poisson distribution with parameter $\lambda$
(d) $Y$ has mean $[1/\lambda]$

**52.** Consider a finite state space Markov chain with transition probability matrix $P = ((p_{ij}))$. Suppose, $P_{ii} = 0$ for all states $i$. Then, the Markov chain is

(a) always irreducible with period 1.
(b) may be reducible and may have period > 1.
(c) may be reducible but period is always 1.
(d) always irreducible but may have period > 1.

**53.** Let $X_1, X_2, \ldots, X_n$ be iid. Normal random variables with mean 1 and variance 1 and let $Z_n = (X_1 + X_2 + \ldots + X_n)/n$. Then,

(a) $Z_n$ converges in probability to 1
(b) $Z_n$ converges in probability to 2
(c) $Z_n$ converges in distribution to standard normal distribution
(d) $Z_n$ converges in probability to Chi-square distribution

**54.** Let $X_1, X_2, \ldots, X_n$ be a random sample of size $n (\geq 4)$ from uniform $(0, \theta)$ distribution. Which of the following is not an ancillary statistic?

(a) $\frac{X_{(n)}}{X_{(1)}}$ (b) $\frac{X_n}{X_1}$

(c) $\frac{X_4 - X_1}{X_3 - X_2}$ (d) $X_{(n)} - X_{(1)}$

**55.** Suppose $X_1, X_2, \ldots, X_n$ are i.i.d. Uniform $(0, q)$, $\theta \in \{1, 2, \ldots\}$. Then, the MLE of $\theta$ is

(a) $X_{(n)}$

(b) $\bar{X}$

(c) $[X_{(n)}]$, where $[a]$ is the integer part of $a$.

(d) $[X_{(n)} + 1]$, where $[a]$ is the integer part of $a$.

**56.** Let $X_1, X_2, \ldots, X_n$ be independent and identically distributed random variables with common continuous distribution function $F(x)$. Let $R_i = \text{Rank } (X_i)$, $i = 1, 2, \ldots, n$. Then, $P(|R_n - R_1|^3 \; n - 1)$ is

(a) 0 (b) $\frac{1}{n(n-1)}$

(c) $\frac{2}{n(n-1)}$ (d) $\frac{1}{n}$

**57.** A simple random sample of size $n$ is drawn without replacement from a population of size $N (> n)$. If $\pi_i$ $(i = 1, 2, \ldots, N)$ and $p_{ij}$ $(i \neq j, i, j = 1, 2, \ldots, N)$ denote respectively, the first and second order inclusion probabilities, then which of the following statements is not true?

(a) $\sum_{i=1}^{N} p_i = n$

(b) $\sum_{i=1}^{N} p_{ij} = (n-1)\, p_i$

(c) $p_i p_j$ £ $p_{ij}$ for each pair $(i, j)$

(d) $p_{ij} < p_i$ for each pair $(i, j)$

**58.** Consider a balanced incomplete block design with usual parameters $v, b, r, k (\geq 2), \lambda$. Let $t_i$ be the effect of the $i$th treatment $(i = 1, 2, \ldots, v)$ and $\sigma^2$ denote the variance of an observation. Then, the variance of the best linear unbiased estimator of $\sum_{i=1}^{v} p_i t_i$, where $\sum_{i=1}^{v} p_i = 0$ and $\sum_{i=1}^{v} p_i^2 = 1$, under the intra-block model is

(a) $\left(\frac{\lambda v}{k}\right)\sigma^2$ (b) $\frac{2\sigma^2}{r}$

(c) $\left(\frac{k}{\lambda v}\right)\sigma^2$ (d) $\left(\frac{2k}{\lambda v}\right)\sigma^2$

**59.** An aircraft has four engines two on the left side and two on the right side. The aircraft functions only if atleast one engine on each side functions. If the failures of engines are independent and the probability of any engine failing in equal to $p$, then the reliability of the aircraft is equal to

(a) $p^2\,(1 - p^2)$ (b) ${}^4C_2 p^2\,(1 - p)^2$

(c) $(1 - p^2)^2$ (d) $1 - (1 - p^2)^2$

**60.** A company maintains *EOQ* model for one of its critical components. The setup cost is $k$, unit production cost is $c$, demand is $a$ units per unit time and $h$ is the cost of holding one unit per unit time. In view of the criticality of the component the company maintains a safety stock of $s$ units at all times. The economic order quantity for this problem is given by

(a) $\sqrt{\frac{2ak}{h}} + s$ (b) $s + \sqrt{\frac{2ak}{h}}$

(c) $\sqrt{\frac{2ak}{h}}$ (d) $\sqrt{\frac{2ak + s}{h}}$

# Part 'C'

**61.** Suppose $\{a_n\}$, $\{b_n\}$ are convergent sequences of real numbers such that $a_n > 0$ and $b_n > 0$ for all $n$. Suppose $\lim_{n\to\infty} a_n = a$ and $\lim_{n\to\infty} b_n = b$. Let $c_n = a_n / b_n$. Then,

(a) $\{c_n\}$ converges, if $b > 0$

(b) $\{c_n\}$ converges only, if $a = 0$

(c) $\{c_n\}$ converges only, if $b > 0$

(d) $\limsup_{n\to\infty} c_n = \infty$, if $b = 0$

**62.** Consider the power series $\sum_{n=0}^{\infty} a_n x^n$, where $a_0 = 0$ and $a_n = \sin(n!)/n!$ for $n \geq 1$. Let $R$ be the radius of convergence of the power series. Then,

(a) $R \geq 1$ (b) $R \geq 2\pi$

(c) $R \leq 4\pi$ (d) $R \geq \pi$

**63.** Suppose $f$ is an increasing real-valued function on $[0, \infty)$ with $f(x) > 0$, $\forall\, x$ and let

$$g(x) = \frac{1}{x}\int_0^x f(u)\, du,\ 0 < x < \infty.$$

Then, which of the following are true?
(a) $g(x) \le f(x)$ for all $x \in (0, \infty)$
(b) $x\,g(x) \le f(x)$ for all $x \in (0, \infty)$
(c) $x\,g(x) \ge f(0)$ for all $x \in (0, \infty)$
(d) $yg(y) - xg(x) \le (y - x)\,f(y)$ for all $x < y$

**64.** Let $f : [0, 1] \to \mathbb{R}$ be defined by

$$f(x) = \begin{cases} x \cos(\pi/(2x)), & \text{if } x \ne 0 \\ 0, & \text{if } x = 0 \end{cases}$$

Then,
(a) $f$ is continuous on $[0, 1]$
(b) $f$ is of bounded variation on $[0, 1]$
(c) $f$ is differentiable on the open interval $(0, 1)$ and its derivative $f'$ is bounded on $(0, 1)$
(d) $f$ is Riemann integrable on $[0, 1]$

**65.** For any positive integer $n$, let $f_n : [0, 1] \to \mathbb{R}$ be defined by $f_n(x) = \dfrac{x}{nx + 1}$ for $x \in [0, 1]$.

Then,
(a) the sequence $\{f_n\}$ converges uniformly on $[0, 1]$
(b) the sequence $\{f_n'\}$ of derivatives of $\{f_n\}$ converges uniformly on $[0, 1]$
(c) the sequence $\{\int_0^1 f_n(x)\,dx\}$ is convergent
(d) the sequence $\{\int_0^1 f_n'(x)\,dx\}$ is convergent

**66.** Let $f : [0, \infty) \to \mathbb{R}$ and $g : [0, \infty) \to \mathbb{R}$ be continuous functions satisfying

$$\int_0^{f(x)} t^2 dt = x^3 (1 + x)^2$$

and $$\int_0^{x^2(1+x)} g(t)\,dt = x, \text{ for all } x \in [0, \infty)$$

Then, $f(2) + g(2)$ is equal to
(a) 0 (b) 5
(c) 6 (d) 11

**67.** Consider $f : \mathbb{R}^2 \to \mathbb{R}$ defined by $f(0, 0) = 0$ and

$$f(x, y) = \frac{x^2 y}{x^4 + y^2} \text{ for } (x, y) \ne (0, 0)$$

Then, which of the following statements is correct?
(a) Both the partial derivatives of $f$ at $(0, 0)$ exist
(b) The directional derivative $D_u f(0, 0)$ of $f$ at $(0, 0)$ exists for every unit vector $\underline{u}$
(c) $f$ is continuous at $(0, 0)$
(d) $f$ is differentiable at $(0, 0)$

**68.** Let $f : \mathbb{R}^2 \to \mathbb{R}$ and $g : \mathbb{R}^2 \to \mathbb{R}$ be defined by

$$f(x, y) = |x| + |y|$$
and $$g(x, y) = |xy|$$

Then,
(a) $f$ is differentiable at $(0, 0)$ but $g$ is not differentiable at $(0, 0)$
(b) $g$ is differentiable at $(0, 0)$ but $f$ is not differentiable at $(0, 0)$
(c) both $f$ and $g$ are differential at $(0, 0)$
(d) both $f$ and $g$ are continuous at $(0, 0)$

**69.** Decide for which of the functions $F : \mathbb{R}^3 \to \mathbb{R}^3$ given below, there exists a function $f : \mathbb{R}^3 \to \mathbb{R}$ such that $(\nabla f)(x) = F(x)$.
(a) $(4xyz - z^2 - 3y^2, 2x^2 z - 6xy + 1, 2x^2 y - 2xz - 2)$
(b) $(x, xy, xyz)$
(c) $(1, 1, 1)$
(d) $(xyz, yz, z)$

**70.** Let $f : \mathbb{R}^n \to \mathbb{R}$ be the function defined by the rule $f(x) = x \cdot b$, where $b \in \mathbb{R}^n$ and $x \cdot b$ denotes the usual inner product. Then
(a) $[f'(x)]\,(b) = b \cdot b$
(b) $[f'(x)]\,(x) = \dfrac{x \cdot x}{2}$, $x \in \mathbb{R}^n$
(c) $[f'(0)]\,(e_1) = b \cdot e_1$, where $e_1 = (1, 0, \ldots, 0) \in \mathbb{R}^n$.
(d) $[f'(e_1)]\,(e_j) = 0$, $j \ne 1$, where $e_j = (0, \ldots 1, \ldots, 0)$ with 1 in the $j$th slot

**71.** Consider the subsets $A$ and $B$ of $\mathbb{R}^2$ defined by

$$A = \left\{\left(x, x \sin\frac{1}{x}\right) : x \in (0, 1]\right\}$$
and $$B = A \cup \{(0, 0)\}$$

Then,
(a) $A$ is compact (b) $A$ is connected
(c) $B$ is compact (d) $B$ is connected

**72.** Let $f = \mathbb{R} \to \mathbb{R}$ be a continuous function. Which of the following is always true?
(a) $f^{-1}(U)$ is open for all open sets $U \subseteq \mathbb{R}$
(b) $f^{-1}(C)$ is closed for all closed sets $C \subseteq \mathbb{R}$
(c) $f^{-1}(K)$ is compact for all compact sets $K \subseteq \mathbb{R}$
(d) $f^{-1}(G)$ is compact for all connected sets $G \subseteq \mathbb{R}$

**73.** Let $A$ be an $n \times n$ matrix, $n \ge 2$, with characteristic polynomial $x^{n-2}(x^2 - 1)$.

Then,
(a) $A^n = A^{n-2}$
(b) rank of $A$ is 2
(c) rank of $A$ is atleast 2
(d) there exist non-zero vectors $x$ and $y$ such that $A(x + y) = x - y$

**74.** Let $A, B$ and $C$ be real $n \times n$ matrices such that $AB + B^2 = C$. Suppose $C$ is non-singular. Which of the following is always true?

(a) $A$ is non-singular
(b) $B$ is non-singular
(c) $A$ and $B$ are both non-singular
(d) $A + B$ is non-singular

**75.** Let $V$ be a real vector space and let $\{x_1, x_2, x_3\}$ be a basis for $V$. Then,
(a) $\{x_1 + x_2, x_2, x_3\}$ is a basis for $V$
(b) the dimension of $V$ is 3
(c) $x_1, x_2, x_3$ are pairwise orthogonal
(d) $\{x_1 - x_2, x_2 - x_3, x_1 - x_3\}$ is a basis for $V$

**76.** Consider the system of $m$ linear equations in $n$ unknowns given by $Ax = b$, where $A = (a_{ij})$ is a real $m \times n$ matrix, $x$ and $b$ are $n \times 1$ column vectors. Then,
(a) there is atleast one solution
(b) there is atleast one solution, if $b$ is the zero vector
(c) if $m = n$ and if the rank of $A$ is $n$, then there is a unique solution
(d) if $m < n$ and if the rank of the augmented matrix $[A : b]$ equals the rank of $A$, then there are infinitely many solutions

**77.** Let $V$ be the set of all real $n \times n$ matrices $A = (a_{ij})$ with the property that $a_{ij} = -a_{ji}$ for all $i, j = 1, 2, \ldots, n$. Then,
(a) $V$ is a vector space of dimension $n^2 - n$
(b) for every $A$ in $V$, $a_{ii} = 0$ for all $i = 1, 2, \ldots, n$
(c) $V$ consists of only diagonal matrices
(d) $V$ is a vector space of dimension $\dfrac{n^2 - n}{2}$

**78.** Let $W$ be the set of all $3 \times 3$ real matrices $A = (a_{ij})$ with the property that $a_{ij} = 0$, if $i > j$ and $a_{ii} = 1$ for all $i$. Let $B = (b_{ij})$ be a $3 \times 3$ real matrix that satisfies $AB = BA$ for all $A$ in $W$. Then,
(a) every $A$ in $W$ has an inverse with is in $W$
(b) $b_{12} = 0$
(c) $b_{13} = 0$
(d) $b_{23} = 0$

**79.** Let $f(z)$ be an entire function with $\text{Re}(f(z)) \geq 0$ for all $z \in \mathbb{C}$. Then,
(a) $\text{Im}(f(z)) \geq 0$ for all $Z \notin \mathbb{C}$
(b) $\text{Im}(f(z)) = a$ constant
(c) $f$ is a constant function
(d) $\text{Re}(f(z)) = |z|$ for all $z \in \mathbb{C}$

**80.** Let $f$ be an analytic function defined on $D = \{z \,||\, z| < 1\}$ such that $|f(z)| \leq 1$ for all $z \in D$. Then,
(a) there exists $z_0 \in D$ such that $f(z_0) = 1$
(b) the image of $f$ is an open set
(c) $f(0) = 0$
(d) $f$ is necessarily a constant function

**81.** Let $f(z) = \dfrac{\sin z}{z^2} - \dfrac{\cos z}{z}$. Then,
(a) $f$ has a pole of order 2 at $z = 0$
(b) $f$ has a simple pole at $z = 0$
(c) $\oint f(z)\, dz = 0$, where the integral is taken anti-clockwise $|z| = 1$
(d) the residue of $f$ at $z = 0$ is $-2\pi i$

**82.** Let $f$ be an analytic function defined on $D = \{z \in \mathbb{C} : |z| < 1\}$. Then, $g : D \to \mathbb{C}$ is analytic, if
(a) $g(z) = f(\bar{z})$ for all $z \in D$
(b) $g(z) = \overline{f(z)}$ for all $z \in D$
(c) $g(z) = \overline{f(\bar{z})}$ for all $z \in D$
(d) $g(z) = \bar{i} f(z)$ for all $z \in D$

**83.** Which of the following statements involving Euler's function $\phi$ is/are true?
(a) $\phi(n)$ is even as many times as it is odd
(b) $\phi(n)$ is odd for only two values of $n$
(c) $\phi(n)$ is even when $n > 2$
(d) $\phi(n)$ is odd when $n = 2$ or $n$ is odd

**84.** Let $p$ be a prime number and $d \,|\, (p - 1)$. Then, which of the following statements about the congruence $x^d \equiv 1 \pmod{p}$ is/are true?
(a) It does not have any solution
(b) It has atmost $d$ incongruent solutions
(c) It has exactly $d$ incongruent solutions
(d) It has atleast $d$ incongruent solutions

**85.** Let $K$ be a field, $L$ a finite extension of $K$ and $M$ a finite extension of $L$. Then,
(a) $[M : K] = [M : L] + [L : K]$
(b) $[M : K] = [M : L]\,[L : K]$
(c) $[M : L]$ divides $[M : K]$
(d) $[L : K]$ divides $[M : K]$

**86.** Let $R$ be a commutative ring and $R[x]$ be the polynomial ring in one variable over $R$.
(a) If $R$ is a UFD, then $R[x]$ is a UFD
(b) If $R$ is a PID, then $R[x]$ is a PID
(c) If $R$ is an Euclidean domain, then $R[x]$ is an Euclidean domain
(d) If $R$ is a field, the $R[x]$ is an Euclidean domain

**87.** Let $G$ be a group of order 56. Then,
(a) all 7-sylow subgroups of $G$ are normal
(b) all 2-sylow subgroups of $G$ are normal
(c) either a 7-sylow subgroup or a 2-sylow subgroup of $G$ is normal
(d) there is a proper normal subgroup of $G$

**88.** Which of the following statements is/are true?
(a) 50! ends with an even number of zeros
(b) 50! ends with a prime number of zeros
(c) 50! ends with 10 zeros
(d) 50! ends with 12 zeros

**89.** Let $X = \{(x, y) \in \mathbb{R}^2 | x^2 + y^2 = 1\}$
$Y = \{(x, y) \in \mathbb{R}^2 | |x| + |y| = 1\}$
and $Z = \{(x, y) \in \mathbb{R}^2 | x^2 - y^2 = 1\}$
Then,
(a) $X$ is not homeomorphic to $Y$
(b) $Y$ is not homeomorphic to $Z$
(c) $X$ is not homeomorphic to $Z$
(d) no two of $X$, $Y$ or $Z$ are homeomorphic

**90.** Let $\tau_1$, $\tau_2$ and $\tau_3$ be topologies on a set $X$ such that $\tau_1 \subset \tau_2 \subset \tau_3$ and $(X, \tau_2)$ is a compact Hausdorff space. Then,
(a) $\tau_1 = \tau_2$, if $(X, \tau_1)$ is a Hausdorff space
(b) $\tau_1 = \tau_2$, if $(X, \tau_1)$ is a compact space
(c) $\tau_2 = \tau_3$, if $(X, \tau_3)$ is a Hausdorff space
(d) $\tau_2 = \tau_3$, if $(X, \tau_3)$ is a compact space

**91.** The initial value problem $\dot{x}(t) = 3x^{2/3}$, $x(0) = 0$; in an interval around $t = 0$, has
(a) no solution
(b) a unique solution
(c) finitely many linearly independent solutions
(d) infinitely many linearly independent solutions

**92.** For the system of ordinary differential equations

$$\frac{d}{dt}\begin{pmatrix} x_1(t) \\ x_2(t) \end{pmatrix} = \begin{bmatrix} 0 & -1 \\ 1 & 0 \end{bmatrix}\begin{bmatrix} x_1(t) \\ x_2(t) \end{bmatrix}$$

(a) every solution is bounded
(b) every solution is periodic
(c) there exists a bounded solution
(d) there exists a non-periodic solution

**93.** The kernel $p(x, y) = \dfrac{y}{y^2 + x^2}$ is a solution of
(a) the heat equation (b) the wave equation
(c) the Laplace equation (d) the Lagrange equation

**94.** The solution of the Laplace equation on the upper half plane, which takes the value $\phi(x) = e^x$ on the real line is
(a) the real part of an analytic function
(b) the imaginary part of an analytic function
(c) the absolute value of an analytic function
(d) an infinitely differentiable function

**95.** The evaluation of the quantity $\sqrt{x+1} - 1$ near $x = 0$ is achieved with minimum loss of significant digits, if we use the expression
(a) $\sqrt{x+1} - 1$ (b) $\dfrac{x}{\sqrt{x+1}+1}$
(c) $\left(1 - \dfrac{1}{\sqrt{x+1}}\right)\sqrt{x+1}$ (d) $\dfrac{x + 2\sqrt{x+1}}{\sqrt{x+1} - 1}$

**96.** If $x(t)$ is an extremal of the functional $\int_a^b \left(\frac{1}{2} m(\dot{x})^2 - cx^2\right) dt$, where $a, b, c$ are arbitrary constants and $\dot{x} = \dfrac{dx}{dt}$, then the function $x(t)$ satisfies
(a) $m\ddot{x} + 2cx = 0$
(b) $m\ddot{x} - 2cx = 0$
(c) $m(x)^2 + 2cx^2 = k_1$ with $k_1$ as an arbitrary constant
(d) $x(t) = k_1 \sin\left(\sqrt{\dfrac{2c}{m}}\, t + k_2\right)$ with $k_1$ and $k_2$ as arbitrary constants

**97.** If $u(x)$ and $v(x)$ satisfying $u(0) = 1$, $v(0) = -1$, $u\left(\frac{\pi}{2}\right) = 0$ and $v\left(\frac{\pi}{2}\right) = 0$ are the extremals of the functional

$$\int_0^{\pi/2} \left\{\left(\frac{du}{dx}\right)^2 + \left(\frac{dv}{dx}\right)^2 + 2uv\right\} dx, \text{ then}$$

(a) $u\left(\frac{\pi}{4}\right) + v\left(\frac{\pi}{4}\right) = 0$ (b) $u\left(\frac{\pi}{3}\right) - v\left(\frac{\pi}{3}\right) = 0$
(c) $u\left(\frac{\pi}{4}\right) - v\left(\frac{\pi}{4}\right) = 1$ (d) $u\left(\frac{\pi}{3}\right) + v\left(\frac{\pi}{3}\right) = 0$

**98.** Consider the integral equation $y(x) = x^2 + \lambda \int_0^1 xty(t)\, dt$, where $\lambda$ is a real parameter. Then, the Neumann series for the integral equation converges for all values of $\lambda$
(a) except for $\lambda = 3$
(b) lying in the interval $-3 < \lambda < 0$
(c) lying in the interval $-3 < \lambda < 3$
(d) lying in the interval $0 < \lambda < 3$

**99.** The solution of the integral equation $\phi(x) = \dfrac{5x}{6} + \dfrac{1}{2}\int_0^1 xt\,\phi(t)\, dt$ satisfies
(a) $\phi(0) + \phi(1) = 1$ (b) $\phi\left(\frac{1}{2}\right) + \phi\left(\frac{1}{3}\right) = 1$
(c) $\phi\left(\frac{1}{4}\right) + \phi\left(\frac{1}{2}\right) = 1$ (d) $\phi\left(\frac{3}{4}\right) + \phi\left(\frac{1}{4}\right) = 1$

**100.** A particle of unit mass is constrained to move on the plane curve $xy = 1$ under gravity $g$. Then,
(a) the kinetic energy of the system is $\frac{1}{2}(\dot{x}^2 + \dot{y}^2)$
(b) the potential energy of the system is $\dfrac{g}{x}$

(c) the Lagrangian of the particle is $\frac{1}{2}\dot{x}^2(1+x^{-4})-\left(\frac{g}{x}\right)$

(d) the Lagrangian of the particle is $\frac{1}{2}\dot{x}^2(1+x^{-4})+\left(\frac{g}{x}\right)$

**101.** Suppose a mechanical system has the single coordinate $q$ and Lagrangian $L=\frac{1}{4}\dot{q}^2-\frac{q^2}{9}$. Then,

(a) the Hamiltonian is $p^2+\left(\frac{q^2}{9}\right)$

(b) Hamilton's equations are $\dot{q}=2p, \dot{p}=-\left(\frac{2}{9}\right)q$

(c) $q$ satisfies $\ddot{q}+\left(\frac{4}{9}\right)q=0$

(d) the path in the Hamiltonian phase-space, *i.e.*, $q-p$ plane is an ellipse

**102.** Let $X_1,\ldots,X_n$ be i.i.d. observations from a distribution with variance $\sigma^2$ ($<\infty$). Which of the following is/are unbiased estimator(s) of $\sigma^2$?

(a) $\frac{1}{n-1}\sum_{i=1}^{n}(X_i-\bar{X})^2$

(b) $\frac{1}{n}\sum_{i=1}^{n}(X_i-\bar{X})^2$

(c) $\binom{n}{2}^{-1}\frac{1}{2}\sum_{i\le 1<j\le n}(X_i-X_j)^2$

(d) $\frac{1}{n}\sum_{i=1}^{n}X_i^2-n\bar{X}^2$

**103.** Let $X_1, X_2,\ldots$ be i.i.d. $N(0,1)$ and let $S_n=\sum_{i=1}^{n}X_i$ be the partial sums. Which of the following is/are true?

(a) $\frac{S_n}{n}\to 0$ almost surely (b) $E\left(\frac{S_n}{n}\right)\to 0$

(c) $\text{Var}\left(\frac{S_n}{n}\right)\to 0$ (d) $\text{Var}\left(\frac{S_n^2}{n}\right)\to 0$

**104.** Let $(X, Y)$ be a pair of independent random variables with $X$ having exponential distribution with mean 1 and $Y$ having uniform distribution on $\{1, 2,\ldots, m\}$. Define $Z=X+Y$. Then,

(a) $E(Z|X)=X+\frac{m+1}{2}$

(b) $E(Z|Y)=1+\frac{m+1}{2}$

(c) $\text{Var}(Z|X)=\frac{m^2-1}{2}$

(d) $\text{Var}(Z|Y)=2$

**105.** A simple symmetric random walk on the integer line is a Markov chain which is

(a) recurrent

(b) null recurrent

(c) irreducible

(d) positive recurrent

**106.** Suppose $X$ and $Y$ are random variables with $E(X)=E(Y)=0$, $V(X)=V(Y)=1$ and $\text{Cov}(X,Y)=0.25$. Then, which of the following is/are always true?

(a) $P\{|X+2Y|\ge 4\}\le\frac{4}{16}$

(b) $P\{|X+2Y|\ge 4\}\le\frac{5}{16}$

(c) $P\{|X+2Y|\ge 4\}\le\frac{6}{16}$

(d) $P\{|X+2Y|\ge 4\}\le\frac{7}{16}$

**107.** Let $X_1,\ldots,X_n$ be a random sample from uniform $(\theta,\theta+1)$ distribution. Which of the following is/are maximum likelihood estimator(s) of $\theta$?

(a) $X_{(1)}$ (b) $X_{(n)}$

(c) $X_{(n)}-1$ (d) $\frac{X_{(n)}+X_{(1)}}{2}-0.5$

**108.** Let $\underline{X}=(X_1,\ldots,X_n)$ be a random sample from uniform $(0,\theta)$. Which of the following is/are uniformly most powerful size $\alpha\left(0<\alpha<\frac{1}{2}\right)$ test(s) for testing $H_0:\theta=\theta_0$ against $H_1:\theta>\theta_0$?

(a) $\phi_1(\underline{X})=1$, if $X_{(n)}>\theta_0$ or $X_{(n)}<\theta_0\,\alpha^{1/n}$
$=0$, otherwise

(b) $\phi_2(\underline{X})=1$, if $X_{(n)}>\theta_0$
$=\alpha$, if $X_{(n)}\le\theta_0$

(c) $\phi_3(\underline{X})=1$, if $X_{(n)}>\theta_0\,\alpha^{1/n}$
$=0$, if $X_{(n)}\le\theta_0\alpha^{1/n}$

(d) $\phi_4(\underline{X})=1$, if $X_{(n)}<\theta_0\,(\alpha/2)^{1/n}$ or $X_{(n)}>\theta_0(1-\alpha/2)^{1/n}$
$=0$, otherwise

**109.** Suppose $\underline{X}_{p\times 1}$ has a $N_p(\underline{O}, I_p)$ distribution. The distribution of $\underline{X}^T A\underline{X}$ is chi-square with $r$ degrees of freedom only if

(a) A is idempotent with rank $r$

(b) Trace $(A)$ = Rank $(A)=r$

(c) A is positive definite

(d) A is non-negative definite with rank $r$

**110.** Let $X_1, X_2,\ldots,X_m$ be i.i.d. random variables with common continuous cdf $F(x)$. Also, let $Y_1, Y_2,\ldots,Y_n$ be i.i.d. random variables with common continuous cdf $G(x)$ and $X$'s and $Y$'s are independently distributed. For

testing $H_0 : F(x) = G(x)$ for all $x$ against $H_1 : F(x) \neq G(x)$ for atleast one $x$, which of the following test is/are used?
(a) Wilcoxon signed rank test
(b) Kolmogorov-Smirnov test
(c) Wald-Wolfowitz run test
(d) Sign test

**111.** Random variables $X$ and $Y$ are such that $E(X) = E(Y) = 0$, $V(X) = V(Y) = 1$, correlation $(X, Y) = 0.5$. Then, the
(a) conditional distribution $Y$ given $X = x$ is normal with mean 0.5 $x$ and variance 0.75
(b) least-squares linear regression of $Y$ on $X$ is $y = 0.5x$ and of $X$ on $Y$ is $x = 2y$
(c) least-squares linear regression of $X$ on $Y$ is $x = 0.5y$ and of $Y$ on $X$ is $y = 2x$
(d) least-squares linear regression of $Y$ on $X$ is $y = 0.5x$ and of $X$ on $Y$ is $x = 0.5y$

**112.** $X$ has a binomial $(5, p)$ distribution on which an observation $x = 4$ has been made. In a Bayesian approach to the estimation of $p$, a beta (2, 3) prior distribution (with density proportional to $p(1-p)^2$) has been formulated. Then, the posterior
(a) distribution of $p$ is uniform on (0. 1)
(b) mean of $p$ is $\frac{6}{10}$
(c) distribution of $p$ is beta (6, 4)
(d) distribution of $p$ is binomial (10, 0.5)

**113.** In a study of voter preferences in an election, the following data were obtained

| Gender | Party Voting for | | Total |
|---|---|---|---|
| | **C** | **B** | |
| Male | 250 | 250 | 500 |
| Female | 250 | 250 | 500 |
| Total | 500 | 500 | 1000 |

Then, the
(a) chi-square statistic for testing no association between party and gender is 0.
(b) expected frequency under the hypothesis of no association is 250 in each cell.
(c) log-linear model for cell frequency $m_{ij}$, $\log(m_{ij}) =$ constant, $i, j = 1, 2$, fits perfectly to the data
(d) chi-square test of no gender-party association with 1 degree of freedom has a $p$-value of 1.

**114.** Let $X$, $Y$ and $N$ be independent random variables with $P(X = 0) = 1/2 = 1 - P(X = 1)$ and $Y$ following Poisson with parameter $\lambda > 0$ and $N$ following normal with mean 0 and variance 1. Define

$$Z = \begin{cases} Y, & \text{if } X = 0 \\ N, & \text{if } X = 1 \end{cases}$$

Then, the characteristic function of $Z$ is given by
(a) $\left(\frac{1}{2} + \frac{1}{2}e^{it}\right) e^{-\lambda(1-e^{it})}\, e^{-t^2/2}$
(b) $e^{-\lambda(1-e^{it})}\, e^{-t^2/2}$
(c) $\dfrac{e^{-\lambda(1-e^{it})} + e^{-t^2/2}}{2}$
(d) $\left(\frac{1}{2} + \frac{1}{2}e^{it}\right)\left(\dfrac{e^{-\lambda(1-e^{it})} + e^{-t^2/2}}{2}\right)$

**115.** A simple random sample of size $n$ is drawn from a finite population of $N$ units, with replacement. The probability that the $i$th $(1 \le i \le N)$ unit is included in the sample is
(a) $n/N$
(b) $1 - \left(1 - \frac{1}{N}\right)^n$
(c) $\left(\frac{N-1}{N}\right)^n$
(d) $\frac{n(n-1)}{N(N-1)}$

**116.** Under a balanced incomplete block design with usual parameters $v, b, r, k, \lambda$, which of the following is/are true?
(a) All treatment contrasts are estimable, if $k \ge 2$
(b) The variance of the best linear unbiased estimator of any normalized treatment contrast is a constant depending only on the design parameters and the per observation variance
(c) The covariance between the best linear unbiased estimators of two mutually orthogonal treatment contrasts is strictly positive
(d) The variance of the best linear unbiased estimator of an elementary treatment contrast is strictly smaller than that under a randomized block design with replication $r$.

**117.** Consider a randomized (complete) block design with $v$ (> 2) treatments and $r$ (≥ 2) replicates. Which of the following statements is/are true?
(a) The design is connected
(b) The variance of the best linear unbiased estimator (BLUE) of every normalized treatment contrast is the same
(c) The BLUE of any treatment contrast is uncorrelated with the BLUE of any contrast among replicate effects
(c) The variance of the BLUE of any elementary treatment contrast is $2\sigma^2/r$, where $\sigma^2$ is the variance of an observation

**118.** The starting and optimal tableaus of a minimization problem are given below. The variables are $x_1$, $x_2$ and $x_3$. The slack variables are $S_1$ and $S_2$.

**Starting Tableau**

| | $Z$ | $x_1$ | $x_2$ | $x_3$ | $S_1$ | $S_2$ | RHS |
|---|---|---|---|---|---|---|---|
| $Z$ | 1 | $a$ | 1 | −3 | 0 | 0 | 0 |
| $S_1$ | 0 | $b$ | 2 | 2 | 1 | 0 | 6 |
| $S_2$ | 0 | −1 | 2 | −1 | 0 | 1 | 1 |

**Optimal Tableau**

| | $Z$ | $x_1$ | $x_2$ | $x_3$ | $S_1$ | $S_2$ | RHS |
|---|---|---|---|---|---|---|---|
| $Z$ | 1 | 0 | −1/3 | −11/3 | −2/3 | 0 | −4 |
| $x_1$ | 0 | $c$ | 2/3 | 2/3 | 1/3 | 0 | $e$ |
| $S_2$ | 0 | $d$ | 8/3 | −1/3 | 1/3 | 1 | 3 |

Which of the following are the correct values of the unknowns $a$, $b$, $c$, $d$ and $e$?

(a) $a = 2, b = 3, c = 1, d = 0, e = 2$
(b) $a = 2, b = -3, c = 1, d = 0, e = -2$
(c) $a = -2, b = 3, c = 1, d = 0, e = 2$
(d) $a = -2, b = 3, c = -1, d = 0, e = 2$

**119.** Consider the following linear programming problem.

Minimize $Z = x_1 + x_2$

subject to $sx_1 + tx_2 \geq 1$

$x_1 \geq 0$

$x_2$ unrestricted.

The necessary and sufficient condition to make the LPP

(a) feasible is $s \leq 0$ and $t = 0$
(b) unbounded is $s > t$ or $t < 0$
(c) have a unique solution is $s = t$ and $t > 0$
(d) have a finite optimal solution is $x_2 \geq 0$

# Hints & Solutions

**21.** (a) Let $a_n = \dfrac{n}{(n+n)^2}$

$$\Rightarrow \quad \lim_{n\to\infty} a_n = \lim_{n\to\infty}\left(\frac{1}{4n}\right) = 0$$

Hence, by Cauchy's first theorem on limits, we have

$$\lim_{n\to\infty}\left(\frac{a_1 + a_2 + \ldots + a_n}{n}\right) = 0$$

$$\Rightarrow \quad \lim_{n\to\infty} \frac{1}{n}\left[\frac{n}{(n+1)^2} + \frac{n}{(n+2)^2} + \ldots + \frac{1}{(2n)^2}\right] = 0$$

$$\Rightarrow \quad \lim_{n\to\infty}\left[\frac{1}{(n+1)^2} + \frac{1}{(n+2)^2} + \ldots + \frac{1}{(2n)^2}\right] = 0$$

Now, $\displaystyle \lim_{n\to\infty}\left[\frac{1}{n^2} + \frac{1}{(n+1)^2} + \frac{1}{(n+2)^2} + \ldots + \frac{1}{(2n)^2}\right]$

$$= \lim_{n\to\infty} \frac{1}{n^2}$$

$$+ \lim_{n\to\infty}\left[\frac{1}{(n+1)^2} + \frac{1}{(n+2)^2} + \ldots + \frac{1}{(2n)^2}\right]$$

$$= 0 + 0 = 0$$

Hence, option (a) is correct.

**22.** (a) We define a sequence $< a_n >$ as

$$a_1 = 1, \quad a_{n+1} = \frac{n}{n-1}, \ \forall\ n \geq 2$$

Then, $\displaystyle \lim_{n\to\infty} a_n = \lim_{n\to\infty} \frac{n}{n-1}$

$$= \lim_{n\to\infty} \frac{1}{1-(1/n)} = 1$$

Hence, by Cauchy's theorem on limits

$$\lim_{n\to\infty} (a_1\, a_2\, a_3 \ldots a_n)^{1/n} = 1$$

$$\Rightarrow \quad \lim_{n\to\infty}\left(1 \cdot \frac{2}{1}\cdot\frac{3}{2}\cdot\frac{4}{3}\cdots\frac{n}{n-1}\right)^{1/n} = 1$$

$$\Rightarrow \quad \lim_{n\to\infty} (n)^{1/n} = 1$$

Hence, sequence $x_n = n^{1/n}$ converges.

Next, let $a_n = n$

$$\therefore \quad \lim_{n\to\infty} a_n = \lim_{n\to\infty} n = \infty$$

Hence, by Cauchy's theorem on limits

$$\lim_{n\to\infty} (a_1\, a_2\, a_3 \ldots a_n)^{1/n} = \infty$$

$$\Rightarrow \quad \lim_{n\to\infty} (1\cdot 2\cdot 3 \ldots n)^{1/n} = \infty$$

$$\Rightarrow \quad \lim_{n\to\infty} (n!)^{1/n} = \infty$$

Hence, option (a) is correct.

**23.** (a) The given set $\{x \in \mathbb{R} : x \sin x \leq 1,\ x \cos x \leq 1\} \subseteq \mathbb{R}$ is bounded and closed in $\mathbb{R}$.

Hence, option (a) is correct.

**24.** (b) Let $f(x) = 1$, then $f : [0, 1] \to \mathbb{R}$ is continuous such that

$$f(t) \geq 0,\ \forall\ t \in [0, 1]$$

Now, $\displaystyle g(x) = \int_0^x f(t)\, dt$

$$= \int_0^x 1\, dt$$

$$= [t]_0^x = x$$

which is monotonic but not bounded. Let us consider another function $f(x) = x$ which is real-valued continuous function on $[0, 1]$ such that $f(t) \geq 0,\ \forall\ t \in [0, 1]$. Then,

$$g(x) = \int_0^x f(t)\, dt = \int_0^x t\, dt$$

$$= \left[\frac{t^2}{2}\right]_0^x = \frac{x^2}{2}$$

Which is monotonic and unbounded function.

Therefore, options (a), (c) and (d) are incorrect.

Hence, option (b) is correct.

**25.** (b) Let $f(x) = 1$, which is continuous function on $[0, 1]$ with $f(0) = 1$.

Then, $\displaystyle G(a) = \frac{1}{a}\int_0^a f(x)\, dx$

$$= \frac{1}{a}\int_0^a 1\, dx$$

$$= \frac{1}{a}[x]_0^a = 1$$

Hence, options (a), (c) and (d) are incorrect.

Therefore, option (b) is correct.

**26.** (a) Let $\displaystyle u_n = \sin\frac{1}{n^2}$

and $\displaystyle v_n = \frac{1}{n^2}$

Now, $\displaystyle \lim_{n\to\infty}\frac{u_n}{v_n} = \lim_{n\to\infty}\frac{\sin(1/n^2)}{(1/n^2)}$

$$= 1 \neq 0 \text{ (finite)}$$

Hence, $\Sigma u_n$ and $\Sigma v_n$ converge or diverge together.

Now, since $\displaystyle \Sigma u_n = \Sigma\frac{1}{n^2}$

Converges, hence

$$\Sigma \sin\left(\frac{1}{n^2}\right) \text{ converges.}$$

Hence, option (a) is correct.

**27.** (a) Since, $\phi(x)$ denotes the integer closest to $x$, $\forall x \in \mathbb{R}$ (If, there are two such integers taking larger one). Then,

$$\phi(x) = \begin{cases} 10, & 10 \le x < 10.5 \\ 11, & 10.5 \le x < 11 \\ 11, & x \le 11 < 11.5 \\ 12, & 11.5 \le x < 12 \end{cases}$$

Therefore, $\int_{10}^{12} \phi(x)\, dx = \int_{10}^{10.5} 10\, dx + \int_{10.5}^{11} 11\, dx + \int_{11}^{11.5} 11\, dx + \int_{11.5}^{12} 12\, dx$

$$= 10\,[x]_{10}^{10.5} + 11\,[x]_{10.5}^{11} + 11\,[x]_{11}^{11.5} + 12\,[x]_{11.5}^{12}$$
$$= 10\,[10.5 - 10] + 11\,[11 - 10.5] + 11\,[11.5 - 11] + 12\,[12 - 11.5]$$
$$= 10 \times 0.5 + 11 \times 0.5 + 11 \times 0.5 + 12 \times 0.5$$
$$= 44 \times 0.5 = 22$$

Hence, option (a) is correct.

**28.** (d) Let $P(x) = x^k + a_1 x^{k-1} + a_2 x^{k-2} + \ldots + a_{k-1} x + a_k$.

Which is a polynomial of degree $k > 0$ with a non-zero constant term. Hence,

$$f_n(x) = P\left(\frac{x}{n}\right), \forall x \in (0, \infty)$$
$$= \left(\frac{x}{n}\right)^k + a_1\left(\frac{x}{n}\right)^{k-1} + a_2\left(\frac{x}{n}\right)^{k-2} + \ldots + a_{k-1}\left(\frac{x}{n}\right) + a_k, \forall x \in (0, \infty)$$

$$\Rightarrow \lim_{n\to\infty} f_n(x) = \lim_{n\to\infty}\left[\left(\frac{x}{n}\right)^k + a_1\left(\frac{x}{n}\right)^{k-1} + a_2\left(\frac{x}{n}\right)^{k-2} + \ldots + a_{k-1}\left(\frac{x}{n}\right) + a_k\right]$$

$$= \lim_{n\to\infty}\left(\frac{x}{n}\right)^k + a_1 \lim_{n\to\infty}\left(\frac{x}{n}\right)^{k-1} + a_2 \lim_{n\to\infty}\left(\frac{x}{n}\right)^{k-2} + \ldots + a_{k-1} \lim_{n\to\infty}\left(\frac{x}{n}\right) + \lim_{n\to\infty} a_k$$

$$= 0 + 0 + 0 + \ldots + 0 + a_k = a_k$$
$$= P(0), \ \forall x \in (0, \infty)$$

Hence, option (d) is correct.

**29.** (d)

**30.** (a) Let $u = (1, 2, 0)$, $v = (2, 1, 3)$ and $w = (3, 2, 0)$, then $u, v, w$ are not lying in any plane containing zero. Now, $u, v, w$ neither mutually orthogonal nor pairwise orthogonal. Also, none of $u, v, w$ is zero. Hence, options (b), (c), (d) are incorrect.

Now, consider

$$\alpha_1 u + \alpha_2 v + \alpha_3 w = 0$$
$$\Rightarrow \quad \alpha_1 (1, 2, 0) + \alpha_2 (2, 1, 0) + \alpha_3 (3, 2, 3) = 0$$
$$\Rightarrow \quad \alpha_1 + 2\alpha_2 + 3\alpha_3 = 0$$
$$2\alpha_1 + \alpha_2 + 2\alpha_3 = 0$$
$$3\alpha_3 = 0$$

On solving, we get

$$\alpha_1 = \alpha_2 = \alpha_3 = 0$$

Hence, option (a) is correct.

**31.** (c) We have, $T: \mathbb{R}^2 \to \mathbb{R}^2$ such that $Ty = \alpha x$ and $Tx = 0$, where $x$ and $y$ are linearly indepenent in $\mathbb{R}^2$. Therefore,

$$T(Ty) = T(\alpha x)$$
$$= \alpha T(x)$$
$$= \alpha \cdot 0 = 0$$
$$\Rightarrow \quad T^2 y = 0$$

Hence, $T$ is a nilpotent linear transformation of index 2. Hence,

$$T = \begin{pmatrix} 0 & 1 \\ 0 & 0 \end{pmatrix}$$

Hence, option (c) is correct.

**32.** (c) Let $A$ be an $n \times n$ real symmetric matrix with eigen values $\lambda_1, \lambda_2, \ldots, \lambda_n$, then

$$\det(A) = \lambda_1 \lambda_2 \cdot \lambda_3 \ldots \lambda_n = \prod_{i=1}^{n} \lambda_i$$

Hence, option (c) is correct.

**33.** (c) Let $f(z) = \sin z$, which is analytic on $D = \{z \in \mathbb{C} : |z| < 1\}$

and $f(0) = \sin 0 = 0$

Hence, $g(z) = \begin{cases} \dfrac{f(z)}{z}, & z \ne 0 \\ f'(0), & z = 0 \end{cases}$

$$= \begin{cases} \dfrac{\sin z}{z}, & z \ne 0 \\ 1, & z = 0 \end{cases}$$

(a) Since, $g$ is continuous at $z = 0$. Hence, option (a) is incorrect.

(b) Since, $g$ is analytic at $z = 0$. Hence, option (b) is incorrect.

(d) Since, $f'(0) = \cos 0 = 1$. Hence, option (d) is incorrect.

Therefore, option (c) is correct.

**34.** (c) We have,

$$|f(z)| = |\sin z|, \forall z \in \Omega$$
$$\Rightarrow \quad f(z) = \pm \sin z, \forall z \in \Omega$$
$$\Rightarrow \quad f(z) = c \sin z, \forall z \in \Omega$$

where $c = \pm 1$ with $|c| = 1$ and $c \in \mathbb{C}$.

Hence, option (c) is correct.

**35.** (b) We have,

$$a_n = 4n^4 - n^3 + 3$$

$$\Rightarrow \quad a_{n+1} = 4(n+1)^4 - (n+1)^3 + 3$$

$$\therefore \quad \frac{1}{R} = \lim_{n\to\infty}\left|\frac{a_{n+1}}{a_n}\right|$$

$$= \lim_{n\to\infty}\left|\frac{4(n+1)^4 - (n+1)^3 + 3}{4n^4 - n^3 + 3}\right|$$

$$= \lim_{n\to\infty}\left|\frac{4\left(1+\frac{1}{n}\right)^4 - \left(\frac{1}{n^3}+\frac{1}{n^4}\right)^3 + \frac{3}{n^4}}{4 - \frac{1}{n} + \frac{3}{n}}\right| = 1$$

Hence, option (b) is correct.

**36.** (a) Let $\mathbb{F} = \mathbb{Z}_2 = \{0, 1\}$

Then, $x^2 = 0$

$\Rightarrow \quad x = 0 \in \mathbb{Z}_2$

and $\quad x^2 = 1 \Rightarrow x = \pm 1$

$\Rightarrow \quad x = 1 \in \mathbb{Z}_2$

but $\mathbb{F} = \mathbb{Z}_2$ does not have square number of elements. Also, order of $\mathbb{F} = \mathbb{Z}_2$ is not a power of 3. Hence, options (b) and (c) are incorrect.

Now, consider the field $\mathbb{F} = \{0, 1, \alpha, \alpha^2\}$ where $\alpha$ is cube root of unity.

Then, $x^2 = a$

$\Rightarrow \quad 0^2 = 0, 1^2 = 1, \alpha^2 = \alpha^2, (\alpha^2)^2 = \alpha^4 = \alpha$

Hence, $x^2 = a, \forall\, a \in \mathbb{F}$ has solution in $\mathbb{F}$ but $\mathbb{F}$ has order 4, which is not prime. Also, the characteristic of $\mathbb{F}$ is 2.

Hence, option (a) is correct.

**37.** (d) Total number of proper subfield of $\mathbb{F}$ with $5^{12}$ elements.

$$= z(12) - 1$$
$$= z(2^2 \times 3) - 1$$
$$= [z(2^2) \times z(3)] - 1$$
$$= (2+1)(1+1) - 1$$
$$= 6 - 1 = 5$$

Hence, option (d) is correct.

**38.** (a) Let $x \in K$. The family $\{x^k : 0 \le k \le n\}$ has more than $n$ elements, so it is not linearly independent over $K$. This means that there exists a family $\{\lambda_k : 0 \le k \le n\}$ of elements of $K$, not all zero, such that

$$\sum_{0\le k\le n-1} \lambda_k x^k = 0$$

In otherwords, the polynomial $S(X) = \sum_{0\le k\le n} \lambda_k x^k$ of $Q[x]$ vanishes at $x$, because $S \neq 0$. Hence, $x$ is algebraic of degree $\le n$ over $Q$. Hence, finite extension $K$ is an algebraic extension over $Q$.

**Alternative Method**

Let $K$ be a finite extension of $Q$ and $\alpha \in K$. Then,

$$[Q(\alpha) : Q] \le [K : Q] < \infty$$

But, if $k$ is an algebraic extension of $Q(\alpha)$ and $Q$ is a subfield of $K$ containing $Q$. Then, $K$ is an algebraic extension of $Q(\alpha)$.

Hence, option (a) is correct.

**39.** (b) (a) We have,

$21 = 3 \times 7$

Hence, $\quad 21 = \text{LCM}(3, 7)$

but $\quad 3 + 7 = 10$

Hence, $S_9$ cannot have element of order 21 on 9 symbols.

(b) We have,

$20 = 2 \times 2 \times 5$

$\therefore \quad 20 = \text{LCM}(4, 5)$

and $\quad 4 + 5 = 9$

Hence, $S_9$ can have element of order 20 on 9 symbols.

(c) We have,

$30 = 2 \times 3 \times 5$

$\therefore \quad 30 = \text{LCM}(2, 3, 5)$

but $\quad 2 + 3 + 5 = 10$

Hence, $S_9$ cannot have element of order 30 on 9 symbols.

(d) We have,

$14 = 2 \times 7$

$\therefore \quad 14 = \text{LCM}(2, 7)$ and $2 + 7 = 9$

$\therefore S_9$ can have element of order 14 on 9 symbols.

Hence, the largest order = 20

Hence, option (b) is correct.

**40.** (b) Since $V$ is a real vector space of dimension 3. Hence, the number of linearly independent vectors in $V$ is infinity.

Hence, option (b) is correct.

**41.** (d) Given differential equation is

$$\frac{dy}{dx} = y^2\ (x, y) \in (\mathbb{R} \times \mathbb{R}) \qquad \ldots\text{(i)}$$

$$\Rightarrow \quad \frac{dy}{y^2} = dx$$

$$\Rightarrow \quad y^{-2}dy = dx$$

On integrating, we get

$$\Rightarrow \quad \frac{y^{-1}}{-1} = x + C$$

$$\Rightarrow \quad x + \frac{1}{y} + C = 0 \qquad \ldots\text{(ii)}$$

(a) Solution (ii) does not defined at $y = 0$.

Hence, option (a) is incorrect.

(b) At $y(1) = 1$, Eq. (ii) gives

$$1 + \frac{1}{1} + C = 0$$

$$\Rightarrow \quad C = -1$$

$$\therefore \quad x + \frac{1}{y} - 1 = 0$$

which is solution of differential Eq. (i) defined in $(-\infty, \infty)$.

Hence, option (b) is incorrect.

(c) At $y(x_0) = y_0, y_0 > 0$

Eq. (ii), gives

$$x_0 + \frac{1}{y_0} + C = 0$$

$$\Rightarrow \quad C = -\left(x_0 + \frac{1}{y_0}\right)$$

Therefore, $x + \frac{1}{y} - 1\left(x_0 + \frac{1}{y_0}\right) = 0$

which does not defined at $y = 0$ and hence, does not defined in $\left(-\infty, x_0 + \frac{1}{y_0}\right)$.

Hence, option (c) is incorrect.

(d) At $y(x_0) = y_0, y_0 > 0$

$$\Rightarrow \quad x + \frac{1}{y} - \left(x_0 + \frac{1}{y_0}\right) = 0$$

which is defined in $\left(x_0 + \frac{1}{y_0}, \infty\right)$.

Hence, option (d) is correct.

**42.** (d) Given second order partial differential equation is

$$(1 - \sqrt{xy})\frac{\partial^2 u}{\partial x^2} + 2\frac{\partial^2 u}{\partial x \partial y} + (1 + \sqrt{xy})\frac{\partial^2 u}{\partial y^2} = 0$$

or $\quad (1 - \sqrt{xy})\, r + 2s + (1 + \sqrt{xy})\, t = 0 \quad$ ...(i)

Comparing Eq. (i) with

$$Rr + Tt + Ss + f(x, y, z, p, q) = 0 \quad \text{...(ii)}$$

we get $R = (1 - \sqrt{xy})$

$S = 2, T = (1 + \sqrt{xy})$

Therefore, $S^2 - 4RT = 4 - 4(1 - \sqrt{xy})(1 + \sqrt{xy})$

$= 4(1 - (1 - xy)) = 4xy$

$\therefore$ Eq. (i) is hyperbolic, if

$$S^2 - 4RT > 0$$

$$\Rightarrow \quad 4xy = 0$$

$\Rightarrow$ either $x > 0, y > 0$ or $x < 0, y < 0$.

Hence, Eq. (i) is Hyperbolic either in first quadrant or in third quadrant.

Next Eq. (i) is elliptic, if

$$S^2 - 4RT < 0$$

$$\Rightarrow \quad 4xy < 0$$

$\Rightarrow$ either $x < 0, y > 0$ or $x > 0, y < 0$

Hence, Eq. (i) is elliptic in second and fourth quadrant.

Therefore, option (d) is correct.

**43.** (d) Given equation is

$$\frac{\partial u(x, y)}{\partial x} + u(x, y) = e^{-x} \quad \text{...(i)}$$

(a) We have

$$u(x, y) = e^{-x} f(y)$$

$$\Rightarrow \quad \frac{\partial u(x, y)}{\partial x} = -e^{-x} f(y)$$

$\therefore$ From Eq. (i), we get

LHS $= -e^{-x} f(y) + e^{-x} f(y)$

$= 0 \neq e^{-x}$

$=$ RHS

Hence, option (a) is incorrect.

(b) We have,

$$u(x, y) = e^{-x} f(y) + xe^{x}$$

$$\Rightarrow \quad \frac{\partial u(x, y)}{\partial x} = -e^{-x} f(y) + e^{x} + xe^{x}$$

$\therefore$ From Eq. (i), we get

LHS $= -e^{-x} f(y) + e^{x} + xe^{x} + e^{-x} f(y) + xe^{x}$

$= e^{x} + 2xe^{x}$

$\neq e^{-x} \neq$ RHS

Hence, option (b) is incorrect.

(c) We have,

$$u(x, y) = e^{x} f(y) + xe^{x}$$

$$\Rightarrow \quad \frac{\partial u(x, y)}{\partial x} = e^{x} f(y) + e^{x} + xe^{x}$$

$\therefore$ From Eq. (i), we get

LHS $= e^{x} f(y) + e^{x} + xe^{x} + e^{x} f(y) + xe^{x}$

$= 2e^{x} f(y) + e^{x} + 2xe^{x}$

$\neq e^{-x} =$ RHS

Hence, option (c) is incorrect.

(d) We have,

$$u(x, y) = e^{-x} f(y) + xe^{-x}$$

$$\Rightarrow \quad \frac{\partial u(x, y)}{\partial x} = -e^{-x} f(y) + e^{-x} - xe^{-x}$$

$\therefore$ From Eq. (i), we get

LHS $= -e^{-x} f(y) + e^{-x} - xe^{-x} + e^{-x} f(y) + xe^{-x}$

$= e^{-x}$

$=$ RHS

Hence, option (d) is correct.

**44.** (b) Given integral is

$$\int_0^4 (2x^3 - 3x^2 + 5x + 1)\,dx$$

$$= \left[\frac{2x^4}{4} - \frac{3x^3}{3} + \frac{5x^2}{2} + x\right]_0^4$$

$$= \left[\frac{x^4}{2} - x^3 + \frac{5}{2}x^2 + x\right]_0^4$$

$$= [128 - 64 + 40 + 4] = 108$$

Now, $f(x) = 2x^3 - 3x^2 + 5x + 1$

$$a = 0,\ b = 4,\ n = 4$$

$$\therefore \quad h = \frac{b-a}{n} = \frac{0-4}{4} = 1$$

| $x$ | $f(x)$ |
|---|---|
| $x_0 = 0$ | $y_0 = 1$ |
| $x_1 = 1$ | $y_1 = 5$ |
| $x_2 = 2$ | $y_2 = 16$ |
| $x_3 = 3$ | $y_3 = 43$ |
| $x_4 = 4$ | $y_4 = 101$ |

Hence, by Trapezoidal rule, we get

$$\int_0^4 (2x^3 - 3x^2 + 5x + 1)\,dx$$

$$= \frac{h}{2}[(y_0 + y_4) + 2(y_1 + y_2 + y_3)]$$

$$= \frac{1}{2}[(1+101) + 2(5+16+43)]$$

$$= \frac{1}{2}[230] = 115$$

and by Simpson's rule, we get

$$\int_0^4 (2x^3 - 3x^2 + 5x + 1)\,dx$$

$$= \frac{h}{3}[(y_0 + y_4) + 4(y_1 + y_3) + 2(y_2)]$$

$$= \frac{1}{3}[(1+101) + 4(5+43) + 2(16)]$$

$$= \frac{1}{3}[102 + 192 + 32]$$

$$= \frac{1}{3}[328] \simeq 109.33$$

Therefore, the Simpson's rule will give more accuracy than the Trapezoidal rule but less accurate than the exact result.

Hence, option (b) is correct.

**45.** (b) The given integral equation

$$g(x)\,y(x) = f(x) + \lambda \int_\alpha^\beta k(x,t)\,y(t)\,dt$$

with $f(x)$, $g(x)$ and $k(x,t)$ as known functions, $\alpha$ and $\beta$ as known constants and $\lambda$ as a known parameter, is a linear Fredholm integral equations.

Hence, option (b) is correct.

**46.** (d) We have,

$$y(x) = f(x) + \lambda \int_a^b k(x,t)\,y(t)\,dt$$

where $f(x)$ and $k(x,t)$ are known functions, $a$ and $b$ are known constants and $\lambda$ is a known parameter. If $\lambda_i$ be the eigen values of the corresponding homogeneous equation. Then the above integral equation has in general either many solutions or no solution at all for $\lambda = \lambda_i$, depending on the form of $f(x)$, because if homogeneous equation has infinite solutions. Then corresponding non-homogeneous equation has either infinite solution or no solutions.

Hence, option (d) is correct.

**47.** (c) Given equation of motion is

$$\frac{d\mathbf{v}}{dt} = -\mathbf{v} - \hat{\mathbf{k}} \qquad \text{...(i)}$$

$$\Rightarrow \quad \frac{d\mathbf{v}}{-\mathbf{v} - \hat{\mathbf{k}}} = dt$$

On integration, we get

$$\int \frac{d\mathbf{v}}{-\mathbf{v} - \hat{\mathbf{k}}} = \int dt + \ln C$$

$$\Rightarrow \quad \ln\left(\frac{1}{-\mathbf{v} - \hat{\mathbf{k}}}\right) = t + \ln C$$

$$\Rightarrow \quad \mathbf{v} = -\left(\frac{1}{C}e^{-t} + \hat{\mathbf{k}}\right) \qquad \text{...(ii)}$$

Now, at $t = 0$, $\alpha(t) = 1$

$$\Rightarrow \quad \mathbf{v} = \alpha\hat{\mathbf{k}} = \hat{\mathbf{k}}$$

$\therefore$ From Eq. (ii), we get

$$\hat{\mathbf{k}} = -\left(\frac{1}{C}e^{-t} + \hat{\mathbf{k}}\right)$$

$$\Rightarrow \quad -\frac{1}{C} = 2\hat{\mathbf{k}} \qquad (\because t = 0)$$

Hence, Eq. (ii) becomes

$$\mathbf{v} = 2\hat{\mathbf{k}}e^{-t} - \hat{\mathbf{k}}$$

$$= \hat{\mathbf{k}}\,(2e^{-t} - 1)$$

$$\therefore \quad |\mathbf{v}| = 2e^{-t} - 1$$

$$\therefore \quad |\mathbf{v}|_{\text{at } t=1} = 2e^{-1} - 1$$

$$= \frac{2}{e} - 1$$

$$= \frac{2-e}{e}$$

Hence, option (c) is correct.

**48.** (c) Given functional is

$$F(u,v) = \int_0^{\pi/2}\left[\left(\frac{du}{dx}\right)^2 + \left(\frac{dv}{dx}\right)^2 + 2u(x)\,v(x)\right]dx \quad \text{...(i)}$$

which involves two dependent variables.

$$\therefore F(x,u,u',v,v') = \left(\frac{du}{dx}\right)^2 + \left(\frac{du}{dx}\right)^2 + 2u(x)\,v(x)$$

$$= u'^2 + v'^2 + 2uv$$

$$\therefore \frac{\partial F}{\partial u} = 2v, \frac{\partial F}{\partial u'} = 2u'$$

$$\frac{\partial F}{\partial v} = 2u, \frac{\partial F}{\partial v'} = 2v'$$

Therefore, the Euler's equations are

$$\frac{\partial F}{\partial u} - \frac{d}{dx}\left(\frac{\partial F}{\partial u'}\right) = 0 \quad \ldots\text{(ii)}$$

$$\frac{\partial F}{\partial v} - \frac{d}{dx}\left(\frac{\partial F}{\partial v'}\right) = 0 \quad \ldots\text{(iii)}$$

$$\Rightarrow \quad 2v - \frac{d}{dx}(2u') = 0$$

$$\Rightarrow \quad 2u - \frac{d}{dx}(2v') = 0$$

$$\Rightarrow \quad v - u'' = 0$$

$$u - v'' = 0$$

$$\Rightarrow \quad u'' - v = 0 \quad \ldots\text{(iv)}$$

$$v'' - u = 0 \quad \ldots\text{(v)}$$

From Eqs. (iv) and (v), we get

$$u^{(iv)} - u = 0$$

$$\Rightarrow \quad u(x) = c_1e^x + c_2e^{-x} + c_3 \cos x + c_4 \sin x \quad \ldots\text{(vi)}$$

$$\Rightarrow \quad u'(x) = c_1e^x - c_2e^{-x} - c_3 \sin x + c_4 \cos x$$

$$\Rightarrow \quad u''(x) = c_1e^x + c_2e^{-x} - c_3 \cos x - c_4 \sin x \quad \ldots\text{(vii)}$$

$\therefore$ From Eqs. (iv) and (vi), we get

$$v(x) = u''(x) = c_1e^x + c_2e^{-x} - c_3 \cos x - c_4 \sin x \quad \ldots\text{(viii)}$$

Now, applying given conditions

$$u(0) = 1, v(0) = -1$$

and $u\left(\frac{\pi}{2}\right) = 0, v\left(\frac{\pi}{2}\right) = 0$

From Eqs. (vi) and (viii), we get

$$1 = c_1 + c_2 + c_3 \quad \ldots\text{(ix)}$$

$$-1 = c_1 + c_2 - c_3 \quad \ldots\text{(x)}$$

$$0 = c_1e^{\pi/2} + c_2e^{-\pi/2} + c_4 \quad \ldots\text{(xi)}$$

$$0 = c_1e^{\pi/2} + c_2e^{-\pi/2} - c_4 \quad \ldots\text{(xii)}$$

On solving Eqs. (ix), (x), (xi) and (xii), we get

$$c_1 = c_2 = c_4 = 0 \text{ and } c_3 = 1$$

Therefore, putting these values in Eqs. (vi) and (viii), we get

$$u(x) = \cos x, v(x) = -\cos x$$

Hence, $u(\pi) = \cos \pi = -1$

$$v(\pi) = -\cos \pi = -(-1) = 1$$

$$\therefore \quad u(\pi) + v(\pi) = -1 + 1 = 0$$

$$u(\pi) - v(\pi) = -1 - 1 = -2$$

Hence, option (c) is correct.

**49.** (d) From the table,

| $x$ | 2 | 5 | 7 | 11 | 13 | 19 | Total 57 |
|---|---|---|---|---|---|---|---|
| $y$ | 0 | 15 | 25 | 45 | 55 | 85 | 225 |
| $x^2$ | 4 | 25 | 49 | 121 | 169 | 361 | 729 |
| $y^2$ | 0 | 225 | 625 | 2025 | 3025 | 7225 | 13125 |
| $xy$ | 0 | 75 | 175 | 495 | 715 | 1615 | 3075 |

$$\text{Now, } r = \frac{\frac{1}{n}\Sigma xy - \left(\frac{\Sigma x}{n}\frac{\Sigma y}{n}\right)}{\sqrt{\frac{1}{n}\Sigma x^2 - \left(\frac{1}{n}\Sigma x\right)^2}\sqrt{\frac{1}{n}\Sigma y^2 - \left(\frac{1}{n}\Sigma y\right)^2}}$$

$$= \frac{156}{6.12 \times 30.62} = 0.83$$

Hence, option (d) is correct.

**Remark** No option is correct. We may tick on option (d) because it is more close to the actual result.

**50.** (c) $X_1$ is not independent with $(Y_2, Y_3)$.

Hence, option (c) is correct.

**51.** (b) The exponential distribution is the continuous analogue of the geometric distribution. If $X$ is an exponentially distributed random variable with parameter $\lambda$, then $[X]$ is a geometrically distributed random variable with parameter $p = 1 - e - \lambda$.

Hence, option (b) is correct.

**52.** (d) The Markov chain will always be irreducible but may have period > 1.

Hence, option (d) is correct.

**53.** (a) This option is true only, if $X_1$ have power −2.

If all variables have power−2, then the correct option will be (a).

**54.** (d) The difference of Max value and Min value among the observations does not depend on the parent uniform distribution. Therefore, it is ancillary statistics.

Hence, option (d) is correct.

**55.** (d) Let us arrange observations into increasing order of there magnitudes

$$X_{(1)} < X_{(2)} < \ldots < X_{(n)}$$

then $0 < X_{(1)} < X_{(2)} < \ldots < X_{(n)} < \theta$ and so the MLE of $\theta$ is $\hat{\theta} = [X_{(n)} + 1]$.

Hence, option (d) is correct.

**56.** (d)

**57.** (c)

**58.** (c) The variance of a linear combination of unbiased estimator's is given by

$$V\left(\sum_{i=1}^{\nu} p_i t_i\right) = \left(\sum_{i=1}^{\nu} p_i^2\right)\left(\frac{k}{\lambda \nu}\sigma^2\right)$$

$$= \left(\frac{k}{\lambda \nu}\sigma^2\right)$$

Hence, option (c) is correct.

**59.** (c) The reliability = $P$ (atleast one engine of both sides works)

$= P$ (atleast one engine works in one side)$^2$

$= (1-p^2)^2$

Hence, option (c) is correct.

**60.** (d)

**61.** (a,d) Since, $\{a_n\}$ and $\{b_n\}$ are convergent sequence of positive real numbers such that

$$\lim_{n\to\infty} a_n = a \text{ and } \lim_{n\to\infty} b_n = b$$

Then $\lim_{n\to\infty} c_n = \lim_{n\to\infty}\left(\frac{a_n}{b_n}\right)$

$$= \lim_{n\to\infty} a_n \left(\lim_{n\to\infty}\frac{1}{b_n}\right)$$

$$= a\cdot\left(\frac{1}{b}\right) = \frac{a}{b}$$

Hence, sequence $\{c_n\}$ converges if $b \neq 0$. Hence, option (a) is correct, while the options (b) and (c) are incorrect.

Now, if $b = 0$, then

$$\limsup_{n\to\infty} c_n = \infty$$

Hence, option (d) is correct.

**62.** (a,b,d)

**63.** (a) Let $f(x) = 1 + x$ which is an increasing real-valued function on $[0, \infty)$ with $f(x) > 0, \forall x$. Then,

$$g(x) = \frac{1}{x}\int_0^x f(u)\,du$$

$$= \frac{1}{x}\int_0^x (1+u)\,du$$

$$= \frac{1}{x}\left[u + \frac{u^2}{2}\right]_0^x$$

$$= \frac{1}{x}\left[x + \frac{x^2}{2}\right]$$

$$= 1 + \frac{x}{2}, \forall x \in (0, \infty)$$

$\Rightarrow g(x) \le f(x), \forall x \in (0, \infty)$

Hence, option (a) is correct.

Now, $x\,g(x) = x + \frac{x^2}{2} \ge f(x), \forall x \in (0, \infty)$.

Hence, option (b) is incorrect.

**64.** (a,d) We know that, if $f : [0, 1] \to \mathbb{R}$ be defined by

$$f(x) = \begin{cases} x^2 \cos\left(\frac{a}{x^\beta}\right), & x \neq 0 \\ 0, & x = 0 \end{cases}$$

where a is constant, then

(i) $f$ is continuous, if $\alpha > 0$

(ii) $f$ is bounded variation, if $\alpha > \beta$

Now, we have $f : [0, 1] \to \mathbb{R}$ defined by

$$f(x) = \begin{cases} x\cos\left(\frac{\pi}{2x}\right), & x \neq 0 \\ 0, & x = 0 \end{cases}$$

Then, $\alpha = 1 > 0, \therefore f$ is continuous function.

Hence, option (a) is correct.

Also, every continuous function, if Riemann integrable.

Hence, option (d) is correct.

Now, since $\alpha = 1 = \beta$. Hence, $f$ is not bounded variation.

Hence, option (b) is incorrect.

Now, $\lim_{x\to 0}\frac{f(x)-f(0)}{x-0}$

$$= \lim_{x\to 0}\frac{x\cos\left(\frac{\pi}{2x}\right) - 0}{x}$$

$$= \lim_{x\to 0}\cos\left(\frac{\pi}{2x}\right)$$

= exists

$\therefore$ $f$ is differentiable but derivative is not bounded.

Hence, option (c) is incorrect.

**65.** (a,c,d) We have for any positive integer $n$, $f_n : [0, 1] \to \mathbb{R}$ defined by

$$f_n(x) = \frac{x}{nx+1}, \forall x \in [0, 1]$$

$\therefore$
$$f(x) = \lim_{n\to\infty} f_n(x)$$

$$= \lim_{n\to\infty}\frac{x}{nx+1}$$

$$= 0, \forall x \in [0, 1]$$

Hence, sequence $\{f_n(x)\}$ converges to 0.

(a) Now, $M_n = \sup_{x\in[0,1]} |f_n(x) - f(x)|$

$$= \sup_{x \in [0,1]} \left| \frac{x}{nx+1} \right|$$

Let $t = \dfrac{x}{nx+1}$

$$\Rightarrow \frac{dt}{dx} = \frac{(nx+1)\cdot 1 - xn}{(nx+1)^2} = \frac{1}{(nx+1)^2} > 0$$

$\forall\, x \in [0, 1]$

Let $y = \dfrac{1}{(nx+1)^2}$

$$\therefore \frac{dy}{dx} = \frac{(nx+1)^2 \cdot 0 - 2(nx+1)\cdot n}{(nx+1)^4}$$

$$= -\frac{2n(nx+1)}{(nx+1)^4}$$

Putting $\dfrac{dy}{dx} = 0 \Rightarrow nx + 1 = 0 \Rightarrow x = -\dfrac{1}{n}$

Now,

$$\frac{d^2y}{dx^2} = \frac{(nx+1)^4(-2n^2) - (2n(nx+1))\,4(nx+1)^3 \cdot n}{(nx+1)^8}$$

$$= \frac{(nx+1)^3\{-2n^3x - 2n^2 - 8n^3x - 8n^2\}}{(nx+1)^8}$$

$$= \frac{-10n^3x - 10n^2}{(nx+1)^5}$$

$$\therefore \left(\frac{d^2y}{dx^2}\right)_{x=-\frac{1}{n}} = \frac{-10n^3\left(-\frac{1}{n}\right) - 10n^2}{\left(n\left(-\frac{1}{n}\right)+1\right)^5}$$

$$= \infty$$

$$\therefore \quad M_n = \infty$$

$$\therefore \quad \lim_{n\to\infty} M_n = \infty$$

$\therefore$ $f$ is an increasing function in [0, 1].

Therefore, $M_n = \dfrac{1}{n \cdot 1 + 1} = \dfrac{1}{n}$

Now, $\lim_{n\to\infty} M_n = \lim_{n\to\infty} \dfrac{1}{n} = 0$

Hence, by $M_n$-test sequence $\{f_n(x)\}$ is uniformly convergent in [0, 1].
Hence, option (a) is correct.

(b) Now, $f_n'(x) = \dfrac{1}{(nx+1)^2}$

and $M_n = \sup_{x \in [0,1]} |f_n'(x) - f'(x)|$

$$= \sup_{x \in [0,1]} \left| \frac{1}{(nx+1)^2} - 0 \right| \qquad [\because f'(x) = 0]$$

$$= \sup_{x \in [0,1]} \left| \frac{1}{(nx+1)^2} \right|$$

Hence, sequence $\{f_n'\}$ of derivatives of $\{f_n\}$ does not converges uniformly on [0, 1].
Hence, option (b) is incorrect.

(c) Since, each $f_n(x)$ is Riemann integrable. Hence,

$$\int_0^1 f_n(x)\,dx = \int_0^1 f(x)\,dx$$

$$= \int_0^1 0\,dx$$

$$= 0$$

$$\therefore \lim_{n\to\infty} \int_0^1 f_n(x)\,dx = \lim_{n\to\infty} 0 = 0, \forall\, x \in [0, 1]$$

Hence, the sequence $\{\int_0^1 f(x)\,dx\}$ is convergent.
Hence, option (c) is correct.

(d) Since, each $f_n'(x)$ is Riemann integrable. Hence,

$$\int_0^1 f_n'(x)\,dx = \int_0^1 f'(x)\,dx$$

$$= \int_0^1 0\,dx$$

$$= 0$$

$$\therefore \lim_{n\to\infty} \int_0^1 f_n'(x)\,dx = \lim_{n\to\infty} 0 = 0, \forall\, x \in [0, 1]$$

Hence, the sequence $\{\int_0^1 f_n'(x)\,dx\}$ is convergent.
Hence, option (d) is correct.

**66.** (d) We have continuous functions $f : [0, \infty) \to \mathbb{R}$ and $g : [0, \infty) \to \mathbb{R}$

Satisfying $\displaystyle\int_0^{f(x)} t^2\,dt = x^3(1+x)^2$ ...(i)

and $\displaystyle\int_0^{x^2(1+x)} g(t)\,dt = x$ ...(ii)

$\forall x \in [0, \infty)$

Then, from Eq. (i), we get

$$\left[\frac{t^3}{3}\right]_0^{f(x)} = x^3(1+x)^2$$

$$\Rightarrow \frac{[f(x)]^3}{3} = x^3(1+x)^2$$

Putting $x = 2$, we get

$$[f(2)]^3 = 3 \cdot 2^3 \cdot (1+2)^2$$

$$\Rightarrow [f(2)]^3 = 216$$

$$\Rightarrow f(2) = 6 \qquad \text{...(iii)}$$

Now, from Eq. (ii), we have

$$\frac{g[x^2(1+x)]}{3x^2 + 2x} = 1 \qquad \text{...(iv)}$$

(differentiating both sides by Leibnitz rule)

Let $\quad x^2(1+x) = 2$

$\Rightarrow \quad x^2 + x^3 = 2$

$\Rightarrow \quad x = 1$

$\therefore$ Putting $x = 1$ in Eq. (iv), we get

$$\frac{g[1^2[1+1]]}{3\cdot 1^2 + 2\cdot 1} = 1 \Rightarrow g(2) = 5 \qquad \ldots(v)$$

Adding Eqs. (iii) and (v), we get

$$f(2) + g(2) = 6 + 5 = 11$$

Hence, option (d) is correct.

**67.** (a,b) We have,

$f : \mathbb{R}^2 \to \mathbb{R}$ defined by

$$f(x, y) = \frac{x^2 y}{x^2 + y^2}, (x, y) \neq (0, 0)$$

and $\quad f(0, 0) = 0$

(a) $$\left(\frac{\partial f}{\partial x}\right)_{(0,0)} = \lim_{h\to 0} \frac{f(0+h, 0) - f(0,0)}{h}$$

$$= \lim_{h\to 0} \frac{f(h, 0) - f(0,0)}{h}$$

$$= \lim_{h\to 0} \frac{f(h, 0)}{h}$$

$$= \lim_{h\to 0} 0 = 0$$

$\therefore \frac{\partial f}{\partial x}$ exists at (0, 0).

$$\left(\frac{\partial f}{\partial y}\right)_{(0,0)} = \lim_{k\to 0} \frac{f(0, 0+k) - f(0,0)}{k}$$

$$= \lim_{k\to 0} \frac{f(0, k) - f(0,0)}{k}$$

$$= \lim_{k\to 0} \frac{f(0, k)}{k}$$

$$= \lim_{k\to 0} 0 = 0$$

$\therefore \frac{\partial f}{\partial y}$ exists at (0, 0).

Therefore, both the partial derivative of $f$ exists at (0, 0).

Hence, option (a) is correct.

(b) $\partial \bar{u}\, f(0, 0) = f(\bar{c}, \bar{u})$

$$= \lim_{h\to 0} \frac{f(\bar{c} + h\bar{u}) - f(\bar{c})}{h}$$

$$= \lim_{h\to 0} \frac{f((0,0) + h(a_1, a_2)) - f(0,0)}{h}$$

$$= \lim_{h\to 0} \frac{f(ha_1, ha_2) - f(0,0)}{h}$$

$$= \lim_{h\to 0} \frac{f(ha_1, ha_2)}{h}$$

$$= \lim_{h\to 0} \frac{h^2 a_1^2 \cdot ha_2}{h(h^2 a_1^2 + h^2 a_2^2)}$$

$$= \lim_{h\to 0} \frac{a_1^2 a_2}{a_1^2 + a_2^2}$$

$$= \frac{a_1^2 a_2}{a_1^2 + a_2^2}$$

***Case* I** When $a_1 = 0$, $a_2 = 1$, we have $\partial \bar{u} = 0$ exists.

***Case* II** When $a_1 = 1$, $a_2 = 0$, we have $\partial \bar{u} = 0$ exists.

Hence, the directional derivative $\partial \bar{u}\, f(0,0)$ of $f$ at (0. 0) exists for every unit vector $\bar{u}$.

Hence, option (b) is correct.

(c) Taking $y = mx^2$. Then

$$\lim_{(x,y)\to(0,0)} \frac{x^2 y}{x^4 + y^2}$$

$$= \lim_{(x,y)\to(0,0)} \frac{x^2 \cdot mx^2}{x^4 + m^2 x^4}$$

$$= \lim_{(x,y)\to(0,0)} \frac{m}{1+m^2}$$

which depends on $m$.

$\therefore \lim_{(x,y)\to(0,0)} f(x, y)$ does not exists. Hence, $f(x, y)$ is not continuous at (0, 0).

Hence, option (c) is incorrect.

(d) Since, $f$ is not continuous at (0, 0). Hence, $f$ is not differentiable at (0, 0).

Hence, option (d) is incorrect.

**68.** (b,d) We have

$$f : \mathbb{R}^2 \to \mathbb{R}$$

and $\quad g : \mathbb{R}^2 \to \mathbb{R}$

defined by $\quad f(x, y) = |x| + |y|$

and $\quad g(x, y) = |xy|$

Now, $\quad |f(x, y) - 0|$

$$= ||x| + |y|| \leq |x| + |y|$$

$$= |x - 0| + |y - 0|$$

take $\quad \delta = \frac{\varepsilon}{1+1} = \frac{\varepsilon}{2}$

$\therefore$ for $\varepsilon > 0$, $\exists\, \delta = \frac{\varepsilon}{2}$ such that

$$|f(x, y) - 0| < \varepsilon$$

whenever $0 < |x - 0| < \delta = \frac{\varepsilon}{2}$

$$0 < |y - 0| < \delta = \frac{\varepsilon}{2}$$

Also, $\lim_{(x,y)\to(0,0)} f(x, y)$

$= \lim_{(x,y)\to(0,0)} |x|+|y|$

$= |0|+|0| = 0$

$\therefore = f(0, 0)$

Hence, $f$ is continuous at (0, 0).

Next, $|g(x, y) - 0|$

$= ||xy| - 0|$

$= |xy|$

$= |x||y|$

$= |x - 0||y - 0|$

$\therefore$ take $\delta = \sqrt{\frac{\varepsilon}{1}} = \sqrt{\varepsilon}$

$\therefore$ for given $\varepsilon > 0$, $\exists\, \delta > 0$ such that $|g(x, y) - 0| < \varepsilon$, whenever

$$0 < |x - 0| < \delta = \sqrt{\varepsilon}$$
$$0 < |y - 0| < \delta = \sqrt{\varepsilon}$$

Also, $\lim_{(x,y)\to(0,0)} g(x, y)$

$= \lim_{(x,y)\to(0,0)} |(x, y)| = 0$

$= g(0, 0)$

$\therefore g(x, y)$ is continuous at (0, 0).

Hence, option (d) is correct.

Next, $f(0 + h, 0 + k) - f(0, 0)$

$= |h| + |k|$

$= 0 \cdot h + 0 \cdot k + h \cdot \frac{|h|}{h} + k \cdot \frac{|k|}{k}$

$\therefore \phi_1(h, k) = \frac{|h|}{h}$

$\phi_2(h, k) = \frac{|k|}{k}$

Now, $\lim_{(h,k)\to(0,0)} \phi(h, k) = \lim_{(h,k)\to(0,0)} \frac{|h|}{h}$ does not exists.

Also, $\lim_{(h,k)\to(0,0)} \frac{|k|}{k}$ does not exists.

Hence, $f$ is not differentiable at (0, 0).

Next, $g(0 + h, 0 + k) - g(0, 0) = |hk|$

$= 0 \cdot \alpha + 0 \cdot \beta + \sqrt{h^2 + k^2} \cdot \frac{|hk|}{\sqrt{h^2 + k^2}}$

$\therefore \phi(h, k) = \frac{|hk|}{\sqrt{h^2 + k^2}}$

Now, $\lim_{(h,k)\to(0,0)} \phi(h, k)$

$= \lim_{(h,k)\to(0,0)} \frac{|hk|}{\sqrt{h^2 + k^2}}$

Let us approaches (0, 0) along $k = mh$, we get

$$\lim_{(h,k)\to(0,0)} \frac{h^2\,|m|}{h\sqrt{1+m^2}} = 0, \text{ exists}$$

Hence, $g$ is differentiable at (0, 0) and

$$g_x = 0, g_y = 0$$

Hence, options (b) and (d) are correct.

**69.** (a,b,d)

**70.** (a,c,d)

**71.** (b,c,d) Given subset $A$ and $B$ of $\mathbb{R}^2$ are

$$A = \left\{\left(x, x \sin\frac{1}{x}\right) : x \in (0, 1]\right\}$$

and $B = A \cup \{0, 0\}$

(a) Limit point of $A = \{0,0\}$, which does not belong to set $A$. Hence, $A$ is not compact.
Hence, option (a) is incorrect.

(b) $A$ is connected subset of $\mathbb{R}^2$.
Hence, option (b) is correct.

(c) Since, $B$ contains the limit point {(0, 0)}. Hence, $B$ is compact.
Hence, option (c) is correct.

(d) $B$ is connected subset of $\mathbb{R}^2$.
Hence, option (d) is correct.

**72.** (a,b,c,d) Let $f : \mathbb{R} \to \mathbb{R}$ is continuous and $U \subseteq \mathbb{R}$ is an open set. Then

$$f^{-1}(U) = \{x \in \mathbb{R} : f(x) \in \mathbb{R}\}$$

Now, if $f^{-1}(U) = \phi$, then it is open set

if $f^{-1}(U) \neq \phi$

Let $x \in f^{-1}(U)$

$\Rightarrow f(x) \in U$

$\Rightarrow \exists \delta > 0$ such that

$f(x) \in S_\delta(f(x)) \subseteq U$

Now, since $f$ is continuous $\exists \varepsilon > 0$ such that

$f(S_\varepsilon(x)) \subseteq S_\delta(f(x)) \subseteq U$

$\Rightarrow x \in S_\varepsilon(x) \subseteq f^{-1}(U)$

$\Rightarrow f^{-1}(U)$ is open set.

Hence, option (a) is correct.

Similarly, if $f : \mathbb{R} \to \mathbb{R}$ is continuous map, then $f^{-1}(C)$ is closed for all closed sets $C \subseteq \mathbb{R}$.

Hence, option (b) is correct.

Also, if $f$ is continuous map. Then $f^{-1}(K)$ is compact for all compact subset $K \subseteq \mathbb{R}$.

Hence, option (c) is correct.

Also, if $f$ is continuous map. Then $f^{-1}(G)$ is connected for all connected sets $G \subseteq \mathbb{R}$.

Hence, option (d) is correct.

**73.** (a,c,d)

**74.** (b,d) Given real matrices $A, B$ and $C$ of $n \times n$ order such that

$$AB + B^2 = C \quad \ldots(i)$$

where $C$ is non-singular matrix.

$\therefore \quad |AB + B^2| = |C|$

$\Rightarrow \quad |B||A + B| = |C| \neq 0 \quad (\because C \text{ is non-singular})$

$\Rightarrow \quad |B| \neq 0, |A + B| \neq 0$

$\Rightarrow B$ and $A + B$ are non-singular matrices.

Hence, options (b) and (d) are correct.

**75.** (a,b,c) Given that $\{x_1, x_2, x_3\}$ is a basis of vector space $V$.

(a) Consider $\alpha(x_1 + x_2) + \beta x_2 + \gamma x_3 = 0$

$\Rightarrow \quad \alpha x_1 + (\alpha + \beta) x_2 + \gamma x_3 = 0$

$\Rightarrow \quad \alpha = 0, \alpha + \beta = 0, \gamma = 0$

$(\because \{x_1, x_2, x_3\}$ is basis of $V)$

$\Rightarrow \quad \alpha = 0, \beta = 0, \gamma = 0$

Hence, the set $\{x_1 + x_2, x_2, x_3\}$ is linearly independent.

Let $X \in V$. Then $\exists\, \alpha_1, \alpha_2, \alpha_3$ such that

$$X = \alpha_1 x_1 + \alpha_2 x_2 + \alpha_3 x_3 \quad \ldots(i)$$

$\{\because \{x_1, x_2, x_3\}$ is basis of $V\}$

Let there exists $\beta_1, \beta_2, \beta_3$ such that

$$X = \beta_1(x_1 + x_2) + \beta_2 x_2 + \beta_3 x_3 \quad \ldots(ii)$$

From Eqs. (i) and (ii), we get

$$\beta_1(x_1 + x_2) + \beta_2 x_2 + \beta_3 x_3 = \alpha_1 x_1 + \alpha_2 x_2 + \alpha_3 x_3$$

$\Rightarrow \quad \beta_1 = \alpha_1, \beta_1 + \beta_2 = \alpha_2, \beta_3 = \alpha_3$

$\Rightarrow \quad \beta_1 = \alpha_1, \beta_2 = \alpha_2 - \alpha_1, \beta_3 = \alpha_3$

Thus, $X \in V$ can be expressed as a linear combination of elements of the set $\{x_1 + x_2, x_2, x_3\}$ which is linearly independent. Hence, the set $\{x_1 + x_2, x_2, x_3\}$ is a basis of $V$.

Hence, option (a) is correct.

(b) Since, the number of linearly independent vector in the basis of $V$ is 3. Hence, dimension of $V$ is 3. Hence, option (b) is correct.

(c) Since, the elements of the basis are pairwise orthogonal. Hence, $x_1, x_2, x_3$ are pairwise orthogonal.

Hence, option (c) is correct.

(d) Since, $(x_1 - x_2) + (x_2 - x_3) = x_1 - x_3$.

Hence, $\{x_1 - x_2, x_2 - x_3, x_1 - x_3\}$ is linearly dependent. Hence, does not form a basis of $V$.

Hence, option (d) is incorrect.

**76.** (b,c,d) We have, a system of $m$ linear equations in $n$ unknowns given by

$$Ax = b$$

where $A = (a_{ij})$ is a real $m \times n$ matirx, $x$ and $b$ are $n \times 1$ column vectors.

Then $Ax = b$ has atleast one solution if $b = 0$ namely trivial solution.

Hence, option (b) is correct.

If $m = n$ and $\rho(A) = n$, then

$$\rho(A) = \rho(A : b) = m = n$$

Hence, the system has unique solution.

Hence, option (c) is correct.

Also, if $m < n$ and

$$\rho(A) = \rho(A : b)$$

Then, the system of equation has infinitely many solutions.

Hence, option (d) is correct.

**77.** (b,d) Given that $V$ be the set of all real $n \times m$ matrices $A = (a_{ij})$ with the property that

$$a_{ij} = -a_{ji}, \forall\, i, j = 1, 2, \ldots, n$$

Then, by putting $i = j$, we get

$$a_{ij} = -a_{ij}$$

$\Rightarrow \quad 2a_{ij} = 0$

$\Rightarrow \quad a_{ij} = 0, \forall\, i = 1, 2, \ldots, n$

$V = \{A : a_{ij} = -a_{ji}, \forall i \neq j \text{ and } a_{ij} = 0, \forall i = j\}$

$\therefore \quad \dim V = \dfrac{n^2 - n}{2}$

Hence, options (b) and (d) are correct.

**78.** (a) Given that, $W$ be the set of all $3 \times 3$ real matrices $A = (a_{ij})$ with the property that

$$a_{ij} = 0, \forall\, i > j$$

and $\quad a_{ij} = 1, \forall\, i$

and $\quad B = (b_{ij})$ be $3 \times 3$ real matrix such that

$$AB = BA, \forall\, A \in W.$$

Let $\quad A = \begin{bmatrix} 1 & a_{12} & a_{13} \\ 0 & 1 & a_{23} \\ 0 & 0 & 1 \end{bmatrix}$

$\therefore \quad |A| = 1 \neq 0$

$\therefore \quad$ Inverse of $A$ exists.

$\therefore \quad A_{11} = (-1)^{1+1}\begin{vmatrix} 1 & a_{23} \\ 0 & 1 \end{vmatrix} = 1$

$$A_{12} = (-1)^{1+2}\begin{vmatrix} 0 & a_{23} \\ 0 & 1 \end{vmatrix} = 0$$

$$A_{13} = (-1)^{1+3}\begin{vmatrix} 0 & 1 \\ 0 & 0 \end{vmatrix} = 0$$

$$A_{21} = (-1)^{2+1}\begin{vmatrix} a_{12} & a_{13} \\ 0 & 1 \end{vmatrix} = -a_{12}$$

$$A_{22} = (-1)^{2+2}\begin{vmatrix} 1 & a_{13} \\ 0 & 1 \end{vmatrix} = 1$$

$$A_{23} = (-1)^{2+3}\begin{vmatrix} 1 & a_{12} \\ 0 & 0 \end{vmatrix} = 0$$

$$A_{31} = (-i)^{3+1}\begin{vmatrix} a_{12} & a_{13} \\ 1 & a_{23} \end{vmatrix} = a_{12}a_{23} - a_{13}$$

$$a_{32} = (-1)^{3+2}\begin{vmatrix} 1 & a_{13} \\ 0 & a_{23} \end{vmatrix} = -a_{23}$$

$$a_{33} = (-1)^{3+3}\begin{vmatrix} 1 & a_{12} \\ 0 & 1 \end{vmatrix} = 1$$

∴ Coefficient matrix of $A$ is

$$\begin{bmatrix} A_{11} & A_{12} & A_{13} \\ A_{21} & A_{22} & A_{23} \\ A_{31} & A_{32} & A_{33} \end{bmatrix} = \begin{bmatrix} 1 & 0 & 0 \\ -a_{12} & 1 & 0 \\ a_{12}a_{23} - a_{13} & -a_{23} & 1 \end{bmatrix}$$

$$\therefore \quad \text{adj}(A) = \begin{bmatrix} 1 & -a_{12} & a_{12}a_{23} - a_{13} \\ 0 & 1 & -a_{23} \\ 0 & 0 & 1 \end{bmatrix}$$

$$\therefore \quad A^{-1} = \frac{\text{adj}(A)}{|A|} = \begin{bmatrix} 1 & -a_{12} & a_{12}a_{23} - a_{13} \\ 0 & 1 & -a_{23} \\ 0 & 0 & 1 \end{bmatrix}$$

$$\Rightarrow \quad A^{-1} \in W$$

Hence, option (a) is correct.

Consider $A = \begin{bmatrix} 1 & 1 & 1 \\ 0 & 1 & 1 \\ 0 & 0 & 1 \end{bmatrix}$

and $B = \begin{bmatrix} 1 & 1 & 1 \\ 0 & 1 & 1 \\ 0 & 0 & 1 \end{bmatrix}$

Then, $AB = \begin{bmatrix} 1 & 1 & 1 \\ 0 & 1 & 1 \\ 0 & 0 & 1 \end{bmatrix}\begin{bmatrix} 1 & 1 & 1 \\ 0 & 1 & 1 \\ 0 & 0 & 1 \end{bmatrix}$

$$= \begin{bmatrix} 1 & 2 & 3 \\ 0 & 1 & 2 \\ 0 & 0 & 1 \end{bmatrix}$$

and $BA = \begin{bmatrix} 1 & 1 & 1 \\ 0 & 1 & 1 \\ 0 & 0 & 1 \end{bmatrix}\begin{bmatrix} 1 & 1 & 1 \\ 0 & 1 & 1 \\ 0 & 0 & 1 \end{bmatrix}$

$$= \begin{bmatrix} 1 & 2 & 3 \\ 0 & 1 & 2 \\ 0 & 0 & 1 \end{bmatrix}$$

but $b_{12} = 1, b_{13} = 1, b_{23} = 1$

Hence, options (b), (c), (d) are incorrect.

**79.** (b,c)

**80.** (a,d)

**81.** (b,c) We have,

$$f(z) = \frac{\sin z}{z^2} - \frac{\cos z}{z}$$

Since, $\lim_{z\to 0}(z-0)\cdot\frac{\sin z}{z^2}$

$$= \lim_{z\to 0}\frac{\sin z}{z}$$

$$= 1 \neq 0$$

and $\lim_{z\to 0}(z-0)\frac{\cos z}{z}$

$$= \lim_{z\to 0}\cos z$$

$$= 1 \neq 0$$

Hence, $f(z)$ has simple pole at $z = 0$

Hence, option (b) is correct.

Now, $\int_{|z|=1} f(z)\,dz$

$$= \int_{|z|=1}\frac{\sin z}{z^2}dz - \int_{|z|=1}\frac{\cos z}{z}dz$$

$$= 2\pi i g'(0) \quad 2\pi i h(0)$$

(where

$g(z) = \sin z$

$\Rightarrow \quad g'(z) = \cos z$

$\Rightarrow \quad g'(0) = \cos 0 = 1$

and

$h(z) = \cos z$

$\therefore \quad h(0) = \cos 0 = 1)$

$$= 2\pi i \times 1 - 2\pi i \times 1$$

$$= 0$$

Hence, option (c) is correct.

Now, since $z = 0$ is a simple pole.

Hence,

$$\text{Res } f(0) = \lim_{z\to 0}(z-0)f(z)$$

$$= \lim_{z\to 0} z\left[\frac{\sin z}{z^2} - \frac{\cos z}{z}\right]$$

$$= \lim_{z \to 0} \left[ \frac{\sin z}{z} - \cos z \right]$$

$$= \lim_{z \to 0} \frac{\sin z}{z} - \lim_{z \to 0} \cos z$$

$$= 1 - 1$$

$$= 0$$

Hence, option (d) is incorrect.

**82.** (c,d)

**83.** (b,c) We know that

$$\phi(1) = 1$$
$$\phi(2) = 1$$
$$\phi(3) = 2$$
$$\phi(4) = 2$$
$$\phi(5) = 4$$
$$\vdots$$
$$\phi(n) = \text{even number}$$

Hence, $\phi(n)$ is odd for only two values of $n$.

Hence, option (b) is correct.

$\phi(n)$ is even when $n > 2$.

Hence, option (c) is correct.

**84.** (b,c,d) Let $p$ be a prime number and $d/(p-1)$. Then

$$X^d \equiv 1 \pmod{p}$$

has exactly $d$ incongruent solution.

Hence, options (b), (c), (d) are correct.

**85.** (b,c,d) Since, $L$ is an extension of field $K$ and $M$ is an extension of field $L$. Hence,

$$[M:K] = [M:L]\,[L:K].$$

Hence, option (b) is correct.

$\Rightarrow$ $[M:L]$ divides $[M:K]$.

Hence, option (c) is correct.

and $[L:K]$ divides $[M:K]$.

Hence, option (d) is correct.

**86.** (a,d)

(a) By Gauss Theorem. If $R$ is unique factorization domain, then $R[x]$ is also a unique factorization domain.
Hence, option (a) is correct.

(b) Since, $Z$ is principle ideal domain but $Z[x]$ is not principle ideal domain because $Z$ is not field. Hence, option (b) is incorrect.

(c) $(Z, ||)$, where $||$ is the absolute value map) is an Euclidean domain but $Z[x]$ is not Euclidean domain as $Z[x]$ is not principle ideal domain.
Hence, option (c) is incorrect.

(d) Every field $\mathbb{R}$ is an Euclidean domain with respect to a $\delta$ defined by $\delta(a) = 1, \forall\, a \neq 0$. Hence, $R[x]$ is also Euclidean domain.
Hence, option (d) is correct.

**87.** (a,d) We have

$$o(G) = 56 = 2^3 \times 7$$

$\therefore$ No. of 7-sylow subgroup

$$= \text{value of } k \text{ for which } 1 + 7k/2$$
$$= 1$$

$\therefore$ 7-sylow subgroup in group by order 56 is unique.
Hence, normal in $G$.

But no. of 2-sylow subgroup

$$= \text{value of } k \text{ for which } 1 + 2k/7$$
$$= 2$$

$\therefore$ 2-sylow subgroup may or may not be normal in $G$.

Hence, options (a) and (d) are correct.

**88.** (a,d) The exponent of 2 in 50!

$$= \left[\frac{50}{2}\right] + \left[\frac{50}{2^2}\right] + \left[\frac{50}{2^3}\right] + \left[\frac{50}{2^4}\right] + \left[\frac{50}{2^5}\right]$$

$$= 25 + 12 + 6 + 3 + 1 = 47$$

The exponent of 5 in 50!

$$= \left[\frac{50}{5}\right] + \left[\frac{50}{5^2}\right]$$

$$= 10 + 2 = 12$$

Therefore, $50! = 2^{47} \times 5^{12} \times 3^a \times 7^b \times \ldots$

$$= 2^{35} \times (10)^{12} \times 3^a \times 7^b \times \ldots$$

Therefore, the number of zeros at the end of 50! is same as the exponent of 10, which is 12 (even).

Hence, options (a) and (d) are correct.

**89.** (b,c)

(a) We know that a square of unit length is homeomorphic to a circle radius 1. Hence, $X$ is homeomorphic to $Y$.
Hence, option (a) is incorrect.

(b) $Y$ is not homeomorphic to $Z$ because $Y$ has only one connected component while $Z$ has two connected component.
Hence, option (b) is correct.

(c) $X$ is not homeomorphic to $Z$ because $X$ has only one connected component while $Z$ has two connected component.
Hence, option (c) is correct.

(d) Since, $X$ and $Y$ are homeomorphic.
Hence, option (d) is incorrect.

**90.** (b,c)

**91.** (b,c) Given initial value problem is

$$\dot{x}(t) = 3x^{2/3},\ x(0) = 0 \quad \text{...(i)}$$

Then, $\frac{dx(t)}{dt} = 3x^{2/3}$

$\Rightarrow \frac{dx}{x^{2/3}} = 3\,dt$

$\Rightarrow x^{-2/3}\,dx = 3\,dt$

On integration, we get

$3x^{1/3} = 3t + C$

Now, $x(0) = 0$, gives

$0 = 0 + C$

$\Rightarrow C = 0$

$\therefore$ Solution of Eq. (i) is

$3x^{1/3} = 3t$

$\Rightarrow \sqrt[3]{x} = t$

Which is unique around $t = 0$.

Hence, options (b), (c) are correct.

**92.** (a,b,c) Given system of equation is

$$\frac{d}{dt}\begin{pmatrix} x_1(t) \\ x_2(t) \end{pmatrix} = \begin{bmatrix} 0 & -1 \\ 1 & 0 \end{bmatrix}\begin{bmatrix} x_1(t) \\ x_2(t) \end{bmatrix}$$

can be written as

$$\frac{d}{dt}X(t) = AX(t)$$

where $A = \begin{bmatrix} 0 & -1 \\ 1 & 0 \end{bmatrix}$ and $X(t) = \begin{bmatrix} x_1(t) \\ x_2(t) \end{bmatrix}$

Now, characteristic equation of $A$ is

$|A - \lambda I| = 0$

$\Rightarrow \begin{vmatrix} 0-\lambda & -1 \\ 1 & 0-\lambda \end{vmatrix} = 0$

$\Rightarrow \lambda^2 + 1 = 0$

$\Rightarrow \lambda = \pm i$

Hence, eigen values of the coefficient matrix are complex conjugate.

Now, take $\lambda = i$. Then,

$[A - \lambda I]\,X(t) = \begin{bmatrix} 0 \\ 0 \end{bmatrix}$

$\Rightarrow \begin{bmatrix} -i & -1 \\ 1 & -i \end{bmatrix}\begin{bmatrix} x_1(t) \\ x_2(t) \end{bmatrix} = \begin{bmatrix} 0 \\ 0 \end{bmatrix}$

$\Rightarrow -i\,x_1(t) - x_2(t) = 0$

$x_1(t)\ i\,x_2(t) = 0$

$\Rightarrow x_1(t) = i\,x_2(t)$

$\therefore$ Eigen vector corresponding to eigen value $\lambda = i$ is

$v = \begin{bmatrix} 1 \\ -i \end{bmatrix} = \begin{bmatrix} 1+0i \\ 0-1i \end{bmatrix}$

$\therefore \quad v_1 = \begin{bmatrix} 1 \\ 0 \end{bmatrix}, v = \begin{bmatrix} 0 \\ -1 \end{bmatrix}$

Hence, the solution is

$$X_c(t) = [c_1\,(u_1 \cos bt - u_2 \sin bt) + c_2\,(v_2 \cos bt - v_1 \sin bt)]\,e^{at}$$

$$= \left[c_1\left\{\begin{bmatrix} 1 \\ 0 \end{bmatrix}\cos t - \begin{bmatrix} 0 \\ -1 \end{bmatrix}\sin t\right\} + c_2\left\{\begin{bmatrix} 0 \\ -1 \end{bmatrix}\cos t + \begin{bmatrix} 1 \\ 0 \end{bmatrix}\sin t\right\}\right]e^{0t}$$

$$= c_1\left\{\begin{bmatrix} \cos t \\ 0 \end{bmatrix} - \begin{bmatrix} 0 \\ -\sin t \end{bmatrix}\right\} + c_2\left\{\begin{bmatrix} 0 \\ -\cos t \end{bmatrix} + \begin{bmatrix} \sin t \\ 0 \end{bmatrix}\right\}$$

$$= c_1\begin{bmatrix} \cos t \\ -\sin t \end{bmatrix} + c_2\begin{bmatrix} \sin t \\ -\cos t \end{bmatrix}$$

Next, take $\lambda = -i$, then

$[A - \lambda I]\,[X(t)] = \begin{bmatrix} 0 \\ 0 \end{bmatrix}$

$\Rightarrow \begin{bmatrix} i & -1 \\ 1 & i \end{bmatrix}\begin{bmatrix} x_1(t) \\ x_2(t) \end{bmatrix} = \begin{bmatrix} 0 \\ 0 \end{bmatrix}$

$\Rightarrow i x_1(t) - x_2(t) = 0$

$x_1(t) + i x_2(t) = 0$

$\Rightarrow i x_1(t) = x_2(t)$

Therefore, the eigen vector corresponding to eigen value $\lambda = -i$ is

$v = \begin{bmatrix} 1 \\ i \end{bmatrix} = \begin{bmatrix} 1+0i \\ 0+1i \end{bmatrix}$

Hence,, $v_1 = \begin{bmatrix} 1 \\ 0 \end{bmatrix}, v_2 = \begin{bmatrix} 0 \\ 1 \end{bmatrix}$

Hence, the solution of the system of differential equation is

$$X_c(t) = [c_1\,(v_1 \cos bt - v_2 \sin bt) + c_2\,(u_2 \cos bt + u_1 \sin bt)]\,e^{at}$$

$$= \left[c_1\left\{\begin{bmatrix} 1 \\ 0 \end{bmatrix}\cos(-t) - \begin{bmatrix} 0 \\ 1 \end{bmatrix}\sin(-t)\right\} + c_2\left\{\begin{bmatrix} 0 \\ 1 \end{bmatrix}\cos(-t) - \begin{bmatrix} 1 \\ 0 \end{bmatrix}\sin(-t)\right\}\right]e^{0t}$$

$$= c_1\left\{\begin{bmatrix} \cos t \\ 0 \end{bmatrix} - \begin{bmatrix} 0 \\ -\sin t \end{bmatrix}\right\} + c_2\left\{\begin{bmatrix} 0 \\ \cos t \end{bmatrix} + \begin{bmatrix} -\sin t \\ 0 \end{bmatrix}\right\}$$

$$= c_1\begin{bmatrix} \cos t \\ \sin t \end{bmatrix} + c_2\begin{bmatrix} \sin t \\ \cos t \end{bmatrix}$$

Thus, both solutions for $\lambda = i$ and $\lambda = -i$ are bounded and periodic.

Hence, options (a), (b) and (c) are correct.

**93.** (a,b,d) **94.** (a,d) **95.** (a,b,c)

**96.** (a,d) Given functional is

$$I[x] = \int_a^b \left(\frac{1}{2} m(\dot{x})^2 - cx^2\right) dt \quad \text{...(i)}$$

$$\therefore \quad F(t, x, \dot{x}) = \frac{1}{2} m(\dot{x})^2 - cx^2$$

$$\therefore \quad \frac{\partial F}{\partial x} = -2cx$$

$$\frac{\partial F}{\partial \dot{x}} = m\dot{x}$$

∴ Euler's Lagrange's equation is

$$\frac{\partial F}{\partial x} - \frac{d}{dt}\left(\frac{\partial F}{\partial \dot{x}}\right) = 0$$

$$\Rightarrow \quad -2cx - \frac{d}{dt}(m\dot{x}) = 0$$

$$\Rightarrow \quad -2cx - m\ddot{x} = 0$$

$$\Rightarrow \quad m\ddot{x} + 2cx = 0 \quad \text{...(ii)}$$

Hence, option (a) is correct.

Now, auxiliary equation of Eq. (ii) is

$$m\lambda^2 + 2c = 0$$

$$\Rightarrow \quad \lambda = \pm\sqrt{\frac{2c}{m}}\, i$$

$$\therefore \quad X(t) = k_1\left(\sin\frac{\sqrt{2c}}{m} + k_2\right)$$

where $k_1$ and $k_2$ are arbitrary constants.

Hence, option (d) is correct.

**97.** (a,d) Given functional is

$$F(u, v) = \int_0^{\pi/2}\left\{\left(\frac{du}{dx}\right)^2 + \left(\frac{dv}{dx}\right)^2 + 2uv\right\} dx \quad \text{...(i)}$$

which involves two dependent variables. Here,

$$F(x, u, u', v, v') = \left(\frac{du}{dx}\right)^2 + \left(\frac{dv}{dx}\right)^2 + 2uv$$

$$= u'^2 + v'^2 + 2uv \quad \text{...(ii)}$$

$$\therefore \quad \left.\begin{aligned} \frac{\partial F}{\partial u} = 2v, \quad \frac{\partial F}{\partial u'} = 2u' \\ \frac{\partial F}{\partial v} = 2u, \quad \frac{\partial F}{\partial v'} = 2v' \end{aligned}\right\} \quad \text{...(iii)}$$

Therefore, the Euler's Lagrange's equation is

$$\frac{\partial F}{\partial u} - \frac{d}{dx}\left(\frac{\partial F}{\partial u'}\right) = 0 \quad \text{...(iv)}$$

$$\text{and} \quad \frac{\partial F}{\partial v} - \frac{d}{dx}\left(\frac{\partial F}{\partial v'}\right) = 0 \quad \text{...(v)}$$

$$\text{or} \quad 2v - \frac{d}{dx}(2u') = 0$$

$$\text{and} \quad 2u - \frac{d}{dx}(2v') = 0$$

$$\text{or} \quad v - u'' = 0$$

$$u - v'' = 0$$

$$\text{or} \quad u'' - v = 0 \quad \text{...(vi)}$$

$$v'' - u = 0 \quad \text{...(vii)}$$

Now, from Eqs. (vi) and (vii), we get

$$u^{(iv)} - u = 0 \quad \text{...(viii)}$$

The solution of Eq. (viii) is

$$u(x) = c_1e^x + c_2e^{-x} + c_3\cos x + c_4\sin x \quad \text{...(ix)}$$

$$\Rightarrow \quad u'(x) = c_1e^x - c_2e^{-x} - c_3\sin x + c_4\cos x$$

$$\Rightarrow \quad u''(x) = c_1e^x + c_2e^{-x} - c_3\cos x - c_4\sin x \quad \text{...(x)}$$

Now, from Eqs. (vi) and (x), we get

$$v(x) = u''(x) = c_1e^x + c_2e^{-x} - c_3\cos x - c_4\sin x \quad \text{...(xi)}$$

Now, applying given conditions

$$u(0) = 1,\ v(0) = -1,\ u\left(\frac{\pi}{2}\right) = 0$$

and $v\left(\frac{\pi}{2}\right) = 0$. On Eqs. (ix) and (xi), we get

$$1 = c_1 + c_2 + c_3 \quad \text{...(xii)}$$

$$-1 = c_1 + c_2 - c_3 \quad \text{...(xiii)}$$

$$0 = c_1e^{\pi/2} + c_2e^{-\pi/2} + c_4 \quad \text{...(xiv)}$$

$$0 = c_1e^{\pi/2} + c_2e^{-\pi/2} - c_4 \quad \text{...(xv)}$$

On solving Eqs. (xii), (xiii), (xiv) and (xv), we get

$$c_1 = c_2 = c_4 = 0 \text{ and } c_3 = 1$$

Putting these values in Eqs. (ix) and (xi), we get

$$u(x) = \cos x,\ v(x) = -\cos x$$

(a) $u\left(\frac{\pi}{4}\right) + v\left(\frac{\pi}{4}\right) = \cos\left(\frac{\pi}{4}\right) - \cos\left(\frac{\pi}{4}\right)$

$$= \frac{1}{\sqrt{2}} - \frac{1}{\sqrt{2}} = 0$$

Hence, option (a) is correct.

(b) $u\left(\frac{\pi}{3}\right) - v\left(\frac{\pi}{3}\right) = \cos\left(\frac{\pi}{3}\right) + \cos\left(\frac{\pi}{3}\right) = \frac{1}{2} + \frac{1}{2} = 1$

Hence, option (b) is incorrect.

(c) $u\left(\frac{\pi}{4}\right) - v\left(\frac{\pi}{4}\right)$

$$= \cos\left(\frac{\pi}{4}\right) + \cos\left(\frac{\pi}{4}\right) = \frac{1}{\sqrt{2}} + \frac{1}{\sqrt{2}} = \frac{2}{\sqrt{2}} = \sqrt{2}$$

Hence, option (c) is incorrect.

(d) $u\left(\frac{\pi}{3}\right) + v\left(\frac{\pi}{3}\right) = \cos\left(\frac{\pi}{3}\right) - \cos\left(\frac{\pi}{3}\right) = \frac{1}{2} - \frac{1}{2} = 0$

Hence, option (d) is correct.

**98.** (b,c)

**99.** (a,d) The given integral equation is

$$\phi(x) = \frac{5x}{6} + \frac{1}{2}\int_0^1 xt\,\phi(t)\,dt \quad \text{...(i)}$$

$$\Rightarrow \quad \phi(x) = \frac{5x}{6} + \frac{1}{2}cx \quad \text{...(ii)}$$

where, $c = \int_0^1 t\,\phi(t)\,dt$

$$= \int_0^1 t\left[\frac{5t}{6} + \frac{1}{2}ct\right]dt$$

$$= \int_0^1 \left[\frac{5t^2}{6} + \frac{1}{2}ct^2\right]dt$$

$$= \frac{5+3c}{6}\int_0^1 t^2\,dt$$

$$= \left[\frac{5+3c}{6}\right]\left[\frac{t^3}{3}\right]_0^1 = \frac{5+3c}{18}$$

$$\Rightarrow \quad c - \frac{5+3c}{18} = 0$$

$$\Rightarrow \quad \frac{15c-5}{18} = 0 \Rightarrow c = \frac{1}{3}$$

On putting the value of $c$ in Eq. (ii), we get

$$\phi(x) = \frac{5x}{6} + \frac{1}{2}\left(\frac{1}{3}\right)x$$

$$= \frac{5x}{6} + \frac{x}{6} = x$$

$\Rightarrow \phi(x) = x$ is the solution of the given integral Eq. (i).

(a) $\phi(0) + \phi(1) = 0 + 1 = 1$

Hence, option (a) is correct.

(b) $\phi\left(\frac{1}{2}\right) + \phi\left(\frac{1}{3}\right) = \frac{1}{2} + \frac{1}{3} = \frac{5}{6} \neq 1$

Hence, option (b) is incorrect.

(c) $\phi\left(\frac{1}{4}\right) + \phi\left(\frac{1}{2}\right) = \frac{1}{4} + \frac{1}{2} = \frac{3}{4} \neq 1$

Hence, option (c) is incorrect.

(d) $\phi\left(\frac{3}{4}\right) + \phi\left(\frac{1}{4}\right) = \frac{3}{4} + \frac{1}{4} = 1$

Hence, option (d) is correct.

**100.** (a,b,c,d) Given plane curve is

$$xy = 1 \quad \text{...(i)}$$

The parametric equation of Eq. (i) is

$$x = t,\ y = \frac{1}{t}$$

$$\Rightarrow \quad \dot{x} = 1,\ \dot{y} = -\frac{1}{t^2} = -\frac{1}{x^2}$$

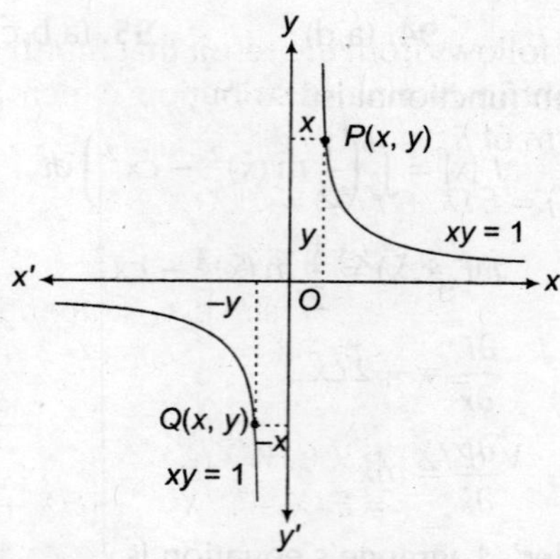


Suppose at time $t_1$ the particle is at $P(x, y)$ and at time $t_2$ the particle is at $Q(x, y)$. Then, kinetic energy of the particle is

$$\text{KE} = \frac{1}{2}(\dot{x}^2 + \dot{y}^2) = \frac{1}{2}\left(1 + \left(-\frac{1}{x^2}\right)^2\right)$$

$$= \frac{1}{2}\left(1 + \frac{1}{x^4}\right) = \frac{1}{2}\dot{x}^2(1 + x^{-1}) = \frac{1}{2}\left(\frac{x^4+1}{x^4}\right)$$

$$(\because \dot{x} = 1)$$

$$= \frac{x^4+1}{2x^4}$$

Hence, option (a) is correct.

The potential energy is $gy = g\cdot\frac{1}{x} = \frac{g}{x}$ $\left(\because y = \frac{1}{x} \text{ given}\right)$

Hence, option (b) is correct.

Now, for Lagrangian of the particle there are two cases arises.

***Case* I** When the particle is moving in first quadrant, then the Lagrangian is

$$L = T - V = \frac{1}{2}\dot{x}^2(1 + x^{-4}) - \frac{g}{x}$$

Hence, option (c) is correct.

***Case* II** When the particle is moving in third quadrant, then the Lagrangian is

$$L = T - V$$

$$= \frac{1}{2}\dot{x}^2(1 + x^{-4}) - \left(-\frac{g}{x}\right) = \frac{1}{2}\dot{x}^2(1 + x^{-4}) + \frac{g}{x}$$

Hence, option (d) is correct.

**101.** (b,d)

**102.** (a,c,d) Result (d) follows from (a) and result (b) is given by

$$E\left(\left(\frac{n}{2}\right)^{-1}\frac{1}{2}\sum_{i,j}^{n}(x_i - x_j)^2\right)$$

$$= \frac{1}{n(n-1)}[n(n-1)E(x_i^2) - n(n-1)E(x_i x_j)]$$

$$= [(\sigma^2 + \mu^2) - \mu^2] = \sigma^2$$

**103.** (a,b,d) (d) follows from the result that fourth moment is constant in Normal distribution which appears in the term of $S_n^2$.

**104.** (a) $E(Z/X) = E(X + Y/X) = E(X/X + Y/X)$

$$= E(X/X) + E(Y/X) = X + E(Y)$$

(since $X$, $Y$ are independent)

$$= X + \frac{m+1}{2}$$

and $V(Z/X) = V(X + Y/X)$

$$= E(X + Y/X)^2 + \{E(X + Y/X)\}^2$$

$$= E(X^2/X + Y^2/X + 2XY/X) - \left(X + \frac{M+1}{2}\right)^2$$

$$= X^2 + E(Y^2) + 2XE(Y) - \left(X + \frac{M+1}{2}\right)^2$$

$$= X^2 + \frac{1}{6}(m+1)(2M+1) + 2X\frac{(M+1)}{2}$$

$$- X^2 - \frac{(M+1)^2}{4} - \frac{2X(M+1)}{2} = \frac{m^2-1}{12}$$

In a similar way, $V(Z/Y) = 1$

Hence, option (a) is correct.

**105.** (a,b)

**106.** (c,d) According to Markov's Inequality

$$P(|X| \geq \varepsilon) \leq \frac{E(X^2)}{\varepsilon^2}$$

So, $$P(|X + 2Y| \geq 4) \leq \frac{E(X + 2Y)^2}{4^2}$$

$$= \frac{E(X^2 + 4Y^2 + 4XY)}{16} = \frac{1 + 4 + 4 \times 0.25}{16}$$

$$= \frac{6}{16}$$

(d) follows from (c).

Hence, options (c) and (d) are correct.

**107.** (a,c,d) (d) follows from the property that mean of MLE's is also MLE.

**108.** (c)

**109.** (a,b) The two options are correct from properties of multivariate chi-square distribution.

Hence, options (a) and (b) are correct.

**110.** (b) The best test for testing equality of distributions is Kolmogorov-Smirnov test.

Hence, option (b) is correct.

**111.** (d) The least squares linear regression equation of $Y$ on $X$ is

$$y - \bar{y} = r\frac{\sigma_y}{\sigma_x}(x - \bar{x})$$

and the linear equation of $X$ on $Y$ is

$$x - \bar{x} = r\frac{\sigma_x}{\sigma_y}(y - \bar{y})$$

Hence, results follows.

**Note** (a) is true only if $Y$ is normal. In that case

$$E(Y/X) = \mu_y + r\frac{\sigma_y}{\sigma_x}(x - \mu_x)$$

and $$V(Y/X) = \sigma_Y^2(1 - \rho^2)$$

Hence, option (d) is correct.

**112.** (b,c) The likelihood function of $p$ based on $X$ is given by

$$L(x; p) = \binom{5}{x} p^x (1-p)^x = 5p^4(1-p)^1$$

given that $x = 4$

therefore the posterior distribution of $p$ is

$$f(p) = k(p^4(1-p))\left(\frac{p^{2-1}(1-p)^{3-1}}{B(2,3)}\right)$$

$k$ is chosen such that $f(p)$ be a pdf.

$$\Rightarrow f(p) = kp^5(1-p)^3$$

$$\Rightarrow f(p) = \frac{1}{B(6,4)} p^{6-1}(1-p)^{4-1}$$

So, $f(p)$ is beta density $B(6, 4)$ with mean $\dfrac{\alpha}{\alpha+\beta}$

*i.e.*, 6/10

**113.** (a,b,c,d)

**114.** (c) The characteristic function of $Z$ is, $\exp(itz)$

$$ch(z) = E(e^{itz})$$

$$= E(e^{ity}/X = 0)\,P(X = 0)$$

$$+ E(e^{itN}/X = 1)\,P(X = 1)$$

$$= \frac{1}{2}e^{-\lambda(1-e^{it})} + \frac{1}{2}e^{-\frac{t^2}{2}}$$

Hence, option (c) is correct.

**115.** (b) $P$(*i*th unit included) $= 1 - P$(*i*th unit is not included in any draw)

$$= 1 - \left(1 - \frac{1}{N}\right)\left(1 - \frac{1}{N}\right)\ldots n \text{ times}$$

$$= 1 - \left(1 - \frac{1}{N}\right)^n$$

Hence, option (b) is correct.

**116.** (b) Higher order treatment contrasts are not necessarily estimable. Covariance between two orthogonal treatment contrasts is zero. and Var (BIBD)> Var (RBD).

Hence, option (b) is correct.

**117.** (b,c,d) **118.** (a) **119.** (b,c)

# Solved Paper

# UGC CSIR

# NET Mathematical Sciences*

## Solved Paper 2024

### PART B

**21** For $t \in R$, define $M(t) = \begin{pmatrix} 1 & t & 0 \\ 1 & 1 & t^2 \\ 0 & 1 & 1 \end{pmatrix}$

Then which of the following statements is true?

1 $\det M(t)$ is a polynomial function of degree 3 in $t$
2 $\det M(t) = 0$ for all $t \in R$
3 $\det M(t)$ is zero for infinitely many $t \in R$
4 $\det M(t)$ is zero for exactly two $t \in R$

**22** Let $\leq$ be the usual order on the field $R$ of real numbers. Define an order $\leq$ on $R^2$ by $(a, b) \leq (c, d)$ if $(a < c)$, or ($a = c$ and $b \leq d$). Consider the subset $E = \left\{\left(\frac{1}{n}, 1 - \frac{1}{n}\right) \in R^2 : n \in N\right\}$. With respect to $\leq$ which of the following statements is true?

1 $\inf(E) = (0, 1)$ and $\sup(E) = (1, 0)$
2 $\inf(E)$ does not exist but $\sup(E) = (1, 0)$
3 $\inf(E) = (0, 1)$ but $\sup(E)$ does not exist
4 Both $\inf(E)$ and $\sup(E)$ do not exist

**23** For a quadratic form in 3 variables over $R$, let $r$ be the rank and $s$ be the signature. The number of possible pairs $(r, s)$ is

1 13 2 9
3 10 4 16

**24** Which of the following is true about subset of $R^2$ with usual topology?

1 A is connected iff closure is connected.
2 Intersection of two connected subsets is connected.
3 Union of two compact subsets is compact.
4 Exactly two function from $Q^2$ to the set $\{(0, 0), (1, 1)\}$.

**25** What is he cardinality of the set of real solutions of $e^x + x = 1$?

1 0 2 1
3 Countably infinite 4 Uncountable

*** Based on Memory**

**26** Let $V$ be a vector space of dimension 3 over $R$. Let $T : V \to V$ be a linear transformation, given by the matrix $A = \begin{pmatrix} 1 & -1 & 0 \\ 1 & -4 & 3 \\ -2 & 5 & -3 \end{pmatrix}$ with respect to an ordered basis $\{v_1, v_2\ v_3\}$ of $V$. Then which of the following statements is true?

1 $T(v_3) = 0$ 2 $T(v_1 + v_2) = 0$
3 $T(v_1 + v_2 + v_3) = 0$ 4 $T(v_1 + v_3) = T(v_2)$

**27** Let $X \subset R$ be an infinite countable bounded subset of $R$. Which of the following statements is true?

1 $X$ cannot be compact 2 $X$ contains an interior point
3 $X$ may be closed 4 closure of $X$ is countable

**28** Which of the following sets is countable?

1 The set of all functions from $Q$ to $Q$
2 The set of all functions from $Q$ to $\{0, 1\}$
3 The set of all functions from $Q$ to $\{0, 1\}$ which vanish outside a finite set
4 The set of all subsets of $N$

**29** Let $(x_n)_{n \geq 1}$ be a sequence of non-negative real numbers. Then, which of the following is true?

1 $\liminf x_n = 0 \Rightarrow \lim x_n^2 = 0$
2 $\limsup x_n = 0 \Rightarrow \lim x_n^2 = 0$
3 $\liminf x_n = 0 \Rightarrow (x_n)_{n \geq 1}$ is bounded
4 $\liminf x_n^2 > 4 \Rightarrow \limsup x_n > 4$

**30** Let $f$ be a polynomial on $0 < |z| < \epsilon, \epsilon > 0$ given by convergent Laurent series $\sum_{n=-\infty}^{\infty} a_n z^n$. Given also that $\lim_{z \to 0} |f(z)| = \infty$, we can conclude that

1 $a_{-1} \neq 0$ and $a_{-n} = 0\ \forall n \geq 2$
2 $a_{-N} \neq 0$ for some $N \geq 1$ and $= 0\ \forall n > N$
3 $a_{-n} = 0\ \forall n \geq 1$
4 $a_{-n} \neq 0\ \forall n \geq 1$

**31** Suppose, $x_1, x_2, ..., x_n$ are $i \cdot i \cdot d$ random variables with characteristics function $\phi(t:\theta): E[e^{itx_1}]$, where $\theta \in R^k$ is the parameter of the distribution. Let $z = x_1 + x_2 + x_3 + x_4 ... + x_n$. Then, for which of the following distributions of $x_1$ would the characteristics function of $z$ be of the form $\phi(t:\alpha)$ for some $\alpha \in R^k = ?$

1 Negative binomial
2 Geometric
3 Hyper geometric
4 Discrete uniform

**32** The value of the integral $\oint_{|1-z|=1} \frac{e^z}{z^2-1} dz$ is

1 0      2 $\pi ie$
3 $\pi ie - \pi ie^{-1}$      4 $e + e^{-1}$

**33** A permutation $\sigma$ of $[n] = \{1, 2, ..., n\}$ is called irreducible, if the restriction $\sigma|_{[k]}$ is not a permutation of $[k]$ for any $1 \le k < n$. Let $a_n$ be the number of irreducible permutations of $[n]$. Then $a_1 = 1, a_2 = 1$ and $a_3 = 3$. The value of $a_4$ is

1 12      2 13
3 14      4 15

**34** Let $X$ be an infinite set. Consider the topology $\tau$ on $X$ whose non-empty open sets are complements of finite sets. Then which of the following statements is true?

1 $X$ is disconnected
2 $X$ is compact
3 No sequence in $X$ converges in $X$
4 Every sequence in $X$ converges to a unique point in $X$

**35** Let $T : C \to M_2(R)$ be the map given by
$$T(z) = T(x+iy) = \begin{bmatrix} x & y \\ -y & x \end{bmatrix}$$
Then which of the following statements is false?

1 $T(z_1 z_2) = T(z_1)T(z_2)$ for all $z_1, z_2 \in c$
2 $T(z)$ is singular if and only if $z = 0$
3 There does not exist non-zero $A \in M_2(R)$ such that the trace of $T(z)A$ is zero for all $z \in c$
4 $T(z_1 + z_2) = T(z_1) + T(z_2)$ for all $z_1, z_2 \in c$

**36** Which of the following partial differential equations is not parabolic for all $x, y \in R$?

1 $x^2 \frac{\partial^2 u}{\partial x \partial y} - 2xy \frac{\partial u}{\partial y} + y^2 = 0$

2 $x^2 \frac{\partial^2 u}{\partial x^2} - 2xy \frac{\partial^2 u}{\partial x \partial y} + y^2 \frac{\partial^2 u}{\partial y^2} = 0$

3 $x^2 \frac{\partial^2 u}{\partial x^2} + 2xy \frac{\partial^2 u}{\partial x \partial y} + y^2 \frac{\partial^2 u}{\partial y^2} = 0$

4 $x^2 \frac{\partial^2 u}{\partial x^2} - 2xy \frac{\partial^2 u}{\partial x \partial y} + y^2 \frac{\partial^2 u}{\partial y^2} + x \frac{\partial u}{\partial x} + y \frac{\partial u}{\partial y} = 0$

**37** Let $X$ be a topological space and $E$ be a subset of $X$. Which of the following statement are correct?

1 $E$ is connected implies $\bar{E}$ is connected.
2 $E$ is connected implies $\partial E$ is connected.
3 $E$ is path connected implies $\bar{E}$ is path connected.
4 $E$ is connected implies $\bar{E}$ is compact.

**38** Let $G$ be a group of order $p^n$, $p$ a prime number and $n > 1$. Then which of the following is true?

1 Centre of $G$ has at least two elements.
2 $G$ is always an Abelian group.
3 $G$ has exactly two normal subgroups (i.e., $G$ is a simple group).
4 If $H$ is any other group of order $p^n$, then $G$ is isomorphic to $H$

**39** Let $f : C \to C$ be a entire function with $f\left(\frac{1}{n}\right) = \frac{1}{n^2}$ for all $n \in N$. Then which of the following statements is true?

1 No such $f$ exists
2 such an $f$ is not unique
3 $f(z) = z^2$ for all $z \in c$
4 $f$ need not be a polynomial function

**40** For $z \in C$, let $f(z) = \begin{cases} \frac{\bar{z}_2}{z} & \text{if } z \ne 0 \\ 0 & \text{otherwise} \end{cases}$

Then which of the following statements is false?

1 $f(z)$ is continuous everywhere
2 $f(z)$ is not analytic in any open neighbourhood of zero
3 $zf(z)$ satisfies the Cauchy-Riemann equations at zero
4 $f(z)$ is analytic in some open subset of $C$

**41** Consider the function $I(u) = \int_a^b F(u, u')dx; u(a) = u_1$, $u(b) = u_2$ $F$ has second order continuous partial derivatives with respect to $u, u'$ and $u_1, u_2$ are given real number.

1 $\frac{\partial F}{\partial u} = 0$      2 $F$ remains constant
3 $F - u' \frac{\partial F}{\partial y'} = \text{constant}$      4 $F - y \frac{\partial F}{\partial u'} = \text{constant}$

**42** Let $x_1, x_2, ..., x_n$ be the $i \cdot i \cdot d$ random variable with common *Pdf*.

$f(x/\theta) = \frac{(\log \theta)^{\theta x}}{\theta - 1}$, for $0 < x < 1$, where $\theta > 1$ is an unknown parameter.

Then, the statics $T = \sum_{i=1}^{n} x_i$ is

1 sufficient, but not complete
2 sufficient, but not minimal sufficient
3 complete sufficient
4 neither complete nor sufficient

**43** For the following system of ordinary differential equations $\frac{dx}{dt} = x(3-2x-2y)$, $\frac{dy}{dt} = y(2-2x-y)$, the critical point (0, 2) is

1 a stable spiral   2 an unstable spiral
3 a stable node   4 an unstable node

**44** Let $y = \phi(x)$ be the extremizing function for the functional $I(y) = \int_0^1 y^2 \left(\frac{dy}{dx}\right)^2 dx$, subject to $y(0) = 0$, $y(1) = 1$. Then $\phi(1/4)$ is equal to

1 1/2   2 1/4
3 1/8   4 1/12

**45** Consider the system of ordinary differential equations $\frac{dx}{dt} = 4x^3y^2 - x^5y^4$, $\frac{dy}{dt} = x^4y^5 + 2x^2y^3$

Then for this system there exists

1 a closed path in $\{(x, y) \in R^2 \mid x^2 + y^2 \le 5\}$
2 a closed path in $\{(x, y) \in R^2 \mid 5 < x^2 + y^2 \le 10\}$
3 a closed path in $\{(x, y) \in R^2 \mid x^2 + y^2 > 10\}$
4 no closed path in $R^2$

**46** Let $u(x, y)$ be the solution of $\frac{\partial^2 u}{\partial x^2} + \frac{\partial^2 u}{\partial y^2} = 64$ in the unit disc $\{(x, y) \mid x^2 + y^2 < 1\}$ and such that $u$ vanishes on the boundary of the disc. Then $u\left(\frac{1}{4}, \frac{1}{\sqrt{2}}\right)$ is equal to

1 7   2 16   3 −7   4 −16

**47** Consider a mass-less infinite straight wire with one end fixed at $O$. Assume that the wire is rotating in a plane about the point $O$ with constant angular velocity $\omega$. Consider a bead of mass $m$ sliding along the wire in the absence of external forces. Let $r(t)$ denote the distance of the bead from $O$ at time $t \ge 0$, and $\frac{dr}{dt}(0) = 0$. Then which of the following statements is true?

1 $\exists M > 0, \alpha > 0$ such that $r(t) > Me^{\alpha t}, t > 0$
2 $r(t) \to 0$ as $t \to \infty$
3 $r(t)$ is a constant function
4 $\frac{dr(t)}{dt}$ changes its sign for some $t > 0$

**48** Consider 35 $i \cdot i \cdot d$ observations $X_1, X_2, X_3, \ldots, X_{15}$ and $Y_1, Y_2, \ldots, Y_{20}$. Let $R$ be the Wilcoxon's rank sum statistic based on the ranks of the $X$'s in the combined sample. Then, the expected value of $R$ is

1 270   2 300   3 360.5   4 330.5

**49** The sum of the series $\sum_{n=1}^{\infty} \frac{1}{(4n-3)(4n+1)}$ is

1 0.25   2 0.40   3 1.50   4 2.35

**50** Suppose data $(X_1, Y_1), (X_2, Y_2), \ldots, (X_n, Y_n)$ are generated as follows $Y_1, Y_2, \ldots, Y_n \sim i.i.d.$ Bernoulli $\left(\frac{1}{2}\right)$ and $X \mid Y_i = y \sim$ Uniform $(0, y + 1)$. Define

$$h(x) = \begin{cases} 1 & \text{if } x \ge 1 \\ 0 & \text{otherwise} \end{cases}$$

Then, which of the following is a correct linear regression model for $m(x) = E(Y_i \mid X_i = x)$, in the sense that the true $m(x)$ is obtained for some values of the parameters $\alpha_0, \alpha_1, \alpha_2$ for all $x$?

1 $m(x) = \alpha_0 + \alpha_1 x$
2 $m(x) = \alpha_0 + \alpha_1 x + \alpha_2 x^2$
3 $m(x) = \alpha_0 + \alpha_1 x + \alpha_2 x h(x)$
4 $m(x) = \alpha_0 + \alpha_1 x + \alpha_2 h(x)$

**51** If $A$ is a (2, 2) matrix over $R$ with $\det(A + 1) = 1 + \det(A)$, then we can conclude that

1 $\mathrm{Det}(A) = 0$   2 $A = 0$
3 $\mathrm{Tr}(A) = 0$   4 $A$ is non-singular

**52** For a quadratic from $f(x,y,z) \in R[x,y,z]$, we say that $(a,b,c) \in R^3$ is a zero of $f$ if $f(a,b,c) = 0$. Which of the following quadratic forms has at least one zero different from (0,0,0)?

1 $x^2 + 2y^2 + 3z^2$
2 $x^2 + 2y^2 + 3z^2 - 2xy$
3 $x^2 + 2y^2 + 3z^2 - 2xy - 2yz$
4 $x^2 + 2y^2 - 3z^2$

**53** Suppose $\begin{pmatrix} X_1 \\ Y_1 \end{pmatrix}, \begin{pmatrix} X_2 \\ Y_2 \end{pmatrix}, \begin{pmatrix} X_3 \\ Y_3 \end{pmatrix}$ are i.i.d observations from the Uniform distribution on the unit square $[0, 1] \times [0, 1]$. What is the probability that the rank correlation between the $X_i$ and the $Y_i$ values is 1?

1 0   2 $\frac{1}{2}$   3 $\frac{1}{3}$   4 $\frac{1}{6}$

**54** Let $X$ and $Y$ be independent Exponential random variables with means $\frac{1}{\lambda}$ and $\frac{1}{\mu}$ respectively with $\lambda \ne \mu$. Let $f_z(z)$ denote the density function of $Z = X + Y$. Then for $z > 0$,

1 $f_Z(z) = (\lambda + \mu) e^{-(\lambda+\mu)z}$
2 $f_Z(Z) = \frac{\lambda\mu}{\lambda + \mu} e^{\frac{-\lambda\mu}{\lambda+\mu} z}$
3 $f_Z(z) = \frac{\lambda\mu}{\lambda - \mu}(e^{-\mu z} - e^{-\lambda z})$
4 $f_Z(z) = \begin{cases} \frac{\lambda\mu}{\lambda - \mu} e^{\frac{-\lambda\mu}{\lambda-\mu} z} & \text{if } \lambda > \mu \\ \frac{\lambda\mu}{\mu - \lambda} e^{\frac{-\lambda\mu}{\mu-\lambda} z} & \text{if } \mu > \lambda \end{cases}$

**55** Let $X_1, X_2, \ldots, X_n (n \geq 2)$ be a random sample from a distribution with probability density function $f_\theta, \theta > 0$, unknown, where $f_\theta(x) = \begin{cases} \frac{2(\theta - x)}{\theta^2}, & 0 \leq x \leq \theta \\ 0, & \text{otherwise} \end{cases}$

Let $\bar{X}_n$ be the sample mean and $X_{(n)} = \max\{X_1, X_2, \ldots, X_n\}$.

Then which of the following statements is correct?

1 $X_{(n)}$ is sufficient for $\theta$
2 $X_{(n)}$ is unbiased for $\theta$
3 $3\bar{X}_n$ is unbiased for $\theta$
4 $3\bar{X}_n$ is sufficient for $\theta$

**56** If $T: R^4 \to R^3$ defined by $T(x, y, z, t) = (x - y + z + t, x + 2z - t, x + y + 3z - 3t)$, then nullity and rank of $T$ are respectively,

1 2, 3    2 4, 3
3 2, 2    4 4, 1

**57** If $1, \omega, \omega^2$ are the cube roots of unity, then $(1 - \omega + \omega^2)^5 + (1 + \omega - \omega^2)^5$ will be

1 4    2 8    3 16    4 32

**58** Let $V = (A \in M_{3 \times 3}(R) : A^t + A \in RI)$, where $I$ is the identity matrix. Consider the quadratic form defined as $q(A) = \text{Trace}(A)^2 - \text{Trace}(A^2)$. What is the signature of this quadratic form ?

1 $(++++)$    2 $(+000)$
3 $(+---)$    4 $(---0)$

**59** Let $(X_1, Y_1), (X_2, Y_2) \ldots (X_n, Y_n), n \geq 5$, be a random sample from a Bivariate Normal $(\mu_1, \mu_2, \sigma_1, \sigma_2, \rho)$ distribution with all parameters unknown. For testing $H_0: \rho = 0$ against $H_1: \rho \neq 0$ if you use the usual $t$-test and your observed sample correlation coefficient is 0, then what is the $p$-value?

1 0    2 0.05    3 0.5    4 1

**60** Let $\{X_n : n \geq 0\}$ be a two state Markov chain with state space $S = \{0, 1\}$ and transition matrix $P = \begin{bmatrix} \frac{1}{2} & \frac{1}{2} \\ \frac{1}{3} & \frac{2}{3} \end{bmatrix}$

Assuming $X_0 = 0$, the expected return time to 0 is

1 $\frac{5}{2}$    2 $\frac{9}{4}$    3 $\frac{3}{2}$    4 3

## PART C

**61** For each natural number $n \geq 1$, let $a_n = \frac{n}{10^{[\log_{10} n]}}$, where $[x]$ = smallest integer greater than or equal to $x$. Which of the following statements are true?

1 $\liminf_{n \to \infty} a_n = 0$
2 $\liminf_{n \to \infty} a_n$ does not exist
3 $\liminf_{n \to \infty} a_n = 0.15$
4 $\limsup_{n \to \infty} a_n = 1$

**62** Let $n$ be a fixed natural number. Then the series $\sum_{m \geq n} \frac{(-1)^m}{m}$ is

1 Absolutely convergent
2 Divergent
3 Absolutely convergent if $n > 100$
4 Convergent

**63** Let $N \geq 5$ be an integer. Then which of the following statements are true?

1 $\sum_{n=1}^{N} \frac{1}{n} \leq 1 + \log N$    2 $\sum_{n=1}^{N} \frac{1}{n} < 1 + \log N$
3 $\sum_{n=1}^{N} \frac{1}{n} \leq \log N$    4 $\sum_{n=1}^{N} \frac{1}{n} \geq \log N$

**64** Let $A \in M_3(R)$ and let $X = \{C \in GL_3(R) \mid CAC^{-1}$ is triangular$\}$. Then

1 $X \neq \phi$
2 If $X = \phi$, then $A$ is not diagonalisable over $C$
3 If $X = \phi$, then $A$ is diagonalisable over $C$
4 If $X = \phi$, then $A$ has no real eigenvalue

**65** Let $U \subseteq R^n$ be an open subset of $R^n$ and $f: U \to R^n$ be a $C^\infty$-function. Suppose that for every $x \in U$, the derivative at $x$, $df_x$, is non singular. Then which of the following statements are true?

1 If $V \subset U$ is open then $f(V)$ is open in $R^n$
2 $f: U \to f(U)$ is a homeomorphism.
3 $f$ is one-one
4 If $V \subset U$ is closed, then $f(V)$ is closed in $R^n$

**66** If a five digit number divisible by 3 is to be formed using the numerals 0, 1, 2, 3, 4 and 5, without repetition, the total number of ways this can be done is

1 $5 \cdot {}^6P_3$    2 216
3 600    4 500

**67** If $y(x)$ is a solution of the equation $4xy'' + 2y' + y = 0$. Satisfying $y(0) = 1$. Then, $y'''(0)$ is not equal to

1 1/24    2 1/12
3 1/6    4 1/2

**68** Consider the function $f(z)=\dfrac{(\sin z)^m}{(1-\cos z)^n}$ for $0<|z|<1$, where $m$, $n$ are positive integers, then $z=0$ is

1 A removable singularity, if $m \geq 2n$
2 A pole, if $m<2n$
3 A pole, if $m \geq 2n$
4 An essential singularity for some values of $m$, $n$

**69** Let $(X, d)$ be a compact metric space. Let $T: X \to X$ be a continuous function satisfying $\inf_{n\in N} d(T^n(x), T^n(y)) \neq 0$ for every $x, y \in X$ with $x \neq y$. Then which of the following statements are true?

1 $T$ is a one-one function.
2 $T$ is not a one-one function.
3 Image of $T$ is closed in $X$.
4 If $X$ is finite, then $T$ is onto.

**70** Which of the following statements are true?

1 Any two quadratic forms of same rank in $n$-variables over $R$ are isomorphic
2 Any two quadratic forms of same rank in $n$-variables over $C$ are isomorphic
3 Any two quadratic forms in $n$-variables are isomorphic over $C$
4 A quadratic form in 4 variables may be isomorphic to a quadratic form in 10 variables

**71** Let $f:[0,1] \to R$ be a monotonic function with $f\left(\frac{1}{4}\right)f\left(\frac{3}{4}\right)<0$.

Suppose $\sup\{x \in [0,1]: f(x)<0\}=\alpha$.
Which of the following statements are correct?

1 $f(\alpha)<0$
2 If $f$ is increasing, then $f(\alpha) \leq 0$
3 If $f$ is continuous and $\frac{1}{4}<\alpha<\frac{3}{4}$, then $f(\alpha)=0$
4 If $f$ is decreasing, then $f(\alpha)<0$

**72** Let $p(x)$ be a polynomial function in one variable of odd degree and $g$ be a continuous function from $R$ to $R$. Then which of the following statements are true.

1 $\exists$ a point $x_0 \in R$ such that $p(x_0)=g(x_0)$
2 If $g$ is a polynomial function then there exists $x_0 \in R$ such that $p(x_0)=g(x_0)$
3 If $g$ is a bounded function there exists $x_0 \in R$ such that $p(x_0)=g(x_0)$
4 There is a unique point $x_0 \in R$ such that $p(x_0)=g(x_0)$

**73** Let $n \geq 1$ and $\alpha, \beta \in R$ with $\alpha \neq \beta$. Suppose $A_n(\alpha,\beta)=[a_{ij}]$ is an $n \times n$ matrix such that $a_{ii}=\alpha$ and $a_{ij}=\beta$ for $i \neq j$, $1 \leq i, j \leq n$. Let $D_n$ be the determinant of $A_n(\alpha,\beta)$. Which of the following statements are true?

1 $D_r=(\alpha-\beta)D_{n-1}+\beta$ for $n \geq 2$
2 $\dfrac{D_n}{(\alpha-\beta)^{n-1}}=\dfrac{D_{n-1}}{(\alpha-\beta)^{n-2}}+\beta$ for $n \geq 2$
3 $D_r=(\alpha+(n-1)\beta)^{n-1}(\alpha-\beta)$ for $n \geq 2$
4 $D_r=(\alpha+(n-1)\beta)(\alpha-\beta)^{n-1}$ for $n \geq 2$

**74** Consider a Markov chain with state space $S$. Let $d(k)$ denote the period of state $k \in S$, which of the following statements are correct?

1 For $i, j \in S$, if $\exists\, n, m>0$ such that $P_{ij}^{(n)}>0$, $P_{ji}^{(m)}>0$,
2 For $i, j \in S$, if $\exists\, n, m>0$ such that $P_{ij}^{(m)}>0$, then $d_{(i)}=d_{(j)}$
3 For $i, j \in S$, if $\exists\, r>0$ such that $P_{ij}^{(m)}>0$, then $j$ cannot be transient.
4 For $i, j \in S$, if $\exists\, r>0$ such that $P_{ij}^{(r)}>0$ and $i$ is null recurrent, then $j$ is positive.

**75** A linear mapping $T$ on the Euclidean space $R^3$ with the standard inner product maps the basis vectors as follows :

$T(0,1,1)=(-1,0,1), T(1,0,1)=\frac{1}{3}(1,-1,4)$ and $T(1,1,0)=(0,1,1)$.

The matrix $T$ relative to the ordered basis $\{e_1, e_2, e_3\}$ where $e_1=(1,0,0)$, $e_2=(0,1,0)$, $e_3=(0,0,1)$, then

1 matrix $T=\begin{pmatrix} 2/3 & -2/3 & -1/3 \\ 1/3 & 2/3 & -2/3 \\ 2/3 & 1/3 & 2/3 \end{pmatrix}$
2 $T$ is orthogonal
3 $T(0,0,1)=\left(\frac{-1}{3},\frac{-2}{3},\frac{2}{3}\right)$
4 $T(1,0,0)=(2,3,-4)$

**76** Let $L^2([-\pi,\pi])$ be the metric space of Lebesgue square integrable functions on $[-\pi,\pi]$ with a metric $d$ given by

$$d(f,g)=\left[\int_{-\pi}^{\pi}(f(x)-g(x))^2\,dx\right]^{1/2} \text{ for } f, g \in L^2([-\pi,\pi])$$

Consider the subset $S=\{\sin(2^n x): n \in N\}$ of $L^2([-\pi,\pi])$
Which of the following statements are true?

1 $S$ is bounded
2 $S$ is closed
3 $S$ is compact
4 $S$ is non-compact

**77** Let $f:[0,1]^2 \to R$ be a function defined by

$f(x,y)=\dfrac{xy}{x^2+y^2}$ if either $x \neq 0$ or $y \neq 0 = 0$ if $x=y=0$

Then which of the following statements are true?

1 $f$ is continuous at $(0,0)$
2 $f$ is a bounded function
3 $\int_0^1\int_0^1 f(x,y)\,dx\,dy$ exists
4 $f$ is continuous at $(1,0)$

**78** Which of the following statements regarding quadratic forms in 3 variables are true?

1 Any two quadratic forms of rank 3 are isomorphic over $R$
2 Any two quadratic forms of rank 3 are isomorphic over $C$
3 There are exactly three non zero quadratic forms of rank $\leq 3$ upto isomorphism over $C$
4 There are exactly three non zero quadratic forms of rank 2 upto isomorphism over $R$ and $C$

**79** Let $C[0, 1]$ be the ring of all real valued continuous function on $[0, 1]$.
Let $A = \{f \in C[0, 1] : f(1/4) = f(3/4) = 0\}$. Then which of the following statements are true?

1 $A$ is an ideal in $C[0, 1]$ but is not a prime ideal in $C[0, 1]$
2 $A$ is a prime ideal in $C[0, 1]$
3 $A$ is a maximal ideal in $C[0, 1]$
4 $A$ is a prime ideal in $C[0, 1]$, but is not a maximal ideal in $C[0, 1]$

**80** Which of the following statements are true?

1 There exist three mutually disjoint subsets of $R$, each of which is countable and dense in $R$
2 For each $n \in N$, there exists $n$ mutually disjoint subsets of $R$, each of which is countable and dense in $R$
3 There exist countably infinite number of mutually disjoint subsets of $R$, each of which is countable and dense in $R$
4 There exist uncountable number of mutually disjoint subsets of $R$, each of which is countable and dense in $R$

**81** Consider the power series $f(z) = \sum_{n=0}^{\infty} (-1)^n \frac{z^{2n+1}}{(2n)!}$

Which of the following are true?

1 Radius of convergence of $f(z)$ is infinite
2 The set $\{f(x) : x \in R\}$ is bounded
3 The set $\{f(x) : -1 < x < 1\}$ is bounded
4 $f(z)$ has infinitely many zeroes

**82** Let $F[X]$ be the polynomial ring in one variable over a field $F$. Then which of the following statements are true?

1 $F[X]$ is a *UFD*
2 $F[X]$ is a *PID*
3 $F[X]$ is a Euclidean domain
4 $F[X]$ is a *PID* but is not an Euclidean domain

**83** Let $f(x) \in Z[x]$ be a monic polynomial of degree $n$. Then which of the following are true?

1 If $f(x)$ is irreducible in $Z[x]$, then it is irreducible in $Q[x]$
2 If $f(x)$ is irreducible in $Q[x]$, then it is irreducible in $Z[x]$
3 If $f(x)$ is reducible in $Z[x]$, then it has a real root
4 If $f(x)$ has a real root, then it is reducible in $Z[x]$

**84** Let $f : C \to C$ be an analytic function. For $z_0 \in C$, which of the following statements are true?

1 $f$ can take the value $z_0$ at finitely many points in $\left\{\frac{1}{n} \middle| n \in N\right\}$
2 $f(1/n) = z_0$ for all $n \in N \Rightarrow f$ is the constant function $z_0$
3 $f(n) = z_0$ for all $n \in N \Rightarrow f$ is the constant function $z_0$
4 $f(r) = z_0$ for all $r \in Q \cap [1, 2] \Rightarrow f$ is the constant function $z_0$

**85** Let $I$ be an ideal of $Z$. Then which of the following statements are true?

1 $I$ is a principal ideal
2 $I$ is a prime ideal of $Z$
3 If $I$ is a prime ideal of $Z$, then $I$ is a maximal ideal in $Z$
4 If $I$ is a maximal ideal in $Z$, then $I$ is a prime ideal of $Z$

**86** Let $U$ be an open subset of $C$ and $f : U \to C$ be an analytic function. Then which of the following statements are true?

1 If $f$ is one-one, then $f(U)$ is open in $C$
2 If $f$ is onto, then $U = C$
3 If $f$ is onto, then $f$ is one-one
4 If $f(U)$ is closed in $C$, then $f(U)$ is connected

**87** Consider $[n] = \{1, 2, \ldots, n\}$ with the discrete topology and let $X = \prod_{N \geq 1} [n]$

be the product space with the product topology. For $x = (a_1, a_2, \ldots) \in X$, define $T(x) = (1, a_1, a_2, \ldots)$. Then which of the following statements are true?

1 Let $x_n \in X$ for $n = 1, 2, 3, \ldots$ be a sequence in $X$. Then it is convergent.
2 $X$ is a compact, Hausdorff space.
3 The map $T : X \to X$ is continuous.
4 The map $T : X \to X$ has a unique fixed point.

**88** Let $F$ be a field. Then which of the following statements are true?

1 All extensions of degree 2 of $F$ are isomorphic as fields.
2 All finite extensions of $F$ of same degree are isomorphic as fields if $\text{char}(F) > 0$
3 All finite extensions of $F$ of same degree are isomorphic as field if $F$ is finite
4 All finite normal extensions of $F$ are isomorphic as field if $\text{Char}(F) = 0$

**89** Let $U \subset C$ be an open connected set and $f : U \to C$ be a non-constant analytic function. Consider the following two sets.
$X = \{z \in U : f(z) = 0\}$
$Y = \{z \in U : f$ vanishes on an open neighbourhood of $z$ in $U\}$
Then which of the following statements are true?

1 $X$ is closed in $U$
2 $Y$ is closed in $U$
3 $X$ has empty interior
4 $Y$ is open in $U$

**90** Suppose that, $M_{P \times P} \sim$ Wishart $p(I, M)$ and $Z \sim N_p(0, \Sigma)$ are independent where $\Sigma$ is positive definite. Let $a \in R^P$ be a fixed $P$-vector such that $a \neq 0$ and define $d = z / \| z \|$. Then, which of the following random variables has a $\chi^2$ distribution, possibly after being scaled by a constant factor?

1 $d^I M^{-1} d$
2 $(d^I M^{-1} d)^{-1}$
3 $a^I M a$
4 $(a^I M^{-1} a)^{-1}$

**91** Two function $f(t)$ and $g(t)$ of real numbers are such that $f(0) = f(1) = 0$ and $g(0) = g(1) = 1$ and $f(1/2) > g(1/2)$, $t \in (0, 1)$

1 $f(t) = g(t)$ at exactly one point in [0, 1]
2 $f(t) = g(t)$ at least one point in [0, 1]
3 $f(t) = g(t)$ at infinitely many point in [0, 1]
4 $f(t) \neq g(t)$ at any point in [0, 1]

**92** Let $\{(X_n, Y_n) : n \geq 1\}$ and $(X, Y)$ be random variables, on $(\Omega, F, P)$. Then, which of the following statements are correct?

1 If $X_n \to X$ almost surely, $Y_n \to Y$ almost surely, then $X_n + Y_n \to X + Y$ in distribution.
2 If $X_n \to X$ in probability, $Y_n \to Y$ almost surely, then $X_n + Y_n \to X + Y$ in distribution.
3 If $X_n \to X$ in probability, $Y_n \to Y$ in probability, then $X_n + Y_n \to X + Y$ in distribution.
4 If $X_n \to X$ in distribution, $Y_n \to Y$ in distribution, then $X_n + Y_n \to X + Y$ in distribution.

**93** A possible initial strip $(x_0, y_0, z_0, p_0, q_0)$ for the Cauchy problem $pq = 1$ where $p = \frac{\partial z}{\partial x}$, $q = \frac{\partial z}{\partial y}$ and $x_0(s) = s$, $y_0(s) = \frac{1}{s}$, $z_0(s) = 1$ for $s > 1$ is

1 $\left(s, \frac{1}{s}, s, \frac{1}{s}, s\right)$ 2 $\left(s, \frac{1}{s}, 1, -\frac{1}{s}, -s\right)$
3 $\left(s, \frac{1}{s}, 1, \frac{1}{s}, -s\right)$ 4 $\left(s, \frac{1}{s}, 1, -\frac{1}{s}, s\right)$

**94** Let $u(x, t)$ be the solution of $\frac{\partial^2 u}{\partial t^2} - \frac{\partial^2 u}{\partial x^2} = xt$, $-\infty < x < \infty, t > 0, u(x, 0) = \frac{\partial u}{\partial t}(x, 0) = 0, -\infty < x < \infty$

Then $u(2, 3)$ is equal to
1 9 2 1
3 27 4 12

**95** The values of $\alpha$, $A$, $B$, $C$ for which the quadrature formula $\int_{-1}^{1} (1 - x) f(x)\, dx = Af(-\alpha) + Bf(0) + Cf(\alpha)$ is exact for polynomials of highest possible degree, are

1 $\alpha = \sqrt{\frac{3}{5}}, A = \frac{5}{9} + \frac{\sqrt{5}}{3\sqrt{3}}, B = \frac{8}{9}, C = \frac{5}{9} - \frac{\sqrt{5}}{3\sqrt{3}}$
2 $\alpha = \sqrt{\frac{3}{5}}, A = \frac{5}{9} - \frac{\sqrt{5}}{3\sqrt{3}}, B = \frac{8}{9}, C = \frac{5}{9} + \frac{\sqrt{5}}{3\sqrt{3}}$
3 $\alpha = \sqrt{\frac{3}{5}}, A = \frac{5}{9}\left(1 - \frac{\sqrt{3}}{\sqrt{5}}\right), B = \frac{8}{9}, C = \frac{5}{9}\left(1 + \frac{\sqrt{3}}{\sqrt{5}}\right)$
4 $\alpha = \sqrt{\frac{3}{5}}, A = \frac{5}{9}\left(1 + \frac{\sqrt{3}}{\sqrt{5}}\right), B = \frac{8}{9}, C = \frac{5}{9}\left(1 - \frac{\sqrt{3}}{\sqrt{5}}\right)$

**96** Assume that $h_1, h_2, g_1$ and $g_2 \in C([a, b])$.

Let $\phi(x) = f(x) + \lambda \int_a^b [h_1(t) g_1(x) + h_2(t) g_2(x)] \phi(t)\, dt$ be an integral equation. Consider the following statements :

$S_1$ : If the given integral equation has a solution for some $f \in C([a, b])$, then $\int_a^b f(t) g_1(t) dt = 0 = \int_a^b f(t) g_2(t) dt$

$S_2$ : The given integral equation has a unique solution for every $f \in C([a, b])$ if $\lambda$ is not a characteristic number of the corresponding homogeneous equation

Then

1 Both $S_1$ and $S_2$ are true
2 $S_1$ is true but $S_2$ is false
3 $S_1$ is false but $S_2$ is true
4 Both $S_1$ and $S_2$ are false

**97** The minimum value of the functional $I(y) = \int_0^{\pi} \left(\frac{dy}{dx}\right)^2 dx$, subject to $\int_0^{\pi} y^2(x)\, dx = 1$, $y(0) = 0 = y(\pi)$ is equal to

1 1/2 2 1 3 2 4 1/3

**98** Consider a mechanical system whose position is described using the generalised coordinates $q_1, \ldots, q_n$. Let $T(q_1, \ldots, q_n, \dot{q}_1, \ldots, \dot{q}_n)$ be the kinetic energy of the system. If the generalized force $Q_j, 1 \leq j \leq n$, acting on the system is zero, then the Lagrange equations of motion are

1 $\frac{d}{dt}\left(\frac{\partial T}{\partial \dot{q}_j}\right) - \frac{\partial T}{\partial q_j} = 0, 1 \leq j \leq n$
2 $\frac{d}{dt}\left(\frac{\partial T}{\partial q_j}\right) - \frac{\partial T}{\partial q_j} = 0, 1 \leq j \leq n$
3 $\frac{\partial}{\partial q}\left(\frac{dT}{dt}\right) - 2\frac{\partial T}{\partial q_j} = 0, 1 \leq j \leq n$
4 $\frac{\partial}{\partial \dot{q}}\left(\frac{dT}{dt}\right) - \frac{\partial T}{\partial q_j} = 0, 1 \leq j \leq n$

**99** Let $y$ be a solution of $(1 + x^2)y'' + (1 + 4x^2)y = 0, x > 0$ $y(0) = 0$. Then $y$ has
1 infinitely many zeros in [0, 1]
2 infinitely many zeros in $[1, \infty)$
3 at least $n$ zeros in $[0, n\pi]$, $\forall n \in N$
4 at most $3n$ zeros in $[0, n\pi]$, $\forall n \in N$

**100** Let $y = y(x) \in C^4([0, 1])$ be an extremising function for the functional $I(y) = \int_0^1 \left[\left(\frac{d^2 y}{dx^2}\right)^2 - 2y\right] dx$, satisfying $y(0) = 0 = y(1)$. Then an extremal $y(x)$, satisfying the given conditions at 0 and 1 together with the natural boundary conditions, is given by

1 $\frac{x}{24}(x-1)^3$  2 $\frac{x^2}{24}(x-1)^2$

3 $\frac{x}{24}(x^3-2x^2+1)$  4 $\frac{x}{24}(x^3+x^2-2)$

**101** Let $X_1, X_2$ and $X_3$ be *i.i.d.* normal random variables with mean $\theta$ and variance $\theta^2$ where $\theta \in R$ is unknown. Then, which of the following statements are correct?

1 $\frac{X_1+2X_2+3X_3}{6}$ is unbiased for $\theta$

2 $\frac{X_1^2+4X_2^2+9X_3^2}{14}$ is unbiased for $\theta^2$

3 $\frac{2X_1+X_3^2}{2}$ is unbiased for $\theta(1+\theta)$

4 $X_2\left(1-\frac{X_2}{2}\right)$ is unbiased for $\theta(1-\theta)$

**102** Let function $f$ does not depend on $x$ explicity i.e., $f=f(y, y', x)$ then,

1 $\frac{\partial f}{\partial x} \neq 0$  2 $f-y'\frac{\partial f}{\partial y} \neq \text{constant}$

3 $f-y'\frac{\partial f}{\partial y'}=\text{constant}$  4 $\frac{\partial f}{\partial x}=0$

**103** The transformation is defined by $q=\sqrt{[2P]}\sin Q$, $p=\sqrt{[2P]}\cos Q$, then

1 it is canonical.
2 it is not canonical.
3 it is canonical, if $[Q, P]=1$.
4 it is canonical, if $[Q, Q]=[P, P]=0$.

**104** Let $\{X_n : n \geq 0\}$ be a Markov chain with state space $N \cup \{0\}$ such that the transition probabilities are given by $p_{ij}=\begin{cases} q & \text{for } j=0 \\ 1-q & \text{for } j=i+1 \\ 0 & \text{otherwise} \end{cases}$

for $=0, 1, 2, \dots$, where $0<q<1$. Then which of the following statements are correct?

1 The Markov chain is irreducible
2 The Markov chain is aperiodic
3 $p_{00}^{(n)}=q$ for all $n \geq 1$
4 The Markov chain is positive recurrent

**105** A random variable $T$ has a symmetric distribution if $T$ and $-T$ have the same distribution. Let $X$ and $Y$ be independent random variables. Then which of the following statements are correct?

1 If $X$ and $Y$ have the same distribution then $X-Y$ has a symmetric distribution
2 If $X \sim N(3, 1)$ and $Y \sim N(2, 2)$, then $2X-3Y$ has a symmetric distribution
3 If $X$ and $Y$ have the same symmetric distribution, then $X+Y$ has a symmetric distribution
4 If $X$ has a symmetric distribution, then $XY$ has a symmetric distribution

**106** Let $\{(X_n, Y_n) : n \geq 1\}$ and $(X, Y)$ be random variables, on $(\Omega, F, P)$. Then which of the following statements are correct?

1 If $X_n \to X$ almost surely, $Y_n \to Y$ almost surely, then $X_n+Y_n \to X+Y$ in distribution
2 If $X_n \to X$ in probability, $Y_n \to Y$ almost surely, then $X_n+Y_n \to X+Y$ in distribution
3 If $X_n \to X$ in probability, $Y_n \to Y$ in probability, then $X_n+Y_n \to X+Y$ in distribution
4 If $X_n \to X$ in distribution, $Y_n \to Y$ in distribution, then $X_n+Y_n \to X+Y$ in distribution

**107** Consider a Balanced Incomplete Block Design $(v, b, r, k, \lambda)$ of $v$ treatments and $b$ blocks of $k$ plots each. Let $N$ be the $v \times b$ incidence matrix of the design. Then which of the following statements are correct?

1 $\lambda(k-1)=r(v-1)$  2 $b \geq v$
3 $\text{rank}(NN')=v$  4 $\text{trace}(NN')=bk$

**108** Suppose in a single service queue, customers arrive at a Poisson rate of one per ten minutes, and the service time is Exponential at a rate of one service per five minutes. Let $P_n$ be the probability that there are $n$ customers in the system in steady state. Then which of the following statements are correct?

1 $P_{n+1}=\frac{1}{2}P_n$ for all $n \geq 0$
2 The expected number of customers in the system is 1 in steady state
3 The expected number of customers in the system is 2 in steady state
4 The expected amount of time a customer spends in the system in steady state is 10 minutes

**109** Suppose the conditional p.d.f. of a random variable $X$ given $\theta$ is $f(x \mid \theta)=\begin{cases} \frac{2x}{\theta^2}, & 0<x<\theta \\ 0, & \text{otherwise} \end{cases}$

where the prior distribution of $\theta$ is Uniform (0, 1). Based on a single observation $x$ from $X$, which of the following statements are correct?

1 The Bayes estimate for $\theta$ under squared error loss function is $-x\log_e x$
2 The Bayes estimate for $\theta$ under squared error loss function is $-\frac{x\log_e x}{1-x}$
3 The Bayes estimate for $\theta$ under absolute error loss function is $x$
4 The Bayes estimate for $\theta$ under absolute error loss function is $\frac{2x}{1+x}$

**110** Let $\{X_i : i \geq 1\}$ be i.i.d. observations with $E(X_i) = 0$ and $\text{var}(X_i) = \sigma^2 > 0$. Then which of the following statements are correct?

1 $\frac{1}{n}\sum_{i=1}^{n}(X_{2i-1} - X_{2i})^2$ is consistent for $\sigma^2$

2 $\frac{1}{n}\sum_{i=1}^{n}(X_i - \bar{X})^2$ is consistent for $\sigma^2$

3 $\frac{1}{n}\sum_{i=1}^{n}X_i^2$ is consistent for $\sigma^2$

4 $\frac{1}{n-1}\sum_{i=1}^{n}(X_i - \bar{X})^2$ is consistent for $\sigma^2$

**111** Suppose that $M_{p \times p} \sim \text{Wishart}_p(I, m)$ and $Z \sim N_p(0, \Sigma)$ are independent where $\Sigma$ is positive definite. Let $a \in R^p$ be a fixed $p$-vector such that $a \neq 0$ and define $d = Z/\|Z\|$. Then which of the following random variables has a $\chi^2$ distribution, possibly after being scaled by a constant factor?

1 $d'M^{-1}d$
2 $(d'M^{-1}d)^{-1}$
3 $a'Ma$
4 $(a'M^{-1}a)^{-1}$

**112** Let $X_1, X_2$ and $X_3$ be i.i.d. Normal random variables with mean $\theta$ and variance $\theta^2$ where $\theta \in R$ is unknown. Then which of the following statements are correct?

1 $\frac{X_1 + 2X_2 + 3X_3}{6}$ is unbiased for $\theta$

2 $\frac{X_1^2 + 4X_2^4 + 9X_3^2}{14}$ is unbiased for $\theta^2$

3 $\frac{2X_1 + X_3^2}{2}$ is unbiased for $\theta(1+\theta)$

4 $X_2\left(1 - \frac{X_2}{2}\right)$ is unbiased for $\theta(1-\theta)$

**113** Suppose $X_1, X_2, \ldots, X_n$ are i.i.d. Uniform $(\theta, 2\theta), \theta > 0$. Let $X_{(1)} = \min\{X_1, \ldots, X_n\}$ and $X_{(n)} = \max\{X_1, \ldots, X_n\}$. Then which of the following statements are correct?

1 $(X_{(1)}, X_{(n)})$ is jointly sufficient and complete for $\theta$

2 $(X_{(1)}, X_{(n)})$ is jointly sufficient but not complete for $\theta$

3 $\frac{X_{(n)}}{2}$ is a maximum likelihood estimator for $\theta$

4 $X_{(1)}$ is a maximum likelihood estimator for $\theta$

**114** Consider the following system with three independent components $u_1, u_2$ and $u_3$.

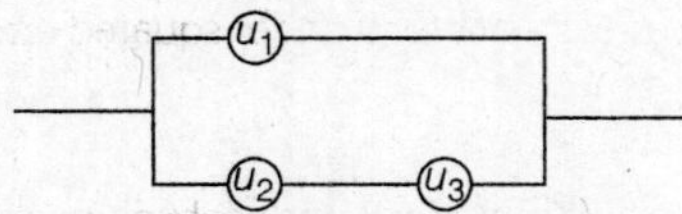


Suppose that the failure probability of each component is $p$, and let $f(p)$ be the probability that the whole system is still functioning. Then which of the following statements are correct?

1 $f\left(\frac{1}{2}\right) = \frac{5}{8}$
2 $f\left(\frac{1}{2}\right) = \frac{3}{8}$
3 $f\left(\frac{1}{3}\right) = \frac{22}{27}$
4 $f\left(\frac{1}{4}\right) = \frac{50}{64}$

**115** Given data $\{(x_i, y_i) : i = 1, 2, \ldots, n\}$ where $n \geq 2$ and not all $x_i$'s are identical, the simple linear regression model $y = \alpha + \beta x + \varepsilon$ is fit. Let $h_i$ be the $i$th diagonal element of the Hat matrix $H = X(X'X)^{-1}X'$, where $X_{n \times 2}$ is the corresponding model matrix. Then which of the following are possible for some choice of $n$ and $x_1, x_2, \ldots, x_n$?

1 $h_{ii} = -1$ for some $i$
2 $h_{ii} = -0$ for some $i$
3 $h_{ii} = 1$ for some $i$
4 All $h_{ii}$ are equal

**116** Consider a Markov chain with state space $S$. Let $d(k)$ denote the period of state $k \in S$. Which of the following statements are correct?

1 For $i, j \in S$, if $\exists\, n, m > 0$ such that $p_{ij}^{(n)} > 0$ and $p_{ji}^{(m)} > 0$ and $i$ is recurrent, then $j$ is recurrent

2 For $i, j \in S$, if $\exists\, n, m > 0$ such that $p_{ij}^{(n)} > 0$ and $p_{ji}^{(m)} > 0$, then $d(i) = d(j)$

3 For $i, j \in S$, if $\exists, r > 0$ such that $p_{ij}^{(r)} > 0$ then $j$ cannot be transient

4 For $i, j \in S$, if $\exists, r > 0$ such that $p_{ij}^{(r)} > 0$ and $i$ is null recurrent then $j$ is positive

**117** Lex $X$ be a discrete random variable with sample space $\chi = \{1, 2, \ldots, 10\}$ and probability mass function $p(x)$, $x \in \chi$. Consider testing the hypothesis $H_0 : p(x) = \frac{1}{10}$, $x \in \chi$ against
$H_1 : p(x) \propto x, x \in \chi$
based on a single observation $X$. Then which of the following statements are correct?

1 The test with critical region $\{X \geq 2\}$ is most powerful of its size.

2 The test with critical region $\{X < 2\}$ is unbiased at level $\alpha = 0.1$

3 If $X = 7$ the $p$-value of the most powerful test is 0.6

4 There exists a nonrandomized test of size 0.05

**118** Let $X$ and $Y$ be real-valued independent random variables on $\Omega$. Then which of the following statements are correct?

1 $E[\cos(tX - uY)] = E[\cos(tX)]E[\cos(uY)] - E[\sin(tX)]E[\sin(uY)]$ for all $t, u \in R$

2 If $X \sim N(2, 1)$ and $Y \sim N(0, 2)$, then $\text{var}(X + Y) = 3$ where $N(\mu, \sigma^2)$ represents Normal distribution with mean $\mu$ and variance $\sigma^2$

3 $\{X = a\} \cap \{Y = b\} = \phi$ for all $a, b \in R$

4 $P(\{X = a\} \cap \{Y = b\}) = P(\{X = a\})\, P(\{Y = b\})$ for all $a, b \in R$

**119** For $t \in R$ define $M(t) = \begin{bmatrix} 1 & t & 0 \\ 1 & 1 & t^2 \\ 0 & 1 & 1 \end{bmatrix}$

Then, which of the following are true?

1 $\det M(t)$ is a polynomial of degree 3 in $t$.

2 $\det M(t) = 0 \ \forall t \in R$.

3 $\det M(t)$ is zero for infinitely many $t \in R$.

4 $\det M(t)$ is zero for exactly two $t \in R$.

**120** Let $M$ be a $3 \times 3$ matrix with real entries such that $M^2 = M + 2I$, where, $I$ denotes that $3 \times 3$ identity matrix. If $\alpha$, $\beta$ and $\gamma$ are eigen values of $M$ such that $\alpha\beta\gamma = -4$, then $\alpha + \beta + \gamma$ is equal to

1 $3C_1$

2 $9\,C_1 \div 3$

3 3

4 4

# ANSWERS

## PART B

| | | | | | | | | | |
|---|---|---|---|---|---|---|---|---|---|
| **21.** 4 | **22.** 2 | **23.** 3 | **24.** 3 | **25.** 2 | **26.** 3 | **27.** 3 | **28.** 3 | **29.** 2 | **30.** 2 |
| **31.** 1 | **32.** 2 | **33.** 2 | **34.** 2 | **35.** 3 | **36.** 1 | **37.** 1 | **38.** 1 | **39.** 3 | **40.** 4 |
| **41.** 3 | **42.** 3 | **43.** 3 | **44.** 1 | **45.** 4 | **46.** 3 | **47.** 1 | **48.** 1 | **49.** 1 | **50.** 4 |
| **51.** 3 | **52.** 4 | **53.** 4 | **54.** 3 | **55.** 3 | **56.** 3 | **57.** 4 | **58.** 1 | **59.** 3 | **60.** 1 |

## PART C

| | | | | | | | | | |
|---|---|---|---|---|---|---|---|---|---|
| **61.** 4 | **62.** 4 | **63.** 1,2,4 | **64.** 3 | **65.** 1 | **66.** 2 | **67.** 1,3,4 | **68.** 1,2 | **69.** 1,3,4 | **70.** 2,4 |
| **71.** 3, 4 | **72.** 3 | **73.** 2,4 | **74.** 1,2 | **75.** 1,2,3 | **76.** 1,2,4 | **77.** 2,3,4 | **78.** 2,3 | **79.** 1 | **80.** 1,2,3,4 |
| **81.** 1,3,4 | **82.** 1,2,3 | **83.** 1,2 | **84.** 1,2,4 | **85.** 1,4 | **86.** 1 | **87.** 2,3,4 | **88.** 3 | **89.** 1,2,3,4 | **90.** 2,3,4 |
| **91.** 2 | **92.** 1,2,3 | **93.** 1,2 | **94.** 1 | **95.** 1,4 | **96.** 3 | **97.** 2 | **98.** 1,3 | **99.** 2,3,4 | **100.** 3 |
| **101.** 1,3,4 | **102.** 3,4 | **103.** 1,3,4 | **104.** 1,2,3,4 | **105.** 1,2,3,4 | **106.** 1,2,3 | **107.** 2,3,4 | **108.** 1,2,4 | **109.** 2,4 | **110.** 2,3,4 |
| **111.** 2,3,4 | **112.** 1,3,4 | **113.** 2,3 | **114.** 1,3 | **115.** 3,4 | **116.** 1,2 | **117.** 1 | **118.** 1,2,4 | **119.** 4 | **120.** 1,3 |